ONTARIO

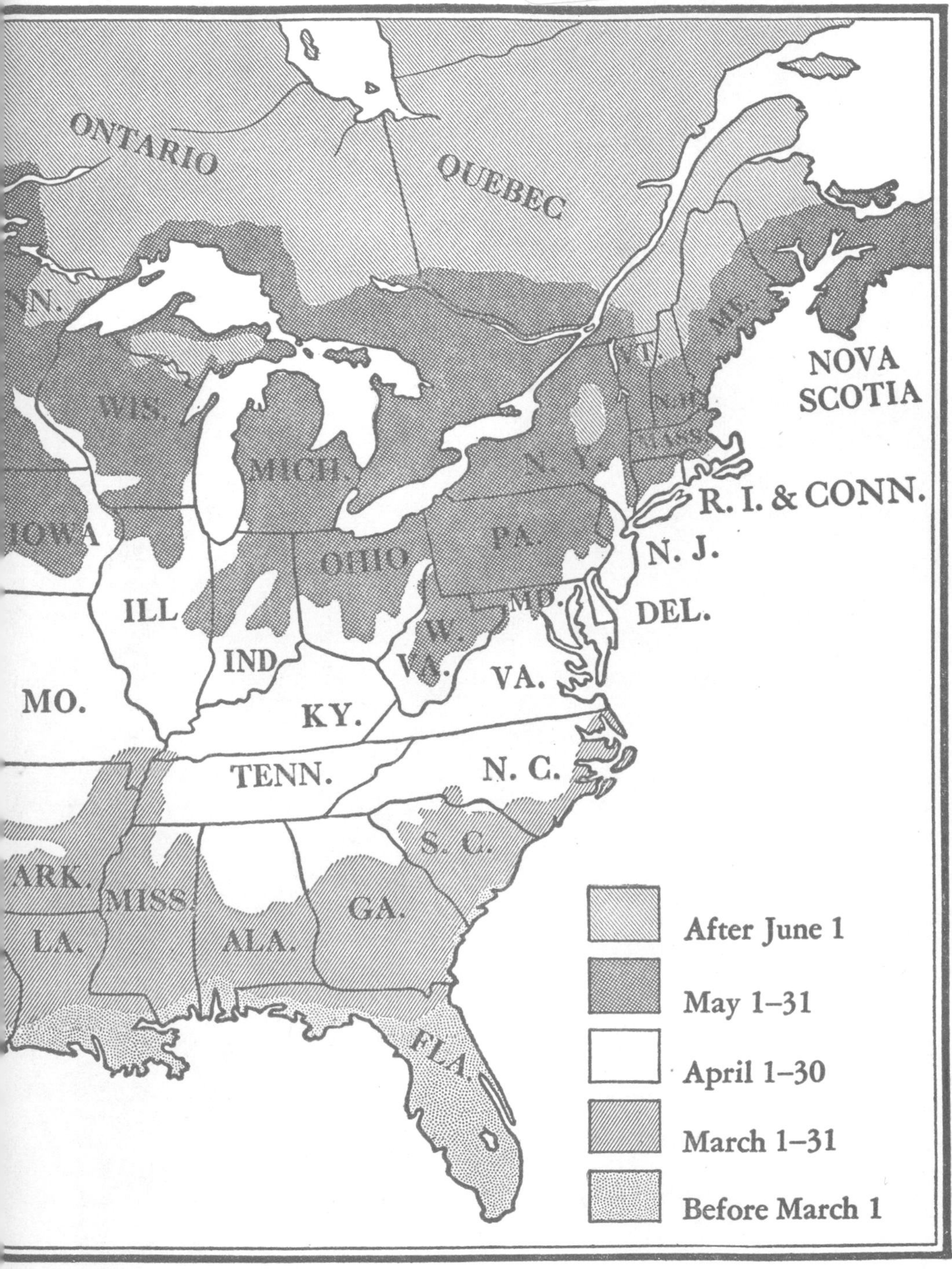

QUEBEC

NOVA
SCOTIA

NN.

WIS

MICH.

VT.

ME.

N. H.

MASS.

N. Y.

R. I. & CONN.

IOWA

ILL

OHIO

PA.

N. J.

IND

MD.

DEL.

MO.

W.
VA.

VA.

KY.

TENN.

N. C.

S. C.

ARK.

MISS.

GA.

LA.

ALA.

FLA.

	After June 1
	May 1–31
	April 1–30
	March 1–31
	Before March 1

TAYLOR'S

Encyclopedia of Gardening

TAYLOR'S
Encyclopedia
of Gardening

HORTICULTURE AND LANDSCAPE DESIGN

Edited by

NORMAN TAYLOR

FOURTH EDITION
COMPLETELY REVISED AND ENLARGED
ILLUSTRATED WITH MORE THAN 500 DRAWINGS
AND 48 PAGES OF COLOR ILLUSTRATIONS

HOUGHTON MIFFLIN COMPANY BOSTON
The Riverside Press Cambridge
1961

Preface to the Fourth Edition

THIS fourth edition of the ENCYCLOPEDIA OF GARDENING has been demanded by the garden public ever since 1948. The Editor and the publishers have long felt an acute obligation to this growing garden audience. Their demands have expanded so greatly since our last edition that more than 850 plants and many new methods are here included for the first time.

Over the years the book has had a wide and ever-increasing reception. That, of course, is a source of profound gratification to its sponsors. But in anything so fluid as gardening no book can rest on past honors, no matter how impressive. Hence this new and completely revised edition. It inevitably prompts the hope that it will be as useful in the future as the older ones appear to have been in the past.

N. T.

Elmwood
Princess Anne, Maryland

FIRST PRINTING

The Riverside Press
CAMBRIDGE • MASSACHUSETTS
PRINTED IN THE U.S.A.

Introduction

THE preparation of this new edition falls into several categories, the most important of which are New Plants, New Methods, Plant Enemies, and Nomenclature.

NEW PLANTS

More than 850 species are included here for the first time. The criterion of whether they should or should not be included is the degree of their acceptance by the garden public. In the recent sixth edition of the *Plant Buyer's Guide* (issued by the Massachusetts Horticultural Society in 1958), all the usually cultivated plants are listed and the nurserymen or seedsmen carrying them are noted. Unless a species is offered by at least five dealers it is reasonably certain that the item is of interest only to specialists and hence is omitted here. Certain exceptions occur among some old-fashioned garden plants and some economic species, which in the judgment of the Editor should be included, although they may not be currently popular among dealers.

The book, then, includes all the commonly cultivated plants likely to interest the amateur gardener in the United States and Canada — a total of over 9000 species, varieties, and named horticultural forms. To have included all species dear to the hearts of specialists would have greatly increased the size and cost of the book. It is regrettable, for instance, to have to exclude hundreds of species and varieties offered by such experts as Samuel Ayres, Jr., of Los Angeles, Edwin A. Menninger of Stuart, Fla., the huge collection of exotics of Julius Roehrs & Company of Rutherford, N.J., and the incomparable seed collections of Rex D. Pearce at Moorestown, N.J.

NEW METHODS

The art of gardening suffers from, and is frequently helped by, a constant bombardment of new ideas. Not so long ago it was hydroponics (a new term for an old technique). More recently have come starter solutions, soluble fertilizers, mist propagation, gibberellic acid, foliar feeding, hormones, iron chelates and many others. All these are entered at their proper place in the ENCYCLOPEDIA with an appraisal of their worth to the average grower — usually based upon tests made by experts at the U.S. Department of Agriculture or by those at the various experiment stations.

PLANT ENEMIES

It has long been the conviction of the Editor that most of us should not be expected to know the intricacies of insect pests and plant diseases, nor the horrendous battery of relatively dangerous chemicals used to control these garden enemies. Few among us can read with profit the textbooks or bulletins on these subjects, any more than sensible people, when illness threatens, read medical books.

The earlier editions of this book contained such directions for dealing with plant pests — and much of it was of doubtful use to the amateur, although technically sound enough. Therefore, the whole section on plant diseases and insect pests has been completely rewritten for this edition.

All pesticides have been reduced to a numbered series and the directions for their use — as at CABBAGE for instance — simply indicate which numbered pesticide to use at such and such a stage. The Editor is profoundly grateful to Dr. Spencer H. Davis, Jr., plant pathologist, and Dr. Leland G. Merrill, Jr., entomologist, both of Rutgers University, who have so expertly dealt with the problem for this edition.

NOMENCLATURE

Forty years ago the Editor was cautioned by his botanical mentors that the correct name for the Douglas fir was not *Abies douglasi,* but *Pseudotsuga douglasi.* Soon it was whispered in the cloistered halls where such things are concocted that *Pseudotsuga douglasi* was wholly wrong and the correct name was *Pseudotsuga taxifolia.* Finally, and only yesterday, it was rumored that this, also, was wrong and that the correct name should be *Pseudotsuga menziesi!*

This nomenclatorial floundering is cited, not because it is exceptional, but because unhappily it is duplicated in hundreds of other cases, to the confusion of everyone.

The purpose of any system of attaching Latin names to plants is, or should be, to give the garden public (including foresters, pharmacists, doctors, and others), a definitive name to which they could cling with some hope of certainty. But in the case of this majestic evergreen tree, *Douglas fir* appears to be a far better name for it than any of the four different Latin ones!

Some of this confusion, but by no means all of it, has been settled by various international meetings of horticultural taxonomists. Their rules, however, are modified from time to time, and may be again. According to one of them, for instance, the Japanese anemone that everyone for a hundred years has called *Anemone japonica* should be called something else, if one is to be "correct."

In this edition of the ENCYCLOPEDIA as few changes of Latin names have been made as possible. In the case of native plants of the northeastern states the names have been made to conform to the new edition of Britton and Brown's *Illustrated Flora,* by Dr. H. A. Gleason, or to the eighth edition of *Gray's Manual* by the late M. L. Fernald.

For the rest of the Latin names the Editor has retained what appears to be the most valid name, and validity here means the one of greatest convenience to the garden public and to the trade, whether or not it pleases some cloistered expert whose idea of "correctness" may be as ephemeral as in the case of the much-named Douglas fir.

Two other suggestions (or are they rules?) have not been followed here, again because they do not seem to advance science and may cause confusion. For years, every gardener knew that the Concord Grape and Dorothy Perkins rose were *varieties* of a grape or rose, and there was no uncertainty about them. There are possibly 50,000 such varieties in cultivation, but experts would now have us call them *cultivars* and instead of writing Dorothy Perkins they insist that it should be 'Dorothy Perkins' (*i.e.,* with inverted commas). The disposition of *cultivar* and *variety* will be found at those entries in the body of the book while the inverted commas appear here and nowhere else! A similar avoidance of such suggestions has been followed by the Royal Horticultural Society's *Dictionary of Gardening* (issued in 1956).

ACKNOWLEDGMENTS

To the new and old contributors, who are listed elsewhere, the book owes much of its value. That they should always agree with each other or with the Editor is as unlikely as that two plants are ever exactly alike. Where possible such inconsistencies have been ironed out, but it seemed better to let informed conflicts persist, rather than make weak compromises. There are only a few such.

The co-operation of all but two of the Agricultural Experiment Stations has resulted in the revision of their original articles on the gardening possibilities of the different states and provinces, together with temperature and rainfall figures. Few features of the book are as valuable and the Editor gratefully acknowledges the efforts of the staffs of the experiment stations both in the U.S. and in the provinces of Canada.

Various individuals and institutions have been lavish in their willingness to help in this revision. At the New York Botanical Garden, Miss Elizabeth Hall, Librarian, and Dr. H. W. Rickett, Bibliographer, have both been of the greatest help. At the Massachusetts Horticultural Society, Mr. Arno H. Nehrling, Executive Secretary, and Miss Dorothy S. Manks, Librarian, have made valuable suggestions. At Rutgers University, Dr. Ernest R. Purvis, Professor of Soils, has kindly read and approved the articles on SOILS and SOIL OPERATIONS. At Harvard University, Professor Norman T. Newton, head of the School of Landscape Architecture, has been helpful in making suggestions for the revision of articles on landscape architecture, and in selecting Mr. Garrett Eckbo of South Pasadena, Calif., to implement them. At the United States National Arboretum, Dr. Henry T. Skinner, the Director, has contributed valuable notes on the zones of hardiness used in the ENCYCLOPEDIA. I am also under pleasant obligation to D. Van Nostrand Company of Princeton for permission to use here parts of my *Fruit in the Garden*, published by them in 1954.

From the publishers the Editor has received nothing but the heartiest co-operation, and especial thanks are due to Messrs. Lovell Thompson and David Harris, and to Evelyn F. Bright, who copy-edited the whole manuscript.

My thanks are especially due Mr. B. Y. Morrison, lately Chief of the Division of Plant Exploration and Introduction, U.S. Department of Agriculture, and to Mr. E. J. Alexander, curator at the New York Botanical Garden, both of whom have read the proofs and contributed many helpful suggestions. Mr. Morrison did a similar service for the first edition of this book in 1936.

More personal thanks are due to three people who have given understanding aid, often unsuspected. The first is my wife, Margaretta Stevenson Taylor, who, for three years, has never failed to ease the burden as much as possible. The second is my friend Shelby H. Jarman, of Brentwood, Princess Anne, Md., whose unflagging interest and helpful suggestions are greatly appreciated. And finally my profound thanks go to Anna H. Scott, also of Princess Anne, who typed all the manuscript and performed many other services. Her keen intelligence and willing co-operation have created that sort of obligation for which one can only say, "Well done — and thank you."

Contributors

The contributors and the initials used to
designate their articles are as follows:

A.F.   **Armistead Fitzhugh**, Landscape Architect, Jamaica, N.Y.

A.H.N. **Arno H. Nehrling**, Executive Secretary, Massachusetts Horticultural Society,
        Boston, Mass.

A.J.W. **Albert J. Winkler**, Professor of Viticulture, University of California, Davis,
        Calif.

B.J.L. **Bryan J. Lynch**, Landscape Architect, Stamford, Conn.

B.Y.M. **Benjamin Y. Morrison**, Pass Christian, Miss.

C.A.   **Cornelius Ackerson**, President, National Chrysanthemum Society, Keyport,
        N.J.

C.B.L. **Conrad B. Link**, Professor of Floriculture, University of Maryland, College
        Park, Md.

C.O.H. **Claron O. Hesse**, Professor of Pomology, University of California, Davis,
        Calif.

D.S.M. **Dorothy S. Manks**, Librarian, Massachusetts Horticultural Society, Boston,
        Mass.

D.W.   **Donald Wyman**, Horticulturist, Arnold Arboretum, Harvard University,
        Jamaica Plain, Mass.

F.W.A. **Frank W. Allen**, Professor of Pomology, Emeritus, University of California,
        Davis, Calif.

G.D.R. **George D. Ruehle**, Vice-director, Sub-tropical Experiment Station, University
        of Florida, Homestead, Fla.

G.E.   **Garrett Eckbo**, Landscape Architect, South Pasadena, Calif.

G.H.P. **George H. Pring**, Superintendent, Missouri Botanical Garden, St. Louis, Mo.

H.A.C. **Harold A. Caparn**, Landscape Architect, New York, N.Y.

H.B.T. **H. B. Tukey**, Head, Department of Horticulture, Michigan State College, East
        Lansing, Mich.

H.C.T. **H. C. Thompson**, Professor of Vegetable Crops, Emeritus, Cornell University,
        Ithaca, N.Y.

H.E.D. **Henry E. Downer**, Horticulturist, Emeritus, Vassar College, Poughkeep-
        sie, N.Y.

H.H.H. **H. Harold Hume**, University of Florida, Gainesville, Fla.

H.M.C. **Mrs. Jay Clark, Jr.**, Worcester, Mass.

H.M.F. **Helen Morgenthau Fox**, Mount Kisco, N.Y.

H.T.   **Henry Teuscher**, Curator, Montreal Botanical Garden, Montreal, Canada

H.W.K. **Harold W. Knowlton**, Past President, American Iris Society, Auburndale, Mass.

I.N.G. **Ira N. Gabrielson**, President, Wildlife Management Institute, Washington, D.C.

J.E.S. **Joel E. Spingarn**, Amenia, N.Y.

J.G.C. **J. Gregory Conway**, Fullerton, Calif.

L.B.W. **Louise Beebe Wilder**, New York, N.Y.

L.D.D. **Luther D. Davis**, Professor of Pomology, University of California, Davis,
        Calif.

L.G.M. Leland G. Merrill, Jr., Extension Specialist, Entomology, Rutgers University, New Brunswick, N.J.

L.Y.K. Mrs. Francis King, South Hartford, N.Y.

M.A. Mary Averill, New York, N.Y.

M.F. Montague Free, Senior Editor, *Flower Grower;* Consultant, American Garden Guild Book Club, Hyde Park, N.Y.

N.G. Norvell Gillespie, Norvell Gillespie & Associates, Berkeley, Calif.

O.E.W. Orland E. White, Director, Emeritus, Blandy Experimental Farm, University of Virginia, Charlottesville, Va.

R.E.G. Ralph E. Griswold, Landscape Architect, Pittsburgh, Pa.

R.E.S. Roy E. Shepherd, Rose hybridist, Medina, Ohio

R.J.G. Robert J. Gillespie, Orchid specialist, Missouri Botanical Garden Arboretum, Gray Summit, Mo.

R.L.F. Robert Ludlow Fowler, Jr., Landscape Architect, New York, N.Y.

R.S.L. Robert S. Lemmon, Wilton, Conn.

R.W. Richardson Wright, West Chatham, Mass.

R.W.H. Robert W. Hodgson, Professor, Sub-tropical Horticulture, University of California, Los Angeles, Calif.

S.H.D. Spencer H. Davis, Jr., Extension Specialist, Plant Pathology, Rutgers University, New Brunswick, N.J.

S.S. Silvia Saunders, A. P. Saunders Hybrid Peonies, Clinton, N.Y.

T.A.W. T. A. Weston, New York, N.Y.

T.R.M. Thomas R. Manley, Gladiolus specialist, Selingsgrove, Pa.

W.P.T. Warren P. Tufts, Professor of Pomology, Emeritus, University of California, Davis, Calif.

Why an Encyclopedia?

BECAUSE plants and what we do with them never follow such an orderly sequence as the alphabet, for instance, one often hears the query: "Why follow the progression of the alphabet rather than the seasons?" Why, in other words, a garden encyclopedia at all?

The real answer to such a question is the reason this book was written. It was planned to be an index to itself, so simply arranged that it is easy to find the things you want with a minimum of groping among momentarily useless features. Thousands of cross-reference items have been inserted to lead one directly to the needed information, and 4732 common or vernacular names are similarly cross-referenced to the article where their culture is discussed.

There is, in this arrangement, another helpful feature, of which much has been made in this book: No words of special import (*i.e.,* the jargon of gardeners, nurserymen, botanists, and such) have been used unless the word is defined at its proper vocabulary entry. In other words, you do not have to go to any other reference work to understand the terms used here. (*See,* below, HOW TO USE THE BOOK.) All such words are, in any case, marked with an asterisk (*), the significance of which will be found as the footnote to all pages.

The unquestioned advantage of the alphabetic arrangement of so much material has, however, one drawback — it gives us no *simultaneous* view either of the whole field of gardening, or of the contents of this book. To meet such a need the titles of the main articles in the encyclopedia have been rearranged here according to the main divisions of gardening. Such a schematic plan, if followed as a reading guide, removes the only cogent reason for asking "Why an Encyclopedia?"

Such an outline may well be divided under ten main heads. It should be understood that it includes only the longer articles in the book, and the culture of all plants of secondary importance should be sought at the proper vocabulary entries, as well as thousands of briefer notes and definitions.

ABBREVIATIONS
USED IN WRITING THE ENCYCLOPEDIA

NOTE: Common horticultural abbreviations are defined at their proper vocabulary entries, *i.e.,* B. & B., P.G., etc. States of the Union and months of the year: usual abbreviations.

Hort. = { Horticultural / Horticulture } according to context.

Cult. = { Cultivated / Culture / Cultivation } according to context.

Af. = Africa	Eng. = England	L.I. = Long Island, N.Y.	S.A. = South America
As. = Asia	Eu. = Europe	N.A. = North America	U.S. = United States
Aust. = Australia	Jap. = Japan	N.Z. = New Zealand	W.I. = West Indies
E.I. = East Indies			

in. = inches   ft. = feet

Main Articles

1. GREENHOUSES, COLD FRAMES, AND HOTBEDS

Greenhouse Cold Frames (including hotbeds)

2. CLIMATE AND HARDINESS

Climate
Wind
Rainfall
Temperature
Snow

Frost and Frost Control
Hardiness
Zones (of hardiness in U.S. and Canada)
Protecting Plants
Windbreaks

3. SOILS AND SOIL OPERATIONS

Soils (general)
Acid and Alkali Soils
Humus
Lime
Manure
Fertilizers
Soil Operations (general)
Soil Conditioners
Draining

Irrigation
Green Manuring (soil improvement)
Compost
Cultivation, Plowing, Harrowing
Raking, Digging, Hoeing, Trenching
Mulch and Mulching
Cover Crops
Organic Gardening

4. SPECIALIZED GARDENS

SEASONAL
Spring Garden
Summer Garden
Autumn Garden
Winter Garden

COLOR GARDENS
Red Garden
Blue Garden
Yellow Garden
Pink Garden
White Garden
Gray and Lavender Garden

SPECIALIZED GARDENS
(ORNAMENTAL)
Bog Garden
Border
Bulbs
Cacti
Ferns and Fern Gardening
Japanese Gardens
Rock Garden
Sand Garden
Seaside Gardens
Shady Garden
Soilless Gardening
Sub-tropical Garden
Succulents
Water Garden
Wild Garden

MISCELLANEOUS
SPECIALIZED GARDENS
Cellar Gardening
Herb Gardening
Kitchen Garden
Window Boxes
Medicinal Plants
Muckland Gardening
Tub Gardening
Lawn

5. GARDEN PLANNING AND DESIGN

PLANNING THE HOME GROUNDS

SPECIAL LANDSCAPE FEATURES

Arbors
Banks
Bridges
Drives

Gates and Gateways
Lighting (night illumination)
Paths and Paving
Steps

Structures
Vista
Walls and Wall Gardening
Water

6. PROPAGATION

Propagation (general)
Seeds and Seedage
Budding

Cuttings
Division

Grafting
Layering

7. PLANT BREEDING

Crossing   Hybridizing   New Varieties   Mutation   And 26 shorter articles

8. PESTS

PLANT DISEASES (and their control)

Fungicides   Damping-off

Also hundreds of brief notes on control at the crops needing it.

INSECT PESTS (and their control)

Insect Friends   Fumigation
Insecticides   Spraying and Dusting

Also hundreds of brief notes on control at the crops needing it.

ANIMAL INJURY (control of rodents, bird nuisances, etc.)

9. MISCELLANEOUS HORTICULTURAL OPERATIONS, SPECIAL TYPES OF GARDENING, AND MISCELLANEOUS ARTICLES

PLANTS	OPERATIONS (except Soil Operations, for which *see* 3, and Propagation, for which *see* 6)	EDUCATIONAL AND REFERENCE
Annuals		Arboretum
Biennials		Botanic Garden
Perennials		Birds
Flowering Shrubs	Planting	Flower Shows
Fragrance	Potting	Garden Books
Aquarium	Pruning	Garden Calendar
House Plants	Storage	Garden Clubs
Grasses	Training Plants	Garden Magazines
Bamboo	Tree Surgery	Garden History
Flower Arranging	Tools and Implements	Garden Questions
Everlastings	Watering	Garden Tables (statistics)
Vines	Weeds and Weeding	Garden Tours
Mushroom	Dwarfing	Weights and Measures
Hanging Baskets	Forcing	Poisonous Plants
Perfume Plants	Retarding	Bees and Bee Plants
	Foliar Feeding	Labels
	Starter Solutions	Quarantines
	Iron Chelates	

10. SPECIAL CULTURAL ARTICLES ON THE BEST VARIETIES AND HOW TO GROW THEM

A. FLOWERS

Special articles on:

Anemone	Cineraria	Fuchsia	Michaelmas daisy	Primula
Aster	Clematis	Gladiolus	Narcissus	Rose
Begonia	Cosmos	Gloxinia	Nasturtium	Snapdragon
Calceolaria	Crinum	Hollyhock	Orchids	Stock
Calla Lily	Crocus	Hyacinth	Pansy	Sweet Pea
Camellia	Cyclamen	Iris	Pelargonium	Tulip
Canna	Dahlia	Lilium	Peony	Violet
Carnation	Daylily	Lily-of-the-valley	Poinsettia	Water Lily
Chrysanthemum	Delphinium	Marigold	Poppy	

B. VEGETABLES. One long general article on Kitchen Garden

Special articles on:

Artichoke	Carrot	Kale	Parsnip	Sea-kale
Asparagus	Cauliflower	Kohlrabi	Pea	Spinach
Bean	Celery (and Celeriac)	Lettuce	Potato	Squash
Beet (and Chard)	Chinese Cabbage	New Zealand Spinach	Pumpkin	Sweet Potato
Broccoli	Corn		Radish	Tomato
Brussels Sprouts	Cucumber	Okra	Rhubarb	Turnip
Cabbage	Eggplant	Onion	Rutabaga	Watercress
Cardoon	Endive	Parsley		

C. Miscellaneous Economic and Ornamental Plants

Ginseng	Rice	Sugar Cane	Smilax	Horse-radish
Hop	Sorghum	Tobacco	Vetch	Tarragon
Peanut	Soybean	Nepenthes	Foliage Plants	

D. Nuts and Trees. Trees (general). Nut Culture (general)

Special articles on:

Almond	Eucalyptus	Magnolia	Pecan	Tung-oil tree
Beech	Fir	Maple	Pine	Walnut
Chestnut	Hazel	Oak	Poplar	Evergreens
Coconut	Hickory	Palm	Spruce	
Elm	Litchi			

E. Ornamental Shrubs

Azalea	Cotoneaster	Privet	Lilac	Hedges
Box	Erica	Rhododendron	Flowering Shrubs	Broad-leaved Evergreens

F. Fruit Culture. General articles, including eastern and western fruit culture; Dwarf Fruit Trees

Special articles on:

Apple	Currant	Guava	Mulberry	Plum
Apricot	Date	Lemon	Olive	Pomegranate
Avocado	Dewberry	Lime	Orange	Prune
Banana	Fig	Loganberry	Peach	Quince
Blackberry	Gooseberry	Loquat	Pear	Raspberry
Blueberry	Grape	Mango	Persimmon	Strawberry
Cherry	Grapefruit	Melon	Pineapple	Watermelon
Cranberry				

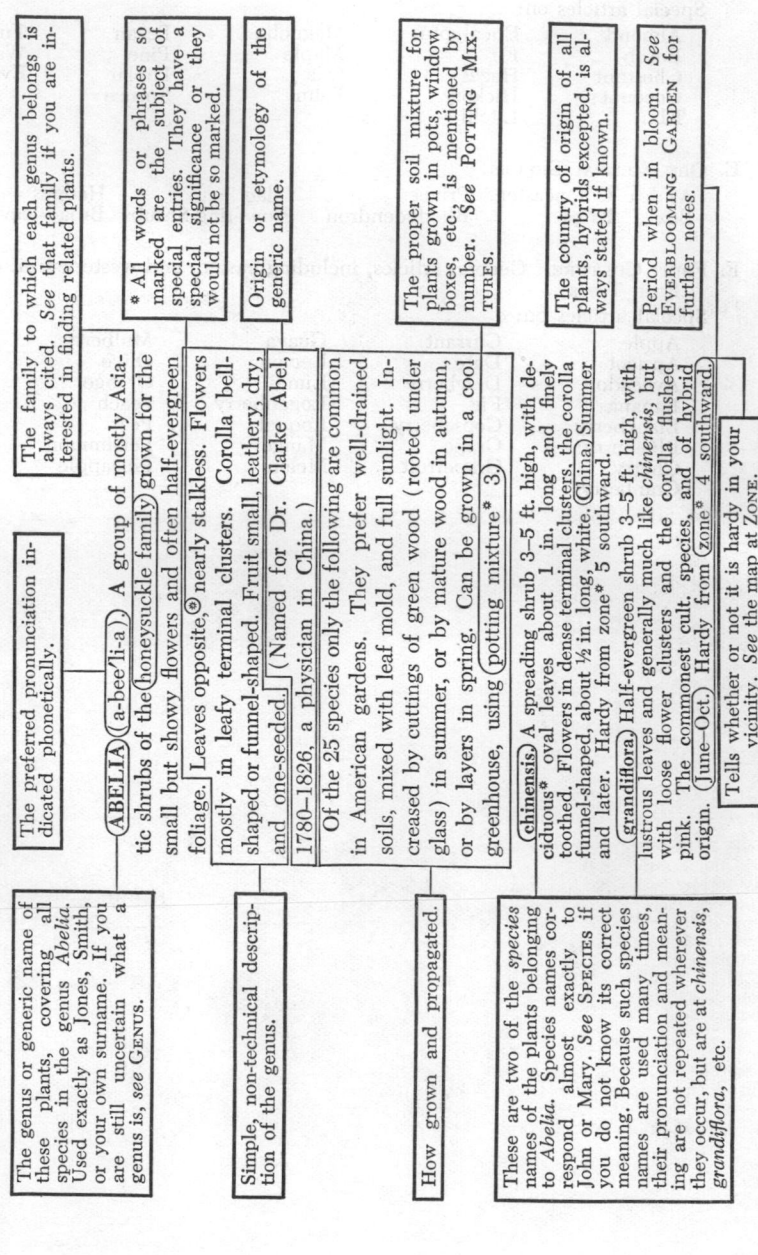

HOW TO USE THE BOOK

As in any other encyclopedia, the items are entered in strict alphabetical sequence. Look for red oak, New England aster, white spruce, **black** oak, **pink** lady's-slipper, etc., under the boldface word, not under oak or spruce or lady's-slipper or aster. They will, of course, be found under oak or spruce or lady's-slipper or aster, but much more quickly and directly (*i.e.*, referred to the exact species) by going to the first word of names that contain two. For all other items the strictly alphabetical entry needs no explanation.

For those who are not familiar with the usual method of arranging plants under their Latin names, a sample of two species in the first genus in the book is given below. *See also* PLANT NAMES.

The genus or generic name of these plants, covering all species in the genus *Abelia*. Used exactly as Jones, Smith, or your own surname. If you are still uncertain what a genus is, *see* GENUS.

The preferred pronunciation indicated phonetically.

Simple, non-technical description of the genus.

How grown and propagated.

These are two of the *species* names of the plants belonging to *Abelia*. Species names correspond almost exactly to John or Mary. *See* SPECIES if you do not know its correct meaning. Because such species names are used many times, their pronunciation and meaning are not repeated wherever they occur, but are at *chinensis, grandiflora*, etc.

The family to which each genus belongs is always cited. *See* that family if you are interested in finding related plants.

* All words or phrases so marked are the subject of special entries. They have a special significance or they would not be so marked.

Origin or etymology of the generic name.

The proper soil mixture for plants grown in pots, window boxes, etc., is mentioned by number. *See* POTTING MIXTURES.

The country of origin of all plants, hybrids excepted, is always stated if known.

Period when in bloom. *See* EVERBLOOMING GARDEN for further notes.

ABELIA (a-bee'li-a) A group of mostly Asiatic shrubs of the honeysuckle family grown for the small but showy flowers and often half-evergreen foliage. Leaves opposite,* nearly stalkless. Flowers mostly in leafy terminal clusters. Corolla bell-shaped or funnel-shaped. Fruit small, leathery, dry, and one-seeded. (Named for Dr. Clarke Abel, 1780–1826, a physician in China.)

Of the 25 species only the following are common in American gardens. They prefer well-drained soils, mixed with leaf mold, and full sunlight. Increased by cuttings of green wood (rooted under glass) in summer, or by mature wood in autumn, or by layers in spring. Can be grown in a cool greenhouse, using potting mixture* 3.

chinensis A spreading shrub 3–5 ft. high, with deciduous* oval leaves about 1 in. long and finely toothed. Flowers in dense terminal clusters, the corolla funnel-shaped, about ½ in. long, white. China. Summer and later. Hardy from zone* 5 southward.

grandiflora Half-evergreen shrub 3–5 ft. high, with lustrous leaves and generally much like *chinensis*, but with loose flower clusters and the corolla flushed pink. The commonest cult. species, and of hybrid origin. (June–Oct.) Hardy from zone* 4 southward.

Tells whether or not it is hardy in your vicinity. *See* the map at ZONE.

Taylor's Encyclopedia of Gardening

A

AARON'S-BEARD = *Hypericum calycinum* (*see* St. John's-wort); also *Saxifraga sarmentosa* and *Cymbalaria muralis*.

AARON'S-ROD = *Thermopsis caroliniana*.

ABACA = *Musa textilis*.

ABAMA = *Narthecium*.

ABELE = *Populus alba*.

ABELIA (a-bee′li-a). A group of mostly Asiatic shrubs of the honeysuckle family grown for the small but showy flowers and often half-evergreen foliage. Leaves opposite,* nearly stalkless. Flowers mostly in leafy terminal clusters. Corolla bell-shaped or funnel-shaped. Fruit small, leathery, dry, and one-seeded. (Named for Dr. Clarke Abel, 1780–1826, a physician in China.)

Of the 25 species only the following are common in American gardens. They prefer well-drained soils, mixed with leaf mold, and full sunlight. Increased by cuttings of green wood (rooted under glass) in summer or by mature wood in autumn, or by layers in spring. Can be grown in a cool greenhouse, using potting mixture* 3.

chinensis. A spreading shrub 3–5 ft. high with deciduous* oval leaves about 1 in. long and finely toothed. Flowers in dense terminal clusters, the corolla funnel-shaped, about ½ in. long, white. China. Summer and later. Hardy from zone* 6 southward.

floribunda. A Mexican evergreen shrub, 3–5 ft. high, the young twigs rusty-hairy. Leaves about 1 in. long, lustrous, and shallowly toothed. Flowers red, pendulous, narrowly funnel-shaped, about 1 in. long. Hardy only from zone* 7 southward.

grandiflora. Half-evergreen shrub 3–5 ft. high with lustrous leaves and generally much like *chinensis*, but with loose flower clusters and the corolla flushed pink. The commonest cult. species, and of hybrid origin. June–Oct. Hardy from zone* 4 southward. The *var.* **sherwoodi** is offered as a more compact shrub, hardly over 3 ft. high. Blooming July–frost.

schumanni. A deciduous shrub, 3–6 ft. high. Leaves ovalish, ¾–1¼ in. long, minutely toothed or without teeth. Flowers few or several, on 1-flowered stalks, pink, about 1 in. long, funnel-shaped. July–Sept. China. Hardy from zone* 6 southward.

zanderi. A deciduous shrub, 5–8 ft. high. Leaves short-stalked, oval-oblong, 1½–3 in. long, hairy on the veins on under side. Flowers in twins, on short stalks, pink, the tube about ½ in. long, the lobes flaring. China. June. Hardy from zone* 4 southward. A variable shrub, evergreen in mild regions and sometimes offered as the *var.* Edward Goucher, which is a hybrid between *grandiflora* and *schumanni*.

ABELIOPHYLLUM (a-bee-li-o-fill′um). A genus of Korean shrubs of the olive family, comprising only one species, **A. distichum,** which in foliage resembles *Abelia* (*see* above), but is a spring-blooming, profusely white-flowered shrub suggesting *Forsythia*, but lower. It is 2–3 ft. high. Leaves ovalish, opposite, without marginal teeth, 1–3 in. long. Flowers in short finger-shaped clusters (racemes*), the corolla about ½ in. wide. Korea. May–June. Hardy from zone* 4 southward. Of easy culture in most garden soils. (*Abeliophyllum* is from *Abelia* and *phyllon,* for its *Abelia*-like leaves.)

Abelmoschus (a-bel-mos′kus) = Musky-seeded. See Hibiscus Abelmoschus.

ABELMOSK = *Hibiscus Abelmoschus*.

ABERIA = *Dovyalis*.

ABIES. See Fir.

ABOBRA (a-bo′bra). A tropical, herbaceous vine of the cucumber family with a tuberous root, grown mostly for its small, showy fruits. Leaves alternate,* cut into linear divisions. Male and female flowers on separate plants, green and fragrant. Female flower solitary, the male usually in clusters. Fruit egg-shaped and berry-like. Stems tendril*-bearing, the tendrils usually forked. (*Abobra* is the Brazilian vernacular name.)

Easily grown from seed but only outdoors in zones* 8 and 9; northward in a warm greenhouse in potting mixture* 3.

tenuifolia. Cranberry gourd. Stems quickly climbing to 20 or 30 ft. Leaves broadly oval in general outline, 2–4 in. long, white-dotted, their much cut segments almost thread-like. Fruit about ½ in. long, bright scarlet. Tropical S.A.

ABORTIVE. Imperfectly developed; especially failing to produce seeds.

---

* Special articles on the subjects indicated by an asterisk (*) will be found at the words so marked.

ABRONIA (a-bro′ni-a). Sand verbena; also called wild lantana. A large genus of herbs, family Nyctaginaceae, mostly from western N.A. and one of them grown for its fragrant flowers that suggest a verbena. Leaves opposite,* stalked, somewhat inequilateral, usually sticky-hairy and with no marginal teeth. Flowers tubular, crowded in a loose head below which are 5 or more colored bracts.* Petals none, but the calyx is petal-like. Fruit leathery, 1-seeded. (Named from *abros,* Greek for delicate, in allusion to the bracts beneath the flower cluster.)

Among the 45 species only the following is of any hort. importance. Although a perennial it is treated as an annual. Seeds which are slow to germinate may be started indoors or in the frame, or sown in place after danger of frost. The plant is useful for the border, rockery or for hanging baskets. *See* ANNUALS.

umbellata. A prostrate, vine-like herb, often rooting at the joints, with long-stalked nearly oval leaves. Flowers about ½ in. long, pink, with usually 10–15 in an umbel*-like cluster that may be 2 in. across. Pacific Coast. June. The variety **grandiflora** has somewhat larger flowers.

abrotanifolia, -us, -um (a-bro-tay-ni-fō′-li-a). Having leaves like the southernwood (*Artemisia Abrotanum*).

ABROTANUM. An ancient name for some fragrant or beautiful plant. *See* ARTEMISIA.

ABRUS (ab′rus). Woody, tropical vines of the pea family, chiefly grown for their scarlet, black-spotted seeds, commonly used in beadwork. Leaves compound,* with 10–15 pairs of small leaflets that fold up in cloudy weather. Flowers small, pea-like, in a stalked, lax cluster that arises in the leaf axil.* Fruit a somewhat woody pod. (Named from *abros,* Greek for delicate, in allusion to the leaflets.)

The only hort. species, the rosary pea, can be grown outdoors in zone* 9, elsewhere in a warm greenhouse in potting mixture* 3. Propagate by seeds, or by cuttings in moist sand. *See* VINES.

precatorius. Rosary pea. Trailing on the ground for 8–10 ft. or on lattice in the greenhouse. Leaflets about ½ in. long, the whole leaf 2–3 in. long. Flowers small, pink, red, or purple, very rarely white. Pod about 1½ in. long. Seeds poisonous but showy, used for a variety of purposes in the tropics. Called also Indian licorice and (the seeds) Jequirity bean.

Absinthium. Classical name of the wormwood. *See* ARTEMISIA.

ABUTILON (a-bū′ti-lon). Flowering maple, also called Chinese bellflower. Over 100 species of tropical shrubs (rarely herbs) of the mallow family, only a few of which are grown in greenhouses, or as bedding plants in frost-free areas. Leaves alternate,* often veined and looking like a maple leaf, in some of the hort. varieties beautifully variegated. Flowers showy, solitary, and borne in the leaf axils,* usually drooping and often trumpet-shaped. Fruit a circle of beaked, dry fruits that split off individually when ripe. (*Abutilon* is from the Arabic for some mallow.)

Grow in cool greenhouse in potting mixture* 4, or outdoors in zone* 8 or 9. Easily propagated by cuttings of young wood in spring or autumn. Very popular pot plants both for flowers and handsome foliage. Occasionally *Malvaviscus arboreus* is incorrectly sold for an abutilon. Plants are sometimes attacked by scale insects and mealybug. The best control is a good commercial preparation of nicotine sprayed according to direction.

hybridum. Of hybrid and uncertain origin but the commonest of all in cultivation. Leaves variable, lobed like a maple leaf or unlobed, green and variously speckled or blotched. Flowers red, pinkish-purple, yellow or white, more or less bell- or trumpet-shaped. Many showy named forms belong here: Boule de Neige (white), Golden Fleece (yellow), Sayitzi (grown for white-edged foliage).

megapotamicum. A drooping plant suitable for hanging baskets. Leaves narrow, 1½–3 in. long, not lobed, but wavy-margined and toothed. Flowers 2–3 in. long, drooping, red with conspicuous yellow, long-protruding stamens.* Brazil.

pictum. Leaves 3-lobed, the central lobe shorter than the others, the margins toothed. Flowers about 1½ in. long, yellow or orange veined with red. Southern S.A.

theophrasti. Velvet-leaf. An annual coarse herb 3–5 ft. high and often a pernicious weed, with hairy, roundish or heart-shaped, tapering leaves. Flowers yellow, ½–1 in. wide. India, but widely naturalized* in N.A.

vitifolium. Sturdy shrub with white-hairy foliage and twigs. Leaves prominently lobed, but roundish or heart-shaped in outline and 4–5 in. wide. Flowers lavender, often 2½ in. across, very showy. Chile.

ABYSSINIAN BANANA = *Musa Ensete.*

abyssinica, -us, -um (a-bis-sin′ee-ca.) From Abyssinia.

ACACIA (a-kā′si-a, also a-kā′sha). An enormous genus of quick-growing shrubs and trees of the pea family found all over the tropical world, and a few in sub-tropical regions. About a hundred species are known to be cult. in America, of which the following are the most common — all but one of them Australian. Some are thorny. Leaves normally twice compound,* the leaflets very numerous and small. In all species marked † there is a simple blade resembling a leaf (actually a modified leafstalk and called a phyllodium) and no leaflets, a common feature in many species of *Acacia.* Flowers very small but crowded into dense finger-shaped or globular clusters, all yellow in the species below. The clusters may be solitary, but more often are arranged in variously branched sprays, and consequently very handsome. Fruit like a pea pod, but often somewhat woody in maturity and sometimes twisted. (Named from the Greek for a point or thorn, in allusion to the many thorny species.) The Australian species are often called wattle.

---

* Special articles on the subjects indicated by an asterisk (*) will be found at the words so marked.

Acacias are attractive, free-flowering shrubs and trees, easily grown outdoors in most of zone* 7 and all of zones* 8 and 9, elsewhere in a cool greenhouse in potting mixture* 3. They are not long-lived trees and this should be taken into account in planning a sub-tropical garden. Propagation by seed, which should be soaked in hot (not boiling) water for a few moments and then allowed to soak in cold water for a day or two. This softens the hard seed-coat. Plant while the seeds are still wet, but even with this treatment some species take four or five weeks to germinate. Propagated also by cuttings of half-ripened wood, with little or no bottom-heat.* From the cuttings or seedlings a taproot* develops which is sensitive to disturbance. Subsequent transplanting must therefore be done with great care. Water freely at first, but as the plants become established they should need little water for most species are drought-resistant.

Some acacias are common show plants in florists' windows, being much grown for their free bloom which is greatest in March and April. *See especially* A. ARMATA and A. PUBESCENS.

In Calif. a nice succession of acacia bloom is secured by planting *A. podalyriaefolia* (Dec. bloom), *A. baileyana* (Jan.), *A. cultriformis* and *A. decurrens dealbata* (Feb.), *A. pravissima* (March), and typical *A. decurrens* in April.

The species marked with a † bear phyllodia (*see* above).

†**alata.** Winged acacia. A prickly, hairy shrub, 4–6 ft. high, its twigs nearly covered by the prominently winged, triangular phyllodia which are about ½ in. wide. Flower heads short-stalked, solitary or in pairs, about ½ in. in diameter, light yellow. Aust. Much planted in Calif.

†**armata.** Kangaroo thorn. A spiny shrub 6–8 ft. high, much grown in greenhouses as a decorative pot plant. Phyllodia about an inch long, usually pressed against the stem, prickle-tipped. Flower heads globular, solitary, about as big as a pea, but very numerous, bright yellow.

baileyana. Cootamundra wattle. Showy shrub or small tree, without spines, and beautiful, feathery, bluish-gray foliage. Leaves doubly compound,* the ultimate leaflets scarcely ¼ in. long, numerous enough to nearly hide the stem. Flower heads globular, only ⅛ in. across, but very numerous in large clusters that exceed the leaf in length. Commonly planted outdoors, and very popular in Calif.

†**cultriformis.** Knife acacia. Stout shrub, with its oblique, blue-gray, knife-shaped phyllodia numerous enough to nearly sheathe the stem and slightly prickle-tipped. Flower heads about ⅛ in. thick, globular, yellow, and very numerous in a terminal, much-branched cluster.

decurrens. Green wattle. Widely planted tree in Calif., often 50–60 ft. high. Leaves twice-compound, the ultimate leaflets very numerous, about ⅓ in. long, always dark green. Flower heads about ¼ in. across, globular, golden-yellow, and arranged in a raceme.* Pods about 4 in. long. In addition to the typical form there are two widely grown varieties: *var.* **dealbata.** Silver wattle, has silvery-gray foliage; var. **mollis.** Black wattle, has white-hairy foliage and attractive purplish pods. All much planted in Calif.

farnesiana. Huisache; called, also, popinac, sponge tree and cassie. Probably American, but planted all over the tropical and sub-tropical world, the huisache is an attractive, very thorny shrub, much-branched and covered with twice-compound* leaves. Ultimate leaflets scarcely ⅛ in. long but very numerous. Flower heads globular, nearly ½ in. thick, deep yellow and fragrant, in rather dense clusters.

floribunda. As offered, usually a form of *A. longifolia.*

†**latifolia.** A tree, the bluish-green phyllodia nearly 6 in. long and a third as wide. Flowers yellow, in globose heads, arranged in a loose cluster (spike) 1–2 in. long. Pods 2–4 in. long. Aust.

†**longifolia.** Golden wattle. Sydney golden wattle. A shrub or small tree, without prickles, the phyllodia nearly 6 in. long and more or less oblong. Flowers in finger-shaped clusters which are about 2½ in. long, and lemon yellow. Pod about 4½ in. long.

†**melanoxylon.** Lightwood. Black acacia. Tall, unarmed tree. Phyllodia more or less inverted lance-shaped about 4½ in. long and an inch wide. Sometimes there are also doubly compound* leaves on young twigs. Flowers in dense, globular heads which are about ¼ in. across, cream-yellow, not particularly showy. Pod about 4 in. long, twisted. This tree yields the famous blackwood of Australia, which is very light. Much planted as a street tree in Calif., but not very lasting.

†**pendula.** Weeping myall. Weeping boree. Resembling the weeping willow in habit, but not over 30 ft. high. Phyllodia narrow, pointed, 2–3 in. long. Flower heads profuse, almost stalkless, the heads yellow, about ½ in. in diameter. Aust. Much planted in Calif.

†**podalyriaefolia.** Mount Morgan wattle. Pearl acacia. A bluish-gray, or even silvery, hairy shrub, much planted in Calif. Phyllodia oval or oblong, about 1½ in. long. Flowers golden-yellow, in ball-like heads that are clustered in long racemes.* Pod about 3 in. long.

†**pravissima.** Much-branched and twiggy tree, usually not over 20 ft. high, the branches drooping. Phyllodia green, ovalish, about 1 in. long, somewhat resembling a helmet in silhouette. Flower heads yellow, scarcely ⅛ in. in diameter, in short clusters scarcely longer than the phyllodia. Pod about 3 in. long, distinctly twisted.

pubescens. Hairy wattle. Handsome shrub with pendulous branches and much grown in greenhouses for its showy bloom. Leaves twice-compound,* the ultimate leaflets usually in 16 pairs, scarcely ⅕ in. long. Flower heads yellow, about ⅓ in. in diameter in lax racemes* longer than the leaves. Pod flat. Common in florist-shop windows and a favorite because of its feathery foliage and free bloom in March or April.

†**retinodes.** A tree, 20–30 ft. high, the twigs angled. Phyllodia narrow, somewhat curved, 3–5½ in. long, scarcely ¼ in. wide, almost prickly-pointed. Flower heads minute, scarcely ¼ in. in diameter, but crowded in dense, showy clusters that in southern Calif. bloom nearly all year. Aust. *Var.* **floribunda** is offered as more profuse flowering but it does not certainly belong here.

†**saligna.** Golden wreath. A shrub or small tree with willow-like phyllodia often 8 in. long. Flower heads nearly ½ in. in diameter, in racemes.* Pod about 5 in. long and constricted between the seeds.

* Special articles on the subjects indicated by an asterisk (*) will be found at the words so marked.

†**verticillata.** Star acacia. A small tree or shrub with very numerous phyllodia, which are needle-shaped, about ¾ in. long and whorled.* Flowers yellow, in finger-shaped spikes which are about 1 in. long and usually solitary, but very numerous as there may be one at each whorl of phyllodia. Pod about 3 in. long.

ACACIA FAMILY. See LEGUMINOSAE.

ACAENA (a-seen'a)ʹ. A small group of perennial herbs of the rose family, nearly or quite evergreen. Of the 40 or more, nearly all from the southern hemisphere, only the following are of much hort. importance. They are used mostly as ground-covers or in the rock garden, in mild climates. Leaves compound,* the pinnate* leaflets toothed. Flowers very small, but crowded in spikes or heads, prickly. Fruit dry. Most of the species are trailing or prostrate. (*Acaena*, Greek for thorn.)

Prefer open sunlight and a sandy soil. Propagation is easy, by cuttings in autumn or spring, or by seeds in early spring over gentle heat.

buchanani. Dwarf trailing perennial grown mostly for its beautiful bluish-gray leaves. Flowers insignificant, in tiny stalkless heads, its spines yellowish. N.Z.

microphylla. New Zealand bur. Growing in large patches, but scarcely 3 in. high. Leaves, greenish, bronzy or slightly silky, but not bluish-gray. Flowers crimson in prickly heads, the spines red. N.Z.

ACALYPHA (a-ka-lee'fa, also a-ka-ly'fa). A very large genus of mostly tropical shrubs of the spurge family; a few weedy herbs in temperate regions. The hort. species are greenhouse plants or used for bedding or even hedges in zone* 9 and, sometimes, in zones 7 and 8. Leaves alternate, usually long-stalked. Flowers imperfect,* very minute, but crowded in a dense finger-thick, often bracted* cluster, hence often very showy. Fruit a 2-valved capsule.* (*Acalypha* was applied by Hippocrates to a nettle, but adopted by Linnaeus for these plants.)

As greenhouse plants grow in a warm house in potting mixture* 4. Outdoors (in zone* 8) they should be protected from occasional frosts. Propagated by cuttings in the autumn taken from bedded plants or from those in the greenhouse, over mild bottom-heat.* Pots of any of the species may be plunged outdoors in the north for summer show, but all are tender and must be in the greenhouse before frost. *A. hispida* is a popular decorative plant for the conservatory, its long tassels of reddish-purple flowers being very striking.

godseffiana. Dense bushy shrub, grown mostly for its cream-margined, rather short-stalked leaves which are ovalish, but heart-shaped at the base and coarsely toothed. Flower spike greenish, half hidden by the leaves. New Guinea. By some considered only as a variety of *A. wilkesiana*.

hispida. Chenille plant. The leading hort. species, much cultivated for its long, drooping, reddish-purple spikes. These are three times as long as the leaves, which are green, broadly oval, about 6 in. long, and hairy-veined. East Indies. There is a variety with branched spikes, and another, more rare, with white spikes.

wilkesiana. Copper-leaf. Grown for its bronzy-green, usually red-mottled foliage. Leaves elliptic or oval, about 6 in. long, in some varieties handsomely mottled with green, white, yellow, brown or orange. Flower spike thinner than in *hispida*, reddish, and scarcely 8 in. long. Pacific Islands. Much planted in the far South for its extremely showy foliage.

ACANTHACEAE (a-kan-thā'see-e). The acanthus family comprises some 175 genera and nearly 2000 species, all but a handful tropical. Most of them are herbs, but there are some shrubs and vines. Leaves opposite,* simple, without stipules.* Flowers nearly always irregular, either 1-lipped or 2-lipped and generally crowded in a leafy cluster of some sort, often a spike. In some genera (*Pseuderanthemum*, *Odontonema*, *Barleria*, and *Crossandra*) the flowers are nearly regular. Fruit a 2-celled capsule, often splitting elastically.

There are about a score of hort. genera, some of wide use in the garden or greenhouse because of showy flowers or bracts or colored foliage. Besides those mentioned above *see also*: ACANTHUS, APHELANDRA, BELOPERONE, FITTONIA, GRAPTOPHYLLUM, HEMIGRAPHIS, PERISTROPHE, RUELLIA, SCHAUERIA, and STROBILANTHES, most of which are herbs or low shrubs, nearly all greenhouse plants in the north. *Thunbergia* comprises mostly twining vines, while among the showiest of the family are *Eranthemum*, *Jacobinia*, *Justicia*, *Pachystachys*, and *Sanchezia*.

Technical flower characters: Stamens 2, or 4, in the latter case in two pairs. Ovary superior,* its long, very slender style usually persistent, even after the corolla has fallen.

Acanthium. Pre-Linnaean* name for the Scotch thistle (*Onopordon Acanthium*).

ACANTHOCEREUS (a-kan-tho-see'ree-us). Little-known trailing or climbing cacti with 3-angled stems, no leaves, and many spines borne at woolly cushion-like depressions. Flowers night-blooming, large, and funnel-shaped. Fruit a berry, which is sometimes spiny. (Named from the Greek for thorn and the genus *Cereus*.)

Grown outdoors in Fla. and Tex. As a greenhouse plant use potting mixture* 6, and a cool house. See CACTI.

pentagonus. Stems sometimes 20 ft. long and rooting at the tips, often half erect without support. Spines about 1½ in. long, usually 4–6 in a cluster. Flowers about 7 in. long, greenish-white and not so attractive as several other night-blooming species of cacti. Berry red. Fla. and Tex. and perhaps to the Argentine.

acanthocoma, -us, -um (a-kan-tho-ko'ma). With spiny hairs.

ACANTHOLIMON (a-kan-tho-lee'mon). Prickly thrift. Low evergreen perennial herbs, family Plumbaginaceae, with prickly or sharp-pointed, densely crowded and rigid leaves. Flowers small, crowded in one-sided racemes* or in a spike, pink or purple (in

---

* Special articles on the subjects indicated by an asterisk (*) will be found at the words so marked.

those below), the tiny flowers usually partly hidden by the many bracts. (Name from the Greek for spine, and limon, the sea lavender.)

Of the 90 species, all from the eastern Mediterranean region, only a handful are in cultivation and only those below are at all common in America. They are chiefly rock garden plants needing open sun, light and sandy soil and are slow growing. Propagation in late summer by cuttings wintered in a frost-protected cold frame, or by layering.* For related and more widely cultivated plants see ARMERIA and LIMONIUM.

glumaceum. Not over 6 in. high, its tufts of slender leaves making a considerable cushion. From this arises the stalk of the flower cluster, which is a one-sided raceme of rose-colored flowers. Summer. Can be grown, also, in the open border.

venustum. About 5 in. high. Leaves rather spiny, bluish-green, and in open rosettes. Flowers rose-pink, in relatively long-stalked dense spikes. Summer. A rock garden species doing best in sandy or gritty soil with perfect drainage.

ACANTHOPANAX (a-kan-tho-pay'nax). A genus of Asiatic shrubs or trees of the ginseng family, having 20 species of which only the following are of hort. significance in America. Leaves compound* in the first and last species, but simple* in A. ricinifolius. Flowers small, imperfect,* greenish-white, in small umbels,* but these sometimes grouped in a large, much-branched cluster. Fruit a black berry. (Named from the Greek for spine and the genus Panax.)

Acanthopanax is chiefly grown for the very handsome foliage. They make striking accents in a shrub border and fine specimen or lawn plants. They have no special soil requirements and are relatively free of pests. Propagation by seeds which should be stratified, or by root cuttings over bottom-heat.

henryi. A shrub 7–9 ft. high, with stiff, slightly recurved prickles. Leaves compound, the 5 nearly stalkless leaflets ovalish, rough to the touch, 1½–2½ in. long. Flowers minute, greenish, crowded in ball-like clusters, 1–1½ in. in diameter, either terminal or from the leaf-joints. China. Aug.–Sept. Hardy from zone* 3 southward.

pentaphyllus. A common name in the trade, but the plant is A. sieboldianus.

ricinifolius. A medium-sized tree with stout, prickly branches. Leaves nearly round in general outline, often a foot or more wide, and with 5–7 lobes, its stalk nearly 2 ft. long. Flowers whitish in small umbels,* but these grouped in a compound terminal cluster that is 15–18 in. wide. Berries about ⅓ in. in diameter. Jap. Summer. Doubtfully hardy in zone* 3, surely hardy from zone* 4 southward. Called by some Kalopanax pictus.

sieboldianus. A shrub usually not over 9 ft. high, usually without prickles. Leaves compound,* the 5–7 leaflets nearly stalkless, and generally wedge-shaped, and arranged fan-fashion. The general leafstalk is about 4 in. long. Flowers greenish-white in solitary, long-stalked umbels.* Berries about ½ in. in diameter. Jap. Summer. Zone* 4 southward. A good plant for smoky places. Some consider that the correct name for this is A. pentaphyllus.

ACANTHUS (a-kan'thus). A genus of perennial herbs, family Acanthaceae, comprising possibly 20 species, only the following of much hort. importance here. Leaves large, much cut, the segments or large teeth almost prickly, somewhat thistle-like. Flowers irregular,* one-lipped, in longish, erect spikes. Fruit a 4-seeded capsule. (Acanthus is Greek for thorn.)

Acanthus needs open sunshine, rich soil, and will not stand much water, especially in autumn and winter. It should be mulched from zone* 3 northward, in winter. Propagation by division* in spring.

mollis. Bear's-breech. A striking plant for the border, upright, its mostly basal leaves about 2 ft. long and half as wide, distinctly hairy on the upper surface. Flower spike about 1½–2 ft. long, the white, lilac, or rose-colored flowers with tiny bracts beneath. Southern Eu. Aug. There is a broader-leaved variety (**latifolius**), taller, and hardier.

ACANTHUS FAMILY = Acanthaceae.

ACAULESCENT. Apparently stemless, actually with the stem below ground. See CAULESCENT.

acaulis, -e (a-call'is). Acaulescent.

ACCLIMATION. The natural process by which plants come to tolerate a definite climate. It differs from acclimatization (which see at HARDINESS) because the latter involves the activities of man.

ACCLIMATIZATION. See HARDINESS.

ACEAE (ã'see-e). A suffix found at the end of the name of most plant families signifying belonging to. Thus to the genus Rosa is added aceae, which then becomes Rosaceae, or the rose family. Aceae is the almost universal termination for plant family names, but there are exceptions like Umbelliferae, Labiatae, Gramineae, Leguminosae, and Compositae.

ACER. See MAPLE.

ACERACEAE (a-sir-ã'see-e). The maple family. The only genus here is the maple. See that entry for the characters of the Aceraceae.

acerifolia, -us, -um (a-sir-ee-fõ'lee-a). Having maple-like leaves.

Acetosa. Pre-Linnaean* name for the common sorrel (Rumex Acetosa).

Acetosella. Pre-Linnaean* name for several plants with acid foliage, especially the sorrel and wood sorrel.

ACHENE (a-keen'). A dry, one-seeded fruit that does not split; typical examples being the fruit of the buttercup and the "seeds" on the surface of a strawberry (which see).

ACHILLEA (a-kil-lee'a). Yarrow. A large genus of perennial herbs, family Compositae, mostly from the north temperate zone and a few grown for their white, pink, or yellow flowers. Leaves toothed or parted or divided, and in some species finely dissected, often aromatic when crushed. Flower heads small, but usually numerous, in often flat-topped clusters. Of the 80

* Special articles on the subjects indicated by an asterisk (*) will be found at the words so marked.

species only the following are of any hort. importance. (Named for Achilles who is supposed to have used some species to heal his wounds.)

Yarrow is easy to grow in ordinary garden soil and the taller species are attractive in the border. Low ones, like *A. clavennae, ageratifolia, nana,* and *tomentosa* are chiefly rock garden* plants. Propagation, which is simple, is by root division in spring or autumn. Many species are rank growers and will crowd out more delicate plants. One (*see* A. PTARMICA below) is perhaps the most widely grown garden plant. In places too sandy or too dry for lawn grasses, some of the low, perennial achilleas make reasonably acceptable lawns, esp. in Calif. For others *see* Grass Substitutes at LAWN.

ageratifolia. Silvery-leaved, tufted, rock garden plant, scarcely 6 in. tall. Leaves cut feather-fashion, the margins crimped. Flowers white. Greece. The variety **Aizoon** (often sold as *Anthemis Aizoon*) has nearly uncut leaves. Summer. *See* ROCK GARDEN for cult.

Ageratum. Sweet yarrow. A border plant that reaches 1–2 ft. high. Leaves merely toothed, crowded in small clusters. Flowers yellow, the clusters slightly dome-shaped. Eu. Summer.

argentea = *A. clavennae.*

clavennae. A rock garden, tufted,* perennial herb with hoary, much dissected leaves. Flower heads ½–¾ in. in diameter, compact, the 7–18 rays* white. Spring–summer. Eu.

clypeolata. A mat-forming perennial, resembling *A. Millefolium,* the hoary leaves deeply dissected. Flower heads yellow, in a concave cluster, these arranged in compound clusters (corymbs*). Greece. Summer.

filipendulina. A stout border plant frequently reaching 4 ft. high, the stems hairy and slightly furrowed. Leaves 6–7 in. long, densely clothing the stem, finely dissected. Flowers yellow, showy. Eurasia. Summer.

Millefolium. Common yarrow, called also milfoil. Stem leafy, scarcely 2 ft. high. Leaves finely dissected. Flowers white. Rarely cult. and in fact a weed (*see* list at WEEDS). The *var.* **roseum,** the rosy milfoil, is grown, however, for its red or pink, attractive flower clusters. Eurasian. July.

nana. A European rock garden plant, scarcely 5 in. high. Leaves white-woolly, cut feather-fashion, distinctly aromatic. Flowers white. June.

Ptarmica. Sneezewort. This, the parent form of widely planted garden varieties, is not very commonly grown. It is a stout herb 1–2 ft. high. Leaves lance-shaped, toothed. Flower heads white, not double, in loose open clusters. North temperate zone. Summer. Its double-flowered varieties, especially The Pearl and Boule de Neige, are very old favorites, free bloomers during most of the summer, and are useful both in the border and for cutting, particularly the former.

taygetea. A border perennial, 15–20 in. high, with handsome silvery foliage. Leaves much cut, 6–8 in. long, the small segments toothed, rather blunt. Flower heads pale yellow, about 3 in. wide, long-lasting and good for cutting. June–Sept. A good plant for dry, sunny places. Not the true *A. taygetea* of the botanists, and possibly of hort. origin.

tomentosa. A rock garden plant from the north temperate zone with green but woolly, cut leaves and yellow flowers. It needs a sandy

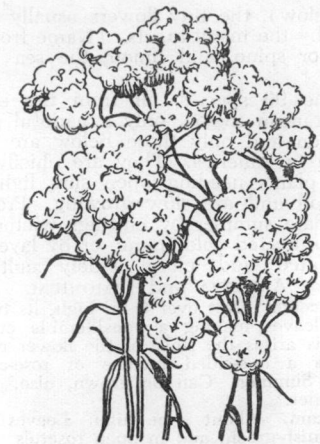

Sneezewort (*Achillea Ptarmica*), a double-flowered form of a hardy perennial, useful for dry or even sandy sites; summer-blooming and white.

soil and will bloom from June to Sept. Moonlight is an excellent hort. var.

umbellata. Resembling *A. clavennae,* but lower and best grown in the rock garden. Foliage silvery, the white flower heads in small clusters (umbels*). Greece. Summer.

ACHIMENES (a-kim′e-neez). Tropical American herbs, family Gesneriaceae, grown either in pots or hanging baskets for their showy gloxinia-like flowers. Of the 25 known species only two are commonly cult. and they have been so much hybridized that those below are more likely to represent the sorts in cultivation than the species themselves. Roots or rootstocks more or less tuberous or scaly. Leaves opposite* or in a whorl,* usually tinted on the lower side, always more or less toothed. Flowers in the leaf axils,* tubular, the tube curved, and with a spreading, somewhat irregular limb.* Fruit a 2-valved capsule. (From the Greek implying that the plants suffer from cold, which they do.)

Achimenes should be grown in the cool greenhouse in potting mixture* 4. When through flowering the tuberous root or rootstock should be taken from the pot, stored in clean sand, without watering, at a temperature of about 45°. In March or April re-pot, put in a greenhouse with a temperature of about 60°. Do not plant them deeply as they are shallow rooted. Give plenty of drainage. Easily propagated by division of the rhizome, or by cuttings in summer in a moist greenhouse, or by planting partly dried root scales. Rhizomes can also be purchased from seedsmen. Summer-flowering.

grandiflora. Stem erect, more or less covered with stiff hairs. Leaves ovalish, a little inequilateral at the base, reddish on the under side, about 3 in. long. Flowers numerous, often more than 1 in an axil,* large and showy, bright red-purple. Mexico and Central America. Summer.

---

* Special articles on the subjects indicated by an asterisk (*) will be found at the words so marked.

longiflora. Stems 4–12 in. long. Leaves oval or oval-oblong, often in whorls* of 3 or 4, usually tinted on the lower side. Flower usually one in each axil, salver-shaped, with a long curving tube, violet-blue (or white in a variety). Mexico to Panama.

Among the named hort. forms of *Achimenes,* not certainly referable to any particular species, are: Dainty Queen (white and pink-eyed), Galatea (deep lavender), Purple King (purple), Supreme (lavender with whitish center), Patens (purple), Big Boy Blue (blue), Margarita (white), Miniata (red), and many others. Most of them are grown outdoors in the warmer parts of the Gulf Coast.

ACHIOTE = *Bixa Orellana.*

ACHRAS (ak'ras). A small genus of tropical American trees, family Sapotaceae, of no interest except for the marmalade plum which can only be grown outdoors in zone* 9. It is grown in the tropics for its fruit, rarely under glass in a warm greenhouse northward. (*Achras* is from Greek for the pear, in allusion to the fruit of the marmalade plum.) The tree is sometimes known as *Calocarpum* and the name *Achras* has also been applied to the sapodilla (*see* SAPOTA).

Zapota. Marmalade plum, called also sapote. A tree up to 60 ft. Leaves without teeth, up to 15 in. long by 4 in. wide, usually clustered at the ends of the twigs. Flowers small, white, nearly stalkless, appearing on the old wood in the axils* of the fallen leaves. Fruit russet, about 5 in. long, somewhat pear-shaped, with thick skin and firm, spicy, reddish flesh. Central America. The tree is also, incorrectly, known as *Lucuma mammosa.* It is sometimes called mamey, but *see,* in this connection, MAMMEA.

ACHYRANTHES. *See* IRESINE.

ACHYRODES = *Lamarckia.*

acida, -us, -um (as'i-da). Tart or acid.

ACID AND ALKALI SOILS. Acidity and alkalinity of soils come from two sources. The first, and probably most important, is the chemical nature of the rock from which the mineral soil is derived. In many specialized habitats, however, such as a bog, or humus* on the forest-floor, the chief source of acidity is the partial or complete decomposition of vegetation. Alkalinity, from the hort. standpoint, is confined to the comparatively limited areas of natural limestone, the salt marshes, and the alkali deserts of the West.

Much has been written on the acidity of soils and the "preference" of certain plants for soils of a definite degree of acidity. Technically, there may be no such preference. Much more accurately we can say that plants are acid-tolerant or alkali-tolerant, which implies that they grow in such places not because they prefer them but because they must.

From the practical gardening standpoint all we need to do is to provide acid-tolerant plants with the degree of acidity in which they mostly grow. This acidity is pretty well known for most of the plants where it is at all significant. But the bog-gardener, or wild-gardener, and often the rock-gardener does need a method of testing his soil to determine with reasonable accuracy whether his site meets these conditions.

SOIL ACIDITY AND ALKALINITY

Of the many and often elaborate methods of determining the degree of soil acidity and alkalinity only one will be described here — the simplest and most convenient. What lies behind the reactions described hereafter belongs to the realm of chemistry — technical and perhaps quite unnecessary information for the gardener. The terms, however, and the nearly universal scale used in measuring acidity have been derived from the soil chemists and it will be necessary to define a few of them and explain what their significance may be.

Water, the common solvent of all soils, is H_2O. That is as near truth as most of us desire, but it is not exact truth, for, while the molecules of hydrogen and oxygen in water are mostly associated or combined with each other, they are not completely so. A small proportion are completely dissociated into positive, hydrogen ions and negative, hydroxyl ions. The latter is characteristic of alkalies, and the hydrogen ions of acids. If the number of hydrogen ions and hydroxyl ions were the same, water, or soil solutions, would be neither acid nor alkaline but neutral — as in distilled water.

If the water, or soil solution, or whatever you are testing, were acid, the hydrogen ions would be more numerous, while the hydroxl ions would, contrariwise, be in the ascendant in alkali solutions. The amount of the divergence from neutral (neither acid nor alkaline) is thus commonly called the hydrogen ion concentration and the universal symbol for it, used here, is pH.

Chemists have devised a scale for measuring the acidity and alkalinity of soils based upon their hydrogen ion concentration or pH value as it is called. It utilizes (in the method below) the known color reaction of certain pH values for certain chemical indicators. Using this method does not need any greater knowledge of what lies behind such tests than most of us know exactly what is behind the figures on a radio dial or a barometer. In other words, we now have a simple scale for measuring acidity and alkalinity, which any gardener can use.

PRACTICAL APPLICATION

This scale is numbered from 4 to 9 which includes the whole range of soil in which plants can grow — 4 being the acid extremity of the scale and 9 the alkaline limits. It is divided into the following intervals:

pH value	4.0	5.0	6.0
	Very acid	Acid	Slightly acid
pH value	7.0	8.0	9.0
	Neutral (neither acid nor alkaline)	Alkaline	Strongly alkaline

---

* Special articles on the subjects indicated by an asterisk (*) will be found at the words so marked.

These intervals may be split into minute subdivisions, and usually are in many industrial applications, but for the gardener these are all we need, and of them 9.0 is confined only to such unhappy hort. sites as the alkali deserts.

Before making a test to determine what the degree of acidity may be, it will be worth while, perhaps even imperative, to see what ordinary soils contain, as to their acidity. For convenience of reference, they are listed below, together with a few special terms not elsewhere used in his book, as being unnecessary for the gardener, but frequently appearing in some publications.

Acid and Alkali Soil Types

pH 4
VERY ACID. Found only in peat bogs covered with sphagnum moss and in the duff under coniferous trees. No lime is found in such places. Called, also, SUPERACID.

pH 5
ACID. Peaty upland soils, rotted wood, some pine-barren sands, and fields or gardens heavily fertilized and scarcely ever limed. Called, also, MEDIACID.

pH 6
SLIGHTLY ACID. Ordinary garden soils in a non-limestone region, including those without much manure and scarcely ever limed. Called MINIMACID.

pH 7
NEUTRAL. Includes ordinary garden soils, especially where they have been limed occasionally, and even some more acid types that have been limed; also most compost, rotted manure, black leaf-mold, etc.

pH 8
ALKALINE. Salt marshes, limestone soils or heavily limed soils. Called, also, MINIMALKALINE.

To the last three categories the general term of CIRCUMNEUTRAL has also been applied.

For all practical purposes 6 and 7 do not concern the gardener because they comprise between them practically all normal garden soils. And most garden plants are very tolerant as to variations within the range of pH 6 and 7. In other words, one scarcely needs to consider by far the most widely occurring of pH values, nor the plants that grow in such places, insofar as their acidity or alkalinity requirements are concerned.

It is otherwise with pH 4.0 to 5.0. This degree of acidity appears to be of such significance that a list of the commonly cultivated plants characteristic of it is recorded below.

Some Acid Soil Plants
(Comprises only those entered in the ENCYCLOPEDIA)
Plants with tolerances of pH 4–5

Abies (see FIR)
Aletris
Alnus incana (see ALDER)
Andromeda (all species)
Androsace (all species)
Anemone nemorosa

Arctostaphylos Uva-ursi
Arenaria groenlandica
Arethusa bulbosa
Arnica montana
Azalea (all species)
Calla palustris
Calopogon pulchellus
Camellia (all species)
Chamaecyparis thyoides
Clethra alnifolia
Clintonia
Coptis trifolia
Corema conradi
Cornus canadensis
Cranberry
Cypripedium (all species)
Darlingtonia californica
Dionaea muscipula
Drosera (all species)
Empetrum nigrum
Epigaea (see TRAILING ARBUTUS)
Erica (all species)
Gardenia (all species)
Habenaria (all species)
Helonias
Heuchera americana
Ilex Aquifolium (see HOLLY)
Ilex opaca (see HOLLY)
Kalmia (all species)
Leiophyllum buxifolium
Ledum (all species)
Linnaea
Lithodora diffusa
Loiseleuria
Lygodium palmatum
Lyonia
Magnolia virginiana
Menziesia pilosa
Phyllodoce
Pinus (all species, see PINE)
Pogonia
Polygala paucifolia
Polygala Senega
Polypodium aureum
Potentilla tridentata
Rhexia
Rhododendron (all species)
Sarracenia (see PITCHER-PLANT)
Sorbus americana (see MOUNTAIN-ASH)
Stenanthium
Streptopus
Vaccinium (for cult. see BLUEBERRY)
Viburnum acerifolium
Xerophyllum
Zantedeschia (see CALLA LILY)

Most of the above are wild garden or bog plants. Very few vegetables or ordinary garden flowers are so particular about the acidity of their soils, so long as it comes within the range of pH 6, 7 or 8. A few crops, however, seem to need special conditions, or at least do better when provided with them. The most important and their apparent pH tolerances are the following:

	pH
Aleurites fordi (see TUNG-OIL TREE)	5–6
Citrullus vulgaris (see WATERMELON)	5–6
Nicotiana Tabacum (tobacco)	5–6
Solanum tuberosum (potato)	5–6
Spinacia oleracea (spinach)	6–8 (Does not do well if pH is below 6.)

For the gardener it is often interesting and may be important to know what the pH of some common garden materials may be. Here is a list:

	pH
Lime	12.0
Bone meal	10.0
Ashes	9.0–10.0
Most city water	8.0– 9.5
Nitrate of soda	9.0
Most animal manures	8.0
Rain water	6.5– 7.0
Tea leaves and coffee grounds	5.0
Cottonseed meal	4.5
Peat moss	4.0
Aluminum sulphate	3.2
Superphosphate (Sulphate of potash, magnesium sulphate, manganese sulphate)	2.0
Sulphur	1.2

* Special articles on the subjects indicated by an asterisk (*) will be found at the words so marked.

TESTING SOILS FOR ACIDITY

As mentioned above, certain chemical indicators give definite color reactions when mixed with soils of a certain degree of acidity. Upon this principle a simple porcelain plate has been devised with a small well at one end, a shallow trough through the center and a much smaller well at the opposite end. On each side of the central trough is a series of colored bands, standardized at exactly the intervals of the pH values from 4 to 9 (*see* above).

All that is done to make a test is to put a pinch of soil (with a spoon, *not* the fingers) in the larger well, and drop enough of the liquid indicator (a few spots) to puddle the pinch of soil. Allow the puddle to stand for 2 or 3 minutes and then gently incline the plate so that the indicator will trickle through the central trough to the smaller well. Its color can then be exactly compared with the colored band that nearest matches it, and from that matching you can read the pH value, for the figures for these are put alongside of each of the color bands.

The above device, known as the Hellige Soil Tester, while the simplest and most direct, is by no means the only one. Others have several different indicators, some require distilled water in which the soil sample must be soaked, and there are a few (much more accurate) electrical devices for determining soil acidity. But, for the practical gardener, the simplicity and directness of the Hellige method will be all he needs.

HOW TO INCREASE OR MAINTAIN SOIL ACIDITY OR ALKALINITY

Having made the test by this method and knowing the acid or alkali requirement of your plants, there remains still one more problem. Is it practicable to make a site more acid or more alkaline? In other words, can we change the soil environment to suit the plants we wish to grow, or should we limit our plantings to existing conditions?

On anything like a large scale there is no doubt that the latter alternative is the correct one, and that it is foolish attempting to make over a large tract. The only exception is the common one of increasing the alkalinity of fields, lawns or garden soil by the periodical addition of lime. This is both practical and effective. (For details, *see* LIME.)

Assuming that your soil now tests pH 6 and you need to make it more acid, use aluminum sulphate at the following rates, depending on the physical texture of your soil.

AMOUNT OF ALUMINUM SULPHATE
NEEDED FOR 1 SQ. YD.

	To make the soil pH 5	To make the soil pH 4
Sandy loam	¾ lb.	1 lb.
Good garden loam	1½ lb.	2 lbs.
Clay or silt soil	4 lbs.	6 lbs.

If you have an isolated plant or shrub that needs more acidity than occurs naturally, a good rule is to put a cupful of aluminum sulphate around the plant and stir it into the soil. Rainfall will leach it down to the roots, and do not water it unless your tap water is neutral or slightly acid. The effects will not be noticeable for a fortnight. If improved leaf color and more vigorous growth are not evidenced within three weeks, the dose of aluminum sulphate should be repeated. It should be remembered that aluminum sulphate has nothing to do with fertility and manure should be used in addition. Do not use commercial fertilizers on these acid-tolerant plants.

Fortunately for the gardener, most cultivated plants are fairly tolerant of pH values from 6 to pH 7 or nearly pH 8. There are some, however, which need the treatment advocated above, or some modification of it, as listed above.

Sulphur or tannic acid may also be used to make neutral or alkaline soils more acid. If sulphur is used it should be applied at ½ the rate given above for aluminum sulphate. Tannic acid can be applied at the rate of one part of commercial tannic acid to 50 parts of water. Neither has any advantage over aluminum sulphate. The use of Epsom salts for increasing acidity has nothing against it except the price. It is a compound consisting of magnesium sulphate, the sulphur being the only effective ingredient.

ACIDANTHERA (as-i-dan'the-ra). Bulbous African herbs of the iris family. Of the 20 species only the following is much grown here. Its summer-blooming, long-tubed flowers are handsome, somewhat resembling gladiolus. Leaves sword-shaped. Flowers in a long, loose, rather leafy spike, the corolla-tube slightly dilated toward the top. Fruit an oblong capsule. (Named from the Greek for a cusp and anther, in allusion to the cusp-like anthers of some species.)

Acidanthera (which is tender) should be treated exactly like gladiolus. Propagation by use of the many cormels* that start about the old corm.*

bicolor. The brownish corm* is about an inch in diameter. Stem unbranched, about 18 in. long. Leaves few, usually only one or two. Spike few-flowered, its leafy sheaths about 3 in. long. Flowers fragrant, cream-white outside, splashed chocolate-brown inside, the slender tube about 4 in. long. Tropical Af. Summer. **murieliae** = *Gladiolus murieliae.*

ACID LEMON. See LEMON.

ACID LIME. See LIME.

acidosa, -us, -um (as-i-do'sa). Acid or bitter.

ACID SOIL PLANTS. *See* the list of them at ACID AND ALKALI SOILS.

acinacifolia, -us, -um (as-i-nas-i-fō'li-a). With scimitar-shaped leaves.

ACOELORRAPHE = *Paurotis.*

ACOKANTHERA (ak-o-kan'the-ra). A genus of African, very poisonous (not by con-

* Special articles on the subjects indicated by an asterisk (*) will be found at the words so marked.

tact) shrubs and trees, family Apocynaceae, one of which is a greenhouse plant with fragrant, whitish-pink flowers. Leaves opposite,° thick, leathery and without teeth. Flowers in small stalkless cymes,° tubular, the limb° slightly twisted to the left. Fruit a berry. (Name from Greek for pointed anthers.) Related, but not hort. species, furnish deadly arrow poisons.

Should be grown in warm greenhouse in potting mixture° 4. Propagation by cuttings in spring over bottom-heat.° The plant is a rich feeder.

spectabilis. Shrub to 10 ft. but often kept as a much smaller pot plant. Leaves oblongish, about 4 in. long, narrowed at the base into a thick leafstalk. Flowers about 1 in. long. Berry ellipsoid about 1 in. long, blackish-purple. Tropical Af. Spring. Also called *Carissa Acokanthera*.

ACONITE. A plant of the genus *Aconitum,* or the sedative derived from them. *See* Monkshood.

aconitifolia, -us, -um (a-ko-ny-tee-fo′li-a). With leaves like a monkshood (*Aconitum*).

ACONITUM. *See* Monkshood.

ACORN. The fruit of an oak (which see).

ACORUS (ak′or-us). Marsh herbs of the arum family, hardy all over the United States and useful only in similar sites. Leaves long, parallel-sided, thickish, but otherwise grasslike, from a thick stout rootstock. Flowers greenish, minute, crowded on a stalkless spadix° that arises from a leaf-like sheath near the end of the stalk. Fruit berry-like, stalkless on the leaf-like stem. (*Acorus* is the classical name of the sweet flag.)

Suitable for bogs, water-sides or marshes, and of the easiest culture. Propagated by division of the creeping rootstock almost at any season. For uses *see* Herb Gardening.

Calamus. Sweet flag. Stout perennial herb, its aromatic rootstock yielding calamus-root. Leaves usually about 2 ft. high, but sometimes twice this in rich soil. Spadix° about 2 in. long, finger-like. Throughout the north temperate zone. A yellow-striped form (*var.* **variegatus**) is more common in cultivation than the typical plant, but unknown wild.

gramineus. Tufted and half the height of the sweet flag, the leaves scarcely ¹⁄₁₀ in. wide. Spadix° 2–3½ in. long. Summer. Jap. *var.* **pusillus** is scarcely 4 in. high, and useful in an aquarium.

ACRE. The common square measure for land. For its exact dimensions *see* Weights and Measures 1. For the number of plants to an acre *see* Garden Tables I.

acris, -e (ak′ris). Sharp.

ACROCLINIUM. *See* Helipterum.

ACROCOMIA (a-kro-ko′mi-a). Very spiny-trunked feather palms, all tropical American, and suitable for outdoor cultivation only in zone° 9 and sheltered parts of zone° 8. Trunk often swollen about halfway up. Leaves pinnate,° the leaflets numerous, often drooping. Flower clusters appearing from amongst the dense crown of leaves, shiny-sheathed, branched and drooping. Fruit

round, thick-skinned. (From Greek for sharp and hair.)

Prefers moist sandy soil. The species below is a handsome palm suitable for lawn specimens but too spiny for street planting.

Totai. This is also the native name for it in Paraguay and the Argentine where it frequently reaches a height of 40 ft. Trunk swollen, its long blackish spines borne in continuous bands around the trunk. Leaves green both sides, the leaflets narrow and rather sharp-pointed. Leaf-stalk felty and somewhat prickly. Fruit about ¾ in. in diameter.

acrostichoides (a-kros-ti-koy′deez; but *see* Oïdes). Resembling a fern of the genus *Acrostichum,* which is scarcely in cultivation.

ACROSTICHUM. *See* Elaphoglossum crinitum.

ACTAEA (ak-tee′a). The baneberries are perennial herbs of the buttercup family, somewhat sparsely scattered over the north temperate zone. Leaves twice- or thrice-compound,° the ultimate leaflets sharply cleft and toothed. Flowers numerous, white, in thick terminal clusters. Fruit a red or white berry. (*Actaea* is the classical name of the elder, but adopted by Linnaeus for the baneberries.)

Useful and attractive herbs for the wild garden, these plants need a woods soil, but not a strongly acid one, and grow best in partial shade. Easily increased by root division in the early spring. The genus has received much attention from systematic botanists, and the names for the red and white baneberry below, while well known to gardeners, are possibly interpreted otherwise by some.

alba. White baneberry, also called white cohosh. Flowers white, in June. Fruit a white, but black-tipped, glistening, poisonous berry on thick stalklets. Common in rich woods throughout eastern N.A.

rubra. Red baneberry, also called red cohosh. Similar to the above but the leaflets thinner, and the flower cluster not quite so elongate. Fruit a cherry-red, poisonous berry on very slender stalklets. Flowers about a week earlier than *A. alba,* and is rarer in the wild state. More common northward.

ACTINEA (ak-tin′e-a). A genus of 15 species of New World, mostly perennial, herbs of the daisy family, usually with resinous-dotted, aromatic foliage. Leaves basal in the first species but borne on the stem in the second. Flower heads radiate, rather showy, usually solitary. (*Actinea* is from the Greek for ray, in allusion to the showy ray flowers.) Also known as *Actinella.*

Actineas are of easy culture in the rock garden or open border, but, as in many western plants, they do not like winter slush at their crown.°

acaulis. Practically stemless, the rosette of basal leaves narrowly oblong, ashy when young, ultimately green, 1–3 in long. Flower heads solitary, the stalk about 6 in. high, the yellow head of 3-toothed rays. Central N.A. May–July. Also known as *A. herbacea.*

grandiflora. About twice the height of *A.*

° Special articles on the subjects indicated by an asterisk (°) will be found at the words so marked.

acaulis, and the densely woolly leaves much cut into fine segments, but almost uncut at the top of the plant. Flower heads nearly 3 in. wide, yellow. Summer. Rocky Mts.

ACTINELLA = *Actinea.*

ACTINIDIA (ak-ti-nid′i-a). A group of 40 species of Asiatic woody vines, family Dilleniaceae, grown for their handsome foliage and ability to cover completely arbors and trellises. They have alternate simple leaves, the stalk of which covers the succeeding winter bud. Leaf-margins toothed. Flowers inconspicuous, cup-shaped, the male and the female often on different plants, or sometimes polygamous (*see* HERMAPHRODITE). Petals 5. Fruit a many-seeded berry. (From Greek for ray, in allusion to the radiating styles.) Some consider the genus as belonging to the family Actinidiaceae; not here maintained.

They may be grown in ordinary garden soil, and climb rather quickly, either in full sun or part shade. Propagation is easily provided for by spring-sown seeds, cuttings of partly ripened wood in summer or matured wood under glass in winter. Layering* is also effective. *See also* stem climbers at VINES.

arguta. Tara vine. A high-climbing, densely leafy, woody vine, its broadly oval leaves about 5 in. long, lustrously green, the stalks about 2 in. long, reddish. Flower cluster shorter than the leafstalk, usually of three brownish-white flowers that are about ¾ in. across. Fruit ellipsoid, about 1 in. long, yellowish, sweet, and edible. Jap. and eastern As. July. Hardy from zone* 4 (and possibly from 3) southward.

chinensis. Yangtao. Often 30 ft. long, its branches and twigs covered with shaggy hairs that are red in youth. Leaves nearly round, about 6 in. in diameter, heart-shaped at the base, green above, paler and felty beneath, the veins with red hairs. Flowers whitish, but ultimately yellowish, about 2 in. wide. Fruit nearly globular, about 2 in. in diameter, hairy, acid, but edible, not unlike a gooseberry in flavor. China. June. Perhaps the handsomest of the four but certainly hardy only from zone* 6 southward, and possibly in protected places in zone* 5.

Kolomikta. Kolomikta vine. Not so high-climbing, rarely over 10 ft., usually about 6 ft. high. Leaves (especially on the male plant) often white or pink-blotched, generally oblongish, about 5 in. long. Flowers white, about ¾ in. across. Fruit oblong or ovoid, about an inch long, greenish-yellow, sweet, and edible. Eastern As. May. Hardy usually from zone* 3 southward, certainly so from zone* 4.

polygama. Silver vine. Sometimes climbing to 15 ft., the silver vine is attractive to cats. Leaves (especially on the male plant) often splashed with silvery white or yellowish blotches, generally oval-oblong, about 6 in. long. Flowers white, about ¾ in. across and fragrant. Fruit ovoid, beaked, yellow, and edible. Eastern As. July. Hardy from zone* 3 southward. Male plants, which bear no fruit, have very attractive foliage.

ACTINOLEPIS CORONARIA = *Baeria coronaria.*

ACTINOPHLOEUS (ak-tin-o-flee′us). A small genus of Australasian feather palms grown outdoors only in zones* 8 and 9, and elsewhere as tubbed specimens in the greenhouse. Leaves pinnate,* the leaflets more or less fringed, or jagged, or cut off obliquely at the tip. Flowers greenish, small, in a branched cluster that appears just below the crown of leaves. Fruit more or less cylindric, blunt-nosed, scarcely ¾ in. long. (From Greek for ray and reed, perhaps because of the ringed stems.)

Both the species below are slender graceful palms, usually suckering and sending up a number of thin prominently ringed stems. The first is usually a bushy plant, the second more graceful and, in its young state, a common pot plant. In the greenhouse grow both sorts in potting mixture* 4, feed well and provide plenty of water. *A. macarthuri* does well outdoors in southern Fla.

macarthuri. Cluster palm. Trunks greenish, scarcely more than 10 ft. high. Leaves about 2½ ft. long, paler beneath than above, the leaflets numerous (often over 36), about 8 in. long, always obliquely cut or jagged at the top. Fruit furrowed or wrinkled in drying. Aust. Identity still in doubt in many collections, as the plant is often offered as *Ptychosperma macarthuri* and *Kentia macarthuri.*

sanderianus. Resembling *A. macarthuri,* but more slender, especially its leaflets, some of which are long and narrow. Aust. Chiefly grown as a pot plant for its graceful foliage, often under the name of *Kentia sanderiana.*

actinophylla, -us, -um (ak-tin-o-fill′a). With ray-like leaves or with leaves arranged in ray-like clusters, as in *Schefflera actinophylla.*

aculeata, -us, -um (a-kew-le-ā′ta). Prickly.

acuminata, -us, -um (a-kew-mi-nā′ta). *See* ACUMINATE.

ACUMINATE. Ending in a sharp, but distinctly tapering point. *See* ACUTE.

acuminatifolia, -us, -um (a-kew-mi-na-ti-fō′li-a). With acuminate leaves.

acuta, -us, -um (a-kew′ta). *See* ACUTE.

acutangula, -us, -um (a-kew-tang′u-la). Sharply angled.

ACUTE. Ending in a sharp, but not a tapering, point. *See* ACUMINATE.

acutifolia, -us, -um (a-kew-ti-fō′li-a). Sharp-leaved.

acutiloba, -us, -um (a-kew-ti-lō′ba). With sharp-pointed lobes.

ADAM-AND-EVE. *See* APLECTRUM HYEMALE (an orchid), and ERYTHRONIUM GRANDIFLORUM (a western dogtooth violet).

ADAM'S-APPLE = *Tabernaemontana coronaria.*

ADAM'S-NEEDLE = *Yucca filamentosa.*

ADANSONIA (a-dan-sown′i-a). Huge tropical African trees, family Bombacaceae, grown as a curiosity only in zone* 9, rarely in the warm greenhouse. Frequently a shade tree in the tropics. Leaves compound,* palmate.* Flowers solitary, hanging on extraordinarily long stalks, from which, later, the huge fruit (known as monkey's-bread) also hangs.

---

* Special articles on the subjects indicated by an asterisk (*) will be found at the words so marked.

(Named for Michel Adanson, 1727–1806, French botanist.)

digitata. Baobab. A huge tree, the trunk sometimes 30 ft. in diameter in the wild state, much smaller in southern Fla. where it is sometimes grown. Leaflets usually 5, and about 5 in. long. Flowers white, nearly 6 in. across, the purple stamens very showy, soon withering. Fruit hard-shelled, white, about a foot long, the pulp mealy and acid. Tropical Af. July. The tree is leafless in the late spring and early summer.

ADDER'S-MOUTH = *Pogonia ophioglossoides.*

ADDER'S-TONGUE. See ERYTHRONIUM.

ADDER'S-TONGUE FAMILY = OPHIOGLOSSACEAE.

ADDER'S-TONGUE FERN = *Ophioglossum.*

ADDER'S VIOLET = *Goodyera pubescens.*

ADELIA = *Forestiera.*

ADENANTHERA (a-den-ăn'the-ra). A small genus of acacia-like trees of the pea family, all from the Old World tropics. The only hort. species is grown outdoors in zone* 9 or in greenhouses northward, for its feathery foliage and yellowish and white flowers. Leaves many times compound,* the leaflets very numerous and small. Flowers in spike-like clusters, some white, others yellowish, in the same cluster. Fruit a linear pod that coils up when ripe. Seeds (often called Circassian seeds) red, showy, and lens-shaped. (From *adeno,* glandular or sticky, and *anther,* in allusion to the glandular anthers.)

The only cultivated species is easily grown in ordinary garden soil in zone* 9. In the greenhouse use potting mixture* 4. Propagation by seeds that have been soaked in warm water.

pavonina. Barbados pride, called also red sandalwood, bear-tree, peacock-flower, and flower fence. A tall tree in the tropics but in cultivated specimens scarcely over 20 ft. Foliage very fine and feathery. Flower clusters in the axils.* Pod about 8 in. long, its seeds used for beadwork. Tropical Af. and As.

ADENOCARPUS (a-den-o-kar'pus). A horticulturally unimportant genus of low trees or shrubs of the pea family cultivated in southern Calif., mostly native in the Orient and the Canaries. Leaves compound,* with only 3 small leaflets. Flowers pea-like, yellow, in terminal clusters. Fruit a sticky, linear pod. (From *adeno,* glandular or sticky, and *carpus,* fruit, in allusion to the sticky pod.)

The species below is grown in open sunlight and sandy soil in southern Calif., rarely in greenhouses where it should have potting mixture* 3. Propagated by cuttings of green wood in the spring or by seeds, or layering.*

viscosus. A sticky-stemmed shrub scarcely over 3 ft. high. Leaflets nearly oblong, often folded. Flower cluster crowded, somewhat sticky. Teneriffe. Hardy outdoors only in zones* 8 and 9.

ADENOPHORA (a-den-off'o-ra). Ladybell. About a dozen species of perennial herbs mostly from eastern Asia, closely related to the bellflowers (*see* CAMPANULA), two species grown for their handsome blue flowers. It differs from *Campanula* only in technical characters, and its cultivation is also like that genus. (Named for the gland-bearing nectary.)

lilifolia. A Eurasian leafy herb 2–3 ft. high. Lower leaves roundish and stalked, the stem leaves longer and stalkless, toothed. Flowers pale blue, fragrant, about an inch long, rather broadly bell-shaped and in pyramid-shaped, terminal clusters. Summer.

potanini. Hairy-stemmed Chinese herb 2–3 ft. high, with oval-lance-shaped leaves that are either coarsely and remotely toothed or without any teeth. Flowers blue, about ¾ in. long, in racemes.* Summer.

adenophylla, -us, -um (a-den-off'il-la). Having sticky leaves.

ADENOSTOMA (a-de-nos'to-ma). A small group of chaparral shrubs of the rose family, common in southern Calif. and not much grown elsewhere. They have very small, evergreen, needle-shaped or heath-like leaves and small white flowers in a terminal truss. Petals 5. Fruit dry, partly enclosed by the calyx.* (From *adeno,* a gland, and *stoma,* mouth, in allusion to the glands on the calyx.)

While the species below will stand some frost, it does not thrive in the comparatively humid east. Suitable mostly for southern Calif. and regions like it. Prefers sandy soil and open sunlight. Propagation by cuttings of green wood in the spring or by seeds.

fasciculatum. Chamiso. As a native, up to 15 ft., in cultivation considerably less. Leaves scarcely ¼ in. long, densely crowded. Flowers very small, nearly stalkless in a dense terminal cluster that is about 3 in. long. Calif.

ADIANTUM (a-dee-an'tum). A very large genus of mostly tropical ferns, the maidenhairs, family Polypodiaceae. A few species reach the temperate zone, notably our common maidenhair (*A. pedatum*). Of the nearly 200 known species, nearly 40 are supposed to be in cultivation in America, but of these only the following are generally grown — some on a great scale as greenhouse favorites.

Stems nearly always polished black or purplish. In all those below, the fronds are twice- or thrice-compound* (simple-leaved species are known). The ultimate segments are characteristically fan-shaped or wedge-shaped in the wild species but often much altered in the horticultural forms. The outer margin is always slightly rolled and, in fertile forms, conceals the spore cases. The latter contains the spores which are the source of new plants (*see* the details at Spores and Reproduction in the article FERNS AND FERN GARDENING), unless the plants can be divided. (*Adiantum* is from the Greek not, and to wet, alluding to the water-shedding character of the leaflets.)

For the culture of the maidenhairs *see*

---

* Special articles on the subjects indicated by an asterisk (*) will be found at the words so marked.

FERNS AND FERN GARDENING, both for the greenhouse (tropical) species and our common maidenhair (*A. pedatum*) which can be easily grown in woods soil under shade. One of the greenhouse species (*A. cuneatum*) is grown by the million for house decoration or for ornamental grouping, its feathery, relatively resistant fronds being very beautiful. So are some of the horticultural varieties of maidenhair noted below. Some are common as florists' decorations.

Capillus-Veneris. Venus's-hair. In Europe this is the true or black maidenhair. It is a slender, somewhat spreading plant, its black unforked leafstalk arising from the slender, somewhat chaffy rootstock. Leaf twice- or thrice-compound,* its ultimate leaflets bright green, stalked, more or less wedge-shaped, about ½ in. wide. Old and New World tropics and rarely in the warmer parts of Eu. and N.A. Largely a greenhouse species, but hardy along the moister parts of the Pacific Coast and in the east from zone* 7 southward. There is a hort. form with fewer, almost crested leaflets.

cuneatum. The common maidenhair of the florists, and a native of Brazil. Stems brownish-black. Leaves twice- or thrice-compound,* the ultimate leaflets very numerous, stalked, dull green, broadly wedge-shaped and about ¼ or ⅓ in. wide. Of its many horticultural varieties the best-known are forms with white-striped leaflets (*var.* **variegatum**); with crested ones (*var.* **grandiceps**); with very much smaller ones (*var.* **gracillimum**); and the *var.* **croweanum**, a florist's favorite because its sturdy fronds keep so well.

farleyense. See *A. tenerum*.

pedatum. The common hardy maidenhair of our rocky woods, somewhat resembling *A. Capillus-Veneris*, but its black-purple leafstalk always forked at the top. Leaves nearly round in general outline, the leaflets oblongish but wedge-shaped at the base, about ¾ in. long. N.A. A good wild garden plant and easy to grow in the shade.

tenerum. A tropical American, almost climbing maidenhair, scarcely known in ordinary greenhouse collections except for its *var.* **farleyense.** The latter is perhaps the showiest of all the greenhouse maidenhairs. It originated, as a supposed hybrid, at the Farley Hill garden, Barbados, produces no spores (in the typical form), so must be increased by division. Leaves 2–3 ft. long and nearly as wide, curving or falling in a spray-like mass. The ultimate leaflets about 2 in. wide, overlapping each other, light green or sometimes tinted pink, the generally wedge-shaped segments cut or fringed at the top.

ADICEA = *Pilea.*

ADLAY. See COIX.

ADLUMIA (ad-loom′i-a). A leaf-climbing, very delicate, biennial,* herb-like vine, family Fumariaceae, of rich woods in eastern N.A., sometimes grown in the wild garden for its spurred flowers. Leaves alternate, thrice-compound,* its ultimate leaflets fragile and cut-lobed. Flowers white or purple, irregular, spurred, drooping in a loose cluster. Fruit a several-seeded pod. (Named for J. Adlum, 1759–1836, an amateur American botanist and grape breeder.)

Easily grown in nearly windless corners of the wild garden, in shade, and rich but not acid humus. Propagated by self-sown seeds. It often escapes.*

fungosa. Climbing fumitory. Often climbing many feet by its slender leafstalks. Flowers about ¾ in. long. Also called Allegheny vine and mountain fringe. Summer.

ADOBE LILY = *Fritillaria plurifolia.*

ADONIS (a-don′is). Annual or perennial Eurasian herbs of the buttercup family, some of them old favorites in the flower garden. Of the 20 known species only three are common in cultivation. They have alternate, dissected leaves and a solitary flower with 5–16 petals. Fruit dry (an achene*) crowded into a roundish head. (Named for Adonis, from whose blood it is fabled to have sprung.)

The plants are of easy cult. in any ordinary garden soil (except *A. amurensis*) and are grown for their flowers, especially the annual species. Sow seeds in the spring for the pheasant's-eye; in spring or fall for the perennials, which may also be increased by spring division.

aestivalis = *A. annua.*

amurensis. A perennial, rock garden plant about 1 ft. high. Leaves crowded, almost fernlike, finely dissected. Flowers golden yellow, about 2 in. across. Eastern As. May. Needs rich loam. A double-flowered form is known.

annua. Pheasant's-eye. Often offered as *A. autumnalis* or *A. aestivalis.* Annual about 18 in. high. Flowers red, about ¾ in. wide, with a prominent dark center. Eurasian. June and often later. The common species in cultivation and useful for the border or for cutting. See ANNUALS.

vernalis. Perennial about 9 in. high, usually, though not necessarily, grown in the rock garden. Flowers 3 in. wide, yellow. Eu. March. Both white and double-flowered varieties are also grown.

adpressa, -us, -um (ad-press′a). Pressed against; *see also* APPRESSED.

ADROMISCHUS (a-dro-misk′us). About a dozen species of South African succulent perennials. Closely related to *Cotyledon* and grown like them. For culture, *see* SUCCULENTS. Leaves alternate, sometimes marbled or variegated, thick and fleshy. Flowers not very showy, in a long slender cluster (raceme*) at the end of a bracted stalk. (*Adromischus* is from the Greek for a strong flower stem, in allusion to the stiffish flower stalk.) All are sometimes offered as *Cotyledon.*

cooperi. Not over 1 ft. high, usually less, the 5–6 leaves mostly basal, 2–3 in. long, gray-green but spotted. Flowers about ½ in. long, red- or pinkish-green. Called also *A. festivus.*

cristatus. Usually less than 10 in. high, the stem covered with reddish, aerial, hair-like roots. Leaves about 1 in. long, wedge-shaped, narrowed to a short stalk, hairy. Flowers about ½ in. long, pink at the tip.

maculatus. A short-stemmed, stout perennial, the roundish flat leaves convex beneath, gray-green but blotched with purple-brown spots. Flowers pink at the base, paler upward.

adstringens (ad-strin′jenz). Astringent.

---

* Special articles on the subjects indicated by an asterisk (*) will be found at the words so marked.

adsurgens (ad-sir'jens). Ascending.

advena, -us, -um (ad-ven'a). Adventive; newly arrived.

ADVENTITIOUS. Arising at an unusual place, as adventitious buds which sometimes arise after severe pruning, or adventitious roots which may arise from the veins of a cut leaf, as in some begonias.

ADVENTIVE. A wild, usually weedy plant that becomes accidentally established, usually only for a brief period. Many foreign weeds are adventives, until they become naturalized. *See also* ESCAPE.

ADZUKI BEAN = *Phaseolus angularis.*

AECHMEA (eek'mee-a). A very large group of stemless South American air plants (*see* EPIPHYTES), family Bromeliaceae, grown only as greenhouse plants for their colored or scurfy foliage and rather handsome flowers in bracted* clusters. Leaves in a basal rosette,* the margins more or less spiny-toothed. Flowers yellow or red, often tipped with blue, in a branched cluster, on a long, often colored and bracted, stalk. Fruit many-seeded, berry-like. (Greek for a point, in allusion to the pointed sepals.)

Of the 130 known species only a handful are of hort. interest, and of these only those below are at all commonly cult. For care, potting mixture, propagation, etc., *see* VRIESIA.

calyculata. A tree-perching Brazilian greenhouse plant, not over 1 ft. high, the leaves strap-shaped, green, about 10 in. long, the blunt tip furnished with a soft prickle or spine. Flowers bright yellow, tubular, in dense heads, the bracts* red. A showy plant for a warm, moist greenhouse.

fasciata. Brazilian epiphyte* with long-lasting pink flowers. Leaves nearly 2 ft. long, remotely toothed, edged and marbled with white on the back. Flowers in close heads on a bracted stalk, each flower in the head with a spiny-toothed, pinkish bract* longer than the flower.

fulgens. A handsome Brazilian foliage plant with a dense rosette of basal leaves that form a nest-like cavity from which the flowering stalk arises. Leaves about 14 in. long and 2½ in. wide, with a few scattered, marginal and spiny teeth. Flower cluster longer than the leaves, branched. Flowers about ½ in. long, red, but blue-tipped, or some segments all bluish-violet. More common in cultivation is *var.* **discolor** with the under side of the leaves red or violet-red, often faintly striped.

miniata. Usually, as offered, a form of *A. fulgens.*

weilbachi. Leaves strap-shaped, 12–18 in. long, green both sides and arranged in a rosette of 12–30 leaves. Flowers long-stalked, lilac, but ultimately blackish, the stalks red. S.A.

AEGOPODIUM (ee-go-po'di-um). A small group of Eurasian perennial herbs of the carrot family, one of which, the goutweed, is planted (mostly in its variegated form) as a non-evergreen edging or ground cover. Leaves twice-compound,* the ultimate leaflets toothed. Flowers small, white, in a compound umbel (*see* UMBEL). Fruit dry,

seed-like, aromatic. (From the Greek for goat and a small foot, possibly from the outline of its leaflets.)

Easily grown in ordinary garden soil, but prefers partial shade. Increased by dividing its slender rootstocks in spring or fall.

Podagraria. Goutweed, called also bishop's-weed. Stout coarse herb about a foot high. Leafstalks, especially the lower ones, winged and clasping. Flowers scarcely ⅛ in. wide, usually 12–15 in each umbel. June. Most popular in *var.* **variegatum** which has white-margined leaflets and is a useful foliage plant.

AEONIUM. *See* HOUSELEEK.

aequinoctialis, -e (ee-kwi-nox-i-ale'is). Relating to the equinox.

aequitriloba, -us, -um (ee-kwi-tryl-o'ba). Equally three-lobed.

AERIAL ROOT. A root borne in the air, as in many epiphytic (air) plants, and on the stems of some vines like the ivy. *See also* VELAMEN.

AERIDES (a-err'i-deez). Thirty tropical orchids from the East Indies region, all air plants (*see* EPIPHYTES), one of which is grown in greenhouses for its profusion of fragrant, purple- or carmine-spotted, white flowers. There is no pseudobulb.* Leaves two-ranked (*see* DISTICHOUS), rather fleshy, more or less clothing the stem. Flowers very irregular, the lip spurred, the profusely flowering pendent cluster appearing from the leaf bases. (*Aerides* is Greek for air in allusion to the epiphytic habit.) For culture *see* ORCHIDS (greenhouse species).

odoratum. Leaves strap-shaped, about 7 in. long. Flower cluster longer than the leaves. Flowers generally white, but some segments carmine-spotted; others, purple-spotted, or even lined and hence very showy, fragrant. Aug.

AESCHYNANTHES (eyes-ki-nan'theez). A genus of about 170 species from tropical Asia and Indonesia, belonging to the family Gesneriaceae. They are fleshy, rather weak-stemmed plants useful for hanging baskets in the warm greenhouse. Leaves opposite, short-stalked, in pairs or clustered. Flowers irregular, 2-lipped, borne in the leaf axils.* Fruit a long pod (capsule*) the seeds many. (*Aeschynanthus* is from Greek to be ashamed and flower.) Formerly called *Trichosporum.* These are warm-greenhouse subjects, needing rich, porous soil, and occasional fertilization with liquid manure.

lobbianus. A somewhat climbing, fleshy plant, 1–2 ft. long, the elliptic, bluish-green, opposite leaves about 1½ in. long, sometimes purple-tinged. Flowers scarlet, yellow-blotched, about 2 in. long and showy. Java.

marmoratus. Weak-stemmed, sprawling plant, the stems 12–20 in. long. Leaves opposite, marbled with deep green above, but reddish below. Flowers green but brown-blotched. A fine foliage plant for hanging baskets. Indo-Malaya.

pulcher. Resembling *A. lobbianus,* but with larger flowers, the green or purplish calyx* nearly 1 in. long. Java.

AESCULACEAE = HIPPOCASTANACEAE.

---

* Special articles on the subjects indicated by an asterisk (*) will be found at the words so marked.

AESCULUS. *See* Horse-chestnut.

aestiva, -us, -um (ess-ty′-va). Summer.

aestivalis, -e (ess-ti-vail′is). Pertaining to summer.

aethensis, -e (eye-thenn′sis). From Mt. Etna, Sicily.

AETHIONEMA (e-thi-o-nee′ma). The stone cresses are dwarfish perennial herbs of the mustard family, mostly from the Mediterranean region. Of the 60 species those below are mostly rock garden plants related to candytuft. They have small, rather narrow leaves and variously colored, but rarely white flowers in terminal racemes.* Petals 4. Fruit a roundish, dry pod, usually winged (*see* Wing). (From Greek to scorch and a filament, in apparent allusion to the brownish stamens of some species.)

The stone cresses are attractive, slightly woody, rock garden plants, all blooming in May or June. For the details of their culture *see* Rock Garden.

armenum. A perennial, not over 4 in. high, and densely tufted. Leaves bluish-green, short and sharp. Flowers in a close cluster (raceme*), pink. Armenia.

coridifolium. About 6 in. high, somewhat bushy, the one-inch, narrow leaves bluish-gray and crowded. Flowers rose or lilac-pink in short compact clusters. Mt. Lebanon. Sometimes sold as *Iberis jucunda.* A var. with deep pink flowers and pink-edged leaves, offered as Warley Rose, appears to belong here.

grandiflorum. About 14 in. high, the stem not much branched. Leaves bluish-gray, 1½ in. long. Flowers about ¼ in. wide, rosy pink. Persia.

persicum. A dealers' name of uncertain origin. Not over 9 in. high, the leaves narrow and bluish-green. Flowers in a profuse, congested cluster (raceme*), dark pink. Habitat unknown.

pulchellum. Resembling *A. coridifolium* but not so bushy and inclined to trail. Flowers in almost headlike clusters, rosy pink. Persia.

schistosum. Dwarf herb, the stems scarcely 2 in. high, but erect. Leaves very small and narrow. Flowers rose-pink, comparatively large for such a small plant. Asia Minor.

warleyense. A form of *A. coridifolium.*

aethiopica, -us, -um (ee-thi-o′pi-ca). From Ethiopia, Africa.

affinis, -e (af-fy′nis). Related or allied to another species.

afra. African.

africana, -us, -um (af-ri-cay′na). From Africa.

AFRICAN CHERRY-ORANGE = *Citropsis schweinfurthi.*

AFRICAN DAISY = *Arctotis stoechadifolia.* The name is also applied to plants in the genera *Dimorphotheca, Gazania,* and *Gerbera.*

AFRICAN HAIR. *See* Chamaerops humilis.

AFRICAN HOLLY. *See* Solanum giganteum.

AFRICAN LILY = *Agapanthus africanus.*

AFRICAN MARIGOLD = *Tagetes erecta.* *See* Marigold.

AFRICAN MILK-BUSH = *Synadenium granti.*

AFRICAN MILLET. The name is applied to three unrelated grasses. *See* Pennisetum glaucum, Eleusine coracana, and Sorghum vulgare caffrorum.

AFRICAN OIL PALM = *Elaeis guineensis.*

AFRICAN TULIP-TREE = *Spathodea campanulata.*

AFRICAN VALERIAN = *Fedia Cornucopiae.*

AFRICAN VIOLET = *Saintpaulia ionantha.*

AFRICAN YELLOW-WOOD = *Podocarpus elongatus.*

AGAPANTHUS (ag-a-pan′thus). A tuberous rooted herb of the lily family much grown in tubs or pots for its showy flowers. Leaves all basal, numerous, long and narrow. Flowers numerous, in a terminal cluster (umbel*) which arises from between 2 sheathlike bracts.* Corolla funnel-shaped, its oblong segments about as long as the tube. Fruit a 3-celled pod. (From Greek for love flower.)

Grown in the greenhouse in potting mixture* 4, in large pots or tubs. Flowers in the summer, after which the plant should be rested over the winter (with little water and in a frost-free place). Very vigorous growers needing a large pot or tub. If kept in the same one they should be fed liberally with liquid manure.

africanus. African lily, called also lily-of-the-Nile, but a native of South Africa. Leaves about 20 in. long, rather thick. Flower stalk longer than leaves, the cluster consisting of about 20 striking blue flowers. It may be grown outdoors in zones* 8 and 9, and flowered outdoors northward as a summer pot specimen. There are many hort. varieties, some larger than the type, some very much smaller, others with variegated leaves and still others with flowers paler blue, or violet, or white.

mooreanus. A listed name for the hardiest of the plants passing as lily-of-the-Nile, but of uncertain origin and parentage. It is a perennial, hardy outdoors in mild climates, 12–18 in. high. Flowers blue, in a terminal cluster. It is by some considered (perhaps wrongly) as a var. of *A. africanus.*

orientalis. Flowering stalk 2–3 ft. high. Leaves numerous, thickish, 12–25 in. long and nearly 3 in. wide. Flowers numerous (often 100–150) in a dense terminal cluster (umbel*), blue. A very showy plant but suited to outdoor culture only in frost-free regions.

AGARICUS. *See* Mushroom.

AGARITA = *Mahonia trifoliolata.*

AGATHAEA = Felicia.

AGATHIS (ag′a-thiss). Dammar pine. Evergreen Australasian and Malayan trees of the pine family, useful outdoors only as indicated below. They have flat, broad (not needle-like) leaves, usually decidedly leathery, without marginal teeth. Male and female flowers on separate trees, the female in broad roundish cones composed of broad

---

* Special articles on the subjects indicated by an asterisk (*) will be found at the words so marked.

overlapping scales, between which are the solitary, winged seeds. (From Greek for ball or globe, alluding to cones of the female tree.)

Rarely grown as greenhouse specimens.

alba. Up to 100 ft. high, but lower in cultivation. Leaves opposite,* about 3 in. long, more or less striated and dull green. Cone nearly globe-shaped, but slightly egg-shaped, about 3 in. long. Malaya. Zone* 8 in Calif. This plant is often sold as *Agathis orientalis.*

australis. Kauri pine. Sometimes 130 ft. high, the bark bluish-gray and flaky. Leaves opposite,* stalkless, more or less oblong and about 1 in. long on young trees, twice the size on old trees. Cone nearly globe-shaped, about 2½ in. in diameter, its scales faintly prickle-tipped. N.Z. Zone* 8 in Calif.

robusta. Tall tree, reaching 150 ft., its branches in whorls.* Leaves oval to oblong, about 3 in. long, faintly striated, usually alternate.* Cones from globe- to egg-shaped about 3½ in. long. Aust. Zone* 8 in Calif. Also known as *A. browni.*

AGATI (a-gay′tee). Comprising only the following species, a medium-sized tree from tropical As. belonging to the pea family, cult. outdoors only in zone* 9 or in greenhouses for its showy flowers and fruit. Leaves compound,* the leaflets numerous, usually in about 25 pairs. Flowers pea-like. Fruit a long pod. (*Agati* is a Latinized derivative of the Hindu vernacular for this plant.)

When grown in greenhouses, use potting mixture* 4.

grandiflora. Pea tree. A short-lived but handsome tree, up to 25 ft. Leaves about 9 in. long, the many leaflets scarcely 2 in. long. Flowers very showy, in short clusters in the leaf axils,* red or white, about 2 in. long. Pod almost woody, flat and narrow, up to 2 ft. long and very striking. The tree is also called *Sesbania grandiflora.*

AGAVE (a-gah′vee). An immense genus of succulent, fleshy-leaved, semi-desert, tropical American plants, family Amaryllidaceae, of importance both in hort. and in industry. Of the 300 species much the best-known is the commonly cult. century plant (*A. americana*), which, like many other species, blooms once and then dies, often leaving a circle of small plants about the base. Other species flower periodically. Leaves in a basal rosette,* usually spiny-margined and often with a strong terminal prickle; persisting for many years. Flowers in a long terminal cluster, at the end of a very long stalk (40 ft. in some species). The flowers are greenish-yellow, funnel-shaped, with 6 segments. Fruit a capsule* with 3 valves. (From the Greek for noble or illustrious.)

Except for the century plant, agaves are not so widely grown as they should be, for they are handsome succulents useful in dry, frost-free regions outdoors, and as cool-greenhouse or house plants where there is plenty of sun. All the species below, in the north, are improved by plunging outdoors during warm weather. Best grown in large pots or tubs in potting mixture* 6, although in young stages they can be started in small pots.

Propagation is easiest by pulling off the usu-ally many suckers* that arise from the base of old plants, especially just before they bloom. Bulbils* are sometimes produced in certain species and these can also be used for propagating. Root the bulbils in potting mixture* 1, but the suckers are already provided with roots and should be potted in the same mixture as mature plants. Seeds are rarely used, for most cult. species set no seeds unless the flowers have been hand pollinated. For general culture *see* SUCCULENTS.

americana. Century plant, also, but incorrectly, called American aloe. Stemless, the large leaves in a basal rosette* of huge size in mature plants. Leaves up to 5 or 6 ft. long, and 6–8 in. wide, decidedly grayish, their tips usually recurved, marginal spines stout and recurved. Stalk of flower cluster (rarely produced in cult. but likely any time after 10 or 15 years) from 25–40 ft. high, rather slender. Flowers about 2½ in. long, very numerous. Probably Mexico, but cult. so long and scarcely known in the wild state, that original habitat is uncertain. Of the hort. varieties one has yellow-margined leaves, another yellow- or white-striped leaves, and a third has a central yellow-ish band. A widely cult. plant, often growing to immense size in large tubs.

atrovirens. Pulque agave. A huge Mexican species widely cult. there as the source of pulque. Leaves up to 9 ft. long and a foot wide, their marginal spines gray, but the leaf generally green. Stalk of the flower cluster (rare in cult.) about 20 ft. high. Flowers about 3½ in. long.

attenuata. Stems 3–6 ft. high, the rosette of leaves usually at the summit, but sometimes basal. Leaves 6–15 in the rosette, without teeth on the margin, but spiny-tipped, 20–30 in. long, about 10 in. wide. Flowers greenish-yellow, about 2 in. long, the stalk of the flower cluster 8–10 ft. high. Mex.

coerulescens. This, in cult. specimens, is *A. lophantha coerulescens.*

decipiens. Stem, when present, 3–4 ft. high, the leaves mainly basal, 3–4 ft. long, stiff, sword-shaped, the spiny, brown tip very sharp. Marginal prickles very short, brownish-black, recurved. Flowers greenish-yellow, the cluster (panicle*) loosely branched. Fla.

fourcroydes. Henequen. Native, and an important plant, in Yucatan, where thousands of acres are devoted to its culture for a fiber resembling sisal. Produces a trunk 8–10 ft. high with a crown of narrow, green, nearly spineless leaves that are about 7 ft. long and 3 in. wide. Stalk of the flower cluster 20 ft., the flowers greenish, fetid, and about 3 in. long.

lecheguilla. Lechuguilla. A Mexican species somewhat grown as a pot plant for its handsome leaves which are bluish-green, pale-banded along the midrib, but striped underneath, usually not over 18 in. long, prickly-margined. Stalk of flower cluster 4–8 ft., the flowers about 1½ in. long. Resembling the next and by some considered a variety of it.

lophantha. Bearing a short trunk and a crown of leaves that are about 3 ft. long and 3 in. wide, shiny green above, striped beneath. Marginal spines not large but variously hooked. Stalk of the flower cluster about 12 ft. high, the flowers 1½ in. long. Mex. In cult. perhaps better known in the *var.* **coerulescens** which has bluish-gray leaves and no stripes beneath.

sisalana. Sisal. This, the commercial source of sisal hemp (mostly in Java and S. Af.), is

---

* Special articles on the subjects indicated by an asterisk (*) will be found at the words so marked.

probably native in the Bahamas. It very much resembles *A. fourcroydes,* but usually produces no trunk, and has shorter leaves. Stalk of the flower cluster about 18 ft. high, the flowers green, fetid, and about 2½ in. long.

stricta. Stemless and small enough to be easily grown as a pot plant. Leaves about a foot long and scarcely ⅓ in. wide, without prickles except for the terminal spine, somewhat triangular in cross-section, forming a dense, rather handsome cluster. Stalk of the flower cluster about 7 ft. high, the flowers about 1 in. long. Mex. Widely cult., especially in some of its hort. forms with bluish-gray or purplish leaves, or in a dwarfish form with a distinct bloom* on the leaves.

tequilana. Tequila mescal. A Mexican stemless plant, one of the sources of mescal, and thus widely cult. Leaves about 2½ ft. long, 3 in. wide and bluish-gray. Stalk of the flower cluster up to 15 ft., the flowers about 2½ in. long.

virginica. False aloe; also called rattlesnake master. Leaves green, narrow, to 2 ft. in length. Flower stems 3–5 ft. high. Flowers short-stalked, about 2 in. long, fragrant, greenish-yellow. The tube is 3 times as long as the segments. The *var. tigrina* has mottled leaves. N. Car. to Mo. and Tex. The hardiest of all the agaves and often called *Manfreda.* It is herbaceous without a woody stem.

agavoides (a-gah-voy′deez; but *see* OÏDES). Resembling a plant of the genus *Agave.*

AGE OF TREES. *See* GARDEN TABLES III.

ageratifolia, -us, -um (a-jur-a-ti-fo′li-a). With leaves like an ageratum.

AGERATUM (a-jur-a′tum). A group of nearly 30 species of chiefly tropical American annual herbs, family Compositae, one of which is perhaps the most popular of all bedding and edging plants. Leaves opposite,* generally oval, the margins with rounded teeth. Flowers blue, rarely pink or white except in some hort. forms, in compact, clustered heads, without rays.* Fruit minute, dry. (*Ageratum* is from the Greek for not growing old, of uncertain application to these plants.) They are sometimes known as floss flower.

Ageratum is as easily grown as it is deservedly popular. It is a tender annual. *See* ANNUALS. They can be used to give sheets of misty blue bloom in the border, but their greatest use is for bedding, for a carpet in which other plants are set, and for low edgings. They flower over most of the summer, and late fall or winter flowering can be had from potted plants, the seed for which is sown in early Sept. Keep these in a cool greenhouse.

houstonianum. Common garden ageratum. Leaves somewhat heart-shaped at the base, the typical form a plant about 14 in. high. Flower heads just over ¼ in. in diameter, blue, the outside somewhat sticky. There are many named hort. varieties of this old favorite, some white or pink, but the most useful are the dwarf sorts which are compact enough to be very valuable for edging.

For a related plant, sometimes called hardy ageratum, *see* EUPATORIUM COELESTINUM, better called mist-flower.

aggregata, -us, -um (ag-gree-gay′ta). Grouped or aggregated.

AGGREGATE FRUIT. *See* FRUIT.

AGLAONEMA (ag-la-o-nee′ma). Tropical Asian and Malaysian herbs of the arum family, one of the 15 species a very popular house plant. Stems lax, with a tendency to climb. Leaves without marginal teeth, always stalked, usually with a thick midrib, often splashed with white. Flowers minute (rare in cult. specimens), crowded on a short spadix,* beneath which is a soon-withering, green, or whitish spathe.* Fruit berry-like. (Greek for bright thread, of uncertain application here.)

The last species below is one of the most widely cult. house plants. It grows perfectly in water, even in comparatively dark, dry rooms. Like any other tropical aroid, however, it will grow much better in a warm, moist greenhouse in potting mixture* 4, to which charcoal has been added. Easily propagated by division of the rootstock, or by cuttings in moist sand.

commutatum. Not over 2 ft. high, the oblongish leaves 6–9 in. long, dark green but blotched with pale or white markings. Spathe* white. Philippines.

costatum. A Malayan short-stemmed plant often branching at the base. Leaves handsome, about 8 in. long, and half as wide, tapering at both ends, the midrib white, and prominently marked with scattered white patches. A very satisfactory foliage plant, because its rather numerous leaves are crowded to make a compact specimen.

pictum. Stems 6–9 ft. high, the elliptic leaves slender, 4–6 in. long, and about 2 in. wide, irregularly white or gray-blotched. Spathe* yellowish. Sumatra. There is a var. with yellow or golden spots on the leaves.

simplex. Chinese evergreen; called, also, Chinese water-plant and Japanese leaf. Erect or laxly spreading stem 3 ft. or more long, in cult. specimens commonly less. Leaves more or less loosely disposed toward the end of the stem, oblongish, nearly 10 in. long, green. Recently introduced but in practically every florist shop in America. It grows easily in water. Also called *A. modestum.*

Agnus-castus. Classical name of the chaste tree (*Vitex Agnus-castus*).

AGONIS (a-go′nis). A genus of Australian shrubs and trees of the myrtle family, one grown outdoors in Calif. for ornament. Leaves alternate,* willow-like (in the species below). Flowers small, crowded in dense, globe-shaped, stalkless clusters. Fruit a leathery or nearly woody many-seeded capsule. (Greek, for gathering, perhaps alluding to its plentiful seed.)

flexuosa. Willow myrtle. A tree to 40 ft. high in the wild, less in cult. Leaves about 6 in. long. Flowers white, the dense globe-like clusters about ½ in. thick, the numerous stamens* prominent. Cult. in southern Calif., scarcely known elsewhere. Sometimes called *Leptospermum flexuosum.*

AGRICULTURE. Farming, as distinguished from horticulture.*

* Special articles on the subjects indicated by an asterisk (*) will be found at the words so marked.

agrifolia, -us, -um (ag-ri-fo′li-a). Scabby or rough-leaved.

AGROPYRON REPENS. *See* Quack Grass in the list at WEEDS.

AGROSTEMMA. *See* LYCHNIS COELI-ROSA.

AGROSTIS (a-gros′tis). Bent grass. A large genus of widely distributed grasses, a few of which are much used in hay and lawn seed, although many wild species are weedy. They are annual or perennial grasses, some of the latter valuable because of their creeping stolons.* Leaves narrow. Flowers in small spikelets that are borne in open, loose panicles.* (*Agrostis* is from the Greek for field and Latin for some grass.)

Most of the species below form part of many pasture or lawn mixtures and are little grown otherwise. *See* the heading Lawn Mixtures at LAWN for the important ones and their value. The botanists and dealers do not agree as to the specific identity of those below. Some apply the name *A. alba* to the redtop and *A. palustris* to the creeping bent. Hence the Latin names used here may not agree with catalogue names and to avoid confusion it is better to use common or vernacular names in ordering seed or stolons.

canina. Brown bent; also called dog bent and velvet bent. A perennial* grass up to 18 in. high. Leaves 2 in. long, scarcely ½ in. wide. N.A. Common in some lawn mixtures. *See* LAWN.

capillaris. Rhode Island bent. A common perennial* pasture grass, resembling redtop (*A. stolonifera*) but smaller and having shorter, more distinctly red flower clusters. Leaves about 6 in. long and ⅕ in. wide. Eu. but commonly naturalized in N.A. Called also *A. tenuis.*

nebulosa. Cloud grass. An annual* grass with very short and narrow leaves. Grown only for its wide cluster of tiny spikelets which are on very slender stalks and persistent enough to be used for dry bouquets. Spain.

stolonifera. Redtop, called also fiorin. A perennial* European pasture grass, naturalized in N.A. and much planted for hay and as an ingredient of lawn mixtures. It reaches a height of about 3 ft. Leaves about 7 in. long and ¼ in. wide. Flower cluster greenish-red. Also called *A. alba* and *A. palustris*. Creeping bent (*A. stolonifera compacta*) is a variety with creeping rootstocks.

AHUEHUETE = *Taxodium mucronatum.*

AILANTHUS (a-lan′thus). A small genus of chiefly Asiatic trees, family Simaroubaceae, one widely grown in cities for its smoke-resistant, insect-free but ill-scented foliage. Leaves compound, with 6–12 pairs of leaflets, and an odd one at the end. Flowers small, yellowish-green, in large terminal clusters, the male and female mostly on different trees. Fruit winged, the seed surrounded by the wing, and rather showy when ripe. (Latinized form of the vernacular name for the tree in the Moluccas.)

altissima. Tree-of-Heaven. Stinkweed; also called *A. glandulosa*. A quick-growing, smooth-barked, medium-sized tree, easily propagated by fresh seed, by root cuttings and from suckers* which readily follow any root injury. Leaflets

about 5 in. long, prominently toothed toward the base. China. Only female or fertile-flowered trees should be cult. as the odor of the male flower is noxious to many. Varieties with red fruit, with large drooping leaves and with purple leafstalks are often preferred to the ordinary ailanthus. No other tree will stand smoke and city conditions so well. In some places it has run wild and become a pest.

AIPHANES. *See* MARTINEZIA.

AIRA: *A. caerulea* = *Molinia.*

AIR LAYERING. *See* LAYERING.

AIR PLANT. *See* BRYOPHYLLUM.

AIR PLANTS. *See* EPIPHYTES.

AIR POTATO = *Dioscorea bulbifera.*

AIZOACEAE (a-eye-zo-a′see-e). The carpetweed family, comprising 150 genera and perhaps 3000 species of widely distributed herbs, is of no garden significance except for the genus *Mesembryanthemum* and for the New Zealand spinach (which see). Leaves often succulent or at least thickish, opposite* or alternate* or in whorls,* in some ice-plants (*Mesembryanthemum*) covered with glittering dots. Flowers regular, lacking petals in New Zealand spinach but with so many in *Mesembryanthemum* as to suggest a daisy-head. Fruit a capsule or nut-like, many-seeded.

Technical flower characters: Calyx 4–5-cleft or 4-parted. Stamens perigynous.* Ovary 3–5-celled, the ovules numerous in each cell.

aizoides (a-eye-zoy′deez, but *see* OÏDES). Resembling a plant of the genus *Aizoon*, which is a relative of the ice-plants but scarcely cult.

AIZOON. *See* AIZOIDES.

Ajacis (a′ja-kiss). Old Greek name, said to relate to the marks on the petal of the rocket larkspur (*Delphinium Ajacis*).

ajanensis, -e (a-jan-en′sis). From Ajan on the coast of Siberia.

Ajax (ā′jacks). Named for the Greek hero, perhaps because of the size of a plant so named.

AJUGA (aj′oo-ga). Bugleweed. Annual or perennial herbs of the mint family, sometimes weedy, but a few cult. in borders and rock gardens for their profusion of white, blue, or sometimes reddish bloom. Flowers irregular* and 2-lipped, in close clusters or spikes. (*Ajuga* is Latin for not yoked, alluding to the calyx.)

The bugleweeds, all European, are of easy cult. in ordinary garden soil. Prop. by spring-sown seeds, by division, and by its freely rooting stems in *A. reptans.*

brockbanki. A long-current dealers' name for a blue-flowered bugle, of unknown origin and parentage; possibly a var. of the next species.

genevensis. Flowers blue, in spiked but interrupted* close clusters. Leaves many-toothed, less than 3 in. long. Called, also, *A. alpina*, and a creeping or prostrate plant, but not developing runners.

reptans. The common blue bugleweed, widely escaped from cult. in eastern N.A. It is

---

* Special articles on the subjects indicated by an asterisk (*) will be found at the words so marked.

4–10 in. high, but the stems are usually half-prostrate and often rooting. Lower leaves narrowed to a short stalk, the upper stalkless. In the typical form the flowers are blue or purplish, but the following are the preferred garden sorts: *var.* **alba**, with white flowers; *var.* **atropurpurea**, with bronze foliage and blue flowers; *var.* **metallica crispa**, with metallic, crisped leaves and blue flowers in uninterrupted spikes. Forms with deep purple (*var.* **rubra**) and white-blotched (*var.* **variegata**) foliage are also known.

AKEAKE = *Dodonaea viscosa.*

AKEBIA (a-kee′bi-a). Four species of Asiatic woody vines, family Lardizabalaceae, only the following cult. for shade and for covering walls or arbors. Leaves almost evergreen, compound,* the leaflets 3 or 5. Male and female flowers separate, spring-blooming, and in loose clusters, the male flowers small and purplish-brown, the females larger and pale fawn. Fruit a black-seeded berry. (*Akebia* is the Japanese vernacular name for these plants.)

Propagation by seeds, by root-division and by cuttings over bottom-heat. *See also* VINES.

quinata. Leaflets 5 and without teeth. Flowers fragrant but small and inconspicuous. Fruit (often wanting in cult.) a purple berry, used as food in Japan. A stout, useful climber from zone* 4 southward, reaching a height of 20 ft. It blooms at night. Often planted in cool greenhouses.

trifoliata. A rather coarse rampant vine reaching 20 ft. high. Leaflets 3, about 2–3 in. long, the margins wavy, the tip notched. The middle leaflet longer-stalked than the lateral pair. Eastern As. April–May. Hardy from zone* 4 southward. Also known as *A. lobata.*

AKEE = *Blighia sapida.*

akitensis, -e (a-kee-ten′sis). From or near Akita, Japan.

ALABAMA. The state flower is the goldenrod, the state tree the Southern pine, and the state bird the yellowhammer. The state lies entirely in zones 5, 6, and 7. Climate of the state is mild, the growing season long, and rainfall plentiful. A varied list of vegetables, fruits, and ornamentals is adapted to the soils and climate.

LAND SURFACE. The surface of Alabama rises as an undulating plain from the level of the Gulf of Mexico in the southwest to foothills in the central part of the state, where there is a sharp rise to the Appalachian Mountains which extend into the northeastern counties. The elevation of the plain areas ranges from near sea level to 400 or 600 feet. Elevation of mountain areas averages 800 feet with some summits rising over 2000 feet. The highest point in the state, Mt. Cheaha in southwestern Cleburne County, is 2407 feet high. In every direction except northeast, there are downward slopes from these highlands into river valleys.

NATIONAL FORESTS. There are three national forests in Alabama: William B. Bankhead, largely in Winston County; Talladega, largely in Talladega, Clay, and Bibb coun-ties; and Conecuh, largely in Covington and Escambia counties.

STATE PARKS. There are 14 state parks. Beginning in the northern part of the state and progressing southward, these parks are: DeSota, near Fort Payne; Joe Wheeler, near Wheeler Dam; Little Mountain, near Guntersville; Monte Sano, near Huntsville; Oak Mountain, near Pelham; Cheaha, near Munford; Chewacla, near Auburn; Mound, near Moundville; Valley Creek, near Plantersville; Chickasaw, near Linden; Little River, near Uriah; Chattahoochee, near Cottonwood; Gulf, near Gulf Shores; and Fort Morgan.

GARDENS. A few of the more interesting gardens and points of interest are: Ave Maria Grotto, near Cullman; Vestavia Gardens, in Birmingham; Jasmine Hill, near Wetumpka; Garden of Memory, at Auburn; the Turn-Around, near Clanton; Live Oak Cemetery, at Selma; Blacksher Garden, and Bellingrath Gardens, which is one of the finest in the U.S., at Mobile. Mobile Azalea Trails are of nationwide interest.

INTERESTING HOMES AND GROUNDS. For a more complete listing of places of interest, historical homes, and private gardens, one should obtain the guide prepared by the Garden Club of Alabama, entitled *Keep Alabama Beautiful.* A few homes of unusual interest are the Helen Keller home, Tuscumbia; Forks of Cypress, Florence; the Joe Wheeler home, Courtland; Arlington, Birmingham; Rosemont, Eutaw; Magnolia Grove, Greensboro; Gorgas, Tuscaloosa; State Capitol grounds, Montgomery; First White House of Confederacy, Montgomery; Teague, Montgomery; Gray Columns, Tuskegee; Oak Leigh, Mobile; Eslova House, Mobile; Jordan Place, Mobile; and Springhill College, Mobile.

GARDEN CLUB. The Garden Club of Alabama is most active. It celebrated its 25th anniversary in 1957. At that time, it had 510 local clubs with total membership of 12,327 and 152 junior clubs with 4671 accredited members and 30,000 participating members. In 1956 Alabama won six national awards, conducted nine flower shows, had 79 nationally accredited flower show judges, and 32 active committees. Its publication, *Hortensia,* is published bi-monthly. Since 1954 the club has offered a $250 award to an outstanding high-school graduate entering Alabama Polytechnic Institute at Auburn and enrolling in horticulture. "Keep Alabama Green" has been the theme of the Garden Club of Alabama for a number of years.

SOILS. The soils of Alabama vary in texture from clay to sands, in color from red to gray, in drainage from well drained to poorly drained, in relief from nearly level to hilly, and in reaction from acid to alkaline.

Alabama soils may be divided into five major areas or provinces based primarily on geological origin. Since the soils within major groups are more or less similar in character, agricultural lands have been thrown into soil provinces. The soil provinces are: Lime-

---

* Special articles on the subjects indicated by an asterisk (*) will be found at the words so marked.

stone Valley, Appalachian Mountain, Piedmont Plateau, Coastal Plain, and Black Belt. The Limestone Valley occupies an area bordering the Tennessee Valley in northern Alabama and two narrow strips crossing Jefferson County into Talladega, Calhoun, and Blount counties. Soils of this area, although derived from limestone, are acid. Decatur and Dewey are the two most important soil series. The Appalachian Province is located in the northeast part of Alabama and is found in 12 to 15 counties, comprising most of Cullman, Blount, and Dekalb counties. Soils of the area were derived from sandstone or shale with the Hartsells and Hanceville being the most important series. The Piedmont Plateau is located in the east-central part of Alabama and follows a line drawn from the Georgia state line northeast of Heflin by Talladega, Sylacauga, Clanton, Wetumpka, Auburn, and back to the Georgia state line at Columbus. Soils in this area were derived from rock such as granite and gneiss, with the most important series being the Cecil and Louisa. The Coastal Plain province covers a wide area of the state. It is about one county wide across Colbert, Franklin, and Marion counties and about two counties wide across Lamar, Fayette, Pickens, and Tuscaloosa counties. In the southern third of the state, this province comprises the whole area. Important series of this area are the Norfolk, Orangeburg, Rustin, Greenville, and Kalmia. The Black Belt province begins at Union Springs, Bullock County, and extends westward to the Mississippi line in a strip varying from 10 to 40 miles wide. The soils of this province are heavy clays, and range from alkaline to acid. Some of the more important series are the Oktibbeha, Lufkin, Eutaw, Houston, and Sumter.

FRUITS. The variations in climatic conditions, soils, and elevation supply conditions favorable for a long list of fruits ranging from apples to satsuma oranges. Apples grow well in the upper half of the state, being especially well adapted to the area of higher elevation in northern Alabama. Pears grow in all sections of the state, but only the fire-blight-resistant varieties should be planted. Cherries are not adapted to this state except in a limited way on the mountains of northern Alabama. Dewberries and blackberries, both native and cultivated, grow throughout the state. Raspberries are not adapted generally to the state, although some are grown in the upper part. Strawberries are produced very satisfactorily in all sections of the state, commercial quantities being grown in Cullman, Escambia, Conecuh, and Chilton counties. Satsuma oranges have been grown quite generally in Mobile and Baldwin counties. Improved varieties of pecans, both for commercial and home use, are grown extensively over the southern half of the state. Bunch grapes are adapted to northern Alabama, but muscadine grapes can be grown in most areas. Rabbiteye blueberries are native to southern Alabama, and the dry-land species is found

ALABAMA

The zones* of hardiness crossing Alabama are those shown on the map located at ZONE, which should be consulted for details. The dates are the average latest killing frost in spring and the first one in the fall. The figures below the dates show the average length of the growing season. Rainfall figures are for total annual rainfall and for that falling in the growing season.

in the mountain areas in northeastern counties. Peaches are adapted to most sections of the state except the heavy prairie soils of the Black Belt and the Gulf Coast counties. Most of the acreage is concentrated in Chilton, Blount, and Jefferson counties. The development of low-chilling varieties has made peach growing possible 100 miles south of Montgomery.

VEGETABLES. Almost all the vegetables commonly grown in the United States are adapted to Alabama. Home gardens, while at their peak in spring and fall months, can be grown the year round. The winters are mild enough even in northern Alabama that some cold-tolerant leafy crops are carried in the garden throughout the winter, and in central and southern Alabama many vegetable crops are planted in December, January, and February. Two crops or more may be grown each year on the same area because of the long growing season. Principal planting activity occurs in February, March, and April, and again in July, August, and September.

ORNAMENTALS. In the extreme southern portion of the state Indian azaleas, camellias, and oleanders are especially known for their beauty. The state has a varied display of native flowering and fruiting plants, including southern magnolia, sweet bay, yaupon, and Carolina jasmine in the southern half of the state, and mountain laurel, rhododendron, and red buckeye in the more mountainous sections. Native azaleas, dogwood, redbud, and American holly are found throughout the state. A long and varied list of evergreens and deciduous shrubs, both

* Special articles on the subjects indicated by an asterisk (*) will be found at the words so marked.

native and introduced, is available for landscape use. Broad-leaved evergreens are especially adapted to the state. Mild winters permit the planting and growth in the fall of many early spring-grown annuals such as larkspur, pansy, sweetpea, cornflower, calendula, stock, poppy, and phlox. The long list of perennials grown successfully in the North is greatly abbreviated under southern conditions. A number of the perennials, however, are successfully grown as biennials. Among the bulbous plants *Narcissus* varieties bloom from early February until May. The bulbs of these may remain in the same area indefinitely, while those of hyacinths must be replaced about every third year. Many of the more tender bulbous plants as gladiolus, amaryllis, and dahlia are grown outside without any winter protection for the roots. *Iris* is especially well adapted to the northern part of the state.

CLIMATE. Alabama has a temperate climate. Summers, while warm, are not oppressive, and heat prostrations rarely occur. Twenty-seven states have higher summer maxima than Alabama. In northern counties higher altitudes help make nights more comfortable. Severe cold weather seldom occurs and freezing temperatures usually do not continue longer than three to four days. Rainfall is favorable for good crop production. Summer soil moisture is usually replenished by July rains, while sunny weather in the fall usually provides favorable conditions for crop harvesting. Irrigation is beneficial at some season each year.

The average annual temperature of the state is 64.9°. In a general way the average January temperatures for the extreme southwestern portion of the state, embracing the southern half of Baldwin and Mobile counties, range from 52° to 54°, for the southern third from 48° to 50°, for the central part 46° to 48°, and for the northern third 42° to 44°. The average July temperature for the state ranges from 78° to 80°. Dates of the last killing frost for the extreme southwestern portion of the state range on average from February 18 to March 5, for the southern third from March 15 to March 20, for the central third from March 15 to March 25, and for the northern third from March 30 to April 10. The average dates of the first killing frost in fall for the corresponding areas range from November 20 to December 10, from November 5 to November 20, from November 5 to November 10, and from October 25 to October 30.

The average number of days without killing frosts is shown on the map, which also shows the average annual rainfall for the state.

Address of the Alabama Agricultural Experiment Station of the Alabama Polytechnic Institute is Auburn, Alabama. The station is always ready to answer questions on gardening.

alabamensis, -e. From Alabama.

ALASKA CEDAR = *Chamaecyparis nootkatensis.*

alata, -us, -um (a-lay′ta). Winged.

Alaternus (a-la-ter′nus). An old generic name for a buckthorn (*Rhamnus*).

alato-caerulea, -us, -um (a-lay-toe-se-roo′-lee-a). Blue-winged.

alba, -us, -um (al′ba). White.

ALBANY IVY. See HEDERA HELIX.

ALBERTA. The Province lies wholly in zones* 1 and 2. Its soil and climatic conditions, and consequently its gardening possibilities, are so similar to the northern part of Idaho that it is needless to repeat them here. See IDAHO. See also BRITISH COLUMBIA.

ALBERTA SPRUCE = *Picea glauca albertiana.* See SPRUCE.

albertiana, -us, -um (al-ber-ti-a′na). From Alberta, Canada.

albida, -us, -um (al′bi-da). White.

albiflora, -us, -um (al-bi-flow′ra). White-flowered.

albiflos (al′bee-floss). White-flowered.

albi-plena, -us, -um (al-bi-plee′na). With double, white flowers.

ALBIZZIA (al-bizz′ee-a). A large genus of tropical trees and shrubs of the pea family, three of which are grown for ornament. Their outdoor culture is mostly confined to zones* 8 and 9, except the first species, and scarcely known in greenhouses. Leaves alternate,* twice-compound,* the ultimate leaflets small, numerous, and more or less oblique. Flowers very small, congested in globe-shaped heads or in finger-shaped clusters. Fruit a large pod. (Named for Albizzi, an Italian naturalist.)

Albizzia closely resembles and is related to acacia. For greenhouse culture *see* ACACIA. The first and third species have very handsome foliage.

Julibrissin. Silk tree. Medium-sized tree not over 30 ft. high, but with a broad spreading crown. Leaves with 12–20 or even 25 major divisions, each of which bears from 40–60 very oblique leaflets that are scarcely ¼ in. long. Flowers light pink, in slender-stalked, compact heads. Pod flat, about 5 in. long and 1 in. wide. Persia to central China. Hardy from zone* 5 southward, and commonly cult. from southern Md. southward on the coastal plain. The tree is often, incorrectly, called a mimosa. There is a deeper pink form, the *var.* rosea, smaller than the type and hardy from zone* 4 southward.

Lebbek. Siris; called also lebbek and East Indian walnut. Tall tree up to 80 ft. in the wild, less in cultivation. Leaves with 5–7 major divisions, each of which bears 12–18 stalkless, oblique leaflets that are about 1 in. long. Flowers greenish-yellow, in dense, small, short-stalked heads that are borne in the axils.* Pod 9–12 in. long, flat, just over an inch wide. Tropical As. and Aust. Hardy only in zone* 9, rarely in zone* 8. Sometimes called woman's-tongue tree.

lophantha. Usually a shrub, but sometimes a tree up to 20 ft. high. Leaves with 16–22 major divisions, each of which bears from 40–60, only slightly oblique, leaflets that are about ⅓ in. long, often making a litter. Flowers

---

* Special articles on the subjects indicated by an asterisk (*) will be found at the words so marked.

greenish-white. Aust. Hardy in zones* 8 and 9.

INSECT PESTS. *A. Julibrissin* is attacked by a webworm in late summer. Control with pesticide #1 or #19. (*See* SPRAYS AND DUSTS.)

DISEASES. In some parts of the country a wilt* disease causes bluish-black streaks in the trunk wood and branches. Trees wilt and die quickly. Planting of resistant strains is the only control.

albo-maculata, -us, -um (al-bo-mac-u-lay′ta). White-spotted.

albo-marginata, -us, -um (al-bo-mar-ji-nay′ta). White-margined.

albo-pleno (al-bo-plee′no). White and double-flowered.

albospina, -us, -um (al-bo-spine′a). With white spines.

albo-variegata, -us, -um (al-bo-vare-i-gay′ta). With white markings.

albula, -us, -um (al′bew-la). Whitish.

Alcea. Pre-Linnaean* name for a mallow, probably *Malva Alcea.*

ALCHEMILLA (al-ke-mill′ya). Of 30 species of this genus of annual* and perennial* herbs of the rose family, only the following two are of any garden importance. They are somewhat weedy plants with lobed or compound* leaves and small greenish-yellow flowers without petals. Fruit small, dry (an achene*), partly enclosed by the withered calyx.* (Latinized form of the Arabic vernacular name for these plants.)

They are of the easiest culture in any ordinary garden soil, and may be increased by division. Grown only for their silvery or grayish leaves. *See* ROCK GARDEN.

alpina. A European rock garden species with silvery, small leaflets, which are toothed toward the tip. It spreads to form a dense mat or carpet. Flowers inconspicuous. July.

vulgaris. Lady's-mantle. Rootstock stout and horizontal, producing a clump of erect, long-stalked, grayish leaves, 4–5 in. wide, that have shallow rounded lobes, toothed throughout. Stalk of the flower cluster about 15 in. high, and bearing many, minute, greenish-yellow flowers. Eu. Summer.

ALCICORNIUM = *Platycerium.*

ALCOCK SPRUCE = *Picea bicolor.* See SPRUCE.

aldenhamensis (all-den-ham-en′sis). From Aldenham House, England.

ALDER. A large group of shrubs and trees belonging to the genus Alnus (al′nus) of the birch family grown as specimens or in the shrub border, especially in places too moist for other woody plants. They have rather handsome, often somewhat burnished or sticky, alternate,* leaves. Flowers in catkins, the male and female on the same plant, the latter becoming small, scaly, woody cones. (*Alnus* is the old Latin name of the alder.)

Of the 30 known species only the following are of much hort. importance, and these are useful only in cool moist parts of America.

All those below bloom before the leaves unfold in spring. Easily grown in wet or moist places, and propagated by cuttings, or suckers, or by spring-sown seeds collected the autumn before. The species of *Alnus* here admitted are:

A. cordata. Italian alder. A handsome tree 70–80 ft. high, the foliage pear-like, the twigs reddish-brown. Leaves dark shiny green, 2–4 in. long, heart-shaped at the base, finely toothed. Catkins 2–3 in. long. Corsica and Italy. Mar.–Apr. Hardy from zone* 4 southward.

A. glutinosa. Black alder. A tree up to 70 ft., its twigs sticky. Leaves nearly round or ovalish, about 4 in. long, coarsely toothed, the teeth themselves also toothed. Eurasia. Commonly planted and often an escape* in eastern N.A. There are several hort. varieties, such as a golden-leaved form, one with much-cut leaves, another with oak-like leaves and one with red leaf veins and stalks. An important timber tree in its wild range and often called *Alnus vulgaris.*

A. hirsuta. A Japanese and Manchurian tree 50–60 ft. high. Leaves ovalish, 3–5 in. long, sharp-pointed at the base, green above but with reddish, soft hairs beneath; coarsely toothed. Hardy from zone* 3 southward. Mar.–Apr.

A. incana. Speckled alder. Usually a shrub, rarely a medium-sized tree, the twigs hairy but not sticky. Leaves broadly elliptic, sharp at the tip, about 3½ in. long, dull green above, paler beneath. Found wild in many parts of the north temperate zone, especially Eu. and N.A. There are several hort. and wild varieties having yellow leaves or reddish twigs, or cut leaves, etc.

A. japonica. Japanese alder. A pyramidal tree 60–70 ft. high, the twigs smooth. Leaves dark green above, paler beneath, narrowly lance-shaped, tapering at both ends, 2–5 in. long, half as wide. Catkins 2–3 in. long. Jap. Mar.–Apr. Hardy from zone* 3 southward, possibly in zone* 2.

A. rhombifolia. A tree 40–70 ft. high, the branches drooping at the tips. Leaves ovalish, 2–4 in. long, finely toothed, green above, softly hairy beneath. Male catkins* 3–5 in. long. Western U.S. Hardy from zone* 5 southward.

A. rugosa. Smooth alder. A branching, somewhat coarse shrub, very rarely a small tree. Leaves nearly elliptic but more or less wedge-shaped at the base, not over 4 in. long, finely toothed all round, green both sides. Common in swamps throughout eastern U.S. and often planted in such sites.

A. viridis. Green alder. Low shrub, not over 4–5 ft. high in cultivation. Leaves ovalish, about 2½ in. long, broader toward the base, green both sides, but paler beneath. Eu., especially in the mountains. Not much grown in U.S. and closely related to an American species, common in the mountains from Labrador to N. Car.

INSECT PESTS. Aphids, mites, lace bugs, and leaf feeders are controlled by pesticide #21 or #1 (*see* SPRAYS AND DUSTS).

DISEASES. Fungus cankers* which develop on the trunk or branches should be cut out and destroyed.

ALDER BUCKTHORN = *Rhamnus Frangula.*

ALDER FAMILY = Betulaceae.

ALEPPO GRASS = *Sorghum halepense.*

ALEPPO PINE = *Pinus halepensis.* See PINE.

---

* Special articles on the subjects indicated by an asterisk (*) will be found at the words so marked.

ALERCE = *Fitzroya cupressoides;* also *Libocedrus chilensis; see* INCENSE CEDAR.

ALETRIS (a-lee'tris). A small genus of perennial herbs of the lily family, one grown for its stiff stalk of white tubular flowers. Leaves in a basal rosette* from which arises the flower stalk. Flowers tubular, in a spike, more or less as though mealy, white (in the species below). Fruit a tiny, beaked capsule enclosed by the withered flower. (Greek for a female slave who grinds meal, in allusion to the mealy flowers.)

Aletris is easily grown in an acid (pH* 5) soil in full sunlight. Its erect stiff spikes are attractive enough to make it worth growing in the wild garden, but not to be attempted in ordinary garden soil.

farinosa. Colicroot; called also star-grass. Leaves broadly grass-like, bitter, flat on the ground, about 3 in. long. Flowers tubular, white, about ⅓ in. long, closely clustered in a slender spike at the end of the stiff stalk. Eastern U.S. July.

ALEURITES. See TUNG-OIL TREE.

alexandrina, -us, -um (a-licks-an-dry'na). From Alexandria.

ALFALFA = *Medicago sativa.*

ALFILARIA = *Erodium cicutarium.*

ALGA (plural algae). A flowerless plant of extremely simple structure, usually green, but, in the seaweeds, often beautifully colored. The algae range in size from the microscopic organisms which cover ponds with green scum (*see* SCUM) to the giant kelp, a seaweed over 100 ft. long. See LICHEN.

ALGAROBA = *Prosopis juliflora.* See MESQUITE.

ALGERIAN IVY = *Hedera canariensis.*

ALGERITA = *Mahonia trifoliolata.*

ALICE'S FERN = *Lygodium palmatum.*

ALISMA (a-liz'ma). Aquatic or marsh herbs, family Alismaceae, one grown along pond edges or in the water for its small white flowers. Leaves very variable, often narrow and grass-like if floating, but in mud forms with a distinct longish-oval blade and stalk. Flowers in a branched cluster (panicle*). Fruit dry, small (an achene*) slightly keeled on the back. (Greek name for this plant.)

Of very easy growth in wet places and care must be taken to see that it does not become a pest in the water garden.

Plantago-aquatica. Water plantain. Leaves from grass-like to strap-shaped to much broader, depending on its site. Flowers white, about ½ in. wide, the stalk of the cluster nearly 3 ft. high and much-branched. Throughout north temperate regions. Some consider the native American species distinct from that of Eurasia, but the differences are of no significance to the gardener.

ALISMACEAE (a-liz-mā'see-e). The water plantain family contains only aquatic or marsh plants, in a dozen genera and perhaps 50 species, scattered all over the world. Leaves (in ours) mostly basal and sheathing, but immensely variable, often arrowhead-shaped. Flowers small, borne in whorls* or close or spreading clusters. Petals 3, white. Sepals 3, often chaffy in age. Fruit a cluster of 6 or more, often beaked achenes.* The family is of little garden significance and *Alisma* (the water plantain) and *Sagittaria* (the arrowhead) are the only hort. genera. The first is nearly always aquatic, while *Sagittaria* is used along edges of pools and streams, or in the bog garden.

Technical flower characters: Receptacle flat or convex. Stamens 6 or more, the anthers 2-celled. Ovary 1-celled, usually 1-seeded.

ALKALI-GRASS = *Zygadenus elegans.*

ALKALI SOILS. See ACID AND ALKALI SOILS.

ALKANET = ANCHUSA. See also LITHOSPERMUM CANESCENS.

Alkekengi. Modern version of the Arab vernacular for *Physalis Alkekengi.*

ALLAMANDA (al-la-man'da). A genus of handsome-flowered South American woody vines, family Apocynaceae, widely grown for ornament. Leaves opposite* or in whorls,* without marginal teeth. Flower funnel-shaped or nearly bell-shaped, its five lobes slightly, but distinctly, twisted. Stamens 5, alternating with the lobes of the corolla. Fruit a two-valved, prickly capsule.* (Named for J. N. S. Allamand, a Dutch scientist.)

Allamandas are popular greenhouse vines, and are also much grown outdoors in zones* 8 and 9. They are profuse bloomers and quickly cover buildings and fences, but they will not cling to walls without being tied. In the greenhouse use potting mixture* 4, water freely and use liquid manure every few weeks throughout the growing season. Reduce watering to almost nothing from late autumn until early spring, when the vines can be cut back and repotted, or left in place if planted in the ground. Easily propagated by cuttings. See VINES.

cathartica. Climbing up to 40 ft. Leaves often in groups of four, elliptic-oval, about 6 in. long, very glossy-green. Flowers about 3 in. wide, yellow, or golden-yellow and streaked with white. Brazil. Summer. There are many hort. varieties, of which the best is *var.* **hendersoni.** This is commonly called the golden trumpet and has more flowers than the type and they are often 5 in. across. This variety is the chief hort. favorite.

neriifolia. Yellow bell. Much shorter than *A. cathartica*, and often merely a sprawling shrub 3–5 ft. high. Leaves oblong or elliptic, about 4 in. long. Flowers golden-yellow, striped brownish-red inside, about 3 in. long and distinctly swollen and greenish at the base. Brazil. Summer.

ALLEGHENY BARBERRY = *Berberis canadensis.*

ALLEGHENY SPURGE = *Pachysandra procumbens.*

ALLEGHENY VINE = *Adlumia fungosa.*

alliacea, -us, -um (al-lee-ace'ee-a). Onion-like.

alliariaefolia, -us, -um (al-lee-air-ee-eye-

---

* Special articles on the subjects indicated by an asterisk (*) will be found at the words so marked.

fo′li-a). With leaves like the genus *Alliaria,* which is of little or no garden interest.

ALLIGATOR PEAR. *See* Persea americana.

ALLIGATOR WAMPEE = *Pontederia cordata.*

ALLIONIACEAE = Nyctaginaceae.

ALLIUM (al′li-um). A large genus of mostly onion-scented herbs which includes both the common onion, the leek, garlic, chives, and shallot, as well as another group of perennial herbs grown for their ornamental flowers. Nearly all bear bulbs, often of considerable size, as in the common onion. Leaves mostly basal, typically hollow, but usually flat in the ornamental species. Flowers few to a great many, always in a cluster (umbel *), the stalklets of which arise at one point and produce a usually ball-like flower cluster, variously colored. Fruit a small capsule. (*Allium* is the classical name of the garlic.)

The ornamental alliums are suitable border plants of easy culture in any ordinary garden soil. Most of the onion tribe produce bulbils * which provide a sometimes too excessive method of propagation. Plant the bulbs in autumn or spring or sow seeds in spring. Some yield an onion-scented honey, especially in Calif.

acuminatum. An ornamental species from the Rocky Mts., usually less than 1 ft. high. Leaves about ½ in. wide. Flowers numerous, the umbels profuse, rose-purple. July.

albopilosum. An ornamental herb from Persia to Turkestan, the flowering stalk 18–30 in. high, and terete.* Leaves white-hairy beneath, 12–18 in. long, 1–1½ in. wide. Flowers numerous in a ball-like cluster often 5–7 in. in diameter, lilac and most handsome. June–July. Called by some *A. christophi.*

ascalonicum. Shallot, sometimes called eschallot. About 1 ft. high and resembling the common onion but with small awl-like leaves, and small, more or less angular bulbs that break up into bulblets.* Flowers not always present in the commonly cultivated form, when present violet or white. Possibly native of As., but may be a cultigen.* For culture *see* Shallot.

azureum = *Allium caeruleum.*

caeruleum. A stout herb 2–3 ft. high, cult. for ornament. Leaves 3-sided. Flower clusters (umbels*) dense, about 2 in. thick, deep blue. Turkestan and Siberia.

carinatum. A European ornamental allium, 1–2 ft. high. Leaves flat, scarcely ⅛ in. wide, finely toothed. Flowers violet-purple, rather sparse in the cluster, often the cluster bearing also bulbils.* Summer. A plant resembling this, known here as *A. oleraceum,* has escaped from cult. in the eastern U.S.

Cepa. Onion. Bulb large. Leaves very various, usually bluish-gray and hollow. Flowering stalk about 18 in. high, the umbels profuse, white or lilac. Western Asia. For culture and garden varieties *see* Onion. There are in addition two well-marked hort. varieties: *var.* **aggregatum,** the potato or multiplier onion, which has separable bulbs used for propagation and a sparse flower cluster; and *var.* **viviparum,** the top onion, commonly propagated by its numerous bulbils,* which has small or undeveloped underground bulbs.

cernuum. The wild onion. *See* the end of the list at Weeds.

cyaneum. A Chinese perennial, 6–12 in. high, the narrow leaves channeled above, scarcely ½ in. wide. Flowers bell-shaped, nodding, blue, the blue stamens° protruding. Summer.

farreri. From 10–15 in. high, the stalk angled or winged, and red below. Leaves 12–15 in. long, keeled and channeled. Flowers bell-shaped, purplish-red, about ⅓ in. long, in a loose cluster (umbel*). China. June. Some prefer to call this plant *A. cyathophorum farreri.*

fistulosum. Welsh onion; called also spring onion. Bulb not much more swollen than the base of the flower stalk. Leaves and flower stalk thick, hollow, about 15 in. high, used for seasoning. Flowers whitish, the umbels very dense. As. The Spanish onion is derived from this species.

flavum. A Eurasian ornamental onion, 12–18 in. high, the leaves narrow, terete,° channeled. Flowers yellow, rather lustrous, in a loose cluster, below which are 2 long bracts.° Summer.

giganteum. Giant garlic. A huge, Asiatic ornamental allium, the flowering stalk often 3–4 ft. high. Leaves bluish-gray, strap-shaped, as long as the flower stalk, about 2 in. wide. Flowers lilac, in a dense, globe-like cluster nearly 4 in. wide. Summer.

karataviense. A very broad-leaved ornamental onion, 6–10 in. high, the leaves as long, but nearly 5 in. wide, bluish-green, sometimes variegated. Flowers white, crowded in a dense cluster (umbel*) about 3 in. in diameter. May–June.

Moly. Lily leek. A decorative species for use in the border or rock garden, usually not over 14 in. high, the leaves flat. Flowers showy, yellow, in a small, compact umbel. Southern Eu. July.

narcissiflorum. A striking perennial, 4–10 in. high, the flat, narrow leaves about ⅛ in. wide. Flowers showy, rose-pink, nodding, but ultimately erect, bell-shaped. Southeastern Eu. July.

neapolitanum. Daffodil garlic. A decorative plant for borders in zone° 7 and southward, elsewhere safer to grow in pots with protection in the cold frame. Leaves flat, a little shorter than the stalk of the flower cluster. Flowers white, the cluster very profuse. Eu. June.

odorum. A common name among nurserymen · but the plants so offered are often *A. tuberosum* or *A. ramosum,* otherwise little known in the U.S.

ostrowskianum. Not over 12 in. high, the 2 or 3 flat, weak leaves sharp-pointed, grayish-green. Flowers rose-pink, in a many-flowered cluster (umbel*). Turkestan. June.

Porrum. Leek. A stout herb, often 2½ ft. high. Leaves flat or slightly keeled, not hollow, 2½ ft. long and just less than 2 in. wide. Flowers white, in dense umbels. Probably a cultigen° of Eurasian origin. For culture and uses *see* Leek.

pulchellum. A Eurasian ornamental onion, 18–24 in. high, the leaves nearly as long but thread-thin, and roughish. Flowers in a loose cluster (umbel*), rose or rose-purple, nodding, and beneath the cluster are 2 long bracts.° Summer.

rosenbachianum. A showy onion from Turkestan, 18–24 in. high, the two leaves much shorter than the flowering stalk, about ½ in. wide, and smooth. Flowers in a large, rather loose-flowered cluster (umbel*), purple, often

---

* Special articles on the subjects indicated by an asterisk (°) will be found at the words so marked.

with a dark stripe in the center of each segment of the corolla.* May–June.

sativum. Garlic. Smaller than A. *Porrum*, its bulb with several, separable parts all enclosed in a pinkish-white, membranous skin. Flowers pinkish. Eu. For culture and uses *see* HERB GARDENING.

Schoenoprasum. Chive. Often forming tufts or sods with roots and few or no bulbs. Leaves flat, grass-like, but hollow. Flowers rose-purple in a close, head-like cluster. Eurasia. For culture and uses *see* CHIVES. *See also* HERB GARDENING.

Scorodoprasum. Giant garlic. Rocambole. A tall garlic-like herb, the leaves about ⅓ in. wide. Flowers dark purple, sometimes wanting or in part replaced by bulbils.* Asia Minor and southeastern Eu. *See* ROCAMBOLE.

sphaerocephalum. A rather coarse Eurasian and North African ornamental allium, 2–3 ft. high, the leaves channeled, nearly terete,* scarcely ½ in. wide. Flowers in small, dense clusters (about 1 in. in diameter), reddish-purple. June–July.

stellatum. A native American decorative plant from the plains of Ohio, Minn., Ill. and westward, usually about 2 ft. high. Leaves almost flat. Flowers pinkish-rose in stalked umbels.* Summer and later. Easily grown in the border.

textile. An ornamental herb from western N.A. grown for its showy, many-flowered white or pinkish umbels.* Not over 1 ft. high, the bulbs fibrous-coated.

tibeticum. A Tibetan herb grown for ornament, not over 6 in. high, the bulbs somewhat fibrous-coated. Flowers deep blue, the stamens* included.* Offered by many dealers but not usually true to name.

tuberosum. Chinese chives. An Asiatic salad plant grown here as an ornamental, the flowering stalk 15–20 in. high. Leaves a little terete,* but not hollow (as in many onions), scarcely ¼ in. wide. Flowers fragrant, white to greenish-white, often with a dark line in the middle of the segment. Summer. Plants offered as A. *odorum* are often A. *tuberosum.*

validum. A western U.S. wild plant grown for its showy umbels of rose or white flowers. Leaves nearly 2½ ft. long, flat, not hollow. Flower stalk erect, the cluster not nodding. Summer. It needs a moist soil and does not thrive in the East.

ALLOPLECTUS (al-low-plek'tus). A group of 75 species of tropical plants, family Gesneriaceae, sometimes grown in greenhouses for the colored foliage and rather showy tubular flowers. Leaves opposite,* one of each pair not quite so large as the other. Flower clusters in the leaf axils,* the clusters often bracted.* Flowers not quite regular,* somewhat sac-like at the base. Fruit a leathery, -valved pod. (*Alloplectus* is from the Greek meaning plaited diversely, in reference to the calyx.) For the plant offered as *Alloplectus lynchi, see* NAUTILOCALYX LYNCHI.

schlimi. A woody herb or sub-shrub. Leaves ovalish, 3–4 in. long, somewhat heart-shaped at the base, purplish-violet below, green above. Flowers red, the calyx tube yellow below and red toward the tip. Colombia.

ALLSPICE = *Pimenta officinalis.*

ALLSPICE FAMILY = Myrtaceae.

ALMOND (*Amygdalus communis*). Almonds are limited in production to areas less subject to cold and late spring frosts than the peach. Their production is confined mainly to Calif., though some are grown in other states west of the Rocky Mountains, where the winters are not too cold and late spring frosts do not occur.

The production of the almond is more limited than that of the peach because of its blossoming habit. The tree is as hardy as the peach, but it blossoms nearly a month earlier. In the almond-growing centers, orchard heating is a common practice in protecting the blossoms from frost. (For details, *see* FROST.)

Almonds are propagated by budding named varieties onto either peach or almond seedlings. The seed is stratified in sand and planted in the nursery row, generally in Feb. When almond seedlings are used, generally the wild bitter almond is used. Any variety of sweet almond will do, but it is more expensive than the bitter seed. In Aug. or Sept. the seedling is budded to the desired variety, using the common "T" or shield bud. The following spring the stock is cut back to the bud, which is allowed to grow for a season. At the end of the growing season, the one-year nursery tree is dug and ready to plant in the orchard.

The almond on almond root requires a sandy, well-drained soil. If the soil is a heavy loam, especially if wet during the growing season, the trees will die. The almond root is commonly used in orchards where crown gall is not a problem, while the peach root is less subject to crown gall and will grow on heavier and more poorly drained soils.

In preparation for planting, if one intends to irrigate, the land should be leveled. The field is laid out and tree positions located. Most people prefer the square system of planting — spacing the trees 20 to 30 feet apart. In planting the trees, injured roots should be cut back and the tree set in the orchard at the same depth at which it grew in the nursery. Great care must be taken to firm the soil around the roots. Almond trees can be planted any time from late Dec. to early Mar., the particular time being determined mainly by the moisture condition of the soil. One should wait until winter rains have moistened the soil, but it should not be so wet that it is sticky.

After planting, the tree should be cut back to 24–30 inches. If the side branches are strong and vigorous they may be headed moderately and saved for framework branches. Generally, however, they are not properly spaced and all are cut off. It is advisable to leave stubs about ¼ inch long when cutting off these side branches. After one season's growth in the orchard the trees should be pruned. Select three branches, preferably 6–8 inches apart and spaced equally around the trunk, for the primary framework. These should be headed lightly, generally to laterals. Care should be taken to see that the topmost primary is not subdued too much or the other two primaries

---

* Special articles on the subjects indicated by an asterisk (*) will be found at the words so marked.

will make more growth and tend to choke it out.

The second winter's pruning, if the trees have made normal, vigorous growth, should consist mainly of a thinning out. One should not try to save more than two secondary branches from each primary, otherwise the framework branches will crowd in later years. Subsequent pruning should consist of a moderate thinning out. Trees pruned as above outlined should begin to bear the third or fourth year.

Almonds, like any other fruit tree, require some type of cultivation. The amount of cultivation will depend a great deal on whether the orchard is irrigated or not. In non-irrigated orchards the cover crop or natural weed growth should be turned under either by disking or plowing fairly early in the spring. Subsequent weed growth should be controlled by sufficiently frequent cultivations for moisture conservation. If the orchard is irrigated, it is not necessary to cultivate as often, as the water used by weeds can be replaced by irrigation. In either irrigated or unirrigated orchards the ground should be cultivated just previous to harvest to facilitate the harvesting operations.

Almonds in general respond to an application of nitrogen; the usual amount used is one pound of actual nitrogen per tree. In a few isolated cases there is a response to potassium, none to phosphorus.

As with other fruits, there are many individual varieties of almonds; however, there are only about five important ones. In their order of ripening, they are: Nonpareil, Davey, Ne Plus Ultra, Peerless, Drake, and Texas. The Nonpareil is the best of them. In planting almonds, it must be remembered that all varieties are self-sterile and will not set fruit when planted alone or in solid blocks. Any two of the above varieties will set fruit on the other. The so-called Jordan almond is an imported nut used in confectionery, and grown in Malaga, Spain.

In the early fall the outer hull of the almond splits open. When most of the hulls in the centers of the trees have started to split, the trees should be harvested. The nuts are knocked off the tree by striking the smaller branches with long poles, or more recently by jarring the nuts off by striking the larger limbs with rubber hammers. To simplify gathering the nuts large canvas sheets are spread under the trees before the almonds are knocked off. Of recent years special mechanical equipment has been designed to pick up the almonds from the smoothed surface of the ground.

After harvesting, the almonds must be hulled. This can easily be done by hand if the almonds have been grown under favorable conditions. However, it is cheaper and faster to use specially designed machines to hull the nuts. The hulled almonds are spread out, preferably in partial shade, to dry. When the kernels have dried so that they will be crisp, they may be sacked and kept a num-

ber of months in a cool, dry place, provided they are kept away from insects. Almonds which are sold commercially in the shell are generally bleached by moistening the shell and exposing them to sulphur fumes for a few minutes. However, care must be taken not to expose them too long or the sulphur fumes will penetrate the kernel and spoil its quality. — W. P. T.

INSECT PESTS. *See* Insect Pests at PEACH.

DISEASES. Where almonds can be grown and a crop matured, a number of diseases may be present. For control of brown rot, shot hole, and leaf blight, apply pesticide #2 (*see* SPRAYS AND DUSTS) during the dormant stage just before bud break, and repeat when tree is in popcorn stage, full bloom, and at petal fall. For control of scab, use pesticide #9 about 5 weeks after petal fall.

ALMOND FAMILY. *See* ROSACEAE.

alnifolia, -us, -um (al-ni-fō'li-a). With alder-like leaves.

ALNUS. *See* ALDER.

ALOCASIA (a-low-kay'zi-a). A large genus of tropical Asiatic and Malayan slightly woody herbs of the arum family, a few of which are grown in greenhouses for their handsome, often colored foliage. Leaves large, with long, sheathing stalks that usually end in or near the middle of the leaf blade (peltate*), which is often arrow-shaped with a heart-shaped base. Sheath of the flower cluster (spathe*) boat-shaped, the spadix* shorter than it. Fruit a reddish berry. (*Alocasia* is an unexplained variant of *Colocasia*.)

Alocasias have a thick rootstock* and, in old plants, a tendency to be woody at the base. They need rich feeding and should be grown in potting mixture* 4 and watered freely. Do not let the greenhouse temperature fall below 60° in winter, and night temperatures of 70° are preferable. All of them need partial shade. Easily propagated by suckers, which are freely produced from the base, grown in sand over bottom-heat. More rarely grown from seed and sown in pots, with a temperature of 75°.

indica. In the typical (seldom grown) form the leaves are green. In *var.* metallica the leaves have a reddish-purplish sheen, while in *var.* variegata they are white-mottled. These are the commonly grown forms. Stem stout, and when full grown up to 6 ft. high. Leaves 2–4 ft. long, triangular-arrow-shaped, the basal lobes acutely pointed. Sheath of the flower cluster yellowish, often red inside. Malaya.

macrorhiza. Stem often 10 ft. tall, the plant handsome and striking. Leaves broadly triangular-oval, 3 ft. long, the basal lobes much shorter than the main part of the blade, green, but in many varieties with a white midrib,* or white-blotched. Sheath of the flower cluster grayish-green or greenish-yellow. India and Malaya.

odora. Stems not over 2½ ft. Leaves arrowhead-shaped, 2–3 ft. long, the margins wavy, the lobes rounded, borne on a stout stalk nearly 3 ft. long. Spathe* boat-shaped, bluish-green, 4–5 in. long. Indo-Malaya.

sanderiana. Much smaller than the other three. Leaves peltate,* about a foot long, the blades triangular or narrower, the basal lobes

* Special articles on the subjects indicated by an asterisk (*) will be found at the words so marked.

blunter than the tip of the leaf, dark metallic green with white veins and white margins above, purplish beneath. Sheath of the flower cluster green. Philippine Islands.

ALOE (commonly ă′low; preferably a-low′-ee). A genus of 200 species of mostly African, succulent plants of the lily family, a few grown in pots or tubs, often as specimen plants, for their striking usually spiny-toothed leaves, and red or yellow* flowers. Most species are stemless, with a rosette of basal leaves, but some have woody stems. Leaves with a sharp point and spiny or at least bony-toothed on the margin. Flowers mostly in a finger-shaped rather dense cluster, tubular or cylindric, often slightly curved, the tip separated into more or less spreading segments. Fruit a 3-angled pod (capsule*). (*Aloe* is the Latin version of alloch, its original Arabian name.)

Aloes are often confused with *Agave* or century plants which they superficially resemble, but the latter are all American. They will not stand much frost and are grown in the cool greenhouse in potting mixture* 6. *See* SUCCULENTS for general account of handling these plants, of which many species besides those below are to be had from fanciers and specialists in succulents. Propagated by suckers, or, in those producing stems, by cuttings.

aristata. A stemless succulent, the basal rosette of leaves 6–8 in. wide. Leaves about 4 in. long, spine-margined, and banded on the back with white tubercles. Flowers long-stalked, in a loose cluster (raceme*), yellowish-red. S. Af.

barbadensis. *See* A. VERA.

beguini. A hybrid between *Gasteria verrucosa* and a non-hort. species of *Aloe.* The leaves in a basal rosette, about 4½ in. long and half as wide, bluish-green and warty. Not much grown outside the collections of fanciers.

brevifolia. A short-stemmed plant with thick fleshy leaves 3–4 in. long and about 2 in. wide, keeled on the back, bluish-green, the margins beset with stout prickles. Flowers red, in a short-stalked cluster (spike*). S. Af.

ciliaris. Stems weak and sprawling, often climbing 2–3 ft. Leaves many, thin, about 5 in. long, narrowed from a broader base, the margin white-toothed. Flowers red but green-tipped, about 1 in. long, the cluster long-stalked. S. Af.

ferox. Stem 9–11 ft., the leaves in rosettes. Leaves fleshy, reddish-green, keeled on the back, 18–30 in. long, and nearly 6 in. wide, with reddish prickles on the margin and under side. Flowers red, in profuse, branched clusters, the inflorescence* often 3–5 ft. high. A showy plant in bloom. S. Af.

humilis. Practically stemless, the very thick leaves in a basal rosette, about 4 in. long and 1 in. wide, the surface warted with white dots on the under surface, and white, marginal teeth. Flowers in long clusters (raceme*) reddish-yellow. S. Af.

nobilis. Stem, when developed, 2–3 ft. high, rarely forked, the leaves lax, nearly 12 in. long and 2½–3 in. wide. Leaf margins with horny, triangular prickles about ⅛ in. long. Flowers about 1½ in. long, red, but green-tipped. S. Af.

variegata. A succulent resembling *Haworthia* in youth, mostly with basal leaves, but ultimately with a leafy stem. Leaves triangular or V-shaped, in three oblique ranks. Flowers red, about 1¼ in. long, the segments green-striped. S. Af.

vera. True aloe, sometimes called Barbados aloe. Stemless, the rosette of basal leaves grayish-green. Leaves 1–2 ft. long, erect, juicy, spiny-margined, and, with other (not hort.) species, the source of bitter aloes. Flowers 1 in. long, yellow, the nodding cluster on a stalk somewhat longer than the leaves. Northern Africa, but widely naturalized throughout the tropical world and widely grown as a greenhouse pot plant. A recent suggestion is that the correct name for this plant is A. *barbadensis,* but it is not native in Barbados although much grown there as a source of bitter aloes.

ALOE FAMILY. *See* LILIACEAE.

aloides (a-loy′deez; but *see* OÏDES). Aloe-like.

aloifolia, -us, -um (a-low-i-fo′li-a). With leaves like an aloe.

ALONSOA (a-lon-zō′a). A small group of tropical American herbs of the figwort family, grown as annuals outdoors, or as greenhouse plants for their attractive red, winter-blooming flowers. Leaves opposite* or in threes. Flowers in terminal finger-shaped clusters, the corolla very irregular, two-lipped,* and turned upside down by twisting of its individual stalklets, its tube nearly lacking. Fruit an oblongish pod (capsule*) with many small seeds. (Named for Alonzo Zanoni, a Bogotá official.) The plants are sometimes known as mask-flower.

Easily grown as summer annuals in any ordinary warm garden soil. For winter bloom sow the seed in potting mixture* 3 and put in cool greenhouse in November.

acutifolia. Bushy herb up to 3 ft. Leaves ovalish, deeply toothed on the margin. Flowers vermilion-red, the cluster leafy and elongated, the upper lip very large. Peru. There is a white-flowered hort. variety.

warscewiczi. Resembling the last but larger, the leaves with double-toothed margins and pale on the under side. Flowers scarlet-red, the cluster looser and not so leafy. Peru. The commonly cultivated plant, and offered with various names such as A. *grandiflora,* A. *compacta* and, perhaps, as A. *mutissi.*

alopecuroides (a-low-pee-cure-oy′deez; but *see* OÏDES). Like the meadow foxtail (*Alopecurus*).

ALOPECURUS (a-low-pee-cure′us). A genus of 25 species of meadow grasses mostly from the cooler parts of the north temperate zone, one widely used in grass mixtures for meadows. The only hort. species somewhat resembles timothy but is lower and has shorter spikes. (*Alopecurus* is Greek for foxtail.)

pratensis. Meadow foxtail. Perennial, the stem unbranched and erect from a creeping base, about 18 in. high. Leaves scarcely 6 in. long, slightly roughish. Spike dense, 1–3 in. long, usually standing above the leaves. Eu., but widely naturalized in N.A. A good meadow or pasture grass but too coarse for lawns.

alpestris, -e (al-pes′tris). Almost alpine.

alpina, -us, -um (al-py′na). Growing above timber line.

---

* Special articles on the subjects indicated by an asterisk (*) will be found at the words so marked.

ALPINE. As a term it is strictly applicable to plants found only above timber line on mountains. By extension it has come to be used for any mountainous plant of high altitude, whether from above timber line or not. They are generally grown in the rock garden (which see). As part of a common name it may mean either and has been widely so used. Among the garden plants so called the following occur in this book:

Alpine azalea = *Loiseleuria procumbens;* Alpine catchfly = *Silene alpestris;* Alpine currant = *Ribes alpinum;* Alpine poppy = *Papaver alpinum.* See POPPY; Alpine savory = *Satureia alpina.* See SAVORY; Alpine wallflower = *Erysimum linifolium.*

ALPINE GARDEN. See ROCK GARDEN.

ALPINIA (al-pin'i-a). There are nearly 150 species of these ginger-like herbs from tropical Asia and the Pacific Islands, at least two of which are cultivated for ornament. They belong to the family Zingiberaceae and are leafy-stemmed herbs, some with colored foliage, and showy irregular* flowers in bracted* spikes. Leaves without marginal teeth, parallel-veined, the stalk or leaf-base more or less sheathing. Flowers very irregular,* orchid-like, in a terminal, ultimately nodding cluster. Fruit a slowly splitting capsule. (Named for Prosper Alpino, Italian botanist.)

Can be grown outdoors only from zone* 7 southward, in rich, moist and partially shaded sites. In the greenhouse use potting mixture* 4, give plenty of water and do not let the temperature fall below 60°. Easily propagated by division, which helps to reduce the otherwise large clumps that ultimately develop.

sanderae. A common greenhouse plant of uncertain identity. Leaves about 8 in. long and 1 in. wide, much like those of some cultivated dracaenas, but striped with white, not white-margined. Rarely flowering and the flowers sterile. Origin unknown. Common as a handsome foliage plant under glass.

speciosa. Shell-flower. A leafy-stemmed herb up to 10 ft. Leaves 1–2 ft. long, oblongish, bright green, not over 5 in. wide. Flowers very showy, orchid-like, the lip* yellow with brownish-red markings, the corolla white and tinged with purple. Eastern As. Often sold as *A. nutans* or as *Renealmia nutans.*

ALSIKE CLOVER = *Trifolium hybridum.* See CLOVER.

ALSINACEAE. See CARYOPHYLLACEAE.

ALSINE. Some cultivated plants so named belong to *Arenaria* (which see); for others, mostly weeds, see STELLARIA.

ALSOPHILA (al-soff'i-la). Tree ferns of wide distribution in the tropics and belonging to the family Cytheaceae. Of the 300 known species only a handful are of hort. significance and of these the one below is the best known. They have tall trunks covered with the remains of the frond stalks. Fronds (leaves) very large, in a handsome crown at the end of the trunk, the stalks often chaffy, the blade twice- or thrice-compound,* its ultimate segments of considerable size. (From Greek for grove-loving, in allusion to their shade tolerance.)

Alsophilas are very handsome tree ferns which can be grown outdoors only in the moister parts of zone* 9. Rather commonly grown in greenhouses for their graceful feathery foliage. For culture *see* Greenhouse Ferns at FERNS AND FERN GARDENING.

australis. Trunk up to 20 ft. Leaves usually 8 or 10 in the crown, from 5–10 ft. long, green above, bluish-green beneath, the primary segments about 18 in. long, the ultimate segments about 4–5 in. long and an inch wide. Foliage thus very showy and almost feathery. Aust.

ALSTROEMERIA (al-stro-meer'i-a). The Peruvian lilies comprise perhaps 50 species of South American herbs, family Amaryllidaceae, a few of which are grown in the greenhouse or outdoors (*see* below) for their showy, lily-like flowers. Roots fibrous or tuberous, the stem slender. Leaves often twisted at the base, narrow. Flowers slightly irregular* in a terminal cluster (umbel*) which is sometimes compound. Petals not united into a tube. Fruit (capsule*) 3-valved and with many seeds. (Named for Claus Alstroemer, a friend of Linnaeus.)

Peruvian lilies *require special conditions* to do well. *A. aurantiaca* can be planted outdoors in the spring, allowed to bloom through the summer, and lifted for storing in a cool, frost-free and dryish place over the winter. It needs some shade, a rich garden soil, and not too dry a site. Hardy everywhere, in summer, but will not survive the winter from about zone* 5 northward. It is, in any case, better to lift it.

The species are not hardy but can be grown in a cool greenhouse in potting mixture* 4. Pot them up very carefully, for the roots are tender, in the autumn, and give occasional feeding with liquid manure. After blooming, store them as noted above.

Alstroemerias greatly increase their roots during a single season and need plenty of pot space. Divide them when lifting for the resting period and replant in pots or outdoors as needed. Propagated, also, but rarely, by spring-sown seeds. Do not disturb the seedlings the first year.

aurantiaca. Flowering stem erect, 2–4 ft. high. Leaves numerous (up to 50), lance-shaped, about 3½ in. long, whorled* under the flower cluster, scattered elsewhere. Umbel* compound, the flowers yellow, green-tipped and brown-spotted. Chile. Mulching will sometimes save it outdoors, but it is better lifted. Rarely persisting more than 2 years.

chilensis. Flowering stems about 3 ft. high, the few leaves scattered, bluish-green and fringed. Flowers rose-red or whitish, larger than in *A. aurantiaca,* but not so many in the umbel. Chile. Mostly a pot plant and rarely persisting more than 2 years.

Pelegrina. A Chilean perennial, 12–15 in. high, the numerous leaves lance-shaped and about 2 in. long. Flowers numerous, in branched clusters, the corolla about 2 in. long, lilac without, purple-spotted within. Summer. Not persisting more than 1 year. There are

---

* Special articles on the subjects indicated by an asterisk (*) will be found at the words so marked.

many hort. forms, among them *var*. **alba,** with white flowers, usually called lily-of-the-Incas.

psittacina = *A. pulchella.*

pulchella. A Brazilian perennial, 2–3½ ft. high. Leaves oblongish, essentially stalkless, about 3 in. long. Flowers in unbranched or sparingly branched clusters, the corolla about 1½ in. long, red, but green-tipped outside, brownish and spotted inside. Summer. One of the hardiest for outdoor cult., but mulching is necessary north of Philadelphia.

altaclarensis, -e (al-ta-clar-en′sis). Grown at the estate, Highclere, of the Earl of Caernavon, Wales.

ALTAI LILY = *Ixiolirion montanum.*

altamaha. Named for the Altamaha River, Ga.

ALTERNANTHERA (al-ter-nan′ther-ra). Low-growing foliage plants, belonging to the family Amaranthaceae, of little interest except to addicts of carpet bedding, who use them widely, often under the name *Telanthera.* They are perennial plants, mostly Brazilian, and not well understood botanically. Of the 20 or more known species only those below appear to be in common cult. They have opposite, narrow, small leaves, often colored, and minute, chaffy flowers in dense clusters in the leaf axils,* but the flowers are rarely produced due to the shearing which must be done to keep them low enough for carpet bedding. (*Alternanthera* is from the Greek for alternate stamens, in allusion to the 5 fertile and 5 sterile stamens.)

These summer-bedding plants are not hardy and cannot be grown without a greenhouse for winter care. Their use as carpet-bedding plants is based upon their ability to stand shearing, which is done to keep them 4–6 in. high or even less. They need a warm, sunny place and not too rich a soil. Propagated by cuttings taken in Aug. and carried through the winter in the greenhouse, rarely in a hotbed. Or the plants may be divided when they are lifted in the fall. Whichever method is followed, the young plants should be potted up in Mar. (in potting mixture* 3) and grown along in the temperate greenhouse until the season for outdoor bedding has arrived. They should then be planted close together and shearing started as soon as they become established.

amoena. A dwarf foliage plant, rarely over 4 in. high. Leaves more or less elliptic, green, but with orange or red blotches, or both. Brazil. There are several hort. forms with variously colored foliage.

bettzickiana. A somewhat higher plant than *A. amoena,* and the most popular for carpet bedding. Leaves narrowly spatula-shaped, mostly cream-yellow or red, but in the numerous hort. forms golden, striped, copper, olive-green, etc., and also available in a very dwarf form naturally, only 2–3 in. high. Probably Brazil.

versicolor. A medium-sized herb, 6–8 in. high. Leaves broadly spatula-shaped or roundish, blood-red or coppery. Brazil.

ALTERNATE. Having the point of attachment, as of leaves, twigs or branches, not exactly opposite each other. *See* LEAF.

ALTERNATE HOST. A plant upon which a plant disease lives for only part of its life cycle, depending on some other, and usually unrelated, plant to complete it. Common examples are various rusts that live alternately on wheat and barberry, shadbush and juniper, cabbage and wild mustard, white pine and currant or gooseberry. The remedy is to remove one of the hosts and so break the life cycle. *See* Control Measures at PLANT DISEASES.

alternifolia, -us, -um (all-ter-ni-fō′li-a). Having alternate leaves.

ALTHAEA. *See* HOLLYHOCK.

ALTHEA. An incorrect but very common spelling for *Althaea,* for which *see* HOLLYHOCK. *Althea,* in some catalogues, is also applied to shrubby species of *Hibiscus,* especially the rose-of-sharon. *See* HIBISCUS.

ALTINGIACEAE = HAMAMELIDACEAE.

altissima, -us, -um (all-tiss′i-ma). Tallest.

ALUMINUM SULPHATE. This is used for increasing or maintaining the acidity of soils. For details *see* ACID AND ALKALI SOILS.

ALUMROOT. *See* HEUCHERA; *see also* GERANIUM MACULATUM.

ALYSSOIDES. *See* VESICARIA.

ALYSSUM (a-liss′some). The madworts comprise a large genus of Eurasian perennial herbs of the mustard family, widely grown for their deservedly popular and profuse bloom of yellow or white flowers. (For an annual sort, *see* SWEET ALYSSUM.) Leaves alternate.* Flowers in dense terminal clusters. (Greek for allaying rage, perhaps in allusion to its fabled quality of so doing; hence, madwort.)

Although most madworts are of easy culture in any ordinary garden soil, their profuse bloom and often prostrate habit have made them favorites in the rock garden, for pavement planting, and in dry walls. Widely used also in the flower border, for edging, and for cutting. Easily propagated by seed, or by fall or spring division of the roots.

alpestre. A European herb, not over 4 in. high, its grayish-white foliage tufted. Flowers yellow, in short clusters. Primarily a rock garden species which makes flat grayish-white masses. July. Often listed as *A. serpyllifolium.*

argenteum. Yellow tuft. Up to 15 in. high, dense and compact, the base a little woody. Leaves silvery-white underneath. Flowers in close, head-like clusters, deep yellow, blooming all summer. Eu. Often listed as *A. rostratum.* Mostly for the rock garden.

maritimum = *Lobularia maritima. See* SWEET ALYSSUM.

montanum. Compact or low and spreading, not over 9 in. high. Leaves ashy-gray, nearly linear. Flowers sweet-scented, yellow, mostly in June. A rock garden species from southern Eu. forming a carpet.

rostratum = *Alyssum argenteum* or *A. montanum.*

saxatile. Gold-dust; called also golden tuft and basket-of-gold. The most popular and widely grown of the madworts and easily grown almost anywhere in open sunlight. Leaves grayish, numerous, the plant forming dense mats

---

* Special articles on the subjects indicated by an asterisk (*) will be found at the words so marked.

Gold-dust (*Alyssum saxatile compactum*), a single spray of the compact, yellow-flowered perennial, much used in the border and in pavement planting.

or clumps. Flowers golden-yellow, in numerous clusters. Eu. May. Known in many named forms, such as Silver Queen and *var.* **compactum**. a particularly fine strain for pavement planting because of its dwarf habit. The *var.* **citrinum**, with lemon-yellow flowers, is also one of the best.

serpyllifolium = *Alyssum alpestre*.

spinosum. Densely bushy and spiny herb, about 12 in. high, the foliage silvery. Flowers white. July. Southern Eu. and northern Af. A rock garden species requiring sandy or gritty soil and full sun.

amabalis, -e (a-mab'a-lis). Lovable or pleasing.

amara, -us, -um (a-ma'ra). Bitter.

AMARANTH. *See* AMARANTHUS. For the globe amaranth *see* GOMPHRENA GLOBOSA.

AMARANTHACEAE (am-a-ran-thā'see-ee). The amaranth family contains about 40 genera and perhaps 500 species, comprising rather weedy herbs and a few woody plants of wide distribution, particularly in the tropics. The only hort. genera include important everlastings, the cockscomb, prince's-feather, love-lies-bleeding and several plants used in carpet bedding for their foliage. Leaves alternate* in *Amaranthus* and *Celosia*, but opposite* in the other genera here mentioned. Flowers small, inconspicuous and without petals, often chaffy. The close-packed clusters in which they occur, however, are often brightly colored and very showy, especially in the cockscomb and prince's-feather. Fruit dry in all our genera except *Deeringia*, where it is berry-like. Besides those already mentioned, *see* GOMPHRENA, IRESINE and ALTERNANTHERA. While the prince's-feather and love-lies-bleeding both belong to the genus *Amaranthus* it contains also some pernicious weeds. (*See* Prostrate Pigweed in the list at WEEDS.)

Technical flower characters: Calyx herbaceous or membranous, 2–5-parted. Stamens 1–5, mostly opposite the calyx segments. Ovary 1-celled.

AMARANTH FAMILY = Amaranthaceae.

AMARANTH-FEATHERS = *Humea elegans*.

amaranthoides (am-a-ran-thoy'deez; but *see* OÏDES). Resembling an amaranth.

AMARANTHUS (am-a-ran'thus). The amaranths are coarse, often weedy, mostly annual herbs, family Amaranthaceae, widely distributed and, except the following, of no garden importance. Leaves alternate,* often colored in the hort. forms, without marginal teeth. Flowers very small, without petals, but often conspicuous because congested in a chaffy, often brightly colored cluster. Fruit small, dry, 1-seeded. (From Greek meaning not fading, from the everlasting-like character of some species.)

The amaranths will grow nearly anywhere. If the soil is too rich the leaves will be larger, but the plant tends to lose its color. Dwarf varieties with variegated foliage are useful bedding plants. All need full sunshine. Sow seed in the border for tall sorts, and in frames for the bedding varieties, which may be transplanted any time after danger of frost is over.

caudatus. Love-lies-bleeding; called also tassel-flower. Erect but spreading, up to 3 ft. high. Leaves ovalish or oblong, pointed both ends, green and stalked. Flower-spikes long and slender, often in branched clusters, drooping, the terminal one like a rat's tail, all deep red. Tropical. A very popular annual with varieties having blood-red foliage, green or yellow spikes, and one with close, head-like, red flower clusters. Called by seedsmen, a variety of other names, such as *A. dussi, A. elegantissima, A. margaritae, A. superbus*, etc. *See* ANNUALS.

gangeticus = *A. tricolor*.

graecizans. Prostrate pigweed. *See* list at WEEDS.

hybridus. A weedy herb not worth cult., except for its *var.* **hypochondriacus**, the prince's-feather. The latter is a showy plant 3–4 ft. high, the foliage reddish. Flower clusters dense, much-branched and chaffy, red or brownish-red. Tropical.

tricolor. Joseph's-coat, called also fountain plant. A very variable garden annual 1–4 ft. high, except in the dwarf forms. Flowers in stalkless, head-like clusters in the leaf axils,* or sometimes spike-like and interrupted. Leaves sometimes blotched and colored, especially in the forms known as Combustion, Molten Fire, etc. Tropical. There are several hort. varieties, one with narrow drooping leaves, another with red foliage. *See* ANNUALS. *See also* TAMPALA.

AMARCRINUM (am-ar-cry'num). A cult. hybrid between *Amaryllis* and *Crinum*, produced in Calif., where, and along the Gulf Coast, it is grown outdoors. As a pot plant it should be treated the same as amaryllis. (*Amarcrinum* is a contraction of *Amaryllis* and *Crinum*.) The only species:

howardi. Resembling an amaryllis. Flowers funnel-shaped, the segments recurving, the cluster dense, on stalks often 4 ft. long, fragrant, shell-pink. Garden hybrid. *See* CRINODONNA.

* Special articles on the subjects indicated by an asterisk (*) will be found at the words so marked.

AMARELLE. *See* CHERRY.

amaricaulis, -e (am-ar-i-call'iss). With a bitter stem.

AMARYLLIDACEAE (am-a-rill-i-day'-see-ee). The amaryllis family contains over 80 genera and 1250 species of mostly tropical plants. Lily-like in aspect, and differing from the lily family only in the technical character of the superior ovary. Many of the hort. genera of Amaryllidaceae are commonly called lilies. They have alternate* or basal leaves, without marginal teeth, but often prickly in *Agave* (century plant). Flowers typically of 6 segments, the three inner obviously petals, the outer ones sepals or often petal-like. Fruit a capsule* in all our genera except *Clivia*, *Curculigo*, and *Haemanthus* which have berry-like or fleshy fruit.

The family contains many garden favorites (*see* SNOWFLAKE, SNOWDROP, TUBEROSE, *Lycoris*, and *Narcissus*), as well as a group of bulbous greenhouse plants with showy, lily-like flowers (*see* AMARCRINUM, AMARYLLIS, AMMOCHARIS, BRUNSVIGIA, CHLIDANTHUS, CRINUM, EUCHARIS, HIPPEASTRUM, HYMENO-CALLIS, NERINE, PANCRATIUM, SPREKELIA, and VALLOTA). Some of these are tropical, many from South Africa, and there are a few native American genera in cultivation, among them *Cooperia*, *Habranthus*, *Hypoxis*, and *Zephyranthes*.

Furcraea is allied to *Agave* (the century plants); *Alstroemeria* comprises summer-blooming, fibrous-rooted South American herbs; *Anigozanthus* and *Doryanthes* are Australian genera grown mostly in Calif.; while *Sternbergia*, native in the Mediterranean region, resembles *Zephyranthes*. *Ixiolirion* is Asiatic. A recent suggestion to include *Allium*, *Brodiaea*, and several other genera, heretofore included in the Liliaceae, in the amaryllis family, is not here adopted.

Technical flower characters: Flowers arising from sheath-like bracts.* Stamens mostly 6, attached to the throat of the corolla or to the base of its segments. Ovary inferior, 3-celled.

AMARYLLIS (am-a-rill'is). Technically a genus of one species, a South African bulbous herb, family Amaryllidaceae. But, by extensive and not unnatural garden usage, plants belonging to the genera *Crinum*, *Hippeastrum*, *Brunsvigia*, *Sprekelia*, *Lycoris*, and *Vallota* are also called amaryllis, some, in hort. literature, always so.

The genus *Amaryllis* has large, showy, lily-like flowers on a tall, solid stalk (hollow in *Sprekelia* and *Hippeastrum*), which bloom before the strap-shaped leaves appear. Flowers funnel-shaped, the tube short, its six segments erect and ascending. Fruit a globe-shaped pod (capsule*), its irregular bursting revealing the few pellet-like seeds. (*Amaryllis* is the classical name of this or a related plant.)

Belladonna. Belladonna lily. Leaves strap-shaped, appearing usually after the plant blooms. Flowers typically rose-red (purple or white in some of the many named forms),

sweet-scented, about 3½ in. long, in dense clusters (umbels*) at the end of a stout, naked stalk that is often 18 in. long. S. Af. Blooms outdoors in summer, but before or after depending on when it is planted. Often offered as *Brunsvigia rosea*.

formosissima = *Sprekelia formosissima*.
halli = *Lycoris squamigera*.
vittata = *Hippeastrum vittatum*.

The garden amaryllises may be considered as a cultural group, comprising all the genera mentioned above, except *Crinum* (which see). All are typically greenhouse subjects, but many of them can be grown permanently outdoors in zones* 8 and 9, and *Lycoris* (which see) is grown both outdoors and under glass. A few, especially *Hippeastrum*, are used as pot plants for the window garden, or in the open border during summer.

These popular plants all agree in needing a prolonged resting period during the winter. Take up the bulbs and store in a cool, frost-free, dryish place. In the early spring, or even as early as January, re-pot (some large ones need tubs) in potting mixture* 3 and put in a greenhouse with a night temperature of 65° or more. Water once a fortnight with liquid manure, especially toward blooming time.

Those that are to go outdoors, or whose bloom is to be retarded, should be kept dormant longer. All have tender roots and must be handled carefully. After the plants bloom it is important to remember that they must be watered and fed so that the leaves will develop properly and that the bulbs will ripen sufficiently to permit of safe storage. This can be in the old pot (gradually dried out) or they may be plunged in clean dryish sand. Do not, however, allow them to shrivel.

Propagation of *Amaryllis* and related genera can be accomplished by cutting the bulb, at about the end of July, in half, and bisecting the halves, continuing to cut so long as there adheres to the cut pieces part of the base and a little of the stem end of the bulb. Plant the pieces in potting mixture* 2, not too deep, and keep in a well-watered greenhouse at about 60° F. In a few months shoots and roots will develop, and subsequently a new bulb for each piece of cut-up old bulb.

The American Amaryllis Society is devoted to the culture of *Amaryllis* and related genera. Its present address is Box 150, La Jolla, Calif.

AMARYLLIS FAMILY. *See* AMARYLLIDACEAE.

AMATEUR BOTANICAL GARDEN. With only a reasonable amount of space (not less than one acre) anyone can make an amateur botanical garden. It must first be decided what kind of a botanical garden will yield most instruction of the kind the seeker wants. While there are extremely handsome botanical gardens, such as Kew in London, the chief function of such gardens is study and research.

---

* Special articles on the subjects indicated by an asterisk (*) will be found at the words so marked.

Even very large botanical gardens, such as Kew and the New York Botanical Garden, find it best to confine their efforts to one or two of the several fields of study that would be expected in a complete garden. For those contemplating making an amateur botanical garden, it would be essential to select from the following types the one which offers the most appeal.

SYSTEMATIC. Here, arranged in beds or borders and interspersed with related trees and shrubs, the attempt is made to illustrate in living plants all the plant families and genera that can be grown outdoors in your climate. Such a grouping is obviously a job for the professional, but the amateur can make a beginning by reading the following articles in the ENCYCLOPEDIA: PLANT FAMILY, GENUS, SPECIES, PLANT NAMES. In addition it would be necessary to get a flora of your region to show the preferred sequence of the plant families. This sequence should be maintained in your plan for a systematic botanical garden.

REGIONAL. An attempt is made to illustrate with living plants the flora of a certain region or country climatically related to your own. This requires much study of floras of such regions as the temperate parts of Europe and especially of eastern Asia. Such gardens may be of absorbing interest, especially if confined to one country. Climatically and floristically the obvious choice would be China or Japan, then any of the countries in central Europe, but these are much less rich than eastern Asia.

ECOLOGICAL. Here one attempts to grow plants from different habitats (see that term). It involves creating in the garden such specialized places as bog, swamp, water, sandy place, rock garden, marsh, etc. (see these terms). The selection of plants fit for such specialized sites may be found at the entries cited above. See also plant list at ACID AND ALKALI SOILS.

MEDICINAL. This is a grouping, either by plant family or by pharmaceutical use, of all the plants that have reputed or actual medicinal value. There are not many suited to outdoor culture in our climate, and much still needs to be done to determine the best method of culture in order to get the highest yield of active ingredients. (See MEDICINAL PLANTS.) The selection and growth of these is a long-time job needing much study.

HORTICULTURAL — probably the most showy and satisfactory of all amateur botanical gardens but perhaps not quite entitled to that term. Unlike all of those outlined above, here one specializes only in testing horticultural varieties. These are legion and for all except those with unlimited space, a selection would have to be made, i.e., iris, rose, gladiolus, lily, rhododendron, etc. Notes on hardiness, period of bloom, color variants, and other significant data can be collected by anyone who adopts this plan, which is of more direct value to the gardener than any of the other four types.

AMATUNGULA = *Carissa grandiflora*.

amazonica, -us, -um (a-ma-zon′i-ka). From the Amazon.

AMAZON LILY = *Eucharis grandiflora*.

AMBARELLA = *Spondias cytherea*.

ambigua, -us, -um (am-big′you-a). Ambiguous or uncertain.

AMBLYODON. An obsolete name for plants now included in *Gaillardia*.

AMBROSIA ARTEMISIIFOLIA = Ragweed. See list at WEEDS.

ambrosioides (am-bro-zee-oy′deez; but *see* OïDES). Resembling the genus *Ambrosia* which contains the ragweed. See the list at WEEDS.

AMELANCHIER (am-e-lank′i-er). These plants are variously called shadbush, serviceberry and June-berry, while the profusion of white bloom is commonly called shadblow. They are shrubs or trees of the rose family, found throughout the north temperate zone, a few grown for ornament. Leaves alternate,* toothed, the buds prominently pointed. Flowers white, in terminal, rather profuse, clusters (racemes*), usually with 5 strap-shaped petals. Fruit like a miniature apple, but bony inside, sometimes used for jellies. (*Amelanchier* is from the French for *A. ovalis*.)

The species below, all American except *A. ovalis*, are of easy culture in any ordinary garden soil. They are very attractive in early spring with their white flowers, later from their profusion of small, often brightly colored fruit. Easily propagated by sowing ripe seeds, or sometimes by suckers. All are hardy from zone* 3 southward. The plants are alternate hosts* for the fungus of some juniper rusts.

alnifolia. A shrub 3–20 ft. high. Leaves broadly elliptic or roundish, from 1–4 in. wide, coarsely toothed. Flowers white, 6–8 in a cluster (raceme*), the petals narrow, strap-shaped. Fruit edible, juicy, sweet, about ½ in. in diameter, black. Central and western N.A. May. Hardy from zone* 2 southward.

canadensis. A tree to 45 ft., but often shrubby. Leaves pointed prominently, white-hairy when young, green in age, about 2–3 in. long. Flower cluster about 2 in. long, blooming before or with the opening of the leaves. Fruit red-purple, nearly tasteless. April and May. Eastern N.A.

grandiflora. A hybrid tree or more often a shrub derived from crossing *A. canadensis* and *A. laevis*. It differs little from either of its parents but has rather larger, sometimes pinkish flowers, which bloom before the leaves unfold. May. Hardy from zone* 3 southward.

laevis. A tree to 30 ft., rarely shrubby. Leaves purplish-green when young, about 3½ in. long, rounded or slightly heart-shaped at the base, ultimately bright green. Flower clusters drooping, appearing with or after the unloading of the leaves, making a striking contrast with the early foliage. Fruit purplish-black, sweet. May. Eastern N.A.

oblongifolia = *A. canadensis*.

ovalis. A European shrub scarcely exceeding 6 ft., the leaves ovalish, whitish beneath when young, green in age. Flower cluster

---

* Special articles on the subjects indicated by an asterisk (*) will be found at the words so marked.

white-hairy, not drooping, blooming about the time the leaves unfold. Fruit bluish-black, with a bloom. May.

stolonifera. Dwarf June-berry. A low, more or less sprawling shrub, about 3 ft. high, often forming patches because of its underground stolons.* Leaves oblongish, or rounder, white-hairy on the under side when young, ultimately greenish throughout. Flower cluster upright. Fruit sweet, black-purple, with a slight bloom. Northeastern N.A. May, but blooming a few days later than A. *ovalis* where they are grown together. Sometimes cultivated for its jelly-making fruit under the name Success. Easily propagated by its stolons.*

There are many wild species of *Amelanchier* in America, any of which may be locally naturalized. Their technical differences are slight and very puzzling to the gardener.

amelloides (a-mell-oy'deez; but *see* OÏDES). Like a plant of the genus *Amellus* (which see).

AMELLUS. A genus name applied to plants of little hort. value. Derived from it is the specific name *Amellus* (*see* ASTER AMELLUS). Both were named from the River Mella, in Italy, where *Aster Amellus* was first found.

AMENT. A catkin.*

americana, -us, -um (a-me-ri-cay'na). From North or South America.

AMERICAN. As an adjective, widely applied to thousands of North or South American plants, usually to distinguish them from similar or related Old World species. The following apply only to the hort. species found in this book, although some of them are also used for other wild species not admitted here:

American abscess-root = *Polemonium reptans;* American aloe = *Agave americana;* American arborvitae = *Thuja occidentalis;* American beech = *Fagus grandifolia* (see BEECH); American box = *Buxus sempervirens* (see Box); American centaury, see SABATIA; American chestnut — *Castanea dentata* (see CHESTNUT); American colombo, see FRASERA; American cowslip, see DODECATHEON; American crab = *Malus coronaria;* American elder = *Sambucus canadensis* (see ELDER); American elm = *Ulmus americana* (see ELM); American globe-flower = *Trollius laxus;* American hazel = *Corylus americana* (see HAZEL); American holly = *Ilex opaca* (see HOLLY); American hop-hornbeam = *Ostrya virginiana;* American hornbeam = *Carpinus caroliniana* (see HORNBEAM); American ipecac = *Gillenia stipulata;* American ivy = *Parthenocissus quinquefolia;* American larch = *Larix laricina* (see LARCH); American linden = *Tilia americana* (see LINDEN); American lotus = *Nelumbo nucifera;* American lungwort = *Mertensia virginica;* American mountain-ash = *Sorbus americana* (see MOUNTAIN-ASH); American mulberry = *Morus rubra* (see MULBERRY); American persimmon = *Diospyros virginiana* (see PERSIMMON); American redbud = *Cercis canadensis* (see REDBUD); American red elder = *Sambucus pubens* (see ELDER); American sanicle = *Heuchera americana;* American senna = *Cassia marilandica;* American smoke-tree = *Cotinus obovatus;* American spikenard = *Aralia racemosa;* American Turk's-cap lily = *Lilium superbum;* American twinflower = *Linnaea americana;* American wayfaring tree =

Viburnum alnifolium; American white hellebore = *Veratrum viride;* American white water lily = *Nymphaea odorata;* American witch-alder, see FOTHERGILLA.

amethystina, -us, -um (a-me-thiss'ti-na). Violet-colored.

AMIANTHIUM = *Zygadenus.*

AMMIACEAE. See UMBELLIFERAE.

AMMOBIUM (am-moe'bi-um). A small genus of Australian herbs, family Compositae, the one below usually grown as an annual everlasting. Leaves white, felty, alternate* or basal. Flowers yellow, in chaffy heads which are solitary at the ends of the small branches and surrounded by silvery-white bracts.* Ray* flowers none. (Greek for growing in sand.)

Easily grown as a summer annual in ordinary garden soil. Sow the seeds where the plants are to stand. Before the flowers are mature cut and hang in a shady, cool place, when, upon drying, they will hold their color almost indefinitely.

alatum. Winged everlasting. Bushy herb up to 3 ft., the branches prominently winged.* Basal leaves shaped like a javelin; the stem leaves smaller and fewer. Heads about 1½ in. thick, the bracts* petal-like and silvery-white. The *var.* **grandiflorum,** with larger heads, is the best sort to grow. See ANNUALS.

AMMOCHARIS (am-mock'ar-is). A small genus of South African bulbous herbs, family Amaryllidaceae, the one below somewhat grown for ornament, mostly in the greenhouse. Bulb large (6–8 in. in diameter). Leaves strap-shaped, produced before the plant blooms. Flowers red, fragrant, perfectly regular,* about 30 in a terminal ball-shaped cluster (umbel*), on a solid stalk. Fruit a capsule.* (Greek, meaning sand beauty.)

Culture is the same as for the plants discussed at amaryllis.

falcata. Leaves 1–2 ft. long. Flowers with a cylindrical and straight tube, the segments clawed* and slightly recurved at the tip. Blooms in summer if grown outdoors, earlier if in the greenhouse. Called by some *Cybistetes longifolia.*

AMMOPHILA (am-moff'i-la). A very small genus of sand-binding grasses of nearly world-wide distribution on sandy beaches and dunes. Of no hort. importance except to the seaside gardeners who have shifting dunes to capture, for which the species below is the best-known remedy. It will grow nowhere else, and will stand any amount of salt spray. Rootstock creeping and deep below the surface. Leaves tough, wiry, with a minutely saw-toothed margin, pale green below, shining and leathery above. Flowering spike (rarely produced) about 1 ft. long. (Greek for sand-loving.)

Rootstocks, which may be dug or purchased, should be divided and planted about 6 in. apart, each way, and about 3 in. deep. Within a year or two the plant will completely stabilize a shifting dune.

arenaria. Beach grass; called also marram. Tough wiry grass growing naturally in isolated

---

* Special articles on the subjects indicated by an asterisk (*) will be found at the words so marked.

tufts or clumps. Leaves about 2 ft. long, the stalk of the flower spike (when produced) overtopping the leaves. By some this plant is considered as of world-wide distribution on sand dunes, but others consider the native American plant different and call it A. *breviligulata*. Horticulturally it matters little, for both are sand-binders *par excellence*.

amoena, -us, -um (a-mee′na). Pleasing.

AMOLE = *Chlorogalum pomeridianum*.

AMOMUM (a-mo′mum). A genus of 90 species of tropical Asian herbs, family Zingiberaceae, only the following sometimes grown for ornament or for its fragrant foliage. It differs only in technical characters from the ginger (*Zingiber*). Stem leafy, the leaves without marginal teeth. Flowers in dense spike-like clusters, the stalks arising directly from the creeping rootstock. (*Amomum* is also used as a specific name for a *Cornus*.)

The species below is cultivated as is the ginger (which see).

Cardamon. In spite of the specific name this is not the true source of cardamon (which see), but furnishes a cheap substitute for it. Herbaceous, fleshy, about 6 ft. tall. Leaves narrowly lance-shaped, 8–12 in. long. Flowering stalk much shorter than the stem of the plant. Flowers about 1 in. long, brownish-yellow, tubular, but with a distinct lip. Fruit a capsule. East Indies. The whole plant is spicy or aromatic.

AMORPHA (a-more′fa). False indigo. The group comprises a genus of 15 species of N.A. shrubs of the pea family, identified by rather technical characters. Leaves compound,* the numerous leaflets arranged feather-fashion, in pairs, but with a single terminal one. Flowers small, pea-like, in a dense, terminal, usually branched cluster. Fruit a small pod which does not split and is faintly sticky. (Greek for deformed, alluding to the imperfectly developed and small flowers.)

The species below are easily grown in ordinary garden soil throughout the climatic zones assigned to them. The plants are not particularly showy, but are sometimes used in the shrub border or as specimen plants, especially in cool regions. Easily propagated by seeds, cuttings, layers, or suckers.

canescens. Lead plant. A white-hoary shrub up to 4 ft. Leaves with 15–45 leaflets that are oblongish, and usually less than an inch long. Flowers blue, the cluster about 4½ in. long. Central N.A. Hardy from zone* 2 southward. Summer.

fruticosa. Bastard indigo. A bushy shrub up to 15 or 20 ft., not grayish. Leaflets 11–25, more or less oval, about 1½ in. long. Flowers dull purplish or bluish, in clusters 6 in. long. Conn. to Fla., west to the central U.S. Hardy from zone* 3 southward. June. There are pale blue, white, and crisped-foliaged hort. varieties.

microphylla. Scarcely 3 ft. high, the foliage green. Leaflets 13–14, more or less oblong, about ½ in. long. Flowers purple, usually in an unbranched cluster that is nearly 6 in. long. Central N.A. Hardy from zone* 2 southward. June. This is often offered as A. *nana*, which is considered by some as the correct name for it.

AMORPHOPHALLUS (a-more-foe-fal′-lus). For a plant often listed as *Amorphophallus rivieri*, see HYDROSME. True species of *Amorphophallus* are little known to gardeners, but the name has long been incorrectly applied to a species of *Hydrosme*. *Amorphophallus Titanum*, a very rare East Indian herb, flowered for the first time in the New World in the greenhouse of the New York Botanical Garden on June 8, 1937. Its gigantic spathe* was four feet across, and described in the newspapers as "the largest flower in the world." Actually its flowers are minute (*see* ARACEAE) and probably the most evil-smelling known.

AMPELOPSIS (am-pe-lop′sis). A genus of woody, tendril*-bearing vines, family Vitaceae, a few much grown for covering walls. All the species are North American or Asiatic and differ from the closely related grape vines mostly by their inedible fruit and by not having the shredding bark of the grape. Leaves simple* or compound,* the tendrils forking and without the sucking-disks* of the Virginia creeper (*see* PARTHENOCISSUS) and its relatives. Flowers small, greenish or yellowish. Fruit a 1–4-seeded berry. (Greek for vine-like.)

These vines, which have no very strong soil preferences, will grow well on walls, but should be tied at first as they lack sucking-disks.* Propagated exactly as in the grape. *See also* VINES.

There is much confusion in the garden names of these vines. Besides the four species below, the following have been listed by some as belonging to the genus *Ampelopsis*. A. *henryana, quinquefolia, tricuspidata,* and *vitacea,* all properly belonging to *Parthenocissus* (which see).

aconitifolia. Tall-growing but slender vine. Leaves compound,* the 5 leaflets long-stalked, about 3 in. long, often divided and with toothed lobes. Fruit orange-yellow when ripe, bluish at first, about ¼ in. in diameter. China. Hardy from zone* 4 southward, possibly from zone* 3.

arborea. Pepper-vine. A slender vine with leaves twice-compound,* the ultimate leaflets broadly oval, about 2 in. long. The terminal leaflet is much longer-stalked than the others. Fruit nearly ½ in. in diameter, purple. Va. to Mex. Hardy from zone* 5 southward.

brevipedunculata. A stout, vigorous vine. Leaves simple,* more or less three-lobed, about 5 in. wide, the lobes coarsely toothed. Fruit pale blue at first, dark blue when ripe; about ¼ in. in diameter. China. Hardy from zone* 3 southward. Sometimes known as A. *heterophylla.* The *var.* maximowiczi has the leaves more deeply 3–5-lobed and longer flower stalks.

japonica. A tuberous-rooted, graceful vine with shining foliage. Leaves compound, with 3–5 leaflets which may be cut nearly to the middle, the terminal leaflet much larger than the others. Fruit blue, about ¼ in. in diameter, faintly dotted. Northeastern As. Hardy from zone* 5 southward. Also called A. *serjaniifolia. See* Wall-top Tumblers at VINES.

INSECT PESTS. Control caterpillars with pesticide #1 (*see* SPRAYS AND DUSTS).

DISEASES. A leafspot* often causes poor foliage and when severe may result in defoliation. Where plants are growing on a frame

---

* Special articles on the subjects indicated by an asterisk (*) will be found at the words so marked.

Color Illustrations

Plate 1
Garden Flowers

The four color plates that follow illustrate 48 different garden flowers, chosen from 48 plant families. The culture of each flower is described in the body of the book, the appropriate entry word being indicated by **boldface** type in the legends below. Each of the flowers was painted especially for this edition by Eduardo Salgado. For related plants in each family, see the cited pages.

1. Common crocus (***Crocus*** *vernus*)
> Iris family (Iridaceae), page 603
2. Showy orchis (***Orchis*** *spectabilis*)
> Orchid family (Orchidaceae), page 842
3. Hardy amaryllis (***Lycoris*** *squamigera*)
> Amaryllis family (Amaryllidaceae), page 31
4. Foxtail lily (***Eremurus*** *elwesi*)
> Lily family (Liliaceae), page 677
5. Ten-weeks **stock** (*Mathiola incana annua*)
> Mustard family (Cruciferae), page 282
6. Oriental **poppy** (*Papaver orientalis*)
> Poppy family (Papaveraceae), page 860
7. **Carnation** (*Dianthus Caryophyllus*)
> Pink family (Caryophyllaceae), page 196
8. Spiderflower (***Cleome*** *spinosa*)
> Caper family (Capparidaceae), page 188
9. **Nasturtium** (*Tropaeolum majus*)
> Nasturtium family (Tropaeolaceae). No related genera
10. **Columbine** (*Aquilegia chrysantha*)
> Buttercup family (Ranunculaceae), page 1002
11. **Mignonette** (*Reseda odorata*)
> Mignonette family (Resedaceae), page 1009
12. Bleeding-heart (***Dicentra*** *spectabilis*)
> Fumitory family (Fumariaceae), page 438

Plate 2
Garden Flowers

For the culture of each flower, see the text entry indicated by **boldface** type below. For related plants in the same family, see the cited pages.

1. Rose mallow (***Hibiscus** Moscheutos*)
   Mallow family (Malvaceae), page 717
2. **Houseleek** (*Sempervivum tectorum*)
   Orpine family (Crassulaceae), page 275
3. Coral bells (***Heuchera** sanguinea*)
   Saxifrage family (Saxifragaceae), page 1074
4. Lupine (***Lupinus** hybrids*)
   Pea family (Leguminosae), page 663
5. Gas-plant (***Dictamnus** albus*)
   Rue family (Rutaceae), page 1057
6. Prairie lily (***Mentzelia** decapetala*)
   Loasa family (Loasaceae), page 693
7. Rose-of-Sharon (*Hypericum calycinum*). *See* **St. John's-wort**
   St. John's-wort family (Hypericaceae), page 583
8. Sun-rose (***Helianthemum** Nummularium*)
   Rockrose family (Cistaceae), page 232
9. Flax (***Linum** narbonnense*)
   Flax family (Cistaccac), page 687
10. Cranesbill (***Geranium** grandiflorum*)
    Geranium family (Geraniaceae), page 482
11. Snow-on-the-mountain (***Euphorbia** marginata*)
    Spurge family (Euphorbiaceae), page 375
12. Garden balsam (***Impatiens** balsamina*)
    Jewelweed family (Balsaminaceae), page 94

Plate 3
Garden Flowers

For the culture of each flower, see the text entry indicated by **boldface** type below. For related plants in the same family, see the cited pages.

1. Sea holly (***Eryngium** amethystinum*)
    Carrot family (Umbelliferae), page 1247
2. Prickly pear (***Opuntia** compressa*)
    Cactus family (Cactaceae), page 163
3. Rocky Mountain garland (***Clarkia** elegans*)
    Evening primrose family (Onagraceae), page 827
4. Purple Loosestrife (***Lythrum** Salicaria*)
    Loosestrife family (Lythraceae), page 707
5. Bunchberry (***Cornus** canadensis*)
    Dogwood family (Cornaceae), page 266
6. **Trailing arbutus** (*Epigaea repens*)
    Heath family (Ericaceae), page 364
7. Leadwort (***Ceratostigma** plumbaginoides*)
    Plumbago family (Plumbaginaceae), page 949
8. English primrose (***Primula** vulgaris*)
    Primrose family (Primulaceae), page 975
9. Periwinkle (***Vinca** minor*)
    Dogbane family (Apocynaceae), page 50
10. Butterfly weed (*Asclepias tuberosa*). *See* **Milkweed**
    Milkweed family (Asclepiadaceae), page 75
11. Shortia (***Shortia** galacifolia*)
    Galax family (Diapensiaceae), page 321
12. Closed gentian (***Gentiana** andrewsi*)
    Gentian family (Gentianaceae), page 479

Plate 4
Garden Flowers

For the culture of each flower, see the text entry indicated by **boldface** type below. For related plants in the same family, see the cited pages.

1. Red valerian (***Centranthus*** *ruber*)
   Valerian family (Valerianaceae), page 1253
2. Garden verbena (***Verbena*** *hortensis*)
   Verbena family (Verbenaceae), page 1258
3. Chinese houses (***Collinsia*** *bicolor*)
   Figwort family (Scrophulariaceae), page 1081
4. Cardinal-flower (***Lobelia*** *Cardinalis*)
   Lobelia family (Lobeliaceae), page 694
5. Chinese forget-me-not (***Cynoglossum*** *amabile*)
   Borage family (Boraginaceae), page 130
6. Peach bells (***Campanula*** *persicifolia*)
   Bellflower family (Campanulaceae), page 184
7. Globe daisy (***Globularia*** *trichosantha*)
   Globe daisy family (Globulariaceae), page 491
8. Stokes aster (***Stokesia*** *laevis*)
   Daisy family (Compositae), page 256
9. Sweet Scabious (***Scabiosa*** *atropurpurea*)
   Teasel family (Dipsacaceae), page 327
10. Hardy gloxinia (***Incarvillea*** *delavayi*)
    Trumpet-creeper family (Bignoniaceae), page 116
11. Baby blue-eyes (***Nemophila*** *menziesi*)
    Phlox family (Polemoniaceae), page 954
12. Petunia (***Petunia*** hybrids)
    Potato family (Solanaceae), page 1123

Plate 5
Garden Shrubs and Vines

The four color plates that follow illustrate 48 garden shrubs and woody vines chosen from 44 plant families. The culture of each plant is described in the body of the book, the appropriate entry word being indicated by **boldface** type in the legends below. Each of the plants was painted especially for this edition by Eduardo Salgado. For related plants in each family, see the cited pages.

1. Wintergreen barberry (***Berberis*** *julianae*)
    Barberry family (Berberidaceae), page 110
2. Laurel (***Laurus*** *nobilis*)
    Laurel family (Lauraceae), page 650
3. **Akebia** (*Akebia quinata*)
    Family Lardizabalaceae, page 648
4. A white-flowered form of the Japanese wisteria (***Wistaria*** *floribunda*)   Pea family (Leguminosae), page 663
5. Star magnolia (***Magnolia*** *stellata*)
    Magnolia family (Magnoliaceae), page 711
6. Witch-alder (***Fothergilla*** *monticola*)
    Witch-hazel family (Hamamelidaceae), page 527
7. Silver-lace vine (***Polygonum*** *auberti*)
    Buckwheat family (*Polygonaceae*), page 956
8. **Clematis** (*Clematis jackmani*)
    Buttercup family (Ranunculaceae), page 1002
9. Dutchman's-pipe (***Aristolochia*** *durior*)
    Birthwort family (Aristolochiaceae), page 67
10. **Deutzia** (*Deutzia scabra*)
    Saxifrage family (Saxifragaceae), page 1074
11. **Chimonanthus** (*Chimonanthus praecox*)
    Sweet-shrub family (Calycanthaceae), page 179
12. A white-flowered form of ***Spiraea*** *Bumalda*
    Rose family (Rosaceae), page 1042

Plate 6
Garden Shrubs and Vines

For the culture of each plant, see the text entry indicated by **boldface** type below. For related plants, see the cited pages.

1. A form of a Chinese **holly** (*Ilex cornuta burfordi*), without marginal spines   Holly family (Aquifoliaceae), page 58
2. Trifoliate orange (***Poncirus*** *trifoliata*)
                              Rue family (Rutaceae), page 1057
3. Boston ivy (***Parthenocissus*** *tricuspidata*)
                              Grape family (Vitaceae), page 1274
4. Rose-of-Sharon (***Hibiscus*** *syriacus*)
                              Mallow family (Malvaceae), page 717
5. **Xanthoceras** (*Xanthoceras sorbifolium*)
                              Soapberry family (Sapindaceae), page 1069
6. Rockrose (***Cistus*** *villosus*)
                              Rockrose family (Cistaceae), page 232
7. Tara vine (***Actinidia*** *arguta*)
                              Silver vine family (Dilleniaceae), page 325
8. Bittersweet (***Celastrus*** *scandens*)
                              Staff-tree family (Celastraceae), page 203
9. Blue blossom (***Ceanothus*** *thyrsiflorus*)
                              Buckthorn family (Rhamnaceae), page 1011
10. Smoke-tree (***Cotinus*** *Coggygria*)
                              Sumac family (Anacardiaceae), page 35
11. **Camellia** (*Camellia Sasanqua*)
                              Tea family (Theaceae), page 1204
12. Tamarisk (***Tamarix*** *pentandra*)
                              Tamarisk family (Tamaricaceae), page 1190

Plate 7
Garden Shrubs and Vines

For the culture of each plant, see the text entry indicated by **boldface** type below. For related plants, see the cited pages.

1. Rice-paper tree (***Tetrapanax** papyrifera*)
   Ginseng family (Araliaceae), page 60
2. **Symplocos** (*Symplocos paniculata*)
   Family Symplocaceae, page 1187
3. Mountain rose bay (***Rhododendron** catawbiense*)
   Heath family (Ericaceae), page 364
4. Crape myrtle (***Lagerstroemia** indica*)
   Loosestrife family (Lythraceae), page 707
5. Gold-dust tree (***Aucuba** japonica variegata*)
   Dogwood family (Cornaceae), page 266
6. **Styrax** (*Styrax japonica*)
   Storax family (Styracaceae), page 1172
7. Fetter-bush (***Leucothoe** catesbaei*)
   Heath family (Ericaceae), page 364
8. Spurge laurel (***Daphne** Laureola*)
   Mezereon family (Thymelaeaceae), page 1209
9. Buffaloberry (***Shepherdia** argentea*)
   Oleaster family (Elaeagnaceae), page 351
10. **Pomegranate** (*Punica Granatum*)
    Pomegranate family (Punicaceae), page 993
11. Mountain laurel (***Kalmia** latifolia*)
    Heath family (Ericaceae), page 364
12. Flame azalea (***Azalea** calendulacea*)
    Heath family (Ericaceae), page 364

Plate 8
Garden Shrubs and Vines

For the culture of each plant, see the text entry indicated by **boldface** type below. For related plants, see the cited pages.

1. **Oleander** (*Nerium Oleander*)
    Dogbane family (Apocynaceae), page 50
2. Tea-olive (***Osmanthus*** *fragrans*)
    Olive family (Oleaceae), page 824
3. Lavender cotton (***Santolina*** *Chamaecyparissus*)
    Daisy family (Compositae), page 256
4. Pink-flowered form of the butterfly-bush (***Buddleia*** *davidi*)
    Family Loganiaceae, page 695
5. Trumpet honeysuckle (***Lonicera*** *sempervirens*)
    Honeysuckle family (Caprifoliaceae), page 188
6. **Elsholtzia** (*Elsholtzia stauntoni*)
    Mint family (Labiatae), page 643
7. Matrimony vine (***Lycium*** *halimifolium*)
    Potato family (Solanaceae), page 1123
8. Blue spirea (***Caryopteris*** *incana*)
    Verbena family (Verbenaceae), page 1258
9. Cross-vine (***Bignonia*** *capreolata*)
    Trumpet-creeper family (Bignoniaceae), page 116
10. **Gardenia** (*Gardenia jasminoides*)
    Madder family (Rubiaceae), page 1052
11. Silk vine (***Periploca*** *graeca*)
    Milkweed family (Asclepiadaceae), page 75
12. Persian **lilac** (*Syringa persica*)
    Olive family (Oleaceae), page 824

Flowers
and
Architecture

The beauty and convenience of any home can be enhanced by the plant life surrounding it, if careful consideration is given to the many possible types of plantings and to their size, shape, location and color. They should all be integrated into a single harmonious scheme. *See* PLANNING THE HOME GROUNDS, page 921.

Trees already on the site can be used to good advantage. An ancient live oak shelters this small ranch house in Southern California. The pleasantly shaded outdoor living area is defined by borders of spring flowers. *See* SPRING GARDEN, page 1144. *Josef Muench*

The length of this lot is minimized in a striking way by the use of identically colored flowering shrubs in the foreground bed and in the borders leading to the front door of the house. *See* FLOWERING SHRUBS, page 409, and COLOR GARDENING, page 253. *Landscape design by Allan Dalsimer. Courtesy of* American Home

Plantings of evergreens, hedges, iris and other perennials make a fitting setting for this colonial-style cottage. *Paul E. Genereux*

Rhododendron, yew, low pines and broad-leaved evergreens provide an effective background for flowering shrubs and herbs. *See* EVERGREENS, page 383, and BROAD-LEAVED EVERGREENS, page 145. *Paul E. Genereux*

A few well-placed shrubs and vines are often more effective than extensive plantings. They also require less attention. Two climbing vines are trained against the side of this Florida home, camellias are growing beneath the bay window, and two tubs of flowers rest at either edge of the terrace. *See* VINES, page 1265, CAMELLIA, page 180, TUB GARDENING, page 1238. *Landscape design by Boynton Landscape Company. Gottscho-Schleisner*

A perennial border, gorgeous in spring and summer, as an approach to a house. For the plants and management of a border, *see* page 131 at BORDER. *Paul E. Genereux*

Borders

An example of a perennial border where the grade requires it to be above the general ground level. For modifications of this *see* WALLS AND WALL GARDENING at page 1277. *Paul E. Genereux*

Perennial Plantings

Central Beds

These flowerbeds, set in paths of crushed stone, take up a relatively small space, yet give a lavish appearance. Colorful perennials will replace spring-flowering bulbs as the season advances. *See* page 891 at PERENNIALS and page 157 at BULBS. *Design by Fred Stege, landscape architect. Gottscho-Schleisner*

Foundation Plantings

Well-chosen foundation plantings harmoniously relate a house to the grounds surrounding it. The plantings are not only attractive in themselves, but by softening the line at the base of the house they also serve to anchor the building to the ground and dignify its position on the site. *See* PLANNING THE HOME GROUNDS, page 921.

Shrubs, carefully selected, are one of the most practical solutions, for they generally need a minimum amount of care. The low silhouette and strongly horizontal shape of the house shown above requires the use of low-growing evergreens and shrubs. At the near corner and at the central chimney the vertical lines of the house are reflected in somewhat taller plants. *Design by Emil Schmidlin and Ellis Leigh. Gottscho-Schleisner*

Clumps of poinsettias set in masses of fern display their scarlet brilliance fully against the white walls of this tile-roofed Spanish-style Florida home. *See* POINSETTIA, page 952. *Gottscho-Schleisner*

Rhododendrons and azaleas help to soften the somewhat severe lines of this modern ranch house. The pink dogwood adds a vertical accent to the horizontal thrust of the roof. *See* Azalea at page 88 and Rhododendron at page 1014. *Paul E. Genereux*

The classical entrance to this spacious home is framed by low evergreens and more widely spaced birch trees on either side. Beds of tulips and perennials conceal the foundations and colorfully unite house and lawn. *Gottscho-Schleisner*

Sub-tropical Gardens

The Mediterranean style of architecture, colorful use of annuals and succulents, an occasional palm, are typical features of Southern California and the Southwest. *See* CALIFORNIA, page 170. *Josef Muench*

A sub-tropical cottage garden, with a profusion of annuals and perennials — dahlias, petunias, poppies and gladioli — in a limited space. *See* SUB-TROPICAL GARDEN, page 1173. *Josef Muench*

Gardens in Dry Country

The deficient rainfall and nearly continuous sunshine of Southern California makes possible a variety of plants — such as *Agave* and *Mesembryanthemum* — that will not grow in the East. *Josef Muench*

Palms, cacti and *Yucca* in a garden near Santa Barbara with a ground cover of pansies and low succulents. *See* Yucca, page 1321, Succulents, page 1174, and Ground Covers, page 519. *Josef Muench*

Desert Garden

A home in the desert resort of Palm Springs, California, with *Agave* at the gateway and *Washingtonia* (the palm) towering above the house, which is brightened by a yellow *Bignonia* vine. *See* AGAVE, page 16, and DESERT GARDEN, page 318. *Josef Muench*

Seaside Garden

Some bright annuals — such as these marigolds, zinnias, and petunias — will thrive in the moist air of the seashore, but exposure to wind, sand, and salt spray imposes limitations. For plants suited to such sites *see* SEASIDE GARDEN at page 1023. *Gottscho-Schleisner*

Swamp or Bog Garden

Many wild flowers, ferns, shrubs, and trees can be grown in a swamp having reasonably good drainage and soil that is not excessively acid. Other plants, such as these azaleas in the Greenfield Gardens in Wilmington, North Carolina, thrive in the more acid soil of a bog. *See* SWAMP, page 1181, BOG GARDEN, page 127, WILD GARDEN, page 1303, and MUCKLAND GARDENING, page 769. *Paul E. Genereux*

A charmingly informal spring garden — pansies in the tubs, magnolia and lilac in the shrub border, and a closed vista at the end. *See* MAGNOLIA, page 709, LILAC, page 677, and VISTA, page 1273. *Paul E. Genereux*

Spring Gardens

See page 1144

Daffodils, either naturalized in the lawn, as here, or planted in drifts in a border, make a lovely display in any spring garden. For their culture and kinds *see* NARCISSUS, page 782. *Paul E. Genereux*

A quiet path through a half-shady summer garden with white birch, rhododendrons, plantain-lilies and other shade-enduring perennials. *See* SHADY GARDEN, page 1099. *Paul E. Genereux*

Summer Gardens

See page 1177

A lavish border of dahlias separating two sections of lawn. Dahlias require full sun. For their culture *see* page 303. *Paul E. Genereux*

29

Autumn Garden

Chrysanthemums, like a number of other late-flowering plants, are marked by luxuriance of bloom and richness of color. Many varieties decorate the well-shaded brick-paved terrace of this Colonial-style Long Island home, with its high-pitched roof, overhanging second story, and diamond-leaded casement windows. Note the whimsical touch of the peacock in clipped-yew topiary work. *See* AUTUMN GARDEN, page 85, and CHRYSANTHEMUM, page 223. *Designed by the owner, Richard K. Webel, landscape architect. Gottscho-Schleisner*

Rock and Wall Gardens

A rock garden in its proper setting, without the contrived massing of rocks that bespeaks artificiality. For the construction of and plants for a rock garden *see* page 1023. *Paul E. Genereux*

A skillfully executed dry wall with tulips above and grape hyacinth below. For other types of walls and the plants suited to them *see* page 1277. *Paul E. Genereux*

Flagstones, irregularly let into the turf, create a feeling of casual informality in this seaside garden. *Paul E. Genereux*

Natural stepping stones form a winding path through a spring garden beside a brook. *Paul E. Genereux*

Garden Walks

See PATHS AND PAVING, page 865, and PAVEMENT PLANTING, page 867

Brick walks are more formal. This one, curving through beds of brilliant tulips, is edged with timbers. *See* EDGING, page 349. *Paul E. Genereux*

If traffic is not a problem, a grassy aisle creates a sense of coolness and tranquility. It will not stand much tramping. *Paul E. Genereux*

Like walks, steps may be made of many different materials and in many different styles. These formal stone steps are in keeping with the flagstone paving and the wall. The flags are edged with low perennials. *See* PAVEMENT PLANTING, page 867. *Paul E. Genereux*

Garden Steps

See STEPS, page 1156

Picturesque steps can be made of old timbers or railway ties, preferably treated with creosote for permanence. The strong horizontal and vertical lines of the earth-backed risers are a good foil for the masses of colorful plants on either side. *Paul E. Genereux*

Garden Fences

See FENCES, page 388

A woven paling fence blends well with the gray of rock and provides a good background for the clear colors of striking plants such as the chrysanthemums shown here. *Paul E. Genereux*

An ordinary white picket fence encloses this colorful seaside garden on Long Island. *Gottscho-Schleisner*

A simple rail fence separates a border of iris, phlox and other perennials from the adjoining meadow. *Garden designed by Mrs. H. I. Nicholas. Gottscho-Schleisner*

An open brickwork fence confining a rose garden. Such a fence is especially useful in hot regions, as it absorbs less heat than does a solid wall. *Landscape design by Mrs. H. I. Nicholas. Gottscho-Schleisner*

Garden Pools

See WATER GARDEN,
page 1286

A beautifully planted garden pool. Hardy water lilies and other aquatic and shoreline plants thrive in such sites. For a list of them *see* page 1287. *Paul E. Genereux*

A smaller garden pool, edged with stones and surmounted by a charming bit of statuary. An even simpler pool can be made by sinking a water-tight half barrel to ground level. *Paul E. Genereux*

Courtyard Gardens

See bottom of page 928

EAST: This courtyard garden is typical of Boston's Beacon Hill. It is useful chiefly during the growing season. *Paul E. Genereux*

WEST: A courtyard garden in Santa Barbara, California, useful nearly throughout the year. *Josef Muench*

SOUTH: A wall garden adds both privacy and interest to this Florida patio with its Japanese teahouse motif. *Design by John L. Volk, architect. Gottscho-Schleisner*

Roof Garden

Bricks set on end in a scalloped pattern edge the terraced borders of this New York City roof garden. A wide variety of flowers and shrubs provide color throughout the season. *See* Penthouse Garden at PLANNING THE HOME GROUNDS, page 925. *Gottscho-Schleisner*

A well-proportioned terrace is restful and adds dignity to a large house, relating it to the natural forms of the surrounding landscape. The generous turf area on this terrace is flanked by tulip beds. In the background are purple lilacs and a flowering crab in full bloom. *Design by Helen Swift Jones, landscape architect. Gottscho-Schleisner*

Terrace Gardens

Masses of blue flowers are reflected in the unusual coral-tinted pool of this modern terrace. *Design by James Rose, landscape architect. Gottscho-Schleisner*

A flagstone terrace with colorful annuals and perennials. *See* ANNUALS, page 44, and PERENNIALS, page 801. *Paul E. Genereux*

Greenhouse

A well-stocked conservatory permits a variety of plants usually unfit for room culture. For the management of a greenhouse and the plants for it, *see* GREENHOUSE, page 514. *Paul E. Genereux*

House Plants

Even without a greenhouse many desirable plants suited to room culture can still be grown, especially in a sunny window. For culture and a list of suitable plants *see* HOUSE PLANTS, page 572. *Paul E. Genereux*

Porch Garden

Many beautiful plants can be grown in an enclosed porch during the winter months. The conditions here and the plants in it should approximate those of a cool greenhouse. *See* page 516 at GREEN-HOUSE. Metal trays on the tiered window shelves permit small potted plants to stand in moist gravel. *Paul E. Genereux*

Window Garden

A sunny window garden, perhaps with an adjustable shelf, is necessary for light-demanding plants. For a list of them *see* page 574 at HOUSE PLANTS. *Paul E. Genereux*

Succulents

In dry, cool, sunny windows some cacti and succulents are favorites, requiring little watering. *See* page 166 for management of cacti in the home, and page 1174 for the kinds and culture of succulents. *Paul E. Genereux*

Window
Gardens

Flowers

Chinese sacred lily, narcissus and cyclamen give color to this window garden. For other suitable plants requiring full sunshine, *see* page 574 at House Plants. *Paul E. Genereux*

Flowers

Contrast the almost violent color of this group of window garden geraniums and the crimson brocade of the draperies with the restrained effect of the cacti and succulents on the opposite page. For the culture of the geranium in the house *see* page 880. *Paul E. Genereux*

Foliage Plants

Foliage plants are grown for their often variegated or colored leaves, as in this bay window. For a list of foliage plants *see* page 421. *Paul E. Genereux*

Spring

This imaginative composition displays yellow tulips and blue iris arranged in plastic containers against a sea-blue background. The medium-sized cylinder holds the tallest tulips and iris, each stem wired to a pin-type holder at the bottom of the container. The larger flowers are secured by a second pin holder in the low plastic container and placed directly in front of the tall stemmed flowers, thus hiding any mechanics. Small white beach pebbles add weight at the base. In the tall cylinder, which reflects the sea-blue background, goldfish are swimming. *Arrangement by Mrs. Homer Cilley. Photograph by Paul E. Genereux*

Summer

This beautiful arrangement, using one kind of flower and its foliage, achieves a monochromatic harmony of tints, tones, and shades of yellow. The flowers are Ivory Fashion, Yellow Gold, and Yellow Dazzler roses. The delicate rose foliage, buds, and half-opened blooms form an asymmetrical line; the larger, more fully opened flowers are placed at the focal area. The handsome silver container, with its tracery of silver leaves, is mounted on a dark stand. A large pin holder in the container secures the plant material. The satiny textures of the roses and the silver harmonize perfectly and the container's leaf pattern is repeated in the foliage. Set against a delicate blue background, this design is a study in elegance. *Arrangement by Mrs. Leslie Vaughn. Gottscho-Schleisner photograph courtesy of Jackson & Perkins*

Seasonal Flower Arrangements

See FLOWER ARRANGING, PAGE 406

Fall

Highly distinctive arrangements can be created through adroit use of the simplest flowers and containers. These garden chrysanthemums, in a variety of autumn colors, are arranged in an urn-shaped wicker basket. Their design is based on the form of a reverse S curve, cleverly emphasized by the distribution of the plant material. The basket container is lined with a copper pan to hold water and a large pin holder secures the flowers and foliage. The color harmony, scale, and texture of the flowers and the basket contribute to the perfect unity of the design. *Arrangement by Mrs. Edward L. Richardson. Photograph by Paul E. Genereux*

Winter

This Christmas composition was inspired by the famous English potter, Josiah Wedgwood (1730-1795). The wreath of cones, nuts and seed pods was constructed on a wooden frame, to which the materials were wired, each one separately. A second layer, consisting of cotton pods, the starlike forms, was added to give depth. The finished wreath was sprayed several times with flat white paint, then superimposed on a tole tray painted Wedgwood blue. The "horns of plenty," inexpensive commercial pottery, were painted the same blue and filled with sand. Pecan nuts sprayed white and wired together to resemble grape clusters, were placed in each container on long florist's picks. After pine cones, eucalyptus and cotton pods were added at the center, a thin coating of melted wax was poured in the top to hold the material in place. The white marble head of a child completes the composition. *Arrangement by Mrs. Chester Cook. Photograph by Paul E. Genereux*

Colonial

Classic Revival

Victorian

Modern

Period Flower Arrangements

See FLOWER ARRANGING, page 406

Colonial

In the spirit of the early Colonial period, this design uses one simple garden flower, the nasturtium, massed asymmetrically in an old pewter pitcher. The triangular arrangement shows flowers in many tints and shades of yellow and orange. The flowers are in different stages of bloom, the buds being placed at the top of the container, the half-opened blooms toward the center, and the fully opened flowers at the base or focal area. The green nasturtium foliage provides contrasting color and lightens the silhouette. The pitcher rests on a black tole tray and the matching pewter plate at the left completes the design. *Arrangement by Mrs. Henry Swaebe. Photograph by Paul E. Genereux*

Classic Revival

This graceful composition of Russell lupines, white lilacs, roses and ivy, with delicate curving stems, restrained colors and contrasting light and dark hues, exemplifies the chaste elegance of the classic revival period in American architecture and interior decoration (1789-1840). The white alabaster container is lined in copper to hold water, and a pin holder secures the stems. The tall stalks of white lupine irregularly placed at the top and sides form a variegated silhouette. The lilacs add weight, while the roses, ranging from pink to light red, create a rhythm of color throughout the design. *Arrangement by Mrs. Chester Cook. Photograph by P. I. Merry*

Victorian

The romantic mood of the Victorian era found expression in ornate décor, heavy mahogany furniture upholstered in velvets and brocades, dark patterned wallpaper, fringed and tasseled curtains, somber oil paintings encased in massive gold frames. In flower arrangements Victorians favored elaborate bouquets of richly textured plants with a profusion of lush solid blooms. The symmetrically massed design shown here contains many kinds of flowers whose colors and textures are in keeping with the period. The lighter and more delicately shaped flowers — the daisies and magenta fuchsias, for example — are placed along the upper edges, while the darker, heavier blooms lie at the central focal area. Harmonizing with the rich colors of the flowers, the white china container, decorated in gold, and the red velvet cloth on which it rests help to recapture the flavor of the time. *Arrangement by Mrs. William J. Breed. Photograph by Paul E. Genereux*

Modern

Boldness — in design, color, plant materials, containers and accessories — is the outstanding characteristic of contemporary flower arrangements. Like the modern houses they adorn, their design is simple and uncluttered, free from all confusing detail, with each element taking its place in a definite pattern. In this naturalistic composition, tawny yellow, rust and brown daylilies form a rhythmical line reaching upward. The dramatic piece of fungus is suited to the plant material in color and texture.(It also conceals a pin-type cup holder which keeps the flowers and foliage fresh and in place.) Through careful placement of materials — the fully opened blooms toward the base and front, those partly opened toward the top and rear — and the resulting spaces between, the composition achieves a forceful three-dimensional effect. *Arrangement by Mrs. Robert Marsh. Photograph by Paul E. Genereux*

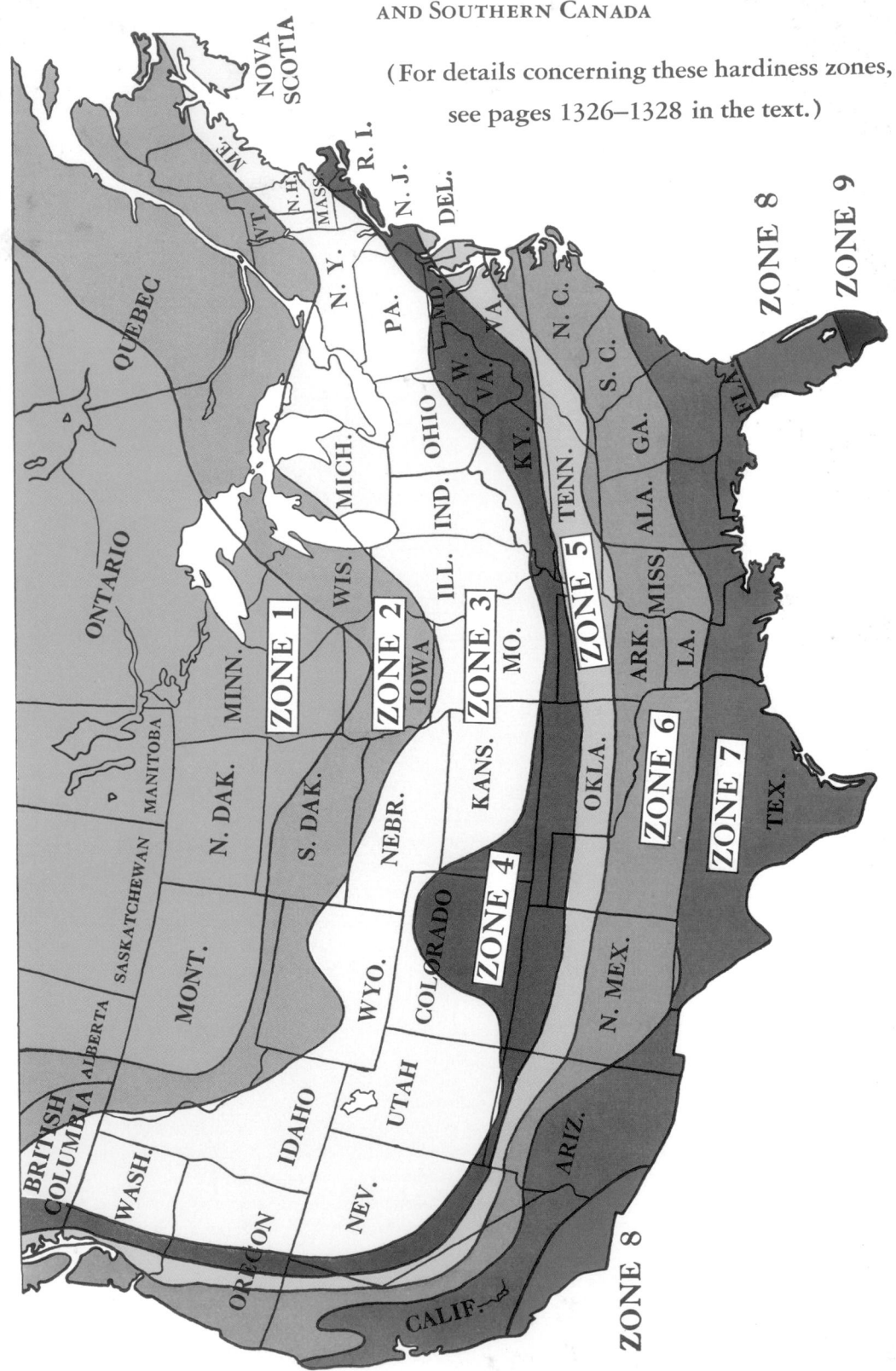

ZONES OF HARDINESS FOR WOODY PLANTS IN THE UNITED STATES AND SOUTHERN CANADA

(For details concerning these hardiness zones, see pages 1326–1328 in the text.)

ZONE 8

ZONE 9

ZONE 1

ZONE 2

ZONE 3

ZONE 4

ZONE 5

ZONE 6

ZONE 7

ZONE 8

NOVA SCOTIA

ME.

N.H.

VT.

MASS.

R.I.

N.J.

DEL.

QUEBEC

ONTARIO

N.Y.

PA.

MD.

W. VA.

VA.

N.C.

S.C.

GA.

FLA.

MICH.

OHIO

KY.

TENN.

ALA.

MISS.

ARK.

LA.

IND.

ILL.

MO.

WIS.

MINN.

MANITOBA

SASKATCHEWAN

ALBERTA

BRITISH COLUMBIA

N. DAK.

S. DAK.

NEBR.

KANS.

OKLA.

TEX.

MONT.

WYO.

COLORADO

N. MEX.

ARIZ.

IDAHO

UTAH

NEV.

WASH.

OREGON

CALIF.

house, it is not possible to use a spray to control the disease. If plants are along paths or on stone walls, apply pesticide #5 (*see* SPRAYS AND DUSTS) as soon as new growth starts in the spring, and repeat 2 or 3 times at 10-day intervals.

amplexicaulis, -e (am-plecks-i-call'is). Stem-clasping.

amplexifolia, -us, -um (am-plecks-i-foe'-li-a). Leaf-clasping.

AMSONIA (am-sown'i-a). A few herbs, the ones below American, the rest Asiatic, belonging to the Apocynaceae, and sometimes grown for ornament. Leaves alternate,* without marginal teeth. Flowers small, funnel-shaped, the lobes long and slender, usually pale blue and in terminal branched clusters. Pods (follicles*) 2, long, slender, and with many seeds. (Named for Dr. Charles Amson, an 18th-century Virginian physician.)

Amsonias are of easy culture in any ordinary garden soil. They are perennials, easily divided in spring or fall.

Tabernaemontana. A bushy perennial up to 2 ft. Leaves taper-pointed, narrow, about 4 in. long. Flowers hairy on the outside, in a dense cluster, but each one scarcely ¼ in. long. Mass. to Tex. Grow in a cool, moist place. Often sold as *A. salicifolia.*

texana. Not over 2 ft. high, the leaves ovalish, about 2½ in. long. Flowers about ½ in. long, smooth on the outside. Tex. and Okla. Will stand drier and more open sites than *A. Tabernaemontana;* also known as *A. ciliata.*

AMUR CORK-TREE = *Phellodendron amurense.*

amurensis, -e (a-moor-en'sis). From Amur, Soviet Russia.

AMUR LILAC = *Syringa amurensis. See* LILAC.

AMUR PRIVET = *Ligustrum amurense. See* PRIVET.

AMYGDALACEAE. *See* ROSACEAE.

amygdalina, -us, -um (a-mig-da-ly'na). Almond-like.

amygdaloides (a-mig-da-loi'deez). Almond-like.

AMYGDALUS (a-mig'da-lus). A very important genus of trees (rarely shrubs) of the rose family. It is of the greatest interest to all gardeners because it contains both the peach and the almond which, by some, are considered to belong to the closely related genus *Prunus* (which see). Leaves alternate,* always toothed. Flowers of 5 petals (except in double-flowered hort. varieties), stalkless or nearly so, and blooming before the leaves unfold. Fruit fleshy, practically always fuzzy as in the peach, the stone pitted or smooth. (*Amygdalus* is the classical name of the almond.)

See ALMOND and PEACH for the hort. varieties and culture of these crops. *A. davidiana* is an ornamental tree with inedible fruit. It has no special soil requirements.

communis. Almond (which see for cult.). A medium-sized tree scarcely ever exceeding 25 ft., the bark gray. Leaves oval-lance-shaped, about 4 in. long, finely toothed. Flowers (in the fruiting trees) about 1½ in. wide, pink. Fruit oblong, 1½ in. long, its stone yielding the edible kernels (almonds). Asia. Because of its showy flowers the tree has many hort. varieties, some white and some double-flowered. The latter bear inedible fruit and are often called flowering almond, a name, however, also applied to *Prunus glandulosa* and *P. triloba.*

davidiana. An ornamental tree, closely related to the peach, and differing only in technical characters. Leaves finely toothed, the stalks sticky. Flowers pink, about ¾ in. across, usually solitary, blooming in March or April. Fruit round, inedible, yellow. China. Hardy from zone* 4 southward.

nana. *See* PRUNUS NANA.

Persica. Peach. Not over 25 ft. high and a short-lived tree. Leaves lance-oblong, narrowly tapering at the tip, about 5 in. long, finely toothed. Flowers pink, usually solitary, very short-stalked or stalkless, blooming well before the leaves unfold. The fruit is the familiar peach (which see for hort. varieties and culture). China, but long cult. in Persia and once thought to have originated there.

There are many ornamental hort. varieties of the peach, grown only for their superb bloom. Some have purple foliage, others double flowers, and white or red forms are also known. Even striped flowers are offered, and as to habit, trees occasionally have weeping branches or a pyramidal outline. Some of them are called flowering peach.

ANACAMPSEROS (a-na-kamp'ser-os). A genus of plants of little interest to gardeners and having fleshy leaves; hence used as a specific name for some plants having fleshy leaves, as in *Sedum.*

ANACARDIACEAE (a-na-kar-di-a'see-ee). The sumac or mango family comprises nearly all tropical shrubs, trees, or vines. A few of the 60 genera and about 600 species, however, reach the temperate zone, especially *Rhus* (sumac and poison ivy) and *Cotinus* (smoke-tree). Leaves alternate,* simple* and often evergreen, or compound* and with many leaflets. Flowers often imperfect,* and in the pistachio (*see* PISTACIA) lacking even petals. Fruit a drupe* but differing widely, relatively large and fleshy in the mango and *Spondias,* usually somewhat dry and much smaller in *Rhus* and *Schinus.* A peculiar fruit is the kidney-shaped one of *Anacardium* (the cashew). Nearly all the plants have resinous bark.

All the hort. genera are tropical except *Rhus, Cotinus,* and possibly *Schinus* (the pepper-tree of Calif.). The mango is much the most important genus.

Technical flower characters: Calyx 3–7-cleft. Stamens as many as the petals or twice as many (5 in *Pistacia*). Ovary mostly 1-celled, rarely 3–5-celled, a single ovule in each cell.

anacardioides (a-na-kar-di-oy'deez; but *see* OÏDES). Resembling the cashew (*Anacardium*).

ANACARDIUM (a-na-kar'di-um). A tropical American genus of shrubs and trees of the sumac family, of garden interest only because it contains the cashew. It is an ever-

---

* Special articles on the subjects indicated by an asterisk (*) will be found at the words so marked.

green tree with simple* rather leathery leaves and many small flowers in terminal clusters. Fruit fleshy, red or yellow, technically part of the receptacle* and commonly called cashew-apple in the tropics. It is about 2½ in. long. The kidney-shaped nut (the true fruit) contains the edible kernel, which, when roasted, is the cashew-nut of commerce. (From Greek, heart-like, in allusion to the shape of the cashew-apple.)

Can be cult. outdoors only in zone* 9, but easily grown there as it appears to need no special soil conditions. It is propagated by seed or by budding. An irritating or poisonous oil in the shell of the nut makes harvesting the nuts a dreadful task. Even the smoke from the burning shells is irritating.

occidentale. Cashew. Not over 40 ft. high. Leaves 4–9 in. long, 2–3½ in. wide. Flowers fragrant, yellowish-pink. "Fruit" (the cashew-apple) more or less heart-shaped, neither edible nor safe when raw. The true fruit, the cashew-nut, must also be roasted before it is edible.

ANACHARIS (a-nack′a-ris). A small genus of American submerged, aquatic, perennial herbs of the family Hydrocharitaceae, useful in aquaria or in pools, but apt to choke both if not kept under control. They have soft leafy stems, the leaves small, opposite* or whorled,* pellucid. Flowers minute, mostly unisexual,* without true petals, the segments sometimes petal-like, less than ¹⁄₁₂ in. wide. Fruit a minute nutlet that ripens under water. (*Anacharis* is from the Greek for very graceful, in allusion to the feathery foliage.)

The plants are of no garden interest except for aquaria, where they are widely popular. Easily grown if rooted in the mud, and very graceful and feathery, underwater plants. Sometimes known as *Elodea.*

canadensis. Water-weed; called also ditchmoss. Leaves about ¼ in. long, scarcely ¹⁄₁₂ in. wide, densely crowded. N.A., but introduced into Eu. and sometimes a pest there. For the plant sometimes called *Anacharis canadensis gigantea see* the next.

densa. Resembling the last, but the leaves less crowded, nearly 1 in. long and ⅕ in. wide. S.A. A better plant for aquaria than the native species.

ANACYCLUS (an-a-cy′clus). A small genus of low or prostrate, annual or perennial herbs of the daisy family, not much grown here except for **A. depressus,** a rock garden perennial from Morocco, useful only in the moraine or scree (*see* ROCK GARDEN). It is a small, prostrate plant, the leaves twice- or thrice-dissected. Flower heads solitary, about 2 in. wide, the rays white, but pinkish-purple beneath. Summer. (*Anacyclus* is from the Greek signifying a flower without a circle.)

ANAGALLIS (a-na-gal′lis). The pimpernels are rather weedy, mostly prostrate herbs, family Primulaceae, comprising perhaps 25 widely distributed species, only two of which are of garden interest. Leaves opposite* or in whorls,* without marginal teeth. Flowers small, mostly solitary in the leaf axils,*

short-stalked, the corolla bell-shaped, its 5 lobes somewhat spreading. Fruit dry (a capsule*), splitting in a circle. (From Greek for delightful.)

There is no difficulty in growing pimpernels, but some difficulty in keeping the first species from becoming a pest. The second is a perennial* or biennial* and a worthy garden plant, propagated by spring-sown seeds or by division.*

arvensis. Scarlet pimpernel; called also poor-man's-weatherglass. A prostrate annual. *See* the list at WEEDS. Otherwise scarcely of garden interest.

linifolia. Erect up to 18 in. high. Leaves narrowly lance-shaped, 1 in. long. Flowers blue, but reddish toward the base, especially on the outside, about ¾ in. wide. Southern Eu. June. There is a hort. variety with oval leaves and another with rose-purple flowers (*var.* **collina**). *A. linifolia* is sometimes sold as *A. grandiflora.*

anagyroides (a-na-ji-roy′deez; but *see* OÏDES). Like a plant of the genus *Anagyrus,* which is scarcely of hort. interest.

ANANAS. *See* PINEAPPLE.

ANAPHALIS (a-naff′a-lis). A large genus of wild everlastings, family Compositae, one of which is common as a weedy herb in America and is sometimes grown for its white, lasting flowers and gray, felty foliage. Leaves stalkless, alternate,* white-woolly throughout at first, ultimately dull green above. Flowers crowded in small heads, the bracts* of which are pearly-white, very numerous and fairly long-keeping. (*Anaphalis* is the Greek name for some everlasting, but lacks precise application to this genus.) The first species is easily grown in any sandy soil, and as easily transferred from the wild. The second is a woolly perennial from the Himalayas.

margaritacea. Pearly everlasting. Perennial erect herb to 20 in. high. Leaves narrow, pointed, about 5 in. long, without marginal teeth. Flower heads in a terminal cluster, the flowers all tubular, the heads about ¼ in. in diameter. For everlastings they are picked before maturity, dried, and by some, dyed various colors. Throughout the north temperate zone. June–July.

triplinervis. A Himalayan perennial, not over 8 in. high, the oblongish leaves white-woolly beneath and as if covered with cobwebs above. Flowers white, the heads about ½ in. in diameter, in loose clusters (corymbs*).

ANASTATICA (a-nas-tä′ti-ca). One extraordinary little desert plant of the mustard family grown for its remarkable ability to respond to alternate moisture and dryness. When moist it unfolds, revealing small, toothed leaves and minute white flowers. When dry or mature, its small branches curve inward, forming a tight ball which, in the deserts of Asia Minor, is driven by the wind. In this resting state it is often sold as a resurrection plant. (*Anastatica* is from the Greek signifying to make to stand [dryness].)

The only species is of easy culture in a warm, sunny place, preferably in a sandy soil. Sow seeds in spring.

---

* Special articles on the subjects indicated by an asterisk (*) will be found at the words so marked.

hierochuntica. Rose-of-Jericho; called, also, resurrection plant. When expanded, a fern-like herb perhaps a foot across, when dry, a tight ball the size of a small orange. In its dry state, it may be kept many years on a shelf but will expand and sometimes continue growth if put in water. Asia Minor. For other plants sometimes called resurrection plants, *see* POLYPODIUM POLYPODIOIDES and SELAGINELLA LEPIDOPHYLLA.

ANATHERUM = *Vetiveria.*

anatolica, -us, -um (an-a-tol′i-ka). From Anatolia, Asia Minor (now Turkey).

ANATTO = *Annatto. See* BIXA.

anceps (an′seps). Two-headed or two-edged.

ANCHISTEA. *See* WOODWARDIA VIRGINICA.

ANCHOR PLANT = *Colletia cruciata.*

ANCHUSA (an-koo′sa). Alkanet; also called bugloss. A genus of perhaps 40 species of Old World herbs, family Boraginaceae, a few of which are grown for their showy flowers. The plants are all more or less hairy, and have alternate* leaves and leafy, usually one-sided, flower clusters not unlike (in some species) those of forget-me-not. Flowers small, trumpet-shaped, but somewhat closed at the throat. Fruit consists of 4 tiny nutlets. (From Greek for a paint for the skin, *i.e.,* rouge.)

Anchusas are of easy cult. in any ordinary garden soil. Some of the hort. varieties of *A. azurea,* a perennial species, are popular plants for the border or for bedding. Easily propagated by spring-sown seeds or by division in spring or fall.

angustifolia = *Anchusa officinalis angustifolia.*

azurea. A stout perennial usually 3½ ft. high or more. Leaves oblongish or lance-shaped, 2–5 in. long, the base clasping or winged.* Flowers bright blue, about ½ in. wide, the cluster graceful and one-sided. Southern Eu. A widely cultivated plant grown for its splendid flowers. Among the best named forms are Dropmore (a lovely bright blue); Opal (sky blue); and Perry's (dark blue), all of which bloom in June and sometimes again in Sept. All are often sold as *Anchusa italica.*

barrelieri. A perennial, 1½–2 ft. high. Leaves ovalish or narrower. Flowers blue, the tube white, but with a yellow throat. Eu. and Asia Minor. Spring.

caespitosa. A rock garden perennial from Crete, low, more or less prostrate, and disliking winter slush at its crown.* Leaves 3–4 in. long, about ¼ in. wide. Flowers blue, with a white eye,* about ½ in. long, in loose, few-flowered, short-stalked clusters.* Summer.

capensis. Cape forget-me-not. A biennial usually less than 18 in. high. Leaves narrowly lance-shaped, about 2½ in. long. Flower buds red, the expanded flower blue, about ¼ in. wide. S. Af. Used mostly as a pot plant. Not hardy in cold regions. There is a white-flowered variety.

italica = *Anchusa azurea.*

myosotidiflora. *See* BRUNNERA MACROPHYLLA.

officinalis. A biennial or sometimes a perennial, usually about 2 ft. high. Leaves lance-shaped, stalkless, about 4 in. long. Flowers

blue, or purple or flesh-colored, in one-sided clusters and opening in pairs. Eu. June, and sometimes again in Sept. There is a narrow-leaved variety (*var.* **angustifolia**).

ANCISTROCACTUS (an-kiss′tro-cac′-tus). A small genus of globular, spiny cacti from the southwestern U.S. and Mex., shallowly ribbed but covered with small tubercles.* Spines numerous, the central one in each group always hooked. Flowers small and inconspicuous. Fruit green, juicy, generally oblong. (*Ancistrocactus* is from the Greek for a fishhook, in reference to the hooked spine.)

scheeri. Fishhook cactus. Scarcely 2 in. in diameter, the spines whitish, about ½ in. long. Flowers greenish-yellow, on the summit of the ball-like plant, not showy. Tex., N. Mex., and Mex. For cult. *see* CACTI.

andicola, -us, -um (an-dick′o-la). From the Andes.

andina, -us, -um (an-dy′na). From the Andes.

ANDIRA (an-dy′ra). Mostly tropical American trees of the pea family, the one below occasionally grown outdoors, only in zone* 9, rarely in greenhouses. Leaves alternate, compound,* the leaflets arranged feather-fashion. Flowers pea-like, fragrant, rather showy, in terminal branched clusters. Fruit a somewhat short, rather fleshy pod. (*Andira* is a Latinized form of a Brazilian name for these trees.)

If grown in the greenhouse use potting mixture* 4, giving plenty of heat and lots of water. The species below is chiefly of interest as the source of angelin. Propagated by cuttings over bottom-heat.

inermis. Angelin; called also cabbage tree. Not over 35 ft., usually less in cult. specimens. Leaflets in pairs, with an odd one at the tip, oval, or oval-lance-shaped. Flowers purple, the branched clusters rather short-stalked. Tropical America. Little grown outside of extreme southern Fla.

ANDORRA JUNIPER = *Juniperus horizontalis plumosa.*

ANDROMEDA (an-drom′i-da). As here, and usually, restricted, a genus comprising only two species of the heath family. One of them, the bog rosemary or moorwort, is a bog shrub with evergreen leaves, the margins of which are rolled. Flowers very small, pink, urn- or bell-shaped in small drooping clusters. Fruit a capsule.* (Named for the mythological character of that name.)

Can be grown throughout the cooler parts of N.A. but only in very acid soils (*see* ACID AND ALKALI SOILS), preferably in the bog garden or in specially prepared soil in the rock garden. Extremely hardy northward. Easily propagated by division or by layering.

glaucophylla. Scarcely over 1 ft. high, with creeping roots and many small branches. Leaves oblong or narrower, about 1½ in. long. Flowers scarcely ¼ in. long, the clusters (umbels*) nodding. Throughout the north temperate zone. Often offered as *A. polifolia.* May–June. The

---

* Special articles on the subjects indicated by an asterisk (*) will be found at the words so marked.

only other species, a close relative, is confined to N.A. and scarcely in cult.

Andromeda, as a word, has suffered much from the attention of the name jugglers. The resulting confusion to gardeners is well illustrated by the following: All, and many others, were once included in *Andromeda*:

Andromeda calyculata. See CHAMAEDAPHNE CALYCULATA.

Andromeda catesbaei. See LEUCOTHOË CATESBAEI.

Andromeda floribunda. See PIERIS FLORIBUNDA.

Andromeda japonica. See PIERIS JAPONICA.

Andromeda ligustrina. See LYONIA LIGUSTRINA.

ANDROPOGON (an-dro-pō′gon). Several wild species of grass, commonly called beard-grass or broom sedge, are properly included in the genus *Andropogon*, but they are of more agricultural than hort. interest. The name *Andropogon*, however, has been used for many other grasses of great interest to the gardener, and now included in *Sorghum* (which see).

ANDROSACE (an-dros′a-see). The rock jasmines comprise a large genus of annual or perennial herbs, family Primulaceae, a few grown in rock gardens and not of particularly easy culture. They are low, often tufted plants, mostly from Eurasian mountains, nearly all with small basal leaves, often in rosettes.* Flowers resembling a miniature primrose, but the corolla constricted at the throat. (Greek for man and buckler, in allusion to the buckler-like anther.*)

For the culture and uses of the species below *see* ROCK GARDEN.

carnea. Scarcely over 3 in. high; perennial. Leaves in rosettes,* very narrow, about ¾ in. long. Flowers about ⅓ in. wide, in clusters of 3–7, rose-pink or whitish, with a yellow eye. Mountains of Eu. May. A popular variety is *var.* **brigantiaca**, with white flowers.

lactiflora. An annual plant, erect, and usually up to 1 ft. Leaves lance-linear, about 2 in. long, mostly in rosettes.* Flowers white, about ½ in. wide, in rather large clusters. Siberia. June–July.

lanuginosa. Prostrate, white-silky, perennial herb. Some leaves basal, others on the short stem, about ¾ in. long. Flowers in a dense cluster, rose-pink, each flower not over ⅓ in. in diameter. Himalayas. June and July.

primuloides. A Himalayan prostrate perennial, the leaves in basal rosettes.* Covered with whitish hairs and not over ⅜ in. long. Flowers pink, about ⅓ in. wide, the flower stalk scarcely 4 in. high. A difficult rock garden plant, best grown in gritty soil, and prefers freedom from winter slush. June.

sarmentosa. A low perennial bearing runners that creep and may be 5 in. long. Leaves in rosettes,* silvery-white when young, about an inch long. Flowers rose-colored, about ¼ in. across in a profuse cluster that stands about 6 in. high. Himalayas. May. The *var.* **chumbyi** is more dense, closely tufted and much more hairy.

sempervivoides. Spreading by short runners, the rosettes of leaves about ⅔ in. wide. Leaves hairy on the margin, sharp-pointed and toothed. Flowers rose-pink, scarcely ¼ in. high,

crowded in a nearly globular cluster (umbel*) that is about 4 in. above the foliage, its stalk sticky. May–June. Himalayas.

villosa. A densely white-woolly perennial, scarcely 3 in. high. Leaves very small, in rosettes.* Flowers in umbels,* fragrant, rose-colored or white, the throat yellowish-red. Eurasia. June–July.

vitaliana = *Douglasia vitaliana*.

androsacea, -us, -um (an-dro-say′see-a). Like a plant of the genus *Androsace*.

androsaemifolia, -us, -um (an-dro-se-mi-fō′li-a). With leaves like the tutsan, a nonhort. species of *Hypericum*.

ANDROSTEPHIUM (an-dro-stee′fi-um). A prairie genus of American bulbous plants of the lily family, one grown for its spring-blooming pretty blue flowers. Leaves all basal, linear or even grass-like. Flowers in a cluster (umbel*) at the end of a naked stalk. Corolla funnel-shaped, 6-parted, with a crown at the throat. Fruit a capsule.* (Greek, referring to the crown in the flower.)

The only hort. species is of easy culture in a sandy soil. Plant the bulbs about 5 in. deep, and protect with a winter mulch of straw or manure. It is not hardy north of zone* 5, and not always so there, and may be increased by division of the bulbs.

caeruleum. Slender perennial, scarcely up to 8 in. Leaves very narrow. Flowers blue, about 1 in. long, each of them stout-stalked, the naked stalk of the cluster about 6–8 in. high. Central U.S. May. Also known as *A. violaceum*.

ANEMONE (correctly, a-nee-moe′nee; usually, a-nem′o-nee). Windflower or anemone, also the pasque-flowers, *Anemone patens* and *A. Pulsatilla*. These most popular garden plants comprise a large genus of perennial herbs of the buttercup family, mostly confined to the north temperate zone. Leaves compound,* or if simple,* divided or dissected, mostly basal. Flowers usually showy, blooming in spring, summer and autumn, without petals, but with petal-like sepals.* The sepals are 5 in most species, but often (in hort. forms) much more numerous. Fruit a cluster of short-beaked achenes,* not so showy as in the long-plumed pasque-flowers formerly included in the genus *Pulsatilla*. (*Anemone* is the classical Greek name for these plants.)

For culture and uses *see* below.

alpina. A showy pasque-flower with tuberous roots, and not over 8 in. high. Leaves cut into 3–6 sharply-toothed segments. Flowers white, nearly 2½ in. wide, but violet or reddish on the outside. Mediterranean region. May–June. The *var.* **sulphurea** has the flowers sulphur-yellow. Does not transplant easily and best raised from seed.

apennina. A tuberous-rooted herb not over 9 in. high. Flowers solitary, about 1½ in. wide, azure-blue. Italy. Mar.–Apr.

blanda. Tuberous-rooted and usually less than 6 in. high; otherwise resembling the last but with larger and darker blue flowers. Greece and Asia Minor. Among the good vars. offered are Fairy (white), Rose (pinkish), Scythinica (blue outside, white inside), Atrocoerulea (dark blue).

---

* Special articles on the subjects indicated by an asterisk (*) will be found at the words so marked.

canadensis. A native American species for the open border or wild garden and moderately showy. Perennial; hairy; not over 2 ft. high, its long-stalked 5–7-parted leaves basal, and above them a long flower stalk. Flowers few, about 1½ in. wide. Eastern N.A. June. Its creeping rootstocks make it an invasive plant; good for planting under shrubbery.

caroliniana. A slender, woodland, native perennial from an almost tuberous root. Leaves 2–3-parted; mostly basal, but also one or two on the flowering stalk. Flowers white or pink, followed by a woolly fruiting head. Not a very showy native. Southeastern and central U.S. Apr.–May.

coronaria. Poppy anemone. This and *A. fulgens* and *A. hortensis* are the leading tuberous-rooted sorts for pot culture and much grown by florists. Roots regularly swollen or tuberous, plant essentially stemless. Leaves compound,* or twice-compound, the ultimate segments narrowly wedge-shaped. Flowers on a smooth stalk 10–18 in. high, solitary, poppy-like, red, blue, or white, or of many shades in hort. varieties, the best known of which are St. Brigid, The Bride and DeCaen. The outdoor cultivation of all of them is confined to Calif. or the South. Southern Eu. Some varieties are double-flowered. This is the "lily of the field" in the Bible.

cylindrica. Native American species resembling *A. canadensis*, but the flower greenish-white. Useful only for the wild garden. June. Its fruiting head is conspicuous, and more showy than the flowers.

fulgens. A French perennial, tuberous-rooted species, related to *A. coronaria* and differing from it chiefly in its brilliant scarlet or vermilion flowers which have conspicuous black stamens. Culture the same as for *A. coronaria.*

globosa. See ANEMONE MULTIFIDA.

halleri. A silky- and white-haired pasque-flower, 6–15 in. high, the leaves finely divided. Flowers hairy on the outside, at first bell-shaped but the sepals* ultimately spreading, purple or white, the flower about 2½ in. wide. Central Eu. May.

hortensis. The garden anemone, with other species. Related to *A. coronaria* and grown like it, differing only in having brownish stamens,* and in the leaves being only once-compound,* or even merely divided. Its flowers are rose-purple or red, and usually single. Southern Eu.

hupehensis. See note at ANEMONE JAPONICA.

japonica. Japanese anemone. One of the most popular garden perennials, and widely grown in the open border. It is a stout, branching plant, about 2½ ft. high, the leaves compound* but with only 3 leaflets. Flower stalks several, the flowers about 2½ in. wide, and, in some of the hort. varieties, of nearly every color except yellow and blue. Eastern As. There are scores of named hort. forms, many of which are double. All flower from Sept. to frost. It is doubtful if *A. japonica* is the correct technical name of this old favorite. Recent studies have revealed that it may be only a variety (or perhaps a hybrid) of *Anemone hupehensis* or *A. vitifolia*. If true, one of these might well be the correct name for the Japanese anemone. Such a suggestion is of more interest to specialists than to the practical gardener and *Anemone japonica* is here retained as probably a group name for the many showy forms of the Japanese anemone.

magellanica. See ANEMONE MULTIFIDA.

multifida. A silky-hairy perennial, 6–12 in. high. Leaves stalked, deeply 3-parted, the lobes much cut into fine segments. Flowers white in the native, N.A. wild form but red in a S.A. form (offered as *A. magellanica*). A handsome plant, native in northern N.A., also, in some forms, south to Tierra del Fuego. A form offered as *A. globosa*, from the Rocky Mts., has larger flowers than the type and bright red sepals.* May–Aug.

narcissiflora. A Eurasian perennial with mostly basal, 3–5-parted, deeply toothed leaves. Flowers suggesting the poet's narcissus, white or cream-white, often pinkish on the outside, about 1 in. wide, in many-flowered clusters (umbels*). Partial to limestone regions. May–June.

nemorosa. European wood anemone. Resembles the common wood anemone of eastern N.A. (*A. quinquefolia*), but it has stouter flower stalks, and, in some forms, purplish flowers. See *A. quinquefolia*. May. Needs a soil of pH 5.

patens. Not much over 6 in. high, but the flowering or fruiting stalk twice divided. Leaves of 3 main divisions, each of which is divided into many narrow segments. Flower bluish-purple, about 2 in. wide, blooming before the leaves develop. Apr.–May. N.A. This is the pasque-flower of N.A., sometimes called *Pulsatilla patens.*

Pulsatilla. Nearly 12 in. high, the leaves divided feather-fashion and appearing with the flowers, which are blue or reddish-purple, bell-shaped and about 2 in. wide. Eurasia. April. There are also some hort. forms with lilac or red flowers and one with variegated foliage. For culture see ROCK GARDEN. Often called *Pulsatilla vulgaris.*

quinquefolia. The common wood anemone of N.A. It is a delicate plant, useful only in the wild garden, and needs protection from too much sun and wind. Leaves compound,* the three leaflets wedge-shaped and deeply cut. Flowers solitary, white, about ¾ in. wide on very slender and weak stalks. May.

ranunculoides. A Eurasian windflower, with a somewhat tuberous root, and 3–8 in. high. Leaves chiefly basal, 3–5-divided, the segments sharply toothed and usually cleft into 3 parts. Flowers golden yellow, generally solitary, about 1 in. wide. Apr.–May.

rivularis. An Indian perennial, found also in Ceylon, 1–3 ft. high, and with a fleshy, turnip-like root. Leaves chiefly basal, a little hairy, 3-parted, the segments also 3-cleft, and toothed. Flower white or blue, about 1½ in. wide, in many-flowered clusters (cymes*). Apr.–May. Needs protection in cold regions and a damp site in summer.

sylvestris. Snowdrop windflower. A beautiful Eurasian perennial suitable for the shaded border or wild garden. Basal leaves thrice cleft or divided, hairy below, the stem leaves long-stalked. Flowers one or two, pure white, about 2 in. wide, sometimes nodding, fragrant. May. See ROCK GARDEN.

vernalis. Not over 6 in. high. Leaves divided feather-fashion, silky-hairy. Flowers about 2 in. wide, the 6 sepals purple outside but white inside. Eu. April. One of the pasque-flowers of Eu.

vitifolia. See ANEMONE JAPONICA.

ANEMONE CULTURE

Anemone japonica and its hybrids are garden flowers making a grand display just before frost in Sept. and Oct. and will grow in almost any soil. They are easily propagated from root cuttings. Dig up a plant, chop off

---

* Special articles on the subjects indicated by an asterisk (*) will be found at the words so marked.

all roots, cut these into pieces 2 in. long, spread them on a flat or in a frame, cover with an inch of soil, and as they send up growths, pot singly, winter in cold frame, and plant out in spring.

Anemone coronaria, A. *fulgens* and A. *hortensis,* the poppy anemones, are most popular and from these most of our present-day hybrids have originated, St. Brigid being the best known. The tubers can be bought at reasonable prices and should be planted in benches or flats in a rich loamy soil in the fall and allowed to grow along in a temperature of 40° to 45°. They come in the most gorgeous colors, the blue shades being particularly beautiful. They are easily raised from seed, and a wonderful assortment of colors in all the pastel shades is one of the desirable advantages in propagating by this means. Save seed from the largest flowers and the best colors, and when mature sow at once in good rich soil.

As the seed is very light a little care will be necessary to sow it evenly. Sow thinly and when the seedlings are large enough prick off into flats 2 in. apart each way, from which they can be transferred to permanent beds in a shady part of the greenhouse. Plant 4 in. apart and allow them to grow undisturbed until they flower. Do not try to hurry flowering by increasing the temperature as they are very impatient of heat and the temperature may be allowed to drop to 35° without any injury; in fact they enjoy it and will respond with better and larger flowers.

The outdoor species enjoy a rich loamy mixture of soil well drained, but partial shade at midday is helpful in keeping the young plants growing vigorously, and upon this will depend final results. Seedlings will start flowering early and keep up a continuous succession of bloom for many weeks if slightly shaded as the weather becomes warm.

If desired, the tuberous kinds can be taken up, well dried, and kept in dry sand for replanting in Sept. Or they may be left in the bench, and after a period of rest, by keeping absolutely dry, may be started again in Sept. for winter flowering.

INSECT PESTS. Anemone is sometimes attacked by leaf tiers and leaf miners. Apply malathion at weekly intervals. *See* SPRAYS AND DUSTS.

DISEASES. Rusts* and smuts* are sometimes a problem causing orange or gray pustules respectively on the leaves. Remove the diseased plants.

anemoneflora, -us, -um (a-nem-o-ne-flow'ra). With flowers like an anemone.

ANEMONELLA (a-nem-o-nell'a), often called *Syndesmon.* A genus of N.A. woodland herbs closely related to *Anemone* and separated only by technical characters. The only species is A. **thalictroides,** the rue anemone, which can be grown best in a wind-sheltered, shady corner of the wild garden in rich woods soil. It is a delicate perennial

with thrice-compound* leaves, the ultimate segments of which resemble those of the meadow rue (*Thalictrum*). Flowers several in a cluster (umbel*), white, about ¾ in. wide, fragile and on weak stalks. (*Anemonella* is a diminutive of *Anemone.*)

ANEMONY = *Anemone.*

ANEMOPAEGMA. *See* BIGNONIA CHAMBERLAYNI.

ANEMOPHILOUS = Wind-pollinated.

anethoides (a-nee-thoy'deez, but *see* OÏDES). Like the dill (*Anethum*).

ANETHUM. *See* DILL.

ANGELICA (an-jell'i-ka). A very large genus of perennial, usually aromatic herbs of the carrot family, only the two following of much hort. interest. Leaves thrice-compound.* Flowers small, white or greenish, in a simple or compound, terminal umbel.* Fruit small, dry, usually aromatic. (Named for their supposed angelic virtue as medicinal plants.)

The first species is practically confined to herb gardens. For its uses and culture *see* HERB GARDENING. The second is a woodland plant of eastern U.S., useful only in the wild garden. Neither is showy.

Archangelica. *See* HERB GARDENING. A stout plant, often 5 ft. high. Leaves twice-compound,* the ultimate segments 3-parted. Flowers greenish, in immense umbels.* Eurasia. July.

triquinata. Woods perennial up to 3½ ft. Leaves twice-compound,* the ultimate segments sharply and irregularly toothed. Umbels* 6 in. wide, the flowers white. Eastern U.S. Aug. This and one or two other wild species are occasionally grown in wild gardens.

ANGELICA TREE. *See* ARALIA; *see also* ZANTHOXYLUM AMERICANUM.

ANGELIN = *Andira inermis.*

ANGELONIA (an-jell-ō'ni-a). Over 20 species of herbs or low shrubs of the figwort family, only the following of garden interest, all tropical American and grown usually only in the greenhouse. Leaves prevailingly opposite.* Flowers blue or purplish in loose racemes.* Corolla prominently 2-lipped,* its tube almost none. Fruit a nearly round pod (capsule*) splitting by its two valves. (*Angelonia* is a Latinized version of a S.A. vernacular for another species.)

Grown in warm (65° or above) greenhouse in potting mixture* 4. Increased by seeds sown in early spring over bottom-heat, or by division of the roots. Outdoor cult. possible only in protected parts of zone* 9.

grandiflora. A sticky, perennial herb about 18 in. high. Leaves nearly without marginal teeth, lance-linear, about 3 in. long. Flowers blue or purplish-white, about ¾ in. wide, the cluster terminal and leafy. Brazil. May.

ANGEL'S-TRUMPET. *See* DATURA.

anglica, -us, -um (ang'li-ka). English, or from England.

ANGOPHORA (an-goff'o-ra). An Australian genus of shrubs and trees of the myrtle

---

* Special articles on the subjects indicated by an asterisk (*) will be found at the words so marked.

family, the one below planted in southern Calif. and Fla. for ornament. The trees are closely related to *Eucalyptus* but have opposite° instead of alternate° leaves. Flowers white in terminal clusters. Fruit a woody pod (capsule°). (*Angophora* is Greek for bearing a vessel, in allusion to the fruit.)

Culture the same as *Eucalyptus*.

lanceolata. Gum-myrtle; also called orange gum and rusty gum. A medium-sized tree with smooth bark. Leaves evergreen, broadly lance-shaped, about 5 in. long. Flowers white, rather showy. Little cultivated outside of Calif.

ANGRAECUM (an-gree′kum). An extraordinary group of tree-perching orchids from the Old World tropics, the one below sometimes cult. in greenhouses for its ivory-white flower which has a spur about 1 ft. long. The extreme length of this spur led Darwin to postulate some insect, then unknown, with a sucking apparatus long enough to reach the nectar at the base of the spur. Years after, such an insect was found. (*Angraecum* is the Latinized version of the Malayan vernacular angerek.)

For culture *see* greenhouse culture at ORCHIDS.

sesquipedale. Stem about 3 ft. long, clothed with two-ranked (distichous°) leaves 1 ft. long and about 2 in. wide. Flower about 5 in. wide, its petals and sepals nearly alike, the spur long and slender. There are usually 2–4 flowers in a cluster about the length of the leaves. Madagascar. Winter-blooming in the greenhouse.

Anguina (an-gwy′na). A species name derived from *anguis*, a serpent.

angularis, -e (an-gew-lar′is). Angled.

angulata, -us, -um (an-gew-lay′ta). Angled.

Anguria (an-gew′ri-a). A specific name derived from a Greek word for a watermelon-like plant.

angusta, -us, -um (an-gus′ta). Narrow.

angustifolia, -us, -um (an-gus-tee-fō′li-a). Narrow-leaved.

ANHALONIUM. Cacti offered as this are usually *Ariocarpus* or *Lophophora*.

ANIGOZANTHUS (a-nig-o-zan′thus). A small genus of greenhouse herbs from Australia, family Amaryllidaceae, one grown for its greenish-red flowers. Rootstock fleshy but not bulbous. Leaves narrow and sword-shaped, mostly basal. Flowers in 1-sided, woolly clusters (racemes°), hairy inside, the tube long and flaring, slightly irregular. Fruit a capsule.° (Greek, an expanded flower, in allusion to the flaring corolla.)

Grow in cool greenhouse in potting mixture° 4. Propagated by division of its fleshy rootstocks, in spring. It needs less water during the winter season, but an ample supply during spring.

manglesi. Not over 3 ft. high, the stem red-woolly. Flowers about 3 in. long, the tube narrow, green at the base, red above, woolly. Usually flowers in May or June in the greenhouse. Little grown.

ANIMAL INJURY. Many small animals are injurious in the garden. Moles and pocket gophers destroy the roots and bulbs of plants; rabbits and woodchucks eat the tops; while rats and mice may do both. Slugs and snails eat the foliage and flowers.

MOLES. Moles are found on the Pacific Coast, and from the Atlantic west to about the one hundredth meridian, being absent from the intervening territory. They dig endless tunnels just beneath the surface, doing mechanical damage to the plant roots and drying out the fine feeding roots, in addition to feeding on the bulbs in a limited way.

Mole trap

Moles can best be trapped with choker, scissor-jaw, or harpoon traps. They travel their runways more or less regularly in search of food. If the runway is blocked, the animal will often rebuild it in its previous location, if not damaged beyond repair. The runway is opened and the trap set in a loose earth fill, the trigger being in such a position as to cause the animal to spring the trap during reconstruction operations. Some gardeners plant bulbs in wire baskets to prevent the ravages of moles. Others treat a 20–40 ft. strip around the garden border with heavy applications of chlordane or similar insecticides which destroy earthworms and insect larvae, the principal food of moles, thereby discouraging the invasion of these animals from adjacent areas.

MICE. Mice may construct small burrows or travel in those built by moles or pocket gophers. They eat succulent roots, cut and eat foliage, and often completely girdle and kill large trees. Whenever serious damage occurs, the mice are usually so abundant that trapping is too slow, and poison must be used. There are ready-mixed poisons on the market, but a freshly mixed bait of rolled oats will usually give better results. The oats should be slightly dampened with water and Karo, and sprinkled with powdered strychnine alkaloid at the rate of one-eighth ounce of strychnine to two and one-half pounds of rolled oats. The bait should

* Special articles on the subjects indicated by an asterisk (°) will be found at the words so marked.

be stirred constantly while the strychnine is added. This should be dropped in mouse holes and scattered along their runways. It is best used in clear weather in fall and early winter.

Two quarts of apples, carrots, or sweet potatoes cut into half-inch cubes and sprinkled with a mixture of one-eighth ounce of powdered strychnine and one-eighth ounce of baking soda makes a good summer bait. The strychnine and soda mixture should be sprinkled over the cut baits with a pepper shaker or similar instrument, stirring constantly to insure an even distribution. Use while fresh, dropping pieces in the small burrows. If available, zinc phosphide may be substituted for the strychnine. It is employed at about a one per cent ratio to the food ingredients.

RATS. Rats are difficult animals to combat and constant warfare is necessary. Poisons or traps should be used until the rodents are destroyed. Further infestations can be avoided by the elimination of places to hide, such as piles of old boards and rubbish. The inexpensive wooden-base snap traps are effective means for dealing with light infestations. Baits, such as bacon, should be fastened to the trigger mechanism. Traps should be placed at right angles to runways so that the trigger portion intersects the route of travel.

There are many excellent rat poisons on the market which will give good results, if used according to the directions on the package. Most contain cornmeal with a small amount of an anticoagulant chemical as the active ingredient. When such baits are consumed daily over an interval of several days, animals die from internal bleeding. It is advisable to place baits in shallow containers in locations where rats are observed to feed and to replenish each station at daily intervals as long as evidence of feeding is noted. Although these poison formulations entail little danger to small children and pets, it is always advisable to place baits in covered feeding stations or sheltered locations.

RABBITS. Rabbits sometimes cause serious loss by eating the tops of valuable plants. Usually only a few animals are involved, and a No. 0 steel trap, set at the point where the animals are feeding, generally will catch the culprits. Box traps, baited with a bait of carrot or lettuce, may be substituted. Other protective measures include placement of a 2-ft.-high poultry-wire netting around individual trees and shrubs or the entire garden area. Several effective repellent sprays and dusts are also on the market. In many cases, the area can be made less attractive to rabbits by the removal of rank grass or other tall vegetation from adjacent locations.

WOODCHUCKS. Throughout many northwestern states these animals at times cause severe local damage. Their presence is often indicated by mounds of dirt and large burrow openings near rock piles and hedgerows, and similar sheltered locations. They may be destroyed by the application of burrow fumigants such as gas cartridges, calcium cyanide, or automobile exhaust fumes.

POCKET GOPHERS. Pocket gophers, like moles, make extensive underground tunnels which cause mechanical injury to roots and bulbs. In addition, the gophers eat the roots of a wide variety of bulbs, herbaceous plants, shrubs, and trees. These animals are found throughout the territory west of the Mississippi and in the Gulf states to and including Florida. They are easily caught by setting a trap in the laterals to the surface mounds, or a pair of them in the main runway. After the traps are set and inserted, the runway may be left open or only partially closed, the trap being designed to catch the animal as it brings earth to plug the opening.

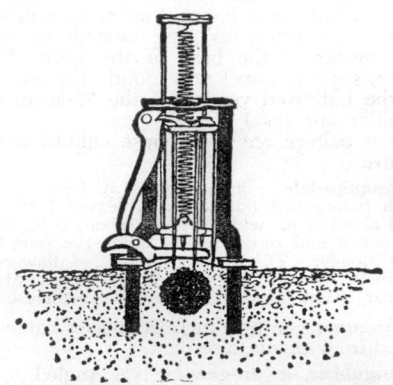

Practical trap for pocket gophers or for moles

Poisoned baits may also be employed, although their effectiveness varies in different parts of the country and during some seasons of the year. Cubed vegetable baits described above for mice may be used. These should be dropped into runways through probe holes made with a broomstick or metal rod. Carefully plug openings after treatment.

The workings of gophers superficially resemble those of moles, but the tunnels usually are deeper, and the mounds decidedly fan-shaped and obviously built from one side, in contrast to the conical mounds of the mole, which are built from the center.

SLUGS AND SNAILS. These persistent garden pests require constant effort if control is obtained. Cleaning up rubbish, rotting vegetation, and weeds will help in keeping down infestation.

A poison bait containing metaldehyde (which attracts slugs and snails) plus either calcium arsenate or sodium fluosilicate has been found effective. Mix 1 ounce of metaldehyde and either 2 ounces of calcium arsenate or 1 ounce of sodium fluosilicate with 2 pounds wheat bran, cornmeal, or similar material. For small gardens apply 1 pound of bait per 1000 square feet. Pellets can be obtained and are preferred for large-

---

* Special articles on the subjects indicated by an asterisk (*) will be found at the words so marked.

scale operations; broadcast at 5–10 pounds per acre. Another method for small gardens is to sprinkle poison on soil or place it in small piles about the size of 50 cent pieces within 5–6 ft. of damaged plants, or dust hiding places with 5 per cent chlordane dust. CAUTION: do not use metaldehyde or chlordane on plants which are to be eaten.

SQUIRRELS. Squirrels, including the red, gray, and fox squirrels of the East and the silver-gray squirrel of the West, occasionally raid fruit trees and corn patches or damage ornamental trees by gnawing the bark from the newer growth. Conifers are most frequently attacked and the damage usually occurs in late winter or early spring when other food becomes scarce. At such times the bark from the leader and the topmost branches are stripped off and the cambium layer eaten, the discarded outer bark being allowed to fall to the ground.

Shooting or trapping the offending individuals is the only sure remedy, although providing food supplies of corn, wheat, nuts, etc., will sometimes reduce the damage. Installation of a metal shield around the tree trunks or application of sticky adhesives to the trunks and branches of fruit trees are helpful measures for preventing crop losses. Further information on control of these pests can be secured from the U.S. Fish and Wildlife Service, Department of the Interior, Washington 25, D.C. For injurious birds, *see* BIRDS. — I.N.G.

ANIMATED OAT = *Avena sterilis.*

anisata, -us, -um (a-ni-say′ta). Anise-scented.

ANISE. The only garden species of the genus **Pimpinella** (pim-pi-nell′a), which comprises many perennial or annual herbs of the carrot family, from the north temperate zone, is the one below, yielding anise. They have twice- or thrice-compound* leaves, the ultimate segments mostly toothed. Flowers small, in a compound unbel.* (*Pimpinella* is possibly a confusion for bi-pinnata; uncertainly applied here.)

P. Anisum. The common anise. Annual, not over 2 ft. high, with long-stalked basal leaves, and shorter-stalked stem leaves. Flowers yellowish-white, the cluster loose. Southern Eu. and Egypt. For culture and uses *see* HERB GARDENING. For the star anise *see* ILLICIUM.

ANISOSTICHUS. See BIGNONIA.

Anisum. An old word for anise; also, apparently, for dill.

ANNATTO = *Bixa Orellana.*

ANNATTO FAMILY. The Bixaceae. *See* BIXA.

ANNONA (a-nō′na). A large genus of tropical trees, family Annonaceae. The species below yield fruits of secondary importance, all of them from tropical America, and are little known in northern markets, because they cannot be shipped when fresh. Leaves alternate,* without marginal teeth. Flowers usually solitary or in clusters, the

calyx tubular, the 6 separate petals in two series of three. Fruit large, fleshy, technically a syncarp.* (*Annona* is a Latinized version of some vernacular name for these trees.)

Of the species below, the cherimoya (*A. Cherimola*) is by far the most important. Originally Peruvian, it is grown to a limited extent in southern Fla., and from Santa Barbara southward in Calif. It matures in late summer, and is quite variable in size and texture. The most favored form has the fruit beset with numerous tubercles, the pulp is white, aromatic and custard-like in texture. It must be eaten fresh.

The cherimoya can be grown in southern Fla., but requires greater elevations than are found there. It can survive light frosts, but bears poorly over most of the cherimoya region in Fla. which extends from about Dade Co. southward. Plants raised from seedlings rarely come true, and the best plan is to cleft-graft or shield-bud desirable varieties upon the hardier stock of *Annona squamosa, glabra* or *reticulata,* all of which are also grown in Fla.

Trees should be spaced about 25 × 25 ft. apart and yield some fruit after the fourth or fifth year. In Fla. they never bear as well as in tropical uplands.

Cherimola. Cherimoya. Medium-sized tree, up to 25 ft., usually spreading, deciduous for part of the year. Leaves ovalish, 3–6 in. long, hairy below, dull green above. Flowers yellowish, fragrant, about 1 in. long. Fruit egg- or heart-shaped, varying from 4 ounces to over a pound, smooth in some, but tuberculate in the best varieties. Andes of Peru.

glabra. Pond-apple. Evergreen tree to 40 ft. Leaves more or less oblong, about 7 in. long. Flowers yellowish-red, about 1 in. long. Fruit ovoid, smooth, about 4 in. long. Tropical America. Fruit of little value, and the tree is useful chiefly as a stock for the cherimoya.

muricata. Soursop, also called guanabana. A tropical American evergreen tree scarcely exceeding 20 ft. in height. Leaves elliptic, about 5 in. long. Flowers yellow. Fruit ovoid, nearly 8 in. long, green and spiny on the outside. The flesh is white, juicy and tart, and used mostly for ices or beverages. The tree is also used as grafting stock for the cherimoya. Hardy only in zone* 9.

reticulata. Custard-apple, called also bullock's-heart. A deciduous or partly evergreen tree up to 30 ft. Leaves oblongish, about 8 in. long. Flowers yellowish. Fruit heart-shaped, up to 8 in. long, smooth, but marked with depressed lines. Its flesh is far inferior to cherimoya. Hardy only in zone* 9.

squamosa. Sweetsop, called also sugar-apple. A deciduous tree with bluish-gray, thin leaves 3–6 in. long. Flowers greenish-yellow. Fruit cone- or heart-shaped, yellowish-green, about 3 in. long, much broken up by its separable divisions (carpels). The flesh is sweet, custard-like and much liked, but it is very perishable. Hardy only in zone * 9 and protected places in zone* 8.

ANNONACEAE (a-no-nay′see-ee). The custard-apple family contains about 70 genera and possibly 600 species of mostly tropical shrubs, vines and trees (one of ours hardy and native), widely cultivated for

---

* Special articles on the subjects indicated by an asterisk (*) will be found at the words so marked.

their often edible fruit in tropical and warm regions. They have alternate* leaves, without marginal teeth, rather inconspicuous flowers with mostly 6 petals. Fruit fleshy and consisting of an aggregation of carpels, or a berry, or even dry and inedible.

The custard-apple family is of little hort. importance in the U.S., and the only genera in this book are *Annona* (custard-apple), *Artabotrys*, *Asimina* (the pawpaw of eastern N.A.), and *Cananga* (ylang-ylang).

Technical flower characters: Sepals 3, or the calyx with 3 lobes; petals 6, their edges meeting but not overlapping; stamens numerous; carpels usually many, mostly distinct and separate.

annua, -us, -um (an′new-a). Annual (which see).

ANNUAL. A plant which germinates, grows, flowers, fruits and dies within a single year. For the many garden plants treated as Annuals, *see* that term. *See also* Biennial and Perennial.

ANNUAL BABY'S-BREATH = *Gypsophila elegans*.

ANNUAL CANDYTUFT = *Iberis amara* and *I. umbellata*. See Candytuft.

ANNUAL MARJORAM = Sweet marjoram.

ANNUAL PHLOX = *Phlox drummondi*.

ANNUAL RINGS. The rings seen in the cross-section of a log or tree trunk, which indicate the annual increment of growth. They are formed just beneath the inner bark (cambium*), one to each year in the temperate zone or even in the tropics if there is a pronounced dry season. Studies of these tree rings indicate the age of the tree (one for each growing season), and the rate of growth as shown by the distance between the rings. In very old trees the outer rings are almost impossible to distinguish because advancing age has meant a waning rate of growth.

ANNUALS. No flower garden is complete without annuals. Their convenience, ease of handling, and variety of color make them of the greatest use for bedding, for mixing in the perennial border, for following spring bulbs, and often they provide the best supply of cut flowers for the house. If they are to be used chiefly for the latter purpose, and a large supply is needed, it is often better to sow seeds in rows as one does vegetables. Such a cutting garden will relieve the flower border which constant picking would otherwise sadly deplete of color.

Annuals are not in fact always annual* plants. Some biennials,* and a number of perennials,* will bloom from seed the first year, just as true annuals must, of course, always do. A few of the plants mentioned below are either biennials* or perennials* that bloom the first year from seed. For practical garden purposes, they are classed as annuals.

While annuals are a boon to both amateur and professional gardeners, they require some

study as to their colors, their adaptability to the place where you wish to plant them, and above all their suitability to your climate.

The last requirement is, of course, the most important. If you live in zone* 4 or north of it some annuals will be unable to bloom in the period after it is safe to sow them outdoors. Such are often called **tender annuals**, a common example being the petunia. Others, somewhat more hardy, but often started in the hotbed or greenhouse, are classed as **half-hardy annuals**. Tender and half-hardy annuals are scarcely very definite categories, but together they are properly set apart from ordinary annuals, the seed of which is sown in the place where they are to grow.

These two groups are so definite and important that in all the lists below, those needing to be started before outdoor planting (*i.e.*, tender and half-hardy annuals) will be marked with a T. All others should be sown where they are to grow.

Tender Annuals. Starting tender (and half-hardy) annuals in the greenhouse, hotbed, or in the kitchen window is almost exactly the same as raising tomato plants from seed (*see* Tomato). In providing needed warmth, in getting stocky plants, in planning their sowing so as to provide outdoor planting material at the proper time, the early culture of these annuals must approximate that of the tomato.

If you read the tomato article carefully, there is no need to repeat its directions here. The only variations from that procedure are that annual flower seeds should be only just covered with soil (instead of ¼ in. deep). You should pot up more seedlings than you think you need at first in order to replace failures. And, most important of all, do not try to beat the weather by setting out tender annuals until soil and air temperatures are definitely those of summer. Most tomato growers will gamble on this, but no grower of tender annuals needs to. Wait for settled warm weather.

When this has arrived, the plants may be knocked out of their pots or boxes and planted where desired. If you can choose a dull instead of a sunny day, do so, and a quiet rather than windy one. If neither can be done, see that each plant gets a cupful of water. In any case, disturb the roots as little as possible. A simple way to avoid this is to thoroughly water the pots the night before they are planted. The moist soil of such plants will hold the shape of the pot, and can be plunged in the ground with little or no root disturbance.

Hardy Annuals. These should always be sown directly where they are to grow. If they come up too thick, the plants can easily be thinned out to the required spacing, which depends, of course, upon the size of each plant. If you are unfamiliar with any of those in the lists, look them up elsewhere in this book. All are entered under the names used in the lists.

* Special articles on the subjects indicated by an asterisk (*) will be found at the words so marked.

If, for some special purpose, you wish the color effect of a hardy annual before its normal blooming season, you can easily get it by treating it as a tender annual (*see* above). Some gardeners do this regularly in order to extend the normal blooming period of some favorite in which case some are sown outdoors, while others, weeks before, have been raised in pots and planted outdoors at the time (or before or after) seed is sown.

The seeds of some annuals are so small that it is difficult to plant them properly. These may easily be handled by mixing the seed with about five times its bulk of fine sand. Stir the mixture thoroughly, then seed and sand may easily be planted together and the seeds properly spaced.

Even with this precaution the plants will be too thick at first. Begin thinning, except as noted below, as soon as the seedlings are three or four inches high, transplanting the thinned seedlings to other sites. The plants should be so spaced finally that they have a chance for proper development.

A few annuals, however, seem to prefer a bit of crowding and are best not thinned. In the list below they are Nos. 14, 15, 16, 20, 21, 24, 30, 33, 35, 36, 56, 62, 64, and 71.

The Seventy-five Best Annuals

In the body of this book there are described probably four hundred plants that are grown as annuals. Not all of them are of equal hort. merit, and many of them are grown only for special purposes. From them the list below has been selected with three things in mind: their value for color or foliage; their relative ease of growing; and their availability. All of them will be found in any good seed catalogue.

They are here listed under the names used in the body of the book and should always be referred to there for additional information. A few seedsmen's names that differ from the ones here used are inserted at their proper vocabulary entry in the body of the book and cross-referenced to the correct name.

Throughout this and subsequent lists the following symbols are used:

† = Useful for cutting.
T = Tender or half-hardy annuals (*see* above for cultural notes). All others, which are hardy annuals, should be sown where they are to grow.

		Height in Inches	Prevailing Color
1.	†Ageratum T	4–9	Blue
2.	Amaranthus caudatus (Love-lies-bleeding)	36–50	Red (foliage)
3.	Amaranthus tricolor (Joseph's-coat)	12–36	Red (foliage)
4.	Ammobium alatum grandiflorum (Winged everlasting)	20–36	White
5.	†Arctotis breviscapa T	low	Orange
6.	†Arctotis stoechadifolia T (African daisy)	30–48	Blue and yellow
7.	Argemone grandiflora	24–36	Yellow
8.	Brachycome iberidifolia T (Swan River daisy)	8–18	Various
9.	Browallia speciosa major	8–12	Blue
10.	†Calendula officinalis T (Pot marigold)	8–20	Yellow and orange
11.	†Callistephus chinensis T (China aster)	8–18	Various (no yellow)
12.	†Candytuft (Iberis, annual species)	6	Various
13.	Castor-oil plant T (Ricinus communis)	48–150	Foliage plant
14.	†Centaurea Cyanus (Cornflower)	12–24	Blue
15.	Centaurea moschata (Sweet sultan)	18–24	Various
16.	†Clarkia elegans	18–36	Various
17.	Cleome spinosa (Spiderflower)	48–60	Rose-purple
18.	†Coreopsis atkinsonia	24–48	Brown-purple
19.	†Coreopsis drummondi T (Goldenwave)	12–24	Yellow
20.	†Coreopsis stillmani T	12–18	Golden
21.	†Coreopsis tinctoria T (Golden coreopsis)	12–36	Yellow
22.	†Cosmos T	60–100	Various
23.	Cynoglossum amabile (Chinese forget-me-not)	18–24	Blue
24.	†Delphinium Ajacis (Rocket larkspur)	12–24	Various
25.	†Delphinium consolida (Field larkspur)	12–18	Blue
26.	†Dianthus chinensis (China pink)	12–18	Various
27.	Dimorphotheca annua T (Cape marigold)	8–14	Various
28.	Eschscholtzia californica (California poppy)	12–40	Yellow
29.	Euphorbia marginata (Snow-on-the-mountain)	8–12	White
30.	Forget-me-not (Myosotis, annual species)	6–9	Blue
31.	†Gaillardia pulchella (Blanket-flower)	12–20	Red and Yellow
32.	†Gilia capitata	18–24	Blue and white
33.	†Godetia amoena T (Farewell-to-spring)	12–30	Various
34.	†Gomphrena globosa T (Globe amaranth)	8–12	Various
35.	†Gypsophila elegans grandiflora (Annual baby's-breath)	10–18	Various
36.	†Gypsophila muralis	6–8	Pink
37.	†Helichrysum bracteatum T (Strawflower)	24–36	Red and orange

* Special articles on the subjects indicated by an asterisk (*) will be found at the words so marked.

38. Hollyhock T 48–60 Various
(Althaea rosea)
39. †Hunnemannia 12–20 Golden
fumariaefolia (Mex-
ican tulip poppy)
40. Impatiens balsa- 18–30 Various
mina T (Garden
balsam)
41. Kochia scoparia T 20–36 Yellow and
(Summer cypress) red
42. Lathyrus odoratus 24–60 All
(Sweet pea)
43. Lavatera trimestris 24–40 Pink
splendens
44. †Linum grandiflorum 12–24 Red
(Flowering flax)
45. Lobelia Erinus T low Blue
(Edging lobelia)
46. Lychnis Coeli-rosa 12–15 Pink
(Rose-of-heaven)
47. Marigold T 15–24 Yellow and
(Tagetes) red
48. †Mathiola bicornis low Purple-black
(Evening stock)
49. †Mathiola incana 12–20 Various
annual (Ten-
weeks stock)
50. †Mignonette low Yellow-green
(Reseda)
51. Mirabilis Jalapa T 14–30 Various
(Four-o'clock)
52. †Nasturtium 7–15 Yellow-red
(Tropaeolum)
53. †Nemesia strumosa 8–18 Various
suttoni T
54. Nemophila menziesi 6 Blue and
(Baby blue-eyes) white
55. †Nicotiana alata 24–40 White
grandiflora (Jasmine
tobacco)
56. †Nigella damascena 12–15 Blue and
(Love-in-a-mist) white
57. Petunia hybrida T 7–12 Various
58. †Phlox drummondi 9–18 Various
T
59. Poppy (Papaver, 12–20 All but blue
annual species)
60. Portulaca grandi- low Various
flora (Rose moss)
61. †Rudbeckia bicolor 12–20 Yellow
superba (Erfurt
coneflower)
62. Salpiglossis sinuata 18–30 Various
T
63. Salvia splendens T 18–30 Scarlet
(Scarlet sage)
64. †Scabiosa atropur- 18–24 Various
purea T (Sweet
scabious)
65. †Schizanthus retusus 18–24 Rose-pink
T
66. †Schizanthus 36–50 Various
wisetonensis T
67. Silene pendula 6–10 Various
68. †Snapdragon T 6–36 All
(Antirrhinum)
69. Sunflower 48–120 Yellow
(Helianthus)
70. Sweet alyssum 6–12 White
(Lobularia mari-
tima)
71. †Trachymene coer- 18–30 Blue
ulea (Blue lace-
flower)
72. †Venidium fastuosum 18–30 Orange
73. Verbena hortensis T low All
(Garden verbena)

74. Vinca rosea T 12–18 White and
(Madagascar peri- rose
winkle)
75. †Zinnia T 18–30 All but blue

Thoughtful gardeners will note the absence in this list of such plants as canna, chrysanthemum, pansy, dahlia, gladiolus, and coleus, all of which are often treated as annuals, and some of them have annual species. For their culture and uses *see* the body of the book. For several annual vines, omitted from the list, *see* VINES.

How one uses the annuals in the above list is almost wholly a matter of personal taste in flower form and color. Conveniently enough, most of them are of average height, ranging from 9 to 24 in. A few much taller ones must be placed at the back of the bed or border. Numbers 13, 17, 22, 38, and 69 are the tallest of the lot, varying from 48–150 in. high.

Slightly less tall (30–50 in.) are numbers 2, 6, 42, and 66.

The annuals so low or even prostrate that they may conveniently be used for ground cover or for edging are numbers 45, 50, 60, 73, and forms of 30. Somewhat higher plants (4–12 in.) are numbers: 1, 5, 9, 12, 36, 48, and 54.

TIME OF BLOOMING

Annuals are primarily plants that bloom in July and August over most of the country. Almost any of them will bloom in the South or in the warm sections of Calif. in other months, depending upon the time of planting them.

For the northern gardener who needs to extend his show of annual color, it is often necessary to plant varieties that bloom earlier and later than the average run of annual flowers. Here are the lists:

Early-Blooming Annuals

(In the north usually in May or early June, often continuing later. For the numbers see the list.)

Cornflower (14). Sweet sultan (15). Forget-me-not (30). Sweet pea (42). *Nemesia strumosa suttoni* (53). Love-in-a-mist (56).

Late-Blooming Annuals

(Flowering in summer but continuing to bloom until overtaken by frost.)

Numbers 5, 6, 10, 11, 12, 16, 21, 22, 23, 28, 29, 33, 39, 49, 58, 63, 69.

Most of the other annuals in the general list are midsummer bloomers not to be expected much before July 1 nor after September 15, although the season and locality may vary both dates.

COLOR

The variety of color among annuals is infinite. Many species, due to the skill of horticulturists, are now found in many other colors than their original one. Such are marked "various" or "all" in the list above. A few annuals, however, come usually only

---

* Special articles on the subjects indicated by an asterisk (*) will be found at the words so marked.

in one definite color and, for convenience, they may be grouped thus:

WHITE: 4, 29, 70.

BLUE: 9, 71.

RED OR PINK: 2, 3, 36, 43, 44, 46, 63, 65.

YELLOW OR ORANGE: 5, 19, 20, 21, 28, 39, 69.

A few of the outstanding annuals that come in a wide range of colors will be found in numbers: 11, 12, 14, 15, 24, 42, 49, 53, 57, 58, 59, 60, 62, 64, 67, 68, 73, and 75.

SOME SECONDARY ANNUALS

Besides the seventy-five leading annuals listed above there are many others of nearly equal worth. Some of these, all of which are in the trade and can be had from some of the larger dealers, are here listed. Further information about them will be found in the body of the book under the names given below:

T = tender or half-hardy annual. For treatment *see* above. All others are hardy and should be sown where needed.

IN VARIOUS COLORS: *Browallia americana, Datura Metel* T, *Downingia pulchella, Gilia tricolor, Godetia grandiflora* T, *Linanthus parviflorus, Lupinus hartwegi, Saponaria Vaccaria, Senecio elegans* T, *Silene Armeria,* and *Zaluzianskya capensis* T.

ROSE-PINK OR RED: *Abronia umbellata grandiflora* T, *Adonis, Helipterum roseum* T, *Linaria maroccana* T, *Malope trifida rosea, Nicotiana sanderae* T, *Polygonum orientale.*

YELLOW AND ORANGE: *Arnebia cornuta, Coreopsis coronata* T, *Emilia sagittata lutea, Helipterum angustifolium* T, *H. manglesi* T, *Layia elegans, Mentzelia lindleyi, Sanvitalia procumbens, Thelesperma burridgeanum, Ursinia anethoides* T, and *Venidium decurrens* T.

ORANGE-RED: *Collomia biflora.*

WHITE OR GREENISH-WHITE: *Artemisia sacrorum viride, Limnanthes douglasi.*

BLUE, VIOLET OR LILAC: *Campanula drabifolia, C. ramosissima, Collinsia bicolor, Dracocephalum Moldavica, Felicia bergeriana, Heliophila leptophylla* T, *Ionopsidium acaule* T, *Lupinus subcarnosus, Nicandra physalodes* T, *Nolana atriplicifolia* T, *Phacelia campanularia, P. tanacetifolia, P. viscida, P. Whitlavia, Sedum caeruleum, Torenia fournieri* T.

Even this supplementary list by no means exhausts the roll of worthwhile annuals. For others, in genera not heretofore mentioned, *see:* ASPERULA, BAERIA, CALANDRINIA, DIASCIA, ECHIUM, ERYSIMUM, EUCHARIDIUM, GAZANIA, HEBENSTRETIA, HELIOTROPIUM, HIBISCUS, LASTHENIA, MALCOMIA, OXALIS, PODOLEPIS, SCHIZOPETALON, SPECULARIA, and TOLPIS.

ANNUNCIATION LILY = *Lilium candidum.*

anomala, -us, -um (a-nom'a-la). Unusual or out of the ordinary. Also, of a species, of uncertain affinity or identity.

ANOMATHECA = *Lapeyrousia.*

antarctica, -us, -um (ant-ark'ti-ka). From or near the Antarctic.

ANTELOPE-BRUSH = *Purshia tridentata.*

ANTELOPE-HORNS = *Asclepiadora decumbens.*

ANTENNARIA (an-ten-ar'i-a). A large genus of hort. unimportant, white-woolly herbs of the Compositae, very common as wild plants, and known as everlasting, cat's-foot, and pussytoes. They have mostly basal leaves and small heads in loose clusters. Flowers all tubular, very minute, dirty-white, sometimes dried and kept for everlastings. (*Antennaria* is derived from antennae, in allusion to the resemblance of the pappus to the antennae of some insects.)

The species are all perennial, mostly somewhat weedy, and of the easiest culture in open, dry, sandy places. Others, besides *A. rhodantha,* are sometimes gathered from the wild, where they are common over much of the country. They spread so rapidly that they may become a nuisance.

dioica. A mat-forming perennial, 6–12 in. high, the leaves hairy, mostly basal and spoon-shaped, about 1½ in. long. Flower heads about ¼ in. wide, not showy, but the bracts* tipped pinkish. Eurasia. May–June. *Var.* **rosea** has pink flower heads.

rhodantha. Scarcely six in. high. Leaves spatula-shaped, about ¾ in. long. Flower heads about ½ in. long, the minute bracts * tipped with red. Wash. and Ore. Summer.

rosea. A perennial of the Rocky Mts. and westward, often confused, in cult., with *A. dioica rosea. See* above.

ANTHEMIS (an'them-is). A very large genus of Eurasian herbs, family Compositae, some cult. for ornament, some like the camomile for fragrant herbage, and a few are weeds. Leaves alternate,* often mostly basal, dissected or cut (in those below), generally strong-smelling. Flower heads with yellow or white rays and yellow disk flowers, not particularly showy except in *A. tinctoria.* (*Anthemis* is Greek for camomile.)

Easily grown in the open border from seeds or by division of the roots in spring or fall. Two plants often offered as *Anthemis* belong elsewhere. They are *A. Aizoon* = *Achillea ageratifolia Aizoon; A. arabica* = *Cladanthus arabicus.*

biebersteiniana. Resembling the camomile (*A. nobilis*) but the leaves silvery-white. Flower heads nearly 1 in. wide, yellow, long-stalked. Mountains of central Eu. Summer. A good subject for the rock garden, but still rare in the U.S.

Cotula. Mayweed. *See* list at WEEDS.

kelwayi. *See* ANTHEMIS TINCTORIA KELWAYI.

montana. A silky-hairy perennial herb, not over 15 in. high. Leaves much dissected. Ray flowers white. Summer. Eu.

nobilis. Camomile. Strong-smelling perennial herb up to 1 ft. Leaves dissected into fine, nearly thread-like segments. Ray flowers white. There is a double-flowered form and another (*var.* **grandiflora**) with larger, sometimes yellow flowers. For culture and uses *see* HERB GAR-

---

* Special articles on the subjects indicated by an asterisk (*) will be found at the words so marked.

DENING. For its use as an unusual grass substitute, *see* Grass Substitutes at LAWN.

Sancta-Johannis. A much-branched, gray-haired, tufted perennial, 12–18 in. high. Leaves twice or thrice cut into fine lobes, the lower ones 4–5 in. long, the upper smaller. Flower heads solitary, orange, about 2 in. wide. Bulgaria. Summer.

tinctoria. Golden marguerite; called also yellow camomile and oxeye camomile. The best garden plant of the genus. Perennial up to 3 ft. Leaves twice-cut, the segments oblongish, not dissected. Flower heads nearly 2 in. wide, golden-yellow. Summer. Eurasia. The *var.* **kelwayi** has dissected leaf segments and darker yellow flowers.

anthemoides (an-them-oy′deez; but *see* OÏDES). Like a camomile (*Anthemis*).

ANTHER. The pollen-bearing part of a stamen. *See* FLOWER.

ANTHERICUM (an-ther′i-kum). A large genus of mostly African herbs of the lily family, only the following grown for their loose clusters of white flowers. Leaves narrow, strap-shaped, basal. Flowers small, white, in a long, loose, leafless cluster (raceme*), each flower nearly stalkless. Stamens* 6. Fruit a 3-celled pod. (*Anthericum* is Greek for flower hedge.)

The St. Bernard's-lily, the only commonly cult. species, is grown as a border plant in the South, elsewhere in the cool greenhouse. Use potting mixture* 4. Easily propagated by division of its rootstock.

Liliago. St. Bernard's-lily. A European, unbranched, perennial herb, up to 3 ft. Leaves rather numerous in a basal cluster, about 10 in. long and an inch wide. Flowers ½–¾ in. wide, flattish, each with small bracts beneath.

ramosum. Resembling St. Bernard's-lily, but lower and with smaller flowers, the stem much branched. Southwest Eu. May–June. Not particularly desirable, but carried by a good many dealers.

For other plants often sold as *Anthericum*, *see* CHLOROPHYTUM.

ANTHESIS. The time of flowering.

ANTHOLYZA (an-tho-ly′za). African gladiolus-like herbs of the iris family sometimes grown for their showy, tubular, but slightly irregular,* flowers in tall spikes. Of the 20 known species only the following are known to most gardeners. They differ from *Gladiolus* mostly in the tube of the flower being long and slender, rather than shorter and broader. (*Antholyza* is from Greek for flower and rage, in allusion to the opening of the corolla resembling the mouth of an enraged animal.)

They are grown exactly as *Gladiolus* (which see).

aethiopica. Corm*-bearing, branching herb up to 4 ft. Leaves about 18 in. long, and 1 in. wide. Spike 6–9 in. long, dense. Flowers reddish-yellow nearly 2 in. long. South Africa. Also known as *Chasmanthe.*

paniculata. Corm* large. Stem 3–4 ft. high, branched. Leaves 18–24 in. long, about 3 in. wide. Spike dense, about 1 ft. long, its stalk wavy. Flowers reddish-yellow, scarcely over

1½ in. long, the tube decidedly curved. Natal. Also known as *Curtonus.*

Anthora (an-thō′ra). A pre-Linnaean* name for some monkshood (which see).

ANTHOXANTHUM (an-thocks-an′thum). A small genus of Old World, mostly aromatic grasses, two of which are often ingredients of meadows or are common escapes* in N.A. They have flat, very narrow leaves, and narrow spike-like flower clusters. (*Anthoxanthum* is from Greek for yellow flower, probably in allusion to the pollen.)

Neither is grown for ornament, but the second species sometimes for its fragrant foliage.

aristatum. European annual grass, scarcely 1 ft. high. Leaves 4 in. long and ⅛ in. wide. Flower cluster (a panicle*) about 1½ in. long, whitish-green, long-bristled. Common as an escape* in eastern N.A.

odoratum. Sweet vernal grass. A Eurasian perennial grass, usually 18–24 in. high. Leaves 6 in. long, rough above, nearly ¼ in. wide. Flower cluster (a panicle*) about 3 in. long, brownish-green. Nearly throughout N.A., mostly in meadows or as an escape.*

ANTHRACNOSE. A plant disease caused by a number of different fungi and displaying different symptoms on various host plants. On the leaves of sycamore, plane tree, oak, and maple, brown or black spots may appear, after which leaves drop prematurely. Anthracnose on tomato does not appear on leaves but causes small, brown, target-like spots on the fruit. The anthracnose disease of snapdragon and some bush fruits produces spots on leaves and stems. For control *see* the various plants.

ANTHRISCUS (an-thris′kus). A small genus of Eurasian herbs of the carrot family, one considerably grown for its foliage, which is used like parsley. Leaves twice-compound,* the ultimate segments very fine. Flowers small, white in compound umbels.* (*Anthriscus* is Greek for flower fence.)

Cerefolium. Salad chervil, but sometimes called merely chervil (which see). A hairy-leaved, Eurasian annual herb, with branching stem not over 18 in. high. Leaves much dissected, parsley-like. Flowers very small, white, in a stiff, compound umbel.* Fruits black and minutely beaked. For culture and uses *see* HERB GARDENING.

ANTHURIUM (an-thoor′i-um). Tail-flower. An immense genus of tropical American perennial herbs of the arum family, some of which are widely grown greenhouse plants cult. for their fine foliage and often striking flowers. Leaves and habit very variable. Some are climbing aroids* with arrow-shaped, often beautifully colored or variegated leaves. Flowers crowded in a dense spike (spadix *), beneath which or surrounding it is an often brightly colored spathe.* (For flower structure *see* ARACEAE.) Fruit berry-like. (*Anthurium* is Greek for tail-flower, in allusion to the tail-like spadix* of most species.)

Anthuriums are widely grown florists'

* Special articles on the subjects indicated by an asterisk (*) will be found at the words so marked.

plants, the first and third species for the showy flower cluster, the second and fourth for the very handsome foliage. They require a moist, warm greenhouse, not much below 60° at night and higher in the day. Give them plenty of water and keep the atmosphere as humid as possible. Use potting mixture* 4, to which should be added chopped-up fern roots or sphagnum moss or both to increase the humus. See that the roots are well covered (they tend to heave). As the plants get older they need re-potting only very occasionally.

andraeanum. A South American aroid* grown for its showy flower cluster. Leaves heart-shaped, green, deeply split at the base, about 12 in. long and 6 in. wide, the stalk as long as the blade. Flower spadix* yellowish-white, its spathe* heart-shaped, leathery, 4–6 in. long, brilliant orange-red.

crystallinum. A showy foliage plant from Colombia. Leaves about 14 in. long and 10 in. wide, more or less heart-shaped, green and white-striped above, pale rose-pink beneath. Flower spathe* narrow, green.

scherzerianum. Flamingo-flower. One of the most widely grown florists' decorative plants, a native of Central America. Leaves oblongish, about 8 in. long and 2 in. wide, leathery, green and with a narrow tip. Flower spadix* coiled, yellow, the spathe* red, yellow, rose, or white (depending upon which of many hort. varieties are grown). Some varieties, also, have scarlet or even white-spotted spathes,* all of which are more or less oval and about 3 in. long.

veitchi. The best-known foliage plant of the group, and a native of Colombia. Leaves oblong, nearly 3 ft. long and 10 in. wide, heart-shaped at the base, metallic-green, and hanging. It has prominent even showy veins on the under side. Flower spathe* scarcely 3 in. long, greenish-white, becoming recurved.

warocqueanum. Somewhat similar to *A. veitchi,* but the leaves not metallic green; velvety, the leaves with pale green or white veins. Spathe* green, about 4 in. long, the spadix* nearly 1 ft. long. Colombia.

anthyllidifolia, -us, -um (an-thil-lid-i-fō′-li-a). With foliage like the kidney vetch (*Anthyllis*).

ANTHYLLIS (an-thil′lis). Old World perennial herbs of the pea family, comprising perhaps 20 species, two of which are of secondary hort. importance. They have compound,* silky leaves, the leaflets arranged feather-fashion, with an odd one at the end. Flowers pea-like, in rather showy spikes or heads. Pod mostly somewhat egg-shaped. (*Anthyllis* is Greek for downy flowers.)

The plants are of easy culture in open places, even if the soil is poor. Propagated by seeds or division of the roots. The first species is somewhat grown in rock gardens, the second scarcely known here but a common forage plant in Eu.

montana. A silky-hairy perennial herb from the Alps, mostly less than 8 in. high and with many leaflets. Flowers purple, in dense heads, below which is a leafy cluster of bracts.* A red-flowered variety (*var.* rubra) is somewhat grown in rock gardens. June.

Vulneraria. Kidney vetch or woundwort; called, also, sand clover. A European perennial herb, about 12 in. high. Leaflets 5, rarely more. Flowers yellow or reddish, small. A clover-like plant, useful for forage in Eu., but occasionally grown for ornament here.

ANTIBIOTICS. Some fungi and molds produce substances which kill or prevent the growth of other fungi and bacteria. The antibiotics have been sold by pharmaceutical companies for a number of years for the control of various diseases of man and animal. More recently, several of these antibiotics have shown promise for the control of a few diseases of plants. Streptomycin is recommended in a number of states for the control of fireblight* disease and penicillin has shown promise for the control of a bacterial disease of cactus.*

ANTIGONON (an-tig′o-non). A small group of showy, tropical American, tendril*-climbing vines, family Polygonaceae, one widely grown for ornament in warm regions where it approaches *Bougainvillaea* in its profuse bloom. Leaves alternate,* without marginal teeth. Flowers small but numerous, in drooping racemes* that come from the leaf axils,* and end in a tendril.* (*Antigonon* means against or opposite an angle.)

Throughout zones* 8 and 9, the species below is common over porches, fences, and walls. Elsewhere, but rarely, it is a greenhouse plant. It is of the easiest culture in poor soils. See VINES. Propagated by seeds or easily rooted cuttings.

leptopus. Coral vine or corallita; called, also, mountain rose, pink vine or Confederate vine. Climbing to 30 ft. or more. Leaves arrow-shaped or heart-shaped, 1–3 in. long, but the lower leaves larger. Flowers pink or white, about ⅜ in. long. Mex. In the southern states it is sometimes called rosa montana.

antillana, -us, -um (an-til-lay′na). From the West Indian Antilles.

antiquorum (an-ti-quor′um). Of or belonging to the ancients.

antirrhinoides (an-ti-ri-noy′deez; but *see* OÏDES). Like the snapdragon (*Antirrhinum*).

ANTIRRHINUM. See SNAPDRAGON.

ANTS. Most ant species are harmless, although they are annoying in houses and on flowers. Some ants attack plants or bore in trees. Other species tend aphids and mealybugs, carrying these pests from plant to plant, causing severe damage. Ants are social insects with various castes such as queens, workers, etc. To kill out ant colonies, the entire population of the hill must be killed. Locate the entrances to the colony by watching movement of ants. Pour chlordane (1 ounce concentrate per gallon) down the holes. In large colonies, treat area for several feet about nest with this mixture or a 5 per cent dust. Poison syrups may be used effectively. Commercially prepared syrups are available or this one may be made up.

(a) Boil together for 30 minutes:

Granulated sugar .... 1¼ pounds
Water .... 1¼ pints
Tartaric acid (crystallized) .... 1 gram
Benzoate of soda .... 1 gram

---

* Special articles on the subjects indicated by an asterisk (*) will be found at the words so marked.

(b) Dissolve sodium arsenite in hot water in the following proportions:

Sodium arsenite (chemically pure) 3½ grams
Hot water .... 1 fluid ounce

When the above solutions have cooled, add (b) to (a) and stir well. Then add ⅔ pound of strained honey and mix. Place POISON label on the container.

Use small tin cans or plastic cups with tops as containers for the poisoned syrup. Crimp opposite sides of the cans or make holes near the top of the cups to provide entrances for the ants. To charge the containers, place several strands of excelsior in them and half fill with syrup. Locate the containers about 20 ft. apart around the house and preferably near ant runs and on trees. Place them high enough to be out of reach of children and pets and fasten them securely to supports. Refill containers about every 3 weeks. — L.G.M.

ANTWERP HOLLYHOCK = *Althaea ficifolia. See* HOLLYHOCK.

apennina, -us, -um (ă-pĕ-ny'na). From the Apennine Mountains, Italy.

apetala, -us, -um (a-pet'a-la). Without petals.

APETALOUS. Without petals, as the flowers of oak, beech, ash, and many other plants. *See* NAKED FLOWER.

APHELANDRA (a-fell-an'dra). A genus of 60 species of showy, tropical American shrubs or woody herbs, family Acanthaceae, the two below much grown in greenhouses for their attractive foliage and handsome, bracted* flowers. Leaves (in those below) opposite, sometimes in opposite pairs, often conspicuously veined or parti-colored. Flowers irregular,* somewhat 2-lipped,* crowded in dense bracted* spikes. Fruit a 4-angled pod. (*Aphelandra* is Greek for simple male, the anthers being 1-celled.)

Grown only in greenhouses where their culture is the same as for poinsettia (which see). Easily propagated by cuttings of partly ripened wood, or by seed, in A. *aurantiaca.*

aurantiaca. Low, perennial herb. Leaves oval or elliptic, 4–6 in. long, more or less wavy-margined, prominently veined, dark green above, paler green beneath. Flowers orange, rarely scarlet-tipped, the bracts* toothed. Mex. A popular greenhouse decorative plant.

tetragona. A shrub 3–4 ft. high, with the lower stems woody, the upper herbaceous and greenish-red. Leaves in opposite pairs, more or less elliptic, 8–12 in. long and about 4 in. wide, green. Flowers in erect, terminal spikes which are branched and profuse in bloom, scarlet, the bracts* merely hairy-margined. Brazil. The showiest species in cult.

APHRODITE. The Greek goddess; often used as a varietal name for strikingly beautiful plants.

aphylla, -us, -um (a-fill'a). Leafless, or apparently so.

APHYLLANTHES (af-ee-lan'theys). A genus of a single species of the lily family from the Mediterranean region, A. mon-

speliensis, a fibrous-rooted perennial suited to the cool greenhouse or outdoors in frostless regions. Leaves small, mostly basal, the flowering stalk naked, rush-like and not over 10 in. high, usually less. Flowers solitary (rarely 2), about 1 in. wide, its 6 segments blue. If in greenhouse, use potting mixture* 4. May–June. (*Aphyllanthes* is from the Greek for leafless flowers in allusion to the rush-like flower stalks.)

APIACEAE. See UMBELLIFERAE.

apiculata, -us, -um (a-pick-you-lay'ta). Tipped with a short, often sharp, point.

apiifolia, -us, -um (a-pi-i-fō'li-a). With celery-like leaves.

APIO = *Arracacia xanthorrhiza.*

APIOS (ā'pi-os). A small genus of tuberous-rooted vines of the pea family, the one below somewhat grown for its brownish flowers. Its roots were an important source of food to the Indians. Leaves compound.* Flowers pea-like, in short clusters, followed by long, flat, thickish, many-seeded pods. (*Apios* is Greek for pair, from the arrangement of the tubers.)

A moderately attractive vine of chief interest because its small tubers were long mistaken for the potato in the early history of that vegetable. Easily grown in any open sandy soil and propagated by seeds or planting the tubers.

americana. Groundnut; called, also, potato bean and wild bean. A vine to 8 ft. long, its tuberous roots in strings like small potatoes. Leaflets 5–7. Flowers brown, with the fragrance of violets. Summer. Eastern N.A. Called also A. *tuberosa.*

APIUM. See CELERY.

APLECTRUM (a-pleck'trum). One North American woods orchid, sometimes transferred from the forest to the wild garden, but not of easy cult. *See* Hardy Orchids at ORCHID. (*Aplectrum* is Greek for spurless.) The only species is A. hyemale, the puttyroot or Adam-and-Eve. It bears late in the summer a single, plaited, oval, many-veined, and winter-persisting leaf, followed early the next summer by the naked stalk of the loose flower cluster. Flowers brown or yellowish-brown, with strap-shaped sepals and a 3-lobed lip. June.

APOCYNACEAE (a-poss-i-nay'see-ee). The dogbane family comprises about 135 genera and over 1100 species of herbs, shrubs, vines, or trees, scattered nearly throughout the world, but largely tropical. They have a milky juice and leaves without marginal teeth. Flowers regular, in clusters (cymes* or panicles*) or solitary. Fruit berry-like or fleshy in *Thevetia, Acokanthera,* and *Carissa,* but mostly a dry pod (follicle *) in the other hort. genera.

The family includes several old garden favorites like the periwinkle (*see* VINCA) and the oleander. Also several showy woody vines like *Trachelospermum, Allamanda, Beaumontia, Dipladenia,* and *Mandevilla,* all

---

* Special articles on the subjects indicated by an asterisk (*) will be found at the words so marked.

tropical or sub-tropical. Among herbs are *Apocynum* and *Amsonia*, all of which are hardy over most of America, but their flowers are not so showy as those of the woody vines. Besides the oleander, there are other hort. genera of shrubs or trees, the frangipani (*see* PLUMERIA) and *Tabernaemontana* widely planted in warm regions for ornament. Some genera have violently poisonous juice, notably *Acokanthera*, used by the natives for arrow poisons. A few genera, especially *Carissa*, bear edible fruits.

Technical flower characters: Calyx 5-parted. Corolla usually bell-shaped or funnel-shaped, its 5 lobes often distinctly twisted. Stamens 5, inserted on the tube of the corolla. Ovaries mostly 2, the seeds in the genera with pods, usually with a tuft of hairs (*see* APOCYNUM).

APOCYNUM (a-poss'i-num). The dog-banes are milky-juiced, tough-stemmed, per-ennial herbs, family Apocynaceae, somewhat grown for ornament, and for medicine. All are from the north temperate zone, those below, American. Leaves opposite,* without marginal teeth. Flowers small, bell-shaped, borne in loose clusters (cymes*). Fruit a long slender pod (follicle*), the seeds with a tuft of hairs. (*Apocynum* is the classical name of the dogbane.)

They are of very easy culture, preferring open, sandy soil. Both those below will stand considerable drought. Propagated by division of the roots in spring or fall.

androsaemifolium. Spreading dogbane; called, also, honey-bloom and wild ipecac. A stout, branching perennial 3–4 ft. high. Leaves 2–3 in. long, about half as wide, pale beneath. Flowers pinkish, about ⅓ in. wide. N.A.

cannabinum. Indian hemp; called also Choc-taw-root. Nearly twice as tall as the above, the stem almost stringy-barked, and once cult. for its fiber. Leaves nearly 5 in. long, about half as wide. Flowers greenish-white, about ¼ in. wide. N.A. The root furnishes an emetic and cathartic.

APONOGETON (a-pon-o-jee'ton). The only genus of the family **Aponogetonaceae** (a-pon-o-jee-to-nay'see-ee), which are aquatic plants of the Old World tropics. Both those below are African and are widely cult. in greenhouse pools or in aquaria. They have tuberous rootstocks and submerged, per-manently skeletonized leaves in the second species, but floating leaves in the Cape pondweed. Flowers very simple, in spikes, the flower parts (petals and sepals) usually only 2. Stamens 6. Ovary of three 1-celled carpels. (*Aponogeton* is of uncertain origin, possibly Celtic for water neighbor.)

These popular aquatics can be grown in water that is kept at or above ordinary room temperatures. Plant the rootstocks, or offsets* in pots of rich loam and submerge at least 8 in. below the water surface, in full sun-light if possible. It is essential that the lace-leaf be grown in clear water to get the full effect of its extraordinary skeletonized leaves. Both species are sometimes sold as *Ouviran-dra*.

distachyus. Cape pondweed or water haw-

thorn. Leaves floating, not skeletonized, long-stalked, narrow, about 4 in. long. Flowers mi-nute, in a branched, emersed spike, white, fra-grant, with one or two bracts beneath each flower. Cape of Good Hope.

fenestralis. Lace-leaf or lattice-leaf. One of the most extraordinary submerged aquatic plants in the world. Leaves broadish-oblong, notched at the tip, usually about 9 in. long and floating just beneath the water surface. The leaf con-sists only of several main parallel veins and a multitude of small lateral, connecting veins, the leaf thus permanently skeletonized. Flowers minute, white, the spikes borne on a stalk about 12 in. long. Madagascar.

APOROCACTUS (a-pore-o-kak'tus). A small group of tropical American cacti, the one below grown for its peculiar habit and crimson flowers. They are vine-like or clam-bering or prostrate succulents with thin, rat-tail-like stems which have 10–12 shallow ribs, brown spines and reddish, bristly fruit. Flowers day-blooming, funnel-shaped, the stamens protruding, gathered in a single, one-sided cluster. (The name is Greek for impenetrable cactus.)

The species below, a popular window plant, is one of the easiest cacti to grow. Plant joints in sandy loam and keep the pots near or in full sunlight. *See also* SUCCULENTS.

flagelliformis. Rat-tail cactus. Stems cylin-dric, about ¾ in. in diameter, erect, prostrate, climbing, or hanging, depending upon age and vigor. Flowers crimson, about 3 in. long, last-ing 3 or 4 days. Fruit ½ in. in diameter. Prob-ably Mex. Often grafted on other cacti and its weak stems trained into grotesque designs.

APOSTLE-FLOWER. See NEOMARICA.

APOTHECARY'S ROSE = *Rosa gallica of-ficinalis*.

APPALACHIAN TEA = *Viburnum cassi-noides*.

appendiculata, *-us*, *-um* (ap-pen-dick-you-lay'ta). Appendaged; *i.e.*, with a crown, crest, hairs, etc.

APPLE (*Malus pumila*). Wherever gen-eral agriculture is practiced in the United States and Canada, the apple is the fruit of fruits. Temperature is the commonest limit-ing factor in its culture in North America. The apple cannot be counted upon to hold its own in regions where the temperature goes down with frequency to 20° below. Long, hot summers are as trying to the apple as cold winters. Dry weather is another limiting factor. The apple cannot be grown with much success in large areas between the Mississippi and the Rocky Mountains where irrigation is not possible but where a low rainfall does permit "dry farming." The rainfall might suffice, but the combination of a dry atmosphere and continuous winds takes too much moisture from apple trees to permit healthy growth.

The local climate as affected by site must be considered to secure freedom from un-seasonable frosts, strong winds, and too great heat. It is well understood that large bodies of water give protection against both frosts and heat, while hills, mountains, and the

---

* Special articles on the subjects indicated by an asterisk (*) will be found at the words so marked.

lay of the land may be selected to modify the sweep of winds. Slopes which give air drainage, irrespective of direction, are better than level lands. These generalities are chiefly directed to orchard enterprises; a good gardener can grow a few apples under very adverse circumstances of climate and location.

If you have only a limited space you can get trees upon which several varieties have been grafted, called "Five-in-one" apple trees. With even less space, you can use only dwarf trees. (See Dwarf Fruit Trees at DWARFING.) And, if you have only a wall, you can get espaliered apples, but they are inclined to be expensive. (See TRAINED FRUIT TREES.)

Not only are apples tolerant of a wide range of climate, but they are equally tolerant of many types of soil. They will not thrive on sand or muck, but almost any reasonably good garden soil will grow apples. Nor is there any good reason for the home grower to put on commercial fertilizer or stable manure. If, as most home growers are apt to do, you grow your apples in the sod, it may pay to mulch each tree with stable manure, put on in late fall, not more than 2 in. thick. On poor soils, evidenced by poor leaf color, small or badly colored fruit, and short shoot growth, it is wise to put around each young tree a heavier mulch of manure. If this is not available, about 2 pounds of ammonium nitrate may be scattered near the trunk of each tree annually. Ammonium nitrate is sold by all fertilizer dealers.

All commercial orchards are kept cultivated; and, if you have more than a few trees, it will be better to keep your orchard cultivated throughout the growing season, not so much for the good of the apple trees as to keep your orchard from becoming a weedy thicket.

If you happen to have a place with old or over-mature apple trees you will have to come to a decision as to what to do about them. They are picturesque or even beautiful in blossom, but generally not much good for fruit. A process known as renovation involves cutting back the old branches as much as one third or even one half, in order to force out a new crop of young wood upon which fruit is more plentiful than on old wood. Few commercial orchardists think the labor is worth while and generally cut down such trees. But the home grower, with only one or a few such over-mature trees, may wish to save them by renovation.

If you decide to renovate, cut back all old branches at least one third of their length, and in old trees practically one half of all old wood should come out. For a year or two the tree will look mutilated, but new growth will ultimately make it more sightly. It will speed renovation to dig up the soil around the trunk, making a circle at least 12 ft. in diameter, and mulch the soil with a layer of manure about 3 in. deep. Whether to renovate or not depends upon the value you put upon the tree and its age. If quite old and with many dead branches, renovation is too costly of time, especially for a tree that in any case will not be worth much in a few years.

That brings us to the age of apple trees and, especially, when you should expect the first fruit crop. Most apple varieties should have some fruit 6 to 8 years after you plant them. They should soon a.ter bear a full crop, and go on doing so for 40 or 50 years. Then they become what the foresters call over-mature, heralded by slower growth, less fruit, and the apples much reduced in size and flavor. As a practical matter such trees should be cut down to make room for younger stock. The only alternative, which is frankly a temporary expedient, is renovation.

VARIETIES. More than one thousand apple varieties are listed in the catalogues of commercial nurserymen in this country. Most of them are known only to a few specialists, and many of them differ little from older and well-tested sorts. Geographically, the apple is more widely grown than any other fruit, and some varieties have been developed to meet the requirements of special regions — as, for instance, the irrigated orchards of Washington, Oregon, and California. Nearly continuous sunshine makes such fruit beautifully colored, but often at the expense of flavor.

For the home grower, the apple varieties can be divided into three categories: (1) Early, (2) Midseason, and (3) Late, which are mostly for winter storage. Some of the varieties are self-sterile* and must be interplanted with other sorts, as explained in the section on Self-Sterile and Self-Fertile at FRUIT CULTURE.

Some of the varieties are excellent both as dessert fruit and for cooking. If you do not have much space, it is better to omit varieties good only for cooking, as such are easily and cheaply available from the shops, whereas good eating apples, ripened on the tree, are available only to the home grower.

A few of the varieties below have given rise to bud sports, differing from the parent, usually in being brighter colored. It is these that some nurserymen feature as novelties, often with lurid colored pictures. Unless you have plenty of space and are willing to pay fancy prices, it is better to avoid such innovations. If they are superior to the parent they will ultimately become generally available. Most of the varieties below are available as dwarfs or as espaliers. (See Dwarf Fruit Trees at DWARFING, and TRAINED FRUIT TREES.)

EARLY APPLE VARIETIES

(Zones* of hardiness are omitted for apples as they can be grown anywhere east of the Mississippi and north of N. Car., and in many other regions.)
Ripening in the vicinity of New York in mid-July or early Aug.

* Special articles on the subjects indicated by an asterisk (*) will be found at the words so marked.

YELLOW TRANSPARENT. Self-sterile. Fruit yellow, conical, slightly acid and one of the first to ripen. Tree shorter-lived than most apples, but very hardy to winter cold.

RED ASTRACHAN. Self-sterile.* Fruit nearly round, crimson and of delicious flavor, but slightly acid. Tree not long-lived.

EARLY MCINTOSH. Very like its famous parent, McIntosh, but earlier. One of the best early red apples.

DUCHESS OF OLDENBERG. Self-sterile.* Fruit streaked with red, round-oval, of fine flavor as dessert fruit, but also a good cooking apple. Often listed as Oldenberg or Duchess.

GRAVENSTEIN. Self-sterile.* Fruit nearly round, streaked with crimson, good for eating and cooking. Tree hardy and very productive.

RED JUNE. Fruit conical to oblong, crimson or yellowish-red, not very large but of fine flavor.

MIDSEASON APPLE VARIETIES

WEALTHY. Fruit ovalish to round, medium-sized or larger, bright red and of good flavor. It does not keep well.

TWENTY-OUNCE. One of the largest apples, the fruit round or slightly conical, red-striped but greenish-yellow, and excellent also for cooking.

FAMEUSE. Often listed as Snow, Snow Queen, or Snow Apple. Fruit nearly round but slightly oval, greenish-yellow, flushed with red or crimson, the flesh extremely good.

MCINTOSH. Self-sterile.* A famous old variety with basically whitish-yellow fruit, overlaid crimson or red, the flavor superb for those who want a slightly acid apple.

SWEET MCINTOSH. Similar to McIntosh, but the fruit sweet and thought by many to be the finest of all sweet apples.

DELICIOUS. One of the latest of the midseason varieties, the fruit yellow, but striped with red, almost oblong, faintly acid but mildly sweet.

LATE APPLES

Fall ripening, and most of the varieties can be stored for use in winter or even up to May 1 of the following spring. The dates indicate the time they can be kept in storage if the latter is properly provided for. Directions for storage are included at the end of the list. In some regions, early autumn frosts may hasten picking in order to avoid frozen fruit.

GRIMES GOLDEN. Feb. 1. Self-sterile. Fruit yellow, roundish-oval, aromatic, rich, slightly acid. Tree not so large as most varieties.

JONATHAN. Mar. 1. Fruit bright red, often yellow-striped, round or round-conical, the flesh mildly acid. Tree very productive.

ROME BEAUTY. May 1. Fruit red, striped with yellow, the flesh pleasantly flavored, aromatic, slightly acid. A medium-sized tree but bearing one of the larger apples.

WINESAP. Apr. 1. Self-sterile. This and its derivative, Stayman Winesap, are among the latest of apples, particularly good for cider. Fruit red, often somewhat striped, the flesh finely flavored, mildly acid, excellent as a dessert fruit and a good keeper in storage. Stayman Winesap is yellowish-red, ripens a little earlier, and does not keep so well in storage.

YELLOW NEWTON. Often called Newtown Pippin. Fruit medium-sized, round-oblong, greenish-yellow, the flesh crisp, mild, and of excellent quality. The tree tends to be a shy bearer.

RHODE ISLAND GREENING. Apr. 1. Self-sterile. A good dessert fruit if allowed to ripen on the tree, but it has become one of the best-known varieties for cooking. Fruit large, greenish-yellow, nearly round, mildly acid. Bears poorly in the off-years.

Winter storage of apples, without refrigeration, is not easy for the average home grower. An ordinary cellar with a heating furnace or a hot water tank is useless, because the air is too warm and dry. Root cellars are ideal, because they generally take the temperature of the ground (about 50° at New York) and hence are cool, dark, and damp. They must not, however, be wet, and there should be no drip from moisture condensed on the sides or the top. Also they must be free of frost. Such conditions are hard to come by. A possible alternative, but not so satisfactory, is a bin in a garage that is kept at about 50° all winter.

Whenever you store winter apples, each fruit should be picked when almost ripe and wrapped in paper, so that no fruit touches another. Fruit stored in bulk, without wrapping, needs a constant temperature of 33–35°. Without such a temperature, and with the fruit touching each other, spoilage is practically certain, especially if the fruit is intended to be kept until the dates indicated on the list of late apples above.

CARE OF APPLE TREES

The apple is the largest of the temperate zone fruit trees. Hence it needs space. Commercial orchardists usually plant the trees 40–45 ft. apart each way, but the home grower can reduce this to 30–40 ft. If you do not have space enough, a possible remedy is to use only dwarf varieties, or, if there is still less room, espaliered trees.

Many apple varieties are plagued with what the orchardists call "off-years." An off-year usually follows a year with a heavy crop of fruit, as though the tree wanted a rest after maturing too much fruit for its strength. This may well be the explanation, especially if the fruit has not been thinned, which should always be done if there is too large a crop. Thinning should be done while the apples are still green, and no fruit, when mature, should be nearer than 3–4 in. to any other.

Another explanation of an apparently "off" year has nothing to do with over-bearing one year and under-bearing the next, but is

---

* Special articles on the subjects indicated by an asterisk (*) will be found at the words so marked.

caused by factors over which we have no control. If, at blossom time, the weather is cold, or if there are hard rains, bees will not be about the business of pollinating apple blossoms, or only sporadically so, and the consequent crop reduction is often blamed on the inherent off-year tendency of some apples. And if there is an erratic late frost at blossom time, there will be practically no fruit that year, although some trees will put out a small, secondary lot of blossoms if the first bloom is frost-blasted.

In regions where the ground can be worked late in the fall, it is better to plant apple trees then, but in the North they should be spring-planted, as early as frost will permit. Most growers will do best with one- or two-year old whips — all of which have been grafted or budded by the nurseryman. This is essential, as few apples will come true from seed, which explains the futility of the efforts of "Johnny Appleseed," who scattered apple seeds all over Ohio and Indiana, few of which ever amounted to anything.

Apples, especially the late varieties have an annoying habit of dropping some of their fruit a few days before ripening. The only remedy is to pick such varieties in time to anticipate this fruit drop. Fortunately it does not occur in all varieties, nor every year, and some authorities attribute it to too liberal use of commercial fertilizers. Little is really known as to its cause.

If your apple orchard is sizable and you keep it in sod (which most professionals never do), it is better to keep such sod mown — at least three times during the growing season. This reduces the hazard of fire, and discourages the mice or rabbits which often gnaw bark. If the place is infested with either animal, wire guards around the trunk or poison bait are correctives. See ANIMAL INJURY for bait recipes.

APPLES IN IRRIGATED DISTRICTS

Apple-growing in the West usually requires irrigation. Among the larger irrigated districts are the Wenatchee and Yakima valleys of Washington, the Hood River Valley of Oregon, the Snake River Valley of Idaho, the western slope of Colorado, and the valley lands of Utah adjacent to Great Salt Lake. In California, apples are not well adapted to the hot interior valleys but do best either near the coast (in the Sebastopol or Watsonville areas) or at elevations of 2000–4000 feet in the Sierra Nevada foothills.

These areas offer the best opportunities for success, and apple trees might well be included in home plantings in many other locations where water is available and where either the summer and winter temperatures are not extremely high or low.

VARIETIES. The varieties grown in the western states are perhaps somewhat more limited than those in other areas. In commercial plantings growers have standardized on those varieties especially adapted to a given area or those for which there is the greatest de-

mand. Commercial production is for the purpose of profit. Home production, on the other hand, is for personal satisfaction, and varieties are chosen primarily according to personal preference. In the northernmost areas one might choose the mild, white-fleshed McIntosh or the Wealthy. In most other areas the choice might be between a sweet variety such as Golden Delicious or one with more acid such as Jonathan. Both of these are equally good for culinary purposes and for eating out of hand. Intermediate in flavor between these two would be Delicious or Red Delicious, generally regarded excellent for fresh consumption (unless overripe and mealy in texture), but not so good for kitchen use. For baking, but not for eating fresh, Rome Beauty is popular. Summer varieties include Yellow Transparent and Gravenstein; for late varieties, Winesap and Yellow Newtown are among the best.

In addition to any or all of these, the home planting may well include some old varieties now little grown, or some new untried sorts which might have a special appeal for the amateur horticulturist.

In small plantings the number of varieties is necessarily limited. However aside from a minimum of two sorts to insure cross-pollination, a succession of varieties from early to late during the season is desirable. This succession may be had either by growing two or more kinds on the same tree or by the use of closely planted dwarf trees. Some nurserymen are now propagating and offering for sale apple trees where each of the main branches has been grafted to a different variety.

DWARF TREES. Where space is limited semi-dwarf and dwarf trees are recommended. Although their cost is about double that of standard trees, they require only half the space, or less. They usually come into bearing several years earlier and are easier to prune, spray, and harvest. Most of the commercial varieties grown can be secured from nurserymen. Others would need to be propagated, either as a special order, or budded or grafted by the grower.

Another possibility of dwarf trees is that of training them by special pruning to an espalier type of tree suitable for growing on a trellis or against a wall or fence. Such trees always attract attention and can be ornamental as well as productive of fruit.

CULTURAL PRACTICES. In sections of the western states having mild winters, planting may be in late fall. In others, plant in the spring as early as the soil can be prepared and before the trees show any signs of growth. Watering at time of planting is advisable to settle the soil around the roots and hasten the establishment of the tree. Because the bark of young trees is tender and sunlight is intense in western areas, a coat of whitewash is applied to the tree trunk to prevent sunburn.

Although annual rainfall may be adequate for apple-growing in some sections, west of

---

* Special articles on the subjects indicated by an asterisk (*) will be found at the words so marked.

the Rockies rain is largely confined to the winter months when the trees are dormant. During the growing and fruiting seasons where temperatures and evaporation are relatively high, additional water is required.

In home plantings the quantity of water needed usually does not exceed that obtainable from the domestic water supply. Larger plantings must depend upon wells, streams, or an irrigation system bringing water down from some mountain source. The amount of water needed varies with climatic conditions, the size of the trees, and the kind and depth of soil. Enough water should be applied at any one time to wet the soil to a depth where it is still moist from the previous rains. Where sprinklers are used they may need to run for a 24-hour period. Wetting to a depth of only a few inches is insufficient. Forcing a small stake or metal rod into the ground is a very good way to ascertain if the soil is wet down to the tree root area — which in the case of bearing trees in good soils may easily extend to a depth of six feet.

Where the basin system of irrigation is used, one inch of water applied to a coarse sandy soil may wet it to a depth of 12–15 in.; with a heavy soil (clay or adobe) of greater holding capacity, to a depth of only 2–3 in. On the intermediate or loam soils one inch may be expected to wet 5–6 in. More water is thus required at each application to wet a heavy soil than a light one. On the other hand, the lighter soils are less retentive of moisture, and water is needed more frequently. Except for the coastal areas of the Pacific States, where irrigation may be unnecessary, from 2 to 5 applications of water may be given annually.

In the home garden, fruit trees need only sufficient cultivation to keep down weeds which compete with the tree for the available soil moisture. Trees growing in a well-watered lawn naturally require no cultivation.

An application of manure or some nitrogenous commercial fertilizer may help the young tree in making its initial growth but excessive use of these in subsequent years may delay the time of fruiting. A good balance should be maintained between vegetative vigor and fruitfulness.

In pruning trees in the home garden the same basic principles apply as with commercial orchards. However with a limited number of trees — and especially with the dwarfs — more attention may be given to shaping and training young trees to a desired form. Light pruning or "pinching" of the new growth during the summer season will aid in this respect. — F.W.A.

INSECT PESTS. The worst pest of apple fruit is the pinkish caterpillar of the codling moth. Adherence to spray schedule will control this pest. Other chewing insects such as cankerworms, tent caterpillars, webworms, green fruit worms, and leaf rollers will damage leaves and fruit if the regular schedule is not followed.

Snout beetles, the plum curculio, and others blemish fruit early in the season. Sprays at petal fall and shortly thereafter control this damage.

Tiny mites of several species feed on leaves in midsummer and later produce a yellow-bronzed leaf which greatly reduces yield and tree vigor. Avoid use of DDT and similar materials unless a mite-killing chemical is included in sprays.

Seldom sprayed, poorly pruned, and unfertilized trees often develop round or flat-headed borers. Leopard moth boring worms may cause serious damage to young trees. All these borers may be killed by wires inserted into holes. Preparations to be injected into borings may be purchased.

Scale insects of several species weaken trees. These insects attach themselves to the bark and cover themselves with a scale which appears grayish on the bark. Regular dormant sprays of oil will control scales of all types.

Aphids of various species distort leaves and fruit and promote sooty mold* on fruit. Pesticide #29 (see SPRAYS AND DUSTS), applied before leaves appear, will kill eggs, and pesticide #1 during the season will control active forms. Root aphids, where present, particularly in the Northeast, can be counteracted by good fertilizing practices.

Apple maggot is present in northern areas. Midseason sprays, particularly those containing lead arsenate, will control adult fruit flies before eggs can be laid. Tunneling of whitish maggots through the fruit produces a knobby apple with brownish trails in fruit.

DISEASES. Choice and adaptibility of apple varieties varies greatly from state to state. Likewise the susceptibility to disease varies among the varieties.

Scab causes black blotches on leaves and fruit. The fungus overwinters on dead leaves on the ground and is controlled only by an intensive spray schedule starting at pink-bud of flowers and continuing through the summer.

Powdery mildew* produces white, powdery masses on the leaves and may envelop whole shoots, causing them to curl. When an entire branchlet is covered with the fungus it should be pruned out to help prevent overwintering of the disease. The more susceptible varieties such as Cortland and Rome may require special sprays early in the spring to hold the disease in check.

Rust* is a fungus disease causing orange-red pustules on leaves and on fruit of some varieties. The fungus spends part of its life on the apple, hawthorn, or quince, and part of its life on the red cedar or juniper tree. For this reason it is best not to grow red cedar and susceptible apple varieties in close proximity. If the disease is serious on apple, add pesticide #11 (see SPRAYS AND DUSTS) to all sprays applied from pink-bud or flower-bud stage up through the spray applied 2 weeks after petals fall.

Fly-speck, causing superficial specks the size of fly-droppings; blotch and sooty-blotch, producing superficial black, irregular spots; bitter-rot and black-rot, causing deep brown or black sooting of the fruit, are all fungus diseases which are controlled by most standard schedules which control scab.

Fireblight* is a bacterial disease which causes sudden wilting and browning and death of entire branches during the early summer. In some states the agricultural experiment stations have had a partial control with the newer antibiotic* spray materials. On susceptible varieties the disease is more severe on trees receiving high rates of nitrogen fertilizer.

---

* Special articles on the subjects indicated by an asterisk (*) will be found at the words so marked.

All cankered and dead branches should be pruned from the tree each year. Some of the fruit-rotting fungi overwinter on these dead branches.

Many commercial orchardists apply 15 or more sprays each year, utilizing 10 or more different chemicals to obtain high-quality fruit. For a plant-hobby person, rather than a commercial grower, the following spray program will give fairly good results. — S.H.D and L.G.M.

APPLE SPRAY PROGRAM

Time	Pesticide
Dormant spray. Before buds show any green and while temperature is above freezing	#29
When bud shows first pink; repeat sprays weekly until the first petals fall	#1 or #2
Petal fall, and 1, 2, 4, and 8 weeks after petal fall	#1, or #2 plus #19

APPLE FAMILY. See ROSACEAE.

APPLE GERANIUM = *Pelargonium odoratissimum.*

APPLE MINT = *Mentha rotundifolia.* See MINT.

APPLE-OF-PERU = *Nicandra Physalodes.*

APPRESSED. Pressing against, as some leaves are appressed against the stem, or the scales against a cone. The botanical term is usually adpressed.

APRICOT (*Prunus Armeniaca*). Besides the U.S., only Australia, the Union of South Africa, Syria, and Persia produce apricots in any considerable quantity, and production in the U.S. is practically confined to Calif., which has about 93 per cent of the total tonnage with Wash. ranking next.

The other western states producing apricots do not seriously compete with the Calif. crop, which is sold dried, canned, and fresh. The earliest season is that of Calif. (May 15 to July 15). The apricot is also grown in British Columbia, and, locally, in Va.

VARIETIES. The ideal apricot variety is suitable for drying, canning, and marketing fresh. It should ripen both halves evenly, be free of the pit, and be well colored when canned or dried. In order of ripening, the four varieties constituting most of the tonnage are Royal, Blenheim, Tilton, and Moorpark.

The old French Royal variety and the English Blenheim were early introduced into Calif., where they are the foundation of the industry. At present no one can surely distinguish between them. In the interior valleys only Royal was planted; in the coastal counties, Blenheim. Royal now stands for a firm, well-colored, freestone apricot, highly flavored and medium to large, suitable for drying, canning, or shipping east. Blenheim, later in season, supposed to have less color and firmness, but better size, serves the same purposes. Trees of both are regularly productive. For the past 20 years, leading Calif. nurseries have increased the confusion by making no clear distinction between the two.

Tilton, a rather large, flat Calif. variety, tends to bear alternately unless carefully grown. It is prolific, having yielded 20 tons of good-sized cannery fruit per acre. In quality it ranks below Royal and Blenheim. It is lighter in color and blooms and ripens somewhat later. Its popularity is waning, no doubt through lack of annual crops of high quality. Although shipped and canned in a limited way, it is mostly dried.

Moorpark, an old English variety, has very large fruit, late and of the highest quality, used for local markets or drying. It is irregular and shy in bearing. The Wenatchee Moorpark variety is most widely grown in all western states except Calif.

For early shipment, Stewart, Derby, Perfection, and others are occasionally planted. The Stewart and Derby, which closely resemble Royal, are commonly shipped as such.

Russian varieties such as Alexander and Budd are grown where winter temperatures are especially severe, but they are small and inferior. These are the so-called hardy apricots grown in the East, of which Doty, Geneva, and Henderson have proved hardy in Ont. and Mich. For the Japanese apricot, *see* PRUNUS MUME.

All varieties except Perfection are self-fertile and can be planted in solid blocks. Any other apricot variety will usually set fruit on Perfection.

LOCATION. In Calif., after the almond, the apricot is first to bloom. It is, however, apparently more susceptible to frost injury in both the flower and the young fruit, so that it must be planted in areas relatively free from frost. Many orchards in Calif. are artificially heated. (*See* FROST.) In order to break the "rest," winter temperatures should not be too mild; otherwise, fruit buds are shed instead of opening, and crops are reduced. With adequate irrigation, the apricot tree thrives in locations ranging from cool coastal to desert. It is more particular in its soil moisture requirements than some other fruits, such as the peach, so far as production is concerned; but the tree itself withstands drought better than the peach. During the growing season, the fruit responds directly to temperatures; it ripens when sufficient heat units have accumulated, whether in 100 or in 130 days, a fact explaining the earliness of certain districts. In most sections, however, temperatures of 103° F. and upward during the ripening season cause "pit burn" — a darkening of the flesh at the pit — which spoils the fruit for selling fresh or canning and lowers its value for drying.

CULTURE. The apricot can be grown successfully on many soils, but apparently prefers a deep, well-drained clay loam. Apricot, peach, and the myrobalan plum are satisfactory rootstocks, although with the myrobalan plum considerable breakage at the graft union occurs unless a congenial strain is secured. Peach root is used on light, well-

---

* Special articles on the subjects indicated by an asterisk (*) will be found at the words so marked.

drained soils; apricot on moderately heavy, well-drained soils; and myrobalan plum on wetter and heavier types. To plant apricots on soils so heavy that the apricot root will not thrive is economically questionable. According to some growers, peach root gives apricots of larger size and earlier maturity. Apricot root is more susceptible to gopher injury. On soils best adapted to apricots, there is probably little to choose between the peach and apricot stocks. Since adequate soil moisture is necessary for regular yields, most apricot orchards are irrigated from 2 to 8 times a season, depending upon age, type of soil, and climate. A permanent cover crop such as alfalfa may be grown, provided adequate irrigation water is available.

Apricot trees are planted from 20 to 30 ft. apart; on good soils 25 ft. should be the minimum. Usually a one-year-old tree is planted and immediately headed to about 30 in. During the next several years, light thinnings encourage an upright, natural habit of growth and first crops that will insure proper spread. Fruits are borne on spurs and new wood. The bearing tree should be pruned for a proper balance between renewal wood and crop — climatic conditions, soil, irrigation, and other factors being considered. Pruning for size of fruit is usually profitably supplemented by thinning of the fruit. Fruits are generally spaced about 4 in. apart.

HARVESTING. Apricots should be hand-picked. Proper maturity is largely determined by color. For distant shipment, for the cannery, and for drying, fruits are picked at successive degrees of firmness and color, being most mature for drying. For this last purpose, they should be fully ripe and yet firm enough to handle. The more nearly complete the ripening on the tree, the higher the sugar content and the consequent quality. After picking, there is no increase in sugar.

DRYING. Apricots should be halved, the pits removed, and placed on trays with cup up, and exposed to the fumes of burning sulphur from 2 to 6 hours and then dried in the sun. After 1 to 3 days, the trays are stacked; and the drying is completed in a week to ten days. A few apricots are artificially dehydrated; about 5 pounds fresh makes 1 pound dry. — W. P. T.

For diseases and insect pests, *see* PEACH.

APTENIA. *See* MESEMBRYANTHEMUM.

AQUARIUM. It is interesting to note the important part aquatic vegetation plays in successful aquarium management. There are five distinct ways in which plants benefit the aquarium, and an additional one which may be turned to the advantage of the aquarist. These values and their relationship to aquarium management may be listed thus:

FIRST. The ability of plants, under the influence of light, to develop free oxygen and to absorb carbon dioxide. Fishes, like other animals, must breathe oxygen. While pure water is composed of two parts of hydrogen and one of oxygen, it is not the oxygen of the water itself which supports fish life. Water absorbs or dissolves air into itself. It is this dissolved air which is absorbed by the gills of the fish and furnishes the oxygen necessary to life. As this oxygen in most aquariums is used by the fish more rapidly than it can be renewed by absorption at the water's surface, plants are most important. In a growing condition and under the stimulation of light, they give off much pure oxygen, most of which is absorbed directly into the water. When the plants are unusually active in this respect they furnish more oxygen than the water can take up, and we see tiny streams of bubbles rising from the leaves. This is to be observed when light is strong. Excessive light, however, is not to be encouraged. The heat which usually goes with it raises the temperature of water. This has the effect of *reducing* oxygen content, for the warmer it gets, the *less* oxygen it can hold. Too much light also tends to turn the water green, and to induce that green mossy growth on the glass and plants — one of the aquarist's chief troubles. In justice to this green scum it should be said that it supplies oxygen and is a food for certain fishes.

The ideal situation for an aquarium is one in which it receives a strong diffused light, such as it would get at a large north window. If facing another direction, one or two hours' direct sunlight is not objectionable.

Before finishing point number one, it should be stated that fishes (again like other animals) exhale carbon dioxide. This is food for the plants, so that a beneficial exchange is thus set up. The term "balanced aquarium" has come into use to express that relationship between plant and fish life.

POINT NUMBER TWO. This also has to do with the chemistry of the aquarium. Fish in order to live must not only breathe; they must eat, and the certain result of eating is the discharge of contaminating substances into the water. These substances are fertilizers to the plants. They absorb them through roots and leaves.

THE THIRD USE for aquarium plants is in helping to keep the water clear. This is accomplished in two ways — by shading and by food competition. Green water is produced by the presence of suspended microscopic vegetal organisms. To exist they must have food and light. Growing plants shade them and successfully compete for the food present in the water. The most effective plants for clearing the water are those which float, forming a green mantle. *Salvinia*, Duckweed, and *Azolla* are the best plants for this purpose. The ideal arrangement is a growth of taller, grass-like plants, rooted in the sand, together with a floating mantle of plants. The disadvantage of small floating plants is that they get into the net when fish must be caught. They do *not* interfere with oxygen absorption — they *furnish* it.

POINT NUMBER FOUR has to do with the

---

* Special articles on the subjects indicated by an asterisk (*) will be found at the words so marked.

very important part plants play in breeding fishes. Goldfishes and many of their cousins among the exotic aquarium fishes deposit their eggs on the finely divided leaves of plants like *Myriophyllum.* A number of the smaller fishes prefer depositing their eggs among loose masses of floating plants, such as *Riccia* or *Utricularia.* Plants of this character are of great value in the breeding of those popular fishes which have their young born alive. In most of those species the parents are cannibalistic and try to eat their new-born young. The babies, however, quickly seek refuge among plants. *Riccia* is particularly good for the purpose. In a few weeks the babies are sufficiently grown to be out of danger of being eaten. *Azolla* is also used for this.

THE FIFTH POINT is by many considered to be the first. That is decorative value. As the aquarium is usually regarded in the light of a miniature bit of aquatic life, re-created in the home in as much completeness as possible, it is self-evident that the beauty of plant life is one of the first considerations. Plants not only give the most natural setting for fishes, but their mellow green furnishes the best possible background for the sparkling colors of the fishes.

The added personal advantage for the aquarist of plants is that there is always a ready market for aquarium-grown specimens. It is a recognized fact that they function better and live longer than do plants of similar species taken from the wild.

As to the most popular aquarium plants, there is no doubt that *Cabomba, Myriophyllum,* and *Anacharis* are the commerical leaders. Each or all of them can be had wherever aquarium fishes are sold. Plants have different capacities in the production of oxygen. These three are fair in that respect. Most expert aquarists are more inclined to favor the two grass-like plants, *Vallisneria* (*see* EEL-GRASS) and *Sagittaria,* but they are not so well suited to aquaria of less than five-gallon capacity. Where the light is not too good, *Cryptocoryne* will be found useful. *See also* NAIAS and NITELLA. Aquarium plants should be rooted in coarse sand in preference to pebbles.

Goldfish do best at temperatures between 60°and 70°, and ought to be fed once a day as much food as they can consume in five minutes. Besides prepared fish-foods they enjoy bits of boiled fish, shrimp, etc.

Exotic fishes (tropicals) should be kept within a range of 70° to 80°, and an average of 75° is satisfactory. At that temperature, or higher, they ought to be fed twice daily. They also should have variety.

No fish should be moved into water of a different temperature. All new water ought to be drawn a day before use, and stored in enamel or glass containers to allow any chlorine to dissipate. Freshly drawn water, especially in winter, may be injurious to plants.

Many other plants, often suggested for aquaria, are quite unsuited to the maintenance of a properly balanced one. Such showy aquatics as the water hyacinth, water lily, water snowflake, and many others are better suited to the water garden (which see) than to aquaria. — C. B. L.

aquatica, -us, -um (a-kwa′ti-ka). Growing in or near water.

AQUATICS. Water plants may be submerged, floating, or merely grow along the edge of a pool. Technically, the term should be restricted to plants that float upon the water (as do most water lilies) or are submerged in it (as is the eel-grass). But hort. usage has stretched the word to include not only true aquatics, but plants of marshes, meadows, swamps, and bogs. For the chief garden aquatics *see* WATER GARDEN.

AQUIFOLIACEAE (a-kwi-fo-li-ā′see-e). The holly family, sometimes called Ilicaceae, comprises only 5 genera, but nearly 300 species of trees and shrubs, of which *Ilex* (the holly) and *Nemopanthus* are the only cult. genera. They have alternate,° often evergreen, leaves, spiny-margined in some of the hollies, and small, inconspicuous, generally greenish-yellow flowers. Fruit berry-like (technically a small drupe°), often showy in some hollies. The family is of hort. importance only because of the fine evergreen foliage of the English, Chinese and American holly trees and for their bright red fruit.

Technical flower characters: Calyx 3–6-parted, often persistent. Petals 4 or 5, distinct and separate, but slightly overlapping, often somewhat united only at the base. Stamens 4 or 5. Ovary superior,° 3- or many-celled.

Aquifolium (a-kwi-fō′li-um). The Latin name for the holly; literally *aqui,* a point, and *folium,* a leaf; in allusion to the spiny-margined leaves of some species.

AQUILEGIA. See COLUMBINE.

aquilegifolia, -us, -um (a-kwi-lee-je-fō′li-a). With foliage like the columbine.

aquilina, -us, -um (a-kwi-ly′na). Aquiline; *i.e.,* eagle-like.

ARABIAN COFFEE = *Coffea arabica*

ARABIAN GENTIAN. See EXACUM.

ARABIAN JASMINE = *Jasminum Sambac.*

ARABIAN PRIMROSE = *Arnebia cornuta.*

ARABIAN VIOLET. See EXACUM.

arabica, -us, -um (a-rab′i-ka). From Arabia.

ARABIS (ar′a-bis). The rock cresses comprise a large genus of herbs of the mustard family, much grown for ornament, especially in the wall garden, the rock garden, and in the open border. Of the hundred species, mostly from the north temperate zone, only the handful below are of garden interest. They have basal or stem leaves, usually hairy, and small, white or purple flowers, often in ample clusters (spikes ° or racemes °). Fruit a long, narrow, usually flattened pod.

° Special articles on the subjects indicated by an asterisk (°) will be found at the words so marked.

(The name is a Latinized form of Arabia, from which some [not hort.] species came.)

The rock cresses are of very easy culture. The perennial sorts are easily propagated by spring or fall division of their roots. All prefer open sunlight and a warm, rather sandy soil, although they will often thrive in poor soils.

albida. Wall cress. A tufted, white-foliaged, hairy perennial from the Caucasus, usually less than 12 in. high. Leaves 1–3 in. long, coarsely toothed toward the relatively broad apex. Flowers white, fragrant, about ½ in. long, in loose clusters. May. There are double-flowered and variegated-leaved forms. A good plant for dry walls or the rock garden.*

alpina. A mountain plant from Eu., lower than the above and less hairy. Leaves more or less oblong, toothed throughout, 1–3 in. long. Flowers about ⅓ in. long, white. Primarily a rock garden species and often confused with A. albida. May. There is a double-flowered form; much finer than the typical one.

androsaca. A silvery-hairy perennial, not over 2½ in. high, the leaves in dense, basal, rosettes; a few on the stem being narrow and toothless. Flowers white, in a short cluster (raceme*). Southeastern Eu. July–Aug.

aubrietioides. A low, densely tufted perennial from Asia Minor, suited only to the rock garden. Leaves felty white or greenish, very small, blunt, and numerous, those on the stem appressed.* Flowers pink. May. Requires a gritty, sandy soil. See ROCK GARDEN.

blepharophylla. A low perennial, unsuited to the East, only 3–4 in. high. Leaves all basal, the margins lined with eyelash-like hairs. Flowers pinkish-purple, the petals rounded at the tip, clawed* at the base. Calif. Apr.

mollis. A form of A. procurrens.

muralis. A biennial or perennial herb, 5–10 in. high, the leaves spoon-shaped and toothed, a little rough; the stem leaves stalkless. Flowers white or rose-purple, in long clusters (racemes*). Southeastern Eu. May–June.

procurrens. A showy, white-flowered perennial,* not over 1 ft. high, creeping by short runners. Leaves oblongish, pointed, without teeth. Flowers in racemes,* the cluster elongating. It thrives in relatively poor soils. Southeastern Eu. May. There is a variegated-leaved form.

ARACEAE (a-ray'see-ee). The arum family (usually called simply aroids) comprises a huge aggregation of more than 100 genera and about 1500 species of herbs, the stems of some, especially in the tropical sorts, becoming woody and even tree-like. The family is often called the arum or Calla family. It contains not only these but such well-known plants as the calla lily, the Jack-in-the-pulpit (see ARISAEMA), the skunk-cabbage, the sweet flag (see ACORUS), and Dracunculus. All these, except the calla lily, are hardy northward, but most of the Araceae are tropical plants. All contain a bitter, often poisonous juice, sometimes milky.

Leaves various, wholly without marginal teeth, but often deeply lobed, very showy in some of the hort. genera, notably Aglaonema, Alocasia, Anthurium, Caladium, Colocasia (elephant's-ear), Dieffenbachia, Nephythytis, Schismatoglottis, Scindapsus, and Spathiphyllum. All of these are handsome, tropical foliage plants of greenhouse culture, a few as summer bedding plants in the North.

There are, besides those above, two or three hardy native plants in Orontium, Peltandra, and Lysichitum. There are 2 tropical aquatics (see CRYPTOCORYNE and PISTIA), and besides the taro (see COLOCASIA), another genus furnishes edible rootstocks (see XANTHOSOMA). For other hort. genera, all tropical, see HYDROSME, PHILODENDRON and MONSTERA, a curious plant with leaves full of holes, and edible fruit.

The flowers of the aroids are difficult for the gardener to fathom. What he calls a "flower," say the "Jack" in Jack-in-the-pulpit, is a collection of almost microscopic ones crowded on a column-like organ (the "Jack") technically known as a spadix. The spadix (which is the "flower" of most gardeners) may be a foot or more long in many tropical species, brightly colored and very showy, especially in Anthurium. See FLOWER.

Below the spadix there is a bract,* leaf-like but often colored in some genera, or funnel-shaped and completely surrounding the spadix as in the "pulpit" of the Jack-in-the-pulpit. This leaf-like or funnel-shaped organ is the spathe,* common (but soon withering in many tropical genera) throughout the Araceae. Fruit fleshy in all genera.

Technical flower characters: Sepals and petals none, or replaced by 4–8 scale-like substitutes. Stamens 1 or many, sometimes united. Ovary 1, with one to many carpels, each with one or more ovules. The individual flowers are extremely minute, and exact identification of the genera consequently difficult.

ARACHIS. See PEANUT.

arachnoidea, -us, -um (a-rak-noy'dee-a). Arachnoid; i.e., like a spider's web.

ARALIA (a-ray'li-a). A genus of 20 species of mostly spiny shrubs and trees, or unarmed perennial herbs, belonging to the ginseng family, and grown for ornament. All but a few are native in N.A. or eastern As. Leaves alternate,* compound,* or twice- or thrice-compound,* often very large and showy. Flowers greenish or whitish, in umbels, the latter often grouped in a large terminal cluster (panicle*). Fruit berry-like, with 2–5 flattened stones. (Aralia is of unknown origin.)

The shrubby and tree aralias, such as the angelica trees and the Hercules'-club, are striking plants for the shrub border or for specimens on the lawn. They need a rich soil and a reasonable amount of moisture. The perennial herbs are largely woods plants suited to the wild garden, where they should have partial shade and a rich humus. Propagation of the woody species is by seeds sown in frames in the spring or by root cuttings over bottom-heat. The perennials are easily divided in the spring.

For some greenhouse decorative plants wrongly but commonly called Aralia, see POLYSCIAS and DIZYGOTHECA.

---

* Special articles on the subjects indicated by an asterisk (*) will be found at the words so marked.

californica. Elk clover. A stout herbaceous perennial 6–10 ft. high. Leaves twice-compound,* the ultimate segments usually doubly toothed, nearly 12 in. long. Umbels* in a spreading panicle* nearly 18 in. long. British Columbia to Calif.

chinensis = A. elata.

cordata. Udo. A perennial herb grown for its young edible shoots which, however, have a turpentine odor unless the shoots have been blanched by earthing up. It is a stout herb 6–8 ft. high, with compound* leaves, provided with 3–5 leaflets. Jap. Only young shoots are palatable and these should be boiled in salty water to help extract the turpentine flavor.

elata. Angelica tree. A stout prickly shrub or small tree, sometimes 25 ft. high. Leaves sometimes 3 ft. long, doubly compound.* the numerous leaflets narrowly elliptic, about 9 in. long, remotely toothed. They are dark green above, but paler beneath. Flower cluster large, hairy, the flowers whitish. Fruit black. Jap. and on the mainland. A very handsome tree with striking, bold foliage. Hardy from zone* 4 southward. There are white- and golden-variegated forms.

elegantissima = Dizygotheca elegantissima.

hispida. Bristly sarsaparilla. A rather coarse perennial herb of eastern N.A., mostly in sandy woods and fit only for the drier parts of the wild garden. It is 12–30 in. high. It has bristles toward the base of the stem. Leaves with generally 5 toothed leaflets. Flowers small, greenish, followed by black fruit. June–July.

japonica = Fatsia japonica

nudicaulis. Wild sarsaparilla. A low herb with a single, long-stalked, compound leaf and a ball-like cluster of greenish-yellow flowers. Eastern N.A. Will grow in a variety of places, and in pure sand. See SAND GARDEN.

papyrifera = Tetrapanax papyriferus.

racemosa. American spikenard; called also spikenard. A branching perennial herb 3–5 ft. high. Leaves twice-compound, the ultimate leaflets few, more or less heart-shaped, about 6 in. long, double-toothed. Flowers greenish, the umbels* arranged in a large cluster (raceme*). Fruit brownish-purple. Eastern N.A. The plant has spicy, aromatic roots.

spinosa. Hercules'-club, called, also, devil's-walking-stick. A North American spiny-trunked tree sometimes 40 ft. high. Leaves twice-compound,* long-stalked, the leaflets prickly, ovalish, about 4 in. long, pale on the under side. Flowers whitish in large, hairy clusters (panicles*). Fruit black. It forms an impenetrable, prickly barrier.

ARALIACEAE (a-ray-li-ā'see-ee). The ginseng family includes only a dozen or so hort. subjects among more than 50 genera of herbs, shrubs, vines, or trees widely distributed over the world. They often have prickly stems among the shrubs and trees, but *Panax* (the ginseng) are unarmed herbs. Leaves simple* in *Hedera* (the English ivy), *Oplopanax, Tetrapanax, Fatsia,* and *Fatshedera,* but the blade may be variously cut or lobed even in these. All the other hort. genera have compound* or even twice- or thrice-compound* leaves, often of great size and consequently very showy.

Of the hardy woody genera (with compound* leaves), *Aralia* and *Acanthopanax* are the best-known. Tropical or sub-tropical genera, mostly of greenhouse culture, include *Dizygotheca, Polyscias,* and the recently introduced *Schefflera,* a valuable house plant.

The flowers of the ginseng family, never showy, are small, usually greenish or greenish-white, borne in umbels, but the latter often congested into a head-like cluster and borne in large, branched, umbel-like clusters (a compound umbel*) or in racemes* or panicles.* Fruit fleshy (a berry or a drupe*).

Technical flower characters: Calyx small, attached to the ovary. Petals 5, their margins touching or overlapping, or even slightly united. Stamens* 5, epigynous. Ovary inferior,* 1- to many-celled.

araucana, -us, -um (or-ro-kay'na). From Araucana, an old name for the southern part of Chile.

ARAUCARIA (or-ro-cay'ri-a). Stately evergreen trees of the pine family, one, the Norfolk Island pine, a widely grown decorative florist's plant in its young state; another, the famous monkey-puzzle. All are natives of the southern hemisphere. Branches in regular tiers. Leaves evergreen, prickly and scale-like or expanded into flat, thick, leathery blades, always stiff. The flowers and seeds are borne between the scales of an egg-shaped or globe-like cone which falls apart in age. (*Araucaria* is from *Araucana,* see above.)

The Norfolk Island pine (*A. excelsa*) is much grown in its young state as a pot plant. It needs a cool greenhouse, partial shade, and is best grown in potting mixture* 3. Propagation is by seed or cuttings of the terminal leader or its successors. Cuttings from lateral growth make unsymmetrical, lopsided plants. Planted in sand, the cuttings will root if kept at about 60°.

The other species are lofty trees, seldom grown in greenhouses, and outdoors only as indicated below, except the monkey-puzzle. This curious evergreen is hardy outdoors from zone* 6 southward, and with protection (see PROTECTING PLANTS), in sheltered places north of this.

araucana. Monkey-puzzle, so called from its habit of inextricable branching. The main branches are in tiers, but the ramifications twist and turn to form an impenetrable and very prickly growth. Leaves persisting for years, prickle-pointed, ovalish, flat, leathery, very stiff, and about 2 in. long when mature, bright green. Cone 6–8 in. in diameter. Hardy outdoors from zone* 6, and often planted for its grotesque habit. Chile. Long sold as A. imbricata.

bidwilli. Bunya-bunya. An Australian tree up to 150 ft., less in cult. and hardy only in zones* 8 and 9. Leaves glossy-green in distinct rows, sharp-pointed, stiff, oblong-oval, about 1½ in. long. Grown outdoors mostly in Calif. and Fla.

cunninghami. Moreton Bay pine, called, also, hoop pine. An Australian evergreen tree up to 150 ft., much less in cult., less symmetrical than the next, but often grown for ornament. Leaves stiff, sharp-pointed, needle-like, about 1½ in. long. There is also a variety with bluish-green foliage. Hardy outdoors only in zones* 8 and 9.

---

* Special articles on the subjects indicated by an asterisk (*) will be found at the words so marked.

excelsa. Norfolk Island pine. As usually grown, a pot plant 2–10 ft. high; at home often 200 ft. high, and an important timber tree. Branches 5–7 in a tier, thickly beset with sharp-pointed leaves that are about ½ in. long and curved at the tip. It practically never flowers or fruits in cult. An extremely popular florist's plant, grown by the million, and an excellent house plant. Norfolk Island (in the Pacific Ocean). Called also star pine.

imbricata = Araucaria araucana.

ARAUJIA (a-raw′je-a). A small genus of mostly Brazilian, woody vines of the milkweed family, the one below sometimes grown as a greenhouse climber. Leaves opposite.* Flowers in sparse clusters in the axils* of the leaves, not very showy, the corolla bell-shaped. Fruit a leathery pod (follicle*). (Named for Araujo de Azevedo, Portuguese statesman.)

A greenhouse plant best grown in potting mixture* 5, in the cool house, and outdoors in zones* 8 and 9. Propagated by cuttings over bottom-heat,* or by seeds sown outdoors in tropical and sub-tropical regions.

sericofera. A tall-growing, woody vine. Leaves oblongish, 2–4 in. long, with a tapering point, mealy on the under side. Flowers pale pink or white, about ¾ in. wide. Southern Brazil.

ARBOR DAY. A day set aside for the planting of trees, usually as a community enterprise, and largely by school children. The plan originated in Neb. in 1872 and is now general, although the day varies in the different states. Arbor Day in most states is in April or early May.

arborea, -us, -um (ar-bore′ee-a). Tree-like; but often, as a specific name, indicating mere woodiness.

arborescens (ar-bore-ress′ens). Almost tree-like.

ARBORETUM. Strictly, a collection of trees grown for study, research, or ornament; now, quite generally, any collection of woody plants so grown. By far the most important arboretum in this country is the Arnold Arboretum of Harvard University at Jamaica Plain, Mass. It occupies several hundred acres, has perhaps the greatest collection of trees, shrubs, and woody vines in the world, and a library and herbarium.*

There are many others in different parts of the country. Those whose collections are outstanding, who issue reports on hardiness and other features of the cultivation of woody plants, and whose collections are labeled for the convenience of the public might include the following. In the titles of them the word "Arboretum" is understood but omitted.

Arizona:
  Boyce Thompson, Superior
California:
  Golden Gate Park, San Francisco
  Los Angeles County, Arcadia
  Rancho Santa Ana, Claremont
Colorado:
  Myron Stratton, Colorado Springs
Delaware:
  Henry F. du Pont, Winterthur

District of Columbia:
  United States National, Washington
Florida:
  Fairchild Tropical Garden, Coconut Grove
  Montgomery Palm Collection, Coconut Grove
Illinois:
  Morton, Lisle
Massachusetts:
  Arnold, Jamaica Plain
  Walter Hunnewell, Wellesley
Michigan:
  Morgan, Ann Arbor
Missouri:
  Missouri Botanical Garden, Gray Summit
New York:
  Bayard Cutting, Oakdale, L.I.
  Cornell University, Ithaca
  Desmond, Newburgh
  New York Botanical Garden, New York City
  Planting Fields, Oyster Bay, L.I.
  Rochester Public Park System, Rochester
Ohio:
  Holden, Mentor
Oregon:
  Hoyt, Portland
Pennsylvania:
  Bartram's Garden, Fairmount Park, Philadelphia
  Morris, Philadelphia
  John T. Tyler, Lima
Virginia:
  Orland E. White, Boyce
Washington:
  University of Washington, Seattle
  Finch, Spokane
Canada:
  Morgan, Macdonald College, Montreal, Quebec
  Queen Elizabeth, Vancouver, British Columbia

Besides these there are many smaller or newer institutions devoted to the cult. of woody plants, scattered in almost every state of the Union and in the provinces of Canada. In addition to the arboretums listed above are others in Calif., Conn., Ga., Mich., Minn., N.J., N. Car., Ohio, Tenn., Tex., Wis., and, in Canada, at Ottawa and Morden. For a complete list see Donald Wyman's *The Arboretums and Botanical Gardens of North America* (Jamaica Plain, Mass., Arnold Arboretum, 1959).

In addition the U.S. Forest Service maintains many tree collections in different parts of the country, mostly for study of silvicultural problems, involving the growing of trees in considerable stands. Such experiments are worth study to those with small pieces of forest on their estates, but lie outside the scope of the usual arboretum. *See also* BOTANIC GARDEN, GARDEN TOURS, and Mount Vernon at TREES.

ARBORICULTURE. The culture of trees (which see).

ARBORS. Arbors are of two general types: one acts merely as a support for vines where the structure is subordinate to the planting; in the other the architectural structure is the important decorative feature, while the planting is secondary.

In construction it is important not to con-

---

* Special articles on the subjects indicated by an asterisk (*) will be found at the words so marked.

A formal architectural arbor

fuse the two types. If the plant effect is to dominate, the design of the structure should be simple and durable. In this case elaborate architectural detail is superfluous, since it is shrouded with vines. The structure, however, should be substantial, because repair work will be difficult after the vines have matured. The main supports of an arbor should be close enough together longitudinally to prevent sagging under weight of the vines. Distance between supports should not exceed eight feet. This same precaution applies to the width of the arbor and its cross-members. When the cross-span is too wide the supporting members must become disproportionately heavy to prevent sagging.

For lightweight structures the longitudinal spacing between supports should be approximately equal to the cross-span. To secure a very light, airy effect the spacing between supports should be lengthened by using light, intermediate side supports and arched cross-spans in place of horizontal members. Since the arch type of arbor combines greater strength with lighter structure, it is more graceful in its effect.

An arbor is merely a repetition of the same unit, depending upon the rhythm of this repetition for its effect. Hence, the cross-members should be reduced to the minimum lest they interrupt the view monotonously and destroy the effect of length. Whenever the longitudinal members of an arbor predominate there is a pleasing sense of continuity.

Details of arbor design are infinite in their variety. It is the purpose here to state general principles of construction, leaving individual ingenuity to develop details.

For the purely vine-supporting structure wood or non-rusting metal are the best materials. From the ornamental viewpoint wood is the most satisfactory. Cypress has proven to be the most durable wood for outdoor arbor construction; next in durability is redwood or fir. If the wood is given two coats of good lead and oil paint before erection, with two more coats after erection, a durable job is assured. To prevent further deteriora-

tion use copper nails and galvanized iron bolts. Wherever possible, wood members should be fitted into each other to be self-supporting without nails. Durability of construction is important because nothing can be more exasperating than the collapse of an arbor when the vines have matured to their full beauty.

Although metal construction combined with wire vine supports can be very attractive it is less ornamental than wood and often burns the vines in very hot climates.

An arbor made chiefly for vines

Wherever the architectural structure is the dominating feature masonry should be used for the main supports. Since the scale of this type of arbor is usually larger than the vine-covered type, both the longitudinal members and cross-spans can be increased in length. The design of masonry arches is a real architectural problem requiring skill in the use of materials and construction. Unless the builder is endowed with creative ability it is wise to refresh his imagination from the many examples of architectural arbor design characteristic of Old World gardens. To insure permanency all supports must be carried below the frost line which averages three feet in the northern states. Unless the structure is securely built many types of vines in maturity will dislodge their supports to suit their growing convenience and the structural design will be destroyed.

Arches are just short arbors and may be treated in much the same way. In its true sense an arch is merely an ornamental opening through a barrier. Therefore, when an arch is used as a gateway it should be flanked by planting so that it is the only opening through which one may pass. It is always inconsistent to see an arch floating in the open where it is just as convenient to go around it as to walk through. — R. E. G.

arbor-tristis, -e (ar-bor-tris'tis). Sad, or grayish, tree.

ARBORVITAE. Properly, the evergreens of the genus *Thuja;* also, not quite so ap-

---

propriately, evergreens of the genus *Thujopsis*. See both genera.

arbutifolia, -us, -um (ar-bew-ti-fō′li-a). With leaves like the strawberry tree (*Arbutus*).

ARBUTUS (ar-bew′tus). A small genus of broad-leaved evergreen trees of the heath family, two of which are grown in warm regions for ornament. Leaves alternate* and stalked. Flowers white or pinkish, urn-shaped, in loose terminal clusters (panicles*). Fruit fleshy, red or orange. (*Arbutus* is the classical Latin name of a European species.)

These plants have nothing to do with trailing arbutus (which see).

Both the species below prefer well-drained, wind-sheltered sites, and the first is an important source of honey to Calif. beekeepers. Propagated by cuttings of partially ripened wood, taken in the fall and under glass, also by layers.

menziesi. Madroña; called also laurelwood and Oregon laurel. A tall tree found wild from British Columbia to Calif. Leaves oblongish, about 4 in. long, grayish-green beneath, and without marginal teeth. Flower cluster about 6 in. long, the flowers white, about ⅓ in. long. Fruit orange-red. June. Hardy outdoors only from zone* 6 southward, generally west of the Rocky Mountains, and seldom planted in greenhouses.

Unedo. Strawberry tree. Less than half the height of the madroña, and a native of southern Eu. Branches sticky-hairy. Leaves elliptic or oblong, about 3½ in. long, toothed. Flower cluster drooping, about 2 in. long, the white or pink flowers about ¼ in. long. Fruit strawberry-like, about ¾ in. in diameter, orange-red, edible but flavorless. Hardy from zone* 6 southward, somewhat north of this with protection, but it does not flourish in a humid climate. Oct.

ARBUTUS FAMILY. The Ericaceae.

ARCHANGELICA. A disused generic name for plants now included in *Angelica*.

ARCHONTOPHOENIX (ar-kon-toe-fee′-nix). King palm. An Australian genus of feather palms, one much planted for ornament in Calif. and Fla., rarely in greenhouses. They have tall trunks, crowned by a large collection of compound* leaves with numerous, sometimes split, leaflets. Flowers with the male and female flowers in separate clusters that are borne considerably below the crown of leaves. Fruit small, nearly round. (*Archontophoenix* is Greek for majestic palm.)

When planted outdoors (only possible in zone* 9 and especially favorable localities in zone* 8) these palms, which are very handsome, require rich soil and plenty of moisture. If the soil is too sandy or dry, dig it out and fill in with rich compost and loam.

alexandrae. A tall palm with a smooth trunk (often 60 ft. high), usually somewhat swollen at the base. Leaves 8–12 ft. long, the leaflets numerous, about 18 in. long and 1½ in. wide, green above but ashy-green beneath. Flower cluster about 12 in. long, the flowers greenish-yellow or whitish. Fruit not quite egg-shaped. A handsome palm sometimes known as *Ptychosperma alexandrae*.

cunninghamiana. This is the palm known to many growers as *Seaforthia elegans* and also as *Loroma*. It resembles A. *alexandrae*, but has no swelling at the base, and the leaves are green both sides, and with wider leaflets. Much more widely grown than the above, and not uncommon as a pot plant in greenhouses. It needs a cool greenhouse and should be planted in potting mixture.* 4.

arctica, -us, -um (ark′ti-ka). Arctic.

ARCTIC DAISY = *Chrysanthemum arcticum*.

ARCTIUM LAPPA = Burdock. *See* list at WEEDS.

ARCTOSTAPHYLOS (ark-to-staff′i-los). A very large genus of woody plants, mostly North American, belonging to the heath family and containing such handsome garden plants as the bearberry and manzanita. They are shrubs or small trees (one a prostrate ground cover), with handsome evergreen leaves without marginal teeth. Flowers small, urn- or bell-shaped, often nodding. Fruit red or dull, fleshy. (*Arctostaphylos* is Greek for bear's grape.)

The tall shrubs or trees below (all natives of the Pacific Coast) have the same cultural and climatic requirements as the genus *Arbutus* (which see). They are useful bee plants in Calif. The bearberry (A. *Uva-ursi*) is a handsome, vinelike, evergreen ground-cover found throughout sandy and rocky places in the north temperate zone. It is difficult to transplant unless one digs frozen clumps and plunges them in a prepared bed of 6 parts clean sand and 4 parts acid humus (*see* ACID AND ALKALI SOILS for details). In the spring the thawing clumps will become established. Potted plants offered by dealers should be put in the same mixture, preferably in early spring or from Aug. 15 to Sept. 15 in the North.

glauca. A tree or shrub, usually less than 20 ft. high. Leaves ovalish, 1–1½ in. long. Flowers white. Southern and Lower Calif.

Manzanita. Manzanita, but the name is also applied to other species in the chaparral* in Calif. A shrub, 8–12 ft. high with crooked and twisted branches. Leaves broadly oval, 1–3 in. long, with a slight prickle at the tip, dull green. Flowers in a profuse cluster (panicle*), white or pink, the fruit brownish-red. Apr.–May. Pacific Coast. Hardy from zone* 6 southward.

pumila. A prostrate, mat-forming, evergreen shrub, the tips of the branches upward-pointing. Leaves ⅝–¾ in. long and half as wide, green above but white-hairy beneath. Flowers in dense clusters (racemes*), white or pink followed by pea-sized, reddish-brown fruit. May. Calif. Hardy from zone* 6 southward.

tomentosa. Woolly manzanita. A tree or shrub rarely exceeding 20 ft. Leaves broadly oval, 1½–2 in., covered with white felt beneath. Flowers pink or white. British Columbia to Calif. Hardier than A. *glauca*. There are many other Californian species which may be in occasional cult.

Uva-ursi. Bearberry; called, also, kinnikinnick. Prostrate, the stems often 5–6 ft. long and rooting at the joints to form large patches of

---

* Special articles on the subjects indicated by an asterisk (*) will be found at the words so marked.

handsome evergreen foliage that turns bronzy in winter. Leaves slightly broader upwards, about 1 in. long and ⅓ in. wide, the margins rolled and minutely fringed with hairs. Flowers white or pink. Throughout the north temperate zone and hardy throughout N.A. For culture *see* above.

ARCTOTIS (ark-toe'tis). A genus of South African, white-woolly, tender annual herbs, family Compositae, the two below widely grown as garden flowers. They have alternate* leaves, usually toothed or deeply cut, and handsome, long-stalked, blue, yellow or orange heads with both ray and disk flowers. (*Arctotis* is Greek for bear's ear, in allusion to the pappus scales.)

Both those below are grown as tender annuals. For culture *see* ANNUALS.

breviscapa. Low, stemless herb with oblongish leaves, 4–5½ in. long, cut feather-fashion. Heads 2 in. wide, the rays orange, the center darker. Flowers from the end of June to frost.

grandis = *A. stoechadifolia.*

stoechadifolia. African daisy. A stout herb 30–48 in. high. Leaves ovalish, or broader toward the tip, about 3 in. long and toothed on the margin. Heads about 3 in. wide, blue and yellow, occasionally white, red, or violet, flowering from end of June to frost. Often sold as *A. grandis.*

Arcturus (ark-tew'rus). The specific name of a few plants named after the star Arcturus.

ARDISIA (ar-diz'i-a). One of the two hort. genera of the family Myrsinaceae, and including one widely grown pot plant (*A. crispa*) cult. for its bright red berries. They have alternate,* leathery, often shining green leaves, and small white or reddish flowers in clusters (cymes* or panicles*). Corolla united, 4–5-lobed, with 5 stamens opposite the lobes. Fruit a drupe.* The genus contains over 200 species of trees and shrubs, all tropical, and often called spearflower. (*Ardisia* is Greek for a point.)

The first species below is a very popular pot plant, where it is a compact, bushy shrub. It should be grown in potting mixture* 5, in a cool greenhouse, and is propagated by spring-sown seeds or by cuttings of half-ripened wood over bottom-heat*. Both species can be grown outdoors in zones* 8 and 9.

crenulata = *Ardisia crispa.*

crispa. A bushy shrub, but as usually grown, a compact, greenhouse pot plant. Leaves oblongish, about 2½ in. long, wavy-margined. Flowers red. Berries scarlet. Tropical As. A fine shrub, when in fruit, for Christmas decoration, and prefers partial shade. There is also a white-fruited var.

paniculata. Marlberry. A tropical American shrub or small tree, wild in southern Fla., but not very common in cult. Leaves more or less oblong, 5–7 in. long. Flowers white. Fruit shiny black.

ARECA (a-ree'ka). A small genus of tropical Old World feather palms, the only species of even secondary hort. interest being the famous betel palm, yielding the betelnut, which is somewhat grown for ornament

in southern Fla. Leaves feather-parted, the leaflets numerous. Flower cluster branched, borne below the crown of leaves, the female flowers toward the base and the male flowers toward the tip of the cluster, fragrant. Fruit egg-shaped or nearly so, orange or red. (*Areca* is thought to be a Latinized version of a Malayan name.)

The species below is not the common areca palm of the florists which is usually *Chrysalidocarpus lutescens*. Other genera also sometimes called *Areca* are: *Dictyosperma, Hyophorbe,* and several others, the name *Areca* having once been widely applied.

For culture *see* CHRYSALIDOCARPUS.

Catechu (spelled, also, **cathecu**). Betel palm. A graceful, unarmed, ring-stemmed, slender palm, sometimes 80 ft. high. Leaves 3–5 ft. long, the numerous leaflets soft, rather wide, irregularly cleft or notched toward the tip, sometimes with the upper leaflets more or less joined. Fruit about 1½ in. long, containing the betelnut, which is so widely used in the Far East that millions of trees are cult. for this purpose. Malaya or tropical As. The seed is sliced, rolled in a leaf of *Piper Betle,* with a sprinkling of lime, and chewed. It stains saliva red, the teeth black, is thought to aid digestion, and is regularly chewed by more than 400 million people.

ARECACEAE = PALMACEAE.

ARECASTRUM (a-ree-kas'trum). A genus of South American feather palms, the only species of which is widely grown for ornament, both in greenhouses and outdoors in zones* 8 and 9. They have ringed trunks, compound* leaves with the leaflets arranged feather-fashion, unisexual* flowers borne in a cluster from the leaf-crown and nearly round fruits about 1 in. in diameter. (*Arecastrum* signifies *Areca*-like.)

Widely cult. by florists for its feathery ornamental foliage, often under the names of *Cocos plumosa* and *C. romanzoffiana*. It needs potting mixture* 4, a warm, moist-atmosphered greenhouse and plenty of water. Its outdoor cult. in Fla. and southern Calif. is very popular as it frequently reaches 40 ft. in height, is a fine avenue or street tree, and relatively hardy up to the limits of zone* 8.

romanzoffianum. Queen palm; called, also, plumy coconut. Trunk ringed, often clothed with a few dead, but persistent, leaves in old specimens. Leaves in mature plants 7–12 ft. long, much smaller in pot or tub specimens, the leaflets very numerous, never more than 1 in. wide. Flower cluster from between a spathe* 2–3 ft. long, the female flowers below the male and toward the tip. Fruits numerous, not over 1 in. in diameter, in large, hanging clusters. Some regard the plant most common in cult. as a variety (*var.* **australe**) of the above, but this is not certain.

ARENARIA (a-re-nay'ri-a). The sandworts comprise a large genus of mostly low herbs of the pink family, a few grown in the border and rock garden for their profuse bloom. Of over 100 species, confined to the north temperate zone, only those below, all perennials, are of hort. interest. They

---

* Special articles on the subjects indicated by an asterisk (*) will be found at the words so marked.

have small leaves and mostly small white flowers, with 5 petals, in variously branched clusters, or solitary. Fruit a tiny dry pod. (*Arenaria* means growing in sandy places.)

The cult. sandworts are usually tufted plants of the open sunshine and require a sandy or gritty soil. They tend to make mats or low tufts and are especially suited to the wall garden or to the rock garden. They are easily propagated by division of the roots. Some of them are occasionally offered as *Alsine* and, more recently, as *Minuartia.*

balearica. Corsican sandwort. Scarcely 3 in. high and prostrate. Leaves ovalish, glossy, rather thick, very small and numerous. Flowers white, solitary. A moss-like plant, preferring moist sites in the rock garden.* July. Balearic Islands. Needs protection north of zone* 4. For cult. *see* ROCK GARDEN.

caespitosa = *Arenaria verna caespitosa.*

grandiflora. A semi-prostrate herb from Europe, with creeping, wiry stems. Leaves awl-shaped, silvery-gray. Flowers white, solitary or in twos or threes. June.

groenlandica. Mountain sandwort; called also mountain starwort. A native, tufted plant suited to the rock garden in cool regions. It makes patches a foot wide and about 5 in. high. Leaves small, very numerous, about ½ in. long and ⅟₁₆ in. wide. Flowers in groups of 1–5. Greenland to mountains of Ga. June. Use gritty soil with pH 5. (*See* ACID AND ALKALI SOILS.)

juniperina. A low, tufted plant with wiry stems, not over 6 in. high. Leaves resembling a juniper, greenish-gray. Flowers white, in small clusters. June. Southern Eu. and Asia Minor. A rock garden species needing protection north of zone* 4.

montana. A European rock garden species scarcely over 4 in. high. Leaves small and narrow. Flowers solitary, white. *See* ROCK GARDEN.

purpurascens. A low, tufted, mat-forming perennial, not over 4 in. high. Leaves ovalish or narrower, pointed. Flowers only 2–3, the stalks hairy. Petals purplish. Spain. June. Best suited to the rock garden.

Saxifraga. A mountain plant from southern Eu. and Asia Minor, used in the rock garden, but needing protection north of zone* 4. Leaves in rosettes, covered with sticky hairs, about ½ in. long. Flowers 2–7 in a cluster. July.

verna. A tufted plant from the European and Rocky Mountains, suited to the rock garden. Leaves flat, very narrow. Flowers solitary on very slender, thread-like stalks. June. The *var.* caespitosa is still lower, compact, and forms dense, moss-like clumps. It is also suited for a rocky wall.

ARENGA (a-ren′ga). A small group of Asiatic and Malayan feather palms, the one below somewhat cultivated outdoors in zone* 9, rarely in greenhouses. Leaves compound,* very large, the leaflets arranged feather-fashion, and having many strong veins, gray beneath and often notched or cut off at the tip. Flower cluster much-branched, the male and female flowers usually in separate clusters on the same tree. Fruit more or less fleshy. (*Arenga* is from the Malayan *areng.*)

The species below rarely flowers and fruits in cult., whether outdoors or in greenhouses, which is fortunate, as the plants die once they have flowered and fruited. The greenhouse cult. is the same as for *Chrysalidocarpus.*

saccharifera. The gomuti, jaggery or sugar palm of Malaya, and widely cult. in the tropics for the sugar made from its sap. Trunk up to 40 ft., generally spineless. Leaves 15–20 ft. long (much less in cult.), with 100 or more leaflets on either side of the leafstalk. Leaflets arranged singly or in small bunches, nearly always toothed toward the tip. Fruit oblongish, nearly 2 in. long, flattened at the top. Sometimes known as *A. pinnata.*

areolata, -us, -um (ar-ee-o-lay′ta). Pitted.

ARETHUSA (a-re-thoo′za). A small group of tuberous-rooted bog orchids, the one below cultivated for its beautiful fringed flowers, but suited only to the more acid sites of the bog garden. It prefers pH 4 or 5 (*see* ACID AND ALKALI SOILS). Besides two Asiatic (not cult.) species, the only other one is the dragon's-mouth or wild pink, **Arethusa bulbosa,** of eastern N.A. It is about 8 in. high, bears a solitary leaf that appears after the plant blooms from the sheaths of the otherwise naked flower stalk. Flower solitary, hooded, rose-purple, fringed with yellow. May. *See* Hardy Orchids at ORCHID. (*Arethusa* was named for the nymph.)

ARGEMONE (are-jem′o-nee). The prickly poppies are tropical American herbs of perhaps 10 species, belonging to the poppy family, one very widely grown as an annual. They are stout herbs with yellow juice, the cut leaves more or less toothed and spiny-margined. Flowers large, with 2 or 3 sepals and 4–6 rather showy petals. Fruit a prickly pod (capsule*), opening by terminal valves. (*Argemone* is a classical plant name of uncertain application here.)

Argemone grandiflora is a very popular hardy annual. For cult. *see* ANNUALS. The other species, also grown as annuals, should be similarly treated.

alba. Mexican horned poppy. A somewhat rare annual from southern U.S. and Mex., 1–3 ft. high, the leaves gray-green, lobed, their margins spiny. Flowers solitary, white, with golden-yellow stamens.* Fruit covered with stiff hairs. It often persists from self-sown seeds.

grandiflora. A stout, Mexican herb, 24–36 in. high, less spiny than the next. Leaves with white veins. Flowers summer-blooming, about 3 in. wide, yellow or white. Fruit about 1 in. long, not very spiny. A very showy, popular annual.

platyceras. Crested poppy. A tropical American herb 24–48 in. high, the stem, leaves and fruit densely clothed with weak or stiffish white spines. Leaves bluish-gray. Flowers about 2½ in. wide or less, mostly white (purple in a hort. form). The hedgehog poppy (*var.* hispida) has distinctly yellowish spines and is bristly as well. There is also a red-flowered variety.

argentata, -us, -um (are-jen-tay′ta). Silvery.

argentea, -us, -um (are-jen′tee-a). Silvery.

argenteo-guttata, -us, -um (are-jen-tee-o-gut-tay′ta). Silvery-spotted.

argenteo-marginata, -us, -um (are-jen-tee-

---

* Special articles on the subjects indicated by an asterisk (*) will be found at the words so marked.

o-mar-ji-nay'ta). Silvery-margined.

argenteo-variegata, -us, -um (are-jen-tee-o-vare-i-e-gay'ta). With silvery patches.

argillacea, -us, -um (are-gil-lay'see-a). Pertaining to clay.

arguta, -us, -um (are-gew'ta). Sharply toothed.

argyraea, -us, -um (are-jy-ree'a). Silvery.

ARGYREIA (are-jy-ree'a). A genus of 40 species of mostly Asiatic tropical vines of the morning-glory family, the one below grown for ornament outdoors in frost-free regions, more rarely in greenhouses. They have alternate, simple, usually large leaves, often hairy beneath. Flowers showy, fugitive, rose-colored in the one below, in a few-flowered cluster, funnel-shaped. (*Argyreia* denotes the often silvery foliage.)

Easily grown outdoors in frost-free parts of Calif. and Fla. In greenhouses the plant may become a rampant nuisance. It is easily grown from seeds, or may be propagated by cuttings over bottom-heat.

splendens. Silver morning-glory. A handsome, tender, tall-climbing vine. Leaves nearly 7 in. long and about half as wide, with an angled base and silvery-hairy beneath. Flowers 1½ in. long, solitary, the stalk 1½–3 in. long. India.

argyrocoma, -us, -um (are-jy-ro-ko'ma). Silvery-haired.

argyroneura, -us, -um (are-jy-ro-new'ra). With silvery veins.

argyrophylla, -us, -um (are-jy-ro-fill'a). Silver-leaved.

Aria (air'i-a). Ancient Greek name for the whitebeam (*Sorbus Aria*).

arietina, -us, -um (a-ri-e-ty'na). Resembling a ram's head.

ARIL. An extra, often colored, coat or appendage to a seed. It is the aril that provides the brilliant color to the bittersweet (*Celastrus scandens*). *See also* TAXACEAE.

ARIOCARPUS (air-i-o-kar'pus). A small genus of top-shaped cacti, mostly Mexican, and often called living-rock. They are small, half-buried succulents, grown as much for their curious habit as for their rose-colored or whitish flowers. Plant spineless, but much-tubercled, the sections sharp-pointed. Flowers arise from the center of the plant. Fruit fleshy, small, with black seeds. (*Ariocarpus* signifies having fruit like the whitebeam.) For culture *see* CACTI.

fissuratus = *Roseocactus fissuratus.*

retusus. Seven-sisters; also called chaute. A low, flat-topped cactus, the plant body 3–7 in. wide and much cut up into tubercles, which are sharp when young but blunt in age, and often with a tuft of white hairs near the tip. Flowers rose-colored, or whitish-pink. Mex.

trigonus. Perhaps only a form of *A. retusus,* but its tubercles are more erect, longer and more pointed. Flowers pale yellow. Mex.

ARISAEMA (a-ri-see'ma). A genus of over 100 species of perennial herbs of the arum family, the ones below suited only to shady, moist places in the wild garden. They have tuberous, acrid roots, divided or compound[*] leaves and tiny flowers crowded on a spadix,[*] which is surrounded by, or has beneath it, a spathe.[*] (*See* ARACEAE for details of flower structure.) Fruit showy, fleshy. (*Arisaema* is Latin and Greek for blood arum, in allusion to the leaf color of some tropical species.)

The only commonly cult. species are plants of rich, moist woods, and they need a good humus soil, shade, and a moist site. With these conditions, their culture is easy. Propagated by division of their roots.

Dracontium. Dragonroot; also called green dragon. A stout, fleshy herb 12–18 in. high, with a single, much, but irregularly, divided leaf, the 7–11 segments oblongish and pointed at the tip. Spathe[*] not pulpit-like (as in the next), green, tapering, and shorter than the long, slender spadix.[*] Eastern N.A. June.

triphyllum. Jack-in-the-pulpit; called, also, Indian turnip. Root very acrid, but used as food, when heated, by the Indians. Leaves usually 2, compound, the three leaflets more or less oval, pointed, about 2 in. long. The erect spadix[*] ("Jack") is surrounded by the spathe[*] ("pulpit") which also arches over the spadix. Eastern U.S. Apr.–May.

aristata, -us, -um (a-ris-tay'ta). Bearded; or with an awn.[*]

ARISTEA (a-ris'tee-a). A group of 15 species of largely South African herbs of the iris family, two of which, while not particularly showy, are grown in Calif. for ornament, rarely in greenhouses. They have alternate or two-ranked, narrow, grass-like leaves and small, blue, rather fleeting flowers, that twist after blooming, and suggest the blue-eyed grass (*Sisyrinchium*). (Fruit a 3-valved pod capsule.[*]) (*Aristea* is derived from *aristata.*)

Their outdoor culture is confined mostly to Calif., where they should be planted in open, sandy loams. Propagated by division of the roots in spring.

capitata. A stout plant 2½–3½ ft. high, the leaves as long, but scarcely ½ in. wide and rather rigid. Flowers about ½ in. long, in narrow clusters. July.

eckloni. Not over 18 in. high, the leaves not rigid and dark green. Flowers about ⅓ in. long, in a small, flat-stemmed, rather profuse cluster. June.

ARISTOLOCHIA (a-ris-toe-loe'ki-a). A genus of 180 species of mostly tropical, woody vines, family Aristolochiaceae, and a few temperate species of vines and perennial herbs. They are widely grown for ornament, and for their extraordinary and usually evil-scented flowers. (*See* ARISTOLOCHIACEAE for details.) They have alternate,[*] often ever-green, and sometimes very handsome leaves. Fruit a capsule.[*] The species are often called birthworts, in allusion (as in *Aristolochia*) to their supposed value in childbirth.

The greenhouse species are handsome tropical vines with large leaves and, in one of them, remarkable flowers nearly 18 in. in diameter, with a tail still longer. They are easily grown in a warm, moist greenhouse

---

[*] Special articles on the subjects indicated by an asterisk (*) will be found at the words so marked.

and should be planted out in a place where their rampant growth will not shade other plants. Any rich soil will do. Propagated by seeds (for *A. elegans*), or by cuttings.

The hardy vines are grown for their fine rich foliage and their ability to cover unsightly obects with considerable speed. *See* Stem Climbers at VINES. The Virginia snakeroot, the only cult. herb, is a woods plant and needs rich humus and a shady, windfree corner of the wild garden. The hardy vines and the last species below should be propagated only by seed.

durior. Dutchman's-pipe; called, also, pipevine. A tall, high-climbing vine of eastern U.S., widely cult. for its fine foliage. Leaves roundish or kidney-shaped, 6–14 in. wide, the stalks about ⅓ of this. Flowers about 1½ in. long, bent like a U, yellowish-brown. Long known as *A. macrophylla* and *A. Sipho* and still offered under either name. *See* VINES.

elegans. Calico-flower. A slender, tropical vine for greenhouses kept about 60°. Leaves kidney-shaped or heart-shaped, rather long-stalked, but only about 2½ in. wide. Flower solitary, long-stalked, not badly scented, its tube yellowish-green and about 1½ in. long, the expanded limb heart-shaped, 3 in. wide, purple, and white-spotted. Brazil. A popular greenhouse vine and also grown outdoors in frost-free regions. *See* VINES.

grandiflora. Pelican-flower. A West Indian greenhouse vine with heart-shaped leaves and extraordinary, solitary flowers. The flower-tube is inflated and yellowish-green, and at its end the broadened limb (6–8 in. wide) is wavy-margined, purple-spotted and purple-veined. At the apex of the limb is a long, slender, rather hairy, and colored tail. In the *var.* **sturtevanti,** which is the usual form in cult., the flower is often 18–24 in. wide and the tail nearly 3 ft. long.

Serpentaria. Virginia snakeroot. A woodland plant of eastern U.S., useful only in the wild garden and cult. more for its medicinal root than for ornament. Not over 18 in. high, the stem rather wiry. Leaves more or less oval or oblong, the tip tapering, the base heart-shaped. Flower small, S-shaped, greenish, borne at or near the ground level. *See* MEDICINAL PLANTS.

ARISTOLOCHIACEAE (a-ris-toe-loe-ki-ā′see-ee). The birthwort or wild ginger family is of little hort. importance, its only cult. genera being *Aristolochia* (mostly vines) and *Asarum* (herbs). Leaves alternate,* stalked, often heart-shaped. Flowers nearly always evil-smelling, the calyx petal-like and curiously tubular or bent (in *Aristolochia* often very large). Petals none. Fruit a capsule.*

Technical flower characters: Sepals united into a tubular, bent, trumpet-shaped or otherwise very irregular calyx, which often has a door-like flap that (at times) covers the opening, and may be tailed. Petals (in the hort. genera) none. Stamens 6–36, inserted on the ovary or joined to the style. Ovary superior,* 4–6-celled.

ARISTOTELIA (a-ris-tot-tee′li-a). A small cult. genus of the family Elaeocarpaceae (ee-lee-o-kar-pay′see-ee), which comprises about 7 genera and over 100 species of mostly tropical shrubs and trees, not dis-

tantly related to the lindens. The cult. genera have alternate or opposite* evergreen leaves and polygamous* flowers with 4–5 sepals, 4–5 petals, many stamens, a superior* ovary, and fleshy, edible fruit. (Named for Aristotle.)

The species below are cult. for ornament in southern Calif. They grow well in the open, prefer sandy loam, and are propagated by layers or cuttings rooted under glass.

macqui. A Chilean shrub 3–6 ft. high. Leaves oblongish, 1½–3 in. long, toothed. Flowers greenish-white, in small clusters. Fruit dark purple, about ¼ in. in diameter, used for wine in Chile. Apr. A variegated-leaved form is also cult. Called by some *A. chilensis.*

racemosa. New Zealand wineberry. A New Zealand shrub or small tree 8–25 ft. high. Leaves oval or nearly so, about 5 in. long. Flowers rose-colored, small, but in profuse clusters. Fruit purplish-black, about ¼ in. in diameter.

ARIZONA. The state flower is the giant cactus. The state lies in zones* 4, 5, 6, and 7, while zone* 8 crosses the small triangle near the mouth of the Gila River.

SOILS. Generalizations cannot be made on the soils of Arizona, as they vary from heavy clays to coarse sands, although the fine sands, sandy loams, and silt loams predominate.

Arizona soils are on the whole quite fertile, provided they can be made to "take water" readily and are kept reasonably well aerated by the introduction of organic matter and by proper drainage. They contain very little organic matter and nitrogen; hence manure (both animal and green) is the most common fertilizer and is used extensively.

White and black alkali salts exist in widely scattered areas over southern Arizona. The reclamation of such areas depends largely upon the subsoil, as good drainage is the first essential for leaching operations. If underlain with sand or permeable substrata the removal of such alkali can be effected without excessive cost.

CHIEF GARDENING CENTERS. The central and southern parts of Arizona, containing the major irrigation projects, comprise the chief gardening centers. These, in order of their importance, are the Salt River Valley, Yuma Valley and Yuma Mesa, the Casa Grande, Safford, Duncan, Verde, Santa Cruz, San Pedro, and the Sulphur Springs valleys. Even in these areas, gardening is limited to land with a reliable source of irrigation water. Garden centers of smaller area in northern Arizona are distributed along the Little Colorado River and its tributaries supplying irrigation water and to the Flagstaff district where rainfall is relied upon for soil moisture.

FRUIT AND GARDEN AREAS. Orchard fruits and vegetable crops are grown for home use in practically all parts of the state where farming operations are at all practicable. At the lower elevations the hardy group of vegetables are grown during the fall, winter, and spring months and many sub-tropical fruits

---

* Special articles on the subjects indicated by an asterisk (*) will be found at the words so marked.

may be planted in the home orchard. At high elevations, vegetable production is limited to the spring, summer, and fall months and the temperate zone fruits must be grown.

The major vegetable crops produced in the state are lettuce and cantaloupes. Several thousand cars of each are shipped annually, chiefly from the Salt River and Yuma valleys. Lettuce is predominant and represents over half of Arizona vegetables.

Other vegetables in the irrigated valleys are white potatoes, onions, peas, sweet potatoes, carrots, and watermelons.

Of the small fruits, strawberries are grown in limited quantity for markets within the state, especially in the Salt River Valley.

Apples, pears, and peaches of excellent quality are grown for Arizona market and home use in many of the higher mountain valleys of northern, eastern, and southeastern Arizona. Apricots, Japanese plums, and peaches succeed well in the lower irrigated valleys.

The *vinifera* grape is grown extensively in home vineyards in the lower valleys of the state. In the Salt River Valley, a number of commercial vineyards of considerable acreage are producing early table grapes of excellent quality — Cardinal and Thompson Seedless — for carlot shipment to eastern markets. American varieties of grapes are being grown successfully in home vineyards at elevations of more than 4000 feet.

Oranges, lemons, and grapefruit of excellent quality and early maturity are produced in the Salt River Valley and on the Yuma Mesa, where increased plantings of lemons, Valencia oranges and specialty citrus varieties have been made. Also, home plantings of citrus are popular in the Tucson area. The choicest of Persian Gulf and North African varieties of dates have been introduced. While the cost of establishing a date garden is greater than for most any other orchard fruit, returns are correspondingly greater. *See* DATE.

Some acreages of the irrigated valley lands have been planted to improved varieties of pecans. A high-quality, large-sized nut is being grown, and production of the groves now in bearing appears to be significantly greater than in the older-established pecan districts of the southeastern states.

At the lower elevations of the state, the winters are sufficiently mild so that the hardy flowers are planted in the fall for winter and spring bloom. Among these are stocks, African daisies, snapdragon, pansies, sweet peas, larkspur, petunias, and many others, including bulbs. These are spring-planted for summer bloom at the higher elevations. In the Yuma area the attractive *Bougainvillaea* flourishes.

Many ornamental trees from China, Japan, Australia, and the Mediterranean region are excellently adapted to the sub-tropical portions of southern Arizona. These include several species of eucalyptus and citrus, several palms, the carob, loquat, Chinese elm, Deodar cedar, olive, tamarisk, and the Aleppo pine. Native poplars, ash, sycamore, elderberry, mesquite, and cypress are widely used for ornamental planting.

In addition to these plants, a number of new plants for southern Arizona are appearing in the nursery trade. A *Rhus* introduced by Dr. Homer Leroy Shantz from Africa has been grown on the University of Arizona campus for 25 years and is widely adapted at elevations below 3000 feet. Other trees have been introduced and proven adapted at the Boyce Thompson Southwestern Arboretum at Superior, Arizona. Emphasis is on plants with low water requirements and a tolerance of alkali and other salts.

Arizona has experienced a tremendous population increase during the past ten years and expects two million people by 1975, mostly in the Salt River Valley and Tucson area. The number of retail nursery establishments has increased correspondingly. A wholesale nursery industry is expanding in the Phoenix area and in the vicinity of Casa Grande. A general line of nursery stock is being grown but the emphasis is on roses. Increasing acreages are under cultivation with several nationally known rose firms producing bushes in Arizona for wide distribution. In the cut-flower industry, field-grown stocks are produced in the Salt River Valley during the winter months for national distribution.

Ornamental shrubs which succeed well are species of the following genera: *Pittosporum, Euonymus, Jasminum, Ligustrum, Rosa,*

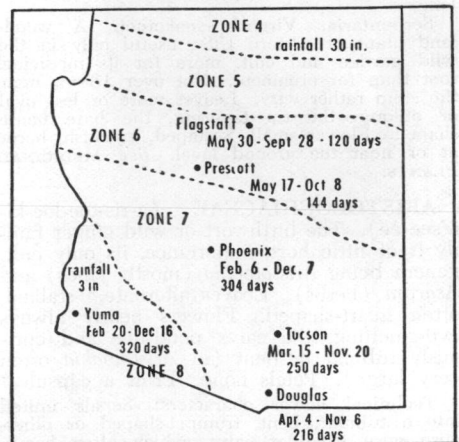

ARIZONA

The zones of hardiness crossing Arizona are those shown on the map located at ZONE, which should be consulted for details. The dates are the average latest killing frost in spring and the first one in the fall. The figures below the dates show the average length of the growing season. Annual rainfall is not over 3 in. in the southwestern part of the state, but nearly 30 in. in the mountainous northern part.

---

* Special articles on the subjects indicated by an asterisk (*) will be found at the words so marked.

Photinia, Punica, Feiioa, Myrtus, Plumbago, Cotoneaster, Pyracantha, Nandina, and many others. At the higher elevations, trees and shrubs grown in the temperate regions of the Middle West and eastern United States are well adapted and commonly grown. The more common of these include the eastern elm, maple, ash, poplar, the sycamore (*Platanus*), both native and introduced, locust, Kentucky coffee-tree, China-tree, walnut; also a number of pines, junipers, and oaks. Shrubs include species of *Thuja, Berberis, Euonymus, Ligustrum, Viburnum, Philadelphus, Spiraea, Cercis, Rhus, Syringa, Tamarix, Lonicera,* and *Rosa.*

Outdoor living areas known as patios are becoming more important in landscaping Arizona homes. The patios are planted to Bermuda grasses for summer use. As these Bermuda lawns become dormant in the fall they are overseeded with annual rye grass for maintaining greenness throughout winter and early spring.

CLIMATE. The climate of Arizona is extremely varied, temperature conditions changing directly with changes in elevation and to a much less extent with latitude. At Yuma, and more particularly on the Yuma Mesa, more than 2 to 5 degrees of frost is rarely experienced in winter, while the summers are long, with the daily maxima ranging from 100° to as much as 118° for a 3 to 4 months' period. Near the other extreme is the Flagstaff district with considerable snow in winter and some sub-zero temperatures, while daily maximum temperatures in summer seldom reach 90°.

Killing frost and growing season data for a few points in Arizona are presented in the Table.

KILLING FROSTS AND LENGTH OF
GROWING SEASON

Station and Elevation	Av. date of last killing frost in spring	Av. date of first killing frost in autumn	Latest date of killing frost in spring
Alpine, 8000	June 21	Sept. 13	July 27
Flagstaff, 6993	May 30	Sept. 28	June 18
Prescott, 5334	May 17	Oct. 8	May 30
Douglas, 3973	Apr. 4	Nov. 6	May 11
Tucson, 2558	Mar. 15	Nov. 20	Apr. 18
Phoenix, 1114	Feb. 6	Dec. 7	Mar. 31
Yuma, 138	Feb. 20	Dec. 16	Mar. 13

Station and Elevation	Earliest date of killing frost in autumn	Av. length of growing season days
Alpine, 8000	Aug. 18	84
Flagstaff, 6993	Sept. 12	120
Prescott, 5334	Sept. 6	144
Douglas, 3973	Oct. 1	216
Tucson, 2558	Oct. 19	250
Phoenix, 1114	Nov. 5	304
Yuma, 138	Nov. 19	320

PRECIPITATION. The mean annual rainfall in Arizona varies from about 3 to 30 inches. It has been found that, in general, rainfall increases with elevation in the state. Arizona, with an elevation of less than 150 feet at Yuma in the southwestern corner, rises more or less like a flight of steps in a northeasterly direction to an elevation of 8500 feet at Greer, the highest weather-observing station in the state. The heavier precipitation on the mountains is often of great economic significance, inasmuch as much of it can be stored in reservoirs and used to irrigate the arid lowlands. A rainfall distribution curve for Arizona shows two distinct rainy seasons, the most important being in July, August, and September when approximately 43 per cent of the entire year's rainfall occurs. The second period (December to March) is one of longer duration, but furnishes less water, as only 35 per cent of the year's rainfall occurs during these 4 months. Summer rains are of a spontaneous nature, short-lived, and are often accompanied by wind, thunder, and lightning. Winter rains, as a rule, are gentle and may be of several days' duration.

IRRIGATION. With the exception of several relatively small areas in the northern part of the state which lie at high altitudes and are farmed without irrigation, all the cropped lands in Arizona require irrigation. In 1956, a total of 1,150,000 acres in 6809 farms were irrigated. The irrigated area is 1.5 per cent of the land area of the state. Eighty per cent of the present irrigated area is in the drainage basin of the Gila River and its tributaries, and 15 per cent is irrigated directly from the Colorado River.

Water supplies for irrigation are obtained from flowing streams, or by pumping from wells, or from minor sources such as springs and artesian wells. Ephemeral flood flows are utilized in some localities. Ground-water supplies and pump irrigation are of relatively high importance in Arizona. Two-thirds of the irrigation is from pumps.

The methods of applying water vary with the crop and, to a lesser extent, with topography and soil. Garden and truck crops are irrigated in furrows between the rows. Orchards are sometimes basined, 1 to 4 trees in a basin, sometimes irrigated by several furrows on each side of the tree row, and sometimes flooded in lands 330 or 660 feet long, the choice depending on the soil and other conditions.

The frequency of irrigation depends on the crop, the soil, and the season. Vegetables and young orchards may require weekly irrigations during midsummer.

CLIMATE AND AGRICULTURE. The mean annual rainfall of but 12.55 inches for the state precludes the possibility of any great amount of dry-farming in Arizona.

Under arid or semi-arid conditions large amounts of water are lost to the soil by plant transpiration, the water requirement of crops being practically double that in humid re-

---

* Special articles on the subjects indicated by an asterisk (*) will be found at the words so marked.

gions. The Hopi and Navajo Indians practice dry-farming in a small way in northern Arizona, but Arizona farmers on the whole have not been entirely successful in attempts to "dry-farm." The Arizona Agricultural Experiment Station abandoned its dry farm at Cochise because the ordinary farm crops could not be satisfactorily grown by dry-farming methods. Dry-farming, however, has possibilities in the higher and moister altitudes. Results of irrigating the valley lands have been highly successful, as most of the once desert land has proved to be fertile. Research on horticultural crops is being conducted at branch experiment stations in the Salt River Valley, Yuma area, Safford, and at Tucson.

The address of the Agricultural Experiment Station which has kindly supplied this information about the state is the University of Arizona, Tucson, Arizona. The Station is always ready to answer gardening questions.

ARIZONA CYPRESS = *Cupressus arizonica.*

ARIZONA FIR = *Abies arizonica.* See FIR.

arizonica, -us, -um (a-ri-zon'i-ka). From Arizona.

ARKANSAS. The state tree is the pine and the state flower is the apple blossom. A wide range of climatic and soil conditions are found in the state of Arkansas, all of which lies in zones* 4, 5 and 6. Average dates of last killing frosts in the spring range from March 20 in El Dorado to April 10 in Fayetteville. The average dates of the first killing frost in the fall range from October 20 in the northwest to November 10 in the extreme south. Average precipitation varies from 44 inches in western Arkansas to 52 inches in the southeastern part. Elevations vary from nearly 3000 feet above sea level to under 100 feet. Nearly half the state is mountainous with the Ouachita Mountains in the southwest and the Ozarks in the north and northwest.

Summers are usually dry and warm with a great deal of the precipitation coming in the fall, winter, and spring months. In most of the state, winters are very moderate with only occasional cold waves extending into the southern half. In the northwest section there are in some years very limited periods of sub-zero weather, usually interspersed with periods of mild weather in which slow plant growth may occur.

Soils vary widely in fertility, but with good care even the poorest will produce good garden crops and flowers. A wide variety of small tree fruits is produced both for home use and for commercial purposes. There is also extensive production of vegetables for commercial marketing.

The wide variety of ornamental plants adapted to climatic conditions throughout the state results in many beautifully landscaped homes. The broad-leaved evergreens are used extensively for planting purposes. Roses are found everywhere. Most of the bulbous plants thrive throughout Arkansas.

There are no public gardens but the state has established ten parks in which the natural beauty of native plants has been largely undisturbed. There is a wealth of native blooming shrubs and trees. Perhaps the most conspicuous are the redbud and flowering dogwood trees and the swamp and mountain azaleas in the spring and the berries on the American holly and deciduous holly in the fall and winter. Many of the native materials are used in landscaping developments.

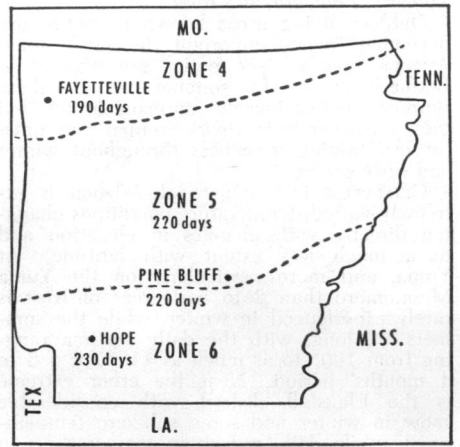

ARKANSAS

The zones of hardiness crossing Arkansas are those shown on the map located at ZONE, which should be consulted for details. The figures show the average length of the growing season, in days. Rainfall of 40–50 in. per year is adequate, but there is sometimes a summer deficiency.

Garden clubs have very active programs in most towns of the state. The office of the Arkansas Federation of Garden Clubs is located at 1301½ Scott St., Little Rock.

The address of the Agricultural Experiment Station, which has contributed this information is Fayetteville, Arkansas.

ARM. Loosely, any branch of a tree. Technically, in grape culture, a branch of a vine that is more than one year old.

armata, -us, -um (are-may'ta). Armed; that is, provided with thorns, prickles, or spines, assumed to be, but not necessarily for, defense.

armena, -us, -um (ar-me'na). From Armenia.

Armeniaca (ar-men-i-ā'ka). An old generic name for the apricot, so called because it was once thought to be native in Armenia.

ARMERIA (ar-meer'i-a). Thrift. Sea pink. Summer-blooming, low, perennial herbs of the family Plumbaginaceae, comprising only a few species, although the names

---

* Special articles on the subjects indicated by an asterisk (*) will be found at the words so marked.

credited to *Armeria* are many. Most of them belong to *Limonium* (which see). The true armerias have small, evergreen leaves in basal rosettes, from which rises a rigid, stiff, flowering stalk, at the end of which is a dense, globe-shaped head of chaffy flowers. Just below the head is a series of membranous colored bracts,* two of them united into a sort of sheath. The arrangement of this flower cluster is the chief difference between *Armeria* and *Limonium,* where the cluster is open and branching. (*Armeria* is an old Latin name of the thrift.) The plants were long known as *Statice* and are still so listed by some dealers.

The thrifts are good plants for the general border, the rock garden, or they are sometimes grown in pots (cool greenhouse) for their long-keeping flowers. They are of easy culture in most garden soils, but do better in light, sandy loams than in heavy clays. Easily propagated by division.

alpina = *Armeria montana.*

caespitosa. This, in some of the forms offered, is likely to be *Armeria juniperifolia.* If it differs from that species it is even lower and the flowers are paler. Spain.

formosa = *Armeria pseudo-armeria*

juniperifolia. A rock garden plant, scarcely 4 in. high and densely tufted. Leaves very narrow and short. Flower heads nearly stalkless, small pink or pale lilac. Pyrenees.

latifolia = *Armeria pseudo-armeria.*

laucheana = *Armeria maritima laucheana.*

maritima. Common thrift. Not over 12 in. high. Leaves very narrow, 1-veined, scarcely ⅛ in. wide, in a dense basal rosette. Flowering stalk smooth, the head about ¾ in. in diameter, pink, purple, or white (in hort. varieties). Eu., also rare in northern N.A. and in Chile. Sometimes offered as *Statice maritima* or *S. vulgaris.* An old garden favorite, and known in several forms. The *var.* **laucheana** and its form known as Six Hills Hybrid are useful in the rock garden; they have light pink flowers. The *var.* **alba** has white flowers.

montana. Perhaps only a form of *A. maritima,* with larger flower heads and a shorter flower stalk. European mountains. It is sometimes known as *Armeria alpina.*

plantaginea. Resembling *A. maritima* but the leaves about ¼ in. wide and 3–5-veined, and the stalk of the flower cluster may be 12–20 in. high. Flower heads about ¾ in. in diameter, pink, purple, crimson, or white. Eu.

pseudo-armeria. A stout perennial 15–24 in. high, the slender leaves 8–10 in. long and about 1 in. wide. Flower heads chaffy, close, about 1½ in. in diameter, pink or white, and, in the form offered as *A. formosa,* of various colors. Southwestern Eu. July–Aug. Commonly cult.

armillaris, -e (ar-mil-lar'is). Ringed, as with a collar or bracelet.

ARMORACIA. *See* HORSE-RADISH.

ARNATTO = ANNATTO. *See* BIXA.

ARNEBIA (ar-nee'bi-a). A genus of perhaps a dozen species of Asiatic and African herbs, family Boraginaceae, the two below grown in the flower garden for their attractive bloom. They have alternate leaves and small flowers in more or less 1-sided clusters.

Corolla nearly regular, its 5 lobes blunt. Fruit of 4 nutlets, hidden by the withered flowers. (*Arnebia* is a Latinized version of an Arabic vernacular.)

The species below are of the easiest culture. Sow seed of the first where it is to stay as it is a hardy annual (*see* ANNUALS). The second species is a perennial, easily propagated by division of its roots, but it requires partial shade.

cornuta. Arabian primrose. A hardy annual from the Orient, rather bushy, and 18–24 in. high. Leaves lance-shaped or narrower. Flowers about ¾ in. wide, orange and black-spotted, fading to red and finally to yellow. Summer. Also known as *A. decumbens.*

Echioides. Prophet-flower. A perennial herb 4–10 in. high. Leaves oblong or slightly wider upward. Flowers in a 1-sided cluster, yellow and purple-spotted, fading to yellow. Southeastern Eu. and Armenia. June. Good for shaded part of a rockery. Called, also, *Echioides longiflorum.*

ARNICA (ar'ni-ka). A large genus of perennial herbs, family Compositae, many from N.A., but the one below European. They are little grown except *A. montana,* which yields tincture of arnica. Leaves opposite. Flowers yellow, the long-stalked heads with conspicuous rays. (*Arnica* is the classical name for these plants.)

Can be grown in the open border, but prefers a distinctly acid soil (pH 4, *see* ACID AND ALKALI SOILS). Best propagated by division of its roots. Best suited to drier parts of the country.

montana. A European herb whose roots yield tincture of arnica; 12–20 in. high. Leaves without teeth, oblongish, smooth. Flowers on branching stalks, the head showy, nearly 3 in. wide. *See also* MEDICINAL PLANTS.

ARNOLD ARBORETUM. *See* ARBORETUM.

AROID. Any plant of the arum family. *See* ARACEAE.

aromatica, -us, -um (a-roe-mat'tick-a). Fragrant or aromatic.

ARONIA (a-rone'i-a). A small genus of North American shrubs of the rose family, often grown in informal shrubberies for their attractive white flowers and persistent, colored, but bitter fruits; hence the name chokeberry. Leaves alternate,* always toothed. Flowers in terminal clusters, blooming early in May, the white petals and black anthers making an interesting contrast. Fruit fleshy, a small berrylike pome.* (*Aronia* is derived from *Aria,* which see.)

The shrubs are of the easiest culture in a variety of soils, and are readily propagated by seeds, cuttings or by layering. They are not particularly showy, but useful because of their early bloom. They are sometimes offered as *Pyrus* from which they are separated only by technical characters.

arbutifolia. Red chokeberry. Not over 8 ft., usually half that. Leaves gray beneath, oblongish, about 2 in. long. Fruit brilliant red, winter-persisting. Mass. to Fla. Fine red foliage in the fall. Zone* 2 and southward. A form

---

* Special articles on the subjects indicated by an asterisk (*) will be found at the words so marked.

carried by many nurseries under the name brilliantissima is said to have even more brilliantly red fruit.

melanocarpa. Black chokeberry. Lower than either of the others, rarely exceeding 4 ft. Leaves without hairs, or only a few, shining. Fruit shining black, but shriveling and soon dropping. Nova Scotia to Fla. Zone* 3 and southward. Called, also, *Aronia nigra.*

prunifolia. Purple chokeberry. Somewhat taller than the first. Leaves merely hairy beneath. Fruit purple-black. Newfoundland to Fla. Zone* 3 and southward. Also called *A. atropurpurea* or *floribunda.*

ARRACACIA (ar-ra-kay'si-a). A large genus of mostly South American herbs of the carrot family, the only cult. species being a parsnip-like plant much grown in the tropics for its edible root. This plant, called apio in Puerto Rico and in S.A. is **A. xanthorrhiza,** a native of the Andes. It has twice-compound* leaves, small, white flowers in compound* umbels, and a thick, branched, yellowish, starchy root. Little known in the U.S. and suited only to zone* 9. (*Arracacia* is the Spanish name of some of the species.) Sometimes known as *A. esculenta.*

ARRHENATHERUM (ar-re-nath'er-rum). A genus of tall, oat-like, perennial grasses of European origin, of no garden interest except as it occurs in meadows. Stems tall, up to 3½ ft. high, the coarse leaves rough on the edges. Flower cluster a narrow panicle, the male spikelets long-awned.* (The name implies a masculine awn, alluding to the male spikelets.)

elatius. Tall oat grass; also called tall meadow oat. Leaves about 12 in. long, ¼ in. wide, and distinctly rough. Flowering panicle 12 in. long, its numerous branches erect, purplish-green. Common as a naturalized grass in the N.A. There is a tuberous-rooted variety (*var.* **tuberosum**) which is sometimes known as *A. bulbosum,* and its variegated-leaved form is the only one of garden interest.

ARROW-ARUM. See PELTANDRA.

ARROWHEAD. See SAGITTARIA.

ARROWROOT = *Maranta arundinacea.*

ARROWROOT FAMILY = Marantaceae.

ARROW-WOOD = *Viburnum dentatum.*

ARTABOTRYS (ar-ta-bō'tris). A genus of woody, climbing plants of the family Annonaceae, all from the tropics of the Old World, the one below cultivated outdoors only in zone* 9, and more rarely in greenhouses. They are generally called tail-grapes from the hooked flower stalks which help them to climb. Leaves alternate and evergreen. Flowers very fragrant, with 6 petals in 2 series. Stamens* numerous. Fruit a collection of plum-like bodies gathered on a common receptacle.* (*Artabotrys* is Greek for suspended grape, in allusion to the hanging fruits.)

The species below should be planted outdoors in rich soil and repays for a yearly mulch of well-rotted manure. If in the greenhouse, use potting mixture* 5 and keep

in a warm house. Easily propagated by seeds.

odoratissimus. Climbing ylang-ylang. A woody vine or half-climbing shrub, with glossy, oblongish leaves 3–6 in. long. Flower stalk hooked, 1–2-flowered, usually opposite a leaf, woody when old. Flowers greenish-yellow. Fruit smooth, yellow and fragrant when ripe. Tropical As.

ARTEMISIA (ar-te-miz'i-a). The wormwoods comprise a very large genus of bitter or aromatic herbs and low shrubs, family Compositae, found in most countries, and cult. since ancient times for their aromatic qualities, for ornament, or as seasoning (*see* TARRAGON). They have alternate,* mostly divided or dissected leaves. Flowers in small heads, wholly made up of disk flowers (*see* COMPOSITAE), not showy except in a few species, prevailingly greenish-yellow. (*Artemisia* is the Latin name of the mugwort.)

Many of the species have silvery coating to the leaves and, like similarly clothed plants, they do not tolerate much winter moisture. Otherwise, except as noted below, they are of easy culture, generally growing better in poor and sandy soils than in rich ones. The perennials are easily increased by division of the roots, the others by seeds. All bloom in the summer, and prefer open sunshine.

Abrotanum. Southernwood; called, also, old man. A grayish-green-foliaged, woody, perennial herb, 2½–4 ft. high. Leaves divided into thread-like sections. Flower heads ⅛ in. in diameter, yellowish-white. Southern Eu. For uses and culture *see* HERB GARDENING.

Absinthium. The classical wormwood, and an ingredient of absinthe. A white-hairy, woody, perennial herb, 2½–4 ft. high. Leaves divided into 2 or 3 oblongish segments. Flower heads ⅛ in. wide, greenish, very numerous. Eu.

albula. Sometimes grown as Silver King artemisia. Not over 4 ft. high. Leaves ovalish, 3–5-lobed, white-felty, the upper ones narrower and unlobed. Flowers inconspicuous. Southwestern U.S.

annua. Sweet wormwood. A quick-growing annual, 4–6 ft. high with pleasantly scented foliage. Leaves 2–3 divided, the divisions deeply indented, pale green. Flower heads minute, but very numerous in profuse clusters (panicle*), yellow. As. Aug.–Sept.

canadensis. Sea or wild wormwood. An American perennial herb, seldom over 2 ft. high, usually grayish, but without hairs. Leaves with 2 main divisions, but these much cut into fine segments. Flower heads about ⅛ in. across, greenish and very plentiful in long, narrow clusters. Eastern N.A. and westward.

canescens = *Artemisia vulgaris.*

Dracunculus. Tarragon; called, also, estragon. A perennial, green, completely smooth herb, the aromatic foliage of which is used for seasoning. Leaves basal and on the stem, the latter narrow and undivided, the basal ones 3-parted toward the tip. Flower heads ⅛ in. wide, whitish-green. Eurasia. For culture *see* TARRAGON.

frigida. Mountain sage; called, also, wormwood sage and wild sage. A perennial herb, 9–15 in. high, with silvery-white foliage. Leaves twice divided, the ultimate segments very narrow. Flower heads yellow, about ¼

---

* Special articles on the subjects indicated by an asterisk (*) will be found at the words so marked.

in. wide, nodding, in racemes.* Western U.S. and As.

glacialis. An alpine perennial for the rock garden, scarcely over 4 in. high, with much-divided leaves and small, golden-yellow flower heads. European Alps. Plant in gritty or sandy soil.

lactiflora = Artemisia vulgaris lactiflora.

pedemontana. As offered, usually a form of A. *pontica.*

pontica. Roman wormwood. A shrubby, perennial herb, 1–2 ft. high. Leaves much dissected into linear segments that are ashy-gray beneath. Flower heads ⅛ in. wide, whitish-yellow, but often failing to develop. Eu.

sacrorum. Russian wormwood. A tall, stiff herb, often 5 ft. high, with whitish, cut, but not dissected leaves and greenish-white, nodding heads in slender racemes. Siberia. The form most worth growing is *var.* **viride,** the summer fir. This is tree-like in habit, grown mostly as a bold foliage plant, and treated as an annual. *See* ANNUALS.

schmidtiana. A Japanese alpine perennial, with much-divided, almost shreddy leaves, usually cult. in the *var.* **nana.** This is a low, cushion-like plant, 4–6 in. high, suited only to the rock garden. Its foliage is soft, silky, and cut into fine, narrow, pointed segments. Flower heads small, not showy.

stelleriana. One of the plants called dusty miller; called, also, beach wormwood and old woman. A densely white-woolly, perennial herb seldom over 24 in. high. Leaves cut, but not dissected, the segments oblong, toothed or sometimes without teeth. Flower heads ¼ in. wide, yellow, crowded in dense racemes.* A splendid beach plant. Coasts of northeastern U.S. and As. For culture *see* HERB GARDENING. *See also* SAND GARDEN.

tridentata. Sagebrush (but the name is applied also to other species). A much-branched shrub, 4–8 ft. high with silvery foliage. Leaves stalkless, narrowly wedge-shaped, ¾–2 in. long, and with 3–7 teeth toward the blunt tip. Flower heads scarcely ⅛ in. in diameter, but numerous in the cluster (panicle*) which is often 12–18 in. wide. Arid parts of western N.A. Aug.–Sept. Hardy from zone* 3 southward. Not easy to grow in the East.

vulgaris. Mugwort. A much-branched, often purplish-stemmed perennial herb, 2–3½ ft. high. Leaves fragrant, white-hairy beneath, cut into oblong, mostly toothed segments. Flower heads yellow, ⅛ in. wide in clustered spikes. Eurasia, naturalized in N.A., and often a troublesome weed. An especially fine form, with white heads, is called *var.* **lactiflora.**

artemisioides (ar-te-miz-i-oy′deez; but *see* OÏDES). Resembling the wormwood (*Artemisia*).

ARTHUR HOYT SCOTT HORTICULTURAL FOUNDATION. *See* BOTANIC GARDEN.

ARTICHOKE (*Cynara Scolymus*). A vegetable, the edible portion of which consists of the unripe flower head and its attendant parts — the scales and receptacle.* It is often known as bur artichoke or globe artichoke, and should not be confused with Jerusalem artichoke, which neither comes from Jerusalem nor is an artichoke (*see Helianthus tuberosus* at SUNFLOWER). For the Chinese artichoke, *see* STACHYS SIEBOLDI.

Globe artichoke is a perennial, does not ordinarily come true from seed, and must therefore be propagated by planting the numerous suckers that arise from the base of old plants. In starting a plantation of them, put these suckers at least 6 ft. apart in rows 8 ft. apart, for mature plants are large and spreading. The suckers should be well cut back and planted 6 or 8 in. deep. While the artichoke may live for many years, it is advisable to renew a plantation every three or four years to ensure not only the largest yield but the tenderest and most juicy heads. They must not be moved once they are planted, so pick a site for them that they will monopolize for the next three or four years.

Frequent cultivation is necessary, and if the plants have been set at exactly the intervals given above, cultivation may well be in both directions. In cultivating, care must be taken not to injure the plants as they become full grown and ready for the harvesting of the heads. Artichoke is a rich feeder. At least 10 tons of stable manure per acre is plowed in after the final crop of heads is harvested and the plants are cut down to the ground. Some growers also use 400 pounds to the acre of nitrate of soda, applied just before the first heads are ready for harvesting.

Artichokes are harvested throughout the latter part of the growing season of the plant. Never allow one of the large buds to become old enough so that its scales get hard or woody, for it is the succulence of these that one seeks in a good globe artichoke. Cut off all old stems that have borne harvested heads, either plowing them in between the rows or feeding them to cattle.

The plant came originally from the southern Mediterranean region, and its climatic requirements have resulted in certain parts of California being the chief places where it is grown, notably in Monterey, San Mateo and Santa Cruz counties. It is primarily a winter vegetable, and, in Calif., the suckers are started so as to ensure winter production of heads. This means an essentially frost-free area in winter, but cool and foggy in summer. Without these peculiar climatic conditions the production of artichokes is not advisable, although the plant, as a perennial herb, may be grown in many frosty regions under the conditions mentioned below.

Throughout the Calif. region of production the plants must be irrigated, but they will not tolerate standing water any more than the heads will stand frost.

Outside of Calif. and a few places along the Gulf Coast, artichoke, as a perennial herb, can be grown if cut down to the ground at the approach of frost. Cover the crown with a box and mulch the box and surrounding soil heavily with manure. Plants not covered with a box or inverted flower pot will gather too much moisture around the crown and probably die. Artichoke protected as described will produce heads, but not very good ones, in the late summer. Few

---

* Special articles on the subjects indicated by an asterisk (*) will be found at the words so marked.

people, outside Calif., take the trouble to grow them.

INSECT PESTS. Control aphids with malathion. Arsenicals or methoxychlor will control chewing pests.

DISEASES. A leafspot* disease which may result in some defoliation, has been controlled with applications of pesticide #5 (see SPRAYS AND DUSTS) although spraying is not usually warranted. The rots which often occur in storage may be retarded if temperatures are kept near 32° F.

articulata, -us, -um (ar-tick-you-lay'ta). Articulated; that is, jointed at obviously, or apparently, separable nodes or joints, as the stems of some bamboos, the joints of a cactus, or the point at which a fruit falls from a stem.

ARTILLERY PLANT = *Pilea microphylla.*

ARTOCARPACEAE. See MORACEAE.

ARTOCARPUS (ar-toe-kar'pus). A large genus of tropical, mostly Asiatic, milky-juiced trees, family Moraceae, the two below grown for their fruit. Leaves alternate,* lobed or unlobed (in ours). Male and female flowers in different clusters on the same plant, the male in spikes, the female in heads, both small. There is no distinction between petals and sepals, which are united to form a small tube. Fruit a syncarp,* edible in the breadfruit, and enormous in the jackfruit. (*Artocarpus* is Greek for breadfruit.)

Outdoor culture possible only in zone* 9; rarely cult. in greenhouses for the handsome stiff leaves and curious flowers and fruit. Propagated by seeds or cuttings, and they should not be moved once they are planted as they do not stand transplanting very well. Both are typically tropical plants of moist lowlands and their culture is thus restricted to extreme southern Fla., and risky even there.

communis. Breadfruit. A tree up to 50 ft., its profuse foliage dense and striking. Leaves 18–24 in. long, thick and leathery, ovalish, but deeply lobed with sharp segments. Male spikes 6 in. long, yellowish, drooping or curving downward. Female cluster nearly globe-shaped. Fruit 4–8 in. in diameter, yellow, the outside weakly spiny, the flesh delicious; seedless in the true breadfruit, but with seeds in a variety known as breadnut. The latter is grown for these seeds which are cooked. Polynesia. It is the fruit made famous by *Mutiny on the Bounty.* See BLIGHIA. The plant is also offered as A. *incisa.*

integrifolia. Jackfruit; called, also, jak. Frequently up to 70 ft. and much cult. in the tropics for its fruit, one of the largest known. Leaves stiff, glossy-green, without lobes, 6–8 in. long. Male spikes 3–4 in. long. Female spike arising only from the bark of the trunk or larger branches. Fruit 1–2 ft. long, often weighing 40 pounds or more, knobby, the flesh edible but insipid. Seeds numerous, edible when cooked, and prized by some tropical natives. Offered, also, as A. *integra.*

ARUM (air'um). Eurasian relatives of the Jack-in-the-pulpit, and requiring the same culture (*see* ARISAEMA), except for the black calla (*see* below). The genus comprises a dozen species of tuberous-rooted perennial herbs with mostly arrow-shaped leaves. The flowers are borne on a naked spadix* which is partly surrounded by the much more showy spathe.* (*See* ARACEAE for minute structure.) Fruit a fleshy berry. (*Arum* is the classical name for these plants.)

italicum. A perennial 12–16 in. high, its arrowhead-shaped leaves about 7 in. long and as broad, the stalk 12–16 in. long. Spathe* stalked, tubular, about 2 in. long, white inside, but the margin purple, green outside. The marginal tip of the spathe* reflexed, 8–9 in. long, about ⅓ as wide. Southeastern Eu. Apr.–May.

maculatum. Lords-and-ladies; called, also, cuckoopint. A fleshy herb about 12 in. high. Leaves more or less arrow-shaped, usually blackspotted, withering in summer, long-stalked. Spathe* 6–10 in. long, pinched at the middle, purple-spotted or purple-margined or both, much exceeding the spadix.* Southern Eu. There are whitish-spathed and all-purple-spathed varieties. Called wakerobin in England. See POISONOUS PLANTS.

palaestinum. Black calla; called also Solomon's lily. A tender, greenhouse plant grown for its handsome foliage and flowers like the calla lily, but blackish-purple inside the spathe.* Leaves 6 in. wide, arrow-shaped and with a heart-shaped base. Spathe green outside, blackish-purple within, the tip often drooping. Palestine. Its soil and culture requirements are the same as for *Caladium* (which see).

ARUM FAMILY. The aroids, as they are often called, comprise an immense family of mostly tropical herbs, but some native plants like the Jack-in-the-pulpit and skunkcabbage. Most of the hort. genera are chiefly greenhouse plants like the anthuriums, the elephant's-ear and the edible-fruited ceriman. For the peculiar flowers of this family and the hort. genera *see* ARACEAE.

ARUNCUS (a-run'kus). A genus of spirea-like herbs of the rose family, differing from the closely related *Spiraea* in having compound* leaves, which are twice- or thrice-compound. Flowers small, white, crowded into showy panicles, the male and female on different plants. Petals 5. Stamens many. Pistils 3 (5 in *Spiraea*). Fruit a collection of follicles.* (*Aruncus* is the classical name of these plants.)

The goatsbeard is an attractive hardy perennial with feathery foliage and masses of small white flowers. It is a fine plant for the border, does best in partial shade, and will grow in any good garden soil. Propagated by division.

dioicus. Goatsbeard. A strong-growing plant 4–6 ft. high. Leaves much dissected, the ultimate leaflets ovalish, sharply and doubly toothed, about 1½ in. long. Flowers about ⅛ in. wide, nearly stalkless on the branches of a widespreading, open cluster 6–10 in. high. N.A. and As. Much confused with *Spiraea* and *Astilbe* and offered under both names and as *Aruncus Sylvester.*

arundinacea, -um (a-run-di-nay'-see-a). Reed-like.

ARUNDINARIA (a-run-di-nay'ri-a). Tall,

---

* Special articles on the subjects indicated by an asterisk (*) will be found at the words so marked.

bamboo-like, but nearly hardy grasses, much grown for their fine foliage and somewhat showy, plume-like flower clusters. They differ from the mostly tropical bamboos (*Bambusa*) only in technical characters, although usually, in temperate climates, *Arundinaria* does not have a woody stem as in the bamboos. Leaves flat, short-stalked, from persistent sheaths. Flowers grass-like, in flattish spikes which are gathered in large, often plumy clusters. (*Arundinaria* is derived from *Arundo.*)

For the culture and garden uses of these handsome plants *see* GRASSES. Some of the species below are credited by some to *Sasa, Semiarundinaria, Pseudosasa,* and *Pleioblastus,* genera not here maintained. Most of them are not hardy above the southern edges of zone* 5. *See also* BAMBOO.

falcata. Stems very slender, 10–15 ft. high, bluish and waxy when young, yellow-green in age. Leaves 3–6 in. long, about ½ in. wide, striped, the margins roughened with minute teeth. Flower cluster a raceme,* which is slightly arched. Himalayas. The stems die down to the ground each year, except in the South.

fastuosa. Stems stout, 20–30 ft. high, usually with purple-brown markings. Leaves 5–7 in. long and about 1 in. wide, green above, bluish-gray beneath. Jap. Stems persisting all year, somewhat woody.

gigantea. Southern cane; called also cane reed. The chief plant of the canebrakes from Md. southward. Stems persistent, 10–25 ft. high. Leaves nearly 12 in. long, about 1½ in. wide, very rough and cutting on the margin. Less showy than the Asiatic species.

japonica. The hardiest of the group and safely planted from zone* 4 southward. Stems 5–8 ft., bluish-waxy. Leaves 4–12 in. long, about 1½ in. wide, green and shining above, whitish and minutely hairy beneath. Jap. Stems dying down each winter in the north.

macrosperma = *gigantea.*

simoni. The handsomest of the group, the stems 10–20 ft. high and usually persisting southward. Leaves 8–12 in. long and about 1 in. wide, often white-striped. There is also a shorter plant with smaller, yellow-mottled leaves. China and Jap.

veitchi. Not over 3 ft. high and hardy, with protection, as far north as the central part of zone* 4. Leaves 5–8 in. long, about 2 in. wide, green above, bluish-gray beneath, the margins often yellowish. Jap.

ARUNDO (a-run′doe). A genus of very ornamental grasses from the Old World, the one below widely planted for ornament. It is not hardy north of zone* 5, rarely in zone* 4 with protection. Stems tall and woody. Leaves long, stiff, and more or less two-ranked on the stems. Flowers grass-like, crowded into a large, silky, plume-like, and striking cluster (panicle*), seldom produced except southward. (*Arundo* is the classical name for the reed.)

For culture and uses in the garden *see* GRASSES.

Donax. Giant reed; called also Italian reed. A stout plant 10–15 ft. high, the stems somewhat woody. Leaves 1–2 ft. long, about 2½ in. wide. Flower cluster spire-like, often 2 ft.

long. Southern Eu. There is a variety with yellow- or white-striped leaves.

arvensis, -e (ar-ven′sis). From cultivated fields.

arvernensis, -e (ar-ver-nen′sis). From or near the Auvergne Mountains in France.

ASARINA. *See Antirrhinum Asarina* at SNAPDRAGON.

ASARUM (ass′a-rum). Woodland perennial plants with aromatic rootstocks and usually kidney-shaped leaves, useful only in shady places in the wild garden. They are usually called wild ginger from their strong scent and flavor. Of 60 known species, belonging to this genus, only a handful are of secondary garden interest; family Aristolochiaceae. Leaves stalked, heart-shaped or kidney-shaped. Flowers brownish-purple, borne at or near the ground and hidden by the relatively dense foliage (for structure *see* ARISTOLOCHIACEAE). Fruit is a rather fleshy capsule.* (The name *Asarum* is of unknown significance here.)

The wild gingers need shade, a humus soil, and plenty of moisture. Given these, they spread readily and will cover considerable areas in a few years. Easily increased by division of their creeping rootstocks. All those below are North American, and some of them are said to belong to the genus *Hexastylis,* not here maintained.

canadense. Leaves 3–6 in. wide, kidney-shaped, the stalk about 6–8 in. long. Flowers 1 in. wide. Eastern N.A. *See* MEDICINAL PLANTS.

caudatum. Leaves 2–5 in. wide, more or less heart-shaped, the stalk 5–7 in. long. Flowers with the lobes prolonged into 2-in. tails. Pacific Coast.

hartwegi. Leaves naturally variegated with white, nearly round or heart-shaped, 3–5 in. wide, long stalked. Flowers ½ in. wide, urn-shaped, the reddish maroon corolla 3-lobed, each lobe with a terminal spur about 2 in. long. Pacific Coast, but hardy in the East if given cool, moist site. May–June.

shuttleworthi. Resembling the first species, the leaves thinner and larger, and differing in flower only by technical characters. In moist woods southeastern U.S. May–July. Called by some *Hexastylis shuttleworthi.*

ascalonica, -us, -um (as-ka-lon′i-ka). Named for Ascalon, a village in Palestine.

ASCENDING. Rising upward, but not stiffly or erectly so.

ASCLEPIADACEAE (as-kleep-i-a-day′-see-ee). The milkweed family, as its name implies, nearly always has a milky juice. Of its 220 widely distributed genera and over 2000 species, only a handful are of any garden significance. Among the most curious are *Stapelia, Huernia,* and *Huerniopsis,* which are succulent, almost cactus-like genera from South Africa. The rest of the hort. genera are herbs, shrubs or vines, the leaves of which scarcely ever have marginal teeth. Flowers regular,* rarely solitary, mostly in terminal clusters, sometimes in the axils.* Fruit a dry pod (follicle*), the seeds with a tuft of hairs.

---

* Special articles on the subjects indicated by an asterisk (*) will be found at the words so marked.

A few are hardy genera (*see* Milkweed, Asclepiodora, Cynanchum, and Periploca), but most of the family are tropical. Among the latter are woody vines in *Araujia, Cryptostegia, Hoya,* and *Stephanotis,* while *Ceropegia* is a prostrate, fleshy-stemmed vine from South Africa.

Technical flower characters: Sepals 5, separate or nearly so. Petals joined to form a united corolla, the 5 lobes of which are usually bent backward. Stamens 5, the filaments usually united into a column.* Between the stamens and petals is usually a crown-like organ (corona*). Ovaries 2, each of them 1-celled but many-seeded, superior.*

asclepiadea, -us, -um (as-kleep-i-ā′dee-a). Milkweed-like.

ASCLEPIAS. *See* Milkweed.

ASCLEPIODORA (as-kleep-ee-o-do′ra). A small genus of North American, milkweed-like, perennial herbs, differing from *Asclepias* (*see* Milkweed) chiefly in technical characters, and in having alternate* leaves. The only species in cult. is A. **decumbens,** called antelope-horns (in N. Mex.) and snakeroot (Tex.). It is a stout herb 18–24 in. high, with short-stalked, oblongish leaves 3–5 in. long, and greenish-purple flowers in a loose cluster (umbel*). Fruit a follicle.* Suitable only for dry, open places. (The name is derived from *Asclepias.*)

ASCYRUM (a-sy′rum). A small genus of mostly North American, shrubby, perennial herbs, family Hypericaceae, only the St. Andrew's-cross of much garden interest. Leaves opposite,* without marginal teeth. Flowers bright yellow, in terminal clusters (cymes*), with numerous stamens and 4 petals. Fruit a small, dry, valved pod (capsule*). (*Ascyrum* is Greek for not hard or rough, and of uncertain application here.)

The St. Andrew's-cross is a pretty little bushy plant, useful in the border and effective when planted in masses. It prefers open sunshine and a decidedly sandy soil. Easily propagated by division or by seeds. They need an annual shearing to keep them tidy.

hypericoides. St. Andrew's-cross. A bushy plant 18–24 in. high. Leaves numerous, oblongish, about 1 in. long. Flowers usually 3 to a cluster, the petals narrowly oblong. Native from Mass. to tropical America, but needs winter covering from zone* 4 northward. Not very long-lived. It is sometimes sold as A. *Crux-andreae.*

aselliformis, -e (a-sell-i-for′mis). Shaped like a wood-louse.

ASEXUAL. Sexless. As applied to flowers, asexual implies that they have no stamens or pollen and no pistil or ovules and are consequently quite sterile. As applied to propagation, asexual reproduction indicates any method of increasing plants except by seeds. *See* Propagation.

ASH. The group of ash trees, all belonging to the genus **Fraxinus** (frax′i-nus) of the olive family, are more important as timber than as ornamentals. Of the 65 known spe-

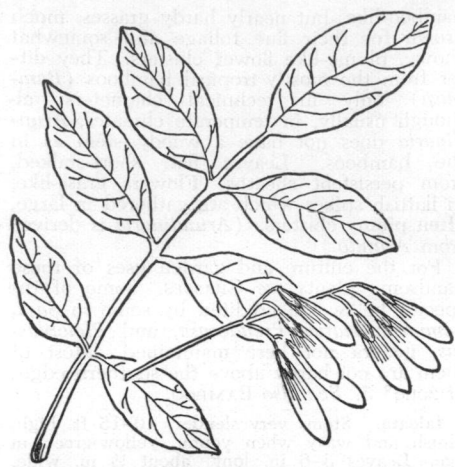

Leaf and fruits of white ash (*Fraxinus americana*)

cies, mostly from the north temperate zone, only six are of hort. interest. These are handsome trees with compound,* opposite* leaves, and (in ours) 5 or more leaflets. Flowers small, greenish or whitish, perfect or unisexual (polygamous*), without petals in all except the flowering ash (*F. Ornus*). Fruit a small nutlet, partly surrounded by an elongated wing (a samara*). (*Fraxinus* is classical Latin for the ash.)

The flowering ash is the only really showy tree of the group. It has large clusters of whitish flowers blooming about the time the leaves appear. The others flower before the leaves unfold and lack petals. All will grow in most ordinary garden soils, but they are not trees for dry sites, especially the black ash, which prefers moist places. Easily propagated from seeds and often becoming a pest from profuse self-seeding.

F. americana. White ash. A tree 60–120 ft. high, the young twigs lustrous-green. Leaflets mostly 7 (rarely 5 or 9), stalked, more or less oval, 3–5 in. long. Fruit oblong, about 1½ in. long. Eastern N.A. Hardy from zone* 2 southward, and not particular as to site.

F. excelsior. European ash. Taller than the last, the twigs smooth but not lustrous. Leaflets mostly 9 (rarely 7 or 11), stalkless, oblongish, 3–5 in. long, dark green above, paler beneath. Fruit very narrow, the wing often notched at the tip, about 1½ in. long. Eu. and Asia Minor. Hardy from zone* 3 southward.

F. lanceolata = *Fraxinus pensylvanica lanceolata.*

F. nigra. Black ash; called also hoop ash. Not over 75 ft. high, the twigs smooth. Leaflets 7–11, usually 9, stalkless, rather broad-oblong, green both sides, 4–6 in. long, and with rusty tufts of hair along the midrib beneath. Fruit narrow-oblong, 1–1½ in. long, the wing surrounding the nutlet. Eastern N.A. Hardy from zone* 2 southward. Prefers moist sites.

F. Ornus. Flowering ash; called also manna ash. A Eurasian round-headed tree, not over 50 ft., usually much less. Leaflets usually 7, stalked, oblong or oval, the terminal one larger

* Special articles on the subjects indicated by an asterisk (*) will be found at the words so marked.

than the others, which are 2½–3½ in. long. Flowers whitish, fragrant, in dense terminal clusters, opening just after the leaves unfold. Fruit about 1 in. long, cut-off or notched at the tip. Hardy from zone° 4 southward. The commonest species in cult. and much the showiest. A sweetish manna is collected from its trunk in Asia Minor and Sicily.

F. pensylvanica. Red or river ash. Much resembles the first but with usually 9 leaflets, and with fruit wing more completely surrounding the nutlet. A variety (**F. pensylvanica lanceolata**) known as green or swamp ash has irregularly toothed leaflets. Both are found wild over much of eastern N.A., and are hardy from zone° 2 southward. The variety is suited to wind-swept regions in the prairie states.

F. quadrangulata. Blue ash. A tree not usually over 70 ft. high, the twigs 4-angled and mostly slightly winged. Leaflets mostly 9 (rarely 7 or 11), short-stalked, yellow-green, more or less narrowly oval, 3–5 in. long. Fruit notched at the tip, winged to the base, 1½–2 in. long. Ont. and central U.S. Hardy from zone° 3 southward. Its foliage turns pale yellow in the fall.

F. velutina. A tree of the southwestern U.S. and adjacent Mex., usually cult. in the *var.* glabra, called the Modesto ash, and suited to dry, semi-arid regions. It may, in nature, reach a height of 40–50 ft. Leaflets 3–5, short-stalked, 1–2 in. long. Useful as a street tree where little else will grow, but only in the arid Southwest.

For other plants sometimes called ash *see* MOUNTAIN-ASH and ZANTHOXYLUM.

INSECT PESTS. *See* borers at INSECT PESTS. *See also* insect pests at APPLE and MAPLE.

DISEASES. Leaves and petioles often have pustules or swellings as a result of a rust° disease. The presence of the disease depends upon proximity to marsh grass — the alternate host for the rust fungus. Use of pesticide #5 (*see* SPRAYS AND DUSTS) has been suggested, but its value is questionable.

ASH AND ASHES. To the gardener ash is the unburnable residue left from the combustion of plant tissue. It contains various chemicals, all of which are part of the food of plants (*see* PLANT FOODS). Practically, however, ash means wood ashes or coal ashes.

To dispose of the latter first, coal ashes have no place in the soil of the garden. Chemically they are useless and physically they are far better replaced by sand. Some people put coal ashes in heavy clay soils to lighten them. This is to be avoided. Use sand instead.

Coal ashes have some value as material in which to plunge° potted plants for the summer, because they are more or less antiseptic and discourage worms.

Wood ashes and the burned vegetable refuse of the garden both yield an appreciable amount of available potash and lime and are therefore valuable. Wood ashes may be used at the rate of a pound to a cubic yard of soil, in heaps, or scattered on the surface at the rate of about 4 ounces per square yard. Those from the fireplace are the best mixed with the compost pile, after screening out the rubbish. They furnish a quick-acting, very soluble form of potash, containing from 4–6% of it.

ASH FAMILY = Oleaceae.

ASHLAR. A type of masonry for garden walls. *See* WALLS AND WALL GARDENING.

asiatica, -us, -um (a-she-at'i-ka). From Asia.

ASIATIC GLOBEFLOWER = *Trollius asiaticus.*

ASIATIC REDBUD = *Cercis chinensis.* See REDBUD.

ASIMINA (as-sim'i-na). A small genus of North American shrubs and trees, family Annonaceae, the one below, the only tree of the group, cult. for its fine foliage, handsome flowers and (to some) desirable fruit. Leaves alternate,° large, without teeth. Flowers in the leaf axils,° green at first, changing to purple, red and yellow. Sepals 3. Petals 6. Stamens numerous. Fruit fleshy, oblong, suggesting an old potato in color and shape. (*Asimina* is a Latinized version of a French and Indian vernacular name for the species below.)

The tree grows in rich woods, and prefers good rich soil and not too much sun. It transplants with considerable difficulty and is best raised from seeds sown in the fall, or stratified (*see* SEEDS AND SEEDAGE) and sown the following spring.

triloba. Papaw; called also custard-apple in the Central States. A medium-sized tree, usually not over 25 ft. high. Leaves more or less oval-oblong, wedge-shaped at the base, 8–12 in. long. Flowers blooming when the leaves expand, about 2 in. wide. Fruit 2–6 in. long, dark brown when ripe, the flesh yellow, aromatic, but banana-flavored, and surrounding the flattish seeds. Eastern and central U.S. Hardy from zone° 4 southward. For another plant called papaw *see* CARICA.

asparagina, -us, -um (as-pa-ra-geen'a). Asparagus-like.

asparagoides (as-pa-ra-goy'deez; but *see* OÏDES). Asparagus-like.

ASPARAGUS (as-pa'ra-gus). An Old World, but chiefly African, genus of 150 species of largely desert herbs and vines, of the lily family. It comprises such unlike plants as the "smilax" of the florist, the common garden asparagus, and the so-called asparagus fern used for trimming countless bouquets. All have tuberous or fleshy roots and no true leaves, which are reduced to scales or wholly lacking, or, in some, like the florist's "smilax," are replaced by flat, leaf-like branches. Flowers very small and greenish. Fruit a berry. (*Asparagus* is the Greek name for the vegetable.)

For the culture of the common garden asparagus, *see* below. For the culture of A. *asparagoides* (the florist's "smilax") *see* SMILAX, 2. The other species below, especially the asparagus fern, are widely grown commercially for their feathery foliage, rivaling in delicacy the finest ferns but, being leafless, are far more resistant to the heat and dryness of an ordinary room. They are thus the most popular material for trimming bouquets and funeral wreaths in America. Their

---

° Special articles on the subjects indicated by an asterisk (°) will be found at the words so marked.

culture is easy in a cool greenhouse, in potting mixture* 4, and they can be propagated from seed which is plentifully produced on old plants.

asparagoides. The "smilax" of the florists. A South African, branching, leafless vine, the leaf-like branches oval, about 1 in. long, bright and lustrous-green. Flowers greenish-white, sparse. Berry dark purple, pea size. For culture and uses *see* SMILAX (2). Often sold as *Myrsiphyllum asparagoides.*

falcatus. Sickle thorn. A tall-climbing, leafless, spiny vine, the leaf-like branches sickleshaped, leathery, 2–3 in. long, dark green. Flowers white, fragrant. Berry brown. South Africa. Cult. in Fla. as an ornamental vine that reaches 40 ft. in height.

officinalis. Garden asparagus. A Eurasian seacoast plant originally very different from the modern vegetable, and perhaps not now in cult. For culture *see* below.

plumosus. Asparagus fern, called also, with as little reason, fern asparagus (it is no fern). A feathery, fern-like, climbing vine from South Africa, the leaves reduced to needle-like bodies about ¼ in. long, and the green stems and twigs functioning as leaves, but wiry. Flowers very small, whitish. Berry purple-black, pea size. In some of its many forms, very widely grown for the florist trade.

sprengeri. A South African low-growing vine, cult. for ornament in greenhouses. Leaf-like branches narrow, linear, about ¾ in. long, freely dropping. Flowers pinkish, in racemes. Berry bright red. An attractive plant for the hanging basket.

verticillatus. A medium-sized, somewhat woody vine sometimes reaching a height of 15 ft. Leaves reduced to thread-like bodies nearly 2 in. long. Flowers whitish-green. Berry red, pea size. Persia and Central As. Hardy outdoors from zone* 6 southward.

ASPARAGUS CULTURE

(*Asparagus officinalis*)

The young tender shoots of asparagus ("grass" to the illiterate) have been used as a vegetable for over two thousand years. It can be grown, and is, in practically every part of the United States, except in areas of extreme heat.

VARIETIES. Several score are known. Of these only a handful have survived the test of public taste and the ravages of various pests. The outstanding sort, often generally called Washington asparagus, is Mary Washington and new selections including Mary Washington 499 and 500, and Raritan.

California (44 per cent) and New Jersey (23 per cent) lead all other states in total asparagus production of U.S., the combined production, of South Carolina, Illinois and Maryland scarcely equaling that of New Jersey. Asparagus production, outside these five states, totals only about 11 per cent of the country's consumption and is grown mostly for local market or home use. It should be noted that most of these regions have winters where the ground freezes at least a few inches and the crop appears to benefit by such conditions.

CULTURE. Asparagus is the most permanent of all vegetable crops. Once established, it used to be assumed, and still is in England, that it will last a lifetime. The best practice now is to renew plantings every 15 years. Because of this it is obvious that the home gardener should plan to put asparagus in areas that do not have to be plowed every year. (For suggestions as to site *see* KITCHEN GARDEN.)

No soil is too rich for asparagus. It will grow in any ordinary good garden soil, but it will not produce tender stalks without liberal supplies of stable manure and plenty of moisture. One of the most successful growers in America grows it on fairly sandy soil, but the permanent water-table is only three feet below the surface and capillarity assures a steady supply to the roots.

For the home gardener it is usually too troublesome to start asparagus from seed. For a moderate price he can purchase dormant one-year-old crowns or roots, thus hastening ultimate production by several years. It takes from 60 to 70 roots for 100 ft. of row. While the old-fashioned idea was to make an "asparagus bed," it is much better planted in rows which should be at least 4–5 ft. apart.

Having selected a rich, well-drained soil, start operations as early in spring as the ground is workable by plowing a deep furrow. This must be deep enough so that when the bottom is smoothed it will still be at least 10 in. below the general ground level. Never start such a plantation on weedy land, because asparagus cultivation has to be limited by the nature of the plant (*see* below).

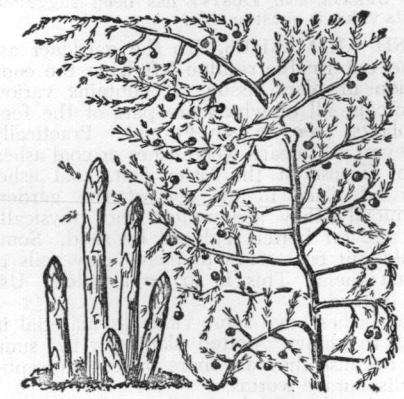

Asparagus ready for harvesting (at left) and the summer condition of the plant.

In this weed-free trench put one crown, with its roots carefully spread out, about every 20 in. Cover, at first, with only 2–3 in. of fine soil, which should be well firmed over the fleshy roots. Put no more soil in the trench until shoots appear, when they are again covered. Repeat the operation until the trench is finally filled. Your plantation

---

* Special articles on the subjects indicated by an asterisk (*) will be found at the words so marked.

is then established, but not yet ready for the harvest. Some prefer to obviate the trench and plant the roots only 1½ in. deep. If soil is rich this may be justified.

ANNUAL MAINTENANCE. For the first year cut no stalks, and some prudent growers cut none until the third year, although a *very moderate* cutting may be made the second year. Left to themselves the tender, juicy stalks will produce a tall, rather wiry, bushy plant that by midsummer completely fills up all the space between the rows. This somewhat brittle growth is easily injured and no machine cultivation is possible once this growth is well developed. Before it starts, and while the shoots are soft, cultivate frequently and keep the plantation as weed-free as possible up to the end of June.

In the fall cut the bushy growth down to the ground, but never cut it away in midsummer, for it is this summer growth that nourishes the roots for next year's production of shoots. Many growers plow in, besides the initial stable manure, extra supplies in the fall or early spring, or top-dress with a liberal application of commerical fertilizer. If manure is plowed in, care must be taken not to injure the roots which, however, are not injured by any amount of surface cultivation.

HARVEST AND YIELDS. A very moderate cutting may be made the second year, and beginning with the third year all stalks should be cut as soon as they are the usual length, but not for more than three weeks. From the fourth year all stalks should be cut throughout the season. Cut just below the ground level with an asparagus knife, or an ordinary knife will do. Care must be taken to cut so that no young, and still buried, shoots are injured.

Cutting can begin as soon as the season will permit, but all cutting must stop by June 20, or at the latest by July 1, when summer growth should be allowed to start. This feathery summer state of the plant is quite unlike the tender spring stalks, but essential to the continued vigor of the plantation.

For those who prefer white stalks some growers heap earth around the emerging shoot. This cuts off the light, and the normally green shoot becomes white, except at the tip.

One hundred feet of row should furnish an ample supply of asparagus for a family of 5, assuming that it is served twice a week and that the plant has been well grown. Good commerical growers expect 2000 bunches per acre, but yields of 3500 bunches are not unknown.

INSECT PESTS. Small beetles feed on and lay eggs on edible spears. Grayish larvae of bluish beetles also feed on spears while larvae of red beetles feed on berries. Apply 1% rotenone dust to shoots, pre-harvest, to control damage. After harvest season is over, promptly on seedling beds, use DDT or lead arsenate.

DISEASES. Rust,* which is the most serious disease of asparagus, causes red pustules on the plant during the early part of the season. In the late summer the pustules are black. Applying pesticide #11 (*see* SPRAYS AND DUSTS) is recommended only for the one-year seedlings to help establish a good root system. Plant the Washington strains which are more resistant to rust. Several root rot diseases may result in reduced yields. Plant healthy roots in soil where asparagus has not been raised previously.

ASPARAGUS BEAN = *Vigna sesquipedalis.*

ASPARAGUS BROCCOLI = *Brassica oleracea italica.* For culture *see* BROCCOLI.

ASPARAGUS CHICORY. See RADICHETTA.

ASPARAGUS FERN = *Asparagus plumosus.*

ASPARAGUS LETTUCE = *Lactuca sativa asparagina.*

ASPEN. See POPULUS.

aspera, -us, -um (as'per-a). Rough.

asperata, -us, -um (as-per-ray'ta). Rough.

asperrima, -us, -um (as-per'ri-ma). Very rough.

ASPERULA (as-per'u-la). A large genus of Old World annual or perennial herbs of the madder family, with square stems, the few below long cult. for ornament, one a pretty, popular annual. Leaves in whorls* of 6 or more. Flowers small, more or less funnel-shaped, and very numerous in forking clusters (cymes*). Fruit leathery but somewhat fleshy, minute. (*Asperula* is diminutive of *aspera*, in allusion to the roughish stems of some species.)

The plants are often called woodruff, and *A. odorata* and *A. tinctoria,* the perennial species, are old favorites in the garden, especially suited to partially shady places. *A. orientalis* is an annual, not so well known as it should be. The perennial species are easily divided in the spring, or raised from seed.

azurea setosa = *Asperula orientalis.*

cynanchica. Squinancy. A prostrate Eurasian perennial, the stems smooth and rather weak. Leaves in 4's, about ⅔ in. long. Flowers white or pink, rather sparse, in a loose cluster. Summer. Once thought to be a cure for quinsy.

odorata. Sweet woodruff. A Eurasian, low-spreading, perennial herb, the dried foliage fragrant. Leaves in whorls* of 8, narrow. Flowers white. Prefers a moist site.

orientalis. A Eurasian, hardy annual easily grown from seed sown in the place they are to grow, not over 12 in. high. Leaves in whorls* of 8, narrow. Flowers blue. A pretty garden flower for open sunlight. See ANNUALS.

suberosa. A low, tufted, rock garden perennial, not over 3 in. high, the foliage silvery. Leaves narrow, 4-clustered. Flowers pink, the cluster (spike*) about 2 in. long. Greece. June–July. Difficult to grow in wet slushy winters.

tinctoria. Dyer's woodruff. A red-rooted, European perennial herb, 18–24 in. long, but straggling. Leaves in whorls* of 4 or 6. Flowers red or pinkish-white. Prefers somewhat moist sites.

---

* Special articles on the subjects indicated by an asterisk (*) will be found at the words so marked.

ASPHODEL. The asphodel of poetry is often a narcissus. The asphodel of the ancients is *Asphodeline lutea.* For another plant, also called asphodel, *see* ASPHODELUS. For the bog asphodel *see* NARTHECIUM AMERICANUM.

ASPHODELINE (as-fo-de-line′e). A genus of 14 species of perennial herbs of the lily family found in the Mediterranean region and of chief interest because it contains the traditional asphodel. This is a yellow-flowered herb differing from the genus *Asphodelus* only in having a leafy flower stalk. (*Asphodeline* means one of the asphodels.) Sometimes called Jacob's-rod.

The culture of the asphodel is easy in any ordinary garden soil, either in partial shade or the open. Propagated by spring or fall division of the roots.

lutea. The traditional asphodel is a thick-rooted herb, 2–3½ ft. high. Leaves 4–10 in. long, rough-margined, mostly basal but also found along the stalk of the flower cluster. Flowers yellow, fragrant, numerous, in finger-shaped clusters (racemes*) 7–15 in. long and about 2½ in. thick, which have membranous and persistent bracts.* Southern Eu. and Arabia. June.

asphodeloides (as-fo-del-oy′deez; but *see* OÏDES). Asphodel-like.

ASPHODELUS (as-fo-del′us). A genus of herbs of the lily family from the Mediterranean region, the one below cultivated for ornament under the name of asphodel (but *see* ASPHODELINE). They are stemless herbs with basal, narrow leaves and lily-like, white flowers in finger-shaped, sometimes branched, clusters (racemes*). Corolla funnel-shaped, of 6 segments, each segment distinctly veined on the back. Stamens 6. Fruit a capsule.* (*Asphodelus* is the classical Greek name of the true asphodel, now included in the genus *Asphodeline.*)

Culture the same as for *Asphodeline.*

ramosus. Often called asphodel. A perennial herb 3–5 ft. high. Leaves all basal, narrow, not so long as the naked stalk of the flower cluster. Flowers white, about ¾ in. long, in a dense, usually branching raceme* which bears also buff-colored bracts. Southern Eu. May. Also called *A. microcarpus* and *A. cerasiferus.*

ASPIDISTRA (as-pi-dis′tra). A small but important genus of foliage plants of the lily family, the one below from southern China, and a most resistant house plant. They have basal, numerous, tough evergreen leaves that arise from a mat of shallow rootstocks (often exposed). Flowers (rare in household plants) solitary, borne at the ground level, thus usually hidden by the foliage, dull brown or purplish-brown, bell-shaped. Stamens 8. Fruit a berry. (*Aspidistra* is Greek for small, round shield, in allusion to the stigma.)

The only cult. species is widely grown for house ornament, for window boxes, and wherever conditions are unfavorable for other foliage plants. It will stand so much abuse that it is often called cast-iron-plant, and is so common in saloons that it is frequently called lager-beer-plant. Florists grow it extensively for decorations that must stand dust, smoke, heat and cold. They are best grown in pots in a cool greenhouse, where they grow rapidly and are easily increased by division of their numerous rootstocks. Use potting mixture* 4.

elatior. Cast-iron-plant. Leaves plentiful, 15–20 in. long, stiff and leathery, deep green, sharp-pointed but more or less oblong and with a stout, channeled stalk about a third the length of the blade. Flowers about 1 in. long. Southern China. Can be grown outdoors in zones* 8 and 9. Often sold as *A. lurida.* There is a variegated (white-striped) variety which loses its stripes if planted in too rich a soil.

ASPIDIUM. A much-confused name for ferns usually, and here, assigned to other genera, especially to *Dryopteris, Polystichum,* and *Cyrtomium.*

asplenifolia, -us, -um (as-plee-ni-fō′li-a). With leaves like a spleenwort (*Asplenium*).

ASPLENIUM (as-plee′ni-um). The spleenworts comprise a genus of over 600 species of widely distributed ferns, family Polypodiaceae, both temperate and tropical, and of great diversity of habit. All those below, except *A. Nidus,* have fronds that are once- or twice-compound,* their ultimate segments small and the foliage thus fine and feathery. *Asplenium Nidus,* the bird's-nest fern, has undivided fronds. The fronds have free (not reticulated) veins along which are the elongated spore cases; *see* FERNS AND FERN GARDENING. (*Asplenium* is Greek for not the spleen, in allusion to their supposed medicinal properties.)

Asplenium bulbiferum and *A. Nidus* are tropical species to be grown in the greenhouse. The other two are hardy ferns for the outdoor fernery or wild garden. See FERNS AND FERN GARDENING for culture of both groups. *See also* ATHYRIUM.

bulbiferum. Mother spleenwort. A curious fern with much-divided fronds 12–18 in. long, the ultimate segments tapering to a point. The fronds often bear bulbils which sprout into new plants while still attached. Tropical Af. and Australasia. Grown by florists for decoration and its proliferating* fronds.

Filix-femina = *Athyrium Filix-femina.*

Nidus. Bird's-nest fern. A handsome tropical fern with undivided fronds without marginal teeth, all of which arise at the ground level and diverge to form a bird's-nest-like clump. Fronds 1–3 ft. long, short-stalked, about 3 in. wide, bright green. A very striking greenhouse fern frequently grown. It is found wild from southern Fla. to Brazil, and in the Old World tropics.

platyneuron. Ebony spleenwort. A hardy American fern with fronds 8–15 in. long. Leaflets 30–35 pairs, each of which has an enlarged, ear-like lobe at the base. A woods fern for the shady nook.

Ruta-muraria. Wall-rue spleenwort. A low fern, not more than 6 in. high, the stalks of the frond green. Fronds 2–3-divided, the ultimate segments distant, toothed, the whole frond 1–2 in. long. Eurasia and N.A., but the native form is called by some *A. cryptolepis.* Not a very desirable cult. species.

Trichomanes. Maidenhair spleenwort. A

* Special articles on the subjects indicated by an asterisk (*) will be found at the words so marked.

hardy, evergreen fern found in rich woods throughout the north temperate zone. Fronds thickly clustered, only once-compound,* about 5 in. long and less than 1 in. wide. Leaflets about ½ in. long, very numerous and crowded, slightly toothed on the upper side. A delicate fern for the shaded part of the wild garden.

ASSURGENT = ASCENDING.

assurgentiflora, -us, -um (as-sir-gent-i-flow′ra). With an ascending flower cluster.

ASTER. As a name *aster* is confusing. To many gardeners it implies the garden or China aster, a popular annual of world-wide cult. This plant, however, does not belong to the genus *Aster* but to *Callistephus,* which see for the garden aster. For a hybrid between *Aster* and a goldenrod *see* SOLIDASTER.

Aster as a genus is an immense group of mostly perennial herbs, family Compositae, very common throughout N.A., much less so in Eu. and As. They are common features of our autumnal landscapes, with a variety of color in their ray flowers (nearly all but yellow). Most of them are stout plants of the woods or fields, easily grown and often too weedy for the border or bed, but useful for bold effects in half-wild sites. Leaves alternate.* Flower heads usually clustered, made up of ray flowers and often yellow disk flowers (*see* COMPOSITAE for details). They differ only in technical characters from *Erigeron.* (*Aster* is Latin for star, hence the little-used name of starwort.)

Of more than 250 species, those below are most likely to be found in cult., although many native species are occasionally dug from the wild. All those below flower in late summer and fall, except those specified otherwise. For the blue garden the hort. forms Blue Gem, Climax, and Feltham Blue are useful. These and many more have been derived from a few, chiefly native American species, from which the English, mostly, have developed a fine strain of hybrid asters called Michaelmas daisies. These are finer garden plants than any of those below, especially as grown in England. See MICHAELMAS DAISY.

acris. A rough-hairy perennial from southern Eu., 2–3 ft. high. Leaves very narrow, without teeth, about 1½ in. long. Ray flowers mauve-blue, the heads about 1 in. wide, clustered. Autumn.

alpinus. Rock aster. Mostly a rock garden species, usually less than 10 in. high. Leaves spatula-shaped or lance-shaped, 1½–2 in. long. Ray flowers blue or violet, the heads solitary, about 1½ in. wide. Mountains of Eurasia and in the Rockies. May. The *var.* **himalaicus** has lilac ray flowers, and is a lower plant. The *var.* **ruber** has rose-pink flowers. For the *var.* **speciosus** *see* ROCK GARDEN.

Amellus. Italian aster. A rough-hairy Eurasian herb 1–2 ft. high, with oblongish leaves with marginal teeth. Ray flowers purple, the heads clustered and about 1½ in. across. The *var.* **bessarabicus** has deeper purple ray flowers. There are several named forms such as Arethusa, Mrs. Perry, etc. August. More recent varieties are King George (lavender) and General Pershing (pink).

cordifolius. Blue wood aster. A much-branched North American herb, 3–5 ft. Basal leaves very large, heart-shaped, and stalked, the stem leaves narrow-oblong, about 5 in. wide and very numerous. Prefers partial shade. A good hort. variety is Silver Spray with pale lilac flowers on arching mahogany-colored stems.

diplostephioides. A Himalayan herb 2–3 ft. high and hairy. Leaves lance-shaped, 2–3 in. long and without marginal teeth. Ray flowers blue or pale purple, the solitary heads nearly 3 in. wide. Some consider this a variety of *A. alpinus,* as offered in the trade.

divaricatus. White wood aster. Somewhat similar to *A. cordifolius* but the ray flowers white. A stout North American species common in dry woods.

ericoides. Heath aster. A wiry, branching herb 2–3 ft. high. Leaves very small and heath-like, seldom over 1½ in. long, but very numerous. Ray flowers white, the heads very small but numerous, and in profuse clusters. U.S.

farreri. A somewhat hairy perennial, 10–18 in. high, the leaves narrow, nearly 6 in. long, toothless but minutely hairy on the margin. Flower heads solitary, but showy, nearly 3 in. wide, the rays deep blue, the center orange-yellow. Tibet and western China.

frikarti. A perennial herb, 2–3 ft. high, with showy lavender-blue heads 2–3 in. wide and fragrant. Aug.–Sept. It is a hybrid between *A. Amellus* and the Himalayan *A. thomsoni,* a plant little known in cult. Among the best of several hort. vars. is Wonder of Stafa, a lavender-flowered form.

grandiflorus. A hairy, much-branched herb 2–3 ft. high, its leaves oblongish, about 1½ in. long and hairy. Ray flowers deep purple or violet, the heads solitary and nearly 2 in. wide. Va. to Fla.

hybridus luteus. *See* SOLIDASTER.

linariifolius. A tough, wiry-stemmed perennial 5–12 in. high, with roughish foliage. Leaves narrow, stiffish, 1–3 in. long, numerous. Flower heads violet, about 1 in. wide, solitary or in few-flowered clusters. July–Sept. Eastern N.A. An excellent plant for dry, sandy soils.

Linosyris = *Linosyris vulgaris.*

novae-angliae. New England aster. A tall branching herb, 3–5 ft. high. Leaves very numerous, lance-shaped, 3–4 in. long. Ray flowers deep purple, the heads crowded and nearly 1½ in. wide. Eastern N.A. One of the finest wild species. *See* MICHAELMAS DAISY for its many named forms.

novi-belgi. New York aster. A perfectly smooth herb 2–3 ft. high, its leaves narrow, pointed, 4–6 in. long. Ray flowers bluish-violet, the heads about 1 in. wide and very numerous in large, branched clusters. Eastern N.A.

porteri. A Rocky Mountain herb seldom over 12 in. high, and suited to the rock garden. Leaves smooth, narrow, 2–3½ in. long. Ray flowers white, the heads small but numerous. July.

ptarmicoides. White upland aster. A North American herb 18–24 in. high. Leaves very narrow, 4–6 in. long, nearly without marginal teeth. Ray flowers white, the heads about 1 in. wide and in profuse, branching clusters. Quebec to Colo.

spectabilis. A low, early-blooming native aster with oval or oblongish leaves 3–5 in. long. Ray flowers bright purple-violet, the heads 1½–2 in. wide and rather sparse. Mass. to Del. and N. Car. Prefers moist sites and open places. July.

subcoeruleus. A rock garden aster seldom over 1 ft. high, the foliage hairy. Leaves oblongish, 1–2 in. long. Ray flowers blue or pale blue,

---

* Special articles on the subjects indicated by an asterisk (*) will be found at the words so marked.

the heads nearly 2 in. wide, showy, but solitary. July. Himalayas. Star of Wartburg, an early-flowering hort. variety, with lavender heads 2 in. wide, is a good alternative to *A. alpinus* in the rock garden.

tataricus. Tartarian aster. The largest of the hort. asters, often 6–8 ft. high and wide-spreading. Lower leaves ovalish or lance-shaped, nearly 2 ft. long, the upper leaves much smaller. Ray flowers blue or violet-purple, the heads 1 in. wide but in numerous and profuse clusters. Siberia. A handsome and striking plant needing plenty of space.

yunnanensis. Resembling *A. alpinus,* the erect stems 6–9 in. high. Flower heads about 2½ in. wide, showy, the rays blue or mauve. Yunnan. June–July.

Various plants are offered from time to time as yellow asters. No true *Aster* is ever yellow so far as known. *See* CHRYSOPSIS for the golden aster, which is sometimes called yellow aster. *See* SOLIDASTER.

ASTERACEAE. *See* COMPOSITAE.

ASTERAGO. *See* SOLIDASTER.

ASTER DAISY = *Chrysanthemum arcticum.*

ASTER FAMILY. *See* COMPOSITAE.

asterias (as-teer′i-as). Star-like.

ASTERMUM. *See* CALLISTEPHUS.

asteroides (as-ter-roy′deez; but *see* OÏDES). Like an aster.

ASTILBE (as-til′be). A genus of spirea-like herbs, of the family Saxifragaceae, widely grown as handsome border perennials and much forced by florists who commonly, but incorrectly, sell them as spirea. They superficially resemble the genus *Aruncus,* but the latter have many stamens, while *Astilbe* has 8–10. Leaves simple,* or twice- or thrice-compound,* the ultimate leaflets cut or toothed. Flowers mostly unisexual.* Petals 4–5, sometimes lacking, white, pink, or reddish. Pistils* 2 or 3. Fruit a group of follicles.* (*Astilbe* is Greek for not shining, in allusion to the leaflets.)

The astilbes are fine garden plants of easy culture in any ordinarily good soil. Their flowers, while small, are borne in profuse, spire-like clusters, blooming mostly in June, but often continuing to August. For forcing in the greenhouse the roots should be potted up in the fall and held in a pit or cold frame. When brought into a moderately warm greenhouse, give plenty of water and allow about 12 weeks until blooming time.

arendsi. *See* ASTILBE DAVIDI.

astilboides. A Japanese herb 2–3 ft. high. Leaves twice- or thrice-compound,* the ultimate leaflets ovalish, sharply toothed, 1½–2½ in. long. Flowers white in dense, spike-like clusters, which are grouped into a panicle.* Often sold as *Aruncus astilboides* and *Spiraea astilboides.*

chinensis. Resembling *A. japonica,* but with a more open flower cluster. Flowers white, but rose-tinged, in short spikes. China. Summer.

davidi. A very showy Chinese herb 4–6 ft. high. Leaves compound,* the leaflets resembling an elm leaf, coarsely toothed, about 2 in. long. Flowers rose-pink (but the anthers*

blue), clustered in long, narrow panicles 12–20 in. long. Under the name of *A. arendsi,* hybrids of this and other species comprise very fine plants, with flowers ranging from purple to white. Some of the best named forms are Meta Immink, America, Gloria, Gruno, Queen Alexandra, and Rose Pearl. *See* PINK GARDEN.

japonica. A Japanese herb 1–3 ft. high. Leaves twice- or thrice-compound,* the ultimate leaflets lance-oval, wedge-shaped at the base, sharply toothed. Flowers white, in terminal, spire-like clusters, or a few clusters in the leaf axils.* A good house plant.

simplicifolia. A low Japanese herb, seldom over 12 in. high. Leaves simple, more or less oval, deeply cut, 2–3 in. long. Flowers white, in slender, narrow clusters. Less showy than the others.

astilboides (as-til-boy′deez; but *see* OÏDES). Like a plant of the genus *Astilbe.*

ASTRAGALUS (as-trag′a-lus). An enormous genus of vetch-like herbs of the pea family scattered over most of the world. Of the 1500 known species, which include some of the cattle-poisoning locoweeds of the West, only a handful are of secondary garden interest. They have alternate,* compound* leaves and small, pea-like flowers in clusters. Fruit a legume,* smaller than in the garden pea. The plants are often called milk vetch. (*Astragalus* is an old Greek name for some shrub, and of uncertain application here.)

The species below are occasionally seen in the border or rock garden. They do not stand transplanting very well and are best raised from seed, but these germinate slowly and poorly. The roots may also be divided, but with care, and see that some of the old soil is transplanted with the divided clump to the new site.

austrinus. A half prostrate or straggling annual or biennial herb 8–12 in. high. Leaflets about ¼ in. long. Flowers purple, in close, head-like clusters (racemes*). Southwestern U.S. and Mex. July.

drummondi. A perennial herb 15–24 in. high, the foliage hairy. Leaflets about ½ in. long. Flowers cream-yellow, in clusters (racemes*) 2–4 in. long. Rocky Mountains. July.

hypoglottis. A low, somewhat prostrate herb scarcely exceeding 6 in. in height. Leaflets numerous (19 or more), oblongish, about ⅓ in. long. Flowers bluish-purple, in small, spike-like clusters that are rarely over 1 in. long. Eu. July. The best-known of the cult. species and sometimes grown in pots for its attractive bloom. Perhaps referable to *A. agrestis, A. goniatus,* or *A. danicus,* none of which are cult. in this country.

mexicanus. Not Mexican but a prairie plant found wild from Ill. to Tex. Perennial, more or less straggling, its leaflets ¼–½ in. long. Flowers cream-white, but blue at the tip. July.

ASTRANTIA (as-tran′she-a). A small group of Eurasian perennial herbs of the carrot family, one commonly cult. as a garden plant for its attractive flower clusters. They have aromatic roots and compound* leaves, with the leaflets arranged finger-fashion, or the upper leaves may be nearly simple.* In both there is a wide-margined or winged* leafstalk. Flowers small (for details *see* UMBELLIFERAE), in tiny umbels,*

---

* Special articles on the subjects indicated by an asterisk (*) will be found at the words so marked.

beneath which are bracts° that often exceed the umbel in length and are attractively colored. (*Astrantia* is derived from *Aster*, in allusion to the star-like bracts.)

The plant below is of the easiest cult. in any ordinary garden soil. It is attractive in June, with its numerous umbels° of small flowers set in the center of the star-like bracts.° Best propagated by division of its roots.

major. Masterwort. A stout plant 2–3 ft. high. Leaves chiefly basal, the 3–5 leaf segments (leaflets) deeply lobed or toothed. Flower clusters (umbels°) pinkish-rose or white, the bracts° beneath usually purplish. Eu.

ASTROPHYTUM (as-trow-fy'tum). A small genus of Mexican cacti, cult. in succulent gardens for their curious, globose or flattened, rarely cylindric, habit. The plant body is ribbed or winged, often giving the plants a star-like appearance, hence their general name of star cactus. They have a few weak spines, or none. The large, quickly fading flowers are borne at the top of the plant; in ours yellow or orange. Fruit fleshy. (*Astrophytum* means star-like plant.) For culture and uses see CACTI.

asterias. Plant body about 3 in. wide, scarcely 1 in. high, with 8 ribs, but no spines, woolly in scattered tufts. Flowers yellow, about 1 in. wide. Mex. and N. Mex.

capricorne. Biznaga. Plant nearly globe-shaped, rarely cylindric, about 8 in. high, usually with 7 or 8 deep ribs. Spines nearly 2 in. long, weak or sometimes wanting. Flower lemon-yellow, about 2½ in. long, its numerous petals spreading, orange at the base.

myriostigma. Mitra. Not over 2 in. high, the globose plant body suggesting a bishop's hood. Ribs mostly 5, lacking spines. Flowers orange-yellow, about 2 in. long, the petals brown-tipped.

ornatum. The most ornamental of the hort. species. Plant body nearly globe-shaped, 10–15 in. high, covered with whitish tufts of hair. Ribs usually 8, armed with spines about 1 in. long. Flowers lemon-yellow, about 3½ in. long and showy.

asturica, -us, -um (as-toor'i-ka). From or near Asturias, Spain.

atalantioides (at-a-lan-te-oy'deez). Like a plant of the non-hort. genus *Atalantia*.

ATAMASCO. North American Indian name for *Zephyranthes Atamasco.*

ATAMASCO LILY = *Zephyranthes Atamasco.*

Atamosco. An untenable generic name (derived from atamasco) for *Zephyranthes.*

ATHEL TREE = *Tamarix aphylla.*

ATHYRIUM (a-thir'i-um). A very large genus of ferns, separated only by technical characters from *Asplenium,* and found almost throughout the world, chiefly in warm regions. Fronds (in ours) once- or twice-compound,° the ultimate leaflets numerous. (*Athyrium* is from the Greek for oblong shield, in allusion to the spore cases.)

The only fern of much garden interest is *A. Filix-femina,* the lady fern, widely grown for ornament in many hort. forms. For cul-

ture and uses see FERNS AND FERN GARDENING.

acrostichoides = *Athyrium thelypteroides.*

angustifolium = *Athyrium pycnocarpon.*

Filix-femina. Lady fern. A delicate, feathery, very popular fern with bright green fronds 24–30 in. long and twice-compound.° Ultimate leaflets very numerous, generally deeply cut or toothed, but of infinite variety in the many hort. named forms, some crested and crisped. Nearly throughout N.A.; also (perhaps a different form), in Eu. and As. Very variable and much cult.

pycnocarpon. Swamp spleenwort. A hardy fern with fronds 18–24 in. long, only once-compound,° the ultimate leaflets nearly 4 in. long, narrow, and nearly without teeth, short-stalked. In rich woods, eastern N.A. Often called A. *angustifolium.*

thelypteroides. Silvery spleenwort. A hardy fern, the fronds 20–30 in. long, twice-compound, on long, yellowish-green stalks. Ultimate leaflets very numerous, toothed. In rich woods, eastern N.A. Sometimes known as A. *acrostichoides.*

atlantica, -us, -um (at-lan'tick-a). From or near the Atlantic; also from Mt. Atlas.

ATLAS CEDAR = *Cedrus atlantica.*

ATRIPLEX (at'ri-plex). A large genus of herbs and salt-tolerant shrubs, of the goosefoot family, of wide distribution. One is a secondary garden vegetable, several are troublesome weeds, and A. *breweri* is a Californian shrub. Leaves mostly alternate,° or rarely opposite,° often mealy or whitish. Flowers inconspicuous, mostly unisexual,° in simple or branched clusters (for flower structure see CHENOPODIACEAE). Fruit dry, partly or wholly hidden by the persistent, tiny bracts.° (*Atriplex* is Greek for orach.) The wild (not hort.) shrubs of the West are commonly called greasewood or saltbush. Some of the wild species are useful in the re-vegetation of arid regions. See also SAND GARDEN.

The garden orach, whose herbage is used like spinach, is an annual whose seeds should be sown in spring in drills 8 in. apart, and thinned, when about 2 in. high, to 6 in. apart in the row. The leaves should be used while young, as they become stringy and tough when old. *Atriplex breweri* is useful for seaside planting along the coast of southern Calif., and for hedges in dry regions of the Southwest.

breweri. Quail-brush. A shrub 3–5 ft. high. Leaves oval or oblongish, silvery-gray, 1–2½ in. long. Southern Calif.

hortensis. Garden orach. A stout, annual herb 1–3 ft. or more. Leaves somewhat triangular or arrow-shaped, or heart-shaped, short-stalked, 4–5 in. long, varying from yellow-green to pale red. As. Sometimes called sea purslane, and mountain or French spinach.

patula. See Orach in the list at WEEDS.

atriplicifolia, -us, -um (at-ri-pli-si-fō'li-a). With leaves like a saltbush (*Atriplex*).

atrocarpa, -us, -um (at-ro-kar'pa). With blackish fruit.

atrocaulis, -e (at-ro-call'is). With blackish (or dark) stems.

° Special articles on the subjects indicated by an asterisk (°) will be found at the words so marked.

ATROPA (at'ro-pa). A genus of only two species of Eurasian herbs of the potato family, the one below a dangerous garden plant, for its berries are poisonous and its sap yields the drugs atropine and belladonna. Leaves large, alternate,* without marginal teeth. Flowers bell-shaped, the calyx* enlarging in fruit, the corolla with 5 rather pointed, short, recurved lobes. Fruit a berry. (Named for Atropos who cut the thread of life.)

Belladonna can be grown in any ordinary garden soil and propagated by division of its roots. The percentage of the alkaloid in its sap, however, under American conditions, does not warrant its culture for atropine. It appears to prefer limestone soils, and north of zone* 4 is apt to be winter-killed. *See* MEDICINAL PLANTS.

Belladonna. Belladonna. A perennial herb 2–3 ft. high. Leaves more or less oval, 3½–5 in. long. Flowers nodding, singly or in pairs, purplish-red, about 1 in. long. Berry black, about ½ in. in diameter, poisonous. Eurasia.

atropunicea, -us, -um (at-ro-pew-niss'i-a). Dark red or dark reddish-purple.

atropurpurea, -us, -um (at-ro-pur-pure'-ee-a). Dark purple.

atrosanguinea, -us, -um (at-ro-san-gwin'-ee-a). Deep blood-red.

atrovirens (at-ro-vy'rens). Dark green.

ATTALEA (at-tay'lee-a). A genus of tropical American feather palms, only one of which is likely to be cult., and this only in frost-free parts of Fla. Leaves compound,* long, graceful, and curving outward at the tip. Leaflets often standing edgewise on the main leafstalk. Flower cluster from among the crown of leaves, issuing from an erect, boat-shaped spathe,* the latter recurved. Flowers unisexual,* mostly yellow. Fruit (in ours) a short-beaked, fibrous-coated drupe,* its nut very hard. (*Attalea* is from the Latin for magnificent.)

The cohune palm can only be grown outdoors in zone* 9, where it prefers low, rich soils. It is too big for pot or tub culture.

Cohune. Cohune palm. An erect palm 50–60 ft. high, with a ringed trunk. Leaves in a tremendous terminal crown, each leaf often 20 ft. long. Leaflets 30–50 pairs, each leaflet about 18 in. long, the leafstalk flat above and rounded beneath. Flower cluster 4–5 ft. long. Fruit about 3 in. long. Central America.

ATTAR OF ROSES. *See* ROSA ALBA SUAVEOLENS and R. DAMASCENA.

attenuata, -us, -um (at-ten-u-ā'ta). Narrowed to a point.

attica, -us, -um (at'tick-a). From Athens, Greece.

AUBERGINE. *See* EGGPLANT.

AUBRIETA (au-bree'sha). A small genus of Old World perennial herbs of the mustard family, the only hort. species very popular as a mat-forming plant for edgings, the rock garden or the open border. They have more or less crowded leaves and relatively large 4-petaled flowers in short terminal clusters (*see* CRUCIFERAE for details). Fruit an oblong pod. (Named for Claude Aubriet, French natural history painter.) The name is sometimes spelled *Aubrietia* and *Aubretia*.

For culture and uses *see* ROCK GARDEN.

deltoidea. Purple rock cress. Usually 3–6 in. high. Leaves more or less triangular, hairy, with one or two teeth, scarcely 1 in. long. Flowers typically purple or violet, the petals with a stalk-like base. Fruit about ½ in. long. Italy and Greece. June. There are many varieties and named forms, some dwarf, others with larger flowers or bigger leaves, and some with pink flowers.

aubrietoides (au-bree-toy'deez; but *see* OÏDES). Like the purple rock cress (*Aubrieta*).

AUCUBA (aw-kew'ba). A small genus of Asiatic, evergreen shrubs, family Cornaceae, very popular as foliage plants, especially for city window boxes in the North, and in the cool greenhouse. Leaves opposite,* without marginal teeth or distantly toothed. Male and female flowers on different plants, small and greenish or red. Fruit a usually orange or scarlet berry. (*Aucuba* is a Latinized form of the Japanese vernacular name for these plants.)

The species below is widely grown by florists for decoration, in the cool greenhouse and in potting mixture* 4. Grown mostly as a pot plant, and propagated by cuttings of half-ripened wood, taken when convenient, and rooted in a cutting bench under glass. The plant is perfectly hardy outdoors from zone* 5 southward, and often in sheltered parts of zone* 4 where it often merely winter-kills without protection. It prefers half-shade and plenty of moisture. Greenhouse plants should be plunged* outdoors in the summer.

japonica. Japanese or Japan laurel. Shrub 4–15 ft. high in the wild, usually much smaller as cult. Leaves glossy, dark green, more or less oval, 4–8 in. long, rather distantly toothed. Berry mostly scarlet, and not produced without male plants. Eastern As. The *var.* **variegata,** often called the gold-dust tree, has yellow-spotted leaves. There are other varieties with narrower leaves, with coarse teeth, and otherwise marked.

Aucuparia (aw-kew-pay'ri-a). A specific name implying bird-catching, from the use of the fruits for this purpose. *See* MOUNTAIN-ASH.

AUDIBERTIA (o-di-ber'shee-a). A genus of mostly Californian perennial herbs or under-shrubs of the mint family and closely related to, and perhaps not distinct from, *Salvia.* They have roughish, opposite, often woolly or hairy leaves, and irregular, 2-lipped flowers in mostly terminal but not profuse clusters. Calyx deeply cleft, almost spathe*-like. (Named for Urbain Audibert, French botanist.) By some the ones below are considered as of the genus *Salvia.*

The plants, commonly called sage in Calif., are cult. more there than in the East, for ornament and A. *stachyoides* as an important

---

* Special articles on the subjects indicated by an asterisk (*) will be found at the words so marked.

bee plant. They are of easy cult. and may be propagated by division.

grandiflora. Crimson sage, called also bee sage. A sticky-hairy perennial 1–3 ft. high. Leaves woolly or felty on the under side, more or less arrowhead-shaped, 3–7 in. long. Flower 1–1½ in. long, crimson-purple or red, the bracts* crowded and showy. Calif.

polystachya. White sage, called also grease-wood (but not the true greasewood). A shrubby herb 4–8 ft. high, its foliage densely white-hairy. Flowers ½–¾ in. long, white, Calif.

stachyoides. Black sage. A stiff, perennial herb 2–3 ft. high and one of the important Calif. bee plants. Leaves green above, grayish beneath, oblongish and short-stalked, 2–3 in. long. Flowers about ⅛ in. long, white or lilac. Calif.

aurantiaca, -us, -um (aw-ran-ty'a-ka). Orange-colored.

aurantifolia, -us, -um (aw-ran-ti-fō'li-a). With leaves like the orange.

Aurantium. An old generic and specific name for the Seville or sour orange.

aurata, -us, -um (aw-ray'ta). Golden.

aurea, -us, -um (aw'ree-a). Golden.

aureo-maculata, -us, -um (aw-ree-o-mac-kew-lay'ta). Golden-spotted.

aureo-marginata, -us, -um (aw-ree-o-mar-ji-nay'ta). Golden-margined.

aureo-regina, -us, -um (aw-ree-o-re-jine'a). Golden queen.

aureo-reticulata, -us, -um (aw-ree-o-re-tick-ew-lay'ta). With golden veins.

aureosulcata, -us, -um (aw-ree-o-sul-cay'-ta). With yellow grooves.

aureo-variegata, -us, -um (aw-ree-o-vair-ee-i-gay'ta). With golden markings.

AURICLE. An ear-shaped organ, often surrounding a leafstalk; or partly sheathing a flower cluster; or an ear-shaped appendage to a petal.

Auricula. A pre-Linnaean* name for plants now included in *Primula.* See PRIMULA AURICULA.

auriculata, -us, -um (aw-rick-kew-lay'ta). Eared; *i.e.,* auricled.

aurita, -us, -um (aw-ry'ta). Eared; *i.e.,* auricled.

australasica, -us, -um (os-tray-lay'zi-ka). From Australasia.

AUSTRALIAN. Many plants from Australia and neighboring islands, wholly unrelated to European plants which they recalled, were, by early settlers, named Australian beech, etc. Of the hundreds so called the following are found here:

Australian beech = *Eucalyptus polyanthemos;* Australian bluebell creeper = *Sollya heterophylla;* Australian brush-cherry = *Eugenia paniculata australis;* Australian fan palm = *Livistona australis;* Australian honeysuckle (*see* BANKSIA); Australian laurel (*see* PITTOSPORUM); Australian lilac = *Hardenbergia monophylla;* Australian oak family = PROTEACEAE; Australian pea = *Dolichos lignosus;* Australian pine (*see* CASUARINA); Australian rye grass = *Lolium multiflorum;* Australian tea-tree = *Leptospermum*

laevigatum; Australian umbrella tree = *Schefflera actinophylla.*

australis, -e (os-tray'lis). Southern.

austriaca, -us, -um (os-try'a-ka). From Austria.

AUSTRIAN BRIER = *Rosa foetida.*

AUSTRIAN COPPER BRIER = *Rosa foetida bicolor.*

AUSTRIAN PINE = *Pinus nigra.* See PINE.

austrina, -us, -um (os-try'na). Southern.

autumnalis, -e (aw-tum-nay'lis). Autumnal.

AUTUMN CROCUS. See COLCHICUM.

AUTUMN FOLIAGE. The fall color of foliage is most gorgeous in the plants of eastern North America and eastern Asia, and it is from these two regions that the gardener must get his best autumnal foliage plants.

Mixing autumn foliage in the border or in vistas requires just as much care as mixing flower color. Taste and individual preference will dictate what one plants. It is well to remember, however, that it is possible to overdo the brilliant scarlet of Japanese barberry, and that a judicious mixture of evergreens, both conifers and broad-leaved evergreens, will help any group planted for autumn color effects.

Some plants not in the tabulation below are planted for their gay twigs, especially Tatarian dogwood of eastern Asia and the native American red dogwood, but these are not primarily fall foliage plants.

From the segregation of colors below, the skillful gardener may get almost any effect within the range from bright scarlet to brown. Scores more could be cited, but the following are the easiest grown and provide all that one needs for autumn foliage effects.

RED OR SCARLET. Sassafras, red maple, sumac, Japanese barberry, red oak, scarlet oak, pin oak, flowering dogwood, sweet gum, sour gum, Virginia willow, and a few native blueberries.

BRONZE. Many broad-leaved evergreens, such as *Mahonia,* some rhododendrons, *Leucothoë, Pieris, Arctostaphylos,* and *Galax.* Some of these will stay green in protected or warm places but become bronzy in exposed or cold sites.

YELLOW OR ORANGE. Sugar maple, Norway maple, *Ginkgo,* larch, witch-hazel, persimmon, moosewood (*see* MAPLE), yellowwood, cucumber tree, wild red cherry, tuliptree, and some wild hickories.

Less showy are the brownish or neutral shades of many oaks, the elms, and hosts of common trees. For other autumn effects in the garden, *see* AUTUMN GARDEN, and the section headed Food Supply in the article BIRDS.

AUTUMN GARDEN. The autumn garden may be marked by opulence of bloom and richness of color if planting is done with this end in view. There are fewer flowering plants and shrubs to call upon than are available in the earlier seasons, but those blossom-

---

* Special articles on the subjects indicated by an asterisk (*) will be found at the words so marked.

ing at the later date are in the main characterized by luxuriance of habit and warmth of hue. Many annuals and perennials linger over from the late summer and add a valuable quota to the autumn assemblage, but the majority of the annuals will be cut off by the early frosts, and reliance should be placed chiefly upon such hardy plants as sunflowers, ironweed, Michaelmas daisies, heleniums, aconites, Japanese chrysanthemums and Japanese anemones, colchicums and rudbeckias whose brightness outlasts many frosts and some of which continue to bloom well on toward December. To increase the splendor of the autumn garden free use should be made of such trees and shrubs as bear decorative fruits or whose foliage colors handsomely. See AUTUMN FOLIAGE.

The autumn-flowering bulbs should also be more widely employed than is commonly the custom. These include *Colchicum, Crocus,* and *Sternbergia.* For the best results they should be planted as early in August as they may be procured.

AUTUMN-FLOWERING PLANTS AND BULBS. *Aconitum autumnale,* 4–5 ft. dark blue, *A. fischeri,* 4 ft. bright blue; *Allium stellatum,* 2 ft. rose; *Anemone japonica* vars., 2–5 ft. pink, rose-white; *Artemisia vulgaris,* 4 ft. cream; *Aster acris* vars. lavender, *A. Amellus,* in varieties of mauve, rose, violet, *A. cordifolius,* 3–5 ft. small flowers, white, lilac, pale rose, *A. ericoides,* 2–3 ft. small flowers, pale blue, white, *A. novae-angliae,* 3–5 ft. purple, deep rose, pink, *A. novi-belgi,* 2–3 ft. all tones of rose, pink, lavender, mauve, purple and white, *A. tataricus,* 6 ft. lavender; *Ceraostigma plumbaginoides,* 18 in. pure blue; *Chrysanthemum arcticum,* 18 in. white, *C. nipponicum,* 2 ft. white, *C.* Japanese vars. white, yellow, orange, bronze, russet, rose, pink; *Cimicifuga simplex,* 3 ft. white; *Colchicum* species and vars., autumnale, bornmuelleri, speciosum, white, rose, purplish; *Cosmos,* 4–6 ft. pink, rose, white; *Crocus* species, longiflorus, nudiflorus, pulchellus, sativus, speciosus, zonatus, white, mauve, lavender, violet; *Dahlias,* many vars. all colors, sizes and heights; *Eupatorium rugosum,* 4 ft. white; *Gentiana andrewsi,* 18 in. blue; *Helenium autumnale rubrum,* 5 ft. russet; *Helianthus* (see SUNFLOWER) Miss Mellish, 6 ft. yellow, *H. maximiliani,* 8 ft. orange-yellow (the latest to flower), *H. salicifolius* 6–8 ft. orange-yellow; *Helleborus niger,* 12–18 in. white; *Hosta lancifolia tardiflora,* 18 in. lavender-blue (see PLANTAIN-LILY); *Kniphofia Uvaria grandiflora* and other species and vars. orange, scarlet, yellow; *Liriope Muscari variegata,* 1 ft. blue; *Lobelia Cardinalis,* 2 ft. scarlet; *Oxalis bowieana,* 1 ft. pink; *Phlox* Jeanne d'Arc, 4–5 ft. white; *Rudbeckia laciniata hortensia,* 6 ft. yellow; *Sedum sieboldi,* pink, *S. spectabile,* 18 in. pink; *Solidago* species and vars. yellow; *Sternbergia lutea,* 6–8 in. yellow; *Tricyrtis hirta,* 2–3 ft. purplish; *Tritonias,* scarlet, orange, yellow; *Vernonia altissima,* 8 ft. purple.

SHRUBS. *Abelia chinensis,* 4–6 ft. pinkish; *Caryopteris incana,* 3–4 ft. lavender or white; *Clerodendron trichotomum,* 10 ft. white; *Elsholtzia stauntoni,* 5 ft. lilac-purple; *Hamamelis virginiana,* 15 ft. yellow; *Lespedeza thunbergi,* 4–5 ft. rose-purple; *Vitex Agnus-castus,* 10 ft. blue. — L. B. W.

Besides autumn foliage effects and the plants listed above, there is a group of shrubs and trees that add color to the fall by their fruits. All those below will be found in their proper place in the ENCYCLOPEDIA and are listed here by color of their fruits, berries or seeds. There are many others but these are the most easily cult.

RED AND SCARLET

Berberis thunbergi	Ilex verticillata (see
Cornus florida	HOLLY)
Cotoneaster divaricata	Ilex opaca (see
Cotoneaster horizon-	HOLLY)
talis	Rosa rugosa
Euonymus atropur-	Viburnum trilobum
pureus	and V. Opulus

ORANGE AND YELLOW

Hippophae rhamnoides	Malus arnoldiana
Crataegus tomentosa	Celastrus scandens

BLUE OR BLUISH-BLACK

Cornus alternifolia	Symplocos paniculata
Cornus rugosa	Viburnum cassinoides
Vaccinium corym-	Viburnum dentatum
bosum	Viburnum prunifolium
Clerodendron tricho-	
tomum	

LILAC OR PURPLE
Callicarpa

AUTUMN PLANTING. Because the season is waning, and dormancy instead of a mass of growth is to follow, fall or autumn is an ideal time to do much planting that the spring rush has left undone.

This applies to most woody plants, except plane trees (*Platanus*), tulip-tree and magnolias, and to the division of many perennial herbs. Of course such work should be completed before hard freezing weather is to be expected, and for the dates of this see the article on your own state.

Within the category of fall planting comes the late summer or early fall planting of coniferous evergreens and such broad-leaved evergreens as *Rhododendron, Kalmia, Pieris, Leucothoë,* and many others. These can be moved with success between Aug. 20 and Sept. 20 nearly throughout zones* 3, 4, and 5. That gives them time to become established before hard frost is to be expected.

Most deciduous* woody plants should not be moved until their foliage is well colored or better yet, dropping. For a general timetable of fall work, as distinguished from autumn planting *per se, see* the fall months at GARDEN CALENDAR.

AUTUMN SQUASH = Winter Squash. See SQUASH.

AUXINS. See HORMONES.

avellana, -us, -um (a-vel-lan'a). From Avellino, in Campania, Italy.

AVENA (a-vee'na). The oats are chiefly agricultural grasses of little interest to the gardener. They are mostly Old World annual plants with flat, grass-like leaves and bristly, long-awned,* usually hanging spikelets which are grouped in loose clusters

---

* Special articles on the subjects indicated by an asterisk (*) will be found at the words so marked.

(panicles*). Fruit the familiar oat, or a modification of it. (*Avena* is Latin for oat.)

The common oat is often a weed in gardens, but easy to control because of its annual habit. Winter oats are hardy strains for autumn planting, maturing the following spring. All others are spring-planted annuals.

fatua. Wild oat. A Eurasian, oat-like grass, 3–4 ft. high. Leaves 6–9 in. long, ¼–½ in. wide. Spikelets drooping, rather broad, grouped in stout panicles* 8–12 in. long. Naturalized on the Pacific Coast.

sativa. The common oat. Foliage resembling A. *fatua,* but the leaves more or less rough. Flower cluster (panicle*) terminal, its flattish, long-awned spikelets spreading on all sides, except in the variety known as side oats, where the spikelets are arranged on one-sided clusters. A cultigen,* perhaps derived from A. *fatua.*

sterilis. Animated oat. A shorter grass from the Mediterranean region, grown chiefly for its curious spikelets, which twist or move when exposed to sudden moisture, due to the hygroscopic action of its awns.* It has a twisted stem.

AVENS. See Geum.

AVERAGE BEARING AGE. *See* Garden Tables I.

AVERRHOA (a-ver-rō′a). A small genus of Asiatic trees, family Oxalidaceae, the one below somewhat planted in Fla. (zone* 9 only) for its pleasant, quince-scented fruit. Leaves alternate,* compound,* the leaflets arranged feather-fashion. Flowers small, fragrant. Petals 5. Stamens 10, five shorter than the other five. Fruit fleshy, drooping. (Named for Averroes, Arabian philosopher.)

The tree needs rich soil and plenty of rainfall. It is propagated by shield-budding or by seeds.

Carambola. Carambola. A symmetrical tree 20–30 ft. high. Leaflets 5–9, increasing in size toward the tip of the leaf, 1–2 in. long, closing when touched or at night. Flowers in the leaf axils,* not over ¼ in. long, white, but purple-marked. Fruit yellowish-brown, smooth-skinned, about 4 in. long, nearly egg-shaped, 3–5-angled or ribbed, thus star-shaped in cross-section. Pulp watery, somewhat acid-sweet, used fresh or for jellies. Malayan region. Like the jackfruit, the fruit is apt to be borne on old wood. *See* Cauliflory.

AVERY ISLAND. *See* No. 16 at Garden Tours.

avicularis, -e (a-vick-kew-lā′ris). Relating to birds.

avium (ā′vee-um). Of the birds; a not inappropriate specific name for the cherry.

AVOCADO (*Persea americana*). This fruit holds high rank among the tropical food fruits and is now extensively cult. in both Fla. and Calif. *Persea* is native to tropical America and, according to place of origin, is divided into the Mexican (var. *drymifolia*), Guatemalan, and West Indian groups or races. The trees require a warm climate, but the races differ somewhat in cold resistance, their hardiness being in the order named. In their native habitats, the trees are not grown in orchards but as scattered seedlings, and it was not until their introduction into the U.S. that orchard plantings were made and propagation of varieties initiated.

The avocado's popularity, especially as a salad fruit, is steadily increasing, and it is now classed as a staple article of diet rather than a novelty. Containing from 7 to 23 per cent fat, 1.5 per cent protein and above 1.5 per cent mineral matter, it is of high nutritional value. The fat percentage varies with variety; highest in the Mexican and lowest in the West Indian races.

In Fla., the West Indian and Guatemalan varieties are chiefly grown, and in Calif. mainly those of the Mexican and Guatemalan races. Fruits of the 3 races are distinct in general appearance, shape, size, fat content, and season of maturity. Wide variation in season gives a succession of ripening fruit extending from early summer until late spring. It has been found that non-setting of fruit is due mainly to an unusual sex-reversal of the flowers that prevents pollination. The difficulty is overcome by interplanting compatible varieties to insure cross-pollination. Varieties have been classified as either "a" or "b" (as below), and selections from the two classes should be interplanted. Of the numerous varieties, the following are among the most popular:

West Indian (season July into Oct.) — Pollock (b), Waldin (a), Trapp (b); Guatemalan (Dec. into Mar.) — Taylor (a), Nabel (b), Hass (?); Mexican (June into Oct.) — Gottfried (a), Puebla (a), San Sebastian (b); Hybrids (Nov. to Feb.) — Booth 8 (b), Lula (a), Fuerte (b).

The trees are adapted to a wide range of soils, but must have an ample supply of soil moisture coupled with good underdrainage. Fertilizers are required. Heavy mulching with organic litter has been especially beneficial, and growing leguminous cover crops is practiced. Planting distances vary with variety, but about 20 × 20 ft. with 30-ft. rows for roadways at intervals is now recommended. Propagation is by seeds and shield-budding or cleft- and side-grafting, the latter method now superseding the former. Nursery stock is propagated for the most part in plant boxes instead of the nursery row to overcome loss in transplanting. — G. D. R.

The large central seed of the avocado fruit, if suspended in a glass of water (by toothpicks or string), will easily germinate if the bottom of the seed is kept just at water-level. When roots develop the seedling should be potted up in potting mixture* 2. It will, in a sunny window, grow into a thriving house plant.

Insect Pests. Several scale insects and whiteflies, often injurious, are controlled by superior oil emulsion sprays of 1.3% oil or pesticide #21 (*see* Sprays and Dusts) or by oil-malathion combination. Red mites are controlled by pesticide #9 dust or by wettable pesticide #9 sprays. Red-banded and greenhouse thrips are best controlled by pesticide #18 or #1 close to harvest. A leaf roller and

---

* Special articles on the subjects indicated by an asterisk (*) will be found at the words so marked.

leaf-eating beetles are controlled with pesticide #19 or #1.

DISEASES. Among the troubles found are scab which attacks the young foliage, shoots and fruits; blotch on foliage and fruits; and powdery mildew* on foliage. All are controlled by use of pesticide #3 (see SPRAYS AND DUSTS). Scab-susceptible varieties need 5 or 6 applications at 3- to 4-week intervals. Varieties not scab-susceptible require only 2 or 3 applications at monthly intervals.

AWL-SHAPED. Gradually tapering from a thickened base to a slender, often prickly, tip, like an awl.

AWN. A bristle-like appendage, sometimes hair-like or stiff, found in the spikelets of certain grasses (oat, etc.), on the fruits of other plants, or even on anthers.

AWNLESS BROME GRASS = *Bromus inermis.*

AXIL. Classically an armpit; in modern botany and hort. the point at which a stalk or branch diverges from the stem or axis to which it is attached. Many flower clusters are borne in leaf axils.

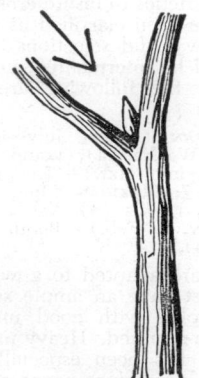

The arrow points to the axil.

axillaris, -e (ax-il-lar'is). Axillary, *i.e.,* borne in an axil.*

AXIS. The main stem of a plant or a flower cluster. The trunk is the axis of a pine tree.

AXONOPUS (ax-o-nō'pus). A small genus of mostly tropical grasses of no hort. interest except for **A. furcatus,** the carpet grass, which is widely used in the South for places where better lawn grasses will not grow. It is a perennial grass which spreads by stolons,* has narrow, grass-like, flat leaves about 4 in. long and ¼ in. wide, and 1-sided clusters of spikelets. It is native from Va. to La. and tropical America; formerly called *A. compressus.* For its use *see* Lawn Mixtures at LAWN. (*Axonopus* is from the Greek for axis and foot, in allusion to the creeping stolons.*)

AXSEED = *Coronilla varia.*

AYRESHIRE ROSE = *Rosa arvensis ayreshirea.*

AZALEA (a-zay'lee-a). A group of well-known garden shrubs and trees of the heath family, perhaps not technically different from *Rhododendron* (which see), but kept distinct from that genus by most gardeners, and here. There are many species and named forms, comprising some of the handsomest flowering shrubs in the world. All are natives of the north temperate zone, chiefly N.A. and eastern As. Leaves alternate* and stalked. Flowers more or less irregular,* usually in terminal, umbel*-like clusters, the stamens often far-protruding. Fruit a dry pod (capsule*), splitting lengthwise, the seeds very numerous and small. (*Azalea* is Greek for dry, in allusion to the old, and false, idea that the plants require dry sites.)

For culture *see* below.

amoena = *Azalea obtusa amoena.*

arborescens. Tree azalea. A native, deciduous* shrub 8–20 ft. high. Leaves more or less oblong, hairy on the margins, 1½–2½ in. long. Flowers funnel-shaped, about 2 in. long, fragrant, white or pinkish, and hairy on the outside. Mountain woods Pa. to Ga. and Ala. Hardy from zone* 4 southward. June.

calendulacea. Flame azalea. A native, deciduous* shrub 6–12 ft. high. Leaves broadly elliptic, 2–3 in. long. Flowers 5–7 together, blooming after the leaves unfold, yellow, orange or scarlet, not fragrant, sticky-hairy on the outside, the stamens* much protruding. Mountains, Pa. to Ga. May–June. One of the most magnificent native shrubs and known in many hort. forms. Often sold as *A. lutea.* Zone* 4 and southward.

californica = *Azalea occidentalis.*

canescens. Mountain azalea. Native American, deciduous* shrub 6–12 ft. high. Leaves oblong or broader above, 2½–4 in. long, grayish-hairy beneath. Flowers nearly odorless, blooming with or before the leaves unfold, pink or white, funnel-shaped, about 1½ in. long. Md. to Fla. and eastern Texas. May. Hardy from zone* 5 southward.

daurica = *Rhododendron mucronulatum.*

gandavensis. Ghent azaleas. A group of hort. important azaleas derived by hybridizing native American species and some from the Old World. There are hundreds of named forms, many of them of unknown parentage, although *A. japonica* is often involved. *See* below.

hinodegiri = *Azalea obtusa* var. *hinodegiri.* One of the Kurume azaleas with scarlet flowers.

indica. A race usually called Indica azaleas and derived from a mixture of Japanese and Chinese species. *See* below at Azalea Culture.

japonica. A Japanese deciduous* shrub 2–5 ft. high. Leaves 2–4 in. long, hairy on the margin. Flowers narrowly bell-shaped, only slightly irregular, orange to scarlet, about 1½ in. long, but numerous, the stamens within the corolla. Hardy from zone* 4 southward. May.

kaempferi = *Azalea obtusa kaempferi.*

ledifolia = *Azalea mucronata.*

lutea. A deciduous shrub, 6–8 ft. high (less as cult.), sticky-hairy when young. Leaves oblong, hairy on the margins and on both sides, sticky when young. Flowers fragrant, numerous, funnel-shaped, yellow, about 2½ in. wide, the stamens* much protruding. May. Eurasia. Hardy from zone* 5 southward. The name *lutea* is often used, incorrectly, for *A. calendulacea.*

---

* Special articles on the subjects indicated by an asterisk (*) will be found at the words so marked.

macrantha. Leaves glossy-green above, pale beneath, 2–3 in. long. Flowers usually 1 or 2 together, broadly funnel-shaped, nearly 3 in. across, white or pink. June. Hardy from protected places in zone* 4 southward. Perhaps only a var. of A. *indica*.

maxwelli. Form of the Indica azaleas. *See* below.

mollis. A beautiful Chinese deciduous* shrub, 2–4 ft. high, with golden-yellow flowers, the young branches hairy. Leaves oblongish, 4–6 in. long, gray and hairy on the under side. Flowers broadly funnel-shaped, about 2 in. wide. Hardy from sheltered places in zone* 4 southward. May.

mucronata. An evergreen, Chinese shrub, 4–6 ft. high, with brilliantly white, fragrant flowers. Leaves more or less elliptic, 1½–2½ in. long, matted with dense, gray or brownish hairs. Flowers 1–3 in a cluster, nearly 2 in. wide. Hardy from sheltered places in zone* 4 southward. May. A very popular azalea with double, and often variously colored flowers in some hort. varieties. It is often sold as A. *ledifolia*.

mucronulata = *Rhododendron mucronulatum*.

nudiflora. Pinkster-flower. A native American shrub, 2–5 ft. high, deciduous,* and growing naturally in rich woods. Leaves green both sides, elliptic or oblongish, 2–4 in. long. Flowers 6–10 in a cluster, appearing before the leaves, pink or whitish-pink, about 1½ in. wide, the stamens* far-protruding. Eastern U.S. Hardy from zone* 4 southward. May. There are white and rose-colored hort. varieties, and the closely related A. *rosea*, with pink flowers, is also cult. It is perhaps only a var. of A. *nudiflora*.

obtusa. In its wild state (seldom cult.) a half-evergreen Japanese shrub 12–30 in. high, and much-branched. Leaves shining dark green above, hairy on the midrib beneath, more or less elliptic, ¾–1 in. long. Flowers 2–3 in a cluster, orange-red or red, about 1½ in. wide. Hardy from zone* 5 southward. Apr.–May.

From this plant many hort. important varieties have been derived by selection and hybridization, largely in Japan. From near Kurume, Japan, have come a beautiful series known as Kurume azaleas. (*See* below.) Some well-known varieties are: *var.* hinodegiri, brilliant scarlet; *var.* amoena, with magenta, often double flowers, and hardier than the typical species; *var.* kaempferi, often called Kaempfer's azalea, with larger and reddish-pink flowers. The number of named, mostly Japanese, forms is legion.

occidentalis. A native American, deciduous* shrub 5–9 ft. high. Leaves oblongish, but with a small, prickle-like point, 2–4 in. long. Flowers white or pinkish, yellow-blotched, about 2 in. wide. Ore. and Calif. Hardy from zone* 5 southward. June–July. Foliage yellow or scarlet in autumn.

pontica = *Rhododendron ponticum*.

poukhanensis = *Azalea yedoensis poukhanensis*.

praecox = *Rhododendron praecox*.

prunifolia. A native, smooth shrub, its bright green, oblongish leaves 1½–4 in. long. Flowers crimson, only 4–5 in a cluster, slightly hairy on the outside, and the latest of all native azaleas to bloom. In southwestern Ga. and much prized there. July–Aug. Hardy from zone* 6 southward.

racemosa. *See* RHODODENDRON RACEMOSUM.

rosea = Perhaps only a form of A. *nudiflora* with rose-colored flowers.

rosmarinifolia = *Azalea mucronata*.

schlippenbachi. A deciduous* shrub 9–15 ft. high. Leaves clustered at the ends of the twigs, green above, pale beneath, ovalish but broader toward the short-pointed tip, 3–5 in. long. Flowers pink, brown-spotted, 3–6 in a cluster, about 2½ in. wide. Eastern As. Hardy from zone* 4 southward. May.

vaseyi. One of the finest native shrubs, 6–12 ft. high, with deciduous* foliage. Leaves oblong or elliptic, 3–5½ in. long, hairy-margined. Flowers distinctly 2-lipped, light rose color, but spotted with orange or brownish-orange, about 1½ in. long. N. Car. Hardy from zone* 4 southward. Apr.–May.

viscosa. White swamp azalea, commonly called swamp honeysuckle. A deciduous* shrub 6–10 ft. high. Leaves ovalish, 1½–2½ in. long, green both sides. Flowers 4–9 in a cluster, glandular-hairy, white or faintly pinkish, very fragrant, nearly 2 in. long, the stamens far-protruding. Swamps and bogs, Me. to Tenn. and Ohio. June. Hardy from zone* 3 southward. There is a variety with rose-colored flowers, and another with bluish-gray foliage.

yedoensis. Korean azalea. A deciduous* or half-evergreen shrub 2–3 ft. high. Leaves narrowly elliptic, 2–3 in. long, pointed both ends, dark green above, paler beneath, evergreen southward. Flowers 1–3 in a cluster, double, rosy-lilac and purple-spotted, about 1½ in. long. Eastern As. Hardy from zone* 5 southward. Often sold as A. *yodogava*. A fine, taller variety, with larger, single, fragrant flowers and more hardy than the type, is var. **poukhanensis**. There are also many named forms.

yodogava = *Azalea yedoensis*.

Most of the above azaleas are unsuited to regions where the rainfall is below 25 in. per year. See the name of your state for rainfall figures in your locality.

AZALEA CULTURE

From the gardener's viewpoint azaleas fall into two sections, deciduous and evergreen, although some of the latter become deciduous, at least in part, if they are grown at the northern limit of their hardiness. In the first group are our native species, several Oriental species, and one from Europe, as well as the garden races resulting from their interbreeding; the second section is essentially Oriental, though most of the races resulting from interbreeding have been produced in Europe and in the United States. All are acid-soil plants, the deciduous species usually more strictly so than the evergreen sorts. They range in size from small, almost prostrate shrubs to tall, slender, almost tree-like forms.

Because of their preference for the humus-rich top layers of soil, they produce relatively shallow, fibrous root masses that are impatient of dry soil conditions, although many of the deciduous forms can adapt themselves to such, if the conditions are uniform throughout the year. All form their flower buds in late summer and early autumn, and some, which are hardy to cold as bushes, have flower buds that succumb to extreme temperatures in the North. Our American species have tubular flowers with five expanded lobes and conspicuously protruding stamens and pistils that add to the beauty of the flower masses. Many of them bloom just be-

---

* Special articles on the subjects indicated by an asterisk (*) will be found at the words so marked.

fore the leaves or with them, though a few are summer-flowering. In color they fall into two series, one white through pink to deep rose-pink, the other white through yellow and orange to deep brick-red or even darker. In many there is a blotch of contrasting color, usually yellow, on the upper lobe.

The Oriental species and their hybrids have wider, more bowl-shaped flowers with the typical five lobes, and range in color from pale yellow to orange and salmon-reds. The conspicuous exception is *A. schlippenbachi,* with exquisite pink flowers that resemble a much enlarged flower of our native *A. vaseyi.*

From the intercrossing of our American species with *A. mollis* and *A. japonica,* and with some use of the Eurasian *A. lutea,* have come the races known as the Ghent azaleas, the Knaphill and Exbury sub-races, all of which are more cold-resistant than the parents, and have far more brilliant flowers. Their limitations in the South have not yet been fully worked out, but in most cases there is not a sufficiently long season of continuous cold to allow them to make normal growth.

The evergreen section has provided some of the most spectacular of all garden shrubs. Many have been in cultivation for more than two hundred years and still are not well known. This section has also provided material for many lines of breeding work in Europe, Japan, and this country. The most widely grown is the group known as the Kurume azaleas, so named for the city where they were first collected in Japan, a somewhat mixed group with probably the interbreeding of several closely related Japanese species. The plants are compact, with fine evergreen foliage, and produce great masses of small flowers, beginning to bloom when very small plants. Colors range from white through every degree of pink to deep crimson, and through lavenders to red-purples. The blooms may be either single or hose-in-hose.* Combined with the florists' tender Belgian azaleas they have given rise to the Pericat azaleas, a few of which have become standard garden plants in the South and florists' plants in the North. Some have been used in the Glenn Dale azaleas, the hybrids from Gable and Yerkes, as well.

Like the Gable azaleas, and to a degree like some of the Yerkes plants, the Glenn Dale azaleas represent a planned effort to produce cold-hardy azaleas that would approximate the size and beauty of the Southern Indicas, recognizing the fact that the latter are no longer widely known in the South or equally large and beautiful among themselves. They were selected after the most critical examination and test for the climatic zone of Washington, D.C. They have proved successful much farther south and, in some clones,* farther north than was originally expected, but have failed at each extreme in hands of persons who insisted on trials. Many represent the best opportunity for extending seasonal bloom, various

heights not obtainable before, and a diversity of color and color-pattern that are not found in other groups of evergreen and semi-evergreen azaleas in the areas for which they were bred.

The other Oriental species that have been important plants in this country are *A. obtusa kaempferi, A. mucronata, A. macrantha, A. yedoensis,* and the somewhat mongrel race known as the Southern Indicas, actually the forerunners of the present-day florists' azaleas from Belgium and nearby countries. *A. yedoensis* is best represented by its single form, *poukhanensis,* and provides fine lavender flowers and a fair show of autumn color in its leaves that are semi-deciduous. Kaempfer's azalea is the most cold-hardy and if grown from seed will yield plants with considerable color variation, all within the field of salmon-red and pink and some variation in flowering times. *A. mucronata* and its several forms give fine white flowers, as well as some tinted with rose and with a blotch of deeper rose. *A. macrantha* is valued chiefly for its late bloom, after all other evergreen azaleas have finished, as well as some dwarf forms, with double flowers. To it are allied the lovely macrantha hybrids from Japan, all late-blooming, many dwarf in stature, and with a fine range of colors. The most commonly met variety is Gumpo, though it is not the best of the many that may be found under the heading of "Chugai" azaleas, an unfortunate term that should be abandoned for the Japanese term "satsuki" azaleas.

The Southern Indicas are the early hybrids from Europe that have long been abandoned there and replaced by the later hybrids now known as the florists' Belgian azaleas. Southern Indicas range in color from white through pinks to lavenders and purples with some startling reds. They vary in hardiness even in the South. The Belgians are impatient of cold and succeed out of doors only in some portions of the Deep South and California. They are mostly used as pot plants in the cool portions of the greenhouse.

All azaleas can be raised from seed, from layers, both branch and mound, and, in the evergreen section, from cuttings of half-ripe wood in sand or sand and peat mixture. A gentle bottom-heat hastens rooting, which occurs along the stem and not at a joint or node. Selected forms of deciduous azaleas can be increased from grafts in winter on seedling stock or piece roots. A few can be raised from cuttings, particularly from certain clones,* and from young basal shoots. Garden forms of azaleas do not come true from seed.

Although all azaleas require considerable moisture, evenly supplied, especially after flowering when new shoots are forming, it is best to reduce watering outdoor plants as summer advances to check new growth and insure ripening of the wood, which will help against bark splitting in winter.

While all flourish in full sun, a light pass-

* Special articles on the subjects indicated by an asterisk (*) will be found at the words so marked.

ing shade overhead helps to prevent sunburning of the delicate colors. None flower freely in dense shade.

All may be grown in pots, and brought into bloom in winter, if they are forced slowly and at relatively low temperatures, which will prevent dropping of foliage and assure an even and simultaneous development of the flowers.

All respond to pruning if this is necessary to check irregular growth. It should be done just after blooming to insure formation of new shoots with flower buds and to insure ripening of the wood. Fertilizer should be given just after blooming time to induce new growth and the proper formation of flower buds. The common combinations of 5–10–5 and cottonseed meal serve well enough, but any fertilizer that has all the proper elements, and will not leave an alkaline residue, will serve. If one needs to increase acidity more than is done by the use of acid leaf mulches and acid peat, a dusting of sulphur will serve well. In areas where the ground is neutral or alkaline, azaleas can be grown if one is willing to make a raised bed with the proper soil and to keep constant watch on the reaction, correcting as needed. The one problem that faces the gardener in heavy soils is that of drainage, for a well-prepared bed in a heavy soil area may serve as a catch basin for soil moisture with harmful results, the solution being a drain away from the bottom of the bed. Humus should be added every year, as leaf mulch or peat moss. The goal should be a soil mixture that will remain moist on a uniform level but never be sodden. — B. Y. M.

The American Rhododendron Society (which includes interest in azaleas) issues a quarterly bulletin and may be addressed at Box 162, Brooks, Oregon. For those who want a more complete account of *Azalea* than is possible here, *The Azalea Book* by Frederick P. Lee is highly recommended. It was issued by the American Horticultural Society, Washington, D.C., in 1958.

INSECT PESTS. Lace bugs stipple leaves by feeding punctures, and stain lower surface of leaves with excrement. Control with pesticide #1 or #21 (*see* SPRAYS AND DUSTS). The latter is also effective against red spiders, a whitefly, leaf miners and leaf-tying caterpillars. *See* RHODODENDRON for boring caterpillars.

DISEASES. For diseases common to both azalea and rhododendron, *see* RHODODENDRON. A disease more common on the azalea is the pinkster gall which causes bladder-like galls on leaves and flowers. These fungus galls are green at first but soon turn pinkish-white. If only a few are present, pick and burn them. If the disease is serious a single application of pesticide #5 (*see* SPRAYS AND DUSTS), just before growth begins in the spring, will give excellent control.

A disease serious in southeastern states is flower spot or petal blight. The fungus causes a sudden browning and collapse of flowers. Sprays of pesticide #11 give excellent control but must be repeated about every 3 days during the blossoming period.

AZALEAMUM. A cushion chrysanthemum.

AZARA (a-zah′ra). A small genus of mostly Chilean evergreen shrubs or vines, family Flacourtiaceae, the two below grown for ornament in Calif., rarely under glass. Leaves leathery, alternate,* short-stalked, one of the stipules* enlarged and leaf-like. Flowers small, fragrant, greenish-yellow, without petals, but with 4–5 persistent sepals. Fruit a berry. (Named for J. N. Azara, Spanish patron of botany.)

The second species is often trained as a vine in Calif., and is handsome in fruit. They need open sunlight and are propagated by seeds or cuttings of ripe wood.

gilliesi. A shrub 8–12 ft. high. Leaves broadly oval, 2½–3 in. long, with coarse, spiny teeth. Flowers in nodding heads. Chile. Blooms Feb.–Mar. in Calif.

microphylla. A sprawling, but erect, shrub 6–12 ft. high, often trained to cover walls. Leaves ½–¾ in. long, somewhat toothed, shining. Clusters few-flowered. Fruit orange. Chile. Flowers in Feb. and Mar. in Calif. Hardy, in the East, from sheltered places in zone* 5 southward.

Azedarach. A pre-Linnaean* name for the China-tree (*see* MELIA).

AZOLLA (a-zol′la). A small genus of minute, floating aquatic, flowerless plants, family Salviniaceae, the one below of little garden interest except to make attractive floating patches on the surface of pools or aquaria. They grow so rapidly and so close together that *Azolla* may also become a scum-like nuisance if not kept in check. The plants have minute stems, fleshy, 2-lobed leaves, upon which the microscopic spores* are borne. (*Azolla* is Greek for destroying by drying.)

caroliniana. Appearing like a reddish, moss-like patch. Plant body scarcely ½ in. long, the leaves much smaller. Its spore characters are technical and microscopic. In quiet water nearly throughout eastern U.S.

azorica, -us, -um (a-zaw′ri-ka). From the Azores.

AZTEC MARIGOLD = *Tagetes erecta.* *See* MARIGOLD.

azurea, -us, -um (a-zoor′ee-a). Sky-blue.

---

* Special articles on the subjects indicated by an asterisk (*) will be found at the words so marked.

B

B & B = Ball and burlap method of handling nursery stock. *See* PLANTING.

BABIANA (bā-bi-ā′na). A genus of chiefly South African herbs of the iris family, comprising over 30 species, of which one is sometimes grown in greenhouses, or outdoors in frost-free regions, for its showy flowers. Leaves mostly basal and sword-shaped, hairy in the one below. Flowers nearly regular, in lax clusters, the slender corolla tube broadening into 6 segments. Stamens 3. Fruit a dry pod (capsule*), splitting into 3 segments. (*Babiana* is from the Dutch for baboon, since baboons eat the corms.) The plants are sometimes called baboon-root. The culture is the same as for *Freesia*.

stricta. A corm*-bearing herb 8–12 in. high, the corm covered with fibers. Leaves shorter than the stem, hairy. Flowering stem slightly twisted, bearing 1–3 spike-like but few-flowered clusters. Flowers red (lilac, blue or yellow in some of the named forms), about ¾ in. long. S. Af. Spring-blooming.

BABOON-ROOT. *See* BABIANA.

BABY BLUE-EYES = *Nemophila menziesi.*

babylonica, -us, -um (bab-i-lon′i-ka). From ancient Babylon, now near Bagdad.

BABY PRIMROSE = *Primula forbesi.*

BABY RAMBLER = *Rosa chinensis minima.*

BABY'S-BREATH. Usually applied to *Gypsophila paniculata* and related species; also to *Galium Mollugo* and *Muscari.*

BABY'S-SLIPPERS = *Lotus corniculatus.*

BABY-TEARS = *Helxine soleiroli.*

baccata, -us, -um (bak-kay′ta). Baccate; *i.e.,* a berry, or berry-like.

BACCHARIS (bak′kar-is). A very large genus of American shrubs, family Compositae, chiefly inhabitants of salt marshes or alkali deserts and of little garden interest except for similar sites. Leaves thick and more or less fleshy. Flowers very small, yellowish or dirty-white, all tubular and crowded in small heads, the fruiting of which is a white and rather showy collection of pappus* bristles (*see* COMPOSITAE for details). (The plants commemorate Bacchus, but without much signification.)

The first species is a salt-marsh shrub useful for seaside planting, less so in ordinary garden soil, although it will grow there if given open sunshine. The last two are Californian species somewhat grown there for ornament, and unsuited to most of the country. All are easily propagated by cuttings and may be dug from the wild.

halimifolia. Groundsel bush or groundsel tree. A much-branched shrub 6–10 ft. high.

Leaves oblongish, short-stalked, 1–3 in. long, wedge-shaped at the base and coarsely toothed, more or less resinous. Flower heads about ¼ in. long, crowded in dense clusters, the fruiting head snowy-white. Mostly in brackish marshes. N. Eng. to Tex.

pilularis. Kidneywort; called also coyote-brush, chaparral broom, and squaw waterweed. An evergreen shrub 2–3 ft. high. Leaves nearly stalkless, broadest toward the tip, scarcely 1 in. long, toothed. On dry hills and dunes, Ore. to Calif.

viminea. Mule-fat; called also guatemote. A leafy, branching shrub, 4–8 ft. high. Leaves willow-like, oblongish, 1–3 in. long (more on sterile shoots). Flowering cluster leafy, the heads in close clusters, which are grouped in a branching inflorescence.* In river-beds, Calif.

BACHELOR'S BUTTON = *Centaurea Cyanus;* also *Bellis perennis,* and *Gomphrena globosa.*

BACK-BULB. One of the old, usually leafless pseudobulbs of an orchid.

BACKCROSS. Result of a hybrid crossed on one of its parents.

BACKYARD GARDEN. The majority of city soils are sour. A soil test will determine the degree of sourness, thus indicating the amount of lime required to sweeten it. (*See* ACID AND ALKALI SOILS.) If the ground is filled with débris, excavate to a depth of approximately one foot in places where you desire plantings; fill in with fresh soil. An excellent mixture is one-third loam, one-third well-rotted manure, and one-third leaf mold. (If unable to obtain manure use a commercial substitute.) After the beds have settled, top-dress with lime if the soil mixture is acid.

Should the ground be merely hard-packed and uncultivated, dig it deeply. In digging, keep the topsoil on one side and the subsoil on the other side of the opening. Loosen up the packed earth at the bottom, then refill with alternate layers of manure and subsoil. Then finish filling in the topsoil. Do not plant until the beds are well settled.

Watering should always be done after sundown, and a thorough soaking given. Sponging off the leaves of broad-leaved evergreens with water to remove soot and grime will often prolong their life. Use a fine overhead spray in order thoroughly to cleanse all the foliage. Plants mentioned in this article are selected because of their suitability for city conditions in the northeastern part of the U.S., especially for their smoke-resistant qualities.

Desirable vines are *Akebia,* trumpet-creeper, *Clematis paniculata,* English ivy, wisteria, and *Polygonum auberti.* Broad-leaved evergreens, such as *Ilex crenata, Mahonia Aquifolium,* and *Pyracantha coccinea,* provide excellent winter effects. The

---

* Special articles on the subjects indicated by an asterisk (*) will be found at the words so marked.

ailanthus is the tree most commonly seen. Smaller trees and shrubs, as hawthorn, magnolia, Cornelian-cherry, Ibota privet, mockorange, common lilac, and snowberry, may be used.

A garden with little or no direct sunlight will sustain only a limited variety of plants. A grass plot is almost an impossibility. Ground covers, such as English ivy, *Pachysandra terminalis,* and *Vinca minor,* may be substituted. Tuberous-rooted begonias, English daisies, annual ageratum, foxgloves, and garden pinks will grow in partial shade.

In a garden with a certain amount of full sunlight numerous aquatics may be grown in a lily pool. Annuals may be bought in flats ready to set out or grown direct from seed. Potted plants and evergreens may always be used for fillers, but they are usually costly, unless bought in special group collections at reduced prices.

If the garden is very small, leave the central plot open. Plant it with grass or ground cover or pave with old flags. Small succulents and tufts of turf may be planted between the flags. *See* PAVEMENT PLANTING. Encourage moss to grow on the paving, as it will absorb the strong sunlight. Plant perennial borders on three sides with iris, peonies, and phlox, to obtain a long succession of bloom and attractive foliage. *Phlox subulata,* pansies, and violets may be used as edgings and ground covers. Small shrubs should be planted at irregular intervals in the background. The following are attractive both winter and summer: *Acanthopanax sieboldianus,* Japanese barberry, *Cornus alba sibirica,* Japanese flowering quince, forsythia, bush honeysuckle, and the mountain currant. For a list of specially smoke-resistant woody plants, *see* SMOKE.

Garden furniture and decorations must conform to the general type of garden created, as an unwise selection creates discord. —G. E. *See also* PLANNING THE HOME GROUNDS and SHADY GARDEN.

The Department of Horticulture of Cornell University has issued valuable lists of plants suited to the unfavorable conditions of the average city backyard in the northeastern states. With some modifications they are listed below. All are treated in more detail at the different articles on the genera mentioned.

SHADE-ENDURING WOODY PLANTS FOR USE IN CITY GARDENS

Acer Negundo	Lonicera japonica halliana
Aesculus parviflora	Lucium halimifolium
Aronia arbutifolia	Mahonia Aquifolium
Celastrus orbiculatus	Pachysandra terminalis
Clematis paniculata	Polygonum auberti
Cornus	Rhamnus cathartica
Euonymus japonicus	Ribes alpinum
Euonymus fortunei	Symphoricarpos orbiculatus
Forsythia	
Hamamelis virginiana	Viburnum acerifolium
Hedera Helix	Viburnum dentatum
Ilex crenata	Vinca minor
Lindera Benzoin	

DRY-SOIL-ENDURING WOODY PLANTS FOR USE IN CITY GARDENS

Actinidia arguta	Mahonia Aquifolium
Ailanthus altissima	Philadelphus (see
Amorpha fruticosa	MOCK-ORANGE)
Berberis thunbergi	Phlox subulata
Campsis radicans	Polygonum auberti
Caragana arborescens	Pyracantha coccinea
Catalpa bignonioides nana	Rhamnus cathartica
	Rhodotypos scandens
Celastrus orbiculatus	Rhus typhina
Cornus Mas	Ribes
Cornus racemosa	Sophora japonica
Elaeagnus angustifolia	Spiraea Bumalda
Forsythia	Symphoricarpos orbiculatus
Hamamelis virginiana	
Hibiscus syriacus	Syringa vulgaris
Ligustrum	Ulmus pumila
Lonicera	Wistaria sinensis
Lycium halimifolium	

BEST VINES FOR USE IN CITY GARDENS

Actinidia arguta	Lonicera henryi
Akebia quinata	Lonicera japonica halliana
Campsis radicans	
Clematis paniculata	Parthenocissus
Euonymus fortunei	Polygonum auberti
Hedera Helix	Wistaria sinensis

SIX GOOD GROUND-COVER PLANTS FOR USE IN CITY GARDENS

Euonymus fortunei minimus	Pachysandra terminalis
	Rosa wichuraiana
Hedera Helix	Vinca minor
Iberis sempervirens	

BACTERIA. Microscopic, one-celled organisms, the cause of most diseases in man, animals, and plants, and popularly called microbes. While many of them are baleful, not a few are of the utmost use to the gardener, because some of them inhabit soils and greatly aid, with fungi, in the decomposition of vegetable matter into humus. Perhaps their most important garden use is the ability of some kinds to aid plants of the pea family in gathering nitrogen from the air (for which *see* LEGUME INOCULATION).

BADIAN. *See* ILLICIUM VERUM.

BADMINTON. A lawn game, the court of which is 44 × 17 ft., or 20 ft. for doubles.

BAERIA (bay'ri-a). Californian yellow-flowered herbs, commonly called goldfields, the two below grown as annuals for their profuse bloom. There are over 20 species, family Compositae, and all have opposite leaves and flower heads with both ray and disk flowers. (Named for K. E. von Baer, Russian naturalist.)

Both species are hardy annuals, the seed of which should be sown where the plants are needed. *See* ANNUALS. The plants are sometimes offered as *Hymenoxis.*

coronaria. A low, weak annual, scarcely exceeding 8 in. in height and used for edging. Leaves compound,* the leaflets arranged feather-fashion, the ultimate segments narrow. Flower heads about ½ in. wide, yellow. Calif. Sometimes known as *Actinolepis coronaria* and as *Shortia californica.*

macrantha. Erect, often unbranched annual, 12–18 in. high. Leaves simple,* very narrow,

---

* Special articles on the subjects indicated by an asterisk (*) will be found at the words so marked.

3–4½ in. long, toothed and hairy on the margin. Flower heads about 1 in. wide, yellow. Calif.

BAG-FLOWER = *Clerodendron thomsonae.*

BAHAMA GRASS = *Cynodon Dactylon.*

baicalensis, -e (by-kal-en'sis). From Lake Baikal, Siberia.

BALAKA (ba-lah'ka). A genus of palms once thought to be in cult. in the U.S. but probably most plants so called are in reality *Ptychosperma elegans* (which see). Plants are sometimes offered as *Balaka seemanni,* but belong to *Ptychosperma.*

BALCONY PETUNIA. *See* PETUNIA.

BALD CYPRESS = *Taxodium distichum.*

baldensis, -e (ball-den'sis). From Mt. Baldo, Italy.

baldschuanica, -us, -um (bald-shoo-ăn'i-ka). From Baldschuan, Bokhara.

balearica, -us, -um (bal-ee-ă'ri-ka). From the Balearic Islands, near the Mediterranean coast of Spain.

BALISIER = *Heliconia Bihai.*

BALL AND BURLAP. *See* PLANTING.

BALL FERN = *Davallia bullata.*

BALLOON-BERRY = *Rubus illecebrosus.*

BALLOON-FLOWER = *Platycodon grandiflorum.*

BALLOON-VINE = *Cardiospermum Halicacabum.*

BALLOTA (bal-low'ta). A genus of 30 species of Eurasian perennial herbs, of the mint family, of little garden interest except for the black horehound, a moderately decorative plant. It has opposite, toothed leaves, a square stem, and small, 2-lipped, irregular* flowers in dense whorls clustered in the leaf axils,* or rarely terminal. (*Ballota* is Greek for the black horehound.)

The black horehound is of the easiest culture in almost any garden soil, and is naturalized* or an escape* in the eastern U.S.

nigra. Black horehound; called also fetid horehound. A strong-smelling, erect, and hairy herb 15–20 in. high. Leaves ovalish, 2–3 in. long. Flowers reddish-purple or paler, about ½ in. long. Eu. June.

BALM. *See* MELISSA. *See also* for plants sometimes called balm, MONARDA, NEPETA, COLLINSONIA, and MOLUCELLA.

BALM-OF-GILEAD = *Populus candicans.*

BALM-OF-HEAVEN = *Umbellularia californica.*

BALSAM. *See* FIR (*Abies balsamea*) for the tree so called. For the garden balsam *see* IMPATIENS.

BALSAM APPLE = *Momordica balsamina.*

balsamea (ball-sam'ee-a). A specific name derived from the genus *Balsamea,* which is of no hort. interest.

BALSAM FAMILY = Balsaminaceae.

BALSAM FIR = *Abies balsamea. See* FIR.

balsamifera, -us, -um (ball-sam-if'fera). Balsam-bearing.

balsamina, -us, -um (ball-sam-eye'na). Balsam or balsam-like.

BALSAMINACEAE (ball-sam-i-nay'see-e). The jewelweed or balsam family contains only two genera, one of which, *Impatiens,* comprises nearly 300 species, among which are our common jewelweeds (or touch-me-not) and a handful of garden balsams. All are rather weak, soft, almost succulent herbs with stalked leaves. Flowers very irregular,* one of the usually 3 sepals petal-like and produced into a long spur. Fruit (in *Impatiens*) an elastically explosive pod (capsule*) that discharges its seeds if touched when ripe.

Technical flower characters: Sepals 3, two of them small and green, the third petal-like and spurred. Petals 5, but often appearing as if three by the union of two pairs. Ovary 5-celled, many-ovuled, the style short and produced into 5 stigmas.

Balsamita. A pre-Linnaean* name for certain plants with the odor of balsam.

BALSAM PEAR = *Momordica Charantia.*

BALSAM POPLAR. *See* POPULUS.

BALSAM TREE FAMILY = Guttiferae.

baltica, -us, -um (ball'tick-a). From the region of the Baltic Sea.

BALTIC IVY = *Hedera Helix baltica.*

BAMBOO. True bamboos are tall, woody, hollow-stemmed grasses of imposing aspect and multifarious uses in regions where they thrive. They belong to the genus *Bambusa* (which see), are nearly all tropical, and grow to such size and with such speed (a foot a day in favorable places) that they are difficult to manage in all but the loftiest greenhouses. Their outdoor culture in U.S. is mostly confined to zone* 9 and to especially sheltered places in zone* 8, although some of the cult. species can be grown up to the limits of zone* 5.

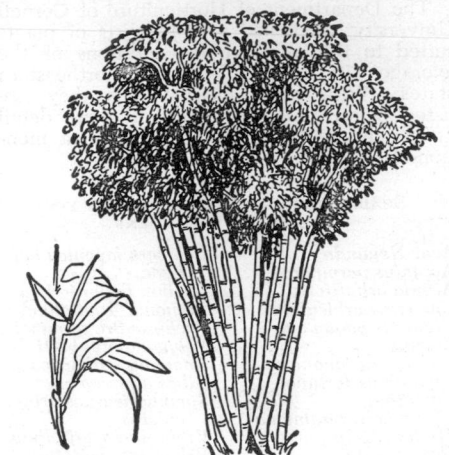

A clump of bamboos and a spray of their foliage

---

* Special articles on the subjects indicated by an asterisk (*) will be found at the words so marked.

The name bamboo is also, somewhat loosely, applied to many other tall-growing, woody grasses, closely related to *Bambusa*, and popularly mistaken for that genus. Some of these are much more hardy than the tropical bamboos, and are widely planted for ornament in many parts of the U.S. For these, and other bamboo-like grasses, *see* ARUNDINARIA, DENDROCALAMUS (mostly tropical), and PHYLLOSTACHYS. For a totally unrelated plant sometimes called bamboo *see* POLYGONUM CUSPIDATUM.

Bamboos, in the broad sense, supply planting material which is duplicated by no other plants. Their tall stems, feathery and handsome foliage, and their slender, arching, often grouped trunks make garden pictures of great beauty. In the tropics, where they frequently reach a height of 100 ft., they make majestic clumps impossible to reproduce in the U.S. But on a reduced scale the same effects may be gained by selecting species from the genera named above.

For the culture of both the tropical and half-hardy sorts *see* GRASSES.

BAMBOO FERN = *Coniogramme japonica*.

BAMBUSA (bam-boo′sa). The true bamboos comprise a large genus of often gigantic, woody, hollow-stemmed, Old World, and chiefly tropical grasses, grown for ornament and for innumerable construction uses in the tropics. The usually polished, hollow stems are interrupted by a partition at the joints which conspicuously ring the trunk. Some species have a few spines on the stem. Leaves short-stalked, parallel-veined or, in some species, netted-veined. Flowers (rarely produced in cult. specimens) in few or many-flowered spikes, which are bunched on the branches of the cluster (panicle°). Stamens 6. Fruit dry, thin-walled (a caryopsis°). (*Bambusa* is a Latinized version of the Malayan vernacular for these plants.)

For culture and uses, *see* GRASSES. The technical names of the bamboos are confusing. Some authorities consider that certain species belong to the genera *Sasa* or *Pleioblastus*, not here maintained. For other grasses, also called bamboo, see ARUNDINARIA, DENDROCALAMUS, and PHYLLOSTACHYS.

disticha. A dwarf species rarely over 3 ft. high. Stems slender, often zigzag, green or tinged with purple. Leaves 2–2½ in. long and about ½ in. wide, minutely toothed on the edges, netted-veined, and borne in paralleled, 2-ranked rows. Japan. Hardy from zone° 5 southward.

multiplex. A rather slow-growing bamboo from Cochin-China, 12–15 ft. high. Stems thick, terete, only thinly clothed with linear, flat, reddish-green leaves that are about 6 in. long. Good for hedges but tardy in growth, especially when young. Not certainly hardy north of zone° 6.

nana. A yellow-stemmed bamboo 8–15 ft. high. Leaves bluish-gray, rough on the edges, 2–3 in. long, scarcely ⅓ in. wide. A very handsome plant with hort. varieties having also variegated (yellow and silvery) leaves. China. Hardy from zone° 5 southward.

palmata. A purple-stemmed grass 3–8 ft. high. Leaves green above, pale bluish-green beneath, about 8 in. long and 2½ in. wide. Japan. Hardy from zone° 5 southward.

vulgaris. The commonest bamboo of the tropics and often reaching (there) a height of 100 ft. It has yellowish stems, often banded lengthwise. Leaves green both sides, 8–10 in. long, about 1 in. wide, and smooth-margined. Probably a native of Java, and will stand no frost.

bambusoides (bam-boo-zoy′deez; but *see* OÏDES). Resembling a bamboo.

BANANA (*Musa sapientum*). Bananas are native to southeastern As. and are now cult. throughout the tropics. They are among the best-known of tropical fruits, and have become a staple food fruit of temperate climates, their popularity being due to their high food value and agreeable flavor, coupled with the year-round season of ripening and availability at all times through refrigerated transportation facilities. Banana culture within the continental U.S. is limited to peninsular Fla., with an occasional plant grown as an ornamental in protected situations in southern Calif. and the coastal area of the Gulf states. Fruit is rarely produced outside of Fla., and there only in local commercial quantity, since severe damage accompanies temperatures below freezing.

The banana plant is large, herbaceous, and tree-like. It suckers freely, but usually only 2 to 4 stalks are allowed to grow in a clump. Each stalk fruits but once, after which it is cut to the ground. New stalks, arising as suckers, give a succession of ripening fruit. In adapted situations growth is rapid and the first fruit matures from 12 to 14 months after planting.

Of the several tall-growing varieties, the Lady Finger (Hart's Choice) is the most popular, with the Apple, Orinoco (horse-banana), and Red Jamaica grown in limited number. Gros Michel, principal commercial variety of the western tropics, is seldom planted. The Cavendish or Chinese banana (*M. cavendishi*), often called dwarf banana, is considered the most resistant to cold and wind and is widely planted; it is but 5 to 7 feet tall, stout-stemmed, and produces good quality but easily bruised fruit.

Fertile, porous soils with a goodly content of organic matter are best suited. The plants require much moisture, but must have adequate drainage, and thrive best in full sun with protection from wind. Heavy mulching and fertilizers are beneficial. Planting distances vary from 8 to 14 or more feet, according to variety and soils. Propagation is by suckers or by sections of the stem "bulb." — G. D. R.

INSECT PESTS. A black snout beetle, the grub-like larva of which bores in the corms, is found in some places in the U.S. Adults may be collected by baits of banana stem. Insect-free planting stock should be used, and the old, dried, outside leaves removed from the plants.

DISEASES. The most serious disease of ba-

° Special articles on the subjects indicated by an asterisk (°) will be found at the words so marked.

nana is wilt* which may kill entire plantings. Soil should be kept in excellent cultural condition and lime should be added where soil is acid. Certain varieties are more resistant to wilt and should be grown according to local recommendations.

Other diseases present on banana are root and stem rot, Moko disease, Sigatoka disease, bonnygate disease, and black head. Aside from suggestions made for wilt control, few preventative measures can be recommended. Spraying with pesticide #3 has been advised in the case of Sigatoka disease.

BANANA FAMILY = Musaceae.

BANANA-SHRUB = *Michelia fuscata.*

BANEBERRY. *See* ACTAEA.

BANGALAY = *Eucalyptus botryoides.*

BANKING. The heaping-up of soil to preserve moisture or coolness in cultivating some crops like potatoes. Or the similar heaping of earth around celery (which see) to aid blanching.*

BANKS. Banks or abrupt slopes are sometimes essential to take care of differences in grade, and other times deliberately created for effect.

When limited space requires that a bank occupy the minimum area it may be as steep as one foot perpendicular to one and one-half feet horizontal. This rate of slope is very difficult to maintain and should be avoided whenever possible. If it must be used it should be planted with a rank, close-growing ground cover such as *Lonicera japonica halliana.* Since the rainfall which accumulates on the bank itself will wash out the planting, no bank of this steepness should exceed eight feet in height without rip-rap protection.

Rip-rap protection is flat field stone almost buried at right angles to the slope of the bank and paralleling the longitudinal direction. Another form of cheap, effective rip-rap is to half bury six-inch logs, paralleling the longitudinal direction of the bank, holding the logs in place by stakes driven down to the top of the logs on the lower side. If the bank is too stony to permit driving wooden stakes, use three-quarter-inch iron pins. Vines planted above these logs will soon cover them, giving the effect of a completely green bank. Locust logs are the most durable, but any wood which will last long enough for the plants to become well established will serve the purpose.

The most commonly used slope for banks where economy of space is necessary is one foot vertical to two feet horizontal. Any extension of slopes beyond these dimensions is unnecessary except for special purposes or appearance. If a bank is to be walked over without steps the minimum slope should be one foot vertical to six feet horizontal.

All banks should avoid a sharply defined edge at the top and bottom. These sharp edges are extremely difficult to maintain and are rarely justified for design effect. Moisture does not reach the grass or plants at the extreme sharp edges of a bank and natural wear and tear breaks down such edges. The ideal bank has a rolled top and bottom, forming a broad letter "S" by the junction of the top and bottom curves with the normal slope of the bank. Do not exaggerate the top curve so that it overhangs the normal slope. Both top and bottom curves should merge easily with the main slope.

For slopes steeper than one foot vertical to three feet horizontal, ground-cover vines or compact cover plants are preferable to turf, which is difficult to mow and water satisfactorily. Types of plants for banks should be of compact growing habit with no tendency to get leggy as they mature. If rank, tall-growing plants are used and kept cut back they ultimately become stubby and unattractive. Ground covers such as myrtle (*Vinca minor*), *Lonicera japonica halliana*, and prostrate roses are most suitable for steep slopes.

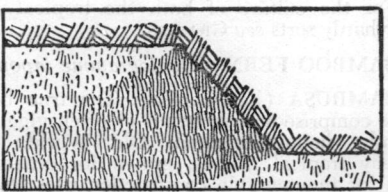

Above — an incorrect bank with sharp edges

Below — a correct one with rolled or rounded edges

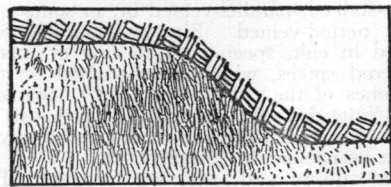

On more gradual slopes such plants as matrimony vine (*Lycium halimifolium*), weeping golden bell, Japanese barberry, Regel's privet, and fragrant sumac (*Rhus aromatica*) are satisfactory. So is *Jasminum nudiflorum*, if it is hardy in your region. *See* JASMINUM.

Pocket planting, which consists of preparing a separate hole of proper size for each plant, is the most satisfactory method of bank planting. Pot-grown myrtle is the best for banks and should be planted in trowel-depth holes at least two to the square foot of surface. The intervening space should be covered with a minimum of four inches of good growing soil. For vines like honeysuckle or roses a spacing of five feet on center is a maximum distance, and for quick covering two and one-half feet is preferable. Plants like barberry or privet should have holes prepared not less than 18 in. deep and 18 in. in diameter. The more generous the

---

* Special articles on the subjects indicated by an asterisk (*) will be found at the words so marked.

prepared growing space the more satisfactory will be the growth. In backfilling the holes around the plants leave a depression on the upper side in order that rain will collect and not run off without soaking in. For the first season it is advisable to mulch deciduous plants with a strawy manure to hold moisture and prevent erosion.

In purchasing stock, two-year vines, 18 in. barberry, 2 ft. privet, and 3 ft. forsythia, are the best sizes for ordinary purposes.

All banks over eight feet in height with a slope greater than one to three should have a gutter along the top adequate to prevent accumulated water from flowing over the bank. Where necessary to prevent water flowing from the bank over other areas a gutter should parallel the foot of the bank. For banks of more than ten feet in height, with slopes greater than one to three, intervening gutters should be placed at intervals of every ten feet of height on the bank. — R. E. G. and G. E.

BANKSIA (banks'i-a). The Australian honeysuckles comprise over 40 species of shrubs and trees of the family Proteaceae, all Australian. One is a sufficiently handsome evergreen plant to be cult. for ornament, mostly in Calif. They are rarely cult. in greenhouses. Leaves alternate,* in those below narrow and not deeply toothed or lobed. Flowers yellow, borne in dense, mostly terminal clusters (spikes*), between rather showy bracts,* followed by a woody, cone-like fruit, bearing winged seeds. (Named for Sir Joseph Banks, noted British botanist.)

The Australian honeysuckles are semi-desert plants that do well in southern Calif., but are scarcely known elsewhere. They do not easily propagate from seed, and cuttings under a bell-jar, with a little bottom-heat,* is the most satisfactory method.

ericifolia. A shrub or small tree under 14 ft. high. Leaves scarcely ½ in. long, very narrow, and with tiny, rolled margins. Flower spikes 6–10 in. long, usually solitary in the axil* of a twig.

integrifolia. A tree 20–30 ft. high. Leaves oblongish, 6–8 in. long, about 1 in. wide, green above, white-hairy or felty beneath. Flower spikes 4–6 in. long, mostly terminal.

BANKS' ROSE = *Rosa banksiae*.

BANNER. *See* STANDARD 2.

BANYAN = *Ficus benghalensis*.

BAOBAB = *Adansonia digitata*.

BAOBOB FAMILY = Bombacaceae.

BAPTISIA (bap-tiz'i-a). The false indigo or wild indigo is a general term for nearly 45 species of perennial herbs of the pea family, all from N.A., a few grown in the flower border for ornament. They are stout plants with compound* leaves, the three leaflets arranged finger-fashion. Flowers pea-like, in showy clusters (racemes*), followed by more or less inflated, short pods. (Named from the Greek to dye, from the indigo-like dye yielded by some species.)

The two below are useful plants in drier parts of the border or wild garden. They need full sun, an open, porous, somewhat sandy soil, and can be increased by division.

australis. Blue false indigo; called, also, rattle-bush. From 3–5 ft. high. Leaflets 1½–2½ in. long, more or less wedge-shaped. Flower blue, the cluster 8–24 in. long. Pa. to Ga. and westward. June.

tinctoria. Clover broom; called, also, shoo-fly. A dome-shaped herb 18–30 in. high. Leaflets about ¾ in. long. Flowers yellow, the clusters sparsely flowered but very numerous. Me. to Fla. July. Turns black in drying.

barbadensis, -e (bar-ba-den'sis). From Barbados, W.I.

BARBADOS. As an adjective, applied to many plants native to or grown in Barbados. The ones of hort. interest and found in this book are:

Barbados aloes = *Aloe vera;* Barbados cherry = *Malpighia glabra;* Barbados flower-fence = *Poinciana pulcherrima;* Barbados gooseberry = *Pereskia aculeata;* Barbados nut = *Jatropha Curcas;* Barbados pride = *Poinciana pulcherrima* and *Adenanthera pavonina;* Barbados royal palm = *Roystonea oleracea.*

barbara, -us, -um (bar'ba-ra). Foreign.

BARBARA'S-BUTTONS. *See* MARSHALLIA.

BARBAREA (bar-ba-ree'a). The winter or upland cresses are rather weedy herbs of the mustard family, of secondary use as substitutes for watercress, and of little ornamental value. They have divided or compound leaves, small yellow flowers in terminal clusters (racemes*) and narrow pods (siliques*). (The name is from St. Barbara, one of the species being anciently known as herb of St. Barbara.)

The plants are of such easy culture as to suggest weeds, which they much resemble.

verna. Early cress; called, also, Belle Isle cress and scurvy-grass. A biennial or perennial herb 12–18 in. high. Leaves irregularly cut, with 5–8 lobes. Flowers scarcely ⅛ in. wide. Pod 1–2 in. long. Eu. One of the earliest blooming weedy plants, sometimes cult. for winter salad, as its foliage is pleasantly acid.

vulgaris. The common winter cress; also called bitter winter cress. Similar to *B. verna,* but with 1–4 lobes or leaflets. Pod 1 in. or less long. Eu. Blooms later than *B. verna* and is widely naturalized nearly throughout N.A. as a weed.

BARBARY FIG. *See* OPUNTIA COMPRESSA.

barbata, -us, -um (bar-bay'ta). Barbed or bearded.

BARBERRY. *See* BERBERIS.

BARBERRY FAMILY = Berberidaceae.

barbinervis, -e (bar-bi-ner'vis). With barbed nerves or veins.

barbinodis, -e (bar-bi-no'dis). Bearded at the joints.

barbulata, -us, -um (bar-bew-lay'ta). Shortly, or somewhat, bearded.

barcinonensis, -e (bar-sin-o-nen'sis). From Barcelona, Spain.

BARK. The outer, usually more or less

---

woody or corky layer of the stems of most woody plants, best exemplified on tree trunks. It appears to have no other function than protection of the tissue within, consequently being of little importance from the standpoint of garden operations.

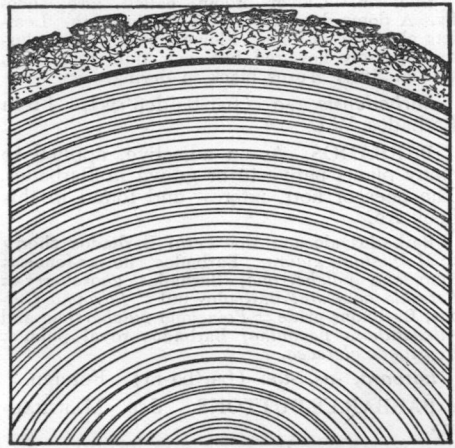

A much enlarged cross-section of a woody stem. Beneath the outer, dead, corky bark is the living, green cambium shown by a dark line. See text for the role of cambium in hort. operations.

It is quite otherwise with the green inner bark, known as cambium. Unlike the outer bark, which is dead, this cambium layer is alive and functionally very important to most woody plants. For it is this layer that carries the foods manufactured in the leaves to the roots. Cutting a complete ring of cambium from a tree trunk will, in most cases, ultimately kill it, a fact well known to the Indians. From this cambium layer also springs all the protective covering which trees throw out over wounds. Sometimes, due to slow growth, the outer bark becomes too old and hard to permit normal growth. Such trees are said to be bark-bound.

BARLERIA (bar-leer'i-a). Greenhouse herbs or small shrubs, of the family Acanthaceae, and comprising over 150 species, nearly all natives of the Old World tropics. The one below is grown for its very showy, bracted* flowers. Leaves opposite,* without marginal teeth. Flowers somewhat irregular,* crowded in the leaf axils* or in spikes, and from between showy, often spiny, bracts.* Corolla tube slender below, its five lobes flaring and somewhat unequal above. Fruit a normally 4-seeded pod (capsule*). (Named for Jacques Barrelier, French botanist.)

It needs a warm, moist greenhouse and potting mixture* 4. Occasionally used as a bedding plant in extreme southern Fla. Propagated by cuttings of young wood over bottom-heat.*

cristata. An herb or low shrub 2–3 ft. high. Leaves ovalish, 1½–3 in. long. Flowers blue, and with spiny bracts.* India.

BARLEY = *Hordeum vulgare.*

BARN OR BARNYARD GRASS = *Echinochloa Crus-galli.*

BAROMETZ. A Tartar word meaning lamb. For centuries the "vegetable lamb of Tartary" was supposed to be a fern (*see* Cibotium). Actually it was cotton.

BARREN STRAWBERRY = *Waldsteinia fragarioides;* also *Duchesnea indica.*

BARRENWORT. See Epimedium.

BARTONIA AUREA = *Mentzelia lindleyi.*

BARTRAM'S GARDEN. The garden of John Bartram, at Philadelphia, is one of the oldest in America. He was a correspondent of Linnaeus* who called him "the greatest natural botanist in the world." There still grow at this famous garden many of the plants which Bartram collected in America or which were sent to him from all over the world. He died in 1777, but the garden is still in existence at 54th Street and Lindley Avenue, and is open to the public.

BASELLA (ba-sell'a). The Malabar nightshades comprise only one or two species of tropical, annual (or rarely biennial) vines, family Basellaceae, the foliage used for greens in the tropics, but the vines cult. for ornament in the North. Leaves succulent, without marginal teeth. Flowers white or red. (See Basellaceae for details.) (*Basella* is a native Malabar name.)

Mostly grown in the greenhouse, but may be started as a tender annual (*see* Annuals) and planted outdoors after danger of frost is past. Propagated by seed.

alba. Perhaps not distinct from the following, but it has leaves longer than broad and white flowers. Tropical As.

rubra. A moderately tall but rampant climbing vine, the stems greenish-purple. Leaves 2–6 in. broad, about as long, nearly round, and somewhat heart-shaped at the base. Flowers in short clusters (spikes*), reddish. Tropical As.

BASELLACEAE (ba-sell-a'see-e). The Madeira-vine family comprises a small group of tropical, herbaceous vines with only two of its six genera of any hort. significance. They have tuberous rootstocks and rather fleshy, alternate leaves without marginal teeth. Flowers regular,* in finger-shaped clusters (racemes*), each with 2 bracts,* the clusters sometimes branched. Fruit small, not splitting, usually enclosed within the withered flower. The only two hort. genera are *Basella* and the much better known *Boussingaultia* (the Madeira-vine), both containing rampant-growing vines grown for their rather ornamental red or white flower clusters.

Technical flower characters: Sepals 2. Petals 5, separate or partly united, scarcely opening. Stamens 5 and opposite the petals. Ovary 1-celled, superior,* with a single ovule, usually with 3 styles.*

---

* Special articles on the subjects indicated by an asterisk (*) will be found at the words so marked.

baselloides (ba-sell-loy'deez; but *see* OÏDES). Like a plant of the genus *Basella*.

BASIL = *Ocimum Basilicum*.

basilaris, -e (bas-il-ar'is). Basal.

BASILICUM (ba-sill'i-kum). Ancient name for the basil (*Ocimum Basilicum*) in allusion to its reputed healing qualities.

BASIN. The depression in an apple, pear, quince, and related fruits at the apex of them; *i.e.*, at the end opposite their stalks.

BASKET FERN = *Nephrolepis pectinata*.

BASKET-FLOWER. Commonly, *Centaurea americana*, but also *Hymenocallis calathina* (*see* SPIDER-LILY).

BASKET GRASS = *Oplismenus compositus*.

BASKET-OF-GOLD = *Alyssum saxatile*.

BASKET PLANTS. See HANGING BASKET.

BASSWOOD = *Tilia*. See LINDEN.

BASTARD BOX = *Polygala Chamaebuxus*.

BASTARD INDIGO = *Amorpha fruticosa*.

BASTARD MAHOGANY = *Eucalyptus botryoides*.

BASTARD SPEEDWELL = *Veronica spuria*.

BATATAS. A very interesting vernacular to all gardeners. It was the aboriginal Haitian word for the sweet potato, and possibly spelled *batata*. From a corruption of the latter came the English word potato. As the specific, Latinized name of plants it has been applied to *Ipomoea* and *Dioscorea*.

BATOKO PLUM = *Flacourtia indica*.

BAUERA (bow-ear'ra). In Australia, where the only three species are known, they call these pretty little shrubs native rose. They are not roses, but small shrubs of the family Saxifragaceae, with evergreen, 3-parted, opposite* leaves and white or pink, slender-stalked, 5-petaled flowers, which may be solitary or in small, terminal clusters. Stamens few or many, borne on a ring-like disk. Fruit a 2-valved pod (capsule*). (Named for Gottfried and Franz Bauer, German painter and professor.)

The only hort. species has long been a favorite cool-greenhouse plant (winter temperature 45–50°). Plant in potting mixture* 3 and do not allow them to become potbound until they reach the size you want, which (for indoor plants) should be 1–2 ft. high. Keep well watered, as the plants naturally grow in wet places. They will bloom most of the winter and early spring under glass, but the pots are best plunged in ashes, in partial shade, during our summer (their winter). Propagated by cuttings of half-ripened wood, in April, preferably under a bell-jar.

rubioides. At home a shrub 4–6 ft., in cult. much less. Leaf segments more or less oblong, ¼–½ in. long, toothed. Flowers pink or white, the petals blunt. Aust.

BAUHINIA (baw-hin'i-a). A large genus of tropical shrubs, trees, and woody vines of the pea family, a few planted outdoors in zones* 6–9 (see below) for their showy flowers and their fine, very interesting foliage. Leaves compound,* with two oblique leaflets, or merely simple* and with 2 oblique lobes, much resembling the redbud, to which it is related. Flowers showy, not pea-like, with 5 rather unequal petals, each narrowed into a claw.* Fruit a long, flat pod. (Named for the brothers John and Caspar Bauhin, noted herbalists, the twin leaflets suggesting the two brothers.)

Bauhinias are slow growing and relatively unsuccessful plants for greenhouse culture. In southern Calif. and Fla. they are handsome but not large trees, their showy flowers being indicated by such names as orchid tree and butterfly-flower. They bloom in the winter and very early spring, after which some species drop their leaves. They need well-drained soils, are easily raised from seed, and no pests are as yet serious.

acuminata. A shrub 5–6 ft. high. Leaves compound,* the 2 leaflets folding at night. Flowers white, 2–3 in. wide. Pod about 5 in. long. Indo-Malaya. Blooms when only a few months old in Fla.

galpini. A half-climbing shrub, its nearly round, only slightly 2-lobed leaves, about 2 in. wide. Flowers scarlet or crimson, about 3 in. wide, and borne in loose clusters (racemes*), hence very showy. Hardy from zone* 6 southward.

grandiflora = *Bauhinia variegata*.

monandra. Butterfly-flower; called also, Jerusalem date. Shrub or small tree, not over 25 ft. Leaves simple,* the 2 lobes broad. Flowers pink, streaked with purple, in showy terminal clusters (racemes*). Pod about 8 in. long. Probably French Guiana.

purpurea. Tree, not over 30 ft., usually less. Leaves simple,* cleft about ⅓ their length into 2 rounded lobes, leathery. Flowers reddish-purple, 2–3 in. wide, in lax clusters, fragrant. Pod about 12 in. long. Indo-China. There is a white variety, and another, called Simpson's Pink, with pink flowers. Both the latter may be varieties of *B. variegata*.

tomentosa. St. Thomas tree. A shrub or small tree, not over 15 ft. high. Leaves simple,* with 2 broad lobes. Flowers yellow, but with one of the petals chocolate-blotched. Pod about 4 in. long. Tropical Af. and As.

triandra = *Bauhinia purpurea*.

variegata. Orchid tree; called also mountain ebony. Tree 10–25 ft. high. Leaves simple, broadly 2-lobed. Flowers lavender or purple, clustered in the leaf axils.* Pod about 9 in. long. Indo-China. One of the most popular of the group in Fla. and often confused with *B. purpurea*.

BAYARD CUTTING ARBORETUM. *See* ARBORETUM.

BAYBERRY. The bayberry of commerce, history, and hort. is *Pimenta acris*. But, in America, the word is quite generally applied to similarly aromatic shrubs of the genus *Myrica*, especially to *M. pensylvanica* and *M. cerifera*.

BAYBERRY FAMILY = Myricaceae.

BAY LEAVES. The leaves of the bay-

---

* Special articles on the subjects indicated by an asterisk (*) will be found at the words so marked.

berry (*Pimenta acris*), used for flavoring (*see* HERB GARDENING). They are the source of bay rum.

BAY POPLAR = *Nyssa aquatica*.

BAY RUM TREE = *Pimenta acris*.

BAY TREE. In history, always the true laurel (*Laurus nobilis*). In California, *Umbellularia californica*.

BAY WILLOW = *Salix pentandra*. See WILLOW.

BEACH ASTER = *Erigeron glaucus*.

BEACH GOLDENROD = *Solidago sempervirens*. See GOLDENROD.

BEACH GRASS = *Ammophila arenaria*.

BEACH PEA. Along the Atlantic Coast, *Lathyrus maritimus;* along the Pacific Coast, *Lathyrus littoralis*.

BEACH PINE = *Pinus contorta*. See PINE.

BEACH PLUM = *Prunus maritima*. See also PLUM.

BEACH WORMWOOD = *Artemisia steleriana*.

BEAD-PLANT = *Nertera granadensis*.

BEAD-RUBY = *Maianthemum canadense*.

BEAD-TREE. See ADENANTHERA and MELIA.

BEAKED HAZEL = *Corylus cornuta*. See HAZEL.

BEAN. To the average gardener the word bean implies only two main types — the string bean (often called snap, kidney, or stringless bean) and the lima bean, both of which are derived from the genus *Phaseolus* (which see). Neither was known before the discovery of the New World, as both types are natives of tropical America.

Beans, however, mean much more than this. The traditional bean of the Old World is *Vicia Faba*, often called the broad bean, and little grown here, except in Canada, mostly as a forage or for the ground meal from its seeds. It is a bushy annual which does not like hot, dry summers. Other plants called beans, grown for ornament, soil improvement, or for forage, will be found in the genera *Dolichos*, *Vigna*, *Glycine* (soybean), and among other species of *Phaseolus*.

CULTURE OF SNAP BEAN (*Phaseolus vulgaris*)

(Commonly called, also, string, kidney, or stringless bean; or haricot)

The snap bean (stringless or nearly so in the best varieties) is cult. more generally than any other plant of the bean tribe, both for its delicious, edible green pods and, later, for the very nutritious seeds. The wax or butter bean is a yellow-podded variety preferred by some, but nothing like as much grown as the common string bean. Both are grown as field crops for commercial production and for canning.

The string bean comes in two main types, a low or bush bean (*Phaseolus vulgaris humilis*) and the pole bean (*P. vulgaris*). Most home growers prefer the bush variety because it avoids the trouble and expense of poles.

VARIETIES. Of the hundreds that are known the consensus of expert opinion indicates the following as most generally successful:

Low or bushy varieties (often called dwarf beans).

Green podded: Tendergreen, Tenderlong, Topcrop, Black Valentine (for the South).

Golden or wax podded: Brittle wax, Pencil Pod, Black Wax.

Pole or high-climbing varieties.

Green podded: Kentucky Wonder (improved strains), Blue Lake, McCaslon.

Golden or wax podded: Kentucky Wonder Wax, Golden Cluster, White Creaseback, Golden Carmine.

SOILS AND FERTILIZER. Beans will grow in almost any soils except heavy muck ones, but will do best in well-drained, warm, garden soils that are sandy rather than heavy, or that have too much clay. The soil should have a moderate amount of humus and plenty of plant food.

The latter is best assured by the application, at planting time, of a 4–8–10 commercial fertilizer (*see* FERTILIZERS) at the rate of 500–600 pounds per acre (2½ pounds per 100-foot row). It may be broadcast or sprinkled in the drills, but in the latter case care must be used to mix it thoroughly with the soil, as the naked fertilizer may injure the seeds. Because all beans gather nitrogen from the air, the nitrogen content of the fertilizer can be lower than for many other crops.

If available, stable manure, plowed in two weeks before planting time at the rate of a ton to the acre, will be a satisfactory substitute for commercial fertilizer. Some growers also make small applications of commercial fertilizer between the rows after the plants have started.

PLANTING. String beans will not stand frost, and should not be planted until two weeks after the last killing frost in your neighborhood (see the name of your state for dates). It takes about ¾ pound of seed for a row 100 feet long, 1½ pounds for a garden 50 × 100 feet, and 8 pounds for an acre garden.

For a succession, plant every ten days or two weeks until about the middle of August. Seed sown after this will probably be caught by early frosts. In the South or other regions of long frost-free periods the bean season may be much longer. Bush beans mature in from 45 to 70 days, depending on heat; pole beans take from 75 to 80 days. Both these periods should be kept in mind in making final plantings. Because early beans are so desirable few gardeners will not gamble a little on the first planting of beans. If you win (*i.e.*, escape the last

---

* Special articles on the subjects indicated by an asterisk (*) will be found at the words so marked.

frost), you may considerably extend the bean season.

For the bush varieties make the drills about 1½ inches deep and 2 feet apart and put the seeds about 2 inches apart in the row. For the tall sorts put the poles (at least 6 feet high) in rows at least 3 feet apart and the poles about 4 feet apart in the row. At each pole plant 5 or 6 seeds (ultimately thinned to 3 or 4 plants). In planting both sorts see that the soil is slightly tamped over the seeds.

CULTIVATION AND YIELDS. Cultivate frequently with a wheel hoe or hand weeder, or with a scuffle hoe. Never do this in the early morning or just about a rain. All evidence points to the foliage of the bean as dangerously likely to spread disease if implements or clothing brush past it while it is wet. Keep this in mind also when picking the crop. (See DISEASES, below.)

Beans must be hand picked, preferably before the pods show much of the outline of the still immature seed, unless it is the latter (shell beans) that are desired, when picking should be delayed. All the varieties are better (i.e., more completely stringless) when picked young. There is a machine picker for large-scale operations.

Bush beans enough for a family of 5 can usually be harvested from 100 feet of row, but more will be needed if there are frequent pickings and several plantings.

CULTURE OF LIMA BEAN (*Phaseolus limensis*)

Even more than the string bean the lima bean is sensitive to frost. Not only should there be no danger of frost, but the ground must have warmed up enough to ensure the proper development of this essentially tropical crop. Safe planting dates for it are generally as follows (but see climatic data at the name of your state):

	Earliest in Spring	Last Planting
Zone* 3	About June 1	June 20
Zone* 4	About May 20	July 1
Zone* 5	About May 1	July 15

In zones* 6, 7, and 8 the season is considerably longer, but in zones* 1 and 2 the culture of the lima bean is generally impossible or extremely risky because of the short growing season and lack of heat.

Many growers, impatient of these climatic restrictions, start the plants in the cold frame or even the greenhouse. Seeds sown in paper pots or old strawberry baskets are started three or four weeks before outdoor planting is safe. When settled warm weather makes planting advisable, the boxes or pots are plunged in the ground at intervals of 6 inches, in rows that are 3 feet apart (for the bush limas). The pole kinds are set out 2 feet apart, in rows 3½ feet apart.

OUTDOOR PLANTING AND SOILS. Soil requirements are the same as for string beans, and so are the fertilizers. Some growers prefer a slightly acid soil (see ACID AND ALKALI SOILS), but this does not appear to be a country-wide factor.

Drills should be 3 feet apart and about 1½ inches deep. Put the seeds about 3½ inches apart in the row, cover, and tamp down slightly. Because the seeds are large it takes about ¾ pound for 100 feet of row (¾ peck to the acre).

CULTIVATION. Same as for string bean (see above).

HARVESTING AND YIELDS. Lima beans take much longer to mature than string beans. It takes from 75–90 days from outdoor planting to harvest, so that over much of the country only one crop can be grown.

They must be hand picked, and as it is the seeds that are used, it is useless to pick until the pod shows indication of some seed formation. Young lima beans, however, are so delicious that many gardeners pick them earlier than the commercial grower would find profitable. If left too long on the plants, lima beans become tough and then are best suited for drying and winter storage.

PREFERRED VARIETIES OF LIMA BEAN.

Low or bush sorts. Fordhook 242, Burpee Improved Bush, Henderson, Triumph.

Tall or pole sorts. Leviathan, Sieva (South), King of the Garden.

Many growers, especially commercial ones, prefer to grow the tall varieties on trellises and in drills, instead of on poles set at intervals. A continuous, fence-like wire trellis 6 ft. high is then constructed, with the wires stretched diagonally up and down, instead of laterally as in a fence. Few home growers will bother with such equipment, or with poles, and bush limas are consequently most preferred. If poles are used they should be rough, preferably with their bark on. (See also KITCHEN GARDEN.)

INSECT PESTS. Mexican bean beetles feed on beans grown in U.S. from Rocky Mountains eastward. A bean-leaf beetle, spotted asparagus beetles, red spider, and several leaf-feeding caterpillars attack foliage. Apply pesticide #21 or #27 (see SPRAYS AND DUSTS) dusts or sprays, paying attention to under surfaces of leaves. Black bean aphids are also controlled by pesticide #21. A combination seed treatment, which includes a fungicide and an insecticide, is available for pre-plant treatment to protect against soil diseases and insects which prevent emergence of seedling. Store seed stock in pesticide #27 or #17 dust to prevent weevil damage.

DISEASES. Several bacterial blights* and a fungus disease known as anthracnose* may appear as problems. Use western seed from dry areas where the disease is not present for best results.

During cool, wet weather a downy mildew* may attack leaves and pods. As soon as disease is first noticed, apply pesticide #7 (see SPRAYS AND DUSTS) and repeat at 7-day intervals.

Particularly where aphids are abundant, the virus disease mosaic* may mar the foliage and stunt plants. Do not grow beans adjacent to overwintering legumes* such as alfalfa.

Several root rot diseases may affect beans, particularly if grown for a number of years in the same soil. Rust* is occasionally present on

---

* Special articles on the subjects indicated by an asterisk (*) will be found at the words so marked.

some varieties. Plant those varieties listed as resistant.

BEAN FAMILY. *See* LEGUMINOSAE.

BEAN TREE. Usually applied to *Catalpa bignonioides;* also to *Laburnum anagyroides.*

BEARBERRY. Commonly applied to *Arctostaphylos Uva-ursi;* in California, to *Rhamnus purshiana.*

BEARBERRY WILLOW = *Salix Uva-ursi.*

BEAR-BUSH = *Ilex glabra.* See HOLLY.

BEARD. A bristle-like awn,° especially a tuft of such. Also, any fringe-like growth on a petal, as in many irises and some orchids.

BEARDED DARNEL = *Lolium temulentum.*

BEARD-GRASS. See ANDROPOGON.

BEARDTONGUE. See PENTSTEMON.

BEAR GRASS. This is applied to several plants with grass-like or sword-shaped leaves, all members of the lily family. *See* DASYLIRION TEXANUM, YUCCA FILAMENTOSA, Y. GLAUCA, and QUAMASH.

BEARING AGE. For the normal time when trees may be expected to bear fruit, etc., *see* GARDEN TABLES I.

BEAR'S-BREECH = *Acanthus mollis.*

BEAR-TONGUE. See CLINTONIA.

BEAUMONTIA (bo-mon'ti-a). A small genus of trees or woody vines, family Apocynaceae, the one below from India, the rest Javanese. Leaves opposite,° without marginal teeth. Flowers large, fragrant, white, and funnel- or triumpet-shaped, the corolla with 5 broad lobes. Fruit long, cylindric, splitting into two follicles.° (Named for Lady Beaumont of Bretton Hall, England.) The herald's-trumpet would be a splendid greenhouse vine if it could be kept within bounds. It cannot be confined to a pot or tub and should be planted in the soil of a greenhouse large enough to contain it. It needs a warm house (65° or more), and plenty of moisture. Some growers regularly thin out its large leaves which might otherwise make a greenhouse into a dusky nook. Can be grown outdoors only in zone° 9.

grandiflora. Herald's-trumpet. A tall-growing, woody vine. Leaves ovalish, 6–9 in. long. Flowers 5 in. long and nearly as wide, spring-blooming in the greenhouse. India, where the floss from its seeds is used as a vegetable silk.

BEAUTY-BERRY. See CALLICARPA.

BEAUTY-BUSH = *Kolkwitzia amabilis.*

BEAVER-POISON = *Cicuta maculata.*

BEAVER-TREE = *Magnolia virginiana.*

BECHTEL'S CRAB. See MALUS IOENSIS.

BEDDING. When plants are grouped together for mass effect they form a planting bed and the term "bedding" is applied to this type of arrangement.

One of these types is called "carpet bedding," which is an arrangement of low, compact, mostly foliage plants in conventional patterns resembling carpet design.

The outline shape of the beds varies from a simple circle to elaborate scroll patterns, and in some cases the bedding plants are used to lay out flags, shields, or other insignia.

Since this kind of bedding remains exactly the same throughout the summer it is too monotonous and also too expensive for private garden use and has, therefore, been confined to public gardens which are seen only occasionally and by different people. In public gardens there are skilled gardeners specially trained for this very difficult type of bedding design. It is beyond the scope of this article to attempt to go into the intricacies of carpet-bedding design.

Another type of bedding, known as parterre work, is well adapted to ornamental planting in private gardens, preferably if it can be viewed from above. The term "parterre" means a geometric arrangement of ornamental shaped beds separated by a pattern of walks or turf areas. Variations in parterre design are unlimited, the simplest form being four beds arranged symmetrically around a central ornamental feature. The shapes of these beds are related one to the other so that they form a complete pattern from which no one bed can be eliminated without having the pattern incomplete.

To lay out a parterre design within any given area, determine first what the major feature in the garden is to be and where it is to be placed. If it is to be a pool, a sundial, or flower bed in the center of the garden, lay out a symmetrical path system leading up to this feature. The resulting shape of the areas in between the paths forms the pattern of the parterre. This pattern should be outlined by formal, trimmed hedges within which the surface may be planted with grass or flowers, according to personal preference.

Sometimes an additional pattern of low hedges, separating beds of different colored flowers, is laid out within the larger areas. Such patterns are often very elaborate scroll designs resembling embroidery, which was characteristic of the French style of embroidery gardening.

If the major feature is to be at one end of the garden the same process of laying out the pattern will apply, but all paths will lead up to this terminal feature.

Annuals are the most suitable plants for parterre bedding because of their continuous profusion of bloom. Any type of plant which has a short season of bloom leaves a blank in the pattern at some one season or another. Typical annuals for parterre bedding are heliotrope, ageratum, single petunias, snapdragons, dwarf annual phlox, geraniums, dwarf marigolds, and lantanas. Colored foliage plants such as *Coleus* and *Alternanthera* are excellent for very formal parterre planting, but less satisfactory among annuals or more informal plants.

The beauty of the parterre is its pattern

° Special articles on the subjects indicated by an asterisk (°) will be found at the words so marked.

design and the flowers are only the color spots which create this pattern. Each division of the pattern should, therefore, be a solid color of a single variety. To see properly the beauty of the pattern it must be viewed from a height sufficient to comprehend the whole pattern. For this reason the parterre is most effective when seen from a terrace or slightly elevated, surrounding walk. If such elevation is not possible, then the pattern should be created with very low-growing plants. Originally these patterns were laid out with boxwood edgings, but *Taxus cuspidata nana* or dwarf forms of *Thuja* are satisfactory evergreen substitutes. *Teucrium Chamaedrys, Nepeta mussini, Euonymus fortunei carrieri,* or *Berberis thunbergi minor* are alternatives.

Spring bedding is similar in design to other types of bedding, but the color is created by spring-flowering bulbs instead of annuals. *See* BULBS.

A "ribbon bed" is a long, narrow-shaped bed with special pattern conforming to its length. Such beds parallel paths or drives, and the pattern is a rhythmic repetition of the same design. The materials used are similar to other types of bedding.

The parterre at the Medici Gardens — the finest type of bedding

The term "flower bed" means any shape of bed within which there may be a great many varieties of flowers, and the bed is not a part of a general pattern. In this case the interest is created by a variety of plants arranged for succession of bloom, color, and foliage composition. There is no limitation of height, type of plant, or arrangement for a flower bed. Perennials and annuals may be intermixed, and since the outline of the bed is secondary in importance to the plants within it there is no necessity for a surrounding hedge. The scattering of unrelated and different-shaped flower beds on a lawn is one of the worst vagaries of amateur design. The parterre is far more artistic. *See also* BORDER.

Low-growing flowers are used around the outside of the bed and built up to higher plants in the center, or if it is a border bed the front is kept low and built up to a high background. In place of a surrounding hedge a border plant should be used to unify the composition.

The only limitation to the size and shape of flower beds is the practical consideration of being able to get into the bed to cultivate the plants. A skillful gardener can easily cultivate a bed twelve feet wide, but a practical width for the ordinary border bed which does not require skillful maintenance is eight feet.

To determine the number of plants required for any kind or size of bed the number of square feet within the bed should be figured. For rank-growing perennials such as larkspur, phlox, and chrysanthemums allow two square feet for the ultimate requirements of each plant; for peonies four square feet; for tea roses three square feet; for hybrid, perpetual roses four square feet; for annuals such as ageratum or petunias one square foot. See GARDEN TABLES IV.

In figuring dwarf hedges count one plant for each six inches in length; for perennial or annual border plants eight to ten inches. The tendency is to overcrowd perennials for immediate effect on new plantings, which results in ultimate stunted growth. It is better to allow adequate room for ultimate growth and interplant with bulbs such as tulips, lilies, or gladiolus for temporary filler. — R. E. G.

BEDSTRAW. *See* GALIUM.

BEE BALM = *Monarda didyma;* also *Melissa officinalis.*

BEECH. These ornamental trees, all belonging to the genus **Fagus** (fay'gus) of the family Fagaceae, comprise only 9 species, all of which are confined to temperate regions of the northern hemisphere. The two below are the only species, so far, of any interest to the gardener, but they are among the most decorative and hardy of all cult. trees (*see* Culture below). Leaves alternate, toothed (in those below). Male and female flowers in separate clusters on the same tree. Male flowers in slender-stalked heads, without petals, but with 4–7-lobed calyx, and 8–16 stamens.* Female flowers usually 2, surrounded by many united bracts. Fruit a triangular or egg-shaped nut in a woody, 4-valved, prickly covering. (*Fagus* is classical Latin for the beech.)

F. grandifolia. American beech; called, also, red or white beech. A tree 90–100 ft. high, with light gray bark. Leaves oblong-oval, broadly wedge-shaped at the base, coarsely toothed, 4–7 in. long, bluish-green above, light green beneath, beautifully silky when unfolding. Eastern N.A.

F. sylvatica. European beech. Somewhat taller than the American beech. Leaves dark, lustrous-green, finely and somewhat remotely toothed, more or less elliptic-ovate, 3½–5 in.

* Special articles on the subjects indicated by an asterisk (*) will be found at the words so marked.

long. Eu. For the many beautiful hort. forms of this *see* below.

CULTURE OF THE BEECH

The beech is among the most beautiful of the larger ornamental trees. Although seven species are hardy in the U.S., only the native and European representatives are well known. The species from China, Japan, and Northern Asia have been in cultivation but a short time, when the natural life span of this group is considered, and are not commonly cultivated.

The beech is quite soil-tolerant, although it prefers a well-drained, light soil. Care in transplanting is the only rigid requirement for successful cultivation. A long taproot is present and should be preserved. For this reason, the moving of large specimens is a dangerous operation unless the tree is first prepared by a gradual process of root pruning. Nurserymen make a practice of transplanting this group regularly to develop a vigorous root system without long taproots. But most old trees also have many shallow roots, which make it difficult to grow anything under a beech.

Propagation is by seed which is planted in the fall in beds which have been screened to keep out rodents. The varieties are grafted on seedlings of the European species. This work is done in the greenhouse during late winter. A cleft graft is sometimes used, although veneer or tongue grafting is more common.

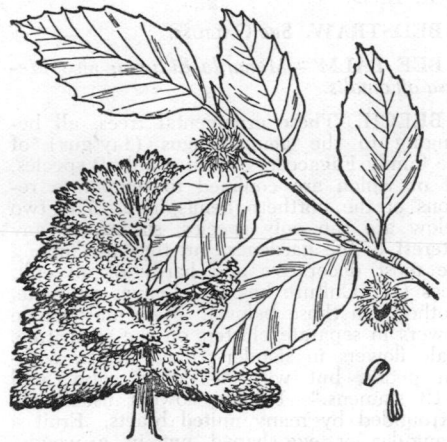

The habit, foliage and fruit of the American beech (*Fagus grandifolia*)

The European beech (*Fagus sylvatica*) is perhaps the most beautiful of the group. Hardy throughout this country, it often reaches a height of more than one hundred feet. When grown as a specimen tree, it forms a huge, broad top with horizontal and ascending branches extending from a generally low, bulky trunk which sometimes measures six feet in diameter. In wooded areas the habit is less broad and the trunk often clean for a height of forty feet. Its smooth, light gray bark and lustrous, dark green foliage combine to furnish a delightful color contrast.

The many varieties of the European beech may be considered as among the most coveted of the ornamental trees. The purple beech, *Fagus sylvatica atropunicea*, is identical with the type, except for its purple leaves, and is one of the finest trees with colored foliage. *Fagus sylvatica cuprea*, the copper beech, although less widely distributed, is identified by its bright copper or rosy-colored leaves. It is slower-growing than the variety *atropunicea*. The pendulous form, *Fagus sylvatica pendula*, has pendulous branches which often completely hide the trunk. A combination of the pendulous-branched and purple-leaved forms is known as *Fagus sylvatica purpurea-pendula*. It combines the characters of both forms, but is rather slow-growing and seldom exceeds forty feet in height. The fern-leaved beech, *Fagus sylvatica laciniata*, has sharply cut, fern-like leaves which cover the tree with a beautiful, dense, shimmering mantle of green throughout the summer. A lesser-known form is the var. *fastigiata*, the upright beech. This tree raises its branches in an almost vertical fashion, forming a narrow, spire-like tree. Many other forms are grown in Europe. Chief among these are a number of varieties with intermediate shades of purple-colored foliage or cut leaves. The European beech holds its green color later in the fall than the American tree, and is thus valuable where late greenery is an advantage.

The American beech (*Fagus grandifolia*) is quite similar in general appearance to the European representative. The bark is a lighter gray and the leaves are larger and duller in color. It is more beautiful in autumn, as its foliage turns a bright yellow, whereas that of the European species turns red. Although most commonly employed as a specimen tree, it is sometimes used for large hedges and is becoming popular for allée work. — D. W.

INSECT PESTS. Woolly aphids on leaves and limbs are controlled by pesticide #21 sprays. Dormant sprays of superior oils control several scale species. *See* oil sprays at INSECTICIDES. Use pesticide #19 (*see* SPRAYS AND DUSTS) for chewing insects.

DISEASES. Canker* often becomes serious following an infestation of woolly aphids* or scale insects. Pinhead or orange pustules of the canker fungus develop on the cankered bark. Various wood-rotting fungi may attack the sapwood or heartwood and then produce bracket-shaped growths on the side of the tree.

Some clones* of beech are particularly susceptible to ravages of hot weather and leaf scorch* results. If the crown is thinned by leaf scorch or heavy pruning, the bark on larger branches may scald.*

In large old specimens of grafted varieties, there often appears to be a breakdown of the wood at the graft union, and general decline of the tree will follow.

* Special articles on the subjects indicated by an asterisk (*) will be found at the words so marked.

All insect-injured, scalded, or mechanically injured bark and wood should be cut out to clean healthy wood and the area treated with a tree paint.

BEECH FAMILY. This includes only shrubs and trees such as the beech, oak, chestnut, and their relatives. For the hort. genera and technical characters *see* FAGACEAE.

BEECH FERN = *Dryopteris Phegopteris.*

BEEFSTEAK BEGONIA = *Begonia feasti.*

BEEFSTEAK GERANIUM. See BEGONIA REX.

BEEFSTEAK PLANT = *Perilla frutescens crispa.*

BEEFSTEAK SAXIFRAGE = *Saxifraga sarmentosa.*

BEEFWOOD AND BEEFWOOD FAMILY. See CASUARINA.

BEE LARKSPUR = *Delphinium elatum.*

BEE SAGE = *Audibertia grandiflora.*

BEES AND BEE PLANTS. While few gardeners combine beekeeping and gardening, enough do to make it worth recording the hort. species and genera which yield the most nectar. Bees are among the most important of all insects in carrying pollen, especially in the fruit trees. See POLLINATION.

Besides such favorites as buckwheat and the lindens, there are a few other genera that yield enough honey so that they are planted in quantity for the purpose, especially in Calif. Among the most important bee plants are:

All clovers (*Trifolium*)	*Cleome serrulata*
Lindens (*Tilia*)	Mesquite (*Prosopis juliflora*)
Nearly all the sages (*Salvia*)	Nearly all milkweeds
Bluecurls (*Trichostema lanceolatum*)	Orange (in Calif. and Fla.)
Buckwheat (*Fagopyrum*)	All sweet clovers (*Melilotus*)
Button-bush (*Cephalanthus*)	Tulip-tree (*Liriodendron*)
Nearly all fruit trees, especially apple	Nearly all wisterias
Eucalyptus (in Calif.)	Lima bean
Alfalfa (*Medicago sativa*)	Toyon (*Heteromeles arbutifolia*) in Calif.
Borago officinalis	*Vitex*
	Ilex glabra. See HOLLY.

Miscellaneous garden flowers, while useful, and regularly visited by bees, are not so attractive to them as the above, some of which should be planted in quantity by those who want to combine gardening and beekeeping.

BEET. The beet and Swiss chard belong to **Beta** (bee'ta), (family Chenopodiaceae), which is a genus of Old World herbs having leaves quite without hairs. Flowers greenish, in spikes or panicles,* without petals, and extremely simple. Usually there are minute bracts* beneath the 5-cleft calyx.* Fruit an aggregate of 2 or more flowers joined together at the base, and forming a dry, corky body (utricle*) which, while not a true seed, is commonly the beet "seed" of the markets.

(*Beta* is the Latin name of the beet.) The only cult. species is:

B. vulgaris. Beet, commonly called beetroot in England. A biennial grown for its much-thickened red (white in the sugar beet) root. Stem produced from the root the second year, rarely seen in cult. specimens, 2–4 ft. high. Leaves oblongish, often red-stalked. Perhaps a cultigen,* but derived from a wild species on the coasts of Eu. The *var.* **Cicla,** the leaf beet and Swiss chard, produces no fleshy root and its foliage, often brightly colored or with white veins or leafstalks, is grown both for ornament and for greens. (See Swiss Chard below.)

Beet Culture (*Beta vulgaris*)

Beets are one of the easiest of vegetables to grow, doing well in almost every type of garden soil, except those too rocky to allow proper root development. A rich, sandy loam, easily worked, is ideal.

While somewhat tolerant of soils, the beet will not grow well in the warm sections of the country, and is primarily a crop for zone* 4 and northward. The commercial production in the South for northern winter markets is based upon the use of the brief cool periods that come before the heat of summer. (*See* CALIFORNIA.)

VARIETIES. Of the many on the market the best varieties of beet for the ordinary garden are, in order of preference: Crosby, Detroit Dark Red, Early Wonder. For winter storage, or for canning, use Long Season, which, unlike the turnip-shaped varieties cited above, is a half-long, more carrot-shaped sort. Early Wonder is one of the quickest from seeding to harvest, averaging, in good soil and favorable climate, about 42 days. The others take from 45–50 days.

PLANTING. If you are to cultivate with a hoe or wheel hoe, the rows should be 12 in. apart. If power cultivation is to be used, the rows should be twice that or even a little more. Make the drills deep enough to allow the seed to be covered with an inch of soil. In planting the seed it is well to remember that the "seed" of the beet is really a fruit containing several seeds. This fruit (hereafter called a seed) is thus likely to sprout with several small plants at each interval. This matters little because the best method is always to sow beet seed thicker than the final stand is to be, and then thin out the plants enough to allow proper root development.

Plant about 10 seeds to a foot of row (at this rate it takes about 2 ounces for 100 ft. of row). Because the seed germinates a little slower than some vegetables, it is a good plan to sprinkle a few radish seeds in the row before covering the beet seed. The radishes sprout quickly, so marking the row plainly for a possible cultivation before the beets are up.

CULTIVATION AND THINNING. Cultivate frequently and deeply at first, being careful not to disturb the young seedlings, however. When the plants get to be 4 in. high you must decide whether you finally want a great

---

* Special articles on the subjects indicated by an asterisk (*) will be found at the words so marked.

many fairly small roots or fewer and larger ones, or a combination of both. Thin to 2 in. apart if you want small roots, and to 5½ in. apart for big ones. Many home growers prefer to let thinning be dictated by how thickly the seed has sprouted, the different development of the individual plants, and whether or not they wish to use the plants they pull out as beet greens. These are a good substitute for spinach. If the larger roots are ultimately desired, it is often possible first to harvest a crop of small roots, and then one or two lots of beet tops, the result being that you have by such harvesting left the final roots spaced so they can develop properly.

Still another use of thinned beets is to transplant them at once. While some growers, with a moist soil or a watering system, can do this successfully, the plants stand moving rather poorly.

In the later stages great care must be used in cultivating to avoid injuring the fleshy roots, which are prone to bleed and become useless if nicked by hoe or cultivator.

Beets are rich feeders, and the soil should be correspondingly rich, especially if quick growth is to be secured, and it should be. Slow growth means tough roots, while quick growth means juicy and tender ones. Do not plow in green or fresh stable manure before planting — use only well-rotted cow or stable manure. If neither is available, broadcast a good commercial fertilizer (3½ pounds to 100 ft. of row). In addition, many find it profitable to broadcast and cultivate in (between the rows), when the plants are 6 in. high, about 8 ounces of nitrate of soda to 100 ft. of row.

SWISS CHARD CULTURE (*Beta vulgaris Cicla*)

Chard (sometimes called the silver beet) is simply a variety of the common beet that develops no turnip-shaped or carrot-shaped root, but whose leaves (due to breeding and selection) are much larger and more succulent than the ordinary beet. A few varieties, often called leaf beet, are variously colored and grown sometimes for ornament. But the chief use is for greens that make a splendid substitute for spinach. This is the ordinary chard of the kitchen garden, sometimes called spinach-beet.

As now developed, some varieties of this have a much-enlarged, white leafstalk which is the only part that many growers use. Others cook the whole leaf (often white-veined), leafstalk and all.

VARIETIES. The best general variety is Lucullus, but if you care only for the stalks, it is better to plant Large-ribbed White. Giant Perpetual has darker green leaves

CULTURE. Chard is planted and cultivated exactly as the beet (see above), but because the plants are very leafy, it is well to thin them to 6 in. apart in the row (using thinned plants for greens). Harvesting can begin whenever the leaves are 6 in. or more long. If the soil is rich, moisture adequate,

and the season not too hot, you can keep on cutting until frost. But if the plants show a tendency to become exhausted (*i.e.*, produce fewer and smaller leaves), it is a good plan to start another crop. This can be done anytime up to 40 days before you expect the first killing frost of autumn (see the name of your state for frost data in your vicinity).

Unlike spinach, chard wilts quickly and cannot be shipped to any great distance. It is thus a home-grown delicacy which is infrequently found in the markets. (*See also* KITCHEN GARDEN.)

INSECT PESTS. Several flea beetles, leaf beetles, webworm caterpillars, and leafhoppers attack beets. Spray with pesticide #1 (see SPRAYS AND DUSTS). To control grasshoppers, cutworms, and slugs, use a poison bait.*

DISEASES. The table beet is relatively free from serious diseases. Damping-off* may be a problem on young seedlings if weather conditions are not conducive to rapid germination. The use of treated seed is advised.

A problem in many areas is a condition known as hollow-heart. It is not caused by an organism, but rather by a lack of available boron in the soil. Use fertilizers with borax added.

BEET FAMILY = Chenopodiaceae.

BEETLEWEED = *Galax aphylla.*

BEGGAR-LICE = *Desmodium canadense.*

BEGGAR-TICKS = *Desmodium canadense;* also *Bidens frondosa* (see the list at WEEDS).

BEGGARWEED = *Desmodium purpureum.*

BEGONIA (bee-gō′ni-a). An immense genus of tropical foliage and flowering herbs, with soft or succulent stems, and the only hort. genus of the family **Begoniaceae** (bee-gō-ni-ā′se-ee). Leaves alternate, often brightly colored or with colored veins, nearly always oblique in general outline. Flowers red, pink, yellow or white, slightly irregular, the male and female separate. Male flowers with 2-5 or more parts scarcely distinguishable as petals and sepals. Ovary inferior,* 2-celled, the fruit a many-seeded capsule.* (Named for Michel Begon, French antiquary and patron of botany.)

As *Begonia* is a genus of perhaps 1000 species, has been widely diversified by breeders, and is now found in a multitude of hort. forms, the names are still in much confusion. Many of the hort. forms have been given Latin names exactly as though they were true wild species, which has simply made the confusion worse.

From the gardening standpoint, those in cult. are best divided into two groups: (a) Tuberous-rooted begonias, and (b) Fibrous-rooted sorts.

(a) Tuberous-rooted begonias (all marked *a* in the list below). Here belong *B. socotrana*, *B. lloydi*, the tuberous begonia hybrids, and *B. evansiana*, the latter the hardiest of all begonias and even standing zero weather. All others are tender plants killed by frost.

---

* Special articles on the subjects indicated by an asterisk (*) will be found at the words so marked.

(b) Fibrous-rooted begonias (all marked *b* in the list below). Here belong *B. bunchi, B. feasti, B. fuchsioides, B. heracleifolia, B. incana, B. manicata, President Carnot, B. Rex, B. sanguinea,* and *B. semperflorens.* The latter includes most of the common bedding begonias.

For culture and uses *see* Culture (below).

angularis (b). A shrubby, much-branched plant, 5–8 ft. high, the branches drooping. Leaves wavy-margined, toothed, ovalish in outline, green above, but with white veins, reddish beneath. Flowers scarcely ⅓ in. wide, white, in profuse, loose clusters. Brazil.

argenteo-guttata (b). Primarily a smooth foliage plant, 2–4 ft. high, and of hybrid origin. Leaves ovalish, but long-pointed, 3–5 in. long, toothed and somewhat angular, shining green but copiously white-spotted. Flowers white or pinkish, small, in clusters arising at the leaf joints.

bunchi (b). A hybrid plant with nearly round, thick leaves, green above, and red beneath, the margins growing out like crests. Perhaps only a var. of *Begonia feasti.*

diadema (b). A fleshy-stemmed plant 18–24 in. high, with numerous, showy, maple-like leaves, deeply cut into segments; the leaves green above, white-blotched, and reddish below as are the leafstalks. Flowers small, pink. Borneo. Primarily a foliage plant.

dichroa (b). A Brazilian begonia of low stature, uncertain identity, and described as "having green leaves and orange flowers." It is offered by many dealers but its true status is in doubt.

evansiana (a). A smooth, branching plant 1–2 ft. high. Leaves more or less oval, but lobed and the lobes toothed, red on the under side. Flowers large, flesh-pink. China and Jap. It is the hardiest of all cult. forms, and stands temperatures of zero at Washington, D.C.

feasti (b). Beefsteak begonia. Leaves red beneath, nearly round, thick and fleshy, from a creeping mass of stems. Leaf margins distinctly hairy. Flowers light pink, long-stalked. Of hybrid origin.

foliosa (b). A fleshy-stemmed, very leafy plant, 18–24 in. high. Leaves numerous, notched and lobed, scarcely ½ in. long, dark green, and arranged in two ranks. Flowers about ½ in. wide, white and often rose-tinted, in rather sparse clusters. Colombia.

frutescens (b). A trade name for a low, spreading begonia, said to have red stems, the leaves green above, red beneath, and white flowers with red stalks. Of uncertain origin and identity.

fruticosa (b). A collective term (in the trade) for a group of possibly hybrid begonias, with very dark green leaves that are red on the under side. Flowers generally white. Of uncertain origin and identity.

fuchsioides (b). A popular greenhouse begonia with slender stem, 2–3 ft. high, the branches shaggy. Leaves lopsided, ovalish, 1–1½ in. long. Flowers suggesting a fuchsia, scarlet, ½–¾ in. wide. Mex. There are several vars., one with pink flowers.

glabra (b). A smooth-stemmed creeping or climbing begonia from thick rootstocks. Leaves ovalish, pointed at the tip, slightly heart-shaped at the base, 2–4 in. long, dark green above but paler beneath, the larger veins with a few hairs. Flowers small, in ball-like clusters, white. Tropical America. Sometimes known as *Begonia scandens.*

haageana (b). A red shaggy-haired plant 2–4 ft. high from a fibrous root. Leaves oval or heart-shaped, 4–10 in. long and about half as wide, wavy-margined, pointed at the tip, the veins red, the under side purplish. Flowers showy, rose-pink, the cluster drooping, 8–10 in. wide. Brazil. Sometimes known as *Begonia scharffi.*

heracleifolia (b). A hairy, creeping-stemmed plant with large leaves on long stalks. Leaves nearly round, nearly a foot wide, deeply cut into 5–9 narrow lobes. Flowers scarcely 1 in. wide, white or pink, on stalks that are 15–20 in. long. Mex.

imperialis (b). A Mexican begonia with thick, creeping, red-shaggy rootstocks. The plant is low, its ovalish leaves 4–6 in. wide, very rough and hairy, green above, the veins white-margined, but brown-green beneath. Flower cluster no higher than the leaves, the flowers about ½ in. wide, white. A fine foliage plant.

incana (b). An upright plant, 1–2 ft. high, the stems, leafstalks and leaves covered with brownish-red hairs. Leaves with the stalk arising near the center of the blade, nearly round, 4–9 in. wide. Flowers white, in long-stalked clusters. Brazil.

manicata (b). A plant with creeping rootstocks, without hairs, except on the margins and veins of the leaves, which are green above, reddish beneath, ovalish, 4–8 in. long and with wavy, toothed margins. Flowers pink, about ½ in. long, the stalk longer than the leaves. Mex. There are crisp-margined forms and others with thin, yellow-mottled leaves.

margaritae (b). A hybrid begonia, 1–2 ft. high and vigorous, the stems hairy and purplish. Leaves ovalish, but heart-shaped at the base, pointed at the tip, the margins wavy and toothed, purplish-green above, red beneath. Flowers showy, rose-colored, in profuse clusters.

metallica (b). A shaggy-stemmed begonia, 2–4 ft. high, the foliage with a metallic sheen. Leaves generally ovalish, about 6 in. long, the margins wavy and toothed, green above but paler beneath. Flowers about 1½ in. wide, pinkish white to rose-colored, in profuse clusters. Brazil.

nitida (b). A smooth-stemmed plant, 4–6 ft. high with shining foliage. Leaves kidney-shaped, or ovalish, 4–6 in. long, bright green, the margins with rounded, blunt teeth. Flowers showy, nearly 1½ in. wide, in profuse clusters, pink or rose-colored. Jamaica.

President Carnot (b). A var. of the rex begonia. *See* Culture (below).

Rex (b). The common rex begonia of many homes and greenhouses. Rootstocks creeping. Leaves large and long-stalked, the stalk shaggy-hairy. Blade marbled, blotched, or banded with metallic markings above, reddish beneath, nearly 9 in. long. Flowers rose-pink, about 1½ in. wide. Occurs in many hort. forms, all derived from a plant from Assam, and is sometimes called beefsteak geranium (not a geranium). For preferred varieties *see* Culture (below).

sanguinea (b). A smooth and shining plant, its several stems red, scarcely over 20 in. high. Leaves green above, red beneath, more or less heart-shaped or oval, about 5 in. long, without marginal teeth. Flowers white, about ¾ in. wide, the cluster usually above the foliage. Brazil.

scandens = *Begonia glabra.*

scharffi = *Begonia haageana.*

semperflorens (b). As usually cult., not over 1 ft. high, mostly less than 8 in., the whole

---

* Special articles on the subjects indicated by an asterisk (*) will be found at the words so marked.

plant nearly without hairs and rather fleshy. Leaves ovalish, glossy-green, 2–4 in. long, very finely toothed, and the margins fringed with minute hairs. Flowers white, pink or red (in some of the many forms), about 1 in. wide, blooming rather continuously when planted out for summer decoration. Brazil. Of the many varieties of this species, the leading bedding begonia, the best are: Corbeille de Feu, Gustav Lind, Ruby Jewel, and Pink Camellia.

socotrana (a). A low begonia from the island of Socotra, interesting for itself, but widely used by hybridizers in the production of hort. forms often credited to other species. Stems not over 1 ft. high, usually branched. Leaves nearly round, 6–7 in. wide, the stalk arising in the middle of the blade. Flowers rose-pink, about 1½ in. wide, in a long-stalked, forking cluster. Among its many named forms the best are: Mrs. Peterson, Melior, and Gloire de Lorraine. Some are called Christmas begonias because they are widely sold then by florists.

speculata (b). A trade name for a begonia of probably garden origin and uncertain identity. It has thick rootstocks and almost round leaves 6–8 in. wide, cut deeply, grayish above and red beneath. Flowers pinkish white. Almost certainly a cultigen.*

sutherlandi (a). A tuberous-rooted begonia, perhaps the most hardy after *B. evansiana*. Stems slender, 1–2 ft. high, purplish or reddish. Leaves narrowly oval, 4–6 in. long, lobed toward the base, toothed on the margin, green, with red veins above, on slender red stalks. Flowers numerous, in branched clusters (cymes*), orange or reddish-orange. Natal (Brazil).

tuberhybrida (a). A group name for many hybrid, tuberous-rooted begonias. They have not more than 2–3 stems. Leaves large, the stalk arising at the base of the blade. Flowers large, in all colors except blue, single or double, some of the forms camellia-like, others narcissus-like.

ulmifolia (b). A shrubby plant, rather rough and shaggy, 2–4 ft. high and branching. Leaves elm-like, green both sides, roughish, toothed and hairy, 3–5 in. long. Flowers numerous, about ½ in. wide, white, in loose clusters. Colombia.

verschaffeltiana (b). A hybrid begonia with large, ovalish, sharply pointed, deeply lobed green leaves. Flowers numerous, in drooping clusters, rose-pink. A cultigen.*

CULTURE AND USES OF BEGONIA

Most of the species above are derived from plants of moist, hot forests. Naturally they thrive best in a greenhouse that approximates these conditions, and, to make their best growth and produce their finest foliage, demand them. Many of them, however, will tolerate a reasonably warm, preferably moist, living room, especially forms of the rex begonia, and those derived from *B. socotrana*, and most of the fibrous-rooted kinds.

All begonias when in active growth are gross feeders and require plenty of liquid manure, but when growth stops they require a short resting period, during which water is reduced and feeding entirely stopped. After new growth begins they may be re-potted in potting mixture* 4.

For those who have no greenhouse, plants wintered over in the living room (a kitchen

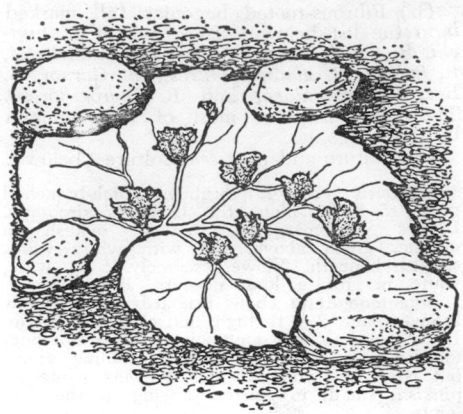

A begonia leaf held down on the sand by stones and forming new plants at the places where the veins were cut.

window, without a gas stove is better) may be brought outdoors after all danger of frost is past, well watered, and kept in partial shade.

Begonias are not good as cut flowers, as they are too delicate. However, nothing is more beautiful than a table piece of tuberous begonias with fern or smilax, while a cascade of flowers of Berthe de Chateauroher or President Carnot is a sight to be remembered.

The rex begonia now comprises hundreds of named garden forms, all hybrids or crosses of other ornamental species and varieties. They are favorites because of their beautiful leaves, variously marked with spots, colored bands, and metallic shadings. The best of the named forms are: Helen Teupel, President Carnot, Can-Can, Merry Christmas, Greenberry, Her Majesty, Gloire de Jouy, and Bodnant. There are also some splendid miniatures.

PROPAGATION. Begonias are grown from stem cuttings, leaf cuttings, division of the tubers, seeds, and in *semperflorens* varieties by root division. These can best be taken as directed below.

STEM CUTTING. Cut below a joint with a sharp knife, insert in moist sand, at room temperature. LEAF CUTTING. Rex begonia leaf cuttings 1½ in. long with main vein running through them, inserted in sand with bottom-heat, will root and form new plants; whole leaves of these varieties placed under benches and kept moist will develop plants on the surface of the leaves. Christmas begonias, hybrids of *B. socotrana*, are propagated by inserting the stalk of the leaf in sand or even in soil, or water. Still another method, especially for *B. evansiana*, is to use the bulbils* which sprout at the apex of the leafstalk where it joins the blade. A quick method is to spread the bulbils over the surface of potting mixture* 1, press down, and cover with glass. The bulbils* will soon

---

* Special articles on the subjects indicated by an asterisk (*) will be found at the words so marked.

produce young plants. DIVISION OF TUBERS. Cut tubers as in potatoes, leaving an eye on each cut, dust with charcoal, cover lightly with peat. When sprouted, plant in potting mixture* 4. SEEDS. These are as fine as dust, and are sown in potting mixture* 1 by placing in a groove of a bent card, which is tapped lightly to give an even distribution. Do not cover with soil, but place a sheet of glass and paper over the pot or pan. Water from below by dipping pot. ROOT DIVISION. The *semperflorens* varieties form clumps with many shoots; these are readily separated into pieces consisting of root and shoot, which may be immediately planted in potting mixture* 4.

The popular tuberous begonias should be started indoors in mid-March or early April in boxes or pots, using potting mixture* 3. Transplant them to a partially moist site only after all danger of frost is over. The modern vars. come in gorgeous colors, the flowers wax-like, single or double, and many vars. have such names as "carnation" begonia, "rosebud" begonia, "camellia" begonia, etc. They are superb summer bedding plants.

The Begonian, a monthly magazine devoted to begonias and other tender plants is published by the American Begonia Society at 3207 West 186th St., Torrance, Calif.

INSECT PESTS. Control whiteflies and mealybugs by repeated applications of pesticide #21 (*see* SPRAYS AND DUSTS).
DISEASES. Gray mold* may cover old dead flowers and advance from them into adjacent leaves and stems. Pick all flowers as soon as they have passed their prime. If gray mold or leafspot* become a problem on outdoor plants or in humid greenhouses, spray with pesticide #1 or #5 (*see* SPRAYS AND DUSTS) at 10-day intervals.

BELAMCANDA (bel-am-kan'da). A single Chino-Japanese, perennial herb of the iris family, usually called the blackberry lily, grown for ornament in the open border throughout the country. It has long, sword-shaped, 2-ranked leaves, and red-spotted, orange flowers. Flower segments 6, scarcely distinguishable as petals and sepals, the three inner ones shorter than the rest. Fruit a 3-valved capsule,* splitting in the autumn and revealing the blackberry-like seeds. (*Belamcanda* is a Latinized form of an Asiatic vernacular.)

chinensis. Blackberry lily. Leopard flower. From 2–4 ft. high. Leaves 10 in. long, 1 in. wide, iris-like. Flowers 1½–2 in. wide, soon withering. Fruit about 1 in. long. Easily grown in any ordinary garden soil and as easily propagated by spring division of its stout rootstock. June.

BELGIAN ELM = *Ulmus hollandica belgica.* See ELM.

belgica, -us, -um (bel'ji-ka). From Belgium.

bella, -us, -um. Handsome or pretty.

Belladonna (bel-la-don'na). From Italian for beautiful woman. One plant so named

contains a red sap used as a cosmetic. *See* ATROPA and AMARYLLIS.

BELLADONNA LILY = *Amaryllis Belladonna.*

BELLE ISLE CRESS = *Barbarea verna.*

BELLFLOWER. See CAMPANULA and OSTROWSKIA.

BELLFLOWER FAMILY = Campanulaceae.

BELL HEATHER = *Erica Tetralix.*

bellidioides (bel-lid-i-oy'deez; but *see* OIDES). Resembling a plant of the genus *Bellium* (which see).

BELLINGRATH GARDENS. *See* No. 4 at GARDEN TOURS.

BELLIS (bel'lis). A small genus of European herbs, family Compositae, one of them cult. for centuries as the true daisy, and a very popular bedding plant. Leaves mostly basal, forming a tuft in the one below. Flower heads solitary, on a naked stalk, its ray flowers, in the typical form, white or pink, the center of the head (disk* flowers) yellow. (The name is from the Latin *bella,* pretty.)

Plants for bedding should be raised from seed sown the previous year. It is a perennial, but often treated as a biennial (*see* BIENNIALS), and often escapes into lawns or borders, or even to roadsides. Its cheerful, early bloom has made it a favorite bedding plant for mass effects and it is also widely used for window boxes. Most of the finer double-flowered varieties, or those with quilled rays, do not come true from seed and should be propagated by division.

perennis. The true daisy of history and literature, but here commonly called English daisy or bachelor's-button. Not over 6 in. high. Leaves broadest toward the tip, in basal tufts. Flower heads nearly 2 in. wide, on stiff, erect stalks. Eu. Among the more desirable named forms, some widely used in city parks, are: Monstrosa, Dresden China, Longfellow, and The Bride. *Var.* ranunculiflora is double and comes in white, pink, and red.

BELLIUM (bel'li-um). A small genus of herbs of the Mediterranean region, family Compositae, sometimes grown in rock gardens for their small, solitary, daisy-like heads of white flowers. Leaves in a basal rosette. Ray flowers white, the disk* flowers yellow. The genus differs from *Bellis* only in technical flower characters. (*Bellium* means resembling a little *Bellis.*)

For culture and uses *see* ROCK GARDEN.

bellidioides. Perennial. Not over 4 in. high and with creeping stolons.* Leaves spatula-shaped. Flower heads about ½ in. wide. June.
minutum. Annual. Shorter, and with narrower leaves. Flower heads about ⅓ in. wide. July.

BELL-JAR. A glass, bell-shaped jar with a knob at the top, often used to give the plant over which it is set uniform atmospheric conditions, and to protect it from draughts or other disturbing factors. A modification of the bell-jar is the cloche, in which

---

* Special articles on the subjects indicated by an asterisk (*) will be found at the words so marked.

a small glass tent is made of separate pieces of glass or plastic clipped together at the edges. *See* CUTTINGS.

BELL PEPPER = *Capsicum frutescens grossum.*

BELLS OF IRELAND = *Molucella laevis.*

BELLWORT. *See* UVULARIA.

BELOPERONE (bel-o-per-own'e). A tropical American genus of 30 species of herbs or low shrubs, family Acanthaceae, only one of secondary interest to gardeners. The genus is separated only by technical characters from *Jacobinia.* Leaves opposite,* without marginal teeth. Flowers tubular but irregular* and 2-lipped, crowded in dense spikes and from between relatively showy, overlapping bracts.* Fruit a capsule.* (*Beloperone* is Greek, in allusion to the arrow-shaped anthers.)

The only cult. species is used as a border plant in zones* 8 and 9, elsewhere rather common as an attractive greenhouse plant. It requires plenty of moisture and liquid manure, and should be planted in potting mixture* 4.

guttata. Shrimp plant. Stems several, 12–18 in. high. Leaves ovalish, 1½–2½ in. long, and tapering to a slender stalk. Flowers in nearly cone-like clusters (spikes*), which are about 3 in. long and beset with numerous, reddish-brown bracts,* from between which the flowers are borne. Flowers about 1½ in. long, white, but spotted with purple. Mex. A form with yellow bracts is known in Calif. and another form is offered as *B. tomentosa.*

BELVEDERE CYPRESS = *Kochia scoparia trichophila.*

BENCH. A raised platform in a greenhouse,* in or upon which plants are grown. *Bench* is often used as a verb meaning that plants or seedlings are transferred from propagating beds, from outdoors, or brought from a resting period and planted in, or their pots put on, the bench.

BENDY TREE = *Thespesia populnea.*

BENE = Benne; *see* SESAMUM INDICUM.

benedictus. Blessed; *see* CNICUS.

BENGAL ROSE = *Rosa chinensis.*

benghalensis, -e (ben-gall-en'sis). From Bengal, India.

BENINCASA (ben-in-kay'sa). A tender annual, pumpkin-like and tendril*-bearing, Asiatic vine, belonging to the cucumber family. It is little known here, except as an ornamental, but in China is the source of the Chinese preserving melon (variously called zit-kwa, tunka and Chinese watermelon). The vine is fleshy, creeping, and has forked tendrils.* Leaves alternate,* large and angled. Flowers solitary, yellow, large, the stamens and pistils never in the same flower. Fruit large, melon-like, but without a hard rind. (Named for Giuseppe Benincasa, who founded the botanic garden at Pisa.)

The vine is grown mostly in warm countries, but can be grown here if treated as we do cucumbers or melons.

hispida. Wax gourd or white gourd (*see* above for other names). A long-trailing vine, the stem brown-hairy. Leaves broadly oval, heart-shaped at the base, 6–9 in. wide and angled on the margins. Flowers 3–4 in. wide. Fruit round-oblong, hairy, 8–15 in. long. Tropical As.

BENJAMIN-BUSH = *Lindera Benzoin.*

BENNE (and **Benny**) = *Sesamum indicum.*

BEN OIL. *See* MORINGA OLEIFERA.

BENT GRASS. *See* AGROSTIS.

BENZOIN (ben'zoin) = *Lindera.*

BERBERIDACEAE (ber-berry-day'see-e). The barberry family comprises perhaps a dozen genera of herbs or shrubs widely scattered over the north temperate zone, rare elsewhere. Much the most important genus is *Berberis*, comprising the barberries. The only other woody plants of garden interest are found in *Mahonia* and *Nandina*, both of which have compound* leaves, while the barberry has simple* leaves and often spiny branches.

All the rest of the hort. genera are herbs. Some have compound* leaves with many leaflets, like *Caulophyllum, Epimedium*, and *Vancouveria.* The rest have simple* leaves that often appear compound because some are lobed, finger-fashion, to or beyond the middle of the blade. (*See* MAYAPPLE, JEFFERSONIA, DIPHYLLEIA.)

Flowers rather large and solitary in the mayapple and *Jeffersonia*, smaller and in variously arranged clusters in all other hort. genera, mostly in racemes.* Fruit a berry or a capsule.* Some consider that the mayapple and *Diphylleia* belong to a newly created family, Podophyllaceae, not here maintained.

Technical flower characters: Sepals and petals with their margins overlapping. Petals often replaced by nectaries.* Ovary superior, 1-celled, its style short or none.

BERBERIDOPSIS (ber-berry-dop'sis). A single Chilean shrub, half vine-like, belonging to the family Flacourtiaceae, and grown outdoors in southern Calif. for its evergreen foliage and red flowers. Leaves alternate,* stalked and toothed. Flowers long-stalked, in clusters (racemes*), the cluster with many bracts. Petals, sepals, and bracts scarcely distinguishable from one another, totaling 9–15 segments. Stamens 7–10. Fruit a berry. (*Berberidopsis* is Greek for like *Berberis.*)

The plant will grow in a variety of soils, but if grown in the greenhouse use potting mixture* 4, and keep in a cool house. Propagated by spring-sown seeds, by green wood cuttings or by layering in the fall.

corallina. A low shrub inclined to sprawl or climb. Leaves oblongish, with a heart-shaped base, 2–3 in. long, spiny-toothed. Flowers nearly round, about ½ in. in diameter, the bracted* raceme about 4 in. long.

---

* Special articles on the subjects indicated by an asterisk (*) will be found at the words so marked.

BERBERIS (ber'ber-iss). The barberries (family Berberidaceae) are of first-rate hort. importance. The genus includes upwards of 400 species of evergreen or deciduous shrubs, all more or less spiny, and scattered throughout the north temperate zone (mostly in As.), with a few in north Af. and S.A. They have yellow wood and inner bark (cambium), and usually 3-branched spines at most of the axils.* Leaves simple,* appearing in small clusters at the ends of short spurs. Flowers yellow, in longish clusters (racemes*) or in closer clusters, all spring-blooming. Petals and stamens 6, the latter irritable and explosively discharging the pollen when touched. Fruit a berry. (*Berberis* is the Latinized form of an Arabic vernacular for the fruit.)

The barberry is used for its foliage, which turns to scarlets, orange, or yellow in the fall, its flowers, and for its handsome fruit, which in *B. sieboldi* and *B. thunbergi,* lasts through the winter. In the others the fruits shrivel or lose their color late in the fall.

A number are evergreens and not quite hardy in extreme winters (*see* hardiness notes below). Others, like the Japanese barberry, are widely planted for hedges or as specimen plants for the gorgeous autumnal foliage and persistent red berries. The box-barberry is a favorite plant for edging, where a low and much cheaper, but deciduous, substitute for real box is desirable.

There is a wide variety of color, stature, and habit to be found in the species below, which are the leading ones of over 50 known to be cult. in America. They are horticulturally so desirable that it is a pity that some must be rigorously excluded from wheat-growing regions. The European and some other barberries are an alternate host* for a serious wheat rust, and have been much exterminated because of this, especially *B. vulgaris.* Those that serve as hosts for rust are so marked below. The others may be considered free of the wheat rust at least, but it should be remembered that plant quarantine authorities will forbid all barberries to enter cereal-growing states.

Most of the species grow readily in ordinary garden soil, and are easily raised from seed. June-made cuttings, also, may be rooted in moist sand, preferably in a shaded hotbed.

For the plants with compound* leaves and no spines, sometimes credited to *Berberis,* see MAHONIA. These are also called barberry. All the species below drop their leaves in the fall unless noted as evergreen.

aggregata. A densely branched deciduous* shrub, 4–7 ft. high, the branches angled, with three-parted slender spines. Leaves oblongish, about 1 in. long, finely spiny-toothed. Flowers yellow, in dense stalkless clusters. Fruit nearly egg-shaped, about ¼ in. long, red but with a faint bloom.* Western China. Hardy from zone* 4 southward. *Var.* pratti has longer, sometimes toothless leaves and longer-stalked flower clusters. Considered by some as a distinct species known as *B. pratti.*

amurensis. From 3–8 ft. high, and related to the common barberry of Eu. (*B. vulgaris*), but with the leaves brighter green and with a more upright habit. Eastern As. Hardy from zone* 2 southward. Sometimes rust-infected.

atrocarpa. An evergreen shrub 2–3 ft. high, the young twigs reddish. Leaves elliptic or oblong, dark green above, paler beneath, spiny-margined, 1½–4 in. long. Flowers about ½ in. wide. Fruit bluish-black. China. Hardy from zone* 5 southward, possibly in sheltered parts of zone* 4.

beaniana. A deciduous shrub, half-evergreen in warm regions, 5–7 ft. high, the twigs reddish when young. Spines about 1 in. long, 3-parted. Leaves elliptic, about 1½ in. long, the margins spiny-toothed. Flowers yellow, about ½ in. wide, 10–20 in a cluster (panicle*). Fruit pea-size, purple, with a bloom. June. Western China. Hardy from zone* 6 southward.

buxifolia. Magellan barberry. Upright, not over 8 ft., and usually less in cult. Leaves evergreen, wedge-shaped at the base, prickle-tipped, ½–1¼ in. long. Flowers only one or two in a cluster, orange-yellow. Fruit dark purple. Southern Chile. Hardy from zone* 4 southward along the Pacific Coast. One of the best of the evergreen sorts and known, also, in a compact dwarf form and also in another where the spines are longer than the leaves.

canadensis. Allegheny or Canada barberry. A native shrub much resembling the common barberry of Eu. (*B. vulgaris*), but with the leaves grayish beneath. In the woods, Va. to Ga. and Mo. Hardy from zone* 4 southward. Sometimes rust-infected and often producing suckers.*

candidula. A low evergreen shrub, related to *Berberis verruculosa,* but dwarfer. Leaves elliptic, about ¾ in. long, the margin rolled and nearly hiding the few marginal spiny teeth; green above, hoary beneath. Flowers about ½ in. wide, solitary, yellow, followed by a small blue fruit with a bloom.* June. Central China. Hardy from zone 5* southward.

chenaulti. A hybrid barberry (*verruculosa × gagnepaini*) somewhat resembling both these plants but having more arching habit, shorter leaves and larger flowers. June. Hardy from zone* 4 southward.

darwini. Handsome evergreen shrub 5–8 ft. high. Leaves oblongish, or broader toward the tip, ½–1½ in., rather remotely, but spiny-toothed, and with a 3-pronged spine at the tip. Flowers golden-yellow in drooping clusters (racemes*). Fruit dark purple. Chile. Hardy from zone* 6 southward along the Pacific Coast. A related, somewhat more hardy species, is *B. ilicifolia.* It has orange-yellow flowers in shorter clusters, and is perhaps hardy in zone* 5. Both are offered by many nurserymen, but the plant sold as *B. ilicifolia* is usually *Mahoberberis neuberti.*

diaphana. A deciduous* spiny shrub not usually over 5 ft. high, the foliage scarlet in autumn. Leaves oblongish or egg-shaped, ¾–1 in. long, finely toothed or toothless, pale bluish-green beneath. Flowers solitary or in a sparse cluster, yellow. Fruit reddish, with a faint bloom. Western China. Hardy from zone* 4 southward.

dictiophylla. A shrub, mostly less than 6 ft. high, the young branches very glaucous.* Leaves deciduous,* oblongish, rounded at the tip, ¾–1 in. long, whitish beneath. Flowers short-stalked, solitary, yellow. Fruit red. Western China. Hardy from zone* 4 southward.

gagnepaini. An evergreen shrub 4–6 ft. high, the branches spreading. Leaves narrow,

* Special articles on the subjects indicated by an asterisk (*) will be found at the words so marked.

lance-shaped, 1–3 in. long, with a wavy, but spiny-toothed margin. Flowers in clusters of 3–10, about ½ in. wide. Fruit bluish-black, with a bloom. Western China. Hardy from zone* 5 southward. Sometimes rust-infected.

hookeri. An evergreen barberry, 4–6 ft. high, the elliptic or oblong leaves 1½–3 in. long, spiny-margined, and white beneath. Flowers in clusters of 3–6, yellowish-green, about ¾ in. wide. Fruit oblong, about ½ in. long, blackish. Himalayas. Hardy from zone* 6 southward. June.

ilicifolia. *See* BERBERIS DARWINI.

julianae. Wintergreen barberry. An upright evergreen shrub 4–6 ft. high. Leaves narrowly elliptic, 1½–3 in. long, the margins toothed and spiny, dark green above, pale beneath. Flowers in close clusters. Fruit bluish-black, with a bloom. Central China. Hardy from zone* 4 southward, the hardiest of the evergreen species, and one of the most popular of all the Chinese species.

koreana. A deciduous* shrub, the young branches grooved, reddish and with a bloom,* ultimately dark brown. Leaves rounded at the tip, wedge-shaped at the base, 1½–3 in. long, pale beneath. Flowers yellow, in dense, nearly stalkless clusters (racemes*). Fruit bright red, holding its color late in the fall. Korea. Hardy from zone* 4 southward.

linearifolia. An evergreen shrub, 3–4 ft. high, its shoots grooved and yellow. Leaves 1½ in. long, scarcely ⅓ in. wide, the margins rolled but not spiny. Flowers 4–6 in a cluster, apricot. Fruit ovoid, about ¼ in. long. Chile. Hardy from zone* 7 southward. June.

mentorensis. A spiny, hybrid barberry (*julianae × thunbergi*), but evergreen in mild regions and a valuable addition to the group. It grows 3–5 ft. high. Leaves elliptic, not much spiny-toothed, 1–2½ in. long, toothed and pale beneath. Flowers 1 or 2 in the cluster, yellow. Fruit dark red, football-shaped. May–June. Hardy from zone* 4 southward. Makes an impenetrable thorny hedge, and will stand drought.

sargentiana. Evergreen, the branches somewhat spreading, not usually over 5 ft. high. Leaves elliptic or oblong, 2–4½ in. long, closely toothed and the teeth spiny, dark green above. Flowers in close clusters, each about ½ in. wide. Fruit bluish-black, with a bloom.* Central China. Hardy from zone* 6 southward.

sieboldi. A low shrub, rarely over 4 ft. high. Leaves oblong or broader toward the tip, 1½–3 in. long, not spiny-margined, but densely fringed along the leaf-edge with hairs. Flowers 3–6 in a cluster. Fruit shining red, winter-persisting. Japan. Hardy from zone* 4 southward. Fall foliage red. Sometimes rust-infected.

stenophylla. Evergreen and from 6–8 ft. high. Leaves narrowly lance-shaped, ¾–1½ in. long, spiny-tipped, but with a rolled margin, dark green above, whitish beneath. Flowers about ½ in. wide in clusters of 2–6, golden-yellow. Of hybrid origin. Hardy from zone* 5, and in sheltered parts of zone* 4 southward but not thriving in the East.

thunbergi. The Japanese barberry more widely cult. than almost any other shrub, and usually 4–6 ft. high when mature. Branches ultimately purple-brown. Leaves variable, usually broader toward the tip, ½–1½ in. long, without teeth. Flowers yellow, but red-tinged outside, about ⅛ in. wide, solitary or in close clusters of 2–5. Fruit bright red, winter-persisting. Japan. Hardy from the southern part of zone* 3 southward. Autumn foliage brilliant scarlet. There are several hort. varieties, some

with variegated leaves. The best-known one, *var.* minor, commonly called box-barberry, is a dwarf, dense form with smaller leaves and rarely exceeds 15 in. in height if trimmed, otherwise it may reach 3 ft.

triacanthophora. Low, evergreen shrub, rarely more than 3½ ft. high. Leaves narrow, 1–2½ in. long, less than ½ in. wide, finely and bristly toothed, green above, bluish-gray beneath. Flowers whitish-yellow, tinged with red. Fruit blue-black, with a slight bloom.* Central China. Hardy from zone* 4 southward.

vernae. A densely branched deciduous* shrub, 4–6 ft. high, the stems grooved and purplish. Leaves inequilateral,* not over 1 in. long, practically without teeth, veiny both sides. Flowers yellow, in dense, nearly stalkless clusters. Fruit round, pale red. Northwestern China. Hardy from zone* 4 southward.

verruculosa. Evergreen and not over 3 ft. high, the branches warty. Leaves ovalish or elliptic, ¾–1½ in. long, glossy-green, remotely spiny-toothed, and pale beneath. Flowers larger than in most barberries, golden-yellow, about ¾ in. wide. Fruit bluish-black, with a bloom. Western China. Hardy from zone* 4 southward.

vulgaris. The common or European barberry. A somewhat arching shrub 5–9 ft. high. Leaves elliptic or oblongish, 1–2 in. long, green but not shining green. Flowers in short-stalked clusters (racemes*). Fruit bright red or purple. Eu. Hardy from zone* 2 throughout the country and frequently naturalized. Much less valuable as a garden plant than most of the others. It resembles *B. amurensis* and *B. canadensis*, and like them is pretty apt to be rust-infected.

wilsonae. A prostrate or erect, half-evergreen, and very spiny shrub, sometimes 6 ft. high. Leaves ⅓–¾ in. long, without teeth, but tipped with a short prickle, pale green. Flowers golden-yellow, about ½ in. wide, in various sorts of small clusters. Fruit coral-red or salmon-colored. Western China. Hardy from zone* 5 southward. Sometimes rust-infected. The variety sold as Tom Thumb, with slightly toothed leaves and prolific red fruit, belongs to this species. There are several others.

BERCHEMIA (ber-kee'mi-a). A small genus of woody vines, family Rhamnaceae, grown for the ornamental foliage. Leaves alternate,* without marginal teeth but with conspicuous parallel veins. Flowers greenish or greenish-white, in branched clusters (panicles*), but small and inconspicuous (for detailed structure *see* RHAMNACEAE). Fruit fleshy. (*Berchemia* was named for M. Berchem, French botanist.)

The species below are moderately decorative, but not high-climbing vines, as cult., and without special soil preferences. They may be propagated by spring-sown seeds or root cuttings or by cuttings of ripened wood in autumn.

racemosa. A woody vine 10–15 ft. long. Leaves ovalish, somewhat heart-shaped at the base, 1½–2½ in. long, green above but paler beneath. Flowers greenish, the clusters about 4 in. long. Fruit red at first, ultimately black. Japan and Formosa. Hardy from zone* 5 southward.

scandens. Supplejack. Climbing to 15–20 ft. in cult., but to the treetops in the wild. Leaves elliptic or oblong-oval, not over 2 in. long. Flowers greenish-white, the clusters

---

* Special articles on the subjects indicated by an asterisk (*) will be found at the words so marked.

scarcely 2 in. long. Fruit bluish-black. In woods Va. to Fla. and Tex. Hardy from zone* 5 southward.

BERGAMOT. See MONARDA and CITRUS BERGAMA.

BERGAMOT LIME = *Triphasia trifolia.*

BERGAMOT MINT = *Mentha citrata.* See MINT.

BERGENIA (ber-gen′i-a). Half a dozen Asiatic, perennial herbs, family Saxifragaceae, three of which are grown in the border for their ornamental foliage and very early-blooming pink or white flowers. They have thickened rootstocks and from them the plants grow in pretty dense clumps or colonies. Leaves mostly basal, thick and fleshy, pitted, half evergreen, the stalks with a sheathing base. Flowers large, in nodding clusters (panicles* or racemes*), the stalk thick and fleshy. (Named for K. A. von Bergen, a German botanist.)

Closely related to *Saxifraga*, grown like them, and all the species below are often offered as *Saxifraga*. The first two are hardy over most of the country, but are better protected with a light straw mulch in the North. *B. ligulata* is not certainly hardy north of zone* 5. The genus is sometimes known as *Megasea*.

cordifolia. A stout, fleshy herb 12–18 in. high. Leaves thick, shining, nearly round, wavy-margined, somewhat heart-shaped at the base. Flowers rose-pink, the clusters among the leaves. Siberia. There are also white and purple-flowered hort. forms.

crassifolia. Siberian tea. Similar to the above, but the leaves longer and with the blade extending down the leafstalk. Flowers rose-pink or lilac, the clusters standing above the foliage. Eastern As.

ligulata. A very showy plant with large leaves nearly round but tapering toward the base, the margins somewhat scalloped and fringed with hairs. Flowers white or rose-purple, in nodding clusters (racemes*). Himalayas. Not certainly hardy north of zone* 5 but sometimes so with protection. There are several named hort. varieties and forms, a very striking one being *var.* **leichtlini,** with crimson leaves and rose-colored flowers.

BERGEROCACTUS (ber′jer-o-kak-tus). A single species of cactus found in southern and Lower Calif. and cult. for its habit of making large colonies or patches and for its day-blooming, yellow flowers. The only species, **B. emoryi,** is an erect-growing plant, 1–2 ft. high, with many closely ribbed, cylindric branches covered with sharp, yellow spines, the stems not over 2 in. thick. Flowers about ¾ in. wide. Useful for decorative plantings in desert gardens and scarcely cult. otherwise. (Named for Alwin Berger, a horticulturist and botanist long interested in succulents.) It is difficult to transplant and is best started from seed sown where wanted.

BERMUDA BUTTERCUP = *Oxalis cernua.*

BERMUDA GRASS = *Cynodon Dactylon.*

BERMUDA LILY. The Easter lily. See LILIUM.

BERMUDA PALMETTO = *Sabal blackburniana.*

bermudiana, -us, -um (ber-mew-di-a′na). From Bermuda.

berolinensis, -e (ber-o-lin-en′sis). From Berlin.

BERRY. A confusing term. Commonly, almost any fleshy fruit such as strawberry, blackberry, raspberry, cranberry, currant, or blueberry, but technically the first three are not berries at all. In the strict botanical sense a berry is a fleshy or pulpy fruit that does not usually split open, has few or many seeds, but no stone. It always develops from a single enlarged ovary. Typical examples of true berries are currant, blueberry, cranberry, grape, tomato, and eggplant. See STRAWBERRY. See also PEPO.

BERRY-BEARING PLANTS. Many shrubs and trees are useful for the autumn color of their fruits or because the fruits are the feed of birds. For the former purpose see the list at AUTUMN GARDEN. For those useful to birds see Food Supply at BIRDS.

BERSEEM = *Trifolium alexandrinum.* See CLOVER.

BERTHOLLETIA (ber-thoe-lesh′i-a). A genus of South American trees, family Lecythidaceae, of no garden interest except to those living in the warmest parts of zone* 9. Of the two known species, one, **B. excelsa,** is the Brazil-nut or Pará-nut, the seeds of which (often called nigger-toes) are the Brazil-nuts of commerce. It is a tall tree, needing heat, moisture and a rich soil for proper development. Leaves leathery, oblong, nearly 2 ft. long. Flowers cream-white, in spike-like clusters (racemes*), with no petals, but colored sepals. Fruit a hard, woody, brown structure about 4 in. in diameter, containing 18–24 of the familiar nuts. (Named for C. L. Berthollet, French chemist.)

BERTOLONIA (ber-toe-low′ni-a). A small Brazilian genus of showy-foliaged herbs, family Melastomaceae, grown in greenhouses for their attractive, opposite,* 3–9-veined and sometimes banded leaves. Flowers rose-colored or purple, in one-sided clusters (racemes*). Petals 5. Stamens 10. Fruit a 3-valved pod (capsule*), enclosed by the persistent calyx. (Named for Antonio Bertoloni, Italian botanist.)

The species below are attractive foliage plants that need a warm (70°) greenhouse, plenty of moisture and a partially shaded section of the house. Use potting mixture* 4. Easily propagated by cuttings in moist sand over bottom-heat.*

maculata. Stems low or creeping, densely covered with rusty hairs. Leaves with magenta or purple bands along the veins, hairy, generally green, but sometimes spotted with color. Flowers rose-pink.

marmorata. Similar but not so hairy-

---

* Special articles on the subjects indicated by an asterisk (*) will be found at the words so marked.

stemmed and with whitish bands along the leaf-veins. Flowers purple.

bessarabica, -us, -um (bess-a-rab′i-ka). From Bessarabia, in eastern Rumania.

BESSERA. A small genus of bulbous herbs of the lily family, perhaps comprising only **B. elegans**, known as coral drops or Mexican coral drops. It is allied to *Milla*, and the plant offered as *Bessera elegans* may often be *Milla biflora*. But *B. elegans* is a taller plant, the 2 or 3 narrow leaves up to 2 ft. long. Flowers in a drooping, long-stalked umbel,* the corolla about 1 in. long, a gorgeous orange-red, marked creamy white inside. Mex. It is a showy herb cult. outdoors in southern Calif., but not certainly hardy in regions of severe winters. (*Bessera* was named for Dr. W. S. J. G. von Besser, a Polish botanist.)

BETA. *See* BEET.

betacea, -us, -um (bee-tay′see-a). Beet-like.

BETELNUT, BETEL PALM. *See* ARECA CATECHU.

BETHLEHEM SAGE = *Pulmonaria saccharata.*

BETHROOT = *Trillium erectum.*

BETONICA. *See* STACHYS

betonicifolia, -us, -um (bee-ton-i-ki-fō′li-a). With leaves like a plant of the genus *Betonica*, especially *B. grandiflora*, here treated as *Stachys grandiflora* (which see).

BETONY. *See* STACHYS.

BETULA. *See* BIRCH.

BETULACEAE (bet-you-lay′see-e). The birch family, often called alder or hazel family, contains only trees and shrubs of the northern hemisphere. Five of its six known genera are cultivated for ornament, or for the nuts, in the hazel. All have alternate* leaves with relatively straight (not curved or arching) veins. Male and female flowers in separate catkins on the same plant. Male catkins, long, in small groups and hanging. Female catkins shorter, almost headlike. Fruit a small nut with membranous wings in the birch (*Betula*) but large and edible, and without the wing, in the hazel (*Corylus*).

The other hort. genera include the hornbeam (*Carpinus*), *Ostrya* (the hop-hornbeam), and the alder (*Alnus*).

Technical flower characters: Petals none. Female catkins with or without a minute calyx; ovary 2-celled, each cavity of it, with a single ovule. Male catkins with a 2–4-parted calyx in the birches and alders, but without a calyx in the hornbeam and hazel.

betulaefolia, -us, -um (bet-you-lee-fō′li-a). With leaves like a birch.

betulina, -us, -um (bet-you-ly′na). Birch-like.

betuloides (bet-you-loy′deez; but *see* OïDES). Resembling a birch.

Betulus. An old name for a birch-like tree, or perhaps for the birch itself. *See* HORNBEAM.

bicolor (by′color, also bick′o-lor). Two-colored.

bicornis, -e (by-cor′nis). Two-horned.

BIDENS (by′denz). A large genus of somewhat weedy herbs, family Compositae, generally called bur-marigold, stick-tight or tickseed. The only species of garden interest is **B. ferulaefolia**, a Mexican annual with yellow flowers. They have usually divided or dissected leaves with toothed segments. Flowers yellow, with bright rays in the one below (often rayless in some native weeds). Fruit a small, flat, 2-pronged and barbed achene,* which, in our weeds, is a familiar fall pest to woolen-clothed walkers. (*Bidens* is Latin for 2-toothed, in reference to the fruit.)

Bidens ferulaefolia is an easily cult. annual. Sow the seeds in any ordinary garden soil, after danger of frost is past. For *B. frondosa* (often called beggar-ticks, bootjack, or Spanish needles), which is a troublesome weed, *see* Beggar-ticks in the list at WEEDS.

ferulaefolia. Smooth and branching annual herb. Leaves dissected into narrow segments. Flower heads about ¾ in. wide, in close or open clusters (corymbs*), bright yellow. Mex. Midsummer.

BIENNIAL. Requiring two growing seasons for the completion of its life. True biennials die after they have set seed. (*See* ANNUAL and PERENNIAL.) For the garden uses and culture of biennial plants *see* BIENNIALS.

BIENNIALS. Plants listed as biennials, as a class, are not difficult of culture. The chief objection to them is their brief period of life. Of the ornamental kinds the majority bloom the second year from seed sown the previous midsummer. A few of the hardier sorts are treated as perennials, seed being sown directly into the ground where they are to remain during their lifetime. This is satisfactory only in localities where winter-killing or rotting of the crowns need not be feared. Foxgloves and Canterbury bells (*see* CAMPANULA MEDIUM) are examples of biennials that nearly always rot when the seed is sown in the aforesaid manner. Short-lived perennials are in many instances, for convenience, classified as biennials and cult. as such. Examples of flowering plants that are commonly grown as biennials are Canterbury bells, hollyhocks, foxgloves, English daisies, some forget-me-nots, honesty, *Lychnis* (some species), horn poppy, verbascums, the improved Sweet Williams, pansies, and Siberian wallflowers.

The best and safest way to treat biennials is to plant the seed in June or July in flats. Later prick out and transplant the seedlings to 3-in. pots and put in the cold frame. Do not transplant them to the garden from the flats. Plunge the pots up to the rim in soil, allowing 8 in. between them. Keep a uniform temperature throughout the winter. Cover with boards or regulation hotbed cover.

---

* Special articles on the subjects indicated by an asterisk (*) will be found at the words so marked.

A light mulch of dry leaves, marsh hay or strawy litter should be placed around the crowns to keep them dry, and among the foliage in such a way that the centers are not smothered. Transfer to beds or borders when the weather permits in the spring. Should you have failed to start your biennials the previous midsummer, try planting them in flats in Feb. Prick them out as soon as the tiny second leaves appear and again transplant, once or twice more, to insure continuous growth. Feb. planting is not, however, so satisfactory a method. If your flats or young plants are grown under the ordinary conditions of home and not in a greenhouse, newspapers may be used as night coverings.

Where biennials are to be included in the mixed border, they must be treated as annual plants. The young seedlings should be placed in the desired position where they are to bloom, and renewed by other plants the following year. Even those biennials which are hardy and self-sowing, such as the hollyhocks, are not to be depended upon. Second-year plants in many cases have a tendency to be weak and straggling, with much smaller blooms. The larger plants should be massed at the back, with the low-growing sorts in the front of the border, to facilitate handling. By so doing the ground may be prepared for their occupancy with the least amount of disturbance of the perennials and hardy shrubs.

Canterbury bells and the "cup and saucer" form are indispensable garden flowers which like a good rich soil and last much longer in bloom if planted in a half-shady place. Sow the seed in flats in separate rows as to color, and water thoroughly, transplanting later to the cold frame. The "cup and saucer" type make excellent pot and conservatory plants for table decoration.

The improved Sweet William (*Dianthus barbatus*) is really a perennial but does much better when treated as a biennial. As a matter of fact, all the perennial species of *Dianthus* should be renewed every two or three years, preferably by seeds when named varieties are not included. The rich color of the flowers produces a splendid effect in beds and borders.

The common foxgloves are usually treated as biennials, seed sown early in the spring producing flowering plants the following year. *Digitalis purpurea* and its horticultural varieties are great favorites for general plantings, making excellent accent plants for the border. Hollyhocks are best used either in massed plantings or as background for low-growing plants.

Forget-me-nots may be planted out of doors, in moderately moist soil, if given winter protection. The annual sorts bloom the first year from seed; the biennials bloom early the second year. Pansies give their best bloom on young plants. Grown as perennials, with care they may survive for many years, but new stock should be kept coming on every year if the large choice blooms are to be had. Seed sown in mid-August gives blooming plants in early spring; seed sown in January makes blooming plants by early summer. Siberian wallflowers are sometimes handled as annuals, as they will bloom during the summer from seed sown early in the spring. Their dwarf height makes them good rock garden subjects.

biennis, -e (by-en'nis). Biennial (which see).

bifida, -us, -um (biff'i-da). Cut into two parts.

biflora, -us, -um (by-flow'ra). Two-flowered.

bifolia, -us, -um (by-fō'li-a). Two-leaved.

bifurcata, -us, -um (by-fur-kay'ta). Twice-forked.

BIGARREAU CHERRY. See CHERRY.

BIG-CONE PINE = *Pinus coulteri.* See PINE.

BIGENERIC HYBRID. The result of a cross between plants belonging to different genera. They are known between *Crinum* and *Amaryllis* (see AMARCRINUM), the radish and cabbage, *Selenicereus* and *Heliocereus* and several other cactus genera, between *Cytisus* and *Laburnum, Sorbus* and *Aronia, Sorbus* and *Pyrus,* and between several orchid genera. See BRASSOCATTLEYA, LAELIOCATTLEYA and BRASSOLAELIA.

BIG LAUREL = *Magnolia grandiflora.*

BIG MARIGOLD = *Tagetes erecta.* See MARIGOLD.

BIGNONIA (big-known'i-a). A beautiful woody vine, usually called the cross-vine, is one of the two species here included in the genus *Bignonia,* once considered as including many other plants (see below). The cross-vine, or **Bignonia capreolata,** or trumpet-flower as it is sometimes called, is an evergreen, high-climbing, woody vine. It has compound* leaves with 2 stalked leaflets which are without marginal teeth, and a terminal tendril.* Leaflets 4–6 in. long. Flowers funnel-shaped, but slightly irregular, about 2 in. long, reddish-orange but pale within, grouped in clusters (cymes*) in the leaf axils.* Fruit a long, narrow, slightly flattened pod, 5–8 in. long. (Named for the Abbé Jean Paul Bignon, court librarian to Louis XIV.) Called also *Anisostichus capreolatus.*

The cross-vine is a handsome creeper (see VINES) found wild from Md. and southern Ill. to Fla. and La. It is hardy from zone* 6 southward, and is usually winter-killed north of this.

chamberlayni. A stout Brazilian climber, often grown in the South, its ovalish leaves shining above but paler beneath. Flowers in clusters (racemes*) at the leaf joints, funnel-shaped, showy, yellow. Aug.–Sept. Hardy from zone* 7 (possibly in protected parts of zone* 6) southward. Called by some *Anemopaegma.*

Other plants of the family Bignoniaceae,

---

* Special articles on the subjects indicated by an asterisk (*) will be found at the words so marked.

once, and sometimes still, credited to the genus *Bignonia*, are:

Bignonia buccinatoria = *Phaedranthus buccinatorius.*
" *grandiflora* = *Campis grandiflora.* See TRUMPET-CREEPER.
" *radicans* = *Campsis radicans.* See TRUMPET-CREEPER.
" *speciosa* = *Clytostoma callistegioides.*
" *stans* = *Stenolobium stans.*
" *tweediana* = *Doxantha Unguis-cati.*
" *Unguis-cati* = " " "
" *venusta* = *Pyrostegia ignea.*

BIGNONIACEAE (big-known-i-ā′see-ee). The trumpet-creeper family, often called catalpa or cross-vine family, comprises nearly 100 genera and over 750 species of widely distributed trees, shrubs, and woody vines, many of which are handsome garden plants. The only herbaceous hort. genus is *Incarvillea.*

While most are tropical, a few well-known ones are temperate zone plants, notably the trumpet-creeper (*Campsis*), the catalpa, and *Bignonia* or cross-vine.

Leaves opposite, simple* or of many leaflets. The only hort. genera with simple leaves are *Chilopsis, Catalpa,* and the calabash (*Crescentia*), all the others having compound leaves and many of the vines having the terminal leaflet replaced by tendrils.* Flowers perfect,* nearly always in showy clusters, more or less tubular or funnel-shaped and always slightly irregular* or two-lipped.* Fruit usually a longish pod, splitting lengthwise, its seeds usually winged.

Upright trees and shrubs of garden interest are found in *Spathodea, Stenolobium, Tabebuia, Jacaranda, Kigelia, Oroxylon,* and *Parmentiera.* But woody vines are among the most handsome of the plants in this family: *see* CLYTOSTOMA, CYDISTA, ECCREMOCARPUS, PANDOREA, PHAEDRANTHUS, PYROSTEGIA, TECOMARIA, and DISTICTIS. *See also* TECOMA.

Technical flower characters: Ovary superior,* the style slender, with a 2-lobed stigma. Calyx tubular, its lobes blunt or 5-toothed. Corolla slightly irregular, its five lobes unequal. Stamens usually 4, rarely 5 or 6, and if so, one or more sterile.

bignonioides (big-known-i-oy′deez; but *see* OÏDES). Resembling the cross-vine (*Bignonia*).

BIG SHAGBARK = *Carya laciniosa.* See HICKORY.

Bihai. A tropical American vernacular name for the wild plantain (*Heliconia Bihai*).

bijuga, -us, -um (by-jew′ga). Yoked; two in a pair.

BILLBERGIA (bill-ber′ji-a). A genus of 50 or more species of tropical American air plants (*see* EPIPHYTES) belonging to the family Bromeliaceae, a few of which are cult. by fanciers for their foliage and showy, bracted* flower clusters. Only those below

are at all common in greenhouse collections and offered by florists. They have spiny, pineapple-like leaves in a basal rosette from which arises a long, branching flower cluster. Flowers with a 3-parted calyx,* 3 petals, and 6 long-protruding stamens.* Beneath the flowers and at many of the joints of the cluster are showy bracts,* scarlet and narrow in the first one below. Fruit fleshy. (Named for J. G. Billberg, Swedish botanist.)

Billbergias need a warm, moist greenhouse (70°–80°) and plenty of moisture at the roots while they are actively growing and blooming (spring and summer). In the winter they need less watering, and when actually in flower, it is better to reduce the amount of water. They should be planted in wooden or latticed boxes, in hanging baskets, or in pans. If pans or pots are used, be sure that there is at least 2 in. of broken flower pots in the bottom. Use one half of potting mixture* 3 and one half fern roots or coconut fiber to which should be added a little charcoal. It is better to hang the boxes or pans about 2 ft. from the greenhouse roof than to grow billbergias on the bench.

nutans. A stemless air plant with long, linear leaves (1–2 ft.) remotely and finely toothed on the margin and finely striped on the back. Flowers 4–8 in a drooping cluster, the flowers green but blue-edged. Brazil.

pyramidalis. Leaves about a dozen, strap-shaped, nearly 2 ft. long and about 2 in. wide, finely spiny-toothed on the margin, white-banded beneath. Flowers red, in dense clusters (spikes*), the petals violet-tipped; bracts* red. Brazil. A very handsome species.

saundersi. Leaves 5 or 6, about 15 in. long and strap-shaped, blunt but with a short, weak terminal prickle, green above, red beneath, white-blotched both sides. Flowers about 2 in. long, in a drooping cluster, reddish-green, and blue-tipped. Brazil.

BILLION DOLLAR GRASS = *Echinochloa Crus-galli frumentacea.*

BILTMORE ESTATE. See No. 15 at GARDEN TOURS.

BINDWEED. See CONVOLVULUS.

BINOMIAL. Having both a generic and specific Latin name. *See* PLANT NAMES.

BIOCHEMICAL GARDENING = Organic Gardening.

BIOTA. See THUJA ORIENTALIS.

bipinnata, -us, -um (by-pin-nay′ta). Twice pinnate* or twice pinnately cut; that is, the segments or leaflets arranged feather-fashion.

bipinnatifida, -us, -um (by-pin-nat-i-fid′a). Twice cut or cleft.

BIRCH. Medium or tall trees (rarely shrubs) of more economic importance for timber or aromatic properties than for ornament. All belong to the genus **Betula** (bet′-you-la), of the family Betulaceae, which comprises over 40 species, mostly North American or Asiatic. Leaves alternate,* always toothed and with relatively straight veins. Flowers without petals, in early-blooming catkins or spikes, or (in the female

---

* Special articles on the subjects indicated by an asterisk (*) will be found at the words so marked.

flowers) in small, cone-like but leafy-bracted clusters (strobiles*), the bracts 3-pointed and dropping at maturity with the minute nut. (*Betula* is the classical name of the birch.)

Most of the birches are not particular as to soil, and few of them are of much value as lawn specimens except the beautiful white-barked sorts from N.A. and the Old World. Unfortunately, all are rather short-lived. Grouped with evergreens the white or paper birch makes beautiful winter pictures. Some of the weeping and cut-leaved hort. forms are also widely planted for ornament. Aromatic, as used below, means the familiar birch-bark odor which is found, however, only in some species. The trees are easily propagated by seeds (fresh sown or stratified); they are also easily grafted. All the birches are wind-pollinated.

B. alba. A common name in nursery catalogues. It applies to the white-barked canoe birch (*B. papyrifera*) of N.A. and the European white birch (*B. pendula*).

B. fontinalis. Red birch, also called black birch. More or less shrubby tree, usually in clumps and (in cult.) not over 25 ft. high, the bark aromatic. Leaves broadly oval, double-toothed, 1–2 in. long, glandular*-dotted on the under side. Female flower cluster (strobile*) nearly as large as the leaves. Alaska to Ore. and Colo. Hardy from zone* 4 northward.

B. lenta. Sweet birch; called also black birch and cherry birch. An aromatic tree up to 75 ft. high, the bark dark, reddish-brown. Leaves oblong-oval, 3–5 in. long, tapering at the tip and heart-shaped at the base, double-toothed. Female flower cluster (strobile*) ⅓ as long as the leaf. Ont. to Ga. and Tenn. Hardy from zone* 3 southward.

B. lutea. Yellow birch. A most important timber tree but less so horticulturally, often 80–90 ft. high, the bark yellowish and characteristically unrolling like shavings, aromatic. Leaves ovalish or oval-oblong, 4–7 in. long, with pale hairs on the veins beneath. Female flower cluster (strobile*) about ⅓ as long as the leaves. Newfoundland to Ga. and Tenn., mostly in the mountains. Hardy from zone* 3 southward, but does not like the heat of the coastal plain.

B. nigra. River birch; called also red birch. A tree 60–80 ft. high, its reddish-brown, ragged bark not aromatic. Leaves somewhat rhombic or ovalish, 1½–3½ in. long, doubly toothed, whitish below when young. Female flower cluster (strobile*) about half as long as the leaves. Mass. to Fla. and westward, and hardy throughout the country, but it needs a moist or even wet site.

B. papyracea = *Betula papyrifera*.

B. papyrifera. Canoe or paper birch; it is the white birch of eastern N.A. A tree up to 90 ft. or more, its brilliantly white bark not aromatic. Leaves more or less oval, but narrowed or wedge-shaped at the base, 3–5 in. long, double-toothed. Female flower cluster (strobile*) about ⅓ the leaf length. Almost throughout the cooler parts of N.A. and preferring zone* 4 and northward in cult.

B. pendula. European white birch. A tree resembling our canoe or paper birch, but not so tall, and in old trees with more or less drooping branches, and with resinous twigs. Leaves rhombic or ovalish, mostly wedge-shaped at the base, doubly toothed, 3–5 in. long. Fe-

male flower cluster (strobile*) 1–1½ in. long. Eu. and As. Minor. Hardy from zone* 2 southward, but not long-lived. This is the commonest white birch of cult. It is found in many attractive forms, especially one with finely divided leaves, another with still more drooping branches (nearly a weeping form) and one with a compact, bushy crown having no drooping branches.

B. populifolia. Gray birch. A weedy and horticulturally useless tree, included here because its similarity to *B. papyrifera* often leads to unscrupulous substitution. The gray birch is (in maturity) much smaller, has dirty-white bark (brilliant white in youth) and its more or less triangular leaves are broadest at the base. Nova Scotia to Va. Useful only where other trees will not thrive. It will grow in very poor, stony soil, or even on sandy or cindery wastes, but is short-lived. Often offered, incorrectly, as *Betula alba*.

INSECT PESTS. In central and eastern U.S., leaf-mining larvae disfigure leaves and cause heavy leaf drop of *B. populifolia* and other species. The adult wasps lay eggs in leaves beginning when largest leaves are about 1 in. across. Control with a lindane spray applied when punctures and small mines become visible. For best results, repeat spray twice at 10-day intervals. This spray will also control gray aphids. *See* SPRAYS AND DUSTS.

BIRCH FAMILY. A small family of shrubs and trees comprising, in the hort. genera, the birch, alder, hazel, hornbeam, and the hop-hornbeam. For the characters of the family *see* BETULACEAE.

BIRD BILLS. *See* DODECATHEON.

BIRD CHERRY = *Prunus Padus*.

BIRD-OF-PARADISE BUSH = *Poinciana gilliesi*.

BIRD-OF-PARADISE FLOWER = *Strelitzia reginae*.

BIRD PEPPER = *Capsicum frutescens*.

BIRDS. Birds are an attractive and very useful garden feature which can be increased by attention to a few fundamentals. Protection, food, water, and nesting sites must be provided.

PROTECTION

About gardens, cats are the worst enemies of small birds. They are natural predators, no matter how well fed. Stray cats may be trapped in box traps and turned over to the humane societies, or killed humanely.

Nest boxes and feeding trays placed in trees or on poles may be made secure against feline depredations by metal bands a foot in width and six feet from the ground. Bird baths and fountains should be of metal, concrete, or stone, and afford the best protection if two or more feet above the ground. Where this is not possible, the fountain should stand away from any bush or plant large enough to afford cover.

Cat-proof fences, while expensive, often prevent neighborhood troubles and save many birds as well. Individual crows, jays, hawks, owls, or other natural enemies which invade the premises, should be killed, and

---

* Special articles on the subjects indicated by an asterisk (*) will be found at the words so marked.

Wren's bird house. If used for chickadees or nuthatches make the hole larger as shown by the dotted lines.

A several-chambered house on a pole or in a tree is preferred by martins and swallows.

starlings and English sparrows often must be vigorously persecuted. Information on combating them will be given in the section "Bird Nuisances."

WATER

Water is an indispensable necessity in attracting birds. The fountain may be of any size, but should have gently sloping sides, otherwise many birds, particularly fledglings, will be drowned.

NESTING SITES

Most birds naturally nest in trees or bushes, and the normal plantings provide their requirements. Ground-nesting birds, likewise, need no special provision. Bluebirds, wrens, swallows, martins, woodpeckers, chickadees, and nuthatches will take advantage of artificial nest boxes. For wrens, boxes should be four inches square and eight inches deep, with an entrance-opening one inch in diameter. Chickadees and nuthatches need

Bluebirds need a larger house than wrens. *See* text for dimensions.

the same size box with one-fourth-inch larger entrance. Bluebirds and swallows should have boxes five inches square, eight inches in depth, with a one-and-one-half-inch doorway, while martins require dimensions a trifle larger, with a two-and-one-half-inch opening.

Swallows and martins will use houses containing several apartments, and prefer them located in the open on a tall pole. All others prefer individual houses which are not too close to those already occupied. These boxes should face away from the prevailing wind and rain, with the entrance-opening well toward the top, leaving the cavity available for the nest. Designs may suit personal taste, although frequently birds prefer structures of natural wood or stained lumber to painted ones. Robins, phoebes, and barn swallows will often build their nests on shelves placed about buildings, or in trees. These can be any type, though those built with a roof and open sides afford the most protection.

FOOD SUPPLY

Even when water, shelter, and protection are available, an adequate food supply must be provided to increase the bird population. This can be accomplished by selecting trees and shrubs that furnish edible berries or fruits.

Among those groups which will grow over most of this country and which will furnish a food supply for summer and early fall are raspberries, blackberries, mulberries, wild cherries, wild grapes, bush honeysuckles, dogwoods, sour gum, elderberries, June-berries, and Virginia creeper. Buckwheat, when in seed, is also an excellent food.

Valuable ornamentals which carry their fruits far into the winter and provide emergency cold-weather rations for birds are barberries, cotoneasters, hawthorns, mountain-ash, roses, sumac, viburnum, snowberries, and holly. In each group are some forms

---

* Special articles on the subjects indicated by an asterisk (*) will be found at the words so marked.

which will grow in almost any part of this country. See these entries for the species best suited to your region.

Food trays and boxes placed on posts, hung in trees, or made as window shelves, will attract juncos, towhees, woodpeckers, chickadees, nuthatches, and many others. These feeding stations should be supplied with suet for insect-eating birds, and wheat, wheat screenings, hemp, sunflower seed, or millet for the seed-eating birds. Sliced apple, dried raisins, and lettuce leaves are also often appreciated by the feathered folk, and water should be provided when not available naturally.

By providing these four essentials one may expect to attract woodpeckers, swallows, thrushes, sparrows, orioles, chickadees, nuthatches, wrens, and thrashers, as nesting birds; while in winter quail, jays, blackbirds, sparrows, thrushes, waxwings, grosbeaks, chickadees, nuthatches, and many others are possibilities. The number and variety attracted will vary according to geographic and climatic conditions.

Bird Nuisances

Comparatively few birds are undesirable. Crows, blackbirds, starlings, brown thrashers, catbirds, cardinal birds, and horned larks are sometimes destructive to seedling corn, peas, and other vegetables. Robins, catbirds, thrushes, starlings, waxwings, bluebirds, and some kinds of woodpeckers attack ripening fruit, especially cherries and strawberries. Purple finches, linnets, and pine siskins eat fruit buds of cherries, apricots, and peaches, sometimes destroying the entire crop. Ring-necked pheasants are frequently bold enough to invade gardens where they do as much damage as domestic chickens in scratching out seedling vegetables and flowers. In such cases wire netting can be placed over the flower beds until the plants have developed to withstand attack. Sometimes it is necessary to shoot or trap the offending individual. For a method of protecting corn seed from crows, *see* CORN.

Starlings and English sparrows frequently drive out more desirable birds in addition to becoming nuisances themselves. If the openings to nest boxes are made in sizes specified above, it will protect wrens, chickadees, and nuthatches from the raids of sparrows and will prevent the starlings from destroying the nests of birds up to the size of bluebirds. Both species may be discouraged by constantly breaking up their nests and, where no local ordinances prevent, by shooting the invading individuals as fast as they appear. A twenty-two rifle shooting dust shot is an effective weapon for this purpose. Many sparrows can also be taken by traps.

Seedlings can be partially protected by streamers of paper or cloth on stakes stuck into the ground at frequent intervals. In small gardens netting may be fastened a few inches above the seed beds until the plants have become several inches tall.

Damage to ripening fruit is more difficult to prevent. Scarecrows in trees do little good, the birds quickly becoming accustomed to them. Single trees or shrubs may be protected by a netting cover. A relatively low-cost woven-paper netting is now available for the protection of blueberries, strawberries, and other high-value crops. It is the most practical measure that can be employed by home gardeners to prevent bird damage to seedbeds, strawberry or blueberry patches, and cherry trees. Although quite expensive, the netting may be used for several seasons if reasonable care is exercised in its handling and storage.

Planting of mulberries which ripen with the cherries is frequently successful in diverting the attention of the birds from the fruit, although it will not entirely prevent damage. Shooting has little effect unless one wishes to continue until the nesting bird population is eliminated. For other animal pests, *see* ANIMAL INJURY. — I. N. G.

BIRD'S-EYE = *Veronica Chamaedrys.*

BIRD'S-EYE PRIMROSE = *Primula farinosa.*

BIRD'S-EYES = *Gilia tricolor.*

BIRD'S-FOOT TREFOIL = *Lotus corniculatus.*

BIRD'S-FOOT VIOLET = *Viola pedata.*

BIRD'S-NEST FERN = *Asplenium Nidus.*

BIRTHROOT = *Trillium erectum.*

BIRTHWORT. See ARISTOLOCHIA; for birthwort family *see* ARISTOLOCHIACEAE.

biserrata, -us, -um (by-ser-ray'ta). Twice or doubly toothed.

BISEXUAL. A flower with both stamens and pistils. See FLOWER.

BISHOP'S-CAP = *Mitella diphylla.*

BISHOP'S-WEED = *Aegopodium Podagraria.*

BISNAGA = *Biznaga.*

biternata, -us, -um (by-ter-nay'ta). Twice-ternate. See TERNATE.

BITTER ALOES. See ALOE VERA.

BITTER-BUTTONS = *Tanacetum vulgare.*

BITTER CRESS. See CARDAMINE; *see also* BARBAREA VULGARIS.

BITTER HERBS. See HERB GARDENING.

BITTER ORANGE. The sour or Seville orange. *See* CITRUS AURANTIUM.

BITTER-ROOT = *Lewisia rediviva.*

BITTER-STEM PALM = *Hyophorbe amaricaulis.*

BITTERSWEET. Generally, in America, *Celastrus scandens,* but also, and certainly first applied to, *Solanum Dulcamara.* The attempt to call *Celastrus scandens* false bittersweet does not make much headway.

BITTERSWEET FAMILY = Celastraceae.

BITTER VETCH = *Vicia Ervilia.*

BITTER WINTER CRESS = *Barbarea vulgaris.*

BITTERWORT = *Gentiana lutea.*

---

* Special articles on the subjects indicated by an asterisk (*) will be found at the words so marked.

BIXA (bick'sa). A single tropical American tree and the only hort. genus of the family Bixaceae (bick-say'see-ee), often called annatto family. They have alternate,° simple° leaves without marginal teeth and rather showy and (in ours) red or pink regular° flowers. Sepals 5. Petals 5, overlapping and twisted in the bud. Stamens many. Ovary superior,° 1-celled. Fruit a reddish, 2-valved, nearly egg-shaped pod (capsule°) which is covered with soft, reddish, weak prickles. (Bixa is a South American vernacular for the tree.)

The annatto can be grown outdoors only in zone° 9, where it is purely an ornamental tree, although in the tropics it is raised as the source of annatto or achiote dye, used for coloring butter and cheese. Easily propagated by seeds or by cuttings.

Orellana. Annatto (also, incorrectly, spelled anatto and arnatto); called also achiote. As cult. in Fla., not over 25 ft. high, and a handsome tree when in flower or fruit. Leaves ovalish, 5–7 in. long. Flower about 2 in. wide. Fruit about 2 in. long, the pulp around the seeds yielding the orange-red dye. Tropical America. It drops its leaves in midwinter in Fla.

BIZARRE CARNATION. See CARNATION.

BIZNAGA. A name for several cacti in the southwestern U.S. and adjacent Mex., most of which have a globular or cylindric, ribbed plant body, plentifully beset with spines. The two hort. species are *Astrophytum capricorne* and *Ferocactus wislizeni* (which see).

BLACK ACACIA = *Acacia melanoxylon.*

BLACK ALDER = *Ilex verticillata* (*see* HOLLY); also *Alnus glutinosa* (*see* ALDER).

BLACK ASH = *Fraxinus nigra.* See ASH.

BLACK BEAD = *Pithecolobium Unguiscati.*

BLACK BEAN = *Castanospermum australe.*

BLACKBERRY (derived from various species of *Rubus*). Wild species of blackberries, of which there are many, are widespread in the north temperate zone in both the Old and the New World, but have been domesticated only in North America. Here they have been under cultivation about one hundred years, but in this brief time at least seven wild types of this fruit have been brought under subjugation. With these facts in mind one may generalize and say that some blackberry may be found for about every agricultural region in North America; and further say that no fruit has proved itself better fitted to fill a place in orchards and gardens, and none varies more rapidly and offers greater opportunities to develop new types.

The blackberry is at home in any climate in which the tree fruits, the hardiest excepted, are grown. Perhaps it is a little more tender to cold than the apple. It is cosmopolitan as to soils, but reaches greatest perfection in strong loams which contain more clay than sand. It is generally agreed that a good soil for this bramble must be retentive of moisture and yet be well drained. A soil too moist or too rich in humus supports a plant so rank in growth that it falls short in fruitfulness; while, on the other hand, light loams and sands will not carry the blackberry through the droughts that accompany every American summer. A cool northern exposure suits this fruit well. Cover crops supply all the humus and fertility that need to be added to a good blackberry soil.

Blackberries are usually propagated from root-cuttings, although suckers naturally spring up and supply new plants for a few varieties. In propagating from cuttings, roots the size of a lead pencil, a little larger if they can be had, are dug in the fall, cut into 4-in. lengths, stratified in sand during the winter, and planted 3 or 4 in. apart in nursery rows in the spring. The following spring these nursery plants are ready for the field. Suckers may well be used for gardens, but are usually too few and cost too much in care for large plantations.

Blackberries are set either in the hills or hedgerows; perhaps hills suit gardeners best, hedgerows, growers for markets. The plants want plenty of roots, sun and air, and 6 × 7 ft. are not too great distances for hills, and 8 ft. between rows and 4 ft. between plants are usual distances in hedgerows.

The soil in a blackberry plantation must be stirred early in the spring and frequently thereafter until the berries are ripe. Perhaps greater care is needed in cultivating blackberries than any other small fruit. The plantation persists for several years and weeds and suckers must be kept down; yet if the cultivator runs a shade too deep the roots are injured and sucker growth is stimulated. The gardener can always use a hoe to advantage, and the owner of a large plantation must hand-hoe it once or twice a year to keep down weeds and suckers.

After the picking season is over, a cover crop must be sown to furnish humus and to check succulent growths which would be winter-killed. Barley, oats, buckwheat, and millet are good cover crops, since none live over winter to plague the cultivator in the spring. Whatever the crop, it should be plowed under in the fall, at which time a heavy furrow should be thrown up to the canes as winter protection. A cover crop, or a mulch in gardens, is all-important to the blackberry, since the limiting factors in fruit production are humus and moisture in the soil. Experiments with fertilizers for this fruit have given only negative results. Nitrate of soda and its equivalents increase cane growth but not the quantity of fruit.

Pruning the blackberry is not difficult but very necessary, and, because of the thorns, is a very disagreeable task. The work of pruning begins by putting on heavy gloves and arming oneself with a brush-hook and long-handled pruning shears. As soon as they

---

° Special articles on the subjects indicated by an asterisk (°) will be found at the words so marked.

have borne a crop, the canes, which are biennials, should be cut out. Promptness in removing and burning old canes helps to keep down insect and fungous pests and permits fuller development of young canes. The blackberry, permitted to have its own way, is a sprawling, unmanageable plant, to avoid which the young canes should be clipped in June with a sickle or pruning-shears to a height of 2 ft. This clipping is very important also because it induces early branching, a stocky growth, and stout laterals which will hold a heavy crop of fruit. In the spring pruning, the fruiting canes are cut back somewhat and laterals reduced to 2 ft. or a little less. Not more than 4 or 5 canes are left in a hill. Gardeners, and some commercial growers, support tall-growing varieties on a trellis of one or two wires.

In cold climates, some winter protection is demanded by the blackberry. A mulch helps, but sometimes the plants must be bent over and the tips covered with earth, a method feasible only for gardeners. The blackberry suffers from drought in winter as well as cold. In the states of the plains, persistent winds dry the canes out unless protection is given and the soil well soaked before winter comes on.

The fruit of the blackberry should be left on the bush until dead ripe; it is not ready to pick when it first turns black. Premature picking has given this fruit an undeserved reputation for sourness. From first to last the berries should be kept cool and dry. The blackberry outyields all other bramble fruits. "Plentiful as blackberries" comes to us from Shakespeare.

Some variety of blackberry can be found for every zone* excepting zones* 1, 8 and 9, extremes of cold and heat. The following varieties are all successfully grown:

ALFRED. An erect plant, and early-fruiting, the berries sweet and firm.

ELDORADO. Erect, and a very satisfactory variety for home use. Fruit medium-sized, sweet, and produced in midseason.

SNYDER. Chiefly of value because of hardiness to cold. Berries medium-sized, rather seedy, but produced in large quantity. Plant erect.

BRAINARD. Semi-trailing, and must be trained on wires. It is a hybrid developed by the U.S. Department of Agriculture between Himalaya and an eastern blackberry, to provide a plant of the semi-trailing habit with the fine fruit of Himalaya. See below.

EARLY HARVEST. Erect, fairly vigorous, and with not so many suckers as some others. Fruit medium-sized, of good quality.

NANTICOKE. A late-fruiting variety, the fruit sweet, soft, and of fine quality. Plant erect, very prickly, and drought-resistant.

McDONALD. Semi-erect and needing wires. Fruit very early, of good quality. Plant is self-sterile, and another variety must be planted with it. Use Early Harvest for this at the rate of one Early Harvest to five McDonald. Not recommended for the northern part of zone* 4.

Besides the foregoing blackberries, all of which have biennial canes, there are two with perennial canes much grown in the Pacific states and somewhat grown in the eastern states, where, however, they are seldom hardy, except south of Pennsylvania. These are: EVERGREEN, with perhaps a half dozen synonyms; and HIMALAYA. Both have large, sweet berries, ripen very late. Canes long and trailing for which reason they are grown on 3 or 4 wire trellises. See also LOGANBERRY, BOYSENBERRY, and DEWBERRY.

INSECT PESTS. Red-spider mites often damage blackberry and related plants severely, particularly in dry seasons. Spray with pesticide #21 (see SPRAYS AND DUSTS) and repeat in 10 days. A caterpillar attacks the canes at the base, causing galling and killing. Apply pesticide #17 at double strength to crown of plant in late summer and again in early fall for control. Control several chewing insects by pesticide #21 or arsenical applications.

DISEASES. See RASPBERRY.

BLACKBERRY LILY = Belamcanda chinensis.

BLACK BINDWEED = Polygonum Convolvulus. See list at WEEDS.

BLACK BIRCH. In the East, Betula lenta; in the West, B. fontinalis. For both see BIRCH.

BLACK CALLA = Arum palaestinum.

BLACKCAP RASPBERRY = Rubus occidentalis. For cult. see RASPBERRY.

BLACK CHOKEBERRY = Aronia melanocarpa.

BLACK COHOSH = Cimicifuga racemosa.

BLACK CORINTH GRAPE. The variety of grape that produces currants. See Vinifera Grapes at GRAPE.

BLACK COSMOS = Cosmos diversifolius.

BLACK CURRANT = Ribes nigrum.

BLACK-EYED SUSAN. Usually some species of Rudbeckia, especially R. hirta, the yellow daisy; also Thunbergia alata.

BLACK GRAM = Phaseolus Mungo.

BLACK GUM = Nyssa sylvatica.

BLACK HAW = Viburnum prunifolium.

BLACK HELLEBORE = Helleborus niger.

BLACK HILLS SPRUCE = Picea glauca densata. See SPRUCE.

BLACK HOREHOUND = Ballota nigra.

BLACK HUCKLEBERRY = Gaylussacia baccata. See HUCKLEBERRY.

BLACK-KNOT. A fungus disease, especially on cherries and plums, which ultimately causes black knots on, or swelling of the wood. It starts with a slight enlargement or swelling of the wood, followed by cracking, and the development of olive-green knots that in the end become black.

BLACKLEG. A disease which causes the stem of the plant to turn black at the soil line. On potato and delphinium the causal organism is a bacterium, while on members of the cabbage family a fungus produces a similar condition.

---

* Special articles on the subjects indicated by an asterisk (*) will be found at the words so marked.

BLACK LOCUST = *Robinia Pseudo-acacia; see* LOCUST; *also Gledistia triacanthos; see* HONEY LOCUST.

BLACK MAPAU = *Pittosporum tenuifolium.*

BLACK MAPLE = *Acer nigrum. See* MAPLE.

BLACK MEDIC = *Medicago lupulina.*

BLACK MUSTARD = *Brassica nigra.*

BLACK NIGHTSHADE = *Solanum nigrum.*

BLACK OAK = *Quercus velutina; see* OAK.

BLACK POPLAR = *Populus nigra.*

BLACKROOT = *Veronicastrum virginicum.*

BLACK SAGE = *Audibertia stachyoides.*

BLACK SALSIFY = *Scorzonera hispanica.*

BLACK SAMPSON = *Echinacea purpurea.*

BLACK SNAKEROOT = *Cimicifuga racemosa.*

BLACK SPOT. The common name of various leaf-spotting diseases on plants such as rose, elm, delphinium, and others. In most cases these diseases are caused by fungi and, if not controlled, may result in defoliation of the plant. In the case of black spot of rose, the fungus responsible for the spotting produces minute quantities of ethylene gas in the leaf. The ethylene is responsible for dropping of leaves even though only a few spots are present.

BLACK SPRUCE = *Picea mariana; see* SPRUCE.

BLACKTHORN. In America, *Crataegus uniflora* (better spelled black thorn), and a very different plant from the blackthorn of the Irish, which is *Prunus spinosa,* the sloe.

BLACK WALNUT = *Juglans nigra* and *J. hindsi; see* WALNUT.

BLACK WATTLE = *Acacia decurrens mollis.*

BLACK WILLOW = *Salix nigra; see* WILLOW.

BLACKWOOD = *Acacia melanoxylon.*

BLADDER-FERN. *See* CYSTOPTERIS.

BLADDER-NUT. *See* STAPHYLEA.

BLADDER-POD = *Vesicaria utriculata.*

BLADDER SENNA = *Colutea arborescens.*

BLADDERWORT. *See* UTRICULARIA.

BLADDERWORT FAMILY = LENTIBULARIACEAE.

BLADDERY. Inflated and usually with papery or thin walls, as in some fruits.

BLADE. The usually flat, expanded part of a leaf, as distinguished from its stalk; less commonly, the similar expansion of a petal which is better called the limb.*

BLADEAPPLE = *Pereskia aculeata.*

BLANCHING. A not unusual garden operation having for its object the reduction or practical disappearance of the green coloring matter of certain plants. This substance (chlorophyll) needs light for proper development, and blanching involves cutting off direct light. It is done by banking up earth, by boards, or by individual plant covers of paper or cardboard. The chief crops in which blanching is a factor are celery, sea-kale, and endive. See these for details.

blanda, -us, -um (blan'da). Mild or bland, not bitter or strong.

BLANKET-FLOWER. *See* GAILLARDIA, especially *G. aristata.*

Blattaria. A pre-Linnaean* name for certain mulleins now included in the genus *Verbascum.*

BLAZING STAR = *Liatris squarrosa, Mentzelia laevicaulis,* and *Chamaelirium luteum. See also* TRITONIA.

BLECHNUM (bleck'num). A very large genus of mostly tropical ferns, family Polypodiaceae, a few of which reach temperate regions. They are rather coarse, stiff-fronded ferns grown for ornament and comparatively immune to the unfavorable conditions of a living room. Fronds with many leaflets or divisions arranged feather-fashion. Along the midrib, on the under side of the leaflets or segments, are the more or less continuous, brown spore cases, containing the spores.* (*Blechnum* is Greek for some ferns, but perhaps not these.)

Blechnums are useful ferns for florists and for house decoration largely because they will stand abuse. This means they can stand a dry atmosphere, but they need water at the roots. Do not sprinkle or syringe the foliage. For soil and greenhouse conditions *see* FERNS. Some species are offered under the name *Lomaria.*

brasiliense. A greenhouse fern with a short trunk (2–3 ft.) and a bushy crown of leaves. Fronds 2–3 ft. long and about 12 in. wide, their segments set at an acute angle. Brazil and Peru. Can be grown outdoors only in zone* 9.

serrulatum. Saw fern. A greenhouse fern without a trunk, the fronds stalked and arising at the ground level. Fronds 12–20 in. long, and about 10 in. wide, their segments many, narrow, stiffish, with nearly parallel edges which are minutely toothed. Fla. to Brazil, mostly in wet places.

Spicant. Deer fern; called also hard fern. A hardy fern suitable for the outdoor fern garden. Fronds evergreen, 2½–3½ ft. long, in a dense cluster. The frond is divided into many small segments which are without marginal teeth or sometimes faintly toothed. In Eurasia and in N.A. from Alaska to Calif.

BLEEDING. Sap pressure in some trees, or sometimes as the result of wounds or pruning, will cause them to bleed, an exudation of sap also known as extravasated sap. It does no harm as ordinary wound response of the tree will usually prevent infection, unless the cavity or wound is too large. In that case *see* TREE SURGERY.

---

* Special articles on the subjects indicated by an asterisk (*) will be found at the words so marked.

BLEEDING-HEART = *Dicentra specta-bilis;* also, in Calif., *D. formosa.*

BLEEDING-HEART FAMILY = Fumariaceae.

Bleo. Brazilian vernacular name for *Pereskia Bleo.*

BLEPHARIGLOTTIS. A once-current name for orchids here included in *Habenaria.*

blepharophylla, -us, -um (ble-far-o-fill'a). Having leaves margined with eyelash-like hairs.

BLESSED THISTLE = *Cnicus benedictus.*

BLETIA HYACINTHINA = *Bletilla striata.*

BLETILLA (ble-till'a). A small group of Asiatic orchids, one suitable to shady parts of the wild garden. Unlike most temperate region orchids, they have a pseudobulb° and a leafy stem. Leaves plaited like a fan. Flowers very irregular, in a terminal cluster (raceme °). Sepals and petals very similar, but the lip° 3-lobed, and the middle lobe toothed. (*Bletilla* is diminutive of *Bletia,* a [non-hort.] genus named for Louis Blet, a Spanish botanist.)

The species below is not well known, but is a desirable plant for the wild garden. It prefers half-shady places, and will form good-sized clumps. Propagated by spring division of clumps.

striata. Pseudobulbs tuber-like and from them the stems rise 8–15 in., along which are 3–6 plaited leaves. Flowers amethyst-purple, and showy. China and Jap. There is also a white-flowered form. Usually offered as *Bletia hyacinthina.*

BLIGHIA (bly'gi-a). Three tropical African trees, family Sapindaceae, one of which is cult. in southern Fla. for its edible fruit (the akee). Leaves compound,° the leaflets arranged feather-fashion. Flowers in racemes,° very fragrant, greenish-white. (For details *see* SAPINDACEAE.) Fruit a 3-celled capsule,° in each cell a single black seed to which is attached the edible white aril.° (Named for William Bligh, commander of the *Bounty. See also* ARTOCARPUS COMMUNIS.)

The akee can only be grown outdoors in zone° 9 as it is susceptible to frost. When the pods split open the furrowed aril° is gathered. From its brain-like appearance it is often called vegetable brain or sesal vegetal. Only ripe arils should be used, preferably fried in butter. Over- or under-ripe arils are apt to be poisonous. The tree is propagated by seeds or by shield-budding.

sapida. Akee. A tree up to 25 ft. or a little more. Leaflets 3, 4, or 5 pairs, more or less oblong and without teeth. Flowers hairy, white, fragrant, the oblong, greenish-white petals somewhat showy. Capsule° 3–4 in. long, yellowish-red. Aril° generally white, but with a pinkish portion (apt to be poisonous) between its white lobes. Tropical Africa.

BLIGHT. An indefinite and loose term for various diseases of plants. In some cases the blight is caused by bacteria while on other plants the same term is used for a fungus disease. Symptoms range from spotting of leaves to death of leaves, twigs, or an entire plant.

BLIND. Failure to produce flowers or fruit, usually from disease, improper nourishment, or too deep or too early planting.

BLIND WOOD. *See* Softwood Cuttings at CUTTINGS.

BLISTER-CRESS. *See* ERYSIMUM.

BLISTER-FLOWER = *Ranunculus acris. See* BUTTERCUP.

blitoides (bly-toy'deez; but *see* OÏDES). Resembling *Blitum,* an old name for the strawberry-blite, which *see* in the list at WEEDS.

BLOODBERRY = *Rivina humilis.*

BLOOD-FLOWER = *Asclepias curassavica. See* MILKWEED.

BLOOD-LEAF. *See* IRESINE.

BLOOD-LILY. *See* HAEMANTHUS.

BLOODROOT. The bloodroot is an ideal wild garden plant where it thrives in rich woods soil (not especially acid) and in partial shade. It is the only known species of the genus **Sanguinaria** (san-gwi-nair'ree-a), belongs to the poppy family, and is confined to the forests of eastern N.A. The only species, **S. canadensis,** has a red, perennial root, red sap, and sends up in early spring a single, lobed leaf which is often 4–6 in. wide. Flower solitary, on a stalk 6–8 in. high. Sepals 2. Petals 8–12, white or pinkish, waxy and about 1 in. long. Stamens many. Fruit a pod about 1 in. long. A very handsome wild flower blooming early in May, but completely dying down by midsummer. It is also called redroot, tetterwort, or Indian plant, and the double-flowered form is a fine plant for the shady garden. (*Sanguinaria* refers to the blood-like juice.) For culture *see* WILD GARDEN.

BLOODROOT FAMILY = Papaveraceae.

BLOODWOOD TREE = *Haematoxylon campechianum.*

BLOODWORT FAMILY = Haemodoraceae.

BLOODY BUTCHERS = *Trillium sessile.*

BLOOM. The delicate powdery coating (sometimes called farina) on some fruits, and occasionally on other parts of plants, of unknown origin and of no known use. Technically bloomy plants or fruits are said to be *pruinose. Bloom,* of course, is also synonymous with blossom.

BLOOMERIA (blue-meer'i-a). A genus of only two Californian bulbous plants of the lily family, one of which is cult. for its summer-blooming flowers that suggest the ornamental species of *Brodiaea.* Leaves all grass-like and basal. Flower cluster an umbel° on a long, naked stalk. Flowers wheel-shaped, orange-yellow, the segments of the

---

° Special articles on the subjects indicated by an asterisk (°) will be found at the words so marked.

corolla parted nearly to the base, about ¾ in. across. (Named for Dr. H. G. Bloomer, an American botanist.)

The only hort. species prefers a well-drained, sandy soil and open sunlight. While it will stand considerable frost, it is safer to cover with straw or light mulch in regions of severe winters. Pot culture is often better than planting in the open ground, especially in cool regions, and it is better, in any case, to dig up the corms after they have ripened (about a month after blooming time), store in a dry place, and replant in the fall.

crocea. Golden stars. A perennial with a crocus-like corm.* Leaf solitary, ¼–⅓ in. wide. Stalk of the flower cluster 6–15 in. high, roughish. Flowers many, golden-orange, the stamens* nearly as long as the petals. Southern Calif. Often offered as *B. aurea.*

BLOOM-FELL = *Lotus corniculatus.*

BLOOMING SALLY = *Epilobium angustifolium.*

BLOSSOM. Any flower, but especially the collection of them when fruit trees are in bloom.

BLOOM ANEMONE = *Hepatica americana.*

BLUE ASH = *Fraxinus quadrangulata.* See Ash.

BLUEBEARD. See Caryopteris.

BLUE BEECH = *Carpinus caroliniana.* See Hornbeam.

BLUEBELL. Many plants are called bluebell, the most common hort. species being *Campanula rotundifolia, Polemonium reptans, Eustoma russellianum,* and *Clematis crispa.* In England, and sometimes here, bluebells is also applied to *Scilla nonscripta.*

BLUEBELL-OF-SCOTLAND = *Campanula rotundifolia.*

BLUEBELLS = *Muscari botryoides; see also* Mertensia and Scilla nonscripta.

BLUEBERRY. Native blueberries of the eastern U.S. can be roughly divided into two groups: the high-bush kinds which are naturally acid-bog plants, or at least grow in low places; and the low-bush sorts which inhabit sandy or rocky acid wastes from Maine to Florida and westward. The high-bush kinds have larger and better berries than the low sorts and all of the cult. varieties are of the high-bush type.

Also, blueberries must be distinguished from the closely related huckleberry which is an inferior fruit and often confused by amateurs. Blueberries all belong to the genus *Vaccinum,* which has many small seeds and often has a bloom on the fruit; the huckleberries belong to *Gaylussacia,* have ten rather bony seeds and are usually black, without a bloom. No huckleberries are cultivated.

Soils. No one should attempt the culture of the high-bush blueberry (hereafter called simply the blueberry) unless he can give it the conditions it demands, or is lucky enough to have them on the place. For best results it must be grown in a soil with a pH of about 4–5 and below pH 4.0, it will not generally thrive. See Acid and Alkali Soils.

Few gardens having such sites, the next step is to create them. If you have ordinary garden loam, dig it all out 18 in. deep, and put in the following mixture: two parts clean sharp sand (not sea sand unless it has been thoroughly washed), and one part loam, and two parts acid peat. The latter can be bought in bales from dealers if you cannot get it from a peat bog. Mix these ingredients thoroughly and test them for acidity. If they are above pH 5 add enough aluminum sulphate, again thoroughly mixed, to bring the whole down to pH 4.5. This may take about ¾ pound of aluminum sulphate to each bushel of the total mixture. It is difficult to know the exact amount of aluminum sulphate, for less is needed on sandy soils and more on heavy ones to bring the mixture to about pH 4.5.

If, on the other hand, you live in a region with naturally acid soils and your mixture is below pH 4.0, a very little lime can be added gradually to bring the mixture to as near pH 4.5 as you can get it.

For most home gardeners, who will probably need only a few plants, it is easier to dig a trench 18 in. deep, 3 ft. wide, and as long as you need to take care of your plants. These should be set 4–5 ft. apart in the row; and, if you have more than one row, there should be 8 ft. between rows. Fill the trench with your tested soil mixture and test it once a year. If it loses acidity it may be top-dressed with as little aluminum sulphate as is necessary to keep the mixture at about pH 4.5. Some growers use sulphur instead of aluminum sulphate for correcting acidity, broadcasting it over the existing soil at the rate of 1 ounce for each 16 square ft. of surface and raking it in. No manure or commercial fertilizer should ever be put on blueberry plants — at least by the home gardener.

Young plants should be set in the trench very early in the spring (or even in winter in the South), and watered at first, preferably with rain water. Do not use tap water for this initial watering if it tests pH 7.0 or 7.5, as many hard waters may do. Ordinary rainfall should take care of subsequent needs.

In estimating the number of plants you need, it is safe to figure that each mature bush will yield 8–10 pints per year, but much less during the first few years and more in later years. The plant is hard-wooded, slow-growing and will not reach maturity until 6–8 years old. It should then bear indefinitely. A few berries may be harvested after the third year.

Because the blueberry is a little difficult to transplant, careful nurserymen wrap shipped plants in moist peat moss, or sometimes dig with a ball of earth. It is well to

---

* Special articles on the subjects indicated by an asterisk (*) will be found at the words so marked.

insist on one or the other method, because the roots never should be exposed to the wind or allowed to dry out.

Much of the improvement of wild blueberries has come from hybridization, mostly in the direction of increasing the size of the berry. Being relatively young as a cultivated plant, berry size is not yet wholly standardized, and it can be controlled by pruning. The plant, or at least some of the varieties, is variable as to berry size. You may have to decide whether you want a greater number of relatively moderate-sized berries, or fewer of considerably greater diameter.

If you want the latter it is well to cut out too vigorous fruit branches, which will reduce the total yield but increase the size of the fruit. Such pruning can be done when fruit-set is completed, well before final harvest.

Blueberries in the home garden do not need to be cultivated. To keep down weeds and conserve soil moisture, it is a good plan to mulch the area between the rows, or around the plants if they are not in rows, with 4–5 inches of sawdust, woodpile chips, or straw — never with strawy manure. Do not smother the stems with this mulch, leaving a clear space of 6–8 inches around each plant.

VARIETIES. The home grower should have at least three plants, an early, midseason, and late sort. Also, while the blueberry is not wholly self-sterile, it is apt to fruit much better if cross-fertilized. It will hence be better to have 6–8 plants, of at least three different varieties.

Because the fruit is relatively new to cultivation it is impossible to assign certain fruit districts where a particular variety is expected to do better than another. Such recommendations are based on years of testing, and there has not been sufficient time in the case of the blueberry.

The varieties below, therefore, have been taken from the latest official report on performance, with the understanding that it is the best that can be done in this comparatively new culture. All the varieties have been tested for at least a few years and are reported upon by the U.S. Department of Agriculture.

ATLANTIC. A late or midseason variety suitable for the region east of Mich. and south to N. Car. Fruit large, not cracking in wet weather, and of fine flavor. Bush vigorous, a little over-productive, and pruning is necessary to increase size of berry.

JUNE. An early variety with medium-sized berries, not much subject to cracking in wet weather. Bush below average size and vigor, but valuable as one of the first available blueberries. Can be grown anywhere in the East, especially along the Atlantic seaboard.

RANCOCAS. A midseason variety, the bush erect, vigorous, and productive. Fruit flat-spherical, medium-sized unless pruned, of more than fair flavor, but cracking badly in rainy spells. Can be grown from Mich. eastward, and south to N. Car.

STANLEY. A midseason variety, the fruit in-

clined to be small, but of the finest flavor, and very aromatic. Best suited to the coastal plain from Va. to N.Y. Considered by many as the finest-flavored of all cultivated blueberries.

BURLINGTON. Next to Stanley considered the best-flavored of cultivated blueberries and superior to it in vigor. It is late-fruiting, medium to large in size, and resistant to cracking in rainy seasons. Suited for all regions east of Mich.

COVILLE. One of the largest and latest of cultivated blueberries, the fruit aromatic, pleasant only when fully ripe, as it is tart when picked before this. Bush vigorous, productive, suited mostly to the Atlantic coastal plain.

Many other varieties are already available, but their acceptance must wait for more extensive tests. The habit of some blueberries to crack in wet weather has not yet been conquered. And some varieties adhere too firmly to the stalk so that their skin is torn in picking or they leave too big a scar at the point of attachment. One of the best for this particular trouble is the Burlington which has only a small, clean scar after picking.

From South Carolina to Florida and along the Gulf Coast the best varieties are derived from the rabbiteye blueberries, which were developed from a southern wild species that is twice the height of those in the list above. They are unsuited to the North, but are heavy yielders in the South. There are at least 10 varieties of rabbiteye, the most notable being Coastal, Callaway, Ethel, and Walker.

Blueberries for the eastern states reach a height of 6–8 feet, and the berries are ripe from June 15–28 (early), June 29–July 20 (midseason), and July 25–August 9 (late). Most cultivated berries should be at least one-half inch in diameter. In good years and with moderate thinning to increase size, the largest fruits may be three quarters of an inch in diameter.

Birds love blueberry fruits and are often such a local nuisance that some growers keep their plants under temporary nets at fruiting time.

INSECT PESTS. Scale insects may be pruned out or killed by dormant oils. Tiny weevils attacking blossoms and plum curculio, which appears after blossom fall, can be controlled by pesticide #21 or #18. Cherry fruitworms attack fruit in late May or June as do leafhopper vectors of stunt. Control with pesticide #21. During harvest, maggots attack berries but can be controlled by pesticide #21. Girdlers can be prevented by soil treatments of pesticide #17. See JAPANESE BEETLE.

DISEASES. The fungus disease, mummy berry, causes fruit to rot and drop. The following spring these diseased berries look like tiny gray pumpkins from which small pinkish-orange cups arise. When these little cups are first seen, spray the ground under each bush with pesticide #4 (see SPRAYS AND DUSTS).

Stunt is a virus disease which, as the name implies, reduces the size of leaves, bush, and crop of fruit. Destroy plants with stunt and replant with certified stock.

A rust* fungus causes witches'-broom* in

---

* Special articles on the subjects indicated by an asterisk (*) will be found at the words so marked.

northern states. Cut out all parts showing these brooms.

BLUE BLAZING STAR = *Liatris scariosa.*

BLUE BLOSSOM = *Ceanothus thyrsiflorus.*

BLUE BONNETS = *Centaurea Cyanus.* See also LUPINUS SUBCARNOSUS.

BLUEBOTTLE = *Centaurea Cyanus.*

BLUE COHOSH = *Caulophyllum thalictroides.*

BLUECURLS. Low herbs in the East, but much taller and somewhat woody in Calif., where some species are widely cult. as bee plants. All belong to the genus Trichostema (try-kos'ti-ma), of the mint family, and are natives of N.A. Leaves opposite.* Flowers blue or purple, irregular and 2-lipped, the long-protruding stamens arched, whence the name bluecurls. Usually the flowers are solitary at the ends of slender stalks or in small clusters in the leaf axils.* (*Trichostema* is Greek for hair and stamen.)

Both these below are little grown outside Calif. They prefer the open sun and will stand much summer heat. Neither is hardy in the East, where they are replaced by several wild species that are scarcely garden plants.

T. **lanatum.** Romero. A shrubby herb to 4 ft. high. Leaves narrow, slender, scarcely 2 in. long, very hairy on the lower surface. Flowers clothed with a blue or purplish wool, about ½ in. long. Calif.

T. **lanceolatum.** Vinegarweed; called also camphorweed. Flowers mostly in the leaf axils,* blue, and blooming from Aug. to frost in Calif. In dry, sandy places Calif. to Ore. A very important bee plant.

BLUE DAISY = *Felicia amelloides.*

BLUE DANDELION = *Cichorium Intybus.*

BLUE DAWNFLOWER = *Ipomoea leari.*

BLUE DICKS = *Brodiaea capitata.*

BLUE DOGWOOD = *Cornus alternifolia.*

BLUE ELDER = *Sambucus caerulea.* See ELDER.

BLUE-EYED GRASS = *Sisyrinchium.*

BLUE-EYED MARY = *Collinsia verna.*

BLUE FALSE INDIGO = *Baptisia australis.*

BLUE FESCUE = *Festuca ovina glauca.*

BLUE FLAG = *Iris versicolor.*

BLUE GARDEN. In planting a blue garden or border the pure blues such as those of gentian and Anchusa and the purple-blues as seen in many campanulas should not be placed side by side. They may be separated by breadths of green or gray foliage or by the intervention of white or some bright-hued flower. A few yellow-flowered plants add immensely to the effectiveness of a collection of blue flowers, and even a touch of orange or scarlet may be introduced with advantage. Woodwork and accessories may be light green, white or yellow. In the following lists the purple-blues are indicated by a dagger (†). All the plants mentioned will be found under their names in the body of this book.

SHRUBS

Amorpha canescens 3–4 ft., Aug.–Sept.; *Caryopteris incana†* 5 ft., autumn; *Hibiscus syriacus coelestis†* 10–12 ft., July–Aug.

TALL PLANTS FOR USE IN BACKGROUND

SUMMER-FLOWERING. *Aconitum fischeri* 4 ft., *A. napellus†* 4–5 ft., A. Spark's Variety† 4–6 ft. (*see* MONKSHOOD); *Anchusa azurea* and vars. 4 ft.; *Campanula pyramidalis†* 4–6 ft.; *Delphinium* hybrids, many vars. 4–6 ft.; *Echinops exaltatus* 4 ft., *E. sphaerocephalus†* 5–8 ft.; *Phlox* Blue Hill† 3–4 ft.; *Salvia azurea* 4–5 ft.

AUTUMN-FLOWERING. *Aconitum autumnale†* 4–5 ft.; *Aster* Blue Gem 4–5 ft., A. Climax† 5 ft.; *Verbena hastata* 4–6 ft.

PLANTS OF MEDIUM HEIGHT

SPRING-FLOWERING. *Aquilegia caerulea* (*see* COLUMBINE) 1½ ft.; *Camassia leichtlini†* 2 ft.; *Linum narbonnense* 2 ft.; *L. perenne* 2 ft.; *Mertensia virginica* 2 ft.; *Polemonium caeruleum* 2–3 ft.; *Pulmonaria angustifolia* 1 ft.; *Tradescantia virginiana†* (*see* SPIDERWORT) 2–3 ft.

SUMMER-FLOWERING. *Adenophora potanini* 18 in.; *Amsonia Tabernaemontana†* 2½ ft.; *Anagallis linifolia* (biennial) 1½ ft.; *Anchusa capensis* (annual) 1½ ft.; *Baptisia australis* 3–4 ft.; *Borago officinalis* 2 ft.; *Browallia americana†* (annual) 2 ft.; *Campanula persicifolia†* 2–3 ft.; *Catananche caerulea* 2 ft.; *Centaurea Cyanus* (annual) 2–3 ft., *C. montana* 2 ft.; *Clematis heracleifolia davidiana* 4 ft., *C. integrifolia* 3 ft.; *Commelina coelestis* 2 ft. (tender); *Cynoglossum amabile* (biennial) 2 ft.; *Delphinium Ajacis* (rocket larkspur) 2–3 ft., *D. grandiflorum* vars. 1–2 ft.; *Echinops Ritro†* 3 ft.; *Eryngium alpinum†* 2 ft., *E. amethystinum†* 2 ft., *E. bourgati†* 1½ ft., *E. oliverianum†* 3 ft., *E. planum* 3 ft.; *Geranium platypetalum†* 2 ft.; *Lupinus polyphyllus* vars. 2–4 ft.; *Pentstemon unilateralis* 2–2½ ft.; *Platycodon grandiflorum* 2½ ft., var. *mariesi* 1½ ft.; *Salvia farinacea†* 3 ft., *S. patens* (half-hardy) 2 ft., *S. pratensis†* 2 ft.; *Veronica austriaca* 2 ft., *V. longifolia* var. *subsessilis* 2 ft., *V. spicata* 2 ft., *V. spuria* 2 ft.

AUTUMN-FLOWERING. *Aster* Feltham Blue† 2 ft.; *Eupatorium coelestinum* 2 ft.; *Gentiana andrewsi* 2 ft.; *Lobelia syphilitica* 2–3 ft.

LOW-GROWING PLANTS FOR FOREGROUND

SPRING-FLOWERING. *Ajuga genevensis*, A. *reptans* (creepers); *Brunnera macrophylla* 1–1½ ft.; *Campanula garganica* vars. 3–4 in.; *Chionodoxa luciliae* 3 in., *C. sardensis* 3 in. (bulbs); *Gentiana acaulis* 3 in.; *Globularia cordifolia* 4 in., *G. trichosantha* 6 in.; *Hyacinthus ciliatus* 3 in., *H. amethystinus* 4–5 in., *H. orientalis* vars. 8–10 in. (bulbs); *Linum alpinum* 6 in.; *Muscari botryoides* 4 in., M. Heavenly Blue 5 in. (bulbs); *Myosotidium hortensia* 12–18 in.; *Myosotis* vars. 4–10 in. (*see* FORGET-ME-NOT); *Phyteuma scheuch-*

---

* Special articles on the subjects indicated by an asterisk (*) will be found at the words so marked.

zeri 1 ft.; *Polemonium richardsoni* 1 ft., *P. reptans* 6 in.; *Primula vulgaris caerulea* 6 in.; *Scilla hispanica* 1 ft., *S. nonscripta* 1 ft., *S. sibirica* 4 in. (bulb); *Sisyrinchium angustifolium* 8 in.; *Veronica gentianoides* 1 ft.; *Vinca minor* (creeping).

SUMMER-FLOWERING. *Asperula orientalis* (annual) 1 ft.; *Convolvulus mauritanicus* (prostrate), *C. tricolor* (annual); *Gentiana cruciata* 6 in., *G. septemfida*; *Jasione perennis* 6–9 in.; *Lobelia* (annual vars.); *Nemesia* Blue Gem (annual) 8 in.; *Nemophila menziesi* (annual); *Nigella damascena* Miss Jekyll 1 ft.; *Pentstemon angustifolius* 1 ft.; *Petunia* Heavenly Blue (annual); *Phacelia campanularia* (annual) 6–8 in.; *Prunella grandiflora†* 9 in.; *Veronica incana* 8 in.

AUTUMN-FLOWERING. *Ceratostigma plumbaginoides* (semiprostrate). — L. B. W.

See also GRAY AND LAVENDER GARDEN.

BLUEGRASS. See POA PRATENSIS.

BLUE GUM = *Eucalyptus globulus*.

BLUE HUCKLEBERRY = *Gaylussacia frondosa*. See HUCKLEBERRY.

BLUE JASMINE = *Clematis crispa*.

BLUE LACE-FLOWER. See TRACHYMENE.

BLUE LILY-TURF = *Liriope Muscari*.

BLUE-LIPS = *Collinsia grandiflora*.

BLUE LOBELIA = *Lobelia siphilitica*.

BLUE LOTUS = *Nymphaea caerulea*.

BLUE MELILOT = *Trigonella caerulea*.

BLUE MYRTLE = *Ceanothus thyrsiflorus*.

BLUE PALMETTO = *Rhapidophyllum hystrix*.

BLUE PHLOX = *Phlox divaricata*.

"BLUE SPIRAL." Florists' name for the cut twigs of *Eucalyptus pulverulenta* (which *see*), and sometimes for *Eucalyptus cordata*, a non-hort. species.

BLUE SPIREA = *Caryopteris incana*.

BLUE SPRUCE = *Picea pungens*. See SPRUCE.

BLUESTEM = *Sabal minor*.

BLUE SUCCORY = *Catananche caerulea*.

BLUE THISTLE = *Echium vulgare*.

BLUETS = *Houstonia caerulea*.

BLUE VERVAIN = *Verbena hastata*.

BLUE VIOLET = *Viola cucullata*.

BLUEWEED = *Cichorium Intybus*; also *Echium vulgare*.

BLUE WING FLOWER = *Torenia fournieri compacta*.

BLUE WOOD ASTER = *Aster cordifolius*.

Boaria. Probably derived from the aboriginal name in Chile for the mayten (*Maytenus Boaria*).

BOAT LILY = *Rhoeo discolor*.

BOCCONIA. A name somewhat common in the catalogues, but it is doubtful if any true *Bocconia* is of much interest to gardeners. For the plants usually listed as *Bocconia*, *see* MACLEAYA.

BOEHMERIA (bo-meer'i-a). A large genus of trees, shrubs or herbs, family Urticaceae, and widely scattered. A few are weedy herbs in N.A., but the one below is widely grown in China, and to some extent in the southern U.S., for the fine fiber taken from its inner bark. Leaves opposite.* Flowers green, without petals, unisexual,* crowded in small heads which are grouped in a spike-like cluster. Fruit an achene.* (Named for G. R. Boehmer, German professor.)

In Fla. and La. the ramie is a shrubby plant, its tall, annual shoots being harvested for the fiber. If grown in the greenhouse the plant becomes tree-like and very handsome. Easily propagated by division. It requires a rich, moist soil, and is not hardy north of zone* 6.

nivea. As cult. for fiber a bushy plant 4–6 ft. high, its stems hairy. Leaves broadly oval, 4–7 in. long, coarsely toothed, rough above, felty-white beneath. As. The common form yields rhea, or China-silk, but a tropical variety yields the true ramie. Ramie, however, as a name, is also applied to the fiber of the typical *B. nivea*, the only form known to be cult. in the U.S.

boerhaaviaefolia, *-us*, *-um* (boor-hah-vi-eye-fō'li-a). With leaves like a *Boerhaavia*, which is scarcely of hort. interest.

BOG ASPHODEL = *Narthecium americanum*.

BOGBEAN = *Menyanthes trifoliata*.

BOG GARDENING. This is somewhat of an English institution which has gained much favor in the United States. This was to be expected, for it is in North America that the major portion of the most useful cultivated bog plants are to be found.

The bog garden is a sanctuary for the wildings that by nature live in wet, acid places, on the sides of lakes, ponds, and streams, or in peaty hollows. The plants are particularly easy of culture. Woody plants, herbaceous perennials, and some species of bulbs furnish the major portion of the plant material used in the development of such a garden. In making a bog garden we must remember that the plants which inhabit the bog will not thrive in any harsh, bare, and dry position. Bog plants are at home only when planted in moist situations, cradled in sphagnum, or other mosses of wet, spongy ground, or in a moist peat soil which is acid in character.

SOIL

A good rich and acid soil is the keynote to success in bog gardening, and correct soil conditions are of more importance to the plants than moisture.

In selecting a soil, preference should be given to one such as is furnished by natural boggy soil. In texture this soil contains a good quantity of decayed humus and is full of fiber, the pH value of the substrata running between 4.5 and 5. (*See* ACID AND AL-

---

* Special articles on the subjects indicated by an asterisk (*) will be found at the words so marked.

KALI SOILS.) Bog plants require an acid soil, and acidity must not be overlooked when the soil is selected. The turf should be cut and laid on a pile and to each two layers of this, add one layer of decayed cow manure. The fall is the best time to prepare the compost. After the pile has laid for a few weeks the turf should be chopped down with a spade in order to cut the fiber mass and thoroughly incorporate the manure. Aluminum sulphate added and well mixed with the compost, using it at the rate of fifty pounds to the ton of soil, will be of great benefit to the plants. The compost, after having been turned a few times, will be ready for use in building the mounds which will be placed here and there throughout the garden.

Nature, in order to retain soil acidity, provides means by utilizing the decaying leaves from the hardwood growths and the needles from the pine growths as soil acidifiers. Dressings of peat moss, decaying leaves, and vegetation, also sawdust from hardwood trees, when used as a top-dressing or mulch, adds acidity and food to the soil.

SITE

The bog garden should be so developed that it will be natural and picturesque in appearance, and it should be so shaped as to fit into the surrounding landscape in a naturalistic manner. A well-designed bog garden is an interesting feature, and it is a continuous source of pleasure to the owner.

Assuming that we have at our disposal a low section of ground inundated part of the year, unfit for garden crops or for the culture of garden flowers, such a spot can be made a thing of beauty at a comparatively low cost and the maintenance afterwards is almost nil. Nature unrestrictedly has clothed her bog gardens with numerous species of moisture-loving plants. Our first duty, then, in developing the garden would be to root out one and all of the undesirable plants, leaving the ones which are ornamental and those which will fit into the composition.

During the process of cleaning the ground it may be necessary to construct temporary trenches to allow the water to drain off, as the removal of brush, roots, and debris is much facilitated if the ground is in a dry and workable condition. After the ground has been cleaned, attention should be given to the soil. In most cases it will not be necessary to add anything to the natural bottom, but it would be best to plow, dig, or cultivate the surface so that the soil will be in good condition for planting. The proper method of working is to draw a plan to scale of the plot, having previously taken the dimensions of the ground and considered its topography, the source of water supply, its inlet and outlet. After deciding upon the plan, stakes are set showing the margin and the depths for excavation.

A well-designed bog garden is usually constructed so that the depression is from 10 inches to one foot below the average surrounding soil. Excavate for the paths running through the garden, utilizing the soil, if good, for the mounds, 12–18 inches high, which will be placed here and there throughout. Place drainage consisting of stones, cinders, brickbats, or other such material below the paths to keep them dry, finishing the surface with three inches of soil in which imbed stepping stones. These will insure a dry walk, giving facilities for the free inspection of the plants at any time without suffering the inconvenience of wet feet. Mounds of various sizes should be made to accommodate the diversified plants which will inhabit them.

TREATMENT OF MARGINS

The margin of the bog is every bit as important as the bog itself and it should receive the same care and consideration in planting. Remember, the bog is the picture and the margin the frame; therefore, in design, try to avoid making one part incongruous to the other. The sloping banks at the edge of the garden will furnish ideal positions to naturalize species of the dwarfer bamboos, alders, willows, birches, and *Ilex verticillata* (*see* Holly). Other good shrubs for such places are: *Myrica Gale, Chamaedaphne calyculata, Andromeda glaucophylla,* and *Kalmia polifolia. Ilex verticillata* is quite conspicuous in the fall and early winter with its display of red berries. Plants of the willow herb (*Epilobium*), purple loosestrife (*Lythrum Salicaria*), *Iris sibirica,* Japanese iris, not forgetting *Iris Pseudacorus,* the eulalia (*Miscanthus sinensis*), and the goatsbeard (*Aruncus dioicus*). The plume poppy (*Macleaya cordata*) is an excellent subject if massed here and there on the slightly higher ground. Other interesting plants most useful for marginal plantings are the marsh marigold (*Caltha palustris*), horsetail (*Equisetum hyemale* and *E. praealtum*), and the knotweed (*Polygonum cuspidatum*), but this is apt to be too rampant if allowed to get out of control. The Asiatic primrose (*Primula bulleyana* and *P. beesiana*), planted on the mounds, makes a charming picture when massed.

BOG PLANTS

In the depressions, and at a lower level, excellent results may be obtained by introducing plants of the royal fern (*Osmunda regalis*), the ostrich fern (*Pteretis pensylvanica*), maidenhair fern (*Adiantum pedatum*), the chain fern (*Woodwardia virginica*), and other species of ferns which by nature are dwellers in wet or boggy soils. Next come the lilies. These should be planted in the prepared mounds in the bog. *Lilium pardalinum, L. canadense,* and *L. superbum,* these three lilies are children of the bog. As companions to the lilies we may place the trilliums, such species as *Trillium grandiflorum, T. erectum, T. stylosum,* and *T. undulatum.* All are pleasingly beautiful when in flower and grow vigorously in a wet-damp situation. Also the foliage of these

---

* Special articles on the subjects indicated by an asterisk (*) will be found at the words so marked.

plants furnishes a mantle to the young growths of the lilies.

Sections of the mounds could be used to naturalize species of the beautiful native orchids: *Cypripedium Calceolus* and its large-flowered form, although the latter is better suited to the wild garden (which see). The showy orchis (*Orchis spectabilis*) and *O. rotundifolia* are also suited to the mounds.

In the depressions: *Cypripedium arietinum, Habenaria ciliaris,* and *H. psycodes* will be at home, as will the rose pogonia. All these plants are moisture lovers and are at their best in an acid soil.

The cardinal flower (*Lobelia Cardinalis*) should be given a prominent place in the bog garden and it is seen to advantage when given the companionship of *Primula sikkimensis*. The bleeding-heart (*Dicentra spectabilis*) is a worth-while subject for the bog garden and is at home when growing in peaty soil. All the varieties of *Astilbe japonica* do best in moist situations and are adaptable to any color combination from warm white to deep pink. The arrowheads (*Sagittaria*) are attractive plants and revel in a position near the margin of the water. The bogbean or buckbean (*Menyanthes trifoliata*) is one of the attractive subjects of the moist bog; its flowers are white, pink or purplish, bearded inside with white hairs.

One of the showy native plants is the pickerelweed (*Pontederia cordata*). Its upright habit of growth and its thick, parallel-veined leaves make it a very worthy subject for any wet position in the bog. In the cool and damp edges surrounding the bog garden the beautiful gentians will thrive; such species as *Gentiana asclepiadea* and *G. andrewsi*. The forget-me-nots (*Myosotis*) are happy dwellers in moist situations, are readily naturalized, and become a beautiful feature of the bog.

Unless the bog is in the immediate vicinity of the flower garden, showy flowering plants massed for effect look at their best when they are detached from each other as they appear in nature. It is much better when planting the bog garden to bear in mind that the naturalistic is to be followed rather than the formal. Nature has no use for the formal in her wild garden arrangement. If the bog adjoins the garden proper, then a more free use can be made of garden plants, but even in this case the emphasis should be placed on natural plantings rather than on the well-groomed appearance of the flower garden.

Mass plantings of cat-tails are appropriate when placed in moist soil near the edge of the bog. Excellent summer effects are produced by a planting of *Cyperus Papyrus*. This plant is not hardy and will require the protection of a cool greenhouse during winter. *Zizania aquatica,* a wild rice, is one of the most interesting of our native hardy plants. It is an annual and will spread rapidly, therefore the young plants should be removed in the early spring where they encroach on other plants.

THE SMALL BOG GARDEN

Where space will not admit the making of a bog garden on the scale of the one discussed, a miniature garden may be constructed by the use of cement pools and barrels cut in half and sunk in the ground. These are best placed in the lowest part of the garden, if low ground is available; if not, they may be kept moist by artificial means. The space where the tubs and bog plants are to be placed should be excavated to a depth of a foot or more. Prepared soil as outlined above should then be filled in. When filling in, the ground should be sunk four or five inches below the level of the surrounding land. This will tend to keep the soil in a fairly moist condition.

Plants recommended for the smaller bog garden are: *Anagallis linifolia, Caltha palustris, Cypripedium Calceolus parviflorum, Drosera longifolia* and *D. rotundifolia, Gentiana andrewsi, Helonias bullata, Menyanthes trifoliata, Myosotis palustris, Parnassia glauca, Pinguicula vulgaris, Rhexia virginica,* and *Sarracenia purpurea* (*see* PITCHER-PLANT). The latter is one of a group of insectivorous plants, most of which grow in bogs. See also DIONAEA, DROSERA, and PINGUICULA.

BOG MYRTLE = *Myrica Gale.*

BOG ROSEMARY. *See* ANDROMEDA.

BOG RUSH = *Juncus effusus.*

BOG VIOLET = *Pinguicula vulgaris.*

BOIS D'ARC = *Maclura pomifera.*

BOKHARA CLOVER = *Melilotus alba.*

BOLDO = *Peumus Boldus.*

Boldus. Latinized form of the Chilean vernacular boldo (*Peumus Boldus*).

boliviensis, -e (bo-liv-i-en'sis). From Bolivia.

BOLTING. The premature or unwanted production of flowers and seeds, often caused by starvation or excessive heat. It happens in lettuce and other plants.

BOLTING TREES. *See* TREE SURGERY.

BOLTONIA (bole-tone'i-a). A small genus of aster-like perennial herbs of the family Compositae, the two below native in the U.S. and planted in the border for ornament. They are erect, leafy plants with alternate* leaves that usually stand vertical by a slight twisting of the essentially stalkless base. Flowers in short-stalked heads, the many rays rather showy, white or violet or purplish. (Named for James Bolton, English botanist.)

These tall, stout, native plants, often called false camomile, false starwort, or thousand-flowered aster, are of the easiest culture. They should be planted in the open sunlight and toward the rear of a bed or border. Their profuse bloom in late summer and early fall makes them attractive garden plants. Easily propagated by spring or fall division. For the plant sometimes offered as *Boltonia incisa,* see CALIMERIS.

---

* Special articles on the subjects indicated by an asterisk (*) will be found at the words so marked.

False Camomile (*Boltonia asteroides*), a native aster-like perennial 3–5 ft. high, and usually with white flowers.

asteroides. From 3–5 ft. high and bushy. Leaves lance-shaped, 3–5 in. long, nearly without marginal teeth, pale green. Flower heads about ¾ in. wide, very numerous, generally white, but sometimes violet or even purple. N.Y. to Ga., mostly near the coast and westward to Ohio. Sometimes sold as *B. laevigata*.
latisquama. Similar, but with larger heads (about 1 in.) that are violet-blue. Mo. to Okla. The commonest species in cult., especially its *var.* **nana**, which is only 2–3 ft. high and has pink flower heads.

BOMBACACEAE (bom-ba-kay'see-ee). The silk-cotton tree family (often called the baobab family) comprises only about 20 genera and possibly 150 species of tropical, often huge, trees. All the hort. genera have compound* leaves, the leaflets arranged finger-fashion. Flowers solitary or in clusters (panicles*), appearing before the leaves unfold in *Adansonia*, *Bombax*, and *Ceiba*. The only other cult. genus is *Chorisia* which has solitary yellow flowers about 3 in. wide.

Few of these genera are much cultivated outdoors in U.S. except as curiosities or for shade in zone* 9. The fruit of the baobab (*see* ADANSONIA) and kapok (*see* CEIBA) are both of interest, and the flowers of *Chorisia* are extremely showy.

Technical flower characters: Calyx 5-toothed. Petals 5. Stamens* 5 or many, often showy. Ovary superior,* the style one, the stigmas 2–5.

BOMBAX (bom'backs). Very large, soft-wooded, tropical trees, family Bombacaceae, its 60 species of little hort. interest outside of the tropics, although the cotton tree is planted outdoors in the southern part of Fla. It is too big for greenhouse culture. They have compound* leaves, the 3–7 leaflets arranged finger-fashion. Flowers large, red, appearing when the tree is leafless, hence very showy. (For flower structure *see*

BOMBACACEAE.) Fruit a capsule,* its seeds embedded in a fluffy mass of cotton-like hairs. (*Bombax* is Latin for cotton or cotton wadding.)

malabaricum. Cotton tree. A spiny tree up to 80 ft. Leaflets 5–7 in. long, but the tree leafless from Dec. to Apr. Flowers nearly 4 in. long, clustered toward the ends of the branches, blooming in Jan. Fruit 4–6 in. long. Indo-Malaya.

Bona-nox (bone-a-nocks'). Good night.

BONAVIST = *Dolichos Lablab*.

BONESET. *See* EUPATORIUM.

BONSAI. *See* DWARFING.

Bonus-henricus (bone-us-hen'ri-kus). Good (King) Henry. *See* CHENOPODIUM.

BOOT-JACK = BEGGAR-TICKS. *See* list at WEEDS.

BORAGE. *See* BORAGO.

BORAGE FAMILY = Boraginaceae.

BORAGINACEAE (bore-aj-i-nay'see-ee). The borage family (often called the heliotrope or comfrey family) contains many well-known garden plants among its 85 genera and over 1500 species. Most of them are herbs of the temperate zone, but *Cordia* and *Ehretia* are tropical shrubs and trees.

Leaves mostly alternate,* the foliage generally rough-hairy. Flowers usually small, but in attractive, 1-sided clusters in most genera, especially in forget-me-not (*Myosotis*), *Anchusa*, *Brunnera*, *Echium*, *Mertensia*, and *Heliotropium*. In some other garden genera the flower cluster is not at all one-sided.

The characters that distinguish the genera of the borage family are mostly technical and based on the tiny, nut-like fruit. From the garden standpoint, the remaining genera are perhaps best grouped thus: *Lindelofia* and *Omphalodes* somewhat resemble forget-me-not; *Lithospermum*, *Lithodora*, and *Moltkia* are closely related to each other; *Pulmonaria* is allied to *Mertensia*; *Arnebia* has spotted, yellow flowers; *Cerinthe* has yellow, but purple-tipped flowers; *Borago* and *Cynoglossum* are usually blue- or purple-flowered; and the remaining garden genera, *Myosotidium*, *Onosma*, and *Symphytum* are variously colored.

Technical flower characters: Calyx and corolla 5-cleft, the calyx often persistent. Corolla often with an appendage.

BORAGO (bore-ray'go). A small genus of European herbs, family Boraginaceae, those below grown in the blue garden for their flowers, which are much liked by bees; also in the herb garden (*see* HERB GARDENING). They usually have stiff-hairy foliage. Leaves alternate.* Flowers blue, more or less wheel-shaped, in a loose, leafy cluster. (*Borago* is derived from the Latin *burra*, rough-hairy.)

The borage is a hardy annual, the seeds of which should be sown where the plants are to bloom. The other is a perennial rock garden plant.

* Special articles on the subjects indicated by an asterisk (*) will be found at the words so marked.

officinalis. Borage. Not over 2 ft. high. Leaves oblongish, 3½–5 in. long, generally narrowed to a winged stalk or base. Flowers about ¾ in. wide, the stamens protruding as much as ¼ in. Southern Eu. and northern Af. Blooming all summer.

laxiflora. A wall or rock garden, drooping or procumbent, perennial herb, with oblong or ovalish, rough leaves. Flowers long-stalked, opal-blue, flowering from April to early autumn. Corsica. If it is not protected by a snow blanket it is best to mulch lightly with straw.

Borbonia (bor-bō′ni-a). An old and now untenable generic name for certain plants included in *Persea* (which see).

borbonica, -us, -um (bore-bon′i-ka). From Reunion (once called Bourbon) Island, in the Indian Ocean. Also applied to some species named for the Bourbon kings of France.

BORDEAUX MIXTURE. A fungicide with an interesting history. It was first used by French grape growers near the town of Bordeaux to discolor the plants to keep children from stealing the fruit. In 1882 a professor at the university noticed that the vines with this mixture of copper and lime not only discouraged the children from picking the grapes but also had less mildew disease. From this accidental discovery the bordeaux mixture became an almost universal fungicide. It was about 1940 when the organic fungicides were first discovered and since that time the bordeaux mixture has been gradually replaced with better materials. (*See* FUNGICIDES.)

BORDER. As generally understood, this term refers to any more or less long and narrow strip of land in the garden, and is not necessarily confined to plantings along the property margins. Borders may be made close to the house, parallel with walks and drives, and designed to form inclosures or garden compartments. They should be laid out with due regard to proportion with the rest of the place, and are best of rather simple outline. Borders are generally planted with a variety of plants arranged for mass effect. The planting may consist entirely of shrubs; of herbaceous or annual flowers, both hardy and tender; or a mixture of shrubs and herbs. A border may be exposed to full sunlight, or be subject to shade in varying degree. In any case a selection of plants may be made that will thrive and give good results, providing the planter has exercised good judgment in choosing.

Flowers appear to best advantage against some kind of background. Shrubs are good if far enough back so as not to smother and rob of food all but the more robust kinds of flowers. A clipped hedge is good if there is a walk or strip of turf between it and the border. Sometimes a wall is ideal, and adds attraction when partly clothed with climbing plants. In some surroundings a picket fence, or one made of more rustic material, will be just the thing for a suitable background on which to drape such plants as roses and clematis. A gravel path or flagstone strip

along the front of the border is a help in upkeep and permits certain dwarf plants to sprawl without causing a problem with the grass.

HARDY FLOWER BORDER

This will consist almost entirely of herbaceous perennials, with some annuals to fill the gaps left by daffodils and tulips where these are admitted. The smaller bulbs that are so welcome in spring are best placed elsewhere if possible, but may be tucked in between the front row dwarfs without too much harm. Inasmuch as a perennial border cannot be really dug each year, it is most important that deep preparation and enrichment of the soil with rotted manure or other good organic material be done before planting.

The following are listed as well-known examples of hardy herbaceous perennials that can be expected to thrive under average garden conditions over a wide area. The height and time of bloom stated are approximate — much depends on soil and climate. Those marked † are tolerant of some shade.

	Color	Height	Month of Bloom
Achillea Ptarmica Boule de Neige	white	2 ft.	6–7
Alyssum saxatile compactum	yellow	8 in.	4–5
Anchusa azurea vars.	blue	3–5 ft.	5–6
†*Anemone japonica* vars.	white, pink	3–5 ft.	9–10
Anthemis tinctoria Moonlight	pale yellow	2–3 ft.	5–9
†*Aquilegia chrysantha* (*see* COLUMBINE)	yellow	3 ft.	6–7
Arabis albida	white	6–8 in.	4–5
Artemisia vulgaris lactiflora	creamy	4–5 ft.	8–9
Asclepias tuberosa (*see* MILKWEED)	orange	2–3 ft.	7–8
Aster frikarti	blue	2 ft.	7–10
†*Astilbe davidi*	various	2–3 ft.	6–7
Baptisia australis	blue	4 ft.	5–6
Boltonia latisquama	pinkish	4–5 ft.	8–9
†*Brunnera macrophylla*	blue	1 ft.	4–5
†*Campanula lactiflora*	pale blue	4–5 ft.	7–8
†*C. persicifolia* vars.	blue, white	2–3 ft.	6–7
Centaurea macrocephala	yellow	3–4 ft.	7–8
C. montana	blue	1½ ft.	5–7
Centranthus ruber	crimson	2–3 ft.	6–7
Cephalaria alpina	pale yellow	5–6 ft.	6–7
†*Chelone lyoni*	deep rose	3 ft.	8–9
Chrysanthemum maximum vars.	white	2–3 ft.	6–7
C. morifolium vars.	various	1–4 ft.	8–11
†*Cimicifuga racemosa*	white	5–8 ft.	7–8
Clematis recta	white	4–5 ft.	6
Coreopsis grandiflora	yellow	2–3 ft.	6–10
Delphinium grandiflorum	blue, white	2–3 ft.	6–9

---

* Special articles on the subjects indicated by an asterisk (*) will be found at the words so marked.

	Color	Height	Month of Bloom
D. hybrids	various	4–8 ft.	6–9
Dianthus plumarius vars.	various	9–15 in.	6–7
†Dicentra eximia	rose-pink	1 ft.	4–10
†D. spectabilis	rosy red	2–3 ft.	5–6
Dictamnus albus	white	2–3 ft.	5–6
Doronicum caucasicum	yellow	1½ ft.	4–5
Dracocephalum virginianum	pink	1–4 ft.	8–9
Echinacea purpurea	reddish	3–5 ft.	7–8
Echinops Ritro	steel blue	2–3 ft.	7–8
†Eupatorium coelestinum	blue	2–3 ft.	9–10
Euphorbia corollata	white	3 ft.	7–8
Gaillardia aristata	yellow	2–2½ ft.	6–10
Geranium ibericum	purple	2 ft.	6–9
Gypsophila paniculata Bristol Fairy	white	3 ft.	7–9
Helenium autumnale	yellow	3–5 ft.	8–9
H. a. pumilum	yellow	2 ft.	8–9
H. a. Riverton Gem	gold and red	4–5 ft.	8–9
Helianthus laetiflorus (see SUNFLOWER)	yellow	3–4 ft.	7–10
†Hemerocallis in variety	various	2–5 ft.	5–8
†Heuchera sanguinea vars.	red, pink, white	1–2 ft.	6–7
†Hosta in variety (see PLANTAINLILY)	white, lavender	1–3 ft.	7–8
Iberis sempervirens Snowflake (see CANDYTUFT)	white	9 in.	5
Iris germanica var.	various	2–4 ft.	5–6
Kniphofia Uvaria	red and yellow	2–4 ft.	7–9
Liatris scariosa	purple, white	4–5 ft.	7–8
Lilium sp. (see LILIUM)	various	2–8 ft.	6–9
Lupinus hybrids	various	3–5 ft.	5–6
Monarda didyma	red	3–4 ft.	7–8
Nepeta mussini	blue	1 ft.	5–8
Oenothera fruticosa (see EVENING PRIMROSE)	yellow	2 ft.	6–8
Paeonia in var.	white, pink, red	2–3 ft.	5–6
Phlox divaricata laphami	lavender	1–1½ ft.	5–6
†P. paniculata vars.	various	2–4 ft.	7–9
†Platycodon grandiflorum	blue, white	2–3 ft.	7–9
Rudbeckia speciosa	yellow	2–3 ft.	7–9
Salvia pitcheri	blue	3–4 ft.	8–10
Scabiosa caucasica	blue shades	1½–2 ft.	6–9
Thermopsis caroliniana	yellow	4–5 ft.	6–7
Veronica incana	blue	1 ft.	6–7
V. longifolia subsessilis	blue	3 ft.	8–9
V. spuria	blue	1 ft.	6–7

In general most herbaceous perennials can be planted to advantage in the fall. Notable exceptions are alyssum, anchusa, Japanese anemone, asters, and chrysanthemums. The soil is in excellent condition in the fall, and new roots are quickly formed to have the plants well set for a good start in spring. Where spring planting is unavoidable it is well to get it done as soon as the soil is dry enough to work; but it may be stretched out where pot plants are available. There is no hard and fast rule concerning arrangement. Much depends on personal taste, but it is well to give thought to succession of bloom, so as to have flowers fairly well distributed throughout the border all during the season. The larger plants may be set singly, the rest in groups of three or more in such a manner as to achieve a free and easy effect.

Elaborate color schemes do not always come out according to plan, but color harmony is doubtless more appealing to the majority of people than vivid contrasts. (See COLOR GARDENING.)

It has often been said that hardy perennials will continue to give a good display year after year with little or no attenion. While true that such as peony, dictamnus, and gypsophila can remain happy for a long time without disturbance at the root, most kinds need to be dug and divided every so often if they are to keep going in vigorous condition. Certain groups, such as phlox, helenium, and aster, are the better for being divided every second or third year; others may go a year or two longer. (See DIVISION.) Double digging and enrichment of the soil is in order whenever this dividing takes place. In most instances the work of renovation can be done in the fall, and of course this is always the time to make any replacements of spring-flowering bulbs.

Where winter protection is needed it should be provided in the form of a not too heavy covering of material that will not pack into a sodden mass. Pine needles and salt hay afford good clean covering, and where evergreen boughs are obtainable there is nothing better for covering those plants with persistent foliage. The important thing is not to cover before winter has really taken possession, and to proceed with caution about removing the material in spring. The real purpose of covering is not to keep the plants warm, but to maintain even conditions about the plants during the periods of freezing and thawing, and to guard against the ill effects which follow extreme weather changes. (See MULCH AND MULCHING.)

A cultural detail worth doing in late fall is to fork lightly over the border just before putting on the winter cover. When taken off in spring a light scratching of the surface will give that well-groomed effect with little danger of injuring pushing shoots of bulbs and other plants.

At this time a sprinkling of bone meal lightly worked in will be an aid to healthy growth throughout the season, and wood ashes are also excellent to apply at this time. If later it appears that extra feeding is required, sheep manure, or some other quick-acting fertilizer, scattered during a rainy time, or watered in, will keep growth moving. Watering in a dry time is helpful when thoroughly done, and the application of a fine mulch after rain or watering helps conserve moisture.

Staking calls for attention early, before growth is far enough along to be injured or broken by storms. The art of staking is to provide support without it being too obvious or detracting from the natural habit of the plants. (See STAKES AND STAKING.)

The prompt removal of faded flowers ensures a trim appearance, and in many cases lengthens the flowering period.

ANNUALS

The use of annuals in the hardy border is taken as a matter of course, and they add greatly to the floral display from midsummer to frost. As fillers they are best established from pots or flats. Ageratum, candytuft, zinnia, petunia, pinks, phlox, and verbena offer colorful varieties to fill gaps along the front. For a little more height, arctotis, calendula, gaillardia, nigella, and snapdragon are good examples. Of larger growth for the background, cosmos, scabious, larkspur, helichrysum, nicotianas, and helianthus are all first-class. *Salvia farinacea*, perennial in a mild climate, can be grown and flowered as an annual. Its long spikes of violet-blue flowers blend well and are very lasting.

A well-planned border of annuals alone can be a source of much beauty and satisfaction. Seeds may be sown in place, and in good soil with ample room for the individual plant to develop, a colorful display may be enjoyed for little expense. (See ANNUALS.)

THE SHRUB BORDER

A border of shrubs gives a year-round effect in the garden, and has some screening and protective value. Some thought should be given to their ultimate size in relation to a particular place in order to avoid drastic use of the pruning shears. Shrubs that are related blend well together and a more pleasing effect is obtained from a limited number of kinds. There are enough good honeysuckles or viburnums to furnish a border that would give fine flower, fruit, and foliage effects all through the growing season. Abelia, weigela, beauty-bush and snowberry would provide a good combination of related plants. Other good border shrubs are to be found among cotoneaster, forsythia, spiraea, shrub-roses, Japanese quince, lilacs, mock-orange, and rose-of-Sharon. Good shrubs for "facing" or tying the planting down are *Abelia grandiflora, Kerria japonica, Spiraea* Anthony Waterer, *Stephanandra incisa,* and *Symphoricarpos chenaulti.*

Rhododendrons and related plants need an acid soil, perpetual mulch, and shelter from winter blasts, and are well worth any extra care in these respects.

The maintenance of a shrub border is not very exacting. The principal thing is to keep old shoots cut out before the plants get all cluttered and unkempt. A mulch of rotted manure or leaves put on in the fall will encourage good growth and can be raked down for a tidy effect in spring.

In some sections certain shrubs may be more or less killed back by severe cold, and respond very well if treated as herbaceous plants, but leaving the cutting-down until spring. Examples are *Abelia grandiflora, Buddleia davidi, Caryopteris incana, Elsholtzia stauntoni, Lespedeza thunbergi, Spiraea* Anthony Waterer, and *Vitex.* These are all valuable for a late flower display, and might be grouped by themselves or in association with such robust herbaceous perennials as aster, baptisia, boltonia, echinops, eryngium, helenium, helianthus, peony, thermopsis, and verbascum. Yucca and some of the lilacs would add interest to such a grouping, as would such little shrubby plants as *Daphne Mezereum,* lavender, southernwood, and rue. For a variety of plants suitable for shady borders, *see* SHADY GARDEN.

SHRUBS FOR MILD CLIMATES

A number of shrubs with evergreen foliage (some with showy flowers as well) may be grown in outdoor borders without protection where winters are mild. Some that can stand a few degrees of frost without much injury are aucuba, Kurume and other evergreen azaleas, camellias, choisya, *Daphne odora, Elaeagnus pungens,* escallonias, *Ligustrum japonicum, Myrtus communis* (the classical myrtle), nandina, olearias, pittosporum, raphiolepis, and *Viburnum Tinus.* While box is not unknown in northern gardens, it is not seen in such perfection as it is in gardens from Maryland south. Rosemary is beloved for its fragrance and sentimental interest. An outstanding deciduous shrub is *Lagerstroemia indica,* better known as crape myrtle.

In those practically frost-free parts of the country, gardens would display a number of shrubs familiar as pot plants in the North. Included would be acalyphas, ardisia, beloperone (shrimp plant), brunfelsia, *Buddleia asiatica,* callistemon, carissa, cestrum, crotons, *Erythrina Crista-galli,* fuchsias, gardenia, *Hibiscus rosa-sinensis,* ixora, lantana, lemon verbena, oleander, poinciana, and poinsettia. — H. E. D.

borealis, -e (bor-ree-a'lis). Northern.

BORECOLE = *Brassica oleracea acephala.* For culture *see* KALE.

BORERS. Grubs or larvae of many beetles, sawflies, etc., work in heartwood or more often in cambium of many trees. Usually, borers attack injured, sick, or dying trees most readily. Preventive bark treatments of pesticide #17 (*see* SPRAYS AND DUSTS) — 3 times normal dosage — applied when adults are active is most effective. For a general borer preventive program in zone*

---

* Special articles on the subjects indicated by an asterisk (*) will be found at the words so marked.

4, treat trunk and major branches (not foliage) 3 times at monthly intervals beginning May 15. Kill established borers by wire, sharp knife, or syringing tunnel with 3 times normal pesticide #20 mixture. — L. G. M.

borinquena, -us, -um (bor-rin-kwen'a). Derived from an old Spanish name for the island of Puerto Rico.

BORONIA (bor-ro'nee-a). A large genus of Australian, fragrant and evergreen shrubs of the rue family, two of which are grown for ornament, mostly in the greenhouse or outdoors in frost-free regions. Leaves opposite, compound* (in the two below), with a few lateral leaflets. Flowers solitary or in twos, borne mostly along the stem, often so thickly as partially to hide it. Stamens 8, four small, yellow and pollen-bearing, the other four large, purple, but sterile. Fruit capsule*-like. (Named for Francesco Boroni, who collected plants in Greece.)

Boronias are very aromatic greenhouse shrubs cult. for their pleasing odor and profusion of flowers. They need a cool greenhouse, not much or certainly not excessive watering, and potting mixture* 5. They should be cut back to the ground after blooming and renewed completely every second or third year. Propagated by cuttings, preferably under a bell-jar.

elatior. A leafy shrub up to 4 ft. high. Leaves stalked, the leaflets 2–6 pairs, with an odd terminal one, very narrow. Flowers rose-purple or red, about ¼ in. wide, very numerous, and often of different colors on the same plant.

megastigma. A sparsely leafy shrub, but twiggy and 12–20 in. high. Leaves stalkless, the leaflets 1 or 2 pairs, with an odd terminal one, about ¾ in. long. Flowers yellow inside, purple outside, nearly ½ in. wide.

BOSTON . FERN = *Nephrolepis exaltata bostoniensis.*

BOSTON IVY = *Parthenocissus tricuspidata.*

BOTANIC GARDEN. Primarily an institution for research in the field of botany, by extension, an institution which may include horticulture, or any of several applications of the science of plant life to practical affairs. The modern, well-balanced botanical garden is apt to have besides research laboratories, a library and herbarium, large collections of growing plants, both outdoors and in the greenhouse. All of the more important ones in America also maintain a department of horticulture and often elaborate gardens to illustrate it.

There are two botanic gardens in the country which from age, endowments, staff, and research are easily the leading institutions of the sort and well worth any gardener's visit. The oldest (established 1860) is the Missouri Botanical Garden at St. Louis, Mo. The largest and most important is the New York Botanical Garden, Bronx Park, New York City, established in 1898.

The Missouri Botanical Garden, besides its systematic collections, has the following features of special interest to gardeners: one of the finest collections of greenhouse orchids in the world at Gray Summit, Mo.; a tropical fruit greenhouse; the best collection of hardy and tender water lilies in the U.S.; a fine formal garden; a special garden of hardy perennials; a large collection of hardy and tropical ferns; and over 11,000 species of plants under cultivation. The garden comprises about 75 acres at St. Louis and fifteen hundred more at its arboretum at Gray Summit, Mo.

The New York Botanical Garden (area over 235 acres), besides its great prestige as a research institution, maintains the following collections of outstanding interest to the gardener: the greatest collection of hardy and tender cacti in the U.S.; large collections of such garden favorites as dahlias, irises, bulbs, daylilies, and roses; very large shrub and tree collections and another of evergreens; and a small model garden. It has nearly 12,000 species of plants in cultivation, both outdoors and under glass.

The Brooklyn Botanic Garden (established 1911, area 50 acres) has the following features of interest to gardeners: Japanese garden; rose garden; a fine collection of Japanese iris.

Two other botanic gardens, both more recent, demand attention. One is the United States Botanic Garden, established 1934. It should have been the culmination of many years of devoted effort to create a real national botanic garden, but it is still of doubtful prognosis. It is in Washington, D.C. The other is Santa Barbara Botanic Garden, Santa Barbara, Calif., which maintains a fine collection of succulents and subtropical ornamentals.

A unique botanic garden is the Rancho Santa Ana, at Santa Ana Cañon, Claremont, Calif. It is devoted to the native plants of Calif., many hundreds of which are in cult. there in an extremely attractive setting. The garden also maintains an herbarium of Calif. plants, a reference library, and co-operates with schools and colleges in an educational program.

Most universities maintain a botanic garden, usually as an adjunct of their work in the classroom. Most of them are an acre or so and, while growing many plants of great interest or merit, their horticultural significance is slight. The leading gardens of this type are at University of Pennsylvania, Yale, University of California, Butler, and at Smith College.

Other botanic gardens, not mentioned above, are to be found as follows, including only the most important:

Huntington Botanical Garden, San Marino, Calif. 200 acres. Mostly desert plants.
Montreal Botanical Garden, Montreal, Canada. 190 acres. Native plants and over 20 greenhouses.
Arizona Botanical Garden (in Papago Park) Phoenix, Ariz. 306 acres. Mostly desert plants.

---

* Special articles on the subjects indicated by an asterisk (*) will be found at the words so marked.

McKee Jungle Gardens, Vero Beach, Fla. 120 acres. Tropical and sub-tropical plants.

Buffalo Botanic Garden, Buffalo, N.Y. Sixteen display greenhouses.

Arthur Hoyt Scott Horticultural Foundation, Swarthmore, Pa. Hardy woody and herbaceous plants.

Fort Worth Botanic Garden, Fort Worth, Tex. Succulents and native plants.

Royal Botanical Gardens, Hamilton, Ontario. Herbaceous and woody plants.

Toronto Botanical Garden, Toronto. Started in 1959.

See also ARBORETUM, GARDEN TOURS, BARTRAM'S GARDEN, and HOSACKIA.

BOTANY. The science of plant life. One of its applications is to horticulture and gardening, the main purpose of this book. Botany, as such, is not. Some features of botany, however, should be known to all gardeners. (*See* LEAF, FLOWER, FRUIT, ROOT, etc.; *see also* the various entries under PLANT.)

BO-TREE = *Ficus religiosa.*

BOTRYCHIUM (bo-trick'i-um). The grape ferns or moonworts, family Ophioglossaceae, are little grown except in the wild garden. Of the 40 known species only two are likely to be cult. They have underground stems from which arises at intervals a single compound* leaf (frond), the leaflets arranged feather-fashion. On an apparently separate stalk, usually exceeding the frond, is a branched, grape-like (but small) cluster of spore cases. This is the fertile frond. (*Botrychium* is Greek for grape-like.)

The species below are both hardy over most of the country. They need the shade of trees or buildings, a good rich woods soil (not acid or only mildly so) and plenty of moisture.

dissectum. An evergreen fern 6–15 in. high, the fronds in 3 main, stalked segments but these dissected, the ultimate segments scarcely 1/16 in. wide. Fertile frond taller than the leaf-like one. Eastern N.A. There is a *var.* obliquum, with much wider ultimate segments. It is sometimes known as *Botrychium ternatum.*

virginianum. Rattlesnake fern. From 6–20 in. high, the fronds with 3 main, stalked segments, the ultimate divisions oblongish and toothed toward the tip. Fertile frond scarcely exceeding the leaf-like one. North temperate zone. The most satisfactory species of the two, but neither is of much garden interest except to fern fanciers.

botryoides (bo-tree-oy'deez; but *see* OÏDES). Grape-like or with grape-like clusters.

Botrys. An old classical name for the feather-geranium (*Chenopodium Botrys*).

botrytis, -e (bo-try'tis). With a grape-like cluster.

BOTTLE-BRUSH. See CALLISTEMON and MELALEUCA.

BOTTLE FERN = *Cystopteris fragilis.*

BOTTLE GARDEN. See TERRARIUM.

BOTTLE GENTIAN = *Gentiana andrewsi.*

BOTTLE PALM = *Hyophorbe amaricaulis.*

BOTTLE-TREE. See BRACHYCHITON.

BOTTOM-HEAT. Heat applied underneath a greenhouse bench in which propagating material is growing. Application of bottom-heat is a common and useful aid in getting cuttings to root, and in the germination of some seeds. It is most widely used in making cuttings of tender plants which root more easily if the soil temperature (due to bottom-heat) is several degrees warmer than the air temperature of the greenhouse. A bench with bottom-heat needs close watching to keep it from drying out.

BOUGAINVILLAEA (boo-gen-vill-ee'a). Perhaps the handsomest, and certainly the most widely planted ornamental vines of the tropics, and a great favorite in the southern U.S. and in Calif. Of the 10 known species, all South American and belonging to the family Nyctaginaceae, the two below are the best-known. They are tall-growing, woody vines with alternate,* stalked leaves. Flowers small and not at all showy, all the color coming from the large, showy bracts,* three of which surround each flower. (For flower characters *see* NYCTAGINACEAE.) Fruit a 5-ribbed achene.* (Named for L. A. de Bougainville, a French navigator.) There are several variations in spelling to be found in the catalogues. Two of the best-known are *Buginvillaea* and *Bouginvillea.*

These vines, for arbors, porches, or for covering the corner of a house, are among the finest creepers known. They will grow in any ordinary garden soil and will stand considerable periods of drought. Outdoors their culture is limited to the most sheltered parts of zone* 7, but they are thoroughly at home in zones* 8 and 9, and, of course, throughout the tropics. Occasionally grown in northern greenhouses, but usually too rampant to be confined. Some florists keep them as trimmed pot plants. They need a cool greenhouse and potting mixture* 4. Propagated by cuttings. There are several hort. forms of the species below, some of them 2-toned and very handsome.

glabra. A vine with a stout, woody and spiny but not hairy, stem often 60–100 ft. long (in the tropics), much less in the U.S. Leaves oblongish, narrowed both ends. Flowers scattered on wand-like, lateral, usually drooping branchlets, the bracts magenta or purple and about 1 in. long, very showy. Brazil. There is a form with variegated leaves and another, *var.* sanderiana, with even more flowers than the typical form. It blooms most of the year.

spectabilis. Similar to *B. glabra,* but the stems densely hairy and with larger and more showy bracts. The bloom does not, however, last as long as in the other species, and the plant is a more rampant climber than *B. glabra.* Bracts reddish in the typical form, but in the variety Crimson Lake, crimson-red. This is the most popular variety in Fla. and Calif. Brazil.

BOULDER FERN = *Dennstaedtia punctilobula.*

BOULDER RASPBERRY = *Rubus deliciosus.*

BOUNCING BET = *Saponaria officinalis.*

---

* Special articles on the subjects indicated by an asterisk (*) will be found at the words so marked.

BOUQUET   LARKSPUR = *Delphinium grandiflorum.*

BOURBON ROSE = *Rosa borboniana.*

BOUSSINGAULTIA (boo-sin-galt′i-a). A small genus of tropical American herbaceous vines, family Basellaceae, one grown for ornament in warm regions and an escape* in Fla. and Tex. They have a tuberous rootstock and alternate* leaves without marginal teeth. Flowers in spike-like clusters (racemes*). Sepals 2; petals 5, and the flower with 2 bracts beneath it. Fruit fleshy, enclosed by the persistent, withered flower. (Named for J. B. Boussingault, French chemist.)

The Madeira-vine is grown outdoors in the South, and its root, with some winter covering, will survive up to zone* 6. North of this the roots should be dug and stored for the winter in a cool, frost-free place.

baselloides. Madeira-vine called also mignonette-vine, from the fragrance of its flowers. A tall creeper with ovalish or heart-shaped, taper-pointed leaves 2–3 in. long. Flowers white (black in age), small, but the slender, drooping racemes* often 12 in. long and showy. Tropical America. It produces tubercles in the axils* of the leaves which, if planted in moist sand, will produce new plants. Also called manetti-vine.

BOUVARDIA (boo-var′di-a). A genus of 30 species of attractive greenhouse shrubs of the madder family, most of them tropical American, and grown for their showy flowers. Leaves opposite* or in whorls.* Flowers tubular, in showy, terminal, flattish clusters (cymes*). Corolla-tube terminated by 4 spreading lobes. Stamens 4. Stigmas 2. Fruit a capsule.* (Named for Charles Bouvard, superintendent of Jardin du Roi, Paris.)

Bouvardias are handsome cult. shrubs, both those below grown by florists, especially the first species, which is fragrant. They need a warm-temperate greenhouse (50°–55°), plenty of water, and should be grown in potting mixture* 5. Home growers can plunge the pots outdoors during summer, but in Sept.–Oct. they need a greenhouse. Propagated by root cuttings, cut to about 1 in. long, in June. Scarcely cover the cuttings with potting mixture* 2 and keep the temperature about 60°.

humboldti. A shrub 2–4 ft. high with opposite, ovalish leaves with a tapering tip. Flowers white, very fragrant, the tube nearly 2½ in. long, the limb about 1½ in. wide. Of uncertain origin, but probably a hort. form.

ternifolia. A shrub 4–6 ft. high, the leaves in whorls* of 3 or 4, more or less lance-oval. Flowers red, hairy on the outside, ¾–1¼ in. long. Tex. to Mex. Called also *B. triphylla.*

BOWER PLANT = *Pandorea jasminoides.*

BOWIEA = *Schizobasopsis.*

BOWLING GREEN. A bowling green is a level, compact turf area 120 ft. square, comparable to a putting green. Since the bowling concentrates wear at the two ends of the rink the play should be alternated from East–West to North–South weekly, to

Bowling Green

allow the end sod to recuperate while the other is being used.

Surrounding the rink is a gutter six inches below the level of the green with a creosoted wooden curb 2 × 8 inches supporting the edge of the gutter next to the green. The curb is held in place by stakes 2 × 4 × 18 inches driven into the ground on 5-ft. centers and nailed to the curb on the inside edge with the top of the stake ½ in. below the level of the green. The width of the gutter may vary from one to two feet, with either a wooden backboard or a turf bank to keep the bowls from rolling beyond. The floor of the gutter should be gravel 18 in. deep, underdrained by a 4-in. agricultural tile.

For bowling, the turf should be absolutely perfect because any undulation counteracts the skill of the bowler. The seedbed should be prepared exactly the same as for a putting green, with perfect underdrainage and at least six inches of good growing topsoil. A mixture of five parts good topsoil to one part peat moss or humus and one part well-rotted manure, with one pound of bone meal to each cubic foot of soil, should be put into a concrete mixer and thoroughly mixed, then laid down in an even, six-inch layer over the subgrade. This should be rolled to a perfect level, seeded with Washington creeping bent (*see* LAWN) which should be raked lightly into the surface, and kept watered daily until satisfactory turf is developed. Just before the first cutting this turf should be rolled, and immediately after the cutting should be top-dressed with a mixture of sifted topsoil and humus, which should be repeated again twice during the first growing season.

Any ornamental planting or shelter around the bowling green depends upon its location and proposed use. For public use a building is necessary for rest rooms, changing of shoes, and storage of equipment. — R. E. G.

BOWMAN'S-ROOT = *Gillenia trifoliata.*

BOWSTRING HEMP. See SANSEVIERIA.

BOX. The box, or as many call it, boxwood, is perhaps our most valuable broad-

BOX 137 BOX

leaved evergreen. Of the thirty known species, all belonging to the genus **Buxus** (bucks′us), family Buxaceae, only two are in common cult. But from these, and their numerous hort. varieties, many historic gardens, especially in Md. and Va., have taken on an atmosphere of grace, charm, and solidity that no other shrubs could give them. And since the days of the Romans it has been the best of all plants for hedges and topiary work.

Leaves opposite,* evergreen, without marginal teeth. Flowers small and inconspicuous, without petals, flowering in April or May, the male and female on the same plant, but not together, and usually the female flowers above the male ones. Female flowers with 6 sepals, the male flowers with 4. Fruit a 3-horned capsule,* usually shedding seed in June. (*Buxus* is classical Latin for the box.) For the Victorian box *see* PITTOSPORUM UNDULATUM.

For culture *see* below.

B. harlandi. An evergreen shrub, related to the next species, but not hardy northward. Its great merit is that it provides a box suitable for places where the summers are too hot and dry for the common box. China.

B. japonica = *Buxus microphylla japonica.*

B. microphylla. A Japanese evergreen shrub, rarely over 3 ft. high, and resembling ordinary box, but with its leaves smaller and broadest above the middle, and with its branchlets prominently 4-angled or winged. This is more hardy than common box, often living up to zone* 4, especially in the *var.* **japonica,** which is also a little taller and with more open habit. The *var.* **koreana** (from Korea) is shorter than the typical form, rarely exceeding 18–20 in., and, like the *var.* **japonica,** more hardy.

B. sempervirens. The common box, including the so-called English and American box, which (in some of its forms) ranges from a dwarf, globular shrub up to a tree 25 ft. high, the latter only in the most favorable sites. Leaves broadest at or below the middle, ¾–1½ in. long, lustrous-green both sides, but darker above, rounded and slightly notched at the tip. A native of southern Eu., northern Af. and western As., consequently not certainly hardy above zone* 4, but often grown there in locally favorable places or with winter protection. Of its many hort. forms there are weeping, pyramidal, globe-shaped, and tree-like varieties, some with variegated foliage. One of the best is *var.* **suffruticosa,** the edging box, a permanent dwarf and used for centuries to edge beds and in formal gardens.

CULTURE OF BOXWOOD

The box is a slow-growing plant, its hard, uniform wood having furnished Albrecht Dürer with material for his woodblocks, and it still does for most artists. Because of its slow growth and evergreen habit it stands moving rather poorly. Its roots must not be exposed to the sun and wind, and it is safest moved with a large ball of earth tightly wrapped in stout canvas, not in porous bagging.

Box is not particular as to soils, and most ordinary garden soils will suit it. If large plants are to be transferred, dig a hole at least a foot deeper and wider than the ball of soil surrounding it. And the bottom of the hole should be of well-tamped, fine garden soil, not sandy or rocky. No matter what the size, the plants should be set a little deeper than their old ground level, and the new soil thoroughly packed around the root ball. Water copiously the first few weeks after planting, which, in the North, should be early in the spring or from Aug. 15 to Sept. 15. Recently transplanted large specimens should be shaded from the sun, winter or summer, until thoroughly established.

In clipping box it should be remembered that well-sheared forms, and, of course, all topiary work, are only secured by regular attention. However, along the northern edge of its hardiness range (*see* notes above), clipping is best done in August or later, as earlier clipping may provoke young growth that will winter-kill if it does not have time to ripen its wood.

The beauty and popularity of box are so great that gardeners are always tempted to grow it beyond its natural range of hardiness. Such venturesome growers should read the articles on zones and on protecting plants.

Box is propagated by cuttings of mature wood taken early in the autumn. If in zone* 5 or 4, they should be kept in a cool greenhouse, in moist sand, without bottom-heat. Farther south the cuttings may be put in a shady place outdoors. It is also sometimes propagated by layers, and, in the edging box, by division. Growing box from seed is interminable.

Nowhere does box do so well as in Md. and Va. For this reason some cultural hints are here reprinted from *Boxwood in Virginia,* by A. G. Smith, Jr., of the Agricultural Extension Service of the Virginia Polytechnic Institute, Blacksburg, Va. Summarized they are:

1. Box is shallow-rooted, hence no digging or cultivation near the plants.
2. Do not apply heavy amounts of fertilizer or manure. If either are needed (not more than every other year), a light application of manure (about 1½ in.) or ¼ cup of 10–6–4 fertilizer to each square yard of root area may be spread in Feb. or Mar. "Often it is best not to fertilize boxwood at all."
3. In pruning or clipping, start cutting weak and crowded branches from the top and center of the mass to allow light and air to penetrate.
4. Box grows well in soils of pH 5.5–7.4, hence liming is unnecessary unless the soil is definitely acid. If lime is needed apply lightly only every 3 or 4 years.
5. If mulch is used, peat, sawdust, or peanut hulls can be spread, but *not more than one inch deep.*

INSECT PESTS. Leaf miners appear in spring. Control with pesticide #17 (*see* SPRAYS AND DUSTS) or #1 when flies are active, in May usually. Mites can be controlled by pesticide #1 or #21 sprays. A psyllid which appears in spring is easily controlled by pesticide #1.

* Special articles on the subjects indicated by an asterisk (*) will be found at the words so marked.

March application of superior-type oil sprays under non-freezing conditions will control oyster shell and other scales.

DISEASES. Canker* is the only serious problem caused by fungi. Small pink or orange pustules form on the bark over the cankered area. All leaves and branches beyond the cankered area will die. Prune out the dead wood and spray with pesticide #8A (see SPRAYS AND DUSTS) when new growth begins in the spring. Repeat 3 weeks later.

Small black dots of fungus growth quickly appear on leaves when winter-killing or mechanical injury has occurred on the stem. Since this fungus is of secondary nature, there is no value in attempting to control it with a pesticide. Clip out all such twigs and spotted leaves.

BOX-BARBERRY = *Berberis thunbergi minor.*

BOX-ELDER = *Acer Negundo.* See MAPLE.

BOX FAMILY = Buxaceae.

BOX-HUCKLEBERRY = *Gaylussacia brachycera.* See HUCKLEBERRY.

BOX-THORN. See LYCIUM.

BOXWOOD. See BOX. The name is also applied to *Cornus florida.*

BOYCE THOMPSON INSTITUTE. The Boyce Thompson Institute for Plant Research, at Yonkers, N.Y., is one of the leading botanical research institutions in the U.S. Most of the experimental work done there is of the first interest to all intelligent gardeners, especially the work on different sorts of light rays, on gases, and on many problems affecting the growth of plants, especially the work on plant hormones. It also maintains the Boyce Thompson Southwestern Arboretum at Superior, Ariz.

BOYKINIA (boy-kin′i-a). A small genus of perennials of the saxifrage family, sometimes grown for the rock garden or wild garden. They have creeping rootstocks,* usually lobed or divided leaves, and small white flowers in open clusters (cymes* or panicles*). Fruit a 2-celled capsule with many seeds. (The genus is dedicated to a Dr. Boykin of Georgia, an American botanist.)

The plants are easily propagated by division of their creeping rootstocks. They need partial shade and woods soil.

jamesi. An alpine perennial, not over 4 in. high. Leaves mostly basal, kidney-shaped, about 1 in. wide and toothed. Flowers in a loose cluster (raceme*), the petals crimson, about ½ in. long. Col. June.

rotundifolia. Not over 2 ft. high, the alternate,* shallowly lobed, and toothed leaves 2–7 in. wide. Flowers in a 1-sided cluster (secund*), the petals scarcely protruding beyond the calyx.* Pacific Coast.

tellimoides. Nearly 3 ft. high, the leaves deeply 7–9-lobed, not over 5 in. wide. Flowers greenish-white, the petals much longer than the calyx.* Japan.

BOYSENBERRY. A relative of the Loganberry, and named for Rudolf Boysen of California where it originated. Its dark, almost wine-red fruit is about ¾ in. in diameter and 1½ in. long. Like the loganberry it is not certainly hardy in the East, especially if trained on horizontal wires or erect trellises. For fruit production the latter is the preferable method, yields of 10 qts. per plant having been harvested from a single plant grown on an erect wire trellis. Plants without horizontal wires or trellises can be easily covered with straw or snow in the East, where they mostly need such protection, but they do not then produce half as much fruit as trellis-grown plants. As the canes are 8–10 ft. high the boysenberry needs plenty of space for proper culture. See LOGANBERRY.

brachyandra, -us, -um (brack-i-an′dra). Having short stamens.*

brachybotrys (brack-ee-bō′triss). Short-clustered, like a bunch of grapes.

brachycera, -us, -um (bra-kiss′e-ra). Short-horned; sometimes short-tipped.

BRACHYCHITON (brack-ee-ky′ton). The bottle-trees, so named for the bottle-like swellings of the trunk, comprise a small genus of Australian trees, family Sterculiaceae, the two below planted for ornament in Fla. and Calif., rarely in greenhouses northward. They have alternate, and (in ours) simple* but deeply lobed leaves. Flowers unisexual* or polygamous,* very showy because of the clusters (mostly panicles*) of scarlet or yellowish bloom. Petals none, but the calyx bell-shaped and corolla-like. Stamens 10–15, in a column surrounding the pistil.* Fruit woody, tardily splitting. (*Brachychiton* is Greek for overlapping hairs or scales.)

These showy trees are hardy outdoors only in zones* 8 and 9, where, especially in Cailf., the first species is much prized. It blooms in midsummer, after which the foliage falls quickly. Neither is particular as to soil, but apparently partial to the shade of larger trees for at least some of the day. Propagated by seeds or by ripe-wood cuttings.

acerifolium. Flame-tree. Frequently 40–55 ft. high. Leaves usually 8–10 in. wide, long-stalked and deeply lobed with 5–7 rounded divisions, or sometimes there are fewer lobes or none. Flowers brilliant scarlet, about ¾ in. long, smooth. Fruit smooth, black, about 4 in. long. Often called *Sterculia acerifolia.*

populneum. Kurrajong. A taller tree, the leaves very variable, scarcely more than 3 in. long, lobed, or unlobed and ovalish. Flowers yellowish-white, but reddish inside, and sometimes dark-spotted on the outside, hairy when young. Fruit 1–2½ in. long. Often called *Sterculia diversifolia.*

BRACHYCOME (bra-kick′o-me). A large genus of mostly Australian herbs of the family Compositae, one, the Swan River daisy, a very popular, tender annual. It has alternate,* rather small leaves, divided, feather-fashion, into narrow segments. Flower heads solitary on the ends of long stalks, the rays white, blue, or rose (in a hort. form). (The name is Greek for short hair, in allusion to the short bristles of the pappus.)

---

* Special articles on the subjects indicated by an asterisk (*) will be found at the words so marked.

For culture *see* Tender Annuals at An-NUALS.

iberidifolia. Swan River daisy. A branching herb 8–18 in. high. Leaves with few, but very narrow, segments. Flower heads about 1 in. wide, the rays blue or white, or rose color in some of the hort. forms. It is an excellent edging plant, and for making an attractive, low covering of bare places in the border.

brachypetala, -us, -um (brack-i-pet'a-la). With short petals.

BRACKEN = *Pteridium aquilinum.* See BRAKE.

BRACT. A small, leaf-like or membranous or even brightly colored organ usually confined to the stalks of a flower cluster or just beneath the flower itself. In many plants they look like miniature leaves and are commonly mistaken for them. Sometimes there are many small bracts surrounding a head, as in the Compositae (there called involucral bracts). But in other plants the bracts are the showiest part of a flower cluster, although a bract is not technically part of the flower. It is the highly colored bracts that make poinsettia, the flowering dogwood, and many plants in the Bromeliaceae, the showy things they are. Bracts are very common throughout the mallow and carrot families, and not unusual in many other garden plants.

bracteosa, -us, -um (brack-tee-o'sa). Bearing bracts.

bracteata, -us, -um (brack-tee-ă'ta). Having bracts.

bractescens (brack-tess'enz). Having bracts.

BRACTLET. A small bract.

BRAHEA (bra-he'a). A small genus of mostly Mexican, medium-sized fan palms, the palma dulce cult. outdoors in southern Calif. for ornament. The stout trunks, toward the top, are usually covered with the persistent but dead and drooping leaves, the lower part ringed and spineless. Leaves divided to the middle or deeper with many slender divisions. Flowers perfect,* the cluster appearing in the crown of leaves, branched and woolly. Sepals and petals 3 each. Stamens 6. (Named for Tycho Brahe, Danish astronomer.)

Outdoors the palma dulce does not need any special soil. If grown in the greenhouse, use potting mixture* 4, give plenty of water and keep in the cool greenhouse. The plant resembles the California fan palm in holding its dead leaves for years.

dulcis. Palma dulce. Usually in groups of several trunks, each 12–20 ft. high and 6–9 in. in diameter. Leaves 4–5 ft. long, its leaflets or segments 36–50, slender and tapering. Flower cluster (spadix*) 6–8 ft. long, hanging. Fruit oblongish, ½ in. long, yellow and edible.

BRAKE. The bracken or brake is a fern of nearly world-wide distribution, but of slight garden interest. It is the only species of the genus **Pteridium** (ter-rid'ee-um), family Polypodiaceae. Fronds on black, polished, and in age, very tough stems, the frond im-mense and twice- or thrice-compound,* its ultimate divisions innumerable and somewhat tough. The only species, P. aquilinum, is about 2–4 ft. high in N.A., thrice that or more in the tropics. Fronds 3–4 ft. wide, the ultimate segments oblongish, sometimes toothed. By some our American form of the brake is considered as comprising three separate vars. of the typical form. (*Pteridium* means *Pteris*-like.) Other plants sometimes called brake are also found in the genus *Pteris.* The true brake will grow almost anywhere and is too coarse a fern except for the most informal plantings.

BRAMBLE. Loosely, any prickly shrub. As used in hort., any plant of the genus *Rubus,* especially the blackberry and raspberry, which are thus often called bramble fruits.

BRAN BAIT. A mixture of bran, a sweetener, and a poison to entice and hence kill certain insect pests. It will also, of course, kill small animals, chickens, etc. For its preparation *see* ANIMAL INJURY.

BRANCH. Any shoot, stalk, or stem that springs from a main axis, as a branch does from a tree trunk, or a secondary axis from the main one in a flower cluster.

BRANCHING BROCCOLI = *Brassica oleracea italica.* For culture *see* BROCCOLI.

BRANDY MINT = *Mentha piperita.* See MINT.

BRASENIA (bra-si'ni-a). A single, nearly world-wide aquatic plant, family Nymphaeaceae, common in still water over most of N.A. and sometimes cult. for its purple flower. It roots in the mud and sends up long, jelly-coated stalks which are attached to the middle of the blade of a floating leaf that is oval and 3–4 in. long. Flowers about ½ in. in diameter, purple, with 3 or 4 narrow petals. Fruit small, club-shaped, not splitting. The only species, B. schreberi (sometimes called B. peltata) is the water shield. (*Brasenia* is of unknown origin.)

brasiliensis, -e (bra-zill-i-en'sis). From Brazil.

BRASSAVOLA (bras-a-vō'la). A genus of 20 species of tropical American, tree-perching orchids, the one below, and perhaps others, grown in the greenhouse for their showy flowers. They have small pseudobulbs* (*see* ORCHIDACEAE) and one or two thick, leathery leaves. Flowers large, solitary in the one below, the sepals and petals spreading, small, and greenish, the lip* white. (Named for A. M. Brassavola, Venetian botanist.)

For culture *see* the article on culture at ORCHIDS.

digbyana. Pseudobulb 3–6 in. long and bearing a single (rarely 2) leaf 5–8 in. long. Flower fragrant, 4–5 in. wide, greenish-white, the lip deeply fringed or bearded. Mex. and Honduras. Blooms in the summer in the greenhouse. Sometimes offered as *Laelia digbyana.*

BRASSIA (brass'i-a). Thirty tropical

---

* Special articles on the subjects indicated by an asterisk (*) will be found at the words so marked.

American, tree-perching orchids, commonly called spider orchids, and cult. for their beautiful and odd flowers. These have narrow, often long-tailed and spreading sepals and petals, a single flower thus suggesting the legs of a spider. The lip* is nearly stalkless, without teeth or a fringe, and much shorter than the sepals. (Named for William Brass, a botanist friend of Robert Brown.)

The brassias are scarcely showy enough to be grown by florists, but their generally yellowish, spider-like bloom makes them attractive to orchid lovers. They have a pseudobulb* with one or two leaves and the flowers in weak, more or less drooping, open clusters. For culture see ORCHIDS. The plants are epiphytes.* Of six known hort. species the following are best known.

lawrenceana. The pseudobulb 4–5 in. long, its two lance-shaped leaves 8–10 in. long. Stalk of the flower cluster 12–20 in. long, and bearing 10–15 flowers. Sepals and petals yellow, brown-spotted, the sepals about 3 in. long. Brazil. In the greenhouse blooms in May or June.

longissima. Pseudobulb 1–3 in. long, its one or two leaves 8–10 in. long and about 2 in. wide. Stalk of the flower cluster 18–24 in. long, bearing 10–15 flowers. Sepals and petals golden-yellow, brown-spotted at the base, the sepals often 9 in. long. Lip white, but spotted with red-brown. Costa Rica. Blooms in June in the greenhouse.

BRASSICA (brass'i-ka). A botanically confusing but horticulturally important genus of temperate Old World annual or biennial herbs of the family Cruciferae, containing not only the mustard, but all the vegetables of the cabbage tribe, as well as rape, turnip, and others (see below). Some, also, are pernicious weeds (see Wild Mustard at WEEDS). They have mostly smooth, often bluish-green, water-shedding leaves which may be cut, lobed, or toothed. Flowers (lacking in most of the vegetables as harvested) yellow or white, with 4 petals, and in terminal clusters (racemes*). Fruit a long pod (silique*), usually stalked. (*Brassica* is the classical name for cabbage.) The exact home of most of the species is lost in antiquity. Many of the vegetables have been cult. over 2000 years.

alba = *Brassica hirta*.

arvensis. Charlock. A weedy plant resembling, in some stages, other plants of this genus. It is an annual, 2–3 ft. high, has green, somewhat stiff-hairy foliage, and small yellow flowers. The pod is about ¾ in. long and tipped by a beak at least ½ in. long. Eurasia, but common as a weed in U.S. Also called *B. kaber*.

caulorapa. Kohlrabi. A biennial, not over 18 in. high, with bluish-green leaves 7–9 in. long borne on a stout stem, the swollen part near the ground level being edible. Flowers cream-yellow. For culture see KOHLRABI.

chinensis. Pak-choi. A Chinese annual or biennial herb, grown there, and a little here, as a pot herb. It has a tight basal cluster (not as tight as cabbage) of leaves which are broadest toward the tip, and have white, margined stalks. The stem leaves are clasping. Flowers cream-yellow. Pods 1½–2½ in. long.

hirta. White mustard. A stout, branching annual, 2–4 ft. high, the foliage sometimes slightly hairy. Leaves ovalish, but divided to or near the midrib, and with a large terminal lobe. Flowers yellow, ⅓–1½ in. wide. Pods ¾–1½ in. long, constricted between the seeds. Eurasia; also a weed in U.S. Not the chief source of mustard (see *B. nigra*). Also called *B. alba*.

juncea. Leaf mustard. An annual, 2–4 ft. high. Lower leaves lobed or divided, the edges scalloped; stem leaves narrower, but not clasping. Flowers yellow. Pod 1–1½ in. long. A well-known form, called Southern Curled, has the leaf margins crisped, and is grown for greens.

Napobrassica. Rutabaga. A biennial with an underground, yellow or white-fleshed, tuberlike swelling (the rutabaga). Leaves very thick, bluish-green, perfctly smooth, rather long and large and with lyre-like divisions. Flowers whitish-yellow. Pods widely spreading, the stalks stout. An agricultural form of it, with large, yellow-fleshed roots is the Swede or Mangel-wurzel. See RUTABAGA.

Napus. Rape or colza. An annual resembling the rutabaga, but with a thin taproot. It is cult. in Eu. as the source of rape seed, but in U.S. mostly as a farm cover crop.

nigra. Black mustard. The chief source of commercial mustard and a tall annual, 4–6 ft. high, with stiff-hairy, mostly green foliage. Leaves lobed or cut, the terminal lobe larger than the lateral ones. Flowers yellow, in many short clusters. Pods about 1 in. long, hugging the stem. Cult. for mustard but also a widely dispersed weed.

oleracea. A thick-leaved, bluish-gray herb, probably native along the coasts of northwestern Eu. but not now cult. in its original form, which appears to have been a biennial or perennial. From it have been derived the following important vegetables: *Var.* **acephala.** Kale, also collards, borecole and cow cabbage. A form with many leaves but not in dense cabbage-like heads or rosettes. For culture see KALE. *Var.* **botrytis.** Cauliflower. A stemless form in which there is a whitish, much-thickened head consisting of a much-modified flower cluster. For culture see CAULIFLOWER. *Var.* **capitata.** Cabbage. A stemless form having a single dense head of consolidated leaves. For culture see CABBAGE. *Var.* **gemmifera.** Brussels Sprouts, called also sprouts and thousand-headed-cabbage. With a stout stem, a terminal or nearly terminal crown of leaves, and button-like heads like miniature cabbages along the stem. For culture see BRUSSELS SPROUTS. *Var.* **italica.** Broccoli, called also sprouting, branching Italian and asparagus broccoli; also calabrese. A form in which the thickened flower branches are in a loose, not compact, head. For culture see BROCCOLI.

pekinensis. Chinese cabbage, but commonly called celery cabbage in the markets, or more rarely, pe-tsai. A plant of Chinese origin in which there is a cylindrical, tender, almost lettuce-like head of whitish, crisp leaves. For culture see CHINESE CABBAGE.

Rapa. Turnip. A biennial with green leaves and a yellow or white-fleshed, tuberous, edible, underground portion. It has long, soft but stiff-hairy leaves, divided lyre-fashion. Flowers yellow. Pods 1½–2½ in. long. There are two varieties. One is *var.* **lorifolia**, the strap-leaved turnip, with nearly unlobed leaves. The other is *var.* **senticeps**, the seven-top turnip or Italian kale, which has no tuberous thickening, but its edible shoots are harvested. For cult. see TURNIP.

---

* Special articles on the subjects indicated by an asterisk (*) will be found at the words so marked.

BRASSICACEAE = Cruciferae.

BRASSOCATTLAELIA (brass-o-cat-lay'-li-a). Interesting orchids resulting from hybridizing the genera *Brassavola, Cattleya,* and *Laelia* — one of the few known trigeneric hybrids. They are cult. by orchid specialists.

BRASSOCATTLEYA (brass-o-cat'lee-a). A bigeneric* hybrid between the orchid genera *Brassavola* and *Cattleya.* More than a dozen such crosses are known, but they are mostly confined to the collections of fanciers and commercial growers.

BRASSOLAELIA (brass-o-lay'li-a). A bigeneric* hybrid between the orchid genera *Brassavola* and *Laelia.* A few crosses have been recorded, but the plants are little known outside the collections of orchid specialists.

BRASSOLAELIOCATTLEYA (brass-o-lay-lee-o-cat'lee-a). A group of trigeneric* hybrid orchids, grown by fanciers, resulting from crossing *Brassavola, Laelia,* and *Cattleya.*

BRAUNERIA = *Echinacea.*

BRAZILIAN GUAVA = *Psidium guineense.* See GUAVA.

BRAZILIAN MORNING-GLORY = *Ipomoea setosa.*

BRAZILIAN PEPPER-TREE = *Schinus terebinthifolius.*

BRAZIL-NUT = *Bertholletia excelsa.*

BREADFRUIT; BREADNUT = *Artocarpus communis.*

BREAK. See MUTATION.

BREAKING. Premature leafing or flowering; as a cion may *break* before it should, or a lily may *break* (flower) before it is expected. The term is also used to indicate shoots forced out by pinching. Such shoots are said to *break.*

BREATH-OF-HEAVEN = *Diosma ericoides.*

BREED. A race or strain and mostly applied to animals. But some plants are so designated, especially if the breed results from the actions of man. In this sense Golden Bantam is a breed of sweet corn. *Variety* is popularly used to designate a breed. See also CULTIVAR.

BREEDING. See PLANT BREEDING.

brevicaulis, -e (brev-i-caul'is). Short-stalked or short-stemmed.

brevifolia, -us, -um (brev-ee-fō'lee-a). Short-leaved.

brevipedunculata, -us, -um (brev-i-pe-dunk-you-lay'ta). With a short flower stalk.

brevipes (brev-i-peez'). Short-stalked.

breviscapa, -us, -um (brev-i-skape'a). With a short scape or flower stalk.

BREVOORTIA (bre-voor'ti-a). A single, California bulbous plant of the lily family, separated from *Brodiaea* only by technical characters. Its only species, **B. Ida-Maia,** the floral firecracker, is a perennial with basal, narrow leaves, a stalk 2–3 ft. high, upon which is a cluster (umbel*) of tubular, scar-

let flowers, tipped with green. (Named for J. C. Brevoort, American naturalist, and for Ida-May, the daughter of a Calif. stage-coach driver who first brought the plant to the notice of Alphonso Wood.)

The floral firecracker has the same cultural requirements as *Brodiaea.*

BREYNIA (bry'nee-a). A small genus of shrubs or trees of the spurge family, the one below from the South Sea Islands and cult. for hedges or ornament in zones* 8 and 9, rarely in greenhouses. Leaves alternate,* without marginal teeth. Flowers without petals, the male and female separate, the female solitary in the leaf axils,* the male in small clusters, and with a turban-shaped calyx* and 3 stamens.* Fruit a berry. (Named for J. P. Breyn, a German botanist.)

The snow bush is grown in Calif. and Fla., where it appears to have no special soil requirements. If grown in the greenhouse, use potting mixture* 4 and keep in a cool house.

nivosa. Snow bush. A loosely branched shrub 3–4 ft. high, the stems somewhat zigzag. Leaves 1½–2 in. long, white-speckled or white-mottled. Flowers greenish, small, inconspicuous. Fruit red. There is a variety with dark purple leaves (*var.* atropurpurea) and another with the leaves mottled with pink and red (*var.* roseopicta). The plant is offered also as *Phyllanthus nivosus.*

BRIAR. See BRIER.

BRICK. See MUSHROOM and also PATHS AND PAVING.

BRIDAL ROSE. See MATRICARIA INODORA PLENISSIMA.

BRIDAL WREATH = *Spiraea prunifolia plena* and *S. vanhouttei,* and possibly *S. trichocarpa.* See also FRANCOA RAMOSA.

BRIDEWORT = *Spiraea salicifolia.*

BRIDGES. For private roads, bridle trails, or even pedestrian walks the arched stone bridge is the handsomest and most permanent type of bridge. Where appearance and permanence are to be considered, stone should always be used in preference

For permanence and beauty the stone arched bridge is unrivaled.

---

* Special articles on the subjects indicated by an asterisk (*) will be found at the words so marked.

to concrete, which is very little cheaper and is much less attractive than stone.

The simplest form of stone bridge for streams with a normal flow less than three feet wide and six inches deep is a culvert type built with large tile. Lay concrete drain tile four or five feet in diameter in the stream bed with the inside of the tile level with the normal bottom of the stream. Use enough lengths of tile to make a bridge at least two feet wider on each side than the path or road crossing the bridge.

Construct a stone wall at right angles to the pipe at both ends, using the pipe as a form for the top of an arch in the stone wall. The wall should rest on a foundation extending three feet below finished grade. This foundation should also carry across the stream bed under the end of the tile to prevent the stream forcing its way under the tile. To conceal the ends of the tile the stone should overhang at least six inches.

The side walls should extend from bank to bank with the bottom of the wall following the natural shape of the ground and the top of the wall following the grade of the path or road. Carry the walls a foot or a foot and a half above the level of the path to act as a guard rail.

After the masonry shell is built fill it in with broken stone, slag, or compact soil to the required level of the path, and lay the path surface in the same way as on the ground.

When the width of the stream is too great for pipe use a regular masonry arch. To construct an arch of eight or ten feet diameter, a form of clay can be built over a temporary drain to take care of the stream flow during construction.

Model the arch opening in clay held in place at the ends by wooden forms. Lay the stone on this clay form just as you would on a wooden form, building from the foundation up to the center of the arch. The stone should be laid with just enough cement mortar to hold it in place and after the arch is completed the whole top of the arch slushed in with very wet mortar. After the mortar is set the clay form and temporary drain should be moved out from under the arch and the joints underneath filled with mortar.

The wing walls connecting the arch with the banks should be constructed over the arch after it is well set.

For bridges with a span of over ten feet a wooden form must be constructed to support the arch during construction. The design and construction of a masonry bridge of this size is a problem requiring the services of a competent designer.

The capacity load of a stone arch bridge when properly constructed is almost unlimited and will stand any ordinary use.

WOODEN BRIDGES. The simple wooden bridge with a span not exceeding fifteen feet may be constructed by laying beams lengthwise from buttress to buttress and nailing the flooring directly onto the cross-beams.

The guard rail may be of some ornamental design, or a simple, protective rail spiked directly onto the outer beams.

For a fifteen-foot span use 8 × 12-in. oak beams two feet on center, cross-braced at the center and ends. The flooring should be two-inch oak or pine planking laid with a quarter-inch opening between planks and securely spiked to the beams. Such a bridge will carry a maximum load of five tons. To increase the strength of this type of bridge a second plank flooring may be laid lengthwise on top of the first floor.

For lighter loads and shorter spans the size of the beams may be decreased proportionately. Common sense will determine the size beams for this small type of bridge quite as adequately as an engineer's calculations. A generous factor of safety is not an extravagance on small structures.

It should be remembered that the entire support of the bridge depends on the ends of the beams. These should be protected by waterproof paint and kept dry.

This type of bridge is not very ornamental. An attractive guard rail will give it added interest, but the flat span is neither graceful nor imaginative.

A timbered bridge for foot passage over a small stream

A more attractive type of construction for simple wooden bridges is some form of truss. The usual form is the inverted "V" truss which is a simple piece of carpentry. More difficult trusses to build are the arched or bowed truss and the more complicated trusses seen in our old-fashioned covered bridges.

There is a prevalent notion that bridges to be picturesque should be rustic. As a matter of fact nothing could be more illogical than a bridge whose real structural form is disguised by gnarled and twisted tree limbs.

The most beautiful wooden bridge is one which is structurally logical, with its members properly proportioned and gracefully fitted into a structural pattern. Rough-hewn timbers of oak or pine, creosoted or filled with boiled linseed oil, far surpass the contortions of so-called rustic work in beauty and picturesqueness. — R. E. G.

BRIER. A term applied to certain roses, better known as sweetbrier, and also to *Erica arborea*, a non-hort. shrub which produces briarwood for pipes.

brigantiaca, -us, -um (bri-gan-ty'a-ka). From Briançon (formerly Brigantium), a town in the French Alps.

BRINJAL. See Eggplant.

BRISBANE BOX = *Tristania conferta.*

BRISTLE-CONE PINE = *Pinus aristata.* See Pine.

BRISTLY SARSAPARILLA = *Aralia hispida.*

BRITISH COLUMBIA. The province lies wholly within zones* 2, 3, 4, 5, and 6, which from the proximity of the mountains and the effect of the sea run approximately north and south instead of east and west as over most of North America. The area is so influenced by diverse factors, however, that any statement of a general nature may well be challenged. In a given district, soils, rainfall, and temperature are so unlike other districts a few miles distant that one area may be producing abundant crops while the other is quite barren. The native flowering dogwood, *Cornus nuttalli,* is the provincial floral emblem.

Vancouver Island Area

The Victoria and Saanich Peninsula area (13,000 square miles) is justly famous as a horticultural center and mixed-farming area, producing such crops as strawberries, loganberries, tree fruits on a limited scale, holly, bulbs, vegetables, cut flowers, greenhouse crops, potatoes, and dairy products. Other fertile areas extending north 175 miles include those of Duncan, Nanaimo, Alberni, and Courtenay. The gulf islands, such as Salt Spring, North and South Pender, Mayne and Galiano, all have their share of farm and garden activities. An excellent detailed description of the whole area is the publication *The Vancouver Island Bulletin Area,* Department of Lands and Forests, Victoria, B.C.

Gardening Centers

The coastal area of the province, best represented by Vancouver Island and the Greater Vancouver area, is famous for beautiful, natural scenery and a wealth of ornamental plants and attractive gardens. The Victoria area includes the world-famous Butchard Gardens which are open to the public. Beacon Hill Park is a most attractive seaside area in which is to be found

great beauty as well as the world's tallest totem pole. The Oak Bay Memorial Rose Garden is a delightful spot. Apart from these public gardens, the very best in garden efforts can be seen in the Spring Garden Festival sponsored each year by the Victoria Horticultural Society. During this festival period — usually during the first or second week in May — some 30 to 35 of the most outstanding spring gardens are visited, exhibiting the best in shrubs, bulbs, and rock plants. The Spring Garden Festival is becoming an increasingly popular event for out-of-town visitors.

A drive around Vancouver and adjacent municipal areas in spring and summer will immediately impress the visitor with the fact that here indeed is a city of gardens blessed by a bountiful nature which helps to set the gardens ablaze with color. Roses are special favorites, but the moderate climate of zone 5 makes many garden treasures possible. The city's 1000-acre Stanley Park is a nature lover's delight. Here in great profusion are to be found roses and bedding-out plants, cultivated trees and shrubs set against a background of giant native firs, cedars, hemlocks, and a great variety of lesser trees. Within a ten-minute drive of the heart of Vancouver one can be in the midst of the forest primeval in Stanley Park.

The Lower Fraser Valley

The soils of this valley region fall into four broad classes. First are the alluvial classes, deltas for the most part and protected by dikes and drainage works. These soils are highly fertile and constitute the main producing area for a wide range of vegetable crops for processing, as well as potatoes and small fruits, particularly raspberries. Second are the upland soils with restricted sub-drainage (Alderwood and Whatcom series). This group closely approaches the alluvial soils in total acreage but, owing to heavy clearing costs and rather steep topography, they are not yet fully developed for agricultural use. However, horticultural production is on the increase in these areas, the principal crops being raspberries, strawberries, and bulbs. The third group of soils is the sandy or gravelly upland series. These cover approximately one-third of the area represented by class two. Drainage is excessive on all of these soils, but fortunately most of them are located over excellent ground-water supplies, thus facilitating irrigation. These soils find wide favor for strawberry production. The peat and muck soils, covering about one-sixth of the total arable area, constitute the fourth class. To the present, development of these organic soils is relatively limited, but the commercial production of blueberries and cranberries is on the increase.

The horticultural possibilities of the Lower Fraser Valley or, as it is so widely referred to, the Lower Mainland Region are very considerable. The region combines agricul-

* Special articles on the subjects indicated by an asterisk (*) will be found at the words so marked.

tural production, homes, and a rapidly expanding industrial development. A pleasant climate coupled with magnificent scenery provides unlimited scope for the talent of the landscape artist.

Forced rhubarb is brought on the market during January, February and March, followed by field rhubarb in April. Strawberries commence ripening late in May and are followed by raspberries, loganberries, blackberries, and boysenberries. The area is not recognized as a commercial producing area for tree fruits; nevertheless a wide range of varieties of apples, pears, cherries, plums, prunes and, in sheltered areas, peaches, are grown for home and local consumption.

The commercial production of filberts is a well-established enterprise. Other nuts, such as walnuts, chestnuts, and hard-shelled almonds, are grown for home consumption.

Early-maturing varieties of grapes, such as Campbell's Early, Seneca, and Portland, are grown for home and local consumption.

The commercial production of bulbs includes narcissi (including daffodils), tulips, hyacinths, bulbous iris, crocus, and scillas. Gladioli-growing is increasing in importance.

Something like two million square feet of glass are used for the growing of house plants, ferns, roses, carnations, chrysanthemums, bedding plants, and other flowers required for the florist trade. In conjunction with the production of greenhouse floral crops, tomatoes and cucumbers are grown for the early market.

The Okanagan District

This is the great apple-producing area of British Columbia. As many as nine million bushels have been shipped in one year. All fruit is grown under irrigation. Vernon, Kelowna, Penticton, and Oliver are the chief centers for this industry. Pears are also grown successfully throughout the same area. Cherries, particularly sweet, are grown from Kelowna south, while peaches and apricots of excellent quality are grown in quantity from Summerland south and in favored areas adjacent to Okanagan Lake. Plantings of grapes are sufficient to supply some local needs and maintain a small winery in Kelowna. Tomatoes, potatoes, and onions are grown in quantity on bottom land from Kamloops to Kelowna. Some truck garden development has taken place on bottom land near Armstrong where celery of excellent quality is shipped.

Gardening is profitably enjoyed throughout the whole Okanagan Valley as well as in other southern valleys of the province. Of particular note are the excellent displays of roses in both public and private gardens, lush growth of tuberous begonias, and fall displays of chrysanthemums. The Experimental Farm, Summerland, and the Parks Board, Kelowna, have both encouraged home beautification with striking results. Amateur horticultural societies are active in all community centers.

The Arrow and Kootenay Lakes

East of the Okanagan Valley lie the Arrow Lakes and Kootenay Valley which have a more extreme climate and somewhat higher precipitation than the Okanagan. For this reason, only apples, pears and cherries can be grown successfully and even these are subject to more disease than in the Okanagan. Commercially, Creston, south of Kootenay Lake, is the only area of importance for tree fruits. Some raspberries and strawberries are also grown here. Other areas are suited to general farming with milk or meat products as a cash crop.

The Northern Interior

This is a vast area, extending north from Kamloops, and represents a large fraction of the 370,000 square miles of the province. It is a hunter's and fisherman's paradise. Mixed farming predominates as an agricultural enterprise. A pleasantly warm summer is followed by a long, cold winter. Horticulturally, other than in native growth, it is not comparable to the other areas described.

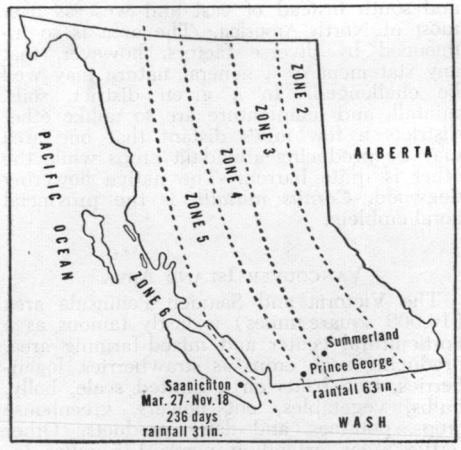

BRITISH COLUMBIA

The zones of hardiness are those described in detail at Zone (which see), but their exact limits are uncertain owing to lack of data for the northern part of the province. The number of days is the length of the growing season at and near Vancouver. Rainfall figures are for total annual rainfall (and snow) at the places shown.

Climatic conditions at the three southernmost Experimental Farms are shown in the tables below. A much more extensive coverage of this subject is given in the provincial publication, *The Climate of British Columbia*.

Saanichton
(43-year average, through 1956)

Yearly Mean Temperature	49.1° F.
Lowest Monthly Mean Temperature, Jan.	36.4°
Highest Monthly Mean Temperature, July	62.2°

* Special articles on the subjects indicated by an asterisk (*) will be found at the words so marked.

Precipitation 30.91 in.
Lowest Monthly Precipitation, July 0.69 in.
Highest Monthly Precipitation, Dec. 5.69 in.
Yearly Bright Sunshine 2066.9 hrs.
Lowest Monthly Sunshine, Dec. 58.2 hrs.
Highest Monthly Sunshine, July 321.2 hrs.
78.49% of precipitation occurs during the winter months (Oct. through Mar.)

AGASSIZ
(65-year average, through 1956)

Yearly Mean Temperature 49.9° F.
Lowest Monthly Mean Temperature, Jan. 34.5°
Highest Monthly Mean Temperature, July 64.2°
Yearly Precipitation 63.55 in.
Lowest Monthly Precipitation, July 1.91 in.
Highest Monthly Precipitation, Dec. 8.41 in.
Yearly Bright Sunshine 1379.4 hrs.
Lowest Monthly Sunshine, Dec. 37.6 hrs.
Highest Monthly Sunshine, July 220.0 hrs.
81% of precipitation occurs from Sept. through Apr.

SUMMERLAND
(41-year average, through 1956)

Yearly Mean Temperature 47.8° F.
Lowest Monthly Mean Temperature, Jan. 25.2°
Highest Monthly Mean Temperature, July 69.7°
Precipitation 10.85 in.
Lowest Monthly Precipitation, Mar. .66 in.
Highest Monthly Precipitation, Dec. 1.29 in.
Yearly Bright Sunshine 1994.2 hrs.
Lowest Monthly Sunshine, Dec. 41.6 hrs
Highest Monthly Sunshine, July 318.4 hrs.

The great variation in climate and soils and the mountainous nature of the province has divided it into many specialized regions. In these areas agricultural and horticultural research is carried out by Experimental Farms at Saanichton, Agassiz, Summerland, Kamloops, Prince George, and Smithers. The Provincial Government Extension Service in Victoria, along with the Experimental Farms, is always ready to assist in matters relating to gardening and agricultural activities in general.

BRITISH OAK = *Quercus Robur.* See OAK.

BRITTLE FERN = *Cystopteris fragilis.*

BRITTLE THATCH = *Thrinax microcarpa.*

BRIZA (bry′za). A group of slender grasses, the spikelets of which are often on hair-thin stalks, hence usually called quaking grass. They are small, annual or perennial grasses, the spikelets suggesting small, flattened hops, often nodding on their thread-like stalks. (*Briza* is Greek for some grain.)

The quaking grasses are sometimes grown in the garden for their attractive panicles* of spikelets. Sow the annuals where they are to stay. The perennial one is easily propagated by division. The dried panicles are used for winter decoration.

maxima. An annual 1–2 ft. high. Leaves 4–6 in. long and ⅓–¼ in. wide. Spikelets ½ in. long,

pale or metallic in age, nodding. Southern Eu. Perhaps the handsomest of the quaking grasses.

media. A perennial 10–18 in. high, with very narrow, slender leaves. Panicle 5–10 in. long, branched, the spikelets broadly oval, purplish, not over ¼ in. long, the stalks stiffish. Eurasia, and naturalized in U.S.

minor. An annual 6–15 in. high. Leaves 3–5 in. long, about ⅛ in. wide. Panicle* compound, broad, about 5 in. long, the spikelets about ⅛ in. long and green. Eu. and naturalized in U.S.

brizaeformis, -e (bry-ze-for′mis). Like a grass of the genus *Briza.*

brizoides (bry-zoy′deez; but *see* OÏDES). *Briza*-like.

BROAD BEAN = *Vicia Faba.*

BROADCAST. The scattering of seeds evenly all over the soil instead of in rows or drills.*

BROAD-LEAVED EVERGREENS. A common designation among gardeners for outdoor plants with relatively broad, evergreen leaves, that do not belong to the cone-bearing plants such as the spruces, firs, pines, yew, etc. (the conifers).

The broad-leaved evergreens are extremely valuable plants to all gardeners. Box, rhododendron, the Japanese holly, *Pachysandra,* the holly, *Leucothoë, Pieris,* the mountain laurel, *Cotoneaster, Daphne,* some species of *Euonymus,* and the evergreen species of *Berberis* provide the choicest plants of this sort for most northern gardeners. *See* each of these for notes on culture and their hardiness in different sections of the country.

Most of them do poorly or cannot be grown at all in regions where the annual rainfall is below 20 in. (*See* the name of your state for rainfall figures.) They grow best in regions of relatively mild winters near the sea. Nearly all of them should have a permanent mulch of leaves.

Farther south there are scores, perhaps hundreds, of plants, not conifers, to which the term could equally well be applied, for they have evergreen or nearly evergreen leaves. But most of them are of tropical affinities, and broad-leaved evergreen, as a term, is not usually applied to them.

BROCCOLI (*Brassica oleracea italica*). Broccoli is a word that has been in some confusion in recent years because two plants are comprised under the one term. In England, and by the technically minded here, the word and vegetable are practically synonymous with the cauliflower (*Brassica oleracea botrytis*). *See* CAULIFLOWER. In America, broccoli means a cauliflower-like plant in which the malformed flower head (the edible part of cauliflower) instead of being white, close and ball-like, is more open, branchy and green. To this now very common vegetable, various names have been applied, such as sprouting broccoli, branching broccoli, asparagus broccoli, Italian broccoli, and calabrese (the original Italian word for it). All these are generally shortened

---

* Special articles on the subjects indicated by an asterisk (*) will be found at the words so marked.

simply to broccoli. The notes below apply only to this sprouting or branching broccoli. For the original and perhaps true broccoli (really a winter cauliflower) *see* CAULI-FLOWER.

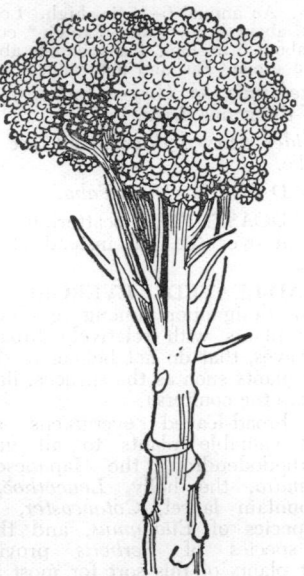

Broccoli ready for harvesting.

Broccoli (as above restricted) is a branching herb about 2 ft. high. Some or all of the lateral branches, and the terminal one, end in a malformed, green, more or less open flower head. This, which should be cut before it actually flowers, and cooked like cauliflower, is a delicious, succulent vegetable, rich in the vitamins of the cabbage tribe to which it belongs. In cooking, however, it lacks most of the tenement house odor of cabbage. Its introduction into America came much later than the cabbage or Brussels sprouts. *Godey's Magazine* for 1858 mentioned it, and Thoreau, on his walking tour of Cape Cod in 1849, saw it in a garden raised "from seeds salvaged from the wrecked Franklin." Its common use here did not materialize until after the beginning of the present century.

CULTURE. The plant prefers coolness and moisture rather than heat and dryness. Unless you are in a particularly favorable place (*i.e.*, along the seacoast or close to the shores of the Great Lakes), broccoli is best treated as a two-season crop. The first is started in the hotbed or greenhouse in February or March (depending on locality) and planted out after the last frost (*see* the name of your state for frost data). The second crop is sown in the seedbed in June or July and transplanted to the garden a month or six weeks later. The latter crop can be harvested through the cool autumn months.

It is absolutely essential to get pure seed of a first-class seedsman if you intend raising your own plants. Considerable instability still exists in the various strains of broccoli (even some weedy, mustard-like plants occasionally appearing). Avoid such accidents by getting the best seed obtainable of the following varieties: Calabrese, Italian Green Sprouting, Dilicco, and Waltham 29.

Because of this uncertainty many home gardeners prefer to buy young plants from a dealer. But even in this case it is well to insist that they be of one of the varieties mentioned.

PLANTING. Seeds sown in the greenhouse, hotbed or seedbed, should be planted in flats or boxes where their management is exactly the same as for cabbage (which see).

When the seedlings are ready to put out in the garden, they should be set 2 ft. apart in the rows which are themselves 2 ft. apart. A single row of fifty plants (100 ft.) is ample for a family of 5, and unless the family has a particularly strong liking for it, the 100 ft. may well be split between the early and late crops (as outlined above).

The plants do well in any ordinary garden soil, but it should be reasonably moist. They are moderately rich feeders and manure or commercial fertilizers should be applied before the plants are set out. (*See* CABBAGE for details.) Some also top-dress with nitrate of soda three weeks after the plants have been set out, at the rate of 1 pound per 100-ft. row and repeat the process just as the plants begin to head.

If the plants have been set out exactly on the two-foot intervals they can, in the early stages at least, be cultivated both ways. In any case, they must be kept free of weeds, and, to conserve moisture, the ground should be kept pulverized, especially after every rain.

HARVESTING. As the plants come to maturity the somewhat abortive and grotesque heads of flowers begin to develop. Some mature quicker than others, but they must be cut well before the true whitish-yellow flowers "break" from the cluster. If the immature heads, which should vary from 4 to 7 in. in diameter, are constantly cut, the plant will force out other heads. This considerably prolongs the harvesting period. The whole flower head and its thick, succulent branches should be green, not white or yellow, when the head is harvested.

For insect pests and diseases, *see* CABBAGE.

BRODIAEA (bro-di-ee′a). An attractive group of 30 species of chiefly Californian herbs of the lily family, with crocus-like corms,* and narrow, grass-like leaves. They are mostly grown in Calif., but can be grown in the South and elsewhere as directed below. Leaves few, narrow. Flowers mostly funnel-shaped, solitary or in loose clusters (umbels*) that arise from spathe*-like membranous bracts.* Petals or colored se-

---

* Special articles on the subjects indicated by an asterisk (*) will be found at the words so marked.

pals 6. Stamens 6, 3 often sterile. Fruit a pod (capsule*), splitting by valves. (Named for James Brodie, Scotch botanist.) Sometimes the species are offered under the name *Triteleia*.

The triplet lilies, as they are often called, are easily grown in Calif., and do well in most soils, except wet or shaded ones, but prefer gritty or sandy sites. In the East they are not hardy outdoors north of Va. without protection, and it is safer to plant them in pans or boxes in the frame. Plant at the same time as for fall bulbs. In the spring they may be taken out of the frame and planted outdoors. After flowering, the corms (in the East) should be dug and stored over the summer, for they will not stand summer humidity nor too much rain. Some, as noted below, are forced in the cool greenhouse.

californica. Not over 1 ft. high. Flowers about 1½ in. long, violet-purple. Southern Calif.

capitata. Blue dicks. Not over 2 ft. high. Flowers about ⅔ in. long, blue, in head-like clusters (umbels*). Ore. to Calif.

coccinea = *Brevoortia Ida-Maia.*

coronaria. From 12–18 in. high. Flowers violet-purple, 1½ in. long. This is often offered as *Hookera* (or even *Hookeria*) *coronaria*, and as *Brodiaea grandiflora*. It is found wild from British Columbia to Calif.

crocea. From 8–12 in. high. Flowers yellow, ½–¾ in. long.

grandiflora = *Brodiaea coronaria.*

hendersoni. Nearly 1 ft. high, the flower cluster flat-topped. Flowers yellow, the corolla* with a purple stripe down the center of each lobe. Oregon.

hyacintha. Not over 2 ft. high, the leaves narrow and nearly grass-like. Flower cluster (umbel*) with 15–20 blooms, the petals white or purplish. Calif. Not certainly distinct from *B. lactea.*

ixiodes. Pretty-face. One of the showiest, and from 10–18 in. high. Flowers salmon or salmon-yellow, streaked with dark purple, ½–¾ in. long. Ore. to southern Calif. Best grown in the cool greenhouse.

lactea. Wild hyacinth. From 10–18 in. high. Flowers lilac or white, ⅓–½ in. long. British Columbia to Calif.

laxa. Triplet lily. Ithuriel's-spear. Not over 2 ft. high. Flowers about 1 in. long, purple or white. Calif.

peduncularis. Two to 3 ft. high, the leaves scarcely ¼ in. wide. Flower cluster (umbel*) with 3–15 blooms, the petals rose-purple or white, not over 1 in. long. Calif.

uniflora. Spring starflower. The best-known and most widely cult. species, usually not over 8 in. high, and somewhat onion-scented. Flowers solitary, white but tinged with blue, about 1 in. long. Argentina. Must be grown in the cool greenhouse in the North. It is also known as *Milla uniflora* and *Leucocoryne uniflora.*

volubilis. Snake lily. Unlike all the others in having a twining stem 3–8 ft. high. Flowers rose-red or pink, ½–¾ in. long. It is sometimes offered as *Stropholirion californicum* and is best grown in the frame or cool greenhouse.

BROME GRASS = BROMUS.

BROMELIA (bro-mee′li-a). A genus of perhaps 25 species of tropical American,

pineapple-like herbs, family Bromeliaceae, with spiny-margined leaves. The only cult. species is the pinguin, **Bromelia Pinguin,** too coarse to grow in greenhouses, but a valuable hedge plant in extreme southern Fla. It has a rosette of long, sword-shaped leaves 4–6 ft. high, very spiny on the margins. Flowers red, in a dense cluster (panicle*) on a mealy, or whitish, stout stalk. Fruit plum-like, acid. (Named for Olaf Bromel, Swedish botanist.) It will grow in pure sand or on bare coral rock in the tropics. Native of the W.I.

BROMELIACEAE (bro-mee-li-ā′see-ee). The pineapple family is exclusively tropical American, with a few stretching into sub-tropical Florida. All are herbs, many of them air plants (*see* EPIPHYTES), and of the 50 genera and perhaps 1000 species, a good number are cult. in greenhouses either for their showy flowers or as extremely handsome, often brightly colored, foliage plants. Not one is a true parasite, although often thought to be from their usually tree-perching habit.

For the only important fruit plant *see* the PINEAPPLE (*Ananas*). All the rest of the garden genera are cult. for ornament, although some genera yield fine fibers. The plants are usually scurfy, have stiffish, sometimes spiny-margined, leaves that are mostly in rosettes. In some genera the rosette and leaf bases hold such considerable amounts of water as to be mosquito breeders in the tropics.

Flowers regular, often very showy, usually in long-stalked, handsome spikes that have colored bracts*; sometimes stalkless. Fruit a dry pod (capsule*) in *Guzmania, Puya, Dyckia, Hechtia, Tillandsia,* and *Vriesia,* and fleshy in all the other garden genera. The flower cluster is prominently stalked in *Aechmea* and *Billbergia,* but close to the rosette of leaves in *Cryptanthus, Nidularium,* and *Canistrum. Dyckia* and *Hechtia* are mostly small desert plants with spiny leaves, while *Bromelia* is the pinguin. One of the most characteristic plants in the pineapple family is the Spanish or long moss that drapes live oak and cypress trees in the southern states (*see* TILLANDSIA).

Technical flower characters: Ovary superior* in the genera that bear capsules; inferior* in the rest. Flowers regular,* of 6 segments, the 3 inner, or the 3 outer, or sometimes both, united into a tube. Stamens 6. Ovary 3-celled.

BROMPTON STOCK = *Mathiola incana.*

BROMUS (bro′mus). Brome grass is a general term applied to this large genus of grasses, most of which live in the north temperate zone. Only one is of secondary garden interest, although others are valuable forage grasses. The cult. species are annuals or perennials with rather coarse, flat leaves. They have large, open, terminal clusters (panicles*) consisting of often drooping spikelets. (*Bromus* is Greek for food, in allusion to a weedy grass long thought to "grow into wheat.")

---

* Special articles on the subjects indicated by an asterisk (*) will be found at the words so marked.

brizaeformis. Quake grass. A useful plant for dry bouquets. It is an annual with leaves up to 8 in. long and about ¼ in. wide. Cluster (panicle*) 6–8 in. long, the branches nodding and with many flattened spikelets that are oblong, about 1 in. long and have no awn.* Eurasia, and naturalized in U.S.

catharticus. Rescue grass. An annual 18–30 in. high. Leaves 8–12 in. long and about ⅓ in. wide. Clusters (panicles*) 6–9 in. long, the spikelets much flattened, the branches of the cluster ascending. Tropical America and northward to our southern states where it is used in pastures. Called also *B. unioloides.*

inermis. Hungarian brome grass; called, also, awnless brome grass. A perennial 2–4 ft. high. Leaves nearly 1 ft. long and about ¼ in. wide. Clusters (panicles*) 8–10 in. long, the branches ascending. Spikelets not awned, oblong, about 1 in. long. Eu. Not much grown except in pastures.

BROOKGREEN GARDENS. *See* No. 19 at GARDEN TOURS.

BROOM. A somewhat confusing term because it has been applied to plants in several different genera and also used as an abbreviation for the witches'-broom (which see). As here used it comprises shrubs of the genus **Cytisus** (sit′i-sus) of the pea family. But this genus contains not only the "genista" of the florists (not the genus *Genista*) but the Scotch broom and several related plants. (For the butcher's-broom *see* RUSCUS, and for the Spanish broom *see* SPARTIUM.)

Cytisus includes perhaps 50 species of generally spineless shrubs, mostly from the Mediterranean region and western As., grown for their profuse bloom of pea-like flowers. They have compound* leaves with 3 leaflets. Flowers yellow, purple or white, solitary or in small clusters (usually racemes*). Calyx irregular* and 2-lipped. Flowers typically pea-like. Fruit a flat pod (legume*). (Cytisus is Greek for some clover-like plant, in allusion to the 3 leaflets.)

All except *C. canariensis* (the genista of the florists) are deciduous shrubs for the open border, but they will not stand much frost and should be planted outdoors only as shown below. They are not particular as to soil, but transplant poorly when mature, so that they should be set out while young in the place they are to stay.

The genista of the florists (*C. canariensis*) should be grown in the cool greenhouse in potting mixture* 4. Keep in a semi-dormant condition during the late fall and early winter by reducing its water. In February or March (earlier if needed) begin more active watering and increase the temperature by a few degrees. The plant will then flower profusely and should afterwards be cut back and re-potted. Put the pots outdoors, partly in the shade, until frost threatens, when they should be brought into the cool greenhouse. This species is widely forced by florists for spring bloom.

C. albus. A low shrub, usually not over 18 in. high. Leaflets broadest above the middle, about 3 in. long. Flowers yellowish-white, nearly 1 in. long in a terminal, close, head-like cluster. Southeastern Eu. June. Hardy outdoors from zone* 4 southward. Sometimes offered as *C. leucanthus.*

C. canariensis. The genista of the florists. An evergreen shrub 4–6 ft. high. Leaflets wedge-shaped, about ⅓ in. long. Flowers slightly fragrant, yellow, about ¾ in. long, in dense terminal clusters (racemes*). Canary Islands. Blooms normally in spring and summer, except when forced. A greenhouse plant (*see* above).

C. decumbens. A sprawling, practically prostrate broom, not usually over 4–6 in. high, often rooting at the branches. Leaves stalkless, not compound,* ¼–½ in. long, oblongish but narrowed at the base; hairy at least on the under side. Flowers 1–3 in a sparse cluster, light yellow, about ¾ in. long. May–June. Southern Eu. Hardy from zone* 5 southward.

C. kewensis. A low plant, nearly prostrate and suited to rock gardens, never over 1 ft. high. Leaflets very narrow, softly hairy, sometimes reduced to only 1. Flowers yellowish-white, about ½ in long or less, mostly on slender, lateral branches. Of hybrid origin, and not certainly hardy north of zone* 4.

C. leucanthus = *Cytisus albus.*

C. multiflorus. Sometimes distinguished as the White Spanish broom, and thought by some to be merely a taller form of *Cytisus albus.* It resembles that plant but may be 4–6 ft. high. May–June. Spain and north Af. Hardy from zone* 5 southward.

C. nigricans. A shrub 4–6 ft. high, its leaflets oblongish and about 1 in. long. Flowers bright yellow, about ¾ in. long or less, in a slender-stalked, terminal cluster (raceme*). Southern and central Eu. June–July. Hardy outdoors only from zone* 4 southward. There is a form (*var. elongatus*) that blooms again in the fall.

C. praecox. Warminster broom. A handsome, hybrid plant, usually with simple* leaves. Flowers yellowish-white or yellow, about ½ in. long. Hardy from zone* 5 southward.

C. purpureus. Not over 2 ft. high and more or less sprawling. Leaflets not over 1 in. long. Flowers scattered along the branches, purple or white, or pink in some hort. forms. Southern Austria. May–June. Hardy from zone* 4 southward. There is a form with pendulous branches which is sometimes grafted high on *Laburnum.* A hybrid of *C. purpureus* and another species, known as *C. versicolor,* has purple and yellowish flowers. It otherwise resembles *C. purpureus,* but is showier.

C. scoparius. Scotch broom. A shrub 4–9 ft. high with green branches. Leaflets ⅓–½ in. long, sometimes reduced to only a single leaflet. Flowers usually one or two together in the leaf axils,* bright yellow, about 1 in. long, blooming profusely in May or June. Eu. Hardy from zone* 3 southward. A lower, more compact form, with sulphur-yellow flowers, is the Moonlight Broom. The *var.* andreanus has the wings of the flower crimson, and is a very handsome plant. There are many other color forms.

C. supinus. An upright or somewhat sprawling shrub, seldom over 3 ft. high. Leaflets elliptic or oblongish, in 3's, about ¾ in. long, very hairy on the under side. Flowers yellow, but ultimately brownish, rather showy and in terminal close clusters about 2 in. wide. July–Aug. Southern and central Eu. Hardy from zone* 5 southward.

C. versicolor. *See* CYTISUS PURPUREUS.

---

* Special articles on the subjects indicated by an asterisk (*) will be found at the words so marked.

BROOMCORN = *Sorghum vulgare technicum.*

BROOMCORN MLLET = *Panicum miliaceum.*

BROOM CROWBERRY. See COREMA.

BROOMRAPE. Brownish or purplish herbs parasitic on the roots of other plants. *See* HOST. They cannot, of course, be cult.

BROOM SEDGE. See ANDROPOGON.

BROUSSONETIA (broo-so-nesh'ee-a). The paper mulberry is the only cult. tree of the three known species of this Asiatic genus belonging to the family Moraceae. It has alternate,* often lobed leaves and the male and female flowers are borne on different trees. Male flowers in hanging catkins. Female flowers in small, compact heads. Neither has any petals. Fruit an aggregate of many carpels (a syncarp*). (Named for T. U. V. Broussonet, French naturalist.)

The paper mulberry (its bark yields a sort of paper) is hardy from zone* 4 southward and will stand considerable abuse as to site. It is occasionally a good street tree in New York, and in gardens often a nuisance because of its propensity to spread. Easily propagated by seeds, suckers, or by layering.

papyrifera. Paper mulberry. A tree 25–40 ft. Leaves generally oval, 6–8 in. long, usually deeply and roundly lobed in young leaves, very rough above. Fruit cluster (syncarp*) densely hairy, about ¾ in. in diameter. China and Jap., sparingly naturalized from N.Y. to Fla. There are cut-leaved, white-fruited, and variegated forms.

BROWALLIA (brow-wall'i-a). A genus of mostly tropical American herbs, belonging to the potato family, several widely grown as very popular, mostly blue-flowered, annuals. Leaves simple,* mostly alternate.* Flowers solitary or in somewhat 1-sided clusters (racemes*). Calyx tubular, usually with 5 teeth. Corolla tubular, the 5-lobed limb* more or less irregular.* Fruit a capsule,* included within the persistent calyx. (Named for Bishop John Browall, a Swedish botanist).

The browallias, especially *B. speciosa major* and *B. americana,* are widely grown hardy annuals. (*See* ANNUALS for culture.) *B. americana,* with bluish-purple flowers, is useful for those who want that color in the blue garden (which see). Seeds sown in pots in midsummer will provide winter bloom if kept in the cool greenhouse, especially *B. speciosa major.*

americana. A branching annual herb 12–20 in. high, its foliage hairy. Leaves round-oval, stalked, 1–2 in. long. Flowers bluish-purple, solitary in the leaf axils,* or in loose clusters, the tube about ½ in. long, the expanded limb a little larger and notched. S.A. There are hort. forms with pure blue and with white flowers. Often called *B. demissa* and *B. elata.*

jamesoni = *Streptosolen jamesoni.*

speciosa. A smooth-branching annual 8–12 or rarely 15 in. high. Leaves alternate* or opposite,* ovalish, but pointed at the tip. Flowers with the tube about 1 in. long, the expanded limb larger and not notched, purplish. S.A. The *var.* **major,** the form most

grown; has steely-blue flowers. There are also hort. forms with violet or with white flowers. *See* ANNUALS.

viscosa. A sticky-hairy annual, 12–20 in. high, the short-stalked, rough-hairy leaves ovalish, and about 1 in. long. Flowers about ¾ in. long, violet-blue, with a white "eye." S.A. Summer.

BROWN BENT = *Agrostis canina.*

BROWN-EYED SUSAN = *Rudbeckia triloba.*

BRUCKENTHALIA (brook-en-thay'li-a). A single species of evergreen shrubs of the heath family, native in southeastern Eu. and Asia Minor, grown for ornament, and sometimes planted in rock gardens. It has narrow, very short leaves, crowded and densely clothing the twigs. Flowers bell-shaped but deeply 4-lobed, in short, dense spikes. Fruit a capsule enclosed by the persistent calyx. (Named for S. von Bruckenthal, an Austrian nobleman.)

A pretty little heath-like shrub needing a gritty soil in the border or rock garden, open sunshine, and a winter mulch of dried leaves in severe places. It can be propagated by seeds or by cuttings.

spiculifolia. Spike heath. Not over 8–10 in. high. Leaves not over ¼ in. long. Flowers pink, about ¼ in. long, the whole spike scarcely ¾ in. long. Hardy from zone* 4 southward.

BRUNFELSIA (brun-felz'i-a). A genus of 25 species of tropical American shrubs or trees of the potato family, those below grown in greenhouses for their extremely fragrant flowers. Leaves alternate* and without marginal teeth. Flowers usually solitary, the calyx bell-shaped, the corolla funnel-shaped, and with a long tube. Stamens 4. Fruit (in ours) fleshy. (Named for Otto Brunfels, one of the earliest German botanists.)

Of the half-dozen species known to be in cult. in America, the lady-of-the-night is the best-known. It needs a warm greenhouse (not below 55° at night) and should be grown in potting mixture* 5. The bloom is better if the plants are kept slightly pot-bound. Easily propagated from cuttings of new wood in spring.

americana. Lady-of-the-night; called also Franciscan nightshade. A shrub 6–8 ft. high. Leaves 3–4 in. long, ovalish. Flowers white, fading to yellow, the tube 3–4 in. long, the expanded part nearly 2 in. wide, especially fragrant at night. Fruit berry-like, yellow, about ¾ in. wide. W.I. Can be grown outdoors in zone* 9 and in sheltered parts of zone* 8.

calycina. An erect or somewhat sprawling shrub, not over 2 ft. high, the leaves oblongish, 2½–4 in. long, bright green above, paler beneath. Flowers nearly 2 in. wide, in a terminal cluster (cyme*), dark purple at first, fading to nearly white. In the greenhouse it may flower almost throughout the year. Brazil.

BRUNNERA (brun'er-ra). An anchusa-like herb of the Caucasus and Siberia, family Boraginaceae, rather commonly cult. as *Anchusa myosotidiflora.* It has large, heart-

---

* Special articles on the subjects indicated by an asterisk (*) will be found at the words so marked.

shaped, basal leaves, erect, somewhat hairy stems, and flowers in a naked cluster. The only cult. species, **Brunnera macrophylla,** is a perennial and should be grown like an *Anchusa.* It is 12–18 in. high and has stem leaves narrower and more tapering toward the top of the plant. Flowers blue, spring-blooming, not over ¼ in. wide, but the clusters showy and handsome. *See* BLUE GARDEN. (Named for Samuel Brunner, Swiss botanist.)

BRUNSVIGIA (bruns-vig'i-a). South African greenhouse herbs of perhaps 12 species, belonging to the family Amaryllidaceae, the one below popular for its showy, lily-like flowers. They differ only in technical characters from *Amaryllis* (which see), and are grown in the same way. (Named for the House of Brunswick.)

josephinae. Josephine's-lily. A perennial with a very large bulb. Leaves sword-shaped, 24–30 in. long, about 1¾ in. wide, ribbed and fleshy. Stalk of the flower cluster naked, stout, solid, about 18 in. high and at least an inch thick. Flowers about 3 in. long, red, in an open umbel,° the tubular part of the flower scarcely more than ½ in. long.

rosea = *Amaryllis Belladonna.*

BRUSH. Twiggy branches used to support peas and other plants. Often used as a verb implying the putting out of such brush. *See* PEA.

BRUSSELS SPROUTS (*Brassica oleracea gemmifera*). This vegetable, called simply sprouts by some and thousand-headed-cabbage by others, is a peculiar member of the cabbage tribe. It is an erect, usually single-stalked herb with some leaves on its stout, thick stalk, but most of them at the summit. At the base of the lower leafstalks the "buttons," or small, ball-like sprouts appear. They are quite stalkless, and in properly grown plants very numerous. Depending on the variety and the success of its culture, the sprouts (which are simply immature but very large buds) should be from 1–1½ or even 2 inches in diameter, close packed and with no loose leaves.

Brussels sprouts are primarily a fall and winter vegetable. The plant will not mature properly in intense heat and dryness. That is why plants set out about August 1 on the cool south shore of eastern Long Island do so well. Plants set out the same day in the interior of the country would be apt to fail.

Some growers (in the East) insist on starting Brussels sprouts at the same time as early cabbage, but even if they mature properly before hot weather (which is not always certain), the harvest comes at the time when most people have given up Brussels sprouts until the following autumn. August-set plants, however, begin bearing about October 1. Because the plant is pretty resistant to cold, the harvest may continue until well after Christmas, at which period it is a most seasonable vegetable.

PLANTING. Upon the theory that most gardeners will prefer to harvest their crop from

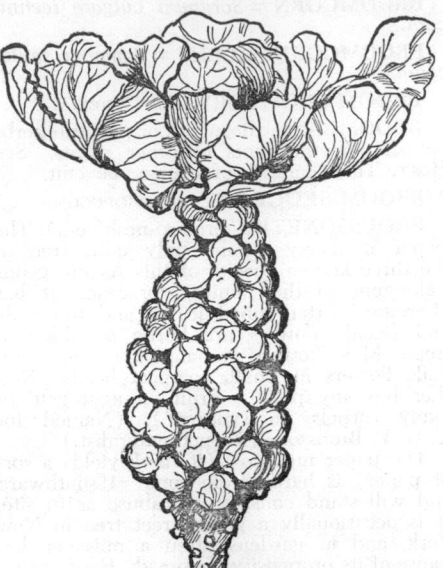

A good Brussels sprouts plant ready for harvesting

October to Christmas or beyond (depending upon locality), the following directions are for plants set out at a time to accomplish this.

The plant is closely related to the cabbage, and Brussels sprouts (for fall use) are, in their early stages, treated exactly like a crop of late cabbage. *See* CABBAGE. Seed sown in the seedbed outdoors in late May should be ready for transplanting to their permanent place in the garden by the latter part of July or early August. They should then be somewhat leggy plants 5–7 inches high.

Pinch off a few of the leaves, and set out the plants about 18 in. apart, in rows that are 2 ft. apart. They should have a rich soil, but most ordinary kitchen garden soils will grow good sprouts if the plants are top-dressed, about 2 weeks after setting out, with nitrate of soda at the rate of 1 pound per 100 ft. of row.

CULTIVATION AND MANAGEMENT. Cultivate frequently, especially after rains. The dust mulch so secured is invaluable for conserving soil moisture, and these plants need moisture, especially if, in spite of late planting, there should be much hot weather. Of course cultivate enough to keep down all weeds.

The sprouts begin forming at the leaf bases of the lower leaves first. To stimulate their production it is a good plan to break off (leaving a stump an inch or two long) most of the lower leaves of the plant, beginning about October 1 or when the buds develop. Be sure to leave the terminal crown of leaves intact. This also forces more food into the forming sprouts, the lowest of which should be picked first. Later sprouts are better flavored than the earliest ones to be picked,

---

° Special articles on the subjects indicated by an asterisk (°) will be found at the words so marked.

as the product is much improved by a few sharp frosts.

Between 50 and 66 plants are usually enough for a family of 5, depending, of course, upon their fondness for them. Each plant should yield a quart of sprouts.

VARIETIES. Long Island is one of the chief commercial centers of production, and the variety called Long Island Improved is by far the best one. Other good varieties are Catskill, Half Dwarf, and Fancymost (for the West). As in all the cabbage tribe, pure seed is essential, whether you start your own plants or buy them ready for transplanting.

WINTER STORAGE. Some gardeners, faced by the destruction of unharvested sprouts when zero weather overtakes them, prefer to store their plants with the sprouts attached. This may be done by pulling up the plants and packing them together, with a little soil at their roots, in a pit or cold frame, where they should be kept cold, but not allowed to freeze much, if at all.

It seems likely that Thomas Jefferson first introduced Brussels sprouts into the U.S.

For insect pests and diseases, see CABBAGE.

BRYONIA (bry-own′i-a). A small genus of mostly Eurasian herbs or (in the one below) tendril*-climbing vines, of the cucumber family. They have tuberous roots, herbaceous stems, unforked tendrils and lobed leaves. Male and female flowers on different plants, greenish. Male flowers in stalked clusters (cymes* or racemes*). Female flowers mostly solitary. Corolla more or less bell-shaped or wheel-shaped. Fruit a round berry. (*Bryonia* is from Greek to sprout, from the annual growth.)

The bryony is little grown in the U.S., but occasionally offered by dealers. In Eu. a cathartic is extracted from its tuberous root. Can be grown in any ordinary garden soil, but not from zone* 3 northward.

dioica. Bryony. A robust climber, quickly covering hedges or fences during the growing season. Leaves rough, 3–5 in. wide, 3–5-lobed, the lobes sharp-pointed, and the margins faintly toothed. Flowers ½–¾ in. wide. Fruit red, about ⅓ in. in diameter.

BRYONY. See BRYONIA.

BRYOPHYLLUM (bry-o-fill′um). As the name implies (it means sprouting leaf), this genus of about 20 species of the family Crassulaceae contains plants that will sprout from a leaf. In the air plant, new plants, starting as bulbils,* will sprout from the notches of a leaf pegged down on moist sand or on blotting paper. They are perennial herbs with opposite,* and in *B. pinnatum,* compound* leaves with 3–5 thick, fleshy leaflets. Flowers in a stalked, drooping cluster, the 4-lobed corolla partly covered by the inflated calyx. Stamens 8. Fruit a cluster of follicles.*

These easily grown and most interesting plants need a cool greenhouse over the winter, or they will do fairly well in a moderately heated living room. They will not stand frost, but may be left outdoors all summer.

Propagation is almost laughably easy due to the great tendency to proliferation at the leaf notches. Sometimes new plants will start while the leaf is still attached to its old stalk, especially in the second species. All of the plants below are also listed as *Kalanchoe.* (*Bryophyllum* is from Greek to sprout and leaf.)

daigremontianum. An erect, smooth, greenish-brown succulent, 12–18 in. high, often producing plantlets from the marginal teeth of the leaves which are thick and oblongish. Flowers yellowish-pink, about 1 in. long. Madagascar.

pinnatum. Air plant; also called life plant and floppers. An herb 2–5 ft. high, its stems round and hollow. Leaflets almost stalkless, ovalish-oblong, 2–5 in. long, notched or wavy on the margins and a new plant likely to spring from each notch. Flowers 1–1½ in. long, the calyx greenish-white and papery, the corolla red. Origin in the tropics but not certainly known where. The best of all plants to illustrate propagation by leaves. Sometimes known as *B. calycinum.*

tubiflorum. A succulent plant, 12–18 in. high. Leaves cylindric, in whorls* of 3, the whorls about 1 in. apart, the leaves 4–5 in. long, about ⅛ in. thick, and grooved on the upper side, the tip 5–7-toothed. Young plants sprout from the tips of the leaves and remain attached until roots form, when they drop off. Flowers pinkish-salmon. Madagascar.

BUBBY-SHRUB. See CALYCANTHUS.

BUCCANEER PALM = *Pseudophoenix sargenti.*

buccinatoria, -us, -um (bew-sin-a-tor′-i-a). Like a crooked horn or trumpet.

BUCHU = *Diosma ericoides.*

BUCKBEAN. See MENYANTHES.

BUCKBEAN FAMILY. See GENTIANACEAE.

BUCKBRUSH = *Symphoricarpos occidentalis; see also CEANOTHUS.

BUCKEYE. See HORSE-CHESTNUT.

BUCKEYE FAMILY = Hippocastanaceae.

BUCKTHORN. See RHAMNUS.

BUCKTHORN FAMILY = Rhamnaceae.

BUCKWEED. See EPILOBIUM ANGUSTIFOLIUM.

BUCKWHEAT. Farm plants of little interest to the gardener unless he keeps bees, which greatly favor the plant. The common buckwheat, also, is one of the best plants for soil improvement or for smothering weeds. Sow as often as possible during the growing season, allowing plants to get about 8 in. high and then plow under, after which a new planting can be made. Buckwheat is one of the sources of rutin.

Buckwheat belongs to the genus **Fagopyrum** (fag-o-py′rum), family Polygonaceae, and comprises about 6, mostly annual, quick-growing herbs with alternate,* usually angled leaves. Flowers small, white, in racemes in those below. Fruit a pointed, triangular achene* which furnishes the buckwheat of commerce.

F. esculentum. The common buckwheat. A weak, fleshy herb, inclined to sprawl in age.

---

* Special articles on the subjects indicated by an asterisk (*) will be found at the words so marked.

Leaves more or less triangular-oval, the stalk stouter than in the next species. Flowers fragrant, white, beloved of bees. Sides of its triangular fruit not grooved. Central Asia.

F. tataricum. India wheat; called also Kangra buckwheat and duckwheat. Similar to common buckwheat but more slender and smaller. Leaves broadly halberd-shaped, the basal lobes wide-spreading. Flowers in a loose cluster and the sides of the fruit with a distinct groove. India. More hardy than the common buckwheat. Sometimes called Tartarian or Iceland buckwheat.

BUCKWHEAT FAMILY = Polygonaceae.

BUDDING. Budding is a form of grafting in which a bud rather than a cion is inserted upon the stock. Since only a single bud is used, it is more economical of wood. It is used to propagate nursery plants and to topwork young trees. Some plants are better adapted to budding than cion grafting, as stone fruits, for the reason that cherry, peach, or plum wood does not split well for grafting, while the bark slips readily for budding.

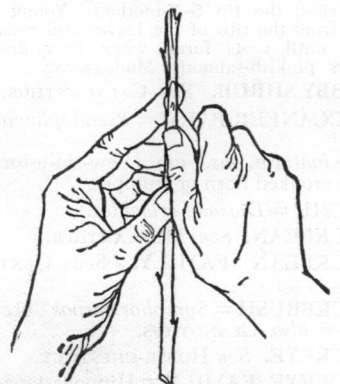

The right way to make the cut in budding, with a slanting, shallow cut

As in any form of grafting, budding depends upon bringing together the growing regions of the "bud" and of the stock under such conditions that they will unite and grow as one (*see* GRAFTING). This growing region, or cambium zone, is at the point where the bark separates from the wood and all operations should be carried on with this thought in mind. Sharp tools, clean cuts, careful matching of cambium regions, snug fitting and tying, and careful protection from drying of tissues both before and after the budding operation, are conducive to success. Although there are various forms of budding, they are essentially the same in general principle, the differences lying in adaptability to some particular material or object in view. Accordingly, June budding refers to the time of the year in which the operation is performed; shield, plate, and patch budding refer to the shape of the bud portion used. T-budding, commonly known as shield bud-

ding, and H-budding, refer to the type cut made in the stock; while up-budding and down-budding refer to the manner of insertion of the bud in the stock.

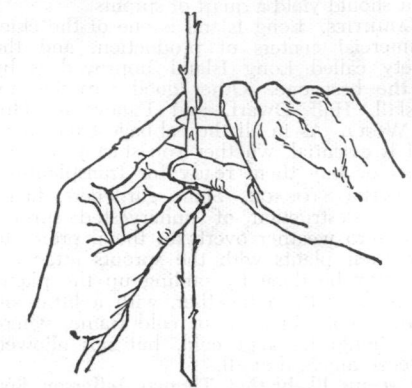

Do not cut a bud with a deep, horizontal stroke of the knife

Budding may be done at any time that the bark of the stock will slip and yet mature buds are available. In general practice this limits the operation to summer after buds of the current season have matured and before the bark of the stock has tightened. Below are given the approximate dates for budding fruit trees and rose stocks in the nursery region of western New York. The dates may be earlier in a dry season or on light soils and in southern regions.

Rose	July 1 to July 15
Pear	July 10 to July 20
Apple	July 15 to Aug. 10
Plum (St. Julien stock)	July 1 to Aug. 1
Plum (Myrobalan stock)	Aug. 15 to Sept. 1
Cherry (Mazzard stock)	July 20 to Aug. 1
Cherry (Mahaleb stock)	Aug. 15 to Sept. 1
Quince	July 25 to Aug. 15
Peach	Aug. 20 to Sept. 10

SHIELD OR T-BUDDING

Shield or T-budding is the most common form of budding, used both for propagating fruit trees and ornamentals in the nursery and for top-working older trees.

Vigorous shoots of the current season's growth are cut for bud wood, the buds in the angles of the leaves having an appearance of maturity and the stick itself having a firm, woody feel. As in grafting, the buds at the tip and base of the year's growth are discarded and only plump, hard buds near the middle are used. The leaves on the budsticks are trimmed away, leaving about ¼ in. of the stem as a handle to the bud. After trimming, the sticks are wrapped in a damp burlap, for once they become dried they are worthless.

At the point where the bud is to be inserted a T-shaped incision is made. the transverse cut being made by a rocking motion of the knife and the vertical one by drawing

---

* Special articles on the subjects indicated by an asterisk (*) will be found at the words so marked.

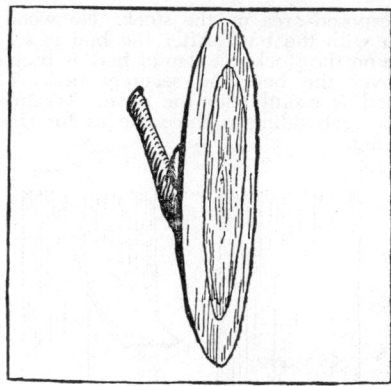

A shield bud

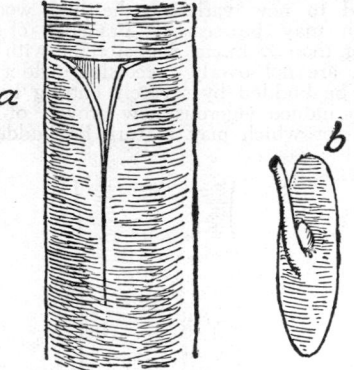

A shield bud (*b*), and T-shaped incision in the bark (*a*), prepared to receive it

the knife upward lightly from a point about an inch below the first cut. Before removing the knife a slight twist of the blade will loosen the edges. Here the advantage of the straight-pointed knife over the curved form is apparent, for the latter could not be twisted to open the bark without boring into and injuring the tender tissue beneath.

The bud is cut from below upward, with a drawing motion of the knife. The entire thickness of the bark is cut at the point of the bud, so that it will not crumple when inserted into the stock.

No wood is cut away with the bud unless just under the "eye"; but, on the other hand, the bud must not be cut so thin that the soft growing tissue between the bark and wood is injured. With fruit plants, one may leave a thin strip of wood, while with roses it is customary to remove all the wood by making the first upward cut very deep and severing the bark by a crosscut above the bud. Grasping the shield firmly between the thumb and forefinger, it is carefully lifted from the wood, without tearing the bud. With the leaf stem as a handle, the bud is inserted into the T-shaped incision and pushed down until its "heel" is flush with the transverse cut. When the T-incision is inverted the bud must be pushed upwards and the operation is called up-budding or reverse T-budding as contrasted with down-budding. Sometimes with plants with large buds, as some pear varieties, a vertical cross is better than a T-incision.

No waxing is necessary, but the bud must be tied. For this purpose raffia and rubber budding strips are used. Raffia is cut into lengths of 18 or 20 inches and moistened to make it flat and pliable. Rubber strips are sold already cut into 2-in. lengths, ⅜ in. in width. The strand is first brought firmly across the upper end of the bud to keep it from working out. Beginning then at the bottom of the slit, the material is wound smoothly upward, covering everything but the eye, and fastened. It is essential that this winding be tight, for it must hold the bud

immovably in place and must be airtight. In from 2 to 4 weeks, depending on the growth of the stock, the tie should be cut to prevent girdling. The bud will not put forth growth, but will lie dormant until the following spring, when the stock is cut away just above the bud. Any new growth from the stock must be removed as soon as it appears.

In the case of nursery trees the bud is inserted on the stock 2 in. above the ground line. The following spring the stock is cut off above the bud. The work may be done in two operations, the first cut being made 2 or 3 in. above the bud so as to leave a stub to which the new shoot may be loosely tied for support. Several weeks later when the new shoot has hardened somewhat, the old stub may be cut off smooth, close to the bud, when the new growth will rapidly heal the wound.

Young trees up to 5 years old are well adapted to top-working by budding, and since budding is economical of wood, it is

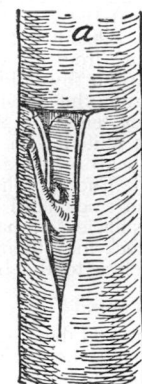

A bud inserted (*a*) bound with raffia (*b*), and ready for growth

---

* Special articles on the subjects indicated by an asterisk (*) will be found at the words so marked.

suited to new varieties, the bud wood of which may be scarce. Branches of trees larger than ½ in. in diameter, or with thick bark, are not overly successful. Older trees may be budded by severely cutting back so as to induce vigorous new growth of small diameter which may in turn be budded.

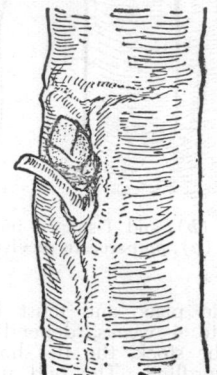

A bud with the raffia removed and thoroughly established in its new home

PRONG BUDDING is similar to shield budding, differing in that a short spur or prong is used in place of a simple bud. No wood should be carried with the bud. The method is adapted to nut trees, the operation being essentially the same as dormant grafting, using dormant buds, cutting off the stock just above the bud, and waxing the wound. *Cion, sprig,* and *twig budding* are erroneous terms for forms of grafting (*see* GRAFTING).

JUNE BUDDING. A special form of shield budding known as June budding is practiced in southern sections of long growing season, where it is possible to force the bud into growth the same season it is set, thus saving a year. Peaches and plums are especially adapted to this method since the rootstock makes sufficient size to be budded the first year from seed, yet other material may also be used to advantage. The difficulty of securing buds sufficiently mature from the current season's growth may be met by holding dormant wood in storage from the previous season until needed. Five or ten days after budding, when the bud has united with the stock, the top should be bent or partially broken so as to force the bud. Enough foliage must be left to maintain the stock until the foliage of the new shoot is sufficient to nourish the entire plant. The stock may then be removed with a clean cut close to the bud.

PLATE AND H-BUDDING

In plate budding, the top and both sides of a rectangle are cut through the bark of the stock, and the resulting flap of bark turned down, exposing a rectangular area. The bud to be united is cut with a similar rectangle of bark attached so as just to fit the exposed area on the stock. No wood is taken with the bud. After the bud is set in place on the stock, the flap of bark is brought up over the bud and securely tied. This method is useful with the olive. Treatment following budding is the same as for shield budding.

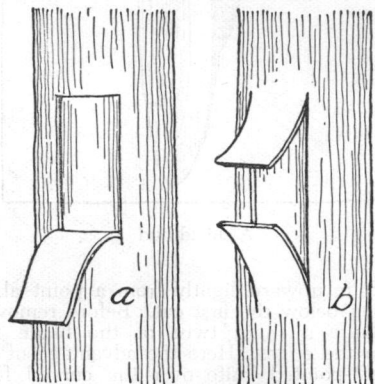

The stock prepared for plate budding (*a*), and H-budding (*b*)

Sometimes a double rectangular cut is made in the bark of the stock to form the letter H, hence the name *H-budding.* Both flaps of bark are turned back, a bud with rectangular shield is placed to match the exposed area, and both flaps turned back over the bud and tied. Where the bark is thick, the H-bud makes a less clumsy job than would simple plate budding.

PATCH BUDDING

Patch budding differs from plate budding in that no hanging strip of bark is left on the stock, otherwise it is essentially the same. A rectangular piece of bark is cut out from the

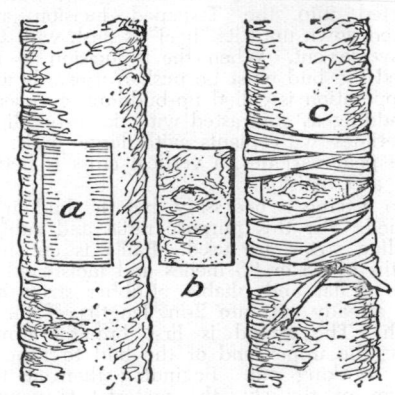

Three stages in patch budding: (*a*) The stock prepared for the bud: (*b*) The bud; (*c*) The bud inserted and bound with raffia

---

* Special articles on the subjects indicated by an asterisk (*) will be found at the words so marked.

stock, and a bud with bark of corresponding size and shape is fitted into the exposed area and tied. Since this method is at present so widely used owing to popular interest in pecans, nut trees in general, mango, and other heavy-bark plants, a special knife is to be had which cuts a rectangle on the stock of identical size as the bud to be inserted. It is patterned after a machinist's die, consisting of a sharp-edged metal box, which when pressed against the stock and the cion, cuts out identical areas. The work is usually done in late spring with dormant buds of the last season's growth, but may be done in summer with buds of the current season's growth.

There are several other modifications of the three main types of budding as described above. Some of them are used by professional fruit growers or nurserymen, but the average home grower will find that all his ordinary budding needs will be met by shield or T-budding, by plate or H-budding, or by patch budding. To list and describe other minor sorts of budding is merely to confuse a comparatively simple operation. — H. B. T.

BUDDLEIA (bud'lee-a). A widely distributed genus of mostly tropical shrubs of the family Loganiaceae, a few of which are outstanding garden plants. Of the 70 known species six are cult. in America. All but one have opposite* leaves and all of them have hairy, mealy, or somewhat scurfy foliage. Flowers in clusters (mostly panicles* or spikes*). Calyx bell-shaped and 4-lobed. Corolla tubular or bell-shaped, 4-lobed, the 4 stamens hidden within it. (They are protruded in *Caryopteris* which some mistake for this genus.) Fruit a 2-valved capsule,* usually surrounded by the withered flower. (Named for Adam Buddle, British botanist.) Sometimes, and perhaps correctly, spelled *Buddleja*.

The shrubs, usually called butterfly-bush, comprise some of the most attractive of late-flowering plants, although some bloom very early. Not all of them are hardy in the North (*see* below), but most of them can be counted upon if given winter protection. If they should be winter-killed, they can be cut back to the ground as the roots nearly always survive. Some growers prefer to cut back most of the cult. species and mulch the crowns with light, strawy manure. They need a rich but not heavy soil and it should be well drained. Easily propagated by cuttings of half-ripe wood and rooted in the fall in the greenhouse. For winter bloom most of them can be grown in the cool greenhouse.

alternifolia. The only cult. species with alternate leaves and a shrub up to 10 ft., thus too big for cutting back. Leaves lance-shaped, 1–4 in. long, green above, grayish and scurfy beneath. Flowers lilac-purple, about ½ in. long, in short, dense, leafy clusters on last year's branches. China. A beautiful plant with arching or pendulous branches and hardy only from zone* 5 southward. June–July.

asiatica. A shrub 2–6 ft. high, the leaves narrow, 5–8 in. long, green above, rusty-hairy or felt-like beneath. Flowers white, fragrant, in slender, drooping clusters that are often 5 in. long. Southern China and India. Not hardy above zone* 5. April–May.

davidii. Orange-eye butterfly-bush. The best known of the cult. species and the hardiest. A shrub 4–10 ft. but often much less in those cut back for the winter. Leaves oval-lance-shaped, 6–9 in. long, finely toothed, green above, white-felty beneath. Flowers lilac, fragrant, orange at the throat, in usually nodding spikes 5–12 in. long. China. Blooms from late July to frost. The *var.* **magnifica** has rose-purple and larger flowers. *Var.* **veitchiana** has mauve flowers with an orange eye. There are several other varieties, all of them and the typical form often called summer lilac.

globosa. A shrub 10–15 ft. high, the foliage nearly evergreen. Leaves elliptic or narrower, 4–9 in. long, densely rusty-hairy beneath. Flowers yellow, small, fragrant, in long-stalked heads, forming a large cluster (panicle*). Peru. Hardy from zone* 7 southward.

lindleyana. Not over 5 ft. high, the branchlets somewhat 4-angled or winged. Leaves oval to oblong, 2½–4 in. long, green both sides, but paler beneath. Flowers purplish-violet in erect, dense spikes. Eastern China. Hardy from zone* 6 southward. Aug.-Sept.

officinalis. A shrub 2–6 ft. high, the branchlets round and gray-scurfy. Leaves lance-oblong, or narrower, 4–7 in. long, grayish above, white or rusty-hairy beneath. Flowers in dense, stalked cymes,* fragrant, lilac with an orange eye. China. April–May. Not hardy north of zone* 6.

BUD DROP. The dropping of flower buds in camellias, gardenias, and other plants may not be a specific disease, but a physiological condition induced by too much water or too sudden changes of temperature, especially in greenhouses. Also highly nitrogenous fertilizers may be the cause. Bud drop is a baffling trouble and perhaps the only remedy is good culture and the avoidance of extremes of temperature and moisture.

BUDS. Nature's protection to undeveloped flowers or leaves. They vary from the eyes on a potato to the delicately tinted rose bud. From the gardening standpoint, the

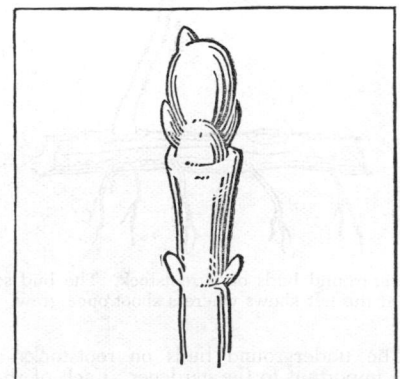

Winter buds, often sticky or varnished, are Nature's best protection for the shoots to follow in spring.

---

* Special articles on the subjects indicated by an asterisk (*) will be found at the words so marked.

most important are the winter buds, which ensure next year's supply of fresh green leaves or flowers. They are often elaborately protected by coatings of hair, scales, felt-like coverings, gums, and some are apparently varnished.

It is upon the knowledge of this function of buds that all grafting, budding, and the making of cuttings is based. For all these operations merely rely upon the bud to develop into a shoot or new plant.

At the left a fruit bud and at the right a leaf bud. In pruning it is often necessary to distinguish between them.

Leaf buds and flower buds are usually formed many months before either will open, and in most temperate climates a winter usually intervenes. It is often a practical matter, therefore, both in pruning and grafting, to know which are flower buds and which will produce only foliage. The accompanying figures tell this better than words.

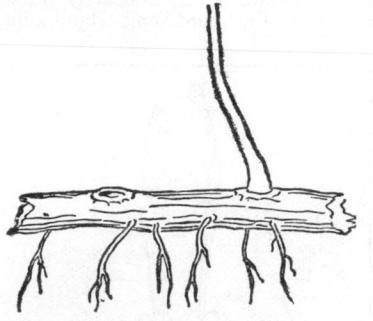

Underground buds on a rootstock. The bud scar at the left shows where a shoot once grew.

The underground buds on rootstocks are also important to the gardener. Each of them will send up a new shoot the following spring, and if the rootstock is cut or divided, a bud must be included in order to ensure a new plant. See also ADVENTITIOUS.

BUD-SPORT. An unusual, and sometimes valuable, variation from the type, originating from the bud of an otherwise normal plant — cause unknown. One of the most famous bud-sports is the navel orange.

BUD STICK. A shoot from which buds are removed for propagation; often called merely a *stick*.

BUD-VARIETY. A bud-sport.

BUFFALOBERRY. See SHEPHERDIA.

BUFFALO BOTANIC GARDEN. See BOTANIC GARDEN.

BUFFALO CURRANT = *Ribes odoratum.*

BUFFALO-GRASS. A native American grass (*Buchloe dactyloides*) used in the West as a turf grass where deficient rainfall will not permit bluegrass lawns. See COLORADO.

BUGBANE. See CIMICIFUGA.

BUGINVILLAEA = BOUGAINVILLAEA.

BUGLE. See AJUGA.

BUGLE-LILY. See WATSONIA.

BUGLOSS = ANCHUSA.

BUGLOSSOIDES. See LITHOSPERMUM PURPUREO-COERULEUM.

BUGS. A general term loosely applied to any insect, but properly, and in this book, applied only to insects that pierce plant tissue and suck their food — hence sucking insects. The commonest examples are the scales, squash bug, plant lice, etc. Some have a sickening odor.

BULB. A much swollen, usually underground stem, of which the onion is a typical example, and from the bottom of which roots always arise. The scale-like coverings are actually much modified, food-storing leaves which completely surround, protect, and feed the bud. True bulbs like onion and tulip always have these scale-like coverings, and sometimes the outermost layer is parchment or skin-like. Such bulbs were once, and are sometimes still, called tunicated bulbs to distinguish them from corms (which see). For the many valuable bulb-bearing garden plants and their uses see BULBS.

bulbifera, -us, -um (bul-biff′e-ra). Bulb-bearing.

BULBIL. A small bulb, differing from a bulblet in being borne above ground, usually among the flowers, as in some onions, but sometimes in the axil* of a leaf.

BULBLET. A small bulb, borne about a larger one, as in many bulbous plants (see MOTHER BULB). The term bulblet is often, but somewhat loosely, applied to a bulbil (which see). See also SET.

BULBOCODIUM (bul-bo-cō′dee-um). A single, crocus-like, European herb of the lily family, grown for its very early spring bloom. They bear corms* which should be planted in the same way and at the same time as crocuses. The only species, **B. vernum**, the spring meadow saffron, bears 1–3 purple, funnel-shaped flowers close to the ground, fol-

---

* Special articles on the subjects indicated by an asterisk (*) will be found at the words so marked.

lowed by a cluster of narrow, basal leaves. (*Bulbocodium* is from the Greek for woolly bulb.)

bulbosa, -us, -um (bul-bō′sa). Bearing bulbs; also applied to other swollen underground stems or even to swollen roots.

BULBO-TUBER. A corm.*

BULBOUS CHERVIL = *Chaerophyllum bulbosum.*

BULBS. Most perennial plants at the time of their dormancy have stems furnished with buds from which will develop shoots, bearing leaves and flowers, and roots from which other roots will develop. There is another group of plants which have a modified structure known as a bulb. These vary somewhat in their structure, but all have a portion that corresponds to the normal stem and is furnished with buds for growth and has a capacity for producing roots which often are only of annual duration. Nearly all have parts that represent modified leaves as in the fleshy scales of the lily. These plants are also characterized by their growth cycle in which dormancy is a longer period than for most plants and is often determined as much by heat and dryness as by cold.

This factor must be clearly recognized in gardening, for it is obvious that it may be unwise to plant bulbs that become dormant in June in the midst of a border that is watered and fed to keep herbaceous plants in active growth until the approach of cold weather.

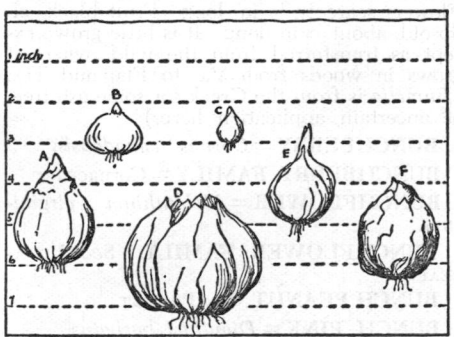

The correct depths for planting common bulbs: (*a*) Narcissus; (*b*) Crocus; (*c*) Snowdrop; (*d*) Lily; (*e*) Tulip; (*f*) Hyacinth

It should be understood that some bulbs renew themselves almost entirely each year, forming a bulb of flowering size annually, and that others are relatively permanent, dividing slowly within their mass until each branch becomes a unit of sufficient size to separate or be separated from the oldest portion of the plant. Tulips and Spanish iris are good examples of the first type and narcissus of the second. This means that the tulip bulb, when planted, must be given

suitable conditions and enough food so that, in addition to flowering, it can immediately form also a new bulb strong enough to flower the next season. Narcissus on the other hand continues to grow from the original base and produces leaves even if there is not food enough to produce flowers. This explains sometimes why tulips that are poorly planted may not flower a second year after planting. It also suggests why tulips are so often treated as annuals and planted for one season's show only, and why narcissus is so often found in deserted homesteads still vigorous but unflowering.

Bulbs, therefore, must be used where they can find food for their continued growth and in sufficient quantity and of proper character to assure annual flowering. This is particularly true of the bulbs of cold climates, for many that come from warm regions, notably members of the Amaryllis family, do not make strictly annual root growth, but have more or less permanent roots that are added to each season.

GARDEN BULBS. In the garden, bulbs are prized because of the prodigality of their blooming and the brilliance of their flowers. Since their flower buds are formed inside the bulb at the time of purchase, the gardener is practically assured of flower the next season unless he commits some signal cultural error.

We commonly group bulbs according to their season of bloom, a purely arbitrary and artificial classification. From the moment snow leaves, they commence with scilla, chionodoxa, snowdrop, crocus, grape hyacinth (*see* MUSCARI), wild tulip, and narcissus until the great army of garden and horticultural forms of hyacinth, tulip, and narcissus bring about the spring climax. This yields in turn to the lilies, amaryllis, lycoris, and nerine of summer and early autumn, with zephyranthes, sternbergia, colchicum, or autumn crocus for late autumn and early winter for northern gardens, to name only the most common of the garden bulbs, a galaxy that can be greatly increased in warmer regions by many of the amaryllis relatives.

All of these plants are discussed at their proper entries, but it is possibly wise to mention both hyacinth and tulip here. The first is essentially a garden plant, the result of years of selection and cultivation. It comes to the garden ready for its best flowering, and then the bulb splits up enough to give only smaller stalks of bloom that each year grow stronger, until they again reach a maximum and the cycle repeats itself. Obviously this points to care in feeding, for the richer the soil the more rapidly the dividing young bulbs will reach their new peak of growth. Being a hungry plant, it enjoys the richly manured soil that would mean ruin to some other bulbs. The tulip, on the other hand, while needing rich food and a warm soil so that it may have a full summer rest, should grow enough to flower well each year. That is why tulips are so often bedded or treated as a crop plant, being lifted and followed by annuals.

In general terms, planting should always recognize these points — food located below the bulb to be reached by the roots annually renewed; drainage to prevent danger of decay of bulb during dormancy; proper location to insure a period of summer dormancy during which growth goes on below ground and within the bulb to insure next year's flowering; and a proper depth to insure full root growth and prevent undue division of the bulb at the expense of all else. The general rule that the bulb should be two and one-half times its depth below the surface is safe except for a few bulbs that must be shallow and are noted elsewhere. In some mole-infested gardens bulbs are occasionally planted in wire baskets to protect against them and other invading rodents.

Bulbs that renew themselves annually are best treated as annuals in garden beds, those that are permanent can be combined with any reasonable amount of herbaceous growth, provided they get their summer rest. Besides use in garden beds, bulbs are successful in lawns, meadows, and near shrubbery where their masses of bloom make spectacular sheets of color and where their maturing foliage, that must not be cut off, can die away normally. They are also useful in pots for forcing, remembering that they must be given time in the dark to develop a fine root system before light is given to bring about leaf and flower. Some, particularly narcissus and hyacinth, are grown in water or in water and pebbles, where the stored-up food in the bulb will bring about the flowering once the roots have fully developed. — B. Y. M.

Growing spring-flowering bulbs (narcissus, tulip, hyacinth, etc.) in the house demands that the bulbs get some chilling before they are brought into a room. Even more important, the bulbs, whether in soil or in pebbles and water, must be kept in the dark until they have developed a good root system. After which, brought into the light and heat, they will flower weeks before their normal blooming period.

INSECT PESTS. Narcissus bulb fly and two or more lesser bulb flies cause widespread losses to narcissus and other bulbs. A preplant treatment of pesticide #16 (*see* SPRAYS AND DUSTS) or #13 at rate of one pint of emulsion concentrate per 15 gallons of water for 10 minutes will protect bulbs from these pests.

Mites can be controlled by heat treatments of bulbs in water containing one half pint of formaldehyde per 12 gallons at 110° F. for 2 to 3 hours. In field, systemics, such as demeton, are effective but dangerous for use by home gardeners.

DISEASES. In addition to diseases specific to various bulbs and corms (*see* TULIP, GLADIOLUS, etc.) there are a number of secondary types of fungi and bacteria which cause rotting in storage. Any bulb with green or white fungus growth on it should not be planted. Likewise, those which are soft and ill-smelling should be discarded. There are various chemicals on the market which may be used as a dip or dust for bulbs and corms. In general, store bulbs and corms under relatively cool, dry conditions.

bulgarica, -us, -um (bul-gare'i-ka). From Bulgaria.

BULLACE = *Prunus domestica insititia.*

BULLACE GRAPE = *Vitis rotundifolia.*

bullata, -us, -um (bul-lay'ta). Bullate; *i.e.,* blistered or puckered.

BULL BAY = *Magnolia grandiflora;* also *Persea Borbonia.*

BULLOCK'S-HEART = *Annona recticulata.*

BULL PINE = *Pinus ponderosa.* See PINE.

BULRUSH. See SCIRPUS and CYPERUS PAPYRUS.

Bumalda (bew-mal'da). An old generic name of uncertain application as a specific name for *Spiraea Bumalda.*

BUMELIA (bew-mee'lee-a). A genus of about 20 species of not very ornamental shrubs and trees, chiefly tropical American, and belonging to the family Sapotaceae. The only species of much cult. interest extends northward to Va. It is a shrub or small tree with hard wood and usually spiny branches. Leaves alternate,* without marginal teeth, persistent and green, but not evergreen. Flowers minute, white, in small, many-flowered clusters. Fruit berry-like. The cult. species is **B. lanuginosa,** variously called gum elastic, chittamwood (also shittimwood), and false buckthorn. Its leaves are 1½–4 in. long, shining green above and rusty beneath. Flowers scarcely ⅛ in. long. Fruit black, ellipsoid, about ½ in. long. It is little grown except as transferred from the wild, where it grows in woods from Va. to Fla. and Tex. (*Bumelia* is from the Greek for some ash tree, of uncertain application here.)

BUNCHBERRY = *Cornus canadensis.*

BUNCHBERRY FAMILY = Cornaceae.

BUNCHFLOWER = *Melanthium virginicum.*

BUNCHFLOWER FAMILY. See LILIACEAE.

BUNCH PEANUT. *See* PEANUT.

BUNCH PINK = *Dianthus barbatus.*

BUNYA-BUNYA = *Araucaria bidwilli.*

BUPHTHALMUM (bewf-thal'mum). A small genus of Eurasian herbs, family Compositae, usually called oxeye, from their yellow, dark-centered flower heads. They are grown somewhat in the perennial border for their rather large flowers. Leaves alternate.* Ray flowers, long and strap-shaped. (*Buphthalmum* is from the Greek for oxeye.)

Both the species below are of easy culture in any ordinary garden soil and may be increased by division.

salicifolium. A perennial herb 1–2 ft. high. Leaves willow-like, toothed and white-hairy, about 3 in. long. Flower heads solitary, about 2 in. wide, the disk darker than the bright

---

* Special articles on the subjects indicated by an asterisk (*) will be found at the words so marked.

yellow rays. Southeastern Eu. Late summer.

speciosum. Taller than the last, the leaves more or less heart-shaped, coarsely toothed, and very large in the lower ones, smaller and ovalish toward the top of the plant. Heads in clusters of 2–5, or solitary. Southern Eu.

BUR. Any prickly or spiny covering or fruit husk, as in the chestnut; also applied to many plants bearing prickly flowers or fruits.

BUR ARTICHOKE. *See* ARTICHOKE.

BURBANK. Luther Burbank (1849–1926), the most widely publicized horticulturist in America, produced many plants of value to orchardists, especially those in Calif., S.Af., and Aust., and some ornamentals. Absurdly wild claims were made for many of his "new creations," which time has proved worthless. So much controversy has raged about the work of Burbank, ranging from "charlatan" to "plant wizard" that it would be impossible for anyone to appraise his true position in American hort., were it not for the work of Dr. W. L. Howard, emeritus dean of the University of Calif. Agricultural Experiment Station. In Bulletin 691, issued in March, 1945, Dr. Howard lists all the varieties put out by Burbank and their subsequent performance. Among several hundreds only a few have stood the test of time.

BUR CLOVER = *Medicago hispida.*

BURDOCK = *Arctium Lappa.* See list at WEEDS.

BUR GHERKIN = *Cucumis Anguria.*

BURGUNDY TREFOIL = *Medicago sativa.*

BURL. An overgrown excrescence or knot found on the trunks of some trees, and sometimes called a knaur. The burls of the redwood (*Sequoia sempervirens*), and of some other trees, will sprout into cutting-like growth if given heat and moisture. Standing the burl in a dish of water will produce the growth in a few days, and such freely sprouting burls make interesting centerpieces.

BUR-MARIGOLD = *Bidens.*

BURN. *See* WATER BLISTER.

BURNET. *See* SANGUISORBA.

BURNET ROSE = *Rosa spinosissima.*

BURNING-BUSH = *Euonymus americanus;* also *Dictamnus albus,* and *Kochia scoparia trichophila.*

BUR OAK = *Quercus macrocarpa.* See OAK.

Bursa-pastoris (bur-sa-pass-tor'is). An old generic name for the shepherd's-purse, which *see* in the list at WEEDS.

BURSARIA (bur-sar'i-a). A genus of only two species of Australian shrubs, family Pittosporaceae, the one below grown in Calif. for ornament, rarely cult. in greenhouses. Branches spiny. Leaves alternate.* Flowers small, white, in clusters, soon falling. Petals, sepals, and stamens each 5. Fruit dry (a capsule*), resembling the shepherd's-purse.

(Named for *Bursa,* a pouch, in allusion to the pod.)

spinosa. Shrub or small tree, the branches pendulous. Leaves oblong-wedge-shaped, ½–1 in. long. Flowers in pyramidal clusters, which are showy, although each flower is very small. Grown outdoors only in Calif., mostly in the southern part of the state.

BURSTWORT. *See* HERNIARIA.

BUSH. *See* SHRUB.

BUSH BEAN = *Phaseolus vulgaris humilis.* For culture *see* BEAN.

BUSH BROOM = *Hypericum prolificum.* See ST. JOHN'S-WORT.

BUSH-CLOVER. *See* LESPEDEZA.

BUSHEL. *See* WEIGHTS AND MEASURES 3.

BUSH FRUITS. A collective term for various small fruits borne on a shrub, notably blackberry, raspberry, gooseberry, and currant. The loganberry and a few others, usually called bramble* fruits, make up the largest part of the bush fruits. For their culture *see* the different entries under the above names.

BUSH HONEYSUCKLE = *Lonicera tatarica, L. Xylosteum,* and any other shrubby *Lonicera,* as distinguished from the vines. See also DIERVILLA.

BUSH HUCKLEBERRY = *Gaylussacia dumosa.* See HUCKLEBERRY.

BUSH LIMA BEAN = *Phaseolus limensis limeanus.* For culture *see* BEAN.

BUSH MORNING-GLORY = *Ipomoea leptophylla.*

BUSH PEA = *Thermopsis mollis.*

BUSH POPPY = *Dendromecon rigidum.*

BUSH PUMPKIN; BUSH SQUASH = *Cucurbita Pepo Melopepo.*

BUSH TREFOIL = *Desmodium canadense.*

BUTCHER'S-BROOM = *Ruscus aculeatus.*

BUTIA (bew'ti-a). A small group of tropical South American feather palms, closely related to the coconut palm. The one below is widely grown by florists as *Cocos australis,* and is also planted outdoors in zones* 8 and 9. Trunk stocky, solitary, not spiny, clothed in nature with the withered leaves or their scars. Leaves rather stiff, drooping beyond the middle, the leaflets curving. Flower cluster arising from between the lower leaves, the male flowers with 6 stamens. Fruit globe-like or somewhat egg-shaped. (Named for the Earl of Bute.)

capitata. The pindo palm. Trunk stout, 12–18 ft. high, nearly 18 in. in diameter. Leaves long and arching, the leaflets many, about 2 ft. long, and grayish beneath, often in bunches of 3 or 4. Fruit nearly egg-shaped, about 1 in. long. Brazil. Common in Fla. and Calif.

BUTNERIA = *Calycanthus.*

BUTOMACEAE (bew-to-may'see-ee). The flowering rush family, of secondary gar-

---

* Special articles on the subjects indicated by an asterisk (*) will be found at the words so marked.

den importance, comprises only 4 genera and perhaps 10 species of aquatic or marsh plants — *Butomus, Hydrocleis,* and *Limnocharis* being the cult. genera. All are closely related to the Alismaceae (which see).

One of the genera is a plant of the pond-edge with iris-like leaves, milky juice, and rose-colored flowers (*see* BUTOMUS), while *Limnocharis* and *Hydrocleis* have yellow flowers and grow in the water. Fruit a cluster of follicles.*

Technical characters: Differs from Alismaceae chiefly in having numerous ovules.

BUTOMUS (bew-tō'mus). A single Eurasian, aquatic or pond-edge herb, family Butomaceae, grown for its rose-colored flowers. It has long, narrow leaves 18–30 in. long and a many-flowered umbel* on a naked, rush-like stalk, 2–3½ ft. high. Flowers rose or pinkish, with 3 petals and 3 sepals, the individual flowers small, but the cluster attractive. The only species, **B. umbellatus,** the flowering rush, is easy to grow in pools or along their edges. It is hardy in all except the coldest regions. (*Butomus* is from the Greek for ox and to cut, in allusion to the leaves being too sharp for fodder.)

BUTTER-AND-EGGS = *Linaria vulgaris.*

BUTTER BEAN. A form of *Phaseolus vulgaris. See* BEAN.

BUTTERBUR. *See* PETASITES.

BUTTER-BUSH = *Pittosporum phillyraeoides.*

BUTTERCUP. The crowfoots or buttercups comprise a large group of mostly north temperate herbs, all belonging to the genus **Ranunculus** (ra-nun'kew-lus), of the family Ranunculaceae. They include, besides the field buttercups, the common florists' ranunculus, which is much grown for winter bloom (*see* below). They have tuberous or fibrous roots, and simple* or compound* leaves, often much cut, lobed or divided. Flowers prevailingly yellow, but white or even red in some hort. varieties. Petals and sepals 5 each. Stamens* numerous. Fruit a tiny cluster of dry achenes.* (*Ranunculus* is Latin for a little frog, in allusion to the meadow habit of many wild species.)

All those below, except the florists' ranunculus, are easily grown outdoors in any ordinary garden soil, and as easily propagated by division in the spring or fall. Some are more weedy than decorative, and one is a weed in one form but a garden plant in another (*see* R. REPENS.

R. aconitifolius. Related to *R. asiaticus,* but taller and with usually branching stems. Flowers about 1 in. wide, often double in the hort. forms, usually white, but yellow in some of the hort. varieties. Eu. Its culture is the same as for the florists' ranunculus (*see* below).

R. acris. The common field buttercup; called also blister-flower and butter-rose. Weedy in the wild state but often double-flowered and handsome in the garden forms. Root fibrous, the stem branched and hairy, 2–2½ ft. high. Leaves divided into three segments, these stalk-less and again thrice-divided or cut. Flowers about ½ in. wide, yellow. Eu., but widely naturalized throughout the U.S.

R. asiaticus. The florists' ranunculus, better called the turban or Persian buttercup. Root bulbous, from which springs a simple (rarely branched) stem 6–15 in. high. Leaves compound,* the three leaflets toothed and somewhat blunt. Flowers 1–4 on a stem, long-stalked, about 1½ in. wide, yellow and mostly double, with broad, blunt petals. Eurasia. For culture and varieties *see* below.

R. bulbosus. The bulbous buttercup, which *see* in the list at WEEDS.

R. geraniifolius. A European rock garden perennial, about 6 in. high, the lower leaves nearly round, the upper 3–5-parted. Flowers yellow, not particularly showy. June. Usually offered here as *R. montanus.*

R. gramineus. A bluish-green perennial from southwestern Eu., the leaves very narrow, grass-like. Flowers pale yellow, long-stalked, the plant 8–14 in. high. May.

R. montanus = *Ranunculus geraniifolius.*

R. repens. Creeping crowfoot or buttercup; called also sitfast. A creeping, weedy plant with long runners, often a nuisance as a weed (*see* the list at WEEDS). It roots at the joints and sends up erect, flowering stems 12–20 in. high. Lower leaves long-stalked and nearly round, the margins wavy. Flowers single, yellow. Eu., but a common weed in U.S. Its *var.* **pleniflorus,** a double-flowered form, is a widely grown garden plant. It has much-doubled, very profuse flowers about ¾ in. wide. It is also called *R. repens flore-pleno* and *R. speciosus.*

R. speciosus = *Ranunculus repens pleniflorus.*

CULTURE OF THE FLORISTS' RANUNCULUS
(*Ranunculus asiaticus*)

This is valuable as a cut flower and for the gay display it may make in the garden. It is recorded by early garden writers, and although it may have lost popularity at one time, today gardeners are returning to an appreciation of its good qualities. In many respects it resembles the poppy-flowered anemone from the Mediterranean region, except that the predominating shades in this anemone are blue, while those of *Ranunculus asiaticus* are orange and yellow. Improved types are offered with larger and more colorful flowers that are very double.

Although the tubers may be planted out of doors after danger of frost has gone, it is in the greenhouse as a winter bloomer that it is most useful. The tubers may be planted in pots or benches in potting mixture* 4 and succeed best under a temperature dropping to 50° at night. They can also be raised from seed sown in May for early spring flowering. As soon as the seedlings are large enough to handle with ease, plant singly in thumb pots in potting mixture* 2, from which they may be transferred when ready, putting three in a 6-inch pot. When the roots become pot-bound in this, apply weak liquid fertilizer once a week.

BUTTERCUP FAMILY. A very large family of plants, nearly all herbs, and containing among its many genera such garden favorites as the larkspur, monkshood, peony, columbine, clematis, and anemone. For the

---

* Special articles on the subjects indicated by an asterisk (*) will be found at the words so marked.

other genera and the characters of the family *see* RANUNCULACEAE.

BUTTERFLY-BUSH. *See* BUDDLEIA.

BUTTERFLY-FLOWER. *See* SCHIZANTHUS; *see also* BAUHINIA MONANDRA.

BUTTERFLY-LILY. *See* HEDYCHIUM.

BUTTERFLY-ORCHID = *Oncidium Papilio.*

BUTTERFLY-PEA = *Clitoria mariana.*

BUTTERFLY-TULIP = *Calochortus.*

BUTTERFLY-WEED = *Asclepias tuberosa.* *See* MILKWEED.

BUTTERNUT = *Juglans cinerea.* *See* WALNUT.

BUTTER-ROSE = *Ranunculus acris.* *See* BUTTERCUP.

BUTTERWORT. *See* PINGUICULA.

BUTTONBALL TREE. *See* PLATANUS.

BUTTON-BUSH. The common buttonbush (called button willow in Calif.) of N.A. is the only American species and the only one worth the gardener's attention in the genus Cephalanthus (sef-a-lan'thus) of the madder family. While growing naturally in swamps, it is perfectly at home in most ordinary garden soils and is hardy over most of U.S. **C. occidentalis,** the cult, species, is a shrub 5–12 ft. high with opposite or whorled* leaves without marginal teeth. From July to late Sept. it has ball-like, fragrant clusters of small, white, tubular flowers. (For technical characters *see* RUBIACEAE.) Easily propagated by seeds or cuttings. (*Cephalanthus* is Greek for flowerhead.)

BUTTON SNAKEROOT. *See* LIATRIS; *see also* ERYNGIUM YUCCIFOLIUM.

BUTTON WLLOW = *Cephalanthus occidentalis.* *See* BUTTON-BUSH.

BUTTONWOOD = *Platanus occidentalis.*

BUXACEAE (bucks-ā'see-ee). The box family is small but horticulturally important because it yields not only box (*Buxus*) but *Pachysandra.* Of its six known genera and about 40 species, the only other one of garden interest is *Sarcococca.* They are widely distributed, but mostly tropical or subtropical.

Leaves alternate* (or opposite in the box) and in hort. genera, evergreen, the plants all shrubs or trees (herb-like in *Pachysandra*). Flowers small, greenish or inconspicuous, without petals. Fruit a pod (capsule*) or fleshy. Much the most important genus is the box (*Buxus*).

Technical flower characters: Flowers monoecious,* without petals. Calyx 4–12-parted, or sometimes none. Ovary superior,* 3-celled. Ovules 2.

buxifolia, -us, -um (bucks-i-fō'li-a). With leaves like the box (*Buxus*).

BUXUS. *See* BOX.

BYRNESIA. *See* GRAPTOPETALUM.

byzantina, -us, -um (bi-zan-ty'na). From Byzantium, ancient name for Stamboul (Constantinople).

C

CABBAGE (*Brassica oleracea capitata*). The cabbage is a cultigen* that originated many centuries ago from *Brassica oleracea,* a mustard-like, mostly seacoast weed of the Old World. Today there are hundreds of varieties found in every country with a temperate climate, and this climatic exclusiveness should not be forgotten in our own culture of the plant. It will not stand extreme heat or dryness, and will grow well only where there is some moisture and coolness. To ensure the latter, cabbage is rightly divided into two groups — early and late. Midsummer crops are not sought at all, or are secondary with this crop.

The seasonal nature of the crop and its wide uses have largely dictated the varieties that are grown here. Some are used for boiling, some only for coleslaw, others only for sauerkraut, some are green, others red, and there is the Savoy Cabbage with blistered, puckery leaves.

VARIETIES. Depending on their use and season, the best varieties are:

Early. Jersey Wakefield (conical head). Charleston Wakefield (larger than Jersey Wakefield). Copenhagen Market, Golden Acre.

Midseason. Glory, Marion Market, Globe, Bonanza.

Late. Danish Ballhead, Flat Dutch, Danish Roundhead, Hollander, Savoy (a Savoy Cabbage).

There are many other varieties, some suited to the special requirements of the market gardener. But the home gardener from the above list, can select those that best fit his needs. For those who want a red cabbage, Red Drumhead or Mammoth Rock Red should be chosen. The Danish Ballhead is one of the best varieties if you wish to store the heads for winter cabbage.

SOILS AND FERTILIZER. Most good garden soil, if it is properly enriched, will produce satisfactory cabbage. Commercially it is grown on soils ranging from sandy loam to fairly heavy clays or even muck. Perhaps more important than texture is the supply of soil moisture. This must be adequate and conserved by constant cultivation (*see* CULTIVATION). Adequate soil moisture may well compensate for long heat spells which cabbage does not like. It will not develop properly if these are too frequent or too long continued.

Most important of all is fertility. No crop

---

* Special articles on the subjects indicated by an asterisk (*) will be found at the words so marked.

Pointed and flat-headed types of cabbage

repays so richly the expenditure for manure or fertilizer. A good grade of commercial fertilizer with a 4–8–10 ratio (see FERTILIZERS) should be applied, before planting, at the rate of one ton to the acre (11 pounds per 100 ft. of row). If well-rotted stable manure is available, spread it 3 in. thick and plow in at least two weeks before the plants are set out.

Some commercial growers, where intensive returns are necessary (8000 heads of cabbage per acre), use both manure and fertilizers.

Home growers will find it will pay also to top-dress, about three weeks after the plants are set out, with nitrate of soda at the rate of 250 pounds to the acre (1¼ pounds per 100-ft. row). The nitrate of soda application is necessary only for the early season varieties (see above).

SEED SOWING. There are several different methods, of which the most practical is the following (for early cabbage): Sow the seeds in fine soil in flats in the hotbed or greenhouse in February or March. Do not make the soil too rich, as it is likely to make the seedlings grow too fast and become leggy. Make small drills about ½ in. deep and 2–3 in. apart, and put 8–10 seeds in each inch of drill. Water and keep in a reasonably cool temperature (50°–60°).

When the seedlings are large enough (3–4 in. high), prick out and replant farther apart in flats or boxes. This ensures stocky instead of spindling plants. The seed-sowing should be timed a month or six weeks earlier than the plants are to be set out.

The method of raising seedlings of the late varieties is exactly the same, except that the flats or boxes are kept outdoors instead of under glass. It will take from four to six weeks to get plants large enough for their permanent location.

Long Island, and the northeastern seaboard generally, the shores of the Great Lakes, and along the Pacific Coast are the preferred cabbage localities, but it is raised very well in many other states. Some quite warm states can grow good crops by picking the coolest season.

SETTING THE PLANTS. Cabbage is set at different intervals, depending on the variety. A useful guide is the following:

Early varieties.	14 in. apart.	Rows 28 in. apart.
Midseason varieties.	16 in. apart.	Rows 30 in. apart.
Late season.	24 in. apart.	Rows 36 in. apart.

To plant much closer may mean crowding and result in smaller heads. If the plants are sold by the head (not by the pound), closer planting may pay, although it makes cultivation more difficult at first and impossible later.

Early varieties can be set out as soon as there is no danger of hard frost (for the dates see the name of your state). Late varieties should, over most of the northern states, be in place by August first.

Depending on the variety, it will take from 67 (early) to 40 plants (for late varieties) for a row 100 ft. long, which is ample, or perhaps too much, for a family of five.

CULTIVATION. To keep down weeds and conserve moisture, frequent cultivation is essential. If only a hoe is used, there need be little trouble about this. But if a wheel hoe or horse or motor machine is used, great care must be taken not to break the rather brittle leaves of the plants.

One way to minimize this is to cultivate only between 10 in the morning and 4 in the afternoon, when the leaves are more pliable, or even partly wilted, than earlier or later, and less likely to injury. Keep up the cultivation as long as possible because, even with the spacing outlined above, the plants will ultimately prevent all but hand weeding. But if cultivation has been clean, the plants properly spaced, and they have grown well, their foliage should keep down the last crop of weeds.

HEADING. If the varieties listed above have been well grown, they should form the well-known, compact head without any extraneous aid. No commercial grower could afford not to have normally heading plants. But if the climate or soil or culture is not up to requirements and the plants are only heading poorly, tie up the outer leaves.

For the preferred position and sequence of cabbage in your garden see KITCHEN GARDEN.

INSECT PESTS. Except for cabbage loopers, cabbage worms will be controlled by pesticide #17. For loopers, pesticide #25–#21 is suggested. Gray aphids are controlled by pesticide #21. Several species of flea beetles are killed by pesticide #17 or #1. Root maggot control is more difficult. Flat paper collars placed snugly about bases of plants are effective in avoiding injury. Dusts of pesticide #15 on plants prior to setting, followed by weekly dusts at base of plant to kill young larvae and flies until plants are 4–5 weeks old, will control damage. Cutworms of many species destroy plants or stunt them by chewing at soil surface. Applications of pesticide #17 or #15 on soil about plants in spring or fall will stop this damage. Cylindrical paper collars about stems will prevent cutworm damage. Wireworms also

---

* Special articles on the subjects indicated by an asterisk (*) will be found at the words so marked.

attack roots. Following sod, pre-planting treatment of soil with pesticide #15 at rate suggested for grub-proofing (*see* JAPANESE BEETLE) will control damage. Within current growing season, little can be done to stop damage after it is noticed. (*See* SPRAYS AND DUSTS.)

DISEASES. Black rot, caused by a bacterium which lives over the winter on the seed, produces a black ring inside the stem and soon kills the plant. Blackleg,* caused by a fungus which penetrates the seed and which also may remain alive in the soil for three years or more, results in a blackening of the outside of the stem near the soil line. This disease may also kill the plants. Another fungus causes black spots* on leaves, as well as causing black areas on the curd of cauliflower. All three of these diseases are best controlled by soaking the seed in hot water (cabbage and brussels sprouts for 25 minutes, broccoli, cauliflower, kale, and kohlrabi for 18 minutes at 122° F.) and by long rotations with non-related crops.

Clubroot* is a formation of many large swellings on the roots and is caused by a slime mold which can live for many years in the soil. The plants may not be killed but they remain small and yield little or no crop. Use pesticide #10 (*see* SPRAYS AND DUSTS) and pour ½ cupful in each hole where a young plant is set.

Wilt* or yellows* is a disease causing the lower leaves of cabbage to turn yellow and die. The most susceptible varieties may fail to yield a crop when the disease is severe. The wilt* fungus lives in the soil for a number of years. Planting wilt-resistant varieties, of which there are several suitable for each specific growing area in the country, is the only control.

A downy mildew* may attack outer leaves or may become serious in the plant beds where seedlings are grown. In some areas broccoli may have the disease not only on the leaves, but in the flowering heads as well. Pesticide #11 applied at 5-day intervals is of value in the plant bed, but no pesticide has proven really valuable in the field.

CABBAGE FAMILY = Cruciferae.

CABBAGE PALM = *Roystonea oleracea.*

CABBAGE PALMETTO = *Sabal Palmetto.*

CABBAGE ROSE = *Rosa centifolia.*

CABBAGE TREE = *Andira inermis;* also *Cordyline australis.*

CABOMBA (ka-bom′ba). A genus of six species of aquatics, family Nymphaeaceae, one widely used in aquaria for its finely divided, submerged leaves, which are good for supplying oxygen to the water. Floating leaves oblong, often lacking. Submerged leaves very finely divided, hair-like, and numerous on the weak stems. Flowers white, with 3 sepals and 3 petals, blooming on the water surface. (*Cabomba* is derived from an aboriginal name for the plant.)

The species are generally called fanwort or water shield and have little use outside of aquaria. Without some soil in the tank the plant will live only a few weeks. It is easily propagated by division, but should be propagated under water.

caroliniana. Washington plant; called also fish-grass and Carolina water shield. Sub-

merged leaves hair-like, about ¾ in. long. Flowers about ⅓ in. wide, white, but with yellow spots at the center. Native from Ill. to Tex. and Fla., often a pest in outdoor pools because of its rampant growth, especially in the South.

CABOMBACEAE. See NYMPHAEACEAE.

CABUYA = *Furcraea gigantea.*

CACALIA. See EMILIA SAGITTATA LUTEA.

CACANAPA = *Opuntia lindheimeri.*

Cacao. Aztec name for the chocolate tree, and still the name for the tree and for chocolate in most tropical countries. See THEOBROMA.

cachemiriana, -us, -um (kash-e-meer-i-a′na). From Kashmir in the Himalayas.

CACTACEAE (kak-tay′see-ee). The cactus family is an immense group of succulent, mostly spiny, desert plants, all but a handful confined to dry or desert regions of the New World. There are perhaps 124 genera and over 1200 species, many of which are cultivated for their grotesque form, their often showy flowers, their sometimes edible fruit, and often because they make good, if odd-looking, house plants.

True leaves with expanded blades are lacking in mature specimens of most cacti, except in *Pereskia.* All the rest have tiny or ephemeral leaves, and the green stem, often separated into leaf-like but swollen joints, functions as do leaves. The stem of some genera is immense, notably in the giant cactus (*see* CARNEGIEA), and in other genera where it stores great quantities of water in barrel-like enlargements. Practically all the genera are spiny, some horribly so, but *Rhipsalis* and *Hatiora* are spineless, and so are the very different plants known as crab cactus, Christmas cactus, and Easter cactus. (*See* SCHLUMBERGERA, EPIPHYLLUM, and ZYGOCACTUS.)

In habit the cacti are often fantastic, sometimes erect and tree-like, sometimes climbing vines, others small and globular growths in the ground. Some, as in *Opuntia,* bear edible fruit; others yield beautiful night-blooming flowers (*see* HYLOCEREUS, SELENICEREUS, and NYCTOCEREUS). Except for the forage value of a few species of *Opuntia,* the cacti have little economic importance, the notable exception being *Nopalea,* which was commercially cult. for the red dye derived from the cochineal insect in Mex. and Guatemala.

From the garden standpoint, the remaining hort. genera may be divided into three groups:

1. *Cereus* and its allies.
2. Globular or low-growing plants without elongated stems.
3. *Echinocactus* and its allies.

The technical differences between these groups are difficult. But so far as the cult. genera are concerned, the three sections may be separated thus:

1. *Cereus* and its allies: Here belong the cacti with obvious stems, sometimes thick, branched and tree-like, or again vine-like, or some prostrate vines. All bear spines, some-

---

* Special articles on the subjects indicated by an asterisk (*) will be found at the words so marked.

times on the ridges of the stem. For the hort. genera in this group see:

MORE OR LESS ERECT, SOMETIMES TREE-LIKE	CLIMBING VINES	PROSTRATE OR LOW
Bergerocactus	Acanthocereus	Chamaecereus
Cereus	Aporocactus	Echinocereus
Cephalocereus	Deamia	Echinopsis
Cleistocactus	Harrisia	Machaerocereus
Escontria		Wilcoxia
Heliocereus		
Lemaireocereus		
Myrtillocactus		
Pachycereus		
Peniocereus		
Trichocereus		

It is mostly from this group that the grotesque desert forms come, and some genera furnish close, spiny, hedge plants in many parts of the Southwest and in tropical America.

2. Globular or low-growing plants without elongated stems: Here belong the small, button-like genera, used for centerpieces, and also some other genera with a larger plant body but no very obvious elongated stem. The hort. genera of this group may be separated thus:

LOW, BUTTON-LIKE OR BALL-LIKE CACTI, OFTEN HALF-HIDDEN IN THE GROUND; SOMETIMES CYLINDRIC	OFTEN A FOOT HIGH OR MORE, BUT BALL-LIKE OR BARREL-SHAPED
Ariocarpus	Escobaria
Astrophytum	Melocactus
Coryphantha	Pediocactus
Epithelantha	
Mammillaria	
Lophophora	
Pelecyphora	
Roseocactus	

3. Echinocactus and its allies: In this group belong cacti with a single, usually unbranched plant body that is stout, cylindric or barrel-shaped, usually too large for pot culture, but the plants are often grown in effective groups outdoors in frost-free areas. The plant body is usually prominently ribbed or grooved and very spiny. The hort. genera in this group are the following: Ancistrocactus, Echinocactus, Echinomastus, Ferocactus, Gymnocalycium, Hamatocactus, Homalocephala, Sclerocactus, Strombocactus, and Thelocactus.

All the cacti are inclined to have very showy flowers, but the petals and sepals are often indistinguishable, as they merge insensibly one into the other. In some genera the flower is tubular; in others, of separate segments. The fruits are nearly always berry-like, and edible in some prickly pears (see OPUNTIA) and in many species of Cereus and its allies.

Besides the spines, some genera bear small tufts of often barbed bristles, and in some the spine arises in a small pit which also is the seat of the tuft of bristles (see GLOCHID). For cactus culture and uses see CACTI.

CACTI. (Plural of cactus.) Most of the cacti native in our southwestern states and in adjacent Mexico are adapted to outdoor cul-

ture in regions where the conditions approximate their own — a low annual rainfall and extremely warm summer temperature. While there are a few hardy sorts, most cacti will not stand much frost, which perhaps explains why only a single wild prickly pear (Opuntia) is native in the northeastern states, and it does not grow much above Cape Cod along the coast. And in all the area east of the 100th meridian and north of Va., there are very few wild species of cacti, all the rest of the U.S. species growing in desert and semi-desert regions, most of which have an annual rainfall of 12 in. or less, sometimes much less, and little of which falls in the winter.

The outdoor culture of most cacti must therefore be confined to these regions of deficient rainfall and summer heat, areas where slush, sleet, fog, and other evidence of winter moisture are lacking. Some hardy collections are kept outdoors by providing a wooden roof to keep off snow and rain, even as far north as Mich. Among the hardiest for outdoor culture up to zone* 4, or even in favorable sites in the southern part of zone* 3, are Opuntia compressa, O. polyacantha, and Pediocactus simpsoni.

OUTDOOR CACTUS GARDEN

Assuming you live within the climatic restrictions as outlined above (see the name of your state for rainfall and frost data), it is not difficult to have an outdoor cactus garden. In it one can grow scores of species from small, button-like plants to the huge, barrel-like or cylindric ones, or even the giant cactus (Carnegiea) if you have the space.

For most of the small kinds it is better to grow them in pots, using potting mixture* 6, and plunge* the pots in the prepared bed. The larger ones had better be planted directly in the bed in a soil mixture approximating potting mixture* 6.

Whether the pots are plunged or the cacti planted in the bed, it is essential that proper drainage be provided. If the local soil is rocky or gravelly, there will be no trouble about this. But if it tends to hold water, dig out to a depth of at least 2½ ft. Fill in about 6 in. of broken stone, cinders or gravel. When this is settled, the rest of the bed should be filled up to the top with the soil that approximates potting mixture* 6, especially if cacti are to be planted directly in it.

Many growers limit their collections to plants that are best grown in pots. Most of the small cacti are easier handled in pots, and these may be plunged so that no pots show. If your cactus collection is only of these potted specimens, the bed for plunging may be filled with sand instead of potting mixture* 6, but the underdrainage is necessary in any case.

What you grow will depend a little upon the region in which you live. If winter rains or spring humidity are even moderate, you should not attempt many genera, especially tropical sorts.

Over much of the outdoor cactus country,

---

* Special articles on the subjects indicated by an asterisk (*) will be found at the words so marked.

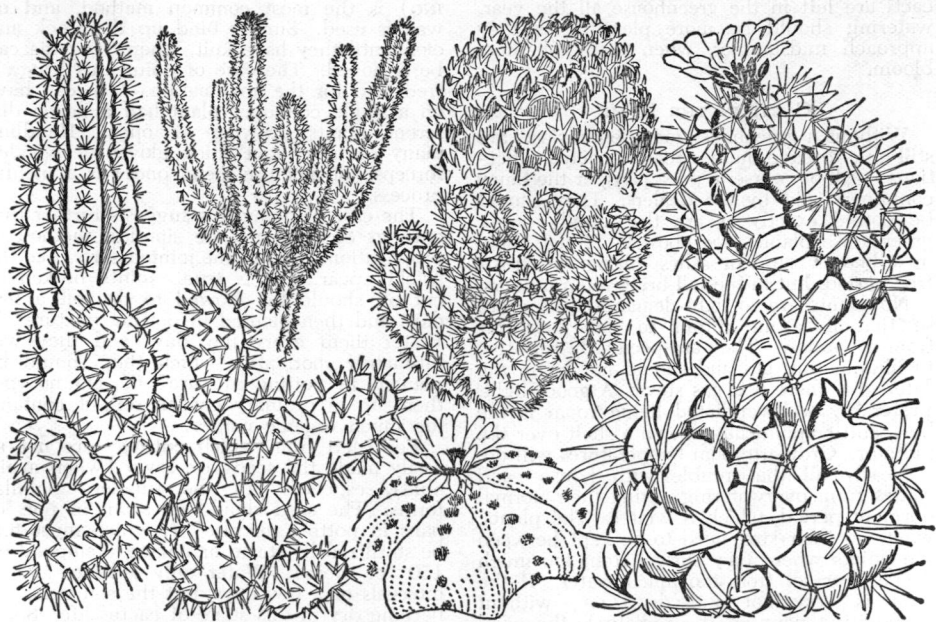

Decorative types of Cacti. Top row (*left to right*): *Pachycereus, Cephalocereus, Mammillaria, Thelocactus.* Bottom row (*left to right*): *Opuntia, Astrophytum, Echinocactus*
The plant in the middle is *Echinocereus.*

however, you can grow at least some species in the genera *Opuntia, Cereus, Cephalocereus, Echinocactus, Echinocereus, Selenicereus, Coryphantha, Melocactus, Astrophytum, Ariocarpus, Roseocactus,* and others. See CACTACEAE for the different genera of this family.

With such a beginning one can get the most grotesque and fantastic effects. Some creep, others climb, some look like burnt buttons, others like a Turk's-head, and there is often a bewildering array of colors in their flowers.

With some genera, notably in the taller forms of *Cereus* and its allies, desert landscapes can be made, with a mixture of ocotillo and *Agave,* neither of which are cacti but are often mistaken for them.

Such an outdoor cactus garden, and some of them in southern Calif., Ariz., and N. Mex. are very extensive and elaborate, needs no water except rainfall if it is in a natural cactus region. In fact a very successful one can be made by collecting the wild plants of such a region. But dealers usually have better plants and, of course, far more species than can be found in any one locality.

Many who do not live in the preferred region for outdoor cactus-growing still insist on having a cactus garden. And this can be done if all plants are grown in pots and plunged in sand as outlined above. But during rainy winter months such plants must be brought into a greenhouse or at least into the living room, which brings us to these features of cacti-growing.

GREENHOUSE CULTURE

Really tropical genera and the plunged specimens needing winter protection are best grown in the greenhouse, which should not go below 50° nor much above 75°. It is not primarily heat that one wants from a cactus greenhouse, but dryness of atmosphere and plenty of fresh air.

Cacti will not stand humidity, and water at their roots. All potted specimens, therefore, should be planted in potting mixture° 6, and have plenty of drainage in the bottom of the pot or tub.

Some growers prefer to plunge the pots in a bed of ashes or sand even in the greenhouse, but this is not necessary if conditions make it difficult. The one thing that the plants need is water in very limited amounts during the dark days of winter. A moderate watering once a week in the winter is all that most of the genera need in the greenhouse. They are all but dormant then, and growth is never very rapid in any of the cacti. If overwatered, no plants will rot so quickly, especially plunged specimens.

As spring approaches and growth is likely to start, the watering can be more frequent and copious, but never forget that you are dealing with a desert plant to which wet feet mean death if continued too long. If the

° Special articles on the subjects indicated by an asterisk (°) will be found at the words so marked.

cacti are left in the greenhouse all the year, watering should be more plentiful as they approach midsummer, when many of them bloom.

Cacti in the Home

Without a greenhouse many enthusiasts are still able to have quite extensive cactus collections — all of course in pots, pans, or the fancy containers sold by the dealers. They should be potted exactly as are the usually larger greenhouse plants (*see* above). Plunge them in a bed of sand or ashes during the frost-free period, but in the fall bring them indoors.

No plants are so light-demanding as cacti, so that it is an affront to put them far from a window. They are peculiarly sensitive to illuminating gas and should not be in the kitchen if there is a gas stove. A good, light, preferably well-ventilated living room is the best, and emphatically not on a shelf over the radiator. Ordinary room temperatures will do.

Nearly all the trouble with house cacti comes from overwatering during their normal dormant period, which is winter. The plants, whatever their size, need to be kept between the points where they shrivel from too much dryness, or rot from too much water. If the room is very hot and dry (*i.e.*, without evaporating pans on the radiator), the cacti will stand more water than in a relatively cool or moister room. No absolute guide can be given. But if planted in the proper mixture and with adequate drainage, they should not need watering more than every six or eight days. And some kinds will last three weeks or more without water.

This does not apply to the genera *Epiphyllum* and *Zygocactus,* long favorite house plants under the name of Christmas or crab cactus. These plants need more water and should be planted in potting mixture* 5. These, too, should be plunged outdoors in summer.

Most of the successful cacti for house culture, especially those suitable for the attractive, miniature desert gardens and for centerpieces, are found in the genera *Ariocarpus, Astrophytum,* and *Mammillaria,* or in the juvenile states of otherwise much larger plants in the genera *Echinocactus, Melocactus, Ferocactus,* and many others. With these, especially in the prepared dishes of the florists, there are often other plants (not cacti) of the genera *Echeveria, Gasteria, Cotyledon,* and especially *Stapelia. See* Succulents.

Propagation and Grafting

Many growers, particularly in the Southwest, have made some of the cacti still more grotesque by grafting structurally different plants upon one another. Unlike most plants, quite unrelated genera can be so united. While the practice started as a fad or stunt, it is now widely done by fanciers and has produced some remarkable results.

The method is perfectly easy, for the joined tissue seems to knit more easily than in most plants. Cleft grafting (*see* Graft-ing) is the most common method, and no wax is used. Simply bind up the stock and cion until they have knit, when the raffia can be removed. The ease of doing this leaves a free field for the imagination. One can have on a single columnar plant half a dozen different plants growing at once. Handling many cacti without thick gloves or wooden forceps (do not use metal ones) is a painful process.

The ease of doing this suggests further that cuttings of cacti are the simplest method of propagation. For all the jointed sorts, like the prickly pear, this is true. Joints broken or cut off should be allowed to dry off a few days and then planted in potting mixture* 1. Water them every few days and they will ultimately root, after which they should be planted in potting mixture* 6. Do not pot them up in ordinary garden soil; it contains too much organic matter.

For cacti from which cuttings are not so easily made the seeds are sown (when available), especially of the smaller, globular forms. The seed should be sown in pots or pans in potting mixture* 1, which must first be sterilized by steam or baking (temperature 150° or more). Water only a little, and at intervals of a few days, but the soil must not become dry in this stage of cactus life. Some sorts will not germinate for months, others in a few days. It is well to sterilize all cacti seeds with Semesan before planting.

When the seedlings are well up, they should be put in pots only just large enough for them, using potting mixture* 6.

The popularity of these plants is so great that there are now many cactus societies whose members exchange specimens and cultural notes. The best known is the Cactus and Succulent Society, 132 W. Union Street, Pasadena, Calif.

Diseases. Cacti grown in the home or greenhouse are relatively free from disease unless plants are overwatered and may then be subjct to various root and stem rots. In warmer areas where cacti grow naturally, the crown gall* may be observed. These large, spongy masses should be cut from the plants.

The giant cactus in Arizona is subject to a serious disease known as bacterial necrosis. Some of the earliest work with the antibiotic*, penicillin, injected into the plants has given promising control.

CACTUS. *See* Melocactus.

CACTUS DAHLIA. *See* Dahlia.

CACTUS FAMILY = Cactaceae.

CACTUS GERANIUM = *Pelargonium echinatum.*

CACTUS SPOON. *See* Dasylirion wheeleri.

caerulea. Dark blue.

CAESALPINIA (see-zal-pin′i-a). A genus of important tropical shrubs and trees of the pea family, not one of which is of much garden interest. One of them is the source of brazil-wood. The name *Caesalpinia,* however, is often incorrectly applied to the fol-

---

* Special articles on the subjects indicated by an asterisk (*) will be found at the words so marked.

lowing cult. trees and shrubs. See their correct names for a description of them:

Caesalpinia gillesi = Poinciana gillesi.
Caesalpinia pulcherrima = Poinciana pulcherrima.
Caesalpinia regia = Delonix regia.

CAESALPINIACEAE. See LEGUMINOSAE.

caesia, -us, -um (see'si-a). Bluish-green (glaucous).

caespitosa, -us, -um (sess-pi-tō'sa). Cespitose; i.e., tufted and forming dense, turf-like clumps or mats.

Caffra. Native South African name for the kei-apple (Dovyalis Caffra).

caffrorum (caff-ror'um). Pertaining or relating to the Kafirs of South Africa.

CAHIOTA = Sechium edule.

Cainoto. West Indian vernacular for the star-apple (Chrysophyllum Cainito).

CAIOPHORA (ky-off'o-ra). A large genus of often climbing, South American herbs, family Loasaceae, only one of secondary garden interest, and beset with stinging hairs. Leaves opposite.* Flowers regular,* but the petals hooded, very showy. Alternating with the petals are 5 scale-like, sterile stamens*; the fertile stamens numerous. Fruit a spirally twisted pod which splits along its valves but is closed at the top. (Caiophora is Greek for burn-bearing, from the stinging hairs.)

The plant below should be treated as a tender annual. See ANNUALS.

lateritia. An annual, climbing vine 10–15 ft. long. Leaves long-stalked, deeply cut, the segments toothed or lobed, 1–3 in. long. Flowers about 1½ in. long, the petals orange-red, the scale-like, sterile stamens greenish-yellow, the flower long-stalked. Fruit 2–3 in. long.

Cajan. A specific name adapted from a Sudanese vernacular for the pigeon pea (Cajanus Cajan).

CAJANUS (kay-jay'nus). A single tropical shrub of the pea family widely cultivated throughout the tropics for its edible seeds. It has compound leaves,* with 3 leaflets that are resinous-dotted beneath. Flowers typically pea-like, in clusters (racemes*) borne in the leaf axils.* Fruit a compressed pod (legume*) with diagonal depressions, the seeds nearly round. (See CAJAN for origin of name.)

The pigeon pea is somewhat grown outdoors in extreme southern Fla. It is also occasionally grown as an annual in the greenhouse for its showy flowers.

Cajan. Pigeon pea. A much-branched, hairy shrub 5–8 ft. high. Leaflets narrowly lance-shaped, about 3 in. long, hairy on both sides. Flowers orange-yellow, brownish on the back or otherwise irregularly colored. Pod about 2½ in. long, its seeds brown with a white "eye," about ¼ in. in diameter. Probably Old World tropics.

CAJEPUT. See CAJUPUT-TREE.

CAJUPUT-TREE = Melaleuca Leucadendron.

Caluba. South American native name for Calophyllum antillanum.

CALABASH. The name calabash is applied to two or more unrelated plants. One is the gourd Lagenaria siceraria (which see), from which calabash pipes are made. The other is a tropical tree of the genus Crescentia (kressen'tee-a), family Bignoniaceae, which bears the huge fruits so widely used for dippers and utensils, and is somewhat grown in Fla. Of the 5 known species, all tropical American, the only cult. one is the calabash tree, Crescentia Cujete, which grows from 25–50 ft. high. It has broad leaves 4–6 in. long, mostly borne in clusters. Flowers solitary, hanging, yellowish but red or purple-striped, tubular. Fruit a hard-rinded berry, more or less oval, or round in some trees, from 6 in. in diameter to 20 in. long. The dried rind is watertight and the split shell has many uses. Hardy outdoors only in zone* 9. (Named for Pietro Crescenzi, an Italian.)

CALABASH GOURD = Lagenaria siceraria.

CALABAZILLA = Cucurbita foetidissima.

CALABRESE = Brassica oleracea italica. For culture see BROCCOLI.

calabrica, -us, -um (ka-lab'ri-ka). From Calabria, Italy.

CALACINUM = MUEHLENBECKIA.

CALADIUM (ka-lay'di-um). An important genus of greenhouse foliage plants widely cult. for their beautifully colored leaves, usually under the gardener's name of fancy-leaved caladiums. Of the 12 or 14 species, all tropical American and belonging to the family Araceae, two are widely known greenhouse subjects. They have thin leaves, the stalk of which (in ours) is joined to, or near, the middle of the blade, not to the base. Leaves variously colored, not usually green, more or less arrowhead-shaped. The flowers (for characters see ARACEAE) and white, berry-like fruit are seldom produced in the greenhouse except by breeders. (Caladium is from a Malay word for a related plant that is not now included in the genus Caladium.)

Caladiums, properly grown, are among our most gorgeously colored foliage plants. They are tuberous-rooted herbs, at home in tropical rain-forests. They, therefore, need heat, moisture and plenty of rich soil. For summer bedding, for which they are very popular, start the tubers in flats, in chopped moss, covering them about one inch. Keep the moss moist and maintain a greenhouse temperature between 75° and 85°. When the tubers have rooted in the moss, remove and pot up each (depending on its size) in a pot only just large enough. Use potting mixture* 2. When they have started good growth, they should be shifted to larger pots, but kept relatively pot-bound; use potting mixture* 3. Keep the temperature 75° or more, and the plants should be as near the glass of the greenhouse as possible. Shade the glass (see SHADING) or the leaves will burn. The air

* Special articles on the subjects indicated by an asterisk (*) will be found at the words so marked.

should be moist at all times, and frequent wetting-down of floors and the benches is advisable. The plants should also be fed with liquid manure every two weeks.

There are perhaps dozens of named hort. forms of caladiums, but the names and identities are in such confusion that there can be no attempt to list them here. Most of them seem to be derived from the following two species, although they are sometimes listed as *Colocasia.*

bicolor. The commonest sort in greenhouses. Leaves ovalish, colored above in various patterns, but bluish-green or metallic beneath, the leafstalk at least 4 times longer than the blade. Tropical America.

esculentum = *Colocasia esculenta.*

picturatum. Leaves more or less lance-shaped, variously colored above but paler beneath. Leafstalks shorter than in *C. bicolor* and variegated. Peru and Brazil.

CALAMINTHA ALPINA = *Satureia alpina.* See SAVORY.

CALAMONDIN ORANGE = *Citrus mitis.*

Calamus (kal′a-mus). A specific name derived from the genus *Calamus* or rattan palms, which are little known to gardeners. Originally the word was from the Latin for reed. See ACORUS.

CALAMUS-ROOT. See ACORUS CALAMUS.

CALANDRINIA (kal-an-drin′i-a). A rather large genus of somewhat fleshy herbs, family Portulacaceae, found in western N.A. and S.A. and of secondary garden interest, although two are grown as annuals. They are commonly called rock purslane in Calif. Leaves alternate* or basal. Flowers somewhat ephemeral, in bracted clusters (racemes*). Petals 3–7, rose-pink or red. Sepals 2 and persistent. Fruit a globe-shaped pod (capsule*) with numerous seeds. (Named for J. L. Calandrini, Geneva botanist.)

The plants are of easy culture if treated as hardy annuals. See ANNUALS.

ciliata menziesi. Red maids. More or less sprawling and 1–2 ft. high. Leaves narrow, not over 2 in. long. Flowers about ½ in. long, rose or crimson. Western U.S. The plant is also called *C. menziesi* and *C. speciosa.* It is not much grown.

grandiflora. A perennial, but grown as an annual and the best-known one in cult. More or less erect and 12–18 in. high. Leaves ovalish, 5–7 in. long. Flowers rose-pink or purplish. Chile.

menziesi. *Calandrinia ciliata menziesi.*

speciosa = *Calandrinia ciliata menziesi.*

umbellata. A perennial, but treated as an annual not over 6 in. high. Leaves all basal and very narrow. Flowers red or crimson-magenta. Peru.

CALANTHE (ka-lan′the). A large genus of mostly tropical orchids, one of which is a favorite greenhouse plant in which the large plaited leaves appear after the showy flowers have passed. In the one below there are pseudobulbs* that are grayish and angled, from which spring a few stalked, plaited leaves. The flowers are borne on a long, hairy and bracted* stalk. Flowers very

showy, yellowish-white in the one below, the petals and sepals similar, but the lip clawed,* flat and lobed. (*Calanthe* is Greek for beautiful flower.) Several Japanese species are hardy outdoors in that country.

vestita. Leaves 18–24 in. long, broadly lance-shaped, the pseudobulbs* 3–5 in. long. Flowering stalk 18–30 in. long, its bracts* conspicuous. Flowers 2–3 in. wide, borne in 6–10-flowered racemes. Petals and sepals cream-white, the lip yellow-orange. Malaya. Blooms in midwinter in the greenhouse.

For culture *see* ORCHID.

CALATHEA (kal-a-thee′a). A genus of over 100 species of handsome foliage plants, family Marantaceae, mostly tropical American, but a few in tropical Africa. The cult. species below are favorite greenhouse plants which suggest, in their finely marked and colored foliage, the fancy-leaved *Caladium,* which, however, belongs to a different family. They differ from *Caladium* in having thicker leaves in which the stalk joins the base of the blade instead of the middle of it, as in *Caladium.* In those below, the leaves are mostly basal and relatively long-stalked, barred, mottled, or striped in various colors, often with a metallic sheen. Flowers (seldom produced in cult. foliage specimens) in cone-like, bracted* clusters among the leaves, not showy. (*Calathea* is from the Greek for basket, in allusion to the basket-like flower cluster.)

The greenhouse cultural requirements are the same as for *Caladium* (which see). In some parts of zone* 8 and in all of zone* 9 *Calathea* can be grown outdoors in rich, moist soil. They should be cut back to the ground and heavily mulched with well-rotted manure. They are gross feeders, and without it their finest coloring cannot be produced. The plants are sometimes offered as *Maranta,* a close relative.

bicolor = *Maranta bicolor.*

leitzi. A slender foliage plant, often sending up erect runners that produce young plantlets. Leaf-blade about 6 in. long, slightly inequilateral, purplish beneath, white banded above, the leafstalk 8–10 in. long. Brazil.

makoyana. A handsome plant 2–3½ ft. high. Leaves broadly oblong, more or less blunt and generally olive-green above, but blotched or ribbed with darker green. The under side is red, but patterned, as is the upper surface. Brazil.

ornata. One of the best-known cult. species, often offered as *Calathea sanderiana.* Stout, compact plant 18–36 in. high. Leaves generally elliptic, but heart-shaped at the base, 12–24 in. long, in maturity plain green above, purple-red beneath. In young or juvenile states (often sold) the leaves are handsomely striped between the veins with pink or white. Northern S.A., but offered in many hort. forms and under a variety of names.

roseo-picta. Small plant not over 8 in. high. Leaves nearly round, about 6 in. long, dark green, but red-ribbed and red-blotched near the margin above, purplish beneath. Brazil. Sometimes mistaken for and offered as *Maranta bicolor.*

---

* Special articles on the subjects indicated by an asterisk (*) will be found at the words so marked.

sanderiana. Mostly forms of *Calathea ornata.*
vittata. Dwarf or rarely up to 3 ft. Leaves lance-elliptic, 8–10 in. long, pointed, light green, but with cross-bands of white on the upper side, green and tinted yellowish-green beneath. Brazil.
zebrina. The zebra-plant and the commonest species in cult. Not over 3 ft., usually less, and of compact habit. Leaves bluntish, more or less elliptic, 12–20 in. long, about half as wide. The upper side is generally velvety green, but from the midrib the side veins are alternately barred with pale yellow-green and much darker green. The lower leaf surface, purplish-red. Brazil.

calathina, -us, -um (kal-a-thy′na). Like a basket.

calcarata, -us, -um (kal-ka-ray′ta). Having a spur.

calcarea, -us, -um (kal-care′ee-a). Pertaining to lime.

CALCEOLARIA (kal-see-o-lay′ri-a). A very large genus of tropical American herbs or shrubby plants of the figwort family and collectively called slipperworts from the slipper-shaped, showy flowers. *Calceolaria crenatiflora* is a very popular florists' flower, and the other two cult. species are occasionally grown. Leaves opposite* or in whorls.* Flowers in irregular, often 1-sided clusters, generally yellow, but often spotted with orange-brown. Corolla very irregular* and 2-lipped, the upper lip small, the lower one large, inflated, and slipper-like. Stamens 2. Fruit a capsule,* splitting at the top. (Name from *calceolus*, Latin for slipper.)
For culture *see* below.

crenatiflora. The usual slipperwort of the florists. An herb 1–2 ft. high, bushy and softly hairy throughout. Leaves simple,* broadly oval, the lower ones 4–7 in. long, the upper ones smaller and stalkless. Flowers about ¾ in. long, yellow, but spotted orange-brown, the large lower lip wavy or fluted. Chile. There are several hort. forms, variously colored. Sometimes called *C. hybrida.*
hyrida = *Calceolaria crenatiflora.*
integrifolia. Shrubby or actually woody and 2–5 ft. high, usually sticky. Leaves simple,* oblong-oval, 1–3 in. long, rough, the margins with wavy teeth. Flowers about ⅓ in. long, yellowish to red-brown, but not spotted. Chile. Rather common in cult. and sometimes used as a summer bedding plant. There are several named forms, some of them hybrids.
scabiosaefolia. An annual herb 1–2 ft. high, the leaves deeply cut or even compound, 5–8 in. long, the base of the leafstalks practically surrounding the stem. Flowers numerous, not over ½ in. long, pale yellow. Chile to Ecuador. Less grown than the other two.

CALCEOLARIA CULTURE

Calceolarias are a very popular florists' flower. Grown from seed, they require careful attention from the time the seed is sown until ready to flower. Seed should be sown in May, and being very small, care must be taken not to bury it in the soil. Potting mixture* 1 finely sifted may be used. Fill the pot or pan two-thirds full of roughage from the sifted soil in which you sow the seed,

and this will give perfect drainage; press it down firmly, fill the pot level with the finely sifted soil, press this gently, particularly around the edge, finishing as level as possible 1 in. below the rim. Should the soil be dry, water with a fine spray and defer sowing until the next day.

Open the seed packet carefully and pour contents on a sheet of white paper, then sow evenly over the surface; no covering of soil will be necessary. Place seed pan up near the light and cover with a sheet of glass. When germination takes place give a little air and encourage the seedlings to grow as sturdy as possible, and as they develop remove glass, always allowing a free circulation of air; avoid direct sunlight at all times. When the plants are large enough to handle, prick off into other pots, pans or flats, using a pointed stick for this purpose. Pot singly when the plants touch each other, using small pots and after the first shift use potting mixture* 4 and pot more firmly.

Slipperwort (*Calceolaria crenatiflora*), a common, very beautiful yellow-flowered, orange-spotted plant from Chile, needing greenhouse culture.

Do not allow the plants to become pot-bound, but as soon as the roots form a network around the pot, shift into a larger size; good plants can be grown in 6-in. pots, but if extra-large specimens are desired an 8-in. may be used for the final potting, which should be completed by Nov. A temperature of 45°–50° should be maintained, and good plants may be grown in cold frames, if kept properly shaded from direct sunlight (a northern aspect being preferable) and given plenty of air, but cold drafts should be avoided. During winter keep on the dry side, but never allow the plants to suffer for want of water, and use as little artificial heat as possible; never allow water to touch the flowers, as they spot very easily.

When the flower spikes appear, liquid fer-

---

* Special articles on the subjects indicated by an asterisk (*) will be found at the words so marked.

tilizer is advisable to feed the mass of fine roots with which the pot should now be filled and to increase the size of the flowers. Neat stakes may be needed to support the flowers, but use as few as possible.

When the plants are mature and ready to flower, plenty of room should be allowed for them to develop into shapely specimens.

The shrubby varieties are not popular, but the Kelway hybrids make very satisfactory pot plants, and the same treatment applies to all varieties. Give plenty of air, keep clean and water carefully.

INSECT PESTS. Control red spiders with pesticide #21 (see SPRAYS AND DUSTS) or #14. See CELERY for leaf tier control.

CALCIFUGE. Plants intolerant of lime, *i.e.*, most plants of the heath family.

CALCIPHILE = Lime-tolerant.

CALCIPHOBE = Calcifuge.

CALCIUM. See LIME.

CALCIUM ARSENATE. A highly poisonous pinkish powder (so colored) used in dusts and sprays. Ready-to-use formulations of this stomach poison are available for control of chewing insects. This mixture is toxic to many plants (see INSECTICIDES) and is now somewhat obsolete.

CALENDULA (ka-len'dew-la). A genus of 20 species of herbs of the family Compositae, chiefly from the Mediterranean region. Only one is of much garden interest, the pot marigold, but it has been cult. for centuries as a popular annual. Unlike other plants known as marigold (which see), the pot marigold has undivided and not strong-smelling leaves, which are alternate,* simple, and faintly toothed. Flower heads large, the rays yellow or orange in the typical forms. (From Latin *calends*, throughout the months, alluding to the long blooming period.)

The pot marigold is one of the most popular of tender annuals (which *see* at ANNUALS for culture). Through breeding and long culture there are many varieties with innumerable shades from whitish-yellow to deep orange. The plant can also be grown for winter bloom in the greenhouse, and outdoors in warm regions. Sow the seeds in pans in August and pot up the seedlings before frost. Grow in a cool greenhouse and by dis-budding the remaining flower heads may be 4 in. wide. See Pinching at TRAINING PLANTS.

officinalis. Pot marigold. A tender annual 12–20 in. high. Leaves oblongish, 2–3 in. long, more or less stem-clasping. Flower heads solitary, stalked, 1–2 in. wide, the day-blooming and night-closing rays usually flattish and or-ange-yellow. Southern Eu. June to frost. Comes in many hort. named forms. Very good for cutting, as the flower heads are lasting.

DISEASES. The calendula is subject to the virus disease known as yellows.* For description and control, see CALLISTEPHUS.

calendulacea, -us, -um (ka-len-dew-lay'-see-a). Like a marigold (*Calendula*) in its brilliant color. See AZALEA.

CALICHE. The crusty layers of soil, impregnated with calcium carbonate, which overlie the stony or sandy soils in arid regions of the southwestern states. Unless broken up, these caliche layers make cultivation of deep-rooted plants almost impossible.

CALICO-BUSH = *Kalmia latifolia.*

CALICO-FLOWER = *Aristolochia elegans.*

CALIFORNIA. As an adjective California is used to designate many plants that grow in that and neighboring states. The ones of garden interest in this book are:

California barberry = *Mahonia pinnata;* California bleeding-heart = *Dicentra formosa;* California bluebell = *Phacelia campanularia* and *P. whitlavia;* California dandelion = *Hypochaeris radicata* (see Cat's-Ear at list of WEEDS); California fan palm = *Washingtonia robusta;* California fuchsia = *Zauschneria californica;* California gold fern = *Pityrogramma triangularis;* California holly (see TOYON); California laurel = *Umbellularia californica;* California lilac = *Ceanothus thyrsiflorus;* California live oak = *Quercus agrifolia* (see OAK); California nutmeg = *Torreya californica;* California pepper tree = *Schinus molle;* California phlox (see GILIA DENSIFLORA); California pitcher-plant = *Darlingtonia californica;* California poppy = *Eschscholtzia californica;* California privet = *Ligustrum ovalifolium* (see PRIVET); California redwood = *Sequoia sempervirens;* California rose = *Convolvulus japonicus;* California scrub oak = *Quercus dumosa* (see OAK); California tree poppy = *Romneya coulteri;* California walnut = *Juglans californica* (see WALNUT); California white oak = *Quercus lobata* (see OAK).

CALIFORNIA. The California poppy is the state flower, and the redwood the state tree. The state lies wholly in zones* 4, 5, 6, 7 and 8, which, instead of running east and west as in most parts of America, run approximately north and south, due to the proximity of high mountains and the Japanese current which flows along the California coast.

SOILS. The soils of California are exceedingly variable in all characteristics, and soils of markedly different value may occur in any given tract of land. Textures range from the fine-textured clays to coarse sands. Some soils vary from high-quality pervious soils to dense claypans and hardpans. A few soils are acid. Many more soils contain sufficient alkali to injure plants, while the great bulk of soils are intermediate or neutral in their reaction and may be expected to give satisfactory results for many crops when properly managed. Every piece of California farm land requires individual examination to determine the actual character and condition of the soils. General statements cannot be made that will apply to any extensive area.

CHIEF GARDEN CENTERS. The oldest garden centers in California are to be found in fertile valleys along the coast from San Diego County northward. Mission San Diego was founded in 1769, and in time 21 Spanish missions were established, extending as far north as Sonoma County. The mission grounds served as demonstration plots where the first American settlers observed the apple,

* Special articles on the subjects indicated by an asterisk (*) will be found at the words so marked.

apricot, fig, grape, peach, pear, olive, almond, walnut, and orange, also such vegetables as peas and beans. Horticulture still flourishes near old missions at San Diego, San Gabriel, Los Angeles, Ventura, Santa Barbara, Santa Ynez, Lompoc, San Luis Obispo, Monterey, Mission San José, Santa Clara and Sonoma.

Several noteworthy contributions to the horticulture of California were made shortly after the Gold Rush of 1849. One of these was the introduction of eucalyptus trees from Australia, which has altered permanently the skyline of the older settled regions of California.

As transportation and irrigation facilities improved, such cities as Pomona, Riverside, Redlands, San Bernardino, Indio, El Centro, Bakersfield, Fresno, Porterville, Merced, Modesto, Stockton, Sacramento, Napa, Santa Rosa, Eureka, Woodland, Marysville, Chico, Red Bluff, and Redding became the centers of thriving horticultural communities. Special impetus was also given to fruit-growing by the early distribution of grafted trees from such counties as Alameda, Contra Costa, Sacramento, Napa, and San Francisco. At the same time early settlers in many districts were growing and testing seedling trees which in time gave rise to many standard varieties of the present day.

While the first Spanish missionaries brought in flower seeds to plant around the missions, the more important ornamentals have been distributed more recently from such cities as San Francisco, Santa Barbara, Santa Monica, Los Angeles, Pasadena, and San Diego where even the tenderest plants could be carefully tested. Nurserymen living outside of the larger cities have also assisted in distributing ornamentals as well as many excellent fruit varieties. Other centers of distribution include some of the city parks, such as Golden Gate Park of San Francisco, and the California Agricultural Experiment Station at Berkeley which began to test and distribute fruits, vegetables, and flowers before 1880. More recently the wholesale seed growers in such counties as Santa Barbara, Los Angeles, Monterey, and Sacramento have supplied a good part of the world's seed requirements and have been centers of garden interest where the latest introductions could be seen under test. Similarly, large nurseries have continued to test and distribute the best the world has to offer.

Since early days the residents of San Francisco, San Mateo, Palo Alto, Berkeley, Oakland, Santa Barbara, Los Angeles, San Diego, and many other cities have brought in seeds and plants from other parts of the world where growing conditions were similar to those found in California. Australia, China, Japan, India, and South Africa as well as the Mediterranean countries have supplied a wealth of plant material which is at home in the mild, semi-arid climate of California which is quite similar to the Mediterranean region in that rainfall comes mostly in the winter months. The United States Department of Agriculture has distributed many new plants to California co-operators. Future introductions will likely continue to come from these other countries rather than from other parts of the United States where climate and other environmental factors are so different.

CROPS FOR THE MAIN FRUIT AREAS. A total of 39 kinds of fruits and nuts is listed for California in the last United States census. This list includes the hardy deciduous fruits, sub-tropical fruits, nuts and the small fruits. Leading nurserymen in the state list over 50 kinds of fruits.

California may be divided into six horticultural areas based largely on climate and other conditions affecting the growth of crops. These divisions are more or less arbitrary, and yet the number of growing days within each of the districts is similar. High mountain or desert areas and areas subject to floods are omitted from consideration. Extremes of heat and cold, rainfall, humidity, and winds should be considered in connection with climate. It should also be remem-

CALIFORNIA

The zones of hardiness crossing California are those shown on the map located at ZONE, which should be consulted for details. The dates are the average latest killing frost in spring and the first one in the fall. The figures below the dates show the average length of the growing season. The figures scattered over the map show the total annual average rainfall in inches in the different regions of the state. In a region of such climatic diversity as California it should be understood that the map is valid only in broad outline. Local conditions of micro-climate often affect plant growth, especially exposure, wind, fog, and the amount and duration of sun and shade.

* Special articles on the subjects indicated by an asterisk (*) will be found at the words so marked.

bered that climate is only one of several factors which control plant growth. The nature of the soil, soil moisture, and topography may be involved within a particular area. A site involving an excessive expenditure might not be suitable, regardless of what crops it would grow. The following lists will give some idea of what crops are important in the six areas here defined. (1) *North Coast,* extending from Marin County on the south, northward to the state line and including Napa and Lake counties; (2) *Sacramento Valley,* bounded on the south by Solano County, the state line on the north, and the mountains on the east; (3) the *Central Valley,* bordered by the counties of Stanislaus, Tuolumne, Amador, and San Joaquin; (4) *Central Coast,* extending from San Mateo County south to San Luis Obispo County and inland through the counties of Alameda, Santa Clara, and San Benito; (5) *San Joaquin Valley,* extending from Merced County on the north to and including Kern County on the south; (6) *Southern California,* which includes the eight counties below the districts described above.

In southern California (district 6) there are two types of desert which are becoming increasingly important, both for agricultural and industrial production, and since the population is increasing in both, there is considerable interest in amateur gardening. The low-elevation deserts of southern California are Death Valley and the Borego, Imperial, and Coachella valleys. There is also a large area of the medium-elevation desert in the great Mojave Desert. Some sections, such as Antelope Valley and Apple Valley, are rapidly becoming used as resort areas or for the manufacture of airplanes. There is a little deciduous fruit production in the medium-elevation desert, but outside of alfalfa and corn, there is not much other agricultural production. The low-elevation deserts produce dates, grapefruit, table grapes, and a wide variety of off-season vegetables.

Fruits for the Leading Horticultural Districts. (The more important kinds listed first — county name mentioned for limited area.)
North Coast. Apples, cherries, grapes, pears, prunes, walnuts, plums, and small fruits such as blackberries, loganberries, strawberries, and gooseberries.
Sacramento Valley. Peaches, plums, almonds, cherries, olives, pears, apricots, figs, grapes, citrus (Butte, Glenn, and Sacramento counties), prunes, walnuts, jujubes, persimmons, and strawberries.
Central Valley. Cherries, grapes, peaches, almonds, apples, apricots, plums, figs, olives, pears, prunes, walnuts, bush fruits, and strawberries.
Central Coast. Almonds, apples, apricots, prunes, cherries, pears, walnuts, grapes, plums, figs, peaches, prickly pears (Santa Clara County), bush fruits, and strawberries.
San Joaquin Valley. Figs, grapes, olives, peaches, citrus fruits (Tulare and Fresno county districts), apricots, plums, apples (mountain valleys), pears, prunes, persimmons, pomegranates, walnuts, bush fruits, and strawberries.
Southern California. Avocados, lemons, oranges, pomelos (grapefruit), walnuts, grapes, peaches, cherries (Riverside and San Bernardino counties), olives, almonds, apricots, pears, figs, plums, prunes, pecans, bush fruits, strawberries, and miscellaneous sub-tropical fruits such as prickly pear and passion fruit (San Diego County), guavas, loquats, persimmons, pomegranates, and dates (Coachella and Imperial valleys).

CROPS FOR THE MAIN VEGETABLE AREAS. About 50 kinds of vegetables are listed in the ordinary seed catalogues, but the United States census enumerates only 32 kinds of California vegetables as being important commercially. Most of these vegetables can be grown at some season of the year in practically all California gardens, although extremes of temperature and moisture may limit the choice or season of certain vegetables such as lettuce, globe artichokes, beans, peas, and squashes. Vegetables grown extensively in the different districts are mentioned below.

Vegetables for the Leading Horticultural Districts.
North Coast. Artichokes (Marin County), green beans, sweet corn, green peas, tomatoes, carrots, parsnips, potatoes, squashes, turnips.
Sacramento Valley. Asparagus (delta region), onions, cabbage, cucumbers, spinach, tomatoes, green beans, sweet corn, lettuce, lima beans, carrots, green peas, sweet potatoes, beets.
Central Valley. Celery (delta region), sweet potatoes, cantaloupes, onions, spinach, tomatoes, watermelons, green beans, cabbage, carrots, parsnips, sweet corn, garlic, lettuce, potatoes, green peas, squashes, beets.
Central Coast. Artichokes, lettuce, cabbage, garlic, spinach, carrots, cauliflower, broccoli, Brussels sprouts, sweet corn, cucumbers, green peas, peppers, tomatoes, green beans, rhubarb, lima beans, beets, cantaloupes, celery, potatoes, onions, squashes.
San Joaquin Valley. Sweet potatoes, onions, potatoes, watermelons, green beans, lima beans, cantaloupes, cucumbers, garlic, asparagus, carrots, parsnips, cauliflower, sweet corn, beets, lettuce, green peas, peppers, tomatoes, squashes.
Southern California. Green beans, lima beans, cantaloupes, carrots, parsnips, cauliflower, broccoli, Brussels sprouts, cabbage, celery, sweet corn, cucumbers, lettuce, peppers, watermelons, onions, green peas, rhubarb, spinach, white potatoes, sweet potatoes, tomatoes, squashes, asparagus, garlic, chayote, eggplant.

ORNAMENTAL FLOWERS, SHRUBS AND TREES. There is probably no place in the world where more kinds of ornamentals can be grown than in California. This may be accounted for by the great extremes of rainfall, snow, temperature, humidity, wind, soil, and elevation within the borders of the state. It is, therefore, not surprising that California has from 800 to 900 species of native woody plants and has more native lilies than any other state. Many exotics find a congenial home some place in the state. Seed catalogues normally mention from 200 to 225 or more genera of flowering plants. Bulb catalogues have listed more than 80 genera. A single nursery catalogue may list 20 genera

---

* Special articles on the subjects indicated by an asterisk (*) will be found at the words so marked.

of conifers, over 100 genera of evergreen trees and shrubs, more than 40 deciduous trees and shrubs and about 20 vines and trailers. It would be a very easy task to list 1000 genera of ornamental plants grown in California and still leave out many natives and the less common exotics.

The evergreen trees and shrubs include both hardy and tender species. Most of the broad-leaved evergreen trees thrive best in districts where there are no killing frosts, as in parts of southern California, in the various coastal areas, and to a limited extent in the warmer parts of the interior valleys. Such conifers as the firs, cedars, junipers, Monterey cypress, pines, redwoods, arborvitae, and spruces are generally hardy against cold but may not thrive with high summer temperatures found in the interior. This is also true of some deciduous trees like the maple, beech, birch, and mountain-ash. The flowering peach and cherry may not break their rest period properly with mild winters. A few conifers like *Araucaria* should not be exposed to freezing winter temperatures. Palms are grown in virtually all areas of California at low elevations from the interior deserts to the ocean. The Washingtonias, the Canary Island date palm, and a few others can be found at the Oregon border near the coast. The more tender sorts are found chiefly in the milder areas of the south coastal region.

Some evergreen shrubs like *Bouvardia, Embothrium, Hibiscus, Gardenia, Grevillea, Iochroma, Lantana, Lavatera, Michelia, Sesbania, Streptosolen, Tibouchina Tipuana,* and *Wigandia* are decidedly sub-tropical in their climatic requirements and should not be planted in frosty situations. Other shrubs like *Abelia, Azalea, Buxus, Cistus, Cotoneaster, Cytisus, Erica, Escallonia, Euonymus, Fremontia, Melaleuca, Nerium, Pyracantha, Rhododendron,* and *Viburnum Tinus* may be expected to stand at least a few degrees of frost. A little frost with short duration in the dormant season may do no serious harm, but prolonged freezing temperatures will cause frost injury to all of the more tender evergreen shrubs.

Deciduous shrubs are for the most part hardy in California. *Lagerstroemia* (crape myrtle) does best in the warm interior. The lilac needs cold winters to break the rest period. This is also true of several other cold-climate trees and shrubs.

Evergreen vines and trailers include both hardy and tender species. *Bougainvillaea, Chorizema, Distictis, Hoya, Passiflora, Solandra,* and *Thunbergia* are popular tender plants, while the bignonias, jasmines, and English ivy are reasonably hardy. Deciduous vines may be considered hardy in California, except when frost occurs during the early growing season.

Several kinds of plants with bulbs or rootstocks live over winter in California and therefore require mild winter temperatures to thrive. The calla lily, *Dierama,* and *Strelitzia* are good examples. The great majority of bulbs will grow in any locality except where the sun is very hot in summer. Such diseases as basal rot of the narcissus may be serious where high summer temperatures prevail.

True annuals which complete their life cycle in one year will be listed in all seed catalogues and can be grown in all parts of California. Some flowering plants often listed as annuals in other states are biennials or perennials in growth in the milder parts of the state. These include such plants as *Antirrhinum* (snapdragon), *Calendula, Calonyction* (moonflower), *Chrysanthemum coccineum* (pyrethrum), *Cobaea scandens, Diascia, Dolichos lignosus* (Australian pea), *Eschscholtzia* (California poppy), *Maurandia,* pansy, petunia, *Quamoclit lobata, Scabiosa atropurpurea,* and *Thunbergia gibsoni.* Most people prefer to treat pansies, snapdragons, and petunias as annuals, even though they may live for more than one year in California gardens.

California has a long list of native wild flowers. Some of the very popular annuals include the following genera: *Clarkia, Collinsia, Eschscholtzia, Gilia, Godetia, Layia, Lupinus, Mentzelia, Nemophila* and *Phacelia.* In addition to these annual wild flowers might be mentioned a large number of native bulbs such as *Bloomeria, Brodiaea, Calochortus, Erythronium, Iris* and *Lilium.*

A larger use of interior decorative plants, both in homes and public buildings, has been a development of recent years. Architects more and more frequently make provision for the use of plants in the integral design, often linking outdoor and indoor plantings with the use of glass. The climate in many areas favors outdoor living and there is a marked Mediterranean influence in gardening. More recently, influences from the Oriental countries, the Hawaiian Islands, and Bermuda are becoming noticeable. Some notable estates are still to be found in California, although they have diminished in recent years.

In the urban areas, a great many private and public gardens too small to justify a full-time gardener are maintained by contract gardeners on a part-time schedule. Gardeners of this class are very numerous.

TURF GRASSES. Although, due to the seasonal character of the rainfall, the maintenance of turf grasses presents some special problems, large areas of lawns and sports fields are maintained. Bermuda grass is the commonest grass of the warmer areas, although St. Augustine grass and the zoysias are sometimes found. Kentucky bluegrass, the fescues, and bents are found in many areas, often growing in mixture with the Bermuda grass, and are becoming increasingly important in the moister and cooler zones. The annual maintenance cost for turf grasses constitutes perhaps the largest outlay in the ornamental field. *Lippia* and, more recently, *Dichondra repens* have been used as substitutes for grass lawns. There has been a

---

* Special articles on the subjects indicated by an asterisk (*) will be found at the words so marked.

tendency to use many different evergreen vines and dwarf shrubs as ground covers for slopes, especially for those too steep for conventional lawn maintenance.

CLIMATE. California possesses all of the climatic variations of other states and has a few more besides. The state has been credited with having the hottest and coldest weather, the wettest and driest, and the sunniest and foggiest. Typical variations in frost conditions are shown below.

Place	Average date of last killing frost in spring	Latest-known killing frost
San Diego	none	Jan. 20
Santa Monica	Jan. 8	March 11
Indio	Feb. 5	March 16
Chico	March 31	April 30
Placerville	April 12	June 15

Place	Average date of earliest killing frost in spring	Earliest-known killing frost
San Diego	none	Dec. 26
Santa Monica	Dec. 27	Nov. 28
Indio	Dec. 4	Nov. 12
Chico	Nov. 20	Oct. 21
Placerville	Nov. 3	Sept. 15

Rainfall in the state varies from none in some years in desert areas to more than 100 inches in exceptional years along the extreme north coast. The summers are typically dry, while during the months of December, January, February, and March about 60 to 75 per cent of the annual precipitation is expected. Humidity also varies widely over the state, being lowest in the hotter inland valleys and highest along the coast. At Fresno the daily range is 39% to 73%, Los Angeles 51% to 77%, Sacramento 50% to 82%, San Francisco 64% to 85% and Eureka 79% to 91%. The low humidity in warm districts tends to make the heat less oppressive but at the same time greatly affects plant selection. Daily moisture stresses may lead to sunburn on such trees as the birch, beech, mountainash, juniper, Monterey cypress, Douglas fir, and several others; consequently these plants may not thrive in the hot, dry, inland valleys away from the moist coastal influences, although these hardy plants will tolerate any reasonable amount of cold. Plants which grow naturally with great moisture variations in the soil are considered drought-resistant. Such drought-resistant plants have been imported from Australia and other countries to supplement similar native plants for such extreme conditions.

The number of days above freezing varies from 365 days along the coast at San Diego, Santa Monica, Santa Barbara, and San Francisco to less than 100 growing days in the high mountain areas. Those areas with 200 or more growing days, as listed on weather maps, will include the primary horticultural districts of the state, but within this large area there is a vast difference in growing conditions. The higher mountains and hills and the desert areas may be excluded from consideration. Even a short distance from a weather-recording station, weather conditions may differ. For example, there may be no frost in ordinary years at the higher elevations in parts of Santa Barbara, which is credited with 325 growing days. In most years the calla lily and other tender plants may grow throughout the winter in mild districts where air drainage is good, as far north as San Francisco Bay.

The so-called frostless belts are scattered throughout southern California and extend along the coast as far north as Marin County. But the more northern districts are much cooler in spite of being frostless in some places. This accounts for differences in the growth of sub-tropical plants. For example, the mean average annual temperature at Santa Monica and Santa Barbara is 60°, while frost-free areas near San Francisco Bay average 56°. Lack of heat rather than excessively low winter temperatures in such cases accounts for the difference in plant growth. In other cases inland districts average a much higher annual temperature, the average being 61° F. at Chico, 63° at Los Angeles, Fresno, and Riverside, and over 73° at Indio. A date palm may fail to mature fruit with an average of 63°, but 10 more degrees average annual temperature at Indio has overcome the deficiency. In a similar way such plants as the jujube, olive, oleander, crape myrtle, and zinnia require considerable heat during the growing season to reach perfection. Such variations in temperatures and temperature requirements help account for the great variety of plants grown over the state.

Fogs, winds, and occasionally snow affect growing conditions. Warm days and cool nights are typical for many parts of the state. Fogs are prevalent at certain seasons of the year in some districts, while only a few miles away fogs may rarely occur. From 80 to 90% of the days are sunny in the drier southern districts, about 75% in the larger interior valleys, 64% at San Francisco, and 45% at Eureka. A few localities exposed to the continuous sweep of strong winds are unsuitable for horticultural purposes. Occasional strong winds, such as the "northers" and "Santa Anas," may require the planting of windbreaks to check the wind velocity. The cool "coast breeze" or sea breeze from offshore in southern California is normally pleasant. Snow is largely limited to the higher elevations. The principal horticultural districts of the main valleys do not have snow except at rare intervals. But such cities as Alturas, Colfax, and Nevada City average a foot or more of snow in winter. The snowfall in the higher mountains is an important source of irrigation water for many areas in California. The type of horticulture developed in each district is generally related to the climatic factors just mentioned.

* Special articles on the subjects indicated by an asterisk (*) will be found at the words so marked.

Specialized horticultural societies are numerous and many floral exhibitions are scheduled regularly. Notable large flower shows have been held in Oakland, and in Inglewood, where the California International Flower Show has been staged.

A quarterly journal is published by the California Horticultural Society, and one of a similar type is issued by the Southern California Horticultural Institute, in co-operation with the Los Angeles State and County Arboretum.

The University of California maintains botanic gardens at Berkeley and Los Angeles. The Strybing Arboretum and Botanic Garden is located in Golden Gate Park in San Francisco. The Santa Barbara Botanic Garden and the Rancho Santa Ana Botanic Garden at Claremont both work exclusively with California native plants.

The address of the Agricultural Experiment Station, which has kindly supplied this information about the state, is the Agricultural Experiment Station of the University of California, Berkeley. Various publications on gardening are obtainable from Agricultural Publications, Room 22, Giannini Hall, University of California, Berkeley 4, California.

There are over 400 chapters of California Garden Clubs, Inc., which is the state organization of the National Council of State Garden Clubs. This group has approximately 15,000 members and publishes a monthly magazine, *Golden Gardens*. There also are chapters of the Garden Club of America, the home office of which is 598 Madison Avenue, New York 22, N. Y.

CALIFORNIA ROSE = *Convolvulus japonicus.*

CALIFORNIAN BLUEBELL = *Phacelia Whitlavia.*

californica, -us, -um (kal-i-for'ni-ca). From California.

CALIMERIS (ka-lim'er-is). A genus of 10 Asiatic perennial herbs, family Compositae, closely related to the genus *Aster*. The only cult. species is grown for ornament in the perennial border. Leaves alternate.* Flower heads with yellow disk* flowers and purple or white ray flowers, the heads solitary at the ends of small branchlets. (*Calimeris* is from the Greek for beautiful arrangement.)

The species below, which is not much grown, is an aster-like herb needing the same culture as the perennials of the genus *Aster* (which see). Easily propagated by fall or spring division.

incisa. A leafy-stemmed, hairy herb 12–20 in. high, branching at the top. Leaves oblongish, more or less irregularly cut or deeply toothed, smaller toward the top and without teeth. Flower heads solitary, about 1 in. wide, the rays usually purple, shading to white. Siberia. Sometimes offered as *Boltonia incisa*. There is also a pink-flowered variety.

CALLA (kal'la). A single species of mud or aquatic herbs of the family Araceae, confined to the north temperate zone and very different from the plant known as calla lily

(which see). The genus *Calla* has long-stalked, oval or heart-shaped leaves, springing from a slender, bitter rootstock. The spathe* is green on the outside but white within. Spadix* cylindric, crowded with the minute green flowers (*see* ARACEAE for structure). Fruit a head of red berries. (*Calla* is the classical name of the only species.)

The water arum is easily grown along the edges of ponds, in the mud or in shallow water, but not in dry soils. It prefers the acid edges of bogs where the muck has a pH of 4–5 (*see* ACID AND ALKALI SOILS).

palustris. Water arum, also called wild calla. Leafstalks 4–8 in. long, fleshy. Leaves coarse, thick, without marginal teeth, 2–4½ in. long. Spathe* not covering the spadix which is about 1 in. long. May. Berries ripe in July.

CALLA FAMILY = Araceae.

CALLA LILY. A group of tropical herbs of the genus **Zantedeschia** (zan-te-desh'i-a) of the arum family (Araceae), quite different from the genus *Calla* (which see). The calla lilies are popular florists' flowers, widely used for decoration. They have thick rootstocks and basal, long-stalked leaves that are chiefly arrowhead-shaped or more or less oval-heart-shaped. They are chiefly grown for the showy, solitary spathes* which are beautifully colored, and suggest a large corolla. (*See* ARACEAE for flower structure.) Fruit berry-like. (Named for Francesco Zantedeschia, an Italian botanist.)

For culture *see* below.

Z. aethiopica. The common calla lily of the florists. A stout herb 18–30 in. high. Leaves smooth, usually arrowhead-shaped, nearly 15 in. long and ⅔ as wide. Spathe* 6–9 in. long, brilliantly white, the upper part tapering to a sharp point. S. Af. Fragrant.

Z. albo-maculata. Spotted calla lily. Resembling the first but smaller and the leaves white-spotted. Spathe* somewhat cream-white or yellowish, tinged purple in the throat, not over 5 in. long. Cape of Good Hope.

Z. elliottiana. Golden or yellow calla lily. Leaves long-stalked, more or less oval-heart-shaped, 7–10 in. long, sporadically white-spotted. Spathe* about 5 in. long, trumpet- or funnel-shaped, golden-yellow, not purple-tinged. S. Af.

Z. melanoleuca. Not over 18 in. high, the white-spotted leaves arrow-shaped and about 12 in. long and half as wide. Spathe* about 3 in. long, pale yellow but with purple-brown spots at the base on the inside. Natal, S. Af.

Z. rehmanni. Red or pink calla lily. Differing from the others in having narrow, tapering leaves which are often white-spotted. Spathe* 3–4 in. long, trumpet-shaped, the limb narrowed to a point, rose-red, rarely white. Natal, S. Af.

CALLA LILY CULTURE

Callas may be grown from divided rhizomes* or corms,* or they may be started from seed. White callas produce rhizomes, and yellow callas produce corms. Offsets are daughter rhizomes (or corms) attached to the mother rhizome (or corm).

The yellow calla is often propagated by seed, but this method of propagation is not

---

* Special articles on the subjects indicated by an asterisk (*) will be found at the words so marked.

necessarily faster than by offsets. Shallow planting of large corms, as well as of offsets, produces a heavy increase of stock, often in one season under outdoor conditions in mild sections of the U. S.

The yellow calla forms seed abundantly under California conditions. The seed may be planted after it has reached full maturity, as indicated by its deep yellow or orange color. Where young seedlings cannot be grown outdoors over the winter, it is better to permit the seed clusters to remain in seed boxes where ripening can continue.

In commercial plantings outdoors, white and pink calla seed is drilled into the soil with a small seeding machine or is sown by hand in field beds. The main commercial fields are located in Santa Cruz County, approximately 75 miles south of San Francisco. It is best to dust the seed before planting with captan, or a suitable fungicide, to prevent damping-off. Frequent and careful watering, together with good drainage, is essential. The seedlings are left in the seed bed or seed flat until they are old enough to transplant to the field or garden. Under commercial growing conditions, or in the mild parts where white callas are grown outdoors in home gardens, division should take place every four or five years. The rhizomes become very large and matted after several seasons of growth.

Greenhouse Culture

Of South African origin, these plants like plenty of food, light, and water. Keep the pots at first under the benches or in a cool, semi-dark spot and do not overwater. Within two or three weeks the roots will be well started and the plants are then shifted to a light, open place in the greenhouse, with plenty of water. Dormant tubers or fleshy roots are usually available by midsummer for potting. In the Southwest, or other sections of the country where the sunlight is very strong, glass should be whitewashed in order to protect against sunburn. Plants respond well to liquid fish fertilizers, applied lightly twice a month, as soon as the pots are filled with roots. Winter temperature under glass should be maintained around 65° F. in the daytime, and 55° F. at night. The pots may be removed outdoors in the spring, after frost danger is over, and sunk in borders. These should be taken in before the weather turns cold.

Should callas be grown for blooms only, the tubers can be planted directly in the greenhouse bench in very rich soil.

The golden yellow varieties of calla lily, as well as the dwarf pink or rose, thrive in a higher temperature. It is best if these remain under glass the year round, except in mild areas of the U.S., as they are less sturdy than the white Z. *aethiopica*.

When the blooming period is finished for the season, the tubers should be rested and dried before repotting for bloom the following year. If plants are to be raised from seed, this should be sown in light soil in November. They can also be propagated from divisions which are potted up in the same manner as the tubers. — N.G.

Diseases. Root rot and soft rot are common diseases of calla lily. The former is a fungus disease which destroys the roots after which leaf margins turn yellow and flowers fail to mature. A bacterium causes the soft rot of the corm and the basal part of leafstalks. Soak the dormant corms for one hour in a suspension of one ounce of New Improved Ceresan in 3¼ gallons of water and plant immediately in individual pots. Use sterilized soil (*see* Soil Sterilization), or that soil in which calla lily has not been grown previously.

Spotted wilt* is a virus disease. Plants with pale yellow streaks in the leaves and green blotches in the flowers should be discarded.

CALLIANDRA (kal′li-an-dra). A large genus of tropical shrubs and trees, family Leguminosae, separated from *Acacia* only by technical characters and of very similar culture. Unlike many acacias, this genus is not usually thorny. Leaves twice-compound,* the ultimate leaflets numerous and small. Flowers small, crowded in dense, globular heads which are covered by the silky, protruding stamens.* Fruit a flattened and sometimes curled legume.* (*Calliandra* is from the Greek for beautiful stamens.)

For culture *see* Acacia.

californica. A much-branched, hairy shrub 3–4 ft. high. Leaves with 7–8 divisions each of which is composed of many, small, oblong leaflets. Flower heads about 1½ in. in diameter, the stamens purple. Lower Calif. and not hardy northward.

guildingi. Much planted in southern Calif., this West Indian tree, 15–25 ft. high, has numerous leaflets, 1–2 in. long. Flowers in dense heads, greenish-white, the long-protruding stamens purple and showy. Hardy only in zone* 9 or protected places in zone* 8.

portoricensis. Pich. A West Indian shrub or small tree with very numerous leaflets that fold up at evening. Flower heads white, in clusters of 3 and blooming at night. Pod straight and narrow. Can be grown outdoors only in zone* 9.

tweedi. A small, Brazilian shrub for the greenhouse or outdoors in zone* 9. Leaflets very numerous, narrow but blunt and shining. Flower heads on slender stalks from the leaf axils,* the showy stamens* purple.

CALLICARPA (kal′li-kar-pa). A large genus of shrubs, family Verbenaceae, the four below grown for ornament, although the fruits are more showy than the flowers. Leaves opposite,* toothed, the teeth often bluntish. Flowers small, tubular, 4-lobed at the top, the four stamens protruding. Fruit nearly globe-shaped, berry-like. (*Callicarpa* is Greek for beauty fruit.)

The bushes are often called beauty-berry, but *C. americana* is commonly called French mulberry, although it is neither French nor a mulberry. They can be grown outdoors as indicated below, preferably in full sun and in a rich soil. If they should winter-kill, they will usually come from the base as in *Buddleia*. They can also be grown in the cool

* Special articles on the subjects indicated by an asterisk (*) will be found at the words so marked.

greenhouse. Easily propagated by seeds or by cuttings of mature wood.

americana. French mulberry. A shrub 4–5 ft. high. Leaves 4–6 in. long, bluntly toothed, green above, rusty beneath. Flowers about ⅓ in. long in a compact, short-stalked cluster (cyme*), bluish, white, purple, lilac, or even red. Md. to Tex. and Okla. and in the W.I. May. The fruit is violet, but a white-fruited form is offered and may be conspicuous in winter, if the fruit does not shatter. Not generally hardy north of zone* 6.

bodinieri = *Callicarpa giraldiana.*

dichotoma. A shrub 2–4 ft. high. Leaves 1–3 in. long, bluntly toothed toward the base, without teeth toward the tip. Flowers pink, about ⅛ in. long, the cluster usually few-flowered. Eastern As. Aug. The fruit is violet or lilac. Hardy to zone* 4. Often sold as *C. purpurea.*

giraldiana. Erect shrub, 6–8 ft. high, the twigs scurfy. Leaves broadly elliptic, 2–5 in. long. Flowers lilac, in a dense cluster (cyme*) about 1½ in. wide, the stamens protruding, the cluster hairy. Fruit handsome, lilac-violet, persisting into Nov. China. July–Aug. Hardy from zone* 5 southward. Usually offered as *C. bodinieri giraldi.*

japonica. Not over 4 ft. high. Leaves 3–5 in. long, finely toothed. Flowers white or pink, about ¼ in. long, the clusters stalked and profuse. Fruit violet. Jap. Aug. A white-fruited variety is also offered. Hardy, with protection, to zone* 5.

purpurea = *Callicarpa dichotoma.*

CALLIOPSIS. See COREOPSIS.

CALLIRHOË (kal-lir′o-ee). The poppy mallows comprise a small genus of North American herbs of the family Malvaceae, well liked for their showy flowers. They have alternate,* usually cleft or dissected leaves. Flowers mostly in the leaf axils,* reddish-purple or pinkish, the petals irregularly cut but not notched at the ends. (Named for the goddess.)

Both the cult. species are easy to grow in ordinary garden soil, and are propagated by spring or fall division of their clumps. They are natives of the prairie region of the central U.S. and prefer dry sites.

digitata. A perennial not over 18 in. high. Leaves usually deeply cut into narrow segments, but not compound.* Flowers 1–2 in. wide, handsome, the petals more or less wedge-shaped, red-purple or violet. Flowers from May to July.

involucrata. Perennial from a deep root-stock, not over 24 in. high and inclined to sprawl. Leaves 3–5-parted, finger-fashion, the segments mostly wedge-shaped. Flowers 1½–2½ in. wide, the calyx leafy, the petals oblongish and pale red-purple. June–Aug.

CALLISIA FRAGRANS. See SPIRONEMA FRAGRANS.

callistegioides (cal-lis-te-je-oi′deez, but see OÏDES). Named for a plant of the obsolete genus *Calystegia.*

CALLISTEMMA = CALLISTEPHUS.

CALLISTEMON (kal-lis-tee′mon). A showy genus of Australian shrubs and trees of the family Myrtaceae, often cult. outdoors in Calif. and in northern greenhouses for their handsome flowers. They have many scattered or crowded, small, but stoutish leaves that are narrow or pointed. Flowers in dense spikes, each flower minute, but the spike very showy from the handsome, protruding and numerous stamens,* hence their common name of bottle-brush. Fruit a somewhat woody capsule.* (*Callistemon* is Greek for beautiful stamens.)

The outdoor cult. of bottle-brushes is popular in Calif., less so in Fla. and Miss., where they can be safely planted in zones* 7, 8 and 9. They are not particular as to soil. Propagated by cuttings of ripened wood or by spring-sown seeds harvested the previous fall. Indoor cult. demands potting mixture* 4 and a cool greenhouse.

lanceolatus. A shrub (rarely a tree in cult.) 10–20 ft. Leaves lance-shaped, about 2½ in. long. Spikes 2–4 in. long, not dense, the bright red stamens about 1 in. long, the spike thus very showy. Also called *C. citrinus.* It is perfectly hardy along the Gulf Coast and thrives on beach fronts.

rigidus. Mostly a shrub 6–10 ft. high, rarely a tree. Leaves very narrow, sharp-pointed and rigid, 2½–5 in. long. Spikes very dense, 2–4 in. long, the stamens red.

CALLISTEPHUS (kal-lis′tee-fuss). A single, extraordinarily variable, Asiatic annual herb, family Compositae, known throughout the world as the China or garden aster. It is not very closely related to the true genus *Aster,* but to most gardeners aster means only *Callistephus.* (For other plants called aster see MICHAELMAS DAISY and ASTER.)

As a garden plant the only species, **C. chinensis,** a native of China and Jap., is a hairy plant from 9–24 in. high, with broadly ovalish, deeply but irregularly toothed leaves. Flower heads solitary at the ends of the relatively long stalks, the rays showy and flat (but *see* below) in the simple types, of nearly every color but yellow, predominately blue or violet. (*Callistephus* is Greek for beautiful crown.) The plant is also sold as *Callistemma.* While there is no true yellow garden aster, a hort. var. called Golden Sheaf has been advertised as such. Its unopened buds are yellow but the expanded rays rapidly become cream color.

CULTURE OF GARDEN OR CHINA ASTER

The plant is a true annual, and for the earliest bloom should always be treated as a tender annual (which *see* at ANNUALS). For the late or main crop, many prefer to sow the seed directly where the plants are to go. This may be done after danger of frost is well over. (For frost data see the name of your state.)

They need a rich, well-drained soil and open sunlight. No plants so well repay clean cultivation and frequent watering if the season is dry, especially in late summer and early fall, when most of the varieties are at their best. But the garden aster is so popular and comes in such a multitude of varieties that it is possible to have aster bloom from early July until frost. Scarcely any other

---

* Special articles on the subjects indicated by an asterisk (*) will be found at the words so marked.

annual is so useful for cutting, and as outlined below they come in many forms, with flower heads ranging from about 2 in. wide (smaller in the dwarfs) to 5 in.

TYPES AND VARIETIES. The original or simple type of the garden aster seems to have been one with flat rays in only one or two rows or circles. It is from this that what we call single asters are derived. They are less showy than some of the strains listed below, but are preferred by many, especially for midseason bloom.

Another class, known as incurved, have many more rays than the single asters, and the rays are curved toward the center of the head. Still another group, known as reflexed, have about the same number of rays, but their tips curve outward. A fourth, and very popular strain, called quilled asters, have the rays all tubular. The latter are divided into two groups: (1) German quilled, in which the quills are very short at the center but longer at the periphery. These are also called Sunshine asters. (2) The other group of quilled has the tubular flowers of approximately even length.

From these four main types have sprung hundreds of named varieties and forms. No attempt can be made here to list them, but the enthusiast should understand that most of them come in early, midseason, and late-flowering strains, and that they are also to be had in dwarf, branching, and tall-branching strains. And, of course, they come in all colors except yellow.

INSECT PESTS. Stalk borers overwinter as eggs on nearby weeds. Destroy weeds and protect plants by early-season applications of pesticide #1 (see SPRAYS AND DUSTS). Slender, large blister beetles which chew flowers and plant parts are controlled by pesticide #1 or #17. Treat soil with 1% pesticide #20 dust and water in to kill root aphids and ant carriers. Pesticide #1 or #21 at weekly intervals controls leafhopper vectors of yellow disease.

DISEASES. The Chinese aster is subject to two serious diseases. Yellows* is a virus disease transmitted by a leafhopper.* Plants at any stage in their growth turn pale yellow and are dwarfed and appear "bunchy" due to many new shoots forming at the leaf bases. Control the leafhopper or cover the plants with a 22 × 22 mesh cloth.

A fungus disease, wilt*, causes death of susceptible varieties. The stem near the soil line becomes woody and plants wilt and die. Plant wilt-resistant varieties. If varieties not resistant to wilt are used, the seeds should be soaked for 30 minutes in pesticide #12 (see SPRAYS AND DUSTS) at a concentration of 1–1000 and then washed in running water. Plant where Chinese aster has not been grown previously.

CALLITRIS (kal-ly′tris). A small group of Australian evergreen trees of the pine family suitable for outdoor culture only in zones* 8 and 9, and usually too large for greenhouse culture. They are commonly called cypress-pines, and have cypress-like leaves that are reduced to scales that cover the angled and jointed branchlets. The male flowers, consisting only of stamens,* are in catkin-like clusters, but the female flowers are borne between the woody scales of a cone. (Callitris is from the Greek for beautiful.)

The cypress-pines are rapid-growing trees, considerably planted for their fine foliage in Fla. and Calif. They have many erect branches, so that the trees make a compact growth not unlike a cedar. They are tolerant of a variety of soils.

cupressiformis. A tall tree, up to 50 ft., its foliage resembling the true cypress. Its cones are scarcely more than ½ in. wide, nearly globular and often borne in clusters. Not so much grown as C. robusta.

rhomboidea = Callitris cupressiformis.

robusta. A pyramidal tree 70–100 ft. high, its branches beginning nearly at the ground level, its foliage light green. Cones nearly globular. ¾–1 in. wide.

callosa, -us, -um (kal-low′sa). Callused (see CALLUS).

CALLUNA. See HEATHER.

CALLUS. The protective or healing tissue that forms over a wound, notably over the cut surface of a cutting or slip. Callus also signifies the hard, knob-like protuberance on some tree trunks. It is from the callused surface that the roots of cuttings arise.

CALOCARPUM = Achras.

calochlora, -us, -um (kal-o-claw′ra). Beautifully green.

CALOCHORTUS (kal-o-kor′tus). A charming group of 50 species of chiefly Californian bulbous herbs of the lily family, grown there for ornament and hardy with protection, as indicated below, in other parts of the country. They bear corms,* erect stems and narrow, grass-like, but somewhat fleshy leaves. Flowers terminal, solitary or in small clusters, usually very showy and almost tulip-like, hence their name of globe tulip and butterfly-tulip, but they are better known as Mariposa lily. The flower has 3 inner and showy segments and 3 outer and sepal-like ones. Stamens 6. Fruit a 3-angled capsule.* (Calochortus is from the Greek for beautiful grass.)

The culture of Mariposa lilies is simple in their native region of western U.S., and in Calif. they do well in a light, sandy, porous soil, preferably slightly acid, but not too rich. Manure is not advised. In the East, while they can stand considerable cold, they do not tolerate alternate freezing and thawing, the mucky conditions of the latter being particularly trying. They are thus best grown in pots in potting mixture* 2, to which should be added a little spent tanbark and charcoal. Plant the corms* in late fall and plunge the pots in a cold frame for the winter. After spring growth and blooming, lift the corms and keep them in a dry place until planting time. In Calif. they can stay in the ground continuously, and C. albus will often live over winter without lifting as far north as Washington in the East. Two of the most satisfactory in the East are C. gunnisoni and C. macrocarpus.

* Special articles on the subjects indicated by an asterisk (*) will be found at the words so marked.

albus. White globe lily. About 2 ft. high. Flowers nodding, more or less globe-shaped, white, the petals purplish at the base, about 1½ in. long. Calif.

amabilis. About 18 in. high, the nodding flowers golden-yellow, about 1 in. long or a little longer, the petals in-arching, their edges hairy. Calif.

catalinae. From 18–30 in. high. Flowers nearly 2 in. long, white or lilac-purple, the petals maroon-red at the base. Southern Calif. and Catalina Island.

clavatus. Nearly 3 ft. high. Flowers 2–3 in. long, deep rich yellow, the petals lined with brown. Calif.

gunnisoni. About 18 in. high, the flowers nearly 1¾ in. long, white but purple-streaked. Central U.S.

luteus. From 15–30 in. high, the stem sometimes branching. Flowers 1½–2 in. long, the petals yellow or orange but brown-spotted at the base, and brown-striped. Calif. There is a variety with lemon-yellow flowers, and another with pure white. Both are brown-spotted.

macrocarpus. Nearly 2 ft. high, the flowers about 2 in. long, purple, but with a green stripe down the center of each segment. Pacific Coast.

splendens. From 15–24 in. high. Flowers numerous (sometimes 30), pale lavender or lilac and unspotted, about 2 in. long. Calif. There is also a reddish-lilac variety.

venustus. White Mariposa lily. Not much over 1 ft. high, usually less. Flowers about 2 in. long, very pale lilac, the petals with a reddish-brown spot at the base. Calif. An improved sort is *var.* **superbus**, and *var.* **roseus** has a rose-colored spot near the tip of the petals.

CALONYCTION (kal-o-nik'tee-on). The moonflowers are perennial vines closely related to the morning-glories, family Convolvulaceae, but bloom at night instead of in sunshine. Of the 3 or 4 species, the two below are perennials only in zones* 8 and 9; otherwise, rather rarely cult. greenhouse vines. They have alternate,* broad leaves and fragrant white or purple, large, salver-shaped flowers. Sepals 5. Corolla with a long, but not dilated tube from which the stamens protrude. (*Calonyction* is Greek for night beauty.)

While the plants are perennial they are mostly grown from seed and will bloom the first year and are commonly so grown as porch climbers over much of the U.S. They will not stand much frost. The hard seeds are slow to germinate. Spread the seeds on, or lightly bury them under wet sand in a closed bell-jar or empty aquarium, kept about 80° F. with an electric bulb. This hastens germination by several days.

aculeatum. A milky-juiced vine with somewhat prickly stems. Leaves broadly oval, 6–8 in. long, sometimes 3-lobed. Flowers white but sometimes green-banded, the tube 5–6 in. long, the expanded part 5–6 in. wide. Tropical America and in southern Fla. Sometimes offered as *Ipomoea Bona-nox*.

muricatum. Similar but smaller and with purplish flowers about half the size of *C. aculeatum.* Tropical America.

CALOPHYLLUM (kal-lo-fill'um). A genus of 60 species of resinous, aromatic, chiefly Asiatic and tropical trees of the family Gutti-

ferae, the one below somewhat grown in zone* 9 or the most sheltered parts of zone* 8 in Fla. Leaves opposite,* evergreen, without marginal teeth. Flowers polygamous,* white, fragrant, in small clusters (racemes*), not showy. Petals, if present, 1–4, often replaced by the colored sepals. Fruit fleshy. (*Calophyllum* is from the Greek for beautiful leaf, from the handsome foliage.)

A very beautiful shade tree in the tropics, but useful only in warm, frost-free regions.

antillanum. Calaba, also called Maria and Santa Maria tree. A tall-branching tree up to 100 ft., casting a very dense shade. Leaves oval-oblong, blunt, 5–6 in. long, bright shiny-green and leathery. Flowers scarcely ½ in. long. Fruit about 1 in. in diameter. W.I. Long known as *Calophyllum Calaba*.

CALOPOGON (kal-lo-pō'gon). A small genus of mostly native American bog orchids, the only one of garden interest being the grass pink, which is also called the swamp pink. This cult. species, **C. pulchellus**, is a tuberous-rooted herb with a single narrow leaf 8–12 in. long. Flowers in a sparse cluster at the end of a naked stalk 6–15 in. long. Sepals and petals similar, rose or purple-pink, the lip beautifully fringed and mostly yellowish-orange. Eastern N.A. The plant can only be grown in an acid bog, preferably with a pH of 4–5 (*see* ACID AND ALKALI SOILS). (*Calopogon* is Greek for beautiful beard, from the fringed lip.) June. The plant is also known as *Limodorum tuberosum*.

CALOTHAMNUS (kal-lo-tham'nus). Australian shrubs of perhaps 25 species, family Myrtaceae, the one below grown outdoors in Calif., rarely in greenhouses elsewhere. They have scattered, rigid, heath-like leaves. Flowers in clusters which, like *Callistemon*, are showy because of the numerous, protruding, colored stamens,* but the spikes do not resemble a bottle-brush as in *Callistemon*. Fruit a woody capsule.* (*Calothamnus* is from the Greek for beautiful bush.)

The culture is the same as for *Callistemon*.

quadrifidus. A shrub 6–8 ft. high. Leaves round in sections, ½–1 in. long, very numerous. Flowers in small, stalkless clusters, the stamens* red, about 1 in. long, and in bundles or clusters.

CALTHA. *See* MARSH MARIGOLD.

CALYCANTHACEAE (kal-ee-kan-thay'-see-ee). The sweet-shrub or strawberry-shrub family contains only two genera of shrubs, both of which, *Chimonanthus* and *Calycanthus*, are cultivated for ornament. They have opposite* leaves without marginal teeth, and solitary flowers on leafy, side branchlets. The fruit consists of many, dry, mostly 1-seeded achenes,* all enclosed in a small, pear-shaped or egg-shaped receptacle.

Chimonanthus is Asiatic and has yellow flowers, while *Calycanthus*, with heavily aromatic, brownish-purple flowers, is the sweet-shrub of N.A.

Technical flower characters: Sepals and petals alike, overlapping in many series. Stamens

---

numerous. Ovaries numerous, each 1-celled, and developing into an achene.

calycanthema, -us, -um (kal-ee-kan'the-ma). With petal-like sepals.*

CALYCANTHUS (kal-ee-kan'thus). Aromatic North American shrubs, so fragrant that they are variously called sweet-scented shrub, bubby-shrub, sweet-shrub, strawberry-shrub, and sometimes merely shrub. Of the four known species three are cult. for their fragrant flowers, which have the sepals and petals similarly colored and either brown or brownish-purple. (*See* CALYCANTHACEAE for details.) (*Calycanthus* is from the Greek for calyx and flower, in allusion to the colored calyx.)

While they have no special soil preferences, these shrubs do best in rich soils with plenty of moisture but also well drained. Easily propagated by layers, suckers, division, or seeds. All of them are occasionally called *Butneria.*

fertilis. A smooth shrub 4–8 ft. high. Leaves oval or oblong, 4–6 in. long, bluish-green beneath. Flowers brownish-purple, 1½–2 in. wide. Pa. to Ga. and Ala., mostly in the mountains. Hardy from zone* 4 southward.

floridus. Carolina allspice. A densely hairy shrub 4–8 ft. high. Leaves oval or elliptic, 3–5 in. long, pale on the under side. Flowers dark purple-brown, about 2 in. wide. Va. to Fla., and Miss., mostly near the coast. Hardy from zone* 4 southward.

occidentalis. Called spicebush in Calif., and a shrub 7–12 ft. high. Leaves oblongish, 6–8 in. long, green both sides. Flowers light brown, 2–3 in. wide. Calif. Hardy only from zone* 5 southward.

calycina, -us, -um (kal-ee-sy'na). Like a calyx.

calycosa, -us, -um (kal-e-ko'sa). Having a conspicuous calyx.*

calyculata, -us, -um (ka-lik-kew-lay'ta). Calyculate; *i.e.,* bearing a calyx,* or within one, as are some fruits.

CALYPSO (ka-lip'so). A single bog orchid of the north temperate zone, of little hort. importance except as grown in the bog garden by enthusiasts in native orchids, and next to impossible to perpetuate. The only species, C. bulbosa (also called *C. borealis*), is a bulbous herb with a single, stalked, round-oval leaf 1–1½ in. wide. Flower solitary at the end of a naked stalk 3–6 in high. Sepals and petals alike, variegated purple, pink, and yellow. Lip large and pouch-like, twice-divided below, and with patch of yellow hairs. (Named for the nymph.)

calyptrata, -us, um (ka-lip-tray'ta). Calyptrate (having a calyptra); *i.e.,* furnished with a cap-like hood or covering.

calustegioides (kal-is-tee-ji-oy'deez; but *see* OÏDES). Resembling a plant of *Calystegia,* another name for *Convolvulus japonicus.*

CALYX. A collective term for all the sepals* of a flower, whether separate or united. While the calyx is usually green and very different from the corolla in color and texture, some flowers have no corolla. Then the calyx is often colored like a corolla and replaces it, as in the common hepatica and in anemone. Some plants are grown for the edible calyx, as in roselle. *See* FLOWER, HOSE-IN-HOSE.

Camara. South American vernacular for *Lantana Camara.*

CAMAS = *Camassia Quamash.*

CAMASSIA (ka-mas'si-a). A small genus of North American bulbous herbs of the lily family, the two below somewhat grown for their showy flowers. They have narrow or grass-like leaves, mostly basal, and a bracted* stalk to the flower cluster (raceme*), which usually over-tops the leaves. Flower not tubular, of six separate segments, each with a stamen* inserted at the base. Fruit a 3-valved capsule,* the seeds black. (Latinized form of the Indian *camas* or *quamash.*) The plants are occasionally called *Quamasia.*

The bulbs should be planted like tulips in the fall and not disturbed. Put them 3–5 in. apart in a loamy soil in which there is some sand. The plants, particularly the second species, are prized in the open border.

cusicki. A large-bulbed perennial, the bulbs rather foul-smelling. Leaves about 1½ in. wide and nearly 20 in. long, bluish-green. Flower stalk 3–4 ft. high, crowned with a terminal spike* of many (50–300) pale blue flowers that are about 1 in. long. Ore.

eculenta = *Camassia scilloides.*

leichtlini. Up to 18–24 in. Leaves narrow, but tough, ¾ in. wide and 3 ft. long. Flowers usually purplish-blue, sometimes whitish, the withered remains tightly clasping the pods. British Columbia to Calif.

Quamash. Camas or bear grass. Usually 2–3 ft. tall, the leaves basal, long and strap-shaped. Flowers blue or white in a long, terminal raceme,* the whole cluster often 1 ft. long, the individual flowers about 1 in. long. British Columbia to Calif. The bulbs of this species were once eaten by the Indians.

scilloides. Wild hyacinth. Not over 20 in. high, the leaves keeled, 10–15 in. long, and scarcely ½ in. wide. Flowers pale blue or even white, about ½ in. long, persistent even after withering. Apr.–May. Central N.A. Often offered as *Camassia esculenta.*

cambrica, -us, -um (kam'bri-ka). From Cambria; *i.e.,* Wales.

CAMBIUM. *See* BARK.

CAMEL GRASS; CAMEL HAY = *Cymbopogon Schoenanthus.*

CAMELLIA (ka-mee'li-a; also in the South, ka-mell'i-a). Asiatic evergreen shrubs or small trees of the family Theaceae, widely grown for their wax-like, very showy and lasting bloom. They have alternate, toothed leaves, and usually solitary, nearly stalkless flowers, red in the typical plant, but of other colors or even double in the many hort. forms (*see* below). Petals mostly five. Sepals 5–7, often falling away. Fruit a woody capsule.* (Named for George J. Kamel or Camellus, a Moravian Jesuit traveler in Asia.)

---

* Special articles on the subjects indicated by an asterisk (*) will be found at the words so marked.

For the tea plant, often offered as *C. sinensis,* see THEA.

For culture *see* below.

japonica. The common camellia. A shrub or rarely a tree up to 25–30 ft. Leaves ovalish, 3–4 in. long, shining dark green. Flowers 3–5 in. wide, waxy, the petals roundish. China and Jap. The plant is sometimes offered as *Thea japonica,* and is often called merely japonica.

japonica × saluensis. A hybrid of chief interest because it has given rise to several new hort. forms of merit. *See* below.

reticulata. A shrub 10–20 ft. high, its dull green, elliptic leaves nearly 4 in. long and about half as wide, their margins toothed. Flowers 4–6 in. wide, very showy, dark rose-colored, the petals soft. China. The source of several hort. forms of merit for greenhouse cult. *See* below.

saluensis. Not over 15 ft. high, the shining green, oblong, blunt, leathery leaves 1–2 in. long and half as wide. Flowers nearly 3 in. wide, white or red. Yunnan. Little cult. but of interest as one of the parents of several desirable hybrids. *See* below.

Sasanqua. Lower than the common sort and more hardy, often being safe outdoors up to zone* 5. China and Japan. There are several named forms. *See* below.

CAMELLIA CULTURE

Seeds germinate readily if planted as soon as mature in late summer and early autumn. Seedlings are grown to secure new varieties and they are used as stocks in grafting. Plants grown from cuttings also are used as stocks. Most plants produced by nurserymen are grown from cuttings, often out of doors in the lower South, and in greenhouses in colder sections. In grafting, the cleft method is used for larger stocks, whip and splice for smaller ones. The optimum time is two or three weeks in advance of the starting of growth in spring. A close frame is used in greenhouses; in the open each individual graft is covered with a glass jar. *C. reticulata* is difficult to grow from cuttings, and propagated by inarching or grafting on japonica and Sasanqua stocks.

Camellias are used extensively as garden shrubs in southern areas from the eastern shore of Maryland to Florida, westward into Texas, and on the Pacific Coast from California to British Columbia. Their culture is being extended northward in many areas with satisfactory results. In warmer sections, camellias usually are planted in gardens during the winter months. Spring planting is best in colder sections to allow plants to become established before growth ceases in autumn. Plants grown in containers or balled and burlapped from open ground should not be set deeper than they grew.

In greenhouses camellias are grown in pots or tubs or planted in beds. Soil used in planting can be made with equal parts of good garden soil, peat, cow manure, and sand. Slightly acid material is best; pH 5.5 to 6.5 or thereabouts is satisfactory. Commercial fertilizer, acid in reaction, is commonly used. Plants in gardens are fertilized twice a year, in spring in advance of growth-starting and about the middle of June. Soil should be kept moist, with little variation, but good drainage is vital. Syringing of foliage is very beneficial. Camellias naturally make shapely plants and need little pruning. Specimens look best branched low. Wayward branches may be cut back and inner growth of small twigs removed. Disbudding is advisable where too many flower buds have developed.

VARIETIES

C. japonica. There is a very large number from which to choose, an amazing number since they are derived from a single species without crossing. Crosses with other species now are being made and beautiful new forms are being secured. Most varieties are fall- or winter-blooming and hence not useful or safe outdoors much above zone* 6.

Adolphe Audusson†	Semi-double, red, early.
Alba-plena	Double, imbricated, white, early.
Arejishi†	Double, irregular, red, early.
Berenice Boddy†	Semi-double, shaded pink, midseason.
Debutante	Double, irregular, pink, midseason.
Donckelarii†	Semi-double, variegated, midseason.
Elegans	Incomplete double, variegated, midseason.
Herme†	Incomplete double, variable, midseason.
Lady Clare†	Semi-double, pink, midseason.
Magnoliaeflora	Semi-double, red, midseason.
Mathotiana†	Double, imbricated, red, midseason.

Those marked with a dagger (†) are suggested for colder climates where midseason varieties usually flower later.

C. RETICULATA

Butterfly Wings	Semi-double, crimson, shaded.
Captain Rawes	Semi-double to incomplete double, rose-madder.
Crimson Robe	Semi-double, crimson.
Lionhead	Incomplete double, variegated, turkey red with white.
Noble Pearl	Incomplete double.
Shot Silk	Semi-double to incomplete double, spinel pink.
Trewithan Pink	Single, rose-bengal.
Willow Wand	Semi-double, rose-bengal.

Reticulata varieties have been found unsatisfactory out of doors in much of the camellia area. Well adapted for greenhouse culture.

C. SASANQUA

Cleopatra	Semi-double, rose-pink, free-flowering.
Crimson Tide	Single, rhodamine-purple.
Hinode-gumo	Single, white, flushed pink.
Jean May	Incomplete double, phlox-pink.
Mine-no-yuki	Semi-double to incomplete double, self white.

---

* Special articles on the subjects indicated by an asterisk (*) will be found at the words so marked.

Ocean Springs	Single, white at center, Tyrian-purple outer parts.
Pink Snow	Incomplete double, phlox-pink.
Showa-no-sakae	Double, irregular, bright pink.

All are early-flowering. Oct.–Dec.—H.H.H.

Varieties of *Camellia japonica*, all spring-blooming, that have proved hardy at least as far north as Milford, Delaware, are:

Jarvis Red, red	Orton Pink, pink
Leucantha, white	Pink Perfection, pink
	Sarah Frost, red

This grower planted them on the west side of the house to protect them from "the sudden thaw of the morning sun," which is more dangerous than cold. Milford is in the northern part of zone* 5. — EDITOR.

The present address of the American Camellia Society is Box 2398, University Station, Gainesville, Florida.

INSECT PESTS. Scales of different species feed on leaves. Control with superior-type oil sprays as recommended by manufacturer or repeated applications of pesticide #21 (*see* SPRAYS AND DUSTS). Use pesticide #1 to control chewing or boring pests.

DISEASES. A flower blight, first reported on the west coast, is now present in some southeastern states. The flowers turn black and drop prematurely. Picking and destroying all blighted flowers will help to reduce the carry-over of the disease. Drenching the soil beneath the plant in the spring, using pesticide #5 (*see* SPRAYS AND DUSTS) is reported to be of value. Use of pesticide #2 on the flowers as they start to open may also help to control the disease.

A canker* or twig blight* may be serious in some areas. Pruning out cankered material, spraying with pesticide #2, or use of resistant varieties is recommended.

CAMLA PHLOX = *Phlox nivalis*.

Cammarum (kam-mar′um). A pre-Linnaean* name for some monkshood.

CAMOMILE = *Anthemis nobilis*. But *Matricaria Chamomilla* is also, not very properly, called camomile. It is better called false or German camomile.

CAMOMILE LAWN. *See* Lawn Mixtures at LAWN.

CAMPANULA (kam-pan′you-la). The bellflowers comprise an important group of garden plants of the family Campanulaceae, over two dozen of its 300 known species being in common cult. for their handsome bloom. While some are perennials for the open border or for the rock garden, a few make handsome pot plants and at least two are annuals.

Basal leaves often unlike the stem leaves, sometimes markedly so, the latter alternate.* Flowers typically bell-shaped, often very showy, mostly blue or white, the calyx* persistent on the egg-shaped pod (capsule*) which opens by a terminal pore in some, by valves in others. (*Campanula* is Latin for little bell.)

The perennial species below (including the related genus *Adenophora*) are of simple culture in any ordinary garden soil, unless they are rock garden species, in which case their culture is treated at ROCK GARDEN. Most of the rest can be grown in the open border and divided in the spring or fall. Or seeds may be started in pans with a glass cover in the greenhouse in February and the seedlings put outdoors after danger of frost.

Some of the biennials are best sown as seeds in summer, transplanted to the garden in early fall and given a mulch of dried leaves for the winter. They will bloom the next season. The annuals should be treated as hardy annuals. *See* ANNUALS.

No garden plants offer such a variety of blue color as the bellflowers. While many of the hort. forms, some of which make fine pot plants for the porch or terrace because of their long-continued bloom, are in other colors than blue, it is the latter which predominates throughout the genus.

One of the best for pot culture is *C. pyramidalis*. Among the rock garden species are *C. bellardi, C. garganica, C. carpatica,* and *C. excisa,* while several of the others are splendid in planning for the blue garden (which see). Most of them bloom in May or June, but a few bloom for several weeks after this. Most of them appear to tolerate some lime in the soil. *See* LIMESTONE PLANTS.

alliariaefolia. A perennial 1–2 ft. high. Leaves oval to heart-shaped, 1–3 in. long, felty beneath, the basal ones long-stalked. Flowers white, ¾–1¼ in. long, nodding. As. Minor and the Caucasus.

attica = *Campanula drabifolia*.

barbata. A rock garden perennial 6–9 in. high. Leaves basal, long-lance-shaped, 4–6 in. long and hairy. Flowers pale blue, 1 in. long, nodding in loose racemes.* Alps.

bellardi. A European perennial plant 4–6 in. high. Flowers blue, solitary, nodding, about ½ in. long. For culture *see* ROCK GARDEN. It is often sold as *C. pusilla* and the true *bellardi* may not be in cult. and may be *C. cochlearifolia*.

caespitosa. A rock garden, tufted perennial, 4–7 in. high with smooth, erect stems and mostly basal, short-stalked leaves that are about ½ in. long, narrowly lance-shaped. Flowers lilac, nodding seldom over 3–5 blooms. Central Eu. Plants offered as this may be *C. cochlearifolia*.

calycanthema. Merely a name for those plants of *C. Medium* with hose-in-hose* type of flowers.

carpatica. Perennial, 9–15 in. high. Leaves ovalish, toothed, about 1 in. long. Flowers solitary, erect, blue, nearly 2 in. wide and very handsome. Eastern Eu. *See* ROCK GARDEN for culture. There are many white and sky-blue varieties.

cochlearifolia. A mat-forming perennial, 2–7 in. high, the chiefly basal, long-stalked leaves ovalish, or roundish, about ½ in. wide, bluntly but sparingly toothed. Flowers violet-blue, about ¾ in. long. Central Eu. June–July. Often offered as *C. pusilla. See* C. CAESPITOSA.

collina. A perennial, 8–10 in. tall, often growing in clumps, the chiefly basal leaves, oblongish or longer, 2–3 in. long, the marginal teeth wavy. Flowers purple, about 1 in. long.

---

* Special articles on the subjects indicated by an asterisk (*) will be found at the words so marked.

Eurasia. Appears to tolerate neutral or mildly acid soils.

drabifolia. An annual 4–6 in. high, useful for the border or rock garden, the foliage hairy. Flowers blue, sometimes with a white tube, solitary and about ½ in. long. Greece and Asia Minor. *See* ANNUALS. Sometimes sold as *C. attica.*

Elatines. A slender, sprawling, nearly vine-like herb with the basal leaves heart-shaped and a little hairy. Flowers rather open, not especially bell-shaped, about ½ in. wide, sky blue. S. Eu. There are several vars. some of which are often offered under other names such as *C. garganica.*

Erinus. Often offered under this name, but the plants are apt to be *C. Elatines* or *C. garganica.* True *C. Erinus* of S. Eu. is probably not in cult.

excisa. An alpine perennial scarcely 5 in. high, with narrow leaves about 1 in. long. Flowers solitary, nodding, about ½ in. wide, pale blue. Alps. For culture *see* ROCK GARDEN.

fragilis. Related to *C. garganica*, but less easy to grow. Plant tufted, prostrate, the leaves kidney-shaped. Flowers pale purplish-blue with a white "eye." Southern Italy. Summer. Rock garden species.

garganica. Somewhat sprawling and about 10 in. long. Leaves ovalish, toothed. Flowers more wheel-shaped than bell-shaped, solitary, blue, about ½ in. wide. Dalmatia. Considered by some as merely a var. of *C. Elatines.* For culture *see* ROCK GARDEN.

glomerata. A hardy, border perennial 12–20 in. high, with large, long-stalked, ovalish leaves 3–5 in. wide. Flowers blue or white, about ¾ in. long, in dense clusters. Eurasia. There is a double-flowered form and a variety with deep violet flowers in large clusters.

isophylla. Ligurian bellflower. A trailing plant useful for hanging baskets, with small, oval, or heart-shaped leaves 1–1½ in. wide. Flowers usually numerous, but not in clusters, shallowly bell-shaped, pale blue and about 1 in. wide. Italy. The *var.* alba has white flowers. Should be wintered over as a house plant in cold regions.

lactiflora. A stout, border perennial 2–4 ft. high. Leaves oval or oblong, 1–3 in. long. Flowers white or pale blue (in a variety), about 1 in. long, in long, terminal, showy clusters (panicles*). Caucasus.

latifolia. A showy Eurasian border perennial, 2–4 ft. high, with broad, toothed, hairy leaves 4–6 in. wide. Flowers purplish-blue, solitary, about 1½ in. long. The *var.* **macrantha** has flowers nearly twice as large.

loreyi = *Campanula ramosissima.*

Medium. Canterbury bells. A much-planted biennial herb from southern Eu., 2–4 ft. high. Leaves hairy, long-oblong, 6–9 in. long, toothed and wavy. Flowers violet-blue, solitary or in loose racemes,* about 1 in. wide. *See* BIENNIALS. It has some interesting forms. In one the calyx and corolla are similarly colored and produce a hose-in-hose* type. Another, known as cup-and-saucer, has a colored calyx, like a saucer, below the cup-shaped corolla.

muralis = *Campanula portenschlagiana.*

persicifolia. Peach bells. A perennial herb 2–3 ft. high and attractive for the border. Leaves narrow, finely toothed, 6–8 in. long. Flowers blue or white, about 1½ in. long, in showy terminal clusters (racemes*). Eu. There are several varieties with larger, white, or double flowers, and many handsome named forms.

portenschlagiana. A Dalmatian perennial, useful for the rock garden and not over 6–8 in. high. Leaves nearly round or kidney-shaped, long-stalked, about 1 in. wide. Flowers few, bluish-purple, about ¾ in. long. For culture *see* ROCK GARDEN.

poscharskyana. A weak-stemmed or sprawling perennial, 12–15 in. high, the mostly basal, long-stalked leaves nearly round, bluntly toothed and 1–2 in. wide. Flowers numerous, lilac, about 1½ in. wide, Yugoslavia. Summer.

pulla. A low, creeping, prostrate perennial, not over 4 in. high, the leaves roundish, short-stalked, the upper ones narrower and stalkless. Flower solitary, nodding, bell-shaped, about ¾ in. long, violet-blue. Eu. June. Needs alkaline site in rock garden.

pulloides. A hybrid bellflower differing from the one above in being about 6 in. high, and with the flowers shorter and broader than in *C. pulla.*

punctata. A hairy-stemmed perennial 1–2 ft. high, with broad, coarsely toothed leaves 3–5 in. wide, the lower long-stalked. Flowers white, lilac-spotted inside, about 2 in. long, solitary and nodding. Asia. In the popular form, known as Marian Gehring, the corolla is pure lilac and unspotted.

pusilla = *Campanula bellardi* or *C. cochlearifolia.*

pyramidalis. Chimney bellflower. A smooth, bushy perennial 3–5 ft. high, useful for the border and for pot plants. Leaves ovalish, about 2 in. long, the lower heart-shaped and long-stalked. Flowers in free-blooming, narrow clusters, pale blue, flat, bell-shaped, about 1 in. long. Southern Eu. There is also a white-flowered variety.

raddeana. A perennial herb 8–12 in. high, with ovalish, toothed leaves, the lower long-stalked. Flowers about ¾ in. long, solitary in the leaf axils,* dark purple. Caucasus.

raineri. Perhaps, as usually offered, a dwarf race or strain of *C. carpatica.*

ramosissima. An annual, not over 12 in. high, with oblongish leaves 1–2 in. long. Flowers solitary, erect, somewhat saucer-shaped, about 1½ in. wide, violet, but whitish at the base. Southeastern Eu. There is also a white-flowered variety. *See* ANNUALS. The plant is sometimes sold as *C. loreyi.*

rapunculoides. A Eurasian perennial, 2–3 ft. high, often an escape* in eastern U.S. Leaves oval or longer, 2–4 in. long, toothed, the lower ones heart-shaped and long-stalked. Flowers blue, 1 in. long, in a loose, terminal, 1-sided cluster. Apt to run wild and often invasive.

rotundifolia. Bluebell or harebell, but better known as the bluebell-of-Scotland. A slender, weak perennial with basal, round leaves and narrow stem leaves, the former often withering. Flowers bright blue, about ¾ in. long, in a lax, few-flowered cluster. Throughout the north temperate zone. There is a white variety and another with apparently double flowers with shredded petals.

sarmatica. An erect perennial 10–20 in. high, its foliage grayish-hairy. Leaves long-stalked, chiefly basal, the base heart-shaped, tapering to a pointed tip, 3–5 in. long, shallowly toothed. Flowers pale lilac, about 1 in. long, rather numerous in the clusters (raceme*). Eurasia. Summer.

Saxifraga. A rock garden crevice plant, hugging the ground or forming tufts, not over 6 in. high. Leaves narrow, hairy on the margins. Flowers solitary on each stalk, but the plant producing 6–12 at once, or even more. Corolla about 1¼ in. across, violet. Caucasus

* Special articles on the subjects indicated by an asterisk (*) will be found at the words so marked.

and Armenia. May–July. Best grown among a litter of stone chips. *See* ROCK GARDEN.

Speculum = *Specularia Speculum-Veneris*.

stansfieldi. A hybrid, rock garden perennial with slender, creeping stems; not over 5 in. high. Leaves oblique, but with parallel sides (rhomboid*), hairy. Flower solitary, nodding, violet or reddish-violet. July. Needs alkaline soil.

Trachelium. Coventry bells. A rough-hairy, Eurasian border perennial, 2–3 ft. high. Leaves narrowly oval, 2–3 in. long, coarsely toothed. Flowers nodding, in a loose cluster (raceme*), the corolla bluish-purple and about 1 in. long. There is also a white variety. A vigorous, often invasive plant and apt to run wild.

turbinata. A form of *C. carpatica*.

CAMPANULACEAE (kam-pan-you-lay'-see-ee). The bellflower family is of considerable garden interest because it contains *Campanula* and *Platycodon*, both widely cult. for their showy flowers. Of the 40 known genera in the family, about a dozen are cultivated in gardens, all of them herbs with alternate* leaves. Some tropical genera of no garden interest are shrubs or even trees.

Flowers regular,* solitary or in clusters, quite often blue or white, and usually more or less bell-shaped. The fruit is a dry pod (capsule*), the splitting of which provides the only, if somewhat technical, difference between the garden genera. Besides those mentioned above, these comprise the following: *Adenophora, Codonopsis, Symphyandra*, and *Trachelium* which resemble the bellflowers (*Campanula*); *Wahlenbergia* and *Edraianthus*, both herbs of the Old World with blue flowers; *Jasione* and *Phyteuma* which have their flowers in dense heads or spikes; *Michauxia* of Asia Minor, a tall herb with flowers 2 in. long; and *Specularia* which has wheel-shaped flowers. *See also* OSTROWSKIA.

Technical flower characters: Flowers hermaphrodite,* the calyx tube united to the usually inferior* ovary. Corolla prevailingly bell-shaped, its lobes 5. Stamens 5. Ovary 2–5-celled. Style 1.

campanularia, -us, -um (kam-pan-you-lay'-ri-a). Bellflower-like.

campanulata, -us, -um (kam-pan-you-lay'-ta). Campanulate; *i.e.*, bell-shaped.

campanuloides (kam-pan-you-loy'-deez; but *see* OïDES). Like a bellflower (*Campanula*).

campechiana, -us, -um (kam-pee-chi-ā'-na). From Campeche on the peninsula of Yucatan.

CAMPERDOWN ELM = *Ulmus glabra camperdowni. See* ELM.

CAMPERNELLE JONQUIL = *Narcissus odorus.*

campestris, -e (kam-pes'tris). Growing in a field or in flat country.

Camphora (kam-for'a). An old and obsolete generic name for the camphor tree.

CAMPHOR TREE = *Cinnamomum Camphora.*

CAMPHORWEED = *Trichostema lanceolatum. See* BLUECURLS.

CAMPION. *See* LYCHNIS; *see also* SILENE.

CAMPO PEA = *Lathyrus splendens.*

CAMPSIS. *See* TRUMPET-CREEPER.

CAMPTOSORUS (kamp-toe-sore'rus). A genus of two species of hardy ferns, family Polypodiaceae, the one below North American and grown only in the wild garden or in ferneries; the other Asiatic and scarcely in cult. Fronds evergreen, undivided, rooting at the tip. Spore* cases narrow, line-like, scattered along the veins of the fronds. (*Camptosorus* is from the Greek for a curved sorus.*)

The walking fern naturally inhabits limestone ledges or limey woods and should only be attempted if one has access to crushed limestone which should be mixed with well-decayed (non-acid) humus. The plants prefer at least partial shade.

rhizophyllus. Walking fern or walking leaf. Fronds basal, evergreen, 7–8 in. long, and narrow, heart-shaped at the base, but tapering at the apex to a long, thread-like tip which roots (hence walking fern). Quebec to Ga. and westward.

camptotricha, -us, -um (kam-to-tree'ka). With bent hairs.

campylocarpa, -us, -um (kam-py'lo-car-pa). With curved fruit.

camtschatensis, -e (kam-chat-ten'sis). From Kamchatka, Siberia.

camtschatica, -us, -um (kam-chat'i-ka). From Kamchatka, Siberia.

CANADA. As an adjective Canada is part of the common name of many plants. Originally most of them were supposed to be confined to Canada, but are now known from many other parts of N.A. The hort. species that appear in this book and their proper equivalents, are:

Canada barberry = *Berberis canadensis;* Canada bluegrass = *Poa compressa;* Canada crookneck squash (*see* CUCURBITA MOSCHATA); Canada moonseed = *Menispermum canadense;* Canada pest (*see* EUSTOMA); Canada plum = *Prunus nigra;* Canada potato = *Helianthus tuberosus* (*see* SUNFLOWER); Canada thistle = *Cirsium arvense* (*see* list at WEEDS); Canada violet = *Viola canadensis.*

canadensis, -e (kan-a-den'sis). From Canada or described as from there (*see* CANADA).

CANAFISTULA = *Cassia Fistula.*

CANAIGRE = *Rumex hymenosepalus.*

canaliculata, -us, -um (kan a-lick-you-lay'-ta). Channeled lengthwise.

CANANGA (ka-nan'ga). Also spelled *Canangium*. A small Malayan genus of aromatic trees, family Annonaceae, one of which, the ylang-ylang, is occasionally grown for ornament in zone* 9. It is hardy nowhere else in U.S. Leaves evergreen, alternate,* without marginal teeth. Flowers hanging, greenish-yellow, very fragrant and the source of perfume in the Pacific Islands. Petals 6. Sepals

---

* Special articles on the subjects indicated by an asterisk (*) will be found at the words so marked.

3. Fruit a collection of stalked, fleshy, and many-seeded carpels.* (*Cananga* is a Latinized version of a native Malayan name.)

odorata. Ylang-ylang. A tree 60–80 ft., much less in extreme southern Fla., the branches drooping. Leaves oblongish, 6–8 in. long, bright green above, a little hairy beneath. Flowers about 2 in. long, the petals narrow. Fruit about 1 in. long, greenish. Indo-Malaya.

canariensis, -e (ka-nay-ri-en′sis). From the Canary Islands.

CANARY-BIRD FLOWER = *Tropaeolum peregrinum.* See NASTURTIUM.

CANARY GRASS = *Phalaris canariensis.*

CANAVALIA (kan-a-val′ee-a). A genus of herbs or vines of the pea family, widely distributed in the tropics. Of the 25 known species the only two of much garden interest are grown from zone* 7 southward, somewhat for ornament but usually for stock food, or the beans occasionally for human food. They have compound* leaves, usually with 3 leaflets. Flowers rather large, showy, typically pea-like, and with a 2-lipped* calyx. Fruit a large, flat, somewhat woody pod (legume*), the seeds white or reddish brown. (*Canavalia* is the Latinized version of an aboriginal name.)

The seeds should be planted in rows 3 ft. apart and put 8–15 in. apart in the rows. The plants need a long growing season to mature.

ensiformis. Jack bean. An annual, erect herb 2–4 ft. high. Leaflets oblong or elliptic, 3–5 in. long, the tip pointed. Flowers purple, about 1 in. long, in showy, drooping clusters 10–12 in. long. Pod 8–12 in. long, slightly curved, white seeds nearly ¾ in. long. W.I.

gladiata. Sword or saber bean. Resembling *C. ensiformis,* but a twining vine with shorter, much-curved pods and the seeds reddish-brown. Old World tropics.

CANDEBOBE = *Lemaireocereus weberi.*

candicans (kan′di-kanz). White-hairy or white-woolly.

candida, -us, -um (kan′di-da). White and shining.

candidissima, -us, -um (kan-di-dis′see-ma). Very hoary or white-hairy.

candidula, -us, -um (kan-did′you-la). Somewhat white and shining.

CANDLE LARKSPUR = *Delphinium elatum.*

CANDLEMAS BELLS. See SNOWDROP.

CANDLE TREE = *Parmentiera cerifera.*

CANDLEWICK = *Verbascum Thapsus.*

CANDLEWOOD. See FOUQUIERIA.

CANDY-STICK TULIP = *Tulipa clusiana.*

CANDYTUFT. These valuable garden plants, belonging to the genus **Iberis** (eye-beer′is), of the mustard family, comprise perhaps 25 species of annual or perennial herbs, mostly from the Mediterranean region. The cult. species are about equally divided between those which are annuals or treated as such and the perennials. Leaves divided or undivided, alternate.* Flowers in flat-topped or finger-shaped clusters, the 4 petals separate. Sometimes the outer flowers of a cluster are sterile. Fruit a nearly round or ovalish pod, flattish and often notched at the tip. (Named from *Iberia,* the ancient name for Spain, where some species are native.)

The annual candytufts can be treated as hardy annuals and the seed sown where needed. They bloom in about 6 weeks from sowing and keep on blooming until frost, except in warm regions. The plants should be thinned to about 6 in. apart. The perennials are easily propagated by division, and are useful plants for edging or for the rock garden. Both sorts tend to run to seed (*i.e.,* stop flowering) if kept too dry, so they are best watered during droughts if bloom is to be maintained, and they are helped by picking.

I. amara. Rocket candytuft. One of the annual species, more or less erect and about 12 in. high. Leaves broadest toward the tip, 3–4 in. long. Flowers fragrant, white, the finger-shaped cluster ultimately getting long. Eu. Much grown, both in the garden and by florists, for cutting, and known in many forms, some dwarf.

I. gibraltarica. A perennial species, not so much grown, and sometimes called the Gibraltar candytuft. Leaves 1–2 in. long. Flowers light purple or lilac, in flat-topped clusters. Spain.

I. jucunda. See AETHIONEMA CORIDIFOLIUM.

I. saxatalis. An evergreen woody perennial or sub-shrub,* 3–6 in. high, usually minutely hairy. Leaves narrow, about ¾ in. long, minutely hairy on the margins. Flowers white, small, but many in a close cluster (umbel*). May. Southern Eu. Hardy from zone* 5 southward.

I. sempervirens. Edging or perennial candytuft. The best perennial species, the foliage evergreen in most regions. Leaves narrow, oblongish, ¾–1¼ in. long. Flowers in longish, finger-shaped clusters, white. Eurasia. A fine hort. form is Snowflake.

I. umbellata. Globe or annual candytuft. The leading annual garden species, more or less erect, 8–15 in. high. Leaves narrow, thin, 2–3½ in. long. Flowers in close clusters, pink, red, lilac, or violet, not fragrant. Eu. Here belong the colored candytufts that are annuals.

CANE. The stem of a bush fruit like the raspberry, or the stem of a rose; more rarely the stem of a bamboo. A special use of the term is the yearling, often bearing, wood of a grape vine or bramble fruit.

CANE PALM = *Chrysalidocarpus lutescens.*

CANE REED = *Arundinaria gigantea.*

canescens (kan-ness′senz). Canescent; *i.e.,* covered with ashy-gray, more or less matted hairs.

canina, -us, -um (kan-eye′na). Pertaining to a dog, as in *Rosa canina,* the dog rose.

CANISTEL = *Lucuma nervosa.*

CANISTRUM (ka-niss′trum). A genus of ten species of scurfy-leaved herbs, family Bromeliaceae, the two below sometimes grown in greenhouses for their rather showy flower clusters. Leaves finely spiny on the margins, borne in a dense, basal, water-hold-

---

* Special articles on the subjects indicated by an asterisk (*) will be found at the words so marked.

ing rosette, but narrow or sword-shaped toward the tip. Flower stalks with a showy, colored whorl* of bracts* beneath the cluster. Flowers yellow-orange or greenish-white. (For structure see BROMELIACEAE.) Fruit a many-seeded berry. (*Canistrum* is from Greek for basket, in allusion to the cup-like whorl of bracts.)

These are showy greenhouse plants, needing a temperature of 60°–75° and plenty of water during spring and summer, but much less in winter, when growth is nearly stopped. Plant in pots or wooden cribs in a soil made up of ⅓ potting mixture* 3 and ⅔ chopped fern roots or other coarse fiber.

amazonicum. Leaves many, the blades 12–18 in. long, about 2½ in. wide, brownish but not spotted. Flowering stalk short, terminated by a dense head of narrow bracts, the flowers greenish-white. Brazil. Sometimes sold as *Nidularium amazonicum.*

aurantiacum. Leaves 10–12 in. long, green but spotted or banded with darker green. Flowering stalk crowned by a head of green and red bracts, the flowers orange-yellow and about 1½ in. long. Brazil.

CANKER. The name applied to various plant diseases. The cankered area is depressed and dead and often results in death of the entire branch or tree trunk above the cankered area. The disease may be caused by bacteria or fungi. In most cases the fungicide sprays are of little or no value. Branches with canker should be cut off, well below the cankered area, and burned.

CANKER LETTUCE = *Pyrola americana.*

CANKER-ROOT = *Coptis trifolia.*

CANNA (kan'na). A very useful and handsome genus of tropical herbs, constituting the family **Cannaceae** (kan-nay'see-ee) which was once included in the Scitamineae. They have mostly tuberous rootstocks and stately, broad, often colored leaves, without marginal teeth, but prominently veined, the leafstalk sheathing. In the garden canna (there are 40 others, mostly non-hort. species) the flowers are very showy, sometimes gorgeous, in a terminal cluster and very irregular.* Sepals 3 and greenish. Petals 3, resembling the sepals. Nearly all the color comes from the much-enlarged, colored, and petal-like, sterile stamens (staminodes). Fruit a 3-angled, roughish pod (capsule*), surrounded by the withered calyx. (*Canna* is an old name for some reed-like plant.)

The lack of species names below is frankly an evasion of the problem of the true parentage and specific identity of the hundreds of named forms of these most popular bedding plants. They have been so much hybridized that it is doubtful if any modern canna can now be assigned definitely to any of its wild ancestors, and even the parentage of many of them is wholly unknown.

CANNA CULTURE AND VARIETIES

Over most sections of the country cannas must be grown as summer bedding plants, as they are tropical plants that will not tolerate frost. In parts of Calif. and the Far South, however, they may be left in the ground and treated like any other perennial herb.

Until a few years ago cannas were mostly grown for their handsome foliage, particularly the old-fashioned Indian Shot (*Canna indica*), with green leaves and often growing 5–7 ft. high. Today we chiefly grow them for the gorgeous flowers that have been developed by the plant breeders, mostly French. These plants are shorter than the Indian Shot, often have bronze-colored leaves and a wide range of color in their very showy flower clusters.

Their culture is easy if one will prepare a bed 18–24 in. deep. They like a good rich soil and if the proposed canna bed is poor or stony dig it out and fill in with any good garden loam to which has been added about ¼ its bulk in well-rotted manure. In making such a bed it is well to leave the center 4–6 in. higher than the edges.

In order to lengthen the canna season it is best to use potted plants instead of planting the rootstocks. The former are cheap and in the markets at the proper time in your locality which is long after all danger of frost is over. The idea is not merely to dodge a sporadic late frost but to put the plants in soil warm enough to be congenial for a tropical plant — in other words, they need summer heat.

Space the rootstocks or potted plants 18 in. apart each way, and, of course, see that tall varieties are at the center of the bed. The foliage and flower color of cannas are so strikingly different from most other garden plants that a canna bed needs careful placing with relation to the rest of your garden. By itself, with a background of shrubbery and trees, or in the center of a formal courtyard, a canna bed may be very stunning. But a scattered clump peppering up the front lawn or a small patch of canna in a perennial border looks, and is, incongruous. Convincing and large patches of them, however, are very striking in a border.

Summer care is very simple. If the bed is kept thoroughly watered over drought periods, and free of weeds, the canna will do well over most of the country, provided there is plenty of heat. When autumn frosts threaten they should be dug up and stored just as one stores dahlias. Their culture is very similar to that of dahlias, except that they require more heat. In the early spring, if you intend raising your own plants, divide the rootstock so that there will be at least one, but not more than two, buds to a piece of rootstock. Pot up the pieces in early April and put in a warm greenhouse. If you have only a hotbed, it is better to wait until May to start the cannas. And if you have neither, the rootstocks may be planted directly in the bed, but not before the soil temperature at 6 in. deep is at least 65°; in other words, tomato-planting time or later. The latter procedure, of course, delays matters so much that most home gardeners prefer to buy pot plants ready for outdoor planting.

---

* Special articles on the subjects indicated by an asterisk (*) will be found at the words so marked.

VARIETIES. If you merely want a handsome, green-foliaged bedding plant, the old-fashioned Indian Shot is one of the best. It has, also, red flowers, but these are nothing like so striking as in the varieties listed below. The plant is about 4 ft. high, has leaves about 18 in. long, and, in the warmer sections of the country, it frequently escapes.*

The modern cannas are all of hybrid origin and the list of named forms is confusing. Often the different dealers will offer the same plant under different names. It is, therefore, of the greatest importance to buy plants or rootstocks from a reputable dealer, whose named forms come true. From hundreds that are offered the following promise the best chances of success, and provide as wide a choice of color and stature as most growers desire. Novelties, at much increased prices, are constantly being offered. Your curiosity and pocketbook are the only limits to trying such.

The relatively standard varieties are:

The Ambassador; 5 ft.; cherry-red flowers; bronze leaves; free bloomer.
City of Portland; 3½ to 4 ft.; clear rose-pink; green foliage; free bloomer.
King Humbert; O. 5 ft.; large, orange-scarlet flowers; bronzy foliage; popular.
Mrs. Alfred F. Conard; 4 ft.; salmon-pink; large-size blooms; bright green foliage.
Mrs. Pierre S. duPont; 4 ft.; watermelon-pink; large flowers; massive trusses.
The President; 4 ft.; crimson flowers; vigorous; free-flowering; green foliage.
Wintzer's Colossal; O. 6 ft.; immense trusses of bright scarlet flowers.
Wyoming; O. 6 ft.; immense spikes of orange flowers; bronze-purple foliage.
Yellow King Humbert; O. 4½ ft.; yellow flowers dotted orange; sport from King Humbert.

Those marked O are the so-called orchid-flowered cannas, in which the petals become re-curved. They are very handsome plants. Other canna varieties, and by some preferred to those above, are:

Hungaria; 3½ ft.; pink; bluish-green foliage.
Eureka; 4½ ft.; white; green foliage.
Copper Giant; 4 ft.; red and old rose; green foliage.

For the number of plants needed for a round bed see GARDEN TABLES IV.

INSECT PESTS. Leaf-feeding insects and leaf-rolling caterpillars can be stopped by regular application of pesticide #1 (see SPRAYS AND DUSTS).

DISEASES. The most serious disease of canna is the bacterial bud rot. The disease starts as a water-soaked leafspot* and stem rot, after which buds and flowers rot. Select planting stock from healthy plants. Soak the dormant rootstocks in pesticide #12 (see SPRAYS AND DUSTS) at a concentration of 1–1000 for 2 hours prior to planting.

cannabina, -us, -um (kan-na-by'na). Hemp-like.

CANNABINACEAE (kan-na-bi-nay'see-ee). There are only two genera in the hemp. family — *Cannabis* and the hop (*Humulus*) — both of which are widely cultivated for fiber, narcotics, for the making of beer, or sometimes for ornament. See VINES.

They have alternate* leaves and small, greenish and inconspicuous flowers. The fruit is a dry achene* in *Cannabis* (the hemp), but a catkin-like or cone-like cluster in the hop. In both genera the male and female flowers are on different plants. From the closely related fig family (Moraceae), with which they are sometimes included, the hemp family is easily distinguished by not having a milky juice.

CANNABIS (kan'na-bis). A single species of annual herb, family Cannabinaceae, a native of temperate As., and of little garden, but great economic, importance because it yields both hemp and hashish. The only species, **C. sativa**, the hemp, is a strong-smelling herb, with a rough, almost woody stem from which the hemp (not Manila hemp) fiber is derived. It has compound* leaves, the 3–7 long, slender leaflets arranged finger-fashion. Flowers green, small, inconspicuous, the male and female on different plants. Widely grown for hemp, then only as an agricultural crop in warm regions. It has little or no garden value and the cult. of female plants is forbidden in many countries because from the sticky gum found among the flower clusters is derived the narcotic hashish, a dilution of which is usually here called marihuana. (*Cannabis* is the classical name of the hemp.)

CANNACEAE (kan-nay'see-ee). The canna family. See CANNA.

CANOE BIRCH = *Betula papyrifera.* See BIRCH.

CAÑON LIVE OAK = *Quercus chrysolepis.* See OAK.

cantabrica, -us, -um (kan-tab'ri-ka). From Cantabria, an old name for northern Spain.

CANTALOUPE. See MELON.

cantalupensis, -e (kan-ta-loo-pen'sis). From Cantalupo, Italy.

canterburyana, -us, -um (kan-ter-berry-ā'na). From Canterbury, New Zealand; rarely from Canterbury, England.

CANTERBURY BELLS = *Campanula Medium.*

cantoniensis, -e (kan-ton-i-en'sis). From Canton, China.

CANTUA (kan'tew-a). A small genus of South American shrubs or small trees, family Polemoniaceae, the one below grown outdoors in Calif. and elsewhere in zones* 8 and 9, rarely in the greenhouse. Leaves opposite,* without marginal teeth (in ours). Flowers in hanging, terminal clusters, the corolla with a long tube and 5 short, spreading lobes. Fruit a 3-valved capsule,* with many seeds. (Name is a Latinized form of a Peruvian vernacular.)

In Calif., where it is sometimes called magic tree, from its quick response to rainfall after a drought, the species below is a handsome, showy garden shrub. For indoor

---

* Special articles on the subjects indicated by an asterisk (*) will be found at the words so marked.

cult. it needs a cool greenhouse and potting mixture* 4. Easily propagated by cuttings.

buxifolia. Shrub 5–8 ft. high. Leaves about 1 in. long, rather crowded. Flowers 2–3 in. long, numerous, the tube pinkish-red but yellow-striped. Andes.

CAPE AND CAPE BULBS. Early hort. literature is full of references to "The Cape" and the Cape bulbs — all referable to bulbous or tuberous plants from the Cape of Good Hope, South Africa. As exploration uncovered the garden treasures of this extraordinary country, the list of Cape Bulbs grew. Among them are *Babiana, Ixia, Freesia, Sparaxis, Lachenalia, Tritonia, Gladiolus,* and many others.

CAPE COWSLIP. See LACHENALIA.

CAPE FORGET-ME-NOT = *Anchusa capensis.*

CAPE FUCHSIA = *Phygelius capensis.*

CAPE GOOSEBERRY = *Physalis peruviana.*

CAPE HONEYSUCKLE = *Tecomaria capensis.*

CAPE JASMINE = *Gardenia jasminoides.*

CAPE MARIGOLD. See DIMORPHOTHECA.

capensis, -e (ka-pen'sis). From the Cape (which see).

CAPE PONDWEED. *Aponogeton distachyus.*

CAPE PRIMROSE. See STREPTOCARPUS.

CAPER = *Capparis spinosa.*

CAPER FAMILY = Capparidaceae.

capillaris, -e (ka-pil-lay'ris). Capillary; *i.e.,* hair-like.

capillata, -us, -um (ka-pil-lay'ta). With capillaries or fine hairs.

Capillus-Veneris (ka-pil-lus-ven'er-is). Venus's-hair. See ADIANTUM.

capitata, -us, -um (ka pi-tay'ta). Capitate; *i.e.,* having flowers or fruits in a dense head (capitulum).

capitulata, -us, -um (ka-pit-you-lay'ta). Having small heads, as in some flower clusters.

cappadocica, -us, -um (kap-pa-dō'si-ka). From Cappadocia in eastern Asia Minor.

CAPPARIDACEAE (kap-par-i-day'see-ee). The caper family consists of over 30 genera and 450 species of mostly tropical or warm region shrubs or herbs, only two of which, *Capparis* and *Cleome,* are of any garden interest. They have usually alternate* leaves, without marginal teeth and a watery sap. Flowers more or less irregular, the four petals often with a claw.*

The fruit is a berry in *Capparis* (the flower buds of which furnish the familiar caper), while it is a dry pod (capsule*), often stalked, in *Cleome,* which is cult. for its handsome flowers.

Technical flower characters: In the garden genera, sepals and petals 4. Stamens numerous in *Capparis;* 6 in *Cleome,* and often long and showy. Ovary 1-celled, with many ovules.

CAPPARIS (kap'par-ris). A large genus of shrubs and trees, family Capparidaceae, widely distributed but mostly tropical, only one of which, the caper, is of any garden interest, and this chiefly in southern Europe where it is cult. for capers. (For flower and fruit characters *see* CAPPARIDACEAE.) The cult. species, C. spinosa, the source of capers, is a spiny, somewhat straggling shrub 3–6 ft. high, with simple,* roundish or oval leaves 1–2 in. long. Flowers (the unopened buds are the capers) white, solitary, borne in the leaf axils* on stout stalks, the petals about 1 in. long. Mediterranean region. Not hardy above zone* 6, but it is sometimes grown northward as a tender annual. (*Capparis* is the classical name of the caper.)

caprea (kap'ree-a). A specific name pertaining to a goat, applied to a willow (*Salix caprea*); of uncertain application there.

capreolata, -us, -um (kap-ree-o-lay'ta). Twining or winding.

capricornis, -e (kap-ri-cor'nis). Like a goat's horn; sometimes, also, applied to plants from or below the Tropic of Capricorn.

CAPRIFIG; CAPRIFICATION. See FIG.

CAPRIFOLIACEAE (kap-ri-foe-li-ā'see-ee). The honeysuckle family, often called the elder or twinflower family, is a large aggregation of herbs, shrubs, woody vines or trees, most of its 350 species growing within the north temperate zone. All of its genera are of garden interest, some, as *Weigela, Lonicera* (the honeysuckles), *Symphoricarpos,* and *Viburnum* being among the most popular shrubs and vines in cult. Leaves opposite*; compound* in the elder (*Sambucus*), but simple in all the other genera. Flowers regular,* and more or less tubular in *Abelia, Abeliophyllum, Kolkwitzia, Leycesteria, Linnaea* (the twinflower), *Triosteum, Weigela,* and *Viburnum,* but more or less irregular* in *Diervilla* and *Dipelta,* and noticeably so in the honeysuckles.

All the genera are shrubs, trees, or woody vines, except *Linnaea* and *Triosteum,* both of which are herbaceous. The fruit is a berry or fleshy in some genera (especially the elder), but dry in others.

Technical flower characters: Overy inferior.* Calyx 4–5-toothed or lobed, its tube joined to the ovary. Corolla 4–5-lobed, the stamens alternating with its lobes. Ovary 1–5-celled.

Caprifolium (kap-ri-fō'lee-um). Pre-Linnaean* name for a honeysuckle.

CAPRIOLA = CYNODON.

CAPSELLA BURSA-PASTORIS = Shepherd's purse. See list at WEEDS.

Capsicastrum (kap-si-kas'trum). Like a pepper of the genus *Capsicum.*

CAPSICUM (kap'si-kum). A confused but hort. important genus of tropical, woody plants of the potato family, yielding red (but not black) pepper, tabasco, and cayenne pepper, as well as the milder peppers commonly

* Special articles on the subjects indicated by an asterisk (*) will be found at the words so marked.

grown for seasoning and as vegetables. Most of the species (or there may be only one with many varieties, as here treated) are from tropical America, but in the North they are grown as tender annuals. Leaves alternate,* simple,* without marginal teeth. Flowers white or greenish-white, usually stalked and solitary or in 2–3-flowered clusters, generally wheel-shaped and 5-lobed. Fruit typically a pod-like berry, with a thickish rind, but much diversified as to shape and color, and easily divided, as to taste, between the mild and very pungent sorts. (*Capsicum* is Latin for a box or chest, apparently in reference to the fruit.)

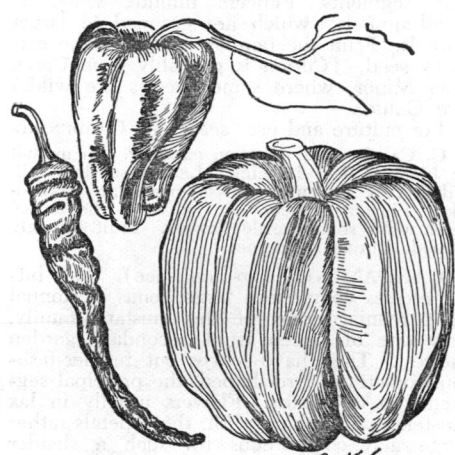

Three common types of peppers. At the left, the red (very pungent) pepper. At the right, the bell pepper. Above, the cherry pepper.

For culture *see* below.

As here, and usually, treated, all the garden peppers are derived from a single species, *C. frutescens* (also called by others *C. annuum* and *C. baccatum*) and probably native in tropical America, although it may have been wild also in the Old World tropics. Its progeny, in scores of forms, are now found all over the tropical world. It is a woody shrub 6–8 ft. tall, with variously shaped leaves, flowers about ½ in. in diameter, and the fruits represented by the bird pepper (also called chili and spur pepper), which is red but scarcely 1 in. long. This plant is rare or altogether lacking among the numerous modern cult. varieties, being chiefly tropical. The varieties derived from it, while of tropical origin, are cult. here as annuals. The chief cult. peppers are:

frutescens cerasiforme. Cherry pepper. Leaves 2–3 in. long. Fruit roundish or heart-shaped, about ¾ in. in diameter, red, yellow, or purplish and very pungent, erect or recurved.

frutescens conoides. Cone pepper. Like the cherry pepper, but the fruit cone-shaped or cylindrical, 1–2 in. long, and erect.

frutescens fasciculatum. Red cluster pepper. Leaves narrow and clustered. Fruit in small bunches, narrow, slender, 3 in. long and pencil-thick, red, very pungent and erect.

frutescens grossum. Bell or sweet pepper. Leaves larger than in the others, oblongish, 4–5 in. long. Flowers nearly 1 in. in diameter. Fruit large, generally bell-shaped or oblongish, more or less puffy, the sides ridged or furrowed, variously colored, but of mild flavor.

frutescens longum. Long pepper. Fruit hanging, 4–10 in. long and tapering to a point, but the base often 2 in. wide, red or yellow. Here belongs the variety yielding cayenne pepper, and other very pungent sorts.

PEPPER CULTURE

From zone* 6 northward peppers are treated as summer annuals, very much like tomatoes. They need more heat than tomatoes and a longer growing season, so that above zone* 4 their culture, while safe enough for household needs, is too risky for commercial production.

If you do not wish to grow your own plants, they can always be purchased at the proper time, which is outdoor tomato-planting time in your locality (*see* TOMATO). If you raise your own plants, the procedure is the same as for tomato.

Whichever method you follow, it is essential to know exactly what sort of peppers you wish to raise and pick them from the following named varieties:

Hot peppers for flavoring, sauces, etc.

Red Chili.
Red Hot. Long, pointed, and fiery hot.
Hungarian Way.
Tabasco. For Calif.

Mild-flavored peppers for stuffing, pickling, or even slicing and eating like tomatoes.

Bull Nose.
California Wonder.
Early California Wonder.

There is still a third category of garden peppers, the pimiento, often incorrectly called pimento. They are raised chiefly in Calif. or south of zone* 6, and the most satisfactory varieties are Perfection (for Calif.) and Panama.

As one approaches the tropics, peppers, instead of being summer annuals, tend to revert to the perennial or woody ancestral form. In some parts of Fla. they are so grown.

INSECT PESTS. Flea beetles which damage leaves badly are controlled by pesticide #1 (*see* SPRAYS AND DUSTS) or #17. In the South and Southwest, pepper weevil, a grayish snout beetle, attacks foliage and particularly fruit. As fruits first appear, protect with pesticide #1 or #17 at weekly intervals. In the Northwest, a maggot attacks fruit. Control adult flies with pesticide #1 or #21 at weekly intervals after fruits are ½ inch in size.

DISEASES. One of the most widespread of the pepper diseases is the bacterial leaf and fruit spot. Severe infections will defoliate the plant and make the fruit unusable. Soak the seeds for 5 minutes in pesticide #12 (*see* SPRAYS AND DUSTS) at a concentration of

---

* Special articles on the subjects indicated by an asterisk (*) will be found at the words so marked.

1–2000, rinse in fresh water, dry, and plant. In some areas the use of streptomycin *plus* pesticide #3 has proven very satisfactory if diseased plants are sprayed while still in the plant bed. Consult your state agricultural experiment station for details for your area.

Several fungi may cause large rotted areas in the fruit. Control with applications of pesticide #1 or #11 as the fruit starts to ripen, and repeat at 10-day intervals.

Several virus diseases cause various mosaic* patterns of yellow in the leaves. Some of these troubles will be prevented if the persons working with the plants use no tobacco while handling plants.

A wilt* disease affects plants in some areas, and various root rots cause death of plants. Although the particular fungus may differ in various parts of the country, the control recommendation of rotating the plantings from year to year will offer best control.

capsularis, -e (kap-soo-lay′ris). Capsular; *i.e.*, bearing a capsule.*

CAPSULE. A dry fruit of more than one, often several, compartments or cells. It always splits open by one or more seams or valves, or rarely by terminal or basal pores. In splitting, it usually does so lengthwise. In a few capsules, it splits around the circumference, hence when split it is in two cup-like sections. Typical capsules are found in iris, all the poppy family, many of the lily family, the trumpet-creeper, the rhododendron, and hundreds of other plants.

CAPTAN. *See* Fungicides.

Caracalla. An obsolete name for plants now included in *Phaseolus.*

caracasana, -us, -um (ka-ra-ka-say′na). From Caracas, Venezuela.

CARAGANA (ka-ra-gay′na). Decorative shrubs and trees of the pea family comprising nearly 50 species which are mostly native in central Asia. Those below are shrubs or small trees with compound* leaves, the numerous leaflets arranged feather-fashion, without an odd one at the end. Flowers typically pea-like, yellow. Legumes* narrow and nearly round. (*Caragana* is a Latinized form of the Mongolian *caragan*, a native name for one of the species.)

The pea tree or pea shrub is a hardy plant easily grown in any garden soil, preferably in full sunlight. As hedge plants for windbreaks and snow traps few plants are superior in regions of intense cold. Propagated by seeds (first soaked in hot water) or by cuttings.

arborescens. Pea tree or pea shrub. Not over 20 ft., usually less, the spines often lacking. Leaves 1–3 in. long, composed of 4–6 pairs of tiny leaflets about ⅛ in. long each. Flowers nearly ¾ in. long, yellow, borne singly, but several close together, hence showy when in bloom. Pod (legume*) 1½–2 in. long, stalked. Siberia. Hardy from zone* 1 southward. There are dwarf forms suitable for hedges, and valuable in regions where privet is not hardy.

frutex. A smooth, upright shrub, 7–9 ft. high, its twigs yellowish. Leaflets 4, oblongish, ¾–1¼ in. long. Flowers bright yellow, 1–3 in a cluster, about 1 in. long, followed by a cylindric pod nearly 2½ in. long. Siberia to

Turkestan. May–June. Hardy from zone* 2 southward.

pygmaea. Resembling *Caragana frutex*, but only 2–4 ft. high, with narrower leaves and solitary flowers, the pods about 1½ in. long. Siberia to China. May–June. Hardy from zone* 2 southward.

Carambola. Vernacular name in the Orient for *Averrhoa Carambola.*

Carandas. Native name for the karanda (*Carissa Carandas*).

CARAWAY. This fragrant condiment is derived from one of about 20 species of the genus **Carum** (kair′um), of the carrot family, all of which are herbs of the temperate zone. Leaves mostly basal, much compounded into tiny segments. Flowers minute, white, in small umbels* which are grouped in larger umbels. Fruit the familiar and aromatic caraway seed. (*Carum* is probably from Caria, Asia Minor, where some species are wild.) *See* Carica.

For culture and uses *see* Herb Gardening.

C. Carvi. The common caraway. An annual or biennial 1–2 ft. high. Leaves so finely divided that the ultimate segments are threadlike. Flowers scarcely ⅒ in. wide, the umbel often with some sterile flowers. Fruit strongly ribbed. Eurasia. Summer.

CARDAMINE (kar-dam′i-nee). The bitter cresses comprise a large genus of annual or perennial herbs of the mustard family, only one of which is of secondary garden interest. They have leaves cut feather-fashion, sometimes lyre-shaped, the principal segments in 3–7 pairs. Flowers usually in lax clusters, white or purplish, the 4 petals rather large and conspicuous for such a slender plant. Fruit a long and slender, somewhat flattened silique.* (*Cardamine* is a classical name for some cress.)

The only cult. species is easily grown in sites that approximate its wild home, which is always in moist or even wet, preferably shaded, places. It will stand open sunlight if kept moist.

pratensis. Lady's-smock; also called cuckoo-flower and milkmaids. An erect, but not stiff, perennial 8–15 in. high. Leaves with the segments scarcely ½ in. long. Flowers in a terminal cluster, rarely double, about ½ in. wide. Cooler parts of the north temperate zone. June.

CARDAMON. The true cardamon is derived from the plant below, which is the only species of the genus **Elettaria** (el-et-tay′ri-a), of the family Zingiberaceae. It is a stout herb, closely related to *Amomum*, and native in tropical As. The only species, **Elettaria Cardamomum**, rarely cult. outdoors in zone* 9, or in a warm greenhouse, is about 5–9 ft. high, with large leaves that are hairy on the under side. Flowering stalk arising from the thick rootstock, and naked, the flowers in loose spikes or racemes, very irregular.* Fruit a capsule,* the seeds being cardamons, except that inferior cardamons are often substituted from the related plant *Amomum Cardamon.* The culture of *Elettaria*, which is a

---

* Special articles on the subjects indicated by an asterisk (*) will be found at the words so marked.

Latinized version of a native Malabar name is the same as for ginger (which see).

Cardiaca (kar-dy'a-ka). Pre-Linnaean* name for the motherwort (*Leonurus*).

CARDINAL-FLOWER = *Lobelia Cardinalis.*

CARDINAL CLIMBER = *Quamoclit sloteri.*

Cardinalis, -e (kar-din-nay'lis). Cardinal-red.

CARDIOCRINUM. *See* LILIUM GIGANTEUM.

CARDIOSPERMUM (kar-dee-o-sper'-mum). A genus of perhaps 15 species of chiefly tropical, herbaceous vines of the family Sapindaceae, one cultivated, mostly in warm regions, for ornament. *See* VINES. Leaves alternate,* twice-compound,* the ultimate leaflets coarsely toothed. Flowers small but numerous, unisexual,* in clusters that bear tendrils. Sepals and petals each 4, the latter slightly irregular* or unequal. Fruit a papery, inflated and veiny capsule,* 3-valved, and with black seeds with a white, heart-shaped spot, hence the common name of heart-seed for these vines. (*Cardiospermum* is from the Greek for heart and seed.)

The balloon-vine is a quick-growing plant useful for trellises and low buildings. While native in the tropics, it can be treated as an annual in the North.

Halicacabum. Balloon-vine. Not usually over 10–12 ft. high. Leaflets ovalish, pointed. Flowers white, the clusters scarcely longer than the leaves. Pod 3-angled, about 1 in. long, the seeds pea-size. Tropical regions, and naturalized in the southeastern U.S.

CARDON = *Lemaireocereus weberi.*

CARDOON (*Cynara Cardunculus*). This thistle-like, spiny-leaved perennial herb is a close relative of the true artichoke, but its edible portion is the thickened (and blanched) leafstalk, which is boiled and used like spinach, or sometimes eaten fresh. Because the leafstalks are somewhat bitter, the cardoon is decidedly one of our secondary vegetables.

Its culture is much like the artichoke (which see) and it has somewhat the same climatic requirements. Being a tender vegetable, it will not ordinarily stand the rigors of a northern winter. Plants must be raised in the hotbed, very much as tomato plants are, and planted outdoors after settled warm weather arrives. Put them about 3 ft. apart each way. In the South or in Calif. the seed may be sown directly outdoors.

In the autumn, draw the leaves together and wrap the stalks in heavy paper, or slip a cardboard cylinder over them. Or any other method of blanching may be used except heaping soil which may rot them. If you want cardoon for winter use, dig up the plants and replant in a frost-free, dark cellar or pit, where blanching will naturally occur.

The plant needs a rich soil and plenty of moisture, but not mucky sites or poorly drained ones.

CARDUACEAE. *See* COMPOSITAE.

Cardunculus (kar-dun'kew-lus). A small thistle. *See* CYNARA.

CARDUUS (kard'you-us). An immense genus of thistles, mostly weedy, and belonging to the family Compositae. They are sometimes called plumeless thistles, and the one below is occasionally cult. in the border for ornament. (For other thistles *see* CNICUS and CIRSIUM.) The only cult. species of much garden interest is **Carduus kerneri,** a biennial or perennial herb 2–3 ft. high, with a winged and spiny stem. It has deeply lobed, spiny-toothed leaves and solitary heads of rose-purple flowers, the head surrounded by a series of spiny-toothed bracts.* There are no ray flowers in the head. The plant is probably native in the Balkans and is easily grown in ordinary garden soil. (*Carduus* is the classical name for a thistle.)

CAREX (cay'rex). The sedges are an enormous genus of grass-like plants of the family Cyperaceae, but of over 900 species scarcely a handful are of any garden interest, and the two below are only seldom cult. for their greenish spikes. From grasses, for which many take them, they are distinguished by having solid (not hollow), 3-angled stems. The two below are tufted perennials with flattish leaves. The flowers are minute, green, and crowded in flattish, spike-like clusters (for flower structure *see* CYPERACEAE), which are grouped at the top of the slender, grass-like stalks. (*Carex* is the classical name for the sedges.)

The first species is native in N.A., and can be grown in the open border. The second, a native of Japan, is sometimes grown as a pot plant in cool greenhouses or for edging greenhouse walks. It is not certainly hardy outdoors north of zone* 5. Propagation, which is simple, is by division of the grass-like clumps.

fraseri. A tufted perennial with flat, lily-like, evergreen leaves, about 18 in. high, and nearly 1½ in. wide. Stalk of the flower cluster about as long. In woods, Va. to S. Car. Also called *Cymophyllus fraseri.*

morrowi. Leaves flat, grass-like, about 12 in. long, evergreen, and sometimes white-striped in cult. forms. Flower spikes flattish, clustered at ends of stalks about as long as the leaves. Jap.

caribaea, -us, -um (kari-i-bee'a). From some island of the Caribbean Sea.

CARICA (ka'rick-a). The papaya is an important tropical American fruit tree and the only cult. genus of the family Caricaceae (ka-ri-kay'see-ee). It is sometimes called papaw (or pawpaw), but this name also applies to another tree (*see* ASIMINA). *Carica* has a straight, palm-like trunk, with a milky juice, topped by a cluster of immense leaves that are deeply lobed, finger-fashion, and very long-stalked. Male and female flowers usually on different trees, only the female producing fruit. Male flowers in slender,

---

* Special articles on the subjects indicated by an asterisk (*) will be found at the words so marked.

long-stalked, hanging clusters (racemes*), yellow, funnel-shaped, and about 1 in. long. Female flowers nearly stalkless, yellow, the 5 petals distinct. Fruit suggesting a yellow or orange melon, in some varieties oblong, in others globe-shaped, the flesh aromatic and delicious. Seeds black. (*Carica* is Latin for Caria, from which the specific name of the edible fig was derived. Caria is a division of southwestern Asia Minor, but neither the fig nor papaya is native there.)

For culture *see* below.

Papaya. The papaya. Not usually over 25 ft. high, bearing trees often being half this. Branches usually none. Leaves nearly 2 ft. across, round, deeply 7-lobed, the lobes again lobed, distinctly pale beneath, the leafstalks hollow and 2 ft. long. Fruit 4–20 in. long. Tropical America, but now naturalized throughout the tropical world, and widely planted there in improved varieties.

Papaya Culture

The tree is safely grown only in zone* 9 and most favored locations in zone* 8. One good frost will kill it, and too much near-frost will prevent its fruiting. It will grow in a variety of soils, but prefers rich ones and a good amount of moisture.

There are thousands of naturalized and relatively worthless papaya trees, the pollen of which infects good cult. varieties in Fla. Care must therefore be taken to root out these strays before planting to good varieties. Plant the trees at 8-foot intervals, using 8 female trees to 1 male tree to ensure pollination by a desirable variety.

The fruit, borne singly on short stems just below the terminal crown of leaves, ripens from midwinter to June in Fla. It is delicious, somewhat mucilaginous, and quickly perishes when ripe. Its milky juice and black seeds are rich in papain, and the juice is often used in tropical countries to soften tough meat.

The trees will respond to a dressing of good commercial fertilizers, but many trees in the tropics that get none are prolific bearers. Each tree should bear from 12–30 fruits a year, and do this for perhaps four years, but not much longer. Some growers only allow the trees to fruit one or two years. Propagation is by seeds, and the tree will bear about 12 months after being transferred from the seed bed to the open ground.

CARICATURE PLANT = *Graptophyllum pictum.*

carinata, -us, -um (ka-ri-nay'ta). Carinate; *i.e.,* keeled.

carinthiaca, -us, -um (ka-rin-thy'a-ka). From Carinthia, Austria.

CARISSA (ka-ris'sa). A genus of 30 species of spiny shrubs of the family Apocynaceae, chiefly South African, two somewhat grown for ornament or hedges, more rarely for their fruit. Leaves opposite,* without marginal teeth. Flowers in stalked clusters (cymes*), the corolla salver-shaped, white or pink. Stamens 5, inserted in the corolla tube.

Fruit a fleshy berry. (*Carissa* is of unknown origin.) For a closely related plant *see* Aco-kanthera spectabilis.

Both species can be grown outdoors throughout zones* 8 and 9, where they are used for hedge plants and are boy-proof from the plentiful spines. Fruits of the second species, the Natal plum, have a reddish pulp suggestive of the raspberry, but are little known outside of Fla., Calif., and the tropics.

Carandas. Karanda. Shrub or small tree, the spines not forked. Leaves oblong-oval, 2–3 in. long. Flowers white or pink, the tube about ¾ in. long. Berry reddish-black, about ¾ in. long, more or less elliptic. India.

grandiflora. Natal plum or amatungula. Very bushy shrub up to 15 ft. high, the spines forked. Leaves ovalish, 1–2½ in. long. Flowers white, nearly 2 in. wide. Berry egg-shaped, red, 1–2 in. long. S. Af.

carlcephalum (karl-seff'a-lum). A manufactured name derived from *Viburnum carlesi* and V. *macrocephalum.*

CARLINA (kar-lee'na). A small genus of Eurasian herbs of the daisy family (Compositae) with generally spiny-toothed, cut leaves, the segments arranged feather-fashion.* Flower heads large, the flowers all tubular, the head surrounded with leaf-like or ray*-like bracts.* The only cult. species, **C. acaulis,** is a stemless perennial herb not over 9 in. high, with much-cut leaves and a huge white solitary head of flowers nearly 6 in. wide. A thistle-like plant from S. Eu., occasionally cult. in the rock garden. (*Carlina* is from the French, carline, a thistle, in allusion to its thistle-like habit.)

CARLUDOVICA (kar-loo-dō'vi-ka). A genus of perhaps 35 species of palm-like, but apparently stemless, tropical American plants, and the only cult. genus of the family **Cyclanthaceae** (sy-clan-thay'see-ee). They have palm-like leaves which are long-stalked and fan-like. Flowers resembling those of the palms (*see* Palmaceae) and differing from them only in technical characters. Fruit a syncarp.* (Named for Carlos IV and Ludovia, king and queen of Spain.)

The species below is not infrequent in greenhouse palm collections, but is of far more hort. interest from the fact that, in Ecuador, it is the plant from which Panama hats are made. The plant is not native at Panama. For greenhouse cult. *see* Palm.

palmata. Jipi-japa; the Panama-hat plant. An essentially stemless, palm-like plant, the leafstalks channeled, arising from the ground, and 4–6 ft. long. Leaves fan-like, the blade split into four main divisions, each of which is again split, and the segments drooping at the tip. Peru and Ecuador.

CARMICHAELIA (kar-my-kay'li-a). Perhaps 20 species of New Zealand shrubs of the pea family, the green, flattened or cylindric branches often functioning as leaves while the latter fall. Leaves compound* (in ours), the few leaflets arranged feather-fashion, soon falling and leaving the plants with bare

---

* Special articles on the subjects indicated by an asterisk (*) will be found at the words so marked.

green twigs. Flowers pea-like, small, in lateral clusters (racemes*). Pod (legume*) small, leathery, nearly round. (Named for Dugald Carmichael, Scotch botanist.)

The two below are somewhat grown for their odd habit and pretty flowers in Calif. They appear to be without much soil preference, but will not stand much frost.

grandiflora. A shrub 4–6 ft. high, very twiggy. Leaflets 3–5, dropping after the plant blooms. Flowers purplish, but with violet veins, about ¼ in. long, 8–12 in a cluster. Pod about ½ in. long.

odorata. Larger than *C. grandiflora*, the branches hanging. Leaves not over ¾ in. long, with 3–7 leaflets or 3–7-parted. Flowers about ⅛ in. long, 10–20 in a cluster, white or lilac. Pod about ¼ in. long.

CARMINE CRABAPPLE = *Malus atrosanguinea.*

CARNATION (*Dianthus Caryophyllus*). To most people the word carnation means a flower which the florists display in their windows from October to May. But this is only part of the truth. *Dianthus Caryophyllus* is just as much a pink as many other species of *Dianthus*, and in some parts of the country can be treated as a hardy perennial. While this is a common method in England, few American gardeners treat the plant in this way. And it can be grown so only in regions of comparatively mild winters. They are grown outdoors successfully in Calif.

While these bedding or border carnations will bloom from seed in 6 or 8 months, they are often treated as perennials, raised from seed or cuttings, and planted out in the early spring. None is really hardy in regions of severe winters. It is among these plants that the fragrant or aromatic clove pink of England is found. They are not so showy as the ordinary carnation of the florists, but have a charm, and particularly a fragrance, that the commercially produced flower ordinarily lacks. Here also belongs the picotee carnation in which each petal is edged with some color that differs from the general color of the petal. Usually the edging is pink. In addition to the popular picotee, two other color designations are used: *Bizarres* for carnations with 2–3 stripes of contrasting color in the petals; and *Flakes* when striped only with one color.

GREENHOUSE CARNATIONS. Anyone with a greenhouse that can be kept during the winter between 50° (night) and 60° during the day can grow the ordinary florists' carnation if the following directions are adhered to. The year-round procedure is this:

(1) In November and December cuttings are made from plants growing in the greenhouse bench (*see below*). They should be taken from prolific-flowering stems, cut about halfway between the swollen joints and rooted in potting mixture* 1, which should take from 4–5 weeks. When thoroughly rooted, the plants should be potted up in potting mixture* 2 and grown along until the next step of the process.

(2) After all danger of frost is past, the potted cuttings should be planted outdoors in rows 16–24 in. apart and the plants set 8–10 in. apart in the row. The plants are then grown all summer very much like any other perennial; that is, the weeds must be kept down and the rows cultivated. Few or no blooms will appear, and if any do, the buds should be pinched off. Some time before frosts are expected the plants should be carefully dug, ready for the final step in their life cycle. Many professional growers omit the outdoor program and plant the cuttings in the greenhouse bench.

(3) The dug plants should be planted out directly in the greenhouse bench. The bench should have been filled several days or a week or two before with rich garden loam or with potting mixture* 3. Never allow the old soil of the previous year to be used the following one. Space the plants 6 in. apart in the rows and have the rows about 12 in. apart. If you want all the flowers you can get from each plant, they can be grown without further attention except plentiful watering and an occasional dose of liquid manure.

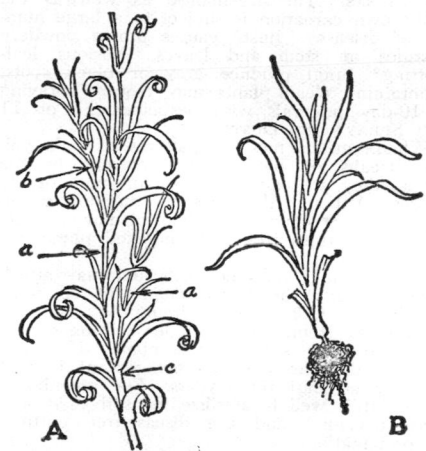

Carnation Cuttings
A. A shoot of carnation showing (*a*) the proper sort of cutting; (*b*) cutting made too high; and (*c*) cutting made too low. B. A sturdy, well-rooted carnation cutting.

Keep the temperature between 50° and 60° — more heat will be most detrimental. If it is necessary to ventilate, however, see that no cold, winter air currents blow on the plants. Assuming that you want the finest blooms rather than quantity, it is necessary to follow the commercial procedure. The plants should be grown to a single stem which is accomplished by pinching off all side shoots. If this is done, the plants should begin blooming about 7 weeks after planting in the bench, and, with successive pickings, keep on

---

* Special articles on the subjects indicated by an asterisk (*) will be found at the words so marked.

blooming until the following May or June. If you have given them the right conditions, each plant should produce 12–18 good flowers. But the number of these and the length of the stem (an important commercial feature) will depend upon the care in growing. The greenhouse glass must be shaded from early in January until the plants are ready to go outdoors. The plants are also extraordinarily sensitive to one of the constituents of manufactured gas — ethylene. If there is the least danger of escaping gas in the greenhouse, test the air with potted tomato plants (*see* TOMATO). Carnation flowers protrude their usually hidden and useless stamens if ethylene is present in the greenhouse in the proportion of 1 part of ethylene to 2 million parts of air — a concentration indetectable chemically. But the flowers are ruined by it.

INSECT PESTS. Red spider mites are most serious pests. Pesticide #14 (*see* SPRAYS AND DUSTS) or Kelthane are effective materials for mite control. Repeated applications may be necessary. Cabbage looper, greenhouse leaf tier, corn earworm and other leaf feeders should be controlled by arsenicals or pesticide #1 before blossoming.

DISEASES. The greenhouse as well as the field-grown carnation is subject to a large number of diseases. Rust° causes brown powdery pustules on stem and leaves. Various leaf-spotting° fungi produce gray or black spots. Maintaining clean plants may require spraying at 10-day intervals with pesticide #1 or 11 (*see* SPRAYS AND DUSTS).

When various mosaic° patterns of pale yellow streaks or blotches are present in the leaves, they are caused by one or more of the viruses. Although the virus may not kill carnation, it may reduce the yield of flowers. Do not take cuttings from virus-infected plants for use in propagation.

Several fungi and one bacterium may attack plants through the roots. Some rot off roots completely. Others grow from the roots up through the stem causing sudden wilting of one branch or one side of the plant. If plants wilt° or die one year, do not replant in that area for at least three years. For greenhouse forcing it is well to sterilize the soil (*see* SOIL STERILIZATION) and use disease-free cuttings for propagation.

If flower buds start to rot before they open, it indicates a fungus bud-rot which is transmitted by grass mites. If open flowers rot with a gray mold,° it indicates leaky glass in the greenhouse. Keep a tight glass over the house and spray with a very fine mist using pesticide #11.

CARNATION POPPY. A form of the opium poppy. *See* POPPY.

carnea, -us, -um (kar'nee-a). Flesh-colored.

CARNEGIEA (kar-nay'gee-a). A single gigantic cactus, the largest in the world, and localized in extreme southeastern Calif., southern Ariz., and the neighboring Mexican state of Sonora. It may be grown in that region and attempted in greenhouses, but it does not take kindly to cultivation. (Named for Andrew Carnegie, in recognition of his aid in establishing the former Desert Laboratory at Tucson.)

gigantea. The giant cactus, locally called suwarro, sahuaro, and saguaro. A huge, post-like, erect plant body 20–60 ft. high, and often 2 ft. thick, with many ribs and stout, strong spines. Old specimens have 3–4, candelabra-like, huge branches that curve upward. Flowers white, produced only at the tips of the stem or branches, 4 in. long, and half as wide. Fruit edible, egg-shaped and as big, red, widely used for sweetmeats. A full-grown plant may weigh 6 tons and be 250 years old.

carnerosana, -us, -um (kar-ner-o-san'a). From the Carnerosa Pass, Mexico.

CARNIVOROUS PLANTS. *See* INSECTIVOROUS PLANTS.

carnosa, -us, -um (kar-nō'sa). Fleshy.

CAROB. This evergreen tree from the eastern Mediterranean region is the only species of the genus **Ceratonia** (see-ra-tone'ee-a) of the pea family, the pods of which are familiar as St. John's-bread (the "wild locusts" of John the Baptist). The only species, **C. siliqua** is a tree 20–40 ft. high. Leaves compound,° with 2–3 pairs of broad, leathery leaflets that are 2–4 in. long. Flowers red, unisexual,° not pealike, without petals. Pods 4–12 in. long, slightly flattened, not splitting, the seeds surrounded by a sweetish, nutritious pulp. Both male and female trees must be planted to ensure fruit. Probably hardy only from zone° 7, certainly frome zone° 8, southward. (*Ceratonia* is from the Greek for horn, in allusion to the fruit.)

carolina, -us, -um (ka-ro-ly'na). From North or South Carolina.

CAROLINA ALLSPICE = *Calycanthus floridus.*

CAROLINA HEMLOCK = *Tsuga caroliniana.* See HEMLOCK.

CAROLINA JASMINE = *Gelsemium sempervirens.*

CAROLINA LILY = *Lilium michauxi.*

CAROLINA MOONSEED = *Cocculus carolinus.*

CAROLINA POPLAR = *Populus canadensis* and its *var. eugenei.*

CAROLINA RHODODENDRON = *Rhododendron carolinianum.*

CAROLINA VANILLA = *Trilisa odoratissima.*

CAROLINA WATER SHIELD = *Cabomba caroliniana.*

carolinensis, -e (ka-ro-ly-nen'sis). From North or South Carolina.

caroliniana, -us, -um (ka-ro-lin-i-ā'na). From North or South Carolina.

CAROSELLA = *Foeniculum vulgare piperitum.* See FENNEL.

Carota (ka-rō'ta). Latin for carrot.

CARPANTHEA. *See* MESEMBRYANTHEMUM.

carpatica, -us, -um (kar-pat'ti-ka). From the region of the Carpathian Mountains.

CARPEL. *See* PISTIL.

° Special articles on the subjects indicated by an asterisk (°) will be found at the words so marked.

CARPENTERIA (kar-pen-teer'i-a). A single shrub of the family Saxifragaceae, native in the southern part of the Sierra Nevada Mountains in Calif. and grown in that region for its handsome white flowers. It differs from *Philadelphus* (mock-oranges) only in technical characters, and in being evergreen. (Named for Wm. M. Carpenter, American physician.)

This shrub, while perhaps able to stand the cold of northeastern U.S., will not stand wet winters. In its own region it is easily propagated by layers or by seeds, and prefers a light, well-drained soil.

californica. Shrub 6–8 ft. high. Leaves opposite,* evergreen, oblongish, 3–4 in. long. Flowers fragrant, showy, white, 2–3 in. wide, and borne singly or in clusters of 2 or 3. June.

CARPET BEDDING. See BEDDING.

CARPET GRASS. See AXONOPUS FURCATUS; see also LIPPIA.

CARPETWEED FAMILY = Aizoaceae.

carpinifolia, -us, -um (kar-py-ni-fō'li-a). With leaves like the hornbeam (*Carpinus*).

CARPINUS. See HORNBEAM.

CARPOBROTUS. See MESEMBRYANTHEMUM.

CARRION-FLOWER. See STAPELIA; see also SMILAX HERBACEA.

CARROT. An important root vegetable derived from an annual or perhaps biennial herb belonging to the genus **Daucus** (daw'-kus) of the family Umbelliferae. Of the sixty species of *Daucus* only one is involved in the cultivated carrot, **Daucus Carota,** the common, weedy Queen Anne's-lace of our roadsides. This is a Eurasian herb, often called the wild carrot, and is without the large root development of the ordinary garden carrot which is known as **Daucus Carota sativa.** The genus *Daucus* has rather bristly, much-divided or compound* leaves, the ultimate segments fern-like. Flowers very small, in a flat-topped cluster (really a compound umbel*), below which is a whorl* of leaflike bracts.* (*Daucus* is from the classical Greek name for this plant.)

Carrot culture is very simple. The ordinary procedure is to sow the seeds rather thickly (germination is slow and poor) in drills about ½–¾ in. deep, the rows being far enough apart for working between them (12–24 in., depending on hand or machine cultivation). Thin the plants to 3–4 in. apart in the row. If the soil is rich and friable there will be no trouble about root development, but remember that young, tender, quick-growing carrots are better flavored than old or slow-growing ones, which are fit only for stock feed. If the soil is not rich, apply a good commercial fertilizer at the rate of 6 pounds per 100 ft. of row. It takes about 1 oz. of seed for a row this length. Good varieties are Red Cored Chantenay, Danvers Half Long, Imperator.

In order to hasten matters, some growers start the plants in the cold frame and transplant later to the garden. This is a troublesome procedure, scarcely warranted unless especially early crops are needed. A succession of ordinary carrots may be sown every two weeks up to the middle of July. Later sowings may not mature before frost.

INSECT PESTS. Carrots are not often damaged by insects. Carrot weevil larvae, legless grubs of a brownish snout beetle, chew carrots through the season. Control with pesticide #17 (see SPRAYS AND DUSTS) on plants and ground beginning in spring with weekly applications. Leafhoppers, particularly in late season, transmit yellows disease. Use pesticide #1 on regular schedule in late summer and fall. In the North, a root maggot destroys carrots on occasion. Combination insecticide-fungicide seed treatments are some help on early infestations. Vegetable weevil is serious in the South. See TURNIP.

DISEASES. The most widespread disease of carrot is yellows* caused by a virus and transmitted by leafhoppers.* The foliage is much reduced in size and is pale yellow. Control of the leafhoppers is often necessary in commercial plantings, but is not usually warranted in the home garden.

Several leaf-blight fungi may turn foliage brown or black. This is readily controlled with applications of pesticide #7 or #11 (see SPRAYS AND DUSTS) applied at 10-day intervals starting when first spots appear.

In the Southwest and West a bacterial disease may cause water-soaked spots on the foliage and eventually kill much of the tops. Rotate the plantings and soak seed for 10 minutes in hot water (126° F.) before planting.

CARROT FAMILY. A huge family of plants, mostly herbs, and containing such diverse garden favorites as carrot, celery, parsley, parsnip, dill, caraway, and anise, as well as the popular blue lace-flower from Australia. For the many kinds and their chief characteristics see UMBELLIFERAE.

CARROT FERN = Onychium japonicum.

carthaginensis, -e (kar-ta-jin-en'sis). From Cartagena, Spain or Colombia.

CARTHAMUS (kar'tha-mus). A genus of 20 species of Old World herbs of the family Compositae, only one of much garden interest. They have spiny, alternate* leaves which decrease in size toward the top and gradually merge with the spiny bracts* beneath the flower heads. The heads are made up of disk* flowers only. (*Carthamus* is a Latinized version of an Arabic vernacular for the plant below.)

The safflower is easily grown as an annual and seeds should be sown where the plants are to stay. Here it is grown for ornament, but it is cult. abroad for the flower heads which yield a drug and a red dye.

tinctorius. Safflower or false saffron. An annual, branching herb 12–30 in. high. Leaves broadly oval, finely spiny-toothed. Flower heads about 1 in. long, orange, the head invested by a series of broad and spiny bracts.* Asia.

carthusianorum (kar-thoose-i-a-nor'um). Named for the Carthusian monks who invented chartreuse.

---

* Special articles on the subjects indicated by an asterisk (*) will be found at the words so marked.

cartilaginea, -us, -um (kar-ti-laj-in'ee-a). Resembling cartilage.

CARUM. *See* CARAWAY.

Carvi (kar'vy). An old name for caraway, derived from its genus *Carum*.

CARYA. *See* HICKORY.

caryophylla, -us, -um (carry-o-fill'a). Relating to the clove; also, and more often applied to the clove pink, a form of the carnation.

CARYOPHYLLACEAE (carry-o-fill-ā'-see-ee). The pink family (which here includes the Alsinaceae or chickweed family) contains many popular garden flowers among its 75 genera and 1200 species, among them the pink and carnation. All are widely distributed herbs having opposite* leaves without marginal teeth, and swollen joints. All, except the carnation, are of outdoor cult., many of them extremely popular annuals or perennial garden plants.

The flowers are regular,* with 4 or 5 petals (fringed in some), often very showy, but wanting in *Herniaria,* and small in *Arenaria, Cerastium, Gypsophila, Sagina, Stellaria,* and *Tunica.* But in several of these, notably *Gypsophila* (baby's-breath), the flowers are so numerous as to make the plants showy. Much larger and handsomer flowers are found in *Dianthus* (the pink and carnation), *Lychnis, Saponaria, Silene,* and *Petrocoptis.* The fruit is a dry pod (capsule*) in all the garden genera.

Technical flower characters: Ovary superior,* usually 1-celled. Sepals and petals 4 or 5, the latter often with a claw,* and in some genera notched or fringed. Stamens 8–10.

CARYOPSIS. A small, 1-seeded fruit that does not split and is so closely invested with its outer husk that the seed inside and the fruit are inseparable. It is characteristic of the grasses, and what is ordinarily called grass seed (*i.e.,* a grain of wheat) is actually a caryopsis.

CARYOPTERIS (carry-op'ter-is). Attractive Asiatic shrubs of the family Verbenaceae, grown for their showy bloom. Of the six species the one below is the best known, usually as bluebeard or blue spirea. Leaves opposite,* short-stalked, and toothed. Flowers in profuse clusters (cymes*), the corolla irregular,* one of its 5 lobes larger than the others and fringed. Stamens 4, protruding (*see* BUDDLEIA). Fruit dry, separating into 4, slightly winged nutlets. (*Caryopteris* is Greek for nut and wing.)

This is a popular greenhouse pot plant and needs a cool house and potting mixture* 3. Outdoors it is hardy from zone* 5 southward, and north of this is frequently planted, but winter-kills. If the shrub is cut back to the ground, as are some buddleias, and well mulched with manure, the new shoots will bloom the next autumn, unless the winter has been very severe.

incana. Blue spirea. A grayish-hairy shrub 1–5 ft. high. Leaves ovalish, coarsely but blunt-ly toothed, 2–3 in. long. Flower clusters showy, mostly in the leaf axils,* bluish-purple or blue. Sept. Eastern As. Often known as *C. Mastacanthus.* A hybrid (*C. clandonensis*) derived from crossing *C. incana* with a non-hort. species is a handsome shrub with nearly toothless leaves, and shorter-stalked, slender clusters (cymes*). Sept. Hardy from zone* 5 southward.

tangutica = *Caryopteris incana.*

CARYOTA (carry-ō'ta). The fish-tail palms comprise a genus of perhaps 12 species of tall feather palms, chiefly from the Indo-Malayan region, some of which sucker from the base and hence have several stems. Leaves twice-compound,* the ultimate segments broad toward the tip and jagged or cut fish-tail fashion. Male and female flowers in different clusters on the same plant, appearing among the lower leaves of the terminal crown and fruiting successively down the trunk. When the flowering and fruiting is completed, the palm dies, but it may take several years to do so. Fruit small, oblongish or globe-shaped, not over ¾ in. in diameter. (*Caryota* is Greek for the date palm and of uncertain application here.)

The toddy palm is well suited for outdoor cult. in zones* 8 and 9, but is likely to be caught by occasional frosts in zone* 8. In Fla. it grows vigorously in almost any good soil and makes very decorative specimens. *Caryota mitis,* a smaller palm, is less known. *C. urens* is widely cult. in India for the delicious wine made from it (12 quarts a day from tapped trunks). The plants are usually too big for all but the largest greenhouses.

mitis. Usually with several smooth stems, the trunk larger than the suckers, not over 25 ft. high. Leaves 4–8 ft. long, the ultimate segments light green, faintly ribbed, the tips irregularly lobed, but generally triangular. Fruit ½ in. in diameter, bluish-black. Indo-Malaya.

urens. Toddy palm or wine palm; called also jaggery palm and kittul. A tall, single-stemmed palm 30–70 ft. high or more (in India). Leaves 12–20 ft. long, the ultimate segments stiff, strongly ribbed, fish-tail-shaped, or some jagged or irregularly cut, the tips mostly drooping. Fruit about ¾ in. in diameter, red. Indo-Malaya.

caryotaefolia, -us, -um (carry-o-ti-fō'lia). With leaves like the fish-tail palms (*Caryota*).

CASABA MELON. *See* MELON.

CASCADE FIR = *Abies amabilis. See* FIR.

CASCARA SAGRADA = *Rhamnus purshiana.*

CASHEW = *Anacardium occidentale.*

CASHEW FAMILY = Anacardiaceae.

cashmeriana, -us, -um (cash-meer-i-ā'na). From Kashmir, India.

CASIMIROA (ka-see-mi-rō'a). Of the four species of this tropical American genus of trees of the rue family, only one, the white sapote, is of much garden value. It can be grown outdoors in zones* 8 and 9, and in Fla. is moderately valued for its fruit. Leaves alternate,* compound,* the leaflets arranged finger-fashion. Flowers greenish

---

* Special articles on the subjects indicated by an asterisk (*) will be found at the words so marked.

and inconspicuous. (For structure *see* RUTA-
CEAE.) Fruit fleshy (a drupe*), its pulp
agreeably sweet and yellow. (Named for
Casimiro Gomez de Ortega, Spanish botanist.)
The white sapote appears to have no soil
preferences in Fla. It will stand occasional
mild frosts, and its fruit begins ripening in
May.

edulis. White sapote; also called Mexican
apple. A tree (in cult.) rarely over 30 ft.
high. Leaflets 3–7, mostly 5, each short-
stalked, pointed both ends, 3–5 in. long. Fruit
tomato-like in size and shape, gray or yellowish-
green on the outside, yellow-fleshed and soft
inside, with usually 3 hard, oblong seeds. Mex.
and Central America.

CASSABANANA = *Sicana odorifera.*

CASSAVA = *Manihot esculenta.*

CASSENA = *Ilex vomitoria.* See HOLLY.

CASSIA (cash'i-a). Under the general
term senna are grouped an immense genus
(perhaps 500 species) of herbs, shrubs and
trees of the pea family, the trees mostly
tropical, but a few herbs in the temperate
zone. They have compound* leaves, the leaflets arranged feather-fashion, and without an
odd one at the end. Flowers not pea-like, but
very nearly regular,* but one of the clawed*
petals often a little larger than the other 4.
(*See* LEGUMINOSAE.) Fruit a flattened or
roundish pod (legume*), usually 4-angled
or winged. (*Cassia* is the old Greek name
for these plants.)

All those below, except *C. marilandica*, are
shrubs or trees that are hardy outdoors only
in zones* 8 or 9, where they are grown for
their usually showy flowers or for interest.
Some of them, especially *C. corymbosa*, are
occasionally grown in the cool greenhouse
and should be planted in potting mixture* 4.
Cassia marilandica is native in the U.S. and
a bold, handsome border perennial of easy
culture.

artemisioides. A compact shrub with silky-
gray foliage. Leaflets 6–8, needle-like, about
1 in. long. Flowers yellow, in racemes* that
arise in the leaf axils.* Aust.

corymbosa. A smooth shrub 4–8 ft. high.
Leaflets 6, oblongish. Flowers yellow, in mostly
flat-topped clusters from the leaf axils. Argentina. A free-flowering, handsome shrub more
grown in the greenhouse than the other tropical
species.

Fistula. Pudding-pipe tree or canafistula;
called, also, golden shower and drumstick tree.
A tree 20–30 ft. Leaflets 8–16, ovalish, about
2 in. long. Flower cluster 1 ft. long, the flowers yellow and blooming before the leaves appear in early spring. Pod cylindric, nearly 2
ft. long. India.

marilandica. Wild or American senna. A
stout, perennial herb 3–7 ft. high. Leaflets 10–
20, oblongish, about 1½ in. long. Flowers yellow, in racemes, some in the leaf axils, some
terminal. Pod narrow, flat, about 3½ in. long.
Pa. to Fla. and westward. Hardy in the perennial border and a striking plant, blooming in
July–Aug.

tomentosa. Shrub 10–12 ft. high, the twigs
felty-hairy. Leaflets 12–18, oblongish, but with
a minute, soft prickle at the tip, gray-hairy

beneath. Flowers nearly 1 in. wide, deep yellow. Pod hairy, flat, nearly 5 in. long. Mex.

CASSIA-BARK TREE = *Cinnamomum Cassia.*

CASSIE = *Acacia farnesiana.*

Cassine. North American Indian name for
the dahoon (*Ilex Cassine*). See HOLLY.

cassinoides (cas-si-noy'deez; but *see*
OÏDES). Like the cassine.

CASSIOPE (cas-sy'o-pee). A small genus
of generally low, alpine or arctic evergreen
shrubs of the heath family, with very small,
scale-like leaves. Flowers solitary, nodding,
often profuse, the corolla small, almost perfectly bell-shaped, followed by tiny, dry fruits
(capsule*) and minute seeds. (*Cassiope* was
named for the mother of Andromeda, but with
little significance as applied to these plants.)
Sometimes known as *Harrimanella.* The cas-
siopes are rock garden subjects that do not
thrive in warm dry regions. They do better
on the Pacific Coast than elsewhere. Open or
filtered sunshine is essential, and drainage
must be perfect.

hypnoides. A low, moss-like perennial,
scarcely 3 in. high, and difficult to find in
alpine fell-fields. Leaves minute, moss-like, but
not closely pressed against the branches. Flowers white or pinkish, about 3⁄16 in. long. Cool
alpine summits, north to the Arctic. July–Aug.
Hardy from zone* 2 northward.

lycopodioides. Resembling a club moss (*Lycopodium*) and with trailing prostrate stems, but
not over 1½ in. high. Leaves minute, closely
pressed against the branches. Flowers white,
nearly ¼ in. long, solitary and nodding. Alpine
and arctic As. and northwest N.A.

mertensiana. Larger than the other species,
often erect or slightly procumbent and 6–8 in.
high. Leaves minute, somewhat loosely pressed
against the branches. Flowers solitary, nodding,
white, about ¼ in. long. Alaska to Calif. May.
Hardy from zone* 4 northward.

cassytha. An obsolete name for dodder-
like (non-hort.), tropical plants, and applied
to *Rhipsalis cassytha,* which somewhat resembles them.

CASTALIA = NYMPHAEA.

CASTANEA. See CHESTNUT.

CASTANOPSIS (cas-ta-nop'sis). A genus
of chiefly Asiatic evergreen trees of the
beech family, the only cult. species being a
native of the Pacific Coast and hardy in
the East only south of zone* 5. It is closely
related to the chestnut. The cult. species,
C. chrysophylla, called giant or golden chinquapin, is a tree up to 100 ft. Leaves without teeth, oblongish, 4–6 in. long, green
above, golden beneath. Flowers in catkins.
Fruit in a spiny bur, the nut (not edible)
usually solitary. Ore. to Calif. and Nev. Little grown in the East. A shrubby, but little
known, form is hardier than the type. (*Castanopsis* is Greek for resembling chestnuts.)

CASTANOSPERMUM (cas-tan-o-spur'-
mum). Two tall trees of the pea family, the
only cult. species being the Moreton Bay
chestnut from Australia, which is grown outdoors only in Calif. and Fla. Leaves com-

---

* Special articles on the subjects indicated by an asterisk (*) will be found at the words so marked.

pound,* the leaflets arranged feather-fashion with an odd one at the end. Flowers not truly pea-like, in loose clusters. Petals 4, the stamens long-protruding. Pod 8–9 in. long, the seeds as big as Italian chestnuts. (*Castanospermum* is from the Greek for chestnut and seed, in allusion to the large seed.)

In Fla. and Calif. (only in zones* 8 and 9) the tree is a handsome ornamental, grown as such rather than for the seeds which are edible only if roasted.

australe. Moreton Bay chestnut; also called black bean. A tree 40–60 ft. high. Leaves 18 in. long, the 11–15 leaflets broad, and thickish. In early spring the tree is covered with its striking yellow-orange flowers in loose racemes. Aust.

CASTILIAN ROSE. A name in Calif. for the damask rose (*Rosa damascena*).

CASTILLA (cas-till′ya). A small genus of Central American milky-juiced trees of the mulberry family, the one below an important source of rubber when the latter is fairly high-priced. It yielded the rubber balls found by Columbus. It can be grown outdoors only in zone* 9 and is occasionally cult. there for interest (not for rubber production, which needs more heat). This cult. species is **C. elastica**, the ule or Mexican rubber-tree. It has alternate* leaves without marginal teeth, and small, unisexual* flowers, without petals. (Named for Juan Castillo y Lopez, Spanish botanist.)

CASTILLEJA (cas-til-lee′ya). Most gardeners will try to grow the painted-cups, a genus of 35 species of gorgeously colored herbs of the figwort family, but they will practically always fail. The plants are partially or wholly parasitic on the roots of other plants, hence nearly impossible of cultivation. They are perennial herbs with alternate* leaves. Flowers small, the corolla tubular, the top very irregular and 2-lipped. The color comes chiefly from the showy bracts,* from between which the flowers are borne in a strikingly beautiful spike. (Named for D. Castillejo, Spanish botanist.) The species most likely to be attempted are:

californica. Indian paint-brush. Erect, 12–18 in. high. Leaves narrow, about 1½ in. long. Flowers red, about 1 in. long, the bracts* red or red-tipped. Calif.

latifolia. Seaside painted-cup. A sticky-hairy herb 12–15 in. high. Leaves thickish, more or less oval, about ¾ in. long. Flowers about ¾ in. long, the bracts* leafy, yellow or red. Calif.

parviflora. Indian paint-brush. A hairy perennial 12–20 in. high. Leaves much cut into narrow segments, or the upper ones uncut. Flowers about 1 in. long, the bracts* red, yellow or white. Western U.S.

The scarlet painted-cup of the eastern U.S. has so far resisted cultivation.

CAST-IRON PLANT = *Aspidistra elatior*.

CASTOR-BEAN. The fruit of the castor-oil plant.

CASTOR-OIL PLANT. A single gigantic herb (tree-like in the tropics), and the only species of the genus **Ricinus** (ris′i-nus) of the spurge family. It is grown as a striking annual foliage plant or for summer bedding, also, far south, for its seeds, which yield castor-oil. The only species is **Ricinus communis**, a native of tropical Africa, often called palma christi in Spanish countries. *See* MEDICINAL PLANTS and POISONOUS PLANTS.

As grown in the North, the castor-oil plant is a tender annual (*see* ANNUALS) 48–150 in. high. Leaves alternate,* often 3 ft. wide, the stalk attached to the middle of the blade, which is divided nearly to the middle by several lobes. Flowers in a dense, terminal cluster often 1–2 ft. high, the individual flowers small, without petals, the sexes separate. Fruit a spiny pod (capsule*) containing the beautifully marked, poisonous seeds. (*Ricinus* is the classical Latin name of this plant.)

The common castor-oil plant is usually grown in the form with green foliage, but there are several other varieties. One has much larger, green leaves. Another has red stems and bluish-gray leaves, and there are several with red and one with variegated leaves. One with white-veined leaves is offered as "mosquito-plant."

CASUARINA (cas-you-a-ry′na). The names beefwood, she-oak, or Australian pine are all applied to this curious group of chiefly Australian trees, the only genus of the family Casuarinaceae (cas-you-a-ry-nay′see-ee). They have apparently leafless twigs, covered with minute, scale-like leaves, the foliage thus suggesting the horsetail. The illusion is further carried out by the twigs being jointed and often ridged, as in some horsetails. True foliage leaves lacking. Flowers extremely simple, lacking true petals or sepals, the flower-parts scale-like, becoming a dry, cone-like or ball-like body. Fruit a winged nutlet, surrounded by 2 bractlets. (*Casuarina* is supposed to refer to the feathery branches being like the feathers of a cassowary.)

The species below make excellent seaside trees along the coasts of frost-free regions such as southern Fla. and Calif. They cannot be grown anywhere else outdoors and are not usually greenhouse subjects.

cunninghamiana. A tree 30–50 ft. high, much resembling the next species, but more desirable, as it carries its branches nearly to ground level. Its cones are smaller, being scarcely ⅓ in. in diameter.

equisetifolia. Horsetail tree; also called beefwood. A tall tree, the drooping branches and leafless twigs swaying wildly in a wind. Branchlets wire-like, jointed, much like the stems of the horsetails (*Equisetum*). Cones stalked, about ½ in. in diameter. Aust., but naturalized in Fla., much planted there, and often suckers.*

stricta. Smaller, or shrub-like, the branches drooping. Branchlets with the joints about ½–¾ in. apart (¼ in. in the other species). Cones about 1 in. in diameter.

catalinae (kat-a-ly′ne). From Santa Catalina Island, Calif.

CATALINA IRONWOOD = *Lyonothamnus floribundus*.

---

* Special articles on the subjects indicated by an asterisk (*) will be found at the words so marked.

CATALONIAN JASMINE = *Jasminum grandiflorum*.

CATALPA (ka-tal'pa). A genus of attractively flowering trees of the family Bignoniaceae, nearly all North American, but some Asiatic, much planted for ornament. They have long-stalked, opposite,* and usually large leaves. Flowers showy, the corolla irregular* and 2-lipped,* the flowers grouped in handsome, branched clusters (panicles*). Fertile stamens only 2. Fruit a long, cylindric, very narrow pod (capsule*), the many seeds with a tuft of white hairs at each end. (*Catalpa* is the North American Indian name for these trees.)

The catalpas are valuable lawn or street trees because of their profuse flowering. It should be remembered, however, that they are quick-growing, soft-wooded trees that reach maturity and then soon begin to fail. Consequently, they should be used with other, more permanent trees in any mass planting. They are easily grown in any ordinary garden soil, and young trees make an astonishing growth in a single season. Easily propagated by seeds, cuttings, root cuttings, or layering.

bignonioides. The common catalpa or Indian bean; also called bean-tree, cigar-tree, and smoking bean tree (from its long pods). A round-headed tree 30–40 ft. high, often less in cult. Leaves broadly oval, 6–8 in. long, bad-smelling when crushed. Flower cluster 6–9 in. long, pyramidal, the flowers about 1½ in. long, white, but yellow-striped inside, and spotted with purple-brown. Pod 9–14 in. long. June–July. Native from Ga. to Fla. and Miss., but naturalized in the northeastern U.S. Hardy from zone* 3 southward. The *var.* **nana,** the umbrella or standard catalpa, is a popular, dwarf, globe-shaped tree (often sold as *Catalpa bungei*). It is a high-grafted plant forming a standard, and most useful for accents along drives, or in formal plantings.

bungei = *Catalpa bignonioides nana*.

kaempferi = *Catalpa ovata*.

ovata. A tree usually less than 30 ft. Leaves broadly oval, 5–7 in. long, often shallowly lobed. Flower cluster as in *C. bignonioides,* but the flowers yellowish-white and orange-striped inside and with violet spots. Pod 10–15 in. long. Eastern Asia. May–June. Hardy from zone* 4 southward.

speciosa. Hardy catalpa. Often up to 60 ft., the bark dark reddish-brown. Leaves oval or oval-oblong, 8–12 in. long, densely hairy on the under side, not malodorous when crushed. Flower cluster rather sparse and open, about 7 in. long, the flowers white, but yellow-striped inside, and inconspicuously spotted purple-brown. Pod 12–20 in. long. Native in central U.S. Hardy from zone* 3 southward. June.

CATALPA FAMILY = Bignoniaceae.

CATANANCHE (kat-a-nann'ke). Of the five known species of this genus (family Compositae) only the blue succory is of garden interest. It is a flower garden perennial grown for its showy blue heads. Leaves mostly basal and narrow. Flowers in handsome, long-stalked heads, the rays flat and slightly toothed. It has dandelion-like heads of fruit. (*Catananche* is from the Greek for ardent incentive as the plant was anciently used as a love potion.)

The blue succory is of easy cult. as a hardy perennial and will grow in any ordinary garden soil. Propagated by division or by seeds.

caerulea. Blue succory; also called Cupid's-dart, and a good everlasting. Not over 2 ft. high. Leaves very hairy, oblongish, with a few scattered teeth. Flower heads nearly 2 in. wide, the rays blue (white or white-margined in a hort. variety). Summer. Southern Eu.

Catappa. East Indian name for the Indian almond (*Terminalia Catappa*).

Cataria (ka-tay'ri-a). Latin for cat. *See* NEPETA.

catawbiensis, -e (ka-taw-bi-en'sis). From or near the Catawba River in the Blue Ridge Mountains of N. Car.

CATBRIER. *See* SMILAX (1).

CATCHFLY. *See* LYCHNIS and SILENE.

Catechu. Asiatic vernacular for several plants yielding tanning extracts; also for the palm yielding the betelnut. *See* ARECA.

CATGUT = *Tephrosia virginiana*.

CATHARANTHUS. *See* VINCA ROSEA.

cathartica, -us, -um (ka-thar'ti-ka). Yielding a purge.

cathayenis, -e (kă-thay-en'sis). From China.

"CATHEDRAL BELLS." *See* COBAEA.

Catjang. Oriental name of *Vigna Catjang*.

CATKIN. A flower cluster typified by the pussy willow and the poplar. It is often called an ament and consists of a scaly spike, the flowers in which have no petals. It is found also in birches and some trees of the beech family.

CAT-MINT = *Nepeta Cataria*.

CATNIP = *Nepeta Cataria*.

CATS. Garden enemies or household pets? They are both. For those who wish to attract them, catnip (*Nepeta Cataria*) is an old favorite; also *Nepeta mussini*. Less known, but most interesting, is the liking shown by

Catkins; poplar at the left, oak at the right

---

* Special articles on the subjects indicated by an asterisk (*) will be found at the words so marked.

cats for the vine *Actinidia polygama* (which see). For those who need to preserve the birds and know that prowling cats are their worst enemies, *see* BIRDS.

CAT'S-CLAW = *Pithecolobium Unguis-cati;* also *Doxantha Unguis-cati.*

CAT'S-EAR = *Hypochaeris radicata.* *See* list at WEEDS.

CAT'S-FOOT. *See* ANTENNARIA.

CAT'S-TAIL SPEEDWELL = *Veronica spicata.*

CAT-TAIL. The cat-tails are marsh rather than garden plants and belong to the genus Typha (ty'fa), the only genus of the family Typhaceae (ty-fa'see-ee). They are reed-like plants with long, narrow, stiffish leaves and thick rootstocks. The flowers are extremely minute, hundreds being crowded in the dense, terminal, brownish spike. They have neither petals nor sepals, which are represented merely by a ring of bristles or hairs. (*Typha* is the Greek name for the cat-tail.)

The plants, easily grown in wet, open places, are suited for no other sites. Care must be taken to keep them from spreading too far or too fast. They are rampant growers.

T. angustifolia. Perhaps not very different from the following, but with generally narrow leaves and an interrupted spike. Nearly throughout the world.

T. latifolia. The common cat-tail, often called flag or reed mace. Growing in dense stands, the leaves 5–9 ft. long, scarcely ¾ in. wide. Flowering spike cylindric, brownish, about 6–8 in. long, continuous at the tip of a stalk as long as the leaves. Throughout the world.

CATTLEYA (kat'lee-a). To most city folk this is *the* orchid. It is the most widely grown of the florists' orchids and is one of a genus of perhaps 40 species of tropical American plants, most of which grow in the trees (true epiphytes*). They have club-shaped, thickened stems very like a pseudo-bulb,* from which arise 1–3 thick, fleshy leaves. Flowers sometimes solitary, often 2 or 3 together or more, large and very showy, the petals and sepals alike, or the petals broader than the sepals. There is a striking, apparently tubular lip,* the summit of which is 3-lobed, with the middle lobe spreading and larger than the side ones. (Named for William Cattley, English plant lover.)

For the culture of cattleyas *see* the section on Tropical Orchid Cultivation at ORCHID. Of the 40 or more known species only a few have contributed to the modern florists' cattleya. But these have been so much hybridized that over 300 named forms are known, many of them of obscure parentage. Of these, 75 are fairly common in the collections of orchid fanciers, but lie outside the scope of this book. The species and varieties that appear to be the most common are listed below. Most of them are considered by many orchid specialists as only varieties of

Cattleya labiata. The flowering months are those under greenhouse culture.

aurantiaca. Pseudobulbs* 12–18 in. long, 2-leaved. Leaves light green, rather fleshy. Flowers 3–15 in the cluster, the individual flower 1½ in. wide, orange, the lip* whitish but crimson-spotted. Guatemala and Mex.

bowringiana. Stems club-shaped, about 12 in. long. Leaves 2, oblongish, 6–8 in. long. Flowers usually 5–9, not over 3 in. wide, the sepals and petals rose-purple. Lip rose-lilac, with a large, white, but maroon-bordered spot in the throat. British Honduras. Sept.–Dec.

citrina. Tulip orchid. Leaves narrow, 8–10 in. long. Flower solitary, on a stalk 8–10 in. long, drooping. Petals and sepals almost tulip-like, yellow, the lip white-edged and wavy. Mex. Oct.–Apr.

dowiana. Pseudobulbs* with only a single leaf, which is 10–12 in. long and nearly 3 in. wide. Flowers fragrant, 3–4½ in. wide, in a sparse cluster or solitary. Petals and sepals brownish-yellow, the lip* fringed on the margin, purple, shading to rose-violet, gold-banded, and very handsome. Costa Rica.

gaskelliana. Perhaps only a var. of *Cattleya labiata,* but summer-blooming. Pseudobulbs* with a solitary leaf nearly 1 ft. long. Flowers nearly 7 in. wide, very showy, the petals pink, the lip expanded and deep crimson. Tropical S.A. May–Sept.

gigas = *Cattleya warscewiczi.*

labiata. The commonest cult. orchid in America. Stem club-shaped, topped by a single, flattish, thickish leaf 5–7 in. long. The stem is green-sheathed when young, furrowed when old. Flowers 2–5, usually about 6 in. wide, the sepals and petals rose-lilac, the petals wider than the sepals. Lip magenta-purple, the throat yellow but orange-spotted, the central lobe of the lip crisped on the margin. Brazil. Oct.–June. This and perhaps 200 named forms and varieties are the chief sources of the cattleya found in the florists' windows. The genus has entered into many hybrids with other genera. *See* BRASSOCATTLAELIA, BRASSOLAELIOCATTLEYA, and BRASSOCATTLEYA.

mendeli. Resembling *C. labiata,* but with larger, white or rosy flowers, the limb of the purple lip wavy, the throat yellow. Colombia. June–Nov.

mossiae. Resembling *C. labiata* and perhaps only a variety of it, but the flowers decidedly larger and rose-colored, the wavy lip with a purplish limb variegated with violet and white-margined. Venezuela. Apr.–July. There is also a variety with violet-blue flowers.

percivaliana. Resembling *C. mossiae,* but the flowers smaller, darker-colored and blooming from Jan. to Mar. It is probably only a variety of *C. labiata.* Venezuela.

skinneri. San Sebastian. Leaves 4–6 in. long, more or less cylindric. Flowers 4–6, not over 4 in. wide, rose-purple, the lip with a yellow throat. Cent. Am. Mar.–June. There is also a white-flowered variety. It is the national flower of Costa Rica, there called guaria morada.

trianae. Next to *C. labiata,* of which it may be only a variety, the most widely cult. of the cattleyas. Leaves oblong 6–8 in. long. Flowers 2 or 3, not over 7 in. wide, rose or rose-purple, the lip purple, its limb wavy and its throat yellow. Colombia. Dec.–Feb. There are several varieties, one with fragrant pink flowers, another with white or lilac-tinged flowers.

warscewiczi. Perhaps only a var. of *Cattleya labiata,* but the flowers larger, often 8–10

---

* Special articles on the subjects indicated by an asterisk (*) will be found at the words so marked.

in. wide, extremely showy, and summer-blooming. Petals violet or rose, the lip dark purple, but yellow-spotted at the throat. May–Sept. Tropical S.A. Often offered as *Cattleya gigas*.

CAUCASIAN LILY = *Lilium monadelphum*.

caucasica, -us, -um (kau-kay′si-ka). From the Caucasus Mountains.

caudata, -us, -um (kau-day′ta). Tailed.

caulescens (kau-les′senz). *See* CAULESCENT.

CAULESCENT. Having an obvious stem, usually above ground; not stemless. *See* ACAULESCENT.

cauliflora, -us, -um (kau-lee-flow′ra). *See* CAULIFLORY.

CAULIFLORY. The bearing of flowers and fruit on the trunk or larger branches. It is mostly found on tropical trees, notably in the chocolate tree, the carambola, and the jack-fruit.

CAULIFLOWER (*Brassica oleracea botrytis*). This, one of the most delicious of the cabbage tribe, is a cultigen,* originating from the European weed *Brassica oleracea*. *See* CABBAGE. Like the others it does not like heat and dryness.

The plant comes in two main types. One is the ordinary cauliflower of the markets. The other is known as winter cauliflower here, and as broccoli in England and also by some here. (*See* BROCCOLI.) Its culture is largely confined to the extreme northwest coastal states. In both sorts we eat the whitened, much enlarged and crowded flower head of the plant, the curd. Ordinary cauliflower will develop in a single season, while winter cauliflower (sometimes called heading broccoli) needs parts of two growing seasons (*see* below).

Cauliflower is more difficult to grow than any other plant of the cabbage tribe. Like most of them it will not stand heat and drought, which limits its culture in this country to areas free of these conditions. Proximity to the sea, and cool uplands of plentiful moisture are ideal. It will not, however, stand as much frost as cabbage or Brussels sprouts, and if there is protracted warm weather, it will not head. Commercial culture is chiefly on Long Island, in Colorado, California, Florida, and about the Great Lakes. It must be grown only in the cool seasons of the South, and northward its cultivation, for the same reason, is divided into an early and late crop, just as in cabbage.

VARIETIES. For ordinary cauliflower the best varieties are: Super Snowball, Holland Erfurt, and Early Snowball.

SOILS AND FERTILIZER. Soil and fertilizer conditions are the same as for cabbage (which see). All growers agree, however, that, assured of the proper degree of coolness and moisture, any good soil will grow cauliflower, sometimes called rich-man's cabbage from the difficulty and expense of growing it.

RAISING YOUNG PLANTS. For both early and late varieties the method of raising young plants and their subsequent management is the same as for cabbage (which see). A possible variation is the much greater expense of cauliflower seed and the consequent need to carefully preserve all thinned seedlings for pricking out. Most home gardeners will prefer to buy rooted plants, but be sure they are true to name and come from a reliable dealer. No crop is more likely to go wrong than cauliflower.

PLANTING OUT. For both early and late varieties set the plants 2 ft. apart in the row and make the rows 3 ft. apart. This will allow 50 heads of cauliflower to a 100-ft. row, which should be more than ample for a family of five.

CULTIVATION AND HEADING. Cultivate frequently and cleanly, being careful not to injure the brittle foliage if machines are used. As in cabbage, if cultivation is confined to mid-day, there is less chance of injury than earlier or later (*see* Cultivation at CABBAGE).

Cauliflower will not usually head of itself. Frequently, if poor seed has been used, or it gets too dry or too hot, the button-like center of the plant will "break," send up a flower stalk, and ruin the plant as a cauliflower. The only way to force the plant to produce a solid white head (the curd) is to start the day the first button-like swelling appears. The safest and most certain method of doing this is to gather the outer leaves and tie them over the center of the plant. Don't pull the cord or tape or raffia tight enough to injure the outer leaves, which must still keep on growing.

A cauliflower head tied up

These leaves are simply bent over the developing head, shield it from the heat of the sun, and gradually (from lack of light) turn it white. Some growers prefer to bend the leaves over the center and pin them with a toothpick, but this method is not so satisfactory as to tie them up.

---

* Special articles on the subjects indicated by an asterisk (*) will be found at the words so marked.

HARVESTING. Cauliflower heads will stand no frost, and when they are ready to be picked (*i.e.*, plump, firm and white), they cannot be left on the plant as a cabbage head may be — perhaps for a fortnight. Harvest at once by cutting well below the head those that are ready to harvest. If freezing weather is likely, all remaining heads should be harvested. The heads are easily damaged and must be handled with great care. They will not keep long in good condition.

WINTER CAULIFLOWER (sometimes called heading broccoli). This is similar to cauliflower, but it needs the late fall and the following very early spring to develop. That limits its culture to parts of the South or the coastal regions of the Northwest. Its chief value is a commercial one — to deliver to the great markets cauliflower that is far out of the normal season of ordinary cauliflower. Winter cauliflower, impossible of growth in regions of cold winters, is therefore of little interest to the average home gardener.

INSECT PESTS AND DISEASES. For general diseases, insects, and troubles, *see* CABBAGE.

Cauliflower is particularly susceptible to a deficiency of boron in the soil. The heads will be yellow or brown instead of white, and the stem will be hollow, dry, and brown. Add borax to the soil at the rate of ½ pound per 1000 square ft. and disk in before planting.

CAULINE. Having a stem.

CAULOPHYLLUM (kau-lo-fill'um). A genus of only two species of perennial herbs of the family Berberidaceae, one Asiatic, the other North American and grown in the wild garden. They have thickened rootstocks and large, thrice-compound* leaves. Flowers greenish-purple, with 6 petals and 6 sepals, and borne in a terminal cluster (panicle*). Fruit berry-like, blue. (*Caulophyllum* is from the Greek for stem and leaf.)

The only cult. species needs a rich woods soil, not particularly acid, and the shade of trees. It is unsuited to open, sunny places. Easily propagated in early spring by division of the rootstocks.

thalictroides. Blue cohosh; also called papoose-root and squaw-root. A perennial herb 1–3 ft. high. Leaves usually 2, one near the flower cluster, the other below it. Leaflets resembling the meadow rue, 3–5-lobed at the tip. Flowers about ⅓ in. long. Fruit nearly round, about ⅓ in. in diameter, on short, stout stalks. Eastern N.A. May.

caulorapa, -us, -um (kau-lo-ray'pa). With a turnip-like stem as in kohlrabi.

cauticola, -us, -um (caw-tick'o-la). Cliff-dweller.

CAVENDISH BANANA = *Musa cavendishi*. For culture *see* BANANA.

CEANOTHUS (see-a-nō'thus). A large genus of very handsome North American shrubs of the family Rhamnaceae, only a few cult., and of these the hardiness is restricted as indicated below. Leaves evergreen in some species, nearly always 3-nerved or veined at the base. Flowers small, blue or white, but showy from the dense, branched clusters in which they are borne. Sepals incurved and often colored. Petals hooded and with a narrow shank. Fruit dry, 3-lobed, and separating into 3 segments when ripe. (*Ceanothus* is from the Greek for a kind of thistle and of uncertain application here.)

These American plants have been more prized in Eu. than here, especially in France where there are many hybrid, named forms. Few of these are hardy here, except in Calif. Those species not quite hardy can often be grown by digging them out before cold weather sets in, and storing them in frost-free pits, either in pots or heeled in. They all prefer open sunlight and a light, porous soil. Propagated by seeds or by cuttings, layering or by grafting the hybrid sorts. In Calif. they are generally called wild lilac or buckbrush.

americanus. New Jersey tea, Indian tea, Walpole tea, and redroot. A shrub not over 3 ft. high. Leaves ovalish, 2–4 in. long, finely but irregularly toothed. Flowers white, in flat-topped, small clusters. Canada to Fla. and westward. Hardy from zone* 3 southward, but the least showy of the cult. species.

arboreus. Tree or island myrtle. An evergreen shrub or tree-like, not over 25 ft. Leaves ovalish, densely white-felty beneath. Flowers pale blue and fragrant. Calif. coast and islands. Hardy only from zone* 7 southward.

coeruleus. A shrub 10–15 ft. Leaves oblong-oval, 2–4 in. long, white-felty beneath. Flowers deep blue in large-branching clusters. Mex. Scarcely hardy except in zones* 8 and 9, but the origin of many fine hybrids that are somewhat hardier.

cyaneus. An evergreen shrub or small tree, not over 20 ft. high, and sometimes trained on walls in Calif. Leaves 3-veined, alternately arranged, more or less oval, 1–2 in. long, its marginal teeth glandular. Flowers blue, in showy clusters (panicle*) that may be 2–5 in. long. Calif. Hardy from zone* 5 southward.

delilianus. A hybrid of *C. americanus* and *C. azureus*, and now found in many forms, among them Gloire de Versailles and Gloire de Plantières. Both, especially the former, are beautiful plants, especially suited to espalier treatment on walls. Flowers profuse, blue. Hardy from zone* 5 southward. July–Aug.

gloriosus. Point Reyes lilac. A prostrate shrub making a good ground cover, with leathery, persistent, but not evergreen leaves that are roundish, about 1 in. in diameter and spiny-toothed on the margin. Flowers purplish or deep blue. Southern Calif. Hardy from zone* 6 southward. The *var.* **exaltatus** is erect and 10–15 ft. high.

prostratus. Mahala mat. A beautiful prostrate shrub with wedge-shaped, evergreen leaves having spiny teeth on the margins. Flowers blue. Pacific Coast. Hardy only from zone* 6 southward.

spinosus. Red-heart. A shrub 8–10 ft. high or tree-like and somewhat higher. Leaves oblong, about 1½ in. long, nearly without marginal teeth. Flowers white or pale blue. Calif. Ha ... m zone* 7 southward.

thyrsiflorus. Blue blossom or blue myrtle; called also Calif. lilac. The finest and most popular of the cult. species. Evergreen and often up to 25 ft. high. Leaves oblong, 1–2½

---

* Special articles on the subjects indicated by an asterisk (*) will be found at the words so marked.

in. long, lustrous. Flowers blue, numerous in lateral clusters (panicles*). Ore. to Calif. Hardy from zone* 5 southward.

verrucosus. A low shrub, the small leaves somewhat larger toward the tip, pale on the under side. Flowers white. Lower Calif. and southern Calif. Hardy only from zone* 8 southward.

CEDAR. A widely used term in botany and hort. For the traditional cedar *see* CEDRUS (which includes the cedar-of-Lebanon). Also commonly called cedars are trees and shrubs of *Juniperus* (which includes the common red cedar). For other plants sometimes called cedar *see* CEDRELA, LIBOCEDRUS, TORREYA, and CHAMAECYPARIS.

CEDAR APPLE. A gall formed on branches of *Juniperus* caused by a rust fungus for which the apple and related plants are the alternate host.

CEDAR MOSS = *Ceratophyllum demersum*.

CEDAR-OF-LEBANON = *Cedrus libani*.

CEDRELA (see-drell'a, also sed-ree'la). A widely distributed genus of trees of the family Meliaceae, one or two of the temperate zone, but most of them tropical. They have alternate,* compound* leaves, the usually large leaflets arranged feather-fashion. Flowers not showy, but small and usually in branched clusters (panicles*). Petals 4–5, keeled inside. Ovary on a short stalk, followed by a capsule* containing many winged seeds. (*Cedrela* is derived from *Cedrus*, in allusion to the wood resembling some cedars.) Some of the species are also called *Toona*.

The only hardy species is *C. sinensis*, which grows well up to zone* 4, or possibly in protected places in zone* 3. It has no special soil preferences. The other two can be grown outdoors only in zones* 8 and 9. and are frequently planted in southern Calif. and Fla.

odorata. Spanish cedar or West Indian cedar. A tree to 100 ft. high. its wood used for cigar boxes. Leaflets 12–20, 4–6 in. long, without marginal teeth, and without an odd leaflet at the end. Flowers yellowish-green, the cluster shorter than the leaves. Tropical America.

sinensis. A hardy tree (*see* above), usually not over 50 ft. high. Leaflets 10–22, without an odd one at the end, 4–7 in. long and remotely toothed. Flowers greenish-white, the cluster a little shorter than the leaves; after seed shedding the cluster rather showy. China. June. The tree somewhat resembles the ailanthus, but the latter has an odd leaflet at the end.

Toona. Toon. Almost evergreen tree 50–70 ft. high. Leaflets 10–20, without an odd one at the end, oval or lance-shaped, 3–6 in. long. Flowers greenish-white, honey-scented, the clusters shorter than the leaves. Himalayas. Often called *Toona ciliata*.

CEDRUS (see'drus). A genus of four species of handsome, evergreen trees of the pine family, three of which are widely cult. for ornament. They are the traditional cedars, the most famous being the cedar-of-Lebanon and the deodar. Leaves stiff, needle-like, 4-angled, scattered or arranged in small, dense clusters. Flowers unisexual,* the male and female on the same tree, wholly without petals or sepals. Cones erect, its scales closely appressed,* the seeds between them triangular and broadly winged. (*Cedrus* is from the old Greek name for a resinous tree.)

The cedars can be grown in the zones indicated for each species. They need open places and ordinary good soil, preferably not too moist. They make handsome specimen evergreens for lawns or parks, and somewhat resemble larches in the arrangement of their leaves, but unlike larches are true evergreens.

atlantica. Atlas cedar. An upright tree 40–100 ft. high (much less as usually cult.), having a main leader or trunk. Leaves bluish-green, just under an inch long, rigid. Cones 1–3 in. long, light brown. Northern Af. Hardy from zone* 5, or in protected sites from zone* 4, southward. There are fine hort. forms or varieties with silvery-white leaves and with drooping branches.

Deodara. The deodar. A tree up to 150 ft. but less as usually cult.; its leading shoot generally pendulous. Leaves dark bluish-green, nearly 2 in. long, not very rigid. Cones 3–5 in. long, reddish-brown. Himalayas. Hardy from zone* 6 southward and a handsome evergreen. Varieties are offered with silvery leaves, with stiff and shorter leaves, and some forms have pendulous branches. The *var.* **crassifolia** is a much shorter, almost stunted tree with shorter and thicker leaves.

libani. Cedar-of-Lebanon. A tree up to 100 ft. (usually less in cult.), with a single trunk or more often splitting into trunk-like branches; its leading shoot generally erect. Leaves dark green, about 1 in. long. Cones 2–4 in. long, brown. Asia Minor and Syria. Hardy from zone* 4 southward. There is a dwarf, compact form (often called Comte de Dijon), and another with silvery or bluish leaves. Formerly known as *Cedrus libanotica*. There is also a form, sometimes designated as *var.* **pendula**, with weeping branches.

CEIBA (say-ee'ba). Gigantic tropical trees, often with widely flaring buttresses, belonging to the family Bombacaceae, one planted in southern Fla. for interest. Leaves compound,* the 7 leaflets arranged finger-fashion. Flowers large and showy, the 5 petals hairy on the outside. Stamens numerous, in one group. Fruit a leathery capsule,* the seeds surrounded by a cotton-like fiber (the kapok of commerce). (*Ceiba* is the native name for them in tropical America.)

pentandra. Silk-cotton tree. A tree 100–150 ft. high, its branches huge and wide-spreading, the twigs often spiny. At the base the trunk flares out into immense, flank-like buttresses which may extend 30 ft. from the trunk. Leaflets oblongish but tapering, 4–6 in. long. Flowers white or pinkish, in clusters that are 6–8 in. long. Fruit 3–6 in. long. Tropical America. A very striking tree, cult. in Fla. for shade (it is deciduous in mid-winter), and in Java as the source of kapok.

CEIBO = *Erythrina Crista-galli*.

CELANDINE = *Chelidonium majus*.

CELANDINE POPPY = *Stylophorum diphyllum*.

CELASTRACEAE (see-lass-tray'see-ee). The staff-tree or bittersweet family comprises

---

* Special articles on the subjects indicated by an asterisk (*) will be found at the words so marked.

about 40 genera and over 500 species of widely distributed shrubs, trees, and woody vines, a few of which furnish valuable garden plants, some of them evergreen. The leaves are alternate* in *Celastrus* (the bittersweet), *Maytenus,* and *Tripterygium,* but opposite* in most of the other garden genera. The flowers are never conspicuous in this family, usually small and greenish or whitish. The fruit is dry or fleshy and in some genera, notably in *Euonymus* and *Celastrus,* very showy from the often brightly colored aril.* Beautiful evergreen vines are found in *Euonymus* (as well as shrubs), while *Pachistima* is a dwarf evergreen shrub with opposite* leaves. All the garden genera are of outdoor cult. over most of America, but *Elaeodendron* is tropical and can be grown outdoors only in zones* 8 and 9, or in the greenhouse.

Technical flower characters: Calyx 4–5-parted or lobed, usually persistent. Petals 4 or 5, their margins overlapping, inserted on a conspicuous disk. Ovary superior* or half inferior.* Style 1, the stigma 3–5-lobed.

CELASTRUS (see-las′trus). While most of this genus are woody vines, they are sometimes called staff-tree, instead of by the better-known name of bittersweet. There are more than 30 species (family Celastraceae), mostly Asiatic, American, or Australian, and three of them are cult. as ornamental vines. (*See* VINES.) They have alternate,* stalked leaves, and small, greenish, mostly unisexual flowers. (For details *see* CELASTRACEAE.) Fruit a usually yellow capsule,* which, upon splitting, discloses the fleshy crimson aril* of the seeds. (*Celastrus* is from the Greek for some evergreen tree.)

These vines are useful for walls, trellises or arbors, not only for the handsome foliage but for the brilliant autumn fruit. They root easily and may be propagated by cuttings or by suckers. Also raised from seed.

loeseneri. Perhaps not specifically distinct from *C. orbiculatus,* but with stems about half as long. Pith of the stems in plates, not solid as in *C. orbiculatus.* Its show of autumnal, orange-red fruit is conspicuous and more profuse than in its close relative. China. Hardy from zone* 4 southward.

orbiculatus. Often reaching 30 ft. and a handsome vine. Leaves nearly round or oblongish, 3–5 in. long. Flowering and fruiting clusters mostly in the leaf axils,* thus often partly hidden. Fruit orange-yellow. Western China. Hardy in protected parts of zone* 4 and southward. Often sold as *C. articulatus. See* VINES.

scandens. Bittersweet, shrubby bittersweet, waxwork, and fever twig. A rampant, but not tall-growing, woody vine very suitable for covering low wall-tops. Leaves oblong-oval, 2½–5 in. long, tapering at the tip. Flower and fruit clusters mostly terminal, hence not much hidden by the foliage. Fruit yellow, the aril* a brilliant crimson. N.A. Hardy from zone* 2 southward. The attempt of the bookish to call this false bittersweet does not make much headway. For another plant called bittersweet *see* SOLANUM DULCAMARA.

CELERIAC. See CELERY.

CELERY. This vegetable and the closely related celeriac both belong to the genus **Apium** (ā′pi-um) of the carrot family, which comprises about 20 species of herbs, mostly from the north temperate zone. They have compound* or twice-compound* leaves, often with sheathing leafstalks (as in celery). Flowers small, white, many in a compound umbel.* Fruit a prominently 2-angled, small carpel. (*Apium* is Latin for parsley, a related plant.)

A. graveolens. Not in cult., and interesting as a Eurasian biennial herb, from which the varieties below have been derived. Var. **dulce.** Celery. A strong-smelling herb without much enlargement of the root. Leaves with many leaflets, the stalks (celery) channeled and sheathing. For culture *see* below. Var. **rapaceum.** Celeriac. Very similar, but cult. for the edible, thickened, turnip-like root. Leafstalks not as in common celery. For culture *see* below.

CELERY CULTURE

The ordinary celery of the markets was derived from *Apium graveolens,* a white-flowered herb from Europe and Asia. Celeriac, often called turnip-rooted celery (*Apium graveolens rapaceum*), is also derived from the same wild plant, but instead of having edible leafstalks, has practically none, but an edible root for which it is cult. *See* Celeriac, below.

Successful celery culture is based on the right climate and the right soils. As to the first, the plant requires coolness. In the commercially important areas, as along the Great Lakes, it gets this for most of the growing season. Elsewhere there are two distinct celery crops, one utilizing the cool spring months for growth; the later and much more important crop matures in the late fall, and, by protection, is extended well through the winter. The very important commercial production of celery in the winter months, as practiced in the South and California, is based upon the use of their brief period of coolness.

SOILS AND FERTILIZER. No garden crop grown is such a rich feeder as celery. The soil must have depth and mellowness and an abundant supply of moisture. If rainfall and moisture retentiveness do not supply this, an overhead watering system or irrigation is essential. It is absolutely impossible to make it grow in hard, dry or sun-baked land. So important is this depth, mellowness, and soil moisture that the most successful commercial growers in the country have utilized drained mucklands for celery farms. In the region about the Great Lakes there are thousands of acres so utilized, and elsewhere mucklands are also highly favored. *See* MUCKLAND GARDENING.

The average home gardener has no muck, but to grow good celery he must approximate the conditions of such places as nearly as possible. This means adding humus for moisture-holding and mellowness and plant food for enrichment.

An excellent method is to plow in 15–20 tons of well-rotted stable manure to the acre (4–5 wheelbarrow loads to a 100-ft. row).

---

* Special articles on the subjects indicated by an asterisk (*) will be found at the words so marked.

This adds humus and plant food, but besides this it is advisable to add 1500 pounds per acre (about 6 pounds per 100-ft. row) of commercial fertilizer with a 4–8–12 ratio (*see* FERTILIZERS). These should be thoroughly and deeply plowed under at least three weeks before the plants are set in the garden. It is almost impossible to get the soil too rich or to plow too deeply for successful celery culture.

VARIETIES. *Pale or Yellow:* Michigan Golden, Cornell 19, Cornell 619. *Green:* Giant Pascal, Utah (many strains), Summer Pascal, Emerson Pascal.

RAISING CELERY FROM SEED. For the average home gardener this is apt to be sufficiently difficult and tedious to suggest the desirability of buying plants ready to be set in his specially prepared soil. Good plants are offered by dealers of both the late and early sorts.

If plants are raised from seed they must be handled very carefully. Celery seed is small, germinates slowly, and a considerable number fail to germinate at all. Germination is hastened by soaking the seeds (in a cotton bag) in water for 24 hours. Then mix the seeds with an equal quantity of fine sand, which greatly facilitates their planting.

Sow the seeds and sand in a fine drill (not over ¼ in. deep), or sow them broadcast if you prefer, covering with about ¼ in. of finely sifted soil. Keep the flats or boxes in which they have been planted moist, or even rather wet. This can be done by covering them for some time, before germination, with wet burlap.

For the early varieties this seed should be sown in the cool greenhouse or hotbed, approximately 8 or 9 weeks before the plants are ready to go to their permanent position. For the late varieties the procedure and timing are the same, except that the seed is sown in flats or boxes outdoors. In either case it will take perhaps 3 weeks before the first plants show above ground.

These young seedlings are very delicate and spindling at first. They are greatly improved by two or three subsequent transplantings, at each move spacing them farther apart. This is an expensive and tedious process, and the loss from wilting and damping-off is considerable. But the survivors are much more stocky and better able to stand conditions in the open garden. If the plants are from seed sown in the greenhouse, it is important that the temperature for the young seedlings be kept around 50° or a little above. Do not let it get down to 40° or 45°.

PLANTING CELERY. The plants should be about 4–5 in. high when set out in the garden, stocky, and with plenty of roots. See that these requirements are met, whether you have raised them yourself or bought them from a dealer.

Set out the plants only when the ground is wet or you can make it so. Setting celery plants in dry soil will certainly kill them. If you have only 100 ft. of celery, the young plants should be watered every day for the first three days — more if you happen to be caught by a dry spell. They should be planted in a trench 3–4 in. deep, which is gradually filled in as the plants grow.

Early varieties should be planted after danger of frost is over (see the name of your state for the dates). Late varieties are best planted from mid-July to August 1.

The plants should be put about 5 in. apart in the row and the rows cannot be nearer than 2½ ft. apart, and 4 ft. is better, as will appear presently, especially for the late crop. The plants must be cultivated frequently and kept absolutely free of weeds. A weedy celery row will greatly increase the difficulty of blanching.

Some growers, in spite of the liberal applications of manure and fertilizer already mentioned, use nitrate of soda in addition. They put on 250 pounds to the acre (1½ pounds to a 100-ft. row) two or three times at intervals of 15 days, starting a week or two after the plants have been put out.

BLANCHING AND HARVESTING. Most of the early varieties are of the sort described as self-blanching, which means that they are supposed to be white and tender without having the light excluded from them. Most of the late (and most desirable) varieties are naturally green and useless without blanching.

For the late varieties the most satisfactory method of blanching is gradually to heap soil about the plants so that only the tops finally show above the raised mounds. This operation must be done carefully and not much before September 15 in most northern localities. No soil must be allowed to fall into the heart of the plant, which, if too spreading,

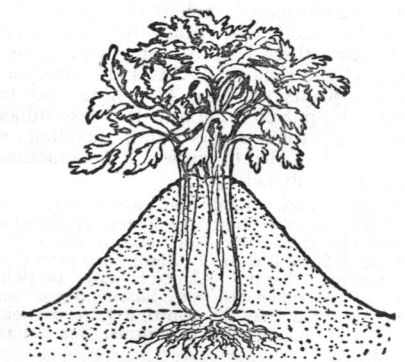

Blanching celery with earth

should be tied up before starting to heap up the soil. It will take considerable, and preferably weed-free soil, to do a thorough blanching job, which is the chief reason for the wide spacing and thorough cultivation.

All the late varieties are better for this soil blanching, and if the tops are protected with a deep dressing of salt hay or straw, the celery may be kept for a good part of the winter and dug as wanted.

* Special articles on the subjects indicated by an asterisk (*) will be found at the words so marked.

The early varieties cannot be soil-blanched, as soil about the stems will almost certainly cause rot. Some prefer paper cylinders slipped over each plant. Others use long boards (a foot wide) each side of the row and pinched nearly together over the plants with wire hooks. Even the self-blanching types are improved by this treatment, and some growers of late celery prefer boards to soil for blanching.

Boards used for blanching celery

Both early and late varieties are harvested by digging out a few plants at a time. A 100-ft. row should yield about 200 plants, or a little more if they are put exactly 5 in. apart.

Celeriac Culture (*Apium graveolens rapaceum*)

The turnip-rooted celery or celeriac is grown in exactly the same way as celery. But because there is no development of leaf-stalk, and the delicious root is the final harvest, the plants need no blanching and the rows can be put 20 in. apart. It is less subject to diseases than celery and, needing no blanching, is easier to grow. It is sometimes known as knob celery.

INSECT PESTS. Leaf tier webs leaves together and injures plant. Repeated applications of pesticide #26 (see SPRAYS AND DUSTS) or pesticide #21 will control. Plant bugs may damage growing "heart." Control with pesticide #20 as recommended on label. Black and green caterpillar may be controlled by pesticide #1 or hand picking of large worms. See SPRAYS AND DUSTS.

DISEASES. Two fungus diseases of leaves of celery are known as early blight and late blight, causing brown or black spots and loss of crop. Because the fungi can live on the seed for at least a year, most commercial growers prefer seed two years old. When this older seed is not available, the fungi may be killed by soaking the seed for 30 minutes in hot water (118° F.) before planting. If leafspot or blight appears on the plants, apply pesticide #7 or #11 (see SPRAYS AND DUSTS) and repeat at 10-day intervals.

Plants with yellowing and wilting, starting with the outer leaves, indicate wilt* disease caused by a fungus in the soil. Secure wilt-

resistant varieties suitable to your area and color preference.

CELERY CABBAGE = *Brassica pekinensis*. For culture *see* CHINESE CABBAGE.

CELERY FAMILY = Umbelliferae.

CELLAR GARDENING. More than a dozen crops will furnish food throughout the winter when grown in a cellar. The only real drawback is the danger of coal, oil, or illuminating-gas fumes. Gas in such minute quantities as to be apparently odorless will kill and stunt the growth of many plants. A temperature of 50 to 60 degrees is best for vegetables. For the growing of those which require darkness, a corner of the cellar may be curtained off, or a box, with a few holes bored for ventilation, turned over the one containing the forced roots.

Rhubarb is the easiest vegetable to force. The clumps must be old and well established, as winter growth is due to the nourishment stored in the roots. Allow the clumps to freeze hard before taking indoors. Store in a cool place. Start a few in Dec. in boxes of earth with a little fresh manure under the roots. Better stalks are obtained by forcing in a dark, moist spot. They will be ready for use in about six weeks.

Dig asparagus roots in the fall and transplant them into boxes of earth. Keep in a light, heated spot; water well. Edible-size stalks will soon appear. If an extra supply of roots is dug, kept in a cool place, and forced at intervals, asparagus may be enjoyed until the new crop arrives.

French endive, sold in expensive restaurants and hotels, is really witloof chicory. Sow seed in the garden in June. In the late fall dig and store the roots in a cool cellar. Start forcing at intervals of two or three weeks. Pack close. Cover the crowns with about 4 in. of sand; water and keep warm. The new tops which push up will be creamy-white, tender, and ready for use in three to four weeks. Do not cut too close to the roots, as second and third cuttings may be made. This plant is commonly, but mistakenly, called simply endive in the shops. See the illustrations at ENDIVE.

Mushrooms, sea-kale, chard, parsley, dandelions for salad, and chives for seasoning also may be grown.

In cellars where the heating apparatus is partitioned off, or where fuel other than coal or gas is used, many plants suitable for the cool greenhouse may be grown. Benches may be placed beneath the windows or artificial, preferably fluorescent, lighting may be used. This is an ideal place in which to start bulbs and other plants for house decoration. Bench planting can be practiced as in ordinary greenhouse culture. Rock garden seedlings and many half-hardy annuals, such as verbenas, can be started and carried through the winter. Small seedlings for next year's plants also do well here through the hot summer. *See also* STORAGE.

---

* Special articles on the subjects indicated by an asterisk (*) will be found at the words so marked.

CELOSIA (sell-ō′si-a). A large genus of tropical herbs or shrubs of the family Amaranthaceae, the chief cult. sorts grown as tender annuals (*see* ANNUALS) for their often fantastic or grotesque, chaffy flower clusters (the cockscombs). Leaves alternate.* Flowers minute and chaffy, crowded into dense spikes which are much enlarged, flattened, crested, or otherwise modified and often brilliantly colored. The minute flower characters are technical. (*Celosia* is from the Greek for burned, in allusion to the brilliant scarlet inflorescence.)

These showy garden plants are of easy culture if treated as tender annuals. They are extremely useful and widely grown to give lasting color in shades of red, yellow, green, purple, or white, and come in many different forms.

argentea. A tropical Asiatic weed, scarcely in cult., with a silvery-white, more or less oblong spike. It is the parent of the *var.* cristata, the cockscomb. This is lower than the type, usually 1–2 ft. Flower clusters very diverse. One common type has a crested or rolled cluster very like a cockscomb and from 3 to 6 in. wide; or congested and monstrous. Some are very broad and fan-like, others spire-like, some open and feathery, all chaffy and in a variety of colors, to which all sorts of names have been applied such as Plumed Knight, etc.

floribunda. A shrubby plant 8–10 ft. high. Leaves triangular or oval, often 7 in. long. Flowers very numerous in tight clusters (panicles*). Lower Calif. and not hardy in the East. Some plants called by seedsmen *C. floribunda* are actually forms of the cockscomb and do not belong here.

plumosa. A plumed form of the cockscomb (*C. argentea cristata*).

CELSIA (sell′zi-a). Thirty species of mullein-like herbs of the figwort family, the two below somewhat grown for ornament, but not hardy over much of the country. They are separated only by technical characters from the mulleins, and have a terminal flower cluster (spike or raceme*) of yellow, usually bracted* flowers. (Named for Olaus Celsius, teacher of Linnaeus.)

The plants are best treated as biennials. Start the seeds in the greenhouse or hotbed and set them out only after settled warm weather has come. While perennials, they often die in cold, wet winters.

Arcturus. Cretan bear's-tail. An erect herb with a single, hairy stem 10–18 in. high. Leaves ovalish and toothed or the lower cut lyre-fashion. Flowers yellow, distinctly stalked, in a loose raceme, the anthers* purple. Crete and Asia Minor.

cretica. Cretan mullein. Hairy and 3–5 ft. high. Leaves ovalish, more or less clasping, the lower ones cut lyre-fashion. Flowers yellow, almost stalkless in the spike, and marked with purple. Mediterranean region.

CELTIS. See HACKBERRY.

CELTUCE. A lettuce-like vegetable, said by its introducer to be native near the Tibetan border of China. For its cult. *see* LETTUCE. It differs from lettuce in being not only used as a salad, but later, as its edible flowering stalk develops, cooked like broccoli.

The leaves are of the Romaine type, not very tightly clasping. The edible stem, flavored like a cross between a mild summer squash and artichoke, is 6–8 in. long and about 1½ in. in diameter. *Celtuce* is a coined term to suggest celery and lettuce. It has nothing to do with the former, being a derivative of or some form of the lettuce (*Lactuca sativa*), perhaps the *var.* asparagina. See LACTUCA.

Cembra (sem′bra). Modern form of the ancient *zember*, the name of the Swiss stone pine.

cembroides (sem-broy′deez; but *see* OïDES) Resembling the Swiss stone pine. (*See* CEMBRA.)

CENCHRUS PAUCIFLORUS. *See* Sandbur in the list at WEEDS.

cenisia, -us, -um (se-nee′zi-a). From Mt. Cenis in the Alps.

CENTAUREA (sen-tor′ree-a). A genus of chiefly Eurasian herbs of the family Compositae, comprising over 400 species, a few of which are among our most popular garden flowers. They are annuals or perennials of diverse leaf-form but with their flowers in heads. The heads contain only tubular flowers, but some, along the edge, are often expanded and ray-like. Below the head is a series of overlapping bracts,* often cut or fringed. (Named for Centaur.)

From the garden standpoint the genus contains rather diverse plants. The annuals like the cornflower, basket-flower, sweet sultan, and *C. imperialis* are best treated as hardy annuals and sown where wanted. Unlike many annuals, they flower better and seem most happy when pretty crowded, so they need little thinning.

All the perennial species, except the dusty millers, can be grown in the open border like any other perennial. They are thrifty plants of apparently no special soil preferences. *Centaurea Cineraria* and *C. gymnocarpa*, both known as dusty millers, are best carried over the winter as cuttings rooted the previous Sept.; or they may be started from fall-sown seed. Their white-felty foliage does not like winter slush and rain. They are most of them summer bloomers.

americana. Basket-flower. Annual, and 4–6 ft. high, the leaves oblongish and mostly without marginal teeth. Heads 4–5 in. wide, the marginal flowers ray-like, hence the head set as though in a rose- or flesh-colored, shallow basket. The bracts below the head have fringed tufts. Central U.S. to Mex. A handsome garden favorite.

Cineraria. Dusty miller. A perennial, 12–18 in. high, its foliage prominently white-felty. Leaves parted into blunt but narrow lobes. Heads large, yellow or purple. Southern Italy. For the garden cineraria *see* that entry.

Cyanus. The cornflower and one of the most popular garden annuals, cult. under such names as bachelor's button, bluebottle, ragged sailor and blue bonnets. A rather sprawling annual 1–2 ft. high, woolly when young, green later. Leaves narrow, nearly 5 in. long, without teeth or the lower sometimes cut. Heads typically pale blue (purple, pink, or white in hort. forms), the marginal flowers expanded and ray-

---

* Special articles on the subjects indicated by an asterisk (*) will be found at the words so marked.

like. Southern Eu. There is also a double-flowered form in nearly all colors.

dealbata. A perennial of the dusty miller type, 18–24 in. high, its white-felty leaves cut into coarsely toothed lobes, the lower leaves sometimes a foot long. Heads with inner flowers red, the outer pink or white. Persia and Asia Minor.

gymnocarpa. Dusty miller. Perennial and white-felty, the leaves twice-cut into narrow, toothless segments. Heads small, rose-purple, grouped in clusters (panicles*), but mostly hidden by the leaves. Capri. A handsome foliage plant, sometimes confused with the cineraria (which see).

imperialis. An annual plant of hybrid origin, thought to be derived from a variety of the sweet sultan. It is 2–4 ft. high, and has fragrant heads in varied colors (white, purple, lilac, or pink).

macrocephala. A perennial, 2–3 ft. high, the ovalish leaves toothed. Flower heads nearly 4 in. wide, yellow, the bracts* below them fringed. Armenia.

montana. Mountain bluet. A European perennial herb, its foliage white-hairy only when young. Leaves oblongish. Heads blue, often 3 in. wide, the marginal flowers much enlarged and ray-like. The bracts beneath the head are black-fringed.

moschata. Sweet sultan. Next to the cornflower the most popular of the annual centaureas. It is smooth, 1–2 ft. high, the leaves toothed or cut feather-fashion. Heads solitary, usually fragrant, yellow, red, purple, pink, or white in some of the hort. forms and very handsome. The marginal flowers are much enlarged, raylike or even fringed. Orient.

nigra. Knapweed; also called hardheads and Spanish buttons. A rough-hairy, rather weedy or coarse perennial, frequent as an escape all over the temperate world. Leaves oblongish, toothed or not, 4–6 in. long. Heads solitary, ball-like, rose-purple, usually less than 1 in. across. Eu.

pulcherrima. A stout perennial, 18–30 in. high. Leaves lance-shaped or sometimes cut into narrow segments, 5–7 in. long and grayish-hairy beneath. Flower heads solitary, purple or rose purple, the bracts* beneath them fringed. Southeastern Eu.

ruthenica. A perennial, 2–3 ft. high, the leaves cut into fine, toothed segments. Flower heads pale yellow, the marginal ones larger than the center flowers, the bracts* beneath the head not toothed or fringed. Eurasia.

centifolia, -us, -um (sen-ti-fō′li-a). Hundred-leaved.

CENTIPEDE-GRASS = *Eremochloa ophiuroides.*

CENTIPEDE-PLANT = *Muehlenbeckia platyclados.*

CENTRADENIA (sen-tra-dee′ni-a). Attractive greenhouse foliage plants of the family Melastomaceae, comprising perhaps half a dozen tropical American species, one not uncommon in cult. Branches 4-winged. Leaves opposite, one in each pair smaller than the other. Flowers rose-pink in a dense cluster (cyme*) that is shorter than the leaves. Calyx tubular, 4-lobed. Petals 4. Stamens 8. Fruit a 4-valved pod (capsule*). (*Centradenia* is from the Greek for spur and gland, referring to a feature of the anthers.*)

The plant below needs potting mixture* 2 and a warm-temperate greenhouse. If grown near the glass (shaded) it will respond with good color in its leaves. Easily propagated by cuttings.

grandifolia. A showy, Mexican under-shrub, not over 2 ft. high. Leaves oval-lance-shaped, but unequal, 4–6 in. long and with generally 5 leading veins, bright red on the under side. Flowers rose-pink, in many-flowered clusters.

centranthifolia, -us, -um (sen-tran-thi-fō′li-a). With foliage like the red valerian (*Centranthus*).

CENTRANTHUS (sen-tran′thus). A small group of mostly perennial herbs of the family Valerianaceae, from the Mediterranean region, the one below an attractive flower garden plant. Leaves opposite,* faintly or not at all toothed. Flowers small, red (in ours), in a dense terminal cluster, the corolla with a slender tube, but spurred at the base, 5-parted at the top. Stamen only 1. Fruit crowned by a bristly crest. (*Centranthus* is Greek for spurred flower.)

ruber. Red valerian or Jupiter's-beard; also called scarlet lightning. A perennial, bushy herb 1–3 ft. high. Leaves oval or narrower, 3–4 in. long, stalkless and broad at the base. Flowers many, fragrant, about ½ in. long, the spur slender, red in the typical form but often crimson or white in some varieties. Eu. and southwestern As. An easily grown and favorite perennial garden plant. Sometimes offered as *Valeriana rubra* or *V. coccinea.*

CENTROPOGON (sen-tro-pō′gon). Of over 100 species of tropical American undershrubs of the family Lobeliaceae, only the following is of much garden interest. It is a favorite plant for hanging baskets, but needs a warm, moist greenhouse for proper growth. Leaves alternate,* stalked and finely toothed (in ours). Flowers scarlet or carmine (in the one below), solitary, on long stalks in the leaf axils,* or in clusters. Corolla tubular, slightly irregular* from being somewhat split. Fruit a berry. (*Centropogon* is Greek for spur and beard, in allusion to the fringed stigma.)

lucyanus. A little woody and 12–20 in. high. Leaves oblongish or oval. Flowers mostly in terminal clusters, rather showy, the corolla about 1½ in. long. Stamens* protruding, the anther* white-bristly.

CENTURY PLANT = *Agave americana;* also, generally, any species of *Agave.*

Cepa (see′pa). Latin name for the onion.

CEPHALANTHUS. See BUTTON-BUSH.

CEPHALARIA (seff-a-lay′ri-a). Coarse, scabious-like herbs of the family Dipsacaceae, comprising over 30 species, mostly from the Mediterranean region, of which two are somewhat cult. in the flower garden. They are tall herbs with coarse, deeply cut leaves and roundish flower heads at the ends of long stalks, the heads surrounded by a series of small bracts.* Flowers very small, densely packed in the head, yellow or white, the corolla 4-parted. Fruit a ribbed achene,* the minute calyx often crowning it. (*Cephalaria*

---

* Special articles on the subjects indicated by an asterisk (*) will be found at the words so marked.

is from the Greek for head, in allusion to the flower heads.)

Both the plants below are suited to the back of the more informal border. They are easily propagated by division, as both are stout perennials.

alpina. Erect, 4–6 ft. high. Leaves much cut, feather-fashion. Flower heads about 1½ in. across, sulphur-yellow. Southern Eu.

tatarica. Stiff, and 5–6 ft. high. Leaves cut feather-fashion into many, toothed segments. Flower heads nearly 2 in. across, white. Western As.

CEPHALOCEREUS (sef-fal-lo-seer′e-us). A striking group of perhaps 50 species of column-like cacti, chiefly Mexican and South American, a few cult. for their odd habit and the interesting, long, white, hair-like "wool" found on the old-man cactus (and some others) near the top of the plant. The plant body has many longitudinal ribs and sharp spines. Flowers chiefly night-blooming, small for the cacti, some of the flower often clinging to the fleshy fruit. (*Cephalocereus* is from the Greek for head and *Cereus*.) They are sometimes known as *Pilocereus*.

For culture see CACTI.

euphorbioides. Usually a single column up to 15 ft. high, and a foot thick, prominently 8-ribbed, the spine-bases cottony. Flowers day-blooming, not over 2 in. long, brownish outside, pinkish in the inner petals. South American (?). Not much known outside the collections of specialists.

polylophus. Tall, columnar, usually unbranched and occasionally 40 ft. high in Mex., much less in cult. Ribs 15–18, the spine-bases felted but not white-woolly. Flowers red, about 2 in. long. Mex.

senilis. Old-man cactus. A popular and widely grown Mexican species, the plant body columnar, 30–40 ft. tall in the wild, usually much less in cult. Ribs 20–30. The top of the plant is crowned with a thatch-like collection of long white hairs. Flowers red outside, whitish within, about 2 in. long. Mex.

cephalonica, -us, -um (sef-fal-lon′i-ka). From Cephalonia, an Ionian Island.

CEPHALOTAXUS (sef-fal-lo-tax′us). The plum-yews are Asiatic evergreen trees of the yew family (Taxaceae), often cult. for their fine foliage, and remarkable for the stalked, plum-like fruit. Leaves needle-like, very numerous and scattered, green above but with 2 bluish-gray bands beneath. For flowers see TAXACEAE. Fruit stalked, not cone-like, but fleshy, more or less egg-shaped and maturing the second season. (*Cephalotaxus* is from Greek for head and *Taxus*, the yew, in reference to the shape of the male flower heads.)

While both the cult. species are trees, they are usually shrubby as grown here. They are handsome evergreens, unsuited to regions of summer heat or dryness, but perfectly at home near the seacoast in the zones indicated below. They much resemble the closely related true yews, but the latter do not have the leaves 2-banded beneath.

drupacea. A tree up to 30 ft., usually shrubby in cult. Leaves 1–2 in. long, pointed. Plum-like fruit green, about 1 in. long. Japan.

Hardy from zone* 4 southward. The two best known of the many horticultural varieties are: *var.* **pedunculata,** with longer leaves and longer-stalked fruit (sometimes sold as *C. harringtoniana*); and *var.* **fastigiata,** with upright, columnar habit.

fortunei. A tree up to 30 ft., usually with several stems, or in cult., shrubby. Leaves spreading nearly horizontally, 2–4 in. long. Fruit purple, about 1 in. long. Central China. Hardy from zone* 5 southward. When perfectly grown it should be a broad-headed tree with the tips of its branches pendulous.

cephalotes (sef-fal-lō′tees). Like a small head.

cerasifera, -us, -um (see-ra-sif′fer-ra). Bearing cherries or cherry-like fruit.

cerasiformis, -e (see-ras-i-for′mis). Cherry-shaped.

cerastioides (see-ras-tee-oy′deez; but *see* OÏDES). Resembling a chickweed (*Cerastium*).

CERASTIUM (see-ras′tee-um). The 100 or so species of chickweed or mouse-ear chickweed, which belong to the pink family, are mostly weedy herbs (sometimes pests), but three of them are attractive garden plants. They have opposite* leaves, without marginal teeth, and slightly swollen joints, the foliage often hairy. Flowers small, white, but relatively showy from being in profuse, forked clusters in the cult. species. Sepals mostly 5. Petals 5, often 2-notched at the tip. Fruit a small capsule.* (*Cerastium* is from Greek for horn, alluding to the shape of the pod.)

The three cult. species are all perennials of the easiest culture, increased by division. Snow-in-summer is an extremely popular prostrate herb, very useful in the rock garden or border for its ground-covering habit, its mats of white foliage and white flowers.

arvense. Starry grasswort or field chickweed. A densely tufted perennial, 6–10 in. high. Leaves very narrow, about 1 in. long. Flowers many, white, about ⅓ in. wide. North temperate zone. Apr.–May. Frequently a mere weed, but one of the earliest of white-flowered plants.

biebersteini. A creeping perennial, not over 6 in. high, the leaves about 1½ in. long and ⅛ in. wide, grayish-woolly. Flowers white, in May and June. Asia Minor.

tomentosum. Snow-in-summer. A popular, prostrate garden plant, not over 6 in. high and forming large patches. Leaves numerous, about ½ in. long and ⅛ in. wide, conspicuously white-woolly. Flowers white, nearly ½ in. wide. June. Eu. It will grow in pure sand. See SAND GARDENS.

vulgatum. See Mouse-ear Chickweed in the list at WEEDS.

Cerasus (ser′a-sus). Classical name for the cherry.

CERATONIA. See CAROB.

CERATOPHYLLUM (ser-rat-o-fill′um). A single, submerged, aquatic plant and the only genus of the family Ceratophyllaceae (ser-rat-o-fil-lay′see-ee). They have finely dissected leaves, with thread-like segments at intervals along a fine, thread-like stem. Flowers extremely minute, without a true calyx or corolla. The only species, C. **demersum,**

---

* Special articles on the subjects indicated by an asterisk (*) will be found at the words so marked.

called hornwort, coon-tail, fish-blankets, or cedar moss, is a delicate, submerged, water plant very useful in aquaria, to which it is easily transferred from the wild, where it grows in ponds or slow streams throughout N.A. (*Ceratophyllum* is from Greek for horn and leaf, in allusion to the stiffish, though very slender, leaves.)

CERATOPTERIS (ser-ra-top'ter-is). The floating or water ferns are the only cult. genus of the family **Ceratopteridaceae.** They are the only really aquatic ferns and have two sorts of fronds. While rooted in the mud, the sterile fronds are usually floating, but the fertile (spore*-bearing) fronds are erect, emersed, and twice or even more compound.* Both sorts are borne in rosettes. (*Ceratopteris* is from the Greek for horned fern.)

These more interesting than decorative plants can be best grown by planting in pots which are just below the surface of the water. They are useful for aquaria or greenhouse pools, but are not hardy where it freezes. The plants must be renewed each year, which may be done by detaching the buds from the leaves. These buds will produce new plants if kept just submerged and planted in good soil.

pteridoides. Sterile fronds floating, short-stalked, broadly triangular, the margins lobed. Fertile fronds divided into whip-like segments. Fla. to Brazil.

thalictroides. Segments of the sterile fronds more or less triangular, the frond long-stalked, floating, but some partly erect. Fertile frond similar, but the segments much finer. Tropics of the Old World.

CERATOSTIGMA (ser-rat-o-stig'ma). A small genus of herbs or low shrubs of the family Plumbaginaceae, from China and Africa, one grown as a border plant for its blue flowers. They have alternate leaves, hairy on the margins, and flowers in loose, head-like clusters which are surrounded by a series of stiff bracts. Corolla tubular, its limb* salver-shaped, the stamens* inserted in the tube. Fruit a 5-valved capsule, inclosed in the persistent, tubular calyx.* (*Ceratostigma* is from the Greek for horn and stigma.)

The only cult. species is an attractive, fall-blooming border plant with no special soil preferences. It is propagated by division.

plumbaginoides. Leadwort. A low or semi-prostrate, shrubby herb or woody, not over 1 ft. high. Leaves 2–3 in. long, broadest above the middle and tapering to the base. Flowers deep blue, not over ½ in. wide. China. Hardy from zone* 4 southward and an attractive plant for the blue garden. Aug.–Sept. Sometimes offered as *Plumbago Larpentiae.* A related Chinese shrub, *C. willmottianum,* with blue, but pink-tubed, flowers is also grown in Calif. and along the Gulf Coast.

CERCIDIPHYLLUM (sir-sid-i-fil'lum). A single, Asiatic tree, commonly called the katsura tree, belonging to the family Trochodendraceae, and frequently cultivated for ornament. Leaves opposite* or nearly so, mostly borne on short spurs, the veins arranged finger-fashion. Male and female flowers on dif-

ferent trees. They are small, have no petals, and are borne on the spurs as the leaves unfold. Fruit a splitting pod, with many seeds. (*Cercidiphyllum* is from *Cercis,* the redbud, and the Greek for leaf.) Placed by some in the family Cercidiphyllaceae.

japonicum. Katsura tree. A tree 30–50 ft., usually less in cult., and often divided into several trunks or stems. Leaves nearly round, heart-shaped at the base, 2–4½ in. long, shallowly and bluntly toothed, pale beneath. Jap. Hardy from zone* 3 southward. The *var.* sinense, with usually a single trunk and longer-stalked leaves, is hardy from zone* 4 southward. These are handsome foliage trees, the leaves purplish when unfolding, changing in the autumn from green to yellow and scarlet.

CERCIDIUM (sir-sid'i-um). A small genus of chiefly tropical American shrubs or trees of the pea family, one of which is wild in the southwestern U.S. and adjacent Mex. and is somewhat cult. in its native region. This cult. species, **C. torreyanum,** is the palo-verde or green-barked acacia, a desert shrub, that is green-barked, spiny and leafless for much of the year. Leaves (when present) alternate,* twice-compound,* falling at the end of spring. Flowers showy, yellow, not pea-like, but nearly regular,* about ¾ in. wide. Pods (legumes*) about 3 in. long. (*Cercidium* means like *Cercis,* the redbud.)

CERCIS. *See* REDBUD.

CERCOCARPUS (sir-ko-kar'pus). In the western U.S., especially in Calif., is a group of evergreen shrubs or small trees of the rose family, commonly called the mountain mahogany, but not related to the true mahogany. Of the 20 known species only two are usually found in gardens and these are not hardy everywhere (*see* below). They have alternate* leaves, and small, greenish-white flowers without petals, usually in small clusters in the leaf axils.* Stamens many, borne on the cup-shaped calyx.* Fruit small, dry, crowned by a long, silky plume. (*Cercocarpus* is from the Greek for tailed fruit.)

The chief attraction of these plants is their feathery, tailed fruits, the early bloom not being showy. The shrubs need open sunlight, a well-drained site, and are propagated by seeds or cuttings.

betulaefolius = *Cercocarpus betuloides.*

betuloides. A shrub, rarely a small tree, with scaly bark. Leaves oblongish, but broadest toward the tip, 1–2 in. long, bluntly toothed. Plume of the fruit 2½–4 in. long. Calif. Hardy from zone* 6 southward.

montanus. A shrub not over 5 ft. high, the bark fissured. Leaves rounded at the tip, 1–2½ in. long, finely hairy and pale beneath, coarsely toothed. Plume of the fruit 3–5 in. long. Western U.S. Hardy from zone* 5 southward.

cerealis, -e (seer-ee-a'lis). Cereal-like, and named for Ceres, the goddess of agriculture.

CEREFOLIUM. An old name for the chervil.

CEREUS (seer'ee-us). As once understood, an immense genus of cacti, of very diverse habit, and popularly including the beautiful night-blooming cereuses, now known

---

* Special articles on the subjects indicated by an asterisk (*) will be found at the words so marked.

to belong to other genera. As now restricted, *Cereus* has about 20 species, mostly South American and West Indian, three of which are cult. in the warmest parts of U.S. or in greenhouses. They are mostly tall, even tree-like, plants with a columnar plant body that is deeply angled or ribbed, spiny, but without the long tufts of white hair found in the old-man cactus. Flowers funnel-shaped, night-blooming, white. Fruit fleshy and naked, edible in some species. (*Cereus* is Latin for a wax candle, perhaps in allusion to the shape of some former species.)

For culture *see* CACTI.

For the plants usually known as night-blooming cereus *see* SELENICEREUS, NYCTO-CEREUS, and HYLOCEREUS.

For other plants hitherto, and by some still called cereus, *see* CHAMAECEREUS, CORY-PHANTHA, HELIOCEREUS, CEPHALOCEREUS, TRICHOCEREUS, ESCONTRIA, PACHYCEREUS, LEMAIREOCEREUS, BERGEROCACTUS, HARRISIA, MACHAEROCEREUS, APOROCACTUS, MYRTIL-LOCACTUS, CARNEGIEA, PENIOCEREUS, ECHINO-CEREUS, WILCOXIA, and DEAMIA.

Jamacaru. Mandacaru. Much-branched, often 20 ft. high and with a woody trunk at base. Ribs 4–6, with many sharp spines. Flowers nearly 12 in. long, white, but green on the outside. Brazil.

peruvianus. Tree-like, much-branched and sometimes 40 ft. high, the branches green or bluish-green, and with 4–9 ribs. Spines long, slender, needle-like. Flowers about 6 in. long, white, but reddish on the outside. Southeastern S.A.

validus. Not over 6 ft. high, more or less shrubby, bluish-green when young. Ribs 4–8, and blunt, the spines 5 in a cluster, short and stout. Flowers white, but reddish on the outside. Argentina.

cerifera, -us, -um (see-rif'fer-ra). Wax-bearing.

CERIMAN = *Monstera deliciosa.*

CERINTHE (sir-rin'the). A small group of Eurasian herbs of the family Boraginaceae, one of them an annual flower garden plant cult. for its showy bloom. Leaves alternate,* often red or white-spotted. Flowers in 1-sided clusters, yellow, borne among numerous purple bracts.* Corolla nearly regular,* tubular. Fruit a group of 2 erect nutlets, very small. (*Cerinthe* is from the Greek for wax flower, the ancients assuming that bees harvested wax from them.)

The only commonly cult. species is a hardy annual, easily grown from seed sown where wanted.

retorta. Honeywort. Not over 18–20 in. tall, the leaves generally bluish-green, the upper nearly stem-clasping by the eared base, gradually passing into the colored bracts* of the flower cluster. Flowers yellow, tipped with purple, protruding beyond the bracts.* Greece.

cernua, -us, -um (sir'new-a). Cernuous; *i.e.,* nodding.

CEROPEGIA (seer-ro-pee'ji-a). Tropical vines, or shrubby plants, comprising over 160 species of the milkweed family, all from the Old World, one of which is a greenhouse vine with wax-like flowers. Leaves opposite* (sometimes none), fleshy. Flowers in pairs (in ours), their long stalks in the leaf axils.* Corolla tubular, a little curved and swollen at the base. Fruit a slender follicle.* (*Ceropegia* is from the Greek for wax fountain, in allusion to the waxy flowers.)

Our only cult. species needs a warm, moist greenhouse and potting mixture* 3. Easily propagated by cuttings over bottom-heat.*

woodi. Prostrate or trailing and needing support for growing on walls. Leaves ovalish or roundish, about ½ in. long, heart-shaped at the base. Flowers pinkish-purple, waxy, about ½ in. long. Fruit smooth, 2–3 in. long. Natal.

CEROXYLON (see-rox'i-lon). Immensely tall feather palms from the northern Andean region, comprising 4 or 5 species, one of which, in the young state, is cult. outdoors in southern Calif. and in greenhouses. The trunk is ringed and spineless, crowned by huge leaves. The leaflets are long, rigid, and sword-shaped. Flowers unisexual,* rather large for a palm. Stamens 9–15. Fruit purplish, berry-like. (*Ceroxylon* is Greek for wax and wood, the trunk being often waxy.)

In southern Calif. the wax palm is somewhat cult., but it does not approach its wild stature. (For greenhouse cult. *see* PALM.)

andicola. Wax palm. Nearly 200 ft. high in the wild, far less in cult., the trunk slightly swollen about the middle, covered (at home) with a whitish, commercially important wax. Leaves 15–25 ft. long, the under side of the leaflets white-scurfy. Fruit purple-red, just less than an inch in diameter. Andes of Colombia and Ecuador.

Cerris (ser'ris). A specific name of uncertain application to the turkey oak; perhaps from the Latin for fringe. (*See* OAK.)

CESPITOSE. *See* CAESPITOSA.

CESTRUM (ses'trum). A fragrant group of shrubs (some vine-like) or low trees, comprising over 200 species of the potato family, all tropical American and a few widely grown for their beautiful bloom. Leaves alternate,* without marginal teeth. Flowers numerous, in clusters at the ends, or the clusters in the leaf axils.* Corolla tubular, the expanded part salver-shaped, the tube sometimes enlarged or contracted near the top. Fruit small, berry-like. (*Cestrum* is from an old Greek name for some plant, of uncertain application here.)

These are handsome greenhouse plants, but also popular outdoors in zones* 8 and 9. They need a cool greenhouse and potting mixture* 4. Some are night-blooming and exceptionally fragrant, and a few are vine-like, especially C. *purpureum.*

aurantiacum. More or less sprawling or half-climbing. Leaves ovalish, 2½ in. long. Flower clusters terminal, the flowers orange-yellow, about 1 in. long, the tips recurved. Guatemala.

diurnum. Day jasmine. A shrub 8–12 ft. high. Leaves oblongish or oval, 2–3½ in. long. Flower clusters on long stems from the axils,* the flowers white, about ½ in. long, very fragrant by day. W.I. Commonly planted in Fla.

elegans = *Cestrum purpureum.*

---

* Special articles on the subjects indicated by an asterisk (*) will be found at the words so marked.

nocturnum. Night jasmine. Queen-of-the-night. A shrub 6–9 ft. high. Leaves oblongish or oval, 6–9 in. long. Flower clusters in the axils,* the flowers about ¾ in. long, greenish-white to cream-colored, very fragrant by night. W.I.

parqui. Willow-leaved jasmine. A shrub 3–6 ft. high, the leaves willow-like, 4–6 in. long. Flower clusters terminal and in the axils,* the flowers whitish or yellowish, about 1 in. long, very fragrant at night. Chile.

purpureum. Coral jasmine; also called purple cestrum. A shrub up to 10 ft. high, often vine-like, its branches softly hairy. Leaves 2–4 in. long, about 1½ in. wide. Flowers in terminal, nodding clusters, the corolla about ¾ in. long, red-purple, and constricted at the throat. Fruit red. Mex. The most popular of the cult. species, with forms also offered with rose-colored flowers and variegated leaves.

CEYLON GOOSEBERRY = *Dovyalis hebecarpa.*

CEYLON MORNING-GLORY = *Ipomoea tuberosa.*

CHAENOMELES (kee-nom'e-lees). All the known species of the flowering quince, which belong to the rose family and come from eastern Asia, are popular garden shrubs, among the earliest to bloom. While closely related to the quince (*see* CYDONIA), it bears many-seeded, aromatic, quince-like fruits used for preserves. Leaves alternate.* Flowers solitary or in small, close clusters, blooming before or with the unfolding of the leaves. Petals 5, showy. Stamens* many. Fruit a pome,* with brown seeds. (*Chaenomeles* is from the Greek meaning to split and apple, applied to these plants under the erroneous notion that they have splitting fruits.)

The flowering quinces are popular as specimen plants and they also are widely used for hedges. While they will not stand so much clipping as privet, their beautiful spring bloom offsets their usual lack of architectural symmetry. They are not particular as to soil and may be propagated by cuttings, layers, or by root cuttings.

japonica. Dwarf Japanese quince. Scarcely more than 3 ft. high, the branches often spiny. Leaves broadly oval, 1½–2 in. long, coarsely toothed. Flowers brick-red, about 1 in. wide. Fruit yellow, about 1½ in. long. Mar.–Apr. Hardy from zone* 3 southward. Often sold as *Cydonia japonica*, and sometimes called merely japonica. It stands smoke.*

lagenaria. Japanese quince, or Japanese flowering quince. A shrub 4–6 ft. high, the branches somewhat spiny. Leaves oval-oblong, 2–3 in. long, finely toothed. Flowers scarlet-red (in the typical form), 1–1¾ in. wide. Fruit yellowish-green, nearly 2 in. long. China. Mar.–Apr. Hardy from zone* 3 southward. There are varieties with pink or white flowers. The best of the flowering quinces for hedges.

sinensis. Chinese quince. A large shrub or small tree 8–20 ft. high and without spines. Leaves elliptic-oval, 2–3 in. long, sharply but finely toothed. Flowers light pink, usually solitary, about 1 in. wide. May. China. Hardy from zone* 4 southward.

CHAEROPHYLLUM (kee-ro-fil'lum). Of 30 or more species of this genus (family Umbelliferae), only the turnip-rooted chervil, or,

as some call it, the bulbous chervil, is of any garden interest. Known as **C. bulbosum**, it is a European biennial which is somewhat cult. for its fleshy, edible root. Leaves compound,* the leaflets arranged feather-fashion. Flowers small, white, in a compound umbel.* The edible, spindle-shaped, tuberous root is blackish, but the flesh is yellowish. It is little grown here. (*Chaerophyllum* is from the Greek for scented foliage.)

CHAETOCHLOA = SETARIA.

CHAFEWEED = *Gnaphalium sylvaticum.*

CHAFF, CHAFFY. The bracts* of many flowers, or sometimes the flower parts themselves, are chaffy or made up of chaff. This is thin, membranous, usually dry, and often brittle. Typical examples are found in the flowers of everlastings and in many grasses. Sometimes it is colored, as in the cockscomb.

CHAIN FERN. *See* WOODWARDIA.

CHALCAS = *Murraya.*

chalcedonica, -us, -um (chal-see-don'i-ka). From Chalcedon (now Kaidikoi), near Istanbul.

CHALICE VINE = *Solandra guttata.*

CHALK. A poor substitute for lime in soil treatment, but common in the literature of gardening that originates in England, where chalk is also common. It has perhaps twice the bulk and half the value of lime (which see).

Chamaebuxus (kam-ee-bux'us). Literally a dwarf box; as used at *Polygala,* meaning like a dwarf box.

CHAMAECEREUS (kam-ee-seer'e-us). A genus of low, small cacti from between Tucuman and Salta, Argentina, containing only **C. silvestri** and resembling a low *Echinocereus.* It is not over 2–3 in. high and consists of small joints with 6–9 ribs and soft, not very prickly, white spines. Flowers funnel-shaped, covered with fine wool. The joints are fragile, easily detached and grow mostly in clumps. For cult. *see* CACTI. (*Chamaecereus* is from the Greek for ground, and *Cereus,* in allusion to their ground-hugging method of growth.)

CHAMAECYPARIS (kam-ee-sip'ar-is). Very valuable timber trees and equally valuable as ornamental evergreen shrubs or trees of the pine family. In their young or juvenile (often permanent) form they are widely planted as retinispora (or retinospora) — perhaps the commonest evergreens in cult., and coming in many named forms. Leaves in mature plants scale-like, minute, closely pressed against the flattened, often fan-like branchlets. In the juvenile (often permanent) state the leaves are needle-like, but softish and stand out from the twigs. In some cult. specimens both sorts of leaves will be found, but in most retinisporas the needle-like leaves predominate. Flowers minute and of no hort. value. Fruit round, maturing the first season, the scales of the small cone pointed or keeled in the middle, the cones not showy as in pines or firs. (*Chamaecyparis* is from the Greek for ground cypress.)

---

* Special articles on the subjects indicated by an asterisk (*) will be found at the words so marked.

These extremely popular evergreens, often called false cypress, are grown throughout the U.S. except in the dry, hot plains and deserts. They do best in regions reasonably near the sea, and better in acid soils than in neutral or alkaline ones. (See ACID AND ALKALI SOILS.) Where used in group plantings it is better to mulch the ground between them with straw or leaves, as the roots of some of the cult. forms are shallow.

For mass evergreen plantings, these and the arborvitaes and cedars are perhaps the finest of our conifers. Because many garden retinisporas die every year is no reason to stop planting them. But we must remember that they need moisture, do not like hot, dry winds, and, in some sections, should be protected during the winter (see PROTECTING PLANTS). Otherwise their culture is no more difficult than any other evergreen, but they repay for feeding, and some of them must be pruned to keep them shapely. See EVERGREENS.

lawsoniana. Port Orford cedar, also called (in the West) Oregon or white cedar. In the forest a timber tree often 150 ft.; in cult. much less and forming a pyramidal tree with branches down to the ground, the bark reddish-brown. Foliage green or bluish-green, the leaves all scale-like, each often minutely white-streaked. Cones about ⅔ in. thick, reddish-brown, often with a bloom. Ore. to northern Calif. Hardy from zone* 4 southward if the rainfall is 30 in. per year or more. Will not stand long summer heat or drought. A magnificent evergreen known, especially in Eu., in over 80 garden forms. Three of the best are *var.* **glauca,** with steel-blue foliage; *var.* **argentea,** with foliage silvery; and *var.* **lutea,** where the young growth is yellow.

nootkatensis. Alaska cedar; also called Nootka, Sitka, or yellow cypress. In the forest taller than the last, but much less in cult., where it is uncommon, and the branches usually droop at the tip. Branchlets or twigs in fan-like growths, particularly toward the upper part of the tree. Leaves flat and scale-like, green both sides, rarely needle-like. Cones about ½ in. thick or less. Alaska to Ore. Hardy from zone* 4 southward, if the summers are reasonably moist. It will not stand high winds and dryness, especially in Feb. and March.

obtusa. Hinoki cypress. This and the next comprise most of the plants offered by nurserymen as retinisporas. It is a tree up to 120 ft. in Japan, much less in cult., where it has a multitude of forms. Leaves scale-like, pressed flat against the twigs in mature specimens, needle-like in the ordinary juvenile cult. forms, green above, faintly white-streaked beneath. Cones about ¾ in. thick, orange-brown, the scales with a sharp, but not prickly, tip. Hardy from zone* 3 southward, but it will not stand drought or hot drying winds.

Of its many hort. forms the following are most worth attention:

Color forms: *var.* **albo-spicata,** young foliage white-tipped
　var. **aurea,** foliage golden-yellow
Habit forms: *var.* **erecta,** columnar form
　var. **gracilis,** compact and pyramidal
　var. **compacta,** a low, broadly conical form and one of the most widely grown
　var. **pygmaea,** a very dwarf form with almost creeping branchlets
pisifera. Sawara cypress. A Japanese tree

up to 150 ft., much lower in cult., where it makes a pyramidal tree of rather loose habit. The branchlets are flattened and fan-like, the closely appressed, scale-like leaves green above, white-streaked beneath. Cones about ½ in. in diameter, dark brown. Hardy from zone* 3 southward, but only in moist regions free from great summer heat and drying winds. It has many color forms, as those with silvery, golden, or variegated foliage. Habit varieties include *var.* **plumosa,** having dense, conical habit, and frond-like, feathery foliage; *var.* **filifera,** a pyramidal form with slender, drooping branches; and *var.* **squarrosa,** a dense bush or small tree, feathery, but the branchlets not flattened or frond-like.

thyoides. White cedar, also called southern white cedar. A bog or swamp tree usually not over 75 ft. high, mostly less, its bark reddish-brown. Foliage dark green, the leaves scale-like, keeled on the back and glandular.* Cones bluish-purple, about ½ in. in diameter. Me. to Fla. and Miss., especially common southward. Not much grown, but the hardiest of all the cult. species; far less attractive than the Asiatic species. Use soil of pH 4–5.

Chamaecyparissus (kam-ee-sip-a-ris′sus). Greek for a dwarf cypress.

CHAMAEDAPHNE (kam-ee-daf′ne). A single, evergreen bog shrub of the heath family, suitable to the bog garden but of little hort. value otherwise. The only species, **C. calyculata,** the leatherleaf, is found throughout the north temperate zone. It has alternate,* leathery, scurfy leaves 1½–2 in. long, and small, white, nearly bell-shaped flowers in a terminal, leafy cluster (raceme*). Stamens 10. Fruit a small, dry pod. (*Chamaedaphne* is from Greek for ground laurel.) The plant was once called *Andromeda calyculata.*

CHAMAEDOREA (kam-ee-dor′ree-a). A large genus of tropical American feather palms, of which many are cult. in Mexico, but only the following much known in greenhouse collections, although it is planted outdoors in southern Calif. and Fla. **Chamaedorea elegans** has a green, reed-like, ringed, spineless stem, usually several in a cluster, and not over 6–8 ft. high. Leaves having several narrow, long-pointed leaflets that are green both sides, not stiff or ridged. Male and female flowers on different plants, often not produced in cult. specimens. The plant is much used as a tubbed specimen for outdoor use, particularly in Fla. and Calif. patios. Also known, and perhaps more correctly, as *Collinia elegans* and, less certainly, as *Neanthe bella.* (*Chamaedorea* is from the Greek for a dwarf gift.) For cult. see PALM.

Chamaedrys (kam-ee′dris). Pre-Linnaean* name for some germander. See TEUCRIUM and VERONICA.

Chamaeiris (kam-ee-eye′ris). A specific name meaning low iris. See IRIS CHAMAEIRIS.

CHAMAELIRIUM (kam-ee-leer′i-um). A single, white-flowered herb of the lily family, found in eastern N.A. and sometimes cult. in the wild garden. The only species is **C.**

---

* Special articles on the subjects indicated by an asterisk (*) will be found at the words so marked.

luteum, the devil's-bit (also called blazing star and fairy wand), a perennial with a bitter rootstock, mostly basal leaves that are broadest above the middle and 2–8 in. long. Male and female flowers on different plants, the spikes borne at the end of a wand-like stalk that reaches up 2–3½ ft. Stamens* (in the male flower) 6. Fruit a 3-lobed and 3-valved pod. (*Chamaelirium* is from the Greek for low lily.) Not much cult., but its tall male spike is showy. It needs a moist, partly shady place, and flowers in June.

CHAMAEROPS (kam'ee-rops). A genus of only two, low, fan palms of the Mediterranean region, one of them widely cult. for ornament and perhaps the hardiest of all known palms. They commonly have several trunks or stems, not over 3 ft. high in cult., higher in the wild. Leaves fan-like, but deeply cut into many segments, the leafstalk slender and usually spiny. Male and female flowers on different plants or sometimes merely unisexual* on the same plant, borne in short, dense clusters among the leaves. Stamens 6–9. Fruit yellowish or reddish, small. (*Chamaerops* is from the Greek for low or dwarf bush.)

The species below is commonly planted outdoors throughout the warm parts of the U.S. almost up to the area of fairly severe frosts. It is also widely cult. in the cool greenhouse, where it is a very serviceable, bushy, foliage plant, well suited for decoration. Also useful for porches or for summer bedding, where it should be plunged. In Eu. and northern Africa it is grown as the source of African hair, a fiber extracted from the leaves.

humilis. Dwarf fan palm; also called European fan palm. As cult. mostly with several or many stems. Leaves bluish-green, the segments stiff, not drooping at the ends which are often deeply cleft. An easy palm to grow. For plants sometimes called *C. excelsa* and *C. fortunei*, see TRACHYCARPUS.

CHAMISE LILY = *Erythronium grandiflorum.*

CHAMISO = *Adenostoma fasciculatum.*

CHAMOMILE = Camomile.

Chamomilla (kam-o-mill'ya). An old name for the wild camomile.

CHAMPNEY ROSE = *Rosa noisettiana.*

CHAPARRAL. The dense, twiggy growth of shrubs and small trees, mostly species of *Arctostaphylos*, especially those known as manzanita in southern Calif. and Mex. See ARCTOSTAPHYLOS.

CHAPARRAL BROOM = *Baccharis pilularis.*

CHAPARRAL LILY = *Lilium rubescens.*

CHAPARRAL SNAPDRAGON = *Antirrhinum coulterianum.* See SNAPDRAGON.

CHARACTER. In ordinary hort. and botanical usage a character is any distinctive characteristic of a plant or its organs, common examples being height, color, texture, and many other *characters*. As a term in genetics character is used as an expression of a gene* or genes in a given environment and is used to designate any form, function, color, or other feature of an organism.

Charantia (ka-ran'shee-a). Pre-Linnaean* name for the plant *Momordica Charantia.*

CHARCOAL. This common form of carbonized wood has some garden uses, especially in sweetening soil mixtures for succulents, sometimes in the cutting bench, and in the rooting of plants like begonia. Ordinary fuel charcoal broken up in small pieces or powdered is all that is necessary. In the soil of the cutting bench it is of use to prevent or check damping-off.*

CHARD. The Swiss chard; for culture *see* BEET.

CHARIEIS (kar-ree'is). A single South African herb of the family Compositae, sometimes grown as a hardy annual in the flower garden. It is of the easiest culture, seeds being sown where wanted. Lower leaves opposite,* without marginal teeth, the upper alternate.* Flower heads solitary, on long stalks, the disk* flowers yellow, the rays usually blue. (*Charieis* is from the Greek for elegant.)

heterophylla. An annual, more or less sprawling herb 6–12 in. high. Leaves oblongish, 1–2½ in. long. Flower heads about ¾ in. wide, the rays blue (occasionally violet or reddish-violet in varieties). Summer. S.Af.

CHARITY = *Polemonium caeruleum.*

CHARLOCK = *Brassica arvensis.*

CHASMANTHE. See ANTHOLYZA AETHIOPICA.

CHASTE TREE = *Vitex Agnus-castus.*

CHAUTE = *Ariocarpus retusus.*

CHAYOTE = *Sechium edule.*

CHECKERBERRY = *Gaultheria procumbens.*

CHECKERBLOOM = *Sidalcea malvaeflora.*

CHECKERED LILY = *Fritillaria Meleagris;* and, in Calif., *F. lanceolata.*

CHEDDAR PINK = *Dianthus gratianopolitanus.*

CHEESES = *Malva rotundifolia.* See Mallow in the list at WEEDS.

CHEESEWOOD = *Pittosporum undulatum.*

cheilantha, -us, -um (ky-lan'tha). Having a lip, or lip-like.

CHEILANTHES (ky-lan'theez). A large genus of mostly rock-loving ferns of the family Polypodiaceae, a few grown in the greenhouse or in the outdoor fern garden. They are widely distributed both in the tropics and in temperate regions. They have no obvious stem, the fronds all arising from the rootstock. Fronds twice- or thrice-compound,* the ultimate segments arranged feather-fashion, often hairy or scaly. The spore* cases are terminal on the veins. (*Cheilanthes* is from the Greek for lip and flower.) Most of them are called lip-ferns.

---

* Special articles on the subjects indicated by an asterisk (*) will be found at the words so marked.

If grown in the greenhouse, care should be used to keep the house cool and well ventilated, and do not let the foliage stay wet. *See* FERNS AND FERN GARDENING.

densa. A tough, stout fern, the fronds not over 13 in. long (including the stalk) and thrice-compound,* the ultimate segments with a rolled margin. Western N.A. Sometimes called *Pellaea densa.*

gracillima. Lace-fern. A tufted, small fern with fronds scarcely more than 4 in. long, the stalk dark brown. Fronds twice-compound,* the ultimate divisions or segments about 9 to each primary division. Western U.S.

lanosa. Fronds 4–9 in. long, the stalk wiry and chestnut-brown, and covered with rusty hairs. The ultimate segments of the frond are more or less triangular or ovalish, regularly toothed, hairy. Conn. to Ga. and westward.

tomentosa. Fronds 4–8 in. long, the stalks densely covered with brown hairs. The ultimate segments of the frond very small, rather distant, the frond thus more open than in the other cult. species. Va. to Ga., Tex., and Mex.

cheilanthifolia, -us, -um (ky-lan-thi-fō′li-a). Having leaves like a lip-fern (*Cheilanthes*).

CHEIRANTHUS (ky-ran′thus). Perhaps a dozen perennial herbs of the mustard family, scattered from Madeira to the Himalayas, one the widely cult. wallflower, **C. Cheiri.** It is a hardy plant 12–13 in. high, covered with minute, forked hairs. Leaves narrow, with few or no marginal teeth, 1–3 in. long and often clustered beneath the flowers, which are in terminal clusters (spikes* or racemes*). Flowers with 4 clawed* petals, yellow or orange-brown, fragrant. Fruit a pod 2–2½ in. long, thickish, angled and with a short, protruding tip. (Origin of the name obscure.)

The wallflower has been a garden favorite from remote antiquity. Originally a native of southern Eu., it has been much improved, so that it now comes also in reddish or reddish-black shades and some forms have double flowers. Some of the special color varieties do not come true from seed and should be increased by division or even by cuttings. The plant does not like wet or slushy winters and in such places is better wintered in the cold frame. The wallflower blooms early in the spring, and, as its name implies, it is useful in the rock wall. But it is also much grown for the border and a bedding plant. In the latter case, seeds sown the previous August are potted up and carried over the winter in the cold frame. For the plant sometimes called *Cheiranthus allioni see* ERYSIMUM ASPERUM; for *C. linifolius see* ERYSIMUM LINIFOLIUM.

Cheiri (ky′ree). An Arabic name for some plant, but of uncertain application to the wallflower. *See* CHEIRANTHUS.

CHELIDONIUM (kelly-dō′ni-um). A single, perennial, somewhat weedy, Eurasian herb of the poppy family, commonly called celandine, killwort, or sightwort. This plant, **C. majus,** is of secondary hort. importance, but frequently escapes* from old gardens. It is 12–30 in. high, and has deeply divided or cleft leaves, distinctly pale bluish-green

beneath. Flowers yellow, in small, stalked clusters (umbels*). Sepals 2. Petals 4, the flower not over ⅔ in. long. Fruit a slender pod, splitting from the base upward. (*Chelidonium* is from the Greek for swallow in allusion to the plant blooming when swallows arrive.) There is also a *var.* **laciniatum** with more finely divided leaves.

CHELONE (kel-lō′nee). A small group of North American perennial herbs of the family Scrophulariaceae, two of which are garden subjects and one, the red turtlehead, a showy plant. Leaves opposite,* toothed. Flowers irregular* and 2-lipped, the upper lip arching and notched. The flowers are stalkless in a compact, terminal spike, only one or two flowering at a time. Stamens 5, one sterile and shorter than the other 4. Fruit a capsule.* (*Chelone* is from the Greek for turtle's head.)

The plants need partial shade and a reasonably moist site, especially the first species, which inhabits swampy woods or moist thickets. They are easily propagated by division.

barbata = *Pentstemon barbatus.*

glabra. Turtlehead; called also snake-head and shell-flower. Not usually over 24 in. high, often half that. Leaves oblong-lance-shaped, 3–6 in. long, short-stalked. Flowers white (rarely pinkish), about 1 in. long. Newfoundland to Ga. and westward. Summer.

lyoni. Red turtlehead. The most desirable for the garden. Leaves ovalish, 4–7 in. long and longer-stalked. Flowers rose-purple, about 1 in. long. Mountains of the Carolinas and Tenn., but hardy much farther north. Summer.

CHEMICAL GARDENING. The feeding of plants with chemicals put directly into irrigation water is long past the experimental stage. It is a highly organized technique suitable only to professionals on a large enough scale to warrant the effort. For the only example of so-called chemical gardening suited to small-scale operations *see* SOILLESS GARDENING.

CHENOPODIACEAE (ken-o-pō-di-a′see-ee). The goosefoot family, often called the beet or spinach family, is of the greatest interest to gardeners because it contains among its 100 genera and perhaps 1000 widely distributed species not only the beet and spinach (which see), but a few garden ornamentals of wide cultivation, as well as many pernicious weeds (the goosefoots). The family contains mostly annual or perennial herbs, and a few shrubby plants, most of them with scurfy foliage and alternate* leaves. Flowers always inconspicuous, prevailingly greenish or whitish, without petals, often unisexual,* and sometimes with male and female flowers on different plants. Fruit dry (an achene* or a utricle*) or berry-like in the strawberry-blite.

Besides the spinach and beet (which includes chard), the garden genera are *Atriplex* (the orach), *Chenopodium* (mostly weedy, but including Good-King-Henry); and *Kochia* (summer cypress). *Salsola* is a salt-tolerant

---

* Special articles on the subjects indicated by an asterisk (*) will be found at the words so marked.

plant of little garden interest, but sometimes planted in saline situations.

Technical flower characters: Plants monoecious* or dioecious,* or at least unisexual.* Calyx 2–5-parted, or merely of 1 sepal, or none. Petals none. Ovary superior,* 1-celled, 1-ovuled, its styles 1–3.

CHENOPODIUM (ken-o-pō'di-um). The goosefoots or pigweeds comprise a genus of 60 species of herbs of the family Chenopodiaceae, many of them pernicious weeds. The two below are of moderate hort. interest. Leaves alternate,* often angled and toothed, usually mealy. Flowers small and inconspicuous. (For details *see* CHENOPODIACEAE.) Fruit small, dry, often enclosed by the persistent calyx. (*Chenopodium* is Greek for goosefoot, in allusion to the shape of the leaves of some species.)

The ones below are of very easy culture and any of them may soon become weedy if not kept under control.

album. *See* Pigweed in the list at WEEDS.

ambrosioides. *See* Mexican Tea in the list at WEEDS.

Bonus-henricus. Good-King-Henry; also called mercury. A rank perennial with a deep rootstock from which arise several stems 12–30 in. high. Leaves spinach-like and sometimes grown for greens, more or less triangular, the margins slightly wavy. Eu.

Botrys. Feather geranium or Jerusalem oak. A rank-smelling annual, much-branched and 12–24 in. high. Leaves more or less wavy-margined or somewhat toothed or cut. Flower clusters profuse, not showy, but much aggregated into sprays or collections of small, head-like clusters. Eurasia and Af., also widely naturalized in N.A.

capitatum. *See* Strawberry Blite in the list at WEEDS. This is also called *Blitum capitatum.*

Cherimola. An adaptation of the vernacular *cherimoya.*

CHERIMOYA = *Annona Cherimola.*

CHEROKEE ROSE = *Rosa laevigata.*

CHERRY. For the home grower, cherries are in much the same category as the plums — they will not thrive in all parts of the country. To save needless repetition look over the climatic preferences outlined for PLUM, as they also apply very generally to cherries.

There are three main groups: sweet cherries that are fine for eating raw; sour cherries that are good only in pies and preserves, and the Dukes, which are hybrids between the sweet and sour groups and combine some of the characteristics of both.

All sour cherries are self-fertile,* but some of the Dukes are self-sterile* and must be interplanted with other Dukes or with sour or sweet cherries which will ensure cross-fertilization. All sweet cherries are self-sterile and must be interplanted only with other sweet cherry varieties. For the significance of self-sterility and self-fertility, *see* the section on this at FRUIT CULTURE.

Cherries, more than most tree fruits, are particular about their soil preferences. Sweet cherries demand a friable, warm soil, do well in a sandy loam, but not so well on gravelly

soil. The sour cherries should have heavier soils, even with an admixture of clay, and the moisture-holding capacity of the soils should be higher than in those chosen for the sweet varieties. The Dukes fall between, and most garden soils will be suitable for them. None of the three groups will tolerate standing water on the surface, nor at their roots; in other words, they must not be grown where the underground water table is too near the surface.

Take special care in planting cherries, because they need it. See that all broken roots are pruned off, that the hole is big enough for the roots, and that the best soil (no subsoil) is used to fill the hole. Sweet cherries and the Dukes should be 25–30 feet apart each way, while the sour varieties will need about 20 feet. At planting time, which should be in spring, the young trees need almost no pruning or heading back, as in nearly all other fruit trees. For later pruning *see* PRUNING.

VARIETIES

SWEET CHERRIES. All varieties are self-sterile* so that two or more other sweet cherry varieties must be planted to ensure cross-fertilization. There are scores of varieties of sweet cherries of which the following six many be chosen, depending on your locality. The trees are larger than in any other group, but most of them are available as dwarfs. See DWARF FRUIT TREES.

BING. Zones* 2, 3, and 4. Fruit dark red or nearly black, late, juicy and sweet, but apt to crack if ripening coincides with heavy rains.

BLACK TARTARIAN. Zones* 2, 3, 4, and 5. Fruit purplish-black, early or midseason, of fine quality. Tree vigorous and productive.

SCHMIDT. Zones* 2, 3, and 4. Fruit black, midseason, rather firm and hence keeps well after picking when ripe; does not crack in rainy spells.

WINDSOR. Zones* 2, 3, and 4. Fruit purplish-red, crisp, sweet and keeps well; the latest and hardiest of all sweet cherries. It is also a commercial variety but excellent for the house if allowed to ripen.

WOOD. Zones* 2, 3, and 4. Also called Governor Wood. Fruit yellow, early, not large but very sweet. A fine home variety, but not always productive.

YELLOW SPANISH. Zones* 2, 3, and 4. Fruit yellow with a red cheek, large, the tree hardy and vigorous.

SOUR CHERRIES. There are only two suited to the home garden, both self-fertile. The fruits are too tart for eating raw, but delicious in pies and preserves. Both are available as dwarf trees.

EARLY RICHMOND. Zones* 2 and 3. Fruit rather small, early, profuse, and light red.

MONTMORENCY. Zones* 2, 3, and 4. Fruit large, bright red, midseason. The standard commercial sour cherry, but often picked too early for its best flavor.

DUKE CHERRIES. Intermediate between the sour and sweet cherries, but generally the fruit tends to tartness. Especially good for the home garden, the juicy fruit being too soft for shipping. Both the varieties are self-

---

* Special articles on the subjects indicated by an asterisk (*) will be found at the words so marked.

sterile, but are fertile to each other, and with any sweet or sour variety.

REINE HORTENSE. Zones* 2, 3, 4, and 5. Fruit early, large, red, delicious and borne on a hardy, vigorous but sometimes unproductive tree.

ROYAL DUKE. Zones* 2, 3, and 4. Fruit later, large, dark red, borne on a very productive tree, which is not quite so hardy as Reine Hortense.

Three things should be remembered by all home growers of cherries. Birds may and often do ravage the fruit crop, the only remedy for which is to pick earlier than complete ripeness, or to plant enough for you and the birds. The second hazard is the tendency of some cherry fruits to crack or split when heavy rains coincide with ripening. There is, of course, no control for this except picking before the fruit is really ripe, which no home grower wants to do.

The third factor may be within your control. All cherry trees are grown upon stock of two wild varieties, upon which the varieties above have been budded by the nurseryman. One of these stocks is known as *Mahaleb*. It is cheap and easy to handle and many nurserymen are hence tempted to use it. The other, and much superior stock is the *Mazzard*. Try to insist that your trees are on the latter stock, and if the nurseryman tries to make you accept the inferior stock, change nurserymen. No experienced expert will tolerate anything but Mazzard understock.

You may find, in some old books and in a few catalogues, certain terms that are confusing and have been omitted from the lists above. "Heart" cherries are simply softfleshed varieties of sweet cherries, which are also sometimes known as "Geans." "Bigarreau" cherries are merely sweet cherries with a somewhat firmer flesh. Among the sour cherries some are called "amarelles" because the fruit is pale red (Early Richmond), others "morellos" because the fruit is darker red (Montmorency). Such terms are unnecessary here.

WESTERN CHERRY-GROWING

Cherry-growing in the Far West is confined mainly to Calif., Ore., Wash., Idaho, and Utah. About 90% of all the sweet cherries produced in the U.S. are grown in these states, and 10% or less of the sour cherries, none of which are produced commercially in Calif. The average annual production of about 80,000 tons of sweet cherries in the West is distributed as follows: Calif. 37%, Wash. 30%, Ore. 26%, Utah 4%, Idaho 3%.

VARIETIES. While a great number of varieties are grown, the important ones are: Bing, Napoleon (Royal Ann), Black Tartarian, Lambert, and Republican. The Chapman and Burbank are grown in the early districts of Calif.

The sweet cherry is subject to many virus diseases. In planting new trees make sure that both the root and top have been propagated from virus-free stock.

The sweet cherry presents a serious pollination problem in that all varieties are self-sterile,* and three important varieties — Napoleon, Lambert, and Bing — are intersterile. Black Tartarian and Republican are quite satisfactory pollinizers for Napoleon and Bing, but most years the Lambert blossoms too late to be pollinized by them. Several other varieties are also used as pollinizers, *e.g.*, the new variety Van.

CULTURE. Most growers practice clean culture during the summer. They may plant cover crops in the fall, or depend upon weed growth which is turned under in the spring. Quite frequent summer cultivations are given, which in many cases may prove to be excessive. Where irrigation water is plentiful, many growers use a permanent cover crop — generally alfalfa. The alfalfa may be cut and removed, left in the orchard to rot, or allowed to grow undisturbed. There seems to be some evidence to indicate that permanent cover-cropping is a desirable practice where it can be followed.

Sweet cherries in general respond to an application of nitrogen; the usual amount used is one pound of actual nitrogen per tree (*e.g.*, 5 lbs. of ammonium sulphate, or 3 lbs. of ammonium nitrate). In a few isolated cases there may be a response to potassium, none to phosphorus.

The sweet cherry crop of the West is either sold fresh as dessert fruit or processed (canned, or brined for Maraschino cherries). Napoleon, a white variety, is the only one used extensively for canning. All the other important varieties grown are black sorts and are disposed of fresh or brined. Black Tartarian is too soft for brining.

The disposition of the crop determines the care in harvesting. Fruit for the fresh market must have the stems attached. Cherries for eastern shipment are picked and handled with the utmost care. Fruit is sometimes taken to the packing house in the picking receptables, but generally in various types of field boxes. All fruit for the fresh market is packed in boxes. Many sizes and styles of packages are used. — W. P. T.

INSECT PESTS. Plum curculio and cherry curculio are bad pests. Control with methoxyclor or pesticide #1 (*see* SPRAYS AND DUSTS) during period following bloom. At least two applications are needed. Scales should be controlled by dormant oil sprays as at APPLE. Peach tree borers should be controlled as at PEACH. Slugs damage leaves by skeletonizing in spring and late summer. Control by pesticide #1 or #21. Maggots which attack fruit should be easily controlled by killing flies which lay eggs. Pesticide #21 or #19 spray at time shucks* reveal young cherries and 10 days later will control maggots and curculio. Pesticide #19-treated cherries should be washed off before eating.

DISEASES. For the description of brown rot of blossoms and fruit, and for the bacterial leafspot or shot hole, *see* PEACH. Black-knot* is more grotesque than it is serious on cherry. A serious fungus disease of both sweet and sour cherry is leafspot* or yellow leaf. Leaves

---

* Special articles on the subjects indicated by an asterisk (*) will be found at the words so marked.

become spotted with the fungus, turn bright yellow, and fall early in the season. Successive seasons of defoliation may kill the trees. Good control will result with presticide #2 (see SPRAYS AND DUSTS) applied just before flowers open, at petal fall, twice more at 10- to 14-day intervals, and again right after harvest.

A number of virus diseases are found on cherry. Symptoms range from a slight yellow mottle of leaves to complete death of the tree. Virus diseases are so severe in some local sections of the country that cherry is no longer planted. When trees are suspected of having a virus disease, they should be removed to prevent insects from transmitting the disease to other cherry trees, peach and plum trees.

CHERRY BIRCH = *Betula lenta.* See BIRCH.

CHERRY FAMILY. See ROSACEAE.

CHERRY LAUREL. See LAUROCERASUS.

CHERRY ORANGE. The African cherry-orange (*Citropsis schweinfurthi,* which see).

CHERRY PEPPER = *Capsicum frutescens cerasiforme.*

CHERRY PIE = *Valeriana officinalis* and *Heliotropium arborescens.*

CHERRY PLUM = *Prunus cerasifera.*

CHERRY TOMATO = *Lycopersicum esculentum cerasiforme.* See TOMATO.

CHERVIL. For the salad chervil *see* ANTHRISCUS CEREFOLIUM. For the bulbous or turnip-rooted chervil *see* CHAEROPHYLLUM BULBOSUM. Both are often called merely chervil.

CHESTNUT. A small group of important nut and timber trees constituting the genus **Castanea** (kas-tay'nee-a) which belongs to the family Fagaceae. They are mostly tall trees with furrowed bark and alternate, toothed leaves that have several parallel veins arising at the midrib. Male flowers in small, erect catkins,* its calyx 6-parted; petals none. The female flower on the lower part of the male catkin. Fruit the familiar chestnut, usually 3 in a prickly bur. Of the eight known species four are in cult. and one or two of them are important. (*Castanea* is the classical Latin name for the chestnut.) In Eu. chestnut usually refers to the horse-chestnut (which see).

For culture *see* below.

C. crenata. Japanese chestnut. Usually not over 30 ft., often considerably less, and shrub-like. Leaves oblong or elliptic, 4–7 in. long, with rounded, not sharp, teeth. Bur about 2 in. in diameter, the nuts 2 or 3. Japan. Hardy from zone* 4 southward. More useful for breeding possibly blight-free hybrids than for its own fruit. Often sold as *Castanea japonica.*

C. dentata. American chestnut. A tree up to nearly 100 ft. high, now nearly exterminated in the northeastern U.S., but freely suckering from the bottom. Leaves oblongish, 5–9 in. long, coarsely toothed. Bur 2–3½ in. in diameter, the nuts usually 3. Ont. to Mich. and Miss. Hardy from zone* 3 southward, but not now planted within the area of the blight (see below).

C. japonica = *Castanea crenata.*

C. mollissima. Chinese chestnut. A tree up to 50 ft. or sometimes shrubby, the twigs hairy, at least when young. Leaves elliptic or oblong, 4–7 in. long, coarsely toothed and white-hairy beneath, at least on the veins. Nuts nearly 1 in. wide, ovoid and pointed. China and Korea. Hardy from zone* 4 southward. It is one of the species used in hybridizing for production of blight-free varieties with acceptable fruit.

C. pumila. Chinquapin. A shrubby, American tree usually not over 20 ft. Leaves oblong-ish, 3–7 in. long, coarsely toothed or the teeth merely bristles, white and felty beneath. Bur about 1½ in. in diameter, the nut mostly solitary. N.J. to Fla. and Tex. Hardy from zone* 4 southward.

C. sativa. Spanish chestnut. A tree up to 90 ft., usually round-headed in age. Leaves oblongish, 7–12 in. long, coarsely toothed, hairy or even felty beneath. Bur 2–4 in. in diameter, the nuts 1–3, nearly twice the size of the native American chestnut. Mediterranean region. Hardy from zone* 5, or in protected places in zone* 4, southward. The finest of all the chestnuts for size of the nut and productiveness. There are several hort. varieties. See below.

CHESTNUT CULTURE

Growing chestnut trees for their fruit is dependent upon freedom from the blight which has destroyed nearly all the native American chestnut trees from central Maine, N.H. and Vt. to most of Mich., and south-westward to include the Alleghenies. In other words, any attempt to grow chestnuts is extremely dangerous or impossible in the following states: Me., N.H., Vt., Mass., R.I., Conn., N.Y., Pa., N.J., Del., Md., Va., West Va., Ohio, Southern Mich., Ind., and in some of the mountainous parts of Ky., Tenn., S. Car., N. Car., Ga., and Ala.

And the blight is constantly spreading so that only last-minute information on your area would be of any value, and should be secured from your local experiment station before attempting a plantation.

In blight-free areas, preferably many miles from the nearest infestation, good crops of the native American species and of the much larger-fruited Spanish chestnut can be raised. The trees are not particular as to soil, except that low wet sites are to be avoided. Rocky, well-drained hillsides are ideal, and they thrive in sandy loams.

Occasional trees of both the European and American chestnuts appear to be immune to blight. These have been worked over by plant-breeding experts, successfully propagated, and used for crossing with Japanese and Chinese varieties which are either immune or nearly immune to the disease.

While many varieties of both the European and American chestnut have been developed in the past, and commercial production of the nuts was important, the blight for years made chestnut cultivation quite hazardous.

Some years of breeding the European, American, Japanese and Chinese chestnuts, especially *C. mollissima,* has resulted in reputedly blight-free varieties having acceptable nuts, several of which are now available.

* Special articles on the subjects indicated by an asterisk (*) will be found at the words so marked.

There are a few successful chestnut orchards left in the Middle West. The most promising feature of an admittedly difficult problem is the research of the U.S. Department of Agriculture in breeding new and disease-resistant varieties.

INSECT PESTS. Snout beetles are controlled by 3 sprays of pesticide #1 (*see* SPRAYS AND DUSTS) or #17 (double dosage) in late summer when weevils first fly into trees. It prevents legless grubs from attacking nuts. Infested nuts can be fumigated with carbon disulphide or methyl bromide. Borers attack tree, and preventive borer trunk sprays, careful pruning, and good fertilization help keep them down. Mites may be controlled by pesticide #14 or #21. It may be best to add either of these to pesticide #17. For filbert worm, *see* HAZEL.

DISEASES. The most important disease of chestnut is the blight or *Endothia* canker for which there is no known cure. Introduced about 1900, this disease has destroyed practically every chestnut tree in the eastern U.S. *See* above. The fungus spores enter through wounds and infect the inner bark. Branches are girdled and the leaves shrivel and appear blighted. Leaves thus killed cling to the tree for months and are useful in recognizing the disease. The fungus does not penetrate below the ground level, hence the tree roots remain alive for a long time. Numerous sprouts arise from these roots and these often give the impression that the tree is recovering. Sooner or later, however, these are killed and their places taken by new shoots. Such sprouts are not likely to develop immunity to the disease, since they are but a part of the old tree which was originally attacked, and the sprouts are in no way different from the parent tree.

CHESTNUT FAMILY = Fagaceae.

CHESTNUT OAK. In the East, *Quercus Prinus* (*see* OAK); on the Pacific Coast, *Lithocarpus densiflora.*

CHIASTOPHYLLUM OPPOSITIFOLIUM. See COTYLEDON SIMPLICIFOLIA.

CHICKASAW PLUM = *Prunus angustifolia.*

CHICKEN-CORN = *Sorghum vulgare drummondi.*

CHICKEN GRAPE = *Vitis vulpina.*

CHICK-PEA. See CICER.

CHICKWEED. See CERASTIUM and STELLARIA; *see also* Chickweed in the list at WEEDS.

CHICKWEED FAMILY = Caryophyllaceae.

CHICKWEED WINTERGREEN = *Trientalis borealis.*

CHICLE TREE = *Sapota Achras.*

CHICORY = *Cichorium Intybus.*

CHILEAN ARBORVITAE = *Libocedrus chilensis.* See INCENSE CEDAR.

CHILEAN BELLFLOWER = *Lapageria rosea* and *Nolana atriplicifolia.*

CHILEAN GUAVA = *Myrtus Ugni.*

CHILEAN JASMINE = *Mandevilla suaveolens.*

CHILEAN TARWEED = *Madia sativa.*

CHILE-BELLS = *Lapageria rosea.*

chilensis, -e (chill-en′sis). From Chile.

CHILI PEPPER = *Capsicum frutescens.*

chiloensis, -e (chill-o-en′sis). From Chile.

CHILOPSIS (ky-lop′sis). A single, rather showy, small tree or shrub of the family Bignoniaceae, found in the southwestern U.S. and adjacent Mex. The only species, **C. linearis,** the desert or flowering willow, is cult. there for ornament, and also in other warm parts of the country. It seldom exceeds 15 ft. Leaves narrow, willow-like, 3–5 in. long. Flowers in a short terminal cluster (raceme°). Corolla crimped, lilac, with a pair of yellow stripes inside, about 1½ in. long. Fruit a cylindric, many-seeded pod, nearly 12 in. long. While the plant grows in dry regions it favors moist sites in them. (*Chilopsis* is from the Greek for lip-like.) It is sometimes called mimbre in N. Mex. and Mex.

CHILOTES. See EPITHELANTHA MICROMERIS.

Chimaera (ky-meer′ra). A specific name of uncertain application, possibly a mythological reference to a flame.

CHIMAPHILA (ky-maf′fil-a). A small genus of low, evergreen herbs of the heath family, the two below natives in N.A., and attractive wild flowers. They are suited only to the wild garden. They are perennials, with slightly woody stems and clustered, leathery leaves. Flowers nodding or spreading, in a sparse terminal cluster, fragrant. Petals 5, concave, somewhat waxy. Stamens 10. Fruit a dry, 5-valved capsule. (*Chimaphila* is Greek for winter-loving, in reference to the evergreen leaves.)

These plants are not of easy culture. They must be grown in rich woods soil, preferably leaf mold that is well decomposed and not too acid. They may also rely on fungus or bacterial organisms at their roots for part of their food supply. Consequently, they must be dug from the wild with plenty of their native soil and even then often fail. See WILD GARDEN. Mr. R. S. Lemmon has developed a method of propagation. Cuttings are made between July 1 and July 10 (in Conn.) of new wood with a slight heel,° and planted in sand. Kept in a cold frame for the rest of the summer and the next winter, about 80% of them strike root and may then be potted up in a mixture of sand and leaf mold.

maculata. Spotted wintergreen, also called rheumatism-root and dragon's-tongue. Stem more or less prostrate, partly underground, sending up occasional flowering and leafing shoots. Leaves lance-shaped, pointed, 1–3 in. long, with distant teeth and mottled white along some of the veins. Flowers white, rarely pinkish, nodding. Quebec to Minn. and southward. Summer.

umbellata. Pipsissewa; also called prince's-pine and wintergreen. Similar to the other species but taller and the leaves blunter and not white-mottled, and the flowers spreading rather

---

* Special articles on the subjects indicated by an asterisk (°) will be found at the words so marked.

than nodding. Nearly throughout eastern N.A. Summer.

CHIMERA. Sometimes, apples occur on a tree representing in one fruit, but in different areas, both cion and stock characters. In other words, the upper half of such apples may be red and slightly acid, indicating their origin from the cion tissue, while the lower half may be sweet and yellow, representing the stock tissue. Such apples are called chimeras. Trees bearing chimeras are grafted trees, and usually certain limbs bear these apples, while other limbs may bear red sour, and still others yellow sweet apples. Chimeras, in such cases, arise through adventitious* buds at the graft union and consist of both cion and stock tissue. Other types have cion skin and a stock core. Chimeric plants often arise naturally through bud sporting, and their occurrence is widespread. Variegated foliage plants of some types are of this nature, *e.g.*, variegated euonymus. — O. E. W. *See* POMATO.

CHIMNEY BELLFLOWER = *Campanula pyramidalis.*

CHIMONANTHUS (ky′mo-nan thus). A genus of Chinese deciduous or evergreen shrubs of the family Calycanthaceae, comprising only 2 species, one of which is cult. for ornament. Leaves opposite,* smooth, without marginal teeth. Flowers appearing before the leaves, the sepals* numerous, overlapping, yellow. Petals none. Stamens* 5–6. (Greek for winter flowering in allusion to its late bloom.)

These shrubs are propagated by layering in the autumn or by seeds in the spring.

praecox. A shrub growing 9–10 ft. high. Leaves 4–6 in. long, ovalish or longer, long-pointed. Flowers fragrant, about 1 in. across, the outer sepals yellow, the inner striped purplish-brown. China. Often listed as *Meratia fragrans.* Not hardy above zone* 5, and in the South blooming nearly all the winter, and very fragrant.

CHINA ASTER = *Callistephus.*

CHINABERRY = *Melia Azedarach.*

CHINA FIR. See CUNNINGHAMIA.

CHINA PINK = *Dianthus chinensis.*

CHINA ROSE = *Hibiscus Rosa-sinensis.* See *also* ROSA CHINENSIS.

CHINA-TREE = *Melia Azedarach;* also *Koelreuteria paniculata.*

CHINA WOOD-OIL TREE. See TUNG-OIL TREE.

chinensis, -e (chi-nen′sis). From China.

CHINESE. As an adjective Chinese has been applied to many plants and other things from China or the region near it. Those occurring in this book and their equivalents are:

Chinese angelica tree (*see* ARALIA); Chinese anise = *Illicium verum;* Chinese artichoke = *Stachys sieboldi;* Chinese banana = *Musa cavendishi* (for culture *see* BANANA); Chinese bellflower (*see* ABUTILON); Chinese cabbage (*see* next main entry below); Chinese chestnut = *Castanea mollissima* (*see* CHEST-

NUT); Chinese chives = *Allium tuberosum;* Chinese date = *Zisyphus Jujuba;* Chinese elm = *Ulmus parvifolia* (*see* ELM); Chinese evergreen = *Aglaonema simplex;* Chinese fan palm = *Livistona chinensis;* Chinese fleece-vine = *Polygonum auberti;* Chinese forget-me-not = *Cynoglossum amabile;* Chinese hat-plant = *Holmskioldia sanguinea;* Chinese houses = *Collinsia bicolor;* Chinese jujube = *Zisyphus Jujuba;* Chinese juniper = *Juniperus chinensis;* Chinese lantern-plant = *Physalis Alkekengi;* Chinese layering = air layering (*see* LAYERING); Chinese loquat (*see* LOQUAT); Chinese monthly rose = *Rosa chinensis semperflorens;* Chinese parasol tree = *Firmiana simplex;* Chinese pistachio = *Pistacia chinensis;* Chinese potato = *Dioscorea Batatas;* Chinese preserving melon = *Benincasa hispida;* Chinese primrose = *Primula sinensis;* Chinese quince = *Chaenomeles sinensis;* Chinese radish = *Raphanus sativus longipinnatus* (*see* RADISH); Chinese sacred lily = *Narcissus Tazetta orientalis;* Chinese scholar tree = *Sophora japonica;* Chinese silk plant = *Boehmeria nivea;* Chinese snowball = *Viburnum macrocephalum;* Chinese tallow tree = *Sapium sebiferum;* Chinese trumpet-creeper = *Campsis grandiflora* (*see* TRUMPET-CREEPER); Chinese water chestnut = *Eleocharis tuberosa;* Chinese watermelon = *Benincasa hispida;* Chinese water plant = *Aglaonema simplex;* Chinese wisteria = *Wistaria sinensis;* Chinese yam = *Dioscorea Batatas.*

CHINESE CABBAGE (*Brassica pekinensis*). This most popular salad vegetable, called in China pe-tsai, and in our markets the celery cabbage, has come into American gardens within the last few years. It is raised commercially in Mich., and for fall and winter use in Calif.

The celery cabbage has little of the cabbage flavor, and when well grown its tender, central core of leaves is crisp, almost lettuce-like, and similarly used. The outer, coarser leaves are used as cooked greens. It is a leaf vegetable, the closely packed cylindric head being 12–18 in. long and 4–5 in. in diameter. A good hort. var. is Chihli.

For early harvest the plants should be raised as for early cabbage and set out in the field as soon as the ground can be worked. It does well on reclaimed muck soils, but will grow in ordinary garden soils if they are deep and rich, and there is plenty of moisture. This early crop is not so likely to be tender as one maturing in late autumn. For this crop, sow the seeds as for late cabbage and set the plants in the field about the last week of July. They should be spaced about 8 in. apart and the rows wide enough to allow frequent cultivation. See MUCKLAND GARDENING.

The finest celery cabbage in the country is now raised in Calif., where magnificent white heads are harvested from Oct. through the winter. The plant is a rich feeder and the soil must be well fertilized. It will not thrive in areas of great summer heat or drought. For its insect pests and diseases *see* CABBAGE.

CHINKAPIN = CHINQUAPIN.

CHINKERICHEE. See ORNITHOGALUM THYRSOIDES, *var.* AUREUM.

---

* Special articles on the subjects indicated by an asterisk (*) will be found at the words so marked.

CHINQUAPIN. In the East, *Castanea pumila,* see CHESTNUT; in Calif. = *Castanopsis chrysophylla.*

CHIOGENES = *Gaultheria hispidula.*

CHIONANTHUS (ki-o-nan'thus). Two handsome shrubs or small trees of the olive family, one widely and the other somewhat cult. for their showy white flowers. Leaves opposite,* without marginal teeth. Flowers in loose, often hanging clusters. Petals 4, strapshaped, slightly united at the base. Fruit fleshy, 1-seeded, blue. (*Chionanthus* is from the Greek for snow and flower. It occurs as a specific name in the genus *Eomecon.*)

These are desirable shrubs (rarely trees), but care must be used in selecting individuals because sometimes male and female flowers are on separate plants. While the male flowers are larger, they produce no fruit. They are easily grown in open, light soils and require no special attention. Propagated by layers or cuttings of plants forced for the purpose. Occasionally grafted on the closely related ash tree.

retusus. Often 10–18 ft. high, usually a shrub, the leaves elliptic or oblongish, 2–4 in. long. Flower cluster about 4 in. long, at the ends of leafy shoots. Petals ¾–1½ in. long. Fruit nearly egg-shaped, about ¾ in. long, dark blue. China. June–July. Hardy from zone* 4 southward.

virginicus. Fringe-tree or old-man's-beard. A shrub or tree up to 25 ft. high. Leaves narrowly elliptic or oblongish, 6–8 in. long. Flower cluster about 7 in. long, from lateral buds at the end of old twigs. Petals 1–2 in. long. Fruit egg-shaped, ¾–1¼ in. long. N.J. to Fla. and Tex. May–June. Hardy from zone* 3 southward.

CHIONODOXA (ki-on-o-dock'sa). Bulbous herbs of the lily family, mostly from Crete and Asia Minor, widely planted in the blue garden or rock garden for their attractive bloom. They are commonly called glory-of-the-snow, from their early flowering. There is a very short stalk from the bulb, narrow, toothless leaves, and small blue flowers in tiny racemes* at the end of the stalk. Corolla bell-shaped, the tube very short, its 6 stamens attached to the throat. Fruit a 3-angled capsule.* (*Chionodoxa* is Greek for glory of the snow.)

For culture *see* below.

luciliae. About 3 in. high, while in flower, longer in fruit. Leaves nearly grass-like, shorter than the stalk of the flower cluster, in fruit longer. Flowers about 5 in a cluster, the lower nodding, blue with a white center. Asia Minor. There is also a pink and a white-flowered variety.

sardensis. Similar, but the blue flowers without the white eye. Asia Minor.

CHIONODOXA CULTURE

Chionodoxas are among the earliest and most beautiful of spring-flowering bulbs. They are perfectly hardy and flourish and increase freely in good soil of a gritty nature, and they like plenty of light and some moisture. Planted in low, sunny sections of the rock garden, or massed closely about such contemporaneous shrubs as *Magnolia stellata,* forsythias, and flowering almond, their blue color shows to perfection. Their best display comes in the years following their first blossoming, so that on no account should they be disturbed, but rather allowed to seed and increase from year to year until a carpet of color is attained. An occasional mulch of old manure in autumn keeps the soil in good condition. *C. luciliae* and *C. sardensis* are the best for general use. The bulbs should be planted in September or October, 3 in. deep and 3 in. apart. — L. B. W.

Chiotilla. Mexican name of the cactus *Escontria Chiotilla.*

CHITTAMWOOD = *Bumelia lanuginosa;* also *Cotinus obovatus* and *Rhamnus purshiana.*

CHIVES (*Allium Schoenoprasum*). An onion-scented, perennial herb that does not produce the bulbs of the typical onion and is grown for its hollow, cylindrical leaves, which are cut and used for seasoning. (*See* HERB GARDENING.) While it is chiefly grown for these leaves, the plant produces attractive, rose-purple flowers, unless cut too much. It needs no special attention and can be grown either in the ordinary soil of the vegetable garden or in the flower border. Every two or three years it should be dug up, divided and replanted, especially if cutting is frequent.

CHLIDANTHUS (cly-dan'thus). A small genus of tropical American bulbous plants of the amaryllis family closely allied to the tender kinds of *Amaryllis* and to be grown as such. Leaves strap-shaped. Flowers (in the one below) fragrant, nearly stalkless in a few-flowered, terminal cluster (umbel*). Lobes of the corolla* 6. (*Chlidanthus* is from Greek for a delicate flower.)

The only species likely to be in cult. in America is the one below, which can be grown outdoors in southern Calif. and other frost-free areas, or planted in the spring and lifted in the fall, when the resting bulbs must be stored in sand in a frost-free place.

fragrans. Bulbs with a parchment-like outer husk. Leaves tongue- or strap-shaped, bluish-green, about 10 in. long, appearing with or before the flowers. Flowers about 3 in. long, in a few-flowered cluster (umbel*), yellow and fragrant. Summer. Andes.

chloodes (klo-ō'deez). Grass-green.

CHLORANIL. See FUNGICIDES.

CHLORDANE. See #4 at INSECTICIDES.

CHLOROGALUM (clow-rog'a-lum). A genus of 3 species of California bulbous plants of the lily family, closely related to *Camassia,* and grown like them. The only cult. species is *C. pomeridianun,* the soap plant or amole, which is an important bee plant in Calif. It has an onion-like bulb and a tall, many-branched stem 3–5 ft. high. Leaves long, narrow and wavy-margined at the base of the stem, diminishing in size and frequency toward the top of the plant. Flowers white,

---

* Special articles on the subjects indicated by an asterisk (*) will be found at the words so marked.

purple-veined, the cluster a terminal panicle.*
Petals 6. Stamens 6. The Indians used the
bulb to make soap. (*Chlorogalum* is from
the Greek for green milk.)

chloropetala, -us, -um (klor-o-pet'a-la).
With light yellow petals.

CHLOROPHYLL. The basic green coloring matter of nearly all plants. For its all-
important function *see* PLANT FOODS.

CHLOROPHYTUM (clow-ro-fy'tum). A
group of 60 species of perennial, tropical herbs
of the lily family, one very commonly grown
in the greenhouse for its numerous, bright
green leaves and for its long-stalked,
branched flower cluster. They differ from
Anthericum only in technical characters,
but the species below has wider leaves than
Anthericum Liliago (which see). (*Chlorophytum* is from the Greek for green plant.)
It is odd that this very common greenhouse
plant has no common name, although it is
locally sometimes called spider plant and ribbon plant. It is of easy, almost rampant
growth in the cool greenhouse in potting
mixture* 3, and is easily propagated by division of its rootstocks, and by its runners.

elatum. Leaves long, flat, often 1 in. wide,
green in the typical form, but white-margined,
variegated, or yellow-banded in some of the
hort. forms. Flowering stem 2–3 ft. long, lax
and inclined to sprawl. Flowers white, about
½ in. long. S. Af. The plant or some of its
forms is also, but incorrectly, called *Anthericum
vittatum, A. mandaianum, A. picturatum,* and
A. variegatum.

CHLOROPICRIN. *See* FUNGICIDES.

CHLOROSIS. A failure to produce the
normal green coloring matter in leaves, causing them to become pale, yellowish, or otherwise unhealthy. It is often caused (not always) by a deficiency of available iron. *See*
IRON CHELATE.
Chlorosis may also be a symptom of a number of virus or fungus diseases of plants.
The virus yellows* will cause the entire plant
to become chlorotic whereas virus mosaic*
and ring spot* will produce chlorotic
streaks or rings in the leaves.

CHOCOLATE. *See* THEOBROMA CACAO.

CHOCOLATE FAMILY = Sterculiaceae.

CHOCOLATE-FLOWER = *Geranium maculatum.*

CHOCTAW-ROOT = *Apocynum cannabinum.*

CHOISYA (shaw'si-a). A single, aromatic,
evergreen shrub of the family Rutaceae,
grown for its fine foliage and for fragrant,
white flowers in early spring. Leaves opposite,* compound,* the three leaflets nearly
stalkless and without marginal teeth. Flowers in 3–6-flowered, slender-stalked clusters
(cymes*). Petals 5. Stamens 10. Fruit of 5
two-lobed carpels. (Named for J. D. Choisy,
Swiss botanist.)
The Mexican orange is a handsome shrub
for the tender border, much grown in Fla.

and Calif. and occasionally hardy up to zone*
6 or even 5 in sheltered places. It has no
special soil preferences and is propagated by
cuttings of old wood in the frame.

ternata. Mexican orange. A shrub 6–8 ft. high.
Leaflets 2–3 in. long. Flowers 1–1½ in. wide.
Mex.

CHOKEBERRY = *Aronia.*

CHOKE CHERRY. Properly, *Prunus virginiana,* but *P. serotina,* the wild black cherry,
is often called choke cherry.

CHOLLA. See OPUNTIA.

CHORISIA (ko-ris'i-a). A genus of South
American trees of the family Bombacaceae,
one planted for ornament but hardy only in
zones* 8 and 9. It is related to the silk-cotton
tree (*Ceiba*) and differs chiefly in the lack of
the huge buttresses of the latter. It has alternate,* compound* leaves, the leaflets arranged finger-fashion. Flowers large (for
details *see* BOMBACACEAE). Fruit a capsule,*
the seeds with a silky floss. (Named for
Ludwig Choris, botanical artist.)

speciosa. Floss-silk tree. A spiny tree up
to 50 ft., occasionally planted for ornament in
southern Fla. Leaflets usually 5, stalked, more
or less lance-shaped and toothed. Flowers solitary in the axils,* nearly 3 in. wide, pink,
purple, or white, appearing in early winter
when the tree is without leaves. Brazil.

CHORIZEMA (core-riz'ee-ma). Of 15
Australian evergreen shrubs of this genus
(family Leguminosae), only one is in general
cult. in the U.S. It is pretty widely planted
outdoors in Calif. and Fla. for its handsome
foliage and showy flowers. Unlike nearly all
plants of the pea family, it has simple*
leaves, which, in the one below, are spiny-
margined. Flowers typically pea-like, in terminal racemes.* Fruit a short pod (legume*). (*Chorizema* is a fanciful Greek
name of uncertain application here.)
If grown in the greenhouse, they need a
cool house, and potting mixture* 4, to which
should be added a little acid peat. They
need plenty of water. Outdoors they need
open sunshine and a well-drained soil. Easily
propagated by cuttings of young wood in
the greenhouse.

cordatum. A weak-stemmed shrub 3–8 ft.
high, often better grown over a small trellis in
the greenhouse, as it tends to sprawl. Leaves
roundish or ovalish, heart-shaped at the base,
about 1 in. long, the margins with small teeth
or prickles. Flowers about ¾ in. long, the
upright standard* scarlet, the rest of the flower
purplish. Very showy, as the flowers are numerous in early spring. Greenhouse plants
should be plunged outdoors in summer, in
partial shade. The plant is sometimes offered
as *C. ilicifolium.*

CHOROGI = *Stachys sieboldi.*

CHRISTMAS BEGONIA. *See* BEGONIA
SOCOTRANA.

CHRISTMAS-BERRY = *Heteromeles arbutifolia* (see TOYON); also *Schinus terebinthifolius,* which is called Christmas-berry tree
in Calif.

---

* Special articles on the subjects indicated by an asterisk (*) will be found at the words so marked.

CHRISTMAS CACTUS = *Zygocactus truncatus*.

CHRISTMAS FERN = *Polystichum acrostichoides*.

CHRISTMAS GREENS. The custom of decking the house with Christmas greens is older than Christmas and survives all attempts of the conservationists to stop it. A better plan is to utilize the foliage of the common native fir of northeastern America, which is worthless from the forestry standpoint. It is also much the best for a Christmas tree. Avoid all spruces and hemlocks, which not only drop their needles very soon in the heat of a room, but are too valuable as trees to warrant trimming or destruction for transitory decoration. Some plantations of Norway spruce are grown for Christmas trees in Mich., however, but the fir is more satisfactory.

There is no justification for wreaths made of ground pine or other native evergreens in danger of extermination and any garden club should exert local pressure upon dealers to stop this. Good wreaths can be made of mountain laurel and other broad-leaved evergreens grown for the purpose and harvested annually.

CHRISTMAS ROSE = *Helleborus niger*.

CHRISTOPHINE = *Sechium edule*.

CHRIST'S-THORN = *Paliurus Spina-Christi*.

CHROMOSOME. The bodies resulting from cell division. They are rod-like, microscopically visible, nuclear, cellular bodies, in which the hereditary units, called genes, are located. Chromosomes are usually definite in number for any given species of plant, and these chromosome numbers have been determined for hundreds of garden flowers. In ordinary flowering plants chromosomes exist in pairs and are hence called diploids. Not infrequently the diploid set is doubled and becomes a tetraploid, which may or may not have desirable variations, of color, size, vigor, disease resistance, etc. In still rarer cases only one of the two diploid sets is doubled, and hence becomes a triploid. Polyploid is a general term for any increase in chromosome number. These terms, and the concepts inherent in them, are of importance to geneticists but of little interest to the amateur. But the term *tetraploid* is frequent in catalogs. The implication that tetraploid plants may be superior to diploids is not necessarily true, although some tetraploids are outstanding, notably in cotton and tobacco and in some garden flowers such as marigolds and snapdragons. — O. E. W.

CHRYSALIDOCARPUS (kris-sal'i-do-karpus). Madagascan feather palms of perhaps 10 species, one of which is the palm perhaps most widely grown by florists, who generally call it areca. They have clustered, smooth, ringed stems, never very high in cult. Leaves compound,* the leaflets numerous, arranged feather-fashion, very graceful and handsome, and drooping at the tip, the plant thus plume-like. Flowers in a short cluster near the leaves, the sepals, petals, and stamens 6 each. Fruit turban-shaped, dark violet or black. (*Chrysalidocarpus* is from the Greek for golden fruit, in allusion to the yellow fruit of another species.)

The florists' areca, better known as cane palm (from its slender, bamboo-like stems), is a favorite tub and pot palm in greenhouses and for house decoration. Not so tough and house-worthy as the kentias (see HOWEA), it is a far more graceful palm. It is widely grown for decoration outdoors in southern Fla. and all over the world in the tropics. In greenhouses it needs the same general culture as *Arenga* and the genus *Areca*. That means a house kept at about 60° at night and 70°–75° during the day. Use potting mixture* 4 and keep the plants, whatever their size, slightly pot-bound. While they need plenty of water, loosely filled pots with meager root development invite stagnant, water-soaked soil and poor growth.

lutescens. The areca of the florists; better called cane palm. Stem clustered, usually not over 10 ft. high, often much less as a pot plant. Leaves olive-green, their stalks yellow, not all at the top of the stem as in most palms. Leaflets 40–60 pairs, about ¾ in. wide or less, with a strong midrib. Fruit about ¾ in. long. Madagascar. Often offered as *Areca lutescens*.

CHRYSAMPHORA = DARLINGTONIA.

chrysantha, -us, -um (kris-san'tha). Golden-flowered.

CHRYSANTHEMUM (kris-san'thee-mum). An important genus of garden plants, comprising about 100 species of the family Compositae, nearly all from the temperate or subtropical regions of the Old World. Some have been in cultivation for over 3000 years in China and Japan, and today the genus includes such unlike plants as the florists' chrysanthemum, the garden pyrethrums, the costmary, and the common white daisy of our fields, as well as the well-known Shasta daisy and Marguerite. They are usually erect herbs (but *C. frutescens* is a little woody), with strong-smelling foliage, and generally much-branched. Leaves alternate,* often more or less divided. Flowers in heads, of all colors except blue and purple, the rays* much modified by long selection and cultivation, the heads usually showy and of immense size in the florists' chrysanthemum, but small and button-like in others. (*Chrysanthemum* is from the Greek for golden flower.) "Mum" is florists' slang for Chrysanthemum.

arcticum. Aster daisy. Arctic daisy. A hardy, border perennial, 12–15 in. high, useful in the autumn garden. Stems more or less prostrate at first, the tips ascending. Flowers white or lilac, the heads aster-like, nearly 2 in. wide. Arctic regions.

Balsamita. Costmary; called also mint geranium, and the leaves are sometimes called "lavender." A hardy perennial 2–3 ft. high. Leaves toothed. Flower heads numerous, scarcely ⅓ in. wide, the white rays very short, sometimes none. Asia. Grown for its aromatic foliage. See HERB GARDENING.

carinatum. A half-hardy annual, smooth and

---

* Special articles on the subjects indicated by an asterisk (*) will be found at the words so marked.

2–3 ft. high, not much branched. Leaves cut into narrow segments. Flower heads about 2½ in. wide, white, red, or yellow, with a differently colored ring at the base of the rays.* Morocco. For culture *see* Tender Annuals at ANNUALS.

coccineum. Pyrethrum. A very popular, summer-blooming, perennial herb, 1–2 ft. high, and little, if at all, branched. Leaves much-divided and fern-like. Flower heads large, very showy, often 2½ in. wide, red, pink, lilac, or white, and sometimes double. Caucasus and Persia. There are scores of named forms, some of them very fine plants for the border, although they are not hardy in severe climates. They are also grown as pot plants by florists. Sometimes known as painted lady or painted daisy.

coreanum. A common name in the literature of chrysanthemum, but of uncertain application. Among gardeners it always means a hardy, white, single-flowered plant, but the origin and nativity of it are unknown.

coronarium. Crown daisy. A hardy annual, stout, branched, and 3–4 ft. high. Leaves deeply divided, the segments also cut or toothed. Flower heads numerous, about 1½ in. wide, sometimes double, yellowish-white. Southern Eu. A variety is grown in Jap. and China for the edible young shoots.

erubescens = *C. rubellum.*

frutescens. Marguerite or Paris daisy. A tender, very beautiful, much-branched herb, 2–3 ft. high, the base usually woody. Leaves rather coarsely divided, a little fleshy. Flower heads daisy-like, 1½–2½ in. wide, white or pale yellow. Canary Islands. Can only be grown in the greenhouse and should be treated the same as the florists' chrysanthemum. *See* below. For a method of increasing the number of flowers, and changing the shape of the plant, *see* Pinching at TRAINING PLANTS.

hortorum. A doubtful name for the group of plants comprising the florists' chrysanthemum, and here listed as *C. morifolium.*

indicum. A hardy border perennial, 2–3 ft. high. Leaves divided, white-woolly on the under side. Flower heads yellow, numerous, about ¾ in. wide, showy only en masse. China. Considered as having contributed in part, to the modern florists' chrysanthemum.

Leucanthemum. Common, white, or oxeye daisy, and often weedy in the fields. Not over 2 ft. high, the stems normally unbranched. Leaves cut or divided. Flower heads long-stalked, usually solitary, about 1½ in. wide, the rays* white, the disk* yellow. Eurasia. Not much grown as a garden plant and sometimes a pest.

majus. A trade name for forms of *C. Balsamita.*

maximum. Chiefly grown in large-flowered hybrid forms known as the Shasta daisy, although originally from the Pyrenees and developed by Luther Burbank. It is a fine perennial border plant, but soon dies out and is best treated as a biennial. (*See* BIENNIALS.) Stems not much branched, 1–2 ft. high. Leaves long, narrow, toothed, but not deeply cut. Flower heads 2–4 in. wide, white and daisy-like. It is widely cult. and there are a variety of named forms.

morifolium. Florists' chrysanthemum. Probably a Chinese perennial herb, originally 2–4 ft. high and much-branched, but often, as grown today, much larger and of various habit (dome-shaped, etc.), due to pinching and disbudding. Leaves broad, strong-scented, lobed, and more or less grayish-hairy. Flower heads

of many forms (*see* below) and colors, often immense. For culture *see* below. Sometimes called *C. hortorum.*

nipponicum. Nippon chrysanthemum or daisy. A hardy, perennial, border plant, 1½–2 ft. high, a little woody at the base, branched above. Leaves thickish, blunt, only slightly toothed toward the end. Flower heads solitary at the ends of the branches, white, 2–3 in. wide. Jap.

Parthenium. Feverfew. A bushy, hardy perennial for the border, the stems leafy, 2–3½ ft. high. Leaves more or less cut, and, in varieties, yellowish or crisped. Flower heads many, scarcely ¼ in. wide, button-like, the rays white, short or lacking altogether. There is also a form with white, ray-like disk flowers. Eurasia. Sometimes offered as *Matricaria capensis* and as *M. parthenioides.*

rubellum. A leafy-stemmed, much-branched perennial, 2–3 ft. high. Leaves 4–6 in. long, divided into 5 lobes that are coarsely toothed or lobed, green above, paler and hairy beneath. Flower heads 2–3 in. wide, the rays pink. Of unknown origin. Summer. Sometimes offered as *Chrysoboltonia pulcherrima.*

segetum. Corn marigold. A much-branched annual herb, to be sown where wanted. Stems 1–2 ft. high. Leaves notched, or somewhat cut, but not deeply so. Flower heads 1½–2½ in. wide, white or yellowish, solitary at the ends of the branches and daisy-like. Eurasia. There are many named forms of this popular annual.

sibiricum. A trade name for forms assigned to *C. coreanum.*

uliginosum. Giant daisy. A hardy, perennial border plant, 4–7 ft. high and much-branched. Leaves narrow and sharply toothed, but not deeply cut. Flower heads solitary at the ends of the branches, daisy-like, about 2½ in. wide. Eu.

TYPES AND CULTURE OF CHRYSANTHEMUMS

The genes* of hardiness contained in the original species are inherent in our modern mums in varying degrees. As a general rule the early-blooming varieties will bloom without protection in the northern plains states, while early, midseason, and late varieties will bloom without protection in the southern states. The ability of any chrysanthemum to survive the winter is not a measure of its hardiness, but rather of the ability of its shallow roots to resist the alternate freezing and thawing which tends to heave the plants out of the ground.

Chrysanthemums were once divided into hardy garden varieties and tender greenhouse varieties. Through breeding, our chrysanthemum specialists have given us many new varieties which equal those grown under glass, and they are hardy throughout the country. Also, many amateurs have discovered that some varieties listed for greenhouse culture will bloom and live over in the outdoor garden. Mature chrysanthemum plants will stand temperatures slightly below freezing; so, as long as frost does not damage the blooms, it is possible to grow many of the later-blooming varieties outdoors, providing some form of frost protection is used to protect the blooms.

The two broad types of chrysanthemums are the multibloom bush types and the single-

---

* Special articles on the subjects indicated by an asterisk (*) will be found at the words so marked.

bloom types. Basically the culture is similar, but the bush types were bred to produce only many sprays of small flowers, while the single-bloom varieties were designed to produce one large bloom on each stem permitted to develop. Some varieties may be grown either way and they will be separately listed as dual-purpose mums in the tables of recommended varieties. A further division of the bush-type mums may be made on the basis of height, for they range from small mounds of bloom barely 1 ft. high to large bushes measuring up to 4 ft. The dwarf varieties are grouped together under the heading Cushion Mums. To some of these taller cushion types the somewhat inappropriate name of Azaleamum has been applied. The height of the taller varieties depends upon the time at which the plants are set out in the garden and the amount of pinching done by the grower.

Outdoor Culture

The only basic requirement for success with mums is a well-drained location which receives full sun for the greater portion of the day.

In the spring many new vegetative growths will develop at the ends of the stolons* surrounding the base of a chrysanthemum plant which has wintered over. Each new growth, with a portion of stolon and its roots, may be cut from the old clump and set out as a new plant. If this "Dutch" cutting, as it is called, is planted no deeper than its original position around the old plant, and is kept watered and shaded until it no longer wilts in the bright sun, it will develop into a sturdy plant. Dutch cuttings may be too tall at normal planting time and they are more susceptible to soil-borne enemies, so many growers prefer to grow new plants from softwood cuttings.* The top 4- to 6-in. section of terminal growth will produce a new plant if the lower 1- to 2-in. section of the stem is placed in moist sand for a period of two to three weeks.

The sand must be maintained uniformly moist, but not soaking wet, at a temperature of approximately 60°. When the cuttings no longer wilt in bright sun, and there are roots on the stems an inch or two long, they may be planted in pots or directly in the garden. Cuttings for outdoor mums may be made anytime between April 1 and July 1. For those who do not have a greenhouse, a cold frame with a sand base and a soil-heating cable beneath it will produce excellent rooted cuttings.

Plants may be grown in beds or borders, or they may be grown in pots. The English plunge-pit method, in which potted mums are plunged into the ground or a sand pit, is excellent for a gardener who wants to move his plants into a greenhouse or sun porch for November blooming. Plants should be shifted from their initial 2- or 3-in. pots to 4-in., and finally into 7-in. blooming pots. When grown in beds it is desirable to limit the width of

the beds to 6 ft. so that plants may be easily reached from either side. Bush-type chrysanthemums will grow leggy if crowded; so the cushion mums should be spaced 1 ft. apart, while taller-growing varieties should be spaced 18 to 24 in. apart. Single-bloom varieties may be spaced as close as 8 in. in the row, with rows 1 ft. apart.

Perennial borders and landscape borders present a problem, for, with the long growing period for mums and their large eventual size, the borders will look bare if the mums are properly spaced. Fortunately mums can be easily transplanted, even while in full bloom. Thus it is often desirable to grow them in an open garden area and transplant them with a good ball of earth at the proper time to make a colorful display. This will permit a better selection of plant heights and blending colors of blooms.

Both bush-type and single-bloom mums look alike when first planted, but the difference in culture occurs after the first pinch. A soft pinch or removal of the top ½ in. of terminal growth by the grower will cause the plant to make breaks or side branches immediately below the point of the pinch, and this should be done as soon as the plant is making active growth, for plants set out in early June. Additional pinches should be made on the breaks of bush-type plants after each one has made 3 or 4 in. of growth. This in turn will cause additional breaks which should be pinched approximately 100 days before the normal blooming date for the variety to insure good stems of terminal sprays.

For mums planted in late June omit the second pinch, but be sure to make the last pinch at least 100 days before the blooming date. Cushion mums require no pinching, for they automatically form false buds which produce breaks. All varieties of mums will do this but judicious pinching of taller bush-type mums will produce a more symmetrical plant than nature had intended.

The strongest break on a single-bloom variety should be retained and all others should be removed. Then this break should be soft-pinched approximately 100 days before the blooming date for the variety. From this "time pinch," as it is called, there will be produced 2 to 4 breaks. The grower must then decide whether he wishes one maximum-sized bloom, two almost as large blooms, or 3 slightly smaller and flatter blooms, for at this time he must remove any excess stems. The bud which then forms on the end of each stem will be either a late crown bud or a terminal bud. Terminal in this sense means the last flowering bud formed. A crown bud will be a cluster of vegetative buds surrounding a central flowering bud, while a terminal bud will consist of smaller flowering buds around a larger flowering bud. In either case all of the buds around the central bud should be rolled away with the thumb as soon as the buds separate and have stalks a fraction of an inch long. This process of disbudding

* Special articles on the subjects indicated by an asterisk (*) will be found at the words so marked.

is essential to produce one large bloom; and, in addition, the smaller stalks of buds which develop in the leaf axils* of single-bloom chrysanthemums must also be removed as soon as they become large enough to snap away from the main stem.

All chrysanthemums have shallow roots, so care must be used in cultivation and in maintaining an adequate supply of moisture in the soil. A mulch is by far the best way to eliminate the need for cultivation and to regulate the supply of moisture. Use a 2-in. layer of leaves which have become wet and compressed through storage in an open bin over the winter. Then, to eliminate weeds and provide an attractive appearance, add a several-inch layer of peat moss. This process is actually sheet composting, which is a very effective way to improve the texture of the soil.

Mums are often called gross feeders, but they like their chemical ingredients in small amounts applied at regular intervals. Either dry or liquid fertilizers may be used on a biweekly schedule in dilutions as recommended by the manufacturer. The use of a leaf mulch will cause a temporary loss of nitrogen as the leaves decompose and this should be compensated for by the addition of extra nitrogen. Ammonium sulphate may be used at the rate of 3 pounds per 100 square ft., applied in 3 or 4 doses over the season. This form of nitrogen will produce the slightly acid soil which chrysanthemums enjoy. Too much nitrogen will produce large green leaves at the expense of large blooms. No application of fertilizer should be made after the buds show color.

Bush-type mums of the taller varieties will require a support of stakes or stretched wires, and large-bloom mums will require support for each stem. For the latter, use strong mason's twine tied with a simple loop knot between two wires stretched along the row. One wire is 6 in. from the ground and the second is 7 ft. from the ground, with each stem held to the string with a plastic-covered wire tie.

For areas where frost usually occurs before the normal blooming dates of the varieties being grown, some form of frost protection will be required. For small beds a sheet or light plastic material may be placed over the beds when frost threatens. For larger plantings, or whenever large-bloom mums are grown for show purposes, it is better to provide a frame of pipe or treated cypress wood over which a vinyl plastic covering may be stretched.

After the blooming season all stalks should be cut down and removed from the garden to lessen the possibility of insect or disease contamination the following year. Then stock plants should be removed to a cold frame, or else, if the garden is well drained, the plants should be mulched with salt hay or straw. Such procedure will insure healthy cuttings for next year.

The tables of varieties below are recommended for outdoor culture in the United States. Blooming dates will vary over the country, since the dates are given for the 40°–45° latitude belt. Blooming will be delayed 3 days for each 5 degrees of southward latitude and increased an equivalent amount for northward latitude.

TABLE I. BUSH TYPES

Variety	Color	Height	Blooming Date
Apache	bright red, overcast with gold	medium	Sept. 15
Avalanche	white	tall	Oct. 1
Baltimore Oriole	golden yellow	medium	Sept. 20
Carnival	burnt orange	medium	Oct. 10
Betty	rosy pink	tall	Oct. 10
Cecil Beed	deep lavender	medium	Sept. 1
Charles Nye	yellow	tall	Oct. 5
Chippewa	aster purple	medium	Sept. 20
Elizabeth Hood	light lavender-rose	medium	Oct. 15
Ginny Lee	white	medium	Oct. 10
Gold Coast	deep yellow	tall	Oct. 25
Huntsman	scarlet-orange	tall	Oct. 5
Jean Treadway	pink, red-tipped center	medium	Sept. 25
Lavender Lady	lavender	tall	Oct. 10
Lee Powell	rich yellow	tall	Oct. 10
Mary McArthur	raspberry rose	tall	Oct. 25
Masquerade	silvery rose	medium	Oct. 10
Red Velvet	deep red	medium	Oct. 10
Reverence	yellow	medium	Sept. 15

TABLE II. CUSHION MUMS
(Including Azaleamums)

Variety	Color	Height	Blooming Date
Amelia	lavender-pink	short	Sept. 30
Bowl O'Gold	canary yellow	short	Sept. 10
Crimson Cushion	wine red	short	Sept. 10
Lipstick	brick red	short	Sept. 28
Marjorie Mills	ruby red	short	Sept. 12
Mischief	red	short	Sept. 30
Pink Surprise	rose pink	short	Sept. 10
Powder Puff	white	short	Sept. 15

Some of these are regularly in bloom by Aug. 1 in southern Maryland.

TABLE III. LARGE BLOOM MUMS

Variety	Color	Type	Blooming Date
Ambassador	white	incurve	Oct. 25
Ambassador Yellow	yellow	incurve	Oct. 25
Blazing Gold	yellow	incurve	Oct. 25
Bunbu	lavender-pink	spider	Nov. 1
Detroit News	light bronze	incurve	Nov. 1
Hilda Bergen	reddish bronze	incurve	Oct. 20
Luyona	yellow	spider	Oct. 25
Major Bowes	lavender	incurve	Oct. 20
Mrs. H. E. Kidder	medium yellow	incurve	Oct. 25
Rex	white	incurve	Oct. 25
Silver Sheen	white	incurve	Oct. 20
Sincerity	white	anemone	Oct. 25

Varieties marked *anemone* have a large disk and regularly arranged flat rays. Those marked *spider* have quilled and hooked-tipped rays.

TABLE IV. DUAL-PURPOSE MUMS

Variety	Color	Height	Blooming Date
Bronze Doty	bronze	tall	Oct. 25
Coral Frost	bronze coral and pink	medium	Oct. 25

* Special articles on the subjects indicated by an asterisk (*) will be found at the words so marked.

Variety	Color	Height	Blooming Date
Doreen Monte	rose-pink	medium	Oct. 20
Frieda	pink-yellow cushion	medium	Nov. 5
Granite State	white	medium	Oct. 20
Lillian Doty	shell pink	tall	Oct. 25
Queen of Pinks	deep pink	medium	Nov. 1
Red Doty	red	tall	Nov. 1
Richard Mandel	white	medium	Nov. 1
Silver Ball	white	medium	Oct. 10
Yellow Doty	yellow	tall	Oct. 25

GREENHOUSE CULTURE

Chrysanthemums are short-day plants which means that they require short days to initiate blooming buds. (See PHOTOPERIODISM.) This requirement opens up a new field for the grower, for by artificially regulating the day length he can have chrysanthemums in bloom at any season.

Since chrysanthemums require full sun, while most other greenhouse plants require some summer shading, it is best to grow them in pots outdoors and move them into the greenhouse for a fall display of bloom. Also, for early blooming of the late varieties it is best to grow them outdoors and produce the short days by shading. In this case a dense black cloth must be fitted tightly over a frame from approximately 5 P.M. to 7 A.M., starting 10 to 12 weeks before the week in which it is desired to have the plants in bloom. For bloom between late November and May a greenhouse is required.

Commercial growers have developed a timing schedule for blooming which is based upon the number of weeks of short days required to initiate bloom.

Response Group Classification	Normal Blooming Dates
6 weeks	Sept. 25–Oct. 1
7 weeks	Oct. 3–Oct. 12
8 weeks	Oct. 15–Oct. 23
9 weeks	Oct. 25–Nov. 1
10 weeks	Nov. 5–Nov. 12
11 weeks	Nov. 15–Nov. 23
12 weeks	Nov. 25–Dec. 3
13 weeks	Dec. 5–Dec. 13
14 weeks	Dec. 15–Dec. 25
15 weeks	Dec. 25–Jan. 5

The amateur grower who wishes to have chrysanthemums in bloom during the winter and spring must root cuttings in August from basal cuttings, if they are available, or from the axillary growths which develop on large-bloom mums in August. The top 4 in. of terminal growth from bush-type mums must be used for cuttings of these varieties. This is a difficult season in which to root cuttings; so more than the required number should be taken, and they should be kept shaded in a humid atmosphere.

Cuttings and potted plants must be lighted from August 15 onward to prevent bud formation. One 75-watt bulb in a wide-angle reflector for each 5 ft. of bench area will do a satisfactory job. For best results the night should be split into two equal parts by having the lights on from 10 P.M. until 2 A.M. A time switch will make this job automatic. The lighting may be discontinued any time after the plants have made sufficient growth to support the blooms. Then each variety will bloom when it has received its quota of short days. The amateur grower can be more flexible with this program than the commercial grower, for he is not too concerned about bloom production on a given date; however, it is not safe to keep mums lighted any later than March 1, for there may be insufficient short days remaining before the long days of spring to initiate blooming buds. Of course a combination of lighting and shading may be used to carry the blooming period into late spring and summer.

Among the other interesting ways in which various types of chrysanthemums can be manipulated in the greenhouse is the spring pot-plant program. This is simple, for it requires no lights or shading. Cuttings of any of the so-called hardy garden mums may be taken in January from stock plants which have been carried over in a cool greenhouse. The rooted cuttings are then placed in 2-in. pots and shifted to 4-in. pots for bloom in late May. After blooming these plants may be planted outdoors for a second crop in the fall.

All of the essentials for good outdoor culture, such as pinching, fertilizing, staking, and disbudding are required for success with mums in a greenhouse. With all of the factors for good growth under the personal control of the operator, it is possible to grow excellent plants in the 60° greenhouse. The blooms however may be slightly inferior to those of the same varieties grown outdoors. With fewer sunny days to add color and fullness to the blooms, it pays to use only those varieties which will do well under adverse light conditions. The following varieties are especially recommended for both a winter-blooming program and a shading program:

TABLE V. OUT-OF-SEASON MUMS

Variety	Color	Type	Response Group
Beauregard	orange-bronze	pompon	10
Bluechip	lavender-pink	pompon	9
Detroit News	light bronze	incurve	9
Giant Betsy Ross	white	incurve	9
Gold Coast	yellow	pompon	9
Good News	golden yellow	incurve	9
Harvester	deep yellow	incurve	11
Indianapolis			
bronze	bronze	incurve	10
golden bronze	golden bronze	incurve	10
pink	pink	incurve	10
white	white	incurve	10
yellow	yellow	incurve	10
Kramer			
bronze	light bronze	pompon	14
peach	peach-pink	pompon	14
pink	deep pink	pompon	14
white	white	pompon	14
yellow	yellow	pompon	14
Mrs. David Roy	red-bronze reverse	incurve	10
Pinocchio	white	pompon	9
Queen's Lace	white	spider	9

---

* Special articles on the subjects indicated by an asterisk (*) will be found at the words so marked.

The present address of the National Chrysanthemum Society is 345 Milton Rd., Rye, New York. — C. A.

INSECT PESTS. Control black and other aphids with pesticide #21 or #20 (see SPRAYS AND DUSTS). Either of these materials will control leaf miners and thrips. Gall midges produce lumpy galls on leaves and warped growth. Inspect planting stock and remove infested leaves. Spray with above materials or with phosphate aerosols if precautions are followed. See CELERY for leaf-tier control.

DISEASES. Although one of the most popular flowers in the garden and greenhouse, the chrysanthemum is subject to a number of serious diseases and many more minor ones. The wilt* disease is caused by a fungus which may live for years in the soil and also may be spread in the cuttings used for propagation. Where the soil is infested with the fungus it is impossible to grow many varieties. Susceptible varieties will be killed, moderately resistant varieties will have a gradual browning of leaves starting at the bottom of the plant, and completely resistant varieties will have no apparent ill effects. Rotate the planting sites and use resistant varieties.

A virus disease, stunt, will reduce plants and leaves to two-thirds or one-half normal size. Plants will flower earlier than normal and colors of some varieties will be altered. The virus cannot live in the soil, but once in a plant will carry the disease to all cuttings used for propagation.

Two different fungi cause brown or black leafspots* starting on the lowest leaves and spreading upward to cause a gradual defoliation. A rust* fungus produces brown powdery pustules on the lower side of leaves in areas where rainfall or irrigation is heavy. These three fungus diseases will be controlled with applications of pesticide #5 or #11 (see SPRAYS AND DUSTS) starting when first spots appear and repeated at 10-day intervals.

Powdery mildew* spots and later covers the leaves with a white, powdery growth. When the disease first appears, apply pesticide #6 or #9 and repeat at 10-day intervals.

During rainy periods in the flowering season, or in greenhouses with poorly fitting glass, the flowers may have black rays, or entire flowers turn brown. If flower blight* starts, spray with pesticide #11, using a very fine mist for the application.

CHRYSOBALANUS (kris-o-bal′a-nus). A small group of tropical trees of the rose family, one sometimes planted in southern Fla., very rarely in greenhouses. The only cult. species is **C. Icaco,** the coco-plum or gopher-plum, which is also wild from southern Fla. to Brazil. It is usually a shrub in Fla. (a tall tree in the tropics) with alternate,* leathery, evergreen leaves, 2–3 in. across and nearly round. Flowers white, in small clusters (cymes*) in the leaf axils.* Petals 5, with a claw.* Stamens many. Fruit dryish, but a fleshy, yellow drupe,* edible but somewhat insipid, about 1 in. long, its stone pointed and ridged. (*Chrysobalanus* is from the Greek for golden acorn, in allusion to the fruit.) It is useful for seaside planting in zone* 9.

CHRYSOBOLTONIA PULCHERRIMA = *Chrysanthemum rubellum.*

CHRYSOGONUM (kris-sog′o-num). A genus of perennial herbs of the eastern U.S., comprising the single species **C. virginianum,** the golden star. It is a low herb, 4–7 in. high, with opposite, long-stalked leaves that are 1½–3½ in. long and bluntly toothed. Flower heads solitary, or a few, about 1½ in. wide, yellow. It is a plant of rich woods and prefers such sites, but will grow in partly shady places. May–June. (*Chrysogonum* is from the Greek for golden joint and is of uncertain application to this plant.)

chrysographes (kris-o-graff′eez). Golden-lined.

chrysolepis, -e (kris-o-lee′pis). Golden-scaled.

chrysoleuca, -us, -um (kris-o-loo′ka). Yellow and pale or whitish.

chrysophylla, -us, -um (kris-o-fil′la). Yellow- or golden-leaved.

CHRYSOPHYLLUM. See STAR-APPLE.

CHRYSOPSIS (kris-op′sis). The golden asters (not true asters, which are never yellow) comprise a group of North American perennial herbs of the family Compositae, almost weedy in the wild state, but occasionally transferred to the garden for their yellow flower heads and their ability to grow in dry, sandy soils. They are low herbs with woolly or hairy leaves and rather large heads of yellow ray and disk* flowers, usually in small clusters at the ends of the branches. (*Chrysopsis* is from the Greek for golden aspect.)

The golden asters are of the easiest culture in any garden soil and may be increased by division in the spring. All bloom in midsummer.

falcata. Ground gold-flower. Not over 1 ft. high, the leaves narrow, crowded, rigid, and hairy, 2–4 in. long. Flower heads about ⅓ in. wide. In sandy soil, Mass. to N.J.

mariana. Golden star. From 12–20 in. high, the leaves oblongish, 2–4 in. long. Flower heads about 1 in. wide, numerous. In dry sand L.I. to Fla. and Tex.

villosa. Rosinweed. From 10–18 in. high, the leaves oblongish, 1–2 in. long. Flower heads about 1 in. wide, rather sparse. In plains and prairies, Minn. to British Columbia and N. Mex.

CHUCHU = *Sechium edule.*

CHUFA = *Cyperus esculentus.*

CHYSIS (ky′sis). A small genus of tropical American tree-perching orchids, not much grown in greenhouses, but very handsome. Without true pseudobulbs,* the stems are somewhat thickened and spindle-shaped, leafy. Leaves less fleshy than in many orchids, soon falling, when the stems thicken still more. Flowers showy, in short clusters (racemes*) produced from the leaf axils,* and usually shorter than the leaves. One of the sepals and the petals are alike in shape, the other sepals forming a foot with the base of the column.* Lip with the lateral lobes erect, and surrounding the column. (*Chysis* is from the Greek for melting, in reference to a technical character of the pollen.)

---

* Special articles on the subjects indicated by an asterisk (*) will be found at the words so marked.

These plants need to be grown in a basket or wooden crib, or in well-drained pans in a tropical atmosphere. For details *see* Culture at ORCHID.

aurea. Flowers 5–8 in a cluster, about 2 in. wide. Sepals and petals oblongish, yellow. Lip with the lateral lobes yellow, the middle lobe downy, white, but red- and yellow-spotted. Brazil.

bractescens. A leafy orchid with drooping stems. Flowers 3–5 in a cluster, about 3 in. wide. Sepals and petals white. Lateral lobes of the lip white outside, yellow within, red-striped. Middle lobe of the lip yellow but red-streaked. Mex.

CIBOL. The Welsh onion; also the shallot.

CIBOTIUM (sy-bō′ti-um). A small group of sturdy tree ferns of the family Cyatheaceae, found in tropical America and in the tropics of the Far East. Two are rather common greenhouse ferns which (under cult.) do not produce the usually shaggy trunk of wild trees. They are coarser-foliaged than other tree ferns but easier to grow and hence (especially *C. schiedei*) popular florists' ferns. Fronds twice-compound,* the ultimate segments narrow. Spore cases at the ends of the veinlets. (*Cibotium* is from the Greek for a little seed-vessel.)

For the culture of these greenhouse ferns *see* FERNS AND FERN GARDENING.

Barometz. Scythian lamb. As cult., a trunkless fern with the large, feathery leaves arising from the ground level, the stalks shaggy and brownish. Ultimate segments of the frond narrowly oblong, 4–6 in. long, pale bluish-green beneath. Indo-Malaya. This was one of the plants to which ancient legend ascribed the production of vegetable wool, hence its name of Scythian lamb. (*See* BAROMETZ.)

schiedei. In the wild, 15 ft. high or more, but often much less and nearly trunkless in cult. Fronds 3–5 ft. long, drooping and graceful, the stalks brown-hairy. Ultimate segments of the frond 5–8 in. long, much cut, bluish-green beneath. Mex. The best-known and most popular as a cult. fern, being well suited to decorations because of its sturdy growth.

CIBOUL = Cibol.

CICER (sy′sir). Perhaps a dozen Asiatic herbs of the pea family of no garden interest except for the chick-pea or garbanzo, a plant long cult. (little in U.S.) for its edible seeds. Leaves compound,* the leaflets arranged feather-fashion with (in the one below) an odd leaflet at the end. Flowers small, but pea-like, solitary and long-stalked. Pod (legume*) short and swollen, with only 1 or 2 seeds. (*Cicer* is the classical name for the chick-pea.)

The chick-pea is an annual long cult. in southern Eu. for food. Unlike the garden pea, it will stand considerable summer heat. Sow the seeds 6–8 in. apart in drills about 2 in. deep, and space the rows at least 2 ft. apart. The plant is of easy culture.

arietinum. Chick-pea or garbanzo. A sticky-hairy annual, 1–2 ft. high and branched. Leaflets 9–15, ovalish, about ½ in. long, finely toothed. Flowers white or pinkish, scarcely ⅜ in. long. Pod nearly 1 in. long and half as wide, the seed wrinkled, about ⅓ in. in diameter, one end pointed as though a ram's horn, white, red or black. Western Asia.

CICHORIACEAE. *See* COMPOSITAE.

CICHORIUM (sick-kor′i-um). A remarkably versatile group of herbs of the family Compositae, containing such unlike garden plants as the chicory, endive, and the witloof or French endive. Leaves alternate (much modified in the endive), usually toward the base of the stem. Flowers in heads, composed only of ray* flowers, the heads sometimes solitary and stalkless, or a few terminal and short-stalked. (*Cichorium* is a Latinized version of an Arabic name for one of the species.)

Endivia. Endive. Annual or biennial, the stem leafy, 2–3 ft. high. Leaves most numerous at the base, oblong, brittle, lobed or cut in the wild form. Flower heads purple, below them a series of leafy bracts that exceed the head. India (?). For culture *see* ENDIVE.

Intybus. Chicory; called also succory, blueweed, blue dandelion, and coffeeweed, the latter from the use of its ground-up root as an adulterant of coffee. A stout perennial 3–6 ft. high, nearly leafless toward the top. Leaves variable, generally oblongish, clasping, the lower ones sometimes dandelion-like. Heads usually blue, sometimes white or pink, about 1½ in. wide. Eu. Summer. For a reputedly annual form *see* RADICHETTA. For culture and for the witloof *see* below.

CHICORY AND WITLOOF CULTURE

The common chicory is abundant as a weed along roadsides throughout N.A. It is cult. as a farm crop in some sections, where its roots are harvested and are the source of commercial chicory. Such culture is easy, the plants being handled like any other perennial. Young roots are planted in spring in rows 3 ft. apart or seed is sown instead, the ground is kept cultivated, and the plants kept spaced about 18 in. apart in the rows.

Less known in U.S., but common in France, is the French endive or witloof. It is a form or variety of chicory in which the blanched leaves are eaten. They may be forced in a cellar after the roots have been dug from the ground in the fall and stored as other root crops. Seed of witloof should be sown in drills in the spring, spaced about 6 in. apart. In the fall cut the tops off and dig the roots.

CICUTA (sy-kew′ta). The water hemlock is scarcely of garden importance, but warn children against its dangerously poisonous roots. It is one of a small genus of perennial herbs of the carrot family found in the north temperate zone, and sometimes **C. maculata** is transferred to pond edges or bogs, where it thrives. Commonly called water hemlock (not the poison hemlock that killed Socrates); it is also known as spotted cowbane, musquashroot, and beaver-poison. It has compound,* rather graceful or feathery leaves, and tiny white flowers in terminal, compound umbels.* Its roots contain a deadly alkaloid. (*Cicuta* is the classical Latin name of these plants.)

cicutaria, -us, -um (sick-kew-tay′ri-a). Like the water hemlock (*Cicuta*).

---

* Special articles on the subjects indicated by an asterisk (*) will be found at the words so marked.

CIDER. In choosing apples for cider it is obvious that the varieties with most juice will give the greatest yield. But early varieties do not make as good cider as late apples. Consequently, choose one of the later varieties in the article on the apple. Also apples with yellow fruit do not make a cider with as good a color as red-fruited varieties. Winesap, McIntosh, Jonathan, Baldwin, and Wealthy are all good cider apples, as well as having many other fine qualities. *See* APPLE.

CIGAR-FLOWER = *Cuphea platycentra.*

CIGAR-TREE = *Catalpa bignonioides.*

ciliaris, -e (silly-a′ris). *See* CILIATA.

ciliata, -us, -um (silly-a′ta). Ciliate; *i.e.,* with marginal hairs as those on the edges of many leaves or petals.

CILICIAN FIR = *Abies cilicica. See* FIR.

cilicica, -us, -um (sil-lis′i-ka). From Cilicia, Asia Minor.

ciliosa, -us, -um (silly-ō′sa). Slightly fringed or ciliate. *See* CILIATA.

CIMICIFUGA (sim-mi-siff′you-ga). The bugbanes are tall, rather showy, summer-blooming perennial herbs of the buttercup family, well suited to the wild garden or the shadiest part of the border. They have large, thrice-compound* leaves. Flowers small, white, with few or no petals, but crowded in a dense, terminal, finger-shaped cluster at the end of a tall stalk, hence striking, and standing well above the foliage. Stamens many and giving the chief color to the flower. Fruit a collection of small, dry pods (follicles*), differing from the closely related and somewhat similar *Actaea,* which has fleshy fruit. (*Cimicifuga* is Latin for bugbane.)

The three species are best suited to the wild garden. The plants grow in the woods and should have similar soil (not especially acid). A good mixture for them is black leaf mold and rotted sods mixed half and half.

americana. Snakeroot. Not over 4 ft. high, usually about 3 ft. Ultimate leaflets oval or oblong, 1–3 in. long, thin, deeply cut or toothed. Flower cluster 1–2 ft. long, usually branched. Fruits about ¼ in. long. N.Y. and Pa. to Tenn. and Ga. Aug.–Sept.

racemosa. Black snakeroot; also called black cohosh. Taller than the others, and sometimes 6 ft. high. Ultimate leaflets thin and tapering at both ends, 2–4 in. long, toothed or deeply cut or both. Flower cluster branched, its main spike 9–24 in. long and showy. Eastern N.A. July–Aug.

simplex. An erect Eurasian perennial, 3–5 ft. high. Leaflets unequally toothed, the terminal one 3-lobed. Flowers white or greenish-white, in a rarely branched, long raceme.* Midsummer. Called by some *C. foetida.*

CINCHONA (sin-kō′na). A genus of perhaps 60 species of mostly Andean trees of the family Rubiaceae, of little garden interest, but important as the source of quinine. The quinine tree is not cult. in the U.S. although attempts have been made to grow it commercially in Guatemala and S.A. Its commercial production centers in Indonesia and the Belgian Congo. A related tree, the one below, is somewhat planted in extreme southern Fla. and is hardy nowhere else. They have opposite,* stalked leaves and small flowers in terminal clusters (panicles*). Corolla tubular, its 5 lobes spreading. (For details *see* RUBIACEAE.) Fruit a capsule,* splitting from the base upward. (Named for Doña Francisca Henriquez de Rivera, wife of the Count of Chinchon, and long, but erroneously, supposed to be the first prominent European to be cured of malaria by quinine, in Lima, in 1630.)

officinalis. A tree long thought to be the best source of quinine, now replaced by Javanese hybrids. Commonly called quina or Peruvian bark. Leaves oval, or longer, 3–5 in. long. Flowers rose-pink, ½ in. long, the clusters 5–6 in. long. Peru and Bolivia. Somewhat planted from Palm Beach southward, but of little decorative value, and of no importance as a source of quinine.

CINERARIA. As a name cineraria is a little confusing. To the florist it means very showy greenhouse plants with usually bright blue flowers. And some of the hort. varieties are of many other colors, except yellow. These are all derived from a single, woolly-leaved, perennial herb from the Canary Islands properly called *Senecio cruentus* (which see for botanical characters).

But cineraria also applies to some plants known as dusty miller, and for these see *Senecio Cineraria.* And cineraria, as a specific name, has also been used for a species of *Centaurea.*

From the hort. standpoint we can dismiss all but the florists' cineraria (*Senecio cruentus*). This is a very widely grown greenhouse plant forced into profuse bloom, especially in the fall. Their culture should not be attempted without a greenhouse, and this must be kept cool (50° at night, not over 60° in the day).

Part of the attraction of a finely flowered cineraria plant is the large truss of flowers well above the handsome foliage. To secure this the following directions should be noted. For fall and winter bloom all the single varieties are started from seed sown in May, preferably in flats in the cold frame or in a cool greenhouse. As the seedlings develop pot them up in successively larger pots, but always keep them on the edge of being pot-bound. By fall most plants should be only in 5- or 6-in. pots, only the largest in 8-in. pots. Use potting mixture* 3.

During growth up to the 6-in. pot stage many of the plants will have a tendency to bloom. This must be checked by pinching out all buds. Also, to keep the plants bushy so that the final truss of flowers will stand well above the foliage, pinch off any branches that will make the plant leggy.

In the case of the double-flowered varieties they are best increased by cuttings that may be made of the vigorous shoots that start after the flowering top is cut off. After root-

---

* Special articles on the subjects indicated by an asterisk (*) will be found at the words so marked.

ing in sand, these are potted up and handled exactly as are the seedlings from single varieties.

Cinerarias make fine window garden plants, but only if the room is a cool one. Any temperature above 65° will quickly spoil them.

INSECT PESTS. *See* aphids and thrips at CHRYSANTHEMUM, leaf tiers at CELERY, whiteflies at BEGONIA and red spider mite at CARNATION. For sowbugs, centipedes, millipedes, snails, slugs, *see* INSECT PESTS.

DISEASES. Plants may, on occasion, have brown pustules on the leaves caused by a rust* fungus. A powdery mildew* may spot the leaves with powdery white areas. Leaves or entire plants may occasionally turn yellow as a result of a virus or wilt* fungus. As a general rule, the cineraria is relatively free from disease.

cinerea, -us, -um (sy-neer'ee-a). Cinereous; *i.e.*, ashy or ash-colored.

cinnabarina, -us, -um (sin-na-ba-ry'na). Vermilion-red.

cinnamomea, -us, -um (sin-a-mō'mee-a). Cinnamon-like, or of cinnamon color.

CINNAMOMUM (sin-na-mō'mum). A genus of commercially important, aromatic, evergreen trees of the family Lauraceae, mostly from tropical Asia, two of them widely grown as the source of camphor and cinnamon. Leaves often distinctly 3-veined from the base. Flowers small, not showy, without petals, the calyx 6-lobed. Stamens* 9 or fewer, in three series together with a fourth series of sterile stamens. Fruit a berry, set in a cuplike receptacle.* (*Cinnamomum* is from the old Greek name for cinnamon.)

The two below are occasionally planted in zone* 9, or the most favorable sites in zone* 8, not so much for ornament as for the interest of their products. Neither is of commercial importance in the U.S., and true cinnamon (*C. zeylanicum*) is rarely cult. here but is an important industry in Ceylon. Outdoors the trees do well in a sandy loam or on a variety of other soils in southern Fla. In the greenhouse they need a warm house (60°–75°) and potting mixture* 5.

Camphora. Camphor tree. Not over 40–50 ft. high. Leaves alternate,* more or less elliptic, but tapering at the tip, 4–5 in. long, pale underneath. Flowers yellow, the clusters shorter than the leaves. China and Japan. Bruised foliage is camphor-scented, and the wood (in Formosa) is the commercial source of camphor. Occasionally planted as a park tree in southern Calif., and the Gulf Coast, where it occasionally escapes.*

Cassia. Cassia-bark tree. A tree 30–45 ft. high with opposite* leaves that are oblongish and 4–6 in. long. Flowers yellowish-white, the densely hairy clusters as long as the leaves. China. Largely grown in the Far East as a fraudulent adulterant of true cinnamon. Little grown here, but occasionally seen in southern Fla. and Calif.

CINNAMON FAMILY = Lauraceae.

CINNAMON FERN = *Osmunda cinnamomea.*

CINNAMON ROSE = *Rosa cinnamomea.*

CINNAMON VINE = *Dioscorea Batatas.*

CINQUEFOIL. *See* POTENTILLA.

CION (sy'on). Often spelled scion. A detached shoot of a woody plant, containing two or more buds to be used in grafting.*

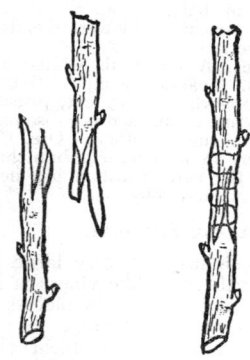

Cion and stock. At the left the cion, above, and the stock, below, cut ready for grafting. At the right, cion and stock waxed and bound ready for uniting.

The purpose of a cion (as distinguished from a cutting which will be rooted) is to insert it in a stock. When cion and stock have completely united the buds of the cion will continue to produce growth similar to the plant from which it was cut, not that of the stock into which it was grafted. Upon this fact has been built the whole reason and technique of grafting.* *See also* BUDDING.

CIRCASSIAN SEEDS. *See* ADENANTHERA.

CIRCASSIAN WALNUT. The wood of the English walnut (*Juglans regia.*) *See* WALNUT.

circinalis, -e (sir-si-nay'lis). Coiled.

circinata, -us, -um (sir-si-nay'ta). Coiled.

CIRCUMNEUTRAL. A term for most ordinary garden soils whose range of soil acidity is indicated by the pH value 6.00–8.00. Most garden plants appear to be relatively indifferent to a soil acidity or alkalinity within this range. For details *see* ACID AND ALKALI SOILS.

CIRCUMPOSITION = Air layering. *See* LAYERING.

CIRSIUM (sir'si-um). Thistles are more often weeds than garden plants. Of 200 known species (family Compositae) scattered over the north temperate zone, only a very few are of any garden interest, and some are most pernicious weeds. They are prickly herbs with alternate* or basal leaves that are nearly always cut or lobed, and horribly spiny-margined. Flowers tiny, tubular (all disk* flowers), crowded in a dense, usually spiny-bracted,* head, and often very handsome. (*Cirsium* is from the Greek for a kind of thistle.)

---

* Special articles on the subjects indicated by an asterisk (*) will be found at the words so marked.

The two garden plants are biennials of easy culture in any garden soil, and their winter rosettes quite handsome. *See* Biennials.

arvense. Canada thistle. One of the worst weeds in N.A. *See* Canada thistle in the list at Weeds.

diacantha. Fishbone thistle. Not over 3 ft. high. Leaves narrowly lance-shaped, not deeply cut, about 4 in. long, smooth above but densely white-hairy beneath. Flower heads purple. Syria. Summer.

occidentale. A beautiful, white-woolly herb 2–3 ft. high. Leaves oblongish, 6–9 in. long, toothed or somewhat deeply cut, prickly. Flower heads about 2 in. across, rose-purple and showy. Calif. and southern Ore. The *var.* **coulteri** differs in having long branches with a single head; the *var.* **venustum** has heads more webby than white-woolly.

CIRUELA. *See* Spondias.

CISSUS (sis′sus). A very large genus of chiefly tropical, grape-like vines (a few non-hort. herbs) of the family Vitaceae, differing from the closely related grape in having an inedible berry, and in technical characters. The cult. species are thick-leaved, handsome-foliaged vines, much grown outdoors in southern Calif. and Fla. (hardy elsewhere only as indicated below) and in greenhouses. Leaves sometimes evergreen, alternate,* simple* and lobed, or compound.* All climb by tendrils.* Flowers small, inconspicuous, with 4 expanding petals. (*Cissus* is from the Greek for ivy.) The cult. species are often known as treebine or grape ivy.

antarctica. Kangaroo vine. An Australian greenhouse vine, the stalked leaves ovalish or oblong, 3–4 in. long, half as wide, shining and more or less leathery. Hardy in zone* 9, possibly in protected places in zone* 8.

capensis. Evergreen grape. Strong-growing evergreen vine, much used in nearly frost-free regions for arbors. Tendrils* forked. Leaves simple,* 4–8 in. wide, strongly 3-veined, the margin broadly wavy or toothed, the young growth rusty. Fruit red-black, about ½ in. in diameter. S. Af. Hardy outdoors only in zones* 8 and 9, possibly in zone* 7 in protected places. Also called *Rhoicissus capensis.*

discolor. A beautiful, slender, greenhouse foliage plant persistently cursed with the name trailing begonia. It has nothing to do with begonia. Leaves simple,* oblongish or ovalish, 4–6 in. long, somewhat tapering at the tip, finely toothed and highly colored. The leaves are generally green above, but blotched with white, pink or red-purple, or all of them; and purple beneath. Java. Needs a warm, moist greenhouse and potting mixture* 4. Not high-climbing, and easily grown over a bamboo trellis.

incisa. Marine ivy. A native of the southern U.S. and a strong-growing vine up to 30 ft. long. Leaves compound* and with 3 leaflets, or simple* and deeply 3-lobed, the ultimate segments about 1 in. long and toothed. Fruit black, about ¾ in. long, on recurved stalks. Mo. to Ariz., Tex. and Fla. Hardy outdoors possibly from zone* 5, certainly from zone* 6, southward.

rhombifolia. A climbing, greenhouse vine, the stems angled. Leaves of 3 oblique, but somewhat heart-shaped, leaflets, the middle one nearly 4 in. long, all rusty-hairy on the veins

beneath. Tropical America. Perhaps the most popular as a house plant.

striata. A low, shrubby, tendril-climbing vine with evergreen, hairy foliage. Leaves compound,* the 3–5 leaflets arranged finger-fashion, usually not over 1 in. long (thrice this on some shoots), toothed. Fruit small, 2–4-seeded. S.A. Hardy outdoors in zones* 8 and 9, elsewhere to be grown in the cool greenhouse in potting mixture* 4.

CISTACEAE (siss-tay′see-ee). The rockrose family is a small one, and of its 7 genera and over 170 species, only *Cistus* and *Helianthemum* are of any garden interest. They are low shrubs or woody herbs, mostly from the north temperate zone, usually with quickly wilting or ephemeral, but often showy, flowers.

Leaves usually opposite,* but the upper ones alternate* in *Helianthemum.* Flowers regular,* usually with 5 petals, solitary or in small clusters. In *Cistus* the flowers are showy, and there are many garden hybrids with white, lilac, or rose-pink bloom. In *Helianthemum* the flowers are usually smaller and of various colors. The fruit in both genera is a dry pod (capsule*) splitting into 3, 5, or rarely 10 valves.*

Technical flower characters: Sepals 5, the three inner often persistent, the two outer ones bract*-like, smaller, and sometimes lacking. Petals mostly 5. Stamens numerous. Ovary superior,* 1-celled, or rarely incompletely 5- or 10-celled, with 2 to many ovules. Style with a 3-lobed or single stigma.

CISTUS (sis′tus). Mediterranean shrubs of low stature and usually called rockrose (family Cistaceae). Long known in Old World gardens, they are less known here, perhaps because they do not stand northern winters. Leaves opposite,* simple,* without marginal teeth,* evergreen or nearly so, generally softly hairy. Flowers large, somewhat suggesting a single rose, with 5 separate petals, but many stamens.* Fruit a capsule splitting by 5 or 10 valves. (*Cistus* is the classical Greek name for these plants.)

The rockroses are handsome garden plants, but need particular attention to soil and climatic restrictions. Most of them are partial to well-drained, open soils, not acid, and preferably somewhat derived from limestone. They must have open sunlight, and will not tolerate slushy, bitter winters. In Calif. and the South they are easily grown, elsewhere only as indicated below. The plants are difficult to move, except when young, consequently seedlings are best kept in pots until ready to be planted out, and then the plants should be let alone. They may also be increased by layering. But an easier method is to make cuttings of non-flowering side shoots, rooted in a sand-filled box covered with glass, preferably from Aug. to Oct. The lower-growing species are excellent rock garden plants.

albidus. From 4–6 ft. high, the foliage white-hairy. Leaves stalkless, oblongish or elliptic, 1–2½ in. long. Flowers about 2 in.

wide, rose-lilac, blotched yellow at the center. June. Hardy from zone° 6 southward.

corbariensis. A hybrid shrub, 18–30 in. high and more or less bushy, the twigs downy, as are the ovalish leaves. Flowers about 1½ in. wide, white, with a yellow "eye." Hardy from zone° 5 southward. Summer.

creticus = *Cistus villosus creticus.*

crispus. Not over 2 ft. high, and a compact shrub. Leaves stalkless, softly white-hairy, more or less elliptic, about 1 in. long and wrinkled. Flowers deep purple-red, about 2 in. across, in a close terminal cluster. June–July. Hardy possibly from zone° 5, surely from zone° 6, southward.

ladaniferus. A sticky-branched shrub scarcely over 4 ft. high. Leaves slightly stalked, green and sticky above, densely white-hairy beneath, lance-shaped, 3–4 in. long. Flowers solitary, white, but purple-blotched at the center, nearly 3½ in. wide. July–Aug. Hardy from zone° 6 southward. The *var.* **maculatus** has a brownish-red center to the flower, and *var.* **albiflorus** has white but yellow-centered flowers.

laurifolius. A shrub 5–8 ft. high. Leaves stalked, ovalish, 1¾–2½ in. long, green above and sticky, densely white or brown-hairy beneath. Flowers nearly 2½ in. wide, in clusters (cymes°), white, with a yellow center. July to Sept. Hardy from zone° 6 southward.

purpureus. A hybrid shrub 3–4 ft. high, the twigs sticky-hairy. Leaves oblongish, 1–2 in. long, nearly stalkless. Flowers showy, 2–3 in. wide, reddish-purple, with a darker "eye." Hardy from zone° 6 southward.

villosus. A compact shrub not over 3 ft. high. Leaves stalked, elliptic or ovalish, 1–2½ in. long, rough and hairy, especially beneath. Flowers about 2½ in. wide, rose or rose-purple, but with a yellow center, borne in a cyme.° June–July. Hardy from zone° 5, and possibly from zone° 4, southward. The *var.* **creticus** has smaller leaves and purple flowers. The *var.* **tauricus** is a lower shrub and has some leaves roundish. It is more hardy than the typical form or than the *var.* **creticus.**

CITRADIA. A citrus hybrid between the orange and *Poncirus trifoliata.*

CITRANGE. A hybrid citrus fruit derived from crossing the sweet orange with *Poncirus trifoliata.* It has little or no value for fresh fruit, but is used somewhat in cooking or for making citrangeade. The plant is hardier than the sweet orange, and can be grown as far north as zone° 7. The fruits, of little importance, are about 2–3 in. in diameter, and are more acid and have a more distinctive odor than the orange. The citrange is chiefly of use as material for professional citrus breeders.

CITRANGEQUAT. An interesting plant to citrus breeders, derived from crossing the citrange and the kumquat. It has yellow, orange, or reddish fruits 1½–2 in. in diameter, of no commercial importance, but used in cooking and for beverages.

citrata, -us, -um (sit-tray'ta). Citrus-like as to color, flavor or odor.

citrifolia, -us, -um (sit-tri-fō'li-a). With leaves like *Citrus.*

citrina, -us, -um (sit-try'na). Like, or colored like, citron.

citriodora, -us, -um (sit-tri-o-door'ra). With the fragrance of the lemon.

citroides (sit-troy'deez; but *see* OÏDES). Citron-like.

CITRON. The preserved rind of *Citrus medica,* or the tree itself. Citron also applies to a form of the watermelon better known as the citron melon or preserving melon. See WATERMELON.

CITRONALIS = *Lippia citriodora.*

CITRONELLA. See COLLINSONIA CANADENSIS, but this is not the source of citronella, for which *see* CYMBOPOGON.

CITRONELLA GRASS = *Cymbopogon Nardus,* the source of citronella.

CITRON MELON = *Citrullus vulgaris citroides.* See WATERMELON.

CITROPSIS (sit-trop'sis). Spiny African trees of the family Rutaceae, one of them of interest to citrus breeders and somewhat as an ornamental in southern Calif. and Fla. Spines usually in pairs. Leaves compound,° the 3–5 leaflets arranged feather-fashion. Flowers much as in the orange, but the petals strap-shaped. Fruit like a lime in appearance but sweet. (*Citropsis* is from Greek for *Citrus*-like.)

schweinfurthi. African cherry-orange. A shrub or small tree. Leaflets broadly lance-shaped, 2–5 in. long. Flowers in clusters of 4–10, not over 1 in. wide. Fruit about 1½ in. in diameter. S. Af. to the Congo. Little known in U.S. as yet.

citrosma, -us, -um (sit-tros'ma). Lemon-scented.

CITRULLUS. See WATERMELON.

CITRUMELO. A citrus hybrid between the grapefruit and *Poncirus trifoliata.*

CITRUMQUAT. A citrus hybrid between the kumquat and *Poncirus trifoliata.*

CITRUS (sit'rus). Here belong the incomparably important citrus fruits, all derived from this genus of only a dozen species of the family Rutaceae. All of them came originally from tropical or sub-tropical Asia or Indo-Malaya, but are now spread all over the world as cult. fruits of the greatest importance, or as innumerable escapes,° many of which are worthless. They are (or were before cult. modified them) often spiny, rather small, highly aromatic trees which have a compound° leaf on which only a single leaflet is found (therefore appearing as if with simple leaves). In most of them there is a distinctly winged leafstalk. Flowers solitary or in few-flowered clusters often very fragrant (orange, especially). Petals 5, white, often waxy. Fruit a special form of berry known as a hesperidium. This is globose or lemon-shaped, often has several compartments separated by the rag,° much pulpy juice, and a spongy rind beset with aromatic oil glands. (*Citrus* is a classical name applied to some other tree, but adopted by Linnaeus for the citrus fruits.) Besides the common citrus fruits there are

---

° Special articles on the subjects indicated by an asterisk (°) will be found at the words so marked.

several other plants in the genus *Citrus* grown for ornament. They are also described below. For the culture and best varieties of the important ones *see* the special articles at ORANGE, LIME, LEMON, and GRAPEFRUIT. In addition to those below there are the interesting hybrids known as citrange, citrangequat, limequat, and tangelo (*see* these terms). See also FORTUNELLA (for the kumquat).

aurantifolia. Lime. A small spiny tree. Leaves elliptic or oblongish, 2–3 in. long, the stalk narrowly winged. Flowers scarcely ½ in. long. Fruit generally round-oval, 1½–2½ in. in diameter, very acid. Asia. For culture and varieties *see* LIME. The sweet lime (*C. Limetta*) is a variety or perhaps a separate species. *See* LIME.

Aurantium. Seville or sour orange. A small tree with long but not especially sharp spines. Leaves oval or oblong, 3–4 in. long, stalk broadly winged. Flowers very fragrant, about ¾ in. long. Fruit acid, the rag* also bitter, flattened-globe-shaped, about 3½ in. in diameter. Cochin-China. Little cult. in the U.S., but in Spain, the finest orange for marmalade. It is more hardy than the common orange. *See* ORANGE.

Bergamia. Bergamot. A spiny tree with oblong-oval leaves, the stalks winged. Fruit sour, pear-shaped, about 3½ in. in diameter. It yields an essential oil, as cult. in Eu., but is little known here.

grandis = *Citrus maxima.*

japonica = *Fortunella japonica.*

Limetta. *See* LIME (the fruit).

Limonia. Lemon. A small tree, its spines or thorns short and stiff. Leaves oblong or elliptic, 2–3½ in. long, finely but bluntly toothed, the stalk very narrowly winged or merely margined. Flowers ⅓–⅔ in. long, white, but pinkish outside. Fruit egg-shaped, but with a nipple-like projection at the end (umbonate), very sour. Asia. For culture and varieties *see* LEMON.

maxima. Shaddock, also pummelo and pompelmous. Tropical tree 15–25 ft. high, not usually spiny. Leaves 4–8 in. long, hairy beneath, the stalk widely winged. Fruit pear-shaped, very large, the flesh coarse and inferior to the grapefruit. East Indies, from which a Capt. Shaddock brought it to Barbados in 1696. Little known here except in southern Fla.

medica. Citron. A shrub or small tree with stiff, short spines. Leaves 4–6 in. long, toothed, the stalk without wings. Flowers about 1½ in. long, white, but purplish outside. Fruit 7–10 in. long, more or less oval or oblong, lemon-yellow, its rough, thick skin highly aromatic and candied to make commercial citron. Asia. Much grown in southern Eu., only occasionally in Fla. and Calif.

mitis. Calamondin orange; called, also, Panama orange, although a native of the Philippines. A nearly spineless small tree with oblongish leaves having narrowly winged stalks. Flowers about ⅓ in. long. Fruit globe-shaped or slightly flattened at the ends, about 1 in. in diameter, the skin loose, the pulp acid. Hardier than the orange, but little grown.

nobilis. King orange. A nearly spineless tree with broadly oval leaves that are only narrowly winged on the leafstalk. Flowers about ⅓ in. long. Fruit orange or reddish, flattened at each end, with a loose, thin skin, and sweet or slightly acid pulp. Cochin-China. Little grown but of interest as the source of two varieties: *var.* **deliciosa,** tangerine, also the mandarin orange. Leaves oval-lance-shaped, 1½–2½ in. long, the stalks scarcely margined. Fruit 2–3 in. in diameter, smooth, reddish-orange, the segments so easily separating that the fruit is sometimes called kid-glove orange, *i.e.*, it need not moisten the hands; *var.* **unshiu,** Satsuma orange. Leaves 3–4 in. long and broader than in the tangerine. Fruit depressed globose, about 2½ in. in diameter, the pulp orange-color, sweet. A very hardy variety.

paradisi. Grapefruit; called, also, pomelo. A tree much like *C. maxima* but larger, and with the leaves not hairy beneath. Fruit 4–8 in. in diameter, usually borne in clusters, the pulp fine-grained, moderately acid. Origin unknown. For culture and varieties *see* GRAPEFRUIT.

sinensis. The common or sweet orange. A medium-sized tree (15–25 ft. as cult.) with a few bluntish spines or none. Leaves oblong-oval, 3–5 in. long, the stalk narrowly winged. Flowers white, fragrant, but not so fragrant as those of the sour orange. Fruit a depressed sphere, 3–5 in. in diameter, the pulp sweet. China. For culture and varieties *see* ORANGE.

taitensis. Otaheite or Tahiti orange. A pretty little miniature orange tree much grown by florists, of unknown origin but not from Tahiti in spite of its widely used common name. Usually not over 2–3 ft. high. Leaves oblongish, 2–3½ in. long, the stalk narrowly winged. Flowers white, but pinkish outside. Fruit bright orange, but lemon-shaped, about 1½ in. long, ornamental because they are numerous, but of insipid taste. A decorative plant well suited for the window garden, but best grown in a cool greenhouse in potting mixture* 4.

trifoliata = *Poncirus trifoliata.*

CITRUS FAMILY = Rutaceae.

CITRUS FRUITS. The chief ones, each the subject of a special article, are orange, lemon, grapefruit, and lime. For other citrus fruits *see* CITRUS.

CITY GARDEN. *See* PLANNING THE HOME GROUNDS and BACKYARD GARDEN.

CLADANTHUS (kla-dan'thus). A single herb of the family Compositae, a native of southern Spain and Morocco and grown as a hardy annual in the flower garden. The only species, **C. arabicus,** is a branching herb 2–3½ ft. high, with strongly scented foliage. Leaves alternate,* parted feather-fashion, the segments narrow and 3-toothed or divided at the end. Flowers yellow, the heads composed of both ray and disk* flowers, the head solitary and the plant often forking beneath it. It is sometimes listed as *Anthemis arabica* and is of easy culture if the seed is sown where the plant is wanted. *See* ANNUALS. (*Cladanthus* is from the Greek for branch and flower, in allusion to its peculiar branching habit.)

cladocalyx (klad-o-cay'licks). With a club shaped calyx.*

CLADODE. A cladophyll.

CLADOPHYLL. An expanded, leaf-like branch, a common example of which is found in the butcher's-broom. *See* RUSCUS.

CLADRASTIS (kla-dras'tis). A small genus of North American and eastern Asiatic decorative trees of the pea family, the na-

---

* Special articles on the subjects indicated by an asterisk (*) will be found at the words so marked.

tive yellow-wood often planted for ornament. They have alternate,* compound* leaves, the leaflets arranged feather-fashion, with an odd one at the end. Flowers fragrant, white (in ours), pealike, in showy clusters (panicles*). Pod (legume*) oblongish, flattened. (*Cladrastis* is from the Greek for fragile and branch, in allusion to the usually brittle twigs.)

The yellow-wood is deservedly popular for its showy bloom, and will thrive in a variety of soils. Easily propagated by spring-sown seeds.

lutea. Kentucky yellow-wood; also called gopherwood. A smooth-barked tree, 30–50 ft. high, its wood yellow. Leaflets 7–9, ovalish and about 3–4 in. long. Flowers about 1 in. long, the cluster 10–20 in. long and drooping. Pod 4–5 in. long. Ga. and N. Car. to Ill. and Mo. Hardy from zone* 3 southward. The tree was for long known as *C. tinctoria.*

CLAMMY LOCUST = *Robinia viscosa.* See LOCUST.

clandonensis, -e (klan-do-nen'sis). From Clandon, Surrey, England.

CLARIN = *Phaedranthus buccinatorius.*

CLARKIA (clark'i-a). Very showy annual herbs of the family Onagraceae, mostly from the western U.S., one of them popular in the flower garden, and the other also much grown. They have alternate,* narrow leaves, without marginal teeth or very small ones, and handsome flowers which are solitary or in few-flowered clusters. Petals 4, clawed,* the upper part widely spreading and sometimes 3-toothed. Fruit a somewhat 4-angled, narrow capsule.* (Named for Captain Wm. Clark of Lewis and Clark fame.)

The two below are of the easiest culture if treated as hardy annuals (*see* ANNUALS). Unlike many others, these should not be thinned out too much, as they appear to bloom better when somewhat crowded. They flower from July 1 or soon after, until Oct.

breweri. *See* EUCHARIDIUM.

concinnum. *See* EUCHARIDIUM.

elegans. Stems erect, reddish, 18–36 in. high. Leaves ovalish, remotely toothed. Flowers purple or rose-colored, but whitish in some hort. forms, nearly 2½ in. wide. Claw* of the petal not toothed. Pod about 1 in. long. Calif. A good named form is Salmon Queen, and a red variety is called Vesuvius.

pulchella. Lower and with narrower leaves. Flowers lilac (white in some hort. forms), the claw* of the petal with 2 recurved teeth. British Columbia to Calif.

There are many hybrids between these two species, some of them double-flowered, and all of them superior to the wild species. They make fine flowers for cutting.

CLARY = *Salvia Sclarea.*

CLASPING. Surrounding the stem, as the leaves of some honeysuckles.

CLASSIFICATION OF PLANTS. See PLANT FAMILY and PLANT NAMES.

Clava-Herculis, -e (kla-va-her'kew-lis). Club of Hercules. *See* ZANTHOXYLUM.

clavata, -us, -um (kla-vay'ta). Clavate; *i.e.,* club-shaped.

CLAW. The long, usually narrow, basal part of a petal, common in some flowers of iris, rose, lily, pink, *Clarkia,* and many others. Such petals are said to be *clawed.*

CLAW-FERN. *See* ONYCHIUM.

CLAY. *See* SOILS and SOIL CONDITIONERS.

CLAYTON FERN = *Osmunda claytoniana.*

CLAYTONIA (clay-tō'ni-a). The spring beauty of our meadows is one of perhaps two dozen species of slender, perennial herbs of the family Portulacaceae, sometimes transferred to the wild garden. Both those below need partial shade and a moist site. They have tuberous roots (corm*), and slender, weak, narrow leaves without marginal teeth. Flowers blooming very early in spring, pink or white, often streaked, borne in few-flowered, lax clusters. Petals 5. Stamens 5. Fruit a small pod with 3 valves. (Named for John Clayton, early American botanist of Virginia.)

Both the plants below will completely disappear by midsummer. They bloom just before the forest canopy comes into leafage, but soon die down. Their culture is easy in moist places under partial shade, impossible on dry sites.

caroliniana. Resembling the next, but with broader leaves and smaller flowers. A mountain plant chiefly in wet woods, eastern N.A. April.

virginica. The common spring beauty, commonly called Mayflower, grass-flower, and good-morning-spring. A slender herb 4–6 in. high. Leaves narrowly lance-shaped, 2–5 in. long. Flowers white, but often tinged with pink or streaked with it, about ⅝ in. wide, very fleeting, and wilting at once if picked. In moist thickets or woods throughout eastern N.A.

CLAYWEED = *Tussilago Farfara.*

CLEAR-EYE = *Salvia Sclarea.*

CLEAVERS. *See* GALIUM.

CLEISTOCACTUS (kly-sto-cac'tus). A genus of over a dozen species of erect or climbing, S.A. cacti with slender, many-ribbed stems, scarcely or only slightly branched, and with many slender but very sharp spines. Flowers lateral on the stem, orange and red, never completely opening, narrowly tubular, the stamens* extending beyond the corolla.* Fruit fleshy and spineless. (*Cleistocactus* is from the Greek for closed and *Cactus,* in allusion to the unopening of the flowers.) For culture *see* CACTI (greenhouse species).

baumanni. A scarcely branched, slender cactus 4–5 ft. high, the stems about 1½ in. thick, and the 12–16 ribs shallow. Spines 15–20 in each cluster, about ¼ in. long. Flowers slightly irregular, numerous, about 3 in. long, but slender. Southern S. A.

straussi. Branching from the base, the stems erect and slender, usually less than 3 ft. high, the many ribs (23–27) shallow, its spines sharp,

---

* Special articles on the subjects indicated by an asterisk (*) will be found at the words so marked.

numerous, bristle-like. Flowers nearly 4 in. long, red. Bolivia.

CLEISTOGAMOUS FLOWERS. Small, often partly underground flowers that never open and are self-pollinated. Some plants, as the violets, have both ordinary and cleistogamous flowers.

clematidea, -us, -um (klem-a-tid′-e-a). Like a clematis.

clematiflora, -us, -um (klem-a-ti-flow′ra). With clematis-like flowers.

CLEMATIS (klem′a-tis). A genus of perhaps 270 species of herbs, or shrubby or woody vines of the buttercup family, widely distributed, but most numerous in eastern As., the Himalayas, and N.A. Leaves opposite, mostly compound,* sometimes simple,* but usually with 3–5, or more, leaflets, the leaf-stalk often curling and acting as a tendril.* Flowers frequently very showy, without petals, but with 4 petal-like sepals, sometimes 5–8. Stamens* numerous, some of them occasionally sterile or even petal-like. Fruit a collection of 1-seeded achenes,* each (in some species) with a plumed, feathery, and often showy, tail-like appeandage. (*Clematis* is from the Greek for a slender vine.) Many of the species are called virgin's-bower.

For culture and many beautiful hybrids *see* below.

alpina. A woody vine, 4–7 ft. high. Leaflets nearly stalkless, ovalish, 1–3 in. long, coarsely toothed. Flowers violet-blue, bell-shaped, about 1½ in. long. Fruits plumed. Eurasia, Apr.–May. Hardy to zone* 2.

apifolia. A woody vine 5–9 ft. high. Leaflets oval-lance-shaped, 2–4 in. long, coarsely toothed or even lobed. Flowers dull white, ½–1 in. wide, in loose clusters (panicles*) in the leaf axils.* Fruits shortly plumed. Jap. Sept.–Oct. Hardy from zone* 1 southward.

armandi. An evergreen, woody vine 10–15 ft. high. Leaflets 3, on twisted stalks, generally oblongish, 3½–5½ in. long. Flowers white, 1½–2½ in. wide, in leafless clusters. Fruits long-plumed. China. May. Hardy in zones* 6 or 7, mostly in Calif.

coccinea = *Clematis texensis.*

crispa. Blue jasmine, called also bluebell, and curly clematis. A shrubby vine, 6–9 ft. high. Leaflets ovalish, 1¾–3½ in. long, sometimes lobed. Flowers nodding, solitary, bell-shaped, blue or bluish-purple to pale pink, ¾–1½ in. long. Fruits with silky, not plumed, appendages. June–Sept. Ill. and Va. to Fla. and Tex. Hardy from zone* 3 southward.

davidiana = *C. heracleifolia davidiana.*

douglasi. Sugar-loaf. An erect herb, 12–20 in. high. Leaves twice- or thrice-compound,* the leaflets narrow. Flowers solitary, about 1 in. long, tubular, purple inside but paler outside. Colo. to Wash. May–July. Hardy up to zone* 2.

durandi. A hybrid. *See* Clematis Culture (below).

Flammula. A woody vine 10–15 ft. high. Leaves twice- or thrice-compound,* the leaflets broadly oval or narrower, ¾–2 in. long. Flowers fragrant, white, nearly 1½ in. wide, in many-flowered clusters (panicles*). Mediterranean region to Persia. Aug.–Oct. Hardy, possibly, from zone* 5 southward.

fremonti. An erect herb 10–18 in. high. Leaves simple,* leathery and stalkless. Flower solitary, nodding, bell-shaped, purple, about 1 in. long. Mo. to Neb. May–Aug. Hardy everywhere.

graveolens = *Clematis orientalis.*

henryi. A common name in the trade for a fine var. of *Clematis lawsoniana* (which see).

heracleifolia. A somewhat woody Chinese perennial, 2–3 ft. high. Leaves with 3 leaflets that are somewhat wedge-shaped, coarsely toothed and a little hairy. Flowers blue, hairy on the outside, in loose clusters, not unlike those of a hyacinth. Most cult. in *var.* **davidiana** which is taller and has deeper blue and fragrant flowers.

integrifolia. An herb or under-shrub, usually not over 2½ ft. Leaves simple, stalkless, oval-oblong, and without teeth. Flowers solitary and terminal, violet-blue (rarely white). 1½–2 in. long, the stamens yellow. Fruit plumed. Eurasia. June–Aug. Hardy everywhere. *See* BLUE GARDEN.

jackmani. A showy, woody climber, perhaps the most widely cult. of all clematis, and of hybrid origin. Leaves compound,* or the upper ones simple, large and ovalish. Flowers usually in threes, sometimes 6 in. and usually more than 4 in. wide, violet-purple. July–Oct. Hardy from zone* 2 southward. For its numerous varieties or named forms *see* below.

jouiniana. A hybrid. *See* Clematis Culture (below).

lawsoniana. A group of hybrid, climbing clematis from which have come many fine hybrids. Best known is the *var.* **henryi** (often offered as *C. henryi*) which has showy white flowers nearly 6 in. wide, with black stamens.* Summer.

ligusticifolia. Hill clematis. A woody climber 10–15 ft. high. Leaves compound,* the 5–7 leaflets ovalish or narrower, 1–3½ in. long. Male and female flowers on different plants, about 1 in. wide, white, in cymes.* Western N.A. July–Oct. Hardy everywhere.

montana. A woody vine up to 20 ft. Leaflets 3, oblong or ovalish, short-stalked, 1½–4½ in. long, deeply toothed (rarely without any). Flowers 1–5, slender-stalked, white, 1½–3½ in. wide. Fruit plumed. China and Himalayas. May. Hardy without protection from zone* 4, with it from zone* 3, southward. The *var.* **rubens** has purplish young foliage and pink flowers. The *var.* **wilsoni** has larger white flowers than the typical form and blooms 1–2 months later. The first variety is somewhat more hardy than the typical *C. montana*, but the second variety a little less so.

orientalis. A woody vine 10–15 ft. high. Leaves compound* or twice-compound,* the leaflets ovalish or oblong, ¾–2 in. long. Flowers yellow, 1½–3 in. wide, solitary or in few-flowered clusters. Fruit long-plumed. Aug.–Oct. Persia to Himalayas. Hardy from zone* 2 or 3 southward. Sometimes called *C. graveolens*.

paniculata. Japanese clematis. A woody climber 20–30 ft. high. Leaflets 3–5, ovalish, 1½–4 in. long, without teeth, but sometimes lobed. Flowers white, fragrant, about 1½ in. wide, in a many-flowered cluster. Fruit plumed. Jap. Sept.–Oct. Hardy from zone* 2 southward. Also known as *C. dioscoreifolia robusta.*

pitcheri. A woody, high-climbing vine. Leaflets usually 3–6, ovalish, 1½–3½ in. long, with a fine, short tip at the end. Flowers urn-shaped, solitary, long-stalked, about 1½ in. long, purplish. Fruit not plumed. Central U.S. June–Sept. Hardy from zone* 3 southward. Sometimes called *C. simsi.*

---

* Special articles on the subjects indicated by an asterisk (*) will be found at the words so marked.

recta. An erect herb 2–5 ft. high. Leaflets 5–9, usually without teeth. Flowers white, fragrant, about 1 in. wide, in many-flowered clusters, mostly terminal. Southern Eu. June–Aug. Hardy everywhere, as are several varieties, one with double flowers.

serratifolia. A woody vine 6–9 ft. high. Leaves twice-compound,* the leaflets ovalish or narrower, 1½–3 in. long, toothed and sometimes 2–3-lobed. Flowers 1–3 together, yellow, 1–1½ in. long. Fruits plumed. Korea. Aug.–Oct. Hardy everywhere.

simsi = *Clematis pitcheri.*

tangutica. Golden clematis. A woody vine 6–9 ft. high. Leaves compound, the leaflets oblongish, 1½–2½ in. long. Flowers solitary, nodding, yellow. Fruits plumed. Northeastern As. June, and often again in the fall. Hardy everywhere.

texensis. Scarlet clematis. A slightly woody vine, 4–6 ft. high. Leaflets 4–8, the uppermost often replaced by a tendril,* broadly oval, 1¾–3½ in. long, bluish-green. Flowers solitary, stalked, urn-shaped, scarlet to rose-pink, about 1½ in. long, constricted near the top. Fruits plumed. Tex. July–Sept. Hardy from zone* 3 southward. Sometimes called *C. coccinea.*

verticillaris. Climbing up to 10 ft. or weak and sprawling without support. Leaflets 3, stalked, ovalish-oblong, 1½–3½ in. long, coarsely toothed or without teeth. Flowers solitary, nearly 3 in. wide, purple or bluish-purple. Fruits long-plumed. Eastern N.A. May–June. Hardy everywhere.

Viorna. Slender, woody vine, 6–9 ft. high. Leaflets 5–7, ovalish or oblong, 1½–3½ in. long, more or less wedge-shaped at the base, sometimes lobed. Flowers solitary, nodding, urn-shaped, dull reddish-purple, about 1 in. long. Fruits with brownish plumes. Pa. and Ga. westward. May–Aug. Hardy everywhere.

virginiana. Woodbine; also called love-vine and old-man's-beard. Climbing, often up to 18 ft. or often sprawling as a wild plant. Leaflets ovalish, 2½ to 4 in. long, coarsely toothed. Male and female flowers on separate plants, white, ¾–1½ in. wide in clusters (panicles*) in the leaf axils. Fruits plumed, the cluster of them nearly 2½ in. in diameter. Eastern N.A. Aug.–Oct. Hardy everywhere.

Vitalba. Traveler's-joy; called, also, old-man's-beard and withywind. A high-climbing, woody vine, sometimes up to 25 ft. Leaflets usually 5, oval-lance-shaped, 1½–4 in. long, coarsely toothed or sometimes 3-lobed. Flowers white, slightly fragrant, about 1 in. wide, in terminal clusters (panicles*) or these sometimes in the leaf axils.* Fruits long-plumed. Eu. and northern Africa. July–Oct. Hardy from zone* 3 southward.

Viticella. Vine bower. Slender, woody vine, not over 12 ft. high. Leaflets ovalish or narrower, ¾–2 in. long, blunt, without marginal teeth, but sometimes 3-lobed. Flowers 1–3, rose-purple or violet, about 1¾ in. wide, the stamens* yellow. Fruit scarcely or not at all plumed. Eurasia. June–Aug. Hardy from zone* 2, perhaps from zone* 1, southward. There is also a white-flowered *var.* alba.

The selection of the species treated above and the specifications of their hardiness in the different zones* are based upon the work of the late J. E. Spingarn, Esq., of Troutbeck, Amenia, N.Y., who also contributed the notes on *Clematis* culture below. The hardiness notes are based upon his collection at Amenia and upon others at Roslyn, L.I.; Bar Harbor, Me.; Montreal; Dropmore, Manitoba; and scattered reports from the South and West.

Clematis Culture

"Many years' experience among my plants," writes Wm. Robinson in the fifteenth edition of his *English Flower Garden,* "makes me more than ever convinced that the clematis is the most beautiful of our northern climbing plants." The genus is distinguished as much by variety as by beauty. It includes nearly three hundred species and an even larger number of beautiful hybrids. The colors include white, yellow, pink, red, lavender, mauve, violet, purple, and a host of intermediate shades. The shapes are almost as diverse, but fall more or less into three general forms, a type with small white flowers in panicles* or loose and irregular spreading clusters (*C. paniculata*), one with bell-shaped or urn-shaped flowers (*C. texensis*), and one with more or less flat or open flowers (*C. montana, C. jackmani*).

Clematis can be made to serve a great variety of purposes. They can be grown on trellises, fences, pergolas, walls, or mounds and tree stumps, or to cover the side of a house. Most of the wild species are found under shrubs or small trees, over which they scramble into the sunlight; and this practice should be more generally followed by gardeners, for nearly all species and varieties love a cool root-run with their heads in the sun.

SMALL- AND MEDIUM-FLOWERED SPECIES. *Clematis* species are scattered all over the world, but are especially numerous in Eastern Asia, the Himalayas, and North America. They are for the most part climbers, growing from five to fifty feet high. Of these every garden should contain at least such slender climbers as *C. tangutica* (yellow), *C. texensis* (scarlet to rose-pink), *C. crispa* (pale purplish-pink), and *C. Viticella* or *C. Viticella alba* (white), as well as the more rampant climbers like *C. montana* (white), *C. montana rubens* (pink), *C. paniculata* (white), and the pale lavender hybrid, *C. jouiniana*. Besides these there are some interesting non-climbers which are admirable for the herbaceous border or the front of the shrubbery, such as *C. recta* (white), *C. integrifolia* (blue with a mass of yellow stamens*), and the attractive blue hybrid *C. durandi*. The gardener need not be dependent on nurseries for the rarer species, for most of them can easily be grown from seed, which can be obtained from American specialists in rare seeds or from European seedsmen; among the delightful sorts that can be grown this way are *C. alpina, C. orientalis, C. serratifolia,* and *C. Viticella*. It is a pity that American gardeners do not take more interest in our native species; two have already been mentioned, *C. texensis* and *C. crispa,* but other sorts, such as *C. virginiana* or its western kinsman *C. ligusticifolia,* are also interesting.

LARGE-FLOWERED HYBRIDS. The large-

---

* Special articles on the subjects indicated by an asterisk (*) will be found at the words so marked.

flowered hybrids are the showiest members of the clematis clan, and are worthy of a place in the proudest garden. The first was produced in 1855, but it was not until *jackmani* was exhibited in 1863 that they captured the imagination of Europe. Since then about 500 varieties have been created, of which about 175 are still listed by European nurserymen; one English nursery alone offers 92 varieties. They were produced by crossing four species, three large-flowered ones from China and Japan (the creamy-white *C. florida,* the white to violet-blue *C. patens,* and the very large pale lavender *C. lanuginosa*) and one medium-flowered species from southern Europe (the rosy-purple *C. Viticella*). The hybrids are grouped into five general types according to the dominant strain in each, four of them receiving their names from the above-mentioned species and the fifth from *jackmani,* which has all the characteristics of a species or established form. The *florida* type and *patens* type bloom on old wood, while the *lanuginosa* type, *jackmani* type, and *Viticella* type bloom on the growing summer shoots. This determines the treatment to be given the plants, the first two requiring little or no pruning, and the last three enduring or in fact requiring more severe pruning.

The hybrids can be propagated by grafting, layering, or from cuttings; but plants on their own roots (that is, from cuttings or layering) should always be preferred when obtainable, and nurserymen should be discouraged from selling grafted plants. Nodal or internodal cuttings of young shoots taken in the greenhouse in January or February usually root in sand more readily than internodal cuttings taken, according to the older method, from half-ripe wood in late summer.

Only a few varieties are obtainable in this country at present, but this was certainly not always the case (one American nursery listed 73 in its 1890 catalogue), and it is not likely to remain the case for long, as the interest in *Clematis* is growing by leaps and bounds. Twenty varieties, most of them hardy as far north as Montreal, are widely accessible, and have proved their adaptability to our climate over a considerable period of years.

(*Note* by EDITOR.) Just before his death Mr. Spingarn selected the twenty best large-flowered hybrid clematis obtainable in the United States.

Variety	Color
Ascotiensis	azure-blue
Belle of Woking	double, silvery-gray
Comtesse de Bouchaud	satiny rose
Crimson King	bright red
Duchess of Albany	scarlet
Elsa Späth	bright blue
Gipsy Queen	dark velvety purple
Henryi	white
Jackmani superba	dark violet-purple
Lanuginosa candida	grayish white
Lady Caroline Neville	delicate mauve with darker bars
Lord Neville	dark plum
Madame Edouard André	velvety purplish red
Mrs. Cholmondeley	light blue
Nelly Moser	pale mauve with red bar
Prince Hendrik	azure-blue
Ramona	blue
Sir Garnet Wolseley	bronzy blue with plum-red bar
Ville de Lyon	reddish purple
William Kennett	deep lavender

All bloom on new wood except Belle of Woking and Sir Garnet Wolseley.

Besides the five types already mentioned, there is a sixth, the *texensis* type, with trumpet-shaped instead of open or flat flowers. This is the result of crossing our native *C. texensis* with some of the large-flowered hybrids; and of the charming varieties of this type, Duchess of York, Countess of Onslow, and Duchess of Albany are available here.

CULTURE. Clematis likes a cool, rich, moist, well-drained soil, preferably with lime in it. Most of the wild species, including those from which the large-flowered hybrids have been derived, are natives of limestone regions, but whether lime or the texture of the soil is of primary importance remains to be determined. Many species and varieties will thrive in a well-drained, lime-free soil, and in some cases grow even under pine trees, but all are apparently benefited by the use of lime. The addition of lime, leaf mold, and sand when planting is therefore recommended; and the plants should never be allowed to become too dry. They should be given a stable support as soon as they are set out, for the stems are brittle and easily broken by swaying in the wind; and shade of some sort should be provided for their root-runs if possible. An annual mulch of well-rotted manure is advisable, especially in the case of the large-flowered hybrids. Directions in regard to pruning have already been given, and it is merely necessary to add that *C. montana* and its varieties, as well as the hybrids, should receive no pruning except the cutting out of dead wood, while other species and hybrids will endure a considerable amount of pruning. But too much pruning is usually more dangerous than too little, and in any event lessens the picturesque effect. — J. E. S.

INSECT PESTS. Borers are best stopped by careful removal with a knife. Monthly spring–summer applications of a strong DDT (3x) to base of plant is suggested as a preventive.

CLEOME (klee-ō′me). Of the 75 known species of *Cleome,* which belongs to the family Capparidaceae, only one is of much garden importance, while another is an important bee plant in the western U.S. They are usually strong-smelling herbs, chiefly tropical, and (in ours) with compound* leaves with 3–7 leaflets arranged finger-fash-

---

* Special articles on the subjects indicated by an asterisk (*) will be found at the words so marked.

ion. Flowers solitary or in clusters, appearing irregular from the 4 long-clawed* petals, the long stamens and the stalked ovary.* Fruit a narrow pod (capsule*) on a long stalk. (*Cleome* is of unknown origin.)

The two below, both annuals, are of the easiest culture if the seeds are sown where the plants are wanted. The spiderflower needs plenty of space, which must be allowed for in thinning out the seedlings.

serrulata. Rocky Mountain bee-plant, also called stinking clover. An annual 2–3 ft. high. Leaflets 3. Flowers pink or white, 2–3 in. long and wide, the petals short-clawed.* Western U.S. and an important bee plant, especially in Calif., where it is planted for the purpose.

spinosa. Annual herb 4–5 ft. high and bushy. Leaflets 5–7, oblongish, long-stalked. Toward the top of the stem the leaves may be simple* and smaller. Flowers 2–3 in. long and wide, rose-purple or white, the petals long-clawed, and the stamens 2–3 in. long. Stalk of the fruit 3–6 in. long. Tropical America. Summer. A very popular garden annual sometimes sold as *C. pungens,* and often called spiderflower.

CLERODENDRON (kler-ro-den'dron).

Also spelled, perhaps correctly, *Clerodendrum.* A genus of perhaps 300 species of chiefly tropical shrubs, vines or trees of the family Verbenaceae, the cult. species often called glory-tree or glory-bower. They have opposite (or whorled*) leaves, often lobed but not compound,* malodorous when crushed. Flowers showy, in clusters (often panicles* or racemes*). Calyx often colored, more or less bell-shaped, and sometimes handsomer than the tubular corolla. Stamens 4, long-protruding and curved. Fruit fleshy, enclosed by the withered calyx. (*Clerodendron* is from Greek for chance and tree, and of no known application here.)

All except *C. trichotomum* are adapted to outdoor cult. only in zones* 7, 8, and 9. Otherwise they must be grown in the cool greenhouse, in potting mixture* 4. They may be propagated by cuttings of half-ripened wood over bottom-heat, in a greenhouse kept at about 70°. Most of them sucker* freely.

speciocissimum. A Javanese, showy, greenhouse shrub 3–4 ft. high, the ovalish, very hairy leaves, heart-shaped at the base, nearly 12 in. long. Flowers in panicles* 12–18 in. long, the bright scarlet flowers nearly 2 in. wide. An extremely handsome shrub suited only to greenhouse cult. except in zone* 9.

thomsonae. Bag-flower. A handsome, woody vine, much grown in greenhouses and outdoors on the Gulf Coast and Calif. See VINES. Leaves ovalish, 3–5 in. long, without teeth. Flowers very showy, in branching clusters, the calyx ivory-white, the corolla crimson. West Africa. It may be winter-killed, but blooms on new wood the next season. There are varieties with rose magenta flowers and with variegated leaves.

trichotomum. A shrub or small tree 7–20 ft. high. Leaves ovalish or elliptic, 3–7 in. long, tapering at the tip. Flowers fragrant, in long-stalked clusters, the corolla white, the calyx conspicuously reddish-brown. Fruit blue, set in the showy, reddish calyx. China and Jap. Aug.–Sept., the fruit lasting into late Oct. Hardy from zone* 4 southward.

CLETHRA (kleth'ra). White-flowered, usually very fragrant shrubs and trees of the heath family, comprising perhaps 30 species, most common in N.A. and eastern Asia, a few tropical. Leaves alternate,* toothed, short-stalked. Flowers in terminal, spire-like clusters (racemes*) with 5 sepals and 5 petals, neither tubular. Stamens 10. Fruit a 3-valved, many-seeded capsule.* (*Clethra* is the classical Greek for alder, which some species suggest.) Commonly called white alder.

The three below, especially *C. alnifolia,* are of the easiest culture in lime-free soils. The first two are native and may often be dug from the wild. Division of young growth is the easiest method of propagation.

acuminata. Shrub or small tree 10–18 ft. high. Leaves oval-oblong, 5–8 in. long. Flower cluster 4–10 in. long, the flowers nodding in the cluster, not fragrant. Pa. and W. Va. to Ga. and Tenn. Aug.–Sept. Hardy from zone* 5 southward.

alnifolia. Sweet pepperbush; also called spiked alder and summer-sweet. A shrub 3–9 ft. high. Leaves oblongish, pointed, 2½–5 in. long. Flowers very fragrant, the clusters numerous, erect, and about 5 in. long. Me. to Fla. and Tex. Aug.–Oct. Hardy from zone* 2 southward. Use soil with a pH of 4–5. There is also a pink-flowered variety.

barbinervis. A Japanese shrub or small tree 10–25 ft. high. Leaves oblongish, 3–6 in. long, tapering at the tip, wedge-shaped at the base. Flowers fragrant in branched, hairy clusters. Aug.–Oct. Hardy from zone* 4 southward.

CLETHRACEAE. See ERICACEAE.

clethroides (kleth-roy'deez; but *see* OÏDES). Like a white alder (*Clethra*).

CLEYERA = EURYA.

CLIANTHUS (kly-an'thus). Showy, Australasian vine-like plants of the pea family often grown on trellises in greenhouses or outdoors in zones* 8 and 9. See VINES. Leaves compound,* the many leaflets arranged feather-fashion, with an odd one at the end. Flowers red, typically pea-like, in profuse or sparse clusters, usually from the leaf axils,* and drooping. Pod (legume*) cylindric and leathery. (*Clianthus* is Greek for glory-flower.)

Greenhouse culture demands a cool house and potting mixture* 3. The plants will sprawl if not tied to a trellis. They are extremely showy plants. Propagation of the parrot's-bill by seeds or cuttings, of the glory-pea by grafts on a stock of *Colutea arborescens.* In the greenhouse they usually bloom in April or May.

dampieri. Glory-pea. Not over 4 ft. high and grayish-green, the stem white-hairy. Leaflets numerous, stalkless. Flower cluster with 4–6 blooms. Flowers nearly 3 in. long, scarlet, but with a black splotch on the lower part of the standard.* Pod silky-hairy. Aust.

puniceus. Parrot's-bill, also called parrot-beak and red kowhai. Taller, and practically without hairs on the stem. Leaflets short-stalked. Flower cluster with about 8 blooms. Flowers 3–4 in. long, crimson but soon fading, somewhat white-streaked at the base of the stand-

---

* Special articles on the subjects indicated by an asterisk (*) will be found at the words so marked.

ard.* Pod smooth. N. Z. There is a white-flowered variety.

CLIFF BRAKE. See PELLAEA.

CLIMATE. The accumulation of all the weathers, and the greatest single factor in the growth of plants. For purposes of analysis the Weather Bureau must separate climate into its significant parts, and for the gardener these are temperature, rainfall, and wind (see these terms). Of these, temperature and rainfall are much the most important. Both affect the suitability of plants for a particular section of the country and the last frost of spring and the first one in autumn dictate the time of many garden operations.

To discuss adequately the climate of the U.S. would take a volume bigger than this one. But the significant details of temperature and rainfall are so necessary to all intelligent gardeners that they have been prepared for each state of the Union and for the Canadian provinces. See the name of your state or province for these details.

How plants respond to the totality of these things — the climate — is quite another thing. It affects their hardiness (which see), and it is responsible for the separation of all the woody plants in this book into definite zones of hardiness. For a complete account of this see ZONE and the map there. See also MICRO-CLIMATE.

CLIMBING FERN. See LYGODIUM.

CLIMBING FIG = Ficus pumila.

CLIMBING FUMITORY = Adlumia fungosa.

CLIMBING HYDRANGEA = Hydrangea petiolaris.

CLIMBING NIGHTSHADE = Solanum Dulcamara.

CLIMBING PLANTS. See VINES.

CLIMBING SAILOR = Cymbalaria muralis.

CLIMBING YLANG-YLANG = Artabotrys odoratissimus.

CLINGSTONE. See FREESTONE.

CLINTONIA (klin-tone′i-a). A small genus of woodland, perennial herbs of the lily family found in N.A. and eastern Asia, not infrequently grown in the wild garden. They have long, underground rootstocks and basal, broad leaves without marginal teeth. Flowers at the end of a short stalk, usually in loose, lax umbels.* Petals and sepals scarcely distinguishable as such, totaling 6, and lily-like. Fruit a fleshy berry. (Named for De-Witt Clinton, Governor of N.Y.) The plants are sometimes called bear-tongue.

They need rich woods soil of pH 4–5, a reasonably moist site, and at least partial shade. Not as difficult to grow as some wild flowers and easily propagated by division of the rootstock. Not suited to open borders or beds.

andrewsiana. A perennial 18–24 in. high, the basal, sharp-pointed, oblongish leaves 6–8 in. long. Flowers bell-shaped, about ½ in. long, deep purple, in a loose, terminal cluster (umbel*). Berries blue. Calif. May.

borealis. Cow-tongue. Leaves broadly oval, but broadest toward the end, 4–7 in. long. Flowers ¾ in. long, greenish-yellow, nodding, the umbel* with 3–6 blooms. Berry blue. Eastern N.A. May.

umbellulata. Dog-plum, also called wild corn. Resembling the cow-tongue, but with smaller, white flowers (more numerous in the cluster) and black fruit. Mountain woods, N.Y. and N.J. to Ga. June.

uniflora. Queen-cup. A perennial, 6–8 in. high, the leaves oval-lance-shaped, the blade longer than its stalk. Flowers downy, usually solitary, 1–1½ in. wide, pure white. Berries blue. British Columbia to Calif. May.

For a totally unrelated plant, often mistakenly named *Clintonia pulchella*, see DOWNINGIA.

CLINTON'S FERN = Dryopteris clintoniana.

CLITORIA (kly-tow′ri-a). A large genus of chiefly tropical, perennial, but not woody vines of the pea family, the ones below natives of the U.S. and As. and sometimes grown for ornament. Leaves compound,* the leaflets arranged feather-fashion. Flowers pea-like, showy, the standard* much larger than the rest of the flower. Pod (legume*) stalked, narrow and flattened. (The origin of *Clitoria* is unprintable.)

Clitoria mariana is almost a weedy vine scrambling over bushes in the wild. It is easily grown in open, sandy soils. *C. ternatea*, a far more showy plant, is tropical and can be grown outdoors only in zones* 8 and 9, where it is an attractive vine.

mariana. Butterfly-pea. A smooth-stemmed vine, not over 4–5 ft. long. Leaflets 3, very veiny, oblongish or narrower. Flowers pale blue, nearly 2 in. long, appearing as if upside down. Pod about 2 in. long. N.J. to Fla. and westward. May–June.

ternatea. Taller, the slender stem hairy. Leaflets 5–7, ovalish, 1–2 in. long. Flowers dark blue, sometimes streaked with lighter blue, about 2 in. long. Pod about 4 in. long. Probably tropical Asia, but now naturalized all over the tropical world. June. Flowers sometimes white and double.

CLIVIA (kly′vi-a). Three South African species of perennial herbs of the family Amaryllidaceae, one a widely popular greenhouse plant and well suited for house decoration when in bloom. They have fleshy roots and a bulb-like swelling of the lower part of the stem formed by the expanded leaf bases. Leaves strap-shaped, evergreen. Flowers in a terminal umbel, the corolla funnel-shaped, the three inner segments wider than the outer ones. Fruit a red berry. (Named for a Duchess of Northumberland, one of the Clive family.)

The species below is a very stout herb needing plenty of space in the pot or tub. Its culture is the same as for *Amaryllis.*

miniata. Leaves thick, two-ranked, more or less strap-shaped and 1–2 in. wide. Flowers

---

* Special articles on the subjects indicated by an asterisk (*) will be found at the words so marked.

10–18 in the cluster, lily-like, scarlet but yellowish inside, the corolla 2–3 in. long. Berry about 1 in. long. Blooms in early spring, as a greenhouse plant. The species is far surpassed by some of the hybrid or improved hort. varieties, notably the *var.* **flava** with yellow flowers.

clivorum (kly-vor′rum). Of the hills.

CLOCHE. *See* BELL-JAR.

CLOCK-VINE = *Thunbergia.*

CLONE (also spelled **Clon**). A group of plants, often many thousands, all of which originated from one seedling plant, from which they have subsequently increased only by asexual reproduction, often by cuttings, by division, or by any method other than by seeds. Many garden plants are considered as units of a clone, notably the Baldwin apple, the Concord grape, and the iris known as Ambassadeur. Because gardeners and botanists have not always recognized the concept of a clone, many clones have been given varietal and specific names. At present there is no simple nomenclatorial machinery for differentiating clones from species or true varieties grown from seeds.

CLOSED GENTIAN = *Gentiana andrewsi.*

CLOSE-FERTILIZATION. *See* SELF-FERTILIZATION.

CLOTH. Commercial growers of summer cut flowers, grown outdoors, have found it profitable, at times, to protect their plants with a covering of cloth. Snapdragon, the garden aster, dahlia, chrysanthemum, gladiolus, *Clarkia,* marigold, and zinnia are among many garden flowers that were benefited.

The advantages are longer stems, larger and better blooms, protection from insect and fungus pests and from heavy rains or violent winds. While commercial growers construct elaborate cloth shelters, with insect-proof doors, most home gardeners will not need such an outlay. A tent-like cheesecloth box, stretched over one's plants, will accomplish the same purpose. If there are high winds or the structure is to be used for long periods, the cloth should be that supplied by dealers in florists' supplies. It should be 6–8 ft. high and sealed at all corners and at the ground level. The most extensive use of cloth is for the growing of tobacco for cigar wrappers. The shade helps to reduce the thickness of the leaf.

CLOTH-OF-GOLD = *Crocus susianus.*

CLOUD GRASS = *Agrotis nebulosa.*

CLOVE. As a hort. term, one of the small divisions of a separable bulb, as in garlic and shallot. The tree producing cloves (the spice) is not much, or perhaps not at all, cult. in the U.S.

CLOVE-PINK = *Dianthus Caryophyllus. See* CARNATION.

CLOVER. Extremely useful agricultural, forage plants of secondary interest to the gardener, except as some of them are constituents of lawn mixtures, and the value of the coarser ones as green manure. The genus **Trifolium** (try-fō′li-um), to which belong all those below, comprises over 300 species of the pea family, nearly all from temperate regions. Leaves compound,* in all of ours with 3 (rarely 4), usually toothed, leaflets, most of them stalkless. Flowers small, pea-like, but so proved only by careful dissection, crowded in dense heads. Fruit small, dry, 1–2-seeded, usually covered by the withered calyx. (*Trifolium* is Latin for 3 leaves.) All are splendid bee plants.

Few or none of those below are garden plants grown for ornament. Their value lies in the fact of their ability to absorb free nitrogen from the atmosphere and add it to the soil. For two thousand years before this was definitely established, clovers were cult. for soil improvement, a practice just as sound today. *See* LEGUME INOCULATION.

T. alexandrinum. Berseem or Egyptian clover. A branching annual 1–2 ft. high. Leaflets oblongish, blunt, ¾–1 in. long, faintly toothed. Flower heads globe-shaped, white or yellowish-white. Egypt and Syria. Grown for soil improvement in alkali and dry regions of Calif. and the Southwest. Not suited to the North and East.

T. hybridum. Alsike clover, called also Swedish clover. Resembling the common white clover (*T. repens*) when prostrate, but in youth an erect perennial, 1–2 ft. high, ultimately sprawling or prostrate. Leaflets ovalish, not notched at the tip. Flower heads globe-shaped, pink. Eu. Much used for soil improvement.

T. incarnatum. Crimson clover, called also Italian clover. An annual 20–30 in. high and branched. Leaflets ¾–1½ in. long, faintly toothed, more or less wedge-shaped at the base. Flower heads oblong, 1½–2½ in. long, crimson. Eu. Perhaps the most widely used for soil improvement and for forage.

T. medium. Zigzag clover, called also cow clover. A perennial 8–15 in. high, its rootstock creeping, the stems zigzag. Leaflets elliptic or oblong, nearly without teeth, not blotched as in the next. Flower heads globe-shaped, stalked deep purple. Eu. Less cult. than the others and sometimes confused with mammoth clover.

T. pratense. Red clover, also called honeysuckle clover. A perennial 1–2 ft. high, but not long persisting. Leaflets ovalish or oblong, 1½–2½ in. long, often notched at the tip and usually white-blotched. Flower heads globe-shaped, rose-purple. Eu. The common clover of our meadows. The *var.* **serotinum**, the mammoth clover, is a stouter plant that blooms later and it does not need such frequent renewal.

T. repens. White or Dutch clover. A low, creeping perennial. Leaves long-stalked, the leaflets notched, minutely toothed. Flower heads solitary, on long stalks arising from the ground, globe-shaped and white. Eu. A low plant forming flat mats. It is the chief clover in grass mixtures and makes a valuable constituent of lawns. On March 17 it annually appears in flats or pans, forced for the purpose as the "shamrock" (which see), but *T. dubium* (a non-hort. species) is also a "shamrock." The *var.* **giganteum**, the Ladino clover, is a larger form with leaflets 4–5 times the size of white clover. It is a valuable ingredient of pasture mixtures especially in the South and is a cultigen* which originated in Lombardy. (Sometimes known as *T. repens latum.*) The *var.* **purpurascens**, often with 4 leaflets and bronzy foliage, makes a neat bedding plant. It is thus sometimes known as a four-leaved clover.

---

* Special articles on the subjects indicated by an asterisk (*) will be found at the words so marked.

Several of these clovers, from wholly unknown causes, occasionally produce leaves with 4, or even 5 or 6 or rarely more leaflets. For other plants sometimes called clover *see* MELILOTUS, MEDICAGO, and LESPEDEZA.

CLOVER BROOM = *Baptisia tinctoria.*

CLUB GOURD = *Trichosanthes Anguina.*

CLUB MOSS AND CLUB MOSS FAMILY. *See* LYCOPODIUM.

CLUBROOT. A disease of all members of the cabbage family. It is caused by one of the lower forms of fungi. The organism lives in the soil, and continuous planting of the cabbage in the same area will usually result in an increase of this disease which produces large knots on the roots and in turn reduces the yield of the crop. For control, *see* CABBAGE.

CLUMP. A cluster or group of shrubs; more usually, in the hort. sense, a mass of roots or rootstocks, such as one divides or moves — as a *clump* of iris.

CLUSIACEAE = Guttiferae.

CLUSTER. As applied to flowers a cluster is an indefinite but convenient designation for inflorescence.* As applied to the stems of shrubs or the trunks of trees it is still more indefinite, suggesting merely a group.

CLUSTERED IVY = *Hedera Helix conglomerata.*

CLUSTERHEAD PINK = *Dianthus carthusianorum.*

CLUSTER PALM = *Actinophloeus macarthuri.*

clypeolata, -us, -um (clip-e-o-lay′ta). Like a broad shield.

CLYTOSTOMA (kly-tos′to-ma). Evergreen woody vines, of the family Bignoniaceae, all the 8 species South American, one of which is popular for outdoor cult. in zones* 8 and 9 (possibly in zone* 7) because of its showy bloom. Leaves compound,* of 2 leaflets, the end of the main leafstalk prolonged into a slender, unbranched tendril.* Flowers in clusters of 2, the calyx* bell-shaped, the corolla funnel-shaped, its lobes wavy. Fruit a prickly capsule.* (*Clytostoma* is from the Greek for splendid and mouth, in reference to the showy corolla.)

The only cult. species is not particular as to soils and makes an attractive, medium-sized vine for Fla., Calif. and other regions of mild climate. It is slow-growing until thoroughly established. Propagated by cuttings of last season's wood.

callistegioides. Leaflets only 2, evergreen, glossy, oblongish 2½–3 in. long. Flowers in terminal pairs, about 3 in. long, light purple or lavender, streaked darker purple inside. Apr.–May. Argentina and southern Brazil. Sometimes known as *Bignonia speciosa.*

Cneorum (nee-ō′rum). Pre-Linnaean* name for some plants of the genera *Daphne* and *Convolvulus;* also a modern genus name for plants little known in cult. and not here included.

CNICUS (ny′kus). A single, thistle-like annual herb, C. **benedictus,** of the family Compositae, and commonly called blessed thistle, Our Lady's thistle, or sometimes, sweet sultan. It is a native of the Mediterranean region, easily grown from seed, and not especially showy or desirable. Stems 1–2 ft. high, branching. Leaves oblong, deeply lobed or toothed, the lobes spiny-margined. Flowers yellow in dense, thistle-like heads about 1 in. in diameter, which terminate the branches and are set in a collection of spiny bracts.* (*Cnicus* is Latin for some thistle-like plant.) The plant is sometimes offered under the names *Carduus* and *Centaurea.*

COACH-WHIP = *Fouquieria splendens.*

coarctata, -us, -um (ko-ark-tay′ta). Crowded.

COAST LIVE OAK = *Quercus agrifolia.* See OAK.

COAST REDWOOD = *Sequoia sempervirens.*

COAST TRILLIUM = *Trillium ovatum.*

COAT FLOWER = *Tunica Saxifraga.*

COBAEA (ko-bee′a). Tendril*-climbing, tropical American woody vines of the family Polemoniaceae, one widely grown for its quick growth and showy bloom when treated as a tender annual. Leaves alternate,* compound,* the leaflets arranged feather-fashion, the terminal one replaced by a branched tendril.* Flowers solitary, on long stalks from the leaf axils.* Corolla bell-shaped, or cylindric, its limb 5-lobed, the stamens protruding. Fruit a leathery, 3-valved capsule.* (Named for Father Cobo, a Spanish Jesuit naturalist.)

scandens. Cup-and-saucer vine; Mexican ivy. Growing from 10–25 ft. high in a single season when sown as an annual in the greenhouse, window box, or outdoors in the South. Leaflets 4–6, oval-oblong, the lowest with an ear-like base and nearly stalkless. Flowers violet or greenish-purple, about 2 in. long, the calyx inflated and leaf-like, the protruding stamens curved. Mex. Seeds are often sold by street hawkers under a variety of catch-penny names such as "Cathedral Bells." See VINES. There is a white-flowered form.

COBNUT = *Corylus Avellana grandis.* See HAZEL.

COBRA-PLANT = *Darlingtonia californica.*

COBWEB HOUSELEEK = *Sempervivum arachnoideum.* See HOUSELEEK.

Coca. Native South American name for the plant yielding cocaine. See ERYTHROXYLON.

COCA FAMILY = Erythroxylaceae. *See* ERYTHROXYLON.

COCAINE PLANT = *Erythroxylon Coca.*

coccigera, -us, -um (kok-kidj′er-ra). Berry-bearing.

coccinea, -us, -um (kok-sin′ee-a). Scarlet.

coccinioides (kok-sin-i-oy′deez). Resembling a plant of the non-hort. genus *Coccinia.*

---

* Special articles on the subjects indicated by an asterisk (*) will be found at the words so marked.

COCCOLOBIS (kok-o-low'bis). Sometimes spelled *Coccoloba*. A genus of 125 species of tropical American shrubs and trees of the buckwheat family, often growing along the sandy beaches, remarkable for their large, leathery leaves which are alternate* and without marginal teeth. Little known as cult. plants outside of Fla., where the sea grape or seaside plum, **C. uvifera**, is both wild and cult. It is a shrub or tree up to 25 ft. high. Leaves nearly round, 6–8 in. wide, heart-shaped at the base. Flowers small, greenish-white, not showy, but in clusters 6–9 in. long (for details *see* POLYGONACEAE). Fruit resembling a bunch of grapes, purple, about ½ in. in diameter and sometimes used for jelly. (*Coccolobis* is from the Greek for a colored fruit.)

COCCOTHRINAX (kok-o-thry'nacks). Tropical American fan palms, often cult. outdoors in zones* 8 and 9 for ornament, rarely in greenhouses outside of botanic gardens. The chief cult. species is **C. argentea**, the thatch-palm or silvertop palmetto (often known as *Thrinax argentea*). It may grow up to 30 ft. high, but as usually cult. it has a short trunk or is practically stemless. Leaves fan-like, nearly round, 2–3 ft. wide, pale green above, silvery beneath, the smooth leafstalk about 3 ft. long. Flowers perfect,* the cluster just at the crown of leaves. Stamens 9–12. Fruit berry-like, black, round and about ⅜ in. in diameter. Native from southern Fla. to the Bahamas and larger W.I. (*Coccothrinax* is Greek for berry and *Thrinax*.)

COCCULUS (kok'kew-lus). A small genus of very widely distributed woody vines or shrubs of the family Menispermaceae, often called moonseed or snailseed. Of the 11 known species two are cult. for ornament, and present no difficulty in any good garden soil, preferably in somewhat moist sites. Leaves alternate,* the veins arranged finger-fashion. Male and female flowers on different plants, small and inconspicuous (for details *see* MENISPERMACEAE). Fruit fleshy (a true drupe*), the stone flattened and ribbed crosswise. (*Cocculus* is a Greek diminutive meaning small berry.)

carolinus. Carolina moonseed. A twining, woody vine 6–12 ft. high. Leaves roundish or triangular-oval, 3–4 in. long, without teeth but often shallowly lobed, pale beneath. Flowers greenish, the clusters 3–5 in. long. Fruit red, about ⅔ in. long. June–July. Va. to Fla., Mo. and Tex. Hardy from zone* 4 southward.

laurifolius. Evergreen shrub and not over 15 ft. high. Leaves leathery, glossy, oblongish, 3–6 in. long. Flower clusters only 2 in. long. Fruit black. Himalayas. Hardy from zone* 7 southward.

cochenillifera, -us, -um (ko-chen-il-lif'e-ra). Bearing cochineal.

COCHINEAL PLANT = *Nopalea cochenillifera*.

COCHLEARIA (kok-lee-ā'ri-a). Of the 20 species of this genus of herbs of the mustard family, only **C. officinalis**, the scurvy-grass, is of any garden interest. It is sometimes cult. as a salad plant, but its rather tarry flavor suggests its medicinal qualities, which are as a cure for scurvy. It is a biennial or perennial herb, usually not over 4–5 in. high, but planted as an annual. Leaves long-stalked, kidney-shaped or heart-shaped, practically all basal. Flowers scarcely ¼ in. wide, white (for details *see* CRUCIFERAE), in a close cluster that elongates as the somewhat inflated pods develop. The plant is wild in the cooler parts of the temperate zone and far northward. (*Cochlearia* is from Greek for spoon, in reference to the shape of the leaves.)

cochlearifolia, -us, -um (kok-lee-ā-ri-fō'-li-a). With leaves like the scurvy-grass (*Cochlearia*).

cochlearis, -e (kok-lee-ā'ris). Spoon-shaped.

COCKLE = *Saponaria Vaccaria*.

COCKSCOMB = *Celosia argentea cristata*.

COCK'S-FOOT = *Dactylis glomerata*.

COCKSPUR GRASS = *Echinochloa crusgalli*.

COCKSPUR THORN = *Crataegus crusgalli*.

COCOA TREE. *See* THEOBROMA.

COCONUT (*Cocos nucifera*). The coconut as a cult. plant has a wide distribution in tropical and some sub-tropical regions of both hemispheres. The trees, strongly wind-resistant and with slender, leaning trunks, reach heights exceeding 80 ft. and are among the most beautiful of the large palms. Probably unexcelled in importance among the world's tree fruits, the coconut yields food, drink and fiber, and is planted to the extent of millions of acres. Most of the cult. acreage is in Asia and the East Indies; only approximately 2 per cent of the total is in tropical America. A frost-free and humid climate is required and planting in the U.S. is limited to the warmest portions of Fla., where the tree thrives but is grown only as an ornamental.

The oily meat of the nut — termed copra when dried — is the source of desiccated coconut and of the coconut oil used extensively in cooking oils, blended fats and soaps; the freshly husked nuts are sold widely; the coir fiber of the husks is utilized for cordage, coarse matting and brushes, and as fiber for planting material; the shells are made into household utensils and high-quality charcoal; and even the leaves are utilized for thatching, mats, and other local uses. Toddy, the sap obtained by tapping the unopened inflorescence, is a sweet and pleasant drink and a source of sugar, alcohol, and vinegar. Fresh coconut meat contains about 30 per cent oil, copra more than twice that amount, and the "milk" about 4 per cent sugar.

There are numerous varieties, several having been introduced into Fla. Propagation is by seeds which are planted in a nursery or in the place where the tree is wanted.

* Special articles on the subjects indicated by an asterisk (*) will be found at the words so marked.

The mature, unhusked nuts are placed on their sides and only partially covered. Most will germinate within 4 to 5 months in moist soil and be ready for transplanting when the sprout is 6 to 12 inches high. Planting distances vary widely, but 70 to 80 trees to the acre is most generally recommended for highest nut production. Fruiting begins within 5 to 7 years and full bearing is reached at about 20 years. Annual tree yields are from 20 to 200 nuts, with the average near the lower figure. The nuts mature over a year-round season. Greatest vigor of growth is obtained by planting in large, well-prepared holes and following with annual applications of complete fertilizers. Additions of organic materials and growing of leguminous cover crops have proved beneficial. The tree thrives on many soil types and even though it grows well on brackish soils close to the sea, neither salt nor close proximity to the ocean is essential to its growth. — G. D. R.

INSECT PESTS. Scale insects are usually controlled by natural enemies unless ants protect them. See ANTS for control. Avoid trunk injuries which attract borers. Control visible borers by use of wires or injection of 3 times normal pesticide #20 (see SPRAYS AND DUSTS). See BORERS.

DISEASES. Bacterial bud rot is a disease of the buds and other tender parts caused by a bacterial organism. Control is accomplished by cutting and burning affected trees. Red ring disease is caused by a nematode worm. The stem and leaves are invaded, the latter turning yellow, orange or brown, while a red ring appears in the stem. Sanitation by the complete removal and destruction of diseased trees, including roots, is the best method of control. Bud rot is a similar disease to the bacterial bud rot, but caused in this case by a fungus. Early recognition and eradication have been effective. Stem rot or stem bleeding is a disease of unknown cause. It responds to careful surgical methods if followed by thorough applications of crude oil or distillate. The treatment should be applied early and trees frequently re-examined.

COCO-PLUM = *Chrysobalanus Icaco.*

COCOS (ko'kos). As originally understood, a very large genus of feather palms, but now considered as including only the coconut palm, **C. nucifera**, a native of the tropical Old World, and introduced into tropical America by the Portuguese and Spanish, and now of world-wide occurrence in tropical regions. It is perhaps the most important of all cult. palms. For a description of the tree and notes on its culture see COCONUT. The fruit of the coconut is technically a drupe,* what is generally called the nut being merely the seed of this drupe, which is fleshy and green when young, but very tough when the nut is ripe.

For the commonly cult. palms formerly included in *Cocos,* see ARECASTRUM, BUTIA, and SYAGRUS.

CODIAEUM (ko-di-ee'um). Gorgeously colored, tropical foliage plants of the family Euphorbiaceae, universally called crotons. Of the six known species, only the one below is of garden interest, but in its many forms it is cult. throughout the tropical world and extensively in northern greenhouses. Leaves alternate,* without marginal teeth, but sometimes lobed, probably green in its original state, but in the cult. forms variously marked, streaked, blotched, or banded with green, white, the reds, and yellow, often spectacularly so when properly grown. Flowers small and inconspicuous (for details see EUPHORBIACEAE). Fruit a roundish capsule,* splitting into 3 2-valved segments. (*Codiaeum* is from Greek for head, in allusion to the leaves being used for wreaths.)

In Fla. and southern Calif. where crotons can be grown outdoors they require no special soil or culture beyond that given to any other shrub. They do better in good soils and with a reasonable amount of moisture, but they need heat most of all. They are widely used in parks and as specimen plants on the lawn and often, as tubbed plants, are showy features of porches or patios.

The greenhouse culture of crotons demands a house kept at 70°–75° at night, more in the day, and the atmosphere must be kept moist by wetting down the paths (not the plants) and the space under the greenhouse bench every three or four hours during the day. Large plants can be grown in tubs, but frequently these become leggy, when cuttings should be made of all bushy shoots, and these grown along in pots until they are fit for exhibition or for summer bedding. They make excellent foliage plants for the latter purpose, coming in so many color combinations that any desired effect can be produced. Do not put outdoors until settled warm weather has arrived.

Use potting mixture* 4, and give plenty of water while the plants are in active growth, but less as growth slackens. To get the finest color, the glass of the greenhouse should be ground-glass or have a thin wash of white paint. Clear glass will burn the leaves and most roller or lath shades make the greenhouse too dark. If possible, the best time to make the cuttings is during the winter months. They need bottom-heat and a house temperature of 80°. Most young plants in the florists' shops and dime stores are grown annually in this way. As house plants they need reasonably moist atmosphere, plenty of heat and regular but moderate watering. See HOUSE PLANTS.

variegatum pictum. The common croton of the florists. A shrub or small tree with smooth, ovalish or oblong (very narrow in some varieties) leaves, which are variously colored (see above). Flower cluster sometimes 7–9 in. long. Fruit white. Java, Aust. and South Pacific Islands. Over a hundred named forms are pretty common in cult. Besides the color variations, some forms have the leaves finely cut, some curled, others crisp-margined, some spirally twisted.

CODONOPSIS (ko-doe-nop'sis). An Asiatic genus of about 20 species of sprawling or trailing perennial herbs of the bellflower family, closely related to *Campanula*. They

---

* Special articles on the subjects indicated by an asterisk (*) will be found at the words so marked.

have thickened rootstocks and alternate* or opposite,* wavy-margined leaves. Flowers bell-shaped, 5-parted, followed by a somewhat fleshy capsule with 3–5 segments. (*Codonopsis* is from the Greek for bell-like, in allusion to the bell-shaped flowers.) They are cult. as in *Campanula,* but need protection with a winter mulch north of zone* 5.

clematidea. Stems not over 1 ft. long, often climbing. Leaves about 1 in. long, ovalish or narrower, short-stalked. Flowers solitary and terminal, about 1 in. long, pale blue but with darker lines and a purple blotch. W. As.

ovata. Stems nearly upright, scarcely longer than 1 ft. Leaves nearly stalkless, oval, about ¾ in. long. Flowers few or solitary, long-stalked, blue, but with dark veins, 1–1½ in. long. Himalayas. Plants offered as this may be *C. clematidea.*

coelestina, -us, -um (see-les-ty′na). Sky-blue.

coelestis, -e (see-les′tis). Sky-blue.

Coeli-rosa (see-li-rō′sa). A species name meaning rose of the sky (heaven). *See* LYCHNIS.

COELOGYNE (see-lo′jen-ee). A very large group of chiefly Indo-Malayan, tree-perching (epiphytic*) orchids, the first a very popular greenhouse flower, the others somewhat grown by orchid fanciers. They have clustered pseudobulbs,* each of which usually bears 2 leaves. Flowers few or many in racemes,* the petals and sepals somewhat similar. Lip* stalkless at the base of the column* and 3-lobed, the side lobes erect, the central one spreading or curved backward. (*Coelogyne* is from the Greek suggesting a depressed or hollow stigma.) *Coelogyne cristata* is a widely grown greenhouse orchid. *C. dayana,* while less known, is a handsome orchid with a drooping flower cluster nearly 3 ft. long. For culture *see* ORCHID.

cristata. The common species in cult. and a fine plant with several drooping clusters of showy flowers. Leaves 9–12 in. long and about 1 in. wide. Flowers 3–4 in. wide, white, the sepals and petals oblong or narrower, sharp-pointed. Throat orange-yellow. The middle lobe of the lip is slightly toothed. Tropical Himalayas. Jan.–Apr., as a greenhouse plant.

dayana. Necklace orchid. Leaves 15–20 in. long, 3–4 in. wide. Flowers nearly 2½ in. wide, the cluster almost 3 ft. long, white, the lip reddish-brown. Malaya. Apr.–June.

flaccida. Leaves leathery, nearly 12 in. long and 1 in. wide. Flowers in pendulous clusters (raceme*), usually 7–12 in each cluster. Individual flower about 1 in. wide, the petals white, the lip* white, streaked yellow, but crimson toward the base. Nepal. In the greenhouse flowering Feb.–Apr.

coerulea, -us, -um (see-roo′lee-a). Dark blue.

coerulescens (see-roo-les′senz). Almost dark blue.

COFFEA (kof′fee-a). The shrubs or trees yielding coffee, of the family Rubiaceae, are of no commercial importance in the U.S., but the two below are often grown for interest in

extreme southern Fla. and occasionally in greenhouses. Leaves usually opposite,* evergreen. Flowers white or cream, the corolla salver-shaped, the stamens* in or below the throat. Fruit a fleshy berry, its seeds the source of coffee and usually (but incorrectly) called coffee berries. (*Coffea* is a Latinized version of the Arabian name for coffee.)

Can be grown (as an ornamental) outdoors only in zone* 9. For commercial production it needs more heat, and preferably a tropical tableland between 2000 and 3000 ft., conditions not found in the U.S. For greenhouse cult. use potting mixture* 4 and keep in a moist, warm (75°) house.

arabica. Common or Arabian coffee. A usually many-stemmed shrub 10–15 ft. high. Leaves oblongish, 3–6 in. long, prolonged into a tip about ½ in. long. Flowers white, faintly fragrant, star-shaped, about ¾ in. long. Fruit red. Tropical Africa; from thence introduced into Arabia and long thought to be native there.

liberica. Liberian coffee. A somewhat similar shrub, but the leaves 9–12 in. long, the flowers about 1 in. long, and with black fruit.

COFFEE. *See* COFFEA.

COFFEEBERRY = *Rhamnus californica.*

COFFEE FAMILY = Rubiaceae.

COFFEE-TREE = *Gymnocladus dioica.*

COFFEEWEED = *Cichorium Intybus.*

Coggygria (kog-ji′gri-a). Old Greek name for the smoke-tree.

COHOSH. Several plants are so called. *See* ACTAEA, CAULOPHYLLUM, and CIMICIFUGA RACEMOSA.

Cohune. Vernacular tropical American name for the cohune palm. *See* ATTALEA.

COIR. *See* COCONUT.

COIX (kō′icks). A small genus of leafy-stemmed grasses of the Indo-Malayan region, one grown in the East for centuries for its edible grain and here for ornament or as a curiosity. Stem obviously jointed. Flower cluster terminal, the male clusters at the end, the female below. From the latter develops the peculiar, white or dirty-white, bead-like structure, inside which is the kernel, the source of the cereal food, adlay, in the Philippines. (*Coix* is the Greek name for this grass.)

Lacryma-Jobi. Job's tears. An annual grass 3–6 ft. high. Leaves 1–2 ft. long, ¾–1¼ in. wide, sword-shaped and with a prominent midrib. Beads about 1½ in. wide, very striking, hard and shiny. Tropical Asia. There is also a variety with yellow-striped leaves. Can be grown as an annual from zone* 7 southward, but north of this it may not fruit.

COLA (kō′la). Tropical African trees comprising over 40 species of the family Sterculiaceae, only one of which is of hort. interest, and this only in extreme southern Fla. This is the tree, *C. acuminata,* that yields the kolanut or Goora-nut, widely used as a stimulant in soft drinks. It is a tree up to 40 ft. high, with alternate,* simple leaves, 6–8 in. long, and without marginal teeth. Flowers unisex-

---

* Special articles on the subjects indicated by an asterisk (*) will be found at the words so marked.

ual,* without petals, the calyx bell-shaped, cream-colored, about ¾ in. wide in the female flower. Fruit a collection of 4–5 woody or leathery pods (follicles*), 5–6 in. long, each containing many seeds (kolanuts). Little grown in the U.S., but an important tree in the tropics. (*Cola* is the African vernacular for these trees.)

colchica, -us, -um (kol′chi-ka). From Colchis, an ancient country now included in Georgia, Transcaucasia.

COLCHICINE. A poisonous alkaloid long used in medicine, but more recently found to have the capacity to alter the chromosomes* of plants. It is derived from an autumn crocus (*Colchicum autumnale*). Its use is confined to expert geneticists, who have announced remarkable changes in stature, flower color and other characters of plants injected with it; many of them tetraploids.

COLCHICUM (kol′chi-cum). A genus of 30 species of mostly autumn-blooming, crocus-like, bulbous herbs of the lily family, very popular in the autumn garden and in the rock garden. Leaves sometimes none at flowering time, but sometimes appearing with the flowers, both arising from the ground, the plant thus apparently stemless. Flowers tubular, the segments 6, and the 6 stamens inserted within the tube. Fruit a 3-valved capsule.* (*Colchicum* is derived from *colchica*, which see.) They are commonly called autumn crocus or meadow saffron, although there are several autumn-blooming plants of the genus *Crocus* (which see).

For culture and color notes *see* below.

autumnale. Leaves in spring 8–10 in. long and about 1½ in. wide, the plant leafless in summer. Flowers 3–4 in. wide. Fruit usually maturing with the leaves in spring. Eu. and northern Africa.

bornmuelleri. Flowers larger, often nearly 5 in. wide, blooming in autumn. Asia Minor. Leaves in spring, about 8 in. long and 2 in. wide.

speciosum. Flowers nearly 6 in. wide. Leaves the following spring, nearly a foot long and 3–4 in. wide. Caucasus. Autumn-blooming. There is also a variety with pure white flowers, *var.* **album.**

Colchicum Culture

This beautiful genus of flowering bulbs has suffered undeserved neglect from American gardeners.

The blooms come, in northern latitudes, from the beginning of September until November, thus giving a succession of flowers for the decoration of house or garden at a time when most of the summer flowers are past. Their general color is a light pink inclining to mauve; but there are varieties in deeper shades, and all the colors are pleasant, many of them lovely. Sometimes the petals are tessellated in white and pink, or light and dark pink.

The only species at all commonly found in cultivation is *C. autumnale;* this bears rather small flowers and is not comparable in beauty with the larger-flowered types. Especially to

be recommended is *C. bornmuelleri,* one of the earliest to bloom, and one of the best. The large, mauve, cup-shaped flowers stand from six to eight inches above the ground. The flower stem goes down to the base of the bulb and if the flowers are pulled up instead of being broken off, most of them will come up with stems about a foot long.

The different forms of *C. speciosum* come later and are equally lovely; particularly good is the rather capricious *C. speciosum album.*

The best forms of *C. autumnale* include the wild pink form so common in southern Europe; also a white single variety, and a double pink and a double white.

Bulbs should be purchased in July or August, when they are dormant. At no other time can they be safely shipped; but for moving about in one's own garden, or for dividing, the clumps may be lifted when in bloom; they should, however, be immediately replanted, as root growth is then active.

The bulbs should be set so that their tops are at least three or four inches below the surface of the soil. They produce their rather coarse leaf growth in spring, hence they should not be put in a position where their lush foliage will mar the appearance of the garden. The best plan is to give them a corner by themselves; a ground cover of *Vinca minor* is both appropriate and useful.

The seeds of the previous year's flowers mature in July when the leaves turn brown. The bed may then be lightly hoed, leaving the ground clear for the flowers which shoot up without any leaves in the autumn. Seeds may be sown when ripe. They often lie dormant until the second or third year; but in time they do germinate, and after three or four years' growth the bulbs reach the blooming stage.

Some extremely good hybrid forms have been put on the market by the firm of van Tubergen in Holland. These are grand additions to the group, and are widely grown. Among the best of these are: Autumn Queen, Lilac Wonder, The Giant, and Water Lily.

COLD. *See* Temperature.

COLD FRAME. Definition of Terms. A frame or garden frame is, ordinarily, a bottomless, box-like structure with a removable top glazed with glass or covered with some transparent material. Frames are used for protecting, propagating or growing plants. A cold frame is any unheated frame; a heated frame is any frame that has a device for heating the air in the frame; a hotbed is a frame that has a device for heating the soil bed of the frame. A heated frame approximates a glasshouse more nearly than the others.

A single frame consists of a frame that will accommodate a single sash.

The sash, or light, is the top of the frame, and the most convenient dimensions are approximately 3 ft. × 6 ft. The most useful noncommercial sizes for frames are of four or six sash.

---

* Special articles on the subjects indicated by an asterisk (*) will be found at the words so marked.

CONSTRUCTION OF FRAME. If the frame is to be movable, a very convenient feature, it is perhaps best constructed of 2-in. planks; the planks may either be rough or dressed. In the case of dressed planks there is a loss of ⅝ in. on all sides, but a much better job can be made of painting. The minimum practicable height for a frame is about 16 in. back, 10 in. front and 6 in. slope. The back and front may be of any convenient height, the slope, however, never need exceed 10 in.

The wood should be the most durable that cost will permit; white cedar, western cedar, redwood, and cypress are excellent, but one often has to make use of pine or other woods, or even of box boarding.

For a frame 6 ft. wide, outside measure, the front may consist of 2 × 10 in. planking, the back of two such planks and the sides of one 2 × 10 in. plank for the lower piece, the top piece of a like plank cut diagonally to provide the slope.

Frames may be double and of any width up to 12 ft.; the ridge is constructed of 2 × 4 in. material on edge supported every 6 ft. by 4 × 4 in. posts. The sash is hinged on the ridge and a 1 × 6 in. board nailed flat on the top of the ridge to form a coping. A double frame 12 ft. wide is too cumbersome for most uses, but if high on the sides and if the hinges have readily removable pins, work such as sowing, pricking-off, digging and harvesting is greatly facilitated. The inconveniences with any frame over 8 ft. wide are greatly increased for watering or harvesting individual plants. In regions where termites are a problem, the outer walls can be made of cinder blocks.

SASH-SUPPORTS. These are best made of 2 × 4 in. lumber and free from large knots. They must be spaced to allow free sliding of the sash; a leeway of about ⅝ in. is usually sufficient. The supports are most effectively fixed by being checked in the planks, but they may be nailed on a rest of 2 × 2 in. material. It is an advantage to nail a 1 × 1 in. strip down the center of the sash support to act as a sash guide. The length of the sash supports for a 6-ft. frame with a 10-in. slope will be 6 ft. 3 in. Mistakes in the exact position of the sash supports may be avoided by placing the sash in a trial position before fastening. If the frames are not portable and cost is very important, the lumber used may be of ship-lap or any kind of 1-in. boarding. In this case the boards are nailed to 4 × 4 in. uprights; if the uprights are on the outside of the frame there will be found to be considerable saving in space, particularly when flats or boxes are used as containers. In districts where the winters are long and severe, take-down frames offer advantages in the matter of convenient storage. A simple method of construction is to make the units of two or three sash sizes. The ends, backs, and fronts are fastened securely by means of cleats; at the end of both back and front a groove of two 2 × 4 in. material is nailed to receive the ends; the back and front may be held firmly

in place by means of stakes; bolts are, however, more workmanlike. The sash supports are made four inches longer (6 ft. 7 in. for 10-in. slope) and a piece of 2 × 2 in. material nailed at both ends to act as lugs. Frames may also be constructed of brick and concrete. Concrete walls must be raised from about a foot below the ground level and may taper from 4 in. to 2½ in. from bottom to top. It is necessary to stabilize the wall by providing concrete piers at 6-ft. intervals below the wall to the depth of 2 ft. The piers are usually 8 × 8 in. × 2 ft. The grout is 4 parts gravel, 2 parts sand and 1 of cement; this is thoroughly mixed and wetted, then poured into the form.

SASH. The 3 × 6 ft. one-man sash glazed with 10 × 12 in. glass is the most desirable. The single-weight strength is sufficient and lightest; double-weight glass is stronger, but unless the district is subject to heavy hailstorms adds unnecessary weight.

A notched stick is the simplest device for ventilating cold frames or hotbeds.

Standard sash material is generally purchasable in populous districts, but the following specifications may help. The sides and upper ends of 3 × 1½ in. material are grooved to receive glass, the lower end of 1 × 5 in. material and the two center strips of 1 × 1½ in. material. Paint the sash twice before glazing and once afterwards. The glass may be butted or lapped, but if lapped the slope needs to be of about 12 in. to shed the water quickly enough. Either putty or a good putty substitute may be used. If difficulty is encountered in obtaining standard or approximately standard lumber, sash may be constructed of dressed 2 × 4 in. material, in this case all but the lower end is ripped. This makes a very neat and rigid sash, and by cutting ⅜-in. grooves for the glass, the sash will be about 35 in. wide.

Various substitutes for glass, such as waterproofed cloth and fine wire netting coated with cellulose, have been used for temporary covering. At the present time, sheet plastic promises good results, both as to cost and the growth of plants. Sash can be made of 1 × 2 in. material to carry either a single sheet of plastic or a reinforced covering of

---

* Special articles on the subjects indicated by an asterisk (*) will be found at the words so marked.

two layers with a 4×4 in. mesh wire between. Being light, it is advisable to secure the sash against the possibility of the wind lifting them off.

LOCATION. For maximum use the frames should slope to the south or thereabouts, to trap as much sun as possible in the early part of the year, and be on ground high enough to prevent surface water from seeping in under normal conditions. Protection from wind is highly desirable, and might be provided by a nearby building, a tight board fence, or shrub hedge.

USES OF COLD FRAMES. Where plants are to be grown directly in the bed of the frame there should be at least 6 in. of good soil made friable with leaf mold and sand if need be, over good under-drainage. If plants are in flats or pots, then a base of coal ashes is better for these to stand on. In spring, before outdoor sowing is possible, seeds of half-hardy annuals may be sown for an early start, also vegetables such as cabbage and lettuce for setting outdoors as soon as soil is workable. Beet and radish may be sown and onion sets planted for early use direct from the frame. After these have been cleared out, the frame can be readied for sowing seeds of biennials and perennials for the flower garden the following year. Early summer is a good time to root cuttings of certain shrubs and herbaceous plants in frames. Cucumbers and melons may be grown for earlier production where this is desirable. Cold frames are invaluable for hardening off tender plants raised in the greenhouse or hotbed, prior to setting them out in the garden. In the fall, plants such as Canterbury bell, English daisy, foxglove, forget-me-not, and pansy, where not reliably hardy outdoors, may be safely carried over winter in frames for early spring planting, while if desired, violets and parsley would give good picking from time to time. Stock plants of chrysanthemum and any perennial of doubtful hardiness can be established in a frame, before hard freezing, to provide cuttings or divisions in spring. Those who like to raise trees and shrubs from seed will find a frame a safe and convenient place in which to keep the flats of fall-sown seed.

MANAGEMENT OF FRAMES. Where winters are severe it is necessary to provide extra protection besides the sash covering for plants wintering over. Banking soil or leaves outside the frame will keep out a good deal of frost, while an inside mulch of light material such as excelsior or pine needles, put on after frost has entered, will help maintain uniform conditions. Board shutters cut to measure, or mats of reed, old quilts, or burlap bags stitched together are desirable covers on the sash during periods of extremely cold weather.

During warm spells in the early part of the year, the mats or shutters may be taken off during the middle of the day, and the sash opened a little for an hour or so to change the air. Outside conditions must be carefully observed to decide when and how much to ventilate. The object is to admit fresh air without a draft, and to control excess humidity. The best way to ventilate at first is with a notched block set under one end of the sash. Gradually more and more ventilation is given, until on very warm days in spring the sash may be pushed off during most of the day. The inside mulch should be taken out as soon as there is evidence of new growth starting, and any decaying leaves promptly removed.

With seedlings in spring, care must be taken to give a little air before the inside temperature gets above 70° on sunny days, also to close the sash when the sun begins to lose power in order to conserve heat for the night. Should there be prospect of freezing, the mats or shutters should be brought into use.

Water must be applied with great care, just enough to keep the soil nicely moist and avoid stagnation. It should be given in the forenoon so that any free moisture will have dried off before the frames are closed for the night. Later on, with full exposure, this is not so important.

HEATED FRAMES. Heated frames are sometimes connected with a greenhouse, making it possible to extend that heating system and provide enough overhead warmth to maintain a temperature a few degrees above freezing. Successful frame heating has also been accomplished by the use of ordinary frosted 25-watt light bulbs, 8 to a frame of ordinary size. The bulbs are attached to a strip which is placed close up under the center of each sash, with bulbs turned down, and regulated by a thermostat. With heated frames it is possible to extend the range of plants that may be grown for greater pleasure and satisfaction. Before going ahead with electrical heating, it would be advisable to confer with the local power company as to costs and details of installation.

HOTBEDS. For many years hotbeds were made so by the fermenting of fresh horse manure with the litter, plus one-third in bulk of unrotted leaves to gain a longer and steadier period of heat. The material was well mixed in a pile and moistened with water. After a few days, when steaming nicely, the pile was thoroughly turned inside out, and after a week or so would be ready for making up. Very often a pit would be dug out inside the frame about 2½ ft. deep. The fermenting material would be evenly spread in 6-in. layers and firmly packed until there was a solid bed 2 ft. thick, on which 6 in. of good friable soil was placed if plants were to be grown directly in the bed, or half that depth if in flats or pots. It is safe to sow seeds when a hotbed thermometer indicates that the bed heat has dropped to 90° F. Sometimes frames would be raised up on a 30-in. pile of the material, which was extended 2 ft. or so beyond the dimensions of the frame. This exposed heap cooled off more quickly than the pit, but there was usually enough fresh material available to bank a new layer all around the outside.

* Special articles on the subjects indicated by an asterisk (*) will be found at the words so marked.

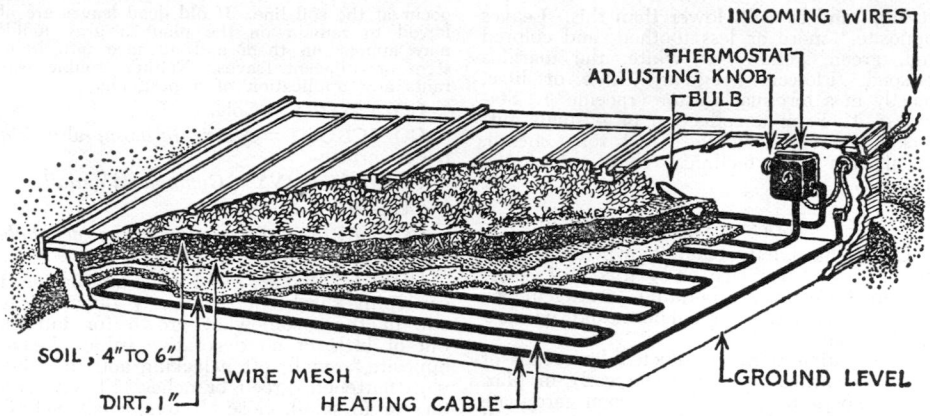

INCOMING WIRES

THERMOSTAT
ADJUSTING KNOB
BULB

SOIL, 4" TO 6"

WIRE MESH

DIRT, 1"

HEATING CABLE

GROUND LEVEL

Cross-section of an electrically heated hotbed.　For details see text.

ELECTRICAL HEAT. With the decline in horses and increase in electric power, the fermenting heap has been pretty well displaced by heating cable. This is a clean and lasting installation, with only soil renewal necessary for several years. An excavation a foot deep is made inside the frame and 6 in. of cinders laid in for heat insulation and drainage, tamped to an even surface, then covered with burlap to keep soil out of the drainage. A 1-in. layer of sand or soil is then placed, on which the flexible cable is laid in lines looped back and forth 6 in. apart, with a 3-in. space from the frame all around. The cable may be protected from injury when the soil is worked by placing a 1-in. mesh wire netting over it, then filling in with 5 or 6 in. of friable soil. If it is intended to raise plants in flats or pots, then a 3-in. layer of sand will suffice.

When the wiring is all hooked up and the thermostat in place, the current is switched on and the frame closed. A thermometer set 2 in. deep in the bed will show the soil temperature next day. The thermostat can then be regulated to maintain the soil at about 65°. A dealer in electrical equipment could advise on cost of installation; that perhaps might vary a bit according to locality, but should not be exorbitant. Power consumption averages about 3½ kilowatt hours per day for a 6 × 6-ft. 2-sash bed.

Hotbeds are managed much like cold frames. Ventilation calls for closer attention, and mats or shutters should be at hand for night covering of the sash when tender plants are started before spring has really arrived. With an electrically heated hotbed a more uniform temperature is maintained with automatic control, a device which also permits the operator to raise or lower the temperature to best suit his purpose.

Winter-stored plants such as tuberous begonia, caladium, canna, and dahlia may be started in a hotbed — the dahlia for cuttings, which root readily under such conditions, as do cuttings of coleus, fuchsia, heliotrope, and other plants of which softwood material may be at hand. Seeds of dwarf strains of dahlia, salvia, and verbena soon germinate, and when transplanted to pots grow into nice plants for summer flowering. For the vegetable garden it is easy to raise tender plants such as tomato, eggplant, and pepper in the preferred varieties. Certain small vegetables like radish, beet, carrot, and lettuce may be grown to maturity in a hotbed.

When the heat has died down or is turned off, a hotbed becomes a cold frame where plants that are to be set out can be hardened off a few days in advance of removal. The summer rooting of shrub cuttings is aided by gentle bottom-heat, which is another advantage of an electrically heated frame. — H. E. D. *See also* PROPAGATING FRAME.

COLE. An indefinite term for plants of the cabbage tribe, including kohlrabi and rutabaga.

COLEONEMA (ko-le-o-nee'ma). A small genus of evergreen shrubs from South Africa of the rue family, closely related to *Diosma* and separated from it only by technical characters. The cult. species is *C. pulchrum* (usually offered as *Diosma pulchra*) an erect shrub 4–6 ft. high, with long slender shoots and very narrow leaves about 1 in. long. Flowers solitary in the upper leaf axils,* rose-pink, about ¾ in. wide, the petals recurved. Fruit a 5-celled capsule. The shrub needs a cool greenhouse or it can be grown outdoors in southern Calif. and similar climates. (*Coleonema* is from the Greek for sheath and a filament, in allusion to a stamen character.)

COLEUS (kō'lee-us). Foliage plants of the Old World tropics comprising about 150 species of the mint family, commonly called *Coleus,* but all through the Middle West called simply "The Foliage Plant." The only cult. species is **C. blumei** from Java, and its *var.* **verschaffelti,** which is the usual garden plant. It is a somewhat weak or soft herb, sometimes shrubby in age, not usually over 3

* Special articles on the subjects indicated by an asterisk (*) will be found at the words so marked.

ft. high and as cult. lower than this. Leaves opposite,* more or less toothed, and colored red, green, yellow, or white, the margins crisped. Flowers irregular,* blue or lilac, mostly in a terminal cluster (raceme*). Stamens* 4. Fruit a collection of 4 small nutlets. (*Coleus* is from the Greek for a sheath, in allusion to a technical character of the stamens.)

COLEUS CULTURE

Coleus have long been known and highly esteemed for their rich and varied leaf coloring in sub-tropical bedding arrangements, and as ornamental greenhouse and window garden plants.

Propagation is easily effected by means of seeds or cuttings. Seeds sown early in Mar. in a temperature of 60–65° F. soon germinate and become ready to pot off singly into small pots. The smallest seedlings often give the best leaf markings and colorings, and from a good strain there will be wide variation. Desirable forms are increased from cuttings whenever shoot tips about 3 in. long are obtainable. These root readily in moist sand under warm, close conditions. Housewives often root them in a glass of water standing in the kitchen window. Being so tender it is not safe to plant coleus outside until all likelihood of frost has passed. Plants nicely established in 4-in. pots soon get going in rich soil and a sunny spot to bring out the colors. One or two pinchings will ensure bushy well-furnished plants.

To grow fine specimen pot plants they must be kept growing in good light without a check, potting on as necessary until in their final pots, 8 in. or more in diameter. Use potting mixture* 3, and pot rather firmly to ensure the desired short-jointed growth. Pinch out the growing points of shoots now and then to obtain well-furnished plants. Nip off flower buds as they appear, until perhaps the plants have attained their full size. Diluted liquid manure or fertilizer now and then will be appreciated when the pots are filled with roots. Large plants do not carry well over winter as a rule. Cuttings rooted in Sept. can be carried along safely in a moderately warm greenhouse if kept rather on the dry side. From these, numerous cuttings will be obtainable in Feb. or Mar., and later on these young plants may be tipped to afford more cuttings if needed.

Only a few of the many named varieties are listed today. *C. blumei* var. *verschaffelti*, with leaves of rich crimson and green frilled edges, is one of the oldest and still outstanding. Others still to be found are Golden Bedder; Candidum (cream with green edges); Pink Brilliant: Her Majesty (bronzed-red, edged orange); Salvador (rose and maroon, edged green); Sun Ray (reddish-purple, yellow and bronze). — H. E. D.

INSECT PESTS. *See* mealybugs at BEGONIA.

DISEASES. The coleus has little trouble with disease. Occasionally, and primarily following injury at time of potting or planting, a rot may

occur at the soil line. If old dead leaves are allowed to remain on the plant a gray mold* may appear on them and advance into living stem or adjacent leaves. Neither trouble warrants any application of a pesticide.

COLEWORT = Cole.

COLICROOT = *Aletris farinosa;* also *Liatris squarrosa.*

COLISEUM IVY = *Cymbalaria muralis.*

COLLAR = CROWN 1.

COLLARDS = *Brassica oleracea acephala.* For culture *see* KALE.

COLLETIA (kol-lee′shi-a). South American spiny shrubs of the family Rhamnaceae, one of them somewhat grown for interest, but of little or no decorative value. Leaves opposite,* small, often lacking and the plant with flattened, green branches. Flowers solitary or in small, close clusters, small, yellowish-white, without petals, the calyx* more or less urn-shaped. Fruit dry and leathery, separating into 3 parts. (Named for Philibert Collet, French botanist.)

The anchor plant is sometimes grown in the cool greenhouse or outdoors from zone* 8 southward. For greenhouse culture it needs potting mixture* 3 and not too much water.

cruciata. Anchor plant. A very spiny shrub, 3–4 ft. high. Spines stout, stiff, more or less triangular. ¾–1½ in. long. Branches flattened. Leaves (frequently wanting) ovalish, about ¼ in. long. Southern Brazil and Uruguay.

collina, -us, -um (kol-ly′na). Growing on hills.

COLLINIA ELEGANS. *See* CHAMAEDOREA ELEGANS.

COLLINSIA (kol-lin′si-a). A genus of 25 species of attractive annual herbs of the family Scrophulariaceae, three often grown in the flower garden. Most of them are natives of western N.A. Leaves opposite* or in threes. Flowers solitary or in small clusters in the leaf axils,* the corolla irregular* and 2-lipped, the calyx bell-shaped. The lower lip is 3-lobed and spreading. Fruit a capsule.* (Named for Zaccheus Collins, Philadelphia botanist.)

The species below may be easily grown if treated as hardy annuals, the seed being sown in spring, after warm weather has arrived, in the place where wanted.

bicolor. Chinese houses. Not over 2 ft. high, the leaves oblongish, 1–2 in. long, toothed. Flowers 1 in. long, nearly stalkless, the upper lip* white, the lower rose-purple or violet. Calif. Summer. The *var.* **candidissima** has pure white flowers.

grandiflora. Blue-lips. From 8–15 in. high, the leaves narrow, ¾–1½ in. long, toothed. Flowers about ¾ in. long, the stalks about the same length, the upper lip* purple or white, the lower blue or violet. British Columbia to Calif.

verna. Blue-eyed Mary. From 1–2 ft. high, the leaves ovalish, 1–2 in. long. Flowers long-stalked, about ⅓ in. long, the upper lip white or purple, the lower blue. N.Y. to Ky. and Wis.

COLLINSONIA (kol-lin-sō′ni-a). Three woodland species of herbs of the mint family, of eastern N.A., one of them grown in the wild garden but not of much decorative val-

---

* Special articles on the subjects indicated by an asterisk (*) will be found at the words so marked.

ue. The cult. species, **C. canadensis**, variously called horse balm, stoneroot, richweed, and citronella, is a strong-smelling perennial 2–4 ft. high. Leaves opposite,* broadly oval, 4–8 in. long. Flowers yellow, lemon-scented, irregular,* about ½ in. long, in a long, terminal, often branched cluster (raceme*). Its culture in the wild garden is easy if kept in woods soil and given shade. (Named for Peter Collinson, British botanist.) It is not the source of citronella. *See* CYMBOPOGON.

COLLOID. *See* SOIL CONDITIONERS.

COLLOMIA (kol-lo′mi-a). Attractive annual herbs of the family Polemoniaceae, found in western N.A. and in S.A., three of them useful plants in the flower garden. They have usually alternate* leaves and flowers suggesting those of *Gilia* from which they are separated only by technical characters. Corolla mostly funnel-shaped, the stamens usually protruding. (*Collomia* is from the Greek for glue, in allusion to the seeds, which are mucilaginous when wet.)

Collomia biflora is a showy-flowered annual well worth a place in the flower garden. This and the other species should be grown as hardy annuals. *See* ANNUALS. They bloom very freely with a minimum of attention.

biflora. Usually not over 9 in., rarely up to 15 in. high. Leaves narrow, 1–2 in. long, toothed or cut. Flowers in leafy clusters, the corolla about 1 in. long, orange-red or scarlet. Bolivia to Chile and Argentina. Sometimes offered as *C. coccinea*.

coccinea = *Collomia biflora*.

grandiflora. Similar to *C. biflora*, but the leaves without teeth and the flowers salmon or buff. Western U.S.

linearis. Not over 15 in. high, the leaves narrow and without teeth. Flowers reddish-purple or pinkish. Western N.A.

COLOCASIA (ko-lo-kay′zee-a). Large, tuberous-rooted, tropical Asiatic herbs of the arum family, commonly known as elephant-ear, and widely grown for their ornamental foliage, and, in the tropics, for the edible tubers of the taro. They have a short, or no, stem and very large leaves with long, fleshy, sheathing leafstalks. The blade of the leaf is usually arrowhead-shaped, or halberd-shaped, deeply cut at the base and the leafstalk attached to or near the middle of the blade (peltate*). Flowers minute (for details *see* ARACEAE), crowded on a spadix,* the boat-shaped spathe* longer than the spadix.* Fruit fleshy. (*Colocasia* is from the Greek for an Egyptian plant resembling the water lily; of uncertain application here.)

As a garden plant the elephant-ear is a striking summer bedding herb, its fine foliage being unlike any plant similarly used. Well-grown specimens should be covered with the large leaves, which should hang nearly to the ground. Plants should not be put outdoors until settled warm weather, and they need plenty of space and the soil cannot be too rich. Keep the bed thoroughly watered, and if it is in shade for part of the day, so much the better. The young plants, ready for summer bedding, can be purchased from dealers, but to raise your own, dig up the tubers from the old plants and store in a frost-free, but cool place all winter. In April plant them in potting mixture* 4, water well and put in a moist, warm greenhouse (75°–80°). They will be ready for bedding out by June.

antiquorum. The common bedding elephant-ear. A stout herb, when properly grown, 6–9 ft. high and as wide, usually less as cult. Leaves green, thick and fleshy, about 2 ft. long, the stalks 4–5 ft. long. East Indies. While this common green form is the most widely grown, there are several varieties, as *var.* **illustris**, with purple leafstalks and larger leaves which are dark-spotted between the veins, and others with violet leaf margins and veins.

esculenta. Taro, eddo, dasheen. A plant very similar to *C. antiquorum*, but its tubers yield an edible, starchy vegetable, a staple food in the Pacific Islands. Little grown in the U.S. except in the South where the form known as dasheen is cult. for food. Small tubers are planted in regions with at least 7 months of warm weather (generally from zone* 7 southward). Put them 2 ft. apart in the row, and the rows about 4 ft. apart. They may be grown, harvested, and stored like sweet potatoes, except that the tubers need no curing. They are cooked and eaten like potatoes. Often known as *Caladium esculentum*.

COLOMBO AGENT = *Scindapsus aureus*.

COLORADO. The columbine is the state flower and the Colorado blue spruce the state tree. The state lies wholly in zones* 3 and 4. More than one-half of Colorado is mountainous; the remainder is plains and high mesas. The Continental Divide approximately bisects the state from north to south. Streams starting in Colorado deliver their waters to the Atlantic, Pacific and the Gulf of Mexico. They flow out of the state to the north, east, south, and west. The eastern two-fifths of the state lies in the Great Plains and is a level or broken prairie crossed by the Arkansas and South Platte rivers and their numerous tributaries. The western part, in the Pacific watershed, contains the largest streams in the state, the Colorado, White, Gunnison, Animas, and San Juan. The surface is broken with high mesas, fertile, narrow agricultural valleys which rise to rugged, picturesque mountains, the Switzerland of America. Here it is that we find that air drainage exerts a greater control over temperatures than does the elevation.

There are four high, large mountain valleys or parks, north to south, near the Continental Divide. They are completely surrounded by high mountains; from north to south they are North Park, Middle Park, South Park and the San Luis Valley. The San Luis Valley is the bed of an ancient lake and the home of the famous Red McClure potato.

Colorado is the seventh largest state in the nation. It is the highest state in mean elevation and this accounts for its being the coldest state. Because of the low humidity there are days when at zero temperatures a light sweater is sufficient for outdoor wear. The elevations of its lands, as measured from sea

---

* Special articles on the subjects indicated by an asterisk (*) will be found at the words so marked.

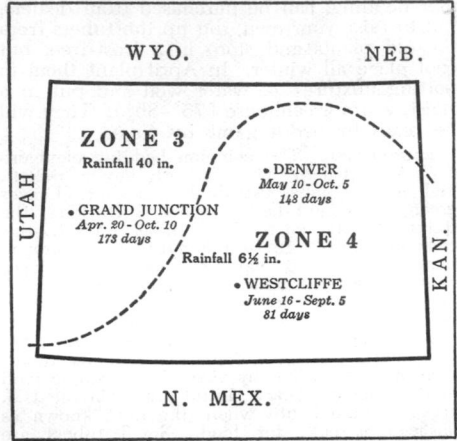

WYO.   NEB.

ZONE 3
Rainfall 40 in.

UTAH

• DENVER
May 10 - Oct. 5
148 days

• GRAND JUNCTION
Apr. 20 - Oct. 10
173 days

ZONE 4
Rainfall 6½ in.

• WESTCLIFFE
June 16 - Sept. 5
81 days

KAN.

N. MEX.

COLORADO

The zones of hardiness crossing Colorado are those shown on the map located at ZONE, which should be consulted for details. The dates are the average latest killing frost in spring and the first one in the fall. The figures below the dates show the average length of the growing season. The rainfall figures show the total annual rainfall, in inches, for two significant localities.

level, ranges from 3387 ft. to 14,431 ft., and there are a lot of hills and valleys between these extremes in elevation. Forty per cent of the area of the state is above 7000 ft. elevation.

Because of the diversified topography there is a remarkable variety of climates, great differences often occurring within short distances. Within a distance of 200 miles mean temperatures may differ as much as 35° F., a difference equal to that between Florida and Iceland. The average snowfall at Cumbres is 264 in. while at Manassa, only 30 miles away, it is 18 in.

In general, climatic features are low relative humidity, a large amount of sunshine, light rainfall largely confined to the warmer half of the year, and a large daily range in temperature. Wind movement is relatively high; high day temperatures are common in summer and in winter there are a few protracted cold spells. Severe cold waves, common on the eastern plains, are comparatively rare in the western part of the state. The prevailing lack of moisture in the air is favorable to increased intensity of the direct rays of the sun; the dry atmosphere also means rapid cooling by evaporation, so that the warmest days are comfortable in the shade and they are followed by cool nights.

Soils in Colorado vary tremendously, with many variations in a small community. There are at least 13 recognized soil types. The majority of the cultivated soils are brown soils which originated under short grasses, bunch grasses, and scattered shrubs in the temperate, semi-arid climate. The surface soil grades

into a calcareous horizon 1 to 3 feet from the surface. The soils are generally high in minerals, low in organic matter, alkaline and capable of high productivity under irrigation. While the pH usually ranges from 7.2 to 7.6 there are many good gardens on soils with a pH of 8.0 and higher. Quick soil tests are not considered reliable on these highly alkaline soils and the use of acidifying agents is not considered practical. Lime is never added to garden soils in Colorado. When sufficient organic matter can be applied, the use of chemical fertilizers is not necessary; however most successful gardeners apply small amounts of low-analysis complete fertilizer each year as insurance. The only minor element likely to be deficient is iron. Certain plants are quite susceptible to iron-induced chlorosis* which in most instances can be corrected by using ferrous iron sulphate or iron chelates.

Family vegetable, flower, and fruit gardens are found at elevations ranging from 3387 to 10,500 ft. Above 9000 ft. frost can be expected every month during the year. Good gardens with many plant species are found where growing seasons range from 59 to 189 days. Natural precipitation will range from 7 to 30 in. The majority, and the better, family gardens are in areas where the natural precipitation ranges from 8 to 18 in. In these good gardening areas, production is largely determined by available water for supplemental irrigation. The value of land is largely determined by "water rights" which go with the land. Most of the supplemental water comes from perennial surface streams; the volume of water they carry fluctuates greatly from year to year, depending upon the amount of snow stored in the mountains. Water is diverted from the streams and stored in large man-made reservoirs for future use. The same water is used over and over as it flows by gravity from stream to storage to use, to stream and back to storage and use again. In several areas of the state, water is pumped from underground streams, and in the San Luis Valley it flows from artesian wells all year round.

Because gardeners can control the water supplied to plants, periods of drought or too much water seldom occur. Water is provided as needed and this means rapid growth and superior quality. The high light intensity also contributes to rapid growth and superior quality and in flowers results in pure, intense colors. The low natural humidity discourages many diseases common in areas of high humidity.

More than 30 different kinds of vegetables and many flower species are grown in Colorado gardens. Gardens in the river valleys and in the plains area where water is available are largely planted to tomatoes, bush beans, sweet corn, root crops, cabbage, cucumbers, and squash. The larger gardens include head lettuce, cauliflower, celery, peas, onions, and potatoes. Gardeners in the lower valleys include melons, peppers, eggplant, and lima

---

* Special articles on the subjects indicated by an asterisk (*) will be found at the words so marked.

beans. The high altitude gardeners are limited to the root and salad, cool, short-season crops. Asparagus and rhubarb are perennials found in most gardens.

The home fruit gardens in nearly all of the state include strawberries; raspberries are found in the larger gardens. Tree fruits east of the mountains are usually limited to sour cherries, apples, and plums. West of the Continental Divide peaches, apricots, sweet cherries, and pears are included in the tree-fruit garden in many areas.

The hybrid tea rose is undoubtedly the most popular flower but the gladiolus is a close second; these flowers are found on nearly every property. Gladioli have been observed blooming in Leadville (the Cloud City) at 10,500 ft. Sweet peas are very popular in the mountain gardens. Paonia, a delightful town in western Colorado nestling in the pleasant Northfork Valley, was named for *Paeonia* and is known as the "peony town." Paonia is also the headquarters for Pan-American Seeds, Inc., and thousands visit their many acres of petunias each season. Zinnias and marigolds are common annuals in most gardens. Up to 200 acres of zinnias are grown for seed each year in the Arkansas Valley to supply retail markets throughout the world. The zinnia seed fields are a rainbow of color and are visited by many in Aug. and Sept. The state is also a large producer of carnations.

Colorado is known for its excellent bluegrass turf. The majority of all home lawns and public turfed areas are 100 per cent bluegrass. Where supplemental water is not available buffalo-grass or the Fairway strain of crested wheat-grass is used for home lawns and public and recreational areas.

Colorado has its own garden magazine, *The Green Thumb*, published by The Colorado Forestry and Horticulture Association. The association also sponsors "Look and Learn Garden Visits" throughout the summer months in the Denver area in addition to many mountain trips. Horticulture House, headquarters for the association, has one of the leading horticultural libraries in the mountain states and is the meeting place for a number of plant societies and other horticultural groups.

There are more than 100 garden clubs in the Colorado State Federation of Garden Clubs, Inc. The garden clubs are active in improving horticultural standards in the state. There are also chapters of the Garden Club of America, the home office of which is 598 Madison Avenue, New York 22, N. Y.

Because gardening in Colorado is different, gardeners experienced in other areas are advised to study *Rocky Mountain Horticulture Is Different*, by George W. Kelly. To assist in recognizing Rocky Mountain wild flowers, trees, and shrubs, the book *Meet the Natives*, by M. Walter Pesman, is recommended.

The state flower, the Rocky Mountain columbine, *Aquilegia caerulea*, is not successful at elevations below 5000 ft.; the intense lavender and pure white colors are at their best in the mountain zone from 8000 to 10,000 ft. It prefers shady, moist places but requires good drainage.

The recognized state tree, the Colorado blue spruce, *Picea pungens*, is a native and is adapted to nearly all of the state. It is used in park landscape in groupings, and in home landscape as an accent or background tree. Its large size does not permit its use in small front yards.

The address of the Agricultural Experiment Station, which has kindly prepared this information, is Fort Collins, Colorado.

COLORADO BLUE SPRUCE = *Picea pungens*. *See* SPRUCE.

COLORADO FIR = *Abies concolor*. *See* FIR.

COLORADO GRASS = *Panicum texanum*.

COLORADO RED CEDAR = *Juniperus scopulorum*.

colorata, -us, -um (kol-or-ray′ta). Colored.

COLOR GARDENING. Taste or preference may at times dictate the carrying out of a garden wholly or in part with plants having flowers in tones of a special color. In this case, while the preferred color will predominate, a more pleasing effect is brought about if a few flowers or foliage plants of harmonizing or contrasting hues are introduced as foils or accents. In such a planting the colors of nearby buildings or walls should be taken into consideration so that they will not bring about a lack of harmony; and all garden accessories such as trelliswork, fences, gates, seats or arbors should be painted or otherwise treated with the general color scheme in view, while care should be taken that jars, pots, umbrellas, and such minor accessories do not introduce a discordant note. The success of a special color garden depends upon keeping all its component parts in pleasant harmony.

If the color garden is a subdivision of a larger garden its effectiveness is greatly enhanced if it is walled or fenced or hedged about so that other portions of the garden do not intervene to detract from the impression it is intended to create. If merely a border it should be placed or screened so that it does not come within the same vision-scope as parts of the garden that would not accord with it. In planting such a garden or border use should be made of flowering shrubs, climbers, bulbs, perennial and annual plants of all types and heights and seasons of blossoming. *See* BLUE GARDEN, RED GARDEN, WHITE GARDEN, PINK GARDEN, YELLOW GARDEN and GRAY AND LAVENDER GARDEN.—L. B. W.

COLQUHOUNIA (ko-hoon′i-a). A small and horticulturally unimportant genus of Asiatic plants of the mint family, C. **vestita** somewhat cult. outdoors, from zone* 7 southward, for ornament. It is an erect, white-woolly plant 3–4 ft. high. Leaves opposite,* large below but smaller and bract*-like above. Flowers irregular,* orange-scarlet, winter-

---

* Special articles on the subjects indicated by an asterisk (*) will be found at the words so marked.

blooming, the corolla about ¾ in. long. The flowers are in whorls in the upper leaf axils.* (Named for Sir Robert Colquhoun, British worthy.)

COLTSFOOT = *Tussilago Farfara.*

colubrina, -us, -um (kol-you-bry′na). Pertaining to or shaped like a snake.

columbiana, -us, -um (ko-lum-bi-ā′na). From British Columbia.

COLUMBINE. Many attractive garden herbs, all perennials, belonging to the genus **Aquilegia** (a-kwee-lee′ji-a) of the buttercup family. Of the 60 known species, all from the north temperate zone, about a dozen are very popular plants for the border or rock garden. Leaves twice- or thrice-compound.* Flowers showy, usually at the ends of the branches. Sepals and petals colored alike, the 5 petals with long, hollow spurs,* some of which are knobbed, others hooked at the end. Sepals shorter than the spurs. In many of the garden hybrids double-flowered forms are common. These are possibly derived from *A. caerulea, A. chrysantha,* or others, but the parentage of some of the finest is uncertain. Fruit a collection of dry, erect pods (follicles*) which split off separately. (*Aquilegia* is of uncertain origin.)

The columbines are well divided into those whose original habitat makes the rock garden their best cult. home, and those, more tolerant, that can be grown in the open border. The latter group includes the long-spurred hybrids as well as several of the Old World species. They do best in open, sandy loam in the perennial border. Many of them resent too much summer rain or watering, and some are apt to die out prematurely. The others, as indicated below, are rock garden species and their culture should be sought there. All the columbines are best increased by division of the clumps in the spring.

A. akitensis. A Japanese perennial, 4–6 in. high, the lower leaves cut into segments (ternate*), the upper undivided, stalkless and narrow. Flowers with long straight spurs, pale purple sepals* and yellow petals. May.

A. alpina. Not over 1 ft. high. Flowers nearly 2 in. wide, blue, the spurs long and incurved. The Alps. July–Aug. For cult. see ROCK GARDEN.

A. bertoloni. An alpine perennial, suited to the rock garden, 8–12 in. high. Leaves small, undivided, bluish-green. Flowers short-spurred, the spurs knobbed, the petals and sepals bluish-violet. Italy. June–July.

A. caerulea. A native American columbine, 2–3 ft. high. Flowers up to 2 in. wide, bluish-purple, the spurs straightish and knobbed at the ends. May–June. Rocky Mountains. A fine border plant, but also grown in the rock garden (which see).

A. canadensis. The common columbine of eastern N.A. A beautiful herb 15–24 in. high. Flowers about 1½ in. wide, the sepals yellow, the spurs red, almost straight, knobbed at the end. Eastern N.A. May. A fine plant for the shady nook in the wild garden, preferably in woods soil. Also grown in the rock garden. See WILD GARDEN.

A. chrysantha. A very showy border colum-

Columbine (*Aquilegia vulgaris*), a Eurasian perennial with usually blue, nodding, long-spurred flowers.

bine, 2–4 ft. high, and branched. Flowers nearly 3 in. wide, yellow, the spurs straight, nearly 2½ in. long. Rocky Mountains to Tex. May–Aug.

A. clematiflora. A group, perhaps of garden origin, having either no spurs or very short ones. Plants perennial, 12–18 in. high. Flowers very showy, often up to 3 in. wide, blue or pink. A commonly offered race or strain, decidedly worth growing, but of uncertain origin.

A. ecalcarata. A badly confused name for columbines said to be either from the Rocky Mts. or from China! The latter plant is a perennial 12–15 in. high, with compound and much-divided leaves. Flowers almost spurless, about 3 in. long, nodding, deep crimson. Western China. May. By some considered as of the genus *Semiaquilegia*, a concept not here maintained.

A. flabellata. Not over 18 in. high, the flowers lilac, nodding, and about 2 in. wide. Spurs rather short, the ends incurved. Jap. July–Aug. There is a much smaller, almost dwarf *var.* **nana** with pure white flowers. For its culture see ROCK GARDEN.

A. formosa. A striking columbine for the open border, 2–3 ft. high. Flowers about 1½ in. wide, nodding, red and yellow, the spurs red, straight, and not knobbed. Western N.A. and Siberia. May–Aug. There are several hort. varieties or forms, some of them of hybrid origin, including dwarfs, a double-flowered form and one with nearly white flowers.

A. glandulosa. A Siberian columbine for the border, usually not over 18 in. high. Flowers nodding, up to 3 in. wide, lilac-blue, the shortish spurs much incurved. June–Aug. The *var.* **jucunda** has whitish, somewhat double flowers.

A. jonesi. A Rocky Mt. tufted, stemless, hairy, perennial, scarcely 3 in. high, its tiny leaves much crowded. Flowers solitary, blue or purple, about 1 in. long, the short spurs slightly curved. June–July.

A. jucunda = *Aquilegia glandulosa jucunda.*

A. longissima. A showy perennial 2–3 ft. high, the foliage silky-hairy. Flowers golden-yellow, nodding, the spurs about 5 in. long. Southwestern Tex. and northern Mex. July–Oct.

A. pyrenaica. A low columbine, usually not

* Special articles on the subjects indicated by an asterisk (*) will be found at the words so marked.

over 12 in. high. Flowers about 2 in. wide, dark blue, the spurs short but distinctly incurved. Pyrenees. Summer.

A. skinneri. A handsome columbine from the mountains of Mex. and Guatemala, often 2½–3 ft. high. Flowers about 1½ in. wide, nodding, the sepals greenish-yellow, the spurs red, nearly 2 in. long and straight. July–Sept. There is also a double-flowered form.

A. vulgaris. Perhaps the best known of the columbines for the open border, and often up to 2 ft. high. Flowers 1½–2 in. wide, nodding, usually blue, but sometimes purple or white, the spurs decidedly incurved and knobbed at the ends. Eurasia. Summer. There are many color forms and hybrids, some dwarf, white and double-flowered, some lilac, and one with yellow-lined leaves.

COLUMBO. See FRASERA.

columellaris, -e (kol-you-mel-lay′ris). Relating to a small collar or to a pillar.

COLUMN. The structure formed by the union of stamens* and pistils in orchid flowers, or of the stamens* in the flowers of the mallow family (Malvaceae).

columnaris, -e (kol-um-nay′ris). Columnar.

COLUMNEA (ko-lum′ne-a). A genus of over 100 species of tropical American, usually epiphytic* shrubs or vines (family Gesneriaceae), grown in the greenhouse for their showy, usually irregular or 2-lipped flowers. Leaves generally opposite, one of the pair often different from the other. Flowers solitary or in sparse clusters, borne in the leaf axils.* Fruit a many-seeded berry. (*Columnea* was named for Fabius Columna, Italian botanist.)

Columnea cult. is relatively easy in a warm greenhouse, with plenty of moisture and in potting mixture* 4, or some prefer to grow them in vermiculite, using nutrient solutions for watering and feeding. See SOILLESS GARDENING. Of the dozen or so cult. species the following are most in demand.

gloriosa. A weak-stemmed plant, best grown in a hanging basket. Leaves dark green or purplish above, reddish-hairy beneath ¾–1½ in. long. Flowers solitary, scarlet, with a yellow patch in the throat of the corolla. Berry about 1 in. wide, whitish. Costa Rica.

hirta. Also a plant for the hanging basket, differing from the last in having stiffer stems, and less colored leaves. Flowers scarlet, scarcely yellow in the throat, nearly 2½ in. long. Costa Rica. Less satisfactory as a basket plant than *C. gloriosa.*

microphylla. Not materially different from *C. gloriosa* except in having much smaller and more numerous leaves, which are scarcely ½ in. long. Costa Rica.

tulae. A weak-stemmed West Indian plant, suited to pot culture or for the hanging basket, its opposite, oblongish leaves 1–1¾ in. long, softly hairy. Flowers solitary in the leaf axil,* yellow in the usually cult. var. commonly called **flava,** nearly 2 in. long. Fruit white.

Colurna (ko-lur′na). Classical name of the hazel.

COLUTEA (ko-lew′tee-a). Eurasian shrubs of the pea family, the one below often grown for ornament, and as a stock for grafting cions of the glory-pea (*Clianthus dampi-*

eri). Of the 10 known species only *C. arborescens,* the bladder-senna, is much cult. It is about 4 ft. high and has compound* leaves, the leaflets arranged feather-fashion, with an odd one at the end. Leaflets without teeth, usually 9–13, and about 2 in. long. Flowers pea-like, bright yellow, about 1 in. long, in long-stalked clusters (racemes*) from the leaf axils.* Pod (not a legume) papery, inflated and not splitting, about 2½ in. long. Southern Eu. May–July. Hardy from zone* 4 southward, and of easy culture in ordinary garden soils. (*Colutea* is from the Greek for some pea-like tree.)

COLZA = *Brassica Napus.*

COMBRETACEAE (kom-bret-tay′see-ee). A family of 16 genera and about 450 species of tropical shrubs, trees and woody vines of little garden interest except for the Indian almond (see TERMINALIA) and the Rangoon creeper (see QUISQUALIS), both of which can be grown outdoors only in frost-free regions.

Leaves mostly alternate* in *Terminalia,* but opposite in *Quisqualis,* a rank-growing, woody vine with rusty young foliage and white flowers that turn pink or red. *Terminalia* is a tall tree with large, glossy leaves and a dry fruit with an edible seed.

Technical flower characters: Flowers in spikes,* panicles,* or heads,* the cluster bracted* at the base. Sepals 4 or 5. Petals (in ours) 4 or 5. Stamens inserted on the calyx, usually 10, in 2 series. Ovary inferior,* 1-celled, with a single style.*

COMFREY. See SYMPHYTUM.

COMFREY FAMILY = Boraginaceae.

COMMELINA (kom-mel-ly′na). The day-flowers are weak, watery-juiced, quickly wilting herbs of the family Commelinaceae, with jointed stems and alternate leaves without marginal teeth. Of the 100 known species, of wide distribution, only 3 are of any garden interest. They have quickly fading flowers, blue in those below, solitary or in small clusters, below which is a boat-shaped bract* or spathe.* Flowers irregular,* the 3 sepals often colored and joined. Petals 3, two of them long-clawed.* Stamens 6, 3 of them infertile. Fruit a 3-celled capsule.* (Named for Caspar and Johann Commelin, Dutch botanists.)

Commelina erecta and *C. diffusa* are hardy, with protection, over most of the country. Both of them tend to sprawl and prefer moist, shady places. *C. coelestis* is more often almost a weed under greenhouse benches, but can be grown outdoors in the blue garden if south of zone* 6. All are easily propagated by rooting bits of their jointed stems in moist sand; all of them spread by self-sown seeds.

angustifolia = *C. erecta.*

coelestis. A perennial up to 2 ft. high, but usually half sprawling. Flowers dark blue, nearly 1 in. long. Common in greenhouses and hardy outdoors south of zone* 6. Mex.

diffusa. More or less creeping perennial, easily rooting at the joints. Flowers blue, scarcely ½ in. wide. A somewhat weedy perennial hardy up to zone* 4. Widely distributed from Del. to S.A. Formerly called *C. nudiflora.*

---

* Special articles on the subjects indicated by an asterisk (*) will be found at the words so marked.

erecta. More or less prostrate, the stems up to 2 ft. long. Leaves very narrow, 3–5 in. long. Flowers blue, the bract* below it purplish. U.S. and W.I. Formerly called *C. angustifolia.*

COMMELINACEAE (kom-mel-ly-nay'see-ee). The spiderwort or day-flower family is familiar to all gardeners from containing the wandering Jew and the spiderwort (which see). All of its 26 genera and over 600 species are fleshy herbs, mostly of warm regions, but *Commelina* and the spiderwort (*Tradescantia*) are also found in the temperate region. Most of the garden genera have fleshy, watery-juiced stems that quickly wilt when picked. Leaves alternate,* without marginal teeth. Flowers regular* or irregular, the 3 petals soon withering, but often rather showy. Fruit a dry pod (capsule*).

Besides those mentioned above, the garden genera include *Dichorisandra, Spironema,* and *Rhoeo,* all tropical plants of greenhouse cult., and *Zebrina,* which contains one of the plants called wandering Jew (for the other *see* SPIDERWORT).

Technical flower characters: Ovary superior,* 2–3-celled, its ovules few or many. Sepals 3, free, or sometimes united into a sheath-like organ, green. Petals 3, free, or rarely united into a short tube (in *Zebrina*), usually brightly colored.

communis, -e (kom-mew'nis). Common or general.

commutata, -us, -um (kom-mew-tay'ta). Changing or changeable.

comosa, -us, -um (ko-mō'sa). Long-haired.

compacta, -us, -um (kom-pack'ta). Compact or dense.

COMPASS-PLANT = *Silphium laciniatum.*

COMPETITION. While garden plants are often assumed to be free of the bitter struggle which wild plants wage for food, water, and a place in the sun, this is only a half-truth. By cultivation, fertilizing, and watering, we remove some of the most difficult of the hazards that wild plants must meet or die. But we should not forget that garden plants are themselves engaged in the age-old warfare of survival. And this competition should not be ignored by the gardener. Space, light, food, and water must be provided, and the greatest use of these is best accomplished by judicious thinning — in other words, destroy the weaklings for the sake of the survivors. *See also* the end of the article at ROOT.

complanata, -us, -um (kom-plan-nay'ta). Flattened.

COMPLETE. A flower is said to be complete when it bears sepals, petals, stamens, and a pistil. *See* PERFECT; *see also* ESSENTIAL ORGANS.

complexa, -us, -um (kom-plecks'sa). Encircled or embraced.

composita, -us, -um (kom-poz'i-ta). Compound.

COMPOSITAE (kom-poz'i-tee). One of the largest family of plants in the world, comprising shrubs, trees, vines, and thousands of herbs, many of which are among the finest garden flowers, such as dahlia, chrysanthemum, coreopsis, marigold, aster, cosmos, and others to be mentioned presently.

It is variously called the thistle, aster, daisy, cosmos, or goldenrod family, but its technical difficulty, because of the tremendous number of other genera involved, is very great. Many specialists consider it is best divided into three families — Carduaceae, Cichoriaceae (often, thence, called the chicory, lettuce, dandelion, or hawkseed family), and the Ambrosiaceae (mostly weeds of little garden interest).

Cross-section of a flower head of the Compositae, showing ray flowers (around the margin) and disk flowers in the center.

Here considered as one big family, the Compositae comprise perhaps 800 genera and over 15,000 species of world-wide distribution. While the leaves are very various — opposite,* or whorled*— the flowers of the Compositae are all alike in being borne in heads,* the individual florets of which are small, often minute, and may consist of *ray* flowers (often supposed to be the "petals" of a daisy) or *disk* flowers (the small, tubular flowers in the center of a head of black-eyed Susan) or of both.

One section of the family (the old Cichoriaceae) has only ray flowers (ligules*). Such flowers are said to be radiate. Most of these plants have a milky juice. Here belong chicory (*see* CICHORIUM), lettuce, *Crepis,* dandelion, *Hieracium, Hypochaeris, Catananche, Malacothrix, Scolymus, Scorzonera, Tolpis,* and *Tragopogon.* Among these garden genera, some are weedy, but *Scorzonera, Tragopogon,* and *Scolymus* furnish vegetables such as black salsify, the Spanish oyster plant and salsify.

All the remaining plants in the Compositae bear disk flowers, or disk flowers and ray flowers, but not ray flowers alone. The disk may be flat or cone-shaped (as it is in the coneflower and many sunflowers). Below the head and usually tightly surrounding it, all plants of the Compositae have a series of small, overlapping and minute, leaf-like, or chaffy scales (involucral bracts).

Among the disk flowers there is usually a

---

* Special articles on the subjects indicated by an asterisk (*) will be found at the words so marked.

Ageratum, a type of Compositae flower head (like many others) that has disk flowers but no ray flowers

collection of minute bristles (the pappus), and upon this, and upon the shape of the involucral bracts and upon still other technical characters, the different garden genera are separated.

Such characters lie outside the scope of this book and if included would exhaust the patience of the most enthusiastic gardener. From the hort. standpoint, the following genera are those of importance and you should turn to those that most nearly meet your garden interest in this complex and huge plant family.

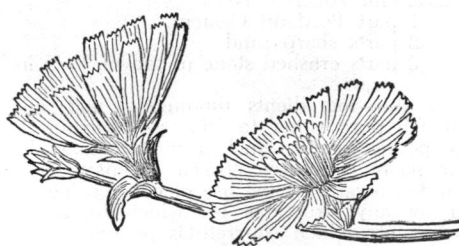

Chicory, a type of Compositae flower head (like many others) that has ray flowers but no disk flowers

The chief garden genera, including only herbs of usually outdoor cultivation, are: *Achillea, Ageratum, Artemisia, Aster, Bellis, Bidens, Boltonia, Brachycome, Calendula, Callistephus, Carlina, Centaurea, Chrysanthemum, Coreopsis, Cosmos, Dahlia, Gaillardia, Helenium, Helianthus* (see SUNFLOWER), *Matricaria, Parthenium, Rudbeckia, Senecio* (including cineraria), *Stokesia, Tagetes* (see MARIGOLD), and *Zinnia.*

Secondary, mostly outdoor, garden genera, nearly all herbs, include the following: *Actinea, Ammobium, Anacyclus, Anaphalis, Antennaria, Anthemis, Arctotis, Arnica, Baeria, Bellium, Buphthalmum, Calimeris, Carthamus, Charieis, Chrysopsis, Cladanthus, Cotula, Dimorphotheca, Doronicum, Echina-*

cea, Echinops, Emilia, Encelia, Erigeron, Eriophyllum, Eupatorium, Gazania, Gnaphalium, Grindelia, Helianthella, Helichrysum, Heliopsis, Helipterum, Inula, Lasthenia, Layia, Leontopodium (see EDELWEISS), *Liatris, Ligularia, Linosyris, Madia, Marshallia, Petasites, Podolepis, Polypteris, Ratibida, Santolina, Sanvitalia, Silphium, Solidago* (see GOLDENROD), *Tanacetum, Thelesperma, Townsendia, Trilisa, Tussilago, Ursinia, Venidium, Verbesina, Vernonia, Vittadinia, Wyethia, Xanthisma,* and *Xeranthemum.*

A few genera are grown chiefly in the greenhouse, or outdoors in the warmer parts of the country: *Felicia* (also outdoors), *Gamolepis, Gerbera, Gynura, Humea, Montanoa, Mutisia, Olearia, Othonna, Piqueria,* and *Tithonia.* Some of these are used as summer bedding plants or even as summer annuals, as well as being grown under glass, and some are tropical shrubs and trees.

Thistle-like or frankly weedy genera include: *Arctium* (see Burdock in the list at WEEDS), *Carduus, Cirsium, Cnicus, Onopordon,* and *Silybum.*

There remain still a few cult. genera in this huge family of plants. *Cynara* (artichoke), *Lactuca* (lettuce), and *Cichorium* (the endive) are the only genera yielding important vegetables, while *Baccharis* is the only hardy shrubby genus of the garden genera. *Olearia* and *Montanoa* include greenhouse plants from the tropics; both are woody and *Olearia* is grown outdoors in coastal Calif.

COMPOST PILE. Compost is a substitute for manure, made up of a variety of fermented or decomposed materials, or refuse matter, adaptable to use as a fertilizer. It may be composed of some or all of the following ingredients: manure, mushroom soil, straw, leaves, lawn clippings, vegetable refuse, peat moss, sod, rubbish, etc., and topsoil, muck, or sand. It is an excellent source of humus, and the best "filler" or base to use in the distribution of commercial fertilizers.

The object in making or keeping a compost pile is to make use of all refuse, vegetable matter, manures, etc., and to have on hand a source of top-dressing highly valuable as an organic fertilizer, used to improve the mechanical condition of the soil.

It may be used to fertilize flower beds, trees, shrubs, etc., and is invaluable as a top-dressing for lawns; especially for turf which is thin and poor or coarse, and which covers soil which is (1) excessively light, (2) excessively heavy, or (3) which contains an excess of decayed vegetable matter. Grass does not like an overabundance of any one ingredient in the soil, and by means of top-dressings it is possible eventually to correct such a condition as far as the uppermost layer of soil is concerned.

A comparatively heavy dressing of compost should be given before winter, a medium-heavy dressing in spring, and a very light

---

* Special articles on the subjects indicated by an asterisk (*) will be found at the words so marked.

dressing several times during the summer, to maintain a healthy, heavy, weed-free turf, or beautiful lawn.

The value of compost depends greatly upon its composition and upon the soil on which it is to be used. For light soils the mixture should contain a large percentage of good topsoil, to aid in the retention of moisture, and, eventually, to give weight to the soil, thereby preventing excessive leaching.

For heavy or clayey soils, a preponderance of sand is best, for this will gradually work down into the soil, making it more porous and absorbent of moisture.

The physical condition of the soil should be the determining factor regarding the correct proportioning of the materials to be used.

Never use materials infected with fungous diseases or infested by insect pests. Burn these immediately when noticed.

The process of decomposition is aided, and leaching to some extent prevented by the addition of topsoil, muck, or sand. Excessive leaching may be prevented by providing a roof of some sort, or by covering the heap with several inches of topsoil. If there is no manure in the compost, a sprinkling of ground limestone will help decomposition.

The pile of earth and manurial matter should preferably be in pyramid section, in order to shed rain. In constructing the storage pile the manure, vegetable matter, or rubbish should be spread in a layer 4 in. thick; the topsoil, muck, or sand 3 in. thick over it. Continue spreading alternate layers in this proportion until the pile reaches a height of 5 or 6 ft. A small amount of a complete commercial fertilizer may be spread over each layer of soil.

If there is danger of foul odor from the compost heap, a small amount of acid phosphate sprinkled over it will correct this condition, and preserve the gasses valuable for plant food, though this is unnecessary where the mixed fertilizer has been added in the process of mixing.

Where a large amount of compost is to be made it is advisable to make the pile long and narrow. This facilitates mixing or stirring the compost, a necessary procedure which aids decomposition and mellows the mixture. The pile should be turned or spaded over occasionally, mixing it thoroughly and completely, yet must be kept compact and sufficiently moist to exclude oxygen and prevent the loss of nitrogen. It should not be allowed to become dry, or fermentation and proper decomposition will cease. Screen compost through a half-inch screen before applying. *See also* Artificial Manure at MANURE and ORGANIC GARDENING.

COMPOUND. As applied to a leaf, compound means having more than one blade to a single leafstalk. A compound leaf is thus composed of from two to any number of leaflets,* as in the rose, locust, ash, and many other plants. Some leaflets are arranged feather-fashion (*see* PINNATE) as in the locust, others finger-fashion (*see* PALMATE) as in the horse-chestnut. Compound is also applied to a flower cluster. See INFLORESCENCE.

compressa, -us, -um (kom-pres′sa). Compressed or flattened.

COMPTONIA (komp-tō′ni-a). A single, highly aromatic shrub of the family Myricaceae, found in sandy or rocky soils throughout eastern N.A. The only species, **C. peregrina**, the sweet-fern or shrubby fern (actually no fern) is also called sweetbush. It is a hairy shrub up to 5 ft., but often much less. Leaves alternate,* stalked, fragrant when crushed, rather narrow and about 4–5 in. long, the margins obliquely cut into rounded lobes. Flowers small and inconspicuous, green, in catkins* (for details *see* MYRICACEAE). Fruit a small nutlet, beneath which are narrow bracts,* the fruit thus burlike. The shrub, suited to open, dry places, is of secondary garden importance, and should be given a sandy or peaty-sandy soil. Also known as *Myrica asplenifolia.* (Named for Henry Compton, Bishop of London.)

conchiflora, -us, -um (konk-i-flow′ra). With shell-shaped flowers.

concinna, -us, -um (kon-sin′na). Neat, natty, or even elegant.

concolor (kon′kul-or). Colored the same throughout.

CONCRETE. The best general-purpose mixture for concrete is:

   1 part Portland Cement.
   2 parts sharp sand
   3 parts crushed stone or gravel, ½–¾ in. sizes

Mix the ingredients thoroughly and add enough pure water to allow the mixture to be poured easily. Such a mixture is useful for pools (but *see* WATER GARDEN for a caution regarding first use of concrete pools) or for any structures for which forms are made into which concrete is poured.

CONDIMENT PLANTS. See HERB GARDENING.

CONE. Typically the flower and fruit cluster of the pine and its relatives. See PINACEAE. Most cones consist of a central stem or axis, around which are arranged a series of overlapping, often woody, scales (the cone scales) between which the naked ovule* is born, and from which the ripe seed is shed. *Cone* is also, somewhat loosely, applied to many cone-shaped organs, such as the fruits of magnolia and the strobiles* of a hop.

CONEFLOWER. See ECHINACEA, RATIBIDA, and RUDBECKIA.

CONE PEPPER = *Capsicum frutescens conoides.*

CONFEDERATE JASMINE = *Trachelospermum jasminoides.*

CONFEDERATE ROSE = *Hibiscus mutabilis.*

---

* Special articles on the subjects indicated by an asterisk (*) will be found at the words so marked.

CONFEDERATE VINE = *Antigonon leptopus.*

CONFEDERATE VIOLET = *Viola priceana.*

conferta, -us, -um (kon-fer'ta). Crowded.

conglomerata, -us, -um (kon-glom-er-ray'ta). Crowded.

conica, -us, -um (kon'i-ka). Conical or cone-shaped.

CONIFERS. The cone-bearing trees and shrubs, especially the pines, spruces, firs, cedars. See PINACEAE. Their overwhelmingly evergreen habit makes the conifers of the greatest garden importance. For this feature of them see EVERGREENS.

CONIOGRAMME (kon-i-o-gram'me). A small genus of useful greenhouse ferns of the family Polypodiaceae, **C. japonica**, the bamboo fern, being grown for ornament. It is found in Jap. and the Pacific Islands, and is excellent for house decoration as it stands ordinary room conditions better than most ferns. Fronds usually compound,* 18–24 in. long, the ultimate segments 6–12 in. long and about 1 in. wide, veiny. Spore* cases extending along the main veins. Grown best in a cool greenhouse in potting mixture* 3 to which about ⅓ its bulk of chopped peat has been added. It is a strong-growing, useful fern. (*Coniogramme* is from the Greek for dust line, in reference to the spore cases along the veins.)

CONIUM. See POISON HEMLOCK.

conjugens (kon'jew-genz). Joined.

CONNECTICUT. The mountain laurel is the state flower, and the white oak the state tree. The state lies wholly in zones* 3 and 4. Its southern shore is bounded by the waters of Long Island Sound which softens the climate of the shorelands. The northwestern highlands, an extension of the Berkshire Hills, are subject to more snow cover and lower temperatures than are other sections of the state. Small valley areas in other parts of the state commonly have early and late frosts and register much colder temperatures than areas that are only a few miles away. Elevations in the state vary from sea level to a high of 2380 ft.

About 60 per cent of the state is wooded. Although Connecticut is one of the smallest states, it has 1000 lakes and 7600 miles of streams and rivers. The shoreline along Long Island Sound is 165 miles in length. There are 69 state parks, totaling 20,015 acres and 26 state forests of 122,162 acres.

SOILS AND CLIMATE. There is a great variation of soil types even within a small area. Light, well-drained soils are common, but some fields have an impervious layer in the lower strata which impedes drainage. The well-drained soils warm up early in the spring and can be cultivated soon after a rain. The soils are low in organic matter and in available phosphorous. Soils are acid, often very acid, with the exception of the

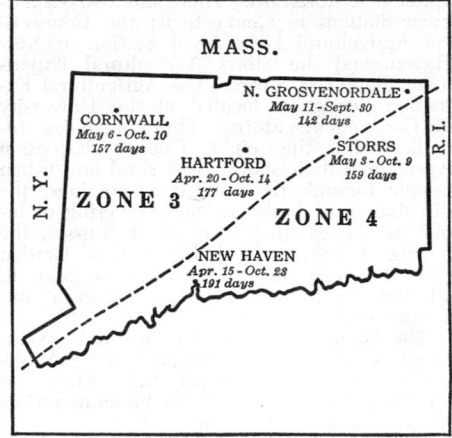

CONNECTICUT

The zones of hardiness crossing Connecticut are those shown on the map located at ZONE, which should be consulted for details. The dates are the average latest killing frost in spring and the first one in the fall. The figures below the dates show the average length of the growing season.

northwestern section of the state where limestone outcroppings are common. It has long been standard practice in this state to lime and fertilize soils, and on the better soils high yields are common when these good cultural practices are followed.

Stony fields prevail in the eastern and western highlands. Numerous stone walls line the secondary roads and the fields that were cleared by earlier inhabitants. The broad river valleys, particularly along the Connecticut River, are quite free of stone and offer highly productive areas for nursery crops and other horticultural enterprises. Commercial nurseries represent the fastest growing agricultural industry.

Rainfall for the state is about 45 inches. The 68-year average rainfall at Storrs is 44.64 in., and for the critical months of the growing season the average is as follows:

April	3.63″
May	3.64″
June	3.22″
July	4.10″
August	4.31″
September	3.83″

FROST DATA

Station	Av. last date 32° or lower	Record late date 32° or lower	Av. first date 32° or lower	Record early date 32° or lower
Putnam-No. Grosvenordale	May 14	June 21	Sept. 27	Sept. 10
Storrs	May 5	May 28	Oct. 6	Sept. 21
Hartford	Apr. 22	May 30	Oct. 15	Sept. 21
Cream Hill (Cornwall)	May 6	June 3	Oct. 7	Sept. 11
New Haven	Apr. 13	May 30	Oct. 26	Oct. 2

* Special articles on the subjects indicated by an asterisk (*) will be found at the words so marked.

SERVICE AGENCIES. There are two Experiment Stations in Connecticut: the Connecticut Agricultural Experiment Station at New Haven, and the Storrs Agricultural Experiment Station at Storrs. The Agricultural Extension Service is located at the University of Connecticut, Storrs. These agencies, together with the eight County Extension Agents and their staffs, assist rural and urban people through demonstration meetings, the distribution of bulletins, the answering of inquiries, the conducting of short courses, the testing of soils, and other activities. Garden clubs are very active in the state and, in addition to regular meetings, sponsor numerous civic projects.

The Garden Club of America has several chapters in Conn. Its home office is 598 Madison Avenue, New York 22, N.Y. There are also over 75 chapters of the Federated Garden Clubs of Connecticut.

Horticultural displays that attract large crowds in Connecticut are the Municipal Rose Garden (oldest one of its kind in the country, established in 1904) at Elizabeth Park, Hartford; Flowering Dogwood Festival in Greenfield Hill (both pink and white dogwoods have been widely planted by all residents); chrysanthemums at Bristol Nursery in Bristol; Laurel Week in Winsted; Spring Flower Show in Hartford; Fall Horticultural Show at the University of Connecticut, Storrs; the Connecticut Arboretum (native plants only) at Connecticut College for Women, New London; and the Harkness State Park in Waterford. Many communities sponsor garden visits at which times private gardens are opened to the public. The money that is collected is donated to some worthy civic project. The Merritt Parkway is well landscaped with extensive plantings of fullgrown native plants. The display of flowering dogwood and mountain laurel is outstanding.

conoides (ko-noy′deez; but *see* OÏDES). Cone-shaped or cone-like.

CONSERVATION. The preservation of forests and other natural areas is primarily a function of governmental agencies, such as the Forest Service and the National Park Service. But garden clubs can often, and should, help in such activities by influencing legislation or public opinion. *See* GARDEN CLUBS.

CONSERVATORY. *See* GREENHOUSE.

consolida, -us, -um (kon-sol′i-da). Solid or stable.

conspicua, -us, -um (kon-spic′kew-a). Conspicuous or showy.

CONSUMPTION-WEED = *Pyrola americana.*

contorta, -us, -um (kon-tort′a). Wrenched or twisted.

controversa, -us, -um (kon-tro-ver′sa). Controversial as to identity or origin.

CONVALLARIA. *See* LILY-OF-THE-VALLEY.

CONVALLARIACEAE. *See* LILIACEAE.

convexa, -us, -um (kon-vex′a). Round-curved.

CONVOLVULACEAE(kon-voll-view-lay′-see-ee). The garden genera of the morning-glory family are all vines, but shrubs and trees are found among its 40 other genera which contain about 1000 species of worldwide, but especially tropical, range. Leaves alternate.° Flowers mostly funnel-shaped or long-tubular, expanded into a broad limb, nearly always twisted in the bud. Fruit mostly a pod (capsule°), but sometimes fleshy.

Of the 7 garden genera, *Ipomoea* (the morning-glory and sweet potato) is the most important, the closely related *Calonyction* (which are night bloomers) and *Convolvulus* coming next. *Argyreia, Jacquemontia, Porana,* and *Quamoclit* are chiefly tropical. While grown occasionally outdoors (in the summer) northward, they are chiefly greenhouse plants, or some can be grown outdoors only in frost-free regions. *See* VINES. *Dichondra* is a grass substitute for Calif. lawns.

Technical flower characters: Flowers regular° and complete.° Calyx with 5 lobes often persistent. Corolla gamopetalous,° its flaring limb usually 5-angled or 5-lobed. Stamens 5, inserted deep in the corolla. Ovary superior,° mostly 2-celled, and with 2 ovules in each cell.

CONVOLVULUS   (kon-voll′view-lus). The bindweeds include a few garden plants and some very pernicious weeds, among the 200 widely distributed species of the family Convolvulaceae. They are trailing or twining plants, rarely shrubby, with alternate° leaves, usually without marginal teeth or lobes. Flowers chiefly day bloomers but sometimes closing by noon, solitary or a few in the leaf axils,° often long-stalked. Corolla bell-shaped or funnel-shaped, usually showy, but not as handsome as the closely related morning-glories (*see* IPOMOEA), from which they differ in having 2 stigmas.° Fruit a 4-valved, irregularly bursting capsule.° (*Convolvulus* is Latin, to entwine.)

All those below are perennials except *C. tricolor,* which is an annual, useful in the blue garden. *C. arvensis* and *C. sepium* are two very troublesome weeds. The other species are of the easiest culture, but even these should be watched to prevent their rampant growth from becoming a nuisance.

arvensis. *See* Field Bindweed in the list at WEEDS.

Cantabrica. An erect or prostrate, rock garden perennial, not over 2 ft. high or long, and usually hairy. Leaves narrowly oblong, sharp-pointed at the tip. Flowers 2 or 3, not over ½ in. wide, pink or rose-colored. Southern Eu. Summer.

Cneorum. A sub-shrub, 2–3 ft. high, the lance-shaped leaves covered with silvery leaves. Flowers pale pink, hairy outside, solitary or in sparse clusters. Southern Eu. and cult. outdoors only in dry, warm sites in Calif. and similar climates.

japonicus. California rose. A perennial climber up to 20 ft., twining by its coiled stems.

° Special articles on the subjects indicated by an asterisk (°) will be found at the words so marked.

Leaves narrowly arrow-shaped. Flowers about 2 in. wide, pink. Eastern Asia. Summer. Sometimes known as *Calystegia pubescens*. Throughout the eastern states there is a double-flowered, sterile form of this which is often a troublesome weed, and is usually prostrate.

mauritanicus. Perennial and prostrate. Leaves roundish or oval, about 1½ in. wide. Flowers blue, or violet-purple, about 2 in. wide. Africa. Useful for hanging baskets or in the blue garden and widely planted in Calif. as a ground cover along parkways.

sepium. *See* Hedge Bindweed in the list at WEEDS.

tricolor. Dwarf morning-glory. An annual with stems more or less erect or semi-prostrate, not over 1 ft. long, usually branched. Leaves narrowly oblong. Flowers about 1½ in. wide, blue, but with the throat yellow, and white-margined. Southern Eu. A good annual for the blue garden, the seeds of which may be sown where wanted.

COOLIE'S-CAP = *Holmskioldia sanguinea*.

COOLWORT = *Tiarella cordifolia*.

COON-TAIL = *Ceratophyllum demersum*.

COONTIE = *Zamia floridana*.

COOPERIA (koo-peer'i-a). There are only six species of the rain lily or prairie lily, two of which are sometimes cult. in the flower garden. They are bulbous herbs of the family Amaryllidaceae, found in the southwestern U.S. and adjacent Mex., with grass-like, basal leaves and night-blooming flowers. Leaves often twisted. Flower fragrant, solitary at the end of the stalk, and beneath it is a bract*-like spathe,* tubular or funnel-shaped. (Named for Joseph Cooper, English gardener.)

Of easy culture in their native region. Elsewhere, especially in regions of slushy winters, the bulbs should be dug in the fall, stored in a frost-free but cool place and planted in the spring. Both species bloom in summer, and bloom repeatedly after rains.

drummondi. Evening star. Bulb about 1 in. in diameter, its leaves erect and about 12 in. long. Flower stalk hollow, weak, 7–12 in. long, the tube of flower 3–5 in. long, its expanded limb about ¾ in. wide, white, but reddish-tinged outside. Tex. and N. Mex. to Mex.

pedunculata. Fairy lily. Stouter and larger than the last, but the tube of the flower shorter, the limb about 1½ in. wide, reddish outside. Tex.

COOTAMUNDRA WATTLE = *Acacia baileyana*.

copallina, -us, -um (ko-pal-ly'na). Gummy or resinous.

COPPER BEECH = *Fagus sylvatica cuprea*. *See* BEECH.

COPPER IRIS = *Iris fulva*.

COPPER-LEAF = *Acalypha wilkesiana*.

COPPER-TIP = *Crocosmia*.

COPRA. *See* COCONUT.

COPROSMA (kō-prŏs'ma). A large genus of chiefly New Zealand shrubs or small trees of the family Rubiaceae, one of them very generally grown outdoors from zone* 7 southward, and sometimes in greenhouses northward. Leaves opposite,* persistent or half-evergreen, thick and shining in the one below. Male and female flowers on different plants, small, greenish-white, in short, dense heads. Fruit fleshy. (*Coprosma* is from the Greek for dung, in allusion to the vile odor of some species.)

The plant below is a favorite specimen and hedge plant in southern Calif., less so elsewhere in the South. It stands clipping very well, and without it makes a handsome bush 10–25 ft. high. In greenhouses it needs a cool house and potting mixture* 4.

baueri. Leaves nearly evergreen, oval or oblongish, 2–3 in. long, usually notched or blunt at the tip. Fruit, on female plants only, orange-yellow, about ⅓ in. long. N.Z. The *var.* variegata has yellow-blotched leaves.

COPTIS (kop'tis). Weak, low, perennial herbs of the buttercup family, one somewhat grown for interest, and, by some, for its medicinal root. Of the eight known species, all from the cooler parts of the north temperate zone, the only cult. plant is C. trifolia, the goldthread, yellowroot, or canker-root, found in northern N.A., Eu., and As. (By some the American plant is called C. *groenlandica*.) It has creeping, golden-yellow, thread-like roots and basal, compound,* long-stalked leaves, with 3 wedge-shaped, toothed leaflets. Flowers small, white, the 5–7 sepals colored like the petals. Fruit a small, dry, pointed pod. The goldthread needs shade, moisture, and a peaty or sandy soil with a pH of 4–5 (*see* ACID AND ALKALI SOILS). It is suited only to the wild garden. (*Coptis* is from the Greek for cut, in allusion to the leaflets.)

COQUITO PALM = *Jubaea spectabilis*.

coracana (kor-ra-kā'na). A Latinized version of a name in India for the African millet. *See* ELEUSINE.

CORAL BEAN = *Erythrina*.

CORAL BELLS = *Heuchera sanguinea*.

CORALBERRY = *Symphoricarpos orbiculatus*.

CORAL DROPS = *Bessera elegans*.

CORAL HONEYSUCKLE = *Lonicera sempervirens*.

CORAL JASMINE = *Cestrum purpureum*.

CORAL LILY = *Lilium pumilum*.

corallina, -us, -um (kor-ral-ly'na). Coral-like; also coral-red.

CORALLITA = *Antigonon leptopus*.

Corallodendron (kor-ral-lo-den'dron). The specific name for the coral tree. *See* ERYTHRINA.

CORAL PLANT = *Russelia equisetiformis* and *Jatropha multifida*.

CORAL TREE. *See* ERYTHRINA.

CORAL VINE = *Antigonon leptopus*.

CORCHORUS (kor'ko-rus). Annual, tropical herbs, belonging to the family Tiliaceae, of no garden but much commercial interest, and sometimes cult. here. They are quick-growing herbs with alternate,* toothed

---

* Special articles on the subjects indicated by an asterisk (*) will be found at the words so marked.

leaves, and stems, in *C. capsularis,* yielding jute. Flowers not showy, small, yellow, usually with 5 petals and 5 sepals. Fruit a 2–6-valved capsule.* (*Corchorus* is from the Greek for an eye remedy which one of the 35 species was supposed to yield.)

Jute is nowhere grown commercially in the U.S., and the plant is of scarcely any other interest. *Corchorus,* as a name, has also been applied by gardeners to two widely cultivated shrubs. *See* KERRIA and RHODOTYPOS.

capsularis. Jute. A usually single-stemmed annual up to 15 ft. high. Leaves oblongish, 2–4 in. long, toothed, the two lower teeth long and sharp-pointed. Capsule globe-shaped, 5-valved. India, but widely escaped in tropical countries.

olitorius. Jew's mallow. Similar, but with the cylindric capsules having 3–6 valves. India.

cordata, -us, -um (kor-day'ta). Cordate; *i.e.,* heart-shaped or with a heart-shaped base.

CORDATE. *See* CORDATA.

CORDIA (kor'di-a). A very large genus of tropical trees of the family Boraginaceae, many of them important timber trees, and the one below cult. outdoors in zone* 9 for its showy bloom. **C. Sebestena,** the geiger tree or sebesten, is native from southern Fla. to tropical America, and is an evergreen tree not usually over 35 ft. high. Leaves alternate,* rough-hairy, ovalish, 6–8 in. long, the margins wavy but not toothed. Flowers in showy clusters blooming most of the year. Corolla tubular or somewhat bell-shaped, 1½–2 in. long, scarlet or orange-red. Fruit fleshy, surrounded by the persistent calyx. Occasionally cult. in the warm greenhouse, where it should have potting mixture* 4 and plenty of room. (Named for Valerius Cordus, German botanist.)

cordifolia, -us, -um (kor-di-fō'li-a). With heart-shaped leaves.

CORDON FRUIT TREES. A method of training fruit trees to grow a single main stem and laterals from it that are usually trained along parallel wires, or in other ways. Cordon trees are very popular in France, but not so well known here. For cordons, and other methods of training and pruning fruit trees, *see* TRAINED FRUIT TREES.

CORDULA. *See* CYPRIPEDIUM.

CORDYLINE (kor-di-ly'ne). Here belong some, but not all, of the handsome foliage plants which the florists call dracaena; others belong to the genus *Dracaena* (which see). *Cordyline* is a genus of perhaps a dozen species of tropical foliage plants, three of which are very popular greenhouse subjects and widely used for summer bedding, ornamental vases, window boxes, and for house plants. In nature they have a single stem or trunk and a terminal crown of leaves suggesting a palm, but usually in the North cult. plants are much shorter. Leaves long and sword-shaped, or broader, wholly without teeth or prickles, in some species the tips gracefully arching. Flowers greenish or whitish, not showy, mostly in small, but sometimes in larger, branched clusters. Corolla tubular or funnel-shaped, its 6 segments scarcely separable into petals and sepals. Fruit a berry. (*Cordyline* is from the Greek for club, in allusion to the thick roots.)

Cordyline and *Dracaena* are separated only by technical characters. Because of this and the fact that both genera contain popular foliage plants, the names have been loosely applied to both genera and are in much confusion. So far as the cult. plants are concerned, the identity of them is best understood by reading the descriptions below and at *Dracaena.*

The culture of both genera is essentially the same. They are grown outdoors in Fla. and southern Calif. and make valuable additions to any sub-tropical garden, because only there is the proper trunk-like habit developed. For house plants, window boxes, porch specimens, and for their wide use as summer bedding plants in the North, a greenhouse is necessary for propagation and best growth.

They should be grown in a warm, moist greenhouse in potting mixture* 3. Their finest color — and the variegated leaves are their chief attraction — is best developed, however, by gradually reducing the heat and watering just before they are to be planted out or used by florist or householder as potted specimens. This is particularly true of *Dracaena fragrans* and *Cordyline terminalis.* Such treatment adds greatly to the ability of these plants to withstand household conditions. Both genera may be propagated by seeds, but the more usual way is to strip off the leaves and cut up the woody stem into pieces about 3 in. long. These are half buried in sand in the propagating bench, bottom-heat* of about 80° applied, and they should be well watered. New plants will soon start from the "eyes" (buds), which can then be separated and potted up for growing.

The cult. species of *Cordyline* are:

australis. Ti tree; called, also, tuft tree and cabbage tree. This is the plant commonly sold by florists as *Cordyline indivisa* and sometimes as *Dracaena australis.* Trunk (outdoors) up to 40 ft. Leaves in a rosette-like, terminal crown, the blades 18–30 in. long, about 1⅓ in. wide, green, without a stalk, but with an abruptly contracted base. N.Z. The *var.* veitchi, much cult., has the midribs and leaf bases bright crimson.

indivisa = Mostly *Cordyline australis,* the true *C. indivisa* of N.Z. being rare or unknown as a cult. plant here.

stricta. From 6–12 ft., the leaves less crowded than in the next. Leaves without a stalk, 12–20 in. long, scarcely 1 in. wide, and narrowed at the base to half this. Aust. There are also colored forms, one bronzy-purple.

terminalis. Not over 10 ft. high. Leaves crowded at the end of the stem, the blades with a distinct, narrowed, channeled stalk, the blade oval-lance-shaped, 12–24 in. long, 2–5 in. broad, tapering to a point both ends. Eastern Asia. The typical form has green leaves, but dozens of hort. forms or varieties have red, pink, white, metallic, purple, and variegated or striped leaves.

* Special articles on the subjects indicated by an asterisk (*) will be found at the words so marked.

coreana, -us, -um (kor-ee-ā′na). From Korea.

COREMA (ko-ree′ma). Two species of heath-like, bushy but low shrubs of the family Empetraceae, **C. conradi**, the broom crowberry, sometimes cult. in the wild garden or rock garden. It is scarcely 18 in. high and native from N.J. to Newfoundland, and can be grown in this or similar regions but only in sandy or rocky soils with a pH of 4–5 (*see* ACID AND ALKALI SOILS). It has crowded, very narrow leaves about ⅛ in. long. Flowers small and inconspicuous (for details *see* EMPETRACEAE). Fruit very small, fleshy (a drupe*), but dryish. (*Corema* is from the Greek for a broom.)

COREOPSIS (ko-ree-op′sis). Handsome garden flowers commonly called tickseed, comprising a genus of about 100 species of the family Compositae, perhaps a dozen of which are widely cult. for their showy bloom. They are annual or perennial herbs, the annuals being the most popular. Leaves generally opposite,* often lobed or dissected but entire* in some. Flower heads solitary or in branched clusters, composed of central, usually yellow disk* flowers, and showy ray* flowers which are prevailingly yellow, but white, pink, or sometimes variegated in certain hort. varieties. There are usually about 8 rays in the single sorts, more in the double varieties. Fruits flattish, but becoming curved, small, dry, crowded in the head. (*Coreopsis* is from the Greek for bug, in allusion to the shape of the fruit.)

Coreopsis is almost weed-like in its ease of culture. Many of those below are tender annuals and should be treated as such. *See* ANNUALS. The perennials are readily divided in spring or fall. All grow in any ordinary garden soil. Most of them are among the most lasting of cut flowers. All are summer bloomers, and many of them are occasionally offered under the name *Calliopsis*.

atkinsoniana. A perennial, but often treated as a hardy annual (*see* ANNUALS), not usually over 36 in. high. Leaves twice- or thrice-compound,* the ultimate segments narrow. Flower heads long-stalked, the rays yellow, but brownish-purple at the base. Western N.A.

atrosanguinea = *Thelesperma burridgeanum*.

auriculata. A hairy perennial, 12–18 in. high, with slender rootstocks, and leafy chiefly toward the base. Leaves stalked, oval or elliptic, or sometimes nearly round, 3–4 in. long, sometimes lobed at the base. Flower heads mostly solitary, about 1 in. wide, golden-yellow. Southeastern U.S. May. The *var.* **nana** is only about 8 in. high.

coronata = *C. nuecensis*.

delphinifolia. A perennial 3–5 ft. high. Leaves suggesting a larkspur, usually 3-parted finger-fashion, about 2½ in. long, each segment divided into narrow, almost thread-like divisions. Heads nearly 2½ in. wide, the disk flowers brownish, the rays yellow. Va. to Ga. and Ala.

drummondi. Golden-wave. A tender annual 12–14 in. high. Leaves divided into narrow lobes Flower heads nearly 2 in. wide, long-stalked, the rays notched, yellow at the ends, brown-

ish-purple at the base, the head thus with a dark center. Texas.

grandiflora. A perennial up to 2 ft. high. Leaves narrow, usually 3–5-parted. Flower heads long-stalked, about 2½ in. wide, the ray* and disk* flowers yellow, the rays often notched or lobed. Southern U.S.

lanceolata. A perennial up to 2 ft. high, often an escape* in eastern N.A. Leaves lance-shaped, mostly basal, undivided. Flower heads very long-stalked, the disk and ray flowers yellow, the ray flowers notched. Eastern N.A. There is a double-flowered variety.

maritima. Sea dahlia. A perennial up to 3 ft. high, with leafy, hollow stems. Leaves much-divided, the segments narrow. Flower heads long-stalked, nearly 3 in. wide, yellow, solitary. Coast of southern Calif. and Mex. Not hardy in regions of slushy winters. Sometimes offered as *Leptosyne maritima*.

nuecensis. An annual, branched herb, not over 2 ft. high, the oblongish, somewhat hairy leaves 2–3 in. long, the lower 2–3-parted but the upper usually unlobed. Flowers 1¾–2 in. wide, the rays yellow, dark-striped. Tex. Sometimes offered as *Coreopsis coronata*.

pubescens. Plants offered as this are apt to be *Coreopsis auriculata*. True *C. pubescens* of the southeastern U.S. is a perennial 2–4 ft. high, resembling *C. lanceolata*, and is doubtfully cult.

rosea. Swamp tickseed. A weak, slender-stemmed perennial up to 2 ft. high. Leaves very narrow, or 3-parted and the segments narrow. Flower heads short-stalked, about 1 in. wide, the rays rose-pink, the center yellow. Eastern U.S. A beautiful wild flower preferring open, sunny, and moist places, but it grows well in the border.

stillmani. A beautiful tender annual, 12–18 in. high, with somewhat fleshy stems. Leaves divided, the segments long and narrow. Flower heads nearly 2 in. wide, golden-yellow. Calif. An annual that blooms best when somewhat crowded. Sometimes offered as *Leptosyne stillmani*.

tinctoria. Golden coreopsis. The best-known and most popular of the annual species. Erect and from 20–36 in. high. Leaves divided into narrow segments. Flower heads long-stalked, red-brown in the center, the ends of the rays notched and pure yellow. Central U.S. Blooming from July 1 to Oct. Do not thin out, as the plant blooms best when crowded. There are forms with all-crimson rays, and with double flowers.

tripteris. Tall coreopsis. An anise-scented perennial herb up to 8 ft. high, usually lower in cult. Leaves lance-shaped, or the lower 3-parted. Flowers yellow in a large corymb.* Eastern N.A. Aug.–Sept. A good, erect plant with the aspect of a rudbeckia.

verticillata. A perennial with ascending stems up to 3 ft. Leaves finely divided, the segments thread-like. Flower heads nearly 2 in. wide, dark yellow, the rays not notched. Md. to Fla. and Ark.

coriacea, -us, -um (kor-ee-ā′see-a). Coriaceous; *i.e.*, thick and leathery.

CORIANDER. Aromatic plants, one of which is grown for the seeds used in seasoning. There are only two species of the genus **Coriandrum** (kor-ee-an′drum), which belongs to the carrot family. One of them, **C. sativum**, is the common coriander, a native of southern Eu. It is an annual herb with twice- or thrice-compound leaves, the

---

* Special articles on the subjects indicated by an asterisk (*) will be found at the words so marked.

lower less divided than the upper which are dissected into very narrow segments. Flowers small, white, in compound umbels,* the outer flowers in each umbel sometimes enlarged and ray-like. Fruit ribbed, the coriander "seed" of the markets. For culture and uses *see* HERB GARDENING. (*Coriandrum* is from the Greek for this plant in allusion to the bedbug-like odor of its foliage.)

CORIANDRUM. See CORIANDER.

CORIARIA (ko-ri-ā′ri-a). A small group of herbs or shrubs, the only genus of the family **Coriariaceae** (kor-ree-air-ree-ā′see-ee), one of them a Japanese shrub, C. japonica, cultivated for ornament. It grows usually to 3, rarely to 7–8 ft. in height and has nearly stalkless, opposite,* ovalish leaves 2–4 in. long and 3-veined. Flowers regular,* greenish, small. Sepals 5. Petals 5, ultimately becoming fleshy and enclosing the fruit. Stamens 10. Fruit fleshy, bright red at first, ultimately black, pea-sized. The plant, not much grown as yet, is hardy from zone* 4 southward. (*Coriaria* is derived from *coriacea,* leathery, in reference to one species used for tanning.)

coridifolia, -us, -um (kor-rid-i-fōli-a). With leaves like a plant of the genus *Coris.*

Coris. A specific name for a St. John's-wort, based upon its similarity to the genus *Coris,* which includes an irregular-flowered plant of the primrose family, scarcely of garden interest.

CORK. Practically the same as bark.* In some plants, notably the cork oak, this bark is much developed and yields the cork of commerce.

CORK ELM = *Ulmus thomasi.* See ELM.

CORK FIR = *Abies arizonica.* See FIR.

CORK OAK = *Quercus Suber.* See OAK.

CORKSCREW-FLOWER = *Phaseolus Caracalla.*

CORKSCREW WILLOW = *Salix Matsudana tortuosa.* See WILLOW.

CORK-TREE. Properly, the cork oak, but cork-tree is more generally applied to *Phellodendron* and to *Entelea arborescens.*

CORKWOOD = *Entelea arborescens.*

CORM. A solid, bulb-like, underground stem, resembling a bulb, without its scales, but sometimes with a membranous coat. Typical examples are the corms of crocus and gladiolus. Corms are often called solid bulbs or bulbo-tubers. They bear roots at the base and nourish the young plant, just as in bulbs, and from the base or apex of them arise young *cormels,* which are commonly detached and grown along as propagating material, ultimately forming mature corms.

CORMEL. See CORM.

CORN. The most valuable food plant contributed by the New World to the Old. Doubt exists as to its true botanical origin, but as now considered, all corns belong to the genus **Zea** (zee′a) of which there is only one species, Z. **Mays.** What the prototype of this may have been is lost in Pre-Incan, Pre-Mayan, and Pre-Aztec antiquity, but *see* EUCHLAENA. Modern corn is a tall, annual grass with a jointed, solid stem (most grass stems are hollow), and bearing numerous, relatively broad, sword-shaped leaves, which in many varieties have a cutting edge. Male flowers in a terminal cluster (spike) which produces plentiful supplies of pollen. Female flowers in small clusters, borne below the males and only one or two in the upper leaf axils.* It is the long, thread-like styles* of these female flowers that constitute corn silk. From these the familiar, heavily sheathed ear of corn develops, the kernels of which are the seeds. (*Zea* is a Greek name for some cereal.)

Common Indian corn or maize is not a garden plant. It is the field corn of agriculture and of enormous economic importance. But several varieties of it are grown in gardens for interest, and the sweet corn is one of the most delicious of American vegetables. (It is almost unknown in Eu.) *See* Culture of Sweet Corn below.

The species and varieties of corn are:

Mays. Common field corn, often called Indian corn or maize. Useless as a garden plant, this is taller (up to 12 ft.), coarser, and more vigorous than any of its varieties. Its kernels contain too much starch and too little sugar to be of any value as sweet corn.

var. **Curagua.** The curagua of Chile, where it yields a kind of popcorn. It is little grown here as an ornamental, being a robust, leafy, green-leaved form.

var. **everta.** Popcorn. Resembling sweet corn, but has small ears which have very hard, pointed seeds that explode when heated. Its culture is the same as sweet corn (*see* below).

var. **indentata.** Dent corn. A tall (8–10 ft.) variety, the seeds of which are yellow or white and indented at the top. Scarcely a garden plant, but occasionally grown.

var. **indurata.** Flint corn; Yankee corn. A medium-sized corn, little grown as a garden plant, with dark yellow, hard, smooth seeds.

var. **japonica.** As an ornamental the most valuable of all the corn varieties. Its leaves are striped up and down with yellow, white, or pink; — a handsome grass.

var. **rugosa.** Sweet corn, and, from the garden standpoint, the most important of all the varieties of corn. Generally lower than field corn its kernels are soft and sweet in the young state, wrinkled when old. For culture and best strains *see* below. Also called sugar corn.

var. **variegata.** A variegated form of *Zea Mays japonica* and a good ornamental grass.

In Mexico, and sometimes in the southern U.S., there are many other varieties or forms of corn to be found, but they are of little interest to the gardener. Some of them appear to be related to the teosinte (*see* EUCHLAENA MEXICANA).

CULTURE OF SWEET CORN (*Zea Mays rugosa*).

Of all the varieties of corn mentioned above, sweet corn is the only one of real interest to the home gardener. Field corn

---

* Special articles on the subjects indicated by an asterisk (*) will be found at the words so marked.

takes too much space in the garden, is useless for the table, and if dried corn is needed for chickens it can be bought cheaper than you can raise it.

Sweet corn, or corn as it is quite generally but not very accurately called, can be raised in every state of the Union having a growing season of 70–80 days and plenty of summer heat. This means that corn can be grown throughout the country at some season, but the best corn is raised in the summer months.

Someone has said that anyone can grow corn, that the Indians and Aztecs (it is purely an American plant) grew it under very primitive conditions, and hence no directions are necessary. Anyone *can* grow it, but to get the best varieties to mature in the shortest time possible requires a bit of planning and considerable attention to cultivation.

SOILS. Any good garden soil (and many poor ones) will grow corn. But it will mature quicker and be more tender if a ton of a 3–5–7 commercial fertilizer (see FERTILIZERS) is used per acre. For a row of 100 ft. use 11 pounds of such a fertilizer. Some growers prefer 8 tons of stable manure to the acre (about 5 wheelbarrow loads to a 100-ft. row), plowed in two weeks before planting time. A few seacoast gardeners still follow the old Indian method of burying a dead fish or two at each hill.

VARIETIES. Getting the first corn in their locality is almost a fetish with home gardeners. To accomplish this, and to maintain a steady supply until frost, means that early and late varieties must each be planted in sufficient amount and at the proper intervals of time. The best varieties are:

EARLY AND MIDSEASON (yellow): Seneca 60, North Star, Marcross, Golden Beauty, Golden Bantam.
LATE: Golden Cross, Iochief, Golden Hybrid, Calumet Golden Security, Country Gentlemen, Stowell Evergreen.

There are also many vars. with black, red, purple, and striped kernels, grown mostly for winter decorations.

Most of the early sorts are fairly short plants (3–4 ft. high), while the later kinds frequently run from 5–7 feet, or even more on rich soils. Because of this it is often a question, in small gardens, whether one should not plant only a succession of the early sorts because of the space saved. Of all the early sorts Golden Bantam has the best-filled ears.

PLANTING. Generally speaking, it is better to plant the early varieties in drills and the late sorts in hills so spaced that cultivating may be done both ways. If, in spite of all directions, your garden is weedy, it is better to plant all varieties in hills, because it is thus possible to control weeds more easily than if the plants are in long rows.

For early varieties make the drills 2½ ft. apart and 1½ in. deep. (If in hills make them 2½ ft. apart each way.) For growing in rows, put a seed every 3 in. in the drill,

with the expectation of thinning to 6-in. intervals, as soon as possible. The thinned plants cannot be transplanted without such a serious check that your next succession will easily overtake them.

If you plant in hills (as you should for the late varieties or on weedy land), put the hills 3 ft. apart each way and plant 6 seeds to a hill. These should soon be thinned to 3 or at the most 4 plants to a hill. Do not make the hill before planting. Simply put the seed about 1½ in. below the general ground level and leave the making of the hill until later.

If you want variety in your corn diet, it will pay to plant the different sorts at 12-day intervals, beginning only after settled warm weather has arrived. A good indicator of this in your locality is to plant the first corn just after the common lilac has definitely passed out of bloom.

The last planting of the late varieties must allow about 75–80 days from seeding to the expectation of the first frost in your locality, and it is safer to allow 80–85 days because of waning heat. (For frost dates see the name of your state.) This requires such perfect timing that many growers prefer to run no risks. They keep on planting early varieties because they mature faster and are less likely to be caught by the first frost.

Crows may scratch out the seed. If they are numerous the seed should be treated with creosote. This should be used at the rate of about a tablespoonful to a half bushel of seed, which has been previously heated with warm water, and then drained. A continued stirring of the grain will eventually permit an even coating of creosote. The seed must then be spread on a dry surface, or drying may be facilitated by the application of some absorbent medium, such as ashes, land plaster, or powdered earth. When thoroughly dried the grain may be used in a planter.

CULTIVATION AND CARE. Clean cultivation is essential, whether your corn is in rows or hills. If in the latter, you can run the wheel cultivator in both directions. In any case see that no weeds are stealing the food your corn should have.

Corn plants, especially the tall, late sorts, nearly always develop a ring of secondary roots just above the level of the ground. These are the well-known prop roots that tend to stiffen the plant in a strong breeze. It much helps the formation and usefulness of these prop roots to draw up on each side of the plants enough soil to cover them. In doing so you make all the "hill" the corn plant needs — usually not over 8 in. high.

In the early varieties (most of which are in rows) the same object is accomplished by a shallow plowing along each side of the row. This, except in very stony land, will usually bury the prop roots about 5–6 in., which is all these shorter varieties need. Some growers do not bother to cover the prop roots of the early varieties at all, upon

Corn showing how the hill of soil provides food
and anchorage for the prop roots

the theory that the plants need the support less and that the roots will penetrate the soil without aid. Both are true, but covering them helps, especially in a violent wind. It can, of course, be done with a hoe, if a wheel cultivator is lacking.

All corn plants tend to send up suckers from the base. Much has been written upon the desirability of pulling or not pulling these suckers. Except in California, most growers are now convinced that suckering is not necessary.

For the preferred position and sequence of sweet corn in your garden *see* KITCHEN GARDEN.

HARVESTING AND YIELDS. No instructions are necessary except the old one that the ears should not be picked before the water for them is boiling. Flavor and succulence are soon lost after picking, which is why those used to home-grown corn are never satisfied with the store kind. The ears are ready to be picked when the kernels are plump. If you are uncertain, pry open a few of the outer husks and see when it is prime. Most corn plants should average two ears to a plant, occasionally 3, and if poorly grown, one or even none. From this you can easily estimate the amount you should grow.

INSECT PESTS. Flea beetles appearing on early corn as seedlings emerge must be controlled by pesticide #17 (*see* SPRAYS AND DUSTS) or similar material to avoid bacterial wilt. To kill earworm and corn borers attacking ear, dust silks 3 times, beginning as they appear, with pesticide #17 or similar material. Use paintbrush with 3-in. bristles and get each ear, or dust with garden duster, concentrating on ear zone of plant. Control chinch bugs with pesticide #17 or #1. *See* cutworms at CABBAGE.

DISEASES. Two diseases, either of which may be serious some years, are smut* and bacterial wilt.* Smut is a fungus which attacks the ear or the terminal tassel. It produces a large, gray, shining, gall-like growth and makes the corn useless if the cob and kernels are attacked. There is a definite correlation between the amount of corn borer present and the intensity of the smut disease. Control the corn borer as described under insects above.

The bacterial wilt disease is carried to the young corn plants by flea beetles. The disease produces wilting and death of young plants and white, broken streaks in the leaves of older plants. Controlling the flea beetle, starting as soon as plants are 1 in. high, as described under corn insects, is the best control for bacterial wilt. Use resistant varieties in those areas where wilt is an annual problem.

Corn is one of the crops which can really repay the grower who uses seed treatments. Any of the commercial preparations for corn seed, containing a fungicide, and an insecticide, will prove beneficial.

CORNACEAE (kor-nay'see-ee). The dogwood or bunchberry family, so far as its garden genera are concerned, comprises only woody plants in 14 genera and includes about 120 species (but *see* the bunchberry *Cornus canadensis*). Most of them are shrubs and trees, some with handsome flowers and showy fruits. Leaves simple,* alternate* or opposite,* often, but not exclusively, without marginal teeth. Flowers in terminal clusters, the cluster sometimes surrounded by showy white bracts* commonly mistaken for flowers. (*See* CORNUS.) Fruit a 1- or 2-seeded drupe,* or a berry.

Two of the cultivated genera, *Nyssa* (which includes the tupelo and sour gum) and *Davidia* (an Asiatic tree), are, with other genera, sometimes considered as a separate family, Nyssaceae, not here recognized as such. The other cult. genera of the Cornaceae are *Aucuba, Cornus,* and *Griselinia,* of which *Cornus* is by far the most important, because it contains all the cornels, the flowering dogwood, and the bunchberry. Many of its species much resemble *Viburnum.*

Technical flower characters: Flowers sometimes unisexual* or dioecious. Calyx 4–5-toothed, sometimes wanting. Petals 4 or 5, or none. Stamens 4–5. Ovary inferior.* Style 1.

CORNEL. *See* CORNUS.

CORNEL FAMILY = Cornaceae.

CORNELIAN CHERRY = *Cornus Mas.*

CORNFLAG = *Gladiolus segetum.*

CORNFLOWER = *Centaurea Cyanus;* less frequently applied to *Uvularia grandiflora.*

corniculata, -us, -um (kor-ni-kew-lay'ta). Horned.

CORNISH HEATH = *Erica vagans.*

CORN LILY. *See* GLADIOLUS.

CORN MARIGOLD = *Chrysanthemum segetum.*

CORN MAYWEED = *Matricaria inodora.*

CORN MINT = *Mentha arvensis.* See MINT.

CORN POPPY = *Papaver Rhoeas.* See POPPY.

CORN SALAD = *Valerianella Locusta olitoria.*

* Special articles on the subjects indicated by an asterisk (*) will be found at the words so marked.

Cornucopiae (kor-new-kō'pi-ee). Like a cornucopia.

CORNUS (kor'nus). The dogwoods or cornels comprise an important genus of garden shrubs and trees (one an herb) of the family Cornaceae, much grown for their handsome flowers, often brightly colored fruits, and in some species for the winter effect of their colored twigs. All the 40 known species are native in the north temperate zone. Leaves generally opposite,* without marginal teeth. Flowers small, with 4 small petals and 4 stamens. In many species these flowers are white and grouped in flat-topped or rounded clusters (cymes*); such resemble viburnums, but the latter have 5 stamens and a united corolla.* In a few species the flowers are inconspicuous, greenish, and set in the midst of several colored bracts* (often mistakenly called petals), as in the flowering dogwood and the bunchberry. One has yellow flowers. Fruit fleshy. (*Cornus* is the old Latin name of the Cornelian cherry.)

Fortunately, most of the cornels are of easy culture in any good garden soil, the exceptions being noted at each species. Propagation by cuttings of old wood or by layering. Some choice varieties are occasionally grafted on commoner sorts.

alba. Tartarian dogwood. A showy shrub, 6–10 ft. high, its twigs bright red. Leaves ovalish, 3–5 in. long, bluish-green beneath. Flowers white, the clusters numerous and about 2 in. wide. Fruit whitish-blue. Eastern Asia. May–June. Hardy everywhere and widely cult., also in the *var.* **argenteo-marginata,** with white-margined leaves; the *var.* **sibirica,** with coral-red twigs; and the *var.* **spaethi,** with yellow-edged leaves.

alternifolia. Blue dogwood; also called pigeonberry. A shrub or small tree 8–15 ft., the only cult. species (except *C. controversa*) with alternate* leaves, which are elliptic or ovalish, 2–4 in. long. Flowers white, the clusters about 2½ in. wide. Fruit bluish, with a bloom. Eastern N.A. and hardy everywhere. May–June.

Amomum. Silky cornel. A shrub 6–8 ft. high, its branches purplish. Leaves ovalish or longer, 2–4 in. long, generally silky beneath. Flowers white, the clusters about 2½ in. wide. Fruit pale blue. Eastern U.S. and hardy everywhere. June.

baileyi. A close relative of *C. stolonifera* and very much like it; useful for seashore planting. *See* SEASIDE GARDENS.

canadensis. Bunchberry, also called crackerberry. Scarcely over 6 in. high, and a woody herb. Leaves in a usually basal whorl,* ovalish, 1–2½ in. long. Flowers greenish, inconspicuous, set among 4–6 large white and petal-like bracts.* Fruit scarlet. Northern N.A. and Asia, and on mountain tops southward. May. A plant for the wild garden. It needs coolness and moisture and often grows wild in sphagnum moss. *See* WILD GARDEN.

controversa. A tree up to 60 ft. in China and Jap., less as cult., and resembling *Cornus alternifolia* in foliage, flowers and fruit. May. Hardy from zone* 4 southward.

florida. Flowering dogwood, also called boxwood. A showy tree up to 30 ft. Leaves oval, 3–5 in. long. Flowers small, greenish, set in the midst of 4 large, showy, white, notched and petal-like bracts.* Fruit scarlet. Eastern U.S. May–June. In its natural state the flowering dogwood is a tree of the under-canopy of the forest. While it can be grown in the open it prefers partially shady sites. There is a very popular red- or pink-bracted *var.*, rubra, commonly called the red dogwood, and cult. here since 1731. There is also a form with weeping branches and another with 6–8 large bracts,* as though "double-flowered." All have bright scarlet autumnal foliage. Not quite hardy north of zone* 4.

Kousa. An Asiatic representative of our flowering dogwood, there called kousa. It is a lower tree, has smaller leaves, very similar flowers and bracts, but its pinkish fruits are in a head-like cluster. Japan and Korea. June. Hardy from zone* 4 southward. The *var.* **chinensis** has longer and more showy bracts.*

Mas. Cornelian cherry. A shrub or small tree, the naked twigs of which are crowded with short-stalked, small, head-like clusters of minute yellow flowers in March or April. Leaves oval or elliptic, 3–4 in. long. Fruit edible, but acid, scarlet, ripening in Aug. Eurasia. Hardy from zone* 3 southward. It stands smoky atmosphere better than most shrubs.

nuttalli. Pacific dogwood. A western representative of the flowering dogwood (*C. florida*), but a much taller tree, and it usually has 6 petal-like white or pinkish bracts,* instead of 4. Fruit red or orange. May. British Columbia to southern Calif. and easily cult. there but, in the East, doubtfully hardy above zone* 6.

paniculata = *Cornus racemosa.*

racemosa. Gray dogwood. A shrub, 6–10 ft. high with gray twigs. Leaves elliptic or narrowly oval, 2–4 in. long, tapering at the tip, but wedge-shaped at the base. Flowers white, the cluster branched, not flat-topped. Fruit white. Eastern U.S. Hardy from zone* 2 southward. June–July.

rugosa. Green osier. A shrub 3–8 ft. high, the twigs green, faintly purple-spotted. Leaves nearly round, about 3 in. long. Flowers small, the flat-topped cluster nearly 2½ in. wide. Fruit blue. May–June. Eastern N.A. Hardy from zone* 2 southward.

sanguinea. Red dogwood. For hort. purposes very similar to *C. alba*, and differing chiefly in having black fruit. Eurasia. May–June. Hardy from zone* 3 southward. *See* SMOKE.

sibirica = *Cornus alba sibirica.*

spaethi = *Cornus alba spaethi.*

stolonifera. Red osier. A shrub, rarely above 6 ft. high, its red branches erect, but spreading by underground, prostrate stems, thus making large clumps. Leaves ovalish or narrower, 3–5 in. long. Flowers white, small, in flat-topped clusters that are often 2½ in. wide. Fruit bluish-white. N.A. May–June. Hardy everywhere. The *var.* **flaviramea** has yellow twigs.

INSECT PESTS. Control borers by pesticide #17 or #18 (*see* SPRAYS AND DUSTS) trunk sprays. Apply 3 sprays at 3-week intervals beginning at full-leaf stage. Remove by hand. *See* BORERS.

DISEASES. The flowering dogwood is subject to several diseases. Anthracnose* causes spotting of leaves and flower bracts. Control with pesticide #2 or #7 (*see* SPRAYS AND DUSTS) applied as flower buds start to open, when flower bracts drop, and again one month later.

Leafspot* attacks only the leaves, and may be controlled with the same sprays used for anthracnose.

During some seasons, if weather is wet during the time flower bracts drop off, a leaf blight*

---

* Special articles on the subjects indicated by an asterisk (*) will be found at the words so marked.

may develop. This is caused by old flower bracts dropping on leaves, after which a gray mold* develops. A single application of pesticide #7 or #11, during the later part of the blooming period, will prevent the leaf blight.

Dogwood is quite subject to leaf scorch* during hot, dry weather, or when grown on poor soil. When conditions are too severe, entire branches may defoliate and die.

cornuta, -us, -um (kor-new'ta). Horned.

COROLLA. The petals, collectively, of a flower. They are often separate, as in a rose, but many plants have a united corolla, as in a bellflower or morning-glory. See FLOWER.

corollata, -us, -um (kor-ro-lay'ta). Corolla-like.

CORONA. Any crown or crown-like appendage in a flower, usually between the petals and the stamens, but often applied also to a crown-like appendage of the corolla as in narcissus.

coronaria, -us, -um (kor-ro-nay'ri-a). Pertaining to a corona,* also to any garland or crown.

coronata, -us, -um (kor-ro-nay'ta). Crowned.

CORONILLA (kor-ro-nil'la). A genus of perhaps 20 species of herbs or shrubs of the pea family, scattered from the Canary Islands to western Asia, a few of secondary hort. interest. They have compound* leaves, the leaflets arranged feather-fashion, with an odd one at the end. Flowers pea-like, in long-stalked clusters (umbels*) from the leaf axils.* Fruit a slender pod (legume*) constricted between the seeds. (*Coronilla* is Latin for a little crown, alluding to the umbels.*)

The four below present no difficulties, but their hardiness should be noted. They are occasionally grown in the cool greenhouse in potting mixture* 3. Propagated by seeds, or by cuttings for *C. Emerus* and *C. glauca*.

cappadocica. A prostrate rock garden perennial, 6–9 in. high. Leaflets 9–11, hairy on the margins. Flowers in a loose cluster (umbel*), yellow. Asia Minor. July–Aug.

Emerus. Scorpion senna. A shrub, usually 3–7 ft. high, its twigs green-striped. Leaflets 7–9, usually broadest toward the tip, not over 1½ in. long. Flowers yellow, about ¾ in. long. Pod about 2 in. long. Southern Eu. May–Sept. Hardy from zone* 4 southward.

glauca. A low shrub 2–4 ft. high. Leaflets 5–7, blunt, bluish-green. Flowers yellow, usually 7–9 in a cluster, heavy-scented. Southern Eu. May–Sept. An attractive border plant, not certainly hardy north of zone* 7, and a favorite in Calif. There is also a variety with variegated foliage.

varia. Crown vetch or axseed. A perennial, usually sprawling, vine-like herb, not over 18 in. high. Leaflets 11–25, oblongish and blunt (but fine-tipped), about ⅝ in. long. Flowers about ½ in. long, pink, in dense clusters. Eu. June–Oct. A useful creeper or sprawling plant for the perennial border.

coronopifolia, -us, -um (kor-ro-no-pi-fō'li-a). With leaves like a weed of the genus *Coronopus*, which is scarcely in cult.

CORREA (kor'ree-a). Australian shrubs or small trees of the family Rutaceae, four of the six known species cult. outdoors in zones* 8 or 9 for their showy flowers, rarely in greenhouses. Leaves opposite,* dotted with resinous glands, and rather thick. Flowers solitary, or 2 or 3 together, hanging, apparently tubular, but actually of 4 separate, hairy petals. Stamens 8. Fruit composed of 4 nearly distinct segments (carpels). (Named for Jose Francesco Correa de Serra, Portuguese botanist.)

Correa speciosa is a valuable shrub for dry, sandy places in Calif. The others are little grown elsewhere, and *C. alba* is even less known outside Calif.

alba. A much-branched, bushy shrub 3–4 ft. high, the twigs rusty-hairy. Leaves generally roundish, blunt, ½–1 in. long. Flowers white or pink, about ½ in. long, the petals ultimately spreading, so that the flower no longer appears as if tubular.

ferruginea = *Correa lawrenciana*.

harrisi. A hybrid shrub, not very different from *Correa speciosa*, and perhaps not distinct from it. Flowers darker red than in *C. speciosa*.

lawrenciana. A scurfy-twigged shrub, rarely a small tree, usually shrubby and 5–6 ft. high and as wide. Leaves ovalish or narrower, wedge-shaped at the base, ¾–1½ in. long, and about ⅜ in. wide. Flowers greenish-yellow, about ¾ in. long, solitary or in 2's or 3's. Winter-blooming in Calif. outdoors, May-blooming in the greenhouse. Also offered as *C. ferruginea* and *C. magnifica*.

magnifica = *Correa lawrenciana*.

speciosa. Compact shrub, 2–3 ft. high, its twigs rusty-hairy. Leaves varying from roundish to oblong, about 1 in. long, wrinkled, whitish beneath. Flowers about 1 in. long, scarlet, remaining as though tubular, and the tips of the petals often greenish-yellow.

corsica, -us, -um (kor'si-ka). From Corsica.

CORSICAN HEATH = *Erica stricta*.

CORSICAN NETTLE = *Helxine soleiroli*.

CORSICAN PINE = *Pinus nigra calabrica*. See PINE.

CORSICAN SANDWORT = *Arenaria balearica*.

CORTADERIA (kor-ta-deer'i-a). Pampas grass is confined to southern S.A. and the genus contains only six species of tall, reed-like grasses. One of them, **C. selloana** (sometimes called *C. argentea*), is cult. for its showy plumes, but is not hardy outdoors north of zone* 7. It grows in clumps, the stems 8–20 ft. high. Leaves numerous, rough-margined, long and narrow, usually not over ¼ in. wide. Male and female flowers on different plants, only the female producing the showy, terminal cluster of feathery, plumed spikes. These are silvery, 1–3 ft. long and, as one traveler has expressed it, pampas grass *en masse* looks like "a rolling sea of silver." (*Cortaderia* is the Latinized version of the Argentine vernacular for this grass.)

cortusoides (kor-tu-zoy'deez; but *see* OÏDES). Like a plant of the genus *Cortusa*,

---

* Special articles on the subjects indicated by an asterisk (*) will be found at the words so marked.

which are primrose-like herbs scarcely in cult.

CORYDALIS (kor-rid′a-lis). A large genus of usually weak-stemmed, often prostrate herbs of the family Fumariaceae, most of them from the north temperate zone. Of the 100 known species only those below are of much garden interest, mostly for the open border, but *C. sempervirens* primarily for shady parts of the wild garden. They have lobed or finely dissected leaves, often bluish-green. Flowers in dense or lax clusters (racemes*), the 4 petals spurred as in the bleeding-heart. Stamens 6. Fruit a slender pod. (*Corydalis* is from the Greek for lark, the spur of the flower suggesting a lark's spur.)

The plants below are not so much grown as they should be. Their handsome, spurred flowers, mostly spring and early summer-blooming, are fine for the border, but not lasting enough for picking. Most of them, except *C. sempervirens,* can be grown in the open border, but preferably in a partly shady section of it. Some of them die down by mid-summer.

bulbosa = *C. cava.*
cava. A single-stemmed herb, not over 1 ft. high, arising from a corm-like solid tuber. Leaves not over 2–3. Flowers deep purple to rose color, in a showy raceme.* Eu. Sometimes offered as *C. bulbosa,* and confused with *C. halleri,* a species scarcely in cult.
cheilanthifolia. A low perennial from a thickened rootstock, the leaves finely dissected and fern-like, nearly 8 in. long. Flowers about ½ in. long, yellow. China.
glauca = *Corydalis sempervirens.*
lutea. Annual or sometimes perennial herb, erect or spreading, not over 8 in. high. Leaves bluish-green, much-divided, the segments generally wedge-shaped. Flowers pale yellow, about ½ in. long. Southern Eu.
nobilis. An erect perennial 6–9 in. high. Leaves deeply cut, the few segments wedge-shaped and toothed. Flowers white, but tipped yellow and purple-spotted, the spur about 1 in. long the clusters terminal and dense. Siberia.
sempervirens. Pink or pale corydalis. An annual with weak, pale, bluish-green foliage, stems straggling. Leaves lobed, the segments spoon-shaped or knife-shaped. Flowers about ½ in. long, in a loose, branched cluster, pink, but tipped with yellow. N.A. Prefers shady site and woods soil in the wild garden, preferably among rocks or boulders. Sometimes known as *C. glauca.*

CORYLOPSIS (kor-ril-lop′sis). A small group of Asiatic shrubs of the family Hamamelidaceae, related to the witch-hazel, but flowering in late winter or early spring before the leaves unfold, hence sometimes called winter hazel. They have alternate,* stalked, prominently veined and toothed leaves. Flowers yellow, in nearly stalkless, nodding clusters (racemes*). Petals 5, clawed.* Stamens* 5. Fruit a 2-beaked pod (capsule*) with 2 black seeds. (*Corylopsis* is from the Greek for like hazel.)

The three below prefer a somewhat peaty, sandy soil, but can be grown in any ordinary garden soil that is not too heavy. Propagated by seeds or by cuttings of green wood under glass.

pauciflora. Shrub up to 6 ft. Leaves ovalish, obliquely heart-shaped at the base, 2–3 in. long. Flowers about ¾ in. long, the cluster sparse. Jap. Feb.–Mar. Hardy from zone* 4 southward.
sinensis. A hairy-twigged shrub 7–12 ft. high, its leaves oblongish, 2½–5 in. long, obliquely heart-shaped at the base, hairy and pale beneath. Flowers fragrant, light yellow, in hanging clusters (raceme*), the petals broadoval. China. Hardy from zone* 4 southward. Feb.–Mar.
spicata. Similar to *C. pauciflora* in height, but with leaves nearly twice the size. Flowers in clusters of 7–10, yellow, fragrant, about ¾ in. long. Jap. Feb.–Mar. Hardy from zone* 4 southward.

CORYLUS. See HAZEL.

CORYMB. A flower cluster in which the individual flower stalks elongate, so that the cluster is nearly or quite flat-topped. It blooms from the edge toward the center of the cluster. Common examples are some of

Corymb

the spireas, the ninebark (*Physocarpus*) and the fire thorn (*Pyracantha*).

corymbosa, -us, -um (kor-rim-bō′sa). Bearing corymbs.

CORYPHANTHA (kor-ri-fan′tha). A group of small, ball-like or button-shaped (rarely cylindric) cacti, mostly from the southwestern U.S. and adjacent Mex., a few of them popular for pot culture, especially for miniature desert gardens in pans. The plant body is covered with small spines borne on raised, knob-like projections or tubercles. Flowers showy, borne near the summit, day-blooming, the gradations between sepals and petals not very obvious. Fruit fleshy. (*Coryphantha* is from the Greek for summit and flower, in allusion to the terminal bloom.) Many of the species are called pin-cushion cactus.

For culture see CACTI.

elephantidens. Plant body nearly globe-shaped, never more than 5 in. Spines 8 to each group, all interlocking, there being no central erect one. Flowers nearly 4 in. wide, rose-pink. Mex.

---

* Special articles on the subjects indicated by an asterisk (*) will be found at the words so marked.

macromeris. Plant body somewhat cylindrical, 6–8 in. long, densely spiny, the spines interlocking except the central black one of each group. Flowers nearly 3 in. wide, purple. Western Tex. and Mex.

recurvata. Plant body a flattened globe, 3–7 in. in diameter, often in masses. Spines many, about 22 to a group, 20 of them interlocking and curved, the two central ones erect. Flowers about 1 in. long, yellow inside, brownish outside. Ariz. and Mex.

robustispina. Devil's-pincushion; called also pineapple cactus. Plant body nearly globe-shaped, 2–4 in. in diameter, practically concealed by the numerous spines. At each spine group are 12–15 interlocking spines, 3 lower and stouter ones, and a central solitary one. Flowers salmon-pink, about 2 in. long. N. Mex., Ariz., and Mex.

runyoni. A ball-like cactus forming clumps 2–3 ft. wide with wide, short, irregular tubercles. Spines yellowish, 6 or more in a cluster, about 1 in. long, with 2–3 central spines that are 2 in. long. Flowers nearly 2 in. wide, purple. Southwestern U.S.

CORYTHOLOMA (kor-rith-o-lō′ma). A large genus of tropical American, tuberous-rooted herbs of the family Gesneriaceae, only one, **C. Cardinalis**, cult. in greenhouses for its showy red flowers. Leaves opposite* or in 3's. Flowers irregular,* the tube often long and curved, its limb 2-lipped,* the upper lip helmet-shaped and projecting, the lower almost lacking. Stamens mostly 4, borne on the corolla. (*Corytholoma* is from the Greek for helmet and throat, in reference to the shape of the flower.) Some have suggested *Rechsteineria* as the correct name for this genus.

Corytholoma and *Alloplectus* (which see) both require the same culture as gloxinia, to which they are related. *See* GLOXINIA.

Cardinalis. Not over 1 ft. high, the stem hairy. Leaves ovalish or heart-shaped, 4–6 in. long, wavy-toothed. Flowers in the leaf axils* or crowded at the summit, the corolla* hairy, red, about 2¾ in. long. Somewhere in tropical America. The plant is sometimes offered as a *Gesneria.*

COS LETTUCE = *Lactuca sativa longifolia.* For culture *see* LETTUCE.

COSMETIC-BARK TREE = *Murraya paniculata.*

COSMIDIUM. *See* THELESPERMA BURRIDGEANUM.

COSMOS (kos′mus). Tropical American garden plants, of the family Compositae, the annual species of the greatest popularity and the easiest culture. Of the 20 known species, mostly Mexican, only three are of garden interest, and all the popular annual varieties have been derived from *C. bipinnatus.* Leaves opposite,* in those below much cut into fine segments. Flowers in heads, the latter solitary and long-stalked or in loose, open clusters. Ray* flowers showy, of many colors, the rays often notched, the disk flowers (center of the head) yellow or red. (*Cosmos* is from a Greek word implying orderliness; *i.e.,* beauty.)

For culture and varieties *see* below.

bipinnatus. The common garden cosmos. An annual 7–10 ft. high, the stems green, not very stout. Leaves cut into fine, almost thread-like segments. Flower heads 1–2 in. wide (wider in some hort. forms), the rays white, pink, or red, the disk* flowers yellow. Mex. *See* below.

diversifolius. Black cosmos. A perennial up to 15 ft. high, but often grown as an annual, with dahlia-like, but smaller tubers. Leaves parted into 5–7 segments, the terminal one much the largest. Flower heads solitary, the rays velvety, dark red or purplish, the disk* flowers red. Mex. Sometimes offered as *Cosmos dahlioides.*

sulphureus. A much-branched, hairy annual, 4–7 ft. high. Leaves up to 12 in. long, twice- or thrice-cut into narrow lobes that are hairy on the margins. Flower heads solitary, long-stalked, both ray* and disk* flowers orange-yellow. Mex.

COSMOS CULTURE

The common annual cosmos, derived from *Cosmos bipinnatus,* is a tall-growing, erect, but weak-stemmed plant from the tableland of Mexico. While it can be planted as a hardy annual (seeds sown where wanted), it is better treated as a tender annual (*see* ANNUALS).

Unlike most garden plants, cosmos does not need a rich, heavily manured soil. If given such conditions, it will grow to great size but produce few flowers. Given relatively indifferent and preferably sandy soils, it blooms profusely from July to frost, and sometimes even a few straggling heads may be gathered in late November if the season hasn't been too severe. Of course no one plant will bloom so long, but by a selection of varieties cosmos flowers may be had from July 1 to the end of the season.

Such a popular garden annual has been much hybridized and selected, so that today there are numerous named forms and strains. Perhaps the most desirable are the old-fashioned single sorts, in which the rays are neither quilled nor doubled. They come in early and late varieties and in red, pink, crimson, and white.

Another race comprises the double or crested cosmos. In these the ray* flowers are unchanged, but the disk flowers are modified into many petal-like enlargements. The outer part of the head is thus single, but the center is double. These are sometimes called anemone cosmos, and come in the same colors and in both early and late strains. Some of the early varieties will bloom in 50 days from seed planting. Such plants, and several of the hort. strains, are apt to be lower than the old-fashioned single cosmos — often not over 3 ft. high. All yellow-flowered varieties are derivatives of *Cosmos sulphureus,* and are to be treated the same as the common kinds.

COSMOS FAMILY. *See* COMPOSITAE.

COSTA RICA NIGHTSHADE = *Solanum wendlandi.*

costata, -us, -um (kos-tay′ta). Ribbed.

---

* Special articles on the subjects indicated by an asterisk (*) will be found at the words so marked.

COSTMARY = *Chrysanthemum Balsamita.*

cotinoides (ko-ty-noy'deez; but *see* OïDES). Resembling the smoke-tree (*Cotinus*).

COTINUS (ko-ty'nus). Two species of shrubs or small trees of the sumac family, both cult. for ornament, and having a strong-smelling juice. Leaves alternate,* short-stalked, without marginal teeth. Flowers yellowish, not very showy, small, polygamous,* in large-branching, terminal clusters. Petals 5, longer than the sepals.* Fruit fleshy (a drupe*), but somewhat dry, slightly lopsided. The fruiting cluster consists mostly of the lengthened stalks of the numerous sterile flowers, which are plumed, silky, and form, in the mass, the most attractive feature of these plants, which are generally known as smoke-tree. (*Cotinus* is an old Greek name for the wild olive, and of uncertain application here.)

Both species are of easy culture in any ordinary garden soil, preferably not too rich or moist. They make handsome lawn specimens, the plumy fruiting cluster suggesting greenish-buff smoke from a distance, especially in the first species. Easily raised from seed, but not easy to get started, hence needing water and attention after planting out. Later they grow easily.

americanus = *C. obovatus.*

Coggygria. A Eurasian shrub, 10–15 ft. high. Leaves ovalish, 2–3 in. long, abruptly narrowed at the base. Fruiting cluster (mostly sterile) much-branched, 7–10 in. long, covered with long, spreading, purplish-green hairs, the actual fruits few, kidney-shaped, scarcely ¼ in. wide. Flowers in July, fruiting cluster in Aug.–Sept. Hardy from zone* 4 southward. Often known as *Rhus Cotinus.*

obovatus. American smoke-tree, also called chittamwood. A small tree 15–20 ft. high. Its foliage resembles the one above, but the leaves are generally wedge-shaped at the base, and the fruiting cluster not so showy. Tenn. and Ala. to Tex. Flowers in July, fruiting cluster in Aug.–Sept. Hardy from zone* 5 southward, perhaps in zone* 4 with protection. Sometimes known as *Rhus cotinoides* and *C. americanus.*

COTONEASTER (ko-tō'nee-as-ter). An important group of garden shrubs or small trees of the rose family, comprising perhaps 50 species, many of which are widely planted for ornament. Leaves alternate,* stalked, without marginal teeth, in some species (specified below) evergreen. Flowers small, white or pinkish, usually in small clusters (corymbs*). Petals 5, upright or spreading. Stamens about 20. Fruit small, fleshy, apple-like, crowned by the persistent calyx,* and with 2–5 stones. (*Cotoneaster* is from the Greek meaning like quince, in reference to the quince-like leaves of some species.)

For culture *see* below. All those below drop their leaves in the autumn unless noted as evergreen. All are spring-blooming.

acuminata. A stout shrub, 8–12 ft. high, not evergreen. Leaves hairy on both sides, ovalish, 1½–4 in. long, very short-stalked. Flowers 2–5 in a short-stalked cluster, pinkish. Fruit red, showy. Himalayas. June. Hardy from zone* 4 southward.

acutifolia. A deciduous* shrub, 8–12 ft. high, the oblong or elliptic leaves scarcely hairy, 1½–4½ in. long, short-stalked. Flowers pink or whitish, 2–5 in a short-stalked cluster. Fruit black. N. China. Hardy from zone* 2 southward. The *var.* **villosula,** with more hairy leaves is hardy only from zone* 5 southward. May–June.

adpressa. A low, prostrate shrub suited to the rock garden. Leaves ½ in. long, wavy-margined. Flowers pinkish, the petals upright. Fruit red. Western China. Hardy from zone* 4 southward. *Var.* **praecox,** is a more vigorous form, a little taller, with distinctly pink flowers and larger fruit.

apiculata. A half-evergreen shrub, not usually over 5 ft. high. Leaves nearly round, with a sharp tip, about ¾ in. in diameter. Flowers mostly solitary, short-stalked, pink. Fruit scarlet, nearly stalkless and essentially round. W. China. Hardy from zone* 4 southward. June.

bullata. A hairy-twigged, deciduous* shrub, 4–6 ft. high. Leaves puckered (bullate*) above, oblongish, 2–3 in. long, somewhat hairy beneath. Flowers white or pink, in a close cluster (corymb*). Fruit nearly round, pea-size, brilliant scarlet and long-persisting. Western China. May–June. Hardy from zone* 4 southward.

congesta. A low shrub, scarcely 3 ft. high, the ovalish leaves less than ½ in. long, whitish beneath. Flowers solitary, scarcely ¼ in. wide, pink or white. Fruit red, pea-sized. Himalayas. Hardy from zone* 5 southward.

conspicua. An evergreen and spreading shrub, 4–6 ft. high, its leaves oblongish, somewhat hairy above, much more so beneath, 3–5 in. long, ending in a minute soft prickle. Flowers white, solitary, nearly ½ in. wide, followed by pea-size, bright red, and winter-persisting fruit. Western China. May–June. Hardy from zone* 5 southward. The *var.* **decora,** the most widely grown form, is practically prostrate.

dammeri. An evergreen, prostrate shrub, its trailing branches often rooting at the joints, and thus a valuable plant for the rock garden. Leaves about 1 in. long, pale beneath. Flowers white, solitary, the petals spreading. Fruit red. Central China. Hardy from zone* 5, or with protection from zone* 4, southward.

dielsiana. An erectish shrub 2–7 ft. high, the branches arching. Leaves 1 in. long, densely hairy beneath. Flowers pinkish, the petals upright. Fruit red, very showy in autumn. China. Hardy from zone* 5 southward.

divaricata. Upright shrub, 3–7 ft. high, its branches wide-spreading. Leaves ¾ in. long, pale beneath. Flowers pinkish, the petals erect. Fruit bright red, profusely borne and showy, ultimately becoming plum-red. China. Hardy from zone* 4 southward.

foveolata. An upright shrub 4–8 ft. high, the branches spreading. Leaves 2½–4 in. long, hairy. Flowers pinkish, the petals upright. Fruit black. Central China. Hardy from zone* 4 southward.

francheti. A partly evergreen, upright shrub, 4–8 ft. high, the branches spreading. Leaves 1–1½ in. long, densely hairy beneath. Flowers pinkish, the petals erect. Fruit orange-red. Western China. Hardy from zone* 5 southward.

frigida. A tall shrub or small tree, 7–20 ft. high with deciduous foliage. Leaves ovalish, 3–5 in. long, dull green above and white-hairy beneath when young. Flowers white, in dense clusters (corymbs*) followed by a brilliantly red fruit that persists for half the winter. Himalayas. May–June. Hardy from zone* 6 south-

---

* Special articles on the subjects indicated by an asterisk (*) will be found at the words so marked.

ward. The *var.* **aldenhamensis** has somewhat narrower leaves.

glaucophylla. Related to *C. salicifolia*, but with its bright-red fruit more football-shaped. China. Hardy from zone° 5 southward.

henryana. An evergreen or half-evergreen shrub, 8–12 ft. high, its grayish leaves 2–4 in. long, decidedly woolly beneath. Flowers about ½ in. wide, in a loose, hairy cluster (corymb°), followed by ovoid, dark-red fruit. China. June. Hardy from zone° 5 southward.

horizontalis. A low shrub, its branches forked and almost trailing. Leaves half-evergreen or dropping in the northern edge of its hardiness range, nearly round, ½ in. long. Flowers pinkish, the petals upright. Fruit red. Western China. Hardy from zone° 4 southward. The *var.* **perpusilla** has smaller but more numerous fruit, and it has many more small branches. Its foliage turns orange-red in autumn.

hupehensis. An arching shrub 4–6 ft. high, not evergreen. Leaves 1–1½ in. long, grayfelty beneath. Flowers white in clusters of 5–12. Fruit scarlet. China. Hardy from zone° 4 southward. May.

lactea. Related to *C. pannosa*, but with whitish-hairy twigs, and more hardy than that species. Hardy from zone° 5 southward.

lucida. An upright shrub, 4–10 ft. high, the branches ascending or erect. Leaves 1–2 in. long, shining above, pale beneath. Flowers pinkish, the petals upright. Fruit black. Northern Asia. Hardy from zone° 3 southward.

microphylla. Rock spray. A low, evergreen shrub, its branches somewhat upright, but the plant forming dense masses. Leaves about ¼ in. long, shining above, pale or grayish-hairy beneath. Flowers white, the petals spreading. Fruit scarlet, profuse. Himalayas. Hardy from zone° 4 southward. The *var.* **thymifolia** has narrower leaves and smaller flowers and fruit.

moupinensis. Closely related and quite similar to *C. bullata*, but with black fruit. China. June. Hardy from zone° 4 southward.

multiflora. A deciduous shrub, 8–10 ft. high, its branches arching. Leaves thin, broadly oval, 1–2 in. long, ¾–1½ in. wide, obviously stalked. Flowers white, ½ in. wide, in a many-flowered, loose, smooth cluster (corymb°). Fruit nearly round, red, about ⅜ in. in diameter. Western China. May–June. Hardy from zone° 5 southward, possibly in protected sites in zone° 4.

nitens. A deciduous shrub, 4–6 ft. high, leafy. Leaves shining green above, ovalish, ½–¾ in. long, paler beneath. Flowers pink, in a sparse cluster, followed by a nearly round, purplish-black fruit about ¼ in. in diameter. China. May–June. Hardy from zone° 3 (?), certainly from zone° 4 southward.

pannosa. Evergreen or half-evergreen shrub, 3–6 ft. high, the branches arching. Leaves 1 in. long, dull green above, white-woolly beneath. Flowers white, in profuse clusters, the petals spreading. Fruit dull red. Southwestern China. Hardy from zone° 6 southward and much planted in Calif.

praecox = *Cotoneaster adpressa praecox*.

prostrata = *C. rotundifolia*.

Pyracantha = *Pyracantha coccinea*.

racemiflora. A shrub 3–6 ft. high, the branches ascending or erect. Leaves nearly round, ¾–1¼ in. wide, whitish-hairy beneath. Flowers white, the petals spreading. Fruit red. Eurasia and northern Africa. Hardy from zone° 4 southward. The *var.* **songarica** from western China has leaves less hairy beneath. There are several other varieties of this most variable species.

rotundifolia. An upright evergreen shrub, 8–10 ft. high, but making dense patches. Leaves ½–¾ in. long, dark green above. Flowers white, the petals erect. Fruit scarlet. Himalayas. Hardy from zone° 5 southward.

salicifolia. An upright shrub 7–12 ft. high. Leaves evergreen southward, half-evergreen northward, 1½–3 in. long, the veins and stalk sometimes reddish. Flowers white, the petals spreading, the clusters densely woolly. Fruit red. Western China. Hardy from zone° 5 southward. The *var.* **floccosa** has the under side of young leaves densely hairy.

simonsi. Upright shrub, 7–12 ft. high, often partly evergreen. Leaves ¾–1¼ in. long, hairy beneath. Flowers white, the petals upright. Fruit scarlet. Himalayas. Hardy from zone° 5 southward.

zabeli. A deciduous° shrub, not over 6 ft. high, the branches spreading. Leaves broadly oval, ½–1 in. long, short-stalked, yellow-felty beneath. Flowers 3–9 in a nodding, hairy cluster, pinkish. Fruit red, about ¾ in. long. Central China. Hardy from zone° 3 southward. May. *Var.* **miniata** has orange-scarlet fruit.

COTONEASTER CULTURE

Cotoneasters form a useful group of shrubs or rarely small trees with deciduous or persistent-to-evergreen leaves. They are valued more for their showy black or red fruits than for their small white to pinkish flowers. They prefer sunny locations in well-drained soils with an alkaline rather than acid reaction. In limited quarters one might choose only the species with red fruits as they are more striking. In growth habit they vary from almost vine-like, prostrate shrubs, such as *C. dammeri*, through low, wide-spreading forms like *C. horizontalis*, wide-spreading bushes such as *C. divaricata* and *C. salicifolia* to erect, almost tree-like forms. Nearly all of the deciduous forms are hardy in the North, while the evergreen sorts are best in the South, as, for example, the handsome *C. pannosa*. The several varieties of *C. salicifolia* are the best evergreen sorts for the North. Nearly all cotoneasters are impatient of moving when once established and should be planted where needed, with preference for spring planting, and potted plants are safer. Propagation is by seed, which is often slow to germinate, or by cuttings of green wood with heat, or half-ripe wood with enough bottom-heat to stimulate root action. — B. Y. M.

INSECT PESTS. See scales at APPLE. Pruning out heaviest infestations will help.

DISEASES. Although not usually a serious problem the bacterial fireblight° will at times kill branches of this plant. See PEAR.

COTTON. See GOSSYPIUM.

COTTON GRASS. See ERIOPHORUM.

COTTON GUM = *Nyssa aquatica*.

COTTON ROSE = *Hibiscus mutabilis*.

COTTONSEED MEAL. A by-product of the oil mills and valuable as a fertilizer on lawns and for acid-tolerant plants, particularly kalmias, etc., at the rate of 3–5 lbs. per 100 sq. ft. The formula is about 6–3–2. (*See* FERTILIZERS; also MANURE.)

° Special articles on the subjects indicated by an asterisk (°) will be found at the words so marked.

COTTON THISTLE = *Onopordum Acanthium.*

COTTON TREE = *Bombax malabaricum.* For the silk-cotton tree *see* CEIBA.

COTTONWOOD. *See* POPULUS.

COTTONY JUJUBE = *Zizyphus mauritiana.*

COTULA (kot'you-la). A genus of herbs of the daisy family from the southern hemisphere, one, **C. squalida,** planted in the rock garden for its fern-like foliage. It is a low perennial, scarcely 2 in. high, but the stems creeping and often 1 ft. long. Leaves alternate,* about 2 in. long, deeply cut into fern-like segments. Flower heads scarcely ¼ in. in diameter, stalked, without rays, the head wholly of minute disk flowers. N. Z. The genus is sometimes called *Leptinella.* (*Cotula* is from the Greek for cup, perhaps in reference to the cup-shaped flower heads.)

COTYLEDON. The first or seed-leaf, folded within the seed. It is obvious upon germination of the common bean, but remains hidden within the seed in many other plants. *See* DICOTYLEDON, MONOCOTYLEDON, and POLYCOTYLEDON.

COTYLEDON (kot-ee-lee'don). A large group of succulent plants of the family Crassulaceae, all from the Old World and many from desert regions of South Africa. Leaves mostly in rosettes,* the latter basal or borne on the stem, thick and fleshy. Flowers in terminal clusters (cymes* or racemes*), the calyx 5-parted, the corolla tubular or urn-shaped. Stamens 10. Fruit a collection of pods (follicles*), each with several seeds. (*Cotyledon* is from the Greek for a cavity, in reference to the cup-like leaves of some species.)

For culture *see* SUCCULENTS. The species are sometimes offered under the name *Umbilicus.*

elegans = *Oliveranthus elegans.*
orbiculata. A shrubby plant 2–4 ft. high, the opposite leaves thick, fleshy, oblongish or even rounder, nearly 4 in. long, red-edged. Flowers about ½ in. long, red or yellowish-red, drooping. July–Aug. S. Af.
paraguayensis. *See* GRAPTOPETALUM.
simplicifolia. Stem erect or creeping, not over 18 in. high. Leaves thick and fleshy, ovalish or rounder, shallowly and irregularly blunt-toothed on the margin. Flowers golden-yellow, small, but attractive in hanging, loose clusters (raceme*). Caucasus. Summer. Recent suggestions that the correct name of this should be *Cotyledon oppositifolia,* or perhaps *Chiastophyllum oppositifolium,* are not here entertained.
umbilica. Navelwort; called, also, penny-wort. Not over 12 in. high, the leaves round, the stalk attached to the middle of the blade, the margins coarsely toothed. Flowers yellowish-green, about ⅓ in. long, drooping, and borne in a raceme. Eurasia. Can be grown in the rock garden southward. Also called *Umbilicus pendulina.*

COUCH GRASS = Quack grass (*Agropyron repens*). *See* list at WEEDS.

COUGHWORT = *Tussilago Farfara.*

COULTER PINE = *Pinus coulteri.* See PINE.

COUNTRY ESTATE. *See* PLANNING THE HOME GROUNDS.

Courbaril (koor-bar'il). South American native name for *Hymenaea Courbaril.*

COURTYARD GARDENS. *See* PLANNING THE HOME GROUNDS.

COVENTRY BELLS = *Campanula Trachelium.*

COVER CROP. A temporary crop to cover the ground, sometimes for protecting the land from erosion, to smother weeds, or for soil improvement. Sown broadcast and fairly thickly, any of the following will accomplish this: rye, oats, millet, and many legumes such as clovers, vetch, and peas. One of the best, for summer use, is soybean. Most cover crops are plowed under in the spring, but some are plowed under as soon as there is danger of their flowering. The legumes are the most valuable because of the nitrogen they gather and add to the soil.

COWAGE = *Stizolobium pruritum.*

COWBANE. *See* CICUTA.

COWBERRY = *Vaccinium Vitis-Idaea.*

COW CABBAGE = *Brassica oleracea acephala.* For culture *see* KALE.

COW CLOVER = *Trifolium medium.* See CLOVER.

COWHERB = *Saponaria Vaccaria.*

COWITCH = *Stizolobium pruritum.*

COW LILY = *Nuphar advena.*

COW PARSNIP. *See* HERACLEUM.

COWPEA = *Vigna sinensis.*

COWSLIP. As a garden plant, *Primula veris;* as a wild flower, *Caltha palustris* (*see* MARSH MARIGOLD). *See also* DODECATHEON and LACHENALIA.

COW-TONGUE = *Clintonia borealis.*

COW VETCH = *Vicia Cracca.*

COYOTE-BUSH = *Baccharis pilularis.*

COYOTE MINT = *Monardella villosa.*

CRAB, CRABAPPLE. *See* MALUS.

CRAB CACTUS = *Zygocactus truncatus.*

CRAB GRASS. Any annual grass of the genus *Digitaria.* It is one of the most pestiferous weeds in a lawn. Once crab grass has germinated it is essential to use sprays designed to kill grasses but not other plants. There are many such sprays on the market, all of them dangerous poisons (to children, pets, etc.), and they must be used only in the concentrations printed on the container. Three of them, in the relative order of effectiveness are PMA (phenyl mercuric acetate); DSMA (disodium methyl arsenate), useful also for chickweed; and potassium cyanate.

All of these should be used when the young seedlings are obvious, and because none of them kill all seedlings, the treatment should be repeated twice or thrice in the summer.

---

* Special articles on the subjects indicated by an asterisk (*) will be found at the words so marked.

After many years of experiment a leading authority has written, "Crab grass cannot be permanently controlled in a lawn by chemicals alone." Seed will inevitably be carried in and become established, especially on poor soils that will not maintain a good lawn. The remedy is to so improve the soil that a strong turf will smother the seedlings of crab grass long before their maturity. Crab grass is also known as finger-grass.

CRAB-TREE. See MALUS.

Cracca (krak′ka). An obsolete generic name applied to several vetch-like plants. *See* VICIA and TEPHROSIA.

CRACKERBERRY = *Cornus canadensis.*

CRAMBE (kram′be). Perhaps 20 species of fleshy-leaved, mostly bluish-foliaged herbs of the mustard family, scattered from the Canary Islands to western Asia, **C. maritima,** the sea-kale, being the only one of garden interest. It is a perennial with cabbage-like leaves nearly 2 ft. long, oblongish, lobed and notched. Flowers white, about ½ in. wide, in a large terminal cluster often 3 ft. high. (For details *see* CRUCIFERAE.) Fruit a hard, pealike body with a single seed in each pod. The original plant is native along the seacoasts of western Eu. For culture *see* SEA-KALE. (*Crambe* is the Greek name for this plant.)

CRANBERRY (*Vaccinium macrocarpon*). The culture of the common cranberry (purely an American species, although the name is also applied to V. *oxycoccus*) is not to be attempted unless one has or can make the specialized conditions it needs for growth. As to climatic requirements, the location of the commercial growers in Mass., N.J. and Wis. should be a guide to anyone.

While climatic conditions are important, the soil is still more so. It cannot be grown on upland soils, so that its culture is confined to a place having a low, relatively flat topography with a sluggish stream in it, or where ditches can be dug. And in addition, it must have an acid muck or peaty soil with a pH of 4.5–5 (*see* ACID AND ALKALI SOILS). A natural site with such a soil will be dominated by wild bog shrubs or herbs such as *Chamaedaphne calyculata,* the cranberry itself, much sphagnum moss, the pitcher-plant (*Sarracenia purpurea*), the sundews, or other acid-tolerant plants. In some places there may even be taller shrubs or trees like the white cedar (*Chamaecyparis thyoides*), or, in the North, tamarack or spruce.

Underlying the soil in which such plants are rooted is generally a layer of hardpan, often, and in the most favorable conditions, about 5 ft. below the surface. This maintains a steady supply of relatively acid water in the upper layer of muck.

To start operations, all live vegetation must be removed by burning or by a complete flooding and submergence for two years. Flooding is such an essential feature of subsequent culture that it is better to build a dam, with gates, at the start, so constructed that it is possible to cover the whole bog, plants and all, as needed.

Once the site is completely cleaned, the cuttings of the vine are planted in a layer of clean, moist sand about 2 in. thick. Put the rows 12–20 in. apart, and usually 2 cuttings are put at each 8-in. interval in the row. It will take them considerable time to cover completely all the ground and in the meantime weeds must be kept down. When once established, little weeding is necessary. Ordinarily it will be 2 or 3 years before such a plantation begins to bear in any quantity. Yields run from 3000–14,000 pounds per acre, depending on the variety and season.

FLOODING. Cranberry is sensitive to frost and the bogs are usually flooded soon after the final picking, which should be over by Nov. 20 or earlier in some regions. They must be flooded (*i.e.,* the plants submerged) from Dec. 15 to May 8 in N.J. and elsewhere to correspond with the worst of the cold weather and late spring frosts.

There are other temporary floodings for pest controls as outlined below. The necessity for these floodings is so imperative that no plantation should be contemplated unless adequate water supplies (*i.e.,* of acid water) are available for storage, and arrangements made for conducting it quickly. Growers will temporarily flood a bog if late afternoon temperatures get down to 28° or 29°. While the berries are able to stand 28° without injury, 24° or 22° will quite likely ruin them.

FERTILIZER. Of course the native growth of wild cranberries gets no special feeding. But commercial growers have found, after a long series of experiments, that their crop is greatly increased by an application of a special fertilizer. Due to the acid soil condition of the site, this fertilizer must be made according to the following formula:

Sodium nitrate	75 pounds
Dried blood	75 pounds
Rock phosphate	300 pounds
Sulphate of potash	50 pounds

A single application of such a mixture at a rate of 500–800 pounds per acre is beneficial, but it should not be done more than once in three or four years. On some cranberry soils even this single application may stimulate vine growth at the expense of fruit production. It is safer, therefore, to experiment on a small part of the bog to determine if your soil type responds favorably to fertilizer.

INSECT PESTS. Any leaf feeders such as fireworms are easily controlled by pesticide #17 or #21. (*See* SPRAYS AND DUSTS.) Holding water on bogs until May makes for fewer insect problems, except for army worms which may increase. Army worms are controlled by pesticide #17. At dangle stage of blossom buds, before bloom, apply pesticide #17 to control leafhopper vector of false-blossom disease. Best time to control most other pests is at stage before blossom buds dangle with pesticide #21-#17 mixture. October floods will control girdlers in roots. Scales are easily controlled in spring by pesticide #21.

DISEASES. Although a number of different fungi cause berry rot, the differences can be

---

* Special articles on the subjects indicated by an asterisk (*) will be found at the words so marked.

distinguished only by an expert. The control recommendations are approximately the same in all instances. Apply pesticide #5 or #11 (*see* SPRAYS AND DUSTS) at about the mid-bloom period and repeat two weeks and four weeks later.

Cranberry false blossom is a disease which produces upright green flower heads rather than the normal hanging red or pink heads. This virus disease, as the name implies, results in a "false blossom" and no fruit develops from it. This disease is best controlled by protecting the plants against attack by the insect which transmits the virus. *See* Insects above.

CRANBERRY BUSH = *Viburnum trilobum.*

CRANBERRY GOURD = *Abobra tenuifolia.*

CRANBERRY TREE = *Viburnum Opulus.*

CRANESBILL. *See* GERANIUM.

CRANESBILL FAMILY = Geraniaceae.

CRAPE JASMINE = *Tabernaemontana coronaria.*

CRAPE MYRTLE = *Lagerstroemia indica.*

crassifolia, -us, -um (kras-si-fō'li-a). Thick-leaved.

crassipes (kras'si-peez). Thick-stalked.

CRASSULA (krass'you-la). A very large genus of succulent herbs or shrubs of the family Crassulaceae, all from the Old World, and most from South Africa. Several of those below are very widely grown as pot plants and in miniature desert gardens, especially in Calif. Leaves opposite,* very thick and fleshy, without teeth (in ours). Flowers (rarely produced in house plants) white or pink, in compact clusters (often cymes*), the petals, sepals and stamens 5, the petals sometimes joined at the base. Fruit dry. (*Crassula* is Latin diminutive of *crassus*, thick.)

For general notes on culture *see* SUCCULENTS. *Crassula argentea* is one of the commonest succulent plants in the U.S., every florist offering specimens that range from only a few leaves to compact, well-grown, bushy plants containing scores of leaves. As a house plant it will stand more abuse than almost any other, but it will not stand overwatering. While it will stand house conditions, it is best grown in the cool greenhouse, as are most of the others below, except in frost-free regions.

arborescens. A shrub 3–5 ft. high, more in its native region. Leaves thick, fleshy, grayish-green, dotted, the margins red, generally round-oval and about 2 in. long. Flowers, often wanting in cult., white but ultimately pink or red. S. Af

argentea. The common species in cult., but without an appropriate common name, the florists' names of Japanese laurel, Japanese rubber-plant and jade plant being misleading. As grown in Calif., a thick-stemmed, branching shrub 6–10 ft. high, as a pot plant much smaller and often unbranched. Leaves very thick and shining, oval to roundish, about 1½ in. long, the broad base appearing as though merged with the stem. Flowers, which may not bloom for years

(or ever in house plants), white or pink. S. Af. Also offered as *C. portulacea.*

coccinea = *Rochea coccinea.*

falcata. A shrub 2–4 ft. high as cult., more in the wild. Leaves sickle-shaped, 2–4 in. long, slightly inequilateral, grayish-green, practically stalkless, or the stem passing through the joined leaf bases. Flowers scarlet, in close flat-topped clusters (corymb*). S. Af.

lactea. A shrubby plant 1–2 ft. high, its white-dotted leaves in opposite pairs. Leaves thick and fleshy, about 1½ in. long, distinctly tapering at the tip. Flowers star-like, white, in a loose terminal cluster (raceme*). Natal and the Transvaal.

lycopodioides. Prostrate or sprawling, its stems quite hidden by the numerous tiny leaves (resembling a club moss). Leaves green, very small, crowded. Flowers greenish, very small and borne from the leaf axils.* S. Af.

multicava. A low, greenhouse herb, but grown outdoors in Calif. Leaves ovalish, 2–3 in. long, the bases of the leaves joining so that they surround the stem. Flowers white. S. Af.

perforata. A shrubby plant, 1–2 ft. high, its opposite leaves joined at the base and surrounding the stem (perfoliate*). Leaves green, about 1 in. long, red-dotted, the margins hairy. Flowers small, yellow, in a showy, interrupted cluster (thyrse*) that may be nearly 12 in. long. S. Af.

portulacea = *C. argentea.*

pseudolycopodioides. Perhaps not distinct from *C. lycopodioides,* but stouter and with grayish-green foliage, and more numerous flowers.

quadrifolia = *C. multicava.*

rupestris. An erect or often procumbent plant with very thick leaves through which the stem appears to pass. Leaves keeled on the back, about ¾ in. long, bluish-green, concave above, red-edged. Flowers small, pinkish or white in a dense, terminal cluster (corymb*). S. Af.

tetragona. A brittle, shrubby plant, the stems easily broken and as easily rooted, 1–2 ft. high. Leaves green, 3-sided, or roundish in cross-section, about 1 in. long, stalkless, and almost joined at the base. Flowers white, in a few-flowered cluster (cyme*). S. Af.

There are many other species to be found in the collections of specialists in succulents.

CRASSULACEAE (krass-you-lay'see-ee). The orpine or stonecrop family is easily recognized if only its garden representatives are considered. They are characteristically fleshy-leaved plants with often handsome, prevailingly red or yellow, rarely white, flowers. They are chiefly grown as pot plants, especially *Rochea, Crassula, Cotyledon, Bryophyllum, Kalanchoe, Pachyphytum,* and *Echeveria,* but many are grown in the open border and some, especially in *Sedum,* are popular rock garden plants.

Leaves (in our genera) thick and fleshy (scale-like in some sedums). Flowers perfect,* nearly always in clusters, often in cymes,* the individual flower small, but the cluster often very showy, especially in *Sempervivum* (*see* HOUSELEEK), *Gormania, Graptopetalum,* and *Oliveranthus.* The only other garden genera are *Monanthes,* from Morocco and the Canaries, and *Adromischus,* from S. Af. The family contains over 1500 species, in perhaps 30 genera, the identification of which

---

* Special articles on the subjects indicated by an asterisk (*) will be found at the words so marked.

is puzzling. For the culture of the garden genera *see* SUCCULENTS.

Technical flower characters: Sepals or lobes of the calyx 4 or 5. Petals 4 or 5, sometimes united into a tube (*Cotyledon, Echeveria, Bryophyllum, Kalanchoe,* etc.). Stamens 4 or 5, or double these numbers. Fruit dry, 1-celled, a follicle.*

CRATAEGUS (kra-tee′gus). Under the name hawthorn, thorn, or thornapple is grouped an enormous genus (perhaps 1000 species) of thorny shrubs and trees of the rose family, found in the north temperate zone but most common in eastern N.A. Less than 20 are really garden plants, although any of the wild species may be transferred to informal plantings. Leaves alternate,* always toothed or lobed, none truly evergreen. Flowers white (red or pink in some hort. forms), nearly always in small clusters (corymbs*). Sepals and petals 5, the stamens 5–25, sometimes the anthers* pink or purple. Fruit resembling a miniature apple, nearly always brightly colored, and a most attractive autumn feature of the group. (*Crataegus* is the old Greek name for these plants, implying strength, from their hard wood.)

The native hawthorns are extremely attractive in flower (May–June) and in fruit (Sept.–Oct.). While most of those below will grow in ordinary garden soil, they prefer limestone regions and an open, sandy loam. Because of their thorns, impenetrable barriers can be made of them, although they do not stand being clipped for hedges. Of the Old World species much the best known is the English hawthorn or May. Propagation is by seeds and a slow process. Allow the pulp of the fruit to decay or soak it off in water, after which the seeds must be stratified (*see* SEEDS AND SEEDAGE). Ordinarily they take two years to sprout. Another and quicker method is by root cuttings (*see* CUTTINGS). All those below can be purchased as rooted plants from nurserymen. Some of them are known as haw.

The flowers are white unless otherwise noted, and the hardiness of the American species is indicated by their wide range.

arnoldiana. A tree up to 20 ft. or even more, the thorns thin, straight, about 3 in. long. Leaves 2–3 in. long, doubly toothed and shallowly lobed. Flowers nearly ¾ in. wide. Fruit pear-shaped, red, about ¾ in. long. Mass. and Conn.

carrieri = *Crataegus lavallei.*

coccinea = *Crataegus intricata.*

coccinioides. A small tree, not over 20 ft. high, sometimes shrubby, the dark purple thorns about 1½ in. long. Leaves ovalish, 2–3 in. long, sharply and deeply toothed or even lobed; short-stalked. Flowers white in dense clusters (corymbs*), the anthers* rose-colored. Fruit nearly round, bright red, about ¾ in. in diameter. Central U.S. May.

cordata = *C. Phaenopyrum.*

crus-galli. Cockspur thorn. A large shrub or small tree up to 30 ft., the thorns numerous, slender, 3–4 in. long. Leaves oblongish, wedge-shaped at the base, 2–3 in. long, toothed in the upper part. Flowers about ½ in. wide. Fruit

nearly round, about ½ in. in diameter. Quebec to Mich. and S. Car.

douglasi. A nearly unarmed shrub or sometimes a tree up to 25 ft. Leaves ovalish, 1–3 in. long, toothed or even shallowly lobed, dark, shiny green. Flowers about ½ in. wide, usually 5–12 in a loose cluster (corymb*). Fruit red at first, ultimately black, about ½ in. thick and oblongish. Northern N.A. May.

intricata. A shrub 5–8 ft. high, the thorns few, curved and 3–4 in. long. Leaves elliptic to ovalish, 2–3 in. long, doubly toothed and also with 3–4 pairs of sharp lobes. Flowers nearly 1 in. wide. Fruit nearly round, reddish-brown. Mass. to Va. and Mich. Sometimes known as *C. coccinea.*

lavallei. A hybrid tree up to 20 ft., the thorns stout and about 2 in. long. Leaves elliptic or oblongish, 3–4 in. long, unequally toothed. Flowers white, with a red disk, about ¾ in. wide. Fruit persisting through the winter, brick red, about ½ in. long. Hardy from zone* 4 southward.

mollis. Red haw. Tree up to 30 ft., the thorns stout and 2 in. long or less. Leaves broadly oval, 3–4 in. long, doubly toothed. Flowers white, with a red disk, about 1 in. wide. Fruit nearly 1 in. in diameter, scarlet. Ont. to Ala. and westward.

monogyna. English hawthorn, but the name applied also to *C. Oxyacantha.* A shrub or small tree, not over 15 ft. high, the thorns about 1 in. long. Leaves broadly oval, cut into 3–5 lobes that are shallowly toothed. Flowers white, about ½ in. wide. Fruit scarlet. Eurasia. Hardy from zone* 3 southward. There are many varieties, some with pink, red, or double flowers, and one with upright branches and columnar habit.

nitida. A round-topped tree, 20–30 ft. high, almost or quite thornless. Leaves oblong or elliptic, 1½–3 in. long, pointed at the tip, sharply toothed, on short, winged stalks. Flowers about ⅝ in. wide, profuse in a branched cluster (corymb*), the anthers* yellow. Fruit nearly round, dark red and about ½ in. in diameter. Central U.S. and possibly a natural hybrid. Often cult. May.

Oxyacantha. English hawthorn, but *see* C. MONOGYNA. A tree up to 30 ft., and with the leaves more deeply lobed and the lobes toothed only in the upper part. Eurasia and northern Africa. Hardy from zone* 3 southward. Often confused with *C. monogyna.* Of the many varieties offered the most noteworthy are those with drooping branches, another with bloom extending into mid-August, and one with fern-like foliage.

Phaenopyrum. Washington thorn. A dense, round-headed tree, 20–30 ft. high, the thorns slender, up to 3 in. long. Leaves broadly triangular, 3–7-lobed, the lobes doubly toothed. Flowers ½ in. wide. Fruit bright red, about ¼ in. in diameter. Pa. to Fla. and Mo. Hardy from zone* 4 southward.

pinnatifida. An Asiatic hawthorn, usually a tree 15–20 ft. high and essentially thornless. Leaves stalked, broadly oval, 2–4 in. long and wide, usually with 2 deep lobes toward the base, mostly hairy on the veins beneath. Flowers white, about ¾ in. wide, in hairy clusters. Fruit dotted, red, round or pear-shaped and about ⅝ in. in diameter. May. A fine hawthorn, especially in fruit, which are edible (in China).

prunifolia. A possibly hybrid tree (one of its assumed parents is from N.A.), not over 15–20 ft., its thorns 1½–3 in. long. Leaves shining dark green, ovalish, 2–3 in. long. Flowers

---

* Special articles on the subjects indicated by an asterisk (*) will be found at the words so marked.

white, about ¾ in. wide in profuse, hairy, clusters 2–3 in. wide, the anthers* pink. Fruit round, about ⅝ in. in diameter, not winter-persistent.

punctata. An open-topped tree 25–30 ft. high, sometimes unarmed, or with a few stout thorns; sometimes thorny on the trunk. Leaves broadest toward the tip, wedge-shaped at the base, toothed toward the base but lobed above the middle, 2–3½ in. long. Flowers numerous, about ¾ in. wide, in profuse, branched, clusters, the anthers* pink or pale yellow. Fruit dotted, red, nearly round or pear-shaped, about ¾ in. in diameter. Eastern N.A. May–June.

succulenta. A tree up to 25 ft., its brownish thorns nearly 2 in. long. Leaves wedge-shaped at the base, generally oval in outline, 2–3 in. long, toothed on the margin, hairy on the upper surface when young. Flowers white, in many-flowered clusters, the anthers* pale yellow or pink. Fruit nearly round, about ⅝ in. in diameter, bright red. Eastern N.A. May.

tomentosa = C. uniflora.

uniflora. Pear haw; also called black thorn. A shrub or small tree up to 15 ft. high, the thorns short or none. Leaves elliptic or oblongish, 3–5 in. long, toothed and sometimes slightly lobed. Flowers about ½ in. wide. Fruit somewhat pear-shaped, orange-red, about ½ in. long. L.I. to Fla. and Tex. Also called *C. tomentosa.*

INSECT PESTS. Aphids are controlled by applications of malathion (*see* SPRAYS AND DUSTS) repeated as necessary. Leaf miners also respond to repeated applications of that material.

DISEASES. Many varieties of hawthorn have severe rust* of foliage and fruit, particularly if growing close to juniper trees which are alternate hosts for the rust disease. Use pesticide #5 (*see* SPRAYS AND DUSTS) applied just as flowering begins, and again immediately after petal fall.

The English hawthorn will defoliate completely during the latter part of the summer in many areas. This is a result of leafspot* disease. Use pesticide #11 just as buds break in the spring and repeat 10 days later.

Fireblight* will cause sudden wilting of leaves and death of entire branches during some years. In some areas, the use of antibiotic* sprays has offered control. Contact your state agricultural experiment station for directions for your locality.

CREAM BUSH = Holodiscus discolor.

CREAM-CUPS. A single, rather attractive, annual Californian herb belonging to the genus **Platystemon** (plat-i-stee′mon) of the family Papaveraceae. The only species, **P. californicus**, covers great areas there and is often grown as an annual in the flower garden elsewhere. It is an erect plant 6–12 in. high, the leaves narrow, clasping the stem and about 2 in. long. Flowers solitary, long-stalked, with 3 sepals and 6 petals, the latter cream-colored or light yellow. Stamens* numerous, some of them flattened and petal-like. Fruit a head of small pods. (*Platystemon* is from the Greek for broad and stamen.) Seeds should be sown where the plant is wanted, but only after warm weather has arrived.

CREEPERS. *See* VINES.

CREEPING. As a descriptive word for plants of prostrate or trailing habit, *creeping* is part of the common name of many plants. Those found in this ENCYCLOPEDIA are:

Creeping barberry = Mahonia repens; **Creeping bent** = Agrostis stolonifera compacta; **Creeping buttercup** = Ranunculus repens (*see* BUTTERCUP. See also Creeping buttercup in the list at WEEDS); **Creeping Charlie** = Lysimachia Nummularia; **Creeping crowfoot** = Ranunculus repens (*see* BUTTERCUP. See also Creeping buttercup in the list at WEEDS); **Creeping fig** = Ficus pumila; **Creeping forget-me-not** = Omphalodes verna; **Creeping Jennie** = Lysimachia Nummularia; **Creeping Juniper** = Juniperus horizontalis; **Creeping lily-turf** = Liriope spicata; **Creeping myrtle** = Vinca minor; **Creeping snowberry** = Gaultheria hispidula; **Creeping thyme** = Thymus Serpyllum (*see* THYME).

crenata, -us, -um (kree-nay′ta). Crenate; *i.e.*, scalloped or with an irregularly waved margin; mostly applied to leaf margins.

crenatiflora, -us, -um (kree-nay-ti-flow′ra). Having flowers with scalloped edges.

crenato-serrata, -us, -um (kree-nat-o-ser-ray′ta). With wavy-margined teeth.

crenulata, -us, -um (kren-you-lay′ta). Somewhat crenate or scalloped.

CREOSOTE. An excellent wood preservative, more lasting than paint, and used also as a repellent for insects. Reports that creosote will injure vines or prevent their climbing over creosote-impregnated fences, pergolas, etc., is apparently true if the material is freshly dipped. When thoroughly absorbed by the wood creosote does not injure plants.

CREOSOTE BUSH = Larrea tridentata.

CRÊPE MYRTLE. *See* LAGERSTROEMIA INDICA.

CREPIS (creep′is). Rather weedy herbs, some actual pests, but one an annual flower garden plant. The hawksbeards, which comprise the genus *Crepis*, include well over 200 species, but only C. rubra is of any garden interest. It is a branching annual 8–18 in. high, with a leafy stem and milky juice. Leaves largely basal, dandelion-like, the lower ones with a winged stalk. Flowers in small, solitary, long-stalked heads, red or flesh-colored. Italy. Summer. A showy annual to be sown where wanted. *See* ANNUALS. For the plant known as Crepis barbata *see* TOLPIS. (*Crepis* is Greek for sandal and of uncertain application here.)

crepitans (krep′i-tanz). Crackling or rustling.

CRESCENTIA. *See* CALABASH.

CRESS. Many plants of the mustard family are known as cress, the most important being watercress (which see). For other cresses *see* LEPIDIUM, BARBAREA, CARDAMINE, and ARABIS.

CRESS FAMILY = Cruciferae.

CRESTED. Bearing a crest. In plants the crest is often a ridge or appendage, sometimes toothed or elevated and irregular. The crest may be on the petals, as in some iris, or it may modify the whole flower cluster as in

---

* Special articles on the subjects indicated by an asterisk (*) will be found at the words so marked.

the cockscomb, or even leaves, as in some crested forms of the fern *Pteris cretica.*

CRESTED DOG'S-TAIL = *Cynosurus cristatus.*

CRESTED IRIS = *Iris cristata.*

CRESTED POPPY = *Argemone platyceras.*

CRESTED SHIELD FERN = *Dryopteris cristata.*

CRESTED WHEAT-GRASS. A good turf grass (*Agropyron cristatum*) of the Old World introduced into the regions of Western U.S. where deficient rainfall will not permit bluegrass lawns. *See* COLORADO.

CRETAN BEAR'S-TAIL = *Celsia Arcturus.*

CRETAN MULLEIN = *Celsia cretica.*

CRETAN SPIKENARD = *Valeriana Phu.*

cretica, -us, -um (kree'ti-ka). From Crete.

CRIMSON CLOVER = *Trifolium incarnatum. See* CLOVER.

CRIMSON FLAG = *Schizostylis coccinea.*

CRIMSON GARDEN. *See* RED GARDEN.

CRIMSON GLORY VINE = *Vitis coignetiae glabrescens.*

CRIMSON RAMBLER. *See* ROSA MULTIFLORA CATHAYENSIS.

CRIMSON SAGE = *Audibertia grandiflora.*

crinita, -us, -um (kry-ny'ta). Long-haired.

CRINKLE-BUSH. The dyed sprays of *Lomatia silaifolia,* an Australian shrub of the family Proteaceae, used by florists and decorators for ornament. It is otherwise of no garden interest.

CRINKLEROOT = *Dentaria diphylla.*

CRINODENDRON (cry-no-den'dron). A small genus of ornamental evergreen trees of the family Elaeocarpaceae, mostly from southern S.A. Leaves alternate or opposite, nearly stalkless. Flowers generally solitary or in 2's, from the leaf joints, urn-shaped or lantern-shaped, generally nodding and long-stalked. Petals 5. Fruit a leathery pod. (*Crinodendron* is from the Greek for lily and tree, in allusion to the fragrant white flowers.) Formerly known as *Tricuspidaria.* There is some doubt as to the application of the name for the Patagua.

These are grown outdoors in coastal Calif. and other frost-free regions, but as they are plants of cool rain-forests they need plenty of moisture. Can also be grown in the cool greenhouse in potting mixture* 3.

dependens = *Crinodendron hookerianum.*
hookerianum. Lantern tree. A beautiful tree, 15–25 ft. high. Leaves short-stalked, leathery, elliptic, 1½–4½ in. long, with a few shallow, blunt teeth on the margin. Flowers about ¾ in. long, urn-shaped, the petals incurved at the tip, deep crimson. Chile. Spring-blooming outdoors in Calif.
Patagua. Patagua. A tree up to 30 ft. or more in the wild, usually less as cult. and a slow grower. Leaves broader than in the species above, 1–3 in. long, sparingly toothed, prominently veined. Flowers cup-shaped, the petals not incurved, white, not quite ¾ in. long

and fragrant. Chile. Does well in the fog area of Calif., poorly or not at all elsewhere.

CRINODONNA. The European, and perhaps correct name for hybrids between *Amaryllis* and *Crinum,* which were first crossed in Europe. Here they are known as *Amarcrinum* (which see).

CRINUM (kry'num). A genus of perhaps 100 species of thick- or bulbous-rooted, lily-like herbs of the family Amaryllidaceae, mostly tropical, a few cult. for their very showy flowers. Leaves persistent or evergreen, thick or almost fleshy, strap-shaped or sword-shaped, stalkless. Flowers in an umbel* at the end of a tall, solid stalk, beneath the umbel 2 spathe*-like bracts. Corolla funnel-shaped, or with a long, slender tube, the summit ending in narrow or broad segments. Fruit an irregularly bursting capsule.* (*Crinum* is the Greek name for a lily.)

These handsome plants, sometimes called crinum lilies, are grown outdoors chiefly in the South, although some of them can be wintered over up to zone* 5 with a good mulch of strawy manure. They are naturally rich feeders and do best in good soils and with plenty of water. In the South they should be left where planted, as they dislike moving and may not flower for two or three seasons after being lifted. If let alone they are apt to make striking, large clumps.

Greenhouse culture is rare because the plants get too big for easy handling. If grown in the greenhouse the roots of most of them should be stored over the winter in a cool but frost-free place, potted up in early March and put in a warm, moist greenhouse, using potting mixture* 4. Greenhouse culture of the evergreen sorts demands that they be potted up continuously but rested by reduction of heat and partial drying-out during the winter.

Most of the species produce small offsets* from the base of the bulb-like root. These can be detached and provide the easiest method of propagation as they root easily. If the plants set fruit, which is seldom, propagation by seeds is possible, but it will take at least 2 or 3 years before the seedlings will bloom.

americanum. Swamp lily (not a true lily, however). Leaves few, long and narrow. Flowers white, the segments long and narrow. Stalk of the flower cluster 18–24 in. long, usually arising before the leaves appear. Fla. to Tex.
asiaticum. A large, strong plant, its bulb-like root often 1 ft. long. From this spring large clumps of closely placed leaves, that are 3 ft. long, 3–4 in. wide, and with a tapering tip. Flowers fragrant, white, at least 20 in the cluster, which is borne on a 2-edged stalk that slightly overtops the leaves. Tropical Asia. Blooming all summer and beyond.
bulbispermum. The commonest crinum in cult. and hardy, with protection, up to zone* 5. Leaves long and narrow, the margins roughish. Flowers white or pink, about 12 in the cluster, 3–4 in. wide, the tube 3–4 in. long and curved. Segments about 1 in. wide. S. Af. Also known as *C. capensis* and *C. longifolium.*
moorei. A larger plant than the last, the

---

* Special articles on the subjects indicated by an asterisk (*) will be found at the words so marked.

leaves at least 3 in. wide and smooth on the edges. Flowers nearly 4 in. wide, white, with a pink stripe. S. Af. Tender above zone* 5.

powelli. A hybrid *Crinum* (*bulbispermum* × *moorei*), with a globular, long-necked bulb, and about 20 narrow leaves, 3–4 ft. long. Flowers curved, about 3 in. long, reddish but green at the base, with 6–8 flowers in a terminal cluster (umbel*) that stands about 2 ft. high. Hardy up to zone* 5.

scabrum. Leaves scarcely 2 in. wide, the margins rough. Flowers white, the back of the segments crimson, the tube greenish, curved and 3–5 in. long, the segments half that length. Tropical Af. Not hardy north.

crispa, -us, -um (kriss'pa). Crisped or curled.

Crista-galli. A specific name meaning a cock's comb or like one, but not applied to the plant cockscomb.

cristata, -us, -um (kriss-tay'ta). Crested.*

crocata, -us, -um (kro-cay'ta). Yellow.

crocea, -us, -um (krō'see-a). Crocus-yellow.

CROCKS. Mostly broken flower pots, the pieces put over the hole in the bottom of a flower pot to provide proper drainage and keep soil from washing out. For its proper use *see* POTTING.

crocosmaeflora, -us, -um (kro-kos-mi-flow'-ra). With flowers like the genus *Crocosmia* (which see).

CROCOSMIA (kro-kos'mee-a). A South African herb of the iris family, having gladiolus-like corms,* and to be grown, in the North, in the same way. The only cult. species, **C. aurea,** the copper-tip, is a branching herb up to 3½ ft. high, with only a few small, scattered leaves, the lower shorter than the upper, sword-shaped. Flowers nearly regular,* bright orange-yellow, the tube about 1 in. long, the segments longer and spreading. The flowers are in spikes and these are sometimes branched. Not much grown in the North. Related to *Gladiolus,* but differing in having the valves of the spathe* not notched. (*Crocosmia* is from the Greek for saffron smell, which is evident when the dried flowers are soaked in water.) It is one of the parents of the common garden montbretia. *See* TRITONIA CROCOSMAEFLORA.

CROCUS (krō'kus). A genus of perhaps 80 species of very popular garden plants of the iris family, ranging from the Mediterranean region to southwestern Asia. They are apparently stemless plants arising from a corm* (the crocus "bulb" of the shops). Leaves narrow or grass-like, appearing before, or with, or after the flowers. Flowers blooming very early in spring or in autumn, but the plant commonly called autumn crocus belongs to the genus *Colchicum.* Crocus flowers are produced at the ground level, are stemless or very short-stalked, and have 6 segments and 3 stamens.* Fruit a capsule,* ripening at or below ground level. (*Crocus* is the Greek name of the saffron, *Crocus sativus.*)

For culture and uses, *see* below. The common garden crocus is *C. vernus.*

asturicus. A fall-blooming bulbous plant, the leaves 8–10 in. long, appearing with the flowers which are 4–5 in. long, violet or lilac, bearded, the base of the flower violet-purple. Spain. Sept.–Nov.

aureus. A spring-blooming sort sometimes called Dutch crocus or simply Dutch yellow. Flowers bright yellow, the segments about 1½ in. long. Southeastern Eu. and Asia Minor. Also called *C. flavus* and *C. moesiacus.*

biflorus. Scotch crocus (but a native of southeastern Eu. and Asia Minor); a useful, spring-blooming plant for the rock garden. Flowers purple-tinged, the outer segments purple-striped, the throat yellow. There are several named forms or varieties, most of them color variants.

chrysanthus. A spring-blooming crocus, the leaves appearing after the bloom. Leaves keeled, about 12 in. long, and very narrow. Flower not bearded, about 3 in. long, orange or bronze. Feb.–Mar. Greece and Asia Minor. There are several good hort. forms, some with darker orange flowers and one or two with nearly brown flowers.

etruscus. A spring-blooming crocus, the leaves appearing with the flowers and very narrow, with a white band. Flowers 2–3 in. long, somewhat bearded, yellow, but purplish inside. Italy. Mar.

imperati. Spring-blooming, the flowers lilac or white, the outer segments purple-striped and about 1½ in. long. One of the first to bloom. Italy.

korolkowi. A very early-blooming crocus, its flowers not bearded. Leaves appearing with the flowers or just after, ultimately 8–10 in. long, much less at blooming time. Flowers fragrant, about 2 in. long, golden-yellow, but darker toward the center. Jan.–Mar., depending on the site. Turkestan.

longiflorus. Autumn-blooming, the flowers lilac, the segments about 1 in. long, the throat slightly bearded and yellow. Southern Eu.

moesiacus. Some consider this the correct name for the Dutch crocus. *See* CROCUS AUREUS, above.

nudiflorus. Autumn-blooming, the flowers lilac, the segments nearly 2 in. long. Southern Eu. This and *C. longiflorus* are good plants for the autumn garden (which see).

pulchellus. Autumn-blooming, the flowers lilac, but faintly striped. Segments about 1½ in. long, the throat yellow. Greece to Asia Minor.

sativus. Saffron crocus; called also vegetable gold. Autumn-blooming, the flowers white or lilac, the segments nearly 2 in. long, the throat bearded, the stigmas* orange. Asia Minor. A common form has a yellow throat. *See* HERB GARDENING.

sieberi. An old garden favorite, spring-blooming crocus, now in many forms, chief among them the *var.* versicolor. Leaves appearing with the flowers, about 8 in. long, white-banded. Flowers 3–4 in. long, not bearded, lilac with the throat deep orange, the stigmas* orange-red. Mar. Greece.

speciosus. A good rock garden, autumn-blooming crocus with lilac or purple-tinged flowers, the segments 2 in. long. Eurasia.

susianus. Cloth-of-gold. Spring-blooming, the flowers orange-yellow, but brownish outside, the segments about 1¼ in. long. Crimea. Called by some *C. angustifolius. See* ROCK GARDEN.

tomassinianus. Spring-blooming, the flowers

---

* Special articles on the subjects indicated by an asterisk (*) will be found at the words so marked.

pale reddish-blue, the segments about 1½ in. long, often dark-spotted at the tip. Dalmatia and Serbia.

vernus. Common crocus, spring-blooming and in a variety of colors (*see* Culture below), the segments about 1½ in. long, bearded. Eu. Very like the last except for the beard.

versicolor. A spring-blooming crocus, the parent of many hort. varieties, the leaves 8–9 in. long and appearing with the flowers. Flowers 4–5 in. long, yellowish-white to purple, often streaked with purple on the outside. Mar. French and Italian Alps.

zonatus. A rock-garden, autumn-blooming crocus, the rose-lilac flowers streaked with purple, and orange-spotted inside. Segments about 2 in. long, the throat yellow and bearded. Asia Minor. Also known as *C. kotschyanus.* *See* ROCK GARDEN.

CROCUS CULTURE

Possibly none of the smaller spring bulbs will make a braver show than crocus if one remembers to plant them in a warm, well-drained soil where the first spring sun will make them open wide their brilliant flowers, accented by showy yellow-to-orange stamens* and pistils.* From the small corms that resemble those of gladiolus, they push up sharp noses from which rises the grassy foliage with silver mid-stripes and masses of bloom — white, white with purple and violet stripes, lavenders, lilacs, gray-blues, rosy purples, and deep, warm purples darkening almost to black, especially in the throat. Recommended varieties are: Jeanne d'Arc and Kathleen Parlow for whites; Pickwick with lilac stripes; Pallas with purple stripes; Excelsior and Little Dorrit, amethyst; Gladstone and Paulus Potter, reddish purples; and old Purpurea Grandiflora, darkest of all. All these are forms of *Crocus vernus.* For yellows one must turn to the species, particularly *C. aureus* which is sold as Dutch Yellow, and *C. susianus,* sold as Cloth-of-Gold.

More and more attention is now given to species crocus and the seedlings raised from them. These can become the basis of a collection, and for the beginner, the forms of *C. biflorus, C. chrysanthus,* and *C. tomassinianus* should be the start, with *C. sieberi* and *C. imperati* in any form that can be had. Then for the autumn bloomers, *C. speciosus* in all its forms and any other available, except *C. sativus* which rarely persists in gardens.

Plant the corms deeply (3–4 in.) so that they will not produce a multitude of small and non-blooming cormlets, unless you want to increase one particular corm. Choose a spot where they may self-sow, with a warm soil, and if planted with other plants, choose ground covers that will not make too dense a mass to hold moisture in summer. In lawns, crocus persists well, though the lawns should not be mowed until the crocus foliage is half ripened. Although most crocus come from areas where there is intense heat in summer, they usually need definite cold in winter, so that the whole genus is not likely to persist in the deep South, except with artificial treatment each season. — B. Y. M.

CROCUS FAMILY = Iridaceae.

CROQUET. A lawn game, the standard area for which is 30×60 ft.

CROSSANDRA (kros-san′dra). Showy greenhouse plants, comprising perhaps 20 species of herbs or shrubs of the family Acanthaceae, all from the Old World tropics. The only one of hort. interest is **C. infundibuliformis,** a shrub 1–3 ft. high from India. Leaves generally opposite,* narrowly oval, 3–5 in. long, more or less wavy-margined. Flowers orange-scarlet, in a large, dense, hairy, 4-sided spike. Corolla tubular, its limb 1-sided, about 1 in. long, each flower from within the leafy bracts,* which are persistent and about as long as the capsules.* The plant needs a warm, moist greenhouse and potting mixture* 3. (*Crossandra* is from the Greek for fringed anthers.)

CROSS-BREED. The result of a cross between plants of varieties of one species. Synonyms are *half-breed, mongrel, variety hybrid.* — O. E. W.

CROSS-FERTILIZATION: CROSS-POLLINATION. A sexually produced seed may result from either cross- or self-pollination and subsequent fertilization. In the former case two plants are involved; in the latter only one. The pollen and egg parent plants may be simply two individuals of the same variety, or plants more distantly related, *i.e.,* representing two varieties, two species or even two genera. Natural cross-pollination is probably more common than self-pollination. — O. E. W.

CROSSING. This involves the artificial transfer of pollen from one flower to another for the purpose of producing a hybrid* and in crossing or hybridizing plants, at least six essentials must be kept in mind: (1) The prevention of self-pollination*; (2) The protection of the pistil and its receptive surface from injury during the removal of the stamens (emasculation); (3) Guarding the pistil from pollen other than that with which it is to be crossed; (4) Using pollen that is both viable and otherwise effective in producing a seed; (5) Using such protective devices on the crossed flower that will not facilitate wilting, mold, or cause it to fall; and (6) Proper labeling.

Many plants self-pollinate themselves in the bud, so that it is necessary to remove or otherwise destroy the effectiveness of the pollen in such cases, before the pollen is shed. This is sometimes done with water and a syringe, but usually the bud is carefully slit with a sharp scalpel and the immature anthers are picked off with a pair of straight tweezers or with a spear-headed dissecting needle. Extreme care is used not to mutilate the flower more than is necessary, since some plants have flowers that are very prone to fall due to their sensitiveness to injury. One soon discovers which these are.

(1) Plants commonly self-pollinated* are wheat, barley, oats, tomatoes, sweet peas,

---

* Special articles on the subjects indicated by an asterisk (*) will be found at the words so marked.

beans, garden peas, commercial tobacco, peanuts and four o'clocks.

(2) Various devices are used to guard the pistil, crossed or uncrossed, from undesired pollination. Among these are square-bottomed manila paper bags of various sizes fastened over the flowers with either string or paper clips; celluloid cylinders with cotton plugs where maximum light is needed to keep flowers from falling; cellophane or glassine bags, or toothbrush or cigar holders; muslin or cheesecloth cages covering the whole plant. In some cases the flower envelope itself can be closed with paper clips. Which device is used depends on the plant involved.

(3) In the case of many self-pollinating species, it is probably most practical, where this can be done, to cross-pollinate them at once, and provide no protection, since the chance of contamination would be rare under these conditions, in such plants as sweet peas and peanuts. Obviously wind-pollinated plants require greater flower protection to prevent undesirable crossing than most insect-pollinated forms, since this type of pollen is more easily and more profusely distributed.

(4) Pollen of different species varies much in its length of life or viability, even under optimum conditions. Pansy pollen is said to be "good" for 26 days, that of the peony and some grape species for 60 days, while date palm pollen is saved from year to year by the Arabs as a precaution against a poor supply or a bad season. Tomato growers save tomato pollen from the summer flowers to use several months later on greenhouse plants. Carnation pollen will live for several weeks, sweet cherry pollen is viable for 28 days, nasturtium pollen for 88 days, while the pollen of some grasses dies in a day or two. The drier pollen is kept (within certain limitations), the longer it lives. Nasturtium pollen, wetted for 2 minutes and then dried, remained alive for 2 days, as against 88 days for the unwetted sample, while sweet cherry pollen in 60 per cent humidity was viable for 25 days as against 126 days in moisture-free air. Shallow, sterilized dishes with covers are often used as pollen containers. Molds are great enemies of stored pollen. Storage is unnecessary where the plants to be crossed are both in bloom.

Pollen may be viable and it may even germinate on the "strange" pistil, but never produce a seed. In general the more closely related plants are, the more likely they are to successfully cross. Thus varieties within a species usually hybridize, but successful crosses between species of a genus are less certain; though in certain genera common (*Rosa, Salix, Gladiolus, Viola*), in others rare (*Lathyrus*). All our varieties of petunia are said to have come from crossing the two species *Petunia violacea* and *Petunia axillaris*. Crosses between genera within a given family are still more problematical, although there are a sufficient number recorded to show there is a chance of securing them. Crosses between orchid genera are comparatively common,

and many have a commercial value. Startling results were obtained from crossing a cabbage (*Brassica*) and a radish (*Raphanus*). As a rule, most profitable and practical results can be expected from crosses between species of a genus or between varieties of a species. *See* BIGENERIC HYBRID.

(5) In using the various devices against undesirable pollination, experiment is necessary, since what works with one may be quite unsuccessful in the case of another species. Paper and cellophane bags may involve too high a temperature, or in the case of paper bags, shut out too much light, thereby causing the flowers to wilt, dry up, or fall. Bags once used should not be used again.

(6) Labeling is usually done with marking tags — only cardboard types should be used — as the others peel when wetted. Besides the date, the tag should indicate the parents involved in the cross, the mother first — Baldwin × Jonathan — either names or numbers being used.

Crossing Technique

The actual mechanics of crossing are simple, once one knows his material. It consists of transferring viable pollen from the flowers of the plant used as father to the receptive stigmatic surface of the flower to be used as the mother. There are many ways of doing this. In the sweet pea and the garden pea, the pistil somewhat reminds one of a miniature toothbrush — the brush end being the stigmatic surface. In crossing such plants, it is most convenient to collect on the stigma of the same flower pollen from the pollen sacs, and transfer it by rubbing the pollen-loaded, brush-like stigma on that of the flower to be crossed. In morning-glories and the four o'clocks the pollen grains are large enough to be handled singly with a small camel's-hair brush or with tweezers. Camel's-hair brushes are often used, but after each type of cross, if accurate knowledge of parentage is important, the brush should be cleansed in alcohol.

In hybridizing such plants as maize and conifers, pollen is collected in paper bags and these are placed over the female flowers, made tight, and shaken, raising within the bag a pollen dust storm. For day-blooming plants, the morning is, in general, the best time to pollinate. For night bloomers, early evening is the most practical. At these times, the stigmas are more likely to be receptive. Likewise the pollen is more plentiful and less spoiled, since the anthers or pollen sacs have just opened. Pollen should be taken only from protected flowers (bagged), since insects are great mixers of pollen. Some plants, such as avocados, are very definitely timed as to anther bursting and stigma receptiveness. — O. E. W. *See* PLANT BREEDING.

CROSS-LEAVED HEATH = *Erica Tetralix.*

CROSS-POLLINATION. The act of transferring pollen from one flower to another on a different plant.

---

* Special articles on the subjects indicated by an asterisk (*) will be found at the words so marked.

CROSS-STERILITY. When, under the most favorable environmental conditions, two normal plants of the same species cannot be crossed, they are said to be cross-sterile. They may belong to different varieties of this species, or they may be members of a segregating hybrid population, involving closely related species. Cross-sterility is widespread among cultivated plants, especially fruits. In Oregon, Napoleon, Lambert, and Bing varieties of sweet cherries are all cross-sterile with each other. Theoretically, it is assumed that both cross- and self-sterility are due to the inability of the pollen to reach the ovary before the pistil dies. — O. E. W.

CROSS-VINE = *Bignonia capreolata.*

CROSS-VINE FAMILY = Bignoniaceae.

CROSSWORT. See CRUCIANELLA.

CROTALARIA (kro-ta-lay′ri-a). A genus of about 275 species of herbs or shrubs of the pea family, largely tropical, but scattered also in the temperate zone, only two of any garden interest and these only in zones* 8 and 9. Leaves alternate,* consisting of only a single leaflet (thus appearing simple-leaved) in the two below. Flowers pea-like, yellow, showy, usually in handsome clusters (racemes*). Fruit a roundish pod, not pea-like, the seeds loose in it, hence the name rattlebox for most of the species. (*Crotalaria* is from the Greek for a rattle.)

The plants below are scarcely grown outside the warmer parts of the Gulf Coast and Calif., where they are sometimes offered as "yellow-flowering pea." The seeds germinate more easily if soaked in warm water for a few hours. They are valuable plants for green manuring in the South.

candicans. A medium-sized shrub, its many branches covered with brownish, silky hairs. Leaves oblongish or ovalish, 2–4 in. long, pointed at the tip. Flowers nearly 1 in. wide, the standard nearly round and silky. Pod 1½ in. long, swollen and a little hairy. India. In Fla. it is winter-blooming.

retusa. An annual herb 1–3 ft. high. Leaves 2–3 in. long, blunt, and broadest toward the tip, grayish-hairy. Flowers ¾–1 in. long, the standard yellow but variegated. Pod 1–1½ in. long, beaked. Indo-Malaya. Grown as an annual cover crop in Fla. and often escaping.

spectabilis. A shrubby plant 3–4 ft. high, the leaves wedge-shaped at the base, without marginal teeth. Flowers purple, in a showy cluster (raceme*) nearly 1 ft. long. Pods about 2 in. long. India. Planted as a cover crop along the Gulf Coast, and in gardens there for its fine bloom.

CROTON. There is a genus *Croton* of the spurge family, but it contains no garden plants. To all gardeners and to many others the word croton means handsome tropical foliage plants. They all belong to the genus *Codiaeum* (which see).

CROWBERRY. See EMPETRUM; for broom crowberry see COREMA.

CROWBERRY FAMILY = Empetraceae.

CROWDED PLANTS. Most garden plants suffer if too closely crowded — suffer from lack of light, air, water, and plant food. The need for thinning is thus obvious. But a few annuals appear to bloom better and more profusely if left a bit crowded. For a list of such *see* ANNUALS.

CROWFOOT. See BUTTERCUP.

CROWFOOT FAMILY = Ranunculaceae.

CROWN. 1. That part of a plant between the root and the stem, usually at or near the ground level; often called the *collar* of a plant.

2. The whole upper foliage of a tree; its *canopy* in the forestry sense.

3. = Corona.*

CROWN DAISY = *Chrysanthemum coronarium.*

CROWN GALL. A bacterial disease which is found on many types of plants. The brown, rough, woody galls,* often resembling a black walnut, may be present on larger roots near the surface of the soil, on the main stem. On some trees, such as the willow,* the galls may appear out on the branches. The disease does not appear to injure large trees, other than to make them grotesque. Small plants such as roses, rhododendron, tomato, etc., should be discarded if crown gall is present.

CROWN GRAFTING. See Bark Grafting at GRAFTING.

CROWN IMPERIAL = *Fritillaria imperialis.*

CROWN-OF-JEWELS = *Lopezia coronata.*

CROWN-OF-THORNS = *Euphorbia splendens.*

CROWN TUBER. See PIP.

CROWN VETCH = *Coronilla varia.*

CROW'S-TOES = *Dentaria laciniata.*

CRUCIANELLA (kroo-si-a-nell′a). The crossworts are annual or perennial herbs of the family Rubiaceae, all Old World, only *C. stylosa* of garden interest, and mostly confined to shady places in the rock garden. It is a prostrate annual, 6–9 in. high, the leaves in whorls of 8–9, generally lance-shaped and stiff-hairy. Flowers small, dark pink or rose-red, crowded in a dense, globe-shaped head about ½ in. in diameter, the corolla funnel-shaped. Fruit dry. (*Crucianella* is Latin for a little cross, in allusion to the arrangement of the leaves.)

cruciata, -us, -um (kroo-si-ā′ta). Cross-like or cross-shaped.

CRUCIFER. Any plant of the mustard family, common examples being the cabbage and its relatives. See CRUCIFERAE.

CRUCIFERAE (kroo-siff′er-ee), often called Brassicaceae, is a family of over 350 genera and perhaps 2500 species, nearly all herbs of wide distribution. It is commonly called the mustard, cabbage, cress, or radish family, but besides these and other important vegetables it contains many popular gar-

---

* Special articles on the subjects indicated by an asterisk (*) will be found at the words so marked.

den plants like candytuft, sweet alyssum, honesty, *Aethionema,* and the stocks.

Leaves prevailingly alternate,* often bitter but never poisonous, simple* or compound.* Flowers always (except in double-flowered forms) with 4 petals arranged cross-fashion (hence Cruciferae = cross-bearing), usually with a claw.* Fruit a dry pod, when long called a silique*; when as broad as long (as in honesty) called a silicle.*

The garden genera of the Cruciferae furnish many important vegetables and condiments. *See* HORSE-RADISH, CABBAGE, CAULIFLOWER, BROCCOLI, MUSTARD, BRUSSELS SPROUTS, TURNIP, KOHLRABI, RADISH, the genera BRASSICA and NASTURTIUM (watercress).

Among the chief ornamental genera are: *Aethionema, Alyssum, Aubrieta, Cheiranthus, Hesperis, Iberis* (candytuft), *Lobularia* (*see* SWEET ALYSSUM), and *Mathiola,* some of which have been garden favorites for centuries. Lesser known and less ornamental genera include: *Arabis, Barbarea* (largely weedy), *Cardamine, Cochlearia, Dentaria, Draba, Erysimum, Hutchinsia, Ionopsidium, Isatis, Lepidium* (largely weedy), *Malcomia, Schizopetalon, Stanleya, Thlaspi,* and *Vesicaria.*

Of the three remaining garden genera two furnish minor vegetables or salad plants — *Crambe* (sea-kale) and *Eruca* (rocket salad). *Anastatica* (which see) includes an extraordinary little desert plant often called Rose-of-Jericho or resurrection plant.

Technical flower characters: Flowers small, usually very numerous in mostly unbranched clusters (racemes*). Sepals 4, soon withering. Petals 4. Stamens typically 6, four long and two short. Ovary superior,* developing into dry pods (siliques* or silicles*).

cruenta, -us, -um (kroo-en'ta). Blood-colored or bloody.

crus-galli (kruss-gal'li). A specific name implying that a plant or its organs are like a cock's spur.

Crux-andrae (krux-an'dree). A specific name implying that the plant is named for St. Andrew's cross.

CRYOPHYTUM *See* MESEMBRYANTHEMUM.

CRYPTANTHUS (krip-tan'thus). Perhaps a dozen terrestrial, South American foliage plants of the family Bromeliaceae, two of which are very common greenhouse subjects. They have practically no stems and a basal rosette of stiff, spiny-margined leaves, in the center of which is nested the stalkless, dense head of white flowers. The outer segments of the flower are united into a tube, the inner ones free and usually narrowed at the base or with a claw.* Fruit dry but berry-like. (*Cryptanthus* is from the Greek for hidden flower.)

Both species, especially *C. zonatus,* are very common foliage plants, much grown by florists. They are best grown in the greenhouse in pots, baskets, or wooden cribs, allowing plenty of drainage. Use potting mixture* 3, to which one half its bulk of chopped fern fibers or coir should be added. During winter the plants need much less water than in spring and summer. The house should be kept between 55° and 65° in winter, but 10° above this when more active growth starts in March. They usually flower in summer under glass.

acaulis. Leaves 6–12 in a basal rosette, 3–5 in. long, about 1 in. wide, the margins prominently wavy and finely toothed. Upper surface green, lower surface whitish and scurfy. Brazil. Sometimes sold as *C. undulatus.* There are several hort. forms with bright green, striped, or variegated leaves.

undulatus = *Cryptanthus acaulis.*

zonatus. Very similar to *C. acaulis,* but the leaves longer (5–9 in.), and with prominent white or brownish bands across the blades. Brazil. The most popular species in cult. because of its handsome variegation. Occasional plants of both species, when well grown, will show a pinkish tinge to the foliage.

CRYPTOCORYNE (krip-toe-core-ry'nee). An Asiatic and Indo-Malayan genus of mostly aquatic herbs of the arum family, with creeping rootstocks and ribbed, linear or ovalish leaves. The minute flowers are borne separately on the spadix* which is completely enclosed by the spathe.* The only two species likely to be found are **C. griffithi,** with ovalish or nearly round, red-lined leaves, and **C. willisi,** with narrower leaves which are reddish-brown but marked with darker spots. Both are useful aquarium plants, especially where the light is not too good. (*Cryptocoryne* is from the Greek for closed or hidden spadix.*)

CRYPTOGAM, CRYPTOGAMOUS. Literally meaning a hidden marriage, but as applied to plants, meaning any that do not produce flowers or seeds in the ordinary garden sense of those terms. Cryptogams reproduce by spores (*see* FERNS AND FERN GARDENING). Common examples of cryptogamous plants are the ferns, club mosses, horsetails, and mushrooms. *See* PHANEROGAMS.

CRYPTOGRAMMA (krip-to-gram'ma). Mostly northern or alpine ferns of the family Polypodiaceae, comprising seven species generally known as rock brakes. One, C. crispa. *var.* acrostichoides, the parsley-fern or mountain parsley, is a native of northern regions and is sometimes grown in the fern garden or in the rock garden. It has a short, stout, chaffy rootstock, and two sorts of fronds — fertile and sterile. The latter are leaf-like, twice-divided or compound,* the ultimate segments rounded, more or less toothed. Fertile fronds longer than the leaf-like ones, similarly divided, but the ultimate segments very narrow, the spore* cases at or near the margin, which is rolled over and hides them before maturity. (*Cryptogramma* is from the Greek and implies hidden spore* cases.)

CRYPTOMERIA (krip-to-meer'ri-a). A single species of Japanese evergreen tree of

---

* Special articles on the subjects indicated by an asterisk (*) will be found at the words so marked.

the pine family, **C. japonica,** known as the Japan cedar or sugi. It is a magnificent, pyramidal tree up to 125 ft. in its native home and much used there for the planting of temple gardens and ceremonial avenues. Here it is much lower, hardy only up to zone° 4, and often failing there, and nearly always turning a bronzy color in winter, but becoming green the following season. Farther south it does much better. Bark reddish-brown and shreddy. Leaves small, awl-shaped, the tips always curved inward, more or less completely clothing the twigs, spirally arranged, and keeled. Cones nearly globe-shaped, about 1 in. in diameter, the scales wedge-shaped but pointed at the tip. (*Cryptomeria* is from the Greek for hidden and part; of uncertain application here.)

The tree is less particular as to soil than to climatic conditions. Near the seacoasts and south of zone° 5 it grows well. It cannot be grown in regions of great summer heat and deficient rainfall, nor anywhere that has bitter winds and zero temperatures. In its proper climatic range a very stately evergreen. There are several important hort. varieties of *C. japonica*:

var. **compacta.** A compact conical form with bluish-green leaves. About as hardy as the typical form.

var. **dacrydioides.** A form having closely set, brownish leaves. Hardiness not certainly known.

var. **elegans.** Densely branched, somewhat bushy form, not very long-lived, but useful for quick effects.

var. **lobbi.** The commonest form in cult. in the U.S., not differing materially from the type, but apparently a little more hardy. Useful for the northern limits of *Cryptomeria* culture.

CRYPTOSTEGIA (krip-tō-stee′ji-a). Handsome woody vines of the milkweed family from tropical Africa and Madagascar, two of them grown for ornament in greenhouses or in the open in zones° 8 and 9, where they are very showy. They have opposite° leaves and a milky juice, and large, funnel-shaped flowers in 3-branched clusters (cymes°). Corolla with a short tube and a corona° of 5 scales attached to it, the stamens° forming a tube around the stigma.° Fruit an angled or winged pod (follicle°). (*Cryptostegia* is from the Greek for conceal and cover, in allusion to the corona.°).

Both species should be grown in the warm greenhouse, preferably planted out in rich, loamy soils rather than in pots. In southern Fla. they grow profusely in most ordinary garden soils. Propagated by cuttings, preferably in spring, over bottom-heat.° In Africa some species yield rubber, and those below do so in Fla., but not in commercial quantities.

grandiflora. Called rubber-vine from the fact that it yields rubber, although not commercially. A sturdy, woody vine, not very high-climbing. Leaves oblongish, 3–4 in. long, thick, glossy, and without teeth. Flowers purplish, about 2 in. wide, the lobes of the corolla not divided. Tropical Africa.

madagascariensis. Somewhat like the last, but the leaves are red-veined, the flowers pink or white, and the corolla lobes are divided. Madagascar.

crystallina, -us, -um (kriss-tal-ly′na). Resembling crystals, or crystalline; *i.e.*, transparent.

CRYSTAL TEA = *Ledum palustre.*

CUBAN LILY = *Scilla peruviana.*

CUBAN PINE = *Pinus caribaea.* See PINE.

CUBAN ROYAL PALM = *Roystonea regia.*

CUBÉ. See ROTENONE.

CUBEB = *Piper Cubeba.*

Cubeba. An obsolete generic name for plants now included in *Piper.*

CUCKOO-FLOWER = *Cardamine pratensis;* also *Lychnis Flos-cuculi.*

CUCKOOPINT = *Arum maculatum.*

CUCKOO SPITTLE. The frothy white secretion found on the stems of low-growing plants, popularly supposed to have been caused by frogs, hence the other name of frog spittle. Actually it is a secretion from spittle insects (which see).

Cucullaria (kew-kew-lay′ri-a). An obsolete generic name for a genus of plants scarcely in cult., signifying a hood, and used as a specific name for a *Dicentra.*

cucullata, -us, -um (kew-kew-lay′ta). Hooded.

CUCUMBER (*Cucumis sativus*). Gardeners with limited space cannot afford to grow cucumbers unless on a trellis. For outdoor culture they must be planted in hills at intervals of at least 4½ ft. each way. (See below.) The plant is a sprawling, tendril-bearing vine. It requires considerable heat, a lot of moisture and a rich soil. Cucumbers are much more sensitive to frost than most vegetable crops. They can only be grown in regions that not only have plenty of heat but a frost-free period of 75–90 days. (See the name of your state for frost data.)

In some regions with insufficient heat cucumbers can be grown in hotbeds which have already been used for raising tomato or other tender plants. Put two vines under each sash and at first, on cool days and every night, put on the glass and, at night, a mat. When settled warm weather arrives, the sash is left off and the plants matured in the frame. This is often an ideal arrangement, for it utilizes the spent manure of the hotbed.

SOILS. Warm, sandy loam, especially if it has a gentle slope southward, is the best soil for outdoor cucumbers. No other method of fertilizing is so satisfactory as putting 2 forks of thoroughly rotted manure (horse or cow) under each hill, and a scant wheelbarrow load is better. Broadcasting manure or fertilizer, for plants spaced so far apart, is merely wasteful.

PLANTING. See that the manure is covered sufficiently so that no seed touches it. This is easily accomplished by forming a circular

---

° Special articles on the subjects indicated by an asterisk (°) will be found at the words so marked.

hill about a foot wide and 4 in. deep over each lot of buried manure, the site of which had better be marked with a stick, if some days intervene between burying it and planting time.

Planting cannot be done until warm or hot weather is assured, a fair criterion for most regions being that catalpa blossoms are budding, or that Japanese iris are beginning to bloom.

Plant six seeds at each hill, expecting to reduce them to three as soon as germination is complete and it is possible to select the three best plants. The seeds should be planted about 1½ in. deep.

Commercial growers often take elaborate precautions to protect the young plants from cold or frost, which they feel forced to ignore in the race to produce the first cucumbers for the market. Most home growers need not bother with such methods, but if they do, any of the small, glass-covered, individual frames or boxes may be put over the young plants on cold days and every night until the vines become too long.

CULTIVATION. As the vines become large they will fill all the space between the hills which should never be less than 4 ft. apart each way, and many put them 5 ft. apart or even more.

This means that while the plants are young, cultivation must be very thorough or you will have a very weedy cucumber patch when it is no longer possible to get between the plants with implements. In the later stages this cannot be done at all, as the vines are very fleshy and easily injured. Hand-weeding is the only sequel to early neglect of thorough, clean cultivation. Some, to avoid this trouble, grow the so-called bush cucumbers, but they are not so prolific as the ordinary sort.

VARIETIES. Cucumbers are grown mainly for two purposes; to slice and eat fresh or cooked, and for pickling. For slicing, the larger-fruited varieties are used, of which the best are Marketer, Ashley, Stono, Niagara, Straight Eight, and Burpee Hybrid. These should be from 5 to 9 in. long when harvested.

For pickling, the small-fruited varieties like Chicago Pickling, National Pickling, Model, and Ohio MR-17 are the most favored. These are usually harvested when the fruits are from 1½–3 in. long. Some cucumber enthusiasts also pickle the large-fruited sorts, cut into longitudinal sections.

Most families will be amply provided for by a dozen hills of ordinary cucumbers. The fruit is indigestible to some and almost a poison to others. It is a not very distant relative of a plant yielding an arrow poison in the Amazon. Growing pickling cucumbers is largely a commercial business.

For the preferred position and sequence of cucumbers in your garden see KITCHEN GARDEN.

INSECT PESTS (all cucurbits). Seed should be treated with combination seed treatment (see INSECTICIDES). Control of beetles in early season is necessary to prevent wilt. Use pesticide #20 or #23 (see SPRAYS AND DUSTS). Aphids may be controlled with pesticide #20 or #27. Pickle worm and melon worm which appear later may be controlled by pesticide #20. Observe label precautions on interval between last application and harvest. Squash bugs may be hand-picked. Young bugs are killed by pesticide #20.

DISEASES. Untreated seed may carry the fungi which will result in a number of leafspot diseases. Dip seeds for five minutes in pesticide #12 (see SPRAYS AND DUSTS), then wash in fresh water and dry.

Young or mature plants may suddenly wilt and die. This is usually the result of a bacterial disease which is transmitted by cucumber beetles. Start the control program for this insect while plants are still in the seedling stage, using the pesticide described above under Insect Pests.

In some areas, during some seasons, a downy mildew* disease may become serious. This fungus disease causes gray or brown spots, starting on the lower surface of the leaves. The entire plant may then appear to "dry up" and as a result there are few fruits matured. Because this disease is so dependent upon precise weather conditions for its development, the United States Department of Agriculture has plant pathologists who "predict" the arrival of the disease in various localities. When your county agricultural agent or the news service warns of this disease, apply pesticide #11 (see SPRAYS AND DUSTS) and repeat at 10-day intervals.

Some years, late in the season, a white powdery coating of powdery mildew* may appear on the upper surface of the leaves. This does not usually warrant the application of a fungicide but if the disease appears to be too severe, apply one or two applications of pesticide #3.

CUCUMBER FAMILY. All the squashes, melons, watermelon, pumpkin, gourds, and several ornamental vines belong to the cucumber family. All the cult. genera have creeping or climbing, herbaceous stems, bear tendrils, and have sometimes showy but rather ephemeral flowers. The fruit is always a modified berry known as a pepo.* For the cult. genera see CUCURBITACEAE.

CUCUMBER TREE = *Magnolia acuminata.*

cucumerifolia, -us, -um (kew-kew-mĕ-ri-fō′li-a). With cucumber-like leaves.

CUCUMIS (kew-kew′mis). A genus of probably 30 species of trailing or climbing vines of the cucumber family, mostly tropical African or Asian, two of them of outstanding garden interest as yielding the cucumber and all the melons (but not the watermelon). The cult. species are frost-tender, annual, tendril*-bearing vines with generally hairy stems and alternate,* usually large leaves. Male and female flowers on the same plant but in separate flowers, which are solitary, but not large as in the closely related pumpkins. Corolla more or less bell-shaped, yellow. Fruit fleshy, smooth or netted or ribbed in the melons, but with weak, fleshy

---

* Special articles on the subjects indicated by an asterisk (*) will be found at the words so marked.

prickles or tubercles in the cucumber. (*Cucumis* is Latin for some plant with a cucumber-like odor.) The tendrils* are not forked in these plants, but branched in the closely related watermelon (which see).

Anguria. Bur gherkin, also called West India gherkin. A trailing vine with angled, rough-hairy stems. Leaves 1½–3 in. long, rough, 3-lobed, each lobe again lobed, the margins wavy and toothed. Flowers less than ½ in. wide. Fruit oval or oblongish, about 2 in. long, its stalks crooked, the skin furrowed and prickly. Southern U.S. to Brazil. While the fruit is called gherkin, the "gherkins" of most pickle mixtures are young cucumbers little known outside of the deep South.

dipsaceus. Teasel gourd. Hedgehog gourd. A prickly-stemmed vine with broadly oval or kidney-shaped, unlobed leaves. Fruits 1–2 in. long, bur-like and bristly, and cult. mostly for interest or ornament. Arabia.

Melo. Melon. Here belong all the cultivated melons except the watermelon (which see). The vines are soft-hairy trailers, seldom climbing, the tendrils* not forked. Leaves roundish-oval, 3–5 in. wide, more or less angled on the margin but scarcely lobed, rough. Flowers about 1 in. wide, usually 1 in a leaf axil.* Fruit the melon. Probably Central Asia. For an account of all the cult. varieties of the melon and how to grow them *see* MELON.

sativus. Cucumber. A trailing, rarely climbing, rough-hairy, annual vine. Leaves triangular-oval, 3–6 in. long, more or less angled or 3-lobed, the middle lobe pointed. Flowers 1–1½ in. wide, the male flowers often several to a leaf axil,* very short-stalked. Fruit the familiar cucumber, which varies from nearly globe-shaped (rare) to the long-cylindric type forced in England. Here the fruit is, when mature, 3–9 in. long (3 ft. in England), always with minute, soft prickles. For culture and varieties *see* CUCUMBER. Its native home is uncertain; possibly from southern Asia.

CUCURBITA (kew-kur′bi-ta). Mostly tender, annual, trailing or climbing vines of the family Cucurbitaceae, comprising perhaps 10 species, the original home of some uncertain, but chiefly tropical. The genus includes the squash, pumpkin, and many ornamental gourds grown for interest (but *see also* GOURDS). They are mostly rough-hairy vines with forked tendrils,* and large leaves, often lobed. Flowers yellow, large, usually more or less bell-shaped, but lobed halfway down the tube. Fruit a large berry of the sort known as a pepo,* smooth-skinned in some, deeply furrowed in others, and, in the various cult. varieties, of great variety as to form (*see* below). (*Cucurbita* is Latin for gourd.) The species are little understood.

For the culture of the ornamental gourds *see* GOURDS. For culture of the squash and pumpkin, *see* those entries.

ficifolia. Malabar gourd. A running or climbing vine grown for ornament, its fruit inedible. Leaves nearly round or kidney-shaped, 7–10 in. wide, the margins wavy or lobed, more or less weakly prickle-toothed. Flower with spreading, large lobes, the tube funnel-shaped. Fruit roundish or oblong, 6–12 in. long, smooth, green, but white-striped, the seeds black. Eastern Asia.

foetidissima. Calabazilla; called also Mis-

souri gourd and wild pumpkin. A perennial, native American, prostrate and long-running vine, with inedible fruit. Leaves triangular-heart-shaped, whitish beneath, finely toothed, long-stalked. Flowers 2½–4 in. long. Fruit smooth, orange-shaped, green and yellow-splashed. Mo. and Kan. to Calif. and Mex. A gourd for the South, but it often fails to ripen fruit in the North. Will stand much heat and a sandy soil.

maxima. Squash. Here belong the autumn and winter squashes, the well-known Hubbard squash, and, sometimes, very large squashes that pass for pumpkins. An annual vine, the stems prostrate, and not very rough or prickly. Leaves roundish or heart-shaped, blunt, but usually not lobed. Flowers yellow, the lobes recurved, or drooping, and soft, the tube bulging toward the base. Fruit very variable, spherical or oblong, sometimes immense, the top of its stalk not swollen. Seeds white. Origin unknown. For culture *see* SQUASH. The turban squash, sometimes called a "squash-within-a-squash," has turban-shaped fruit. It is the *var.* **turbaniformis.**

moschata. Canada crookneck squash; winter crookneck squash; cushaw. A soft-hairy annual vine, the leaves more or less limp, somewhat velvety, more or less broadly oval or roundish, usually not lobed, often white-blotched. Flowers large, the corolla lobes wide-spreading and crinkly. Fruit very variable, often crook-necked, the stalk distinctly bulged at the point of attachment. The fruits, often called pumpkins, are harvested for autumn and winter use. Origin unknown.

Pepo. The common field pumpkin belongs here, but so does the vegetable marrow. A confusing species of harsh, annual, prostrate vines, with prickly stems and leafstalks. Leaves triangular-oval, usually prominently lobed, 6–12 in. long, and pointed at the tip. Flower large, the corolla lobes pointed, erect or spreading, not recurved. Fruit large, furrowed, usually orange, not keeping as in the winter squashes, the stalk enlarged at the point of attachment. Origin unknown. The *var.* **Melopepo** includes the bush pumpkins or squashes, which are more or less compact plants without tendrils. The fruits are summer-maturing and include such well-known types as the Pattypan, scallop, and summer crookneck squash. The *var.* **ovifera** includes running vines producing hard-shelled, ornamental yellow gourds which are inedible but showy. For culture of the pumpkin, *see* PUMPKIN. For the squashes, *see* SQUASH.

CUCURBITACEAE (kew-kur-bi-tay′see-ee). The cucumber family is often called (with equal reason) the gourd, melon, or squash family. It comprises about 90 genera and perhaps 750 species of mostly tropical, generally fleshy-stemmed vines, all of which usually bear tendrils, except *Ecballium.*

Leaves alternate,* usually broad and simple,* but sometimes cut, or divided or even compound.* Flowers regular, often large and showy, but in some genera small, greenish and inconspicuous, funnel-shaped or with 5 separate petals. The fruit is large, fleshy and usually with a rind in *Citrullus* (*see* WATERMELON), *Cucumis, Benincasa, Cucurbita* (which contains the squash and pumpkin), *Luffa, Sechium, Lagenaria,* and *Sicana.* These genera contain all the important garden plants in the family, because they in-

---

* Special articles on the subjects indicated by an asterisk (*) will be found at the words so marked.

clude the cucumber, gourds, melons, squash, pumpkin, and chayote.

Less well known, and with much smaller fruit, usually fleshy, are *Abobra, Bryonia, Cyclanthera, Ecballium* (the squirting cucumber), *Echinocystis, Momordica,* and *Trichosanthes.* Most of these are cult. only for ornament.

Technical flower characters: Plants with male and female organs mostly in separate flowers on the same plant. Corolla united and more or less funnel-shaped, or of 5 separate petals. Calyx joined to the 5-lobed ovary. Stamens 5, but with 2 pairs united, thus with apparently only 3 stamens.

CUDWEED. *See* GNAPHALIUM.

Cujete (kew-yee′te). Brazilian vernacular name for the calabash (*Crescentia Cujete*).

CULINARY HERBS. *See* HERB GARDENING.

CULTIGEN. A plant assumed to have originated in cultivation, and unknown as a wild plant. Cabbage and cauliflower are cultigens, as well as many other garden plants.

CULTIVAR. A named hort. variety as distinguished from a natural variety of a species. Pride of Rochester is a cultivar of *Deutzia scabra,* Dorothy Perkins a cultivar of one of the rambler types of roses. While the term has a certain currency its use is more popular with the professionals than with the garden public. *See* PLANT NAMES and VARIETY.

CULTIVATION. Like many other garden terms cultivation has a double meaning — the cultivation of a crop and the cultivation of the soil. This book is packed with notes on the cultivation of various crops, consequently this phase of cultivation will be ignored here.

Soil cultivation, however, is one of the most important of gardening operations. It is to be distinguished from those soil operations which usually precede planting, such as plowing, rolling, raking, harrowing, etc. Cultivation, as here treated, and as ordinarily understood by gardeners, means the cultivation or tillage of the soil while occupied by a crop and for its benefit.

BENEFITS. There are two main reasons for soil cultivation — to conserve moisture and keep down weeds. Both are important enough to warrant separate treatment.

The conservation of soil moisture makes certain dry areas of America possible as garden sites, and there is no garden that is not improved by cultivation with this as the chief object. Wherever practiced, it is based upon a purely physical characteristic of soils and soil water which every gardener should understand.

Soil water, or what soil scientists call the water table, usually lies a long way below the roots of most garden plants. Here lies the permanent water reservoir of the soil which only appears at the surface in pools, lakes, marshes, or bogs. In all other garden soils the water table is far below the surface and reaches the roots of plants only by capillarity. Water rises in soils just as it will rise if put at the base of a lump of sugar. On its way up to the surface this soil moisture is absorbed by the roots of whatever plants grow there, and the rest reaches the surface to be lost by evaporation.

Upon the continuity of this capillary water all plants, except aquatics, depend for their moisture supply. And upon the breaking of this capillarity depends the prevention of water loss by excessive evaporation at the surface. Cultivation does this more effectively than anything else, in the following manner:

DUST MULCH. Thoroughly pulverized surface soil is dried almost at once by the sun and wind. Even roughly cultivated soil dries out pretty rapidly. And in the process of drying it creates a dust mulch, which, depending on the type of soil and on how well you have done the job, will vary from one inch to several inches thick. Through this dusty upper layer, capillary water finds it very difficult to penetrate and escape into the air as water vapor. In other words, the dust mulch, if it does not completely stop the ascent of capillary water, stops so much of it that roots growing under a dust mulch have far more available water than without it. Upon this fact rests the whole theory and practice of cultivation. In other words, successful cultivation means the creation of an effective dust mulch. Weeds play no part in such a program, but in properly carrying it out, most weeds are necessarily destroyed.

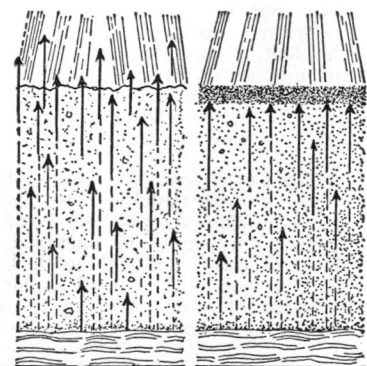

How the dust mulch (the black layer) prevents evaporation of soil moisture (*at the right*) and the water lost by evaporation without the dust mulch (*left*).

MAKING THE DUST MULCH. Various methods of cultivation (the creation of the dust mulch) are in vogue, depending upon the size of the soil particles, presence of stones, the weather, and the size of the area to be cultivated. For very small gardens with reasonably stone-free soil, any of a number of small hand cultivators are available at

---

* Special articles on the subjects indicated by an asterisk (*) will be found at the words so marked.

any seedsman's. The principle upon which all of them work is the same. Teeth, or spikes, or knives are so arranged that they scratch or scuffle up the surface soil, leaving it pulverized instead of in the normal packed or caked condition of untouched surface soil. A simple precaution is to so plan your work that cultivated soil is ahead (*i.e.*, finished) and uncultivated soil is behind you. In other words, don't walk over freshly cultivated soil (*see* below).

The time to cultivate, because its object is the conservation of soil moisture, is after every good soaking rain. In heavy soils with much clay or silt this cannot be done at once or your implements will become mud-caked, and you can also do more harm than good by packing the soil into cement-like hardness. A good test of when to start is to take a handful of soil and press it into as hard a cake as you can with one hand. Let the cake fall and if it breaks apart it is usually safe to begin. If the cake sticks together, it is better to wait a few hours or days.

Between rains there is less reason for cultivating, except to keep down any weeds that may not have been killed by the last cultivation. Some gardeners keep up cultivating, however, according to a schedule, regardless of when the last rain happened to come. They know that dew and wind may have slightly packed the old dust mulch, and to maintain its effectiveness they cultivate even an apparently dry soil. The theory is absolutely sound, and most good commercial growers follow it, but it means, of course, more time and labor. In periods of long drought, or in regions where rainfall is always deficient, these between-rain cultivations are imperative. There is, paradoxically enough, no better moisture conserver than dry surface soil. For other methods of conserving soil moisture *see* MULCH AND MULCHING.

DEPTH TO CULTIVATE. For most ordinary garden soils a dust mulch of one inch is sufficient. For some deep-rooted crops and with machine cultivators in operation, the upper layer of dusty soil will be thicker — up to 3 or 4 inches. The depth is far less important than the thoroughness of pulverization — dusty, not lumpy, soil is what is needed.

EQUIPMENT. For all small gardens, tubs, cold frames, and hotbeds, small hand cultivators are the most convenient and effective. Next in simplicity and for larger-scale operations are the different types of long-handled hoes. The ordinary draw hoe you can use only by drawing it toward you, a disadvantage in cultivating overcome by the scuffle hoe which you use by pushing it away from the operator.

For vegetables or anything else planted in rows, the most effective tool is a single-wheel cultivator to which are fitted various blades that scuffle up the soil and cut weeds at the same time. Its easiest method of op-

eration is to push it ahead of you and this has the disadvantage that you are constantly walking over the soil just cultivated. Some operators, to avoid this, work backwards. They cultivate by a few thrusts of the knives forward and backward, and then walk backwards, repeating the operation. This is more tedious, but at the end of the row you have walked on no cultivated soil. If this seems a needless precaution, it is well to remember that your footprints destroy the dust mulch by partially restoring capillarity, and that you may firm down an uprooted weed just enough to let it get a fresh start.

In using any type of wheel cultivator, whether man- or power-driven, it is necessary to be very careful about fleshy-rooted crops, which are easily injured by tools. The rows must be straight and spaced for whichever type of cultivator you use. In large gardens with motor-driven tractor cultivators such as one sees on farms, the rows must have been spaced for them. To most home gardeners the loss of planting space, in order to accommodate such cultivators, precludes their use.

cultora, -us, -um (kul-tor'a). Assumed to be derived from cultivation. *See* CULTIGEN.

cultriformis, -e (kul-tree-for'mis). Knife-shaped.

CULTURE SOLUTIONS. *See* SOILLESS GARDENING.

CULVER'S-ROOT = *Veronicastrum virginicum.*

CUMIN = *Cuminum Cyminum.*

CUMINUM (kew-my'num). A single species of annual herb of the carrot family, **C. Cyminum,** the cumin, a native of the Mediteranean region, long cult. for its aromatic fruit. (*See* HERB GARDENING.) It is a delicate little herb, scarcely 6 in. high, the leaves dissected into thread-like segments. Flowers very small (for details *see* UMBELLIFERAE), in compound umbels,* usually white, rarely pinkish. Fruits dry, bristly, scarcely ¼ in. long, aromatic. June. (*Cuminum* is the old Greek word for this plant.)

CUMMIN = Cumin.

cuneata, -us, -um (kew-nee-ā'ta). Cuneate; *i.e.,* wedge-shaped, usually with the narrow end downward.

cuneifolia, -us, -um (kew-nee-i-fō'li-a). With wedge-shaped leaves.

CUNNINGHAMIA (kun-ning-ham'i-a). Two Asiatic evergreen trees of the pine family, the one below cult. for ornament from zone* 6 southward, possibly also in protected places in zone* 5. The only cult. species is **C. lanceolata,** the China fir, which is sometimes offered as *C. sinensis.* It is a noble evergreen up to 75 ft. high, with brownish outer, and reddish inner bark, the branches spreading and inclined to droop at the ends. Leaves crowded, narrow, about 2 in. long, broad at the base, but sharply pointed at the tip, green above, and with 2

* Special articles on the subjects indicated by an asterisk (*) will be found at the words so marked.

white bands beneath. Cones nearly round, about 2 in. long, persisting after the shedding of the seeds, 3 of which are at each scale. The tree resembles *Araucaria* in habit. (Named for J. Cunningham, British explorer in Asia.)

CUP-AND-SAUCER. See CAMPANULA MEDIUM.

CUP-AND-SAUCER VINE = *Cobaea scandens*.

CUP FERN = *Dennstaedtia punctilobula*.

CUPFLOWER. See NIEREMBERGIA.

CUPHEA (kew'fee-a). A large group of chiefly tropical American herbs or shrubs of the family Lythraceae. Of over 200 species only 4 are of any garden interest, and they are mostly greenhouse plants grown for their attractive flowers. They are also, but rarely, grown outdoors in zones* 7 to 9. Leaves opposite* or crowded. Flowers irregular,* the calyx* tubular and corolla*-like, often exceeding the 6 unequal petals, sometimes swollen and pouch-like, or curved at the base. In one species there are no petals. Stamens generally 11. Fruit a capsule,* enclosed by the persistent calyx.* (*Cuphea* is from the Greek for curved, in reference to the curved calyx* of some species.)

The cigar-flower is a popular greenhouse plant considerably cult. by florists. It and the others need a cool or warm-temperate greenhouse and potting mixture* 3. They are of easy cult. and best propagated by cuttings, or by seeds, from which blooming plants may be had in one season.

hyssopifolia. A much-branched, hairy, small shrub. Leaves crowded, very narrow, usually less than ½ in. long, stalkless. Flowers numerous, stalked in the leaf axils,* scarcely ¼ in. long, violet-white, the calyx* tube straight. Mex. and Guatemala.

ignea = *Cuphea platycentra*.

Llavea. A stiffly-hairy shrub, with numerous stems, not over 2 ft. high. Leaves essentially stalkless, ovalish, ½–1½ in. long, rough. Flowers red, in a leafy cluster (raceme*). Mex. Cult. in southern Calif. and similar climates.

micropetala. An erect shrubby herb 1–4 ft. high. Leaves stalked, oblongish, 2–5 in. long. Flowers in a long, leafy, terminal cluster (raceme*). Calyx* tubular, about 1½–2 in. long, yellowish, but scarlet at the base, longer than the minute petals, but shorter than the protruding red stamens.* Mex.

platycentra. Cigar-flower. A popular pot plant, often used for summer bedding. It is a shrub (but may be grown as a tender annual) 8–15 in. high. Leaves lance-shaped, 1–2½ in. long. Flowers solitary, slender-stalked and chiefly in the leaf axils.* Calyx tube about ¾ in. long, spurred at the base, red but with a darker ring near the tip and an ash-white mouth; petals none. Mex. Often sold as *C. ignea.*

CUPID'S-DART = *Catananche caerulea*.

CUP-PLANT = *Silphium perfoliatum*.

cuprea, -us, -um (kew'pree-a). Coppery.

cupreata, -us, -um (kew-pree-ā'ta). Copper-colored.

CUPRESSACEAE. See PINACEAE.

cupressifolia, -us, -um (kew-pres-si-fō'li-a) With cypress-like leaves.

cupressiformis, -e (kew-pres-si-for'mis). Resembling the cypress (*Cupressus*).

cupressina, -us, -um (kew-pres-sy'na). Cypress-like.

cupressoides (kew-pres-soy'deez; but *see* OÏDES). Resembling the cypress (*Cupressus*).

CUPRESSUS (kew-pres'sus). Magnificent evergreen trees of the pine family (the true cypress), mostly from the warmer parts of the Old World, a few from western N.A., most unfortunately not hardy over great stretches of the U.S. Of the 12 known species, half are in common cult. over most of the warmer sections of the world. They have aromatic foliage and the branchlets are densely clothed with small, usually 4-angled leaves that are pressed against the twigs. The very small leaves are opposite,* scale-like. Sometimes, on young plants or shoots, the leaves are longer and spreading, otherwise they hug the twigs. Cones nearly globe-shaped, composed of 6–12 woody scales, often nearly prickly at the scale-tip, at each scale many narrowly winged, flattish seeds. (*Cupressus* is the classical name of the Italian cypress.)

Outdoor culture of those below is only possible in the indicated zone* or south of it. The trees are closely related to *Chamaecyparis.* See EVERGREENS.

arizonica. Arizona cypress. An evergreen tree up to 40 ft., its foliage pale bluish-green. Leaves thick, keeled, pointed and resinous. Cones about 1 in. in diameter, bluish-green. Ariz. Hardy from zone* 6 southward, and particularly good for exposed places and for windbreaks.*

duclouxiana. A medium-sized tree closely related to the Italian cypress but the branches more slender and bluish-green, and generally more spreading. Leaves very small (¹⁄₁₂ in.), closely pressed against the twigs. Cones about ¾ in. wide, mostly with 8 scales. China. Hardy from zone* 5 southward.

funebris. Mourning cypress and much planted in cemeteries along the Mediterranean. A beautiful tree up to 60 ft. high, its main branches drooping. Twigs flattened, the leaves sharp-pointed, light green. Cones about ½ in. in diameter. China. Hardy from zone* 7 southward.

lusitanica. Portuguese cypress. Both the Latin and common names of this Mexican tree are misleading, but it was long thought to be native in Portugal. Tall tree (40–60 ft.), its main branches drooping. Leaves sharp-pointed, bluish-green. Cones about ½ in. in diameter, with a bloom. Hardy from zone* 7 southward.

macnabiana. Macnab cypress, also called white cedar and Shasta cypress. A bushy tree up to 35 ft., usually less, often with several stems, its branches very slender. Leaves dark green, blunt, resinous. Cone about 1 in. in diameter. Ore. and Calif. Hardy from sheltered places in zone* 4 southward. The hardiest of all the cypresses. There is a variety with yellow twigs.

macrocarpa. Monterey cypress. A tree up to 75 ft. high, broad and spreading in age, pyramidal in youth. Leaves blunt or 4-sided

---

* Special articles on the subjects indicated by an asterisk (*) will be found at the words so marked.

(rhomboid*), dark green. Cones nearly 1½ in. in diameter. Calif., south of Monterey. Hardy from zone* 6 southward. There are several hort. varieties, one with the young foliage yellow.

sempervirens. Italian cypress, and the cypress of history. A tree up to 75 ft., its branches erect or horizontal. Branchlets or twigs flattened, the leaves dark green, blunt, 4-sided (rhomboid*). Cones nearly 1½ in. in diameter. Southern Eu. and southwestern As. Hardy from zone* 6 southward. The *var.* **horizontalis** has branches that spread out in a flat plane. The *var.* **stricta,** a common form in cult., has a columnar habit.

Curagua (kew-rah'gwa). Chilean name for a kind of popcorn. See CORN.

curassavica, -us, -um (cure-ras-săv'i-ka). From Curaçao, West Indies.

Curcas (kur'kaz). Pre-Linnaean* name for the purging-nut (*Jatropha Curcas*).

CURCULIGO (kur-kew-ly'go). Perhaps a dozen species of greenhouse herbs of the family Amaryllidaceae, one a well-known foliage plant needing a warm, moist greenhouse, never much below 75°, and potting mixture* 4. The only cult. species, **C. capitulata** (also known as *C. recurvata*), a native of tropical Asia and Aust., is a stemless herb which makes a cluster of handsome foliage. Leaves all basal, the blade plaited like a fan, recurved, 1–3 ft. long, 2–6 in. wide, the stalk channeled. Flowers yellow, nearly ¾ in. wide, borne on short, recurved stalks, the cluster near the ground level and half hidden by the foliage. (For details *see* AMARYLLIDACEAE.) Fruit somewhat fleshy. (*Curculigo* is from Latin for a weevil, in allusion to the beaked ovary.)

CURCUMA (kur-kew'ma). A genus of about 50 species of aromatic, perennial herbs of the family Zingiberaceae, all from the tropics of the Old World, two sometimes cult. for interest here, but the turmeric widely grown in India. They are ginger-like herbs with thick rootstocks, and stout leafy stems, the leaves generally large, lance-shaped, and sheathing at the base. In many cult. plants there is no stem, the leaves arising at the ground level. Flowers in a dense, bracted* spike, two irregular* flowers at each bract,* the top of the spike with a cluster of large, colored bracts. Corolla funnel-shaped, its summit 2-lipped.* Some of the stamens* are sterile and petal-like. Fruit a spherical, 3-valved capsule. (*Curcuma* is a Latinized version of an Arabic name for the turmeric.)

These plants need a warm (70°–80°) greenhouse and moist air as well as plenty of moisture at their roots. Use potting mixture* 4. Little grown outdoors and only possible in zone* 9. In the Far East turmeric is widely grown as an ingredient of curry powder.

longa. Turmeric. Rootstock stout and source of the turmeric. Leaves oblongish to lance-shaped, 12–18 in. long, 4–8 in. wide, the sheathing stalk about as long. Flower spike 4–7 in. long, nearly 2 in. thick, the showy bracts*

white, pink-tipped, the stalk from within the leaf sheaths. Flowers pale yellow. India.

petiolata. Smaller in all its parts than *C. longa,* the leaves rounded at the base. Flowers yellowish-white, the tuft of bracts* at the end of the spike purple. Eastern Asia.

CURD. The edible and often whitish flower head of plants like cauliflower and broccoli. It is, of course, a much modified and monstrous form of flower cluster.

CURDWORT = *Galium verum.*

CURING. Few vegetables need curing in the sense that sweet potatoes must be cured to be kept. The process involves the introduction of heat, the forcing out of excess moisture and provision for the elimination of the latter as water vapor rather than its accumulation on the walls of the curing room. For the details of curing *see* SWEET POTATO.

CURLED DOCK = *Rumex crispus.* See the list at WEEDS.

CURLED MALLOW = *Malva crispa* and *M. verticillata.*

CURLY CLEMATIS = *Clematis crispa.*

CURLY-GRASS = *Schizaea pusilla.*

CURLY PALM = *Howea belmoreana.*

CURRANT (*Ribes*). The red currant is a modern fruit, its domestication having taken place within the last three or four hundred years in several widely separated regions and from at least three species. All red currants are natives of cool, moist climates and their culture is restricted to northern latitudes and regions where summer rainfall is fairly copious. Currants do not thrive in the Gulf states and grow but poorly under the dry, hot summers of the plains states.

Any gardener can propagate currant plants easily, but nurserymen grow them so cheaply that home propagation is seldom worth while. In home propagation hardwood cuttings are taken in the autumn after leaves have dropped. Customarily they are 8 or 10 in. long and are planted at once 6 in. apart in nursery rows. Or they may be tied in bundles and stored, butts up, in moist sand and held until early spring. The cuttings are grown in nursery rows two seasons.

Currants are very hardy and may be grown north of fruit-tree latitudes without fear of injury. A cool, moist, well-drained loam or clay, even a stiff clay, are the most suitable soils for currants. Light soils and southern exposures are unsuitable. In the South and the prairie states the shade of buildings or trees sometimes makes currant-growing possible.

The plants are best when set in the fall, as plants often open their buds in the spring before the ground can be made ready for planting. In the North, at least, a furrow should be plowed up to the newly set rows to prevent heaving. Distances apart vary with the soil and the variety. Strong-growing varieties need a distance of 6 × 6 ft.; for weaker-growing sorts, 5 × 5 ft. suffice. A plantation lasts for many years.

---

* Special articles on the subjects indicated by an asterisk (*) will be found at the words so marked.

Cultivation should be shallow since currant roots are surface feeders. In home gardens and small plantations, mulching with grass or straw may take the place of cultivation. Stable manure will furnish both a mulch and a fertilizer. Currants need organic matter and cover crops of barley, buckwheat, or oats, crops which do not live through the winter, should be turned under in the fall. Several experiments seem to show that currants do not make a satisfactory response to chemical fertilizers.

Pruning is simple but very necessary. The aim in pruning should be to maintain an abundant supply of young wood, since the currant bears fruit on the base of one-year canes and on spurs of older wood. All canes over three years old should be cut out as well as very weak ones and those that sprawl on the ground. Usually there should be 6 or 8 strong canes, according to the vigor of the bush. Heading back is a poor practice, since it makes the bark too dense. Pruning is best done in early winter.

Currants are most used for jelly and for this purpose must be picked before fully ripe. The berries should be dry when picked and should not be stripped from the cluster stem. Ripe currants hang on the bushes for several weeks, and should be picked just befor using.

The culture of black currants does not differ from that of red currants except that the plants require more room. The cultivation of black currants is forbidden in some states because the bush is a host plant to the pine blister rust.

Five red currants may be recommended. Cherry is an early sort with very large, dark-red berries. Diploma is one of the handsomest and best in quality. Red Lake is a midseason variety. Perfection is an early midseason currant liked best of all for table use. White Imperial and White Grape are the best white currants. Naples is the best black. One thrives as well as another in plant zones* 1, 2, 3, 4, and 5 and 6 in the Pacific states. Dried "currants" are usually the dried fruits of the Black Corinth grape. See *vinifera* varieties at GRAPE. For restriction on planting currants, *see* GOOSEBERRY.

INSECT PESTS (Currant and Gooseberry). As plant comes into full leaf, greenish worms attack leaves. Control with pesticide #1 or #21 (*see* SPRAYS AND DUSTS). Greenish aphids curl leaves badly. Control with pesticide #21 or #20. Control scales with oil sprays as at APPLE. Plant bugs, reddish to green in color, attack new growth and leaves. Control with pesticide #21 or #20. Borers which attack canes should be pruned out and destroyed in spring. Pesticide #17 sprays at bottom of canes in June and July (avoid fruit) will control adult moths.

DISEASES. If experience during previous years indicates that leafspot* is serious in your area, or if tips of canes die from anthracnose* disease, a spray schedule may be necessary. Apply pesticide #5, or #11 (*see* SPRAYS AND DUSTS), immediately after bloom and repeat in 14 to 20 days. If leafspot appears, follow with a third application immediately after fruit has been picked.

The currant and gooseberry are alternate hosts for the white pine blister rust* (*see* under Gooseberry) and in some localities they must not be planted.

CURRANT TOMATO = *Lycopersicum pimpinellifolium.* See TOMATO.

CURTONUS. See ANTHOLYZA PANICULATA.

CURUBA = *Sicana odorifera.*

curvifolia, -us, -um (kur-vi-fō'li-a). With curved leaves.

CUSHAW = *Cucurbita moschata.*

CUSH-CUSH = *Dioscorea trifida.*

CUSHION PINK = *Silene acaulis.*

CUSHION PLANT. See TUFTED.

CUSHION SPURGE = *Euphorbia epithymoides.*

cuspidata, -us, -um (kus-pi-day'ta). Having a sharp, stiff point (cusp).

CUSTARD-APPLE. In the Central States, *Asimina triloba;* in Fla. and the tropics, *Annona reticulata.*

CUSTARD-APPLE FAMILY = Annonaceae.

CUT-AND-COME-AGAIN. See *Helianthus annuus* at SUNFLOWER.

CUT FLOWERS. No one needs to have a list of the common florist's offering of cut flowers. They are shown with the greatest profusion during the changing seasons and one never need be without flowers from this source.

For the home gardener, however, nothing quite replaces the things he can raise himself, and if properly planned, the flower garden will yield a supply for all months including winter. Not all garden flowers, however, keep well when cut. Some wilt too soon, and others never should be picked at all, for they seem more at home on the plant than you can ever make them in the house.

Annuals are always the best source of cut flowers, for they can be raised like vegetables, in rows, if large quantities are needed. Those best suited to picking, their colors, and the times to expect their bloom, are all designated in the list at ANNUALS.

Among perennial garden flowers the following have proved the most satisfactory for cutting. Notes on the culture and best varieties of each are scattered throughout the ENCYLOPEDIA and should be consulted for these details. The names in the list are the same as those under which they are entered in the ENCYCLOPEDIA:

Achillea	Foxglove	Mignonette
Anchusa	Galega	Monkshood
Anemone	Gypsophila	Peony
Boltonia	Helenium	Phlox
Campanula	Hemerocallis	Platycodon
Candytuft	Heuchera	Poppy (some
Chrysanthemum	Iris	sorts)
Columbine	Kniphofia	Rudbeckia
Coreopsis	Limonium	Scabiosa
Dahlia	Lilium	Snapdragon
Delphinium	Lupinus	Sweet Alyssum
Dianthus	Marigold	Sweet Pea
Forget-me-not	Milkweed	

* Special articles on the subjects indicated by an asterisk (*) will be found at the words so marked.

There are some annuals in certain of the plants listed above, but many more good ones will be found in the list at ANNUALS.

To annuals and perennials should be added the bulbous plants like tulip, hyacinth, and, for summer, the gladiolus. Less well known bulbous plants, many of them suited for cutting, will be found at BULBS.

Cut flowers should be cut, not torn off the plant. Make a clean cut with a good, stout pair of shears, never leaving the stems out of water for more than a few minutes and it is far better to plunge them at once in a pail of water. More flowers wilt in consequence of the first few minutes of neglect than one would ordinarily expect. Cutting, after all, is a shock, and it should be done early in the morning or late in the afternoon, never at midday nor in a wind. And carry your treasures into the shade of a tree or indoors as soon as possible.

While most cut-flower stalks are best plunged immediately into cold water, it is better to put dahlias, heliotrope, poinsettias, and oriental poppies in water of about 170° at once, after which they may be put in water of room temperature. Also do not submerge any more leaves than is necessary, for they soon decay and induce wilting. Aspirin, salt, and sugar are useless in spite of newspaper notices to the contrary. If any chemicals are useful in prolonging the freshness of cut flowers, and there is still doubt about it, hydrozene sulphate appears to be the best. Mix one ounce of the chemical in a quart of water as a stock solution (too strong for direct use). Dilute the stock solution at the rate of one quarter cup to 12 qts. of water. Each day the ends of flower stalks should be cut, as the old end tends to heal and cut off water entrance.

Flowers may be kept fresh in the refrigerator, but blooms so stored will not last long when brought to heated rooms. If they are put in the refrigerator the best temperature is 45°–50°, except for roses, carnations, tulips, and gardenias which are better kept at 40°–45°.

What you do with cut flowers is a reflection of your taste in color, form, and arrangement. No one can dictate that to you, but the main principles of it are well known. See FLOWER ARRANGING.

CUTLEAF BEECH = *Fagus sylvatica laciniata.* See BEECH.

CUTLEAF BLACKBERRY = *Rubus laciniatus.*

CUTTAGE. The making and care of cuttings (which see).

CUTTING BENCH. A bench in a greenhouse for rooting cuttings. It is ordinarily sand-filled, is often covered with a frame and sash, and sometimes provided with bottom-heat.*

CUTTINGS. A cutting is a piece of a plant without roots but induced to produce roots after it has been severed from the parent plant. Layers, suckers, etc., already have roots when they are cut off. The term *slip* applies to softwood cuttings because the side-shoots of which they frequently consist are sometimes pulled or slipped off the main stem without the use of a knife.

ADVANTAGES OF PROPAGATING BY CUTTINGS

Propagation by cuttings is a cheap and convenient way to increase a stock of plants. Sizable plants are usually much more quickly obtained in this manner than from seeds. Besides, many garden varieties and hybrids vary greatly if raised from seeds, while from cuttings one is sure to obtain a very uniform set of plants which resemble the parent plant in every way. Certain plants, also, do not readily produce seeds in cultivation or, as is the case for instance with willows and poplars, are rather difficult to propagate from seeds.

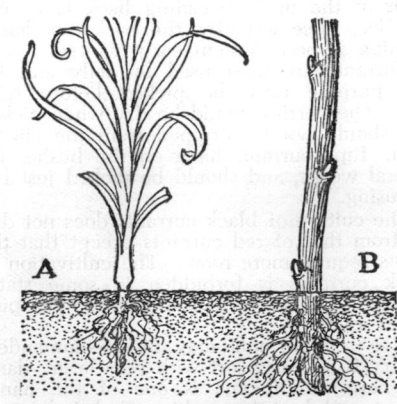

A softwood cutting (A) and a hardwood cutting (B)

Skilled propagators claim that there is no plant which cannot be propagated from cuttings. This, unquestionably, is true, but certain plants, notably most of our fruit trees, grow so much better and are so easy to propagate from buds or grafts that with them these latter methods are preferred.

TYPES OF CUTTINGS

We can distinguish between the following types of cuttings:

a. Stem cuttings, consisting of parts of the stem, to be divided into:
   1. Softwood or green cuttings, taken from the plant while it is in leaf and growth, thus providing half-ripened wood.
   2. Hardwood cuttings, taken from the leafless, dormant plant, after it has finished and ripened its yearly growth.
   3. Single-eye cuttings, consisting of only one bud or eye with not more than a part of the stem attached.
b. Leaf cuttings, consisting only of a leaf, with or without its stalk.
c. Root or rootstock cuttings.

---

* Special articles on the subjects indicated by an asterisk (*) will be found at the words so marked.

Softwood Cuttings

Easiest and most frequently used is the softwood cutting. For best results, cuttings of this type should be taken when the plant is at a certain intermediate stage of growth — that is, when the cuttings are neither too soft and succulent nor too mature. If the young shoots, when bent, neither snap off like glass nor crush without breaking, they are in the right condition to use. For only a few plants does this rule not hold true. Lilacs and azaleas, for example, have been found to root most readily when the cuttings are very soft, while others, like varieties of *Weigela* and *Hydrangea,* give better results if the cuttings are almost mature. June to August are the months in which outdoor plants may be propagated in this manner. Softwood cuttings of greenhouse or bedding plants are usually taken in early spring.

The shoot chosen for a cutting must be healthy and in good condition and must show the characteristics which are typical for the variety we wish to propagate. The most vigorous shoots, however, never make the best cuttings. The best results are usually obtained with side-shoots of intermediate strength, and if these are cut directly at their base, they will root most readily. The frequently recommended "heel," a small slice of the main stem left on the base of the side-shoot cutting, is with many plants more a hindrance than a help. Only with certain hollow-stemmed alpines has the heel been found to be of definite advantage.

With certain plants not all side-shoots make equally desirable cuttings. On carnations, for instance, only the side-shoots from the center of the stem make flowering plants of good habit.

With roses, cuttings of side-shoots — so-called flowering wood — give earlier and more free-flowering plants than do tip cuttings, so-called blind wood.

If small side-shoots are not available, we have to use the tips of longer shoots, and with them we find that usually the cuttings root best if the basal cut is made from ¼ to ½ inch below a leaf or a pair of leaves, as the case may be, since it is from the part of the stem below the node* that roots are most likely to arise. The old and long-accepted rule that all cuttings should be cut at a node,* that is, directly below a leaf, has been disproved by recent extensive experiments. Only a few of our hardy shrubs, such as box, *Caragana, Clethra, Cotoneaster, Kolkwitzia, Laburnum, Photinia,* and *Pyracantha,* give decidedly better results if the cut is made at a node. The weigelas and some of the privets root most readily if the cut is made slightly above a node,* leaving a long internode beneath the first pair of leaves.

An important point with softwood cuttings is that they must be put into the cutting bench as soon as they are cut and before they have had a chance to wilt. To put cuttings in a pail of water in order to keep them fresh, however, is a mistake, since the water has an undesirable effect on the cut surface, preventing the formation of a protective fatty layer for which the oxygen of the air is necessary, and rendering the cutting susceptible to rot. Cuttings which are collected outdoors may be wrapped in a moist cloth and in this manner be kept fresh for an hour or two.

Also, in the future treatment of the cuttings it is absolutely essential that they never be allowed to wilt. Frequent sprinkling — on hot days several times during the day — is necessary. On the cutting bench in the greenhouse the cuttings may be covered with cheesecloth over which the sprinkling may take place until callus has been formed. The cutting bench must have bottom-heat* and should have a temperature of 60°–65° F. The electrically heated frame, now obtainable in the trade at a reasonable price, will be found a great help by the amateur who does not have a greenhouse. (*See* Cold Frame.) An even simpler device for use in the house is the Propagating Frame (which see).

The *best medium* in which to root cuttings is a mixture of sand and peat in equal parts, surfaced with about a quarter-inch of pure sand. Vermiculite and perlite in medium grades, or perlite and peat moss mixed in equal parts, are excellent media also. There are only a few plants which root better in pure sand, such as *Euonymus, Magnolia, Daphne* and most of the dwarf spruces, while pure peat is a rather unsatisfactory medium, since it provides poor aeration. The surface of the rooting medium is smoothed and is gently but not too firmly pressed down. Then the cuttings are inserted in rows, so far apart that their leaves barely touch. Their lowermost leaves may be cut off, if they interfere. It is advisable not to use a dibble in putting in the cuttings, since this may easily leave an air space beneath the cutting, which is a serious disadvantage.

Taking the cutting between three fingers of one hand, a slight downward pressure will be sufficient for inserting it in the rooting medium deeply enough to make it stand upright, though never more than half its length. After all cuttings are in place, the rooting medium is settled firmly around them by a thorough soaking with water. This is better than to firm it down with the fingers or with a piece of wood.

A Simple Aid in Propagation

The amateur without a greenhouse will find the following simple arrangement effective for small amounts of cuttings:

In a seedpan (6–7 in. diam.) a smaller pot (2½–3 in. diam.) with closed drainage hole is inserted. The drainage hole of the seedpan must be kept open. The space between the two pots holds the rooting medium (peat and sand). The cuttings are in-

---

* Special articles on the subjects indicated by an asterisk (*) will be found at the words so marked.

serted close to the rim of the small inner pot, which is kept filled with water. Since the moisture seeps slowly through the pores of the pot, no direct watering of the cuttings is necessary. A large bell-jar* covering the seedpan, or a plastic bag pulled over the pan from above and tied with a string around the rim of the pan, will prevent wilting of the cuttings. It must be shaded if set in a sunny window.

The root development of the cuttings can easily be watched by taking out the center pot from time to time with a twisting movement which prevents disturbance of the soil.

ROOTING SOFTWOOD CUTTINGS UNDER MIST

Propagation under mist is assuming considerable commercial importance because it permits the use of very soft cuttings in early summer and results in rapid rooting of many types of trees and shrubs which previously were considered very difficult to propagate in this manner. The principle of this method is to prevent the cuttings from wilting by keeping their leaves damp under a mist-fine spray, while still exposing them to the full light of the sun. A wind-sheltered spot must be chosen, or at least partial wind shelter must be provided. An open sunken pit serves also. The propagating bed must be well drained by means of a subsurface layer of gravel, and a medium-grade perlite serves particularly well as rooting medium. The fog nozzles should be from 3 to 3½ ft. above the surface of the bed and should be placed 3 to 4 ft. apart since each covers an area of about 3 × 3 or 3 × 4 ft. Continuous or constant mist, employed in earlier experiments, has not been found fully satisfactory, because it results in leaching the leaves of the cuttings as well as of the rooting medium, and, though rooting is satisfactory, the cuttings usually succumb afterwards. Interrupted or intermittent mist gives better results and may be controlled either by means of a so-called "electronic leaf" which automatically turns on the mist spray whenever the leaves of the cuttings commence to become dry, or by a clock which can be set so as to turn on the mist for a few seconds in every minute. The latter setup actually is more satisfactory because it permits gradual lengthening of the intervals between the mist applications as the cuttings start rooting. Even the intermittent mist, however, results in a certain amount of leaching and therewith weakening of the cuttings which in addition are likely to produce mainly water-roots, making their later establishment in soil difficult. This handicap can be largely overcome by soaking the rooting medium once a week with a mild nutrient solution and by applying a foliar nutrient spray to the cuttings several times when they are commencing to root. The amateur can employ this procedure also by setting up one fog nozzle over a box with cuttings in a wind-sheltered spot.

HARDWOOD CUTTINGS

One advantage of hardwood over greenwood cuttings is that they are much easier to handle, being less perishable, and may even be shipped safely over great distances. Many hardy deciduous shrubs can be propagated in this manner, and, though various ways of handling are advocated, the following is probably the simplest and most effective.

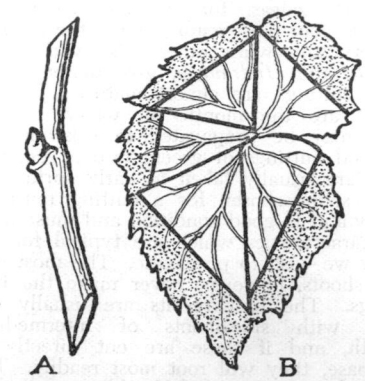

A single-eye woody cutting (A) and a leaf cutting of begonia (B). The dark lines on the inset enlargement of the veins show where they should be cut to induce new plants to sprout. See BEGONIA.

The mature shoots of last season's growth are collected as soon as the leaves have fallen, usually in October or November, and are cut up into sticks 6–10 in. long. The cut on the lower end should be just below a node. Tied in small bundles, they are set upright in trenches about 1 ft. deep, preferably in a cold frame.* The trenches then are filled with sand to not more than 1 in. above the tips of the cuttings. There they are left to form callus. In the spring they may either be rooted in the cutting bench in the greenhouse or lined out in beds outside, where they must be buried to the uppermost pair of buds and planted 4–6 in. apart. *Deutzia, Forsythia*, privet, *Lonicera*, mock-orange, *Populus, Ribes*, willow, spireas, and other shrubs may be propagated in this manner.

CONIFER CUTTINGS are generally recommended to be taken from mature wood during November. However, contrary to common belief, this is probably the worst time of the year, and such cuttings are very slow to root. The best time for conifer cuttings is either during March or April, just before the plants are ready to start their spring growth, or from the middle of June to the middle of July, when the spring growth is completed but before it hardens. Short side-shoots, cut at the very base, or with a small heel,* are usually most successful. They may be rooted in the cutting bench or

---

* Special articles on the subjects indicated by an asterisk (*) will be found at the words so marked.

in small quantities in the double-pot arrangement mentioned under softwood cuttings. The rooting medium and general treatment are also the same as mentioned there. *Cephalotaxus, Chamaecyparis, Juniperus, Taxus,* and *Thuja* are readily rooted in this manner, though some of them, in particular *Juniperus* and some of the *Chamaecyparis,* may take a few months before they produce roots. Excessive callus formation to which they are inclined hinders the production of roots. If this is observed, it is advisable to pare off part of the callus with a sharp knife. Spruces and pines are difficult to root from cuttings mainly because of the resin which is exuded at the cut surface and which hinders callus and root formation. This may be overcome by dipping the lower ends of the cuttings for a few minutes in fairly hot water (130°–150° F.) before they are inserted in the cutting bed.

Broad-leaved evergreens, such as *Aucuba,* box, *Euonymus, Osmanthus, Phillyrea, Stranvaesia,* heathers, and holly, etc., are readily rooted in the same manner and at the same times as the conifers. Most of them also give excellent results under mist.

BUD CUTTINGS

Bud cuttings, consisting of only one single bud with a part of the stem, are employed particularly with grapes. In November the bud-sticks are collected and cut up into single-eye pieces, about ½ in. above and ½ in. below the eye. The stem is then split lengthwise through the center and the halved stems with the eye up and the cut surface downward are placed in boxes filled with peat and sand.

A stem cutting of dracaena

The cuttings are pressed only lightly into the rooting medium and covered thinly with pure sand until only the eyes show. Sphagnum moss is then spread over the sand to the thickness of 1 in. and the box, covered with a pane of glass, is stored for at least 6–8 weeks in a cool greenhouse or cellar to form callus. After that the box is removed to a warmer place to induce root formation.

LEAFBUD CUTTINGS may be used for quick increase of dahlias, but this is done in the spring from shoots which have been forced from the tubers in the greenhouse in February. In this case the leafstalk and at least half of the leaf-blade form part of the cutting besides the bud, and usually only a small slice of the stem is left at the base. Various other plants may be so propagated in an emergency.

LEAF CUTTINGS

Propagation by leaf cuttings is widely practiced, especially with *Begonia Rex.* Large, well-matured leaves are selected, and are cut off with or without a small part of the stalk. The principal veins are cut on the under side in a few places and the leaf is placed flat on the sand bed in a warm propagating house, and weighted down with sand or small pebbles. If carefully shaded, young plants will develop from each incision.

Other begonias are usually propagated from leaf cuttings in November or December. Healthy, well-matured leaves are cut off with their stalks and the stalks are inserted in the sand bed to at least half their length. The individual leaves should be spaced in such a manner that they do not touch each other, or they will start to rot. The danger of damping-off* may be further reduced by sprinkling charcoal dust over the sand of the cutting bed. A temperature of 70° is required for best results.

Gloxinias and saintpaulias and other members of the same family (Gesneriaceae) are frequently propagated from leaf cuttings, but gloxinias only if one particularly fine form is to be perpetuated. In their case the leaf is cut with about 1 in. of its stalk and inserted in the cutting bench so that a small part of the leaf-blade also is covered with sand. They must be kept rather dry and should not be sprayed with water, although the air in the greenhouse should be always moist.

Lachenalias, old-fashioned but rather pretty bulbous greenhouse plants, may also be propagated from leaf cuttings. About half a dozen leaves may be inserted about 1 in. deep in a 5-in. pot, filled with sand, and kept moist and shaded in the propagating case. Within a month each one will produce five to ten tiny bulblets at its base. Succulents of the family Crassulaceae grow readily from leaf cuttings also.

ROOT CUTTINGS

Pieces of true roots are a ready means of increase, especially for all those plants which are inclined to sucker from their roots, such as blackberries and raspberries, trumpet-creeper, Osage orange, *Wistaria, Plumbago, Phlox, paniculata,* Oriental poppies, *Rhus, Ailanthus,* etc. This method is quite effective also with certain other trees and shrubs from which stem cuttings do not root readily, for example: *Acanthopanax, Gymnocladus,* locust, *Sophora, Xanthoceras,* etc.

---

* Special articles on the subjects indicated by an asterisk (*) will be found at the words so marked.

The roots are dug up in the autumn, as soon as the leaves have fallen, cut into 1–3 in. pieces and stored in boxes in moist sand either in the cold frame or in a cold but frost-proof cellar. The root cuttings of those varieties which are slow to respond to this treatment have to be brought into the greenhouse in February, where with gentle bottom-heat they may be induced to form buds. All others may be lined out in beds in the spring, the distance depending on the variety, but far enough apart to allow the young plants to develop.

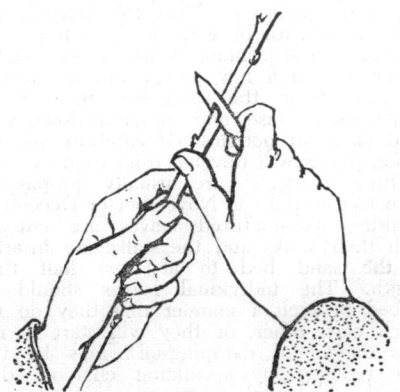

A clean, slanting cut with a sharp knife is best for making slips or cuttings.

The creeping rootstocks of many perennials may also be used for propagation. During the resting period of the plant, which with the spring-flowering plants usually is in midsummer, the rootstocks are dug up and cut into small pieces (2 in. long will usually do), and are stored in sand in a cool place. Their further treatment is like that of root cuttings.

The Basement Propagating Box

Cuttings of many plants can readily be rooted in a closed box equipped with two 40-watt tubes of cold-white fluorescent light and set up in the basement. The light tubes should be about 12 in. above the rooting medium, and the lights must be left on for approximately 12 hours of each 24. One of the long sides of the box should open on hinges. The cuttings may be inserted in flats filled with vermiculite or perlite or sand and peat moss, and the cutting-filled flats then are placed into the box under the lights. Syringing as needed is important. If the temperature of the basement is less than 65° F. an electric, thermostatically controlled, heating unit must be installed in the bottom of the box. *See also* Propagating Frame.

Rooting Hormones

A number of synthetic plant hormone preparations, which induce or stimulate the production of roots on cuttings, are on the market under various trade names. With their help many varieties of woody plants can be raised successfully from cuttings which otherwise give only a very low percentage of rooting or produce poor-quality roots. With easily rooting kinds the progress is speeded up. Not all of these preparations work equally well on all kinds of cuttings. Some even are supplied in a range of different concentrations and the manufacturer supplies a list of the plants which best respond to each. In any case, the manufacturers' directions must be carefully followed. — H. T. See Hormones.

CUTWORM. Dull-gray fat worms ¾–1½ in. long, very destructive because of their habit of biting through the stems of herbaceous plants at the ground level mostly in the evening. They can often be poisoned with a bait made of ¼ pound of Paris green to 5 lbs. of wheat bran to which enough water is added to moisten it. This should be scattered around the ground near the plants. Pesticide #17, #15, #18 (*see* Sprays and Dusts) and others, as spray or dust about the base of plants, kill caterpillars. To protect individual plants, a collar of cardboard should be slipped around the stem, 1 in. below the soil and 2 in. above it. — L. G. M.

cyanoclada, -us, -um (sy-an-ok′la-da). Blue-twigged.

Cyanus (sy-an′us). An old generic name for the cornflower (*Centaurea Cyanus*), signifying blue.

CYATHEA (sy-ăth′ee-a). An immense genus of tall tree ferns of the family Cyatheaceae, mostly tropical, and one of them much cult. by florists for its feathery foliage. **C. dealbata** grows in New Zealand up to 30–40 ft., but as cult. in greenhouses usually less than half this. The trunk is stout and crowned with a dozen or less very graceful fronds, 5–9 ft. long and 2–4 ft. wide. Frond thrice-compound,* the ultimate segments 2–4 in. long and usually toothed, yellowish-green above, whitish beneath. Spore* cases on the lower surface of the fronds, brownish and conspicuous. For the cult. of this handsome greenhouse fern *see* Ferns and Fern Gardening. (Cyathea is from the Greek for cup, in allusion to the spore* cases.)

CYATHEACEAE (sy-ath-ee-ā′see-ee). The tree fern family includes, among garden plants, only 4 genera of arborescent ferns of great beauty, cult. only in greenhouses or in the most sheltered parts of zone* 9. All of its 7 genera and over 800 species are plants of moist, warm, or hot tropical forests. For their culture *see* Ferns and Fern Gardening.

The leaves (fronds) are often of great size, being twice- or thrice-compound,* and the ultimate segments often deeply cut or lobed, the foliage thus being of great beauty and of feathery texture. The leafstalk is often smooth or polished, but in some genera prick-

---

* Special articles on the subjects indicated by an asterisk (*) will be found at the words so marked.

ly. The minute technicalities that separate *Alsophila, Cibotium, Cyathea,* and *Dicksonia,* the only hort. genera, and Cyatheaceae from the Polypodiaceae are quite outside usual garden practice and may be left to the experts. Some of the tree ferns which, in cult. specimens, do not have much of a trunk (but often 60 ft. high in the tropics), are widely grown by florists.

CYBISTETES. *See* AMMOCHARIS FALCATA.

CYCAD. Any plant of the family Cycadaceae.

CYCADACEAE (sy-ka-day'see-ee). The cycas or sago palm family, geologically very ancient, has only 9 existing genera and perhaps 75 species of woody, fern-like or palm-like plants that once nearly covered the earth. They are, however, quite unlike ferns in bearing cones and seeds. The only cult. genera are *Cycas* (which contains the common, and funereal, sago palm), and *Zamia* which is American and includes the coontie. All are of greenhouse cult. or planted outdoors only in zones* 8 and 9.

They are ornamental, evergreen plants with a trunk or trunk-like base, compound,* usually leathery leaves that, in opening, uncoil like a fern frond. The leaves are usually borne in a crown or rosette* at the top of the trunk, and are often very handsome (notably in the sago palm, *Cycas revoluta*).

Technical characters: Plants gymnospermous,* the male and female flowers usually borne naked between the scales of a cone-like structure that mostly arises in the center of the rosette of leaves. Fruit fleshy.

CYCAS (sy'kas). A group of fern-like or palm-like plants of the family Cycadaceae, comprising about 8 species, chiefly from Asia and Australasia. Two of them are widely cult. greenhouse plants and grown outdoors in Fla. and Calif. They have a stout, unbranched, but not very tall, trunk-like stem and a large crown of frond-like leaves, for which they are mostly cult. Leaves long and stiffish, divided feather-fashion into innumerable rigid, often pointed segments which have no veins but the midrib. Male and female flowers on different plants, neither with any petals, but crowded in cone-like structures, between the scales of which are borne the naked male and female organs of reproduction. (*Cycas* is from the Greek for some palm tree, which these are not.)

The second species is more widely grown for funeral wreaths than any plant in America, its crossed fronds tied with a ribbon being nearly universal. Both need a warm, moist greenhouse (65°–75°) and plenty of water. Use potting mixture* 3. Young plants do not have a trunk, but old ones have trunks of considerable height, mostly concealed beneath the persistent bases of the old leaves. Propagated by suckers which should be detached when dormant — that is, between the periods when the plant is forcing out a new crop of leaves, all of which appear at once, often in May–June when planted outdoors, but forced at will by the florists.

circinalis. Palm-like, the trunk 10–12 ft. Leaves in a terminal crown, 5–8 ft. long, the stalk spiny at the base. Ultimate leaf segments alternate,* 10–12 in. long, the margins flat. Male cone nearly 2 ft. long and 5 in. in diameter (rarely produced in cult.). Tropical Africa to the islands of the Pacific.

revoluta. This, the commonest cycad in cult., is universally called sago palm in spite of the fact that it does not produce commercial sago nor is it a palm. It is palm-like, with a trunk 6–10 ft. high. Leaves in a terminal crown, 2–7 ft. long, somewhat arching at the tip, glossy-green, the ultimate segments numerous, crowded, stiff, spine-tipped, 3–5 in. long and with rolled margins. Male cone 18–20 in. long. China and East Indies. Common as a specimen plant in sub-tropical gardens and hardier than *C. circinalis. See* above for its use for funeral wreaths.

CYCAS FAMILY = Cycadaceae.

CYCLAMEN (sy'kla-men, also sick'lamen). About 20 species of tuberous, stemless, perennial herbs of the family Primulaceae, mostly from central and southern Eu., one a very popular florists' pot plant, grown for its handsome flowers. Leaves all basal, long-stalked, the blade roundish or kidney-shaped. Flowers solitary on each stalk, which is less than 12 in. high. Calyx with 5 divisions. Corolla with a very short tube, the 5 lobes much longer, contorted, and with strongly recurved tips. Fruit a 5-valved capsule* splitting from the top downward. (*Cyclamen* is the classical name for these plants.)

For culture *see* below.

atkinsi. A hybrid cyclamen, relatively hardy and spring-blooming. Leaves similar to those of the next species, but with white markings. Flowers pale pink or whitish, spotted or streaked with red. May–June.

coum. A perennial herb resembling *C. indicum,* but hardy. Leaves nearly round, or kidney-shaped. Flowers smaller than in *C. indicum,* purple-spotted and odorless. Southeastern Eu. Spring.

europaeum. A relatively hardy cyclamen with kidney-shaped leaves that are almost evergreen in mild regions. Flowers deep red, not over 1 in. long, on a stalk about the length of the leaves. Central Eu. and western As. Aug.–Sept.

hederaefolium = *Cyclamen indicum.*

indicum. The common cyclamen of the shops. A stemless herb, the leaves roundish-heart-shaped, 2½–3 in. wide, the margins with rounded teeth. Flower stalk 6–8 in. high, the flower about 2 in. wide, white or rose, dark purple at the mouth (much variation exists in some of the hort. varieties). Greece to Syria. Blooming in early spring where grown outdoors, but winter-flowering as grown under glass by florists. There are many forms in cult. One has flowers nearly twice the normal size. Others have double flowers and some have the petals crested or shredded.

neapolitanum. A late summer-blooming perennial herb with large, black-skinned tubers. Leaves roundish or eared, wavy-margined. Flowers pink or rarely white, the petals twisted. Southern and eastern Eu.

persicum = *Cyclamen indicum.*

---

* Special articles on the subjects indicated by an asterisk (*) will be found at the words so marked.

repandum. A relatively hardy cyclamen with heart-shaped wavy-margined leaves that are silvery above but reddish beneath. Flowers bright red, but darker at the throat. Southern Eu. May–June.

Cyclamen Culture

Cyclamen indicum, the common cyclamen of the florists, needs a greenhouse for best results. The other species can be grown as hardy perennials, being suited especially to the rock garden or shaded borders. They are generally hardy up to zone* 4, and need good garden loam and moisture.

Cyclamen coum is a spring-bloomer, while *C. neapolitanum* blooms in the late summer or early fall. These two relatively hardy cyclamens cannot usually be grown outdoors without protection in the East. But in Calif. they will bloom on the bare soil, before the leaves appear. Cult. in places with not too cold and wet a soil is relatively easy if the situation is free of alternate freezing and thawing.

The common cyclamen of the florists needs rather special attention. For good bloom the plants should be started from seed, allowing 18 months from that time until they are ready to flower. Seeds should be sown in flats in July or August, in potting mixture* 2, and the young seedlings transferred to other flats with potting mixture* 3 when large enough to move. Only on the last move should the plants be transferred to pots. They need plenty of water, but will rot if the drainage is not good. Keep the greenhouse about 55° during the period of active growth, and do not allow the plants to be shaded in winter either by trees outside, or by a wash on the greenhouse glass. During the summer the glass should be shaded.

Just before the blooming period the temperature should be reduced to 45°–50°, to prevent too short a flowering period, which is likely to happen if the temperature is too high. Cyclamens are occasionally raised from seed in cold frames and brought to maturity as house plants.

INSECT PESTS. Microscopic mites twist plants and stunt growth. Use uninfested stock. Fumigate greenhouse before planting. Immersion of plants for 15 minutes at 110° F. will control. New miticides are being developed. Consult your state agricultural experiment station. See black vine weevil at TAXUS and thrips at CHRYSANTHEMUM.

DISEASES. Leafspot,* caused by a fungus, may occasionally mar the appearance of leaves but does not become serious enough under normal conditions to prevent growing the plant. During very humid weather gray mold* may become serious, rotting the crown or center of the cluster of leaves. Apply pesticide #5 or #11 (see SPRAYS AND DUSTS) and repeat once or twice at 10- to 14-day intervals.

CYCLANTHACEAE. See CARLUDOVICA.

CYCLANTHERA (sy-klan'theer-ra). A group of over 30 species of chiefly tropical American vines of the cucumber family, **C. pedata** being the only one of much garden interest. It is an herbaceous vine grown as an annual and reaches up to 10 ft. or beyond. Leaves alternate,* compound* or nearly so, the 5–7 segments or leaflets arranged feather-fashion, lobed or toothed. Flowers small and inconspicuous, the male and female separate, but on the same plant, greenish-white. (For details see CUCURBITACEAE.) Fruit oblongish, about 2 in. long, short-stalked, its yellowish-white husk covered with soft prickles. The vine grows quickly and soon covers fences or a lattice screen. (*Cyclanthera* is from Greek for circle and anther, in allusion to a stamen character.)

CYCLOPHORUS (sy-klof'for-us). Mostly tropical Indo-Malayan ferns of the family Polypodiaceae, of the 100 known species **C. lingua,** the tongue-fern or Japanese fern, commonly grown in greenhouses. It has slender, shaggy rootstocks from which arise many undivided fronds that are lance-shaped, 5–6 in. long, half of which is stalk. The under side of the frond is rusty-colored, and often almost completely covered with the conspicuous, circular spore* cases. There is a form with the tip of the frond crested,* and another with variegated fronds. For culture see FERNS AND FERN GARDENING. (*Cyclophorus* is from Greek for circle-bearing, in reference to the shape of the spore cases.) It is sometimes known as felt-fern.

CYDISTA (sy-dis'ta). A single species of tropical American woody vine of the family Bignoniaceae, related to the trumpet-creeper, and grown in the far South for its showy flowers. The only species, **C. aequinoctialis,** is a tendril-bearing vine with opposite,* compound* leaves composed of only 2 leaflets and a terminal tendril.* Leaflets leathery, wavy-margined, 4–6 in. long. Flowers in racemes,* the corolla funnel- or trumpet-shaped, nearly 3 in. long, white or purplish. Fruit a slender pod 9–12 in. long. It is a popular vine in Fla. but little known and not hardy much north of it. (*Cydista* is from the Greek for most glorious, in reference to the beautiful flowers.)

CYDONIA. See QUINCE. For the flowering quince see CHAENOMELES.

cylindrica, -us, -um (sil-lin'dri-ka). Cylindrical.

CYMBALARIA (sim-ba-lay'ri-a). A genus of 10 species of generally prostrate, Old World herbs of the family Scrophulariaceae, one very common as a greenhouse vine or in hanging baskets, the other two less grown. They have herbaceous stems and alternate* or opposite* leaves, sometimes lobed and veined finger-fashion. Flowers solitary in the leaf axils,* irregular* and spurred, usually small, the throat nearly closed. Stamens 4. Fruit a small capsule, shedding its seeds through small pores. (*Cymbalaria* is from the Greek for cymbal, in allusion to the leaf-shape of some species.)

All those below are often listed as of the genus *Linaria.*

* Special articles on the subjects indicated by an asterisk (*) will be found at the words so marked.

The Kenilworth ivy is a popular, widely grown plant for hanging baskets and for small trellises in the living room, conditions it withstands very well. It is almost weedy under many greenhouse benches. While a perennial, it often persists as a self-sown escape outdoors. The other two are chiefly plants for the cool greenhouse, or outdoors in the South, or in the rock garden.

aequitriloba. Creeping perennial herb, the leaves opposite,* 3–5-lobed or unlobed. Flowers small, pale mauve, the top of the corolla reddish-purple. Southern Eu. See ROCK GARDEN.

hepaticifolia. Prostrate, the leaves usually opposite,* slightly 3-5-lobed or unlobed. Flowers nearly ½ in. long, lilac-blue, the upper part of the corolla yellowish inside. Corsica.

muralis. Kenilworth ivy; called also Coliseum ivy, Aaron's-beard and climbing sailor. A creeping vine easily rooting at the joints. Leaves generally alternate,* roundish or kidney-shaped, more or less shallowly 3–7-angled or lobed. Flowers about ⅓ in. long, lilac-blue, the upper part of the corolla yellowish inside. Eu. Sometimes persisting or naturalized outdoors in eastern N.A. There are white and pink-flowered varieties and one with larger flowers. A useful vine for hanging baskets or window boxes, never growing more than 3 ft. or so.

CYMBIDIUM (sim-bid'i-um). Nearly 50 species of handsome, tree-perching (epiphytic*) orchids of the Old World tropics, many of its scores of hybrids much grown by orchid fanciers, and two rather generally in greenhouses. The commonly cult. species, **C. lowianum,** has a compressed, oblongish pseudobulb,* from which arise narrow, sharp, curved leaves 2–3 ft. long, which are usually persistent. Flowers very showy in an arching cluster (raceme*) that may have 20 blooms. Flowers 3–4 in. wide, the sepals and petals alike, greenish-yellow with brown or reddish streaks. Lip* yellowish-tan on the side lobes, the front lobe maroon with a yellow margin. Burma. For culture see ORCHID. A recent fine introduction is **C. insigne.** A showy orchid with nearly globose pseudobulbs.* Leaves bluish-green, 1½–3 ft. long and about ½ in. wide. Flowers in erect spikes, 3–4 ft. long, the individual flower 3–4 in. wide, whitish-rose, crimson-spotted, the lip* white, but crimson-lined and spotted. Indo-China. (*Cymbidium* is from the Greek for boat, in allusion to the shape of the lip.*)

cymbiformis, -e (sim-bi-for'mis). Boat-shaped.

CYMBOPOGON (sim-bo-pō'gon). Tropical Old World, mostly perennial grasses, often aromatic, of the 40 known species the three below grown for their fragrant oil, or rarely for ornament. Here they are little known, but they are the source in India of perfumes and drugs. They have grass-like leaves and flowers in twin spikelets, the spikelets grouped in a branched, often hairy, cluster (panicle*). Sometimes the spikelets are awned.* (*Cymbopogon* is Greek for boat and beard, in reference to the spikelets.)

The three below can be grown outdoors only in the warmest parts of the U.S. They are scarcely cult. otherwise.

citratus. Lemon grass. Differs from *C. Nardus* chiefly in technical characters of the spikelets and in the lemon-scented foliage. Origin unknown, but cult. in India for centuries.

Nardus. Citronella grass, its roots and herbage the source of citronella oil. A perennial grass 4–6 ft. high. Leaves 2–3 ft. long, about ¾ in. wide, bluish-green. Flower cluster 1½–2½ ft. long, usually branched. Tropical As., but naturalized in tropical America.

Schoenanthus. Camel hay or camel grass. Resembling *C. Nardus*, but rarely over 2 ft. high. Foliage very fragrant. Joints of the flowering cluster hairy. Southern As. and northern Af.

CYME (syme). A broad, often flat-topped, branching flower cluster that blooms from the center toward the edges, and in which the main stalk or axis is always terminated by a flower. Typical examples are many plants of the pink and gentian families. Such clusters are said to be cymose.

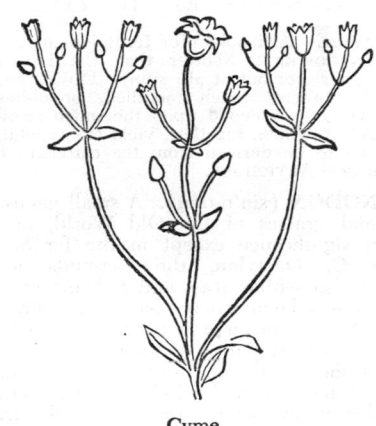

Cyme

Cyminum (sym-my'num). A variant spelling of *Cuminum*, the cumin.

CYMLING. See SQUASH.

CYMOPHYLLUS. See CAREX FRASERI.

cymosa, -us, -um (sy-mō'sa). Cymose; see CYME.

cynanchoides (sy-nan-choy'deez; but see OIDES). Resembling the mosquito-trap (*Cynanchum*).

CYNANCHUM (sy-nan'chum). A genus of Old World perennial herbs of the milkweed family, one of them, **C. acuminatifolium,** known as the mosquito-trap or mosquitoplant, and of easy cult. in any ordinary garden soil. It is a Japanese herb, often somewhat vine-like at the tip. Leaves opposite,* arrow-shaped, grayish and hairy on the under side. Flowers whitish, sometimes entrapping small insects. (See ASCLEPIADACEAE.) Fruits resembling the common milkweeds. The plant is sometimes known as *Vincetoxicum acuminatum*, and is of only secondary garden

---

* Special articles on the subjects indicated by an asterisk (*) will be found at the words so marked.

interest. (*Cynanchum* is from the Greek for dog-strangling, of remote application here.)

CYNARA (sin'a-ra). Perhaps a dozen coarse, thistle-like herbs of the family Compositae, mostly from the Mediterranean region, two of them yielding garden vegetables. Leaves large, more or less lobed or cut or both, sometimes spiny, in one of them with thickened, edible leafstalks. Flowers in large, dense heads, one of which terminates most of the larger branches. Flowers all tubular and disk° flowers, there being no rays. Below and surrounding each head is a cluster of bracts° in many series (much modified in the artichoke), spiny-tipped in the cardoon. (*Cynara* is from the Greek, implying that the spiny bracts are like a dog's tooth.)

Cardunculus. Cardoon. Stout perennial up to 6 ft. high. Root and thickened leafstalks edible. Leaves large, very deeply cut, grayish-green above, but white-felty beneath, densely spiny. Flower heads with spiny-tipped bracts,° the flowers purple. Southern Eu. For culture *see* CARDOON.

Scolymus. Artichoke (for Jerusalem artichoke *see* SUNFLOWER). Shorter than the last, the leaves not so, or not at all, spiny. Flower heads with the bracts° much modified, broad-based and compactly crowded upon the much swollen receptacle,° which, together, yield the vegetable. Supposed to be derived from the cardoon. For culture *see* ARTICHOKE.

CYNODON (sin'o-don). A small genus of perennial grasses of the Old World, of no garden significance except in the far South where **C. Dactylon,** the Bermuda grass (called also scutch grass and Bahama grass), will make a lawn where many other grasses cannot live. It has a creeping rootstock which spreads rapidly in dry and sandy soils. Leaves short and flat, mostly near the base of the stems, which rise 3–16 in. high. There are also many leaves arising directly from the rootstocks. Flower cluster of flattened spikelets, without an awn,° arranged somewhat finger-fashion. A useful, but sometimes a weedy grass in warm regions, much planted in Fla. and Calif. *See* LAWN. In gardens it is a practically ineradicable weed, often called wire grass. (*Cynodon* is from Greek for dog-tooth, perhaps in allusion to the teeth-like sheaths on the runners.)

CYNOGLOSSUM (sin-o-gloss'um). A genus of 75 species of widely scattered herbs of the family Boraginaceae, most of them pretty weedy, but the two below often grown in the flower garden for their blue, purple, or pink flowers. They have alternate,° undivided, often roughish leaves, and small flowers in often arching, always one-sided clusters (racemes°). Corolla funnel-shaped, its limb with 5 rounded lobes. Fruit a collection of small, minutely prickly nutlets. The wild plants are commonly called hound's-tongue, and some of the species are occasionally credited to the genus *Omphalodes.* (*Cynoglossum* is from the Greek for hound and tongue, in allusion to the roughish leaves.)

Cynoglossum grande is a perennial of easy culture in any ordinary garden soil, and is propagated by division in spring or fall. The first species is the more desirable garden plant, and, while a biennial, will bloom from seed the first year and is usually grown as a hardy annual. *See* ANNUALS.

amabile. Chinese forget-me-not. Biennial, but grown as an annual, 18–24 in. high. Leaves oblongish or narrower, 2–3 in. long, rough. Flowers about ⅓ in. long, in a relatively showy cluster, usually blue, but a pink form is known. Eastern As. Blooms from July 1 to Oct.

grande. Perennial, 2–3 ft. high, the leaves mostly basal and ovalish. Flowers nearly ½ in. long, blue or purple, but the center white. Pacific Coast of U.S. Not much grown in the East.

cyparissias (sip-a-riss'i-as). Greek name of some cypress-like plant.

CYPERACEAE (sy-per-ray'see-ee; also sip'er-ray-see-ee). The sedge family comprises 75 genera and about 4000 species of grass-like plants, differing from true grasses in technical characters, and, usually, in the more easily recognized triangular, solid stem, instead of a hollow round one. They are found throughout the world, usually in moist places.

The only cult. genera are *Carex, Cyperus, Eleocharis,* and *Scirpus,* all of minor garden importance, although *Cyperus Papyrus,* often grown in pools, is the paper-making papyrus of the Egyptians. Sometimes *Eriophorum* is grown in the bog garden.

The flowers are small, green, inconspicuous, and crowded in usually tightly bracted° spikes. Like the grasses they are wind-pollinated. Fruit a tiny, dry, usually 3-sided achene.°

CYPERUS (sy-peer'us). An enormous genus, with perhaps 600 species of grass-like herbs, of the family Cyperaceae, only three of any garden interest. The cult. species are of very different origin and aspect. *C. alternifolius* and *C. Papyrus* are tall-stemmed, practically aquatic sedges suited to greenhouse pools or pots, while *C. esculentus* is a dryland, hardy perennial that bears edible tubers. Flowers inconspicuous, borne in crowded spikelets, these often arranged in large, branching clusters. (*Cyperus* is the old Greek word for these sedges.) The species, especially the chufa, are often called galingale.

alternifolius. Umbrella plant. A common pot plant, but requiring much moisture at its roots. It usually has several stems from a mass of roots. Stems slender, 2–4 ft. high, essentially leafless but having brownish sheaths. At the top of each stem is an umbrella-shaped cluster of leaves, from which the flower spikelets arise. Africa. Widely grown in greenhouses and easily propagated by detaching the leaf-crown, which, in moist sand, will send up a new plant from most of the axils.° The *var.* **gracilis** has shorter terminal leaves (2–3 in. long), and the *var.* **variegatus** has white-margined foliage.

esculentus. Chufa; called also earthnut and earth almond. A common sedge of sandy places over most of the north temperate zone. It is a perennial 2–3 ft. high, rising from an edible

---

° Special articles on the subjects indicated by an asterisk (°) will be found at the words so marked.

rootstock, pieces of which are planted in spring for harvesting in the fall. Leaves mostly at the ends of the stem and in a crown-like cluster just below the nearly stalkless spikelets. More cult. in Eu. than here.

Papyrus. The papyrus of the Egyptians from which they made paper, and hence sometimes called paper plant. An aquatic sedge, the stems 6–8 ft. high, essentially leafless but clothed with sheaths. Terminal cluster of flower spikelets umbel*-like, with 50–100 drooping rays that are thread-like, 12–18 in. long, and longer than the leaves beneath them. Southern Eu. and northern Af. A striking plant for greenhouse pools, supposed to be the "bulrush" of Moses.

CYPHOMANDRA (sy-fo-man′dra). Perhaps 30 species of South American herbs, shrubs, or trees of the potato family, only **C. betacea**, the tree tomato, of hort. interest. It is a tree-like shrub, 8–10 ft. high, with alternate,* heart-shaped or ovalish, soft-hairy leaves 8–12 in. long. Flowers pinkish, fragrant, about ½ in. wide, mostly in small clusters (cymes*). Corolla bell-shaped, its lobes long and narrow and spreading. (For details *see* SOLANACEAE.) Fruit a smooth, dull-red, egg-shaped berry about 3 in. long, the flesh somewhat tomato-like in flavor, but acid. Somewhat cult. for its fruit in zones* 8 and 9, but of secondary interest. (*Cyphomandra* is from the Greek for hump and man, in reference to an anther character.)

CYPRESS. The traditional cypress belongs to the genus *Cupressus.* Many other evergreen trees are so called, or cypress makes part of their name. *See* TAXODIUM, METASEQUOIA, and CHAMAECYPARIS.

CYPRESS GARDENS. *See* No. 3 at GARDEN TOURS.

CYPRESS-PINE. *See* CALLITRIS.

CYPRESS SPURGE = *Euphorbia Cyparissias.*

CYPRESS-VINE = *Quamoclit pennata.*

CYPRIPEDIUM (sip-pri-pee′di-um). Very beautiful orchids, nearly always growing in the ground, and cult. both in the greenhouse and outdoors for their showy flowers. As here understood, the lady's-slippers, as they are generally called, comprise a genus of several hundred species, scattered in temperate regions and in the tropics. Certain of the tropical species have been separated into the genera *Cordula, Paphiopedilum, Phragmipedium,* and *Selenipedium,* all of which are orchids of greenhouse culture, reserving for the hardy plants the name *Cypripedium.* As here inclusively considered, *Cypripedium* comprises all these genera, which are stemless or stemmed orchids with fleshy, usually brittle root systems, sometimes fibrous-rooted. Leaves usually plaited like a fan, many-nerved, generally with a sheathing base. Flowers solitary or few. Sepals 3, two of them often united, erect, and showy. Petals mostly spreading, oblong, or narrower. Lip very striking, much enlarged, sac-like or pouch-like (hence the name lady's-slipper), often beautifully colored. Fruit a 3-valved

capsule.* (*Cypripedium* is a corruption of the Greek for Venus and shoe.)

†All the species below marked with a dagger are greenhouse orchids. *See* the culture of greenhouse orchids at ORCHID. The others are hardy plants for the bog garden, wild garden, or other special sites or soils as indicated.

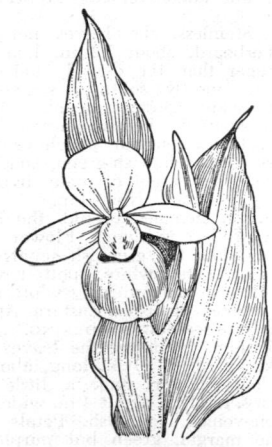

Showy Lady's-slipper (*Cypripedium reginae*). A woodland orchid, not easy to grow, with white and crimson highly irregular flowers in May–June.

acaule. Moccasin flower; pink lady's-slipper. A stemless perennial herb with two basal, ovalish leaves, 6–8 in. long. Flower solitary at the end of a scurfy-hairy stalk 6–10 in. long, nearly 4 in. wide, the lip pink (rarely white), the petals yellowish-green. In dry woods, N.A. May–June. Needs a dry soil with a pH of 4–5 (*see* ACID AND ALKALI SOILS). Difficult to grow and maintain. *See* WILD GARDEN.

arietinum. Ram's-head lady's-slipper. A slender-stemmed orchid bearing 3 or 4 lance-shaped leaves, which are nearly smooth. Flower about 1½ in. wide, the 3 sepals separate, narrow and purple, the lip whitish but crimson-streaked. In bogs or moist woods, northeastern N.A. and China. May–June. Needs a moist soil with a pH of 4–5 (*see* ACID AND ALKALI SOILS). *See also* BOG GARDENING.

†**barbatum.** Stemless, the leaves marked like a checkerboard, usually less than 6 in. long. Flower solitary or 2 at the end of a hairy stalk, about 3 in. wide. Sepals white or purplish, greenish at the base. Petals narrow, purple at the tip, black-dotted on the upper margin. Lip helmet-shaped, brownish-purple, the lobes spotted. Malaya. Feb.–June. The parent of many hybrid greenhouse plants, one of them being *harrisonianum.*

Calceolus. Yellow lady's-slipper. A showy native orchid with a leafy stem, 10–25 in. high, the leaves ovalish, 2–8 in. long and about half as wide. Flowers about 2 in. wide, the sepals and petals greenish, flushed purple, the lip* yellow. Eastern N.A. May–June. There are at least two forms of this: (a) A small-flowered, bog-inhabiting form (sometimes called *C. parviflorum*) and (2) a large-flowered plant of rich woods (sometimes called *C. parviflorum pubescens*) and one of the easiest of the native orchids to grow. *See* WILD GARDEN.

---

* Special articles on the subjects indicated by an asterisk (*) will be found at the words so marked.

†**callosum.** Leaves oval or oblong, 6–9 in. long, dark-blotched. Flowers 1 or 2, nearly 2½ in. wide, the white sepals crimson-striped, the petals greenish-purple, warted, the lip brown-purple. Flowers very showy and long-lasting. Cochin-China.

†**harrisonianum.** Commonly grown by florists, resembling *barbatum*, but with the upper sepal nearly black-purple, and white-margined. Lip pale purple, but darker-veined. Hybrid origin. Jan.–Mar.

†**insigne.** Stemless, the leaves not marked like a checkerboard, about 12 in. long and ¾ in. wide, longer than the densely hairy flower stalk. Flowers mostly solitary, sometimes 2, about 4 in. wide, glossy. Sepals white and green, brown-spotted. Petals narrow, spreading, wavy, yellow-green but purple-veined, the margins hairy. Lip yellowish-green, shaded with brown. India. The parent of many hybrid species and very variable. Nov.–Jan.

japonicum. A stemmed orchid, the leaves 2 to a stem, and 3–5 in. long. Flower solitary, about 2½ in. wide, the greenish sepals spotted red at the base. Petals white, spotted with red-brown at the base. Lip generally white and red-spotted, sometimes pinkish. Eastern As. May–June. For culture *see* Bog Gardening.

†**lawrenceanum.** Stemless, the leaves marked like a checkerboard, 8–10 in. long, about 2 in. wide, the hairy flower stalk a little longer. Flower solitary, rarely 2, about 4 in. wide. Sepals white, purple-veined, roundish. Petals narrow, hairy on the margin, green but purple-tipped, warty on the margin. Lip dull purple, green underneath but brownish above. Borneo.

†**leeanum.** Stemless and resembling *C. insigne*, but with purple spots on the upper sepal, the lower one green, and with the lip yellowish-brown. Of hybrid origin. Jan.–May.

macranthum. A Siberian orchid, the stems with 3–4 leaves. Flowers solitary, large, the sepals and petals purple, the lip dark red and contracted at the mouth. May–June. For culture *see* Bog Gardening.

montanum. A native orchid not over 20 in. high, the leaves lance-shaped, hairy, about 6 in. long and half as wide. Flowers very showy, solitary or in sparse clusters, nearly 4 in. wide, the petals red-brown the lip* whitish-yellow, but purple-streaked. Pacific Coast. Summer. Not suited to cult. in the East and Midwest, as it needs coolness and moisture, also partial shade.

parviflorum. See *C.* Calceolus. *C.* **parviflorum pubescens.** See *C.* Calceolus.

reginae. Showy lady's-slipper. Stemmed and up to 2 ft. high. Leaves several, 5–7 in. long, ovalish. Flowers nearly 3 in. wide, the sepals and petals white. Lip much inflated, white, but crimson-magenta in front. Eastern N.A. May–June. Prefers moist, mossy places in the shade. Difficult to grow. See Wild Garden.

spectabile = *C. reginae.*

†**spicerianum.** Stemless, the leaves not checker-board-marked, 8–12 in. long, about 2 in. wide, nearly equaling the smooth flower stalk. Flower solitary, nearly 3 in. wide. Sepals white, crimson-banded, a green-spotted blotch at the base. Petals greenish-brown. Lip violet. India.

CYRTOMIUM (sir-tō'mi-um). A small genus of ferns from the Old World tropics, of the family Polypodiaceae, the one below a very popular greenhouse plant well suited to the living room. The genus differs only in technical characters from *Polystichum*. They have rather stiff, firm fronds which are divided feather-fashion, and the large, brown spore cases are scattered over the leaf segments. (*Cyrtomium* is from Greek for arching and merging, in allusion to the behavior of the veins.)

The holly fern is easily grown in any reasonably moist greenhouse, and is commonly cult. by the florists because of its lasting qualities under unfavorable room conditions. It is hardy outdoors along the Gulf Coast. For culture *see* Ferns and Fern Gardening.

falcatum. Holly fern. A stiff, erect fern, 1–2 ft. high, the leafstalks very shaggy. Fronds with alternate, deep green and glossy segments that are short-stalked, 2–4 in. long, somewhat suggesting a holly leaf. Widely dispersed in warm regions of the Old World. There is also a *var.* **compactum** which is shorter and denser in habit. The plant is often offered as *Polystichum falcatum.*

CYSTOPTERIS (sis-top'ter-is). The bladder-ferns comprise a small genus of plants of the family Polypodiaceae, of little garden significance except in the outdoor fern garden (which see for culture). They are delicate ferns with twice- or thrice-compound* leaves, the ultimate segments cut-toothed. Spore cases on the veins, on the back of the segments. (*Cystopteris* is from the Greek for bladder and fern.)

bulbifera. Common bladder-fern. Fronds 18–24 in. long, the many segments tapering, toothed or cut on the margin, bearing on the upper surface small bulbils* from which new plants can be germinated. Eastern N.A., mostly on limestone rocks in the woods.

fragilis. Brittle fern, called also bottle fern. Fronds shorter and grayish-green, the stalk very brittle. Segments ovalish, or narrower, irregularly cut or toothed, the stalklet usually margined or winged. Rocky woods nearly throughout N.A.

Cytherea (sith-eer'ee-a). A plant name derived from that of the goddess.

CYTISUS. See Broom.

---

* Special articles on the subjects indicated by an asterisk (*) will be found at the words so marked.

D

DABOECIA (dab-ee′shi-a). A small genus of heath-like, low shrubs, of the family Ericaceae. The only cult. species, **C. cantabrica**, the Irish heath, and a native of Western Eu., is cult. for its evergreen foliage and nodding purple flowers. It is suited to the rock garden or other sites where a sandy, peaty, moderately acid soil can be mixed for it, and the plant is seldom hardy north of zone* 4 without protection. It is an upright shrub about 18 in. high, the leaves alternate* but numerous, elliptic, and about ½ in. long. Flowers in a terminal cluster (raceme *), from June–Oct., the corolla bell-shaped or urn-shaped, about ½ in. long. Fruit a small, 4-valved pod. There are variously colored forms, one a beautiful white, and one a dwarf variety with smaller leaves. (Named for St. Dabeoc and sometimes called St. Dabeoc's-heath.) Sometimes sold as *Menziesia polifolia* or *D. polifolia.*

dacrydioides (day-krid-i-oy′deez; but *see* OÏDES). Like a plant of the genus *Dacrydium.*

DACRYDIUM (day-krid′i-um). A genus of chiefly Australian evergreen, tender trees of the family Taxaceae, little known outside of Calif., where they are sometimes grown for ornament. The leaves are scale-like, suggesting a juniper, on old twigs, but often needle-like on the young growth. Male and female flowers on different trees (for details *see* TAXACEAE). Cones much modified in some, but with cone scales and more typically cone-like in others. Seeds nut-like, surrounded by an aril.* (*Dacrydium* is from a Greek diminutive for a tear, with allusion to the tear-like gum.) The trees are commonly called mountain pine in N. Z. and Aust. They have the general aspect of *Podocarpus.*

cupressinum. Rimu. A tall tree, up to 100 ft., its branches drooping when young. Leaves scale-like on old twigs, about ¼ in. long, smaller and needle-like on young growth. Nutlet nearly ⅛ in. long in an aril.* N. Z.

franklini. Huon pine. A tall tree up to 100 ft. its branches horizontal but the branchlets drooping. Leaves all scale-like and scarcely ½₀ of an in. long, closely pressed against the twigs. Cones very small, composed of 4–8 tiny scales. Tasmania.

dactylifera, -us, -um (dak-til-lif′fer-a). Finger-bearing or finger-like.

DACTYLIS (dak′til-is). A single species of Old World perennial grass, **D. glomerata**, the orchard grass or cock's-foot, widely naturalized in N.A. and an ingredient of many pasture grass mixtures. It is of no garden interest except rarely for a silvery-margined variety sometimes cult. for ornament. It is a stout perennial, 2–3 ft. tall and usually forming dense, tussock-like clumps. Leaves flat, about ⅓ in. wide, rough. Grass-like flowers in a large, terminal, branching cluster (panicle*) often 6 in. long. (*Dactylis* is from the Greek for finger, and of uncertain application here.)

Dactylon (dak′till-on). Finger-like.

DAFFODIL. *See* NARCISSUS.

DAFFODIL GARLIC = *Allium neapolitanum.*

DAGGER FERN = *Polystichum acrostichoides.*

DAHLIA (dahl′ya, also day′li-ya). A small but very important genus of tuberous-rooted herbs of the family Compositae, the source of all the garden dahlias. Of the dozen or so species, the ones below have contributed to the making of the modern dahlia, and all are from the uplands of Mexico and Guatemala. A few other species are Central American or from northern S.A. Ours are perennials with tuberous roots and opposite* leaves which are often compound* or twice-compound,* the leaflets or segments toothed or cut. Flowers very various, due to breeding, but the wild types always with both ray* and disk* flowers. For details *see* below. (Named for Andreas Dahl, Swedish pupil of Linnaeus.)

The exact identity of the species below is open to much question. The description of them, being based on cultivated plants, is more apt to reflect the hort. development of them than it does their actual wild prototypes.

For the different classes of modern dahlias and their culture *see* below.

imperialis. A tall herb, woody at the base, from 6–18 ft. high and one of the plants known as tree dahlia. Leaves large, thrice-compound,* the ultimate segments ovalish, 1–2 in. long, stalkless, sharp-pointed and with incurved teeth. Flower heads long-stalked, nodding, 4–7 in. wide, white, but red-tinged, the rays* about 8, narrow and not notched at the tip. Mex.

juarezi. Cactus dahlia. Resembling the common dahlia (*D. pinnata*), but the rays* with recurved margins, of unequal length, and overlapping. Perhaps of hybrid origin, but supposed to be based upon a wild plant from Mexico and Guatemala.

mercki. A low, slender, smooth herb 2–3 ft. high. Ultimate leaf segments 1–2 in. long and about as broad, toothed. Flower heads erect (not nodding), the rays* short, blunt, lilac, not over 2 in. long, usually less. Mex.

pinnata. Common garden dahlia, usually 4–8 ft. high. Leaves usually grayish underneath, the ultimate segments ovalish, more or less blunt-toothed, and the axis of the leaf usually winged.* Flower heads more or less nodding, at least 4 in. wide, but much wider in some of the classes (*see* below), and less than this in the smallest form, originally with 8 rays,

---

* Special articles on the subjects indicated by an asterisk (*) will be found at the words so marked.

and rose or lilac, but much modified as now cult. Mex.

Dahlia Culture

Dahlias, as they occur in the wild state in the mountains of Mexico, Central America, and northern S.A., are nearly always "single-flowered" plants, using the word "flower" in the popular sense. As a result of cultivation and of crossings of perhaps two or three natural species and of their numerous hort. varieties, a great number — at least 14,000 of named garden varieties — most of them double-flowered, have been introduced to the trade. The flowers of any seedling very rarely match accurately the flowers of the seed-parent (the pollen-parent, in actual practice, is commonly unknown), so it has been customary to give hort. names to any seedlings that are considered worthy of introduction. Exhibitors and commercial growers require classifications, which differ to some extent in different countries. No classification is wholly satisfactory or ever can be. The latest classification recognizes fourteen groups, as follows, with definitions here slightly abbreviated and modified:

1. *Single.* Open-centered flowers, with only one row of ray florets* ("petals").
2. *Mignon.* Flowers as in *Single*, but the plants not exceeding 18 inches in height.
3. *Anemone.* Open-centered flowers, with only one row of ray florets and with tubular disk florets* elongated, forming a pincushion effect.
4. *Collarette.* As in *Single*, but with the addition of one or more rows of petaloids,* usually of a different color, forming a collar around the disk.
5. *Duplex.* Open-centered flowers, with only two rows of ray florets.*
6. *Peony.* Open-centered flowers, with not more than four rows of ray florets, with the addition of smaller curled or twisted floral rays around the disk.
7. *Incurved Cactus.* Fully double flowers, with the margins of the majority of the floral rays turned back for half or more of their length, the rays tending to curve toward the center of the flower.
8. *Recurved and Straight Cactus.* As in 7, but the floral rays recurved or straight.
9. *Semi-cactus.* As in 7 or 8, but with the margins of the majority of the floral rays turned back for less than half their length.
10. *Formal Decorative.* Fully double flowers, with margins of the floral rays slightly or not at all turned back, the rays generally broad, the outer tending to recurve and the central tending to be cupped, all in a somewhat regular arrangement.
11. *Informal Decorative.* As in 10, but the floral rays generally long, twisted or pointed, and usually irregular in arrangement.
12. *Ball.* Fully double flowers, ball-shaped or slightly flattened, floral rays in spiral arrangement, blunt or rounded at tips and quilled or with markedly turned-in margins, the flowers more than three inches in diameter.
13. *Miniature.* All which normally produce flowers not exceeding four inches in diameter, *Pompons* excluded, to be classified according to the foregoing definitions.
14. *Pompon.* As in *Ball*, but, for show purposes, not more than two inches in diameter.

The tendency in the U.S., has been toward the development of large-flowered exhibition varieties of the Decorative classes, but a distinct trend toward the popularization of the Miniatures and Pompons and of low-growing, bedding sorts is recognizable. These are more amenable to inclusion in a general flower-border planted for succession and are also considered more suitable for household bouquets than are the giant-flowered kinds.

Dahlias thrive best on a well-drained loam. They like plenty of water after they begin to bloom, but, like roses and peonies, they seem to resent "wet feet." As a rule, they do better on a slope than on level ground. Sunny positions are preferred, though dahlias often perform very well when they have only five or six hours of direct sunlight a day. A heavy clay soil that bakes hard in the summer is distinctly unfavorable, but such may be improved by spreading on sand to a depth of four or five inches and mixing it well with the soil.

Fertilizers. Bone meal is commonly recommended as a safe and effective fertilizer. It is valuable for its phosphorus compounds; these, however, are more immediately available from commercial superphosphate (acid phosphate), which is more directly soluble. Most soils are said to be well supplied with potash, yet, in many cases, a healthier, more vigorous growth is obtained by applications of muriate of potash or of unleached wood-ashes, which contain the same substance. One pound of the muriate (or 10 lbs. of wood-ashes) and 5 lbs. of raw bone meal (or 2 lbs. of superphosphate) for each 100 square ft. may be raked deeply into the surface after spading or plowing in the spring. Or, instead, a balanced mixed fertilizer may be broadcast to the amount of about 10 lbs. to 100 sq. ft. and raked in as directed above. If cow or horse manure is used, it is better to apply and turn it under in the autumn. Manuring "in the hill" at the time of planting is not to be recommended, for close contact of the tuberous root and animal or chemical fertilizers is often injurious.

Dahlias seem to thrive best when fed from the surface, after they have made a good start. It is a good plan to use a top-dressing about Aug. 15. For every 10 hills, one may apply 2 lbs. raw bone meal, and ½ lb. of muriate of potash, keeping it away about six inches from the base of the plant and raking into the surface. For producing large exhibition flowers, one may repeat this treatment two weeks later, or may use dilute liquid manure in a shallow trench a foot from the plant. The healthiest stock comes from field-grown plants that have had

---

* Special articles on the subjects indicated by an asterisk (*) will be found at the words so marked.

no special feeding. Dahlias are tolerant of a mildly acid soil, but results are often improved, especially in newly turned land and in ground rich in humus, if lime is added at the rate of 1 lb. for 20 or 30 sq. ft.

PLANTING AND CULTIVATION. Where the growing season is short, dahlias should be put out as soon as safe from freezing and, in some cases, should be previously started in the house or in cold frames. Where a longer season is assured, as along the mid-Atlantic seaboard, the last of May and the first week of June are the preferred planting dates. On the Pacific Coast of the U.S., planting is done considerably earlier than in the East. In ordinary field culture, the rows are commonly 3 or 4 ft. apart, with the plants 2 to 3 ft. apart in the row, but for the development of large exhibition flowers, the plants should stand at least 4 ft. apart in all directions.

It is desirable to stake all except the dwarf varieties and it is well to drive the stakes before the actual planting is done. The root should be laid down horizontally, eye upward and toward the stake, in a hole about six inches deep. Cover two or three inches at first, drawing the soil in later, as the shoot grows, leaving the general surface level, or, in most soils, a little concave to facilitate watering. Let only one, or at most two, shoots develop. Stir the soil freely — once a week — up to the middle of August. At this time, or by Sept. 1, the fine feeding roots are close to the surface and hoeing may do more harm than good. A mulch of stable manure, compost, or granulated peat at about this time helps to hold the moisture and supply food. If desirable to do artificial watering, as is usually the case in the blooming period, it is better to apply the water copiously, once a week, perhaps — so that it will soak down a foot — than to water lightly every evening. However, after a hot day, a good sprinkling of the leaves seems to have a cooling and healthful effect.

DIVISION OF ROOT CLUMPS. The enlarged underground parts of a dahlia are sometimes called "bulbs" or "tubers," but, properly speaking, they are always *tuberous roots.*

Beginners often make the mistake of planting a whole clump of roots, which, in most cases, is not only a waste but the results are usually not so good as when the clump is properly divided. All of the eyes are in the "crown" or upper end, which is essentially a part of the base of last year's stem. Sometimes there are more roots than there are eyes and sometimes more eyes than roots. Amateurs with a few root clumps divide them in May or late in April. If the roots are still dormant, and really alive, one may hasten the visibility of the eyes by keeping them moist and moderately warm, or, if danger of freezing is past, may heel them in out of doors, before dividing. Or one may take chances

in dividing and treat the divisions in a similar way to find out which have good eyes. Long sprouts should be carefully cut back to a length of about a quarter-inch. Roots of medium size are the best. Large ones should have the lower half or two-thirds removed.

SEEDS AND SEEDLINGS. It is from the planting of seeds that the new varieties originate. It is a common belief, not yet fully substantiated, that the double, large-flowered dahlias do not set seed to their own pollen. Many of the originators of new varieties raise only a few of the better kinds and allow the bees to do the cross-pollinating. Others, more particular and wishing to know the pollen-parent, carefully remove all the stamens in the 100 to 300 florets in a head before any pollen is set free, cover the "flower" with a paper bag to keep away pollen-carrying insects, bring pollen-dust from the desired male parent, sift it on the stigmas when mature and receptive, and then restore the covering for a few days. If, under these circumstances, viable seeds are obtained, one may feel fairly certain that the desired cross has been made. (*See* CROSSING.) Seeds, if planted in a greenhouse in March, commonly make plants that flower the same season and develop plenty of tuberous roots for carrying the variety over the next winter. The more critical of the growers of seedlings often consider only four or five out of a thousand to be worthy of naming and preservation.

PRUNING AND DISBUDDING. Certain varieties (and others when not thriving properly) have a dense, shrubby growth, and in such cases a freer blooming may often be induced by removing one-half or two-thirds of the branches, allowing better lighting and better circulation of air. The bud terminating the main stem commonly produces the best flower, and its size and beauty are enhanced and better stems for cutting are developed if the lateral buds and branches for two, three, or four pairs of leaves directly underneath are soon snipped out. Growers of exhibition flowers often develop "standards," or only one flower to a plant, all laterals being removed. Many growers, especially of large fields, "crown out" or "top" their plants when they have formed three pairs of good leaves. Removal of the terminal bud then allows six lateral branches to develop and take the place of the single main stem. If these six are disbudded, one gets six large, long-stemmed flowers to a plant. Crowned-out plants do not grow so tall as normally and they require less staking. The operation sets back the opening of the first flower about two weeks, and it should rarely be attempted in the more northern regions.

SELECTION OF VARIETIES. Of the 14,000 dahlia varieties that have been introduced, perhaps 2000 are on the market at the present time. Few of these date back more

---

* Special articles on the subjects indicated by an asterisk (*) will be found at the words so marked.

than 15 years, so that any selected list of the "best varieties" is soon outmoded.

For most amateur growers six of the 14 types are of outstanding interest, and only a few varieties under each category can be included here. They are:

SINGLES AND DUPLEX — Orange Gold (orange), Purity (white), Scarlet Lady (scarlet), Snow Princess (white), Garnet Poinsettia (scarlet), Newport Wonder (raspberry), Pequot Yellow (yellow).

DECORATIVE — Jersey Beauty (pink), Jane Cowl (buff, gold, and rose), Lord of Autumn (yellow), Murphy's Masterpiece (red), Arelda Lloyd (yellow and pink), Betty Cotter (salmon-red), Thomas A. Edison (violet-purple), White Wonder (white), Forest Fire (red), Blue Train (blue), Purple Mist (pinkish purple), Red Sunset (pink).

CACTUS — Coral Cactus (pink), Golden Standard (orange-yellow), Adries Orange (orange), Frau O. Bracht (yellow), Ivory Princess (white), Michigan White (white), Pink Mum (pink), Sarett's Pink Flamingo (pink), Son of Satan (scarlet), Jersey Dainty (white), Lady in Red (red).

POMPON AND MINIATURE — Amber Queen (pale yellow), Little Edith (yellow and carmine), Little David (russet-orange), Bronze Beauty (bronze), Honey (yellow and red), Yellow Gem (yellow), Joe Fette (white), Baby Royal (salmon-pink), Bishop of Llandaff (red), Morning Mist (rose-lavender), Albino (white), Little Jerry (purple).

It should be understood that many of these varieties may become obsolete within a short time as the production of new forms is constantly presenting a challenge to growers. But some like Jane Cowl and Jersey Beauty have been popular for many years.

STORAGE. Soon after the first killing frost, the roots should be lifted carefully, with as little breaking of necks as possible. Cut off stump a second time, down to about one inch in height, dry off three or four hours in sunshine, cover stump copiously with sulphur, filling hollow, if any, and pack away. The largest clumps keep better if stump is split. In a furnace-heated cellar, dahlia roots need some kind of covering to prevent excessive shrinkage and possible death. Sand, granulated peat, ashes, newspapers, gunny sacks, etc., are commonly used. Strike a happy medium, learned by experience, between too much covering and too little. A storage temperature of 35–50° F. is the most favorable.

The American Dahlia Society publishes a *Bulletin* containing much practical information and notes of new varieties. The society welcomes as members any interested in dahlias. Its officers change from time to time, but its present address is 10 Crestmont Road, Montclair, N.J.

INSECT PESTS. Control leaf feeders with pesticide #1 (*see* SPRAYS AND DUSTS). Tarnished plant bug is killed by pesticide #20 sprays. European corn borer attacks in late season. Control with pesticide #17 as eggs hatch in your area. Repeat weekly for 3 to 4 weeks.

DISEASES. Of the diseases on dahlia, the virus infections are the most serious. Yellow blotches or patterns in the leaves are characteristic of the names of the various virus diseases: mosaic,* ringspot, oak leaf and stunt. Infected plants should be destroyed so that insects will not transmit the disease to healthy dahlia plants. Keep aphids under control as directed. The virus cannot persist from year to year in the soil, but infected plants will retain the virus and should not be used for propagation.

The fungus causing wilt* may build up in the soil if dahlias are grown continuously in the same area.

If wet, humid weather persists at flowering time, the blooms may have a brown, wet rot. Use pesticide #11 (*see* SPRAYS AND DUSTS) and gently "mist" over the flowers at 3- or 4-day intervals.

DAHOON = *Ilex Cassine.* See HOLLY.

DAHURIAN LARCH = *Larix gmelini.* See LARCH.

dahurica, -us, -um (da-hoor′ik-a). From Dahuria, Siberia.

DAIKON = *Raphanus sativus longipinnatus.* See RADISH.

DAISY. The traditional daisy is *Bellis perennis,* commonly called English daisy here. For the many other plants to which the name daisy is also applied *see* CHRYSANTHEMUM, TOWNSENDIA, ARCTOTIS, ASTER, and RUDBECKIA. *See also* COMPOSITAE.

DAISY FAMILY. See COMPOSITAE.

DAISY TREE. See OLEARIA.

DALBERGIA (dal-ber′ji-a). A large genus of tropical vines or valuable timber trees of the pea family, only one, **D. Sissoo,** the sissoo, of any garden interest and this only in zones* 8 and 9. It is a tree up to 80 ft. high. Leaves compound* and comprising 5 nearly round leaflets, narrowed at the tip, 3–4 in. long. Flowers small, pea-like, yellowish-white, in short clusters (panicles*) which arise at the leaf axils. Fruit a flattened pod (legume*) about 3 in. long. India, but planted for ornament in Fla. (Named for Nils Dalberg, Swedish botanist.)

DALIBARDA (dal-i-bar′da). A single species of perennial herbs of the rose family, found in rich woods in eastern N.A. and of garden interest only for shaded places in the wild garden. The only species, **D. repens,** the false violet or dewdrop, is a tufted,* half-prostrate herb with long-stalked, scalloped leaves that are heart-shaped at the base, roundish, and about 1½ in. in diameter. Flowers white, long-stalked about ½ in. in diameter, with 5 rounded petals and many stamens. Near the base there are also one or two cleistogamous* flowers. Fruit a collection of 5 dryish, drupe*-like bodies, enclosed by the persistent calyx. (Named for T. F. Dalibard, French botanist.)

dalmatica, -us, -um (dal-mat′i-ka). From Dalmatia, Yugoslavia.

damascena, -us, -um (da-ma-see′na). From Damascus, Syria.

DAMASK ROSE = *Rosa damascena.*

---

* Special articles on the subjects indicated by an asterisk (*) will be found at the words so marked.

DAME'S-ROCKET and **DAME'S-VIO-LET** = *Hesperis Matronalis.*

DAMEWORT. *See* HESPERIS.

DAMMAR PINE = *Agathis.*

DAMPING-OFF. Damping-off is the term applied to death of seedlings either before they emerge from the soil or during the early days after they emerge. The group of fungi which causes damping-off may persist in the soil and attack young plants after they have passed the tender seedling stage. This disease is then called root rot. A young seedling, showing typical symptoms of damping-off, suddenly topples over at the soil line. Closer examination will disclose a good white root and a green set of leaves, but a black or dark-brown line around the stem just at the soil line. If examination of the recently killed seedling does *not* have the black area at the soil line, and it *does* have brown roots, it is likely that too much fertilizer is in the soil or that the soil is too wet or too dry.

Many seed-houses now treat the seeds with a fungicide or combination fungicide-insecticide before they are sold. If the gardener harvests his own seed he will do much to prevent damping-off by applying one of many "seed protectants" now on the market which contain captan, phygon, spergon, thiram, or some similar fungicide.* A small quantity of the "seed protectant" should be placed in a bag or jar with the seed and shaken for a few minutes so that all seeds are well coated.

The fungicide "seed protectant" will keep the plant healthy during its very early stages of growth but soil sterilization may be necessary for longer-lasting benefits. Soil which has been heated with steam until it reaches a temperature of 180° F. and that temperature maintained for one-half hour is sterilized. If steam is not available, formaldehyde may be used to sterilize soil, pots, and flats. Dilute commercial formaldehyde or formalin, using 50 parts of water to 1 part formaldehyde. Drench the soil and cover with paper or plastics for 24 hours. After removing the cover, stir the soil and allow to "air" until *absolutely* no smell of formaldehyde remains before planting seeds or plants. It must be remembered, however, that a trowel or other soil-working tool or even hands, which have non-sterilized soil attached, will recontaminate sterilized soil.

If damping-off appears after young seedlings start to push through the soil, a drench will often arrest the spread of disease. Apply pesticide #2A, or #5A, using a sprinkling can so that each square foot of soil area receives about one pint of the fungicide mixture. *See* SPRAYS AND DUSTS.

The fungi which cause damping-off require a lot of moisture and attack the plant at or just beneath the surface of the soil. For this reason it is best to keep the surface as dry as possible. Watering should be done in the morning so that the surface has an opportunity to dry somewhat before night.

The application of a light film of sand or pulverized sphagnum moss (*see* SPHAGNUM) to the surface of the soil immediately after seeds are planted will help to decrease damping-off. — S. H. D. For a recent review of the damping-off problem, see "The University of California System for Producing Healthy Container-grown Plants," by K. F. Baker (Univ. of Calif. Division of Agricultural Science, March, 1957).

DANDELION. The common dandelion, one of the six known species of the genus **Taraxacum** (ta-raks'a-kum), is chiefly noted as a weed, but others have spoken of it as the "tramp with a golden crown." It belongs to the section of the family Compositae which have milky juice and only ray flowers in the head. Perennial herbs with a deep taproot (in ours), the leaves in a basal rosette, the blades cut into more or less triangular sections, the tips of which are curved or bent downwards (runcinate). Flower head solitary at the end of a hollow stalk. Below the head is a series of calyx-like bracts,* some bent downward, the inner ones erect. Rays numerous, golden-yellow. Fruit a collection of minute, plumed achenes,* the mass forming a globe-shaped cluster. (*Taraxacum* is from the Greek for disquiet or disorder, in allusion to the medicinal qualities of the herbage.)

T. officinale. The common dandelion. For its eradication *see* Dandelion in the list at WEEDS. It is of European origin, but naturalized everywhere in U.S. A larger-leaved form is sometimes cult. for its bitter-juiced foliage used as greens.

DANDELION FAMILY. *See* COMPOSITAE.

DANGLEBERRY = *Gaylussacia frondosa.* *See* HUCKLEBERRY.

DAPHNACEAE. *See* THYMELAEACEAE.

DAPHNE (daf'nee). Sometimes evergreen, very desirable Eurasian shrubs of the family Thymelaeaceae, a few widely grown for their pretty flowers, some of which bloom before the leaves unfold. Leaves generally alternate,* without marginal teeth, evergreen in those so specified below. Flowers in small clusters (racemes or umbel*-like heads), without petals, but the usually bell-shaped calyx* corolla-like. Stamens 8 or 10, in two rows, not protruding. Fruit leathery or fleshy, a 1-seeded drupe.* (*Daphne* is the Greek name for the true laurel and of misleading application to these plants.)

Daphne comprises beautiful shrubs for low borders or for the rock garden, but some of the best of them are not hardy over much of the country. They prefer a loose loam with a fair amount of sand, although some of them will grow in ordinary garden soil, preferably somewhat alkaline, especially *D. Mezereum.* If grown in the greenhouse, use potting mixture* 3 to which ⅓ its bulk of chopped-up peat has

---

* Special articles on the subjects indicated by an asterisk (*) will be found at the words so marked.

been added. They may be propagated by layers or by hardwood cuttings, or seed may be used, but it should either be sown at once or stratified. (*See* SEEDS AND SEEDAGE.)

burkwoodi. A hybrid evergreen shrub, 2–4 ft. high, with oblongish leaves, 1–2½ in. long and pale beneath. It is usually grown under the varietal name of Somerset, which is a very fragrant shrub, the flowers at first white, but fading to pink. Hardy from zone* 5 southward. Apr.

Cneorum. Low-creeping, evergreen shrub forming large mats, useful as a ground cover on in the rock garden. Leaves crowded, more or less oblong, about 1 in. long, blunt at the tip and with a minute point. Flowers fragrant, pink, about ⅓ in. wide, in terminal clusters. Fruit yellow-brown. Mountains of Eu. Apr.–May. Hardy from zone* 4, and, with protection, from zone* 3, southward. Sometimes called garland-flower.

Genkwa. A stout, branching shrub, 1–3 ft. high, the twigs silky when young. Leaves generally opposite,* oblongish, 1½–2 in. long, expanding after the flowers bloom. Flowers in sparse clusters, each flower about ½ in. wide, lilac-white, scarcely fragrant. Fruit white. China and Korea. Apr.–May. Hardy from zone* 5, southward.

Laureola. Spurge laurel. An erect, bushy shrub, 18–30 in., the foliage evergreen. Leaves oblongish, 2–3 in. long, gradually narrowed at the base. Flowers yellowish-green, in nearly stalkless clusters (racemes*). Fruit bluish-black. Pyrenees. Mar.–Apr. Hardy from zone* 5, and, with protection, from zone* 4, southward. Prefers partial shade and a pH of 5.

Mezereum. Mezereon. An upright shrub 18–36 in. high, the foliage not evergreen. Leaves oblongish, 2–3 in. long, wedge-shaped at the base. Flowers in stalkless clusters of 3, blooming before the leaves unfold, lilac-purple or rosy-purple, and very fragrant. Fruit scarlet. Eurasia, sometimes an escape* in eastern N.A. Mar.–Apr. Hardy from zone* 3 southward. Prefers partial shade and moderately alkaline soil.

odora. An evergreen shrub 3–5 ft. high. Leaves oblongish, or elliptic, 2–3 in. long, narrowed at both ends but bluntly-pointed. Flowers rosy-purple, fragrant, in dense head-like, terminal clusters. Japan and China. Mar.–Apr. Hardy from zone* 5 southward. There is a var. **marginata** with yellow-bordered leaves.

DAPHNIPHYLLUM (daf-ni-fill′um).

Twenty-five species of evergreen, Asiatic shrubs or trees of the spurge family, only **D. macropodum** much known here. It is a shrub or small tree, rarely up to 30 ft., with alternate,* stalked leaves and red twigs. Leaves oblong, 4–7 in. long, dark green above, paler or bluish beneath, the stalk and midrib often red. Flowers pale green and inconspicuous (for details *see* EUPHORBIACEAE). Fruit fleshy, oblong, 1-seeded, about ½ in. long. Cult. chiefly for its handsome foliage. Hardy from zone* 6, possibly from zone* 5 (with protection), southward, but most at home in Calif. and the South. Eastern As. (*Daphniphyllum* is from Greek for laurel and leaf.)

daphnoides (daf-noy′deez; but *see* OïDES). Like a plant of the genus *Daphne*.

DARLING PEA. *See* SWAINSONA.

DARLINGTONIA (dar-ling-tō′ni-a). A single species of insect-catching herbs of the family Sarraceniaceae, sometimes sold as *Chrysamphora*. **C. californica,** the California pitcher-plant or cobra-plant, the only species, is sometimes cult. for its interesting habit. It is a bog plant needing acid moss of pH 4–5 (*see* ACID AND ALKALI SOILS) and plenty of water. It can be grown outdoors north of zone* 5, in the East, only with protection; otherwise, in the cool greenhouse. Native from Ore. to Calif. The plant has a basal rosette of tubular, water-holding leaves, 12–30 in. long, capped by an arched, white-spotted, hooded flap, and a forked appendage. Flowers solitary, yellowish-purple, about 1¼ in. long. (For details *see* SARRACENIACEAE.) *See also* INSECTIVOROUS PLANTS. (Named for William Darlington, American botanist.)

DARLINGTON OAK = *Quercus laurifolia.* *See* OAK.

DARNEL = *Lolium temulentum.*

DASHEEN = *Colocasia esculenta.*

dasycarpa, -us, -um (das-i-kar′pa). Thick-fruited.

DASYLIRION (das-i-lir′i-on). Attractive desert plants of the lily family, from the southwestern U.S. and adjacent Mex., cult. there and in greenhouses northward for their foliage and tall-stalked, flowering clusters. They have a superficial resemblance to agave when young but as the trunk develops they have a terminal crown of leaves more like a dracaena. Generally called sotol in the Southwest. Leaves very narrow, prickly margined in those below, often shreddy at the tip or margin. Male and female flowers on different plants, always in large, branched clusters at the end of a very tall (12–18 ft.) stalk. Flowers lily-like, the male flowers with 6 protruding stamens. Fruit dry and not splitting. (*Dasylirion* is from Greek for tufted lily.)

All the plants below will stand a little frost, but not slushy, wet winters. Outdoors they must have sandy or rocky soils, brilliant sun, and much summer heat. For greenhouse culture *see* SUCCULENTS.

glaucophyllum. Trunk not tall, the leaves 3–4 ft. long and about ½ in. wide, bluish-green, the prickles yellowish-white. Flowering stalk 12–18 ft. high, the flowers small, white. Fruit about ⅜ in. long. Mex.

texanum. Bear grass. Trunk short, partly underground. Leaves glossy-green, 2–3 ft. long, about ½ in. wide, the prickles yellowish-brown. Flowering stalk 9–15 ft. high. Fruit about ¼ in. long. Tex.

wheeleri. Trunk not over 3 ft. high, usually absent in cult. specimens. Leaves nearly 3 ft. long and about 1 in. wide at the spoon-shaped base. Stalk of the inflorescence* about 15 ft. high. Southwestern U.S. and adjacent Mex. The leaves, unfortunately, are harvested for the so-called "cactus spoons."

dasyphylla, -us, -um (das-i-fil′la). With thickly hairy leaves.

---

* Special articles on the subjects indicated by an asterisk (*) will be found at the words so marked.

Dasystemon (da-sis′te-mon). With thick stamens.

DATE (*Phoenix dactylifera*). The date palm can be cultivated in any warm, frost-free part of the U.S. or in a conservatory, but such trees will not bear fruit unless they can get the requisite amount of heat during the fruiting period. Its demands for heat exceed almost any other cult. plant, so much so that the U.S. Department of Agriculture made careful studies of the summer climatic needs of the date in Egypt.

These show that the date will not ripen nor produce good fruit here unless the mean temperature is somewhere near that of at least a dozen famous date plantations in Egypt. The figures are critical. It also needs dryness during the ripening period.

MEAN TEMPERATURES (= MAXIMUM + MINI-MUM ÷ 2) FOR EGYPTIAN DATE PLANTA-TIONS AND FOR THE ONLY POSSIBLE DATE REGIONS IN THE U.S.

	Egypt	South Ariz.	Near Mecca, Calif.
April	76–84	66	70
May	78–92	73	77
June	88–92	82	85
July	82–90	88	90
Aug.	82–90	86	90
Sept.	76–86	81	83

The kernel of these temperature figures lies in the fact that just when the date needs a good deal of heat, in April and May, the U.S. localities are deficient in it by 10 degrees on the average. And another unfavorable U.S. climatic feature in our only possible date regions is the prevalence of night dews and, in irrigated regions, too high a water-table. The date is a palm of desert regions of extreme heat, so that its cult. in U.S. is always something of a problem.

There are date plantations in Ariz., Calif., and in parts of Texas in spite of the climatic handicaps. The trees are set on 30-ft. intervals, usually started from suckers, and begin bearing within 5 or 6 years, but full bearing will not be reached for 15 years and may then yield 100–200 pounds of dates for many years. The suckers are produced freely by old plants and should be gradually removed, whether needed for new plants or not. If they are to make new plants, they should be gathered when 3–4 years old, well headed back, and planted directly in the field. Only a few suckers from each old tree should be taken at a time — to take all at once may prevent the old plant from setting fruit for a couple of years. Most suckers are produced from the base of fairly young trees, but suckering may occur well up on the trunks of old trees. The latter should not be used for propagating.

The male and female flowers of the date are on different trees (the suckers are the same sex as the parent tree). Consequently, pollination is a problem. Naturally they are wind-pollinated, but this is too precarious for commercial production. The best prac-

tice is to plant one male tree for every 70 females and hand-pollinate the latter. This is done by tying a piece of pollen-producing inflorescence (a few inches long) to the female flower cluster. It is safer to repeat the process in a few days. More expert pollination is practiced in Arabia where bottled pollen of especially fine varieties brings high prices and is used sparingly on only the finest female clusters.

The fruits ripen on the trees if the season is favorable, but most commercial growers prefer to ripen them off the trees in heated rooms. Some criterion of the ability of our climate to ripen dates is shown by the fact that dates usually fail to ripen at Fresno, Calif., and Tucson, Ariz., but complete that process, usually, at Phoenix and Tempe, Ariz., and at Mecca, Calif. The leading varieties for the U.S. are the Saidy and Deglet Noor.

While the plant needs an intensely dry, hot atmosphere, it also needs some moisture at its roots, but not too much. This is accomplished in the oases of Egypt and in our Southwest by irrigation.

INSECT PESTS. Several scale species are controlled by superior oils. Clean fiber away from trunk. Mites can be controlled by pesticide #21 or #14 (*see* SPRAYS AND DUSTS). Thrips are controlled by pesticide #1 or #21, as are leaf-footed bugs and mealybugs.

DISEASES. Heart rot or black scorch is caused by a fungus which enters through wounds or attacks weakened trees. The hearts turn black and new leaf growth is curled and shortened. Secure planting stock from healthy plants.

A leafspot* which is usually of minor importance may be held in check with pesticide #3 (*see* SPRAYS AND DUSTS).

DATE YUCCA = *Samuela.*

DATE PLUM = *Diospyrus Lotus.* See PERSIMMON.

DATURA (dah-toor′ra). A genus of only 12 or 15 species of the potato family, ranging from annual weeds to tropical trees. Some are poisonous, especially the jimson-weed, and all have foliage which is malodorous when crushed. Leaves alternate,* often coarsely but remotely toothed. Flowers usually trumpet-shaped, solitary, usually from the leaf axils.* Calyx* with a long tube splitting lengthwise or across. Corolla with a spreading limb.* Fruit a large capsule,* often prickly or spiny; rarely the fruit is fleshy. (*Datura* is a Latin version of an East Indian vernacular for some species.)

Only *Datura Metel* is of much garden interest. It is to be grown as a tender annual (*see* ANNUALS). The jimsonweed merely needs eradication and a warning about its poisonous juice. *D. arborea* and *D. suaveolens* are tropical shrubs or trees and can be grown outdoors only in zones* 8 and 9. Sometimes grown in the warm-temperate greenhouse where they should have potting mixture* 4.

arborea. Angel's-trumpet. A showy, medium-sized Peruvian tree. Leaves of various

---

* Special articles on the subjects indicated by an asterisk (*) will be found at the words so marked.

shapes, but of two sizes, one a third shorter than the other. Flowers 6–9 in. long, white but green-striped, the corolla lobes long-pointed. Fruit about 2 in. long, without prickles.

Metel. Tender annual herb, 3–5 ft. high. Leaves ovalish, oblique at the base, 7–9 in. long, or some considerably smaller. Flowers about 7 in. long, the calyx* purple and tubular, the corolla white, violet or yellow. Fruit about 1½ in. long, prickly. India. Resembling the jimsonweed, but with larger flowers. There are double-flowered varieties, and some have variously colored flowers.

Stramonium. Jimsonweed, also called thorn-apple. A tropical, annual herb, 3–5 ft. high, naturalized as a weed over most of the country, only its juice poisonous, but deadly so when the plant is wilted. Leaves more or less lobed, 5–8 in. long. Flower erect, about 4 in. long, white or violet. Fruit very spiny, about 2 in. long. A dangerous weed against which children should be warned. Sometimes called Jamestownweed.

suaveolens. Angel's-trumpet, also called floripondio. Closely related to *D. arborea*, but leaves up to 1 ft. long. A shrub 10–15 ft. high, the solitary, nodding, white flower sometimes 12 in. long. Fruit spindle-shaped, 2½–5 in. long. Brazil.

DAUBENTONIA (do-ben-tō'ni-a). A genus of tropical shrubs and trees of the pea family, only **D. punicea** of much hort. interest. It is a South American shrub 5–9 ft. high, which is grown for ornament, and has escaped along the Gulf Coast from Fla. to Miss. and Ga. Leaves compound,* the 12–14 leaflets about 1 in. long, without an odd one at the end. Flowers pea-like, rusty-red, scarcely over ¼ in. long, but the clusters (racemes*) showy, about 4 in. long, from the leaf axils.* Fruit a 4-winged pod nearly 4 in. long. The plant is sometimes known as *Sesbania punicea*. (Named for L. J. M. Daubenton, French naturalist.)

DAUCUS. *See* CARROT

daurica, -us, -um (dau'ri-ka). Same as dahurica.

DAVALLIA (da-val'li-a). A genus of perhaps 80 species of tropical Old World ferns of the family Polypodiaceae, three rather popular as greenhouse ferns. Most of them have thin, pliant rootstocks that tend to creep along the surface or even over the edge of whatever they grow in, thus being ideal for hanging baskets, and commonly used to make fern balls. Fronds very much divided and feathery, more delicate than most cult. ferns, the spore cases on or near the margins of the leaf segments. (Named for Edmund Davall, Swiss botanist.) Some of them are called hare's-foot fern.

All are greenhouse ferns. For culture *see* FERNS AND FERN GARDENING.

bullata. Ball fern, also called squirrel's-foot fern. The commonest species in cult. and often used in fern balls. A slender fern, its fronds 6–12 in. long and about half as wide, at least 4 times compound,* the ultimate segments sharply toothed, not narrow as in *D. fejeensis*. Indo-Malaya and Jap. Its fronds usually droop and fall off in age.

dissecta. A stouter plant than *D. bullata*,

its rootstocks strongly creeping. Leaves (fronds) 12–18 in. long, 4 times compound,* the ultimate segments somewhat wider than in *D. bullata*. Java. Less grown than the last, but offered sometimes as *D. elegans* and a very beautiful finely dissected fern.

fejeensis. An evergreen fern, its fronds drooping but persistent. Fronds 4 times compound, its numerous ultimate segments very narrow, the leaf more delicate and feathery than the other cult. species. Fiji Islands. The most beautiful of the davallias, and cult. in several forms, one, *var.* **plumosa**, having especially feathery and gracefully drooping fronds.

DAVIDIA (day-vid'i-a). A single species of Chinese tree of the family Cornaceae, grown for ornament. **D. involucrata**, the dove tree, is an upright tree, up to 50 ft., branching like a linden, with alternate,* short-stalked, toothed leaves that are broadly oval, 4–6 in. long, and silky-hairy underneath. Flowers small and inconspicuous, without petals, in dense heads, beneath which are 2 showy, cream-white bracts,* which make the tree very attractive in bloom. One of the bracts* is nearly 6 in. long, the other about half this, both drooping. Fruit fleshy, green but with a bloom, pear-shaped, about 1½ in. long. May–June. Hardy from zone* 5, in protected parts of zone* 4, southward. (Named for Armand David, French missionary and botanist in China.)

davurica, -us, -um (da-voor'i-ka). Same as dahurica.

"DAWN REDWOOD" = *Metasequoia glyptostroboides*.

DAY-FLOWER. *See* COMMELINA. For day-flower family *see* COMMELINACEAE.

DAY JASMINE = *Cestrum diurnum*.

DAYLILY. The term is applied to the plantain-lily (which see), and to the plants below, all of which belong to the genus **Hemerocallis** (hem-mer-o-kal'lis), which comprises about 15 wild species of herbs, found from Central Eu. to Jap., and many hybrid forms, all belonging to the lily family. Roots somewhat fleshy, the leaves nearly all basal, narrow, sword-shaped and keeled. The stem or stalk of the flower cluster is often branched and usually exceeds the leaves. Flowers funnel-form or bell-shaped, widely expanding above. Stamens 6, inserted on the throat of the corolla. Fruit (which is rare) a capsule. (*Hemerocallis* is from the Greek for beautiful for a day.) Several species, other than those below, have been described. For varieties and culture *see* below.

H. altissima. A tall-growing plant, 4–8 ft. high, the flowers pale yellow, night-blooming. Jap. Aug. It is the parent of new, tall races.

H. aurantiaca. Leaves up to 3 ft. long and 1 in. wide. Flowers burnt-orange or salmon-orange, not fragrant. Jap. Spring and summer.

H. citrina. Up to 4 ft. high, the leaves about 3 ft. long and 1 in. wide. Flowers light lemon-yellow, nearly 5 in. long, fragrant. China. Summer.

H. dumortieri. Scarcely over 1½ ft. high, the leaves 1 ft. long, about ½ in. wide.

---

* Special articles on the subjects indicated by an asterisk (*) will be found at the words so marked.

Flowers pale orange, about 2½ in. long, the tube short. Jap. Spring.

H. flava. Lemon daylily. Flowering stalk 2–3 ft. high, the leaves less and about ¾ in. wide. Flowers yellow, 3–4 in. long, the stalks weak and arching. Eastern As. Rarely an escape* in eastern U.S. Spring and summer. By an over-meticulous application of the rules of hort. nomenclature, this well-known old favorite should now be called *H. Lilioasphodelus*, a suggestion not followed here.

H. fulva. Up to 5 ft. high, the leaves 2 ft. long and 1⅛ in. wide. Flowers not fragrant, 3–5 in. long, rusty-orange-red, often with dark lines. Eurasia. Summer. Quite common as a roadside escape* in the eastern U.S. The *var. rosea* has rose-colored flowers. *See* below for other forms.

H. goldeni. Perhaps merely a garden race or strain of *Hemerocallis fulva.*

H. middendorffi. Scarcely over 1½ ft. high, but the leaves about 1 in. wide. Flowers pale orange, about 2½ in. long, the segments curving backward in age. Siberia. Spring.

H. minor. About 20 in. high, but the leaves scarcely ¼ in. wide. Flowers yellow, about 4 in. long, fragrant. Eastern As. Spring and summer.

H. multiflora. A much-branched very floriferous Chinese herb, the flowers small, orange. Aug.–Sept. Many excellent varieties have been derived from it.

H. thunbergi. About 3 ft. high, the leaves 2 ft. long and about ¾ in. wide. Flower stalk stiff, somewhat 3-angled. Flowers lemon-yellow, 2–3 in. long, night-fragrant. Jap. Summer. One of the commonest species in cult., mostly night-blooming.

DAYLILY CULTURE

Daylilies are important herbaceous perennials, valued for their free flowering, ease of culture, hardiness, and freedom from disease. They thrive in sun or partial shade and are most adaptable as to placement. Individual clumps look well in the flower garden and in association with shrubs, while they seem equally at home when massed on dry slopes or in moist soil by the waterside.

The long narrow green leaves are attractive all through the growing season. Some kinds are evergreen. While these may survive a northern winter with protection without much injury, they are better suited for the South. In growth, there is variation from small and graceful, with flower stalks to about 18 in., to robust clumps with flower stalks to 5 ft. tall. Some may flower a second time in the season. Individual flowers last only a day, but others follow on the branched stems to prolong the display many days. By a thoughtful selection of varieties it is possible to have some plants in flower from late spring until fall.

Daylilies are readily increased by division. Clumps sometimes remain undisturbed for several years, but whenever growth gets too congested it is time to divide and replant. This is best done in late summer or early spring. Pry off divisions of about 3 growths from the outside of the clump and replant in well-worked soil to which some organic material has been added. Trim the foliage back about half when done in summer. To

protect against heaving the first winter, spread a mulch of litter, after the ground has frozen. Sometimes plantlets are developed on the flower stem. If detached and planted, these will grow and flower like the parent. Hybridizers raise many thousands of seedlings annually, and select only a few for naming and distribution. Seedlings may be expected to bloom when 2 or 3 years old.

SELECTION OF DAYLILIES. Of the species, *Hemerocallis flava* (lemon daylily) is the best known, having been grown in gardens for centuries. It is still popular for its early fragrant flowers. *H. fulva* is an escape from gardens and a familiar roadside plant in many parts of the eastern U.S. Cultivated double forms of this are Kwanso, *flore-pleno,* and *variegata. H. dumortieri* and *H. minor* are well-known early-flowering dwarfs, and the taller *H. thunbergi* is widely planted for midsummer bloom.

But it is named seedlings that have created the popular interest in daylilies. The first hybrids were produced in England in the 1890's. Apricot is the first listed named clone,* and it is still a good one. Since then, in ever-increasing numbers, new varieties have been named by the thousands. The only way to keep up-to-date is through the annual listings in catalogues and garden magazines. Listings in a work of this kind are chiefly of historical interest years hence. To satisfy personal preferences, especially as to color shades, there is nothing like first seeing plants in flower.

The following 100 are popular varieties of the present time, grouped as early, intermediate, midseason, and late bloomers, as actual flowering dates vary according to regional differences. Those marked † are fragrant.

EARLY. † Dr. Regel, orange; Gold Dust, bronzy-yellow; Blanche Hooker, red and orange; Baggette, pale lemon and rose; Brocade, amber rose, open in evening; Belle of Georgia, yellow, peach suffusion; Little Cherub, light yellow; Queen of Gonzales, orange; Tangerine, deep orange; Brunette, orange-brown and tan.

INTERMEDIATE. Baronet, red, evening bloomer; Caballero, yellow and vermilion; Colonel Joe, yellow; Dido, apricot; Duchess of Windsor, cream and gold; Fascinating, soft yellow and apricot; Gay Troubador, red and yellow bicolor; Golden Chimes, clear yellow; Lady Bountiful, soft yellow; Maid Marian, pink; Mrs. Hugh Johnson, bright red; North Star, pale yellow to cream; Purple Waters, rosy-wine; Mrs. B. F. Bonner, yellow, evening bloomer; Halo, yellow, frilled, evening bloomer; Easter Morn, blend; Colonial Dame, yellow; † Princess, yellow; Raven, red; Revolute, greenish yellow, evening bloomer; Royal Beauty, red; † Sachem, dark red and orange, evening bloomer; Salmon Sheen, cinnamon and pink, evening bloomer; Spitfire, red and yellow; Sweetbrier, pink and yellow; Taruga, lemon yellow and cinnamon, evening bloomer; † Wau Bun, light yellow, splashed red; Tasmania, coral and gold.

MIDSEASON. Afterglow, buff and pink; Athlone, buff and yellow bicolor; Black Prince, very dark, yellow throat; Bold Courtier, red and yellow; Chloe, deep yellow and cinnamon;

---

* Special articles on the subjects indicated by an asterisk (*) will be found at the words so marked.

Crimson Glory, red; Ballet Dancer, pint tints; Carved Ivory, cream-white; Copper Colonel, coppery; Cool Waters, pale yellow, nocturnal; † Dauntless, bright yellow; Erie, buff-pink; Evelyn Claar, pink; Helen Fischer, apricot and reddish; † Hesperus, lemon-yellow; Hyperion, canary yellow; High Noon, deep yellow; J. T. Russell, red and gold; Linda, yellow and buff; Mabel Fuller, red; † Ming, gold to cream; Mission Bells, light yellow; Midwest Majesty, light yellow; † Moonbeam, creamy yellow; Naranja, orange; Primula, soft yellow; † Ophir, golden yellow; Orange Beauty, orange; Picture, rosy-purple and yellow; Prima Donna, peach; Honey Redhead, coppery red and gold; Patricia, lemon yellow, greenish throat; Pink Dream, bright pink; Pink Damask, rosy-pink; Potentate, purple; Royal Ruby, crimson; Theron, purple.

LATE. August Orange, bright orange; August Pioneer, chrome-yellow, orange-red flush; Autumn King, deep yellow; Autumn Prince, light yellow; Autumn Red, rich red; Boutonniere, yellow and pale rose; Calypso, lemon yellow, nocturnal; Canari, soft yellow, evening bloomer; Chengtu, orange-red; Comet, brownish-red and yellow; Crinoline Belle, pink; Galatea, bright pink; † Golden West, golden yellow; Hankow, yellow, scarlet eye; Jean, brick-red and yellow; Pink Charm, coral pink; Queen Esther, bright red; Rajah, bright red and orange; Moonray, pale yellow, evening bloomer; Scarlet Sunset, red, evening bloomer; Starlight, pale yellow, evening bloomer; Valiant, rich orange; Windsor Tan, buff and tan. — H. E. D.

The present address of the American Hemerocallis Society is 416 Arter Avenue, Topeka, Kansas.

DDT. A very effective insecticide for eradication of mosquitoes and flies in buildings. Its indiscriminate use as an insecticide on plants, especially those subsequently to be eaten, is not advised. It is No. 4 in the list of INSECTICIDES, and should be used only for those plants where it is definitely recommended by the entomologist and plant pathologist responsible for such entries in this book.

DEADLY NIGHTSHADE = *Solanum nigrum.*

DEAD NETTLE. See LAMIUM.

dealbata, -us, -um (dee-al-bay′ta). Nearly white.

DEAMIA (deem′i-a). A single species of climbing cactus found from southern Mex. to Colombia, once called *Cereus* but now called **Deamia testudo,** and cult. for interest and for its huge, day-blooming flowers. It climbs naturally over rocks and trees, its stems or joints about 4 in. wide, with 3 (rarely 5–8) high ribs or wings. Spines 10 or more to a cluster, brown and spreading. Flower yellowish-white, nearly a foot long, slender, hairy tube expanding into many narrow corolla segments and with many stamens* (for details *see* CACTACEAE). Fruit fleshy. A very handsome cactus needing greenhouse culture (*see* CACTI). (Named for Charles C. Deam, American botanist.)

debilis, -e (deb′il-is). Weak or frail.

DE CAEN. See ANEMONE CORONARIA.

DECAISNEA (de-kane′i-a). A small genus

of Asiatic shrubs of the family Lardizabalaceae, with alternate, compound leaves, the leaflets without teeth. Flowers with the sexes often in different flowers on the same shrub. Male flowers with the stamens* united into a short tube. Female flowers inconspicuous, followed by a blue fruit. The only cult. species is **D.** fargesi, a shrub 10–12 ft. high with leaves 2–3 ft. long, the 6–12 pairs of leaflets 3–6 in. long. Flowers in drooping clusters, yellowish-green. Fruit a fleshy, edible pod (follicle*) 3–4 in. long, its black seeds embedded in a white pulp. June. Western China. Hardy from zone* 4 southward. (*Decaisnea* was named for Joseph Decaisne, once director of the Jardin des Plantes, Paris.) The shrub is of easy cult. in most soils and is propagated by seeds.

decandra, -us, -um (de-kan′dra). With ten stamens.*

decapetala, -us, -um (dek-a-pet′a-la). With ten petals.

decidua, -us, -um (de-sid′you-a). See DECIDUOUS.

DECIDUOUS. Dropping its leaves, petals, fruits, etc. Most broad-leaved trees are deciduous, as distinguished from plants whose leaves are persistent or evergreen, but even these ultimately shed their leaves.

decipiens (de-sip′ee-enz). Deceptive or at least not obvious.

DECK TENNIS. A lawn game needing a space 40 × 18 ft.

DECODON (dek′ko-don). A single species of woody herb of the family Lythraceae, found in bogs and swamps of eastern N.A. and of little garden interest except for similar sites. Commonly called swamp loosestrife, water willow, or wild oleander, **D. verticillatus** makes large clumps of gracefully arching stems 3–8 ft. high, rooting at the tip. Leaves opposite* or in opposite pairs, narrow, willow-like, 2–5 in. long. Flowers pink-purple, in a dense, nearly stalkless cluster at the leaf axils,* half the 10 stamens prominently protruding, the others hidden. Fruit a 3–5-chambered capsule. Of easy culture in wet places and rooting freely from its arching tips, hence soon covering large areas. (*Decodon* is from the Greek for ten-toothed, in allusion to the toothed calyx.*)

decora, -us, -um (de-cō′ra). Becoming; comely.

decorata, -us, -um (de-cor-ray′ta). Decorative.

DECUMARIA (de-koo-mare′ee-a). A small genus of woody vines of the family Saxifragaceae, related to *Hydrangea*, but without the sterile flowers. Of the two known species one is Chinese, the other, **D. barbara,** is a stem-climbing vine (*see* VINES) hardy from zone* 5 southward, and native from Va. to Fla. and La. It has peeling, shreddy bark, its stem often climbing up to 30 ft. Leaves opposite,* ovalish, 2–4 in. long, nearly or quite without marginal teeth, often

---

* Special articles on the subjects indicated by an asterisk (*) will be found at the words so marked.

half-evergreen. Flowers small, white, in terminal clusters (corymbs*). Calyx turban-shaped, its 7–10 sepals small. Petals 7–10. Stamens* 20–30. Fruit a small, ribbed capsule, splitting between the ribs. It prefers moist, low situations. (*Decumaria* is derived from the Latin for 10, in allusion to the flower parts.)

decumbens (dee-kum'bens). Decumbent; *i.e.*, trailing, but the tips upright.

decurrens (dee-kur'renz). Decurrent; *i.e.*, a leaf base or other organ that merges with or runs into the stem or stalk below it.

decussata, -us, -um (dee-kus-say'ta). Decussate; *i.e.*, arranged in pairs, but each pair diverging at right angles to the pair above and below it.

DEER FERN = *Blechnum Spicant.*

DEER GRASS = *Rhexia virginica.*

DEERHORN CACTUS = *Peniocereus greggi.*

DEER'S-TONGUE = *Frasera speciosa.*

DEER VINE = *Linnaea americana.*

DEHISCENCE. The splitting or other mode of opening of a seed pod for the release of seeds; or the opening of an anther to discharge pollen. Fruits or anthers that never split are called indehiscent.

DELAWARE. The peach blossom is the state flower and the American holly the state tree. The state lies wholly in zones* 4 and 5. Except in the northern part of the state the topography is level or gently rolling and is characteristic of the Atlantic Coastal plain. The northern part of the state is hilly.

SOILS. In general the soils are of a loamy, or sandy loam, or loamy sand type and are often deficient in lime, nitrogen, phosphoric acid, and potash. Crops generally quickly respond to applications of commercial fertilizer. Along the western side of the state many areas are poorly drained. The eastern side of the state adjacent to the Delaware River has a fringe of tidal swampy land.

CLIMATE. The climate of Delaware is humid temperate, with hot summers and mild winters. The mean annual temperature ranges from 55° in New Castle County to 56° in Kent and Sussex counties.

The average monthly temperatures by climatological divisions (Division 1 — northern Delaware or New Castle County, and Division 2 — southern Delaware or Kent and Sussex counties) are:

	Div. 1	Div. 2
Jan.	34.3 F.	37.4 F.
Feb.	34.2	37.1
Mar.	42.2	44.3
Apr.	52.0	53.3
May	63.0	63.8
June	71.5	72.3
July	76.1	76.6
Aug.	74.2	74.9
Sept.	68.0	68.9
Oct.	57.3	58.5
Nov.	45.9	47.8
Dec.	35.7	38.1

The average annual precipitation ranges from 44 inches in northern Delaware to 47 inches in southern Delaware. Freezing temperatures at several places will occur on or preceding the dates given with chances as indicated below:

Date of last min.	Chance	Wilmington	Newark	Dover
32° or less in spring.	9 in 10	May 3	May 14	May 3
Date of first min. 32° or less in fall.		Nov. 11	Nov. 5	Nov. 12

Date of last min.	Chance	Milford	Bridgeville	Millsboro
32° or less in spring.	9 in 10	May 7	May 13	May 15
Date of first min. 32° or less in fall.		Nov. 11	Nov. 7	Nov. 7

The average length of the growing season based on a minimum temperature higher than 32° ranges from about 175 to 195 days.

The winter climate of Delaware is intermediate between the cold of the Northwest and the mild weather of the South.

The average frost penetration ranges from about 5 inches in southern Delaware to about 10 inches in northern Delaware. The annual average number of days with snow cover of one inch or more varies from about 5 days in southern portions to about 15 days in northern portions.

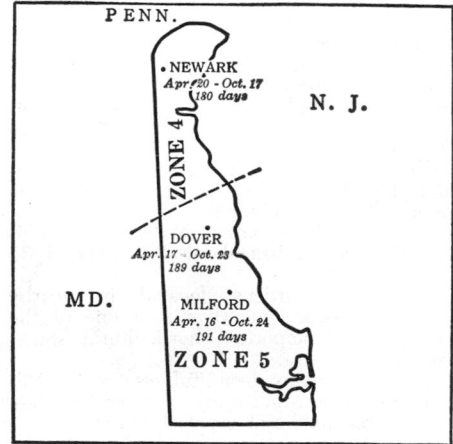

DELAWARE

The zones of hardiness crossing Delaware are those shown on the map located at ZONE, which should be consulted for details. The dates are the average latest killing frost in spring and the first one in the fall. The figures below the dates show the average length of the growing season.

* Special articles on the subjects indicated by an asterisk (*) will be found at the words so marked.

Summer weather is characterized by considerable warm weather, including at least several hot, humid periods. Precipitation occurs mostly in the form of showers with occasional scattered, locally heavy amounts. Although rainfall amounts are generally sufficient to grow good crops, the unequal distribution of summer showers and occasional dry periods at critical stages of crop development makes irrigation necessary for maximum crop yields in some years.

ORNAMENTAL PLANTS. Delaware is situated at the northern limit of many of the southern ornamental plants. The following plants do well in Delaware in most years but occasionally are injured by severe winter weather.

Camellia japonica	Evergreen magnolia
Camellia Sasanqua	Franklinia
Crape Myrtle	Ornamental pomegranate
Mimosa (Albizzia)	Evergreen Privet
	(Ligustrum lucidum)
Evergreen Barberry	

This is only a partial list of borderline ornamentals grown in Delaware.

Ornamental plants which are well suited to Delaware conditions include most annuals, hardy bulbs, most perennials except those which prefer cool temperatures, shrubs such as azaleas, rhododendron, yews, holly (including American, Chinese and Japanese), boxwood, deciduous magnolia, cherry laurel, dogwood, roses, barberry, and privet. There are, of course, many other evergreen and deciduous plants suitable for the state.

Most northern plants will thrive in Delaware but some northern mountain plants are not suited to southern Delaware.

OUTSTANDING GARDENS IN DELAWARE.

Winterthur Farms, Winterthur. One of the showiest collections of azaleas in the country. Open to the public during the flowering period.

Valley Garden Park, Wilmington. Contains a large display of spring-flowering bulbs.

Jasper Crane Rose Garden, Wilmington. Contains over 1000 roses of 60 varieties.

The Josephine Garden, Wilmington. Contains 118 Japanese cherry trees which surround a beautiful fountain.

Kirkwood Rose Garden, Wilmington. This beautiful garden has about 400 roses of 30 varieties.

Longwood Gardens, located in nearby Kennett Square, Pennsylvania, is one of the nation's most important horticultural showplaces.

There are many beautiful estates in Wilmington, Dover, and other parts of the state open to the public at events listed below.

FLOWER SHOWS AND GARDEN EVENTS

Spring Flower Show. Held at the University of Delaware, Newark, Delaware, the first weekend in June, by Delaware Garden Committee.

Wilmington Garden Day. Second Saturday in May features tours to some of the outstanding estates and small gardens in Wilmington and vicinity.

Dover Day. Held the first Saturday in May at Dover, Delaware. Features dogwood and azaleas surrounding many historical homes.

New Castle Day. Third Saturday in May. Features many colonial homes, and gardens of beautiful boxwood plantings.

Flower Show. Held annually in May in Rehoboth or Lewes, Delaware. Sponsored by the Sussex Gardeners.

Odessa Day. Second Saturday in October. Many historic places open to the public.

Delaware Orchid Society Show. Usually scheduled in fall or spring in Wilmington.

The Greens Show. Held annually in late November or early December in Christ Church, Greenville, Delaware. Features Christmas decorations and is open to the public.

ORGANIZATIONS

The Delaware Garden Committee, federation of most of the garden clubs in the state; The Delaware Orchid Society; The Peninsula Horticultural Society, composed of fruit and vegetable growers on Del-Mar-Va Peninsula; Wilmington branch of the National Association of Gardeners; Delaware Roadside Council.

For information concerning officers and offices of above societies, write Delaware Agricultural Extension Service, University of Delaware, Newark, Delaware.

deliciosa -us, -um (del-ish-i-ō'sa). Delicious.

DELONIX (dee-lon'icks). The royal poinciana, peacock-flower, or flamboyant is admittedly the most showy tree cult. in the warmer parts of Fla. and Calif. Sometimes known as *Caesalpinia regia* or *Poinciana regia*, this Madagascan tree of the pea family is better known as **Delonix regia**. It is a broad-headed tree and not over 40 ft. high. Leaves twice-compound.° 1–2 ft. long, composed of scores of small, oblong leaflets, of which there is no odd one at the end of each series. Flowers not pea-like, 3–4 in. wide, the 5 long-clawed° petals brilliant scarlet, or one of them yellow-striped. The flowers are in clusters (racemes°) and these are so numerous that the flame-like color may be seen far off. Fruit a flat, woody pod (legume°) about 2 in. wide and 8–20 in. long. This most gorgeous of cult. trees will stand a variety of soils, but can be grown outdoors only in zones° 8 and 9. It blooms in summer and is usually leafless in spring. (*Delonix* is from the Greek for long claw, in reference to the petals.) It is sometimes known as flame-of-the-forest.

delphinifolia, -us, -um (del-fin-i-fō'li-a). With leaves like a larkspur.

DELPHINIUM (del-fin'i-um). The larkspurs comprise a genus of about 200 species of annual or perennial herbs of the buttercup family, all from the north temperate zone,

---

° Special articles on the subjects indicated by an asterisk (°) will be found at the words so marked.

and they include some of the finest of hardy garden flowers. Leaves always lobed or divided finger-fashion and alternate.* Flowers very showy, generally in a long, terminal cluster (raceme* or spike*), these sometimes on stalks several feet high, but lower in some of the annual sorts. The flowers are prevailingly blue, but of other colors in some cult. forms, and very irregular.* Sepals 5, petal-like, one of them produced into a long spur.* Two of the petals are also short-spurred, the other petals (sometimes wanting) are short, small, and usually clawed.* Stamens numerous. Fruit a collection of small, splitting follicles.* (*Delphinium* is from the Greek name for a larkspur.) All of them have a poisonous juice. *See* POISONOUS PLANTS.

For the culture of the common, perennial, garden larkspur *see* the article below. The identity and parentage of this garden favorite are in so much confusion that it is still impossible to assign definite Latin names that mean very much. The other perennial species are also in some doubt as to their identity, and the names here given are likely to be changed, as the group is better understood. The annual larkspurs, *D. Ajacis* and *D. consolida*, may be treated as hardy annuals (*see* ANNUALS), or if earlier bloom is desired, they may be started earlier and treated as tender annuals.

Ajacis. Rocket larkspur. An annual, 12–24 in. high, erect and branching. Leaves usually bunched at the joints and rather finely divided. Flowers violet, rose, pink, blue or white (in some of the many garden strains). Southern Eu. June–Aug.

Belladonna. *See* DELPHINIUM CHEILANTHUM.

Bellamosa. *See* DELPHINIUM CHEILANTHUM.

cardinale. Scarlet larkspur. An erect or arching perennial herb, 2–3 ft. high. Leaves thickish, divided into many narrow, almost line-like segments. Flowers scarlet, but the petals yellowish, the spurs* long, the flowers borne in long, open or lax-flowered racemes.* Calif. Summer.

cashmerianum. A leafy-stemmed perennial, 1–2 ft. high. Leaves nearly round in outline, but cut into broad, toothed lobes. Flowers blue, hairy, in a broad cluster (corymb*), the spurs short and somewhat curved. Fruits hairy. Himalayas. Summer.

cheilanthum. Garland larkspur. An erect perennial, usually branched and 2–3 ft. high in the wild form but much taller in some of its derivative hybrids. Mostly cult. in the *var.* **formosum,** which has extremely showy blue flowers, 2–3 in. wide. The hort. forms usually offered as "Belladonna" or "Bellamosa" hybrids, belong to the *var.* **formosum.** Eastern As.

chinense = *Delphinium grandiflorum.*

Consolida. Field larkspur, also called knight's-spur. A forking annual herb 12–18 in. high. Leaves scattered, cut into long, narrow segments. Flowers in sparse clusters at the ends of the branches, nearly 1 in. wide, blue or violet. Fruit smooth. Eu. Often confused with *D. Ajacis.*

cultorum. The garden larkspur (*see* below).

elatum. Candle larkspur; also called bee larkspur. A perennial herb up to 6 ft. high, the branches upright. Leaves cut into broad segments that are sharply cut or toothed at the tip. Flowers in a long, terminal, spike-like raceme,* each flower scarcely over 1 in. wide, blue, smooth, the spurs not very long, slender, and somewhat curved. Petals small and closing over the throat. Fruits only slightly hairy. Eurasia. Summer. Perhaps not cult. in its true wild form, but it may be one of the parents of the tall garden larkspurs.

formosum. *See* DELPHINIUM CHEILANTHUM.

garden larkspur. Of uncertain origin, but almost certainly comprising a group of hybrids. Many Latin names have been applied to the presumed parents and to the finished product, which is the perennial garden larkspur of today. None of these names can be used with certainty and they are therefore omitted here. *See* below.

grandiflorum. Siberian larkspur; also called bouquet larkspur. A branched perennial, 2–4 ft. high, often blooming from seed the first year. Leaves much divided into very narrow, nearly feathery segments. Flower clusters lax, open, and more or less scattered. Flowers blue or whitish, 1–1½ in. wide, the spur longish. Fruits hairy. Eastern As., and widely grown.

nudicaule. Red larkspur. A slender, perennial herb 12–24 in. high, resembling *D. cardinale,* but the leaf segments broad and blunt. Flowers red, the spurs long, the much smaller petals yellow. Fruit hairy at first, smooth later. Ore. and Calif.

sibiricum = *Delphinium grandiflorum.*

sinense = *Delphinium grandiflorum.*

DELPHINIUM CULTURE

The perennial garden *Delphinium* is a confused hybrid of uncertain origin and probably several European and Siberian species are the foundation of this popular garden flower. This garden hybrid is quite easy to grow in the North and isn't exacting as to soil, provided it is deep enough for the roots to penetrate freely to their full length.

Of recent years the garden *Delphinium* has had an enormous vogue in America and is spoken of as being temperamental and difficult, but the basic fact is that it is a northern-region, cold-country plant that does not take kindly to warm climates and hot soils.

Delphinium is raised easily from seed best sown as soon as ripe in the late summer or early fall. Much complaint about the poor viability of *Delphinium* seed is due to improper storage conditions through the winter. It keeps best in totally sealed packets and preferably at a temperature around 50°.

Though in Europe named varieties are well established and commonly grown, and such can also be had in Canada, in the other parts of the American continent it is most satisfactory to raise plants constantly from seed. Such named varieties as are offered are usually field selections from mixed sowings from selected strains.

Propagation of particular varieties is possible and not really difficult by division of the clumps in the spring or fall or even by cuttings of the young shoots in the spring. It is so much easier to raise seedlings, however, that vegetative propagation is rarely resorted

---

* Special articles on the subjects indicated by an asterisk (*) will be found at the words so marked.

to. Under average conditions seeds sown in fall will give plants that flower sparsely the following summer when selections of the desired types can be made and the following year the plant gives its best bloom.

If the flower stalk is cut down as soon as the blooms fade, a second flowering in fall will be quite satisfactory although not as good as the early bloom. The ordinary practice is to discard the plants after this second bloom, but this is purely a cultural convenience, because of the difficulty of getting them permanently established and carrying them through for later years. Strenuous effort is being made to introduce some native American species into the garden strains, but progress along this line is only just beginning. *Delphinium cardinale* and *D. nudicaule* appear to need a summer rest and are hence not good garden plants.

The plant is valued in the garden for its height and stature, and there has thus been a tendency toward selection of tall-growing individuals which, however, often need staking to prevent damage from wind. Some specialists, therefore, prefer a lower stature and more heavy type of stem that will withstand the storms.

PLANTING. For permanent planting, open up the earth 2 ft. deep and allow 2 ft. of space for each plant, putting a liberal quantity of old manure with the soil in the lower part of the hole. After setting, tamp well. In heavy soils make holes deeper and put an undertrench in the extra space of coarse gravel or stony rubble. Have plenty of humic matter in the soil that is filled in. Incorporate sand with clay soils to prevent caking. Set the crowns 2 in. below the surface. Plant in an open, airy place not heavily overshadowed by trees or buildings or where there are roots of trees.

When growth starts in spring stir the soil around each plant, uncovering the ground shallowly, and add at this time a mixture of commercial plant food, but keep it away from the crowns. Water regularly, preferably by flooding the ground rather than showering overhead. As the flower stalks develop, tie lightly to stakes and after blooming cut spikes away to prevent seeding. If seed is desired select only one or two of the early good flowers on a given spike and prevent all others from ripening.

The type of flower cluster varies from a strict cylindrical column to pyramidal with lateral branching, which includes the Wrexham strain. An ideal type is one in which the flowering stalk is about two-thirds of the whole height with foliage well up to the lowest flowers. The type of individual flower varies from single, semi-double (most popular) and fully double or ranunculus-flowered in which the bloom is a rather tight rosette. The semi-double type in which the conspicuously colored sepals form a nearly solid circle is preferred, and the base of the petals may be white, brown, yellowish, or black.

The leading strains offered today are selections of English growers which again have formed the basis of strains offered by American specialists. Particularly on the Pacific Coast, the breeding of American strains of larkspur holds most promise. The object of this is to give to the American garden a plant that will withstand the average conditions of all America — a wiry stem to endure winds, combined with a constitution to resist the onslaught of insidious diseases. Rather than a plant that grows to a height of eight or nine feet, our ideal would seem to be a plant of lesser stature but greater stability. Mere height can hardly be an ideal of accomplishment.

In the transition stage, such as we are going through at the present time with the delphinium, strains and types will vary with local conditions as well as with the ideals of the individual grower. If the gardener wants a simple pyramidal spike for garden accent, he can have it in the Pudor strain. Or, again, if his desire be for one that will show a strong development of lateral branchlets that will give abundance of short-stemmed flowers for cutting, he can find that in the Pacific and other strains. All these are from the Pacific Coast.

The individual strains are fairly well determined, and there are three recognized classes of flower forms:

1. *Single:* one row of sepals and at least five petals forming the eye.
2. *Semi-double:* two rows of sepals; eyes present or absent.
3. *Double:* more than two rows of sepals: eyes present or absent.

The Wrexham delphinium, an especially fine English or Welsh strain, is very popular here, and is best raised from imported seed. The spike is more spire-like than columnar and very handsome. While named *Wrexham* from a village in Wales, this strain originated in Somerset, England, about 1908. They are often called hollyhock delphiniums.

The American Delphinium Society is active in furthering interest in the larkspur and its culture, and welcomes members in sympathy with its aims. Its present address is 38253 Wilson Mills Road, Willoughby, Ohio.

INSECT PESTS. Control leaf feeders by arsenicals or pesticide #21 (*see* SPRAYS AND DUSTS). Stem borers can be held back by cleaning out weeds and rubbish in early spring. *See* mite at CYCLAMEN, red spider at CARNATION. Control leaf miners with pesticide #21. Foliage is sensitive to certain insecticides, including DDT.

DISEASES. Delphinium grown in the same location year after year may soon become almost a complete loss due to one of several root-rotting organisms. If diseased plants are pulled from the soil and small, round, white, tan, or brown objects about the size of a pinhead are attached to the root system near the stem, the plants then have southern blight. Drenching the soil around the adjacent plants with pesticide #10 (*see* SPRAYS AND DUSTS) will help to arrest this disease. If the small objects characteristic of southern blight are not found, the plants may then have a bacterial

---

* Special articles on the subjects indicated by an asterisk (*) will be found at the words so marked.

crown rot, or a rot due to other fungi. No pesticide has proven very beneficial for these other diseases. Practice rotating the site of planting for best results.

Powdery mildew° causing a white, powdery fungus growth on the leaves may be controlled on most varieties with pesticide #9. On some varieties such as Belladonna the sulphur is of little value and pesticide #6 must be used.

Black spots on the upper surface of the leaves are symptoms of bacterial leafspot.° Although a number of chemicals have been recommended to control this disease we know of none which does the job. Burning the dead brush of delphinium in the fall probably does as much good as anything.

DELTOID. Triangular, usually with a broader base than sides; delta-shaped.

deltoidea, -us, -um (del-toy′dee-a). Deltoid.

deltoides (del-toy′deez; but *see* OÏDES). Deltoid.

demersa, -us, -um (de-mer′sa). Submerged.

DEMETON. See #6 at INSECTICIDES.

demissa, -us, -um (de-mis′sa). Weak or low.

DENDROBIUM (den-dro′bi-um). Next to *Cattleya* the most popular greenhouse orchids in cultivation, although they lack a common name. Of over 900 species, chiefly from the steaming forests of the Indo-Malayan region, few are in cult., but from them have been developed scores of hort. important hybrids and named forms much prized by orchid fanciers and by florists. All are tree-perching (epiphytes°), without true pseudobulbs,° but with often thickened stems that are usually jointed and leafless at flowering time. Leaves various, but neither strap-shaped nor folded like a fan. Flowers extremely showy, in all those below in few or many-flowered clusters (racemes°) which are terminal, or from along the sides of the stem. Sepals nearly equal in length, the two side ones forming a spur-like sac. Petals resembling the odd sepal. Lip° joined to the base of the column.° (*Dendrobium* is from the Greek for tree and life, in allusion to their epiphytic habit.)

For the culture of these greenhouse orchids *see* ORCHID.

densiflorum. Stems 4-angled, club-shaped, 12–18 in. long and leafy. Leaves 3–5, leathery, about 6 in. long. Flowers golden-yellow, or whitish and with an orange-yellow lip, about 2 in. wide, the many-flowered, showy hanging cluster 7–10 in. long. Himalayas. Mar.–Apr.

formosum. Stems round, about ⅓ in. thick, 12–18 in. long, in youth bearing a few blackish hairs on the sheath. Leaves oval-oblong, about 5 in. long, more or less stem-clasping. Flowers 2–3 in. wide, white, but with a yellow-marked lip,° usually only 3–5 blooms in the cluster, which is near the end of the stem. Himalayas. Feb.–May. A *var.* **giganteum** has flowers 4–5 in. wide.

nobile. Much the commonest dendrobium in cult., and frequently offered by florists. Stems round, 1–2 ft. long. Leaves lasting 2 years, ovalish or narrower, 3–4 in. long. Flowers about 2½ in. wide, usually only 2

or 3 in a cluster, white or rosy-purple, the lip edged white, with a rose-purple tip and dark-purple throat. Himalayas. Mar.–June. There are innumerable varieties, the colors and markings of which are too variable to make it worth cataloguing them here.

Phalaenopsis. Stems finger-thick, 12–20 in. long, leafy, especially at the end. Flower cluster nearly 2 ft. long, terminal, containing 8–15 flowers that are about 3 in. wide, and white, rose, and purple, the lip maroon-purple. A very showy plant. East Indies and Aust.

pulchellum. Stems 2–3 ft. long, finger-thick. Flowers 6–9, or more, in a hanging cluster, yellowish-brown, with a purple spot in the throat. Sepals much narrower than the petals. India. Apr.–June.

wardianum. Stems 2–3 ft., pencil-thick, the leaves about 3 in. long. Flowers only 2–3 in the cluster, white but rose-tipped, the lip with a yellow throat and two deep purple spots. The flowers are nearly 4 in. wide and when blooming the stems are leafless. Burma. Mar.–June.

DENDROCALAMUS (den-dro-kal′a-mus). Indo-Malayan, tree-like grasses usually called giant bamboos (*see* BAMBOO), and of outdoor cult. only in zones° 8 and 9. Of the 16 known species, the two below are somewhat cult. in southern Fla. and Calif., and one of them is an imposing plant. They have jointed, greenish, or yellowish, usually hollow stems, and leaves wider than in most grasses. Flowers in globe-shaped clusters, which are grouped in long, branching clusters (panicles°). Stamens 6. Fruit small and hard (a caryopsis°). (*Dendrocalamus* is from the Greek for tree reed.)

For culture *see* GRASSES. See *also* BAMBOO.

latiflorus. A very straight-stemmed bamboo 60–70 ft. high. Leaves 7–10 in. long, 1–2 in. wide, tapering at the tip, very short-stalked, with a prominent midrib° and about 9 veins on either side of it. India to Cochin-China. A popular bamboo in southern Calif.

strictus. Male bamboo. Stems often solid or partly so, 40–50 ft. high, bluish-green in youth, ultimately greenish-yellow. Leaves 4–9 in. long, about 1 in. wide, softly hairy when young, with 3–6 veins on either side of the midrib,° and with the tip of the leaf slightly twisted. After flowering only once the plant dies. India, Burma, and Java.

dendroidea, -us, -um (den-droy′dee-a). Woody or tree-like.

DENDROMECON (den-dro-mee′kon). A small genus of Californian shrubs of the poppy family, **D. rigidum**, the tree or bush poppy, often cult. there for its handsome yellow flowers. Its culture in the East is infrequent and difficult, probably because its usually evergreen habit and fondness for dry, sandy sites suffer from the wet, slushy winters and alternate thawing and freezing. Even in Calif. it occasionally loses most of its leaves and should then be cut back to the ground. A stiff, rigid shrub 2–8 ft. high, and very leafy. Leaves lance-shaped, stiff, leathery, veiny, generally persistent or evergreen, and pale green. Flowers solitary, 1–3 in. wide, golden-yellow, with 2 sepals,° 4 petals, and many stamens.° Fruit a narrow, curved, and grooved pod, 2–4 in. long, splitting by 2

° Special articles on the subjects indicated by an asterisk (°) will be found at the words so marked.

valves. Some authorities have split the tree poppy into 20 species. (*Dendromecon* is from the Greek for tree and poppy.)

DENNSTAEDTIA (den-stet′i-a). A large genus of chiefly tropical ferns of the family Polypodiaceae, **D. punctilobula**, the hay-scented, cup, or boulder fern common in eastern N.A. and sometimes transferred to the hardy fern garden (*see* FERNS AND FERN GARDENING for culture). It is a fern with minutely hairy fronds and grows in moist, shady places and on rocks. Fronds thrice-compound,* nearly 3 ft. long and 9 in. wide, the ultimate segments thin, cut-toothed, sweet-scented (especially when dry). Spore* cases round, brownish, each at the end of a vein and borne near the margin of the leaf segments. A very handsome wild fern. (Named for August Wilhelm Dennstaedt, German botanist.)

densa, -us, -um (den′sa). Dense or compact.

dens-canis (denz-kay′nis). A dog's tooth, or like it.

densiflora, -us, -um (den-si-flow′ra). With dense flowers or a densely compacted flower cluster.

DENTARIA (den-tay′ri-a). Perhaps 30 species of chiefly woodland, perennial herbs of the mustard family from the north temperate zone, the two below natives and sometimes grown in the wild garden. They have toothed or scaly rootstocks (hence the name toothwort) and few leaves that (in ours) are deeply divided, but not compound.* Leaf lobes usually 3, bluntly and irregularly toothed. Flowers in a loose, open, few-flowered, terminal cluster, the petals 4. Stamens 6. Fruit a very narrow, flat pod (silique*) splitting from the bottom upwards. (*Dentaria* is derived from Latin *dens*, a tooth, in allusion to the toothed rootstocks.)

The toothworts are of easy culture in woods soil, in partly or wholly shady places, in the wild garden, but useless in the open border. Easily propagated by division of their rootstocks in fall or very early in spring. They flower both early in May and late in April.

diphylla. Crinkleroot, also called pepper-root. Rootstock strongly toothed, the plant 6–12 in. high. There are 2 stem leaves, 3-lobed and toothed, as well as the similar but basal leaves. Flowers white inside, flushed pinkish outside, about ½ in. wide. Eastern N.A.

laciniata. Pepper-root, also called crow's-toes. Rootstock thicker, deeper in the ground, tuber-like. Stem leaves 3, the lobes deeply cleft and toothed. Basal leaves (sometimes wanting) similar. Flower purplish or white, about ¾ in. wide. Eastern N.A.

dentata, -us, -um (den-tay′ta). Dentate; *i.e.,* toothed.

DENT CORN = *Zea Mays indentata*. See CORN.

denticulata, -us, -um (den-tick-you-lay′ta). Slightly toothed.

denudata, -us, -um (dee-noo-day′ta). Naked.

DEODAR = *Cedrus Deodara*.

Deodara (dee-o-dar′ra). Native name in India for the deodar.

depressa, -us, -um (de-pres′sa). Depressed or flattened.

DERRIS. See ROTENONE.

DERRIS (der′ris). A genus of tropical woody vines or shrubs of the pea family, of secondary garden interest except for the one below. The only cult. species is **D. scandens**, the Malay jewel-vine, a native of the Malayan region and cult. for ornament in Fla. It is a woody climber with compound* leaves, the leaflets stalked, about ½ in. long, and usually 5–13 to a leaf. Flowers small, white, pea-like, showy because they are borne in large clusters, sometimes exceeding the leaves in length. Pods (legumes*) about 3 in. long. A handsome vine, but only suitable for zone* 9. It is not the plant which yields rotenone (which see). (*Derris* is from the Greek for a leather covering, perhaps in allusion to the pod.)

DESCANSO GARDENS. See No. 17 at GARDEN TOURS.

DESERT CANDLE. See EREMURUS.

DESERT GARDEN. For the plants suited to the desert garden and for some of the conditions that make for success in such sites, see the articles on cacti and succulents. For additional plants suited to the desert *see also* AGAVE, FOUQUIERIA, HAWORTHIA, YUCCA, STAPELIA, MESQUITE, MESEMBRYANTHEMUM, EUPHORBIA; also the families Amaryllidaceae and Crassulaceae.

Technically there is no true desert (*i.e.,* absolutely rainless) in the U.S. What we call the desert has a rainfall of from 3–10 in. a year. See the name of your state for rainfall figures in your vicinity, and if the annual precipitation is much over 15 in., it is better not to try growing many desert species. They will stand extremes of heat and, in some kinds, considerable cold, but few will tolerate much winter moisture.

DESERT GUM = *Eucalyptus rudis*.

DESERT WILLOW = *Chilopsis linearis*.

DESMODIUM (des-mō′di-um). A very large but horticulturally secondary genus of herbs of the pea family, mostly tropical, but a few reaching temperate N.A., where they are weedy plants of indifferent garden interest. Leaves compound.* the leaflets usually 3, the central one often longer-stalked than the lateral pair. Flowers small, pea-like, usually in branched, sometimes sparse clusters. Fruit a prominently jointed legume (loment*), the segments of which may become detached separately and, in the native species, often stick to the clothing, hence their names of tick trefoil and tick clover. (*Desmodium* is from the Greek for a chain, in reference to the jointed pods.)

See cultural notes at each species.

canadense. Bush trefoil; called, also, beggar-lice and beggar-ticks. A perennial herb

---

* Special articles on the subjects indicated by an asterisk (*) will be found at the words so marked.

3–5, rarely up to 8 ft. high. Leaflets oblongish, about 1½ in. long. Flowers about ¾ in. long, purple, the cluster rather showy. Pods about 1 in. long, with 3–5 joints. Eastern N.A. A plant of open, sandy woods and of the easiest culture in loose, warm soils. Easily propagated by division. *See* SAND GARDENS.

gyrans = *D. motorium.*

motorium. Telegraph plant. A tropical Asiatic perennial herb (often grown as an annual in the warm greenhouse) of interest for the movements of its leaflets. It grows 2–4 ft. high, the terminal leaflet larger than the lateral pair which constantly (but slowly) move in all directions. Flowers purple or violet, about ¼ in. long. Pods about 1½ in. long, 6–10-jointed. A greenhouse curiosity long studied by Darwin for the telegraph-like regularity of the movement of its leaflets. Best raised from seed.

penduliflorum = *Lespedeza thunbergi.*

purpureum. Beggarweed. A West Indian perennial herb, grown as an annual cover crop in the far South and practically unknown elsewhere. It is 5–7 ft. high, and its leaflets are ovalish or oblong, 3–4 in. long and have a minute, soft prickle at the tip. Flowers blue or purple, scarcely ⅓ in. long. Pods about 1 in. long, the joints 2–6. Grown from seed as a forage or cover crop, preferably in moist soil, but of the easiest cult. and freely seeding itself.

DETERMINATE. A term applied to tomato plants in which terminal growth is stopped by the production of a terminal flower (and fruit) cluster. Such plants bear nearly all their crop at one time, a distinct advantage in short-season regions. *See* IN-DETERMINATE.

DEUTZIA (doot′zi-a). A group of garden shrubs of the first importance, comprising perhaps 50 species, 2 from Mex., all the rest Asiatic, and belonging to the family Saxifragaceae. They have usually hollow twigs and mostly shreddy bark. Leaves opposite,* short-stalked and toothed. Flowers mostly in terminal clusters (cymes* or panicles*), generally white. Calyx* with 5 teeth. Petals 5 (more in some double-flowered hort. forms). Stamens 10. Fruit a 3–5-valved capsule,* its seeds minute. (Named for Johan van der Deutz, Dutch patron of botany.)

These well-known shrubs, which have no common name, are of the easiest culture in any ordinary garden soil. They provide a fine display of bloom in bushes from 12 in. to several feet in height, mostly in the spring. Besides the species below there are many named garden forms, some of hybrid and uncertain parentage. Greenwood or hardwood cuttings, which root easily, are the best method of propagation. They can be forced to bloom in the greenhouse if kept at about 50°, but the process is not likely to succeed more than once.

campanulata = *Deutzia rosea campanulata.*

candida. A shrub 6 ft. high and of hybrid origin, the shreddy bark brownish. Leaves ovalish, or oval-oblong, 1½–2½ in. long, finely toothed and slightly rough. Flowers white, nearly 1 in. wide, in rather loose clusters 1½–3 in. wide. Hardy from zone* 4 southward.

crenata = *Deutzia scabra.*

gracilis. Much the best known of all the

deutzias and a shrub not over 5 ft., usually lower and bushy, its bark not very shreddy and yellowish-gray. Leaves oblong or narrower, 1½–2½ in. long. Flowers very numerous, white, about ¾ in. wide, the clusters loose. Jap. One of the best-known shrubs in cult. and often forced for late winter bloom. For the pink-flowered form sometimes called *D. gracilis rosea* see DEUTZIA ROSEA. Hardy from zone* 3 southward.

kalmiaeflora. A hybrid shrub up to 6 ft. high. Leaves oval-oblong, 1–2 in. long, a little hairy beneath. Flowers cup-shaped, nearly 1 in. wide, white, but flushed carmine outside in rather loose 5–12-flowered clusters. Hardy from zone* 4 southward.

lemoinei. The best-known of the taller deutzias and a hybrid shrub up to 7 ft. high. Leaves elliptic or narrower, 3–4 in. long, sharply toothed. Flowers pure white, about ¾ in. wide, very numerous in pyramidal or flattish clusters 2–4 in. wide. Petals broadest toward the tip. Hardy from zone* 3 southward. Here belong many named garden forms, among them the old favorite Boule de Neige.

magnifica. A hybrid shrub, 6–8 ft. high, not very different from *Deutzia scabra*, but the flower cluster less spire-like, shorter and broader. June. Hardy from zone* 4 southward.

parviflora. Shrub 4–6 ft. high. Leaves ovalish, 3–4 in. long, somewhat wedge-shaped at the base, unequally but finely toothed. Flowers pure white, about ¾ in. wide, the clusters 2–3½ in. wide. A handsome, free-flowering shrub from China and hardy from zone* 3 southward.

purpurascens. A shrub 4–6 ft. high, the shreddy bark brownish. Leaves oblong or ovalish, 1½–2½ in. long, rounded at the base and roughish above. Flowers nearly 1 in. wide, star-shaped, white, but distinctly purplish on the outside. Western China. Hardy from zone* 5 southward.

rosea. A shrub much resembling *D. gracilis*, but the flowers pinkish and decidedly bell-shaped. Of hybrid origin and hardy from zone* 4 southward. The *var.* **campanulata** (often sold as *D. campanulata*) has bell-shaped but white flowers that are nearly 1½ in. wide.

scabra. A widely cult. shrub, especially in a double-flowered variety known as Pride-of-Rochester. It is a branching, more or less arching shrub 5–8 ft. high, the shreddy bark reddish-brown. Leaves ovalish, 2–3 in. long, hairy both sides. Flowers white, or pinkish outside, nearly 1¼ in. wide, the clusters spire-like and 3–5 in. long. Eastern Asia. June-July. Hardy from zone* 4 southward. There are many hort. forms, especially dwarf ones and others with white-dotted or white-marbled leaves. It is a good shrub for a smoky atmosphere.

DEVIL-IN-THE-BUSH = *Nigella damascena.*

DEVIL'S APPLE = *Mandragora officinarum.*

DEVIL'S-BIT = *Liatris spicata;* also *Chamaelirium luteum.*

DEVIL'S-CLAW = *Proboscidea louisianica.*

DEVIL'S-CLUB = *Oplopanax horridus.*

DEVIL'S-IVY = *Scindapsus aureus.*

DEVIL'S-PAINTBRUSH = Orange hawkweed. *See* list at WEEDS.

* Special articles on the subjects indicated by an asterisk (*) will be found at the words so marked.

DEVIL'S-PINCUSHION = *Coryphantha robustispina*.

DEVIL'S-TONGUE = *Hydrosme rivieri*.

DEVIL'S WALKING-STICK = *Aralia spinosa*.

DEVILWOOD = *Osmanthus americanus*.

DEWBERRY. The dewberry is simply a prostrate form of the blackberry, the trailing stems of which root at the joints or at the tip and make, consequently, rather unmanageable patches, if not kept under control. The only real difference between blackberry and dewberry from the hort. standpoint is that the fruits of dewberry are generally ripe from one to two weeks earlier than the ordinary tall blackberries.

While botanists are not agreed upon the specific identity of most dewberries — purely an American fruit — they are, generally speaking, prostrate forms of the genus *Rubus*, possibly derived from *R. flagellaris* and *R. trivialis*. They have blackberry-like fruits and are more at home in the southeastern and southern states, as a garden crop, than the upright blackberries. Texas and some of the states to the eastward are thus the chief dewberry-producing areas. *See also* BOYSENBERRY and LOGANBERRY.

The culture of dewberry is the same as for blackberry (which see), except that the prostrate canes must either be trained on wires or kept in control if allowed to sprawl. Training on wires strung between posts is expensive, but makes cultivation easier. The alternative is to confine the vines, by cutting off the tips, into flat patches, between which one may walk for cultivating or harvesting. The chief vars., mostly of hybrid origin, are Lucretia, Mayes and Young. Most of the cult. dewberries do indifferently as far north as Ohio, although several wild species are found in the North.

DEWDROP = *Dalibarda repens*.

DEW PLANT = *Drosera rotundifolia*.

diacantha, -us, -um (dy-a-kan'tha). Two-spined.

DIACRIUM (dy-ak'cree-um). A small genus of tropical American orchids, related to *Epidendrum* (which see). The only cult. species here admitted is **D. bicornutum** of Trinidad and Brazil. It is an extremely showy, fragrant orchid with cylindric, hollow pseudobulbs* that are 7–12 in. long. Leaves only 3–4, leathery, persistent, 4–7 in. long. Flowers nearly 2 in. wide, in a terminal, 4–12-flowered spike, the petals and sepals white, the lip* 3-lobed, white but purple-spotted and with a yellow crest. For cult. *see* ORCHID. (*Diacrium* is from the Greek for *through* and *point*, alluding to the sheaths on the stalk of some species.)

diadema, -us, -um (dy-a-dee'ma). Crown or diadem-like.

DIAMOND FLOWER = *Ionopsidium acaule*.

DIAMOND-LEAF LAUREL = *Pittosporum rhombifolium*.

dianthiflora, -us, -um (dy-an-thee-flow'ra). With flowers like a pink (*Dianthus*).

DIANTHUS (dy-an'thus). About 300 species of annual or perennial herbs of the family Caryophyllaceae, mostly Eurasian, some, as the pink, Sweet William, and carnation being important garden plants. They have opposite,* usually narrow leaves and swollen joints. Flowers terminal, solitary in the carnation and some others, but usually grouped in small, often dense, clusters (cymes* or panicles*). Calyx veiny, and with 5 teeth, often with 2 or more bracts* beneath it. Petals 5 (much doubled in some hort. forms), fringed or toothed in some species, always with a longish basal shank (claw*). Stamens 10. Fruit a 4-valved capsule.* (*Dianthus* is from the Greek for flower of Jove.)

There are many valuable garden plants in *Dianthus*, of which several types demand comment. For *D. Caryophyllus* and its culture *see* CARNATION. All the others are hardy, and all except those designated otherwise are perennials. These are of the following types: (1) the grass pinks (*D. plumarius*) which are low, tufted herbs, usually with fragrant foliage; (2) the maiden pinks (*D. deltoides*) which make turf-like mats and have small flowers; (3) the Sweet William (*D. barbatus*) and its allies which have dense, nearly globular flower clusters; (4) species of pinks grown less frequently than any of the above groups.

The culture of the perennials is usually easy in any ordinary garden soil, especially in warm, somewhat sandy ones, but they are inclined to die out if left alone for two or three years. To avoid this, keep a fresh stock coming along by division, layering or by cuttings, all of which are easily managed, as the plant roots freely. In the mat-forming sorts it is better to cut off all flowering stalks in the fall, nearly to the base of the plant. Also, cut off all faded flowers. Of the 80 or so species of *Dianthus* known to be cult. in the U.S. the following are the best known. Most of them are spring-blooming.

allwoodi. A group of hybrid pinks (*Caryophyllus × plumarius*), generally tufted, with narrow, bluish-green foliage, and varying from 4–20 in. high. Flowers of many colors, the petals fringed or not. Offered in a variety of forms, often of uncertain identity.

alpestris. A European alpine plant chiefly suited to the rock garden. Leaves narrow, shorter than the stalk of the flower cluster, which has 1 or 2 deep pink or rose-colored flowers about 1 in. wide, the petals notched and without fragrance. Also called *D. furcatus*.

alpinus. A tufted plant scarcely 4 in. high, useful only in the rock garden (which see for culture). Leaves short, broad and blunt. Flowers usually solitary, rose or purplish and crimson-eyed, nearly 1½ in. wide, not fragrant. Mountains of Eurasia.

arenarius. A tufted plant with many slender stems 6–15 in. high. Flowers white, not very fragrant, long-stalked, the petals finely cut or almost fringed. Central Eu.

arvernensis. A grayish, mat-forming pink of

---

* Special articles on the subjects indicated by an asterisk (*) will be found at the words so marked.

hybrid origin (*monspessulanus* × *sylvaticus*), 4–15 in. high, usually branched upward. Leaves broadly linear. Flowers solitary or 2 or 3 together, the petals mostly unfringed but fringed in a hort. var. Some of the plants offered as this may be *D. monspessulanus.*

barbatus. Sweet William; called bunch pink. A popular garden plant with many named forms, such as the Newport Pink. While a perennial, it is better grown as a biennial, especially for the improved sorts (*see* BIENNIALS). The seedsmen also have strains that bloom from seed the first year and such can be treated as hardy annuals (*see* ANNUALS). The typical form is a smooth herb 12–24 in. high, with green, flat, and broader leaves than in most pinks. Flowers not fragrant, in dense, close heads, red, rose-purple, white or sometimes varicolored, and in a few forms double-flowered. Eurasia and sometimes an escape* in eastern U.S.

caesius = *D. gratianopolitanus.*

carthusianorum. Clusterhead pink. An erect perennial, 8–20 in. high with usually green foliage and a 4-angled stem. Leaves scarcely 1/16 in. wide, slightly roughened on the margin. Flowers numerous, small, packed into a tight head that is 2–3 in. wide, mostly purple, rarely white. There are many garden forms with a variety of generally uncertain names. Central Eu. May–June.

Caryophyllus. Carnation; also the clove pink. A smooth-tufted* herb 1–3 ft. high, the foliage grayish, the stems stiffish. Flowers usually solitary, very fragrant, about 2 in. wide (more in nearly all the much-doubled forms of the carnation), the petals cut or slightly fringed. Eurasia. For the culture of the carnation and hardy derivatives of it *see* CARNATION.

chinensis. China pink, also called Indian pink. A green-foliaged, tufted* plant 12–18 in. high, its stems erect and stiffish. Flowers faintly fragrant, red, white, or lilac, solitary or in sparse clusters, 1–2 inches wide. Eurasia. Sometimes sold as *D. sinensis,* and as *D. seguieri,* by some considered the European form of *D. chinensis.* For cult. *see* ANNUALS, although the plant is a biennial or perennial.

cruentus. A tufted,* grayish-foliaged herb, its stems forked and 8–15 in. high. Flowers deep red, in small, dense, head-like clusters, the petals toothed. Eastern Eu.

deltoides. Maiden pink; called also meadow pink and spink. A turf-forming plant forming mats of green foliage, the leaves scarcely 1 in. long and very narrow. Flowering stalks forked, 4–12 in. high, the flowers scarcely 3/4 in. wide, red, or pink (white with a crimson eye in some hort. forms). Western Eu. to eastern As. The var. *glaucus* has bluish-gray foliage. For culture *see* ROCK GARDEN, but it may also be grown in the open border.

giganteus. Probably a large-flowered form of *D. carthusianorum,* but thought by some to be a distinct species from southeastern Eu.

glacialis. A rock garden tufted herb 3–4 in. high, the stems unbranched and with 1–2 flowers that are about 1/2 in. wide, not fragrant, reddish-purple, the petals toothed, and yellowish underneath. Mountains of southern Eu. Sometimes offered as *D. neglectus,* which is a closely related plant.

graniticus. A rock garden plant with 4-angled stems 4–7 in. high. Leaves chiefly basal, very narrow. Flowers solitary (rarely 2 or 3), about 3/4 in. wide, the petals purplish and toothed but paler beneath. Pyrenees.

gratianopolitanus. Cheddar pink. A low, mat-forming plant, its bluish-green, numerous

stems usually unbranched and 3–9 in. high. Flowers usually solitary, fragrant, rose-colored, very handsome and with fringed petals. Eu. By some called *D. caesius.* For culture *see* ROCK GARDEN.

knappi. A rough-stemmed border plant 8–16 in. high, unbranched, the foliage bluish-gray. Flowers yellow, not fragrant, about 3/4 in. wide, in a dense, solitary cluster at the end of each stem. Southern Eu.

latifolius. Probably a hybrid between the Sweet William and the China pink. An erect, branching herb, 9–18 in. high, the foliage green and roughish, the leaves 2–3 in. long and about 1/2 in. wide. Flowers in a few-flowered head, rose-pink, shading to dark red (double in some varieties).

monspessulanus. A somewhat stiff perennial, a little woody at the base and 5–12 in. high. Leaves bright green, rather stiff and upward-pointing. Flowers solitary or only 2–3, the petals deeply fringed, red or white (in some hort. forms), the lower leaves often absent at flowering time. Southern Eu. May–June.

neglectus. A plant closely related to *D. glacialis,* and sometimes sold for it, but *neglectus* always packs a solitary flower, the bracts* below the calyx 4. Southern Eu. For culture *see* ROCK GARDEN.

noeanus. A stiff-leaved, densely-tufted Eurasian perennial, 4–10 in. high, its foliage bright green. Leaves sharp-pointed, spreading, about 3/4 in. long. Flowers about 3/4 in. wide, 1–5 in a loose cluster, the petals white and cut almost to the center. Summer.

petraeus. Tufted, usually mat-forming herb with smooth, slender, sometimes forked stems 6–15 in. high, the leaves green and 3-veined. Flowers about 3/4 in. wide, fragrant, the petals fringed. Eastern Eu.

plumarius. Grass pink and including many common garden pinks; sometimes called Scotch pink. Mat-forming herb with smooth, bluish-gray foliage, the stems erect, sometimes forked, 9–18 in. high. Flowers 2–3, fragrant, rose-pink to purplish or white or with variegated colors, the petals fringed. Eurasia. An old garden favorite, known in many named forms and varieties, some double-flowered. The var. *semperflorens,* with long-continuing bloom, includes many of the common garden pinks.

seguieri. See DIANTHUS CHINENSIS.

sinensis = *Dianthus chinensis.*

subacaulis. A rock garden dwarf pink, scarcely 3 in. high, its foliage bluish-green. Leaves very short and stiff, minutely hairy on the margins. Flowers very small, pink, the petals only slightly or not at all fringed. Southwestern Eu. Summer.

superbus. A border pink 1–2 ft. high, its stems branched and smooth. Leaves flat, narrow, 3–5-veined. Flowers fragrant, nearly 1 1/2 in. wide, lilac or pale rose, the petals deeply fringed and bearded. Eurasia.

winteri. A current trade name for a plant of the border carnation type, the status and origin of which is unknown.

DIAPENSIACEAE (dy-a-pen-si-ā'see-ee). The galax or pyxie family consists of only 6 genera of evergreen, low shrubs or herbs, all from the north temperate zone, four of which are of garden interest. *Galax* is found in every florist shop in America, its glossy, evergreen leaves being much used in funeral wreaths.

Leaves simple,* very small and crowded in *Pyxidanthera,* long-stalked and much

---

* Special articles on the subjects indicated by an asterisk (*) will be found at the words so marked.

larger in *Galax* and in *Schizocodon,* a Japanese relative of the American *Shortia.* Most of these garden genera are of rock garden culture. Flowers solitary in most of the cult. genera, white or pink. Fruit a dry pod (capsule*), with many minute seeds.

Technical flower characters: Flowers regular,* the calyx and corolla more or less bell-shaped, 5-lobed. Stamens 5, borne on the corolla. Ovary superior,* 3-celled.

diaphana, -us, -um, (dy-aff'a-na). Transparent.

DIASCIA (dy-ass'si-a). A large genus of South African herbs of the family Schrophulariaceae, only **D. barberae,** the twin-spur, of secondary garden interest. It is a tender annual (*see* ANNUALS for cult.), 8–15 in. high, with opposite,* toothed, ovalish leaves 1–1½ in. long. Flowers irregular* and 2-lipped,* rose-pink but yellow-throated, about ½ in. long, the lower lip with 2 spurs. The plant is showy because of the terminal flower cluster (raceme*) which is often 6 in. long. Fruit a roundish pod. (*Diascia* is from a Greek word meaning having two spurs.)

DIBBER (or **DIBBLE**). A pointed stick, with a metal sheath and a curved handle, useful for making holes for bulbs or seedlings.

DICENTRA (dy-sen'tra). A small genus of slender, rather weak, somewhat watery-juiced herbs of the family Fumariaceae, some Asiatic, the rest from N.A. They have fleshy rootstocks, and feathery, much dissected, often basal leaves which are sometimes compound.* Flowers in terminal racemes,* very irregular,* the petals joined into a heart-shaped or long-spurred corolla. Fruit a slender, 2-valved pod, the seeds minutely crested.* (*Dicentra* is from the Greek for two-spurred, in allusion to spurred corolla.) The first and third species should only be grown in the deep shade of the wild garden, preferably in a wind-free place. After their early bloom, the leaves die down and the plant is not seen until the following season. The others may be grown in open borders or in the rock garden, and present no special difficulty. All are increased by division in early spring.

canadensis. Squirrel-corn or turkey-corn. Very similar to *D. Cucullaria,* but with the flower spurs not diverging. In rich woods, eastern N.A.

chrysantha. Golden eardrops. A stout, leafy-stemmed herb 3–5 ft. high, the foliage bluish-green. Flowers yellow, the spurs very short, the flower cluster large and often branched. Calif. Not much cult. and difficult to grow in the East.

Cucullaria. Dutchman's-breeches; called also white eardrops. A delicate. stemless herb, the feathery leaves all basal. Flowering stalk 5–8 in. high, the cluster sparse. Flowers white but tipped with yellow, about ¾ in. long, the two spurs diverging, the flowers appearing forked. Rich woods, eastern N.A.

eximia. Wild bleeding-heart. A native herb suited to the rock garden (which see for cult.).

Leaves all basal. Flowers nodding, in a branched cluster, rose-colored or pink, the spurs short and rounded. In woods, N.Y. to Ga. A related species, *D. formosa,* commonly called California bleeding-heart, may not be distinct, but it has rose-purple (rarely white) flowers.

formosa. See DICENTRA EXIMIA.

oregana. A perennial with much-cut foliage; not over 12 in. high. Leaves silvery, nearly all basal. Flowers in a hanging cluster (raceme*), generally creamy-yellow, but faintly purple-spotted. Ore. Summer.

spectabilis. The common garden bleeding-heart, and a leafy-stemmed herb 12–24 in. high. Flowers in a usually unbranched, 1-sided cluster, rose-colored or red, the spurs short and rounded. Jap. An old garden favorite of the easiest cult. in the open border. Sometimes sold as *Dielytra spectabilis.*

DICHLONE. See FUNGICIDES.

DICHONDRA (dy-kon'dra). A small genus of prostrate, creeping tropical vines of the morning-glory family, of no hort. interest except for **D. repens,** which is widely used in Calif. and other desert regions for lawns where lawn grasses will not grow. It is a creeping perennial, with inconspicuous flowers, and small roundish leaves less than ½ in. in diameter. It makes a dense growth, will stand mowing, and along the Gulf Coast is a pestilential weed. (*Dichondra* is from the Greek for double and grain, in allusion to a fruit structure.)

DICHORISANDRA (dy-kor-i-san'dra). About 30 species of tropical American perennial herbs of the family Commelinaceae, the two below infrequently grown in greenhouses for their fine foliage and blue flowers. They have erect or somewhat sprawling, usually unbranched stems which bear the few leaves at or near the top. Leaves without teeth, nearly stalkless, and with a sheathing base. Flowers blue, borne in a dense cluster (panicle*). Sepals and petals each 3. Stamens usually 6. Fruit a 3-angled pod, with few seeds. (*Dichorisandra* is from the Greek and refers to a technical stamen character.)

Should be grown in the warm greenhouse in potting mixture* 4. During the growing season give plenty of water, but after blooming the plant dies down to the ground until it puts forth a new shoot (usually only 1) the following spring. It may not do this unless kept a bit pot-bound.* During dormancy reduce its watering materially. Easily propagated by division, preferably during winter dormancy or when re-potting.

mosaica. Stem lower than in the next, and spotted. Leaves broadly elliptic, about 6 in. long, 3–4 in. wide, white-lined above, rich purple beneath. Flower cluster short and dense, but often wanting in cult. Peru. A very handsome foliage plant, which in the *var. gigantea* has blue flowers more sure than in the typical form. Called by some *Geogenanthus undatus.*

thyrsiflora. Stems stout, 3–6 ft. high. Leaves green both sides, 6–10 in. long, about 2 in. wide. Flower cluster showy, usually branched, sepals and petals blue, or the sepals some-

---

* Special articles on the subjects indicated by an asterisk (*) will be found at the words so marked.

times greenish. Brazil. More showy in bloom, but a less desirable foliage plant.

dichotoma, *-us*, *-um* (dy-kot'o-ma). Dichotomous, *i.e.*, forked in pairs.

dichroa (dy-crow'a). Two-colored.

DICKSONIA (dik-sõ'ni-a). A small genus of comparatively hardy tree ferns of the family Cyatheaceae, **D. antarctica** frequently grown in the warm-temperate or cool greenhouse for ornament. It is an Australian fern with a trunk 30–40 ft. high in the wild, much less as usually cult., the stem plentifully studded with leaf bases. Leaves (fronds) thrice-compound,* not over 6 ft. long, the ultimate segments lance-shaped, toothed, and about 2 in. long. Spore* cases near the margin and at tips of the veins. One of the most useful of the tree ferns for decoration. Not so feathery as some, it is much more able to stand unfavorable conditions. For culture *see* FERNS AND FERN GARDENING. (Named for James Dickson, English botanist.) The plant offered as *Dicksonia punctilobula* is *Dennstaedtia punctilobula* (which see).

DICOTYLEDON. A plant having two cotyledons* or seed leaves. Dicotyledonous plants usually have netted-veined leaves, and the parts of their flowers (petals, stamens, etc.) in fours or fives or multiples of these. Most garden plants except the palms, aroids,* lilies, grasses, iris, amaryllis, and their allies are dicotyledons. *See* MONOCOTYLEDON and POLYCOTYLEDON.

DICTAMNUS (dik-tam'nus). A single species of hardy, Eurasian, perennial herb of the family Rutaceae, long cult. for ornament in the open border where it may persist for generations. The only species is **D. albus**, variously called gas-plant, dittany, fraxinella, and burning-bush. It is called gas-plant because the strong vapor of its foliage and flowers will faintly ignite if a lighted match is put to it on a windless summer evening. It is a somewhat woody herb, 2–3 ft. high, its leaves compound,* the 9–11 leaflets ovalish and leathery. Flowers in a terminal cluster (raceme*), white, about 1 in. long. Petals 5. Stamens 10. Fruit a 5-divided, hard, almost woody capsule.* Of the easiest culture, but not tolerating change, so it is better planted where wanted permanently, and avoid dividing if possible. Seeds sown in the fall, outdoors, will sprout the next spring and provide the easiest method of propagation. *Var.* **purpureus** has purple, and *var.* **rubrus,** red flowers. (*Dictamnus* is the classical Greek name of the plant.)

dictiophylla, *-us*, *-um* (dick-ti-o-fill'a). With netted-veined leaves.

DICTYOSPERMA (dik-ti-o-sper'ma). A single species of feather palm (some say 2 others are known) from the Mascarene Islands, much grown for ornament in greenhouses or outdoors in the warmer parts of Fla. and Calif. It is a spineless palm with large, feathery, gracefully arching leaves. Flowers in a short-stalked cluster, the branches of which are rope-like and upon which the flowers are in scattered bunches of 3, of which the central one is female, the two others male. Stamens 6. Fruit fleshy, somewhat olive-shaped. (*Dictyosperma* is from the Greek for netted seed.) The genus is also called *Linoma*, and some of the forms are often sold as arecas.

The young state of the species below is a fairly common pot palm with the florists. For its greenhouse cult. *see* PALM. In Fla. and Calif. it grows fairly rapidly in a variety of soils, but should not be planted outdoors except in zone* 9 and the more favorable sites in zone* 8.

album. In Fla. about 30 ft. high, much less under glass, and twice that in its own home, bulging at the base. There is a striking terminal crown of 10–15 gracefully drooping leaves about 10 ft. long, the long, drooping segments arranged feather-fashion, 2–3 in. wide, light green. The *var.* **rubrum** has reddish veins and leafstalks in youth, and the *var.* **aureum** is similarly yellow-tinged. All of them are very attractive palms whether as juvenile pot plants or in maturity.

DIDISCUS. See TRACHYMENE.

didyma, *-us*, *-um* (did'i-ma). In pairs.

DIE-BACK. A general term referring to death of tips of plants. It may be caused by various bacterial, fungus, or virus diseases. In many cases, however, the die-back is the result of some climatic condition such as heat, drought, or low winter temperatures.

DIEFFENBACHIA (dee-fen-bak'i-a). Handsome tropical American foliage plants of the family Araceae, much grown in greenhouses for their attractive leaves. They are erect, shrubby plants (apparently stemless in youth), bearing near the summit a few oblong, large leaves without marginal teeth and with sheathing leafstalks. Flowers minute, unisexual,* crowded on an erect spadix,* about as long as the oblong spathe* (for details *see* ARACEAE). Fruit fleshy. (Named for J. F. Dieffenbach, German botanist.)

These popular aroids* need a warm greenhouse (70°–80°) during the growing season, plenty of water, and should be planted in potting mixture* 4. They prefer a partially shaded greenhouse and moist atmosphere. Easily propagated from cut sections of the partially dormant stems, which should be half buried, lengthwise, in moist sand over bottom-heat. The rooted stem cuttings can then be potted up. The plants are rich feeders and respond well to occasional doses of liquid manure. All have an acrid, some a poisonous, juice.

amoena. A Central American thick-stemmed aroid.* Leaves oblong, pointed at the tip but roundish at the base, with long, whitish-yellow stripes along the main veins on upper and lower surfaces. A fine foliage plant for the house.

bausei = form of D. *picta.*

magnifica = *Dieffenbachia picta magnifica.*

---

* Special articles on the subjects indicated by an asterisk (*) will be found at the words so marked.

picta. Not over 4 ft. high. Leaves oblong or elliptic, at least 3 times as long as broad, the sheathing leafstalks nearly as long as the blade, which is green, but with many irregular, oblongish or narrower, lighter-colored, usually yellowish markings between the veins. S.A. There are at least 2 dozen named forms of this popular foliage plant, perhaps the best being *var.* **magnifica,** with white markings. The others are variously banded, feathered, or blotched with white or yellow.

Seguine. Dumb cane, so called because chewing it causes temporary speechlessness. A taller, stouter plant than *D. picta* and less well known in cult. Leaves about twice as long as broad, slightly heart-shaped at the base, green, irregularly spotted with unequal sized and shaped yellowish blotches or dots or both. W.I. There are few cult. varieties, but one has a yellow stripe along the midrib.*

DIELYTRA SPECTABILIS = *Dicentra spectabilis.*

DIERAMA (dy-ray′ma). A small genus of South African herbs of the iris family, which are cult. outdoors in southern Calif., rarely in greenhouses northward. They have gladiolus-like corms,* but culturally they must be grown the same as *Ixia* (which see), outside of Calif. and neighboring regions. Leaves chiefly basal, long and rigid. Flowers large, showy, usually in branched spikes, the corolla funnel-shaped but expanded at the throat. Stamens* 3. Fruit a 3-valved capsule.* (*Dierama* is from the Greek for funnel, in allusion to the shape of the flowers.)

pendula. Nearly 4 ft. high, the chiefly basal leaves 12–20 in. long, about ¼ in. wide. Flowers about 1 in. long, grouped in slender, drooping clusters (spikes*), white to lavender.

pulcherrima. Nearly 4 ft. high, the leaves stiff, 12–20 in. long, about ¼ in. wide. Flowers about 1½ in. long, in drooping clusters (spikes*), reddish-purple. Sometimes sold as *Sparaxis pulcherrima.*

DIERVILLA (dy-er-vil′la). A small genus of low shrubs of the honeysuckle family, mostly North American, two of them of secondary garden interest. They are useful under shade or in the wild garden, where they make rather extensive patches from the spreading of their underground stems. Leaves opposite,* short-stalked and toothed. Flowers yellow, funnel-shaped, mostly in small, leafless clusters, from the leaf axils.* Corolla irregular,* slightly 2-lipped. Stamens 5. Fruit a 2-valved capsule* crowned with the narrow lobes of the calyx. (Named for Dierville, French surgeon in Canada.) The plants are usually called bush honeysuckle. For related plants, much more important as decorative shrubs, *see* WEIGELA.

The species below are of the easiest culture, preferring shade, but doing pretty well in open sunshine. They grow freely from suckers or may be increased by division.

Lonicera. Gravelweed. Never over 3 ft. high, usually about 2 ft. Leaves ovalish or oblong, 2–4 in. long, taper-pointed. Flowers usually 3 to a cluster, the corolla about ¾

in. long. June. Que. to Del. and westward, and hardy everywhere.

sessilifolia. Somewhat taller and with longer, narrower leaves. Flowers usually 3–7 to a cluster, the corolla shorter than in *D. Lonicera.* In mountain woods N.C. to Tenn., Ga., and Ala. June. Hardy from zone* 3 southward.

trifida = *Diervilla Lonicera.*

diffusa, -us, -um (dif-few′sa). Diffuse; *i.e.,* spreading.

DIETES. *See* MORAEA.

DIGGER PINE = *Pinus sabiniana. See* PINE.

DIGGING. The simplest, best, but most laborious method of turning the soil in anticipation of planting. All machine or horse-implement substitutes have the disadvantage of the operator of the machine walking over the turned-up earth, which never happens in spading or forking because one necessarily walks backward as digging progresses.

Forking is simply digging with a spading fork, which one does if the roots of plants are apt to be cut with the broad blade of a spade. It is also easier to fork in manure than to spade it in.

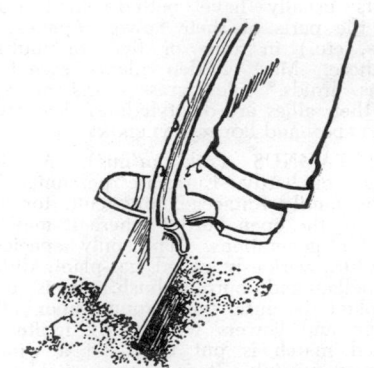

Right angle to dig

Wrong angle to dig

---

* Special articles on the subjects indicated by an asterisk (*) will be found at the words so marked.

Whether the operation is digging or forking, it would scarcely seem necessary to give any directions for a process as old as gardening. It would not be, except that there is a right and a wrong way to dig, both for the operator and for the soil.

The main objects of digging are to loosen up the soil, allow it to aerate, and in the process to cover up all weeds, vegetable trash, or spent manure. This cannot be done properly by shallow (*i.e.*, slantwise) digging, but is usually successful if the spade or fork is driven almost vertically into the ground and nearly or quite the depth of its blade. While the illustrations show the right and wrong ways to dig, they cannot convey the fact that the wrong method is much the most laborious.

There is also the obvious caution about the time to dig. Late fall is good if the turned-up soil is left in the rough over the winter. Frost and snow are good for it. Many fall-dug soils will be ready for raking and planting in spring, especially if they are light, loamy, or sandy loam soils, which will not pack over the winter. If there is much clay or silt, digging is best left to the spring and even then must be approached with caution.

Heavy clay or silt soils pack badly when wet and may be unworkable by midsummer if you begin digging them too soon. Wait until a clod of earth breaks or crumbles when dropped off the spade. If it packs or sticks together, it is too early to dig. If you insist, the penalty may be unmanageable chunks of cement-like hardness by the time your soil should be in its most friable condition for root development and for cultivation.

DIGITALIS. See Foxglove.

DIGITARIA. See Crab Grass.

digitata, -us, -um (dij-i-tay'ta). Digitate; *i.e.*, with the leaflets,* or with the lobes of a simple leaf, all arising from one point, as in the horse-chestnut. See Pinnate.

dilatata, -us, -um (dy-la-tay'ta). Expanded.

DILL. The common dill, the fruits of which are used for seasoning, is one of two species of the genus Anethum (a-ne'thum) of the carrot family, native in the Old World. The only cult. species is A. graveolens, the dill, which is an annual or biennial herb of perhaps 2½-ft. stature with finely dissected, usually thrice-compound* leaves. Flowers very small, yellowish, the petals soon falling, arranged in a large umbel* which is smooth and without bracts.* (For detailed flower structure *see* Umbelliferae.) Fruit aromatic, flattened, some of the ribs winged.* (Anethum is classical Greek for the dill.) For culture *see* Herb Gardening.

DILLENIACEAE (dil-leen-i-ā'see-ee). The silver vine family has only two genera of garden interest among its 12 genera and 200 species of mostly trees, shrubs, or woody vines, all of which are tropical except Actinidia. This genus of woody vines, often grown for ornament, is sometimes included in Actinidiaceae, a family not here maintained.

Leaves mostly alternate.* Flowers unisexual* in Actinidia, perfect* in the other cult. genus, mostly rather showy. The fruit is fleshy and sometimes edible in Actinidia. The only other cult. genus is Hibbertia.

Technical flower characters: Petals 5, their margins overlapping, as do the 5 sepals which are persistent and sometimes enlarged in fruit. Stamens numerous. Ovary superior,* the styles spreading.

DIMORPHOTHECA (dy-more-fo-thee'ka). The Cape marigolds comprise perhaps 20 species of annual or perennial South African herbs of the family Compositae, one a popular, tender annual. They have alternate* or basal, few-toothed leaves and showy, solitary, long-stalked flower heads. Rays* long and strap-shaped, chiefly yellow, orange, or white, the disk flowers yellow, blue, or orange. (Dimorphotheca is from the Greek for two-formed achenes, in allusion to a technical fruit character.)

While *D. aurantiaca* is a perennial, it will bloom from seed the first year, and, like *D. annua*, is best treated as a tender annual. *See* Annuals. The exact botanical identity of the plants below is in grave doubt, as there has been much crossing of these popular flowers. Sometimes grown in the greenhouse and bedded out in summer. They are sometimes called African daisy.

annua. A rough-hairy herb 8–14 in. high, the leaves oblongish, practically stalkless. Flower heads showy, the rays white, yellow, or orange, but somewhat purplish below, and in some hort. forms double. As the flowers wane, the head is nodding. Summer. Also known as *D. pluvialis*. Of this, or possibly of the next, there are many fine, showy, garden forms, but their identity or parentage is very doubtful.

aurantiaca. A perennial, in age somewhat woody at the base. Leaves narrowly oblong, a little rough but not, or only a little, hairy. Flowers generally orange-yellow (white, bluish, or red in some hort. forms). Easily flowered from seed in a single season if treated as a tender annual, but it requires a long season and plenty of heat.

eck'onis. A leafy, somewhat woody perennial, 12–20 in. high, usually branched upward. Leaves lance-shaped or narrower, 2–3 in. long, without, or with a few, marginal teeth. Flower heads long-stalked, 2–3 in. wide, the rays white above but purple beneath, the head with a violet-blue center. Not hardy above zone* 5.

DINITRO. See Fungicides.

DIOECIOUS (dy-ee'shus). Having male and female flowers on separate plants, as in the willow, in Aucuba, and many other plants. See Monoecious.

dioica, -us, -um (dy-ō'i-ka). Dioecious.

DIONAEA (dy-o-nee'a). A single, remarkable, insectivorous plant of the family Droseraceae, found only in North and South

---

* Special articles on the subjects indicated by an asterisk (*) will be found at the words so marked.

Carolina, and cult. for its interesting method of catching and digesting insects. The only species, **D. muscipula**, the Venus's-flytrap, can be grown outdoors in its native region, but is easier managed in the frame or cool greenhouse. It grows perfectly in wet sphagnum moss with a pH of about 4.0 or 4.5 (*see* ACID AND ALKALI SOILS) or in a similarly acid mixture of sand and peat, both kept saturated. The plant is a perennial with a basal rosette of flat-stalked leaves, the blade of which consists of two hinged lobes which are fringed with bristles. The lobes close together when irritated with a pencil or by an insect, completely trapping the latter, which is subsequently digested. Flowers white, small, in a terminal cluster (umbel*), the stalk of which is 8–12 in. long. (For structure of flowers *see* DROSERACEAE.) Fruit a capsule.* (*Dionaea* is a Greek name for Venus.) *See also* INSECTIVOROUS PLANTS.

DIOSCOREA (dy-os-kor-ree′a). A very large genus of chiefly herbaceous, twining vines of the family Dioscoreaceae, most of them tropical and a few cult. for food (the yam) or ornament. (*Yam* is also applied, incorrectly, to the sweet potato.) They have usually large underground tubers (the air potato has them in the foliage) and rather various, but prevailingly alternate* leaves. Flowers small, white or greenish, usually in spikes* or racemes.* (For details *see* DIOSCOREACEAE.) Fruit a strongly 3-angled or 3-winged, sometimes inflated, seldom a fleshy, pod. (Named for Dioscorides, one of the Greek fathers of botany.)

The yams grown for food must be confined to zone* 7 or southward, as they need a long season and considerable heat. Those grown for ornament are hardy up to zone* 4 or possibly to zone* 3, as their tops die down, but the roots persist. All are of the easiest culture, preferably in sandy, warm soils. The tubers may be planted almost at any time of the year in the South, preferably in spring in the North.

Batatas. Chinese yam or potato; usually called cinnamon vine in the North where it is cult. for ornament. Tubers 2–3 ft. long, deep in the ground. Stem angled, sometimes twisted, tall-climbing. Leaves opposite.* often with small tubers in the axils,* ovalish, but broad or angled at the base. Flowers cinnamon-scented, in small clusters from the leaf axils.* China.

bulbifera. Air potato. An Indo-Malayan vine, tender in the North, and without the large underground tuber of most yams. Stems round, often bearing in the leaf axils* large tubers 8–12 in. long and weighing several pounds. Leaves alternate,* heart-shaped or roundish, the stalk longer than the blade. Flowers in many drooping, slender spikes. Chiefly grown for the aerial tubers.

trifida. Yampee, also called cush-cush. Underground tubers, not large, but prized for their flavor. Stem more or less winged or angled, without tubers. Leaves 3–5-lobed, the lobes extending nearly to the middle. Flowers in racemes* (male flowers) or the female ones

in spikes. S.A. Can be grown only far south.

villosa. Wild yam. A native vine with a woody but not large rootstock. Leaves ovalish, heart-shaped at the base, with 9–11 main veins. Flowers in drooping clusters. Almost a weedy vine, native from Conn. to Fla. and Tex. and Minn. Little cult. and hardy to zone* 3.

DIOSCOREACEAE (dy-os-kor-ree-ā′see-ee). The yam family would be of no garden interest if it were not for the food value of the yam (*Dioscorea*). Like the other 8 genera and upwards of 600 species, this is a herbaceous vine, often with tremendous underground (rarely in the air) tubers which furnish the yams of commerce.

Leaves alternate* or opposite.* Flowers small, greenish or whitish, usually in clusters (spikes* or racemes*), nearly always unisexual.* Fruit a decidedly 3-angled or winged capsule.* The single genus is cult. mostly for the edible tubers, but some vines in *Dioscorea* are decorative.

Technical flower characters: Flowers regular,* the 6 segments not easily separable as sepals and petals. Stamens 6 or 3. Ovary 3-celled, its styles 3 and distinct.

DIOSMA (dy-ōs′ma). Aromatic, small, heath-like, South African shrubs of the family Rutaceae, only **D. ericoides**, the breath-of-heaven or buchu of much garden interest. It is a tender border shrub in Calif. and Fla., more often grown as a greenhouse plant needing potting mixture* 4 and a cool house. It is a much-branched, bushy shrub, 1–2 ft. high. Leaves alternate,* scarcely ½ in. long, needle-shaped and much crowded. Flowers about ⅕ in. wide, in clusters of 1–3 but the clusters very numerous. Petals 5, reddish. Calyx deeply 5-parted. Fruit a collection of 5 carpels, ultimately separable as 5 distinct capsules,* each 1-seeded. An attractive and floriferous little bush. (*Diosma* is from the Greek for divine fragrance, from the aromatic foliage.) For the plant offered as *D. pulchra, see* COLEONEMA.

DIOSPYROS. *See* PERSIMMON.

DIPELTA (dy-pel′ta). A small genus of Chinese shrubs of the honeysuckle family, only **D. floribunda** of interest to the shrubbery enthusiast. It is 8–15 ft. high and has shreddy bark. Leaves opposite,* short-stalked, ovalish or narrower, 2–4 in. long, mostly without marginal teeth. Flowers fragrant, in slender, nodding clusters of 2–6 blooms. Corolla pale rose, but orange in the throat, tubular but a little 2-lipped,* about 1½ in. long. Beneath the flower is a series of bracts* of unequal size. Stamens* 4. Fruit a capsule,* partly enclosed by the persistent bracts. An ornamental shrub, resembling beauty-bush, blooming in May, hardy from zone* 4 southward, and tolerant of most ordinary garden soils. (*Dipelta* is from the Greek for twice and shield, in allusion to the unequal bracts.*)

dipetala, -us, -um (dy-pet′a-la). With two petals.

---

* Special articles on the subjects indicated by an asterisk (*) will be found at the words so marked.

diphylla, -us, -um (dy-fil'la). Two-leaved.

DIPHYLLEIA (dy-fil-lee'ya). A genus of two species of the family Berberidaceae, one Asiatic, the other, **D. cymosa**, the umbrella leaf, a woodland perennial herb of the southeastern U.S., cult. in the wild garden. It is an erect, stout herb with a single, basal, long-stalked leaf 12–20 in. in diameter, and 2 stem leaves, shorter-stalked. Both sorts are deeply 2-lobed, the lobes more or less cut or lobed also, and the leafstalks arise from or near the middle of the blade (peltate°). Flowers white, in a small, terminal cluster (cyme°), the 6 petals and 6 sepals similar. Stamens 6. Fruit a blue berry about ½ in. in diameter. The plant needs shade and woods soil and prefers mountain forests to sandy lowlands. (*Diphylleia* is from the Greek for double-leaf, in allusion to the two stem leaves.)

DIPLACUS. *See* MIMULUS.

DIPLADENIA (di-la-dee'ni-a). Forty species of tropical American woody vines of the family Apocynaceae, two sometimes cult. in the greenhouse or outdoors only in zone° 9. Leaves opposite,° without marginal teeth, their juice milky. Flowers large, showy, in few-flowered clusters (racemes°). Corolla funnel-shaped, slightly twisted, the 5 stamens° inserted in its throat. Fruit a pair of divergent, narrow pods (follicles°). (*Dipladenia* is from the Greek meaning double gland, in reference to a technical character of the disk.°)

These are very handsome woody vines which in youth are somewhat shrubby and only climb later. They need a warm-temperate greenhouse and potting mixture° 3 to which is added about ½ its bulk in charcoal. Propagated by cuttings over bottom-heat.° In extreme southern Fla. they appear to thrive on a variety of soils.

boliviensis. Leaves 2–3 in. long, narrowed at the base, and stalked. Flowers about 1½ in. long, white, the throat yellow, the stalk of the cluster shorter than the leaves. Bolivia.

splendens. Leaves elliptic, 4–8 in. long, the heart-shaped base nearly stalkless. Flowers nearly 4 in. long, white or rose-flushed, the throat purple, the stalk of the cluster longer than the leaves. Brazil. The most popular in cult. and often sold under a variety of names.

DIPLOID. *See* CHROMOSOME.

diplostephioides (dip-low-stee-fi-oy'-deez; but *see* OÏDES). Like a plant of the genus *Diplostephium*, which is of little garden interest.

DIPPER GOURD = *Lagenaria siceraria.*

dipsacea, -us, -um (dip-say'see-a). Teasel-like.

DIPSACACEAE (dip-sa-kay'see-ee). The teasel family, closely related to the Compositae, contains mostly weedy herbs in perhaps 8 Old World genera and about 160 species. The only cult. genera are *Cephalaria, Morina, Scabiosa,* and *Dipsacus,* the latter yielding fuller's teasel from its spiny-tipped fruiting head.

Leaves usually opposite° or whorled.° Flowers small, in bracted° heads, except in *Morina* where they are in interrupted spikes. Unlike the Compositae, there are no ray flowers, all being tubular in the Dipsacaceae. Fruit dry, small (an achene°).

The only important hort. genus is *Scabiosa,* one species of which is the parent of popular flower garden annuals.

Technical characters: Flowers mostly in heads, the heads bracted. Ovary inferior,° 1-celled, the calyx-tube poined to it. Ovules 1.

DIPSACEAE = Dipsacaceae.

DIPSACUS (dip'sa-kus). Coarse, thistle-like, Old World herbs of the family Dipsacaceae, none of any real garden interest, but one of them cult. for the peculiar fruiting head, known as teasel and used to raise the nap on woolen cloth. It is **D. Fullonum,** the fuller's teasel, a biennial European herb 4–6 ft. high, coarse and hairy. Leaves opposite,° nearly 1 ft. long, the bases connected and cup-like. Flowers pale lilac, all tubular and minute, crowded in a dense, cylindric head, somewhat resembling those in the Compositae. The head is provided with a number of hooked bracts,° which are spine-tipped (the teasel). Once grown commercially for these teasels near woolen factories. (*Dipsacus* is Greek for thirst, in allusion to the water-holding leaf-bases.)

diptera, -us, -um (dip'ter-ra). Two-winged.

dipterocarpa, -us, -um (dip-ter-ro-kar'pa). Having two-winged fruit.

DIRCA (der'ka). Two species of North American shrubs of the family Thymelaeaceae, the alternate° leaves having no marginal teeth. The only cult. species is **D. palustris,** commonly called leatherwood, leather bush, wicopy, or rope bark. It is a tough-wooded, but pliable shrub, 3–5 ft. high, the leaves elliptic, 2–3 in. long, short-stalked. Flowers blooming before the leaves unfold (March–April), yellow, without petals but the calyx° petal-like, grouped in small, nearly stalkless clusters in the axils° of old wood. Fruit fleshy, egg-shaped, reddish or green. The shrub is wild in eastern N.A., mostly in moist places, but it can be grown in any ordinary garden soil and is hardy from zone° 3 southward. (*Dirca* is Greek for a mythological fountain, perhaps in allusion to their moist sites.)

DIRT GARDENER. Really to understand the fundamentals of gardening everyone should be a dirt gardener. In no other way can one get the feel and texture of soil. How you treat it will decide whether you should be a gardener at all. Its needs and handling are the foundation of all successful gardening. *See* the series of articles on SOILS and SOIL OPERATIONS.

DISBUDDING. The pinching of certain

° Special articles on the subjects indicated by an asterisk (°) will be found at the words so marked.

buds for the benefit of those left to grow. It has in reality two phases. The first is the pinching-off of leaf buds that would otherwise form perhaps unwanted shoots. It is easy to control the shape and branching of woody plants by this process. But as its objects are the same as pruning, this feature of disbudding will be found at the article PRUNING. It is also possible to change very greatly the form or growth of herbaceous plants by pinching out certain buds. *See* Pinching at TRAINING PLANTS.

A plant needing disbudding

The pinching of flower buds is in a somewhat different category. While the object is to increase the chances of the remaining flowers, it does not ordinarily change the habit or permanent shape of the plant as pinching off leaf buds always does.

Disbudding for better bloom is so common among professional gardeners that it is extraordinary how many amateurs all but ignore it. At the blooming stage, plants are at the peak of their activity and Nature is usually perfectly reckless about the number of blossoms produced, perhaps upon the sound theory that the more blooms the

Same plant disbudded for the sake of the remaining bloom

greater the chances of survival from a large crop of seeds. Disbudding is the interruption of this process.

No absolute rules can be given for disbudding because conditions vary so much in different plants and in different seasons. A little practice will inform any observant gardener whether he wants 6 fair blooms or 2 splendid ones. Scattered throughout the cultural articles in this book there are notes on the need for reducing the number of blooms for the sake of the remainder. The only general, necessary direction is that if you are to disbud, do it early. Then a minimum of the plant's strength will have passed into flower buds that are to be pinched out.

DISC = Disk.

disciformis, -e (dis-kee-for′mis). Disk-shaped.

discolor (dis′color). Of different, and usually of two distinct colors.

DISHCLOTH GOURD. *See* LUFFA.

DISH GARDEN. A terrarium (which see) without the glass top is the usual container in which so-called dish gardening is done. It involves the growing of plants that will resist ordinary room temperatures, even in steam-heated apartments, which is the most unfavorable environment of all indoor attempts to grow plants. In choosing a dish, of whatever design, be sure it has holes in the bottom to permit of proper drainage. The soil for most dish gardens can be potting mixture* 3, unless the plants used are cacti, in which case use potting mixture* 6. Dwarf forms of box, *Sarcococca ruscifolia, Myrtus, Pittosporum,* and *Serissa foetida* are useful plants for the dish garden.

disjuncta, -us, -um (dis-junck′ta). Not quite joined.

DISK (also spelled **Disc**). The structure which bears the central flowers in the head of plants of the family Compositae (which see). *See also* RECEPTACLE.

DISK FLOWER. *See* COMPOSITAE.

DISKING. *See* HARROWING.

DISPORUM (dy-spore′um). A genus of perennial herbs of the lily family, some Asiatic, the two cult. species North American. They are sometimes called fairy bells and are woodland herbs with creeping rootstocks, suited to shady places in the wild garden, preferably in rich (not very acid) humus. Leaves somewhat downy, nearly stalkless, alternate* on the stem. Flowers bell-shaped, the six segments scarcely identifiable as petals or sepals. Stamens* 6, thread-like. Fruit a fleshy red berry. (*Disporum* is from the Greek for double seed, in allusion to a technical ovary character.)

These are scarcely of much garden interest, as their flowers are too ephemeral, but they are sometimes cult. by wild-flower enthusiasts. Both bloom in the spring.

---

* Special articles on the subjects indicated by an asterisk (*) will be found at the words so marked.

lanuginosum. Liverberry. Not over 30 in. high, usually less. Leaves taper-pointed, roundish at the base, 3–4½ in. long, about 2 in. wide. Flowers greenish-yellow, about ½ in. long, solitary or in small umbels.* Eastern N.A.

oreganum. Not quite so tall as the last, the leaves smaller and heart-shaped at the base. Flowers white, about 1 in. long, solitary or in small umbels.* Western U.S.

dissecta, -us, -um (dis-sek'ta). Dissected, *i.e.,* divided into numerous fine, sometimes almost thread-like, segments.

dissitiflora, -us, -um (dis-si-ti-flow'ra). Loosely flowered; not compact.

distachya, -us, -um (dy-stack'ee-a). Two-spiked.

disticha, -us, -um (dis'ti-ka). Distichous.

DISTICHOUS. Arranged in two vertical rows or ranks on opposite sides of a stem, often called two-ranked. The leaves of some iris and of the traveler's-tree are distichous. It results in a flat, fan-like arrangement.

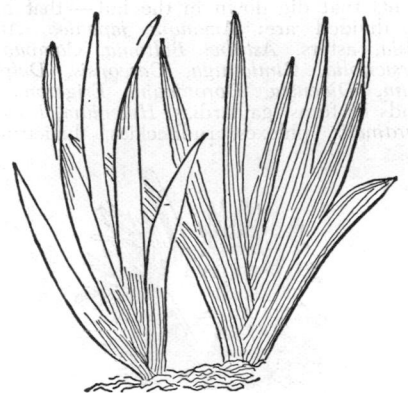

A two-ranked (distichous) arrangement of leaves

DISTICTIS (dis-tick'tis). A small genus of tropical American woody vines of the family Bignoniaceae, **D. lactiflora** somewhat cult. in Calif. for its showy clusters of purple flowers. It is a high-climbing, tendril*-bearing vine with twice — or thrice — compound* leaves. Leaflets 2 or 3, without teeth, ovalish and 1–2 in. long. Flower purple, the corolla funnel- or bell-shaped, 2–3½ in. long. The flower cluster is branched (panicle*) and very handsome, usually at the ends of the twigs. Fruit a smooth pod 2½–3½ in. long. The plant is not hardy above zone* 8, and is sometimes sold as *D. cinerea.* (*Distictis* is from Greek for twice-dotted.)

DITCH-MOSS = *Anacharis canadensis.*

DITTANY. See DICTAMNUS ALBUS.

diurna, -us, -um (dy-er'na). Day-flowering.

divaricata, -us, -um (dy-var-i-kay'ta). Divergent; spreading widely.

diversifolia, -us, -um (dy-ver-si-fō'li-a). With variable leaves or with different ones.

diversiloba, -us, -um (dy-ver-si-lō'ba). Variously lobed.

DIVIDED. Parted or cut to the base or center, as the segments of some leaves. However deeply divided, such leaves are not compound,* and bear no leaflets.

DIVISION. Division is an important method of propagation used for all kinds of plants that increase in size by suckers, rhizomes, or underground growths. The

Divide asters and similarly rooted plants as shown above.

majority of herbaceous plants spread by the development of eyes or growth buds, each of which, though attached to the parent root, makes independent growth the following season. Most bulbs also increase by division, but in a different way, the parent bulb splitting up into several. Some shrubs likewise spread by underground sucker-like shoots or root eyes which develop into independent plants though attached to the parent.

While practically all such plants can be and usually are propagated commercially from cuttings because of the greater numbers possible, division is the simplest and quickest method of propagation for the amateur. Almost all the hardy perennials lend themselves to division, including the fleshy-rooted subjects like the peony. Lift an old

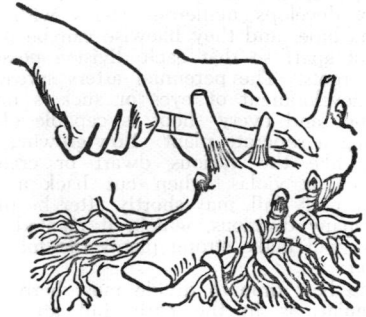

Peony rootstocks should be cut so as to provide several eyes and roots.

---

* Special articles on the subjects indicated by an asterisk (*) will be found at the words so marked.

peony root and it will be seen that it is composed of a number of crowns, each having several eyes or growth buds. These crowns may be pulled apart or severed with a knife, so that several independent pieces, each with roots, are secured. Of a different character is the dahlia, which has fleshy, tuber-like roots with the eyes or growth buds on the stems to which are attached the fleshy roots. The latter, unlike true tubers, have no eyes and will not grow if severed from the stem. A large dahlia root with several stems may be pulled apart, but the division of a one-stemmed root necessitates the use of a knife, so that each fleshy root has a portion of the woody stem attached.

The herbaceous perennials vary in their root formation. The *Delphinium* root with several stems must be divided by a knife, each stem at the base having several eyes.

Violet clumps are easily divided by pulling apart.

aid of two digging forks; tearing or pulling apart is better than chopping with a spade or axe. Evergreen low-growers can be pulled apart with the fingers. For some subjects that have woody or fleshy roots and few crowns, a spade if carefully used is the best tool.

Tallish-growing herbaceous perennials — plants that die down in the fall — that may be divided are: *Anemone japonica, Artemisia,* asters, *Astilbe, Boltonia, Campanula persicifolia, Cimicifuga, Coreopsis, Delphinium, Dicentra, Doronicum, Erigeron,* all kinds of ferns, gaillardias, *Helenium, Lobelia Cardinalis,* phloxes, rudbeckias, thalictrums,

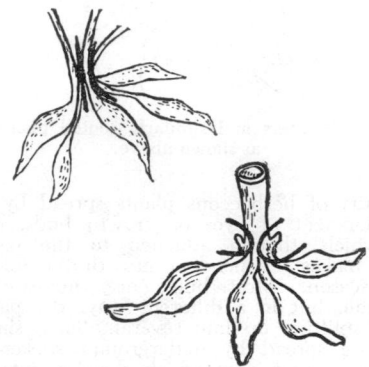

In dividing dahlia roots it is essential to see that part of the bud-bearing stem (*i.e.*, with "eyes") is secured. The upper figure shows a clump which may or may not have eyes; the lower figure has eyes and should be divided where indicated.

Phlox and similar clumps are best divided by cutting with a spade.

Helleborus niger, like the peony, develops crowns, but in larger numbers, and these may readily be pulled or cut apart. Some irises, too, can easily be divided. The tall phlox develops numerous stems with eyes at the base, and they likewise can be pulled or cut apart so that each division possesses some roots. The perennial asters spread by the development of eyes or suckers underground, and every shoot is capable of becoming a separate plant. Low-growing subjects, like the various dwarf or creeping phloxes or violas, when cut back a little in the early fall, may shortly after be pulled into many divisions, which, if planted right away, will make strong plants the following season.

The best time to divide most herbaceous perennials is in the early fall after they are through blooming or early in the spring. Cut them to the ground and lift, and if large and woody, tear them apart by the

Trollius, and *Veronica longifolia subsessilis* and *V. spicata.* A few low-growing, more or less evergreen subjects easily divided are: *Androsace, Arabis, Aubrieta, Campanula gar-*

Shrubs that bear suckers or creeping roots should be divided by cutting as indicated

---

* Special articles on the subjects indicated by an asterisk (*) will be found at the words so marked.

ganica and kindred types, geums, heucheras, *Phlox subulata* and kindred sorts, primulas, pyrethrums, saxifrages, sedums, sempervivums, and violas.

Some perennials have tuber-like roots which are readily separated, among the most common being aconitums, *Liatris,* and montbretias. Corm-rooted subjects like *Gladiolus* may be divided or cut into several pieces, but it is not practiced except when rare forms have to be increased more rapidly than the natural increase by bulblets allows. Shrubs that spread by underground shoots are *Symphoricarpos albus, Kerria japonica, Clethra alnifolia,* etc. Cut off at the point of union, these shoots quickly make plants. — T. A. W. See also PROPAGATION.

DIZYGOTHECA (di-zee-go-thee′ka). Tender, greenhouse foliage plants of the family Araliaceae, probably from the Pacific Islands, but of uncertain identity, as they rarely flower in cult. They are shrubby plants with no spines and compound* leaves, the leaflets arranged finger-fashion and very variable. Sometimes the leaflets are broad and leathery, others, on the same plant or at a different age, being graceful, threadlike and drooping. Whether any of the plants below really belong here is still uncertain. (*Dizygotheca* is from the Greek for having double the usual number of anther* cells.) Often offered as *Aralia.*

elegantissima. Leaflets 7–11, narrow or thread-like, drooping, the leafstalk mottled white.

kerchoveana. Leaflets 7–11, broad (up to ½ in. wide), the margins conspicuously notched, the leafstalks mottled.

veitchi. Leaflets 9–11, wavy-margined or toothed, about ¼ in. wide, reddish beneath. There is also a variety with much narrower leaflets, white-striped along the midrib.

DOCK. See RUMEX.

DOCKMACKIE = *Viburnum acerifolium.*

DODDER. Sprawling, yellow, thread-like plants, parasitic on the foliage of other plants, often completely smothering them. See HOST. As a garden pest dodder is to be controlled only by pulling it out.

dodecandra, -us, -um (do-deck-an′dra). Having 12 stamens.

DODECATHEON (do-deck-kath′ee-on). Beautiful North American wild flowers comprising perhaps 30 species, family Primulaceae, a few of which are cult. in the wild garden or in the rock garden. They are perennial, essentially stemless herbs with basal leaves and cyclamen-like, nodding flowers. Leaves wavy-margined, without teeth, usually narrowed at the base into a winged stalk. Flowers in a small terminal cluster (umbel*) at the end of a stalk arising from the ground. Sepals* 5, turned backwards. Corolla with a very short tube, the 5 lobes turned backwards. Stamens* 5, the anthers* united into a characteristic cone-shaped structure. Fruit a 5-valved capsule. In various sections of the country these plants are called shooting star, Ameri-

can cowslip, and bird bills. (*Dodecatheon* is from the Greek for 12 gods and of no significance here.)

The woodland species cannot be grown successfully in the open border nor in heavy soils. They prefer rich, sandy, woods soil and partial shade. Those suited to the rock garden are so indicated and their culture should be sought at ROCK GARDEN. Easily propagated by division.

alpinum. Not over 6 in. high, the leaves about 4 in. long. Flowers purple, whitish toward the yellow-zoned base and with a purple band. Pacific Coast mountains. A rock garden species.

clevelandi. A perennial herb from southern Calif. and of uncertain culture elsewhere. Leaves 2–2½ in. long. Flowers purple or whitish, the base yellow. The stamens* are purplish, but the cone-like collection of anthers* is yellow.

dentatum. Resembling *D. Meadia,* but the leaves toothed. Flowers white, the base of each petal purple-spotted. Utah to Ore., and best grown in the wild garden or rock garden.

hendersoni. Mosquito bills; called also sailor caps*. Somewhat similar to the last, but the anthers* deeper yellow. The plant is also of easier cult., as it is native from Calif. to Wash.

jeffreyi. Sierra shooting star. Leaves nearly 12 in. long. Flowers deep reddish-purple throughout. Western N.A., best grown in the rock garden.

latilobum. Perhaps only a western var. of *D. Meadia.* Leaves nearly 10 in. long. Flowers yellowish-white, the anthers* purple. Ore. and Wash.

Meadia. Shooting star; also called prairie pointer. Leaves 4–6 in. long. Flowers rose-pink, whitish at the base. Stamens reddish-yellow, but the cone-like collection of anthers* purple. A wild garden plant native from Pa. to Tex. and Wis.

pauciflorum. A smooth perennial, not over 8 in. high. Leaves spoon-shaped or narrower, about 3 in. long, rarely with marginal teeth. Flowers few in a cluster (umbel*), mostly pale lilac, but yellow on the tube and purplish at the throat. Western N.A. June.

radicatum. A rock garden herb, the leaves 4–5 in. long. Flowers rose-pink or reddish, the cone-like collections of anthers purple. Central and southwestern U.S.

vulgare = *D. pauciflorum.*

DODONAEA (do-do-nee′a). A genus of 50 species of tropical and chiefly Australian shrubs and trees of the family Sapindaceae, two grown for ornament in zones* 8 and 9, but of secondary hort. significance. They have alternate* leaves, not compound in those below, without marginal teeth. Flowers small, often of one sex only, without petals, the 3–7 sepals inconspicuous. Stamens 8. Fruit an angled capsule.* (Named for Rembert Dodoens, Dutch physician.)

These bushes, which usually have sticky foliage, are not uncommon in sub-tropical gardens, especially in Fla. and Calif. They are of easy cult. and not particularly attractive. In Aust., and sometimes here, they are called hop-bush.

cuneata. A much-branched shrub, the leaves oblongish, ½–1 in. long, wedge-shaped at the

---

* Special articles on the subjects indicated by an asterisk (*) will be found at the words so marked.

base. Flowers mostly in terminal, sometimes branched clusters (racemes*), not showy. Aust.

viscosa. Akeake. A shrub, 8–12 ft. high. Leaves oblongish, 3–4 in. long, about an inch wide. Flowers in generally terminal clusters (racemes*), not showy. Resistant to smog and drought in Calif. Of uncertain nativity, perhaps tropical American, but certainly wild in New Zealand from whence comes the vernacular akeake.

DODONAEACEAE. See SAPINDACEAE.

DOGBANE; DOGBANE FAMILY. See APOCYNUM and APOCYNACEAE.

DOG BENT. See AGROSTIS CANINA.

DOGBERRY = *Ilex verticillata.* See HOLLY.

DOG FENNEL = Mayweed. See the list at WEEDS.

DOG-HOBBLE = *Leucothoë catesbaei.*

DOG-PLUM = *Clintonia umbellulata.*

DOG ROSE = *Rosa canina.*

DOGS. To prevent dogs from injuring plants, either by burying bones or urinating on foliage, there are several repellants on the market, which must be used only as directed on the container as some of the chemicals are injurious to plants in improper concentrations. For the fondness of dogs for tree trunks, *see* STREET TREES.

DOGTOOTH VIOLET. See ERYTHRONIUM.

DOGWOOD; DOGWOOD FAMILY. See CORNUS and CORNACEAE.

dolabrata, -us, -um (do-la-bray′ta). Hatchet-shaped.

DOLICHOS (dō′li-kos). A large genus of tropical, mostly herbaceous vines of the pea family, important in the tropics as forage plants, but of secondary hort. interest. They have compound* leaves with 3 leaflets. Flowers pea-like, showy, often solitary or a few clustered in the leaf axils.* Fruit a curved, flat, often beaked legume.* (*Dolichos* is an old Greek name for a bean.)

Grown only as ornamental vines in the U.S., where the seeds should be sown as for any annual vine. See VINES. They require more heat than is found in the North, and are most successful from zone* 7 southward.

Lablab. Hyacinth bean; also called bonavist and lablab. A perennial (grown as an annual) vine, the stems often 30 ft. long, but usually half this. Leaflets broadly oval, the side ones lopsided, and 3–6 in. long. Flowers purple or white, ¾–1 in. long. Pod flat, 1–2½ in. long, papery and beaked, the seeds black or white. Old World tropics and of considerable economic importance there; *i.e.,* food, forage, acids, etc.; here only an ornamental.

lignosus. Australian pea. Less common in cult., and an evergreen, somewhat woody vine. Leaflets more or less triangular oval, 1–1½ in. long. Flowers white or rose-purple, ⅓ in. long. Pod about 1 in. long, the seeds black. Probably tropical Asia, but now widely distributed.

DOMBEYA (dom′bee-a). Extremely showy, African shrubs and trees of the fam-

ily Sterculiaceae, comprising over 100 species, two of which are cult. in zones* 8 and 9 for their very handsome flowers, rarely in greenhouses northward. They have large, angled, alternate* leaves, often long-stalked. Flowers usually in dense heads, sometimes in loose clusters (cymes*), below which are often 3 bracts.* Petals 5 and flat. Stamens many, some infertile, others joined into a tube. Fruit a 5-valved capsule.* (Named for Joseph Dombey, French botanist.)

These valuable, quick-growing shrubs and trees are popular in Fla., where they are grown on a variety of soils. Easily propagated by seeds, or by cuttings over bottom-heat.* They bloom in winter in Fla.

punctata. A shrub 6–10 ft. high. Leaves angled or toothed on the margin, densely hairy beneath. Flowers pink, fragrant, in umbel-like but not profuse clusters. Mauritius.

wallichi. A tree up to 30 ft. and the most popular in cult. Leaves somewhat 3-lobed, roundish, nearly 12 in. wide, long-stalked. Flowers pink, about 2 in. wide, in dense, umbel*-like, hanging clusters. Madagascar and tropical Africa.

domestica, -us, -um (do-mes′ti-ka). Domesticated; not wild.

DOMINANT. The exclusion or partial exclusion of any effect from the other member of a cross; the opposite from *recessive.* A character is often referred to as dominant or recessive as tall (dominant) and dwarf (recessive) garden peas or as the *dominance* of tall over dwarf. Dominance is seldom complete, most hybrids showing imperfect dominance, or, as it is often called, blending. In such cases, the height is intermediate between the parents, or the color of the flower may be diluted. Thus yellow × white in certain four-o'clock crosses is light yellow. Dominant variations are far less common than recessive variations, and most of the valuable characteristics that distinguish wild from cultivated plants are recessive variations.—O. E. W.

Donax (dō′nacks). Classical name for the reed, which may have been the cat-tail; now applied to another plant. See ARUNDO.

DOODIA (doo′di-a). A genus of chiefly Australasian, dwarf, dense-growing ferns of the family Polypodiaceae, **D. aspera,** the hacksaw fern, popular as a window box and house plant. It is not usually over 12 in. high, often half this, and has rigid, stiffish fronds that are deeply cut into fine segments, but not compound.* Segments 1½–3 in. long, very rough. Spore cases in one or two rows between the midrib and the margins of the segments. Aust. Of easy culture in the cool greenhouse, but it does not like water standing at its roots and the glass should be shaded. *See* FERNS AND FERN GARDENING. (Named for Samuel Doody, London apothecary.)

DORMANCY. See HARDINESS.

DORONICUM (do-ron′i-kum). Eurasian perennial herbs of the family Compositae,

---

* Special articles on the subjects indicated by an asterisk (*) will be found at the words so marked.

comprising 20–30 species, of which a few are widely grown garden plants under the name leopard's-bane. They are stout, often unbranched herbs with basal, and with alternate* stem leaves, the latter often clasping. Flower heads yellow, long-stalked, with a single row of ray* flowers. (*Doronicum* is a Latinized version of the Arabic name for these plants; it is also a specific name for a *Senecio*.)

The leopard's-banes are of very simple cult. in the border or flower bed, and are considerably grown, especially in the well-filled perennial border; doing better in the north than southward. Easily propagated by division. They are mostly spring-blooming.

caucasicum. A single-stemmed herb 1–2 ft. high, the leaves coarsely toothed and hairy, the basal ones heart-shaped and long-stalked. Flower head usually only 1, about 2 in. wide, long-stalked at the end of the main stem. Caucasus and elsewhere in southern Eu.

clusi. Nearly 2 ft. high, the stem leaves clasping or partly so, remotely or not at all toothed. Flower heads solitary. Southern Eu.

plantagineum. The most popular of the cult. leopard's-banes, and often somewhat branching, 18–30 in. high. Stem leaves stalkless, but not clasping, the basal leaves ovalish or oblong, the base narrowed into a winged stalk. Flower heads more numerous, terminating most branches, 1½–4 in. wide. Eu. There are several named forms, some with many more than a single row of rays and more handsome garden plants than the typical species.

DOROTHEANTHUS. *See* MESEMBRYANTHEMUM.

DORSAL. The back, or outside, or under side of an organ; as the dorsal side of a leaf is the under side of it. *See* VENTRAL.

DORYALIS = *Dovyalis*.

DORYANTHES (dor-i-an'theez). A genus of Australian desert plants of the family Amaryllidaceae, little known in the U.S. outside of Calif. or Fla., where they are cult. for ornament. They much resemble the century plant (*Agave*) in having a basal rosette of thick, fleshy, but not prickly-margined, leaves. There is an immense central stalk topped by a large cluster of showy, red flowers. Petals and sepals distinct. Fruit a capsule.* (*Doryanthes* is from the Greek for spear and flower.) They are commonly called spear lily.

For culture *see* AGAVE, to which they are related.

excelsa. Torch lily. Leaves sword-shaped, 2–4 ft. long, numerous. Flowering stalk 12–18 ft. high, the flowers 4 in. long, in dense heads nearly 1 ft. wide, its bracts* green.

palmeri. Leaves very narrow, up to 6 ft. long, the outer arching, the inner erect and hugging the flowering stem which may be 25 ft. high. Flower cluster branched (a panicle*), nearly 3 ft. long, the flowers about 21 in. long, scarlet. An extremely handsome plant in bloom.

DOUBLE FLOWERS. Producing more, and usually much more, than the usual number of petals. The ordinary single flower has, usually, a definite number of petals (or rays in a head), which are pretty apt to be uniform. There are, for instance, 5 petals in an ordinary wild rose. But for some cause, mostly quite unknown, a plant will occasionally produce a flower with more than the usual number of petals. Such plants are a boon to the breeder, whether they happen to be garden possibilities at the moment or not. For they have the capacity to vary in the direction of producing more petals. Most of the double-flowered garden plants have been derived from such variants. The production of petals goes so far that some flowers have lost stamens or pistils, or even both. Double flowers are very common in the rose, peony, garden aster, dahlia, and hundreds of others. Double flowers are extremely rare among wild plants.

DOUBLE ORANGE DAISY = *Erigeron aurantiacus*.

DOUBLE WORKING = Double Grafting. *See* GRAFTING.

DOUGLAS FIR. *See* PSEUDOTSUGA.

DOUGLASIA (dug-las'si-a). A small genus of European and N.A. alpine plants of the family Primulaceae, suited to the rock garden. They are tufted,* more or less prostrate perennial herbs with a basal rosette of small, narrow, hairy leaves. Flowers 1 or 2, at the end of a short stalk 2 in. high, arising from the rosette. Corolla yellow or red, the tube long. Fruit a small capsule. The plants resemble *Androsace* and need the same culture. *See* ROCK GARDEN. (Named for David Douglas, Scotch botanist who explored the Northwest.)

laevigata. Leaves scarcely ¼ in. long, imbricated.* Flowers in a sparse umbel,* the tube long, bright red. Ore. and Wash. Suited only to the rock garden.

montana. A densely tufted perennial, with basal, tiny leaves that are scarcely ⅓ in. long and tightly overlapping. Flowers solitary (or 2 or 3 rarely), scarcely ½ in. long, rose-purple. Alpine summits of western U.S. May–June.

vitaliana. A prostrate perennial, the stems tipped with rosettes of small, narrow leaves which are somewhat hairy. Flowers nearly stalkless, yellow, solitary, or a few in a sparse cluster. European Alps and Pyrenees. Sometimes offered as *Androsace vitaliana*.

DOVE FLOWER; DOVE ORCHID = *Peristeria elata*.

DOVE TREE = *Davidia involucrata*.

DOVYALIS (do-vi-ā'lis). A genus of 12 species of Old World tropical shrubs or small trees of the family Flacourtiaceae, two of them cult. in Fla. and Calif. as the source of minor fruits. They have alternate,* short-stalked leaves and inconspicuous, small flowers, the male and female on different plants. (For details *see* FLACOURTIACEAE.) Fruit an edible, but acid, berry. (*Dovyalis* is of unknown origin.) Often called *Aberia* and sometimes spelled *Doryalis*.

Both of those below must have male plants interspersed with female ones to ensure the

---

* Special articles on the subjects indicated by an asterisk (*) will be found at the words so marked.

latter setting fruit. They are not particular as to soils, doing very well on the sandy soils of Fla. The kitambilla can be grown up to the northern edge of zone* 8, but the kei-apple is not so hardy. Propagated by seeds or by shield budding.

Caffra. Kei-apple; also called umkokolo. A thorny shrub or small tree 10–20 ft. high, the thorns long and stiff. Leaves often clustered at the base of the thorn, 1½–2 in. long. Flowers greenish. Fruit nearly round, about 1 in. in diameter, yellow, the juicy pulp also yellow, cranberry-flavored and good only when cooked. S. Af.

hebecarpa. Kitambilla; also called Ceylon gooseberry. About the same size as *D. Caffra*, but more branched. Leaves 3–4 in. long. Fruit about 1 in. in diameter, velvety, maroon-purple, less acid than the kei-apple. India and Ceylon.

DOWNINGIA (down-in'ji-a). Rather showy, low-growing, annual herbs of the family Lobeliaceae, the two cult. species from the Pacific Coast, others in S.A. Leaves alternate,* without teeth, diminishing upward into small bracts.* Flowers stalkless in the axils* of the upper bracts. Corolla irregular * and 2-lipped, but tubular below. Upper lip much narrower than the 3-lobed lower lip. Stamens 5. Fruit a capsule splitting lengthwise, tipped by the leafy, persistent lobes of the calyx.* (Named for Andrew Jackson Downing, American horticulturist.)

These attractive little summer-blooming plants are hardy annuals. For their culture *see* ANNUALS.

elegans. Not over 7 in. high. Leaves oblongish, ½–¾ in. long. Flowers light blue, but white-throated and the throat streaked green or yellow, the stamens* long-protruding. Wash. to Calif.

pulchella. From 4–6 in. high. Leaves oblongish or ovalish, about ½ in. long. Flowers deep blue, the center of the lower lip white, splotched yellow and purple, the stamens scarcely protruding. Ore. to Calif.

DOWNY. Softly and weakly hairy.

DOWNY MILDEW. A disease caused by a specific group of fungi and not to be confused with powdery mildew.* The downy mildew diseases usually cause a sudden blackening of spots on the leaves. Very often a gray fungus growth will then appear on the lower surface of the leaf directly beneath the black spot. The disease may be serious on grape, lima bean, and melons (which see). A similar disease on tomato and potato is referred to as late blight even though it is actually a downy mildew.

The downy mildew disease is spread by wind-blown spores* and is rather easily controlled by proper applications of zineb or maneb (*see* FUNGICIDES and SPRAYS AND DUSTS).

DOWNY MYRTLE = *Rhodomyrtus tomentosa*.

DOXANTHA (docks-an'tha). Two species of tropical American woody vines of the family Bignoniaceae, one of them, **D. Unguis-cati**, the cat's-claw, grown in the South and in greenhouses northward. It is a handsome vine with compound,* evergreen leaves composed of 2 leaflets and a terminal, 3-parted, claw-like tendril* by which it clings to supports. Flowers showy, solitary or in small clusters (racemes*), the corolla trumpet-shaped, about 2 in. long, yellow, but the throat orange-streaked. Fruit a narrow pod nearly 12 in. long. Argentina. It is hardy up to the edge of zone* 7, and north of this should be in the cool greenhouse in potting mixture* 4. An extremely handsome vine sometimes offered as *Bignonia Unguis-cati* or *B. tweediana*. (*Doxantha* is from the Greek for glory flower.)

DRABA (drah'ba). Whitlow grass is a general name for perhaps 250 species of small, usually tufted,* herbs of the mustard family, a few of which are cult. in the rock garden, rarely in borders. They are mostly spring-blooming annuals or perennials from the north temperate zone, with the small leaves chiefly in basal rosettes, and nearly always hairy. Flowers small, but usually numerous and grouped in racemes*; white, yellow, or pinkish-purple. Petals 4. Fruit a small pod. (*Draba* is an old Greek name for some cress.)

All of the drabas below are suited only to the rock garden (which see for their culture).

aizoides. A tufted perennial, not over 4 in. high. Leaves narrow, pointed, without teeth, about ½ in. long. Flowers yellow. Mountains of southern Eu.

cuspidata. A tufted perennial, not over 4 in. high. Leaves narrow, blunt, about ½ in. long. Flowers purplish-pink. Mountains of southern Eu.

fladnizensis. A tufted perennial, making flattish cushions not over 3 in. high. Leaves oblongish, blunt, scarcely ½ in. long. Flowers greenish-white. Mountaintops of Eu. and N.A. and in the Arctic.

hirta. A perennial 5–10 in. high. Leaves narrow, sometimes toothed at the tip, ½–¾ in. long. Flowers white. Northern Eurasia.

olympica. A cushion-like, tufted perennial, 2–4 in. high. Leaves scarcely ¼ in. long, hairy on the margins. Flowers orange. Southern Eu.

repens = *Draba sibirica*.

rigida. A low tufted perennial, the clumps not over 3 in. wide. Leaves scarcely ½ in. long, stiff, almost prickly, hairy on the margin. Flower stalk scarcely 3 in. high. Flowers small, in a dense cluster (corymb*), golden yellow. Southeastern Eu. May–June.

sibirica. Stems more or less prostrate and often 12 in. long. Leaves not in rosettes, oblongish, hairy, pointed and without teeth. Flowers yellow on slender, upright stems. Siberia and in the Caucasus.

drabifolia, -us, -um (dra-bi-fō'li-a). Having leaves like the genus *Draba*.

DRACAENA (dra-see'na). Handsome foliage plants of the lily family, chiefly from the Old World tropics, comprising perhaps 50 species, of which a few are popular greenhouse subjects. They are tree-like, with a crown of leaves suggesting a palm, or more often shrubby and grown in pots for their handsome foliage. Leaves narrow and sword-shaped or wider and with a distinct stalk.

---

* Special articles on the subjects indicated by an asterisk (*) will be found at the words so marked.

Flowers small, greenish, yellowish or red, rarely produced in greenhouse specimens. They differ only in technical characters from *Cordyline,* with which the cult. species are often confused. Petals and sepals 6 in all, not easily separable as such. Stamens 6. Fruit a 1–3-seeded berry. (*Dracaena* is from the Greek for female dragon, in reference to the second species.)

The dracaenas, especially popular for house decoration and for summer bedding, are only to be grown in the greenhouse in the North, but do well outdoors in southern Fla. and Calif. For their culture and propagation see CORDYLINE.

australis = *Cordyline australis.*

deremensis. A branched shrub-like plant, 8–15 ft. high, with unpleasantly scented leaves 18 in. long and about 2 in. wide, narrowed into a stalk-like base. Flowers small, red, ill-scented, in a large branched cluster (panicle*). Tropical Af. The form usually offcred is the *var.* **warnecki,** which is of uncertain status.

Draco. Dragon tree. Rare in cult., but interesting as being the famous dragon tree of the Canary Islands, known to the Greeks before the Christian era. It is a gigantic tree, not over 60 ft. high, but the trunk nearly 20 ft. in diameter. Leaves bluish-green, about 2 ft. long and 1½ in. wide. Flowers greenish. Fruit orange. Canary Islands. Planted outdoors in Calif., but rare in greenhouses and very slow-growing. It was long thought to be the source of commercial dragon's blood.

fragrans. A very common greenhouse plant, usually small and unbranched, but in maturity tree-like, up to 20 ft., and branched. Leaves handsome, in a terminal, rosette-like cluster, about 3 ft. long and 4 in. wide, green, or, in several hort. varieties, variously whitestriped or yellow-margined, but not banded crosswise. Flowers (rare in greenhouse plants) yellowish, fragrant. Central Af.

godseffiana. Somewhat similar, but the leaves not over 10 in. long, about 2½ in. wide, narrowed into a channeled stalk, green and irregularly ₒplotched or banded crosswise with white. Flowers, when produced, greenish-yellow. Central Af. A popular foliage plant.

goldieana. Leaves long-stalked, ovalish, 4–8 in. long, about 4 in. wide, short-pointed, green, but banded crosswise with gray-green. Flowers (rare in the greenhouse) white. Central Af.

sanderiana. A showy, commonly cult. greenhouse or house plant with slender stem and white-margined leaves 7–10 in. long and about 1 in. wide, the leafstalks 1–3 in. long. Central Af. In cult. in the greenhouse it is likely to become leggy,* and should then be propagated by cuttings.

dracaenoides (dra-see-noy′deez; but *see* OÏDES). *Dracaena*-like.

Draco (dray′ko). A specific name meaning dragon and applied to the dragon tree. See DRACAENA.

DRACOCEPHALUM (dra-ko-seff′a-lum). The dragonheads, so called from the shape of their flowers, comprise about 40 species of herbs of the mint family, a few grown in the flower garden. The cult. species are summer-blooming, moderate-sized herbs with opposite* leaves and square stems. Flowers irregular,* 2-lipped,* crowded in dense heads in the leaf axils* or in terminal spikes (for details see LABIATAE). The upper lip is arched and notched, the lower 3-divided. (*Dracocephalum* is Greek for a dragon's head.)

All those below, except *D. Moldavica,* are perennials of easy culture in the open border, but prefer partial shade and a fairly moist site. They can be divided in spring or fall.

grandiflorum. A handsome Siberian herb 6–12 in. high. Leaves oblongish, toothed, diminishing upward. Flowers nearly 2 in. long, blue, hairy, in terminal spikes.*

Moldavica. A hardy annual, 12–18 in. high. Leaves lance-shaped, toothed, 1–1½ in. long. Flowers bluish-violet, or white, usually less than 1 in. long, in a long, leafy cluster (raceme*). For culture see ANNUALS. Eurasia.

nutans. A perennial 8–12 in. high. Leaves ovalish or oblong, 1–2 in. long, toothed. Flowers about ½ in. long, blue, in short, terminal spikes. Siberia. There is also a white-flowered variety which is shaded with blue.

sibiricum. A stout perennial, 1–3 ft. high, the oblong leaves 2–4 in. long, toothed, green above, minutely golden glandular beneath. Flowers in interrupted whorls,* the cluster 5–10 in. long. Corolla bluish-lavender, about 1 in. long. Eastern As. Usually offered as *Nepeta macrantha.*

virginianum. False dragonhead or obedient plant is a tall (4 ft.), wand-like herb with 4-sided stems and opposite,* oblongish, toothed leaves, 3–5 in. long. Flowers purple-red, often rose-pink or even lilac, in a terminal, leafy cluster (spike*), nearly 8 in. long and showy. Corolla tubular, inflated upward, 2-lipped,* but the lips small. The *var.* **album** has white flowers; *var.* **giganteum** grows up to 7 ft. high; and the *var.* **grandiflorum** has bright pink flowers. All are rather commonly cult. in the flower border and are of easy culture. They may be propagated by division of the clumps. Eastern N.A. Summer. Sometimes known as *Physostegia.*

DRACONTIUM (dra-kon′she-um). A specific name derived from the genus *Dracontium,* which is of little garden interest. See ARISAEMA.

DRACUNCULUS (dra-kun′kew-lus). A small group of putrid-smelling aroids* from the Mediterranean region, **D. vulgaris,** the green dragon, sometimes cult. in the greenhouse or outdoors south of zone* 7. It has a tuberous rootstock and a few, basal, long-stalked leaves that are deeply cleft into 11–15 segments, the whole leaf often 12 in. wide. Flowers crowded upon a spadix* (for details see ARACEAE), which is surrounded by a spathe* that is tubular, green and purple-striped at the base, but purple at the apex and nearly 12 in. long. When in bloom, the odor is offensive. Fruit fleshy. More a curiosity than a garden asset. (*Dracunculus* is Latin for a dragon; also a specific name at *Artemisia.*)

DRAGONHEAD. See DRACOCEPHALUM.

DRAGONROOT = *Arisaema Dracontium.*

DRAGON'S-MOUTH = *Arethusa bulbosa.*

DRAGON SPRUCE = *Picea asperata.* See SPRUCE.

---

* Special articles on the subjects indicated by an asterisk (*) will be found at the words so marked.

DRAGON'S-TONGUE = *Chimaphila maculata.*

DRAGON TREE = *Dracaena Draco.*

DRAINING. The underdraining of land is usually too expensive to be worth undertaking. But there are tracts where the water-table is so near the surface that it must be carried off or lowered to prevent ordinary garden plants from being killed by water suffocation.

While the regulation of excess water under the surface demands an engineer or surveyor if it is to be done on any large scale, the home gardener can often do for himself all that is necessary. First of all, determine, after a dry spell, how much of the site is really water-soaked. This can easily be seen, as capillarity will keep the surface soil moist or even muddy in such places, long after the rest of your garden is already showing a dry or dryish surface.

Having determined the area of water-soaked soil, the next step is to see if, upon your own land, there is an outlet low enough to be well below the lowest part of your proposed drainage system. If these two factors are favorable, it will be possible to make an effective system. And even if there is no natural outlet such as a stream or pond, it is sometimes possible, especially in suburban areas, to empty your drainage system into a town main.

Assuming that the area is known and a drainage outlet is provided for, there then comes the question of grade and depth and spacing of the tile drains and their diameter. These tiles are made for the purpose, without collars or sleeves, and baked enough so that practically no water enters through their pores as it does through the side of a flower pot.

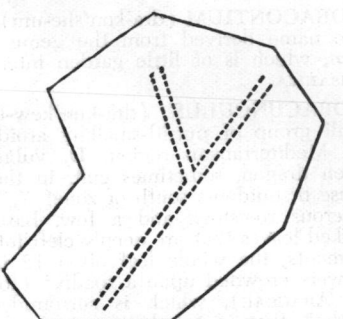

A simple plan for draining a small area. Usually only a few lateral branches are needed.

If the wet area is a small one (25 × 25 ft.), a single line of tile drains will often be enough. But if the area is larger, especially if of irregular shape, a more elaborate system of laterals will be necessary.

Some gardeners prefer to solve the draining difficulty by merely digging a ditch. Others improve upon this by filling up the ditch with loose stones. Such makeshifts are inadvisable, on the score both of looks and efficiency. Tile drains properly laid are buried out of sight and will last almost indefinitely.

DEPTH AND PITCH. Drains should not be nearer than 2 ft. below the surface, nor, except in special cases, more than 3 ft. deep. It is better not to use drains of less than 4 in. diameter, and if there is to be only a single line, it is better to use 6-in. pipe.

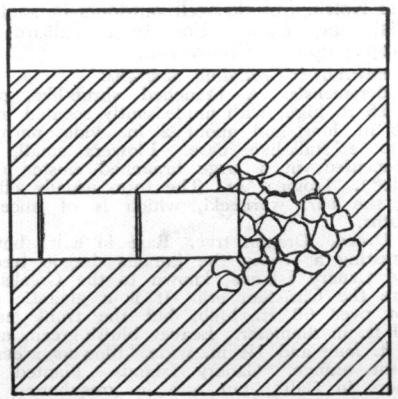

See that the upper end of the tile drain is set in a collection of stones or loose gravel to allow water but not soil to get in.

The pitch at which the system is laid is naturally of the greatest importance. Sometimes the general grade of the land will determine this, but usually the area to be drained is level enough to hold too much standing water and the pitch of the system can be arranged as desired.

A good general rule is that the system shall fall at least 3 in. in each 100 ft. That allows a free flow through the tile and a current sufficiently active to carry off any fine soil particles that may seep into the system. It requires considerable ingenuity to determine accurately the proper levels, but it can be done with a spirit level and a string stretched tightly over the trench. Of course an engineer will do it better, but any intelligent gardener can plan his own system with a little care.

Assuming that only one line of tile is to be laid, dig a trench of the proper depth and pitch to carry off the excess water. If in a nice garden, separate topsoil and subsoil as you dig, so that refilling will not leave the subsoil on the top. Then place the drains end to end as closely as possible. They are not made to "nest" like sewer pipe, but they must be so tightly placed end to end that only water and not soil will seep in at the joints.

Having laid the tile, it is wiser, before rough filling of the trench, to cover every joint carefully with a little coarse soil or

* Special articles on the subjects indicated by an asterisk (*) will be found at the words so marked.

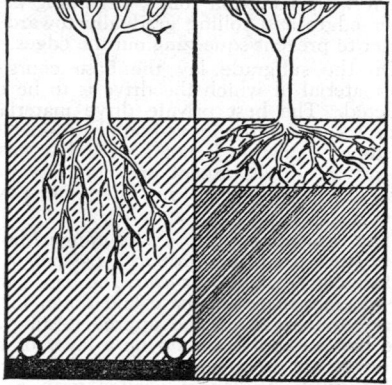

At the right a root system prevented from developing by a water table too high. At the left the same area drained so the roots can develop.

cinders or tar paper. And any irregularity in the bottom of the trench must be taken up as each tile is laid. Either scoop out enough, or if too deep, put the tile on a stone or brick to bring it exactly at the desired depth below your taut string. All this needs care and patience. But properly done, it will transform boggy, useless land into a garden site.

There then remains only the final filling of the trench which may be cinders below but earth above. See also that the outlet is kept free of leaves and debris. The system will then be in operation. It will work no wonders at first. But as the years go on, the underdrainage will gradually be carried by your system instead of seeping through the ground generally.

DRAW; DRAWING. A term of somewhat limited application in the propagation of the sweet potato (which see). A draw is a slip in the propagating bed and drawing is the pulling of such slips, with their roots, for planting in the field.

DRAWN. *See* LEGGY.

DRESSING. The trimming and preparation of nursery stock for grafting, budding, or for making cuttings. *See* these articles for the details. It is also applied to the spreading of manure, lime, fertilizer, etc.

DRIED FLOWERS. Most of the everlastings (which see) and a few of the finer grasses that hold their panicles (*see* AGROSTIS NEBULOSA, BRIZA, ERAGROSTIS, and PANICUM) make good subjects for dried flowers. Their use is dependent upon their holding their color or form or both when perfectly dry. The best method is to dry them slowly, in the shade, and not over artificial heat. Hang them with heads down in an ordinary living room (not over a radiator) until they are brittle, after which they must be handled carefully. The only real

objection to them is the dust they gather. *See also* HONESTY and SYNGONANTHUS.

The fad for dyeing dried flowers has little to recommend it, but is widely practiced. Various aniline dyes can be used, a common one being the green used for carnations on St. Patrick's Day. And the foliage of the butcher's-broom (*Ruscus aculeatus*) is generally colored red for Christmas decorations, after first being bleached white. The dyes should be sprayed on the dried flowers if they are fragile, but many can simply be dipped in a bath of the desired dye. *See* DYEING FLOWERS.

DRIED FRUITS AND VEGETABLES. Except in the desert regions, it is usually impossible to dry fruits and vegetables outdoors in the U.S. Artificial heat is therefore necessary, but this must not be too violent, as drying, not cooking, is the object. For the home gardener the best drying apparatus is the kitchen range if it burns coal or cheap electricity. Put the fruit in slat racks, which will allow plenty of air circulation, as the process involves driving off much moisture.

The racks can be put in the oven, leaving the door open and keeping the temperature between 160° and 190°. A slower method is to suspend the racks over the stove where, of course, there is merely a warm-air current passing through them. When thoroughly dry, the material must be stored in some place where there will be no re-absorption of moisture. Among the best for drying are apple rings, halved pears, apricots (in Calif.), currants, beans, shredded carrots, and peas. The process is troublesome but worth the effort to preserve an excess harvest.

DRILL. A trench in which seeds are planted. Short and shallow ones can be made with a hoe or sharp stick. But much better drills can be made with a proper attachment to a wheel cultivator. Do not, generally speaking, make your drills until ready to plant them, otherwise they become sun-baked and dry.

DRIMYS. A genus of perhaps 20 species of evergreen shrubs and trees of the magnolia family, only one, **D. winteri**, the Winter's bark, of any hort. interest. It is found from Mex. to Cape Horn, and was once used in medicine. It is a tree up to 50 ft. in the wild, but shorter as cult. where it must be confined to zone* 9 or sheltered places in zone* 8. Leaves elliptic, without teeth, highly aromatic. Flowers jasmine-scented, about 1 in. wide, borne in small umbels.* Fruit a berry. It was named for a Captain John Winter who first discovered it at the Straits of Magellan in 1579. (*Drimys* is from the Greek for acrid or bitter, in allusion to their bitter bark.)

DRIP. Rain water dripping off certain trees has a bad effect upon some garden plants and often on the lawn. Tests of the run-off from oaks, pines, firs, beeches, spruces, and the walnut show clearly that the acid dissolved from bark, twigs, or leaves is so highly concentrated that it injures some garden plants. This is especially true of the first run-off following a prolonged drought. Nothing, of course, can be done about this, but in planting the tree it is well to keep its run-off in mind. The acidity of the run-off may be tested in the same way as soil (see ACID AND ALKALI SOILS). The often poisonous drip from city-smoke-infested trees, is more serious. For a list of plants that will stand this worst form of drip see SHADY GARDEN. Many rock garden plants do not tolerate drip.

DRIVES. There are five essential factors in the design of drives — alignment, width, grade, road-bed construction, and drainage.

To determine the alignment of a drive the points of entrance from the highway and arrival at the house must first be fixed. Between these two known points the drive should follow the easiest grade along the most direct and attractive route without unnecessary winding. Curves should be used only when they appear logical, to follow the natural shape of the ground, or to avoid permanently fixed obstacles.

The connection with the main highway should be at right angles wherever possible and where this is not possible the angle should favor the direction from which the property is most often approached. Widen the drive at the highway connection by flaring the drive edges on a 30-foot radius. This radius should meet the drive and highway edges at their points of tangency.

Set stakes along the proposed center line of the road at 25-foot intervals. Line the stakes by eye into a pleasing alignment free from abrupt changes in direction, and, after a satisfactory center line is established, set side-line stakes opposite each center stake. Avoid curves less than 90-foot inside radius and grades exceeding 10%.

For drives involving considerable grading an engineer will have to be called in.

Around curves the inside curve should be at least 1 foot lower than the outside. If the curve is on a steep grade it should be banked even more. For a 90-foot radius on a 10% grade make the inside curve 18 inches lower than the outside.

For a single-way drive 10 feet is ample width for practical driving. For two-way passage 15 feet is the minimum width for comfortable passing. Greater width is unnecessary except for curves, parking, or special design effects. Around curves the drive should be widened in proportion to the radius of the curve. Around a 90-foot radius the width should be at least 18 feet.

Modern cars can take a straightway 14% grade in high gear if the surface provides even traction. Curves and uneven surfaces make it necessary to shift into second gear on anything over a 10% grade. Any grade over 10% is hazardous for winter driving.

To construct the road bed the subgrade should be graded exactly like the finished surface. After a rough subgrade is established roll it with a ten-ton roller, beginning at the outer edges and rolling gradually toward the center to prevent squeezing out the edges.

On the subgrade lay the base course of the material of which the drive is to be constructed. The best private drive material is some form of bituminous-bound crushed slag or stone. Concrete is not a desirable surface for private drives except on short city property drives and even in this case paving block or brick is more suitable.

The essentials for a bituminous-bound macadam drive for ordinary passenger car and delivery truck wear are: The base should be an eight-inch slag base laid down in two layers or courses on the approved subgrade. The bottom course should be a layer of two-and-one-half to five-inch hard heavy slag which, when thoroughly rolled with a ten-ton roller, must be four inches thick, and have the same crown or bank as the finished section.

The second or upper course of the base must be a layer of the same slag, which, when thoroughly rolled with a ten-ton roller, should be four inches thick and have the same crown or bank as the finished section. The layer should then be penetrated with an application of two gallons of asphalt or tar to each square yard of surface area. While the bituminous binder is still warm, a layer of limestone chips, clean and free from dust, should be spread over the surface to fill the voids and the layer then given its final rolling. The surface should be swept clean of all free chips.

DRIVE SURFACE. This surface course consists of a three-inch (after final compression), one-course wearing surface, composed of slag and bituminous binder, with a bituminous seal coat and stone-chip covering constructed on the prepared base course.

The slag, one and one-quarter to two and one-half inches, should be spread evenly over the base and then thoroughly rolled with a ten-ton roller until keyed and solid. This layer should be three inches thick and penetrated with the bituminous binder at the rate of two gallons to the square yard of surface covered. While the bituminous binder is still warm, enough limestone chips should be spread over the surface to fill all the voids and the drive thoroughly rolled again. All excess chips should be brushed off and then the entire surface given a seal coat of bituminous binder at the rate of one-half a gallon to each square yard of surface covered. Before this is cold the surface should be covered with a thin layer of limestone chips and rolled lightly. The entire surface must be thoroughly rolled after this application and additional chips applied as required to take up all excess bituminous material and leave the finished surface uniform and conforming to grades.

Variations in surface treatment may be substituted for the above specifications to meet special requirements. For a smoother, more perfect surface a pre-mix material such as Amiesite or Colprovia may be used in place of a penetration surface. To disguise the macadam texture granite chips of various colors, or silica gravel, may be rolled into the surface.

The life and durability of a drive depend on its drainage. To keep water off the surface, crown the drive two to three inches higher in the middle than at the edges, and provide gutters adequate to collect all surface drainage from the drive and any slopes pitching toward the drive.

Water must be kept out from under the drive base. A wet base means a soft road bed and frost will soon destroy the most perfect construction under such conditions. — R. E. G.

DROPWORT = *Filipendula hexapetala.*

DROSERA (dros'sir-ra). Interesting insectivorous plants, commonly called sundew from their glistening foliage. The genus comprises over 90 species, widely distributed, but most abundant in Aust. All those below are found in N.A., where they grow in sphagnum bogs, on the sandy shores of them, or even in open fields. All require similar conditions to thrive under cult., although a good substitute is a sphagnum-filled pot in the cool greenhouse. Whether indoors or out, the mixture in which they grow must be about pH 4 (*see* ACID AND ALKALI SOILS for details). They are small, perennial herbs with a basal rosette of much-modified leaves covered with glistening, sticky hairs. Flowers in a sparse cluster at the end of a short stalk arising from the rosette of leaves (for details *see* DROSERACEAE). Fruit a capsule.* (*Drosera* is from the Greek for dewy, in allusion to the glistening leaf hairs.)

For their methods of digesting insects *see* INSECTIVOROUS PLANTS.

filiformis. Leaves long and thread-like, 6–9 in. long, green, but the hairs purplish. Flower cluster about as high as the leaves, or a little more, the flowers pinkish-purple, about ¼ in. wide. Mass. to Fla.

intermedia. Leaves broadest toward the tip, narrowed to a very slender base, usually about 1½ in. long, green or reddish, the hairs reddish-purple. Flowers white, the cluster 6–8 in. high. North temperate zone.

rotundifolia. Common sundew; called also dew plant and rosa solis. Leaves close to the ground and having a round, flat blade, about ¾ in. in diameter, narrowed to a flat stalk, the whole red or green, the hairs always reddish-purple. Flowers white or pinkish, the stalk 4–10 in. high. North temperate zone.

DROSERACEAE (dros-sir-ray'see-ee). The sundew family is one of the few plant families having the ability to digest animal matter directly (*see also* NEPENTHACEAE and SARRACENIACEAE). Of its six known genera, two are often cult. for their interesting habit of catching and digesting insects. *Drosera,* the sundew, does this by the sticky-glistening hairs on its foliage, while *Dionaea,* the Venus's-flytrap, has hinged, hairy, valve-like leaves that close on its prey. Both are plants of low places; *Drosera* being cosmopolitan, but *Dionaea* localized in N. Car. and S. Car.

Leaves unlike ordinary foliage leaves (*see* DROSERA and DIONAEA). Flowers usually in small clusters, white or pinkish (in ours), followed by a small pod (capsule*).

Technical flower characters: Flowers regular. Sepals and petals 5, the stamens 5 or more. Ovary superior,* 1-celled, the single style rather long, the ovules 3 to many.

DROUGHT-RESISTANT PLANTS. Regions with deficient or seasonal rainfall present difficult problems to the gardener. There is no need here to repeat information on the plants suited to such localities. *See* the articles on CACTI, SUCCULENTS, SAND GARDENS, DESERT GARDENS, and the rainfall data at the name of your state or province. *See also* RAINFALL.

DRUMMOND PHLOX = *Phlox drummondi.*

DRUMSTICK TREE = *Cassia Fistula.*

drupacea, -us, -um (droo-pay'see-a). Bearing drupes.

DRUPACEAE. See ROSACEAE.

DRUPE. A fleshy, 1-seeded fruit that does not split. The seed is enclosed in a bony stone, hence such fruits are often called stone fruits, common examples being peach, plum, cherry, and olive.

DRUPELET. A little drupe, often one of many, as in the raspberry.

DRYAS (dry'as). Rock garden herbs of the cooler parts of the north temperate zone, family Rosaceae, two of the half dozen known species sometimes grown in the rock garden. They are somewhat woody, perennial herbs with alternate,* usually evergreen leaves, and rather showy, solitary flowers borne at the end of slender stalks. Sepals 8–10, more or less persistent. Petals 8–10, yellowish or white. Stamens* many. Fruit a collection of feathered or plumed achenes,* suggesting *Geum.* (*Dryas* is from Greek for wood nymph.) The plants are sometimes called mountain avens.

For culture *see* ROCK GARDEN.

octopetala. Densely tufted, prostrate plant, the leaves oblongish, about 1 in. long, and white-felty beneath. Flowers about 1½ in. wide, white, upright. Fruiting plumes about 1 in. long. Mountain and northern parts of Eu., As. and N.A.

suendermanni. Somewhat similar, but the flowers yellow in the early stage, ultimately white, nodding. Of hybrid origin.

DRYING OFF. A common greenhouse procedure consisting of the gradual withdrawal of water until the bulb, tuber, or corm goes into a dormant state fit to store until it is again started into growth. Drying off is also practiced with potted plants that need a resting period, usually by tipping their pots on one side and stopping or nearly stopping their water supply.

drymifolia, -us, -um (dry-mi-fō'li-a). With leaves like the genus *Drimys.*

---

* Special articles on the subjects indicated by an asterisk (*) will be found at the words so marked.

DRYMOCALLIS GLANDULOSA = *Potentilla glandulosa*.

DRYOPTERIS (dry-op'ter-is). The shield ferns, of nearly world-wide distribution, and containing over 1000 species of the family Polypodiaceae, are, so far as the cult. plants are concerned, chiefly hardy ferns for tne outdoor fern garden. For other plants sometimes included here *see* POLYSTICHUM. Some of the shield ferns are also still called *Aspidium* and *Thelypteris* by dealers. They have usually erect, handsome fronds that may be twice- or thrice-compound,* the ultimate segments somewhat or very much toothed. Spore* cases near the center or along the edges of the segments that bear them. (*Dryopteris* is from Greek for oak fern.)

For culture of these chiefly hardy ferns *see* FERNS AND FERN GARDENING.

acrostichoides = *Polystichum acrostichoides*.

clintoniana. Clinton's fern. Much resembling the next and perhaps only a variety of it, but the ultimate frond segments are 4–6 in. long. N.A. and northern Eu.

cristata. Crested shield fern. Fronds 18–30 in. long, erect and striking, twice-compound,* the ultimate segments 2–3 in. long, finely toothed, the foliage thus beautifully feathery. North temperate zone.

disjuncta. Oak fern. Fronds more or less triangular, about 11 in. long and as wide, twice-compound,* the ultimate segments narrow and wavy-toothed or nearly without teeth. North temperate zone. Also called *D. linnaeana*.

Filix-mas. Male fern. Leaves (fronds) in dense crowns, nearly evergreen, 2–3½ ft. long, and almost 1 ft. wide, twice-compound,* the ultimate segments deeply toothed or cut. N.A. and Eu. A popular fern garden plant, offered also in a crested and in a dwarf form.

goldiana. Goldie's fern. Fronds in a dense crown, each leaf 2½–4 ft. high, nearly 18 in. wide and twice-compound.* Ultimate segments dark green, broadest at the middle, toothed. Eastern N.A. and one of the finest of our native ferns.

hexagonoptera. A lower and more open fern, the fronds more or less triangular in outline, about 15 in. long and 12 in. wide, and only once-compound, often somewhat sticky beneath. Ultimate segments oblongish and a little toothed, but the lowermost pair much longer than the others and deeply lobed or toothed. Eastern N.A.

linnaeana = *D. disjuncta*.

marginalis. Evergreen wood fern. Marginal shield fern. Fronds growing in a dense crown, nearly evergreen, 8–24 in. high, twice- or thrice-compound.* Ultimate segments lobed or without lobes, the spore cases conspicuously dotted along the margins. Eastern N.A. Very common in woods and much gathered for florists' decorations. Of easy cult. in the shade. *See* FERNS AND FERN GARDENING.

noveboracensis. New York fern. Fronds pale green, the lowest pairs of leaf segments gradually smaller than the others and recurved, the whole frond up to 2 ft. long. Eastern N.A. and west to Ark. A good fern for the shady wild garden.

Phegopteris. Beech fern. Fronds more or less triangular, about 9 in. long and 8 in. wide, once-compound.* Ultimate segments mostly without teeth, but the lowermost pair recurved and standing forward. Spore cases near the margin. North temperate zone.

spinulosa. Fronds about 18 in. long and half as wide, persistent or nearly evergreen, twice-compound,* the ultimate segments deeply cut. North temperate zone.

Thelypteris. Marsh fern. Rootstock creeping, the erect fronds very graceful, nearly 30 in. long, and about 6 in. wide, once-compound,* the ultimate segments deeply cut, the margin slightly rolled. North temperate zone, especially in open, wet places. It needs less shade and more moisture than the others.

DRY STRAWBERRY = *Waldsteinia fragarioides*.

dubia, -us, -um (doo'bi-a). Doubtful, especially as to identity or name.

DUCHESNEA (doo-shay' nee-a). Two Asiatic species of perennial herbs of the rose family, **D. indica** of secondary garden interest. It is commonly called the mock strawberry or Indian or barren strawberry from its *Fragaria*-like aspect. It is a trailing herb with runners, the compound* leaves with 3 leaflets, which are ovalish and coarsely toothed. Flowers yellow, solitary, about ¾ in. wide, the petals 5. Fruit red, surrounded by the persistent calyx, suggesting a strawberry, but inedible. It is established as a weedy plant in various parts of the U.S. and is of the easiest cult. Of some use as a ground cover. (Named for Antoine Nicholas Duchesne, French student of the true strawberry.)

DUCKWEED. *See* LEMNA.

DUCK WHEAT = *Fagopyrum tataricum.* *See* BUCKWHEAT.

DUDAIM MELON = Pomegranate melon. *See* MELON.

DUDLEYA = *Echeveria*.

DUKE CHERRY = *Prunus avium regalis*.

Dulcamara (dul-ka-mā'ra). Latin for bitter-sweet. *See* SOLANUM.

dulcis, -e (dul'sis). Sweet.

DUMBARTON OAKS. *See* No. 8 at GARDEN TOURS.

DUMB CANE = *Dieffenbachia Seguine*.

dumosa, -us, -um (doo-mō'sa). Shrubby.

DUNE GRASSES. For the best sand-binding grass on sea-beaches *see* AMMOPHILA ARENARIA, which will grow in salt-impregnated sand. On inland dunes that are free of salt *see* ELYMUS ARENARIUS, which, however, will also grow on seacoast dunes in places a little farther from the beach than *Ammophila*.

duracina, -us, -um (du-ra-sy'na). With hard fruit or berries.

DURANTA (du-ran'ta). Perhaps a dozen species of tropical American shrubs and trees of the family Verbenaceae, **D. repens** (sometimes called *D. plumieri*) cult. outdoors in Fla. and Calif. for ornament. It is commonly called tropical lilac, pigeonberry, golden dewdrop, or sky-flower, and is a shrub or small tree 12–20 ft. high, its

---

* Special articles on the subjects indicated by an asterisk (*) will be found at the words so marked.

4-angled branches often drooping or even trailing. Leaves generally opposite* (sometimes whorled*), ovalish, about 3½ in. long, toothed or without teeth. Flowers in a terminal cluster (raceme*), showy, but the corolla* only about ½ in. wide, lilac, slightly tubular, its five lobes, slightly oblique, minutely hairy on the edges. Fruit fleshy, yellow, 8-seeded, about ½ in. in diameter. Fla. to Brazil. Rarely cult. in northern greenhouses, where it needs a warm-temperate house and potting mixture* 4. Along the Gulf Coast it may winter-kill, but flowers the next season, especially a white-flowered form. (Named for Castor Durantes, Roman botanist.)

durius, -or (dur'ee-us). Harder or tougher.

duriuscula, -us, -um (dur-ee-us'kew-la). Rather hard or tough.

Durra. Native name in Egypt for *Sorghum vulgare Durra.*

DUST AND DUSTING. Some insecticides and fungicides are better used in the form of dust than as liquid sprays. For the average gardener the preparation of dusts is inconvenient and sometimes impossible, but there are good commercial mixtures ready for use. They can be safely used in accordance with directions on the container. For the application of dusters and the necessary equipment *see* SPRAYING AND DUSTING.

DUSTY CLOVER = *Lespedeza capitata.*

DUSTY MILLER. An old plant name of rather wide and somewhat confusing application. Perhaps it should be confined to *Senecio Cineraria* or *Artemisia stelleriana,* but it is also used for *Centaurea Cineraria, C. gymnocarpa, Lychnis coronaria,* and many other wild plants.

DUTCH BULBS. A loose designation for bulbs raised in Holland, notably tulip, hyacinth, crocus, etc.

DUTCH CASE-KNIFE BEAN = *Phaseolus coccineus albus.*

DUTCH CLOVER = *Trifolium repens. See* CLOVER.

DUTCH CROCUS. *See* CROCUS AUREUS.

DUTCH CUTTING. *See* Outdoor Culture at CHRYSANTHEMUM.

DUTCH ELM = *Ulmus hollandica. See* ELM.

DUTCH ELM DISEASE. *See* ELM.

DUTCH HOLLY. *See Ilex Aquifolium* at HOLLY.

DUTCH IRIS. *See* IRIS XIPHIUM.

DUTCHMAN'S-BREECHES = *Dicentra Cucullaria.*

DUTCHMAN'S-PIPE = *Aristolochia durior.*

DUTCH RUSH = *Equisetum hyemale.*

DUTCH YELLOW. *See* CROCUS AUREUS.

DWARF. As an adjective *dwarf* is part of the name of many garden plants, usually signifying low stature or small parts. Those found in this book, with their proper equivalents, are:

Dwarf alder = *Fothergilla gardeni;* **dwarf banana** = *Musa cavendishi* (for culture *see* BANANA); **dwarf crested iris** = *Iris cristata;* **dwarf elm** = *Ulmus pumila* (*see* ELM); **dwarf fan palm** = *Chamaerops humilis;* **dwarf ginseng** = *Panax trifolius;* **dwarf goldenrod** = *Solidago nemoralis* (*see* GOLDENROD); **dwarfing** (*see* next main entry); **dwarf Japanese quince** = *Chaenomeles japonica;* **dwarf June-berry** = *Amelanchier stolonifera;* **dwarf laurel** = *Kalmia angustifolia;* **dwarf lima bean** = *Phaseolus limensis limeanus* (for culture *see* BEAN); **dwarf morning-glory** = *Convolvulus tricolor;* **dwarf nasturtium** = *Tropaeolum minus* (*see* NASTURTIUM); **dwarf palmetto** = *Sabal minor;* **dwarf pea** (*see* PEA); **dwarf poinciana** = *Poinciana pulcherrima;* **dwarf Russian almond** = *Prunus nana;* **dwarf sumac** = *Rhus copallina.*

DWARFING. Many naturally dwarf forms of tall plants exist, there being sports or mutations that retain their dwarf character. Thus we have extremely dwarf varieties of antirrhinums, petunias, and other annuals that come true from seed, the dwarf habit being fixed by prolonged selection. There are also many dwarf varieties of coniferous evergreens which, while retaining the general characteristics of the parent species, persist in remaining dwarf, their short-jointedness and slow growth resulting in a stature that is only a fraction of the normal type of the same age.

The dwarf evergreens for which Japanese gardeners are famous are, however, artificially produced. Some of these specimens growing in shallow dishes or earthernware urns may be anywhere between 10 and 200 years old, possessing all the gnarled, aged appearance of full-grown specimens of the same age, though they be no more than two feet tall. Infinite patience is required to obtain such specimens, and some examples, imported from Japan before the Quarantine Law forbade the entry of plants growing in soil, represented the work of three or four generations of gardeners. Such specimens now existing in the United States are few and

An old pine dwarfed by years of effort

are in the hands of skilled gardeners who can give them the necessary attention.

Few occidental gardeners are inclined to devote years to growing artificially dwarf trees of this character, but the process is more a matter of patience than anything else. Seedlings or rooted cuttings, healthy but not the most vigorous, should be chosen, and they should be kept in the smallest pots possible. Before potting into 2-in. pots, cut off part of the tap root, and pot very firmly, using a heavy soil and a bit of moss at the bottom to prevent clogging of the drainage hole. Cut away any roots that push through the bottom of the pot, and keep the latter in a larger pot packed with moist moss to prevent drying out. Allow to stand outdoors sheltered from hot sunshine during the summer and keep in a frost-free house during the winter. Give no more water at any time than is essential and only fertilize in minute doses. Some Japanese growers, however, water constantly, apparently on the theory that over-watering impoverishes the soil, by leaching. Constant pinching of the growths is necessary, and to encourage an aged appearance the various branches should be tied down or twisted as fancy dictates. Re-potting should be done in the spring, each shift being into a pot only slightly larger than the previous one, which means that root pruning must be vigorous. Pines, firs, taxodiums, junipers, cryptomerias, etc., may be dwarfed in this way, as may some of the hard-wooded, flowering shrubs, such as azaleas, *Pieris, Pyracantha,* Japanese cherries, and Japanese quinces, as well as foliage shrubs such as cut-leaf maples, hollies, *Osmanthus,* and *Rhus typhina laciniata.* These very old and grotesque dwarfs, nearly always grown in ornamental containers, are known in Jap. as *bonsai* (a tray or shallow container) and the term is now common in the U.S. A good recent book about them, *Miniature Trees and Landscapes,* by Yuji Yoshimura and G. M. Halford, was distributed in 1958 by the American Horticultural Society, 1600 Bladensburg Road, Washington 2, D.C. — T. A. W.

An interesting new method of dwarfing, developed at the Arnold Arboretum by Dr. Karl Sax, involves the inversion of a ring of bark taken from the young tree and replaced upside down. In some cases two rings are so reversed, separated by a band of undisturbed bark. The inversion of the bark interrupts the flow of nutrients from the leaves to the root and thus results in a retarding of subsequent growth. Whether such stunting is permanent or not is still to be demonstrated.

DWARF FRUIT TREES. In the article on FRUIT CULTURE it is noted that many standard (*i.e.,* full-sized) fruit trees were apt to be too large for the small place, particularly apple, pear, and cherry trees. Plum and peach trees are smaller and will fit into most gardens, but even plum trees now come in dwarf or semi-dwarf form.

It is well for the grower to understand not only the exact significance of the terms *dwarf* and *semi-dwarf,* but how they are produced, and why some unscrupulous dealers palm off mere runts as dwarfs, when they are really only ill-thriven, stunted specimens of standard trees, and will never bear anything but inferior fruit.

Dwarfing depends upon grafting the desired variety upon a stock which is naturally dwarf or semi-dwarf. In the case of apples, an experiment station near Maidstone, Kent, England, known as the East Malling Research Station, worked for years upon many dwarfing stocks and nearly all those known today are derivatives of these. They produced at least a dozen different dwarfing stocks, known in America as Malling I, Malling II, etc. For our purposes Malling IX is used for dwarf apple trees (5–6 feet high) and Malling I, II, IV, and VII for semi-dwarfs, which should be 8–10 feet high. As dwarf trees are relatively expensive, it is well to insist that your dwarf or semi-dwarf apples meet these specifications. Failure to do so may mean that years hence, when it is too late to correct the error, your "dwarf" may be a full- or half-grown standard.

Dwarf pear trees are not grafted upon Malling stock, but upon the Angers quince. Not all pear varieties will grow upon quince stock, so that after a pear that *will* grow on it has made a strong union, the first pear cion (upper part of the graft) acts as the *stock* for the variety of pear that is finally desired. Such pears are known as double-worked or double-grafted. It is well to have the nurseryman specify whether the dwarf pear is simply grafted on quince or is double-worked, as it makes a difference in how it is treated in the years to come. The second graft, if there is one, may be 18–24 inches above the lower, which is essentially at ground level.

From central North America comes a small wild tree or shrub known as the sand cherry (*Prunus besseyi*). Its fruit does not amount to much, but it has been found to be one of the best stocks upon which to dwarf plums. Another dwarfing stock for plums is *Prunus tomentosa* from China. Neither of these is quite so satisfactory as Malling stock for apples, but it is well to have your nurseryman specify which he uses, as they are the best available for plums.

Cherries are usually dwarfed upon a low-growing variety of another sort of cherry and are apt to be less satisfactory, as dwarfs, than apples or pears. Peaches, if you need dwarf varieties, are dwarfed on the same stock as plums, using mostly *Prunus besseyi.* There is little real need for dwarf peach trees, for they are naturally small trees and too short-lived to be worth the expense of dwarfing.

Dwarf trees cost from three to four times the price of young standard trees, and the home grower should buy them with care, from a reliable nurseryman, and keep in mind the relative value of the understocks

---

* Special articles on the subjects indicated by an asterisk (*) will be found at the words so marked.

outlined above. Real dwarf trees take time to produce, expert grafting skills, *i.e.*, compatibility of stock and cion, and we must pay accordingly. Almost any good nursery carries some dwarfs and semi-dwarfs.

The advantages of them on the small place are several. They take up less room, usually begin fruiting earlier, and are far easier to prune and spray; picking the fruit of dwarfs does not ordinarily require a ladder, and only a stepladder is needed for semi-dwarfs. Watching out for pests is so much easier than with standard trees that for most small gardens dwarfs seem the only solution.

It would be quite so were there not a disadvantage to all dwarf trees, especially apples. The Malling stocks are shallow-rooted, and both dwarf and even some semi-dwarf apple trees are prone to be blown in a wind. For that reason all dwarf apples, and many semi-dwarfs, should be fastened to a stout stake, driven into the ground at planting time, especially if the site happens to be windy. If the dwarf trees are protected from winds it may be safe to omit the stake.

Also all dwarf trees, because they are grafted a little higher than standards, are apt to snap off in a wind at the union of the graft, especially when they are young and the union has not completely "set" — something like a newly set fracture. It is consequently safer to stake all dwarfs and semi-dwarfs for the first three years, and permanently if they are on Malling stocks. Double-grafted pear trees are particularly subject to this danger.

It is for these reasons that few commercial fruit growers have ever made a success of dwarf fruit trees in this country, as open orchards are too vulnerable to the wind hazard, and large growers have found other faults with them such as much decreased yield.

These need not restrain the home grower, nor have they affected the commercial growers in France. Dwarf trees fill a useful niche, and, with the hazards understood and the understocks carefully specified, the home orchardist is usually willing and eager to pick his own fruit from a tree sometimes one fifth the size of a standard.

PLANTING AND CARE

Dwarf apple trees must be planted with more care than ordinary fruit trees. Follow the usual procedure for planting as outlined at FRUIT CULTURE, but with an important, and in fact an essential, difference. Standard trees are planted at the same depth as they were in the nursery, but no dwarf or semi-dwarf apple tree should ever be.

Find out the exact place of the union between the understock and cion,* which can usually be felt as a slight swelling, even if there is no difference in the color of the bark. In planting see that this union is as near 2 inches above permanent ground level as possible, allowing for some settling of the tree in its hole. If the tree settles too much,

from failure to pack the soil properly, or because of heavy rains soon after planting, scrape away enough soil so that the union of understock and top is just 2 inches above any soil.

This precaution is so essential because the grafted base of your tree, if actually in or too near the soil, may send down roots of its own. When that happens, especially if it passes notice for a year or two, your "dwarf" tree may shoot up because it is thriving on its own roots instead of being dwarfed by its proper understock. In other words, inspect your dwarf trees once or twice a year and cut off all unwanted roots. Also of course, cut off all suckers from the understock, which may spring up from any fruit rootstock. What you want is the variety you are paying for and only this, properly dwarfed by its understock. It cannot be without watchfulness.

In the case of double-grafted dwarf pear trees there is also an additional contingency to be looked out for. All that is stated above is true of pear trees, and should be followed strictly, also, with those that have been double-worked. But the stem between the lowest graft (2 inches above ground) and the upper graft (18–24 inches above the lower one) is a variety that you do not want. Hence see that all leaves, twigs, or branches that spring from that part of the stem between the upper and lower grafts are permanently suppressed.

Generally, because grafted dwarf trees take more time to grow than the whips of standard trees, you will be planting a dwarf that is already 2–3 years old. Its general pattern or skeleton will have been fixed by the nurseryman. This means that dwarf trees need little or no pruning the first year or two after you plant them. Later all you need to do is to cut off straggling branches, and keep the crown of the tree open enough to let the sunlight ripen the fruit.

Dwarf and semi-dwarf fruit trees may be planted much closer together than standards. It will depend a little on the variety, but a safe general guide may be as follows:

	Dwarf	*Semi-Dwarf*
Apples	10–12 feet	12–18 feet
Pears	10–12 feet	12–18 feet
Plums	10–12 feet	12–18 feet
Quince	10–12 feet	12–18 feet
Cherry	12–15 feet	15–20 feet

Trees should not be closer than these intervals, and if you have the space they should be a little farther apart. Because cherries do not dwarf as well as apples, they need more space than the latter, both in dwarf and semi-dwarf form.

VARIETIES

Not all the varieties mentioned below will be available at any one nursery, so that it will be well to get the catalogues of half a dozen of the leading dealers in fruit trees before placing an order. Dwarf and semi-dwarf trees are emphatically not items to be

---

* Special articles on the subjects indicated by an asterisk (*) will be found at the words so marked.

picked up at any roadside stand, the risks are too great and the cost is too high. Some very reputable dealers charge as much as $5.00 for a 3-year-old dwarf, and five times that for a 5-year-old specimen.

The following varieties are available both as dwarfs and semi-dwarfs, either as 2- or 3-year-old trees. Average price $4.00–$5.00 each, for 3-year specimens. Cheaper stock is offered but is not always safe as to variety, and especially as to the skill of the grafter.

APPLES

Early: Yellow Transparent, Red Astrachan, Duchess of Oldenberg, Gravenstein, Red June.

Midseason: Wealthy, Fameuse, Delicious.

Late: Jonathan, Rome Beauty, Winesap, Yellow Newton, Rhode Island Greening.

PEARS

Kieffer (but scarcely worth it), Seckel, Bartlett, Conference, Beurre Bosc, Winter Nelis, Gorham.

QUINCE

Orange, Champion.

PLUMS

European or Domesticas: Bradshaw, Arctic (Moore's Arctic), Italian Prune, Reine Claude (Green Gage), Stanley.

Damsons: Shropshire.

Japanese: Abundance, Burbank, Formosa, Red June.

American or hybrid: None.

CHERRIES

Sweet: Black Tartarian, Bing, Schmidt, Windsor, Yellow Spanish.

Sour: Early Richmond, Montmorency.

Duke: None.

PEACHES

Because peach trees are short-lived and relatively small trees, the expense of dwarfs does not seem justified. The following varieties, however, are available:

Belle (Belle of Georgia), Carman, Champion, Early Crawford, Crawford, Elberta, Golden Jubilee, Halehaven, J. H. Hale.

NECTARINES

Sure Crop, Hunter.

Many other varieties of dwarf or semi-dwarf fruit trees are available, but have been excluded here because it seems safer for the amateur to stick to varieties the performance of which is known. It should also be remembered that the varieties chosen should be checked for self-sterility* before planting. See the section on self-fertility and self-sterility at FRUIT CULTURE. For other notes on the fruit tree dwarf of your choice see the various articles on APPLE, PEAR, PEACH, etc., which may be essential for climatic fitness of the various varieties. It is suggested that those who want to dwarf their own trees get Bulletin 783 of the Agricultural Experiment Station, Geneva, N.Y., entitled "Rootstocks and Methods Used for Dwarfing Fruit Trees," issued in April, 1959.

DYCKIA (dike'i-a). Over 75 species of desert, succulent, South American plants of the pineapple family, two of which are sometimes cult. outdoors in Fla. and Calif., more rarely in northern greenhouses. They resemble miniature century plants in having a basal rosette of spiny-margined leaves. Flowers (in those below) yellow or orange in a bracted cluster which arises from the leaf rosette (for details of flower structure see BROMELIACEAE). Fruit a capsule.* (Named for Prince Salm-Dyck, German botanist.)

For culture see SUCCULENTS.

rariflora. Leaves 4–6 in. long, about ⅕ in. wide, the spines sharp and upward-pointing. Flowers nearly stalkless in the cluster, orange, about ½ in. long, the cluster nearly 18 in. long. Brazil.

sulphurea. Leaves 5–8 in. long, about ⅓ in. wide, the spines smaller. Flowers yellow, about ⅓ in. long, distinctly stalked in the cluster, which may be up to 12 in. long. Brazil.

DYEING FLOWERS. The passion for dyeing flowers appears to be ineradicable. If there is any necessity to "improve" on nature's colors it can easily be done, whether they are fresh flowers or dried. Various inks or aniline dyes are readily absorbed by cut flowers, esp. the gardenia. It works best, of course, on white flowers, a familiar example being the green St. Patrick's Day carnations.

For dipping already dried flowers, grasses, etc., the following solutions will be found useful:

Deep Shell Pink — Dissolve one-quarter teaspoon of mercurochrome crystals with four teaspoons of powdered alum in a pint of hot water. Very good on Bristol Fairy and dried gypsophila.

Salmon Pink — Use Sanford's cardinal red ink (not royal red). Use rain or well water only in this solution in July and August to avoid the chemicals used in city water.

Deep Pink — Use Sanford's or Higgins' red stamp-pad ink; a two-ounce bottle will make one quart. Use eight teaspoons of powdered alum.

Royal Purple — Use Waterman's patrician purple ink (in small bottles only). This is extra good on freesias. Tint the flowers with blue first.

Violet, Orchid, Lavender — Use Waterman's or Sanford's violet ink. Tint the flowers with pink for orchid, blue for violet. Dip the white flowers for light lavender.

Blue-Green — Use Parker's green ink for St. Patrick's green or use Waterman's tropic green ink (in small bottles only). Dip twice.

Flag Blue — Use Parker's permanent blue-black ink and Parker's permanent royal blue ink mixed half and half. Dip twice or tint the flowers with lavender.

Medium Blue — Use Parker's or Waterman's permanent blue ink. Dip twice or tint the flowers with lavender.

Peach, Apricot, Orange — Different shades of yellow chrysanthemums dipped in salmon-pink solution produce the above shades.

When mixing the solutions above use the smallest size of ink bottle, pouring the contents into a pint container to which four

---

* Special articles on the subjects indicated by an asterisk (*) will be found at the words so marked.

teaspoonfuls of alum and enough cold water are added to make a pint.

To color dried material to resemble silver, gold, bronze, etc., it is necessary to dip them in diluted solutions of metallic paints, which can be bought at any paint store. In diluting the paints use turpentine for flat effects and linseed oil or varnish if they are to be shiny.

DYER'S GREENWEED = *Genista tinctoria*.

DYER'S WOAD = *Isatis tinctoria*.

DYER'S WOODRUFF = *Asperula tinctoria*.

DYNAMITE. An unusual, but very useful, garden adjunct, to be employed only by an experienced, usually professional, operator. There is no substitute for it in destroying layers of hardpan or other compacted material. Such a subsoil often makes tree-growing impossible, but a stick of dynamite exploded where each tree is to be planted will shatter the most refractory material.

It is also commonly employed for making tree holes in stony or rocky land, especially where layers of impervious rock underlie an orchard or garden site. Needless to add is the caution to remove to a safe place all topsoil before the charge is exploded.

E

EARDROPS. See Dicentra.

EARLY. A common hort. designation for crops that mature quickly, regardless of when they are planted. Early corn, for instance, may take 45 days from seeding to harvest, while late corn requires from 55–65 days. The term *early* thus has two distinct meanings in the garden world: the usual one of being early in the season and this somewhat special one which relates to speed of maturity.

EARLY CRESS = *Barbarea verna*.

EARLY DWARF PEA = *Pisum sativum humile*. See Pea.

EARLY MEADOW RUE = *Thalictrum dioicum*.

EARLY PERENNIAL PHLOX = *Phlox carolina*.

EARLY SAXIFRAGE = *Saxifraga virginiensis*.

EARTH ALMOND = *Cyperus esculentus*.

EARTHING-UP. Hilling up of corn (*see* illustration at Corn). While it is a necessary operation for corn, and is also common in celery-growing to accomplish blanching, the amateur practice of indiscriminate earthing-up of shrubs, etc., is of no value and may do harm. It encourages root production on the hill which is harmful in periods of drought.

EARTHNUT = *Cyperus esculentus*.

EARTHWORMS. True earthworms do not belong to the same branch of the animal kingdom as insects, crabs and spiders. They inhabit moist, fertile soils in most of the humid regions. Because their habits of mixing the soil by burrowing, and of bringing bits of decaying vegetable matter into the soil, tend to increase soil fertility, they are listed among beneficial organisms. Their usefulness as fish bait is well known. Occasionally, however, they cause complaint by making little heaps of soil on the surface of lawns and interfering with the playing qualities of golf greens, and this sometimes leads to requests for control methods.

Best means of control is by adding 1 pound of active chlordane per 1000 sq. ft. to soil as dust or in fertilizer. One treatment lasts for years and will control most other soil pests. Apply as at Japanese Beetle. — L. G. M.

EASTER-BELL = *Stellaria Holostea*.

EASTER CACTUS = *Schlumbergera gaertneri*.

EASTER DAISY = *Townsendia exscapa*.

EASTER LILY = *Lilium longiflorum eximium*.

EAST INDIAN LOTUS = *Nelumbo nucifera*.

EAST INDIAN ROSE BAY = *Tabernaemontana coronaria*.

EAST INDIAN WALNUT = *Albizzia Lebbek*.

EBENACEAE (ee-be-nay'see-ee, also ebb-e-nay'see-ee). The ebony or persimmon family, largely tropical, contains only 6 genera of unusually hard-wooded trees or shrubs. One of its few genera found in the temperate zone is *Diospyros* (*see* Persimmon), widely cult. for its edible fruit.

Leaves alternate,* without marginal teeth, mostly rather leathery. Male and female flowers often on separate trees, but always separate even if on the same tree, solitary or in small clusters in the leaf axils.* Fruit (in the cult. genera) fleshy.

The persimmon is the only cult. genus.

Technical flower characters: Calyx 3–7-lobed, sometimes persistent and much enlarged in fruit. Corolla more or less bell-shaped or tubular, 3–7-lobed. Stamens inserted on the base of the corolla, the same number as the corolla-lobes or twice as many, some (or all in the female flowers) sterile. Ovary superior,* 2–16-celled. Styles 2–8.

EBONY FAMILY = Ebenaceae.

---

* Special articles on the subjects indicated by an asterisk (*) will be found at the words so marked.

EBONY SPLEENWORT = *Asplenium platyneuron.*

ecalcarata, -us, -um (e-kal-ka-ray′ta). Without a spur.

ECBALLIUM (ek-bal′lee-um). The squirting cucumber, E. Elaterium, is the only species in this curious genus of vines of the family Cucurbitaceae. It is grown more for its remarkable fruits than for ornament (but *see* VINES). It is a hairy, perennial, herbaceous vine from the Mediterranean region, with alternate,* triangular-ovalish leaves, 3–4 in. long and grayish-felty beneath. Male and female flowers separate on the same plant, both yellow. Female flower solitary, the male flowers in racemes,* sometimes both in the same leaf axil.* Fruit an oblongish berry, 1½–2 in. long, rough-hairy, which at the moment of detachment from its stalk squirts out its brownish seeds with explosive force. (*Ecballium* is from the Greek to eject.)

ECCREMOCARPUS (ek-krem′o-kar-pus). A small genus of Andean vines of the family Bignoniaceae, **E. scaber** grown for its very handsome flowers. It is a stem-climbing, tendril*-bearing vine with opposite, twice-compound* leaves. Leaflets ovalish, about 1 in. long. Flowers orange-red, in a showy, summer-blooming, terminal raceme.* Corolla about 1 in. long, tubular, but the limb 2-lipped, hence slightly irregular.* Fruit a slender pod (capsule*) about 1½ in. long. Chile. Hardy as a perennial vine from zone* 7 southward, but in the North it blooms from seed if treated as a tender annual (*see* ANNUALS). (*Eccremocarpus* is from the Greek for pendulous fruit.)

ECHEVERIA (ech-e-veer′i-a). A large genus of tropical American, chiefly Mexican, succulent plants of the family Crassulaceae, a few grown as summer bedding plants and in the greenhouse. They have thick, often grayish leaves, chiefly in a basal rosette, resembling the houseleeks. Flowers in a cluster at the end of a stalk that arises at the leaf rosette. Calyx tubular and 5-parted, usually nearly as long as the 5 petals, which are rarely or only slightly united into a tube. Stamens* 10. Fruit dry. (Named for Atanasio Echeverria, botanical artist in Mexico.) Some are often offered as *Dudleya.*

All the plants below can be grown in the cool greenhouse (*see* SUCCULENTS). They are often used for summer carpet bedding. While they grow perfectly outdoors in Calif. and the Southwest, they cannot stand the wet, slushy winters of much of the North. *Echeveria secunda* and *E. glauca* are nearly hardy as far north as Washington, D.C.

agavoides. Low-growing plant with short, thick stem. Leaves in a rosette overlapping each other, ovalish, to 2 in. long, the midrib ending in a spine. Flowering stalk crowded with small leaves. Flowers in coiled clusters. Corolla red-dish, tipped yellow. Mex. Also known as *Urbinia agavoides.*

derenbergi. A rosette-forming succulent, the leaves all basal, more or less spoon-shaped, about 1½ in. long and red-edged. Flowers about ½ in. long, orange-red, with a darker red keel. Mex.

elegans. A stemless succulent, the leaves in a basal rosette and the flower stalk 6–8 in. high. Leaves very fleshy, white, about 2 in. long, the green margins translucent. Flowers pink, yellow-tipped, about 5–7 in a loose cluster. Mex.

gibbiflora. A branching plant 1–2 ft. high. Leaves somewhat wedge-shaped or oblongish, 5–7 in. long, grayish-blue or becoming pinkish, mostly in a basal rosette, but a few clustered toward the ends of the branches. Flowers red, about ½ in. long, in a 1-sided cluster. Mex. Var. *metallica* is a form with the bluish-purple leaves having a metallic luster.

glauca. Leaves all basal, nearly round, about ¾ in. wide, pale bluish-green, the terminal point purplish. Flowers about ½ in. long, pink outside, yellowish inside, the stalks reddish, the cluster 1-sided. Mex. Sometimes offered as *E. secunda glauca.*

harmi. See OLIVERANTHUS.

metallica = *E. gibbiflora metallica.*

multicaulis. A woody-stemmed, branched, succulent, 2–3 ft. high, leaves in rosettes, but not all basal, spoon-shaped, 4–6 in. long, dark green but scarlet-edged. Flowers yellow inside, red outside, the branches of the flower cluster rose-pink. Mex.

paraguayensis. See GRAPTOPETALUM.

pulvinata. A low succulent, the white-hairy leaves clustered in a terminal rosette, the plant not over 5–7 in. high. Leaves about 1 in. long, spoon-shaped but blunt at the tip except for a soft prickle; sometimes red-haired on the margin. Flowers in a leafy cluster (raceme*), scarlet. Mex.

secunda. Similar to *E. glauca*, but the leaves reddish along the margins, and with red flowers. Mex.

ECHINACEA (ek-in-ā′see-a). Almost weedy, North American perennial herbs of the family Compositae, commonly called coneflower or purple coneflower and sometimes offered under the name *Brauneria.* They are coarse herbs with black, pungent roots, stout, hairy stems, and alternate* leaves, the basal ones long-stalked. Flower heads solitary on long stalks at the end of the stems, the center of the head distinctly conical. Ray flowers not numerous, rose or rose-purple, withering but persistent. Below the head is a close-set series of small bracts,* the tips of which are finally recurved. (*Echinacea* is from the Greek for hedgehog, in allusion to the sharp bracts.*)

The two below are of the easiest culture in the open border. Both are native in the U.S. and grow wild in a variety of sites. They will stand sun and wind, are easiest propagated by division, and are summer bloomers.

angustifolia. Purple daisy. Usually not much branched, 1–2 ft. high. Leaves broadly lance-shaped or narrower, about 8 in. long, narrowed at the base into a long stalk, without marginal teeth. Ray flowers 1–2 in. long, 2-toothed at the tip. Central cone of the head nearly 1 in. high. Central and western N.A.

---

* Special articles on the subjects indicated by an asterisk (*) will be found at the words so marked.

purpurea. Hedgehog coneflower; called also Black Sampson. Usually branched, 2–3 ft. high. Leaves broader, ovalish, toothed, the long stalk winged° or not. Flower heads similar to *E. angustifolia,* but more numerous. Central U.S.

echinata, -us, -um (eck-i-nay′ta). Prickly or bristly, like a sea urchin.

ECHINOCACTUS (ee-ky′no-kak-tus). A small but badly confused genus of generally globular, or columnar, ribbed cacti, ranging from the southwestern U.S. to Mex. Botanists have attributed nearly a thousand different species to the genus, all but 9 of which are now considered as of other genera (*Ferocactus, Astrophytum, Echinomastus, Thelocactus,* etc.). While some of the species of *Echinocactus* are cult. by fanciers, the ones of chief interest are those below. For culture *see* CACTI. (*Echinocactus* is Greek for spine and cactus.)

grusoni. A large, orange-shaped cactus, 16–30 in. in diameter, with many ribs and numerous golden-yellow spines. Flowers at the summit of the plant, red and yellow, day-blooming, 1½–2½ in. long, partly hidden by the dense wool that clothes the top of the plant. Fruit oblongish, ½–¾ in. long, white-woolly, its seeds black and shining. Mex.

horizonthalonius. A globular or nearly globular cactus, not over 10 in. high, with 8 ribs, the 8–9 reddish spines about 1½ in. long, the central one longer, all flattened and stout. Flowers solitary, terminal, pink, about 2½ in. wide. Southwestern U.S. and adjacent Mex.

ingens. A large, globular cactus nearly 5 ft. high and 4 ft. thick, 8-ribbed when young, but with more ribs in age, woolly at the top. Spines in clusters of 8, brownish, and with a single spine in the center of the 8. Flowers only ¾ in. long, yellow. Mex.

texensis = *Homalocephala texensis.*

ECHINOCEREUS (ee-ky-no-seer′ee-us). A genus of nearly 60 species of generally low, prostrate or hanging cacti, all from the southwestern U.S. and Mex., several grown for ornament or interest in desert regions or in the greenhouse. They usually form large clumps, the stems cylindrical or nearly globular, strongly ribbed, sometimes jointed. The ribs are plentifully beset with spines. Flowers solitary, borne on the sides but toward the top of the branches, day-blooming, more or less funnel-shaped or bell-shaped, the tube spiny. Fruit fleshy, thin-skinned, edible in some species. (*Echinocereus* is Greek for spine and *Cereus.*)

More than 30 species are known to be in cult., most of them confined to the collections of experts or fanciers. For the cult. of those below, which are the commonest in the trade, *see* CACTI.

engelmanni. Forming large clumps, the cylindric stems 5–12 in. long, 2–3 in. in diameter, with 11–14 ribs. Spines yellowish brown, 10 in each group, with 5–6 stouter, curved spines in the center of each group. Flowers purple, 2–3 in. long, wider when expanded. Southwestern U.S. and adjacent Mex.

enneacanthus. A clump-forming cactus, not over 5 in. high and about 2 in. in diameter, with 7 or 8 ribs. Spines in groups of 8, yellowish, with a single longer one in the center. Flowers

purple or reddish, about 2 in. long. Southwestern U.S. and adjacent Mex.

fitchi. Not over 4 in. high and 2 in. thick, the plant body cylindric, with 8–12 shallow ribs. Spines white, in groups of 20, short and spreading. Flowers nearly 3 in. wide, pink. Tex.

knippelianus. Not over 8 in. high and nearly as thick, dark green, with 5–7 obvious ribs. Spines short, weak, only 1–3 in each cluster. Flowers pink, about 1 in. long. Mex.

pectinatus. Stems usually unbranched, cylindric, 4–6 in. long, about 1½ in. in diameter. Ribs about 20, covered with many interlocking spines, which are in groups with about 30 laterals and a few erect at each center. Flowers 2–3 in. long, purple. Mex.

pentalophus. A prostrate or procumbent cactus, the tips of its branches ascending, but not over 5 in. high, and with 4–6 ribs. Spines 4–5 in a cluster, white, short, sometimes also with a single central spine. Flowers reddish-violet, 3–5 in. long. Tex. and Mex.

polyacanthus. One of the cacti with edible fruit called pitahaya. It is a low plant forming dense clumps of 20–50 pale, reddish-tinged stems. Ribs about 10, not very prominent. Spines yellow or grayish, becoming purplish in age. Flowers crimson, about 2 in. long, the tube spiny and woolly. N.M., Ariz. and Mex.

reichenbachi. A roundish cactus, the stems 6–8 in. long and about 3 in. thick, the ribs 12–19. Spines hugging the plant body, 20–30 in each group, with 1 or 2 central spines, all white or brownish. Flowers fragrant, 2–3 in. long, pale purple. Tex. and Mex.

rigidissimus. Rainbow cactus. An erect, stiff, nearly cylindric cactus 4–8 in. high and half as thick with 18–22 ribs. Spines numerous, interlocking, 16 in each group but with no central spine. Flowers pink, 2–3 in. long. Ariz. and Mex.

stramineus. A clump-forming cactus, the mass 1–3 ft. high. Stems 8–12 in. long, 1–3 in. thick, with about 13 ribs. Spines straw-colored, 7–14 in each group, with 3–4 central spines that are longer, often 3–4 in. long. Flowers showy, 3–5 in. long, purple. Southwestern U.S. and adjacent Mex.

ECHINOCHLOA (ee-ky-nock′lo-a). Rather weedy grasses of little or no garden interest, but often cult. for forage, and sometimes persisting in the garden as weeds, especially in the South. Of the dozen species only *E. crus-galli* is likely to be met. It is commonly called barn, or barnyard, or cockspur grass and is an annual stout, coarse grass 3–6 ft. high, very leafy, and usually branched. Leaves 18–24 in. long, about 1 in. wide. Flowering cluster terminal, the spikelets awned. There is a *var.* **frumentacea,** the Japanese barnyard millet or billion dollar grass, also known as Sanwa millet, with edible seeds, which has denser clusters and purplish spikelets without awns.° (*Echinochloa* is from the Greek for hedgehog grass.)

ECHINOCYSTIS (ee-ky-no-sis′tis). Herbaceous, usually quick-growing vines, comprising about 25 species of the cucumber family, all from N.A. or S.A., only one of secondary garden interest. It is *E.* **lobata,** the wild balsam apple, often called wild or mock cucumber. It is an annual, North American tendril°-bearing vine, often reaching 20 ft. and useful for quick covering.

° Special articles on the subjects indicated by an asterisk (°) will be found at the words so marked.

Stems slender, angled. Leaves alternate,* more or less ovalish-heart-shaped, 3–5 in. long, 3–7-lobed, the lobes with a minute soft prickle. Flowers small, whitish, in branched racemes* (for structure see CUCURBITA-CEAE). Fruit a puffy, rather papery, weak-spined pod about 2 in. long. (*Echinocystis* is from the Greek for hedgehog and bladder, in allusion to the spiny pod.) Sometimes offered as *Micrampelis.* See GOURDS.

ECHINOMASTUS (ee-ky-no-mas'tus). A small genus of chiefly Mexican cacti, two of them sometimes grown in desert gardens or in northern greenhouses. They are small, nearly globular or short-cylindric cacti, with many rather low ribs which are divided into tubercles. Spines several at each cluster, but often without a central spine or with few. Flowers central, usually purple. Fruit small, scaly, becoming dry. (*Echinomastus* is from the Greek denoting spiny breast, in allusion to the spiny tubercles.)

For culture see CACTI.

intertextus. Nearly globular and about 4 in. in diameter. Ribs 13. Spines 16–25 at each cluster, with 4 erect, central ones. Flowers purple, about 1 in. long. Tex., Ariz. and Mex.

macdowelli. Nearly globular, but about 3 in. high and a little more in diameter. Ribs 20–25. Spines 15–20 at a cluster with 3 or 4 erect, darker-colored, central spines. Flowers rose-purple, nearly 1½ in. long. Northern Mex.

ECHINOPANAX (ee-ky-no-pay'nacks) = *Oplopanax.*

ECHINOPS (ek'i-nops). Decidedly handsome, thistle-like, Old World herbs of the family Compositae, commonly called globe thistle and useful plants in the hardy border. Of the 75 known species the ones below, especially *E. Ritro* and *E. exaltatus,* are useful both for their handsome, white-woolly foliage and blue flowers. See BLUE GARDEN. Leaves alternate,* more or less prickly toothed or lobed, the under surface white. Flower heads densely beset with spiny bracts* and each flower in the head so furnished, the bracts usually metallic blue. (*Echinops* is Greek for like a hedgehog, in allusion to the spiny heads.)

These bold, showy plants are of easy culture in any ordinary garden soil, and may be increased by division or raised from seed like any other perennial or biennial. They need plenty of space.

exaltatus. A biennial,* 3–4 ft. high, scarcely branched, the stem cobwebby. Leaves unevenly cut, the spines small. Flower head large, blue, some of its bracts hairy on the margin. Russia. Late summer.

humilis. A perennial, 3–4 ft. high, usually unbranched and with a single spiny flower head. Leaves cobwebby above, white-felty beneath, lobed or cut, but wavy-margined and not very spiny. Siberia. Summer.

Ritro. A perennial 1–3 ft. high and the most widely cult. of the four. Stems branched and white-felty. Leaves nearly smooth above, white-felty beneath, cut into narrow segments. Flower heads blue. Eurasia. July–Sept.

sphaerocephalus. A stout perennial, 5–8 ft. high, and branched. Leaves roughish and green

above, hairy beneath, cut into triangular, spiny lobes. Flower head nearly 2 in. wide, blue. Eurasia and northern Af. Aug.–Oct. Sometimes confused with *E. Ritro.*

ECHINOPSIS (e-kin-op'sis). Sea urchin cactus. A genus of about 20 species of S. A. cacti, generally with low, ridged or fluted plant bodies, mostly sharp-angled. The only commonly cult. species is E. **multiplex,** from southern Brazil. It is about 8–12 in. in diameter in the wild, but smaller in cult., with 12–14 ribs and numerous, yellowish spines. Flowers very showy, rose-red, 10–14 in. long. For cult. see CACTI. It is a good plant for window sill or dish garden. A recently introduced species is E. **calochlora,** a round or ovalish cactus, about 4 in. high and nearly as thick, with 12 sharp ribs. Spines 14–22 in a cluster, sharp, straight and yellowish-brown, about ½ in. long and with 3–4 stouter central spines. Flowers 4–6, ½ in. long, white. Brazil.

ECHIOIDES (ek-ee-oy'deez; but see OïDES). Like a blueweed (*Echium*).

ECHIUM (ek'i-um). A genus of over 35 species of Eurasian herbs or shrubby plants of the family Boraginaceae, a few grown for ornament, and *E. vulgare,* a common roadside, naturalized weed in eastern N.A. They have rough foliage, with alternate,* simple leaves. Flowers rather showy, prevailingly blue, in forked or unforked, one-sided spikes.* Corolla funnel-shaped or trumpet-shaped, its limb somewhat oblique, the flower hence a little irregular.* Stamens 5, nearly always protruding. Fruit a collection of 4, erect, wrinkled nutlets. (*Echium* is from the Greek for viper, some of the species being called viper's-bugloss.)

The first species is a shrub suited to outdoor cult. only in Calif. and similar regions. The others are of easy culture anywhere and may be raised from seed. Flowering in summer.

fastuosum. Shrub 4–6 ft. high, the foliage gray-hairy. Leaves lance-shaped. Flowers purplish or dark blue, the stamens* red. Canary Islands.

plantagineum. An annual or biennial 15–20 in. high, but usually grown as a hardy annual. See ANNUALS. Leaves ovalish or oblong, diminishing upward into bracts.* Flowers blue, rarely light purple. Southern Eu.

vulgare. Blueweed, called also blue thistle. A somewhat weedy biennial 18–30 in. high. Leaves oblongish, 2–6 in. long. Flowers at first pink, in maturity brilliant blue, about ½ in. long and very handsome. Eurasia, but common as a weed and little grown as a garden plant.

EDDO = *Colocasia esculenta.*

EDELWEISS. A much publicized but not particularly beautiful alpine herb comprising the genus **Leontopodium** (lee-on-to-pō'di-um), native in the mountains of Eurasia and S.A. The only cult. species is L. **alpinum,** the edelweiss of the Alps, which is sometimes sold as *Gnaphalium Leontopo-*

---

* Special articles on the subjects indicated by an asterisk (*) will be found at the words so marked.

dium. It is a white-woolly perennial herb with erect or ascending stems usually about 6 in. high. Leaves lance-shaped but broader toward the tip, ultimately shedding the white wool from the upper surface. Flower heads solitary at the ends of the branches, wholly of yellow disk* flowers, not showy, but beneath which is a series of dry, silvery bracts,* much longer than the width of the head. For culture *see* ROCK GARDEN. (*Leontopodium* is Greek for lion's-foot.)

EDGEWORTHIA (edj-wor'thi-a). A small genus of Asiatic shrubs of the family Thymelaeaceae, one of secondary garden interest. It is the paper tree or paper bush, **E. papyrifera**, which is also called by some *E. gardneri* and *E. chrysantha,* and is a Chinese and Japanese shrub, the source of mitsumata paper. Leaves alternate,* mostly crowded at the ends of the twigs, oblongish, 4–5 in. long, unfolding after the yellow flowers appear. Flowers in dense, head-like clusters, fragrant, rather small (for details *see* THYMELAEACEAE). Fruit fleshy but somewhat dry. The bark yields a paper-making fiber in China and Japan. Not hardy north of zone* 6, nor does it like the extreme summer heat of much of the Middle West. (Named for M. P. Edgeworth, English botanist.)

EDGING. A border of flowers, wood, brick, metal or stones used to define the edge of a lawn, drive, path, or flower bed.

Whether composed of plants or other materials, edgings are the features that first strike the eye. Metal edgings, of rolled steel and zinc, as well as iron, are obtainable in various sizes to fit all spaces. A standard size of one-quarter inch by five inches is preferred in most cases. These

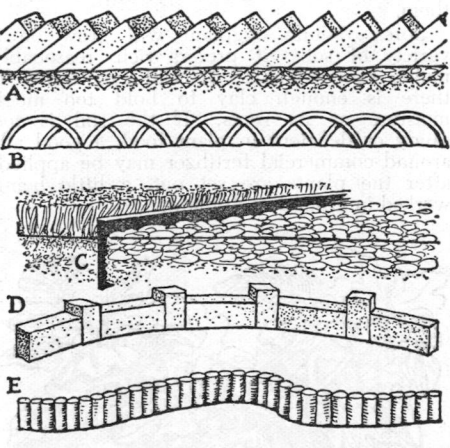

Edgings. (A) Bricks. (B) Wire hoops. (C) Steel edging for edge of path or road. (D) Wooden edging. (E) Wooden cylinders set on end. None of these are to be compared with plant edgings, but (C) is often necessary on drives.

are used to retain the soil in raised beds, to obtain clean-cut lines on walks and drives, and to confine gravel or loose-stone paths and roadways within their proper limits. Cement, stone, or brick curbs may be used if preferred. Turf is often used as a border edging, although constant care is required to keep it from acquiring a ragged appearance. There are also attractive wooden edgings, but they are not permanent.

An informal edging of low plants

Upon the width and type of the border depend to a large extent the plants used as edging material. Low, compact-growing plants must be used with small or formal borders, while taller, less formal, massed plantings may have as an edging the plants that often make up the small border proper. Long borders, either straight or winding, are usually edged with a variety of plants varying in form and color, but sometimes a ribbon of one variety runs the entire length.

The edging strip is an excellent place for low-growing annuals which provide a bril-

A formal clipped edging of low shrubs such as box or box barberry

---

* Special articles on the subjects indicated by an asterisk (*) will be found at the words so marked.

liancy not found in many perennials. Very early-blooming bulbs, such as *Muscari*, snowdrops, crocuses, and tulips may be used to prolong the season of bloom, by filling in the space later with petunias, dwarf snapdragons, ageratum, *Lobelia Erinus* and pansies, to cover the dying foliage. Of the quickly maturing annuals, sown where they are to bloom, the most popular is the sweet alyssum. Other good annuals for edgings are abronia, the annual candytufts, dwarf coreopsis, dianthus, godetia, nemophila, nigella, phlox, and portulaca.

Perennial edgings, such as the violas and dwarf campanulas, cannot be changed each year. Variety may be obtained by replacing old or winter-killed plants with new seedlings or substituting taller-growing specimens for mat-like species. Good perennials for both sun and shade are *Dianthus gratianopolitanus*, *Veronica incana*, and *Iberis sempervirens* (see CANDYTUFT).

Romanzoffia is a garden plant which does well in shady or half-shady situations. It succeeds very well when used in conjunction with brick or stone edgings. Box° is one of the most popular of all edgings, and the most desirable for formal plantings, especially in the dwarf edging form (see Box). A good substitute, and much cheaper, is the box barberry (see BERBERIS THUNBERGI MINOR).

EDGING BOX = *Buxus sempervirens suffruticosa*. See Box.

EDGING CANDYTUFT = *Iberis sempervirens*. See CANDYTUFT.

EDGING LOBELIA = *Lobelia Erinus*

EDIBLE-PODDED PEA = *Pisum sativum macrocarpon*. See PEA.

EDRAIANTHUS (ed-dry-an'thus). A small genus of herbs of the family Campanulaceae, mostly from the Mediterranean region, E. **tenuifolius** sometimes cult. in the rock garden (which see). It is sometimes known as E. *dalmaticus*. It is a perennial, tufted° herb, scarcely 6 in. high, with alternate,° very narrow leaves, and blue flowers in dense terminal, and bracted clusters. Corolla bell-shaped, the upper part 5-lobed. Fruit a 2–5-valved capsule.° Another species, perhaps more desirable than the above, is E. **graminifolius**. It is a densely tufted perennial, 2–4 in. high, the leaves linear, pointed, about 1 in. long. Flowers in a few-flowered head, the corolla° hairy, purple, bell-shaped, with bracts° beneath. Albania and Italy. (*Edraianthus* is from the Greek for [essentially] stalkless flower.)

edulis, -e (ed'you-lis). Edible.

EEL-GRASS. Common submerged, aquatic herbs of the genus **Vallisneria** (val-lis-neer'i-a) of the family Hydrocharitaceae, of no garden interest except for aquaria, but of absorbing fruiting habits. The only cult. species is **V. spiralis,** often called tape-grass or wild celery, a favorite feed of wild ducks. It has long, very narrow, tape-like leaves

and minute flowers, the male and female on different stalks. (*See* HYDROCHARITACEAE.) Male flowers white, at first submerged and on short stalks near the bottom, ultimately released and reaching the surface detached. Here they fertilize the female flowers which are on long, coiling stalks that ultimately contract. Fruit minute, many-seeded and ripening far beneath the surface. The American representative of this nearly world-wide aquatic is sometimes designated as *V. americana*. (Named for Antonio Vallisneri, Italian naturalist.) Many of the wild plants are in danger from a disease which does not yield to control measures.

EELWORM. A microscopic worm better known as nematode (which see). They cause root knots, galls, etc.

effusa, -us, -um (eff-you'sa). Loosely spreading.

EGGFRUIT = *Lucuma nervosa*.

EGGPLANT (*Solanum Melongena esculentum*). The eggplant, sometimes, in one of its varieties, called snake eggplant, is essentially a tropical crop needing heat for its proper development. While it can be grown as far north as zone° 4, its best development is in the warmer parts of the country. Other names for it are aubergine, brinjal, Jew's-apple and mad-apple.

Because it will not stand the cold, it is better to plant seed in the hotbed or in the greenhouse, allowing 6–8 weeks from seeding until the plants are ready to be put outdoors, which should not be before settled warm weather has arrived. Its early handling is very much the same as for the garden peppers or for tomatoes, but the plant is even more sensitive to cold than either of them.

SOILS. While eggplant will grow on a variety of soils, it prefers rich, reasonably moist, sandy loams. It will not thrive if there is enough clay to hold too much moisture at its roots. If the soil is too sandy or deficient in plant food, a good all-around commercial fertilizer may be applied, after the plants are set out, a little being worked in around each plant.

Eggplant

° Special articles on the subjects indicated by an asterisk (°) will be found at the words so marked.

While the eggplant needs humus, it is better not to use stable manure, unless it is old and thoroughly composted. Some commercial growers prefer to get humus through plowing in a leguminous crop the season before.

PLANTING. Having raised your seedlings to the stage of being about 6 in. high, preferably each in its own pot, you are ready for outdoor planting, assuming the seedlings have been gradually hardened-off as with tomato plants (which see). Put the plants 3–4 ft. apart each way, and if it is a dry period, give each a little water. If, however, you are using potted plants, these may be given a thorough soaking the night before planting and then should show little effects from the shift to outdoor culture.

YIELDS AND VARIETIES. For the South, use Black Beauty and Florida Highbush. For the North, and especially for the home gardener, the preferred varieties are Fort Myers Market, Black Magic, and also Black Beauty. For the South, Florida Market and Florida Beauty. A good plant, with the right soil and plenty of heat, will bear 3–8 fruits, often less, but sometimes more under favorable conditions. The fruit is so heavy it should be cut, not torn, from the plant.

INSECT PESTS. Lacebug may be controlled by pesticide #21, #20 or #1 (see SPRAYS AND DUSTS). For other pests, see POTATO.

DISEASES. A fungus disease which causes blighting of young plants, leaf and stem spots on older plants, and rotting of fruit may be carried on the seeds. Soaking the seed for 25 minutes in hot water (122° F.) will rid the seed of the fungus. If a rot of the fruit starts to develop, spray at 10-day intervals using pesticide #11 (see SPRAYS AND DUSTS). The eggplant varieties Florida Market and Florida Beauty are resistant to blight.*

A wilt* disease may cause wilting and death of eggplant, particularly if grown in the same soil during successive years.

EGLANTERIA (egg-lan-teer'i-a). A Latinized version of an old French name for the sweetbrier.

EGLANTINE = Rosa Eglanteria. For another plant sometimes called eglantine see LONICERA PERICLYMENUM.

EGYPTIAN CLOVER = Trifolium alexandrinum. See CLOVER.

EGYPTIAN LILY = Calla lily (Zantedeschia aethiopica).

EGYPTIAN LOTUS. See NELUMBO NUCIFERA. Also the white lotus (Nymphaea Lotus) and the blue lotus (N. caerulea) are both called Egyptian lotus.

EHRETIA (er-ree'shi-a). A genus of nearly 50 species of chiefly tropical shrubs and trees of the family Boraginaceae, one grown for ornament. They have alternate* and (in ours) toothed leaves and small, white flowers in terminal clusters. Corolla shortly funnel-shaped, its 5 spreading lobes blunt. Stamens 5, inserted on the tube

of the corolla. Fruit fleshy, with 4 nutlets. (Named for G. D. Ehret, German botanical artist.)

While E. thyrsiflora will survive in the North as indicated below, it is most at home in central and northern Fla., where it flowers and fruits much more freely than in the North.

acuminata = Ehretia thyrsiflora.

thyrsiflora. A tree 20–45 ft. high. Leaves oblongish or broadest above the middle, 4–7 in. long, toothed. Flowers about ⅓ in. wide, the clusters (panicles*) 5–7 in. long and showy. Fruit orange, ultimately brownish-black. Eastern Asia. Hardy in protected sites from zone* 5 southward. June–July. Popular in Fla.

EICHHORNIA. See WATER HYACINTH.

ELAEAGNACEAE (ell-ee-ag-nay'see-ee). All of the three known genera of the oleaster family contain plants of garden interest. They are shrubs or trees mostly of warmer parts of the north temperate zone, but some species of Elaeagnus extend far northward. Most of the plants have scurfy or golden-brown foliage.

Leaves alternate* in Elaeagnus and Hippophae, but opposite* in Shepherdia, without marginal teeth in all genera. Flowers not very showy, in small clusters in the leaf axils,* or solitary, or in racemes.* Fruit actually a dry nut or achene,* but appearing fleshy because the fleshy receptacle* encloses the true fruits. This fleshy receptacle is often incorrectly called a berry (see GUMI at Elaeagnus multiflora). The shrubs of this family are widely planted for their ornamental, often silvery foliage, and for their brightly colored, often edible "fruits" (i.e., receptacles*).

Technical flower characters: Flowers hermaphrodite* in Elaeagnus, but mostly dioecious* in the other two genera, without petals. Calyx tubular, 2–4-lobed, petal-like. Stamens 2–4, or twice as many. Ovary 1-celled, with long style and a single ovule.

Elaeagnos (el-e-ag'nos). Resembling an oleaster (Elaeagnus).

ELAEAGNUS (eel-ee-ag'nus). A handsome genus of shrubs or trees of the family Elaeagnaceae, comprising perhaps 40 species of the north temperate zone, several cult. for their ornamental foliage and for their decorative or edible fruits. Leaves alternate,* short-stalked, more or less dotted with silvery or scurfy scales. Flowers not showy, without petals, the calyx* tubular or bell-shaped, 4-lobed. Stamens 4. Fruit berry-like but not a true berry (actually the modified receptacle*). (Elaeagnus is from the Greek for olive and the chaste tree.)

These are hardy, wind-resistant shrubs or small trees, useful as windbreaks in the prairie states, and they will grow easily in a variety of dry sites. They are easily propagated by root cuttings, layers or by grafting. Stratified seeds sown the second season will also yield new plants.

angustifolia. Oleaster; called also Russian

* Special articles on the subjects indicated by an asterisk (*) will be found at the words so marked.

olive and Trebizond date. A Eurasian, sometimes spiny tree 10–20 ft. high. Leaves silvery beneath, oblongish, 2–3½ in. long. Flowers greenish, 1–3 together. Fruit egg-shaped, about ½ in. long, yellow but silvery-scaled, the flesh sweet but mealy. June. Hardy from zone* 2 southward. There are varieties with spiny branches and with larger, greenish leaves.

argentea = *E. commutata.*

commutata. Silverberry, also called wolfberry. An erect shrub 8–12 ft. high, spreading by stolons.* Leaves short-stalked, ovalish to oblong, 1–4½ in. long, silvery. Flowers fragrant, silvery-yellow, about 1 in. long, in clusters of 1–3. Fruit silvery, short-stalked. May–July. Northern N.A. Hardy everywhere.

longipes = *Elaeagnus multiflora.*

multiflora. Gumi. A spreading shrub 4–9 ft. high. Leaves more or less elliptic, 1–3 in. long, silvery beneath. Flowers yellowish-white, silvery and brown-scaly on the outside. Fruit red, scaly, of a pleasant acid flavor. Apr.–May. Eastern As. Hardy from zone* 3 southward. There are several varieties with minor foliage differences. The plant is also offered as *E. longipes.* It is smoke-resistant.

pungens. A usually spiny, spreading shrub 10–15 ft. high, the foliage evergreen. Leaves wavy-margined, silvery beneath, oblongish, 2½–5 in. long, stalked. Flowers 1–3, hanging, silvery-white and very fragrant. Fruit brown at first, then red. Japan. Oct.–Nov. Hardy from zone* 5 southward and commonly cult. in the south. The *var.* **aurea** has yellow-margined leaves; *var.* **maculata** has yellow-blotched leaves; *var.* **variegata** has white or yellowish-white-margined leaves; the *var.* **reflexa** has wavy-margined leaves, brown-scaly beneath; the *var.* **simoni** has somewhat larger leaves, scarcely scaly beneath.

umbellata. A branching shrub 10–18 ft. high, the branches brown-scaly. Leaves elliptic to oval-oblong, 1–3½ in. long, silvery beneath, the margins often crisped. Flowers fragrant, yellowish-white, scaly on the outside, about ¾ in. long. Fruit brown, then red. May–June. Eastern As. Hardy from zone* 3 southward.

ELAEIS (ee-lee′is). A single species of feather palms from tropical Af., E. **guineensis,** the African oil palm, cult. outdoors only in zone* 9. Economically important in the African oil trade, it is of little hort. importance in the U.S., although it is a handsome palm, up to 70 ft. (less in cult. here), in the young state resembling a *Phoenix.* Leaves 10–15 ft. long, often long-persistent even when dead. Leaflets very numerous, ridged, stiffish. Flowering cluster among the crown of leaves, branched, short and head-like, sometimes spiny. Fruit egg-shaped or conical, about 1 in. long, red or orange-yellow. (*Elaeis* is Greek for olive, in allusion to the fruit.)

ELAEOCARPACEAE (ee-lee-o-kar-pay′-see-ee). A family of about 8 genera and perhaps 150 species of tropical shrubs and trees, not distantly related to the lindens. Leaves opposite or alternate, never compound.* Flowers with separate petals, sometimes showy, mostly in racemes* or panicles.* Petals and sepals 4 or 5, the petals sometimes wanting. Fruit a capsule in *Crinodendron,* but a berry in *Aristotelia,* the only cult. genera here considered.

ELAEODENDRON (ee-lee-o-den′dron). A genus of 45 species of warm-country shrubs or trees of the family Celastraceae, one grown for ornament in Calif. and other nearly frost-free places, and in the greenhouse. They have leathery leaves and small, whitish or greenish flowers in small clusters in the leaf axils.* Of several species in cult., **E. orientale,** the false olive, is most likely to be of interest. It is a handsome shrub, the juvenile and mature leaves being very different. Mature leaves oblongish, scalloped, 2–3 in. long, the young ones narrower and very graceful, the shrub chiefly grown for them. Fruit olive-like, but inedible. Use potting mixture* 5 and grow in a warm greenhouse. (*Elaeodendron* is from the Greek for olive tree.)

ELAPHOGLOSSUM (e-laff-o-gloss′um). Nearly 400 species of tropical ferns of the family Polypodiaceae, with undivided fronds and creeping rootstocks. Only one, **E. crinitum,** the elephant-ear fern of tropical America, is of any garden interest, and is widely grown in the greenhouse for its hardy, resistant foliage. Sometimes known as *Acrostichum crinitum.* Fronds stout, thick, 12–20 in. long, the stalk conspicuously shaggy, the blade without teeth, paddle-shaped and nearly 7 in. wide, often hairy on the margins. Spore cases completely covering the under side of some of the narrower fronds, felt-like and brownish. The plant needs greenhouse culture, with plenty of water but perfect drainage. See FERNS AND FERN GARDENING. (*Elaphoglossum* is from the Greek for deer tongue, in allusion to the fronds.)

elastica, -us, -um (ee-las′ti-ka). Elastic or rubber-producing.

elata, -us, -um (ee-lay′ta). Tall.

Elaterium (ell-a-teer′i-um). Old Greek word implying to drive. See ECBALLIUM.

Elatines (e-la-ty′neez). Named for a non-hort. genus *Elatine.*

elatius, -or (ee-lay′ti-us). Taller.

ELDER. Attractive shrubs comprising the genus **Sambucus** (sam-bew′kus) of the honeysuckle family. There are perhaps 20 species, of which those below are in common cult. for their flowers and some for their fruit used for making both wine and jelly. They have pithy branches and opposite,* compound* leaves, the leaflets arranged feather-fashion with an odd one at the end, all toothed. Flowers small, white, in terminal, much-branched, often flat-topped clusters (corymb* or panicle*). Corolla small, wheel-shaped, the calyx very small or nearly abortive. Fruit berry-like, with 3–5 one-seeded nutlets. (*Sambucus* is the classical Latin name of the elder.)

The elders, or, as they are often called, the elderberries, are rather showy shrubs but inclined to be sprawling and more suited to informal shrubberies than for speci-

---

* Special articles on the subjects indicated by an asterisk (*) will be found at the words so marked.

men plants. Some of the cut-leaved varieties of *S. racemosa* are, however, valued for their foliage. And the fruits of *S. canadensis* were once very widely gathered for wine-making. All are of the easiest culture, although most of them do better in moist sites than in dry ones. They are easily increased by cuttings or by suckers,* which are very common in most of them.

S. caerulea. Blue elder. A shrub or small tree 10–40 ft. high in the wild, less as cult. Leaflets 5–7, oblongish, 2–5½ in. long, sharply toothed and smooth. Flowers yellow-white in a convex close cluster (cyme*) that is 4–6 in. wide. Fruit bluish-black, with a bloom. Western N.A. July–Aug. Hardy from zone* 4 southward.

S. canadensis. American elder or elderberry. A very common North American shrub 6–10 ft. high, its branches brittle. Leaflets mostly 7, short-stalked, 2½–6 in. long, tapering at the tip. Flowers small (about 1/10 in. wide), the cluster slightly convex but essentially flat-topped, nearly 4 in. across. Fruit purple-black, about ⅙ in. in diameter. June–July. Hardy from zone* 2 southward. There are golden-leaved varieties, and the *var.* **acutiloba** has dissected leaflets. All forms stand smoke better than most shrubs.

S. nigra. European elder. A shrub up to 25 ft. high, sometimes tree-like. Leaflets mostly 5, elliptic to ovalish, short-stalked, 2–5½ in. long. Flowers yellowish-white, heavy-scented, the essentially flat-topped cluster about 3 in. wide. Fruit black, about ¼ in. in diameter. Eurasia and northern Af. Hardy from zone* 3 southward. The *var.* **aureo-variegata** and the *var.* **albo-variegata** have golden-yellow and white-blotched foliage, respectively.

S. pubens. American red elder. A spreading shrub 8–12 ft. high. Leaflets 5–7, generally ovalish or oblongish, 2½–4 in. long. Flower cluster pyramid-shaped. Fruit scarlet, inedible. Eastern N.A. but west to Ore. May. Hardy from zone* 3 southward and possibly in protected parts of zone* 2. Not much grown, but common in moist, mountain woods.

S. racemosa. Red-berried elder. A commonly cult. Eurasian shrub, perhaps the best of the five, scarcely over 10 ft. high. Leaflets 5–7, practically stalkless, ovalish or elliptic, 2–3½ in. long, tapering at the tip. Flowers yellowish-white, the cluster not flat-topped. Fruit scarlet. Apr.–May. Of its many varieties two are: *var.* **laciniata**, with the young foliage green and the leaflets dissected; and *var.* **plumosa**, with the young foliage purplish and the leaflets cut to nearly the middle.

For other plants sometimes called elder *see Acer Negundo* at MAPLE, and STENOLOBIUM STANS.

ELDERBERRY = Elder, especially *Sambucus canadensis. See* ELDER.

ELDER FAMILY = Caprifoliaceae.

ELECAMPANE = *Inula Helenium.*

ELECTRO-HORTICULTURE. Twenty years of experiment in the use of electricity for plants has resulted in much of practical importance. Most of the experimental work has been with light rays of different color, intensity, or duration. Astonishing response to such stimuli, especially long-continued night illumination, has demonstrated that the speed of growth can, in certain plants, be tremendously accelerated, usually to the plant's disadvantage. Increasing the length of winter days, by the judicious use of electric illumination is practical and widely used by commercial florists.

The substitution of electric coils for heating hotbeds instead of using stable manure is now common. For details *see* COLD FRAME. *See also* PROPAGATING FRAME.

elegans (el′lee-ganz). Beautiful or elegant.

elegantissima (el-lee-gan-tiss′i-ma). Most beautiful or elegant.

ELEOCHARIS (el-e-ock′a-ris). A large genus of rush-like sedges, family Cyperaceae, of no garden interest except **E. tuberosa**, the Chinese water chestnut, which is sometimes called *Scirpus tuberosus.* It produces an edible corm,* rich in sugar and protein and these are much used in China and in Chinese restaurants here. The corms, which may be procured from Chinese markets, should be planted in rich muck, preferably with cow manure, in 6-in. flower pots and then submerged in water. Corms will mature in six months and the pots must be brought indoors or into a greenhouse before cold weather. This has nothing to do with the water chestnut for which *see* TRAPA. (*Eleocharis* is from the Greek for *marsh* and *grace* in allusion to the marsh habit of most species.)

ELEPHANT-EAR. *See* COLOCASIA.

ELEPHANT-EAR FERN = *Elaphoglossum crinitum.*

elephantidens (el-ee-fan′ti-denz). Large-toothed.

ELETTARIA. *See* CARDAMON.

ELEUSINE (el-you-sy′ne). Perhaps half a dozen species of Old World grasses, one yielding a minor grain, one a weed, and none particularly ornamental. Ours are annuals, or treated as such, with tufted* stems and narrow, grass-like leaves. Flowers minute (for details *see* GRAMINEAE), usually arranged in 1-sided spikes which are grouped in a terminal, umbel*-like cluster. (*Eleusine* is Greek for the town where Ceres, the goddess of agriculture, was worshiped.)

Eleusine coracana is somewhat grown here for ornament, but in the Old World its grain is a secondary cereal. Like the others it is easily raised as an annual.

barcinonensis = *Eleusine tristachya.*

coracana. African millet. From 1–4 ft. high. Leaves 8–12 in. long, about ¼ in. wide. Flowering spikes erect, about 1½ in. long and ¼ in. wide. Fruit (a caryopsis*) nearly round, with a loose husk. As. and Af., probably.

indica. Wire grass. A weedy, sometimes troublesome Old World grass naturalized* in N.A., not over 2 ft. high. Leaves 8–12 in. long, about ¼ in. wide. Flowering spikes spreading, 2–4 in. long.

tristachya. Usually less than 12 in. high. Leaves 3–7 in. long, about 1/16 in. wide. Flowering spikes about 1 in. long and ⅛ in. wide. India.

* Special articles on the subjects indicated by an asterisk (*) will be found at the words so marked.

ELGIN BOTANIC GARDEN. *See* Ho-SACKIA.

ELK CLOVER = *Aralia californica.*

ELK-GRASS = *Xerophyllum tenax.*

elliptica, -us, -um (el-lip′ti-ka). Elliptic; *i.e.,* oval, but narrowed toward the rounded ends.

ELM. No trees could replace elms in the American landscape. They all belong to the genus **Ulmus** (ul′mus) of the family Ulmaceae, and of the 25 known species, all from the north temperate zone, nearly half are in pretty common cultivation for their beautiful habit and fine foliage. They are mostly tall trees with alternate,* short-stalked leaves that are usually somewhat oblique and doubly toothed. Flowers without petals, the calyx* bell-shaped and inconspicuous. Fruit a compressed nut surrounded by a flat, often hairy wing (a samara). (*Ulmus* is the classical Latin name of the elm.)
For culture *see* below.

U. americana. American elm, also called white elm and water elm. A magnificent tree, vase-like in outline when mature, up to 120 ft. in height and with light gray, scaly, but deeply fissured bark. Leaves oval-oblong, 3–7 in. long, unequal at the base, smooth or roughish above, sometimes hairy beneath. Flowers small, on stalks ½–¾ in. long, 3 or 4 together. Fruit about ¾ in. long, notched at the tip, hairy on the margin. N.A., east of the Rocky Mountains. Flowering before the leaves unfold. Hardy everywhere. A hybrid of the American elm and another (unrecorded) species is said to grow faster and be immune to disease, both statements lacking verification. The *var.* **pendula,** often called the weeping American elm, has the ends of the main branches drooping. Both are widely planted as street trees.
U. campestris = *Ulmus procera.*
U. carpinifolia. Smooth-leaved elm. A tree rarely over 75 ft. high. Leaves very oblique, smooth both sides, glossy-green, 2–4 in. long. Flowers in dense clusters. Fruit elliptic, but wedge-shaped at the base, the seed close to the closed notch. Eurasia and northern Af. Hardy from zone* 3 southward. There are several varieties in cult., the best known being *var.* **umbraculifera,** with a globe-shaped crown, and *var.* **wheatleyi,** the Jersey elm, which has stiffer, more erect branches.
U. foliacea = *Ulmus carpinifolia.*
U. fulva = *Ulmus rubra.*
U. glabra. Wych elm. A smooth-barked tree up to 120 ft. Leaves short-stalked, oblongish or elliptic, 3½–7 in. long, rough above, but usually hairy beneath. Flowers in dense clusters. Fruit broadly elliptic, over 1 in. long, smooth. Eurasia. A widely planted tree for lawns or parks, hardy from zone* 3 southward. Of its many cult. varieties the following are best liked: *var.* **atropurpurea,** with dark purple young foliage; *var.* **camperdowni,** the Camper-down elm, which has drooping branches; *var.* **crispa,** with twisted and incurved leaf teeth; and *var.* **fastigiata,** with upright branches forming a columnar tree.
U. hollandica. Dutch or Holland elm. A hybrid elm, intermediate in characters between the wych elm and the smooth-leaved elm. It is best known in two varieties long cult. for orna-

ment: *var.* **belgica,** the Belgian elm, a tall tree with upright branches and a broad crown, its leaves more or less elliptic, 3½–5½ in. long, somewhat rough above, and very oblique at the base. The *var.* **vegeta,** usually known as the Huntingdon elm, is a tall tree, usually with a forking trunk, the leaves very oblique at the base, smooth above, 4–7½ in. long, generally elliptic. Both the Dutch elm and its two varieties are hardy up to zone* 3.
U. parvifolia. Chinese elm. A small, smooth-barked tree usually not over 40 ft. high, and inclined to forking. Leaves more or less elliptic, 1–2½ in. long, shining above, hairy beneath at first, at length smooth. Flowers in small clusters, blooming in Aug.–Sept. Fruit about ½ in. long, notched at the tip. Eastern As. A small, quick-growing tree, hardy from zone* 3 southward, the fall foliage red or purple in the North, but persistent and green southward. Sometimes known as *U. chinensis.*
U. procera. English elm. A tall tree, more round-headed than the American elm, often 100–150 ft. high. Leaves oval or elliptic, 2½–4 in. long, very oblique at the base, rough above, softly hairy beneath. Flowers short-stalked, appearing before the leaves unfold. Fruit nearly round, about ¾ in. in diameter, not hairy. Eu. Somewhat planted here, but surely hardy only up to zone* 3. Sometimes known as *U. campestris.* There are many varieties of this handsome tree, some with variegated foliage, some purple-tinged, and some with more erect branches than the typical plant.
U. pumila. Siberian elm. Dwarf elm. Somewhat resembling *U. parvifolia,* but much taller, the bark rough, the flowers appearing before the leaves unfold, and the branches still more inclined to fork. Leaves 1½–3½ in. long, smooth both sides. Fruit nearly 1 in. long. Northeastern As. Hardy from zone* 3 southward. Unfortunately the name dwarf elm became attached to this species, although it reaches a height of 80 ft. in its native home. It is often called (incorrectly) the Chinese elm, and both are widely used for shelterbelt planting in the West.
U. racemosa = *Ulmus thomasi.*
U. rubra. Slippery elm. Rarely over 60 ft. high. Leaves very oblique at the base, rough above, hairy beneath, 5–9 in. long. Flowers short-stalked, but in dense clusters. Fruit nearly round, almost 1 in. long, hairy in the center. Eastern N.A. Hardy from zone* 2 southward, but not much planted. Its bruised twigs have a characteristic odor. Often called *Ulmus fulva.*
U. thomasi. Rock elm, also called cork elm. A tree up to 90 ft. high, its twigs corky-winged. Leaves roughish above, oblongish, 2½–5 in. long, unequal at the base. Flowers in small, hanging clusters (racemes*). Fruit elliptic, ¾–1½ in. long, slightly notched at the tip, hairy. Eastern N.A. Not much planted, but handsome in the fall when its foliage turns yellow. Hardy from zone* 2 southward. Often called *Ulmus racemosa.*

ELM CULTURE

The Elm is without doubt the most commonly planted ornamental tree in the northeastern states. About fifteen species and many varieties are hardy. This group is easily transplanted and is not particular as to soil requirements. Neither does it mind severe pruning. Its greatest drawback is its susceptibility to insect attack and disease.

* Special articles on the subjects indicated by an asterisk (*) will be found at the words so marked.

At the present time, plantings in this country are in great danger due to an infection known as the Dutch elm disease. This disease has become so serious, especially in the northeastern states, that thoughtful owners are already on the lookout for elm substitutes. There is, of course, no real substitute for the incomparable branching of the American elm. Good shade trees, however, can be found among the lindens, oaks, maples, and many others.

The American Elm is the most common of the group. At the present time several upright forms are being propagated in large numbers for situations that require a narrow tree and for street work. All species of elm are susceptible to the Dutch elm disease but recently the U.S. Department of Agriculture has been distributing some varieties that are thought to be more disease-resistant than others. These are Christine Buisman and Bea Schwarz but neither of these European varieties has the vigorous growth and desirable vase-shaped habit of our native *Ulmus americana*. Hence they probably will not be widely planted. However, Augustine, a variety of *U. americana*, is becoming increasingly popular because of its upright columnar habit, much desired in planting narrow streets.

Ulmus rubra, the Slippery Elm; *Ulmus glabra*, the Wych Elm; and *Ulmus procera*, the English Elm, are all hardy and fast-growing. The hybrid, *Ulmus hollandica*, is commonly used for street ornamentation in Europe and to some extent in this country. It cannot compete, however, with the American Elm in size or rate of growth in the northeastern states.

The Camperdown Elm, *Ulmus glabra camperdowni*, a rounded or flat-headed form with pendulous branches, is generally grafted head-high and is an excellent small tree for the garden.

Several of the Asiatic species such as *Ulmus pumila* and *parvifolia* are now commonly planted. The former is especially noted for its fast growth. However, because of its brittle wood, it is not a clean tree, and cannot be recommended for avenue ornamentation. As a fast-growing tree it has merit, especially in dry, poor soils.

All elms have a majority of their feeding roots close to the soil surface, hence they can be voracious feeders in the garden, robbing the soil in plant beds and borders of nutrients and moisture. Where possible, it is inadvisable to plant elms in a garden where rich, deep soil is needed for growing smaller plants. Rather the elm should be planted in the lawn or street areas where plenty of room for root expansion is available.

The Elm is most commonly propagated by seed which is sown immediately after it ripens in June. Germination takes place soon after it is sown and the following year the seedlings will be six inches to more than a foot high. They are then lined out in nursery rows. The varieties and hybrids are generally budded on the American Elm. Some propagators prefer grafting, but it can hardly be recommended as it is more expensive and does not produce as good a tree as budded stock. In rare instances, layering and softwood cuttings are used, but the results are seldom satisfactory when carried out on a large scale. In recent years it has become the custom with many nurserymen to bud the American Elm in order to obtain standardized trees, a practice to be particularly recommended where the material is to be used for street plantings. — D. W.

INSECT PESTS. Various scales and cockscomb-gall aphids are controlled by dormant superior oils. Pesticide #21 (*see* SPRAYS AND DUSTS) will control leaf aphids. Sticky tree-bands in fall and spring suppress cankerworm (inchworm) but pesticide #19 or #21 sprays may be needed for this and other leaf feeders such as tussock moth and including elm leaf beetle which is a notorious household invader in fall and late summer. Bark beetles carry Dutch elm disease. Control with thorough late dormant heavy sprays or mist applications of pesticide #17. Municipal campaigns to control this pest are the most satisfactory. Mites, scales, and aphids may increase following the use of pesticide #17. Pesticide #14 will kill mites, pesticide #21 aphids.

DISEASES. In the northeastern states the most serious disease is Dutch elm disease. This disease, caused by a fungus and spread from elm to elm by the elm bark beetle, has killed an untold number of trees. During the early summer, one or more branches will exhibit a wilting and browning of leaves. If the bark is peeled from these branches, brown streaks will be seen running the length of the diseased branch. Once a tree has Dutch elm disease there is little or no hope for recovery, regardless of any treatment given the tree. The best preventative is an application of pesticide #17 at 12% DDT (*see* SPRAYS AND DUSTS) during the dormant period before leaves come out in the spring. This will con-

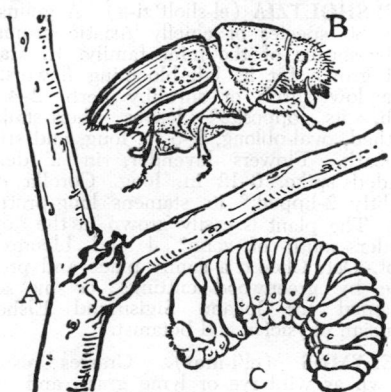

Dutch Elm Disease. (A) The incision made by the European bark beetle; (B) The beetle; (C) The grub. (Both much enlarged.) The beetle is the carrier of the disease.

* Special articles on the subjects indicated by an asterisk (*) will be found at the words so marked.

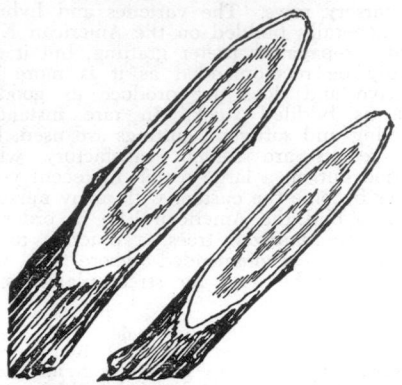

Discolored elm twigs attacked by the
Dutch elm disease

trol the elm bark beetle and prevent the transfer of the fungus causing the disease.

A virus disease, known as phloem necrosis,
has killed many elm trees in the Ohio Valley
and is now extending outward from that valley
area. The virus is transmitted from diseased
elms to healthy elms by a leafhopper. The infected tree will die quickly. There is no control for this disease.

Of minor importance, contrasted to the two
diseases previously described, is black spot
of elm. This is a fungus disease which causes
small black spots on the leaves, after which
leaves turn yellow and drop. Even though this
disease may defoliate a tree each year, it will
not cause death of the tree. Control with applications of pesticide #5, starting at bud break
in the spring and repeat twice at 10- to 14-day
intervals.

ELM FAMILY = Ulmaceae.

ELODEA (ee-low'dee-a) = *Anacharis*.

elongata, -us, -um (ee-lon-gay'ta). Elongate; *i.e.*, lengthened or stretched out, as in
many leaves.

ELSHOLTZIA (el-sholt'zi-a). A genus of
over 30 species of chiefly Asiatic aromatic
under-shrubs of the mint family, E. stauntoni grown for its late-blooming flowers. It
is a low shrub or shrubby herb, 2–4 ft.
high, its opposite* leaves short-stalked,
toothed, oval-oblong, 3–5 in. long, and sticky
beneath. Flowers lavender, in a dense,
1-sided spike, 6–12 in. long. Corolla only
slightly 2-lipped,* its stamens long-protruding. The plant is easily grown in the open
border south of zone* 4 and blooms in
Sept.–Oct. Choose a sunny place and propagate by greenwood cuttings, or by seed.
(Named for Johann Sigismund Elsholtz,
Prussian physician and botanist.)

ELYMUS (el'i-mus). Grasses usually
known as wild rye or lyme grass, and comprising over 40 species, all from temperate
regions. They are perennial grasses of secondary garden interest, although E. arenarius
is a good sand-binder. They have flat, grass-
like leaves and a dense terminal spike, usu-

ally unbranched. (*Elymus* is from the
Greek to roll up, in reference to a technical
flower character.)

Elymus arenarius, a Eurasian species, is
well adapted for binding shifting dune sand.
The other species is occasionally grown for
ornament.

arenarius. Sea lyme grass. Dune grass. A
stout perennial grass 5–8 ft. high. Leaves
about 12 in. long and ⅛ in. wide, rough on
the upper surface, the margin rolled in age.
Flowering spikes about 8 in. long, not awned.*
By some the native form is distinguished as
var. villosus, or as *E. mollis.*

glaucus. An ornamental grass 3–5 ft. high.
Leaves about 12 in. long, nearly ⅛ in. wide,
bluish-green. Flowering spike 5–7 in. long, with
rather stiff, long awns.* Turkestan.

emarginata, -us, -um (ee-mar-ji-nay'ta).
Emarginate; *i.e.,* shallowly notched at the
tip, as in some leaves and fruits.

EMASCULATION. *See* CROSSING.

EMBOTHRIUM (em-bo'three-um). A
small genus of chiefly S.A. shrubs and
trees of the family Proteaceae, with evergreen leaves and extremely showy flowers.
Leaves without marginal teeth (in ours),
and arranged alternately. Flowers in dense
clusters (racemes*), the fruit a many-seeded
pod (follicle*). The only cult. species is
the firebush, E. coccineum, a small Chilean
tree or shrub (as cult.) 10–20 ft. high
(tree-like in the wild and 40–50 ft. high),
with leaves 2½–4½ in. long, generally
ovalish. Flowers very handsome, nearly 2
in. long, brilliant scarlet, the lobes recurved
and exposing the long-protruding style.*
May–June. A most desirable plant, suited
only to Calif. and similar climates. (*Embothrium* signifies "in a little pit," in allusion to arrangement of the anthers.*)

EMBRYO. The minute plantlet within
the seed, and sometimes called the seed-
germ, a term to be frowned upon.

Emerus. Pre-Linnaean* name of uncertain application. *See* CORONILLA.

EMILIA (e-mil'i-a). Perhaps a dozen species of chiefly tropical herbs of the family
Compositae, one a rather widely grown flower-garden annual sometimes offered as
Cacalia. The only cult. species, E. sagittata,
the tassel-flower or Flora's paintbrush, is
sometimes offered under the perhaps correct
name of *E. flammea.* It is a showy, erect
annual, 1–2 ft. high, with alternate,* more or
less elliptic leaves that are narrowed to a
winged stalk. Flower heads loosely clustered,
about ½ in. in diameter, without rays, red or
scarlet. Tropical America. More popular is
the *var.* lutea, with yellow or golden flowers.
Both are of the easiest culture if treated as
hardy annuals. *See* ANNUALS. (*Emilia* is
probably named for someone, but for whom
is unknown.)

EMMENANTHE (em-me-nan'thee). A
small genus of the family Hydrophyllaceae,
grown in the flower garden for their loosely

---

* Special articles on the subjects indicated by an asterisk (*) will be found at the words so marked.

branched clusters of cream-yellow flowers. The only cult. species is **E. penduliflora**, the yellow bells, golden bells, or whispering bells found wild from Calif. to Mex. It is a rather sticky-foliaged, branching herb 12–18 in. high. Leaves cut into fine segments, but not compound.* Flowers bell-shaped, persistent, about ½ in. long, hanging on longish stalks, the whole cluster loose but much-branched. Fruit a 2-valved capsule. Should be grown as a hardy annual, or as a tender annual, if early bloom is desired. *See* ANNUALS. (*Emmenanthe* is from Greek for abide and flower, from the lasting corolla.)

EMPETRACEAE (em-pe-tray'see-ee). The crowberry family contains only 3 genera of low, evergreen, heath-like shrubs, two of which, *Empetrum* and *Corema*, are sometimes grown under the specialized conditions necessary for both genera.

Leaves very small, crowded, deeply grooved or furrowed on the under side. Flowers very small, without petals, regular.* The flower is solitary and the fruit fleshy in *Empetrum*, but in *Corema* the flowers are in tiny heads and the fruit is dry. Of little hort. but of considerable botanical interest, *Empetrum* extends to the Arctic Circle. *Corema* (one species) is localized from Newfoundland to N.J.

Technical flower characters: Flowers polygamous* or dioecious* without petals. Sepals 2 or 3 (or sometimes wanting), a little petal-like. Stamens 2 or 3, often colored. Ovary superior,* 2–9-celled, the 2–9 stigmas parted or fringed; all very minute.

empetriformis, -e (em-pee-tree-for'mis). With the form or aspect of the crowberry (*Empetrum*).

EMPETRUM (em-pee'trum). Evergreen, prostrate, or mat-forming shrubs, comprising only 5 species of the family Empetraceae, only **E. nigrum**, the crowberry, likely to be in cult. It is an alpine plant of the northern hemisphere and the Andes, adapted only to the rock garden and frequently makes patches 2–3 ft. across. Leaves very numerous, heath-like, narrow, about ½ in. long. Flowers solitary in the leaf axils,* mostly unisexual* (for details *see* EMPETRACEAE), purplish, not over ¼ in. long. Fruit black, berry-like, about ¼ in. in diameter. There is also a variety with purple fruit. May. In cult. it needs a strongly acid, rather gritty soil of pH 4–5, preferably cool moisture at its roots, and it will not stand continued summer heat. In the Gaspé Peninsula, however, it is known to grow wild on limestone. (*Empetrum* is old Greek for on rocks.) *See* ROCK GARDEN.

EMPRESS TREE = *Paulownia tomentosa*.

ENCELIA (en-see'li-a). A group of herbs or under-shrubs of the family Compositae, ranging from western N.A. to Chile, two grown in Calif. and the Southwest for their showy heads of yellow flowers. Leaves alternate* or opposite,* sometimes silvery, and usually strong-scented. Flower heads with conspicuous yellow rays,* the disk* flowers sometimes purple, the heads on naked stalks. (Named for Christopher Encel, who wrote about oak galls in 1577.)

californica. A strong-smelling, woody, perennial herb 3–4 ft. high. Leaves ovalish or a little narrower, 2–2½ in. long. Flower heads solitary, nearly 2½ in. wide, the disk* flowers purple, the rays golden-yellow. Calif., and little grown outside that state.

farinosa. Incienso. A showy, desert, shrubby plant, 3–5 ft. high, the clumps very handsome when in bloom. Leaves ovalish, 1¾–2½ in. long, generally silvery. Flower heads yellow throughout, about 1 in. in diameter, in branched clusters (cymes*). Calif., Ariz. and Mex.

encelioides (en-see-li-oy'deez, but *see* OÏDES). Like a plant of the genus *Encelia*.

ENCINA = *Quercus agrifolia*. *See* OAK.

ENDEMIC. Native in and confined to a particular area, as the big-tree is *endemic* in Calif.; opposed to exotic.

ENDIVE (*Cichorium Endivia*). This delicious salad plant is troublesome to bring to perfection. It is grown for the rosette of leaves, which when tied up and blanched constitutes practically the whole plant.

Common and true endive; a frilled variety is often called escarole.

While endive is chiefly fancied in the cool autumn or early winter months, it may also be had in midsummer by sowing the seeds in April or May. The frilled sort is sometimes known as escarole, a name not applied, however, to the French endive, a very different plant. Good vars. are Batavian, Full Hearted, Green Curled, White Curled, and Full Heart.

Generally, seed may be sown 2 weeks apart from June 10 to August 20, which will provide a succession from early fall well into cold weather. They may be sown in shallow drills directly in the garden or raised as seedlings much like young lettuce and transplanted to the row, preferably about 9 in. apart in the row, and the rows 18–24 in. apart.

During the early stages endive needs no more attention than any hardy vegetable beyond rather constant cultivation and, of course, freedom from weeds. But as the

---

* Special articles on the subjects indicated by an asterisk (*) will be found at the words so marked.

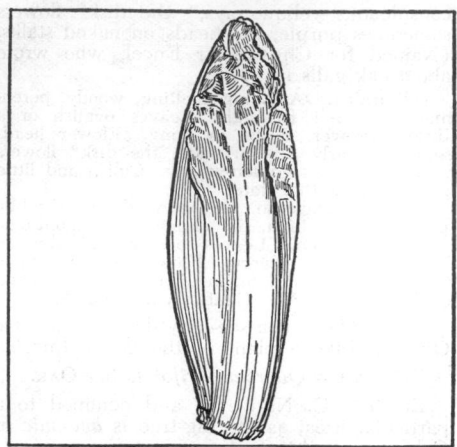

French endive (Witloof chicory). This
plant is commonly called endive in vegetable shops.

plants approach maturity, the necessity for
blanching arrives and this is both troublesome and hazardous. The leaves will not
turn white nor become crisp without excluding the light. Many good growers prefer to
tie up each plant by hand. Others put boards
each side of the row, pinch them together
over the endive and thus cut off all light.
The real difficulty in either method is that if
drops of water are left, or subsequently get
into the heart of the plant, it will probably
rot before it blanches. Great care is needed
in this operation, and some professional
growers even open up the heart of the plant
after each rain to allow drops of water to
dry off before letting the blanching process
go on.

Also, if the late crops are likely to be
overtaken by frost, which they cannot stand,
they must be carefully lifted and brought into
a cold frame and covered with mats every
night. By doing this, blanching may often
be carried on until the weather gets too
severe for further endive culture.

For the culture of the plant known as
French endive, which is really Witloof chicory, *see* CELLAR GARDENING.

Endivia. An East Indian word adapted
into Latin, and, with *Intybus,* applied to
chicory and endive; the application to both
being quite uncertain.

ENDYMION. *See* SCILLA.

ENGELMANN CREEPER = *Parthenocissus quinquefolia engelmanni.*

ENGELMANN'S SPRUCE = *Picea engelmanni. See* SPRUCE.

ENGLISH. As an adjective *English* has
naturally been applied to many plants, things,
gardens, etc., which originated in, or have
long been associated with, England. Those
that occur in this book, and their proper
equivalents, are:
English **box** = *Buxus sempervirens* (*see* BOX);
English **daisy** = *Bellis perennis;* English **dogwood** = *Philadelphus grandiflora* (*see* MOCK-
ORANGE); English **elm** = *Ulmus procera* (*see*
ELM); English **gooseberry** = *Ribes Grossularia;*
English **hawthorn** = *Crataegus monogyna* and *C.
Oxyacantha;* English **holly** = *Ilex aquifolium* (*see*
HOLLY); English **iris** = *Iris xyphioides;* English
ivy = *Hedera Helix;* English **laurel** = *Laurocera-
sus officinalis;* English **meadow grass** = *Lolium
perenne;* English **oak** = *Quercus Robur* (*see*
OAK); English **primrose** = *Primula vulgaris;*
English **walnut** = *Juglans regia* (*see* WALNUT);
English **yew** = *Taxus baccata.*

ENKIANTHUS (en-ki-an'thus). Asiatic
shrubs of the heath family, three of the ten
known species cult. for ornament, but not
widely, although they are handsome shrubs
for the border and turn a fine color in the
fall. Leaves alternate,* mostly clustered at
the ends of the twigs, stalked and finely
toothed. Flowers usually nodding, in terminal
clusters (umbels* or racemes*). Corolla bell-
shaped or urn-shaped, the 10 stamens not
protruding. Fruit a 5-valved capsule.*
(*Enkianthus* is from the Greek for pregnant
and flower, from the colored involucre* of
one [non-hort.] species, where there appears
to be a flower within a flower.)

These shrubs need a well-drained soil, very
much like that needed for *Azalea* and *Rhododendron,* moderately acid (*see* ACID AND
ALKALI SOILS). They do not stand moving
very well and should be left in place when
once established. Propagated by seeds, or
by cuttings or layers.

campanulatus. A shrub 15–25 ft. high.
Leaves elliptic or somewhat 4-sided, 1–3 in.
long, the small, marginal teeth minutely bristly.
Flowers about ⅝ in. long, yellowish-orange
but veined with red. Pod oblongish or egg-
shaped, about ¼ in. long, green at first, ultimately rusty brown. Jap. May. Hardy from
zone* 3 southward.

cernuus. A shrub 5–12 ft. high. Leaves
elliptic or oblongish, ¾–1½ in. long, shining
green above, the marginal teeth rounded. Flowers white, about ⅓ in. long, the clusters
(racemes*) hairy. Jap. May. Hardy from
zone* 3 southward. There is also a particularly
fine, red-flowered variety.

perulatus. A handsome, much-branched
shrub 3–5 ft. high. Leaves more or less elliptic or oblongish, 1–2½ in. long, bright green
above. Flowers white, about ⅓ in. long, nodding, in small umbels.* Jap. Early May.
Hardy from zone* 3 southward. The fall foliage is attractively colored yellow and scarlet.

enneacantha, -us, -um (en-nee-a-kan'-
tha). With 9 spines.

enneaphylla, -us, -um (en-nee-a-fill'a).
Nine-leaved or with nine leaflets.

ensata, -us, -um (en-say'ta). Sword-like.

Ensete. Abyssinian vernacular for *Musa
Ensete.*

ensifolia, -us, -um (en-see-fō'lee-a). With
sword-shaped leaves.

ensiformis, -e (en-si-for'mis). Sword-
shaped.

<hr>

* Special articles on the subjects indicated by an asterisk (*) will be found at the words so marked.

ENTELEA (en-tee'lee-a). A single New Zealand tree, **E. arborescens,** usually called cork-tree or corkwood, somewhat grown in southern Calif. for ornament, but little known elsewhere. It belongs to the family Tiliaceae and scarcely exceeds 20 ft. in height. Leaves alternate,* ovalish or heart-shaped, 9–12 in. long, sometimes 3-lobed, and usually toothed. Flowers white, about 1 in. wide, the stamens numerous. Fruit a capsule,* covered with weak bristles or stiffish hairs. (*Entelea* is from the Greek for complete in allusion to the fertility of all the stamens.)

ENTIRE. Whole; as wholly without teeth, as are many leaf margins.

ENTOMOPHILOUS. Pollinated by insects.

ENVIRONMENT. The total influences arising outside a given plant, such as soil, temperature, light, disease, moisture, fertilizer, wind, sunshine, insects, and other plants. Certain types of characters are much more influenced by environment than others. Examples are height and size. Flower and fruit colors and shapes are much less likely to be affected, depending on the nature of the soil ingredients. Thus, certain varieties of hydrangeas in some soils or with certain chemicals applied are either pink or blue. The relation of heredity and environment is best illustrated by the farmer and his three cornfields planted with Boone County White. He planted one with poor seed, but cultivated it well and fertilized it well. The yield was 30 bushels per acre. (Poor heredity, good environment.) Field 2 he planted with the best seed to be had, but it was neither cultivated nor fertilized. The yield was 30 bushels per acre. (Good heredity, poor environment.) The third field was given the best of seed and the best of care and the yield was 60 bushels. (Good heredity, good environment.) — O. E. W.

EOMECON (ee-o-mee'kon). A single, Chinese herb of the poppy family, **E. chionanthum** rather commonly and easily cult. under the name snow poppy. It is a showy perennial with a stout, creeping rootstock and basal, long-stalked leaves that are heart-shaped, wavy-margined, and 4–6 in. wide. Flowers white, poppy-like, nearly 2 in. wide, blooming in spring. Petals 4. Stamens numerous. Fruit a capsule. (*Eomecon* is Greek for eastern poppy, in reference to its Chinese nativity.)

EPAULETTE-TREE = *Pterostyrax hispida.*

EPHEDRA (ef-fee'dra). Remarkable little plants and the only cult. genus of the family **Gnetaceae** (ne-tay'see-ee), cult. for thousands of years in China, where one of them yields ma-huang, a source of ephedrine. They are chiefly low or climbing, essentially leafless, desert shrubs, the green twigs resembling the horsetail (*Equisetum*). The plants are not of much garden importance, for the minute flowers are very primitive and the red, berry-like fruit is rarely produced in cult. specimens. Male and female flowers on separate plants, consisting of only 2–4 very small, scarcely petal-like organs, 2–8 stamens (in the male flower), and the female flower consisting of a single upright ovule.* (*Ephedra* is an old Greek name, probably of a horsetail.)

Of the 30 known species, commonly known as joint-fir, only 2 are likely to be found in cult. The plants are easily propagated by division of the clumps.

altissima. A sprawling or climbing shrub from northern Af., suited only to the desert regions of the Southwest. Unlike most of the other species, it has definite leaves that are nearly 1 in. long, and scattered along the bluish-green, jointed stems.

distachya. A low, nearly prostrate, shrubby plant, the dark green, jointed stems scarcely 1/12 in. thick, and less than 2 ft. long. Leaves reduced to opposite* scales, which sheathe the stems. Eurasia. Hardy from zone* 4 southward.

EPHEMERAL. Lasting only one day, as some flowers. *See* FUGACIOUS.

EPIDENDRUM (ep-i-den'drum). An enormous genus (over 800 species) of tropical American tree-perching orchids, a few of which are cult. in ordinary greenhouses, but many more in the collections of orchid specialists. The few below are the ones most likely to interest the average grower. All have pseudobulbs,* and often quite showy, but not large flowers in loose clusters (racemes,* panicles,* or spikes*). They have equal-length sepals, and often quite similar petals, the lip* being clawed.* For cult. *see* ORCHID. (*Epidendrum* is from the Greek for on trees, in allusion to their epiphytic habit.)

atropurpureum. Pseudobulbs* ovalish, 2–3 in. long, its two leaves 12–15 in. long and leathery. Flowers 5–15 in a cluster, the individual flower about 2½ in. wide. Sepals and petals rose-purple but green-tipped, slightly incurved. Lip* rose-colored, crimson-blotched. Brazil.

ciliare. Pseudobulbs* compressed oblong, about 7 in. long, with one or two leathery leaves 6–10 in. long. Flowers fragrant, usually blooming throughout the year, in sparse clusters (racemes*), the petals greenish yellow, the lip* white but yellow-spotted. Tropical America.

nemorale. Pseudobulbs* nearly globose, 2–3 in. in diameter, 2-leaved. Leaves 10–12 in. long. Flowers in an arching cluster (panicle*), the individual flower 3–4 in. wide, rosy-lilac, the lip violet-striped. The showy cluster of flowers may be 2–3 ft. long. Mex.

obrienianum. A hybrid orchid derived from crossing two non-hort. species. It is a climbing plant, sometimes 8–10 ft. long, with essentially stalkless leaves. Flowers about 1¼ in. wide, long-lasting, orange-red, in a long cluster (raceme*). Lip* 3-lobed.

vitellinum. Pseudobulbs* egg-shaped, about 2 in. long, 2-leaved. Leaves bluish-green, 6–9 in. long. Flowers in a terminal lax cluster (spike*), often 20-flowered. Petals and sepals similar, cinnabar red, the lip* orange-yellow. Guatemala and Mex. The *var.* **majus** has shorter pseudobulbs* and more brightly colored flowers.

EPIGAEA. *See* TRAILING ARBUTUS.

---

* Special articles on the subjects indicated by an asterisk (*) will be found at the words so marked.

EPILOBIUM (ep-i-lō′bi-um). The willow-herbs are usually herbaceous, but some a little woody, and comprise perhaps 100 species of the family Onagraceae, widely distributed in temperate regions. Those below are grown for ornament and by beekeepers, and one of them in the rock garden. Leaves usually willow-like, often, but not always, toothed. Flowers in showy terminal clusters or sometimes only a few in the leaf axils.* Petals 4, broadest toward the end. Stamens 8, of unequal length. Fruit a long, 4-sided pod (capsule*), its seeds with a tuft of silky hairs. (*Epilobium* is from the Greek for upon the pod, in allusion to a technical flower character.) Both are perennials.

The first species is the famous fireweed that follows so many forest fires, but the plant is also cult. in Calif. as an important bee plant. The last species is a rock garden plant, for which *see* ROCK GARDEN.

angustifolium. An erect herb 3–4 ft. high, wand-like in the wild, but often branched in cult. Leaves alternate,* narrow, 2–6 in. long. Flowers rose-purple, in a showy, terminal cluster, the petals widely spreading. Pod 3–4 in. long. Summer. Throughout the north temperate zone, especially after forest fires, and of the easiest culture. The plant has a variety of names, as fireweed, giant willow-herb, French willow, blooming Sally, rose-bay, and in Calif., buckweed.

nummularifolium. A creeping and tufted herb, the stems 6–9 in. long. Leaves opposite,* nearly round, about ½ in. wide. Flowers about ⅓ in. wide, pink or white, solitary or few in the leaf axils. N.Z. For culture *see* ROCK GARDEN.

EPIMEDIUM (ep-i-mee′di-um). Rather woody, perennial herbs of the family Berberidaceae; of the 20 known species, all from the north temperate zone, three widely cult. for their fine flowers. They have compound* leaves, the leaflets finely toothed and arranged feather-fashion. Flowers in simple or branched clusters, either terminal or opposite the leaves. Sepals 8 and petal-like. Petals 4, mostly in the form of spurs* that are sometimes longer than the sepals. Stamens 4. Fruit a few-seeded capsule.* (*Epimedium* is from the Greek for like Medion, a plant thought to grow in Media.) The plants are called barrenwort.

Chiefly of use in the rock garden (which see), and valuable as ground cover. They prefer partial shade, and, with a little protection, their foliage may keep green over the winter. Propagated by division, but the first two species are slow to increase.

alpinum. A European herb, usually less than 1 ft. high, not much cult. except in the *var.* **rubrum,** which has red-margined leaflets and red flowers with short spurs. May–June.

grandiflorum. An erect herb 6–9 in. high. Leaves thrice-compound.* Flowers with outer segments red, the inner violet, the spurs white, and nearly 1 in. long. Jan. May–June. The *var.* niveum has pure white flowers; the *var.* violaceum has the spurs violet. Known also as *E. macranthum.*

macranthum = *Epimedium grandiflorum.*

pinnatum. Leaves only twice-compound.*

Flowers brilliant yellow, the short spurs red. Persia and the Caucasus. The *var.* **colchicum** has yellow flowers throughout, and is offered by some as *sulphureum,* or *E. versicolor sulphureum.* It spreads rapidly by its stem-like rootstocks.

rubrum = *Epimedium alpinum rubrum.*

EPIPACTIS = *Goodyera.*

EPIPHYLLUM (ep-i-fill′um). Tree-perching (epiphytic), usually spineless cacti, ranging from Mex. to Brazil, very popular for greenhouses, window gardens, or as potted plants on porches. They are leafless in age, but the jointed, flattened branches are green and leaf-like, and are sometimes winged. Flowers showy, but often not blooming as house plants, the many stamens long and handsome. For details of flower structure *see* CACTACEAE. (*Epiphyllum* is from the Greek for on a leaf, in allusion to the leaf-like branches which bear the flowers.)

While these are true cacti, they are not desert plants, but inhabitants of much moister climates. They need a richer soil and more water than most cacti (which see). Some of the plants below are occasionally offered under the names *Nopalxochia, Phyllocactus,* and *Zygocactus.* The latter includes the Christmas or crab cactus, often mistaken for some of the plants below. In addition to the four species there are many fine hybrids or clones,* over 40 in all.

ackermanni. Stems many, up to 3 ft. long, inclined to droop at the tips. Branches usually less than 12 in. long, the midrib and side ribs obvious. Flowers day-blooming, 4–6 in. wide, scarlet outside, carmine inside, the throat greenish-yellow. Of unknown, perhaps hybrid, or Mexican, origin.

crenatum. Stems nearly 3 ft. high, erect, the margins strongly scalloped, the midrib thick. Flowers about 8 in. long and 4 in. wide, day-blooming, fragrant, white but yellow in age. Central America.

oxypetalum. A much-branched, flat-stemmed cactus, the joints thin and wavy-margined. Flowers nocturnal, white, but reddish outside, 8–10 in. long, showy, and often incorrectly called "night-blooming cereus." Tropical America.

stenopetalum. A tree-perching cactus, 6–10 ft. high in the wild, the joints flattish, deeply wavy-margined, about 4 in. wide. Night-blooming, the extremely showy flowers are fragrant, 6–10 in. long, reddish-white, but the style* pinkish. Mex. The nocturnal flowers remain open in the morning.

truncatum = *Zygocactus truncatus.*

EPIPHYTES. Plants that grow on other plants is the exact meaning of this term, but by extension it has come to include all the air plants or tree-perchers. The epiphytic habit is so common in the tropics and so rare in the temperate zone that a few words regarding it may be useful to all who grow plants from both regions.

A true epiphyte is a plant driven by demands for light or moisture to seek a perch upon a tree rather than succumb upon the dark forest floor. Thousands of orchids, aroids,* ferns, and other plants are epiphytes, and their need for that sort of an environment

---

* Special articles on the subjects indicated by an asterisk (*) will be found at the words so marked.

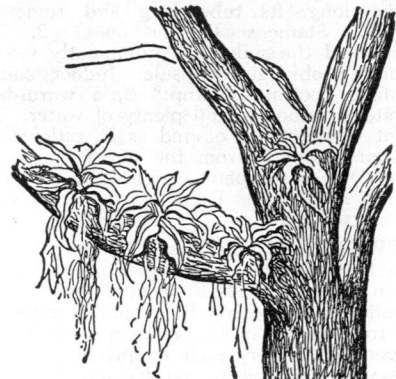

Tree-perching (epiphytic) plants at home
in the tropics

we translate into greenhouse practice every
day. *See* the articles on culture of ORCHIDS.
See also BROMELIACEAE.

Epiphytes are often rooted in moss or debris in the fork of a branch; very rarely are
they actually rooted upon the green surface
of another plant. But no myth of the vegetable world is harder to kill than the assumption that epiphytes are parasites.° They never
are, for they steal not food (as would a true
parasite), but merely a place to perch in
the light. Hence they are here often called
tree-perching to avoid the technical term of
epiphyte. So little do they rely upon the
nature of the support that, in the tropics,
many epiphytes cling to telegraph wires or
the eaves of buildings.

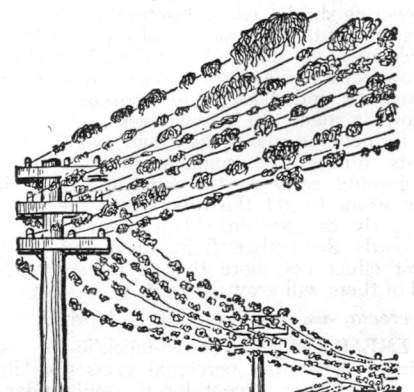

Epiphytic tillandsias on telegraph wires are sufficient proof that air plants do not get food from
their perch.

Many of them have special mechanisms for
absorbing atmospheric moisture, which most
plants never do. *See* VELAMEN.

EPISCIA (ep-piss'i-a). Thirty species of
tropical American herbs of the family Ges-

neriaceae, **E. cupreata** widely grown in hanging baskets, but it needs a warm, moist
greenhouse. Stems slender, branching, rooting at the joints, the tips drooping. Leaves
opposite,° unequal, rough-hairy above, reddish beneath, nearly round or ovalish, the
margin scalloped. Flower solitary in the leaf-
axils,° scarlet, about ¾ in. wide, the corolla
somewhat irregular° and sac-like. A very
handsome plant for the greenhouse, needing
support or a chance to droop. Colombia and
Venezuela. There are many fine hort.
forms to which names have been attached,
such as Chocolate Soldier (dark chocolate
leaves), Emerald Queen (silvery midrib),
Metallica (metallic pink leaves, etc.) Besides these hort. forms **E. fulgida** from Colombia has recently become available. It is
scarcely 6 in. high but has handsome vermilion, hairy flowers about 2 in. long, which
are solitary in the leaf axils.° Foliage sometimes coppery. A handsome plant. (*Espiscia*
is from Greek for shady, in allusion to their
habitat preference.) For the plant offered
as *Episcia tessellata, see* NAUTILOCALYX BUL-
LATUS.

EPITHELANTHA (ep-i-thel-an'tha). A
single, small globe-shaped cactus, **E. micromeris** of western Tex. and Mex., often cult.
for interest, especially in small desert gardens or as a centerpiece decoration. It has
a tubercular plant body usually less than 2½
in. in diameter, almost globe-shaped, but
flattened somewhat at the ends and a little
depressed at the top. Spines numerous, white.
Flowers from near the center of the plant,
surrounded by spines and wool, scarcely ¼
in. wide, white or light pink. Fruit edible,
but slightly acid, known to the natives as
chilotes. For culture *see* CACTI. (*Epithelantha* is from the Greek meaning upon a nipple,
in allusion to the flowers being borne on
tubercles.)

epithymoides (ep-i-thy-moy'deez, but *see*
OÏDES). Like the genus *Epithymus,* which
is of no garden interest.

equestris, -e (ee-kwes'tris). Pertaining to
a horse.

EQUISETACEAE. *See* EQUISETUM.

equisetifolia, -us, -um (ek-kwee-see-ti-fo'-
li-a). With leaves like a horsetail (*Equisetum*).

equisetiformis, -e (ek-kwee-see-ti-for'mis).
Shaped like, or resembling a horsetail
(*Equisetum*).

EQUISETUM (ek-kwee-see'tum). The
only genus of the horsetail family, **Equise-
tacae** (ek-kwee-see-tay'see-ee), now of little
importance, but covering the earth in the
Carboniferous period and forming gigantic
forests which largely contributed to the coal
measures. The present-day remnants of the
horsetails comprise rush-like, perennial herbs
with striped, hollow stems, and no true leaves,
the latter reduced to mere sheaths at the
joints. The group belongs to the fern allies,
bears no flowers, but spores borne in a cone-

° Special articles on the subjects indicated by an asterisk (°) will be found at the words so marked.

like spike at the ends of some of the stems. (*Equisetum* is the classical name of the horsetails.)

These plants are of much more historical than garden interest, for they link modern plants with an incredibly ancient type of vegetation. The first two are of easy culture in any ordinary garden soil, preferably a moist one. *E. arvense*, common along railway embankments, is often a nuisance. Only a single (non-hort.) Brazilian species is treelike.

arvense. Common horsetail. *See* list at WEEDS.

hyemale. Scouring rush; called also Dutch rush, and many other names, all implying that its tough, wiry, rough stems are used for scouring. Stems furrowed, evergreen, 3–4 ft. high. Scale-like leaves pointed, clustered at the joints. The cone-like spikes that bear the spores are pointed. Throughout the north temperate zone, mostly in moist places.

praealtum. An evergreen, rush-like plant, the tough, wiry stems 3–10 ft. high, nearly 1 in. in diameter. Scale-like leaves pointed, the base of the sheath of which they are part blackgirdled. Western N.A.; also in As. Sometimes known as *E. robustum*.

robustum = *Equisetum praeltum*.

EQUITANT. Said of leaves, the bases of which overlap, often making a flat, fan-like arrangement as in some forms of *Iris*.

ERAGROSTIS (e-ra-gros′tis). A genus of over 100 species of annual or perennial grasses of minor economic importance, but a few somewhat grown for their delicate, spray-like flower spikes. All those below are annuals and should be sown where wanted. The small flower spikes are borne in open, lax, branching clusters (panicles*), the spikes not awned. (*Eragrostis* is from the Greek for love grass and of uncertain application here.)

abyssinica (or abessinica). Teff. A North African, fragrant grass, there yielding a cereal grain (teff), but grown here only for ornament, and 1–3 ft. high. Leaves grass-like, 4–6 in. long, about ⅒ in. wide. Flowering cluster nearly 1 ft. long, its hair-like branches more or less erect. In Abyssinia teff is an important cereal grain.

elegans = *Eragrostis interrupta*.

interrupta. Usually 1–2 ft. high, rarely 3 ft. Flower cluster nearly half the height of the plant, narrow, rather interrupted, its spikelets very numerous but small. Jap. Sometimes known as *E. elegans* or *E. japonica*.

suaveolens. A delicate grass sometimes grown for dry bouquets. It resembles *E. abyssinica*, but it is not fragrant and its cluster of flowering spikes is less spreading, and the spikelets more compact. Western As.

ERANTHEMUM (ee-ran′thee-mum). Tropical Asian shrubs or woody herbs of the family Acanthaceae, **E. nervosum** of India a popular ornamental greenhouse shrub 2–4 ft. high, which can also be grown outdoors in zones* 8 and 9. It has thickish, prominentlyveined, ovalish leaves, 4–8 in. long, faintly toothed and long-stalked. Flowers blue, in closely bracted* spikes, either terminal or in the leaf axils.* Corolla nearly regular,* about

1 in. long, its tube long and somewhat curved. Stamens (fertile ones) 2. The bracts* of the spike are prominently veined. Fruit an oblongish capsule. Indoor culture demands potting mixture* 3, a warm-temperate greenhouse, and plenty of water. The plant is sometimes offered as *E. pulchellum*. (*Eranthemum* is from the Greek for lovely flower.) For the plant occasionally known as *E. reticulatum, see* PSEUDERANTHEMUM RETICULATUM.

ERANTHIS (e-ran′thiss). Tuberous, Eurasian herbs of the buttercup family. Of the seven known species E. hyemalis, the winter aconite, is a deservedly popular plant for the rock garden or border because its yellow flowers bloom very early in spring or even in late winter if the season has not been too severe. It is an erect, usually unbranched perennial, 3–8 in. high, the leaves all basal, roundish, long-stalked, and much cut into fine segments. Flower solitary, the petals none or much reduced. Sepals 5–8, yellow and petal-like, about ⅝ in. long. Fruit a collection of small pods (follicles*), somewhat resembling a miniature bean pod. For culture *see* below. (*Eranthis* is Greek for flower of spring.) It is sometimes called New Year's Gift. A recent hybrid. E. **tubergeni**, resembles *E. hyemalis*, but has larger, brilliant, golden-yellow flowers.

WINTER ACONITE CULTURE

Winter aconite thrives in any good, welldrained garden soil. One of its recommendations is that it will flourish in shade, and a woodland bank suits it well. Being a free seeder in such a position, it increases rapidly, and may be left undisturbed year after year. It may also be planted thickly beneath earlyflowering shrubs, where the bright color showing during the first months of the year is very welcome. If mingled with such bulbs as snowdrops, *Scilla sibirica*, chionodoxas, *Crocus imperati*, and *Hyacinthus azureus*, a brave show is made for many weeks. After seed is formed the plants die down and the tuber rests during the summer months, growth beginning early in the autumn. It is thus important to get the tubers into the ground as early as possible. Plant them in August or early September, 3 in. deep and for the best effect not more than 3 in. apart. Not all of them will grow. — L. B. W.

erecta, -us, -um (ee-rek′ta). Upright.

EREMOCHLOA (e-ree-mock′lō-a). Asiatic or Australian perennial grasses of little garden interest, except for **E. ophiuroides** of China, commonly called centipede-grass, and useful for lawns in places too warm or sandy for ordinary lawn mixtures. It creeps by runners, from the ends and joints of which arise the bluish-green leaves that are about 3 in. long and ¼ in. wide. Flowering spikes terminal, rather narrow, somewhat arching, composed of many 1-sided, small spikelets. (*Eremochloa* is from the Greek for lovely grass.) *See* Southern Lawns at LAWN.

---

* Special articles on the subjects indicated by an asterisk (*) will be found at the words so marked.

EREMURUS (e-ree-mure'us). Magnificent Asiatic, perennial herbs of the lily family, with thick, cord-like or fibrous roots, comprising about 30 species. They need careful culture, but few border herbs are so striking or showy. They are generally known as foxtail lily or desert candle, perhaps from the very tall, flowering stalk. Leaves all basal, rather narrow, without teeth, and forming tufts or rosettes. Flowering stalks from 4–10 ft. high, the spire-like cluster (raceme*) usually 1–3 ft. long. Flowers very numerous, bell-shaped, but the petals only slightly connected at the base, usually with 1 prominent vein. Stamens 6, sometimes protruding. Fruit a capsule.* (*Eremurus* is from the Greek for lonely tail, probably in reference to the solitary flower cluster.)

The foxtail lilies are among the most striking garden plants, the tall, flowering cluster often containing several hundred flowers. Because they have peculiarly brittle roots they must be planted very carefully, and the cord-like branches of the root must be spread out very gently, looking when planted not unlike a starfish. Plant at least 6–9 in. deep in a rich, well-drained soil. They are voracious feeders and the soil can scarcely be too rich. Fall planting is best, after which top-dress the soil with strawy manure, and this is best repeated each year, for the plants are not quite hardy north of zone* 4, and a good mulching is always safer. Of the species below the best known are *E. himalaicus* and *E. robustus,* and they are the easiest to grow. But some of the others, and particularly some of the newer hybrids, are even better worth growing. All are most attractive when planted against a background of shrubbery. The Shelford hybrids come in copper, bronze, or pink; usually 4–5 ft. high.

Eremuri can also be raised from seed, although it is a slow process. Plant the seeds when they are ripe, usually in Aug. or Sept., and leave outdoors until after the necessary fall and winter chilling of the seeds. In early spring (March–April) put the pots in a cool greenhouse and give them the ordinary care of other plants raised from seed. Germination is slow. If you have no greenhouse leave the seed pans or pots in a cold frame, protected with mats or leaves over the winter. In the spring the seeds will then germinate.

aurantiacus. Perhaps not distinct from the next species, but the flowers orange. Turkestan. July.

bungei. Leaves narrow, about 1 ft. long. Flowering stalk 4 ft. high, the cluster about 5 in. long. Flowers yellow or orange. Persia. July.

elwesi. Leaves ovalish-oblong or narrower, bluish-green. Flowering stalk 10–12 ft., the cluster nearly 2½ ft. long. Flowers pink. Of unknown, but probably of hybrid origin. The *var.* **albus** has white flowers.

himalaicus. Leaves narrow, about 18 in. long. Flowering stalk 6–8 ft. high, the cluster 18–30 in. long. Flowers white. Himalayas. June. The best-known in cult.

robustus. Leaves strap-shaped, up to 2 ft.

long. Flowering stalk 8–10 ft. high, the cluster 2–3 ft. long and nearly 5 in. thick. Flowers bright pink. Central As.

shelfordi. A group of extremely showy hybrid forms, some of them pink, orange, yellow, or white. The plants are normally about 4 ft. high. July.

tubergeni. A hybrid between *E. himalaicus* and *E. bungei.*

warei. A hybrid, often 8 ft. high, related to *E. bungei,* but with smaller, orange flowers in a more slender spike. Perhaps a natural hybrid from Turkestan.

ERFURT CONEFLOWER = *Rudbeckia bicolor superba.*

ERIANTHUS (e-ri-an'thus). Perhaps 20 species of chiefly tropical grasses, usually called plume grass, most of them perennials and **E. Ravennae,** the Ravenna grass, commonly grown for ornament. It is a stout, strong-growing grass, 8–12 ft. high, the stems smooth and stiff. Leaves nearly 3 ft. long, about ½ in. wide, the veins roughish, the sheath at the base hairy and very rough. Flowering plume much-branched, very silky and showy, much resembling pampas grass (*see* CORTADERIA). Southern Eu. to India. Scarcely hardy above zone* 4, but easily grown in any ordinary garden soil. (*Erianthus* is from the Greek for wool-flower, in allusion to the silky plume of inflorescence.)

ERICA (e'ri-ka). The true heaths comprise a genus of over 500 species of the family Ericaceae, largely from South Africa and the Mediterranean region, a few scattered elsewhere. They are sometimes tree-like, more often low shrubs and some are nearly prostrate. Leaves characteristically heath-like, *i.e.,* small, narrow, and needle-like, usually in clusters of 3–6, but so numerous as to be often densely crowded, prevailingly evergreen. Flowers sometimes solitary, more often in small clusters (umbels* or spikes*), often nodding. Corolla urn-shaped or bell-shaped, never large, with 4 small lobes. Stamens 8. Fruit a many-seeded capsule. (*Erica* is from the Latin for heath.)

For culture *see* below. All those marked with a dagger (†) can be grown only on the Pacific Coast, and the zone numbers apply only to the Pacific Coast. The other species are hardy in the East as indicated.

† **arborea.** Tree heath. A shrub or small tree 10–20 ft. high, the twigs hairy. Leaves in 3's. Flowers white, about ⅕ in. long, fragrant, in large, branching clusters. Not hardy north of zone* 6. Southern Eu. Source of briarwood for pipes.

† **australis.** Spanish heath. An upright, open-branched shrub 5–8 ft. high, its tiny, sometimes hairy leaves in 4's, and about ¼ in. long. Flowers about ¼ in. long, in dense umbel*-like clusters, pinkish-red. Spain and Portugal. May. Hardy from zone* 5 southward.

carnea. Spring or winter heath. Not over 12 in. high, mostly prostrate. Leaves in 4's. Flowers red, about ¼ in. long, in 1-sided clusters. March–May, or earlier with protection. *See* WINTER GARDEN. Southern Eu. Hardy up to zone* 3. The *var.* **alba** has white, and the *var.* **rosea,** rose-colored flowers. All are

---

* Special articles on the subjects indicated by an asterisk (*) will be found at the words so marked.

often grown in the rock garden (which see).

ciliaris. Fringed heath. Not over 12 in. high, mostly prostrate. Leaves in 3's, hairy on the edges. Flowers rosy-red, about ½ in. long, the terminal clusters (racemes*) about 5 in. long. Eng. to Spain. Spring. Hardy up to zone* 6, possibly to zone* 5 with protection.

cinerea. Twisted heath; also called Scotch heath (for the heather see CALLUNA). A dense, much-branched shrub 12–18 in. high. Leaves in 3's. Flowers rosy-purple, about ¼ in. long, the clusters about 3 in. long. Western Eu. June–Sept. Hardy up to zone* 3, and naturalized at Nantucket.

† **darleyensis.** A hybrid heath not over 2 ft. high, the minute leaves in 4's, their edges rolled. Flowers pink, scarcely ¼ in. long, urnshaped, in showy clusters (racemes*) that are 3–6 in. long. Winter-blooming and suited only to frostless regions, but a fine shrub for such areas.

mediterranea. A shrub 6–10 ft. high. Leaves in 4's or 5's. Flowers deep red, about ¼ in. long, the stamens* protruding. Spring. Western Eu. Hardy from zone* 5, and, with protection, from zone* 4, southward. The *var.* **alba** has white flowers.

† **melanthera.** A South African heath, rarely over 2 ft. high. Flowers in 3's. Flowers winterblooming, rose-red, very profuse at the ends of the twigs, the corolla scarcely ⅓ in. long. For culture and hardiness see below.

stricta. Corsican heath. A shrub 6–9 ft. high, the leaves usually in 4's. Flowers rosypurple, about ¼ in. long, summer-blooming. Southern Eu. Hardy only up to zone* 6.

† **subdivaricata.** Garland heath. A South African heath never over 2 ft. high. Flowers rosered (or white in a variety), about ⅛ in. long, borne in terminal racemes* in spring. For culture and hardiness see below.

Tetralix. Cross-leaved heath. Bell heather. Not over 2 ft. high, the branches mostly prostrate. Leaves in 4's, hairy on the edges. Flowers rose-red, about ¼ in. long, in dense terminal clusters. Eu. June–Oct. Hardy up to zone* 3 and naturalized in Mass.

vagans. Cornish heath. A spreading, but not prostrate, shrub, 8–12 in. high. Leaves in 4's or 5's. Flowers pinkish-purple about ⅓ in. long, in leafy clusters that may be 6 in. long. Western Eu. Aug.–Oct. Hardy from zone* 4 southward.

† **ventricosa.** A South African heath 4–6 ft. high. Leaves in 4's, hairy on the edges. Flowers red, pink, or white, up to ⅔ in. long, in dense clusters (umbels*). For culture see below.

† **verticillata.** A South African heath 3–5 ft. high. Leaves usually in 4's or 6's, not hairy on the edges. Flowers more tubular than bellshaped, nearly ¾ in. long, in dense racemes.* For culture see below.

williamsi. A hybrid, low heath not unlike its parents (*Tetralix* × *vagans*) with tiny urnshaped, rose-pink flowers in tight clusters (umbels*). Summer. Hardy from zone* 4 southward.

ERICA CULTURE

The heaths are represented by two groups, those of Europe, particularly southern Europe, and those from South Africa that were once more used than now as pot plants for winter bloom. The hardy heaths, all evergreen shrubs, vary from white through pink to deep rose and the tender heaths add yellow and orange to the range.

All require firm mixtures of peat and sand. The hardy forms, such as *Erica carnea, ciliaris, cinerea, stricta, Tetralix* and *vagans* are best used in masses with callunas and other related plants, either in the open or with passing shade. The taller Mediterranean forms are most useful in California, as are some of the South African species. The latter, however, particularly *melanthera* for winter and *verticillata, ventricosa,* and *subdivaricata* for late winter and early spring, are best suited to pot culture, using potting* mixture no. 5, growing them in a house with a temperature of about 45° F., with ample ventilation and no excess of moisture.

All are easily propagated by cuttings of halfripe wood in sand, or sand and peat, with mild bottom-heat. All should be trimmed from time to time to cause the formation of new shoots and prevent the bare appearance of the lower part of the plant. — B. Y. M.

ERICACEAE (e-ri-kay'see-ee). The heath family, often called the arbutus, heather, or wintergreen family, is of outstanding garden importance because it includes both azalea and rhododendron, as well as the showy South African and European heaths, and many valuable hort. genera, including splendid, broad-leaved evergreens.

As here understood it is a very large family of herbs, shrubs or, rarely, small trees, largely evergreens, comprising over 70 genera and 1500 species, most of which are plants of somewhat, or decidedly, acid soils and are confined mostly to the north temperate zone.

By many authorities this large family is split into four:

Clethraceae, or white alder family, which includes only *Clethra.*

Pyrolaceae, or shinleaf family, which (in the garden genera) includes only *Chimaphila, Pyrola,* and *Moneses.*

Vacciniaceae, or huckleberry family, which includes only (in the garden genera) the huckleberry and *Vaccinium* (the blueberry).

Ericaceae, or heath family, here considered as including not only the plants sometimes restricted to it but all those often included in the three above.

The Ericaceae (as a whole) have alternate,* very rarely opposite* but sometimes much-crowded leaves. Flowers often very showy (as in azalea and rhododendron and many cult. genera), regular,* or highly irregular* in *Azalea,* solitary or in various sorts of clusters, quite often bell-shaped or urnshaped, but sometimes of separate petals. The fruit is a dry pod (capsule*) in the Ericaceae proper, but fleshy in the huckleberry, blueberry (*Vaccinium*), and its relatives.

The garden favorites in the heath family, all of outdoor culture over most of the U.S., are *Azalea, Calluna*(see HEATHER), *Kalmia* (the mountain laurel), *Leucothoë, Pieris, Rhododendron,* and the beautiful *Rhodora,* and *Lyonia.*

Among the lesser known garden genera, some of which require specialized culture,

---

* Special articles on the subjects indicated by an asterisk (*) will be found at the words so marked.

dealt with at each genus, are: *Andromeda, Arctostaphylos, Bruckenthalia, Cassiope, Chamaedaphne, Daboecia, Epigaea* (see TRAILING ARBUTUS), *Gaultheria, Ledum, Leiophyllum, Loiseleuria, Menziesia, Pernettya* and *Phyllodoce.*

There are in addition a few shrubs and tree genera, which instead of being evergreen, drop their leaves in the fall, among them being: *Enkianthus, Oxydendrum* (a tree), and *Zenobia.*

The only genera of greenhouse culture are *Erica* (in part) and *Arbutus,* both of which are also mostly hardy from zone* 6 southward outdoors.

Technical flower characters: Ovary superior* in most genera, except the blueberry and its relatives, where it is inferior.* Corolla bell-shaped or urn-shaped or more or less tubular in nearly all genera, but of separate petals in *Ledum, Leiophyllum,* some azaleas, *Clethra,* and partly so in *Chimaphila* and *Moneses.* Calyx 4–5-parted. Stamens as many as the petals or corolla lobes or twice as many, the anthers opening mostly by terminal pores. Ovary 2–5-celled, in the genera with dry fruit (see above), many-seeded.

ericaefolia, -us, -um (e-ri-see-fo′li-a). With heath-like leaves.

ericoides (e-ri-koy′deez, but see OÏDES). Like a heath (*Erica*).

ERIGERON (e-rij′er-on). The fleabanes comprise perhaps 200 species of annual or perennial herbs of the family Compositae, of wide distribution, but mostly of temperate regions. A few are fine garden plants, much resembling wild asters, from which they differ only in technical characters, and some are merely weedy. Plants sometimes nearly stemless and with basal leaves, but the taller sorts have alternate* leaves. Flower heads solitary or in branched clusters, the disk* flowers yellow, but the rays* numerous, mostly violet-purple, yellow, or rose-red, but white in a few weedy species. (*Erigeron* is from the Greek for old man in spring, in allusion to the hoary leaves of some species.)

The ordinary border fleabanes are of very simple culture in any usual garden soil, and may be propagated by division in spring or fall. A few, such as *E. alpinus, E. aurantiacus,* etc., are, as indicated below, best suited to the rock garden (which see). All bloom in summer.

alpinus. A rock garden plant from the mountains of Eurasia and the Rocky Mountains, over 1 ft. high. Leaves narrow, without marginal teeth. Flower heads mostly solitary, about ¾ in. wide, mostly purple, sometimes whitish.

aurantiacus. Double orange daisy. A rock garden perennial from Turkestan, and not over 10 in. high. Leaves narrow, broadest toward the tip. Flower heads solitary or 2, about 1 in. wide, orange yellow.

compositus. A tufted perennial, 5–8 in. high, the foliage grayish. Basal leaves cut into narrow segments, clammy-hairy. Flower heads solitary, about ¾ in. wide, the rays white or pinkish. Western N.A. Summer. Suited only to the rock garden.

coulteri. A stout perennial 12–20 in. high

and useful in the open border. Leaves lance-shaped, or broader toward the tip, somewhat toothed. Flower heads solitary, about 1½ in. wide, whitish or purplish-white. Western U.S. There are one or two named forms in the trade.

glabellus. A smooth perennial 10–18 in. high, with showy flower heads. Lower leaves broadly lance-shaped, the upper narrower and stem-clasping, all finely hairy on the margins. Flower heads 2 or 3, about 2 in. wide, the many rays narrow, purple. Western U.S. June–July.

glaucus. Beach aster or seaside daisy. A seaside plant of the Pacific Coast, not much grown elsewhere and not hardy in the East. Leaves chiefly basal, oblongish, without marginal teeth. Flower heads solitary, about 1½ in. wide, violet or lilac.

karvinskianus. A rock garden or border perennial, not over 18 in. high, the stems mostly creeping or trailing. Leaves about 1 in. long, toothed or lobed, especially toward the tip. Flower heads several, but solitary on each stalk, about ¾ in. wide, pinkish-white. Tropical America. Not hardy northward and sometimes used as a summer bedding plant, as it blooms from seed the first year. Offered as *E. mucronatus,* but more often as *Vittadinia australis.*

macranthus. A perennial 12–20 in. high, the stem leafy to the top. Leaves lance-shaped to ovalish, those on the stem about 1 in. long. Flower heads about 1½ in. wide, in loose clusters (corymbs*). Rays numerous, narrow, blue or purplish. Rocky Mts. Summer.

mucronatus = *Erigeron karvinskianus.*

multiradiatus. Himalayan fleabane. A rock garden perennial, 6–18 in. high. Leaves oblongish or narrower, without marginal teeth. Flower heads solitary, very showy, purple, nearly 3 in. wide. Himalayas.

pulchellus. Poor Robin's-plantain or Robin's-plantain. A border herb, almost weedy, but rather showy, 12–20 in. high, producing off-sets.* Leaves chiefly basal and tufted, more or less oblong. Flower heads 1–6, in a loose, terminal cluster, violet or violet-purple, about 1½ in. wide. Eastern N.A.

speciosus. A showy border perennial from western N.A. and the best-known of all the cult. species. It grows from 15–30 in. high, and has narrow leaves without teeth. Flower heads dark violet, about 1½ in. wide, numerous in showy corymbs.* There are many named forms, especially with larger, double, or rose-colored heads.

trifidus. Not very different from *E. compositus,* but not over 4 in. high and hairy throughout. Flower heads about ½ in. wide, the rays white or purplish. Western N.A. May–June. A rock garden species.

erinacea, -us, -um (e-ri-nay′see-a). Hedgehog-like.

erinoides (e-ri-noy′deez, but see OÏDES). Resembling the genus *Erinus.*

ERINUS (e-ry′nus). A single, tufted, spring-blooming, perennial herb of the figwort family, found in the mountains of Europe and suited chiefly for the rock garden, where the cult. of E. alpinus is noted. The plant is scarcely 3½ in. high, and has basal, coarsely toothed leaves about ½ in. long. Flowers purple, about ½ in. wide, the cluster (raceme*) about 2 in. long. Corolla slightly irregular.

---

* Special articles on the subjects indicated by an asterisk (*) will be found at the words so marked.

Stamens 4. There are white- and red-flowered varieties. (*Erinus* is from the Greek indicating early bloom.)

ERIOBOTRYA (e-ri-o-bō'tri-a). A small genus of Asiatic evergreen trees and shrubs of the rose family, E. japonica, the loquat, widely cult. for its fruit, and as an ornamental. It is a tree up to 20 ft. high, the leaves nearly stalkless, thick, stiff, nearly 1 ft. long, and rusty-hairy beneath. Flowers fragrant, white, about ½ in. wide, in hairy clusters (panicles*) nearly 6 in. long. Petals 5, clawed.* Stamens about 20. Fruit fleshy (a pome*), plum-shaped, 1-2-seeded, its yellow flesh agreeably acid. Some of the improved cult. varieties have fruits nearly 3 in. long. There is also a variegated-leaved form grown chiefly for ornament. For culture *see* LOQUAT. The tree is hardy, with protection, up to zone* 6, and is commonly grown far southward, rarely in the cool greenhouse. (*Eriobotrya* is from the Greek for woolly cluster, in allusion to the hairy flower cluster.) In the South often called Japanese plum (it is not a plum).

ERIOCAULACEAE. *See* SYNGONANTHUS.

ERIODICTYON. *See* NAMA.

ERIOGONUM (e-ri-og'o-num). A genus of 140 species of western American, mostly woolly herbs of the buckwheat family, decidedly of secondary garden interest except for their culture in Calif. as bee plants. They have chiefly basal leaves without teeth, the stem leaves, when present, alternate* or whorled.* Flowers small, inconspicuous, in various sorts of close clusters. (For detailed flower structure *see* POLYGONACEAE.) Fruit a 3-angled achene.* (*Eriogonum* is from the Greek for woolly joint, in allusion to the hairy stems.)

These are not easy to grow in eastern gardens because of the cold, wet winters. While the plants can stand intense, dry cold, their woolly foliage is unsuited to slush and winter rains. In the West they thrive in dry, open soils, thoroughly drained. The third species does well, however, in the East, as far north as Washington, D.C.

fasciculatum. Wild buckwheat; called also flat-tops in Calif., in which state and Nev. it is native. Stems woody at the base, 2-3 ft. high. Leaves oblongish or narrower, about ¾ in. long, densely white-woolly on the under side. Flowers white, the cluster a simple or compound umbel.*

subalpinum. Perhaps not distinct from E. *umbellatum*, but the flowers pale yellow, sometimes ultimately rose-pink, and the flowering stalk a little taller. Western N.A. Aug.–Sept.

umbellatum. Sulphur-flower. Not over 1 ft. high, the leaves chiefly basal, ovalish, about 2 in. long, white-woolly on the under side. Flowers golden-yellow, the umbels* simple. Pacific Coast.

eriophora, -us, -um (e-ri-off'o-ra). Woolly.

ERIOPHORUM (e-ri-off'o-rum). The genus *Eriophorum*, the cotton grasses, are sometimes planted in the bog garden. They are grass-like plants belonging to the sedge family, with cottony, terminal heads; mostly native in cool-region bogs.

ERIOPHYLLUM (e-ri-o-fill'-um). Western North American herbs of the family Compositae, often called woolly sunflower, from their often white-woolly foliage and sunflower-like heads. They have alternate,* and, in ours, deeply lobed leaves. Flower heads small, resembling a miniature sunflower, the disk* and ray* flowers yellow. (*Eriophyllum* is from the Greek for woolly leaf.)

The woolly sunflowers are not happy in our eastern, usually slushy or wet, winters. In the Far West they are occasionally transferred to open, sandy borders where they do well.

caespitosum = E. *lanatum*.
lanatum. A perennial 9-18 in. high. Leaves deeply 5-7-parted or lobed, the segments oblongish or narrower. Flower heads chiefly solitary, about 1 in. wide, golden-yellow. Idaho and British Columbia to Calif. Summer.

ERODIUM (ee-rō'di-um). Nearly 60 species of widely distributed herbs of the family Geraniaceae, a few grown for ornament, some weedy, a few planted for forage in dry regions, and one or two fairly important as bee plants in Calif. They are closely related to the genus *Geranium* (not the garden geranium), from which they differ in having the outer stamens* bearing no anthers,* while all the 10 stamens of *Geranium* are anther-bearing. Leaves generally divided or compound,* feather-fashion. Petals 5. Fruit a collection of spindle-shaped carpels, all attached to the styles which coil up in age. The plants are commonly called stork's-bill or heron's-bill. (*Erodium* is from the Greek for heron's-bill.)

Erodiums are of very easy culture in open, sandy or loamy soils. Outside of their use as forage, they are of secondary garden interest, and are readily raised from spring-sown seed or increased by division.

chamaedryoides. A rock garden perennial, scarcely 4 in. high, the leaves roundish, wavy-margined and about ½ in. long and long-stalked. Flowers solitary, very short-stalked, small, white but faintly veined with pink. Majorca and Corsica. Summer. It does best in partial shade.

cheilanthifolium. A perennial not over 4 in. high. Leaves basal, twice-compound,* gray-felty. Flowers about ¾ in. wide, white, veined with rose. Southern Spain and Morocco. Useful in the rock garden..

chrysanthum. A silvery-leaved, tufted perennial best suited to the rock garden, and not over 4 in. high. Leaves twice-compound,* chiefly basal. Flowers ½ in. wide, yellow. Greece.

cicutarium. Alfilaria; called also filaree and pin-clover. The best known of the heron's-bills and widely cult. for forage, and in Calif. for bees. It is an annual, erect or sprawling, 6-15 in. high, and with chiefly basal, much-divided leaves. Flowers ¼ in. wide, purplish-pink. Southern Eu., but naturalized in the U.S.

macradenum. A perennial 8-12 in. high, the leaves all basal and only once-compound.* Flowers nearly ½ in. wide, light purple but dark-spotted. Pyrenees. Rock garden plant.

---

* Special articles on the subjects indicated by an asterisk (*) will be found at the words so marked.

erosa, -us, -um (ee-rō'sa). Jagged or gnawed.

EROSION. In regions of little or no forest cover, steep slopes, and sandy soil, the washing of soil in rainy weather is a serious menace. To overcome such, on any considerable scale, the attention of trained foresters and engineers is needed. Local erosion in a garden is best stopped by sodding, or, if that is impossible, *see* the methods and plants mentioned at BANKS.

erubescens (er-roo-bes'senz). Blushing.

ERUCA (ee-roo'ka). A small genus of Eurasian annual or biennial herbs of the mustard family, E. **sativa** rather rarely grown here as a salad plant under the name of rocket salad, roquette, or simply rocket. It is a mustard-like, half-hardy annual, branching, 18–30 in. high, and does not like summer heat. Leaves large, deeply toothed or cut. Flowers yellowish-white, about ¾ in. long, the 4 petals with purple veins, the flower cluster erect, terminal, and a raceme.* Fruit an erect, flattish, beaked pod (silique*). Sow seeds as for early and late cabbage; *i.e.*, avoid midsummer heat. The leaves should be ready for harvesting in about 65 days from sowing the seed. Quick growth and a cool season help to reduce the peculiar odor that makes many dislike the plant. (*Eruca* is the classical name of some mustard-like plant, but perhaps not this one.)

ERVATAMIA CORONARIA = *Tabernaemontana coronaria.*

ERVIL = *Vicia Ervilia.*

Ervilia. Ancient classical name, used by Pliny for some legume, but now a specific name for a vetch. *See* VICIA.

ERYNGIUM (er-rin'ji-um). Very striking and handsome, chiefly perennial, spiny-leaved herbs of the carrot family, widely cult. for the border or rock garden, and commonly called eryngo or sea holly. Of over 100 species the following seven are very popular as tall, bold plants, especially for the blue garden (which see). Unlike most plants of the carrot family, eryngo has simple* leaves, generally cut or lobed, and the margins usually spiny. Flowers prevailingly blue in the cult. sorts, but sometimes white or green, crowded in dense, bracted,* head-like clusters. Calyx showy, spiny-toothed, the petals less conspicuous, erect and stiffish. Fruit egg-shaped, without ribs, several in a cluster. (*Eryngium* is Greek for some spiny plant.)

The sea hollies thrive in any ordinarily good garden soil, preferably a reasonably moist one. They may be increased by division or by sowing fresh seed. Extremely handsome plants for the border, but they need plenty of space. Most of them are summer-blooming.

alpinum. About 2 ft. high, the plant bushy. Leaves triangular-heart-shaped, bluish, the up-

per ones often 3-lobed. Flower heads bluish-purple, rarely white, about 1½ in. wide, below a series of finely divided bracts.* Eu.

amethystinum. A perennial, not over 2 ft. high. Leaves deeply lobed or sometimes quite compound.* Flower heads about ½ in. long, bluish-purple, the bracts* below them lance-shaped. Eu. Sometimes confused with *E. planum.*

aquaticum = *E. yuccifolium.*

bourgati. Scarcely over 18 in. high. Leaves nearly round, stiff, spiny-toothed, and divided finger-fashion into 3–5 segments. Flower heads ½ in. long, bluish-purple, the bracts* beneath long and spine-tipped. Southern Eu.

giganteum. Five to seven feet high and much-branched. Leaves heart-shaped or triangular, the upper ones 3-lobed. Flower heads nearly 4 in. wide, blue or pale green, the bracts beneath long, stiff and much cut. Caucasus. A very handsome plant.

oliverianum. A perennial 2–3 ft. high. Leaves various, the lower undivided, the upper 4–5-parted or lobed, finger-fashion. Flower heads about 1½ in. wide, blue or bluish-purple, the bracts* below rigid, very narrow and stiff. Of hybrid origin.

planum. Not over 3 ft. high, the lower leaves undivided, the upper 3–5-parted. Flower heads blue, about ½ in. wide, the bracts* beneath rigid, narrow and stiff. Eurasia.

yuccifolium. Button snakeroot; also called rattlesnake master. A stout, bushy herb 4–6 ft. high. Leaves stiff, rigid, very narrow, bristly margined. Flower heads pale blue or whitish. Southeastern U.S. Also called *E. aquaticum.*

ERYNGO. *See* ERYNGIUM.

ERYSIMUM (e-riss'i-mum). A large genus of Old World herbs of the mustard family, closely related to the common wallflower (*see* CHEIRANTHUS) and differing only in technical characters from it. *Erysimum*, usually called blister-cress, contains a few flower garden plants, somewhat resembling stocks, with yellow, lilac, or blue flowers, usually in terminal clusters (racemes*) that lengthen considerably as the long, 4-sided pods (silique*) ripen. The pods are usually beaked. (*Erysimum* is from the Greek to draw blisters.)

The blister-cresses are of very easy culture in any garden soil. The plants are almost weedy in their ability to withstand unfavorable conditions. Under usual garden culture they flower profusely. Sow the annuals where wanted, while the perennials and biennial species should be sown the season before they are to be planted out. The Latin names below are still in much confusion.

asperum. Siberian wallflower. A North American perennial herb, best treated as a biennial (*see* BIENNIALS). Leaves rather narrow, 2–4 in. long, the lower ones remotely toothed. Flowers orange-yellow. Pods slender, 2–4 in. long. Often sold as *Cheiranthus allioni* and long thought to be Asiatic.

linifolium. Alpine wallflower. A grayish, perennial herb, 6–12 in. high, but the branches somewhat prostrate. Leaves narrow, nearly line-like. Flowers lilac or mauve. Spain. Often sold as *Cheiranthus linifolius.*

murale. An old, flower garden, hardy annual (*see* ANNUALS), grown or offered under a variety of names, one of the most widely

---

* Special articles on the subjects indicated by an asterisk (*) will be found at the words so marked.

used being *E. perofskianum* (a name properly applied to another non-hort. species). It is a showy herb 12–18 in. high, leafy, and with the leaves little, if at all, toothed. Flowers golden-yellow, in compact clusters. Pods not much over 1 in. long, rather thick. Eu. A much-confused species as to name, but long in cult.

perofskianum. *See* ERYSIMUM MURALE.

pulchellum. A tufted, perennial herb 12–24 in. high, the stem erect. Leaves oblongish, toothed or with lyre-shaped lobes, the upper ones narrower and deeply toothed. Flowers dark orange. Pod slender and erect. Asia Minor and Greece. Also called *E. rupestre*. Sometimes the plant offered as this is *E. murale*.

ERYTHEA (e-ri-thee'a). Mexican fan palms, two of the eight known species grown for ornament outdoors in zones* 8 and 9, especially in Fla. and Calif. They are not very tall, the trunk without spines but sometimes very shaggy, as in the not distantly related California fan palm. Leaves fan-like, the stalk sometimes prickly, the blade split into many (20–80) segments, the tips of which often droop. Flowers perfect,* the cluster from among the leaf crown, the spadix* provided with a spathe.* Stamens 6. Fruits about ¾ in. long or a little less. (Named for one of the Hesperides, The Daughter of Evening.)

For culture *see* PALM.

armata. Mexican blue palm. Not over 40 ft. high, the trunk covered by the remains of the withered leaf bases and their attendant shag. Leaves bluish-green, waxy, cut deeply into nearly 50 segments, the leafstalk spiny. Flowering cluster long, protruding beyond the crown of leaves. Fruit nearly round, fleshy. Baja Calif. The tree is also offered as *Glaucothea*.

edulis. Guadalupe palm. A stout, ringed palm, usually less than 30 ft. high, the trunk not shaggy. Leaves green both sides, but paler beneath, cut about ⅓ to the middle into 70–80 segments that are about 1 in. wide, and deeply cleft at the tip. Leafstalk usually without spines. Fruit globe-shaped, black, about ⅞ in. thick, in a long cluster. Guadalupe Island and Baja Calif. Commonly planted in Calif. and Fla.

ERYTHRINA (e-ri-thry'na). A genus of about 30 species of handsome tropical shrubs or trees (rarely herbs) of the pea family, of many uses in the tropics, but planted only for ornament in zones* 8 and 9, where their usually showy flowers are mostly borne before or after, not with, the leaves. Commonly called coral trees because of their striking flowers. Leaves compound,* the leaflets usually only 3 and broad. Flowers almost pea-like, very handsome, borne in large clusters (racemes*). Pod (legume*) long, somewhat woody, usually constricted between the seeds, which are usually brightly colored, hence sometimes called coral bean. (*Erythrina* is from the Greek for red, in allusion to the flower color.)

The two below, all tropical American, are somewhat grown in zone* 9 or protected parts of zone* 8 in Fla., where they are highly prized. They appear to have no spe-

cial soil preferences. Propagated by seeds or cuttings. Both of them are thorny and winter-blooming.

americana. Not over 20 ft. high, usually prickly. Leaflets more or less rhomboid.* Flowers scarlet, the cluster loose, but very handsome. Pod about 4 in. long, the seeds black-spotted, but scarlet. Tropical America. Also called *E. Corallodendron*.

Crista-galli. Ceibo. A shrub or small tree, not over 15 ft. high. Leaflets often spiny on the midrib and sometimes on the stalk. Flowers crimson, the cluster loose. Brazil and Argentina, of which it is the national flower.

herbacea. In the southeastern U.S. a woody herb, 3–4 ft. high, but in tropical America a spiny-trunked tree or shrub, 3–10 ft. high. Leaflets 3, ovalish, the stalks prickly. Flowers slender, scarlet, in a showy raceme* 1–2 ft. long. Seeds scarlet, poisonous. Native and commonly planted along the Gulf Coast.

erythrocarpa, -us, -um (e-ri-throw-kar'pa). Red-fruited.

ERYTHRONIUM (e-ri-throw'ni-um). About 20 species of generally woodland, bulbous, spring-blooming herbs of the lily family, all but one North American. They have 2, often mottled, basal leaves and rather handsome flowers that are nodding, usually in small clusters or solitary. Petals and sepals not easily distinguishable as such, but the segments separate. Stamens* 6. Fruit an oblongish, somewhat 3-angled pod. The plants are generally called dogtooth violet, adder's-tongue, trout flower or trout lily. (*Erythronium* is from the Greek for red flower.)

Except for the rock garden species, noted as such below, all the dogtooth violets are best suited to the wild garden, where they do well in partial shade, and in moist woods soil, not especially acid. They are best propagated by offsets, although they may be raised from seed if one is willing to wait for 3–4 years for the first flowers. Some of them are among the most attractive of American wild flowers, the western ones best treated as bulbous plants that need a long rest after blooming.

albidum. Spring or fawn lily. Not over 12 in. high. Leaves green or brown-mottled. Flowers white or pinkish-purple, about 1½ in. long, the segments curved backward. Eastern N.A.

americanum. The common dogtooth violet or yellow adder's-tongue. Leaves 4–6 in. long, the blade mottled with brown. Flowers yellow, about 1½ in. long, the segments curved backward. Eastern N.A., especially in rich, moist woods. Often grown in the rock garden (which see), but also suited to the wild garden.

californicum. Fawn lily. About 1 ft. high, the leaves strongly mottled with brownish or whitish spots. Flowers 1½ in. long, cream-white. Native in Calif. but will grow well in the East.

dens-canis. Dogtooth violet of Eu. A blotched-leaved perennial 5–7 in. high, the ovalish, stalked leaves with a slender point. Flowers nodding, nearly 2 in. wide, purple or pink. Eurasia. May. There are several vars. with variously colored or spotted flowers.

giganteum. Plants offered as this are usually *E. oregonum,* or they may be *E. californicum.*

grandiflorum. Adam-and-Eve; called, also, in Calif., the chamise lily, and little grown outside that state. It grows nearly 24 in. high and has unmottled leaves and bright yellow flowers nearly 2 in. long, the flower segments strongly bent backward. Western N.A., but grows well in the East.

hendersoni. Not over 12 in. high, the leaves mottled. Flowers about 1½ in. long, purple, the segments strongly bent backward. Southern Ore., but grows well in the East.

johnsoni. By some considered only a variety of *E. revolutum,* but the leaf mottling is darker brown and the leaves look as though varnished. Flowers dark rose-color, the center orange. Calif. For culture *see* ROCK GARDEN.

oregonum. A perennial 10–15 in. high, the leaves mottled with brown or white or both colors, their stalks margined. Flowers nearly 2 in. wide, cream-white or yellowish, often brown- or green-spotted. Pacific Coast. May.

revolutum. A fine, rock garden, bulbous herb, up to 12 in. Leaves mottled. Flowers lavender-white, ultimately turning purple. British Columbia to Calif. For culture *see* ROCK GARDEN.

tuolumnense. A perennial, 10–12 in. high, its foliage bright green and not mottled. Leaves 8–10 in. long, broadly lance-shaped, the stalk clasping. Flowers about 1¼ in. long, yellow, but greenish-yellow or paler at the base. Calif., but grows well in the East. May–June.

ERYTHROXYLON (e-ri-throx'i-lon). The only cult. genus of the coca family, **Erythroxylaceae** (e-ri-throx-i-lay'see-ee), and comprising over 90 species of South American shrubs or small trees. The only cult. species is **E. Coca,** the coca plant, which is the only source of cocaine. It can be grown only in zone* 9 or the most favorable places in zone* 8, and nowhere in the U.S. does it produce leaves worth cocaine extraction. It is a shrub 8–12 ft. high, with alternate* leaves about 2 in. long, which nearly all Andean Indians chew to relieve fatigue. Flowers small, regular, yellowish, scarcely ¼ in. wide. Fruit a reddish drupe* about ⅓ in. long, the stone furrowed. Best propagated by cuttings over bottom-heat.* (*Erythroxylon* is from the Greek for red wood, true of some non-hort. species.)

ESCALLONIA (es-ka-low'ni-a). Handsome, chiefly evergreen shrubs and trees of the family Saxifragaceae, unfortunately not hardy in the North, but widely grown southward. Of the 60 known species, mostly from the Andes, those below are popular in Calif., but can be grown northward only as indicated below. Leaves alternate,* toothed. Flowers white, red, or pink, in terminal clusters (racemes* or panicles*) or these occasionally in the leaf axils.* Sepals 5, the tube turban-shaped. Petals with a long claw.* Stamens 5. Fruit a 2–3-valved capsule.* (Named for Escallon, Spanish traveler.)

These useful and handsome shrubs are very popular in Calif., where their late autumn or winter bloom is most welcome. They do not need any specialized soil con-

ditions, but do better in rich soils than in poor ones. Some of them are trained on walls or trellises. Best propagated by autumn cuttings rooted in a cold frame and planted out the following spring, a procedure possible only in mild climates. They have not done well in the sub-tropical, moister climate of Fla.

alba = *Escallonia montevidensis...*

macrantha. A densely leafy, compact shrub 7–10 ft. high. Leaves thickish, broadly oval, 2–3 in. long. Flowers crimson, about ½ in. long, in short, leafy clusters. Chile. One of the best-known of the cult. species and offered under a variety of names, such as *rosea, alba,* etc. Hardy only up to zone* 7.

montevidensis. A shrub and often procumbent, the leaves oblongish, 2–4 in. long, slightly notched at the tip. Flowers white, about ½ in. long, the cluster rounded. Uruguay and southern Brazil. Hardy only up to zone* 7. Common on walls in Calif.

organensis. Not over 6 ft. high, the branches resinous or sticky. Leaves narrowly oblongish, sometimes red-margined, 2–3 in. long. Flowers about ½ in. long, rose-red, in short, dense clusters. Brazil, in the Organ Mountains. Hardy only up to zone* 7.

pulverulenta. A densely sticky shrub 9–12 ft. high. Leaves oblongish, tapering toward the base, 2–4 in. long, finely toothed, shining on the upper surface. Flowers white, small, crowded in a tail-like cluster nearly 9 in. long. Chile. Hardy, with protection, up to zone* 6, and a very handsome shrub.

punctata. A sticky shrub 7–9 ft. high. Leaves 1–2 in. long, tapering both ends, and toothed chiefly toward the tip. Flowers crimson, solitary in the leaf axils,* or more generally in sticky, terminal clusters. Chile. Hardy, with protection up to zone* 6.

rosea. A trade name of uncertain application, often merely forms of the next species or of other pink- or red-flowered plants.

rubra. An evergreen shrub, 10–15 ft. high, its foliage sticky, the twigs reddish. Leaves broadly lance-shaped, tapering both ends, 1–2 in. long. Flowers red, about ⅓ in. wide, in loose clusters (panicles*) that are about 2½ in. long. Chile. Summer. Hardy only up to zone* 7.

ESCALLONIACEAE.. See SAXIFRAGACEAE.

ESCAPE. A cultivated plant that has run wild and maintains itself without further cultivation. Common examples of garden escapes are found in phlox, lily-of-the-valley, some pinks, many bulbous plants and fruit trees. See ADVENTIVE.

ESCAROLE. See ENDIVE.

ESCHALLOT = Shallot.

ESCHSCHOLTZIA (esh-sholt'zi-a). Very popular flower garden annuals (or treated as such) of the poppy family, all from western N.A., **E. californica,** the California poppy, being the finest, and a widely grown favorite. It is 8–12 in. high, perennial, but grown as an annual (*see* ANNUALS), and has finely dissected, long-stalked, bluish-green leaves. Flower long-stalked, solitary, very showy, 3–4 in. wide, orange-yellow, opening in sunshine, the 4 petals each with a deep-orange spot at the base. Fruit a strongly ribbed pod (cap-

---

* Special articles on the subjects indicated by an asterisk (*) will be found at the words so marked.

sule*) 3–4 in. long. A splendid garden annual blooming from July 1 to Oct. (Named for J. F. Eschscholtz, who sailed with Otto von Kotzebue to the Pacific Coast in 1816.) There are many fine hort. forms, some with nearly white, pink, rose or reddish flowers.

ESCOBARIA (es-ko-bay′ri-a). A small genus of cylindric or somewhat globe-shaped cacti from Mex. and the Southwest, E. **tuberculosa** cult. for ornament and interest in the cactus garden (*see* CACTI). It grows in clumps, the plant body more or less cylindric, 8–10 in. high, crowded with spirally arranged tubercles. Central spines brownish or blackish, few; the lateral spines white and numerous at each spine cluster, never hooked. Flowers about 1 in. wide, pink, appearing at the top of the plant. Fruit oblong, red, about ¾ in. long. (Named for Escobar y Mendoza, Spanish Jesuit.)

ESCOBITA = *Orthocarpus purpurascens.*

ESCONTRIA (es-kon′tri-a). A striking Mexican cactus called there the jiotilla or chiotilla, comprising only the species E. **Chiotilla.** It is tree-like, much-branched, and up to 20 ft. high, the few-ribbed branches bright green, rather weak and easily broken. Ribs 7–8, rather sharp-edged. Spines of 2 sorts at each cluster, a central group with one longer than the others, and 7–10 lateral, shorter, and slightly hooked spines. Flowers yellow, about 1 in. long, borne near the ends of the branches (for details *see* CACTACEAE). Fruit about ½ in. in diameter, edible, and sold in Mexican markets. Little cult. and suited only to the warmest cactus regions. *See* CACTI. (Named for Señor Don Blas Escontria of Mexico.)

esculenta, -us, -um (es-kew-len′ta). Edible.

ESPALIER. A method of training fruit and other trees. *See* TRAINED FRUIT TREES.

ESSENTIAL ORGANS. In flowers, those upon which the perpetuation of the species depends. Flowers can get along without petals or sepals, and some have neither (*see* NAKED FLOWER), but most plants cannot produce seed unless their flowers contain the essential organs of stamen* and pistil.* *See* COMPLETE, PERFECT.

ESTIMATING TREE HEIGHT. *See* GARDEN TABLES III.

ESTRAGON = *Artemisia Dracunculus. See* TARRAGON.

ETHERIZATION. The subjecting of dormant plants, both perennial herbs and shrubs and trees, to the effects of ether vapor in order to hasten their starting into growth. Much experimental work has been done on this, and the period of normal dormancy can be shortened by the use of ether, especially on woody plants like maple, horse-chestnut, birch, barberry, redbud, deutzia, spirea, etc. Ordinary procedure calls for exposure to ether fumes for about 48 hours, split into 2 equal periods and separated by a day of ether-free atmosphere. Concentrations of one

part of ether to 400–500 parts of air seem to be the best, and even this concentration becomes less effective as the plant approaches the natural end of its dormancy. Etherization is useful, if at all, early in January.

ETHYLENE. A poisonous, colorless gas, forming a considerable constituent of manufactured gas, and with a remarkable effect upon plants. Concentrations of one part ethylene to one million parts of air will force stamens and pistils of carnations above the petals, hence making them unsalable. Its use in hort. is still experimental, but it appears, in certain concentrations, to stimulate fruit ripening, promote growth of certain vines, and accelerate root production. In all but carefully controlled experiments where proper concentrations are maintained, ethylene will quickly kill most plants as does manufactured gas. *See also* GAS INJURY.

ETIOLATED. The blanched condition of the leaves of plants grown in the dark.

etrusca, -us, -um (e-truss′ka). From or near Tuscany, Italy.

EUCALYPTUS (you-ka-lip′tus). An enormous genus of chiefly Australian, sometimes gigantic, very aromatic, evergreen trees of the myrtle family, widely planted in zones* 8 and 9, and even in sheltered parts of zone* 7, for their striking flowers and foliage, but not hardy elsewhere. They are especially popular in Calif., where many of the over 400 known species have been introduced from Aust., and are prized for their freedom from pests, and some for their use as bee trees. Leaves prevailingly alternate* (opposite* in the closely related cult. genus *Angophora*), without marginal teeth, often very variable on the same plant. Flowers usually in the leaf axils,* often in small umbels,* but sometimes in branched clusters, white, yellow, or red. Calyx bell-shaped or turban-shaped, the calyx-lobes and petals forming a lid at flowering time, and separating from the calyx-tube. Fruit a capsule* opening at the top by 3–6 valves. The fruits and leafy branches are often colored and sent East as winter decorations. (*Eucalyptus* is from the Greek for well and to cover, in allusion to the lid-like arrangement of the flowers.)

The trees are generally called gum tree or stringy-bark, and of over 70 species known to be in cult. here (mostly in Calif.), the following are perhaps the best selection for the average grower. No attempt is made here to include many valuable timber trees, although some are cult. on a great scale for this purpose as they grow quickly and some to an incredible height (300 ft. or more). For culture *see* below.

amygdalina. Peppermint gum. A fibrous-barked tree up to 300 ft., the foliage peppermint-scented. Leaves lance-shaped. Flowers small, in profuse umbels.* Fruit about ¼ in. wide.

botryoides. Bastard mahogany; also called bangalay. Not over 150 ft. high, the bark persistent and furrowed. Leaves lance-shaped.

---

* Special articles on the subjects indicated by an asterisk (*) will be found at the words so marked.

Flowers nearly stalkless, large. Fruit about ⅓ in. wide.

camaldulensis. A trade name for a variety of *Eucalyptus rostrata.*

citriodora = *Eucalyptus maculata citriodora.*

cladocalyx. Sugar gum. A tree 80–120 ft. high, the bark smooth but deciduous.* Leaves ovalish or lance-shaped. Flowers nearly ½ in. wide in umbels* of 7–12 blooms. Fruit about ¼ in. wide.

cornuta. Yate-tree. A tree up to 80–120 ft. high. Leaves oblongish or broadly lance-shaped. Flowers greenish-yellow, in dense, head-like umbels.* Fruit about ⅓ in. wide.

ficifolia. Scarlet-flowered gum; also called scarlet bloom. Not much over 30 ft., the bark dark and furrowed. Leaves ovalish or narrower. Flowers white, pink or scarlet, nearly 1½ in. long. Fruit nearly 1½ in. wide.

gigantea = *Eucalyptus obliqua.*

globulus. Blue gum, and one of the most widely cult. It may reach 300 ft. in height, the trunk smooth and bluish-white. Leaves broad and very bluish on young growth, later narrower. Flowers about 1½ in. wide, solitary or a few together. Fruit nearly 1 in. wide.

maculata. Not over 150 ft. high, the bark peeling off in patches. Leaves lance-shaped. Flowers about ½ in. long, in a many-flowered, branched cluster. Fruit about ½ in. wide. The *var.* citriodora, the lemon-scented gum, has lemon-scented foliage and is often offered by dealers as *E. citriodora.*

obliqua. Tasmania stringy-bark. A tree up to 300 ft., the bark persistent but fibrous. Leaves ovalish, very oblique. Flowers small, in umbels.* Fruit about ⅓ in. wide. Sometimes offered as *E. gigantea.*

polyanthemos. Red box; also called Australian beech. A tree up to 150 ft. high, the bark persistent. Leaves ovalish or even roundish, gray-green. Flowers small, in a profuse, branched cluster. Fruit about ½ in. wide.

pulverulenta. A small tree, not over 30 ft. high, the bluish-green leaves nearly round, opposite, stalkless, and about 2½ in. wide, without marginal teeth. Flowers in 3's from the joints of the leaf, white, each flower about 1 in. long. Planted outdoors in Calif. and in similar climates, its cut twigs sold in florist shops as "blue spiral."

resinifera. Red mahogany. A tree scarcely over 100 ft., the bark rough and persistent. Leaves lance-shaped, thickish. Flowers small, in umbels.* Fruit about ⅓ in. wide.

robusta. Swamp mahogany; also called mahogany gum. A widely planted tree, not over 100 ft. high, with rough, persistent bark. Leaves ovalish or lance-shaped. Flowers about ¾ in. wide, in umbels.* Fruit about ½ in. wide.

rostrata. Red gum. A popular tree in Calif., 150–200 ft. high, the smooth gray bark deciduous.* Leaves narrowly lance-shaped. Flowers nearly ½ in. wide, in umbels.* Fruit about ¼ in. wide.

rudis. Desert gum. Not over 100 ft. high, the rough, gray bark persistent. Leaves lance-shaped. Flowers about ½ in. wide, in umbels.* Fruit about ½ in. wide.

Sideroxylon. Red ironbark. Not over 100 ft. high, the dark red or blackish rough bark persistent. Leaves narrowly lance-shaped, the young growth even narrower. Flowers yellowish-white, in umbels.* Fruit about ½ in. in diameter. There are also red or rose-colored forms and one with silvery foliage.

tereticornis. Gray or slaty gum. Up to 150 ft. high, the smooth, gray bark deciduous.*

Leaves broadly lance-shaped or even ovalish. Flowers nearly ¾ in. wide, in umbels.* Fruit about ¼ in. wide.

umbellata. A name originally given to some Australian *Eucalyptus,* without description and unidentifiable. The modern use of *Eucalyptus umbellatus* appears to be equally untenable.

viminalis. Manna gum. A beautiful tree, up to 300 ft. high, the branches hanging. Leaves lance-shaped. Flowers about ½ in. wide, in umbels.* Fruit about ¼ in. wide.

EUCALYPTUS CULTURE

The culture of eucalyptus in Calif. is simple, as they do well in a variety of soils. The easiest method of propagation is by seeds. Take the unopened fruits from the trees and put them in a dry place until the small seeds are loosened. Then sow in flats in potting mixture* 2, preferably in July or Aug. Press the seeds in gently and sprinkle a little charcoal dust over them, cover the flat with a sheet of glass and put in the shade. They should germinate, if the seed is reasonably fresh, in about 5 days. This is much better than trying to propagate by cuttings, budding, or grafting.

The southern Calif. skyline is dominated by gum trees, especially *E. amygdalina, globulus, rudis, robusta,* and the lemon-scented gum. The latter is also grown in the cool greenhouse for its fragrant foliage. Of lesser height, at least as grown in Calif., are *Eucalyptus ficifolia, cladocalyx, cornuta,* and *resinifera.* Young twigs of *E. pulverulenta* are much harvested for shipment to florists as "blue spiral."

EUCHARIDIUM (you-ka-rid′i-um). Californian annual herbs of the family Onagraceae, two of the three known species rather popular flower garden annuals, closely related to *Clarkia,* and often offered as that. Leaves alternate.* Flowers showy, in terminal clusters (mostly spike-like racemes*). Petals 4, with a long claw,* the broadly expanded limb 3-lobed. Stamens 4. Fruit a 4-angled, 4-valved, many-seeded capsule.* (*Eucharidium* is from the Greek for charming.)

Both those below should be grown as hardy annuals. *See* ANNUALS.

breweri. Fairy fans. Not over 9 in. high, the leaves lance-shaped. Flowers deep pink, fragrant, the petals fan-shaped, one of the lobes longer than the other two.

concinnum. Red ribbons. Twice as tall as the above, the leaves ovalish or oblong. Flowers rose-purple, the petals with the three lobes nearly equal. A very handsome plant sometimes offered as *E. grandiflorum.*

grandiflorum = *Eucharidium concinnum.*

EUCHARIS (you′kar-is). South American bulbous herbs of the family Amaryllidaceae, *E. grandiflora,* the Amazon lily, a popular greenhouse and pot plant, and grown outdoors in southern Fla. and Calif. It has a stout bulb, nearly 2 in. in diameter, from which spring the leaves and stalk of the flower cluster which is 1–2 ft. high. Leaves 8–12 in. long, about half as wide, the slender leafstalk 8–12 in. long. Flowers pure white,

---

* Special articles on the subjects indicated by an asterisk (*) will be found at the words so marked.

fragrant, in a terminal umbel.* The stalk round. Corolla cylindric and tubular below, the lobes spreading, in all about 2½ in. wide and very showy. Stamens 6, inserted in the throat of the corolla and shorter than its segments. Fruit a 3-lobed capsule.* Colombia. Its culture is the same as for *Amaryllis* (which see). (*Eucharis* is from the Greek for very graceful.) Often sold as *E. amazonica.*

EUCHLAENA (you-klee′na). A genus of corn-like Mexican or Central American grasses of secondary garden significance, except for **E. mexicana,** the teosinte, which may have been a remote ancestor of, or perhaps derived from, modern corn. The teosinte today is chiefly grown for forage in the South, and is an annual grass 6–10 ft. high, with a very leafy stem. Leaves 3–5 ft. long, about 1½ in. wide, the midrib prominent. Male and female flowers in separate clusters, the male in terminal spikelets, the female in clusters in the upper leaf axils, as in corn, from the husks of which the silk-like styles* protrude. The grain (seed) is about ¼ in. long and shining, not borne in "ears" like corn, but on a jointed spike enclosed by the husk. (*Euchlaena* is from the Greek for well-covered, from the husk-enclosed fruit.)

euchlora (you-claw′ra). Well, *i.e.,* thoroughly green.

EUCOMIS (you-kō′mis). A small genus of South African bulbous herbs of the lily family; only **E. comosa,** the pineapple-flower, of garden interest. It is a greenhouse plant related to *Scilla,* and 1–2 ft. high. Leaves brown-spotted beneath, nearly 2 ft. long and 3 in. wide, in a basal rosette. Flowers greenish-white, borne in a leafy-topped, terminal raceme,* the flower about ½ in. long, its segments separate. Stamens 6. Fruit a 3-valved capsule. South of zone* 6 the bulbs may be allowed to stay in the ground over the winter, but in the North they should be handled as pot subjects in the cool greenhouse. Sometimes offered as E. *punctata.* (*Eucomis* is from the Greek for beautiful topknot, from the leafy tuft at the end of the flower cluster.)

EUCOMMIA (you-kom′mi-a). A single Chinese tree, the only genus of the family **Eucommiaceae** (you-kom-mee-a′see-ee) and of more interest as the only hardy woody plant producing rubber than as an ornamental. (The rubber is of no commercial importance.) The only species, **E. ulmoides,** is an elm-like tree up to 50 ft. high. Leaves alternate,* stalked and toothed, elliptic or oblongish, 2–3 in. long. Flowers unisexual,* blooming in April before the leaves unfold, without petals or sepals. The male flowers with red anthers,* the female consisting only of a 1-celled ovary. Fruit a stalked, 1-seeded, and winged nutlet. Hardy from zone* 4 southward, and of easy culture. (*Eucommia* is from the Greek for well and gum, in allusion to the rubber it contains.)

EUGENIA (you-jee′ni-a). Perhaps a thousand species of chiefly tropical, generally aromatic, shrubs and trees of the myrtle family, of great economic and garden interest, both for the often edible fruits and for the fine ornamental plants used throughout the tropical and sub-tropical world, especially in Calif. and Fla. Leaves opposite,* evergreen. Flowers solitary in the leaf axils* or in few-flowered clusters (cymes*). Calyx* turban-shaped, the sepals 5. Petals 4–5. Stamens numerous, in several series, usually longer than the petals. Fruit a berry. (Named for Prince Eugene of Savoy, plant patron.)

South of zone* 7 these plants are of easy culture in any usual soil and are propagated by seeds or by cuttings over bottom-heat or in the frame outdoors. They are not usually cult. in the greenhouse.

apiculata. A shrub 4–5 ft. high. Leaves ovalish, ¾–1 in. long. Flowers white, in 3′s, nearly ½ in. wide. Fruit black. Chile.

hookeriana = *Eugenia paniculata.*

Jambos. Rose-apple; also called jambu. A branching, broad-headed tree, usually not over 30 ft. Leaves narrowly lance-shaped, tapering both ends, 6–8 in. long. Flowers 2–3 in. wide, greenish-white, the numerous stamens* showy. Fruit edible (as preserves), greenish-yellow, about 2 in. in diameter. Tropical Asia.

myrtifolia = *Eugenia paniculata australis.*

paniculata. A widely popular ornamental tree, especially in Calif. Leaves oblongish, 2–3 in. long, tapering both ends. Flowers about ½ in. wide, white, the stamens numerous and showy. Fruit edible (for jelly), purple, about ½ in. in diameter. Aust. Often sold as *E. hookeriana.* Even more popular is var. **australis,** the Australian brush cherry (often sold as *E. myrtifolia*), which is a bushier form, popular in Calif. for topiary work, but its flowers and fruits are less desirable than in the typical form.

uniflora. Pitanga; called also Surinam cherry. A shrub or tree not over 25 ft. high. Leaves ovalish or narrower, 1–2 in. long. Flowers fragrant, white, about ½ in. wide. Fruit edible, crimson, ribbed. Brazil.

eugenioides (you-jee-nee-oy′deez; but *see* OÏDES). Resembling the genus *Eugenia* (which see).

EULALIA = *Miscanthus sinensis.*

EUONYMUS (you-on′i-mus). Also spelled *Evonymus.* Shrubs, vines, or trees of the greatest garden importance and belonging to the family Celastraceae. Of the 120 known species, generally called spindle-tree, over a dozen are very popular garden plants, although their flowers are inconspicuous. They are grown either for their showy fruits or often evergreen foliage, or both, and some are extremely valuable vines (which see). Leaves opposite,* stalked, nearly always smooth. Flowers greenish, white, or yellowish, small, in small clusters (cymes*) in the leaf axils.* Sepals and petals 4–5. Fruit a capsule,* often lobed, the splitting of which discloses the seeds which are enclosed or partly surrounded with a showy,

---

* Special articles on the subjects indicated by an asterisk (*) will be found at the words so marked.

fleshy, orange or red aril.* (*Euonymus* is the old Greek name for the spindle-tree.)

These valuable plants are not particular as to soil, nor exposure, but all are not hardy, as indicated below . They may be propagated by stratified seeds, or by cuttings taken of the old wood, which in evergreen sorts should be rooted under glass. All are spring-flowering (May–June), and set their attractive fruits from July to frost. All are deciduous,* unless mentioned as evergreen.

acutus = *Euonymus fortunei acutus.*

alatus. Winged spindle-tree. A stiff, spreading shrub 6–9 ft. high, the twigs corky-winged. Leaves elliptic to ovalish, 1½–3 in. long. Flowers yellowish. Fruit purplish, about ½ in. long. Eastern As. Hardy from zone* 3 southward. The *var.* **compactus** is an almost globose shrub with brilliantly red fall foliage.

americanus. Burning-bush; called also strawberry-bush and skewerwood. A sparsely branched shrub 5–8 ft. high. Leaves oval or oblongish, 1½–4 in. long, wavy-toothed. Flowers greenish. Fruit pinkish, warty, about ½ in. thick. N.Y. to Fla. and Okla. Hardy from zone* 4 southward.

atropurpureus. Wahoo or burning-bush. A shrub or small tree 8–20 ft. high. Leaves elliptic or ovalish, 2–5 in. long, finely toothed, and hairy beneath. Flowers greenish-purple. Fruit scarlet, 4-lobed, the aril* crimson. Ontario to Va. and Tex. Hardy from zone* 3 southward. The crimson fruit and the shrub are often facetiously called "hearts-bustin'-with-love." There is also a variegated-leaved form.

bungeanus. A shrub or small tree, not over 18 ft. high. Leaves elliptic or ovalish, 2½–5 in. long, wedge-shaped at the base. Flowers yellowish. Fruit when open disclosing the showy, orange aril* of the seeds. China. Hardy from zone* 2 southward.

europaeus. Spindle-tree; also called prick-timber. A shrub or small tree 9–20 ft. high. Leaves oblongish, 1½–4 in. long, wavy-toothed, wedge-shaped at the base. Flowers yellowish-green, larger and more showy than in the others. Fruit 4-lobed, red or pink, nearly ¾ in. wide, the aril* orange. Eurasia, sometimes an escape in the U.S. Hardy from zone* 3 southward.

fortunei. A trailing or climbing evergreen vine and the finest of all the cult. species, especially in some of its varieties. Leaves ovalish or broadly elliptic, ¾–2½ in. long. Flowers greenish-white. Fruit nearly round, pale-pink. Eastern As. Hardy from zone* 4, and, with protection, from zone* 2 southward, and occasionally hardy farther north. By some the various forms are still called *E. radicans*, an old and now invalid name. Of the many varieties the best are: *var.* **argenteo-marginatus**, with silvery-margined leaves; *var.* **acutus**, with smaller leaves, and an especially good climber; *var.* **carrierei**, a low, shrubby form, with showy fruit, useful for bedding; *var.* **minimus**, a very small-leaved form, the veins whitish, useful in the rock garden (which see, sometimes sold as *var.* **kewensis**); and *var.* **vegetus**, a somewhat shrubby form.

japonicus. An evergreen shrub up to 15 ft. or more, the twigs a little angled. Leaves narrowly elliptic or broadest toward the tip, 1–3 in. long, bluntly toothed. Flowers greenish-white. Fruit nearly round, pinkish, the aril* orange. Southern Jap. Hardy from zone* 5 southward. An extremely popular plant also offered in *var.* **albo-marginatus**, with yellow-

margined leaves; *var.* **aureo-marginatus**, with yellow-margined leaves; *var.* **compactus** is as tall as the type, but almost ball-like in its compact habit. Its autumnal foliage is a gorgeous red; and *var.* **microphyllus** (often offered as *E. pulchellus*), with smaller leaves and dwarf stature is an acceptable substitute for box, esp. as an edging plant. It will stand sub-zero temperatures.

kewensis = *Euonymus fortunei minimus.*

kiautschovicus. Evergreen or half-evergreen shrub, 4–8 ft. high, the lower branches sometimes prostrate and rooting. Leaves oblongish, 2½–4 in. long, bluntly fine-toothed. Flowers greenish-white. Fruit nearly round, about ⅝ in. wide, pinkish, the aril* orange-red. China. Hardy from zone* 5, or, with protection, from zone* 4 southward. Also and often called *E. patens.*

latifolius. A Eurasian shrub or small tree 9–20 ft. high. Leaves oblongish, 3–5½ in. long, broadly wedge-shaped at the base, the teeth rounded. Flowers greenish. Fruit bright red, nearly 1 in. wide, 4-winged, the aril* orange. Hardy from zone* 4 southward.

nanus. A low, partially procumbent shrub, the tips of the branches often erect and 2–3 ft. high. Leaves narrow, ¾–1½ in. long, the margins slightly rolled. Flowers small, brown-purple, followed by a 4-lobed pink fruit. Eurasia. May. Hardy from zone* 2 southward.

obovatus. Running strawberry-bush. A prostrate or procumbent shrub, never over 18 in. high. Leaves elliptic or broadest toward the tip, 1½–3 in. long, blunt-toothed. Flowers greenish-purple. Fruit crimson, 3-lobed, warty, the aril* scarlet. Eastern N.A. Hardy from zone* 2 southward.

oxyphyllus. A small tree or shrub 10–20 ft. high, the foliage deciduous.* Leaves ovalish or oblong, 1½–3 in. long, pointed at the tip, the margins with small, incurved teeth. Flowers greenish-brown, inconspicuous. Fruit nearly round, 4–5-ribbed, about ½ in. thick, the aril* bright red. Jap. Fruit showy in Oct. Hardy from zone* 4 southward.

patens = *E. kiautschovicus.*

pulchellus = *E. japonicus microphyllus.*

radicans = *E. fortunei.*

sieboldianus. Not very different from *E. bungeanus*, but with unlobed fruit. The plant offered as this may often be *E. bungeanus* or *E. kiautschovicus.*

yedoensis. A large Asiatic shrub 4–10 ft. high, the leaves oblongish or broadest toward the tip, 3–5½ in. long, bluntly fine-toothed. Flowers yellowish. Fruit deeply 4-lobed, pinkish, the aril* orange. Hardy from zone* 2 southward. Fall foliage brilliant scarlet. By some considered as a *var.* of *E. hamiltonianus*, a species not here maintained.

INSECT PESTS. Control scale with delayed, dormant, oil application. Two broods of young appear, one in late spring, the other at mid-summer. Pesticide #21 sprays repeated once 2 weeks later will control them (*see* SPRAYS AND DUSTS). Pruning out is desirable.

EUPATORIUM (you-pa-toe'ri-um). The bonesets or thoroughworts comprise a genus of over 500 species of chiefly tropical American herbs of the family Compositae, a few reaching temperate regions, and grown in the flower garden, and the only sorts here treated. Some of the tropical species are occasionally grown in the greenhouse, but are little known to the average greenhouse

---

* Special articles on the subjects indicated by an asterisk (*) will be found at the words so marked.

owner. The hardy species are perennial herbs with opposite° or whorled° leaves. Flowers showy in numerous small heads crowded in various sorts of clusters, some of them arching and lax, others close and dense. Ray flowers none, as the head is composed of many small, tubular flowers suggesting the garden ageratum, to which *Eupatorium* is closely related. The minute branches of the styles° usually protrude beyond the general level of the head, which thus appears roughish and accounts for the name mist-flower for some species. (Named for *Eupator*, King Mithridates VI of Pontus, who is supposed to have used some related plant for healing.)

All the bonesets are of easy culture in ordinary garden soils. They are grown for their profuse, usually late summer or autumn bloom. Propagated by division in spring.

aromaticum. Wild hoarhound; also called poolroot. A stout herb much resembling *E. rugosum*, but the leaves thicker, blunter, and usually hairy. Flowers white. Mass. to Fla. along the coast, and especially suited to sandy soils. Not aromatic.

coelestinum. Mist-flower, blue boneset, and often called the hardy ageratum. It is a perennial up to 2 ft. Leaves stalked, more or less triangular-ovalish, thin and coarsely toothed. Flower heads numerous, small, but very attractive, light blue or violet blue, and late-blooming. N.J. to Kan. and southward. *See* BLUE GARDEN.

hyssopifolium. A low herb with whorled,° narrow leaves and a terminal, flat-topped cluster of small, white flower heads. It is of no garden interest except for the fact that it will grow in pure sand (*see* SAND GARDEN). Eastern U.S.

perfoliatum. Boneset; called, also, Indian sage and feverwort. A coarse, stout herb, 3–6 ft. high, somewhat rank-smelling. Leaves pointed at the tip, but broadening toward the base and united with the leaf opposite it. Flower heads white, in a dense, flat-topped cluster. Nearly throughout N.A. and preferring low grounds. Long cult. as a domestic medicine.

purpureum. Joe-pye-weed; also called purple boneset. A rank-growing herb 7–9 ft. high, less in dry ground. Leaves in whorls° of 5 or 6, oblongish or ovalish, coarsely toothed and taper-pointed. Flower heads purple, in a roundish, much-branched and showy terminal cluster. Nearly throughout N.A., in some of its forms, mostly in moist places.

rugosum. White snakeroot; called also Indian sanicle and richweed. A branching herb 2–4 ft. high, the leaves smooth or nearly so and thin, long-stalked, ovalish, but broad toward the base, sharply toothed. Flower heads in a loosely branched cluster, white. Eastern N.A. and blooming from midsummer to frost. Causes milk-poisoning to cattle and should be eradicated from pastures. *See* AUTUMN GARDEN.

urticaefolium = *E. rugosum*.

EUPHORBIA (you-for′bi-a). Probably over 1500 species of wide distribution and great diversity of habit, belonging to the family Euphorbiaceae, some tropical, cactus-like succulents, others weeds, the popular flower garden annual snow-on-the-mountain and the gorgeous poinsettia. The cactus-like plants from Africa and the East Indies, such as *E. lactea*, are widely planted for hedges in warm regions, and are usually as leafless as most cacti. *E. splendens* is a prickly, creeping plant from Madagascar, but bears a few leaves, and is a greenhouse favorite. *E. marginata*, *E. corollata*, and *E. epithymoides* are herbs. The flowers in all of them have no petals or sepals and would not be showy if it were not for the often highly colored bracts.° (For structure *see* EUPHORBIACEAE.) Fruit a capsule,° which often opens explosively. All the plants have a milky juice and in some the juice is poisonous. (*Euphorbia* is from a Greek word of uncertain significance as applied to these plants.)

The plants are of such diverse habit and origin that cultural notes are appended for each. Some of them are called spurge, especially the herbs.

corollata. Flowering spurge; also called milk purslane. A hardy, perennial herb best grown for cutting, or as a bedding plant. It is 18–30 in. high, sparsely branched. Leaves ovalish-oblong, 1–2 in. long, diminishing upward and opposite near the flower cluster. Flower cluster with showy white appendages, for which the plant is grown. Eastern N.A., especially in sandy soil. *See* SAND GARDEN.

Cyparissias. Cypress spurge. A lusty perennial, 8–10 in. high, apt to spread where not wanted, and, if grown, to be kept confined. Leaves very numerous, bright green, about 1½ in. long, crowded. Flowers greenish-yellow, quite small, but crowded in a dense cluster (umbel°). Eurasia. May–July. Often escaping as a weed nearly throughout N.A.

epithymoides. Cushion spurge. A European, hardy, perennial herb, the 12-in. stems usually forming a cushion-shaped or roundish clump. Leaves oblongish, green, becoming yellow near the flower cluster when the latter blooms. A good accent plant for the border, its bracts and foliage very attractive.

fulgens. Scarlet plume. A Mexican shrub to be grown in the greenhouse as one does poinsettia (which see for culture). It is a small bush with slender, usually drooping branches. Leaves long-stalked, green, generally lance-shaped. Bracts° of the flower cluster bright scarlet and very showy.

grandicornis. A much-branched S. Af. succulent, 4–6 ft. high, the usually leafless stems 3-angled, apparently winged and nearly 6 in. thick, more or less spiny, the gray spines in pairs and about 2 in. long. Flowers yellow, small, stalkless, borne between the spines. A greenhouse subject or for desert, frostless regions.

hermentiana. Not unlike *E. lactea* but not so tall, and the branches wider. West Af.

heterophylla. Mexican fire-plant. A showy annual herb, 1–3 ft. high. Leaves varying from ovalish and unlobed to lobed or fiddle-shaped. The upper leaves pass into the bracts which are red at the base or mottled red and white. In the Mississippi Valley from southern Ill. to Fla. and southward to Peru. Sometimes known as *Poinsettia heterophylla*.

lactea. A tall, branching, candelabra-like and cactus-like plant, frequently 20 ft. high, but less as clipped for hedges in the warm sections of Fla. and throughout the tropics. Joints broadly but bluntly winged, plentifully beset with light-colored spines, 1–2 in. long.

° Special articles on the subjects indicated by an asterisk (°) will be found at the words so marked.

Through the middle of each joint there is generally a white-marbled area. Leaves very small, soon falling and for months the plant is leafless. It requires the same treatment as tree-like cacti (which see). East Indies.

maculata. *See* the Spotted Spurge in the list at WEEDS.

mammillaris. A S.Af. succulent, 1–3 ft. high, its cylindrical branches spiny, nearly 2 in. thick, with 7–17 tubercled* angles. Leaves (mostly absent) minute and scale-like. Spines about ½ in. long. Flowers many, small, with purplish bracts* beneath them. A greenhouse plant or cult. outdoors in frostless regions.

marginata. Snow-on-the-mountain. Ghost-weed. A prairie plant widely grown as one of the most popular of flower garden annuals. For culture *see* ANNUALS. It is a bushy herb 8–15 in. high, much-branched. Leaves oblongish, 1–3 in. long, the lower green, the upper white-margined. The bracts* of the flower cluster, for which the plant is grown, are also white and very showy. S. D. to Tex. July 15–Oct. An old garden favorite, and sometimes sold as *E. variegata*. Its milky juice is a skin irritant to some.

mili. *See* EUPHORBIA SPLENDENS.

Myrsinites. A European, hardy, perennial herb, the many stems almost prostrate. Leaves numerous, fleshy, bluish-green, oblongish, pointed and a little concave. Bracts* of the flower clusters yellow. Useful for dry walls or in the rock garden.

obesa. An unusual S. Af. succulent, the nearly leafless plant body almost globular, about 5 in. in diameter, with 8 spineless ribs, the plant body alternately striped with dark green bands. Flowers small, greenish, short-stalked, borne only at the apex or along upper part of the ribs. It needs little water and will stand conditions in warm sunny rooms. Use potting mixture* 6.

pseudocactus. A half-buried succulent, the 4–5 stems producing a clump 4 ft. wide. Stems angled, about 2 in. thick, with spines ½ in. long, in pairs and yellow V-shaped markings on the joints. Flowers yellow. Natal. (Af.) A greenhouse plant or cult. outdoors in frostless regions.

pulcherrima. The common poinsettia of the florists; sometimes called painted-leaf. In the wild a shrub 2–10 ft. high or even more; as cult. a handsome winter-blooming pot plant, usually 2–4 ft. high, grown in the greenhouse or outdoors in frostless regions. Leaves ovalish, or elliptic, 3–6 in. long, usually shallowly lobed or wavy-margined and weakly toothed, the upper leaves passing into the brilliantly colored, vermilion bracts.* Flowers and attendant structures green and yellow. Tropical America. Often known as *Poinsettia pulcherrima*. For the hort. varieties and cult *see* POINSETTIA.

splendens. Crown-of-thorns. A creeping, spiny, greenhouse plant, best trained over a small trellis, its stems not over 6 ft. long, usually dull purple-brown, but the young growth often green. Spines about 1 in. long, thick and stout. Leaves oblongish, thin, 1–2 in. long, rather sparse and the plant often leafless. Flower clusters long-stalked, the bracts* brilliant red. Madagascar. It blooms most of the year, but most freely in the winter. Treat as a greenhouse succulent (which see). By some the correct name is considered to be *E. mili*, a name not here maintained.

variegata = *Euphorbia marginata*.

EUPHORBIACEAE (you-for-bi-ā′see-ee).

The spurge or poinsettia family, while of huge size and diverse habit, furnishes only a few genera of garden significance. Of its 280 genera and over 7000 species, world-wide in their distribution, only 19 are of hort. interest, and of these *Codiaeum* (the garden crotons), *Ricinus* (*see* CASTOR-OIL PLANT), *Aleurites* (*see* TUNG-OIL TREE), *Euphorbia*, and *Acalypha* are much cult.

The family comprises herbs, shrubs, or trees (some cactus-like, nearly leafless succulents), many of which have a milky (often poisonous) juice and alternate* leaves. The true flowers (*see* below) are usually small and inconspicuous, but the bracts around or beneath them are extremely showy in some genera, notably in poinsettia, in some euphorbias, and in *Pedilanthus*. The fruit in nearly all genera is a dry, 3-lobed capsule,* but fleshy in *Breynia* and *Daphniphyllum*, neither of which, though in cultivation, is of much garden importance.

A few tropical genera are of outstanding importance. They include *Hevea* (rubber), *Hura* (sandbox tree), and *Manihot* (cassava). The other cult. genera are *Jatropha*, *Mercurialis*, *Phyllanthus*, *Sapium*, and *Synadenium*.

Technical flower characters: Flowers monoecious* or dioecious.* The naked female flower is often surrounded by several male flowers. This whole cluster is, in some genera, surrounded by a series of brightly colored bracts* (often mistaken for flowers in poinsettias and snow-on-the-mountain). Calyx and corolla both sometimes wanting, of separate petals or sepals when present. Stamens many or 1. Ovary superior,* 3-celled.

EUPHORBIOIDES (you-for-bee-oy′deez, but *see* OÏDES). Like a plant of the genus *Euphorbia*.

EUPHORIA (you-foe′ri-a). Half a dozen Asiatic tropical trees of the family Sapindaceae, E. **Longana**, yielding the longan or lungan, which are fruits of secondary interest for outdoor culture only in zones* 8 and 9. It is a tree 30–40 ft. high, the leaves compound* and composed of 2–5 pairs of blunt, oblongish or narrower leaflets. Flowers small, yellowish-white, in small terminal clusters, or these in the leaf axils.* (For details *see* SAPINDACEAE.) Fruit nearly round, about 1 in. in diameter, yellowish-brown, the outer husk thin and shell-like, the white, juicy pulp edible. India. As grown in Fla. and Calif. the trees are indifferent to soils, and will even stand slight frosts, but they do better in the shade of larger trees than in full sunlight. Propagated by seeds or by grafting. (*Euphoria* is from the Greek for carries well, in allusion to the fruits.)

EUPRITCHARDIA. *See* PRITCHARDIA.

EUPTELEA (you-tee′lee-a). Three Asiatic species of shrubs or small trees of the family Trochodendraceae, two of them grown for ornament. Leaves alternate,* toothed, appearing after the flowers bloom. Flowers not showy, without petals or sepals, small, crowded in small, head-like clusters or ra-

* Special articles on the subjects indicated by an asterisk (*) will be found at the words so marked.

cemes.* Stamens many. Fruit a small, winged nut (samara*) or a splitting pod (follicle*). (*Euptelea* is from the Greek for well or handsome and elm, in allusion to the fruit.)

Both those below are chiefly grown for the young foliage, which is reddish, changing to green and, in the fall, a bright yellow or red. They do well in well-drained, moist soils, and may be increased by seeds or root grafts.

francheti. Resembling the next, but the leaves rather regularly toothed and the fruit a samara.* China. Hardy from zone* 3 southward.

polyandra. A large shrub or small tree not over 40 ft. high. Leaves roundish-oval, 3–5 in. wide, with a point at the tip, coarsely and irregularly toothed. Fruit a slender, stalked pod (follicle*), about ¾ in. long. Jap. Hardy from zone* 3 southward.

europaea, -us, -um (you-ro-pee'a). From Europe.

EUROPEAN. As an adjective *European* has been part of the name of many European plants, especially since the discovery of America, where most of the names below are in pretty common use. All will be found at the proper entry in this book:

European ash = *Fraxinus excelsior* (*see* ASH); European aspen = *Populus tremula;* European barberry = *Berberis vulgaris;* European beech = *Fagus sylvatica* (*see* BEECH); European birch = *Betula pendula* (*see* BIRCH); European bird cherry = *Prunus Padus;* European black currant = *Ribes nigrum;* European chestnut = *Castanea sativa* (*see* CHESTNUT); European elder = *Sambucus nigra* (*see* ELDER); European fan palm = *Chamaerops humilis;* European fly-honeysuckle = *Lonicera Xylosteum;* European goldenrod (*see Solidago Virgaurea* at GOLDENROD); European globeflower = *Trollius europaeus;* European hazel = *Corylus Avellana* (*see* HAZEL); European hornbeam = *Carpinus Betulus* (*see* HORNBEAM); European larch = *Larix decidua* (*see* LARCH); European linden = *Tilia europaea* (*see* LINDEN); European mallow = *Malva Alcea;* European mountain-ash = *Sorbus Aucuparia* (*see* MOUNTAIN-ASH); European raspberry = *Rubus idaeus;* European sweet cicely = *Myrrhis odorata;* European twinflower = *Linnaea borealis;* European white birch = *Betula pendula* (*see* BIRCH); European white hellebore = *Veratrum album;* European white water lily = *Nymphaea alba;* European wood anemone = *Anemone nemorosa.*

EURYA (your'i-a). A genus of over 45 species of evergreen shrubs and trees of the family Theaceae, found in the warmer parts of Asia and America and grown for ornament in the greenhouse or outdoors in the South. Leaves alternate,* rather leathery. Male and female flowers chiefly on different plants, solitary or in clusters in the leaf axils,* small and not showy. Petals and sepals 5 each. Stamens* usually many. Fruit a berry. (*Eurya* is Greek for broad or large and of little or no significance as applied to these plants.)

The indoor and outdoor culture of the two below is the same as for camellia (which see),

to which they are related. But they lack the showy flowers of camellia; *Eurya* is valued chiefly for its foliage. Both are sometimes offered under the name *Cleyera.*

japonica. A smooth, smallish shrub. Leaves short-stalked, more or less elliptic and irregularly toothed. Flowers greenish-white, in small clusters. Eastern As. A variegated form has white-blotched leaves.

ochnacea. Somewhat similar to *E. japonica,* but the leaves without marginal teeth and with cream-white, fragrant, but small flowers. Berry red. Himalayas to Jap. There is also a variegated-leaved variety.

EUSTOMA (you-stō'ma). A small genus of North American prairie herbs of the gentian family, **E. russellianum** sometimes grown in the flower garden, although in its native home (Neb. to Tex.) it is rather inappropriately called Canada pest by some. It is an attractive hardy annual (*see* ANNUALS) 2–3 ft. high, with bluish-gray foliage and opposite* leaves that are ovalish and 2–3 in. long. Flowers pale purple, but with dark purple blotches at the base, usually in a branched cluster (panicle*), the corolla nearly bell-shaped, but flaring, and about 2 in. long and wide. Fruit a many-seeded capsule.* It may also be treated as a biennial, as well-established seedlings may be carried over winter in the cold frame. (*Eustoma* is from the Greek for good mouth, in allusion to the flaring corolla.) In Tex. it is called bluebell and prairie gentian.

EUTOCA. See PHACELIA VISCIDA.

EVAPORATION. See TRANSPIRATION.

EVENING BLOOM. See NOCTURNAL FLOWERS.

EVENING CAMPION = *Lychnis alba.*

EVENING PRIMROSE. The evening primroses and their day-blooming relatives, the sundrops, both belong to the genus **Oenothera** (ee-no-thee'ra, also ee-nōth'er-ra), which comprises nearly 150 species of herbs of the family Onagraceae, all American. They have been credited to various other genera at times, especially to *Hartmannia,* but all are here treated as of the genus *Oenothera.* Leaves alternate.* Flowers very showy, day- or night-blooming, prevailingly yellow, but also white or rose-color in some species, generally one or 2 in the leaf axils.* Calyx* tubular, usually 4-sided, its 4 lobes often bent backward and usually soon falling. Petals 4, mostly very broad. Fruit a 4-lobed or 4-angled capsule, splitting by 4 valves. (*Oenothera* is from the Greek for wine-scenting and of uncertain application here.)

The evening primroses are of easy culture if given an open, sandy, or loamy site. All the perennial kinds can easily be increased by division. Some are biennials, but seed so freely that they are easily maintained. The sundrops are day-bloomers, and so are some others, as indicated below. The others bloom at night or on dark days. All bloom in the summer and many are rather weedy.

O. acaulis. A biennial sundrops, apparently

---

* Special articles on the subjects indicated by an asterisk (*) will be found at the words so marked.

stemless, but ultimately producing prostrate stems. Leaves much cut, the terminal segment larger than the others. Flowers nearly 4 in. wide, white or pink, the tube long. Chile. It is the plant put out by Burbank as America.

O. biennis. Evening primrose. A weedy, biennial herb 3–5 ft. high, of less garden interest than for its wide use by plant breeders to illustrate principles of that science. Flowers yellow, 1–2 in. wide. Nearly throughout N.A. and widely naturalized in Eu. The *var.* **grandiflora**, chiefly from the southern states, has larger flowers and is a better garden plant, but its botanical identity is uncertain.

O. caespitosa. An essentially stemless perennial or sometimes biennial with a woody base, and narrow, hairy leaves with wavy margins or even cleft into narrow segments. Flowers very showy, nearly 3 in. wide, white or pink, night-fragrant. Fruit winged on the capsules. Central U.S.

O. fruticosa. Sundrops. A perennial herb, 1–3 ft. high, usually woody at the base, the stems reddish. Leaves lance-oblong, usually short-stalked, 1–2 in. long. Flowers yellow, nearly 2 in. wide. In dry soil nearly throughout eastern U.S. The *var.* **major** has more profuse bloom and is bushier. *Var.* **youngi** is a strong, stocky form, and a profuse bloomer with larger leaves.

O. glauca. A sundrops related to *O. fruticosa* and perhaps only a form of it, but the foliage usually bluish-green, and the leaves essentially stalkless.

O. hookeri. A biennial from the high Sierras in Calif., but grows well along the coast and elsewhere. It is 2–5 ft. high, with ashy foliage. Leaves 7–9 in. long, ovalish or narrower. Flowers day-blooming, yellow, nearly 4 in. wide and showy. Flower buds pinkish.

O. lamarckiana. An evening primrose closely related to *O. biennis*, but with larger flowers, broader and crinkled leaves, and a stem that is red-dotted. Unknown as a wild plant, but long cult. in old gardens. Perhaps the *O. erythrosepala* of some authors.

O. lavandulaefolia. A grayish-hairy, tufted perennial, 6–8 in. high. Leaves very narrow and without teeth. Flowers funnel-shaped, yellow, day-blooming, 2–3 in. long. Dry regions of western U.S.

O. missouriensis. Missouri primrose. A perennial, day-blooming herb, not over 12 in. high, the base a little woody. Leaves hairy, narrowly oval, 3–5 in. long. Flowers yellow, showy, nearly 4 in. wide. Fruit 2–3 in. long and nearly that wide. Central U.S. A garden favorite, but less known eastward than in the prairie states.

O. perennis. A common perennial sundrops throughout the eastern N.A., often known as *O. pumila* or *O. pusilla*, the latter name indicating its habit of often blooming when scarcely 3 in. high. Normally the plant is 12–24 in. high, and has lance-oblong leaves without marginal teeth. Flowers yellow, about 1 in. wide.

O. rosea. A half-prostrate biennial (blooming from seed the first year), with hairy stem and ovalish or narrower leaves. Flowers rose-purple, about ½ in. wide, night-blooming, and also blooming the next day. Central U.S. to S.A.

O. speciosa. Showy primrose. A fine, day-blooming, garden perennial, the stems erect or nearly so, and finely hairy. Leaves lance-shaped or narrower. Flowers nearly 3 in. wide, white, but changing to pink. Central U.S. Sometimes offered as a *Hartmannia*. In most gar-

dens the plant is so rampant as to become a pest.

O. serrulata. A woody-stemmed perennial, 10–18 in. high, its leaves hairy or smooth, narrow, toothed and 1–3 in. long. Flowers day-blooming, yellow, about 2 in. wide, the petals wavy-margined. Western N.A.

O. trichocalyx. A day-blooming biennial or perennial, 6–12 in. high, the stem silky-hairy. Leaves narrowly lance-shaped, wavy-toothed, 1–2 in. long. Flowers white, about 2 in. wide. Colo., Wyo., and Utah.

O. youngi = *Oenothera fruticosa* var. *youngi.*

EVENING PRIMROSE FAMILY = Onagraceae.

EVENING STAR = *Cooperia drummondi.*

EVENING STOCK = *Mathiola bicornis.*

EVERBLOOMING GARDEN. Most gardeners would like to have continuous bloom in the garden but think it impossible unless they live in the tropics or at least in southern Calif., the Gulf Coast, or in peninsular Fla. Not counting shrubs and trees with showy autumnal fruit (*see* AUTUMN GARDEN) there are more plants than the amateur suspects that provide bloom for every month of the year. This is true for all of zones* 3, 4, and 5, and even up into the southern part of zone 2. (*See* ZONE.) Of course, in zones 6, 7, 8, and 9 there is such a wealth of material that continuous bloom in the garden is easy.

It is not quite so easy in zones 3, 4, and 5, especially in the interior of the country, and at high elevations. Even an elevation of 1500–2000 ft. may invalidate some of the plants suggested below. Otherwise all the plants in the lists are perfectly hardy unless specially noted. The culture of them will not be repeated here and should be sought at the proper entry. The first name used below is the same as that used in the body of the book, so that cross-referencing from here to there is easy. It is suggested that before planting any of them the reader look up the articles on HARDINESS and ZONE.

Generally, only plants hardy in the area covered by zones 3, 4, and 5 are included here, and some of these, especially those whose northern range of winter safety is in zone 5, should not be attempted in either zones 3 or 4.

The lists are not all-inclusive, and they include no annuals. Hundreds of other plants might be found that would bloom in the different months, and for these the seeker will find their usual blooming period noted at their proper entry word. The time when the plants are in bloom is that of the latitude of New York. North of this the dates will be later and southward earlier. The variation is about one week for each degree of latitude.

WINTER MONTHS

From the middle of Nov. to the end of Feb., roughly from Thanksgiving to Washington's Birthday, the selection of garden flowers and shrubs is much restricted. Few herbs bloom then and among the scanty list of shrubs, none is spectacular. But bloom

---

* Special articles on the subjects indicated by an asterisk (*) will be found at the words so marked.

of any kind is so welcome that we can only echo the wonder of the late Alfred Rehder, who wrote of one of the shrubs that "the delicate petals withstand zero weather without injury." This was at Boston in January!

WINTER-BLOOMING SHRUBS

Hamamelis virginiana. Witch-hazel. Nov.–Dec. (sometimes earlier) Yellow.
Hamamelis vernalis. Witch-hazel. Dec.–Feb. Yellow, reddish at the base. Fragrant.
Hamamelis japonica. Witch-hazel. Jan.–Mar. Yellow.
Hamamelis mollis. Witch-hazel. Jan.–Mar. Yellow. Fragrant.
Corylopsis spicata. A Japanese relative of the witch-hazels. Feb.–Mar. Yellow. Fragrant.
Lonicera fragrantissima. Chinese honeysuckle. Feb. or later. White. Fragrant.
Chimonanthus praecox. No common name. Jan.–Mar. Yellow. Fragrant. Not hardy north of zone 5.

WINTER-FLOWERING HERBS

Helleborus niger. Christmas rose. 6–8 in. Nov.–Feb. White or pinkish white.
Eranthis hyemalis. Winter aconite. 6–8 in. Jan.–Feb. Yellow.
Snowdrop (*Galanthus nivalis*). 7–12 in. Feb. White.
Snowdrop (*Galanthus elwesi*). 10–18 in. Oct.–Feb. White.
Crocus pulchellus. 3–4 in. Nov.–Dec. Lavender.
Crocus imperati. 3–4 in. Feb. Lilac or white.

eral species and varieties, from 8–12 ft., mostly yellow-flowered.

PERENNIAL HERBS

Tussilago Farfara. Coltsfoot. 8–10 in. Golden yellow; somewhat weedy.
Bergenia crassifolia. Siberian tea. 10–15 in. Rose-pink.
Bergenia ligulata. Bergenia. 10–15 in. Rose-pink or white. Not certainly hardy north of zone 5, without a winter mulch.

BULBS

Chionodoxa luciliae. Glory-of-the-snow. 3–4 in. Blue.
Scilla sibirica. Siberian squill. 4–6 in. Blue.
Iris reticulata. 8–10 in. Red-purple; fragrant.
Snowflake (*Leucojum vernum*). 9–12 in. White; fragrant.
Bulbocodium vernum. Spring meadow saffron. 4–6 in. Purplish rose.
Tulipa kauffmanianna. 10–12 in. Whitish yellow. Much earlier than the usual garden tulips.
Crocus. Any of many horticultural forms, in nearly all colors but yellow. 2–4 in. See CROCUS.
Crocus aureus. Dutch yellow. 2–3 in. Yellow.
Crocus susianus. Cloth-of-gold. 2–3 in. Golden yellow.
Scilla hispanica. Spanish squill. 8–12 in. Blue.
Scilla nonscripta. Bluebells of England. 6–10 in. Blue.

MARCH

While this is often a month of bitter winds and freezing temperatures there is one favorable factor in the steadily increasing length of the day. At New York, for instance, there is a difference of 2 hrs. and 34 min. in the amount of possible sunlight between the first and last of March. This has an appreciable effect upon the melting of snow, and particularly on the signs of spring, which will not really be evident for three weeks or more, depending on elevation and proximity to the sea.

Increasing light and some increase in the temperature bring many shrubs, trees and herbs into bloom, of which the following lists are a guide.

TREES

Cornus Mas. Cornelian cherry. 8–15 ft. Yellow flowers on naked twigs. Often shrubby northward.

SHRUBS

Jasminum nudiflorum. Winter jasmine. 3–5 ft. Yellow. Not hardy north of zone 4.
Chaenomeles lagenaria. Japanese flowering quince. 4–6 ft. Red.
Daphne Mezereum. Mezereon. 2–3 ft. Rosy purple; fragrant.
Daphne odora. Daphne. 1–2 ft. Rosy purple; fragrant. Not hardy above zone 5. Evergreen.
Daphne Cneorum. Daphne. 8–15 in. Pink; fragrant. Not hardy above zone 4. Evergreen.
Magnolia stellata. Star magnolia. 4–8 ft. White. Often flowering in late Mar. or early Apr., and blossoms sometimes blasted by late frosts.
Forsythia. See FORSYTHIA. Shrubs in sev-

APRIL

That "uncertain glory of an April day" is often wrecked by an unseasonable frost. That is why some of the shrubs and trees noted below may have their flowers blasted about one April in three. This is especially true away from the coast, at high elevations and in low valleys where cold-air drainage at night can devastate the bloom in a peach orchard, without, however, doing any permanent damage to the tree.

Far more plants are in bloom in April than in March, and it is more difficult to make a selection that, while providing continuous bloom in April, will not be so complicated as to discourage the seeker.

TREES

Japanese flowering cherries (see PRUNUS LANNESIANNA, PRUNUS SERRULATA, and PRUNUS YEDOENSIS). Magnificent flowering trees, in many varieties. 12–40 ft. Red, pink or white. Among the most popular varieties are:
Rosebud. Weeping.
Kwansan. Rose-pink and double-flowered.
Yoshino. Single, pink flowers; very profuse.
Fujisan-sakura. White.
Kofugen. 40 ft. Double-flowered and pink.
Double-flowered peach (see AMYGDALUS PERSICA). A small tree or large shrub, with wax-like, superb, double flowers in pink or scarlet.
American redbud (*Cercis canadensis*). 10–30 ft. Rosy pink.
Chinese redbud (*Cercis chinensis*). 10–30 ft. Rosy purple. Not certainly hardy north of zone 4.

* Special articles on the subjects indicated by an asterisk (*) will be found at the words so marked.

Magnolia denudata. Yulan. 15–40 ft. White; fragrant.

Magnolia soulangeana. Magnolia. 15–20 ft. Purplish. In several varieties, and often shrubby.

SHRUBS

Viburnum carlesi. No common name. 3–5 ft. White and very fragrant.

Viburnum carlcephalum. No common name. 6–7 ft. White and very fragrant.

Spiraea thunbergi. Spirea. 3–5 ft. White.

Spiraea prunifolia plena. Bridal wreath. 5–7 ft. White and double-flowered.

Spiraea vanhouttei. Bridal wreath. 4–6 ft. White.

PERENNIAL HERBS

Adonis vernalis. A perennial relative of the pheasant's-eye. 6–9 in. Yellow; also a white variety.

Anemone Pulsatilla. Pasque-flower. 10–15 in. Reddish purple.

Anemone patens. American pasque-flower. 12–18 in. Bluish purple.

Primrose. See PRIMULA. Only the English primrose (*Primula vulgaris*), 4–6 in. and yellow, or the oxlip (*Primula elatior*), 6–8 in. and also yellow, should be tried unless conditions for the many others are ideal.

Iris cristata. Crested iris. 3–5 in. Lilac.

Iris pumila. A Eurasian bearded iris. 3–5 in. Various colors, and blooms a week later than *Iris cristata.*

Pulmonaria angustifolia. Lungwort. 6–12 in. Blue. First blooms in April; continues into June.

Violet. See VIOLA. The best of the native sorts is *Viola priceana*, the Confederate violet, 6–8 in. Flowers pale blue, striped and dark violet.

Phlox subulata. Ground pink. Prostrate ground cover. Flowers magenta or white, or pink in the variety Alexanders pink.

BULBS

Muscari botryoides. Grape hyacinth. 6–9 in. Blue, but varieties are available in white and pink.

Puschkinia scilloides. Striped squill. 8–12 in. Blue.

Narcissi. See NARCISSUS. Of the many kinds the following three will provide bloom throughout April. Arranged in order of blooming they are:

Jonquil (*Narcissus Jonquilla*). 12–18 in. Yellow.

Poet's narcissus (*Narcissus poeticus*). 12–18 in. White; red-edged.

Trumpet narcissus (*Narcissus Pseudo-narcissus*). The commonest kind and in all shades of yellow or white. 12–18 in.

MAY

Several hundred plants could be selected for this month, but the complexities of such a list would defeat the purpose of the list below, which is restricted to as few plants as possible. By rigid selection, even among these, the average amateur can be assured of continuous bloom in May, and some of the perennials will stretch their bloom into June or even later.

TREES

Crab or crabapple. See MALUS. A group of gorgeous flowering trees, which hold their bloom for a fortnight. Among the many ornamental kinds are the following:

Malus spectabilis. 20–25 ft. Rosy pink. The var. *albiplena* is white and double-flowered. Var. *riversi*, pink and double-flowered.

Malus floribunda. Showy crabapple. 15–25 ft. Rose-red, fading to white. There are many named horticultural forms of the crabapple, some of them extremely showy.

Cornus florida. Dogwood. 20–40 ft. White. There is a pink-flowered form (*Cornus florida rubra*).

Horse-chestnut (*Aesculus Hippocastanum*). 50–100 ft. White, tinged with red.

Crataegus Oxyacantha. English hawthorn. 20–30 ft. White.

SHRUBS AND VINES

Lilac (*Syringa*). See LILAC. Of the many named horticultural forms of the common lilac, the following are suggested.

White, single-flowered: Vestal, Mont Blanc, Marie Legraye.

White, double-flowered: Ellen Willmott, Edith Cavell.

Red: Congo and Monge (single-flowered); Charles Joly (double-flowered).

Purple or lilac-purple: Colbert and Charles Sargent (double-flowered); Descaine (single-flowered).

Especially fragrant varieties: Lamartine (pink), Leon Gambetta (rose-salmon), Ludwig Spaeth (red), President Grevy (blue).

Azalea. See AZALEA. Arranged approximately in the order of their blooming may be listed.

Azalea vaseyi. May 5–10. 6–10 ft. Light rose.

Kurume azaleas. May 9–15. 1–1½ ft. In all colors but yellow, in over 50 named varieties. Not hardy north of zone 4.

Mollis azaleas. May 15–20. 2–5 ft. Many varieties in yellow, orange, salmon-pink, etc.

Ghent azaleas. May 20–25. 6–9 ft. Many varieties in nearly all colors. Not hardy north of zone 4.

Flame azalea (*Azalea calendulacea*). Late May into June. 6–15 ft. Yellow, orange or scarlet.

Deutzia gracilis. No common name. 18–30 in. White.

Deutzia lemoinei. No common name. 4–7 ft. The var. Boule de Neige is especially showy.

Viburnum Opulus sterile. Snowball (Guelder rose). 8–12 ft. White.

Wisteria (*Wistaria floribunda*). Woody vine, often up to 30–40 ft. Violet-blue; also white in a named variety.

PERENNIALS

Peony. See PEONY. A very large group of varieties, from which a good selection might include the following.

White: Festiva Maxima, Le Cygne, Victory.

Light Pink: Therese, Moonstone, Minuet.

Pink: M. Jules Elie, Walter Faxon, Mrs. Livingston Farrand.

Red: Richard Carvel, Kansas, Tempest. Yellow peonies will be found among the varieties of the tree peony. See PEONY.

Iris. May-blooming iris are mostly the tall-

---

* Special articles on the subjects indicated by an asterisk (*) will be found at the words so marked.

bearded or German iris. Of the over 1500 varieties, excluding expensive, recent novelties, a good selection might include the following.

White (sometimes marked with other colors): New Snow, Matterhorn, Tranquility, Snow Flurry.

Blue (prevailingly): Great Lakes, Blue Rhythm, Sable.

Pink to red-purple: Master Charles, Ranger, Quechee.

Yellow: Jasmine, Treasure Island, Gold Imperial.

Blending colors: Sunset Blaze, Cordovan, Inca Chief.

Aubrieta deltoidea. Purple rock cress. 4–6 in. Pinkish purple.

Lily-of-the-valley (*Convallaria majalis*). 6–8 in. White; fragrant.

Columbine (*Aquilegia caerulea*). 2–3 ft. Blue.

Columbine (*Aquilegia chrysantha*). 2–4 ft. Yellow.

Poppy (*Papaver orientale*). 3–4 ft. Scarlet, but in many horticultural color forms.

Pinks. See DIANTHUS.

Dianthus barbatus. Sweet William. 18–24 in. Variously colored.

Dianthus plumarius. Grass pink. 9–18 in. Rose-pink (in other colors also in some varieties).

Dianthus deltoides. Maiden pink. 4–12 in. Red or white (variously colored in some varieties).

BULBS

Tulip. *See* TULIPA. Of the hundreds of named forms and species, a selection of the two main divisions could include the following.

COTTAGE TULIPS: 15–20 in.

Carrara (white), John Ruskin (rose), Mrs. Moon (yellow).

DARWIN TULIPS: 18–30 in.

Bartigon (scarlet), The Bishop (violet), Nephotos (yellow).

Hyacinth. *See* HYACINTHUS. 8–12 in. Of the scores of varieties the following will provide good contrasting colors.

Blue: King of the Blues, Oxford Blue, Queen of the Blues.

Red: Roi des Belges, Jan Bos.

Yellow: City of Haarlem, Yellow Hammer.

White: L'Innocence, Queen of the Whites.

Pink: Lady Derby, Princess Irene.

JUNE

The month may be deceptive. Hundreds of plants rush into bloom in this best of all spring months, but a few shrubs and most trees appear to know that toward the end of the month days will be getting shorter. This reduction in the length of the day, accentuated of course in July and Aug., decreases the number of things in bloom during midsummer, and even in June there are far less shrubs and trees in bloom than in May.

There is, however, such a wealth of flowering material in June that only a selection of it is possible here.

TREES

Laburnum anagyroides. Golden chain. 10–20 ft. Golden yellow.

Magnolia grandiflora. Evergreen magnolia.

40–70 ft. White. Not hardy north of zone 5.

Tulip-tree (*Liriodendron tulipifera*). 60–100 ft. Greenish yellow.

Honey locust (*Gleditsia triacanthos*). 70–100 ft. Greenish white.

Mountain-ash (*Sorbus Aucuparia*). 30–50 ft. White.

SHRUBS

Deutzia scabra. Pride of Rochester. 5–9 ft. Pinkish white.

Kalmia latifolia. Mountain laurel. 4–20 ft. Pinkish white.

Mock-orange or syringa (*Philadelphus coronarius*). 6–10 ft. White.

Styrax japonica. Storax. 10–15 ft. (Sometimes tree-like). White.

Kerria japonica. No common name. 4–6 ft. Yellow. A double-flowered form is handsomer and often called Japanese rose.

Kolkwitzia amabilis. Beauty-bush. 4–6 ft. Pink with yellow throat.

Roses. See ROSE.

Of the hundreds of varieties a brief selection will be found at ROSE and need not be repeated here.

Rhododendrons. See RHODODENDRONS. 6–9 ft. Of the scores of showy, June-blooming shrubs are the following hybrids.

Red or scarlet: Kettledrum, H. W. Sargent, Caractacus.

Pink: Abraham Lincoln, Henrietta Sargent, Delicatissimum.

Purple: Purpureum elegans, Purpureum grandiflorum, Everestianum.

White: Album grandiflorum, Album elegans, Boule de Neige.

PERENNIALS

There are so many June-blooming perennials that it is difficult to restrict the list to only the following dozen.

Foxglove (*Digitalis purpurea*). A biennial, 2–4 ft. Purple-spotted; also white or pink in hort. forms.

Chrysanthemum maximum. Shasta daisy. 1–2 ft. White.

Pentstemon barbatus. Beardtongue. 4–6 ft. Red or pink.

Nicotiana alata grandiflora. Jasmine tobacco. 3–5 ft. White; fragrant. (Grown as an annual.)

Daylily. *See* DAYLILY. 2–3 ft. Of the scores of varieties the following will provide June bloom.

Dr. Regel (orange), Tangerine (dark orange), Belle of Georgia (golden yellow), Brunette (orange-brown).

Lily. *See* LILIUM. June-flowering kinds, which may extend into July, might include the following.

Lilium Martagon. Martagon lily. 3–4 ft. Brown-purple.

Lilium candidum. Madonna lily. 3–5 ft. White.

Lilium elegans. 1–2 ft. Crimson or yellow; and in other colors in some varieties.

Lilium concolor. Star lily. 3–4 ft. Red.

Heuchera sanguinea. Coral bells. 1–2 ft. Red; but pink or white varieties are available.

Campanula portenschlagiana. No common name. 6–8 in. Bluish purple.

Catananche caerulea. Blue succory. 1–2 ft. Blue.

Japanese iris. *See* IRIS. 18–30 in.

---

* Special articles on the subjects indicated by an asterisk (*) will be found at the words so marked.

Lupinus. See LUPINUS.
  Russell hybrids. 2½–3½ ft. The finest of the garden lupines, coming in blue, red, yellow, maroon and purple colors.
Dicentra eximia. Bleeding-heart. 1–2 ft. Rose or pink.

JULY

This month well illustrates the waning of trees and shrubs that come into bloom during July, although there is a wealth of summer-blooming perennials.

TREES

Cladastris lutea. Yellow-wood. 30–50 ft. White; fragrant. Sometimes known as *Cladastris tinctoria,* and blooming at N.Y. in late June or July.
Koelreuteria paniculata. Pride-of-India. Varnish tree. 20–30 ft. Yellow.
Cotinus. American smoke-tree. 15–20 ft. Yellowish. Doubtfully hardy north of zone 5.

SHRUBS

Spiraea alba. Meadowsweet. 4–6 ft. White.
Spiraea Bumalda. Spirea. 1–2 ft. Rose-red.
Spiraea billiardi. Spirea. 4–6 ft. Red. A good variety is Anthony Waterer.
Spiraea margaritae. Spirea. 3–5 ft. Pink.
Buddleia davidi. Butterfly-bush. 4–10 ft. Lilac.
Genista tinctoria. Woadwaxen. 2–3 ft. Yellow.
Vitex Agnus-castus. Chaste-tree. 6–20 ft. Lilac-blue.
St. John's-wort (*Hypericum patulum henryi*). 2–3 ft. Evergreen. Yellow.
Button-bush (*Cephalanthus occidentalis*). 5–12 ft. White. Often extending into Aug. Pink.
Sorbaria aitchisoni. False spirea. 6–10 ft. White.
Clematis. See CLEMATIS.
  Of these very handsome climbing vines there are many species and scores of varieties. Among the best are the hybrids, most of which start blooming in July and continue for weeks. See CLEMATIS.

PERENNIALS

Of the scores of summer-blooming perennials only the following dozen can be included here.
Gladiolus. See GLADIOLUS.
  Nearly all the hybrid varieties listed below have essentially no odor. But one species, *Gladiolus tristis,* 1–2 ft. with purple-streaked, yellowish flowers, is beautifully night-fragrant. The hybrids for July bloom and later are:
  White: Snow Clad, Snow Velvet.
  Red: Charm, Red Radiance.
  Lavender: Campanile, Princess.
  Yellow: Gold, Prospecter.
  Smoky: Brown Lullaby, Gunsmoke.
Dahlia. See DAHLIA.
  An enormous group comprising over 14,000 varieties separated into several classes. Of these only three are listed here, with the following varieties.
  DECORATIVE DAHLIAS: Lord of Autumn (yellow), Murphy's Masterpiece (red), Jersey Beauty (pink), Lord of Autumn (white).
  CACTUS DAHLIAS: Frau O. Bracht (yellow), Royal Sussex (red), Coral Cactus (pink).
  POMPON AND MINIATURE DAHLIAS: Snow Sprite (white), Little Edith (yellow),

Baby Royal (pink), Bronze Beauty (bronze).
Chrysanthemum coccineum. Pyrethrum. 1–2 ft. Colors various; prevailingly red.
Veronica spicata. Speedwell. 1–2 ft. Blue.
Veronica incana. Speedwell. 6–8 in. Blue.
Sedum spurium. Stonecrop. Prostrate. Pink.
Sedum album. Stonecrop. Prostrate. White.
Sedum reflexum. Yellow stonecrop. Prostrate. Yellow.
Monkshood (*Aconitum Napellus*). 2–4 ft. Blue.
Hollyhock. (*Althaea rosea*). 2–6 ft. Variously colored, prevailingly pink. A biennial or annual. See HOLLYHOCK.
Lily. See LILIUM.
  Besides those mentioned for June, some of which may still be in bloom, the following superb species begin to bloom in July:
Lilium auratum. 3½–5 ft. White, gold-banded.
Lilium chalcedonicum. Scarlet Turk's-cap lily. 3–4 ft. Scarlet.
Lilium pardalinum. Leopard lily. 5–7 ft. Orange, purple-spotted.
Lilium regale. Royal lily. 3–5 ft. White, rose-striped.
Lilium sargentiae. 4–6 ft. White, the throat yellow.
Campanula Medium. Canterbury Bells. A biennial, 2–4 ft. Blue (and in other colors).
Campanula persicifolia. Peach Bells. 2–3 ft. Blue or white.
Campanula pyramidalis. Chimney Bellflower. 3–5 ft. Blue (and in other colors).
Achillea Ptarmica. Sneezewort. 1–2 ft. White. Good varieties are The Pear and Boule de Neige.
Lythrum Salicaria. Purple loosestrife. 2–3½ ft. Purple. A pink variety is Morden's Pink.
Liatris pycnostachya. Prairie button snakeroot. 3–5 ft. Rose-purple.

AUGUST

August is definitely the herald of autumn. Waning sunlight, night and morning, reduces the length of the day by just over 1 hr. as between the beginning and end of the month. This has such a profound effect upon woody plants that only a handful come into bloom during the month. Perennials seem less affected by waning daylight, but the meager list of shrubs and trees reflects the fact that "from that full meridian of my glory, I haste now to my setting."

TREES

Sophora japonica. Japanese pagoda tree. 40–60 ft. Yellowish white.
Aralia spinosa. Hercules'-club. 15–30 ft. Whitish.

SHRUBS

Lagerstroemia indica. Crape myrtle. 5–25 ft. Pink, red or white. Not hardy above zone 5.
Clethra alnifolia. Sweet pepperbush. 3–9 ft. White and fragrant.
Heather (*Calluna vulgaris*). 9–15 in. Purple or pink or white.
Stewartia ovata. Mountain camellia. 10–15 ft. White.
Tamarix pentandra. Tamarisk. 10–15 ft. Pink.
Hibiscus syriacus. Rose-of-Sharon. 5–15 ft. Prevailingly magenta, but the following

---

* Special articles on the subjects indicated by an asterisk (*) will be found at the words so marked.

varieties are better-colored:

Jeanne d'Arc (white), Snowstorm (white), Rosea (white with red center), Speciosa plena (pink), Rubis (red).

St. John's-wort (*Hypericum prolificum*). 4–5 ft. Yellow.

Hydrangea paniculata grandiflora. Hydrangea, 8–20 ft. White. Often tree-like.

Callicarpa dichotoma. Beauty-berry. 2–4 ft. Pink; the showy fruits violet or lilac.

Clerodendron trichotomum. No common name. 7–15 ft. White and crimson.

PERENNIALS

Stokesia laevis. Stokes aster. 12–30 in. Lavender-blue; varieties in white and pink.

Helenium autumnale. Yellow star. 4–6 ft. yellow; and variously colored varieties.

Chrysanthemum. See CHRYSANTHEMUM. Most of these bloom in Sept. and later, but some begin flowering in Aug.

Chelone lyoni. Red turtlehead. 10–20 in. Rose-purple.

Salvia patens. Blue sage. 18–30 in. Blue.

Salvia azurea. Pale blue sage. 4–5 ft. Pale blue, or white.

Michaelmas daisy. See MICHAELMAS DAISY. 2–3 ft. Most of these are Sept. bloomers or even later but some bloom late in Aug.

Phlox. See that entry. Many fine annuals and perennials, showy all summer.

Clematis texensis. Scarlet clematis. 4–6 ft. Scarlet or rose-pink.

Lilies. See LILIUM.

Lilium speciosum. Japanese lily. 3–5 ft. White or pinkish, red-spotted.

Lilium tigrinum. Tiger lily. 4–5 ft. Orange-red and purple-spotted.

Tritonia crocosmaeflora. Montbretia. 3–4 ft., mostly August-blooming.

Sedum spectabile. Stonecrop. 1–2 ft. Pink.

Rudbeckia laciniata hortensia. Golden Glow. 8–12 ft. Yellow.

SEPTEMBER

The obvious effects of shorter daylight and cooler night temperatures are well shown by the meager list of shrubs and trees, although there is still a goodly number of perennials and a few bulbs that give color in a Sept. garden.

TREES

Gordonia altamaha. Franklinia. 10–25 ft. White and fragrant. Tree from zone 5 southward, more often shrubby in zone 4; not safe in zone 3.

SHRUBS

Caryopteris incana. Blue spirea. 1–5 ft. Blue. Not winter-hardy above zone 4.

Abelia chinensis. Abelia. 3–5 ft. White. Not hardy above zone 5.

Elsholtzia stauntoni. No common name. 2–4 ft. Lavender. Not hardy north of zone 5.

Polygonum auberti. Silver-lace vine. White. A high-climbing vine (10–35 ft.).

PERENNIALS

Anemone japonica. Japanese anemone. 2–2½ ft. Of the many varieties a good selection might include:

September Queen (rosy red), September Charm (silvery pink), Prince Henry (rosy red), Queen Charlotte (white), Alice (rose-pink), Prince Heinrich (crimson).

Liatris spicata and *L. scariosa.* Gay-feather. 4–6 ft. Rose-purple.

Vernonia noveboracensis. Ironweed. 3–7 ft. Dark purple.

Ceratostigma plumbaginoides. Prostrate. Blue. Blooms sometimes in Aug.

Aster. See ASTER. Of the native asters, two are worth growing: *Aster acris*, 2–3 ft., mauve-blue; and *Aster ericoides*, 3–5 ft., white. Far more showy are the hybrid Michaelmas daisies, which see.

Chrysanthemum. See CHRYSANTHEMUM. Among the scores of varieties the following should begin to bloom in Sept.:

Ruth Hatton (white and a pompon), Jean Cumming (white), Apollo (rose-salmon), Louise Schling (crimson and rose), Mars (red), R. Marion Hatton (pompon and yellow).

Gentiana andrewsi. Closed or bottle gentian. 12–20 in. Blue. The only native gentian reasonably easy to grow.

Sunflower (*Helianthus decapetalus* and other species). 6–12 ft. Yellow.

BULBS

Snowflake (*Leucojum autumnale*). 7–9 in. White; red-tinged.

Crocus. See CROCUS. Autumn-flowering sepcies are:

Crocus longiflorus. 3–8 in. Lilac.

Crocus nudiflorus. 3–8 in. Lilac.

Crocus speciosus. 3–8 in. Purple or lilac.

Colchicum autumnale. Autumn crocus. 3–5 in. Pink.

Colchicum bornmuelleri. Autumn crocus. 3–5 in. Mauve, the flowers nearly 5 in. wide.

Lycoris radiata. 8–14 in. Pink to red.

OCTOBER

Scarcely any shrubs or trees come into bloom in this month, unless you live in zone 6 or south of it, where there are many autumn- or winter-blooming plants impossible to grow in the region covered by this list. Even the two plants below are not safe north of zone 5.

TREE

Arbutus Unedo. Strawberry-tree. 20–30 ft. White or pink, the fruits more showy than the flowers. Not hardy north of the central part of zone 5.

SHRUB

Camellia Sasanqua. 4–6 ft. In many colors according to the variety chosen. Not hardy north of zone 5.

PERENNIALS

Many chrysanthemums and Michaelmas daisies that bloomed in Sept. will still be in flower, and to them can be added the following:

Chrysanthemum. This is *the* month for these showy perennials, of which many vars. are listed at CHRYSANTHEMUM, together with the expected time of blooming.

Helenium hoopesi. Sneezeweed. 2–3 ft. Yellow.

Lespedeza thunbergi. Bush clover. 3–6 ft. Rose-purple.

BULBS

Tuberose (*Polianthes tuberosa*). 12–30 in. White and very fragrant.

Sternbergia lutea. Winter daffodil. 8–12 in.

---

* Special articles on the subjects indicated by an asterisk (*) will be found at the words so marked.

Yellow. Often blooms in Sept. in favorable sites.

EVERGLADE PALM = *Paurotis wrighti.*

EVERGREEN. Holding its foliage over the winter, or, in the tropics, over the dry season. For the garden uses of such plants, *see* EVERGREENS.

EVERGREEN CHERRY = *Prunus ilicifolia.*

EVERGREEN GRAPE = *Cissus capensis.*

EVERGREEN IVY = *Hedera Helix*

EVERGREEN MAGNOLIA = *Magnolia grandiflora.*

EVERGREEN WHITE OAK = *Quercus engelmanni.* See OAK.

EVERGREEN WOOD FERN = *Dryopteris marginalis.*

EVERGREENS. No woody plants can replace the evergreens. No matter what the size or extent of the garden, its winter attractiveness is tremendously enhanced by the judicious use of these plants.

As a term, evergreens is somewhat confusing, for in ordinary hort. speech it means two things, and maybe three. The first comprises the non-cone-bearing, broad-leaved evergreens, which form an important group of garden plants. But all belong to other families than the evergreens as here treated, and for their culture and kinds, *see* BROAD-LEAVED EVERGREENS.

The second, and to the northern gardener, the least important group, comprises those tropical plants that hold most of their foliage continuously. Such plants are truly evergreen, but the term is seldom applied to them.

By far the most important group of evergreens comprise the subject of this article. All of them are gymnosperms,* so that we do not cultivate them for their flowers, because they have none in the garden sense of flower. Nearly all of them bear cones, the commonest example of which is the familiar pine cone. But some, especially the yews, junipers, and some others, have fleshy fruits not in the least cone-like. So many of the evergreens are cone-bearing, however, that the group is commonly called conifers and no one is confused by the term *coniferous* tree for a pine, hemlock, spruce, or fir.

From the garden standpoint, it is their winter-persisting foliage that makes the evergreens so important. But, as in so many things botanical, there are exceptions. The larch, the bald cypress (*see* TAXODIUM) and *Metasequoia* all drop their leaves in autumn, but are universally included among evergreens because of their cones.

Evergreens do well in most ordinary garden soils. They do not bear transplanting as well as plants that drop their leaves. Consequently, most careful nurserymen will deliver them with a ball of earth tightly wrapped in bagging. They cannot stand drying of the roots, and climatically there are restrictions to their culture in a country as large as ours.

Many of the firs and spruces range far northward in Eurasia and N.A. and will stand much cold. But they cannot stand a deficiency of summer moisture. It is chiefly

SOME TYPES OF
EVERGREEN OUTLINES

The first and third from the left are good examples of the fastigiate* outline of columnar cedars and cypress. The second and fourth, the more usual type of spruce and fir outlines.

for this reason that evergreens are really unsuited for great sections of the country. Generally speaking, they are precariously happy, or impossible, in regions that have 25 in. of rain a year or less. *See* the name of your state or province for the rainfall in your locality. It is also important that the moisture be distributed throughout the year.

Some evergreens, especially *Chamaecyparis* and the arborvitae, have a tendency to lose inner shoot branches, generally in August. As they die out amateurs think the whole plant will die. Usually a thorough soaking will correct the trouble, which is due to midsummer heat and lack of moisture. A mulch* will often help.

There are special cultural articles on the pine, spruce, hemlock, and fir. See these entries for the details, as these comprise the most important group of evergreens. All the other evergreens in this book will be found listed at the entries Pinaceae, Taxaceae, Ginkgoaceae, and a related, but not hardy family, the Cycadaceae. Among other especially important genera are *Chamaecyparis, Juniperus, Thuja,* and *Taxus,* some of which are widely used for foundation planting. (There is also an extraordinary newcomer, *Metasequoia,* which see.)

Propagation of evergreens, especially the trees, is usually by seeds which germinate readily if kept stratified, or sometimes they are planted fresh. Sow them in rows about 6 in. apart in flats or boxes, in which the

* Special articles on the subjects indicated by an asterisk (*) will be found at the words so marked.

soil should be fine, mellow, and preferably a little sandy. Cover the flats with pine needles or a light, strawy mulch, and keep them moist. All this is best done in the cold frame. When the seedlings are a few inches high, they should be spaced to allow for proper development, but they must be grown for the first year under a lath screen or under some other shade. Keep them constantly moist, but not wet. As they get older, they will stand more exposure, but it must not be forgotten that evergreens do best along the Atlantic Coast and in regions like Oregon and Washington, where there is abundant moisture, much fog, and a consequent reduction of direct sunshine.

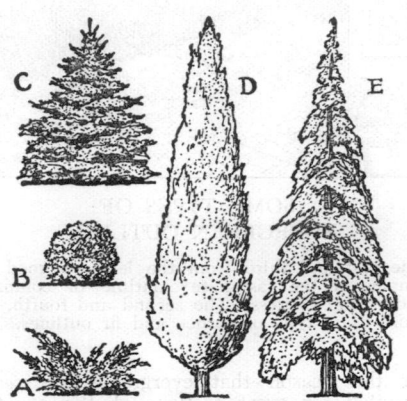

FORMS OF EVERGREENS

(A) *Juniperus chinensis pfitzeriana.* (B) Low-growing arborvitae. (C) Colorado blue spruce. (D) Italian cypress. (E) Incense cedar.

Some of the ornamental sorts, especially the forms of peculiar habit or with variegated or colored foliage, will not come true from seed. Such are propagated by cuttings. For the details of this process see CUTTINGS.

While most of the evergreens do well in ordinary garden soil, the larches, bald cypress, and some species of *Chamaecyparis* are especially suited to lower and moister sites, as is the arborvitae (see THUJA). Pines and spruces do better on drier sites. All of them should be kept clear of weeds in their young state, and a mulch of leaves or strawy manure often helps to conserve moisture. The insect and fungus pests of evergreens are treated at the description of the different sorts.

EVERLASTING. Valuable garden plants for winter decoration because their chaffy or papery flower parts hold their color when thoroughly dry. For the details of drying see DRIED FLOWERS.

The best everlastings will be found in the genera *Ammobium, Anaphalis, Antennaria, Catananche, Gomphrena, Helichrysum,* *Helipterum, Armeria,* and *Xeranthemum.* All are the subject of special articles. To them are often added the plumes of certain of the grasses like the pampas grass, and the fine panicles of grasses like *Briza* and *Panicum.* Also the fine colored fruits of some species of *Physalis* are a welcome addition, as well as the pods of honesty.* For an interesting addition to everlastings see SYNGONANTHUS.

EVERLASTING PEA = *Lathyrus grandiflorus* and *L. latifolius.*

EVERLASTING THORN = *Pyracantha coccinea.*

everta, -us, -um (ee-ver′ta). Turned inside out.

EVODIA (ee-vō′di-a). Sumac-like trees or shrubs of the family Rutaceae, comprising nearly 50 species from Asia and Aust., two somewhat grown for ornament. Leaves opposite,* compound* in ours, the leaflets arranged feather-fashion. Flowers small and not showy, mostly in panicles* or corymbs.* Sepals and petals usually 4, the stamens* 4–5. Fruit a collection of 4–5 pods, each 2-valved. (*Evodia* is from the Greek for pleasant odor, in allusion to the aromatic foliage.)

These trees are easily grown in any ordinary garden soil and propagated by seed, or cuttings of half-ripened wood.

danielli. A small tree, the twigs reddish. Leaflets 7–11, more or less ovalish, 2–4½ in. long, very finely toothed. Flowers scarcely ⅛ in. long, whitish, the clusters hairy and nearly 8 in. long. Pods with a hooked beak. Eastern As. June. Hardy from zone* 3 southward. Much liked by bees.

hupehensis. A tree up to 25 ft. Leaflets 5–9, oblong or ovalish, 3–4½ in. long, oblique at the base. Flowers pinkish, nearly ¼ in. long, the cluster pyramidal and nearly 6 in. thick. China. June. Hardy from zone* 3 southward.

EVOLUTION OF FLOWERS. Flowers are comparatively recent in the history of the world. There were none during the Carboniferous, when only the ancestors of our modern ferns and pines covered the earth. When the first recognizable flower evolved no one exactly knows, but it appears to have been some ancestor of *Magnolia* or a relative of it, and was a flower with *separate* petals. This first appears in the fossil record millions of years after the remains of the flowerless plants of the Carboniferous were already making coal.

From plants with separate petals, like magnolias, buttercups, and roses, those with a *united* corolla, like bellflowers, morning-glories, and many others, are assumed to have been derived, and those with irregular* flowers, like snapdragon and the lobelias, are still more recent. Last of all, as the evolutionists picture the story, came the huge family of the Compositae* (the daisy, aster, and relatives), which are probably our most recent flowering plants.

Whether the development of grasses, lilies, palms, and their allies (the monocotyle-

---

* Special articles on the subjects indicated by an asterisk (*) will be found at the words so marked.

dons*) came before or after the rest of our flowering plants is still a disputed point. But all agree that the final and most recent development of this chapter of floral history is the perfection of floral structure, complexity, and beauty found in the orchids. See ORCHIDACEAE.

Far older, in fact many millions of years older, are plants which rely upon spores for reproduction. Among these are the algae,* fungi,* mosses,* and ferns,* none of which bear flowers and are considered as very ancient ancestors of flowering plants.

EVONYMUS = Euonymus.

EXACUM (ecks'a-kum). A genus of 20 species of herbs or under-shrubs of the gentian family, all from the Old World tropics, the two below grown for ornament in the greenhouse or outdoors in zones* 8 and 9. Leaves opposite,* mostly stalkless or very short-stalked, without marginal teeth. Flowers in forked clusters (cymes*), the calyx* 4–5-parted. Corolla more or less twisted, its lobes usually 5 and blunt or pointed. Stamens 4–5, attached to the throat of the corolla. Fruit a roundish, 2-valved capsule.* (Exacum is of wholly uncertain application here.)

These are best treated as warm-greenhouse plants in potting mixture* 3. Sow seeds in pots in March for E. affine, and they should bloom in August. Or they may be treated as greenhouse perennials and plunged outdoors in the summer and in the shade.

affine. A much-branched herb 1–2 ft. high. Leaves elliptic or ovalish, not over 1½ in. long, faintly 3–5-veined. Flowers bluish, about ¾ in. wide, the corolla lobes pointed. Socotra. Some, without much reason, have called this Arabian violet and Arabian gentian.

macranthum. Only slightly branched and less than 2 ft. high. Leaves oblongish, strongly 3-veined. Flowers purplish-blue, nearly 2 in. wide, the corolla lobes blunt. Ceylon.

exaltata, -us, -um (ecks-all-tay'ta). Very tall.

excelsa, -us, -um (ecks-sell'sa). Tall.

excelsior. Taller.

EXHIBITIONS AND SHOWS. See FLOWER SHOWS.

eximia, -us, -um (ecks-im'i-a). Out of the common run; distinguished.

excisa, -us, -um (ecks-sy'za). Excised; i.e., cut away.

EXOCHORDA (ecks-o-kor'da). A small but important genus of Asiatic shrubs of the rose family, E. racemosa, the pearl bush, being a very popular garden plant, and useful for forcing (which see). It is a spreading shrub, 5–10 ft. high, the leaves alternate,* more or less elliptic-oblong, 1–3 in. long, generally without marginal teeth. Flowers white, nearly 2 in. wide, in a showy, terminal, but not very profuse, cluster (raceme*). Sepals 5. Petals 5, broad but with a short claw.* Stamens 15. Fruit a 5-angled capsule.* China. Apr.–May. Hardy from zone* 3 south-

ward and often sold as E. grandiflora. This handsome shrub is of the easiest culture in any ordinary garden soil. Propagated by seeds, layers, or by softwood cuttings. A recently introduced species is E. giraldi, which is similar to E. racemosa and separated from it only by technical characters, and cult. mostly as the var. wilsoni, which is a more upright shrub and more floriferous than the type. Northwestern China. Apr.–May. Hardy from zone* 4 southward. (Exochorda is from the Greek for an external cord, in allusion to a technical ovary character.)

exoniensis, -e (ecks-o-ni-en'sis). From Exeter, England.

exotica, -us, -um (ecks-ot'i-ka). Exotic; i.e., not native; from another region.

expansa, -us, -um (ecks-span'sa). Expanded.

EXPERIMENT STATIONS. The state experiment stations and the U.S. Department of Agriculture do more for the gardener than any other agencies dealing with the growth of plants. While some of them, especially the National Government, carry on much original research, their chief function is the preparation of first-hand, practical directions on how to grow plants and how to combat the pests that attack them.

You will find the name and address of your own experiment station under the name of your state or province in the ENCYCLOPEDIA OF GARDENING, where you will also find an account of the garden possibilities of your state contributed by the experiment station. Few other features of the ENCYCLOPEDIA are so useful.

EXPOSURE. Within the general hardiness range of whatever plant you wish to grow, there are places where it will do better or worse, depending on many contributing factors. One of the most important of these secondary contributors to success or failure is exposure. Whether your plant will be exposed to too much sun or wind, or have to stand cooler nights, depends in great measure upon the place you finally select for it. No hard-and-fast rules can be given, but it is well to study the wild range and cultivated hardiness of your proposed plant, and to read the articles on SITE, HARDINESS, MICROCLIMATE, and ZONES, before you choose what the exposure will be.

exscapa, -us, -um (ecks-skay'pa). Without a stalk (scape).

EXSERTED. Protruding. Exserted is the usual technical term for stamens* or pistils* that protrude beyond the corolla.

EYE. A bud on a cutting, or a bud on a tuber, as the eyes on a potato. Eye is also very commonly applied to the differently colored center of a flower, very conspicuous in some pinks, forget-me-nots, and in Hibiscus oculiroseus, which has a white flower with a conspicuous red eye (center). Many garden flowers have them.

EYEBRIGHT = Mimulus ringens.

---

* Special articles on the subjects indicated by an asterisk (*) will be found at the words so marked.

F

F_1, F_2, F_3. Symbols used to indicate first, second, and third hybrid generations from a given mating or cross, F meaning filial. The original parents are often designated P_1 and P_2.

Faba (fay'ba). Classical name of the bean.

fabacea, -us, -um (fay-bay'see-a). Bean-like.

FABACEAE. *See* LEGUMINOSAE.

FABIANA (fay-bi-ā'na). Low, heath-like, South American shrubs of the potato family, comprising perhaps 20 species, of which **F. imbricata**, the false heath, is often grown for ornament in greenhouses or outdoors in Calif. and Fla. It is an erect, branching shrub 4–7 ft. high, the branches numerous and softly hairy. Leaves small, crowded, heath-like or scale-like. Flowers nearly stalkless, white, solitary, but many of them at the ends of short spurs. Corolla tubular, not over ½ in. long, the 5-lobed limb scarcely evident. Stamens* 5, of unequal length. Fruit an oblong, 2-valved capsule.* Peru. Of easy culture in the cool greenhouse in potting mixture* 3, and outdoors in any frost-free area. Propagated by cuttings taken in Aug. (Named for Francisco Fabiano, Spanish botanist and Archbishop.)

FACTOR. *See* GENE.

FAGACEAE (fay-gay'see-ee). The beech family is, with equal reason, called also the oak or chestnut family. See these three trees for the chief genera. The only other genera are *Castanopsis* and *Lithocarpus*, but of the 400 species known in the whole family less than 50 are of much garden importance, although many furnish valuable timbers, and the nuts of the chestnut are widely harvested for food.

Leaves alternate* (evergreen in some trees). Flowers without petals, all the male flowers in catkins,* the female solitary or in small clusters, both on the same tree, and always wind-pollinated. Fruit a 1-seeded nut, partly enclosed in a cup (in oaks), or completely surrounded by a bur (in the chestnut), and by bracts* in some other genera.

Technical flower characters: Petals none. Calyx extremely simple, 4–8-lobed. Stamens 4–20. In the female flower the calyx is joined to the 3–7-celled ovary. Styles 3–7.

FAGOPYRUM. *See* BUCKWHEAT.

FAGUS. *See* BEECH.

FAILURE TO BLOOM. Many are the disappointments caused by the failure of favorite flowers to bloom, or the failure of fruit trees to flower as freely as they should. In the latter case, it is often a case of im-proper pruning. *See* PRUNING. *See also* Self-sterile and Self-fertile at FRUIT CULTURE.

Failure to bloom should be separated into woody and herbaceous examples of it, for the underlying causes are often different.

In the case of herbs, few annuals, unless diseased, ever fail to produce flowers at the normal time. But not a few perennials, especially the peony, bloom poorly or not at all the first season after planting. There is no remedy for this, except to leave the plants alone. After the second or third season there is usually no trouble about this. The same is true of many slow-growing, long-lived perennials. Time is the only cure. But sometimes they have too much nitrate of soda or other nitrogenous fertilizer, which tends to produce leafage at the expense of flowers. Phosphorus and potash will usually correct this. *See* FERTILIZERS. Too deep planting of perennials also retards bloom.

In the case of all woody plants, there are occasional or periodic "off years" when there is little or no bloom. The cause and the remedy are as yet unknown. Many early-flowering shrubs and trees fail to bloom because a late frost may have caught their flower buds — notably the peach and apricot. But the chief cause in woody plants is improper pruning. This is discussed in detail in the article on pruning.

Disease and poor culture will, of course, tend to reduce bloom, and improper site, such as too much or too little sunlight. The notes on habitat and country of origin should be studied with this in mind for any plant that habitually fails to bloom. Often it is simply too weak to do so.

Another cause of failure to bloom is that sometimes a plant on its own roots does not do so well as when grafted upon a different stock. A common example is the wisteria. Plants on their own roots will often postpone blooming for years, while properly grafted plants will flower readily. It is important to see that purchased nursery stock of such plants as wisteria have been grafted to ensure bloom. Most good nurserymen do so, but it is well to be sure of it.

FAIRY BELLS. *See* DISPORUM.

FAIRY CUP = *Mitella diphylla.*

FAIRY FANS = *Eucharidium breweri.*

FAIRY GLOVE = *Digitalis purpurea.* See FOXGLOVE.

FAIRY LILY = *Zephyranthes Atamasco;* also *Cooperia pedunculata.*

FAIRY PRIMROSE = *Primula malacoides.*

FAIRY ROSE = *Rosa chinensis minima.*

FAIRY WAND = *Chamaelirium luteum.*

---

* Special articles on the subjects indicated by an asterisk (*) will be found at the words so marked.

falcata, -us, -um (fal-kay'ta). Falcate; *i.e.,* sickle-shaped.

FALL COLOR. *See* AUTUMN FOLIAGE and AUTUMN GARDEN.

FALL GARDEN. *See* AUTUMN GARDEN.

FALL PLANTING. *See* AUTUMN PLANTING.

FALSE. As an adjective *false* is linked with the names of many plants, usually indicating that they are like, or may be mistaken for, some other plant. Those that occur in this book, and their proper equivalents, are:

False acacia = *Robinia Pseudo-acacia* (*see* LOCUST); False aloe = *Agave virginica;* False alumroot = *Tellima grandiflora;* False anemone = *Isopyrum biternatum;* False aralia (*see* DIZYGOTHECA); False arborvitae = *Thujopsis dolabrata;* False bittersweet (*see* BITTERSWEET); False bugbane = *Trautvetteria carolinensis;* False camomile (*see* MATRICARIA and BOLTONIA); False cypress (*see* CHAMAECYPARIS); False dragonhead = *Dracocephalum virginianum;* False flag (*see* NEOMARICA); False heath = *Fabiana imbricata;* False hellebore (*see* VERATRUM); False indigo (*see* BAPTISIA and AMORPHA); False ipecac = *Gillenia trifoliata;* False Jerusalem cherry = *Solanum Capsicastrum;* False loosestrife (*see* LUDWIGIA); False mallow (*see* SIDALCEA and SPHAERALCEA); False mermaid family = Limnanthaceae; False mitrewort (*see* TIARELLA); False olive = *Elaeodendron orientale;* False saffron = *Carthamus tinctorius;* False Solomon's-seal (*see* SMILACINA); False spirea (*see* SORBARIA); False starwort (*see* BOLTONIA); False sunflower = *Helenium autumnale* and *Heliopsis helianthoides;* False tamarisk = *Myricaria germanica;* False violet = *Dalibarda repens.*

FANCY GERANIUM = *Pelargonium domesticum.*

FANCY-LEAVED CALADIUM. *See* CALADIUM.

FAN PALM. A palm with fan-like leaves. *See* the illustration at PALMACEAE.

FAN TRAINING. *See* TRAINED FRUIT TREES.

FANWORT. *See* CABOMBA.

FANWORT FAMILY. *See* NYMPHAEACEAE.

FAREWELL-TO-SPRING = *Godetia amoena.*

Farfara (far'fa-ra). Pre-Linnacan* name for the coltsfoot (*Tussilago Farfara*).

FARFUGIUM. *See* LIGULARIA.

FARINA. *See* BLOOM.

farinacea, -us, -um (far-ri-nay'see-a). Farinaceous; *i.e.,* starch-yielding.

farinosa, -us, -um (far-ri-nō'sa). Mealy.

farleyensis, -e (far-lee-en'sis). From Farley Hill Gardens, Barbados.

farnesiana, -us, -um (far-nee-zi-a'na). Named for the Farnesian Garden, Rome.

fasciata, -us, -um (fay-see-a'ta). Fasciated.

FASCIATED; FASCIATION. An abnormal widening and flattening of the stem, often of a flower stalk. While generally of unknown origin, it is sometimes due to disease. Fasciation is not at all uncommon among garden plants, particularly in the genus *Nicotiana,* and in *Celosia* and *Lilium.*

fasciculata, -us, -um (fa-sick-kew-lay'-ta). Fascicled; *i.e.,* in a close, dense cluster.

fastigiata, -us, -um (fas-tij-ji-a'ta). Fastigiate.

FASTIGIATE. With the branches turning upward and relatively close to the trunk. It is rare or unknown among wild trees but hort. forms such as the Lombardy poplar are common enough. Fastigiate trees may also be found among the maples, beech, oak, and of course the columnar form of the Italian cypress (*Cupressus sempervirens stricta*).

fastuosa, -us, -um (fast-you-o'sa). Proud.

FATHER HUGO'S ROSE = *Rosa hugonis.*

FATSHEDERA (fats-hed'e-ra). A bigeneric* hybrid, derived from crossing the English ivy with *Fatsia japonica,* family Araliaceae. The only species is **Fatshedera lizei,** a shrub with rusty-hairy twigs in youth, not over 6 ft. high, its evergreen leaves somewhat resembling the English ivy, but larger, often 5–10 in. wide. Flowers small, light green, in dense clusters (umbels*) that are grouped in a large, showy, branched cluster (panicle*) that may be 8–10 in. long and half as wide. Sept.–Oct. Hardy from zone* 6 southward. Propagation is by cuttings. (*Fatshedera* is a combination of *Fatsia* and *Hedera,* the English ivy.)

FATSIA (fat'si-a). A single, evergreen, Japanese shrub or small tree of the family Araliaceae, much planted south of zone* 7 for its tropical-looking foliage. The only species, **F. japonica,** is an unarmed, bushy shrub or small tree 10–20 ft. high. Leaves alternate,* its stalks 8–12 in. long, the blade nearly round in outline, 9–15 in. wide, cut into 5–9 ovalish, broad, toothed lobes, shiny and stiff. Flowers small, whitish, in small umbels,* many of which are grouped in a large, very showy, branched cluster. (For details *see* ARALIACEAE.) Fruit black, berry-like about ¼ in. in diameter. The plant grows well in nearly every type of soil, but prefers rich, sandy ones. Propagated by seeds, o: by cuttings in spring. Often offered as *Aralia japonica.* There is also a form with variegated leaves. For a related plant sometimes offered as *F. papyrifera, see* TETRAPANAX PAPYRIFERUS. And for the plant sometimes offered as *F. horrida, see* OPLOPANAX HORRIDUS. (*Fatsia* is derived from a Japanese vernacular for the plant.)

fatua, -us, -um (fat'you-a). Simple; or, in horticultural usage, simply insipid.

FAUCARIA. *See* MESEMBRYANTHEMUM.

FAWN LILY = *Erythronium albidum* and *E. californicum.*

FEATHER-BALL = *Mammillaria plumosa.*

FEATHER-FASHION. With the leaflets

---

* Special articles on the subjects indicated by an asterisk (*) will be found at the words so marked.

of a compound leaf arranged as are the segments of a bird's feather, *i.e.*, arising from opposite sides of a common axis.* The technical term is pinnate (which see).

FEATHER-FLEECE = *Stenanthium gramineum.*

FEATHER-GERANIUM = *Chenopodium Botrys.*

FEATHER-GRASS. See STIPA.

FEATHER-HYACINTH = *Muscari comosum monstrosum.*

FEATHER PALM. A palm in which the segments of the leaf are arranged feather-fashion; not like a fan. *See* the illustration at PALMACEAE.

FEDERATED GARDEN CLUBS. See GARDEN CLUBS.

FEDIA (fee′di-a). A single, annual herb of the family Valerianaceae, native in the Mediterranean region, and grown chiefly for ornament, and rarely as a salad plant. The only species, **F. Cornucopiae**, the African valerian, is a stout, purplish-stemmed, leafy herb, 10–15 in. high. Leaves opposite,* ovalish or spatula-shaped, 2–4 in. long, shiny and green. Flowers red, small, in dense terminal clusters (cymes*), the corolla tubular but slightly 2-lipped.* Stamens 2. Fruit like a grain of wheat. To be grown as a hardy annual (*see* ANNUALS). (*Fedia* is of unknown origin.)

FEEDING PLANTS. See FERTILIZERS. *See also* MANURE. For Feeding Trees *see* TREE SURGERY.

FEIJOA (fa-jo′a). A small genus of South American shrubs or small trees of the myrtle family, **F. sellowiana**, the pineapple guava grown in Fla. and Calif. for its delicious, white-fleshed fruit. It is hardy surely only south of zone* 7, although it stands an occasional drop to 14°. Leaves opposite,* oval-oblong, 2–3 in. long, white-felty beneath. Flowers solitary, ¾–1½ in. long. white-felty outside, purplish inside, long-stalked, blooming in April. Petals 4. Stamens* many, red, protruding and showy. Fruit (ripe in Aug.–Sept.) a greenish-red berry, 2–3 in. long. The pineapple guava is grown both in the dry Calif. climate and in the moister one of Fla. They do well in sandy, rich loam, and should be planted 15–20 ft. apart each way. Seeds germinate 2–3 weeks after sowing. Cuttings and layers are both very slow. To ensure a good set of fruit it is well to stagger varieties in the row, some of the best being Andre, Coolidge, Choice, and Superba. Otherwise, pollination may fail. (Named for J. da Silva Feijo, a Spanish naturalist.)

feijeensis, -e (fee-jee-en′sis). From the Fiji Islands.

FELICIA (fe-liss′i-a). A large genus of chiefly South African under-shrubs (rarely annuals) of the family Compositae, with alternate or opposite leaves and showy, usually blue, radiate flower heads. The first

species is rather tender but can be grown outdoors in mild regions. (Named for a Herr Felix, a German official.)

amelloides. The blue daisy or blue Marguerite, a popular greenhouse plant grown for ornament, sometimes under the name *Agathea coelestis.* It is a bushy shrub 1–3 ft. high, the leaves opposite,* more or less elliptic, mostly without teeth, and tapering at the base to a winged stalk. Flower heads solitary, daisy-like, about 1 in. wide, the numerous rays* blue, the small disk* flowers yellow. It is a handsome plant to be grown in potting mixture* 3 and in the cool greenhouse, but is hardy outdoors from zone* 5 southward. Oct.–Nov.

bergeriana. Kingfisher daisy. A tender annual, 4–8 in. high, the slender, grass-like leaves about 1½ in. long and hairy. Flower heads bright blue, solitary, about ¾ in. wide. A useful plant for window boxes. S. Af.

coelestis = *F. amelloides.*

FELT-FERN. See CYCLOPHORUS.

FEMALE. Male and female are common terms among gardeners, indicating flowers with stamens* and pistils,* respectively. The preferable, but botanical, terms, staminate (for male) and pistillate (for female), appear unlikely to replace male and female as the usual garden terms for the reproductive organs of plants. *See* FERTILIZATION.

FENCES. Fences should harmonize with their surroundings, combining decorative design with practical usage. A fence, to act as a screen, and not just a barrier, must have no openings. French hand-riven chestnut palings, pointed at the top and closely woven together, are best for this purpose, but they rot if buried in the soil. This fence is durable, economical, cannot be seen through, and fits into the landscape. With formal houses of brick, stone, or stucco, house and garden may be tied together by using this type in panels between piers, plain or ornamental, built of the same material as the house walls. In small gardens where every inch of space is precious but privacy is desired, solid board or thin masonry fences may be used. There are many variations of the latter, the most common being of metal lath fastened to tee irons set into concrete

Good type of woven-paling fence

---

* Special articles on the subjects indicated by an asterisk (*) will be found at the words so marked.

at intervals of six to eight feet. The entire structure is then stuccoed and a stucco base and top molding added. Stone or brick may be used for a heavy fence.

Lattice, with large or small openings, or a combination of both, intricate designs, and ornamental finials and moldings, serve a variety of purposes. The wood hurdle fence and the heavy post and rail fence are ideal for country boundaries. The old-fashioned picket fence is well adapted to the Colonial style of architecture. Pickets may vary in width, shape, and spacing; they may be flat and wide with pointed tops, square, or round. Pine, white or red cedar, and locust make excellent durable posts. Give a priming coat of lead and oil to all parts before erecting, or have them creosoted.

Common types of wooden fences and railings. The split-rail type of fence at the bottom encloses some of the finest gardens in America at East Hampton, L.I., usually covered (only partly) with honeysuckle, clematis or climbing roses.

For protection, especially on country estates, heavy metal chain link or woven wire fences are best. They do not provide privacy, but climbers or dense hedges of privet or shrubs may be grown inside them.

fenestralis, -e (fen-es-tray'lis). Having window-like openings.

FENNEL. The common garden fennel is one of 4 species of European herbs of the genus **Foeniculum** (fe-nick'you-lum) of the carrot family, and is grown for its aromatic fruits and foliage. It has twice-compound* leaves, the leaflets arranged feather-fashion, and small, yellow flowers in compound umbels* (for details *see* UMBELLIFERAE). (*Foeniculum* is a Latin diminutive for hay, in allusion to the odor of its foliage.)

Of the four known species, the only one of garden interest is the common fennel and its varieties. For culture and uses *see* HERB GARDENING.

F. officinale = *Foeniculum vulgare.*
F. vulgare. Common fennel. A perennial, but grown usually as an annual or biennial. Stems 3–5 ft. high, bluish-green. Ultimate leaflets very numerous, thread-like. Flower-cluster (umbel*) large, the number of flowers in each umbel 15–25. Summer. The *var.* **dulce**, the Florence or sweet fennel, which is also called finnochio, has the leaf base enlarged, and, when blanched, is used as food, and is considerably grown in Calif. The *var.* **piperitum**, the carosella, is grown for its tender, young stems which are eaten, and sometimes made into a glace confection.

FENNEL-FLOWER = *Nigella sativa.*

FEN ORCHIS = *Liparis loeseli.*

FENUGREEK = *Trigonella Foenum-Graecum.*

FERBAM. See FUNGICIDES.

FERN ALLIES. The fern allies are not true ferns but like them in being reproduced by spores. Not many fern allies are of much garden significance. For those in this encyclopedia, *see* EQUISETUM, LYCOPODIUM, MARSILEA, SALVINIACEAE, and SELAGINELLA.

FERN ASPARAGUS = *Asparagus plumosus.*

FERN BALL. A compact, pudding-shaped mass of the rhizomes* of certain ferns, notably *Davallia bullata,* mostly made in Japan and imported in a dry, dormant condition. The mass is tightly tied together, and when soaked in water and hung in a warm, moist, partly shaded greenhouse will soon be covered with the beautiful, feathery foliage of *Davallia.* Subsequent care is the same as for any greenhouse fern. (See FERNS AND FERN GARDENING.) Fern balls may well replace hanging baskets on a summer porch, but it must not be a windy or dry one. Watering is most easily done by dipping the whole fern ball, foliage and all, in a bucket of water. They must be kept moist.

FERNLEAF BEECH = *Fagus sylvatica laciniata.* See BEECH.

FERNS AND FERN GARDENING. Ferns are perennial, flowerless plants of more than 10,000 species, divided into several families, which are widely distributed throughout the temperate and tropical regions of the world. Long before the Age of Man, gigantic ancestors of our ferns formed mighty forests, while higher plant life gradually evolved above them. Today the extinct species of ferns far outnumber the living.

Two groups are recognized by gardeners. The hardy kinds are chiefly terrestrial species from temperate regions, which may be planted in gardens if given conditions approximately like those of their natural habitat. The greenhouse kinds, of tropical regions, include the epiphytic* varieties, which require special growing facilities approximating their environmental conditions. The popularity of ferns as garden subjects has waned considerably since our first edition,

---

* Special articles on the subjects indicated by an asterisk (*) will be found at the words so marked.

but all those mentioned below are still available.

SPORES AND REPRODUCTION

Ferns pass through two complete stages in their life cycles. The first consists of a tiny, green, flattened body, often heart-shaped, connected with the soil by hair-like roots and bearing on its lower surface both of the reproductive organs. This is termed a *prothallus*. The union of these reproductive organs does not, as in flowering plants, form seed. Instead of seed-formation, the germ-cell in the fern develops into the second stage, or fern-plant proper. The first fronds are very small and simple,* quite unlike the later ones. For a time the little plant is nourished by the prothallus, but as soon as it is sufficiently vigorous to shift for itself, the prothallus dies away, and the fern maintains an independent existence. This fern plant, in turn, develops the spores which produce the prothallus, thus completing its life cycle.

PROPAGATION

Ferns are propagated by division, by the buds or offsets* that form on the fronds of certain varieties, and by means of spores. These spores are collected in spore cases clustered in dots or lines, usually on the back of a frond or leaf, or along its margin. Spores differ from seeds in that they are not the immediate result of the interaction of reproductive organs; they resemble seeds in that they are expelled from the spore cases upon attaining maturity, and germinate on contact with moisture. Ripened spores may be taken from the parent plant, and put in sacks of paper to dry. Sow in one or two weeks in flats or pots on light, moist, well-sifted soil. Equal parts of garden loam and leaf mold, with sand for drainage, make a good mixture. Do not cover the spores with earth or water on top; the flat or pot should be kept in a frame or house at a temperature of about 60 degrees. After the tiny prothalli appear, a little more air may be given. When large enough to be handled easily, prick out little sporelings and transplant them, later re-transplanting them individually into separate pots. From ten months to a year are required to produce good ferns by this method.

HARDY FERNS

To many people ferns have an aesthetic value in the landscape not surpassed by any class of flowering plants. Their immense variety and geographical distribution make it possible to select species adapted to almost any location. Almost all may be introduced into our gardens if their preferences are consulted, and reasonable attention given to their simple cultural requirements. The majority are terrestrial in habit; a few climb; some prefer dry, sunny places, and others are at home in humid, moisture-laden swamps. Being so varied in their characteristics, they are adapted to a

wide variety of purposes — exposed northern spots where flowers will not grow, massed plantings, walk edgings, rock gardens, bog gardens, sunny walls and banks. Many of the plants will thrive under ordinary conditions, but a little leaf mold added to common soil, will in general prolong the life of all ferns. Early spring or late fall is to be preferred for planting, as the roots are then least apt to be disturbed. Autumn planting, with a mulch of leaves during the cold months to give protection and to retain moisture in the soil until the rootlets have started to grow, is probably the best.

Some types of hardy ferns. Above, *Dryopteris marginalis* (left) and *Woodsia*; below, the Christmas fern (*left*) and the cinnamon fern.

The spots in our garden that cause us the most worry and trouble are those where flowers do not thrive — the north side of the house, wall and foundation plantings, bare spots under trees, or any place where light is not abundant.

The evergreen wood fern, *Dryopteris marginalis*, as its name signifies, flourishes throughout the winter, and comes nearer being a "tree" fern than any other of our northern species. It requires deep shade and has a liking for rocks or stones. It grows equally well in neutral or acid soil. An excellent companion for massing under shrubs, to form an evergreen ground cover, is *D. spinulosa*, which requires more moisture than *D. marginalis*. The crowns should be placed just at the surface, about a foot apart. The Christmas fern, *Polystichum acrostichoides*, is easily grown in dry, shady places and is indifferent to soil. *Polystichum brauni* will succeed in any rich, neutral soil. It prefers shaded locations.

Some ferns will grow in either sun or shade. Regardless of soil, exposure, or moisture, the lady fern is one of our most graceful and valuable hardy plants. For the best results a little shade is desirable. It makes good undercover,

* Special articles on the subjects indicated by an asterisk (*) will be found at the words so marked.

a background for smaller ferns, and transplants readily. The hay-scented fern is a favorite wild-garden subject. It has no preference as regards soil or moisture. One of the easiest to cult., the ostrich fern is propagated by means of underground runners, and soon forms dense growths of almost tropical luxuriance. These ferns thrive best in a mixture of swamp muck and fine loam; a portion of the crown should be left above the surface.

In moist, shady places in open woods, deep ravines and river banks, grow some of our loveliest native ferns. Even though we may not have the identical landscape facilities, nearly all gardens have certain spots where we can use some of them.

The foliage of certain wild flowers much resembles that of our northeastern maidenhair, which is the most popular of all ferns. Easily cult., it prefers a rich, moist soil and well-drained location. If planted in masses, place them 8 in. apart; cover the roots lightly with leaf mold. The spleenworts are indifferent as to soil, if the roots are not covered too deeply; place them 1 ft. apart. *Dryopteris cristata* is splendid for edging walks in damp woodlands; its larger relative, *D. clintoniana*, is desirable for the fern bed. Set so the crowns are above the surface; both are indifferent to soil. All of this group may be propagated by division.

For wet ground, such as lake borders, bogs, and meadowland, the royal fern is the most beautiful. Like others of the *Osmunda* group it prefers full sunlight. They will flourish in still water of 2 or 3 in., provided the crowns are above the high-water line. *Osmunda claytoniana* requires the same cult.

Dry, rocky ledges and rock gardens are always glad to welcome low-growing, hardy plants which may be used as backgrounds. The common polypody forms dense mats when set 4 in. apart. *Woodsia ilvensis* and *W. obtusa* are good covers for bare spots, easy of cult. and need little moisture. Cover the crowns partially in planting. For a dry, limestone wall, *Pellaea atropurpurea* is an attractive and unique plant. Propagation by the creeping rootstocks or spores.

Although southern Fla. and the tropics are blessed with a number of climbing species of the fern family, we of the North must be content with one only, *Lygodium palmatum*. Potted plants bought from dealers and set out in an acid soil of pH4–4.5 (*see* ACID AND ALKALI SOILS), preferably among mountain laurel and blueberry bushes, will grow and flourish. Each season give a heavy mulch of oak leaves; the bushes will protect it from a too-hot sun. *Polystichum munitum*, an evergreen species known as giant holly fern, is hardy in the Northeast.

GREENHOUSE FERNS

The most commonly grown ferns in conservatory and greenhouse are found in the genera *Adiantum, Alsophila, Blechnum, Cibotium, Cyathea, Cyrtomium, Davallia, Dicksonia, Lygodium, Nephrolepis, Platycerium, Polystichum,* and *Pteris*.

In general the night temperature should be a minimum of 55 degrees, with a rise of 10 to 15 degrees during the day. Extremes of heat and cold should be avoided. Standing water must never be left in the pots. Never use stable manure or fresh commercial fertilizer. Watch closely for signs of pot-binding; re-pot often. Do not use clay soil. Propagation chiefly by division; break the crowns in small pieces and place in a pan of live sphagnum moss. Cover with glass. Keep at a temperature of 65 to 70 degrees. When the eyes develop and one or two fronds appear, pot and place in shaded house. Ventilate, but keep atmosphere moist and even. In a few cases where propagation is by bulbils,* as in the hardy *Cystopteris bulbifera,* separate and put directly into small pots.

Many ferns grown in the North as house and greenhouse plants are hardy in central and southern Fla. and Calif. With the slight protection of a lath-house, practically all will do well there. Tree ferns are unable to withstand more than slight frost and dislike extreme heat and drought. Whether in pots or gardens, they must have perfect drainage and a neutral soil. Use potting mixture* 5; add a little charcoal. *Alsophila australis* is commonly grown under glass; *Cyathea dealbata* does well in sheltered gardens; *Cibotium schiedei* is beautiful but so slow-growing it may be used as a house plant. Damp down the house often; a humid atmosphere is essential.

The maidenhair ferns of this class do best under shelter. A liberal supply of water must be given during the growing season. Use potting mixture* 4 with broken pots for drainage, and add charcoal. Keep a fairly moist atmosphere of about 65 degrees and protect from full sun. *Adiantum cuneatum* and its varieties are the best known and most important of the genus and make good house plants.

The leathery texture of the foliage of the

Greenhouse ferns: Above, *Pteris cretica* (*left*) and *Cyrtomium falcatum:* below, the bird's-nest fern (*left*) and the Boston fern.

---

* Special articles on the subjects indicated by an asterisk (*) will be found at the words so marked.

spleenworts and their ease of cult. make these species popular. Under glass they must not be exposed to strong sunlight. If kept too wet they lose color in the dormant season. Use potting mixture* 4. *Asplenium bulbiferum* is propagated by bulbils.* *A. Nidus*, the bird's-nest fern, is well suited for the greenhouse. Do not re-pot this species very often. After pot is well filled with roots, give occasionally a little very weak liquid manure.

A few species of blechnums are cultivated chiefly as backgrounds for orchids. They are good specimen plants. Average temperature 60 degrees. Dry atmosphere, with plenty of moisture at the roots. They are practically free from pests. While they will grow in any soil, it is better to use potting mixture* 5. Excellent for outdoor cult. in Fla.

The sword-ferns are greenhouse, house, and porch subjects, sometimes grown in baskets. The epiphytic species do well in conservatories; *Nephrolepis cordifolia* grows on palms; *N. exaltata*, of which the Boston fern is a variety, grows luxuriantly on the trunks of palmettos, live oaks and other moss-covered trees in Fla. All varieties of the Boston type make excellent living room plants. Propagation by means of rooting runners.

Platycerium does not appear to be a fern at all. They are striking-looking plants when old and well grown. Propagation may be by suckers as well as spores. The common staghorn, *P. bifurcatum*, is an excellent conservatory plant. It may be grown on a piece of tree-fern trunk if given a little peat and moss for a foothold. Add a little bone meal now and then and occasionally some charcoal. These plants will, in the open, endure a temperature of 40 degrees.

The claw-ferns remain fresh longer and are as attractive, when used with cut flowers, as maidenhair ferns. *Onychium japonicum* is excellent for a conservatory, and its small size makes it suitable for a centerpiece. Use potting mixture* 4.

Polypodiums are both terrestrial and epiphytic, many being hardy in Fla. and Calif. They will do well in either potting mixture* 4 or 5, as they are not particular as regards soil. Propagate by division of clumps or spores. The golden polypody is a good, hardy, house plant. This particular species grows on palms, where it self-sows by means of spores. The rootstocks adhere tightly to the trunk. It grows well in pots in patios in the Southwest. *Polypodium polypodioides*, the resurrection fern, is the most abundant of all the epiphytic ferns along the Gulf Coast. Many of these are sold by the trade, as the dry, shriveled fronds expand when put in water and become as beautiful as ever. The tongue-fern (*Cyclophorus*), often called felt-fern, is much like the polypody and is often listed as such. This plant does not stand dry weather well, if grown in the open. It requires plenty of moisture in the greenhouse, and does not always do well even there. However, it is worth growing because of its beautiful, variegated foliage. Otherwise cult. the same as polypody.

The cyrtomiums are half-hardy or glasshouse ferns of easy culture, thriving admirably in places where light is not abundant. For this reason forms of *Cyrtomium falcatum*, are, next to the Boston fern, the best for apartment use. A dwarf variety, *compactum*, makes a good centerpiece. Same cult. as the spleenworts.

Pteris is among the best of all fern types for northern greenhouse cult. They thrive in lath houses in deep, rich soil in Fla. and Calif. Potting mixture* 4 will suit the majority, although they are not fastidious as regards soil. Some few burn easily when placed in full sunlight at midday. The crested forms are in great demand for pan and fern dishes and for table decorations, particularly *Pteris cretica* and *P. serrulata* and their varieties. *P. serrulata* grows wild in Fla. on limestone ledges and old walls in full sun. It dislikes shade and heavy rains. These ferns do well in terrariums* and in window gardens, under ordinary conditions.

The davallias are popular for hanging-basket and fern-ball use. *Davallia bullata* is hardy in Fla. and Calif. These plants are deciduous, shedding their dry leaves in winter. If grown in a basket, the rootstocks should be bound over sphagnum moss by the use of copper wire. If the fern-ball type is preferred, a good plan is to soak thoroughly before hanging, as the plants will be received in a dormant condition. Propagation is by division of the old plants and spores; keep at a temperature of 65 degrees.

The asparagus fern, commonly grown in conservatories and apartments, is not a fern. It is *Asparagus sprengeri* or *A. plumosus* and belongs to the lily family.

All the genera of ferns in this encyclopedia will be found listed at the entries POLYPODIACEAE, CYATHEACEAE, OPHIOGLOSSACEAE, OSMUNDACEAE, and SCHIZAEACEAE. *See also* CERATOPTERIS and FERN ALLIES.

Fern lovers are welcome as members of the American Fern Society, a national organization devoted to ferns. It publishes a journal, and its present address is Department of Botany, Syracuse University, Syracuse, N.Y.

FEROCACTUS (fer'o-kak-tus). Horribly spiny cacti from Mexico and the southwestern U.S., comprising perhaps 30 species, of which two, and sometimes more, are cult. in the desert garden, less commonly in the greenhouse. They have a cylindric or globe-shaped, often large plant body, prominently ribbed and plentifully beset with stout or needle-like spines. Flowers not usually large, funnel-shaped, mostly borne just above a spine-cluster (for details *see* CACTACEAE). Fruit thick-walled and dry, the seeds black and pitted. (*Ferocactus* is from fierce and cactus, in allusion to the spines.)

For culture *see* CACTI.

glaucescens. Plant body nearly globe-shaped, 9–15 in. in diameter, bluish-green and with 11–15 prominent ribs. Spines in clusters of 7, one solitary and erect, the others spreading, all straight. Flowers nearly 1 in. long, yellow. Mex.

---

* Special articles on the subjects indicated by an asterisk (*) will be found at the words so marked.

wislizeni. Biznaga. Fishhook cactus. Roundish in youth, cylindric and nearly 6 ft. high in age, the prominent ribs at least 25. Spines in large clusters, several erect but most of them spreading, all long and needle-like. Flowers 2–3 in. long, yellow. Western Tex., Ariz., and Mex.

ferox (fe′rocks). Fierce or wild.

ferruginea, -us, -um (fer-rew-ji-nee′a). Rusty.

FERTILE. As to flowers, bearing both stamens* and pistils* and thus able to produce seed. As to soil, *see* FERTILITY.

fertilis, -e (fer′till-iss). Fertile; *i.e.*, having both stamens* and pistils.*

FERTILITY. Soil fertility is a combination of many things. Chief among them are the proper ingredients for plant growth, the right soil texture, the acidity or alkalinity of it, and the proper conditions of soil moisture.

There is no simple chemical test for fertility, because the ability to produce a satisfactory crop is a combination of all the four factors outlined above, and a fifth, the presence of soil organisms like the microscopic fungi. The best test for fertility is to grow plants, preferably under carefully controlled conditions. These should consist of corn sown in pots, thinning the seedlings to 4 in a pot. After 3 weeks measure the growth and compare with a sample pot in which potting mixture* 3 has been used. If the crop is poor, study the articles on soils, and also the following: CULTIVATION, ACID AND ALKALI SOILS. To increase the amount of plant food in the soil some sort of fertilizer or manure is indicated. *See* FERTILIZERS, MANURE, PLANT FOODS.

There are various chemical tests for the amount of nitrogen, phosphoric acid, and potash in soils, but they are somewhat complicated and are better left to the soil chemists at the experiment stations. For the average home grower the pot culture of plants under uniform conditions provides the best ready measure of fertility.

FERTILIZATION. The process, in flowering plants, after pollination,* which results in the impregnation of the ovule by the sperm (male) cell. Immediately after it is placed upon a stigma,* the pollen begins a (microscopic) process of downward elongation, forming the pollen tube which carries the sperm cell. The growth of the pollen tube inside the tissue of the style* is culminated by the impregnation of the ovule by the sperm cell. Only when this is completed is fertilization accomplished and a future seed assured. Sometimes, but loosely, this final union of male and female elements is called pollination, but the latter process is merely a preliminary to fertilization. *See* POLLINATION and the account of the fertilization of ferns at FERNS AND FERN GARDENING.

FERTILIZERS. As here and usually understood, fertilizers include the so-called artificial, or chemically prepared, commercial fertilizers, but not manure (which see), the latter being of animal origin.

A complete fertilizer should theoretically contain all the plant food that could be derived from a perfect soil. But plants use so many different chemical elements and their compounds, and so many of them are present in more than adequate amounts in all soils, that a complete fertilizer is now understood to contain the three most essential elements only — nitrogen, phosphoric acid, and potash. It is upon these three, especially nitrogen, that the fertility of most soils depends, and all commercial fertilizers contain these substances in varying ratios, depending upon the crop and the soil to which the fertilizer will be added. For the complete list of substances that make up the food of plants, *see* PLANT FOODS. Here we shall deal only with the three that are often deficient, and which, in varying amounts, are found in all fertilizer mixtures.

No one today needs to buy fertilizers blindly. They are forced to contain a specified amount of available nitrogen, phosphoric acid, and potash, and their claims are checked by the chemists of the agricultural experiment stations. Most of the stations publish annually a list of fertilizers which shows what they claim and what was actually found in them. All seedsmen and supply houses carry standard brands with a guaranteed formula on the bag. To buy any others is to invite deception and in the old days deception was rife in the fertilizer business — some of the samples being inert or actually detrimental substances, such as borax, for instance. All high-priced, small-packaged brands, without a formula, should be purchased with caution. Even when they are of value, their cost is generally far too high.

FERTILIZER MIXTURES. The uninitiated, however, can still be misled, or can buy fertilizers wastefully, by not understanding exactly what the figures on a fertilizer bag mean. It is, for instance, a common thing to see a bag labeled 4–8–4, or 2–5–7, or 3–5–9, or almost any other combination of three numbers separated by hyphens. Throughout the U.S. such figures always mean that the first figure is the percentage of nitrogen, the second figure the percentage of phosphoric acid, and the third figure the percentage of potash, in the mixture. Represented diagrammatically, such a simple formula as 4–8–4 would thus mean:

| = 4% of Nitrogen | = 8% of Phosphoric acid | = 4% of Potash |

Throughout this encyclopedia, and in horticultural literature generally, especially in experiment station bulletins, these symbols of fertilizer constituents are used, the significance of which is important to all gardeners. For the right kind of fertilizer often means success, while the wrong kind, if it does not spell failure, at least means a useless waste of money.

Many intelligent gardeners often ask, why use commercial fertilizers at all, considering that it is only since the rise of industrial chemistry that they have been available. This is true, and if manure in sufficient quantities could be found, chemical fertilizers

---

* Special articles on the subjects indicated by an asterisk (*) will be found at the words so marked.

would not be needed. But the motor age and the passing of the horse have made animal manure available only near large cities or on stock farms, and its cost far exceeds what one pays for even the finest commercial fertilizers. But manure is still the best for the soil and is an extremely valuable plant food. See MANURE.

Before coming to specific fertilizer suggestions for different crops, it will make them more intelligible to understand the role of the chief constituents.

NITROGEN. The most valuable, most expensive, and soonest exhausted of all fertilizer constituents. Outside of the nitrogen gathered from the air by plants of the pea family, there is no other method of replacing the nitrogen which the current crop has used, except by fertilizers or manure. Of course some sort of a crop can be grown without applying nitrogen, just as wild vegetation must rely upon the nitrogen naturally in the soil. But to get the best crops, there must be a renewal of nitrogen, for this is the substance that stimulates vegetative growth (as distinguished from flowering and fruiting). Hence crops like cabbage, Brussels sprouts, kale and kohlrabi, celery, endive, Swiss chard, and asparagus thrive on a fertilizer with a high nitrogen content.

The quickest-acting and most effective source of nitrogen is nitrate of soda. It is available almost as soon as applied to the ground as it dissolves at the first rain and is immediately available thereafter. Its disadvantage is that, once applied, it is soon lost (i.e., absorbed by the crop) and consequently builds up little or no residue of nitrogen for later crops. But other sources of nitrogen will supply this deficiency.

One of them is bone meal. This ground-up bone dust dissolves much more slowly than nitrate of soda and is consequently of value in small gardens, as top-dressing for pots, frames, or for feeding house plants. And because of its slow action, it is safer to use than nitrate of soda, an overdose of which can easily injure or even kill a crop. See the formulas below. Bone meal also contains much phosphoric acid.

Other valuable sources of nitrogen are tankage and dried blood, both prepared by-products of the slaughter houses, and, like bone meal, more useful for permanent enrichment than for quick effects. Calcium nitrate, sulphate of ammonia, and urea are also valuable sources of nitrogen.

PHOSPHORIC ACID. This, mostly supplied by rock phosphates and superphosphates, is, next to nitrogen, the most valuable of fertilizer constituents. Its special function is the stimulation of cereal crops, but it is also absolutely necessary for most vegetable and flower crops. Many soils are deficient in phosphorus and the lack of it often slows up final crop production. Various basic slags and ground-up acid phosphates, carrying from 12–20% of phosphoric acid, are available. Still another source of it is bone meal.

POTASH. The chief use of potash is the stimulation of root crops like beets, carrots, turnips, radishes, and parsnips. But as part of the balanced ration for perfect growth, potash must be a constituent of all fertilizer mixtures. It is used chiefly in the form of muriate of potash (mostly for vegetables), sulphate of potash for potatoes, kainit for asparagus and a few other succulent vegetables, and as carbonate of potash. Most wood ashes contain from 4–6% of potash.

While different plants need different amounts of these three substances, only nitrate of soda is usually applied alone, and this for the quick stimulation of leafage as outlined above. Most fertilizers contain judicious mixtures of the three, hence the common advertising of so-called "complete fertilizers." There never can be a really complete one, but long experience has shown that the following come as near being complete as one can expect.

THE COMPLETE FERTILIZER. There is available today the greatest range of fertilizer ratios. From them every fertilizer need can be met and a few of the most important mixtures and their uses are outlined below. The application of any of them would be a simple matter if all of their constituents were to be used by the end of the season. But there is always a residue, and what is left has an effect upon the soil that cannot be ignored by any intelligent gardener. Sulphate of ammonia (a common source of nitrogen), muriate of potash, sulphate of potash, and acid phosphate all tend to leave a soil more acid; in other words, they are acid-residue fertilizers. But nitrate of soda, carbonate of potash, and some of the commercial phosphates are inclined to leave the soil more alkaline. Repeated applications of these, in the same ratios, would have a bad effect upon the soil, even though they might have benefited successive crops. For the acid-residue fertilizers, and to some extent all fertilizers, have a tendency to exhaust the humus content of the soil. This may do more harm than no fertilizer at all. And overdoses of fertilizers may also have the same effect. The remedy, of course, is rotation of crops, an occasional season of fallow land, and the use of different mixtures in successive years.

With these cautions the following fertilizer mixtures have been found helpful. (For the meaning of the figures see Fertilizer Mixtures, above.) All of them should be used at the rate of about 2–3 lbs. per 100 sq. ft., or a cupful to each individual plant.

5–8–7. A widely used mixture for potatoes, for root crops, and for general purposes.

4–8–4. An all-round mixture, especially valuable for sweet corn and the vegetable garden.

4–12–4. A good general-purpose mixture for lawns, flower gardens, and the kitchen garden.

6–6–6. A special mixture found valuable for celery.

4–2–10. A special lettuce mixture.

---

* Special articles on the subjects indicated by an asterisk (*) will be found at the words so marked.

FERTILIZER RECOMMENDATIONS FOR GARDEN FLOWERS

Plants	Recommended Fertilizer	Amount of Application	Time of Application
Annuals	Manure, also superphosphate, or mixed fertilizer 4–12–4; 5–10–5 when strawy manure is used.	Manure: 4 bu. per 100 sq. ft. Superphosphate: 5 lbs per 100 sq. ft. 4–12–4; 5–10–5: 2 to 3 lbs. per 100 sq. ft.	Worked into top 5 inches of soil every second year.
	Inorganic nitrogen.	1 lb. per 100 sq. ft.	Applied just previous to time of flowering (two applications for types with long flowering period).
Biennials and Perennials	Prepare as for annuals; mixed fertilizer 4–12–4; 5–10–5.	4–12–4; 5–10–5: 2 or 3 lbs. per 100 sq. ft.	Applied each year after the first, in the spring. Second application in July or August for later blooming types.
Bulbs	Prepare as for annuals; peat is preferred to manure for organic matter.	Peat: 2 bushels per 100 sq. ft.	Soil should be prepared in spring previous to planting if manure is used.
Roses (climbers and hybrid perpetuals)	Manure.	5 bushels to 100 sq. ft. worked into the soil.	Before planting.
	Mixed fertilizer 4–12–4; 5–10–5.	4–12–4; 5–10–5: 2 to 3 lbs. per 100 sq. ft.	Apply when growth starts in the spring and again at flowering time.
	Manure.	5 bushels to 100 sq. ft.	Before planting.
Roses (hybrid teas and polyanthas)	Mixed fertilizer 4–12–4; 5–10–5.	4–12–4; 5–10–5: 2 or 3 lbs. per 100 sq. ft.	Apply when growth starts.
	Inorganic nitrogen in liquid form.	1 lb. to 10 gal. of water applied to 100 sq. ft. of soil.	At flowering time apply every two weeks from spring to August.

Some of the mixtures above would scarcely interest the ordinary home gardener, for they were made by specialists who had to make every fertilizer penny yield a profitable return. Two of the best all-round mixtures are ratios of 5–8–7 and 4–8–4 applied at the rate of 2–3 lbs. per 100 sq. ft., or a cupful to each individual plant.

Another important feature of fertilizers is the proper distribution of them. All commercial fertilizers contain a legally determined amount of "filler" (inert matter, usually sand), which is thoroughly mixed with the salts and helps to ensure their even distribution. But even with this filler, raw fertilizer should never be put directly at the roots, nor against germinating seed. It is better to rake or harrow in the fertilizer a day or two before planting, or else top-dress between the rows after the plants are up. For regular and even distribution the use of a fertilizer spreader is by far the best.

In quick-acting fertilizers like nitrate of soda, the only method should be top-dressing after the crop is up. Specific directions for the use of nitrate of soda will be found at the cultural notes on each crop.

The use of fertilizers does not offset good tillage nor will it produce crops if ordinary care is not used. Study the group of articles at Soil, Cultivation, Lime, and Acid and Alkali Soils. For the recent high-formula fertilizers used as starter solutions and in foliar feeding, see Foliar Feeding and Starter Solutions. The idea that radioactive fertilizers would be of any value has been completely disproved, after much testing by the U.S. Department of Agriculture.

FERULA (fer'you-la). A genus of 80 species of Eurasian and northern African herbs of the carrot family, only F. communis, the giant fennel, of any garden interest. It is a stout perennial plant 8–12 ft. high, grown occasionally for its handsome foliage and large clusters of small, yellow flowers. Leaves twice- or thrice-compound,* the basal sheaths very large, the ultimate leaflets fine and thread-like. Flowers small (for details see Umbelliferae), in umbels* which are grouped in a large, compound umbel,* the central umbel nearly stalkless, all the other umbels* in the cluster long-stalked, the latter mostly male flowers. Fruit flattened, about ½ in. long. Southern Eu. and northeastern Af. A striking plant of simple culture easily propagated by division. It flowers in the spring. (Ferula is perhaps from the Latin for ferule, a stick, in allusion to the tall stems.)

* Special articles on the subjects indicated by an asterisk (*) will be found at the words so marked.

ferulaefolia, -us, -um (fer-you-lee-fō′lee-a). With leaves like the giant fennel (*Ferula*).

FESCUE GRASS. *See* Festuca.

festalis, -e (fes-tal′is). Agreeable or gay.

festiva, -us, -um (fess-ty′va). Festive or gay.

FESTUCA (fess-too′ka). The fescue grasses comprise a genus of nearly 100 annual or perennial, usually tufted,* grasses mostly from the temperate regions, some of them found in pasture or lawn mixtures, and a few of moderate interest as ornamentals. They are generally small grasses, the leaves flat and typically grass-like, but in some with rolled or coiled leaves that thus appear very fine and thread-like.* Flowering cluster usually a narrow panicle,* the spikelets generally not awned.* Stamens* 1–3. (*Festuca* is an old Latin name for some grass.)

For meadows and pastures the leading fescue grasses are the tall fescue (*F. elatior*), the sheep's-fescue (*F. ovina*), and the red fescue (*F. rubra*).

duriuscula = *Festuca ovina duriuscula.*
elatior. Tall or meadow fescue. An upright perennial grass, the stems smooth and 2–4 ft. high. Leaves flat, grass-like, nearly 12 in. long, about ⅛ in. wide, a little rough. Flowering cluster (panicle*) 3–8 in. long, not much branched. Eu., but commonly naturalized nearly throughout N.A., and sometimes called *F. pratensis.* Common in meadow and pasture mixtures.
glauca = *Festuca ovina glauca.*
ovina. Sheep's fescue. A low grass, its many stems very fine and slender, tufted,* 8–20 in. high, producing no stolons.* Leaves rolled, thread-like, not over 6 in. long. Flowering cluster (panicle*) 2–6 in. long, often 1-sided. North temperate zone, and useful in dry places. Often entering poor lawns. The *var.* **duriuscula,** the hard fescue, has stiffish leaves; *var.* **glauca,** the blue fescue, has silvery-blue foliage; *var.* **capillata** has awned* spikelets and still narrower leaves. It is a good variety for shady places. *See* Lawns.
pratensis = *Festuca elatior.*
rubra. Red fescue. A perennial grass creeping by stolons,* the stems 8–30 in. high and reddish at the base. Leaves rolled, very narrow, somewhat finely hairy, shorter than the stems. Flowering cluster (panicle*) 2–5 in. long, green, reddish, or bluish-green. North temperate zone, and found mostly in meadows.
tenuifolia = *Festuca ovina capillata.*

FETERITA = *Sorghum vulgare caudatum.*

FETID. Evil-smelling, as are some flowers of the arum family and a few other plants.

FETID HOREHOUND = *Ballota nigra.*

FETTER-BUSH = *Leucothoë catesbaei* and *Lyonia lucida.*

FEVERFEW = *Chrysanthemum Parthe-ium.*

FEVER-TWIG = *Celastrus scandens.*

FEVERWORT. *See* Triosteum and Eu-patorium perfoliatum.

FIBER PLANTS. Those that produce fibers in the leaf, stem, fruit, etc. Common examples are cotton, jute, abaca, sisal, flax, and kapok.

ficifolia, -us, -um (fy-si-fō′li-a). With fig-like leaves.

FICUS (fy′kus). A huge genus (over 600 species) of chiefly tropical trees, shrubs, or vines of the family Moraceae, one of which is the common fig, but including also many ornamentals like the banyan and the much-domesticated rubber-plant. Some of them are epiphytes* at first, some are strangling trees in the tropics, and many, like the banyan, produce numerous aerial roots, whip-like at first, but ultimately reaching the ground and becoming trunk-like in age. Nearly all have a milky juice. Leaves alternate.* Flowers and fruits (achenes*) minute, borne on the inside face of a closed, fleshy receptacle (syncarp), which is edible in the common fig, but in few others. *See* Fig. (*Ficus* is classical Latin for the fig.)

The ornamental figs are hardy only in zones* 8 and 9, but are popular in Calif. and Fla., where they grow in a variety of soils. Two species are widely grown as greenhouse plants, *F. lyrata* and *F. elastica,* and the latter, the household rubber-plant, is one of the most widely known tender plants grown in the U.S. While it will do best in a warm, moist greenhouse, it will stand a surprising amount of abuse. Do not over-water it during the winter, and preferably plunge* it outdoors, in the shade, during warm weather. It is easily propagated by air layering (*see* Layering). Household plants that become leggy may be shortened, and a new crop of young plants obtained by air layering the ends of the shoots. "Fruits," as used below, means the whole syncarp (*see* Fig).

aurea. A banyan-like tree, well-suited to seashore planting in sub-tropical regions (zones* 8 and 9). While at first an epiphyte,* it ultimately becomes a tree up to 50 ft. high. Leaves oblongish, narrowed both ends. Fruit nearly stalkless, yellow, about ⅓ in. in diameter. Southern Fla.
benghalensis. Banyan. A widely spreading tree with many aerial roots that ultimately become additional trunks (one such tree in India covers nearly an acre). Leaves broadly oval, 4–8 in. long. Fruit red, about ½ in. long, borne in pairs. India.
benjamina. Java fig. Java willow. A large, perfectly smooth tree with spreading and drooping branches. Leaves ovalish or oblong, 2–4 in. long, the tip tapering, without marginal teeth and rather leathery. Fruit nearly round, about ½ in. in diameter. Indo-Malaya. A good street tree, but only in frostless regions.
Carica. The common fig. An irregularly branching tree, usually not over 25 ft. high. Leaves deeply 3–5-lobed, rough above, hairy beneath. Fruit the edible fig. Mediterranean region. For cult. *see* Fig.
elastica. The common household rubber-plant, naturally a large tree, but as usually grown a pot plant. Leaves oblong-elliptic, 6–11 in. long, green and glossy. Fruit yellowish, ½ in. long. Malaya. The *var.* **variegata** has white-blotched leaves. It was once an important source of rubber and still yields india rubber. For the true rubber tree *see* Hevea.

---

* Special articles on the subjects indicated by an asterisk (*) will be found at the words so marked.

lyrata. A medium-sized tree in the wild, but usually a pot plant as cult., and much grown by florists for its large, fiddle-shaped, lasting leaves which are often 15 in. long, the veins white-streaked. Fruit nearly 2 in. in diameter. Sometimes sold as *F. pandurata*.

macrophylia. Moreton Bay fig. A large Australian tree, very popular in Calif. It has gray bark, bulging roots and broadly oblong leaves, nearly 10 in. long and brownish underneath. Fruit stalked, purplish but white-spotted, about 1 in. in diameter.

nitida = *Ficus retusa.*

pandurata = *Ficus lyrata.*

pumila. Climbing or creeping fig. A popular greenhouse vine that grows flat against walls, except for the fruiting branches. Leaves very numerous, oval-heart-shaped, about ¾ in. long, except on the fruiting branches where 2–4 in. long. Fruit pear-shaped, yellowish, about 2 in. long. Tropical As. and Aust. A widely grown plant both in the greenhouse and outdoors in the South (*see* VINES). Long, but incorrectly, known as *F. repens.*

religiosa. Peepul; also called bo-tree. A fig sacred to many millions in India, and sometimes planted in Fla. and Calif. Leaves roundish or ovalish, 4–6 in. long, the tailed tip 2–3 in. long. Fruit purplish, about ½ in. long. India.

repens = *Ficus pumila.*

retusa. A popular Indo-Malayan tree, much planted in the warmer parts of Fla. Leaves broadly ovalish, 2–4 in. long. Fruit yellowish-red, about ¼ in. long. Sometimes offered as *F. nitida.*

Ficus-indica, -us, -um (fy-kus-in'di-ka). The Indian fig. *See* OPUNTIA.

FIDDLENECK = *Phacelia tanacetifolia.* The term is also applied to the young, coiled growth of many ferns.

FIELD BALM = *Glecoma hederacea. See also* Ground Ivy in the list at WEEDS.

FIELD BINDWEED = *Convolvulus arvensis. See* list at WEEDS.

FIELD CHICKWEED = *Cerastium arvense.*

FIELD LARKSPUR = *Delphinium Consolida.*

FIELD MINT = *Mentha arvensis. See* MINT.

FIELD PEA = *Pisum sativum arvense. See* PEA.

FIELD SALAD = *Valerianella Locusta olitoria.*

FIELD SCORPION GRASS = *Myosotis arvensis. See* FORGET-ME-NOT.

FIESTA FLOWER = *Nemophila aurita.*

FIG (*Ficus Carica*). What we call the "fruit" of an ordinary fig is a syncarp (a fleshy receptacle), and without an understanding of its structure and function, fig culture is next to impossible. Upon the inside of the "fruit," which in most varieties never opens, are scores of minute male and female flowers which thus bloom and mature wholly in the dark interior. There is, however, in most varieties a tiny terminal pore or opening, which is sometimes a clear passageway and in other varieties a passage-

way well blocked, or apparently so blocked, by a series of minute, overlapping scales. The female flowers ultimately develop into the "seeds" so familiar in the commercial fig, but these "seeds" are actually small fruits (achenes*) which in some varieties can only develop after pollination.* This looks like an impossible process, and would be quite so were not a pollen-coated insect able to force its way through the terminal pore of the "fruit" and accomplish this. Such insects are bred for the purpose in Calif. and carry into the immature fruit a load of pollen from another kind of fig. This fertilizes the desired kind and mature fruits result from the process. This is known as caprification from the fact that the insects come pollen-laden from the caprifig, a variety otherwise useless, but grown for the fact that it produces much pollen and is a suitable temporary home for the insects that carry it.

A branch of the common fig with foliage and "fruit." In the upper left-hand corner a cross-section of the receptacle ("fruit") showing the true fruits inside. See text for explanation of fruit structure and caprification.

In the notes below, the varieties that will set "fruit" only by aid of caprification are marked with a dagger (†), and it is useless to grow such without providing a supply of caprifigs. The others produce edible, but of course sterile, fruits without caprification.

The tree will stand occasional cold weather, and by pruning, the branches may be kept low enough to be bent down and covered with earth during the winter, up to the limits of zone* 5 or even farther north. But the preferred climatic localities for fig culture are southern Calif. and the Gulf Coast of Tex. where all the commercial production is centered. Soils vary from

---

* Special articles on the subjects indicated by an asterisk (*) will be found at the words so marked.

open, sandy ones in Calif. to the much heavier and blacker soils of the Tex. fig region. Summer heat and freedom from long-continued winter cold are more important than soil conditions.

VARIETIES. In Calif. the figs of the Smyrna type are represented by †Calimyrna, †Kassaba, and †Bardajie, mostly used for drying figs. Other valuable sorts are Adriatic and Kadota. The Mission, sometimes called Black Mission, is a black fig, popular only for drying. †Turkey is grown chiefly for fresh figs. One of the most popular varieties is Magnolia, the only sort grown in Tex. and usually successful without caprification. For the home orchard, Osborn's Prolific, Ronde Noire, and White Genoa are preferred, at least in Calif. The leading varieties of caprifigs, grown only as a source of pollen and a breeding place for the pollen-carrying insect, are Roeding No. 1, Milco, Roeding No. 3, and Stanford. The caprifigs are not interplanted with the regular sorts but are kept separate, and the fruits picked and carried to the vicinity of the trees to be pollinated. Usually the insects will complete their work within 24 hours. But care must be taken to see that the caprifigs are plentifully supplied with pollen before the regular kinds are exposed to the insect visitors. Sterility will otherwise be the only result of all the trouble.

Figs of a sort can, of course, be grown without the above somewhat elaborate precautions. They often are, and occasional fig trees may be found as far north as New York or Mich. where, however, they need winter protection. Some small trees are pulled down and covered with soil or bagging for the winter. They are perfectly hardy in southern Md. on the Eastern Shore. They are interesting curiosities more than anything else, because successful fig production is chiefly based upon summer heat and caprification. The best method of propagation is by cuttings which root easily.

INSECT PESTS. Root-knot nematodes attack roots. Starting with certified nematode-free plants is best. Fig scale is the most serious pest. Control it with 3% dormant oil sprays, or oil plus pesticide #21 (see SPRAYS AND DUSTS). Two per cent light summer oil in May is effective. Pesticide #14 or ovex sprays will control red spiders. Rust mite can also be controlled by delayed dormant oil sprays.

DISEASES. For the various canker* diseases which attack fig, the only recommendation is pruning out diseased branches, making the cut at least 6 in. below the cankered area.

Rust,* leafspots, and anthracnose* should be controlled with pesticide #5 or #11 (see SPRAYS AND DUSTS) applied at 10-day intervals, starting when disease first becomes apparent.

FIG FAMILY = Moraceae.

FIG-MARIGOLD. See MESEMBRYAN-THEMUM.

FIGWORT. See SCROPHULARIA.

FIGWORT FAMLY. A huge aggregation of herbs, shrubs, and trees from all over the world. The best-known garden plants are snapdragon, mullein, foxglove, and the calceolarias, but the veronicas of Australia are favorite greenhouse plants. For a complete list of the garden genera see SCROPHULARIA-CEAE.

FIJI FAN PALM = *Pritchardia pacifica*.

FILAMENT. The slender, shank-like, or thread-like part of a stamen which supports the anther.*

filamentosa, -us, -um (fill-a-men-tō'sa). Thread-like.

FILAREE = *Erodium cicutarium*.

FILBERT = *Corylus maxima*. See HAZEL.

filicaulis, -e (fill-i-caw'lis). With thread-like stems.

filicifolia, -us, -um (fil-iss-i-fō'li-a). Fern-leaved.

filifera, -us, -um (fy-liff'e-ra). Bearing threads.

filiformis, -e (fill-i-for'mis). Filiform; *i.e.,* thread-like.

FILIPENDULA (fill-i-pen'dew-la). A genus of free-flowering herbs of the rose family, all from the north temperate zone, half of the ten species grown for ornament in the border and sometimes sold as spirea. They have alternate,* compound* leaves, the leaflets alternate, arranged feather-fashion with an odd one at the end which is sometimes lobed. Flowers numerous in large terminal clusters (panicles* or corymbs*), the individual flowers small and usually with 5 petals. Stamens* numerous. Fruit a collection of small, capsule*-like but non-splitting bodies. (*Filipendula* is from the Latin for hanging thread, in allusion to the root-tubers of some species hanging together by threads.)

All the species below are of easy culture in any ordinary garden soil and may be propagated by division of the clumps in early spring.

camtschatica. A stout herb 5–8 ft. high. Terminal leaflet oval or heart-shaped, more or less 3–5-lobed, the other leaflets often lacking. Flowers white. Northeastern As. Sometimes sold as *Spiraea camtschatica*.

hexapetala. Dropwort. A perennial herb 2–3 ft. high, the rootstocks tuberous. Leaves finely dissected and fern-like, the leaflets numerous and much cut. Flowers white. Eurasia. Sometimes offered as *Spiraea filipendula*. The *var.* flore-pleno has double flowers.

palmata = *Filipendula purpurea*.

purpurea. A perennial herb 2–4 ft. high. Terminal leaflet* large, 5–7-lobed, the other leaflets much smaller and unlobed or wanting. Flowers pinkish-purple. Jap. The *var.* alba has white flowers and the *var.* elegans has white flowers with red stamens.*

rubra. Queen-of-the-prairie. A stout but graceful perennial herb 4–7 ft. high. Terminal leaflet* large, 7–9-lobed, and the other leaflets also lobed. Flowers magenta-pink. Eastern U.S. The *var.* venusta has deep pink flowers.

Ulmaria. Queen-of-the-meadow. A feathery, beautiful herb 3–5 ft. high. Terminal leaflet* 3–5-lobed, the other leaflets smaller, toothed,

---

* Special articles on the subjects indicated by an asterisk (*) will be found at the words so marked.

and white-felty beneath. Flowers white. North temperate zone, mostly in moist places. Sometimes offered as *Spiraea Ulmaria*. The *var.* flore-pleno has double flowers.

filipendulina, -us, -um (fill-i-pen-dew-ly'na). Like the genus *Filipendula* (which see).

Filix-femina (fy-licks-fem'i-na). The lady fern. See ATHYRIUM.

Filix-mas (fy-licks-mas'). The male fern. See DRYOPTERIS.

FILLER. Inert matter (often sand) used in fertilizers to ensure an even distribution of their constituents. See FERTILIZERS.

FILMY FERN. Any extremely delicate, thin-leaved fern of the family Hymenophyllaceae, none of which are likely to be in cult. They are common as tree-perching ferns in tropical rain-forests.

fimbriata, -us, -um (fim-bri-ā'ta). Fimbriate; *i.e.,* fringed.

fimbriatula, -us, -um (fim-bri-at'you-la). Somewhat fringed.

FINES HERBES. See Cooking with Herbs at HERB GARDENING.

FINGER-FASHION. Arranged as are the fingers on the hand; *i.e.,* all arising from approximately the same point. The technical term is palmate (which see). *See also* FEATHER-FASHION and PINNATE.

FINGER-FLOWER = *Digitalis purpurea.* See FOXGLOVE.

FINGER-GRASS. See CRAB GRASS, which is the more usual name for this weed.

FINGER-LIME = *Microcitrus australasica.*

FINNOCHIO = *Foeniculum vulgare dulce.* See FENNEL.

FIORIN = *Agrostis stolonifera.*

FIR. Magnificent evergreen trees comprising perhaps 40 species of the genus Abies (ah'bee-āz); also ā'bees) of the family Pinaceae, all from the north temperate zone, and many of them among our finest cultivated evergreens. They are generally of pyramidal habit, with whorls[*] of graceful branches. Leaves narrow, line-like, wholly without marginal teeth, stalkless and persistent when dry (the spruces shed their leaves when dry), flattened, but usually grooved beneath and with 2 pale whitish bands. They are often arranged as though 2-ranked, the spray of foliage hence flattened. Cones erect (hanging in the spruces), the cone-scales never prickle-tipped. (*Abies* is the classical Latin name of the fir.)

For culture *see* below; *see also* EVERGREENS.

A. alba. Silver fir. A tree up to 150 ft., the bark grayish. Leaves just over 1 in. long, slightly notched at the tip. Cones reddish-brown, 3–5 in. long. Eu. Hardy from zone[*] 4 southward, but *see* notes below. Sometimes offered as *A. pectinata* and as *A. nobilis,* although the latter name, as here used, belongs to the plant here entered as *A. nobilis.* The *var.* pyramidalis, the sentinel fir, has upright branches and is hence of more columnar habit.

A. amabilis. Cascade fir. A tree up to 200 ft., with silvery-white bark. Leaves nearly 1 in. long, notched at the tip. Cones purplish, nearly 6 in. long. British Columbia to Ore. *See* notes below for hardiness.

A. arizonica. Arizona or cork fir. A tree resembling *A. lasiocarpa* and thought by some to be only a variety of it; differing in having silvery bark and leaves whiter on the under side. Ariz. and N. Mex.

A. balsamea. Balsam fir; the only species native in the northeastern states. It is most unsatisfactory as a cult. tree, being difficult and sometimes impossible to establish. Not over 70 ft. high, usually less. Leaves about ¾ in. long. Cones 2–2½ in. long, violet-purple. Labrador to the mountains of W. Va. west to Iowa. Our chief and best Christmas tree.

A. cephalonica. Greek fir. A tree up to 90 ft., the bark grayish-brown. Leaves about 1 in. long, sharp-pointed. Cones brownish, nearly 7 in. long. Greece. Hardy from zone[*] 4 southward.

A. cilicica. Cilician fir. A handsome tree up to 90 ft., the bark ashy-gray. Leaves about 1 in. long, slightly notched at the tip. Cones reddish-brown, 7–9 in. long. Asia Minor and Syria. Hardy from zone[*] 3 southward. One of the largest and oldest specimens in the U.S. was until recently, at Watermill, L.I.

A. concolor. White or Colorado fir. One of the most satisfactory of the cult. firs and widely planted (*see* below). It is a grayish-barked tree up to 125 ft. Leaves nearly 2 in. long, not notched. Cones 3–5 in. long, greenish-purple. Colo. to N. Mex. and northern Mex. There are several hort. varieties with variously colored young foliage. It is the best fir for city planting.

A. fraseri. A southern representative of the common balsam fir (*A. balsamea*), and a much more satisfactory cult. tree. It differs only in technical characters from *A. balsamea.* Mountains of N. Car., W. Va. and Tenn. Hardy up to zone[*] 3.

A. grandis. Giant fir. A magnificent tree up to 300 ft. high, much less as cult. Leaves nearly 2½ in. long, rounded and notched at the tip. Cones greenish, 3–4 in. long. Vancouver to northern Calif., east to Mont. Not hardy in the East (*see* below).

A. homolepis. Nikko fir. An extremely valuable Japanese tree, widely and deservedly planted, rarely over 75 ft. high. Leaves about 1 in. long. Cones 2–4 in. long, purplish. Hardy from zone[*] 3 southward. *See* below.

A. lasiocarpa. Rocky Mountain fir. A fine fir, up to 90 ft. high, but not suited to the eastern states. Leaves nearly 1½ in. long, not notched. Cones purplish, 3–4 in. long. Alaska to the Rocky Mountains. For hardiness *see* below. *See also* A. ARIZONICA.

A. nobilis. A magnificent fir of the forests of Wash., Ore., and northern Calif. unsuited to the East in its typical form which may reach 250 ft. The *var.* glauca, usually a semi-dwarf form, with beautiful bluish-green leaves 1–1½ in. long, is hardy in the East up to zone[*] 3 and is a valuable hort. fir. Cones (rarely produced in the East) 6–9 in. long, purplish-brown.

A. nordmanniana. Nordmann fir. A popular and very widely planted evergreen, rarely over 125 ft. high. Leaves 1–1½ in. long, rounded and notched at the tip. Cones reddish-brown, 4–6 in. long. Asia Minor, Caucasus and Greece. Hardy from zone[*] 3 southward.

A. pectinata = *Abies alba.*

---

[*] Special articles on the subjects indicated by an asterisk ([*]) will be found at the words so marked.

A. Pinsapo. Spanish fir. An evergreen tree 40–75 ft. high. Leaves spreading, about ¾ in. long, gray-green, with pale bands on the under side. Cones about 4½ in. long, and about 2 in. thick, brownish-purple. Spain. Hardy from zone* 5 southward.

A. procera. Thought by some to be the correct name for the tree here maintained as *Abies nobilis.*

A. veitchi. A valuable fir, and one of the most easily cult., rarely over 70 ft., but handsome, especially when young. Leaves about 1 in. long, notched at the tip. Cones bluish-purple, 1½–2½ in. long. Jap. Hardy from zone* 2 southward.

Fir Culture

The fir is one of our most valuable economic trees and, for ornamental work, leaves little to be desired. Unfortunately, it does not enjoy a wide distribution, as its dislike for smoke or dust and hot, dry climates limits its successful cultivation mostly to the Pacific Coast and Atlantic seaboard where, even in these localities, it must be kept away from industrial centers if a healthy specimen is desired. To many the fir is looked upon as a sort of spruce and is, in fact, sometimes known by that name. Differentiation between the two is quite simple (*see* above).

The firs are without doubt the most particular of all of the conifers as regards proper conditions for good growth. Practically all members of the group are inhabitants of high altitudes and, in some instances, will not succeed on low land. *Abies lasiocarpa,* from the Rocky Mountains, is rarely a success in the East. Their great need of good air and light is clearly evidenced by the fact that most of the species in cultivation lose their lower branches and become scrawny after they reach the two-score mark. To a large extent this condition is impossible of cure with many of the species, but it can be held off for a considerable time if the tree is given full advantage of sun and light. This does not mean undue exposure to dry winds or scorching sun, for no conifer is more sensitive to drought than the fir.

Probably the best combination for the successful cultivation of this group is a planting on a north slope with surrounding specimens of other conifers set sufficiently close to break the wind without hindering a free circulation of air or light. In like manner does the fir demand exactness in the condition of the soil. Fertility is not paramount and, while many species will grow on poor land, good drainage without dryness is an absolute necessity. Fertility will, of course, aid greatly and may be accomplished by the application of well-rotted manure spaded in about the base of the tree every few years.

For general planting in the temperate parts of this country, several species recommend themselves highly. *Abies concolor,* from the Rocky Mountains, will thrive in locations too difficult for any other species. *Abies homolepis* and *A. veitchi* from Japan are among the finest of our exotic trees and appear hardy in practically all parts of the country. *Abies*

nordmanniana and *cilicica,* from the Caucasus and Asia Minor, are excellent trees for the Middle Atlantic states. The Pacific Coast species, *Abies amabilis* and *grandis,* do not thrive in the East. Unlike most of the conifers, the fir is not represented by a great number of varieties or forms, although one of our western species is best known by a semi-dwarf, bluish-leaved form which is indeed beautiful. Known as *Abies nobilis glauca,* it is the one representative of the species which thrives in the East.

Transplanting of the fir follows the usual method of most conifers. The roots must not be permitted to dry out and, hence, are moved with a ball of earth. This operation is greatly facilitated by systematic root pruning for one or two seasons previous to moving for the purpose of developing a large number of fibrous roots within a small area. Pruning the fir is seldom necessary except for the removal of dying branches near the base and the removal of secondary leaders. In some cases medium-sized specimens grow too fast and do not develop their lateral branches properly. This condition, which creates a bare, open appearance, may be easily corrected by pinching out the terminal buds on the longer branches, thus forcing lateral growth. Do not remove the buds on the main leader.

As most of the firs are represented by species, propagation from seed is most common. The seed is sown in late spring and carefully shaded during the first two years. Seedling firs are very sensitive to strong sun and must be well protected. Forms of the species are veneer-grafted in the greenhouse during Jan. and the plants set out in propagating frames in late spring. — D. W. For the Douglas fir *see* Pseudotsuga.

INSECT PESTS. Control disfiguring aphids with pesticide #21 (*see* Sprays and Dusts). Sawfly larvae yield to pesticide #21 or arsenicals. Pesticide #17 controls budworm, which feeds on bud in spring, but may bring on red spider mite problems. Use pesticide #14 for mites.

DISEASES. The various species of fir tree are relatively free from serious diseases. Occasionally a rust* fungus may cause pustules on the needles or needle-cast* may cause some defoliation. There is no control for these troubles. The greatest problems with fir are brought about by trying to grow them too far south of their natural habitat.

FIR BARK. The chopped-up bark of the Douglas fir, now largely replacing *Osmunda* fiber in potting orchids.

FIREBLIGHT. A bacterial disease of apple, pear, firethorn, hawthorn, and related plants. The disease causes sudden browning and death of small branches or entire limbs of trees of susceptible varieties. The bacteria live through the winter in cankers* in diseased trees. In the spring, bees and other insects visit the canker areas and then go to blossoms, carrying the bacteria which then infect the blossoms. Within a few weeks the entire branch may die.

---

* Special articles on the subjects indicated by an asterisk (*) will be found at the words so marked.

The disease cannot be controlled with the common fungicides. In some states the agricultural experiment stations have had success in controlling the disease by using some of the antibiotic* materials such as streptomycin. At least three applications of one of these antibiotics are usually necessary during the blossoming period. Contact your state agricultural experiment station for local recommendations. — S. H. D.

FIREBUSH = *Kochia scoparia* and *Embothrium coccineum.*

FIRE-LILY = *Xerophyllum tenax.*

FIRE-PINK = *Silene virginica.*

FIRE-PLANT. See POINSETTIA.

FIRE-THORN. See PYRACANTHA.

FIREWEED = *Epilobium angustifolium.*

FIR FAMILY = Pinaceae.

FIRMIANA (fir-mi-ā′na). Ornamental, Asiatic trees, comprising about 10 species of the family Sterculiaceae, **F. simplex,** the Chinese parasol tree or phoenix-tree, also called Japanese varnish tree, being the only cult. species. It is planted for ornament from zone* 7 southward and is a round-headed tree up to 40 ft. Leaves alternate,* nearly round or heart-shaped, almost 12 in. wide, and split into 3–5 sharp-pointed lobes. Flowers small, greenish-white, usually in branched clusters (for structure see STERCULIACEAE). Fruit a collection of follicles,* each of which splits into a leaf-like expansion to which cling the still unripened seeds. A handsome, green-barked tree, popular in Fla. and Calif. because of its showy foliage and peculiar fruits. It is not particular as to soil. (Named for Karl Joseph von Firmian, governor of Lombardy.)

FISH-BLANKETS = *Ceratophyllum demersum.*

FISHBONE THISTLE = *Cirsium diacantha.*

FISH GERANIUM = *Pelargonium hortorum.*

FISH-GRASS = *Cabomba caroliniana.*

FISHHOOK CACTUS = *Ferocactus wislizeni* and *Ancistrocactus scheeri.*

FISH-TAIL PALM. See CARYOTA.

fissurata, -us, -um (fiss-your-ray′ta). Cleft, as the fissure in a cliff.

fistula. See FISTULOSA.

fistulosa, -us, -um (fist-you-lō′sa). Fistulose; *i.e.,* cylindrical and hollow, as is a reed or pipe (fistula).

FITTONIA (fit-toe′ni-a). Tropical American foliage plants of the family Acanthaceae, **F. verschaffelti,** which may be the only species, widely grown in the greenhouse for its handsome leaves. It is a low herb with creeping, shaggy or hairy stems. Leaves opposite,* without marginal teeth, ovalish, 3–4 in. long, more or less heart-shaped at the base, dark green above, but red-veined beneath. Flowers small, yellow, not showy, in scaly spikes*

(for details *see* ACANTHACEAE). Fruit a long-stalked capsule.* The *var.* **argyroneura** has white-veined leaves. These plants are of the easiest culture in a warm (60°–75°), moist greenhouse. They need plenty of water and root so easily from cuttings that the plants often become established from broken bits that root under the greenhouse bench. Use potting mixture* 3. (Named for Elizabeth and Sarah Fitton who wrote "Conversations on Botany.")

FITZROYA (fitz-roy′ya). A single, Chilean, evergreen tree, or as cult., usually shrubby, belonging to the pine family, and grown outdoors only from zone* 7 southward. The only species, **F. cupressoides,** the alerce, is sometimes called *F. patagonica* and is related to the arborvitae and the genus *Chamaecyparis.* It has deeply furrowed, reddish bark and small, usually overlapping leaves about ⅛ in. long, dark green above, keeled, and with 2 white lines beneath. Cones (*see* PINACEAE) nearly globe-shaped, about ⅓ in. in diameter, the cone-scales with a prominent but blunt projection (umbonate). Occasional specimens are found north of zone* 7, but as cult. the plant is slow-growing and inclined to be straggly. (Named for Captain R. Fitzroy of the British navy.)

FIVE-SPOT = *Nemophila maculata.*

flabellata, -us, -um (fla-bel-lay′ta). Flabellate; *i.e.,* having fan-like parts.

flabellifer (fla-bell′i-fer). Fan-shaped.

flabelliformis, -e (fla-bel-li-for′mis). Fan-shaped.

flaccida, -us, -um (fla′sid-a). Flabby.

FLACOURTIA (fla-koor′ti-a). Old World tropical, often spiny shrubs or trees of the family Flacourtiaceae, comprising perhaps 15 species, only **F. indica,** a secondary fruit tree, of any garden interest. It is grown in Fla. and Calif. (zones* 8 and 9) as the ramontchi, governor's-plum, or Batoko plum, and is sometimes called *F. ramontchi.* Not over 25 ft. high and often shrubby. Leaves alternate,* ovalish or elliptic, 2–3 in. long, the teeth rounded. Flowers unisexual,* small, yellowish, without petals, and mostly in small clusters (*see* FLACOURTIACEAE). Fruit fleshy, nearly globe-shaped, about ¾ in. in diameter, dark red, somewhat resembling a plum. Commonly grown in Fla., but care must be taken to grow several plants together as the plant is dioecious* and solitary specimens will not fruit. Easily propagated by seeds. Native of Madagascar and southern As. (Named for Etienne de Flacourt, once a governor of Madagascar.)

FLACOURTIACEAE (fla-koor-ti-ā′see-ee). The Indian plum family is wholly composed of tropical shrubs and trees in about 70 genera and perhaps 500 species. Of these only *Azara, Dovyalis, Flacourtia,* and *Berberidopsis* are of garden interest, chiefly because the edible kei-apple and Indian plum are derived from two of them.

---

* Special articles on the subjects indicated by an asterisk (*) will be found at the words so marked.

Leaves (in ours) alternate.* Flowers regular,* without petals in all the garden genera, but the sepals colored like petals, or greenish in *Azara*, not showy in any of the cult. genera. Fruit fleshy and edible in *Flacourtia* and *Dovyalis*, a showy but inedible berry in *Azara*. *Berberidopsis* and *Xylosma* are cult. for ornament, outdoors in relatively frost-free regions, while *Idesia* is hardy from zone* 4 southward. *Flacourtia* and *Dovyalis* can be grown outdoors only in zones* 8 and 9.

Technical flower characters: Flowers dioecious* in *Dovyalis*; mostly hermaphrodite* in the other genera. Sepals 4 or more, their edges overlapping. Petals none in cult. genera. Stamens many, some often sterile. Ovary superior* or essentially so, 1-celled.

fladnizensis, -e (flad-ni-zen'sis). From Fladungen in northwestern Bavaria.

FLAG. Many plants are called flag, or with various combinations, blue flag, yellow flag, etc. For those in this book *see* CAT-TAIL, IRIS, SCHIZOSTYLIS, ACORUS.

flagellaris, -e (fla-jell-ar'is). Whip-like.

flagelliformis, -e (fla-jell-i-for'mis). Whip-shaped.

FLAKE. See CARNATION.

FLAMBOYANT = *Delonix regia.*

FLAME AZALEA = *Azalea calendulacea.*

FLAME FLOWER. See KNIPHOFIA.

FLAME-OF-THE-FOREST = *Delonix regia.*

FLAME-OF-THE-WOODS = *Ixora coccinea.*

FLAME-TREE = *Brachychiton acerifolium.*

FLAME-VINE = *Pyrostegia ignea.*

FLAMINGO-FLOWER = *Anthurium scherzerianum.*

flammea, -us, -um (flăm'ee-a). Flame-colored or flame-like.

Flammula (flăm'you-la). A pre-Linnaean* name for *Clematis Flammula*, signifying a little flame.

FLANNEL-BUSH = *Fremontia californica.*

FLANNEL-LEAF = *Verbascum Thapsus.*

FLAT PALM = *Howea forsteriana.*

FLAT-TOPS = *Eriogonum fasciculatum.*

flava, -us, -um (flay'va). Yellow.

flavescens (flay-ves'zens). Yellowish.

flavicoma, -us, -um (flay-vick'o-ma). Yellow-haired.

flaviramea, -us, -um (flay-vi-ray'me-a). Yellow-branched.

flavissima, -us, -um (flah-viss'i-ma). Very yellow.

FLAVOR. The distinctive flavor of most fruits is instantly identified but impossible to define. It is the result of concentration of what the botanists call cell-sap. No definite rules can be given for increasing that concentration, except the obvious one that, as fruit is maturing, the plant's water supply is best reduced. Much fruit naturally ripens toward the end of summer, and Nature takes care of this reduction of water supply by a usually diminished rainfall. It is this that makes non-irrigated fruits, picked when ripe, of such fine flavor.

In irrigated trees the reduction of water as the fruit is ripening is imperative. Again, no rule can be given because varieties and soils and sunshine vary so much. But overwatering during this ripening period may well result in mealy or watery fruit, while a reduction of water would nearly always allow the proper concentration of cell-sap and a fine flavor.

flavovirens (flay-vo-vy'renz). Yellowish-green.

FLAX. Common flax (*Linum usitatissimum*) is raised as a farm crop in this country chiefly for the oil expressed from the seeds (linseed or flaxseed oil). The fiber of the stem, from which linen is made, does not attain the perfection here that it does abroad; consequently, flax-growing for linen production does not amount to much in the U.S. For several other sorts of flax, grown only for ornament, *see* LINUM. For New Zealand flax, *see* PHORMIUM TENAX.

FLAX FAMILY = Linaceae.

FLAX LILY = *Phormium tenax.*

FLEABANE. See ERIGERON.

FLEECE-VINE = *Polygonum auberti.*

flexilis, -e (flecks'il-is). Pliant or flexible.

flexuosa, -us, -um (flecks-you-ō'sa). Flexuose; *i.e.*, more or less tortuous or zigzag; usually applied to stems.

FLINT CORN = *Zea Mays indurata.* See CORN.

FLOATING ARUM = *Orontium aquaticum.*

FLOATING FERN. See CERATOPTERIS.

FLOATING HEART = *Nymphoides cordatum.*

floccosa, -us, -um (flock-kō'sa). Woolly.

FLOCCULATE. The joining of fine particles of clay or silt into larger ones; often the result of liming or the use of soil conditioners. See LIME.

FLOPPERS = *Bryophyllum pinnatum.*

FLORAL EMBLEMS. See STATE FLOWERS; also NATIONAL FLOWERS.

FLORAL FIRECRACKER = *Brevoortia Ida-Maia.*

FLORA'S-PAINTBRUSH = *Emilia sagittata.*

FLORENCE FENNEL = *Foeniculum vulgare dulce.* See FENNEL.

florentina, -us, -um (flo-ren-tee'na). From or near Florence, Italy.

flore-pleno (floor-re-plee'no). Double-flowered; often abbreviated Fl. Pl.

FLORET. One of the individual, and usually small flowers, that comprise the flower head* in plants of the Compositae (which

---

* Special articles on the subjects indicated by an asterisk (*) will be found at the words so marked.

see). Also, but less correctly, any small flower in a dense cluster of them.

floribunda, -us, -um (floor-i-bun'da). Blooming freely; floriferous.

FLORICULTURE. Strictly speaking, the raising of flowers, as distinguished from general horticulture (which see). By extension, and now quite generally, *floriculture* has come to mean any branch of horticulture that has to do with plants grown chiefly for ornament, whether trees, shrubs, or herbs. In this broad sense floriculture is synonymous with ornamental horticulture.

florida, -us, -um (flo'ri-da). Freely flowering.

FLORIDA. The state flower is the orange blossom, the state tree the cabbage palmetto. The state lies wholly in zones* 7, 8, and 9.

SOILS. Surface soils are mostly sandy, having been derived from unconsolidated marine sands. Some small areas are of limestone origin, while others have developed as organic soils in lakes and marshes. The Norfolk soils, comprising the most extensive uplands, and closely related series, together with the various hammock lands, are adapted to a wide range of truck, fruit, and farm crops. Most of the grassy flatwoods and marl areas, when drained, are good truck and farm lands. The organic soils, of which the Everglades of approximately 5,000,000 acres is the largest uniform body, consist of peat and muck and usually are quite fertile when drained. Swamps, savannahs and river flood plains are rarely cropped.

The production centers for vegetables are localized in such places as are particularly adapted for the production of particular crops. Thus, Hastings is the center of an area in which potatoes are produced; Sanford of a region in which celery is the principal crop, although lettuce, endive, and peppers are also shipped; Sarasota, on the west coast, is another important celery-production center. Manatee County, also on the west coast, produces a number of vegetable crops, the most important being tomatoes, lettuce, peppers, and celery. Alachua County is the center of an area for watermelons, spring cucumbers, beans, cabbage, and potatoes. Marion County, located directly south of Alachua, produces watermelons, tomatoes, green beans, lettuce, and cabbage. Plant City, in Hillsborough County, is the strawberry center of Florida, the Starke–Lawtey area producing in lesser quantity. Tomatoes, peppers, and green beans are also raised in this area. Leesburg, in Lake County, is the center of the earliest watermelon-producing area within the United States.

In the southernmost part of the state there are three important regions. The coastal areas of Palm Beach, Broward, and other adjoining counties produce large quantities of tomatoes, peppers, green beans, and eggplant. The production region known as the Everglades is situated on the southeastern shores of Lake Okeechobee. Green beans have been the most important crop in this area. Large quantities of green peas, tomatoes, potatoes, and cabbage also are grown. In coastal glades of Dade County potatoes and tomatoes are the principal crops, with an increasing amount of miscellaneous crops, as rhubarb, Chinese cabbage, broccoli, and cauliflower, being produced.

A great variety of fruits can be grown in Florida, the kinds depending on the climatic zone. Citrus fruits can be grown throughout the state, but are very limited in kind in the northern area. In this section the home garden may have satsuma and calamondin oranges, kumquat, peach, pecan, pear, plum, Oriental persimmon, fig, oranges, blueberry, and strawberry. In the central part of the state, orange, grapefruit, lemon, tangerine, avocado, litchi, pitanga, strawberry guava, and jaboticaba may be grown, besides kumquat, persimmon, and grape. In the southern section, besides the above citrus kinds, may be had lime, avocado, mango, litchi, papaya, pineapple, pitanga, guava, jaboticaba, sapodilla, banana, raspberry, and peach, the latter two of kinds especially adapted, besides many little-known tropical fruits. *See also* TUNG-OIL TREE.

The small and bush fruits are just as varied as the tree fruits. Blackberries and dewberries occur throughout central, north and west Florida, while blueberries are grown in the western section. Muscadine and bunch grapes

GA.

ZONE 7

JACKSONVILLE
* Feb. 20 - Dec. 1
284 days

TALLAHASSEE
Mar. 20 - Nov. 20
245 days

ORLANDO
Feb. 15 - Dec. 15
303 days

TAMPA
Jan. 15 - Dec. 20
339 days

ZONE 8

ZONE 9

MIAMI

KEY WEST

FLORIDA

The zones of hardiness crossing Florida are those shown on the map located at ZONE, which should be consulted for details. The dates are the average latest killing frost in spring and the first one in the fall. The figures below the dates show the average length of the growing season. From the northern edge of Zone 9 southward killing frosts are rare (but liable in half the years), except at and near Key West where a killing frost has never been recorded.

* Special articles on the subjects indicated by an asterisk (*) will be found at the words so marked.

are to be found in the central north and west sections.

ORNAMENTALS. The wide diversity of its plant life is one of Florida's great attractions, in addition to a wealth of native material, which is representative of the southeastern United States and the West Indies. A number of exotics from all over the world have been introduced. Well over 1500 species of flowers and ornamental plants, some with striking flowers and others with exotic foliage or fruit, are adapted to Florida's climate. Only a few deciduous and coniferous species are used in ornamental plantings in the state. Most of the common herbaceous annuals and perennials are grown, many of the former flowering during the winter months.

Some of the outstanding gardens and places of horticultural interest include:

McKee Jungle Gardens, Vero Beach: A naturalistic development of 120 acres of tropical and sub-tropical plants; over 100 varieties of hibiscus, collections of water lilies, and an orchid collection are on display all during the year.

Fairchild Tropical Gardens, Coconut Grove (Miami): Open all year but the best display is during the winter months; over 80 acres of tropical and sub-tropical plants from all over the world, including many rare and exotic species.

Sub-Tropical Experiment Station, Homestead: Plantings and experimental plots of tropical and sub-tropical plants and fruits, many of which have been introduced.

Orchid Jungle, Homestead: A 35-acre display of 15,000 species and varieties of orchids and many hybrids, some grown under protection; open all year.

Highland Hammocks State Parks, Sebring: A natural park of 3800 acres containing native plants of the cypress swamp and hammock of Central Florida.

Cypress Gardens, Winter Garden: Open all year, the best from Jan. to Mar. for plantings of native and exotic plant material combined in excellent landscape effects.

Edison Botanical Gardens, Fort Myers: Composed of 5 acres of gardens and 9 acres of experimental and observational plantings of over 300 varieties of plants from all over the world; of year-round interest.

Killearn Gardens, Tallahassee: Open the year round but best from Mar. to Apr. as an extensive landscape development of ornamental plants adapted to West Florida.

The production of flowers and ornamental plants contributes about 40 million dollars annually to Florida's agricultural economy. The ornamental crops produced include gladioli, chrysanthemums, fern and cut foliage, foliage plants, woody shrubs, trees and palms, caladiums, lilies, amaryllis and narcissus bulbs. See also PALM, BAMBOO, and SUBTROPICAL GARDEN for a list of the plants most suited to the state.

CLIMATE. The geographical location of Florida favors long summers and moderate winters. The Gulf of Mexico and the Atlantic Ocean have a tempering effect on the summer as well as winter temperatures. The many lakes within the state tend to modify the local temperature and frequently pre-vent the occurrence of frost or freeze damage. Average seasonal temperatures for the state are: Summer, 81; Autumn, 72; Winter, 60; and Spring, 70.

The normal annual rainfall for the state is 52.35 inches, seasonally divided as follows: Spring, 3 inches; Summer, 7 inches; Autumn, 4 inches; Winter, 3 inches a month. One-half of the rainfall occurs from June to September. While Florida is so situated as to justify the expectation of sufficient rainfall the state is not immune from drought. Many of the horticultural crops are produced during the dry period of the year. Thus the artesian water supply available in the state south of Tampa and Orlando and on the east coast south of Jacksonville is often used for irrigation purposes. Many lakes in the state are also used as a source for irrigation waters.

The principal horticultural crops are produced during the fall, winter, and spring months. Therefore, the occurrence of frost and freezes is of vital importance. The southern half of the state is normally free from serious freezes, although the mainland areas of the state have been subjected to occasional freezing temperatures. The significant frost dates for various localities are:

Town	Average date of last killing frost	Latest-known killing frost
Tallahassee	February 28	April 6
Jacksonville	February 15	April 10
Orlando	February 10	March 23
Tampa	January 31	February 6
Miami†	†	March 9

Town	Average date of earliest killing frost in fall	Earliest-known killing frost
Tallahassee	November 25	November 3
Jacksonville	November 30	November 17
Orlando	December 8	November 10
Tampa	December 5	November 21
Miami†	†	November 21

† Frost occurs infrequently at this locality, the greater part of the year being entirely free from frost.

The address of the Agricultural Experiment Station, which has kindly supplied this information about the state, is Gainesville.

Garden club activities include clubs of the Garden Club of America, the home office of which is 598 Madison Avenue, New York 22, N.Y. There are also over 285 clubs in the Florida Federation of Garden Clubs.

FLORIDA ARROWROOT = *Zamia integrifolia.*

FLORIDA CAT'S-CLAW = *Pithecolobium Unguis-cati.*

floridana, -us, -um (flo-ri-day'na). From Florida.

---

* Special articles on the subjects indicated by an asterisk (*) will be found at the words so marked.

FLORIDA VELVET BEAN = *Stizolobium deeringianum.*

FLORIFEROUS. Bearing many, or a few large, flowers.

FLORIPONDIO = *Datura suaveolens.*

FLORIST. One who sells, and sometimes grows, cut flowers and potted plants. While the florist business aggregates many millions of dollars annually, such a purely commercial aspect of floriculture lies outside the scope of this book. The chief flowers offered by florists can, however, be raised by anyone willing to take the trouble. The cultural articles at camellia, carnation, sweet pea, rose, chrysanthemum, *Lilium, Viola,* buttercup, orchid, and ferns and fern gardening will be found useful. *See also* FREESIA, FUCHSIA, GARDENIA, and SNAPDRAGON. Some plants that florists offer are sold under names that are often confusing. *See* the next few entries.

FLORISTS' CHRYSANTHEMUM = *Chrysanthemum morifolium.*

FLORISTS' GENISTA = *Cytisus canariensis. See* BROOM.

FLORISTS' GERANIUM = *Pelargonium.*

FLORISTS' SMILAX = *Asparagus asparagoides. See* SMILAX (2), for cult.

FLORISTS' SPIREA. *See* ASTILBE, FILIPENDULA, ARUNCUS.

FLORISTS' VIOLET = *Viola odorata.*

Flos-cuculi (floss-kew′kew-li). Cuckoo flower. *See* LYCHNIS.

Flos-jovis (floss-joe′vis). Flower of Jove. *See* LYCHNIS.

Flos-reginae (floss-re-jy′nee). The queen's-flower.

FLOSS FLOWER. *See* AGERATUM.

FLOSS-SILK TREE = *Chorisia speciosa.*

FLOWER. An absolutely essential organ in all seed plants, usually brightly colored, often very beautiful. While it caters to man's conceit to assume that flowers were created for his enjoyment, their true function is far more important. Without them most vegetation would perish in a generation or two, for flowers contain within them the mechanism of perpetuation. No one who raises them for pleasure should, and absolutely no plant breeder can, ignore the fact that flowers are the seat of sexual activity in all flowering plants. *See* PLANT BREEDING. And this necessary reproductive function is usually enclosed within one, or generally two, series of outer coverings, the calyx and corolla.

In a complete* flower the outermost, usually greenish, series of organs are the sepals (collectively called the calyx) and it is these that often cover the unopened flower bud. Inside them is the second series of floral envelopes, the petals (collectively called the corolla). It is these that usually give color to a flower, and sometimes the petals are

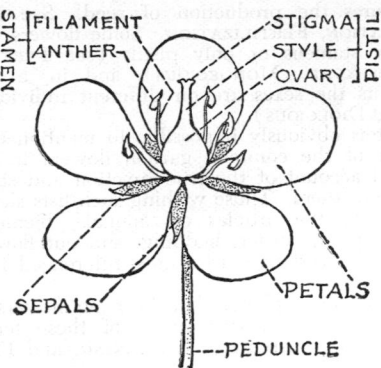

Diagram of a perfect and complete flower

separate, as in a rose or buttercup, or they are united and tubular or bell-shaped or even 2-lipped and irregular.* Many flowers have no petals, as in some ash trees, and in some the lack of petals is made up by the sepals being colored and petal-like, as in the common hepatica. *See* APETALOUS.

But within the calyx and corolla are the really essential organs (which see) of a flower. These consist of the male and female organs of reproduction. The female is usually in the center and consists in the typical case of a swollen base, the ovary,* within which are the ovules,* a shank-like style,* and a club-shaped, forked or swollen tip, the stigma.* Around the style and stigma, and hence next to, or often inserted on the petals, are the male organs of reproduction — the stamens.* A typical stamen consists of a thread-like or club-shaped shank, the filament,* and a terminal organ of various shapes, the anther,* within which the male fertilizing element, the pollen,* is produced. It is the union of this, usually yellow, dust-like pollen and the ovule that

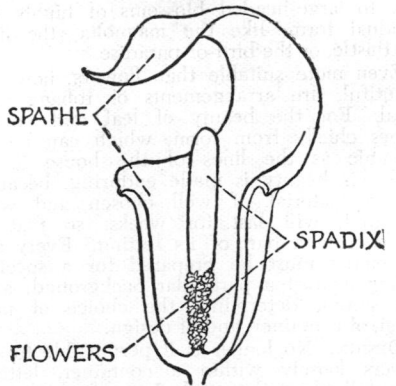

The flowering apparatus in the Jack-in-the-pulpit, a type of flower cluster found in the arum family. For details *see* ARACEAE.

---

* Special articles on the subjects indicated by an asterisk (*) will be found at the words so marked.

ensures the production of seed. *See* Pollination, Fertilization. Some flowers bear
only stamens or only pistils (*see* Perfect,
Unisexual, Monoecious) and in a few
plants the sexes are on different individuals
(*see* Dioecious).

It is obviously impossible to mention even
part of the common garden flowers in this
brief account of the true function and structure of them. Those wishing such lists should
turn to the articles on annuals, biennials,
perennials, border, bedding, and cut flowers,
and the various entries cross-referenced from
them.

For those plants that bear no flowers or
seeds, in the garden sense of these terms,
see Ferns and Fern Gardening, and Fern
Allies.

FLOWER ARRANGING. For most
women the business of flower arrangement
today is easier than it was twenty-five years
ago. There is abundant help from garden
clubs, books and periodicals, and lecturers;
and the changed pattern of domestic architecture demands simplicity of decoration.
The house and the garden today are one
unit. Large windows, walls of glass, terraces, permanent planters, enclosed patios
— all these features of modern design have
made flowers and foliage a part of the
structure. The clean-cut lines of the modern
house and the almost total absence of architectural trimming compel a corresponding
simplicity of furnishings and accessories. The
flower arrangement, consequently, must seem
an essential detail of the room.

Primary Factors. The area is the first
determining factor, for the flower arrangement is a decoration and therefore must
beautifully, yet suitably, adorn its position.
Contemporary architecture with its flat planes
requires little floral display. The strength
of modern building materials — of steel, of
solid timber, of inset stone, and of glass
— calls for a corresponding strength of design in ornamentation. The tiny flowers, so
familiar in the old-time bouquet, now give
way to large-headed blossoms of highly individual form, like the magnolia, the lily,
the thistle, or the bird-of-paradise.

Even more suitable than flowers, however
beautiful, are arrangements of foliage material. For the beauty of leaf and bough
comes chiefly from form, which can be as
dynamic as the lines of the house itself.
And this beauty is made enduring, because
foliage material, if well chosen and well
prepared, will last for weeks, so that it
seems truly a part of its setting. Every arrangement must be prepared for a specific
setting against a particular background; and
this setting determines the choice of material, of container, and of design.

Design. No longer is it permissible to set
flowers loosely within a container, letting
them fall where they will. In conformity with
the exactitude of line in the modern house,
each piece of plant material must be precisely placed in a thought-out pattern. Ar-

rangements are either vertical, horizontal,
circular, or triangular in form. Because vertical compositions suggest strength and force,
they are highly suitable for the modern
home to relieve the bareness of a plain, flat
wall or to reinforce the dignity of a partition-
ing column.

Horizontal compositions imply quiet and
repose. They look well on low tables. Circular designs also are intended to be viewed
from above. Both the horizontal and circular patterns may be used as centerpiece
designs for table arrangement, particularly
if the occasion is informal or the table is
small.

The triangular design is most frequently
used because it is flexible and can be
adapted to almost any setting where height is
admissible. The symmetrical triangle is the
most formal of all patterns. It finds many
uses. A mantel, a table in a formal entry way,
or an occasional table in a large living room
are suitable locations for a single arrangement. The symmetric triangle is used for
centerpieces on a formal dining table if the
plant material is well spaced so that it does
not present an obstacle to conversation across
the table. The large formal arrangement is
particularly effective on a tea table where
height and massed display do not interfere
with social courtesy. Church arrangements
are also made in formal triangles. The asymmetrical triangle looks well on a corner table
or at one end of the buffet table. Two
matching asymmetrical designs placed in reverse suggest the classic dignity of formal
pattern but provide interesting variation.
They can be used in any two-paired setting,
such as the ends of a mantel or a long table.
They are well suited to religious settings
near the pulpit or as altar decoration.

Because of the severity, the formality, and
stark functionalism of the modern home, the
principles of Oriental design are as effective
as the more familiar patterns of Western
devising. Two Japanese styles are always
good. The Shōkwa is an upright arrangement consisting of three principal placements whose length and directional curves
are rather rigidly determined by rule. The
Moribana is intended to represent a landscape effect or the principles of natural
plant growth. The usual three placements
are apparent but not so precisely measured
as in Shōkwa arrangements.

Principles. Whatever the general form of
the design, the pattern is made up of lines,
masses, and spaces. One of the difficulties
in manipulating the line placements is to
secure the feeling of depth. To produce
a three-dimensional effect, work from front
to back and set the stems in recessive angles. Then strengthen these lines with additional material. This filling-in process will
produce the rounded contours of three-dimensional form. The spaces, or voids, will
help in creating a feeling of depth. They
also serve to isolate the significant plant
material which should be given appropriate

---

* Special articles on the subjects indicated by an asterisk (*) will be found at the words so marked.

emphasis and to provide rhythmic movement through the design.

The manipulation of texture is an important principle of plant arrangement. The surface of plant materials is always interesting and often beautiful. Slick materials reflect light, therefore add brilliance. Rough, prickly materials suggest informality or strength. Texture must be considered more carefully in arrangements of foliage than in combinations of flowers and foliage; but it is most important in designs made of fruit or vegetables where a harmony or a contrast of surface qualities is as essential as a consideration of form.

COLOR. The contemporary floral artist uses color discreetly. Designers base their color patterns on the twelve-step color wheel: red, red-orange, orange, yellow-orange, yellow, yellow-green, green, blue-green, blue, blue-violet, violet, red-violet. A design may consist of only one hue. This monochromatic arrangement may comprise both light and dark values of the chosen color. Such a simple pattern is satisfying through its quiet charm. Or it can be enlivened by the use of flowers that differ in form, size, and texture, yet are of the same color. Variety of this sort vivifies the pattern.

A design of closely related hues is called an analogous harmony. Any such combination as red-orange, orange, and yellow-orange, or green, blue-green, and blue, has a unity of color that is very attractive. If the hues are not skillfully blended, the arrangement may seem spotty; but spottiness can be avoided by so placing the colors that the transitions from hue to hue pass easily through the composition.

The most dramatic color pattern is the complementary harmony, or the combining of opposites; that is, of hues that stand opposite each other on the color wheel, like blue and orange. Because there is no unity in blue and orange, an arrangement built entirely of these hues is almost too noticeable for the average room. The violence of the complementary harmony can be softened by modifications of the scheme. A color pattern that goes by the name of near-complementary is good. It also uses two hues; but the second hue, instead of being the direct complement of the first, is the hue adjacent to the complement. If, then, blue is the first hue, the second hue will be red-orange or yellow-orange instead of orange. Another modification, the split-complementary, uses with the first hue the two hues bordering the complement; that is, with blue, both red-orange and yellow-orange. These two modifying harmonies are more successful than the pure complement because the blends suggest the presence of an additional color which, though not actually present, is felt sufficiently to ensure color transitions throughout the design.

The last color harmony is the triad, which uses a hue from each of the three main segments of the color wheel; for example, orange, green, and violet. Because of its variety the triad design is vivid and animated.

CONTAINERS. The container is selected for its appropriateness to the material it is to hold and the setting it is to occupy. Like plant material it is judged by its form, color, and texture. Good containers are so simple that they do not attract attention to themselves, and they are in harmony with their contents. Large, heavy plant material belongs in a container whose size, form, and texture suggest strength; small, dainty arrangements, in delicate vases of fine substance.

The usual containers are made of ceramics, glass, and metals. The most useful containers for the average home of modest means are ceramics. Simple, vertical shapes, together with a few low bowls, will meet most needs. A few pieces of total glaze, some with brilliant surface, others of dull finish, are desirable. Vases of thin clay are best for delicate plants, while heavy cuttings of foliage belong in containers of greater weight and thickness. The color of the vase will be determined by the color pattern of the arrangement. The opaqueness of pottery successfully conceals the mechanics of arrangement and therefore is desirable for the unskilled designer.

Glass is very lovely for choice material. The most serviceable glass containers are vertical forms, plain in line and uncolored. A footed or pedestaled vase is always good because it raises the bottom of the design above the table. In a glass container the stems within the water are a part of the design and should be made conspicuous. The pedestaled foot helps in this display of the lower part of the vase. Low glass bowls are good for low tables; therefore they make good centerpieces where a small and relatively simple arrangement is desired. The water in glass containers must always be clear. Disintegrating plant material, then, cannot be left within the vase; and stems which secrete latex, or heavy, milky plant fluid, must be drained of this juice before they are placed in the container. Foliage material must not be stuffed inside the container to conceal the holder or the stems. Only leaves which serve as a part of the design may be introduced under water. Sometimes a heavy-textured leaf gives a pleasing accent at the base of the design and consequently is more attractive than the bare stems.

Many of the metal containers are choice, but present an additional problem for the designer. Silver is always beautiful, especially for centerpieces. But it must be clean and shining, which requires constant effort. Colored metals, such as brass, copper, and gold, are suitable only with flowers of the yellow order — orange, yellow-green, and the like. The texture of metal interposes another problem because the surface of metal is very conspicuous. Soft-petaled blossoms should not be set in polished metal con-

---

* Special articles on the subjects indicated by an asterisk (*) will be found at the words so marked.

tainers. Brilliant-surfaced vases are compatible with satin-sheened flowers and foliage. The most modern designers are beginning to use iron for containers as they use it for other interior furnishings; but the average homemaker will choose very carefully among these novelties.

Baskets and vases set within shapes of wood are useful.

HOLDERS. The pin-type holder is probably the most helpful for the home designer because it can be made to function with most of the vases found in the average home. It is always good with low bowls. It can be used in a deep vase, such as an urn, by placing layers of cloth within the container and then setting the pin-type holder on top of the cloth far enough below the rim so that the mechanics do not show. In a transparent container or a bowl so low that the holder shows, pebbles, rocks, or interesting shapes of wood can frequently be piled about the holder to conceal the needles.

The Y-shaped holder, long used by the Japanese, is the best device for vertical containers. Cut a small crotch from a shrub, as if for a slingshot, and fit it horizontally to the top of the vase opening, slightly below the rim. Then cut slantwise the ends of the stems of the material to be used so that the stem will be braced against the side of the vase after it has been inserted within the Y-opening.

For glass containers where the stems are to show it is often possible to build a lattice effect of several twigs wedged together, then set at the edge of the water. Contrivances of wire mesh are sometimes placed at the top of the container, but if these are firm enough to hold the stems immovable, there is danger that they may scratch the glass. Arrangements that are not too heavy can be made, then held firmly while the stems are wrapped first with wire, then with plumbers' lead. A short end of the lead must be left to fasten to the edge of the vase at one side.

ACCESSORIES. Floral designers make extensive use of figurines to complete their compositions. The little statue must harmonize with the plant material, the pattern, and the setting. It may substitute for a plant placement by supplying a dominant line of the design or reinforce a line established by a plant form. But it must be an integral part of the design and not an added detail stuck into a complete composition. Figures of the Madonna and the saints must be given reverent treatment with plants suited to their spiritual tradition. Figures of lay interest are particularly useful for holiday arrangements. The market affords a large choice of objects for New Year's and Christmas, for Saint Valentine's Day, Mother's Day, Halloween, and all other festivals. The same principles of choice apply as for containers. Color and texture are important. The figure must fit into the color pattern of the design. Its texture determines the choice

of plant material. Delicate floral material must not be combined with heavily folded draperies.

In addition to figurines, interesting accessory material may be found in rocks, driftwood, bits of bark, weathered roots, sea shells, and other lifeless forms.

Contemporary designers are creating abstract figures from metal and wood that are useful for modern plant compositions which disregard traditional meanings. Because they are not realistic they must be selected and used with caution. But they are significant of the new trends exemplified in contemporary architecture — J. G. C.

FLOWER BED. *See* BEDDING. For the number of plants needed for beds of different shapes, *see* GARDEN TABLES IV.

FLOWER BOX. *See* WINDOW BOXES.

FLOWER FENCE = *Adenanthera pavonina.*

FLOWER GARDEN. To the average American this term connotes a collection of perennials or annuals, or both, arranged in beds. For several reasons, practical and esthetic, these beds tend to be of formal pattern. The plants are easier to care for if assembled into clearly defined beds. If assembled, their collective effect becomes greater and may be made continuous, from early spring until late fall. And if the shape of the beds is good, it may be emphasized by a border of box or other plants, so that it remains a decorative feature throughout the year, except when covered with snow.

The most common and useful layout of a flower garden is rectangular, which continues or repeats the lines of the house. Patterns of beds should be simple. It might seem that flower gardens of few and simple beds would soon get monotonous by repetition of similar or near-similar patterns, but this is not the case. There is no more reason for monotony in two rectangular gardens than in two rectangular rooms. There may be a central or terminal feature, a fountain or figure. The garden may be enclosed by a hedge, wall, or fence with vines with or without a border planting of shrubs or flowers.

Border and accent plants may be evergreen or deciduous or both. Size, proportions of beds and intervening spaces, character of setting, by which is meant the building and planting along the boundaries, construction of paths, garden furniture, and the planting in the beds themselves, may and do vary endlessly.

It is far better to concentrate the flowers (perennials and annuals) into one place than to scatter a few here and a few there. Isolated beds in the lawn generally look as if they had been dropped casually to be left till called for, and if put in the borders of the shrubbery, leave bare spaces before and after they develop.

This does not mean that annuals and perennials cannot be used informally, or

---

* Special articles on the subjects indicated by an asterisk (*) will be found at the words so marked.

that there cannot be a good informal flower garden. When successful, informal flower gardens are usually made on rolling or irregularly shaped sites, and there are many situations where it would be better to make an informal flower garden than to level off the surface for the reception of a formal pattern. For a formal pattern should be laid down on a flat surface or on level terraces, or it loses its formal character and becomes neither formal nor informal, but merely shapeless.

In an informal flower garden the flowers are usually better for a background of foliage, and a mass planting of shrubs and trees should, generally speaking, follow, rather than cross, the contours of the ground, *i.e.*, lines of shrubs on a convex surface should be convex, on a concave surface concave. Flowers suited to the situation may be set effectively in the recess of such plantations. The successful design and maintenance of an informal flower garden requires especial judgment and knowledge of plant material, one reason being that lines are less definite than in a formal garden and more dependent on the plant material itself.

A common error in flower planting is to scatter them around and about the shrubbery with long bands of tulips, narcissus, and annuals along the edges. This kind of thing soon cheapens the flowers and makes them tiresome by repetition. It also greatly increases the upkeep. But flowers concentrated in a relatively small area gain by contrast with long bands of tulips, narcissus, and grounds.

A tantalizing characteristic of a perennial garden is the short duration of bloom of most of the plants: but this is also part of its charm, for before one kind of flower has had time to become stale it disappears, only to be followed by others. If the garden is well planned, there is something new almost every week. In midsummer there is apt to be a period of scarcity of flowering perennials, and the empty spaces may be filled with bedding plants such as ageratum, cockscomb, heliotrope, geraniums, salvia. The use of these is highly debatable, and each must decide whether their use in the flower garden is desirable or not.

Some of the colors are hard to reconcile with other colors: but, if care be taken to keep reds, oranges, and pinks apart, there are likely to be few clashes of hues in the beds that the sunlight and a little distance will not harmonize. In considering the effect of a flower garden one should not concentrate on local color combinations, but on the impression produced by the whole. Better, for the most part, are annuals, the most popular of which seem to be zinnias, marigolds, and candytuft, although these are the least easy to reconcile with their perennial neighbors. *Phlox drummondi*, petunias, hunnemannia, snapdragons, centaurea, alyssum, annual larkspurs, shirley poppies, stocks, and asters are much more sympathetic.

It is not possible to give precise directions as to the arrangement of plants in a flower garden. The large masses of one kind, advocated by many, are striking in themselves and may be used in informal plantings with shrub backgrounds effectively, but in formal beds they tend to cut the beds into visual sections and thus concentrate on themselves the attention that should be given to the garden. When their flowering season is over, they leave large, unsightly, blank spaces.

Groups of plants should vary with the size and shape of the beds. Thus, in a long border, the groups would tend to be long and narrow: in a square or round bed they would not differ much in length and width. When using a large number of plants of one kind in a formal bed it is better to distribute them up and down the bed in groups of different sizes so that the eye may be carried from one to the other. Taller plants may be brought near the edge of the beds at irregular intervals forming bays containing lower plants. Varieties should be distributed through a bed so that, as far as may be, there is something in bloom in different parts of the bed throughout the season. For the details of what to plant, *see* COLOR GARDENING, ANNUALS, BIENNIALS, PERENNIALS, and BULBS. — H. A. C.

FLOWERING ALMOND. *See* PRUNUS GLANDULOSA, P. NANA, and P. TRILOBA. *See also* AMYGDALUS COMMUNIS.

FLOWERING ASH = *Fraxinus Ornus*. See ASH.

FLOWERING BEAN = *Phaseolus coccineus*.

FLOWERING CHERRY = *Prunus lannesiana, P. serrulata*, and *P. yedoensis*.

FLOWERING CRAB; CRABAPPLE. See MALUS.

FLOWERING CURRANT = *Ribes aureum* and *R. sanguineum*.

FLOWERING DOGWOOD = *Cornus florida*.

FLOWERING FLAX = *Linum grandiflorum*.

FLOWERING MAPLE. *See* ABUTILON.

FLOWERING MOSS = *Phlox subulata, Sedum pulchellum*, and *Pyxidanthera barbulata*.

FLOWERING PEACH. See AMYGDALUS PERSICA.

FLOWERING PLUM. *See* PRUNUS MUME.

FLOWERING QUINCE. *See* CHAENOMELES.

FLOWERING RASPBERRY = *Rubus odoratus* and *R. deliciosus*.

FLOWERING RUSH = *Butomus umbellatus*.

FLOWERING RUSH FAMILY = Butomaceae.

FLOWERING SHRUBS. All shrubs must, of course, bear flowers of some sort, but many of them have small or inconspicuous

---

* Special articles on the subjects indicated by an asterisk (*) will be found at the words so marked.

ones and are hence grown mostly for foliage or fruits. But some genera are noteworthy for the beauty of their flowers. Among the best flowering shrubs, all of which are the subjects of special articles, are (the predominantly tender ones, in the East, are marked with a dagger [†]):

†Abelia	Daphne	Lilac
†Acacia	Deutzia	Lonicera
Azalea	Diervilla	Magnolia
†Bauhinia	Elder	Malus
†Broom	†Erica	Mock-orange
Buddleia	Exochorda	†Osmanthus
†Callistemon	Forsythia	†Pittosporum
Calycanthus	†Fuchsia	Prunus
†Camellia	†Gardenia	Rhododendron
Caryopteris	†Grevillea	Ribes
†Cassia	Heather	Rosa
†Ceanothus	Hydranga	†Solanum
Cercis	Itea	Spiraea
†Cestrum	†Ixora	Symphoricarpos
Chaenomeles	†Jasminum	†Veronica
†Clerodendron	Kalmia	Viburnum
Cornus	†Lagerstroemia	Vitex
Crataegus	†Lantana	Weigela

FLOWERING SPURGE = *Euphorbia corollata.*

FLOWERING TIME. *See* Phenology for the factors that control it.

FLOWERING WILLOW = *Chilopsis linearis.*

FLOWERING WINTERGREEN = *Polygala paucifolia.*

FLOWER-OF-AN-HOUR = *Hibiscus Trionum.*

FLOWER-OF-JOVE = *Lychnis Flos-jovis.*

FLOWER-OF-TIGRIS = *Tigridia.*

FLOWER POTS. The best permanent container for most potted plants is the common clay flower pot, porous, unglazed, and with a hole in the bottom to allow the escape of excess water. They come in sizes from 1¾ in. to 14 in. diameters, the standard sizes for which are as follows:

STANDARD FLOWER POTS

Inside diameter (inches)	Inside diameter (inches)	Inside diameter (inches)
1¾	3¾	6½
2 Thimble pot	4	7
2¼	4½	8
2½ Thumb pot	5	9
3	5½ Lily pot	10
3½	6	12
		14

From such a series one can take care of nearly every potting need from the pricking out of seedlings to a potted plant needing the largest of the standard sizes — 14 in. Above this diameter the cost and breakage of clay pots become so great that tubs are more economical.

There are some growers, especially bulb growers, who prefer shallower pots than those of the standard sizes. For such, the following are to be had in the sizes specified below:

THREE-QUARTER OR AZALEA POTS. These are clay pots much like the ordinary ones but only three-quarters the regulation depth. They come in all sizes from 6-in. to 12-in. diameters.

CYCLAMEN POTS. The same as three-quarter pots, but with 5 holes in the bottom. They come only in 5–6–7-in. diameters.

PANS (often called Bulb or Seed Pans). These are clay pots of about half the depth of standard flower pots, and have many uses for shallow-rooted plants, for bulbs, or for pricking out seedlings. They are to be had in all diameters from 5 in. to 12 in.

SAUCERS. In rooms, and sometimes in the greenhouse, flower pots must stand in some sort of a saucer which collects excess water or sometimes holds water that is applied at the base of the pot. Clay saucers are made in all sizes from 3- to 14-in. diameters. Because of the downward flare of all flower pots, a 6-in. saucer will fit a 6-in. pot.

Only fancy and one's pocketbook need dictate the use of many glazed, glass, colored, enamel, or metal containers for the growing of plants. But they are expensive and not so practical as the common clay flower pot.

To keep pots clean, especially to free them from the green scum or moss so common in moist greenhouses, they should be soaked in a solution of 2½ ounces of carbonate of copper, and 1½ pints of ammonia in about 20 gallons of water, given a good scrubbing, and then rinsed in clear water.

PAPER POTS. For all temporary purposes paper pots are most useful. They come in all the smaller sizes, are far cheaper than clay pots, and for the few weeks they are needed answer every purpose. They will not stand much wear, but for young vegetable plants or tender annuals waiting for outdoor planting, paper pots are very satisfactory. Even cheaper substitutes are the discarded paper drinking cups, especially the corrugated sort with a rim. Empty tin cans are sturdy, but ugly, and do not allow aeration, for which only clay pots properly provide. More recently plastic and pressed fiber pots are available.

FLOWERS FOR INDOOR DECORATION. *See* Cut Flowers and Flower Arranging.

FLOWER SHOWS AND EXHIBITIONS. A great public interest in horticulture has developed with the tremendous growth in the garden club movement and the many new suburban home owners. With this has come an increased interest in flower shows and exhibitions, not only in the big, well-established, nationally known shows, but in many new, smaller shows on the local level which are mushrooming all over the country.

1. ORGANIZATION. In planning and staging it is essential to determine the type show to be held, its purpose and value, and the financial backing available, and then select a competent committee empowered to proceed with plans and arrangements. An efficient chairman or co-ordinator, through whom all matters must channel, and a dependable secretary to maintain accurate rec-

---

* Special articles on the subjects indicated by an asterisk (*) will be found at the words so marked.

ords are of first importance for a smoothly operating group.

The schedule, staging, judging, hospitality, publicity, tickets, and any special projects must all be properly assigned, with the duties of each committee chairman clearly and specifically defined. In a small show one chairman may handle several jobs.

2. SCHEDULE AND PRIZES. Most schedules are made up of four groupings including horticulture and arrangement classes, a section for juniors, and special educational exhibits. The horticulture classes include collections or display groups to cover a specified area, as well as specimen classes. Include classes suitable for the exhibitors you will draw from, and contain enough variety in the classes to insure an interesting show, both from the standpoint of competition and the viewer. In making out the schedule be explicit and concise, using correct horticultural terms, defining words about which there might be any question. In smaller shows include show rules with the schedule, stating them clearly, anticipating and thereby avoiding misunderstandings; list time entries must be in, time exhibits must be staged, removal time, whether class is for amateurs or professionals, whether multiple entries are permissible, and how long a house plant must be owned by an exhibitor to be entered in competition. In all classes be specific so the exhibitor will have no difficulty understanding and complying with the requirements of the class.

If cash prizes are not offered, ribbon prizes are frequently given, blue for first, red for second, and yellow for third. A special or sweepstake prize is frequently awarded the exhibitor winning the greatest number of points in the show. Five points are given for each first award, three points for each second, and one point for each third prize.

The following sample schedule for a show to be held in September may be changed to cover any season.

SAMPLE SCHEDULE

Section I

HORTICULTURE CLASSES

Exhibits in these classes must be grown by the exhibitor. All specimens must be correctly labeled.

CLASS   *Annuals*
1. Collection of annuals to cover 10 sq. ft.

China Asters
2. Single, 5 blooms.
3. Double, 5 blooms.

Chrysanthemums
4. Any type, 3 sprays.
5. Collection consisting of 12 varieties.

Dahlias
6. Decorative, 3 blooms, 1 variety, on long stems.
7. Single, 3 blooms, 1 variety, on long stems.
8. Specimen, 1 bloom, any color, any type, finest dahlia in show.

9. Display to cover 25 sq. ft. Any or all types, not less than 5 varieties.

Gladiolus
10. Exhibition type, 1 stalk, any color.
11. Primulinus type, 1 stalk, any color.

Marigolds
12. Single, 5 blooms.
13. Double, 5 blooms.

Petunias
14. Single, 3 sprays.
15. Double, 3 sprays.

Roses
16. Hybrid Teas, 3 blooms, 1 variety, any color.
17. Floribundas, 3 sprays, 1 variety, any color.
18. Any other type of rose, 3 blooms or 3 sprays.

Shrubs
19. Valuable for both spring blossom and fall fruit or color — An arrangement of branches.

Trees
20. Valuable for both spring blossom and fall fruit — An arrangement of branches.

Zinnias
21. Collection of pastel colors, to cover 10 sq. ft.
22. Collection of other colors, to cover 10 sq. ft.

Section II

ARRANGEMENT CLASSES

23. Silhouette — A line arrangement of flowering branches in a low container staged against a light green background measuring 42″ high, 32″ wide, and 40″ from the floor.
24. One Color Predominating — An arrangement featuring color, staged same as Class 23.
25. Flowering material combined with fruit and/or vegetables. Staged in a lighted niche with a sunlight-yellow background. 40″ high, 30″ wide and 40″ from the floor.
26. Miniatures staged in framed openings 4″ high, 3″ wide, with a curved light-green background, depth 2½″ and 40″ from the floor.
27. Luncheon table seating eight, 36″ long, 30″ wide, and 30″ from the floor. Arrangement to be viewed from all sides. Use one place table setting.
28. Dinner table set for six. Table 72″ long, 36″ wide, and 30″ from the floor. Arrangement to be viewed from all sides.

Invitation classes for well-known arrangers are frequently scheduled.

Section III

CLASSES FOR JUNIORS
(For kindergarten through the third grade)
29. Any arrangement in a favorite container.
30. A collection of gourds.
    (For fourth through sixth grades)
31. An arrangement in a pumpkin, using grasses, weeds and "mums."

---

* Special articles on the subjects indicated by an asterisk (*) will be found at the words so marked.

32. Arrangement for a Scout meeting.
     (For junior high school)
33. A dish garden.
34. An arrangement of berried branches.

Section IV

SPECIAL EDUCATIONAL EXHIBITS

Pruning exhibit — State Extension Service
Conservation exhibit — State Department of
     Natural Resources
Correct foundation planting — Local nursery

3. ENTRIES. When mailing the schedule with
rules and general information to prospective
exhibitors, enclose an entry blank so it may
be filled out and returned on time.

The general information and rules should
give a deadline for returning entry forms,
listing clearly the name and address of the
person to whom it should be sent. All classes
the exhibitor proposes to enter must be listed
on the form.

ENTRY FORM

Exhibitors must make their entries on this
official blank and file same on time with the
secretary or chairmen of entries.

Class No.	Description of Class

Date entry was received

Each exhibitor agrees to conform to all the
rules governing this exhibition.

Exhibitor

Address

READ THE SCHEDULE
AND THE RULES CAREFULLY

There is a very simple, practical, and
completely informative method of recording
and tabulating entries. Keep a class book.
In a small show, any blank book with ruled
pages will suffice. Each page should be devoted to one class, with the class number
listed at the top of the page. On the left-
hand side of the page, rule off a one-inch-
wide column the length of the page. As
the entries come in, enter each exhibitor's
name and address under each class in which
he or she proposes to compete, using a
number for each exhibitor in the left-hand
column. The exhibitor whose entry is first
recorded in a class will be number one in
that class, although he or she may be number two, five or ten in other classes, if others
are already registered in the class. The entries for a given class are all recorded on its
special page or sheet and from this the show
manager will know the number of entries
and can judge the space necessary for staging the class.

Exhibitors' cards for each individual exhibit are made out from the class book and
placed in an envelope, with only the class

number and exhibitor's number showing on
the envelope. The exhibitor must place his
entry card beside his exhibit.

Exhibitor's Card

CLASS

EXHIBITED BY

ADDRESS   DATE

4. RULES AND REGULATIONS. Read the rules
carefully, for they will be strictly enforced
and are necessary for the success of any
show, small or large, to avoid both confusion
and friction.

A distinction should be made between
professional and amateur growers with separate sections and classes for each group.
If there are classes open to all, this fact
should be clearly stated.

Those responsible for staging the show
must know in advance what entries to expect in order to plan intelligently and allot
each class sufficient staging space. Therefore,
a closing date when all entries must be in
must be stipulated. This should never be
less than 24 hours in advance of the opening day; in large shows at least two or three
days is essential.

All exhibits must be ready for judging at
the time specified in the schedule and
exhibitors must leave the hall at the hour
when judging begins and may not return
until the show is opened to the public.

Exhibitors should not be permitted to remove an exhibit nor any part thereof until
the end of the show.

Exhibitors must conform to the specified
conditions. Judges do not like to disqualify
a prize-winning exhibit because there are 11
or 13 blooms in the vase in a class which
calls for 12. It is wise to bring along a
few extra flowers in case of breakage or an
accident, but it is the exhibitors' responsi-
bility to stage in exact accordance with the
requirements.

Reasons for disqualifying an exhibit must
be indicated on the entry card and on the
judges' report sheet.

Judges should be instructed not to award a
first prize to an exhibit scoring less than 75
points, even when it is the only entry in
the class. An exhibit is not entitled to a prize
or other award unless it possesses merit.

The show management should supply uniform cards or labels for most pleasing effect.

The exhibitor must keep his or her exhibit
in good condition until the close of the
show.

5. JUDGING. From the class book the judges'
book is prepared by writing in the class
numbers and number of entries entered under each class. The judges record the awards
made against the entry numbers in their
book, never seeing the exhibitors' names.
The judges should sign their book upon completion of their duties and return it to the

---

* Special articles on the subjects indicated by an asterisk (*) will be found at the words so marked.

secretary or proper authority. Corresponding entries of the awards are then made in the class book and it becomes a complete record of all entries and winners.

After the judging, the secretary, a clerk, or the chairman of judges, whoever has been assigned the duty, removes the entry card from its envelope and, with any award received properly attached, places the card neatly in front of the exhibit where it can be easily seen, so the public may know both the class and the exhibitor. In small shows, an ordinary $3'' \times 5''$ card may be used, placed face down with the entry. The class and exhibitor's numbers are on the back of the card for the judges to see.

There should be three judges in each set or group, to offset differences of opinion. Select one set of judges who know horticulture, another set who are qualified to judge arrangements. Care in selection is very important and when possible it is wise to choose judges not familiar with the exhibitors. Judges should not enter the show until everything is ready for judging and only official attendants should be permitted to remain in the show until judging is concluded.

In competitive shows judging is a very important function and everything possible should be done to make the awarding of prizes as fair and just as is humanly possible. As a helpful aid toward that end, scales of points have been adopted and are in general use. With experienced, competent judges this point system is, of course, only a means to an end and serves the judges best when two exhibits are so near the accepted standard of perfection that a review of the scale of points will help ascertain in what particular specification the one exhibit has a slight advantage over the other. Applying the scale to these two exhibits serves as a means of justifying why one was awarded first over the other. In the last analysis, it is often the intangible something not measurable by points which influences true judgment. There is an old adage, "trifles make perfection, but perfection is no trifle," which is a truth apparent to all good exhibitors.

The following scales of points for judging are taken from the *Rule Book for Exhibitors and Judges* at the exhibitions of the Massachusetts Horticultural Society. They are helpful and informative to the extent that they show the relative qualities and proportionate values which competent judges consider essential.

SCALES OF POINTS FOR JUDGING
No. 1 — Groups of Foliage Plants

Staging and Arrangement 35
Cultural Perfection 30
Distinctiveness 10
Color Effect 10
Rarity 10
Correct and Suitable Labeling 5
                                        ———
                                        100

No. 2 — Groups of Flowering Plums

Staging and Arrangement 35
Cultural Perfection 30
Color Effect 20
Quality and Suitability of Accessories 10
Correct and Suitable Labeling 5
                                        ———
                                        100

No. 3 — Groups of Miscellaneous Plants

Staging and Arrangement 35
Cultural Perfection 30
Variety and Rarity 15
Color Effect 15
Correct and Suitable Labeling 5
                                        ———
                                        100

No. 4 — Groups of Succulents or Cacti

Staging and Arrangement 35
Cultural Perfection 30
Variety 20
Rarity 10
Correct and Suitable Labeling 5
                                        ———
                                        100

No. 5 — Groups of Orchid Plants

Staging and Arrangement 20
Cultural Perfection 20
Condition of Flowers 20
Variety and Rarity 15
Color Effect 10
Quality and Suitability of Accessories..... 10
Correct and Suitable Labeling 5
                                        ———
                                        100

No. 6 — Orchid Plants — Single Specimen

Size of Plant 25
Cultural Perfection 25
Condition of Flowers 20
Color 15
Floriferousness 15
                                        ———
                                        100

No. 7 — Specimen Foliage Plants

Cultural Perfection 60
Form 15
Distinctiveness 15
Rarity 10
                                        ———
                                        100

No. 8 — Specimen Flowering Plants

Cultural Perfection 40
Form and Size of Plant 20
Floriferousness 15
Color 15
Foliage 10
                                        ———
                                        100

No. 9 — Garden Exhibits

Design and Consistency to Scale 30
Suitability and Quality of Plant Material .. 25
Color Harmony 10
Seasonability 10
Quality and Suitability of Accessories 10
Condition of Plant Material 10
Correct and Suitable Labeling 5
                                        ———
                                        100

No. 10 — Naturalistic Planting or Garden

Naturalistic Reproduction 40
Condition of Plants 20
Suitability of Plants 15
Arrangement of Plant Material 10
Seasonability 10
Correct and Suitable Labeling 5
                                        ———
                                        100

---

* Special articles on the subjects indicated by an asterisk (*) will be found at the words so marked.

No. 11 — Garden Features

Charm and Atmosphere	25
Quality and Suitability of Plant Material	25
Design and Consistency to Scale	20
Color Harmony	15
Condition of Plant Material	10
Correct and Suitable Labeling	5
	100

No. 12 — Rock Garden Exhibits

Selection and Arrangement of the Rocks	25
Placing of Plants and Color Harmony	25
Quality of Plant Material	15
Suitability of Plant Material	10
Variety of Plant Material	10
Seasonability	10
Correct and Suitable Labeling	5
	100

No. 13 — Bird Feeding Stations

General Design	30
Suitability and Arrangement of Plant Material	25
Suitability and Arrangement of Accessories	20
Consistency to Scale	20
Correct and Suitable Labeling	5
	100

No. 14 — Displays of Cut Flowers

Cultural Perfection	35
Staging and Arrangement	35
Quality and Suitability of Accessories	15
Condition	10
Correct and Suitable Labeling	5
	100

NOTE: Where the scale of Points No. 14 is used for judging Displays of Cut Branches of Trees and Shrubs the 35 points allowed for Cultural Perfection will be for Quality of Plant Material.

No. 15 — Cut Roses
Adopted by the American Rose Society

Form	25
Substance	20
Color	25
Stem and Foliage	20
Size	10
	100

No. 16 — Cut Carnations
Adopted by the American Carnation Society

Color	25
Size	20
Stem	20
Substance	15
Form	10
Calyx	5
Fragrance	5
	100

No. 17 — Cut Peonies
Adopted by the American Peony Society

Color	25
Form	15
Size	15
Distinctiveness	15
Substance and Texture	10
Stem	10
Fragrance	10
	100

No. 18 — Cut Sweet Peas
Adopted by the American Sweet Pea Society

Size	25
Length of Stem	25
Color	20
Number of Flowers on Stem	15
Substance	15
	100

No. 19 — Cut Irises
Adopted by the American Iris Society

The Flower		
Color According to Variety	10	
Size	5	
Form	10	
Substance	10	35
The Stalk		
Number of Open Flowers	15	
Branch Balance, Bud Placement	15	30
Condition		
Grooming of Specimen	15	
Cultural Perfection	20	35
		100

No. 20 — Cut Chrysanthemums Standards
Adopted by the Chrysanthemum Society of America

Size	30
Color	15
Fullness	15
Form	15
Depth	15
Stem	5
Foliage	5
	100

No. 21 — Cut Chrysanthemums — Pompon, Anemone and Single Varieties
Adopted by the Chrysanthemum Society of America

Color	40
Form	20
Substance	20
Stem	10
Foliage	10
	100

No. 22 — Cut Gladioli

Individual Florets:	Exhibition	Decorative
Color	15	30
Substance	5	10
Size	15	3
Form	5	5
Entire Spike:		
Harmony	15	15
Arrangement	10	10
Florescence	20	8
Length of Stem	7	5
Foliage	3	4
Vigor	0	5
Condition	5	5
	100	100

No. 23 — Cut Dahlias
Adopted by the American Dahlia Society

	Small	Medium	Large
Color	20	20	20
Form	15	15	20
Distinctiveness	5	5	5
Size	0	0	10
Stem	20	20	20
Foliage	20	15	20
Substance	10	15	5
Uniformity	10	10	0
	100	100	100

* Special articles on the subjects indicated by an asterisk (*) will be found at the words so marked.

No. 24 — Cut Delphiniums
Adopted by the American Delphinium Society

Color	25
Flower Spike:	
Length	10
Symmetry	10
Florets:	
Size	10
Form	10
Placement	10
Substance	5
Foliage	10
Special Features	10

(Fragrance, new types of sepals and petals, new types of spikes, new colors, etc.)

                               100

No. 25 — Cut Tulips

Color	25
Substance and Texture	20
Culture	20
Form	15
Stem	10
Condition	10
	100

No. 26 — Cut Daffodils (Narcissi)

Substance of Perianth	25
Culture	25
Color	20
Size Suitable to the Variety	15
Balance Between Crown and Spread of Perianth	15
	100

No. 27 — Cut Camellias
Adopted by the American Camellia Society

Substance and Texture	25
Size	25
Color	15
Form	15
Condition	10
Foliage	10
	100

No. 28 — Table Arrangements

Harmony of Arrangement with Container(s) and Accessories	35
Distinctiveness	20
Condition	20
Proportion	10
Color Effect	10
Suitability to the Occasion	5
	100

No. 29 — Arrangements of Cut Flowers

Arrangement of Flowers	25
Quality and Condition	20
Color Harmony	15
Distinctiveness	15
Proportion and Balance	15
Container	10
	100

No. 30 — Shadow Boxes

Distinctiveness of Composition	30
Color Harmony	20
Proportion and Arrangement	20
Container and Accessories	20
Condition	10
	100

No. 31 — Porch or Window Boxes

Arrangement and Color Harmony	35
Container	20
Adaptability of Plant Material	20
Cultural Perfection	20
Correct and Suitable Labeling	5
	100

No. 32 — Arrangement of Flowers, Fruits and/or Vegetables adapted to a definite purpose such as a mantel, wall, porch, table or the like

Selection and Quality of Plant Material	35
Condition	35
Design and Arrangement of Planting	25
Correct and Suitable Labeling	5
	100

No. 33 — Terrariums

Design and Arrangement of Planting	35
Suitability of Material	35
Quality and Condition	25
Correct and Suitable Labeling	5
	100

No. 34 — Group of Aquarium Plants

Arrangement and Color Effect	40
Quality and Condition of Plant Material	25
Variety	20
Fish and Other Accessories	10
Correct and Suitable Labeling	5
	100

No. 35 — Aquariums

Arrangement of Plants and Accessories	20
Variety and Rarity of Fish	15
Variety of Plant Material	15
General Artistic Effect	15
Design of Aquarium	10
Quality and Condition of Plant Material	10
Other Aquatic Fauna	10
Correct and Suitable Labeling	5
	100

No. 36 — Miniature and Dish Gardens

Design and Consistency to Scale	30
Quality and Type of Plant Material	25
Distinctiveness and Originality of Design	20
Accessories	10
Perfection of Detail	10
Correct and Suitable Labeling	5
	100

No. 37 — Grapes

Form of Bunch	30
Flavor	20
Freedom from Blemishes	15
Color	15
Size of Bunch	10
Firmness	5
Bloom	5
	100

No. 38 — Apples, Pears and Quinces

Quality	25
Uniformity	25
Freedom from Blemishes	25
Color	15
Size	10
	100

No. 39 — Plums

Quality	25
Uniformity	20
Freedom from Blemishes	20
Color	20
Size	15
	100

No. 40 — Peaches and Cherries

Quality	25
Uniformity	20
Freedom from Blemishes	20
Color	15
Size	10
Form	10
	100

* Special articles on the subjects indicated by an asterisk (*) will be found at the words so marked.

No. 41 — Melons

Quality	50
Depth of Flesh	15
Size	10
Form	10
Color of Flesh	10
Freedom from Blemishes	5
	100

No. 42 — Plates and Specimens of Apples and Pears

Quality	30
Uniformity	25
Color	20
Size	15
Form	10
	100

No. 43 — Display of Fruits

Quality and Arrangement	50
Staging	30
Variety	15
Correct and Suitable Labeling	5
	100

No. 44 — Collection of Fruits

Quality	40
Color	25
Uniformity of Individual Specimens	25
Size	5
Correct and Suitable Labeling	5
	100

No. 45 — Display of Vegetables

Staging and Arrangement	35
Quality and Color	30
Variety	20
Trueness to Type	10
Correct and Suitable Labeling	5
	100

No. 46 — Collection of Vegetables

Quality and Color	25
Trueness to Type	25
Size	15
Uniformity of Individual Specimens	15
Freedom from Blemishes	15
Correct and Suitable Labeling	5
	100

No. 47 — Display of Vegetables and Flowers

Staging and Arrangement	30
Quality and Color	25
Variety	20
Trueness to Type	25
Uniformity	10
Correct and Suitable Labeling	5
	100

No. 48 — Collection of Vegetables and Flowers

Quality and Color	20
Arrangement	20
Trueness to Type	15
Size	15
Uniformity	15
Freedom from Blemishes	10
Correct and Suitable Labeling	5
	100

No. 49 — Roadside Stands

Design and Utility	35
Arrangement of Material	25
Quality and Variety	25
Customer Appeal	10
Correct and Suitable Labeling	5
	100

No. 50 — Collection of Herbs

Educational Value	40
Variety of Material	25
Quality	15
Arrangement	15
Labeling	5
	100

NOTE: In the judging of fruits, taste will be considered as a part of "quality."

The person assigned the duty, with a good committee, is responsible for securing enough competent judges for the show, giving them the necessary information and instructions they need, securing clerks and instructing them, having stickers and ribbons at hand, and writing thank-you notes to the judges after the show is over. This committee may also serve as the hospitality group, taking care of any local transportation the judges may require, their luncheon at noontime, and in general making them comfortable and showing the proper appreciation for their contribution to the show. A hospitality committee provides hostesses, any refreshments or music wanted, and an information center where questions about the show may be correctly answered. If an authority is present to answer horticultural questions, that is of added value.

6. STAGING. Local available facilities will, of course, necessarily determine where the show is to be held. During the summer months some outdoor shows are held with success, but unpredictable weather always makes for uncertainty and problems. A large hall or spacious rooms with enough area to accommodate the contemplated exhibits is recommended. A cool building with plenty of available water is desirable and, of course, it is an advantage if the floor can be hosed down, both for cleaning purposes and to keep the atmosphere moist. In a large show, a floor plan of the hall showing all openings, posts, or partitions and using accurate measurements is advisable.

A planned unity or harmony throughout the show is pleasing and effective. For this reason a general theme is frequently planned. With good-quality material and the artistic know-how an attractive display should result, although a good show involves a tremendous amount of detail and hard work.

Simple tables made with board tops placed over ordinary trestles or horses are excellent for staging house plants and cut flowers, either as specimens or in groups. The table should not exceed 4 or 5 ft. in width if not to be viewed from both sides. Large plants and tall cut-flowers 3 ft. or more in height may be staged on the floor since it is usually more effective to look down upon them.

Plan sufficient space to display each specimen entry properly yet keep the entries in each class together to facilitate judging. The allotted space is usually specified in the schedule for group classes. Leave a space of about 2 ft. between these exhibits

---

* Special articles on the subjects indicated by an asterisk (*) will be found at the words so marked.

to show and accentuate the group effect desired. All these details must be thought out and prepared in advance of the exhibitors' arrival with their entries.

Before the exhibitors arrive to set up their entries, it will save much time and confusion to chalk off accurately the exact space for the different classes and number them all correctly.

The use of suitable material, appropriate in color and texture, to cover and improve the appearance of the tables, or for use as a good background, must be decided by the management and not left to individual exhibitors, so there will be a harmony and pleasing general over-all effect. A wide 8-ft. table with exhibits facing both ways may advantageously have a central dividing line of dark-green burlap tacked to a light framework, extended to a height of about 4 ft. above the table, but the management must make the decision so the whole table is treated uniformly.

The table-tops should be covered with a waterproof paper. Burlap in a neutral tint makes a satisfactory drape for the sides of the tables.

At seasons when short-stemmed flowers predominate and exhibits lack of sufficient height to permit effective staging, a step table solves this problem. A two- or three-step, shelf-like arrangement, simple and easy to make, can be placed on a table. It should be set back one or two feet from the front of the table, with a two- or three-step rise, each 12 to 18 in. in height, carrying a 12- to 18-in.-wide shelf. This will permit the effective display of three or four rows, one above the other, and show the exhibit to a much better advantage.

7. FRUITS AND VEGETABLES. If the season permits, provide classes for fruits and vegetables. A display of edible fruits and berry-bearing trees and shrubs can be made most attractive. A prize for the largest tomato, cabbage, or pumpkin creates a competitive spirit and serves as a stimulus for better cultivation. With such classes you may interest a new group of people in your shows.

NOTES ON EXHIBITING AND JUDGING VEGETABLES

1. *Type.* It is important in vegetable exhibits that the specimens represent the type of the variety. For example, Bonny Best tomato has several strains or types, some distinct from others. All one type should be shown.

2. *Size.* Specimens should be of uniform size and representative of the varieties. Box exhibits should, as a rule, be of the size most desirable for market, while plate exhibits may more nearly represent the size most desirable for table use. As a rule oversize means coarseness, while undersize means waste and often lack of typical color.

3. *Uniformity.* Uniformity in size, shape, color, and maturity are important. The ideal is reached when one specimen cannot be told from another.

4. *Freedom from blemishes.* Freedom from the effects of insects, diseases, and mechanical injuries is important. Bruises or any kind of injury to the skin or foliage should not be present.

5. *General.* Stems and roots should be either "all off" or "all on." Tops should all be cut even.

DISPLAYS OF VEGETABLES

Displays of vegetables should be so arranged that not only the quality of the individual specimens is apparent but that the whole arrangement is in harmony. Backgrounds of vegetable foliage should be used, such as green cornstalks, kale, fennel, or parsley. Other foliage is permissible. Containers should be in keeping with the material exhibited. Crowding should be avoided. The use of high-handled baskets is discouraged. Unusual and original arrangements in good taste are encouraged. Due regard to color combination is essential. Varieties in all exhibits should be labeled.

Displays of vegetables may be made as attractive as exhibits of flowers. In box or commercial exhibits it is important to conceal the boxes as much as possible. Vegetable foliage may be used for this purpose. Highly colored vegetables like tomatoes should be used to break up the monotony of those with neutral coloring.

The packing of exhibition vegetables is very important. Careful protection against bruising in transit should be given all delicate specimens like eggplants, tomatoes, squash, etc. Always bring some extra specimens to replace injured ones.

SPECIMEN VEGETABLES

Asparagus. Stalks should be of the same length, green, with close heads of the same diameter at the butt and tapering uniformly. Large size is desirable, as it denotes quick growth and high quality.

Artichokes. The rule of uniformity in color should apply in both varieties of artichokes. Medium size in Jerusalem artichokes is best, while with true artichokes moderately large size usually means higher quality.

Beets. The desirable qualities in beets are tenderness and color. Oversize should be avoided. It is difficult to give the most desirable size in inches but, as a rule, beets from two to two and one-half inches are best, provided there has been quick growth. Color for the variety is very important. Dark-colored beets showing white streaks should be penalized. If tops are to be shown, they should be small and free from rusty leaves.

Beans. Shell beans should be shown with the pods of equal size. The pods must not be dried. High color is required in horticultural strains. Snap beans should be under-rather than over-mature, keeping in mind that quality is the first requisite. Long,

---

straight specimens of the same length and color should be selected. Avoid stringiness, as this counts against them.

Broccoli (Italian). Close heads, dark green and not over six inches of stem are preferable. Do not tie broccoli in bunches. Avoid any tendency to yellowing.

Brussels Sprouts. Firmness and medium size are very important. Avoid all soft and leafy specimens. Color should be uniform for the variety.

Cabbages. The type is important in judging. Exhibitors should not peel the leaves too closely. When some of the leaves are allowed to remain, they prevent bruises. Color varies with the variety. Firmness is very important.

Carrots. Should be kept to type, using short, half long and long in their places. Oversize is to be avoided; quality is best in medium-sized specimens. Color is very important. Avoid exhibiting greenish or pale-yellow specimens. Irregular and coarse carrots will be penalized.

Cauliflower. Should be pure white, solid, and with no leaves appearing through the head. The side leaves should be trimmed about two inches above the center of the head. Avoid yellow leaves and discolorations.

Celery. Should be exhibited without roots. The outside leaves should be removed until the inside is uniform in color. Avoid split and pithy stalks. Wash carefully and avoid cutting roots too closely.

Cucumber. Oversize should be avoided. Avoid the extremes of immaturity and over-ripeness. Immature specimens are likely to be too spiny. Overripe ones show a tendency to turn yellow. Type and color are very important. Be sure not to mix types.

Eggplant. Specimens should not be too large. Maturity is largely determined by color. Avoid greenness in specimens. Give protection in transit.

Endive. Plants should be of the same size, leaves uniformly curled and centers blanched.

Lettuce. Should be crisp and fresh, firm, free from sunscald and exhibited with roots in water.

Onions. Should not be peeled down to the green. At late season exhibitions, onions must be thoroughly ripened off, with the necks dry.

Parsley. Close-curled varieties are best for exhibition. Select plants of about the same age, for then the color will be similar. Avoid any tendency to yellow leaves. Exhibit with roots in water.

Parsnips. Should be white, smooth, tapering, and true to type.

Peas. Be sure specimens are uniform, true to the variety type, under- rather than over-mature and of the same color and length of pod.

Peppers. All specimens should have the same number of lobes. All specimens in plate exhibits should be of one color and true to type.

Potatoes. Select only specimens of medium, uniform size. Oversize is to be avoided. Skins should be the color for the variety, tender and smooth, without scab, mosaic, or bruises. Potatoes for exhibition should be dried carefully and the soil brushed off lightly. Do not wash.

Radishes. The value of radishes lies in their color and crispness. Selections should be made, keeping these points in mind. Type, however, is very important and types must be kept distinct. Choose small-size, uniform specimens of right color for variety. Exhibit with foliage. Pithy specimens should be avoided.

Spinach. Only entire plants of spinach should be shown. They should be cut close to the ground. The stalks should be short and the leaves broad and deep green. Wash spinach carefully. Do not bruise the leaves.

Squash. Summer squash must be tender and of medium size. Specimens must be of even color and true to type. Winter squash should be of large size for the variety, although extreme size is of no advantage. A typical Blue Hubbard for exhibition should not weigh over 35 pounds, and other varieties in proportion. Specimens should be mature and the skin firm. They should be free from blemishes and insect injury. Stems should be cut at the vine. (*See* Vegetable Marrows, below.)

Sweet Corn. Should be shown only in the edible stage. Ears should be taken to the exhibition in full husk. Strip off one-third of the husk and remove the silk. Be sure that the tips are well filled-out. Corn should be true to type. The kernels should be even in size and color and each cob of the same length, thickness, and color.

Tomatoes. Should be firm and colored all over. Type is especially important. Do not mix varieties or types. Be sure there are no cracked specimens or green ends. Remove the stems.

Turnips. The three types of turnips should be kept distinct. Egg varieties should have the typical egg shape, while flat specimens should be selected for their conformity to type. Purple-top varieties should be purple all the way around the top. Rutabaga or Swedish turnip should be exhibited with the fine roots as well as the main tap root cut off. All turnips should be firm and yet not woody. Uniformity in size is very important.

Vegetable Marrows. Vegetable marrows are not true squashes and must not be exhibited in squash classes. They include many types of varying sizes and shapes. For exhibition they should be picked while tender and shown with their stems on.

---

* Special articles on the subjects indicated by an asterisk (*) will be found at the words so marked.

NOTES ON EXHIBITING AND JUDGING FRUITS

1. Some judges overemphasize the value of size in fruits shown for exhibition, especially in plate classes. This is to be guarded against. Large size may indicate especially good culture but it should not rank with high color and freedom from blemishes. This does not mean that fruit specimens should be undersized. On the contrary, judges are encouraged to favor specimens which are slightly above the average size of the particular variety under consideration.

2. When fruits are exhibited in England great importance is placed upon taste and skill in arrangement. This is a matter which should receive more attention. Not only should the fruit shown be as nearly perfect as possible but it should be staged attractively. Judges should keep this matter in mind.

3. In the case of a new variety, extra specimens should be available for tasting by the judges.

4. Fruits which show insect injury, traces of disease, bruises or malformations of any kind should not be exhibited. Judges should penalize or disqualify exhibits which offend noticeably in this respect.

5. In so far as possible the bloom on grapes, plums, apples, and nectarines should be preserved, as this adds greatly to the natural beauty of these fruits. Polishing of apples is allowed only in the displays.

6. Large size in melons for the variety is important, denoting quick growth, which usually means quality in outdoor varieties. Judges should sample melons. Uniformity in size, netting, and color are important. Melons for exhibition should be ripe.

DISPLAYS

In displays of fruit avoid the use of large baskets with high handles or highly colored splints which do not harmonize with the color of the fruit. The use of proper foliage in displays is very important. Fruit-tree foliage or fruiting berried shrubs are to be preferred over other kinds of decorative material. Many of the fruits of the ornamental apples and pears are ideal for decoration in fruit displays.

Backgrounds are very important in bringing out the color of fruits. A dark background is much better than a light one for most apples, while light backgrounds bring out the color in grapes and plums.

Do not crowd exhibits. Harmony in fruit displays is just as important as in flower displays.

APPLE EXHIBITS

1. *Form.* Specimen apples should be smooth, regular, and typical of the variety.

2. *Color.* In judging color, the following points should be considered:
   a. Depth and attractiveness of ground color.
   b. Characteristic overcolor.
   c. Amount of overcolor.

3. *Uniformity.* Specimens should be of the same form, size, color, and ripeness.

4. *Quality.* This should include both texture and flavor.

5. *Size.* The following scale of sizes in well-known apples is intended to be a guide to exhibitors in choosing specimens. The measurements given are the largest transverse diameter.

Baldwin	3 –3¼ in.
Cortland	3 –3¼ "
Delicious	2⅞–3⅛ "
Early McIntosh	2⅞–3⅛ "
Fall Pippin	3⅛–3⅜ "
Fameuse	2⅜–2⅞ "
Golden Delicious	2⅞–3⅛ "
Gravenstein	3 –3⅜ "
†Grimes Golden	2¾–3 "
Jonathan	2⅛–3¼ "
Kendall	2⅞–3⅛ "
King	3¼–3⅜ "
Macoun	2⅞–3⅛ "
Maiden Blush	3 –3¼ "
McIntosh	2⅞–3⅛ "
†Newtown Pippin	2⅞–3⅛ "
Northern Spy	3⅛–3½ "
Oldenburg	2⅞–3⅛ "
Opalescent	3¼–3½ "
†Palmer Greening	3 –3¼ "
†Porter	2⅝–2⅞ "
†Rhode Island Greening	3⅛–3⅜ "
Richard	2⅞–3⅛ "
Rome Beauty	3 –3¼ "
Roxbury Russet	2⅞–3⅛ "
Stark	3 –3¼ "
Starking	2⅞–3⅛ "
Sutton	2⅞–3⅛ "
Tolman	2⅞–3⅛ "
Twenty Ounce	3½–3⅞ "
Wagener	3 –3¼ "
Wealthy	2⅞–3¼ "
Winter Banana	3 –3½ "
Wolf River	3½–4 "
Yellow Bellflower	3 –3¼ "

NOTE: *In varieties with a dagger (†) the presence or absence of blush are not considered in judging.*

8. **MEANING OF TERMS COMMONLY USED.**

Accessories. Cut foliage and foliage plants, stands and containers, baskets, as well as sundials, bird baths, garden furniture, textile backgrounds, draperies, etc., are classed as accessories.

Amateur. An amateur is one who does not engage in the sale of plants for any part of his livelihood and who does not accept pay as a gardener, garden consultant, or landscape architect.

Annual. A plant that normally completes its outdoor growth cycle in one year.

Arranged for Effect. This term is used to emphasize the necessity of staging a group or display to create an attractive and aesthetic impression. The proper selection and use of accessories is important in such exhibits.

Artistic. Pleasing to the eye, conceived with taste and executed with skill.

Biennial. A plant that requires two growing seasons to complete its growth cycle.

Blooms. Individual flowers, one on a stem.

---

* Special articles on the subjects indicated by an asterisk (*) will be found at the words so marked.

Charm. An inner quality which gives an exhibit an intangible appeal.

Cluster. Several blossoms or fruits growing close together on the same stem. The rambler rose Dorothy Perkins is an example. Plum tomatoes and grapes are others.

Collection. Several varieties of plants, flowers, fruits, or vegetables in one exhibit. It differs from a group in that the number of different varieties is an important factor. Artistic arrangement is desirable and implied even though not called for in the schedule.

Color. The natural color and not any variation produced by dyeing, rubbing, or polishing. In the case of apples, an exception is made, polishing being permitted in displays but not in competitive classes.

Color Harmony. The orderly combination of colors resulting in an aesthetically pleasing general effect.

Commercial Grower. One who grows plants, flowers, or other garden products for sale.

Condition. The quality or the nearness to perfection at the time of judging — not what the material probably looked like the previous day nor what it may look like the following day.

Display. Unless otherwise specified in the schedule, a display calls for an exhibit of cut flowers, vegetables, or fruits artistically arranged to create an effect. Accessories, including cut foliage and foliage plants, are permitted.

Distinctiveness. A quality of elegance and finish that makes an exhibit stand out above the ordinary.

Foliage. When the term "own foliage" is used, it means the kind produced by the species of plant exhibited and not necessarily the foliage of the particular flower being shown. The words "any foliage" are to be interpreted as natural foliage. Gypsophila, stevia, etc., are sometimes used as accessory foliage but are not permitted unless the schedule so specifies.

Form. The normal type or shape of the species or variety.

Freedom from Blemish. Bruises, loss of stem, spray discoloration, any injury by insects or diseases, and any malformation detracting from the appearance of a specimen are called blemishes.

Group. An exhibit of one or more species or varieties of plants. Artistic arrangement is of great importance.

Herbaceous. A plant which does not develop woody tissue and which dies to the ground each winter. (*See* Perennial, below.)

Kinds. Flowers, fruits, or vegetables of a different genus. Thus, in a collection of vegetables, beans, cabbages, carrots, and turnips are kinds. There are exceptions. Snap beans are to be considered as different kinds from shell beans and the Savoy as distinct from other cabbages.

Meritorious. An exhibit that compels admiration, possesses high horticultural value as measured by judgment on points, has exceptional artistic quality and individuality, is distinctive and that shows high culture.

Novelty. A variety of recent introduction or still undisseminated and not previously shown at an exhibition.

Originality. The quality of being independently conceived without undue exaggeration. This does not mean bizarre or freakish.

Outstanding. The most conspicuous or spectacular exhibit which combines quality of material with artistic arrangement.

Perennial. An herbaceous plant that lives from year to year. A group or collection of perennial plants or flowers includes perennial bulbs and so-called biennials but not woody plants. The term perennial applies in the schedule only to plants which are hardy in this section.

Professional Gardener. A person who, because of his training and experience, qualifies for horticultural employment.

Rock Garden. A landscape composition designed and built to simulate natural rocky surroundings for the culture and harmonious display of rock plants, alpines, and other plants of similar habit and character.

Seasonability. Plants which naturally flower about the same season although not necessarily at the time of year when the show is held. For instance, where the schedule calls for a garden in bloom on a specified date such as "the end of May," three weeks either side of this date is permitted under the term seasonability. It must be remembered that in staging flower shows reasonable latitude with respect to season is for the benefit of the show and the drawing of too sharp a line is merely pedagogical.

Shrub. A woody plant of low growth, as distinct from a tree.

Size. Exhibition flowers, fruits, or vegetables may be somewhat above the average size of the particular variety but the selection of abnormally large-sized specimens should be avoided, especially when size tends to impair quality.

Specimen. A single fruit, vegetable, plant, bloom, spike, or stalk.

Spike. A thick, upright stem carrying several flowers. The gladiolus, foxglove, and delphinium are examples.

Stalk. A stiff stem carrying one or more flowers and buds. It may be branched. The bearded iris is an example.

Substance. Firmness and texture as characteristic of the flower at its best.

Suitability. Appropriateness; in keeping with the purpose and character of an exhibit.

Undisseminated. A variety or a clone is

---

* Special articles on the subjects indicated by an asterisk (*) will be found at the words so marked.

considered undisseminated until the time it is sold by the originator or his agent, with or without restrictions.

Uniformity. All specimens on a plate or flowers in a vase, etc., should be as nearly as possible alike in size, form, and color.

Varieties. Named variations in plant species.

Woody. Plants which are covered with bark and do not die back. Shrubs and trees are classed as woody plants.

9. PUBLICITY, ADVERTISING, TRADE EXHIBITS. Publicity is important to any show. People must know about it to attend. Garden and society editors, local newspapers, TV and radio stations are most co-operative with community, nonprofit projects put on for the benefit of the community. Actually you are after free publicity in the small, free shows. Larger shows will find it profitable to pay for some advertising. Competitive posters made by local school children in their art classes always create interest, and the posters bring parents and friends to the show. If admission is charged, you may find it profitable to give complimentary tickets to the press and other important personalities you want to visit the show. Their presence is newsworthy and will give the show publicity. The publicity chairman is responsible for the show stories, arranging for publicity pictures and interviews, and must send out announcements of the show to neighboring clubs, florists, and garden centers. A list of the prize-winners should be prepared and given to the local newspapers. A scrapbook should be kept of all stories, pictures, and publicity for future reference.

If tickets are to be used, the publicity committee may handle that too, unless the show is large. Advance sales are always good insurance against bad weather.

As a source of income, many flower shows find it profitable to invite commercial concerns to have trade booths for which a rental fee is charged. These booths should feature only horticultural products or closely related items such as vases, flower holders, etc., with restrictions as to background, signs, etc., so the theme or atmosphere of the show will be maintained. — A. H. N.

Two good books for sponsors of shows, recently issued, are *Handbook for Flower Shows* (Box 4965, Philadelphia 19, Pa.) and *Flower Show Exhibitors and Judges Handbook* (145 Tanglewood Drive, Urbana, Ohio).

With reference to the last sentence of the above article, some large metropolitan shows have succumbed to a tendency that is to be deplored. They sell space for exhibitions that have nothing to do with horticulture. A warning against this was sounded by Mr. F. F. Rockwell in the *Home Garden* for May, 1947. Because little attention was paid to it we reprint Mr. Rockwell's remarks below (in part): — EDITOR.

Unless there's a change in the policy behind these biggest shows, they are on their way out — at least so far as the real horticultural public is concerned. There has been a tendency to put more and more emphasis on "Show" and less and less on "Flower." Cut flowers, super-Grade-A-glass-grown florists' flowers, there are, of course . . . but that is not what the "Flower" in Flower Show means.

The feature particularly lacking, or particularly on the decline, in these big shows is horticulture — especially amateur horticulture — and exhibits of genuine educational value. The few such features still to be found are stuck away in corners or on upper floors. They should be given a share of the spotlight. . . . Flower arrangements alone will not take their place.

The "big" shows for this spring are now past history. The thousands of little ones throughout the land, to be held in late spring or in autumn, are in the making. Less dramatic, less publicized, than the big ones, they nevertheless are, in their combined effect, more important.

Let us hope that the managers and the schedule makers of these county, local, and garden club shows will not forget that the primary purpose of a flower show is to foster an interest in *gardening*, and to help educate those who attend them to become better gardeners. Commercial cooperation may be essential to success — but it should remain cooperation and not become *coercion*.

Those who run the shows hold the keys. Let us hope they'll see that the door is locked before the horse is stolen.

FLOWER SOCIETIES. There are many local or national flower societies devoted to the culture or improvement of various flowers, *i.e.*, dahlia, chrysanthemum, cactus, etc. They are noted at the name of the flower to which they are devoted.

FL. PL. Short for *flore-pleno; i.e.,* double-flowered.

fluitans (flew'i-tanz). Floating.

fluminensis, -e (flew-min-nen'sis). Named for the flumen (river) at Rio de Janeiro, when it was supposed that the harbor of that city was part of a river. *See* SPIDERWORT.

FLY-HONEYSUCKLE. *See* LONICERA.

FOAM FLOWER = *Tiarella cordifolia.*

FOENICULUM. *See* FENNEL.

Foenum-Graecum (fee-num-gree'kum). Literally, Greek hay. *See* TRIGONELLA.

foetida, -us, -um (fe'ti-da). Evil-smelling.

foetidisssima, -us, -um (fe-ti-diss'i-ma). Most evil-smelling.

FOG FRUIT. *See* LIPPIA.

FOG MIST. *See* rooting of softwood cuttings under mist at CUTTINGS.

foliacea, -us, -um (foe-li-ā'see-a). Foliaceous; *i.e.*, leafy or leaf-like. Many bracts* are foliaceous, others are colored.

FOLIAGE PLANTS. As generally used, foliage plants refers to greenhouse subjects grown primarily for their handsome leaves, some of which are variegated or otherwise colored. Among the best greenhouse ones are plants in the genera *Begonia, Bertolonia, Episcia, Calathea, Dieffenbachia, Aglaonema, Ficus, Grevillea, Pandanus, Hoffmannia, Sonerila, Dracaena, Cordyline, Araucaria,*

---

* Special articles on the subjects indicated by an asterisk (*) will be found at the words so marked.

Peperomia, Philodendron, Xanthosoma, Maranta, Caladium, and *Polyscias;* all of which are described at their generic names. *See also* Ferns and Fern Gardening and Palms, some of which are among our finest foliage plants. For the finest collection of illustrations of tropical foliage plants, *see* A. B. Graf's *Exotica,* published by Roehrs Co., Rutherford, N.J., in 1957 (second edition, 1959). It contains over 4000 illustrations.

Among hardy plants or summer bedding ones, those grown chiefly for their foliage are less numerous than the tropical genera. But the castor-oil plant, *Coleus, Colocasia,* and a variety of *Ligularia* are mostly so grown. So are some of the bamboo-like grasses. *See* Bamboo. Other hardy plants, some species of which have especially fine foliage, are the maples, some of the vines (*see* Vines), *Acanthopanax, Oplopanax,* and box. *See also* Evergreens and Broad-leaved Evergreens.

FOLIAR FEEDING. When the Atomic Energy Commission began releasing radioactive isotopes for biological and medical experimentation they provided a new tool to the plant physiologists. Formerly it was believed that foliage would not absorb nutrients other than gases, through the cuticle of the leaf. By spraying the leaves of plants with various nutrient solutions, to which radioactive isotopes were added, experimenters were able by X-ray photography and other techniques to trace the absorption and translocation of these nutrients within the tissues of the plant because they were "tagged" by the radioactive isotopes. The results were revolutionary.

Using at first various trace* elements, and ultimately the main fertilizer ingredients, it has been possible to demonstrate that plants can absorb through their leaves nutrients such as nitrogen, phosphoric acid, and potash which had hitherto been assumed to enter the plant only through the roots.

What does such a concept mean to the average gardener? For centuries we fed plants with manure, and since the rise of chemical fertilizers, with their chemical ingredients, both of which were of use only by their absorption through the root hairs. *See* Root. Perhaps the ability of leaves to absorb some of the plant nutrients directly through the cuticle might be of much practical importance. It might save the costly and messy distribution of manure or fertilizers in the soil and replace such drudgery by the clean, easily applied spraying with properly balanced nutrients dissolved in water.

A tremendous amount of work has been done on this new facet of plant nutrition. Nearly every experiment station in the country has studied it — some with profound skepticism, others with enthusiastic, and often fervent, advocacy. One of the leaders of the latter contingent wrote (in 1955): "If we apply these materials to the leaves in soluble forms, as much as 95% . . . may be used by the plant. If we apply a similar amount to the soil we find about 10% of it to be used."

A somewhat chilling rejoinder to such a claim came from the other school of thought. They pointed out that less than 5 per cent of the plant's total nitrogen requirement *could* be absorbed by the leaf and 95 per cent would come only through the roots. Others pointed out the obvious fact that nutrient solutions sprayed on leaves must, in ordinary garden practice, drip down to the soil, which would then be merely a combination of root feeding and foliar feeding. They also pointed out that what the leaf had absorbed it could lose by leaching in heavy rains. This, too, has been demonstrated beyond doubt.

Faced with such a dilemma, what is the average gardener to do? A reasonable appraisal of all the evidence shows quite certainly that:

1. Plants can absorb nutrient solutions through their leaves. This is especially true of trace* elements and where one of these is lacking (a rare contingency) such leaf-feeding is apparently justified.
2. Leaves cannot absorb solutions high enough in nutrients to be very effective, because when such solutions are made in the necessary strength they injure the plant.
3. At certain periods, especially when the soil is cool or cold, and root activity is retarded, foliar feeding may be justified. This has been tried experimentally on strawberries and apples with apparent success.
4. Foliar feeding, as "tagged" by radioactive isotopes, is relatively rapid and fleeting. Hence spraying of nutrient solutions has to be repeated at least "once a month."
5. Permanent translocation of nutrients sprayed on the leaves is scanty. In the case of phosphorus, less than 5 per cent of that sprayed on the leaves in four applications could be found in the root — which led one experimenter to liken such minimal movement of this nutrient to "feeding a pig one grain of corn at a time."
6. Many plants make maximal growth in the first four to six weeks of their life, when about half of their total nutrient requirements are absorbed through the roots. Hence "foliage sprays for the most part are too little and too late."

The ability to trace the absorption and translocation of plant nutrients sprayed on the leaves provided a technique entirely unknown to the scientists until the advent of radioactive isotopes. But the above summary shows quite clearly that the discovery of this, which is purely a problem in plant physiology, may or may not be of much importance to the gardener. Heated and extravagant claims on both sides have stirred up a mass of writing on what should perhaps have been an interesting feature of plant

---

* Special articles on the subjects indicated by an asterisk (*) will be found at the words so marked.

life, maybe best confined to the laboratory. That it has done far more than this is of importance to every gardener.

Soon after the news "broke," enterprising and not always ingenuous manufacturers began putting out a spate of literature and products to cater to a public that was admittedly confused over the conflicting testimony. Nearly every large fertilizer company began putting out mixtures suitable for foliar feeding, and thousands of gardeners have tried them. The formulas for these may be summarized thus:

1. A high phosphate formula — 10–52–17. (See FERTILIZERS for the meaning of these figures.)
2. Medium phosphate mixture — 15–30–15.
3. Equal ingredients — 20–20–20.

As will be seen, these formulas are far higher in nutrients than those applied in the dry state, and consequently vastly more expensive. One experiment station has pointed out that some commercial formulas can be made for about $200 per ton, but as packaged and advertised they cost the consumer at the rate of nearly $2000 per ton.

If in spite of the cost, and the controversial nature of the evidence, you decide to try these sprays on your garden foliage it is imperative to follow the directions on the box precisely. Nothing will kill your plants quicker than too concentrated a solution of these foliage sprays. One expert grower of camellias and azaleas reports that foliar feeding in the former produces good foliage, but poor roots. In azaleas it "keeps growth going until mid-July, and then no more." See also STARTER SOLUTIONS.

foliosa, -us, -um (fo-lee-o′sa). Leafy.

FOLLICLE. A usually dry, one-chambered fruit, which, unlike a legume (pea), splits only along one seam. The fruits of peony, monkshood, and the milkweed are follicles. In *Decaisnea* the follicle is fleshy and edible.

FONTANESIA (fon-ta-nee′zi-a). Asiatic shrubs of the olive family, both the two known species cult. for ornament, although their flowers are not particularly showy. Leaves opposite,* without, or nearly without, marginal teeth, and short-stalked. Flowers small, in leafy clusters (panicles*), the calyx* very small and 4-parted, the 4 petals also small and narrow. Stamens* 2, a little longer than the petals. Fruit a small, flat, winged nutlet. (Named for Rene Louiche Desfontaines, French botanist.)

Both the shrubs below are of easy culture in any ordinary garden soil. They may be increased by seeds, or by layering.

californica = *Fontanesia fortunei.*

fortunei. A slender, smooth, upright-branching shrub, 6–12 ft. high. Leaves lance-shaped, or ovalish, shining green, 2–4 in. long. Flowers greenish-white. Fruit oval, nearly ¾ in. long. China. May–June. Hardy from zone* 4 southward.

phillyreoides. Closely related to *F. fortunei,* but lower, and with smaller and more oblongish leaves, which are minutely toothed on the margin, and gray-green. Fruit nearly round, ½–¾ in. in diameter. Hardy from zone* 5 southward.

fontinalis, -e (fon-ti-nay′lis). Pertaining to a spring.

FOOD PLANTS. Outside the cereals, which are agricultural rather than garden crops, many food plants come within the scope of this book. See the several articles on fruit culture, kitchen gardening, herbs, and herb gardening. See also the name of your state or province, for the chief food plants suitable to your region.

FORCING. The forcing of flowers, fruits, and vegetables out of season is not a new innovation, it having been in practice in European countries for many years.

In America the forcing of vegetables, potted plants, and cut flowers has developed into an enormous industry and many acres of land are covered with greenhouses and frames in order to produce various specialized crops out of season for the markets.

Probably no horticultural industry requires more skill than that of forcing plants in order to harvest the crops when in most demand. In the case of an amateur grower having a small greenhouse at his disposal, success can be achieved in the forcing of plants if the following simple general instructions are followed:

a. See that the plants are well rooted and in a good healthy condition.

b. Commence with a minimum temperature, increasing a few degrees weekly until the maximum is reached. See RETARDING.

c. Maintain a buoyant atmosphere in the forcing house by the liberal use of water sprayed under the benches and walks and, less often, on the foliage of the plants.

d. Administer air during all seasonable weather, avoiding drafts, closing the ventilators in the early afternoon.

e. Do not allow the plants to become dry from the time forcing has commenced.

f. Fumigate or vaporize regularly to keep down insect pests. See FUMIGATION.

BULBS. Hyacinths, tulips, narcissus, and lilies. Use potting mixture* 3. Place the bulbs as soon as received in pots or pans 4–8 inches in diameter, allowing one to ten bulbs in each. As soon as potted, water thoroughly and place where they can be kept cool in order to give the roots an opportunity to develop. If a frame is convenient they may be placed in that or they may be placed in a block outside where they will be shaded from the sun. Cover with three or four inches of sand or coal ashes. This will keep the pots from drying out. As soon as the bulbs develop a good root system they may be taken out and placed in the greenhouse in a temperature of 50° F., later increasing the temperature to 60° –65°.

AZALEA, RHODODENDRON. Use potting mix-

---

* Special articles on the subjects indicated by an asterisk (*) will be found at the words so marked.

ture* 5. These plants should be kept in a cool house until wanted for forcing, 40°–45° at night, with plenty of air through the day. When the buds have developed forcing may begin. Place in a temperature of 55° to start, increasing to 60°–65°. Frequent watering and syringing will be necessary. Do not at any time allow the plants to get dry at the roots. Best results are obtained in a well-ventilated and lightly shaded greenhouse. It is important to keep the buds of the rhododendrons moist to encourage evenness in breaking. Spray the foliage with the hose at least twice on all bright days.

HYDRANGEA. Use potting mixture* 3. As a house plant *Hydrangea macrophylla,* the hortensia, is very popular. Flowering at Easter, it has become one of the most useful florists' plants, as it lends itself readily to forcing. The young plants are bedded out during the summer and in late September or October are taken up, potted, and placed in a block outside on the dry ground. This is done to check the vigorous growth and to encourage its ripening. Force as recommended for azaleas.

Hydrangeas are great water-lovers, therefore they should not be allowed to become dry. They are also gross feeders and an occasional watering with liquid manure is very beneficial to them. Force in a temperature 50° F., increasing to a maximum of 60° F.

HARDY PLANTS. Use potting mixture* 3. Hardy plants have been forced for many years in Europe; it is, however, a relatively new industry in this country. The flowers of many of these plants are most useful for cutting, and many lend themselves admirably for decoration in the home when grown as pot plants. A number of the species of the hardy shrubs are well adapted for forcing, the best results being obtained from those flowering early in the season.

Well-grown and shapely plants should be selected that have been prepared for the purpose. They require a resting period of from two to three months before they are brought into the forcing house. Among the most useful for forcing are: *Zenobia pulverulenta, Pieris floribunda, Azalea mollis, Kalmia latifolia, Exochorda racemosa, Spiraea vanhouttei, Viburnum tomentosum sterile, Viburnum Opulus sterile, Deutzia gracilis, Deutzia lemoinei, Deutzia scabra, Lagerstroemia indica, Clethra alnifolia, Daphne Cneorum, Syringa vulgaris* (see LILAC), *Buddleia alternifolia, Kolkwitzia amabilis, Viburnum carlesi, Forsythia intermedia spectabilis, Philadelphus virginalis* (see MOCK-ORANGE) and *Hamamelis vernalis.*

Young stock should be planted in the nursery or garden rows and grown for two or three seasons, transplanting each year to ensure a mass of fibrous roots that will adapt them for their growth in pots. Pruning should be attended to in order to shape the plants. When strong and vigorous enough for forcing they may be dug as the leaves fall. Place in pots of a suitable size. Water

thoroughly and plunge* in a frame or in a sheltered spot outside. Water occasionally as their needs require. Early in January the first plants may be started, bringing in other plants at intervals of two weeks for succession.

Place at first in a cool greenhouse, 45° F., increasing the temperature gradually until a maximum of 60°–65° F. is reached. Spray frequently on all sunny days to encourage a free and even breaking of the growths.

FORCING PLANTS IN FRAMES. The frame method of forcing has been in use for many generations, decaying manure or electricity being the medium from which the heat is furnished, supplemented with the rays of the sun. For the details of hotbed and cold frames *see* COLD FRAME.

Many excellent crops can be grown in frames if care is taken with regard to watering, protection and ventilation. Crops such as lettuce, radish, carrots, and cucumbers may be grown in the hotbed.

FORCING HOUSE. Any greenhouse in which plants are forced into harvest out of season. *See* FORCING.

FORESTIERA (fo-res-ti-ee′ra). A genus of 20 species of New World shrubs of the olive family, only two of rather secondary ornamental value. Often sold as *Adelia,* they have opposite,* short-stalked leaves, and small, unisexual,* greenish flowers, without petals, which bloom before the leaves unfold in *F. acuminata.* Sepals 4–6, unequal, often soon falling, thus apparently wanting. Stamens* 2–4. Fruit small, black, fleshy (a drupe*), mostly 1–seeded. (Named for Charles Le-Forestier, French naturalist and physician.)

The swamp privet, as its name indicates, will thrive best in moist places, while *F. ligustrina* is more tolerant of drier sites. Both the cult. species are native in the southeastern U.S. and are hardy only as indicated below. Easily propagated by seeds or by layering.

acuminata. Swamp privet. Usually a shrub up to 9 ft., rarely tree-like and up to 25 ft. Leaves ovalish-oblong, 2–4 in. long, tapering at the tip. Flowers very small, the male in bracted* clusters, the female in panicles.* Fruit oblongish, about ½ in. long. Southern Ill. to Fla. and Tex. Apr.–May. Hardy from zone* 4 with protection and from zone* 5 without it, southward.

ligustrina. A shrub, never over 9 ft. high. Leaves oblong or elliptic, blunt at the tip, 1–1½ in. long. Flowers almost stalkless. Fruit egg-shaped, about ⅝ in. long. Ky. to Ga. and Fla. Aug. Hardy from zone* 6, or with protection from zone* 5, southward.

FORESTRY. While commercial forestry lies outside the scope of this book, the management of small woodlands on country estates is often important. Unless one is a trained forester, the selection of trees and management of cutting are likely to be of little permanent value. It is urged that most owners call in a professional for this, supplied by many states from their Department of Forests.

---

* Special articles on the subjects indicated by an asterisk (*) will be found at the words so marked.

FORGET-ME-NOT. Mainly blue-flowered, but sometimes pink- or white-flowered, annual or perennial herbs of the genus **Myosotis** (my-o-so'tis) of the family Boraginaceae, most of the 40 species European, but a few throughout the north temperate zone. They are usually branching, often weak or prostrate, generally hairy, plants of very easy culture. Leaves alternate,° without marginal teeth. Flowers small, in branched or unbranched, sometimes 1-sided, clusters. Calyx short, tubular, 5-toothed at the top. Corolla salver-shaped, 5-lobed, the throat crested and often of a different color (with an eye°). Fruit a collection of 4 small, smooth nutlets. (*Myosotis* is from the Greek for mouse-ear, in allusion to the leaves.)

Most garden forget-me-nots, especially *M. arvensis* and *M. sylvatica*, are best treated as hardy annuals or biennials. See ANNUALS; BIENNIALS. Some, like *M. scorpioides*, are true perennials and should be so grown, and may easily be divided in early spring. The beautiful color and low growth make the forget-me-nots very attractive bedding plants, especially as a carpet under tulips or other bulbs. All of them do better when a bit crowded, the annuals especially, and most of them prefer partial shade and plenty of moisture. Can also be grown in the greenhouse for winter bloom.

M. alpestris. A common name in the catalogues but the plant, and its white and pink-flowered forms, are usually *M. sylvatica*. The true *M. alpestris* is scarcely known in gardens.

M. arvensis. Field scorpion grass. An annual or biennial, somewhat sprawling, but occasionally up to 18 in. high. Leaves oblongish, ¾–1 in. long. Flowers blue or white, about ⅕ in. wide. North temperate zone.

M. dissitiflora = *Myosotis sylvatica*, so far as cult. plants are concerned.

M. palustris = *Myosotis scorpioides*.

M. scorpioides. Common perennial forget-me-not of the gardens, the stems more or less prostrate and up to 12 in. long. Leaves oblongish or narrower, about 1 in. long. Flowers blue, but with a yellow, pink, or white eye.° Eurasia. Spring. The *var.* **semperflorens** is a lower form which blooms through the summer.

M. sylvatica. A Eurasian annual or biennial, not over 9 in. high, usually less. Leaves oblongish or narrower, about ¾ in. long. Flower blue, but sometimes pink or white, the eye differently colored, often yellow. May–Aug. Usually offered, also, as *M. alpestris*.

FORMALDEHYDE. See Formaldehyde at FUNGICIDES.

formosa, -us, -um (for-mo'sa). Handsome.

formosana, -us, -um (for-mo-say'na). From the island of Formosa.

formosissima, -us, -um (for-mo-sis'i-ma). Most showy or handsome.

FORSYTHIA (for-sĭth'i-a; *also* for-sy'thi-a). Very handsome, spring-blooming, Asiatic shrubs of the olive family, widely planted for their profuse, usually yellow, flowers that bloom before or with the unfolding of the leaves. Commonly called golden bell, the shrubs are inclined to be arching or spreading, and some varieties root at the ends of the pendulous branches. Leaves opposite,° stalked. Flowers in clusters of 1–6 in the leaf axils,° practically stalkless, and so numerous as nearly to cover the stems in some varieties. Calyx 4-lobed and persistent. Corolla bell-shaped below, but split into 4 strap-shaped lobes which look casually like 4 separate petals. Stamens 2. Fruit a 2-celled capsule.° (Named for William Forsyth, British horticulturist.)

Fortunately, the golden bells are of the easiest culture in any garden soil. They root as easily as privet, and cuttings of the stems, or uprooting the usually plentiful supply of suckers, will always provide new plants. They are extremely effective when planted in large masses, especially against an evergreen background. All are hardy up to zone° 2, but sometimes slightly winter-killed,° especially the flower buds, which are more sensitive than the leaf buds. Most of them stand smoke better than such decorative shrubs usually do.

intermedia. A hybrid between *F. suspensa* and *F. viridissima* and by far the best of the golden bells. It is a shrub up to 9 ft. high, with arching or spreading, pithy branches. Leaves oblong or ovalish, 3–5 in. long, sometimes 3-parted, but usually merely toothed. Flowers yellow, usually several at each cluster, about 1½ in. long, the clusters very numerous. The *var.* **primulina** has pale yellow flowers, which are more numerous toward the ends of the branches. The *var.* **spectabilis** has more flowers at each cluster and each corolla may be up to 1½ in. long. This variety is probably the finest *Forsythia* in cult. It is useful for forcing (which see).

ovata. A Korean shrub, not over 5 ft. high, the branches arching. Leaves broadly oval, 2–3 in. long. Flowers solitary,° but very numerous, amber-yellow. Mar.–Apr., usually blooming before any of the others. Hardy from zone° 3 southward, possibly in zone° 2.

suspensa. Weeping golden bell. An upright shrub up to 12 ft. high, the tips of the long, arching, hollow branches often pendulous and, in age, rooting at the tip. Leaves oval-oblong, toothed, 3–5 in. long. Flowers golden-yellow, about 1 in. long, mostly 1–3 at each cluster. China. If left unpruned this may sometimes act like a vine over a wall. See VINES. The *var.* **atrocaulis** has dark purple, young branches; *var.* **fortunei** is chiefly erect and has few or no pendulous branches; *var.* **sieboldi** has slender, almost trailing branches.

viridissima. A nearly erect shrub up to 10 ft., the branches pithy. Leaves 4–6 in. long, toothed only toward the tip. Flowers greenish-yellow, about 1 in. long, usually only 1–3 at each cluster. China. Less grown than the other two, but a variety from Korea is welcomed by some. It has bright yellow flowers. The *var.* **bronxensis** is said by its sponsor to be dwarf — scarcely 15 in. high.

FORTUNELLA (for-tew-nel'la). Evergreen Chinese trees or shrubs, commonly called kumquat, belonging to the family Rutaceae and closely related to the orange. Leaves alternate,° compound,° but reduced to a single leaflet with a margined or winged stalk and prominently dotted with

---

° Special articles on the subjects indicated by an asterisk (°) will be found at the words so marked.

glands on the under side. Flowers star-like and flat (*see* Citrus). Fruit orange-like, but small, its cells 3–7 (8–15 in the orange), aromatic and eaten fresh or used for preserves. (Named for Robert Fortune, English traveler who introduced the kumquat into Eu.)

The kumquats should be grown in the same way as oranges, but they will stand more cold than the common sweet orange. *See* Orange. They are usually grown on the stock of *Poncirus trifoliata*, when they are still more frost-resistant. They have been crossed with other citrus fruits and the citrangequat* and limequat* both have kumquat blood in them.

crassifolia. Meiwa kumquat. A shrub or small tree 8–15 ft. high, sometimes spiny. Leaves thick, the stalks narrowly winged. Fruit nearly egg-shaped, about 1½ in. in diameter, its cells 6 or 7.

japonica. Round kumquat; also called Marumi kumquat. A shrub or small tree 7–10 ft. high, usually much-branched. Leaves bluntish, broad, about 2½ in. long. Fruit globe-shaped, about 1¼ in. in diameter, its cells 5 or 6. Sometimes offered as *Citrus japonica*.

margarita. Oval or Nagami kumquat. A spineless shrub or small tree, the leaves narrow-oblong, 3–4 in. long, pointed at the tip. Fruit ovalish-oblong, about 1 in. thick, the cells 4 or 5. Hardier than the other species, and with sweet and acid flesh.

FORT WORTH BOTANIC GARDEN. *See* Botanic Garden.

FOTHERGILLA (foth-er-gil′la). A small genus of North American shrubs of the family Hamamelidaceae, commonly called witch-alder or American witch-alder, related to the witch-hazel, but lacking petals. Leaves coarse, toothed, alternate,* resembling those of the witch-hazel. Flowers small, white, in small terminal heads or spikes, without petals, the only showy feature being the numerous white stamens.* Fruit a beaked capsule. (Named for John Fothergill, English physician.)

The witch-alders are rather ornamental shrubs blooming in April or May, and prefer rather low, moist places. Propagated by seeds or by root cuttings, or suckers.

carolina = *Fothergilla gardeni.*

gardeni. Dwarf alder. A low shrub, usually under 3 ft. high, the broadly wedge-shaped leaves 1–2 in. long, bluish-white and hairy on the under side. Flowers white, the spikes oblongish and about 1 in. long, blooming before the leaves unfold. Va. to Ga. Hardy from zone* 4 southward. Sometimes offered as *F. carolina.*

major. A shrub 7–10 ft. high, the nearly round or ovalish leaves 2–5 in. long, pale and a little hairy on the under side. Flowers white, the clusters 1½–4 in. long, blooming with the unfolding of the leaves. Ga. Hardy from zone* 4 southward. Its foliage turns orange or scarlet in autumn.

monticola. A spreading shrub 4–6 ft. high. Leaves broadly oval, 3–4 in. long, hairy on the veins on the lower surface. Flowers conspicuous, blooming with the unfolding of the leaves, the spikes nearly 3 in. long. N. Car. to Ala. May. Hardy from zone* 4 southward.

FOUNTAIN-GRASS = *Pennisetum ruppeli.*

FOUNTAIN-PALM = *Livistona chinensis.*

FOUNTAIN-PLANT = *Russelia equisetiformis* and *Amaranthus tricolor.*

FOUQUIERIA (foo-kwee-ee′ri-a). The only cult. genus of the family **Fouquieriaceae** (foo-kwee-air-ee-ā′see-ee), the torch tree family, which comprises cactus-like, fantastic, desert plants from Mex. and the adjacent U.S. The only cult. species is **F. splendens**, which is usually called ocotillo, coach-whip, vine cactus, candlewood, or Jacob's staff. It is cactus-like and consists of several very prickly, rigid stems 8–20 ft. high, which are apparently leafless, although there are clusters of small leaves in the axils* of the spines in early spring. Flowers scarlet, tubular, about 1 in. long, with 5 sepals and a 5-lobed corolla, beyond which the 10–17 stamens* protrude. Flower clusters very showy, often branched and 6–10 in. long. Fruit a capsule about ¾ in. long. A showy, desert, hedge plant, fine for the desert garden or in a greenhouse suitable for cacti (*see* Cacti). It is not hardy northward. (Named for Pierre E. Fouquier, French professor of medicine.)

fourcroydes (foor-croy′deez; but *see* Oïdes). A name derived from, and meaning like, the genus *Furcraea.*

FOUR-LEAVED CLOVER. Any of the normally trifoliolate clovers may, very rarely, produce a leaf with 4 leaflets. One that does so more or less habitually is *Trifolium repens purpurascens.* See that plant at Clover.

FOUR-O'CLOCK = *Mirabilis Jalapa.*

FOUR-O'CLOCK FAMILY = Nyctaginaceae.

foveolata, -us, -um (foe-vee-o-lay′ta). Slightly pitted.

FOXBERRY = *Vaccinium Vitis-Idaea.*

FOX GERANIUM = *Geranium robertianum.*

FOXGLOVE. Handsome, sometimes poisonous or medicinal herbs comprising the genus **Digitalis** (di-ji-tay′lis) of the figwort family, some of them deservedly popular garden flowers. Of the 25 known species, all Eurasian, only a few are in cult. and of these the common garden foxglove (*D. purpurea*) is by far the most important. They are erect, biennial or perennial herbs, with alternate* leaves or the lower ones sometimes crowded. Flowers in long, terminal, often 1-sided clusters (racemes*), often very showy, usually purple, yellow, or white. Corolla more or less bell-shaped at the base, the tube a little inflated, the top slightly 2-lipped. Stamens 4. Fruit a capsule.* (*Digitalis* is Latin for the finger of a glove, in allusion to the shape of the corolla.)

All the foxgloves below are either perennials or biennials, but most of them, especially

---

* Special articles on the subjects indicated by an asterisk (*) will be found at the words so marked.

the common garden sort, tend to die out and are best treated as biennials. *See* BIEN-NIALS. If they are treated as perennials they may be divided in spring. All are of simple culture in ordinary garden soil, but the common *D. purpurea* does much better in relatively cool, moist climates, especially along the seacoast of New England and in Wash. and Ore. It is one of the handsomest of garden plants, its leaves yielding an important heart remedy.

D. ambigua. Yellow foxglove. A hairy herb 2–3 ft. high. Leaves stalkless, toothed, oval-lance-shaped. Flowers nearly 2 in. long, yellowish but brown-marked. Eurasia. Sometimes sold as *D. grandiflora.*

D. grandiflora = *Digitalis ambigua.*

D. laevigata. A perennial herb up to 3 ft. high. Flowers yellow but purple-marked. Southern Eu. A handsome species but not much grown.

D. lanata. A biennial or perennial, rarely over 3 ft. high. Flowers white, but with fine veins. Southern Eu. Little known in cult.

D. lutea. A perennial 12–20 in. high. Flowers yellowish-white, scarcely more than ¾ in. long, in 1-sided clusters. Eu.

D. purpurea. Common foxglove of the gardens and called by many other names such as purple foxglove, fairy glove, and finger-flower. It is generally a biennial, 2–4 ft. high, but much higher in favorable places; along English roadsides often 5–8 ft. high. Leaves roughish, the lower long-stalked, the upper shorter-stalked and smaller. Flowers 2–3 in. long, hanging, purple but spotted, borne in a 1-sided raceme 12–24 in. long. Western Eu. The finest of the foxgloves and planted in several forms, especially the *var.* **alba**, with white flowers; *var.* **gloxiniae-flora**, with longer flower clusters; and *var.* **maculata superba**, the leopard foxglove, which is a showy, spotted form.

FOXGLOVE BEARDTONGUE = *Pentstemon Digitalis.*

FOXGLOVE FAMILY = Scrophulariaceae.

FOX GRAPE = *Vitis Labrusca.*

FOXTAIL. *See* ALOPECURUS.

FOXTAIL LILY. *See* EREMURUS.

FOXTAIL MILLET = *Setaria italica.*

FRAGARIA. *See* STRAWBERRY.

fragarioides (fra-gay-ri-oy′deez, but *see* OÏDES). Strawberry-like.

fragiformis, -e (frag-e-form′is). Strawberry-like.

fragilis, -e (frä′ji-lis). Easily broken or, often, easily wilted.

FRAGRANCE. Fragrance adds so much to the pleasure derived from a garden that special effort should be made to insure a succession of sweet-scented flowers throughout the growing season, both for cutting and for garden decoration. It is quite possible to fill a garden with fragrant flowers alone and for those who like to specialize, a small enclosed "nose-garden" or border devoted to them is both practicable and pleasant. But it is commonly more satisfactory to distribute the fragrant flowers generously among the others in order that the choice of material

shall not be limited, but the whole garden impregnated by agreeable odors. In any collection of plants those with aromatic leaves should be prominently featured. They are especially useful in bouquets and nosegays of unscented blooms. Climbers with sweet-scented flowers may be trained about the windows of the dwelling and over porches and arbors, and if there is a favorite walk its verges may be planted with shrubs and herbs giving forth pleasant aromas.

Many flowers are fragrant only at night, like the evening stock, and the sweetness of many others is greatly increased with the coming of dusk. This is true of the tuberose and honeysuckles. If the night-scenting plants are massed in the vicinity of the dwelling their fragrance is carried into the rooms on the night breezes. Some flowers give off their sweetness freely to the air, others release it most readily under a hot sun, or after rain, or in a warm room. The garden is most full of scents when the air is mild and somewhat damp. Certain leaves that must ordinarily be crushed to loose their aromas give it forth readily after a rain. This is true of the sweetbrier and the box. Heliotrope and many sweet herbs are intensely fragrant after a light frost.

Flower scents are of many types and not all are pleasing to all persons, but few will be found to be unpleasant in the open air or to clash with each other. Each week of the growing year has its special scents and with a little forethought these may be given pre-eminence.

Early scents come from snowdrops, daffodils, jonquils, poet's narcissi, *Crocus imperati*, hyacinths, grape hyacinths, some tulips, especially of the early and Cottage varieties; from *Viola odorata*, wallflowers, primroses, cowslips, *Arabis*, lily-of-the-valley, and from such shrubs as *Daphne Mezereum, Lonicera fragrantissima, L. standishi, L. syringantha, Viburnum carlesi*, flowering currant, *Magnolia stellata, M. denudata, Mahonia Aquifolium*, azaleas, *Corylopsis*, English hawthorn, Carolina allspice, and many flowering fruit trees, both domesticated and exotic. Later-flowering shrubs are mock-oranges, lilacs, and the fringe-tree. Sweet-scented climbers include *Akebia quinata, Wistaria*, and *Clematis montana* and its variety *rubens*.

With the coming of summer arrives a wealth of roses, irises, peonies, garden heliotrope, fraxinella, pinks, hardy carnations, *Lilium candidum*, and *Clematis recta*. Later come *Clematis ligusticifolia*, tall phlox, *Lilium regale, L. speciosum*, and *L. auratum*, white plantain-lily, *Campanula lactiflora, C. pyramidalis, Malva moschata*, meadowsweet, and many annuals. Among the annuals are heliotrope, sweet alyssum, sweet peas, sweet sultan, sweet scabious, mignonette, four-o'clocks, stocks, snapdragons, verbenas, petunias, *Abronia*, candytuft, lupines, and daturas. At this season also we have the pungent odors of marigold, tansy, *Calendula*, and chrysanthemums. Summer-flowering

---

* Special articles on the subjects indicated by an asterisk (*) will be found at the words so marked.

shrubs and trees are *Clethra alnifolia, Magnolia virginiana,* and *Elaeagnus angustifolia.* Climbers include honeysuckles, moonflower, and *Clematis paniculata.*

Some sweet-scented, late-flowering bulbs are *Lycoris squamigera, Crocus longiflorus, Colchicum speciosum,* and *C. bornmuelleri.*

Important among night-scenting flowers are bouncing Bet, evening stock, *Nicotiana, Hesperis matronalis, Lychnis alba, Akebia quinata, Lonicera heckrotti, Zaluzianskya villosa, Schizopetalon walkeri* (annual), *Gladiolus tristis.*

Plants and shrubs with fragrant leaves are the following: sweet geraniums (tender), lemon verbena (tender), bergamot, mints, thymes, southernwood and other artemisias, lavender, rosemary (tender), sweet marjoram, sweet basil, tansies, winter and summer savory, costmary, balm, *Teucrium Marum, Nepeta mussini,* camomile, feverfew, yarrow, *Micromeria,* hyssop, rue, bayberry, *Sassafras,* and sweetbriers.

Southern gardens may enjoy a variety of jasmines, pittosporums, *Osmanthus, Gardenia,* myrtles, tender daphnes, and magnolias, as well as *Gelsemium, Azara microphylla,* and *Choisya ternata;* also *Acacia, Boronia megastigma, Camellia, Cestrum nocturnum, Murraya exotica,* camphor tree, clerodendrons, *Diosma ericoides, Eriobotrya japonica, Escallonia, Cytisus fragrans* (*see* BROOM), sweet bay, oleander, and the laurustinus. — L. B. W.

fragrans (fray'granz). Fragrant.

fragrantissima, -us, -um (fray-gran-tiss'i-ma). Most fragrant.

FRAGRANT SUMAC = *Rhus aromatica.*

FRAME. See COLD FRAME.

FRANCISCAN NIGHTSHADE = *Brunfelsia americana.*

FRANCOA (fran-ko'a). Chilean perennial herbs of the family Saxifragaceae, two grown outdoors in Calif. and in similar climates, or rarely in the greenhouse, for their white or pink flowers, in long-stalked spikes or racemes.* Leaves mostly basal, lyre-like, and coarsely toothed. Flowers about 1 in. wide, the cluster very floriferous, the 4 petals broad, but with a claw.* Stamens 4. Fruit a 4-angled capsule.* (Named for Doctor F. Franco, a Spanish patron of botany.)

While chiefly suited to warm or mild regions, the francoas can be wintered in the cold frame in the East, and are sometimes grown in the cool greenhouse in potting mixture* 3. Propagate by division of the thick rootstocks.

appendiculata. A perennial herb 18–30 in. high, the leaves long-stalked, the lowest lobes of the leaf far from the base of the stalk. Flowers pink or paler, the petals sometimes spotted.

ramosa. Maiden's-wreath, sometimes called bridal wreath. A showy, perennial herb 20–36 in. high, often grown in pots for Calif. patios. Flower spikes showy, white, often 2 ft. long and nearly an inch thick. Leaves prominently crinkled.

FRANGIPANI. *See* PLUMERIA.

Frangula (fran'gew-la). An old name for the alder buckthorn (*Rhamnus Frangula*).

FRANKLINIA = *Gordonia altamaha.*

FRASERA (fray'zer-ra). Stout North American herbs of the family Gentianaceae, commonly called columbo or American columbo, and suited only to shady parts of the wild garden. They are sometimes known as *Swertia,* and are large, perennial herbs with chiefly basal leaves without marginal teeth, if on the stem then opposite,* or whorled.* Of the 15 known species the two cult. sorts are from the Far West. They are fine plants for the open border in Calif. and the Pacific Coast, but not much grown elsewhere. They have rather large flowers in terminal clusters (panicle* or thyrse*), the calyx 4-parted and the corolla wheel-shaped, the 4 corolla lobes each with a fringed gland. Fruit a somewhat leathery, 2-valved, flattened capsule.* (Named for John Fraser, a noted botanical collector in America.)

The plants are of easy culture in the region west of the Rockies, but they are not partial to the cold, wet winters in the East. Propagated by division.

parryi. Not over 36 in. high, the chiefly basal leaves nearly 8 in. long and white-margined. Flowers greenish-white, the corolla lobes black-spotted, the clusters nearly 1 ft. long. Southern Calif.

radiata = *Frasera speciosa.*

speciosa. Deer's-tongue. A stout herb 3–5 ft. high, the chiefly basal leaves green and sometimes 12 in. long. Flowers greenish-white, the corolla lobes purple-spotted, the clusters (panicles*) narrow and nearly 2 ft. long. Mont. to Ore. and Calif. A very handsome plant often sold as *Frasera* (or *Swertia*) *radiata.*

FRAXINELLA = *Dictamnus albus.*

FRAXINUS. *See* ASH.

FRAZERIA. A somewhat common error for *Frasera.*

FREESIA (free'zi-a). Very fragrant and beautiful South African branched herbs of the iris family, deservedly popular for their winter-blooming flowers. They are of greenhouse culture and bear bulb-like corms,* and mostly narrow, basal, sword-shaped leaves. Flowers typically white or yellow, in terminal, not very floriferous clusters (spike-like racemes*), which are mostly at right angles to the stem. Corolla funnel-shaped, or tubular, the limb* slightly irregular.* Stamens 3. Fruit a small capsule.* (Named for F. H. T. Freese, a pupil of the christener of the genus.)

Freesias are extremely popular florists' flowers, but may be grown by anyone with a cool greenhouse, and the culture of the related *Babiana* and that of *Lachenalia,* which belongs to the lily family, are the same. The corms* should be planted in potting mixture* 3 about the middle of Aug. Keep in a cool greenhouse, and even during the winter the night temperature should not be above 45°–50°. Keep them reasonably moist,

* Special articles on the subjects indicated by an asterisk (*) will be found at the words so marked.

and in about 3½ months the first flowers of the earliest varieties should appear, when they should be watered freely. If a succession of bloom is desired, delay the planting of some for 2–3 weeks. As the flowering spike elongates, the plants had better be staked, for they are weak-stemmed. If the bulbs are held in a cool, moist place, they may be started in Feb. for window-box blooming in spring. Whenever they have finished blooming, reduce the water, and when the leaves are dying, shake out the corms* and store in a cool, moist, dark place until the following Aug.

While freesias are typically white or yellow, they have been much hybridized, and some of the newer hort. forms are pink but lack the wonderful fragrance of the older sorts. The first two below are considered, by some, as mere variants of *F. refracta,* and there are over 40 named forms, mostly produced by English or Dutch hybridizers, but some American forms were sponsored by the late Walter van Fleet.

armstrongi. Resembling *F. refracta,* but with the white corolla orange at the base, and with the segments rose-purple on the margins.

hybrida. Here are grouped many hort. hybrids, probably all derived from *F. refracta,* and having much variation in flower color, notably tinted or veined with pink, purple, blue, orange, and even brown. Not generally as fragrant as the next.

refracta. A corm*-bearing herb up to 18–20 in. high, the leaves long, narrow, sword-shaped or even grass-like. Flowers about 2 in. long, yellow or greenish-yellow (white in *var.* **alba,** in which the tube is gradually narrowed). There are several other varieties, all yellow, but differing in the corolla tube being abruptly narrowed.

FREESTONE. Peaches, nectarines, and some plums are divided by the fact that in some varieties the flesh clings to the stone (clingstone), while in others the flesh slips easily from the stone (freestone). These differences have existed ever since the peach was first grown by the Chinese, perhaps 2500 b.c.

FREMONTIA (free-mon'ti-a). A small genus of chiefly Californian, evergreen shrubs of the family Sterculiaceae, suited only to climatically similar regions, but hardy in the East only up to zone* 6. The only cult. species is **F. californica,** variously called flannel-bush, leatherwood, mountain leatherwood, and, in Calif., the slippery elm (no elm, however). It is a shrub 6–10 ft. high, with alternate,* lobed leaves about 1 in. long and felty-hairy beneath. Flowers yellow, showy, nearly 2 in. wide, solitary in the leaf axils* (for details *see* Sterculiaceae). Fruit a capsule.* It is best propagated by seeds or by cuttings of green wood over bottom-heat.* (Named for John C. Fremont, an explorer, who discovered the plant.)

FRENCH ENDIVE. For botanical identity *see* Cichorium. For culture *see* Cellar Gardening.

FRENCH HONEYSUCKLE = *Hedysarum coronarium.*

FRENCH LAVENDER. See Lavandula Stoechas and L. Spica.

FRENCH MARIGOLD = *Tagetes patula.* See Marigold.

FRENCH MULBERRY = *Callicarpa americana.*

FRENCH NETTLE = *Lamium purpureum.*

FRENCH ROSE = *Rosa gallica.*

FRENCH SPINACH = *Atriplex hortensis.*

FRENCH TAMARISK = *Tamarix gallica.*

FRENCH WILLOW = *Epilobium angustifolium.*

FRIABLE. Easily crumbled or pulverized. A soil is friable when it can be easily cultivated or dug, which cannot be done to wet clay or silt soils which become friable with difficulty after a downpour. *See* Tilth.

frigida, -us, -um (fri'ji-da). Growing in cold regions.

FRINGE-BELL = *Schizocodon soldanelloides.*

FRINGE-CUPS = *Tellima grandiflora.*

FRINGED GALAX = *Schizocodon soldanelloides.*

FRINGED GENTIAN = *Gentiana crinita.*

FRINGED HEATH = *Erica ciliaris.*

FRINGED LOOSESTRIFE = *Steironema ciliatum.*

FRINGED MILKWORT = *Polygala paucifolia.*

FRINGED ORCHIS. See Habenaria.

FRINGE-FLOWER. See Schizanthus.

FRINGE-TREE = *Chionanthus virginicus.*

FRITILLARIA (fri-til-lay'ri-a). Fine, old-fashioned garden flowers of the lily family, all from the north temperate zone and usually called fritillary, although *F. imperialis* is the well-known crown imperial. Of the 80 known species only the following are much cult. They are bulbous, mostly unbranched herbs with alternate* or whorled* leaves, sometimes in a terminal cluster above the flowers, which are mostly early-blooming. Flowers lily-like, pendent, the 6 segments alike (there is no apparent calyx*). Stamens 6. Fruit a many-seeded, 3-valved capsule.* (*Fritillaria* is from the Latin for dicebox, in reference to the flower markings of some species.)

The Old World fritillaries, especially the crown imperial, are old garden favorites which persist for years and are of simple culture in most ordinary garden soils. *F. Meleagris* is best grown in the rock garden.* All of them pay for dividing and re-setting every second or third season, but there should be no delay between digging and re-setting. Best propagated by offsets. Most of the western species are not very partial to the cold, wet winters of the eastern U.S.

---

* Special articles on the subjects indicated by an asterisk (*) will be found at the words so marked.

imperialis. Crown imperial. A stout, strong-smelling herb, 2–4 ft. high, the stem purple-spotted. Leaves many, some in a terminal whorl* above the flowers, usually lance-shaped. Flowers nearly 2 in. long, purplish, or yellow-red, or terra-cotta-colored, the segments veined. Persia.

karadaghensis. A purple-stemmed bulbous herb, its 6–14 narrow, linear leaves 2–3 in. long and scattered on the stem. Flowers about 1 in. long, bell-shaped, greenish-yellow, but with a green stripe on each segment, the whole corolla more or less purplish, but faintly so. Persia. Not suited for outdoor cult. in the East.

lanceolata. Checkered lily. Not over 2 ft. high, the leaves ovalish or lance-oval. Flowers about 1½ in. long, in few-flowered clusters (racemes*), the segments dark purple but mottled greenish-yellow. British Columbia to Calif. Not happy in eastern gardens.

Meleagris. Toad or checkered lily; called also snake's-head or guinea-hen flower. An erect herb 12–18 in. high. Leaves few, oblongish or narrower. Flowers usually solitary, bell-shaped, 2–3 in. wide, the segments checkered and veined purplish or maroon. Eurasia. There are also white- and yellow-flowered forms. For culture see ROCK GARDEN.

pallidiflora. A handsome bulbous perennial, 6–14 in. high, the lower leaves opposite and oblong, the rest narrower and scattered, all bluish-green. Flowers mostly at the upper leaf joints, about 1½ in. long, bell-shaped, white but green tinged outside, and with reddish-purple dots on the inside. Southern Siberia.

pluriflora. Adobe lily or pink fritillary. Not over 12 in. high, the leaves oblongish or lance-shaped. Flowers about 1½ in. long, in a 6–12-flowered raceme,* the segments pinkish-purple. Calif. and not much suited to the East.

pudica. Yellow fritillary. Not over 9 in. high, the leaves narrow, but broader toward the tip. Flowers about ¾ in. long, only 1–3 in a cluster, the segments orange-yellow, but purple-tinged. British Columbia to Calif. and N. Mex.

recurva. Scarlet fritillary. A stoutish herb 15–30 in. high, the leaves narrowly lance-shaped. Flowers about 1½ in. long, in a cluster of 3–6, the segments brilliant scarlet, but yellow-checkered. Southern Ore. to Calif. A showy plant, but not suited to most eastern gardens.

FRITILLARY. See FRITILLARIA.

FROG'S-BIT = *Hydrocharis Morsus-ranae.*

FROG'S-BIT FAMILY = Hydrocharitaceae.

FROND. Properly, a fern leaf, but the term is also applied to the leaves of some palms.

frondosa, -us, -um (fron-do′sa). Leafy.

FROST AND FROST CONTROL. Destructive or killing frosts should not be confused with white or hoar frosts, which may do little or no damage, except to the tenderest plants. And the killing frosts of autumn usually do little damage, as most plants are in any case approaching dormancy.

It is quite otherwise with the late or unseasonable frosts of spring, which may ruin the flowers of early-blooming fruit trees, especially the apricot, almond, peach, and some citrus fruits. For these and a few other plants the frost hazard is great. For critical dates of spring frosts see the general map

at GARDEN CALENDAR, and the more detailed ones at the name of your state. Somewhat elaborate and effective measures are taken to reduce frost damage. Successful control can be based only upon rather accurate knowledge of what frost is and how it works.

Upon still, calm nights, especially in dry climates, there begins about sundown a rapid, and sometimes violent radiation of heat from the air just above the ground level. This process goes on for an hour or two until the loss of heat, which, of course, rises, begins to affect the air at considerable elevations (500–1000 ft.) above the surface. When this is well under way there starts an inversion which results in the much colder, upper air finally reaching the ground, a process usually known as cold-air drainage. It is this, if the general temperature is near 32°, which may cause a killing frost to occur sometime in the early morning.

Effective fighting of such a condition requires careful reading of accurate thermometers put all over the orchard and especially on the edges of it. Some thermometers, also, should be put at elevations (if possible) of 30, 60, and 100 ft. above the surface. If the temperatures between sundown and 10 P.M. indicate that cold-air drainage may be serious within a few hours, frost control must be started at once.

FROST CONTROL. For many years it was supposed that smoky fires or smudges were the best means of preventing cold-air drainage, but scientific fruit growers have found it cheaper and more effective to use heat. Nor does this involve the apparent absurdity of heating all outdoors. It is based solely upon the fact that to stop radiation of heat will prevent cold-air drainage or so reduce it that little or no damage will result. When the hourly readings of the thermometers show that radiation from the surface is very rapid, the grower must start his fires. Because the control is expensive, the fires should not be burned an hour longer than necessary, which usually means that they are not started until the rate of falling temperature indicates that a killing frost is an hour or two away. They must, of course, be started if the temperature is anywhere near 32°, although some fruits will stand temperatures as low as 27°.

Various types of small, portable, oil-burning furnaces are the best for general use. Orchard-heating-oil, sold for the purpose, is available wherever frost control is feasible. And the furnaces, which should hold enough fuel to burn all night, are also available in frost-control regions.

It will need about 400–600 gallons of oil per acre for citrus fruits and about half this for deciduous fruits, in a single night of serious frost hazard. The number of heaters or furnaces varies from 20 to 100 per acre, depending upon topography (*i.e.,* danger of cold-air drainage), the temperature, and the crop to be protected. See the different

---

* Special articles on the subjects indicated by an asterisk (*) will be found at the words so marked.

cultural articles for frost susceptibility of the different fruit crops.

If there is a general hard freeze, or a wind, no frost control by heating can be effective, but it saves much fruit in Calif., where the operation is well managed on a large scale. In the East it seldom pays, where moisture conditions of the atmosphere or wind make frost control very often impossible. It is, for instance, generally ineffective in the citrus region of the lower Rio Grande valley in Tex., largely because of the wind, but along the Gulf Coast heat applied *all* night often prevents injury even if the temperature is 28–30°. For frost protection of individual plants, *see* PROTECTING PLANTS.

FROST GRAPE = *Vitis vulpina.*

FROSTWEED. *See* HELIANTHEMUM.

fructescens (fruk-tess′zens). Fruitful.

FRUIT. The term fruit has two somewhat specialized meanings. In the ordinary garden sense a fruit is any edible development from a flower, such as a peach, apple, pear, or plum. For fruits in this sense *see* FRUIT CULTURE.

Fruit, as a botanical term, is of much wider significance. It is technically important in all schemes of plant classification because the seed-bearing organs of plants vary much less than the foliage. Upon this relative stability of the form and structure of fruits and the flowers that produce them depends the classification of plants into families and genera, and sometimes even species in the same genus have decidedly different fruits.

A fruit in this restricted, wholly botanical sense is the ripened ovary and the seeds within or upon it, together with other parts of the flower, which often change materially in the process of ripening. In the apple, for instance, the only development of the ovary is the papery core and its seeds, all the rest of the fruit being the much-enlarged and juicy development of the receptacle* and part of the calyx.*

Fruits in this sense may be edible or not; usually they are worthless in the hort. sense. But it makes much of the descriptive matter in this book more useful to understand the classification of the more important fruits in the botanical sense as given below. All with an asterisk are defined at their proper entries.

Dry Fruits which split: Legume* (pea), Capsule* (Iris), Follicle* (peony), Silique* (mustard). (All these are the product of a single ovary.)

Dry Fruits which do not split: Achene* (buttercup), Utricle* (Chenopodium), Caryopsis* (wheat), Samara* (maple), Schizocarp* (mallow), Nut* (acorn). (All these are the product of a single ovary.)

Fleshy Fruits: Berry* (grape), Drupe* (plum), Pome* (apple). (All these are the product of a single ovary.)

Aggregate Fruits: Strawberry, Raspberry, Magnolia. (All these are the products of the several ovaries of a single flower.)

Collective Fruits: Mulberry, Fig, Pineapple. (All these are the products of the fused ovaries of several flowers.)

This comparatively simple table does not comprise all the fruits recognized by the systematic botanist, but it does include most of those of any interest to the gardener. For other specialized fruit structures *see* CITRUS (for a hesperidium), LOMENT, SILIQUE (for a silicle), PEPO.

Another important botanical feature of the fruits that split is the way they do so. Some, like the iris, split lengthwise along their seams or valves. Others split around the capsule, as in the common weedy plantain. Still others discharge their seeds through pores, as in the poppy.

FRUIT CULTURE. Some gardeners wonder if home-grown fruit is possible on a small plot. Others have, very likely, heard of the difficulties of pest control. Still others are bothered by such terms as whips, stocks, cions, espalier, cordon, spurs, and a dozen others — all of them necessary to the professional fruitgrower, but admittedly confusing to the amateur. These terms are defined at their entry words in the body of the book or cross-referenced to a definition.

One feature of fruit-growing must be decided at the outset. Fruit and berry plants take more care than most ornamental shrubs and trees. Unless one has the time and inclination to give them that care, it is better not to start — for failure follows neglect with unerring regularity. Not only must they get this care at planting time, but there is a yearly program of pruning, spraying, thinning, and harvesting. Each operation is a heavy expense to commercial growers, but if your home fruit garden is not too large, each of the yearly tasks can be a pleasurable use of leisure time. Then, too, some varieties need little spraying, and that saves one from a yearly chore.

Another point that must be decided before you plan the home fruit garden is how much space you can afford to give to it. Fruit trees are roughly divided, according to the room they need, into *standard* and *dwarf.* The former is the natural height and spread of a mature tree. But dwarfs and semidwarfs are much lower, usually grafted on slow-growing and often worthless stocks chosen because they dwarf the top. Some idea of the difference between them is shown in the table.

	Height in Feet	Spread	Planting Distance Between Trees in Feet	Years Before Fruiting
Standard apple	30–40	30	35	6–8
Dwarf apple	6–8	10	10–12	2–4
Standard pear	35–45	30	30	5–7
Dwarf pear	6–10	8–10	10–12	3–5

If you have sufficient room, at least 50 × 50 feet, by all means choose *standard* trees. If your fruit area is much less than

---

* Special articles on the subjects indicated by an asterisk (*) will be found at the words so marked.

this, you may have to omit all standard fruit trees. But fortunately there are dwarf and semi-dwarf varieties of many common fruits, and, for those cases where space is still more restricted, there are the espaliers, cordons, etc., which are based on the techniques of French orchardists who are perhaps the most skillful in the world. The exact significance of dwarf fruit trees, espaliers, cordons, etc., that are available in this country, and the cultural directions for them are found at Dwarf Fruit Trees at DWARFING, and at TRAINING PLANTS.

Another important feature of fruit-growing is where you live. All temperate-zone tree-fruits need a period of dormancy during the winter. So important is this winter chilling of dormant fruit trees that it is impossible to grow satisfactory crops of apples, pears, peaches, cherries, or plums where the winters are too warm. Generally speaking (there are exceptions in highlands), our ordinary fruits should not be attempted south of the coastal plain regions of Georgia, and along the Gulf Coast to eastern Texas (Georgia peaches do not come from the coastal plain). Nor can the peculiar and enormously productive orchard practice in the west be considered here, because the varieties, climate, and procedure differ too much from that of any other region in the country. See the article entitled FRUIT WEST OF THE ROCKY MOUNTAINS which follows.

Although winter cold is thus necessary, and winter warmth a barrier, there are parts of the northern United States where winter cold is too severe for peaches, and for many varieties of other fruits. If there are likely to be even moderately prolonged periods of temperatures 10–20° below zero, many varieties cannot be grown.

The cultivation of hardy fruits east of the Rocky Mountains is localized in several great regions, the most perfect of which is the vast area extending from Nova Scotia on the northeast, west to Lake Michigan, south to Virginia, and west to Illinois. In parts of this great area, all the hardy fruits grow with vigor, are long-lived, healthy, and produce fruits in abundance of high quality and of great beauty. High lands in the states south of Virginia, in southern Illinois, in the Ozarks of Missouri and Arkansas, and in the mountains and foothills of the plains region provide some splendid lands for hardy fruits. The strawberry is at home not only in the regions named but in the lowlands of the Gulf and South Atlantic states.

Fruits, even more than vegetables, and greatly more than farm crops, are grown by small landowners, and give vastly greater pleasure to collectors and gardeners than other food products of the soil. Indeed, those who grow fruits as a business but poorly supply the necessaries of a wholesome and a palatable fruit diet. The human palate seeks a greater variety of flavors and aromas and the human eye delights in more shapes

and colors in fruits than commercial growers provide. Through the many varieties found in collections more purposes can be served, the season for these products can be lengthened, and new habitats can be found. For these reasons fruit-growing is the chief agricultural hobby, "an elegant branch of agriculture," as one old writer puts it.

SOILS

There is scarcely a soil type in this country that will not grow satisfactory fruit. The only possible exceptions are sands that are too porous to hold enough water for growth, and layers of clayey hardpan below the small landowners, and gave vastly greater surface, which hold too much water. Notably acid or alkali soils are best avoided, and if you do not know how to determine acidity or alkalinity, see ACID AND ALKALI SOILS. Nor will most fruits grow in swamps.

Generally speaking, any soil that will grow potatoes or a vegetable garden will grow good fruit. Of course the soil must not be too thin, i.e., a skimpy layer on a flat rock. That would be dooming the tree to be blown down at the first gale. Nor should very stony land be chosen if it is possible to avoid it. All that is needed is a reasonably rich soil, deep enough to dig the necessary hole for planting. As most orchards should be started from whips, which are yearlings, single-stemmed, slender young trees, the hole for planting may not need to be more than a foot deep.

As to whether or not to add commercial fertilizer or manure, there is still some controversy. It will no doubt induce lush growth, but it may be mostly leafy twigs rather than fruit. This is to be avoided in standard trees, but among dwarfs, espaliers, and cordons, which are rigorously pruned for fruit production, manure or fertilizer is more than justified. The experts in Normandy and Brittany heavily manure their trees, but pruning for fruit production is drastic.

Some commercial growers think it pays to put about half a pound of nitrate of soda around each tree that is 1–2 years old, and 2–3 pounds for a tree 8–10 years old, annually. Others that are equally successful use only stable manure, about 2 inches deep and dug into the soil around the tree. Still others who believe that available food is sufficient in most soil, see that the humus content of it is kept up by digging in grass-cuttings, leaves, cornstalks or any other green refuse that will, when decomposed, help the moisture-holding capacity of any soil. And, finally, there are those who think that any kind of fertilizer or manure is unnecessary for fruit culture, except on the poorest and sandiest soils.

For the home fruitgrower the only sensible plan, which will be dictated by the kind of soil you have, is to try a little (not more than one-half pound) of a commercial fertilizer to each young tree, and watch the result.

---

* Special articles on the subjects indicated by an asterisk (*) will be found at the words so marked.

SELF-FERTILE AND SELF-STERILE

Nature works in devious ways to make the process of fertilization rather complicated. (*See* POLLINATION.) She apparently hit upon the principle that steady fertilization of a flower with its own pollen might lead to sterility, and it would quite certainly retard the production of hybrids, with their supposed greater vigor and their undoubted capacity to produce interesting new strains or even species. Whatever the motive, if there was one, there grew up in the plant world a wilderness of flowers that became perfectly sterile to their own pollen, thus depending for their survival upon pollen coming from a different flower of the same species — a process, commonly, but not quite correctly, called cross-fertilization.

It is precisely this self-sterility that afflicts many fruit trees. In order to produce fruit they *must* get pollen from another tree of the same species. In fruit blossoms this is a fairly simple operation, although the timing of it has to be precise. When the stigma is receptive, which may last only a few hours, rarely a few days, the foreign pollen must be available, and must be carried from the flower that produces it to the one waiting to receive it.

This always happens if there is a favorable wind or, most important of all, if there are plenty of insects. These busy creatures, especially bees, are constantly at work visiting all the blossoms they need for a load of nectar. In such traffic they become coated with pollen and cannot help rubbing some of it off on the receptive stigma. Only a single pollen grain is necessary for ultimate fertilization, for the ovule is quite literally monogamous, and there is thus a prodigal wastage of the male units of reproduction. But Nature has accomplished her purpose — the production of a fruit with foreign pollen and within which will be seeds that are not the result of self-fertilization. Sometimes during storms, pelting rain, or unseasonable cold during blossom-time, there will be no chance for insects to ensure cross-fertilization. Such unhappy accidents result in a poor yield of fruit that year, or none at all if the conditions are severe. It also accounts for the so-called "off-year" habit of some trees, although other factors are often involved in this intermittent production of fruit.

The implications of all this are obvious to any fruitgrower. Not all varieties are self-sterile, but many are, and for them we must provide other, closely related trees so that pollen will be available when needed. The terms *self-sterile* and *self-fertile* must be understood *before* you plan a fruit garden, although as far as possible self-fertile varieties will be selected. But it is impossible in many highly desirable fruits to find *all* self-fertile varieties, notably among pears, plums, cherries, strawberries, etc. Most peaches, however, and many apples are self-fertile.

Notes of self-sterility and self-fertility will be found in all the articles on the different fruits, whenever necessary, and they must be followed carefully to ensure a good crop. If there is no mention of either it means that the tree is self-fertile, which most amateurs take for granted, but as we have seen this is by no means a safe assumption.

PLANNING THE FRUIT GARDEN

If the space you can devote to fruit is about 50 × 50 feet, you can grow sufficient fruit to keep the average family well supplied during the season, give some away, and have enough left over for storage, canning, and deep-freezing, if you have the equipment.

Planning a fruit garden is primarily dictated by the tastes of the family, and by the capacity to save surplus fruit for later use. Hence an "average" plan is impossible. But, as a guide in planning a fruit garden, it is safe to assume that it should contain the following:

3 apples
3 pears
3 peaches
2 cherries
2 plums
1 nectarine
2 varieties of raspberry ⎫
1 variety of blackberry ⎪ Low or bush fruits,
3 varieties of straw- ⎬ of which several or
berry ⎪ dozens of plants will be
2 varieties of currant ⎪ needed. *See* the articles
1 variety of gooseberry ⎪ on these low fruits.
3 varieties of blueberry ⎭
3 varieties of grapes to
be grown on wires,
fences, or arbors

In commercial orchards the ground between the fruit trees will be cultivated once or twice during the growing season, and often a cover crop of vetch or the clovers will be sown broadcast, and plowed under in spring or fall. In the home fruit garden this is unnecessary, and sod or a lawn is the only ground cover needed for the taller trees. Either should be mown, when necessary, for neatness and to keep down weeds.

PLANTING AND AFTER CARE

The planting of fruit trees is the same as for ornamental ones. All fruit trees are grafted or budded on to a vigorous root-stock; and this union, having been made by the nurseryman, generally at ground levels, you may not notice unless you look sharp. Its only significance to the fruitgrower is to see to it that no shoots spring up from the rootstock, which sometimes happens; and, if they do, cut such shoots (usually called suckers) off at or just below ground level. The need to do this is obvious, because, if the sucker were allowed to grow, it might well replace the grafted top (cion), and ultimately the tree would be as worthless as the stock from which it sprang. In other words, you purchase fruit trees only for the grafted (or budded) cion which will develop into the tree of your choice.

In starting a fruit garden it is far better

---

* Special articles on the subjects indicated by an asterisk (*) will be found at the words so marked.

to purchase 1- to 2-year-old whips (slender, often unbranched and usually yearling trees, often called maidens) rather than older, probably branched, and much more expensive ones. From the whip, which will grow surprisingly fast, you can guide the future branching of the tree, and the chances of loss from the shock of planting are far less with young trees than with older ones.

In getting trees from a nursery it is well to study the catalogues of several rival firms before placing an order. While it would be unfair to say that nurserymen are more unscrupulous than other businessmen, it is a fact that the catalogues of some of them suggest precisely this. Lurid color, wildly improbable claims, many so-called letters of approval from satisfied customers — all are the stock-in-trade of the patent-medicine barker of fifty years ago. Throughout this book there are definite named varieties of fruit, all of them tried and tested over a period of years. The amateur would do well to insist upon these varieties, see that he gets them, and leave all expensive novelties (some of them are even patented!) to the appraisal of the experts.

In planting standard fruit trees, put them in at about the same level they occupied at the nursery. You can easily see this by noticing the difference in the color of the exposed and formerly buried stem. Dig a hole deep enough to plant the tree at the proper level (*i.e.*, the old one) and wide enough to take care of its present root-spread. If there are any broken roots cut them off at the break with a sharp knife or pruning shears. Then fill in the hole with the best soil you have (avoiding or breaking up lumps) until it is about two-thirds full. Then shake the whip gently to filter the soil down close to the buried roots, and tramp down the soil firmly, with the feet or a stout piece of timber. When thoroughly packed down, fill up the hole with water, and after this has settled, put in enough more soil to fill the hole up to within an inch or so of the ground level. This will leave a shallow well for subsequent watering if the tree needs it. If there is normal rainfall, the tree will not need watering.

When the whip is planted, it will probably be 4–5 feet high. From the whip, cut off about one-third of the tip, and no other pruning should be done the first year. For the subsequent pruning of standard fruit trees and ultimate spacing and direction of the main branches, *see* PRUNING.

For the specific cult. and varieties of fruit *see* the separate articles on them at APPLE, PEAR, PEACH, STRAWBERRY, etc.

† This and several other articles on fruits are reprinted, in part, from *Fruit in the Garden* by the Editor, published in 1954 by D. Van Nostrand Co., who have kindly permitted its use here.

FRUIT WEST OF THE ROCKY MOUNTAINS. The West is noted for the size and diversity of its fruit industries. Many species of fruit are grown over wide areas of the western states which are little known and not grown in other parts of the nation. The Western gardener therefore has a wide choice in the fruits he can successfully grow, except in areas with climatic limitations. In the more favored locations he may be able to grow almost any of the common deciduous and sub-tropical tree fruits, brambles, vines, and other small fruits. This results from the widely diverse climatic situations which obtain within limited distances over much of the West. (*See* individual states for climatic zones.) Certain fruits are favored by the long, dry, clear summers which add materially to the total number of species which can be successfully produced as compared to equal latitudes in the East.

In the Northwest, east of the mountain ranges, low winter temperatures are the limiting factors in fruit production. Only the most hardy species, such as apple, European plum, Labrusca grapes, and small fruits, may do well. Along the coastal regions of the Northwest, low summer temperatures and high rainfall effectively limit the production of many fruit crops. Those favored by these conditions, as many of the brambles and strawberries, do exceedingly well in this area. The high desert areas of the West are not adapted to fruit culture because of long, extremely hot, dry summers, and lack of water for irrigation. Late spring frosts may further limit the production of many tree fruits. Nevertheless, in favored areas within this range, where water is available, peaches, apricots, European plums, apples, and bush fruits are grown. In the Southwest climatic conditions favor the sub-tropicals, especially citrus fruits. Deciduous trees may be limited by the lack of winter chilling which is required for their normal growth. (*See* the special articles on the various trees.) In California the climatic zones tend to parallel the coast, giving a wide range of climates from coastal to inland locations. Therefore a large portion of northern and central California provides climatic situations which are intermediate between the more severe winter conditions of the Northwest and the extreme heat and dryness of the Southwest. In this area, particularly, many kinds of fruit are adapted. Citrus may be grown as far north as 40° latitude where advantage can be taken of benches and hillsides which provide good air drainage and temperature inversion. On the other hand, in southern California where sub-tropicals are well adapted, some deciduous fruits can be grown well, especially at high altitudes or if they are adapted to the mild winter conditions.

Only apples, pears, and some of the small fruits are well adapted to strictly coastal exposures along the north and central coast of California. In the interior valley and in the coastal valleys of central and northern California, the summers are warm and dry, the winters not too cold, and the area therefore particularly favored for the production of a

---

* Special articles on the subjects indicated by an asterisk (*) will be found at the words so marked.

wide variety of fruits. Thus, in much of California all the temperate-zone fruits and nuts may be grown, especially in the garden when special care can be given and maximum production is not essential. In two states, California and Arizona, all the subtropical fruits can be grown, and in the warmest parts, tropical crops such as the mango have occasionally ripened well.

WINTER INJURY: In the mountain states a large percentage of the total area may occasionally experience temperatures low enough to cause killing of wood of temperate-zone fruit and nut trees. In these areas only the hardiest species should be grown, such as apples, European plums, and pears. In the commercial fruit sections of the Pacific Northwest, especially eastern Washington, winter injury to the species such as pear, sweet cherry, and peach is occasionally known. However, killing temperatures are infrequent enough to warrant growing these somewhat tenderer species in the garden. In California and Arizona, except at high elevations, there are no winter temperatures that kill wood of a common temperate-zone fruit. Citrus fruits grown in the northern range of adaptation may suffer from low winter temperatures, but are still well above the limits for injury to deciduous fruit species.

FROSTS: During the spring growth period, when trees are flowering or the fruits are young, much of the western area is subject to frosts. Temperatures may drop to the mid or low 20's during clear nights. Under these conditions damage is usually limited to the killing of flowers or young fruits of the deciduous species, but fruit, foliage, and young wood of citrus species may be injured. The risk of loss from frost is usually less in the garden than in commercial orchards because of the protective presence of buildings nearby. In addition the gardener may effectively combat moderate frost conditions. (See FROST AND FROST CONTROL.)

SOILS: Deciduous tree fruit crops uniformly do best on deep soils of medium to light texture. The latter generally require more frequent irrigation and often a more intensive fertilization program. Some species, particularly the peach, nectarine, and almond, do poorly on heavy or shallow soils. Other species, such as the apricot, are not well adapted to heavy soils but may be grown by use of Myrobalan rootstocks which are tolerant of such conditions. All fruit species suffer from water-logged soils; in order of increasing resistance to such sites are peach, almond, apricot (on peach or apricot rootstocks), apples, figs, plums (on Myrobalan rootstocks), pears, and quince. Shallow soils — 18 to 24 inches — are poor for tree fruit production; trees can be grown but will not equal those on deeper, more fertile soils, and require greater care and culture, especially irrigation. Sub-tropical fruit species, especially the citrus, do well on soils of 3- to 4-foot depths, although deeper soils are desirable. For citrus trees, medium to light soils are best, and they particularly should be well drained.

IRRIGATION: Except for coastal areas from northern California to the Canadian border, most western sites lack sufficient summer rainfall to insure good growth of tree and fruit without summer irrigation. The term *irrigation* is here used for emphasis: flowers and lawns, shallow-rooted garden plants, may be watered — trees should be irrigated! In the drier areas of the Southwest, and the central valley of California and eastern Washington, summer irrigations are a necessity.

Irrigations should be sufficient to wet the soil to 4 to 6 feet, or to the full depth of shallow soils, repeated as often as necessary to maintain normal growth. In cooler locations and on heavier soils fewer irrigations, perhaps only one, will be necessary. On sandy soils in hot locations irrigations may be needed at 10-day or shorter intervals. In garden locations special care of the trees may prove necessary, the watering of lawns and flower beds being too shallow to provide the tree with needed moisture in the root zone. Irrigation should be continued until early fall even though the fruit has long since ripened.

Citrus and many sub-tropical fruit plants do not tolerate over-irrigation. On shallow or heavy soils irrigation should be such as to insure against waterlogging even for short periods of time. It is also generally best to keep water off the trunk at the crown line.

Water may be applied efficiently in basins, furrows, and by sprinklers. However the area wet should encompass the spread of the tree branches.

In all the arid areas of the West, native soils tend to be of neutral to alkaline reaction and low inorganic matter. The addition of organic matter is usually neither harmful nor helpful to tree growth and vigor, but may greatly improve soil tilth. Under garden conditions trees are usually allowed to root closer to the surface than in cultivated orchards, and this may be helpful to their general growth and nutrition, for it allows the roots to develop into the shallower, and for some mineral elements, richer layers of soils.

FERTILIZATION: Under most conditions in western areas nitrogen is the element most likely to be deficient. Short annual growth, yellowish foliage, and light crops of small but highly colored fruit results. As a good general rule, for an average-size tree like peach or apricot, the nitrogen requirement is seldom more than one pound of actual nitrogen per year. Larger orchard trees, as apples, may require proportionately more. In some areas of the West other elements may prove deficient. Zinc, potassium, iron, magnesium, manganese, and copper have all been found to be needed in local situations. Corrections of these deficiencies usually require expert advice and specialized correction because the elements are readily fixed in the soil and do not become readily

---

* Special articles on the subjects indicated by an asterisk (*) will be found at the words so marked.

available following soil applications. In other areas elements like boron, sodium, and chlorine have been found to be in excess and to cause harm to trees. Excesses can be corrected only by leaching the harmful element with excess water.

SUMMER, SUNSHINE AND TEMPERATURE: In most of the fruit-growing districts of the western states there is little cloudiness in the summer, and the sunshine tends to be more intense than in eastern locations. There is a tendency for both fruit and wood to be firmer in the Pacific slope states except at high elevations. Whether this is due to abundant sunshine and resulting abundant food supply or to high temperature we cannot be certain. This greater firmness is sometimes associated with a milder, more pleasant flavor in varieties which tend to be tart, and more insipid flavor in varieties that are naturally mild.

High summer temperatures do not prevail in all western districts. Near the Pacific Ocean the summers are cool. Even in some districts where sub-tropical fruits are grown, the summers are moderately cool and the fruit may ripen several months later than fruit of the same variety grown a few miles farther from the coast. Farther north in some coastal districts, owing partly to fog, the summer temperature is lower than in any other fruit-growing districts in the mountains or in the East. Many kinds of temperate-zone fruits will not develop normal flavor.

In mountain districts, where the summer temperatures tend to be moderate, western mountain fruit tends to resemble eastern fruit of the same varieties, but is often more highly colored.

HIGH WINTER TEMPERATURE: For most of the southwest area where citrus is grown the locations are nearly frost-free, or experience only occasional frosts of a mild nature. Here the climate during the remainder of the year is conducive of good growth and high quality of fruit. However, under these conditions, deciduous fruits fail to leaf and bloom normally in the spring. For deciduous fruits subject to this harmful effect of mild winters, approximately 800–1000 hours below 45° F. must be experienced during the fall and winter months to insure normal bloom and leafing. With successively less accumulation of these hours of relatively low temperatures, the trees suffer more severely from the symptoms mentioned, even to the point of failing to leaf and grow until midsummer so that the trees are weakened and eventually succumb to secondary infections caused by sunburn of the bare limbs. Under severe conditions, fruit buds may drop rather than open. However, there are several kinds of deciduous fruits such as the Japanese persimmon, fig, most varieties of Vinifera grapes, blackberries, and some small fruits which apparently require so little winter chilling that all warm winter situations are favorable for them. Varieties of peaches, nectarines, Oriental plums, and apples have

been developed which do well under these mild winter conditions. Some species like the apricot and sweet cherry may develop normal foliage early enough in the season to make good vegetative growth year after year but seldom if ever produce a crop.

This adverse effect of warm winters is seen only rarely north of latitude 35° except mildly, in which cases it causes only a beneficial delay in bloom and leafing, enabling the tree to escape some spring frosts.

VARIETIES: For each kind of fruit a selection of varieties is available. For particular recommendations, see article under each named fruit. Certain general principles are given which help as guides in selecting varieties.

For deciduous trees, starting in central California and going northward, select successively hardier species and varieties having relatively high chilling requirements and (or) late bloom. The same applies to higher elevations. For interior locations varieties with quite differing times of maturity may be successfully grown, for the summers are normally warm to hot. For coastal areas select early-ripening varieties, for the summers are cool and not enough heat is accumulated to ripen normally midseason-to-late varieties.

In southern California, except at high elevations, only the special varieties of deciduous fruit with low chilling requirements can generally be successfully grown. This is particularly true near the coast. Few deciduous fruits are adapted to the desert, Vinifera grapes being an important exception. At middle elevations in some areas of the Southwest, peaches and Oriental plums may grow well.

Winter cold is usually the limiting factor for citrus. In coastal locations grapefruit does not produce quality fruit. Inland, in areas of hot summers, all citrus except lemons do reasonably well. Oranges are among the hardiest of citrus species, lemons among the more tender. Tender evergreens, such as avocado, cherimoya, mango, and papaya require frost-free winters and relatively mild summers, and hence production is limited to the coastal Southwest.

CROPPING. None of the fleshy tree fruits should be overcropped. Unfavorable results are decreased tree vigor, weak foliage, dieback of branches, and small, poorly flavored fruit. Cropping is usually regulated by pruning and, more especially, by thinning. Peaches, plums, apricots, and apples are usually thinned. Cherries, prunes, and pears are not usually thinned, but overcropping sometimes occurs and could be alleviated by thinning. Grapes may be bunch-thinned or the bunches berry-thinned, often with considerably improved berry size and quality. Sub-tropical fruits are seldom thinned.

The earlier thinning is done, the greater the benefit derived. The usual time is when

---

* Special articles on the subjects indicated by an asterisk (*) will be found at the words so marked.

the fruits can be easily seen and removed without tearing the fruiting wood or spurs in its removal.

PRUNING. In general, trees are pruned somewhat more heavily in western states than in the East. Pruning may be used 'o keep trees in bounds in a small yard. But for maximum production, pruning should be as light as is conducive to maintenance of good annual shoot-growth, and to remove interfering and crossing branches. The peach and nectarine bear primarily on last year's shoot-growth, hence pruning is relatively heavy to insure strong annual renewal of fruit-bearing area. For spur-bearing species, pruning consists primarily of thinning out the annual shoot-growth and removal of barren limbs.

HARVEST. For most fruits, changes in color, softening, and improvement of edible quality adequately determine harvest-time for the gardener who seldom wants to pick fruit in the firm-ripe or green-ripe condition often necessary commercially.

If fruit is to be stored, harvesting on the firm side is preferable, however. It will ripen better off the tree, whereas fully ripe fruit would soften sooner and deteriorate.

Except for long periods of cold storage, moderate storage temperatures, such as a cool basement, afford good ripening and holding temperatures. The more tender fruits, such as apricots, cherries, peaches, and nectarines, can be held for a few days only. Some soft fruits, such as a few varieties of European plums, may be held up to two months under basement storage conditions. Fall-maturing varieties of common fruits, like peaches and plums, are often better when harvested firm ripe and ripened off the tree as described than when allowed to soften on the tree.

Fruits to be dried should be fully ripe before a harvest or should be ripened off the tree as for pear (*see* below).

Pears and some apple varieties need to be harvested before softening and color changes are obvious. A convenient guide to the gardener is ease of separation from the tree. If the stem breaks readily when the fruit is lifted and twisted slightly, it will ripen to full quality when stored at moderate temperatures, as in a basement.

Winter pears usually develop best quality if held in cold storage (32° to 40° F.) for a month or six weeks before ripening at a moderate temperature of approximately 65° to 70° F.

Pears and apples to be cold stored should be stored as harvested and ripened after storage. Soft fruits have short storage lives and always deteriorate in quality in storage. For soft fruits, best quality is obtained if the fruit is ripened before it is stored. — C. O. H.

FRUIT DOTS. See SORUS.

frumentacea, -us, -um (froo-men-tay'see-a). Grain-bearing.

frutescens (froo-tess'zens). Shrubby.

frutex (froo'tex). A shrub.

fruticans (froo-ti-kanz'). Shrubby.

fruticosa, -us, -um (froo-ti-ko'sa). Fruticose; *i.e.,* shrubby.

fruticulosa, -us, -um (froo-tick-you-lō'sa). Somewhat shrubby.

FUCHSIA (few'sha, but properly fuke'-zi-a). A genus of perhaps 100 species of showy shrubs of the family Onagraceae, all but a handful tropical American, the rest from New Zealand. They are very popular as greenhouse plants, for summer bedding, and for window boxes, but may be grown outdoors all year in zones* 8 and 9, where they are very handsome, especially in Calif. Leaves simple,* opposite* or alternate.* Flowers usually very showy, often hanging, and mostly in small clusters, or solitary in the leaf axils,* red, purple, blue, or white, or sometimes all four. Calyx* tubular or bell-shaped, the limb with 4 spreading tips. Petals usually 4 (wanting in *F. procumbens*). Stamens 8, usually unequal and nearly always long-protruding and showy, as is the style.* Fruit a 4-celled, pulpy berry. (Named for Leonhard Fuchs, a German botanist and physician, 1501–1566). The plants are sometimes called lady's-eardrops.

As commonly grown by florists or by amateurs with a cool greenhouse, fuchsias are annually propagated each year from softwood cuttings rooted in pots or in the propagating bench. They need potting mixture* 3 and a greenhouse temperature of 50°–60°. They are usually trained to a central stem or into a bushy crown, largely by pinching. Outdoors, or if kept over the blooming season, they become much larger. If this is done, they bloom more freely if the branches are cut back after the current blooming season. The height dimensions below are for plants as grown permanently outdoors, the usual greenhouse specimens being much smaller. Fuchsias make good house plants, and during the summer they may be plunged outdoors, preferably in the shade.

The American Fuchsia Society welcomes those interested in this flower. Its present address is 1633 Moreland Drive, Alameda, Calif.

For the California fuchsia *see* ZAUSCHNERIA.

boliviana. A shrub 3–5 ft. high, the tips of the branches drooping. Leaves ovalish or elliptic, rather large, hairy, and the margins toothed. Flowers 2–3 in. long in showy drooping clusters (corymbs*), the petals red, the sepals* paler, and the protruding filaments* red. Bolivia. Needs a cool greenhouse.

hybrida. A hybrid plant and including most of the common fuchsias in cult., probably derived from *F. magellanica* and a Mexican species. It differs from the former species in having sturdier twigs, broader leaves, and larger flowers. As a greenhouse plant always shrubby. Calyx crimson, but the petals white, rose, yellow, or purple, and shorter than the calyx*-lobes.

Some hort. varieties have flowers 3 in. long. *See* Pinching at TRAINING PLANTS.

magellanica. As grown on walls or trained on a trellis, often 20 ft. high in Calif., where it is very popular, much lower in the greenhouse. Leaves opposite* or in 3's, oval-lance-shaped, 1½–2 in. long, wavy and toothed on the margin. Flowers 1–2 in. long, the calyx* red and the petals blue, the stamens long-protruding. Peru to southern S.A. The *var.* **conica** has a scarlet calyx* and purple petals; *var.* **globosa** has small, reddish-purple flowers, the buds of which are globe-shaped; and the *var.* **gracilis** is a lower, more slender shrub with a scarlet calyx and purple petals.

The *var.* **riccartoni** is the hardiest of all the commonly cult. fuchsias, standing frost up to New York if in sheltered site. If winter-killed it will send up flowering shoots the following summer.

procumbens. Trailing fuchsia. A prostrate or trailing plant useful for hanging baskets. Leaves alternate,* roundish-oval, long-stalked, about 1 in. long. Male and female flowers on different plants, solitary in the leaf axils,* erect, not over ¾ in. long, the calyx orange-purple, the petals none. N.Z.

FUCHSIA FAMILY = Onagraceae.

fuchsioides (fuke-zi-oy′deez, but *see* OÏDES). Fuchsia-like.

FUGACIOUS. Soon withering or falling off, but not truly ephemeral (which see).

fulgens (ful′jenz). Glistening or shining.

fulgida, -us, -um (ful′ji-da). Shining.

FULLER'S TEASEL = *Dipsacus Fullonum.*

Fullonum (full-lō′num). Of or pertaining to the fullers (of cloth), the Latin for whom was *fullo.*

fulva, -us, -um (full′va). Of a tawny or smoky orange-yellow.

FUMARIA. *See* FUMITORY.

FUMARIACEAE (few-mare-i-ā′see-ee). The fumitory or bleeding-heart family comprises only 5 genera and about 165 species, four of which contain garden plants, and one, *Dicentra,* the ever-popular bleeding-heart and Dutchman's-breeches. The other cult. genera are *Adlumia, Corydalis,* and *Fumaria* (*see* FUMITORY).

All are relatively weak herbs with more or less glistening foliage and highly irregular* flowers with a conspicuous spur, sometimes very showy.

Leaves simple* and much cut, or compound,* and sometimes thrice-compound. All the plants have a watery juice (unlike the often milky juice of the closely related poppy family). Fruit a dry pod (capsule*) which splits by valves in all the genera except *Fumaria,* which bears a small, nut-like fruit.

Technical flower characters: Sepals 2, small and scale-like. Petals 4 in two series. One or both of the outer series prolonged into a spur or merely swollen. Stamens 6. Ovary superior.*

fumariaefolia, -us, -um (few-mare-i-ee-fō′li-a). With fumitory-like leaves.

fumarioides (few-mare-i-oy′deez, but *see* OÏDES). Like the fumitory.

FUMIGATION. Horticulturists are most interested in greenhouse plant fumigation and fumigation of soils before planting. Many insect pests can be controlled by the use of fumigant insecticides, and soil pests such as centipedes, grubs, nematodes, and diseases respond to fumigation and heat treatment.

AEROSOL BOMBS; SPACE FUMIGANTS. Aerosols are fine aerial dispersions of insecticides which are produced by the rapid volatilization of a compressed and liquified gas to which has been added 10–20 per cent of a non-volatile solution of one or more insecticides. As the liquefied gas volatilizes, it releases a very finely-divided insecticide particle into the air. Many forms of aerosols are available, from large thick-walled cylinders to lightweight cans. The use of the aerosol bomb containing synthetic organic chemicals has largely replaced the use of hydrocyanic acid and nicotine formulations.

A wide variety of chemicals are formulated in aerosols. Chiefly, the phosphate-type materials such as parathion, dithion, TEPP, and malathion are formulated for insecticidal activity with a mite-killing chemical such as ovex, Aramite, Kelthane, or Dimite to produce a wide-range pest killer.

Labels on aerosol bombs usually state the number of pounds of aerosol formulation to be applied per 1000 cubic feet of space. Use as labelled to avoid injury. Normally, aerosols should be applied over the plants, not directly upon them, to avoid injury. After a period of fumigation, as recommended on the label, a complete ventilation is recommended to vent poisonous fumes. With the more toxic materials, use of a gas mask or approved respirator, rubber gloves, and protective equipment is mandatory.

Most mites, chewing, sucking, and rasping insects succumb to aerosol applications. The young of scale insects may be controlled as well. Routine aerosol applications are a regular practice in most fine greenhouses.

OLDER FUMIGANTS. Hydrocyanic acid is a gas which is most deadly to all insects, higher animals, and man. Its use is declining. Plant injury often follows its use, and except for fumigation of flour mills, furniture, and equipment, little is used horticulturally.

Nicotine formulations as smokes are being replaced by the new synthetics. Carbon disulphide is a foul-smelling liquid which evaporates to a heavy gas at normal temperatures. Seeds infested by weevils may be freed of pests by using 1 to 2 pounds of the liquid per 100 cubic feet.

Napthalene (with crystals) and paradichlorobenzene (PDB) are used to combat carpet beetles and clothes moths in fabrics. PDB will kill established peach tree borers (*see* PEACH).

SOIL TREATMENTS. Several excellent soil sterilants are available to kill most soil pests. Among these are methyl bromide, Vapam, Mylone, V-C 13 Bedrench and others. These chemicals when used specifically as recommended on the label will control **most**

---

* Special articles on the subjects indicated by an asterisk (*) will be found at the words so marked.

weeds, nematodes, insects, fungi, and incidental pests. Most materials require soil conditions equivalent to these for optimum planting before treatment. Afterwards, a waiting period plus soil aeration are necessary. With volatile materials such as methyl bromide, a plastic sheet to confine the vapors to the soil is needed. Follow label directions in all cases, as improper application can cause serious root injury.

A general rule of thumb is to sterilize all greenhouse soils prior to seeding or transplanting.

HEAT. Insects succumb readily to exposure to moderate heat; few can withstand temperatures of 120° to 130° F. for very long. It is difficult to apply heat to living plants without injuring them; however, it is practicable in some cases, as in the control of cyclamen mites on various plants. Bulbs can be freed of some pests by immersion in warm water (110° F.) for 3 hours. Soil that is to be used for the growing of plants can be sterilized by steaming or otherwise heating, and greenhouse pipes or tiles can easily be arranged to steam soil in beds before planting. — L. G. M.

FUMITORY. An old garden plant, the only cult. species of 25 herbs of the genus **Fumaria** (few-may′ri-a) of the family Fumariaceae, all from the Old World temperate regions. The only one of even secondary garden interest is **F. officinalis,** which is also called hedge fumitory, wax dolls, and a dozen other names. It is an annual or biennial herb with finely dissected, almost fern-like leaves and a weak stem. Flowers small, in racemes,* the 4 petals purplish but crimson at the tip, one of them spurred. Stamens 6. Fruit small, stalked, not splitting, the lower ones usually ripe before the upper flowers of the cluster have finished blooming. The plant is of the easiest culture in any garden soil. It was once widely grown as a remedy for scurvy. (*Fumaria* is from the Latin for smoke, in allusion to the smoky odor of some species.) *See also* ADLUMIA FUNGOSA.

FUMITORY FAMLY = Fumariaceae.

funebris, -e (few-nee′bris). Funereal.

FUNGI (fun′jy). Plural of fungus (which see). For the edible fungi *see* MUSHROOM. For the harmful fungi *see* PLANT DISEASES.

FUNGICIDES. A fungicide is a chemical which kills or inhibits the growth of fungi (*see* FUNGUS). Most fungicides are used as protectants — to prevent a plant from becoming diseased, rather than as eradicants which stop a disease once the plant is infected. The fungicides are available as liquids, wettable powders, and dusts. The liquids are added to water and applied as a spray or drench. The wettable powders are mixed with water and also applied as a spray or drench. The dust forms are for use in various types of dusting machines or for applying a protective coating of dust to seeds.

Most amateurs, and some professional gardeners, find it more convenient to purchase commercial preparations of fungicides and insecticides, sold under various trade names. Their use avoids buying stock chemicals, their storage, their preparation, and the waste of the unused residue that often follows a spraying operation. It is important to select good commercial preparations made by a reliable manufacturer. All the better ones have accurate directions for use and these should be followed exactly, as all fungicides contain poisons which, at improper concentrations, will do more harm than good. For small gardens these prepared fungicides are strongly recommended by the experts at the agricultural experiment station in each state.

Because a specific fungicide is often better for a specific job of plant disease control (*see* control recommendations under each plant or crop) some gardeners prefer to keep various materials on hand. Most fungicides are formulated by a number of manufacturers and are sold under the manufacturer's brand name. For this reason, the plant pathologists have grouped the fungicides and suggest their use under a common name rather than specifying brand names. According to federal and state laws, the common name must appear on each package sold. The most used fungicides (*see* SPRAYS AND DUSTS for methods and amounts of application) are given here:

BORDEAUX MIXTURE. A combination of copper sulphate and lime used as a protectant spray for foliage. The copper causes some plant injury, particularly in cool damp weather, and for this reason bordeaux mixture (written bordo by some authors) is no longer a general recommendation. When a suggestion is made for this material, it is usually expressed as three numbers — for example, Bordeaux 2–4–50 — and indicates 2 pounds of copper sulphate, 4 pounds of spray lime, in 50 gallons of water.

CAPTAN. A mercapto compound used for sprays and dusts and seed treatments. It has been particularly useful in the control of apple scab as well as other diseases.

CHLORANIL. A quinone compound used mostly as a seed treatment and as a dust or dip for bulbs and corms.

CHLOROPICRIN. Tear gas is a liquid which is used in soil sterilization and fumigation.

COPPER. This material formulated as carbonates, oxides, etc., is available under many brand names. Copper is still one of our best fungicides for the control of plant diseases. However, it is somewhat injurious to the host plants in many instances, although not so injurious as the bordeaux mixture. For the most part, the copper compounds are being replaced by the newer, less injurious, organic fungicides.

CORROSIVE SUBLIMATE. A poison used as a seed treatment, as a dip for some corms and bulbs, and in various other manners for disinfecting. It may be purchased at drug-

* Special articles on the subjects indicated by an asterisk (*) will be found at the words so marked.

stores under the name corrosive sublimate or bichloride of mercury. The material is usually sold in tablet form. One tablet (of approximately 7.3 grains) dissolved in one pint of warm water will give a concentration referred to as 1–1000 corrosive sublimate or bichloride of mercury. Mark the storage bottle POISON and keep both the tablets and liquid solution above the hands of children. The liquid should not be made up in metal containers because, as the name implies, it is corrosive.

DICHLONE. A napthoquinone formerly called phygon, it is used as a seed treatment, a dip for bulbs and corms, and as a spray.

DINITRO. The dinitrocresol and dinitrophenol materials are liquid or wettable powder materials used as eradicant sprays. The spray must be applied while the host plant is in a dormant stage because the chemical is so strong that it would burn leaves and flowers.

FERBAM. This iron carbamate fungicide was one of the first of the organic fungicides to be used for the control of plant diseases. It is a good general protectant, used as a spray, dust, or drench, and is particularly useful for the control of rust diseases. The one drawback with ferbam is the black residue on the plant.

FORMALDEHYDE. This material, often called formalin, is bought as a liquid and is diluted with water, usually using one part of the commercial formalin in 50 or 100 parts of water. It is used as a soil disinfectant, and as a dip for seeds and bulbs. The odor is extremely disagreeable and the fumes are very injurious to growing plants. If it is used as a soil disinfectant, make sure that no odor is discernible in the soil when the seed or plants are set.

GLYODIN. A glyoxalidine material, this liquid fungicide is particularly good for control of apple scab, cherry leaf spot, and some other diseases of fruit and foliage.

KARATHANE. A dinitrocrotonate which is excellent for the control of powdery mildew but is of little value for other diseases.

MANEB. This manganese carbamate fungicide has a wide range of use for control of diseases of vegetables and some fruit.

MERCURY. There are many brand names for various organic and inorganic mercury compounds. These materials are of primary value as seed protectants, bulb and corm dips, and general disinfectants. Many of the fungicides for turf diseases belong to the mercury family. All mercury compounds are poisonous and should be so labeled, and kept beyond the reach of children.

METHYL BROMIDE. This highly poisonous soil fumigant is excellent for control of many pests in the soil.

NABAM. A sodium carbamate, this liquid is usually used in combination with zinc sulphate. The combination produces a zinc carbamate (see Zineb below) which is a good fungicide for control of many vegetable diseases.

PHENYL MERCURY. This special group of the mercury fungicides has value in control of diseases of fruit and ornamentals. It has some eradicant value and thus will stop some diseases of plants after the infection has occurred. (Most fungicides have no eradicant value and must be applied before infection takes place.) It is of particular value in the control of apple scab and the anthracnose disease of plane tree and sycamore.

PHYGON. See Dichlone above.

SPERGON. See Chloranil above.

SULPHUR. Specially prepared sulphur is sold as paste, wettable powder, and dust under many trade names. Sulphur is one of the earliest known fungicides and still has wide use for control of disease of apple, peach, and powdery mildew on many plants.

TERRACLOR. A nitrobenzene compound which is particularly good for control of some soil-inhabiting fungi.

THIRAM. A thiuram disulphide material usually classified as one of the carbamates. It has had wide usage as a turf fungicide as well as a seed treatment for many vegetables and ornamentals.

ZINEB. A zinc carbamate used either as a spray or dust. It has a wide range of effectiveness against many fungus diseases of fruit, vegetables, and ornamentals. It is particularly useful as a spray on blossoms since no objectionable residue may be seen.

ZIRAM. Another in the group of zinc carbamates but with a much narrower range of usefulness. In recent years the ziram materials have been replaced by zineb to a great extent. — S. H. D.

fungosa, -us, -um (fun-go′sa). Related to or resembling a fungus; also, spongy.

FUNGUS (fun′gus). Plural fungi.* One of a huge group of flowerless plants, of little interest to the gardener except for the mushroom (which see) and for the many plant diseases* caused by the microscopic forms. Unlike nearly all flowering plants, the fungi contain no green coloring matter and are therefore wholly parasitic or else live on the dead remains of other plants (see SAPROPHYTE). They bear no flowers, but are reproduced by microscopic spores, a common example being the cloud of such given off by a puffball. While the great majority of the fungi can only be seen under the microscope, *en masse* even these are very noticeable, as in the mold on bread or jam, or the blights on leaves. Others, however, are large, as in the mushroom and toadstools, or the often very large bracket fungi on tree trunks. See WOOD ROT.

FUNKIA. See PLANTAIN-LILY.

FURCRAEA (fur-kree′ya.) Tropical American plants of the family Amaryllidaceae, resembling the century plants in habit, and the benefit derived. The usual time is when grown like them. See AGAVE. They have fleshy, long, sword-shaped leaves in a basal rosette from which springs a tall flowering stalk with a terminal cluster (panicle*) of

---

* Special articles on the subjects indicated by an asterisk (*) will be found at the words so marked.

greenish-white flowers, after the blooming of which the plant dies. Corolla° more or less wheel-shaped, the 6 segments spreading but united at the base. Stamens 6. Fruit (sometimes bulbiferous) an oblong, 3-sided capsule.° (Named for Antoine François de Fourcroy, French chemist.)

gigantea. Giant lily; called also cabuya, and sometimes Mauritius hemp for which it is grown commercially. Leaves nearly 8 ft. long and 6–7 in. wide, very fleshy and with only a few, distant, marginal teeth. Flowering stalk about 20 ft. high, the flowers about 1½ in. long. Brazil. Called by some *F. foetida.* There is a hort. variety with variegated, wholly spineless leaves. Both are very striking plants for the desert garden They seldom or never produce a trunk, the leaves all being basal.

Selloa. Leaves about 4 ft. long and 3 in. wide, the rosette basal or at the end of a short, stout trunk. Marginal leaf-prickles curved. Flowering stalk 15–20 ft.

FURZE. Very showy, spiny, yellow-flowered, mostly Eurasian shrubs comprising the genus **Ulex** (you'lex) of the pea family, and often called gorse or whin. Of the 15 known species only the two below are much cult. They are low shrubs, mostly leafless, or the leaves represented only by a thorny leaf-stalk. Flowers pea-like, mostly in the axils° of thorns, but inclined to be crowded at the ends of the twigs. Fruit a small, egg-shaped legume.° (*Ulex* is the classical Latin name for this plant or one like it.)

Furze is not easy to transplant and should be let alone once it is established. Some growers prefer to sow seeds directly where the plants are wanted. They prefer a sandy, slightly acid soil, and when once established they are fine plants for sandy banks or open wastes. They are not hardy everywhere (*see* below), but are sometimes a pest or even a fire hazard when dry.

U. europaeus. A much-branched, twiggy and spiny shrub 2–3 ft high, the leaves scale-like, none, or reduced to spines. Flowers about ¾ in. long, bright yellow, fragrant. Pod about ½ in. long, brown and hairy. Eu. Apr.–July (all the year in Calif.). Hardy from zone° 4 southward.

U. nanus. A dwarf, spiny shrub, 12–20 in. high, sometimes half prostrate, very twiggy. Flowers golden-yellow. Pod about ½ in. long, enclosed by the persistent calyx. Aug.–Sept. Eu. Hardy from zone° 5 southward.

fusca, -us, -um (fuss'ka). Brown.

fuscata, -us, -um (fuss-kay'ta). Brownish.

fusco-rubra, -us, -um (fuss-ko-roo'bra). Brownish-red.

FUSIFORM. Spindle-shaped; *i.e.*, narrowed both ends from a swollen middle.

G

GACHIPAES = *Guilielma Gasipaes.*

GAILLARDIA (gay-lar'di-a). Showy North American herbs of the family Compositae, the three below very popular flower garden plants from the western U.S. They are leafy, erect, branching herbs with alternate° or basal leaves which are more or less dotted. Flower heads extremely handsome, the rays 3-toothed or almost fringed, yellow, orange, or orange-red (white in a hort. form), the head appearing fringed. Disk° flowers purple. (Named for Gaillard de Marentonneau, French botanist.)

The annual blanket-flower (*G. pulchella*) and *G. amblyodon* are both hardy annuals and should be grown as such. See ANNUALS. The blanket-flower is a widely grown garden favorite, especially fine for cutting. The other species is a perennial and, like the annuals, is partial to light, open soils and full sunlight. It is propagated by division, spring or fall. They are chiefly summer-bloomers.

amblydon. A leafy-stemmed, hairy annual, 12–24 in. high, the foliage rough-hairy. Leaves oblongish, stalkless, more or less eared at the base. Flower heads about 2 in wide, the rays brownish-red. Tex.

aristata. Blanket-flower. A popular flower garden hardy perennial, 2–3 ft. high, more or less rough-hairy. Leaves nearly 5 in. long, more or less lance-shaped, sometimes deeply cut. Flower heads 3–4 in. wide, the rays yellow. Western N.A.

drummondi = *Gaillardia pulchella.*

grandiflora = *Gaillardia aristata.*

pulchella. Annual blanket-flower; Indian blanket. A very showy, popular flower garden annual, 12–20 in. high, the foliage softly hairy. Leaves oblongish, 3–4 in. long. Flower heads 2–3 in. wide, the rays yellow at the tip, rose-purple at the base, the head thus with a dark eye.° Central U.S. A popular form is var. **picta,** with the rays in various shades of red, yellow, or white. Burgundy is a good red variety; there are many others.

galacifolia, -us, -um (gay-las-i-fō'li-a). With the leaves of *Galax* (which see).

GALANTHUS. See SNOWDROP.

GALAX (gay'lacks). A single, perennial, evergreen herb of the family Diapensiaceae, the only species being **G. aphylla,** the beetleweed, a native in mountain woods from Va. to Ga. and Ala. It is a stemless, tufted herb, the leaves nearly round, 3–4½ in. wide, green, but bronze in age, and widely used for funeral decorations. Flowers white, in a spike-like cluster (raceme°), the slender stalk of which may be 25 in. high. Petals 5. Stamens 10, five of them sterile and petal-like. Fruit a 3-valved capsule.° The plant is suited only to the moister and shadier parts of the rock garden or wild garden, and prefers a rich, woods soil, not too acid. (*Galax* is from the Greek for milk, perhaps in allusion to the white flowers.) For the fringed galax *see* SCHIZOCODON.

° Special articles on the subjects indicated by an asterisk (°) will be found at the words so marked.

GALAX FAMILY = Diapensiaceae.

Gale. Ancient European name, of uncertain origin, applied to the sweet gale (*Myrica Gale*).

GALEGA (ga-lee′ga). A small genus of Eurasian perennial herbs of the pea family, G. officinalis, the goat's-rue, a good garden plant and of easy culture in any ordinary soil. It is an erect herb 2–3 ft. high, with compound* leaves, the leaflets arranged feather-fashion and with an odd one at the end. Leaflets oblongish, 1½–2 in. long. Flowers pea-like, purplish-blue, about ½ in. long, arranged in terminal clusters (racemes*) or these in the leaf axils.* Summer. The *var.* carnea, with rose-pink, double flowers is fine for cut flowers. There are also white-flowered and variegated-leaved forms. All are readily propagated by division. (*Galega* is from the Greek for milk, as some species were supposed to increase its flow.)

galegiflora, -us, -um (ga-lee-gi-flow′ra). With flowers like the goat's-rue (*Galega*).

Galeobdolon (gay-le-ob′do-lon). An old generic name for plants now included in *Lamium*.

GALINGALE. See CYPERUS.

GALIUM (gay′li-um). Weak, almost weedy, perennial herbs, commonly known as bedstraw or cleavers, and comprising a widely distributed genus of perhaps 300 species of the family Rubiaceae. They are suited only to informal plantings in the border or rock garden, are of the easiest culture, and are of only secondary hort. interest. Stems often prostrate or arching, 4-sided, often finely barbed. Leaves stalkless, usually 4–10 in a whorl.* Flowers very numerous, but small, white, yellow or maroon, the corolla wheel-shaped or deeply 4-parted. Stamens 4. Fruit small, dry, not splitting, 2-lobed, sometimes minutely prickly. (*Galium* is from the Greek for a plant supposed to curdle milk.)

boreale. Northern bedstraw. Forming mats or patches, the stems smooth, 1–3 ft. long. Leaves 4 at a joint, narrow, ¾–1 in. long, sometimes with smaller leaves in the axils.* Flowers scarcely ⅒ in. wide, white. Eurasian but naturalized in N.A. Summer.

Mollugo. White bedstraw; called, also, wild madder and baby's-breath. A smooth-stemmed herb, erect or arching, 1–3 ft. high. Leaves 8 or rarely 6 at a joint, not over 1 in. long. Flowers about ⅒ in. wide, white, in practically leafless clusters. Eu., but naturalized in eastern N.A. Summer.

rubrum. Not over 18 in. high, sprawling, and like other bedstraws apt to become invasive and weedy. Leaves mostly in groups of 6, very narrow and bristle-tipped. Flowers red. Southern Eu. Summer.

verum. Yellow bedstraw; also called curd-wort or (Our) Lady's-bedstraw. A perennial herb with narrow leaves about 1 in. long that are bristle-tipped and minutely barbed on the margins. Leaves 8 or 6 at a joint. Flowers about ⅛ in. wide, yellow. Eu., but naturalized in eastern N.A. June–Oct.

GALL. Galls are peculiar malformations of plants usually caused by insects, or by rust

Some common types of insect galls. Oak gall (*left*), wart gall on oaks (*center*), and a midrib gall on a leaflet of the ash. Galls are not serious garden pests.

fungi that are sometimes carried by insects. Common examples are the cedar apple, various oak galls (see the illustration), and the less conspicuous ones on herbaceous plants. Most galls are of secondary importance in gardens.

gallica, -us, -um (gal′li-ka). From France.

GALTONIA (gall-tō′ni-a). A small genus of South African bulbous herbs of the lily family, G. candicans, the summer hyacinth or giant summer hyacinth, a garden plant with showy white flowers. It has strap-shaped, basal leaves 2–3 ft. long and 1–2 in. wide, and an erect, flowering stalk 2–3 ft. high, terminated by a long, rather sparsely flowered raceme.* Flowers short-tubed, fragrant, about 1 in. long, narrowly bell-shaped, the segments longer than the tube. Stamens 6. Fruit a somewhat 3-sided capsule.* The plant is not really hardy north of zone* 5 unless well mulched. Increased by offsets, and often sold as *Hyacinthus candicans.* (Named for Sir Francis Galton, British anthropologist.)

GAMES. For the minimum space requirements of lawn games see BADMINTON, BOWLING GREEN, CROQUET, DECK TENNIS, and TENNIS.

GAMOLEPIS (gam-ol′e-pis). South African herbs or shrubs of the family Compositae, the only cult. species being G. Tagetes, a tender annual grown for its yellow or orange-yellow flowers. It is a wiry, much-branched herb 4–6 in. high, and has alternate,* usually cut leaves, the segments toothed. Flower head solitary, about ¾ in. wide, the bracts beneath it forming an urn-shaped involucre.* It is best treated as a tender annual (*see* ANNUALS), and is often used for low edging. (*Gamolepis* is from the Greek meaning united scales, in allusion to the urn-shaped involucre.)

GAMOPETALOUS. Having the petals

---

* Special articles on the subjects indicated by an asterisk (*) will be found at the words so marked.

united to form a one-piece, or nearly one-piece corolla,* as in the bellflower and many other plants. The opposite term, *polypetalous,* indicates that the petals are separate, as in the rose and hundreds of garden flowers. Whether flowers are gamopetalous or polypetalous is of greater botanical than hort. importance, for upon the character of separate or united petals the botanists have classified whole sections of the plant world.

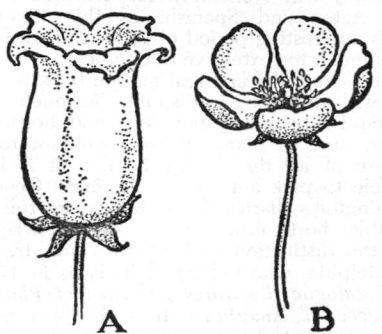

A   B

(A) A united (gamopetalous) corolla. (B) A flower with separate petals (polypetalous).

gandavensis, -e (gan-da-ven′sis). From Ghent, Belgium.

GARAMBULLO = *Myrtillocactus geometrizans.*

GARBANZO = *Cicer arietinum.*

GARCINIA (gar-sin′i-a). A large genus of Old World tropical trees of the family Guttiferae, only one, **G. Mangostana,** the mangosteen, suitable for outdoor cult. in the U.S., and this only in the warmest sections of zone* 9. It is a handsome tree up to 30 ft., with opposite,* thick, leathery, shining green leaves, 6–9 in. long, that have several prominent cross-veins. Flowers rose-pink, nearly 2 in. wide, usually polygamous.* Petals and sepals 4. Stamens* many. Fruit reddish-purple, about 2½ in. in diameter, its outer rind thick, but the 5–7 orange-like, white segments of flesh, juicy, of superb flavor, and highly prized in the Indo-Malayan region where the tree is native. Grown here only occasionally in extreme southern Fla., where it needs a moist, well-drained soil. It may be propagated by seeds, budding, or by inarching (*see* GRAFTING). (Named for Laurence Garcin, French botanist.)

GARDEN. Traditionally, a more or less enclosed place in which to grow plants, nearly always in conjunction with a house. This restricted, old meaning of the term is now stretched to include almost any outdoor collection of plants, and easily merges with one's concept of a small farm, such, for instance, as a commercial market garden. In spite of this stretching of its meaning, *garden* still implies a home garden to most of us, whether a backyard or a country estate.

What we do *with* a garden is a reflection of our taste, knowledge, and pocketbook. No rule can be stated that would apply for everyone. In the ENCYCLOPEDIA OF GARDENING are many articles designed to guide the seeker. Perhaps the surest way toward one's garden hopes and aspirations is to scan the list of subjects below, all of which have special articles about them:

Soils	Rock Garden
Kitchen Garden	Wild Garden
Annuals	Trees
Biennials	Shrubs
Perennials	Vines
Fruit Culture	Water Garden
Herb Gardening	Ferns and Fern
Planning the Home	Gardening
Grounds	

For what we do *in* a garden, and the daily routine of garden management, *see* the various subjects treated at GARDEN OPERATIONS.

GARDEN ANEMONE = *Anemone hortensis.*

GARDEN BALSAM = *Impatiens Balsamina.*

GARDEN BOOKS. Books about gardening are almost as old as the art itself, and they are legion. At the beginning there are, of course, only the rudest inscriptions to tell us of the first rescue of wild plants by our still wilder ancestors.

But long before the Christian Era, cultivated Greeks not only developed beautiful gardens but wrote books about them. One of the greatest was Theophrastus of Eresus, born 370 B.C., and a favorite pupil of Aristotle. He is thought to have written over 200 books, but only two of them survive, the *History of Plants* and the *Causes of Plants,* and these only in part. But the remarkable thing about them and their author, who also developed the first known botanical garden, is that, almost alone, they carried Greek learning about plants and gardens to the Renaissance. No greater glory in the history of hort. literature can exceed this — to have impressed one's knowledge and standards upon the world for close to 16 centuries. And many of the observations of Theophrastus are current right down to our own time.

He had many elaborators, copyists, and some pupils. Today their writings give us much light on gardening and the plants grown for pleasure and use over two thousand years ago, but none of them left such an impress upon garden literature as the genius of Theophrastus. Chief among the Greeks who followed their master was Dioscorides, whose *Materia Medica* has been issued in countless editions. Another was Crenatus who illustrated the first herbal. Then came Claudius Galen, born 130 B.C., a talented Greek physician who wrote an herbal, *De Simplicium,* of which only 83 out of 400 parts have been preserved but that fragment influenced all subsequent writing

* Special articles on the subjects indicated by an asterisk (*) will be found at the words so marked.

about medicinal plants down to almost modern times.

EARLY ROMAN. Of the many Roman books about gardens and flowers only a few need notice here. While the art of gardening and the development of country estates made far greater progress in Rome than in Greece, the writers on it were mostly elaborating upon the writings of Theophrastus. Two Romans stand out especially. They were Pliny, who wrote a *Natural History*, and Marcus Porcius Cato, whose *De Re Rustica* is a remarkable garden book full of sound advice on topiary work, olive trees, pools, fountains, and the kitchen garden.

HERBALS. From the Greeks and Romans to the Renaissance there stretch what are popularly called the Dark Ages. So far as the printed or written word is concerned perhaps they were. But it should not be forgotten that the art of gardening was carried through these dark centuries almost wholly by the Church. In many a cathedral and cloister garden, not only the plants and methods, but the very books themselves of the talented Greeks and proud Romans were preserved for the flowering of the Renaissance, which was soon to astonish a sluggard world.

One of the first evidences of a revival of garden learning was the publication in 1471 of *Opus Ruralium Commodorum* by Pietro Crescenzi, an Italian lawyer, who became enamored of country life after the Roman plan of centuries earlier. Published in Latin, the book was quickly translated into Italian, French, and German. While it borrowed heavily from the Greeks and Romans, especially from Cato's *De Re Rustica*, its great merit was that it showed to a relatively gardenless world the pleasures of having a garden and how to go about making one. While not an herbal in the usual sense of that term, Crescenzi's book was followed by many that were. And in fact garden books within the next century or two became as popular as they are today.

Among the herbals, which are systematic accounts of the plants known at the time, especially their "virtues" as medicine and condiment, the following English examples should be consulted by all students of the development of garden literature:

William Turner's *Herbal*; 1568.
John Gerard's *Herball or Generall Historie of Plantes*; 1597.
John Parkinson's *Herbal*, but called by him *Paradisi in Sole Paradisus Terrestris*; 1629.

There were, in addition, many other herbals, mostly by the German fathers of botany, and hundreds of books on gardening were published in England between 1500 and 1700. But, with the settlement of America and the beginnings of gardening here, came the first truly American hort. literature.

AMERICA. While most of us think that American gardening began in Mass. or Va.

soon after 1600, the Spanish and Portuguese had long before brought the incomparable art of the Moors to Mexico, Central America, Peru, and Brazil. Upon an elaborate system of Aztec and Inca horticulture they reared a garden structure of which too little is known. To the New World cultivation of corn, tobacco, chocolate, potato, and many other plants, they brought wheat, rye, sugar cane, banana, the olive, fig, the citrus fruits, and many Old World flowers. The literature, both Aztec and Spanish, of this tremendously interesting period of American gardening is much too extensive to cite here.

Who wrote the first real garden book in the U.S. will always be in dispute. So much was written by botanists, travelers, and horticulturists, and so many of the books were a mixture of all three subjects, that it is impossible to pick out one as the first. George Washington's diaries, for instance, are full of valuable horticultural notes. Some writers give the distinction to William Yong, Jr., of Philadelphia, who published in Paris in 1783 his *Catalogue d' Arbres Arbustes et Plantes Herbacées d' Amérique*. It is chiefly a catalogue of plants he grew in his garden with notes on their culture. But others credit a Mrs. Martha Logan of Charleston, S.C., with the first real garden book, *The Gardener's Kalendar*. It may have been only a pamphlet, but of its existence there is no doubt. She died in 1779 and her book was published soon after, so that it may well antedate the catalogue of William Yong, Jr.

If both these early claimants are excluded, the earliest hort. book, written by an American, and published here, is Robert Squibb's *Gardener's Kalender*, Charleston, 1787. In Boston, in 1799, was published an American edition of *Introduction to the Knowledge and Practice of Gardening*, an English book by the Rev. Charles Marshall. The second really American garden book was printed at Washington, D.C., in 1804. It was entitled *The American Gardener* and was written by John Gardiner and David Hepburn.

With the opening of the nineteenth century, American gardening and books about it grew as rapidly as the country. There is no space here to catalogue that literature, which includes hundreds of titles. Some of the landmarks, however, issued between 1900 and 1959 are listed below in the order of their publication. They have been selected not only for their importance, but for diversified subject matter.

1900–02 Liberty Hyde Bailey. *Cyclopedia of American Horticulture*. New York.

1903 Helena Rutherford Ely. *A Woman's Hardy Garden*. New York.

1907 Mabel Cabot Sedgwick, assisted by Robert Cameron. *The Garden Month by Month*. New York.

1908 Ulysses Prentiss Hedrick. *The Grapes of New York*. Albany.

1911 Ulysses Prentiss Hedrick. *The Plums of New York*. Albany.

---

* Special articles on the subjects indicated by an asterisk (*) will be found at the words so marked.

1915 Ulysses Prentiss Hedrick. *The Cherries of New York.* Albany.

1917 Ulysses Prentiss Hedrick. *The Peaches of New York.* Albany.

Ernest Henry Wilson. *Aristocrats of the Garden.* New York.

Henry Vincent Hubbard and Theodora Kimball. *Introduction to the Study of Landscape Design.* New York.

1921 Ulysses Prentiss Hedrick. *The Pears of New York.* Albany.

1924 John McLaren. *Gardening in California, Landscape and Flower.* San Francisco.

Liberty Hyde Bailey. *Manual of Cultivated Plants:* a Flora for the Identification of . . . Plants Grown in the Continental United States and Canada. New York.

1925 Ulysses Prentiss Hedrick. *The Small Fruits of New York.* Albany.

1927 Alfred Rehder. *Manual of Cultivated Trees and Shrubs Hardy in North America, Exclusive of the Subtropical and Warmer Temperate Regions.* New York.

1928 Louise Beebe Wilder. *Pleasures and Problems of a Rock Garden.* New York.

Susan Delano McKelvey. *The lilac,* a monograph. New York.

1928–37 Ulysses Prentiss Hedrick. *The Vegetables of New York.* Albany.

1930 Liberty Hyde Bailey. *Hortus; a Concise Dictionary of Gardening, General Horticulture and Cultivated Plants in North America,* compiled by Liberty Hyde Bailey and Ethel Zoe Bailey. New York.

1931–34 Garden Club of America. *Gardens of Colony and State: Gardens and Gardeners of the American Colonies and of the Republic before 1840.* Compiled and edited by Alice G. B. Lockwood. New York.

1932 Ephraim Porter Felt. *Insects and Diseases of Ornamental Trees and Shrubs.* New York.

1936 Selman A. Waksman. *The Soil and the Microbe.* New York.

1936 Clement Gray Bowers. *Rhododendrons and Azaleas.* New York.

1936 Norman Taylor. *The Garden Dictionary.* Boston.

1946 H. Harold Hume. *Camellias in America.* Harrisburg, Pennsylvania.

1949 Donald Wyman. *Shrubs and Vines for American Gardens.* New York.

1951 Donald Wyman. *Trees for American Gardens.* New York.

1954 Thomas H. Everett. *American Gardener's Book of Bulbs.* New York.

1955 Thomas D. Church. *Gardens Are for People.* New York.

1957 A. B. Graf. *Exotica.* Rutherford, New Jersey.

1957 Harold E. Moore. *African Violets, Gloxinias and Their Relatives.* New York.

1958 Frederic P. Lee. *The Azalea Book.* New York — D. S. M.

GARDEN CALENDAR. The map below shows by belts the average dates on which the last killing frost in spring may be expected to occur. The earliest date from which it is possible to show the *average* time of the last killing frost is March 1 and the last date is June 1. Either before or after these dates the times of killing frosts are too irregular to base any accurate figures upon. In high elevations in the West large areas, which are used for sheep and cattle grazing, are subject to frosts after June 1.

Variations in frost dates are smaller near the Atlantic Coast and in the strip of country lying east of the Rocky Mountains. There will be, of course, in all areas a variation of a few days each year from the given average. The greatest variations are in sections west of the Rocky Mountains and in regions where frost is less common, such as parts of Florida and the Gulf Coast. The only absolutely frost-free area in the United States is near Key West, Florida.

Plantings must be made late enough to be safe from too great a risk of spring frost and early enough for the crops to mature before being in danger from autumn frosts. In general, the frost-free period is, depending entirely upon the location, between 15 and 50 days longer than the average number of days fit for ordinary garden operations.

Common sense must be applied to all gardening problems; remember that many plants are often tolerant of wide differences in soil and other conditions under which they will grow. Many of the items listed in the calendar are treated more fully in other sections of this book.

The calendar is arranged according to the months of the year. It is divided into sections for four large areas of the country. These areas are roughly divided as follows: the NORTH, the states of the Northeast, south to Virginia, north of the Ohio River and west to the Rockies; the SOUTH, the states south to the Gulf; the NORTHWEST, those of the north Rockies and west; and the SOUTHWEST, the states west of Texas to, and including, California. There is also a section on what to do indoors and in the greenhouse. For the sequence of bloom in the garden *see* EVERBLOOMING GARDEN.

The North. Check to see that winter mulch is still in place over the plants you

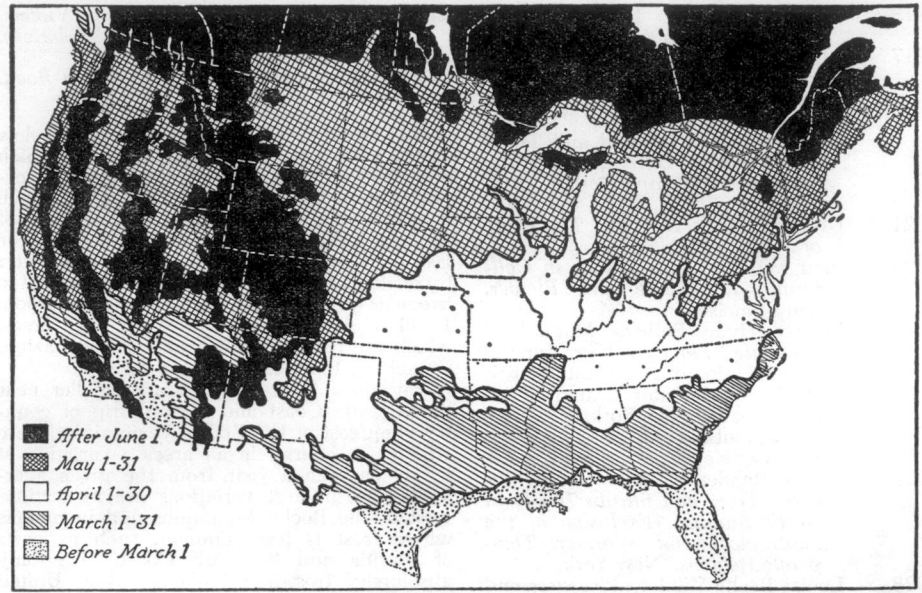

Legend:
- After June 1
- May 1-31
- April 1-30
- March 1-31
- Before March 1

THE ONSET OF SPRING

The map shows the average dates of the last killing spring frosts, which coincide with the beginning of many garden operations, as outlined in the introduction to the Garden Calendar. Canadian gardeners should be guided by data found at the name of each province.

have protected. If the wind has blown some away, add more leaves or peat. Old Christmas trees and other evergreen branches make excellent material for mulching purposes.

Protect Christmas roses with branches or a small frame so that you can easily find the flowers and not have them broken with snow.

Following snowstorms, gently knock the snow from evergreens, especially the broad-leaved types. Use a pole or rake and raise or shake the branches gently. If snow has frozen on the plant or the plant is covered with ice, it is better to take a chance; it may melt off with less damage than if you try to break it off.

During mild days, toward the end of the month, pruning may be started on deciduous plants.

Now is the time to plan the flower and vegetable plantings for the year. It is garden catalogue time and there is no more optimistic reading on a cold winter day.

Look over the stored bulbs, gladiolus, and dahlias. Do not keep them too moist or too cold, which will cause injury, or too warm, which may encourage premature growth.

The South. It is time in the milder sections of this area to begin planting of trees and shrubs. This should be done in the milder weather and when the soil is moist and in a workable condition.

Broad-leaved evergreens may be planted now. They are dug and handled with a ball of soil. Azaleas may be transplanted now before they flower although many gardeners prefer to wait until such plants are in flower in order to achieve the effect they desire.

Prune deciduous plants such as shade trees, and shrubs before new growth begins.

Roses should be pruned and general spraying begun before new growth starts. Roses are ready for transplanting. Prepare the soil thoroughly, make sure it is well drained and that some organic matter has been added.

In the lower areas of the South, it is time for the first planting of gladiolus, calla, ginger-lily, and the tuberous-rooted begonias. Other bulbs will include the lilies such as the regal lily, *Lilium speciosum* and its many varieties, and *Lilium auratum*.

The Southwest. Planting of deciduous plants such as roses, shrubs, shade trees, fruit trees, berries and perennials is done this month. Prepare the soil thoroughly before planting. Conifers and broad-leaved evergreens should also be transplanted before they resume a more active growth. Newly transplanted plants will benefit by a screen or protection until they get started. It will help to prevent drying out of the branches.

Perennials are divided and transplanted this month. Plan the garden where they are to go so that you can get the desired picture.

January is the month for pruning. Prune

* Special articles on the subjects indicated by an asterisk (*) will be found at the words so marked.

carefully to develop the type of plant growth you want. Early-flowering shrubs may be pruned after they have flowered.

Ground-cover plants are excellent in places where grass is difficult to grow or become established. These may be planted this month and in this way they will have a good chance of becoming established before warm weather.

Pansies should be fertilized to keep them blooming. Use a liquid fertilizer over 2 to 4 weeks. A mulch of leaf mold or peat over the soil will help to prevent drying out and will encourage growth and continued flowering.

Gladiolus plantings may be started. Varieties range from 90 to 120 days from planting to bloom, which means that those planted now would flower in May. Later plantings, growing in warmer weather, will flower in a shorter time.

The Northwest. Pruning of woody plants such as deciduous shrubs, fruit trees, flowering shrubs, and grapes is timely. This is usually done by the end of the month. Roses are better left unpruned until later in the spring, although they can have the canes shortened if they blow around excessively.

Dormant spraying should be completed by the end of the month. It should be done before there is any new growth.

A nitrogen fertilizer such as ammonium sulphate should be applied to rhododendron, camellia, and other shrubs to give them a chance to absorb it before new growth. Well-fertilized plants do not brown as much during the winter, and leaf drop is reduced.

Indoors and Greenhouse. Cut branches of early-flowering shrubs such as forsythia, pussy willow, flowering quince, and early-flowering crabapples or cherries may be brought in. Put them into containers of water and in a warm place until the buds begin to swell and show color. Then remove them to light so that color will develop more intensely.

Poinsettias that have lost their attractiveness should be put aside and not watered. They are rested until April or May when, after cutting back, they are again started into growth. They will store better if the temperature is below 50°F.

This is the month to begin bringing in the bulbs that were potted last fall, such as tulips, hyacinths, and narcissi. Make sure they have a well-developed root system. Start them in a 60° to 65° temperature.

Avoid overwatering plants, especially in the home. Overwatering may favor root rot or root injury or a trouble known as oedema which is characterized by water-soaked areas in the leaves.

The first planting of tuberous begonia and gloxinia may be made. Start them in moist sphagnum moss or peat, and when roots begin to start, pot them in a soil well supplied with organic matter.

Amaryllis are potted usually in a 4- to 5-inch pot with the tip of the bulb extending above the pot. Bulbs from previous years that are dormant may be transplanted, but kept in a relatively small pot. Watch for growth of those in storage, and when there are signs of new leaves or a bud, then bring to a warm temperature for flowering.

The North. Pruning of deciduous plants may be started if the weather is mild. Remove weak and straggly branches as well as those broken or damaged by winter storms. It is a good time to shape up deciduous shrubs, trees, and hedges.

Large deciduous trees and shrubs may be transplanted with a ball of soil at this season and, if it is done carefully, they will not show signs of transplanting injury.

Perennials that may have heaved from the soil through alternate freezing and thawing should be gently pressed back. Add additional protection.

Garden tools and furniture should be cleaned, repaired, and made ready for use when the time comes.

It is time to order seeds and plants for spring. Make a plan so you know where to plant when the time comes.

February is the month when the first flowers may be found outdoors. During mild periods you may find the first snowdrop, winter aconite, *Helleborus, Hamamelis mollis,* or winter jasmine.

Fruit trees are pruned this month. Cut off large branches by first undercutting so there will be little or no injury to the bark as the branch falls.

The South. This is the time for planting of trees and shrubs. Transplant before active growth begins. In the most southern areas this is as late as it is practical to transplant deciduous plants without a ball of soil.

Pruning is done now on all plants excepting those early-flowering kinds where pruning is delayed until after bloom. Roses should be pruned by the middle of the month or later, depending on weather conditions. Once that has been done, begin the summer fertilizer program.

Azaleas are blooming and should be fertilized after they have finished flowering and new growth begins.

Camellias are given treatment similar to the azalea. They should be fertilized after bloom. Pruning is done then but is usually kept to a minimum, merely to keep the plant shapely or remove injured branches.

Lawns are beginning to grow and fertilizer should be applied. Use a type high in nitrogen as a 10–5–4. Trees and shrubs should be fertilized with the same material.

---

* Special articles on the subjects indicated by an asterisk (*) will be found at the words so marked.

Hardy annuals and vegetables are sown. Annual flowers include larkspur, cornflower, lupine, poppy, alyssum, and California poppy. Early vegetables include beet, cabbage, carrot, lettuce, onion, pea, radish, and spinach.

The Southwest. February is the month for planting. Soils are moist and temperatures not excessive. Root growth should get started before top growth. Prune back newly planted deciduous plants as much as is practical in order to encourage root growth. Keep the soil moist.

Trees and shrubs that have been dug with a ball of soil or have been grown in pots or cans need similar attention after planting. Plant with a small depression or basin around the plant so water will soak into that area.

Pruning of woody plants is done now before active growth begins. Early-flowering plants are pruned after flowering. Cut out the oldest canes from the blackberry and boysenberry and fasten those remaining on a trellis.

Seed of many annuals may be sown; these include alyssum, calendula, stock, and sweet pea.

The Northwest. Pruning of deciduous plants is begun as the weather becomes more mild. Remove dead and injured branches. When the tops have not proved winter-hardy, the plants should be cut off close to the ground, especially in hydrangea and buddleia. Roses in the milder areas are pruned severely to encourage strong vigorous new growth. In the colder sections pruning is delayed according to the weather conditions.

The first planting of deciduous plants is done depending on local weather conditions.

Seed of hardy annuals, such as garden peas and sweet peas, is sown outdoors.

Indoors, seeds of perennials or tender annuals are started, later to be planted outdoors. Tuberous begonias and gloxinia are started indoors for later use, inside or out. The begonias may be planted outdoors after danger of frost. More cold-resistant bulbs may be planted outdoors in well-drained areas.

Indoors and Greenhouse. Potted spring-flowering bulbs are brought from their storage and placed at a window or in the greenhouse. A temperature of 60° to 65° F. is best at the start, but it may be raised once new top growth begins.

House plants should be fertilized again. During the winter (mid-Nov. to early Feb.) the light intensity is low and growth of plants is slow, so that fertilizing is usually stopped. This month fertilizing is begun again as the light intensity increases and growth of most plants is resumed.

Many of the slow-growing annuals are sown this month, such as snapdragons, double and large-flowering petunias, *Vinca rosea*, and *Salvia splendens*.

Chrysanthemum plants from the garden may be lifted and put in pots or boxes to encourage growth. These are used as stock plants from which to take cuttings.

Azaleas are brought from storage and put in a 55° to 60°F. temperature to force. The temperature may be raised 10° to 15° providing the humidity is high. The Kurume and Indica or Belgian types are easiest to force.

Lilies being forced for Easter should be at a 62° to 65° temperature at night.

Take cuttings of geraniums, lantana, begonia, and *Iresine* for small plants to put out in May or June.

Cut branches of forsythia, pussy willow, flowering quince, and cornelian cherry may be forced into flower.

The North. This is the month to plant trees and shrubs before new growth begins. Plant carefully and prune.

Pruning of established plants may be done, preferably before new growth is active; this includes fruit trees and grapes. Evergreens may be cut back slightly, depending upon the kind.

Remove winter mulch gradually; that is, the coarse material on the surface at one time and then the remainder a little later.

Hardy bulbs that are covered should have this covering removed. Clean up such garden refuse and add it to the garden compost area. Mulch materials can be used for this compost.

Perennials and roses should be fertilized if the soil has thawed. In more northern areas this is delayed until April.

Hybrid tea and floribunda roses should be pruned. Old leaves and trash from the rose bed should be cleaned away and destroyed.

Perennials of many kinds that have started to grow may be dug and transplanted.

Lawns should be fertilized. Select a fertilizer high in nitrogen. Lime should not be applied unless a soil test indicates a need of it. Bare spots may be reseeded.

Toward the end of the month in the milder areas of the North certain annuals and vegetable seed may be sown. Plant, in a well-drained area, seed of annual flowers such as cornflower, gypsophila, larkspur, lupine, or sweet pea, and vegetables such as radish or peas.

The South. Spring is advancing rapidly. Planting of trees and shrubs continues, especially plants that are dug with a ball of soil or that have been grown in containers. Magnolias and dogwood are best replanted in the spring. Evergreens are also transplanted before new growth.

Pruning is continued providing new growth

* Special articles on the subjects indicated by an asterisk (*) will be found at the words so marked.

is not too far advanced. Early-flowering shrubs that have finished bloom should be pruned.

Sow seed of most kinds of annuals and vegetables, especially in the more southern sections and progressively to the north as the season advances. Sow sweet peas, especially the Cuthbertson strain which is more heat-tolerant.

Most perennials may be dug, divided, and replanted, particularly chrysanthemum, dianthus, heuchera, pyrethrum, and Shasta daisy.

After roses have been pruned, they should be fertilized and sprayed.

Boxwood and other evergreens may be sheared or pruned carefully as long as the shape is retained.

Most varieties of camellias are finished bloom by now. Fertilize them when they are finished flowering, with a complete fertilizer such as those for acid-tolerant plants, or one high in nitrogen. Mulch such plants with peat moss, leaf mold, pine needles or similar material. Old camellia flowers should be raked up and destroyed.

Lawns should be fertilized and reseeded if necessary. Fertilizer should be a high nitrogen type, as 10–6–4.

The Southwest. In the more southern areas this is the end of the season for planting of dormant plants. After this it is best to transplant with a ball of soil. In more northern sections planting of dormant plants continues throughout the month.

Fertilize shrubs, trees, perennials, and the lawn. Use complete fertilizers and work them into the soil around the plants. A program of fertilization through the irrigation water is practical. By using soluble materials, they become immediately available to the plant. On lawns, fertilizer with herbicides included is practical.

Seed of annuals may be sown outdoors in frames and later planted in the open garden when cold temperatures are past.

After the danger of frost is past, subtropical plants may be planted out, such as hibiscus, avocado, fuchsia, and bougainvillaea. Prune the tops to induce compact growth. Tuberous begonias are planted in cool, shaded areas. They will benefit by being mulched with some material to keep the soil moist. Sprinklers to water the plant and to maintain the humidity are desirable.

Camellias are finished flowering and the old flowers should be cleaned up and destroyed. This is to prevent the flower blight from being carried over for the next year. The disease is not yet widespread but this precaution is good garden practice.

The Northwest. March is the month for most active planting of deciduous trees and shrubs and, in the colder areas of this section, evergreens that are winter-hardy. Roses are also planted.

Tender annual seed should be sown indoors or in a protected frame and the seedlings transplanted to the garden later. More hardy kinds of annuals or those that do not transplant readily, such as allysum, California poppy, clarkia, or godetia, are sown outdoors. Pansy can be sown now for summer and fall bloom.

Planting season begins in the mild areas for gladiolus corms. By beginning now and planting at 10- to 14-day intervals until late June, a succession of flowers may be had all summer and fall. Dahlias usually are not planted until about the time of last frost and maybe until late June.

Tuberous begonias and fancy-leaf caladiums are started indoors in moist peat and when they have begun to form roots are planted outdoors, if the weather permits, or potted and planted out later. Starting in this manner is more certain than planting directly in the open.

Indoors and Greenhouse. The days are longer and sun more intense. This means that the greenhouse temperature will need to be watched more closely. Apply a light shade to the glass to reduce this intensity. Foliage plants and certain others will benefit by a reduction in light intensity.

Hyacinth, narcissus, or other spring-flowering hardy bulbs that have flowered may be saved by allowing the foliage to remain on the plant and grow. Plant them out early in the spring or allow them to mature the foliage, then keep them dry until time for planting in the fall.

House plants should be fertilized regularly. Plants may be shifted to larger pots if they need more soil.

Continue to take cuttings of carnations, chrysanthemums, coleus, lantana, and other plants that are to be used outdoors in the summer.

Tuberous begonias are started by placing the roots in moist sphagnum moss or peat. When active growth starts, pot them up into small pots. Fancy-leaf caladiums are handled in the same way, or potted directly.

Young seedlings from seed sown in January or February may be large enough to pot into small pots or flats. Kinds that do not need warm temperature may be put out in hotbeds once they have become established.

Seeds of slower-growing annuals and perennials should be sown this month.

The North. April is a time for a general cleanup. Remove winter mulch and save the material for the compost; leaves and old plant tops are all good.

Planting time continues in April. Deciduous trees, shrubs, and evergreens may be transplanted. Prepare the soil thoroughly and dig the hole large enough to accommodate the root system. Most perennials may be

---

* Special articles on the subjects indicated by an asterisk (*) will be found at the words so marked.

transplanted now before they begin growth. Those kinds that begin to grow early should be transplanted first. Early-flowering kinds may be transplanted before growth or in the fall.

Pruning should be finished before new growth starts. Early flowering shrubs such as the cornelian cherry and forsythia are pruned when the flowers fade and before new growth begins.

Soil for annuals and other planting should be well prepared and fertilized. Spade this in together with organic matter.

Seed of many annuals should be sown — those tolerant of cool temperatures, such as the California poppy, cornflower, larkspur, and annual poppies.

Pansy plants are planted out. They are a good plant to cover areas that have spring-flowering bulbs.

Hybrid tea, hybrid perpetuals, and floribunda roses are pruned now. Prune out the dead, injured and diseased canes.

Lawns should be fertilized as early as possible and any reseeding done if necessary. Early sowing is essential to good growth of young grass.

The South. Annual flowers may be sown outdoors and annual plants set out after the danger of frost is past. This will include many tender plants, among them alternanthera, coleus, geranium, and lantana.

Chrysanthemum plants are planted out, and once they have become established, the tips should be topped to induce branching. Most kinds of summer-flowering bulbs and corms are planted. These include caladium, canna, crinums, dahlia, hymenocallis, gladiolus, montbretia, and tigridia. Plantings of the gladiolus may be made at intervals until July or later, depending on location, to give a long season of bloom. Dahlia-planting continues into June. Tuberous begonias are planted outdoors in a shaded area for summer flowering.

Early-flowering shrubs and trees are pruned after they have finished flowering. Evergreens of all kinds should be pruned or sheared to encourage a bushy compact growth.

Azaleas may need special attention. If pruning is to be done, it should be after the flowers have dropped and before new growth starts. Prune only to keep the plant in shape or to remove broken branches.

Lawns should be fertilized not later than the early part of the month to get them well established and growing. Weed killers should be applied for the control of broad-leaved weeds. Grass started from sprigs or plugs, such as zoysia, Bermuda or St. Augustine grass, is planted when the weather becomes mild.

Vegetable planting is well under way. Seed of most kinds may be sown in the open, such as beets, carrots, corn, lettuce, peas and radishes. Plants of cauliflower, eggplant, peppers, tomatoes, and sweet potatoes are put out after frost danger is past.

The Southwest. Planting of shrubs and trees continues, especially those grown in cans or containers. After frost danger, tropical and semi-tropical material is planted out. The material should be carefully removed from the container at planting time.

Dahlias are planted out. Stake the plants at the time of planting so there will be no damage to the roots later. Dwarf types and most pompons do not need staking if they are well-branched plants.

Planting or transplanting of chrysanthemum should proceed. Prepare the soil thoroughly and continue then to top, disbud, and fertilize plants. Other perennials such as coreopsis, delphinium, dianthus, gaillardia, and perennial phlox are planted out.

April is also planting time for seeds of annual flowers and vegetables. Plants of most kinds, including vegetables, are planted out after danger of frost is past.

The Northwest. The gardening and planting schedule of this region will have to be fitted to the location and elevation.

Planting and pruning continues for trees and shrubs. Pruning should keep the plants well shaped and free from old or injured branches. Evergreens may need shearing or clipping to encourage bushy growth. Such woody plants need to be fertilized at least once each season. Early-flowering shrubs will need to be pruned immediately after bloom and before new growth begins.

Prepare soil for annuals. Fertilize perennials before new active growth. Lawns should be included in a fertilizing program, with the control of weeds by herbicides.

Annual seed is planted this month, for both flowers and vegetables. Tender plants or those started early, both indoors or in the greenhouse, are then planted out after frost danger is past.

Spring-flowering bulbs must be allowed to retain their foliage in order to manufacture food for next year. Old flowers or seed pods should be removed.

April is planting time for dahlias, gladioli, and other bulb types. Dahlias are planted now and for the next month, depending upon the location. Gladiolus plantings are made at intervals until about July 1. This provides flowers throughout the summer and early fall.

Azaleas, rhododendron, and camellias are fertilized now and the plants mulched. Use materials that will leave an acid reaction.

Indoors and Greenhouse. Greenhouse temperatures go up quickly with the strong intensity of the sun. Ventilate freely. Many foliage and flowering plants will benefit by having shade put on the greenhouse to reduce the light intensity. Whitewash or other shading compounds are effective.

Propagation for outdoor planting continues. Cuttings are made of ageratum, chrysanthemum, coleus, and other bedding plants. Seeds of many annuals may be sown, such as marigolds, petunias, salvia, snapdragons, torenia, and zinnias.

---

* Special articles on the subjects indicated by an asterisk (*) will be found at the words so marked.

April is the time to take cuttings of certain plants such as carnations, fuchsia, hydrangea and *Piqueria,* for flowering next winter.

Cut back overgrown foliage plants; cuttings may be made from the tips or even stem pieces. Old plants may be repotted, or planted out for the summer, to be used for more cuttings or lifted in the fall again and potted.

Dahlia roots may be started by placing the roots on moist sphagnum or other moist, well-aerated medium. New shoots are removed, rooted, and potted. Once they are established they can be planted outdoors after frost danger is past.

The North. Seed of annual flowers and vegetables may be sown outdoors. Sow seed in well-drained areas and add some organic matter to the seed bed to loosen the soil.

When danger of frost is past, tender plants like the begonia, coleus, geranium, and lantana, and annuals started indoors, are planted out. Allow them to have sufficient space so they will develop into well-shaped plants. After annuals become established remove the tip bud to encourage branching of the plant.

Fertilize peonies with a complete fertilizer early in the month. Disbud the flower stems to allow only the tip bud to remain. When the side buds are removed, the growth goes into the main flower which will be larger. Stake the plant to hold the large flowers upright.

Seed of perennials and biennials may be sown. These may be sown from now until September, for plants for next year's flowering. Early sowing results in stouter plants.

Tender plants such as the canna, dahlia, tuberous begonia, montbretia, and caladium may be planted outdoors. Gladiolus may be planted from early May until the end of June which will give a succession of flowers during the summer and fall. Plant in a loose, well-drained, fertile soil.

Sow vegetable seeds of beets, carrots, celery, onion, bean, corn, and radish, or set out plants of cabbage, cauliflower, celery, or tomato.

The South. Container-grown plants of trees and shrubs may be planted in the landscape plantings even when in full bloom. Prepare the planting soil, and water regularly.

Mulching should be done on any acid-tolerant plants. Use well-rotted leaf mold or peat.

Young plants set out this spring should be protected, if necessary, from strong winds or intense sun. Young camellias, azaleas, rho-dodendron, and other broad-leaved plants will benefit from some protection or shade.

Seeds of most kinds of annuals may be sown outdoors. Tender plants started indoors or in the greenhouse may be planted out.

Young perennials planted now will give good bloom next year. Chrysanthemums started from cuttings will be more satisfactory than old clumps.

Perennial and biennial seed sown from now until July is generally most satisfactory.

Summer-flowering bulbs should be planted. These include caladium, canna, dahlia, gladiolus, ginger-lily, and tuberous begonia. Gladiolus may be planted at intervals to prolong the period of bloom.

Fertilize and mulch roses.

Apply herbicides for the control of broad-leaved weeds and crab grass, but *see* Crab Grass.

Lawns need regular mowing; set the mower to cut higher as the season becomes warmer. Rapid-growing kinds such as zoysia, St. Augustine, and Bermuda grasses will respond to regular fertilization throughout the season.

The Southwest. Plants grown in cans or containers may still be planted in the garden. Palms may be transplanted. They should have support until they become well established. Cacti and succulents are often excellent plants to be included in a landscape planting. Their care is somewhat less than for many other plants, but they do require water at times.

As the season progresses and there is dry weather, plants need to be irrigated. Water thoroughly so the soil around the roots is well moistened. Mulch plants to reduce the need for watering.

Early-flowering annuals that have finished bloom in more mild areas should be replaced with others. Dwarf or bedding dahlias, chrysanthemums, marigolds, or zinnias are useful, or others that grow rapidly in a warm temperature.

Chrysanthemums are excellent plants for fall bloom. Those propagated from cuttings and growing in pots or pans may be planted with little check in growth. Use starter* solutions at the time of planting. Once they are started, the tips should be removed to hasten branching.

Dahlias will need topping, as do the annuals, to induce or encourage branching. The large-flowering kinds of dahlias, that are staked individually, usually are trained to 4 main stems per plant.

The Northwest. May is the end of the planting season for most woody plants. Make sure they are well watered and mulched if possible. They should not be allowed to dry out.

Annual seed of rapidly-growing kinds may be sown outside in protected areas. When the danger of frost is past, the tender kinds can be sown. Sow pansy seed for fall and early winter bloom.

The general garden practice of topping or "pinching" of the shoots of annuals and

---

* Special articles on the subjects indicated by an asterisk (*) will be found at the words so marked.

some perennials is done to induce branching. One topping is sufficient in most cases.

Seed of perennials and biennials is sown in May and as late as August. The small plants may be ready for flowering next spring.

Spring-flowering bulbs are still in need of their foliage. Do not remove it until it begins to yellow.

Planting of gladioli and dahlias continues. Set the stakes as the dahlias are planted so there will be no damage later to the roots. Montbretia, canna, and tigridia are also planted.

Tuberous begonias help to add color to the garden. Use them in containers or plant them in a sheltered area.

Remove the old flower heads of woody plants instead of allowing them to mature. Rhododendron, camellia, and lilac are treated in this manner.

Indoors and Greenhouse. May is the month for transferring plants to the garden or to a cold frame for a few days, and then outdoors when danger of frost is past.

Pot seedlings that are ready or rooted cuttings from the propagating bench. Annual seed may be sown in small pots or flats for rapid germination and growth. Seed sown now may produce plants for later summer flowering.

Foliage or flowering plants should be fertilized regularly. Many kinds are pruned back in the spring to encourage branching and to develop a more bushy plant by fall. The prunings may be used for propagation.

Sow seed of snapdragons for cut flowers in August, *Begonia semperflorens* for early winter; ornamental peppers for next December; *Primula obconica* for January and later flowering; and *Anemone coronaria* for next winter.

Cuttings taken now include chrysanthemum for fall bloom, bouvardia for next winter, and *Piqueria* for November.

Many house plants may be planted out for the summer, or plunged outdoors in a partially shaded spot near a building, or protected by large shrubs or trees.

Poinsettia plants are pruned back severely and started into growth. The new growth is allowed to grow until it is 4 to 6 inches tall, when the tip is removed to induce many branches which later will be used as cuttings in August and September.

Callas are allowed to dry off and become dormant by withholding water. They are then rested in the pots until fall.

The North. Planting of all annuals outdoors is completed this month. Fertilize such

plantings with a complete soluble fertilizer such as 10–10–10 to give them a good start.

Remove old flowers from perennials that have finished blooming. On some kinds this may encourage repeated blooming, but in any case the garden will be more attractive.

Seed of perennials and biennials may be sown now for young plants to flower next year. Most kinds may be sown now and through August, outdoors in seed beds. Early sowing will produce larger plants by fall.

The old flowers should be removed from spring-flowering bulbs so the seed pods do not develop. Do not remove the foliage until it has yellowed and dried. Foliage is essential in order for the bulb to manufacture food for next year.

Gladioli and dahlias may be planted until the end of the month.

Hybrid tea and floribunda roses should be fertilized again after the first crop of flowers is gone. Use a complete fertilizer as used on annuals or perennials.

With warmer weather, raise the lawn mower so it does not cut too closely. Lawn watering, if done, should be thorough and infrequent. Use herbicides on the lawn. Crab grass killers should be used early on the young seedlings to get best control. *See* Crab Grass.

Cabbage and cauliflower seed may be sown for a fall crop. Lettuce seed sown now must be of the heat-resistant types.

The South. Use a summer mulch of whatever material is available for annuals, perennials, and roses. Evergreens, especially broad-leaved kinds, benefit by this practice.

Perennial seeds may be sown for next year's bloom, as well as some of the more rapidly growing annuals for flowering in the fall. Gladioli and dahlias may still be planted.

Tropical water lilies are planted in June, after the water has warmed up.

Fertilize roses after their first crop of flowers. Select a complete fertilizer. Apply and soak thoroughly.

Protect newly planted broad-leaved evergreens, such as azalea, boxwood, and rhododendron, with a screen the first year after planting.

Planting of the summer, vegetatively propagated grasses, such as St. Augustine and Bermuda, is done during June.

Lawns need special attention. Water thoroughly. Use herbicides early to be effective on the control of weeds and crab grass.

Summer crops of vegetables to be planted include corn, melons and okra. Side-dress vegetables with fertilizer to encourage good growth.

The Southwest. Use a mulch around the garden wherever possible to conserve moisture and reduce water loss.

Water newly planted shrubs or roses. Large plants may still be planted from containers.

Sow seed of perennials and biennials for

* Special articles on the subjects indicated by an asterisk (*) will be found at the words so marked.

bloom next winter and spring. Sow outdoors in specially protected areas or in pots or boxes indoors.

When cutting flowers of gladiolus, remove only a minimum of foliage with the flower spike.

Summer pruning may be done carefully on large shrubs to maintain an attractive plant.

Fuchsia, tuberous begonias, and other shade plants are at their best now. Provide plenty of moisture and light shade. Water plants in containers or pots carefully.

Weed control should be followed through on lawns now for effective control.

The Northwest. Mulch perennials, annuals, and other plants in order to reduce maintenance and loss of water, as well as to make the garden attractive.

Prune back leggy growth of annuals or perennials to make a more attractive plant. Remove old flowers of shrubs such as the lilac and rhododendron.

Plant annuals in, among, or over the early spring bulbs such as tulip and narcissus. Set out plants or sow seeds of fast-growing annuals. Allow the bulb foliage to mature naturally before removing.

If spring-flowering bulbs are to be transplanted, do it as the foliage turns yellow. If it is necessary to transplant these before the foliage is mature, dig and replant, keeping the foliage in place. Usually bulbs dug after they have matured are stored in a dry place and replanted in the fall.

There is still time to plant gladiolus and dahlia this month. Sow seed of perennials for large plants for next spring.

Plant cabbage, cauliflower, corn, beans, kale, melons, and squash for later summer vegetables.

Roses should be fertilized and mulched.

Indoors and Greenhouse. June is the time for putting outdoors as much from the house or greenhouse as possible. Prune back and plant or plunge outdoors. Most foliage plants are placed where they are in the shade for most or all of the day. Plants remaining in the greenhouse should be pruned as necessary to develop an attractive plant by fall. Many, like the philodendron, may be propagated more rapidly during the summer.

Poinsettia stock plants should be fertilized regularly to encourage growth. Keep plants topped to cause branching.

Chrysanthemum cuttings planted this month should flower in September or October, depending on the variety.

Seed of cineraria sown in June will produce flowering plants for January. *Primula malacoides* seed sown now will flower in January in 5- or 6-inch pots; sowings may be made until September, and the plants will flower later. Gerberas are planted out or divided and replanted in benches or pots. Cyclamen sown now will flower in about 18 months.

This is a good time to give the greenhouse a general cleanup. Replace dirty gravel or sand on the benches. Clean up under the benches and plan for replacing glass and repainting.

The North. Watering should be done infrequently but a thorough soaking given each time. This applies to the lawn, flowers, or woody plants.

Cultivate annuals and perennials to keep weeds from competing for the soil nutrients and the moisture. Keep old flowers removed to encourage new growth and flowers.

Bearded iris are dug, divided, and replanted if they are becoming crowded. They are more or less dormant at this time of the year and will begin new growth again in the fall. Plant with the rhizome only slightly covered.

Perennial seed of campanula, coreopsis, dianthus, delphinium, and perennial herbs is sown. Seed freshly gathered is satisfactory for some kinds while year-old seed often is more satisfactory for others. Seed of hybrid varieties does not normally come true to type, such hybrids being propagated vegetatively.

Continue to top chrysanthemums until about August 1 to encourage branching.

Roses will benefit by the use of a summer mulch. This reduces the need of watering. Prune climbing roses after flowering. Remove the old flowers of the rose without taking off extra foliage.

Cut back strong shoots of wisteria to check growth and to encourage flowering for next year.

Sheared hedges of privet, yew, hemlock, and others will need shaping and shearing at this time.

The South. Water perennials and annuals thoroughly and apply a summer mulch on as many as possible.

Sow seed of portulaca in bare spots of the garden. Water regularly until the young plants are well established.

Bearded iris should be transplanted. Do not plant too deep.

Perennial and biennial seed is sown this month. Cuttings of many shrubs — azalea, camellia, gardenia, holly, and photinia — may be taken at this time. Layering may be done on many kinds of plants. *See* LAYERING.

Chrysanthemums and dahlias should be disbudded and kept staked to be at their best at blooming time.

Continue to remove the old flowers of annuals and perennials.

Prune hedges to keep them in shape and attractive. Espaliered plants will need

---

❋ Special articles on the subjects indicated by an asterisk (❋) will be found at the words so marked.

pruning to keep them in their desired pattern.

Lawn mowers should be raised to cut the grass higher for the hot weather.

Vegetables to be planted include beans, beets, carrots, and spinach, and plants to set out include broccoli, Brussels sprouts, cabbage, and cauliflower.

The Southwest. Soluble fertilizer, dissolved in water, is a simple way of getting nutriment to plants and watering at the same time. *See* Foliar Feeding.

There is still time to plant pot-grown plants. Fuchsias, geraniums, and tuberous begonias may be used to fill in some rather vacant spot.

Perennial seed, such as columbine, hollyhock and primrose, is sown this month. Annuals that may be sown now for late-winter and spring bloom include Iceland poppy, pansy, and snapdragon. Marigolds and zinnias sown now will flower in the fall.

Iris should be transplanted at this time of the year. Cut the rhizomes into divisions of one or two fans of leaves. Plant them shallowly with the rhizome lightly covered.

Spring-flowering bulbs, such as the hyacinth, narcissus, and tulip, may be dug when the foliage has yellowed, and stored for fall planting. The narcissi do well if left undisturbed for several years while the tulips are better dug and replanted each year.

Lawns will need regular mowing, watering, and fertilizing. Herbicides should be used now for crab grass control. *See* Crab Grass.

The Northwest. Regular watering may be necessary in order to have continued growth. Water thoroughly and infrequently. Hydrangeas need much water. Azaleas and rhododendron are forming flower buds for next season and must not lack for moisture.

Rapidly growing annuals may be sown to fill in areas where earlier flowering kinds are gone. Dwarf marigolds are satisfactory for this. Chrysanthemums, dahlias, and gladioli may be planted until about the middle of the month.

Stake tall-growing plants such as dahlias, hardy asters, and lilies, and provide support for chrysanthemums.

July is the time to divide and replant some of the early-flowering perennials such as the bearded iris, lily-of-the-valley, primula and violets.

Softwood cuttings of azaleas, some kinds of rhododendron, and deciduous shrubs are made this month. Select fully developed shoots for cuttings.

Any of the spring-blooming bulbs that are now dormant may be lifted and stored for replanting in new places in the fall.

Corn, endive, kale, rutabaga, and snap beans may be sown. Plants of broccoli, cabbage, and celery are set out for a fall crop.

Indoors and Greenhouse. Keep the shade on the greenhouse roof. Replace it if rains wash some away. Some plants may need extra shade, and a covering of cheesecloth on the inside of the greenhouse is an easy and effective way of providing it.

Foliage plants such as Chinese evergreen, dracaena, and dieffenbachia that are too large may be cut back. The tip may be used as a cutting and the cane or stem cut up into stem-cuttings. Philodendrons are handled in the same manner except that the stems are cut up as leaf-bud cuttings for propagation.

During the summer do not neglect regular fertilization of plants — those in the home or greenhouse, or those planted or plunged outdoors that are to be brought back indoors in the fall. A completely soluble fertilizer is easy to use.

Chrysanthemum cuttings planted now should flower in November. Carnations should be planted by now. Keep them topped to induce branching until about mid-August.

Perennial and biennial seeds are easily cared for if started in flats in the greenhouse and then later taken outdoors.

Seed of calceolaria are sown for bloom next spring; *Begonia semperflorens* for Christmas; kalanchoe for February flowering, snapdragons for November and December; and, in late July, sweet peas for December and January flowering.

The North. Late-flowering annuals and perennials that are tall-growing should be staked so the stems will be straight when they flower.

Disbudding is necessary on chrysanthemum and dahlia for large flowers.

Perennials that have finished bloom are now cut back, but allow some foliage to remain. Others, like the bearded iris, are transplanted.

Lilies, such as the Madonna lily, that are dormant may be planted.

Flowers and grasses that are suitable for drying are cut at their prime and hung in small bunches upside down in a dark place. When dry, they are ready for use in arrangements. Such kinds include celosia, strawflower, and the quaking grass (*see* Briza).

Lawns may need watering to keep them growing. Use herbicides, if necessary, to control lawn weeds. New lawns are prepared, ready for seeding later.

This is the last month in which to sow seed of bean, endive, lettuce, and rutabaga.

The South. Rapidly growing annuals such as ageratum, alyssum, marigolds, and zinnias may be seeded for bloom before frosts.

Pansy seed is sown for winter bloom as

---

* Special articles on the subjects indicated by an asterisk (*) will be found at the words so marked.

well as such perennials as campanula, dianthus, hollyhock, foxglove, poppy, pyrethrum, and Sweet William for next year's flowering.

Fall-blooming plants such as the dahlia and chrysanthemum should be watered regularly and fertilized. Early August is the time for the last topping of chrysanthemums.

Many perennials are divided and transplanted after they have finished flowering. These include daylilies, iris, and Shasta daisy.

Early-flowering bulbs, such as colchicum, the Madonna lily, lycoris, oxalis, and, in mild areas of the South, callas, are available for planting this month.

Continue to mow the lawn high until rains come, or irrigate it regularly.

New plantings of strawberries are made in August. Spade the soil thoroughly and turn under organic matter.

Vegetables such as beets, broccoli, carrots, lettuce, spinach, turnip, and the wax bean may still be sown in the more northern areas of this section, and in the more southern areas, these plus lima beans, okra, peppers, and sweet corn.

The Southwest. Continue to fertilize annuals, begonias, geraniums, fuchsia, and other plants to keep them growing.

Sub-tropical species transplant readily if they are dug with a good ball of soil. Pruning of the top is necessary to compensate for the loss of roots.

Seed of calendula, forget-me-not, snapdragon, stock, and sweet pea is sown now for winter bloom. Perennial and biennial seed may also be sown for next year's flowering. Delphinium and pansy seed will germinate more readily if stored in the refrigerator a month before planting.

Cut back lightly, straggly plants of lantana, pelargonium, petunia, and verbena to encourage a more compact growth.

Plant bulbs such as the Dutch iris, freesia, lycoris, Madonna lily, tritonia and watsonia.

Wisteria will bloom more freely if vigorous growth is checked by shortening the branches. Root-pruning of a non-flowering plant also will check the growth of the plant.

Trees and shrubs that were newly planted in the spring should be kept well watered until thoroughly established.

The Northwest. Sow seed of forget-me-not, pansy, and viola in the garden for later transplanting.

Perennials such as iris, poppy, primula, Shasta daisy, and some of the spring-flowering kinds may be dug and replanted.

Remove the old flowers from perennials to keep the plants and the garden more attractive. It will prevent them from going to seed. Annuals will benefit from the same treatment.

Bulbs of colchicum and fall crocus are planted this month for bloom in September or October.

August is a time for taking cuttings of azaleas, camellia, daphne, pieris, rhododend-ron, and many of the deciduous shrubs.

Canes of the bramble fruits, such as blackberry, loganberry, and raspberry, that have fruited this year are pruned out as they are finished with a crop.

Strawberry plants are planted out this month in a well-drained, well-prepared soil.

Sow head lettuce, spinach, turnip, carrots, and set out plants of cabbage.

Indoors and Greenhouse. This is a time in which to get many plants ready for winter. Carnations are topped for the last time this month. Chrysanthemums may be topped until about August 10 for normal fall-flowering.

August is the time to finish any painting or repairs for the greenhouse. A clean-up fumigation may be desirable before bringing in plants for the winter. Repairs to the heating system should be made.

Propagation, by cuttings, of many plants is done this month. Greenhouse plants include geranium, poinsettia, lantana, philodendron, and other foliage types. Woody plants propagated now include azaleas and rhododendron, daphne, boxwood and holly.

Pinch any house plants that are outdoors so they will be well branched when brought in later.

Perennial seed, such as delphinium and primula, may be started in a greenhouse and later planted outdoors.

Seed to be sown this month for growing in a cool greenhouse (45° to 50° F.) includes calendula for early winter; calceolaria for April flowering; forget-me-not, snapdragon, baby primrose, cineraria, stock, and sweet peas for February and March; and for late-winter and early-spring flowering, annual lupine, annual chrysanthemum, and winter-flowering marigold.

The North. Planting and transplanting season for deciduous and evergreen shrubs and trees begins this month and continues into November, depending on the local area.

Prepare areas for fall planting of roses, perennials, or bulbs.

Sow seed of winter-hardy annuals such as cornflower and larkspur.

Perennial and biennial seedlings should be transplanted when large enough, from the seed bed to areas for growing on, or into the border. Pansies are good to plant in areas when annuals are gone.

Early-blooming perennials, such as the bleeding-heart, lily-of-the-valley, peony, and phlox, are divided and transplanted.

Order spring-flowering bulbs for October

* Special articles on the subjects indicated by an asterisk (*) will be found at the words so marked.

planting. In addition to the large-flowering kinds, include some of the crocus, grape hyacinths, snowdrops, species tulips, and squills. The smaller kinds are most effective when used in masses.

Lilies may be planted this month in a loose, well-drained soil.

Dahlias and gladioli are dug after a frost. They are put in shallow boxes to dry or cure for several days before storing.

Hedges are pruned or sheared for the last time this season.

Fertilize the lawn early this month. Areas that need reseeding should be moistened if dry, raked or spaded, then seeded.

The South. Fall planting of shrubs and trees begins this month. If the deciduous types are still in leaf, either wait until the leaves dry or dig with a ball of soil.

Prepare areas for fall planting. Add organic matter to the soil as well as fertilizer. These areas will then be ready for later planting of bulbs, perennials, and roses.

Perennials may be divided and transplanted, especially the spring- and early-summer-flowering kinds. Early transplanting gives them a chance to become well established by spring.

Chrysanthemums are fertilized for the last time after the flower buds show.

In the more southern parts of this area, many half-hardy bulbs are planted, such as the paper-white narcissus. In other areas, plant anemone, bulbous iris, lycoris, ranunculus, and spring-flowering bulbs.

Roses should be fertilized again this month as they begin growth again following the heat of summer.

Lawns should be fertilized and areas reseeded as necessary. Use a complete fertilizer or, on well-established lawns, a nitrogen fertilizer alone may be sufficient. Annual grass may be overplanted on centipede, Bermuda, and St. Augustine lawns.

Fall and winter crops of vegetables may be sown in the mild areas. These include sowings of beets, carrots, collards, kale, lettuce, spinach, and turnip.

The Southwest. This is a good month in which to transplant trees and shrubs. Prepare the soil thoroughly and keep well watered. Areas for roses and other fall planting should be fertilized and organic matter added.

Sow seed of sweet peas for winter bloom, using the multiflora or winter-flowering varieties.

Dig dahlias when their bloom is past their prime. Dry these tubers and then store.

Disbud camellias when the flower buds are large enough to distinguish from the leaf buds. Flower buds in clusters are thinned to one bud, or at least so that buds do not touch. Water the plants if the soil is dry.

Order spring-flowering bulbs for October planting.

Lawns will need to be watered and fertilized regularly in order to maintain good green color.

Cool-season vegetables, such as cabbage, carrots, swiss chard, lettuce, onions, peas, and spinach, can be seeded now.

The Northwest. Fall cleanup should start. Destroy rubbish and disease- or pest-infected plants. Leaves and other plant refuse can be added to the compost heap.

Peonies and other perennials are dug and replanted. Seedlings of those kinds started earlier, such as the Canterbury bell, English daisy, foxglove, pansy, primrose, and others, are planted in the flower border.

Fall-blooming bulbs are planted as soon as they are received. Lilies are ready for planting. Most of the spring-flowering bulbs are planted next month.

Dig and prepare for storing dahlias, gladioli, and other non-hardy bulbs and tubers.

Roses should be fall-fertilized with a complete fertilizer by the middle of the month.

Lawns that are newly made or that are reseeded will need to be kept watered. Such planting should be done by the end of September.

Late vegetables such as the turnip may be sown if there are still at least 6 weeks for maturity.

Indoors and Greenhouse. Lift and pot those plants that have been growing outdoors and that are to be used indoors during the winter. Be prepared to bring them in as the temperatures become cool.

Propagate by cuttings coleus, begonia, *Iresine*, lantana, and other tender plants.

Soil should be prepared for use in the winter. Make up the potting mixtures that are to be used. *See* POTTING MIXTURES. Sterilize before storing for winter use.

Freesias are either potted or planted in a bench from now until November. Callas are potted from now until November in large pots, in a soil mixture well supplied with organic matter.

Poinsettia cuttings are taken by the middle of the month. Small plants from earlier propagations are potted, several to a larger pot.

Bulbs should be ordered for winter forcing — tulips, hyacinths, and narcissi as well as tender kinds like amaryllis, brodiaea, veltheimia, anemone, lachenalia, and ranunculus.

As outdoor temperatures become cooler during the day, stop overhead sprinkling on foliage plants.

Seed to be sown in September includes everblooming begonias to flower in February; calceolaria and cineraria for March and April; calendula for January and February; larkspur and lupine for April; snapdragon and stock for March, at a 50° temperature; sweet pea from Christmas to March and blue lace-flower for February and March.

---

* Special articles on the subjects indicated by an asterisk (*) will be found at the words so marked.

The North. Save leaves, old plants and other garden litter and use it to make a compost pile. This composted material is valuable to add to the soil, to use as summer mulch, and for other garden purposes. To hasten decomposition sprinkle some complete fertilizer over the materials as they are being stacked. A few shovelfuls of topsoil will also be beneficial.

Dig and cultivate all beds so there will be no carryover of perennial weeds.

After frost, spade the garden, add organic matter and superphosphate.

Dig caladium, canna, dahlia, gladiolus, tuberous begonias and other plants that are not winter-hardy. Dry off for several days and then put into their winter storage. Tuberous begonias are stored in dry peat or dry sand.

This is the time to plant spring-flowering bulbs. Select a well-drained area. Smaller-growing bulbs, such as crocus, snowdrops and squills, do well under trees. They grow and flower before the shade of the tree would interfere with their growth. The depth of planting depends on the kind of bulb. *See* BULBS.

Transplanting of trees and shrubs may be done this month and on into early December if weather permits.

Mow lawns late in the season and rake up any leaves. Edge the beds to give the lawn a finished appearance all winter.

The South. Seed of hardy annuals, as cornflower, California poppy, larkspur, and sweet pea, may be sown.

Perennials, especially the early-flowering kinds, are divided at this season of the year. Pansy plants are transplanted to their place of flowering.

It is time for planting of the spring-flowering bulbs, especially in the more northern sections of this area.

Camellia Sasanqua and the earliest varieties of *C. japonica* begin to flower this month. Make sure they are well watered, and mulch them if possible.

Shrubs and trees may be given an application of a complete fertilizer.

Dig and store dahlias and gladiolus as well as other non-hardy bulbs.

Annual ryegrass may be sown in Bermuda-grass lawns or on hot-weather lawns.

Vegetables planted this month include beets, carrots, kale, turnips, and spinach.

The Southwest. Now is the time to plant seeds of pansy, viola, and other annuals to flower in the winter months, such as the calendula, snapdragon, stock, and sweet pea.

Roses should be fertilized to encourage new growth and flowering. When cutting flowers, always leave 2 to 3 nodes on the plant from which new shoots will develop.

Dahlias, gladioli, and other fleshy roots or bulbs should be dug and stored.

In the warmer sections of this area late-flowering kinds of tulips and narcissi are generally the best kinds to select.

Deciduous shrubs and trees should be watered regularly until the foliage naturally drops.

Camellias may now begin to flower. Make sure they are well watered and mulched.

Lawns are reseeded or new ones made at this season. Select grasses that are known to do well in your area. *See* LAWN.

The Northwest. Annuals for early spring flowering are sown this month, directly where they are to flower, among them alyssum, cornflower, larkspur, and Shirley poppies. Kinds such as calendula, dianthus, and snapdragon may be sown in beds and transplanted in the spring.

Perennials may still be transplanted providing you are in an area with mild winter temperatures, where they have a chance to get established. Fall-blooming kinds are transplanted in the spring. Mulch fall-planted perennials.

Bulb planting continues this month. Plant only in a well-drained area.

This is the month to dig many of the plants such as canna, dahlia, gladiolus, and tuberous begonias and store them for the winter. Gladioli and dahlias may be left outdoors until the tops are killed by frost.

Rose planting is an October job. Planting now gives the plant an opportunity of becoming established before the push of the spring growth.

Fuchsias used outdoors in the mildest sections of this area should be mulched and protected in exposed sites.

Indoors and Greenhouse. As chrysanthemums come into flower, do not wet the blooms, especially in the late afternoon as moisture on them is favorable for the development of disease.

Bulbs for winter forcing are potted this month and stored under cool conditions to encourage root growth. Plunge pots in a well-drained area outdoors. Cover with an inch or two of sand and then several inches of soil and later with straw or other covering in the coldest areas. Such outdoor storage is practical only for winter-hardy kinds. Tender kinds as the amaryllis, freesia, and veltheimia are stored in places not subject to cold.

Store hortensia hydrangea in a 38° to 45° storage until about the first of the year, for spring forcing.

The Glory lily, *Gloriosa rothschildiana*, is potted now for spring bloom, 2 to 3 tubers to an 8-inch pot. Grow at a 60° temperature.

Seed to be sown this month includes: aster for April flowering with additional lights to provide a long day; calceolaria and cineraria for May; cyclamen for one year later; feverfew for early May or, if given long days, then April; stock for April; schizanthus

* Special articles on the subjects indicated by an asterisk (*) will be found at the words so marked.

for spring flowering; and sweet pea for February through May.

The North. This is cleanup month. Collect and pile leaves, tops of annuals, perennials, and other garden refuse into a compost pile or use for winter mulching and protection on late-planted bulbs or woody plants. Burn disease- or insect-infested plants.

Areas where only annuals or vegetables have been growing should be spaded or plowed. Add lime or organic matter if possible. Leave soil in rough condition.

A late sowing of larkspur may be made in a well-drained soil to germinate early in the spring.

Do not cut off the tops of perennials that are green and alive. Dead leaves may be taken off. Wait until late in the month or early December to mulch perennials and roses.

Loose canes of vines should be tied to their trellis or supports so they are not injured by wind during the winter.

This is the last chance to plant spring-flowering bulbs. Mulch the soil to delay freezing and to enable the bulbs to produce roots before cold weather. Label or mark areas of planting.

Deciduous plants may still be transplanted. Large sizes should be moved with a ball of soil.

The South. In the upper South sow seed of larkspur, cornflower, sweet pea, phlox, and poppies for early bloom.

Perennials may still be divided and transplanted. Pansy plants are planted out where they are to flower.

Dig and store tender bulbs and tubers for the winter period. These include dahlias, fancy-leaf caladium, gladiolus, hymenocallis and tuberose.

In the lower South plant refrigerated tulip bulbs in late November or early December. Also sow seed of alyssum, annual gaillardia, calendula, California poppy, snapdragon, and stock.

Rose planting is best done now and into December. Trees and shrubs of all kinds may be transplanted.

Mulch plants such as the azalea, camellia, and rhododendron with leaves, pine needles, peat, or partially rotted sawdust.

The Southwest. Old plants, leaves, grass clippings are all useful for the compost pile to build up a supply of organic matter to incorporate into the soil.

Sweet peas sown in November should now have a trellis provided and be fertilized.

Perennials are transplanted. Cut back the old tops. Plant annuals in among perennials to add color. Such kinds as calendula, pansy, primula, and stock are all satisfactory.

Bulb planting is in progress. Plant tulips, amaryllis, montbretia, tigridia, and callas. Gladiolus may be planted at intervals beginning now for a succession of bloom. Lilies are planted as soon as received so as not to dry out.

Add mulch to azaleas and camellias. Keep the soil moist.

Fertilize lawns with a high nitrogen fertilizer to help keep a good green color and encourage growth.

Crab grass controls are effective if used now. Select kinds that prevent seed from starting next spring. *See* Crab Grass.

The Northwest. Clean up the garden and put old plants, leaves, and other garden refuse on the compost pile.

Protect plants that are transplanted late or as the temperature gets colder this month or next.

Seed of sweet peas, cornflower, larkspur and other annuals is sown now for early spring flowering.

Cut back the tops of chrysanthemums and other perennials that have become dormant. In milder areas they may still be transplanted.

Bulbs and tubers that are not winter-hardy are dug and stored. These include caladium, canna, dahlia, gladiolus, and tuberous begonias. Store in dry peat or vermiculite.

Winter-hardy bulbs are planted in November and into December.

Planting of trees and shrubs continues. Larger deciduous plants may be handled with ball of soil.

Use herbicides on lawns to kill broad-leaved weeds. The response is slow in cool weather but still effective.

Indoors and Greenhouse. Most greenhouse plants will need all or most of the shade removed from the glass. On orchids or many foliage plants a little may be left to break the intensity of the sun.

Poinsettias should be kept at 60° to 62° at night in order to have them in flower for Christmas.

Begonias are propagated by leaf or tip cuttings for next spring.

Chrysanthemums that have flowered are cut back and put in a cool place over winter.

Maintain temperatures in the greenhouse at night. Cool temperatures may check the growth of the plants.

Plant tender bulbs of amaryllis, veltheimia and others when they are received. Plant in pots only an inch or so larger in diameter than the bulb. Water sparingly until growth starts. Begin fertilization after flowering.

Bring in soil, sand, organic matter and other materials so it will be available for winter use.

Water house plants carefully. Overwatering is prevented by placing gravel or other material under the pot to provide a place to which the excess water may drain

---

* Special articles on the subjects indicated by an asterisk (*) will be found at the words so marked.

without being in direct contact with the pot.

November is the time of potting paper-white narcissus. They will flower in about 6 weeks. Keep dormant bulbs in a cool place and make several plantings for continued bloom.

Azaleas to be forced are put in a cold frame to hold for winter forcing.

Sow seed of calendula for April flowering; clarkia and stock for March bloom; calceolaria for May; pansy for spring bloom in the greenhouse; snapdragon for mid-April flowering and winter flowering; sweet peas to flower from April to hot weather. Seed of achimenes, gloxinia, and tuberous begonias sown now will produce plants to flower next spring and summer. Sow seed thinly on a loose, well-prepared soil mixture.

The North. Garden work for the year is about done. One more final cleanup of the leaves and trash will keep it for a while. Lawn edges will give a finished appearance for months.

Finish mulching perennials and late-planted roses or other shrubs. Apply after the soil has become frozen.

Clean up the garden tools, sharpen (or have it done) shears, mowers, and hoes. The mower should be cleaned, sharpened, and oiled, ready to use.

Pansy plants are given a loose mulch of straw or cut evergreen branches for protection.

Cut back tall canes of roses so they do not whip around in the winter wind and loosen the plant.

Newly planted broad-leaved evergreens should be given some winter protection the first winter. A burlap or lath screen is satisfactory.

Evergreen plants can be carefully pruned in order to obtain cut branches or twigs for Christmas decorations. Tie together or support the branches on any of the evergreens that would be bent over or spread apart by snow.

The South. The last garden cleanup for the year. Check plants and remove dead foliage. Clean up perennials that have completed growth.

Planting of trees and shrubs, including roses, may be done this month. Now is a satisfactory time.

Bulbs to plant include amaryllis, calla, gloxinia, and tuberous begonias.

Hardwood cuttings may be made of many deciduous shrubs such as crape myrtle, deutzia, forsythia, philadelphus, and weigela.

Fertilize camellias, if it was not done last month. Plants will absorb the fertilizer and be ready to grow later with much vigor.

Prune deciduous fruit trees and grapes in December or early next month. Strawberry and the bramble fruits are planted now.

Christmas decorations from the garden are varied. Careful pruning will provide much material for such purposes. Many broad-leaved evergreens or red-berried plants may be cut. Holly, magnolia, evergreen privet, and nandina all furnish attractive decorations.

In the lower South, plant broccoli, carrots, cabbage, kale, mustard, lettuce, parsley, and turnips. Annual flowers for planting in this area include alyssum, candytuft, calendula, cornflower, larkspur, pansy, petunia, snapdragon, stock, and verbena.

The Southwest. Be prepared for frost protection as may be needed for semitropical or tropical kinds of plants. Burlap, muslin, or heavy paper coverings may be effective for short periods.

Sow sweet peas (the multiflora or Spencer types), California poppies and baby-blue-eyes now for spring flowering.

Plant young plants of annuals in order to provide color. Alyssum, forget-me-not, and pansy are all useful to fill in empty spots in the garden.

Early-dug gladiolus may be replanted now and at intervals in order to continue a supply of bloom.

Prepare for planting of trees, shrubs, and roses as they become available later in this month or next.

Camellia japonica may be transplanted before it comes into flower.

Cut carefully selected branches from evergreen plants to provide Christmas decorations. Holly, especially the Chinese and English kinds, is useful. These may be used as decoration as small plants and then planted out. Berried plants or branches of pyracantha are useful in decorations.

The Northwest. General garden cleanup should be completed for the year. Tools need to be cleaned and oiled, lawn mowers sharpened, and repaired. Stakes and other garden equipment need to be cleaned, painted, and stored.

Complete digging of dahlias, clean the roots and store in a cool, dry place in peat, sand, or vermiculite. Dust with sulphur before storing.

In mild areas, transplanting of deciduous shrubs and trees is still possible. Stake tall plants. In the colder sections, late-planted material should be protected with a mulch and supported to prevent wind whipping.

Hardwood cuttings of deciduous shrubs are made now, stored in bundles, at 40° to 50° in moist sand, or sand and peat, until ready to set out in the spring. Plants include crape myrtle, forsythia, deutzia, philadelphus, privet, spirea, and willow.

Pruning of trees and shrubs is done, especially to remove long shoots that are not wanted and in order to shape the plant. More severe pruning is delayed until spring.

Indoors and Greenhouse. House plants should be kept in a warm window with as much light as practical. Plants used within a room away from light should be rotated occasionally with plants at a window.

Fertilize house plants early in the month. This should be sufficient to last until late January.

For a cool greenhouse, take cuttings of evergreens and broad-leaved evergreens for young plants in the spring.

Avoid excess watering of poinsettia. Keep at a night temperature of 60° to 62°.

After Christmas bring in hortensia hydrangeas from storage, also the first of the azaleas for forcing.

Pot Easter lilies late in the month for April flowering.

Cacti and succulents and others that are less active in growth should be watered infrequently during the winter months.

Sow seed of larkspur, stock, and sweet peas for April bloom; trachymene for May; tuberous begonias and gloxinia for May flowering: pansy for April, and annual gypsophila for April.

NOTE: All the plants mentioned in this calendar will be found in the body of the book, where culture and hardiness should be sought. — C. B. L.

GARDEN CHEMICALS. Many chemical substances enter into modern garden practice or into the life history of the plant itself. There is no need to list them here for all are noted where they belong. *See* FERTILIZERS, INSECTICIDES, FUNGICIDES, Weed Killers (at WEEDS AND WEEDING), PLANT FOODS, HORMONES and GIBBERELLIC ACID.

GARDEN CLUB OF AMERICA. *See* GARDEN CLUBS.

GARDEN CLUBS. Second only to the experiment stations, the garden clubs are the greatest single agency for the advancement of gardening in America. Their lectures, test gardens, and influence for better standards of the art of horticulture are of incalculable value. Some of their lecture courses are as complete as a first-class school of horticulture. Overwhelmingly they are managed by women who thus exert an immense influence for civic betterment, school gardens, flower shows, conservation, and for the general raising of the standards of garden art.

Unfortunately, there is no one national organization or amalgamation of the garden clubs of the country. United they could do more, especially with legislation, than is possible under present conditions.

All the clubs mentioned below are women's activities, but there are a few clubs for men only. The leading women's garden club amalgamations, in the order of their establishment, are:

GARDEN CLUB OF AMERICA. A national association of garden clubs, formed in 1913 and scattered over most of the country. It wields potent influence for good, issues a journal devoted to gardening, and has affiliated clubs in most of the states of the Union. Its national headquarters and permanent office are at 598 Madison Avenue, New York 22, N. Y.

FEDERATED GARDEN CLUBS. A national association or amalgamation which includes nearly all the local garden clubs not affiliated with the Garden Club of America. There are over 10,000 clubs scattered practically throughout the country, and the total membership is well over 360,000. Some, but not all, of these clubs are affiliated with The National Council. It is obviously impossible to list here all the clubs in this large federation of widely scattered clubs. *See* the name of your state for the garden club possibilities in your region. The address of the National Council of State Garden Clubs is 160 Central Park South, New York 19, N. Y.

MEN'S GARDEN CLUBS. While all of the organizations mentioned above are primarily feminine, there are scores of men's garden clubs. Starting in New York, about 1936, the movement has spread to nearly all large cities and many smaller ones. Their annual conventions are attended by hundreds and not the least admirable of their activities is to stage informative exhibits at some of the larger spring flower shows.

GARDEN CRESS = *Lepidium sativum.* *See also* WATERCRESS.

GARDEN CURRANT = *Ribes sativum.*

GARDEN ENEMIES. The only serious ones are all the subjects of special articles. *See* INSECT PESTS, PLANT DISEASES, ANIMAL INJURY, and Bird Nuisances at BIRDS.

GARDENER'S-GARTERS = *Phalaris arundinacea picta.*

GARDEN EXPERIMENTS. No inquisitive gardener can help making some yearly experiments, for knowledge of the art of gardening has come chiefly by this route. Depending upon your bent, they may take various forms.

If they have to do with the suitability of plants for certain soils, it will help to read the general article on soils and all the cross-references there suggested.

If, however, it is climate and hardiness which chiefly interest you, *see* the articles under HARDINESS, ZONE, and the cross-references there suggested. *See also* PROTECTING PLANTS.

GARDEN FLY-HONEYSUCKLE = *Lonicera tatarica.*

GARDEN GERANIUM. *See* PELARGONIUM.

GARDEN GOOSEBERRY = *Ribes Grossularia.* For culture *see* GOOSEBERRY.

GARDEN HELIOTROPE = *Valeriana officinalis.*

GARDEN HISTORY. Gardens first appeared when primitive man, no longer depending on the chase of migratory stock-raising for his sustenance, settled down in one chosen spot. Here, alongside his hut, his womenfolk scarred the ground with a crotched stick or a hoe made by lashing a shell or animal shoulder-blade to a length of branch. To this patch they brought wild edible grains and roots collected from the meadows, and soon found that better crops resulted from intensive cultivation. A fence of woven branches or thorns or a cactus hedge kept out straying cattle. As water was necessary, the garden was usually located either by a brook or around a water hole. From this source, runnels carried water to the plants.

In these primitive attempts we see the beginnings of the fenced or hedged garden, irrigation, and horticulture. These first gardens were made for no aesthetic reasons, however. They were gardens of necessity. Not until man "built finely," as Bacon put it, did he begin to garden for the delight of his eye. His crops were food crops and such herbs as were necessary for family doctoring.

Climate, the nature of the soil, and religious beliefs were further factors in the evolution of the garden from those primitive conditions to the various garden forms we know today. Thus in Persia and India, where intense heat required much water to cool the air and fill bathing tanks, water was much in evidence. This style, carried to Spain, was developed in Saracenic gardens, which were the progenitors of Spanish gardens as we know them today in Florida and California.

Religious taboos and predilections also gave rise to garden forms and garden adjuncts. From the totem and Tree of Life set up in gardens by primitive man for purposes of worship, we can trace the lineage of garden statuary and fountains. The effect of Buddhism, as it spread over through the East by way of the Straits Settlements and China to Japan, brought about a taste for gardens that copied the features of Nature, and from these, in turn, we have inherited the informal style of garden design.

The nature of the soil, together with climate, decided what plants grew in gardens. For a long time the plants used in decorative gardens were such as grew naturally in the locality, together with some few brought in by conquests or commerce. Commerce was responsible for the distribution of plants almost up to the threshold of our own times, when plant explorers and traveling botanists made a special business of plant importation.

EGYPTIAN GARDENS were produced by a peculiar local condition. The Nile, the main source of water, was dammed, and the flood gates opened at certain required seasons. Consequently, Egyptians made their gardens for ease of irrigation, i.e., formal in patterns and divided by irrigation ditches. The grapevine was an early favorite plant of Egyptians, and its proper cultivation required the vines being raised on wooden supports. From these supports grew the pergola that the Romans later developed into a decorative

feature and which is a commonplace adjunct of gardens today.

Both Egyptian and Sumerian temples were situated on either natural or artificial hills called *ziggurats*, and the surrounding area given over to the cultivation of trees and herbs especially adapted. As most of these early temples were also the meeting place of the priest-physicians, they served as the ancestors of those later monastic enclosures in which the herb garden, for the cure of the ailing, was a necessary feature. From the ziggurats can be traced the garden mount which appeared in Roman gardens and many centuries later was made a feature in gardens of mediaeval Europe and Tudor England. Used first as a lookout or a spot from which to enjoy a panorama of the garden and the surrounding country, it was later topped by a pavilion for entertainment.

Throughout the Near East the plane and the palm were the trees most grown. The latter was especially valued since so many necessary products were derived from it. Though the Persians allowed their trees to grow naturally, the Egyptians clipped them into columnar forms, thus affording the first instance of topiary work.

GREEK GARDENS, in the beginning, were not extensive, nor can the early Greeks be said to have advanced garden practices. The usual home garden was in the rear of the house, enclosed by two projecting wings. On these three sides was built a covered terrace or peristyle. Sometimes the peristyle ran around all four sides. When it was not built on the fourth, the ground was banked up and lined with trees. In this enclosure was laid out a formal garden. In the center was a water basin, into which roof water drained and which served as a source for watering the garden. Around it were beds of fragrant flowers, since it was believed that fragrant plants had prophylactic properties, keeping the air pure and warding off disease. Between the columns of the peristyle were set deep flower boxes and on the walls behind were trained vines. However, if vines would not grow in this shade the walls were painted with garden scenes. This use of garden perspectives cropped up again in seventeenth-century France.

Two other garden features, of which gardens of subsequent civilizations were the heirs, first appeared in Greece — grottoes and the Adonis garden. Originally believed to be the abode of nymphs, grottoes were made to serve as cool retreats in hot weather. Built of rock and decorated with shells and often watered by a spring, they were comfortable adjuncts to the garden. As they copied nature, they also were almost the only naturalistic effects in these classical Greek gardens.

The Adonis garden consisted of small pots of quickly growing seeds set around a statue of Adonis either in the garden or on the housetop. Adonis was the god of the growing world; in autumn when winter brought death

---

* Special articles on the subjects indicated by an asterisk (*) will be found at the words so marked.

to plants, he was believed to disappear into the bowels of the earth; in spring he reappeared again. To celebrate his reappearance these gardens were made. From them can be traced the Mediterranean custom of clustering potted plants around the foot of a statue or the basin of a fountain. Roof gardens may also find some semblance of a heritage in this custom, since the Adonis garden, made for a short display at a particular season, gave rise to rooftop gardens, made for all the seasons. However, the crowding of cities and the restricted areas of cultivatable space also were factors in the evolution of the roof garden.

After the conquests of Alexander, the Greeks began to enjoy some of the luxuries of Persian living; they began developing country villas, and when they planted their colonies in Sicily and along the Mediterranean, these settlements soon became famous for the luxury of their gardens.

ROMAN GARDENS carried on the heritage of Greece and developed it further. Whereas the Greeks preferred city life, country living came naturally to the Romans, and the art of horticulture was part of their national tradition. The early writers on land improvement — Cato and Varro and Columella — were among the farm heroes. Rome was early a garden city. Nobles developed much of the lands within the city limits into elaborate estates. These were laid out formally. Two features appeared in them — the *gestatio* or area for taking a "constitutional," and the *hippodromo* or horse-pacing ring. Even the poor citizen had his window-box garden — which can still be seen in the poor quarters of Italian cities. Where tillable space was scarce, Romans planted their housetops into roof gardens or *sylvae in tectus*.

The crowded condition of Rome caused the city to spill over into the Campagna and the nearby hills. This countryward movement was quickened by the publication of Virgil's Georgics. A man of ordinary means had a *suburban inn* or little country place where he kept a *villicus* or farm manager and his wife. Those with more means might possess either a *villa rustica*, a farm on which special crops were grown and where the owner went at harvest times; or he might have a *villa urbana*. The latter was an elaborate country place with building designed in the manner of city dwellings, and where little or no farming was pursued. Such pleasure gardens the Younger Pliny maintained on the seashore at Laurentium and on his larger place in the Tuscan Hills. His letters describing them afford us the most authentic records of country living and garden design of the times.

In these Roman country gardens were found two features that handed on their lineage — water-tricks and topiary work. Neatly calculated garden benches, when one sat on them, sprayed water on the sitter or caused it to flow in a fantastic design. Even more popular was shrub-sculpture or topiary clipping of trees and shrubs into amusing and decorative effects. A large estate would keep a special gardener or *topiarius* to care for these; at the same time actual statuary was not neglected, and indeed the Roman garden was well populated with figures of the gods and national heroes.

Eventually both in Rome itself and in the surrounding countryside garden luxury grew to such proportions that agriculture was neglected. When Alaric descended on Rome he found some 1700 villas with gardens. At the arrival of invaders owners of these estates fled to the cities and their country places fell into ruin. Southern Europe entered on the Dark Ages, during which the only garden light that burned was found in monastic gardens.

MONASTERY GARDENS in Europe first followed the form of Roman gardens, since many of them were located in *villae urbanae* and *villae rusticae*. Before this, the cenobites of Egypt had their vegetable patches. When the monastic ideal was adapted for western Europe by St. Benedict, gardening was made one of the required labors. Benedict's rule set the pattern for subsequent regulations of both monasteries and convents.

The convent gardens, tended by women, could scarcely be expected to grow field crops that entailed heavy manual labor; consequently, within these enclosures the monks grew flowers and herbs with which to deck their chapels and from which they decocted specifics and cosmetics. These arts they taught to women.

The garden of a well-equipped monastery, such as St. Gall on Lake Constance, of which we have plans, contained four parts — a physic garden, a cloister garth, a vegetable garden and a combined orchard-vineyard and burial ground. Altar flowers were grown in the cloister garden or else the sacristan had his own patch devoted to this purpose. Many of the flowers which we grow for decorative purposes today, in those times were used for making medicine. Among the many services the monastery rendered gardens in the Dark Ages was the preservation of strains of fruit and vegetables that, without their care, would have disappeared. In later times the monastery also afforded new varieties of fruit, some of which are still grown today.

CASTLE GARDENS. In this same era the domestic garden of the castle and the burgher home alike was restricted in size, being laid out in the narrow limits between castle and town walls. Returning Crusaders and other travelers from the East brought home new concepts of gardens and new plants to grow in them. As safety in country living became more assured, gardens crept beyond the walls, increased in size, and were equipped with structures and amenities that both gave them a marked architectural pattern and suited them for outdoor living. This medieval pattern was formal — a series of geometric beds around a central fountain, and the

---

* Special articles on the subjects indicated by an asterisk (*) will be found at the words so marked.

garden was square, oblong or circular, a wall or fence marking its limits.

RENAISSANCE GARDENS were produced by two main influences — humanistic thought, which aroused interest in old Roman traditions, and an awakening appreciation of the beauties of nature. These, together with the increasing safety of the countryside, revived country living and brought the country villa into prominence once more. By gradual steps the garden passed from the old house terrace of the Romans to those elaborate patterned gardens dominated by architectural effects that well-nigh submerged horticultural effort. At the same time the revived interest in tradition brought into the garden old Roman statues or copies of them and all manner of classical embellishments and water effects.

Though architecture was its main feature, nevertheless an interest in new plants began to appear in Renaissance gardens. This was the dawn of the age of exploration, and from distant corners of the world came roots, seeds, and plants that the botanically minded tried to grow in their gardens. This age also saw the rise of the botanical garden, a service to science and the public which continues down to our own day.

From Italy the Renaissance garden spread to France, Germany, Spain, Holland, and England, each country making its own interpretations and adaptations of the style, according to its environment. Thus the grand proportions of Renaissance gardens could not be copied in Holland, nor did the public interest tend in that direction. Holland early became the nursery of Europe and produced many new plants. The French clung to their medieval moated castle gardens for a long time, then eventually, with the assistance of Italian garden designers and water engineers, began to evolve an elaborate Renaissance style, the parterre being an especial subject for development into complicated designs. England, on the other hand, was evolving its own style of garden.

THE ENGLISH MEDIEVAL contained the same features found in medieval French gardens — the pleached bower, the turf seats, the flower-spangled lawns, the sanded walks, the herbary and the orchard — but not until the late Renaissance did the pleasance appear as a separate entity. Up to that time it had been combined with the orchard or the physic garden. The gardens described by Chaucer are medieval and early Renaissance; those found in Shakespeare show later influence. One of the most pronounced influences was the diversity of flowers that were planted in gardens. England began to awaken to the natural beauties of her own countryside and at the same time to those foreign plants that were trickling in. Not for several centuries, however, did new plants affect the form of gardens.

LE NÔTRE, with the gardens in the grand manner he created at Vaux de Vicomte and Versailles and other magnificent places, dis-played the ultimate flowering of the Renaissance. His style was formal and required extensive space.

The main features of his style were the planting of bosquets or groups of trees to make decorative arbors in which were placed architectural or water effects; the goose-foot styles of allées, i.e., several allées radiating from a central point; the elongated water canal; the complicated and decorative use of water in cascades and fountains; the abundance of statuary to which the greatest artists of the time contributed; the development of treillage or architectural latticework for backgrounds and garden structures; and the relegation of flowers to especial spots for immediate effect. At the same time he did not neglect the more utilitarian parts of the garden, for the vegetables and fruits at Versailles, entrusted to the care of Jean de la Quintinie, set the style for an interest in these matters that was reflected not alone in other French estates but in other countries as well. Both as a horticulturist and as a garden author, de la Quintinie was one of the greatest figures of all time, as LeNôtre was in the world of garden designing.

This influence of Le Nôtre soon spread over the continent, although in England it did not appear to have been generally accepted. There the taste ran more to the small formal garden or the garden in the Dutch manner, in which the living plant was the object of more solicitude than the setting given it. Moreover, since England was reaching out to empire limits by its explorations and colonizations, it became the home of plants found in those far-flung countries, as countless books on the subject attest. From the multitude of authors and gardeners who contributed to the advancement and appreciation of gardening and plants in this era, three stand out supreme — John Gerard, John Parkinson, and the Tradescants.

ORIENTAL GARDENS of China and Japan began to make their influence felt at this stage and acted as a counter-influence to the formality of Le Nôtre. Returning missionaries and travelers brought news of the naturalistic gardens found in the East. As we saw previously, the followers of Buddha were worshipers in natural groves and their temples were set in naturalistic gardens. This lost its influence to the types of domestic and palace gardens that were made for many centuries in China and Japan. A favorite glimpse of a mountain or a stream was scaled down to the limited proportions of a home garden. Soon each of its elements was given a name and a symbolic significance, a custom developed into a highly complicated ritual of garden design by the Zen Buddhist priests in Japan. Meantime a deep love for the beauty of particular flowers was growing. The peony, the peach blossoms, the chrysanthemum were all subject to hybridization, tender care, and poetic adulation. See JAPANESE GARDEN.

This Oriental influence came to Europe at

---

* Special articles on the subjects indicated by an asterisk (*) will be found at the words so marked.

exactly the right time. Formalism reached its apex and was going into a decline; the naturalism of the Orient was seized on enthusiastically.

To this Oriental influence can be traced the later stages of the naturalistic garden movement in England and the rococo taste in France.

THE NATURALISTIC GARDEN of England first appeared as a revolt against the trifles and formality of the Dutch garden, together with an enthusiasm for the painting of Salvator Rosa, who depicted Nature in all her grandeur, and an awakening to the beauties of Nature as found in the writings of Rousseau. Gardens were supposed to copy that grandeur. Great formal gardens were destroyed that they might give place to the rustic visions of "Capability" Brown and Humphrey Repton that made gardens appear a part of the surrounding countryside. In its later phase this movement adopted all sorts of picturesque effects — ruins, Gothic chapels, and hermitages. It also gave rise to the fancy farm. The taste was quickly copied in France. The hameau at Versailles, made to please the fancies of Marie Antoinette, still stands as a reminder of this taste.

At the same time, in both England and France, there appeared the pronounced Chinese taste in the design of garden structures. This gave rise to the Oriental rococo that, for more than fifty years, maintained its influence. At the same time interest in Chinese plants increased as the English and Dutch imported them to their gardens.

Since much of the early exploration went to tropical countries, the first plants brought from distant lands could be raised only in warm climates. However, in England the desire to grow them soon gave rise to the development of the greenhouse in which oranges and other warm-climate fruits and flowers were eventually grown to perfection.

The threshold of our own time finds the garden inheriting several traditions — classical formalism and its opposite, informal naturalism. Advances in horticultural technique and the study of plants preceded a wider appreciation of the material grown in gardens. Nevertheless garden styles were still marked by pronounced nationalistic influences. The gardens Spanish conquistadors and their descendants made in Spanish colonies showed marked influences from the homeland. The same was true of gardens in Dutch colonies and in those settled by the English. The gardens of Early America, indeed gardens made here until almost the present time, are directly traceable to English influence. The early settlers brought their own seeds from the Old Country and grew many of the plants they had known at home. In the Georgian era, the estate gardens laid out along the Atlantic seaboard were patterned after gardens of that time in England. When the naturalistic English school began spreading its influence, the same sort of gardens appeared in the United States.

The later years of the nineteenth century saw England combining many types of garden in one place — there would be an Italian garden, a bit of Spain, something from Holland, and a reminiscence of France. This taste also is found today in the United States. However, another factor brought about specialized gardens.

SPECIAL PLANT GARDENS were produced by the better understanding of the requirements of plants. The contemporary rose garden, water garden, rock garden, naturalistic planting of daffodils, bog garden, and garden of wild flowers, all represent an effort to produce on the home grounds the environments in which special groups of plants naturally thrive. Interest in these plants has caused the founding of special societies and an extensive body of literature. Today gardeners are apt to be specialists, choosing one group of plants and making them dominate the garden.

In more recent years we have witnessed a revolt against the informalism of the naturalistic type of garden and a gradual creeping in of traditional garden shapes and architecture. Gardens have lost their pronounced nationalistic atmosphere and become eclectic. Our gardens today combine features from all the gardens of the past, and in them are grown flowers from all countries of the world.

ROOF GARDENS, however, can be called America's latest contribution to garden practice. Here again we have only revived an ancient art. The stepping back of architecture in high buildings, necessitated by the demand for sunlight in the lower floors and on the street, caused a series of flat terraces suitable for rooftop gardens. Most of the plants are grown in pots or deep boxes of soil, and in this respect they repeat the experience and technique of the Babylonians when they made their hanging gardens and the custom of the Greeks when their women set potted gardens around the statue of Adonis, to celebrate the return of spring. See Penthouse Garden at PLANNING THE HOME GROUNDS. — R. W.

GARDEN HUCKLEBERRY. See SOLANUM NIGRUM. See also HUCKLEBERRY.

GARDENIA (gar-den′i-a; also gar-din′-i-a). A genus of over 60 species of tropical Old World shrubs and trees of the family Rubiaceae, one a very popular, fragrant, florists' flower. They have opposite* evergreen leaves, some of which are occasionally found in 3's at a single joint. Flowers large, white (in ours), usually solitary in the leaf axils* (always so when disbudded by the grower). Calyx tubular. Corolla salver-shaped or short-tubular, its limb with 5–11 spreading, more or less twisted, waxy, petal-like lobes. Stamens 5–9. Fruit stalkless, leathery, or fleshy. (Named for Doctor Alexander Garden, Charleston physician and friend of Linnaeus.) For cult. see below.

---

* Special articles on the subjects indicated by an asterisk (*) will be found at the words so marked.

florida = *Gardenia jasminoides.*
fortunei = *Gardenia jasminoides fortuniana.*
jasminoides. Cape jasmine and the common gardenia of the florists. A shrub 2–5 ft. high. Leaves generally lance-shaped or broader toward the tip, 3–4 in. long, thick, leathery, and occasionally variegated. Flowers 2–3½ in. wide, very fragrant. China, but long supposed to come from the Cape of Good Hope, hence its common name. The *var.* **fortuniana** is a larger flowered form and is sometimes called *G. veitchi.* This is hardy outdoors from zone* 6 southward. A var. known as Belmont, with larger flowers, was granted Plant Patent No. 93.
radicans. A low form, with smaller flowers, of *Gardenia jasminoides.*
Thunbergia. A shrub, 4–6 ft. high, with narrowly elliptic leaves, 4–6 in. long and arranged in groups of 4–5. Flowers terminal, solitary, white, fragrant, 3–4 in. wide and long-tubed, followed by a woody fruit crowned by the persistent calyx.* S.Af. Mostly winter-flowering and suited to cool greenhouse.
veitchi = *Gardenia jasminoides fortuniana.*

CULTURE

Gardenias are grown from hardwood or softwood cuttings, 6 to 8 inches long, taken from healthy plants. Hardwood cuttings of previous season's growth or older, made in winter, are planted in rows in the open in the lower South. Softwood cuttings, made in early summer, are best handled in a frame or greenhouse, using clean, sharp sand as a rooting medium. When rooted they are potted. After growth of one season, plants are ready for transplanting, usually in March, spaced 4 to 5 feet apart each way in open ground, one-half the distance in greenhouse beds. Soil with uniform moisture, as adjacent to a lake or stream, but not subject to overflow, is excellent. Unless it is virgin soil, it should be sterilized for own-rooted plants to make sure it is reasonably free from nematodes. For greenhouse culture a soil made with good garden soil, peat, cow manure, and sand, in equal parts, is suitable. This should be mixed and sterilized before filling beds, 5 to 6 inches deep. Best soil reaction is pH 5.5 to 6.5. Commercial fertilizer, such as is used for camellias, is used to maintain fertility at high level. An application of a quarter of a pound to a square yard at two-month intervals will increase growth and size of flowers. Flowers are most valuable during winter months; they can be secured at that season by keeping plants in good growing condition and disbudding until autumn. They should be well budded by October and November. If too many flower buds form, their number should be reduced. Temperature of 65° and above should be maintained in greenhouses. A limited number of varieties have been selected and propagated. — H. H. H.

G. jasminoides fortuniana is summer-blooming outdoors on the Eastern Shore of Md. and Va. — EDITOR.

DISEASES. A canker* disease may cause death of a branch or entire plant. When propagating from cuttings, mix one ounce of ferbam, wettable powder (*see* FUNGICIDES) with 25 pounds of sand, and use this for rooting medium for cuttings. After plants are potted, spray three times at monthly intervals with pesticide #5 (*see* SPRAYS AND DUSTS).

GARDEN MAGAZINES. Of the 450 or more U.S. magazines devoted at least in part to some phase of gardening, those most likely to be of general interest are listed below. Those marked with a dagger (†) are only partly devoted to gardening. The place of publication and date of establishment together with frequency of issue are also noted.

African Violet Magazine Quarterly. Knoxville, Tenn. 1947.
American Camellia Quarterly. Gainesville, Fla. 1946.
American Daffodil Yearbook. Washington, D.C. 1935.
American Fuchsia Society Bulletin. Quarterly. San Francisco. 1944.
American Gesneria Society Journal. Quarterly. San Francisco. 1953.
†American Home. Monthly. New York. 1905.
American Horticultural Magazine. Quarterly. Washington, D.C. 1922.
American Iris Society Bulletin. Quarterly. Nashville, Tenn. 1920.
American Peony Society Bulletin. Annual. Rapidan, Va. 1915.
American Primrose Society. Quarterly. Portland, Ore . 1948.
American Rock Garden Society Bulletin. Quarterly. Ramsey, N.J. 1943.
American Rose Annual. Columbus, Ohio. 1916.
American Society for Horticultural Science. Semi-annually. Ithaca, N.Y. 1903.
Arnold Arboretum Journal. Quarterly. Jamaica Plain, Mass. 1941.
Begonian, The. Monthly. Los Angeles. 1934.
†Better Homes and Gardens. Monthly. Des Moines, Iowa. 1922.
Cactus and Succulent Journal. Bimonthly. Pasadena, Calif. 1929.
California Garden. Quarterly. San Diego, Calif. 1909.
California Horticultural Society Journal. Quarterly. San Francisco. 1940.
Chrysanthemum Society of America Bulletin. Quarterly. Ashtabula, Ohio. 1933.
Fairchild Tropical Garden Bulletin. 8 per year. Coconut Grove, Fla. 1945.
†Farm and Garden. Monthly. New York. 1914.
Florists Exchange (commercial) Weekly. New York. 1888.
Flower and Garden Magazine. Monthly. Kansas City, Mo. 1956.
Flower Grower. Monthly. Albany, N.Y. 1914.
Garden Journal (N.Y. Botanical Garden). Bi-monthly. New York. 1951.

---

* Special articles on the subjects indicated by an asterisk (*) will be found at the words so marked.

Gesneriad Journal. Quarterly. San Leandro, Calif. 1953.

Gladiolus Magazine. Quarterly. Hudson, N.H. 1937.

Hemerocallis Society Yearbook (also News letter). Nashville, Tenn. 1947.

Horticulture. Monthly. Boston, Mass. 1904.

†House and Garden. Monthly. New York. 1901.

†House Beautiful. Monthly. New York. 1900.

Minnesota Horticulturist. Monthly. St. Paul, Minn. 1866.

National Council State Garden Clubs Bulletin. Monthly. New York. 1930.

North American Lily Society. Quarterly Bulletin. Oyster Bay, N.Y. 1947.

†Organic Gardening and Farming. Monthly. Emmaus, Pa. 1949.

Plants and Gardens. Quarterly. Brooklyn, N.Y. 1945.

Popular Gardening. Monthly. New York. 1950.

Subtropical Gardening. Monthly. Brooksville. Fla. 1938.

†Sunset Magazine. Monthly. San Francisco. 1898.

†Town and Country. Fortnightly. New York. 1846.

†Tropical Living. Monthly. Miami, Fla. 1956.

Among outstanding British publications are the *Journal* of the Royal Horticultural Society, *Gardener's Chronicle, Gardening Illustrated*, and the *Kew Bulletin*, all of London. In Canada there is *Canadian Homes and Gardens*, published at Toronto.

GARDEN MEASURES. For sizes, volumes, weights and measures, *see* WEIGHTS AND MEASURES. For plants, yields, amount of seed, plants per acre, etc., *see* GARDEN TABLES.

GARDEN MINT = *Mentha spicata.* See MINT.

GARDEN NASTURTIUM = *Tropaeolum majus. See* NASTURTIUM.

GARDEN OPERATIONS. What has to be done in a garden comprises the different skills one learns from the seeding to harvesting of the final crop. Naturally these different garden operations divide themselves into things that are done to the soil or to the plants themselves. And there is no need to repeat in detail here all the things that are treated extensively in other parts of the book.

But suggestions of where to find these special articles are helpful enough to summarize here.

SOIL. For all details having to do with the soil, *see* SOILS (and the cross-references there mentioned). *See also* CULTIVATION, DRAINING, DIGGING, FERTILIZERS, WATERING.

PLANTS. In the treatment of your plants, whether herbs or trees, there are certain things you must know about their care, protection from pests, or perpetuation. *See,* especially, the articles on PLANTING, PROPAGATION, WATERING, FORCING, ANIMAL INJURY. There are also many cultural notes on special crops which should be looked for under their common names (*i.e.,* apple, cabbage, carnation, fig, etc.).

GREENHOUSE OR COLD FRAME. For the things to do in daily management of a greenhouse or a conservatory, *see* GREENHOUSE. For the management of a hotbed or a cold frame, *see* COLD FRAME.

HOUSE PLANTS. *See* that entry.

GARDEN ORACH = *Atriplex hortensis.*

GARDEN PHLOX = *Phlox paniculata.*

GARDEN PORTULACA = *Portulaca grandiflora.*

GARDEN QUESTIONS. No lecture ever ends without inevitable questions by members of the garden club. Several thousands have accumulated in the past, most of which have ultimately reached the editorial office either in the form of printed lists or in direct queries. Sifting them out gives one a cross-section of the doubts and perplexities of the average gardener.

To list them here is impossible. To sort them into categories and steer the seeker to the proper reference in this book seems not only possible but perhaps the most helpful way of answering them. Most garden questions have to do with (1) specific plants; (2) the soil in which they grow; (3) their pests; (4) their suitability for the place in which you wish to grow them.

(1) SPECIFIC PLANTS. All the plants in this book are listed under their generic names and under as many vernacular names as are in common use. If you know the Latin or common name of the plant in question, turn to that entry and you will soon learn its culture and the varieties most worth growing, its diseases or insect pests, and much other useful information on propagation. There are also special articles on the culture of all the important fruits, vegetables, flowers, and trees.

(2) SOILS. Read the article on SOILS and the cross-references there suggested. *See also* FERTILIZERS, PLANT FOODS, ACID AND ALKALI SOILS, SOIL OPERATIONS.

(3) PESTS. Read first the general articles on INSECT PESTS, PLANT DISEASES, and ANIMAL INJURY. If your query is about a specific pest on some plant, turn to that plant, where you will find an account of the control of all insects or fungous pests thought worth including by the Contributing Editors in charge of this section.

(4) SUITABILITY. The whole question of a plant for your locality is tied up with your local climate and the hardiness of the plant involved. *See* HARDINESS, ZONE, PROTECTING PLANTS, and, especially, the climatic data on temperature and rainfall at the name of your state or province.

If, in spite of these possible question answerers, there are still problems that puz-

---

* Special articles on the subjects indicated by an asterisk (*) will be found at the words so marked.

zle you, *see* the Classified List of Main Articles in the Introduction.

GARDEN ROCKET = *Hesperis matronalis.*

GARDEN ROOM. A garden room should be an intimate area containing plant material and sufficiently defined in extent and purpose to be a recognized entity.

Garden room which encloses a lily pool and a tea house

Garden rooms extend from a simple open area beneath the canopy of great spreading tree branches to a highly organized architectural unit forming an integral part of a garden scheme.

The purpose of a garden room is to provide a place accessible, yet apart, and amid natural growing things where one may be quiet and free to sit and think or to meditate on the heart's desires.

Its intimate use gives the place a certain distinction. Interesting variations in ground level and frank recognition of existing dominant features adjacent to the site, such as a building or large tree, add an air of permanence and suggest a sympathetic relationship between landscape elements. To be convincing, such a unit area should obviously suggest its function. The treatment of its various features should all contribute toward successfully carrying out the general purposes of the garden room, which is detachment and privacy outdoors.

The choice of materials employed to create the setting of such an area is governed by individual requirements and is usually dependent upon local conditions.

Floor areas are generally paved with flagstone or brick, and a carpet of turf is also used where dampness and mosquitoes are not deterrent factors.

The enclosure strikes the dominant note in the composition of the room. For formal effect, a wall or hedge usually serves as a

A simple outdoor garden room, paved or not, and close enough to the house to be convenient.

boundary, and occasionally an arbor or covered seat is used, or a combination of such elements. For informal effects, the limits are not so severely defined. A dry stone wall or flanking mass of shrubs may be used, or a group of trees or possibly one large low-branched tree.

Supplementing necessary furniture, such as seats and tables, the judicious use of potted or tubbed plants, sculptural ornament, and the use of water, all definitely contribute to the character and atmosphere of the place, providing they are in keeping with the spirit of the room.

Where feasible and desirable, electric outlets can be provided for a portable electric stove or a percolator. Also for evening occasions, electric illumination of the garden room has proved an interesting feature and the effects are quite adaptable to the mood desired. *See* LIGHTING. — A. F.

GARDEN SCHOOLS. Nearly every state university has a well-equipped department of horticulture, the most notable being at Cornell, Iowa, Rutgers, Wisconsin, Illinois, Florida, Michigan, Pennsylvania State College, Virginia Polytechnic Institute, Purdue, University of California, and Ohio State University.

Special courses in various garden subjects are offered from time to time by the botanic gardens (which see), especially the New York Botanical Garden and the Missouri Botanical Garden. There are, in addition, a few special schools of horticulture or courses offered in gardening, of which the most noteworthy are:

Caldwell College for Women, Caldwell, N.J. (Horticulture.)
California School of Gardening for Women, Hayward, Calif.
Horticultural Society of New York. New

* Special articles on the subjects indicated by an asterisk (*) will be found at the words so marked.

York, N.Y. (Courses for amateur and professional gardeners.)

Lowthorpe School of Landscape Architecture for Women. Groton, Mass.

School of Horticulture for Women. Ambler, Pa.

State Institute of Applied Agriculture. Farmingdale, Long Island, N.Y. (Courses in horticulture.)

GARDEN TABLES. There is apt to, but need not be, confusion between this entry and WEIGHTS AND MEASURES. At the latter entry look for all statistics having to do with the standard dimensions or contents of things, like a mile, foot, yard, bushel, acre, pint, or the contents of a cistern, etc.

But here are grouped many tables that most gardeners need to consult from time to time. For ready reference they may be separated into various sections:

I. Yields, Plants per Acre, Average Bearing Age, Seeds Needed for 100 Feet of Row and for an Acre.

II. Weight of Seeds, Viability of Seeds, Percentage of Seed Germinating.

III. Tree Height, Age or Longevity of Trees, Rate of growth, How to Estimate Tree Height.

IV. Number of Plants for Oval, Round, or Square Flower Beds.

I
AVERAGE YIELDS

The average yields per acre of various garden crops are given below. They vary, of course, with locality, cultural methods, and the variety grown.

Artichoke	200 to 300 bushels
Beans, String	75 to 120 bushels
Beans, Lima	75 to 100 bushels of dry beans
Beets	400 to 700 bushels
Carrots	400 to 700 bushels
Corn	50 to 75 bushels, shelled
Cranberry	100 to 300 bushels
Cucumber	About 150,000 fruits per acre
Currant	100 bushels
Eggplant	1 or 2 large fruits to the plant for the large sorts, and from 3 to 8 fruits for the smaller varieties
Gooseberry	100 bushels
Grape	3 to 5 tons
Horse-radish	3 to 5 tons
Kohlrabi	500 to 1000 bushels
Onion, from seed	300 to 800 bushels
Parsnips	500 to 800 bushels
Pea, green in pod	100 to 150 bushels
Peach	In full bearing, a peach tree should produce from 5 to 10 bushels
Pear	A tree 20 to 25 years old should give from 25 to 45 bushels
Pepper	30,000 to 50,000 fruits
Plum	5 to 8 bushels may be considered an average crop for an average tree
Potato	100 to 300 bushels
Quince	100 to 300 bushels
Raspberry and Blackberry	50 to 100 bushels

Salsify	200 to 300 bushels
Spinach	200 barrels
Strawberry	75 to 250 or even 300 bushels
Tomato	8 to 16 tons
Turnip	600 to 1000 bushels

PLANTS PER ACRE

Plants Needed for an Acre of Land when Set the Indicated Number of Inches Apart

NOTE: *To estimate for smaller areas figure that a plot 33 × 66 ft. is exactly 1/20 of an acre.*

Inches	Plants	Inches	Plants
1 × 1	6,272,640	9 × 10	69,696
1 × 2	3,136,320	9 × 12	58,080
1 × 3	2,090,880	10 × 10	62,726
1 × 6	1,045,440	10 × 12	52,272
1 × 9	696,960	10 × 15	41,817
1 × 12	522,720	10 × 18	34,848
2 × 2	1,568,160	10 × 20	31,362
2 × 3	1,045,440	10 × 24	
2 × 4	784,080	or 2 ft.	26,132
2 × 6	522,720	10 × 30	20,908
2 × 8	392,040	10 × 42	14,935
2 × 10	313,632	10 × 48	
2 × 12	261,360	or 4 ft.	13,068
3 × 3	696,960	10 × 60	
3 × 4	522,720	or 5 ft.	10,454
3 × 6	348,480	15 × 15	27,878
3 × 8	261,360	15 × 20	20,908
3 × 10	209,088	15 × 36	
3 × 12	174,240	of 3 ft.	11,616
4 × 4	392,040	15 × 48	
4 × 6	261,360	or 4 ft.	8,712
4 × 8	196,020	15 × 60	
4 × 10	156,816	or 5 ft.	6,969
4 × 12	130,680	18 × 18	19,360
5 × 5	250,905	18 × 24	
5 × 7	179,218	or 2 ft.	14,520
5 × 9	139,392	18 × 36	
5 × 12	104,544	or 3 ft.	9,680
6 × 6	174,240	18 × 48	
6 × 8	130,680	or 4 ft.	7,260
6 × 10	104,544	20 × 20	15,681
6 × 12	87,120	20 × 24	
7 × 7	128,013	or 2 ft.	13,168
7 × 10	89,609	20 × 36	
7 × 12	74,674	or 3 ft.	8,712
8 × 8	98,010	20 × 48	
8 × 10	78,408	or 4 ft.	6,534
8 × 12	65,340	20 × 60	
9 × 9	77,440	or 5 ft.	5,227

PLANTS PER ACRE

Plants Needed for an Acre of Land when Set the Indicated Number of Feet Apart

NOTE: *To estimate for smaller areas figure that a plot 33 × 66 ft. is exactly 1/20 of an acre.*

Feet	Plants	Feet	Plants
1 × 1	43,560	12 × 60	60
1 × 2	21,780	15 × 15	103
1 × 3	14,520	15 × 18	161
1 × 4	10,890	15 × 20	145
1 × 5	8,712	15 × 24	121
1 × 6	7,260	15 × 30	96
1 × 8	5,445	15 × 36	80
1 × 10	4,356	15 × 42	69
1 × 12	3,630	15 × 48	60
2 × 2	10,890	15 × 54	53
2 × 4	5,445	15 × 60	48
2 × 6	3,630	18 × 18	134
2 × 8	2,722	18 × 20	121
2 × 10	2,178	18 × 24	100
2 × 12	1,815	18 × 30	80

* Special articles on the subjects indicated by an asterisk (*) will be found at the words so marked.

PLANTS PER ACRE (continued)

Feet	Plants	Feet	Plants
3 × 3	4,840	18 × 36	67
3 × 6	2,420	18 × 42	57
3 × 8	1,815	18 × 48	50
3 × 10	1,452	18 × 54	44
3 × 12	1,210	18 × 60	40
4 × 4	2,722	20 × 20	108
4 × 6	1,185	20 × 24	90
4 × 8	1,361	20 × 30	72
4 × 10	1,089	20 × 36	60
4 × 12	907	20 × 42	51
5 × 5	1,742	20 × 48	45
5 × 7	1,244	20 × 54	40
5 × 9	968	20 × 60	36
5 × 11	792	24 × 24	75
5 × 12	726	24 × 30	60
6 × 6	1,210	24 × 36	50
6 × 8	907	24 × 42	43
6 × 10	726	24 × 48	37
6 × 12	605	24 × 54	33
7 × 7	888	24 × 60	30
7 × 8	777	30 × 30	48
7 × 9	691	30 × 36	40
7 × 10	622	30 × 42	34
7 × 11	565	30 × 48	30
7 × 12	518	30 × 54	26
8 × 8	680	30 × 60	24
8 × 9	605	36 × 36	33
8 × 10	544	36 × 42	28
8 × 11	495	36 × 48	25
8 × 12	453	36 × 54	22
9 × 9	537	36 × 60	20
9 × 10	484	38 × 38	30
9 × 11	440	38 × 40	28
9 × 12	403	38 × 42	27
9 × 14	345	38 × 48	23
9 × 15	322	38 × 50	22
9 × 18	268	38 × 54	21
9 × 20	242	38 × 60	19
10 × 10	435	40 × 40	27
10 × 12	363	40 × 42	25
10 × 15	290	40 × 48	22
10 × 18	242	40 × 50	21
10 × 20	217	40 × 54	20
10 × 24	181	40 × 60	18
10 × 30	145	42 × 42	24
10 × 36	121	42 × 48	21
10 × 42	103	42 × 54	19
10 × 45	96	42 × 60	17
10 × 48	90	48 × 48	18
10 × 54	80	48 × 54	16
10 × 60	72	48 × 60	15
12 × 12	302	50 × 50	17
12 × 15	242	50 × 54	16
12 × 18	201	50 × 60	14
12 × 20	181	54 × 54	14
12 × 24	151	54 × 60	13
12 × 30	121	60 × 60	12
12 × 36	100	70 × 70	8
12 × 48	75	80 × 80	6
12 × 54	67	90 × 90	5
12 × 42	86	100 × 100	4

AVERAGE BEARING AGE OF FRUIT PLANTS FROM TIME OF SETTING OUT TO FIRST FULL CROP

	Years		Years
Apple	5–20	Peach	2
Blackberry	1	Pear	4–7
Citrus fruits	3–6	dwarfs	3–5
(oranges,		Persimmon,	
lemons, etc.)		or Kaki	1–3
Cranberry	3	Plum	3–5
Currant	1–2	Quince	2–3
Gooseberry	1–2	Raspberry	1–2
Grape	4	Strawberry	1–2

SEEDS NEEDED PER 100 FEET OF ROW, PER ACRE, AND PER FOOT OF VARIOUS CROPS

Crop	Seeds per 100-ft. row	Seeds per acre	No. of seeds per foot
Asparagus	1–2 oz.	4–6 lb.	7–10
Beans, String	8 oz.	1 bu.	5–8
Beans, dry shell	4–8 oz.	¾ bu.– 1½ bu.	5–8
Beets	½ oz.	4 lb.	10
Brussels Sprouts	¹⁄₂₀ oz.	½ lb.	5–8
Cabbage	¹⁄₂₀ oz.	½ lb.	5–8
Carrot	¹⁄₁₀ oz.	2 lb.	15–20
Cauliflower	¹⁄₂₀ oz.	¼–½ lb.	5–8
Celery	¹⁄₂₀ oz.	¼–1 lb.	10–20
Cucumber	¼ oz.	1–2 lb.	5–6 (per hill)
Eggplant	¹⁄₂₀ oz.	¼–½ lb.	6–8
Endive	¹⁄₁₀ oz.	4 lb.	8–10
Lettuce	¹⁄₁₀ oz.	3 lb.	8–10
Muskmelons	¼ oz.	2 lb.	5–6 (per hill)
Onion	½ oz.	4–5 lb.	10–15
Onion sets	1–2 lb.	8–12 bu.	5–6
Onions, Winter	1–2 lb.	8–12 bu.	5–6
Parsley	¹⁄₁₀ oz.	3 lb.	8–10
Parsnips	¼ oz.	3–5 lb.	8–10
Peas	½ lb.	1½–4 bu.	5–8
Peppers	¹⁄₂₀ oz.	¾–1 lb.	4–5
Potatoes	5–6 lb.	12–15 bu.	
Radish	½ oz.	10–12 lb.	8–10
Rutabaga	¹⁄₁₀ oz.	2–3 lb.	8–10
Salsify	½ oz.	6–8 lb.	5–8
Spinach	½ oz.	12–20 lb.	10–12
Squash, Winter	1 oz.	3–5 lb.	5–6 (per hill)
Sweet Corn	¼ lb.	10–15 lb.	3–4
Tomatoes	¹⁄₂₀ oz.	2–4 oz.	6–8
Turnips	¹⁄₁₀ oz.	1–2 lb.	5–8

For the amount of vegetable seed needed for gardens 100 × 50 ft. and 200 × 100 ft., *see* KITCHEN GARDEN.

II

AVERAGE WEIGHT OF SOME COMMON GARDEN AND TREE SEEDS

These weights are apt to vary with the variety and the thoroughness with which the seeds have been dried.

Garden seeds	Weight of a quart of seed in ounces	Garden seeds	Weight of a quart of seed in ounces
Anise	11.6	Chicory	15.5
Balm	21.3	Coriander	12.4
Basil	20.5	Corn	24.8
Bean	24.2–	Cucumber	19.4
	33.0	Dill	11.6
Beet	9.7	Eggplant	19.4
Borage	18.7	Endive	13.2
Broccoli	27.1	Fennel, Com-	
Cabbage	27.1	mon or Wild	17.4
Caper	17.8	Fennel, Sweet	9.1
Caraway	16.3		
Cardoon	24.4	Hop	9.7
Carrot with		Horehound	26.4
the spines	9.3	Hyssop	22.3
Cauliflower	27.1	Kohlrabi	27.1
Celery	18.6	Leek	21.3
Chervil	14.7	Lettuce	16.6

* Special articles on the subjects indicated by an asterisk (*) will be found at the words so marked.

Garden seeds	Weight of a quart of seed in ounces	Garden seeds	Weight of a quart of seed in ounces
Marjoram, Sweet	21.3	Sage	21.3
Muskmelon	13.9	Salsify	8.9
Nasturtium, Tall	13.2	Savory, Summer	19.4
Nasturtium, Dwarf	23.3	Savory, Winter	16.6
Okra	24.0	Spinach	14.5
Onion	19.4	Spinach, New Zealand	8.6
Pea	27.1– 31.0	Squash	16.6
Peanut	15.5		
Pepper	17.4	Strawberry	23.3
Pumpkin	9.7	Sweet Cicely	9.7
Radish	27.1	Tansy	11.6
Rhubarb	3.1– 4.6	Thyme	26.4
		Tomato	11.6
Rosemary	15.5	Turnip	26.0
Rue	22.5	Watermelon	17.8

Approximate Number of Some Tree Seeds to a Pound

Tree seeds	Approximate number of seeds to a pound	Tree seeds	Approximate number of seeds to a pound
Apple	12,000	Norway Maple	7,231
Cherry (pits)	1,000	Sugar Maple	7,488
Peach	200	Red Cedar	8,321
Pear	15,000	White Ash	9,858
Plum	600	Osage Orange	10,656
Quince	15,000	Box Elder	14,784
Mulberry	200,000	Catalpa	19,776
Butternut	15	Ailanthus	20,161
Black Walnut	25	White Pine	20,540
Hickory	78	Red Maple	22,464
Chestnut	90	Green Ash	22,656
Silver Maple	2,421	Black Locust	28,992
Honey Locust	2,496	Slippery Elm	54,359
Black Cherry	4,311	American Elm	92,352
Black Ash	5,629	Mountain-ash	108,327
Linden	6,337		

Viability of Seeds

While some seeds, under specialized conditions, will hold their germinating power for many years, the average period is rather short. All tales of seeds from Egyptian mummies still holding the power to germinate are false. The extreme viability of wheat is about 30 years, usually far less. The average and extreme longevity of some typical garden seeds are as follows:

	Average: in years	Extreme: in years
Angelica	1 or 2	3
Anise	3	5
Asparagus Bean	3	8
Aster	1 to 3	13
Balm	4	7
Basil	8	10+
Bean	3	8
Beet	6	10+
Borage	8	10+
Broccoli	5	10
Cabbage	5	10
Caraway	3	4
Cardoon	7	9

	Average: in years	Extreme: in years
Carrot	4 or 5	10+
Cauliflower	5	10
Celery	8	10
Chervil	2 or 3	6
Chicory	8	10+
Coriander	6	8
Corn	2	4
Cucumber	10	10+
Dandelion	2	5
Dill	3	5
Eggplant	6	10
Endive	10	10+
Fennel, Common or Wild	4	7
Fennel, Sweet	4	7
Gourds	6	10+
Hop	2	4
Horehound	3	6
Hyssop	3	5
Kohlrabi	5	10
Leek	3	9
Lettuce	5	13
Lovage	3	4
Marjoram, Sweet	3	7
Marjoram, Winter	5	7
Muskmelon	5	10+
Mustard	4	9
Nasturtium, Tall	5	5
Nasturtium, Dwarf	5	8
Okra	5	10+
Onion	2	7
Orach	6	7
Parsley	3	9
Parsnip	2	4
Pea	3	8
Pepper	4	13
Pumpkin	4 or 5	9
Purslane	7	10
Radish	5	10+
Rhubarb	3	8
Rosemary	4	(?)
Rue	2	5
Sage	3	7
Salsify	2	8
Savory, Summer	3	7
Savory, Winter	3	6
Spinach	5	7
Spinach, New Zealand	5	8
Squash	6	10+
Strawberry	3	6
Tansy	2	4
Thyme	3	7
Tomato	4	13
Turnip	5	10+
Watermelon	6	10

Average Percentage of Vegetable Seed Usually Germinating under Ordinary Garden Conditions

Kind of seed	Per cent	Kind of seed	Per cent
Artichoke	70	Okra	70
Asparagus	80	Onion	75
Beans	85	Parsley	60
Beets	70	Parsnip	65
Cabbage	80	Peas	85
Carrot	70	Pepper	60
Cauliflower	70	Pumpkin	75
Celery	60	Radish	85
Chicory	70	Rutabaga	80
Cress	70	Salsify	70
Cucumber	80	Spinach	65
Eggplant	65	Squash	80
Endive	75	Sweet Corn	80
Kale	70	Swiss Chard	75
Kohlrabi	75	Tomato	75
Lettuce	75	Turnip	80

* Special articles on the subjects indicated by an asterisk (*) will be found at the words so marked.

III

TREE STATISTICS ARE GROUPED UNDER THREE HEADS

AVERAGE HEIGHT OF SOME MATURE TREES UNDER REASONABLY GOOD CULTURE

	Height in feet
White pine (*Pinus Strobus*)	70
Pitch pine (*Pinus rigida*)	40
Austrian pine (*Pinus nigra*)	70
Scotch pine (*Pinus sylvestris*)	75
Larch (*Larix laricina*)	50
White spruce (*Picea glauca*)	60
Blue spruce (*Picea pungens*)	50
Douglas fir (*Pseudotsuga taxifolia*)	150
Balsam (*Abies balsamea*)	40
Cilician fir (*Abies cilicia*)	60
Hemlock (*Tsuga canadensis*)	60
Arborvitae (*Thuja occidentalis*)	40
Red cedar (*Juniperus virginiana*)	35
Redwood (*Sequoia sempervirens*)	250
Big Tree (*Sequoia gigantea*)	220
Ginkgo (*Ginkgo biloba*)	70
White poplar (*Populus alba*)	50
Aspen (*Populus tremuloides*)	35
Balm-of-Gilead (*Populus candicans*)	45
Lombardy poplar (*Populus nigra italica*)	70
Butternut (*Juglans cinerea*)	30
Walnut (*Juglans nigra*)	60
English walnut (*Juglans regia*)	70
Hop-hornbeam (*Ostrya virginiana*)	30
Ironwood (*Carpinus caroliniana*)	25
Black birch (*Betula lenta*)	60
Yellow birch (*Betula lutea*)	75
Paper birch (*Betula papyrifera*)	60
American beech (*Fagus grandifolia*)	65
European beech (*Fagus sylvatica*)	75
White oak (*Quercus alba*)	65
Bur oak (*Quercus macrocarpa*)	60
Swamp white oak (*Quercus bicolor*)	50
Chestnut oak (*Quercus montana*)	45
Red oak (*Quercus rubra*)	70
Pin oak (*Quercus palustris*)	45
Scarlet oak (*Quercus coccinea*)	45
Black oak (*Quercus velutina*)	60
Slippery elm (*Ulmus rubra*)	70
English elm (*Ulmus procera*)	85
American elm (*Ulmus americana*)	30
Hackberry (*Celtis occidentalis*)	30
Red mulberry (*Morus rubra*)	30
White mulberry (*Morus alba*)	35
Cucumber tree (*Magnolia acuminata*)	45
Umbrella tree (*Magnolia tripetala*)	25
Tulip-tree (*Liriodendron tulipifera*)	65
Sassafras (*Sassafras albidum*)	45
Sweet gum (*Liquidambar styraciflua*)	50
Plane tree (*Platanus occidentalis*)	75
London plane (*Platanus acerifolia*)	60
Black cherry (*Prunus serotina*)	40
Common cherry (*Prunus avium*)	50
Sour cherry (*Prunus Cerasus*)	30
Peach (*Amygdalus Persica*)	15
Honey locust (*Gleditsia triacanthos*)	50
Locust (*Robinia Pseudo-acacia*)	30
Ailanthus (*Ailanthus glandulosa*)	60
Eucalyptus (various species)	30–250
Sugar maple (*Acer saccharum*)	75
Silver maple (*Acer saccharinum*)	55
Red maple (*Acer rubrum*)	50
Norway maple (*Acer platanoides*)	50
Sycamore maple (*Acer Pseudo-platanus*)	50
Box elder (*Acer Negundo*)	45
Horse-chestnut (*Aesculus Hippocastanum*)	65
American linden (*Tilia glabra*)	70
European linden (*Tilia vulgaris*)	75
Flowering dogwood (*Cornus florida*)	25
Black gum (*Nyssa sylvatica*)	45

	Height in feet
White ash (*Fraxinus americana*)	60
Black ash (*Fraxinus nigra*)	70
Catalpa (*Catalpa speciosa*)	50
Paulownia (*Paulownia tomentosa*)	60

AGE OR AVERAGE LONGEVITY OF TREES

The big trees of Calif., the ahuehuete, and the Dragon tree of the Canary Islands may well be among the oldest of living things, certainly 2000–3000 years old. But most ordinary trees are far younger when disease or old age overtakes them. Not many accurate records have been kept of cultivated trees, but a few are known, at least for fruit trees and a few ornamental species.

Apple	40–100
Beech	200–400
Citrus	50–60
Cryptomeria	300–700
Olive	300–600 (some known to be over 1500 years)
Peach	8–12
Pear	50–75
Persimmon	25–40
Plum	20–25
White oak	300–700
Yew	200–800

RATE OF GROWTH OF SOME COMMONLY PLANTED TREES

The following, if given reasonably good care, and assuming that they were each planted as saplings of 3 in. in diameter, should, in 20 years, have the following diameters:

	Inches		Inches
White elm	19	Red maple	16
Plane tree	18	Silver maple	21
Tulip-tree	18	Sugar maple	13
Linden	17	Horse-chestnut	13
Catalpa	16	Red oak	13
Ailanthus	16	Pin oak	13
Cucumber tree	15	Scarlet oak	13
Chestnut	14	White oak	12
Common locust	14	White ash	12
Honey locust	13	Hackberry	10

HOW TO ESTIMATE THE HEIGHT OF TREES

While professional foresters use an instrument known as a hypsometer for measuring the exact height of a tree without putting a tape measure on it, the gardener or landscape architect is often satisfied with a reasonably close approximation of the true height, which can be determined with no more equipment than a yardstick and the sun.

1. Measure the exact distance from the trunk to the extremity of the shadow of the tree (on level ground, if possible).

2. At the extremity of the shadow stand a yardstick (3 ft.) as nearly erect as possible.

3. Measure the exact length of the shadow of the yardstick, which, of course, projects beyond the shadow of the tip of the tree.

4. Divide the length of the tree shadow by the length of the yardstick shadow and multiply by 3, which gives the height of the tree.

---

* Special articles on the subjects indicated by an asterisk (*) will be found at the words so marked.

Example: A tree throws a shadow 20 ft. long; the shadow of the yardstick is 4 ft. 20 divided by 4 = 5 ft. × 3 = 15 ft., which is the height of the tree.

IV
NUMBER OF PLANTS FOR ROUND, OVAL, OR RECTANGULAR FLOWER BEDS

PLANTS NEEDED FOR A ROUND OR CIRCULAR BED

Diameter of bed	Plants 6 in. apart	Plants 12 in. apart	Plants 18 in. apart	Plants 24 in. apart	Plants 30 in. apart
3 feet	28	7	..	..	..
4 feet	48	12	6	..	..
5 feet	80	20	8	..	..
6 feet	112	28	13	7	..
7 feet	152	38	17	9	..
8 feet	200	50	23	12	..
9 feet	256	64	28	16	..
10 feet	320	80	36	20	13
11 feet	380	95	42	24	16
12 feet	452	113	50	28	18
13 feet	528	132	59	33	22
14 feet	612	153	68	39	25
15 feet	704	176	78	44	28
16 feet	804	201	89	50	32
17 feet	904	226	100	57	36
18 feet	1016	254	113	63	40
19 feet	1132	283	126	71	46
20 feet	1256	314	139	78	50

PLANTS NEEDED FOR AN OVAL BED

Assuming that the bed is a perfect oval, *add* the breadth and length of the bed and *divide* by 2. The result is exactly the same as though the bed were round and the above table for round beds should then be used.

Example: An oval bed is 9 × 7 ft.

Add 9 + 7 = 16 which divided by 2 = 8.

Use the table for a round bed 8 ft. in diameter.

PLANTS NEEDED FOR A RECTANGULAR BED (SQUARE OR OBLONG)

1. Determine the exact area of the bed.
2. Determine what fraction of an acre (*see* WEIGHTS AND MEASURES) the bed may be.
3. Use the table at I (Plants per Acre) to see how many plants will be needed for your fraction of an acre.

A somewhat simpler, but not so accurate method is illustrated thus:

A rectangular bed is 12 × 10 ft. and plants are to be 6 in. apart and 6 in. from all edges.

Along the 12-ft. edge 23 plants will be needed.

Multiply this by the 19 needed along the 10-ft. edge 19 × 23 = 437 plants.

GARDEN TOURS. Nearly everyone, no matter how simple or elaborate their own garden, and many who have none at all, like to see the gardens of others. Fortunately, there are many opportunities to visit fine or famous gardens, some private and others open free to the public. Among the latter are the botanic gardens. A list of the most important will be found at BOTANIC GARDEN. Likewise the garden-pilgrimage enthusiast should see the fine collections of shrubs and trees in the various arboreta. For a list of these *see* ARBORETUM. In addition there are various public parks in certain cities that are noteworthy from the hort. standpoint. Among them are the incomparable Vale of Cashmere at Prospect Park, Brooklyn, N.Y.; the unique collection of lilacs and thorns at the parks at Rochester, N.Y.; Golden Gate Park at San Francisco; and the municipal rose gardens in many large cities, notably at Hartford, Conn., Portland, Ore., Allentown and Hershey, Pa., Providence, R.I., etc.

Gardens of outstanding merit are also open to the public for a small fee and some twenty-two of the most noteworthy are:

1. Magnolia Gardens, near Charleston, S. Car. John Galsworthy wrote of this: "I specialize in gardens and freely assert that none in the world is so beautiful as this." It is incomparably rich in azaleas and camellias.

2. Middleton Place, near Charleston, S. Car. One of the most beautiful formal gardens in the country, famous since 1740 when it was started. Michaux first introduced *Camellia japonica* into America at Middleton Place.

3. Cypress Gardens, near Charleston, S. Car. A beautiful island-studded lagoon, through which one travels in small boats to see the huge development of azaleas and other plants. The dark, quiet stillness of these gardens is assured by the great cypress trees that are wild all through the lake.

4. Bellingrath Gardens, near Mobile, Ala. A fine old estate, noted for the camellia parterre, rose garden, rock garden, and an azalea trail. This, now that its perpetuation is assured, is perhaps the finest garden in America. Visitors often number over forty thousand on a single Sunday at camellia or azalea time.

5. McKee Jungle Gardens, Vero Beach, Fla. Mainly a rich collection of tropical and sub-tropical plants that are restricted to warm regions. It comprises over 120 acres. Many hundreds of species and varieties are cult. there in naturalistic settings.

6. Viscaya Art Museum, Biscayne Bay, Miami, Fla. A magnificent estate developed by James Deering, and acquired by Dade Co. in 1952. Its Italian gardens are probably the finest in the U.S.

7. Stanley Park, Vancouver, British Columbia. Outstanding shrubs and trees and one of the finest rock gardens in North America.

8. Dumbarton Oaks, Georgetown, Washington, D.C. Some of the finest old box collections, vistas, and huge old trees. Architecturally a gem.

---

* Special articles on the subjects indicated by an asterisk (*) will be found at the words so marked.

9. Lambert Gardens. Portland, Ore. Ten outstanding gardens, among them a Spanish garden, sunken rose garden, informal gardens, canyon garden, etc.

10. Pierates Cruze Gardens, Mount Pleasant, S. Car. Camellias (Jan. 15–April 1) and azaleas (Mar. 15–Apr.1) are the chief features of this fine old garden, across the harbor from Charleston.

11. Longwood Gardens, near Kennett Square, Pa. A 1000-acre estate developed by Pierre S. du Pont and given by him to the public. Greenhouses cover about three acres (the largest in the world) and hold monthly shows. Outdoor collections are famous for formal gardens, water garden, and a unique collection of flowering crabapples.

12. Kingwood Center, Mansfield, Ohio. A 47-acre estate now devoted to gardening and the arts. It plants and tests many thousands of tulips each year, in huge naturalized drifts.

13. Sherwood Gardens, Baltimore, Md. Fine old box, 5000 azaleas, and 100,000 bulbs (planted annually) are the chief features.

14. Winterthur, Winterthur, Del. Estate of Henry F. du Pont, open to the public for a fee. Noted for naturalistic planting of azaleas and many other shrubs and trees. Site of the world-famous museum of antiques (entrance to the museum by appointment only).

15. Biltmore Estate, Asheville, N. Car. A magnificent estate with many historic trees and shrubs.

16. Avery Island, Iberia, La. Probably the finest iris collections in the U.S. and also famous for camellias. A subtropical bird sanctuary.

17. Descanso Gardens, La Canada, Calif. Over 50,000 mature camellias, in 400 varieties, a rose garden and an old Spanish garden (San Rafael).

18. Orchid Jungle, Homestead, Fla. Over 100,000 orchids and tropical exotics.

19. Brookgreen Gardens, Georgetown, S. Car. Old southern plantation of 10,000 acres of native plants and a unique collection of garden sculpture.

20. Norfolk Botanic Garden, Norfolk, Va. A new garden in a city famous for its unexcelled display of camellias and azaleas.

21. International Friendship Gardens, Michigan City, Ind. Over 100 acres of woodland and Greek, Swedish, English, Polish, French, Italian, Swiss, and Turkish gardens.

22. Sterling Forest Gardens, near Tuxedo, N.Y. A garden of 125 acres in Sterling Forest, a 30,000-acre woodland tract. There are continuous floral displays from May to November, featuring massive plantings of Dutch bulbs, azaleas, iris, peonies, roses, delphinium, lilies, Kniphofia, Michaelmas daisies and chrysanthemums.

There are also many garden tours, mostly to large private estates near the larger cities. The itinerary, dates, and fees for such garden tours can be secured from the local garden club or from current newspapers.

garganica, -us, -um (gar-gan′i-ka). From or near Gargano, Italy.

GARLAND CRABAPPLE = *Malus coronaria.*

GARLAND-FLOWER = *Hedychium coronarium* and *Daphne Cneorum.*

GARLAND HEATH = *Erica subdivaricata.*

GARLAND LARKSPUR = *Delphinium cheilanthum.*

GARLAND SPIREA = *Spiraea arguta.*

GARLIC (*Allium sativum*). The dried bulblets or cloves* of an onion-like plant, familiar enough as sold in vegetable shops, where they hang in dried braids. For culture *see* HERB GARDENING.

GARNISHES. See Cooking with Herbs at HERB GARDENING.

GARRYA (gă′ri-a). A small genus and the only one of the family **Garryaceae** (ga-ri-ă′-see-ee), comprising perhaps 15 species of evergreen shrubs chiefly from the western part of N.A., and sometimes cult. for ornament. The only species of much garden interest is **G. elliptica,** the silk-tassel tree, which is also called tassel-tree or quinine bush (it does not yield quinine). It is a hairy-branched shrub up to 6 ft. high. Leaves opposite,* without marginal teeth, leathery, elliptic or oblong, 2–3 in. long and densely hairy beneath. Male and female flowers on different plants, without petals, and in catkin*-like, rather long clusters (racemes*). Sepals 4. Stamens 4. Fruit a nearly round, velvety berry. Jan.–Mar. Hardy only in the region from Ore. to Calif., and considered by some as one of the ten best Calif. shrubs. (Named for Nicholas Garry, secretary of the Hudson's Bay Company.)

GARRYACEAE. See GARRYA.

GAS INJURY. Common manufactured gas is death to most plants, if in concentrations sufficient to be detected by odor, and sometimes in concentrations so minute that no one can smell it. One of the constituents of manufactured gas is ethylene, which, strangely enough, may actually stimulate the growth of some plants. One part of ethylene in two million parts of air, a concentration too weak to be detected chemically, will force the stamens of carnations to protrude. Natural gas does not contain ethylene.

From a practical garden standpoint the chief danger from gas is from leaky pipes, especially where street trees are near them. Sometimes the first warning will be a sudden yellowing of leaves, much too rapid to be the result of a fungous pest. Prompt stopping of the leak is the only remedy. If it is allowed to go on, the plants will certainly be killed.

Another example of the danger of leaking

---

* Special articles on the subjects indicated by an asterisk (*) will be found at the words so marked.

gas is that under frozen ground. It will often seep along below the frozen layer and come up through the unfrozen soil in a greenhouse. At the slightest hint of such trouble it is best to bring into the greenhouse a few potted tomato plants. They are more sensitive to gas poisoning than almost anything else. If enough tomato plants are scattered about the greenhouse, it is usually possible to localize the trouble, for the plants will show discoloration or droop within a few hours in a gas leakage so slight that no one can smell it. *See* the note at TOMATO and at ETHYLENE.

Gasipaes (gă′si-peez). Latinized form of gachipaes, a tropical American native name for the palm *Guilielma Gasipaes*.

GAS-PLANT = *Dictamnus albus.*

GASTERIA (gas-steer′ri-a). South African desert plants of the lily family, suitable for desert gardens outdoors in Calif. and the Southwest, the two below also grown for interest or ornament in the greenhouse. Of the 40 known species, several are grown by fanciers, the two below most commonly. They are essentially stemless plants with a dense, basal rosette of thick, 2-ranked, often dotted leaves. Flowers greenish, but the tips red or pink, in rather loose, lax clusters (racemes°). Corolla with a curved tube, swollen at the base. Fruit a capsule. (*Gasteria* is from the Greek for belly, in allusion to the swollen flower.)

The gasterias are aloe-like plants, but usually smaller, and need the same culture. *See* ALOE. *See also* SUCCULENTS.

acinacifolia Leaves very fleshy, 8–12 in. long, about 2 in. wide, not much dotted, more or less 3-edged. Flower cluster nearly 4 ft. long, sometimes branched, the flowers about 2 in. long, not much inflated.

verrucosa. Leaves 4–5 in. long, about ¾ in. wide, the surface conspicuously white-dotted, more or less 3-sided. Flower cluster about 2 ft. long, usually unbranched, the flowers pink, about 1 in. long, swollen. The most popular species in cult. and a good house plant. There are several varieties, mostly differing in the shape or wartiness of the leaves.

GATES AND GATEWAYS. A gateway is an opening in a wall or enclosure, made for purposes of entrance and exit, and capable of being closed with a barrier. A gate is the barrier which closes a gateway. Generally, the term "gate" is used to indicate the opening, together with its barrier, as one unit.

A gate has two, double functions: one, to exclude and retain; the other, to permit access and egress. Where privacy is desired, the gate should clearly express its function of exclusion, by its narrowness, by its height, or by the strength and solidity of is consturction. These same characteristics will also serve to hold one's attention within the enclosed area and prevent it from wandering to some less pleasing area beyond. Such a gateway is eminently suited to the walled city garden, adjacent to a street or service walk, or to any similar situation where

A simple but effective garden gate of iron

it is desirable to avoid intrusion from without and to limit one's perceptions to the pleasant area within. Inherent in any gateway is a slight suggestion of discrimination, a hint that someone or something is to be excluded, but in many situations this feeling should be subdued until the dominant note is one of welcome — beckoning one onward. Such a character is suitable to the entrance gateway of a country home where hospitality is the keynote of daily life, or to the gateway between a quiet garden and a woodland walk, where the essential spirit of the two areas is very similar, and an interruption in transition from one to the other undesirable.

A high wall and a wooden gate, suitable for screening an entrance court or service yard from the garden

A generous width of opening, a light and open gate structure, or even the use of piers without any actual barrier will give the gateway the character here desired. Between these two extremes of openness and guarded

---

° Special articles on the subjects indicated by an asterisk (°) will be found at the words so marked.

seclusion there are gradations of feeling which may be expressed in gate design.

It is desirable that the gate be in character with the wall, fence, or hedge in which it forms a passage, the gate and enclosure combining in a harmonious unit. Both should express the character of the area enclosed. An entrance gateway should conform in feeling to the house to which it gives access. It should be simple and unpretentious if it leads to a small, unassuming house, but given a dignified architectural treatment if it leads to a large, imposing building. Often the same structural materials are used in the entrance gate as in the house itself, creating a harmony of relationship between the two. A garden gateway may be delicately graceful, severely architectural, rugged, or rustic, depending upon the character of the garden itself. Occasionally the gateway may be given something of the character of each of two areas between which it forms a connecting link, suggesting slightly some pleasing quality of each.

While it would be absurd to place a gate where it could not possibly have any real use, it may nevertheless be employed in situations where its decorative qualities far overshadow its actual usefulness as an exit or barrier. An enclosed garden with but a single means of entrance and exit would create in the mind a disturbing sense of confinement. But a gateway at the far end, while it might seldom be used as an exit, would give a feeling of spaciousness and freedom, and at the same time could be made a dominant decorative feature. A gate can be successfully used as the terminus of a garden or as the terminus of a minor- or cross-axis. It may close the end of an allée or serve as the frame for a vista. Sometimes its chief purpose is to relieve a blank expanse of wall, its open grillwork contrasting pleasantly with the wall's smooth, unbroken surface.

There is an almost limitless variety of forms which a gate may take, depending upon the function to be served and the materials used in its construction. The latter should be chosen with due regard to the former, but necessity for economy is sometimes an influential factor.

Gates may be high or low, single or double, depending upon function and proportional relationship to walls, etc. The materials chiefly employed in their construction are wood and iron. Wooden gates may be of either solid or open construction. They may be plain or they may be decorated with pickets, panels, moldings, perforations, latticework, spindles, or applied ironwork. Iron gates may be extremely simple or they may assume the infinitely varied and complicated forms peculiar to wrought-iron work. Gates may also have supporting posts or piers of wood, brick, stone, or ironwork. These likewise may be plain, or may be decorated with such ornaments as caps, moldings, tiles, finials, or sculptured figures and escutcheons.

Careful thought and good taste can do much to achieve suitability and harmony of design in a gateway, but for best results the advice of a trained designer is indispensable. — A. F. and B. J. L. *See also* Lych Gate.

GAULTHERIA (gaul-theer'ri-a). Beautiful evergreen shrubs (some herb-like) of the family Ericaceae, most of the 100 species from the Andes, a few from eastern As. and North America. They are low or prostrate plants with usually alternate,* toothed leaves. Flowers solitary in the leaf axils* or in small, terminal clusters. Calyx* ultimately becomes fleshy, colored, and enclosing the fruit, which is really a capsule, although the fruit is apparently berry-like. Corolla urn-shaped. Stamens 10. (Named for a Doctor Gaultier, a physician in Quebec.)

All the plants below need a decidely acid soil and are best grown in the wild garden or rock garden, preferably in partial shade. They do not transplant easily, and it is better to plant potted specimens than to attempt transferring them from the wild. They may be propagated by cuttings of half-ripened wood, or by seeds sown in peaty sand under a bell-jar. But the seeds are extremely minute and hard to handle.

hispidula. Creeping snowberry, moxieberry or running-birch. It has a creeping, slender stem, and small, alternate leaves that are ovalish and scarcely ¼ in. long. Flowers white, bell-shaped, not over ⅕ in. long, solitary and nodding in the leaf axils.* Fruit aromatic (birch flavor), white, berry-like, and scarcely ⅕ in. in diameter. It grows in cold bogs and wet, often evergreen, woods in the northern part of N.A., and is suited only to similar places in the wild garden or rock garden. Formerly called *Chiogenes hispidula.*

miqueliana. A low shrub, scarcely over 12 in. high, the stems inclined to sprawl. Leaves ovalish, about 1 in. long, the margins with blunt, glandular* teeth. Flowers small, urn-shaped, white, crowded in terminal clusters (racemes*) followed by a pea-sized white fruit. Jap. June. Hardy from zone* 5 southward.

nummularoides. A low, prostrate shrub, its hairy branchlets much intertwined. Leaves

An inviting wooden garden gate, effective because of the arch and planting

---

* Special articles on the subjects indicated by an asterisk (*) will be found at the words so marked.

nearly round, about ½ in. long, with minute, bristly teeth, and a small glandular (sticky) tip. Flowers minute, from the leaf joints and mostly hidden by the foliage, pink or white. Fruit fleshy and blue-black. Himalayas. Hardy from zone* 5 southward.

procumbens. The common wintergreen of our dry woods; called also checkerberry, teaberry, ground holly, and spiceberry. A prostrate, herb-like, evergreen, woody plant, the stems half underground, the tips upright and about 4 in. high. Leaves ovalish, about 1¾ in. long, the marginal teeth often bristly. Flowers solitary, nodding, white or pinkish, about ¼ in. long. Fruit scarlet, pea-size. Eastern N.A. May–July. Hardy everywhere.

Shallon. Salal. A Pacific Coast, evergreen shrub, more or less spreading and not over 18 in. high. Leaves round-oval, 3–5 in. long. Flower cluster terminal, 2–5 in. long, the corolla pink or white, about ½ in. long. Fruit purplish-black, nearly ½ in. in diameter. Alaska to Calif. May–June. Hardy from zone* 4 southward, but chiefly suited to the rock garden.

GAURA (gau′ra). Perhaps 20 species of rather coarse, chiefly perennial, North American herbs of the family Onagraceae, the two below somewhat grown for ornament in the more informal border. They are stout herbs with alternate* leaves and white or pink, summer-blooming flowers in terminal clusters (spikes or racemes*). Calyx* tubular below, but its 4 lobes separate and bent backward. Petals slightly unequal, separate, the base narrowed into a claw.* Fruit 4–5-ribbed, nut-like. (*Gaura* is from the Greek for superb.)

Both species are of the easiest culture in any ordinary garden soil, and are readily increased by spring or fall division. The first species is more hardy than *G. lindheimeri,* which needs a mulch north of zone* 5.

coccinea. Wild honeysuckle (not a true honeysuckle). A perennial herb 12–30 in. high. Leaves oblongish, about 1 in. long. Flowers about ½ in. long, pink, red, or white. S. D. to Mex.

lindheimeri. A perennial herb, 2–4 ft. high and bushy. Leaves lance-shaped, 1½–3½ in. long, white. La. to Tex. and Mex.

GAY-FEATHER = *Liatris scariosa* and *L. spicata.*

GAYLUSSACIA. See HUCKLEBERRY.

GAY ORCHIS = *Orchis spectabilis.*

GAY-WINGS = *Polygala paucifolia.*

GAZANIA (ga-zay′ni-a). Showy, South African flower garden herbs of the daisy family, comprising about two dozen species, a few long cult. for their handsome flower heads. Leaves alternate,* but the plants often nearly stemless and the leaves thus basal. Flower heads solitary, long-stalked, day-blooming, but closing at night or in cloudy weather. Rays yellow, golden, or white (in ours), often with a dark spot at the base, the head thus with a dark eye.* (Named for Theodore of Gaza, a translator of Theophrastus.)

Gazania longiscapa is a fine, summer-blooming plant, best treated as a tender

annual. (*See* ANNUALS.) The other two are perennials, not quite hardy north of zone* 5 without mulching. In the South they may bloom nearly all year. Propagated by division, or by cuttings of basal shoots taken in Aug. and rooted in sand. They are sometimes called African daisy.

longiscapa. Practically stalkless. Leaves more or less deeply cut, feather-fashion, felty-white beneath. Flower heads golden-yellow, dark-eyed, the flower stalk smooth, 6–8 in. long.

rigens. A perennial herb, the stems leafy, short, and branched. Leaves spatula-shaped, felty-white beneath. Flower heads about 1½ in. wide, the stalk smooth, the rays* orange, but with a black spot near the base.

splendens. Perhaps a hybrid plant and unknown in the wild. An erect perennial 9–18 in. high, the leaves silky, and very narrow. Flower heads large and showy, the rays orange, but with a black and white spot at the base.

GAZEBO. See STRUCTURES.

GEAN. See CHERRY.

GEIGER TREE = *Cordia Sebestena.*

GELSEMIUM (gel-see′mi-um). Two (or perhaps three) evergreen, woody vines of the family Loganiaceae, one Asiatic, the other, **G. sempervirens,** of the southeastern U.S., and famous as the Carolina or yellow jasmine, although it is not the true jasmine (*see* JASMINUM). It is a beautiful vine, climbing 10–20 ft. high, the leaves usually opposite,* oblongish, 2½–4 in. long and shining. Flowers bright yellow, very fragrant, in a dense cluster (cyme*) usually in the leaf axil.* Corolla funnel-shaped, about 1 in. long. Stamens 5, alternating with the 5 short lobes of the corolla. Fruit a flattened, short-beaked pod (capsule*) about ¾ in. long, its seeds winged. This beautiful porch-climbing vine, very popular from Charleston southward can be grown in any ordinary garden soil, and can be propagated by seeds or cuttings. Once established it spreads by suckers.* It is not hardy north of zone* 6, and its juice is dangerously poisonous. (*Gelsemium* is a Latinized version of *gelsomino,* the Italian for jasmine.)

geminiflora, -us, -um (jem-i-ni-flow′ra). Twin- or several-flowered.

geminispina, -us, -um (jem-i-ni-spy′na). Twin- or several-spined.

gemmifera, -us, -um (jem-mif′er-ra). Bearing buds.

GENE. The unit of inheritance, sometimes called a factor or determiner. It is the lowest amount that hereditary material is ordinarily divided into and corresponds somewhat to the chemical atom. Genes may differ in size, and they are contained in the chromosomes* in linear arrangements.

GENERA. Plural of genus (which see).

GENETICS. See HEREDITY.

genevensis, -e (je-nee-ven′sis). From Geneva, Switzerland.

GENIP = *Genipa americana* and *Melicocca bijuga.*

---

* Special articles on the subjects indicated by an asterisk (*) will be found at the words so marked.

GENIPA (jen′i-pa). A small genus of chiefly West Indian shrubs or trees of the family Rubiaceae, one, **G. americana**, the genip or genipap, somewhat grown in extreme southern Fla. for its edible fruits. It is not hardy north of zone* 9. It is a tree 30–50 ft. high, with opposite,* short-stalked, leathery, oblongish leaves that are nearly 12 in. long. Flowers yellowish-white, in few-flowered cymes.* Corolla salver-shaped, about 1 in. wide, its 5–6 blunt lobes slightly twisted to the left. Fruit a russet-brown berry about 2½ in. in diameter with large, dark-brown seeds. The tree, sometimes called marmalade box, is popular in the tropics, but not much known in the U.S. It needs heat and moisture for proper growth. The juicy fruit is largely used for preserves or in making beverages. (*Genipa* is the Brazilian vernacular for the tree.)

GENIPAP = *Genipa americana*.

GENISTA (je-niss′ta). Low, rather handsome, often evergreen or nearly leafless shrubs of the pea family, all from temperate or mild regions of the Old World, and comprising over 100 species. Of these only those below are much cult. in this country, and some are not hardy northward. While some of them are called broom, the common broom is a *Cytisus* (*see* BROOM), and the common genista of the florists is *Cytisus canariensis* (*see* BROOM). The genus name *Genista* is properly applied to the plants below. They are sometimes spiny, usually green-barked shrubs with compound* leaves, the leaflets often reduced to one (rarely 3), and without teeth. Flowers typically pea-like, yellow or white, usually borne in terminal clusters (racemes* or heads*), rarely in the leaf axils.* Fruit a longish, flattened pod (legume*), usually several-seeded. (*Genista* is the classical Latin name of these plants.)

The shrubs do well in dry, open places, but they do not transplant easily and should not be moved when once established. They can be increased by seeds or by layering.*

aethnensis. An apparently leafless shrub, 10–15 ft. high, the solitary leaflet silky and soon falling. Flowers almost stalkless in a loose cluster (raceme*), golden-yellow, about ½ in. long. Fruit a curved pod, about ½ in. long, densely hairy in youth. Sicily. Summer. Hardy from zone* 6 southward.

canariensis = *Cytisus canariensis*. See BROOM.

germanica. A rather spiny shrub, not over 18 in. high, the twigs hairy. Leaves elliptic or oblong, hairy, about ¾ in. long, deep green. Flowers small, in a short cluster (raceme*) followed by a silky-hairy pod about ⅓ in. long. Eu. May. Hardy from zone* 4 southward.

hispanica. Spanish broom. A densely branched, spiny, often leafless shrub, not over 18 in. high, usually less. Leaflet one, ovalish, about ½ in. long, often soon deciduous.* Flowers golden-yellow, in a dense head of 2–10 blooms. Pod hairy. Southern Eu. May–June. Hardy from zone* 4 southward. The *var.* **nana** is about half as high, and often used to plant

sloping banks. For another plant called Spanish broom, *see* SPARTIUM.

horrida. A low, very spiny shrub, scarcely over 2 ft. high, its leaves with 3 leaflets which are narrowly linear, about ½ in. long and silky. Flowers in dense, small, closely packed heads, yellow. Pyrenees. Summer. Hardy from zone* 6 southward.

monosperma. A nearly leafless shrub 3–8 ft. high. Flowers fragrant, white, in clusters in the leaf axils. Spain and northern Africa. Mar.–Apr. Hardy from zone* 6 southward. Little known in this country.

pilosa. Prostrate and warty, the leaflets one, oblongish, scarcely ½ in. long. Flowers yellow in sparse clusters in the leaf axils. Pod nearly 1½ in. long, silky. Southern Eu. May–July. Hardy from zone* 4 southward.

radiata. Somewhat resembling *G. horrida,* but the plant not spiny, and up to 3 ft. high. Leaves evergreen (in mild climates), the 3 leaflets about ½ in. long and silky. Flowers yellow, in small heads. Central and eastern Eu. June–Aug. Hardy from zone* 5 southward.

sagittalis. Nearly prostrate shrub, chiefly suited to the rock garden, its branches 2-winged. Leaflets one, ovalish or narrower, nearly 1 in. long. Flowers yellow, in terminal clusters. Eurasia. June. Hardy from zone* 4 southward. For culture *see* ROCK GARDEN.

tinctoria. Woadwaxen (or woodwaxen); called also dyer's greenweed, and the best-known species in cult. It is an upright shrub 24–36 in. high, with a single leaflet to each leaf. Leaflets oblongish, ½–1½ in. long, smooth, but fringed with hair on the margin. Flowers yellow, in profuse clusters. Pod narrow-oblong, often slightly hairy. Eurasia. June–Aug. Hardy from zone* 3 southward. There are several hort. forms, mostly varying in habit, some of them dwarf. The *var.* **plena** had double flowers.

villarsi. A low, spineless shrub, much intertwined, its branches often rooting at the joints and hence making broad patches. Leaflets solitary, densely hairy, nearly stalkless and scarcely ½ in. long. Flowers yellow, hairy, in loose clusters (racemes*), followed by a small, silky pod. Southern Eu. June–July. Hardy from zone* 6 southward.

GENTIAN. See GENTIANA.

GENTIANA (jen-she-ā′na). The gentians comprise a genus of perhaps 400 species of herbs, family Gentianaceae, some of them choice plants for the rock garden, border or wild garden, and all of them needing somewhat specialized culture. While most of them are perennials, a few, like our fringed gentian, are biennials, and some are annuals. They are chiefly plants of cool, moist regions, especially mountain meadows and some on alpine summits. Leaves opposite,* rarely in 3′s, stalkless in the main, and without marginal teeth. Flowers showy, often solitary or in few-flowered clusters, prevailingly blue, but occasionally purple, yellow, red or white. Corolla 4–5-lobed, often with teeth between the lobes, which in some (the fringed gentian) are beautifully fringed. Stamens 5, inserted in the tube of the corolla. Fruit a capsule.* (Named for King Gentius of Illyria, who is credited with faith in the medicinal value of gentians.) Some of the Asiatic species are

---

* Special articles on the subjects indicated by an asterisk (*) will be found at the words so marked.

credited to the genus *Gentianella,* a suggestion not here adopted.

Cultural directions are difficult because the plants have such diverse habitat preferences. Those suited to the rock, wild, or bog garden are specified below and their culture should be sought at ROCK GARDEN or BOG GARDEN or WILD GARDEN. For the others there are special cultural notes. *See also* BLUE GARDEN.

acaulis. A perennial rock garden plant and the common blue gentian of European mountains. Not usually over 4 in. high, with elliptic or narrower leaves. Flower solitary, deep blue, about 2 in. long, sometimes spotted inside. Mountains of the Alps and Pyrenees. Summer. Various other names for this plant, such as *G. excisa,* have been suggested. For its forms, or perhaps species, and their culture, *see* ROCK GARDEN.

andrewsi. Closed gentian, or bottle gentian. A North American perennial herb 12–20 in. high. Leaves ovalish or narrower, 1–2 in. long. Flowers about 1½ in. long, purplish-blue, more or less permanently closed; *i.e.,* the corolla inarching and not open. Eastern N.A. Aug.–Oct. It is the easiest to grow of all our native gentians; choose a cool, moist, shady place.

asclepiadea. A European perennial herb, 12–18 in. high and suited to the shadier parts of the herbaceous border. Leaves ovalish to lance-shaped. Flowers dark blue, about 1½ in. long, usually solitary in the leaf axils,* or in small clusters resembling leafy racemes.* Southern Eu. Summer.

calycosa. A branched and erect perennial, 8–12 in. high, with ovalish blunt-tipped leaves about 1 in. long. Flowers solitary or a few, bell-shaped, about 1½ in. long, dark blue but green-spotted. Pacific Coast. Autumn. Prefers moist or wet site.

clusi. A European perennial, not over 4 in. high and best suited to the rock garden. Leaves mostly in a basal rosette, leathery, more or less stiff and elliptic. Flower solitary, funnel- or bell-shaped, about 2 in. long, deep blue but paler at the throat. June.

crinita. Fringed gentian. A beautiful biennial, North American meadow herb that should never be dug from the wild, and will not grow if it is. Leaves lance-shaped or broadest toward the tip. Flowers bright blue, usually solitary and terminal, about 2 in. long and very showy, the lobes of the corolla beautifully fringed. Eastern N.A. Sept. and Oct. For its difficult cult. from seed *see Wild Flower Gardening* by Norman Taylor (Princeton, N. J.: D. Van Nostrand Co., 1955), pp. 116–18.

cruciata. A Eurasian perennial herb 4–10 in. high. Leaves ovalish or narrower. Flowers with a corolla about ¾ in. long, dark blue, usually in small clusters in the leaf axils.* Suited to the hilly regions north of zone* 4. *See* BLUE GARDEN.

farreri. A more or less prostrate perennial herb, the ascending stems not over 4 in. high. Leaves very narrow or line-like, usually partly united at the base. Flowers deep blue, solitary, about 1½ in. long, the corolla lobes with a white or yellowish band. China. Aug.–Sept.

gentianella. A listed name for rock garden species, but of uncertain application. By some it is considered as a form of *Gentiana acaulis* (*see* that species at ROCK GARDEN).

gracilipes. A decumbent perennial, often rosette-forming, the stems scarcely 10 in. long. Basal leaves narrow, nearly 6 in. long, the

stem leaves less. Flowers solitary and terminal, about 1 in. long, green outside but purplish-blue inside. China. Aug.–Sept. Some of the plants offered by the trade as *Gentiana purdomi* belong here.

hascombensis. A fairly common name in the catalogues, the plants said to be derived by hybridization in England. But the recently issued *Dictionary of Gardening* by the Royal Horticultural Society does not mention *Gentiana hascombensis.*

lagodechiana = *Gentiana septemfida.*

linearis. A slender bog perennial 12–20 in. high, with narrow leaves. Flowers in terminal clusters, blue or white, the corolla nearly 2 in. long. Eastern N.A. Should be grown in the bog garden (which see) or on wet, rocky ledges. Sept.

lutea. Yellow gentian or bitterwort. A perennial, often 3–4 ft. high, and cult. for centuries in Eu. for its bitter, tonic rootstock. Leaves coarse, plaited, 9–12 in. long, pointed both ends and resembling those of the white hellebore (*Veratrum album*). Flowers yellow, about 1 in. long, the calyx resembling a small spathe.* Eu. and Asia Minor. Little grown in the U.S., but suited to the perennial border.

macaulayi. A hybrid gentian — *sino-ornata* × *farreri,* with the leaves of the latter. Flowers deep blue, nearly 2½ in. long, funnel-shaped. A perennial of garden origin. Sept.–Oct.

menziesi. Erect and not over 1 ft. high. Leaves oblong or elliptic, about ¾ in. long. Flowers with the calyx* split down one side, purple or bluish, about 1 in. long. Northwestern N.A. Sept.

parryi. An erect perennial, 12–16 in. high, the narrow lance-shaped leaves about 1½ in. long. Flowers showy, nearly 2 in. long, bright blue. Utah to Wyo. Aug.–Sept.

Pneumonanthe. A Eurasian perennial herb 5–14 in. high, and suited to the open border. Leaves oblongish or narrower. Flowers dark blue, but green-striped on the outside, about 1½ in. long. Aug.–Sept.

Porphyrio. A slender perennial from the pine barrens from N.J. to S. Car., its opposite, very narrow leaves 1–3½ in. long. Flowers solitary and terminal, about 2 in. long, funnel-shaped and bright blue. Autumn. Prefers a definitely acid soil and a moist site.

purdomi. It is doubtful if this Chinese gentian is much cult. in the U.S. Most of the plants offered under this name are apt to be *G. gracilipes* (which see).

septemfida. An Asiatic rock garden perennial, sometimes grown in the border (*see* BLUE GARDEN). It is erect, 9–15 in. high. Flowers dark blue, about 2 in. long, and grouped in a terminal cluster. Aug.–Sept. For culture *see* ROCK GARDEN.

sino-ornata. A handsome perennial, about 6–8 in. high, spreading by stolons.* Leaves narrowly lance-shaped, borne in rosettes. Flowers solitary, terminal, 1½–2 in. long, the corolla whitish-yellow, irregularly splotched with purple. China.

tibetica. A Himalayan perennial 10–20 in. high, the leaves lance-shaped. Flowers about 1½ in. long, yellowish-white, but lilac-tinted, mostly crowded in the upper leaf axils.* Aug. For culture *see* ROCK GARDEN.

verna. A rock garden, tufted* perennial, scarcely more than 3 in. high, the small leaves ovalish. Flowers about 1 in. long, terminal, solitary and dark blue. Eu.

walujewi. A rock garden perennial not over 8 in. high, the leaves elliptic or lance-shaped.

---

* Special articles on the subjects indicated by an asterisk (*) will be found at the words so marked.

Flowers whitish, but blue-dotted, usually crowded in a terminal cluster. Turkestan. Aug.–Sept. For culture see ROCK GARDEN.

GENTIANACEAE (jen-she-a-nay′see-ee). The gentian family, mostly herbaceous, contains 70 genera and over 800 widely distributed species of often showy plants, but few of the genera are much known in the garden. Two of them, *Menyanthes* and *Nymphoides*, are aquatic or bog plants, sometimes, but not here, considered as belonging to a separate family, the Menyanthaceae. Both have alternate° leaves.

Leaves otherwise opposite,° without marginal teeth. Flowers usually showy, often grouped in cymes,° the corolla more or less tubular or spreading, sometimes beautifully fringed (see GENTIANA). Fruit a 2-valved pod (capsule°).

Less than a dozen genera are of garden interest. *Eustoma* is the Canada pest and attractive in spite of its name. *Exacum* contains Old World herbs not hardy in cold regions; *Frasera* contains the columbo; while *Sabatia* is mostly confined to salt marshes. Of all the cult. genera *Gentiana* is by far the most important, many of the species being rare and interesting plants from mountain meadows and summits.

Technical flower characters: Corolla regular, 4–5-lobed (more in *Sabatia*). Calyx 4–12-parted, often persistent. Stamens 4–12, inserted on the corolla. Ovary superior,° 1-celled or rarely 2-celled, with numerous ovules.

GENTIAN FAMILY = Gentianaceae.

gentianoides (jen-she-a-noy′deez, but see OÏDES). Gentian-like.

GENUS (plural, genera). The simplest grouping or category of plants, so classified because they are more like each other than like any other group. Common examples are *Rosa* (genus name for all the roses), *Quercus* (genus name for the oaks). No one needs to be confused by the use of such generic names for an easily recognized category of plants, but many gardeners and all beginners are apt to confuse genus and species.

A genus is a group of species (which see), linked together by usually obvious, but sometimes rather puzzling, botanical characters. To take a simple illustration: the genus name of the larkspur is *Delphinium*, a generic name properly printed in italics and with a capital *D*. This typography for genus names is followed throughout this encyclopedia (unless the generic name is the usual bold-face entry word or a cross-reference). To this genus *Delphinium* belong all the larkspurs, each one of which is a separate species. In this book there are eight species of larkspur noted under *Delphinium*, but as in most reference works, the name *Delphinium* is not repeated at each of the eight, but it is understood to cover all of them. Also, as in practically all reference works, *Delphinium* is abbreviated to *D*. after the first use of the full name.

Some genera have only a single species. Common examples of such monotypic genera, as they are called, are *Sanguinaria,* which contains only the single species *canadensis,* the bloodroot. Another is *Chamaedaphne,* with only the species *calyculata,* or leather-leaf. But most genera have several or many species, and some are enormous (see CAREX, SOLANUM, EUPHORBIA, and CRATAEGUS).

In the ENCYCLOPEDIA OF GARDENING there are nearly 1800 genera of sufficient hort. interest to demand inclusion, but there are thousands of other genera of ferns and flowering plants known in the world.

Another feature of generic names that sometimes leads to confusion is the type in which they are printed when they have become so common that everyone uses them as the common name of the plant. Examples are *Rhododendron* (a generic name) and rhododendron (the common name for these plants). There are many other such generic names, of which a few are:

Aster and aster.
Chrysanthemum and chrysanthemum.
Cosmos and cosmos.
Delphinium and delphinium.

This difference in typography between generic names and common ones derived from the genus is maintained throughout this encyclopedia. *See also* SPECIES, PLANT NAMES, PLANT FAMILY.

geometrizans (jee-o-met′ri-zans). In a geometrical pattern.

GEORGE PEABODY ARBORVITAE = *Thuja occidentalis lutea.*

GEORGIA. The Cherokee rose is the state flower and the live oak the state tree. The state lies in zones° 6 and 7.

SOILS. Silt loam soils predominate in the limestone valley of northwest Georgia. Shallow soils are found on the steep slopes of the northern and northeastern mountain area, with rich, loamy soils in the valleys. The Piedmont plateau in the north-central part of the state is characterized by red Cecil-clay loams and sandy loams. The coastal plain, comprising the lower half of Georgia, consists mostly of Norfolk and Tifton sandy loams in the northern and middle sections and of Norfolk sand in the flatwood areas near the coast. River valleys and delta areas of the coastal plain generally contain deposited silts and fine sands.

CLIMATE. The long-term mean temperature for January ranges from 40° F. in the extreme north to 55° F. in the southern border counties. The long-term mean for July ranges from 74° F. in the north to approximately 82° F. at several central and southern stations. The average daily range in temperature varies from 20 to 28 degrees with the widest ranges occurring in spring and fall. Maximum temperatures of 100° F. or more have been recorded in all parts of the state but readings that high are very unusual in the extreme north. The highest temperature recorded in Georgia was 112° at

---

° Special articles on the subjects indicated by an asterisk (°) will be found at the words so marked.

Louisville in July 1952. Record low temperatures range for 15° in the extreme south to the all-time low of 17° below zero in Floyd County in January 1940.

Freeze Dates

Town	Median Date of Last Freeze in Spring (32° F. or less)	Latest Freeze (32° F. or less)	Median Date of First Freeze in Fall (32° F. or less)	Earliest Freeze (32° F. or less)
Clayton	Apr. 16	May 21	Oct. 19	Oct. 1
Dahlonega	Apr. 2	Apr. 23	Nov. 1	Oct. 7
Athens	Mar. 29	Apr. 21	Nov. 10	Oct. 18
Griffin	Mar. 28	Apr. 21	Nov. 12	Oct. 24
Thomasville	Mar. 1	Apr. 16	Nov. 26	Oct. 30

RAINFALL. The average annual rainfall ranges from 75 inches in the northeast corner of the state to 42 inches in parts of the east-central section. The long-term averages for the nine climatological divisions of the state are given below. The northern third of the state has its greatest rainfall during the winter months, with a secondary maximum in midsummer. In the south, there is a definite summer maximum in the rainfall distribution. Most summer rainfall occurs in connection with thunderstorms which have their greatest frequency in this part of the state. Rainfall is more evenly distributed through the year in central Georgia, but all sections have their least rainfall in autumn.

Average Annual Precipitation, Georgia (1931–1955)

Division	Average in inches
Northwest	52.26
North Central	51.13
Northeast	53.24
West Central	49.62
Central	46.36
East Central	42.76
Southwest	50.28
South Central	46.15
Southeast	47.87

GARDENING. Gardening is a well-organized and popular pastime in Georgia. The Ladies Garden Club of Athens, organized in 1891, is considered to be the first formal garden club of America. Since its founding the movement has grown and spread throughout the state. In all there are approximately 700 ladies' garden clubs in Georgia, with eleven men's garden clubs (1958). Garden club activities also include clubs of the Garden Club of America, the home office of which is at 598 Madison Avenue, New York 22, N.Y., and the Men's Garden Club of America, whose Executive Secretary is Mr. George Spader, Morrisville, New York.

Gardening, especially vegetable and fruit gardening, is also encouraged by the 4-H and FFA or FHA clubs. Organized home and civic improvement projects sponsored by the Agricultural Extension Service in co-operation with various industries and civic groups stress landscaping and maintenance of ornamental plantings. There are approximately 41,580 individual gardening or home beautification projects among 4-H young people in Georgia each year. In addition there are some 3000 garden projects among FFA and FHA boys and girls.

ORNAMENTAL HORTICULTURE. The varied climate of Georgia permits the use of a great diversity of ornamental and garden plants over the state as a whole. In the extreme southern part and along the Atlantic Coast some of the hardier citrus fruits and palms are useful whereas such cold-climate plants as hemlock, white pine, rhododendron, peony, and raspberry thrive in the mountainous area.

TREES. The principal large shade and ornamental trees of the coastal plain are the live oak, the longleaf pine, white oak, water oak, willow oak, elm, camphor tree, magnolia, yellow poplar (tulip-tree), pecan, the black and sweet gums, and red maple. The dogwood, American holly, cassine, cherry laurel, mimosa, and palmetto are desirable small trees. In the Piedmont, the most popular large shade and ornamental trees are the water, pin, red, and white oaks, the loblolly pine, yellow poplar, ginkgo, magnolia, sweet gum, black gum, river birch, and pecan. Smaller favorite trees are the hackberry, mimosa, redbud, dogwood, American holly, dwarf maple, hawthorn, and flowering crabapple. In the mountainous area the most satisfactory large trees are the hemlock, white pine, chestnut oak, red oak, yellow poplar, black birch, and weeping willow. Smaller trees include the sourwood, redbud, serviceberry, and crabapples.

Some of the above warrant special comment. The live oak is undoubtedly the most satisfactory large tree in the sandy soils of the lower half of the state. It is evergreen, graceful, long-lived, tough, fairly rapid-growing, adaptable, and practically immune to diseases and insects. It will grow as far up as the lower Piedmont but does not assume its most graceful form and shape out of the coastal plain. The water oak, a rapid-growing tree, is widely planted throughout the lower two-thirds of the state. In recent years, however, a serious defoliating disease has lessened its popularity. The yellow poplar (tulip-tree) is found throughout the state and has been planted to a limited extent in parks and on large estates. The yellow poplar, like the pines and gums, is more likely to be found in new subdivisions and parks where it has been saved from the original trees present at the time of the development. Pecans are especially desired as shade trees on farms and around suburban homes and are found as residual trees from commercial groves that have been turned into subdivisions. Dogwoods grow most satisfactorily as understory trees, and are not at their best when planted

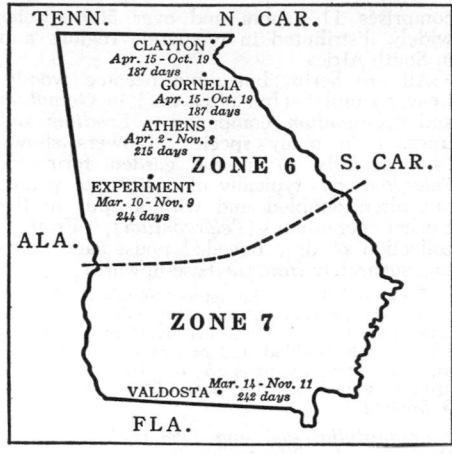

TENN.   N. CAR.

CLAYTON
Apr. 15 - Oct. 19
187 days

GORNELIA
Apr. 15 - Oct. 19
187 days

ATHENS
Apr. 2 - Nov. 3
215 days

ZONE 6   S. CAR.

EXPERIMENT
Mar. 10 - Nov. 9
244 days

ALA.

ZONE 7

VALDOSTA
Mar. 14 - Nov. 11
242 days

FLA.

GEORGIA

The zones of hardiness crossing Georgia are those shown on the map located at ZONE, which should be consulted for details. The dates are the average latest killing frost in spring and the first one in the fall. The figures below the dates show the average length of the growing season.

in full sunlight. The mimosa tree is very popular throughout the lower three-fourths of Georgia, but the widespread fusarium wilt disease makes it advisable to plant only wilt-resistant strains.

SHRUBS. Georgia is blessed with a wealth of beautiful shrubs, either indigenous or adapted. In the spring the entire coastal plain is ablaze with Indica azaleas and the Piedmont with Kurumes, hardy hybrids, and native deciduous azaleas. One native species, *Azalea prunifolia,* reserves its beauty for July and August. Rhododendrons, both native and hybrid, and mountain laurel are a riot of color in the mountains in May and early June. *Camellia japonica* and *Camellia Sasanqua* bloom from September to March from the lower Piedmont to the southernmost boundaries of the state. In the Piedmont a few early varieties can be counted on for blooms before severe freezes, and some of the hardier kinds will bloom in occasional years in midwinter or early spring. The foliage of most varieties is hardy even in the Piedmont. Gardenias and hydrangeas can be depended on for summer flowers throughout most of the state. Oleander thrives on the sea islands and adjacent mainland, and provides a variety of summer color for these areas. Crape myrtle blooms in summer throughout most of the state and is typical of the Southland. Other popular and satisfactory flowering shrubs include winter jasmine which blooms in January or early February, flowering quince, golden bell, Scotch broom, spirea, yucca, and roses of all kinds.

Typical evergreen foliage shrubs of widespread use and popularity include the American and Oriental hollies, tea olive, boxwood, euonymus, the large-leaved privets, abelia, photinia, *Eurya,* nandina, aucuba, low-growing juniper, and arborvitae.

Fragrant-leaved or fragrant-flowered shrubs, such as the banana shrub, tea olive, and Chinese anise (*Illicium verum*), are old favorites in Georgia gardens.

VINES. English ivy, smilax, Carolina jasmine, wisteria, clematis, Banksia rose, Virginia creeper, and honeysuckle are prized in landscaping for various uses.

GROUND COVERS. *Vinca minor* (periwinkle) and *Vinca major,* English ivy, liriope (various varieties), *Euonymus fortunei,* creeping juniper, and galax (mountains only) are popular and valuable ground covers and border plants.

LAWNS. The most widely used and popular grass for sunny locations is common Bermuda overseeded with Italian rye grass each August or September. This combination, when it is properly maintained, gives a very satisfactory year-round green lawn throughout most of Georgia. Several new Bermuda varieties make a finer turf and are superior for certain uses, but none of them can be overseeded with rye grass as satisfactorily as common Bermuda. The best new varieties are Sunturf (for the Piedmont), Tifgreen, Tiflawn, and Tiffine.

The zoysia grasses (*Zoysia Matrella*) and Meyer zoysia are excellent summer grasses for both sun and shade. They are slow to cover but tend to crowd out other grasses and weeds and require less maintenance for equal elegance. Zoysias "green up" faster in the spring and stay greener longer in the fall than Bermudas.

St. Augustine grass is a popular wide-bladed grass for the coastal plain and lower Piedmont. It is a fast grower and crowds out other grasses and many weeds. It is shade- and salt-tolerant and for the latter reason grows well along the coast and on the sea islands.

Centipede is another important medium-wide-bladed grass for the coastal plain. It is aggressive and low-growing, and tolerates acid soil. Its fertility requirement is low, and it grows in partial shade in adapted areas. Carpet grass is used throughout the state in low areas in sun or shade. It is very wide-bladed. Kentucky bluegrass and the fescues do well in the mountains and upper Piedmont when provided with ample moisture, high fertilization, and high lime.

ANNUALS, BIENNIALS, AND PERENNIALS. Practically any important garden flower grown in the United States, except strictly alpine or tropical plants, can be successfully grown in some part of Georgia on the proper site with appropriate culture. Only a few of the most typical and important will be mentioned.

Dahlias are popular and thrive in the upper two-thirds of the state. They are one of the most widely exhibited plants in fairs

---

* Special articles on the subjects indicated by an asterisk (*) will be found at the words so marked.

and fall flower shows. Chrysanthemums of all types are likewise popular and widely grown. They are also the chief greenhouse commercial crop of the state. Hemerocallis, an old summer favorite, has been revived in recent years by the introduction of many new varieties. Peonies do well in the mountains and some varieties thrive as far south as Atlanta. Columbine and foxglove are also favorites.

Spring-flowering bulbs are a riot of bloom throughout Georgia. Snowdrop, hyacinth, narcissus, and Dutch iris are widely planted. Varieties of daffodils and jonquils remain and increase around old homesites and along cultivated areas and roadways. Tulip, anemone, ranunculus, and crocus make a splendid show in the mountains and upper Piedmont, but most varieties must be re-planted from bulbs from more northern regions every year or two for best results.

Native iris, gladiolus, Easter lily, amaryllis, canna, caladium, and spider lily are other favorites.

Of the annuals, verbena, marigold, petunia, annual phlox, larkspur, salvia, celosia, and zinnia are popular.

FRUITS. The peach has rightfully made Georgia famous. The Fort Valley area in the central-southern Piedmont is a concentrated early-peach area. Carloads of peaches start moving north from here in middle or late May. Peaches are grown throughout the Piedmont with concentrated areas in Meriwether and Spalding counties and in the vicinity of Commerce. Georgia is also the largest producer of improved varieties of pecans. There is said to be a pecan tree for every person in Georgia. There are trees in every county, but the largest areas are in the lower Piedmont and upper coastal plain. There is a small but thriving apple industry in the mountain counties. Certain varieties of apples grow as far south as Atlanta and the earliest apples on the market come from the northern Georgia area. Muscadine grapes are typical of the Southland and are grown for local market and in home gardens. The American bunch grape thrives only in the mountains of northern Georgia where it is grown to a limited extent for wine and for local market. Improved rabbiteye blueberries, blackberries, dewberries, and strawberries are grown throughout the state. Georgia is also one of the principal producers of vegetables for northern markets.

The address of the Agricultural Experiment Station, which has kindly supplied this information about the state, is University of Georgia, Athens, Georgia.

GERANIACEAE (ger-ray-nee-ā′see-ee). The geranium or cranesbill family is of great hort. interest because it contains the common garden geranium (*Pelargonium*) and the cranesbill or wild geranium which belongs to the genus *Geranium*. The only other cult. genus is *Erodium*, but the family comprises 11 genera and over 500 species widely distributed in temperate regions and in South Africa.

All are herbs, but some become woody. Leaves simple* (but often cut) in *Geranium* and *Pelargonium*, compound in *Erodium* and fragrant in many species. Flowers showy (spectacularly so in the garden forms of *Pelargonium*), typically of 5 separate petals, but often doubled and with a spur in the garden geranium (*Pelargonium*). Fruit a collection of dry, 1-seeded pods, each splitting separately from the base upward.

Technical flower characters: Sepals 5, distinct from one another. Petals (typically) 5, separate, but with the margins overlapping, sometimes much doubled and one or more produced into a spur. Stamens 5 or 10, rarely 15, usually joined at the base. Ovary superior,* 3–5-lobed.

geraniifolia, -us, -um (ger-ray′ni-i-fo-li-a). With geranium-like leaves.

GERANIUM (ger-ray′ni-um). Hardy perennial, biennial, or rarely annual herbs, commonly called cranesbill, and comprising about 275 species of the family Geraniaceae. The genus does not include the common garden geranium, as this belongs to *Pelargonium* (which see). The genus *Geranium* includes several plants of garden interest, mostly suited to the border or to the wild garden. They are generally low, often half-prostrate herbs, with forking stems and more or less dissected or lobed, roundish leaves divided finger-fashion. Flowers regular, not spurred as in *Pelargonium* (the garden or common geranium), the petals 5, the stamens 10. Fruit a collection of elastically splitting, beaked carpels* which persist for some time. (*Geranium* is from the Greek for a crane, the beaked fruits resembling a crane's bill.)

The cranesbills are of easy culture, and the perennial species are readily increased by division of the clumps in spring or fall. The only annual, *G. robertianum*, should be raised from seed sown where wanted. Some of them, as noted below, are woodland plants, and such should be grown in partially shaded parts of the wild garden. Nearly all of them bloom in early spring.

argenteum. A biennial or perennial herb, scarcely over 6 in. high, the white-silvery leaves 5–7-parted. Flowers about 1 in. wide, pink, but darker-veined. Northern Italy. For culture *see* Moraine at ROCK GARDEN.

cinereum. An almost stemless perennial, not over 6 in. high, its chiefly basal leaves 5–7-parted, bluish-green, their lobes wedge-shaped. Flowers about 1 in. wide, the dark-veined petals pink. Pyrenees. June.

endressi. A perennial 12–18 in. high. Leaves 5-parted or lobed nearly to the middle. Flowers about 1 in. wide, rose-pink. Pyrenees.

grandiflorum. A perennial herb 8–15 in. high. Leaves deeply 5-parted nearly to the middle. Flowers almost 1½ in. wide, blue, but with purple veins. Northern As.

ibericum. A perennial 10–20 in. high. Leaves 7-lobed almost to the middle. Flowers nearly 1½ in. wide, purple. Southwestern As. There is also a white-flowered variety.

---

* Special articles on the subjects indicated by an asterisk (*) will be found at the words so marked.

incisum. A perennial 12–20 in. high. Leaves 3–5-parted, the segments also cut or coarsely toothed. Flowers about 1 in. long, pinkish-purple. British Columbia to Calif.

lancastriense. A prostrate form of G. *sanguineum* with light pink flowers.

macrorrhizum. An aromatic perennial (when crushed), 12–18 in. high, its leaves deeply 5–7-parted, its roots thick. Flowers magenta or pink, the petals not notched. Southern Eu. June–July.

maculatum. Wild geranium of eastern woodlands; also called alumroot and chocolate-flower. A perennial 12–20 in. high. Leaves 3–5-parted nearly to the middle. Flowers about 1 in. wide, rose-purple. Apr.–May. Eastern U.S., especially rocky woods. Grow in the wild garden.

platypetalum. A Chinese perennial 12–24 in. high and well suited to the border. See BLUE GARDEN. Leaves deeply 5-parted. Flowers about ¼ in. wide, purplish-blue.

pratense. A stout Eurasian perennial 18–30 in. high and well suited to the open border. Leaves 7-parted. Flowers about ½ in. wide, purple.

robertianum. Herb Robert; called, also, red shanks and fox geranium. A nearly prostrate annual or biennial, the stems sometimes erect or sprawling and as much as 15 in. high. Leaves 3-parted, the segments deeply cut or toothed. Flowers numerous, about ¼ in. wide, reddish-purple. North temperate zone and northern Africa, mostly in woods or thickets. Grows best in the wild garden.

sanguineum. A commonly grown Eurasian perennial, 12–18 in. high, the foliage white-hairy. Leaves 5–7-parted. Flowers about ¾ in. wide, reddish-purple. The best of the cranesbills for the open border. There is a white-flowered variety and one with prostrate habit and lighter-colored flowers. A low form, with light pink flowers, is often offered as G. *lancastriense.*

subcaulescens = *Geranium cinereum.*

wallichianum. A prostrate, Himalayan perennial, best suited to the rock garden (which see). Leaves 3–5-parted, the segments deeply toothed. Flowers nearly 2 in. wide, purple.

zonale = *Pelargonium, i.e.,* the Garden Geranium.

For other plants sometimes called geranium, or where geranium is part of the name (*i.e.,* strawberry geranium, etc.), *see* SAXIFRAGA SARMENTOSA, CHENOPODIUM BOTRYS, CHRYSANTHEMUM BALSAMITA, PELARGONIUM.

GERANIUM FAMILY = Geraniaceae.

GERARDIA (ger-rar′di-a). A genus of which no species appear to be in cult., although many are beautiful wild flowers.

GERBERA (ger′ber-ra); also spelled *Gerberia.* A genus of perhaps 40 species of South African or Asiatic, mostly stemless herbs, of the family Compositae, only **G. jamesoni,** the Transvaal or Barberton daisy, of any hort. interest. It is an erect, hairy herb, with leaves in a basal rosette. Leaf-blade about 8 in. long and considerably cut or parted feather-fashion, very woolly on the under side. Flower heads solitary at the ends of long, hairy stalks, the head nearly 4 in. wide, the rays a brilliant orange or orange-red in the typical form, but in the *var.* **hybrida,** white, pink, salmon, or violet.

South Africa. Not hardy outdoors north of zone° 6, but often grown in the cool greenhouse in potting mixture° 3, for its very showy, usually winter-blooming flowers. (Named for Trang Gerber, German naturalist.) Often called by florists the African daisy. Propagated by seed sown in Oct. in the greenhouse for transplanting by the following April. Sow seeds about an inch apart each way, and cover the pot or flat with glass. Keep the greenhouse about 60°. Use potting mixture° 6.

GERMAN CAMOMILE = *Matricaria Chamomilla.*

GERMAN CATCHFLY = *Lychnis Viscaria.*

GERMANDER. See TEUCHRIUM.

GERMANDER SPEEDWELL = *Veronica latifolia.*

germanica, -us, -um (ger-man′i-ka). From Germany.

GERMAN IRIS. See IRIS "GERMANICA."

GERMAN IVY = *Senecio mikanioides.*

GERMAN MILLET = *Setaria italica stramineofructa.*

GERMAN TAMARISK = *Myricaria germanica.*

GERMINATION. For a general account of the things that help seeds to sprout or germinate *see* SEEDS AND SEEDAGE. For the average percentage of germination of some garden seeds *see* GARDEN TABLES II.

GESNERIA. There seem to be no cult. plants in the true genus *Gesneria.* For some cult. plants often incorrectly credited to Gesneria *see* GESNERIACEAE.

GESNERIACEAE (jez-near-i-a′see-ee). A large family of mostly tropical herbs (rarely woody plants), without any well-recognized common name, but yielding many fine greenhouse plants, among them the gloxinia (*Sinningia*). Of its over 80 genera and perhaps 1100 species, about a dozen are in cultivation, nearly all of them herbs of greenhouse culture. The leaves are simple° in all genera.

Some are popular plants for hanging baskets, especially *Episcia* and *Columnea.* Two genera, *Haberlea* and *Ramonda,* are European and can be grown outdoors in some parts of the U.S. But most of the cult. genera contain showy-flowered greenhouse plants, the most important being *Aeschynanthus, Achimenes, Alloplectus, Corytholoma, Episcia, Isoloma, Naegelia, Nautilocalyx, Saintpaulia* (the African violet), and *Streptocarpus.* Fruit dry or fleshy. The recent monograph on this family by H. E. Moore, Jr., is suggested for further study. The adoption here of the many changes there proposed might confuse the garden public — at least until the suggestions of Dr. Moore have achieved permanent acceptance.

Technical flower characters: Calyx tubular, 5-parted or 5-lobed. Corolla tubular (often with a considerable tube), the five lobes usu-

---

° Special articles on the subjects indicated by an asterisk (°) will be found at the words so marked.

ally unequal, and often definitely 2-lipped and strikingly irregular.* Stamens mostly 4, two shorter than the others. Ovary superior* (in *Episcia, Alloplectus, Aeschynanthus, Streptocarpus,* and *Saintpaulia*), more or less inferior in the other genera.

GEUM (jee'um). Perennial herbs of the rose family, most of the 60 known species from the cooler parts of the north temperate zone, and usually called avens. A few are grown in the border or rock garden for ornament, although only one, *G. chiloense,* is at all popular. They have chiefly basal leaves which are compound* or so deeply cut or lobed as to appear so, the terminal segment or leaflet much larger than the others. There are often a few smaller leaves on the stem. Flowers solitary or a few, in corymbs,* yellow, white, or red. Calyx usually bell-shaped, its 5 lobes alternating with 5 bractlets. Petals 5, rather broad. Stamens* numerous. Fruit a collection of silky-plumed achenes which are often as showy as the flowers. (*Geum* is of unknown significance here.)

The avens are of simple culture in most garden soils, and are readily increased by division. Some of the taller ones are striking plants for the border, but the best of the avens is *G. chiloense,* which is rarely over 2 ft. high. Mostly summer-blooming. An absurd, but phonetic, plural for *Geum* is "gums," which has some currency among the illiterate.

atrosanguineum = *Geum chiloense.*

borisi. A hybrid avens derived from a cross between two species of *Geum* (*bulgaricum*× *reptans,* which is non-hort.). It is a perennial, 8–10 in. high. Flowers, nodding, bright yellow, about 1 in. wide. Summer. Of garden origin.

bulgaricum. Not over 2 ft. high. Leaves with a large, heart-shaped end leaflet or segment, and many smaller side leaflets. Flowers bright orange or yellow, about 1 in. wide, nodding. Bulgaria.

chiloense. Not over 2 ft. high. Terminal leaflet or segment much larger than the numerous side ones, all hairy. Flowers nearly 1½ in. wide, bright scarlet. Chile. A popular border perennial known also in several forms, one double-flowered. Others, like Mrs. Bradshaw, have long been favorites.

ciliatum = *G. triflorum.*

coccineum. The garden plants so called are mostly *Geum chiloense,* the true *G. coccineum* being not much cult.

heldreichi = *Geum montanum.*

montanum. Not over 12 in. high, the terminal leaf segment or leaflet much larger than the many smaller side ones. Flowers nearly 1½ in. wide, golden-yellow. Southern Eu. Often offered as *Geum heldreichi.*

sibiricum. A plant listed in some catalogues. It may be a form of *G. chiloense,* although it is a lower plant and the flowers are coppery-red. There is no true *Geum sibiricum* known to be in cult.

triflorum. Prairie smoke; also called Johnny smokers A North American perennial 12–18 in. high, its leaves much cut into silky segments. Flowers about ½ in. wide, purplish, not so handsome as the fine head of silky-plumed fruit.

GHENT AZALEA. *See* AZALEA GANDAVENSIS.

GHERKIN. Usually a gherkin is a young cucumber used for pickling; but *see also* CUCUMIS ANGURIA.

GHOSTWEED = *Euphorbia maculata.*

GIANT. As an adjective *giant* enters into the name of many plants. Those occurring in this encyclopedia and their proper equivalents are:

Giant arborvitae = *Thuja plicata;* **Giant arrowhead** = *Sagittaria montevidensis;* **Giant bamboo,** *see* DENDROCALAMUS; **Giant cactus** = *Carnegiea gigantea;* **Giant chinquapin** = *Castanopsis chrysophylla;* **Giant daisy** = *Chrysanthemum uliginosum;* **Giant fennel** = *Ferula communis;* **Giant fir** = *Abies grandis* (*see* FIR); **Giant garlic** = *Allium Scorodoprasum* and *A. giganteum;* **Giant granadilla** = *Passiflora quadrangularis;* **Giant holly fern** = *Polystichum munitum;* **Giant lily** = *Furcraea gigantea;* **Giant reed** = *Arundo Donax;* **Giant sequoia** = *Sequoia gigantea;* **Giant snowdrop** = *Galanthus elwesi* (*see* SNOWDROP); **Giant summer hyacinth** = *Galtonia candicans;* **Giant sunflower** = *Helianthus giganteus* (*see* SUNFLOWER); **Giant willow-herb** = *Epilobium angustifolium.*

GIBBERELLIC ACID. A relatively new growth-promoting substance derived from a Japanese microscopic fungus, *Gibberella fujikuroi* (and perhaps from *Fusarium moniliforme*), variously called gibberellin or Gibrel, the latter a trade-marked product. In this form it is a potassium salt of gibberellic acid, which itself is a metabolite of the fungus. Its sponsor denies that it is a nutrient, fertilizer, or plant hormone, and the mechanism of its action is still uncertain.

Twenty years ago Japanese scientists noted the effects of this, and some other fungi, upon diseased rice plants, which just before death put out unexpected elongation of their stems. This is the chief value of gibberellic acid today although its reputed other effects include increasing the vigor and color of turf grasses and many greenhouse plants, increasing the speed of seed germination, breaking of dormancy, advancing flowering time of several perennials, and many other horticultural objectives, some of which may be dubious: *i.e.,* increasing the leafstalk of a normally short-stalked leaf. Such elongation has sometimes come with a weakening of tissue and even discoloration.

Extremely weak concentrations are used, ranging from 10 to 100 parts of gibberellic acid to one million parts of water. Some toxicity to plants has been reported and care must be used in its application, especially to crops that may be eaten. Various fantastic claims have been made for it, but the fact remains that it has remarkable growth-stimulating properties, the value and range of activity of which need much further study. The compounds derived from it are expensive, and a recent study of it at the University of California reports: "We know gibberellic acid will increase a plant's growth rate, but we find many undesirable effects

* Special articles on the subjects indicated by an asterisk (*) will be found at the words so marked.

when it is applied to the above-ground portions of a plant." (May, 1959.) So far, the spraying of foliage appears to be the preferred method of application. Naturally the directions on the packet (in powder or liquid) must be followed accurately to secure the correct (and safe) dilution. For a good technical review of it see *Transactions* of the New York Academy of Sciences, vol. 20 (June 1958), pp. 717–32, and *Economic Botany,* vol. 12 (Sept. 1958), pp. 213–55.

gibbiflora, -us, -um (gib-bi-flo′ra). Having flowers with a pouch-like swelling on one side.

GIBRALTAR CANDYTUFT = *Iberis gibraltarica.* See CANDYTUFT.

gibraltarica, -us, -um (gib-ral-tar′i-ka). From or near the Rock of Gibraltar.

gigantea, -us, -um (ji-gan′tee-a). Large or immense.

giganticaerulea, -us, -um (ji-gan-ti-see-roo′-le-a). Large and blue.

GILIA (gil′li-a). A genus of nearly 100 species of herbs of the family Polemoniaceae, most of them from the western U.S., a few rather showy garden annuals, or occasionally biennial or perennial. They have alternate* or opposite* leaves, usually without marginal teeth, but some with dissected or divided leaves. Flowers rather various, mostly in clusters. Corolla more or less bell-shaped or funnel-shaped, the stamens* attached to the tube of the corolla. Fruit a 3-valved capsule. (Named for Philipp Salvador Gil, Spanish botanist.) For related plants sometimes offered as *Gilia see Collomia.* Some are also offered as *Linanthus.*

Gilias are showy plants, most of which are best treated as hardy annuals. (*See* ANNUALS.) Even biennial or perennial plants like *G. rubra* will often flower from seed within a single season, although some prefer fall-sown seed, and wintering of the seedlings, as in a biennial. (*See* BIENNIALS.) All of them need open sunny places.

abrotanifolia. A Californian annual, 12–20 in. high. Leaves divided into very narrow, line-like segments. Flowers blue, in a dense terminal truss. Also known as G. *achilleifolia.*

aggregata. Skyrocket. Resembling *Gilia rubra,* but a biennial, not over 2½ ft. high, its dissected leaves thread-like. Flowers fragrant, fiery red (rarely white) in a long cluster (thyrse*). Calif. Summer.

californica. Prickly phlox. A perennial Californian herb or woody shrub 2–3 ft. high. Leaves divided, finger-fashion, into 5–9 rather rigid, stiff segments that are about ½ in. long. Flowers nearly 1½ in. wide, in few-flowered clusters. Corolla rose-pink or lilac. Not suited to the cold, slushy winters of the East, unless grown in a cold frame. Often sold under the name *Leptodactylon.*

capitata. An extremely popular flower-garden annual, 18–24 in. high. Leaves divided or dissected, feather-fashion, into very narrow segments. Flowers light blue or white, in stalked, head-like clusters that are about 1 in. wide. Wash. to Calif. Flowers fine for cutting.

coccinea = *Collomia biflora.*

coronopifolia = *Gilia rubra.*

densiflora. A sprawling annual herb, 1–2 ft. high. Flowers about 1 in. long, prevailingly lilac, but sometimes pinkish-white, borne in dense, head-like clusters. Calif. Frequently offered as *Linanthus densiflorus,* or *Gilia grandiflora,* and some catalogues call it California phlox (not a true phlox).

grandiflora = *G. densiflora.*

parviflora. A popular annual, generally 4–8 in. high. Flowers about 1½ in. long, more salver-shaped than funnel-like, purplish-yellow, orange or pink, and borne in leafy clusters. Calif. Often offered as *Leptosiphon,* and under such names as "aureus," "hybridus," "luteus," etc., to designate the many different forms, all of which appear to be *G. parviflora.* Also called *G. lutea.*

rubra. A showy perennial or biennial, 3–5 ft. high, and known by a variety of names, of which tree cypress, standing cypress, Texas plume, and trailing fire are the best known. Leaves dissected, feather-fashion, into thread-like segments. Flowers in a narrow cluster (panicle*), very showy. Corolla scarlet outside, but yellow and red-dotted inside. S. Car. to Fla. and Tex.

tricolor. Bird's-eyes. A Californian annual, 18–24 in. high, and next to *G. capitata* the most widely grown of the annual gilias. Leaves finely dissected into narrow segments. Flowers fragrant in loose clusters, the corolla lilac or violet above, the tube yellowish but purple-streaked. There is a variety with rose-pink flowers.

GILLENIA (gil-len′i-a). North American perennial herbs of the rose family, both the known species occasionally cult. in the wild garden and commonly called Indian physic. They are erect, branching plants having compound* leaves with 3 leaflets, or simple* ones which are deeply 3-parted. There are often, in addition, 2 leaf-like stipules,* the whole leaf thus appearing as with 5 leaflets or segments. Flowers white, in loose, terminal clusters (panicles*). Petals 5, narrow and spreading, a little unequal. Stamens 10–20, not protruding. Fruit a collection of 5 follicles,* each of which is 2–4-seeded. (Named for Arnoldus Gillenius, a German botanist.)

Both the species are woodland plants suited to the wild garden, preferably in partial shade, and they should have rich woods soil, not too acid. In such places they are of easy cult. Propagated by division of the clumps in spring.

stipulata. American ipecac. A wand-like herb, 2–4 ft. high. Leaves usually 3-parted, sometimes compound, the two stipules* prominent and leaf-like. Flowers about ½ in. wide. N.Y. to Ga. and Texas. July.

trifoliata. Bowman's root; also called false ipecac and Indian hippo. Much resembling *G. stipulata,* but with compound* leaves and with the leaflets toothed. Stipules* small and very narrow, hence not so leaf-like as in the other species. Eastern U.S. June.

GILLIFLOWER = Gillyflower.

GILL-OVER-THE-GROUND = *Glecoma hederacea.* But *see also* Ground ivy in the list at WEEDS.

GILLYFLOWER = *Mathiola incana.*

GINGER. The common ginger is derived from an herb of the genus **Zingiber** (zin′gi-

---

* Special articles on the subjects indicated by an asterisk (*) will be found at the words so marked.

ber), of the family Zingiberaceae. Of the 50 or more species, all from moist tropical forests in southeastern Asia, only the ginger, **Z. officinale**, is likely to be cult. in the U.S., and its outdoor cult. must be confined to frost-free regions of Fla. where there is abundant moisture and a rich soil. It is chiefly grown as an ornamental, as commercial ginger production needs more heat than is found anywhere in the U.S. It has a stout cane-like stem 3–4 ft. high, rising from a thick rootstock (the source of ginger). Leaves sheathing at the base, oblongish or narrower, 8–12 in. long. Flower cluster a bracted spike, the bracts* usually persistent and with one flower at each. Flower irregular,* yellowish-green, about ¾ in. long, the irregular lip* purple, but yellow-spotted. Fruit a capsule.* While the plant is not much grown outdoors, it is frequent in greenhouse collections. Together with the closely related *Amomum*, it needs a warm (70°–80°) greenhouse, potting mixture* 3, and a large pot or tub to take care of its stout rootstock. During nine months of the year it needs plenty of water and will repay an occasional application of liquid manure. But during the winter the plant should be allowed to become half dormant by reducing the heat and keeping it as dry as possible. (*Zingiber* is a Latinized version of the Sanskrit name for ginger.) For the wild ginger, *see* ASARUM.

GINGER FAMILY = Zingiberaceae.

GINGER LILY. See HEDYCHIUM.

GINKGO (gink′o, jin′ko). A remarkable, deciduous,* Chinese tree, the only species and only genus of the family **Ginkgoaceae** (gink-ko-ā′see-ee), once a widely distributed group stretching back to the Carboniferous, but now a dwindling family with only this survivor which is unknown as a wild tree, all the cult. specimens having been derived from trees preserved around Chinese temples. It is a resinous tree with deciduous, fan-shaped leaves. Male and female flowers on separate trees, both without sepals or petals. The male flowers consist of naked pairs of anthers* in catkin-like clusters. Female flowers consist only of a naked ovule, which, unlike all other trees, is fertilized by motile sperm-cells, as in the ferns. Fruit fleshy, drupe*-like, foul-smelling, but the kernel edible. (*Ginkgo* is the Chinese name for the tree.)

The ginkgo or maidenhair-tree is one of the finest street and specimen trees in the temperate world. Only male trees should be planted, because of the foul odor of the fruit. For the first few years it is gawky, but in age it is a magnificent, round-headed, full-foliaged tree. Practically immune to all pests and standing street conditions very well.

biloba. Ginkgo or maidenhair-tree. A smooth tree up to 120 ft. Leaves alternate,* fan-shaped, more or less cut at the broad tip, wedge-shaped at the base, 2½–3½ in. wide, and much resembling a segment of the frond of a maidenhair fern. The foliage turns a soft

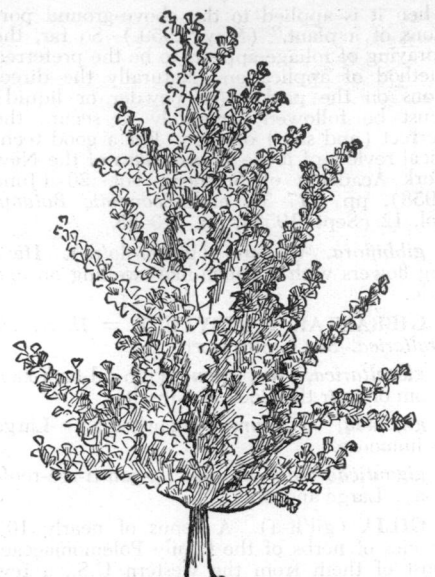

It will take nearly 20 years for this ginkgo to lose its gawky habit of branching and become a round-headed tree.

yellow in autumn. Fruit yellow. China. Hardy from zone* 3 southward. The *var.* aurea has yellow leaves, at least in youth; *var.* fastigiata has upward-pointing branches and columnar in habit; *var.* pendula has hanging branches; *var.* variegata has yellow-blotched leaves.

Ginnala (gin-nay′la). Asiatic vernacular name for the maple, *Acer Ginnala*. See MAPLE.

GINSENG. Two species of *Panax*, one, native to this country, *Panax quinquefolius*, the other, *Panax Schinseng*, indigenous to eastern Asia, are the source of ginseng. The roots are much prized by the Orientals and are used for medicinal purposes with no known reason except superstition and ignorance. The native American species is chiefly grown and harvested in the United States and Canada for export.

SOIL. Ginseng grows naturally on the slopes of ravines and in other situations where the drainage is good and when the soil is slightly acid, brought about by the decaying leaves of hardwood trees.

For cultivated ginseng, the soil should be well drained, fairly light; a soil suitable for growing early vegetables would be in right condition for its culture, substituting decayed leaves for manure. Sandy soil should not be used, as it is apt to produce plants whose roots are fibrous and hard and of inferior value.

The plant is grown from seeds which are slow in germination. When gathered, they should never be permitted to become dry. They may be stratified by mixing them with

---

* Special articles on the subjects indicated by an asterisk (*) will be found at the words so marked.

Ginseng growing under a lath shade.

twice their bulk of moist sand, fine loam, or old sawdust and stored in a cool, damp building until they are planted in early spring. As a rule the seeds do not germinate until a year from the summer following their ripening, and they do not reach a marketable size until about the sixth year from seed. Autumn and spring are the proper times for transplanting to permanent beds. Plants are usually placed at a distance of five inches apart each way.

FERTILIZERS. The best fertilizers to use are woods soil or well-decayed hardwood leaves, well spaded into the soil. Raw bone meal is also beneficial to the plants, used at the rate of 1 lb. to each square yard of bed.

SHADE AND CULTIVATION. Ginseng grows naturally in rather dense shade; therefore it will be necessary to grow the plant under lath houses or frames covered with lath screens. It requires little cultivation, the mere pulling out of grass and weeds from the beds and a light cultivation to leave a dust mulch on the bed to keep it from caking being sufficient. A winter mulch is also advisable; this prevents the heaving by frost. Hardwood leaves, applied to the depth of four inches when freezing weather sets in, prove the best protection to the plants.

MARKETING. Late in September to mid-October is the most favorable time. The drying of the roots is best effected in a heated storage with a temperature of 60° to 90° F. Approximately a month is required to cure the larger roots.

DISEASES. The wilt* disease which attacks chrysanthemum, snapdragon, and other plants may become a serious problem on ginseng. Soil should be steam sterilized (*see* SOIL STERILIZATION) where seed is sown and where the young plants are set out.

Various blights* and leafspots* may be held in check with pesticide #5 (*see* SPRAYS AND DUSTS) if these diseases become a problem.

GINSENG FAMILY. Besides the ginseng itself, this family comprises shrubs like the greenhouse aralias, trees like the Hercules'-club, and vines like the English ivy. *See* ARALIACEAE.

GIRASOLE = *Helianthus tuberosus* (the Jerusalem artichoke). *See* SUNFLOWER.

GIRDLE. To strip a ring of bark from a tree, a practice well known to the Indians. It cuts off the food supply and will ultimately kill most trees. *See* BARK.

glabella, -us, -um (glay-bell′la). Nearly smooth.

glaber (glay′ber). Same as *glabra.*

glabra, -us, -um (glay′bra). Smooth.

glaberrima, -us, -um (glay-berr′i-ma). Very smooth.

glabrata, -us, -um (glay-bray′ta). Glabrate; *i.e.,* somewhat smooth.

GLABROUS. Completely smooth, *i.e.,* altogether lacking hairs, pustules, warts, or any sort of roughness; mostly applied to leaves and stems. The opposite of pubescent (which see).

glacialis, -e (glay-see-ā′lis). Growing on or near a glacier.

GLAD. Florists' slang for gladiolus.

gladiata, -us, -um (glay-dee-ā′ta). Sword-like.

GLADIOLUS (gla-dy′o-lus, also glad-i-ō′lus). Very popular, summer-blooming plants of the iris family, many of them from South Africa, but a few from tropical Africa and elsewhere. More than 240 species are known, and from a few of them the breeders have developed several thousand named forms among which are very striking plants. The gladioli bear corms from which grows a usually erect, unbranched, leafy stem. Leaves commonly sword-shaped, long, and narrow, handsome. Flowers very showy, in a long, terminal, spike-like cluster composed of leafy bracts (spathe*) between every two of which there is a single, stalkless flower (for color variations *see* Culture below). They bloom from the bottom upward. The flowers are more or less funnel-shaped, but with the tube dilated, and usually curved upward. Flower segments 6, the upper three larger than the lower, hence the flower is slightly irregular. Stamens 3. Fruit a large capsule,* its seeds usually flattened or winged. (*Gladiolus* is Latin for a small sword, in allusion to the shape of the leaves.) Old names for them are sword lily and corn lily.

It is almost impossible to assign the modern gladiolus of the garden to any of the botanical species below. The list is therefore more of a guide to the species that have been used in *breeding* the modern flower than a list of species actually in cult. in gardens today. With thousands of named forms, and the parentage of many of the hybrids quite uncertain, any list of species of *Gladiolus* is

---

* Special articles on the subjects indicated by an asterisk (*) will be found at the words so marked.

frankly tentative. For a discussion of the leading classes and varieties and how to grow them *see* Culture below.

anatolicus. Probably plants offered as this are *Gladiolus illyricus.*

blandus. About 2 ft. high, the stems sometimes branched. Leaves usually 4, nearly 12 in. long and ½ in. wide. Flowers 4–8 in the spike, white, or red-tinged, or pink, the segments pointed, the upper one about ¾ in. wide. S. Af.

byzantinus. Most of the material offered as this is apt to be *Gladiolus illyricus.*

cardinalis. Usually unbranched and 3–4 ft. high. Leaves 2–3 ft. long, bluish-green. Flowers 5–10 in the spike, crimson or scarlet, the upper segment larger and hooded, the lower ones blotched with white. S. Af. Thought to be one of the parents of *G. gandavensis.*

colvillei. Usually not over 2 ft. high. Flower spikes short, early-blooming, the flowers scarlet and with oblong blotches. It is supposed to be a hybrid between a form of *G. tristis* and *G. cardinalis.*

dracocephalus. Not over 2 ft. high, the stem unbranched. Leaves about 18 in. long and nearly 1 in. wide. Flowers 3–5 in the spike, yellow-green, but purple-spotted, the tube much curved and nearly 2 in. long. S. Af.

gandavensis. A hybrid, very popular and long-cult. garden gladiolus, perhaps derived by crossing *G. psittacinus* and *G. cardinalis* or *G. oppositiflorus.* It is late-blooming, has broad leaves and a rather long, dense, flowering spike. Flowers prevailingly red or reddish-yellow, often streaked or penciled. It is certainly the origin of many named forms.

grandis. Probably, as offered here, a variety of *Gladiolus tristis.*

illyricus. Plants offered as *G. anatolicus* and *G. byzantinus* are apt to be *G. illyricus,* which is a cormous herb 12–20 in. high, with only 2 or 3 narrow leaves, 6–10 in. long. Flowers in a loose, 1-sided spike, the tube slightly curved, red or pink, changing to blue. Eu. Summer.

murieliae. Often offered as *Acidanthera murieliae,* this tall Abyssinian herb may be 2½–3 ft. high. Leaves erect, nearly 2 ft. long and about 1½ in. wide. Flowers showy, fragrant, nearly 5 in. long, white fading to pink at the base, the tube slightly curved. Aug.

oppositiflorus. Occasionally branched, the stem 3–4 ft. high. Leaves usually 4, nearly 18 in. long and 1 in. wide. Flower spike 2-sided, the flowers numerous, nearly 3 in. long, white. S. Af.

primulinus. One of the most important parents of many garden forms, and a tender species from the moist regions of tropical Africa.

psittacinus. Probably one of the parents of *G. gandavensis,* and with a usually unbranched stem 3–4 ft. high. Flowers numerous in the spike, the tube nearly 3 in. long, the lower flower segments red and yellow and smaller than the larger upper one, which is crimson. S. Af.

saundersi. A South African gladiolus which has entered into several hybrid forms or strains. It is 2–3 ft. high, usually unbranched. Leaves, 4–6, nearly 2 ft. long and 1 in. wide, prominently ribbed. Flowers scarlet, 6–8 in the spike, the three lower segments white-blotched.

segetum. Cornflag. A cormous herb from the Mediterranean region, 18–24 in. high, the leaves scarcely ½ in. wide. Flowers in a loose 1-sided spike, the corolla about 1½ in. long, purple, the segments flaring. May.

tristis. Not over 2 ft. high, unbranched. Leaves 3, round in section, about 18 in. long and ribbed. Flowers night-blooming, white or yellowish-white, but purple-streaked and very fragrant, the tube about 2 in. long. S. Af. There is a *var.* **concolor** with pure white flowers.

GLADIOLUS CULTURE

It is probable that *Gladiolus blandus,* *G. cardinalis,* *G. dracocephalus,* *G. psittacinus,* *G. oppositiflorus* and *G. primulinus* have contributed most to the creation of the varieties now generally known. But *Gladiolus gandavensis* is considered the original of the large-flowered or exhibition type, while the introduction of *G. primulinus* blood has probably brought about the forms in which small size, charm, and daintiness have created a classification called Small Decorative.

The origin and history of gladiolus reach far into the past. As late as A.D. 1000 gladioli were known as sword lilies and about A.D. 200 Dioscorides described several different *corn* lilies, which today we know were gladiolus species.

CULTURE. The corms, erroneously called bulbs, are planted from early spring to midsummer. Plant when maples are leafing, to a time in July or August which will allow a 90-day growth till the first killing frost.

The size of the corm will determine the planting depth; small corms, ½ inch or less, 3 inches deep; medium corms, ½ to 1 inch in diameter, 4 to 5 inches deep; and large corms, 1¼ inches and up, 6 to 8 inches deep. Deep planting holds large plants erect, avoiding staking, when they are in bloom. Deep-planted corms do not split or produce as many cormels as those shallow-planted.

For early bloom, corms may be sprouted by placing them in a warm place for 30 to 40 days earlier than dormant planted corms. Once dormancy is broken, growth continues even in cold wet soil.

A well-drained, deeply prepared soil is necessary for optimum growth. Full sunlight and freedom from competition by other deep-rooted plants are also necessary. The trench should be opened 2 inches deeper than the prescribed planting depth to place fertilizer, 5–10–10, 4–12–12 or their equivalents, plus bone meal, if available, for top-quality spikes. Use a cup of fertilizer and bone meal per 10 inches of row. Cover fertilizer with 2 inches of soil so that the corm will not touch it and be burned.

Plant corms from 3 to 6 inches apart; wider spacing produces taller plants and larger flowers. Rows in the cutting garden should be from 24 to 30 inches apart. Allow 6 inches between plants in a border planting. Cover corms with several inches of soil and work in soil as plants grow, thus smothering weeds in the row. Hilling is advantageous for large-flower types or in commercial plantings. Cultivate to keep plants free of weeds.

The emergence of the seventh leaf signifies that the bloom spike is emerging above the

---

* Special articles on the subjects indicated by an asterisk (*) will be found at the words so marked.

ground level. Water is essential for maximum spikes and is necessary when the spike is elongating. Soak, not sprinkle, the soil every third day till the first flower opens if the season is dry. Water produces longer spikes, better placement and larger flowers. Clean cultivation is necessary for fine spikes.

For cutting purposes, cut the spike when the first flower opens and place in water in a cool room for 24 hours to allow it to develop; then it may be used in an arrangement or placed on exhibition. When cutting, allow at least 5 leaves to remain on the plant to provide growth and food for the developing corm. Low cutting will produce immature, undersized corms.

Corms may be harvested 4 to 6 weeks after blooming; it is not necessary to allow the plants to die. Cool weather speeds up corm development; thus late-blooming corms will produce corms in a shorter period than those blooming in early summer. Cut the leaves from the corm as soon as dug; remove them flush with the top of the corm. Destroy or compost the foliage, which could harbor insects and fungus diseases of the gladiolus.

Place the corms in an open container to cure; remove the old corm and cormels as soon as they will separate easily. Place new corms in an open container, and dust in accordance with the directions at Diseases (below). Then store in a cool, dry, well-ventilated cellar.

In temperate zones, cool weather causes the corms to become dormant; however, in warm regions it is necessary to place corms in cold storage for a period of 3 months to induce dormancy and a sufficient rest period for good growth.

In the South, where more than 11,000 acres of gladiolus are grown for cut flowers during the winter months, plantings may be made at any time of the year with dormant corms. For continuous bloom, make successive plantings 10 to 14 days apart; corms of different sizes, or varieties of different maturity periods and days to bloom may be used.

Corms are graded commercially into 6 sizes: #1 and #2 (large), #3 and #4 (medium), #5 and #6 (small). Bloom may be obtained from any of these corms; however, the size and quality decrease with the size of the corm. Sizes below #3 in most varieties will not produce spikes of acceptable commercial quality. Few varieties like Sans Souci, Morning Kiss, and Salman's Sensation will produce quality spikes from #4 corms. Numbers 5 and 6 (commercially designated as planting stock) are generally grown from new corms. Usually these will produce large to jumbo corms.

Gladioli are propagated by planting the cormels found clustered around the corm. These pea-sized corms are covered with a thick protective husk; frequently two layers of husk are present. Thus speedy growth is usually a problem. While the amateur can crack and remove this husk from his expensive cormels, this is not practicable for the commercial grower. Several methods are used: (1.) Store the cormels at 40° for 60 days, then raise the temperature to 70° for 60 days or till planting time. (2.) Soak cormels for several days prior to planting, using a detergent soap in the water to remove oils in the husk and increase greater water penetration. (3.) After soaking, some growers allow the cormels to begin growth by keeping them moist and warm. CAUTION: plant before root growth begins or many cormels will die. (4.) Cormels may be treated with a starter* solution or plant hormone,* or planted, soaked or dry, then the soil over the row covered with paper or burlap to insure continuous moisture.

Cormels are planted thickly in a band 4 to 6 inches wide, usually 2 to 3 inches deep, depending on soil type; *i.e.*, heavy soils, shallower planting. Thick planting controls weeds in the row, always a hazard to these fragile plants. Frequent cultivation and regular irrigation will produce corms of all sizes including #1 corms. The size will vary with the variety. Cormels should be dug when the foliage is green or many small ones will be lost, as they break from the plant easily.

Seed culture requires several seasons to produce blooming-size corms. Those with time and patience will find this a most interesting hobby as a cross will produce an endless variety of colors. The chances of obtaining an acceptable type are rather small. Gather seed when pods begin to split, remove seed, dry and store in a dry place until spring. A well-prepared seed bed, high in organic matter is necessary. Plant seed thickly, 1 inch deep. Firm soil, keep weed-free, and water regularly. Dig while plants are green in early October. Screen soil for small corms, dry and store. Handle as small corms the following season until they flower.

Gladioli are no longer forced in greenhouses due to the extensive plantings in Florida and Costa Rica which supply blooms much cheaper than those grown under glass. Growers may plant corms in a heated cold-frame outside in February. Plastic covering or sash can be used during cold weather or late spring frosts to keep plants from freezing. Blooms in mid-May can be obtained from these plantings. Plant corms 3 inches deep and 4 inches apart in the hotbed. Night temperatures should not drop below 50° for continuous growth. Varieties that respond to forcing are Snow Princess, Friendship, Myrna Loy, Rhett Butler, Yellow Herald, Apple-Blossom, Rose Charm, Hopman's Glory, Red Charm, and Gail.

VARIETIES OF GLADIOLUS. The North American Gladiolus Council conducts an annual symposium which features the best varieties in each color class. There are many thousands of varieties on the market today with about 200 new introductions each season. The outstanding ones are few, but they are soon evident.

The following varieties are the finest avail-

---

* Special articles on the subjects indicated by an asterisk (*) will be found at the words so marked.

able today, but may not be in a few years, as gladiolus breeders are very active.

White. Snow Clad, Snow Velvet
Cream. Lorelei, Apple-Blossom
Yellow. Prospector, Gold
Buff. A. B. Coutts, Patrol
Salmon. Salmon Queen, Picardy
Scarlet. Sans Souci, Valeria
Pink. Friendship, Ruffled Dream
Red. Red Charm, Red Radiance
Rose. Rose Spire, Innocence
Lavender. Campanile, Princess
Purple. King David, Emperor
Violet. Violet Charm, Salman's Sensation
Smoky. Brown Lullaby, Gunsmoke.

Horticultural classification established in 1944 by the North American Gladiolus Council provides the basic classification of all gladiolus varieties. The basic classification is published each year with the addition of some 150 to 300 new varieties.

SIZES

Miniature Glads	100	Flowers under 2½ in.
Small Glads	200	2½ in. up to 3½ in.
Medium Glads	300	3½ in. up to 4½ in.
Large Glads	400	4½ in. up to 5½ in.
Giant Glads	500	5½ in. and larger

The future of the gladiolus appears to be one of breeding for increased disease resistance, greater substance, better germinating qualities of cormels, wider range in color and better keeping qualities. The form of the gladiolus is almost endless, with ruffled, waved, crimped, laciniated, horned, frilled, recurled, needle-pointed, ruffled and plain-petaled flowers. The desire to produce fragrant varieties has resulted in many faintly scented varieties, namely: Yellow Rose, Sweet Cream, Sweetie, Perfume, Sachet, and Red Scent, which lose their fragrance rapidly as the flowers age. Hybridization continues with a promise for fragrance in the future.

Although size is important for cut flowers, the home gardener and flower arranger prefers the small decorative type. Many hybridists are working for better Miniatures. The following represent the best available today:

White. Gracy Y, Daintiness
Yellow. Statuette, Yellow Bird
Orange. Little Gold, Peter Pan
Scarlet. Atom, Osage
Pink. Little Sweetheart, Puck
Red. Zig Zag, Fifth Avenue
Rose. Tweedledum, Little Pal
Lavender. Camarie, Petunia
Violet. Parma Violet
Smoky. Little Joe, Old South

The address of the National Gladiolus Society is 3200 Cheverly Avenue, Cheverly, Md. — T. R. M.

INSECT PESTS. Thrips should be controlled by dusting stored corms with 5% pesticide #17 or 1½% pesticide #18 (*see* SPRAYS AND DUSTS). Spray or dust pesticide #18 or #17 on plants in field to prevent damage there, particularly in hot, dry weather.

DISEASES. Small sunken spots with a varnish-like coating are symptoms of bacterial scab. If only a few spots are present, corms may be planted and good results expected. If large decayed areas are present on corms it indicates one of the fungus diseases such as hard rot, dry rot, or storage rot. Discard these corms. When plants turn yellow and die before flowering it is usually due to fungus yellows.* Gladiolus should not be planted in that area for at least three years. If light-gray streaks develop in the leaves, and the flower has abnormal white streaks in the petals, the corms should be discarded because it indicates the mosaic* virus. During humid weather, leaves and flowers may develop spots of gray mold.* Spraying with pesticide #1, or #11 (*see* SPRAYS AND DUSTS), at weekly intervals will prevent further spotting. For general health of gladiolus, after digging, dry the corms and remove the old mother-corm (discard it) and dip or dust the new corm with pesticide #1 or #2 and place in cool, dry storage. In the spring remove the husks before planting corms.

GLADIOLUS FAMILY = Iridaceae.

GLAND, GLANDULAR. Minute, often sticky or glistening bodies common on the stems, leaves, petals, or flower stalks of many plants. The gland itself is often too small to see, but its secretions, especially those of the glandular hairs of some plants, make them very sticky. Typical examples are seen on the stems of tomato or the flowers of *Azalea viscosa*.

glanduliflora, -us, -um (glan-dew-li-flow'-ra). With glandular flowers.

glandulosa, -us, -um (glan-dew-lō'sa). Glandular.

GLASS. A general term for hotbeds, cold frames,* greenhouses,* or conservatories; it usually occurs in the phrase *under glass*, implying that the plant is not grown in the open.

GLASSHOUSE. A greenhouse.*

GLASS SUBSTITUTES. *See* Sash at COLD FRAME.

GLASS WOOL. *See* MULCH AND MULCHING.

glauca, -us, -um (glaw'ka). Glaucous (which see).

glaucescens (glaw-ses'senz). Glaucescent; *i.e.*, almost, or becoming glaucous (which see).

GLAUCIUM (glaw'si-um). Stout, biennial or perennial herbs of the poppy family, usually with bluish-green or grayish foliage and yellow juice. Of the 20 known species, which are often called sea or horn poppy, all from the Mediterranean region, only G. flavum is of much garden interest. It is a branching biennial, 2–3 ft. high, often planted in the border. Lower leaves cut or lobed and stalked, the stem leaves clasping and wavy-toothed or lobed, all bluish-gray. Flowers solitary, long-stalked, orange-yellow, nearly 2 in. wide. Sepals 2. Petals 4. Stamens* numerous. Fruit a narrow capsule 8–12 in. long. For culture *see* BIENNIALS. The plant is showy, but its

* Special articles on the subjects indicated by an asterisk (*) will be found at the words so marked.

flowers do not last long. It is naturalized, especially along sea beaches, in eastern N.A. (*Glaucium* is from the Greek for glaucous,* in allusion to the foliage.)

glaucophylla, -us, -um (glaw-ko-fill'a). With glaucous* leaves.

glaucopsis (glaw-kop'sis). Nearly glaucous.

GLAUCOTHEA = *Erythea armata.*

GLAUCOUS. Covered with a minute whitish or grayish powder that will often rub off, as it will in the bloom on some fruits. Glaucous leaves are, due to the green beneath the powder, conspicuously blue-green or gray-green, as in the common blue spruce.

GLECOMA (gle-ko'ma). A small genus of weedy herbs of the mint family, mostly Eurasian, and of little garden interest except **G. hederacea**, the ground ivy, gill-over-the-ground, or field balm. A creeping perennial, with low-growing, branching, prostrate stems which make a dense mat, every joint producing roots from which new plants may grow. Leaves roundish, with scalloped margins, 1–2½ in. across, dark green. Flowers light to dark blue, about 1 in. long, in scattered clusters. Will grow either in sunny or shady places. Suitable for ground cover or hanging over rocks. The *var.* **variegata**, with variegated leaves, is sometimes used as an edging plant. Eurasia, but naturalized in N.A. *See also* the list at Weeds. (*Glecoma* is an old Greek name for a mint.) Also called *Nepeta hederacea.*

GLEDITSIA. *See* Honey Locust.

GLENN DALE AZALEA. *See* Azalea.

GLOBE AMARANTH = *Gomphrena globosa.*

GLOBE ARTICHOKE. *See* Artichoke.

GLOBE CANDYTUFT = *Iberis umbellata.* *See* Candytuft.

GLOBE DAISY = *Globularia.*

GLOBEFLOWER. *See* Trollius.

GLOBE MALLOW. *See* Sphaeralcea.

GLOBE THISTLE. *See* Echinops.

GLOBE TULIP. *See* Calochortus.

globifera, -us, -um (glō-bif'fe-ra). Bearing globe-like or head-like clusters.

globosa, -us, -um (glo-bō'sa). Globe-shaped.

GLOBULARIA (glob-you-lay'ri-a). Globe daisy. A small group of chiefly blue-flowered, Eurasian herbs, and the only cult. genus of the family **Globulariaceae** (glob-you-lair-ee-ā'see-ee). They are often cult. in the border or rock garden (*see* Blue Garden) for their early spring bloom. The ones below are all low or prostrate herbs, sometimes a little woody, with alternate* leaves. Flowers small, in dense, globular heads and crowded between small bracts.* Corolla 2-lipped,* the upper lip 2-lobed,

the lower one 3-lobed. Stamens* 2–4. Fruit a tiny nutlet included within the persistent calyx. (The name is derived from the arrangement of the flowers in globular heads.)

All those below do better in partial shade, and are easily grown in the border or rock garden if provided with it and a reasonably well-drained soil. They are readily propagated from seeds or by division of the plants in early spring.

cordifolia. A prostrate, woody herb or under-shrub, not over 4 in. high. Leaves about 1 in. long, broader toward the end and notched at the tip. Flower heads about ½ in. wide, blue. May. Southern Eu.

nana = G. repens.

nudicaulis. More or less erect, and sometimes 8–10 in. high. Leaves nearly 3 in. long, without teeth or notches. Flower heads nearly ¾ in. wide, blue. Southern Eu. May.

repens. A prostrate, somewhat woody herb, with tiny, club-shaped leaves that are scarcely ⅕ in. long. Flower heads about ½ in. wide, pale blue. Southern Eu. April–May.

trichosantha. The best-known species in cult. and a nearly erect perennial up to 8 in. high. Leaves about 1 in. long, finely toothed. Flower heads about ½ in. wide, blue. Asia Minor. June.

GLOBULARIACEAE. *See* Globularia.

globulus (glob'you-lus). A little globe.

GLOCHID. One of the barbed bristles found on the joints of some cacti, especially the prickly pears. Sometimes the spines arise near the glochids. *See* Cactaceae.

glomerata, -us, -um (glom-er-ray'ta). Glomerate; *i.e.*, in dense, often globe-shaped and compact clusters.

glomulifera, -us, -um (glom-you-lif'-fer-ra). Bearing small, globe-shaped heads or clusters.

GLORIOSA (glow-ri-ō'sa). Glory-lily. Weak-stemmed, tuberous-rooted, showy vines of the lily family, natives of tropical Af. and As., mostly grown in the greenhouse, but suited to outdoor culture in the Far South. (*See* Vines.) They have narrow leaves, the tips of which are prolonged into tendril*-like organs by which the plants climb. Flowers lily-like, solitary in the upper leaf axils,* mostly red or yellow, the segments separate, rather narrow, sometimes crisped. Stamens* 6. Fruit a capsule.* (*Gloriosa* is from the Latin for glorious, in allusion to the showy flowers.)

Greenhouse culture demands a warm-temperate house (day temperature of 55°–65°), and potting mixture* 3. The tubers should be potted soon after Jan. and will then bloom in late summer and autumn, after which they need a rest (reduce their water). It is often, in the North, grown as a summer annual, the tubers of which, of course, must be stored over winter. It needs for outdoor cult. a long growing season, and they must be staked. Propagated by division of the tubers during dormancy.

rothschildiana. A climbing vine, 4–6 ft. high,

---

* Special articles on the subjects indicated by an asterisk (*) will be found at the words so marked.

the leaves broadly lance-shaped. Flowers bent downward, 2–3 in. long, yellowish-white near the base, crimson toward the tip, the segments not crisped, but sometimes wavy. Tropical Af. Spring-blooming outdoors.

superba. More high-climbing than the last, usually 10–12 ft. Leaves narrowly lance-shaped. Flowers 2–3 in. long, yellow, but changing to red, the segments narrow, much-crisped and appearing as though twisted. Tropical Af. A very handsome plant and the most widely grown of the genus, flowering in the fall outdoors.

GLORY-BOWER. See CLERODENDRON.

GLORY-BUSH = *Tibouchina.*

GLORY-LILY = *Gloriosa.*

GLORY-OF-THE-SNOW = *Chionodoxa.*

GLORY-OF-THE-SUN = *Leucocoryne ixioides.*

GLORY-PEA = *Clianthus dampieri.*

GLORY-TREE. See CLERODENDRON.

GLOXINIA. The florists' gloxinia is one of a small group of chiefly Brazilian herbs belonging to the genus **Sinningia** (sin-nin'ji-a) of the family Gesneraceae. They are tuberous-rooted, nearly stemless herbs with opposite, long-stalked leaves. The only cult. species is S. **speciosa,** the common gloxinia of the greenhouses, long cult. for its very showy flowers. It has oblongish or oblong-oval, toothed leaves, 6–8 in. long. Flowers solitary or a few in a cluster, the corolla tubular or bell-shaped, somewhat swollen on one side, nearly 3 in. long, usually violet or purple, but sometimes reddish and white-spotted. Stamens 5, not protruding. Fruit a 2-valved capsule.* (Named for Wilhelm Sinning, German gardener.) Gloxinias are offered under a variety of incorrect names such as G. *erecta, hybrida, robusta,* etc.

GLOXINIA CULTURE

The culture of gloxinia, and of the related genera *Alloplectus, Isoloma,* and *Corytholoma,* is essentially the same. They are plants of the warm, humid rain-forests and need, during their growing season, a warm greenhouse (70°–80°). Because they are plants primarily of the lower canopy of the forest or of the forest floor, they must have shade and this must be provided by painting the greenhouse glass or by the roller type of shades. Also, after blooming, which corresponds with the beginning of a dry season in their natural environment, they need a resting period. This means that after the blooming period, the corm-like tubers should be taken up and stored in a temperature of about 45°, in the dark, until Feb. or early Mar., when they may be started up again.

Then they should be potted up or put in pans in potting mixture* 3 and put into the warm greenhouse. Be careful to give them plenty of water, but see that none of it gets on the foliage. Liquid manure may be given every three weeks, especially as they approach the flowering period.

Gloxinias, and in fact most of the family Gesneriaceae to which they belong, are more easily propagated by leaf cuttings than by any other method. (*See* Leaf Cuttings at CUTTINGS.) They may also be increased by seeds, but either method needs a propagating bench, shade, moisture, and heat. Both methods should produce plants ready to flower within a year. Gloxinias make good house plants.

The address of the American Gloxinia Society, which publishes a journal, is 4139 S. Rockford Place, Tulsa, Okla.

gloxiniaeflora, *-us,* *-um* (glocks-in-ee-flow'ra). With flowers like a gloxinia.

gloxinioides (glocks-in-i-oy'deez, but *see* OÏDES). Like a gloxinia.

glumacea, *-us,* *-um* (gloo-may'see-a). Bearing chaffy scales or glumes.*

GLUME. A chaffy bract* or scale, especially one of the two empty bracts* often found at the base of a grass spikelet.

glutinosa, *-us,* *-um* (gloo-ti-nō'sa). Glutinous; *i.e.,* sticky or gluey.

GLYCINE. See SOYBEAN.

GLYCYRRHIZA. See LICORICE.

GLYODIN. See FUNGICIDES.

glyptostroboides (glip-to-stro-boy'deez). Like an evergreen of the non-hort. genus *Glyptostrobus.*

GNAPHALIUM (na-fā'li-um). Cudweed. Few, or perhaps only one, of this genus of the family Compositae, are of much interest to the gardener. They are woolly-foliaged plants resembling an everlasting, and one of them, G. *sylvaticum,* is so grown occasionally in the hardy border. There are over 120 widely distributed species of usually perennial herbs in the genus, with alternate* leaves and rather dirty-white flower heads arranged in corymbs,* spikes, or other clusters. There are no ray* flowers, the heads being composed only of disk* flowers, and rather compact and button-like. (*Gnaphalium* is from the Greek for wool, in allusion to the woolly foliage of most species.)

The wood cudweed is easily grown in open, sandy soil, and can be increased by division of the clumps in early spring. As noted below, some plants credited to *Gnaphalium* belong elsewhere.

lanatum = *Helichrysum petiolatum.*

Leontopodium = *Leontopodium alpinum.* See EDELWEISS.

sylvaticum. Wood cudweed; also called owl's-crown and chafeweed. A rather weedy, perennial herb 6–18 in. high, the stem mostly unbranched. Leaves narrow, sharp-pointed, about 1½ in. long. Flower heads numerous, about ¼ in. wide, in a more or less leafy spike. North temperate zone and common in northeastern N.A. July.

GNETACEAE. See EPHEDRA.

GOATSBEARD. See ARUNCUS and TRAGOPOGON.

GOAT'S-RUE = *Tephrosia virginiana* or *Galega officinalis.*

---

* Special articles on the subjects indicated by an asterisk (*) will be found at the words so marked.

GOAT WILLOW = *Salix Caprea. See* WILLOW.

GOBO = *Arctium Lappa. See* list at WEEDS.

GODETIA (go-dee'she-a). A genus of perhaps 25 species of New World, prevailingly annual herbs of the family Onagraceae, some of them very popular as flower garden annuals. They have alternate,* stalkless or short-stalked leaves, and showy, day-blooming flowers in leafy clusters (racemes*) or in spikes. Calyx* tubular, often colored like the petals which are 4, usually pink, lilac-purple or white, and sometimes crimson- or purple-spotted. Stamens* 8, 4 shorter than the others. Fruit a 4-valved capsule, its seeds numerous. (Named for C. H. Godet, Swiss botanist.)

All those below are best grown as tender annuals. (*See* ANNUALS.) The first species is extremely popular and makes a fine plant for cutting. Like a few other annuals, it blooms more profusely if the plants are a bit crowded; in other words, do not thin them out too much.

amoena. Farewell-to-spring. A slender, branching herb 12–30 in. high. Leaves lance-shaped or narrower, ¾–2 in. long, often with smaller ones in the axils.* Flowers 1–2 in. wide, the petals satiny, lilac-crimson or reddish-pink. Fruit roundish in cross-section. Mid-July to Oct. British Columbia to Calif. There are many fine garden forms, some white, some double-flowered, and one crimson-blotched. A very showy and desirable annual.

bottiae. Resembling *G. amoena,* but the buds nodding, and the petals light pink or light crimson, and the pods flattish. Southern Calif. Summer.

grandiflora. Satin-flower. An unbranched annual 8–14 in. high, its leaves oblongish, tapering both ends. Flowers in a short spike, the corolla 3–5 in. wide, red but deeper red-blotched at the center. There are also pure white, crimson, and carmine forms. Pods 4-sided. Calif. Summer.

viminea. A showy, stiffly-branched annual, not over 3 ft. high, the stems pale. Leaves without teeth, narrow lance-shaped. Flowers red or purple about 1 in. long, with a dark eye* at center. Ore. and Calif.

GOLD-DUST = *Alyssum saxatile* and *Sedum acre.*

GOLD-DUST TREE = *Aucuba japonica variegata.*

GOLDEN. As an adjective, *golden* is part of the name of many plants with yellow, orange, or golden-colored flowers or fruit. Those in this encyclopedia and their proper equivalents are:

Golden aster (*see* CHRYSOPSIS); Golden bamboo = *Phyllostachys aurea;* Golden bell (*see* FORSYTHIA); Golden bells = *Emmenanthe penduliflora;* Golden calla lily = *Zantedeschia elliottiana* (*see* CALLA LILY); Golden chain = *Laburnum anagyroides;* Golden chinquapin = *Castanopsis chrysophylla;* Golden clematis = *Clematis tangutica;* Golden club = *Orontium aquaticum;* Golden coreopsis = *Coreopsis tinctoria;* Golden crownbeard = *Verbesina encelioides;* Golden cup = *Hunnemannia fumariaefolia;* Golden currant = *Ribes aureum;*

Golden dewdrop = *Duranta repens;* Golden-ear-drops = *Dicentra chrysantha;* Golden-eyed grass = *Sisyrinchium californicum;* Gold fern (*see* PITYROGRAMMA); Golden flax = *Linum flavum;* Golden garden (*see* YELLOW GARDEN); Goldenglow = *Rudbeckia laciniata hortensis;* Golden gram = *Phaseolus aureus;* Golden larch (*see* PSEUDOLARIX); Golden loosestrife = *Lysimachia vulgaris;* Golden marguerite = *Anthemis tinctoria;* Golden Mock-orange = *Philadelphus coronarius aureus* (*see* MOCK-ORANGE); Golden moss = *Sedum acre;* Golden osier = *Salix vitellina* (*see* WILLOW); Golden polypody = *Polypodium aureum;* Golden queen = *Trollius ledebouri;* Golden ragwort = *Senecio aureus;* Golden-rain tree = *Koelreuteria;* Goldenrod (*see* second main entry below); Goldenseal (*see* fourth main entry below); Golden shower = *Cassia Fistula;* Golden Spider-lily = *Lycoris aurea;* Golden star = *Chrysopsis mariana* and *Chrysogonum virginianum;* Golden stars = *Bloomeria crocea;* Golden thistle = *Scolymus hispanicus;* Golden-top = *Lamarckia aurea;* Golden trumpet = *Allamanda cathartica hendersoni;* Golden tuft = *Alyssum saxatile;* Golden violet = *Viola pedunculata;* Golden wattle = *Acacia longifolia;* Golden-wave = *Coreopsis drummondi;* Golden wonder millet = *Setaria italica stramineofructa;* Golden wreath = *Acacia saligna.*

GOLDEN GATE PARK. *See* GARDEN TOURS.

GOLDENROD. Coarse, rather weedy herbs belonging to the genus **Solidago** (sol-i-day'go) of the family Compositae. All but a handful of the 100 known species are from the New World, with scattered species in Eu. and As. They are usually perennial herbs, often branched or arching, and have alternate,* usually toothed leaves. Flower heads mostly yellow (white in one hort. species), the small heads very numerous and crowded in sometimes one-sided clusters, or these branched and consisting of compound panicles* or racemes.* While the whole inflorescence is often showy, the plants are little used in the garden outside of the more informal borders. (*Solidago* is from the Latin implying to strengthen or draw together, in allusion to supposed medicinal value.)

The goldenrods are of very easy culture and make attractive groupings with native asters (*see* ASTER) and other fall-blooming wild flowers. While they improve with cultivation, the soil should not be too rich, or they may develop more foliage than flowers. They can easily be divided; some species spread so fast that they must be watched. *See* SOLIDASTER.

S. bicolor. Silver-rod, or white goldenrod. Not usually over 3 ft., the stems wand-like, or sometimes branched. Leaves oblongish, 2–4 in. long, hairy and toothed. Flower heads white, in a narrow, spike-like cluster 5–7 in. long. Eastern N.A.

S. brachystachys. *See* S. VIRGAUREA.

S. caesia. Wreath goldenrod. A smooth-stemmed, often bluish-green herb 1–3 ft. high. Leaves lance-shaped, 3–5 in. long, and toothed. Flower heads yellow, in clusters in the axils,* the whole flower cluster thus leafy. Eastern N.A. and west to Tex.

S. canadensis. Rock goldenrod; also called yellow-weed. A tall, striking, branching plant

---

* Special articles on the subjects indicated by an asterisk (*) will be found at the words so marked.

often 4–6 ft. high. Leaves narrowly lance-shaped, 3–5 in. long, prominently 3-veined, but without teeth. Flower heads yellow in very large, terminal, 1-sided clusters. Eastern N.A.

S. cutleri. An alpine perennial suited only to the rock garden; 3–12 in. high. Leaves chiefly basal, elliptic or spoon-shaped, 1–6 in. long, scarcely ½–¾ in. wide. Flower heads in a loose cluster (corymb*), the heads small and not very showy. Alpine summits of New England and N.Y. July–Aug.

S. nemoralis. Dwarf or gray goldenrod. A grayish-hairy, wand-like plant not over 2 ft. high. Leaves broadest toward the tip, 4–6 in. long, the margins wavy-toothed. Flower heads yellow, in congested, prominently 1-sided, terminal clusters. Eastern N.A. A fine plant for dry, sandy banks.

S. rigida. A course, stiff-hairy herb 3–5 ft. high, its leaves oblongish or oval, 1½–3 in. long, mostly without teeth. Flower heads yellow, mostly in terminal clusters (corymbs*) that are not conspicuously 1-sided. Mass. to Ga. and Tex.

S. sempervirens. Beach or seaside goldenrod. A completely smooth, stout, thick-stemmed herb 5–8 ft. high. Leaves thick or even fleshy, oblongish, 6–10 in. long, without teeth. Flower heads yellow, in large, branched, terminal and 1-sided clusters. On sea beaches or salt marshes, eastern N.A. and south to Mex. A fine plant for the seaside garden, although it will also grow in any good sandy loam.

S. Virgaurea. European goldenrod. A stout perennial, 1–3 ft. high, and little known here, except for a dwarf form offered as *S. brachystachys.* This is the smallest of all known goldenrods, usually 5–7 in. high, its chiefly basal leaves in a rosette, from which springs a flowering stalk about 5 in. high, the small heads golden-yellow. Not unlike *S. cutleri.* Eu. Sept.–Oct. Suited to the rock garden.

GOLDENROD FAMILY. See COMPOSITAE.

GOLDENSEAL. Two species of perennial herbs of the genus **Hydrastis** (hy-dras′tis) of the buttercup family, one Asiatic, the other **H. canadensis** of the richer woods of the eastern U.S., and cult. in the wild garden under the name of yellow puccoon, yellowroot, orangeroot, and Indian dye. It has a thick, yellow, medicinal rootstock, for which it is often cult. commercially. Leaves chiefly basal, nearly 8 in. wide and deeply 5–9-lobed. Stem leaves usually 2, the upper one just beneath the flowers and stalkless. Flowers about ¼ in. wide, greenish-white, without petals, but with 3 petal-like sepals.* Stamens* numerous. April–May. Fruit a collection or head of red berries. Its culture for ornament should be in the shadier part of the wild garden. Its commercial culture is the same as for ginseng (which see). A considerable commercial plantation of goldenseal, raised for the extraction of the alkaloid hydrastine, is on the Seattle-Vancouver Highway in Wash. *See also* MEDICINAL PLANTS. (The origin of the name is unknown.)

GOLD FERN. See PITYROGRAMMA.

GOLDFIELDS. See BAERIA.

GOLD-FLOWER = *Hypericum moserianum.* See ST. JOHN'S-WORT.

GOLDIE'S FERN = *Dryopteris goldiana.*

GOLDILOCKS = *Linosyris vulgaris.*

GOLD MOSS = *Sedum acre.*

GOLDTHREAD. See COPTIS.

GOMESA (go-mee′za). Brazilian tree-perching orchids, little known in cult. except **G. planifolia**, which is best grown in a moderately cool greenhouse. *See* Greenhouse Orchids at ORCHIDS. It bears pseudobulbs* that are about 2 in. long, and from which spring 2–3 narrow leaves. Flowers yellowish-green in hanging clusters (racemes*) that are profuse-flowered and about 8 in. long. One of the sepals* and the petals alike, partially united and wavy. Lip* shorter than the sepals, with 2 crests. In the greenhouse it blooms in June–July. (Named for Bernardinus A. Gomes, Portuguese surgeon interested in Brazilian botany.)

GOMPHRENA (gom-free′na). A genus of about 70 tropical Old World herbs of the family Amaranthaceae, **G. globosa,** the globe amaranth, a deservedly popular flower garden annual, grown for its fine bloom which is so lasting when dried that the plant is one of the more useful everlastings. It is 8–20 in. high, and superficially resembles a clover. Leaves opposite,* oblongish or elliptic, 2–4 in. long, without teeth, but margins minutely hairy. Flowers chaffy, in dense, long-stalked, clover-like heads of red, pink, white, or orange flowers without petals. Fruit 1-seeded, dry (a utricle*). The globe amaranth, which is found in many hort. forms, is a fine plant for summer and later bloom, and for cutting. It should be treated as a tender annual. (*See* ANNUALS. *See also* DRIED FLOWERS, for the best method of preserving these everlastings.) (*Gomphrena* is an old name for some amaranth, but possibly not for this one.) Occasionally called bachelor's button.

GOMUTI = *Arenga saccharifera.*

GOOBER. See PEANUT.

GOOD-KING-HENRY = *Chenopodium Bonus-henricus.*

GOOD-MORNING-SPRING = *Claytonia virginica.*

GOODYERA (good-year′a). Woodland orchids suitable only for specialized sites in the wild garden. Of the 25 known species, mostly from temperate regions, only the three below are likely to be grown. They have a basal rosette of often variegated leaves and an erect, often bracted or sheathed flower stalk terminated by a small, often 1-sided spike of very irregular* flowers, which have 2 free sepals and one united with the petals into a small, hoodlike structure. (Named for John Goodyer, British botanist.) Also called *Epipactis.*

For culture *see* Hardy Orchids at ORCHIDS.

pubescens. Rattlesnake plantain; also called

---

* Special articles on the subjects indicated by an asterisk (*) will be found at the words so marked.

adder's violet. Leaves 1–2 in. long, margined toward the winged base, prominently and regularly white-mottled. Flowering stalk 7–18 in. high, densely sticky-hairy, the flowers greenish-white, about ¼ in. long. Eastern N.A., mostly in dry woods. July–Aug.

repens. Squirrel's-ear. Leaves ½–1 in. long, rather irregularly white-blotched, the base a sheathing leafstalk. There are also a few leaves on the lower part of the stem. Flowering stalk 5–9 in. high, densely sticky-hairy, the spike decidedly 1-sided. Flowers scarcely ⅛ in. long, greenish-white. Eastern N.A.

tessellata. Leaves oblongish or oval, 1–1½ in. long, tapering to a winged base, green but conspicuously white-blotched. Flowering stalk 6–9 in. high, the flowers white, about ⅙ in. long. Eastern N.A., mostly in evergreen woods. Aug.–Sept.

GOOLS = *Caltha palustris.* See MARSH MARIGOLD.

GOORA-NUT = *Cola acuminata.*

GOOSEBERRY (*Ribes*). The gooseberry is a neglected fruit in America. Perhaps not more than a dozen varieties are grown in the United States and Canada, whereas in Great Britain not less than a thousand sorts have been listed for British gardeners, with whom it is a great favorite. Americans seem not to have acquired or cultivated a taste for the gooseberry.

Gooseberries do not "strike" readily from cuttings and so are usually propagated from mound layers. In this operation vigorous, healthy bushes, 5 or 6 years old, are cut back closely in the dormant season. About the middle of July friable earth is piled up around the bushes until only the tops of the shoots are uncovered. Shoots of American varieties are well rooted by the following fall, but English sorts are left a year longer. The rooted shoots are set in nursery rows for 1 or 2 years after being detached. Rich, moist, well-drained clay soils suit gooseberries best. This is a fruit that cannot be coaxed to thrive in sands or light loams. It is just as particular about climate. English gooseberries find the hot sun of any part of America trying and refuse to grow in any part of the country except the north Atlantic and north Pacific seaboards and close to the Great Lakes. If the soil is suitable, a gooseberry will stand more shade than any other cultivated fruit, and in trying climates cannot be grown without it.

Perhaps the gooseberry is best transplanted in autumn, and if in spring it must be early, since the buds open with the first burst of spring warmth. The plants are spaced variously, depending upon the soil and the vigor of the varieties. Five feet apart each way is a fair average. Some growers like to set them close in the row with greater distances between rows. Plants well cared for last many years, and ground should be in good tilth* before planting.

In commercial plantations, gooseberries should receive shallow cultivation, but in gardens they thrive under mulches of straw or grass. Barnyard manure supplies a good mulch and a fertilizer as well. Chemical fertilizers seldom pay for their cost. If the culture of gooseberries is attempted in the interior states it is a good practice to plant them in the shade of trees, fences, or grapevines. Under shade the plants should be grown with open heads to discourage mildews.

Pruning and training is very simple but quite necessary. The fruit is borne for the most part on 2- and 3-year-old wood, and pruning is close with the view to keeping a vigorous supply of bearing wood. Cut out canes older than three years and feeble ones of lesser age. Gooseberries can be trained to single stems, but the bush form is better. A sprawling habit can be corrected by cutting back. Sometimes it is necessary to prune out the tops to lessen mildew and thin the crop.

Gooseberries, especially American varieties, are nearly always picked green, an unpleasant task, since the canes and shoots bristle with thorns. The berries are best picked by raising and steadying a cane with one hand and stripping the pendent berries off with the other — gloves on both hands.

Gooseberries belong to two quite distinct species, which gardeners classify as American and European. Downing, ripening in midseason, is the most commonly grown American sort. Josselyn (Red Jacket of some) is a good early variety. Poorman is noteworthy for its large productive bushes and handsome fruits of high quality. Out of several hundred European varieties Chautauqua and Fredonia are best and these may be grown only in the eastern parts of zones* 2 and 3, and on the Pacific Coast in zone* 4. Gardeners trained in Europe, who know this fruit well, can, with a little care, grow a good many of the splendid English varieties.

For pests *see* CURRANT.

A restriction on the cult. of currants and gooseberries is enforced by law in some states. Both of these shrubs, especially the gooseberry, harbor a microscopic parasite which lives the other half of its life on a white pine tree, which it usually kills.

Once this white pine blister rust infects the tree, nothing can be done to save it, and so serious is this to forest and ornamental plantings of white pine that the U. S. Government passed stringent quarantine laws that forbid the planting of currants and gooseberries in critical areas. This prevents the organism from completing its life cycle on these bush fruits, and saves the immensely more valuable white pine forests of the country.

If you live in any of the following states

WHITE PINE BLISTER RUST STATES		
Connecticut	Michigan	Rhode Island
Delaware	Minnesota	Tennessee
Georgia	New Hampshire	Vermont
Illinois	New Jersey	Virginia
Kentucky	New York	West Virginia
Maine	North Carolina	Wisconsin
Maryland	Ohio	
Massachusetts	Pennsylvania	

* Special articles on the subjects indicated by an asterisk (*) will be found at the words so marked.

you *must* apply to the experiment station in your state to find out whether you can plant currants or gooseberries. Do this before ordering plants from the nursery.

Not all parts of every one of these states are under the ban — only where the danger to white pine is critical. In other words, you cannot have white pines and gooseberries or currants in the same vicinity. But in many sections of at least some of the states you will be free to grow them.

GOOSEBERRY FAMILY. See SAXIFRAGACEAE.

GOOSEBERRY-TREE = *Phyllanthus acidus.*

GOOSEFOOT. See CHENOPODIUM.

GOOSEFOOT FAMILY. Besides many weeds, this large family of plants includes a few shrubs, often of desert or alkali regions, and such well-known garden plants as the beet, spinach, summer cypress, and the orach. For the other genera and a description of the family *see* CHENOPODIACEAE.

GOPHER-BERRY = *Gaylussacia dumosa.* See HUCKLEBERRY.

GOPHER-PLUM = *Chrysobalanus Icaco.*

GOPHERS. See ANIMAL INJURY.

GOPHERWOOD = *Cladrastis lutea.*

GORDONIA (gor-dō′ni-a). Rather rare, and botanically interesting, late-blooming shrubs or trees of the family Theaceae, all but two of the species Asiatic, but both the native ones grown for ornament. They have half-evergreen, or completely evergreen, alternate,* stalked leaves without marginal teeth, or remotely toothed. Flowers large, solitary, white, the 5 sepals unequal, the petals sometimes partly united. Stamens* many. Fruit a woody capsule, its seeds flat. (Named for James Gordon, English nurseryman.)

The first species has a remarkable history. It was introduced into cult. in 1770, but has never been seen again in the wild state, although it was recently reported (erroneously) as rediscovered. Both species need low, moist, peaty soils. They may be propagated by seeds, layers, or by cuttings.

altamaha. A shrub or small tree, not over 25 ft. high, the branches erect. Leaves oblongish, 5–7 in. long, remotely toothed, long-persistent, but ultimately bright crimson in the late fall. Flowers cup-shaped, fragrant, about 3½ in. wide. Fruit nearly globe-shaped, ½–¾ in. in diameter. Ga. Sept.–Oct. Hardy from zone* 5, or, with protection, from zone* 4 southward. Usually known as *Franklinia.*

Lasianthus. Loblolly bay; also called tan bay. An evergreen tree up to 60 ft. high. Leaves 5–6 in. long, oblongish, turning reddish before they fall, which is irregularly. Flowers fragrant, 2–3 in. wide, long-stalked. Fruit egg-shaped and slightly pointed. Va. to Fla. and Miss. July–Aug. Hardy from zone* 6 southward, and considerably planted in Fla. for ornament.

GORMANIA (gor-man′i-a). Succulent plants of western N.A., related to and resembling *Sedum,* and belonging to the family Crassulaceae. They have chiefly basal, roundish, blunt leaves, those on the stem fewer and smaller, but otherwise similar. Flowers in terminal clusters, red or yellowish, the 5 petals more or less united at the base. Stamens* 10. Fruit a collection of follicles.* (Named for M. W. Gorman, of Portland, Ore., a collector of plants from the Pacific Northwest.)

For culture, *see* SEDUM.

obtusata. Not over 6 in. high, the foliage sometimes bluish-green. Leaves about ¾ in. long, broadest toward the blunt tip. Flowers yellowish, the segments of it pointed, the cluster rather narrow. In the Sierras of Calif. Sometimes offered as *Sedum obtusatum.*

oregana. Not over 6 in. high, always green. Leaves less than ¾ in. long, more or less wedge-shaped at the base, broader toward the tip. Flowers yellow, fading to pink or reddish, the cluster nearly 3 in. wide and branched. Alaska to Northern Calif. Sometimes offered as *Sedum oreganum.*

watsoni. A perennial, creeping by its flat, horizontal rootstocks. Leaves spoon-shaped, blunt at the tip or with margin notched, nearly 1 in. long. Flowers lemon yellow, in a longish cluster (cyme*). Ore. Also known as *Sedum watsoni.*

GORSE. See FURZE.

GOSMORE = *Hypochaeris radicata.* See Cat's-ear in the list at WEEDS.

GOSSYPIUM (gos-sip′i-um). While cotton is in no sense a garden plant, its huge commercial culture for fiber, and the fact that the different species are occasionally grown for interest or ornament, make a brief note on them necessary here. The flowers are also favorites of the bees, although it is scarcely cult. for that purpose, except possibly in parts of Calif. The genus contains perhaps 30 species, belonging to the family Malvaceae, some of them woody herbs, but some tree-like. Practically all of them are grown as annuals in the U.S. All are of tropical origin and need a long season and much heat to produce seed. Consequently, their commercial culture is confined to the cotton belt, which roughly coincides with the region from zone* 7 southward, although the plant will flower much farther north. Leaves alternate,* more or less lobed or ribbed finger-fashion, often dotted. Flowers usually solitary in the leaf axils,* large, showy, generally white, yellow, or pinkish-purple, but often changing color soon after opening. Below the flower is a collection of 3–7, often fringed or cut, bracts.* Calyx* 5-lobed. Petals 5. Stamens numerous, joined together to form a tube around the style.* Fruit a capsule* (the cotton boll), containing the seeds, to which is attached the fiber (cotton). (*Gossypium* is a very old name for the cotton plant.) There are now many valuable named forms of the species below, and these are the ones chiefly grown commercially.

arboreum. Tree cotton; also called Indian tree cotton. An erect plant 8–10 ft. high, the branches glossy and purple. Leaves leathery, 3–7-lobed, sometimes deeply so. Flowers small, pale yellow or whitish-pink, sometimes

---

* Special articles on the subjects indicated by an asterisk (*) will be found at the words so marked.

blotched at the center (with an eye*). Fruit egg-shaped or ovalish, the lint of the seeds dull white or reddish. Old World tropics. Not one of the commercial cottons in the U.S.

barbadense. Sea-island cotton; sometimes called tree cotton, and widely grown commercially here and in Egypt. It is a shrubby plant 5–8 ft. high. Leaves as broad as long, 3–5-lobed, the lobes pointed, the base more or less heart-shaped. Flowers yellow, but purple-tinged. Fruit 3–4-valved, the lint of the seeds yielding fine long-staple cotton. Tropical America, but described first from Barbados, W.I.

herbaceum. Levant cotton. Stem not woody, annual. Leaves generally heart-shaped, 5–7-lobed, the lobes not deeper than half the distance to the center. Flowers yellow, the center purplish. Fruit 4–5-celled, the lint of the seeds grayish. Asia Minor or Arabia, probably. Not grown commercially, but assumed as one of the parents of certain short-staple U.S. cotton varieties.

hirsutum. Upland cotton and a commercially important source of both long- and short-staple varieties. Mostly an annual, much branched, reddish-stemmed plant 2–5 ft. high. Leaves 3–6 in. wide, 3-lobed, the lobes broad below but pointed at the tip. Flowers yellowish-white, but soon turning purplish-pink. Fruit 1½–3½ in. long, 4-celled, the lint white. Tropical America.

mexicanum. Mexican cotton. A shrubby plant of no commercial importance in the U.S., 3–5-lobed leaves that are divided only about ⅓ the distance to the center. Flowers yellowish-white tinged with pink. Lint or fuzz of the seeds grayish. Mex.

punctatum. Jamaica cotton. A shrubby, noncommercial cotton, the stems 4–5 ft. high. Leaves softly hairy, divided halfway to the middle, strongly dotted. Flowers yellow, the center brown. Lint or fuzz of the seeds grayish or rusty. Tropical America and Africa.

GOURD FAMILY = Cucurbitaceae.

GOURDS. As distinguished from the edible melons, pumpkins, squashes and cucumbers, the ornamental gourds are chiefly grown for show. All belong to the family Cucurbitaceae, and their need for heat, moisture, and rich soil is the same as for the melons (which see for cultural directions).

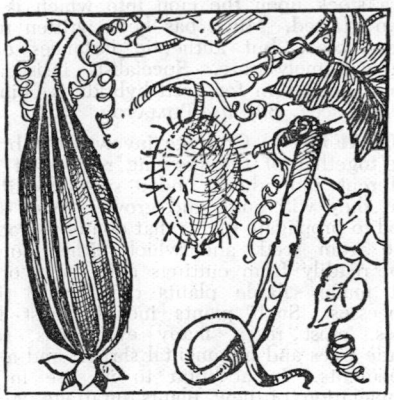

Gourds. At the left, the dishrag gourd; in the center, the mock-cucumber, a hardy, native gourd; at the right, the snake gourd.

All the ornamental gourds in this book are described at the following genera: *Abobra, Cucumis, Cucurbita, Lagenaria, Luffa,* and *Trichosanthes.* Some of them have grotesque fruits, as shown in the illustrations, while others are extremely decorative and are grown to cover porches, screens, or fences, which they do in a very short time. (*See* VINES.) While they can be treated as tender annuals, they do not bear transplanting well, and are better sown where wanted, after settled warm weather has arrived. If grown in an open bed some sort of a rough-barked, twiggy post, or trellis must be provided for them. All are tendril-bearing vines, which, without support, will sprawl like a pumpkin vine. Some of their fruits make handsome table decorations.

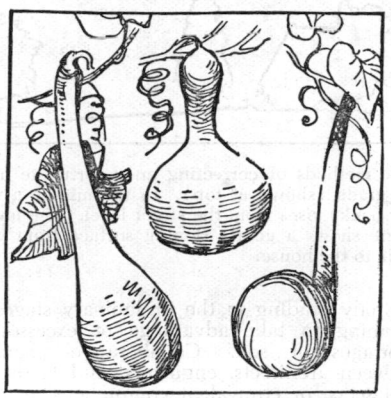

Various forms of the bottle gourd

A hardy, native one is *Echinocystis lobata,* the mock-cucumber. The Gourd Society of America welcomes those interested in these plants. Its present address is Horticultural Hall, Boston 15, Mass.

GOUTWEED = *Aegopodium Podagraria.*

GOVERNOR'S-PLUM = *Flacourtia indica.*

gracilipes (gra-sill′i-peez). Slender-stalked; literally slender-footed.

gracilis, -e (grass′i-lis). Slender and graceful.

gracilistylis, -e (gra-sill-i-sty′lis). With slender styles.*

gracillima, -us, -um (gra-sill′i-ma). Very slender or graceful.

GRADING LAND. In reshaping land for use the term grading is used in engineering practice where utility is the primary purpose. Grading as applied to landscape design should be more than an engineering operation, it should be a process of modeling land primarily for appearance. Wherever it is necessary to change the natural shape of land for practical use the remodeling is quite as essential to landscape beauty as any other

* Special articles on the subjects indicated by an asterisk (*) will be found at the words so marked.

phase of composition. No amount of planting or architectural ornamentation will compensate for ugly grading.

Two methods of correcting an unfortunate natural grade (shown at top). In the middle a wall (or bank) rises from the street level. The lowest figure shows a gently sloping surface from sidewalk to the house.

Study grading in the preliminary stages of planning to take advantage of excesses or shortages of soil. Collaborative planning between architects, engineers, and landscape architects, or equivalent comprehensive planning by individuals, is essential to efficient and well-designed grading.

Use excavation from building foundations, roads or walls as subsoil to create terraces or improve the general grade. Gardens and ter-

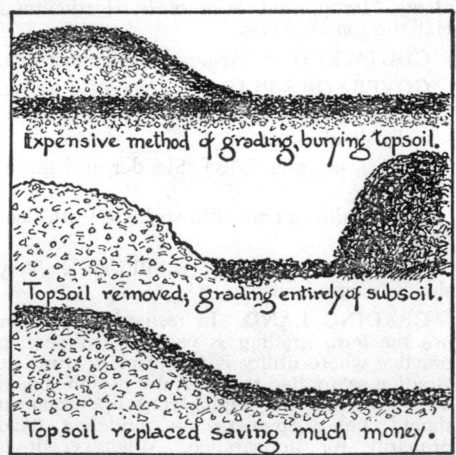

Much money is wasted in grading if expensive topsoil is buried. Study the two lower figures to see how this can be avoided.

races can usually be made to utilize excess excavation or, when necessary, to provide extra fill. When such adjustments are left to afterthought, opportunities for utilizing these differences to advantage are often lost. With modern engineering equipment it is possible to anticipate and utilize the exact amount of grading involved in any construction operation. Before starting any subgrading, conserve all existing topsoil and pile in convenient piles out of the way of all construction. On large operations a power shovel can skim soil as thin as six inches. On smaller jobs plow to the depth of good soil and use a scoop to collect the soil in piles. A haul of over 100 yards is not efficiently done by scoops; for longer hauls load on 2-ton dump trucks.

The subgrade should be modeled to conform to the finished grade, allowing six inches for topsoil on lawn areas, and at least 24 inches for planting beds. Planting pockets may be distributed before topsoil is replaced. If possible, mix manure with topsoil when it is piled and if weeds grow in the pile keep them cut to avoid weed seeds.

The solution of the drainage system is a part of the grading problem and they should be planned together. Unless they are equally well planned one or the other is bound to be unsatisfactory. One of the practical reasons for grading is to control drainage. Whenever possible open drainage gutters should be avoided in landscape grading. By providing frequent drain inlets, water can be carried away in underground lines cheaper than constantly repairing surface gutters. Properly modeled land surfaces should be drained effectively without causing erosion or allowing water to accumulate where it can cause damage. Inadequate drainage will result in erosion, and unsatisfactory grading will result in drains being clogged or washed out. — R. E. G. and G. E.

graeca, -us, -um (gree'ka). Grecian.

GRAFT-HYBRID. The assumed influence of a stock upon the cion into which it has been grafted. Much has been written upon this subject, but authentic instances of it are extremely rare. Specialists insist that the correct term for graft-hybrids is chimera (which see). *See also* POMATO.

GRAFTING. Graftage involves the bringing together of the growing regions of two different individuals under such conditions that they will unite and grow as one. It is used to propagate plants that do not reproduce true from seed, and which either do not root readily from cuttings and layers or do not make salable plants quickly by these processes. Such plants include most fruit trees, most roses, many evergreens, some shade trees and ornamental shrubs, and a few succulents. In addition to its use in the propagation of new plants, graftage is also used to change the top of an established plant, as by top-working bearing fruit trees; to correct an injury, as by bridge-grafting and inarching girdled trees; to alter the

* Special articles on the subjects indicated by an asterisk (*) will be found at the words so marked.

behavior of the top, as by propagating a fruit variety upon dwarf roots to dwarf the entire plant; and to adapt a plant to otherwise unfavorable conditions, as the propagation of apples upon roots resistant to root rot.

A graft is composed of **stock** and **cion**. The stock is a plant or portion of a plant upon which the graft is to be made. The cion is the part inserted upon the stock. **Union** is accomplished by placing the **cambium region** (*see* BARK), the region where the bark separates from the wood, of stock and of cion against each other. Growth of both stock and cion in the cambium region results in so-called union, by an interlacing and dovetailing of tissues. Sharp tools, clean, straight cuts, careful matching of cambium regions, snug fitting and fastening, and careful protection from drying of tissues, both before and after the grafting operation, are conducive to success.

The union of plants with one another by grafting is limited by their congeniality, a fact which can be determined solely by experience. In general, only plants closely related botanically can be made to grow together, such as peach on peach, apple on apple, spruce on spruce, and walnut on walnut. Yet the peach may be grafted upon its near relative, the plum, with a fair degree of success, and the pear upon the quince, while the McIntosh apple fails completely upon a selected apple rootstock upon which the Northern Spy variety succeeds. In some instances of uncongeniality **double-working** is resorted to, in which the uncongenial cion and stock are made to succeed by the interposition of a portion of stem from a third species or variety, with which the uncongenial cion and stock are both congenial, as the use of a stem-piece of Beurré Hardy pear between a quince root and a Bartlett pear cion.

The best time for grafting many woody plants out of doors is in early spring just before growth starts, yet if the cions are maintained dormant by storage under cool, moist conditions, grafting may be done even after the stock has begun new growth. With grafting of plants in full leaf and active growth, success is dependent largely upon keeping the cion from drying out, as by enclosing the grafted plants in closed frames with high humidity.

Cion wood of deciduous woody plants should be dormant both when it is collected and when it is used. Wood should be taken from vigorous shoots of the past season's growth, 12 in. or more in length. It is possible, however, to use 2- and even 3-year-old wood. It should be collected in late fall or early winter, tied in bundles, packed in sawdust or peat moss, and stored in a cool, damp place such as a cool cellar. A temperature of 40° is best. Two or 3 in. of the base and a portion of the tip of the shoot should be discarded, since the buds at the base of the shoots are frequently poorly developed, while the tip is frequently

soft. If it becomes necessary to collect frozen wood, it should be carefully handled and should be thawed slowly, as in a cool room, but not in water.

Grafts are classified and named according to:

(1) Time, as summer grafting, winter grafting, or dormant grafting;

(2) Place, as root graft, crown graft, stem graft, and top graft;

(3) Part used, as root graft, twig graft, sprig graft;

(4) Description of method or type of cut, as cleft graft, bridge graft, bark graft, saddle graft, veneer graft, side graft, and tongue graft. Accordingly, a plant may be root grafted by tongue grafting, it may be top grafted by cleft grafting, and so on. **Budding,** in which a single bud is used in place of a cion, may quite properly be included as a method of grafting, but is treated separately. *See* BUDDING.

There are endless modifications of the principal forms of graftage, each named by its originator or user for convenience, or because it describes a method found successful with some particular material or in some particular locality. Most of them are merely variations of the forms described under the following general headings.

CLEFT GRAFTING

The cleft graft is most often used on large trees. Trees of more than 8 years of age are better top-worked during more than one season because of the severe pruning incident to cleft grafting. Work the center and top of the tree the first season, otherwise the grafts may be shaded; and work the sides and lower portions the next and succeeding seasons.

The most favorable time for cleft grafting is just before growth starts, although it may be done both during the winter and also after growth has started. The cion wood, however, must be dormant. Choose branches ranging from 1 to 4 in. in diameter; those about 1½ to 2 in. across are the most convenient and satisfactory. For very large limbs the *bark graft*, described later, is preferred. The limb should be sawed off squarely and split with a grafting chisel and mallet.

In making the split, care should be taken to see that it does not run into a knot, but extends straight down on either side of the limb. In cases where four or more cions are wanted, the extra clefts should be made parallel to the first and not across it. The two halves of the limb are spread apart by the wedge on the grafting chisel.

Cions should bear two or three buds, preferably three, although it is possible to use only one when economy of wood is essential. Beginning on either side of a bud, with two strokes of the knife cut the lower end of the cion in the form of a wedge, one side

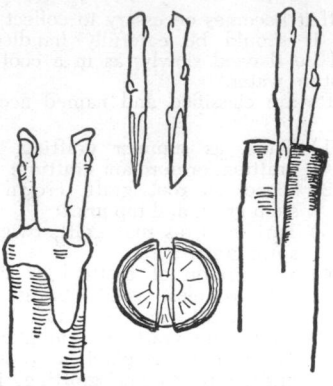

Cleft grafting, showing (*top center*) the two cions and (*bottom center*) the stock, both cut ready for grafting. At the right, the cions inserted in the stock. At the left, the finished graft with its coating of wax.

of which should be slightly narrower than the other. If the sides of the cion are not cut clean and straight so as to taper evenly, the point of contact may be only at the thickest portion of the cion rather than through its length. The wedge of the cion is then inserted into the cleft with its narrower side toward the center of the stock, thus allowing the outer and thicker edge of the cion to be firmly gripped when the parts of the stock spring together. Utmost care should be taken to match the growing layer, or inner bark, of the cion with that of the stock. They must come in contact. If the cion is set too far toward the center of the cleft, the cambium zones will not match.

The final step is waxing. The wax should be spread in a thin coat over all the cut surfaces, including the tip of the cion, and extending down the limb on both sides covering the cleft. For its preparation *see* GRAFTING WAX. Some prefer paraffin (which see).

A variation of the cleft graft may be used to propagate varieties of grapes of both American and European species upon phylloxera-resistant or more vigorous roots, and also to change a bearing vine to another variety. The work may be done after active growth has passed, or preferably, just before growth starts in early spring. Established vines, preferably not over 6 or 8 years old, are sawed off at the ground. With a thin-bladed saw a cleft is cut down through the center of the stock for about 2 in. Cions are cut with two buds, with the wedge starting at the lower bud. A single cion is then inserted in the cleft as already described for fruit trees. Two cions may be used if the stock is large. No wax is used, and it is usually not necessary to tie the graft except with young vines. Dry dirt is mounded over the graft, covering the top of the cion, so as to keep the graft uniformly moist and at a more even

temperature. Two or three times during the summer the mound should be removed to cut away any sprouts which come from the stock and any roots which come from the cion.

WEDGE GRAFTING. This is the same in general principle as the cleft graft, differing in that a wedge is cut in the stock rather than merely splitting it. It generally involves herbaceous or soft-wooded plants, both stock and cion being of nearly the same size, and the cion being held in place by tying.

WHIP GRAFTING

The whip graft, also called **tongue graft,** is used for small limbs, for grafting grapes, and for root grafting nursery stock. It is easily made, and because of the several uniting edges, forms a good union. In the case of trees, the stock should be cut off with a slanting cut 1½ in. long. Half an inch down from the cut end of the stock, cut, but do not split, a tongue downwards about half an inch. The objection to splitting the tongue is that it leaves a rough surface which will not fit the cion.

The base of the cion is prepared in the same way as the stock, and the two are then fitted to match the growing parts along one side. The union should be bound with common twine, grafting tape, or, if available, waxed string or waxed cloth strips, and then thoroughly waxed. After growth is well started, usually in June, the strings under the wax should be cut to prevent girdling. This is best done by drawing a sharp knife up the back side of the graft.

In grafting the grape, the procedure is similar, the best results being secured in March. For the stock, sections of 1-year canes should be used, 8 to 10 in. in length and at least ¼ in. in diameter, the top cut being made 1½ in. above the top bud and all buds removed so as to lessen sucker growth. The cion is made with one bud, the lower cut being made 2½ in. below the bud and the upper cut 1½ in. above. The stock and cion are joined as described above, and tied with wax string. The resulting grafts are packed upright in a box in wet sawdust and stored at 70° to 75°. They are planted out in the nursery row before the buds have started.

ROOT GRAFTING

In the case of root grafting with nursery stock, seedling roots are cut into pieces 4 or 5 in. long and cions are prepared of the same length and of as nearly the same diameter as the roots as possible. The process is the same as in top-working, except that no wax is used, while grafting tape and waxed string are preferred for tying. The grafts are packed away in damp moss or sand in a cool cellar until spring when they are planted in nursery rows leaving only the upper bud above ground. Careful matching of stock and cion will reduce loss from callus knot formation. Sometimes a whole root is used instead of short pieces, when the graft is known as a **whole-**

---

* Special articles on the subjects indicated by an asterisk (*) will be found at the words so marked.

root graft, as contrasted with **piece-root graft.**
In cases where it is desired to secure a cion-
rooted plant, a **nurse-root graft** may be used,
in which the cion of a root graft is planted
deep so as to encourage rooting of the cion,
after which the nurse root is cut off. A copper wire may be placed just above the union
so as gradually to constrict the nurse root and
automatically cut it off without the necessity
of digging the entire plant to remove it.

There are various modifications of the whip
graft of which the **side whip graft** is one,
in which the cion is placed on the side of a
stock rather than on the end of it. The cut
end of the cion may be left long or the tie
allowed to hang down so as to rest in a
container of water and supply water by absorption while the graft is uniting. This is
sometimes called **bottle grafting,** more interesting than useful.

SPLICE GRAFTING

Splice grafting, used for tender wood which
does not split readily, and for small shoots,
is perhaps the simplest form of grafting.
The cion and stock are cut with a
diagonal cut as for whip grafting, the tongue
being omitted, and tied together. Sometimes
a pin is placed vertically in the stock, and
the cion pressed down upon it, so as to

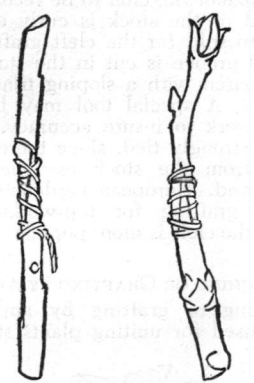

At the right, a saddle graft; at the left,
a splice graft

make the graft more firm. With cions which
have a terminal bud, and with some soft and
herbaceous plants, as cacti, the stock is cut
flat wedge-shaped and the cion, with a split
or wedge-shaped cut in the lower end, placed
upon it, whence the name **saddle graft.**

SIDE GRAFTING

The side graft is a form of grafting used
with both dormant and full-growing plants,
in which the cion is inserted in the side of
the stock, the stock being cut off just above
the point of insertion either immediately after
grafting, at a later time, or not at all, as the

case may demand. It is used in grafting
woody ornamentals with slender stems, particularly potted junipers, arborvitae, and
spruce; and because of the rapidity of the
method it may be used in top-working fruit
trees. In the case of evergreens, potted
stocks 2³⁄₁₆ to ³⁄₁₆ in. in diameter are used.
A cut is made in the side of the stock about
1½ in. long, running just inside the wood, the
flap of bark and wood being left attached
at the lower end. The cion is prepared
wedge-shaped, with smooth cuts of similar
length, and the two cut surfaces placed carefully against each other, the flap of bark
and wood from the stock being brought
up along the cion and the graft and securely
tied. In 3 or 4 weeks part of the stock is
cut off so as to force the cion into growth,
and four weeks later the remainder is removed just above the union.

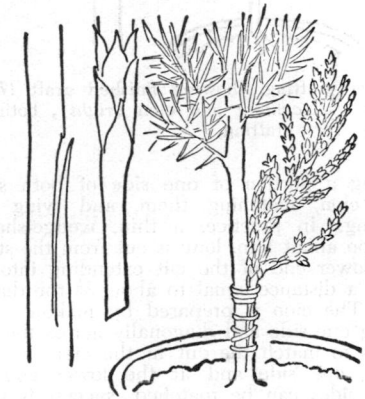

The side grafting of evergreens. At the left, the
stock cut to receive the cion (*in the center*).

In its use in top-working fruit trees during
the dormant season small branches not over
¾ in. in diameter are best. A downward-
slanting cut is made nearly to the pith, and
the cion is prepared wedge-shaped as already
described. The stock is then bent so as to
open the cut, the cion pushed down into it,
the stock cut off just above the cut, and the
entire graft waxed. No tying is necessary,
since the spring of the wood holds the cion
in place.

There are several minor forms of grafting
which are but variations of the side graft,
suited to particular material. One of these is
the **shield graft** or **sprig graft,** used advantageously in grafting the mulberry with
dormant cions in early spring, and for the
weeping and purple beech in fall with
freshly cut cions. A T-shape incision is cut
in the bark of the stock as for budding (*see*
BUDDING). Into this incision, a wedge-shaped
cion is inserted, tied in place, and waxed,
the stock being headed back and eventually
cut off just above the cion.

---

* Special articles on the subjects indicated by an asterisk (*) will be found at the words so marked.

Veneer Grafting

The veneer graft is a very useful form of side graft used largely with ornamentals, as evergreens, *Rhododendron,* and Japanese maples. In general principle it consists in ex-

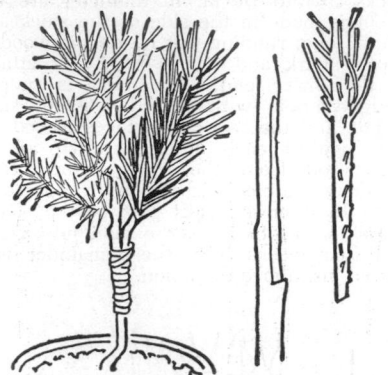

Veneer grafting, showing finished graft (*left*), the stock (*center*) and cion (*right*), both cut ready for grafting.

posing a portion of one side of both stock and cion, matching them, and tying and waxing. In practice, a thin, wedge-shaped section about 1 in. long is cut from the stock, the lower end of the cut extending into the stem a distance equal to about ⅓ the diameter. The cion is prepared by making a cut along one side and diagonally across the end so as to match the cut in the cion, at least along one side and at the lower end. If both sides can be matched, success is more likely. The union is tied and waxed, and subsequent care is as described under side graft.

Bark Grafting

Bark grafting is employed in place of cleft grafting with material the bark of which does not split well, as the cherry, and when the stock is much larger than the cion. The work is done in the spring when the bark will slip. The cion must be dormant. The stock is cut off, as for the cleft graft, and a slit made downward in the bark for about 1½ in. from the end of the stub in the positions where the cions are to be placed. The cions are cut flat and wedge-shaped on one side and pushed down between the slit bark, held in place with slender brads, and the entire graft covered with wax. The cions may be prepared quite thin by cutting a shoulder in them so that they will slip under the bark more easily. The bark graft is used in rehabilitating trees of large diameter cut off near the crown, whence it has been unfortunately called **crown graft.**

Inlaying

Inlaying refers to a refinement in various forms of grafting to adapt that method to particular material. It consists in carefully removing a definite area of the stock and preparing a similar area of the cion so that it will exactly fit into the stock. It is a useful refinement in the case of the bark graft and the bridge graft, where the stock has heavy bark, and will not split readily. In such cases a piece of bark is cut from the stock just the size of the cion to be received. Where the wood of the stock is curly or otherwise difficult to split for the cleft graft, a sloping, V-shaped groove is cut in the stock, and the cion prepared with a sloping triangular edge to match. A special tool may be procured for this work to insure accuracy. The cions must be strongly tied, since there is no such support from the stock as when the cleft graft is used. European gardeners prefer this form of grafting for top-working, but in America the cleft is more popular.

Inarching or Grafting by Approach

Inarching or **grafting by approach** is a method used for uniting plants still attached

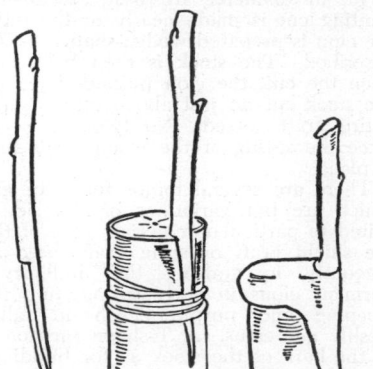

Bark grafting. Cion (*left*), stock (*center*) with cion inserted near the bark, and the finished, waxed job at the right.

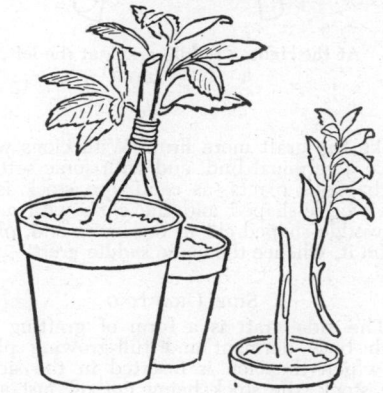

Inarching or grafting by approach. *See* text for explanation.

* Special articles on the subjects indicated by an asterisk (*) will be found at the words so marked.

to their own roots, and is useful for plants which are otherwise difficult to unite, for rapid propagation of rare specimens, and for repairing and bracing injured or weak trees and crotches. Either the veneer or the tongue graft may be used, the principal feature being to expose the cambium regions of both plants and fasten them together in such a position that they will unite. When union has been accomplished one plant may be severed from its own roots just below the union. Merely twisting together and tightly fastening young shoots from opposite forks of a crotch will produce a natural graft for strengthening the crotch, although best results are secured by exposing the cambium regions of both shoots by thinly slicing the bark from where the shoots are in contact. Grafting by approach has been used to secure early flowering of seedling roses in breeding work, in which the new plants, while only a few weeks old from seed, are grafted to a vigorous potted stock.

CUTTING-GRAFTAGE

Cutting-graftage combines the rooting of cuttings with the operation of grafting, useful with plants which are difficult to root, are uncongenial, or are otherwise difficult to unite. Nurse-rooting grafting (*see* Whip Grafting) is a form of cutting-graftage. Still another mode is to permit the cion or "cutting" to project downward beyond the point of union with the stock and to stand in moist soil, a dish of water, or damp peat moss so as to keep the cion fresh until union has been accomplished. The lower projecting portion of the cion is later cut off.

BRIDGE GRAFTING

This form of grafting is used to preserve trees injured or girdled by rodents or suffering from winter injury or disease. Ragged edges and loose bark should be cleanly cut away. In case the injury extends to the roots, the earth must be removed from the base of the tree and the larger roots until sound bark is uncovered. A longitudinal slit is made in the bark, both above and below the wound, and the edges of the slits loosened. With older trees with thick bark, make two parallel slits as far apart as the cion is wide so as to lift a tongue of bark. A cion should then be cut 2 or 3 in. longer than the space to be bridged, one side beveled off at both ends, and inserted in the slits, beveled face against the wood of the trunk. When the space to be covered is more than 12 in., the cion should be long enough to stand out an inch from the trunk when in place. In order to guard against any accidental displacement, it is well to drive a small brad through each end of the cion, which, however, must not be split in the operation.

Other cions in a like manner may be inserted at intervals of about 2 in. around the injured surface, taking care to ensure cions directly under the main branches. The ends of the cion should be covered with wax, but it is not necessary to cover all of the bridge portion of the trunk. If the tree is so small as to wave in the wind, it should be tied to a strong stake.

With old trees having very thick bark, and on old roots, the method of inlaying is used, in which a piece of bark is removed 3 or 4

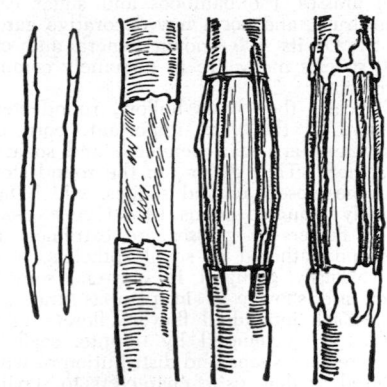

Bridge grafting. For details *see* text.

in. long and as wide as the end of the cion. The cion is cut flat on one side and fitted into place in the stock prepared to receive it and is fastened with small brads driven through it.

In cases of extensive injury, young trees may be grafted by approach by planting around the injured tree and their tops either inserted or veneer grafted above the wound. —H. B. T.

GRAFTING WAX. An essential feature of this material is that it will "work" without becoming "tacky." One way to avoid both troubles is to keep the fingers greased while using the wax. But unless of the proper consistency, no grafting wax is likely to be very workable. A good formula for the average grafting wax:

    1 lb. of tallow
    2 lbs. of common beeswax
    4 lbs. of resin

These should be melted together and thoroughly mixed, after which the mixture should be poured into a tub of cold water. Before it thoroughly hardens it should be "pulled" just as molasses candy is pulled, after which it can be stored almost indefinitely. It will, of course, harden somewhat after long storage, but, if properly made, will soften up enough through the heat of one's hand to be workable.

There are also several prepared, commercial substitutes for the above. If they exclude the air for the necessary time and do not harden too much, they save the trouble of making the above mixture.

GRAM. *See* PHASEOLUS AUREUS and P. MUNGO.

---

* Special articles on the subjects indicated by an asterisk (*) will be found at the words so marked.

graminea, -us, -um (gra-min'i-a). Grass-like.

GRAMINEAE (gra-min'ee-ee). The grass family (often called Poaceae) is an immense aggregation of plants of world-wide distribution and of supreme importance because it yields the world's cereals, all its forage and lawn grasses, the bamboos and sugar cane, some drugs, and not a few decorative garden plants. Of its 400 known genera and over 6000 species many are in extremely common cultivation.

Typically they have hollow, round stems, but two of the most important, corn and sugar cane, are solid-stemmed, and so are a few others. They differ (in the round stem) from the closely related sedges, which have typically 3-angled stems (*see* Cyperaceae).

The flowers of grasses are extremely minute and gathered in small spikelets, which are variously grouped in clusters, some of which are showy, as in pampas grass and corn. Each individual flower (floret) in the spikelet is surrounded by minute, scale-like structures, the shape and distribution of which are used as diagnostic characters to separate the different genera — a study far outside the scope of this book and the equipment or patience of the average gardener. For this reason no attempt will be made here to list all the cult. genera, nor to describe their wholly technical distinctions at their vocabulary entries.

From the purely hort. standpoint the chief cult. grasses may be grouped thus:

Cereals: *Euchlaena, Zea* (*see* Corn), *Oryza* (*see* Rice), *Secale* (*see* Rye), *Avena, Coix, Pennisetum, Triticum, Hordeum, Eleusine,* etc.

Pasture and Lawn Grasses: *Alopecurus, Agrostis, Arrhenatherum, Axonopus, Bromus, Dactylis, Festuca, Cynodon, Lolium, Phleum, Poa,* etc.

Bamboo and its Relatives: Tall and woody. *Bambusa, Arundinaria, Phyllostachys, Dendrocalamus,* etc.

Ornamental Grasses, without much economic value, and grown chiefly for show: *Miscanthus, Vetiveria, Anthoxanthum, Erianthus, Cortaderia, Phragmites, Lamarckia, Tricholaena, Uniola, Stipa, Lagurus,* etc.

Sugar-producing: *Saccharum* (sugar cane) and some sorghums (*see* Sorghum).

Besides these there are many other cult. genera, and not a few grasses are pernicious weeds (*see* the list at Weeds).

graminifolia, -us, -um (gra-mi-ni-fō'li-a). With grass-like leaves.

granadensis, -e (gran-a-den'sis). From Granada, Spain, or Nicaragua.

GRANADILLA. *See* Passiflora.

Granatum (gra-nā'tum). Pre-Linnaean* name for the pomegranate.

grandicornis, -e (grand-i-kor'nis). Large-horned.

grandiflora, -us, -um (gran-di-flaw'ra). Large- or showy-flowered.

grandifolia, -us, -um (gran-di-fō'lee-a). Large-leaved.

grandis, -e (gran'diss). Large or showy.

granitica, -us, -um (gra-ni'ti-ka). Growing on granite or in granite crevices.

GRAPE. The grape of history, the classics, and Bacchus came only from the vine. Ever since they have been called *vinifera* grapes, because they stem from a European or Persian species known as *Vitis vinifera,* the latter name meaning wine-bearing. This is *the* grape of California, now found in scores of varieties, and produces wine, table grapes and raisins, but it cannot safely be grown east of the Rocky Mountains.

This limits the home grower (and all the professionals) in the East to grape varieties that have been mostly developed from native wild species and their hybridized progeny. Among them are old favorites like the Concord and Catawba, and these, with other varieties to be mentioned presently, must be our compensation for not being able to grow the admittedly superior varieties that have made California the greatest grape-growing region in the New World. Very superior table grapes and some of our driest sherries are produced from those grape varieties that can be grown in the East, and New York State champagne is not inferior to many French products.

The grape, in nature, is an immense woody vine, often climbing to the top of the tallest trees, and producing a woody stem almost trunk-like in age. All garden varieties for the East have been derived from such vines, but we must control this vegetative exuberance for the very good reason that fruit is borne only on canes that are 2 years old, which should then be removed after fruiting.

It is the annual production of these 2-year-old canes that makes grape pruning a necessity, whether you train the vines on wires, which is the best method, or grow them on arbors, which is decidedly next best, but dear to the hearts of youngsters and many oldsters with nostalgic memories. Keep in mind that grapes are never produced on old wood, so that long, woody vines may give shade (on an arbor), but will produce only as many grapes as there happen to be 2-year old canes on such an old and neglected vine.

Whether you train them on wires or on an arbor, grapes should not be planted less than 8 feet apart; and, if grown on wires, the rows should be at least that distance apart, or even more. Neither wires nor arbor need to be constructed the first year, because the vines are allowed to sprawl for one growing season, and no grapes will be harvested until later.

When the plants arrive from the nursery and have been planted in early spring, select only one or two of the thickest stems to leave, cutting off all weak and spindling ones. During the following winter select the best

---

* Special articles on the subjects indicated by an asterisk (*) will be found at the words so marked.

cane you have, cutting it back to about 5 feet in length if you grow it on wires, or 7 feet if on arbors. This will ultimately make the permanent stem or "trunk" of your vine. All other canes should be cut off, except one other which may be allowed to grow for a year or two as a possible substitute in case the main stem fails. Later such substitute canes should be removed, if the permanent one is thrifty, as the ultimate aim is to produce only one main stem for each plant.

As soon as possible tie this to the lowest wire (which should be 2½ feet above the ground) and later to the top wire (which is 5 feet from the ground). If you grow them on an arbor 7 feet high, let the main stem (and only this one) grow to that height. Both wires (which should be stretched tightly between posts set 20 feet apart) and arbors should be put up in the late summer or autumn of the second year.

It is in the winter of the second year that pruning is most important, because you then begin the production of canes that will produce fruit the third year. The trunk should by that time have reached the topmost wire (or the top of the arbor) and should be securely tied. It will, in the meantime have produced several or many lateral canes, all but four of which should be removed. Let these grow laterally, one on each wire, to the left and right of the trunk. Tie the four to the wires (or arms of the arbor) but do not let these laterals interfere with the laterals that come from neighboring trunks. Cut them back so that they have 10–12 buds per cane and no more. From these buds shoots will spring and bear grapes that season, but not again.

After the canes have borne fruit they should be removed, and new young canes be allowed to take their place for fruiting next year. You must, to get the best fruit, be constantly cutting off old fruiting canes so that they can be replaced with new ones. Left to itself any grapevine will produce far more canes than it needs, but by proper pruning you can keep it to the four-cane method, which is universally used by most professionals and is by far the easiest method for the home grower. It is known as the 4-cane Kniffen system and without it, or some modification of it, grapevines become unmanageable or over-bear with inferior fruit. Your plant at this stage, if grown on wires, should look very like the illustration.

The grape is quite adaptable to many sorts of climate, and thus some variety can be found for all fruit districts except the extreme North. In the coastal plain and southeastern states most of the best varieties cannot be grown. But from wild grapes of this region several varieties have been developed, notably the Scuppernong, which is good eating and produces a sweet, musky wine.

In the home garden, assuming you have a reasonably good soil, fertilizers or manures should not be used — they merely promote a lush, vegetative growth which you are try-

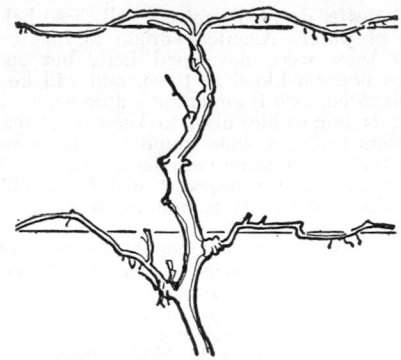

The Four-cane Kniffen System of pruning and training grapes, used for most varieties except *vinifera* grapes. *See* below.

ing to reduce by pruning. The plant wants plenty of summer heat, a sandy or even a gravelly loam, and not too much humidity. These conditions, which prevail in France and California, are impossible to imitate in the East, but our ideal grape regions and culture methods approach them. That is why grapes grow better in the Middle West than along the Atlantic seaboard, especially south of Delaware.

One thing grapes will not tolerate is too much moisture at their roots. That is why so many commercially successful vineyards are on well-drained hillsides.

All the varieties to be mentioned presently are self-fertile, but many grapes are self-sterile. If you plant a variety not in the list below (there are scores to choose from), always inquire from the nurseryman whether or not it is a self-fertile sort. If not, it must be interplanted with some other variety.

VARIETIES

No true *vinifera* grapes can be recommended for the eastern states, although experimental planting of them in warm, dry sections of the South is perhaps justified. Nor can zones[*] 1 and 2 be recommended for the varieties suitable for the East. The growing season (the time between the last killing frost in spring and the first in the autumn) is too short for proper maturity of fruit, and early spring frosts often do damage.

For the remainder of the East the selection of varieties suffers from a plethora of material. Many native American grapes were sent to France years ago because they were more immune to the dreaded phylloxera disease than the *vinifera* varieties of that country. The American sorts were used as stocks upon which to grow *vinifera* grapes, and were sometimes crossed with the latter. Back-crosses of some of these French hybrids were made with native American varieties, so that today the parentage of many grape varieties is decidedly mixed. All those below are of purely American origin in the sense that they were developed here, but some have *vinifera* blood in them, and will be so designated, as it is important culturally.

It is impossible, also, to know how many readers prefer a wine grape to a table sort, but fortunately some varieties are suitable for both. In the list below it will be specified whether the variety is best for white or red wines.

CONCORD. The most popular grape in cultivation for the home garden. Fruit black, with a bloom, large, foxy and aromatic, midseason, the skin thick and somewhat tough.

FREDONIA. A black-fruited variety originating in New York in 1915, covered with a heavy bloom. Juice somewhat foxy, sweet, aromatic. An early grape, good for eating and for red wine.

NIAGARA. A good green table grape, suited to the highland regions of the Southeast and hardy up to zone* 4.

IVES. Originated in Ohio in 1841 (?). Fruit blue-black, not so good for table, but one of the best for red wine.

CATAWBA. Known in the District of Columbia as early as 1823 and contains some *vinifera* blood. Fruit purplish-red, with a bloom, aromatic, reasonably sweet, late-season, and fine for dessert. It is one of the best, also, for all white wines.

BROCTON. A medium-sized fruit, green to amber-colored, the pulp juicy, sweet, delicately flavored, the skin rather thin and tender. Midseason. Very good, also, for white wines. Has *vinifera* blood in it.

ONTARIO. Fruit medium-sized, amber to greenish, with a light bloom, the pulp juicy, sweet. An early variety with *vinifera* blood in it and especially good for dessert. Not a wine grape.

DELAWARE. Known in Ohio as early as 1849. Fruit light red, with a thin pale bloom, the pulp juicy, above the average in sweetness, aromatic and vinous. One of the best for table use and a good grape for white wines. Has *vinifera* blood in it.

GOLDEN MUSCAT. Fruit green to amber-colored, larger than most, the pulp tender, juicy, sweet, and distinctly tinctured with the flavor of muscatel (a musky wine of France), although it is not a wine grape. Its only drawback is that the vine is not very vigorous. Has *vinifera* blood in it.

SHERIDAN. One of the earliest of black table grapes, the skin thick and somewhat tough, the pulp juicy, aromatic, and mediumsweet. Good, also, for all red wines. A vigorous, hardy, and productive grape with *vinifera* blood in it.

CLINTON. Fruit somewhat small, but very numerous, black, with a bluish bloom. Not a table grape but one of the best for grape jelly and for all red wines.

Of the eleven varieties, selected from literally scores, six have *vinifera* blood in them, which means that somewhere in their ancestry they were crossed with a *vinifera* variety.

Having the blood in them of the finest grapes in the world, however dilute, they are especially welcome in a region unfit for true *vinifera* varieties.

All varieties contain varying amounts of grape sugar (dextrose), upon which depend the sweetness of the juice and its ability to ferment. The amount of dextrose increases rapidly as the fruit ripens, so that thoroughly ripe grapes, fresh from the vine, are a luxury that only the home grower can enjoy. All commercially produced fruit must be picked days before ripening, because ripe fruit would spoil in transit.

For dessert use and for wine, it is better to allow complete ripening before picking. Some varieties, especially the Clinton, contain, also, various amounts of pectin, upon which jelly-making depends. If picked for jelly-making it is better to harvest the fruit a few days before complete ripeness, even if the dextrose is not up to maximum, as cane sugar can easily be added, and the pectin appears to be best developed a few days before maturity.

VINIFERA GRAPE-GROWING

The production of *vinifera* grapes in the United States is practically confined to the states of California, Arizona, and Oregon.

In California grapes are grown principally in the great central valley and in the coastal valleys below 1000-feet elevation. Variations in climate caused by various combinations of temperature, rainfall, and atmospheric humidity make it possible to divide the grape-growing areas of the state into a number of regions as follows:

THE COAST REGION comprises the coastal valleys from Mendocino County to San Diego. The temperatures are moderate and have a relatively small range between day and night and between summer and winter. Fogs are frequent during the spring and early summer but diminish in duration from north to south and with distance from the ocean. The rainfall varies the same way, being ample toward the northern limit and somewhat deficient toward the southern. This region is commonly subdivided into the north coast and south coast. The former includes the counties around San Francisco Bay and the adjoining counties of Mendocino, San Benito, and Monterey. This is the great "Dry-Wine Region" and is not well suited for the commercial production of either table or raisin grapes. The south coast includes the coast counties from Santa Barbara to San Diego and the western portion of Riverside and San Bernardino counties. It is also a dry-wine region, but a few table grapes and even raisins are successfully produced in the warmest locations.

THE GREAT INTERIOR VALLEY, extending from Shasta to Kern County, is characterized by hotter summers and cooler winters than the Coast Region and by greater difference between day and night temperatures. The rainfall, on the other hand, is less and

---

* Special articles on the subjects indicated by an asterisk (*) will be found at the words so marked.

varies from just about enough at the north to a negligible amount at the extreme south. Spring and summer fogs are rare. It embraces three sub-regions: (1) the *San Joaquin Valley region,* from Bakersfield to Modesto, (2) the *Central Valley region,* from Modesto to Sacramento, (3) the *Sacramento Valley region,* extending from Sacramento to Redding.

In the *San Joaquin Valley* the average temperature increases from north to south. It is favorable for varieties of grapes that need abundant heat. The annual rainfall decreases gradually from about 14 inches at Modesto to four or five inches at Bakersfield, hence irrigation is everywhere necessary. This is the great raisin-producing region but also produces many excellent table grapes.

The *Central Valley* is the coolest part of the interior valley and has a moderate rainfall of from 14 to 20 inches. It owes its relative coolness to the influence of the ocean breezes which pass through the gaps in the coast range north and south of the Golden Gate. It is the great Tokay region but also has limited areas of several other commercial table grapes and large areas of heavily producing wine grapes.

To the north of the Central Valley lies the *Sacramento Valley.* As we proceed north through this valley, the influence of the ocean breezes gradually diminishes and the average seasonal temperature increases so that Chico has nearly the same temperature as Fresno. The rainfall also increases from south to north, reaching about 24 inches at Chico and 36 inches at Redding. Irrigation, though favorable, is not in all cases necessary. Grape-growing in this region has been less developed than in the San Joaquin Valley. There are, however, many scattered vineyards of wine grapes and some raisin vineyards in the central part of the valley. The climatic conditions of the area in Oregon where *vinifera* grapes are grown are similar to those of the upper Sacramento Valley.

The *Desert Region* of the Imperial and Coachella valleys is the hottest grape-growing area of California. The Thompson Seedless and Perlette are the principal varieties grown. Raisins are not made, because the table grapes ripening in June and early July are more profitable, and because the grapes produced under such severe conditions of temperature are not suited to the production of raisins. The climatic conditions of the Salt River Valley, where the majority of Arizona's grapes are produced, are intermediate between those of the hot desert and the southern end of the San Joaquin Valley regions.

VARIETIES. In the vineyards and collections of California there are growing probably eight hundred or more varieties of *vinifera* grapes. Of this horde, a small number, not more than one hundred and fifty, are grown in commercial quantities.

Vinifera grapes can be divided into three large classes, (1) raisin grapes, (2) table grapes, and (3) wine grapes.

RAISIN GRAPES

MUSCAT OF ALEXANDRIA. Berries large, white, egg-shaped, pulpy, with a strong, Muscat flavor; maturing in midseason. It is the variety from which the Muscat raisins of California are made. It has no rival for quality as a "cluster" or dessert raisin. It is grown most extensively from Madera south to Kern County in the San Joaquin Valley and the interior of the South Coast region. It is also a very good table grape.

THOMPSON SEEDLESS. Berry medium to small, oval, yellow, seedless; early maturing. From this grape the Seedless raisins of California are made, as are the Sultana raisins of Smyrna and Australia. It is at present the most largely grown grape in California. It is grown throughout the grape areas of the San Joaquin, Sacramento and hot desert regions. It ranks second to Tokay in volume shipped as table grapes.

BLACK CORINTH. Berry very small, nearly spherical, black or dark purple, seedless; very early maturing. It is from this grape that the dried "currants" are made. It succeeds well in California when girdled and given the requisite special care, but has not generally been found profitable. It is adapted to the cooler areas of the raisin-producing region.

TABLE GRAPES

TOKAY. Berry large, irregularly short ovoid; maturing in late midseason. Its most valuable quality is its brilliant red color, which it attains, however, only in limited localities, of which the principal one is the Central Valley region. In the cooler regions its ripening is late and irregular and in the hotter regions it fails to color sufficiently even when ripe.

THOMPSON SEEDLESS. *See* Raisin Grapes.

EMPEROR. Berry large, long, oval, rose-purple or red; maturing very late. This variety, like the Tokay, has a limited range wherein it is successful. In both cases it is a matter of attaining a desired color. The Emperor has been most profitable in localities where it reaches only a light purplish-red color. The principal Emperor region is near the Sierra foothills, along the east side of the San Joaquin Valley, in Fresno and Tulare counties.

PEARLETTE. Berry medium small, round, yellow, translucent; seedless; ripening ahead of Thompson Seedless. Clusters large and over–compact unless thoroughly berry-thinned.

ALMERIA (Ohanez). Berry large, cylindrical, white; very late maturing. It is of fair quality when well grown and ripe, but its chief value lies in its keeping qualities. It has been grown for many years in California in the Emperor district on a small scale with indifferent success, both in quality and productiveness.

MUSCAT. *See* Raisin Grapes.

RISH BABA. This is one of several varieties of white grapes which are often referred to as "Ladyfingers." It is of very attractive appear-

---

* Special articles on the subjects indicated by an asterisk (*) will be found at the words so marked.

ance, long, spindle-shaped, and matures early. It requires skillful packing to carry well and is produced by only a few growers in the Central Valley region.

OLIVETTE BLANCHE. Berry very large, fusiform elongated, white; late maturing. This is another of the so-called "Ladyfingers." It bears well and ships better than the Rish Baba. It does well in the hotter parts of the interior valleys.

RED MALAGA (Molinera). Berry large, spherical, deep red; maturing in early midseason and has a hard, crisp texture. It has a very attractive red color, but does not equal the brilliant red of the Tokay. It can, however, be grown successfully in localities that are somewhat too hot for the Tokay, and is earlier.

CORNICHON. Berry large, elongated, ellipsoidal, black, often somewhat flattened on one side; maturing in late midseason. Its irregularity of bearing with ordinary methods of pruning and its inferior quality should restrict further plantings. It does best in the Central Valley.

RIBIER (Alphonse Lavallée). Berry very large, irregularly spherical, black; maturing early to early midseason. It is the principal black variety grown. This is a hot-region grape, doing best in the San Joaquin Valley.

CARDINAL. Berries large, round to oval, brilliant cherry red; early maturing. A strong competitor of Red Malaga.

WINE GRAPES

The number of wine varieties is so large and the differences employed in identifica-

The head system of pruning and training *vinifera* grape varieties. The figure at the left is after the third winter pruning, the central one after the fourth winter pruning, and the right one after the fifth winter pruning.

tion are so small that it is beyond the scope of this treatise to attempt a separation of the varieties. — A. J. W.

CULTURE OF VINIFERA GRAPES

The culture of the *vinifera* or European grape differs somewhat from that of the native Eastern species. *Vinifera* grapes are grown extensively in the Western states, especially in California and Arizona. Generally the table varieties used for dessert purposes, which the gardener will want to grow, require long, hot summers to properly mature the fruit. In cool districts, as along the California coast and in coastal areas of the Northwest, only the earliest-maturing varieties such as Pearl Csaba, Pearlette, and Delight are adapted, though many of the finer wine varieties do best in the coastal valleys of California. In warm interior valley and the lower desert areas, table grapes reach highest quality. Varieties of the American grape species usually are grown in the Northwest.

In the areas in which the *vinifera* table grapes are grown, the vines require irrigation. They are injured by water standing on the soil for long periods, and therefore irrigation should be relatively shallow but frequent. Generally only the upper two to three feet of soil needs to be wet at each irrigation. Only on very unfertile soils does the grape respond markedly to fertilization with nitrogen.

The training and pruning of *vinifera* grapes differs somewhat from that of the Eastern grape species, especially in requiring more care in forming the vine and in pruning to prevent over-bearing, which is particularly devitalizing to *vinifera* varieties.

TRAINING THE YOUNG VINE. A rooted cutting is usually planted to start a new vine. It is planted so that only the top bud is level with the ground and this may be covered with a mound of soil. During the first summer the buds which emerge from the rooted cutting are allowed to grow undisturbed. At the end of the first year, at the time of the first dormant pruning, all but one strong cane is pruned from the vine, and the cane retained is cut back to two or three buds. During the second summer a single strong shoot which will form the trunk of the vine is selected. This shoot is tied loosely up along a stake, which is placed by the vine, preferably at the time of planting. Lateral shoots from this cane are allowed to develop but suckers from the roots and crown are removed. If low-growing laterals tend to outgrow the upright cane, they should be pinched at the tip to slow their growth.

Three methods of training are applicable to *vinifera* grapes: training to a head, training to canes, and cordon training. The first is simplest, requires the least space, and no further support but the stake along which the trunk-forming cane was tied. Vines to be trained to be cane or cordon systems require a trellis, which usually consists of two wires, one about 3 feet from the ground and the other 1 foot to 15 inches higher.

TRAINING TO A HEAD. After the second summer, vines to be trained to a head have the upright cane cut at the top of the supporting stake, usually a height of 2½ to 3½ feet, and the top tightly tied to the stake.

* Special articles on the subjects indicated by an asterisk (*) will be found at the words so marked.

The trunk cane may be loosely tied about midway to the ground. All lateral canes below the middle of the trunk are removed entirely, and weak laterals above this point are best removed. Two to four strong laterals are retained and cut to two or three buds each. The greater the vigor of vine growth and the larger the diameter of the selected canes, the more buds can be retained. During the third summer all canes arising below those selected at the second dormant pruning should be rubbed off and canes growing from near the ground should be removed. At the end of the third summer remove all but four to six canes, depending upon vigor of the vine. The retained canes are cut to two to four buds, again depending upon cane vigor. These will be fruiting spurs. They should be symmetrically spaced around the trunk and up and down the upper portion of the trunk. As the type of pruning described is continued each year, the old spur systems will form "arms" near the top of the vine. At each winter pruning, strong new canes are selected and treated as described above — that is, cut back to two to four buds. As the vine grows older the number of spurs retained each season may be gradually increased until, on large head-trained vines, 10–20 spurs may be retained annually. Production of fruit is balanced with vine vigor by leaving fewer or more fruiting spurs.

TRAINING TO CANES. Cane-pruned vines are handled in much the same fashion as head-trained vines except that canes of 6 to 18 buds, depending upon variety and cane vigor, are retained for fruiting after the second dormant pruning. Selection is made so as to form the arms along the trellis in a fan shape rather than symmetrically around the trunk. At the third dormant pruning, two such canes are selected and all others are removed. The selected canes are tied along the trellis wire. These canes will produce the fruit. From the base of the canes strong lateral shoots will arise. At the following dormant pruning two to four of the strongest of these laterals are retained and cut back to two buds; the rest of the fruiting cane is cut off. Always remove the canes which have borne fruit. These spurs will develop the fruit canes for the following year. From such spurs kept the preceding season, new fruiting canes are selected and tied along the trellis wire. As the vine grows older the number of fruiting canes retained may be increased to four or six. If the vine is to be trained high against a wall or on a pergola, the number of canes may be increased to fill the space, for the vine will have much more leaf surface and can therefore carry more fruit.

CORDON-TRAINED VINES. The trunk of the cordon-trained vine is formed as was described for head-trained vines except that during the second summer, if growth has been vigorous, two strong laterals, or the main shoot and a strong lateral, are chosen to form the cordons (long arms). All other laterals are pinched back to slow growth — as is the main cane if it has not been chosen for one of the cordons. A single cordon may be used, in which case it is training in one direction only along the trellis wire; more commonly, two arms are formed by training two canes in opposite directions along the trellis from the trunk. The selected canes are brought up to the lower trellis wire from the trunk in a smooth curve of about 6- to 8-inch radius, and are tied along the trellis wire to form the cordon. The canes are tied at successive intervals through the summer as they elongate, but not too close to the growing tip. Cordon arms about five to six feet long are satisfactory, at which point they may be pinched back to establish their final length. If the canes are not vigorous enough to make the required growth during the second summer, choose two canes in proper position and cut them to two buds each during the following dormant pruning, and form the cordons the third summer. At the time of the third dormant pruning, lateral shoots along the canes selected to form the cordon arms are pruned to two or three buds, depending upon the vigor of the canes. The retained spurs should be spaced 8 to 12 inches apart along the cordon arms. At this time it is best to retie the cordon arms, straightening them as much as possible and taking special care to remove any sags which have developed.

During the following summer the strong canes arising from the fruiting spurs should be tied to upper trellis wire to avoid bending or twisting the cordons. Growth of the canes can be kept even by judicious pinching of overly vigorous canes. Each following year new fruiting spurs are formed by selecting and pruning strong canes which have grown along the cordon, in the manner described above.

During the training and early fruiting years of cordon-trained vines, new growth from the arm bends and along the vine trunk should be rubbed off as it appears.

Most *vinifera* table varieties are spur-pruned. Training may be either to the head or cordon system, but the commonest practice is cordon training. However, Flame Tokay, Muscat, and Black Muscat are generally head-trained. The popular Thompson Seedless should be cane-pruned, for the basal buds are relatively unfruitful.

The severe pruning given *vinifera* grape varieties is directed toward balancing fruiting with vegetative growth. The production of quality bunches of grapes requires adequate leaf area; overproduction in the *vinifera* table grape is devitalizing to the vine. Longer spurs or even canes of several buds in length may be retained if fruit-thinning is followed. However, even with the recommended types of pruning, fruit-thinning will often materially increase the quality and appearance of the bunches.

Thinning may be done by removing flower clusters at the time of flowering, or by thin-

---

* Special articles on the subjects indicated by an asterisk (*) will be found at the words so marked.

ning out the bunches shortly after the fruit has set, when the individual berries are about the size of buckshot to peas. Flower cluster removal, practiced at the time of bloom, tends to result in heavier berry-set on the remaining clusters. It should be used only on varieties which tend to set poorly or set loose bunches. Cluster-thinning after fruit-set enables the gardener to remove small and poorly set clusters. For some varieties, especially those that tend to set tight, heavy clusters, berry-thinning will give the most favorable results. Berry-thinning is done soon after the berries set and is accomplished by cutting off the upper third of the bunch and by removing one or more of the branches of the cluster. This type of thinning changes the shape and reduces the size of the individual bunch, but opens them up and allows better development of the individual berry. Berry-thinning is especially adapted to varieties which tend to set compact clusters.

Seedless varieties, as Thompson Seedless, normally have bunches with small berries. Girdling the vine about a week or two after bloom will greatly increase the size of the individual berries borne by seedless varieties. If girdling is practiced, berry-thinning should also be done to loosen the cluster and allow space for the greater size of the remaining individual berries. Girdling is done by cutting out a strip of bark around the vine trunk, arm, or cane. The girdle should be about 3/16 inch wide and the bark should be removed, but the cut should not be scraped. Girdles should heal in from three to six weeks. Failure to heal will cause the death of the portion of the vine beyond the girdle. Properly healed girdles appear to have no deleterious effect on the vines, but girdled vines should not be allowed to produce as much fruit as those grown ungirdled. Usually the crop is reduced by about 1/3 by cluster removal.

HARVESTING AND HANDLING. As grapes mature they become sweeter, less acid, and acquire the characteristic flavor and color of the variety. The black varieties change color rapidly; green varieties become yellowish or whitish. The cluster stems often become brown or woody in appearance. The cluster should be clipped from the vine and over-ripe or diseased berries removed at the time of harvest. Most table grapes will hold well for several days or longer if stored in a cool, relatively dry place. Grapes to be dried for raisins should be allowed to remain on the vines longer than those for fresh use, as their sugar content will continue to increase, resulting in a higher quality raisin. — C. O. H.

INSECT PESTS. Early season flea beetle attack on buds is controlled by pesticide #17 (see SPRAYS AND DUSTS). Later in season, Japanese beetle, root worm adults, rose chafer and many cutworms attack plants. Control with pesticide #21 or #1. See cutworm control at CABBAGE. Leafhoppers cause poor foliage appearance. Control with pesticide #21 or #1.

Most serious pest of fruit is grape-berry moth. After bloom, apply pesticide #1 or #17 twice at 10-day intervals. A second brood may appear nearer to harvest. Use pesticide #21 at that time. Galls of phylloxera, an aphid, are often present on leaves in the East. In the West, aphids may cause severe damage to roots, hence, Eastern rootstocks are preferred.

DISEASES. Destruction of the fruit by black rot is the most common disease of grape. Raking up and destroying the rotten fruit in the fall will help to prevent the disease. Following the spray schedule will give much better control.

If leaves have pale yellow spots with a mold growth on the lower surface of leaves and mold in clusters of grapes, the disease is downy mildew.°

In western states, dead arm may be a serious problem. Use pesticide #4 (see SPRAYS AND DUSTS) while canes are still dormant, followed by one application of pesticide #2 when new growth is not over 4 in. long. If powdery mildew° is a problem, use pesticide #9 when growth is 6 and again when 12 in. long and repeat at 14-day intervals up to time of ripening.

The following spray program will control other common insects as well as the more common grape diseases such as black rot and downy mildew.

GRAPE SPRAY PROGRAM

	TIME	MATERIAL	
1.	As buds open	Pesticides #	11 and 17
2.	Growth 8 to 12 in. long	"	11 and 17
3.	After blossoms fall	"	11 and 17
4.	Two weeks later	"	11 and 21
5.	Two weeks later	"	11
6.	One month later	"	21

GRAPE FAMILY = Vitaceae.

GRAPE FERN = *Botrychium.*

GRAPEFRUIT. Grown first in Florida and later extended to California, Arizona, and Texas, the grapefruit or pomelo (*Citrus paradisi*) is now the second most important citrus fruit. It is believed to have originated in the West Indies and to have developed from the thick-skinned and worthless pummelo or pompelmous (*Citrus maxima*), which in this country is known as the shaddock. In any event the grapefruit as we know it is of modern origin and is known in the eastern hemisphere only as an introduced fruit.

Like the other citrus fruits, the grapefruit is a tender sub-tropical evergreen. In frost resistance it stands intermediate between the sweet orange and sour orange, though closer to the former than the latter (see ORANGE). For this reason a comparatively small part of the acreage is provided with frost protection. (For details see FROST.) The grapefruit requires a high total amount of heat for the production of good-quality fruit; it succeeds better than any other citrus fruit in the tropics and in the desert, in the latter, of course, only with irrigation.

In California the best-quality fruit is produced in the desert sections where the amount of heat is sufficient to ripen the fruit 9 or 10 months after bloom; this fruit ripens at the same period as does that in Arizona,

° Special articles on the subjects indicated by an asterisk (°) will be found at the words so marked.

Texas, and Florida. In the other citrus-growing regions of California more than one growing season is required to ripen the grape-fruit. Advantage is taken of this fact, however, and by growing this fruit in four climatic zones, differing mainly in amount of heat, tree-ripened grapefruit is available every month in the year.

The grapefruit is less affected by heat and more resistant to wind than any other citrus fruit. It therefore has a wider range of climatic adaptation. Its culture in the United States is limited to central and south Florida, the lower Rio Grande Valley of Texas and areas of mild winters in Arizona and California.

There is no pollination problem in grape-fruit culture for, like other citrus fruits, it does not require seed formation for fruit setting, unpollinated fruits being seedless. The major variety, Marsh, is commercially seedless because it normally has few functional ovules; all other varieties are regularly seedy. Two other varieties, Thompson and Ruby, and several others exhibit pink-colored flesh and juice, and have a pink blush on the rind.

PROPAGATION. Like other citrus fruits, the grapefruit is propagated by budding on seedling rootstocks and the nursery trees are usually planted as year-old budlings. In Florida the rootstock most used is the rough lemon (see LEMON), which seems not to cause the undesirable effects associated with the use of this rootstock for the orange (see ORANGE). In Texas, and on the heavier soils in Florida, the sour orange is preferred because of its resistance to root and bark diseases. The sweet orange is also used to some extent in California.

The planting of bare-rooted nursery trees is the regular practice in Florida but elsewhere the use of balled trees is preferred. Fall and early-spring planting are practiced in Florida and Texas; in California and Arizona spring planting is preferable, and protection against sunscald is advisable.

SOILS. The grapefruit appears to have an even wider range of soil adaptation than do the other citrus fruits. It does not require deep soils, for its root distribution is comparatively shallow; it is sensitive to alkali and excessive moisture, however, and requires good drainage. It is essential that only irrigation water of good quality be used.

For satisfactory yields and high-quality fruit regular fertilization is required. The usual program employed is similar to that used for the orange, though the application of chemical fertilizers in early spring to favor the setting of the fruit is not considered so important. A total application of 200 pounds of nitrogen per acre per year is considered adequate, not less than half of which is supplied from bulky organic substances. The usual practice consists in the application, in summer or fall, of manures, and, in the winter or spring, of chemical fertilizers.

In California winter cover crops are usually grown, and also summer cover crops where the water supply permits. Tillage operations are usually confined to the turning under of cover crops, weeds, and fertilizers, and furrowing or basining for irrigation. Pruning is of less importance than with other citrus fruits.

VARIETIES. The most important variety is Marsh, seedless and late-ripening. Pink-fleshed varieties include Thompson, Ruby, and Foster. Seedy varieties are of importance in Florida. — R. W. H.

INSECT PESTS and DISEASES. See ORANGE.

GRAPE-HYACINTH. See MUSCARI.

GRAPE IVY. See CISSUS.

GRAPTOPETALUM (grap-toe-pet'a-lum). A small genus of chiefly Mexican, succulent plants of the family Crassulaceae, one of them much grown in the southwest desert gardens. Of the 3–4 species, the most likely to be grown is G. paraguayensis, which is not a native of Paraguay, and has been, and may still be, offered as Byrnesia, Sedum weinbergi or even as Cotyledon paraguayensis, or as an Echeveria. It has fleshy, bluish-green leaves in a basal rosette, or sometimes the rosette at the end of a short stem. Leaves oblongish, pointed, keeled beneath, about 2 in. long. Flowers white, but red-spotted, in small clusters (cymes*), often wanting. The plant is not hardy in the North, but is grown in desert gardens in Calif. and Ariz. For greenhouse cult. see SUCCULENTS. (Graptopelatum is from the Greek for variegated petals, in allusion to the spots on them.)

GRAPTOPHYLLUM (grap-to-fill'um). A small genus of tender foliage plants, family Acanthaceae, mostly from tropical India, one of them, G. pictum, the caricature plant, a popular greenhouse shrub grown for its handsome variegated leaves. It is 6–8 ft. high in the wild, usually much lower as cult., with opposite* leaves without marginal teeth, more or less elliptic and blotched irregularly along the central vein with yellow. Flowers crimson, in nearly stalkless whorls* in the leaf axils.* Corolla hairy, widely gaping, the tube inflated, but the limb 2-lipped,* the lower lip 3-parted. Stamens* 2. Fruit an oblongish capsule. Nativity unknown. It should be grown as a pot plant in a warm, moist greenhouse, preferably in potting mixture* 3. While the leaves are usually yellow-marked as indicated, the plant is very variable as to this and some have leaves with marginal yellow markings. (Graptophyllum is from the Greek signifying variegated foliage.) Sometimes known as G. hortense. There is a form with purplish-red leaves with bright red-purple blotches and veins.

GRASSES. The grass family supports the temperate and tropical world, for it contains wheat, corn, rice, rye, barley, oats, and also the sugar cane. Horticulturally, it is nothing like so imposing as the world crops found within it; most grasses, outside the bamboos, being of secondary decorative value. An exception to the latter statement are the beautiful silky plumes of the pampas grass

---

* Special articles on the subjects indicated by an asterisk (*) will be found at the words so marked.

and the genera *Arundinaria, Arundo,* and *Phragmites,* as well as some grown for their value in dry bouquets. *See* DRIED FLOWERS.

It is impossible to list here all the genera of grasses found in this ENCYCLOPEDIA, for they have already been listed at the description of the family. (*See* GRAMINEAE.) But some of the horticulturally more important grasses are found in so many gardens that notes on their culture and uses are quite essential. Nor can we repeat here the merits of the many grasses that enter into lawn or meadow mixtures. For this feature of grasses *see* LAWNS.

GARDEN USES. For bold, tropical effects none of the grasses excel the bamboos and related genera. While many of them can only be grown in the warmer sections of the country, some bamboo-like grasses are hardy northward, and should be planted in large masses by those seeking such effects. *See* BAMBOO.

Lower, and not so striking, are many other grasses that are widely grown for special garden compositions — some for their decorative foliage, as in a variety of *Coix,* and in the variegated or colored-leaved form of sweet corn. (*See* CORN.) Others are, of themselves, of little value, but in masses or as edgings they are decorative enough. Among genera especially suited for such purposes are: *Anthoxanthum, Axonopus, Elymus, Eragrostis, Lamarckia, Miscanthus, Pennisetum, Setaria, Tricholaena,* and *Uniola.* Some of these are annuals of which the seed should be sown where needed.

The perennial grasses are best grown as are any perennial garden flowers. Seeds sown in flats in the cold frame in Aug. will be ready to set out permanently the following spring. After the second or third year they may then be easily divided in spring or fall, and often they should be, to prevent too rapid encroachment into other parts of the bed or border.

Grasses are so world-wide in their distribution that, as a family, they tolerate nearly every sort of soil. This freedom from soil preferences is reflected in the variety of garden soils in which they will grow. Most cult. grasses will grow in any ordinary garden soil, and, once established, need very little attention, except to keep them from spreading too fast. This is particularly true of the low-growing sorts that will form a sod if not checked.

Garden grasses are chiefly grown for their often feathery habit and foliage, rather than for the flowers which are minute, wind-pollinated, and conspicuous only because they are crowded in dense or branching clusters (usually panicles*). These, especially in the genera *Briza, Bromus, Eragrostis,* and *Panicum,* are first dried and then dyed various colors. Some of these dyed grasses are common in florists' shops and, to some, have decorative value. But the form and branching of most grass clusters are their chief charm, to which little or nothing is added by dyeing. *See* DRIED FLOWERS.

As noted at the different genera (*see* GRAMINEAE), a few cult. grasses are essentially tropical. This tropical distribution may dictate hardiness if the grass is a perennial species, but many tropical annuals will, if sown outdoors in the North, usually produce fine plants during a single season.

Annual grasses, not necessarily all tropical, may be sought in the genera *Avena, Bromus, Coix, Echinochloa, Euchlaena, Lagurus, Panicum, Phalaris,* and *Zea* (*see* CORN). These can all be sown where wanted, or if needed earlier, they may be sown in flats or pots in the hotbed or greenhouse and transplanted, just as are tender annuals. *See* ANNUALS.

A few grasses are grown more for interest than for ornament, two especially being mostly so grown. One is the curious animated oat (*see* AVENA) and the other is the well-known Job's-tears (*see* COIX), with its bead-like fruits. For a good dune-binding grass *see* AMMOPHILA.

INSECT PESTS. Grub-proofing with pesticide #15, #18 (*see* SPRAYS AND DUSTS), or other standard grub-killing chemical may be necessary if six or more grubs per foot are encountered. These materials, as dust or spray, kill chinch-bug lawn pests.

DISEASES. Most gardeners believe that every brown spot in the lawn is "disease spot." In our experience, the vast majority of the dead spots are caused by drought, wet soil, acid soil, fertilizer burn, lack of proper fertilizer, insect damage, dog injury, improper use of weed killers, or even improper use of fungicides. In those cases where spots are actually caused by fungi* the gardener does not usually have the proper equipment to apply a fungicide. Recommendations for application of fungicides range from ½ to 2 ounces of material per 1000 square feet. Improper application rates may do as much or more harm than the disease. For these reasons we suggest that gardeners do not use turf fungicides unless they are prepared with proper spray equipment and a willingness to follow directions to the letter. Also, they should follow a preventive spray schedule rather than attempt control of the disease after it appears.

Brown patch produces dead areas 6 in. to 3 ft. in diameter and is most serious in midsummer on overfed lawns. Copper spot may attack under similar conditions, producing dead areas one inch in diameter with a copper color. In late spring, or early fall, dollar spot may cause one-inch, straw-colored dead areas in lawns which lack sufficient nitrogen. Snow mold attacks in late fall, through the winter and early spring, causing small or large dead areas, particularly where snow collects on leeward side of hedges and fences or is piled along paths and driveways. Melting-out, fading-out, and pink patch, are other diseases which may attack grass. Most of the better turf fungicides are proprietary materials which are bought only under the manufacturer's brand name, and should be used according to manufacturer's directions.

A common sight on lawns is slime mold* which does not injure the grass but is unattractive for a period of several weeks. Mowing, brushing or hosing at high pressure will remove the gray mold on the grass blades.

GRASS FAMILY. *See* GRAMINEAE.

GRASS-FLOWER = *Claytonia virginica.*

GRASS-OF-PARNASSUS. *See* PARNASSIA.

---

* Special articles on the subjects indicated by an asterisk (*) will be found at the words so marked.

GRASS PANSY = *Viola pedunculata.*

GRASS PINK = *Dianthus deltoides;* also *Calopogon pulchellus.*

GRASSWORT. See CERASTIUM ARVENSE.

gratianopolitana, -us, -um (gra′ti-an-o-pol-i-tay′na). From or near Grenoble, France.

gratissima, -us, -um (gra-tiss′i-ma). Most pleasing or agreeable.

GRAVELWEED = *Diervilla Lonicera.*

graveolens (gra-vee′o-lenz). Strong-smelling.

GRAY AND LAVENDER GARDEN. Gardens planted in tones of lavender, violet, and purple, with a few pale pink and pale yellow flowers and a plentiful admixture of gray foliage, are very lovely and restful in effect. Stone walls make a fine background for such gardens or borders, and the trellises, arbors, and seats that are made of wood are best painted silver-gray, or, when near the sea, allowed to weather. Besides the plants given in the following lists, those marked with a dagger at BLUE GARDEN may be made use of.

SHRUBS

Buddleia davidi, 8–12 ft., summer; *Callicarpa dichotoma,* 3 ft., purple berries in autumn; *Cercis canadensis,* small tree, spring; *Cytisus purpureus* (see BROOM), semi-prostrate, spring; *Daphne Mezereum,* 3–4 ft., spring; *Hibiscus syriacus coelestis,* 8–10 ft., summer; *Lonicera syringantha,* 5–8 ft., spring, *L. thibetica,* 5 ft., spring; *Rhododendron* hybrids and many varieties; *Syringa* (Lilac) *persica, S. vulgaris,* many hybrid varieties, mauve, lilac, purple, etc.; *Vitex Agnus-castus,* 6 ft., late summer.

TALL PLANTS FOR USE IN BACKGROUND

SUMMER-FLOWERING: *Aster,* various forms; *Boltonia latisquama; Campanula latifolia; Delphinium,* lavender varieties; *Iris,* Japanese varieties; *Ostrowskia magnifica; Thalictrum dipterocarpum.*

AUTUMN-FLOWERING: *Aster grandiflorus, A. novae-angliae, A. novi-belgi, A. tataricus; Vernonia crinita.*

PLANTS OF MEDIUM HEIGHT

SPRING-FLOWERING: *Aquilegia,* long-spurred hybrids (see COLUMBINE); *Geranium grandiflorum; Nepeta mussini.*

SUMMER-FLOWERING; *Ageratum* (annual); *Aster acris, A. cordifolius;* China aster (annual); *Campanula Medium* (Canterbury Bells); *Delphinium* annual varieties; *Trachymene caerulea; Erigeron speciosus; Geranium pratense; Galega officinalis; Gilia capitata* (annual); *Hesperis matronalis; Hosta fortunei, H. sieboldiana; Iris,* tall-bearded varieties; *Limonium latifolium; Monarda fistulosa; Pentstemon diffusus; Phlox maculata; Salpiglossis* (annual); *Salvia nemorosa, S. Sclarea; Scabiosa* (annual); *S. caucasica, S. japonica; Stokesia laevis; Thalictrum aquile-*

gifolium purpureum; Verbascum phoeniceum.

AUTUMN-FLOWERING: *Aster ericoides,* and other species (see ASTER); *Cheloni lyoni.*

DWARF PLANTS FOR FOREGROUND

SPRING-FLOWERING: *Anemone, Pulsatilla; Aquilegia vulgaris* (see COLUMBINE); *Aster alpinus; Aubrieta* (lavender); *Campanula portenschlagiana; Crocus imperati, C. tomassinianus, Crocus,* Dutch varieties; *Erysimum linifolium; Iris* (dwarf-bearded); Pansies; *Phlox arendsi* Louise, *P. divaricata, P. subulata; Primula denticulata; Viola cornuta, V. gracilis.*

SUMMER-FLOWERING: *Ageratum* (dwarf annual varieties); *Alyssum* (annual); *Aster acris, A. subcoeruleus; Iberis gibraltarica* (see CANDYTUFT); *Petunia,* Heavenly Blue, Violet Queen, and Balcony Blue; *Phlox drummondi; Primula capitata; Sedum caeruleum* (annual).

AUTUMN-FLOWERING: *Colchicum autumnale,* double and single, *C. speciosum* (bulbs); *Crocus longiflorus, C. nudiflorus, C. speciosus, C. zonatus* (bulbs).

CLIMBERS

Akebia quinata (spring); *Clematis crispa, C. jackmani* (summer); *Dolichos Lablab;* Morning-glory (annual); Sweet Peas (annual); *Wistaria sinensis, W. floribunda macrobotrys.*

PLANTS WITH GRAY FOLIAGE

Arabis alpina (prostrate); *Artemisia Abrotanum,* 2 ft., *A. vulgaris,* 3–4 ft., *A. stelleriana,* 2 ft.; *Cerastium tomentosum* (prostrate); *Dianthus plumarius,* 1 ft.; *Elymus arenarius,* 2 ft.; *Eryngium* and *Echinops; Festuca ovina glauca,* 6–8 in.; Lavender; *Ruta graveolens,* 2 ft.; *Salvia argentea; Santolina chamaecyparissus; Stachys lanata,* 8–10 in.; *Thalictrum glaucum,* 5 ft.; *Thymus Serpyllum lanuginosus* (creeping); *Verbascum olympicum,* 8 ft. For the culture and hardiness of all these plants see the various genera cited above. — L. B. W.

GRAY BIRCH = *Betula populifolia.* See BIRCH.

GRAY DOGWOOD = *Cornus racemosa.*

GRAY GOLDENROD = *Solidago nemoralis.* See GOLDENROD.

GRAY GUM = *Eucalyptus tereticornis.*

GRAY PINE = *Pinus banksiana.* See PINE.

GREASEWOOD. In the west, *greasewood* is applied chiefly to *Larrea tridentata* and to species of *Atriplex.* But to most gardeners, greasewood is *Audibertia polystachya.*

GREAT BURDOCK = *Arctium Lappa.* See the list at WEEDS.

GREATER STITCHWORT = *Stellaria Holostea.*

GREAT LAUREL = *Rhododendron maximum.*

GREAT LOBELIA = *Lobelia siphilitica.*

---

* Special articles on the subjects indicated by an asterisk (*) will be found at the words so marked.

GREAT NETTLE = *Urtica dioica. See* NETTLE.

GREAT SOLOMON'S-SEAL = *Polygonatum canaliculatum. See* SOLOMON'S-SEAL.

GREAT WHITE TRILLIUM = *Trillium grandiflorum.*

GREEK FIR = *Abies cephalonica. See* FIR.

GREEK GARDEN. There is plenty of evidence from Homer, Plato, and Theophrastus that the Greeks were passionately devoted to flowers, but little or nothing tells us what kinds of gardening were practiced, and of their design we know very little. As one of the chief historians of Greek gardens well put it: "In ancient Greece we have no tomb paintings or sculpture preserving for us any adequate idea of gardens."

In spite of this lack, so different from the history of gardens in Rome, we learn that Theophrastus had the first botanical garden in the world, mostly for study, though of its design we may not even infer.

We do know that small properties were separated by hedges of "thorns, brambles or barberry," and we read in Plato of the love of flowers, especially fragrant ones like the jasmine, that resulted in many comparatively poor families planting such things so that fragrance was wafted into their homes.

The climate and soil of Greece was, and still is, highly unfavorable for lush gardens. Not quite a desert, much of the country has a deficient summer rainfall. In spite of this handicap, the Greeks grew the cypress, cedar, oak, angus-castus, myrtle, olive, fig, rosemary, and myrtle, as well as many perennials.

Most of this plant material is suited here chiefly to California. This fact, plus our ignorance of plan and design, makes it impossible to reproduce a facsimile of a Greek garden here. That Plato, Socrates, and Aristotle held many of their classes in the garden is a fact that makes it frustrating to read only about "beds of white violets, irises, hyacinths, ranunculus, asphodel and carnations" with edgings of parsley and rue — but no word of how such beds were arranged, nor of their setting. Ornate and splendid gardens, such as were developed in ancient Rome, do not appear to have existed in Greece.

But smaller, private gardens did exist and what they were like is outlined at the section on Greek gardens at GARDEN HISTORY.

GREEK JUNIPER = *Juniperus excelsa.*

GREEK VALERIAN = *Polemonium caeruleum.*

GREEN ALDER = *Alnus viridis. See* ALDER.

GREEN ARROW-ARUM = *Peltandra virginica.*

GREEN ASH = *Fraxinus pensylvanica lanceolata. See* ASH.

GREEN-BARKED ACACIA = *Cercidium torreyanum.*

GREENBRIER. *See* SMILAX (1).

GREEN DRAGON = *Dracunculus vulgaris* and *Arisaema Dracontium.*

GREEN GRAM = *Phaseolus aureus.*

GREEN HELLEBORE = *Veratrum viride.*

GREENHOUSE. As generally understood today, the term *greenhouse* applies to any form of glass structure erected for growing plants, with the exception of cold frames and pits, which see.

A conservatory is a distinct type of greenhouse, usually attached to the dwelling as a show place for plants that could be enjoyed by entering from the living or drawing room. Tree ferns, palms, and a variety of tropical plants, including climbers to adorn columns and hang from the roof, are set out in beds or tubs as more or less permanent plants, with a constant flow of flowering plants in pots from growing-houses as needed to maintain a continuous floral display. The conservatory has now almost disappeared, along with large estates. A notable example, open to the public, is still maintained in beautiful condition, at the du Pont estate of Longwood, Kennett Square, Pennsylvania.

A greenhouse may be large or small, depending on location, the plants to be grown, method of culture, and the amount of money available. If it is long enough to be divided into two or more compartments with glass partitions, it is possible to segregate plants of cool, temperate, and tropical regions for easier care; but most home greenhouses will be of one compartment only, and it is wonderful what a variety of plants have been grown in such.

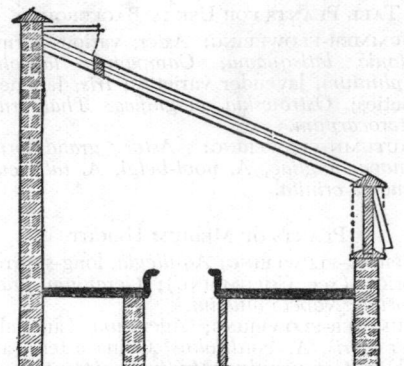

Cross-section of the most economical of greenhouses — the lean-to. In some the bench near the inner wall is arranged in steps so that the plants at the rear may be nearer the glass. Note the ventilators both at the top and side.

The most economical in construction and upkeep is the lean-to, in which the roof has but one slope and is attached to a back

---

* Special articles on the subjects indicated by an asterisk (*) will be found at the words so marked.

wall. For most plants it should have a south or southeast exposure for maximum light, and be well removed from trees. However, a north exposure is not impossible for such flowering plants as African violet, begonia, camellia, cyclamen, primula, and for ivies, philodendron, and other foliage plants. Should there be a sloping roof above, it will be necessary to place wire guards to protect the glass from sliding snow and ice. The three-quarter span or hip-roof style is sometimes erected to conform to a peculiar grade condition, but whenever possible the best growing-house is the free-standing even-span type, with one end attached to the potting shed. Curved eaves prevent the accumulation of snow and ice.

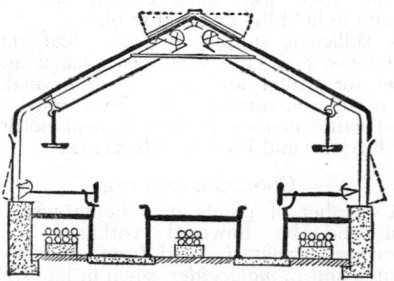

Cross-section of even-span greenhouse, showing preferred arrangement of ventilators, benches for plants, with heating pipes below them, the paths, and the best method of constructing the walls.

A good foundation is important, especially in cold climates, where it is advisable to build side walls of brick, cinder blocks or poured concrete about 2 ft. above grade. Cypress and redwood are the most lasting woods for greenhouse construction. Small prefabricated greenhouses are available in sections that are easy to erect and to extend, if need be. A recent introduction is an all-aluminum greenhouse which needs no putty or paint, thus simplifying upkeep.

Experiments have been made with plastic in place of glass, and for some purposes it appears to be very useful. Orchids have been well grown in a house constructed of large panels of fiberglass, aided by special heating, ventilating, and humidifying devices.

The maintenance of proper temperature and ventilation have been made easier by the use of automatic controls. Hot water provides steady heat and, by using fin tubes instead of plain pipe, less piping is required to get the same amount of heat. Good heaters that use natural gas, oil, or electricity are obtainable. Which fuel is best depends on cost in different areas. Warm-air blower-type units suspended from the roof are used in some places where electric rates are low, and give clean, controlled, and efficient heat. It is well to consult a greenhouse firm or heating expert as to the capacity of the heating unit to provide the desired temperature. Where

there is a cellar window, it may be possible to keep a small greenhouse attached to the dwelling warm enough by blowing in heat from the cellar with an electric fan. For plants in a cool house a night temperature of 45° to 50° F. will do; in a temperate house, 50° to 55°; in a warm house, 60° to 65°. A drop of a few degrees on very cold and windy nights is not harmful.

The installation of automatic ventilator control saves a lot of running on changeable days and, better yet, makes it possible for the owner to be away during the day and feel assured that the plants are not liable to be roasted or chilled. Day temperatures may rise 10 degrees or more, depending on the weather, and a gradual rise and fall is preferable. A recent development eliminates ventilating sash by placing vent turrets containing exhaust fans on the roof ridge of the greenhouse. Automatic control provides a complete change of air every few minutes.

Required humidity will vary with the kind of plant and conditions. Desert plants require less humidity than tropical jungle plants. For plants requiring high humidity, wetting of the walks and area about the staging may be necessary several times on bright days and when the heat is on full, and perhaps spraying of the foliage after watering. Again, automatic devices are available to take care of this as needed.

Simple aluminum greenhouse without brick or cement walls. (Courtesy of Lord & Burnham.)

Watering must be done with discrimination. Not all plants need to be watered at the same time, and the requirement varies according to their state of growth; they need plenty when active, less when resting. It is impossible to overwater a calla lily in growth, but a geranium is easily harmed with too much water. In cool houses especially, watering is best done before noon, so as to avoid excessive and often harmful,

* Special articles on the subjects indicated by an asterisk (*) will be found at the words so marked.

moisture condensation at night. *See* WATER-ING.

Cleanliness should prevail at all times and in all places. Keep trash cleaned up promptly and do away with hiding places for insects and diseases. Overcrowding is a common fault from which many plants suffer. Each individual should be given ample room for proper development. Sickly specimens that do not respond to treatment are best disposed of for their space. A watchful eye should be kept to detect insect pests and plant diseases at the beginning, and immediate steps taken to apply measures of control and to correct bad conditions if need be. For details of treatment, see the notes on control at the entry covering the plant involved.

A type of roller shades for the outside of the greenhouse.

SHADING. Although a site allowing the maximum amount of sunlight is the most desirable, some shade is necessary for most plants under glass during hot weather. This is not only to protect from sunburn, but also to help maintain more uniform conditions of temperature and moisture. Lath blinds on rollers are most satisfactory in every respect. With these it is possible to give the plants the advantage of full light on dull days, while lowering them on cold, windy nights will check heat loss and so, to a certain extent, cut fuel costs. In early spring only certain plants may need the protection of temporary shading, and this can be given on the inside by the use of paper or scrim. The slapdash method of spraying limewash all over the glass and framework is not recommended. A good temporary shading to apply on the glass is a thin mixture of whiting and gasoline. For a shading to last all summer, substitute white lead for the whiting. If a green tint is desired, add a little Brunswick green to the mixture. A powdered preparation known as Summer Cloud, obtainable in white or green, mixed according to directions, also makes a satisfactory shading. Whatever is applied to the glass,

the best effect is obtained by stippling it on with a wide brush.

Internal arrangements of staging and growing space will vary to suit the kinds of plants to be grown and the method of culture to be followed. For some plants a solid bed a foot or so above the walk level serves well; a raised bench of wood or concrete 6 in. deep is well adapted for growing cut flowers. The best table for pot plants is made up of an angle-iron frame supported on pipe legs, with a bottom of slate or tile rather than wood. This is covered with a layer of crushed stone, gravel, or screened cinders on which to stand the pots, and which is frequently wet down to evaporate moisture about the plants. The rim of the angle iron need extend only high enough to hold the material in place.

A sufficient supply of loam, leaf mold, peat moss, and sand should be placed under cover for winter and spring use in making up potting mixtures — plus bone meal and dried cattle manure to add at final pottings. *See* POTTING and POTTING MIXTURES.

COOL GREENHOUSE

A number of plants may be grown from seed and be flowered within a year. Calceolaria, cineraria, and forms of *Primula sinensis* and *P. malacoides*, sown in late spring or early summer, give fine pot plants for winter and spring display. Cyclamen seed sown in Aug. gives flowering plants about 18 months later. Others sown in Aug. for pot or bench culture (the latter especially for cut flowers) are antirrhinum, calendula, clarkia, nemesia, pansies, Drummond phlox, schizanthus, stock, and sweet peas. Pots of daffodils and tulips, brought in at intervals from their cold quarters early in the year, are always welcome. Other bulbous plants such as freesias, *Gladiolus tristis*, iris, ixia, and lachenalia grow well under cool conditions, but must not be exposed to frost. Carnations thrive under cool conditions.

Examples of hard-wooded flowering plants that can be kept growing from year to year under cool treatment are certain acacias and azaleas; also boronia, camellia, cytisus, and erica. These are benefited by being plunged outdoors under lath or other light shade for the summer. *Buddleia asiatica* is easily grown from spring cuttings for winter bloom, and just one plant will fill the house with fragrance. Fancy pelargoniums and fuchsias grow from cuttings into good specimens within a year, and can be grown for several years if cut back annually when rested after flowering. Chrysanthemums are indispensable for fall bloom. Vines add to the attractive furnishing of any greenhouse. Among those that will flourish under cool conditions are antigonon, lapageria, manettia, Cherokee rose, and the woody solanums.

If desired, such vegetables as beets, carrots, lettuce, radish, and spinach may be grown in a bench for extra-early use. During the summer, tomatoes, cucumbers and melons may be grown, and will be finished in time to prepare the house for new occupants in the fall.

WARM-TEMPERATE GREENHOUSE

There is a large group of plants that prefer conditions between cool and tropical. These thrive in what is known as a warm-temperate house, with a night temperature of 50°–55° F. Many of these are more or less permanent, but it is a good plan to keep up a stock of vigorous plants from cuttings. A genial, moist atmosphere is required during their season of active growth, and in the summer free ventilation with shading. A varied selection can be made from begonias, featuring attractive form, foliage and flowers. Achimenes, gloxinia, isoloma, and strepto-carpus are plants with attractive flowers that can be grown along year after year if rested under cooler conditions after flowering, while the related African violet (*Saintpaulia*) continues in growth and flower the greater part of the year. Good plants for winter bloom grown annually from cuttings are impatiens, jacobinias, tender salvias, and eupatoriums. Examples of woody plants worth growing for their flowering qualities are acacia, abutilon, bouvardia, centradenia, pseuderanthemum, strobilanthes, and streptosolen. Desirable vines are clerodendron, dipladenia, gloriosa, and stephanotis.

TROPICAL GREENHOUSE

Tropical plants require more heat and moisture in the atmosphere than the other groups. For best results a night temperature of 60°–65° F. should be maintained. Frequent damping of the walks and staging, with overhead spraying on bright days, gives just the right growing atmosphere. The resting time is in winter, when less moisture is needed at the roots, but a dry atmosphere must be avoided, especially near the heating pipes.

Most of the re-potting takes place toward spring, and care must be taken to avoid constant saturation of the soil until new roots are active. The soft-wooded plants prefer more shade than the hard-wooded ones, and this may be managed to a certain extent by careful arrangement in the house. Early shading is necessary, and here, roller blinds, run down and up as conditions require, are especially good. Ventilation must be closely watched and sparingly given until hot weather arrives.

Numerous fine foliage plants belong in this group. Such kinds as alocasia, calathea, codiaeum (garden crotons), cordyline, dieffenbachia, dracaena, fittonia, pandanus, sanchezia, and xanthosoma provide a colorful display of varied leaf forms. Anthuriums, with their brightly colored spathes, should also have a place as well as an assortment of philodendrons for leaf variation. The pineapple family (Bromeliaceae) offers many kinds with interesting leaf form and color, as well as showy bracts and flowers. Good woody flowering plants can be selected from acalypha, hibiscus, ixora, medinilla, pentas, posoqueria, and rondeletia. A few plants of nepenthes, the tropical pitcher-plants, suspended in baskets will add to the interest. If vines can be accommodated, such kinds as allamanda, bougainvillaea, passiflora, and thunbergia will give colorful displays.

For greenhouse orchid culture, *see* ORCHID. — H. E. D.

GREEN MANURING. No soil-improvement scheme should be without at least one phase of green manuring, for the process supplies humus to the soil in the cheapest and most effective way. Particularly is this true where stable manure is impossible to get or too expensive to use on the necessary scale. *See* HUMUS.

OBJECTS. Green manuring has for its primary object the increase in the water-holding capacity of the soil. Any ordinary subsoil, which is usually without humus, will hold only as much water as its particles will absorb, which, in the case of sandy or gravelly ones, is not much. Even fairly good garden soils will not hold as much water as they should. And the capacity of all, except muck soils, to hold adequate amounts of soil moisture is tremendously increased by the humus that green manuring adds to them.

The process, in short, involves the plowing under of green crops, usually grown for the purpose. It may well begin by plowing under the initial weed crop, preferably in late May or early June, before many of them have gone to seed. Try to cover the weeds

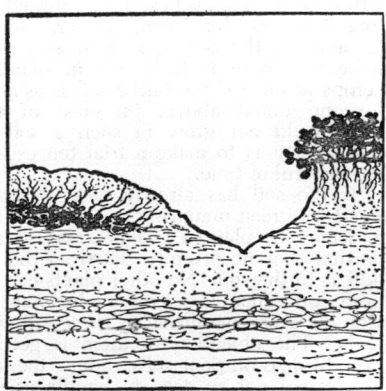

Diagrammatic outline of the green crop (*at right*), the furrow (*center*), and the buried green crop (*at the left*), the complete covering of which is essential in correct green manuring for soil improvement.

with soil as completely as possible, so that decay may start at once and to prevent a few of them from sprouting again. This initial plowing should be as deep as possible with an ordinary plow. Or on a small scale, dig the weeds in as thoroughly as possible.

---

* Special articles on the subjects indicated by an asterisk (*) will be found at the words so marked.

SUCCESSIVE STEPS. Assuming the worst — that the land you are to improve consists only of subsoil, or contractors' fill — in other words, a weedy lot — after the first plowing in of all possible weeds, allow the rough furrows to stand as they are for 10–15 days. Then disk harrow or coarsely rake the area and sow very thickly a crop of ordinary buckwheat. Even on pretty poor land the buckwheat will make a fair stand and should be allowed to grow only about 8 in. high when it too is turned under. Wait another 10 days and sow another crop of buckwheat as before, which will germinate and grow considerably better than the first one.

This rotation of buckwheat can be repeated as often as possible until the final crop is plowed under, which should be, in the North, about Sept. 20. Then let the land lie fallow until about Oct. 15, when a heavy seeding of winter rye should be given. This will germinate before heavy frosts and go through the winter looking much like a coarse lawn. In the spring, plow under the rye when it is about 9 in. high. Then, if necessary begin the buckwheat series again.

Not all green-manuring schemes will need to be so intensive as the one just outlined. Sometimes only a crop or two will suffice to add all the humus the particular soil will need. And there are some regions of heavy rainfall where decay may be too sluggish, in which case there should be a light application of lime only once in the season.

NITROGEN GATHERERS. While the rotation just outlined does a tremendous amount for the physical texture of a soil, it adds little real plant food to it. This is best accomplished by planting legumes like pea, clover, vetch, alfalfa, and, in the South, *Lespedeza striata* or soybean. There is little use in planting such crops at once if the initial soil is as poor as the one noted above, for most of the legumes would not grow in such a soil or grow so poorly as to make a trial too expensive or wasteful of time.

But if the soil has already been partially improved by green manuring, then one of the legumes may be planted. Their great advantage is that they absorb nitrogen from the air and add it to the soil. No other plants can do this, and consequently, no other plants are as valuable for green manuring as these nitrogen gatherers. The objection to them is getting them established on poor soils. Some, too, are perennials and not so easy to handle as rye and buckwheat.

GREEN MINT = *Mentha spicata*. See MINT.

GREEN OSIER = *Cornus rugosa*.

GREEN ROSE = *Rosa chinensis viridiflora*.

GREENS. See CHRISTMAS GREENS. See *also* SALAD PLANTS.

GREEN WATTLE = *Acacia decurrens*.

GREENWOOD CUTTING. A softwood cutting. See CUTTINGS.

GREVILLEA (gre-vil′lee-a). Australasian shrubs or trees of the family Proteaceae, comprising about 230 species, but only the following of much garden interest. They are planted south of zone* 7 for street or avenue trees or specimen plants, but *G. robusta* is often used as a pot plant in northern greenhouses for its fine foliage. Leaves alternate,* sometimes small and heath-like, or much larger and divided or deeply parted, feather-fashion, into five segments. Flowers in close clusters (racemes* or heads), without petals, but the calyx* more or less tubular, the 4 lobes joined even after the flower has opened. Stamens 4. Fruit a woody follicle.* (Named for Charles F. Greville, British patron of botany.)

The chief feature of the grevilleas is the long, showy styles* which protrude much above the general level of the flower cluster. The plants are easily raised from seed sown as soon as ripe in warm, moist sand. In Calif., where they are widely grown, the species are at home in a variety of soils, and stand the summer drought very well. In greenhouses *Grevillea robusta* needs potting mixture* 3 and a temperature of 50°–60°.

banksi. A shrub or tree, not over 20 ft. high. Leaves about 4 in. long, split into 3–11 narrow segments, silky beneath. Flowers red, very showy, in 1-sided, terminal clusters that are 2–4 in. long. There is also a white-flowered variety. Both are planted for ornament in Fla.

robusta. Silk-oak. In outdoor cult. a tree 100–150 ft. high, but as grown in the juvenile state in the greenhouse 2–3 ft. high. Leaves twice-divided into graceful, feathery, fern-like segments. Flowers orange, in 1-sided clusters (racemes*) that are up to 4 in. long, and borne on leafless branches. A popular street tree in southern Calif., but brittle and hence littering the ground.

rosmarinifolia. A shrub 6–7 ft. high, its foliage resembling the rosemary, the leaves about 1½ in. long, practically stalkless and silvery beneath. Flowers crowded in dense, short, terminal clusters (racemes*), the styles* red. Aust. Hardy in zone* 9 and in protected sites in zone* 8, and commonly planted in southern Calif.

thelemanniana. A shrub not over 5 ft. high, the leaves about 2 in. long and divided into many narrow segments. Flowers pinkish, tipped with green, the clusters terminal, 1-sided, and not over 1½ in. long.

GREYIA (gray′ee-a). A genus of only 3 species of South African trees of the family Melianthaceae, **G. sutherlandi** grown for ornament in Calif. It is a small tree with alternate,* simple,* toothed leaves that are roundish or oval-oblong, 2–3 in. long and deeply heart-shaped at the base. Flowers bright scarlet, about 1½ in. long, very profuse in showy racemes* 8–10 in. long. Sepals and petals both 5, not united. Stamens* 10, both they and the style long-protuding. Fruit a 5-valved, membranous capsule.* It does well in Calif. on a variety of soils and blooms plentifully long before it is fully grown. Propagated by cuttings of partially ripened wood, or by seeds. (Named for Sir George Grey, Governor of Cape Colony.)

* Special articles on the subjects indicated by an asterisk (*) will be found at the words so marked.

GRIDIRON TRAINING. *See* Trained Fruit Trees.

GRINDELIA (grin-dee'lee-a). New World, resinous or gummy herbs, of the family Compositae, most of the 20 known species from the western U.S. and of little hort. interest, although some non-hort. species furnish medicines. Commonly called gum plant or tarweed, they are often woody at the base and have decidedly sticky foliage. The only cult. species of much garden interest is **G. robusta,** a perennial herb 1–2 ft. high, with alternate,* clasping, ovalish or lance-shaped leaves 1–2 in. long and toothed. Flower heads solitary, gummy, about 1½ in. wide, both the rays* and disk* yellow. Calif., and not much suited to regions with wet, cold winters. The *var.* **latifolia** (sometimes known as *G. latifolia*) has broader and more clasping leaves. (Named for H. Grindel, Riga professor.)

grisea, -us, -um (gri'see-a). Gray.

GRISELINIA (gri-se-lin'ee-a). Attractive evergreen shrubs and trees of the family Cornaceae, mostly from New Zealand and Chile, the two below somewhat grown for ornament south of zone* 6, especially in Calif. They are related to and suggest *Aucuba.* Leaves alternate,* rather leathery and shiny. Male and female flowers on different plants, small, greenish, inconspicuous and sometimes (in the female flowers) without petals. In both those below the flowers are borne in small, branched clusters (panicles*). Fruit a berry. (Named for Franc Griselini, Venetian botanist.)

They need a light, moderately rich loam, and do well near the Pacific Coast.

littoralis. Kapuka. A tree 20–40 ft. high, the twigs brown-hairy. Leaves oblongish or wedge-shaped, 2–4 in. long. Flowers in panicles* 1½–3 in. long, chiefly in the leaf axils.* New Zealand. There is a variegated-leaved form.

lucida. Puka. A shrub or small tree, 5–20 ft. Leaves oblongish, 5–7 in. long, unequal at the base. Flower clusters (panicles*) nearly 6 in. long, the flowers without petals. New Zealand.

GRIT CELLS. *See* Stone Cells.

groenlandica, -us, -um (green-lan'di-ka). From Greenland.

GROMWELL. *See* Lithospermum.

grossa, -us, -um (gro'sa). Great or large.

GROSSULARIA. *See* Ribes.

GROSSULARIACEAE. *See* Saxifraga-ceae.

GROUND CEDAR = *Lycopodium complanatum.*

GROUND CHERRY. *See* Physalis.

GROUND COVERS. On the best-ordered property there are places that refuse to be pleasant ones to look upon. Under shady trees the absence of light and the heavy drip of every rain obliterates grass year after year. In another place the surface roots of forest trees have taken up all nourishment intended for the lawn grasses.

There may be steep banks facing the noon-day sun, and these are constant sources of expense and trouble. New turf shrivels up and becomes a prey to crab grass; if it is seeded a rain often carries new seed and prepared soil into the gutters below. Or a wood clearing of brush requires a cover to restore the natural effects.

With these vexations to overcome it is a relief to know that there are good plant materials that will provide covers for every condition. Weeds and fickle grass can be replaced by plants that are both happy and attractive. One of the finest is the bearberry, but it is difficult to get established. *See* Arctostaphylos.

The shade and drip of trees are not an ideal condition for most plants, but some native herbs and shrubs can be made to grow. And often no more expense is involved than for the work of clearing. *See* Shady Garden.

The materials listed are those suitable for shade and woods; for moist places; for full sun, and for sun and shade at choice. Whenever possible, choose shrubs that have edible berries; many of these have a threefold feature in spring flower, summer foliage, and autumn fruit. See the body of the Encyclopedia for cultural notes on the different species, and for their hardiness. Here only their names and flower color are given.

Ground Covers for Shady Places:

Lily-of-the-valley. *Convallaria majalis.* White, spring.

St. John's-wort. *Hypericum calycinum.* Yellow, summer.

Leiophyllum buxifolium. White, May, evergreen.

Sarcococca ruscifolia. Evergreen, spring or late fall, fragrant white flowers.

Ground ivy. *Glecoma hederacea.* Blue, May to Sept., but weedy.

Navelwort. *Omphalodes verna.* Blue, March.

Sedum spurium. Dense evergreen carpet. For cult. see Rock Garden.

Speedwell. *Veronica Chamaedrys.* Blue, all summer.

Periwinkle. *Vinca minor.* Blue, summer.

Euonymus fortunei minimus. Small evergreen leaves.

Moneywort. *Lysimachia Nummularia.* Yellow.

Ground Covers for Partially Shady Places:

Allegheny spurge. *Pachysandra procumbens.* Deciduous.

Japanese spurge. *Pachysandra terminalis.* Evergreen.

Ground hemlock. *Taxus canadensis.* Evergreen.

Creeping thyme. *Thymus Serpyllum.* Evergreen, May–June.

Bugleweed. *Ajuga reptans variegata.* Blue and white, summer. Deciduous.*

---

* Special articles on the subjects indicated by an asterisk (*) will be found at the words so marked.

Lily-turf. *Liriope.* Evergreen grass-like leaves.
Pachistima canbyi. Leaves dark green, but purplish in winter. Evergreen.
Hedera Helix baltica. Evergreen.
Wintergreen. *Gaultheria procumbens.* Evergreen.
Honeysuckle. *Lonicera japonica.* Evergreen in the South, and dangerously invasive.
Creeping barberry. *Mahonia repens.* Yellow, all summer, evergreen.
Mazus japonicus. Blue, summer, evergreen.
Nertera depressa. Good for Calif.; not hardy eastward.
Leadwort. *Ceratostigma plumbaginoides.* Blue flowers, late summer.

GROUND COVERS FOR SUNNY PLACES:
Snow-in-summer. *Cerastium tomentosum.* Silvery foliage, white flowers in spring.
Dianthus arenarius. White flowers in June.
Candytuft. *Iberis sempervirens.* White, spring, evergreen.
Phlox amoena. Purple, spring.
Polemonium reptans. Blue, spring.
Silene maritima. White, June.
Veronica repens. Blue, July.
Veronica latifolia prostrata. Blue, summer.
Cytisus kewensis. White, May. For culture see ROCK GARDEN.
Galax aphylla. White, June, leaves purple in winter.
Berberis verruculosa. Foliage bronzy in winter.
Buxus microphylla koreana. See Box.
Dryas octopetala. White, summer.
Rosa wichuraiana. Pink, red and white; and forms a dense mat of glossy foliage.

GROUND COVERS FOR MOIST PLACES:
Phlox divaricata. Blue, spring.
Phlox stolonifera. Purple, spring.
Swamp dewberry. *Rubus hispidus.* White, June.
Bergenia crassifolia. Pink, spring; large foliage.
Epilobium nummularifolium. Pink, July.
Star violet. *Houstonia serpyllifolia.* Blue, spring.
Partridge-berry. *Mitchella repens.* White, April; red berries all summer.
Forget-me-not. *Mysostis scorpioides.* Blue, all summer.
Woodland ferns. — D. W.

GROUND GOLD-FLOWER = *Chrysopsis falcata.*

GROUND HEMLOCK = *Taxus canadensis.*

GROUND HOLLY = *Gaultheria procumbens.*

GROUND HONEYSUCKLE = *Lotus corniculatus.*

GROUND IVY = *Glecoma hederacea.* See also the list at WEEDS.

GROUND LAUREL = *Epigaea repens.* See TRAILING ARBUTUS.

GROUND LILY = *Trillium cernuum.*

GROUNDNUT = Peanut; also *Apios americana.*

GROUND PINE. See LYCOPODIUM.

GROUND PINK = *Phlox subulata.*

GROUND RATTAN = *Rhapis excelsa.*

GROUNDSEL. See SENECIO.

GROUNDSEL BUSH, OR TREE = *Baccharis halimifolia.*

GROWTH PROMOTING CHEMICALS. See HORMONES and GIBBERELLIC ACID.

GROWTH RINGS. See ANNUAL RINGS.

GUADALUPE PALM = *Erythea edulis.*

Guajava. The name in Spanish America for the guava.

GUAMACHIL = *Pithecolobium dulce.*

GUANABANA = *Annona muricata.*

GUANO. See MANURE.

GUARIA MORADA = *Cattleya skinneri.*

guatemalensis, -e (gwa-te-ma-len'sis). From Guatemala.

GUATEMOTE = *Baccharis viminea.*

GUAVA. A group of perhaps 150 species of the genus **Psidium** (sid'i-um), family Myrtaceae, all tropical American shrubs and trees, the three below, especially *P. Guajava,* widely cult. in warm regions for their fruit, which is the common guava and the source of such widely used products as guava jelly and guava paste (the guayabada of the Brazilians). They are medium-sized trees or tall shrubs with opposite° leaves. Flowers large and showy, usually 1–3 on stalks that are often in the leaf axils° or on the sides of the branches, never terminal. Calyx,° or its base, bell-shaped or pear-shaped, its lobes 4–5. Petals 4–5. Stamens° numerous, in several series. Fruit a berry, the tip crowned with the persistent calyx lobes or sepals. (*Psidium* is the Greek name for the pomegranate which the fruit somewhat resembles.) For culture and varieties *see* below.

P. cattleianum. Strawberry guava. A shrub or small tree, not over 25 ft. high, the bark smooth and grayish-brown. Leaves elliptic or broadest toward the tip, leathery, 2–4 in. long, the veins not prominently depressed. Flowers about 1 in. wide, white, the stamens° about as long as the petals. Fruit roundish, 1–1½ in. long, purplish-red, the flesh white. Brazil.

P. Guajava. Common guava. A shrub or tree not over 30 ft., the twigs 4-angled, the bark brownish-green and scaly. Leaves oblongish, 3–6 in. long, the veins prominently depressed above, ridged beneath. Flowers about 1 in. wide, white. Fruit egg-shaped or pear-shaped 2–4 in. long, yellow, the flesh whitish-yellow or pinkish. Tropical America.

P. guineense. Brazilian guava, but once supposed to be African, hence the specific name of *guineense.* A shrub, usually not over 8–10 ft. high. Leaves oblongish, 3–5 in. long. Flowers in clusters of 2–3. Fruit about 1½ in. long, greenish-yellow, the flesh white. S.A.

P. littorale. By some considered the correct name for *cattleianum.*

° Special articles on the subjects indicated by an asterisk (°) will be found at the words so marked.

Guava Culture

Culture of the common guava, a native of tropical America, is restricted to a limited area of southern Calif. and to peninsular Fla. where it has become naturalized in many places. It is primarily a jelly and preserve fruit, the high pectin and acid content of sour varieties making possible a yield of 3½ lbs. of jelly from each pound of fruit. It is also eaten fresh, cooked and canned, and made into butters, paste, relishes, catsups, and chutneys. High in both mineral value and vitamin C, the guava is important in the diet, but because of the characteristic odor the fruit is not at first relished in the fresh state by everyone.

The plants fruit at an early age and bear regularly and abundantly. Beginning in early summer, a succession of ripening fruit is produced over a season of several weeks. There are two distinct fruit types, the pyriform (pear guava) and globose (apple guava), but several named hort. varieties are now grown. Many seedling forms are planted and are differentiated mainly according to shape, flesh color — white and yellow to deep pink, and degree of acidity — sour to sweet. Acid varieties are chosen for jellies and pastes, and those of large size with meaty fruit and sub-acid flavor are preferred for other uses.

Plants of the red-fruited strawberry guava (*Psidium cattleianum*) bear little or no resemblance to the common guava and are included in ornamental as well as fruit plantings. They are much hardier, the range extending to the protected areas of the Gulf Coast and southern Calif. Like the common guava, they are precocious and prolific but the fruits are small and used principally for jelly-making.

Guavas thrive on nearly any except marsh soils. Good drainage is desirable, although ample soil moisture must be available throughout the season of growth and fruit development for maximum yield. Several planting distances, varying with soils and variety from 10 × 15 ft. to 25 × 25 ft., are used, but the closer spacing ultimately results in crowding of mature trees. Either clean culture, with cultivation, or mulching* is practiced, and material benefits are derived from both manures and commercial fertilizers.

Propagation is mainly by seeds and air layering, and to a much lesser extent by root cuttings, budding and grafting. Sprout growth from desirable varieties may be forced by severing roots of large plants 2 or 3 ft. from the main trunk and allowing to grow in place until large enough for transplanting. — G. D. H.

Insect Pests. Guava fruit is attacked by a tiny moth, the larva tunneling through the flesh. Pesticide #17 (*see* Sprays and Dusts) sprays have given some control. Scale insects, whiteflies and plant bugs can be controlled by sprays of pesticide #21 combined with 1.3% oil emulsion.

Diseases. Algal spot on leaves and fruit can be controlled with an application of pesticide #3 or #11 (*see* Sprays and Dusts).

GUAVA FAMILY = Myrtaceae.

GUAYULE. See Parthenium argentatum.

GUELDER ROSE = *Viburnum Opulus sterile*. See also Kerria japonica pleniflora.

GUERNSEY LILY = *Nerine sarniensis*.

GUILIELMA (gwe-li-el′ma). Chiefly Brazilian, spiny, feather palms, comprising perhaps 3 species, only G. Gasipaes, the pejibaye or gachipaes, known to be in cult., and confined to the warmest parts of peninsular Fla. It has one or several trunks, 30–50 ft. high, usually spiny. Leaves in a showy terminal crown, each leaf 8–12 ft. long, with many strongly ribbed leaflets that are deeply 2-toothed at the tip, the ribs and margins with stiff bristles. Flower cluster from just beneath the crown of leaves, the stalk spiny, the male and female flowers separate in the same cluster. Stamens* 6. Fruit 1–2 in. long, yellowish-orange, more or less top-shaped, the flesh edible and much prized in tropical America, where there is also a seedless variety. The plant is sometimes known as *G. utile*. (Named for Queen Guilielma Carolina of Bavaria.)

GUINEA GRASS = *Panicum maximum*.

GUINEA-HEN FLOWER = *Fritillaria Meleagris*.

guineensis, -e (gi-ne-en′sis). From Guinea, West Africa.

GUMBO = *Hibiscus esculentus*. For culture, *see* Okra.

GUMBO LILY = *Mentzelia decapetala*.

GUM ELASTIC = *Bumelia lanuginosa*.

GUMI = *Elaeagnus multiflora*.

gummosa, -us, -um (gum-mō′sa). Gummy.

GUMMOSIS. A gummy exudation, usually attributed to injury or disease, often found on the trunks of certain trees, especially on plum, cherry, and on citrus fruits. It is not often serious and good cult. often avoids it.

GUM-MYRTLE = *Angophora lanceolata*.

GUM PLANT. See Grindelia.

GUMS. An uncommon, illiterate, and phonetic attempt to construct a plural for *Geum* (which see).

GUM TREE. See Eucalyptus. Trees of the genus *Nyssa* are also so called, but are better known as sour, tupelo, or black gum. See also Sweet Gum.

GUNNERA (gun′ner-ra). Very showy foliage plants little known in American gardens, but interesting as being large herbs in a family, the Haloragidaceae, otherwise aquatic. Of the 30 known species, all from the southern hemisphere, the following are occasionally grown for bold effects in the border or on a lawn. They are perennial

---

* Special articles on the subjects indicated by an asterisk (*) will be found at the words so marked.

herbs with stout, creeping rootstocks, the
leaves all basal, stalked, usually very large
and striking. Flowers unisexual* or polygamous* in often dense spikes or panicles,
the cluster sometimes spadix*-like. Petals
2, or none. Stamens 1 or 2. Fruit a drupe.*
(Named for J. Ernest Gunner, Swedish
bishop and botanist.)

The gunneras are extremely handsome
foliage plants that need much space, a moist,
rich soil, and, north of zone* 6, a thick winter mulch of straw or strawy manure. It is
useless to attempt growing them in poor or
dry soil. Propagated by division of the rootstocks.

chilensis. A stout herb, the leafstalks green,
6 ft. long, and covered with stiff, bristly hairs.
Leaf blade nearly 6 ft. in diameter, roundish
or heart-shaped, divided finger-fashion into
many large segments. Flower cluster a spike
nearly 3 ft. long, the individual flowers small and
without petals. Fruit red. Ecuador, Colombia,
and Chile. Sometimes known as *G. scabra.*
manicata. Resembling the above but larger,
the leaves considerably larger and with the red-
dish-spiny leafstalk attached to the middle of the
leaf blade. Southern Brazil.
scabra = *Gunnera chilensis.*

Gutta. East Indian vernacular for many
plants yielding products like rubber or gutta-
percha. See PALAQUIUM.

GUTTA-PERCHA TREE = *Palaquium
Gutta.*

guttata, -us, -um (gut-tay'ta). Speckled.

GUTTIFERAE (gut-tiff'er-ree). The balsam tree or mamey family, sometimes called
the Clusiaceae, includes only tropical shrubs
and trees, few of which are cultivated. Of
the many genera and perhaps 1000 species
only 3 are known to gardeners in the extreme South, *Calophyllum, Garcinia,* and
Mammea. The two latter are of interest only
for the edible fruit (mangosteen and the
mamey).

They are resinous or aromatic trees with
opposite* leaves having no marginal teeth,
rather showy, sometimes waxy flowers which
are solitary or in clusters, and (in ours)
fleshy, usually edible fruit. See also HYPERI-
CACEAE.

Technical flower characters: Flowers mostly
polygamous* or dioecious.* Sepals and petals
separate and free, usually 4, but sometimes 2
or 6. Stamens usually very numerous, some
sterile, and often joined into groups at the
base. Ovary superior,* with 2 or more cells.

GUYING TREES. See PLANTING.

GUZMANIA (guz-man'i-a). A genus of
about 85 species of handsome tropical American plants of the family Bromeliaceae, one
or two grown in greenhouses for their handsome foliage and the white or yellow flowers
borne in usually stalked clusters among the
foliage. Leaves stiffish, in a dense basal rosette in the practically stemless *G. musaica,*
but the rosettes on the stout stems of *G.
lingulata.* Flower clusters with showy bracts,*
the flowers more or less tubular. (See BRO-

MELIACEAE.) Fruit a capsule.* (Named for
A. Guzmann, Spanish naturalist.)

For culture *see* TILLANDSIA.

lingulata. A tree-perching, stout-stemmed
plant, the numerous leaves scurfy, sword-shaped,
remotely toothed, 12–18 in. long and about
1 in. wide. Flowers yellowish below, the tip
purplish, crowded in a dense, red-braced* cluster. Tropical America.
musaica. Normally growing in the ground
and stemless. Leaves 12–20 in. long and 2–3
in. wide, round-tipped, with wavy cross-bands
that are dark green on the upper side and
purple on the lower surface. Flowers yellowish-
white, the cluster 2–3 in. long, its bracts* greenish and red-striped. Colombia.

gymnocarpa, -us, -um (jim-no-kar'pa).
Naked-fruited.

GYMNOCLADUS (jim-nock'lay-dus). A
genus of only two species of trees of the pea
family, one of them Chinese; the other, **G.
dioica,** the Kentucky coffee-tree (often called
simply coffee-tree) which is scattered from
N.Y. and Pa. to Neb., Okla., and Tenn., and
sometimes cult. for ornament. It is a tree up
to 90 ft. high (less in cult.), with twice-compound* leaves, the leaflets arranged feather-
fashion, in 3–7 pairs, more or less ovalish,
without teeth, 2–4 in. long. Male and female
flowers (in ours) on separate trees, or the
flowers polygamous,* in terminal clusters, not
pea-like but more or less regular. Calyx*
tubular, 5-lobed. Petals 5, oblongish, greenish-white. Fruit a thick, flat, pulpy legume,*
8–12 in. long, the seeds large and flattened.
The plant is of easy cult. in most ordinary
garden soils, but it is certainly hardy only
from zone* 3 southward. It is best propagated from root cuttings, or by seed. (*Gymnocladus* is from the Greek for naked and
branch, in reference to some of the branches
which are without twigs.)

GYMNOGRAMMA = *Pityrogramma.*

GYMNOSPERM. The exact meaning of
the term is naked-seeded, but the botanical
and hort. significance of gymnospermous
plants is greater than the mere meaning of the
term would imply. Nearly all flowering

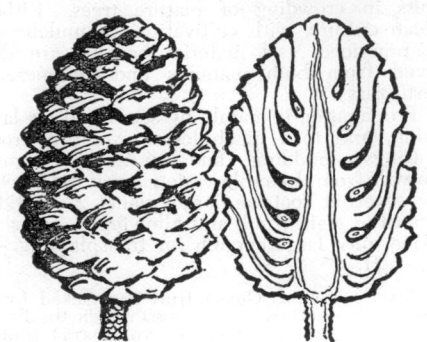

A pine cone (a gymnosperm), the cross-section
showing the position of the naked ovules (the
future seeds) between the cone scales.

---

* Special articles on the subjects indicated by an asterisk (*) will be found at the words so marked.

plants have ovules* in a closed ovary,* the development of which results in some sort of a fruit with the seeds (developed ovules) inside. Gymnosperms have no ovary, no petals, sepals, nor any "flower" in the ordinary hort. sense of that word. Instead they have naked ovules typically borne between the scales of a cone as in the common pine. Or the male flowers consist merely of naked, pollen-bearing organs in various sorts of clusters. Upon fertilization the naked ovules (the female flowers) develop into seeds which are common in pines, spruces, and other cone-bearing plants. For the genera in the ENCYCLOPEDIA OF GARDENING that are included in the gymnosperms see PINACEAE, TAXACEAE, CYCADACEAE, GINKGO, META-SEQUOIA, and EPHEDRA.

GYNURA (jy-noor'ra). Handsome, greenhouse foliage plants of the family Compositae, most of the 20 species from tropical Asia or Africa. The only cult. species, **G. aurantiaca**, the velvet plant, is a native of Java, and is grown in the warm greenhouse for its handsome foliage. It is a shrubby, but somewhat fleshy herb, 2–3 ft. high, more or less velvety, with violet or purple hairs. Leaves alternate,* soft, ovalish, raggedly toothed, the blades narrowed at the base into winged stalks. Flower heads in loose clusters, not very showy, the flowers all in the disk and yellow or orange. The plants need a good light in order to bring out the color of the leaves, for which these plants are grown. (*Gynura* is from the Greek for tailed stigmas,* in allusion to a technical flower character.)

GYNANDRIUM. A structure found only in orchid flowers whereby the male and female organs are united into a column. *See* ORCHIDACEAE.

GYPSOPHILA (jip-sof'fill-a). Handsome, although small-flowered, annual or perennial herbs of the pink family, some of the 50, chiefly Eurasian, species very popular garden plants, known generally as baby's-breath from the profusion of mostly small, white or pink flowers. They are bluish-green herbs with opposite,* small leaves and slightly swollen joints. Flowers many, in usually profuse branched clusters (panicles*). Calyx* 5-toothed. Petals 5, sometimes toothed, usually with a minute claw.* Stamens* 10. Fruit a 4-valved capsule.* (*Gypsophila* is from the Greek for gypsum-loving, in reference to the tolerance of some species for limey soils.)

The annual and perennial species of *Gypsophila* are very popular garden plants because of their ease of culture and the profusion of bloom which makes snowy (or pink) patches in the border or bed, and are most useful as trimming for bouquets. While *G. cerastioides* and *G. repens* are most at home in the rock garden (which see), *G. elegans* and *G. muralis,* both annuals, are of the simplest cult. if the seeds are sown where wanted. Both will bloom more freely if not thinned out too much, as, like some annuals, they seem to prefer a bit of crowding. The perennial species are easily propagated by division. All of them need full sunlight and open, not too rich, soils.

acutifolia. Very like the common baby's-breath (*G. paniculata*), but the foliage less bluish-green, and the leaves only slightly 3-veined. Flowers white or pink. Caucasus.

cerastioides. A perennial with prostrate habit and creeping stems not over 4 in. high and downy. Lower leaves long-stalked, the upper nearly stalkless and broadest toward the tip. Flowers nearly ¾ in. wide, white, but pink-veined. Himalayas. For culture *see* ROCK GARDEN.

elegans. Annual baby's breath. Upright, forking, and 10–18 in. high. Leaves sharp-pointed, lance-shaped, a little fleshy. Flowers small, long-stalked, white or pinkish, the petals slightly notched. Caucasus. Blooms from June 15 to Oct. The *var.* **grandiflora** has larger, white, pink, or rose-colored flowers and is the usual form in cult. The *var.* **carminea** has carmine flowers.

fratensis = var. *rosea* of *G. repens.*

muralis. An annual pink-flowered herb, more or less sprawling and not over 8 in. high. Leaves narrowed at both ends. Flowers usually solitary in the leaf axils,* the tiny petals more or less wavy-margined. Eu. and rarely escaped in the eastern U.S. June 15–Oct.

pacifica. Perhaps only a form of *G. paniculata,* but with pink flowers, and taller.

paniculata. Baby's-breath; called also gypsum pink and mist. The best-known of the perennial species and often much-branched and 20–30 in. high. Leaves 2–4 in. long, much smaller on the flowering branches, 3-veined. Flowers very numerous, small, white, the clusters (panicles*) much-branched. Spring and summer. Eurasia. There are also double-flowered, named forms of the *var.* **flore-pleno.** Among these is Bristol Fairy, a common florists' plant. It is propagated by grafting upon stock of single-flowered *G. paniculata.*

repens. A perennial scarcely 6 in. high, the foliage pale blue-green. Leaves very narrow, smooth. Flowers nearly ½ in. wide, white or pinkish, the clusters rather few-flowered. Mountains of Eu. For culture *see* ROCK GARDEN. The *var.* **rosea** has rose-pink flowers, and the *var.* **monstrosa** is merely a larger form.

GYPSUM. A whitish mineral (calcium sulphate) better known as land plaster. Its chief hort. use is as a filler in various dusting mixtures for the control of pests. Its use on the land has been replaced by agricultural lime.

GYPSUM PINK = *Gypsophila paniculata.*

gyrans (jy'ranz). Gyrating or revolving.

GYROTHECA = *Lachnanthes.*

---

* Special articles on the subjects indicated by an asterisk (*) will be found at the words so marked.

H

HABENARIA (ha-be-nay′ri-a). A large and showy genus of orchids, mostly of the temperate regions, and commonly called fringed orchis from the beautifully fringed flowers of all the cult. species. All those below are wild flowers of N.A., needing rather special conditions for successful cult. They have (in ours) leafy stems and fleshy or tuberous roots, the leaves usually with a sheathing base. Flowers few or several in a terminal, bracted* spike, very irregular* and spurred. Sepals broad or spreading, the lip usually fringed or 3-parted, and toothed. Spur* longer than the lip. Fruit a capsule.* (*Habenaria* is from the Greek for rein, in allusion to the long, narrow spur of some species.)

It is useless to attempt growing the species of *Habenaria* without supplying the conditions they demand. All of them need a decidedly acid soil mostly from pH 4.0 to 5.0 (*see* ACID AND ALKALI SOILS). Where noted below, the bog is the best place for some species, but others are acid-soil plants of drier sites. There are many other wild species, some of them without the beautiful fringed flowers of the cult. sorts. While the average grower will prefer to buy roots from a dealer, it is possible to dig them from the wild. If the latter plan is adopted, it is better to mark wild plants when in flower and dig them out, with ample soil about their roots, at least 6 weeks after they are through blooming. But such digging should be done with discretion, as orchids are rare flowers worth preserving in their native habitat.

Blephariglottis. White fringed orchis. A bog orchid differing from *B. ciliaris* in having longer spurs, but generally smaller and pure white flowers. Eastern N.A. Should only be grown in an acid bog. July–Aug.

ciliaris. Yellow fringed orchis; also called rattlesnake master. A slender orchid 12–28 in. high, the leaves lance-shaped, 4–8 in. long, the upper smaller and merging into the bracts.* Flowers showy, orange-yellow, the lip* much-fringed, the spur 1–1½ in. long. In meadows or bogs, eastern N.A. July–Aug. For culture *see* BOG GARDEN.

cristata. A bog orchid 8–20 in. high, the leaves narrow, 2–8 in. long. Flowers orange or yellow, the lip* deeply fringed, but not 3-parted, the spur scarcely ⅓ in. long. In pine-barren bogs, Mass. and N.J. to Fla. and Tex.

fimbriata. Purple fringed orchis; also called meadow pink. A very beautiful native orchid 12–36 in. high. Leaves ovalish or lance-shaped, 5–10 in. long, the base more or less stem-clasping. Flowers fragrant, purplish-lilac, the tip deeply 3-parted and each of the segments fringed, the spur 1–1½ in. long. In woods or moist places, eastern Canada to Tenn. June–July.

psycodes. Pink fringed orchis; also called soldier's-plume. Resembling the last, but the flowers pinkish or lilac, smaller, and less fringed. The spur is shorter than in *H. fimbriata* and has a knob at the end. In woods or bogs, eastern N.A. July–Aug.

HABERLEA (ha-ber-lee′a). A small genus of tufted, perennial herbs of the family Gesneraceae, only the two below sometimes grown in the rock garden. They are low herbs with rosettes of basal leaves and slightly irregular,* nodding flowers borne on a naked stalk, the corolla generally tubular and irregularly 5-lobed. Fruit a capsule.* (Named for Karl Konstantin Haberle, Austrian botanist.)

These are attractive little herbs suited to the rock garden. They are related to *Ramonda,* the cult. of which is discussed at ROCK GARDEN (which see, also, for the cult. of *Haberlea*).

ferdinandi-coburgi. Resembling the next, but smaller and with the leaves smooth above and the flowers smaller and dark blue. Balkans.

rhodopensis. A perennial herb scarcely 6 in. high. Leaves somewhat broader toward the tip, hairy above, 2–3 in. long and coarsely toothed. Flowers pale lilac, about 1 in. long. Balkans.

HABITAT. The site in which a wild plant grows, as woods, bogs, dunes, etc., is its *habitat. Habitat* is thus different from *distribution* in that the latter defines the *range* of a species, *i.e,* from Canada to Florida and westward. *Habitat,* by the careless, is often used to define *distribution,* but the latter term is far more inclusive than habitat which, correctly, merely describes the conditions under which a wild plant is usually found.

HABRANTHUS (ha-bran′thuss). A small genus of bulbous herbs from S.A. belonging to the amaryllis family, the two below of greenhouse cult. or in frostless regions outdoors. Closely related to *Hippeastrum* and *Zephyranthes,* from which they are separated only by technical characters. They have coated bulbs, narrow leaves and showy, but rather fleeting flowers. Petals recurved at the tip (erect in *Zephyranthes*). Fruit a 3-lobed pod. (*Habranthus* means delicate flower.) For cult. *see* AMARYLLIS. Both the plants below may be offered as *Hippeastrum* or *Zephyranthes.*

brachyandrus. Bulb football-shaped, about 1 in. thick. Leaves about 12 in. long, sparse. Flowering stalk about 12 in. high, topped by a solitary, funnel-shaped flower which may be 3 in. wide, pink above, but shading to a much darker, almost blackish base. Southern Brazil.

robustus. Lower than the preceding, the narrow leaves appearing after the flowers, and inclined to be recurved. Flowers nearly 3 in. long, almost without a tube, lavender-pink, the flower stalk stout. Argentina. Along the Gulf Coast it self-sows and repeats its bloom.

HACKBERRY. Elm-like, but usually medium-sized, round-headed trees comprising

---

* Special articles on the subjects indicated by an asterisk (*) will be found at the words so marked.

the genus **Celtis** (sell'tis), of the family Ulmaceae, only a few of the 70 widely distributed species cult. for ornament. They are much less attractive than the closely related elms. Leaves alternate,* stalked, more or less oblique at the base and 3-veined. Flowers inconspicuous, unisexual* or polygamous,* without petals and with a 4–5-lobed calyx.* Stamens* 4–5. Fruit a greenish or blackish, bony, egg-shaped or roundish drupe, the pulp scanty. (*Celtis* is the classical Greek name for a tree with a sweet fruit, but not certainly applicable to these trees.)

The hackberry is of the easiest culture in any ordinary garden soil, but they are hardy only as indicated below. Propagation is easiest from fall-sown seeds or from cuttings taken in the fall. The species much resemble one another and are hard to distinguish.

C. australis. A tree 40–70 ft. high. Leaves ovalish, 4–6 in. long, sharply toothed, more or less pale and hairy beneath. Fruit purplish-green. Eurasia and northern Af. Little grown outside of Calif. and similar climates, and not hardy north of zone* 5.

C. laevigata. Sugarberry. A tree 50–90 ft. high. Leaves almost without marginal teeth, oblongish, but long-tapering at the tip, 2½–4 in. long. Fruit at first orange-red, ultimately black-purple, almost ⅓ in. in diameter. Central U.S. to Fla. and Tex. Hardy from zone* 3 southward. Sometimes known as *C. mississippiensis*.

C. mississippiensis = *Celtis laevigata*.

C. occidentalis. The common hackberry of eastern N.A., and a tree up to 100 ft., usually lower and round-headed. Leaves ovalish or oblongish, 3–5 in. long, tapering at the tip, but roundish at the base, usually toothed except toward the base. Fruit greenish-orange, but ultimately blackish-purple nearly ⅓ in. long, somewhat pear-shaped. Eastern N.A. Hardy from zone* 2 southward and standing poor soil, high winds, smoke, and dust better than most trees. Called also nettle tree. Very subject to witches'-broom (which see).

HACKMATACK = *Larix laricina*. See LARCH.

HACKSAW FERN = *Doodia aspera*.

HAEMANTHUS (hy-man'thus). Bloodlily. Showy, bulbous, African herbs of the family Amaryllidaceae, comprising over 50 species, those below grown in greenhouses for their handsome flowers. They have chiefly basal, broad, blunt leaves and a somewhat flattened, solid flower stalk, crowned by a dense head of usually red flowers beneath which is a whorl* of spathe*-like bracts. Flowers more or less tubular, the segments erect or spreading. Stamens* sometimes showy and protruding. Fruit berry-like, not splitting. (*Haemanthus* is Greek for blood flower, in allusion to the red flowers of many species.)

The blood-lilies should be grown in a cool greenhouse (not over 55° night temperature) in potting mixture* 3. Grown in such a house, they flower in late summer and early autumn, when the bulbs should be rested through the winter and started into growth in the spring. The bulbs may be dug and stored in a cool, dark, frost-free cellar, or the pots gradually dried off and similarly stored.

albiflos. Not over 12 in. high, the thick, fleshy leaves 6–8 in. long and nearly 4 in. wide, hairy on the margins. Flowers about ¾ in. long, white, crowded at the end of the solid stalk in dense clusters (umbels*) that may be 3 in. wide. S. Af.

coccineus. Leaves thick and fleshy, nearly 20 in. long and 8 in. wide. Flowering stalk about 12 in. high. Flowers red, about 1 in. long, the cluster about 3 in. wide. S. Af.

katherinae. Leaves thin, 10–14 in. long and about 6 in. wide. Flowers bright red, nearly 2½ in. long, the cluster nearly 9 in. wide and very showy. S. Af.

multiflorus. Twelve to 18 in. high, the leaves oblongish, nearly 12 in. long, borne on a short, spotted stem. Flowers about 1 in. long, 80–100 crowded in a dense terminal cluster (umbel) that may be 6 in. wide and hence very showy. Flower stalk 1–3 ft. high, solid. Tropical Af. Rare in the trade, but not uncommon as a garden escape* in Fla.

haematodes (hy-ma-toe'deez). Blood-red.

HAEMATOXYLON (hy-ma-tocks'i-lon). A small genus of tropical American, spiny trees of the pea family, of little hort. interest, but **H. campechianum**, the logwood or bloodwood tree, occasionally planted in extreme southern Fla. as a curiosity. Its wood is the source (in Yucatan and Campeche) of a dark dye that has resisted all attempts of the synthetic chemists to replace it. The tree is rarely over 40 ft. high and has alternate, compound* leaves, with 2–4 pairs of broad, wedge-shaped leaflets about 1 in. long. Flowers yellow, irregular* but not pea-like, bad-smelling, and borne in racemes* in the leaf axils. Fruit a flattened pod (legume*), about 1½ in. long. Central America and the W.I. (*Haematoxylon* is from the Greek for blood and wood, in allusion to the red wood.)

HAEMODORACEAE (hy-mo-door-rā' see-ee). The bloodwort family comprises about 17 genera and 100 species, largely confined to the southern hemisphere, but *Lachnanthes*, the redroot, common in bogs from N.S. to Fla. They are nearly all tuberous-rooted herbs, with regular, perfect flowers, having 6 petals (or sepals), 3 stamens* in the cult. genera, and a 3-celled pod (capsule*). The only other cult. genus is the Southern African *Wachendorfia*, which is widely grown outdoors in Calif. In both the cult. genera the roots are red-juiced.

HAIRBRUSH CACTUS = *Pachycereus pecten-aboriginum*.

HAIRY WATTLE = *Acacia pubescens*.

HAKEA (hă'kee-a). A genus of over 100 species of evergreen Australian shrubs of the family Proteaceae, useful for outdoor cult. only from zone* 7 southward, a few of them popular plants in Calif. Leaves alternate,* in the cult. species either flat or needle-like. Flowers crowded, in pairs, in a dense, globe-shaped or finger-shaped cluster. Corolla tube slender, its 4 lobes joined even after the tube has opened. Fruit a hard, woody, 2-valved

---

* Special articles on the subjects indicated by an asterisk (*) will be found at the words so marked.

capsule.* (Named for Baron von Hake, German patron of botany.)

While popular in Calif., *Hakea* is little grown elsewhere, although it can stand an occasional frost. Mostly they are useful in semi-desert conditions and thrive there in a variety of soils, but prefer well-drained, light ones. Propagated by seeds, which are very slow to germinate, as they are extremely hard, and are best kept in a cool place for a year before being planted. Also the capsules will not discharge their seeds for some time unless kept in a warm, dry place.

laurina. Sea urchin; called, also, pincushion-flower. A tall shrub or small tree, sometimes up to 25 ft. high. Leaves elliptic or narrower, 5–6 in. long, about ¾ in. long, narrowed at the base into an obvious stalk, 5–7-veined. Flowers crimson in dense, stalkless, nearly globe-shaped clusters. Fruit egg-shaped, about 1 in. long, short-beaked.

saligna. A shrub 5–8 ft. high, the foliage grayish. Leaves oblongish, 4–6 in. long, short-stalked, the tip with a small, callused point. Flowers white, the clusters dense and stalkless. Fruit about 1 in. long, more or less warty.

suaveolens. A round-headed shrub, 6–10 ft. high. Leaves needle-like, spiny-tipped, often divided into several needle-like, spiny segments. Flowers fragrant, white, in short-stalked clusters, the corolla smooth. Fruit about 1 in. long, corrugated, the small beak incurved.

halepensis, -e (ha-le-pen'sis). From Aleppo, Syria; or from the region anciently so called.

HALESIA (ha-lee'zi-a). Five species of rather showy, medium-sized trees of the family Styracaceae, one Chinese, all the others from the southeastern U.S. and cult. for ornament. They have alternate,* stalked, toothed leaves. Flowers in small, hanging clusters from the twigs of the previous season. Corolla bell-shaped, prevailingly white, 4-lobed. Stamens* 8–16. Fruit an oblongish, rather fleshless, winged, and dry drupe,* the stone with 1–3 seeds. (Named for Stephen Hales, an early botanical author.)

Some of these handsome trees are called silver-bell or snowdrop tree, from their profusion of white flowers in early spring. They are chiefly trees of the under-canopy of the forest and prefer sheltered to windy sites, and a rich, well-drained soil. If raised from seed, this should be stratified for one season, or they may be propagated from layers or by root cuttings. They are sometimes offered as *Mohrodendron.*

carolina. Silver-bell tree; also called snowdrop tree. Not over 40 ft., usually half this as cult. Leaves ovalish or oblong, 2–4 in. long, finely blunt-toothed. Flowers 2–5 in a cluster, the stalks about ¾ in. long. Corolla white, about ¾ in. long. Fruit oblongish, 4-winged. May. W. Va. to Fla. and Tex. Hardy from zone* 3 southward. Sometimes sold as *H. tetraptera.*

diptera. Snowdrop tree; also called silver-bell tree. A tree or large shrub, rarely over 20 ft. high. Leaves elliptic or wider toward the tip, 2½–5 in. long, remotely wavy-toothed. Flowers 3–6 in a cluster, or this with more flowers and raceme*-like. Corolla about 1 in. long, white, deeply lobed. Fruit nearly 2 in. long, 2-winged. May. S. Car. to Fla. and Tex.

Hardy from zone* 5 southward; possibly in zone* 4 if in a sheltered place.

monticola. Tisswood. A larger tree than the others, 90 ft. in the wild, and about half this as usually cult. in the South. Leaves elliptic or oblongish, tapering at the tip, 5–9 in. long. Flowers 2–5 in a cluster, the corolla white, about 1 in. long, deeply lobed. Fruit nearly 2 in. long, 4-winged. May. N. Car. to Tenn. and Ga. Hardy from zone* 4 southward. Var. **rosea** is a rare but desirable pink-flowered form.

tetraptera = *Halesia carolina.*

HALF-BREED. See CROSS-BREED.

HALF-HYBRID. The result of a cross between a species and a variety of another species.

Halicacabum (ha-li-ka-kay'bum). Pre-Linnaean* name for the balloon-vine. See CARDIOSPERMUM.

halimifolia, -us, -um (ha-li-mi-fō'li-a). With leaves like the genus *Halimium.*

HALIMIUM. See HELIANTHEMUM HALIMIFOLIUM.

HALIMODENDRON (ha-li-mo-den'dron). A single species of salt-tolerant shrubs of the pea family, known as the salt tree, although it is a shrub scarcely 5 ft. high. The only species, H. Halodendron, has compound* leaves, having 2–4 pairs of stalkless, rounded leaflets that are 1–2½ in. long, the main leaf-stalk often spiny. Flowers pea-like, pale purple, about 1 in. long, the clusters (racemes*) usually with only 2–3 flowers. Fruit a pod (legume*), 1–2 in. long, the clusters (racemes*) usually with only 2–3 flowers. Fruit a pod (legume*), 1–2 in. long, inflated and brownish-yellow. May–June. Vicinity of Turkestan. While an original inhabitant of alkali deserts, it is a fine ornamental shrub for ordinary gardens from zone* 4 southward, and may be propagated by seeds or by cuttings over bottom-heat,* rarely by grafting on *Laburnum* or *Caragana.* (*Halimodendron* is from the Greek for maritime and tree, in allusion to its saline habitat.)

HALL'S HONEYSUCKLE = *Lonicera japonica halliana.*

Halodendron (ha-lo-den'dron). An obsolete generic name for *Halimodendron* (which see).

HALORAGIDACEAE (hal-or-ra-ji-day'see-ee). The water milfoil family is a puzzle to gardeners who cannot see the relationship of its only two cult. genera. One, *Myriophyllum,* is the beautiful submerged aquatic known as parrot's-feather, while *Gunnera* comprises huge herbs with very large, expanded leaves. There are six other genera and about 90 species of wide distribution.

Leaves hair-like in *Myriophyllum,* nearly always submerged, but often 6 ft. across and on stalks 6 ft. long in *Gunnera,* which is grown as a decorative foliage plant. Flowers very small, inconspicuous, but in *Gunnera* often crowded in dense clusters, nearly always unisexual.* Fruit dry and nut-like in *Myriophyllum,* fleshy in *Gunnera.*

Technical flower characters: Flowers uni-

---

* Special articles on the subjects indicated by an asterisk (*) will be found at the words so marked.

sexual* or polygamous.* Calyx joined to the ovary, or none. Petals 2–4, or none, if present very fleeting. Ovary inferior,* 1–4-celled.

HAMAMELIDACEAE (ha-ma-mell-i-day'-see-ee). The witch-hazel family, except for the cult. genera, is chiefly tropical or subtropical. It comprises about 20 genera and possibly 100 species of trees or shrubs, none except the sweet gum (*Liquidambar*) and the winter- or fall-blooming witch-hazel being particularly handsome.

Leaves alternate* and simple, the veins arranged finger-fashion in *Liquidambar* (*see* SWEET GUM), but feather-fashion in the rest of the cult. genera. Some writers consider that the sweet gum and a few other (non-hort.) genera should be included in a separate family, Altingiaceae, not here so considered.

There are no petals in *Parrotia* and *Fothergilla*, but all the other cult. genera have them, and *Fothergilla* is showy from its plentiful stamens.* The only other showy garden plants are *Hamamelis* (witch-hazel) with yellow flowers, *Loropetalum*, an evergreen Chinese shrub, with mostly white flowers, and *Corylopsis* whose yellow flowers appear in spring before the leaves unfold. Fruit is a woody capsule* which explosively discharges the seeds in the witch-hazel.

Technical flower characters: Sepals 4 or 5, sometimes 6 or 7. Petals 4–7, often strapshaped, or lacking. Stamens 4 or 5, rarely none. Ovary inferior* or nearly so. Styles 2.

HAMAMELIS (ha-ma-mell'is). A small genus of rather coarse shrubs, family Hamamelidaceae, confined to N.A. and eastern As., usually called witch-hazel or winter-bloom, the latter in allusion to their blooming from Oct. to April, while the twigs are bare. Leaves alternate,* short-stalked, oblique at the base, more or less wavy-toothed. Flowers yellow or reddish, crumpled in the bud, the 4 petals strap-shaped. Stamens* 4. Fruit a 2-valved, explosively splitting capsule, which shoots its 2 black, shining seeds for a considerable distance. (*Hamamelis* is an old Greek name for a plant with a pear-shaped fruit, perhaps the medlar, and of little applicability to the witch-hazel.)

The witch-hazels are of the easiest cult., for they thrive in any ordinary garden soil, although preferring moist sites to dry ones. As the seeds take two years to germinate, the plants are most easily propagated by layers. They are good plants for the shrub border or for a border screen.

japonica. A shrub or small tree 10–25 ft. high. Leaves roundish or broadly oval, 3–4 in. long. Flowers about ¾ in. long, bright yellow. Jap. Jan.–Mar. Hardy from zone* 3 southward. The *var.* **arborea** is more tree-like in habit, and has golden-yellow flowers.

mollis. A shrub or small tree 10–25 ft. high. Leaves roundish or broadest toward the tip, 3½–7 in. long, finely toothed, and grayish-hairy beneath. Flowers golden-yellow, but reddish at the base, about ¾ in. long. China. Feb.–Mar. Hardy from zone* 3 southward.

vernalis. A shrub, often with many stems, usually less than 6 ft. high. Leaves oblongish, or broadest toward the tip, 3–5 in. long, coarsely toothed above the middle. Flowers about ½ in. long, dark yellow, or reddish toward the base. Central U.S. to La. Jan.–Mar. Hardy from zone* 4 southward. A useful shrub for forcing (which see).

virginiana. Common witch-hazel. A coarse shrub up to 15 ft. high. Leaves elliptic or broadest toward the tip, 4–6 in. long, coarsely toothed. Flowers bright yellow, about ¾ in. long. Eastern N.A. Sept.–Nov. Hardy from zone* 2 southward.

HAMATOCACTUS (ha-ma-toe-kak'tus). A single species of globe-shaped or oblongish cactus, H. setispinus, from southern Tex. and adjacent Mex. It is scarcely 6 in. high and has usually 13 rather thin ribs. Spines 12–16 in a cluster, with 1–3 central and larger spines in the center of each spine cluster. Flowers funnel-shaped, yellow, 2–3 in. long, its outer scales somewhat fringed. Fruit red, small, berry-like. The plant is cult. outdoors in the desert regions of the U.S. and in greenhouses. *See* CACTI for details of culture. (*Hamatocactus* is from the Greek for hook and *Cactus*, in reference to the hooked central spines.)

HAMBURG PARSLEY. *See* PARSLEY.

HAMELIA (ha-me'li-a). Showy, evergreen, tropical American shrubs of the family Rubiaceae, favorite garden plants in the tropics, but cult. outdoors in the U.S. only in zones* 8 and 9, especially in Fla. They have generally opposite* leaves and handsome, tubular, red or yellowish flowers in terminal, branching clusters (cymes*). Corolla regular, 5-lobed. Stamens usually 5, not protruding. Fruit a berry. (Named for Henry L. Duhamel du Monceau, French botanist.)

The hamelias are very fine garden shrubs in warm regions and respond to rich soils and plenty of moisture, although they will grow in a variety of less favorable sites. Propagated by cuttings of partially ripe wood rooted under glass, or by seeds.

erecta. Rat-poison plant. A stout, branching shrub 8–20 ft. high, more or less grayish-hairy on the twigs. Leaves ovalish, 4–6 in. long. Flowers about ¾ in. long, usually scarlet, but sometimes orange. Fruit about ¼ in. long, reddish-purple, more or less egg-shaped. Fla. to Brazil. Sometimes mistaken for *Ixora* (which see). Sometimes called scarlet-bush.

patens = *Hamelia erecta*.

HAND CULTIVATOR. *See* No. 7 at TOOLS AND IMPLEMENTS.

HAND POLLINATION. *See* Crossing Technique at CROSSING.

HANDSOME HARRY = *Rhexia virginica*.

HANGING BASKET. A basket-like contrivance of wood or wire, suspended from the roof, and filled with soil and suitable plants. Its chief value is decorative, and in the greenhouse or hanging from a porch roof, a series of well-filled hanging baskets may be very handsome.

While very showy, painted, wooden baskets

---

* Special articles on the subjects indicated by an asterisk (*) will be found at the words so marked.

are to be had from the dealers, the most lasting and practical are made of wire stout enough to hold the weight of soil and plants. Also, wire baskets stand daily watering better than wooden ones. Another type is the so-called self-watering basket. It is made of iron with a double bottom, the space below the

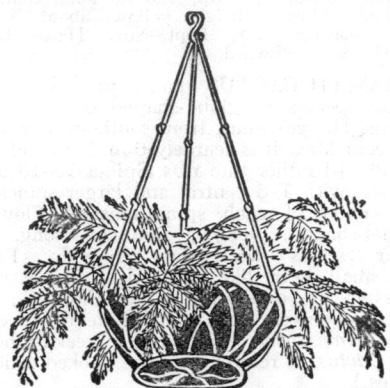

Old-fashioned, moss-lined hanging basket with fern

soil container being filled with water which is poured down a tube that projects up to the soil level. Such baskets are thus sub-irrigated and avoid the inevitable drip that follows ordinary watering as outlined below. They are more costly than wire baskets, and do not need watering until the reservoir is dry.

It adds to the attractiveness of wire baskets, and also holds the soil, to line them next to the wire with fresh slabs of green moss. See that the moss completely covers the inner side of the basket, and it is better to fit the moss a bit at a time as the soil is put in. For most hanging baskets, potting mixture* 3 will be the best. Pack the soil reasonably well so that the moss is tightly pressed against the wire. Then dip the basket in a pail of water and allow the soil to settle for a day or so. Then fill in any holes that may have developed and you are ready for planting.

BASKET PLANTS. Very attractive hanging baskets can be made by using plants like dwarf nasturtiums, sweet alyssum, *Browallia, Vinca major,* the English ivy, *Cobaea scandens, Thunbergia, Saxifraga sarmentosa,* wandering Jew, or the Kenilworth ivy. These, and more desirable plants to be mentioned presently, will form drooping sprays, without which a hanging basket looks rather naked. These trailing or drooping plants should be planted near the edge or even plunged in the sides of the basket, which may be done with a dibble if the plants are young. In fact most hanging-basket plants are best started elsewhere and transplanted into the basket when still quite young.

Usually the center of the basket should have some erect plant, or several if they are small,

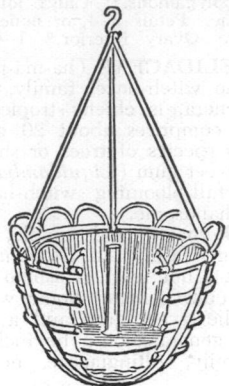

So-called self-watering hanging basket with a basal reservoir and pipe. For details *see* text.

around which are grouped the smaller or trailing species. Good plants for the center are geraniums, petunia, *Cordyline, Dracaena,* begonia, coleus, *Cuphea,* platycentra, fuchsia, and ferns. Some very fine hanging baskets consist only of the Boston fern and its drooping variety.

While an all-fern basket is often very attractive, there are some very fine greenhouse plants with beautiful flowers that are suited to hanging baskets. They must be purchased from the florist or grown in one's own greenhouse. And the plants listed below will not stand too much wind or dry air. Hanging baskets containing them should therefore be put in quiet, wind-free porches or kept in the greenhouse. Some of these choicer basket plants are:

Centropogon lucyanus	*Convolvulus*
Begonia lloydi	*mauritanicus*
Fuchsia procumbens	*Episcia cupreata*
Abutilon megapotami-	*Solanum jasmin-*
cum	*oides*
Columnea gloriosa	

WATERING. Because they are exposed to the air on all sides, hanging baskets dry out much more quickly than ordinary flower pots. If they are in a sunny or windy place, they will need a thorough watering at least every other day and often every day. Much the most satisfactory method is to dip the basket, plants and all, in a tub of water, but begonia leaves should not be submerged. Watering from a ladder with a watering pot is apt to wash out the soil, especially in freshly planted baskets, where the roots of the plants have not yet bound to the soil. If the plants in your basket show signs of yellowing, they may need fertilizer. The best plan, so as not to disturb the plants, is to work into the soil a little complete fertilizer (*see* FERTILIZERS), or water with liquid manure. *See also* FERN BALL.

HANGING GARDEN. No garden really hangs, but the term hanging gardens has been applied to roof gardens from the days

---

* Special articles on the subjects indicated by an asterisk (*) will be found at the words so marked.

when elaborate ones were made in Babylon to the modern penthouse garden.

HANSEN BUSH CHERRY = *Prunus besseyi*.

HAPLOID. The normal number of chromosomes basic for any particular plant. For what happens after fertilization, *see* CHROMOSOME.

HARDENBERGIA (har-den-ber'ji-a). A small genus of Australian woody vines of the pea family, the two below much grown in Calif. and south of zone* 7 for their long clusters of small flowers. They have compound* leaves, the leaflets 3–5, or reduced to 1 in *H. monophylla.* Flowers pea-like, very small, but in long, showy racemes.* Fruit a swollen or flat pod (legume*). (Named for Franziska Countess of Hardenberg.)

While popular as outdoor vines in Calif., both can be grown in the cool greenhouse. Use potting mixture* 3, to which about ⅓ its bulk should be added of peaty, slightly acid humus. They are best propagated by greenwood cuttings taken in spring and kept under glass.

comptoniana. Leaflets mostly 3, rarely 5, ovalish or narrower, 1½–3 in. long, blunt-tipped. Flowers blue or violet blue, scarcely ½ in. long. Pod flattish, 1½–2 in. long.

monophylla. Leaflet only 1, ovalish or oblong, 2–4 in. long, blunt at the tip. Flowers scarcely ½ in. long, violet or rose-color. Pod more or less swollen. The *var.* **alba** has white flowers and the *var.* **rosea** has pink ones.

HARDENING OFF. This is a gardener's term used to describe the process of making plants ready for outdoors. All plants raised in frames or greenhouses, whether from seeds, cuttings or otherwise, are necessarily tender at first, and if exposed to outdoor conditions without being hardened off, would suffer severely from sunscald or chilly winds. Hardy annual or hardy perennial seedlings if raised in the open may be transplanted without much fear of damage, even from light frost. If raised in a greenhouse, or even a cold frame, the same plants would, if put outdoors right away, lose much of their foliage and perhaps be severely cut back by late frosts. Geraniums, petunias and similar tender subjects that are raised under glass would likewise suffer injury, even if not planted out until the end of May.

Hardening off, therefore, means making such plants hardy enough to withstand outdoor conditions. If raised indoors or in a greenhouse, the usual plan is to place the plants in a cold frame, keeping the sash closed for two or three days, then gradually allowing more and more air until eventually the sash is removed entirely. The hardening process takes about two weeks — that is, if the plants are to be set out at the end of May, they should spend two weeks in the frame, the sash being dispensed with the last few days.

If no frame is available the plants, whether in pots or boxes, should be stood outdoors in a partially shaded, sheltered place when weather permits, either covering with a temporary canvas arrangement or bringing them indoors at night, especially if frost threatens. By degrees the plants may be brought more into the open until they are thoroughly inured to sun and wind.

The time for hardening off depends largely upon the class of plants and when they are to be planted out. Most half-hardy annuals such as petunias, verbenas, salpiglossis, etc., are sown in heat in March and are not safe outdoors until mid-May; therefore the hardening process should begin the latter part of April. Geraniums and similar plants wintered indoors are usually planted out after the end of May, and therefore should be given their hardening treatment from the middle of that month, special precautions against cold winds and night frosts being taken. If the nights are very cold, mats on the frame are advisable at night.

Vegetable and even flowering plants raised in a hotbed, if space is lacking for full hardening off in frames, may be planted outside and covered with paper cones known as Hotkaps. These paper cones ward off both wind and hot sunshine and serve as miniature greenhouses. The plants can gradually be ventilated until it is safe to remove the protector entirely. Hotkaps are largely used by vegetable growers, even for the raising of cucumbers, melons, etc., the seeds being sown under the covers, which are allowed to remain until the plants no longer can be protected by them. — T. A. W.

HARD FERN = *Blechnum Spicant.*

HARD FESCUE = *Festuca ovina duriuscula.*

HARD-FLESHED CHERRY = *Prunus avium duracina.*

HARDHACK = *Spiraea tomentosa;* also *Potentilla fruticosa.*

HARDHEADS = *Centaurea nigra.*

HARDINESS. No terms are more common in hort. literature than hardy, tender, and half-hardy, and none more difficult to define. For we try to reduce to such terms many factors that determine the climatic fitness of a plant for outdoor culture. The difficulty is that in their own home all plants are hardy, while the average garden has dozens of plants that come from a variety of climates. Some are hardy, some merely root hardy (which means they may winter-kill*), while others are tender. And some are hardy for one season but not for others.

Hardiness, for most ordinary purposes, means trying to answer the question, "Will it live over the winter?" In other words, hardiness is a temperature response, and only this, to most gardeners. While this is true in a general way, so many other things besides winter cold contribute to hardiness, that they are worth noting.

DORMANCY. For all woody plants, except evergreens, there comes a period of winter dormancy, coinciding with leaf-fall and the onset of cold weather in the fall, and ending

---

* Special articles on the subjects indicated by an asterisk (*) will be found at the words so marked.

with the onset of spring. For all wild plants, in any locality, this periodic dormancy is automatic, or the plants, instead of being acclimated, would have long since perished.

This dormancy is a very definite physiological response to cold. The plant cells, the air spaces between them, and the concentration of cell-sap change materially during cold weather — mostly in the direction of lessened water content. The effectiveness of this dormancy also depends upon a rather delicate balance which can withstand sudden warm spells in midwinter, when an untimely bursting into leaf would be fatal. But no native plant ever does this, nor do they change by more than a few days their yearly rhythm of dormancy. Resistance to cold is based upon these facts, although the physiology of what goes on in the dormant wood is more complicated than there is space to enlarge upon here.

When this is thoroughly understood, hardiness takes on a somewhat different meaning. If resistance to cold depends not only upon the intensity of winter temperature, but upon water content and concentration of the cell-sap, it is imperative to know more about these very important factors of hardiness.

Woody plants enter the winter with a water content dictated by the amount and distribution of summer rainfall. If there has been a gradual slackening of rainfall as mid-August or September approaches, then the season's growth will tend to ripen and the plant will enter the winter as well prepared to meet it as possible.

If, on the other hand, there is much late-summer rainfall, the season's growth will continue green, there will be little ripening of wood, and the plant will enter the winter in the worst possible state to meet its rigors. Such a plant will almost surely winter-kill, and it may be killed outright. In other words, it is not "hardy."

With many plants their hardiness is thus a matter of summer rainfall rather than winter cold. A study of their condition during the early fall will tell us much about their chances of winter survival. If their growth is too lush and if the wood has not ripened, then pruning or protection is advisable. See PROTECTING PLANTS.

INCREASING HARDINESS. While, as we shall see presently, it is impossible to make tender plants (i.e., climatically unsuited ones) hardy, there are many things that a resourceful gardener can do to increase the hardiness of plants that are on or near the edge of their hardiness range. All of them point in the same direction, the gradual slackening of the plant's activity as it enters the winter. The chief things to remember are:

1. Do not cultivate the soil after late summer; it may induce a lot of new shoots that will enter the winter unprepared for it. For the same reason do not use nitrogen fertilizers (see FERTILIZERS) late in the season, and do not overwater after Aug. 15, especially on rich but poorly drained soils.

2. Do not, if possible, allow shrubs to suf-

fer from midsummer drought, which usually checks growth, induces a premature ripening of wood, and may be followed by a lush fall growth that will be unfit to face the winter.

3. If you have allowed a smothering overgrowth or a crowded plantation to go through the summer without thinning, do not clean it up in the fall. This merely means that you expose tissue which was not given the proper chance to ripen. For the same reason vigorous summer pruning may induce a lot of fresh and therefore vulnerable growth.

4. The popular notion that plants raised from cuttings grown in a region climatically similar to your own are preferable to ones from a different climate may not always be true. Mutation within a species may often produce plants, the hardiness of which is unexpectedly effective. Thus, experiments at the University of Virginia have shown that many plants from the South will grow in regions far north of their regular range, and thus are "hardy" in zones* beyond their expected range of hardiness. For a more detailed discussion of this little-known phase of hardiness, see a paper by O. E. White in Carylogia, Vol. 6, pp. 1146–49, from the Proceedings of the 9th International Congress of Genetics, Bellagio, Italy, 1953.

5. Some plants known to be tender or only half-hardy may often be used if one studies the site or exposure. In regions where cold-air drainage naturally reaches the lowest part of your grounds with the greatest intensity, avoid such sites for your questionably hardy plant. (See MICRO-CLIMATE.)

6. The really important feature of hardiness in nearly all woody plants is to grow them in a well-drained soil, get their ordinary spring growth well ripened, and then trust to their going through the winter with a minimum of damage. They will do this if they are climatically suited for your region. In other words, do they come within certain climatic zones of hardiness, outside of which it is impossible to grow them?

ZONES OF HARDINESS. It is possible, and has been done for most woody plants in the ENCYCLOPEDIA, to assign them to definite zones of hardiness, north of which it is unreasonable to expect them to grow. While, as we have seen, the hardiness of a plant in a particular site is a compound of many things besides temperature, it is still true that winter cold is the chief factor which dictates the climatic zonation of vegetation from the Arctic to the tropics. While many refinements of method have been used for plotting such zones, perhaps the most readily workable one is the plan evolved by Alfred Rehder of considering the lowest mean temperature of the coldest month. Concentrated in such periods are the extremes of unfavorable temperatures, the plant's survival of which will probably mean its continued growth.

For the ENCYCLOPEDIA an extension of the Rehder system had to be made to cover the whole country, as his published map only includes, roughly, the region north of a line

* Special articles on the subjects indicated by an asterisk (*) will be found at the words so marked.

from N. Car., Ark., northern Tex. and westward. The plan here adopted separates the region north of Mex. into 9 zones.* For a complete description of them and a map *see* ZONE.

While such a scheme certainly operates over large areas, many local conditions of hardiness are affected by slope, site, exposure, and by some of the purely hort. operations of cultivation, pruning, watering, and fertilizing, such as are outlined above. For all herbs there is also the protection of a snow blanket, or of a mulch (which see). Both so change the cold hazard that it is impossible to assign most herbs to any of these countrywide zones of hardiness.

There are some plants, too, especially a group of Californian bulbs and certain cacti which, while able to stand pretty severe winter temperatures (10°–23°) in their own region, succumb at once in a higher temperature in the East when this is accomplished by winter slush or rain. Whether such a condition of winter dryness is properly considered as hardiness is a moot point. That is why there are notes at most such genera explaining their peculiar climatic requirements. While these may well be outside the scope of hardiness, the term also covers the ability of a plant to survive, no matter whether the hazard it must overcome is too much cold or heat or unfavorable factors such as drought.

The same is true of the unfitness of certain conifers and many broad-leaved evergreens for large sections of the country due to insufficient rainfall. *See* EVERGREENS, BROAD-LEAVED EVERGREENS. The survival of such plants is due to a combination of moisture and temperature to which hardiness should perhaps be applied in a sense far from the usual one of being able to withstand winter cold.

HARDPAN. A layer of compact clay or silt below the usual penetration of the roots of most shallow-rooted plants. It often prevents the penetration of shrub or tree roots, and especially taproots. Hardpan may cause an accumulation of relatively stagnant water, which, in some dry regions, is a benefit. But to most gardeners, in a reasonably moist cli-

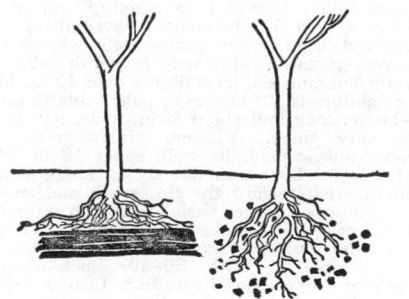

At the left, a root system driven laterally by hardpan. At the right, the root system developing normally after removal or breaking-up of hardpan.

mate, hardpan is a nuisance to be destroyed by digging or dynamite.*

HARDY. *See* HARDINESS.

HARDY AGERATUM. *See* EUPATORIUM COELESTINUM.

HARDY AMARYLLIS = *Lycoris squamigera.*

HARDY CATALPA = *Catalpa speciosa.*

HARDY GLOXINIA. *See* INCARVILLEA DELAVAYI.

HARDY ORANGE = *Poncirus trifoliata.*

HAREBELL = *Campanula rotundifolia.*

HARE'S-FOOT FERN. *See* DAVALLIA. *See also* POLYPODIUM AUREUM.

HARE'S-TAIL GRASS = *Lagurus ovatus.*

HARICOT = *Phaseolus vulgaris.* *See* BEAN.

HARISON'S YELLOW ROSE = *Rosa harisoni.*

HARLEQUIN FLOWER = *Sparaxis.*

HARRISIA (har-riss′i-a). Night-blooming, mostly climbing or vine-like cacti, most of the 20 known species from the W.I. and S.A., none from Mex. or the southwestern U.S. They have angled or fluted and 8–10-ribbed branches which bear at intervals a group of straight spines. Flowers solitary, funnel-shaped, the tube scaly but not spiny, the sepals* greenish-pink, the petals white. Fruit fleshy, spineless but tubercled or deeply warty. (Named for William Harris, Superintendent of the Public Gardens of Jamaica.)

The cult. species are tropical cacti to be grown in the greenhouse or outdoors only in extreme southern Fla. or Calif. *See* CACTI for details of soil and handling.

bonplandi. Climbing, often 8–10 ft. high. Branches 2–3 in. in diameter, 4-angled. Spines 6–8 at each cluster. Flowers 8–9 in. long, usually closing after sunrise. Southern S.A.

eriophora. Not much over 12 in. high, the branches about 1½ in. in diameter, 8–9 ribbed. Spines dark-tipped, 8–9 at a cluster. Flowers nearly 9 in. long, pinkish outside. Cuba.

gracilis. High-climbing (15–20 ft.) and much-branched, the branches with 9–10 ribs. Spines black-tipped, 10–16 at a cluster. Flowers about 8 in. long, the outer scales hairy in their axils.* Jamaica.

martini. A climbing cactus 6–8 ft. long in the wild, usually less as cult., the stems nearly round. Spines short, few, or none in age, the central one solitary, about 1 in. long. Flowers very showy, nearly 8 in. long, with many white or pink-tinged petals. Argentina.

tortuosa. An erectish but arching, not high-climbing cactus, its branches about 1½ in. in diameter and 7-ribbed. Spines 6–10 at each cluster. Flowers 5–6 in. long. Argentina.

HARROWING. What we do to the soil by hand raking, harrowing does with a machine. Whether the machine is horse-drawn or motor-driven does not matter, but the operation can be done most effectively by recognizing a few simple facts. Harrowing practically always follows plowing, and it is best to harrow as soon after plowing as convenient. The

---

* Special articles on the subjects indicated by an asterisk (*) will be found at the words so marked.

soil is most workable then and we shall accomplish the greatest object of harrowing, which is thoroughly to pulverize the soil. Hand raking does this for small areas, but for anything over ¼ acre, harrowing is far easier and just as effective.

When the land is left in furrows by the plow, it is best to use first the disk harrow, the rotating knives of which break up the lumps and begin the process of smoothing out the ridges left by plowing.

Some operators run a disk harrow several times over a field and in different directions, but this is not usually necessary. And it saves time to begin harrowing with an ordinary toothed harrow immediately after one or two disk harrowings. The toothed or spring-toothed harrow has a series of spike-like teeth so arranged that as the implement is dragged over the land it acts much like a rake. Run it as long as necessary in order to make finely pulverized soil, for this is the only real object of raking or harrowing. In other words, both operations usually precede planting and have nothing to do with cultivation, which is a soil operation that follows planting.

Like any other soil operation, harrowing can not be done successfully if the land is wet. See CULTIVATION for a discussion of the handling of soils after a rain.

HARTFORD FERN = *Lygodium palmatum.*

HARTMANNIA SPECIOSA = *Oenothera speciosa.* See EVENING PRIMROSE.

HART'S-THORN = *Rhamnus cathartica.*

HARTSTONGUE FERN = *Phyllitis Scolopendrium.*

HARVESTING. One of the reasons for having a garden is to have fresher flowers, fruit, and vegetables than come from the shops. All commercially produced products must be picked before they are fully ripe to prevent spoilage in transit. It is precisely this time lag which intelligent home harvesting avoids. When, exactly, to harvest all your crops only experience will tell. Varieties, soil, climate, and your own idea of perfect ripening, especially for fruits, will dictate the preferred time of harvesting.

HASHISH. See CANNABIS SATIVA.

Hasjoo. Japanese name for the Yokohama bean; see STIZOLOBIUM.

hastata, -us, -um (has-tay′ta). Hastate; *i.e.,* shaped like the head of a spear or arrow, but the basal lobes widely spreading.

HATCHET-CACTUS = *Pelecyphora aselliformis.*

HATIORA (ha-ti-or′ra). A small genus of tree-perching, spineless cacti, found in tropical American forests, and unlike most cacti, not true desert plants. They have round, usually pencil-thick branches, which are much-branched, and the small terete branchlets are more or less club-shaped and about 1 in. long in the only cult. species, H. salicornioides. Its main branches are frequently 6 ft. long and

pendulous. Flowers day-blooming, about ⅓ in. long, more or less wheel-shaped, the petals erect and salmon-colored. Fruit mistletoe-like. Brazil. This is a cactus of greenhouse culture, where it blooms in late winter, and is closely related to *Rhipsalis,* where notes on how to grow both will be found. (*Hatiora* is an anagram of *Hariota,* an untenable name.)

HAULM. The stem; especially of peas, beans, or grasses. The term is more common in England than here.

HAUSTORIA. The root-like sucking contrivances used by parasitic plants to suck their food from the host. See HOST.

HAUTBOIS STRAWBERRY = *Fragaria moschata.* See STRAWBERRY.

HAW. See VIBURNUM and CRATAEGUS.

HAWKSBEARD. See CREPIS.

HAWKWEED. Very showy and handsome, but pestiferous, weeds belonging to the genus *Hieracium.* The two worst are the orange hawkweed and the mouse-ear hawkweed, both of which will be found in the list at WEEDS.

HAWKWEED FAMILY. See COMPOSITAE.

HAWORTHIA (ha-wor′thi-a). Generally stemless, South African succulent plants of the lily family, comprising over 70 species, often grown in desert gardens and in miniature groups of cacti and other succulents for table decorations. They have mostly a basal rosette* of thick, fleshy leaves, which are often white-warty or tubercled, and in some species crowded on a short stem. Flowers greenish or whitish, usually in sparse clusters (panicles or racemes*) at the end of a slender stalk that arises from the leaf rosette.* Corolla tubular, its limb slightly irregular.* Stamens* 6. Fruit a 3-valved capsule, its numerous seeds flat and somewhat angled. (Named for A. H. Haworth, English succulent fancier and botanist.)

For culture see SUCCULENTS.

attenuata. Leaves 30–40 in a rosette,* the thick blades white-warty on the back, 2–3 in. long and about ¾ in. wide. Flowers greenish-white, with brownish veins, the stalk of the cluster nearly 2 ft. long.

coarctata. Leaves in a rosette,* but at the end of a stem 5–7 in. long. Leaves about 2 in. long and ¾ in. wide, prominently white-warty. Flowers greenish-white, with brownish veins, the cluster unbranched, its stalk not over 12 in. high.

cymbiformis. Leaves pale bluish-green, 1–1½ in. long and about ¾ in. wide, not warty, but very thick. Flowers pinkish-green, the cluster unbranched, its stalk about 12 in. high.

fasciata. Leaves about 2 in. long, slender and tapering toward the tip, green and smooth on the upper surface, keeled and with transverse bands of whitish tubercles beneath. Flowers in a loose cluster (raceme*), whitish-green.

margaritifera. With 30–40 much-tubercled leaves in a dense basal rosette.* Leaves 2–3 in. long, about 1 in. wide. Flowers whitish, the cluster (raceme*) long-stalked and about 6 in. long.

Radula. Leaves covered with minute tubercles on both surfaces, 2–3 in. long, less than

---

* Special articles on the subjects indicated by an asterisk (*) will be found at the words so marked.

1 in. wide, tapering at the tip. Flower cluster 12–15 in. high, the flowers green- or rose-lined.

tessellata. Leaves almost triangular, thick, about 1½ in. long, nearly as wide, the margins shallow-toothed, dark green with paler green lines above, rough and with minute tubercles beneath. Flower cluster (raceme*) nearly 12 in. long, the flowers not over 1 in. long.

turgida. Leaves 20–30 in a basal rosette,* the thick, keeled blades scarcely 1 in. long, ⅓ in. wide, the upper side lined with pale green toward the tip. Flowers very short-stalked in a spike-like raceme,* which is few-flowered.

HAWTHORN. See CRATAEGUS. For other plants sometimes called hawthorn *see* APONOGETON and RAPHIOLEPIS.

HAY-SCENTED FERN = *Dennstaedtia punctilobula.*

HAZEL; HAZELNUT. The hazel (*hazelnut* is best restricted to the fruits) is a general term comprising all the shrubs and trees of the genus **Corylus** (kor′i-lus) of the birch family, all the 15 species being found in the north temperate zone. Some of them yield hazelnuts and filberts, both of which are cult. commercially for the nutritious nuts. Leaves alternate,* doubly toothed, stalked, and generally hairy. Male and female flowers in separate clusters on the same plant, both without petals. Male flowers in scaly catkins,* the female in a partially enclosed, stalkless, head-like, dense cluster, only the red styles* protruding, both blooming before the leaves unfold. Stamens 4–8. Fruit an egg-shaped, roundish or oblong nut with a hard, smooth shell, partly or wholly surrounded by a leafy, sometimes tubular, structure (involucre*). (*Corylus* is the classical name for the hazel.)

For culture *see* below.

C. americana. American hazel. A shrub 5–8 ft. high. Leaves broadly ovalish, 3–5 in. long, irregularly double-toothed. Fruits 2–6 in the cluster at the ends of the twigs, the leafy, lobed involucre* twice as long as the nut, which is nearly round and about ⅝ in. wide. N.A. Hardy from zone* 2 southward. Nuts of little value.

C. Avellana. European hazel. A shrub 10–15 ft. high. Leaves roundish or broadest toward the tip, 3–4 in. long, heart-shaped at the base. Fruits 1–4, the leafy, deeply lobed involucre* as long as or shorter than the nut which is about ¾ in. long. Eu., and commonly grown there for the nuts, but here mostly for ornament. Hardy from zone* 2 southward. The *var.* **aurea** has yellowish leaves; *var.* **fuscorubra** has purplish or brownish-red leaves. The *var.* **grandis,** the cobnut, is usually grown for the nut, which is larger than the typical form. Var. **atropurpurea** is *var. fuscorubra.* Var. **contorta** has the branches twisted and curled.

C. Colurna. Turkish hazel. A tree up to 60 ft. and grown chiefly for ornament, its branches corky. Leaves broadly oval, heart-shaped at the base, 3–5 in. long. Fruits clustered, the leafy involucre* divided into narrow, sticky lobes, the nut about 1 in. wide. Western As. and southeastern Eu. Hardy from zone* 3 southward. Used, also, for grafting stock for the filbert.

C. contorta = *Corylus Avellana contorta.*

C. cornuta. Beaked hazel. A shrub 3–8 ft.

high. Leaves ovalish or broadest toward the tip, 2½–4½ in. long, densely double-toothed. Fruits 1–2 in a cluster completely hidden by the long, tubular, leafy involucre* which is nearly 3 times as long as the nut. The latter is thin-shelled, about ⅝ in. long, and more or less egg-shaped. Eastern N.A., but west to British Columbia. Hardy from zone* 3 southward. Formerly known as *C. rostrata.* The nuts are nearly worthless.

C. maxima. Filbert. A shrub 10–30 ft. high, sometimes tree-like (*see* below), the twigs and foliage sticky-hairy. Leaves roundish-oval, suddenly tapering at the tip, 3–5½ in. long. Fruits 1–3 in the cluster, the leafy, tubular, usually lobed involucre* about twice as long as the nut, which is oblongish, its kernel with a red or whitish skin. Western As. and southeastern Eu. Hardy from zone* 3 southward. The *var.* **purpurea,** chiefly grown for ornament, has dark-purple leaves.

HAZEL CULTURE

Growing shrubs of *Corylus americana* and *C. cornuta* presents no difficulties, for both are common on a variety of soils in many parts of eastern N.A. But the nuts of both species are inferior to the filberts of the Old World which are imported into this country on a large scale.

Hazelnuts, which are chiefly the product of these two American and some Old World species, are generally roundish, and include also the cobnut, a variety of *Corylus Avellana.* They are, from the commercial standpoint, not worth cultivating, but will always be collected from the wild.

Filberts, on the other hand, include various hort. varieties of *Corylus maxima,* widely grown in Europe for the nuts, which are decidedly oblong and far better than our hazelnuts or the cobnut. Unfortunately, the plant does not grow so well in the eastern U.S. and its commercial production in the U.S. is chiefly limited to Washington and Oregon. There the plant is trimmed to a tree-like form and often reaches a height of 20–30 ft. It is planted upon 25-ft. intervals.

While it can be propagated by stratified seeds, most of the better varieties are budded or grafted upon stock of *Corylus Colurna* or sometimes on *C. Avellana.*

The culture of filberts in the East seems to be in an experimental stage, although many new American and European hybrids are being produced, and offer better chances of success with the hazel than formerly, especially in the East. The plant does much better in the moist coolness of Washington and Oregon than in New York, where experimental plantings are still to demonstrate their value. Small plantations show that some of the varieties are at least hardy, but they should not be planted on southern or warm sites because the warmth may force them into flower, only to have a late frost kill all chances of a later crop of nuts.

VARIETIES. For Washington and Oregon the outstanding variety of filbert is Barcelona, there allowed to become tree-like, but usually a shrub as grown in the East, where it is also the best variety for general purposes. It may be the same as the Barcelona variety of Spain, which produces large crops of Old World nuts.

---

* Special articles on the subjects indicated by an asterisk (*) will be found at the words so marked.

Other varieties of promise are Kentish Cob (a cobnut), Daviana, and Red Lambert, but all of them do better in the Pacific Northwest than in the East. Winter injury to or premature flowering of the male catkins is a trouble of nearly all varieties in the East, as well as disease.

INSECT PESTS. Aphids and lace bugs are controlled by pesticide #1 (*see* SPRAYS AND DUSTS) or #21. Dormant sprays of lime-sulphur or early-season miticides control bug-bud condition, caused by a tiny mite. Dormant sprays of oils will prevent scale build-up. Early spring sprays of pesticide #1 will control a flea beetle. Tent caterpillars can be stopped with pesticide #1. Filbert-worm is controlled by pesticide #19 or #17 applied when eggs hatch (mid-July) and repeated three weeks later.

HAZEL FAMILY = Betulaceae.

HEAD. Any tight or head-like flower cluster. Technically, *head* should perhaps be restricted to the flower clusters of the daisy, chrysanthemum, aster, and all the other plants of the huge family of Compositae (which see for details). But to most gardeners a head is any close cluster of flowers. For *head* in the sense of a head of lettuce *see* the next entry.

HEADING. A few plants, notably lettuce, endive, cabbage, cauliflower, and Chinese cabbage and some others, have, by selection and the work of the plant breeder, developed a more or less congested head of leaves, or of flowers, as in the cauliflower. All but the outside leaves of such heads are cut off from light and consequently produce no green coloring matter.

This fact means that the production of such an abnormal thing as a head puts a tremendous burden upon the functionally normal leaves. It is the latter that support the development of the head, for it is ordinary green leaves that produce plant food, while the head merely produces food for us.

It is for this reason that the cultural notes on cabbage, cauliflower, lettuce, etc., stress the fact that the only way to insure good heading is good, quick growth. Sluggish growth, weedy gardens, too much shade, and any other major disturbance of the plant's economy will make heading difficult and it may make it impossible. Do not forget that heading is something man has forced upon some plants, and to get the best results from such an unusual process, the best of care must be given.

In a few, like endive and cauliflower, no amount of good care will force the plants to head properly. Such have to be tied up, a laborious process described at both crops.

HEADING BROCCOLI = *Brassica oleracea botrytis*. See CAULIFLOWER.

HEAD LETTUCE = *Lactuca sativa capitata*. For culture *see* LETTUCE.

HEAL-ALL = *Prunella vulgaris*. *See also* the list at WEEDS.

HEART CHERRY = *Prunus avium juliana*. See CHERRY.

HEARTNUT = *Juglans sieboldiana cordiformis*. See WALNUT.

"HEARTS-BUSTIN'-WITH-LOVE." *See* EUONYMUS ATROPURPUREUS.

HEARTSEASE. *See* VIOLA TRICOLOR HORTENSIS.

HEART-SEED. *See* CARDIOSPERMUM.

HEATH. *See* ERICA.

HEATH ASTER = *Aster ericoides*.

HEATHER. A single, remarkably variable, low shrub, comprising the genus **Calluna** (ka-loo′na) of the family Ericaceae, found all over Eu. and in Asia Minor, and widely cult. for its evergreen foliage and profusion of small, nodding, rosy-pink flowers (in the typical sort). The only species, **C. vulgaris**, the common heather or ling, usually grows in dense masses, and is mostly less than 18 in. high. Leaves small, opposite,° stalkless, keeled, mostly in 4 ranks and so numerous as to completely clothe the twigs. The leaves are scarcely ¹⁄₁₀ in. long. Flowers in dense, terminal spikes. Corolla bell-shaped, 4-parted above, ultimately becoming membranous and long-persisting. In the closely related genus *Erica* the corolla falls off after blooming. The corolla of the heather is exceeded also by a bell-shaped colored calyx.° Stamens° 8, included within the corolla. Fruit a small 4-valved capsule° which is hidden by the persistent corolla. (*Calluna* is from the Greek to sweep, in allusion to the ancient use of the twigs to make brooms.) *See also* ERICA TETRALIX.

The heather makes a splendid plant for naturalizing on sandy banks or slopes, and has become naturalized in the northeastern U.S. in a few places having such conditions, notably at Nantucket. For details of its culture *see* ERICA, as it needs the same conditions as the hardy specimens there noted. The heather, which blooms from July to Oct., has been so long cult. and is so popular that many hort. varieties are to be had. The best of them include:

C. vulgaris alba. White-flowered.

C. vulgaris alporti. Crimson-flowered and taller than the typical form.

C. vulgaris aurea. Foliage golden-yellow.

C. vulgaris carnea. Flowers pink.

C. vulgaris coccinea. Flowers deep red. Sometimes know as *C. vulgaris rubra*.

C. vulgaris cuprea. Summer foliage golden; winter foliage bronzy.

C. vulgaris hammondi. Flowers white; taller than the typical form.

C. vulgaris hirsuta. Foliage gray-hairy.

C. vulgaris humilis. Lower than the typical form; flowers white.

C. vulgaris nana. Scarcely 6 in. high; flowers purple.

C. vulgaris rubra = *C. vulgaris coccinea*.

C. vulgaris searlei. Flowers white; taller and of looser growth than the typical form.

HEATHER FAMILY = Ericaceae.

HEATH FAMILY. Horticulturally an important family of woody plants, because it includes heath, heather, mountain laurel, rhododendron, azalea, trailing arbutus, wintergreen, rhodora, shinleaf, cranberry, blueberry,

---

° Special articles on the subjects indicated by an asterisk (°) will be found at the words so marked.

and huckleberry. Most of them have showy flowers and a few produce edible fruits, but some are poisonous. The family furnishes many broad-leaved evergreens of great garden value. For all the cult. genera and a description of the technical characters of the family, *see* ERICACEAE.

HEAVENLY BAMBOO = *Nandina.*

HEAVING. Many soils with a considerable amount of clay or silt in them, and any soils that are water-soaked, are likely to heave in the spring. It is caused by the alternate thawing and freezing of the upper layer of the soil. Such frost or soil heaving will likely throw out loosely rooted perennials, especially ones planted the fall before.

Heaved-out roots that have no chance to get anchored, because of shallow or indifferent planting

It is a minor nuisance in the garden because it exposes the roots of such plants to the cold or dryness and kills many of them. This is true not only of recently planted perennials but of some long-established ones if they happen to have shallow and fleshy, but few, fibrous roots.

One remedy is to practice spring transplanting in heavy or wet soils. If this is impossible,

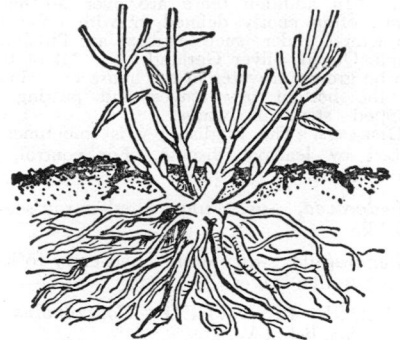

Perennials planted deeply and firmly enough do not heave

try to be especially careful to plant securely, and even a little too deep, those plants which may be heaved out in the spring. Another is to mulch* the plants with manure or straw which will prevent alternate thawing and freezing. But care has to be used in mulching very wet soils, as the mulch may cause rotting if not taken off in time.

HEBE. *See* VERONICA.

hebecarpa, -us, -um (he-be-kar'pa). Hairy-fruited.

HECHTIA (heck'ti-a). A genus of 30 species of chiefly Mexican, semi-desert, spiny-toothed plants of the family Bromeliaceae, the two below cult. in the greenhouse for their foliage. They have dense rosettes* of spiny-margined leaves that are purple above, toward the tip, but silvery beneath. Male and female flowers on separate plants, white but not showy, scarcely ⅓ in. wide, borne in small, bracted,* interrupted clusters on a slender stalk about 2 ft. high. (Named for J. G. H. Hecht.)

argentea. Leaves about 12 in. long, silvery, stiff, and spiny. Flowers white nearly stalkless, but numerous in each of the many small clusters. Mex.

glomerata. Leaves 12–18 in. long and about an inch wide at the base, leathery and rigid, but gradually narrowed toward the sharp-pointed tip. Flowers white. Not such a good foliage plant as *H. argentea.* Mex.

HEDEOMA. So far as hort. plants are concerned, *Hedeoma* is not cult. *H. pulegioides,* the American or false pennyroyal, is a weedy herb of eastern N.A. For the true pennyroyal *see Mentha Pulegium* at MINT.

HEDERA (hed'er-ra). This genus of evergreen, woody vines of the family Araliaceae comprises only 7 Eurasian and North African species, generally called ivy, but one of them (*H. Helix*) cultivated throughout the temperate world as the English ivy, although it is native from England to the Caucasus. They have woody stems and climb by aerial rootlets which cling very easily to brick or masonry, but less so to wood. Leaves alternate,* evergreen, stalked, usually more or less lobed or coarsely toothed. Flowers green-

Rooting ivy cuttings in sand (or water) is one of the simplest of hort. operations.

---

* Special articles on the subjects indicated by an asterisk (*) will be found at the words so marked.

ish, not very conspicuous, and produced only on the oldest specimens of the English ivy, mostly in small umbels,* but these often in branched clusters on bushy branches. Petals 5, the sepals small or obsolete. Stamens* 5. Fruit a 3–5-seeded berry. (*Hedera* is the classical name of the ivy.)

The English ivy is one of the most valuable of evergreen vines, useful for walls, rocks, and any rough surface like the bark of a tree, and is often trained on decorative trellises. It is fine for hanging baskets or window boxes, but it should be remembered that it does not like open, sunny places and does best under shade, on the sides of buildings where the walls are in shade for part of the day, or it will make a splendid ground cover under trees where grass cannot be maintained.

The plant is perfectly hardy up to the limits of zone* 4, and even in many parts of zone* 3, if not planted in full sun and if the moisture conditions are right. The latter feature of its needs is well taken care of in places near the sea from Boston southward and along the Pacific Northwest. In many sections of the interior the summers are too hot and dry for it.

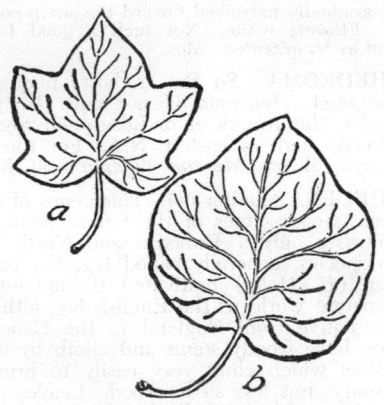

The juvenile form (*a*) and the fruiting or mature form (*b*) of the English ivy. Most ivy plants never get beyond the juvenile stage.

Ivy is easily propagated by cuttings, many of which are already provided with aerial roots. The cuttings may be started in sand in the greenhouse in winter, or almost any time during the growing season in frames or outdoors in sandy soil. Of the three species noted below only *H. Helix*, the English ivy, and its varieties are much grown in the U.S., where millions of plants are propagated for landscape and cemetery planting, for house plants, or for window boxes. For the latter purposes it is better to buy potted plants, although its propagation is easy if one has a stock from which to make cuttings.

canariensis. Algerian ivy. Perhaps only a form of *H. Helix* found on Madeira and Canary Islands and in North Africa and hardy only from

zone* 7 southward. It is a stout, high-climbing vine with roundish or heart-shaped, usually 5–7-lobed leaves that are 2–6 in. long. Fruit black, larger than in the English ivy (*H. Helix*).

colchica. A high-climbing vine, the leaves broadly oval or elliptic or on some branches oblongish, 5–10 in. long and usually not lobed, dark green and leathery. Fruit black. Caucasus, Asia Minor, and Persia. Not hardy above zone* 6.

Helix. The common English or evergreen ivy. Creeping, or if allowed to climb frequently reaching a height of 80–90 ft. and completely covering walls in favorable places. Ordinary leaves 3–5-lobed, 2–5 in. long, dark green above, yellowish-green beneath. On flowering branches (mostly produced only in very old plants) the leaves are larger and squarish but not lobed. Flowers green, inconspicuous, the umbels* globe-shaped. Fruit nearly round, almost ½ in. in diameter, black. For its hardiness and uses see above. There are many hort. varieties of this plant, some for special places and with different degrees of hardiness. The best-known ones are:

var. **arborescens.** An upright shrub with essentially unlobed leaves; perhaps originating from cutting of only flowering branches.

var. **argenteo-variegata.** Vine-like, the leaves white-variegated or white-margined.

var. **aureo-variegata.** Leaves yellow or variegated with yellow.

var. **baltica.** A small-leaved form very useful for a ground cover (which see); also more hardy than the typical *H. Helix* or than any other of its varieties.

var. **conglomerata.** A slow-growing, creeping form with small, crowded, unlobed or only 3-lobed leaves. For culture *see* Rock Garden.

var. **gracilis.** A small-leaved form, the foliage turning bronzy in winter. One small-leaved form is commonly sold as Japanese ivy.

var. **minima.** A very popular form with small leaves having wavy margins.

Many varieties including those above are offered, to which various names have been attached, notably Algerian ivy (*H. canariensis*); Baltic ivy (*H. Helix baltica*); Albany ivy (an erect form of the English ivy); so-called Heart-leaved ivy (*H. Helix cordata*); Clustered ivy (*H. Helix conglomerata*), a form of the English ivy that does not climb; and Irish ivy (*H. Helix hibernica*), a good form for a quick ground cover. In addition there are over 30 named forms, often poorly defined or with ephemeral characters under such names as Pittsburgh, Maple Queen, Silver Garland, etc. All of them can be grown in water in the house by stripping off the bottom few leaves and putting the stripped stem in water.

Diseases. The English ivy is sometimes attacked by leafspot disease. For control, *see* Ampelopsis.

hederacea, **-us, -um** (hed-er-ray'see-a). Ivy-like.

hederafolia, **-us, -um** (hed-er-ry-fō'li-a). With ivy-like leaves.

HEDGE BINDWEED = *Convolvulus sepium.* See list at Weeds.

HEDGE FUMITORY = *Fumaria officinalis.* See Fumitory.

---

* Special articles on the subjects indicated by an asterisk (*) will be found at the words so marked.

HEDGEHOG CONEFLOWER = *Echinacea purpurea.*

HEDGEHOG GOURD = *Cucumis dipsaceus.*

HEDGEHOG POPPY = *Argemone platyceras hispida.*

HEDGES. A clipped or informal hedge is in many ways better than a wooden or wire fence. For the purely architectural features of hedges see the section devoted to this below. Here we are concerned only with hedge plants, their care, clipping, and advantages and disadvantages.

All the plants mentioned below are entered in other parts of this book and should be looked for at their regular entries for additional details about them, especially for the notes on their hardiness. It is needless to repeat these details here, but neglect of them may mean failure in the case of some of the rarer and finer hedge plants.

In making a hedge it is important to decide which type of plant will be used, whether they will be closely planted or whether they are large enough to make individual holes necessary. For privet and most small plants that will be planted a foot or less apart, the best plan is to dig a trench 2 ft. wide and 2 ft. deep and fill it in with good topsoil into which dig a 3-in. layer of well-rotted manure. Let the soil settle until after the first good rain and then fill up to the general ground level if there has been much sinking. Some prefer to make such a trench for evergreens or larger plants, but these can be planted in separate holes if expense is a factor.

PLANTING. For all hedge plants that drop their leaves, planting can be done in the usual spring or fall planting time in your locality. For evergreens the planting should be done either in early spring or between Aug. 15 and Sept. 15 over most of the country. In subtropical regions the planting of hedges will naturally follow the very different conditions in such places. *See* the different sections under each month at GARDEN CALENDAR.

For most small plants it is better to stretch a line so as to insure straight planting, and it may be well to use a line for larger ones, although if it gets in the way of handling them, drive stakes where the larger plants are to go and remove the line. Plant in single, not double, rows. For all but large plants and evergreens, a good average distance apart is 12 in., but many fine privet hedges are planted only 6 in. apart.

Privet and most small hedge plants are better set a little deeper (2–3 in.) than the soil-line of their old site, but evergreens should be planted at approximately their old soil-line. Always start the hedge with comparatively young plants (2–3 years for privet). The wholesale moving-in of large hedge plants is very expensive and if a few of them fail, it may leave bad holes in the hedge, difficult to re-fill with similarly sized plants.

All hedge plants that drop their leaves (all except the evergreens) should be severely cut back at planting time. Cut back privet and barberry at least ⅓ of their length. No feature of hedge planting is so important as this, because "leggy" plants will never make a bushy hedge, which is the object of all early clipping and shearing. Evergreens, because they are delivered with a ball of earth and a burlap covering, need not be cut back so severely.

CLIPPING OR SHEARING. It is a mistake to let a young hedge get tall before clipping it. The taller it gets in the young state the less chance there is of making it fill out toward the base. During the first year after planting, cut it back two or three times in the growing season, the permanent height of the clipped hedge being increased only a few inches after each clipping. This will force out a lot of new growth toward the base of the hedge and permit the start of the most important feature of the properly shaped hedge.

When there is an ample growth of twigs near the base and the hedge (in the case of privet) is still only 3–4 ft. high, begin trimming so that the base of the hedge will always be a little wider than the top. If the reverse is done (a common failing in amateur hedge-shearing), the top will be wider than the bot-

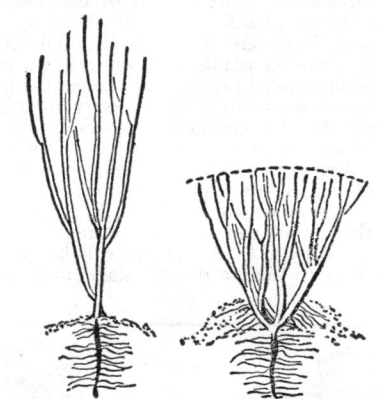

Start the young hedge properly by forcing it to produce twigs from the base. Cut at first as shown at the right.

tom, and enough light will be screened off the base of the hedge to kill or partially suppress the twigs near the base. This is why so many old hedges are naked at the bottom but fine enough at the top. No matter how high or wide the hedge may become, always plan its trimming so that the top is left slightly narrower than the bottom. Such a hedge also sheds snow more easily.

While for small hedges clipping is best done with an old-fashioned hedge shears, there are, for extensive hedges, several types of electrically driven hedge-clipping machines. They remove one of the chief objections to hedges. Three times in a growing season is enough for clipping most hedges, unless they are wanted

---

* Special articles on the subjects indicated by an asterisk (*) will be found at the words so marked.

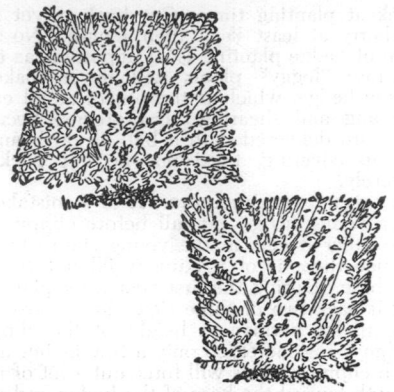

As it matures see that the hedge is slightly narrower at the top, not broader at the top as shown in the lower figure. *See* text for details.

in the most perfect symmetry, when they will need clipping more often. It all depends upon the season and the plant itself.

HEDGE PLANTS

Well-sheared, perfect hedges can only be made from plants that will stand regular clipping. Very fine, but more informal hedges can be made of plants that will stand a good deal of occasional pruning, but resent the more or less constant clipping necessary for plants like privet and boxwood. These informal hedge plants are far more numerous than the sorts which thrive upon regular clipping, but they cannot be molded into architectural forms such as privet and the others. In the list below those that can be clipped regularly are marked with a †. All others can be pruned from time to time, a disadvantage, in a hedge

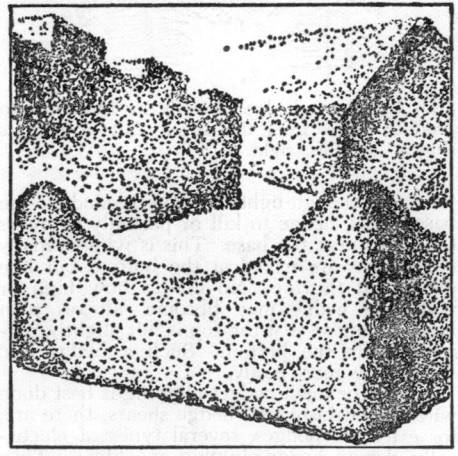

Some rather common but not particularly desirable kinds of hedge shearing. Compare with the next illustration.

plant, perhaps overcome by the fact that many of them flower profusely. Few clipped hedge plants do so.

Note: See the entries in the ENCYCLOPEDIA OF GARDENING under which the plants are listed below, for essential notes on hardiness.

† = Can be clipped as much as necessary. All others may be more or less shaped by occasional pruning.

†Privet (*Ligustrum*). The best all-round hedge plants in the U.S., especially *L. ovalifolium*, the California privet, which holds its leaves most of the winter. Other good privets are *Ligustrum obtusifolium*(the ibota privet) and *L. obtusifolium regelianum* (Regel's privet). The common privet (*L. vulgare*) is not so good as California privet as it drops its leaves long before *L. ovalifolium*. In the South *L. japonicum* makes beautiful evergreen hedges.

†Box (*Buxus*). The finest evergreen hedge plant, but slow-growing and expensive. Not hardy everywhere. *See* Box.

†*Taxus.* The yews make magnificent hedge plants, but are generally slow-growing. *See* TAXUS.

†*Thuja occidentalis* (arborvitae). One of the best of the coniferous evergreen for hedges, but useless near big cities. Old hedges are often 20 ft. high and 10 ft. thick. For low arborvitae hedges use some of the dwarf varieties. *See* THUJA.

Hemlock (*Tsuga canadensis*). A splendid evergreen, but useful only in regions where it thrives. *See* HEMLOCK. It will not thrive in or near big cities nor in regions of extreme summer heat. Will not stand severe clipping, especially when young, but it may be pruned and shaped fairly well. As a tall, hedge-like screen, the hemlock is fine.

Spruce (*Picea glauca*). The white spruce is a beautiful evergreen, very similar to the hemlock in its growth requirements, and will do well in the North or along the seashore, but not in the South. Needs careful pruning to shape it. Will not stand steady shearing in youth.

Berberis thunbergi. The Japanese barberry makes a fine informal, round-headed hedge plant. Its fine foliage and red berries are especially attractive. Will not stand close shearing, but it needs little because of its close, twiggy growth. There is also a dwarf variety. *See* B. THUNBERGI. Another fine barberry is *B. julianae.*

Berberis vulgaris. The common barberry is less desirable than the Japanese one, but grows taller. A purple-leaved variety is especially fine. Will stand, and needs, for hedge purposes, a good deal of pruning, but not close shearing.

Chamaecyparis. Several of the lower-growing species and varieties make fine informal, evergreen hedges, but they will not stand shearing. *See* CHAMAECYPARIS.

†*Acanthopanax pentaphyllus.* Will stand clipping when old, and severe pruning in youth.

Poncirus trifoliata. Hardy orange. A fine,

---

* Special articles on the subjects indicated by an asterisk (*) will be found at the words so marked.

prickly, defensive hedge plant, not hardy northward. *See* PONCIRUS.

†*Elaeagnus angustifolia.* Russian olive. Good for open, wind-swept places.

Rosa rugosa. A good hedge plant which will stand severe pruning but not shearing. Very attractive in flower and for its showy fruits.

†Hornbeam (*Carpinus Betulus*). The European hornbeam is a tall-growing, stout hedge plant. It needs very careful clipping to make it well furnished with foliage at the base. Perhaps a better substitute is *Ulmus pumila.*

Besides these there are many other plants suitable for hedges. Some of them are lilac, mock-orange, beech, *Chaenomeles japonica* (flowering quince), *Deutzia gracilis* and *D. lemoinei, Maclura, Osmanthus ilicifolius, Crataegus,* several spireas (*see* SPIRAEA), *Viburnum cassinoides, V. Tinus* and *V. dentatum, Kerria japonica,* and *Caragana arborescens.* The latter is the best of all hedge plants for regions of long, severe winters, such as the northern prairie states and far into Canada, where privet is often killed outright or severely winter-killed. Most of them, except the flowering quince, need careful pruning in youth to make them satisfactory hedge subjects. In the South the crape myrtle is often used for hedges, although it is not a good hedge plant.

GARDEN USES

A hedge is a line of trees or shrubs formalized in semblance to a wall or fence, and usually serves to define the limits of a given area.

It is desirable that the height and form of a hedge be in character with the function, size,

The beauty and dignity of a hedge
rightly used

and shape of the area it bounds, as well as with the nature of the general surroundings. The use to which an area is to be put plays an important part not only in dictating the general type of hedge to enclose it, but also the texture and density of its foliage mass. Treated architecturally, for formal effects, a hedge may be regulated to definite lines and clean-cut surfaces. Used more informally, it may be allowed to grow freely as a thicket, within its natural limitations.

As an element in landscape design, a hedge may be employed to act as a windbreak, barrier, screen, edging, background, or an enclosure for privacy. As a boundary barrier, it may serve as a protection and screen from neighboring grounds, or be used to provide a feeling of seclusion. A hedge may create a sense of unity by separating a given space from any unrelated features which otherwise would visually intrude and tend to distract the eye and mind from the essential purpose of the area as designed.

As a contributing element in relating structural features to the landscape, by seemingly tying a building to the ground, a hedge is often used as a dominant horizontal line. It accentuates the base lines and defines and recalls certain architectural space relationships in softer, more dynamic texture and in a natural vital color. To frame a formal vista, or to act as a definite yet unobtrusive foreground for a broader view, a controlled and regulated line of shrubs or trees is most useful.

A low, compact hedge may bound a flower bed, a lawn area, or a walk or terrace, clearly defining in the third dimension the pattern of the area enclosed. As a quiet background for perennials, a hedge presents an ideal surface of uniform texture and color to contrast with the delicate forms and shadings of the flowers.

The play of light and shade gives the hedge a distinct appeal by outlining ever-changing patterns, whose subtle variations in hue and color are a constant source of interest and delight. — A. F.

HEDGE SHEARS. *See* No. 10 at TOOLS AND IMPLEMENTS.

HEDRAIANTHUS = *Edraianthus.*

HEDYCHIUM (he-dich′i-um). Tropical Asiatic (one Madagascan) herbs of the family Zingiberaceae, comprising 40 species, often called ginger-lily or butterfly-lily, grown in the greenhouse, or from zone* 6 southward outdoors, for their ornamental foliage and very fragrant flowers. They have large, 2-ranked leaves, without marginal teeth, and sheathing at the base. Flowers showy, irregular,* borne from between bracts* in a terminal cluster (spike or panicle*). For details of flower structure *see* ZINGIBERACEAE. Fruit a capsule.* (*Hedychium* is from the Greek for sweet snow, in reference to the often white, fragrant flowers.)

The ginger-lilies, which differ only in technical characters from the true ginger, have stout underground rootstocks by which they are propagated and which should be divided every two or three years. They need a warm greenhouse, potting mixture* 3, and plenty of water. Some, like *H. coronarium,* can even be submerged up to the crown. They also require liberal applications of liquid manure, because they are gross feeders. After blooming, the plants should be gradually dried off,

---

* Special articles on the subjects indicated by an asterisk (*) will be found at the words so marked.

and when the foliage is browned, the pots had better be rested for two months or so, after which the growth should be renewed by liberal watering. They will stand no frost, although their rootstocks may be left in the ground all year below zone* 6, even if the tops are ruined by frost. They are popular bedding plants throughout the tropics, where 15 or more species may be grown. In the U.S. the three below are the most likely to be seen. Most of them bloom in the late fall.

coronarium. Garland-flower, and by far the most widely grown species. Stems 4–7 ft. high, the leaves 15–30 in. long, about 5 in. wide. Flowers 2–3 in. long, white, very fragrant, the bracts of the cluster whitish-green firm. The lower part of the lip* is usually yellow-tinged. Tropical As. Petals edible.

flavum. From 3–5 ft. high. Leaves 8–14 in. long, tapering to a slender point. Flowers nearly 2½ in. wide, yellow, with an orange spot on the base of the lip. India.

gardnerianum. Not over 6 ft. high, the leaves 9–18 in. long, but nearly 6 in. wide. Flowers nearly 2 in. long, the corolla yellow, but the long-protruding stamen red. The flowering spike is nearly 18 in. long. India. A very showy plant, but a shy bloomer.

HEDYSARUM (hed-i-sar′rum). A large genus of chiefly Old World herbs of the pea family, perhaps a dozen of its 70 species found in N.A. They are perennial herbs or under-shrubs with compound* leaves, the leaflets arranged feather-fashion and with an odd one at the tip. Flowers small, pea-like, mostly in showy racemes.* Fruit a jointed legume (a loment*), usually flattened. (*Hedysarum* is from the Greek for sweet smell, in allusion to the fragrance of some species.)

Both the species below are of easy culture in open, preferably sandy soils. The first species is an old garden plant, but not so much grown as formerly. Readily propagated by seeds or by division.

coronarium. French honeysuckle; called, also, sulla clover. A bushy, perennial herb 2–4 ft. high, and long cult. in old gardens. Leaflets in 3–7 pairs, elliptic or roundish, hairy. Flowers deep red, fragrant, densely crowded in spikes or racemes* from the leaf axils.* Eu. Summer. A white-flowered variety is also offered.

pabulare. A prairie herb not over 30 in. high. Leaflets in 4–7 pairs, oblongish, about ¾ in. long. Flowers purplish, nearly ½ in. long. Mont. to N. Mex. Summer.

HEDYSCEPE (hed-i-see′pe). A single species of unarmed feather palm from Lord Howe's Island in the Pacific. The only species is **H. canterburyana**, often called umbrella palm, and sometimes offered as *Kentia canterburyana*. It is somewhat grown for ornament in Fla. and southern Calif., more often in the greenhouse for its fine foliage. Mature plants may be 30 ft. high (much lower in the greenhouse), the gracefully arching or drooping leaves in a dense crown at the top of the trunk. Leaf-segments numerous, narrow, but broader at the base than at the tapering and drooping tip. Flowers in a dense, branched cluster from the leaf-crown, the male and female in different parts of the cluster. Fruit more or less egg-shaped, about 2 in. long. For its greenhouse culture *see* PALM. (*Hedyscepe* is from the Greek for sweet covering.)

HEEL. The basal end of a cutting, tuber, or other propagative material, especially if there is some of the old stock taken with it.

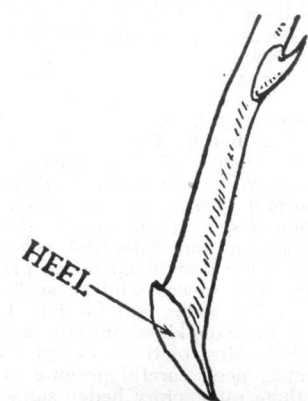

Heel of a cutting. Most practical gardeners do not attach much importance to the heel in propagating. *See* CUTTINGS.

HEEL-IN. To cover temporarily with soil the roots of plants awaiting permanent planting. It should always be done upon the arrival of nursery stock. An old term for it is *to sheugh*. *See* the illustration at PLANTING.

HE-HUCKLEBERRY = *Lyonia ligustrina*.

HEIGHT OF TREES. *See* GARDEN TABLES III.

HELENIUM (hell-lee′ni-um). The sneezeweeds are rather tall, coarse, New World herbs of the family Compositae, comprising about 40 species, useful chiefly toward the rear of the informal herbaceous border, or in open places in the wild garden. All the cult. species except the last are stout perennials with alternate* leaves and profuse heads of yellow or brownish flowers (red in a hort. variety), the heads containing both ray* and disk* flowers. Clusters usually flat-topped, the flowers mostly blooming in late summer and fall. They have a superficial resemblance to sunflowers. (Named for Helen of Troy; and *Helenium* is also used as a specific name for *Inula*.)

Almost any garden soil will suit sneezeweeds, which, in the case of *H. autumnale*, may need curtailing, as it tends to become weedy. Easiest propagated by spring division of the clumps.

autumnale. Yellow star; false sunflower. Stout, branching perennial 4–6 ft. high. Leaves lance-oval, 3–5 in. long, toothed, the base decurrent* on the stem. Flower heads nearly 2 in. wide, the rays* lemon-yellow, the disk* flowers darker yellow. Eastern U.S. The *var.*

* Special articles on the subjects indicated by an asterisk (*) will be found at the words so marked.

grandiflorum has larger flowers; *var.* **pumilum** (sometimes offered as *H. pumilum*) is only about 2 ft. high; *var.* **rubrum** has deep-red flowers and is a useful plant for the autumn garden (which see). There are also many desirable named hort. forms, such as Riverton Gem, with red and gold heads, and Riverton Beauty, with lemon-yellow heads.

bigelovi. A Californian perennial, not over 4 ft. high. Leaves lance-shaped, 6–9 in. long, narrowed into a decurrent* base. Flower heads about 2 in. wide, the rays* yellow, the disk* flowers brownish.

hoopesi. A perennial, not over 3 ft. high. Leaves lance-shaped or narrower, 4–6 in. long, without marginal teeth and not decurrent* at the base. Flower heads nearly 3 in wide, solitary or a few in a cluster, yellow. Rocky Mountains westward to Ore. and Calif.

peregrinum. A common name in the catalogues applying mostly to red-flowered varieties of *H. autumnale* (which see).

pumilum magnificum = *Helenium autumnale*.

tenuifolium. A rather weedy annual, 12–30 in. high, the leaves grass-thin, about 1 in. long, and mostly basal. Above the foliage extend the thin stalks of the flower head which is 1–1½ in. wide. Rays 3-cleft at the tips, yellow. Southeastern U.S. Summer.

HELIANTHELLA (he-li-an-thell'la). Western American, sunflower-like, perennial herbs of the family Compositae, only one of the 13 known species at all likely to be cult. This is **H. quinquenervis**, a nearly smooth, essentially unbranched herb 2–4 ft. high, its leaves mostly opposite, 4–8 in. long, the upper ones stalkless. Flower heads showy, 3–5 in. wide, solitary or in few-flowered clusters, pale yellow. Rocky Mountains. Summer. The plant is of easy culture in most garden soils, and can be increased by division. (*Helianthella* is Latin for a small sunflower.)

HELIANTHEMUM (he-li-an'thee-mum). Usually prostrate or sprawling woody plants or herbs of the family Cistaceae, comprising perhaps 100 widely distributed species, of which only a few are cult. in the garden for their roselike flowers. They are chiefly suited to the rock garden in the East, but are very popular in Calif., a climate that suits them well. They are usually called frostweed or sun-rose, and have evergreen, usually opposite* (sometimes alternate*) leaves without marginal teeth. Flowers very fleeting, in few-flowered clusters or solitary, prevailingly yellow, and of two kinds. Some flower earlier than the others and are larger and with showy petals, while the later flowers are smaller and may have no petals. Large-flowered petals usually 5. Stamens* numerous. Fruit a 3-valved capsule.* (*Helianthemum* is from the Greek for sun and flower, in allusion to their day-blooming.)

For culture *see* Rock Garden.

apenninum. A Eurasian woody herb or subshrub, 1–2 ft. high, the foliage white-downy. Leaves elliptic or narrower, about 1 in. long. Flowers white, about 1 in. wide, the petals slightly eroded at the tip. Calyx* white-hairy. Summer. The *var.* **roseum** (often offered as *H. rhodanthum*) has rose-colored flowers.

Chamaecistus = *Helianthemum nummularium*.

halimifolium. Not over 2 ft. high. Leaves oblongish or narrower, conspicuously white-felty when young. Flowers yellow, about 1½ in. wide, the petals dark-spotted. Southern Eu. and northern Af. Summer. By some considered as belonging to the genus *Halimium*.

Nummularium. The commonest sun-rose in cult. and coming in many hort. varieties. The typical form is usually less than 12 in. high. Leaves ovalish or narrower, 1–2 in. long, grayhairy on the under side. Flowers about 1 in. wide, yellow. Mediterranean region. Summer. Often offered as *H. Chamaecistus* and *H. vulgare*. For the many hort. varieties of this popular plant and their culture *see* Rock Garden.

rhodanthum = *H. apenninum roseum*.

Tuberaria. A perennial herb with mostly basal leaves that are ovalish, or narrower, 1–3 in. long, minutely toothed and white-hairy on the under side. Flowers about 1½ in. wide, yellow, in sparse, terminal clusters, the petals slightly eroded at the tip. Southern Eu. Summer.

vulgare = *Helianthemum nummularium*.

helianthoides (he-li-an-thoy'deez, but *see* Oïdes). Sunflower-like.

HELIANTHUS. *See* Sunflower.

HELICHRYSUM (hell-i-kry'zum). One of the better-known groups of everlastings, and comprising a genus of over 300 species belonging to the family Compositae, all from the Old World. They are herbs or shrubs with chiefly alternate* leaves without marginal teeth. Flower heads wholly of disk* flowers, the parts chaffy, mostly yellow (red, orange, or white in hort. varieties of the strawflower), and holding their color long after drying. The bracts* of the involucre* beneath the heads are also colored, almost petal-like. (*Helichrysum* is from the Greek for sun and gold, in allusion to the gay flower heads.)

The second species is the well-known strawflower from Australia and one of the most satisfactory plants for winter bouquets as its chaffy flower heads will hold their color for months. *See* Dried Flowers. It is a tender annual and should be grown as such. *See* Annuals.

bellidioides. An almost prostrate, somewhat woody perennial 3–5 in. high, the ovalish or spoon-shaped leaves, ½–1 in. long and whitedowny beneath. Flower heads chaffy, silverywhite, about ½ in. across, solitary and terminal. N.Z. Summer. Not certainly hardy north of zone* 5.

bracteatum. Strawflower. A tender annual from Australia, 24–36 in. high, usually branched. Leaves oblongish or narrower, 2–5 in. long, roughish. Flower heads 1–2 in. wide, the bracts of the involucre* petal-like, red, yellow, orange, or white (in some of its varieties), the true disk* flowers yellow. Widely grown for its bloom, which besides its use for dry bouquets is good for summer cutting.

petiolatum. A South African, shrubby, perennial herb, somewhat woody at the base, the stems woolly, its slender shoots vine-like. Leaves ovalish, woolly. Flower heads (often lacking in cult. specimens) in branching clusters (corymbs*), the disk* flowers yellow, the bracts of the involucre* cream-white. Must be grown in the cool greenhouse in potting mixture* 3, or may be plunged outdoors in the summer. Chiefly an interesting foliage plant. Sometimes known

---

* Special articles on the subjects indicated by an asterisk (*) will be found at the words so marked.

as *Gnaphalium lanatum* or as *Helichrysum lanatum*.

HELICONIA (hell-i-kō'ni-a). Large, tropical American, banana-like herbs of the family Musaceae, comprising over 30 species, the only cult. species being **H. Bihai**, the wild plantain or balisier. It is a large herb, 10–15 ft. high, its leaves banana-like, transversely ribbed. The leafstalks are very long, all arising from the ground, the plant thus differing from the banana and without a true stem. Flowers borne on long stalks, showy, but still more striking are the scarlet, boat-shaped bracts often 5–10 in. long, from between which the flowers are borne. Corolla irregular,* its tube short. Fruit a bluish capsule* which ultimately separates into berry-like segments. There is a variety (or perhaps a separate species) with yellow striped or splashed leaves. The culture of the wild plantain, outdoors, is the same as for banana (which see). Also grown in the tropical greenhouse, where it needs plenty of moisture, a humid atmosphere, and rich soil. (Named for Mt. Helicon, seat of the Muses and purely fanciful as applied to these plants.)

HELIOCEREUS (he-li-o-seer'ee-us). A small genus of chiefly Mexican and mostly climbing or sprawling cacti, only of secondary hort. interest. They are sometimes erect as cult. in the greenhouse, and have strongly angled or ribbed branches, and mostly needle-like spines that are all alike. Flowers day-blooming, showy, funnel-shaped, prevailingly scarlet. The plants differ only in technical characters from *Cereus*. (*Heliocereus* is from the Greek for sun and *Cereus,* in allusion to their desert habitat.)

For culture *see* CACTI. The plants are of less interest as ornamentals, especially *H. speciosus*, than as material for making interesting cactus crosses. Some breeders have used this species as one of the parents in a cross with *Selenicereus pteranthus,* which produces a bigeneric* hybrid.

elegantissumus. Branches or stems (as cult.) usually less than 1 ft. high, sometimes sprawling, nearly 2 in. thick and 3–4-angled. Flowers nearly 6 in. long, scarlet, the lobes of the stigma* white. Mex.

speciosus. Santa Marta. More or less branching, the stems seldom erect, 3–5-angled or with 3–5 ribs. Flowers 6–7 in. long, scarlet, the lobes of the stigma* red. Mex. and Central America.

HELIOPSIS (he-li-op'sis). Perennial, sunflower-like, North American herbs of the family Compositae, useful for the informal border or wild garden, but otherwise rather coarse, tall, yellow-flowered, summer-blooming plants. They have opposite,* rather coarsely toothed, 3-veined leaves, often very rough on one or both surfaces. Flower heads long-stalked, showy, the long rays* generally yellow, the disk* flowers darker. (*Heliopsis* is from the Greek for like the sun, in allusion to the yellow flower heads.)

There is no difficulty in growing either of the species, both of which are wild and almost weedy throughout most of the eastern U.S. Propagated by division. The plants are called oxeye by some, but the name is better applied to some daisies.

helianthoides. False sunflower. Three to five ft. high and with an essentially smooth stem. Leaves oblong or ovalish, 3–5 in. long, rough above, smooth beneath. Flower heads 1½–2½ in. wide, yellow, rays* about 1 in. long. The *var.* **pitcheriana** has deeper yellow flowers.

scabra. Orange sunflower. Similar to the last, and perhaps merely a form of it, but the leaves very rough on both sides and the flower heads fewer and orange-yellow. There are several hort. varieties, some with the flower heads double, and others with paler yellow flowers. One of the best is *var.* **zinniaeflora,** which is double-flowered.

HELIOTROPE. See HELIOTROPIUM. For the garden heliotrope *see* VALERIANA OFFICINALIS, which is perhaps better known as the common valerian. For winter heliotrope *see* PETASITES FRAGRANS.

HELIOTROPE FAMILY = Boraginaceae.

HELIOTROPIC. Turning toward the sun, as do many leaves and flowers.

HELIOTROPIUM (he-li-o-trō'pi-um). A genus of over 200 species of mainly tropical or sub-tropical herbs (some woody) of the family Boraginaceae, one of them a widely cult. garden plant grown for its fragrant flowers. Leaves mostly alternate,* usually hairy. Flowers rather small, borne in forking, usually 1-sided clusters (sometimes cymes*). Calyx* tubular, as long as the corolla in some species. Corolla tubular, regular, the stamens not protruding from it. Fruit a collection of 4 small nutlets surrounded by the persistent calyx. (*Heliotropium* is from *heliotropic,* which see.)

The cult. heliotropes may be treated as greenhouse plants or as tender annuals (*see* ANNUALS). For fragrance it is better to grow them in the greenhouse, but still as annuals. They need plenty of heat and a rich soil. If grown as tender annuals outdoors, the stems may be pegged down, especially young shoots, which will root. They may also be propagated by cuttings.

arborescens. Common heliotrope. A perennial herb 2–10 ft. high, usually grown as a tender annual. Leaves ovalish or oblong. Flowers small, purple or violet (white in a hort. variety), scarcely ¼ in. long, strongly vanilla-scented. Peru. Sometimes offered as *H. peruvianum,* and is called by some cherry pie (but *see also* VALERIANA OFFICINALIS).

corymbosum. Not very different from *H. arborescens,* but with narrower leaves, and the flowers narcissus-scented. Peru (?). It may be only a form of *H. arborescens.*

peruvianum = *Heliotropium arborescens.*

HELIPTERUM (hell-lip'ter-rum). An important group of 40 species of garden everlastings from South Africa and Aust., belonging to the family Compositae, and widely grown as tender annuals for dried bouquets (*see* EVERLASTINGS; *also* DRIED FLOWERS). They have alternate,* often white-felty leaves without marginal teeth. Flower heads wholly

---

* Special articles on the subjects indicated by an asterisk (*) will be found at the words so marked.

of disk* flowers, generally yellow, chaffy, and holding their color for long periods. Below the flower head are bracts of the involucre* that are green, or petal-like and white, yellow, or rose-pink. (*Helipterum* is from the Greek for sun and wing, in reference to a technical pappus character.) The plants are sometimes offered under the names of *Acroclinium* and *Rhodanthe*.

These are fine flower garden everlastings or immortelles, and are best grown as tender annuals (*see* ANNUALS), although the seed may be sown in place if planted after settled warm weather has come.

anthemoides. A green-leaved, perennial herb scarcely 12 in. high, with very narrow leaves. Flower heads nearly 1 in. wide, mostly solitary, the bracts of the involucre* white, but brownish-tinged. Aust.

humboldtianum. A white-felty herb 8–18 in. high, the leaves very narrow. Flower heads small, yellow, in branched clusters, the bracts of the involucre* yellowish-green. Aust. Sometimes offered as *H. sanfordi.*

manglesi. Swan River everlasting. A green-leaved herb 8–15 in. high, the leaves ovalish. Flower heads mostly solitary, 1½ in. wide, the bracts of the involucre* white or pink (spotted red in *var.* maculatum). Aust. The most popular of the cult. species, sometimes known as *Rhodanthe.*

roseum. A green-leaved herb 12–20 in. high, the leaves lance-shaped or narrower. Flower heads usually solitary, nearly 2 in. wide, the bracts of the involucre white or rose-colored. Aust. Often offered under the name *Acroclinium roseum.*

sanfordi = *Helipterum humboldtianum.*

Helix (he'licks). Latin for ivy.

HELLEBORE. For the plant *see* HELLEBORUS. For the plant yielding a poison, which is properly known as false hellebore, *see* VERATRUM.

HELLEBORUS (hell-e-bore'rus). A small genus of Eurasian perennial herbs of the buttercup family, one of them the ever-popular Christmas rose, so called from its very late bloom. They are nearly stemless plants with thick but fibrous roots and chiefly basal, long-stalked, compound*or divided leaves, the leaflets or segments arranged finger-fashion. Flowers solitary or few, showy, and with 5 petal-like sepals.* Petals very small and mostly hidden by the numerous stamens. Fruit a collection of papery or leathery follicles.* (*Helleborus* is the classical name of the Christmas rose.) These are the true hellebores, yielding drugs, and the root of the third species is also a violent poison. *See* POISONOUS PLANTS.

The Christmas rose will grow in most garden soils, but it prefers moist ones and partial shade. It may be propagated by division of the roots in Aug.–Sept. Division must be done carefully, for the roots are brittle. The plant may also be forced in the greenhouse. *See* FORCING.

corsicus = *H. lividus.*

foetidus. A somewhat woody perennial, 12–18 in. high, the foliage evergreen. Leaves cut into 7–10 narrow, toothed segments, rather

The Christmas Rose, a winter-flowering perennial (*Helleborus niger*), with evergreen leaves and white or pinkish-green flowers.

leathery. Flowers cup-shaped, about 1 in. long, green but sometimes purplish, unpleasantly scented. Western Eu. Mar.

lividus. A rather woody, perennial, evergreen herb 12–18 in. high, its leaf long-stalked, the segments leathery, toothed, and bluish-green. Flowers nodding, nearly 2 in. wide, greenish-yellow, borne in a profuse cluster of 15–20 flowers. Islands of the western Mediterranean. Mar.–Apr.

niger. Christmas rose; also called winter rose. Leaves evergreen, its 7 or more leaflets or segments oblong. There are also a few small leaves or bracts on the stem. Flower nearly 2½ in. wide, white or pinkish-green. Eu. Depending on locality the plant will bloom in late fall (*see* AUTUMN GARDEN), at Christmas, or in the early spring, sometimes under the snow. It is also called black hellebore. The *var.* altifolius is a finer and taller plant, its stalks red-spotted and its pink-tinged flower nearly 4 in. wide. For a related winter-blooming plant *see* ERANTHIS.

orientalis. Lenten rose. Related to the last, but differing in having a cluster of 2–6 flowers on a branched, leafless stem. It has basal leaves similar to *H. niger.* Asia Minor. Not much grown here, but very popular in Eu., especially in Germany, where there are numerous fine hort. varieties.

helodoxa (he-lo-dox'a). Splendor of the marsh.

HELONIAS (hell-lō'ni-as). A single, perennial, bog herb of the lily family, *H. bullata,* the swamp pink, found wild in bogs from southern N.Y. to Ga. It has basal leaves nearly 15 in. long and 2 in. wide, without marginal teeth. Flowers pink, fragrant, scarcely ¼ in. long, borne in a dense cluster (raceme*) about 3 in. long, which terminates a 2-ft. hollow stalk. Fruit a 3-valved capsule.* Its outdoor culture is usual only in the bog garden (which see), where it needs

---

* Special articles on the subjects indicated by an asterisk (*) will be found at the words so marked.

a very acid soil (pH 4–5; *see* Acid and Alkali Soils). Propagated by division. (*Helonias* is from the Greek for a swamp [bog], in allusion to its habitat.)

HELXINE (hell-zy'nee). A single, Sardinian and Corsican, prostrate, moss-like plant of the family Urticaceae, mostly grown in the cool greenhouse for its minute foliage. The only species, **H. soleiroli**, the baby-tears or Corsican nettle, is an extremely delicate plant with very numerous, somewhat inequilateral, moss-like leaves of very unequal size, but none over ¼ in. long, and generally roundish. Flowers extremely minute, greenish, solitary and stalkless in the leaf axils° (for details *see* Urticaceae). In warm regions it can also be used to cover rock walls, but it needs plenty of moisture. (*Helxine* is Greek for the pellitory, a related plant.)

HEMEROCALLIS. *See* Daylily.

HEMIGRAPHIS (hem-i-graff'is). A genus of 30 species of chiefly tropical, Asian perennial herbs of the family Acanthaceae, one of them, **H. colorata**, of some hort. importance. It is a prostrate or trailing plant with opposite simple° leaves, 2–3 in. long and purplish. Flowers tubular, more or less irregular,° white, about ¾ in. long, borne between large bracts in a dense terminal head. The plant is little grown outside of Fla., where it is sometimes used as a basket plant or as a ground cover. It will not stand frost. Java. (*Hemigraphis* is Greek for half-written, and of no application here.)

hemisphaerica, -us, -um (hem-i-spheer'-i-ka). Shaped like half a sphere.

HEMLOCK. In the U.S. beautiful evergreen trees, as noted below, but generally in Eu. *hemlock* means the poison hemlock which killed Socrates. For this plant *see* Conium. For the water hemlock *see* Cicuta. For the ground hemlock *see* Taxus canadensis.

The evergreen trees called hemlock in America all belong to the genus **Tsuga** (soo'ga) of the pine family, which comprises only 10 species. chiefly from N.A. and eastern As., at least six of which are valuable trees in any garden landscape. Some are magnificent trees with more or less horizontal or pendulous branches and deeply furrowed bark. Leaves 2-ranked, very numerous, their arrangement resulting in the foliage being in flattish, fan-like sprays. The leaves (which drop off quickly when dry) are flattish, minutely grooved on the upper surface, and with 2 white lines on the lower side. Cones usually small, the scales somewhat woody, but not stiff. Seeds 2 under each scale. (*Tsuga* is the Japanese name for one of the Asiatic hemlocks.)

While the common hemlock of eastern N.A. is a very hardy tree, like most of the others below it dislikes open, wind-swept places. They will thrive in many different soil types, but generally they are trees of moist, rich woods. In the great bulk of the central, wheat-growing section of N.A. the hemlocks will grow with difficulty or not at all, for they cannot

Habit, foliage and cones of the common hemlock (*Tsuga canadensis*)

stand great summer heat nor a deficiency of summer rainfall. East of the Alleghenies and along the northern coastal region of the Pacific states they do well, but there is little use trying them in or near big cities, as few evergreens are so sensitive to dust and smoke. With these restrictions in mind, they are magnificent lawn or estate trees, and *T. canadensis* can be made into a fine evergreen hedge. The acid drip after a rain, and the shade beneath hemlocks, make the cult. of most plants impossible beneath them.

T. canadensis. The common hemlock of northeastern N.A., and often called hemlock spruce (it is not a spruce). It may reach 90 ft., but is usually shorter as cult., the branches gracefully drooping in age. Leaves lustrous dark green above, bluish beneath, about ⅝ in. long, sometimes slightly notched at the tip, never over 1/16 in. wide, almost microscopically saw-toothed on the margins. Cones short-stalked, slightly egg-shaped, about ¾ in. long. Eastern N.A. Hardy from zone° 2 southward, but often failing in cult. because of unfavorable moisture conditions. Useful for hedges (which see). The *var.* **compacta** is a dwarf, cone-shaped tree; *var.* **gracilis** is a slow-growing form with shorter leaves and the smaller branches drooping at the tip; *var.* **pendula** is a compact, bushy form, usually broader than high, with pendulous branches. This, usually called Sargent's Weeping Hemlock, appears to have originated near Fishkill, N.Y., and thence propagated rather widely so that it is now in many of the finer conifer collections. Discovered about 1860, its introduction into gardens was largely due to the late Henry W. Sargent.

T. caroliniana. Carolina hemlock; sometimes called spruce pine, although it is no spruce or pine. Resembling the last, but generally lower, the leaves very similar, but without the minute marginal teeth. Cones oblongish 1–1¾ in. long. Mountains of W. Va. to Ga. Hardy from zone° 3 southward, and often doing better in cult. than *T. canadensis*.

T. diversifolia. Japanese hemlock. A pyramidal-headed tree rarely over 80 ft. high, less in cult. specimens. Leaves less than ½ in.

° Special articles on the subjects indicated by an asterisk (°) will be found at the words so marked.

long, about ⅟₁₆ in. wide, notched at the tip, dark, glossy, and green above. Cones practically stalkless, more or less egg-shaped, about 1 in. long. Jap. Hardy from zone* 3 southward and a fine evergreen.

T. heterophylla. Western hemlock; also called hemlock spruce. A Pacific Coast evergreen tree of noble stature, but not well suited to the East. Trunk often 220 ft. high. Leaves dark green and glossy above, not notched, about ¾ in. long. Cones stalkless, about 1 in. long. Hardy in the East only from zone* 4 southward, and often failing because of insufficient summer moisture and too much heat.

T. mertensiana. Mountain hemlock. A tree up to 90 ft. or even more, the branches drooping. Leaves bluish-green, not notched, ¼–¾ in. long. Cones stalkless, oblongish, 1½–3 in. long, generally purplish. Alaska to Mont., Idaho, and Calif. Resembling *T. heterophylla* in general aspect, sometimes confused with it, and with the same climatic requirements.

T. sieboldi. A tree up to 80 ft., the branches spreading horizontally. Leaves notched at the tip, ¼–¾ in. long, nearly ⅟₁₆ in. wide, dark and glossy-green above. Cones stalked, more or less egg-shaped, about 1 in. long. Jap. Hardy from zone* 4 southward.

HEMLOCK SPRUCE. In the East, *Tsuga canadensis;* in the West, *T. heterophylla.* Neither is a true spruce. See HEMLOCK.

HEMP. The true hemp is *Cannabis sativa* (which see). For other plants called hemp, or where hemp is part of their names, *see* SANSEVIERIA, APOCYNUM, MUSA TEXTILIS (the Manila hemp), and the next few entries.

HEMP FAMILY = Cannabinaceae.

HEMP PALM = *Trachycarpus fortunei.*

HEMP TREE = *Vitex Agnus-castus.*

HEN-AND-CHICKENS = *Sempervivum tectorum.* See HOUSELEEK.

HENBANE. See HYOSCYAMUS.

HENEQUEN = *Agave fourcroydes.*

HENNA. See LAWSONIA INERMIS.

HEPATICA (he-pat′i-ka). Low, perennial herbs of the buttercup family, comprising only a few species from the north temperate zone, generally called hepatica, liverleaf, or liverwort. They should only be grown in rich woods soil (not too acid) and in shadier parts of the wild garden. Leaves basal, long-stalked, 3-lobed, evergreen through the winter, but a new crop developing after the plant blooms. Flowers solitary, without petals, the sepals petal-like, and below them a calyx-like involucre* of 3 bracts. Fruit a collection of small achenes.* (*Hepatica* is from the Greek for liver, in allusion to the shape of the leaves.)

The hepaticas are charming little wild flowers, but not suited to open places (*see* above). They are easily propagated by division. They bloom early in the spring. For culture *see* WILD GARDEN.

acutiloba. Resembling the next species, if indeed distinct from it, the only difference being the sharper lobes of the leaf. Eastern U.S.

americana. The common hepatica of eastern N.A., often called Mayflower and blue anemone,

and for long named *H. triloba.* It is a perennial herb, usually under 6 in. high, the stalk of the leaves and flowers silky-hairy. Leaves 3-lobed, the lobes rounded. Flowers about ¾ in. wide, lavender-blue, white, or even rose-pink. Eastern N.A., west to Minn.

angulosa = *Hepatica transilvanica.*

nobilis. A European representative of the last, also once called *H. triloba.* It differs from *H. americana* in having less hairy stalks and in the larger flowers. Little grown in the U.S. There are double-flowered varieties in Eu.

transilvanica. A Central European hepatica, not unlike *H. americana,* but taller and with flowers nearly 2 in. wide, the sepals sometimes 3-toothed.

triloba. Long the name of the common hepatica of N.A., now known as *H. americana.* Also *H. triloba* was once incorrectly applied to the European hepatica, now known as *H. nobilis.*

HEPATICA FAMILY = Ranunculaceae.

hepaticifolia, -us, -um (he-pat-i-see-fō′li-a). With leaves like the hepatica.

heracleaefolia, -us, -um (her-ra-klee-ee-fō′li-a). With leaves like the genus *Heracleum* (which see). Sometimes spelled *heracleifolia,* as at Begonia.

HERACLEUM (her-ra-klee′um). The cow parsnips comprise a genus of about 70 species of tall, coarse herbs of the carrot family, chiefly from the north temperate zone, and of little hort. interest except for moist places in the wild garden or for very informal border plantations. They are perennials, with immense, thrice-compound* leaves, the stalks of which are often sheathed. Flowers small, usually white, crowded in huge, compound umbels* (for details *see* UMBELLIFERAE). Fruits flattened and grooved. (*Heracleum* was named for Hercules.)

There is no difficulty in growing the cow parsnips. All they need is open sunshine and a moist site. The first is weedy in wet places nearly throughout N.A. Propagated by division.

lanatum. Cow parsnip; also called masterwort. Nearly 8 ft. high and nearly as wide. Leaves at least 18 in. wide, the leaflets broadly oval, toothed and lobed, felty beneath. Flowers white, the compound clusters (umbels*) 12–20 in. wide. N.A. Summer.

mantegazzianum. Nearly 9 ft. high, the leaves 3 ft. long, the leaflets deeply cut. Flower cluster nearly 4 ft. wide (a compound umbel*), the flowers very small, white. Caucasus. Summer.

HERALD'S-TRUMPET = *Beaumontia grandiflora.*

HERB. A plant without a permanent woody stem. Most herbs have fleshy stems and die down to the ground over the winter. But some herbs are evergreen, and a few, like the banana, attain the size of trees, although they still have a fleshy stem. Some, like the castor-oil plant, are herbs as grown in the North, but immense, tree-like shrubs in the tropics.

Most herbs come up year after year, and are then called perennial (which see). Others live two years, while a few complete their

---

* Special articles on the subjects indicated by an asterisk (*) will be found at the words so marked.

growth and die within a single year. *See* ANNUAL; BIENNIAL.

As garden plants herbs furnish us with most of our color. For the uses of herbs in the garden *see* ANNUALS, BIENNIALS, PERENNIALS, and BORDER. To some *herb* means only the plants discussed at HERB GARDENING.

herbacea, -us, -um (her-bay'see-a). Herbaceous (which see).

HERBACEOUS. Having a stem that is fleshy and often green. Most herbs have herbaceous stems, which in some sorts are stiff, but usually not woody as in shrubs or trees. *Herbaceous* is also used, more rarely, to designate an organ that is green and leaf-like, instead of being membranous or scarious, as an *herbaceous* bract.*

HERBAL AND HERBALIST. Old, usually pre-Linnaean* books of the greatest possible interest to the gardener, although their authors (the herbalists) made many quaint mistakes about plants and what they called "their virtues." The great value of these books, most of them 16th-century English and German works, is that they contain a complete description of what was cult. at the time. Many of them were illustrated. Although the names they used for plants are confusing today, the pictures make identification of these garden plants of long ago fairly certain. The three best collections in America of these priceless old books are at the New York Botanical Garden, the Missouri Botanical Garden, and the library of the U.S. Department of Agriculture. *See also* Herbals at GARDEN BOOKS.

HERBARIUM. A collection of dried specimens of plants, usually, in America, mounted on stiffish paper or thin cardboard, 11½ × 16½ in. While all systematic studies of the wild flora of the different countries are based on herbarium specimens, there are few such for garden plants, the most notable being that at the Bailey Hortorium, Ithaca, N.Y.

An herbarium specimen should consist of as much of the plant as possible, but to be of real use as a permanent record it must have leaves and flowers, or if not, leaves and fruit. Each specimen should be ticketed with the names of the plant and its collector, the date, locality, the color of the flower, and any other helpful notes that may aid identification. The specimens must be pressed flat and thoroughly dried between blotters before mounting. Such collections are an invaluable record of plants which may long since have died.

HERB GARDENING. Herbs are plants the stems of which die down to the ground after flowering, as distinguished from woody plants with persistent stems. The plants here noted are a special class of herbs, most of them used as condiments, and selected for the aromatic properties of their roots, stems, leaves, seeds, flowers, or flower buds. As in all definitions there are many exceptions, and a few of the herbs such as the artemisias,

thymes, sages, perennial savories and rue have woody stems which die back only a little in the cold winter months. Herbs differ from vegetables in that the herbs are used to flavor other dishes, while vegetables are eaten for themselves. But here too are exceptions, for example, the celery, carrots, and onions, which although considered vegetables, are also used to flavor other dishes, whereas such herbs as fennel, angelica, and lovage can be eaten as vegetables. The basils, savories, or chervil are sweet herbs with pleasant-tasting leaves, seeds or roots, while bitter herbs taste either bitter or sharp. Wormwood is said to be the bitterest of all. When it comes to matters of taste and smell people react very differently, and although coriander has a pleasant-tasting seed, it is eaten at the Jewish Feast of Passover as one of the bitter herbs, while rue, generally considered decidedly bitter, is eaten with bread by the Italians and Spanish.

The herbs here included can be used to-day for flavor or fragrance by the amateur cook or distiller and can be grown by him in his garden. A few have been added to our list because of their sentimental associations. Herbs used only for medicine are not included, because almost every plant has been used medicinally at some time and the list would be far too long. A "simple" is a medicinal herb or the medicine made from it. (*See* MEDICINAL PLANTS.)

LIST OF HERBS

Note: All these plants appear elsewhere in the Encyclopedia under their Latin and English common names. See these entries for additional information.

Angelica, *Angelica Archangelica*, persists until it sets seed. The seed has to be sown while it is fresh. Stems are candied for decorating pastry; seeds and stems are used for flavoring. The blanched stalks were formerly eaten as a vegetable. Oil distilled from root flavors liqueurs.

Anise, *Pimpinella Anisum*, annual. Leaves in salads or as a garnish, seed for flavoring. Oil from seeds in perfumes and also liqueurs.

Balm, *Melissa officinalis*, perennial. Leafy tips flavor drinks, dried leaves make tea. Oil distilled from the whole plant in perfumes. Called, also, lemon balm.

Basil, *Ocimum Basilicum*, annual. Same uses as balm.

Bee balm, *Monarda didyma*, perennial. Dried leaves for tea, but leaves of *M. fistulosa* and *M. citriodora* make better teas. Oil from *M. didyma* formerly used in perfumes.

Borage, *Borago officinalis*, annual. Flower sprays and leafy tops impart flavor of cucumber to cool drinks. Leaves when cooked can be eaten as spinach.

Burnet, *Sanguisorba minor*, perennial. Young leaves for salads, and to flavor cool tankards.

Camomile, *Anthemis nobilis*, perennial. Dried yellow disk flowers make tea for medicine and as a cosmetic.

Caraway, *Carum Carvi*, biennial. Roots

---

* Special articles on the subjects indicated by an asterisk (*) will be found at the words so marked.

eaten as vegetable, leaves for garnish and in salads, seeds as a condiment. Oil distilled from seeds in liqueurs, sachets and perfumes.

Carnation, *Dianthus Caryophyllus*, perennial. Flowers formerly conserved, and also flavored wine and vinegar.

Chervil, *Anthriscus Cerefolium*, annual. Leaves flavor salads, soups and are an ingredient of *fines herbes*. (*See* below.)

Chives, *Allium Schoenoprasum*, perennial. Leaves are condiments.

Clary, *Salvia Sclarea*, biennial. Leaves formerly flavored many varieties of drinks; also put into omelettes. Flowers make tea. Oil distilled from plant used in perfumery. Leaves used in sachets.

Coriander, *Coriandrum sativum*, annual. Seeds when crushed a condiment, also an ingredient in curry powder, mixed spices, and liqueurs. Oil distilled from seeds in toilet waters.

Costmary, *Chrysanthemum Balsamita*, perennial. Leaves for flavorings, and for tea.

Cowslip, *Primula veris*, perennial. Flowers make a narcotic tea, formerly made into wine. Leaves can be eaten in salads. Flowers and leaves used as a pot herb in England.

Cumin, *Cuminum Cyminum*, annual. Seeds flavor cheese, bread, sauerkraut. An ingredient of curry powder. Oil distilled from seeds flavors liqueurs.

Damask Rose, *Rosa damascena*, shrub. Petals make a jam and scent potpourris. When distilled they yield rose oil for perfume and condiment.

Dill, *Anethum graveolens*, annual. Leaves, flowering tops, and seeds are condiments. Oil from seeds perfumes soaps.

Fennel, *Foeniculum vulgare*, annual. Stems of flowering plant eaten, seeds and leaves a condiment.

Fennel-flower, *Nigella sativa*, annual. Seeds a condiment. Oil from seeds in perfumery.

Florence Fennel, *Foeniculum vulgare dulce*, annual. Thickened stem bases a vegetable, also used to aromatize wine. Seeds a condiment.

Fraxinella, *Dictamnus albus*, perennial. Leaves make a tea.

German Camomile, *Matricaria Chamomilla*, annual. Oil distilled from plant used in perfumes and for coating glass and porcelain.

Horehound, *Marrubium vulgare*, perennial. Juice from boiled plants made into horehound candy, given for colds. In England beer is made from the plant.

Hyssop, *Hyssopus officinalis*, perennial. Leaves and flowering tops a condiment. Leaves make a tea. Oil extracted from green portions an ingredient of eau de cologne.

Lavender, *Lavandula Spica*, perennial. Calyx of flowers yields oil for perfume. Dried flower buds highly fragrant.

Lemon verbena, *Lippia citriodora*, shrub in South, pot plant in North. Leaves for flavoring drinks, fruit cups and when dried for tea.

Lovage, *Levisticum officinale*, perennial. Young stems a condiment, leafstalks and stem bases when blanched eaten as a vegetable,

seeds are condiments and roots used medicinally.

Pot Marjoram, *Origanum vulgare*, perennial. Leaves for flavoring, also in sachets and with tobacco. *See also* OREGANO in the body of the ENCYCLOPEDIA.

Sweet Marjoram, *Majorana hortensis*, annual. Leaves for seasoning, as a garnish, cooked with spinach. Oil from plant highly fragrant and present in perfumes.

Mustard, black. *Brassica nigra*, annual. Leaves mixed with salads, bruised seed flavors sauces. Oil from seeds used for making soaps and in East for lighting.

Mustard, white. *Brassica hirta*, annual. Same as above.

Nasturtium, *Tropaeolum minus* and *T. majus*, annuals. Flowers as garnish, stems and young leaves can be eaten in salads; seeds, chopped, used in sauces as a condiment.

Old Woman, *Artemisia stelleriana*, perennial. Used medicinally and as a charm by the Chinese.

Parsley, *Petroselinum crispum*, biennial. Leaves for condiment and garnish; seed and root for medicine.

Peppermint, *Mentha piperita*, perennial. Leaves and flowering tops flavor drinks; leaves make tea. Oil from plant flavors toilet articles and chewing gum.

Opium Poppy, *Papaver somniferum*, annual. Seeds for flavoring; opium gum comes from the juice of the unripe pod, but is not found in the seeds.

Pot Marigold, *Calendula officinalis*, annual. Rays flavor puddings and color butter; also, a substitute for saffron.

Provence Rose, *Rosa gallica*, shrub. Same use as damask rose.

Rose Geranium, *Pelargonium graveolens*, shrub in South, pot plant in North. Leaves flavor jellies and desserts. Oil distilled from leaves is used in perfumery.

Rosemary, *Rosmarinus officinalis*, a shrub. Leaves flavor certain foods, notably soup. Oil extracted from leafy portions of plant and flowers used medicinally and in perfumery.

Rue, *Ruta graveolens*, perennial. Leaves for flavoring by some people, but are very strong. Oil distilled from leafy portions of plant in toilet preparations.

Saffron Crocus, *Crocus sativus*, perennial. Dried stigmas for perfume, flavor, and formerly for coloring.

Sage, *Salvia officinalis*, perennial. Leaves a condiment, and make tea for sore throats and colds. Oil distilled from whole plant perfumes soaps.

Summer Savory, *Satureia hortensis*, annual. Leafy portions of plants and flowering branches flavor foods; also make medicinal teas.

Winter Savory, *Satureia montana*, perennial. Same as above, only less delicate as a flavoring.

Sesame, *Sesamum indicum*, annual. Seeds as a condiment and food. Oil extracted from seeds used in cooking in East and Latin America and medicinally everywhere.

---

* Special articles on the subjects indicated by an asterisk (*) will be found at the words so marked.

Southernwood, *Artemisia Abrotanum,* perennial. Dried stems and leaves said to keep moths and ants away. Also used medicinally.

Spearmint, *Mentha spicata,* perennial. Leaves flavor vinegars, cold drinks, and certain vegetables. Oil extracted from plant used medicinally, as a condiment and for toilet preparations.

Sweet flag, *Acorus Calamus,* perennial. Leaves flavor certain desserts. Pulverized roots made into sachet powders. Bark of root yields oil used in perfumery.

Tansy, *Tanacetum vulgare,* perennial. Leaves in puddings; said to destroy fleas; have long been used medicinally, but reputed poisonous.

Tarragon. *See* TARRAGON, in the body of the ENCYCLOPEDIA.

Thyme, *Thymus vulgaris,* perennial. Leaves and flowering tops a condiment. Oil distilled from them used medicinally and for perfume.

Violet, *Viola odorata,* perennial. Flowers sometimes candied, used as a dye and for perfume.

Wintergreen, *Gaultheria procumbens,* perennial. Berries in brandy make a drink like bitters. Leaves used formerly for tea. Oil distilled from leaves used medicinally, for perfume, and for candy flavoring.

Wormwood, *Artemisia Absinthium,* perennial. Dried leaves an ingredient in absinthe. Fruit in beer. Was formerly used medicinally.

EARLY HISTORY

Herbs were used long before the days of written history, and man may have learned his first herb lore by watching the animals, who take certain of them, such as fennel, as purgatives and others as emetics. Herbs were so important in the life of early man that in their wanderings the Indo-Europeans undoubtedly carried them from Europe to India and the Eastern tribes brought others to western Europe.

Magical properties were attributed to them because of their medicinal potency, and as time went on superstition gradually obscured much of the original herb lore. The Chinese use *Artemisia vulgaris* as a charm, while in France babies of the Middle Ages were rubbed with the juice of *Artemisia Abrotanum* so they never would feel cold. The Brahmins regard the basils as holy and women pray to a basil plant every day. The Greeks and Romans thought one should curse when sowing the basil to insure its germination. In Italy a maiden stands a pot of basil in her window as a signal to her lover that he is expected. As with the basil, so most herbs have many superstitions and old customs associated with them.

The first men and women gathered the fragrant thymes, rosemary, and lavender from the rocky ledges on the hillsides, sweet woodruff in the woods, fennel from the seacoast and others wherever they grew wild. But as people settled down into an agricultural and stationary life, they planted herbs in their gardens. Seeds of coriander were found in

Egyptian tombs of the twenty-first dynasty, and of caraway among the debris of the Lake Dwellers of Switzerland.

Mint, lavender, rue, wormwood, anise, and cumin are mentioned in the Bible, and Theophrastus, the Greek, who lived in the fourth century B.C., wrote delightfully of saffron crocus and thyme growing on the Grecian hills and roadsides. He gives recipes for making perfumes and cosmetics which contain the same ingredients as are used today. Galen, another Greek who wrote about the medicinal use of plants, was the first to make cold cream. His writings and those of Dioscorides were transmitted by the monks, who copied books by hand, and were studied and followed until the Renaissance, as were the writings of the Roman gentleman Pliny.

Although monks and educated people knew of these old formulae, the common people were unaware of them and used the herbs according to traditions handed down by word of mouth. The herb women still gathered the herbs from the woods and fields, probably to sell to people without gardens, but the thrifty housewife grew, dried, and stored her own. Mothers, cooks, and herb gatherers all made a tea of sage for sore throat, of balm leaves to cause sweating, of camomile flowers for indigestion, used anise water to cleanse the complexion, and the oils of lavender, rosemary, and others for their stimulating and pleasant qualities. Besides their medicinal uses, these sweet-smelling herbs had for long been associated with religious and magical practices, also to flavor foods, and often to disguise the disagreeable odors of putrefaction. Fragrant oils were burned and carried through hospitals, partly to counteract unpleasant odors, but also for their supposed healing properties.

Charlemagne, about the year 800, promulgated an order telling what vegetables to grow, and this gives us a picture of the gardens of his day, which, with few exceptions, contained what the European peasant grows in his combination vegetable-flower-and-herb garden today. In Charlemagne's time few flowers were grown for ornament, because the gardens were primarily practical. There would be lilies and violets, and, after the thirteenth century, the Damask and Provence roses. But there were always the flowers of hyssop, borage, opium poppies, the fennels, anise, the mints, sage, and others. The cottage gardens were probably either a front or a back yard where the vegetables were grown, margined with neat lines of basil, chives, or thyme.

INTRODUCTION INTO AMERICA

When the colonists came to North America they brought along the customs of their home lands. They carried seeds, roots, and cuttings, of which many were herbs and simples. In the first newspapers were advertisements of herb seeds for sale, such as anise, caraway, chervil, fennel, mustard, and savory.

The Indians showed the settlers where the

---

* Special articles on the subjects indicated by an asterisk (*) will be found at the words so marked.

Some examples of English knot gardens, now again in vogue among herb gardeners. All are from Leonard Meager's *The Complete English Gardener*, 1704.

native bee balms and wintergreen grew, and how to make teas from their leaves and medicines from other plants. The Indians used few flavorings in their food except the leaves of bee balm and of wild mint with the meats they dried for winter use. The roots of wild ginger (*Asarum canadense*) seasoned cakes made of hominy, and disguised the taste of meat and fish no longer fresh. They thought ginger was an antidote against the poison in decaying foods. The squaws gathered herbs and brought them into the New England villages until quite late. Some of these were used to flavor the Colonial beers, preserves, and foods, as well as for medicine.

In time the colonists found wild onions, garlic, and strawberries and used them as they had the related plants growing at home. They also used the native artemisias for medicine, and the native angelica and rose hips.[*] By 1643 Adrian Van der Donck was growing in his Yonkers gardens such herbs as angelica, *Acorus Calamus, Malva, Origanum,* geranium, *Althaea,* violet, iris, indigo, coriander and leeks.

Living in a wilderness, there was no other source of supply than one's own kitchen, and as it was essential for the Colonial housewife to have a well-stocked larder, she grew her own herbs with her vegetables and fruits. There must have been a constant preserving and drying going on all through the growing season in the Colonial kitchens. Many of the herbs were used to flavor the conserves, wines, and homemade drinks, as they had been in Europe, and the housewives often kept manuscript recipe books where the recipes which "Mother used to make" were handed down from one generation to the next.

Sassafras gave a special flavor to New Orleans gumbo, rose water was in many recipes, thyme was popular with southern cooks, and the French colonists in the South flavored their food with saffron, bay leaves, thyme, cloves, garlic, cayenne pepper, mustard, tomato, and parsley. The Spanish colonists in the West and Southwest were fond of the taste of marjoram and also used thyme, parsley, coriander, saffron, cumin, anise, and sesame. Sesame, used for its oil in China and as a cereal throughout the Orient, was brought to the colonies by the Negroes.

As the different nationalities came, each brought their favorite flavorings from home. Greeks were partial to sage, the Italians always flavor their soups and other dishes with basil. The French like chives, and the Negroes, who are our best cooks, are fond of many herbs and use them well.

In time, new plants, unknown in Europe before the voyage of Columbus, took their places with the herbs of the Old World, such as the peppers from Central and South America. They were first used in the South and Southwest in the Spanish colonies. Peppers are said to be good for a sluggish stomach, for they stimulate the digestive juices. Nasturtium is a native of South America, and its seeds are often substituted for capers. Lemon verbena is another South American

[*] Special articles on the subjects indicated by an asterisk ([*]) will be found at the words so marked.

plant, the leaves of which have a lemon flavor. However, practically all of the herbs are native to the Old World, and the ones used here for flavoring are, with few exceptions, imported.

CULTURE

There have been a few attempts to grow herbs for profit, the most extensive being that of the Shaker communities in Massachusetts and New York in the middle of the nineteenth century. Mint is grown commercially in the Far West and in New York. There was a halfhearted attempt, in Florida, to raise fragrant-leaved geraniums commercially, which was not a success. At the present, it does not seem practical to grow them here on a large scale, but it is decidedly advantageous for the amateur, because home-grown and home-dried herbs and seeds are more fragrant than the ones which come from abroad.

The herbs are not difficult to grow. Most of them belong either to the parsley, the mint, or the composite families. On the whole, they germinate readily and can be raised without any special horticultural skill. Of course there are the usual exceptions, but they are few in number.

All but a few seem to thrive in a well-drained, sunny, friable* soil which is not too rich. The mints like a damp soil and after the frost has killed back the stems they can be cut down to the ground and the plants buried with compost which acts as a fertilizer. Tarragon likes a fairly rich soil and not too hot a sun. The bed for the herbs should be prepared as one does the soil for vegetables, except that no manure is applied. It should be trenched for eighteen inches or two feet and forked over several times to render it well aired and friable*, then smoothed down, leaving the top not too hard.

Seeds should be sown thinly. A bed measuring two by four feet is sufficient for each kind of herb for a private family, and seeds can cover the whole bed, being sown about half an inch apart. After sowing, cover the seeds by lightly strewing soil over them and press down with a board. For commercial growing the herbs can be planted in rows.

The young seedlings do not require watering, for most herbs are natives of hot, dry regions. The weeds should be removed, if possible, by hand, because less damage is done that way, and as the season advances, a fine dust mulch around them will preserve the moisture in the soil. If the plants become too thick, they should be thinned. After cutting back the stems and leaves, it is a good plan to stir a little fertilizer around the roots so they will continue to produce more leafy stems. Too rich a soil, however, causes the plants to become leggy.* In herb culture a compact, bushy plant will produce more of the essential oil which gives it flavor and that is why a fairly lean soil is the best for them.

The annual members of the parsley family, such as coriander, cumin, anise, dill, and fennel all grow quickly and take from two to three months from seed time to harvest. If planted early in May out of doors, they will be bearing seeds in August or early September. All the annuals will ripen the first season, but a few, such as opium poppy and sesame, should have an earlier start than can be given them in northern gardens. It is a good plan to start them indoors, or in a hotbed or greenhouse, transplanting them into the garden after all danger of frost is past. Poppies are difficult to transplant because they have a slender taproot, but it can be done with skillful fingers. The best way is to prick out the seedlings into paper pots and plunge* the latter without disturbing the roots at all. From zone* 6 southward the poppies should be planted out of doors in February or March.

Annuals, such as the basils, summer savory, and borage, can be started out of doors. There are eight sorts of basil; two of these have red leaves and one has twisted leaves. The two most attractive are the bush basil and sweet or common basil. Sweet marjoram and marigold should be started indoors in cold climates.

Caraway and clary are biennials and do not produce seeds until the second season. Angelica sometimes takes two years to flower, but dies after this. Parsley is a biennial too, and germinates slowly, but since it is more often grown for its leaves than its seeds, it can be harvested the first season. It is not hardy in cold climates.

Most perennial herbs are hardy, except rosemary which dies out of doors north of zone 4. Tarragon does not set seed and has to be increased by dividing the roots. Thymes too can be increased by dividing the roots. Sages, geraniums, and rosemary can be increased by stem cuttings made in late summer. Most other perennial herbs come readily from seeds. If these are started indoors in February they will often be large enough to be planted out of doors in May. Damask roses should be replaced after five years. Most perennials have a given life span and are not permanent fixtures in the garden, although so many beginners think they are.

Fragrant-leaved geraniums, such as the rose, nutmeg, and some forty others, are not hardy, nor is the lemon verbena. In southern climates they grow to be shrubs, but north of Washington have to be handled as pot plants.

HERBS AS PART OF THE GARDEN PICTURE

Herbs can be grown in a walled garden all to themselves, in small, rectangular beds. The beds of marjoram, hyssop, or rue can be outlined with chives, parsley, or basil. Or one can grow them in rows in a portion of the vegetable garden or in little beds strung together, separated by walks. Some of them are so decorative that they add to the charm of the herbaceous border. Among these are the hyssops, thymes, lavenders, winter savory, the artemisias, borage, the monardas, rue, violet, and marigold. The anise and coriander

---

* Special articles on the subjects indicated by an asterisk (*) will be found at the words so marked.

are pretty in a dainty way, and angelica is a handsome plant with its lush leaves and ball-like inflorescence.

A few of the herbs, such as the mustards, are too weedy for the garden. The leaves of the young plants are peppery and tart in salads, but they are a fertile lot and growing them is courting an invasion. *Artemisia Absinthium* makes a strong, shrubby growth and has to be cut to the ground once during the summer, for it spreads. Tansy is a strong grower and forms huge clumps. Camomile makes a mossy-looking ground cover and was so used in the gardens of Shakespeare's day and earlier, but it, too, will spread far and wide. There is an old saying that camomile keeps the garden healthy.

The herb garden has a uniform fluffy, somewhat grayish, appearance, for so many of the herbs have a similar foliage and habit of growth. The basils, thyme, winter savory, the dwarf lavender and others are good edging plants. In the South, rosemary makes a fragrant and lovely edging for the garden. A dry wall, the chinks of which are filled with good garden soil, is a fine place in which to grow the thymes and savories. So are the spaces between steps and stone pavements.

HARVESTING

It is important to harvest herbs when the plants are richest in essential oils. After the flowers have opened, there is less of the volatile oil present, so that the time to harvest plants to be used for their leaves and flowering branches is just as the buds are about to open or after the first one has unfolded its petals. The herbs should be cut while the dew is still on them, on the morning of what promises to be a hot summer's day. Carry your harvest indoors, where branches are washed and shaken dry, the leaves stripped from the stems, and the flowering truss cut off. Place the harvest scantily on trays of wire mesh and put in a shaded room, where the air can circulate around it. Every morning the leaves should be stirred about so all of them will be exposed to the air. In three or four days the plants should be thoroughly dry and ready to pack into air-tight containers. Of course damaged or diseased leaves or stems are thrown out. Hanging plants to dry from the rafters was an old custom, but is an excellent way to collect dust. Drying out of doors causes the leaves to shrivel and blacken.

Rose petals, violets, or lavender calyces are picked and dried in the same way. Rose petals should have their white claws* cut off. Pick early in the morning of the day they open and never if they have opened the day before. The lavender should be picked when the buds have formed, for the calyx is the most fragrant part.

Seeds are collected as soon as they are ripe and before they fall to the ground. They too are washed, dried, and packed away for future use. Roots are dug either in the fall or spring, cut into small pieces, and dried as one would apricots or peaches.

The leaves to be dried for teas should be kept whole, but many people crumble the other herbs into powders, which never look as pretty, for they do not show in the food. When herbs are used for flavoring in beans or rice pudding, it is attractive to see the little black specks or tiny stems. For making pot-pourris the herbs are dried this way too, but if it is intended to extract the oil from the plants, the fresh stems and leaves are used.

How to Use Herbs

Every perfume, sachet, or potpourri has to have an element in it known as a fixative and, since Theophrastus's day and perhaps earlier, these have been ambergris, civet, musk and gum benzoin, all of them, except the last, expensive. The French perfumers have been using clary sage, which can be grown in the garden, as a fixative. Gum benzoin can be purchased at the druggist's.

Herb Teas. In Colonial times there was an active propaganda for the use of herb teas. The people were called upon to drink home-made teas instead of those from China as a protest against the British tax. The following are only a few of the many Colonial herb teas: Sweet marjoram with a little mint; thyme and a little hyssop; sage with balm leaves, to which was added lemon juice; rosemary and lavender; clover and camomile; the leaves of a red rose and sweet myrtle; strawberry leaves and the leaves of sweetbrier; goldenrod and betony with honey; peppermint and yarrow.

Besides these, the following have been found to make pleasant teas: The leaves of costmary, balm, *Monarda fistulosa*, and fraxinella. Teas can be made from the flowers of camomile. As one becomes adept one can mix and combine different herbs into teas. All teas made of herbs are green, because the leaves are dried quickly and not allowed to ferment as are the leaves of black teas. Since these teas are green, they are not a dark color even when strong, but a pale green or yellow, so in brewing them the strength should be judged by the taste and not the appearance.

Cooking with Herbs. To cook with herbs no other implements than the usual cooking utensils are needed except for a mortar and pestle. When using them as a condiment, since their flavor is very penetrating, only a little of the herbs is required to give the dish the aromatic scent or taste. When infusing the herbs which have a peppery or spicy taste into a dish, very little salt and no pepper is needed. A dash of orange juice intensifies the flavor of some herbs. Dried herbs are just as potent as fresh ones if they have been properly stored, but they are not so pretty.

It has been found that butter, eggs, cheese, milk, or stock take up the herb flavoring quickly. So first measure out any of these ingredients to be used and mix the herbs into them and if possible let them stand for a few hours before making up the dish. A few herbs such as coriander seeds and angelica seeds should be bruised in a mortar before using

---

* Special articles on the subjects indicated by an asterisk (*) will be found at the words so marked.

them. When flavoring soups, the dried herbs should cook in the soup for a while longer than the fresh ones, which should be put in just for a few minutes before serving. In flavoring cold fruit drinks or iced tea, the herbs should be boiled in the hot syrup first, which is then cooled before it is added to the drink. After flavoring a soup with rosemary or thyme, it looks pretty to drop a tiny sprig of the herb in each plate.

Herbs make attractive garnishes. The basils, chervil, thyme, sage, rose geranium, and lemon verbena are every bit as pretty as the ever-present parsley, but more difficult to obtain. The French *fines herbes* consist of four different herbs combined variously according to the dish they flavor. Generally chives is one of them and parsley another, but any of the others, such as the savories, basils, chervil, sage, or thyme can be added. Thyme, basil, summer savory, and chives are a pleasant combination of *fines herbes* for omelettes, soups and meats. Chives with thyme, winter savory, and fennel taste good in flavoring the butter sauce to go with fish. Basil, thyme, sweet marjoram, and parsley are another delicious combination. Some people cannot digest chives and for them they must be omitted, but the good cook knows that members of the onion family are the best undertone for flavoring every dish except desserts. The French cooks rub the chives or garlic around the empty salad bowl before putting in the lettuce which they then dress in the bowl. The tops and leaves of borage, which have a flavor of cucumber, are used for flavoring drinks, as are the leaves of spearmint, peppermint, and of balm.

Tarragon has a very decided flavor, as has rosemary, and should preferably not be mixed with other herbs. Jellied eggs are flavored with tarragon by placing the leaves on the eggs before the jelly is poured over them. Vinegar is aromatized with tarragon and gives the flavor of the herb to the salad dressing. Vinegar can also be aromatized with fennel and dill. Tarragon leaves chopped and scattered over the salad give them a strong flavor. Rosemary flavors a chicken broth thickened with cream.

FINES HERBES. Stirred into cream or cottage cheese these make delicious sandwich fillings as do mint leaves chopped finely, mixed with chives worked into butter with a little orange juice and sugar. The leaves of rose geranium, boiled, flavor custards, blanc mange and jellies, especially apple jelly. The juice of boiled mint leaves flavors jellies colored green to serve with roast lamb. Dill and fennel leaves flavor fish. In dishes where tomatoes are used, basil leaves give a delicate flavor. Thyme, sage, and marjoram have long been added to the stuffings and dressings for poultry, veal, and pork. Sage is said to help digest the fat of certain meats and vegetables. Nowadays we flavor fruit salads with it, and iced tea, but as said above, the leaves should be boiled in the hot syrup and not scattered over the dish at the last moment.

HERB RECIPES

FRUIT AND HERB DRINK

Juices of 3 oranges and 2 lemons
½ cup of sugar syrup
1 cup of tea, very strong
1 sprig of balm, first pounded in a mortar
5 sprigs of borage
A bunch of mint
1 sprig of burnet
3 anise leaves
A pinch of salt

Pour the hot tea and syrup over the fruit juices and herbs. Cover the pitcher and allow the mixture to stand for an hour or more. Strain into another pitcher which is partly filled with ice. Add wine or White Rock and serve, first floating a few flowers of borage in the mouth of the pitcher.

GREEN PEA SOUP WITH MINT

1 quart of fresh peas
1 onion
A few sprigs of mint
1 teaspoon of spinach juice
1 teaspoon of salt
1 teaspoon of sugar
2 tablespoons of butter
2 egg yolks
½ cup of cream

Boil the pods of the peas for two or three hours in water in which other vegetables have been cooked. Strain. To three pints of this strained water add the fresh peas, the onion, mint, salt, and sugar. Cook until the peas are tender, then rub through a sieve, add butter, spinach juice, and bring to the boiling point. Season more if needed and just before serving add the egg yolk diluted with cream. Cook, stirring constantly, for five minutes but do not allow the liquid to boil. Strain and serve with croutons or fried bits of toast. This soup may also be made with one pint of dried peas which have been soaked.

PARSLEY SOUP, also called *Soupe à la Bonne Femme*

2 cups of milk
1 cup of water
1 teaspoon of salt
2 tablespoons of butter
2 tablespoons of flour
1 medium-sized onion

Melt the butter, add flour and salt and the liquids and onion. Cook slowly for one hour. Remove the onion, add ½ cup of finely chopped fresh parsley. Stir well and serve.

EGGPLANT STUFFED WITH HERBS

1 onion
A small bunch of parsley
A little thyme
1 cup of bread soaked in milk
1 egg
Salt and pepper
1 tablespoon of bread crumbs

Cook the eggplant in boiling water until it is soft, then cut off a piece from the top and re-

---

* Special articles on the subjects indicated by an asterisk (*) will be found at the words so marked.

move the inside. Then add the onion which has been fried in butter; mix all the ingredients together and put them back into the eggplant and scatter the bread crumbs on top. Put it in the oven for a half an hour until the top is brown. Then serve.

COLD STUFFED EGGS, for hors d'oeuvres
Hard-boiled eggs
Cold tomato ketchup
Salt and pepper
Basil and savory
Mayonnaise

Cut the eggs in half, remove the yolks, and mix them with ketchup and other ingredients. Fill the halved whites with the mixture. And over this put mayonnaise mixed with the ketchup.

CHOPPED MEAT BALLS
½ pound of chopped meat (beef, veal, or pork)
1 teaspoon each of chopped chives, thyme, marjoram, and parsley mixed
1 tablespoon of flour mixed with salt and pepper
Butter

Into the meat work the chopped herbs; form into balls; roll in seasoned flour; fry in butter until well browned.

ROSE-GERANIUM JELLY
Prepare apples as for a usual jelly. Boil the juice from the pulp for twenty minutes. To each pint of juice add one pound of sugar and place in a kettle over the fire. Stir until all the sugar has melted, then add two or three rose-geranium leaves, bring to the boiling point and boil rapidly for two minutes, removing any scum which may rise to the surface. Turn into jelly glasses, removing the leaves, but place a fresh leaf in each glass. — H.M.F. The Herb Society of America welcomes those interested in these plants. Its present address is Horticultural Hall, Boston 15, Mass.

HERBICIDES. *See* Weed Killers at WEEDS AND WEEDING.

HERB MERCURY = *Mercurialis annua.*

HERB OF GRACE. *See* RUE.

HERB PATIENCE = *Rumex Patientia.*

HERB ROBERT = *Geranium robertianum.*

HERCULES'-CLUB = *Zanthoxylum Clava-Herculis* and *Aralia spinosa.*

HERD'S GRASS = *Phleum pratense.*

HEREDITY. Plants are described in terms of characters. Characters result from ancestrally inherited genes,* which may or may not express themselves under a given set of environmental conditions. In other words, by no means all of a plant's inheritance appears. Heredity is what a plant possesses from the beginning, at real birth, when egg and sperm unite. Environment is all that surrounds this inherited gift from conception to death. It is air, smoke, water, fertilizer, temperature,

light, other living things, and myriads of different entities. Variations are simply differences, contrasts. They may be hereditary (germinal mutations) or may be environmental (*see* ENVIRONMENT). Thus we see that *environment,* *heredity* and *variation** are, in a sense, inseparable in an attempt to understand clearly their significance in breeding work.

The science of *genetics* is the study of these three phenomena and their interrelations. The most striking and fundamental fact in all genetics is that living things — both plants and animals — are made up of these independent units called genes,* and that these are transmitted through the succeeding generations in an orderly and predictable manner. It is upon this fact that all plant breeding rests. For the other factors involved *see* MUTATION, CROSSING, PLANT BREEDING, INBREEDING and SELECTION. — O. E. W.

HERMAPHRODITE. The normal condition of most garden plants and implying that both male (stamens*) and female (pistil*) organs of reproduction are within a single flower. Some plants, however, are polygamous, which means that they bear both hermaphrodite flowers and others which are only male or female, as in the ash and sumac. *See also* MONOECIOUS and DIOECIOUS.

HERMODACTYLUS (her-mo-dak′ti-lus). A single iris-like bulbous herb from southern Eu., differing from *Iris* chiefly in its 1-celled pod. The only species is **H. tuberosus,** the snake's-head iris, which is about 15 in. high. Leaves somewhat 4-angled, about 2 ft. long, bluish-green. Flower solitary, the outer segments dark purple, the inner greenish, not over 2 in. long. Southern Eu. (*Hermodactylus* is from the Greek for Hermes and *dactylos,* a finger, in allusion to the shape of the root.) The plant is grown exactly as are the bulbous species of *Iris* (which see).

HERNIARIA (her-ni-ā′ri-a). Herniary. A genus of prostrate or trailing herbs of the pink family, all from the Old World, two of the 10 known species of secondary garden interest. Both the hort. species are low, perennial, short-lived herbs with stalkless, small, opposite* leaves, and swollen joints, and usually much-branched. Flowers inconspicuous, in small clusters in the leaf axils* (for details *see* CARYOPHYLLACEAE). Fruit a small capsule enclosed within the persistent calyx.* (*Herniaria* is from the Greek for hernia, in allusion to their supposed efficacy for rupture. The plants are sometimes called rupturewort or burstwort.)

Both species prefer a sandy soil as their original habitat is along the seacoast. They are sometimes used for carpet bedding or for covering rocks, and are of easy culture. While the flowers are too minute to be of interest, the foliage is attractive, and in warm regions persists through the winter and turns bronzy-red.

glabra. Prostrate, the stems not over 6 in.

* Special articles on the subjects indicated by an asterisk (*) will be found at the words so marked.

high, usually spreading over the ground. Leaves oblongish. Flowers greenish, in stalkless, leafy clusters in the leaf axils. Eurasia.

hirsuta. Somewhat similar to *H. glabra* but the foliage hairy. Eu.

HERNIARY. See Herniaria.

HERON'S-BILL. See Erodium.

HESPERALOE (hes-per-ă'loe). A small genus of stemless desert plants of the lily family found from Tex. to Mex. and usually suited only to similar climates although it is reported as hardy in Ind. It is also grown in the cool greenhouse. They differ from the closely related *Yucca* (which see) only in having rose-colored flowers. The only cult. species, **H. parviflora** of Tex., has basal, thread-margined leaves nearly 4 ft. long and about 1 in. wide. Flowers day-blooming (mostly night-blooming in *Yucca*), rose-pink, nodding, about 1½ in. long. The *var.* **engelmanni** has bell-shaped and smaller flowers. (*Hesperaloe* is from the Greek for evening, *i.e.*, toward the sunset, and *Aloe*, in allusion to their being New World and western representatives of the Old World aloe.)

HESPERIDIUM. See Citrus.

HESPERIS (hes'per-is). Attractive, Old World, biennial or perennial herbs of the mustard family, comprising about 25 species, and generally called rocket or damewort. One is a widely grown flower-garden plant long known in cult. They are erect, branching plants with alternate,* usually finely toothed leaves, and showy purplish or white, fragrant flowers in long, terminal clusters (racemes*). Petals 4. Fruit a long, slender pod (silique*), contracted at intervals. (*Hesperis* is from the Greek for evening, in allusion to their marked fragrance at night.)

They should be grown as ordinary garden perennials or biennials, the seeds started a season before they are expected to bloom. *H. matronalis* is often a biennial and a supply should be kept to replace plants that die out after blooming.

matronalis. Dame's-rocket; called, also, dame's-violet and garden rocket. A branching herb 2–3 ft. high. Leaves lance-shaped or ovalish, 2–4 in. long, tapering at the tip, but nearly stalkless and broad toward the base. Flowers normally purple or lilac-purple, delightfully night-fragrant. Pods 3–4 in. long, beaked. Eurasia. A double-flowered form is sometimes called, especially in England, the Whitsun gillyflower. White-flowered forms are also known, sometimes under the name *var.* **nivea.**

nivalis. A perennial herb up to 1 ft. high. Leaves oblongish, 1–2 in. long, without marginal teeth. Flowers pale, pure white, in a loose raceme.* An alpine species from the mountains of Persia, and probably only a white-flowered form of *H. matronalis*.

HESPEROYUCCA (hes-per-o-yuck'a). A single, Californian desert plant of the lily family, **H. whipplei**, there called the mountain queen or Quixote-plant, and formerly known as *Yucca whipplei*. It is almost stemless, but with a short, woody base from which arises a rosette of rigid, sword-like leaves 12–20 in.

long and about ¾ in. wide, prickle-tipped and with fine, marginal teeth. Flowering stalk 10–12 ft. high, the cluster at the end branched. Flowers white, nearly 2 in. long, nodding. The plant needs the same conditions as for *Agave* (which see), and cannot be grown in frosty, wet regions. (*Hesperoyucca* is from the Greek for evening, *i.e.*, toward the sunset, and *Yucca*, in allusion to its far western range.) Also called Our Lord's candle.

HETEROCENTRON (het-er-o-sen'tron). Tropical American perennial herbs or under-shrubs of the family Melastomaceae, one of its 4 species a fairly common greenhouse plant, grown for its attractive flowers. Leaves opposite,* more or less lance-shaped and without marginal teeth. Flowers (in the hort. species) rose-pink or purple, in rather showy clusters (panicles*). Petals 4. Stamens 8, of unequal length. Fruit a 4-valved capsule.* (*Heterocentron* is from the Greek for unlike spurs, referring to the unequal anthers.*)

The only cult. species needs a warm, moist greenhouse and potting mixture* 3. It is an attractive pot plant with a profusion of small flowers. In frostless regions it can be grown outdoors.

elegans = *Schizocentron elegans.*
mexicanum = *Heterocentron roseum.*
roseum. Not over 2 ft. high (as cult.), the branches 4-angled. Leaves 1 in. long, conspicuously stiff-hairy on the margins. Flowers rose-pink (white in a hort. variety), about ½ in. long. Mex. Often known as *H. mexicanum*.

HETEROMELES. See Toyon.

heterophylla, -us, -um (het-er-o-fill'a). With variously shaped leaves.

HETEROSIS or hybrid vigor. Crosses between different varieties or races of plants often increase the size, vitality, floriferousness, and fruit yield of their immediate offspring. This phenomenon probably accounts for the vigor, general health, and desirability of many cultivated plants asexually propagated, and its use is increasing in commercial pursuits, notably among tomato and sweet-corn growers of canners' seed, among growers of fancy field-corn seed, and to some extent in the lumber and wood-pulp trade.

Many species crosses produce weak progeny, but in many cases the F_1 progeny exhibit remarkable hybrid vigor, as illustrated by Burbank's walnut species hybrids Paradox (California walnut × Persian) and Royal (California black × Eastern black), which grew several times more rapidly than the parents. Increased hardiness, greater longevity, greater ease of vegetative propagation and earlier maturity are other characters often associated with this phenomenon. Experimenters have often noticed higher percentage of germination among such crossed seed. The proverbial hardihood of the mule is a familiar example of heterosis in animals. In the application of heterosis to plant-breeding problems, a wide and little-exploited field, rich in possibilities, exists, particularly in re-

---

* Special articles on the subjects indicated by an asterisk (*) will be found at the words so marked.

gard to increasing yields, longevity, more rapid growth, and earlier maturity. — O. E. W.

HEUCHERA (hew'ker-a). Alumroot. Attractive, North American perennial herbs of the family Saxifragaceae, comprising over 70 species, chiefly from the Rocky Mountain region. They have stout rootstocks and mostly basal, long-stalked, often roundish or lobed leaves. Stalk of the flower cluster arising from the rootstock, often leafy, and crowned with a narrow panicle* or raceme* of bell-shaped or saucer-shaped, green, white, red, or purple flowers. Petals small or narrow and inconspicuous, most of the color coming from the conspicuous 5-lobed calyx. Stamens* 5, attached to the petals. Fruit a 2-valved capsule.* (Named for Johann Heinrich von Heucher, German botanist.)

Coral bells (*Heuchera sanguinea*) is a very popular garden perennial suited to a variety of soils, but generally preferring some shade to full sunlight, as do most of the alumroots which are naturally woodland plants, preferring rocky cliffs. The most adaptable of all to general garden culture is *H. sanguinea*, the others being chiefly suited to the wild garden or rock garden. All may be propagated by division. A hybrid between *H. lithophila* and *Tiarella cordifolia* was made in England, under the name *Heucherella;* little known here.

americana. Common alumroot; also called American sanicle. A woodland herb, the flowering stalk often 2 ft. high. Leaves roundish, mottled in youth, the marginal teeth rounded. Flowers greenish-white, the stamens protruding. Eastern U.S. June. Not suited to the open, and best grown in the shady part of the wild garden in a soil of pH 4–5.

brizoides = *Heuchera lithophila.*

cylindrica. A perennial 15–24 in. high, the kidney-shaped leaves with marginal teeth and also hairy on the margin, the leafstalks densely hairy. Flowers small, the petals often wanting, greenish-yellow, in a spike-like cluster (panicles*). Northwestern U.S. *Var.* **glabella** has smooth leafstalks.

lithophila. A beautiful plant from the mountains of Calif., suited chiefly for the rock garden. Flowering stalk up to 28 in., the cluster a narrow panicle.* Flowers pinkish, about ⅛ in. long, very delicate. Sometimes offered as *H. brizoides.* Not certainly hardy in the East.

micrantha. A white-flowered plant, the stalk of the flower cluster not over 2 ft. high, sticky-hairy. Flowers small, but the cluster is beautifully light and airy. British Columbia to Calif. Not certainly hardy in the East.

sanguinea. Coral bells. Much the best known and easiest cult. of all the alumroots. It grows from 1–2 ft. high, the leaves all basal and shorter-stalked than in the other species. The flowering stalk is crowned at the top by a loose, often somewhat 1-sided, cluster of small, red, bell-shaped flowers that are scarcely ⅓ in. high. N. Mex., Ariz., and Mex. It is a perfectly hardy perennial, blooming most of the summer, well suited for the open (partly shaded) border. It is also commonly forced by florists and can be by the amateur. See Forcing. There are many popular varieties of this well-known favorite, among the best being *var.* **gracillima**, which is more slender; *var.* **gracillima rosea**, slender and rose-pink; *var.* **alba**, white-flowered; *var.* **hybrida**, more

robust. A good white-flowered named form is Perry's White.

villosa. An almost stemless perennial, the stalks of the leaves and flowers densely clothed with rusty hairs. Leaves nearly round, heart-shaped at the base, the margins angled and toothed. Flowers white or pinkish, minute, but numerous in a spike-like cluster which is shorter than the foliage. Southeastern U.S. Summer. Suited only to moist, shady sites in the wild garden.

HEVEA (he'vee-a). Amazon valley trees of the spurge family, of no hort. interest except as grown in extreme southern Fla. Even there it is neither hot nor moist enough to grow properly this leading rubber plant of the world as a commercial crop. It is **H. brasiliensis**, commonly called Pará rubber tree or seringera. It made millionaires of some Amazon River rubber dealers fifty years ago, but 90 per cent of the world's rubber is now from English and Dutch plantations in the Indo-Malayan region. The tree grows up to 60 ft. as cult. (much more in the Amazon Valley), and has a milky juice which is the source of rubber. Leaves alternate,* compound,* the 3 leaflets oblongish, 4–6 in. long (as cult.), rarely up to 1 ft. long. Flowers greenish, inconspicuous (for details *see* EUPHORBIACEAE). Fruit a capsule.* For another rubber plant *see* FICUS ELASTICA. (*Hevea* is a Latinized form of a Brazilian name for the tree.)

hexagona, -us, -um (hecks-ag'o-na). Six-angled.

hexagonoptera, -us, -um (hecks-a-go-nop'-ter-ra). With six wings or angles.

hexandra, -us, -um (hecks-an'dra). With six stamens.*

hexapetala, -us, -um (hecks-a-pet'a-la). Six-petaled.

hexaphylla, -us, -um (hecks-a-fill'a). Six-leaved.

HEXASTYLIS. See ASARUM.

HEYDERIA. See *Libocedrus decurrens* at INCENSE CEDAR.

HIBA ARBORVITAE = *Thujopsis dolabrata.*

HIBBERTIA (hib-ber'ti-a; also hib-ber'-shi-a). Rather showy, chiefly Australian, woody vines of the family Dilleniaceae, of its nearly 100 species only **H. volubilis** of much garden interest. It is a high-climbing woody vine with alternate,* oblongish leaves 2–3 in. long, more or less clasping at the base and silky-hairy beneath. Flowers solitary, terminal, yellow, unpleasantly scented. Sepals 5. Petals 5, spreading and making rather an open flower. Stamens* numerous. Fruit a collection of 5 ripened carpels. Its culture is confined to southern Calif. (Named for George Hibbert, English patron of botany.)

hibernica, -us, -um (hy-ber'ni-ka). From Ireland.

---

* Special articles on the subjects indicated by an asterisk (*) will be found at the words so marked.

hibiscifolia, -us, -um (hy-bis-ki-fō'li-a). With leaves like *Hibiscus.*

HIBISCUS (hy-bis'kus). An important genus of over 200 species of herbs, shrubs, and trees of the mallow family, of great hort. interest because it yields garden annuals, musky-seeded perfume plants, some foods, many showy perennials, a few shrubs, and some gorgeously colored tropical trees. Leaves alternate,* always with the veins arranged finger-fashion, sometimes lobed or parted. Flowers usually large, generally bell-shaped, of 5 petals and sepals, or sometimes the sepals united to form a 5-toothed calyx.* Stamens* united into a tubular structure which surrounds the style.* Fruit a dry, 5-valved capsule. The plants are generally called mallow or rose mallow, and, as in other genera of the Malvaceae, there is often a series of bracts* beneath the calyx.* (*Hibiscus* is Vergil's name for a mallow.)

The diversity of *Hibiscus* is so great that it is impossible to give general cultural notes that apply to all species. Those mentioned as annuals can be treated as hardy annuals and the seeds sown where wanted. For the others *see* the notes appended to each.

Abelmoschus. The abelmosk or musk mallow. A tropical Asiatic annual or biennial hairy herb 2–6 ft. high. Leaves lobed, often deeply so, and the lobes toothed. Flowers nearly 4 in. wide, yellow but with a crimson eye.* Fruit oblongish, about 3 in. long, its seeds musky and used for perfume. India. Grown mostly for its seeds, and needs more summer heat than is found in most parts of the U.S., but it will flower in the North.

coccineus. An extremely showy perennial, 6–8 ft. high, its long-stalked bluish-green leaves cut into 5 slender lobes. Flowers 5–6 in. wide, brilliant scarlet, its fine petals and long-protruding stamens* producing a flower suggesting that of the tropical Rose-of-China. Low grounds, Fla. and Ga. Hardy up to northern edge of zone* 5, and perhaps beyond.

esculentus. Okra or gumbo. A garden-vegetable annual grown for its immature, mucilaginous pods. It is 2–6 ft. high, with 3–9-lobed or divided leaves that may be 1 ft. wide. Flowers solitary in the leaf axils,* 2–3 in. wide, yellow, with a red eye.* Pods ribbed and beaked, 4–12 in. long. Old World tropics. For culture *see* OKRA.

grandiflorus. A southern representative of the next species, but with larger, pink, and red-eyed flowers. Ga., Fla., and Miss. Useful for seaside planting along the Gulf Coast and in Fla.

Moscheutos. Rose mallow; called also swamp mallow and sea hollyhock, the latter in allusion to its normal salt-marsh habitat. The plant is also, incorrectly, called marsh mallow, a name that properly belongs to *Althaea officinalis* (*see* HOLLYHOCK). A hairy, perennial herb, 3–7 ft. high. Leaves generally ovalish, sometimes slightly angled or lobed, 3–7 in. long, generally, in the wild form, white-felty beneath. Flowers 4–7 in. wide, useless for picking as they wilt within an hour, white or pink, but with no eye.* Fruit about 1 in. long. In brackish marshes, Mass. to Va., rarely in fresh marshes westward to Ill. Aug.–Sept. Forms with narrower leaves are called *H. palustris* by some.

The rose mallow, while typically a salt-marsh plant, can be dug from the wild and transplanted directly to ordinary garden soil with complete success. Few grow it today because from it have been derived much finer plants, mostly the result of selection and crossing with other (non-hort.) species. These improved mallows, with hollyhock-like flowers often 6 in. wide, are of easy culture in most rich garden soils, but need plenty of room. They come in a variety of colors, ranging from pure white to deep crimson. Some have an eye.

mutabilis. Cotton rose; also called Confederate rose, but a native of China. A shrub or sometimes tree-like. Leaves broadly ovalish, 4–8 in. wide, 3–5-lobed, the lobes triangular and round-toothed or scalloped. Flowers 3–4 in. wide, opening white or pink, but soon changing to deep red, hairy on the outside. Fruit globe-shaped, hairy, about 1 in. in diameter. A common bush in the South but not hardy north of zone* 7.

oculiroseus. White rose mallow. Perhaps not really distinct from *H. Moscheutos,* but differing constantly in having a red eye. Marshes, L.I. and Staten Is., to N.J. and D.C. An interesting plant and perhaps the source of the eye* in the improved mallows noted at *H. Moscheutos.* Some prefer to consider this as the true *H. Moscheutos.*

Rosa-sinensis. Rose-of-China; called also China rose and shoeblack plant, the latter indicating the use of its flowers by tropical bootblacks, to polish shoes. A gorgeous, tropical Asiatic shrub, often 20–30 ft. in the tropics, less as widely grown in Fla. and southern Calif. It will stand a little frost. Leaves broadly oval, 3–4 in. long, tapering at the tip, unlobed but often toothed. Flowers usually solitary in the upper leaf axils,* 4–6 in. long, typically rose-red (but *see* below), flaring and spectacularly showy both on account of its petals and the long column of stamens.* Fruit egg-shaped, beaked.

The Rose-of-China is a familiar plant all over the tropical world, and is widely planted in frost-free parts of the U.S. There are many forms of it, some double-flowered, others with the petals cut or fringed, when, from a distance, the flowers suggest a huge scarlet spider. White-apricot, salmon-pink, and yellow-flowered forms are also known.

It is also grown in warm, moist greenhouses,

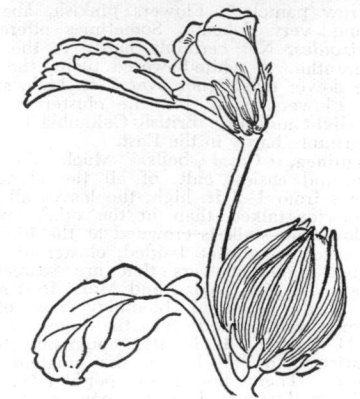

Roselle, an unusual plant grown for its acid calyx* and bracts.*

---

* Special articles on the subjects indicated by an asterisk (*) will be found at the words so marked.

where it needs rich feeding with liquid manure and potting mixture* 4. One of the glasshouse varieties has white- and red-splashed leaves.

Sabdariffa. Roselle; called also red sorrel and Jamaica sorrel, although it is a native of the Old World tropics. An annual, 4–7 ft. high, much-branched from the base, and with reddish stems. Leaves (the upper ones) 3–5-parted, 3–4 in. wide. Flowers stalkless, solitary in the leaf axils,* the petals yellow, longer than the thick, red calyx and its bracts,* for which the plant is grown.

Roselle is a tropical annual, the cult. of which in the U.S. is confined to the warmest parts of the southern states. It may be grown in such places very much like eggplant (which see for details of spacing and cultivation). The immature calyx and its bracts are harvested for their much-prized acid, which supplies, in regions where the cranberry cannot be grown, a fair substitute. It is especially used for the making of acid jellies and drinks, but must be harvested before the parts become relatively juiceless and woody.

schizopetalus. A tropical African, medium-sized, smooth shrub. Leaves ovalish, toothed. Flowers hanging, the petals deeply incised, brilliantly orange-red, on long, slender stalks, the showy stamens* protruding. Much cult. in Fla. and often hybridizing with *H. Rosa-sinensis.*

syriacus. Rose-of-Sharon; also called shrubby althaea, and sometimes listed as *Althea.* The only really hardy shrub of the genus and a valuable garden subject because of its late bloom. It is a shrub 5–15 ft. high with ovalish leaves 2–5 in. long, sharply toothed, some 3-lobed and some unlobed, often on the same plant. Flowers solitary, short-stalked, 3–5 in. long, red, purple, violet, or white, broadly bell-shaped and most showy on dark days. Fruit a 5-valved capsule. China. Aug.–Oct. Hardy from zone* 3 southward, and offered in many forms. Some of them have names like coelestis (lavender-blue), totus-albus (white), monstrosus (white with purple eye*), and several others, some double-flowered and some with variegated leaves. A good, double-flowered white form is Jeanne d'Arc, and a single white is Snowstorm.

Trionum. Flower-of-an-hour. A flower-garden annual 18–24 in. high, the seed of which should be sown where wanted. Leaves 3–5-parted or lobed, the middle lobe much the largest. Flowers pale yellow or yellowish-white, with a dark eye.* Fruit a capsule, surrounded by the stiff-hairy, dark-striped calyx.* Central Af. Summer.

HICCAN. See HICKORY.

HICKORY. Valuable timber and nut trees comprising the genus **Carya** (kă′ri-a) of the walnut family, all of its 20 species North American except two in China. They are tall trees with alternate,* compound* leaves, the leaflets arranged feather-fashion with an odd, and usually larger, one at the end. Male and female flowers on the same tree but in different clusters, the male in pendulous catkins, without petals, and with 3–10 stamens. Female flowers also without petals, and consisting of an ovary enclosed by a 4-lobed involucre.* Fruit a fleshy drupe,* becoming hard and woody in age, and separating into 4 woody valves, within which is the usually edible nut (the hickory nut and pecan). The

genus was long called *Hicoria,* a Latinized form of the old Indian name for the trees or their nuts. (*Carya* is from the Greek for the walnut, a related tree.)

For culture *see* below.

C. illinoensis = *C. Pecan.*

C. laciniosa. Shellbark hickory; also called big shagbark. A tree up to 120 ft., its light-gray bark shaggy. Leaflets 7–9, oblongish, 6–9 in. long, tapering at the tip, toothed, and hairy beneath. Nut nearly round, but obscurely 4-angled, pointed at the ends, its shell cracking with difficulty, the kernel sweet. N.Y. to Iowa, Tenn. and Okla.

C. ovata. Shagbark or shellbark hickory. Taller than the last and with more shaggy, gray bark. Leaflets usually 5 (rarely 7), oblongish, 4½–7 in. long, tapering at the tip, the margins decidedly fringed with hairs. Nut elliptic or inverted egg-shaped, slightly flattened and angled, the shell thinner than in *H. laciniosa,* the kernel sweet. Quebec to Minn., Fla., and Tex.

C. Pecan. The pecan. A tree up to 130 ft., its bark deeply furrowed. Leaflets 11–17, short-stalked, oblongish, toothed, 5–7 in. long. Nut oblongish, 1¼–2½ in. long, the shell easily cracking, the kernel sweet. Central U.S. south to Ala., Tex., and Mex. For culture and varieties *see* PECAN.

HICKORY CULTURE

There are many other wild species of hickory than the three listed above, but they have nuts too small, or too bitter, to be worth cult. Hickory cult. is scarcely a garden operation in any case, but much land too rough or hilly for gardens can appropriately be planted to these hardy trees. The pecan, which is less hardy, is considered elsewhere.

These two species of hickory, especially *C. ovata,* have been developed by nut breeders and there are now available various hort. varieties, most of them grafted trees. It is better to purchase such from a reliable dealer than to attempt the somewhat technical job of hybridizing these wind-pollinated trees and the subsequent isolation of desirable varieties by vegetative reproduction. It is useless to plant nuts of desirable hickories because they hardly ever come true from seed, so great is the tendency to natural hybridization.

VARIETIES. Most nut breeders have attempted to make the shell easier to crack or thin enough to crack in the fingers, and to increase the amount and flavor of the kernel. At present only a few of these improved varieties are available, because of the time needed to develop a stock of them. A few of the best which may be had are:

Hales. Originated in N.J. Shell thin and reasonably easy to crack. Kernel plump, deeply corrugated, sweet.

Kentucky. Originated in Ky. Medium-sized nut, the shell moderately easy to crack. Flesh plump, angled, rich, and sweet.

Kirtland. More or less angular, rather large nut, the shell thin and moderately easy to crack. Kernel plump and rich.

---

* Special articles on the subjects indicated by an asterisk (*) will be found at the words so marked.

Vest. Originated in Va. A quadrangular nut of medium or small size, the shell thinner than in most hickories. Kernel deeply corrugated.

Weiper. Originated in Pa., probably from *C. laciniosa*. Nut elongated, the shell thick but reasonably easy to crack. Kernel plump and of good flavor.

Over 20 other varieties are known and improvements are to be expected yearly, so that it is advisable to get the latest catalogues of the specialists in nut culture before deciding upon which variety to choose. It naturally takes many years to correct an initial error. Hybrids between the hickory and pecan, known as hiccans, mature the nuts earlier than the pecan. Two varieties of hiccan are Burlington and Bixby which produce the largest nuts of any of the hybrids, but are not heavy bearers.

Hickory trees have a deep taproot and care must be taken to see that they are planted with no injury to it. They do not transplant easily in any case. Put no manure in the hole which should be filled very carefully only with good topsoil. Never allow the roots to become dry, even for a few moments, or failure is pretty certain. Heel-in* or cover with wet bagging all trees waiting to be planted.

After planting, cut back the growth at least one third, and tie to a stout stake to prevent the wind from loosening the tree's hold on the soil. A swaying tree will probably die, at least the first year or two after planting. Water the young trees if there is a dry spell, but as they become established, this is no longer necessary.

If the trees are in a place where it can be done, it is advisable to cultivate the soil for the first year or two. Also, unlike some nut trees, hickories respond to an occasional mulch of well-rotted manure, especially when young, and during the summer. Remove or dig in the mulch before the winter, as it may harbor rodents who gnaw the bark.

INSECT PESTS. Nut weevils similar to those attacking chestnut can be controlled by sprays as at CHESTNUT. Fall webworm damages foliage (*see* PERSIMMON) as do walnut caterpillars (*see* WALNUT). Control a twig girdler by destroying twigs as they fall. *See* INSECT PESTS for control of several species of borers. Many species of insects produce galls on leaves. These galls, while deforming, do not ordinarily harm the tree.

DISEASES. Leafspot* causes brown areas up to one inch in diameter. It is controlled with pesticide #11 (*see* SPRAYS AND DUSTS) applied when buds first open and repeated twice at 10- to 12-day intervals. A witches'-broom* may occasionally appear and should be cut from the tree.

HICKORY FAMILY = Juglandaceae.

HICKORY PINE = *Pinus aristata*. See PINE.

HICORIA = *Carya*. See HICKORY.

HIERACIUM (hy-er-ray'see-um). A very large genus of showy herbs of the family Compositae, much grown abroad for their handsome flowers but here known only as extremely troublesome weeds, usually called hawkweed. Two of the worst are the orange hawkweed (*H. aurantiacum*) and the mouse-ear hawkweed (*H. Pilosella*). For both *see* the list at WEEDS.

HIEROCHLOË (hy-er-rock'lō-e). A genus of grasses of little hort. interest except for the sweet-scented **H. odorata**, the vanilla grass, sometimes called holy grass or Seneca grass. It is a perennial grass with flat leaves and a terminal panicle* which may be 8–15 in. high and brownish. It is easily grown from division of its creeping rootstocks. While of little decorative value, it is hallowed in the memory of many from being strewn on the pavement of countless church doors on saints' days. It is wild throughout northern Eu., and in N.A. along the New England coast and about the Great Lakes. (*Hierochloë* is from the Greek for sacred and grass, in allusion to its chief use.)

hierochuntica (hy-er-ro-chun'ti-ka). Hierochuntica was the old name of Jericho, hence the specific name *hierochuntica* for the Rose-of-Jericho or resurrection plant. See ANASTATICA.

HIGH-BUSH BLUEBERRY = *Vaccinium corymbosum*. For culture *see* BLUEBERRY.

HIGH-BUSH HUCKLEBERRY = *Gaylussacia baccata*. See HUCKLEBERRY.

HIGH CRANBERRY = *Viburnum trilobum*.

HILL CLEMATIS = *Clematis ligusticifolia*.

HILL GOOSEBERRY = *Rhodomyrtus tomentosa*.

HILLOCK-TREE = *Melaleuca hypericifolia*.

HILLS-OF-SNOW = *Hydrangea aborescens grandiflora*.

HILUM. The scar or mark (actually the navel) on a seed, showing its former point of attachment to the walls or partitions of the ovary.

himalaica, -us, -um (him-a-lay'i-ka). From the Himalayas.

HIMALAYA-BERRY = *Rubus procerus*.

HIMALAYAN FLEABANE = *Erigeron multiradiatus*.

HIMALAYAN MUSK ROSE = *Rosa brunoni*.

HIMALAYAN PINE = *Pinus griffithi*. See PINE.

HINOKI CYPRESS = *Chamaecyparis obtusa*.

HIP. *See* ROSE HIP.

HIPPEASTRUM (hipp-e-ăs'trum). Amaryllis-like, tropical American, bulbous herbs, family Amaryllidaceae, comprising 70 or more species and many garden hybrids, the hort. sorts commonly called amaryllis and grown like them. They differ from the true *Amaryllis* chiefly in technical characters, but also in having a hollow stalk to the flower cluster. Leaves basal and, in the hort. kinds,

* Special articles on the subjects indicated by an asterisk (*) will be found at the words so marked.

strap-shaped. Flowers large, showy, lily-like, prevailingly red or sometimes white-lined, generally funnel-shaped and borne in a large, terminal umbel.* Fruit a globe-shaped capsule.* Some of the plants are sometimes known under the name *Habranthus* (which see). (*Hippeastrum* is from the Greek for horse and star, but of no known application here.)

The garden hippeastrums have been so much hybridized that it is doubtful if any of them are now referable to any particular wild species. Those below appear to be, however, the leading ones involved. For culture *see* AMARYLLIS.

equestre = *Hippeastrum puniceum.*

johnsoni. An old hybrid plant produced by a London watchmaker named Johnson. It may not now be in cult. in America, but is certainly the origin of many cult. varieties.

puniceum. One of the commonest species in cult. Bulb globe-shaped, the strap-shaped leaves produced from it after the plant has bloomed. Flowers few in the cluster, 4–5 in. long, red or salmon color, the throat greenish. Stamens* not protruding. Mex. and the W.I. to S.A. Often sold as *H. equestre.*

reginae. An old garden plant, the bulb globe-shaped and 3 in. in diameter. From it, after the plant blooms, develop the strap-shaped leaves which are 2 ft. long and about 1¾ in. wide. Flowers only 2–4 in a cluster at the end of a 2-ft. stalk. Corolla 4–5 in. long, bright red, but white-blotched in the throat. Mex. to Brazil.

vittatum. Much resembling the last, but the leaves fewer and the stalk of the flower cluster nearly 3 ft. long. Corolla 4–5 in. long, red, the short tube greenish. Brazil. One of the best known in cult. and with several hort. varieties, mostly minor variations in color. Sometimes offered as *Amaryllis vittata.*

HIPPOCASTANACEAE (hip-poe-cass-ta-nay'see-ee). The horse-chestnut or buckeye family (sometimes, but not here, called Aesculaceae), comprises only three genera. One of them is Chinese, and not a garden plant. Another, *Aesculus,* comprises the well-known horse-chestnut and the buckeyes. They are very ornamental trees or shrubs with compound* leaves, showy flowers in profuse clusters, and large seeds (horse-chestnuts) in a more or less prickly husk. *See* HORSE-CHESTNUT.

Hippocastanum (hip-po-kas'ta-num). The Latin name of the horse-chestnut.

HIPPOCREPIS (hip-po-creep'is). A small genus of shrubs or herbs of the pea family with compound leaves, the leaflets without marginal teeth. Flowers pea-like, yellow, in drooping clusters (racemes* or umbels*), followed by flat, curved pods with easily separable, horseshoe-shaped joints. Of the dozen species only **H. comosa** is of much hort. interest. It is a perennial, 12–20 in. high. Leaves with 3–5 pairs of leaflets. Flowers in a close cluster (umbel*) which is long-stalked. Southern Eu. A rock garden plant, reputed to do best in alkaline soil. (*Hippo-*

crepis is from the Greek for horse and shoe, in allusion to the shape of the pod segments.)

HIPPOPHAE (hip-pof'fay-ee). Two Eurasian spiny shrubs or small trees of the family Elaeagnaceae, one of them **H. rhamnoides,** the sea buckthorn, cult. for its foliage and the orange-yellow fruits. It is a shrub, sometimes tree-like, 10–25 ft. high. Leaves alternate,* lance-shaped or narrower, 1–3 in. long, and more or less silvery in youth, later greenish on the upper surface. Flowers yellowish, inconspicuous, the male and female on different plants, both without petals. Fruit fleshy, but somewhat hard, not quite egg-shaped, about ¼ in. long, orange-yellow and persistent for most of the winter. The shrub is tolerant of most kinds of soil, and is thoroughly hardy up to the limits of zone* 2. To ensure fruit, which is one of its most attractive features, it is necessary to plant both male and female kinds in close proximity. Propagated by seeds, cuttings, or layers. (*Hippophae* is an old Greek name for some spiny bush, but not certainly this one.)

hippophaeoides (hip-pof-eye-oy'deez). Like a sea buckthorn (*Hippophae*).

hircina, -us, -um (hir-sy'na). Goat-like, or smelling like one.

hirsuta, -us, -um (hur-sue'ta). Hirsute; *i.e.,* more or less covered with stiff, coarse hairs.

hirsutula, -us, -um (hur-su'tew-la). Somewhat stiffly hairy.

hirta, -us, -um (hur'ta). Hairy.

hispanica, -us, -um (his-pan'i-ka). From Spain.

hispida, -us, -um (hiss'pi-da). Hispid; *i.e.,* with bristly hairs.

hispidula, -us, -um (hiss-pid'you-la). Somewhat bristly.

HOARHOUND = Horehound.

HOARY. Covered with ashy-gray or whitish hairs.

HOBBLEBUSH = *Viburnum alnifolium.*

HOEING. One of the oldest skills in gardening, in fundamentals changing very little from the half-savage irritation of the soil to our modern tools for the same purpose. Some very skillful modern gardeners say that with a spade and a hoe they have the only two really essential tools, and if they could have only one, it is the hoe they would keep.

The reason is clear. With the ordinary hoe many things can be done. Its sharp blade is set at an angle at the end of a long handle, and with the corner of it one can dig small holes* or make a drill,* or dig deeper ones for planting potatoes. Its greatest use is for chopping down weeds or for any operation like hilling up corn or drawing the soil up around potatoes.

In cultivating with a hoe, and in fact with

---

* Special articles on the subjects indicated by an asterisk (*) will be found at the words so marked.

Common hoe, often called a draw hoe

all operations of this essential tool, the action is a steady chopping *toward* one, hence its other name of draw hoe. Unless it is turned upside down, it is next to impossible to use a hoe for shoving soil *away* from the operator. For this reason, and for the more important one that a different sort of hoe would be better for cultivating, the D or Dutch hoe, sometimes called the English scuffle hoe, was developed.

The English scuffle hoe, often called a
D or Dutch hoe

This tool allows the operator to cultivate by pushing the blade both away from and toward him. It is so set that the blade, by a series of short strokes, slides just beneath the surface, cutting off all weeds and leaving the soil in a good state of tilth.* The D hoe will not do as many things as an ordinary hoe, but it is one of the best all-round hand tools for cultivating. With one can always see what one is doing, and it will reach into a broad bed without disturbing the plants.

Whichever sort of hoe is used, an important point is not to walk over the hoed land. Begin at the end of a row and walk over the un-hoed land. For the reasons for this, and the general theory of cultivating with a hoe or any other tool, *see* CULTIVATION.

For large gardens hoeing is often too ex-

pensive an operation to be considered. To meet this condition there are various types of wheel hoes or machine cultivators, to be seen at all supply houses.

HOFFMANNIA (hoff-man'ee-a). Tropical American foliage plants of the family Rubiaceae, a few of the 45 species grown in the greenhouse for their very showy leaves. They are herbs or under-shrubs with opposite* or whorled* leaves, which are usually more or less colored, especially along the veins. Flowers small, the corolla tubular, with mostly 4, blunt or narrow, lobes. Stamens 4. Fruit a many-seeded, oblongish berry. (Named for Georg Franz Hoffman, German botanist.)

These handsome foliage plants need a warm, moist greenhouse and should be grown in potting mixture* 3. Unless well grown, their leaves will not develop the fine color which is their chief attraction. Easily propagated by cuttings over bottom-heat.*

discolor. Hairy, not over 6 in. high, but generally drooping over the edge of the pot, the stems purplish. Leaves green above, purple or greenish-purple beneath, short-stalked, nearly 5 in. long. Flowers red and red-stalked, growing in long-stalked, curving clusters (racemes*). Mex.

ghiesbreghti. A smooth under-shrub, not over 4 ft. high, the stems 4-angled. Leaves oblongish, nearly 12 in. long, the base decurrent,* green above and very veiny, purplish-red beneath. Flowers yellow, but red-spotted, the short clusters crowded in the leaf axils.* Mex. A hort. variety has handsomely mottled leaves.

refulgens. A Central American under-shrub, the stems purplish. Leaves roundish or ovalish, green above, purplish-red beneath. Flowers reddish, in stalkless clusters in the leaf axils.* A good foliage plant.

HOG CABBAGE PALM = *Pseudophoenix sargenti.*

HOG PLUM = *Spondias Mombin.*

HOHERIA (hoe-heer'i-a). New Zealand shrubs or trees of the mallow family, perhaps consisting of only one variable species, but cult. in Calif. under the three names below and possibly distinct. They have alternate,* stalked, toothed leaves, often differing in age and youth, and numerous small, white flowers in small clusters in the leaf axils.* Petals 5, notched at the tip, oblique. Stamens* 20. Fruit of separate segments, each of which is winged. (*Hoheria* is a Latinized version of the N.Z. native name for these trees, meaning to bind a captive, in allusion to the use of the bark in making rope.) They are called ribbonwood and lacebark in N.Z.

The hoherias are grown only in Calif. in the U.S., and mostly in the San Francisco Bay region. They prefer well-drained but moist soil and partial shade. Propagated by hardwood cuttings or by seeds.

angustifolia. A tree up to 25 ft. Leaves oblongish or narrower, 1–2 in. long, the margins spiny-toothed. Flowers about ½ in. wide.

populnea. A little shorter than the last, the leaves ovalish, 3–5 in. long and doubly

---

* Special articles on the subjects indicated by an asterisk (*) will be found at the words so marked.

toothed. Flowers nearly 1 in. wide, in very profuse clusters, mostly on old wood. Aug.

sexstylosa. Usually about 25 ft. high, the leaves lance-shaped, 3–5 in. long, sharply toothed. Flowers about ¾ in. wide.

HOLCUS = *Sorghum.*

HOLLAND ELM = *Ulmus hollandica. See* ELM.

hollandica, -us, -um (hol-lan'di-ka). From Holland.

HOLLY. Extremely valuable, mostly evergreen trees and shrubs comprising the genus **Ilex** (eye'lecks) of the family Aquifoliaceae. Of perhaps 400 species, widely scattered in temperate and tropical regions, a few are among the most valuable of our broad-leaved evergreens, and a few others which drop their leaves are grown for their showy fruits. They have alternate,* sometimes spiny-toothed leaves, and inconspicuous white or greenish flowers usually in small clusters in the leaf axils.* Sepals 3–6, and petals 4–5, both small. Fruit berry-like, often showy, actually a drupe* with 2–5 stones. (*Ilex* is derived from the old Latin name of the holm oak, *Quercus Ilex.*) As the sexes of most hollies are borne on separate plants, it is essential to have male and female plants in reasonable proximity in order to ensure a crop of berries.

For the sea holly *see* ERYNGIUM. For the mountain holly *see* NEMOPANTHUS. For the California holly *see* TOYON.

Culturally the hollies are divided between the evergreen and deciduous* species. The latter, which drop their leaves, are of simple culture in any good garden soil and present no difficulties in transplanting, although not all of them are hardy everywhere (*see* the notes at each species).

The evergreen hollies should be carefully packed with a ball and burlap, and in planting it is better to knock off most of their leaves, and prune severely.

The evergreen kinds are far more valuable and need greater care. Purchased plants will come with a ball of soil wrapped in bagging. Keep it moist until the specimen is planted. Most of the evergreen kinds are slow-growing and difficult to get established. Water them freely the first year or so after planting. If old plants are to be moved, most of their leaves should be knocked off before they are dug, and pruned freely after planting. A slow method of propagation is by seeds, but they must be stratified and even then usually take 2–5 years to germinate. A quicker method for the evergreen sorts is to make cuttings of young ripe wood and plant them in sand in the cool greenhouse. They should root in a few weeks, but are slow to get really started, unless the base of the cutting is dipped in a plant hormone which must be used in concentrations stated on the container. There are several root-promoting hormones on the market. In spite of these difficulties, the evergreen hollies are very popular garden subjects, but expensive, as befits their worth and slow growth.

The evergreen species of holly, especially *I. Aquifolium, I. opaca* and *I. crenata,* are splendid for hedges and screens, and any of them can be grown as dwarfs. (*See* DWARFING.) For those to be used as hedges it is essential to begin pruning quite early, to force those that would normally be trees to put out extra stems in order to get a well-furnished thick hedge. For the best account of the hollies see *Handbook of Hollies,* published by the American Horticultural Society in January 1957, under the direction of H. W. Dengler, with several contributors, among them Dr. Shiuying Hu, of the Arnold Arboretum.

I. altaclarensis. A hybrid holly derived from crossing the English holly with *I. Perado* (a non-hort. species). It resembles the English holly but the leaves are flatter at the margin which has more numerous and more regular teeth. Cult. as for *I. Aquifolium.*

I. Aquifolium. English holly. An evergreen tree up to 40 ft. high, usually much less as cult. in America. Leaves short-stalked, dark lustrous-green above, ovalish or oblong, 1½–2½ in. long, the margin wavy and with large, triangular, spiny teeth, sometimes lacking in age. Fruit nearly round, pea-sized, bright red, usually in clusters. Eurasia and northern Af. Precariously hardy in zone* 4, generally hardy southward, but it does not like hot, dry summers. It grows best in the U.S. in Ore. and Wash. Use soil of pH 4–5. Long cult. and found in over 100 hort. varieties. Two of the best are *var.* **albo-marginata,** with silvery-margined leaves, and *var.* **aureo-regina,** with yellow-margined, gray-mottled leaves. To ensure getting plants that will certainly produce fruit it is best to select a named form like the Van Tol or Dutch holly as it is called. It is a grafted variety and always fruits if given proper care.

I. aquiperneyi. A reputed hybrid between *I. Aquifolium* and *I. perneyi,* with leaves like the latter but nearly twice the size, originating from Stewartstown, Pa., by J. B. Gable. Cult. as for *I. Aquifolium.*

I. bullata = A form of *Ilex crenata convexa* with puckered leaves.

---

* Special articles on the subjects indicated by an asterisk (*) will be found at the words so marked.

I. burfordi = *Ilex cornuta burfordi.*

I. Cassine. Dahoon; called also, yaupon, but this is more correctly applied to the last species. An evergreen shrub or small tree up to 25 ft. Leaves oblongish, 2–3 in. long, shallowly toothed or without them. Fruit globe-shaped, red or yellowish, borne on the current season's twigs. N. Car. to Fla. and La. Hardy from zone* 6 southward.

I. convexa = *Ilex crenata convexa.*

I. cornuta. A handsome, Chinese relative of the English holly, the oblongish, evergreen, angular, lustrous leaves with 3 spines at the tip and one or two along the sides. Fruit globe-shaped, red, stalked, nearly ½ in. in diameter. Hardy from zone* 4 southward. The *var.* **burfordi** has bright green, wedge-shaped leaves that have only a few spines at the tip of the leaf. There are several other hort. forms of *I. cornuta,* which tolerates heat and dryness, among them *var.* **rotunda** a dwarf, male form, recently become available.

I. crenata. Japanese holly. An extremely handsome evergreen shrub with box-like habit and foliage. Leaves generally oblong, but broadest toward the tip, 1–2½ in. long, more or less wedge-shaped at the base, dark green and very finely toothed. Fruit black. Jap. Hardy from zone* 4 southward, sometimes in zone* 3 with protection. The *var.* **latifolia** has elliptic or oblongish leaves and is perhaps the most common form in cult.; *var.* **microphylla** has smaller leaves and is hardier than the type; *var.* **fortunei** is a trade name for typical *I. crenata; var.* **convexa** has the leaves convex above but concave beneath. A form of this, offered as *I. bullata,* has more puckered leaves.

I. decidua. Possum haw. A deciduous shrub, 10–20 ft. high, rarely a tree, its leaves ovalish, 1½–4 in. long, wedge-shaped at the base, blunt at the tip, with many small, rounded teeth, generally hairy on the upper surface. Fruit red (or orange in youth), about ½ in. in diameter. Southeastern U.S. May. Hardy from zone* 5 southward.

I. glabra. Inkberry; also called winterberry and bearbush. Evergreen southward but only half evergreen northward and then turning a rusty green in the late fall. Usually not over 6 ft. high, mostly 3–4 ft. Leaves oblongish, but broadest toward the tip, wedge-shaped at the base, 1–2½ in. long. Fruit pea-sized, stalked, black. Typically a bog shrub, native in eastern N.A., but growing in any reasonably good, sandy loam in the garden. Hardy from zone* 3 southward. A mulch of leaves is better than trying to cultivate the soil for this shrub, which is a good bee plant.

I. laevigata. Smooth winterberry; called also, hoopwood. Not evergreen, and planted chiefly for its showy, orange-red fruits. It grows 5–8 ft. high, and has ovalish or narrower leaves 1½–2¾ in. long which are more or less wedge-shaped at the base and very finely toothed. Me. to Pa. and Ga. Hardy from zone* 3 southward. Often mistaken for *I. verticillata,* but a more desirable plant than the latter.

I. montana. A deciduous shrub or small tree 10–35 ft. high, the leaves ovalish or narrower, 3–7 in. long, with a long-tapering tip, and sharply but finely toothed on the margin. Fruit red, about ⅜ in. in diameter. Eastern U.S., mostly in the highlands. May–June. Hardy from zone* 3 southward.

I. monticola = *Ilex montana.*

I. opaca. American holly; called also, white holly. The New World cult. representative of the English holly, but not such a handsome plant. It is a spreading tree, up to 40 ft. Leaves evergreen, elliptic, 1¾–3 in. long, dull green above, yellowish-green beneath, the marginal teeth remote and spiny. Fruit usually solitary, pea-sized, red. Mass. to Fla. west to Mo. and Tex. Hardy from zone* 4 southward. It grows naturally in acid soils (pH 4–5; *see* ACID AND ALKALI SOILS) and is difficult to transplant. Its chief garden merit is that it is hardier than the much finer English holly. And it is now found in over 70 hort. named forms.

I. pendunculosa. An evergreen shrub or small tree, 8–20 ft. high, the ovalish or elliptic leaves 1½–3 in. long, without marginal teeth, shining green above. Fruit nearly round, pea-size, scarlet, solitary or in sparse hanging clusters, rather persistent through Nov. Jap. Hardy from zone* 4 southward. Foliage bronzy in winter.

I. perneyi. An evergreen holly, usually a shrub, rarely a small tree up to 25 ft. Leaves crowded and numerous, almost quadrangular, ¾–1½ in. long, with 1–3 spines on each side and a larger terminal one. Fruit clustered, red, about ½ in. in diameter. China. May. Hardy from zone* 4 southward.

I. rotunda. A shrub or small tree (as cult.), 8–20 ft. high, the evergreen leaves broadly elliptic, 2–3 in. long, without marginal teeth. Fruit football-shaped, about ¼ in. long, red, borne in dense clusters (umbels*) in the axils of the leaves. Eastern As. Hardy from zone* 6, and in protected sites in zone* 5 southward.

I. serrata. A Japanese relative of *Ilex verticillata,* but shorter and smaller in all its parts. Fruit red, pea-size. Jap. May. Hardy from zone* 4 southward.

I. verticillata. Black alder; also called winterberry and dogberry. Not evergreen, and usually a spreading shrub up to 8 ft. high, grown mostly for its bright red fruits, which are more profuse than in any other holly and persist over most of the early winter. Leaves ovalish or narrower, wedge-shaped at the base, 1½–2¾ in. long, very finely toothed. Eastern N.A. Hardy from zone* 3 southward.

I. vomitoria. The true yaupon; sometimes called cassena, and occasionally mistaken for *I. Cassine* (the dahoon). It is an evergreen tree 15–25 ft. high, with short-stalked, elliptic or oblongish leaves about 1½ in. long, the margins wavy-toothed. Fruit scarlet, borne on the old wood. Va. to Fla. and Tex. Hardy from zone* 6 southward. The parched leaves were used by the Indians in making a ceremonial tea, called the "black drink" by English colonists.

INSECT PESTS. Leaf miners can be controlled by lindane or malathion sprays applied as new leaves appear and repeated twice at 10-day intervals. Scales can be controlled by 2% dormant oil emulsion sprays. Red mites can be controlled by malathion or ovex (*see* SPRAYS AND DUSTS).

DISEASES. Three "troubles" with American holly probably cause more concern than all diseases combined. A condition we have come to call "spine spot" results from spines of leaves puncturing the blades of the adjacent leaves. The resultant spots are circular or elliptical with gray or tan center and a purple halo. A second trouble is purple blotch which is thought to be associated with weather conditions and perhaps nutrient deficiencies in the soil. The purple blotches are irregular in shape and may appear on upper, lower, or both surfaces of the leaf. The third trouble is scald.*

* Special articles on the subjects indicated by an asterisk (*) will be found at the words so marked.

This is a white or tan dead area with definite margins appearing on the leaves. It may result from intense sunlight while water or ice is present on the leaves.

In some sections of the country a leafspot* or tar spot causes black, tar-like areas on the leaf. The disease is not usually serious enough to warrant an annual preventive spray program. In some southeastern states a spray program with dichlone (*see* FUNGICIDES) is suggested.

Lower inside branches on rapidly growing plants will occasionally die. Although a fungus is associated with it, the trouble is considered to be primarily a result of winter injury.

HOLLY FAMILY = Aquifoliaceae.

HOLLY FERN = *Cyrtomium falcatum.*

HOLLYHOCK. Old and popular flower garden plants belonging to the genus **Althaea** (al-thee′a) of the mallow family, and including, besides the garden hollyhock, the true marsh mallow and the Antwerp hollyhock. The genus comprises only about 15 species of tall, leafy-stemmed annual, biennial, or perennial herbs, all from the temperate regions of the Old World. They have usually hairy, often felty, alternate* leaves and a terminal, spire-like cluster (mostly racemes*) of very showy flowers, the 5 petals usually notched, originally red or white, but variously colored in the hort. forms. Below the calyx* is a series of 6–9 bracts.* Fruit a collection of 1-seeded carpels, which are at first united in a circle, but ultimately separate from it and from each other. (*Althaea* is the Greek name of the marsh mallow.)

For culture *see* below.

A. ficifolia. Antwerp hollyock. A biennial* herb related to the common hollyhock, but the leaves deeply divided into 7 narrow, irregularly toothed segments. Flowers showy, lemon-yellow or orange, in terminal spikes, double or single. Eu. Not much grown in the U.S., and it may be only a form or variety of the common hollyhock.

A. officinalis. Marsh mallow; also called sweatweed. A perennial* herb 3–4 ft. high, more or less downy. Leaves sometimes unlobed but usually 3-lobed, generally ovalish or heart-shaped, the middle lobe much larger than the other 2. Flowers solitary or a few together in the leaf axils,* not over 1 in. wide, pinkish. Eu., and naturalized in the salt marshes of the eastern U.S. Little grown here, but its roots yield a mucilage in Eu.

A. rosea. The common garden hollyhock. Originally a tall, Chinese perennial herb, but grown mostly as a biennial and even as an annual (*see* below). It is erect, 5–9 ft. high, the stem leafy, spire-like and hairy. Leaves generally roundish, long-stalked, rough, wavy-angled on the margin or shallowly 5–7-lobed. Flowers essentially stalkless, in long, stiff, but wand-like, terminal clusters, typically single, and red or white, but the hort. forms of many colors and often double. It flowers from the bottom upward. China.

A common misspelling for *Althaea* is *Althea*, and the latter is sometimes used in catalogues both for the hollyhock and for the Rose-of-Sharon. *See* HIBISCUS SYRIACUS.

HOLLYHOCK CULTURE

The hollyhock had been cult. in China for perhaps a thousand years before it was introduced into England in 1573. Typically a short-lived perennial, it is now universally grown as a biennial or even as an annual.

Records show that soon after the colonists reached America they cultivated hollyhocks in their simple Colonial gardens, mostly red, pink, or white varieties with single flowers. Then, as now, it gave a note of aspiring and gay color to many otherwise bare places, especially fitting under windows, along picket fences, or against the walls of a house. It is better not to group hollyhocks in the general border. They are too striking and, if their lower leaves are too much shaded by surrounding vegetation, they do not thrive so well as out in the open sunlight.

CULTURE. Nearly any ordinary garden soil will suit hollyhocks. If they are to be treated as biennials, sow the seed in the frame or in flats outdoors in July or Aug. for plants to bloom next year. Prick out the seedlings and grow them along until frost time, when they should be lightly mulched and left in the frame or wherever they are growing, without any heat.

The following spring the seedlings should be moved to their permanent location. In planting, see that their naturally downward-pointing roots are left pointing downward; otherwise, they are much liable to frost heaving (*see* HEAVING) the following winter. Also plant them a little deeper than they were in the seed bed. Both these precautions should be taken to prevent their roots from becoming exposed, which they resent more than most plants, and to anchor properly such a tall, stately plant.

Many of the newer strains of hollyhocks may be treated as tender annuals. Sow the seed in Feb.–Mar. in the greenhouse or on

One of the best places for a planting of hollyhocks.

---

* Special articles on the subjects indicated by an asterisk (*) will be found at the words so marked.

a window ledge, and when outdoor planting time arrives, the seedlings can be planted in their permanent place. Such plants will bloom the first season, but later than old ones and later than those started as biennials the season before.

VARIETIES. Because hollyhocks have been naturally and artificially much hybridized, the varieties of them are most unstable. This is especially true in the forms sold as annuals, which are also generally shorter than the normal biennial type. Of the annual sorts perhaps only 50% will come true from seed; also some will be single, some double, and some semi-double. A packet of annual hollyhock seed is therefore very much of a gamble.

It is somewhat less so with the sorts to be treated as biennials, although considerable instability is likely even in these. Named varieties are of fleeting permanence, but the following colors can usually be relied upon: crimson, pink, rose, salmon-pink, scarlet, yellow, and white. As to form there is the common single-flowered type, double, and semi-double forms, and some with curled or fringed petals. Traditionally, hollyhocks were single-flowered and many prefer them so today, as they seem more fitting to the simplicity of the garden pictures than the newer types. In many catalogues these biennial hollyhocks are still listed as perennials, which, as we have seen, is historically correct, but horticulturally misleading.

INSECT PESTS. Red spider is the most serious pest. Can be controlled by pesticide #14 or #21 sprays or dusts. Leaf-feeding caterpillars are controlled by pesticide #1. (See SPRAYS AND DUSTS.)

DISEASES. The most serious trouble with this plant is rust.* Once the disease attacks a clump it usually persists as long as the plant grows in that spot, because the fungus over-winters on the underground parts. Dig out the clump and start from seed. Pesticide #5 (see SPRAYS AND DUSTS) will control the disease if started on the new plants and repeated three or four times at 10- to 12-day intervals.

HOLM OAK = *Quercus Ilex. See* OAK.

HOLMSKIOLDIA (holm-skee-ol'dee-a). A small genus of tender shrubs of the family Verbenaceae, **H. sanguinea,** of the warmer part of the Himalayas, occasionally grown in the greenhouse under the name of Chinese hat-plant, from its widely spreading calyx.* It is a somewhat sprawling or straggling evergreen shrub or small tree, 10–30 ft. high in the wild, much less in cult. It has oval, opposite* leaves, 2–4 in. long, and short-stalked. Flowers tubular, red, the 5 corolla lobes slightly oblique, thus somewhat irregular, about 1 in. long. Below the corolla is the brick-red, membranous, widely flaring calyx* which is nearly 1 in. wide. Fruit a 4-lobed drupe,* seated within the large calyx.* Outdoor cult. of this beautiful shrub is confined to southern Fla. (Named for Theodor Holmskiold, Danish botanist and

nobleman.) In the South often called coolie's-cap.

HOLODISCUS (ho-lo-dis'kus). Rock spirea. American, mostly hairy shrubs of the rose family, two of the 14 species of secondary garden interest, and grown for ornament. They have alternate,* stalked, usually toothed leaves, sometimes slightly lobed. Flowers white, very small, but numerous in a branching cluster (panicle*). Calyx tube cup-shaped, the sepals 5. Petals scarcely longer than the sepals.* Stamens numerous, a little protruding. Fruit a collection of 5 achenes.* (*Holodiscus* is from the Greek for entire disk, in allusion to the disk of the flower.) Sometimes sold as *Schizonotus*.

Both the species below prefer open, sandy loams and full sunlight. The first is especially handsome in bloom, as its gracefully arching branches are a mass of creamy-white, spirea-like trusses. Propagated by seeds or by layers.

discolor. Cream bush. A spreading shrub 6–12 ft. high, its branches arching. Leaves oval, 2–4 in. long, white-felty beneath. Flower cluster about 9 in. long, very showy. British Columbia to Calif. and Mont. July. Hardy from zone* 4 southward. A variety with the leaves grayish-green beneath, instead of white, is the most likely form to be in cult.

microphyllus. Scarcely over 3 ft. high, the leaves elliptic, about ¾ in. long, more or less wedge-shaped at the base, white-silky beneath. Flower cluster about 3 in. long. Colo., Wyo., and Utah. July. Hardy from zone* 4 southward.

Holostea (ho-los'stee-a). Ancient Greek name for a chickweed-like plant. *See* STELLARIA.

HOLY CLOVER = *Onobrychis viciaefolia.*

HOLY FLAX. *See* SANTOLINA VIRENS.

HOLY GHOST FLOWER = *Peristeria elata.*

HOLY GRASS = *Hierochloë odorata.*

HOLY THISTLE = *Silybum Marianum.*

HOMALOCEPHALA (ho-mal-o-seff'a-la). A single species of cactus from Tex., N. Mex., and Mex., known there as manca caballo and to science as **H. texensis.** It is allied to *Echinocactus* and has the shape of a flattened orange, so that while it is only about 6 in. high, its width is nearly 12 in. The plant body has 13–27 ribs, and on them at intervals are spine clusters. There is one central and longer, erect spine and 6–7 shorter ones that divaricate. Flowers about 2 in. long, orange or scarlet below, but pink or even white at the tip, bell-shaped. Fruit fleshy, irregularly bursting. The plant is suited only to outdoor desert gardens in its own region or to greenhouse culture northward. *See* CACTI. (*Homalocephala* is from the Greek for like or similar and head, in allusion to the shape of the plant.)

HOMALOCLADIUM. *See* MUEHLENBECKIA.

HOME GROUNDS. *See* PLANNING THE HOME GROUNDS.

---

* Special articles on the subjects indicated by an asterisk (*) will be found at the words so marked.

HOMERIA (ho-meer'i-a). A small genus of S. Af. bulbous plants of the iris family, with a usually basal solitary leaf and others on the stem. Flowers in a leafy cluster, the flower funnel-shaped or cup-shaped, but its segments free and spreading, the stamens* forming a united tube. Of the 6–8 species only **H. collina** is much cult., its growth and cult. similar to *Ixia* (which see). It is about 18 in. high, has its stem leaves concave, and they are sword-shaped and about 2 ft. long. Flower orange-red and yellow, about 1½ in. long. In Calif. it seeds freely and is apt to be invasive. (*Homeria* was named for Homer.)

homolepis (home-o'lep-is). Having structurally similar parts, as scales, leaves, buds, etc.

HONESTY. Two Eurasian herbs of the mustard family, long cult. for the satiny, parchment-like divisions of their pods, which are favorite winter decorations and are used in dried bouquets. *See* DRIED FLOWERS.

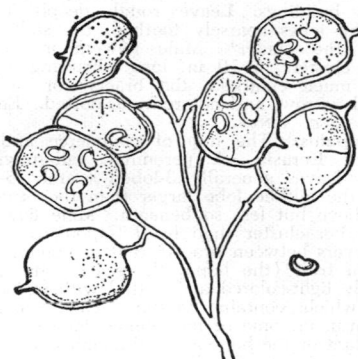

The parchment-like partition of the pods of honesty

They belong to the genus **Lunaria** (loo-nay'-ri-a) of the mustard family. One is a biennial as cult., but it may be an annual; the other is a perennial. Leaves sometimes opposite,* most of them alternate,* more or less ovalish and stalked. Flowers violet-purple or white, in a terminal cluster (raceme*). Petals 4, long-clawed. Fruit a large, flat, roundish pod (silicle*), its valves falling away in age and leaving a satiny, paper-like remnant for which the plants are grown. (Named for the moon which the color and shape of the septum* suggest.)

Of very easy culture in most ordinary sites. The first is treated as a biennial (*see* BIENNIALS), while the second is a perennial that may be increased by division of its roots.

L. annua. Honesty; moonwort, satinpod, or satinflower. An annual, but grown as a biennial, from 18–30 in. high. Leaves coarsely toothed. Flowers fragrant, purplish, nearly 1 in. long. Pod thin and flat, nearly round, about 1½ in. wide. May–June. Much the best for dried

bouquets. Also called silver shilling and St. Peter's-pence.

L. rediviva. Perennial honesty. A perennial, the leaves sharply but finely toothed; otherwise as in the last, but the pods are oblongish, 2–3 in. long and not so showy as in the common honesty. May–June.

HONEY BELL = *Mahernia verticillata*.

HONEY-BLOOM = *Apocynum androsaemifolium*.

HONEY-BUSH. See MELIANTHUS.

HONEYDEW. In midsummer it is common to find the leaves of certain plants, especially Norway maples, lindens, and roses, covered with a sticky exudation that is sometimes so plentiful as to fall off in minute drops. The condition, long thought to be a "bursting of the plant's vessels," is honeydew, so called because the sticky material is sweet, and in Calif. a source of honey for bees.

Honeydew is actually a rather complicated affair. In periods of intense heat and dryness, certain aphids and scale insects secrete this fluid more freely than in cooler and moister periods. The secretion furnishes an eagerly sought food for certain ants and for some fungi. The latter are not parasitic on plants but they form a fiber over the honeydew, which accounts for the fact that many leaves affected with honeydew look sooty. Before this happens, they look varnished, from the completeness of the film. Usually a rain or cool spell will clear up the trouble. Do not park a car under infected trees, as drip from them badly stains enamel. *See* SOOTY MOLD. *See also* the honeydew at MELON.

HONEY-FLOWER = *Melianthus major*.

HONEY LOCUST. Very thorny trees of the pea family, comprising the genus **Gleditsia** (gle-dit'si-a), which has only about a dozen species, chiefly American and Asiatic, but one in tropical Africa. They are usually tall trees, the trunks and branches of which are armed with often-branched thorns. Leaves compound,* the leaflets arranged feather-fashion, with no odd one at the tip, and often irregularly wavy-toothed. Flowers not pea-like, usually greenish, polygamous (*see* HERMAPHRODITE), and mostly in racemes.* Petals 3–5, nearly equal. Fruit a large, usually flattened pod (legume*), sometimes sickle-shaped and twisted. (Named for G. Gleditsch, director of the Berlin Botanical Garden, but the generic name spelled as above by Linnaeus.)

The honey locusts are handsome trees, but do not compare with the common locust (which see) in the beauty of their flowers. The honey locust is not particular as to soils, but propagating it by seeds involves soaking them in hot (not boiling) water for a few hours to help their otherwise slow germination. For another plant sometimes called honey locust *see* MESQUITE. *See also* LOCUST. Those below flower in May–June.

G. aquatica. Water or swamp locust. A tree

* Special articles on the subjects indicated by an asterisk (*) will be found at the words so marked.

up to 60 ft. Leaflets 12–18, oblong, 1–2 in. long, usually notched at the tip. Occasionally there are leaves that are twice-compound. Pod long-stalked, thin, 1½–3 in. long, more or less ovalish and 1-seeded. N. Car. to Fla. and Tex. Hardy from zone* 4 southward.

G. horrida = G. japonica.

G. japonica. A tree up to 75 ft. high, the thorns somewhat flattened and usually branched. Leaflets 16–20, oblongish, about 2 in. long. Pod a foot or more long, twisted and puckered. China and Jap. Hardy from zone* 5 southward. Sometimes sold as G. horrida.

G. triacanthos. The common honey locust of the eastern U.S., often called black locust or three-thorned acacia. In maturity it may reach 130 ft., lower as usually cult., the trunk and branches armed with long, usually branched thorns. Leaflets 20–30, oblongish, 1–1½ in. long. Sometimes there are also twice-compound leaves with smaller leaflets. Pod sickle-shaped, twisted, nearly 18 in. long and persisting for months. Hardy from zone* 3 southward. The var. inermis has few or no thorns and is a more slender tree. Trade names for unarmed honey locusts include Moraine locust and Imperial locust.

HONEY MESQUITE = *Prosopis juliflora glandulosa.* See MESQUITE.

HONEY PLANTS. See BEES AND BEE PLANTS.

HONEYSUCKLE. See LONICERA. The name is sometimes applied also to the swamp honeysuckle. See AZALEA VISCOSA. For the bush honeysuckle *see* DIERVILLA. For other plants occasionally called honeysuckle *see* TECOMARIA, HEDYSARUM, PASSIFLORA LAURIFOLIA.

HONEYSUCKLE CLOVER = *Trifolium pratense.* See CLOVER.

HONEYSUCKLE FAMILY. A large family of mostly shrubs, trees, or vines, such as the honeysuckle, elder, snowball, and *Abelia*, but it also contains, among cult. herbs, the twinflower and *Triosteum*. For the garden genera and their characteristics *see* CAPRIFOLIACEAE.

HONEYWORT. See CERINTHE.

HOOKERA or HOOKERIA CORONARIA = *Brodiaea coronaria.*

HOOP-ASH. *Fraxinus nigra.* See ASH.

HOOP-COOP PLANT = *Lespedeza striata.*

HOOP-PETTICOAT NARCISSUS = *Narcissus Bulbocodium.*

HOOP PINE = *Araucaria cunninghami.*

HOOPWOOD = *Ilex laevigata.* See HOLLY.

HOP. Valuable economic plants, but of secondary garden interest except as quick-growing but not very handsome vines. All belong to the genus **Humulus** (hew'mew-lus) of the family Cannabinaceae, and are rough-stemmed annual or perennial vines, all of the three known species being natives of the north temperate zone. Leaves opposite,* more or less lobed. Male and female flowers green, on separate plants, only the latter producing the hops used in beer-making. Male flowers in catkin-like racemes,* with a 5-parted calyx,* no petals and 5 stamens. Female flowers in pairs, each pair beneath a large bract,* the collection of which at maturity forms the cone-like body of "hop." It is the latter which contains lupulin, valued in beer-making. Fruit a small achene,* which is surrounded by the persistent calyx.* (*Humulus* is a Latin name of uncertain application to these plants.)

The first species, which is useless for the commercial production of hops, is an annual vine grown for a quick covering of unsightly objects. The second is the hop of commerce and is widely grown for brewing. Its culture, however, is an agricultural operation and scarcely a hort. subject for this book. In fact, where the common hop occasionally escapes, it can become a garden nuisance because of its rampant growth. For commercial culture trellises or poles must be provided, as it is a tall-growing vine. Commercial hop-yards are chiefly found in N.Y. and Ore.

H. japonicus. An annual, quick-growing, stem-climbing vine, useful for covering fences or unsightly buildings. Leaves rough, deeply 5–7-lobed, the lobes coarsely toothed, the stalk as long as the blade.* Male flowers in long, hanging clusters, 6–10 in. long. Fruiting cluster not much enlarged, the bracts* or scales long and narrow, and not resinous-dotted. Eastern As. See VINES.

H. Lupulus. The hop of commerce and a native of Eurasia. A perennial, tall-growing vine, its leaves generally 3-lobed (rarely 5–7-lobed), the middle lobe larger than the others, rough above but less so beneath. Male flowers in a smaller cluster than in *H. japonicus*. Female flowers between bracts* that are much enlarged in fruit (the hop), the scales thin and ultimately light-colored and dotted with resinous glands which contain lupulin. The common green form, in some of its commercial varieties, is the plant of the hop-yards, although a yellow-leaved form is occasionally grown for ornament.

An interesting form of this is called *H. americanus*, which differs only in minor characters from *H. Lupulus*. It is supposed to be native in the central or western U.S., and is of interest chiefly because it has entered into some of the commercial varieties grown in Ore., especially the Oregon Cluster hop.

INSECT PESTS. Aphids and mites, the major pests, are controlled by pesticide #21, repeated if necessary. Pesticide #1 will control leaf feeders as they appear. Borers in tips of vines should be clipped out when noticed. (*See* SPRAYS AND DUSTS.)

DISEASES. Various leafspot* diseases may be present on hop, but are not usually serious enough to warrant control measures. Wilt,* as described under chrysanthemum, may cause a gradual decline and final death of hop plants. Do not replant hop where wilt is present.

Two mildew* diseases may be serious enough to require pesticides. Powdery mildew,* causing white spotting and curling of leaves, is controlled with pesticide #9 (*see* SPRAYS AND DUSTS) applied at 10-day intervals. The downy mildew,* which blackens the cones and kills plants, may be controlled with pesticide #11 applied at 7-day intervals.

---

* Special articles on the subjects indicated by an asterisk (*) will be found at the words so marked.

HOP-BUSH. *See* DODONAEA.

HOP-CLOVER. *See* MEDICAGO.

HOP FAMILY = Cannabinaceae.

HOP-HORNBEAM. *See* OSTRYA.

HOP-TREE. *See* PTELEA.

HORDEUM (hor'dee-um). A genus of perhaps 20 species of annual or perennial grasses, widely distributed in temperate regions, the only two cult. species comprising a troublesome weed and the barley, which is only of agricultural interest. They have flat, grass-like leaves and terminal, more or less cylindric flower clusters, mostly dense spikes with conspicuous awns.° The individual spikelets are 1-flowered, three of the spikelets at each node° of the jointed stalk. Due to the infertility of some spikes, the resulting cluster may be 2-rowed or 4-rowed, an important feature in the barley. (*Hordeum* is the classical Latin name of barley.)

jubatum. Squirrel-tail grass. A perennial, seldom grown for ornament and more often a troublesome weed, usually 12–25 in. high, mostly unbranched. Leaves short, not over 5 in. long and about ⅛ in. wide. Spikes about 4 in. long, the awns° slender and nearly 3 in. long. North temperate zone.

vulgare. Barley. An annual cereal grass usually about 30 in. high. Leaves nearly 12 in. long and about ¾ in. wide. Flowering cluster almost 4 in. long, the long, bristly awns° nearly 6 in. long. A cultigen° of Old World origin, and perhaps cult. for over 2000 years.

HOREHOUND; also spelled **HOARHOUND.** The common horehound is one of perhaps 30 species belonging to the genus **Marrubium** (mar-rew'bi-um) of the mint family, cult. for its aromatic oil. *See* HERB GARDENING. The only cult. species is **M. vulgare,** the common horehound, sometimes called the hound's-bane. It is a perennial, hairy, aromatic herb with square stems and opposite,° white-woolly, ovalish leaves ½– 1¾ in. long, narrowed at the base to a short stalk. Flowers in profuse, nearly stalkless clusters in tight whorls° in the leaf axils.° Calyx° tubular, the lobes with sharp teeth. Corolla irregular° and 2-lipped, whitish, and very small. Fruit a collection of small nutlets. The plant is Eurasian, but widely escaped° in N.A. For its culture and uses *see* HERB GARDENING. (*Marrubium* is the old classical name of the horehound and refers to its bitter flavor.)

horizontalis, -e (hor-ri-zon-tay'lis). Horizontal.

HORIZONTAL TRAINING. *See* TRAINED FRUIT TREES.

horizonthalonia, -us, -um (hor-ri-zon-thal-o'ni-a). Horizontal.

HORMINUM (hor-my'num). A single species of perennial herb of the mint family, **H. pyrenaicum,** native in the Pyrenees and the Tyrol and occasionally grown in the rock garden (which see). It has a few basal leaves, but an essentially leafless stem about 10 in. high, the upper leaves reduced to bracts° among the usually 1-sided flower clusters. Corolla purple-violet, somewhat 2-lipped, scarcely protruding from the irregular° calyx. June–July. (*Horminum* is an old Greek name for sage [*Salvia*], which is a related plant.)

HORMONES. Rather recently it was discovered that certain chemicals, in minute quantities, some actually secreted by the plant itself, have a marked effect upon plant growth, especially in promoting root production on cuttings. Much experimental work was done on these responses and the materials responsible for them were at first called *auxins,* or growth-promoting substances.

All of these were chemicals, and the action of these auxins on plants, and the minute amounts of the chemicals involved, was so suggestive of true hormone action that they have become known, perhaps misleadingly, as plant hormones. Actually, they are minute concentrations of indolebutyric acid, indoleacetic acid, ascorbic acid, and over 30 other chemicals tested in the laboratories. Such work is beyond the patience and perhaps the competence of most gardeners who are apt to ask "What does it mean to us?"

It means considerable, for the proper use of these plant hormones will induce cuttings to root with much greater ease and speed than without them. Tests on hundreds of plants normally propagated by cuttings show quite remarkable response to the use of these substances — notably holly, azalea, rhododendron, rose, blueberry, most coniferous evergreens, and many others. The cuttings are dipped in the solutions or powders and then planted in the ordinary way.

It being impossible for the average gardener to prepare these hormone-like substances, it is fortunate that dealers now have ready-made preparations. It is, however, absolutely essential to follow directions on the container, because different plants react very differently to varying concentrations of the chemicals. Used intelligently, especially on notoriously difficult plants such as holly, these substances make propagation much easier than without them.

Some of these preparations are used as a liquid, others as a dusting powder. The necessity to follow instructions on the container most accurately is imperative, as overdoses may be fatal.

There are other hormones which appear to control fruit drop and flower drop and, as in the case of cuttings, the directions on the container must be carefully followed. Other hormones are also used to promote the setting of fruit, and for control of dormancy; in the latter connection *see also* GIBBERELLIC ACID. For the use of the well-known hormone 2,4-D as a weed killer, *see* WEEDS AND WEEDING.

HORNBEAM. Hard-wooded, slow-growing, usually small trees or shrubs belonging to the genus **Carpinus** (kar-py'nus) of the

---

° Special articles on the subjects indicated by an asterisk (°) will be found at the words so marked.

birch family and cult. for ornament, although their flowers are inconspicuous. Of the 25 known Eurasian and North American species only 3 are of any hort. interest. They have smooth, gray, close-fitting bark and are twiggy enough, in the European cult. species, to make it a hedge subject. Leaves alternate,* but more or less 2-ranked, sharply toothed. Male and female flowers in different clusters on the same tree, both without sepals or petals. Male flowers in drooping, scaly catkins which are 2-forked at the tip. Between each scale are 3–13 stamens.* Female catkins terminal. Fruit a ribbed nutlet, beneath and close to which is a flat, 3-lobed bract (it is more or less bladdery in the related hop-hornbeam; *see* OSTRYA). Both species bloom before the leaves unfold. (*Carpinus* is the ancient name of the hornbeam.)

The three below will grow in most ordinary garden soils, but the American species is a tree of the under-canopy of the forest, and hence prefers some shade and protection from wind. They are otherwise hardy but slow-growing trees. Propagated by stratified seeds, or the varieties by grafting on the parent stock.

C. Betulus. European hornbeam. A tree up to 50 ft., but much lower and more bushy as grown here, especially in the young state. Leaves ovalish to oblong, birch-like, 3–4 in. long. Female catkin 2½–4 in. long, the bract* beneath each nutlet nearly 2 in. long, the middle lobe much larger than the other two. Eu. to Persia. Hardy from zone* 3 southward, and suited for hedges if trained for it. *See* HEDGES. The *var.* **columnaris** has a column-like habit and is even more slender than *var.* **fastigiata**, where the branches are upright, forming a narrow, pyramidal tree. There are several other varieties of this long-cult. tree, some of them with deeply lobed leaves and another with the young foliage purplish.

C. caroliniana. American hornbeam; also called blue beech, ironwood, and water beech. Not very different from the last, but usually not tending to have a continuous trunk, the latter soon divaricating into several main branches, never over 30 ft. high, usually less. Leaves ovalish, or oblong, 3–4 in. long. Fruiting catkins 3–4 in. long, the bract* beneath the nutlet only about 1 in. long, the middle lobe of the bract* somewhat larger than the other two. Eastern N.A. but west to Tex. and Minn. Hardy from zone* 3 southward.

C. japonica. A medium-sized tree, rarely over 35 ft. high, with spreading branches, the young shoots hairy. Leaves heart-shaped at the base, long-tapering at the tip, 2–4 in. long, sharply toothed. Fruiting catkin 3–4 in. long, more or less ovoid. Jap. Hardy from zone* 4 southward.

HORNED RAMPION. *See* PHYTEUMA.

HORNED VIOLET = *Viola cornuta.*

HORN POPPY. *See* GLAUCIUM.

HORNWORT; HORNWORT FAMILY. *See* CERATOPHYLLUM.

horrida, -us, -um (hor′ri-da). Horrid; usually horribly spiny.

HORSE BALM = *Collinsonia canadensis.*

HORSE BEAN = *Vicia Faba* and *Parkinsonia aculeata.*

HORSE BRIER = *Smilax rotundifolia.*

HORSE-CHESTNUT. Highly prized street and lawn shrubs and trees belonging to the genus **Aesculus** (es′kew-lus) of the family Hippocastanaceae, some of them called buckeye. Of the 25 known species, which are chiefly North American and Eurasian, several are much cult. and the common horse-chestnut is one of the most widely planted trees in the U.S. They have very scaly and, in the spring, gummy-coated buds, and large, compound,* long-stalked leaves, the 5–9 leaflets arranged finger-fashion (digitate*), and toothed. Flowers very showy in a large, many-flowered cluster (thyrse*), the calyx bell-shaped or tubular and 4–5-toothed. Petals 4–5, narrowed into long claws.* Stamens 5–9. Fruit a large, 3-valved, often spiny capsule containing one or two very large seeds, the horse-chestnuts. (*Aesculus* is the classical Latin name of an oak that bears edible acorns, and applied to the horse-chestnut by Linnaeus, although its seeds are worthless.)

The common horse-chestnut casts the densest shade of almost any cult. tree. It is for this reason a welcome street tree, although many object to the litter of its many flowers and fruits. Also, in warm regions, heat from pavements may induce leaf scorch or even leaf fall. Few trees are so handsome in flower, especially some of the hort. forms. Most of those below are tolerant of all ordinary garden soils. They can be propagated by stratified seeds, and the shrubs also by mound layering, especially *AE. parviflora.* (*See* LAYERING.) Some of the shrubby species are extremely handsome specimen plants for the lawn, or in the shrubbery, but they need plenty of room. In Europe, especially in Paris and London, they are commonly called chestnut, a name here mostly restricted to *Castanea* (*see* CHESTNUT).

AE. carnea. Red horse-chestnut. A hybrid tree (*Hippocastanum × Pavia*), very similar to the common horse-chestnut, but with red flowers, somewhat reddish foliage and the tree stands drought better than the common sort. May. Hardy from zone* 3 southward.

AE. glabra. Ohio buckeye. A tree not over 30 ft. Leaflets 5, elliptic or broadest toward the tip, 3½–5 in. long. Flowers pale yellowish-green, about ¾ in. long, the clusters 4–6 in. long. Fruit inverted egg-shaped, 1–2½ in. long. Pa. to Ala. and west to Neb. May. Hardy from zone* 4 southward, possibly in protected places in zone* 3.

AE. Hippocastanum. Common horse-chestnut. A tree up to 100 ft. high, usually broad and, in youth, dome-shaped. Leaflets 5–7, stalkless, wedge-shaped at the base, broader upward, 5–9 in. long. Flowers white, tinged with red, about ¾ in. wide, the cluster 8–15 in. long, and very showy. Fruit about 2 in. thick, spiny. Balkans. May–June. Hardy from zone* 3 southward. There are hort. varieties or hybrids with variegated leaves, with deeply cut leaflets, with weeping branches, and one with flesh-colored or red flowers. The *var.* **baumanni** has double, and hence sterile, white flowers, and

---

* Special articles on the subjects indicated by an asterisk (*) will be found at the words so marked.

thus is useful in parks where some object to the litter of fruit in the typical horse-chestnut.

AE. octandra. Sweet buckeye. A tree reaching 60 ft. or more. Leaflets 5, elliptic or broadest toward the tip, 4½–7 in. long. Flowers yellow, about 1¼ in. long, the cluster 4½–7 in. long. Fruit nearly globe-shaped, about 2¾ in. thick, without prickles. Pa. to Ga. and Ill. May–June. Hardy from zone* 3 southward.

AE. parviflora. A widely spreading shrub 8–12 ft. high. Leaflets 5–7, practically stalkless, elliptic to oblongish, but a little broader at the tip, 3½–8 in. long. Flowers white, about ½ in. long, the clusters cylindric, nearly a foot long. Stamens* pink, protruding and showy. Fruit inverted egg-shaped, about 1¾ in. high. S. Car. to Ala. and Fla. Aug.–Sept. Hardy from zone* 4 southward. A valuable lawn shrub and the latest of all the *Aesculus* to flower.

AE. Pavia. Red buckeye. A shrub or more rarely a small tree 10–30 ft. high. Leaflets 5, short-stalked, oblongish, 3½–5 in. long. Flowers bright red (both the calyx and petals), the cluster loose, 4–7 in. long. Fruit roundish or egg-shaped. Va. to Fla. and La. June. Hardy from zone* 4 southward.

AE. turbinata. Japanese horse-chestnut. A tree 60–80 ft. high. Leaflets 5–7, more or less wedge-shaped, 9–14 in. long, pale beneath. Flowers about ¾ in. wide, yellowish-white, but with a red sport. Fruit pear-shaped, about 2½ in. thick, warty. Jap. June. Hardy from zone* 3 southward.

HORSE-CHESTNUT FAMILY = Hippocastanaceae.

HORSE GENTIAN. See TRIOSTEUM.

HORSE GINSENG = *Triosteum perfoliatum.*

HORSEHEAL = *Inula Helenium.*

HORSE MINT = *Mentha rotundifolia.* See MINT. See also MONARDA.

HORSE NETTLE = *Solanum carolinense.* See list at WEEDS.

HORSE-RADISH. Perhaps the most pungent-rooted of garden plants, and belonging to the genus **Armoracia** (ar-more-ray'she-a) of the mustard family. There are only a few species of Eurasian perennial herbs in the genus and only the common horse-radish, **A. rusticana,** is cult. It is much grown near big cities, for there is a steady demand for the freshly grated root. The root is parsnip-like, but white, and always branched below. Stems coarse, 18–30 in. high, the leaves long-stalked and dock-like, often notched or more or less cut or fringed, especially the younger ones. Flowers scarcely ½ in. wide, white, borne in a long terminal cluster (raceme*). Fruit a short-oblong pod, often failing to mature and its seeds generally infertile. The plant has been called by many other names, among them *Radicula* and *Roripa Armoracia.* (*Armoracia* is an old Latin name for the horse-radish.)

For centuries horse-radish has been grown to tickle the jaded appetites of the overfed. Because it habitually fails to set viable seed, and the deep perennial root is the part harvested, an unusual method of propagation has been practiced to perpetuate the plant. During spring and summer the plant goes

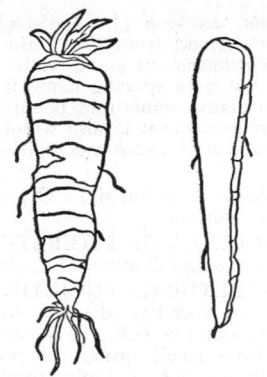

Horse-radish root and a piece cut for propagation

on developing its stout root, the pungent qualities of which are best matured as cool or even cold weather sets in. The roots are then dug and must be marketed very soon, for their pungency is soon lost. Home gardeners can dig a few at a time, as the root is perfectly hardy if left in the ground all winter.

Next year's supply of plants comes from root cuttings. These are made lengthwise, the strips of cut root being 4–6 in. long and about ¼ in. thick. These should immediately be planted, the large end up (to plant them small end up means failure), about 12 in. apart. Such root cuttings will be ready to harvest a year hence. Cultivate and keep down the weeds, as with any other crop.

Horse-radish has no particular soil preferences, except that it does better in rich loam. It will not thrive on light, sandy soils. Also its roots during the summer are inferior or worthless, so that no roots should be dug until Oct. If a summer supply is wanted, store the fall-dug roots in a dark, cool rootcellar.

The plant is a weedy escape* in many parts of eastern N.A. Children are occasionally poisoned by eating the white root of the poke which grows in similarly moist places. The poke plant does not in the least resemble horse-radish, but the roots have a dangerous similarity. See PHYTOLACCA.

INSECT PESTS. Harlequin cabbage bug can be controlled by pesticide #17, as is the flea beetle. Repeat applications. (See SPRAYS AND DUSTS.)

HORSE-RADISH TREE = *Moringa oleifera.*

HORSE SUGAR. See SYMPLOCOS TINCTORIA.

HORSETAIL. See EQUISETUM. See also the list at WEEDS.

HORSETAIL CREEPER = *Porana paniculata.*

HORSETAIL FAMILY. The Equisetaceae. See EQUISETUM.

HORSETAIL TREE = *Casuarina equisetifolia.*

* Special articles on the subjects indicated by an asterisk (*) will be found at the words so marked.

Hortensia, -us, -um (hor-ten'si-a). A species name derived from the Latin *hortus,* a garden. *Hortensia* means literally a woman gardener, but as a specific name it has been applied to many, sometimes beautiful plants. As a common name it is also widely used by gardeners for *Hydrangea macrophylla* (which see).

hortensis, -e (hor-ten'sis). Of, or belonging to, the garden.

HORTICULTURAL LITERATURE. *See* GARDEN BOOKS and GARDEN MAGAZINES.

HORTICULTURAL SOCIETIES. There are scores of societies devoted to horticulture throughout the U.S. They range in importance from small groups of people who meet to discuss garden topics to the Massachusetts Horticultural Society with a large building of its own and the best horticultural library in the country. A few of the leading horticultural societies, all of which issue publications, are:

American Horticultural Society. Washington, D.C.
California State Board of Horticulture. Sacramento, Calif.
Horticultural Society of New York. 157 West 58th Street, New York City.
Illinois State Horticultural Society. Normal, Ill.
Indiana Horticultural Society. Indianapolis, Ind.
Kansas State Horticultural Society. Manhattan, Kan.
Kentucky State Horticultural Society. Lexington, Ky.
Massachusetts Horticultural Society. Boston, Mass.
Minnesota State Horticultural Society. St. Paul, Minn.
New Jersey State Horticultural Society. New Brunswick, N.J.
Ohio State Horticultural Society. Wooster, Ohio.
Pennsylvania Horticultural Society. West Chester, Pa.
Saratoga Horticultural Foundation. Saratoga, Calif.
Wisconsin State Horticultural Society Madison, Wis.

Perhaps more important than any of them is the Royal Horticultural Society, Vincent Square, London, whose *Journal,* published for many years, is the leading horticultural periodical in the world.

HORTICULTURE. The main purpose of this book. It embraces the growing of plants whether for ornament or food, usually, but not always, upon a smaller scale than the production of field crops, which is the chief business of agriculture.

A large-scale, wholly horticultural business like fruit-growing and an agricultural operation like the raising of cotton or corn often make it difficult to draw an inflexible line between horticulture and agriculture. And large-scale market gardening could be quite reasonably assigned to either.

If a true distinction actually exists, it may perhaps be found in the root of the word horticulture, *i.e., hortus,* a garden, and *culture.* Reduced to its simplest elements, horticulture is thus the culture of a garden as distinguished from a farm.

Horticulture, as thus restricted, or as stretched by the usage of time, has well-marked divisions. While they are plain enough, the pedantic have attached special names to them as follows.

Fruit culture (which see) is called Pomology.

Vegetable culture (*see* KITCHEN GARDEN) is called Olericulture.

Flower culture, and by extension, the culture of any plant grown for ornament, is Floriculture, often called Ornamental Horticulture. The latter involves Landscape Architecture.

hortorum (hor-to'rum). Of the garden.

hortulana, -us, -um (hor-tew-lay'na). Belonging to the garden.

HORTULAN PLUM = *Prunus hortulana.*

HOSACKIA (ho-zack'ĭ-a). A genus of over 50 species of perennial herbs or undershrubs of the pea family, mostly from the Pacific slope of the U.S., and of secondary hort. interest. The only cult. species is **H. gracilis,** the witch's-teeth, native from Wash. to Calif. It is a weak-stemmed herb about 12 in. high, with compound* leaves, its 3–7 oblongish leaflets arranged feather-fashion. Flowers pea-like, borne in small umbels* in leaf axils. Corolla about ¾ in. long, rose-pink, but the upper petal yellow. Fruit an oblongish pod (legume*). The plant is also referred to as *Lotus formosissimus.* (Named for David Hosack, New York physician and botanist, who founded the Elgin Botanic Garden, subsequently deeded to Columbia University and now the site of Radio City, New York.)

HOSE. *See* No. 9 at TOOLS AND IMPLEMENTS.

HOSE-IN-HOSE. That condition in a flower wherein the calyx and corolla are

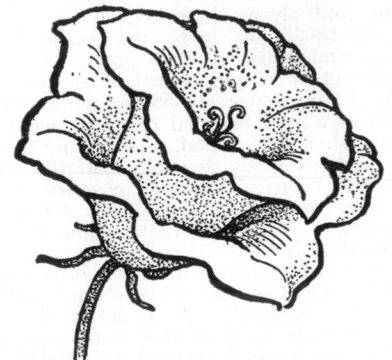

Hose-in-hose, or appearing as if one flower grew in another

---

* Special articles on the subjects indicated by an asterisk (*) will be found at the words so marked.

colored alike, resulting in one flower appearing to grow within another. It is found in some primroses, in certain Kurume azaleas, and in forms of the Canterbury bell.

HOST. A somewhat euphemistic term for the victim of a parasite.* Among the flowering plants, hosts are usually plants infected by some parasitic disease. But the oak is a common host to mistletoe, and there are several other parasitic flowering plants who live off their hosts, notably dodder and the broomrape.

HOSTA. *See* PLANTAIN-LILY.

HOTBED. A heated cold frame. *See* COLD FRAME.

HOTHOUSE. *See* GREENHOUSE.

HOTTENTOT FIG = *Mesembryanthemum edule.*

HOT WATER TREATMENT. Many tubers, roots, corms, etc., may be freed of insect pests by soaking in hot water for a specified time before planting. It is essential, however, that the water be kept at the required temperature (usually 110–120 degrees) throughout the time of soaking (anywhere from 5 min. to one hour). Wherever necessary this hot water treatment is mentioned at the plant involved, and time and temperature directions (with a good thermometer) should be carefully followed to prevent injury to the dormant tubers.

HOUND'S-BANE = *Marrubium vulgare.* *See* HOREHOUND.

HOUND'S-TONGUE. *See* CYNOGLOSSUM.

HOUSELEEK. Attractive and interesting succulent plants of the Old World belonging to the genus **Sempervivum** (sem-per-vee'vum) of the family Crassulaceae, many of them grown in the rock garden, in succulent collections in the greenhouse, and a few shrubby, tender species in Calif. All except the latter have dense rosettes of basal, thick, often gray or whitish leaves, and some of them produce many offsets,* by which they are readily propagated. Flowers yellow, red, or purple, mostly in terminal clusters (cymose panicles*), the often bracted* stalk of which arises at the leaf rosette.* Petals 6 or more, separate, but the flower often apparently tubular. Stamens* twice as many as the petals. Fruit a collection of 1-celled follicles.* (*Sempervivum* is Latin for live forever, in allusion to the lasting quality of some species.)

The houseleeks are primarily foliage plants, as their flowers are less showy than in the closely related sedums. All but a handful are stemless plants often used for elaborate carpet-bedding schemes in public parks, but widely grown also for the rock garden and for open, sandy places. They do not like too rich a soil nor too much moisture, especially in the winter. Some of them are very interesting plants. S. *tectorum*, the commonest species in cult., is

often called the roof houseleek from the fact that it grows on the roof of many thatched cottages abroad. S. *arachnoideum*, the cobweb houseleek, has the rosette of leaves covered with a network of cobweb-like hairs, which the plant produces for no known cause.

The culture of most of them is simple, and those that need rock garden conditions are noted below. Most houseleeks are summer-bloomers. Two commonly used names in the trade are S. *atroviolaceum* and S. *violaceum*. Both are of uncertain identity and of no botanical standing.

Sempervivum haworthi and S. *spathulatum*, both from the Canary and Madeira Islands, are tender, shrubby species, not to be grown outdoors outside of southern Calif., where they are popular in desert gardens. By some, these and related tender species are considered as belonging to the genus *Aeonium*, not here maintained.

S. arachnoideum. Cobweb houseleek. A small plant with about 50 leaves in a dense, globular rosette, the leaves about ⅝ in. wide and very cobwebby. Stalk of the flower cluster 3–4 in. high, leafy and hairy, forking at the top into a 9–12-flowered cluster. Flowers about 1 in. wide, red. Southern Eu. The *var.* **laggeri** has smaller rosettes. The *var.* **doellianum** has fewer leaves to a rosette and fewer cobwebby strands. For culture *see* ROCK GARDEN.

S. arenarium. Rosettes globe-shaped and composed of 50–60 generally lance-shaped leaves, the outer ones about ¾ in. long and reddish on the back. Flowering stalk leafy and hairy, the cluster globe-shaped, nearly 3 in. thick, its flowers yellow. Tyrol.

S. brauni. Rosettes about 2 in. in diameter. Leaves about 1 in. long, sticky, slightly broader above the middle and with a soft prickle at the tip. Flowering stalk about 9 in. high, crowned with a close cluster nearly 4 in. wide. Flowers about 1 in. wide, yellow, but the petals green-keeled. Tyrol.

S. fauconnetti. Rosettes about 1½ in. wide, the leaves about ¾ in. long and tinged reddish-purple, and with a tuft of hairs at the tip. Flowering stalk about 8 in. high, the flowers nearly 1 in. wide, bright red. Eastern France in the Jura Mountains. For culture *see* ROCK GARDEN.

S. fimbriatum. A hybrid houseleek. Rosettes about 1½ in. wide, the leaves broadest above the middle, the outer ones reddish, all tipped with a bunch of hairs. Flowering stalk about 10 in. high, the cluster open, the flowers bright red and about 1 in. wide.

S. glaucum. Rosettes about 3 in. wide, the leaves bluish-gray, with a brown spot toward the wider tip. Flowering stalk nearly 12 in. high, hairy, the cluster 3–4 in. long, the flowers about 1 in. wide and red. Central Eu. Perhaps only a form of S. *tectorum*.

S. globiferum. A plant of uncertain origin and identity. What commonly passes for it has rosettes about 3 in. wide, rather flattened in age, but globe-shaped in youth, the leaves gray-green and tipped with a soft prickle. Flowering stalk about 12 in. high, the flowers yellow and about 1 in. wide. Russia (?). Confused with S. *soboliferum*.

S. haworthi. A tender, shrubby species from the Canary and Madeira Islands, sometimes referred to the genus *Aeonium*. It has a

---

* Special articles on the subjects indicated by an asterisk (*) will be found at the words so marked.

shrubby trunk or stem 1–2 ft. high, with short, thick branches. Leaves thick, ovalish, but sharp-pointed. Flowers yellowish-rose, very numerous in a terminal cluster. Suited to outdoor culture only in southern Calif. and similar climates.

S. mettenianum. Rosettes about 2 in. wide, the leaves tipped and more or less blotched with red-brown. Flowering stalk about 6 in. high, the flowers rose-pink. Central Eu. For culture *see* ROCK GARDEN.

S. montanum. Rosettes compact and scarcely 1¾ in. wide, the leaves about 1 in. long and hairy on the margins. Flowering stalk about 6 in. high, ending in a hairy cluster about 2 in. wide, the flowers mauve-red or purplish. Pyrenees and the Alps. For culture *see* ROCK GARDEN.

S. soboliferum. A low plant with globular rosettes forming pill-like offsets which are attached by short, slender threads which break and allow the offsets to roll away and form new colonies. *S. montanum* is sometimes confused in the catalogues with *S. soboliferum.* For culture *see* ROCK GARDEN.

S. spathulatum. A tender, shrubby species from the Canaries and Madeira, and sometimes considered as of the genus *Aeonium.* Stems thick and woody, 1–2 ft. high, the leaves marked with red-brown. Flowers yellow in a profuse panicle.* Its outdoor culture is limited to southern Calif. and similar climates.

S. tectorum. The common houseleek and more widely cult. than all the others, often called roof houseleek (*see* above), hen-and-chickens, or old-man-and-woman, from its frequent offsets.* Rosettes 3–4 in. wide, the leaves many, wedge-shaped and tipped with a soft prickle. Flowering stalk about 12 in. high, dividing into 1-sided clusters of pinkish-red flowers that are about 1 in. wide, and have 12 petals. The stalk and branches of the cluster are hairy. Eurasia, and occasionally escaping* in the U.S.

S. triste. Perhaps only a form of *S. tectorum.*

HOUSE PLANTS. Plants which are suitable for interior decoration must grow easily and satisfactorily in a residence without any special treatment other than ordinary care. Modern architecture, with its emphasis on more light in the house, has increased the number of kinds useful as house plants.

FAILURE WITH HOUSE PLANTS

There are four primary causes to which failure with plants grown for home decoration generally may be attributed.

LACK OF KNOWLEDGE OF PLANT NEEDS. Many difficulties connected with the successful growing of plants in the house may be overcome by a careful study of the actual requirements of the different kinds. Each plant requires food and water in certain proportions continually, the proper kind of soil, and sufficient light and heat necessary for its proper development.

UNSUITABLE PLANTS. Choosing plants which are not suited to the condition of the room in which they are to be grown, is oft-times the cause of failure. Proper lighting in a room with little sun is difficult to achieve and varieties should be chosen which will do best with little or no sun. Moisture-loving plants should not be attempted in a dry or uneven atmosphere, nor those which require

a high temperature when there are facilities for growing cool house plants only.

NEGLECT. There are no hard and fast rules as regards growing conditions which apply equally to all plants, but there are certain fundamentals which must be observed with all plants if they are to survive. All specimens, regardless of type, must be given constant attention, particularly as to the proper amount of water at the proper time, additional fertilizer when needed, re-potting when necessary, and freedom from insect pests.

INJURIOUS GASES. Proper ventilation will to a large extent prevent loss of plants due to poisonous vapors. Some plant species are extremely sensitive to coal gas — the Jerusalem cherry, for example, dropping its leaves and fruit very quickly if coal gas is present. Illuminating gas does little harm to the tough-leaved varieties, such as rubber plants and aspidistra, but the tender kinds such as begonias, coleus, and geraniums are stunted and eventually killed. Primrose and carnation buds either fail to mature or the opened flowers close and then drop off, even in many cases where the amount of gas is so slight that the nose does not detect it.

SUCCESS WITH HOUSE PLANTS

LIGHT. No other factor governing the growth of plants is so important as that of light. The amount required varies, of course, with different plants. The majority will do best in a window facing south or southwest, and moderately well in eastern light, but usually only foliage plants such as ferns, aspidistras, ivy, and palms should be placed where they receive north light. Sunlight is absolutely essential to develop buds to maturity on such blossoming plants as begonias, fuchsias, and geraniums. Unless, of course, you grow them under an electric light; a frosted 100-watt bulb is best. Earlier blooms may sometimes be obtained also in this manner. *See* ELECTRO-HORTICULTURE.

HEAT. Violent fluctuations in the tempera-

What happens when house plants are not turned every few days so that they do not become lopsided from one-sided illumination.

---

* Special articles on the subjects indicated by an asterisk (*) will be found at the words so marked.

ture should be avoided as much as possible, as every plant has a definite range in which it makes its best growth. In general, a daytime heat of 60 to 70 degrees is best; plants which require a temperature of more than 70 degrees do not make satisfactory house specimens. During the night the plants must be cooler, but the drop should be about 10 or 15 degrees only. In extreme cold weather they might be given slight additional protection by covering with paper or some other nonconducting material.

HUMIDITY. Modern heating systems are often equipped with a humidifying device, or radiator covers contain water-holding compartments. But under ordinary conditions the atmosphere of most dwelling houses is too dry to suit a large number of plants. Various makeshifts may be employed to obviate this situation. Bowls filled with water may be placed upon the radiators or set among the potted plants, or bulbs grown in pebbles and water will add a decorative as well as useful touch. Spraying the foliage frequently will serve the purpose also, as well as keeping the plants clean, although the hairy-leaved sorts as African violets and gloxinias must never be treated thus. Care must be taken also to see that no water remains in the crowns of such plants as the cyclamen, as this would cause them to rot. An inexpensive substitute for a sprayer would be an ordinary bulb syringe, although a fine mist which can be evenly distributed over the foliage is to be preferred.

VENTILATION. All plants like plenty of fresh air but they must not be subjected to draughts or sudden chilling. Cold air blowing directly on many plants will cause them to lose their foliage and even, in the sensitive species, to die. Fresh air should be admitted gradually for a few minutes morning and afternoon, a good plan being to open a door or window in an adjoining room rather than in the one where the plants are kept. Even in very warm weather it is best not to open the windows directly beside them.

WATERING. "When and how shall I water my plants?" one is frequently asked. And to this the reply must be "Whenever the plant is in need of water." No hard and fast rule can be given, but a good test is to rub some of the soil between the fingers. If it pulverizes without caking, it requires water; if it cakes, it requires none. During the dormant or rest period less water must be given than during their growing season, while in sunny weather they will dry out much more quickly than on moist, dull days. The type of pot must also be taken into consideration, as the unglazed varieties are porous, while the glazed ones hold all the moisture, unless they contain a drainage outlet. The latter containers retain so much moisture that the plant may often be watered as seldom as once a week.

When watering a plant, do it thoroughly — not just a little today and a little the next day — but a good, thorough soaking and then not again until you test the soil and find it

actually needs it. The roots must be thoroughly soaked; the excess moisture will run out of the drainage hole in the bottom of the container and this excess must not be allowed to stand in the saucer, except in the case of plants which ordinarily grow in water. Standing water must never be allowed in jardinieres. If the plants are very dry or of extreme size, let the pots stand in water to within an inch or so of the brim; when the soil is thoroughly soaked remove them. Plants which cover the topsoil with leaves may be watered from below by keeping the saucer filled until the plant and soil refuses to take any more. For weekenders, who must leave their plants without water the wick system is available. See WICK WATERING.

SOIL AND FERTILIZERS. Although all plants will not do equally well in the same potting mixture, nearly all will thrive moderately well in any well-balanced soil by adapting themselves to the varying conditions that are forced upon them. For general potting, where a medium-rich mixture is desired, use potting mixture* 3; this will do very well for all plants of the order of fuchsias, geraniums, palms, and chrysanthemums. Many of the ferns, begonias, and plants which require more humus are best grown in potting mixture* 4. When the plants are well established, additional fertilizer may be given to increase growth and strengthen the plant throughout. This may be mixed with the soil or applied in the form of liquid fertilizer; if the latter, be careful not to use it too strong, as there is danger of burning the roots with a strong solution. Water-soluble fertilizers come packaged, but must be used only according to the directions on the container; plants are easily killed by too concentrated solutions.

DRAINAGE. Next to light, perhaps the most important factor in the successful growing of house plants is drainage. Most pots, however small, have a drainage hole at the bottom which is to provide an escape for excess

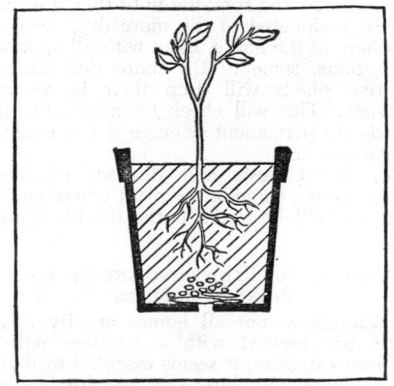

In potting house plants be sure to put broken crocks (potsherds) over the hole at the bottom. These allow proper drainage and aeration of the soil.

* Special articles on the subjects indicated by an asterisk (*) will be found at the words so marked.

moisture. The best method is to put a piece of arched crock over the hole, which is all that is necessary in small pots. As the size of the pot increases, the amount of drainage will increase, so that in a ten-inch pot, for example, two or three inches of drainage, comprised of broken crock at the bottom with gravel, cinders, or pebbles placed above the crocking, is not excessive.

RE-POTTING. Most plants begin their most active season of growth in late spring, and the period just previous is, as a general rule, the best time for re-potting. The shock of re-shifting is then easily overcome during the summer outdoors. Examine the roots carefully before deciding to pot into a larger container. *See* POTTING.

REST PERIOD. All plants have a definite rest period. During this time they require less light, heat, and water than when in their period of active growth. Fertilizer should never be given to any plant during the rest period, as it forces it to unnatural growth at the sacrifice of health and vitality.

SUMMER CARE OF HOUSE PLANTS

During the warm summer months all house plants should be placed out of doors, preferably in the shade.

PLUNGING. This is the best method of caring for house plants during the summer months. Sink the plants in their pots to the rim in the garden. Never remove the plant from the pot. A shady location is best for ferns and foliage plants; a sunny place will be required for many of the flowering species, such as geraniums and heliotropes. Water must be given regularly unless rainfall is adequate.

PREPARATION FOR WINTER. Before frost all the plants must be lifted from the garden, removed from the pots and examined to make certain that drainage facilities are unimpaired. If possible, do not disturb the roots.

After they are established in their winter living quarters, special attention must be given to ventilation and spraying until they are thoroughly acclimated to the more dry, close atmosphere of the house. Even with all apparent precautions, some of the more delicate and sensitive plants will drop their leaves and blossoms. This will check them slightly, but will do no permanent damage if the cause is not continuous.

For insect pests and diseases of house plants, *see* the name of the plant where control measures will be found if the trouble is serious.

VARIETIES OF FLOWERING AND FOLIAGE PLANTS AND BULBS

Inasmuch as not all homes or city apartments are blessed with a window with a southern exposure, it seems essential to divide house plants into those that require full sun to produce blossoms, those that will do well with partial sun, and the ones that are content with plenty of light, but little or no sun. Plants may be moved about to secure their requisite amount of light or sun, but this requires time and patience, and it seems better to grow only such species as are suited to their environment.

FULL SUN. The following list is not complete but is intended as a guide to the type of flowers which require at least five hours of sunlight each day. *Amaryllis, Aechmea, Vriesia, Astilbe japonica,* Indica azalea, Cactus varieties, Calla lily, *Calceolaria,* Cape bulbs,* Cineraria, Dutch bulbs, *Euphorbia splendens, Gardenia,* Geraniums, Heliotrope, *Impatiens,* Jerusalem cherry, *Poinsettia,* and Shrimp plant.

PARTIAL SUN. Plants requiring two to three hours of sunlight each day: Begonias, *Coleus* (a few of the Cape bulbs might be included), Dracaena, Crotons, *Anthurium,* Flowering maple, *Fuchsia, Cyclamen,* Primrose in varieties, African violet, tuberous Begonia, Periwinkle, and any of the foliage plants in the following list.

LITTLE OR NO SUN. This list includes the foliage plants with inconspicuous or no flowers, such as ferns, palms, dracaenas, pandanus, vines such as Wandering Jew, and many others; also *Begonia Rex,* Chinese evergreen, Hen-and-Chickens (*Sempervivum tectorum*), Norfolk Island pine (*Araucaria excelsa*), *Philodendron,* Rubber plants, *Aspidistra,* Snake plant, Dieffenbachia, and *Asparagus plumosus.*

BULBS FOR FORCING. With careful planning in autumn it is possible to have a succession of blossoming bulbs from Thanksgiving Day past Easter. The Dutch bulbs, which include such as narcissus, hyacinth and tulips, remain in bloom for ten days to two weeks. Buy your bulbs early, so they may be potted at one time. Either soil or fiber can be used as a pot-

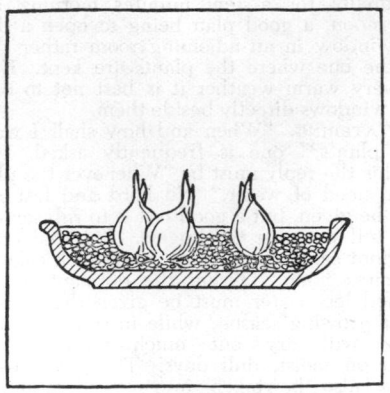

Cross-section of a gravel-filled dish and bulbs for forcing in the house. The line shows the level at which water should be kept.

ting mixture, and these bulbs need a period of outdoor storage before being brought into the house. *See* BULBS. Lily-of-the-valley is easily grown and makes lovely table decorations. Tropical bulbs, such as freesias, ixias

* Special articles on the subjects indicated by an asterisk (*) will be found at the words so marked.

and sparaxias, amaryllis, clivia, are more easily grown than the Dutch bulbs, as they require no period of cold before forcing.

CARE OF HOLIDAY PLANTS

Ferns, palms, poinsettias, primroses, dracaenas, Jerusalem cherry, Christmas cactus, and dozens of other plants are given each year as holiday gifts. Being forced plants the food supply in the soil will soon be exhausted and liquid fertilizer should be given every two or three weeks. Other care is the same as for ordinary house plants except for poinsettia (which see). Ferns in particular make excellent gifts.

PLANTS THAT GROW IN WATER. We are not concerned here with the true aquatics (*see* AQUARIUM) but with those vines, bulbs, and plants which will live and thrive in water. English ivy, once established, requires practically no care and will climb stucco walls or trail from a mantel with beautiful effects. Nasturtiums, cut before frost, will bloom indoors all winter if fertilizer is added to the water each week. Paper-white narcissus, Chinese sacred lily, Dutch and Roman hyacinths, and the Chinese evergreen (*Aglaonema simplex*) are all easily grown in water; add a little charcoal to sweeten. *See also* DISH GARDEN.

HOUSTONIA (hoos-tō'nĭ-a). Spring-flowering, delicate, and beautiful North American wild flowers of the family Rubiaceae, only two of the 25 known species of much hort. interest. The cult. species are low, perennial herbs, usually tufted or growing in large patches with chiefly basal leaves but a few opposite* on the delicate stems, without marginal teeth. Flowers solitary, blue or white (in ours), the corolla regular, more or less funnel-shaped and small. Stamens 4. Fruit a capsule* which opens near the top. (Named for a Doctor William Houston, a botanical collector in Mex. and the W.I.)

Both the plants below are suited only to moist places in the wild garden. Few plants like to have their roots in cool water as much as these. They grow naturally on flat, wet rocks or in moist, grassy meadows. Easily propagated by division of the clumps, which may also be dug from the wild.

caerulea. Bluets; also called Quaker ladies and innocence. Not over 7 in. high, usually about 5 in. Leaves scarcely ½ in. long, oblongish. Flowers usually pale blue, rarely violet or white, with a yellow eye,* solitary at end of a slender stalk, not over ½ in. wide. Eastern N.A.

serpyllifolia. Star violet. A perennial, the stems mostly creeping. Leaves nearly round, about ½ in. in diameter. Flowers deep blue, about ½ in. wide, the flowering stems usually about 8–10 in. high. In mountain meadows and along stream banks, Pa. and W. Va. to Ga. and Tenn.

HOVENIA (ho-veen'ĭ-a). A single species of Chinese tree of the family Rhamnaceae, somewhat grown for its handsome foliage, although the Japanese, who grow it for the purpose, consider the fleshy fruiting stalks as edible. The only species is **H. dulcis**, the Japanese raisin tree, which grows about 25 ft. high and has alternate,* long-stalked, broadly oval leaves, 4–9 in. long, and 3-veined at the base. Flowers small, greenish, in cymes* that are terminal, or in the leaf axils.* Fruit 3-celled, but drupe*-like, its stalks reddish, thick, and twisted at maturity. July–Sept. Hardy from zone* 3 southward, and prefers a sandy loam. Propagated by seeds or by root cuttings. (Named for David Hoven, a Senator at Amsterdam.)

HOWEA (how'ee-a). Two feather palms, perhaps the most widely grown of all palms by florists, as they are better suited for decoration and house plants than almost any other (but *see* CHRYSALIDOCARPUS). Generally known as *Kentia*, the only two species of the genus are graceful, unarmed, ringed palms of medium height, crowned with a beautiful cluster of deep-green, rather tough, gracefully curving leaves, made up of many slender, drooping leaflets or segments, their tips long-pointed but split at the extremity into two hanging ends. Flowers (never produced on small pot plants) from among the lowest leaves, the cluster with a long, usually unbranched, pitted stalk, within each pit 3 flowers, the central one female and the other two males. Stamens 30–100. Fruit more or less olive-shaped, but larger (pecan-sized), 1-seeded. (Named for Lord Howe's Island, east of Australia, where both species are native.)

The outdoor culture of these palms is nothing like so important as the use of them by florists. While grown in Fla. and Calif., many other palms are much more thought of than these kentias. As greenhouse subjects they range in size from small plants in 5-in. pots to large, tubbed specimens 30 ft. high. The dimensions given below are for full-sized mature plants which are rare in the U.S. For their culture *see* PALMS.

belmoreana. Curly palm. A tree not over 40 ft. high. Leaves about 7 ft. long, plumy, the many segments about 1 in. wide, abruptly rising from the main leafstalk, but ultimately hanging very gracefully at the tip, the whole leaf thus not flattish.

forsteriana. Flat palm. A tree up to 60 ft. Leaves about 10 ft. long, not so plumy as the last, the many segments about 1 in. wide, standing out horizontally from the main leafstalk, ultimately drooping more than in the last, but the leaf generally flattish.

HOYA (hoy'ya). A large genus of rather brittle, somewhat fleshy, tropical vines of the milkweed family, native from Asia to Australia, **H. carnosa**, the wax-plant, much grown in the greenhouse and outdoors in Fla. and Calif. It is not hardy north of zone* 8. It is a vine 6–10 ft. high, climbing by many aerial* roots. Leaves opposite,* ovalish or oblong, short-stalked, very thick and fleshy, without marginal teeth, 2–4 in. long. Flowers white, pink-eyed, waxy and fragrant, about ½ in. wide, in small, nearly stalkless clusters in the leaf axils.* Corolla wheel-shaped and within it is a crown of 5 fleshy scales. Stamens* united

---

* Special articles on the subjects indicated by an asterisk (*) will be found at the words so marked.

and covering the stigma* with their joined tips. Fruit a collection of smooth follicles.* Use potting mixture* 4 and grow in a warm (60°–70°), moist greenhouse, but reduce the heat and moisture during the dark winter months. It can also be grown in the house with proper care, *i.e.*, attention to heat and moisture. (Named for Thomas Hoy, 18th-century gardener to the Duke of Northumberland.)

HUAMUCHIL = Guamachil. *See* PITHE-COLOBIUM DULCE.

HUBAM CLOVER = *Melilotus alba annua.*

HUCKLEBERRY. Fruit-bearing, or ornamental, sometimes evergreen, North American shrubs comprising the genus **Gaylussacia** (gay-loo-say′she-a) of the heath family, containing about 50 species, the fruiting ones commonly mistaken for the blueberry (which see), a far more valuable fruit. Leaves alternate,* usually without teeth, often resinous-dotted, evergreen in *G. brachycera*, but falling in all the rest. Flowers in small clusters (racemes*) mostly in the leaf axils.* Corolla bell-shaped or urn-shaped, the 5 shallow lobes usually bent backward. Stamens 10. Fruit fleshy (a drupe*) with 10 seed-like nuts. While edible it is not a true berry and lacks the fine flavor of the blueberry. (Named for J. L. Gay-Lussac, French chemist.) The plant in every florist shop and sold for foliage under the incorrect name of "huckleberry" is *Vaccinium ovatum* (which see).

The fruit-bearing species are scarcely worth cultivating, most of the fruit reaching the markets being collected from the wild. The exception is the nearly prostrate *G. brachycera*, an evergreen shrub with worthless fruit but valuable as a ground cover in shaded, peaty places. Except for the need for partial shade, the huckleberries need the same acid soil as the blueberry (which see).

G. baccata. Black huckleberry; also called high-bush huckleberry. A shrub not over 3 ft. high, the young growth sticky and resinous. Leaves oblongish, 1–3 in. long, yellowish-green above, resinous-dotted beneath. Flower clusters drooping, the corolla orange-red, about ⅓ in. long. Fruit edible, black and shining, about ⅜ in. in diameter. Eastern N.A. May. Hardy from zone* 2 southward. Sometimes called *G. resinosa.*

G. brachycera. Box-huckleberry; also called juniper-berry. A nearly prostrate evergreen shrub, not over 18 in. high, the stems creeping but turning up at the tips. Leaves many, elliptic, 1–1½ in. long, smooth and not resinous-dotted. Flowers white or pink, about ¼ in. long. Fruit blue. Del. to Tenn. May. Hardy from zone* 3 southward.

G. dumosa. Bush huckleberry; also called gopher-berry. Not usually over 18 in. high, the twigs sticky-hairy. Leaves nearly stalkless, oblongish, 1½–2 in. long, resinous beneath. Flower cluster with several small leafy bracts.* Corolla white or pink, about ⅜ in. long. Fruit insipid but edible, black. Newfoundland to Fla. and La., mostly in sandy bogs. May. Hardy from zone* 3 southward.

G. frondosa. Dangleberry (or tangleberry);

also called blue huckleberry. A spreading shrub up to 6 ft. high, the twigs smooth. Leaves more or less elliptic, 1½–2½ in. long, green above, noticeably paler and hairy beneath. Corolla broadly bell-shaped, nearly ½ in. long, greenish-purple. Fruit blue, with a bloom, nearly ½ in. in diameter, edible. N.H. to Fla. and La. May. Hardy from zone* 3 southward.

G. resinosa = *Gaylussacia baccata.*

HUCKLEBERRY FAMILY. *See* ERICA-CEAE.

HUERNIA (hur′nee-a). A small genus of succulent, leafless herbs of the milkweed family, all African, only **H. penzigi** from the Nile region of much hort. interest. It somewhat resembles *Stapelia* and is a small succulent, scarcely 3 in. high, the stems angled and toothed, about ½ in. thick, the blunt teeth nearly ½ in. long. Flowers evil-smelling, blackish-purple, warty, about ¾ in. wide, mostly borne in small cymes* at the base of young shoots. The plant is suited to the desert gardens of southern Calif. or to the greenhouse. *See* SUCCULENTS. (Named for Justus Huernius, the first collector of South African plants.)

HUERNIOPSIS (hur-nee-op′sis). A single species of the three known South African succulent herbs of the milkweed family, **H. decipiens**, differing from *Huernia* in technical flower characters. It is a small, more or less prostrate, fleshy-stemmed, leafless plant, the stems club-shaped, not over 3 in. long, 4-angled and coarsely but bluntly toothed. Flowers evil-smelling, in clusters of 2–3, borne at the middle or toward the top of the stem, about 1 in. wide, yellowish-green, but streaked and spotted with purple on the outside, the inside brownish-red but yellow-spotted. Its outdoor cult. is confined to desert gardens in Calif., but it may be grown in the greenhouse elsewhere. *See* SUCCULENTS. (*Huerniopsis* means *Huernia*-like.)

HUGO ROSE = *Rosa hugonis.*

HUISACHE = *Acacia farnesiana.*

HUISQUIL = *Sechium edule.*

HULL. Loosely, the outer shell or covering of any fruit, often called its husk; specifically, the enlarged calyx* of the fruit of the strawberry.

HUMBLE PLANT = *Mimosa pudica.*

HUMEA (hew′mee-a). Australian plants of the family Compositae, the only cult. species, **H. elegans**, often called amaranth-feathers from its mass of reddish disk flowers. It is a biennial herb 4–6 ft. high, the stems widely branching. Leaves oblongish, wrinkled, 7–10 in. long. Flowers of a cedar-like or strawberry-like fragrance, very numerous in long, feathery, drooping clusters (corymbs* or panicles*), the heads very small. Seed should be sown in the cool greenhouse in the late summer for next season's bloom. They should be grown, after the seedling stage, in potting mixture* 3 in flats or small pots and later transferred to 5-in. pots. Fill the pots nearly full of soil to prevent overwater-

---

* Special articles on the subjects indicated by an asterisk (*) will be found **at** the words so marked.

ing, which the plants will not stand, but they must not be allowed to dry out. As they approach flowering time they need plentiful applications of liquid manure. After warm weather has arrived, they may be put in the border or left as pot plants, as they make very decorative plants for porches or to set about a patio. (Named for Lady Hume.)

HUMIDITY. The amount of moisture in the atmosphere, and of the greatest importance to plants. Except in the greenhouse (which see), and the living room (*see* HOUSE PLANTS), it is impossible to control humidity, which depends upon rainfall or proximity to a large body of water. *See* RAINFALL.

humilis, -e (hew'mi-lis). Low-growing or dwarf.

HUMMINGBIRD'S-TRUMPET = *Zauschneria californica.*

HUMULUS. *See* HOP.

HUMUS. Humus is partly or thoroughly decomposed vegetable matter, but the simplicity of such a definition does not begin to state its importance to the gardener and the nation.

Perhaps no country, except China, has been so reckless in the destruction of such a priceless asset as our own. Forest fires have annually destroyed thousands of tons of rich woods soil, 80% of which is humus of the most valuable kind. In recent years the Forest Service has attempted to control these fires, well knowing that upon the maintenance of an adequate humus layer, the perpetuation of the forest depends. It is just as important to the gardener.

Ordinary mineral soil (the subsoil) is without any humus. Topsoil contains varying amounts of humus mixed with the mineral soil, while the humus layer under many forests may contain from 80–90% of vegetable matter. The implications of this to the gardener are important.

Moisture-holding capacity of soils. (A) A subsoil or inferior topsoil, holding 20% of water. (B) A fair garden topsoil, holding 60% of water. (C) Pure humus, which may hold several times its own weight of water. Black indicates the amount of humus in each sample.

Take some mineral soil, some topsoil, and some woods soil, or leaf mold as it is often called, and allow each to be dried (not burned) in an oven. When, by weighing, it is found that no more water can be driven out of any of them, weigh out exactly a pound of each of the oven-dry samples. Then allow each to soak up (by capillarity) as much water as it can, and weigh again. Under ordinary conditions, the mineral soil will absorb perhaps 20% of its own weight, the topsoil perhaps 60%, but the woods soil may easily, depending upon the sort of humus in it, absorb water from 300–500% of its weight.

Such a crude, simple experiment (the figures will vary much according to the soil type) demonstrates why humus is so important. Pure 100% humus is like a sponge for holding water, while mineral soils, except clay, give it off rather easily.

HUMUS IN THE GARDEN. Long before these fundamentals were understood, farmers plowed cover crops and vegetable refuse into the land. The humus so added enriches the soil far more than the chemical constituents of the plowed-under material might indicate, and this not only because the humus has raised the water-holding capacity of the soil. It does much more. For in the process of decay there is a whole series of microscopic organisms involved, which do things for the soil that nothing else will.

Ordinary garden topsoil contains a reasonable amount of humus, usually indicated by a darker color than the subsoil beneath it. If you use nothing but commercial fertilizers, some of which actually destroy humus, see to it that some cover crop is plowed in to overcome the deficiency (*see* GREEN MANURING), or else import humus and use it like manure.

COMMERCIAL HUMUS. Many firms gather humus from different sources and sell it by the bag or carload for just this contingency. Some of them are baked, weed-free products of the greatest value. But in purchasing them one must be careful for what purpose they are wanted.

Thoroughly decomposed humus is usually black and is either neutral or only slightly acid (*see* ACID AND ALKALI SOILS). Such can be safely and most beneficially added to any ordinary garden soil. It is splendid for potted plants in the house. Usually a layer about 1½ in. thick is enough and it should be worked into the existing soil. It is also good as a top-dressing for lawns. *See* LAWN.

If acid humus is needed, as it should be for rhododendrons, azaleas, and many other plants of the heath family, and for a lot of places in the wild garden or bog garden, it is necessary to supply humus of a very different sort. Acid humus is usually not thoroughly decomposed and is apt to be brownish or tan in color. More important still, it should test to pH 4.5–5.5 (*see* ACID AND ALKALI SOILS). Dealers who know their business will be glad to meet these specifications. Many produce acid humus baled up ready to use.

---

* Special articles on the subjects indicated by an asterisk (*) will be found at the words so marked.

All of which shows that the intelligent gardener should not add "just humus" to his garden. Study the existing soil, the plants you wish to grow, and choose the sort of humus you need. Plowing in cover crops is the cheapest, but takes the most time. Manure always adds humus to the soil. The alternative is to supply commercial humus, some of which come fortified with commercial fertilizers, and some even have bacterial cultures in them to hasten decomposition. *See also* PEAT.

HUNDRED-LEAVED ROSE = *Rosa centifolia.*

HUNGARIAN BROME GLASS = *Bromus inermis.*

HUNGARIAN GRASS = *Setaria italica nigrofructa.*

HUNGARIAN LILAC = *Syringa Josikaea.* See LILAC.

HUNNEMANNIA (hun-nee-man-ĭ'-a). A single species of Mexican perennial herbs of the poppy family, generally known as Mexican tulip-poppy or golden cup, and to science as H. fumariaefolia. In the garden it can be treated as a hardy annual (*see* ANNUALS), but see below. It is a showy herb 12–20 in. high, the leaves bluish-green and much dissected into blunt but narrow segments. Flowers 2–3 in. wide, yellow, but the many stamens orange and showy. Petals 4, sepals 2. Fruit a 2-valved capsule,* nearly 4 in. long, splitting from the bottom upward. A popular flower garden annual, blooming from July 15 to Oct. and related to the California poppy. (Named for John Hunneman, English botanist.) If early plants are needed it pays to start seedlings in the greenhouse or sunny window early in March. Sow the seeds in paper pots, later transferring them to 4-in. flower pots in which they are left until ready for outdoor planting in late May. This procedure is better than treating them as ordinary annuals, as their roots are brittle and the use of pots helps to preserve the roots when transplanting to permanent site.

HUNTER'S ROBE = *Scindapus aureus.*

HUNTINGDON ELM = *Ulmus hollandica vegeta.* See ELM.

HUNTSMAN'S-CUP = *Sarracenia purpurea.* See PITCHER-PLANT.

HUON PINE = *Dacrydium franklini.*

hupehensis, -e (hoo-pay-en'sis). From Hupeh, China.

HURA (hew'ra). A genus of poisonous, milky-juiced, tropical American trees of the spurge family, H. crepitans, the sandbox-tree, an interesting but horticulturally little-known tree. It is spiny-trunked and reaches 80–100 ft. high and has alternate,* broadly ovalish, toothed leaves nearly 2 ft. long. Male and female flowers separate on the same tree, red, without petals, rather inconspicuous. Fruit a many-ribbed, woody capsule,* explosively splitting when ripe, sometimes with a loud report. It is grown in the warmest parts of southern Fla. (zone* 9), and prefers a light, sandy loam. (*Hura* is the South American name of the tree.) Its name of sandbox-tree came from the sections of its fruit being used for the ink-drying sand that preceded modern blotters.

HURSINGHAR = *Nyctanthes Arbor-tristis.*

HUSK. See HULL.

HUSK TOMATO. See PHYSALIS.

HUTCHINSIA (hut-chin'see-a). A small genus of Eurasian herbs of the mustard family, only H. alpina of any garden interest. It is a tiny, perennial, tufted herb, 1–4 in. high, suitable only to the rock garden (which see). Leaves mostly basal, ¾–1 in. long, divided into ovalish or oblong segments. Flowers very small, white, in a close raceme (*see* CRUCIFERAE for details). Fruit an ovalish or short-oblong pod (silicle*). (Named for a Miss Hutchins, an Irish student of flowerless plants.)

HYACINTH. See HYACINTHUS. For the grape-hyacinth *see* MUSCARI. *See also* SCILLA AMOENA, EICHHORNIA, and BRODIAEA LACTEA.

hyacintha, -us, -um (high-a-sin'tha). Hyacinth-like.

HYACINTH BEAN = *Dolichos Lablab.*

HYACINTH FAMILY = Liliaceae.

hyacinthina, -us, -um (hy-a-sin-thy'na). Like a hyacinth.

HYACINTHUS (hy-a-sin'thus). A genus of perhaps 30 species of bulbous herbs of the lily family, chiefly from the Mediterranean region, and from tropical and South Africa. The chief hort. species is the common garden hyacinth, the other two below being more rarely grown. They have a deep, large bulb, narrow, basal, sometimes almost grass-like leaves without marginal teeth. Flowers fragrant in a showy, stiff, regular, terminal cluster (raceme*), each of the individual flowering stalks with a narrow bract* at the base. Corolla more or less bell-shaped, its 6 lobes or segments spreading or turned backward. Stamens* 6. Fruit a 3-angled capsule.* (Named from the mythological character.) For culture *see* below.

amethystinus. A slender, graceful, hardy, bulbous herb, 4–5 in. high, well suited for the rock garden, and providing a fine blue, early-flowering subject for the blue garden (which see). Its flowers are nodding, light blue, and bell-shaped. Spain.
azureus = H. ciliatus.
candicans = Galtonia candicans.
ciliatus. Nearly 5 in. high, the leaves bluish-green and channeled. Flowers blue, in a dense, short cluster resembling the grape-hyacinth, but the lobes of the corolla not incurved. Mediterranean region. Sometimes offered as *Muscari azureum.* A good plant for the blue garden (which see).
orientalis. Common garden hyacinth. Flowering stalk up to 15 in., the leaves nearly 12 in. long and about ¾ in. wide. Flowers of many colors (*see* below) and sometimes double blooming early in spring, always with a single

---

* Special articles on the subjects indicated by an asterisk (*) will be found at the words so marked.

cluster to each plant. Greece to Asia Minor. The *var.* **albulus**, mostly white (but *see* below), is the Roman hyacinth. It is a smaller plant, blooms earlier, and has several flower stalks to each plant, but these have fewer blooms and are not so stiff as the common hyacinth. It is not so hardy as the common sort.

Hyacinth Culture

Garden hyacinths are all forms derived under cultivation from *Hyacinthus orientalis*, and show what variation one may derive from a single species. Although the bulb is reasonably cold-hardy, it must be planted deeply (5–6 in.) and in good soil, rich in food. In the North a winter mulch, applied late in autumn, may be needed to protect the young shoots as they push through the soil. Given this treatment the plants are quite hardy and permanent. The bulbs will not give equal performance each year, as the bulb offered in the market is one that has been grown up to a definite age when it will produce a bloom stalk that may be classified as First, Second, or Exhibition size. The second year in the garden the bulbs must begin the cycle again, and if fed and cared for will again come to the same size and stage as when first purchased. This is not often understood and the bulbs are said to "go back." Some natural multiplication also occurs at this time, so that one gets several smaller flower stalks, that are very charming in themselves. Food is the answer, and hyacinths are about as hungry as potatoes.

The range of varieties changes from season to season, and since there have been some tetraploid* varieties produced, that are not indicated in lists, one is free to choose larger or smaller flowers as he wishes. The varieties with deep rose and with yellow coloration produce smaller spikes than the others. The varieties are: Arentine Arendsen and L'Innocence for whites; Delft Blue and Myosotis for light blue; Queen of the Blues, a little darker; City of Haarlem, yellow; Oranje Boven, apricot-salmon; Delight and Princess Irene, light pink; Jan Bos and Tubergen's Scarlet, deeper to almost scarlet; King of the Blues, still a good dark blue-purple.

When planted in gardens they should be used in clumps through the low-growing perennials and bedding annuals of the season, not in huge masses of color. All may be grown in lines but are less effective in that way. Since all have heavy and delightful scents, their use may be dependent on the reaction of the owner of the garden to the cloying scent.

Hyacinths force well in pots but must not be hurried until the roots have filled the bottom of the pot. Best forcing dates are given in all good catalogues. When ready, bring the pots into the light, under the greenhouse bench or on the floor, which will help develop the flower stalk that must not be overtopped by the foliage. They may also be grown in water, in hyacinth glasses, keeping them in the dark until the base of the glass is well filled with roots.

Where it is cold-hardy, the Roman hyacinth makes a charming garden plant as it always has many slender stalks with few bells. It is most commonly known in its white form. In many Southern gardens there are other hyacinths that resemble the Roman hyacinth but usually are found in various hues of lavender and purple, less often in pink and rose. There is one charming double pink known locally as Southern Belle.

Two other species of hyacinth, often grown, present no cultural problems, *H. amethystinus* and *H. ciliatus*. They respond to the treatment given snowdrops and scillas, and the latter will self-sow widely when once established. — B.Y.M.

Diseases. Plants growing in wet soil may occasionally wilt suddenly and die. The bulb may be soft and rotten as a result of bacterial soft rot. In wet or dry soil a similarly wilted plant may have a solid bulb under it but the neck of the bulb will have small, hard, black objects adhering to it. This indicates one of the fungus rots and the bulb should be dug out and destroyed. If these bulb rots become serious after several years of continuous planting in the same area, do not replant with hyacinth for at least three years.

HYBRID. The offspring or progeny of a cross-fertilization between parents differing in one or more genes.* This definition makes hybrids much more common, and rightly so, than is generally appreciated. Hence the offspring of crosses between two individuals of the same variety or race (Shirley poppies), between different varieties, species and genera are hybrids. Hybrids may or may not breed true. Hybrids are often remarkably fertile; in other cases as remarkably sterile. Many, possibly the majority of our cultivated plants, have resulted either from artificial or natural hybridization. Striking results of artificial hybridization are found among roses (involving many species), gladioli, lilacs, and irises. For hybridization technique, *see* Crossing. — O.E.W.

hybrida, -us, -um (hib′ri-da). Hybrid.

HYBRIDIZING. *See* Crossing.

HYBRID VIGOR. *See* Heterosis.

HYDRANGEA (hy-dran′jee-a). Important garden shrubs and woody vines of the family Saxifragaceae, many of the 80 species cult. for their showy flower clusters. Most of the garden sorts are Asiatic or North American, but the genus ranges to S.A. and Java. Leaves opposite,* stalked, usually toothed. Flowers small, prevailingly white, blue, or pink, arranged in dense, flat-topped or globe-shaped clusters, the outer flowers of the cluster often without stamens or pistils (sterile*) and with larger petals than the inner, fertile flowers. Petals usually 5, rarely 4. Stamens mostly 10, rarely 8–20. Fruit a 2–5-valved capsule* splitting at the top. (*Hydrangea* is from the Greek for water vessel, in allusion to the shape of the fruit.)

---

* Special articles on the subjects indicated by an asterisk (*) will be found at the words so marked.

The common hydrangea (*H. paniculata grandiflora*) has been so much planted as to become tiresome to many. Its large masses of midsummer white bloom are very handsome, however, and its ease of growing and cheapness will make it popular long after the critics of it have turned to something else.

One of those below is a vine (*H. petiolaris*), little grown, but worth more attention by the gardener. A relative, also a vine, will be found at the genus *Schizophragma*.

Most of the others are shrubs, hardy as noted below, but the forms of *H. macrophylla*, widely called hortensia, demand notes on culture and uses. Originally a Japanese shrub, where it has been cult. for centuries and where there are many named varieties, it is now *the* hydrangea of the florists who force it in pots or tubs for spring bloom. While it will occasionally winter-kill in parts of zone* 4, it is perfectly hardy along the coast from N.Y. southward, and north of this if protected with straw or bagging. In the commonly cult. form it has huge globe-shaped clusters of blue or pink flowers, all of which are sterile. An occasional white-flowered form is found, and another with a flat-topped cluster in which only the marginal flowers are sterile. Pink-flowered, globe-shaped specimens may sometimes be changed to blue by putting bits of iron or alum in the soil.

The winter or early-spring blooming of hortensia is from pot plants started from cuttings made the previous Feb. or Mar. Start them in shallow boxes or pans, over gentle bottom-heat,* and when rooted, plant them in small pots in potting mixture* 3. Plunge* the pots outdoors during the summer and re-pot as the plants increase in size. See that the plunged pots do not dry out and give them an occasional dose of liquid manure. By Sept. they are ready to be put in 8-in. pots, and after the first frost they should be brought into the cool greenhouse and kept there until Jan. Then increase the heat to 50°–60°, when they should be ready to flower by Easter. Just before flowering time, reduce the temperature again to harden them off, as forced plants may resent a sudden change to other conditions.

Large tubbed specimens of hortensia, widely used on porches and for accents along drives, should be left out until after the first frost has killed the leaves. Then move into a frost-free but cool pit, where they should be kept rather dry. In the spring re-pot them in fresh soil (potting mixture* 3) and put outdoors after hard frosts are passed. They need liberal watering and liquid manure during the growing season. The cult. species of *Hydrangea* are:

arborescens. Wild hydrangea; also called sevenbark. An upright but open, straggling shrub 3–5 ft. high. Leaves ovalish, more or less rounded or heart-shaped at the base, 3–6 in. long. Flowers white, the cluster 2½–5½ in. wide, flattish or a little rounded, all fertile except a few marginal, sterile flowers. N.Y. to Iowa and southward. June–July. Hardy from zone* 3 southward. The *var.* **grandiflora**, called hills-of-snow, has all the flowers sterile and in a ball-like cluster.

bretschneideri. A shrub 5–9 ft. high, the bark peeling and the twigs hairy. Leaves ovalish or elliptic, more or less wedge-shaped at the base, 3–5½ in. long. Flowers white, the cluster 4–7 in. wide, slightly arched, the sterile marginal flowers becoming purplish. China. July. Hardy from zone* 4 southward.

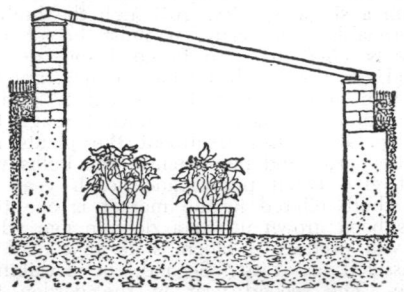

Wintering hortensia hydrangeas in a pit. Most growers do not put them in the pit until all the leaves have fallen.

hortensis; Hortensia. See Hydrangea macrophylla.

macrophylla. Hortensia, the common forcing hydrangea of the florists, and much grown in tubs. In the wild, a shrub up to 12 ft., less as usually grown. Leaves broadly oval, shortly tapering at the tip, 3–6 in. long, coarsely toothed, shining green above, lighter beneath. Flowers normally pink or blue (rarely white), all sterile in the form with globe-shaped clusters, only the marginal ones sterile in the form with flat-topped clusters. Jap. For hardiness and cult. *see* above. Sometimes known as *H. opuloides*. There are many varieties, of which the following are perhaps the best known:

    var. **caerulea.** Flowers deep blue, or occasionally some marginal ones white.

    var. **Hortensia.** All flowers sterile, cluster globe-shaped, blue or pink. The most usual form in cult.

    var. **mandshurica.** Stems dark purple or almost black. This form is sometimes catalogued as *H. opuloides cyanoclada*.

    var. **Otaksa.** A lower dwarf form.

    var. **rosea.** A flat-clustered, pink-flowered form.

    var. **veitchi.** Flowers a deep-rose-pink.

opuloides = *Hydrangea macrophylla*.

Otaksa = *Hydrangea macrophylla Otaksa*.

paniculata. The commonest hardy hydrangea in cult., but almost universally grown in its *var.* **grandiflora**, which is commonly abbreviated to P.G. or even pcegee. This form is a tree-like shrub 8–25 ft. high, the leaves elliptic or ovalish, rounded or wedge-shaped at the base, 3–5 in. long. Flower cluster 8–12 in. long, dense, white, later changing to pink and purple, long-persistent, nearly all the flowers sterile. Eastern As. Summer. Hardy from zone* 2 southward, possibly in zone* 1. It is better to prune the shrub a little each spring. It is still the best all-round, hardy hydrangea in cult.

petiolaris. Climbing hydrangea. A woody vine climbing by aerial rootlets up to 50–60 ft.

---

* Special articles on the subjects indicated by an asterisk (*) will be found at the words so marked.

Leaves broadly oval, more or less rounded or heart-shaped at the base, 2–4 in. long. Flower clusters loose, white, 6–12 in. wide, some of the marginal flowers sterile and thrice wider than the fertile ones. Eastern As. July–Aug. Hardy from zone* 3 southward. A fine vine for clinging to brick or masonry walls or to tree trunks. See VINES. Sometimes sold as *H. scandens* or *H. volubilis*, and known also as *H. anomala*.

quercifolia. A shrub not more than 6 ft. high, the twigs reddish and hairy. Leaves 3–7-lobed, almost oak-fashion, the lobes toothed, white-felty beneath. Flower cluster a panicle,* 4–10 in. wide, many of its flowers sterile, white and 2 in. wide. Later they turn purple. Ga. to Fla. and Miss. June. Hardy from zone* 5 southward, and perhaps in protected parts of zone* 4.

radiata. A remarkably handsome shrub 5–7 ft. high, its leaves ovalish, tapering to the tip, 3–5 in. long, green above, but conspicuously white-hairy beneath. Flowers white, in a flat cluster (corymb*) which may be 5–6 in. wide, often fringed by ray-like sterile flowers, the whole cluster thus encircled by supplementary flowers. N. Car. and S. Car. Summer. Hardy from zone* 4 southward. Perhaps only a form of *H. arborescens.*

scandens = *Hydrangea petiolaris.*

serrata. Tea-of-heaven. A shrub 3–5 ft. high, the leaves elliptic or ovalish, 2–4 in. long, tapering at the tip, but wedge-shaped at the base. Flower cluster flat or slightly arched, 2–3½ in. wide, only a few of the flowers marginal and sterile, blue or white. Jap. and Korea. July–Aug. Hardy from zone* 4 southward. Perhaps only a form of *H. macrophylla.*

volubilis = *Hydrangea petiolaris.*

HYDRANGEACEAE. See SAXIFRAGACEAE.

HYDRANGEA FAMILY. See SAXIFRAGACEAE.

hydrangeoides (hy-dran-jee-oy'deez, but *see* OïDES). Like a hydrangea.

HYDRASTIS. See GOLDENSEAL.

HYDROCHARIS (hy-drok'ar-is). Spongy-leaved, floating aquatic plants of the family Hydrocharitaceae, **H. Morsus-ranae,** the frog's-bit, frequently grown in pools or aquaria. It is a Eurasian plant with very fine, thread-like and silky roots and floating stems with long-stalked, ovalish, spongy, thick leaves about 2 in. wide. Flowers minute, usually unisexual,* white. The plant dies outdoors over the winter, but may be propagated by cuttings of its runner-like stems, or by thickened winter buds which the plant produces in the fall. A graceful and interesting aquatic for the aquarium. (*Hydrocharis* is from the Greek for graceful water plant.)

HYDROCARYACEAE. See TRAPA.

HYDROCHARITACEAE (hy-dro-kăr-i-tay'see-ee). The frog's-bit family is wholly aquatic, all its cult. genera being submerged or floating water plants suited only to aquaria or pond culture. There are 14 genera and perhaps 85 species, found all over the world, some (non-hort.) in the sea.

In the four cult. genera the leaves are submerged and ribbon-like in *Vallisneria* (*see* EEL-GRASS), a popular aquarium plant, but scarcely ½ in. long in *Anacharis,* where, however, they are very numerous. In *Hydro-*

charis and *Stratiotes,* both floating aquatics, the leaves are thick and spongy.

Technical flower characters: The flowers are very small, inconspicuous and extremely simple. They have 3 minute sepals and 3 equally small petals, an inferior* ovary and 3–12 stamens. Fruit minute, nut-like.

HYDROCLEIS (hy'dro-cleez). Also spelled *Hydrocleys.* Brazilian, aquatic herbs of the family Butomaceae, one of the three known species cult. for the aquarium, for greenhouse pools, or outdoors south of zone* 7. The only cult. species is H. nymphoides, the water poppy, which is sometimes offered as *Limnocharis humboldti,* more rarely as *Hydrocleis commersoni.* It has creeping stems which root in the mud and long-stalked, ovalish or narrower, floating leaves. Flowers on long stalks arising from joints of the stem, floating, about 2½ in. wide. Sepals 3, leathery and persistent. Petals 3, light yellow. Fruit a collection of 5–7 carpels which are not united. If grown in a tub, fill it about ⅔ full of potting mixture* 4 and plant the roots in it, covering them with a layer of sand about ½ in. thick. Fill the tub with water and put in a warm, sunny place. Only 2 or 3 roots are needed for each tub. Outdoor planting or that in a greenhouse pool may be directly in the mud, but not over 2½ ft. below the water surface, and preferably less. It will spread rapidly, but will stand no frost. (*Hydrocleis* is from the Greek for water and key, but the exact application here is unknown.)

HYDROGEN ION CONCENTRATION. See ACID AND ALKALI SOILS.

HYDROPHYLLACEAE (hy-dro-fill-lay'-see-ee). The waterleaf family comprises 18 genera and about 275 species of chiefly herbs, very abundant in N.A., but found widely elsewhere; all the cult. genera grown for ornament.

Leaves mostly opposite* (alternate in some nemophilas), often lobed or deeply cut. Flowers regular, but mostly in terminal or lateral, 1-sided clusters resembling a forget-me-not in aspect. They are showy in *Nemophila, Hydrophyllum, Phacelia, Nama,* and *Emmenanthe,* all of which are herbs of outdoor culture. *Wigandia* is a tropical American shrubby plant with small, tubular flowers, grown as a foliage plant, and *Romanzoffia* is a perennial herb from Calif. to Alaska with the habit of saxifrage. The fruit of all genera is a 2-valved pod (capsule*).

Technical flower characters: Flowers hermaphrodite,* the united calyx 5-parted. Corolla regular,* mostly 5-lobed or 5-parted. Stamens chiefly 5, arising on the corolla and alternate with the lobes of it. Ovary superior,* mostly 1-celled. Styles 2.

HYDROPHYLLUM (hy-dro-fill'um). North American, mostly perennial herbs of the family Hydrophyllaceae, commonly called waterleaf, two of the six known species cult. in the wild garden. They have chiefly basal, divided or cut leaves, and terminal,

---

* Special articles on the subjects indicated by an asterisk (*) will be found at the words so marked.

1-sided clusters (cymes*) of chiefly blue, lavender, or white flowers. Calyx* 5-parted, often with a small appendage between each lobe. Corolla more or less bell-shaped, but sharply 5-toothed or cleft. Stamens* (in ours) much protruding. Fruit a 2-valved capsule,* its seeds globe-shaped. (*Hydrophyllum* is from the Greek for water and leaf, but of no known application here.)

These herbs are of simple culture if given a partly shaded place in the wild garden, preferably planted in rich woods soil. They can easily be increased by division, and they bloom in summer.

canadense. Waterleaf. Leaves with the segments aranged finger-fashion, the lobes 5–7. and more or less rounded, unequally toothed. Flowers white, the stalk of the cluster shorter than the leafstalks. The whole plant is about 18 in. high and nearly smooth. Eastern N.A.

virginianum. Waterleaf; also called Indian salad and Shawnee salad. A perennial herb about 18 in. high, the 5–7 leaf segments arranged feather-fashion, more or less oblongish, pointed, and sharply cut or toothed. Flowers white or violet-purple, the stalk of the cluster longer than the leafstalk. Eastern N.A.

HYDROPONICS. *See* Soilless Gardening.

HYDROSME (hy-dros'me). Tropical, very evil-smelling, rather fleshy herbs of the arum family, the few known species scattered in the East Indies, Africa, and Asia. Only one of them, H. rivieri, the snake palm (it is not a true palm) or devil's-tongue, is occasionally cult. in the tropical greenhouse under the name *Amorphophallus rivieri.* It is a rank-growing herb 3–4 ft. high. Leaves nearly 4 ft. wide, the long, fleshy stalk spotted with brown and white. The leaf blade is divided, finger-fashion, into 3 main divisions, each of which is again divided into more or less triangular, irregularly cleft lobes. The leaves do not develop until the plant is through flowering. Flowers minute (*see* Araceae), crowded on a dense spadix,* which is set in the middle of a spathe* that suggests the calla lily, but dark red and carrion-scented, the whole inflorescence on a stout, fleshy stalk, 3–4 ft. high, dark-colored and red-spotted. The plant grows from a large, bulbous rootstock, and should be planted in potting mixture* 4 and given plenty of water. After it has flowered and leaved, it should be rested over the winter by reducing the water and lowering the temperature to about 50°. Re-pot and put in the tropical greenhouse about the end of March. Sometimes the pots may be plunged* outdoors in a shady place for the summer. (*Hydrosme* is from the Greek and apparently refers to its fondness for plenty of moisture.) The plant is also somewhat grown outdoors from zone* 6 southward. *See also* Amorphophallus.

hyemalis, -e (hy-e-may'lis). Relating to winter.

HYGROMETER. An instrument for measuring the humidity of the air. It is little used by gardeners, but foresters use it as a measure of the humidity of the forest-floor conditions, which much affect the establishment of tree seedlings. The same factors also affect the growth of plants in the wild garden. Most ordinary garden plants are also affected by humidity, but less so than those of the forest.

HYLOCEREUS (hy-lo-seer'ee-us). Showy, tropical American night-blooming cacti, mostly climbing and some tree-perching (epiphytic*), widely grown for their magnificent bloom, one of them commonly called night-blooming cereus (for others *see* Selenicereus and Nyctocereus). They have long, 3-angled or 3-winged stems which bear aerial roots, but only a few, short, stout spines. Flowers large, white (in ours), the outside crowded with leaf-like scales, but without spines or wool as in some related genera. Fruit fleshy, edible in some species. (*Hylocereus* is from the Greek for wood, and *Cereus,* in allusion to their woody stems.)

In Fla. these plants are very popular for covering low walls, or they will climb to a height of 25 ft. if given support. They are also used for hedges. Their immense, night-blooming flowers are among the showiest of the cacti, which see for culture in northern greenhouses. They root easily from cuttings of the stem, preferably with aerial* roots attached.

tricostatus = *Hylocereus undatus.*

undatus. The commonest of the plants known as night-blooming cereus, the stem high-climbing, its ribs or wings thin and wavy-margined. Flowers nearly 12 in. long, pure white, but the outer scales yellowish-green. Fruit oblongish, 4½ in. long, red, edible and often called strawberry pear or pitahaya. Tropical America.

HYMENAEA (hy-men-ee'a). Tropical American trees of the pea family, of little hort. interest, but one of them, H. Courbaril, the West Indian locust, occasionally planted in zone* 9. It is a valuable tree in tropical America, yielding a copal or resin used in varnish, and grows about 60 ft. high, or less in cult. Leaves alternate,* compound,* the leaflets only 2, stalkless, very oblique, but generally oblongish, about 3 in. long. Flowers not pea-like, the sepals 4. the petals 5, not much longer than the sepals, about ¾ in. long, yellow, but purple-striped. Fruit an oblong. woody pod, 3–4 in. long, that does not split (*see* Leguminosae). filled with an acid pulp eaten by the Brazilian Indians. It is rare in cult. in the U.S. (*Hymenaea* is from the Greek for nuptial, in allusion to the paired leaflets.)

HYMENOCALLIS. *See* Spider-lily.

hymenosepala, -us, -um (hy-men-o-see'-pa-la). With membranous sepals.

HYMENOSPORUM (hy-men-o-spore'rum). A single species of Australian evergreen shrubs or trees, family Pittosporaceae, H. flavum cult. for ornament in Calif., but unsuited to most sections of the country. It

---

* Special articles on the subjects indicated by an asterisk (*) will be found at the words so marked.

may reach 50 ft. in the wild, more often a shrub as cult. Leaves alternate,* without teeth, somewhat broader toward the tip, but generally ovalish, 4–6 in. long. Flowers yellow, nearly 1½ in. wide, more or less tubular and felty, and borne in a loose, terminal cluster (umbel*-like). Fruit a capsule about 1 in. long, its seeds winged. Its culture is the same as for the closely related genus *Pittosporum* (which see). (*Hymenosporum* is from the Greek for membrane and seed, in allusion to the winged seeds.)

HYMENOXIS. See BAERIA.

HYOPHORBE (hy-o-for′bee). Pignut palm. A small genus of feather palms from the Mascarene Islands, noteworthy because of their bulging trunks, hence their name of spindle palm or bottle palm. Two of them are planted outdoors in southern Fla. (zone* 9), but little known otherwise. They have handsome crowns of leaves, the many segments of which are set close together on the main leafstalk. Flowering cluster arising just below the crown of leaves, its many branches making a bushy cluster. Flowers small, 3–7 together, the lower 2 in each cluster female. Stamens 6. Fruit oblongish, purple, usually less than 1 in. long (a drupe*). (*Hyophorbe* is from the Greek for food for swine, in allusion to the fleshy fruits.)

As grown in Fla., both the species below make a reasonably rapid growth and thrive in both shade and sunshine on a variety of soils.

amaricaulis. Bottle palm; also called bitter-stem palm. Not usually over 40 ft. (higher in the wild), the trunk swelling near the base of the plant. Leaves 4–7 ft. long, the stalk about 1 ft. long, the segments or leaflets about 18 in. long, strongly veined.

verschaffelti. Spindle palm. As cult. usually 25–30 ft. high, the trunk swelling near the middle or toward the top of the trunk. Leaves 3–6 ft. long, the segments or leaflets about 2 ft. long, only the midrib prominent.

HYOSCYAMUS (hy-o-sy′a-mus). Very poisonous (or medicinal), coarse and clammy herbs of the potato family from the Mediterranean region, **H. niger**, the henbane, and most dangerous of them, occasionally cult. It is a biennial or annual herb 18–30 in. high, with spindle-shaped roots. Leaves alternate,* oblongish, 5–7 in. long, more or less cut or toothed, and narrowed at the base into a clasping stalk. Flowers funnel-shaped, greenish-yellow, but black-veined, nearly stalkless in the leaf axils,* or the upper ones in a small, leafy cluster. Fruit a capsule, enclosed by the persistent and much-enlarged calyx.* The plant is somewhat weedy, easily grown in almost any soil, and is occasionally naturalized in eastern N.A. (*Hyoscyamus* is from the Greek for hog and bean, in reference to its assumed poisoning of hogs.) See POISONOUS PLANTS.

HYPANTHIUM. See RECEPTACLE.

HYPERICACEAE (hy-perry-kay′see-ee). The St. John's-wort family, as here restricted, comprises over 300 species in only three genera, two of which, *Hypericum* and *Ascyrum*, are shrubby herbs, some of which are handsome garden plants of outdoor culture. By some the family is included within the Guttiferae (which see), but that family is here considered as including only tropical shrubs and trees with mostly edible fruit.

Plants of the Hypericaceae have opposite, mostly stalkless leaves, usually prominently spotted with resinous dots. They have regular flowers, mostly yellow or white (rarely pink), sometimes solitary, but typically in branched clusters (cymes*). In the only two cult. genera the sepals and petals are 4 in *Ascyrum*, but 5 in *Hypericum* (see ST. JOHN's-WORT). Fruit a dry, many-seeded pod (capsule*).

hypericifolia, -us, -um (hy-perry-si-fō′li-a). With leaves like a St. John's-wort (*Hypericum*).

hypericoides (hy-perry-koy′deez, but *see* OÏDES). Like a St. John's-wort (*Hypericum*).

HYPERICUM. See ST. JOHN's-WORT (at Saint).

hypnoides (hip-noy′deez). Moss-like.

HYPOCHAERIS (hy-po-keer′is). Weedy, somewhat dandelion-like, chiefly Old World herbs of the family Compositae, one of the cult. species sometimes grown for ornament, the other a weed. They have mostly basal, cut or toothed, dandelion-like leaves and solitary or few heads of yellow flowers, all of which have only ray* flowers. Fruit a small, 10-ribbed achene,* plumed. (*Hypochaeris* is an old name of uncertain application here.)

There is no trouble about growing either of those below, but the first is sometimes a troublesome weed.

radicata. Cat's-ear; also called California dandelion (not native there) and gosmore. A coarse perennial herb, the stems nearly 2 ft. high, the leaves deeply toothed or lobed. Flower heads solitary, about 2 in. wide, deep-yellow. Eu., but common as a weed in N.A. See list at WEEDS.

uniflora. A perennial herb 12–18 in. high and hairy. Leaves oblongish or narrower. Flower heads mostly solitary, about 1 in. wide, yellow. European mountains. Rare in cult.

hypochondriaca, -us, -um (hy-po-kon-dry′-a-ka). Morbid.

hypogaea, -us, -um (hy-po-jee′a). Underground, or developing underground, as in the peanut.

hypoglottis, -e (hy-po-glot′tis). With a swollen tongue.

HYPOXIS (hy-pocks′is). A widely distributed, but chiefly tropical, genus of 100 species of grass-like, perennial herbs, family Amaryllidaceae, commonly called star-grass. The only cult. species is H. hirsuta, the yellow star-grass, more often called yellow-eyed grass. Its grass-like, ribbed leaves are nearly

---

* Special articles on the subjects indicated by an asterisk (*) will be found at the words so marked.

12 in. long and about ⅟₁₆ in. wide, arising from a stout rootstock. Flowers yellow, star-like, about ½ in. wide, only a few in a terminal cluster on a leafless stalk, the outside of the flower greenish. Of very easy culture in open, sandy soil. July. N.Y. to Fla. and westward. (*Hypoxis* is the Greek name for some plant with sourish leaves, but probably not this one.)

HYSSOP. See Hyssopus.

HYSSOP FAMILY = Labiatae.

hyssopifolia, -us, -um (his-sop-i-fō'li-a). With hyssop-like leaves.

HYSSOPUS (his-soap'us). A single species of Eurasian under-shrubs of the mint family, widely grown for ornament and as an herb for flavoring. The only species is **H. officinalis**, the hyssop. It is somewhat woody, 12–18 in. high, the stems 4-sided. Leaves opposite,* oblong or narrower, 1–2 in. long, without teeth. Flowers irregular,* 2-lipped,* about ½ in. long, blue, in 1-sided, terminal spikes 3–5 in. long. Fruit a collection of 4 egg-shaped, somewhat 3-angled nutlets. For culture and uses *see* Herb Gardening. The *var.* albus has white flowers; *var.* ruber, red flowers; and the *var.* grandiflorus has considerably larger flowers. (*Hyssopus* is a very old name for the hyssop, but whether the sacred hyssop of the Jews is this plant or not is uncertain.)

hystrix (hiss'tricks). Bristly, like a porcupine.

I

iberica, -us, -um (eye-beer'i-ka). From Spain or Portugal.

iberidifolia, -us, -um (eye-ber-id-i-fō'li-a). With leaves like a candytuft.

IBERIS. See Candytuft.

IBIDIUM = *Spiranthes.*

IBOLIUM PRIVET = *Ligustrum Ibolium.* See Privet.

Ibota (eye-bo'ta). Japanese name for the ibota privet (*Ligustrum obtusifolium*). See Privet.

IBOZA (eye-bō'za). A genus of African shrubs or herbs of the mint family, **I. riparia**, cult. for ornament outdoors in zones* 8 and 9, sometimes under the name of *Moschosma.* It is a stout herb, 3–5 ft. high, with square stems, and opposite,* aromatic, broadly ovalish leaves 1–2 in. long, coarsely toothed and also notched at the base. Male and female flowers on separate plants, both very small, cream-white, numerous, in erect, terminal clusters (panicles*) which stand above the foliage. Corolla only slightly irregular, its limb 4–5-lobed. Stamens* 4. The plants should be cut to the ground after blooming. If grown under glass, give them a cool greenhouse, where they should bloom in winter. Propagated by cuttings. (*Iboza* is a Latinized version of a Kafir name for these plants.)

Icaco (i-kā'ko). The Spanish name of the coco-plum. See Chrysobalanus.

ICELAND BUCKWHEAT = *Fagopyrum tataricum.* See Buckwheat.

ICELAND POPPY = *Papaver nudicaule.* See Poppy.

ICE-PLANT = *Mesembryanthemum crystalinum.*

idaea, -us, -um (eye-dee'a). From Mt. Ida, Asia Minor.

IDAHO. The mock-orange is the state flower. The state lies in zones* 2 and 3.

Soils. The soil types of Idaho are as varied as its topography and climate, and exert an important influence on the character of the horticulture practiced in different parts of the state. Some of the glacial and residual soils of the northern panhandle, varying from fertile, deep silt loams and clay loams to sand and gravel are exceedingly productive; while others, of a morainic character, are so low in organic matter and natural fertility that they are unsuitable for crop production. The aeolian or "wind-blown" soils of the Palouse country are usually deep and fertile, and, where erosion has not been excessive, produce high yields of cereals, peas, and potatoes. The desert soils of the irrigated valleys and plateaus of southern Idaho are typified by the productive soils of the Boise-Payette region and the Snake River valley. Here the soils, mostly aeolian in origin, are often deep and fertile but sometimes are deficient in organic matter and nitrogen. Small, scattered areas of high alkali concentration, or "slick spots," within this region are unproductive. On the whole, the irrigated soils of the southern parts of the state are well adapted to the production of fruits, vegetables and alfalfa.

Chief Gardening Centers. The Snake River from Saint Anthony to Weiser describes the arc of a semicircle that passes through, or borders on, the principal fruit and vegetable areas of Idaho. Apples comprise the most important fruit crop, principally in an area embracing Weiser, Caldwell, and Boise, and in the Twin Falls-Burley region. The Italian prune, marketed largely as a fresh fruit, is the second most important fruit

---

* Special articles on the subjects indicated by an asterisk (*) will be found at the words so marked.

crop. Sweet cherries are grown on a limited scale in these southern districts, while both cherries and apples are produced in commercial quantities on the plateaus overlooking Lewiston, where the Snake River leaves the state border to enter Washington. Apples are now grown only to a limited extent under dry-land conditions in Latah and Kootenai counties, where, in earlier days, apples were a major crop. Peaches and pears are grown to a limited extent at Lewiston for local markets, and on bench lands in the Payette-Emmett region both for local markets and for a limited out-of-state trade. Strawberries, brambles, and American grapes are grown for home consumption in most parts of the state at altitudes of 6000 feet or less.

Onions are produced in abundance for distant and near-distant markets. The principal area for onions is the southwestern part of the state. A great variety of vegetables is grown for local markets in the fertile bottom lands and bench lands near Boise, Weiser, Caldwell, Twin Falls, Lewiston, Coeur d'Alene and other large towns and cities. Vegetable-seed production is an important commercial industry, centering in Canyon County, near Caldwell. In general it might be stated that many kinds of vegetables and most of the temperate-zone fruits can be grown to perfection throughout extensive areas of southwestern Idaho. In total income produced by Idaho farm products the potato ranks first.

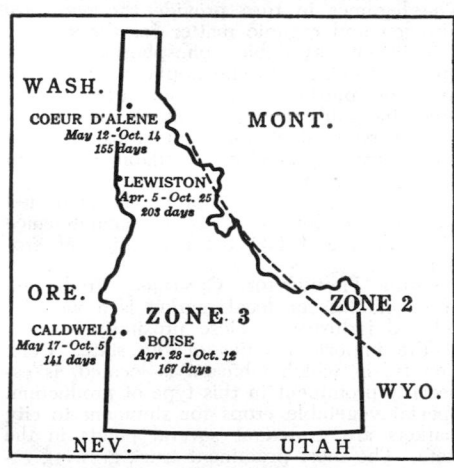

IDAHO

The zones of hardiness crossing Idaho are those shown on the map located at ZONE, which should be consulted for details. The dates are the average latest killing frost in spring and the first one in the fall. The figures below the dates show the average length of the growing season. Annual rainfall near Salmon may not be over 10 in., while at Burke it is over 40 in.

BEST ORNAMENTAL PLANTS. With the exception of arid and semi-arid regions of the state, most parts of Idaho enjoy a wide variety of attractive native flowers, ornamental shrubs and trees. Outstanding among the ornamentals are the common wild rose (*Rosa nutkana*), mock-orange, snowberry, Oregon grape, red osier, golden currant, and cream bush. Among the particularly desirable, native, small trees or large, shrub-like forms might be mentioned the chokecherry, serviceberry, hawthorn and some of the willows. If larger trees are desired for shade or background planting the aspen, birch, alder, mountain-ash, cottonwood, Douglas fir, and Englemann spruce offer a good selection. Among the most striking of the flowering annuals and perennials, especially abundant in the northern parts of the state, are fireweed, dog-tooth violets, wild iris, wild geranium, *Clarkia*, and the lupines. Many cultivated flowers and shrubs, not native, thrive in most of the agricultural regions of the state.

FRUIT. For home use a wide variety of tree fruits and small fruits are successfully grown in most of the more heavily populated parts of the state. Apples, pears, sour cherries, plums, raspberries, and strawberries can be grown almost anywhere at altitudes under 3000 ft., and in the more southerly portions their range may sometimes be extended to over 5000 ft. if only the hardier varieties are planted. The culture of sweet cherries is limited by low winter temperatures. They are not generally satisfactory in the northern parts of the state at altitudes above 2800 ft., nor in the southern portions above 3800 ft. The distribution of peaches and grapes is limited more by low summer temperature than by severe winters. These fruits attain their best quality in the northern half of the state at elevations under 2000 ft., and in southern areas under 3000 ft. Both reach perfection in the hotter river valleys as at Lewiston, and in Canyon, Payette, Gem, and Adams counties. In the warmer sites in those places some of the European grapes do fairly well. Apricots are grown where peaches thrive, but they are likely to be unsatisfactory because of their early blooming habit which makes them especially subject to damage by spring frost.

CLIMATE. The extent of the state from south to north and the ruggedness of its topography give to Idaho a wide range of climatic conditions. Some of the higher mountainous regions to the east, at altitudes exceeding 11,000 feet, enjoy cool nights and warm days in summer and suffer extreme cold in winter. At lower altitudes, as in the vicinity of Lewiston, summers are very hot but winters are short and mild. The following list of frost dates indicates the extremes in length of growing seasons at different altitudes and latitudes within the state.

Rainfall over much of the southern part of the state is deficient for crop production without irrigation. In many of the northern counties dry-land farming is practiced but only early-maturing crops are grown. Rain-

Station	Av. date of last killing frost in spring	Latest-known killing frost	Av. date of earliest killing frost in fall	Earliest-known killing frost
Boise	Apr. 28	June 16	Oct. 12	Sept. 11
Caldwell	May 17	June 9	Oct. 5	Sept. 14
Lewiston	Apr. 5	Apr. 29	Oct. 25	Oct. 5
Coeur d'Alene	May 12	June 12	Oct. 14	Aug. 31

fall in the mountains is relatively high. Extremes between the arid and rainy regions are represented by Salmon with an annual rainfall of 9.6 inches, and Burke with an annual rainfall of 44.2 inches. Space does not permit discussion of seasonal distribution of rainfall, which varies so greatly among different locations that averages for the state have no meaning.

The address of the Agricultural Experiment Station, which has kindly supplied this information about Idaho, is Moscow, Idaho. The station is always ready to answer gardening questions.

IDAHO POTATO. See POTATO.

IDA-MAIA. See BREVOORTIA.

IDESIA (eye-dee′zee-a). A single tree from Eastern Asia, family Flacourtiaceae, often cult. more for interest than ornament. The only species, **I. polycarpa**, is a medium-sized tree, with grayish-white bark, alternate, long-stalked leaves, the blade ovalish, its margins wavy-toothed. Flowers fragrant, in loose clusters, yellowish-green, the sexes on different trees or in different clusters on the same tree. Fruit an orange-red berry, borne in large clusters, very handsome. May. Hardy from zone° 4, or safer, from zone° 5 southward. (*Idesia* was named in honor of Eberhard Y. Ides, a Dutch explorer who went to China about 1720.)

ignea, -us, -um (ig′nee-a). Colored like flame; fiery.

ILEX. See HOLLY. *See also Quercus Ilex* at OAK.

ILICACEAE = Aquifoliaceae.

ilicifolia, -us, -um (il-li-see-fō′li-a). With leaves like the holly (*Ilex*).

illecebrosa, -us, -um (ill-le-see-brō′sa). Growing in the shade.

ILLICIUM (il-li′si-um). A genus of 20 species of shrubs and trees of the family Magnoliaceae, all of them natives of Asia, except two found in the southeastern U.S. They have aromatic, evergreen, alternate° leaves, usually short-stalked and without marginal teeth. Flowers yellowish or purplish-red, solitary or in few-flowered clusters in the leaf axils.° Sepals (which soon fall away) 3–6. Petals 9 or more. Stamens numerous. Fruit a collection of woody, slowly splitting follicles,° sometimes star-like. (*Illicium* is Latin for something enticing, in allusion to their pleasant aroma.)

Neither of the plants below, both Asiatic, is hardy north of zone° 7. The native species, wild in Fla. and La., seem not to be in general cult.

anisatum. A shrub or small tree, not over 12 ft. high. Leaves more or less elliptic, 2–3 in. long. Flowers about 1 in. wide, yellowish-green, the stalk bracted,° the petals many and narrow. Jap. Sometimes known as *I. religiosum.*

religiosum = *Illicium anisatum.*

verum. Star anise; also called Chinese anise. A shrub or small tree, usually 9 ft. high or less. Leaves elliptic or slightly broader at the tip. Flowers purplish-red, the petals about 10. Fruits making a star-shaped cluster (of follicles°), anise-scented, carminative, and generally known as badian. China. The plant is rare in cult. in the U.S.

ILLINOIS. The violet is the state flower, the oak the state tree. The state is wholly in zones° 2, 3, and 4. The climate and soils are well adapted to the production of a wide range of horticultural plants, both from an amateur and a commercial standpoint.

SOILS. In characterizing the soils of Illinois one notes first the great profusion of varieties. No less than 214 distinguishable soil types have, to date, been identified by the State Soil Survey. These types represent all degrees of productiveness ranging from barren wastes to highly fertile land. Fortunately, the latter predominate.

The material most frequently required for soil improvement is limestone, in order to insure the successful growth of legumes. The legumes in turn provide the necessary nitrogen and organic matter for the soil.

Sufficient available phosphorus is frequently lacking and the application of some form of phosphate is often attended by profitable gains in crop yields. With the continuous removal of abundant crops from the soil, a growing need for available potassium is also apparent.

The two outstanding problems connected with Illinois soils are (1) the maintenance of fertility, and (2) the prevention of erosion.

CHIEF PRODUCTION CENTERS. Production of vegetables for local market is a well-developed industry in close proximity to each of the important cities of the state. Cook County, in which Chicago is located, is especially prominent in this type of production. Special vegetable crops for shipment to city markets are grown at several points in the state. The most prominent truck-growing region is in Union and adjacent counties in the southern end of the state. Here tomatoes, cucumbers, snap beans, squash, and sweet potatoes are especially important. Asparagus is also extensively grown in Madison, Ogle, and La Salle counties. Watermelons thrive on the sandy soil along the Wabash, Illinois, and Mississippi rivers, and muskmelons are grown to some extent in the same regions and also in certain other parts of the state. Sweet corn for canning is produced in large quantities in the central and northern parts of the state, as are peas.

° Special articles on the subjects indicated by an asterisk (°) will be found at the words so marked.

Commercial grape production is most highly developed in Hancock and St. Clair counties. Strawberries are produced principally in Pulaski, Union, Fayette, and Edgar counties.

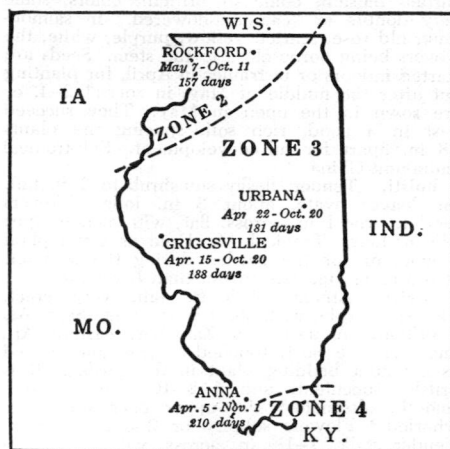

ILLINOIS

The zones of hardiness crossing Illinois are those shown on the map located at ZONE, which should be consulted for details. The dates are the average latest killing frost in spring and the first one in the fall. The figures below the dates show the average length of the growing season. Rainfall is adequate.

ORNAMENTAL PLANTS AND HOME GARDENS. The nursery business has been conspicuous in Illinois since an early date. Formerly fruit trees predominated, but more recently the production of ornamentals has been emphasized.

The American elm was probably the most popular street tree in Illinois, but the Dutch elm disease has reduced it greatly. Hackberry and sycamore have largely replaced it. The hard maple is also a favorite in some parts of the state. Shrubs and vines in wide variety enhance the beauty of the landscape in both public and private grounds. Flowering bulbs, herbaceous perennials, and annual flowers thrive in great profusion wherever they are given proper care.

Home vegetable gardens are a source of pleasure and profit on Illinois farms and suburban places. The long-row farm garden, recommended by the College of Agriculture, University of Illinois, is especially well adapted to Illinois conditions.

CLIMATE. Since Illinois comprises an area nearly four hundred miles long, north and south, there is considerable difference in temperature and in the length of the growing season in different parts of the state. Frost data for four different locations are presented in the accompanying table. The

DATES OF FROSTS IN FOUR ILLINOIS LOCALITIES

Name of town	Av. date of last killing frost in spring	Latest-known killing frost
Anna (Union County)	April 5	May 1
Griggsville (Pike County)	April 15	May 7
Urbana (Champaign County)	April 22	May 25
Rockford (Winnebago County)	May 7	May 27

Name of town	Av. date of earliest killing frost in fall	Earliest-known killing frost
Anna (Union County)	Nov. 1	Sept. 30
Griggsville (Pike County)	Oct. 20	Sept. 22
Urbana (Champaign County)	Oct. 20	Sept. 14
Rockford (Winnebago County)	Oct. 11	Sept. 14

mean annual temperature at Anna, in the southern part of the state, is 57.1° F., at Griggsville 53.9° F., at Urbana 51.5° F., and at Rockford 48.8° F. The average length of the growing season (that is, the period between the latest killing frost of spring and the earliest killing frost of fall) at Anna is 210 days, at Griggsville 188 days, at Urbana 181 days, and at Rockford 157 days.

The average annual rainfall is considerably greater in the southern than in the northern part of the state, being 46.67 inches at Anna and 33.51 inches at Rockford. However, a larger percentage of the total precipitation occurs during the period from April to September inclusive in the northern part of the state, being 62 per cent at Rockford, as compared with 55 per cent at Anna. Thus the average precipitation during the growing season is 20.97 inches at Rockford and 25.79 inches at Anna.

RAINFALL IN CERTAIN ILLINOIS LOCALITIES

Town	Total annual		
	Av.	High	Low
Anna	46.67	64.93	32.75
Griggsville	37.07	57.36	24.09
Urbana	35.34	55.93	23.47
Rockford	33.51	43.30	22.87

Town	April to Sept. incl.		
	Av.	High	Low
Anna	25.79	35.63	13.14
Griggsville	23.59	45.92	12.08
Urbana	21.00	35.30	9.88
Rockford	20.97	30.17	13.41

The address of the Illinois Agricultural Experiment Station, which has kindly supplied this information about the state, is

* Special articles on the subjects indicated by an asterisk (*) will be found at the words so marked.

Urbana, Illinois. The station is always ready to answer gardening questions.

Garden club activities in Illinois are extensive. There are several clubs of the Garden Club of America, the home office of which is 598 Madison Avenue, New York 22, N.Y. The Garden Club of Illinois, Inc., also has over 200 chapters.

illustris, -e (il-lus′tris). Brilliant or lustrous.

illyrica, -us, -um (ill-ir′i-ka). From the ancient kingdom of Illyria, now Yugoslavia.

ilvensis, -e (il-ven′sis). Described first as from the Island of Elba. Applied to *Woodsia ilvensis* (which see), now known to be a widely distributed fern.

imbricaria, -us, -um (im-bri-cay′rĭ-a). Imbricate.

imbricata, -us, -um (im-bri-kay′ta). Imbricate; *i.e.*, overlapping as though shingled.

IMMORTELLE. An everlasting (which see); specifically often applied to *Xeranthemum annuum.*

IMPATIENS (im-pay′shens). A genus belonging to the balsam family, represented by nearly 500 species widely distributed, found in As., tropical Af. and N.A. They are tender, succulent annuals and perennials with irregular,* spurred* flowers which may be solitary or clustered in the axils* of the leaves. The fruit, a pod, will burst easily, often scattering the seeds, the plants deriving therefrom the names — touch-me-not, snapweed. (*Impatiens* is from the Latin for impatience, in allusion to the bursting of the pods.)

Garden Balsam (*Impatiens Balsamina*), a tender annual with flowers of nearly all colors except blue in its many hort. forms.

They are easily started from seeds. The species grown as house plants, or for bedding, are also propagated by cuttings, especially when varieties with striking colors

have developed, in order to assure their coming true.

Balsamina. Tender annual, 24–30 in. tall, stiff and erect. Stem brittle and succulent, leaves smooth, lanceolate. Flowers of cultivated varieties of this species called lady′s-slipper or garden balsam, come in brilliant colors, some very double or "camellia-flowered," in salmon-pink, old rose, scarlet, yellow, purple, white, the flowers being borne close to the stem. Seeds are started indoors or in frames in April, for planting out after the middle of May, in zones* 2–4, or are sown in the open in May. They succeed best in a good, rich soil, spacing the plants 18 in. apart for full development. Sub-tropical India and China.

holsti. Tender, fleshy sub-shrub to 3 ft. tall, the leaves ovate, about 3 in. long. Flowers scarlet, over 1 in. across, flat, with slender spur 1½ in. long. Tropical Af. Used as a pot plant indoors or for the garden during the summer. It is a more vigorous grower than *I. sultani.*

roylei. Annual, 4–5 ft. tall, very erect. Flowers purple, with short spur. Aug.–Sept. As.

sultani. A native of Zanzibar, eastern Af., and therefore easily touched by frost and treated as a tender bedding plant in the garden. It is brittle, succulent, and 1–2 ft. high. Leaves smooth, alternate,* the upper ones sometimes whorled.* Flowers solitary or 2–3 on a short, slender stalk, 1–1½ in. across, with thin, long spur curving up. Bright scarlet in the original form, hybrids and sports in shades of pink, salmon, purple, white.

Jewelweed and snapweed are the names applied to N.A. species *I. biflora* and *I. pallida*, which are scarcely garden plants.

impedita, -us, -um (im-ped-dy′ta). Tangled.

imperati (im-per-ray′ti). Showy; imperial.

IMPERFECT FLOWER. One having stamens* or pistils,* but not both. *See* PERFECT.

imperialis, -e (im-peer-ĭ-ā′lis). Fine or showy; imperial.

IMPERIAL JAPANESE MORNING-GLORY. *See* IPOMOEA NIL.

IMPERIAL LOCUST = *Gleditsia triacanthos inermis. See* HONEY LOCUST.

IMPREGNATION. *See* FERTILIZATION.

INARCHING. *See* GRAFTING.

INBREEDING. When a plant is selfed,* and its progeny selfed, and so on for several generations, the procedure is called inbreeding, and the results are inbred plants or strains of plants. This example illustrates the most intense type of inbreeding. Where selfing is not possible or practicable, brother-sister crossing may be practiced, involving two closely related plants. Inbreeding is a matter of degree. Close inbreeding in many plants, especially normally cross-fertilized plants such as maize, often results in decreased vigor, size, and yield, though this is not necessarily so. Actually, inbreeding tends to sort out pure breeding types, so that in a comparatively few generations the inbred lines cease to show any effect from inbreeding — the sorting process has stopped because everything is sorted. These sorted-out types may be good, poor, or indifferent. Many of our very valuable plant varieties have resulted from crossing and subsequent inbreeding. — O. E. W.

incana, -us, -um (in-kay'na). Whitish or grayish-white.

incarnata, -us, -um (in-kar-nay'ta). Flesh-colored.

INCARVILLEA (in-kar-vil'lee-a). Tender herbaceous perennials belonging to the family Bignoniaceae. Leaves alternate,° 2-3-pinnate,° segments narrow. Flowers trumpet-shaped, five-lobed, spreading, somewhat irregular,° in terminal clusters, red to yellow. Species native to Tibet and China. Fruit a capsule. (Named for Father Incarville, French Jesuit in China.)

They should be given a sheltered position, in a sunny and warm spot in the garden. A well-drained soil, preferably sandy, enriched with humus, is best suited for their culture. They require special winter protection and are not hardy from zone° 3 northward.

delavayi. Semi-hardy perennial with graceful, pinnate leaves to 1 ft. long, each leaf with as many as 15–21 segments. Flower stalk to 2 ft. tall, rising above the foliage, bearing from 2 to 12 large, trumpet-shaped flowers, rosy-purple, the individual flower 1 to 2 in. long and as wide. Tube yellow inside and outside, the 2 upper lobes somewhat smaller than the 3 lower ones. Also called hardy gloxinia. Propagated by seeds and by division. Native of China.

delavayi grandiflora = *Incarvillea grandiflora*.

grandiflora. Similar to *I. delavayi*, but not as robust in growth. Leaflets shorter, the flowers fewer, but larger and with deeper trumpets. Deep rosy-red. The *var.* **brevipes** has brilliant crimson flowers.

variabilis. A somewhat woody perennial, 18–30 in. high, the leaves twice or thrice pinnate,° the segments finely dissected. Flowers about 1 in. wide, rose-pink, often 8–10 on each plant. Blooming most of the summer, and flowering the first year from seed. China.

INCENSE CEDAR. The incense cedars belong to the genus **Libocedrus** (lee-bo-see'-drus), a small group in the pine family. They are handsome evergreen trees of pyramidal or spreading habit and with small, scale-like leaves on flattened branches; quite suggestive of arborvitae. Cones oblong, with 4–6 woody scales. (*Libocedrus* is from the Greek for drop, and cedar, referring to the oozing resin.)

Only one species can be grown outdoors in the North. Where hardy they are splendid ornamental trees, and in their native countries are widely used for their durable timber. A rather open, well-drained situation seems to be preferred. Propagation is mainly by seeds sown in the spring. *See* EVERGREENS.

L. chilensis. Alerce. Chilean arborvitae. A compact, pyramidal tree attaining 60 ft. Leaves small and spreading, glaucous, with a white line beneath; branchlets flattened. Cone oval, about ½ in. long. Chile. Hardy only in zones° 8 and 9.

L. decurrens. Incense cedar. White cedar. Columnar or narrow pyramidal tree growing 50–100 ft. high, occasionally higher. Bark red-brown, loose or scaly. Leaves small, scale-like, opposite. pressed close to the stem except at tip, dark glossy-green. Branches upright, flattened vertically. Cones ¾–1 in. long, oval or oblong. Ore. and western Nev. to southern Calif. in the mountains. Hardy from zone° 4 (3 in some places) southward. Some prefer to call this *Heyderia decurrens.*

INCHWORM. Most common of these measuring worms or inchworms which travel by a looping gait are the cankerworms. These pests feed on leaves of many trees, causing much damage. Pesticide #1 or #19 will control them easily. Females of fall and spring species are wingless and must climb trees to lay eggs in fall or spring, according to species. Banding trees with a sticky chemical in later summer and late winter will prevent ascent of females to trees and egg-laying. (*See* SPRAYS AND DUSTS.) — L. G. M.

INCIENSO = *Encelia farinosa.*

incisa, -us, -um (in-sy'za). Incised; *i.e.*, cut or slashed more or less deeply and irregularly.

INCLUDED. Not protruding beyond the corolla. Many stamens° are included; others are exserted or protruding.

INDEHISCENT. Not splitting. *See* DEHISCENCE.

indentata, -us, -um (in-den-tay'ta). Indented or toothed.

INDETERMINATE. A term applied to tomato plants in which terminal growth is not prevented by flower (and fruit) clusters at the apex. Such plants grow and bear until frost, a disadvantage in a short-season region. *See* DETERMINATE.

INDIAN. As part of the name of many plants *Indian* is both very common and a little confusing. It was applied, after the discovery of America, to many plants used by or identified with the North American Indians, but it had also long been used to designate plants from India or once thought to grow there. Those that occur in the ENCYCLOPEDIA OF GARDENING with their proper equivalents, are listed below, the unmarked ones from the New World, those with a † from the Old World.

†Indian almond = *Terminalia Catappa*; Indian apple = *Podophyllum peltatum* (*see* MAYAPPLE); Indian bean = *Catalpa bignonioides*; Indian blanket = *Gaillardia pulchella*; Indian breadroot = *Psoralea esculenta*; Indian cherry = *Rhamnus caroliniana*; Indian cress = *Tropaeolum majus* (*see* NASTURTIUM); Indian cucumber-root = *Medeola virginiana*; Indian cup = *Silphium perfoliatum*; Indian currant = *Symphoricarpos orbiculatus*; Indian dye = *Hydrastis canadensis* (*see* GOLDENSEAL); Indian fig = *Opuntia Ficus-indica*; †Indian hawthorn = *Raphiolepis indica*; Indian hemp = *Apocynum cannabinum*; Indian hippo = *Gillenia trifoliata*; †Indian jujube = *Zizyphus mauritiana*; Indian lettuce = *Pyrola americana*

° Special articles on the subjects indicated by an asterisk (°) will be found at the words so marked.

and *Montia perfoliata*; †Indian licorice = *Abrus precatorius*; †Indian millet = *Pennisetum glaucum*; †Indian mulberry = *Morinda citrifolia*; Indian paint = *Sanguinaria canadensis* (*see* BLOODROOT); Indian paintbrush = *Castilleja californica* and *C. parviflora*; Indian physic (*see* GILLENIA); †Indian pink = *Dianthus chinensis*; Indian pink = *Silene virginica*; Indian pitcher = *Sarracenia purpurea* (*see* PITCHER-PLANT); Indian poke = *Veratrum viride*; Indian potato = *Helianthus giganteus* (*see* SUNFLOWER); Indian plum family = Flacourtiaceae; Indian rice = *Zizania aquatica*; Indian sage = *Eupatorium perfoliatum*; Indian salad = *Hydrophyllum virginianum*; Indian sanicle = *Eupatorium rugosum*; Indian shot (*see* CANNA); †Indian strawberry = *Duchesnea indica*; Indian tea = *Ceanothus americanus*; †Indian tree cotton = *Gossypium arboreum*; †Indian trumpet-flower = *Oroxyton indicum*; Indian turnip = *Arisaema triphyllum*. See also PSORALEA.

INDIANA. The state flower is the zinnia, and the state tree is the tulip-tree. The state lies wholly in zone* 3.

The soils of Indiana are divided into about five principal soil types, so far as fruits and vegetables are concerned. There are several hundred thousand acres of muck soils in northern Indiana, bordered with considerable quantities of a rich sandy loam. South of the sandy loam area lie the fertile prairie soils that extend as far south as central Indiana. A major portion of south-central and southern Indiana is made up of unglaciated clay, including the more hilly or knob region to the southeast and the low sandy area which lies to the southwest, especially along the White and Wabash rivers.

INDIANA

The zones of hardiness crossing Indiana are those shown on the map located at ZONE, which should be consulted for details. The dates are the average latest killing frost in spring and the first one in the fall. The figures below the dates show the average length of the growing season.

The state is ideally situated for the growing and marketing of horticultural crops. The chief gardening centers are located near the larger industrial cities, such as Indianapolis, Gary, South Bend, Fort Wayne, Richmond, Muncie, and Terre Haute. Numerous greenhouses for both flowers and vegetables are found throughout the state in most cities and towns with 3000 or more population. Sweet corn, tomatoes, beans, popcorn, and pumpkin are the main crops processed.

The fruit-growing sections for small fruits and tree fruits are distributed over the state except on the muck soils. The area covered in a radius of 75 miles from Vincennes and the northern tier of counties produce the most peaches.

The muck soils of northern Indiana are devoted mostly to potatoes, peppermint and spearmint oil production, general outdoor vegetable crops, and onions. The sandy soils of the south-central and southwestern part of the state harvest large acreages of muskmelons, watermelons, tomatoes, peppers, cabbage, and some sweet potatoes for the early market.

An ample supply of water for irrigation purposes is available from deep wells, streams, lakes, and farm ponds to supplement the rainfall. The average rainfall is slightly over 40 inches, varying from 35 inches in the north to 47 inches in the south.

A wide range of flowers may be cultivated in Indiana. Many ornamental trees and shrubs will grow readily under Indiana conditions, including:

TREES	SHRUBS
Oak	Cercis canadensis
Hickory	Barberry
Maple	Cornus stolonifera
Beech	Hydrangea
Gum	Lilac
Walnut	Philadelphus (*see* MOCK-ORANGE)
Sycamore	Forsythia
Tulip-tree	Lonicera
Flowering	Ceanothus
dogwood	Spiraea
Hop-horn-	Viburnum
beam	
Hornbeam	

Town	Frost Data Av. date last killing frost in spring	Av. date earliest killing frost in fall
South Bend	May 6	Oct. 11
Indianapolis	Apr. 23	Oct. 15
Evansville	Apr. 15	Oct. 20

The Agricultural Experiment Station is located in West Lafayette and any inquiries mailed to the Director of the Station will be forwarded to the proper department. The Horticulture Department is always ready to

---

* Special articles on the subjects indicated by an asterisk (*) will be found at the words so marked.

answer questions pertaining to fruits, flowers, vegetables, nuts, and native fruits.

There are 167 active garden clubs in the state affiliated with the Federated Garden Clubs of America. Further information on the garden clubs and horticultural activities may be obtained by writing to the Department of Horticulture.

INDIA WHEAT = *Fagopyrum tataricum.* See BUCKWHEAT.

indica, -us, -um (in'di-ka). From India, but many plants described as from India were subsequently found in widely scattered regions, once generally called "the Indies."

INDIGEN. A native plant, then said to be indigenous, not exotic. See CULTIGEN.

INDIGO. See INDIGOFERA.

INDIGOFERA (in-di-goff'er-a). Herbaceous perennials and shrubs, belonging to the Leguminosae, with about 300 species widely distributed through the tropical regions of the world, especially in As., Af. and the southern part of N.A. Leaves compound.* Flowers pea-like, in axillary racemes, fruits mostly cylindrical pods. (*Indigofera* means indigo-bearing.)

Most of them are not hardy in zones* 1 to 4 and are therefore treated as ornamental conservatory plants. Some species were formerly used in the manufacture of indigo dye by extracting the indigo from the herbage. Propagated by seeds and cuttings.

gerardiana. A low, much-branched shrub, 4–6 ft. high, with silvery-hoary branches. Leaves 1 to 2 in. long, the 9–17 pairs of leaflets about ½ in. long, pale white, firm. Flowers rosyred, hoary outside, in 13–21 flowered racemes.* Pod to 2 in. long. India.

kirilowi. Sub-shrub, 3–4 ft. high. Flowers in axillary racemes,* borne upright, longer than the leaf, bright rose-colored, individual flower 3 in. deep. Leaves with 7–15 pairs of leaflets, which are about 1½ in. long. Propagated by division, suckers, and cuttings. Does not produce seeds readily when in cultivation. Native of northern China and Korea. Hardy from zone* 4 southward. There is also a white-flowered form.

potanini. Shrub to 5 ft. high. Leaves 1½ in. long, the leaflets in 5–7 pairs. Flowers lilac-pink, about ⅓ in. deep, arranged in racemes,* which are longer than the leaves. China.

indivisa, -us, -um (in-di-vy'za). Undivided.

indurata, -us, -um (in-dew-ray'ta). Hardened.

INEQUILATERAL. Unequal-sided; as a leaf which has more of its blade on one side of the midrib than on the other.

inermis, -e (in-er'mis). Unarmed.

INFERIOR. As applied to flowers, the term indicates that the ovary is beneath the point of insertion of the calyx.* It occurs in many plants, notably in flowers of the rose family, in the blueberry, and in the amaryllis family. In the fruits of some of these the

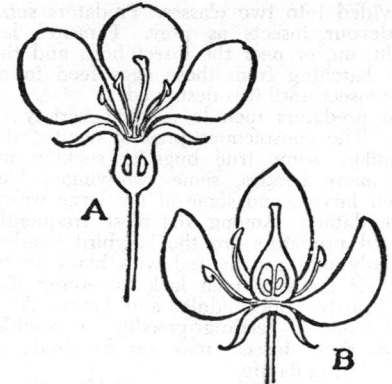

(A) An inferior ovary, the sepals and petals inserted above it. (B) A superior ovary, with the other organs inserted beneath it.

withered calyx persists on the apex of the fruit. See SUPERIOR.

inflata, -us, -um (in-flay'ta). Inflated or swollen.

INFLORESCENCE. The arrangement of flowers in a cluster. It may be simple and solitary, as in the tulip. More often the cluster is compound and variously branched. Of the many types, the leading ones likely to be distinguished by the gardener are all described and figured at PANICLE, RACEME, SPIKE, THYRSE, CYME, and UMBEL. For a special sort of inflorescence, see also ARACEAE.

infundibuliformis, -e (in-fun-dib-you-ly-for'mis). Funnel-shaped.

ingens (in'jenz). Very large.

INKBERRY = *Ilex glabra.* See HOLLY. The name is also applied, more rarely, to *Phytolacca americana* (which see).

INLAYING. See GRAFTING.

INNOCENCE = *Houstonia caerulea.*

innominata, -us, -um (in-nom-in-nay'ta). Hitherto unnamed.

INOCULATION. See LEGUME INOCULATION.

INODES = *Sabal.*

inodora, -us, -um (in-o-door'ra). Not fragrant.

INSECT FRIENDS. Insects pollinate many plants, and furnish food for useful animals, including birds, fish, poultry, and livestock. They produce some important commercial substances, including silk, honey, dyestuffs, wax, and shellac. It has been well said that a world without insects would be strangely lacking in many ways. Some insects perform an important service in killing injurious insects, and many pests are checked by their insect enemies.

The insects that attack other insects may

---

* Special articles on the subjects indicated by an asterisk (*) will be found at the words so marked.

be divided into two classes. Predators seize and devour insects as prey. Parasites lay eggs in, on, or near the insect host, and the larvae hatching from these eggs feed in or on the insect until it is destroyed.

The predators include a great variety of forms. The conspicuous praying mantis, the dragonflies, some true bugs or sucking insects, many beetles, some two-winged flies or their larvae, and some of the large wasps are predators. Among the most frequently observed predators are the ladybird beetles, (the ladybug) usually red with black spots, and their larvae, which look something like little lizards. Both adults and larvae do a useful work in feeding greedily on aphids. One of these insects may eat hundreds of aphids during its life.

Most parasites belong to two of the insect groups, the two-winged flies and the group containing the bees and wasps. The latter parasites are usually small, but on close inspection can be seen to resemble wasps. The different species of parasites vary in size according to the size of the host in which they develop. Even a little aphid may give forth an adult parasite, which has developed to full size inside it. Several small parasites may develop in one large host. A parasite often noticed is the one that affects the large green tomato worm and the caterpillar of the catalpa sphinx. A dead or sick larva may often be seen covered with white cocoons, which are the cocoons of little parasitic larvae that developed inside it. — L. G. M.

INSECTICIDES. (*Note*: It is advisable to read INSECT PESTS in conjunction with this section.) Tremendous progress has been made in this field since the discovery of DDT's unprecedented insecticidal properties in 1939. Development is constant and will be announced from time to time. The major categories of chemicals, and the individual properties and names of most common materials are given here.

1. **Label Instructions: a valuable guide.** New legislation requires accurate and helpful labeling of all insecticides. The proper dosage for use, precautions to be followed in handling, and specific directions for application on food crops is given on the label. Before gardeners use any material, the label must be consulted. Most labels offer a list of injury-susceptible plants.

2. **Inorganic Poisons: arsenicals, fluorine compounds.** Lead and calcium arsenate are commonly used as stomach poisons for chewing insects. Both materials may injure foliage of plants, particularly snap beans and peaches and other stone fruits. Paris green and magnesium arsenate are no longer used in sufficient quantity to merit discussion here.

Lead arsenate is used on most vegetables and herbaceous and woody plants very effectively. Use the acid lead arsenate form which is the most available. The pink powder is used in water. As a dust, it is already formulated with hydrated lime.

Calcium arsenate is also a pink-colored powder which is somewhat more toxic to plants than lead arsenate. It is usually applied as a dust or as a spray with lime.

Arsenical compounds can be removed from vegetables and fruit by washing. Unlike DDT and some related compounds, arsenicals do not tend to produce aphid and mite problems (*see* DDT below) and are also somewhat fungicidal against leaf diseases.

Cryolite and other fluorine compounds are little used now in garden practice.

Sulphur compounds are much less used than formerly. Uncombined sulphur is usually formulated with rotenone or other materials because of some mite-killing properties. Lime-sulphur is a complex mixture of calcium polysulphides. Formerly prepared by the user, only small amounts are now employed. Commercial lime-sulphur is still employed to some extent against scale insects on shade and orchard trees in the dormant stage. Its paint-staining properties work against its use near homes.

3. **Botanical Poisons: pyrethrins, rotenone, nicotine.** Pyrethrins are extractives from pyrethrum flowers. Several chemical substances make up this group. Sprays of pyrethrins alone or in combination with a synergistic agent such as piperonyl butoxide (or others) are used as a quick "knockdown agent" or contact insecticide against many pests. Because of this quick knockdown power, pyrethins, a synergist, and other slower acting insecticides such as DDT are often combined. A synthetic chemical, allethrin, closely related to pyrethrins, is now being used effectively. Pyrethrin combinations are used against aphids, small caterpillars, and various types of flies.

Rotenone, a fish poison, is obtained from roots of plants of the genera *Derris*, *Lonchocarpus* and others. Dusts containing 1% of rotenone are most commonly used. Rotenone is very effective against many insect species, particularly at high temperatures. Four to 5% wettable powders are also employed. Rotenone applications do not create a toxic residue on plants and for this reason are valuable.

Nicotine sulphate is a salt of the alkaloid extracted from the tobacco plant. The 40% solution in water is marketed commonly as an aphicide. Nicotine sprays leave no residue on vegetables and when used with soap are most effective. Less nicotine is being used than formerly. Fixed nicotine, nicotine dusts, and low-pressure fumigators are rarely employed.

4. **Synthetic Organic Hydrocarbons: DDT, BHC and others.** DDT is an excellent material for control of numerous insect pests. Available in many formulations, DDT gives a long-lasting residue which kills by contact or stomach action. DDT does not kill mites, some species of aphids, and chewing insects. In fact, DDT application will produce troubles with aphids and mites, hence, an aphicide or miticide is often needed

---

* Special articles on the subjects indicated by an asterisk (*) will be found at the words so marked.

where DDT is used. For many uses, DDT is not superior to rotenone or arsenicals for this reason. Vegetables should not be sprayed closer to harvest than indicated on the label. Residues of DDT are not readily removable from produce by even most stringent means.

Methoxychlor is a closely related compound which is less toxic than DDT to man and animals but still quite useful as a garden insecticide when used as directed. Methoxychlor is often included as a general insecticide in general-purpose spray mixtures. TDE (DDD) is very similar to DDT in effectiveness and will control hornworms of tomato and tobacco better than DDT.

Lindane is one form from the crude chemical BHC which is widely used to control aphids, ants, certain beetles, and grubs. Lindane is more volatile than DDT and its close relatives and will give a certain fumigating effect.

Chlordane is a widely used material to control ants, grubs in lawns, weevils, and many household pests. Heptachlor, one of the chemicals in technical chlordane, is more volatile than chlordane and widely used in agriculture. Aldrin and dieldrin, members of this terpene group, will find some use in control of grubs, wireworms, and ants. All these materials are available in many formulations. In general, these materials are more toxic than DDT and should be handled with due care.

5. Synthetic Organic Phosphates, Malathion, etc. For the non-commercial gardener, only malathion in this group is safe enough for handling without special precautions. Malathion is available in many formulations and will kill aphids, mites, and many sucking and chewing pests. Malathion residues last only a few days and except for its odor, it is an excellent chemical. Other phosphates, such as parathion, are equally effective but not recommended for general use unless protective clothing, rubber gloves, special respirator, and boots are worn. Several other phosphates are in the development stage, such as diazinon, trithion, and others.

All phosphate materials will cause slight injury to tender foliage. Liquid formulations are more injurious and kerosene formulations are sometimes quite toxic. Wettable powders are safer; dusts will produce injury by use of excessive quantities.

6. Systemic Insecticides: demeton, etc. These materials show an entirely new method of insect control by spraying plants or treating soil with materials, which are translocated through the plant and kill insects feeding on tissue, which has been developed. Far more satisfactory than the old sodium-selenate soil treatments, a group of phosphate chemicals have been employed. Currently, only demeton (Systox) and thimet see much use. They are not safe to handle unless stringent precautions are followed. Mites, aphids, leaf miners, and certain boring insects are controlled.

7. Oil sprays. The use of highly refined "superior" dormant oils at 2 or 3% during dormant season just before bud break in the spring is very effective. These oils should meet the following specifications. Scales, mite eggs, and other pests are well controlled. Certain maples, spruces, *Chamaecyparis,* and other evergreens may be injured by oils.

Summer oils are highly refined light oils which do not ordinarily damage plants and are applicable in the growing season. Oils should be specified as "superior" dormant, or summer oils.

8. Combination Seed Treatment. For control of insects and diseases on seeded plants, the use of a combination seed treater is advised. Liquid or dry mixtures of lindane or dieldrin with a fungicide such as captan or thiram should be applied to all seeds, particularly bean, cucurbits, corn, and other large-seeded plants. Check seed source to be sure it has not already been treated.

9. Poison Baits. A workable poison bait can be prepared to control army worm, cutworms and other pests.

Wheat bran	25 lbs.
Paris green	1 lb.
Molasses	2 qts.
Water	½–2 gals. approx.

Mix bran and Paris green dry. Add the molasses to the water. Then moisten the bran-Paris green with liquids and mix thoroughly.

For slugs and snails, prepared baits containing metaldehyde or even a 15% metaldehyde dust are preferable.

10. Aerosols. *See* FUMIGATION.

11. Combinations of Materials. Most modern materials mix satisfactorily with one another. Oils, sulphur, and lime are materials often not compatible with other chemicals. Some chemicals break down other materials and occasionally a plant-injurious chemical is produced. All combination sprays or dusts mentioned in this book are compatible and safe to use, and for their application *see* SPRAYS AND DUSTS. — L. G. M.

INSECTIVOROUS PLANTS. Only a few plants are able to digest, directly, such nitrogenous substances as meat or the bodies of insects. The few that do so are not all closely related botanically, but they all have somewhat elaborate mechanisms for trapping insects and subsequently digesting them. Darwin devoted much time to studying the habits of these carnivorous or insectivorous plants before writing what is now the classic book *Insectivorous Plants.*

By no means all insectivorous plants are cult. Of those that are, the following will be found in this book, where notes on their culture should be sought: *Darlingtonia, Dionaea, Drosera, Nepenthes, Pinguicula, Sarracenia* (see PITCHER-PLANT), *Utricularia.*

As to their methods of catching insects the plants are easily divided into three categories: (1) Those that drown them, as in *Sarracenia, Nepenthes,* and *Darlingtonia;* (2) those that

Pitcher-plants: Common pitcher-plant (*Sarracenia*) at the left, *Darlingtonia* in the center, and *Nepenthes* at the right.

have sticky hairs in which the insect becomes enmeshed and is killed by a secretion of the plant, as in *Drosera* and *Pinguicula*; and (3) those that have a trap-like or movable parts which imprison the insect as in *Dionaea* and *Utricularia*.

The first group, which drown their prey, are the plants usually called pitcher-plants, of which much the commonest here is *Sarracenia*. All agree in having the leaves modified into a pitcher-like organ, mostly fringed on the inside with down-pointing hairs. These allow the insect to crawl in but not out. At the bottom of the pitcher is a watery liquid in which the victim is drowned and finally digested and absorbed by the plant.

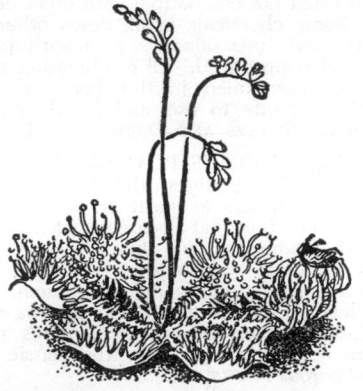

Sundew (*Drosera rotundifolia*)

The insectivorous plants that rely upon sticky hairs are the sundews (*Drosera*) and the butterwort (*Pinguicula*), which, however, operate very differently. In the sundews the insect cannot get away because the foliage is covered with glistening, often reddish, very sticky hairs. Few small insects, which

are attracted by the chance of food, can ever escape once they are caught. For the more they struggle, the greater number of hairs they touch, each making the victim more firmly entrapped. When all is over, the plant secretes enough digestive juices so that the insect is finally completely absorbed. In the butterwort (*Pinguicula*) the much more normal leaf is also covered with sticky hairs in which the insect becomes mired. But the leaf then rolls its margin over the victim and finally absorbs him by digestion much as in the sundews. The ability to roll the leaf margin seems to connect the butterwort with the third group which have trap-like parts or movements.

This third group of insectivorous plants is the most remarkable of all. *Dionaea*, or the Venus's-flytrap, has the leaf divided into two hinged, valve-like segments, the inner face of which is beset with hairs. When an insect lands within these jaw-like valves, they close up and crush the insect, holding him, in the process, by the stiff hairs. Once the trap is shut (you can induce its closing with a toothpick), the insect is digested and the trap opens for another victim.

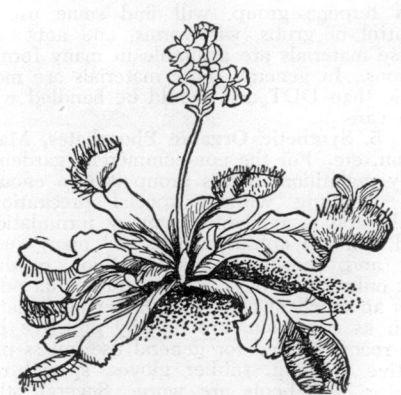

Venus's-flytrap (*Dionaea muscipula*)

The remaining cult. insectivorous plant is the bladderwort (*Utricularia*). It is a submerged aquatic with small bladders provided with a trap door that cannot be opened from the inside. Minute water insects or other aquatic life push their way through the open door, which closes after them. It does not open until they have been digested. The plant is common in quiet pools and often grown in aquaria.

INSECT PESTS AND THEIR CONTROL. Injury by insects is one of the greatest problems of plant growing. About 15% of all crops in the U.S. are destroyed by insects each year. It is estimated that the annual losses from the leading insect pests amount to about 4 billion dollars.

Several hundred thousand species of insects are known to exist in the world, and several

* Special articles on the subjects indicated by an asterisk (*) will be found at the words so marked.

thousand kinds may be found in a single locality. Most of these are harmless and of little interest to man. Some are even helpful, for they perform such tasks as pollinating flowers, furnishing food for animals, producing honey, wax, silk, or shellac, and destroying harmful insects and noxious weeds. Many kinds, however, are injurious, and every plant species we value is attacked by some insects. Injury is done by the insects feeding on parts of the plant or its juices, and also, sometimes, by carrying plant diseases.

Insects and Closely Related Forms

Insects occur throughout the world, in many situations. They are of varied appearance and habits, and range in size from almost microscopic to several inches, and in length of life from a few days or weeks to several years. However, all are built on the same basic pattern. They are an important class in the large group of animals with jointed bodies and a number of jointed legs, which have no true internal skeleton, but are supported by a stiff body wall on the outside. They are distinguished from other members of this group by having only three pairs of legs. Other characteristics are the possession of one pair of antennae or feelers, and usually a pair of compound eyes and one or two pairs of wings. Breathing is done through a number of pores, usually along the sides of the body, and air is carried through the body by a system of air tubes. Of other classes in this large group, one includes crabs, crayfish, and the common gray sowbug found on damp ground under boards; another includes the centipedes and millipedes (thousand-legs); and a third includes the spiders, mites and ticks. The members of this third class have eight legs and no feelers, and some of them are very injurious. Certain kinds of mites are among our plant pests.

Important Groups of Insects

Insects are divided by specialists into more than 20 groups, distinguished by the form of the wings, the mouth parts or jaws, and the method of growth. Some of these are of interest only to students; but a few of the important groups contain nearly all our plant pests.

In some the jaws are suited for biting or chewing food; in others the mouth parts are fitted together to form a tube or beak, for piercing, sucking, or drinking. This difference is important in determining methods of control.

Most insects hatch from eggs, although a few kinds are born alive. In growing, young insects shed their skins several times. In some cases the young look something like their parents when hatched, and the resemblance increases with each molt, until after the last one they appear as adults. Such young are called nymphs and are active at all stages. This may be called development by gradual change. In other orders the young, called larvae, appear much different from their

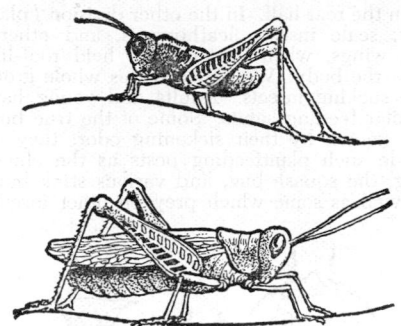

Insect Pests: Grasshopper and locust types are chewing or biting insects.

parents, and are worm-like until full grown, when they suddenly change to pupae, a quiescent form which does not move or eat; a little later the pupae give forth the adults. This may be called development by sudden change.

Seven orders contain most of the plant pests. These seven may be described briefly as follows:

(1) **Grasshoppers, Crickets, Roaches, etc.** Mouth parts suited for biting and chewing; front wings leathery, when present, covering hind wings, which are folded like fans; development gradual. This order has comparatively few kinds of pests, but some species of grasshoppers are among the most destructive insects known. They are especially injurious in the drier parts of the world.

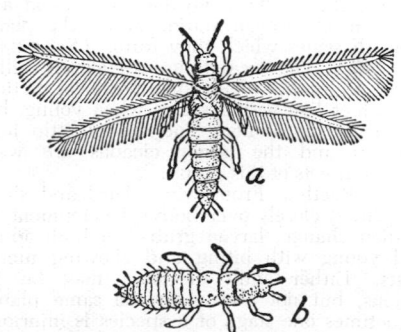

Insect Pests: (a) Adult and (b) nymph* of the onion thrips

(2) **Thrips.** Very small insects; wings fringed when present; mouth parts for rasping and sucking; development gradual. Several species are pests on leaves, flowers, or bark, either injuring the plants or spoiling their appearance.

(3) **True Bugs and Allies.** Piercing and sucking mouth parts; gradual development. In one division (true bugs) the front wings are leathery, fitted closely over the body, and most commonly with the front half thicker

---

* Special articles on the subjects indicated by an asterisk (*) will be found at the words so marked.

than the rear half. In the other division (plant lice, scale insects, leafhoppers, and others) the wings, when present, are held roof-like over the body. We may call this whole group the sucking insects. Adults and young have similar feeding habits. Some of the true bugs are known by their sickening odor; they include such plantfeeding pests as the chinch bug, the squash bug, and various stink bugs, as well as some which prey on other insects.

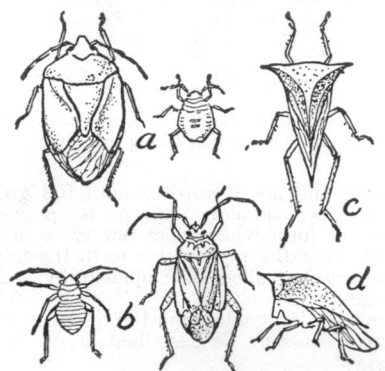

Insect Pests: The true bugs. (*a*) Green soldier bug and young nymph.* (*b*) Tarnished plant bug and nymph.* (*c* and *d*)Two views of a tree-hopper.

The frail little aphids, or plant lice, clustering on leaves, grow and increase rapidly, sometimes a hundredfold in two weeks. The scale insects, except the newly hatched young and adult males, remain stationary on the plants beneath scales which they form. (*See* SCALE INSECTS.) The mealybugs are closely allied to the scales, but retain some power of motion. Whiteflies live within scales when young, but are active as adults. The active little leafhoppers and the larger cicadas are well-known insects of this group.

(4) **Beetles.** Front wings hard and shell-like, fitted closely over body; development by sudden change, larvae grub-like; both adults and young with biting and chewing mouth parts. Either adult or larva may be injurious, but not always to the same plants. Sometimes one stage of a species is injurious, while another stage is harmless or beneficial. Pests of this order are too numerous to mention, and there are also many harmless, colorful, and interesting forms. A few examples of the order are the leaf beetles, which include the Colorado potato beetle and the tiny flea beetles; the June bugs, whose young are the root-feeding white grubs; ladybird beetles, many of which feed on aphids and scale insects; blister beetles; wood borers; and snout beetles. The well-known Japanese beetle is of the June bug family (for control *see* JAPANESE BEETLE), and the Mexican bean beetle is a plant-feeding ladybird beetle. The Asiatic beetle, a relative of the Japanese beetle,

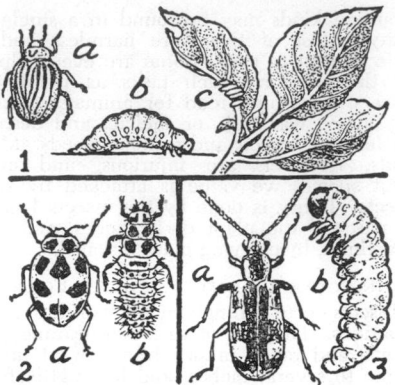

Insect Pests: Beetles. (1) Colorado potato beetle: (*a*) adult; (*b*) larva; (*c*) eggs. (2) Spotted ladybird beetle: (*a*) adult; (*b*) larva. (3) Asparagus beetle; (*a*) adult; (*b*) larva.

attacks lawns. Its control is the same as for Japanese beetle (which see).

(5) **Moths and Butterflies.** Wings large, with a velvety coating of scales; development by sudden change, larvae worm-like, called caterpillars; larvae with biting mouth parts, adult mouth parts in the form of a coiled tube suited only for drinking liquids. In this order are many handsome and conspicuous species sought by collectors. As a rule the pests are among the more inconspicuous forms. The butterflies differ from the moths in having feelers enlarged at the tips, and usually are slower fliers and active only by day. The adults of moths and butterflies are not in-

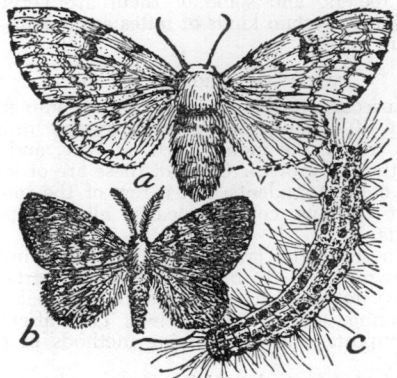

Insect Pests: Gypsy moth. (*a*) female; (*b*) male; (*c*) caterpillar.

jurious, but the larvae are important plant feeders. Some are leaf miners, some bore into the stems or fruit and many feed on the leaves or other parts of the plant. A number of larvae tie up leaves with web, thus making a protecting nest in which to feed. A few

---

* Special articles on the subjects indicated by an asterisk (*) will be found at the words so marked.

important pests of this order are the codling moth, oriental fruit moth, gypsy moth, bagworm, fall webworm, tomato worm, various species of cutworm, corn ear worm, cabbage worm, and European corn borer. The army worm, a striped caterpillar, gets its name from the fact that it moves in huge numbers like an army and destroys everything in its path. The only control in a small garden is a poison bait (*see* #9 at INSECTICIDES for bran bait), or on a larger scale they may be kept from moving over your land by a creosote or tar barrier.

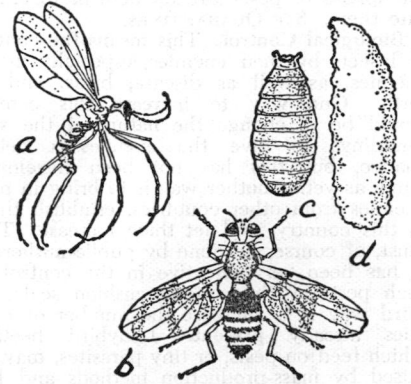

Insect Pests: Two-winged flies. (*a*) pear midge adult; (*b*) apple maggot fly; its pupa at (*c*), and the larva or maggot at (*d*).

(6) **Two-winged Flies, Mosquitoes, and Gnats.** Front wings membranous, hind wings undeveloped; growth by sudden change; footless larvae called maggots; larval mouth parts suited for rasping and sucking; adult mouth parts tubular, suited for piercing and sucking in some species, only for drinking in others. Some adults bite or annoy man and animals. Larvae vary in habits; some feed in filth, some are useful parasites of insects, and some are plant feeders. The plant feeders include root maggots, leaf miners, gall formers, and fruit flies.

(7) **Bees, Ants, Wasps, Sawflies, etc.** Four wings, membranous; development by sudden change; adults and larvae with mouth parts fitted for biting, but often modified for drinking also. The habits in this group are various; many species rear their young in nests, and many others are parasites which help hold destructive insects in check. The parasite lays its egg in or on the insect host, and the parasite larva develops in or on it, killing it. Some members of this order, especially the sawflies, are plant pests. Some of the sawfly larvae are borers, but most of them are leaf feeders.

The majority of the plant pests are included in three of these orders, sucking insects, beetles, and moths and butterflies. Some other orders of insects are dragon-

flies, mayflies, termites, bird lice, sucking lice, and fleas.

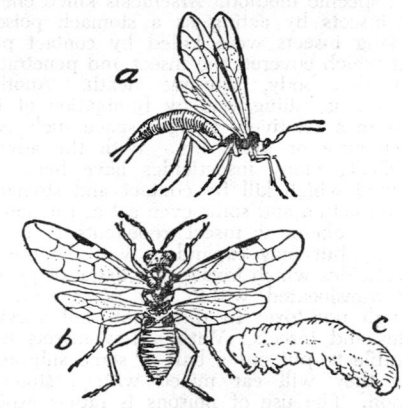

Insect Pests: (*a*) A minute parasite of the tent caterpillar; (*b*) rose-sawfly with its larva (*c*).

CONTROL OF INSECT PESTS

By control of a pest we mean reducing its numbers to such an extent that its injury becomes unimportant. In our struggles with insects we have learned how to check a great many of them, though our knowledge is far from complete. The value of a crop has much to do with the methods we can use. For a crop such as wheat, raised on a large area with a low value per acre, we cannot use expensive methods. For crops such as apples, tomatoes, or greenhouse flowers, with a high value per acre, more costly control methods can be used if necessary. Control methods include killing insects with poisonous substances, use of mechanical devices, modifications of ordinary farming operations, utilization of the insects' natural enemies, and the placing of quarantines.

Natural Control. Nearly all insects have such a great power of increase that if not checked enormous numbers would result within a few generations. Their numbers are reduced by death from adverse weather, lack of food, disease, insect enemies, and other causes. A great many species are thus held down to small numbers all or nearly all the time, and even our bad pests are kept from increasing as much as they otherwise would. This is called natural control. Our efforts to control insects would be much harder if it were not for this natural control. Where valuable crops are involved, however, to depend entirely on such uncertain help would result in severe losses.

Use of Poisons. This has been called chemical control. It will be discussed more in detail under the headings INSECTICIDES, SPRAYING, and FUMIGATION; only the basic principles will be mentioned here. The chemicals used should be deadly to insects, mites, and their allies and do little or no harm to the host plant. Formerly, insect con-

---

* Special articles on the subjects indicated by an asterisk (*) will be found at the words so marked.

trol by chemicals was based on use of specific materials which killed chewing insects by a specific method. Arsenicals killed chewing insects by acting as a stomach poison. Sucking insects were killed by contact poisons which covered the insect and penetrated into the body, causing death. Another method of killing was by fumigation of insects in a relatively airtight space such as a greenhouse or grain bin. With the advent of DDT, many insecticides have been developed which kill by contact and stomach-poison action and some even act as fumigants. Use of chemical insect repellents is in its infancy but may expand as will the use of insecticides which invade the tissue of plants, are translocated within the plant and, although non-toxic to the plant, kill sucking mites and insects. With a few insects it is possible to put out a bait of some substance that they will eat mixed with a stomach poison. The use of poisons is rather expensive, as they usually require a special outlay for material, equipment, and extra labor.

Mechanical Methods. Several simple control devices may be considered as mechanical. Collection and destruction of insects by hand is the oldest control method, and is still a good one where large, conspicuous insects are attacking a few prized plants. For example, tomato worms in small vegetable gardens or bagworms on a few shrubs can easily be controlled by hand picking. Barriers or traps are useful in checking the attacks of some insects. Sticky bands on trees will protect against cankerworms (*see* Insect Pests at Elm). Trap bands help in controlling the codling moth. Immature chinch bugs are kept out of cornfields by barriers such as dust furrows or lines of repellent material. Machines for collecting insects have had some use, chiefly against grasshoppers in the West but are now obsolete in the U.S.

Farm Practices. On farms the regular control operations can be carried on in such a way as to be unfavorable for insects. Rotation of crops is effective, especially where fields are large. Sometimes insect injury can be kept down by the use of resistant varieties of the plant. With some pests relief is obtained by slight modifications in time of planting the crop. The operations of draining and flooding cranberry fields can be conducted in such a way as to check cranberry insects. Early fall plowing reduces the numbers of some soil-inhabiting insects. Livestock and poultry sometimes aid in destroying pests. The most effective farm practices, however, consist of what is called "cleanup" practices — destroying plants after the crop has been picked, cleaning up trash which serves as winter shelter to the insects, and destroying wild plants on which pests will develop and spread to crops. In a home garden, radish plants that are going to seed may keep aphids alive to spread to young fall turnips. Outbreaks of the garden webworm may be traced to pigweeds growing near by. In southern orchards, cowpeas

used as a cover crop foster stink bugs, which later damage fruits and pecans; some other cover crop should be used. Control by cultural practices is suited not only to field crops but also in horticulture, and this type of control is relatively inexpensive.

Quarantine. A large proportion of our worst pests were originally brought in from abroad, and insects in a new country or territory away from their natural enemies, are often worse pests than in their old home. Public authorities try, by plant quarantine and inspection, to prevent new pests from coming in, and in certain cases, to hold back the spread of pests already here or to eradicate them. *See* Quarantines.

Biological Control. This means the control of insects by their enemies, especially insect enemies, as well as disease, birds, and so forth. One way to increase this control would be to change the nature of the surroundings to give the enemies a better chance, but this has not been developed much as yet. Another way is to bring in new enemies from other countries, establish them in this country, and let them increase. This must, of course, be done by public authority. It has been very effective in the control of such pests as the cottony cushion scale. A third way is to increase the number of enemies already present. Ladybird beetles, which feed on pests, or tiny parasites, may be raised by mass-production methods and liberated among the crops. This has been done in a few cases by public authorities, and even undertaken commercially.

Our horticultural crops are of such value that we can usually afford the more expensive control measures, such as use of poisons, better than losses from insects, and these methods will be our main reliance. However, other methods should not be neglected; cleanup measures are helpful in preventing infestation, and mechanical methods are applicable in some cases. In all cases, watchfulness and prompt action will prevent loss and give full value for investments in control. — L. G. M.

insignis, *-e* (in-sig′nis). Distinguished or remarkable.

insititia, *-us,* *-um* (in-si-tish′i-a). Grafted.

integra, *-us,* *-um* (in-tee′gra). Entire or whole; *i.e.,* not cut.

integrifolia, *-us,* *-um* (in-tee-gri-fō′li-a). With uncut leaves.

INTERCROPPING. *See* Kitchen Garden.

intermedia, *-us,* *-um* (in-ter-mee′di-a). Intermediate in color, form, habit, etc.

INTERNATIONAL FRIENDSHIP GARDENS. *See* No. 21 at Garden Tours.

INTERNODE. *See* Node.

INTERRUPTED. Not continuous, especially not continuously furnished with leaves or flowers on a stalk; scattered.

---

* Special articles on the subjects indicated by an asterisk (*) will be found at the words so marked.

INTERRUPTED FERN = *Osmunda claytoniana.*

An interrupted flower cluster. Sometimes leaves are interrupted, as in the interrupted fern.

intertexta, -us, -um (in-ter-tecks′ta). Intertwined or interwoven.

intorta, -us, -um (in-tor′ta). Twisted.

intricata, -us, -um (in-tri-kay′ta). Tangled; often densely branched.

Intybus (in′ti-bus). See ENDIVE.

INULA (in′you-la). Hardy herbaceous perennials of rather coarse habit of growth, belonging to the Compositae, with daisy-like flowers ranging in color from yellow to orange. Of about 60 species, natives of As., Eu., and Af., some are cultivated and even naturalized in N.A. Leaves mostly hairy, alternate or basal. Flower heads solitary or few, yellow, seldom white. (*Inula* is the classical name for these plants.)

They are of easy culture, thriving in ordinary garden soil, but preferring a sunny position. Propagated by division.

    ensifolia. To 2 ft. tall, leaves linear-lanceolate. Flower heads yellow, 1½ in. across, July–Aug., a hardy border plant which will bloom the first year if sown early. Eu. and northern As.

    glandulosa. Native of Caucasia and a hardy perennial, 2 to 4 ft. high. Leaves hairy, oblong, entire.* Flower heads solitary, yellow. June–July. Propagated by division and seeds. The *var.* **laciniata** has golden-yellow, fringed, drooping rays.

    Helenium. Elecampane. A stout herb 4–6 ft. high, the leaves oblong to 2 ft. long, rough above, velvety beneath. The roots are thick and coarse and are used medicinally. For this purpose the roots are dug when 2 years old, in August, before becoming too woody. They require a sunny position. Propagated by seeds or division. Also called horseheal. Native of Eu., and As. and naturalized in eastern N.A.

    orientalis = *Inula glandulosa.*

    royleana. A showy, large-flowered herb, 1–2 ft. high, the leaves ovate, 8–10 in. long, hairy beneath. Flowers orange-yellow, numerous in each head. It requires a sheltered place in the garden. Himalayas.

involucrata, -us, -um (in-vol-you-kray′ta). Provided with an involucre (which see).

INVOLUCRE. A collection, often whorled,* of small leaves or bracts.* It may be of several different forms. The most common one is the series of involucral bracts* which surround the base of the head or flower clusters of the daisy and related plants (*see* COMPOSITAE). In other plants it may be merely scale-like appendages between the otherwise naked cluster, as the involucre

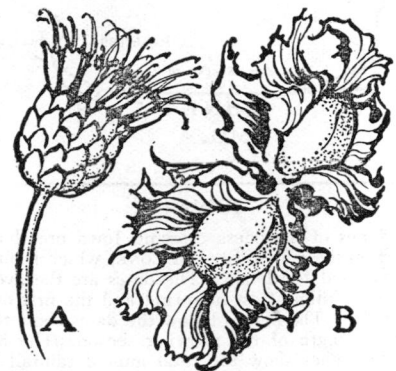

Two types of involucre. (A) The series of involucral bracts* on the head of a cornflower. (B) The leafy bracts* comprising the involucre around the hazelnut.

which covers the ovary in the female flowers of the hickory. And quite often the involucre is decidedly leafy, as in the leafy involucral bracts which surround the fruit of the hazel.

ioensis, -e (eye-o-en′sis). From Iowa.

ionantha, -us, -um (eye-o-nan′tha). Violet-flowered.

IONOPSIDIUM (eye-on-op-sid′i-um). A single species of annual herbs of the mustard family. **I. acaule**, the diamond flower, is from Portugal and is a very small rock garden herb, sometimes grown also in pots in the cool greenhouse. It is a creeping plant scarcely 3 in. high, the leaves alternate,* long-stalked, nearly round, and about ½ in. wide. Flowers minute, violet or white, at the end of slender thread-like stalks 3–4 in. long. Petals 4. Fruit an oblongish or globe-shaped pod (silicle*), slightly notched at the tip. For culture *see* ROCK GARDEN. (*Ionopsidium* is from the Greek for violet-like, in allusion to the flower color.)

IOWA. The state flower is the wild rose. The state lies mainly in zone* 2. Zone 1 takes in approximately the northern 25 per cent of the state, and the southernmost westerly and easterly extremities are included in zone 3. Because of extreme variations in snow cover and intensity of cold, only the most hardy plants should be used for ornamental and fruit plantings, especially in the northern half of the state.

---

* Special articles on the subjects indicated by an asterisk (*) will be found at the words so marked.

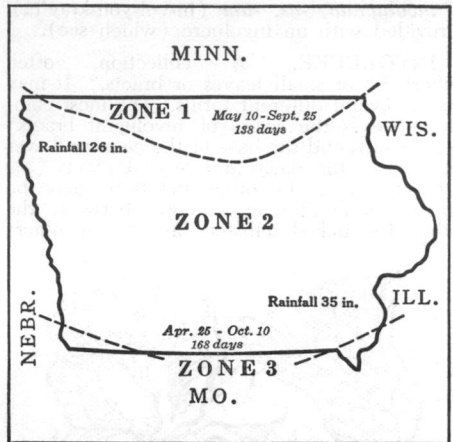

IOWA

The zones of hardiness crossing Iowa are those shown on the map located at ZONE, which should be consulted for details. The dates are the average latest killing frost in spring and the first one in the fall. The figures below the dates show the average length of the growing season. The figures in inches show the total annual rainfall at the places indicated.

SOILS. Iowa has a higher percentage of tillable land than any other state in the nation. Over 95 per cent of the land in Iowa is crop land. Iowa also has about 25 per cent of the nation's grade A land. Five distinct soil types are found within the state. They are either of glacial drift or windblown (loessal) origin. The loess* soils are mainly in southern Iowa and in general are excellent for fruit.

The topography of most of northern Iowa is level or gently rolling. The soil varies from a heavy muck to a light sandy loam. Many gravel deposits are found in the subsoil of this area.

FRUIT. Apples, Iowa's leading fruit, can be grown in all sections of the state, providing suitable varieties are selected for planting. Most of the production, however, is in the southern half of Iowa, along both the Missouri and Mississippi rivers and around Des Moines. Jonathan and Red Delicious are the leading varieties, although Yellow Delicious is also of importance.

Sharon, a variety introduced by Iowa State College in the early 1940's, is gaining wider acceptance in Iowa and surrounding states. Jonadel, another variety developed and introduced by Iowa State College in 1958, is gaining wide attention nationally. A cross between Jonathan and Delicious, Jonadel is proving hardier than either parent, has an excellent bright, dark cherry-red color, and has proven to be highly resistant to fireblight (a disease to which Jonathan and other varieties have shown high susceptibility). Many other apple and fruit tree varieties are successfully grown in this area, both for commercial and home production.

Grapes can be grown for home use all over the state. Concord and Fredonia are the main varieties except in northern Iowa where the more hardy varieties such as Moonbeam, Red Amber, and Blue Jay are more successful.

Strawberries are the leading small fruit, being produced for home use in all sections of the state.

Most of the production of pears, plums, cherries, and raspberries is for home use, although raspberries are commercially produced in a few areas. Blueberries definitely *are not* adapted to Iowa because of the soil pH and unfavorable climate. Also, sweet cherries are not productive in Iowa because of the climate.

VEGETABLES. Home vegetable gardens are found on most of the farms, and many urban home owners maintain a vegetable garden. Vegetable varieties grown in Iowa gardens are as follows:

†Indicates varieties suitable for freezing.
Asparagus — Mary Washington†
Beans, Snap — Top Crop†, Stringless Green Pod†, Wade†, Contender†
†Beans, Bush Wax — Pencil Pod Black Wax†, Round Pod Kidney Wax†
Beans, Lima — Henderson Bush†
Beans, Pole — Kentucky Wonder
Beets — Detroit Dark Red, Early Wonder, Crosby Egyptian
Broccoli — DeCicco†, Calabrese†
Cabbage — (early) Marion Market, (mid-season) Globe, (late) Wisconsin All-Season
Carrots — Red Cored Chantenay, Danvers Half Long, Tendersweet
Cauliflower — Early Snowball†
Chinese Cabbage — Pe Tsai
Cucumber — (slicing) Marketer, Smoothie, Burpee Hybrid; (pickling) National Pickling, Ohio MR-25
Pumpkin (used as squash) — Butternut†, Acorn (Table Queen)
Pumpkin (summer squash type) — Zucchini, Crookneck, Caserta
Radish — Cherry Belle, Scarlet Globe, Sparkler, White Icicle
Rhubarb — McDonald†, Canada Red†, Ruby†
Salsify — Mammoth Sandwich Island
Spinach — America†, Bloomsdale Longstanding†
Squash — Buttercup†, Golden Delicious†, Hubbard†
Eggplant — Black Beauty
Endive — Full Heart Batavian
Kale — Dwarf Blue Scotch†
Kohlrabi — White Vienna
Lettuce — Salad Bowl, Black Seeded Simpson, Oak Leaf
Muskmelon — Hearts of Gold†, Hale's Best†, Queen of Colorado†
Mustard — Tendergreen, Prize Winner
Okra — Clemson Spineless, Dwarf Green Long Pod

---

* Special articles on the subjects indicated by an asterisk (*) will be found at the words so marked.

Onions — Early Harvest, Epoch, Elite, Brigham Yellow Globe, Sweet Spanish, Iowa Yellow Globe No. 44
Parsley — Moss Curled
Parsnips — Hollow Crown
Peas — Alaska, Little Marvel†, Freezoniant
Peppers — California Wonder, World Beater, Harris Earliest
Potatoes — Warba, Irish Cobbler, Cherokee, Pontiac
Pumpkin — Sugar Pie
Sweet Corn — (early) Marcross, (second early) Carmel Cross, (midseason) Ioanat, Iochieft, Golden Crosst, Victory Goldent
Sweet Potatoes — Orange Little Stem, Goldrush, Nemagold, Orliss
Swiss Chard — Lucullust, Rhubarbt
Tomatoes — (early) Sioux, (main crop) Rutgers, Clinton Hybrid, Marglobe, (yellow) Golden Jubilee
Turnip — Purple Top White Globe
Watermelon — Kleckley Sweet, New Hampshire Midget, Dixie Queen, Charleston Gray, Crisscross

ORNAMENTALS AND FLOWERS. There has been increased interest in home gardening as the result of the activities of the Plant Iowa program and the Federated Garden Clubs. At the present time there are nearly 325 active garden clubs in the state, with more than 10,000 members. Most of them are affiliated with the Federated Garden Clubs of Iowa. Iowa has a State Horticultural Society composed of affiliated societies including garden clubs, nurserymen, fruit growers, vegetable growers, beekeepers, golf course superintendents, rose growers, gladiolus growers, etc.

A wide range of ornamental plants may be successfully grown. Listed below are a few of the more commonly grown ornamentals that are hardy enough to stand Iowa's rigorous winters. There are numerous other species and varieties which are used for ornamental planting.

TREES.
Evergreen — Large (40–100 ft.)
Abies concolor (White Fir)
Picea Abies (Norway Spruce)
Picea glauca densata (Black Hills Spruce)
Picea pungens (Colorado Blue Spruce)
Pinus nigra (Austrian Pine)
Pseudotsuga taxifolia (Douglas Fir)
Evergreen — Medium (15–40 ft.)
Juniperus virginiana keteleeri
Deciduous — Large (75–100 ft.)
Acer nigrum (Black Maple)
Acer saccharum (Sugar Maple)
Celtis occidentalis (Hackberry)
Tilia americana (American Linden)
Ulmus americana (American Elm)
Deciduous — Small (20–45 ft.)
Acer Ginnala
Acer tataricum
Cercis canadensis (American Redbud)

Crataegus mollis (Red Haw)
Crataegus Phaenopyrum (Washington Thorn)

SHRUBS.
Evergreen — Large (5–10 ft.)
Juniperus chinensis pfitzeriana (Pfitzer Juniper)
Evergreen — Small (under 5 ft.)
Juniperus horizontalis plumosa (Andorra Juniper)
Juniperus procumbens
Deciduous — Large (8 ft. and over)
Euonymus alatus (Winged Spindle-tree)
Lonicera tatarica (Tartarian Honeysuckle)
Prunus triloba (Flowering Almond)
Spiraea vanhouttei (Bridal Wreath)
Syringa persica (Persian Lilac)
Viburnum Lantana (Wayfaring-tree)
Viburnum prunifolium (Black Haw)
Deciduous — Medium (6–8 ft.)
Ligustrum obtusifolium regelianum (Regel's Privet)
Lonicera morrowi
Syringa vulgaris (Lilac varieties)
Viburnum dentatum (Arrow-wood)
Deciduous — Small (4–6 ft.)
Berberis thunbergi (Japanese Barberry)
Chaenomeles lagenaria (Flowering Quince)
Philadelphus lemoinei (Lemoine Mock-orange)
Ribes alpinum (Alpine Currant)
Spiraea arguta (Garland Spirea)

VINES.
Celastrus scandens (Bittersweet)
Clematis paniculata (Japanese Clematis)
Parthenocissus quinquefolia (Virginia Creeper)

PERENNIAL FLOWERS.
Spring Flowering
Arabis alpina (Alpine Rock Cress)
Dicentra spectabilis (Bleeding-heart)
Iris germanica (Tall Bearded Iris)
Paeonia albiflora (Peony)
Phlox divaricata (Wild Sweet William)
Early Summer Blooming
Chrysanthemum maximum (Shasta Daisy)
Delphinium grandiflorum (Siberian Larkspur)
Gaillardia aristata (Blanket-flower)
Hemerocallis (Daylily)
Iris sibirica (Siberian Iris)
Sedum (Stonecrop)
Late Summer Blooming
Campanula persicifolia (Peach Bells)
Coreopsis grandiflora
Phlox paniculata (Perennial Phlox)
Veronica (Speedwell)

* Special articles on the subjects indicated by an asterisk (*) will be found at the words so marked.

Autumn Flowering
   Aster (varieties)
   Chrysanthemum (varieties)
   Sedum spectabile (Stonecrop)

BULBOUS PLANTS.
  Spring Flowering (plant in the fall)
   Narcissus (Daffodil, Jonquil, Narcissus)
   Scilla sibirica (Siberian Squill)
   Tulipa (Tulip)
  Summer and Fall Flowering (plant fall or spring)
   Lilium auratum
   Lilium candidum (Madonna Lily)
   Lilium elegans
   Lilium pumilum (Coral Lily)
  Spring Flowering (plant in the fall)
   Lilium regale (Royal Lily)

CLIMATE. Precipitation in Iowa ranges from slightly less than 26 inches along the Big Sioux River in the extreme northwest to slightly more than 36 inches at places along the Mississippi River. Approximately 70 per cent of the annual precipitation occurs in the warm season, April to September, and 50 per cent in the months of May to August at a time of greatest crop growth. The cold season is the dry season, during which all of the state, except along the Mississippi and lower Des Moines rivers, has had at some time 100 days or more with 1 inch or less of precipitation. Only a few droughts have covered the entire state.

The average annual relative humidity in Iowa is 72 per cent. April and May are the months of lowest relative humidity and January the highest.

The average growing season for the state is 158 days, from May 2 to October 7. Light frosts have been observed in all summer months. The average date of last killing frost in spring ranges from about April 25 in several southern areas, to about May 10 in several northern areas; the average date of the first killing frost in autumn ranges from about September 25 in the extreme northwest, to about October 10 in several southern areas.

Iowa's Agricultural Experiment Station and Agriculture Extension Service is located at Ames. This information about the state was furnished by Iowa State College. The College is always ready to answer your gardening questions. For this, and the nearest garden club or other organization, you can send your request to the Horticulture Department, Iowa State College, Ames, Iowa.

IPOMOEA (ip-po-mee'a). Morning-glory. Mostly twining vines of the family Convolvulaceae, many of the 400 species of tropical origin, and a few of them of much garden importance as the source of the sweet potato and the common morning-glory. They are mostly annual or perennial, often milky-juiced, vines, the perennials frequently with enormous roots. Leaves alternate,* generally stalked, simple,* or compound* and with several leaflets. Flowers large and showy, usually solitary or a few in the leaf axils.* Calyx* lobed or parted. Corolla chiefly funnel-shaped, rarely bell-shaped, more or less 5-pointed or 5-angled at the top. Stigma* club-shaped or 2-lobed (forked in the closely related *Convolvulus*). Fruit an egg-shaped or roundish capsule.* (*Ipomoea* is from the Greek for *worm* and *similar,* in allusion to the twining habit.)

The annual morning-glories, which are the chief ornamental kinds, are best sown where wanted. They are among our quickest and showiest of annual vines, and will grow easily in almost any soil. The perennial species are not always root-hardy in the North, as noted below. The roots of these tender sorts must be dug and stored over the winter in a cool, frost-free place, and planted outdoors when danger of frost is passed. Morning-glory seeds are very hard and germinate more readily if notched with a file or soaked in tepid water for eight hours. For a still quicker method *see* CALONYCTION. Two fine hort. forms are Heavenly Blue and Rose Marie (pink).

Batatas. Sweet potato. A sprawling perennial vine, rooting at the joints. Leaves lobed or unlobed, or sometimes divided finger-fashion, 4–6 in. long. Flowers rose-pink or violet-rose, about 2 in. long, but scarcely ever produced in the U.S. Probably tropical America. For culture *see* SWEET POTATO.

Bona-nox = *Calonyction aculeatum.*

coccinea = *Quamoclit coccinea.*

grandiflora = *Calonyction aculeatum.*

hederacea. An annual, hairy, twining vine, the leaves ovalish or heart-shaped at the base, 2–3½ in. long, often 3-lobed. Flowers about 2 in. long, blue to pale purple, the sepals narrow and with recurved tips. Tropical America. Called by some *Pharbitis hederacea.*

horsfalliae. A tropical perennial vine not hardy in the North (*see* above). Leaves compound,* finger-fashion, the leaflets* 5–7, thick, nearly 4 in. long. Flowers rose or pale purple, nearly 2½ in. long. The *var.* **briggsi** has crimson-magenta flowers.

imperialis = *Ipomoea Nil.*

leari. Blue dawn-flower. Tropical American perennial vine, its roots not hardy northward (*see* above). Leaves 6–8 in. long, generally ovalish or heart-shaped, sometimes 3-lobed, hairy beneath. Flowers 4–5 in. wide, very showy, blue but the tube white, ultimately turning pink.

leptophylla. Bush morning-glory. A shrubby perennial with an enormous root (20–100 lbs.); not over 4 ft. high, its narrow leaves about 3 in. long, scarcely ¼ in. wide, without teeth. Flowers funnel-shaped, about 3 in. wide, pinkish-purple. Tex. and N.Mex. Summer. Not hardy above zone* 5.

Nil. A tropical, hairy, perennial vine, the roots not hardy in the North (*see* above). Leaves broadly heart-shaped, 4–6 in. wide, more or less 3-lobed. Flowers about 4 in. wide, purple, blue, or rose-pink, often double. Sometimes offered as *I. imperialis,* and including among its many forms the Imperial Japanese morning-glories, which are larger-flowered, very bright-colored and variously striped and margined.

pandurata. Manroot; also called wild sweet potato, man-of-the-earth and scammony. A native perennial vine, the root sometimes weigh-

---

* Special articles on the subjects indicated by an asterisk (*) will be found at the words so marked.

ing 100 pounds and hardy in the North. Leaves broadly ovalish or heart-shaped, 4–6 in. long, rarely fiddle-shaped. Flowers nearly 4 in. wide, white, but the throat purple. Eastern N.A.

purpurea. The common morning-glory and an annual vine with a hairy stem. Leaves broadly oval or heart-shaped, 4–5 in. long, not lobed. Flowers nearly 3 in. long, purple, pink, or blue, the tube paler. There are forms with double flowers and with white flowers. Tropical America. In Mex., there is also a double, yellow-flowered variety.

setosa. Brazilian morning-glory. A tropical perennial vine, the roots not hardy northward (*see* above), the stem covered with purplish and stiffish hairs. Leaves nearly 10 in. wide, 3-lobed and resembling the grape. Flowers about 3 in. long, rose-purple.

tricolor. A perennial, tropical American vine which blooms from seed the first year and can be grown as an annual. Leaves 4–5 in. long, unlobed, generally ovalish or heart-shaped. Flowers nearly 4 in. wide, purplish-blue, but the tip red before opening, the tube white.

tuberosa. Ceylon morning-glory. A tropical, perennial vine, scarcely known in cult. here but the source of the so-called wooden roses found in many dry flower arrangements. Leaves nearly 8 in. wide, cut into 5–7 narrow segments. Flowers yellow. Fruit ultimately a woody pod, which with its persistent, woody sepals* form the "wooden rose" that may be 2½–4 in. wide. India. Cult. in most tropical countries.

IRESINE (eye-re-sy′ne). Ornamental foliage plants (as grown) of the family Amaranthaceae, chiefly tropical. Of the 20 known species the two below are mostly grown as summer bedding plants. They will stand no frost and their winter care needs a greenhouse where they must be grown as is *Coleus* (which see). Leaves opposite,* stalked, generally ovalish. Flowers (rarely produced as grown) woolly, the parts rather chaffy or membranous, small, whitish, crowded in dense spikes* which are gathered in branched clusters (panicles*). Fruit 1-seeded, dry (utricle*). (*Iresine* is Greek for a woolly harvest garland, in allusion to the woolly flowers.)

As usually grown for bedding plants *Iresine* does not ordinarily produce flowers, and is propagated by cuttings wintered in the house or greenhouse. They are good, showy, summer-bedding, foliage plants. Florists often offer them under the name *Achyranthes.*

herbsti. Nearly 6 ft. high when full grown, the leaves 4–5 in. long, yellow-veined, but generally purplish-red, or green, notched at the tip. S.A.

lindeni. Leaves and stems mostly dark red, rarely green, the leaves pointed, not notched, more or less lance-oval, the veins prominent. Ecuador.

IRIDACEAE (eye-ri-day′see-ee). The iris family, often called the crocus or gladiolus family, is of outstanding garden importance. For besides these three popular favorites it contains the freesias and many other hort. genera of wide cultivation.

The family contains over 55 genera and perhaps 1400 species, scattered over most of the world, and of these over 20 genera are to be found in gardens or greenhouses throughout the country. All the garden genera are herbs, with chiefly basal, grass-like or sword-shaped leaves and usually very handsome flowers which arise from between 2 membranous bracts.* Nearly all the plants have an obvious stem, but *Crocus* is apparently (not actually) stemless.

The garden genera divide themselves, culturally, into three groups:

1. Hardy plants, wintering successfully in most regions: *Belamcanda, Crocus, Iris* (most species), *Hermodactylus, Lapeyrousia* (with protection), and *Sisyrinchium.*

2. Summer-blooming plants of warm regions, planted after danger of frost, and their underground parts lifted and stored over the winter; *i.e.,* culture as for *Gladiolus; Acidanthera, Antholyza, Crocosmia, Gladiolus, Tigridia, Tritonia,* and *Watsonia.*

3. Tender plants of greenhouse culture or grown outdoors only in the frost-free (or nearly frost-free) South: *Aristea, Babiana, Dierama, Freesia, Homeria, Ixia, Libertia, Moraea, Neomarica, Schizostylis, Sparaxis,* and *Streptanthera.*

The fruit in all genera is a 3-valved, many-seeded pod (capsule*).

Technical flower characters: (For *Iris,* see that entry.) Flowers otherwise regular in about half the genera, but very irregular in *Gladiolus* and its allies. Sepals 3, often petal-like and not easily distinguished from the 3 petals. The flowers in many genera are tubular, in others apparently (not actually) of separate petals. Stamens 3. Ovary inferior,* 3-celled, its usually 3 stigmas sometimes expanded and petal-like (*Iris* and *Moraea*).

iridifolia, -us, -um (eye-rid-i-fō′li-a). With iris-like leaves.

iridioides (eye-rid-i-oy′deez, but *see* OÏDES). Iris-like.

IRIS (eye′ris). A large genus of herbs of the family Iridaceae, comprising over 150 species, mostly from the north temperate zone, and thousands of horticultural varieties which to the gardener are far more important than any of the species listed immediately below. But over 100 of these species of iris are grown by fanciers and hybridizers, and those listed below are included because many of them have been the parents of most garden irises.

Iris is a genus of perennial herbs, with stout rhizomes or bulbous rootstocks and narrow, often sword-shaped leaves, but in some kinds the leaves are almost grass-like. Flowers are in six segments, and arise from spathe*-like bracts.* The three outer segments are reflexed and generally called the "falls," while the inner three are usually smaller and erect, and are known as "standards." Both the falls and standards have at the base a narrow claw,* often called the haft. The flowers are followed by a large,

---

* Special articles on the subjects indicated by an asterisk (*) will be found at the words so marked.

3-celled, many-seeded pod (capsule*). (*Iris* was named for the goddess.)

The uncertainty and complexity of iris nomenclature has been so great that it is difficult to define *Iris* species. To obviate some of the complexity many schemes have been suggested of separating the various species into groups. Of these at least a dozen have been suggested, but for those species below only six appear to be applicable. It is suggested that the seeker become familiar with these groups before attempting to identify any particular species.

The six sections are:

1. Beardless irises (often called Apogon). Here belong our common blue flag, the fleur-de-lis, the Japanese irises, the Louisiana hybrids, and many others. All are characterized by the absence of any sort of beard on the petals. All grow from rhizomes.*

2. Crested irises (often called Evansia). Here belong our common crested iris from the eastern states, the roof iris of China and Japan, and a few other species. The petals do not have a beard, but the falls have a central ridge or crest. All grow from rhizomes.*

3. Bearded irises (often called Eupogon or Pogoniris). Here belong all the thousands of varieties variously called tall bearded, medium bearded, German, etc., all of which have a copious beard on the falls. Also included in the group are many species which have been the source (by hybridization) of most of the horticultural varieties. To many gardeners these varieties are the only irises they grow, for they are finer garden subjects than any others. All have sword-shaped leaves in a fan-like arrangement (equitant). All grow from stout rhizomes.*

4. Oncocyclus irises. Containing only (as here limited) the single species *I. susiana,* the mourning iris. It arises from a rhizome,* has a broad beard, and only one flower. Has been used in crossing with the bearded irises.

5. Pardanthopsis irises. Containing only (as here limited) the single species *I. dichotoma,* of eastern Asia, which arises from a rhizome.* Late-flowering and usually dies thereafter.

6. Bulbous irises (often called Xiphion). Here belong the Spanish, English, and Dutch irises and a few others, all of which have narrow, not sword-shaped, leaves and arise from bulb-like structures (corms*). They never have a beard.

For the culture and best varieties of these *see* the final section of this article.

All the *species* of iris immediately below have after the name a number in parentheses. This shows to which of the above sections each species belongs, and avoids useless repetition of sectional characters.

The Japanese irises bloom in late June or July but all the others are spring bloomers, except where noted as otherwise.

albicans (3). An Arabian iris of little interest to the amateur, but probably entering into the production of tall bearded irises. It grows well along the Gulf Coast. *See* IRIS "GERMANICA."

Chamaeiris (3). Stems 2–10 in. long. Leaves clustered in a 4–6-leaved tuft, 3–6 in. long, pale green. Flowers solitary or two, the falls about ¾ in. long, blue, purple, white or yellow, brown-veined. Northern Italy and adjacent France. It has been used in the production of dwarf bearded irises.

chrysographes (1). Stems 12–18 in. high, and hollow, bearing 1 or 2 small leaves, the other, and basal, leaves 12–18 in. long and about ½ in. wide. Flowers velvety, violet-purple, gold-veined on the claw* of the falls. Western China.

cristata (2). Dwarf crested iris. Crested iris. A low, native iris, 4–6 in. high, the light green or faintly bluish-green leaves slightly curved, 5–8 in. long, about ¾ in. wide. Flowers blue, the crest yellow, faintly fragrant. Eastern U.S., west to Okla. A fine iris for edging or a ground cover. There are white and light blue hort. varieties.

cyanea (3). A plant, possibly of hybrid origin, and the reputed parent of some vars. of dwarf bearded blue-flowered irises. Origin unknown.

danfordiae (6). A tender short-stemmed iris not over 4 in. high, the stem brown-spotted. Leaves appearing after the bloom, 8–12 in. long, 4-sided and hollow. Flowers yellow, the standards reduced to bristle-like structures about ¾ in. long. Hardy from zone* 6 southward and also grown in the cool greenhouse. Asia Minor. Jan.–Feb.

dichotoma (5). A striking iris from eastern As., the stems nearly 2 ft. high and the white-edged leaves 9–12 in. long in fan-like clusters. Flowers in forked clusters (racemes*), greenish-white flaked with lavender, opening only once in the afternoon and then spirally twisted, but so profuse that the plant often dies after blooming. Aug.

douglasiana (1). An evergreen iris unsuited to cult. in the East, the stems and leaves pink-tinged at the base, 6–12 in. high. Leaves about ½ in. wide. Flowers 1–2 in. long, lilac to white (variable), the falls with four dark lines. Calif. and Ore. May.

ensata (1). An Asiatic iris, forming dense clumps, the flattened stems 6–15 in. high. Leaves narrow, scarcely ½ in. wide, ultimately 18–20 in. long. Flowers solitary or in clusters of 1–3, generally white or lilac, with purple veins, the standards a little darker than the falls, the stalks shorter than the foliage.

flavissima (3). A Eurasian iris of little interest to the amateur but reputed to have entered into the production of miniature dwarf bearded irises. Not over 4–6 in. high, the flowers (in the native plant) yellow.

florentina (3). *See* IRIS "GERMANICA."

foetidissima (3). Gladwin or stinking gladwin. A European iris the bruised, evergreen foliage of which is offensive. Stems 2–3 ft. high, the leaves one half this and about 1 in. wide. Flowers inconspicuous, small, bluish-purple, followed by a splitting capsule filled with showy red or orange-red seeds, for which the plant is chiefly grown.

foliosa (1). A native iris of little interest to the amateur, but reputed to have entered into

---

* Special articles on the subjects indicated by an asterisk (*) will be found at the words so marked.

the production of the Louisiana hybrids. *See* The Beardless Group in the section at Cult. which ends this account of iris. It is a plant with a zigzag stem, 12–18 in. high, and bluish-purple flowers. Ky. to Kan.

fulva (1). Copper iris. A stout, native iris, 2–3 ft. high, and exceeding the sword-shaped leaves. Flowers copper-colored or tawny, rarely yellow, with blue or green variegation. Gulf Coast to southern Ill. Apr.–May. It has entered into the production of Louisiana hybrids.

"germanica" (3). An old and probably incorrect designation for the assumed parent of the garden tall bearded irises, of which there are thousands of hort. vars., the parentage of which is still in much doubt. Among the reputed ingredients of the tall bearded irises (formerly called German iris) are *I. albicans, florentina, pallida,* and probably other species.

giganticaerulia (1). A huge, native iris, 3–4 ft. high, with musk-scented, violet-blue flowers, reputed to have entered into the production of Louisiana hybrids. (*See* The Beardless Group in the section on cult.) It grows in the swamps of La. and is little known as a garden plant, except for its hybrids.

gracilipes (2). A crested, Japanese iris, the branched stem 4–6 in. long. Leaves sword-shaped, 9–12 in. long and not over ⅓ in. wide. Flowers pale lavender, veined, with a white blotch on the falls and a yellow crest. For cult. *see* ROCK GARDEN.

graminea (1). Stems 2-edged, 7–9 in. high, the glossy leaves a little longer, usually only 4 and tufted. Flowers only 1 or 2, fragrant, lilac-purple, 1½–2 in. long, half hidden by the foliage, the throat veined, the claw* yellow. Asia Minor to central Eu.

innominata (1). A sturdy iris, not over 30 in. high and unsuited to cult. in the eastern states. Leaves numerous, grass-like, about ⅛ in. wide, dark green. Flowers dark yellow, purple-streaked on the falls, very showy, nearly 2 in. long. Ore.

japonica (2). A profusely flowering, many-branched iris, the stems 12–18 in. high. Leaves evergreen, 12–16 in. long, shining green above, paler beneath, sword-shaped. Flowers 1–1½ in. long, lavender-blue, the crest orange-yellow on the falls, the margins of which are wavy. Eastern As. Hardy in Calif. and along the Gulf Coast.

kaempferi (1). An Asiatic iris scarcely known in cult. in the wild form, but with other species, the source of scores of varieties of the Japanese iris. *See* The Beardless Group at the section on cult. below. They have very large, flattish flowers that bloom in late June or July, and a leaf with a prominent midrib.

laevigata (1). Like the preceding, little grown in its original form, but included here as it has entered into the production of some Japanese irises. Eastern As. The original form has bluish-purple flowers, and a leaf without the prominent midrib of *I. kaempferi.*

missouriensis (1). A slender-stemmed perennial from western N.A., the stem usually unbranched, 8–20 in. high. Leaves from 12–18 in. long, scarcely ½ in. wide. Flowers bluish-white, but violet-veined, standing well above the leaves. May–June.

monnieri (1). A stout iris, the stems round and 3–4 ft. high. Leaves nearly erect, 18–24 in. long. Flowers fragrant, yellow, about 3 in. high, in loose clusters, the falls eroded at the tip. Variously credited to Crete and as of garden origin, and apparently closely related to *I. ochroleuca.*

ochroleuca (1). Stem 3–4 ft. high, the

slightly twisted leaves 2–3 ft. long and 1 in. wide. Flowers generally white, the falls with a golden patch, the standards pale yellow. Asia Minor. Perhaps not distinct from *I. monnieri.* There are several hort. forms but they are not well defined.

pallida (3). Scarcely known in its wild form, but listed here as one of the important ingredients of the tall bearded irises. See IRIS "GERMANICA."

prismatica (1). Slender blue flag. A native iris found in wet places in eastern N.A. closely allied to our common blue flag (*I. versicolor*) but with narrower, grass-like leaves. Flowers bluish-violet, the falls purple-veined. June–July.

Pseudacorus (1). Water flag. Yellow flag. An Old World iris commonly naturalized in moist places nearly throughout eastern N.A., and the European yellow counterpart of our common blue flag. It is a stout perennial, 1–3 ft. high, the leaves a little longer and slightly bluish-green. Flowers yellow, about 2 in. wide, the falls often violet-veined. There are many named hort. vars.

pumila (3). Related to *I. Chamaeiris* but practically stemless. Flowers 2–3 in. long, yellow to lilac, the beard dense on the lower part of the falls. The standards as large as the falls, a little paler. There are several hort. color forms. Eu. and Asia Minor.

reticulata (6). A stemless iris (until the fruit matures), its 2–4 narrow, grass-like, 4-sided leaves in a tuft, the blades ultimately up to 12 in. long. Flower solitary, violet-purple, fragrant, the falls with an orange ridge, bordered with white, the tube of the flower 3–6 in. long. Caucasus. Feb.–Mar. Not certainly hardy in frosty regions and best grown in cool greenhouse.

ruthenica (1). A nearly stemless iris, the stem rarely as long as 6 in., the leaves grass-like, about 6 in. long. Flowers with the falls whitish but blue-veined or blue-dotted, the standards purple-violet. Eurasia.

sibirica (1). The parent species of many forms and hybrids. It is a hollow-stemmed iris, the stem much exceeding the narrow leaves that are scarcely ¼ in. wide. Flowers 2–5 in a terminal or lateral cluster (head), blue or lilac-blue or purplish-blue, about 3 in. high. Eurasia.

spuria (1). A Eurasian and North African iris with a stem 1–2 ft. high. Leaves narrow, about 12 in. long, of offensive odor when bruised. Flowers blue-purple or lilac, the standards somewhat darker-colored. There are many hort. forms of various colors.

stylosa = *Iris unguicularis.*

susiana (4). Mourning iris. An iris from Asia Minor and Persia, the stem 1–1½ ft. high, the pale green leaves about 12 in. long and 1 in. wide. Flower solitary, grayish, the falls 3–4 in. long, with a conspicuous black patch and a brownish beard. The standards are smaller, lighter-colored and lilac-spotted. Not easy to grow and needing protection from winter slush and from summer rain while it is dormant.

tectorum (2). Roof iris. Stems 8–12 in. high, the evergreen leaves a little longer and nearly 2 in. wide. Flowers with the segments nearly or quite horizontal, lavender-blue or bluish-purple, the falls nearly round, about 2 in. wide, dark mottled, the crest violet-white. China and Jap. There is a white-flowered variety. Needs a winter mulch in frosty regions.

tenax (1). A beardless iris from the Pacific coast and unsuited for cult. in the eastern states. Stem 8–12 in. high, the narrow leaves

---

* Special articles on the subjects indicated by an asterisk (*) will be found at the words so marked.

with tough fibers. Flowers solitary (rarely 2) purple or darker (rarely lighter), the falls scarcely 1 in. wide, the standards about ¼ in. wide. The leaf fibers are so tough that the Indians used them in weaving.

tuberosa = *Hermodactylus tuberosus.*

unguicularis (1). A tufted, almost stemless perennial from the Levant and North Africa, its basal leaves evergreen, narrow, erect, firm, and 16–24 in. long, hardly ⅓ in. wide. Flowers lilac, nearly 3 in. high, the falls yellow-keeled, the standards similar, but narrower and the flower with a long tube. Winter-blooming and suited only to mild regions or the cool greenhouse; hardy at Washington, D.C. Also known as *I. stylosa.*

verna (1). Violet iris. A native iris, not much cult., with grass-like leaves about 8 in. long, the stem less than half this. Flower solitary, violet-blue, the falls about 1½ in. long, the claw° yellow. Standards erect, a little smaller. Sandy woods from Pa. to Ga. west to Miss. Apr.–May.

versicolor (1). Blue flag. The commonest of our native irises, ubiquitous in wet places from eastern N.A. to Manitoba and south to Va. where it is replaced by the closely related *I. virginica.* Stems 2–3 ft. high, sometimes branched, the leaves bluish-green, and a little shorter, about 1 in. wide. Flowers solitary or few, varying from blue to purple or even white, nearly 3 in. long, the standards smaller. An especially fine *var.* is **Kermesina**, with almost crimson flowers.

xyphioides (6). English iris, but not native there and originally from the Pyrenees. A bulbous iris imported to Bristol, England, and thought by the Dutch to be native there and hence called the English iris. They have narrow, channeled leaves, about equal to the stem which may be 8–15 in. long. Flowers 2 or 3, deep purple-blue, usually golden-patched, the falls wedge-shaped. Can be grown outdoors in mild climates, but not easily.

Xyphium (6). Spanish iris. Not very different from the preceding, but the falls fiddle-shaped, the flower blue-purple (in the wild form) with a yellow or orange patch. Mediterranean region. There are many hort. forms, from among which has arisen the Dutch iris, which is one of the best for forcing for winter bloom and much used by florists. Also good for outdoor cult. in mild climates, and now in many fine vars.

Iris Culture and Varieties

Nearly all of our garden irises belong in the rhizomatous group, which is subdivided into sections, the largest and most important of which are the Apogon (the beardless irises) and the Pogon, or, as it is now called, the Eupogon (the true bearded irises). Beardless irises are the most widely distributed, extending through America, Europe, North Africa, and Asia. The bearded irises are native to central Europe and North Africa, and east to China.

The Eupogon group is the most important for gardens, as the bearded irises are spectacular, adaptable to various garden conditions, vigorous, and with a blooming season from early spring to summer. They are hybrids so that seedlings vary, crosses are easily made, first blooms come in two or three years, and every grower of iris is a potential hybridizer. In some parts of the

southern United States bearded irises are difficult to grow, and certain forms of beardless irises are widely grown, especially those commonly called Louisiana irises. Other forms of beardless irises commonly grown are the sibiricas, the kaempferi (Japanese irises), and spurias. On the West Coast are several beautiful species of beardless iris, notably *I. tenax, innominata,* and *douglasiana,* which are not hardy in the Northeast.

Bearded Irises. The bearded irises are divided roughly into three groups — dwarf, intermediate (lately sometimes called "median"), and tall. As a general rule the dwarfs are the earliest to bloom, followed by the intermediate, with the tall bearded coming last. However, interbreeding between groups, and particularly crossing with new species of iris, is spreading the bloom season. So we may look for late dwarfs and early talls, some of which are already here.

Formerly irises were classified as *variegata, pallida,* and other designations based on their botanical derivation. But of recent years varieties belonging to many new species have been crossed with our various garden irises, and many new kinds of hybrids have been created which cannot be distinguished readily on the basis of botanical and garden characteristics. This has led to the adoption by the American Iris Society of a new classification which is based exclusively on the height of the bloom stalk. Varieties with bloom stalks less than 15 inches in height are classed as dwarfs; those with stalks from 15 to 28 inches are classed as intermediates; and varieties which are 28 inches or more in height are classed as tall bearded irises. More recently the society has divided the dwarfs into two series, those 4–10 inches in height being called miniature dwarfs, and those 10–15 inches high are named standard dwarfs (Lilliputs). It has also tentatively subdivided the intermediates into three subclasses — intermediate hybrids, table iris, and border iris.

Miniature Dwarf Bearded. These are the earliest-blooming bearded irises and form a natural division, the stems usually unbranched, flowers small and usually above the leaves, leaves often falcate (curved or sickle-shaped). They are largely from *I. pumila, Chamaeiris, flavissima,* and other small species. Many of them have interesting spots of color on the falls, with widely flaring or horizontal falls and clear colors. They grow best in full sun with a light soil and good drainage. A well-grown clump makes a bright spot of color in early spring. Some good varieties are: Veri-gay (variegated), Sparkling Eyes (blue and white Amoena), Tampa (strawberry red), Sun Drop (yellow), Blazon (purple), Cup and Saucer (striped purple and white), Path of Gold (deep yellow), Ylo (yellow, very floriferous), Tony (deep purple).

Standard Dwarf Bearded (Lilliputs). Plants are 10–15 inches high and bloom generally later than the miniatures. This class in-

---

° Special articles on the subjects indicated by an asterisk (°) will be found at the words so marked.

cludes a group, often called Lilliputs, which are hybrids of *I. pumila* and tall bearded varieties. They are of rampant growth and free-flowering. Included in this group are Garnet Treasure (dark garnet), Pogo (a very distinct form, yellow with red spot on the falls), Pigmy Gold (clear yellow), Happy Thought (light yellow), Little Shadow (dark blue-purple with a blue beard), Small Wonder (light blue), and Lilliput (light blue with a darker spot on the falls). Also in this group are Fairy Flax (clear light blue), Greenspot (white with green markings at the haft), Baria (light yellow) and Brite (cream white). This group is fertile and is of increasing importance in the garden.

INTERMEDIATE BEARDED HYBRIDS. This is a group of hybrid origin, blooming between the dwarfs and the tall bearded, stems rigid, branched, and extending above the erect foliage. It is a limited group of much reduced fertility including such old garden favorites as *"germanica," florentina, kochi* and *albicans,* as well as such widely grown varieties as Golden Bow, Crysoro (yellow), Snow Maiden, Eleanor Roosevelt (purple), Crimson King, Alaska (white), and Andalusian Blue.

Tall Bearded Iris. Hundreds of named hort. forms of this ever popular perennial are available in all colors. For a list *see* text.

MINIATURE TALLS (TABLE IRIS). The use of irises in flower arrangements and for cut flowers has brought about increased interest in these miniature tall bearded irises. They have graceful, slender, flexuous stems with small flowers. They bloom with the tall bearded irises from which they are derived. Examples include Pewee (white), Daystar (cream, bright beard), Tom Tit (blue-purple), Siskin (lemon yellow), Warbler (yellow), Widget (white-dotted lavender), Mary Williamson (standards white, falls purple), Two for Tea (orchid-pink), Billet Doux (pale blue), Bunting (blue).

BORDER IRISES. These are the shorter tall bearded irises, 15–28 inches tall, which are very useful for the front of the border. They have stiffly erect stems of strong growth, and bloom later than the intermediate hybrids. They are a distinct addition to the border which have not been sufficiently emphasized. Among them are some of the most beautiful varieties such as Black Forest (blue-black with a sheen), Priscilla (white with a white beard), Gay Hussar (yellow and maroon), Lodestar (yellow and red-brown), Pearl Cup (white standards, light-blue falls), Buttonhole (yellow), Amigo (blue bitone), Pink Ruffles (orchid-pink), Mary E. Nicholls (cream with yellow haft).

STANDARD TALL BEARDED IRISES. The tall bearded irises are those over 28 inches in height. They bloom generally after the intermediate hybrids and are the most popular of all the garden irises. Hundreds of new varieties are raised and introduced each year. Twenty years ago they were hardy diploids.* The introduction of tetraploid* varieties has resulted in gorgeous, large, well-branched flowers on tall, sturdy stems, some of which vary in their adaptability to the wide differences of climate in the United States and Canada. The hybridizers are continually striving to produce irises that do well everywhere, and with considerable success. Modern blooms have a richness and clarity of color which was undreamed of a few years ago. This is particularly true in the yellow flowers, which now come in clear colors from palest lemon almost to orange, and without the dull shadows of many of the early kinds. Branching and branch balance are important. Many of the favorite kinds are ruffled, fluted, or with crimped or lacy edges. Domed standards and semi-flaring falls are esteemed by most fanciers, but there is no set standard of perfection and many fine varieties are rounded in form. Floriferousness, substance, and texture (which includes weather-resistance) are important items.

Bearded irises come in several patterns and are usually divided into five divisions:

1. Self. Flower all of one color.
2. Plicata or fancy. Standards and falls white or light in color, overlaid with stitching, veining, or mottlings of a darker color.
3. Bitone. All one color, but standards a different tint or shade from the falls.
4. Bicolor. Standards one color and falls another color. Other terms often used for bicolors are
     (a) Amoena. Standards white, falls another color, usually blue, purple, or yellow,
     (b) Variegata. Yellow standards and red falls.
5. Blend. Two or more colors or tones which blend into each other.

The American Iris Society lists over 25,000 names in its check lists and of these from 1000 to 2000 are in general commerce today. Each year from the votes of the 500 judges

---

* Special articles on the subjects indicated by an asterisk (*) will be found at the words so marked.

of the Society, a symposium of 100 favorites is compiled. The number of good varieties is legion, and selection is largely a matter of personal taste. The best method is to see them growing in gardens, but the following list contains many excellent varieties. It must be realized, however, that the procession moves fast and today's favorites are certain soon to be supplanted by new ones.

TALL BEARDED IRISES

Blue-white	*Medium Yellow*
Snow Flurry	Goldbeater
	Solid Gold
	Truly Yours
	Golden Sunshine
	June Sunlight

White	*Yellow-orange*
New Snow	Ola Kala
Matterhorn	Rocket
Spanish Peaks	Zantha
Cliffs of Dover	Top Flight
Tranquility	

Light Blue	*Red*
Helen McGregor	Solid Mahogany
Distance	Ranger
Rehobeth	Pacemaker
Starshine (cream and	Quechee
blue blend)	

Medium Blue	*Orchid-pink*
Great Lakes	Dreamcastle
Blue Rhythm	Lavanesque
Chivalry	Pink Plume
Lady Ilse	Chantilly (pale
Blue Sapphire	ruffled)
	Radiation

Dark Blue	*Flamingo Pinks*
Pierre Menard	Pink Cameo
(blue-violet)	Happy Birthday
Sable	June Meredith
Sable Night	Cathedral Bells
(red-black)	
Black Hills	
(blue-black)	

Blue Bitone	*Rose Tones*
Amigo	Mulberry Rose
Lothario	Mary Randall
	Queen's Taste

Cream, Light Yellow	*Violet*
Amandine	First Violet
Desert Song	Violet Harmony
Limelight	Blumohr (once
Mystic Melody	bred)
(bitone)	Frances Craig
Palomino	
(pale blend)	

Purple	*Plicata* (white ground)
Elmohr	Blue Shimmer
Master Charles	(edged blue)
	Minnie Colquitt
	(edged purple)
	Raspberry Ribbon
	(edged dark
	violet)
	Port Wine
	(edged dark
	violet)

Amoena (white	*Blends* (brown and
standard)	copper
Pinnacle (with	Sunset Blaze
yellow falls)	Copper Medallion
Wabash (with	Argus Pheasant
purple falls)	Cordovan
	Inca Chief
Bicolors (variegata)	Cascade Splendor
Staten Island	
Extravaganza	
Gay Head	
Accent	

THE BEARDLESS GROUP. The beardless group most commonly grown in gardens are the sibiricas, Louisianas, spurias, and Japanese. They quickly make large clumps of many tall, slender stalks if grown in a rich and moist soil. At the back of the garden or along the banks of a pond or brook they are at their best.

The Siberians have a fibrous root system and narrow, grassy foliage with tall, hollow stalks topped with blue, white, or reddish-purple flowers. Most of the popular varieties are hybrids with larger, more ruffled flowers than the wild species from which they came. Favorites are Tycoon (large blue), Caesar's Brother (dark purple), Royal Ensign (deep purple with a blue blaze), Tropic Night (clear blue), Eric the Red (wine-red), Gatineau (flaring blue and white), and Snow Crest (white). *I. Pseudacorus* is a yellow species which combines well with the Siberians.

Following closely are those commonly called Louisianas, made up of *I. fulva, foliosa, giganticaerulea,* and their hybrids, which were first found in the swamps and bayous of Louisiana and are extensively grown in the southern states. They require a heavy, rich soil and quantities of water, but are grown satisfactorily in gardens and do not require bog conditions. They are hardy as far north as Massachusetts. In the South they make growth in the winter months, while in the North the growth is in the warmer months of summer. The discovery a few years ago of large flowers called Abbeville reds have given us hybrids of size and vigor. Some good varieties are Cajan, Joyeuse (rose-pink), Elizabeth Washington (bright blue), Dorothea K. Williamson (red blend), Sunny (yellow), and The Kahn (blue and gold).

The spurias are very tall and stately, blooming late in the season. They are of a strong growth and, like the Louisianas, the rhizomes spread out in all directions and should be given plenty of room. Wadi Zem Zem is a large, pale yellow, Bathsheba and Larksong are attractive yellow-edged white. Two Opals (lavender and cream), Dutch Defiance (blue with yellow signal patch), and Bronzspur (dark yellow-bronze) are all excellent varieties.

The Japanese iris (*kaempferi*) produce many gorgeous blooms with immense flattened flowers on stiff, slender stems. They bloom late, after most other irises are past. In Japan they have been grown in gardens for centuries and many forms were developed,

---

* Special articles on the subjects indicated by an asterisk (*) will be found at the words so marked.

but much confusion in variety names resulted. Recently our hybridizers have been listing varieties which are true to name, and are producing enormous ruffled, double varieties which are becoming increasingly popular. They give best results in a heavily enriched soil with abundant moisture. They will not tolerate lime. They come in shades of lavender, blue, and white, with yellow signal patches in solid colors, bicolors, bitones, stripes, and dots. If planted so they can be viewed from above, as is often done in Japan, the effect is spectacular. For varieties the reader is referred to the catalogues of specialists. Proven varieties of many years' trial are Gold Bound (white and gold), Mahogany (red-purple), and Purple and Gold (ruffled double, very striking).

SOME OTHER BEARDLESS IRISES. Most interesting for semi-shaded spots is *I. cristata,* a native light-blue iris with a yellow crest. It is low-growing and makes a splendid ground cover. A dainty form is *I. gracilipes* which makes clumps of narrow leaves with miniature pale-lavender flowers on slender branched stems about five inches in height. *Iris tectorum,* the Japanese roof iris, comes in lavender-blue with darker markings, and a white form (*tectorum alba*) with crests marked with gold. *I. graminea* has narrow, glossy leaves with bright lilac, purple, and blue flowers hidden in the foliage. They make attractive subjects for arrangements. *I. versicolor,* the blue flag, has in the *var.* Kermesina a color form that varies from red-purple to almost crimson.

CULTURE OF BEARDED IRISES. For centuries the bearded irises have been the most important garden group of irises and there is no reason to suppose that other groups will supplant them in popularity, in wide distribution, and in general garden usefulness. All bearded irises have the beard-like growth along the center line of the haft of the fall, from which the group gets its name. The leaf is wide and sword-like. The rhizome is comparatively large and normally grows near or partially above the surface of the ground. They demand good drainage, sun, and freedom from the roots of other plants. Do not plant under shrubs or trees and expect them to bloom. For good drainage raise the beds above the surrounding ground, and if the soil is heavy, add sand. Garden compost is ideal for conditioning the soil by making it friable. Any good garden soil will grow irises. Do not use manure next to the rhizomes as it may cause rot. However, in setting new plants, if a hole is dug and a shovelful of well-rotted manure placed at the bottom and covered with dirt, it tends to hold moisture and draw the roots downward. On established plants a double handful of bone meal, superphosphate, or a commercial fertilizer, applied separately or as a mixture, should be scattered around each plant in early spring or after the fall growth has started and scratched in lightly. The soil should be neutral or slightly on the acid side. If too acid, light applications of lime may be made, but do not overdo it.

Soon after blooming the iris plants become dormant, the old roots shrivel, and the new rhizomes begin to grow. Once a rhizome has bloomed it is dead, new rhizomes fan out from it and the next year's flowers come from the new rhizomes. Irises are best planted soon after blooming (generally in July or August) which gives opportunity for the new roots to become established before winter. After three or four years the clumps become crowded and do not give good blooms. Then they should be dug, divided, and the largest of the young rhizomes replanted. Usually the leaves are shortened to about six inches when replanted. This reduces transpiration and gives a neater appearance. Division down to single rhizomes is recommended unless they are very small, in which case double-nosed roots may be used. Single roots may be set about 18 to 24 inches apart. If several roots are placed in a group for clump effect, they may be set about 6 to 8 inches apart. It is better to face the rhizomes all one way, although some growers prefer to point the growing fans toward the center of the group. If pointed out from the center, the clump soon shows an open center. Groups should be from 2 to 3 feet apart. Place the rhizomes just below the surface of the ground with roots well spread. Never plant too deep. Be sure to firm the soil around each rhizome. The first year after planting a light winter mulch applied after freezing weather prevents heaving, which is the cause of many losses. In the colder sections of the country this winter mulch is strongly recommended. It may be marsh hay, oak leaves held down by chicken wire, pine needles, cranberry vine clippings, or other material. The covering is not to prevent freezing, but to prevent heaving and breaking of roots caused by thawing.

Cultivation should be shallow as the fine feeding roots in the growing season are very near the surface. Keep free from weeds and do not allow other plants to cover the rhizomes. As the outer leaves ripen off and become brown, they should be stripped off. While irises will live in arid conditions, they appreciate a reasonable amount of moisture, especially the newly set plants. Be sure to label your named varieties and keep a chart. Labels in the garden get lost and obliterated. — H. W. K.

The latest address of the American Iris Society is in care of Clifford W. Benson, Secretary, 2237 Tower Grove Boulevard, St. Louis, Mo.

INSECT PESTS. Iris borer, the major pest, can be controlled by removing and burning rubbish in fall or early spring. Spray with pesticide #17 when leaves are 5 to 6 in. tall. For lesser bulb fly, *see* BULBS. Pesticide #1 will control thrips, aphids, and general leaf feeders. (*See* SPRAYS AND DUSTS.)

DISEASES. Dead tips of leaves cannot be prevented by spraying. They indicate some root trouble or soil problem. Brown, oval spots in leaves are called leafspot* and may be

---

* Special articles on the subjects indicated by an asterisk (*) will be found at the words so marked.

prevented by raking up dead leaves in the fall and spraying with pesticide #1 or #11 (*see* SPRAYS AND DUSTS) the following spring. Start spraying when new growth is 3 in. high and repeat 3 or 4 times at weekly intervals. A bacterial soft rot usually follows injury by iris borers. Dig the rhizome in Aug., cut out the diseased portion, and soak rhizome for 10 minutes in pesticide #12 at rate of 1–1000.

IRIS FAMILY. Besides the iris itself this large family of plants produces many other garden favorites, among them gladiolus, crocus, freesia, blue-eyed grass, *Ixia*, and *Tigridia*. For the other cult. genera and a description of the family *see* IRIDACEAE.

IRISH HEATH = *Daboecia cantabrica*.

IRISH IVY = *Hedera Helix hibernica*.

IRISH JUNIPER = *Juniperus communis hibernica*.

IRISH YEW = *Taxus baccata fastigiata*.

IRONBARK. *See* EUCALYPTUS SIDEROXYLON.

IRON CHELATE (key′late). Iron in very small concentrations is a necessary element for plant growth, especially in the proper functioning of the green coloring matter in leaves (chlorophyll). *See* PLANT FOODS. In most cases iron is found in available form in the soil, and plants do not suffer from a deficiency of available iron. When they do the symptoms are obvious — lack of green color, paleness of leaves, yellowing of leaves that should be dark green. Such deficiency may be found in a soil too alkaline for proper growth or it may be some other soil factor that promotes this chlorosis (lack of green in leaves). The chemical determination of the causes of chlorosis is outside the competence of all but soil scientists, but the symptoms anyone can see and correct.

Iron chelate (a preparation of iron sulphate) has been found to be effective in correcting chlorosis, often with considerable speed. It must be supplied with care, sometimes in a fertilizer or mixed with sand or poured on the soil in which the plant grows. Often it is used as a spray on the foliage, which, of course, allows the solution to drip to the ground. Several commercial preparations are on the market and it is essential that manufacturers' directions be carefully followed. If they are properly used, iron chelates produce almost dramatic correction of chlorosis, but their improper use can result in burning of the foliage or death of the plant.

The list of ornamental plants that may be helped by iron chelates, if chlorosis is present, include roses, gardenias, camellias, rhododendron and azalea, box, turf, and most shrubs and trees, including *Citrus*. As a foliage spray one ounce of iron chelate in 10 gal. of water is safe, but such sprays must not be stronger than this, and as different brands may have different concentrations it is important to follow directions with accuracy.

IRON-TREE. *See* METROSIDEROS.

IRONWEED. *See* VERNONIA.

IRONWOOD. Many hard-wooded trees are so called in all parts of the world. Those in cultivation include: *Ostrya virginiana, Metrosideros, Carpinus caroliniana* (*see* HORNBEAM).

IRREGULAR FLOWER. A flower that is unsymmetrical, due to the parts being of different sizes, or because some part is lacking, mostly because the flower is spurred or 2-lipped, as in the snapdragon. All orchid flowers are irregular. *See* REGULAR FLOWER.

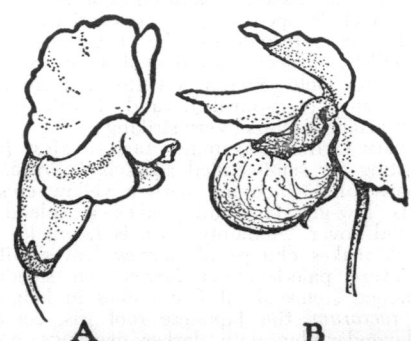

A   B

Two types of irregular flower.
(A) Snapdragon. (B) Lady's-slipper.

IRRIGATION. Many places in the U.S. cannot be certain of growing crops without supplementing an inadequate or poorly distributed rainfall. While this applies chiefly to the region west of the 100th meridian, there are many places in the East where summer droughts may be disastrous if a supplementary water supply is not forthcoming.

The remedy for such rainfall deficiency is irrigation, which for purposes of this discussion may be divided into overhead systems, and the sort used in the West, where the land itself is flooded. The latter system is in wide use in states where the annual rainfall is less than 10 in., and in many others where summer rainfall is almost lacking. *See* the name of your state for rainfall figures in your locality. There are many places, too, where a reasonably good winter rainfall (10–18 in.) will be followed by periods of from 130–250 days in which there is no effective rainfall, *i.e.*, capable of wetting the soil. Growing anything but desert plants in such regions, without irrigation, is practically impossible, although their soils may be fertile enough. The Imperial Valley, much of the Calif. fruit areas, and the apple orchards at Wenatchee in Wash. are examples of irrigated districts that would be worthless without it.

WESTERN IRRIGATION. In regions such as these, large amounts of water must be brought to the garden or orchard during the growing season. It is impossible in a general article to specify whether driven wells, a local water company, or a state irrigation system will be the most economical source of supply. Some-

---

* Special articles on the subjects indicated by an asterisk (*) will be found at the words so marked.

times irrigation water can be purchased for an agreed percentage of the final crop.

Assuming an adequate water supply, it must be conducted to every part of the garden or orchard, usually in tightly jointed iron pipes, but often in open ditches or by flumes, which are reasonably watertight, V-shaped, wooden troughs. Whichever method is used, there must be provision for necessary outlets, so spaced that all parts of the plantation will be covered. In many irrigated districts the outlets are put 6–8 ft. apart for small crops, but 10–20 ft. apart for fruit trees.

No part of the irrigation system is more important than the ground level. If too steep, irrigation is impossible. If too flat, a large number of outlets are necessary properly to distribute the water over even such a small piece of land as an acre.

In moderately sloping land, a system of basins or ridges should be constructed which will hold enough water in comparatively small areas — a plan known as basin or check irrigation. But by far the best method is for the land to slope so gently in one direction that the water may flow directly but slowly between the rows of plants.

The amount and frequency of applying the water depend upon the kind and age of the crop, the kind of soil, the heat and the velocity of the wind, and the time since the last effective rain. They depend, also, in some states, upon the cost of the water. No definite rule can be given, but a few general principles should be understood.

When water is to be turned on, see that the whole area is thoroughly puddled, more for trees, of course, than for shallower-rooted crops. It may take an inch or 2 in. of water to do this, in some places more. When the soil is dry enough, cultivate* it thoroughly, for irrigation is not a substitute for cultivation, but an adjunct of it. Weeds must be kept down or they will steal some of the expensive water.

Many fruit growers plan to use, in rainless summers, about 4–5 applications of water, averaging 1½–2½ in. each. It is well known that too much or too frequent watering is harmful to the crop, and especially to the soil, which appears to lose some plant food by excessive water applications. See LEACHING. Again, no general rule is possible, but the rule of common sense and watching the crop and the weather always applies.

EASTERN IRRIGATION. Supplying gardens or trees with water on such a scale is never necessary in the East. But many shallow-rooted crops, like vegetables, are often caught by summer heat and droughts. And many commercial and private growers have found that some overhead sprinkling system more than pays for itself.

One of the best of these overhead watering plants is the device known as the Skinner system. It consists of galvanized pipes, elevated so as to throw a fine spray in both directions far enough to meet the spray of the next line of pipe. This means that the pipes are from 6–8 ft. above the ground level and must be supported about every 25 ft. with posts or iron pipe.

Water merely forced through holes in a pipe cannot be properly distributed. The merit of the Skinner system is that at each outlet (they should be 4 ft. apart) a patented nozzle is attached, and it is this that ensures a fine, mist-like spray. One can buy pipes already provided with the nozzles, or can drill the holes (with a patented drilling machine) and put the nozzles in. Also, when the system is moved, as it can be readily, a patented union for the piping is necessary.

There is no soil washing, no packing and no injury to the crops, as may come from careless hosing. There are, of course, several other systems in use, some of which operate at ground level.

Water must be kept at a definite pressure and the diameter size of the pipe varies with its length and with the pressure.

There is still another system of irrigation better than any so far noted. It works upon the principle that in nature capillarity supplies the roots of plants with water drawn from below. Sub-irrigation does the same thing It involves delivering water below the surface of the ground. For details of it *see* WATERING, as it is chiefly applied to greenhouse benches, frames, window boxes, and hanging baskets (which see).

ISATIS (eye′sa-tis; also eye-say′tis). Rather unimportant herbs of the mustard family, chiefly from the Mediterranean region. Of the 30 known species only the two below are in cult., generally under the name of woad. Before the days of synthetic dyes they were of interest as the source of a blue dye. They are erect, usually branching herbs, with alternate,* often stem-clasping and mostly undivided leaves. Flowers small, in rather open, loose clusters (panicled racemes*), the 4 petals yellow. Fruit not splitting, key-like, hanging, oblongish or narrower, usually minutely notched at the tip. (*Isatis* is the classical name for some healing herb, but not necessarily of these plants.)

The first is a perennial, and seed of it should be sown the year before bloom is expected. *Isatis tinctoria* is a biennial and must also be sown the previous Aug.-Sept. for bloom the next season. Both are of easy culture in any garden soil.

glauca. A perennial herb 2–4 ft. high, the foliage very bluish-gray. Basal leaves blunt, oblongish, those of the stem nearly stalkless, but the base narrowed and not stem-clasping. Flowers many, the terminal cluster large and branched. Fruit more or less oblongish about ½ in. long. Persia and Asia Minor. June–July.

tinctoria. Common woad; also called dyer's woad. A biennial herb, 18–36 in. high. Basal leaves oblongish, usually without hairs and bluish-green, the stem leaves narrower, the base stem-clasping, with narrow auricles.* Flowers in compound racemes,* small. Fruit about ⅝ in. long, about ⅔ as wide. Eu. Once commonly raised for its blue dye.

ISLAND MYRTLE = *Ceanothus arboreus.*

---

* Special articles on the subjects indicated by an asterisk (*) will be found at the words so marked

ISLAY = *Prunus ilicifolia.*

ISMENE CALATHINA = *Hymenocallis calathina.* See SPIDER-LILY.

ISOLEPIS GRACILIS = *Scirpus cernuus.*

ISOLOMA (eye-so-lō'ma). Tropical American herbs or shrubs of the family Gesneriaceae, comprising over 50 species, of which the two below, or hybrids of them and other species, are favorite greenhouse plants. They have creeping roots or rootstocks and opposite, usually softly hairy and very handsome leaves. Flowers mostly scarlet or orange, borne singly or in small clusters in the leaf axils,* or in a leafy terminal cluster (raceme*). Corolla more or less tubular, but somewhat swollen toward the top, its limb* not quite regular* and 5-lobed. Stamens 4, sometimes with an odd sterile one. Fruit a capsule.* (*Isoloma* is from the Greek for equal and throat, in allusion to the throat of the corolla.) By some, and perhaps correctly, *Kohleria* is considered the approved name for *Isoloma*, here retained because of long usage among gardeners.

They should be grown in the warm-temperate greenhouse (*see* GREENHOUSE), in potting mixture* 4. Otherwise, their culture and propagation are the same as for *Gloxinia* (which see).

amabile. A hairy, perennial herb 12–30 in. high. Leaves stalked, more or less oval, sharply toothed, more or less purple-veined and with scattered purple blotches. Flowers hanging, the corolla slightly curved, the tube purple-blotched and pale within, the limb* dark red, but purple-dotted. Colombia. Also known as *Kohleria amabilis.*

hirsutum. A hairy, shrubby plant 2–4 ft. high. Leaves short-stalked, ovalish or narrower, tapering at the tip, bluntly toothed. Flowers nodding, solitary in the leaf axils, the corolla tube curved, hairy on the outside, purple, but the 5-cleft limb* spotted. W.I. Also known as *Kohleria eriantha.*

isophylla, -us, -um (eye-so-fill'a). Equal-leaved; or with similar leaves.

ISOPLEXIS (eye-so-plecks'is). Two undershrubs from the Canary Islands, of the family Scrophulariaceae, their outdoor cultivation confined to Calif. or similar climates. Leaves alternate,* usually thick and persistent. Flowers yellow, mostly in a dense, terminal cluster (raceme*). Corolla tubular, curved, the tube swollen, the limb* mostly 2-lipped,* the upper and lower lips* of about equal size. Stamens 4, slightly protruding. Fruit an ovalish capsule.* (*Isoplexis* is from the Greek for equal and cut, in allusion to the nearly equal lips* of the corolla.)

The plants are closely related to the perennial forms of the foxglove (*Digitalis*), and are grown in much the same way. See FOXGLOVE.

canariensis. A stiff, erect plant 3–4 ft. high, the leaves thick, lance-shaped, 4–6 in. long, and shining. Flower cluster (raceme*) nearly 12 in. long, the flowers about 1 in. long, yellowish-brown.

sceptrum. Resembling the last, but the leaves are larger, the flowers drooping, and the corolla not 2-lipped,* its 5 lobes nearly equal.

ISOPYRUM (eye-so-py'rum). Dwarf herbaceous perennials, belonging to the Ranunculaceae. Of the 30 North American and Asiatic species, only the false anemone, *I. biternatum*, is likely to be cult. Flowers white, solitary or in panicles, without petals, but with 5–6 sepals. (*Isopyrum* is the classical name of a *Fumaria*, and of no known application here.)

biternatum. False anemone. Leaves twice-compound,* the leaflets 3-lobed and with slender stalks. Flowers ¾ in. wide, the clusters appearing in spring. Ont. to Fla. and Tex. Suitable for the rockery in partial shade, and propagated by seed or by division.

ITALIAN ALDER = *Alnus cordata.* See ALDER.

ITALIAN ASTER = *Aster Amellus.*

ITALIAN BROCCOLI = *Brassica oleracea italica.* For culture *see* BROCCOLI.

ITALIAN CHICORY. *See* RADICHETTA.

ITALIAN CLOVER = *Trifolium incarnatum.* See CLOVER.

ITALIAN CORN SALAD = *Valerianella eriocarpa.*

ITALIAN CYPRESS = *Cupressus sempervirens.*

ITALIAN HONEYSUCKLE = *Lonicera Caprifolium.*

ITALIAN JASMINE = *Jasminum humile.*

ITALIAN KALE = *Brassica Rapa septiceps.*

ITALIAN REED = *Arundo Donax.*

ITALIAN RYE GRASS = *Lolium multiflorum.*

ITALIAN STONE PINE = *Pinus Pinea.* See PINE.

italica, -us, -um (i-tal'i-ka). From Italy.

ITEA (it'ee-a). A small genus of shrubs or trees of the family Saxifragaceae, one cult. for its showy flowers. Leaves alternate,* rather narrow. Flowers in clusters (racemes*), white, with five narrow petals and five persistent sepals.* Fruit a 2-valved capsule.* A few species in eastern As., one in N.A. (*Itea* is from the Greek for willow.)

virginica. Virginia willow. Sweet spire. A shrub 3–5 ft., sometimes 8 ft. high. Branches slender, upright, reddish when young. Leaves oval, 2–3 in. long, turning red in fall. Flowers fragrant, showy. June–July. N.J to Fla., Mo. and Tex. Hardy from zone* 3 southward. Prefers moist, good soil, but is adaptable; easily propagated by division.

ITEACEAE. See SAXIFRAGACEAE.

ITHURIEL'S-SPEAR = *Brodiaea laxa.*

IVY. The ivy of tradition and history, as well as hort., is *Hedera Helix* (which see). *See also* PARTHENOCISSUS. For other plants, in which ivy is part of their name, *see* SENECIO MIKANIOIDES, GLECOMA HEDERACEA, CYMBALARIA MURALIS, CISSUS INCISA, and the next few entries.

IVY ARUM = SCINDAPSUS.

IVY GERANIUM = *Pelargonium peltatum.*

* Special articles on the subjects indicated by an asterisk (*) will be found at the words so marked.

IXIA (ick′sĭ-a). South African bulbous herbs of about 30 species, belonging to the family Iridaceae, the corms producing grass-like leaves and flower spikes with pendulous, bell-shaped flowers. Leaves generally 2-ranked. Flowering stalk mostly longer than the leaves. Fruit a small capsule.* (*Ixia* is from the Greek for bird lime, possibly referring to the juice of some species.)

Hardy generally only in zones* 5 to 9; with protection, occasionally safe northward, but prone to make fall leaf growth that is not frostproof. Elsewhere treated as greenhouse-bloomers, planting the corms of blooming size in 4- or 5-in. pots or pans in the fall, 4 to 7 to a pot, and treating them as crocus or grape-hyacinths forced for early spring bloom. They grow readily out of doors in southern Calif., where they multiply quickly. There are many named hort. forms, some of them finer than the species listed below.

columellaris. Grows 2 ft. high. Flowers lilac or lavender, with blue throat. Corms 1 in. or less in diameter. Perhaps not distinct from the next.

maculata. Leaves linear, ribbed, 6 to 12 in. long. Flowers bright yellow, in dense and erect spikes, with black mark in the throat.

viridiflora. Not over 20 in. high, usually less as cult. Leaves narrowly sword-shaped. Flowers about 1 in. long, numerous in a lax spike, the corolla pale green, but with a black spot at the base, the filaments* of the anthers* also black. May–June.

ixioides (icks-i-oy′deez, but *see* Oïdes). Like the genus *Ixia* (which see).

IXIOLIRION (ix-i-o-lir′i-on). A genus of Asiatic herbs of the amaryllis family, with blue or violet, spring-blooming flowers. They are little known in cult. and of uncertain identity. The only species likely to be in cult. is **I. montanum**, known as Altai lily. It is about 1 ft. high, with 4 basal, persistent leaves. Flowers in umbels,* lilac, the corolla about 1 in. long. Western Asia and Siberia. Not certainly hardy in the North and the bulbous rootstock should be stored over the winter in a cool, dry, frost-free place, for planting the following spring. Often listed as *I. pallasi.*

ixocarpa, -us, -um (icks-o-kar′pa). Sticky-fruited.

IXORA (icks-ō′ra). Tropical, mostly Asiatic shrubs and trees comprising about 150 species, belonging to the family Rubiaceae, cultivated in the open only in Calif. and Florida, and grown as a conservatory plant elsewhere. Leaves opposite* or whorled.* Flowers red to white, in compact bunches, individual flower long-tubular, with 4–5 spreading lobes. Fruit a berry. (*Ixora* was named for a Malabar deity.)

Commonly grown for ornament and in a variety of soils, especially in Fla. For greenhouse culture use potting mixture* 4 and do not let the night temperature go below 65°. Some people confuse shrubs of this genus with *Hamelia erecta*. The most certain identification is through the fruit, which is 2-seeded in *Ixora*, but many-seeded in *Hamelia*.

coccinea. Flame-of-the-woods; called, also, jungle geranium. Evergreen shrub, the leaves oblong, 4–5 in. long. Flowers red, to 1¾ in. long, in dense clusters. East Indies.

fulgens. Shrub with narrow, oblong leaves 4–6 in. long, shiny above. Flowers orange-scarlet, to 1¾ in. long, in large, sessile bunches. India and in the East Indies.

incarnata = *Ixora coccinea.*

J

Jaburan (jab′ur-ran). Oriental vernacular for *Ophiopogon Jaburan.*

JACARANDA (jack-a-ran′da). Tropical American shrubs and trees of the family Bignoniaceae, comprising more than 50 species, of which two are cult. for ornament, outdoors in zones* 8 and 9, and occasionally in the greenhouse. (It is not the genus yielding the valuable cabinet wood known as jacaranda′, which is rosewood and derived from the non-hort. tree *Dalbergia nigra* of the pea family.) Leaves opposite,* twice-compound, the leaflets arranged feather-fashion, numerous, the foliage thus handsome. Flowers showy, blue or violet, the clusters (panicles*) terminal or in the leaf axils.* Corolla tubular, its limb* slightly 2-lipped,* the flower thus a little irregular.* Stamens* 4, often with an odd sterile one. Fruit an oblongish or ovalish capsule.* (*Jacaranda* is the Brazilian name for these trees and for those yielding the cabinet wood mentioned above.)

J. mimosifolia is one of the most popular flowering trees grown in Fla. and southern Calif. It stands many different sorts of soils, and even if hit by occasional frosts, it can be pruned back and used, in its young stages, as a handsome bedding shrub or as specimens on the lawn. It is widely so used in regions where it will not attain tree size. If grown under glass, put in the warm-temperate greenhouse and use potting mixture* 4. Propagated by cuttings of half-ripened wood.

acutifolia. A Brazilian tree probably not in cult., the plants so offered being *J. mimosifolia.*

cuspidifolia. Not usually over 30 ft. high, often shrubby, its leaves nearly 2 ft. long, smooth, and composed of 8–10 main divisions, each of which bears 10–15 pairs of leaflets which are about 1 in. long. Flowers bluish-

---

* Special articles on the subjects indicated by an asterisk (*) will be found at the words so marked.

violet, not over 1½ in. long. Brazil and the Argentine.

mimosifolia. A tree up to 50 ft. high (less as cult.), holding its leaves until early in the spring. Leaves hairy, fern-like, with 16 or more pairs of main divisions, each of these with 14–24 pairs of oblongish leaflets which are about ½ in. long. Flower cluster nearly 8 in. long, the flowers blue, about 2 in. long. Brazil. April–June (in Fla.). A very showy tree, sometimes know as *J. ovalifolia*, and usually offered under the incorrect designation of *J. acutifolia*.

ovalifolia = *J. mimosifolia*.

JACK BEAN = *Canavalia ensiformis*.

JACKFRUIT = *Artocarpus integrifolia*.

JACK-IN-THE-PULPIT = *Arisaema triphyllum*.

JACK-IN-THE-PULPIT FAMILY = Araceae.

JACK PINE = *Pinus banksiana*. See PINE.

Jacobaea, -us, -um (jack-o-bee′a). A specific name applied to several plants, perhaps named for Saint James or derived from the Latin *Jacobus* (James). See SENECIO and LOTUS.

JACOBINIA (jack-o-bin′i-a). A genus of 40 species of showy tropical American herbs and under-shrubs, of the family Acanthaceae, grown in the open only in warm climates, from zones* 7 to 9, but often grown as conservatory plants. They are closely related to *Justicia* and differ from it only in technical characters. Leaves opposite.* Flowers showy, irregular, 2-lipped, in dense, bracted* clusters or solitary. (*Jacobinia* is perhaps named after Jacobina, near Bahia, Brazil.)

Jacobinia and *Justicia* should be grown in the warm greenhouse, in potting mixture*4, and given plenty of water. They root easily from cuttings.

carnea. A shrub 2–3 ft. high. Leaves ovalish or oblong, 6–7 in. long. Flowers rose-purple or flesh-colored, the dense, terminal heads nearly 4 in. long. Brazil. Often offered as *Justicia magnifica* and *Justicia carnea*, and a good house plant.

coccinea = *Pachystachys coccinea*.

pauciflora. Sub-shrub to 2 ft. high, the leaves oblong to oval, about ¾ in. long. Flowers scarlet, tipped with yellow, ¾ in. long, solitary and nodding. Brazil. A floriferous plant, as easily grown as fuchsia.

JACOB'S LADDER = *Polemonium caeruleum*.

JACOB'S ROD. See ASPHODELINE.

JACOB'S STAFF = *Fouquieria splendens*.

JACQUEMONTIA (jak-kwe-mon′she-a). Twining, chiefly tropical American vines of the family Convolvulaceae, much resembling the morning-glory, but not so good as it. Only **J. pentantha** of the 60 known species is at all usual in cult., and it can be grown outdoors only in zones* 8 and 9, as it is native from Fla. to S.A. It is a perennial vine with a slightly woody base. Leaves alternate,* more or less ovalish or heart-shaped, 1½–2 in. long. Flowers blue, about 1 in. long in clusters (cymes*), the stalk of which usually

exceeds the length of the leaves. The plant differs only in technical characters (2 flattened stigmas*) from the closely related *Ipomoea*, and is grown like the tender species of that genus. (Named for Victor Jacquemont, French naturalist.)

JADE PLANT = *Crassula argentea*.

JAGGERY PALM = *Caryota urens*; also *Arenga saccharifera*.

JAK; JAKFRUIT = *Artocarpus integrifolia*.

Jalapa (jal′a-pa). Latinized form of *jalap*, once thought to be derived from the four-o'clock (*Mirabilis Jalapa*).

Jamacaru (ja-mack′a-roo). A Brazilian vernacular for a cactus from which the natives made their huts. See CEREUS.

JAMAICA COTTON = *Gossypium punctatum*.

JAMAICA GOLD FERN = *Pityrogramma sulphurea*.

JAMAICA HONEYSUCKLE = *Passiflora laurifolia*.

JAMAICA SORREL = *Hibiscus Sabdariffa*.

JAMBERRY. See PHYSALIS.

JAMBOS. Adaptation of the Hindu name for the rose-apple (*Eugenia Jambos*).

JAMBU = *Eugenia Jambos*.

JAMESIA (james′i-a). Three species of western American shrubs of the family Saxifragaceae, **J. americana** grown for its foliage, which turns bright orange and scarlet in the fall, and for its fragrant white flowers. It is an upright shrub 3–4 ft. high, with shreddy bark and opposite,* short-stalked, oval and elliptic leaves that are 1½–2½ in. long and white-felty beneath. Flowers white, or pinkish on the outside, in many-flowered clusters (cymes*) that are 1–3 in. long. Petals 5, hairy on the inside. Stamens* 10. Fruit a 3–5-valved capsule. The shrub is wild from Wyo. to Utah and N. Mex., and is hardy from zone* 4 southward. It prefers open, sunny sites and well-drained soils. Easily propagated by seeds or by cuttings of its ripe wood. (Named for Doctor Edwin James, botanical explorer of the Rocky Mountains.)

JAMESTOWNWEED = Jimsonweed. See DATURA STRAMONIUM.

JAPAN CEDAR = *Cryptomeria japonica*.

JAPAN CLOVER = *Lespedeza striata*.

JAPAN LAUREL = *Aucuba japonica*.

JAPAN PLUM. See LOQUAT.

JAPANESE. As part of the name of many plants or things that come from Japan or its vicinity, *Japanese* is common. Those that occur in the ENCYCLOPEDIA OF GARDENING, and their proper equivalents, are:

Japanese alder = *Alnus japonica* (see ALDER); **Japanese anemone** = *Anemone japonica*; **Japanese angelica tree** (see ARALIA); **Japanese apricot** = *Prunus Mume*; **Japanese**

---

* Special articles on the subjects indicated by an asterisk (*) will be found at the words so marked.

artichoke = *Stachys sieboldi;* **Japanese barberry** = *Berberis thunbergi;* **Japanese barnyard millet** = *Echinochloa crus-galli frumentacea;* **Japanese beetle** (*see* next main entry below); **Japanese black pine** = *Pinus thunbergi* (*see* PINE); **Japanese burnet** = *Sanguisorba obtusa;* **Japanese chestnut** = *Castanea crenata* (*see* CHESTNUT); **Japanese clematis** = *Clematis paniculata;* **Japanese dwarf trees** (*see* DWARFING); **Japanese evergreen oak** = *Quercus acuta* (*see* OAK); **Japanese fern** = *Cyclophorus lingua;* **Japanese flowering cherry** = *Prunus lannesiana,* P. *serrulata,* and P. *yedoensis;* **Japanese flowering quince** = *Chaenomeles lagenaria;* **Japanese garden** (*see* second main entry below); **Japanese hemlock** = *Tsuga diversifolia* (*see* HEMLOCK); **Japanese holly** = *Ilex crenata* (*see* HOLLY); **Japanese honeysuckle** = *Lonicera japonica;* **Japanese horse-chestnut** = *Aesculus turbinata* (*see* HORSE-CHESTNUT); **Japanese iris** (*see* IRIS KAEMPFERI); **Japanese ivy** = *Parthenocissus tricuspidata;* also *Hedera Helix gracilis:* **Japanese larch** (*see* LARCH); **Japanese laurel** (*see* CRASSULA ARGENTEA); also *Aucuba japonica;* **Japanese lawn grass** = *Zoysia japonica;* **Japanese leaf** = *Aglaonema simplex;* **Japanese lily** = *Lilium speciosum;* **Japanese maple** = *Acer palmatum* (*see* MAPLE); **Japanese medlar** (*see* LOQUAT); **Japanese mint** = *Mentha arvensis piperascens* (*see* MINT); **Japanese morning-glory** (*see* IPOMOEA NIL); **Japanese pagoda tree** = *Sophora japonica;* **Japanese pear** = *Pyrus pyrifolia;* **Japanese persimmon** = *Diospyros Kaki* (*see* PERSIMMON); **Japanese plum** = *Prunus salicina* (*see* PLUM), also the loquat; **Japanese quince** = *Chaenomeles lagenaria;* **Japanese raisin tree** = *Hovenia dulcis;* **Japanese red pine** = *Pinus densiflora* (*see* PINE); **Japanese rose** = *Kerria japonica pleniflora;* **Japanese rubber-plant** (*see* CRASSULA ARGENTEA); **Japanese snowball** = *Viburnum tomentosum sterile;* **Japanese spurge** = *Pachysandra terminalis;* **Japanese tree peony** = *Paeonia suffruticosa* (*see* PEONY); **Japanese varnish tree** = *Firmiana simplex;* **Japanese white pine** = *Pinus parviflora* (*see* PINE); **Japanese wisteria** = *Wistaria floribunda;* **Japanese yew** = *Taxus cuspidata* (*see also* PODOCARPUS).

JAPANESE BEETLE. This introduced pest has spread over large areas of the eastern part of the United States. Eggs are deposited by beetles in sod during midsummer. Young are small, soil-inhabiting white grubs, among many species, which damage lawns extensively. During winter, grubs descend below frost line and in spring, ascend and continue feeding. During June, grubs transform to pupae and adult beetles, which emerge soon.

To control adults, spray with pesticide #19, hydrated lime, #17 or #1. Area spraying of trees and shrubs will suppress over-all population.

An introduced bacterial disease, milky disease, kills many grubs in areas where spores have been spread. Over long periods of time, spore treatment of large areas will effectively suppress beetle populations. See your local county agricultural agent or state agricultural experiment station for source of spore powder.

Grub-proofing of lawns with newer insecticides will give excellent grub control but will not necessarily keep out migratory adults. Use pesticide #15, #18, #16 or #13 at the strength recommended on label, applied in dry form or spray to grass in early spring or fall. Water in chemicals. Spring applications will not kill mature larvae but will kill young larvae hatching that summer and fall. *See* SPRAYS AND DUSTS. — L. G. M.

JAPANESE GARDENS. A Japanese garden should not be judged by Western standards. Western gardens are designed as an attractive setting for flowers and shrubs. Japanese gardens are designed to represent natural scenery, complete without the aid of flowering plants — equally beautiful at all seasons of the year. But in the season when there are no flowers, Japanese gardens retain more beauty than Western gardens.

With the intense love of nature possessed by the Japanese, it is impossible for them to live contentedly in crowded cities, without a suggestion of the out-of-doors. This passion

JAPANESE LANTERNS

Kusuga, one of the standard variety, at the left. It takes its name from a Shinto deity. Snow-scene lantern or legged lantern, in the middle, wide-roofed to hold the snow. Enshu, named after Kobori Enshu, highest authority on tea ceremony. The form of this lantern suggests the long cranium of Fukurokuju, one of the seven gods of fortune.

for the beauties of nature finds expression in a garden. The smallest space, back of a city house or shop, is used for a garden. The *Sho-ji,* or sliding doors, are pushed back, and before you is a glimpse of natural loveliness, too diminutive to walk about in, but sufficiently large to carry one's thoughts far from the city sounds and confusion. From these tiny gardens, like a natural landscape picture, developed the larger, rarely beautiful gardens in temple enclosures, the *Cha-niwa,* or tea garden, surrounding the houses of the *Cha-no-yu,* or ceremonial tea masters, and the larger, more elaborately planned gardens, adjoining the old palaces, and on the old estates of noblemen and statesmen. The literary and artistic men, as well as the wealthy merchants, all plan and revere their gardens.

ENVIRONMENT. In Japan the placing of a garden does not depend on the character of the land. The garden may represent mountain scenery in a seaside environment, or the designer of the garden may wish to reproduce some historical spot of beautiful scenery which he has mentally cherished, though years have passed since he visited this scene. This, to a Westerner, might seem incongruous, but placed in the same land, the garden fittings and style of construction are so typically Japanese that it appears most natural. There are many sections of New England, as well as of Westchester County, New York, of New Jersey and California, where a Japanese garden will fit perfectly into the environment. We have all seen marvelous natural gardens of iris and ferns combined with rock of such beauty that only a small degree of human aid will transform it into a perfect Japanese garden. Rocks do for lanterns and bridges, and there must be an abundance of water. However, there are many Japanese gardens in America which are so disturbingly out of place that they create in those who behold them a general dislike for all Japanese gardens.

THE OBJECT OF A JAPANESE GARDEN is to bring natural beauty to your very door; to refresh the mind by a complete change of outlook; to bring peace of mind by the contemplation of beautiful surroundings.

HISTORY. We know the existence in Japan of gardens as far back as the beginning of the third century A.D. As in all the arts, the making of gardens was imported either directly from China, or through Korea to Japan. Garden-making, coming from China, showed a strong Buddhist influence. Until the sixteenth century the gardens of Japan were Chinese in design, but at this period all foreign influence was thrown off. A style purely Japanese developed under the successive direction of the priests, the Cha-no-yu masters, of whom Kobori-Enshiu (1579–1647) was the greatest designer, and finally the Niwa-shi, or professional gardeners. Down to the present day the gardens of Japan hold an important place in the hearts of the people, reflecting their love of nature, plus exquisite taste.

CLASSIFICATION. The many forms of Japanese gardens fall under two general heads:

TSUKI-YAMA, ARTIFICIAL HILLS, *and* HIRA-NIWA, LEVEL GROUND

Shima, meaning island, was the name applied to the ancient form of gardens. These gardens were without design, consisting merely of a lake, an island connected to the mainland by a bridge. The island is to give depth and variety to the garden. The one island multiplied to a large variety of islands, too numerous to enumerate, in spite of the interesting names by which they are distinguished. A few of these names follow, for although they sound poetical, they describe the form and character of the islands. The word *Shima* is changed to *Jima* for the sake of euphony. This happens frequently in the Japanese language. *Matsa-jima* (pine island) is much used even in a small lake. It frequently holds only one pine of beautiful form. *Iso-jima* (rock island) — the smallest of the islands, often just a group of rocks placed in water to suggest an island and not connected to the mainland. *Kumo-gata-jima* (cloud-shaped island) — this island is formed completely of white sand, and gives the illusion of a cloud passing over the lake at that special point. *Horai-jima* (Elysian isle) is only seen in gardens of great dimension. This island is in the form of a turtle, and planted with pine trees.

LAKES, WATERFALLS, AND STREAMS. Lakes are important in making the garden appear larger and creating reflections. The earth dug out to make the lake, with some additional soil, should be used to make the hills. The lake should not be too regular in shape. Banks should be so curved that with the aid of trees, well planted, the full extent of the lake is not seen from any one position. Waterfalls form the central feature of many gardens. They should be located far from the main house, from which the garden is viewed. They are usually made to fall from a valley between hills, with higher hills or

STONES IN THE JAPANESE GARDEN

Stone of Two Deities at the right, the Guardian Stone at the left, and the worshiping stone in the center.

* Special articles on the subjects indicated by an asterisk (*) will be found at the words so marked.

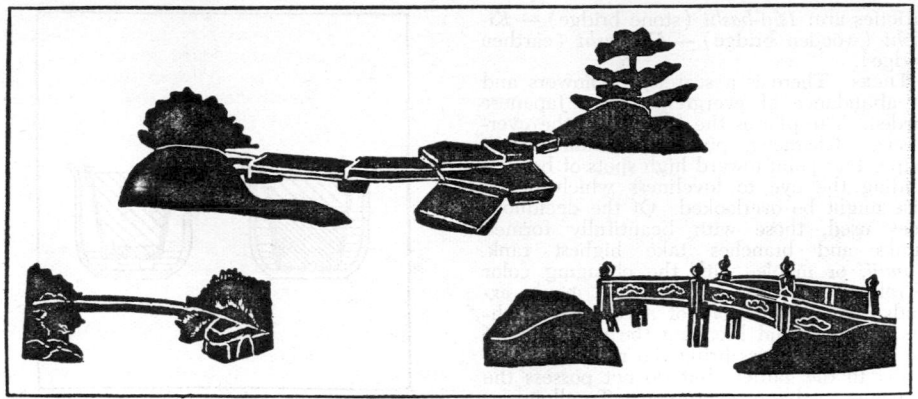

In the middle, Gangyo-bashi or stone bridge formed like a wedge of flying wild ducks. At the left, a bridge formed of one slab of stone. At the right, a wooden bridge used as an approach to temple or shrine.

forest trees for a background. There must be a basin with rocks for the water to dash into. Streams — in the level gardens a spring is made to issue from among moss-covered rocks to form the origin of a stream. The direction of the stream should be determined by the grade of the land. It should flow between naturally curved banks and aid in the drainage. Even when there is no water available for a cascade — a rocky bed is made to give the appearance of the fall having dried up, which is apt to occur in nature during a dry season. The natural forms of cascades have been closely studied. Every variety of fall is reproduced in the gardens of Japan: *Tsutai-ochi* (glide-falling) — the water falling down the surface of inclined rocks. *Nuno-ochi* (linen-falling), when it falls in a thin sheet; *Kata-ochi* (uneven-falling), in which the water falls more from one side than the other. The Japanese delight in placing these falls, when possible, where sunshine and moonlight enhance their beauty.

STONES are too great a subject to be dealt with here. They are chosen for their size, shape, color, texture; according to their forms, they are divided into five varieties, "statue," "low-vertical," "flat," "recumbent," and "arching stones." A distinction of sex is applied to rocks and stones, which aids in obtaining a fitting contrast in grouping them. In a large garden there are as many as one hundred and thirty-odd stones, each with its special name, and its own function to perform, in addition to a large number of others of secondary importance. In a small garden five rocks are sufficient, including always the "guardian stone," "stone of worship," "stone of two deities." These stones are illustrated.

LANTERNS. One of the most striking features of a Japanese garden is the lanterns. They stand in the garden symbolizing light dispelling darkness. In placing, this should be kept in mind, and the lantern not considered only ornamental. Lanterns are made of almost every kind of material, but those of stone are most popular. A lantern should not stand alone in full exposure. There should be set, close to it, a stone to step upon when putting in the light, and it should be guarded by a tree with a branch extending to the front partly to conceal it. The many different styles of lanterns are determined by shape, carved decoration, and proportions. The two styles most used are the standard and the snow-scene or legged. From its original use, to light the way of the Cha-no-yu teachers or as memorials in temple enclosures, it has become a favorite garden ornament, although seldom lighted.

BRIDGES should not be crossed hastily, for, lingering on the bridge, a different view may be had than from the shore. There are many styles of bridges. The three most common

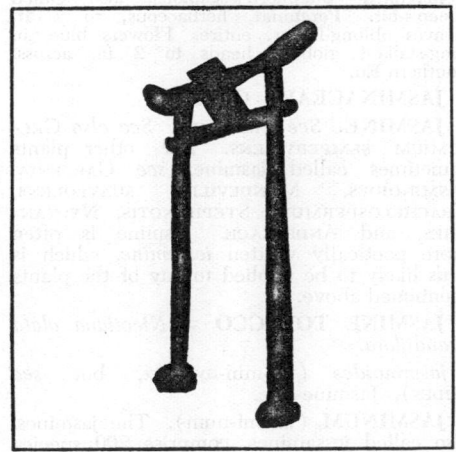

A torii. *See* text.

* Special articles on the subjects indicated by an asterisk (*) will be found at the words so marked.

varieties are: *Ishi-bashi* (stone bridge) — *Ki-bashi* (wooden bridge) — *Do-bashi* (earthen bridge).

TREES. There is a scarcity of flowers and an abundance of evergreens in a Japanese garden. The pine is the favorite of the evergreens. Character pines are trained into shapes that point toward high spots of beauty, guiding the eye to loveliness which otherwise might be overlooked. Of the deciduous trees used, those with beautifully formed trunks and branches take highest rank. *Momiji,* or maple, with the changing color of foliage, is highly esteemed. A maple extends a branch in front of a cascade, catching the spray and breaking the monotony of the fall. Fruit trees bring the refreshment of spring to the garden, but do not possess the permanent value of evergreens. To allow enjoyment of the music of rain, trees, such as palm or *Cycas revoluta,* are placed near the house.

TORII. At the front of many Japanese temples there often stand one or more archways, formed of two uprights and two horizontal beams, often beautifully colored or carved. As the name torii signifies, it was originally a perch for the birds offered to the gods, and was erected at any side of a temple, very rarely in the water.

With the introduction of Buddhism the original significance of the torii was forgotten, and they then came to be placed in front of temples and used as a gateway. Today, these interesting structures, which may be of stone, bronze or wood and sometimes painted red, are often a feature of larger Japanese gardens. — M. A.

japonica, -us, -um (ja-pon'i-ka). From Japan. *Japonica* is also a very common name for the camellia (which see), and is occasionally used for the dwarf Japanese quince. *See* CHAENOMELES JAPONICA.

JARDINIERE. A thoroughly misleading term, for it is from the French for a gardener, while most jardinieres work mischief to potted plants. It is no accident that experience has proved the benefit of clay flower pots, for plants need air and drainage at their roots. Jardinieres, as used by most people, defeat that aim. However beautiful and costly, they are all alike in being of some watertight and airtight material. Into such a receptacle a pot is slipped, its shoulder often sealing the air at the top. And the bottom stands on the bottom of the jardiniere, often with fatal results. For excess water slowly rises from careless watering and soon the flower pot is standing in a puddle of foul water. With no fresh air from the top and with its feet in stagnant water, the plant soon responds by dying.

The remedy is to stand the pot upon an inverted saucer or piece of wood, so that the bottom of the pot will be at least an inch above the bottom of the jardiniere. Also see that the flower pot is small enough to allow at least a ¾ in. space between its rim and

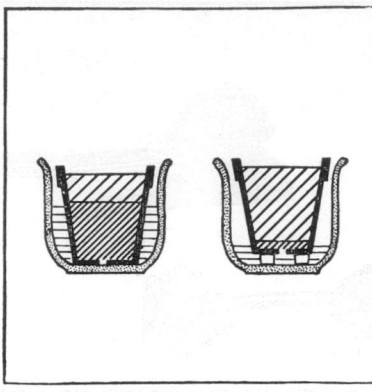

At the left, a water-soaked jardiniere; at the right, one properly arranged to prevent this. *See* text.

the edge of the container. With these precautions, only your taste and purse need limit the use of jardinieres. *See* HOUSE PLANTS.

JASIONE (jas-ee-ō'nee). European annual and perennial herbs of the Campanulaceae comprising 12 species, useful for the rock garden and flower border. They have alternate,* simple leaves, and small white or blue flowers, borne in heads. Corolla cut into 5 very narrow segments, the heads thus resembling a composite, but *Jasione* is easily distinguished from the Compositae by having capsules for fruit. (*Jasione* is of no known application to these plants.)

Of easy culture in most garden soils if grown in full sun or in partial shade. Propagated by division and seeds.

humilis. A dwarf perennial, 6 to 9 in. high. Leaves linear. Flowers blue, on short stalks. July–Aug. Pyrenees.

perennis. Shepherd's-scabious, also called sheep's-bit. Perennial, herbaceous, to 1 ft. Leaves oblong-linear, entire. Flowers blue, in long-stalked globose heads to 2 in. across. Southern Eu.

JASMINACEAE = Oleaceae.

JASMINE. *See* JASMINUM. *See also* GELSEMIUM SEMPERVIRENS. For other plants sometimes called jasmine, *see* GARDENIA, JASMINOIDES, MANDEVILLA SUAVEOLENS, TRACHELOSPERMUM, STEPHANOTIS, NYCTANTHES, and ANDROSACE. Jasmine is often more poetically written *jessamine,* which is thus likely to be applied to any of the plants mentioned above.

JASMINE TOBACCO = *Nicotiana alata grandiflora.*

jasminoides (jas-min-oy'deez, but *see* OÏDES). Jasmine-like.

JASMINUM (jas'mi-num). The jasmines, also called jessamines, comprise 200 species of shrubs or vines of the olive family, chiefly tropical and sub-tropical, found in Eurasia

---

* Special articles on the subjects indicated by an asterisk (*) will be found at the words so marked.

and Af., one in the New World. They are climbing or spreading shrubs with compound* opposite or alternate leaves (sometimes with only 1 leaflet), and often green, angled stems. Flowers generally about 1 in. across, in many-flowered clusters, yellow or white in ours. Calyx* bell-shaped. Corolla tubular, but with 4–9 spreading lobes. Fruit a small berry. (*Jasminum* is from the Persian name for jasmine.)

Widely cultivated and esteemed for their attractive, fragrant flowers. They make fine conservatory plants and in mild climates may be grown outdoors. Some species, mainly *J. nudiflorum, floridum,* and *officinale,* are useful for training on walls. See VINES. They are of easy culture, preferring a sunny position and loamy soil. Propagated by layers* and cuttings* of nearly ripe wood.

beesianum. A low shrub, scarcely over 3 ft. high, rarely climbing to 6 ft., with solitary leaflets, and remarkable for its naturally pink or rose-colored flowers. These are about 1 in. long and borne in a sparse cluster. China. May. Hardy from zone* 6 southward.

dichotomum. A tropical evergreen vine with thick glossy leaflets that are 2–3 in. long. Flowers night-fragrant, white, about 1 in. long. Tropical Af. Blooming most of the year. Suited only to zone* 9 or a warm greenhouse.

floridum. Half-evergreen shrub with angled, smooth branches, upright and arching. Leaves alternate,* with 3–5 oval leaflets, ½–1½ in. long. Flowers golden-yellow in large terminal clusters. Calyx* lobes about ¼ length of corolla tube. Fruit a small black berry. China. July. Hardy from zone* 5 southward.

gracillimum. Graceful, sometimes climbing shrub from northern Borneo. Branches many from near the base, arching, hairy. Leaves opposite, about 1½ in. long, oval to heart-shaped, bright green above, hairy beneath. Flowers in large dense heads, white, fragrant, the corolla with about 9 lobes. Blooms in winter. Hardy from zone* 6 southward.

grandiflorum. Spanish jasmine. Catalonian jasmine. A species from India resembling *J. officinale* and often considered a var. of it. More erect than most of the species though with arching, angled branches and growing about 4 ft. high. Leaves opposite* with 5 to 7 elliptic or oval leaflets. Flowers white, tinged crimson on the outside, freely borne and very fragrant. An excellent greenhouse plant and widely cultivated as an ornamental and for perfumery.

humile. Italian jasmine. An evergreen or half-evergreen shrub with angled branches and of loose, spreading habit. Leaves alternate, composed of 3 to 7 rather thick oblong leaflets that are dark green above, paler beneath, and whose edges are slightly rolled under. Flowers bright golden-yellow, fragrant, summer or fall. Commonly cultivated in greenhouses and hardy outdoors where it is sometimes trained on walls as a vine. Hardy from zone* 5 southward. Much variation occurs in this species and the different forms are sometimes listed as *J. reevesi, J. revolutum, J. triumphans,* and *J. wallichianum.* Tropical As.

mesnyi. Primrose jasmine. An evergreen shrub of rambling habit growing 6–10 ft. high. Branches green, four-angled; the leaves are opposite and composed of 3 rather thick and shiny leaflets, 1–2 in. long. Flowers are borne along branches of the previous season, yellow

with darker eye, often double. Blooms in spring with the leaves. China. Hardy from zone* 5 southward. This species is closely related to *J. nudiflorum* and may be only a form of it.

nudiflorum. Winter jasmine. Upright shrub with stiff, arching four-angled branches. Leaves opposite, dark green with 3 oval leaflets about 1 in. long, falling in autumn. Flowers yellow, ¾–1 in. across, solitary along branches of previous season, appearing in winter or spring before the leaves. China. Hardy from zone* 4 southward. In mild places blooms nearly all winter, but in North flower buds often frozen.

officinale. Common white jasmine. Usually deciduous shrub with long spreading branches that require support and sometimes reach 40 ft. Leaves opposite, leaflets 5–7, glossy, ½–2½ in. long, terminal one larger and stalked. Flowers white, very fragrant. Summer. Kashmir, Persia, China. Hardy from zone* 5 southward. Very attractive shrub cultivated for centuries.

parkeri. A low, evergreen, rock garden shrub, rarely over 12 in. high, with 3–5 ovalish leaflets that are about ¼ in. long. Flowers solitary, about ½ in. wide, yellow. Himalayas. June. Hardy from zone* 5 southward, and with protection considerably farther north, including one report of its hardiness at Boston.

primulinum = *J. mesnyi.*

pubescens. A climbing, hairy shrub with opposite somewhat heart-shaped leaves that are dark green and about 2 in. long. Flowers white with broad lobes, occasionally double, fragrant, about 1 in. across in many-flowered clusters; calyx lobes with spreading yellow hairs. India. August. Good conservatory plant.

reevesi = *J. humile.*

revolutum = *J. humile.*

Sambac. Arabian jasmine. Zambac. Climbing shrub with angled, hairy branches. Leaves opposite or in threes at the ends of the flowering branches, shiny, often ovate, rounded or pointed at the tip. Flowers white, turning purple with age, borne in 3–12 flowered clusters, very fragrant and widely cultivated in the East on this account; used in making jasmine tea. There is a group with very double flowers sometimes known as *J. trifoliata.* India. Hardy only where there is no frost.

stephanense. A hybrid jasmine (*J. grandiflorum* × *beesianum*), with the habit and fragrance of the first parent and the pink flowers of *J. beesianum.* Yunnan. May. Hardy from zone* 6 southward.

triumphans = *J. humile.*

wallichianum = *J. humile.*

JATROPHA (jat'row-fa). A large genus of mostly tropical herbs, shrubs, or trees of the spurge family, having a milky, usually poisonous, juice. Of the 160 known species only the one below is of hort. interest, and of secondary importance. They have alternate* leaves, usually long-stalked, and often somewhat lobed or divided finger-fashion. Male and female flowers separate, but on the same plant, with petals in *J. Curcas* and *J. multifida,* without them in others. Sepals 5, more or less joined at the base. Stamens* usually 10, in two series. Fruit a capsule.* (*Jatropha* is from the Greek for physician and food, in allusion to the medicinal value of some species.)

The only cult. species are tropical trees of

---

* Special articles on the subjects indicated by an asterisk (*) will be found at the words so marked.

easy culture, but only in zone° 9 or the most favored parts of zone° 8, and may be propagated by seeds or cuttings.

Curcas. Physic-nut; also called purging-nut and Barbados nut. A tree not usually over 20 ft., more often lower and shrubby. Leaves long-stalked, 3–5 in. wide, lobed and ivy-like. Flowers small, yellow or yellowish-green, and borne in branched clusters (cymes°). Petals present. Fruit olive-shaped, 1–1½ in. long, its 2 black seeds yielding a purgative oil dangerously poisonous in quantity. For these seeds the plant is cult. in the tropics, although in the U.S. the plant is mostly an ornamental, or used for informal hedges. Tropical America. **multifida.** Coral plant. A tree, with much larger leaves and scarlet flowers, which are very showy; much grown in Florida. S.A.

JAVA FIG or WILLOW = *Ficus benjamina.*

javanica, -us, -um (ja-van′i-ka). From Java.

JEFFERSONIA (jef-fer-so′ni-a). Herbaceous perennial herbs, belonging to the Berberidaceae, native in eastern N.A. and As., one of the two known species used as an ornamental plant in the wild garden. The usually cult. species is **J. diphylla**, the twin-leaf or rheumatism root. It is a woodland herb, 10 to 12 in. high, the leaves 2-parted into kidney-shaped, or lobed divisions. Flowers white, about 1 in. wide, with 4 sepals and 8 oblong, flat petals. Fruit a pear-shaped pod. (Named for Thomas Jefferson.) A close, blue-flowered relative, from China, **J. dubia**, is known among rock garden enthusiasts.

JEFFREY PINE = *Pinus jeffreyi.* See PINE.

JEQUIRITY BEAN = *Abrus precatorius.*

JERSEY ELM = *Ulmus carpinifolia wheatleyi.* See ELM.

JERUSALEM ARTICHOKE = *Helianthus tuberosus.* See SUNFLOWER. It is neither an artichoke nor does it come from Jerusalem, being one of the few plants really cultivated by the North American Indians.

JERUSALEM CHERRY = *Solanum Pseudocapsicum.*

JERUSALEM CORN. A form of durra. See SORGHUM VULGARE DURRA.

JERUSALEM CROSS = *Lychnis chalcedonica.*

JERUSALEM DATE = *Bauhinia monandra.*

JERUSALEM OAK = *Chenopodium Botrys.*

JERUSALEM SAGE. See PHLOMIS.

JERUSALEM THORN = *Parkinsonia aculeata;* also *Paliurus Spina-Christi.*

JESSAMINE. See JASMINUM. For other plants so called *see* JASMINE, the spelling here preferred.

JESUIT'S-NUT = *Trapa natans.*

JETBEAD = *Rhodotypos scandens.*

JEW BUSH = *Pedilanthus tithymaloides.*

JEWELWEED. See IMPATIENS.

JEWELWEED FAMILY = Balsaminaceae.

JEW'S-APPLE. See EGGPLANT.

JEW'S-HARP = *Trillium cernuum.*

JEW'S MALLOW = *Corchorus olitorius.*

JEW'S MYRTLE = *Ruscus aculeatus.*

jezoensis, -e (ye-zo-en′sis). From Hokkaido (formerly Yezo), Japan.

JIMSONWEED = *Datura Stramonium.*

JIOTILLA = *Escontria Chiotilla.*

JIPI-JAPA = *Carludovica palmata.*

JOB'S-TEARS = *Coix Lacryma-Jobi.*

JOCONOSTLE = *Lemaireocereus stellatus.*

JOE-PYE-WEED = *Eupatorium purpureum.*

JOHNNY APPLESEED. A hort. visionary (John Chapman, 1775–1843) who scattered fruit tree seeds in the Ohio Valley, innocent of the fact that few of them could come true from seed. See Care of Apple Trees at APPLE.

JOHNNY-JUMP-UP. See VIOLA TRICOLOR HORTENSIS.

JOHNNY SMOKERS = *Geum triflorum.*

JOHNSON GRASS = *Sorghum halepense.*

JOINT. See NODE.

JOINT-FIR; JOINT-FIR FAMILY. See EPHEDRA.

JONQUIL = *Narcissus Jonquilla.* See also N. JUNCIFOLIUS and N. ODORUS.

JOSEPHINE'S-LILY = *Brunsvigia josephinae.*

JOSEPH'S-COAT = *Amaranthus tricolor.*

JOSHUA TREE = *Yucca brevifolia.*

JOSS FLOWER = *Narcissus Tazetta orientalis.*

JUBAEA (jew-bee′a). A single (or perhaps 2) species of Chilean, very stout-trunked, unarmed, feather palms, found farther south than almost any palm from the New World and hence able to stand a little frost. The only cult. species is **J. spectabilis**, the coquito or wine palm, often called the monkey-coconut. In Chile it grows up to 90 ft. high, much less as cult. in Calif. and in greenhouses, where it is often grown as a tub or pot plant. Trunk usually clothed with, or bearing the scars of, the expanded leaf bases. Leaves 6–12 ft. long, their segments many, about 2 ft. long and 1 in. wide, split at the tip. Flower cluster (rarely produced in cult. specimens) from the lower leaves, drooping and long. Male flowers with 15–30 stamens, and usually at the upper end of the cluster. Female flowers lower, the fruit roundish or egg-shaped, yellow, about 1½ in. long, its single seed yielding a sort of sugar or honey. Its culture in Calif. has been successful in the lower part of the state and in Fla. it is described as "thrifty." For greenhouse cult. see PALM. Sometimes known as *J. chilensis.* (Named for King Juba of Numidia.)

° Special articles on the subjects indicated by an asterisk (°) will be found at the words so marked.

jubata, -us, -um (jew-bay′ta). Crested*; or with a mane-like crest.

jucunda, -us, -um (jew-kun′da). Pleasing or agreeable.

JUDAS-TREE. *See* Redbud.

JUGLANDACEAE (jug-lan-day′see-ee). The walnut or hickory family, ours all trees, comprise only 6 genera and about 55 species, all confined to the temperate or warm regions of the northern hemisphere. There are only three cult. genera, one of them, *Juglans* (*see* Walnut), of outstanding importance. The others are *Carya* (*see* Hickory) and *Pterocarya*, grown only for ornament.

Leaves alternate,* compound,* the leaflets arranged feather-fashion with an odd one at the tip. The male flowers are in drooping catkins, the female solitary or in clusters (racemes*). Both appear with or just after the unfolding of the leaves. The fruit in the walnut and hickory is fleshy (a drupe*), what is ordinarily called a nut being the seed of this fruit. In *Pterocarya* the fruit is a true nut and is winged. All genera are wind-pollinated.

Technical flower characters: Flowers monoecious.* Male flowers with several stamens, no petals and sometimes with no sepals. Female flowers with a 3–5-lobed calyx. Ovary inferior,* mostly 1-celled.

JUGLANS. *See* Walnut.

Jujuba (jew-jew′ba). A Latinized version of the ancient vernacular for the jujube (*Zizyphus*).

JUJUBE. *See* Zizyphus.

Julibrissin. Persian vernacular for the silk tree (*Albizzia Julibrissin*).

juliflora, -us, -um (jew-li-flō′ra). With downy flowers.

JUMPING BEAN. The seeds of species of the non-hort. genus *Sebastiania*, family Euphorbiaceae, of tropical America. The movement or "jumping" of the seeds is due to the erratic movements of the contained larvae of a moth, which cause the seeds to "jump," especially if put in a warm place.

JUNCACEAE (jun-kay′see-ee). The rush family comprises grass-like herbs of which few are of any garden interest. The only cult. genus is *Juncus* (which see), and this is of minor hort. significance.

juncea, -us, -um (jun′see-a). Rush-like.

JUNCUS (jun′kus). A very large genus, and the only cult. one, of the family **Juncaceae** (jun-kay′see-ee), known generally as rushes, and of little garden interest. They have grass-like, round or 3-sided leaves, often jointed, and compact clusters of small greenish or brownish flowers in spikelets. The only cult. species, of over 300 known, is **J. effusus**, the common, soft or bog rush. It is a tufted perennial, 2–4 ft. high, more or less pliant, its grass-like stems with a small cluster of brownish-green flowers near the tip, and apparently attached laterally. In marshy ground, throughout the north temperate zone, and suited only to similar sites. The fibrous stems are used to make mats. (*Juncus* is the classical name for the rushes.)

JUNE-BERRY. *See* Amelanchier.

JUNE GRASS = *Poa pratensis.*

JUNGLE GERANIUM = *Ixora coccinea.*

JUNIPER. *See* Juniperus.

JUNIPER-BERRY = *Gaylussacia brachycera. See* Huckleberry.

juniperina, -us, -um (jew-nip-er-ry′na). Resembling a juniper.

JUNIPERUS (jew-nip′er-us). Juniper. The junipers form a genus of 55 species of evergreen trees and shrubs of the pine family. They vary in habit from low, prostrate shrubs to tall, slender trees, and are widely cultivated. The leaves are of two types: needle-shaped, and usually borne in 3's, and small, scale-like leaves that are opposite and pressed close to the twigs. On young plants and vigorous branches the needle-shaped leaves predominate, while the scaly leaves are characteristic of the adult plant. On older plants, however, both types are often found together and many species, especially in the *communis* group, retain the needle-like leaves permanently. The flowers

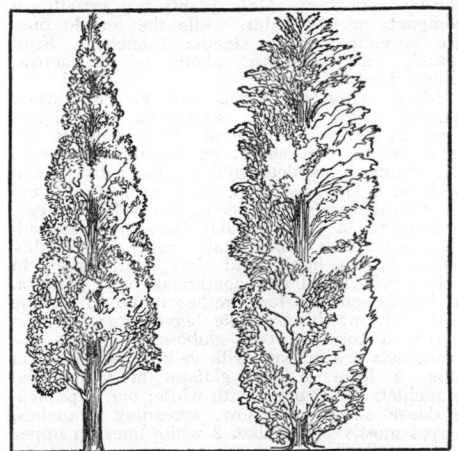

Common red cedar at the left (*Juniperus virginiana*), and at the right the columnar form of the Irish juniper (*J. communis hibernica*).

are insignificant; male flowers are borne in small, oval clusters (catkins*); the female flowers are composed of little scales on which the ovules are borne; these scales later become fleshy, grow together and form a berry-like fruit that takes 1–3 years to ripen, depending on the species. (*Juniperus* is the old Latin name for these plants.) By some considered as belonging to the family Cupressaceae.

The junipers have a wide distribution in

---

* Special articles on the subjects indicated by an asterisk (*) will be found at the words so marked.

the northern hemisphere from the arctic regions to the sub-tropics. Their diverse habits make them valuable ornamental plants; the tall, columnar types are conspicuous planted singly or in groups, while the low, spreading types are excellent for plantings around buildings. An aromatic oil is obtained from the berries and branchlets of certain species; the wood is durable and usually fragrant. Although a moderately moist, loamy soil is preferred, some species, as *J. communis,* will thrive in dry, rocky places. Propagation is by cuttings, seeds, layering and sometimes grafting. For cult. *see* EVERGREENS.

barbadensis. An irregular and rather widely branched tree growing about 70 ft. high, pyramidal when young, becoming round-topped and broader than high with age. The needle-like leaves are sharply pointed, nearly flat and whitish above, green beneath; the scaly leaves are blunt, overlapping and closely appressed. The thin gray bark peels off in long strips. Fruit dark blue, bloomy, about ¼ in. across, broader than high. Bermuda, Barbados, Antigua. The most abundant and characteristic tree of Bermuda. Perhaps hardy in zones* 8 or 9. Also called *J. bermudiana.*

chinensis. Chinese juniper. A quite variable species ranging in habit from low, almost prostrate, shrubs to trees 60 ft. high. The linear leaves are spreading, sharply pointed, have two white lines above and are usually whorled; the scale-like leaves are obtuse and closely appressed. Male plants are usually of compact, upright habit, while the female ones are spreading, with slender branches. Fruit round, purplish-brown, about ⅓ in. across. China, Mongolia, Jap.

Many attractive forms are in cultivation; among them are *var.* **variegata,** a compact form in which the tips of the branchlets are often white; *var.* **aurea,** an upright form with the young branchlets golden-yellow; *var.* **pyramidalis,** a narrow, pyramidal shrub with upright branches and glaucous, linear leaves; *var.* **pfitzeriana,** a very popular form with spreading, sometimes horizontal branches, roughly pyramidal in habit, and dark, dull green in color: will stand city conditions; *var.* **globosa,** a dwarf, compact form rather round in outline and with mostly scale-like leaves; *var.* **globosa aurea,** a form of *var. globosa* in which the branchlets are marked with yellow; *var.* **globosa alba,** a form of *var. globosa* in which the branchlets are marked with white; *var.* **japonica,** a dense shrub with low, spreading branches, leaves mostly needle-like, 2 white lines on upper surface, whorled.*

communis. Common juniper. An upright tree or shrub usually growing about 6–12 ft. high, though occasionally it attains 40 ft. The leaves are all needle-like, with a broad white band above, sharply pointed, spreading and in whorls. The fruit is about ¼ in. in diameter, bluish-black, bloomy, used to flavor gin. N.A. south to Pa., Ill., and in the mountains of N. Mex. and northern Cal. Also in Eurasia. Hardy from zone* 1 southward.

This species is quite variable and has many good varieties. *Var.* **depressa,** the prostrate juniper, is a wide-spreading, low-growing form that rarely exceeds 3 or 4 ft. in height; it does well in dry, rocky soil; *var.* **depressa aurea** is a form of *var. depressa* in which the young growth is often yellow; *var.* **hibernica,** Irish juniper, a narrow, columnar form with upright,

erect-tipped branches and rather short, dark green leaves, a good accent plant, often needs support; *var.* **oblonga-pendula,** a graceful, columnar shrub with narrow leaves and upright branches whose tips are pendulous; *var.* **suecica,** Swedish juniper: a columnar form with bluish-green leaves, the ends of the twigs drooping.

conferta. A prostrate shrub with sharply pointed leaves, usually in threes, having a narrow white band and groove on the upper surface. Fruit black and bloomy, about ⅓ in. across. Japan, Saghalin. Hardy from zone* 5 southward. Suited to sandy soils.

excelsa. Greek juniper. A slender-branched tree of pyramidal habit growing about 60 ft. high. Leaves bluish-green, usually scale-like, pointed at tip, opposite; the needle-like leaves are opposite and have two white bands on the upper surface. Fruit bloomy, purplish-brown. Southwest Eu., Asia Minor, Caucasus. Hardy from zone* 5 southward. *Var.* **stricta.** A narrow, upright form with glaucous, short, needle-like leaves; useful in the rock garden and as an accent plant. The plant sold in the U.S. under the name is not certainly the Greek juniper.

horizontalis. Creeping juniper. A prostrate shrub with long, spreading branches. The leaves are glandular and of two types, needle-like and slightly spreading and on mature branches scaly and overlapping, bluish-green or gray-blue. Fruit on a short stem, blue, sometimes bloomy, about ⅓ in. across. Nova Scotia to British Columbia, south to N.J., Minn. and Montana. Hardy from zone* 1 southward. Grows well in sandy, rocky soil; *var.* **douglasi,** Waukegan juniper, a trailing form with blue-gray leaves that turn grayish-purple in the fall; *var.* **glomerata,** very low, dwarf form with short, compact branches and small, scale-like leaves; *var.* **plumosa,** Andorra juniper, a low, depressed form with flattened top and horizontal branching.

japonica = *Juniperus chinensis japonica.*

occidentalis. Yellow cedar. Western juniper. A round-headed tree to 40 ft., occasionally 60 ft. high, sometimes a shrub. Leaves predominantly scale-like, in 3's, overlapping and pressed close to the stem, with a conspicuous gland on the back; needle-like leaves are about ⅛ in. long, sharply pointed and ridged on the back. Fruit rather oval, blue-black, bloomy, about ⅓ in. long. Wash. to southern Calif. Hardy from zone* 4 southward.

procumbens. A low, prostrate juniper, often planted as a ground cover (in Iowa), the branches ascending, up to 20–30 in. high, the twigs bluish-green. Needles (leaves) in 3's, spiny-tipped, about ½ in. long, greenish-blue above, but with a green midrib, paler beneath, and with 2 white spots near the base. Fruit globose, about ¾ in. in diameter. Jap. Hardy from zone* 2 southward. Considered by some as a var. of *J. horizontalis.*

Sabina. Savin. Shrub with ascending or spreading branches, usually about 4–5 ft. high, though sometimes attaining 10–15 ft. Leaves dark green and of two types: needle-like in pairs, concave and glaucous* above; on mature branches scale-like, rather thick and with a gland on the back. Fruit globular, about ¼ in. long, brown covered with bluish bloom. Mountains of central and southern Eu., western As. to Siberia. Hardy from zone* 3 southward. One of the handsomest dwarf evergreens, it stands city conditions and likes limey soil. The whole plant has a strong, slightly disagreeable odor; *var.* **cupressifolia,** a low, almost prostrate form, usually with overlapping, scale-like leaves;

---

* Special articles on the subjects indicated by an asterisk (*) will be found at the words so marked.

var. tamariscifolia, a low form in which the leaves are mostly needle-like and borne in 3's.

scopulorum. Western red cedar, also known as Rocky Mountain red cedar and Colo. red cedar. A round-topped tree, usually low, but sometimes growing 35–40 ft. high. Trunk short, often dividing near the ground; bark red-brown, shredding. Leaves of two types, mainly scale-like and opposite, pointed and closely pressed to stem. Male flowers with 6 stamens. Fruit blue, bloomy, about ⅓ in. across, ripening second year. British Columbia and Alberta south to Tex. and northern Ariz. in the mountains. Hardy from zone* 3 southward. The western representative of *J. virginiana*, from which it differs mainly in habit, bark and nature of fruit; stands dry and difficult situations; *var.* **argentea,** form with glaucous,* silvery leaves and of narrow, upright habit; *var.* **viridifolia,** habit upright, leaves bright green.

One of the best of all the prostrate junipers, *Juniperus chinensis pfitzeriana*

squamata. A low shrub with reclining, spreading branches that turn up at the ends. Leaves predominantly needle-like and in 3's, slender, pointed, slightly spreading, whitish above and grooved below. Fruit purple-black when mature, 1-seeded, oval, about ⅓ in. long, ripens second year. Himalayas and China. Hardy from zone* 3 southward. An attractive shrub with bluish leaves and compact habit; *var.* **meyeri,** a form with upright branches and very attractive, glaucous* leaves; becomes leggy with age; suited to the rock garden.

virginiana. Red cedar. Tree, columnar or pyramidal when young, becoming broader and spreading with age, usually grows about 40–50 ft. high, though occasionally to 100 ft.; bark red-brown, peeling off in long strips. Leaves of two types: needle-like, glaucous* above, pointed, opposite or in 3's on young plants and branches, on mature branches and plants small and scale-like, pointed, overlapping. Male flowers with usually 12 stamens. Fruit oval, about ⅓ in. long, dark blue, slightly bloomy. A common tree in dry, rocky fields from Canada to Fla., east of the Rockies. Hardy from zone* 1 southward. The wood is fragrant. A variable species with many varieties: *var.* **canaerti,** a form with dark

green foliage and compact, pyramidal habit; *var.* **elegantissima,** in which the tips of the branches are golden-yellow; *var.* **glauca,** a form with silvery-gray foliage; *var.* **keteleeri,** a compact, upright form with dark green, scale-like leaves; *var.* **kosteri,** a low plant with spreading branches; *var.* **schoti,** a narrow, upright tree; *var.* **tripartita,** a low, rather dense shrub with spreading branches and mostly needle-like leaves *var.* **venusta,** an upright form with shiny, dark leaves.

INSECT PESTS. Scale is most common pest (*see* SCALE INSECTS and True Bugs at INSECT PESTS). A webworm is controlled by pesticide #19 or #1. (*See* SPRAYS AND DUSTS.)

DISEASES. Twigs may blight* or, in the case of small plants, the entire seedling may die as a result of a fungus disease. Small black spots are produced on the dead needles. Spray with pesticide #3 (*see* SPRAYS AND DUSTS) as soon as new growth starts in the spring and repeat 4 or 5 times at about 10-day intervals.

A rust* may produce galls* on twigs, particularly if growing close to apples, hawthorn, or quince. The disease may be unsightly on the juniper during early spring, but it is not too detrimental to this host. A single application with pesticide #4 while the juniper is still dormant in the spring will prevent formation of the orange horns of spores which cause the disease to spread to alternate hosts.

JUPITER'S-BEARD = *Centranthus ruber.*

JUSSIAEA (juss-si-ee′a). The cult. species of this chiefly tropical genus of the family Onagraceae are erect or creeping water plants or marsh herbs generally called primrose willow. Of the 50 known species only the two below are likely to be found in cult. They have alternate,* willow-like, toothed leaves and usually solitary, yellow flowers (in ours), found in the leaf axils.* Petals 4–6, separate and spreading. Stamens* 8–12, in two rows. Fruit a round or 4-angled, many-seeded capsule.* (Named for Bernard de Jussieu, French systematic botanist and originator of a natural system of plant classification.)

The primrose willows will not stand frost, and are grown as summer-blooming, tender annuals. But their seeds must be sown in pans or shallow boxes, which must be kept an inch or so below water. Cover the seeds with a little sand to keep them from floating to the surface. After germination they should be potted up in small pots, which need not be submerged, but must be kept wet or at least very moist. They may be grown in the greenhouse or outdoors (in summer), but constant attention to their water needs is easier in the greenhouse.

longifolia. An erect, smooth herb with a 3-angled stem, not over 2 ft. high. Leaves lance-linear, 3–4 in. long, more or less glandular along the margins on the lower side. Flowers yellow, the petals faintly notched at the tip. Brazil.

repens. A prostrate herb, the creeping stems rooting at the joints. Leaves ovalish or spatula-shaped, 2–3 in. long. Flowers yellow, about ½ in. long. Tropics.

JUSTICIA (jus-tiss′i-a). A genus of rather showy-flowered herbs or under-shrubs of the family Acanthaceae, grown in the greenhouse for ornament. From the closely related *Jacobinia* they are separated only by technical characters. Their similarity to other genera has led to much confusion in the names of these plants (as shown below). They have opposite* leaves, without marginal teeth, and a showy, bracted,* terminal cluster of irregular,* 2-lipped* flowers. Stamens 2. Fruit a capsule. Of many species only *J. secunda* appears to be cult. (Named for James Justice, Scotch gardener.)

For culture *see* JACOBINIA.

carnea = *Jacobinia carnea*.
magnifica = *Jacobinia carnea*.
secunda. A shrubby plant 4–6 ft. high. Leaves ovalish or oblong, 4–6 in. long, tapering to a long point. Flowers red, showy, about 1½ in. long, deeply 2-lipped,* grouped in narrow, branched clusters (panicles*). Northern S.A.

JUTE = *Corchorus capsularis*.

JUVENILE FORMS. The young leaves of many plants are very different from those developed at maturity. The common English ivy, for instance, is known to most people only in the juvenile state. Later, when ready to flower or fruit, it produces larger, unangled leaves. The same is true of many other commonly cult. species, notably the climbing fig (*Ficus pumila*), some of the greenhouse plants in the family Araliaceae, and in *Berberis, Eucalyptus,* and *Acacia*.

But juvenile foliage forms are most common in the evergreens, especially the juni-

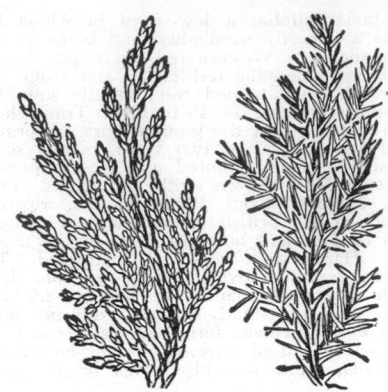

Mature (*left*) and juvenile (*right*) forms of juniper foliage

pers, in *Chamaecyparis, Thuja,* and *Cupressus*. Often these foliage differences are so great as to lead to confusion in the identity of the plant. Some juvenile forms are more desirable horticulturally than the mature state, and where this is true, they are propagated by cuttings, layering, or other non-sexual methods. This results in millions of plants being produced, not one of which ever produces mature leaves, as in the usual forms of the English ivy (*see* HEDERA HELIX).

K

KADSURA (kad-soor'a). A small genus of woody climbers, mostly from tropical Asia, belonging to the magnolia family. Only one species is hardy; this is a handsome climber, evergreen in the South but losing its leaves in northern winters. The flowers are inconspicuous, but when the heads of the scarlet fruits are produced in the fall the plant is an arresting sight. It seems to prefer a sunny position and fairly good, loamy soil. Propagation is by cuttings. (*Kadsura* is the Japanese name for these plants.)

japonica. Climbs 10 ft. or more. Leaves alternate, thick, toothed, 2–4 in. long. Flowers yellow-white, with 9–15 sepals, and petals ½–¾ in. across, dioecious,* usually borne singly in the leaf axils during summer. Fruit clustered, scarlet. Japan, Korea. Hardy from zone* 5 (possibly 4) southward.

KAEMPFER'S AZALEA = *Azalea obtusa kaempferi*.

KAFIR = *Sorghum vulgare caffrorum*.

KAFIR-BEAN TREE = *Schotia latifolia*.

KAFIR LILY = *Schizostylis coccinea*. See also CLIVIA.

KAIDO CRABAPPLE = *Malus micromalus*.

KAINIT. *See* Potash at FERTILIZERS.

Kaki (kah'kee). Japanese vernacular for the persimmon.

KALANCHOE (kal-an-ko'ee). A large genus of succulent, sometimes woody herbs of the family Crassulaceae, many from South Africa, the others chiefly Asiatic. Of the 100 known species, *K. laciniata* from South Africa is one of the chief species in cult. It is grown in desert gardens in warm regions, or in the greenhouse. Corolla with a longish tube, swollen at the base, the 4 lobes wide-spreading and sharp-pointed. Fruit a follicle.* For culture *see* SUCCULENTS. For other plants sometimes listed as *Kalanchoe, see* BRYOPHYLLUM. (*Kalanchoe* is thought to be derived from the Chinese name of one species.) Other, but less well-known species, include the following, the cult. of which is the same as for *K. laciniata*.

blossfeldiana. A many-stemmed succulent, 8–12 in. high, its leaves 1–3 in. long, ovalish, toothed toward the tip, and red-edged. Flowers numerous, small, in branched clusters, scarlet.

---

* Special articles on the subjects indicated by an asterisk (*) will be found at the words so marked.

Madagascar. Often known as *K. globulifera coccinea* and considered by some as of the genus *Bryophyllum.*

daigremontiana = *Bryophyllum daigremontianum.*

fedtschenkoi. A smooth perennial, not over 12 in. high, the nearly round, fleshy leaves, short-stalked, and with rounded marginal teeth. Flowers purple, nodding, in terminal clusters (corymbs*). Madagascar.

globulifera coccinea = *K. blossfeldiana.*

laciniata. An erect succulent, 12–24 in. high, with ovalish, wavy-margined leaves, 3–4 in. long. Flowers fragrant, pink, about ½ in. wide, in a terminal, branched cluster (cyme*). S. Af.

lanceolata. *See* K. TOMENTOSA.

marmorata. A branching succulent with stout stems, the blotched leaves ovalish, sharply toothed, about 4 in. wide. Flowers white, 3 in. long. Abyssinia.

pilosa. *See* K. TOMENTOSA.

pinnata = *Bryophyllum pinnatum.*

somaliensis. An erect, branched succulent, its brown-blotched leaves about 6 in. long and 4 in. wide, whitish-green and toothed. Flowers nearly 3 in. long, white. Somaliland.

tomentosa. A hairy-stemmed, erect, branching succulent, 1–3 ft. high, the leaves in a terminal rosette. Leaves about 1½ in. long, half as wide, the marginal teeth brown, the leaf surface white-felty. Flowers not showy, and not always produced. This handsome succulent has been variously offered as *K. lanceolata* and *K. pilosa,* and is widely cult.

tubiflora = *Bryophyllum tubiflorum.*

verticillata = *Bryophyllum tubiflorum.*

KALE (*Brassica oleracea acephala*). As its Latin name indicates, kale is a kind of cabbage that does not produce a head. There are at least three varieties of kale, one of them being collards, a sort that stands more heat than cabbage or ordinary kale, and is consequently grown in the South. Common kale has a profusion of erect, long, finely cut or curled or crisped leaves, the latter being preferred. In the home garden these may be harvested a few at a time, but for market the whole plant is cut. Its culture is the same as for cabbage (which see) and it is primarily a fall and winter vegetable which does not like heat. South of zone* 5, however,

Kale

it can stand out all winter, furnishing a good supply of pot-herbs. Other names for it are borecole and cow cabbage.

A variety of it, known as Scotch kale, differs only in having light green and tightly curled leaves. Its culture is the same as for common kale, but it likes even less summer heat.

Collards is chiefly grown in the South. It, too, is a variety of kale, but is best treated as a biennial. Unlike true kale, it produces a short, trunk-like stem (10–30 in. high) which is crowned by a loose cluster of cabbage-like leaves that do not form a head. It may be grown as a winter annual by planting seeds in Sept. and transplanting the seedlings to the garden. Such plants stand out all winter in

Collards

the South and the harvest of their leaves, a few at a time, begins in the spring. Or the seeds may be sown in the spring and the leaves harvested all the following fall and winter. A var. with frilled leaf-margins, in various colors, is sometimes grown for ornament and for food. *See also* SEA-KALE.

INSECT PESTS. Kale is affected by cabbage, radish, and turnip insects, especially aphids. These should be prevented from getting a start on young kale by following the pest directions at CABBAGE.

KALMIA (kal′mĭ-a). Shrubs, mostly evergreen, from N.A. comprising 8 species and belonging to the heath family. The leaves are entire* and may be opposite,* alternate* or whorled.* Flowers purple, pink or white, usually showy and borne in terminal or lateral clusters, flat or cup-shaped, 5-lobed, with 10 slender stamens that are caught in the corolla and spring up when touched or disturbed, discharging their pollen. Fruit a round, 5-celled capsule.* (Named for Peter Kalm, a Finnish botanist who traveled in North America.) *See* POISONOUS PLANTS.

Kalmia latifolia is an exceptionally handsome plant when in bloom; it is splendid for massing or as a single specimen. The other

---

* Special articles on the subjects indicated by an asterisk (*) will be found at the words so marked.

species are of indifferent ornamental value, useful in wild plantings or mixed with other evergreens.

Kalmias prefer a somewhat shaded position in moist, peaty, decidedly acid soil (*see* ACID AND ALKALI SOILS). They often grow well in comparatively dry and exposed places, but need a permanent mulch* of, preferably, oak or beech leaves. Propagation is by seed but cuttings of young wood in an acid soil, with bottom-heat* usually succeed.

angustifolia. Sheep laurel, sometimes called lambkill and dwarf laurel. Evergreen shrub of thin, open habit usually growing 2–3 ft. high. Leaves opposite or in 3's, oblong, 1–2 in. long, considered injurious to grazing animals. Flowers lavender-rose in lateral clusters. June. Labrador to Ga. and westward. Hardy from zone* 1 southward.

glauca = *Kalmia polifolia.*

latifolia. Mountain laurel, laurel, calicobush. Round-topped shrub usually growing 4–10 ft. high. though occasionally becoming a small tree. Leaves evergreen, oval, alternate or sometimes whorled, 2–4 in. long. Flowers rose to white, about ¾ in. across, in large, terminal clusters. May–June. New England to Fla. and La. Hardy from zone* 3 southward. An excellent shrub for wild or formal plantings; sometimes forced. *See* FORCING.

polifolia. Swamp laurel; pale laurel. Low, thin shrub about 2 ft. high, branchlets 2-edged. Leaves opposite, almost stemless, oval or linear-oval, white beneath, ½–1½ in. long, the edges rolled under. Flowers rose-colored in terminal clusters. May–June. Labrador to Pa. and Minn. and from Alaska to Wash. Hardy from zone* 4 northward. Sometimes known as *K. glauca*, and suited only to the bog garden.

INSECT PESTS. *See* RHODODENDRON.

DISEASES. The mountain laurel often has one of two leafspot* diseases. The small gray spot with purple border and the brown spot are caused by fungi. Use pesticide #5 (*see* SPRAYS AND DUSTS) as new leaves begin to grow and repeat twice at 10-day intervals.

The mountain laurel is subject to chlorosis* which may be controlled by making the soil more acid, or by adding iron chelates (which see).

kalmiaeflora, -us, -um (kal-mǐ-ee-flō'ra). With flowers like the genus *Kalmia* (which see).

KALOPANAX PICTUS. *See* ACANTHOPANAX RICINIFOLIUS.

kamtschatica, -us, -um (kam-chat'i-ka). From Kamchatka, Siberia.

KANGAROO THORN = *Acacia armata.*

KANGAROO VINE = *Cissus antarctica.*

KANGRA BUCKWHEAT = *Fagopyrum tataricum. See* BUCKWHEAT.

KANSAS. The state flower is the sunflower. The state lies wholly in zones* 3 and 4. Its elevation increases gradually from 800 feet above sea level in the east central part to 3500 feet on the western boundary 400 miles away. Nearly three weeks are required for the march of spring across the state from southeast to northwest.

Kansas has a great diversity of soils ranging from the thin, prairie soils in the famous "bluestem" region to the loess (wind-blown) soils of the northeastern part of the state into which tree roots penetrate to a depth of 20 feet. The soils vary from slightly acid in the northeast to alkaline in most other areas of the state. Garden sites are numerous throughout the state for vegetables, flowers, ornamentals, and strawberries. Tree fruits are grown more generally in the eastern half. However, the dwarf-type trees are being grown in some gardens in the western part of the state. Therefore, the variations in soil conditions do not limit the production of garden crops in general.

Climatic conditions in Kansas are extremely variable, especially as to length of growing season and rainfall. Irrigation facilities, which are available for gardens in many areas of the state, tend to offset the low rainfall. High wind velocity is a problem for many gardeners, but this may be partially overcome by the planting of windbreaks. Summer protection is needed on the south and west sides of garden areas and winter protection on the north and west. The last killing frost at Manhattan is about the last week of April on the average, but may occur as late as May 15. The season is usually about 10 days earlier in the southeast and up to two weeks later in the northwest section of the state.

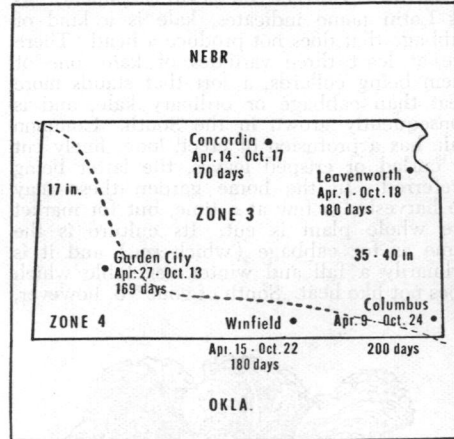

KANSAS

The zones of hardiness crossing Kansas are those shown on the map located at ZONE, which should be consulted for details. The dates are the average latest killing frost in spring and the first one in the fall. The figures below the dates show the average length of the growing season. The figures in inches show the average annual rainfall in the eastern and western parts of the state.

Vegetables are grown throughout Kansas in home gardens. About 30 different vegetables may be successfully grown if given the proper care. However, in most cases, less than half that number are included. City gardeners are usually limited for space and will only include those vegetables which have a relatively high unit value, those in which the quality decreases rather quickly, and crops which require a small area for growth. The number one crop is probably tomatoes, along with the salad crops, peas, summer squash, and peppers. Farm gardens range up to one-half acre and include a wider variety of crops, many of which are suitable for processing and storage. Many city and farm gardeners grow strawberries and grapes along with the vegetables.

Trees and shrubs are grown throughout Kansas, but there is much difference in the adaptability of species to the various areas. Most species which are adapted to the Mississippi Valley can be grown in the eastern third, but only those which are native to the plains area are hardy in the western two-thirds of the state. More emphasis is being placed on the use of trees and shrubs for climate control in both summer and winter. Home owners should make such plantings, where possible, both on farms and in towns. The use of ornamental plants for aesthetic purposes should also be combined with those for climate control. Many of the annual and perennial garden flowers are adapted.

There are many native wild flowers, and improved varieties of both annuals and perennials, which are very useful for garden plantings. However, those plants which require acid soils are limited to southeastern Kansas.

Information concerning the adaptability, use and culture of the various horticultural crops can be obtained by writing to the Department of Horticulture, Kansas State College, Manhattan, Kansas, which has kindly supplied this article on the garden possibilities of the state.

Garden club activities in the state include over 50 chapters of the Kansas Association of Garden Clubs, the latest address for which is 309 West 22nd Street, Hays, Kansas.

KANSAS GAY-FEATHER = *Liatris pycnostachya*.

KAPOK. *See* Ceiba pentandra.

KAPUKA = *Griselinia littoralis*.

karadaghensis, -e (ka-raad-a-gen′sis). From or near the Karadag Mountains, Asia Minor.

KARANDA = *Carissa Carandas*.

karataviensis, -e (ka-ra-ta-vi-en′sis). From Kara Tyube, near the Caspian Sea, Russia.

KARATHANE. *See* Fungicides.

KARO = *Pittosporum crassifolium*.

KASHGAR TAMARISK = *Tamarix hispida*.

KATSURA TREE = *Cercidiphyllum japonicum*.

KAURI PINE = *Agathis australis*.

KEEL. The ridge, suggesting the keel of a boat, on the back of many petals and some leaves. In a more special sense the *keel*

constitutes the two front and united petals in the flowers of the pea.

KEG GARDENING. *See* Tub Gardening.

KEI-APPLE = *Dovyalis Caffra*.

KELP. *See* Manure.

KENILWORTH IVY = *Cymbalaria muralis*.

KENTIA. A common Latin name for certain cult. palms, but of the true genus *Kentia* there appear to be none in cult. For plants called *Kentia* by the florists *see* the following:
Kentia belmoreana = Howea belmoreana.
Kentia canterburyana =Hedyscepe canterburyana.
Kentia forsteriana = Howea forsteriana.
Kentia macarthuri = Actinophloeus macarthuri.
Kentia sanderiana = Actinophloeus sanderianus.

KENTUCKY. The goldenrod is the state flower. The state lies wholly in zones* 3, 4 and 5.

The soils of the state range from sandy to medium clay and silt. An irregular area approximately 50 miles in diameter centering around Lexington is known as the Blue Grass section. The soils of this area contain large amounts of phosphorus, but in all other parts of the state the phosphorus content of the soil is rather low.

KENTUCKY

The zones of hardiness crossing Kentucky are those shown on the map located at Zone, which should be consulted for details. The dates are the average latest killing frost in spring and the first one in the fall. The figures below the dates show the average length of the growing season.

The chief garden centers are located around the larger cities, especially around Lexington and Louisville, where there are over 1500 acres of finely landscaped parks.

Orcharding is important in the counties ad-

---

* Special articles on the subjects indicated by an asterisk (*) will be found at the words so marked.

jacent to the Ohio River and particularly so in Boone, Jefferson, Henderson, Union, and Mc-Cracken counties, although orchards are found throughout the state. Apples and peaches are the principal tree fruits, but the strawberry is the leading fruit of the state. Most of the acreage is located in the western or lower part of the state. Most of eastern Kentucky is mountainous.

Since the state lies midway between the North and the South a wide range of plants thrive in this climate. The number of native flowers, trees, and shrubs is exceeded by few other states. Notable are the bur oaks and elms in the vicinity of Lexington.

Among native shrubs and trees of decorative or economic value are willows (10 species), ash (6 species), hickories (7 species), oaks (19 species), elms (3 species), magnolia (3 species), and over 10 species of coniferous evergreens. In the mountains azalea and rhododendrons are especially fine. Persimmon, black walnut, and *Asimina triloba* (papaw) are all of importance, especially the walnut.

Frost Data

Significant dates of the last killing frosts in spring and the first ones in autumn show the differences between the mountainous and lowland parts of the state, and dictate hort. operations accordingly.

Town	Average date of last killing frost in spring	Latest-known killing frost
Beattyville	April 23	May 10
Maysville	April 20	May 15
Greensburg	April 21	May 10
Louisville	April 11	May 14
Paducah	April 7	April 23

Town	Average date of earliest killing frost in fall	Earliest-known killing frost
Beattyville	Oct. 18	Sept. 26
Maysville	Oct. 18	Sept. 30
Greensburg	Oct. 15	Sept. 14
Louisville	Oct. 22	Sept. 26
Paducah	Oct. 24	Oct. 9

In eastern Kentucky the length of the growing season averages 176 to 188 days. In western Kentucky the length of the growing season averages 177 to 200 days.

Rainfall

The annual rainfall averages 40 to 45 inches for the state. The average rainfall by months is well distributed throughout the year, but a dry period lasting from 4 to 6 weeks usually occurs some time between June 1 and Oct. 1, with occasional very dry summers.

The address of the Agricultural Experiment Station is Lexington, Kentucky. The station is always ready to answer gardening questions.

Garden club activities include clubs of the Garden Club of America, the home office of which is at 598 Madison Avenue, New York 22, N.Y., and clubs of the Garden Club of Kentucky.

KENTUCKY BLUEGRASS = *Poa pratensis.*

KENTUCKY COFFEE-TREE = *Gymnocladus dioica.*

KENTUCKY YELLOW-WOOD = *Cladrastis lutea.*

KERNEL. The whole grain or seed of cereals; the inner, sometimes edible, part of a nut or pit, as the kernel of a stone fruit. Kernel in the latter sense comprises the embryo and its surrounding tissue.

KERRIA (ker'ri-a). A genus of shrubs of the rose family with but one species. It is rather commonly cultivated for its bright appearance and attractive flowers and is quite useful in borders and foundation plantings. *Kerria* grows quite easily, seeming to thrive in ordinary garden soil. Young growth is often winter-killed but the injury is usually not serious; the old stems should be thinned out every few years. Propagation is by division and cuttings. (Named for W. Kerr, a plant collector.)

japonica. Shrub with slender, green branches growing 4–6 ft. high. Leaves alternate, tapered-oval, 1½–4 in. long, toothed. Flowers at the end of short, lateral branches, yellow, 5-petaled, ¾–1½ in. across. April–May. China. Hardy from zone* 3 southward. Sometimes listed under *Corchorus.* Var. **picta.** Usually lower and less robust, leaves edged with white. Var. **pleniflora,** the Japanese rose, is a taller, more vigorous form, with large, double flowers, and is sometimes, incorrectly, called guelder rose.

kerrioides (ker-ri-oy'deez, but *see* OïDES). Resembling the genus *Kerria* (which see).

KETELEERIA (kee-tel-eer'ï-a). Evergreen Chinese trees of the pine family, comprising only 2 species, and closely allied to the firs. The leaves are linear, flat or ridged, pale green below and often pointed on young trees, blunt on older ones. Cones 4–6 in. long, upright, the male flowers clustered. (Named for J. B. Keteleer, a French nurseryman.)

Handsome, tall trees, pyramidal when young, becoming flat-topped with age. They are rare in cultivation and hardy only in mild climates.

davidiana. Tree, 100 ft. or more. Leaves linear, 1–2 in. long, rounded or notched at apex, midrib raised on both sides. Cones cylindric, upright, 4–8 in. long, scales recurved at tip. China. Hardy from zone* 6 southward.

fortunei. Tree, 90–100 ft. high. Leaves linear, ¾–1¼ in. long, ridged on both sides. Cones oval, 3–7 in. long. China. Hardy from zone* 6 (possibly 5) southward.

kewensis, -e (kew-en'sis). From the Royal Botanic Gardens, Kew, England.

KEY FRUIT. *See* Samara.

KEY LIME. *See* Acid Lime at LIME (the citrus fruit).

KHUS-KHUS = *Vetiveria zizanioides.*

KID-GLOVE ORANGE. The tangerine. *See* CITRUS NOBILIS DELICIOSA.

---

* Special articles on the subjects indicated by an asterisk (*) will be found at the words so marked.

KIDNEY BEAN = *Phaseolus vulgaris*. For culture *see* BEAN.

KIDNEY VETCH = *Anthyllis Vulneraria*.

KIDNEYWORT = *Baccharis pilularis*.

KIGELIA (ky-gee'lĭ-a). Two extraordinary tropical African trees of the family Bignoniaceae, one of them, **K. pinnata**, the sausage-tree, widely grown in warm regions for its odd fruit. It is a tree 20–40 ft. high with

Sausage-tree

compound* leaves, the 7–9 oblongish leaflets 4–6 in. long. Flowers nearly 4 in. long, purplish-red, more or less bell-shaped, but slightly irregular,* or bent to one side. Fruit sausage-shaped, 1–2 ft. long, swinging on long, cord-like stalks. The fruits weigh 5–12 pounds each, and are so woody that they must be sawed open to find the many pale seeds which are embedded within. In Fla. it grows on a variety of soils, but only in the warmest parts of the peninsula. (*Kigelia* is a Latinized form of an African vernacular for the tree.)

KILLWORT = *Chelidonium majus*.

KING-CUP = *Caltha palustris*. See MARSH MARIGOLD.

KINGFISHER DAISY = *Felicia bergeriana*.

KING ORANGE = *Citrus nobilis*.

KING PALM = *Archontophoenix*.

KING'S CLOVER = *Melilotus officinalis*.

KINGWOOD CENTER. *See* No. 12 at GARDEN TOURS.

KINNIKINNICK = *Arctostaphylos Uva-ursi*.

KITAMBILLA = *Dovyalis hebecarpa*.

KITCHEN GARDEN. The kitchen garden is a valuable asset to any home, whether in the country or in the village and small cities. On the farm and in many small towns and villages fresh vegetables frequently are not available unless they are grown at home. Many vegetables are more tasty and more valuable from the dietary standpoint when fresh. One who has not eaten sweet corn within an hour or two after it has been picked knows little about the flavor of this product. As soon as sweet corn is picked its sugar begins to change to starch, thus resulting in loss in sweetness, increase in toughness of the skin of the kernel, and a change in the consistency of the cooked product. Many other products decrease in

The kitchen garden need not be kitchen-minded. An attractive vegetable garden in New England, modeled after the English plan.

---

* Special articles on the subjects indicated by an asterisk (*) will be found at the words so marked.

quality after harvest owing to loss in sugar, increase in toughness, or a decrease in succulence.

A garden of one eighth of an acre well planned, well planted and well cared for will supply fresh vegetables for a family of four for a large part of the growing season and leave some for processing and storing. A garden of this size should yield a gross return of at least $75 and returns of $100 from an eighth of an acre are not unusual. Of course, the gardener should use retail prices when computing the value of his home-grown vegetables since this is the price he pays if he buys instead of produces them. For dimensions of gardens *see* Acre at Weights and Measures.

It is frequently asserted that one can buy vegetables cheaper than he can produce them. This may be true under some conditions, if one has to rent the land and hire all of the labor for preparing the soil, planting and caring for the garden. For the indoor worker the kitchen garden offers good wholesome exercise in the fresh air and sunshine and, at the same time, gives a valuable return for the time spent. On the farm a good kitchen garden yields returns greater than most other enterprises, and, for many farms, is the only reliable source of fresh vegetables.

Planning the Garden

It is desirable, especially for the beginner, to make a garden plan on paper, and this should be done long in advance of the time of planting the garden. The plan should show what crops are to be grown, the space to be occupied by each, the direction of the rows, and the distance between the rows. Before making the plan one must decide on the direction of the rows. If the ground slopes much the rows should run across the slope, not up and down it. On level land the rows may run in any direction. Rows running north and south give equal sunlight to both sides, and this is desirable where the slope and the layout of the garden permit it. If the rows run east and west, tall crops, such as corn and pole beans, should be planted on the north side so that they will not shade smaller growing crops too much.

Should the rows run the long way or the short way of the garden? In a small garden, cultivated by hand, it makes little difference, but in a large garden, where tractor cultivation is to be given, long rows are preferable to short ones. With rows running the long way of the garden there will be fewer rows, hence less space will be taken up in turning at the ends.

Arrangement of the Garden

In deciding where to plant the various crops the following points should be given consideration:

1. Perennial crops, those that will remain in one place for several years, should be planted at one end or one side of the garden, so they will not interfere too much with plowing, harrowing and cultivation. Such crops are asparagus, rhubarb, and perennial onions. If small fruits such as raspberries, blackberries, currants, and gooseberries are to be grown in the garden, they should be planted at one side or one end also.

2. Tall crops and those that spread very much should be planted toward one side, where they will not shade or overrun smaller crops. These include sweet corn, pole beans, tomatoes, cucumbers, melons, winter squashes, and pumpkins.

3. Small-growing crops and those that occupy the land about the same length of time should be grouped together, where convenient, so that the area occupied by them may be prepared as a unit for other crops succeeding them the same season.

4. Crops that occupy the land most or all of the growing season should be grouped together. Such crops include parsnips, salsify, chard, onions grown from seed, and New Zealand spinach.

These points have been considered in the plans given, but it is not feasible in any one plan to follow all of them to the letter.

Distance Between the Rows

If the garden is to be cultivated by tractor cultivators, the rows should be at least 2½ feet apart, and for large-growing plants greater spacing should be given. The distance between the rows, shown in the plan of the larger garden, are satisfactory for home gardens under most conditions and are given as a guide. Where hand cultivation is to be given, the rows for most crops do not need to be as far apart as for tractor cultivation. For small-growing crops, such as lettuce, spinach, onions, beets, carrots, parsnips, salsify, radish, turnip, and others of similar size, a space of 15 to 18 inches between the rows is sufficient; for slightly larger crops, as snap beans, cabbage, small varieties of sweet corn, and the like, 2 to 2½ feet spacing is sufficient, while for larger plants greater space is needed, as shown in the plan.

What Crops to Grow

There are many things to consider in selecting the crops to grow in a home garden, the most important being (1) the size of the area available, (2) the relative returns for the space occupied, (3) the food value of the crops, (4) the likes and dislikes of those who are to consume the vegetables, (5) the soil and climatic conditions and the skill of the gardener. In small gardens it is better to plant small-growing crops, such as beets, carrots, lettuce, and beans, rather than sweet corn, cucumbers, and squashes. We should aim to have in the garden a continuous supply of the leafy crops, lettuce, spinach, chard, New Zealand spinach, cabbage, and the like. These are rich in minerals and vitamins and add bulk to the diet. Snap beans, asparagus, and peas are similar to the leafy crops in nutritive value. Carrots, beets, onions, turnips, parsnips, or salsify, and, if the garden is large enough, peas, sweet corn, and potatoes should be included. The tomato is one of the most im-

* Special articles on the subjects indicated by an asterisk (*) will be found at the words so marked.

portant vegetable crops and should be grown in all kitchen gardens regardless of the size. Radishes and cucumbers have little food value but are eaten for their flavor.

The crops giving the highest returns in terms of nutritive value for the space occupied are snap beans, tomatoes, carrots, beets, parsnips, spinach, kale, chard, New Zealand spinach, lettuce, and green onions. Peas, sweet corn, and potatoes do not give high returns for the space occupied and should not be grown in the very small garden unless the gardener can obtain readily a supply of the other vegetables. Freshness is of such great importance with peas and sweet corn that the gardener may wish to sacrifice returns that might be obtained from other vegetables for high quality in these.

The climate of the region determines to some extent the crops that can be grown successfully. For example in zone* 1 the season is too short and too cool for sweet potatoes, pole lima beans, and for all but the quick-maturing varieties of muskmelons, watermelons, and peppers. The same is true of much of zone * 2 and even the cooler parts of

zone* 3. However, in most of zone* 3, except in the higher elevations, nearly all of the common vegetable crops can be grown. In the other zones there is practically no limitation, except that in parts of zones* 6, 7, 8, and 9 the cool-season crops, such as spinach, turnips, beets, carrots, parsnips, cauliflower, and others, cannot be grown successfully in the hottest part of the summer. In fact, in the milder regions these crops are grown mainly in the winter.

THE GARDEN PLAN

Detailed plans for gardens of two different sizes are given in the charts. The small garden, 50 by 100 feet, is suitable for a small family living in a village or a small city, while the larger one, 100 by 200, is suitable for a farm garden or for a small country estate. It is assumed that the small garden would be cultivated by hand and that the larger one would be cultivated by tractor. Some gardeners may wish to cultivate by hand the small-growing crops in the larger garden, in which case the rows do not need to be as far apart as is shown in the chart.

TABLE SHOWING QUANTITY OF SEED AND NUMBER OF PLANTS FOR 100 FEET OF ROW, FOR A GARDEN 50 BY 100 FEET AND FOR A GARDEN 100 BY 200 FEET

Kind of crop	Quantity of seed or number of plants		
	For 100 feet of row	For garden 50 by 100 feet	For garden 100 by 200 feet
Asparagus	60 plants	120 plants	200 plants
Beans, snap	¾ lb.	1½ lbs.	4 lbs.
Beans, lima	½ lb.		
Beets	2 oz.	2 oz.	½ lb.
Broccoli	50 plants		50 plants
Cabbage, early	66 plants	33 plants	133 plants
Cabbage, late	66 plants or 1 pkt. seed	66 plants or 1 pkt. seed	266 plants or 1 pkt. seed
Carrot	½ oz.	¾ oz.	2 oz.
Cauliflower	66 plants		
Celery	200 plants		
Cucumber	½ oz.	1 pkt.	½ oz.
Eggplant	66 plants		
Endive	1 oz.		
Kale	¼ oz.		
Lettuce	¼ oz.	¼ oz.	½ oz.
Muskmelon	½ oz.		½ oz.
Mustard	¼ oz.		
Onion sets	2 lbs.	3 lbs.	4 to 8 lbs.
Onion seed	1 oz.		2 oz.
Parsnips	½ oz.	¼ oz.	1 oz.
Peas	1 lb.	2 lbs.	4 lbs.
Peppers	66 plants	18 plants	36 plants
Potatoes	5 to 8 lbs.	7 to 12 lbs.	30 to 48 lbs.
Pumpkin	1 oz.		
Radish	1 oz.	1 pkt.	½ oz.
Rhubarb	35 roots	10 roots	30 roots
Rutabaga	¼ oz.		
Spinach	1½ oz.	1½ oz.	2½ oz.
Spinach, New Zealand	1 oz.	1 pkt.	1 oz.
Squash, summer	½ oz.	1 pkt.	½ oz.
Squash, winter	½ oz.		
Sweet corn	2 oz.	6 oz.	1¼ lbs.
Swiss chard	1 oz.	1 pkt.	1 oz.
Tomato, staked	50 plants	62 plants	150 plants
Tomato, not staked	33 plants	40 plants	100 plants
Turnip	½ oz.	½ oz.	1 oz.
Watermelon	1 oz.		

* Special articles on the subjects indicated by an asterisk (*) will be found at the words so marked.

In the event that these crops are planted for hand cultivation, several additional rows would be available for growing more kinds of crops, or more of some of the kinds included in the plan. Celery, cauliflower, kohlrabi, lima beans, and other crops might be added to the list, or more space might be used for potatoes and other crops that keep well in storage.

It is not expected that the plans given here will be followed in detail and to the letter, but rather that they will serve as a guide. However, in making the plans there has been taken into consideration the quantities of vegetables of various kinds that would be needed for the family. It is very important to have a planting large enough to provide sufficient at any one time for the number of persons that are to be served. This is particularly important with such crops as asparagus, beans, and peas.

QUANTITY OF SEED AND NUMBER OF PLANTS

A table is given showing the quantity of seed or the number of plants required for 100 feet of row, for a garden 50 by 100 feet, and for a garden 100 by 200 feet. The quantities are based on the spacing recommended for vegetables grown in the home garden and for the number of feet of row of each crop as shown in the plans. In this table several crops are listed that are not included in the plans. Some gardeners may wish to grow other crops than those shown in the plans, or to make substitution in some cases. The information given in the second column of the table will enable the gardener to estimate the quantity of seed needed of any crop listed for any given length of row. Where only a very small quantity of seed of any one variety and kind is needed it is suggested that the gardener buy a standard seedsman's packet.

VARIETIES OF VEGETABLES FOR THE KITCHEN GARDEN

With many kinds of vegetables there are many good varieties and, in some cases, several strains of the same variety, but there is no "best" variety. A good variety for one area may be worthless for another area or region, because of differences in climate or because of the prevalence of serious diseases. The varieties in the following list are, in the main, of good quality and can be grown in nearly all sections of the United States where the crop is produced. There are, however, some exceptions. Some long-season varieties of tomatoes, muskmelons, watermelons, and lima beans cannot be grown successfully in regions having a short growing season. Some varieties of other crops cannot be grown successfully in certain regions because of unfavorable length of day at the time the crop is grown. Note is made of these facts in connection with the varieties in question.

ASPARAGUS: Mary Washington and new selections including Mary Washington 500 and 499 and Raritan.

BEANS:
Snap, green-podded bush: Tendergreen, Tenderlong, Topcrop.
Snap, wax-podded bush: Brittle Wax, Pencil Pod Black Wax, Cherokee, Top Notch Golden Wax.
Snap, pole: Kentucky Wonder (improved strains), Blue Lake, McCaslan.
Lima, bush: Fordhook 242, Burpee Improved Bush, Henderson, Triumph.
Lima, pole: King of the Garden, Sieva (Butter Bean of the southern states).

BEETS: Crosby, Early Wonder, Detroit Dark Red.

BROCCOLI: Italian Green Sprouting, or Calabrese (many strains), DiCicco, Waltham 29.

BRUSSELS SPROUTS: Catskill, Long Island Improved, Half Dwarf and Fancymost (grown in West).

CABBAGE:
Early: Copenhagen Market, Golden Acre, Jersey Wakefield, Charleston Wakefield.
Midseason: Glory, Marion Market, late strains of Copenhagen, Globe, Bonanza, Succession.
Late: Danish Ballhead, Danish Roundhead, Hollander, Flat Dutch, Savoy (good edible quality).

CARROTS: Nantes, Red Core Chantenay, Danvers Half Long, Imperator.

CAULIFLOWER: Super Snowball, Early Snowball, Holland Erfurt.

CELERY:
Yellow varieties: Michigan Golden, Cornell 19, Cornell 619.
Green varieties: Giant Pascal, Utah (of which there are many strains), Summer Pascal, Emerson Pascal.

CHARD OR SWISS CHARD: Lucullus, Large Ribbed White, Giant Perpetual.

CUCUMBER:
Pickling: Chicago Pickling, Model, Ohio MR 17, National Pickling.
Slicing: Marketer, Ashley, Stono, Niagara, Straight Eight, Burpee Hybrid.

EGGPLANT: Black Beauty, Florida High Bush, Fort Myers Market, Black Magic.

ENDIVE: Full Heart, White Curled, Green Curled, Batavian Full Heart, Pancalier.

KOHLRABI: White Vienna, Purple Vienna.

LETTUCE:
Butterhead type: White Boston, Bibb, Mignonette.
Crisp-head type: Great Lakes, Pennlake, Imperial strains, Cornell 456.
Leaf type: Slobolt, Grand Rapids,

---

* Special articles on the subjects indicated by an asterisk (*) will be found at the words so marked.

Prize Head, Salad Bowl, Simpson.

MUSKMELON (Cantaloupe): Hale Best, Delicious, Honey Rock, Harvest Queen, Hearts of Gold, Crenshaw (in West), No. 45 (West and Southwest), Pride of Wisconsin, Smith Perfect (South).

OKRA: Perkins Spineless, White Velvet, Clemson Spineless, Louisiana Green Velvet.

ONIONS:
Green bunching: Beltsville Bunching, Egyptian or Tree, any variety from sets.
Mature bulbs: Various hybrids — Abundance, Early Harvest, Epoch, and many others.
Open-pollinated* varieties — Brigham Yellow Globe, Ebenezer, Yellow Globe Danvers.
For short-day regions and for winter production in lower South: Yellow Bermuda, Grano, Granex, Crystal Wax.

PARSLEY: Moss Curled, Double Curled.

PARSNIP: Model, Hollow Crown.

PEAS:
Early: Little Marvel, Greater Progress.
Late: Alderman, Giant Stride, Stratagem, Asgrow 40, Wando, Victory Freezer.

PEPPERS: California Wonder, Pennwonder, Early California Wonder, Yolo Wonder, Sunnybrook.

POTATOES:
Early: Cobbler, Cherokee, Bliss Triumph.
Late: Katahdin, Kennebec, Chippewa, Sebago, White Rose (in California), Russet Burbank or Netted Gem (in West), Russet Rural.

PUMPKIN: Connecticut Field, Small Sugar, Winter Luxury.

RADISH: Early Scarlet Globe, Cavalier, White Icicle (long).

RHUBARB: Victoria, Linnaeus or Strawberry, MacDonald, Valentine, Crimson Winter.

RUTABAGA: Laurentian, Long Island Improved, American Purple Top.

SALSIFY: Mammoth Sandwich Island.

SOUTHERN PEA (Cowpea): California No. 5, Calva No. 3 (standard blackeye types). Bush Conch, Texas Cream, Brown Crowder (Alabama Crowder).

SPINACH: Early Hybrid, Long Standing Bloomsdale, Virginia Savoy, King of Denmark.

SQUASH:
Summer: Yellow Straightneck, White Bush Scallop, Yellow Bush Scallop, Caserta, Cocozelle, Zucchini, Black Zucchini (used chiefly in West).
Winter: Buttercup, Butternut, Boston Marrow, Blue Hubbard, Golden Hubbard.

SWEET CORN:
Early and midseason yellow: Seneca 60, North Star, Marcross, Golden Beauty.
Late: Golden Cross, Iochief, Golden Hybrid, Calumet, Golden Security, Victory Garden.
(All of above are hybrids)
Open-pollinated varieties:* Golden Bantam, Golden Early Market, Bantam Evergreen, Country Gentleman (white), Stowell Evergreen (white).

TOMATO:
Early: Victor, Fireball, Valiant, Early Hybrid, Sioux, Moreton Hybrid.
Midseason and late: Stokesdale, Marglobe, Rutgers, Manalucie, Long Red.

TURNIP: Purple Top White Globe, Yellow Globe, White Egg, Shogoin (grown for greens), Seven Top (grown for greens in South).

WATERMELON:
For short-season regions: Golden Honey Cream, New Hampshire Midget, Early Kansas, Baby Rhode Island Red.
For long-season regions: Any of the above, Klondike, Florida Favorite, Stone Mountain, Charleston Gray, Black Diamond.

PREPARATION OF THE GARDEN SOIL

The soil for the kitchen garden should be thoroughly prepared before attempting to plant seeds or plants, for no amount of cultivation will make up for poor preparation. The soil should be plowed or spaded to the depth of 6 to 8 inches and smoothed by harrowing or raking. Before sowing seed or setting plants the surface should be smooth, friable* and free from clods or lumps. A very small garden usually is spaded or dug by hand and then the surface is smoothed and prepared with a hand cultivator and a rake or with a rake alone. A large garden ordinarily is plowed and harrowed, and even small ones sometimes are so prepared. After the soil has been plowed and harrowed, further preparation for planting can be done with hand tools. The surface soil should be kept loose and free from weeds until time for planting, and this requires frequent going over with the harrow, hand cultivator, or rake. (*See* PLOWING, DIGGING, HARROWING and RAKING.)

TOOLS FOR THE KITCHEN GARDEN

Not many tools are needed for the small garden. A spade or spading fork, a hoe, and a rake are essential, and a small hand weeder, a trowel, and a garden line are desirable additions to any garden. A wheel hoe or hand cultivator is a great labor saver for either the small or the large garden and a hand sprayer or hand duster is very desirable. After the

* Special articles on the subjects indicated by an asterisk (*) will be found at the words so marked.

land is prepared for planting all labor can be done with the tools mentioned, even in a half-acre garden. On the farm, plows, harrows, and tractor cultivators are available and they are commonly used in the farm garden. Where plows and harrows are not used for other work than preparing the garden soil the home gardener should hire someone who has the necessary equipment to plow and harrow his garden. If a small cultivator is not used for other work on the farm it is desirable to obtain one for the garden, since larger cultivators are not desirable or practical for the family garden.

IMPROVEMENT OF THE SOIL

It is seldom that the land available for the kitchen garden is entirely satisfactory for the purpose without improvement of the soil. Most areas are lacking in one or more fertilizing elements and many lack all of the three important ones, nitrogen, phosphorus, and potash. Heavy soils, such as clays and clay loams, can be made lighter and more friable* by the addition of humus-forming material, and sandy soils are improved in texture and in their water-holding capacity by the same material. Stable manure supplies both humus and the common fertilizing elements. Where this material is available in sufficient quantities it might be applied at the rate of 10–20 tons to the acre. This should be supplemented with about 400 pounds of 20 per cent superphosphate to the acre, since manure is somewhat deficient in phosphorus.

Where manure is not available the texture of the soil can be improved by growing and turning under some soil-improving crop. Rye is a good crop to grow for turning under in most regions, but in regions of the South, where the soil-improving crop might be grown in the summer, cow peas may be planted to improve the soil. (See GREEN MANURING and SOIL MANAGEMENT.) In addition to the soil-improving crop it is desirable to supply a complete fertilizer, which is one that contains nitrogen, phosphorus, and potash. The quantity to apply should be governed to some extent by the natural fertility of the soil. On an infertile soil it is desirable to make an application of 1500 to 2000 pounds or more to the acre of a 5–10–5, or 5–10–10, or some similar fertilizer. (See FERTILIZERS.) This means 5 per cent nitrogen, 10 per cent phosphoric acid and 5 or 10 per cent potash. On a moderately fertile soil the application might be reduced and on a rich soil little or no fertilizer need be applied. Even where stable manure is used a light application of fertilizer is desirable. The most feasible method of applying fertilizer to the soil of the kitchen garden is to sprinkle it broadcast over the entire area after the soil is plowed or spaded. The fertilizer should then be mixed with the surface soil by harrowing or by raking. Coarse manure should be applied before the land is plowed or spaded and should be well turned under so as not to interfere with further preparation and with planting. Well-rotted manure may be applied after the land is plowed, in which case it should be harrowed in or raked in.

Most vegetable crops thrive best on a soil that is slightly acid, but many do not grow well on a very sour soil. Lime is used to correct soil acidity, but garden soil should not be limed unless it has been tested to show whether it is needed, and, if so, the quantity to apply. If spinach and beets grow well the soil probably does not need lime. (See LIME.)

GROWING PLANTS FOR TRANSPLANTING IN THE GARDEN

Several kinds of vegetable plants are practically always started in a specially prepared seed bed, from which they are later transferred to the garden. (See SEEDS AND SEEDAGE.) These include cabbage, cauliflower, Brussels sprouts, celery, eggplant, pepper, tomato, and sweet potato. Others, such as lettuce, onions, beets, muskmelons, watermelons, and lima beans, are sometimes started under protection in greenhouses and hotbeds. In regions having short growing seasons, or where an early crop is desired, seeds of these are generally sown under protection, as in a box in a sunny window of the dwelling house, in a cold frame, hotbed, or in a greenhouse. (See COLD FRAME.) In regions having a short growing season, as in all of zone* 1, in most of zone* 2 and in the cooler parts of zone* 3, good yields of tomatoes, eggplant, and pepper cannot be obtained unless the plants are started under protection several weeks before it is safe to plant them in the garden. For an early crop of the other vegetables mentioned, it is desirable to start the plants under protection in these zones and in zones* 4 and 5 and in most of 6. In sections of the United States where the growing season is sufficiently long the plants for all of these crops might be started in a cold frame or even in a specially prepared bed in the open. Late cabbage, late cauliflower, and late celery are nearly always started in open beds. See the name of your state or province for frost data.

When an early crop of cabbage, cauliflower, celery, and lettuce is desired in regions where the winters are too severe to grow them in the open, seed should be sown 6 to 8 weeks in advance of the time to set the plants in the garden. In zone* 4 this should be from Feb. 1 to 15; in zone* 3 Feb. 15 to Mar. 1; in zone* 2 Mar. 1 to 15; in zone* 1 Mar. 15 to 30; and in zone* 5 Jan. 15 to 30. In part of zone* 6 and in all of zones* 7, 8, and 9 the plants ordinarily would be grown in the open during the fall. Seeds of tomato, eggplant, and pepper are usually sown 8 to 10 weeks in advance of planting in the garden. In zones* 1 to 5 the date of sowing seed of these crops should be 2 to 3 weeks later than for cabbage. In zone* 6 and the cooler parts of 7 seeds of these ordinarily would be sown in Feb. In the milder parts of zone* 7, as in the Gulf Coast region of Texas, and in zones* 8 and 9, these

---

* Special articles on the subjects indicated by an asterisk (*) will be found at the words so marked.

crops can be grown during the winter and spring, so that the time of sowing seed depends on the time the crop is desired.

It should be borne in mind that elevation and proximity to large bodies of water modify the climate and, because of this, the dates given for starting plants in the various zones are only approximate. The reader should consult the name of his state or province where the dates of the last killing frost in spring, the first killing frost in fall, and the length of the frost-free period are all given in detail.

In the growing of early plants for setting in the garden it is a common practice to transplant the seedlings once before they are taken to the garden. This is called pricking-out and is usually done when the plants develop their first true leaves and are from one to two inches tall. The purpose of this transplanting is to give the seedlings more space for development and to develop a more branched root system.

Planting the Garden

The time for planting seeds or setting plants in the garden in most sections depends largely on the dates of the last killing frost in spring for the first planting and the last killing frost in fall for the latest safe date for planting. It is desirable to plant as early as possible in order to get a succession of crops. Some crops must be planted early to avoid hot weather, while others thrive best in warm weather. Some crops will grow before the soil gets warm and are not injured by light frosts, while others will not grow in a cool soil and are severely injured or killed by frost. The following grouping can be used to guide the gardener in planning his planting.

1. Crops that may be planted in the open 3 to 4 weeks before the last killing frost in spring are onion sets, spinach, radish, turnip, kale, mustard, lettuce (seed and plants), peas, early potatoes, asparagus, and rhubarb roots. In most sections of northern United States these crops may be planted as soon as the ground can be prepared in the spring. In zone* 4 this would be about the middle of March, correspondingly later in zones* 1 and 2 and earlier in zones* 5 and 6. In the milder regions of zone* 6, in most of 7 and in all of zones* 8 and 9 these crops can be grown all winter.

2. Crops that may be planted a little before the last killing frost in spring are beets, carrots, chard, onion seed, parsnip, salsify, cauliflower plants, and celery plants. In regions having severe freezes these may be planted about two weeks later than the group mentioned above, while in milder regions they may be planted at approximately the same time.

3. Crops to be planted after the danger of *killing* frost has passed are snap beans, sweet corn, and New Zealand spinach. It may be worth while to take chances on a light frost with these crops.

4. Crops to be planted after *all* danger of frost is over and after the soil has become warm are tomatoes, eggplant, pepper, cucumber, muskmelon, watermelon, squashes and pumpkins, lima beans, and sweet potato. These crops are injured by light frosts and stunted by low temperatures even when there is no frost.

By consulting the frost data at the name of his state the reader can determine the approximate date of the last killing frost in spring in his locality. From this and from the suggestions given above, the gardener can arrive at the time for making the first planting of the various crops.

In many sections of the South, as in most of zones* 5 and all of zones* 6, 7, 8, and 9, the cool-season crops do not thrive in the hottest part of the summer. This is true of spinach, turnips, kale, and peas in most of zones* 2, 3, and 4. However, where the temperature is modified by elevation or by the cooling effects of large bodies of water these crops can be grown even in midsummer.

More than one planting should be made of many crops. There should be a continuous supply of snap beans, beets, carrots, cabbage, lettuce, and sweet corn from the garden throughout the growing season, from the time the earliest is ready for the table until crops are killed by frost in the fall. This will require about three plantings of snap beans and three of sweet corn (or one planting each of an early,* a medium and a late variety); three or more of lettuce, two each of beets, carrots, and cabbage. Two plantings of peas about two or three weeks apart, or one planting each of an early and a late variety, will be sufficient in most regions, as this crop does not thrive in hot weather. Turnips, spinach, and kale may be planted early in the spring and again in late summer and early fall for fall and winter use in most sections where they will not withstand winter weather. In milder regions where these crops are grown in the winter 3 or 4 plantings might be made to advantage. Two plantings of celery and cauliflower, one early and one late, are frequently made, one for early summer and the other for fall use. In most regions only one planting is made of lima beans, cucumbers, eggplant, pepper, melons, summer squash, winter squash, pumpkin, parsnip, tomato, sweet potato, as these continue to bear until killed by frost, unless they happen to be destroyed by disease, insect, or other means.

The garden plans suggest the arrangement of the plantings and the distance between the rows for gardens of two different sizes. (For details of the depth of planting, methods of planting and spacing of plants in the row *see* special articles on all the chief vegetable crops at Cabbage, Onion, Potato, Pea, etc.)

Cultivation, Hoeing, and Weeding

Vegetable plants cannot compete successfully with weeds. The garden, therefore, should be given sufficient cultivation,* hoeing, and weeding to keep weeds under control. The best time to destroy weeds is before they have become well established, for they can then be destroyed by shallow cultivation or hoeing, which merely breaks the crust and stirs the

---

* Special articles on the subjects indicated by an asterisk (*) will be found at the words so marked.

PLAN OF A VEGETABLE GARDEN (100 × 50 feet)

← 50 feet →

Row	Label	Spacing
Asparagus		42 in.
Asparagus		42 in.
Asparagus		42 in.
Asparagus	Rhubarb	42 in.
Sweet corn, third planting or late variety		36 in.
Sweet corn, third planting or late variety		36 in.
Sweet corn, third planting or late variety		36 in.
Sweet corn, first planting	Sweet corn, second planting	30 in.
Sweet corn, first planting	Sweet corn, second planting	30 in.
Sweet corn, first planting	Sweet corn, second planting	30 in.
Tomatoes	Peppers	42 in.
Tomatoes		42 in.
Tomatoes		42 in.
Cucumbers	Summer squash	42 in.
Potatoes		42 in.

← 50 feet →

Spacing	Crop	
36 in.	Potatoes	
36 in.	Potatoes	
36 in.	Potatoes	
30 in.	Snap beans, first planting	
30 in.	Snap beans, first planting	
30 in.	Snap beans, second planting	
30 in.	Snap beans, second planting	
30 in.	Peas, early (followed by late cabbage)	
18 in.	Peas, early (followed by late cabbage)	
18 in.	Peas, later (followed by fall spinach or kale)	
18 in.	Peas, later (followed by fall spinach or kale)	
30 in.	Cabbage, early	
30 in.	Parsnips or salsify	
18 in.	Beets, early (followed by turnips)	
18 in.	Carrots, early (followed by turnips)	
18 in.	Beets, late	
18 in.	Carrots, late	
18 in.	Carrots, late	
18 in.	Onion sets for green onions	
18 in.	Onion sets for green onions	
18 in.	Onion sets for bulb onions	
18 in.	Onion sets for bulb onions	
18 in.	Lettuce, early, early (followed by lettuce)	Radishes
18 in.	Spinach, kale or mustard, early	
18 in.	Spinach, kale or mustard, early	Turnips
18 in.	New Zealand spinach or chard	

50 feet

PLAN OF A VEGETABLE GARDEN (200 × 100 feet)

|← — 200 feet — →|

Crop (left)	Crop (right)	Width
Asparagus		48 in.
Asparagus	Rhubarb, horse-radish	48 in.
Bush fruits (raspberries, blackberries, currants)		48 in.
Strawberries		48 in.
Strawberries		48 in.
Sweet corn, early variety	Sweet corn, second planting	36 in.
Sweet corn, early variety	Sweet corn, second planting	36 in.
Sweet corn, early variety	Sweet corn, second planting	36 in.
Sweet corn, late, large variety		36 in.
Sweet corn, late, large variety		48 in.
Tomatoes	Peppers, eggplant	48 in.
Tomatoes		48 in.
Cucumbers	Melons or summer squash	48 in.
Potatoes		48 in.
Potatoes		36 in.
Potatoes		36 in.
Peas, early (followed by late cabbage)		36 in.
Peas, second planting		36 in.
Cabbage, early (followed by fall spinach)		36 in.
Beans, snap, first planting		36 in.
Beans, snap, second planting		30 in.
Parsnips or salsify		30 in.
Chard or New Zealand spinach	Sprouting broccoli	30 in.
Beets, second planting		30 in.
Carrots, second planting		30 in.
Onion seed or sets for bulb onions		30 in.
Onion sets for green onions (followed by late cabbage)		30 in.
Carrots, early (followed by fall spinach and lettuce)		30 in.
Beets, early (followed by turnips)		30 in.
Spinach, spring (followed by beans)		30 in.
Spinach, spring	Lettuce, radishes	30 in.

(right side: 100 feet)

surface. By the proper use of the hand cultivator and hand hoe, pulling weeds by hand ought not to be necessary except to remove those near the plants. All cultivation and hoeing should be shallow in order to keep root destruction to the minimum. (For details *see* Cultivation, Weeds, Hoeing.)

IRRIGATION

In arid and semi-arid regions irrigation is essential, and in humid regions artificial watering frequently is desirable, especially during periods of drought. In setting plants in the garden in any region it is the common practice to apply water around the plant unless the soil is well supplied with water. In irrigated regions water is always applied at the time of setting plants. The most common methods of applying water to the garden are by spraying or sprinkling from above and by trench or furrow irrigation between the rows. When water is applied it is desirable to apply enough to soak the soil to the depth of several inches and then withhold it until the crops need it again. Merely sprinkling the surface is useless. (For details *see* Irrigation.)

* Special articles on the subjects indicated by an asterisk (*) will be found at the words so marked.

ROTATION OF CROPS

The term rotation or "crop rotation" means the systematic sequence of crops grown on the same land for a period of years. Rotation is important in vegetable-growing in aiding in the control of diseases and insects and in equalizing the drain on the nutrients in the soil. In general, it is not desirable to grow the same crop or closely related crops on the same land year after year. For example, cabbage, cauliflower, and broccoli should not follow each other since many of the same diseases attack all of them. Likewise cucumbers, muskmelons, watermelons, and squashes and pumpkins should not follow each other. A good general plan is to follow foliage crops, celery, cabbage, lettuce, spinach, and others, by root crops, such as beets, carrots, and parsnips, and to follow these by fruit and seed crops, such as tomatoes, eggplant, peppers, beans, and peas. However, in following such a system of rotation, care should be taken to avoid following a foliage crop with a root crop that is attacked by the same diseases. In a home garden it is seldom feasible to follow an ideal system of rotation because of the large number of crops grown and the difference in the size of the area devoted to the various ones. It is important, however, to keep in mind the general principles, and in case disease becomes serious on some crop this crop and others attacked by the same disease should be grown in a section of the garden that is free from the organism.

SUCCESSION CROPPING

Succession cropping means the sequence of crops grown on the same land the same year, where more than one crop is so grown. The same general principles apply to succession cropping as apply to rotation. In planning the garden the cropping system for the entire season should be taken into consideration, and this has been done in the plans. Where the area of land is limited, the garden should be planned so as to utilize it to the utmost throughout the season. The kind and number of crops to be grown are determined by the length of the growing season. As examples of succession cropping the following are given: (a) Early lettuce followed by snap beans or root crops, such as beets and carrots; (b) early cabbage followed by late potatoes, where the growing season is long enough; (c) early peas followed by late planting of beets, carrots, or cabbage; (d) spring spinach or kale followed by tomatoes. In many regions three crops can be grown on the same land in one season.

INTERCROPPING OR COMPANION CROPPING

When two or more crops are grown on the same land at the same time the system is known as intercropping or companion cropping. This may embrace succession cropping as in the planting of cabbage, lettuce, and radishes at the same time on the same area. The radishes will mature and be harvested first and lettuce harvest will follow and both will be out of the way before the cabbage plants need all of the space. For intercropping to be successful there must be an abundance of nutrients and water.

In planning for intercropping the gardener should consider the time each crop is to be planted, the time each will mature and the space needed by each at various stages of growth. In nearly all plans small-growing, quick-maturing crops, sometimes called catch crops, are planted with larger, later-maturing ones. One common plan is to plant lettuce plants between the rows of cabbage and also between the plants in the row. Radishes and carrots may be grown together, the former being planted between the rows of the latter. Many other combinations can be worked out by the thoughtful gardener.

HARVESTING VEGETABLES FOR HOME USE

The garden has not one harvest time, but many. Crops are harvested throughout the growing season as they reach edible maturity and are either consumed at once or else are canned or otherwise preserved. There should remain in the fall crops to be stored for winter use. Some crops, as asparagus, peas, and sweet corn, must be harvested soon after they reach edible maturity or they deteriorate in quality. Asparagus spears branch out in a day or two after they come through the ground and peas and sweet corn lose sugar and become hard unless they are harvested soon after they reach edible maturity. Other crops, as snap beans, lima beans and tomatoes, remain in edible condition for several days, while still others, such as beets, carrots, parsnips, cabbage, celery, eggplant, and peppers, remain in edible condition for several weeks. However, the length of time that any of these products remain in edible condition depends on the temperature. In general, the warmer the weather the shorter the time any of these products remain of good quality. Some crops, such as spinach, kale, New Zealand spinach, chard, and lettuce, may be harvested at any time after they reach sufficient size, until they become old and tough, or until they shoot to seed. The root crops — beets, carrots, parsnips, and turnips — may also be harvested at any stage after they reach edible size until they become tough and woody. Frequently the home gardener allows these plants to grow thickly in the row until they reach sufficient size to use as food and then makes his early harvest a thinning process. Beets and turnips are often pulled for their foliage before the roots are large enough to use.

Summer squash should be harvested before the rind begins to harden, but may be harvested at any size desired. Winter squashes and pumpkins should be allowed to ripen completely in the field. Snap beans are best when harvested before the seeds develop to full size and lima beans should be harvested before the pods get yellow. Tomatoes should be left on the vines until color is well developed. Muskmelons and watermelons are of the

---

* Special articles on the subjects indicated by an asterisk (*) will be found at the words so marked.

highest quality when allowed to ripen on the vines. It is difficult to determine when a watermelon is ripe and only by experience can one become able to do so. The sound emitted when the melon is thumped with the finger is an index of maturity. A dull, dead sound is emitted when the melon reaches maturity, but varieties differ in this respect. One must, therefore, cut many melons before he can correlate the sound emitted on thumping with the stage of maturity. (For details of harvesting methods for the various vegetables see the special crop articles.) — H. C. T.

KITTUL = *Caryota urens.*

KLEINIA. See Senecio.

KNAPWEED = *Centaurea.*

KNAUR. A burl.*

KNAWEL = *Scleranthus annuus.* See list at Weeds.

KNIFE ACACIA = *Acacia cultriformis.*

KNIFFIN SYSTEM. See Grape.

KNIGHT'S-SPUR = *Delphinum Consolida.*

KNIPHOFIA (nip-ho′fi-a). African herbaceous perennials belonging to the Liliaceae, called torch lily, flame flower, or poker-plant, comprising about 24 species. They have thick, fleshy roots, and long, linear, basal leaves. Flowers rising in long, red or yellow spikes or racemes,* above the leaves, and blooming from June to frost. Corolla drooping, tubular. Stamens* 6. Fruit a capsule.* (Named for J. J. Kniphof, German professor.) Often sold as *Tritoma,* and now found in many fine hort. forms, some with apricot-colored flowers. For culture see the last species.

foliosa. Leaves broad, in a dense basal rosette, 3–4 in. broad at base, tapering into a long point. Flower stalk stout, erect, 2 to 3 ft. long. Flowers yellow, in a dense cylindrical raceme,* 6 to 12 in. long. Tropical and South Af.

rufa. Leaves to 1½ ft. long and ⅓ in. across. Flowers yellow, the upper ones tinged red. Stamens* protruding. June to frost. Natal.

tucki. Leaves to 1½ ft. high, about ¾ in. wide. Flowers about ½ in. long, yellow, tinged with red, the cluster nearly 6 in. long. South Af.

Uvaria. Red-hot poker. A handsome plant 2–4 ft. high. Leaves nearly 3 ft. high. Flowers scarlet or the lower ones yellow, the cluster nearly 10 in. long. The *var.* **floribunda** flowers earlier; in *var.* **grandiflora**, the flowers are larger; and the *var.* **pfitzeri** blooms longer. Can be wintered over in the open in the North only if a heavy mulch of salt hay, which does not mat down and cause rotting, is applied. Often wintered over in boxes in the cellar. Propagated by division, offsets, and seeds.

KNOB CELERY = Celeriac. For culture see Celery.

KNOT GARDENS. The intricate patterns, once so well liked, in the arrangement of flower beds. They are scarcely ever seen today, except in some herb gardens which try to perpetuate the arrangement of many old gardens of herbs. See the illustrations at Herb Gardening for some examples of Knot Gardens.

KNOTROOT = *Stachys sieboldi.*

KNOTWEED. See Polygonum. See also the list at Weeds.

Kobus (kō′bus). Japanese name for *Magnolia Kobus.*

KOCHIA (ko′ki-a). Of the 35 species of this chiefly Eurasian genus of the family Chenopodiaceae, only one is cult., but it is a widely grown tender annual valued for its bushy habit and brilliantly colored foliage. Usually called summer, standing or Belvedere cypress, it is known to science as **K. scoparia** of which the *var.* **tricophila** is one commonly grown. It is an erect, much branched, bushy herb, 20–36 in. high, sometimes nearly globe-shaped. Leaves extremely numerous, alternate,* often hairy, without teeth, very narrow, and nearly round in cross-section. They may be red, green, or yellow, but turn purple-red in the fall. Flowers greenish, inconspicuous, very small, and a few in the leaf axils.* (For details see Chenopodiaceae.) Fruit a utricle.* The summer cypress is best treated as a tender annual (*see* Annuals), but seeds may be sown in place if delayed until the ground is warm. It is a showy plant for the border and holds its leaf color all summer. In the South it self-sows and is apt to become weedy, promotes hay fever and is sometimes called burning bush or firebush. The Chinese make brushes from it. (Named for W. D. J. Koch, German botanist.)

KOELREUTERIA (kel-roo-teer′i-a). Golden-rain tree. A small genus of Asiatic trees of the family Sapindaceae; *K. paniculata* often grown for ornament, the yellow summer-blooming flower clusters being very handsome. Leaves alternate,* compound,* the leaflets arranged feather-fashion with an odd one at the end, all more or less irregularly toothed. Flowers in a large, terminal cluster (panicle), the corolla somewhat irregular.* Petals 4, with a claw* and with 2 upward-pointing appendages to each. Stamens 8 or fewer. Fruit a bladder-like 3-valved pod (capsule*) with black seeds. (Named for Joseph G. Koelreuter, German professor.)

The second species is not uncommon in the finer gardens but the first is scarcely known, and is not hardy in the North. They do well on a variety of soils but seem better suited to open sunshine than to shade. Propagated by stratified seeds, or by root cuttings.

formosana. A tree 30–50 ft. high, the leaves twice-compound, nearly 18 in. long. Leaflets ovalish or narrower, rather shallow-toothed. Pods nearly 2 in. long, papery. Formosa. Hardy only in zones* 8 and 9. Little known in the U.S.

paniculata. Pride-of-India; also called China-tree and varnish-tree. Not usually over 30 ft. high and of dome-like form. Leaves 9–14 in. long, the leaflets 7–15, ovalish-oblong and coarsely toothed, or even deeply cut near the base. Flower cluster 12–18 in. long, showy, each flower about ½ in. long. Pods about 2 in. long, papery, brilliantly colored before dropping.

* Special articles on the subjects indicated by an asterisk (*) will be found at the words so marked.

Eastern Asia. July–Aug. Hardy from zone* 3 southward.

KOHLERIA. See ISOLOMA.

KOHLRABI (*Brassica caulorapa*). This is a minor member of the cabbage tribe, the erect stem of which is swollen just above the ground level. The swollen part, while still tender and juicy, has a fine flavor, liked by some, but later it becomes hard, bitter, almost woody, and useless. Kohlrabi (often called the turnip cabbage or turnip-rooted cabbage or even stem cabbage) is closely related to the turnip and by some considered superior.

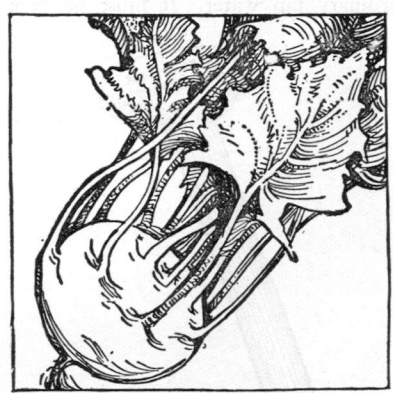

Kohlrabi

Its culture is exactly the same as for early cabbage (which *see* at CABBAGE) except that kohlrabi is set 8 in. apart in the row and the rows (except for motor cultivators) can be 18 in. apart. Its insect and fungus pests are the same as those of cabbage. For their control *see* CABBAGE.

VARIETIES. The best varieties are Purple Vienna and White Vienna. As the names indicate, the vegetable is more popular abroad than here, where its use is largely among the foreign-born.

Some, who want kohlrabi in the late fall, start a second crop exactly as late cabbage is grown. (*See* late cabbage at CABBAGE.) Whether early or late crops are grown, it is important to secure quick growth and to cut the whitish, thickened stems before they become tough and woody. The plant will not stand great heat.

Koidzumi (koyd-zoo'mi). Native name in Formosa for *Pyracantha Koidzumi.*

KOLANUT = *Cola acuminata.*

KOLKWITZIA (kolk-wit'zi-a). A single species of Chinese shrubs of the honeysuckle family, much cult. for its showy bloom under the name of beauty-bush. The only species, **K. amabilis** is a shrub 4–6 ft. high with opposite* ovalish leaves 2–3 in. long. Flowers in flattish clusters (corymbs*) nearly 3 in. wide, the corolla bell-shaped, pink, but with a yellow throat, about ½ in. long, the stalks and sepals* bristly. Fruit dry, both it and the stalk covered with bristly hairs. June. Hardy from zone* 3 southward. The plant is an attractive sight in bloom, which may be forced in the greenhouse weeks before outdoor flowering is due. (*See* FORCING.) Propagated by cuttings of green wood. (*See* CUTTINGS.) (Named for R. Kolkwitz, German professor of botany.)

Kolomikta (ko-lo-mik'ta). Native name in Asia for *Actinidia Kolomikta* (which see). It is here commonly called kolomikta vine.

KONIGA. See SWEET ALYSSUM.

koraiensis, -e (kor-i-en'sis). From Korea.

koreana, -us, -um (kor-i-a'na). From Korea.

KOREAN AZALEA = *Azalea yedoensis.*

KOREAN CHRYSANTHEMUM. See CHRYSANTHEMUM.

KOREAN LAWN GRASS = *Zoysia japonica.*

KOREAN LESPEDEZA. See LESPEDEZA STRIATA.

KOREAN PINE = *Pinus koraiensis.* See PINE.

KOSTER'S BLUE SPRUCE = *Picea pungens kosteriana.* See SPRUCE.

Kousa (cow'sa). Japanese native name for *Cornus Kousa.*

KOWHAI. See CLIANTHUS PUNICEUS.

KRAUHNIA = *Wistaria.*

KUDZU-VINE = *Pueraria thunbergiana.*

KUMQUAT. See FORTUNELLA.

KURRAJONG = *Brachychiton populneum.*

KURUME AZALEA. See AZALEA OBTUSA.

KURUM OIL TREE = *Pongamia pinnata.*

KUSSAIE LIME. See LIME (the citrus fruit).

---

* Special articles on the subjects indicated by an asterisk (*) will be found at the words so marked.

L

LABELLUM. The lip* of an irregular flower.

LABELS. For herbaceous plants or for those grown in pots or tubs, the best temporary label is the ordinary pot label as shown in the figure. They come in sizes from small ones useful for the smallest pots to larger ones that are a foot long and correspondingly wider. Anything written on their smooth wooden face with a soft lead pencil will usually last as long as such temporary labels are needed. They are cheap, well made, and in common use by all professional growers. On some better types of wooden labels (*i.e.*, with better wood), India ink will last 4–6 years.

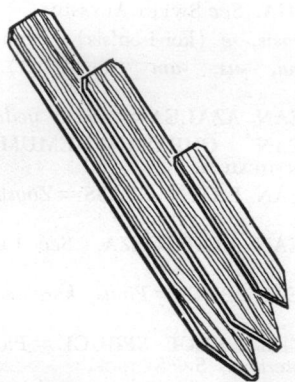

Wooden pot labels, useful also in the garden for temporary marking

If more permanent labels are needed for herbs or for marking varieties in the vegetable garden, they must be of metal, preferably of zinc. Such labels have, in the best forms, a channeled shank which anchors the label firmly in the ground, and a flattened, tilted upper part upon which the record is written. If such zinc labels are left out in the rain for a few days, the slightly oxidized surface can then be easily written upon with a soft lead pencil, and such writing will last for years. It will not last, however, unless the oxidizing is sufficient to coat the zinc with a whitish film which takes pencil marks very well.

INK FOR LABELS. The only objection to pencil marks on zinc labels is that they are sometimes hard to read. To overcome this difficulty an ink is preferred by many. One of the best is a formula used at the Missouri Botanical Garden. It is 1 dram acetate of copper, 1 dram ammonium sulphate, ½ dram lamp black, and 10 drams of water. Such an ink must be applied to the fresh, burnished metal (rubbed up with emery paper) and only a glass or quill pen can be used, or a fresh metal pen for each batch of labels. This ink etches an indelible record on the zinc and can only be removed with sandpaper. Another good ink, useful only on freshly sandpapered zinc, is made with 15 grains of platinum chloride and 4 oz. of ordinary tap water. It must be kept in

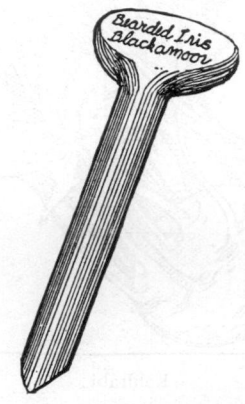

Permanent type of zinc label for herbaceous plants. About one-half of the shank should be in the ground.

glass or rubber-stoppered bottles and applied only with a gold-coated pen. On pure zinc, but not on poorly galvanized labels, such ink will provide lettering that will last 20 years.

WOODY PLANTS. All labels for woody plants must be wired to the twigs in such a way as to prevent girdling them as the twigs grow. Wooden, wired labels, such as come on nursery stock, are all right for temporary mark-

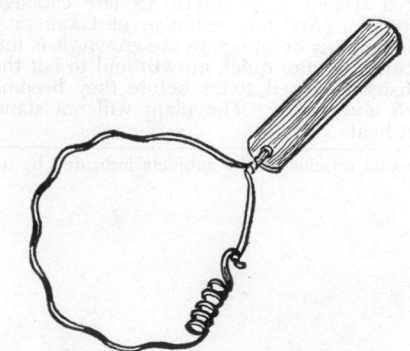

A wooden wired label for shrubs and trees; good for a season or two

---

* Special articles on the subjects indicated by an asterisk (*) will be found at the words so marked.

ing, but their wires are usually twisted around the twigs too tightly and should be removed at planting time.

If the shrub or tree needs a permanent label, get one of the copper labels with an ample wire. Loop this as loosely but securely as possible around a twig, preferably between branchlets, so it cannot be blown away. The best type of copper labels are thin sheets of metal upon which the writing is dug into the metal with a stylus, preferably with a pad of paper under the label while printing it. Such etching is as near permanent as any record can be. When such labels become weather-stained, they are not easy to find, and it is thus better to put them on the same side of all shrubs and trees. One large institution in the country, with thousands of such labels,

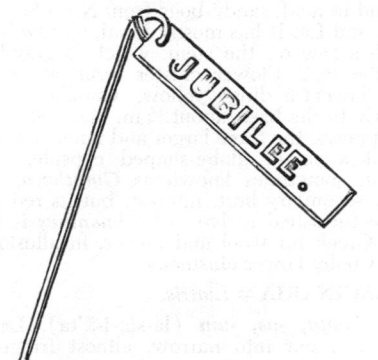

A metal wired label good for woody plants or herbs and lasting for years

puts all of them on the south side of the shrub or tree to facilitate finding them. Other sorts of labels are shown in the illustrations. An interesting rock garden label, known in England, consists of pieces of limestone, sandpapered smooth on one side, and painted with a fine brush. These are stuck in the ground and are more attractive in such a collection than wood or metal labels. They need retouching from time to time. Many modern plastic labels are scarcely time-tested as yet.

labiata, -us, -um (lay-bee-ā′ta). Labiate; *i.e.*, having flowers with a lip,* as in the mint family.

LABIATAE (lay-bee-ā′tee). The mint, hyssop, salvia, or rosemary family is also, but not here, called the Menthaceae and Lamiaceae. It is an enormous group or family of plants comprising at least 160 genera and over 3500 species of mostly herbs (some tropical shrubs), nearly all with fragrant foliage and a square or at least 4-angled stem.

Leaves opposite* (rarely whorled*). Flowers always irregular,* commonly 2-lipped,* often arranged in tight, head-like clusters, but in many genera in open, branched

spikes* and racemes*, the cluster often rather leafy in some of these genera. The fruit consists of 4 one-seeded nutlets, often, but incorrectly, called seeds, which are commonly found surrounded by the often persistent calyx.

The garden uses of the mint family are many. One group of genera are chiefly grown for the fragrant foliage, for seasoning, or for making various condiments. They are: *Hyssopus, Lavandula, Majorana* (see SWEET MARJORAM), *Marrubium* (see HOREHOUND), *Melissa, Mentha* (see MINT), *Nepeta, Ocimum, Origanum, Rosmarinus* (see ROSEMARY), *Satureia* (see SAVORY), and *Thymus* (see THYME). For the uses of these see also HERB GARDENING.

The chief ornamental perennials (a few annual), of easy culture outdoors over most of the country, are: *Ajuga, Audibertia, Elsholtzia, Micromeria, Moluccella, Monarda, Perilla* (foliage plant), *Perovskia, Phlomis, Salvia* (but *see* below for tender species), *Stachys,* and *Teucrium* (some tender).

A secondary group of generally hardy genera are less grown, partly because they are often weedy. Some are adapted to the wild garden, others to the rock garden, and others only to the less desirable parts of the border. This group comprises (w = wild garden; r = rock garden; h = more or less weedy or coarse herbs): *Ballota* (h); *Collinsonia* (w); *Dracocephalum* (w); *Glecoma* (h); *Horminum* (r); *Lamium* (w); *Leonurus* (h); *Monardella* (r); *Prunella* (h); *Pycnanthemum* (h); *Scutellaria* (w); and *Trichostema* which includes the bluecurls.

There are a few tropical shrubs or herbs, all tender. Some are grown only in the greenhouse or in frost-free parts of Calif. and Fla. Others, especially *Coleus* and the Mexican salvias, are used as summer bedding plants throughout the country. These valuable garden genera are: *Coleus* (foliage plant), *Colquhounia* (shrub), *Iboza, Leonotis, Prostanthera,* and *Salvia* (but *see* above for hardy species).

Technical flower characters: Flowers hermaphrodite.* Calyx regular* or 2-lipped,* usually 5-toothed or 5-parted, corolla irregular,* nearly always 2-lipped.* Stamens* 4, two longer than the others. Ovary superior,* deeply 4-lobed, ultimately separating into four 1-seeded nutlets.

Lablab. Egyptian vernacular for the hyacinth bean (*Dolichos Lablab*).

LABRADOR TEA = *Ledum groenlandicum.*

Labrusca (la-brus′ka). Latin name for a wild vine, but not necessarily for a grape to which it was applied. See VITIS LABRUSCA.

LABRUSCA GRAPE. A cultivated variety of the fox grape (*Vitis Labrusca*).

LABURNOCYTISUS. A bigeneric* hybrid between *Cytisus* and *Laburnum.* The only known case of it is the plant called *Laburnum adami,* which is of more scientific than hort. interest.

---

* Special articles on the subjects indicated by an asterisk (*) will be found at the words so marked.

LABURNUM (la-bur'num). A small genus of deciduous trees or shrubs in the pea family. The alternate° leaves are composed of three leaflets. The flowers are pea-like, borne in terminal, usually pendulous clusters (racemes°) and followed by linear pods. (*Laburnum* is the Latin name used by Pliny.)

The trees are handsome objects in the spring when the clusters of bright yellow flowers are produced. They are of quite simple culture, growing even on rocky slopes and standing some shade, effective in shrub borders or as a single specimen. Seed usually germinates freely and is the simplest means of propagation. All parts of the plant, especially the young fruits and the seeds, are poisonous if eaten.

adami. *See* LABURNOCYTISUS.
alpinum. Small trees of stiff, upright habit growing about 20–30 ft. high. Leaflets 3, oval, 1½–2½ in. long, usually glabrous. Flowers yellow, about ¾ in. across in slender pendulous clusters sometimes to 15 in. long. June. Mountains of southern Europe. Hardy from zone° 3 southward.
anagyroides. Golden chain, or bean tree. Shrub or small tree growing about 20 ft. high, though occasionally higher; often branching close to the ground. Leaves composed of 3 leaflets, downy beneath. Flowers yellow, about ¾ in. across in racemes° 4–12 in. long; pod about 2 in. long. May–June. Southern Europe. Hardy from zone° 3 southward. This species has shorter racemes than the preceding and blooms perhaps two weeks earlier. The *var.* **aureum** is a form with yellow leaves.
vossi = *L. watereri.*
vulgare = *Laburnum anagyroides.*
watereri. A hybrid tree (*anagyroides* × *alpinum*), not very different from *L. alpinum*, but the leaves and stems of the flower clusters hairy. *L. watereri* also has longer flower clusters (racemes°) and the flowers are nearly golden yellow. May–June. Hardy from zone° 5 southward and in protected sites in zone° 4. A very handsome tree.

LACEBARK. *See* HOHERIA.

LACE-FERN = *Cheilanthes gracillima.*

LACE-FLOWER. *See* TRACHYMENE.

LACE-LEAF = *Aponogeton fenestralis.*

LACERATE. Torn into shreds or divisions.

LACE-VINE = *Polygonum auberti.*

LACHENALIA (lack-en-ā'lĭ-a). South African greenhouse and bulbous herbs of the lily family, two of the 40 known species grown in pots for their showy flowers, and usually called Cape cowslip. Leaves 1 or 2, or few, basal and without marginal teeth. Flowers red and yellow, drooping (in ours), borne in a terminal cluster (spike or raceme°) at the end of a stalk that rises from the leaves. Corolla cylindric, tubular, its outer 3 segments shorter than the 3 inner. Stamens° 6. Fruit a 3-angled capsule.° (Named for Werner de Lachenal, Swiss professor.)

The culture of the Cape cowslips is the same as for *Freesia* (which see). They are propagated by offsets, and, more rarely, by seeds, but they may also be increased by leaf cuttings. *See* Leaf Cuttings at CUTTINGS.

pendula. A stouter plant than the next, the leaves nearly 2 in. wide. Flowers about 1½ in. long, the outer segments yellow below but red above, and nearly as long as the inner ones, which are red-purple at the tip. Also called *L. bulbifera.*
tricolor. Not over 12 in. high, the leaves 2 to each plant, not over 1 in. wide, but as long as the flowering stalk, often purple-spotted. Flowers many in the cluster, the corolla about 1 in. long, its shorter outer segments yellow but green-tipped, the inner ones yellow but red-tipped. There is also a form, *var.* **nelsoni**, with yellow flowers, but with all of the segments green-tipped. Also called *L. aloides.*

LACHNANTHES (lack-nan'theez). A single bog herb, of the Haemodoraceae or bloodwort family. It is **L. tinctoria**, the redroot, found in acid, sandy bogs from Nova Scotia to Fla. and La. It has mostly basal, narrow leaves with a few on the stem, which is gray-hairy at the top. Flower cluster terminal, woolly, the flowers a dingy yellow. Corolla 6-parted nearly to the base, about ½ in. long. Stamens° 3, opposite the three larger and inner segments. Fruit a small, globe-shaped capsule.° The plant, sometimes known as *Gyrotheca*, is of only secondary hort. interest, but its red roots once furnished a dye. (*Lachnanthes* is from the Greek for wool and flower, in allusion to the woolly flower clusters.)

LACINARIA = *Liatris.*

laciniata, -us, -um (la-sin-ĭ-ā'ta). Laciniate; *i.e.*, cut into narrow, almost fringe-like segments.

laciniosa, -us, -um (la-sin-ĭ-ō'sa). Much torn or fringed.

Lacryma-Jobi (lack-ri-ma-joe'bi). A specific name meaning Job's tears. *See* COIX.

lactea, -us, -um (lak'tee-a). Milk-white.

lactiflora, -us, -um (lack-ti-flō'ra). With milk-white flowers.

LACTUCA (lak-too'ka). A large genus of milky-juiced herbs of the family Compositae, mostly from the north temperate zone, most of them weedy, but one species important as the source of lettuce. Leaves alternate° (except in the much-modified lettuce), usually cut or divided, often with the margin softly prickly. Flower heads small, usually nodding, mostly in large, terminal, branching clusters (panicles°), the florets all ray° flowers, yellow, pink, blue, or white (never produced in properly grown head lettuce). The bracts° beneath each head form a cylindric, apparently tubular involucre.° Fruit a flat achene° (the lettuce "seed"). (*Lactuca* is from the Latin for milk, in allusion to the milky juice.)

Except for lettuce, the genus comprises very weedy plants of no garden interest. One of them is the prickly lettuce, which is a common pest in gardens. *See* WEEDS.

perennis. A perennial, weedy herb 15–30 in. high. Leaves deeply lobed, the segments narrow, the upper leaves stem-clasping. Flower

* Special articles on the subjects indicated by an asterisk (°) will be found at the words so marked.

heads blue or pale violet, long-stalked. Southern Eu.

sativa. Lettuce. An annual herb, its flowering stalks 3–4 ft. high, but only produced after the common garden lettuce has produced its head of leaves. The lower leaves are normally long, narrow, or sometimes nearly roundish, but much modified in the crispy, curled leaves of the cult. lettuce. Flowers yellow. It is supposed to be a cultigen* of Eurasian origin. In its wild form the plant is practically unknown or rarely cult. by experts for breeding. So far as garden forms are concerned they fall into four varieties:

var. **asparagina.** Asparagus lettuce. The thickened stem is used for food. Rare in cult. See CELTUCE.

var. **capitata.** Common head lettuce. The leaves are in a compact head; actually it is a dense, shortened rosette.

var. **crispa.** Garden or leaf lettuce. Leaves loose, not head-forming, crisped or crinkled.

var. **longifolia.** Cos lettuce or Romaine lettuce. A form with long, loose, but rather columnar heads.

For culture *see* LETTUCE.

Scariola = Prickly lettuce. *See* list at WEEDS.

lacunosa, -us, -um (lak-kew-nō'sa). Pitted.

ladanifera, -us, -um (la-da-nif'fer-a). Bearing labdanum, a dark-colored, soft, fragrant resin.

LADIES'-TRESSES = *Spiranthes cernua.*

LADINO CLOVER = *Trifolium repens giganteum.* *See* CLOVER.

LADY BANKS' ROSE = *Rosa banksiae.*

LADYBELL = *Adenophora.*

LADY FERN = *Athyrium Filix-femina.*

LADY-OF-THE-NIGHT = *Brunfelsia americana.*

LADY'S-BEDSTRAW = *Galium verum.*

LADY'S-EARDROPS. See FUCHSIA.

LADY'S-MANTLE = *Alchemilla alpina.*

LADY'S-SLIPPER. See CYPRIPEDIUM and IMPATIENS.

LADY'S-SMOCK = *Cardamine pratensis.*

LADY'S-THISTLE = *Silybum Marianum.*

LADY'S-THUMB = *Polygonum Persicaria.* *See* list at WEEDS.

LADY WASHINGTON GERANIUM = *Pelargonium domesticum.*

LAELIA (lay'le-a). Tropical American, tree-perching orchids, comprising perhaps 35 species, a few much grown in greenhouses for their showy flowers, and several others, together with many hybrids, prized by orchid fanciers. They have pseudobulbs* which are short, or longer and stem-like, and bear 1 or 2 stiffish, rather long leaves without marginal teeth. Flowers one, few, or several in a long-stalked cluster (raceme*). Sepals* nearly of equal length, free, and petal-like. Petals wider than the sepals, more spreading. Lip* more or less 3-lobed, the lateral ones smaller than the broad, expanded, central one. (*Laelia* is named for a vestal virgin or for Gaius Laelius, a Roman statesman.)

For culture *see* the epiphytic orchids among the greenhouse species at ORCHID.

anceps. Much the most widely grown and not uncommon in the florists' shops. Pseudobulbs* oblongish and flattened. Leaves 6–9 in. long, oblongish, thick and rather stiff. Flowering stalk arising at the end of the pseudobulb,* 18–30 in. long, more or less jointed and with a few bracts.* Flowers 2–5, rarely only 1, in a cluster, nearly 4 in. wide, very showy, and pale rose-purple, but the lip yellowish inside. The front lobe, also, is deep purple (and white-marked) and with a yellow keel.* Mex. Blooming Nov.–Jan. in the greenhouse. There are many named forms and hybrids.

digbyana = *Brassavola digbyana.*

grandis. Pseudobulbs* nearly 10 in. long, and bearing only 1 leaf nearly or quite as long. Flowers in pairs, nearly 6 in. wide, very handsome. The sepals and petals are both brownish-yellow. Lip wavy-toothed, generally white but veined or striped with violet. Brazil. Blooming April–June in the greenhouse.

LAELIOCATTLEYA (lay-lĭ-o-cat'lee-a). A group of bigeneric* hybrids between species of *Laelia* and *Cattleya.* Over four dozen of these showy orchids are known to orchid specialists, but they are not much grown by the average owner of a greenhouse.

laeta, -us, -um (lee'ta). Bright or vivid.

laetiflora, -us, -um (lee-ti-flaw'ra). Beautiful-flowered.

laetivirens (lee-ti-vy'renz). Light green.

laevicaulis, -e (lee-vĭ-kaw'lis). Smooth-stemmed.

laevigata, -us, -um (lee-vĭ-gay'ta). Smooth.

laevis, -e (lee'vis). Smooth.

LAGENARIA (laj-en-ā'rĭ-a). A single species of annual, Old World tropical vines of the cucumber family, widely planted for its hard-shelled fruits commonly called calabash gourd (the source of calabash pipes), dipper gourd, and many other names. The only species, **L. siceraria**, the white-flowered gourd, is a musky-scented, quick-growing vine with a sticky-hairy stem and branched tendrils.* Leaves alternate,* broadly oval or kidney-shaped, 6–10 in. wide, not lobed or only faintly so. Male and female flowers separate but on the same plant, white, rather showy, usually withering by midday, 2–4 in. wide. Petals 5. Fruit very variable, 3–36 in. long, round or flattish, crooknecked, bottle-shaped, dipper-shaped, club-shaped, or like a dumbbell, the hard rind used for many purposes in the tropics. The plant is easily raised from seed sown where wanted, but it needs heat and a long growing season to produce its fruits. Also called *L. vulgaris.* See GOURDS. (*Lagenaria* is from the Latin for a bottle, in allusion to its fruit. *Lagenaria* is also a specific name at *Chaenomeles.*)

LAGER-BEER PLANT = *Aspidistra elatior.*

LAGERSTROEMIA (lay-ger-stree'mĭ-a). A genus of about 30 species of decorative shrubs and trees of the family Lythraceae, all from warm regions of the Old World, one widely cult. for its showy bloom. They have opposite* leaves, or the uppermost alternate,* without marginal teeth. Flowers in showy

---

* Special articles on the subjects indicated by an asterisk (*) will be found at the words so marked.

terminal clusters (panicles*), pink, purple
(or white in some **varieties**), the calyx more
or less turban-shaped. Petals 6, usually with
a long claw,* the limb* crinkled or fringed.
Fruit a capsule.* (Named by Linnaeus for his
friend Magnus von Lagerstroem.)

For culture *see* below.

Flos-reginae = *Lagerstroemia speciosa.*

indica. Crape myrtle; also spelled crêpe
myrtle. A shrub or tree up to 20 ft., the bark
shreddy in summer, the twigs 4-angled. Leaves
nearly stalkless, elliptic to oblongish, 1–2 in.
long. Flowers pink, about 1½ in. wide, the
cluster 4–9 in. long. China. Blooms all summer,
according to variety. Hardy from zone* 5 southward and perfectly hardy on the eastern shore of
Md. from Easton southward. Considered by
many as the most spectacularly showy deciduous, summer-flowering shrub; also with fine
autumnal foliage. For culture *see* below. There
are several varieties, of which *var.* **alba** has
white flowers; *var.* **purpurea,** purple flowers; and
var. **rubra,** red flowers.

speciosa. Queen's-flower. A tree up to 50 ft.
and extremely showy in bloom. Leaves ovalish
to oblong, nearly 12 in. long, thick and leathery.
Flowers purplish, almost 3 in. wide. India to
Aust. Hardy only in zones* 8 and 9, and
planted in Fla. and Calif.

CRAPE MYRTLE CULTURE

Crape myrtles are easily grown from seed
and plants sometimes bloom the first season.
Seedlings cannot be depended upon to reproduce true to flower color of the tree from
which seed was gathered, but by growing
from seed, new or different colors and growth
forms may be secured. Dormant cuttings root
readily when set in open ground in warmer
parts of the country and such cuttings, of
course, can be rooted in a greenhouse in the
usual way. Greenwood cuttings taken in summer also are satisfactory for propagation under
glass. Plants secured from cuttings can usu-

Crape Myrtle (*Lagerstroemia indica*). A magnificent shrub, flowering in midsummer and later
in white, pink, and red shades, but not hardy
above zone 5.*

ally be depended upon to bloom in the
second season. Sorts that do not root readily
from cuttings can be grafted (cleft or whip
method) using easily rooted sorts as stocks.
These make good plants.

Widely different soils have been found satisfactory for growing crape myrtles. A goodly
amount of moisture and high fertility give
best results by increasing growth and size of
flower trusses. Farm manures and such commercial fertilizers as are used in growing
other shrubs and trees are satisfactory.

Size of crape myrtles is controlled readily
by pruning and they may be grown as shrubs
or trees. Since flowers are produced on new
growth, the right time to prune is in winter
or early spring before growth starts. At that
time small specimens may be cut back to the
ground and grown as shrubs with several stems
or they can be kept at any height desired by
cutting back to the same level year after
year. This results in developing an enlarged
end of the trunk from which new growth and
larger trusses of flowers are produced. If
trees are grown, only one trunk is allowed
to form and grow. Frequently it is possible
to secure a second set of flowers in a single
season by cutting back branches as soon as the
first flowering is over. — H. H. H.

NOTE: In the Editor's garden, near Princess
Anne, Md., close to the Manokin River there
is a crape myrtle over 25 ft. high, with several
trunks 5–8 in. in diameter. It has repeatedly
withstood winter temperatures of 5°–10°, has
never been pruned, and flowers extravagantly
every year.

LAGUNARIA (lag-you-nair'ĭ-a). A single
species of Pacific Island and Australian evergreen tree of the family Malvaceae, of hort.
interest, as planted in southern Calif. and Fla.
for ornament. The only species is **L. patersoni,**
often called tulip-tree, although it has nothing
to do with the native tulip-tree (which
see). It is a tree up to 50 ft. high with alternate,* oblongish or oval, thick leaves, 3–4
in. long, without marginal teeth, and grayish
beneath. Flowers about 2 in. wide, pale rose-
pink, mostly solitary in the leaf axils.* (For
structure *see* MALVACEAE.) Fruit a capsule*
which splits into 5 parts. Propagated by cuttings, taken in the spring, over bottom-heat.*
An attractive tree resembling hibiscus, but
not hardy above zone* 7. (Named for Andres
de Laguna, Spanish botanist.)

LAGURUS (lag-you'rus). A single species
of annual grass, **L. ovatus** of the Mediterranean region, commonly called hare's-tail
grass or rabbit's-tail grass, and grown for
dried bouquets. It is an erect grass 12–24 in.
high, its narrow, grass-like leaves softly hairy.
The flowering cluster is an oblongish head,
1–2 in. long, and comprised of many 1-flow-
ered spikelets, all softly woolly, and with
slender, protruding awns* about ½ in. long.
Seed may be sown where wanted and culture
is of the easiest. Sometimes grown in pots
for its attractive, long-keeping flowering cluster. (*Lagurus* is Latin for a hare's tail.)

* Special articles on the subjects indicated by an asterisk (*) will be found at the words so marked.

LAMARCKIA (la-mark'ĭ-a). A single species of annual grass, **L. aurea** of the Mediterranean region, commonly grown in the garden under the name of golden-top, for its handsome spikelets. It is a tufted grass about 12 in. high, the leaves numerous, flat, and grasslike, soft to the touch, its sheaths inflated. Spikelets golden-yellow, or even violet, crowded in dense, raceme*-like, drooping clusters which are grouped in a 1-sided cluster, 1–3 in. long. Seed may be sown where wanted, and the plant is of easy culture in any garden soil. It is sometimes offered as *Achyrodes*. (Named for J. B. Lamarck, French naturalist.)

LAMBERT GARDENS. *See* No. 9 at GARDEN TOURS.

LAMBKILL = *Kalmia angustifolia*.

LAMB'S-EARS = *Stachys lanata*.

LAMB'S-LETTUCE = *Valerianella Locusta olitoria*.

LAMB'S-QUARTERS = Pigweed. *See* list at WEEDS.

LAMIACEAE = Labiatae.

LAMIUM (lay'mi-um). Dead nettle. A genus of somewhat weedy Old World herbs of the mint family, of secondary garden interest, although three of its 40 known species are occasionally grown in the herbaceous border. They have opposite,* stalked leaves and a square stem. Flowers in close clusters (whorls*) crowded in the leaf axils,* or terminal. Corolla irregular and 2-lipped,* the lower lip 3-lobed. Stamens* 4. Fruit a collection of small nutlets surrounded by the withered calyx.* (*Lamium* is from the Greek for throat, in allusion to the shape of the corolla.)

The plants below are of the easiest culture in any ordinary garden soil. *Lamium maculatum* and *L. Galeobdolon* can be increased by division, while the seed of *L. purpureum*, an annual, may be sown where it is to stay.

aureum = *L. Galeobdolon*.
Galeobdolon. Yellow archangel. A perennial, 12–18 in. high. Leaves ovalish, about 1½ in. long, the margins doubly toothed, the teeth crenate.* Flowers yellow, about ¾ in. long, in dense clusters in the leaf axils.* Eu. Summer.
maculatum. An erect or half-straggling perennial herb, the tips of its branches more or less upright. Leaves ovalish or heart-shaped, silver-marked, 1–2 in. long. Flowers purple-red, rarely white, nearly 1 in. long, the upper lip* of the corolla distinctly arched. Eu. June–Aug.
purpureum. Red dead nettle; also called French nettle. An annual, more or less sprawling herb 9–15 in. high. Leaves ovalish, ¾–1½ in. long. Flowers purple-red, about ½ in. long. Eurasia, but naturalized in N.A. Summer.

LAMPRANTHUS. *See* MESEMBRYANTHEMUM.

lanata, -us, -um (la-nay'ta). Lanate, *i.e.*, woolly or wool-like.

lancastriensis, -e (lan-kast-ri-en'sis). From Lancaster, England, or Lancaster, Pa.

lanceolata, -us, -um (lan-see-o-lay'ta). Lanceolate (which see).

LANCEOLATE. More or less lance-shaped; *i.e.*, much longer than broad and tapering toward a slender, pointed tip. Typically lanceolate leaves are those of the peach or willow.

lancifolia, -us, -um (lan-si-fō'li-a). Having lanceolate* leaves.

LAND PLASTER. *See* GYPSUM.

LANDSCAPE ARCHITECTURE. *See* PLANNING THE HOME GROUNDS.

LANDSCAPE GARDENING. For centuries men who practiced what, in America, is called landscape architecture were proud of a profession which Wordsworth called the greatest of the arts. But they called themselves landscape gardeners, a term in disrepute among garden designers in America. They say that a landscape gardener here may be an itinerant laborer with a pushcart, a lawn mower, and a box of geraniums — scarcely a designer. It remains true, however, that in England, France, and Germany very talented designers of gardens still prefer to call themselves landscape gardeners. And so did Le Nôtre, the designer of Versailles, and the greatest of all landscape architects.

LANDSCAPE MODELS. *See* MODEL GARDENS.

lanosa, -us, -um (la-no'sa). Woolly.

LANTANA (lan-tā'na). Tropical or subtropical shrubs of the family Verbenaceae, one of the 50 known species much planted outdoors from zone* 7 southward, and frequently grown as a pot plant or for summer bedding for its profuse bloom. They are generally opposite*-leaved shrubs, usually with a hairy, sometimes prickly, stem. Flowers small, borne in dense clusters (spikes or heads) which may be terminal or in the leaf axils.* Calyx minute. Corolla tubular, 4–5-parted, slightly irregular,* but not 2-lipped.* Stamens 4. Fruit fleshy (a drupe*), with 2 hard seeds. (*Lantana* is an old name of uncertain application here; also applied as the species name of a *Viburnum*.)

The first species is a very ornamental shrub throughout the South and in Calif., where it thrives in every sort of soil. Northward it must be grown in the cool greenhouse in potting mixture* 3 and is widely used as a summer bedding plant in the North. It is also a rugged house plant. It can be forced into bloom almost at any time by increasing the heat. *See* FORCING. Cuttings of softwood root easily. For a method of training it *see* Pinching at TRAINING PLANTS.

Camara. Red or yellow sage. Not usually over 4 ft. high, much more in the tropics, occasionally prickly. Leaves ovalish or heart-shaped, 2–6 in. long, with rounded teeth, roughish above and hairy beneath. Flower clusters 1–2 in. wide, flat-topped, usually on stalks longer than the leafstalks. Flowers about ⅓ in. wide, yellow at first, then orange or red, sometimes all three colors simultaneously in a single cluster. Tropical America, north to Tex. and Fla. Hardy from zone* 7 southward. Foliage unpleasantly scented.
delicatissima = *L. montevidensis*.
flava. Common in some catalogues, but ap-

---

* Special articles on the subjects indicated by an asterisk (*) will be found at the words so marked.

parently a yellow-flowered form or state of *Lantana Camara.*

montevidensis. A vine-like shrub (*see* VINES), but not tall-growing, and mostly used as a trailer. Leaves ovalish, about 1 in. long. Flowers pinkish-lilac, the clusters about 1½ in. wide. S.A.

sellowiana = *L. montevidensis.*

LANTERN-PLANT. See PHYSALIS.

LANTERN-TREE = *Crinodendron hookerianum.*

lantoscana, -us, -um (lan-tos-cay′na). From Lantosque in the Maritime Alps.

lanuginosa, -us, -um (lan-you-ji-nō′sa). Downy.

LAPAGERIA (lap-a-jeer′ĭ-a). A single species of showy Chilean vine of the lily family, L. rosea, the Chilean bellflower (for another *see* NOLANA). It is grown outdoors from Ore. to Calif. and in Fla., more rarely in the cool greenhouse. It is a tall-growing, handsome vine with alternate,* rather leathery, 3-veined, short-stalked leaves. Flowers rose-colored, solitary or a few together, 3–4 in. long, trumpet-shaped, but with separate segments. Fruit berry-like, beaked. There is a *var.* **albiflora** with white flowers, and another with red flowers. It needs partial shade and does not like open, sunny or windy places. Propagated by layering (which is the easiest method) or by seeds. (Named for Marie Josèphe Tascher de la Pagerie who became the Empress Josephine.)

LAPEYROUSIA (la-pay-roo′si-a). Also spelled *Lapeirousia.* South African bulbous herbs of the iris family comprising 20 species, related to *Freesia,* but more hardy. They have small corms* and mostly basal, narrow, 2-ranked leaves. Flowers small, not fragrant, red or blue, summer-blooming, from between spathe*-like bracts.* Corolla tubular, slender, slightly swollen where the spreading, nearly equal segments diverge. Fruit a small, 3-valved capsule.* (Named for Philippe Picot de la Peirouse, French savant.) Sometimes called *Anomatheca.*

Corms should be planted 3–4 in. deep in the spring, in any ordinary garden soil. The plants are perfectly hardy from zone* 5 southward, but north of this they should have a winter mulch of straw or litter. They should be divided every few years or they become too crowded. Wherever hardy they self-sow freely.

cruenta. Leaves 6–10 in. long, thin and flat. Flowering stalk about as long, the few flowers in a 1-sided cluster (spike or raceme*). Corolla red, nearly 1½ in. long, the tube very slender. Also known as *L. laxa.*

juncea. Leaves 5–8 in. long and about ¾ in. wide. Flowering stalk 12–20 in. long, the few flowers in loose clusters (spikes). Corolla pale red, about ¾ in. long.

Lappa (lap′pa). Classical name for a bur. *See* Burdock in the list at WEEDS.

lapponica, -us, -um (lap-pon′i-ka). From Lapland.

LARCH. Trees in the pine family belonging to the genus **Larix** (lar′icks), comprising about 10 species. They have the typical pine habit, a cone-shaped head and more or less horizontal branches, but with leaves that are dropped in the fall. The leaves are narrow and needle-like; on actively growing branches they appear singly and are spirally arranged; on the short, lateral spur-like growths they are crowded into terminal clusters. The male and female flowers are borne separately on the same tree; the cone scales are woody and persistent. (*Larix* is the ancient name of the larch.)

The larches are valuable timber trees and are widely cultivated as ornamentals because of their attractive habit. They do well in almost any soil, preferring an open site where there is moisture and good drainage; the American larch usually grows in acid bogs. Propagation by seed is the best method. A rather serious insect trouble is the larch sawfly. It hibernates over the winter in cocoons in surface litter and in this stage is ʽᵉre to be ignored. The sawflies appear in May or June and may strip the foliage. The best remedy is to spray with pesticide #1 or #19 (*see* SPRAYS AND DUSTS) in May or June.

L. americana = *Larix laricina.*

L. dahurica = *Larix gmelini.*

L. decidua. European larch. Tree of 100 ft. or more, the habit pyramidal when young, later becoming irregular. Branchlets slender, yellow-gray, not downy. Leaves narrow, about 1 in. long, midrib raised on lower surface. Cones oval, to 1½ in. long with 40–50 rounded scales, downy on the back. Northern and central Europe. Hardy from zone* 2 southward.

L. europaea = *Larix decidua.*

L. gmelini. Dahurian larch. Tree of about 90 ft. with wide-spreading, horizontal branches; branchlets brown. Leaves narrow, an inch or more long. Cones small, ovoid, ¾–1 in. long with about 20 scales that are downy on the back; pink when young. Northern Asia. Hardy from zone* 1 southward; *var.* **japonica**, a form in which the branchlets are downy and usually red; northern Jap.; *var.* **principis-ruprechti**, cones larger, to 1½ in. long and with 30–40 scales; northern China.

L. kaempferi = *L. leptolepis.*

L. laricina. American larch, often called tamarack or hackmatack. Tree of rather narrow, cone-shaped form, growing 60 ft. or more. Young shoots brownish, glabrous, and sometimes bloomy. Leaves slender, blunt, to 1½ in. long. Cones oval or rounded, to ¾ in. long, scales 12–15. Labrador south to W. Va. and westward. Hardy from zone* 1 southward.

L. leptolepis. Japanese larch. A tree up to 90 ft. high, its scaly bark leaving red scars. Leaves flattened, ¾–1½ in. long, blunt, bluish-green, white-banded below. Cones egg-shaped, ¾–1¼ in. long. Jap. Hardy from zone* 3 southward. A very handsome, quick-growing larch, sometimes offered as *L. kaempferi* and occasionally confused with *Pseudolarix amabilis* (which see).

LARDIZABALACEAE (lar-diz-a-ba-lay′-see-ee). A small family of mostly woody vines, comprising 8 genera and about 20 species, three genera of which, *Akebia, Decaisnea,* and *Stauntonia,* are grown for ornament. All are Asiatic. *See also* VINES.

---

* Special articles on the subjects indicated by an asterisk (*) will be found at the words so marked.

Leaves alternate* and compound* in all the cult. genera with the leaflets arranged finger-fashion. Flowers unisexual* or polygamous,* not very showy, without petals, but in *Akebia* often attractive and brownish-purple, nearly always in racemes.* Fruit a berry in *Stauntonia*, but a fleshy, black-seeded pod in *Akebia* and *Decaisnea*.

Technical flower characters: Sepals 6 in *Stauntonia*, 3 in *Akebia*, petal-like. Petals none. Stamens 6. Ovary superior,* usually with many ovules.

LARGE-LEAVED CUCUMBER TREE = *Magnolia macrophylla*.

LARGE-LEAVED LINDEN = *Tilia platyphyllos*. See LINDEN.

LARGE-LEAVED TOMATO = *Lycopersicum esculentum grandifolium*. See TOMATO.

LARGER YELLOW LADY'S-SLIPPER. *See* CYPRIPEDIUM CALCEOLUS.

LARGE-TOOTHED ASPEN = *Populus grandidentata*.

laricina, -us, -um (lar-i-sy′na). Larchlike.

Laricio (lar-iss′ĭ-o). An old name for some larch-like evergreen. *See Pinus Laricio* at PINE.

LARIX. *See* LARCH.

LARKSPUR. *See* DELPHINIUM.

LARREA (lar′re-a). A genus of 5 or 6 species of heavily scented desert shrubs from the southwestern states and adjoining Mexico, and the only cult. representatives of the family **Zygophyllaceae** (zy-go-fil-lay′see-ee). The family includes about 26 genera and over 250 species of herbs, shrubs, or trees, mostly from warm or tropical regions, usually with opposite* compound* leaves, the leaflets arranged feather-fashion. In the genus *Larrea*, only **L. tridentata**, the creosote bush or greasewood, is of any garden interest, and then only for desert gardens within its natural range. It is an evergreen, balsam-scented, much-branched and resinous shrub, 5–8 ft. high. Leaflets 2, stalkless, more or less oblique and ovalish, about ⅓ in. long. Flowers yellow, solitary, terminal, about ¼ in. long, the petals separate. Stamens* 8–10. Fruit a globe-shaped, white-felty small capsule.* The plant needs a light sandy soil and intense sunlight. (Named for J. A. de Larrea, a Spanish patron of science.)

LARVA (plural larvae). The worm-like or grub-like and wingless stage in the life-history of many insects. The larvae of some moths and butterflies are among the most destructive of the garden pests, and in this stage are usually called grubs, maggots, or caterpillars. *See* INSECT PESTS.

lasiacantha, -us, -um (lay-sĭ-a-kan′tha). Woolly-spined.

lasiandra, -us, -um (lay-sĭ-and′ra). With woolly stamens.*

lasiantha, -us, -um (lay-sĭ-an′tha). Woolly-flowered.

lasiocarpa, -us, -um (lay-sĭ-o-kar′pa). Woolly-fruited.

LASTHENIA (las-thee′ni-a). A small genus of Pacific Coast annual herbs of the family Compositae, one of them, **L. glabrata**, a tender annual, but not of primary hort. interest. It is a slightly fleshy herb 12–18 in. high, with opposite* narrow leaves, 1–2 in. long, the bases of which are joined around the stem. Flower heads yellow, about 1 in. wide, composed of both ray* and disk* flowers. Below the head the bracts* are joined to form a cup-like involucre.* It should be grown as a tender annual. *See* ANNUALS. The *var.* **californica** (sometimes offered as *Lasthenia californica*) is a form in which the leaf bases are not united. (Named for a woman pupil of Plato.)

LATANIA (la-tay′ni-a). A small genus of medium-sized fan palms of the islands of the Indian Ocean, two of them occasionally grown in Fla. and Calif. for ornament. Florists also apply the name *Latania borbonica* to the Chinese fan palm, a widely cult. greenhouse plant better known as *Livistona chinensis* (which see). The true latanias have unarmed trunks, although the long, stiff leafstalks are occasionally prickly on young plants, as are also the leaf margins. The leaves are large, with many pointed segments. Flower clusters from among the crown of leaves, usually several feet long. Male and female flowers on separate trees, only the female fruiting. Male cluster comprised of dense spikes, the 15–30 stamens* in sunken pits. Female cluster looserflowered. Fruit somewhat fleshy, yellow, 1–2½ in. long. (*Latania* is a Latinized version of a native vernacular for these trees.)

For culture *see* PALM.

borbonica = *Livistona chinensis*, so far as the usual cult. plants are concerned. The true *L. borbonica* is scarcely known in cult. The plant grown under that name is usually the next species.

commersoni. Not over 40 ft. high. Leaves nearly 5 ft. wide, the stalk and ribs crimson, especially on young plants. Leaf segments nearly 3 in. wide at the base (on old plants). Fruit nearly globe-shaped, ribbed. A very handsome but little cult. palm, occasionally planted in Fla. Mauritius.

loddigesi. A taller palm, but as cult. usually not over 10–20 ft. high. Leaves 3–5 ft. wide, bluish-green, the veins slightly reddish, especially on young plants. Leaf segments mostly less than 3 in. wide at the base, about 2 ft. long. The leafstalk is often spiny on young plants, merely hairy in age, 3–4½ ft. long. Fruit pear-shaped, 3-angled. Mauritius. Sometimes planted in Fla.

LATE. *See* EARLY.

LATERAL. Borne on or at the side; not central nor terminal.

lateritia, -us, -um (la-ter-rĭ′she-a). Brickred.

LATERITIC SOIL. *See* Origin of Soils at SOILS.

LATEX. *See* SAP.

LATH HOUSE. A "greenhouse" without glass and made of laths or slats so placed that

---

* Special articles on the subjects indicated by an asterisk (*) will be found at the words so marked.

there is ample circulation of air, but only about half the usual amount of light. The laths are usually about 1 in. apart. Lath houses are much used in tropical and sub-tropical regions for growing orchids and ferns,

Lath house

which find congenial quarters within the shaded, wind-free lath house. They are also used in temperate regions for plants needing shade, like the ginseng.

LATH SCREEN. See TRELLISES.

LATHYRUS (lă'thi-russ). An important group of annual or perennial herbs of the pea family, comprising over 160 species, chiefly from the north temperate zone. One of them is the ever-popular sweet pea, and several others are also widely grown for ornament. All our cult. species, except *L. vernus* and *L. splendens,* are tendril-bearing, vine-like plants, usually with winged or angled stems. Leaves alternate,* compound,* the leaflets usually few. Flowers typically pea-like, often very showy, especially in the cult. strains of the sweet pea. (For details of the typical pea flower *see* LEGUMINOSAE.) Fruit a flattish pod (legume*). (*Lathyrus* is an old Greek name for some plant of the pea family, but perhaps not for these.)

For the culture and varieties of *Lathyrus odoratus see* SWEET PEA. The perennial species (noted as such below) are of easy culture in most garden soils and bloom most of the summer. Some of them are very popular stem-climbing vines (*see* VINES) for covering porches. Two of them, *L. maritimus* and *L. littoralis,* are sea-beach plants suited only to sandy soils. The easiest way to increase any of them is by seeds, but the young pods should be picked off the plants that are to produce the most and best flowers, leaving only a few pods for seed supply. All except *Lathyrus vernus* and *L. splendens* have only 2 leaflets. For the garden pea *see* PEA. Some of the small species are occasionally called vetchling.

grandiflorus. Everlasting pea. A perennial, climbing by tendrils* up to 6 ft. or more. Leaflets ovalish, 1–1½ in. long. Flowers 2–3 together, on a long stalk, rose-purple, somewhat fragrant, nearly 1½ in. wide, very showy. Pod about 3 in. long. Southern Eu. *See* Stem Climbers at VINES.

latifolius. Perennial pea; also called ever-lasting pea. A perennial, climbing by tendrils up to 9 ft. or more. Leaflets ovalish or narrower, 2–4 in. long. Flowers several in a long-stalked cluster, rose-pink (or white or darker in some hort. forms), 1–1½ in. wide. Pod 3–5 in. long. Eu. A common garden plant coming in various colors, and so rampant that, without control, it can become a nuisance.

littoralis. Beach pea (in Calif.). A sprawling, perennial seashore plant, suited chiefly to its native region from Wash. to Calif. Leaflets wedge-shaped or oblongish, silky-hairy. Flowers 2–6 in a cluster, about 1 in. wide, purple and white. *See* SAND GARDEN.

maritimus. Beach pea (along the Atlantic coast). A sprawling perennial, sand dune plant suited only to open sandy soils. Leaflets oblongish or ovalish, perfectly smooth. Flowers in clusters of 6–10, showy, about 1 in. wide, violet-purple. Coasts of the north temperate zone. *See* SAND GARDEN.

odoratus. The common sweet pea. An annual vine-like plant, 4–6 ft. high. Leaflets ovalish or oblong, 1–2 in. long, usually with a short, softly spiny tip. Flowers fragrant, 1–3, rarely 4, in a cluster, often 2 in. wide in some hort. varieties, of many colors as now cult., perhaps originally only purple. Pod about 2 in. long, hairy. Seeds nearly globe-shaped, hard, and grayish-brown. Italy. For culture and best varieties *see* SWEET PEA.

splendens. Pride-of-California. Campo pea. A perennial, more or less shrubby and not high-climbing. Leaflets ovalish or oblong, about 1 in. long, usually in 2–5 pairs. Flowers 6–12 in a stout-stalked cluster, pale rose-pink, or violet, or even magenta, very showy, about 1 in. wide. Pod 2–3 in. long, smooth and beaked. Southern Calif. and little known elsewhere.

vernus. Spring vetchling. A perennial herb, not climbing, and rarely over 2 ft. high, without tendrils.* Leaflets 2–3 pairs, ovalish, but tapering, 1½–3 in. long, prominently 2-veined. Flowers 5–8 in the cluster, nodding, bluish-violet, about ¾ in. long. Pod about 1½ in. long, smooth. Eu.

latiflora, -us, -um (la-ti-flo'ra). With wide flowers.

latifolia, -us, -um (la-ti-fō'li-a). Broadleaved.

latiloba, -us, -um (lat-i-low'ba). Broadlobed.

latisquama, -us, -um (la-ti-skway'ma). Having broad, scale-like leaves or bracts.*

latiuscula, -us, -um (lat-i-us'kew-la). Somewhat broad.

LATTICE-LEAF = *Aponogeton fenestralis.*

LATTICE-PLANT FAMILY = Aponogetonaceae. *See* APONOGETON.

LAURACEAE (law-ray'see-ee). The laurel, often called the cinnamon or sassafras family, is a very large one. Of its 50 genera and possibly 1000 species, nearly all are trees or shrubs of the tropics, a few of warm regions, and only a handful from the temperate zone. Of the latter the most familiar and widely cult. are *Sassafras, Lindera, Umbellularia* (the California laurel), and *Laurus* (the true laurel of the ancients, not the mountain laurel). The only other cult. genera are *Persea,* which yields the avocado or alligator pear, and

* Special articles on the subjects indicated by an asterisk (*) will be found at the words so marked.

Cinnamomum, which yields the cinnamon and camphor, both chiefly tropical.

All have alternate* leaves (some evergreen) and all are impregnated with a highly aromatic oil, hence the fragrant foliage of the Lauraceae. Flowers usually not very showy, more so in *Persea* and *Lindera* than in the others, chiefly yellow or yellowish-green. Fruit fleshy, a berry* in *Persea*, a drupe* in most other genera.

Technical flower characters: Flowers perfect* (in *Persea* and *Umbellularia*), unisexual* (in *Sassafras* and *Lindera*) or both in the other genera. Petals and sepals scarcely distinguishable as such; combined they usually total 6 more or less petal-like, or at least colored parts. Stamens 9 or 12, some often sterile. Ovary mostly superior.*

LAUREL. The laurel of history and hort. is probably *Laurus nobilis* (which see), commonly called the bay tree (not the bayberry). But laurel is also very frequently applied to other plants: *see* KALMIA, RHODODENDRON, UMBELLULARIA, LAUROCERASUS, DAPHNE LAUREOLA (which may be the laurel of the ancients), and the next few entries.

LAUREL CHERRY = *Laurocerasus caroliniana*.

LAUREL FAMILY. A large group of generally aromatic shrubs and trees containing such diverse plants as the sassafras, spicebush, the true laurel (*see* LAURUS), the cinnamon, the avocado, and many others. For the cult. genera *see* LAURACEAE.

LAUREL OAK. Properly, *Quercus laurifolia*, but sometimes *Q. imbricaria* is so called. See OAK.

LAUREL WILLOW = *Salix pentandra*. See WILLOW.

LAURELWOOD = *Arbutus menziesi*.

LAURESTINUS = Laurustinus.

laurifolia, -us, -um (law-ri-fō′li-a). With leaves like the true laurel (*Laurus*).

laurina, -us, -um (law-ry′na). Like the true laurel (*Laurus*).

LAUROCERASUS (law-ro-se′ra-sus). Evergreen shrubs or trees of the rose family, often considered as part of the genus *Prunus* (the plums and cherries), but here kept separate for their hort. uses. They are usually called cherry laurel because their foliage is evergreen and suggests the true laurel, while no cult. plants of the genus *Prunus* are similarly endowed. Flowers white, in finger-shaped clusters (racemes*) which are leafless at the base. Fruit inedible, a more or less egg- or cone-shaped, 1-seeded drupe.* (*Laurocerasus* is a combination of the Latin names for laurel and cherry.)

These are handsome evergreen shrubs or trees prized for their lustrous green foliage even more than for the small white flowers. They are not hardy in the North, as noted below, but are favorite plants in suitable climates, where they grow well on a variety of soils. Propagated easily by seed or by cuttings of mature wood under glass. Can be sheared for hedges or other formal effects.

caroliniana. Laurel cherry; also called mock-orange, cherry laurel, and wild orange (it is no orange). A tree up to 40 ft. high. Leaves oblongish or narrower, almost without marginal teeth. Flowers small, scarcely ¼ in. wide, the cluster slender, milky-white. Fruit black and shining, about ½ in. long. N. Car. to Tex. Hardy from zone* 5 southward. Often called *Prunus caroliniana*.

lusitanica. Portuguese cherry laurel. Much resembling the next, but with the toothed leaves shorter than the flower clusters; also it is a taller tree. Spain and Portugal. Hardy from zone* 5 southward. Often called *Prunus lusitanica*. The *var.* **variegata** has white-margined leaves.

officinalis. The common cherry laurel; sometimes called English laurel (but it is not the true laurel). An evergreen shrub or small tree up to 20 ft. high. Leaves oblongish, 2½–6 in. long, remotely or not at all toothed, short-stalked. Flowers fragrant, white, about ⅓ in. wide, the cluster shorter than the leaves. Fruit dark purple, about ½ in. long. Southeastern Eu. to Persia. Hardy from zone* 5 southward and a much-planted bush. The *var.* **angustifolia** has narrower leaves; *var.* **rotundifolia**, roundish ones; and the *var.* **pyramidalis** is a pyramid-shaped, almost cone-shaped form; *var.* **schipkaensis** is merely a shrubby form; *var.* **zabeliana** is one of the hardiest of all the varieties. There are many other forms of this very popular plant which has been cult. for centuries, often under the name of *Prunus Laurocerasus*.

LAURUS (law′rus). A small but important genus of evergreen trees of the family Lauraceae, natives in the Mediterranean region. There are only two species, the cult. one being **L. nobilis**, probably the true laurel of history and the poets, but commonly called bay, bay tree, and sweet bay by gardeners. In Greece it is tree-like and from 40 to 60 ft. high. But as universally grown here it is perhaps the most popular of all tubbed evergreens, usually in the form of standards,* cones, pyramids, or any other shape, as it stands shearing very well. It has stiff, alternate,* oblongish leaves, 3–4 in. long, and without marginal teeth. Flowers small, inconspicuous (*see* LAURACEAE). Fruit a small berry. (*Laurus* is the classical name of the laurel.)

BAY TREE CULTIVATION. (LAUREL)

While the laurel will stand considerable frost, it is not certainly hardy north of zone* 6, and is planted out as part of the shrubbery only south of this. Elsewhere it is grown, perhaps by the million, as a showy evergreen tub plant which needs winter protection. As a decorative, outdoor tub plant from April to October it is very widely used for porches, formal gardens, pools, courtyards, and public buildings, but it is not a good indoor subject as it dislikes dry heat.

Young plants should be potted up in potting mixture* 5 and given plenty of water. As they grow they can finally be sheared into almost any desired shape and put into tubs of a size to be handled without too much effort — for all bay trees in the North must be moved twice a year. They are slow-growing and it takes several years to produce a specimen plant.

In the fall, before hard frosts are due (*see*

---

* Special articles on the subjects indicated by an asterisk (*) will be found at the words so marked.

the name of your state or province for the dates), the laurel tubs should be packed as closely together as they reasonably can be in a shed or deep pit, or in a heavily shaded greenhouse when the temperature can be kept between 38° and 45°. They need little water during the winter, but must not be allowed to dry out. Re-pot in the spring if neces-

Globe-shaped and conical forms of the bay tree, which may be easily sheared to any desired outline.

sary, but do not increase the size of the tub unless absolutely necessary. If the tops are kept sheared to the desired form, the only reason for re-potting is to renew worn-out soil.

The common green bay tree flourishes with considerable neglect, but it does best with plenty of moisture, and care must be taken to see that the tubs do not dry out during the active growing season. Occasionally a variegated or crisp-leaved form is seen, but the common green laurel is the most popular.

LAURUSTINUS = *Viburnum Tinus.*

LAVANDULA (la-van′dew-la). Lavender. Aromatic, Old World perennial herbs or shrubs of the mint family, chiefly grown for their aromatic oil, although the flowers of some species are attractive. Of the 20 or more known species, the true lavender is the only one widely grown and it has been cult. for centuries. Leaves opposite,* without marginal teeth (in ours), and narrow. Flowers lavender or dark purple, crowded into dense clusters in the leaf axils* Corolla irregular,*the upper lip 2-cleft, the lower one 3-cleft. Stamens* 4. not protruding. Fruit a collection of dry nutlets. (*Lavandula* is from the Latin to wash, in allusion to its use in bath water.)

For cult. and uses of the common lavender *see* HERB GARDENING. The only other cult. species is *Lavandula Stoechas*, a shrub which is rarely grown in southern Calif., and is unsuited to most other regions.

officinalis = *Lavandula Spica.*

Spica. The common lavender. An undershrub or woody herb 1–3 ft. high. Leaves narrow, lance-shaped or narrower, 1–2 in. long, often with smaller ones in the axils,* all white-felty and with rolled margins. Flowers about ⅓ in. long, the clusters interrupted.* Mediterranean region. For cult. and uses *see* HERB GARDENING. Sometimes known as *L. officinalis* and *L. vera.* This and the next are both known as French lavender. In mild climates beautiful hedges can be made of lavender.

Stoechas. A shrub 2–3 ft. high, its foliage gray-felty. Leaves narrow and line-like, about ½ in. long. Flowers in dense clusters (spikes), among which are conspicuous purple bracts.* Corolla dark purple. Mediterranean region. Grown in southern Calif. Abroad it is known as stechados or French lavender.

vera = *Lavandula Spica.*

lavanduliaefolia, -us, -um (la-van-du-ly-fōl′i-a). With lavender-like leaves.

LAVATERA (la-va-tee′ra). Tree mallow. A genus of herbs of the family Malvaceae, mostly from the warmer regions of the Old World, a few grown for ornament in the flower garden. Of the 25 known species, the four below are annual, biennial, or perennial herbs, although others are shrubs or even trees. They have hairy stems and alternate,* somewhat maple-like, angled or lobed leaves. Flowers rather showy, pink or purplish in the cult. sorts, and below them a cluster of 3–9 bracts,* united to form an involucre,* Petals 5, notched or cut off at the tip, the base with a claw.* Fruit a collection of beakless, dry, pod-like bodies (schizocarp*). (Named for the brothers Lavater, Swiss naturalists.)

Cultural notes at each species.

arborea. A biennial herb, but forming a tree or shrub-like plant 4–10 ft. high. Leaves 4–9 in. long, nearly as broad, long-stalked, with 5–9 rounded lobes and downy both sides. Flowers about 2 in. wide, pale purplish-red, but purple-veined at the base, born in profuse, short, leafy clusters (racemes*). Eu. Seed should be started the season before bloom is wanted. *See* BIENNIALS. Perhaps the most commonly cult. form is *var.* **variegata,** with white-mottled leaves.

assurgentiflora. A perennial or shrubby plant 6–12 ft. high, confined to the islands off the southern Calif. coast and one of the few American species. It grows there, and in similar climates, often 6 ft. high and blooms the first season from seed. Leaves 3–6 in. wide, the 5–7 more or less triangular lobes coarsely toothed. Flowers about 2 in. wide, purple, stalked, 1–4 in the leaf axil.* Petals with a tuft of hairs on the claw.* Not hardy outside of southern Calif., but used for temporary hedges there because of its quick growth.

cachemiriana. An upright perennial, downy and with a branched stem. Leaves broadly ovalish, long-stalked, 3–5-lobed, the central lobe much the longest. Flowers solitary at the leaf joints, long-stalked, about 2 in. wide, pink. Kashmir.

trimestris. A widely grown, branching annual, 2–3 ft. high, especially in the *var.* **splendens,** which is an improved garden form of the wild species. Leaves irregularly round-toothed. Flowers usually solitary, nearly 4 in. wide, red or rose-pink, and very showy. Mediterranean region. A summer-blooming, hardy an-

---

* Special articles on the subjects indicated by an asterisk (*) will be found at the words so marked.

nual. *See* ANNUALS. There is also a *var.* **alba,** with white flowers.

LAVENDER. The true lavender is *Lavandula Spica* (which see). But *see also* CHRYSANTHEMUM BALSAMITA. For the sea lavender *see* LIMONIUM.

LAVENDER COTTON = *Santolina Chamaecyparissus.*

LAVENDER GARDEN. *See* GRAY AND LAVENDER GARDEN.

LAWN. There is no perfect substitute for a well-kept lawn, but there are many places in the U.S. where fine lawns are impossible. The different grasses that make up the standard lawn mixtures require far less annual rainfall than do trees and shrubs, but they do need an adequate supply during the growing season. If the total rainfall during the growing season falls below 18 or 20 inches, it is next to impossible to have a really fine lawn without more or less constant watering. One can have a lawn of a sort even in these unfavorable places, but it cannot be made of the grasses that are the basis of all the best lawn mixtures as outlined below. For such places there are special kinds of grasses, as there must be also for the South, where summer heat is too much for the best lawn grasses.

So important is this basic rainfall requirement for really fine lawns that anyone contemplating the making of one should verify his local rainfall during the growing season. This is discussed toward the end of each article on the different states and will be found at the name of your state or province.

If your rainfall for the growing season is 18–20 in. or more, you are safe in assuming that you can have a fine lawn if you are willing to observe the few simple rules necessary to have one. If, on the other hand, you live in an unfavorable region, then your lawn must be made of hardier and coarser grasses, which are discussed later.

The basic requirements of a good lawn, assuming adequate rainfall or the ability to overcome an inadequate one by irrigation, are the right sort of soil and the proper mixture of lawn grasses.

SOIL REQUIREMENTS

Any good garden loam will grow a good lawn. The best evidence for such a statement is that of over 200 soil types recognized and named by the U.S. Bureau of Soils, lawns are found on every one. The tolerance of lawn grasses for different sorts of soils stops, however, if they are markedly acid or predominantly sand. If the acidity of the proposed lawn soil is below pH 5.5, it would be foolish to seed down such a site without correcting that acidity. Usually all that is necessary is to broadcast enough agricultural lime just to cover the soil and thoroughly rake it in. This is at the rate of about 75 lbs. per 1000 sq. ft. *See* LIME. If, after a rain or two, the soil still tests acid, it is better to treat it more heavily with lime, as outlined at ACID AND ALKALI SOILS, where there is also a discussion on how

to make the tests. The best of all lawn grasses is particularly intolerant of acidity, so that if your soil is even moderately acid, you should apply agricultural lime a little thicker.

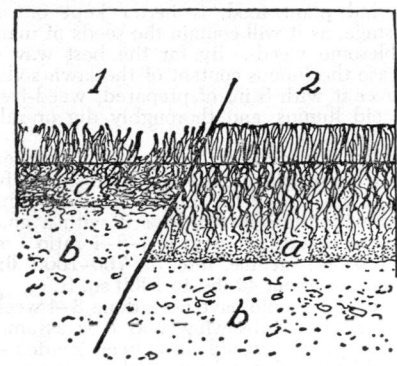

Lawn soils. 1. Topsoil too shallow for proper root development. 2. Topsoil (*a*) deep enough (6–8 in.) to cover properly the subsoil (*b*) and make a good lawn possible.

Soils too high in sand are also unfavorable. They should be either avoided or else treated according to the articles on green manuring and humus, for their humus content must be far better than that of sand to ensure the lawn's survival over a summer drought.

Assuming that you have neither acidity nor sand to contend with, there remains one of the major causes of lawn failure — inadequate depth of soil.

Many statements are made that as grasses are essentially shallow-rooted plants, 4 or 5 in. of good topsoil are all that are needed. If your summer rainfall is very high or you can sprinkle through all droughts, the statement is correct. But it is absolutely incorrect if your region is a more normal one, subject to summer droughts, and you have no facilities for lawn sprinkling. While it is true that most lawn grasses are comparatively shallow-rooted plants, it is much more nearly the truth to say that many thin-soiled sites drive them to be more shallow-rooted than they normally would be.

Good permanent lawns that will survive summer heat and dryness should be grown on not less than 7–8 in. of topsoil, and a foot will do no harm. In such a soil the grasses get a firm, deep hold, which means that their roots are in the coolest and moistest layer of the topsoil. It is impossible to overemphasize the importance of this proper depth of topsoil. If you haven't got at least 7 in., it would be better to improve the soil by crop rotation or green manuring (which see), or else bring in enough topsoil from another place to make the site of the lawn at least 7–8 in. deep. An alternative is to top-dress with a good commercial humus. *See* HUMUS.

PREPARING THE SOIL. Given the proper depth of the right sort of topsoil, the next

---

* Special articles on the subjects indicated by an asterisk (*) will be found at the words so marked.

step is its preparation for the final seeding of the lawn mixture. If the site has been heavily cropped with vegetables or flowers, there is a fair chance that it is somewhat depleted of plant food. Stable manure, while it adds humus and plant food, is better kept out at this stage, as it will contain the seeds of many troublesome weeds. By far the best way to increase the humus content of the lawn soil is to cover it with 3 in. of prepared, weed-free, non-acid humus, and thoroughly dig or rake it in. *See* Humus.

While this adds an important ingredient to any lawn soil, humus is no substitute for plant food. After the humus is thoroughly mixed with the soil, top-dress it with a good commercial fertilizer with a 4–8–4 ratio (*see* Fertilizers) at the rate of 700–1000 lbs. per acre, or about 40 lbs. to 1000 sq. ft.

All of this should have been done 3–4 weeks before actual seed-sowing, and it is assumed that the ground would have been spaded or plowed long before this, as in the preparation of any other soil for a garden crop. Such spading or plowing, especially in the case of preparing for a lawn, should be done carefully enough so that no coarse subsoil is brought to the surface.

Preparation of Seed Bed. Because of the nature of young grass shoots, lawn soil needs more final preparation than that of the vegetable garden. On large areas much time can be saved by disk-harrowing and following this with a spring-tooth or ordinary harrow.

But neither of these will leave the land smooth or fine enough for a good lawn, and the only remedy is a final hand raking. See that all lumps are broken up and the soil left in as smooth and fine condition as possible.

It is not advisable to rake a large area, perhaps leaving the seeding to a later date, because the seed will "take" better on freshly raked land. If the area is large, do the final hand raking in squares of about 20 × 20 ft., and seed immediately; then rake and seed another piece, and so on.

Sowing Grass Seed. Grass seed is so fine that it cannot be sown on a windy day. Early-morning sowing is often practiced by experienced lawn makers to avoid the winds which often freshen enough later to make sowing impossible. For inexperienced sowers it is a good plan to mix the grass seed with an equal volume of fine sand, as the mixture is more easily and more evenly spread than pure grass seed. In any case, scatter the seed as widely and thickly as possible (within the limits outlined below) and rake it in lightly. The seed should then be rolled lightly, or if the area is small and you have no roller, it may be lightly tamped with a board or the back of a spade.

On a new lawn it is important to get as thick a stand of grass as possible. There is no better remedy or cure for the weeds that are bound to come up in a new lawn than for them to be crowded out by the grass itself. To help make the initial distribution of grass seed as thorough as possible, it is well to divide it in half. Walk in one direction while

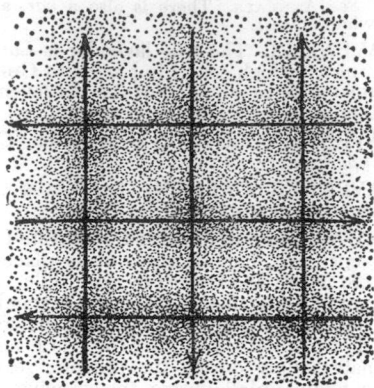

Sow grass seed in two lines, as shown by the arrows.

sowing the first half and then sow the other half on the same area, but walk in the opposite direction while sowing. Such a crisscross sowing will be far more thorough than one done by simply walking in one direction. This, of course, can be obviated by using a mechanical seed sower, which scatters seed more evenly than without it. But most small lawns need such a machine only once, and hence it is a questionable piece of equipment for the average gardener.

The amount of seed necessarily differs on different soils and with different grass mixtures. For most soils in the North and using the standard mixtures as outlined below, at least 5 lbs. of seed should be used on 1000 sq. ft., and the cost of grass seed is so trifling that it would be better to use 7–8 lbs. on an area of that size. A niggardly policy in sowing grass seed is sure to bring much later trouble, especially in spring-sown seedings, which are most likely to be weed-infested, and this brings us to the preferred time of sowing.

There is no question that fall-sown seed has a better chance of making a good lawn than that sown in the spring. The reason is obvious enough. In the spring and early summer the young grass has to compete with all the weed seedlings that spring up with the grass. As summer heat comes along the scarcely established young lawn is in far from the best condition to withstand a possible drought or the competition of weeds. On small areas, which can be kept watered and hand weeded, there is, however, no objection to spring sowing. If this plan is followed, sow the seed somewhere between March 20 and May 1, the earlier the better.

Fall sowing should be done as soon as possible after really hot weather is over, which usually means about Sept. 15. Of course the seeded area should have been thoroughly cleared of the summer accumulation of weeds and just as thoroughly prepared as for spring planting. But it has the added advantage that the new lawn enters the winter with

* Special articles on the subjects indicated by an asterisk (*) will be found at the words so marked.

the young grass in practically exclusive possession of the soil. This is the ideal condition.

Lawn Mixtures

Unless lawn making is a large-scale operation of at least several acres, it scarcely pays to buy separately and mix the different species that make up the best lawn mixtures. The basis of all mixtures for regions of adequate summer rainfall is Kentucky bluegrass (*Poa pratensis*), sometimes known as June grass. Because this grass does not get thoroughly established the first season, it is mixed with other species of quick, though not lasting growth. The latter make a good showing the first year or two, but are ultimately crowded out by Kentucky bluegrass.

A good general-purpose lawn mixture may contain something like the following percentages of the three leading grasses used:

Kentucky bluegrass (*Poa pratensis*)	80%
Redtop (*Agrostis palustris*)	10%
Rhode Island Bent (*Agrostis capillaris*)	10%

The exact proportions are of much less importance than purity of seed. Many cheap grass mixtures may be anywhere from ⅕ to ¼ chaff, weed seeds, or undesirable grasses. Naturally only a poor lawn can be expected from the use of such. Buy the best and most expensive (*i.e.*, cleanest) mixture you can get from a first-class dealer. The cost, except on large-scale operations, is trifling and failure pretty certain with cheap and dirty seed.

Whether or not you add common white clover to any mixture depends upon soil conditions partly, and upon preference. It stains children's clothing much more than any grass, and is objectionable to many on this account. On most good garden soils it is not absolutely necessary, although it adds nitrogen to the soil, which no grass will do. If the soil is sandy, white clover should be used, at the rate of about 1½–2 ounces of clover seed for every 300 sq. ft. The seed is so heavy that it sinks to the bottom of any container of grass seed, and should therefore not be mixed with the grass seed and sown with it. Sow it separately, immediately after the grass seed, and then a reasonable distribution of the clover is more likely. Such comparatively standard mixtures as the above, or trifling variations of them, are useful for nearly all regions (1) where there is adequate summer rainfall; (2) where the soil is not too acid; (3) where there is no shade; (4) which are not south of zone 6 or 7. For these specialized conditions it is necessary to use grasses of a different sort, because Kentucky bluegrass will not stand great heat, or shade, or an acid soil. Two useful grasses for regions of only moderate rainfall are crested wheat-grass and buffalo-grass, both of which are used in the West. *See* Colorado.

Shade Grasses. Most grasses are light-demanding and will not stand shade, even though there is adequate summer moisture. Under the shade of most trees a shade mixture can be used, however, so long as the trees are not evergreens, or those like the horse-chestnut and some lindens under which it is practically impossible to grow any grass. For such places other plants must be used. *See* Ground Covers.

Another factor of importance in getting a lawn under the shade of trees is the immense amount of available water and plant food taken by the shallow-rooted trees at the expense of the grass. In such places watering and top-dressing with humus or occasional applications of commercial fertilizer are imperative. For details *see* Care of Lawns below.

Under moderate or even fairly heavy shade the best grasses are:

Poa trivialis (a relative of Kentucky bluegrass)
Festuca ovina capillata
Poa compressa
Poa nemoralis

Usually, for small-scale operations, it is better to buy prepared shade mixtures from a reputable dealer, as they will contain a reasonable mixture of the above and of a few other shade-enduring species.

Acid Soil Grasses. Where the soil is too acid to make Kentucky bluegrass a success, other species of lawn grasses are used. Slight and perhaps temporary acidity or sourness can be corrected by using lime as outlined above. But over considerable sections of the country the whole soil reaction is sufficiently acid to make it better to adapt the grass to it rather than to try to change the acidity. (*See* Acid and Alkali Soils for details of making tests.)

In places too acid for Kentucky bluegrass, by far the best lawn grasses are various kinds of creeping bent (*Agrostis maritima*, but often sold as *A. stolonifera*). This is the grass used also on fine putting greens, bowling greens, tennis courts, etc. Its great merit is that due to its habit and the way it is planted it will make a perfect lawn in 6–7 weeks. Its great defect is that it is very shallow-rooted, needs constant watering to survive droughts, and its foliage is so thin and slender that only the closest mowing will keep it trimmed.

No finer turf in the world can be made than with creeping bent, of which there are several commercial varieties on the market. But for ordinary lawn purposes it is advised only in acid soil localities where Kentucky bluegrass will not grow. The maintenance, feeding, watering, etc., of a bent lawn must be as intensive as on a golf course where nightly watering of the greens is not unusual.

Creeping bent lawns can be made from seed which is raised on the Pacific Coast, but it is far quicker to plant stolons.* Good varieties are Cocos, Metropolitan, Seaside, and Washington. The grass rootstocks creep all through the upper layers of the soil as do the stolons* along the surface. Bits of these vegetative pieces are usually planted instead of seed. The job is far more laborious than sowing grass seed, as each bit of the creeping bent must be slightly covered with soil, tamped

---

* Special articles on the subjects indicated by an asterisk (*) will be found at the words so marked.

down and sprinkled. A usual interval is to plant the bits 3 × 4 in. apart, or 3 ×5 in. As in seeding, a niggardly policy is not economical in the long run, although creeping bent is far more expensive to buy and plant than ordinary grass seed. The results, however, are remarkable and quick. An even finer bent, still more expensive, is *Agrostis canina,* usually called dog or velvet bent. It is handled in the same way as creeping bent.

GRASS SUBSTITUTES. In regions where insect or other troubles make the keeping of a grass lawn impossible, an interesting substitute is the camomile (*Anthemis nobilis*), a rather weedy plant. But seed sown broadcast, as is grass seed, will soon produce an abundant growth. It will stand rolling and mowing, and if these are done regularly it makes a turf. While camomile lawns are rare in America, they were once common in England. They have been successful near Philadelphia, but they do not thrive in dry places, nor where it is too cold and windswept. *Thymus Serpyllum* is also a possible grass substitute, as are low, perennial species of *Achillea* (which see), and *Lippia canescens* in Calif. Another is the turfing daisy (*Matricaria tchihatchewi*), which makes a low, close mat, grass-like but useful only in dry places, as it will not stand moisture. Its flower heads may be prevented from blooming by clipping with a lawn mower. It should be emphasized that none of these lawn substitutes are as good as grass.

SOUTHERN LAWNS. In places of great heat or considerable drought, none of the grasses so far mentioned are of any use, unless constant watering is possible. Usually, as in most gardening operations, it is better to choose the plant for the site than to keep up a constant fight in order to maintain more desirable species.

The chief grasses for these unfavorable places are:

St. Augustine grass (*Stenotaphrum secundatum*).
Bermuda grass (*Cynodon Dactylon*). This is a valuable turf grass in hot regions and is very popular in the Gulf States, especially in the varieties such as Sunturf, Tifgreen, Tiflawn, and Tiffine. In Calif. and other warm regions the winter brownness of Bermuda grass is overcome by annual sowing of Italian rye grass over the lawn, thus ensuring winter verdure.
Centipede-grass (*Eremochloa ophiuroides*); also a variety of it known as St. Lucie grass.
Carpet grass (*Axonopus furcatus*).

All of these are suited to warm, dry regions and will make a lawn, but none of them compare with Kentucky bluegrass. They are not mixed, but should be used alone, according to the sort of soil. In sandy, rather dry places it is better to use St. Augustine grass (also good for shade) or centipede-grass. In moist sand, carpet grass is the best; while for heavy or clayey soils, Bermuda grass is preferable.

In all of these grasses for the South it is better to plant bits of the stolons* than to try seed sowing. They may be planted as in the directions for creeping bent given above, but because of the heat, even greater care is needed until they become established. Do not let the bits of stolon get dry either before or after planting. When established these lawns should be able to take care of themselves, except in periods of great drought.

ZOYSIA. For regions of long summer heat and deficient rainfall, one of the most useful grasses is Zoysia 51 (a form developed by the U.S. Department of Agriculture from *Zoysia,* which see). It is planted from "plugs," *i.e.,* sections of the rootstock, set 8–10 in. apart in the prepared bed. It will, within a year or two, spread so that it makes a tough, weed-free sod in regions where better turf grasses are impossible. It is a true perennial, needs little or no mowing, turns brown in winter, but revives in the spring.

There are, of course, many places in the U.S. where even these grasses will not grow, so that a grass lawn is impossible. The only remedy is the use of *Lippa canescens* (which see), or *Dichondra repens,* both of which are widely used in southern Calif. Both are prostrate and can be mown. Still another is the turfing daisy mentioned above under Grass Substitutes.

CARE OF LAWNS

Once the lawn suited to your climate and soil is established, only about half the job is completed, for upon its subsequent neglect or care will depend the final result. Such care ranges from a mere mowing of the grass to the practice of that fanatical Englishman who prized his turf so highly that he lifted it each fall and carried it through the winter in the cool greenhouse. Reasonable care of a good lawn may be divided into (1) Mowing and Rolling; (2) Feeding and Watering; (3) Weeds and Repair.

Before taking these up in detail a word of caution about the initial treatment of a new lawn is necessary. When the new grass is about 3 in. high, mow it for the first time, leaving the mowings on the lawn. Thereafter follow the general directions under Mowing below. Also, no matter how well or carefully you have prepared the seed bed, it is certain to settle unevenly, and this should be corrected as soon as the first mowing is done. Fill up all depressions or holes with fine topsoil and reseed immediately — this not only for the looks of the lawn but because every bare spot is a possible point for weeds to get ahead.

MOWING AND ROLLING. Throughout the region where there are alternate days of freezing and thawing in early spring, which is over a good part of the country, the minor heaving of lawns is inevitable. As the season advances these irregularities will tend to disappear, but before they do so are apt to leave some grass roots hung above the soil, when, of course, they will dry out. To avoid

---

* Special articles on the subjects indicated by an asterisk (*) will be found at the words so marked.

Rolling in the spring to smooth down
frost heaving

such troubles and for the general firming of the
whole lawn it is better to roll it as soon as the
season will permit. Never roll a thoroughly
wet lawn, but wait until there is no danger
of packing the soil into a cement-like layer.
On reasonably well-drained sites this should
be a day after a soaking rain.

Use a roller weighing not over 300 lbs. and
roll the lawn only once. This will take care
of any frost heaving without packing the
soil too much, a quite likely contingency if
the soil is a heavy one with considerable clay
or silt in it.

As to mowing, no hard-and-fast rule can be
given. During rainy spring weather it may
have to be done every 5 days; later in the summer it had better be done only as often as
absolutely necessary to keep a fine sward.
This may bring mowings 9–15 days apart
during a dry August.

Do not set the knives of the lawn mower
too low. It is far better to have them set about
1 in. high than to cut too close. In the case
of creeping bent, however, the machine cannot be set too low. But in ordinary lawns, cutting too close unnecessarily exposes the crown
of the plant to too much direct sunlight, which
does it no good. A good rule is to mow
often enough so that a properly set mower will
clip only about ½–¾ in. off the top. After
such a cutting it is neither necessary nor desirable to rake the lawn, for the short mowings will filter down among the grass and
help create a mulch over the roots. Properly
managed lawns should thus need no raking.
But if the grass has gone too long and the
cutting is consequently heavy, it will have to
be raked off or caught in one of the basket-like
devices fitted to mowers for this purpose. In
either case do not destroy the clippings, as they
are valuable for the compost pile. See COM-
POST. The lawn should be mown as late in the
season as growth continues.

FEEDING AND WATERING. Grass exhausts
plant food just as do other crops. To overcome
this it is well to top-dress the lawn twice a
season with a 4–8–4 fertilizer (see FERTILI-

ZERS), but do not use more than about 15 lbs.
per 1000 sq. ft. Rake it in thoroughly, preferably before a rain. Top-dressing with even
well-rotted stable manure is not recommended
because it will be certain to bring in a lot of
weed seeds. If the lawn needs humus, and
few lawns do not, it is far better to cover it
with about ¾ in. of a prepared, neutral,
weed-free commercial humus. See HUMUS.
Rake it in thoroughly, as its chief value is down
at the base of the plant. Such humus is not
a substitute for plant food — it simply does
very well the job of creating a humus layer
where the grass needs it most.

If you live in a region of adequate summer
rainfall and have made your lawn on a proper
depth of topsoil, it ought not to need watering except in some period of extreme summer
heat and drought. Such a statement does not
apply to any creeping-bent lawns, which need
pretty constant watering to keep them in
fine condition. It is also true that if the lawn
is in the middle of a city or any other built-
up area, the heat and dryness of such a condition may make watering a necessity.

The principles of lawn sprinkling are extremely simple. Mere surface sprinkling is
worse than useless, for it encourages the grass
roots to seek moisture near the surface and thus
makes constant sprinkling a necessity, or the
roots will otherwise dry out.

If watered at all, a lawn should be so thoroughly soaked that the soil will be wet through
down to where the grass roots ought to be —
7–8 in. below the surface. One such thorough
watering is of the greatest benefit during a
long dry spell. Watering in such a way should
not need to be done more than once a week,
but it takes a lot of time to move sprinklers or
a hose in such a way as to cover a whole lawn.
Use only sprinklers, or a movable hose nozzle,
that cast a fine, mist-like spray, and run them
as much as possible in the early morning, late
evening, or during the night. Midday sprinkling wastes a lot of water through evaporation.

LIME. Many amateurs top-dress their lawns
every year or so with a sprinkling of lime.
There is no evidence that this does any particular good, and it may do harm. The proper
time to use lime is when the soil is being prepared for a lawn and then only if its reaction
is acid. See the account of lawn soils above.

WEEDS AND REPAIR. A well-kept lawn,
sown thickly enough to make a fine sward,
ought to have no weeds — an ideal seldom, if
ever, attained. Weed seeds will inevitably
blow in and they must be coped with or they
will soon make an unsightly place of the lawn.

All annual weeds are taken care of by constant mowing, which prevents their ever
flowering or seeding unless they are the
prostrate sorts that hug the ground so closely
that no mower will reach them. See CRAB
GRASS. Most perennials, unless they are of
the prostrate type, are similarly prevented from
seeding by constant mowing. Few weeds will
stand steady mowing, but a few deep-rooted
perennials will, and it is these that make the

most trouble. Dock, dandelion, and any other weed with a deep taproot will not be starved by any number of mowings. Such should be cut off as deeply as possible below ground with an asparagus knife or an old carving knife. Fill up all holes so made with soil or, better yet, with the mixture mentioned below, for any general repairing of the lawn.

If weeds are numerous and of the broad-leaved type, some of the commercial weed killers may be used. *See* WEEDS AND WEEDING.

To repair holes made by removed weeds, or to fill up ruts made by careless motorists, it is well to keep in the tool house a dry mixture of ½ fine topsoil and ½ grass seed, thoroughly mixed. Fill up all depressions with this, tamp it down, and water it gently but thoroughly. There is no cure for weeds so good as more grass, and careful people keep this mixture handy and use it frequently.

Prostrate weeds that spread in spite of mowing often make patches in the lawn. The only real remedy is to rake or dig them out and reseed. *See also* Lawn Troubles below.

Lawn Troubles

In spite of the greatest care there are still things that can make a lawn unsightly. A few of them and their remedies are suggested below.

BLACK ANTS. For control pour a teaspoonful of carbon bisulphide into small holes punched 2 in. deep, spaced about 12–18 in. apart, and plug with moist soil to prevent evaporation. Carbon bisulphide is poisonous and explosive.

GRUBS. *See* discussion at end of GRASSES.

MOLES. These often make unsightly, ridged tunnels in even the finest lawns. Once the moles have been eradicated the ridges should be tamped down and depressions refilled before reseeding. To eradicate moles traps are the best of the older methods (*see* Moles at ANIMAL INJURY), but chemical controls have proved useful, especially chlordane.

SPOTS IN THE LAWN. Sometimes brownish spots from a foot across to several times that will appear in a lawn. If they first show in periods of drought, they are probably caused by a boulder too close to the surface or by some rubbish under the topsoil which destroys capillarity. The only remedy is to water such spots copiously.

If such spots appear in moist weather or after protracted watering, they are nearly always caused by a fungus disease, of which there is a general discussion at the end of the article on GRASSES.

MOSS IN THE LAWN. In some lawns, particularly partly shady ones, there are often encroachments of mosses which carpet the ground to the exclusion of grass. Often they are attractive enough to leave alone, but if they are to be replaced by grass, comb out all moss with a steel rake or dig it out. Fill in with fresh topsoil of which about ⅒ of its bulk is ordinary agricultural lime. Then reseed thickly and be sure to water and look

after such spots especially. Do not use on them any fertilizer containing much nitrogen, but instead sow some common white clover. If fertilizer is necessary — it should not be if fresh soil has been added — top-dress only with fertilizers containing mostly phosphoric acid. Later, when the trouble has been corrected, ordinary treatment can be resumed.

SLOPES. It is impossible to seed successfully slopes too steep to hold the soil while the grass is germinating. For such places sodding is the only remedy. For details of this *see* TURF. If the bank is too steep for sod, then some other plant will have to be used and the soil held in place while it captures the place. For details of this *see* BANKS. For a simple method of repairing holes or edges of lawns by turfing them *see* the illustration at TURF.

For Insect Pests and Diseases *see* GRASSES.

LAWN GAMES. For the minimum space requirements *see* BADMINTON, BOWLING GREEN, CROQUET, DECK TENNIS, and TENNIS.

LAWN MOWINGS. *See* COMPOST.

LAWSONIA (law-sō′ni-a). A single species of often spiny shrubs of the family Lythraceae, L. inermis, the mignonette-tree, the leaves of which are the source of henna. It is a native of northern Af., Asia, and Aust. and is sometimes cult. in greenhouses for interest. It has opposite,° short-stalked leaves, more or less lance-shaped and about 1 in. long. Flowers heavily fragrant, usually white but sometimes red or rose-pink, about ¼ in. wide, borne in a loose terminal cluster (panicle°). Fruit a capsule about ¼ in. diameter. Can be grown outdoors only in zones° 8 and 9 and is cult in Fla. and southern Calif. (Named by Linnaeus for John Lawson, a traveler in N. Car. who was burned by the Indians.)

laxa, -us, -um (lack′sa). Loose and open, as are many flower clusters.

laxiflora, -us, -um (lax-i-flōr′a). With a loose flower cluster.

LAYERING. Propagation by layering is the rooting of branches of woody plants while they are still attached to the parent plant. In nursery practice this method is used especially with varieties which have to be propagated vegetatively because they do not come true from seeds, and which are slow or unsatisfactory to grow from cuttings or grafts. For the amateur this simple and safe method is of particular importance, since it necessitates no special equipment and no great skill or experience is required to succeed with it. Layering is often called marcottage, especially in Quebec.

There are only two main requirements, and both can be easily met in the garden. First: The soil, which in the various methods described below is used to cover the shoots which are to be rooted, must be loose and fluffy so that it can be packed tightly without excluding air altogether; and it must be rich in humus to induce root formation. Sec-

---

° Special articles on the subjects indicated by an asterisk (°) will be found at the words so marked.

ond: The layered plants must be watered regularly in dry weather, since satisfactory root development will take place only in soil which is sufficiently moist.

PREPARATIONS. The nurseryman takes care of these needs by planting a special block of mother-plants which are used only for layering, and by selecting for them a low-lying place where rich humus soil is present. This place is plowed deeply in the fall after manure has been spread. In the spring healthy young plants are set out, far enough apart to allow ample room for the layering operation. The rows are carefully cultivated and weeded for two or three years, after which the mother-plants will be strong enough to be ready for layering. The amateur, in most cases, will want to utilize an old established plant without moving it from its present locality. His practice will vary from that of the nurseryman also in that he will usually want to raise only a few layers from one shrub. Also he will not wish to ruin the shape and beauty of the mother-plant, while the nurseryman utilizes his mother-plants to the fullness of their capacity for a number of years; then he discards them and starts again with young plants. With most plants the best results are obtained only with strong one-year-old shoots. Where these are not present, their production must be induced. The nurseryman does this by cutting his mother-plants down to ground level and afterwards removing all weak growth which may develop. The amateur will always have a few suitable young shoots on his older plants, if he has pruned them regularly and has cared for them with proper feeding and watering. If neglected old shrubs, without suitable young growth, are the only specimens available for layering, they must first be restored to vigor by sharp pruning, cutting out all old and weak growth, and by feeding them liberally with manure.

BEST TIME FOR LAYERING. True layering, for which the shoots of the previous season are used, always has to be done in the early spring, as soon as the ground can be worked and before growth has started. Mound or stool layering, as far as it uses the growth of the current season, has to wait until the young shoots are at least a few inches long.

1. TRUE LAYERING

SIMPLE LAYERING, which results in one plant from each layer. In this operation only the upper end of the shoot is buried in a slit in the ground which is made by inserting the spade about six inches deep and moving it back and forth a few times. The distance of the slit in the ground from the plant depends upon the length of the shoot. The shoot must be bent down as flat as possible. To avoid its tearing off at the base it is advisable to bend it in the opposite direction from that in which it grows and to twist it slightly when bending it. The shoot is anchored in the ground with a forked branch or a bent willow twig or a piece of wire. After that its tip is turned up sharply again and the slit in the ground is closed

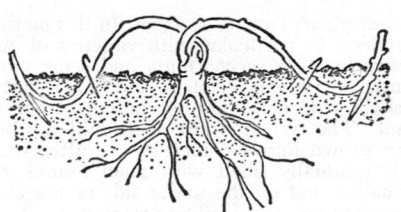

Twigs bent down, buried, and anchored
for true or common layering

tightly over the bent shoot with a stamp of the foot. The tip should protrude at least three inches above the surface.

To facilitate rooting, the shoot may be ringed by removing a narrow strip of bark all around or a shallow cut may be made on its under surface, or it may be girdled by drawing a piece of wire tightly around it. The best place at which to induce callus* formation by such an injury is — facing the plant — shortly behind the upward bend of the tip.

Strong shoots of the previous season are used in this method, which succeeds with a large variety of shrubs. Only with *Rhododendron, Azalea,* etc., which do not produce this type of shoot, are old branches bent to the ground. The two- to three-year-old twigs are then drawn into the soil and buried at least four inches deep, or to the base of the previous year's growth. In Europe, and sometimes here, the whole plant of rhododendron is dug up and replanted flat on the ground with the top spread fanwise, which provides much more layering material.

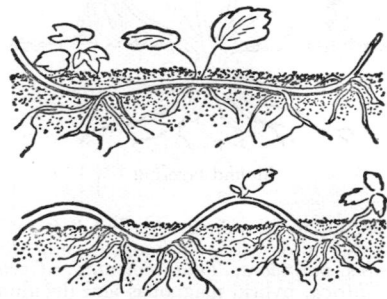

Above, continuous layering; below,
serpentine layering

In the late fall of the same year the layered branches of most varieties will be rooted and should be severed from the mother-plant. The young plants, however, may be left where they are until spring, when they should be transplanted to the nursery. Some layers, for instance, those of *Rhododendron* and *Hamamelis,* take two or three years before they develop sufficient root system to make it safe to sever them from the parent plant.

CONTINUOUS LAYERING, which results in

---

* Special articles on the subjects indicated by an asterisk (*) will be found at the words so marked.

several plants from each shoot. In this method, practiced in particular with varieties of *Acer Negundo, Acer saccharinum* and some viburnums, the whole shoot is laid down flat in a shallow trench, running radially from the plant. The trench is left open until the buds have grown into 4–5 inch shoots, after which it is gradually filled with good humus soil. A shallow cut on the under side of the shoot at each node* will facilitate rooting.

SERPENTINE LAYERING, as practiced in particular with *Wistaria,* climbing honeysuckles, *Clematis* and other vines, is very similar to continuous layering. But in this case the shoot is not laid down flat but is bent up and down in a serpentine, always burying one node* and leaving the next above ground.

ARCHING LAYERS or TIP LAYERING is practiced especially with *Forsythia,* black raspberries and blackberries, which are by nature inclined to root at the tips of their branches. In their case all that is necessary is to peg the tips to the ground so that wind swaying cannot interfere with their rooting.

2. MOUND OR STOOL LAYERING

This method is employed mainly with low bushy shrubs, such as: *Ribes alpinum, Spiraea Bumalda, Prunus glandulosa, Prunus nana,*

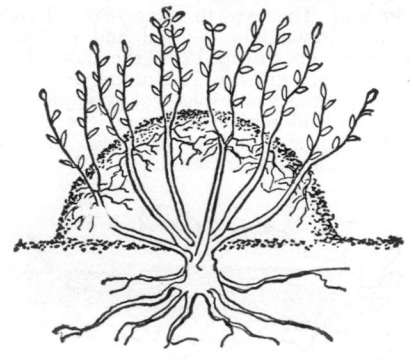

Mound layering

azaleas, Japanese quince, etc., but it is rather successful also with *Hydrangea paniculata, Aesculus parviflora, Tilia tomentosa, Cornus alba sibirica,* hybrid magnolias and deciduous azaleas.

In mound layering, as contrasted with true layering, the shoots are not laid down but are left to grow upright, and in this position are buried eight to ten inches deep in rich humus soil. If last year's shoots are used, it is advisable to ring or girdle them at their base to induce callus* formation, then the soil is heaped up around and packed well between them. This operation is carried out in early spring before growth has started. The treatment of the rooted shoots is the same as recommended under true layering.

Better results, however, are obtained in this method with the shoots of the current sea-

son which have to be buried in three successive stages as they extend in length. Three or four inches of soil is added each time. No ringing is needed in this case.

STUMPING, as practiced, for instance, with the large-fruited blueberries, is very similar to mound layering. Old shoots are cut off at ground level, and a mixture of peat and sand is heaped over the stumps to a depth of four inches. The sand, through which the young shoots have to push their way, may be held in place with a board frame and must be kept continually moist to assure success.

3. AIR LAYERING

This very old practice, which is also called pot layering, Chinese layering, and circumposition, has acquired new interest and importance since the advent of polyethylene plastics. Formerly this procedure was employed only with certain greenhouse plants, such as crotons, rubber-plant, and other species of Ficus, etc., which were slow or difficult to root from normal cuttings. The shoot to be rooted was girdled with a tightly drawn wire, or a T-shaped incision was made on both sides of the stem about 8 or 10 inches below its tip and sphagnum moss was tied around this place. The trick then was to keep the sphagnum moss continually moderately moist. It should not be too wet and it must never be allowed to dry out. Occasionally the sphagnum moss was covered with a piece of burlap. Callus and roots then would form on the injured place, and as soon as the roots were well developed the rooted tip was severed from the stem and potted.

Polyethylene plastic has greatly widened the field of application of this method which now can be employed also outside in the garden. Polyethylene plastic permits air to pass but confines the humidity. The main requirement for success is even but moderate moisture. Therefore, one must make sure that from the beginning the sphagnum moss is not wet but only moderately moist, and it is very important that especially the upper end of the plastic covering is tightly sealed with tape so that rain water cannot enter. If the moss gets too wet, no roots will be formed. It is generally recommended to remove a ring of bark, ½ to ¾ inch wide, all around the branch which is to be rooted and even to scrape the wood so as to remove the slippery cambium. A rooting hormone* powder may be sprinkled very thinly on the upper exposed edge of the bark, but only as much must be left as remains after the branch has been shaken a few times. Too much of the hormone powder will defeat its purpose.

This procedure does not work with all trees and shrubs but some have given excellent results, among them *Cornus florida, Corylopsis, Cotinus, Cotoneaster, Halesia, Gordonia, Ilex, Koelreuteria,* many crabapples, some *Prunus,* some rhododendrons, *Tamarix,* some of the viburnums, *Wistaria,* and *Zelkova,* which are not easy to propagate

---

* Special articles on the subjects indicated by an asterisk (*) will be found at the words so marked.

except from seeds. Outside air layering is carried out in late spring after the leaves have developed, and the rooted branches are removed and potted in late fall. — H. T.

LAYIA (lay′ĭ-a). A genus of mostly Californian herbs of the family Compositae, comprising perhaps 15 species, two of which are popular flower garden annuals grown for their showy flower heads. Leaves alternate,* generally without marginal teeth. Flower heads solitary, the stalks terminal. Ray* flowers handsome, 8–20, yellow or white and 3-toothed. Disk* flowers tubular. (Named for George T. Lay, a naturalist on Beechey's voyage.)

Both are hardy annuals and should be grown as such. *See* ANNUALS.

elegans. Tidy-tips. A branching, hairy herb, 1–2 ft. high in the wild, usually less in cult. Leaves very narrow, 1½–3 in. long. Heads showy because the usually yellow ray* flowers are each tipped with white. Calif. Summer.

glandulosa. White daisy. Not much branched, the stem sticky-hairy. Leaves lance-shaped or narrower, not over 1½ in. long. Flower heads nearly 1½ in. wide, the rays white or rarely pinkish-rose. British Columbia to Idaho and Mex.

LEACHING. Rain water has the power to dissolve out many chemical substances in the surface soil and carry them in solution to greater depth. While it is practically impossible to measure such losses, they should not be lost sight of in maintaining soil fertility, especially in irrigated districts. *See* IRRIGATION. Serious effects of leaching, however, are not experienced outdoors, but in potted or tubbed specimens. Few amateurs water such with sufficient care to prevent some water passing out of drainage holes at the bottom. Every scrap of such excess water carries with it some appreciable amount of plant food from the soil. Overwatering thus makes for soil exhaustion in potted plants, due wholly to leaching. For the leaching of nutrients from foliar-fed plants, *see* FOLIAR FEEDING.

LEAD ARSENATE. *See* No. 2 at INSECTICIDES.

LEADER. The growing apex of a shrub or tree. If it is broken, height-growth is stopped, but this can be prevented by bending and tying upward the strongest of the upper branches. Such a branch will form a new leader in a few years, and some plants do it naturally.

LEAD PLANT = *Amorpha canescens.*

LEADWORT. *See* PLUMBAGO and CERATOSTIGMA.

LEAF. The ordinary foliage organ of most flowering plants and ferns, but in the latter usually called a frond. A typical leaf comprises an expanded blade, a stalk (the petiole*), and often a pair of small bract*-like, leafy organs at the base of the stalk known as stipules. Leaves may be simple* or compound,* depending upon whether there is a single blade or whether it is split into any number of leaflets (which see). The shape,

A complete leaf showing blade (*a*), petiole or leafstalk (*b*), and stipules (*c*).

veining, etc., of leaves have great value in the classification of plants as does their method of arrangement. Some, like the mint family, have only opposite* leaves. In others leaves are always alternate.* For the function of leaves and for their use in the garden *see* LEAVES.

LEAF BEET = *Beta vulgaris Cicla.* *See* BEET.

LEAF CURL. The term applied to curled leaves resulting from various diseases and, on peach, a fungus disease. Leaves of many plants may also curl as a result of soil which is too wet or too dry. Leaves of *Rhododendron* curl naturally in the winter — the lower the temperature, the tighter the leaf curl.

LEAFLET. One of the ultimate segments of a compound* leaf. Typical examples are the leaflets of the ash, hickory, rose or poison ivy. *See* COMPOUND.

LEAF LETTUCE = *Lactuca sativa crispa.* For cult. *see* LETTUCE.

LEAF MOLD. *See* HUMUS.

LEAF MUSTARD = *Brassica juncea.*

LEAFSPOT. The term applied to various spots and blotches on leaves. The leafspot diseases are caused by bacteria and fungi which live through the winter in dead leaves on the ground. In the spring the fungi produce spores* which are splashed or blown to the new leaves and thus continue the diseases. It is often beneficial to rake and burn leaves in the fall to prevent the fungi from starting a new disease cycle the following spring. Most leafspot diseases can be prevented by spraying two or three times about 10 days apart, starting as soon as new leaf growth begins in the spring.

LEAFSTALK. A petiole.*

LEATHER BUSH = *Dirca palustris.*

LEATHERLEAF. *See* CHAMAEDAPHNE.

LEATHERWOOD = *Fremontia californica.* *See also* DIRCA.

---

* Special articles on the subjects indicated by an asterisk (*) will be found at the words so marked.

LEAVES. The functional importance of leaves cannot be overstated. Their green coloring-matter or chlorophyll is the only substance in the world that can make starch or sugar, both primary products in the economy of all plants as well as of man. Chlorophyll accomplishes this quite complicated feat only in the presence of light, air, and the plant foods that have been derived from the soil and the atmosphere. Leaves thus are of enormous importance to the gardener, quite apart from their beauty or diversity of coloring, for upon their proper functioning, free from wilting, disease, or smoke, depend all the subsequent transformations of the primary food they alone can make. In other words, flowers, fruits, seeds, wood, gums, resins, rubber, and hundreds of other plant products would be impossible without the normal functions of leaves. For the uses of fallen leaves in the garden *see* MULCH and COMPOST.

Lebbek (leb'beck). Arabian vernacular for the siris (*Albizzia Lebbek*).

lecheguilla (letch-e-gweel'ya). Adapted from the Mexican vernacular *lechuguilla,* the name of a fiber-yielding *Agave.*

LECHUGUILLA (letch-e-gweel'ya) = *Agave lecheguilla.*

LECYTHIDACEAE (les-i-thi-day'see-ee). Exclusively tropical trees, comprising 18 genera and perhaps 220 species. The family is of no garden interest, except for *Bertholletia* (the Brazil-nut). It is rarely cult. in large greenhouses, or outdoors in the warmer parts of Calif. and Fla.

Leaves alternate,* but often crowded toward the ends of the branchlets. Flowers in clusters (racemes*), white. Fruit a hard woody pod in *Bertholletia* with thick walls. Inside are 18–24 nuts (Brazil-nuts).

Technical flower characters: Flowers regular.* Sepals 4 or 6, sometimes replacing lacking petals. Petals (when present) 4 or 6. Stamens numerous, in several series or groups. Ovary inferior,* 2 or more-celled.

ledifolia, -us, -um (lee-di-fō′li-a). With leaves like the genus *Ledum* (which see).

LEDUM (lee′dum). A small but interesting genus of bog shrubs of the heath family, all the cult. species suited only to very acid sites in the bog garden. They have alternate,* evergreen, short-stalked leaves, without teeth, but with the margins often rolled, and generally sticky-hairy or felty on the under side. Flowers small, white, in umbel*-like, terminal clusters. Petals 5, spreading. Stamens* 5–10. Fruit a capsule.* (*Ledum* is the Greek name for the plants now put in the genus *Cistus,* very different plants from *Ledum.*)

All these can only be grown well in the bog garden, either in sphagnum moss or wet peat with an acidity reaction of pH 4.00– 5.00 (*see* ACID AND ALKALI SOILS). All are shrubs of the colder parts of the north temperate zone and should not be grown in regions of long, hot summers. Propagated by spring-sown seeds or by division. The second and third species may often be transplanted from cold mountain bogs.

columbianum. A shrub 4–5 ft. high, the leaves oblong, 1½–2½ in. long, the margins only slightly rolled. Flowers white, the petals nearly round. Stamens* 5–7. Capsule* oblongish, under ½ in. long. May–June. Wash. to Ore. Hardy from zone* 5 and northward, but not in the East where the summers are too dry for it.

groenlandicum. Labrador tea. An upright bog shrub scarcely over 3 ft. high, its oblongish leaves 1½–3 in. long, rusty-hairy beneath and with the margins strongly rolled. Flowers about ¾ in. wide, white, the petals oblong. Capsule about ⅜ in. long. In cold bogs, Greenland to Pa. and westward. Hardy from zone* 4 northward. May–June. Often called *L. latifolium.*

latifolium = *Ledum groenlandicum.*

palustre. Wild rosemary; also called crystal tea. An upright bog shrub, never much over 3 ft. high. Leaves oblongish or narrower, ¾–2 in. long, the margins strongly rolled, the under surface rusty-hairy. Flowers ½–¾ in. wide, the petals oval. Fruit scarcely ⅓ in. long. Cold bogs throughout the north temperate zone and northward to the Arctic Circle. May–June. Hardy from zone* 3 northward. The var. **decumbens** is a more or less prostr.e form with narrower leaves.

LEEA (lee′a). A small genus of 60 species of tropical Old World shrubs and trees of the family Vitaceae, hence related to the grape but not vine-like. They are grown only occasionally in the greenhouse, still more rarely outdoors in zones* 8 and 9. Leaves alternate,* compound,* the leaflets arranged feather-fashion. Flowers greenish or yellowish, not showy, arranged in small clusters (cymes*). For details of flower structure *see* VITACEAE. Fruit a berry. (Named for James Lee, Scotch nurseryman.)

The plants are grown primarily for their beautiful foliage and need a tropical greenhouse (*see* GREENHOUSE) and potting mixture* 4. The chief growth is in spring and early summer; during the winter the plants should be partially rested by reducing their water and giving them less heat.

amabilis. Leaflets 5–7, more or less lance-shaped, toothed, green and bronzy, but white-striped and with white veins. Borneo. The var. **splendens** has red-marked leaves.

sambucina. Leaves twice-compound,* the ultimate leaflets toothed, bronzy but variegated or veined red. Aust. and tropical As.

LEECHEE = *Litchi chinensis.*

LEEK (*Allium Porrum*). A hardy, onion-like plant, but milder than the onion and more hardy. Both the rather soft bulb and the leaves are used in cooking. It may be grown like the onion (which see), but in mild parts of the country it may stand out all winter and be harvested as needed. Often the lower part of the plant is blanched by hilling up the soil around it, especially at the approach of cold weather. If the weather gets very severe in the winter, leeks may be dug and stored in a cool, frost-free cellar, preferably being heeled-in.*

---

* Special articles on the subjects indicated by an asterisk (*) will be found at the words so marked.

LEGGY. A common term in hort. for a plant that becomes gawky or "too long in the leg" from overfeeding, or often, in the greenhouse, from being too far from the glass. It is a common condition, too, among vegetable plants like tomatoes, which have been crowded too much in youth. The energy which should have produced a stocky plant has gone into making a spindling, leggy one. It can usually be corrected by pinching, or, in the greenhouse, by growing the plants nearer the glass. Leggy plants are often called "drawn."

LEGUME. Typically a pea pod, a type of fruit that splits into two valves and has the seeds attached to the lower seam. *See* LEGUMINOSAE.

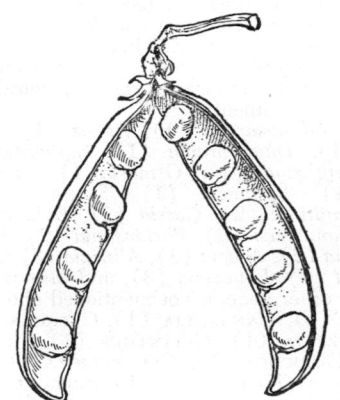

The common pea pod is a typical legume.

LEGUME INOCULATION. Many plants of the pea family will not grow satisfactorily unless the bacteria usually associated with their root tubercles are in the soil or can be put there. Often the organism is found in the soil due to the residue from a former crop. However, it is safer to buy cultures of the particular bacteria of each leguminous crop needing them. These cultures are sold by commercial firms and by some experiment stations, with specific directions for their use. They are particularly valuable for soils upon which, for the first time, the following crops are to be grown: soybeans, sweet clover, alfalfa, cowpea, and some clovers.

LEGUMES. A group name for many plants of the pea family or Leguminosae, usually and perhaps best restricted to those with edible pods or seeds like pea, bean, lentil, etc. It is often used to characterize any herbaceous plant of the pea family, such as vetch, clovers, alfalfa, etc. The legumes are often called pulse crops and they are of great economic importance. *See* LEGUMINOSAE for the different genera and their uses.

LEGUMINOSAE (le-gew-mi-nō'see). The pea family, as here considered, is perhaps the most important group of garden plants in the world. Its range and diversity are somewhat indicated by its having been variously called the bean, vetch, peanut, wisteria, and locust family, while the botanists have, at times, called it Fabaceae and Papilionaceae.

Actually it includes three groups of plants, excluding non-hort. genera. All of these have been considered by some as separate families. They are the pea family itself, with typically pea-like flowers; the Mimosaceae, often called mimosa or acacia family, with small, not very pea-like flowers in dense clusters; and the Caesalpiniaceae, often called the senna, redbud, or tamarind family, which has nearly, but not quite, regular flowers. All of them have, as fruit, a pod or legume, of which the garden pea is the best example. But in many genera it is very small, in a few freakish genera it does not split (*see* HYMENAEA), and in many tropical trees it is an immense woody pod, although a true legume (which see).

Considering the Leguminosae as a whole there are about 495 genera and upwards of 14,000 species, world-wide in distribution and comprising (in the cult. genera) herbs, shrubs, vines and often gigantic trees. While the family is comparatively easy to recog-

Three types of flowers in the pea family: acacia (*below*), sweet pea (*upper left*), and *Cassia* (*upper right*).

nize, the distinctions between even the cult. genera are mostly highly technical. The groups below are therefore wholly upon the basis of their use as garden plants for ornament or food, disregarding here the wide economic importance of the drugs, dyes, timbers, gums, oils, resins, etc., found in many non-hort. genera.

Leaves alternate* and typically compound* (sometimes reduced to a single leaflet) the

---

* Special articles on the subjects indicated by an asterisk (*) will be found at the words so marked.

leaflets arranged feather-fashion in some, as in wisteria, or finger-fashion in others like the lupines; sometimes twice- or thrice-compound, as in many acacias.

The flowers, usually very showy, are of three types. (1) Typically pea-like, with an upstanding petal (the standard* or vexillum), two lateral ones (the wings) and two lower, more or less united petals which form the keel. (2) Not pea-like, but irregular enough to suggest it. This group comprises the genera formerly included in the Caesalpiniaceae. (3) Not pea-like, but small, regular* and often crowded in dense clusters. This group is considered by many as the family Mimosaceae.

There are technical differences between the three groups based upon the stamens. In (1) the 10 stamens are in two groups, a single one free and the other nine united into a tube (monadelphous*). In (2) there are 10 or less stamens, all free (not united). In (3) the stamens are usually more than 10 and all free or united in groups.

There are nearly a hundred cult. genera of the Leguminosae. All of them have root tubercles, which, with the aid of certain bacteria, allow the plants of this family to absorb free nitrogen from the air. It is this faculty which makes alfalfa, clover, vetch, and some tropical genera such valuable cover crops. For centuries before this relationship was discovered, they had been plowed into the land for enrichment, a practice still as sound as when the Romans did it. See LEGUME INOCULATION, GREEN MANURING.

The genera below (not including some relatively unimportant ones entered at their proper place in the ENCYCLOPEDIA) are grouped wholly upon their use in the garden or for food. To help the student, each genus has a number, corresponding to the groups in the discussion of the flowers. They are:

(1) Pea tribe or family proper (the old Papilionaceae or Fabaceae)

(2) Senna tribe or family (the old Caesalpiniaceae)

(3) Mimosa or acacia tribe or family (the old Mimosaceae)

It will be noted that some genera are in two or more groups.

I. EDIBLE PLANTS.

Arachis (1) (*see* PEANUT), *Cajanus* (1), *Cicer* (1), *Lens* (1) (*see* LENTIL), *Pachyrhizus* (1), *Phaseolus* (1), *Pisum* (1) (*see* PEA), *Vicia* (1), *Vigna* (1), *Ceratonia* (2) (*see* CAROB), *Tamarindus* (2).

II. FORAGE OR COVER CROPS GROWN MOSTLY FOR ANIMAL FOOD OR FOR SOIL IMPROVEMENT BY PLOWING IN.

Glycine (1) (*see* SOYBEAN), *Lotus* (1), *Medicago* (1) (includes alfalfa), *Melilotus* (1), *Onobrychis* (1), *Trifolium* (1) (*see* CLOVER), *Vicia* (1), *Trigonella* (1).

III. GARDEN FLOWERS, MOSTLY ANNUALS* OR PERENNIALS.* Hardy outdoors over most of the country; but see in-

dividual genera for specific hardiness notes.

Anthyllis (1), *Astragalus* (1), *Baptisia* (1), *Coronilla* (1), *Desmodium* (1), *Galega* (1), *Hedysarum* (1), *Lathyrus* (1), *Lespedeza* (1), *Lupinus* (1), *Ononis* (1), *Oxytropis* (1), *Petalostemon* (1), *Psoralea* (1), *Thermopsis* (1), and *Cassia* (2), but some of the latter are trees.

IV. SHRUBS, TREES, OR WOODY VINES. Hardy outdoors over most of the country; but see some individual genera for specific hardiness notes.

Amorpha (1), *Cladrastis* (1), *Colutea* (1), *Cytisus* (1) (*see* BROOM), *Genista* (1), *Laburnum* (1), *Maackia* (1), *Prosopis* (1) (*see* MESQUITE), *Robinia* (1) (*see* LOCUST), *Sophora* (1), *Spartium* (1), *Ulex* (1) (*see* FURZE), *Cercis* (2) (*see* REDBUD), *Gleditsia* (2) (*see* HONEY-LOCUST), *Glymnocladus* (2), and *Wistaria* (1).

V. VARIOUS TROPICAL PLANTS OF GREENHOUSE CULTURE, or grown outdoors only in warm regions, mostly for ornament.

Adenocarpus (1), *Abrus* (1), *Derris* (1), *Daubentonia* (1), *Dalbergia* (1), *Erythrina* (1), *Ormosia* (1), *Pueraria* (1), *Sesbania* (1), *Swainsona* (1), *Bauhinia* (2), *Cassia* (2), *Delonix* (2), *Hymenaea* (2), *Parkinsonia* (2), *Poinciana* (2), *Acacia* (3), *Albizzia* (3), *Tipuana* (1), *Leucaena* (3), and *Mimosa* (3).

For other genera, not mentioned above *see:* APIOS (1), CANAVALIA (1), CARAGANA (1), CHORIZEMA (1), CLIANTHUS (1), CLITORIA (1), DOLICHOS (1), GLYCYRRHIZA (1) (*see* LICORICE), HIPPOCREPIS (1), INDIGOFERA (1), STIZOLOBIUM (1), ADENANTHERA (3), and PITHECOLOBIUM (3).

LEGUMINOUS. Bearing legumes* or belonging to the Leguminosae*; sometimes the term is used, rather loosely, for any pea-like plant.

leimanthoides (lī-man-thoy'deez, but *see* OÏDES). Resembling the obsolete genus *Leimanthium* now referred to *Melanthium* (which see).

LEIOPHYLLUM (ly'o-fil'lum). Low, evergreen, North American shrubs of the heath family. They have small, glossy, dark green leaves that may be opposite or alternate and attractive clusters of white flowers that are pink in bud. They are neat, compact shrubs worthy of cultivation, though sometimes difficult; suited to the rock garden or evergreen plantings. A moist, peaty, and acid loam suits them well. Propagation by cuttings in midsummer or by seed. (*Leiophyllum* is from the Greek for smooth leaf, in allusion to the glossy foliage.) *See* WILD GARDEN.

buxifolium. Sand myrtle or sleek-leaf. Compact upright shrub about 18 in. high though sometimes more. Leaves usually alternate,* oval, smooth, to ½ in. long. Flowers white, in terminal clusters. They have 5 petals and 20 stamens. Fruit a many-seeded capsule. May to

* Special articles on the subjects indicated by an asterisk (*) will be found at the words so marked.

June. N.J. to S. Car. and Ky. Hardy from most parts of zone* 3 southward. Use soil of pH 4–5.

lyoni. Very much like the preceding species, and sometimes considered only a variety of it. It differs mainly in its low, dense and somewhat spreading habit; leaves usually opposite.* Mountains of N. Car. and Tenn.

prostratum = *Leiophyllum lyoni.*

LEMAIREOCEREUS (le-mare'ee-o-see-ree-us). A large genus of tree-like or shrubby, ribbed cacti, the plant body usually large, column-like, and mostly furnished with many stout spines. The group differs only in technical characters from *Cereus.* Flowers day- or night-blooming, not very large, white, pink, or reddish, more or less bell-shaped or funnel-shaped, and not much flaring. Fruit fleshy, but in youth covered with spines. (Named for Charles Lemaire, French student of the cacti, and *Cereus.*)

For culture *see* CACTI. All the cult. species, except *L. thurberi,* need tropical desert conditions.

beneckei. A much-branched cactus, 10–15 ft. high, the branches with 7–8 strongly tuberculed ribs. Spines 1–7, usually only 1 or 2, about 1 in. long, brown or black. Flowers night-blooming, not over 2½ in. long, whitish-yellow. Fruit red, tubercled, about ¾ in. thick. Mex.

dumortieri. A tree-like cactus 18–40 ft. high, but with a short, thick trunk and many erect bluish-green branches. Ribs usually 6. Spines 10–20 in each group, straw-colored with mostly a single central spine. Flowers about 2½ in. long, white. Mex.

griseus. Trunk 1 ft. thick and 20–25 ft. high, or the plant sometimes branching from the base. Ribs 8–10, the spines needle-like. Flowers pinkish, about 3 in. long. Venezuela and islands in the vicinity.

hollianus. A usually unbranched columnar cactus, 10–15 ft. high, generally 8–12-ribbed. Spines red at first, ultimately gray, usually 12 in a cluster, scarcely ¾ in. long; the central spines 3–5, nearly 5 in. long, and with a swollen base. Flowers white, about 5 in. long. Mex.

marginatus. *See* PACHYCEREUS MARGINATUS.

pruinosus. An erect, branched cactus, 15–20 ft. high, the ribs on the branches 5 or 6. Spines 5–7 in a cluster, brownish, the central spine solitary, about 1½ in. long. Flowers about 4½ in. long, white. Fruit football-shaped, spiny. Mex.

stellatus. Joconostle. A shrub-like cactus 6–8 ft. high, mostly branching from the base, the branches 8–12-ribbed and bluish-green. Spines in clusters, the central ones long and erect, the 10–12 lateral spines shorter. Flowers reddish, about 1½ in. long, slimly bell-shaped. Southern Mex.

thurberi. Pitahaya; also called sweet pitahaya. A tall cactus, 15–20 ft. high, usually branching from the base, the branches often 8 in. in diameter, and 12–17-ribbed. Spines long and needle-like. Flowers nearly 3 in. long, pinkish-purple, the petals white-margined. Southern Ariz. and Mex.

weberi. Cardon; also called candebobe. A huge cactus often 30 ft. high with innumerable erect branches which are mostly 10-ribbed. Spines in clusters of 1 central, erect, long spine and 6–12 smaller and lateral ones. Flowers nearly 4 in. long, white. Mex.

LEMNA (lem'na). Minute, floating, aquatic plants, commonly called duckweed, and the only cult. genus of the family **Lemnaceae** (lem-nay'see-ee). Outdoors they are frequently a nuisance as they may completely and rapidly cover the surface of a pool. They are, however, much prized in the aquarium (which see). They are minute stemless plants, without true leaves, these replaced by a tiny, floating, frond-like organ, beneath which are hair-like, short roots. Flowers and fruit practically microscopic. They are the smallest known flowering plants. (*Lemna* is an old Greek name for some water plant, but not certainly for this one.)

LEMON. Three kinds of lemons, all assigned to *Citrus Limonia,* are grown in the United States; the common or acid lemon, the botanical variety or hybrid rough lemon, and the sweet lemon. The first named is the commercial fruit, the culture of which is so important in California; the second is a vigorous-growing form much used for rootstock purposes in Florida; and the third, like the sweet lime with which it is often confused, is merely an interesting horticultural curiosity. The so-called Ponderosa, Chinese, and Meyer lemons do not appear to be true lemons; the first two are probably lemon-citron hybrids, of little value, and the last a lemon-orange hybrid which is distinctly hardier to frost and also an acceptable substitute for the lemon.

COMMON OR ACID LEMON. The lemon, like the lime, is a tender evergreen subtropical tree which thrives in tropical and semi-tropical climates, and in true sub-tropical regions is grown only with the aid of irrigation. Its commercial culture is restricted to regions of sub-tropical climate because of the prevalence of diseases of the rind in regions of summer rainfall, and difficulties in "curing" the fruit; these result in a much lower quality of product. The lemon is slightly more frost-resistant than the lime but is distinctly tenderer than either the orange or grapefruit. While temperatures of 28° to 30° may apparently cause no injury, they are sufficient to occasion heavy shedding of the young fruits set from the fall bloom and this is the fruit which, maturing in spring and summer, normally is in greatest demand. Temperatures of 26° to 28° nearly always result in the killing of the young fruits and new growth; at lower temperatures the trees are seriously injured. The young fruits, and also those approaching maturity, are especially sensitive to sudden heat waves (temperatures of 95 to 100 degrees); with the former the effect produced is shedding, with the latter it is sunburn which may either destroy the fruit or render it virtually worthless. In this respect the lemon is even more sensitive than the lime. The rind of the fruit is easily bruised and the result is a scabby condition; for this rea-

---

* Special articles on the subjects indicated by an asterisk (*) will be found at the words so marked.

son comparative freedom from wind is necessary. Because of its sensitiveness culture of the lemon is restricted largely to the coastal region of southern California where the mild winters and cool summers make possible high yields and favor the production of fruit maturing in spring and summer.

Under favorable climatic conditions the lemon is almost everblooming and matures fruit continuously. There are two main periods of bloom, however, spring and fall, and two corresponding periods of peak production, winter and summer. The amount of fall bloom, and hence summer fruit, varies greatly and depends on the variety and climatic conditions. Many of the flowers are imperfect and non-functional, yet the number of normal flowers seems always to be sufficient to set satisfactory crops. There is no pollination problem for, like other citrus fruits, the lemon does not require seed formation for fruit-setting and development. Unpollinated flowers normally set seedless fruit; indeed the commercial varieties are seedless, or practically so, which is a highly desirable characteristic.

PROPAGATION. The lemon is propagated by budding on seedling rootstocks; shield budding is the common and preferred method. The trees are usually planted as year-old budlings, at which stage the root system ranges in age from 24 to 30 months. Until recently the rootstock most used has been the sour or Seville orange (*Citrus Aurantium*), which is practically immune to the foot-rot and gummosis diseases. Widespread decline of bearing trees in recent years, attributed to the use of this rootstock, has occasioned its virtual abandonment in favor of the sweet orange (*Citrus sinensis*), grapefruit (*Citrus paradisi*), and rough lemon rootstocks. With these rootstocks special precautions must be taken to prevent infection from the diseases mentioned above; these include budding the rootstock seedlings high — 6 to 8 inches, the avoidance of planting too deep, special care in irrigation, and preventive soil treatments.

SOILS. This fruit, like the other citrus fruits, has a wide range of soil adaptation, succeeding almost equally well on light soils and moderately heavy soils. Heavy and poorly drained soils should be avoided because of its sensitiveness to excess moisture and the likelihood of root diseases. It is also highly sensitive to alkali salts and to borax, for which reason such soils should be avoided and only irrigation water of good quality be used. Because of its shallow root distribution, a depth of four feet of good soil, well-drained, will suffice.

PLANTING. Special care is required in the planting operations to prevent injury to the roots from desiccation. The use of balled nursery trees is almost universal and insures good results. Early spring is the best time for planting though it can be done at nearly any time of year, if balled trees are used. The best practice involves their heading, usually to a height of 24 to 30 inches, a few weeks before they are dug and balled. Planting distances range from 24 to 30 feet. *See* Ball and Burlap at PLANTING.

Irrigation and fertilization are the soil management practices of greatest importance. An adequate soil moisture supply must be maintained at all times and this usually requires from 4 to 10 irrigations per year. The total amount required is determined by the climate and the size and spacing of the trees; the period between irrigations depends on weather conditions and the nature of the soil. Fertilization is necessary to maintain satisfactory yields. Experience indicates that an adequate fertilization program consists of about 200 pounds of nitrogen per acre per year, half from chemical sources and the balance from decomposable organic matter. Tillage is necessary only to turn under weeds or fertilizers and to facilitate irrigation. The lemon requires more pruning than other citrus trees, which is employed to provide a compact form, in order to minimize wind-injury, and to increase the amount of crop which reaches picking size while still immature. These aims are accomplished by shortening in to laterals and thinning.

The fruit is picked by clipping, while still immature and green, and held in storage until colored and ready for use.

VARIETIES. The principal varieties in California are Eureka and Lisbon. The former is less vigorous but matures more of the crop during the spring and summer months. Villafranca is intermediate and of minor importance. The fruits are indistinguishable. — R. W. H.

INSECT PESTS and DISEASES. *See* ORANGE.

LEMONADE SUMAC = *Rhus trilobata.*

LEMON BALM = *Melissa officinalis.*

LEMON DAYLILY = *Hemerocallis flava.* *See* DAYLILY.

LEMON GRASS = *Cymbopogon citratus.*

LEMON MINT = *Monarda citriodora.*

LEMON-SCENTED GUM = *Eucalyptus maculata citriodora.*

LEMON THYME = *Thymus Serpyllum vulgaris. See* THYME.

LEMON VERBENA = *Lippia citriodora.*

LEMON VINE = *Pereskia aculeata.*

LENS. *See* LENTIL.

lenta, -us, -um (len'ta). Tough but pliant.

Lentago (len-tā'go). Pre-Linnaean* name applied to the genus *Viburnum;* now the specific name of V. *Lentago.*

LENTEN ROSE = *Helleborus orientalis.*

LENTIBULARIACEAE (len-tib-u-lair-ĭ-ā'-see-ee). The bladderwort family, all aquatics or marsh herbs, comprises perhaps 5 genera and 300 species of widely distributed insec-

---

* Special articles on the subjects indicated by an asterisk (*) will be found at the words so marked.

tivorous plants. *Uticularia* is occasionally culti-vated in aquaria or pools, mostly for its beauti-ful submerged foliage, the fine flowers, or for its interesting method of catching insects. *Pinguicula,* which contains mostly marsh herbs, is sometimes grown in the rock garden. *See* INSECTIVOROUS PLANTS.

Leaves dissected into thread-like seg-ments and submerged in *Utricularia;* more normal, but slimy and basal in *Pinguicula,* which is not submerged. Flowers, always produced above the water, showy, very irregular* and prominently 2-lipped.* Fruit a pod (capsule*). Stamens 2. Ovary superior,* 1-celled.

LENTIL. A pea-like edible-seeded legume, much grown for food in Eu., but not often seen here. It belongs to the genus **Lens** (lenz') of which there are only about a half-dozen species scattered along the Mediterranean region to western As. The only cult. species is the common lentil, **Lens esculenta,** a branching annual 10–18 in. high. Leaves com-pound,* the 4–14 leaflets arranged feather-fashion, oblongish or narrower, about ½ in. long. Flowers scarcely ¼ in. long, pea-like, whitish, usually only 1–3 on a slender stalk from the leaf axil.* Pod (a legume*) nearly ¾ in. wide and long, its 2 seeds lens-like, dark-colored. Its culture is the same as for the pea (which see). (*Lens* is the classical name of the lentil, and the ori-gin of the English word *lens,* so named from the shape of the seed.)

LENT LILY. *See* NARCISSUS.

LEONOTIS (lee-o-nō'tis). A genus of Af-rican herbs of the mint family, comprising a dozen species of which **L. Leonurus,** the lion's-tail or lion's-ear, is the only one likely to be in cult. It is a shrub-like, perennial herb, 3–6 ft. high, or lower in a dwarf form, with a hairy stem and opposite,* ob-longish or narrower leaves, 1–2 in. long, and coarsely toothed. Flowers (in ours) yel-low or orange-red (white in a hort. form), in dense clusters (whorls*) in the leaf axils.* Corolla irregular* and 2-lipped, the lower lip with 3 nearly equal lobes. Stamens* 4, generally curved. Fruit a col-lection of 4 nutlets, surrounded by the 8–10-ribbed, persistent calyx.* As an out-door subject the plant is hardy only south of zone* 7, but it can be cult. outdoors north-ward all summer and then brought into the cool greenhouse, where it will flower in Nov.–Dec. If the latter plan is followed, it is better to make cuttings in the early spring and, when rooted, grow the plants outdoors until the fall, when they must be brought into the cool greenhouse. (*Leono-tis* is from the Latin for lion's ear, which the flowers are supposed to resemble.)

LEONTOPODIUM. *See* EDELWEISS.

LEONURUS (lee-o-new'rus). Eurasian, rather weedy herbs of the mint family, of little hort. importance, but **L. Cardiaca,** the motherwort or lion's-tail, occasionally

grown in the informal border for orna-ment, although it is a commonly naturalized weed over much of N.A. It is a coarse, peren-nial herb, 3–5 ft. high, with opposite,* more or less coarsely toothed or divided leaves, 2–4 in. long, the upper ones decidedly narrower than the lower. Flowers small, woolly on the outside, white but pink-spotted, crowded in dense clusters (whorls*) in the leaf axils. Stamens* 4. Fruit a collection of 4 small nutlets. Of very easy culture in any ordinary garden soil, and readily propagated by division. (*Leonurus* is from the Greek for lion's tail, and a pre-Linnaean* name for the plant now known as *Leonotis Leonurus,* which see.)

LEOPARD FLOWER = *Belamcanda chin-ensis.*

LEOPARD FOXGLOVE = *Digitalis pur-purea maculata superba.* See FOXGLOVE.

LEOPARD LILY = *Lilium pardalinum.* See also SANSEVIERIA.

LEOPARD PLANT = *Ligularia kaempferi aureo-maculata.*

LEOPARD'S-BANE = *Senecio Doronicum.* See also DORONICUM.

LEPACHYS = *Ratibida.*

LEPARGYREA = *Shepherdia.*

LEPIDIUM (lep-id'i-um). Pepper-grass. Nearly 100 species of widely distributed, weedy herbs of the mustard family, of little garden interest except for **L. sativum,** the garden or upland cress, which is an Asiatic annual herb, 1–2 ft. high. It is grown oc-casionally as a sharp-flavored salad plant. Leaves alternate,* the basal ones more or less cut and toothed, the upper narrower and without teeth. Some of the hort. forms (the chief ones grown) have curled or crisped leaves. Flowers white or greenish, very small, in a terminal cluster (raceme*). Fruit a roundish, somewhat notched, flattish pod (silicle*), the cluster elongating in age. One of the numerous plants known as cress, and, to distinguish it from watercress, often called upland cress. (*Lepidium* is from the Greek for a little scale, in allusion to the small fruits.)

lepidophylla, -*us,* -*um* (lep-id-o-fill'a). Having scaly leaves.

LEPIDOTE. Scurfy or scaly, as are some leaves.

leporella, -*us,* -*um* (lep-o-rell'a). A little hare.

LEPTANDRA VIRGINICA = *Veronicast-rum virginicum.*

LEPTINELLA = *Cotula.*

leptocaulis, -*e* (lep-to-kaw'lis). Thin-stemmed.

LEPTODACTYLON. *See* GILIA CALIFOR-NICA.

leptolepis, -*e* (lep-tol'ĕ-pis). Thin-scaled.

leptopa, -*us,* -*um* (lep'to-pa). Having a thin or weak stalk or stem.

---

leptophylla, -us, -um (lep-to-fill'a). Thin-leaved.

leptosepala, -us, -um (lep-to-see'pa-la). With thin sepals.*

LEPTOSIPHON. See GILIA.

LEPTOSPERMUM (lep-to-sper'mum). Tea-tree (but it has nothing to do with the tea plant). Australasian shrubs and trees of the family Myrtaceae, comprising over 30 species, several of which are widely cult. in Calif. and elsewhere below zone* 7. Leaves alternate,* small, rigid, often almost prickle-like. Flowers numerous, but solitary or 2 or 3 together in the leaf axils,* white or reddish in those below. Calyx* more or less bell-shaped, its lobes 5. Petals 5. Stamens* many, not protruding. Fruit a leathery capsule.* (*Leptospermum* is from the Greek for slender or thin seed.)

Leptospermum is a popular genus in Calif. In Aust. *L. laevigatum* is widely planted for reclamation of shifting sand. They are of easy cult. in the right climate and are propagated by seeds, or by cuttings. Some of them are grown in the cool greenhouse, where they need potting mixture* 3. They should be kept there until Feb.–Mar., when the temperature should be raised to 55°–60°, which will force them into bloom. In Calif. *L. laevigatum* is by far the most widely grown, although fine specimens of *L. scoparium* are to be seen in Golden Gate Park.

flexuosum = *Agonis flexuosa.*

laevigatum. Australian tea-tree. A tree up to 30 ft., usually shrubby as cult. Leaves very numerous, blunt, about 1 in. long and ½ in. wide. Flowers white, about ¾ in. wide. Aust. Widely planted in Calif.

pubescens. A usually silky-hairy shrub or small tree. Leaves about ⅓ in. long, blunt. Flowers white, nearly ¾ in. wide. Aust.

scoparium. Tea-tree, and the best-known species in cult., but not so commonly planted in Calif. as *L. laevigatum.* A tall shrub or small tree, 12–25 ft. high, or occasionally dwarf and only 1–2 ft. high, the foliage silky when young. Leaves very numerous, about ⅓ in. long, almost prickle-tipped. Flowers about ½ in. wide, white. N.Z. and Aust. Several varieties are cult., of which *var.* **bullatum** has larger flowers; *var.* **juniperinum** has drooping branchlets and narrower leaves; *var.* **nichollsi** has carmine flowers and bronzy foliage.

LEPTOSYNE. See COREOPSIS.

LESPEDEZA (les-pe-dee'za). Bush clover. A genus of about 40 species of annual or perennial herbs or shrubs of the pea family common in N.A. and As., a few in Aust. Some are grown for their showy flower clusters, while *L. striata* is grown in the South for forage and green manuring (which see). They have alternate,* compound* leaves, with mostly 3 leaflets that are without marginal teeth. Flowers small, but showy from the profuse clusters, of two kinds in many species. One set is pea-like, showy, and usually sterile*; the other without petals but fertile. Fruit a very short pod (loment*), usually reduced to 1 joint, half hidden in the persistent calyx,* and with a single seed. (Named for a Governor Lespedez, once Spanish governor of Fla., by his friend Michaux.)

Lespedeza bicolor and *L. formosa* are Asiatic shrubs valued for their late bloom. They prefer open, rather sandy soils and are not difficult to grow. Both are propagated by cuttings. *L. capitata* is a somewhat weedy North American herb which will grow in the poorest soils, and may be increased by division. *L. striata,* the Japan clover, is an annual suited only to the South, where seed may be sown in the early spring as for clover.

bicolor. A shrub 6–9 ft. high. Leaflets 3, ovalish, ¾–1½ in. long. Flowers purple, or rose-purple, the clusters (racemes*) grouped in a large, showy, branching cluster (panicle*). Eastern As. Aug.–Sept. Hardy from zone* 3 southward.

capitata. Bush or dusty clover. A perennial herb 3–5 ft. high, the foliage silvery and silky. Leaflets 3, oblongish. Flowers purple-spotted, but generally yellowish-white, not showy, in dense, head-like clusters. Summer. Sandy soil in eastern N.A.

formosa = *L. thunbergi.*

japonica. Perhaps not specifically distinct from *Lespedeza thunbergi,* but with white flowers. Jap. Sept.–Oct. Hardy from zone* 4, possibly from zone* 3 southward.

sieboldi = *L. thunbergi.*

striata. Japan clover; also called hoop-coop plant. An annual herb not over 18 in. high, grown for forage and as green manure in the South. Leaflets many, scarcely ¾ in. long, nearly stalkless. Flowers pinkish-purple, small, only 1–3 in each leaf axil.* China and Jap., sometimes naturalized in the southern states.

thunbergi. A shrub 3–7 ft. high, but often dying to the ground each winter, hence herb-like. Leaflets 3, oblong-elliptic, the middle one longer-stalked than the other two. Flowers rose-purple, the clusters (racemes*) long and drooping. Eastern As. Sept.–Oct. (*See* AUTUMN GARDEN.) Hardy from zone* 4, possibly from zone* 3 southward. Also known as *Desmodium penduliflorum.*

LESSER WINTERGREEN = *Pyrola elliptica.*

LETTUCE (*Lactuca sativa* and varieties). Crisp, tender lettuce, the most desirable of all salad plants, can only be grown with the strictest attention to its moisture, soil, and climatic requirements. Originally a Eurasian annual* (unknown in the wild state), the plant has been developed into many strains or races each having dozens of named forms or varieties.

For the home gardener lettuce may be divided into three categories: (1) Tight, crisp, nearly white head lettuce with a cabbage-like head. A modification of this is the Butterhead type, of which the Bibb is the most famous and the best. It was originated in Ky. about 1850, by a Jack Bibb, and has a small head of dark-green color and superlative flavor. It is inclined to bolting* in warm weather and hence is often grown in the cool greenhouse. (2) Loose, so-called leaf or garden lettuce which,

---

* Special articles on the subjects indicated by an asterisk (*) will be found at the words so marked.

although it has a head, is looser and has many more outer green leaves. (3) Cos or Romaine lettuce, which is cylindric, has long, relatively loose leaves and forms (in some varieties) a head without being tied up, but often it has to be tied. *See also* CELTUCE.

The order in which these types are listed is no accident. The first is by far the most desirable, but the most difficult to grow. The second is less desirable, but so much easier to grow that most beginners will do well to select one of its varieties. The third is the easiest of all and the only type that makes any pretense of standing summer heat.

And heat is what all the really desirable varieties will not stand. They can easily endure several degrees of frost, especially in the seedling stage, which greatly facilitates the handling of lettuce in the early spring. It is in this respect more hardy than cabbage. But midsummer heat, more than

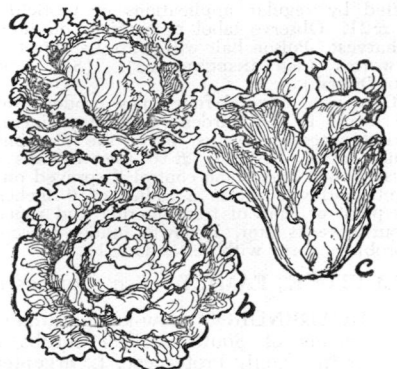

Types of lettuce: (*a*) Crisped type of head lettuce; (*b*) a typical non-crisped head lettuce; (*c*) Cos or Romaine lettuce.

several other things to be mentioned presently, will throw the plant into flower. This ruins its chance of heading, because the tall flower stalk (18 in. or more) is forced up through what should be the head, *i.e.,* bolting.*

It is obvious from this that lettuce is a cool-season crop only (except Cos lettuce), and is consequently grown in early spring and late summer, or in favored localities where it is cool all the growing season. Lettuce commercially produced in the South and California is grown in their winter season when only greenhouse culture (widely practiced) is possible in the North.

VARIETIES. The home grower can ignore the many varieties that shipping requirements and adaptability to greenhouse culture have developed. All of them are highly specialized sorts much favored by commercial growers in different sections of the country. For ordinary garden uses the best varieties are:

(1) BUTTERHEAD TYPE: White Boston, Bibb, Mignonette.
(2) CRISPHEAD TYPE: Great Lakes, Pennlake, Imperial strains, and Cornell 456.
(3) LEAF TYPE: Slobolt, Grand Rapids, Prize Head, Salad Bowl, and Simpson. Here belongs Cos or Romaine lettuce.

SOILS AND FERTILIZERS. Any good garden soil will grow lettuce of a sort. But the most favored soils are rich, sandy loams. Some varieties, like Grand Rapids, do best on heavy soils with considerable clay in them. Some of the largest commercial growers in the country use reclaimed muck soils, not because they are particularly fertile (this is greatly augmented by fertilizers), but because muck soils usually have abundant soil moisture easily available by capillarity with proper handling. Lettuce soils should not be acid. If they are they should be limed. *See* LIME; *see also* MUCKLAND GARDENING.

More important than the texture is soil moisture. If this is not available, do not attempt to grow lettuce unless you can supply the needed moisture by irrigation or an overhead sprinkling system. Both methods are widely used by commercial growers.

Plenty of soil moisture will help to induce quick growth, and no slow-growing lettuce is any good. But it will only grow rapidly if the soil is rich in plant food. To make it so, plow in liberal supplies of well-rotted stable manure (not filled with straw) at the rate of 15–20 tons to the acre (5 or 6 wheelbarrow loads to 100 ft. of row). In addition use 1500 pounds to the acre of a good general-purpose commercial fertilizer (about 5 pounds to 100 ft. of row). If you can use only one of these, try to make it the stable manure, for it adds much humus to the soil and thus heightens its moisture-holding capacity as well as enriching it.

Needless to say, almost, is the necessity of getting these materials thoroughly plowed under and the soil brought to as mellow a condition of tilth* as possible. Once the plants are set out, especially the spring crop of the head lettuce type, it will be a race against the arrival of hot weather in any case. Soil moisture, plenty of plant food and perfectly worked soil will greatly help to force lettuce to head before summer heat makes heading impossible.

STARTING LETTUCE PLANTS. Sowing lettuce seed should be timed so that they are transplanted to the garden just as soon as the ground can be worked. You need not wait for the last (usually erratic) frost of spring in order to set out the seedlings, because, especially in their early stages, they will easily endure several degrees of frost. Count, as your possible outdoor planting date, the average date when the last frost in your locality occurs (see name of your state for frost dates).

Having determined your earliest safe date for outdoor culture, allow 6–7 weeks

* Special articles on the subjects indicated by an asterisk (*) will be found at the words so marked.

before this to begin indoor operations. Start by sowing the seed broadcast or in tiny drills in flats or boxes in a cool greenhouse or hotbed. If you have neither, put the box in your kitchen window (no gas stove). Cover the seeds with about ¼ in. of finely sifted soil. In a few days the plants will be up and as soon as they are 2 in. high, they must be pricked out and spaced about 2 in. each way. A second and third shifting, each more amply spaced, is advisable but not obligatory. Mice are fond of the seedlings and should be coaxed away with corn soaked in strychnine solution.

Gradually harden off the plants by reducing the temperature to something like those they must meet when shifted outdoors. This can easily be done in the hotbed or cold frame.

OUTDOOR PLANTING. The young seedlings are then set out in any garden, preferably on a dull day, and in any case, they must be watered until they recover from the move. Put the plants 10 in. apart in the rows and have the rows 14 in. apart. Keep a few seedlings to replace some, more or less certain, failures. Cultivation and adequate moisture should then do the rest. If you have been thorough, this crop should supply you with head lettuce before warm weather.

In addition to this, it is advisable to sow lettuce seed directly in the garden at about the time, or just after, the indoor plants have been set out. It can be sown broadcast or in very shallow drills, in either case covered very lightly with the finest soil which the rake will pulverize.

Slightly tamp the soil and water it with a fine, mistlike spray (a hose stream without a fine nozzle will wash out the seeds). The plants will come up far too thick for permanent spacing. But as they grow they can be thinned to the intervals given above, and the thinnings are useful house greens.

In many favorable (i.e., cool) localities this outdoor-sown seed will provide good

Good head lettuce, in rich soil, and
properly spaced

lettuce after the indoor plants have been harvested. And in especially cool regions a similar sowing may be made 12 days after the first. But in most regions summer heat puts a stop to all but one or two spring sowings.

For the fall crop exactly the same procedure is followed as for the early crop of indoor seedlings, except that the flats or boxes are put outdoors in a cool, shaded place. Young plants should be ready to set out about August 15 over most of the North.

In the far North, lettuce may be grown throughout the brief, but cool growing season. This applies only to zones* 1 and 2, or to regions of great elevation and plenty of summer moisture (or irrigation). Both plants started indoors and outdoor-sown seed may be used, the latter sown about every 12 days for a succession.

For the preferred position and sequence of lettuce in your garden see KITCHEN GARDEN.

INSECT PESTS. Leafhoppers and leaf feeders that transmit the yellows disease can be controlled by regular applications of pesticide #1 or #21. Observe label precautions on interval to harvest. Poison bait will control spring or fall cutworms (see INSECTICIDES). (See SPRAYS AND DUSTS.)

DISEASES. Several fungi may produce rot of the heads in the garden. If disease increases during successive years, move the planting to a new area. Pesticide #10 (see SPRAYS AND DUSTS) will offer some control if sprayed on the plants and soil within a radius of 6 inches of the plant at time of transplanting and repeated about 2 weeks later. If downy mildew* becomes a problem, spray with pesticide #11.

LETTUCE FAMILY. *See* COMPOSITAE.

LEUCADENDRON (lew-ka-den'dron). A large genus of South African shrubs and trees of the family Proteaceae, **L. argenteum,** the silver tree, widely planted in Calif. and similar climates for its beautiful silvery and silky foliage. Leaves scattered, without marginal teeth, but hard-tipped, 3–6 in. long, nearly stalkless. Male and female flowers on different plants, the male flowers numerous in dense, stalkless, head-like clusters, nearly 2½ in. wide. Female flowers in cone-like heads, beneath which is a series of woody bracts.* Both sorts of flowers have no petals, but 4 sepals. Fruit a nut. Propagated by seeds. (*Leucadendron* is from the Greek for white tree, in allusion to the silvery foliage. *Leucadendron* is also a specific name at *Melaleuca.*)

LEUCAENA (lew-see'na). A small genus of mostly tropical American shrubs and trees of the pea family, related to and somewhat resembling species of *Acacia.* The only cult. species, **L. glauca,** the white popinac, is an evergreen, spineless tree up to 30 ft. and of very easy culture in zones* 8 and 9, but not hardy north of this. It has twice-compound* leaves, the ultimate leaflets very numerous, oblongish or narrower, bluish-green or even grayish. Flowers white, not pea-like, crowded in a dense, globe-

---

* Special articles on the subjects indicated by an asterisk (*) will be found at the words so marked.

shaped cluster which is about 1 in. in diameter. Stamens* 10, protruding. Fruit a stalked, flat pod (legume*) 5–6 in. long. Tropical America, but naturalized and a somewhat weedy tree in Fla. (*Leucaena* is from the Greek for white, in allusion to the white flowers.)

leucantha, -us, -um (lew-kan'tha). White-flowered.

Leucanthemum (lew-kan'the-mum). Pre-Linnaean* name for the common white daisy, now called *Chrysanthemum Leucanthemum.*

leucaspis (loo-kas'pis). Having (a structure like) a white shield.

LEUCOCORYNE (loo-co-cor-ry'ne). Chilean bulbous herbs of the family Liliaceae, closely related to *Brodiaea*, with which the one below is often confused. They have bulbs or corms,* narrow leaves, and flowers in a terminal cluster (umbel*). Fruit a 3-grooved capsule. (*Leucocoryne* is from the Greek for white club, in allusion to the sterile anthers.*)

It can be grown outdoors only in southern Calif. where it is planted in the open sun, 4–6 in. deep, in Sept. or Oct. It should be allowed to stay in the ground so that it will rest during the dry season. The plant is sometimes forced for winter bloom in eastern greenhouses, and for this follow directions at *Freesia.*

ixioides. Glory-of-the-sun. Not over 1 ft. high, the flowers blue-tipped and whitish. It does not flower very profusely. *Var.* **odorata** has fragrant blue flowers with a white center.

uniflora = *Brodiaea uniflora.*

LEUCOCRINUM (lew-ko-kry'num). A single, rather bulbous-thickened, practically stemless herb of the lily family, L. **montanum**, the sand or star lily, native from Neb. to Calif. and Ore. It is not often seen in cult., but is occasionally transferred from the wild. It has a swollen, bulbous-thickened rootstock. Leaves basal, thick, flat, 4–7 in. long, scarcely ¼ in. wide. Flowers practically stalkless, borne at or near the ground, white and fragrant, the corolla funnel-shaped, partly buried. (*Leucocrinum* is from the Greek for white lily.)

LEUCOJUM. *See* Snowflake.

leuconeura, -us, -um (lew-ko-newr'ra). White-veined.

LEUCOPHYLLUM (loo-ko-fill'um). A small genus of rather showy, evergreen shrubs of the figwort family from Tex. and adjacent Mex. They have alternate leaves without marginal teeth, and bell-shaped flowers only slightly irregular,* solitary at the leaf joints. Fruit a dry capsule. The only species likely to be cult. is the Texas ranger, **L. texanum** (also known as *L. frutescens*), a shrub 6–8 ft. high. Leaves oblongish, about 1 in. long, white-woolly on the under side. Flowers about 1 in. long, violet-purple, hairy on the inside. Tex. Summer. Little cult. outside its wild range, but used there for hedges. (*Leu-*

cophyllum is from the Greek meaning white leaf.)

LEUCOTHOË (lew-koth'o-ee). Ornamental shrubs of the heath family, only a few of which, from U.S. and Japan, can be considered hardy. The leaves are alternate* and deciduous or evergreen. In the hardy species the flowers are white, occasionally tinged pink, urn-shaped with 5 little teeth at the top, and borne in clusters along, or at the tip of, the branches. The fruit is a dry, round, 5-celled capsule.* (Named for the daughter of Orchamus, mythological king of Babylonia.)

The leucothoës are handsome shrubs having good foliage and attractive flowers. The evergreen species (particularly *L. catesbaei*) are especially ornamental and desirable. They are of low habit, with graceful, arching branches and thick leaves that turn red or bronze in winter. For use with other evergreens, in foundation plantings, or borders they are invaluable. They grow well in light woods, and the sprays make very attractive winter bouquets.

Their chief cultural need is a moist, peaty soil or a sandy loam with plenty of humus. Propagation is by division, cuttings, or seed.

axillaris. Evergreen shrub with arching branches, growing about 5 ft. high. Leaves leathery, ovoid-lance-shaped, 2–4 in. usually short-pointed and with a stalk of ¼–½ in. Flowers white, in clusters 1–2 in. long borne in the leaf axils.* April–May. Va. to Fla. and Miss. Hardy from zone* 4 southward. Very similar to the following species, but is less hardy and has smaller, abruptly pointed leaves with shorter stalk.

catesbaei. Fetter-bush, also called dog-hobble. Evergreen shrub to 6 ft. high with slender, arching branches. Flowers white in drooping clusters along the branches. May. Va. to Ga. and Tenn. Hardy from most parts of zone* 3 southward. It is the hardiest of the evergreen leucothoës. Called by some *L. editorum.*

davisiae. An evergreen shrub 2–3 ft. high with smooth twigs and short-stalked ovalish leaves 1–3 in. long. Flowers nodding, small, urn-shaped, in a showy terminal cluster (panicle*). Fruit a small capsule. Calif. and Ore. June. Hardy from zone* 5 southward.

keiskei. A Japanese evergreen shrub, the leaves ovalish or oblong, 1½–3½ in. long. Flowers white, larger than in any of the others, nodding, the clusters terminal or in the leaf axils.* Hardy from zone* 6 (possibly from zone* 5) southward.

racemosa. Pepper-bush, sweetbells or white osier. Deciduous* shrub of upright, bushy habit growing 4–6 ft. or sometimes 12 ft. high. Leaves oblong or oval, toothed, 1–3 in. long. Flowers white, abundant, in clusters usually terminating short branches of the previous season. May–June. Mass. to Fla. and La. Hardy from zone* 3 southward.

LEVANT COTTON = *Gossypium herbaceum.*

LEVERWOOD = *Ostrya virginiana.*

LEVISTICUM (le-vis'ti-kum). A single species of perennial herb of the carrot

---

* Special articles on the subjects indicated by an asterisk (*) will be found at the words so marked.

family, **L. officinale** of southern Eu., the well-known lovage, which has been cult. for centuries for its aromatic fruits. It is a stout herb 3–6 ft. high, its leaves thrice-compound, the ultimate segments more or less wedge-shaped and coarsely toothed toward the tip. Flowers greenish-yellow, very small (*see* UMBELLIFERAE), but numerous in a compound cluster (compound umbel*). Fruit flattened and ribbed, the ribs more or less winged. For culture and uses *see* HERB GARDENING. (*Levisticum* is of uncertain origin.)

LEWISIA (lew-is'ĭ-a). A genus of 12 species of fleshy, perennial, practically stemless herbs of the family Portulacaceae, all from western N.A., a number cult. for ornament, mostly in the rock garden. They have thick, starchy roots and basal, narrow leaves in rosettes, usually club-shaped and without marginal teeth. Flowers solitary or in branched clusters at the end of a short stalk arising at the leaf rosette. Sepals* 2–8, mostly persistent. Petals 3–16. Fruit a many-seeded capsule.* (Named for Captain Meriwether Lewis of Lewis and Clark fame.)

The best-known of all the species is the bitter-root, *L. rediviva*, which is grown in succulent collections. All of them need a gritty soil such as that in some sections of the rock garden (which see). The plants are widely grown, mostly in the rock garden. The heights given are for the flowering stalk.

brachycalyx. Leaves rather fleshy, in rosettes,* not evergreen, 2–3 in. long. Flowers solitary, nearly 2 in. wide, white, the stalk scarcely 2 in. high, with 2 bracts* near the flower. Hardy in the northeastern U.S. Native in Southwestern U.S.

columbiana. About 12 in. high, the leaves narrow or spatula-shaped, 1–2 in. long. Flowers about ⅓ in. long, in loose clusters (panicles*), the 4–7 petals white or pink, but red-veined. Mountains of Wash. and Ore.

Cotyledon. About 8–10 in. high, the leaves spatula-shaped, 2–3 in. long. Flowers about ½ in. long, in loose clusters (panicles*), the 7–10 petals white, but pink-veined. Calif.

finchi. About 12 in. high, the leaves 2–3 in. long and about half as wide. Flowers in a profuse cluster (cyme*), the petals pink, but white-margined. Calif.

heckneri. Leaves keeled,* fleshy, and with fleshy teeth, 2–3 in. long, purplish on the under side. Flowers in clusters, the corolla about ¾ in. wide, red, the stalk about 4 in. high. Northern Calif.

howelli. About 6 in. high, the leaves oblong or ovalish. Flowers in cymes.* the 7–10 petals deep rose-red. Southwestern Ore. Largely grown for its handsome flowers.

rediviva. Bitter-root. A stemless, fleshy plant, the succulent leaves scarcely 1 in. long, the flowering stalk about as long. Flowers about 1 in. long, rose-pink or white. When through flowering, the plant is most inconspicuous and quite likely to be weeded out. It cannot stand much winter moisture and needs perfect drainage at all times. Its starchy root, edible in the spring, was once a food for the Indians, but by midsummer it becomes very bitter. Rocky Mountains to British Columbia.

tweedyi. Not over 4 in. high, the root very thick. Leaves more or less oblong, 2–4 in. long. Flowers 1–3, pink, about 2½ in. wide, showy. Alpine summits such as Mt. Rainier and others in Wash. Suited only to the rock garden.

LEYCESTERIA (ly-ses-teer'ia). Himalayan shrubs of the honeysuckle family, comprising only two species, one of them, **L. formosa**, cult. for ornament. It is a smooth shrub, 4–6 ft. high, with hollow stems and opposite,* stalked, broadly oval leaves, 2–7 in. long, and tapering at the tip. Flowers in drooping spikes, each flower from between purplish-red bracts.* Corolla funnel-shaped, purplish, ⅔–1¼ in. long. Stamens* 5. Fruit a many-seeded berry. A handsome shrub, blooming from May–Sept. and hardy from zone* 6 southward. Chiefly conspicuous because of the showy bracts.* Little is known of its cultural requirements. (Named for William Leycester, a Bengal judge.)

LIANA. A high-climbing, usually woody vine, more common in the tropics than in the U.S., although some wild grapes are lianas. So are the poison ivy and some herbaceous vines.

LIATRIS (ly-ā'tris). A genus of perhaps 30 species of North American, rather weedy, but very showy, perennial herbs of the family Compositae, those below often grown in open, sandy, or otherwise poor sites in the wild garden, or in formal borders. They are rather coarse plants with often resinous-dotted, alternate,* usually stiffish, narrow leaves and button-shaped heads of exclusively disk* flowers, the head close and surrounded by many, appressed,* greenish bracts.* The heads are borne in spikes or racemes,* and are handsome. All bloom in summer or early fall and are prevailingly rose-purple. The plants are commonly called button snakeroot and are sometimes offered under the name *Lacinaria*. (*Liatris* is of unknown origin.)

All are of the easiest culture in open, light soils, and may be increased by division. *See* SAND GARDEN.

graminifolia. A perennial herb, 10–30 in. high, with narrow, grass-like leaves 2–8 in. long, minutely hairy on the margins toward the base. Flower heads top-shaped, about ½ in. in diameter, purple, scattered in a spike-like, terminal cluster. N.J. to Ala., mostly in sandy woods and useful in such sites. Aug.–Oct.

odoratissima = *Trilisa odoratissima*.

punctata. A stout herb 12–20 in. high, with narrow, almost prickle-pointed leaves. Flower heads about ¾ in. long, numerous in a dense spike. Prairies of the central U.S.

pycnostachya. Prairie button snakeroot; also called Kansas gay-feather. A stout herb 3–5 ft. high, the stems wand-like. Leaves narrowly lance-shaped, becoming thread-like but stiffish toward the top. Flower heads about ½ in. long, dense spikes. Prairies of the central U.S. July–Aug.

scariosa. Gay-feather; also called rattlesnake master and blue blazing star. A hairy-stemmed herb, 3–5 ft. high, the leaves oblongish or narrower. Flower heads nearly 1 in. wide, but not numerous, bluish-purple, mostly in interrupted* racemes.* Pa. and W. Va. to S. Car. July–Aug.

---

* Special articles on the subjects indicated by an asterisk (*) will be found at the words so marked.

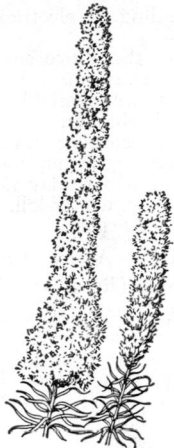

Prairie Button Snakeroot (*Liatris pycnostachya*), a robust prairie perennial with profuse spikes of rose-purple flower heads. Good for dry sites.

spicata. Gay-feather; called also prairie pine and devil's-bit. A very leafy-stemmed herb, 4–6 ft. high, the lower leaves 3–5-veined, narrow, and nearly 12 in. long, much diminishing upward. Flower heads about ½ in. long, the dense spike nearly 15 in. long. Eastern N.A. Sept. Sometimes offered as *L. callilepis*.

squarrosa. Blazing star; also called rattlesnake master and colicroot. Not over 2 ft. high, the stem hairy. Leaves very narrow, nearly 6 in. long. Flower heads nearly 1½ in. long, not numerous, the cluster of them more or less interrupted. Eastern U.S. and west to Tex.

libani (lee′ba-ni). From Mt. Lebanon.

libanotica, -us, -um (lee-ban-nō′ti-ka). From Mt. Lebanon.

LIBERIAN COFFEE = *Coffea liberica.*

liberica, -us, -um (ly-beer′i-ka). From Liberia, Africa.

LIBERTIA (li-ber′she-a). A small genus of plants of the iris family, chiefly Australasian, but the only commonly cult. species, **L. formosa,** a native of Chile. It has a short, creeping rootstock and 2-ranked, rather rigid leaves, 12–18 in. long, the flowering stalk 2–3 ft. high. Flowers in nearly stalkless clusters (umbels*), of which there are many, the individual flowers about ⅝ in. long, white outside, greenish-brown within. Fruit a 3-valved capsule.* The plant is not hardy north of zone* 6, and requires a moist site. Propagated by division of the rootstock. (Named for Marie A. Libert, Belgian botanist.) More recently *L. grandiflora* from N.Z. has come into cult. It is 2–3 ft. high and has white flowers.

LIBOCEDRUS. *See* INCENSE CEDAR.

LICHEN (ly′ken). Curious flowerless plants of little interest to the gardener, but of unusual food habits. The common lichens which hug rocks and tree trunks consist of a flattish, usually brown or ashy plant body looking much like a patch. Within it are an alga and a fungus which live off each other. The process involves complicated chemical reactions, some of which result in the extremely slow disintegration of rocks into soil. Lichens are thus one of the first agencies in changing rock into soil. Sometimes used in terrariums.*

LICH GATE = Lych Gate.

LICORICE. This long-known cough remedy and flavor for tobacco is derived from the only cult. species of the genus **Glycyrrhiza** (gly-ki-ry′za) of the pea family, chiefly from the Mediterranean region. The only cult. species is **G. glabra,** the common or Spanish licorice, which is a perennial herb 2–3 ft. high, with compound* leaves having 4–8 pairs of ovalish leaflets. Flowers blue, pea-like, in short clusters (spikes or racemes*) in the leaf axils.* Fruit a flattish pod (legume*), 3–4 in. long. The plant is suited only to Calif. and similar climates, but the harvest of its roots, which produce the licorice, is not certainly profitable in America. *See* MEDICINAL PLANTS. (*Glycyrrhiza* is from the Greek for sweet root.)

LIFE PLANT = *Bryophyllum pinnatum.*

LIFTING. The transplanting of specimens from one place to another. It is a planting operation and directions will be found at PLANTING.

LIGHT. The prime requisite for all garden plants; for, even with plenty of food and water, most plants will die without an adequate amount of light. While it is true that many forest plants have become shade-tolerant and in fact would perish in full sunlight, the fact still remains that only in the presence of light will leaves perform their function of making starch and sugar — a process absolutely essential to all plants with green leaves. *See* the work of chlorophyll at PLANT FOODS.

So important is solar influence to the growth of plants that much experimental work has been done on the composition of sunlight, and the effects of utilizing the different sorts of light rays found in it upon plants. Experimentally, plants can be made to do queer things by subjecting them to different kinds, amount, and duration of light (*see* ELECTRO-HORTICULTURE). *See also* PHOTOPERIODISM.

One practical feature of the light question is the great improvement in glass now used for greenhouses (*see* GREENHOUSE). It allows more and better illumination for plants growing under it than the old type.

LIGHTING. The purpose of garden illumination is to reveal certain aspects of light by rendering visible out of the darkness of night subtle patterns in garden forms, textures, and colors. Light, a definite medium of visible expression, affords a subjective approach to creative design. Play of light and shade may interpret "song in light" as motifs modify the quality of light and control its distribution. As we sense values in shades and shadows, we become conscious of light, and as we discriminate certain objective illusions from more positive phases of subjective reality, we may discern that "light is the positive of dark," and subjective reality may shine forth as an overtone of optical illusion. Hence garden lighting may reveal in the quiet darkness of evening some hidden enchantment too elusive for the full boldness of day.

The general distribution of the sources of garden lighting and placement of light outlets are technical considerations of the utmost importance for successful illumination. In this matter there seem to be two schools of thought. First, those who prefer their light straight and direct and desire to maintain an obvious fixture and source of light; and second, those who are partial to indirect lighting. In a subtle combination of these two methods it is possible successfully to avoid tiresome stunts and trickiness. Reflected color, however, never has the power of direct color or light.

Where obvious source-lights are used the location and distribution of fixtures are dictated by the type of picture-patterns one is attempting to develop. They are subject to modifications affecting physical display, emotional appeal, and intellectual stimulus. Source outlets to be considered for general installation cover such functions as guide lights to illuminate a pathway, sentinel lights along a vista, and specially featured light fixtures and outlets for spot and flood lighting.

Artificial lighting effects should be controlled to portray the dramatization of such distinctive features in the garden as may be worthy of special selection. It is assumed that only such areas would be featured as would lend themselves readily to this sort of dramatization.

The question of color is difficult and controversial. Warm, positive red may induce certain emotional reactions, whereas the cold higher vibrational light of blue may be more soulful in appeal, but this all depends on local enviroment, both physical and psychological. Yellow — the golden mean — we have become psychologically adjusted to and have considered it as normal in our modern electric-lighting systems. The wave length of red is about twice that of violet, and blue vibrates twice as fast as red. Blue, therefore, fades out the quicker, except at dusk when blue seems to be almost luminous. In the matter of color tones, warm, direct light causes cool shadows and cold light causes warm shadows. For natural lighting effects, structures such as walls and buildings are usually coldly lighted at night, whereas flowers and foliage masses take the complement to coldness — a warm light with an orange cast.

Light is the great revealer — constant, penetrating, and abstract — and we may eventually know its source and the significance of its integrating power through the right understanding of electrical phenomena. — A. F.

To implement the above suggestions needs a practical electrician. Various garden lighting fixtures are available from General Electric Co., Lightolier, and other firms. Night lighting of gardens must not be overdone as too much light may induce abnormal growth, some of which may not ripen properly and hence be winter-killed. It also attracts insects. — EDITOR.

LIGHTWOOD = *Acacia melanoxylon.*

lignosa, -us, -um (lig-nō′sa). Woody.

LIGULARIA (lig-you-lay′rĭ-a). Handsome Eurasian perennial herbs of the family Compositae, cult. in the cool greenhouse or in the flower garden for their showy flower heads or (in a variety) for the variegated foliage. They have alternate,° or often basal and long-stalked leaves which are roundish or kidney-shaped, those on the stem sheathed and smaller. Flower heads usually nodding, arranged in branched or unbranched clusters (racemes° or corymbs°), the rays° usually yellow and strap-shaped. (*Ligularia* is from the root of *ligulate,* meaning strap-shaped, in allusion to the shape of the ray° flowers.)

The plants, which are closely related to *Senecio,* are of simple cultural requirements, doing well in ordinary garden soil. The leopard plant (*L. kaempferi aureo-maculata*) is chiefly grown for its foliage and is rather common as a window-garden plant. Propagated by cuttings or by division.

clivorum. A stout perennial, 3–4 ft. high, rusty-hairy in youth, ultimately nearly smooth. Lower leaves kidney-shaped or roundish, long-stalked, nearly 20 in. wide, sharply but remotely toothed. Flower heads numerous, orange-yellow, nearly 4 in. wide. China and Jap. Often sold as *Senecio clivorum.*

kaempferi. Rootstock prominent; and from it arise many roundish or heart-shaped or kidney-shaped leaves, 6–10 in. wide on slender, white-woolly stalks. Flower heads 1½–2 in. wide, light yellow, in branched clusters that are on white-woolly stalks 2–3 ft. long. Jap. Often sold as *Senecio kaempferi* or *Farfugium kaempferi,* but more commonly cult. in the *var.* aureo-maculata which has yellow, white, or occasionally pink-blotched leaves and is a favorite plant for window boxes; known as leopard plant, and not hardy over the winter above zone° 6. Also known as *Farfugium japonicum* and *L. tussilaginea.*

veitchiana. A usually unbranched, stout perennial, 3–6 ft. high, the lower leaves more or less heart-shaped or kidney-shaped, nearly 12 in. wide and angularly toothed. Flower heads yellow, about 2½ in. wide, numerous. Jap.

wilsoniana. Nearly 5 ft. high, the basal leaves heart-shaped or kidney-shaped, sharply toothed and 12–18 in. long. Flower heads about 1 in. wide, yellow, in long, column-like spikes. China.

ligulata, -us, -um (lig-you-lay′ta). Strap-shaped.

LIGULE. 1. A strap-shaped ray° flower in certain flower heads of the Compositae (which see). 2. A sheath-like organ found

---

° Special articles on the subjects indicated by an asterisk (°) will be found at the words so marked.

on the stems of some grasses and a few other plants.

LIGURIAN BELLFLOWER = *Campanula isophylla.*

ligusticifolia, -us, -um (ly-gus-ti-si-fō'lĭ-a). With leaves like the genus *Ligusticum* which are weedy plants of the carrot family and of little hort. interest.

ligustrina, -us, -um (ly-gus-try'na). Privet-like.

LIGUSTRUM. See PRIVET.

LILAC. A large group of decorative shrubs and trees belonging to the genus **Syringa** (sir-ring'a) of the olive family. They are Old World plants with opposite,* usually unlobed leaves and showy clusters of flowers that are borne in spring and early summer, chiefly in thyrses.* The flowers are tubular, with 4 spreading lobes and 2 stamens.* They may be white, pink, lavender, or purple and are often fragrant. The fruit is, in most cases, a brown, flattened, oval capsule.* (*Syringa* is probably from the Greek for pipe, and refers to the hollow stems of *Philadelphus* which was originally called *Syringa*.)

For culture *see* below.

S. amurensis. Amur lilac. A small tree, more often a shrub 5–15 ft. high, its leaves broadly ovalish, nearly 5 in. long and smooth. Flowers whitish-yellow, the cluster nearly 6 in. long. Eastern As. June. Hardy from zone* 3 southward. The *var.* japonica has larger, hairy leaves and may become a tree up to 30 ft. high.

S. chinensis. Rouen lilac. A hybrid shrub (*persica* × *vulgaris*), usually densely branched, rarely over 10 ft. high. Leaves ovalish, about 2 in. long, smooth, with a tapering tip. Flowers fragrant, lilac-purple, in looser clusters than in the common lilac. May. Hardy from zone* 4 southward.

S. japonica = *L. amurensis japonica.*

S. Josikaea. Hungarian lilac. Shrub up to 12 ft. high. Leaves oval, 2–5 in. long, sometimes tapered at the ends, whitish beneath. Flowers deep lilac to violet, in slender clusters, slightly fragrant. June. Hungary. Hardy from zone* 3 southward. Late but not particularly showy.

S. microphylla. A spreading, slender-branched shrub, growing about 5 ft. high. Leaves ½–1½ in. long, roundish-ovate, hairy beneath. Flowers lilac, fragrant, small, in short clusters 1–3 in. long. May–June. China. Hardy from zone* 3 southward. A species distinguished by the small size of its leaves and flowers; a scattered bloom is often produced in the fall.

S. oblata. Shrub, occasionally tree-like, to 12 ft., resembling the common lilac in habit. The leaves are broad-oval to kidney-shaped, often broader than long and sharp-pointed, reddish when young and becoming red in the fall. Late April–May. China. Hardy from zone* 3 southward. One of the earliest lilacs to bloom. *Var.* dilatata is a form with oval, rather long-pointed leaves to 4½ in. long; and the flowers are more slender and the cluster less compact.

S. pekinensis. A handsome, spreading shrub, 10–15 ft. high, its young twigs brownish-red. Leaves ovalish or narrower, 2–4 in. long, smooth, wedge-shaped at the base. Flowers yellowish-

white, in large, smooth clusters that may be 6 in. long, unpleasantly scented. China. June. Hardy from zone* 4 southward.

S. persica. Persian lilac. A compact shrub with slender, arching branches, usually about 5–6 ft. high though occasionally higher. Leaves lance-shaped, about 2½ in. long and sometimes lobed or divided. Flowers pale lilac, fragrant, in short, broad clusters about 3 in. long. May. Persia to northwestern China. Hardy from zone* 3 southward.

S. prestoniae. A cross between *S. villosa* and *S. reflexa* with whitish to pink flowers appearing two weeks after those of *S. vulgaris.* Several extremely hardy and popular varieties have been recently introduced from Canada, where they originated.

S. pubescens. A slender-branched shrub, sometimes round-headed, usually about 6 ft. high, rarely to 12 ft. Leaves broadly ovate, short-pointed, about 3 in. long, hairy on the veins beneath. Flowers fragrant, pale lilac, tube slender and petals narrow, clusters about 5 in. long. May. Northern China. Hardy from zone* 3 southward.

S. reflexa. Nodding lilac. An unusual and very handsome lilac that grows about 12 ft. tall and has nodding, buddleia-like clusters, 4–8 in. long, of deep pink flowers. The leaves are 3–6 in. long, usually oval-oblong and tapered at the base. June. China. Hardy from zone* 3.

S. swegiflexa. A hybrid lilac (*reflexa* × *sweginzowi*), not very different from *S. reflexa*, but the flowers deep red in youth, ultimately pink.

S. sweginzowi. An upright shrub with purplish-brown branches and oblongish or ovalish leaves, 2–4½ in. long. Flowers fragrant, reddish or paler lilac, the corolla about ½ in. long. Northern China. June. Hardy from zone* 3 southward. The *var.* superba is more profusely flowering. Of chief value because of its late bloom.

S. velutina. A small shrub, 3–8 ft. high, the leaves elliptic to oblongish, 2–3 in. long, about half as wide, the leafstalk and twigs often glandular, the lower surface of the leaf densely hairy. Flowers in hairy clusters (panicles*), lilac. Northern China and Korea. May. Hardy from zone* 3 southward.

S. villosa. An upright, strong-growing shrub, attaining 9 or 10 ft. Leaves 3–6 in. long, more or less oval and pointed at the ends, whitish beneath. The flowers are lilac-pink or paler, and are borne in terminal clusters after most of the common lilacs have passed. May–June. China. Hardy from zone* 3 southward.

S. vulgaris. Common lilac. A handsome, widely cultivated shrub growing about 20 ft. high, sometimes becoming a small tree. The leaves are heart-shaped to oval, 2–6 in. long. The flowers are in clusters 6–8 in. long, very fragrant and usually lilac, though in many horticultural forms there are white, pink and purple flowers. Southeastern Europe. May. Hardy from zone* 2 southward. *See* below for the many hort. forms.

LILAC CULTURE

Syringa vulgaris, persica, and *Josikaea* from southern Eu. and northern As. contribute most of the common garden forms. The remaining species are found mostly in China or Korea and are largely of recent introduction. Among these are: *Syringa reflexa* with dull, rosy, pendulous flower clusters which are quite different from those of the better-known forms;

---

* Special articles on the subjects indicated by an asterisk (*) will be found at the words so marked.

Syringa microphylla which sometimes blossoms a second time in Aug. and has large, loose clusters of lilac flowers. The first to bloom is *Syringa oblata* and its variety, *dilatata.* Although not over-conspicuous in the quality of their flowers, the fact that they bloom two to three weeks before the others makes them valuable. *Syringa villosa* with pale lavender flowers is the last of the shrubby types to show color. The only strong-scented lilac is *Syringa pubescens* with pale lavender flowers. The marked fragrance of this plant guarantees it a prominent place in any planting of the group. The Rouen Lilac (*S. chinensis*), a hybrid between *S. persica* and *vulgaris,* is a large, spreading bush with purplish-lilac flowers. President Grevy is one of the largest-growing of the garden forms and often reaches a height of sixteen feet.

Most of the garden varieties are forms of *Syringa vulgaris* and have come into being through seedling selection and plant breeding. Practically all the possible color combinations are available in either single- or double-flowered forms. They have been divided into 7 color groups:

SINGLE-FLOWERED FORMS: Vestale and Mont Blanc, white; De Miribel and Cavour, violet; President Lincoln and Decaisne, blue to bluish; Jacques Callot and Christophe Colomb, lilac; Lucie Baltet and Macrostachya, pinkish; Congo and Capitaine Baltet, magenta or reddish purple; Ludwig Spaeth and Monge, purple or deep purple.

DOUBLE-FLOWERED FORMS: Ellen Willmott and Edith Cavell, white; Maréchal Lannes and Violetta, violet; Olivier De Serres and President Grevy, blue to bluish; Victor Lemoine and Leon Gambetta, lilac; Katherine Havemeyer and Madame Antoine Buckner, pink to pinkish; Paul Thirion and Mrs. Edward Harding, magenta or reddish purple; Adelaide Dunbar and Paul Hariot, purple.

Some hybrids between *S. villosa* and *S. reflexa* have recently been reported by Miss Isabella Preston of Ottawa, among them Isabella, Donald Wyman, and Miranda.

CULTIVATION. The cultivation of the lilac is not difficult. Almost any well-drained soil will suffice but, if vigorous growth and good flowers are desired, the plant should be fertilized every two years. Well-rotted cow manure is best and may be applied in early spring. Cover an area about the plant four inches deep and equal in diameter to the height of small plants or about two-thirds the height of mature specimens. Work the manure well into the soil and continue to spade this area every two or three weeks throughout the summer. Prepared fertilizers of a chemical nature should not be used, as they often stimulate woody growth to such an extent that the plant does not form flower buds for the next season.

Pruning is very important, especially if quality rather than quantity is desired in the flowers. In all cases the old blossoms should be removed as soon as they begin to fade. Pruning work may be done any time during the winter. Remove all weak wood which does not bear flower buds. Flowering branches are easily identified during the winter by the presence of several large buds at the tips. Only those branches which have vigorous buds should be left. If this method of pruning is carried out faithfully every three years a regular sequence of bloom will result. The first year the quantity will be reduced but each cluster will be very large. The second season the flowers will increase in number and will be of good size. Finally, the third year will bring still more clusters but smaller than those produced the first year. In many cases a two-year sequence of pruning is followed as it provides excellent quality of bloom at all times and requires the removal of less wood at each operation.

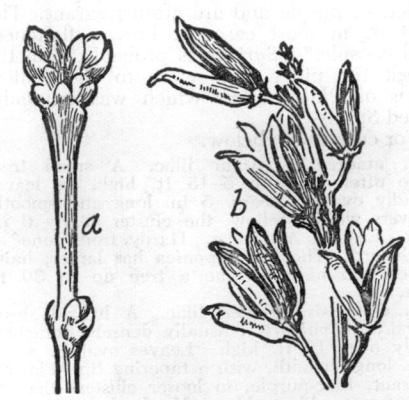

In pruning the lilac, allow flower buds (*a*) to remain, but prune away twigs with last year's fruits (*b*).

PROPAGATION. The lilac can be, and is, grown by almost every known method of propagation. The species are grown from seed, although asexual methods, such as grafting, are equally as common. Grafting is the most common method of propagating the varieties. Lilac seedlings or privet are used as stock and the work done in April and May. Budding on seedling lilacs in July is also practiced. None of these methods can be recommended, however, because of the constant trouble caused by the suckering of the stock. Root grafting on privet is more acceptable. The lilac cion is cleft grafted on a small piece of privet root in Jan. and stored in sand in the root cellar until spring. It is then planted out with the cion set deep in the ground. After three or four years a plant of sufficient size for permanent planting will result. Examination of the root at this time will generally show that the privet root has dried up and that the lilac is on its own roots. If the privet still persists it should be severed from the plant. Layering is the most simple method of propagation. The plant is cut back severely to induce suckering, and after one season each new branch is cut from the plant with a section of root attached and lined out in the nursery. Softwood cuttings are taken in late June and rooted in sand under glass. While lilacs are more or less hardy throughout the North, they are unsuited to the deep South. — D. W.

INSECT PESTS. Control boring caterpillar by double-strength pesticide #17 or #18 sprays on branches only. When leaves appear, repeat twice at two-week intervals. Leaf-mining caterpillars can be controlled by pesticide #1 or #21 at a later time as they feed on leaf surface. Oyster-shell scales, when heavy, should be pruned out. Control with dormant oil sprays or with pesticide #21 sprays when young hatch in late spring with a repeat spray 3 weeks later. *See also* leopard moth at MAPLE. (*See* SPRAYS AND DUSTS.)

DISEASES. Powdery mildew* is the most common disease of lilac. Spray with pesticide #6 or 9 (*see* SPRAYS AND DUSTS) as soon as new growth begins in the spring. Repeat 3 or 4 times at about 10-day intervals.

Occasionally during spring or early summer, particularly on young plants forced with high nitrogen fertilizers, a blight* may cause some shoots to brown and die quickly. Sprays have not proven very satisfactory in the control of either the fungus or bacterial blight. Cut off diseased shoot several inches below the most advanced portion of the blight.

LILAC FAMILY = Oleaceae.

lilacina, -us, -um (ly-la-sy'na). Lilac-like, either in form or color.

LILIACEAE (lil-ĭ-ā'see-ee). The lily family is of more garden importance than even its 240 genera and over 3600 species might suggest. It is sometimes called the aloe, hyacinth, or tulip family, and it has been split by botanists into four families:

1. Lily family proper (Liliaceae)
2. Lily-of-the-valley family (Convallariaceae), often called Solomon's-seal or wakerobin family.
3. Bunchflower family (Melanthaceae)
4. Smilax family (Smilaceae)

As here considered, all these are grouped in one big family, the Liliaceae. They are often bulbous herbs, but some are vines (*Smilax*), and woody or even tree-like plants occur in *Yucca, Samuela, Hesperoyucca, Phormium, Cordyline, Dasylirion, Dracaena,* and *Aloe,* most of which come from warm regions. Garden vegetables are found in *Asparagus* and *Allium.* But the family is noteworthy for the showy bloom of most of its numerous garden genera, especially *Lilium, Brodiaea, Bulbocodium, Calochortus, Chionodoxa, Colchicum, Convallaria* (*see* LILY-OF-THE-VALLEY), *Eremurus, Erythronium, Fritillaria, Hemerocallis, Hosta, Hyacinthus, Kniphofia, Leucocoryne, Muscari, Ornithogalum, Scilla, Tulipa, Trillium, Urginea,* and *Zygadenus.*

Some genera are chiefly greenhouse plants, notably *Agapanthus, Anthericum,* *Aphyllanthes, Aspidistra, Chlorophytum, Eucomis, Gasteria, Gloriosa, Haworthia, Lapageria, Littonia, Reineckia, Rohdea, Ruscus, Sanseviera, Schizobasopsis, Tulbaghia,* and *Veltheimia.* Many of these are grown outdoors along the Gulf Coast and in Calif.

There are, in addition, a few genera which contain native American plants, often in the woods in the East, and on prairies or the Pacific Coast in the West. They are suited to the wild garden, bog, or to other special sites. (*See* each genus for details.) They are: *Aletris, Androstephium, Bessera, Bloomeria, Brevoortia, Camassia, Chamaelirium, Chlorogalum, Clintonia, Disporum, Hesperaloe, Helonias, Leucocrinum, Maianthemum, Medeola, Melanthium, Milla, Narthecium, Polygonatum* (*see* SOLOMON'S-SEAL), *Smilacina, Stenanthium, Streptopus, Uvularia,* and *Xerophyllum.* Many of these have attractive flowers and are well worth the gardener's attention, but they are not so widely grown as better-known genera.

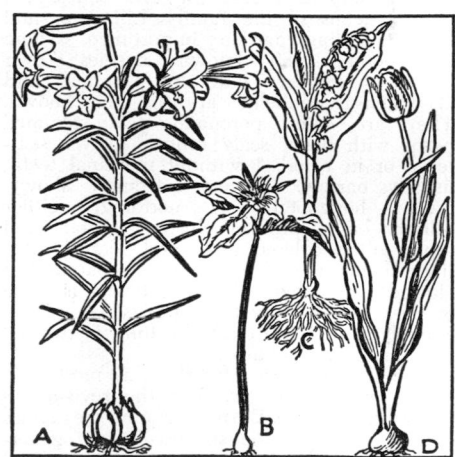

Four types of flowers in the lily family: (*a*) Easter lily; (*b*) trillium; (*c*) lily-of-the-valley; (*d*) tulip.

The only other plants of hort. interest are found in: *Asphodeline, Asphodelus, Galtonia, Lachenalia, Liriope, Ophiopogon, Paradisea, Puschkinia, Tricyrtis,* and *Veratrum.*

The Liliaceae has alternate* (whorled* in some lilies) leaves, nearly always stalkless, generally without marginal teeth. In nearly all the herbs the stem arises from a bulb, very prominent in the onion and tulip, less so in some other genera, and replaced by a rootstock in many genera (*see* SOLOMON'S-SEAL).

Flowers nearly always very showy, typically of 6 segments, indistinguishable as to calyx or corolla, or in some genera tubular. While solitary flowers are not uncommon (tulip, *Erythronium,* etc.), generally the flowers are in clusters, the raceme* being the

---

* Special articles on the subjects indicated by an asterisk (*) will be found at the words so marked.

most common form of inflorescence. But umbels or umbel-like clusters occur in *Smilax, Allium,* and several other genera. The ovary is superior* in all but two genera (*Liriope* and *Ophiopogon*), and this is the chief difference between this family and the Amaryllidaceae which has an inferior* ovary. Stamens* mostly 6, rarely 3. Fruit a berry or a capsule.* It has been suggested to assign *Allium, Brodiaea,* and several other genera to the Amaryllidaceae, but it is not here entertained.

LILIAGO (lil-i-ā′go). An old, now obsolete, generic name for the St. Bernard′s-lily. See ANTHERICUM.

Liliastrum (lil-ĭ-as′trum). Pre-Linnaean* name for *Paradisea Liliastrum.*

liliflora, -us, -um (lil-i-flow′ra). With lily-like flowers.

lilifolia, -us, -um (lil-eye-fō′lĭ-a). With lily-like leaves.

LILIUM (lil′i-um). A large genus of showy, bulbous herbs, the true lilies, the typical genus of the family Liliaceae, and of outstanding garden importance. There are perhaps 80 known species, over 50 of which are cult. in America, and of which those below are the best known. They are erect, perennial, leafy-stemmed herbs with deep, scaly bulbs. Leaves scattered or in whorls,* without marginal teeth, usually narrow. Flowers extremely showy, erect, horizontal or nodding, either solitary or in profuse clusters. Petals and sepals often colored alike and scarcely distinguishable as such, sometimes separate and clawed* or united, when the flower is more or less funnel-shaped. Stamens* 6. Fruit a many-seeded capsule.* (*Lilium* is the old Latin name of the lilies.)

The nomenclature of *Lilium* is most confusing to the amateur. For the revision in this edition of the ENCYCLOPEDIA, the names and identities of the species follow, generally, those admitted in the recent second edition of the *Dictionary of Gardening,* 4 vols. and Supplement, issued by the Royal Horticultural Society, London, in 1956. It should hardly be necessary to point out that among the many hybrid lilies there are far finer plants than will be found among the list of *species* of lily immediately below. For the best varieties and culture, see the article that follows the enumeration of the species.

amabile. Not over 3 ft. high, the stem hairy. Flowers drooping, about 2 in. long. red and dark-spotted, the segments recurved. Korea. The *var.* **luteum** has yellow flowers.

auratum. One of the favorite sorts, 4–6 ft. high. Flowers fragrant, somewhat drooping, nearly 10 in. wide, white, but crimson-spotted, and with a central yellow band. Jap. The *var.* **platyphyllum** has broader leaves and flowers with fewer spots; *var.* **rubrum** has the flowers red-banded. The *var.* **rubrovittatum** has the central bands of the corolla deep crimson. July.

batemanniae. See L. MACULATUM.

bolanderi. A Californian lily, 1–3 ft. high, with clustered bluish-green leaves and 1–4 rather small, horizontal reddish-purple flowers, spotted darker red inside. It is doubtful if the true *L. bolanderi* is offered in the trade, much of the material being *L. kelloggi* or other species.

browni. Not over 4 ft. high. Flowers more or less horizontal, nearly 9 in. long, white inside but rose-purple outside, somewhat fragrant. China. The *var.* **colchesteri** has very fragrant flowers.

bulbiferum. Not over 4 ft. high, often producing bulbils* among the leaves. Flowers about 3½ in. wide, orange-red, dark-spotted, but the center yellow. Eu. The *var.* **croceum,** the orange lily, has yellow-orange flowers. For a confusing tangle as to the correct name of this plant, *see* LILIUM MACULATUM.

callosum. From 1 to 2 ft. high. Flowers about 2 in. wide, bright scarlet, but dark-spotted. Jap.

canadense. Meadow lily. A native lily of secondary garden importance, and best grown in the bog garden (which see). Flowers drooping, about 3 in. wide, orange-yellow or red and dark-spotted. Eastern N.A.

candidum. Madonna or Annunciation lily. Not over 4 ft. high. Flowers pure white, more or less waxy, horizontal, and about 3 in. long. Eurasia. June. The *var.* **plenum** is loosely double-flowered and without stamens* or pistils.*

centifolium. See LILIUM LEUCANTHUM CENTIFOLIUM.

cernuum. From 18–24 in. high. Flowers fragrant, nodding, about 1½ in. long, lilac, but purple-spotted. Eastern As.

chalcedonicum. Scarlet Turk′s-cap lily. Flowers nodding, more or less ill-scented, about 3 in. wide, deep scarlet and rarely spotted, the tips of the petals recurved. Greece. July.

columbianum. From 3–4 ft. high. Flowers nodding, about 2 in. long, orange-red, but copiously dark-spotted, and with the petals recurved. British Columbia to Calif.

concolor. Star lily. From 3–4 ft. high. Flowers erect, somewhat fragrant, about 1½ in. wide, bright red, but unspotted. Jap. June. The *var.* **pulchellum** has somewhat spotted flowers.

croceum. Orange lily. Nearly 6 ft. high. Flowers erect, about 3 in. long, orange, but crimson-spotted. Mountains of southern Eu. Of doubtful status. See LILIUM MACULATUM.

dauricum. About 3 ft. high. Flowers erect, sometimes 5 in. wide, orange-red, but dark-spotted. Siberia. There are forms with unspotted flowers and with the flowers brown-spotted. Of doubtful status. See LILIUM MACULATUM.

davidi. Nearly 6 ft. high. Flowers nodding, about 3 in. long, red, but black-spotted. China.

duchartrei. Not over 4 ft. high. Flowers nodding, fragrant, about 3 in. long, white, but purple-spotted. Western China.

elegans. A very common lily in gardens, usually not over 2 ft. high. Flowers erect, nearly 6 in. wide, orange-red, somewhat dark-spotted. Jap. June. There are many cult. varieties or forms of this old favorite, some with larger, apricot-colored flowers, some with salmon and unspotted flowers, and some in other color patterns.

formosanum. Closely related to L. *philippinense* but with the corolla more flaring at the top, white and fragrant. Formosa. July–Aug. The *var.* **pricei** has fewer and smaller flowers, reddish-purple outside, and is sometimes offered at *L. philippinense.*

---

* Special articles on the subjects indicated by an asterisk (*) will be found at the words so marked.

giganteum. An immense lily, 8–12 ft. high. Flowers somewhat drooping, fragrant, nearly 6 in. long, white, but green-tinged outside and with reddish-purple stripes inside. Himalayas. Thought by some to belong to the genus *Cardiocrinum* and perhaps correctly so, but here retained in *Lilium* for convenience of most gardeners.

hansoni. From 4–5 ft. high. Flowers drooping, fragrant, about 1½ in. long, orange-yellow, but purple-spotted. Jap.

harrisi = *Lilium longiflorum eximium*.

henryi. From 7–9 ft. high. Flowers drooping, about 3 in. wide, orange, but brown-spotted, the petals recurved. China. Needs staking.

humboldti. From 5–6 ft. high. Flowers drooping, about 3½ in. long, reddish-orange, but dark-spotted, the margins of the petals slightly rolled. Calif. The *var.* **magnificum** is larger. The Bellingham hybrids, developed in the Northwest, are especially fine. See Lily Culture, below.

japonicum. Not over 3 ft. high. Flowers more or less horizontal, fragrant, nearly 6 in. wide, rose-colored or pale pink. Jap.

kelloggi. A Pacific Coast lily, 2–3 ft. high, with a brownish stem, clustered, lance-shaped leaves and red-spotted, pinkish flowers about 2 in. long that are yellow-banded. July.

leichtlini. From 4–6 ft. high. Flowers drooping, about 3 in. long, lemon-yellow, but dark-spotted, the tips of the petals recurved. Jap. The *var.* **maximowiczi** is taller and more floriferous.

leucanthum. A little-known lily in cult., mostly replaced by the *var.* **centifolium** (usually offered as *Lilium centifolium*). It is a very showy lily, 6–8 ft. high, with numerous, narrowly elliptic leaves, 5–7 in. long. Flowers 10–20, horizontal, funnel-shaped, 4–6 in. long, white, but yellow in the throat and purplish-keeled on the back. China. July–Aug. Needs staking.

longiflorum. White-trumpet lily. An old and well-liked species, not over 3 ft. high. Flowers more or less horizontal, fragrant, pure white, trumpet-shaped and nearly 7 in. long. Jap. Much better known in the *var.* **eximium**, the Easter lily (often called "Bermuda lily" although not native there), which is taller and has even longer flowers. It, and other forms such as Creole and Estate, are finer than the type. The Croft lily, developed in Oregon, is a newer variety preferred by florists for forcing, often under the name *L. harrisi*.

maculatum. A highly confused name in the genus *Lilium*, probably comprising plants of hybrid origin, but preferred by some as a name including *Lilium bulbiferum*, *L. croceum*, and *L. dauricum*. Over 30 named hort. forms are credited to *L. maculatum*. *L. batemanniae* is also credited here by some.

Martagon. Martagon lily; also called Turk's-cap lily. From 4–6 ft. high. Flowers drooping, about 2 in. long, rose-purple and dark-spotted, the tips of the petals strongly recurved. Eurasia June. The *var.* **album** has white flowers; the *var.* **cattaniae**, from Dalmatia, has dark-purplish, unspotted flowers and is extremely handsome; the *var.* **dalmaticum** has nearly black flowers. There are many other hort. forms.

michauxi. Carolina lily. A native lily, 20–30 in. high, the bluish-green, lance-shaped leaves 3–8 in. long, and generally in clusters of 3–7. Flowers nodding, orange-red, 3–5 in. long and purple-spotted. Southeastern U.S. Aug.

michiganense. Perhaps a mere western form of the Turk's-cap lily (*L. superbum*), flowering a little earlier, but otherwise not significantly different to the gardener.

monadelphum. Caucasian lily. Nearly 6 ft. high. Flowers drooping, almost 5 in. wide, golden-yellow, rarely spotted or tinged with purple, the tips of the petals recurved. Persia. Caucasus.

myriophyllum. Not over 4 ft. high. Flowers nodding, fragrant, about 1 in. long, greenish-white outside, but sometimes with a red keel,* yellowish inside. China. It often produces bulbils* among the numerous leaves.

nepalense. A purplish-stemmed lily, 2–3 ft. high, with short-stalked scattered, smooth leaves. Flowers fragrant, nearly 6 in. long, drooping, greenish-yellow but purplish-tinged in the throat. Nepal. June–July.

pardalinum. Leopard lily. From 6–8 ft. high. Flowers drooping, about 4 in. wide, orange-red, but purple-spotted, yellow at the base, the tips of the petals strongly recurved. Calif. Suited to the bog garden (which see). July.

parryi. Not over 4 ft. high. Flowers more or less horizontal, fragrant, about 4 in. long, lemon-yellow, but spotted on the inside. Calif.

parvum. Sierra lily. A tall-growing, Pacific Coast lily, sometimes reaching a height of 5 ft. Flowers about 1¼ in. long, nearly orange-red, but purple-spotted, and yellow at the base. Ore. to Calif.

philadelphicum. Wood lily. Mostly about 2 ft. high. Flowers erect, about 4 in. wide, the petals with long claws,* orange-red, but dark-spotted. Eastern N.A.

philippinense. Not over 18 in. high. Flowers more or less horizontal, fragrant, nearly 10 in. long, white, but greenish-tinged. Philippine Islands. *See also* L. FORMOSANUM.

pumilum. Coral lily. Not over 2 ft. high. Flowers nodding, about 2 in. wide, bright scarlet and only occasionally spotted, the tips of the petals recurved. Eastern As. Also known as *L. tenuifolium*. Especially fine hort. forms are Golden Gleam, Red Star, and Yellow Bunting.

pyrenaicum. Stem not over 3 ft. high, with very numerous, narrow leaves somewhat silver-edged. Flowers nodding, yellow, purple-spotted, about 2 in. long, unpleasantly scented. Pyrenees. June.

regale. Royal lily. From 4–5 ft. high. Flowers usually horizontal, fragrant, about 6 in. long, lilac or purplish outside, white inside but yellow at the base. Western China.

rubescens. Chaparral lily. Nearly 6 ft. high. Flowers erect, about 2 in. long, at first pale lilac, ultimately rose-purple. Ore. to Calif.

sargentiae. Almost 6 ft. high. Flowers horizontal, fragrant, about 6 in. long, rose-purple outside but white inside. Western China. July. Often produces bulbils.*

speciosum. Japanese lily; an old garden favorite. About 4 ft. high. Flowers drooping, fragrant, about 4 in. long, white or blush, spotted with rose-red. Jap. There are many garden forms, especially *var.* **album** with nearly white flowers; and *var.* **rubrum** with carmine-pink flowers.

superbum. Turk's-cap lily of eastern U.S. From 5–8 ft. high. Flowers drooping, about 4 in. wide, orange-red, but dark-spotted, the tips of the petals recurved. Can be grown in the bog garden (which see).

tenuifolium = *L. pumilum*.

testaceum. Nankeen (or Nankin) lily. From 5–7 ft. high. Flowers drooping, fragrant, about 3 in. wide, apricot-colored or yellowish, often pink-tinged, usually unspotted, the tips

---

* Special articles on the subjects indicated by an asterisk (*) will be found at the words so marked.

of the petals recurved. A hybrid between *L. candidum* and *L. chalcedonicum.*

tigrinum. Tiger lily. From 4–6 ft. high. Flowers drooping, nearly 5 in. wide, orange-red or salmon-red, and black-spotted, the tips of the petals recurved. China and Jap. An old garden favorite and sometimes an escape* in eastern N.A. It often produces bulbils* among the leaves. There are many forms in cult., among the best being *var.* **fortunei** which has a densely hairy stem; *var.* **flore-pleno** has double flowers; *var.* **splendens** has more and larger flowers.

umbellatum. Thought by some to be probably referable to *L. maculatum,* and some of the material may be a form of *L. philadelphicum.* A badly confused name in the trade, although many forms are offered as *L. umbellatum.*

warleyense = *Lilium davidi.*

washingtonianum. Washington lily. From 4–6 ft. high. Flowers horizontal, fragrant, about 4 in. long, white, but often purple-spotted. Ore. and Calif. The *var.* **purpureum** = *Lilium rubescens.*

LILY CULTURE

Lilies are highly decorative for the garden because of their graceful forms, exquisite perfume, and outstanding coloring. Moreover, they have a long and interesting history in Europe as well as in Asia. The Madonna lily (*L. candidum*), native to the Mediterranean littoral, was depicted in decorations on pottery and mosaics from earliest times. In Renaissance paintings of Europe, it was the symbol representing the Annunciation to the Virgin. In the United States more of *Lilium longiflorum* and its varieties Croft, Ace, and Estate are grown than of any other lily. *L. longiflorum* originated from the Ryukyu Islands. The bulbs of these lilies are grown principally in Washington and Oregon, are dug in early fall, and shipped to commercial growers who first put them in cold storage and then force them in the greenhouses or, in the South, plant them out of doors. They are used as a cut flower, for funerals, and principally for Easter.

Lilies are a difficult group to grow and in order to maintain the population in the garden they have to be renewed constantly. The principal difficulty in growing them is to find exactly the right place for them, and next to keep them healthy. They all prefer light, loamy soil and require perfect drainage. Some do better in partial shade, others in the sun, and none of them will grow in deep shade. Most of them benefit by having a ground cover from one foot to eighteen inches high to shade their roots and leave the upper portions of stem and flowers in the sun.

PROPAGATION. Raising lilies from seed provides a large number of bulbs with comparatively little expense and not too much work, but it requires patience, for with few exceptions, it takes from two to four years to obtain a flowering plant. Lilies are subject to mosaic which is not carried by seeds.

The amateur gardener can plant seeds indoors in a greenhouse or out of doors in a cold frame or even in a well-prepared seed bed. In the Northeast it is best to sow most lily seeds in the early spring. Elsewhere fall planting is safe, provided there is no alternation of thawing and freezing.

There are three classifications of behavior of lily seedlings. In the first, germination is immediate and the seed leaf is soon pushed above the ground. To this group belong *L. amabile, callosum, cernuum, concolor, davidi* and its varieties, *formosanum, leichtlinni, leucanthum* var. *centifolium, longiflorum, philippinense, pumilum, regale, sargentiae,* and *tigrinum.* The second group has delayed germination and includes *L. chalcedonicum, candidum,* and sometimes *henryi.* In the third group a little bulb is formed under the ground the first year. Seeds of these require first summer, then winter, and again part of a summer before the seed leaf rises above the ground. These seeds can be first subjected to warmth of 70 degrees for three months, then be placed either out of doors in the cold or in a refrigerator for several months. By summer the little bulbs will be ready to send up their seed leaves. The best soil for lily seed is composed of one part sand, one part loam, and one part rotted leaves. This last provides a slight acidity to the soil, good for all seedlings. In a cold frame or garden this mixture need not be deeper than eight inches but the ground under it should be well spaded and consist of good soil to a depth of at least a foot. The situation must be well drained. The seed bed should preferably be shaded, but if in a sunny situation the young seedlings should be covered with a lath shade or some other device until after the leaves have been above ground at least for six weeks. They can then be exposed to the sun gradually. Seeds sown out of doors should be planted far enough apart so they will not have to be moved the first year; that is about one inch in the row and each row four inches from the next. Commercial growers now often use vermiculite instead of soil.

Indoors lily seeds are sown much closer, and when the bulbs are about an eighth to a quarter of an inch long they can be transplanted into cold frames, having fresh soil consisting of two parts loam to one of rotted leaves with a slight addition of fertilizer, either in commercial powdered form, or thoroughly rotted crumbly manure. Out-of-door seedlings of quick germination will not have to be moved until they have been in the ground one summer, one winter, and a second summer. Most of them will then be found to be large enough to move to beds and borders in the flower garden, but those still tiny can be replanted as a reserve for another year. The slow germinators take a year longer when they have not been hurried along.

---

* Special articles on the subjects indicated by an asterisk (*) will be found at the words so marked.

Lilium hansoni and *L. tigrinum* do not set seed to their own pollen, and hybrids as a rule do not come true from seed, so these are best increased through bulb scales, a method which can be used to propagate all lilies. This is done by pulling the scales away from the parent bulb, and planting them in sand which is kept moist. The flats or pans are stacked on top of each other and in six months the scales will each have produced a little bulblet which can be planted directly in sandy soil. In some species such as *Lilium tigrinum, sargentiae,* and *bulbiferum,* bulbs grow in the leaf axils. These can be removed and planted the same as a true bulb. The best time of year to plant mature lily bulbs is after the foliage has died down, and no roots should be removed any more than they would be from other perennial plants. The bulbs should be out of the ground as short a time as possible, so as not to dry out. Once established, lily bulbs should not be moved until the clumps become too thick, when they are dug up very gently, separated, and the excess bulbs planted elsewhere immediately. Lilies are heavy feeders and can be given fertilizer, to encourage larger plants, perhaps twice in spring. If the season is dry the ground should be kept moist, not wet, by watering thoroughly once a week, until they flower. After flowering they like a time to dry.

OUT-OF-DOOR CULTURE. In the garden, lilies grow best when there is some shade over their roots. The sepals of some lilies such as *L. hansoni* and *L. henryi* bleach when the sun shines brightly on their flowers and keep their color only when grown in slight shade. All lilies resent being crowded and it is advisable not to put them in among strong-growing shrubs but either with low ground covers such as *Teucrium Chamaedrys,* dwarf blue veronicas, low campanulas, perennial salvias, or bushy thymes. *Lilium regale* and *L. candidum* look well with lavender. The yellow and orange flowers of some lilies look handsome with shrubby hypericums and helianthemums. The foliage and stems of these shrub plants protect the young lily shoots as they come out of the ground in early spring. However, strong perennials such as phlox, hemerocallis or peonies would smother them. Lilies can be planted behind or to one side of these plants and produce an effect of companionship without actually intermingling. *L. concolor, pumilum, amabile,* and *cernuum,* all small, low-growing lilies, can be grown in rock gardens, provided their roots are shaded.

When planting lilies the bulbs should always be three times as deep below the surface of the ground as the bulb is high. That is, if the bulb is two inches high, its top should be four inches below the level of the ground. Most lilies have stem roots but need not be planted deeper on that account. As the bulb grows in circumference and depth, contractile roots pull it deeper into the ground. *Lilium candidum* and its hybrids is an exception to this rule for depth of planting and should have only one inch of soil above the top of the bulb. Also, bulbs which form mats, such as *L. pardalinum,* should not be planted deeper than *L. candidum.* Before planting bulbs, it is a good precaution to roll them in sulphur or copper oxide to discourage moles and mice during the first year.

LIST OF TWENTY LILIES FOR THE GARDEN

Hybrids are included, for in many instances they are hardier and handsomer than their parents.

Amabile var. *luteum.* One and a half to three ft. high. July. Bright yellow, nodding blossoms.

Auratum var. *platyphyllum.* Four to six ft. high. Huge saucer-shaped white flowers, few spots, strong scent. Aug.–Sept. Var. *rubrum.* Sepals have yellow band running through center, beginning yellow and ending in red as if powdered on. Spots bright red, as are anthers. Several other forms are good, notable among them a group called Esperanza Seedlings.

Auratum × *speciosum.* Cameo hybrids 2–3 ft. high. Pink with gold band down center.

L. × *aurelianense,* parents *L. henryi* × *sargentiae.* Flowers yellow-orange to pale yellow, each stalk differently shaded; open blossoms with reflexed segments, on stems bending forward; 6 ft. high. Aug.

Aurelian strain of Oregon Bulb Farms, results from crosses of *L. henryi, sargentiae, myriophyllum, aureliense,* and T. A. Havemeyer. There are many good strains of this, all late-blooming, tall; most need staking. Strains suggested are Aurelian Pastel Trumpets (cream to light yellow) and Aurelian Golden Trumpets (greenish yellow).

Backhouse hybrids, results of *L. Martagon* × *hansoni,* are yellow and rose, among them Sutton Court, yellow-shaded pink with purple spots; grows 4–5 ft. high and blooms in June. Flowers in spires, nodding and waxy.

Bellingham hybrids, results of crossing *pardalinum* × *humboldti magnificum* and *parryi* × *humboldti magnificum,* are 4–7 ft. high, come in reds, oranges, and yellows and are spotted. Flowers nodding, leaves in whorls. Bloom in late June and July.

Canadense. Two to five ft. high; flowers shaped like bells, nodding, come in yellow, orange, and occasionally red, and are spotted. June to early Aug.

Candidum. June-blooming, 3½ ft. high; blossoms face sideways, broadly campanulate, exceedingly sweet-scented, glistening white. It requires shallow planting and a little shade.

Cernuum. Nodding pink, and reflexed,

---

* Special articles on the subjects indicated by an asterisk (*) will be found at the words so marked.

spotted flowers, 1–2 ft. high. June–July.

Concolor. Very like *L. pumilum,* only flowers are upright. June.

Henryi. To 7–9 ft., arching stems; flaring orange flowers with dark spots grow on stems that branch several times at right angles from main stem. Aug.–Sept. bloom.

Longiflorum. Long, white tubular flowers, stems 1–3 ft. high; flower in July, August, sometimes later.

Martagon var. *album,* white form, and var. *cattaniae,* burgundy-red, flowers are both handsomer than the type. Stem 3–6 ft. high, topped by spire of nodding, glossy flowers with unpleasant smell. Blooms early and mid–June.

Monadelphum. Four to six ft. high, end of May–June; pale yellow, nodding flowers.

Preston hybrids resulting from crossing of *L. dauricum* × *maculatum.* Blooms June, July; 3½–4 ft. high; flowers generally face sky, come in reds, orange, and yellow; better than either of their parents.

Pumilum. Eighteen in. high, nodding Turk's-cap flowers, lacquer red; thin leaves. June.

Regale. Royal lily; flowers grow in whorl; stems 4–5 ft. high. End of June, July; white trumpets with yellow throats.

Speciosum. Has saucer-shaped white flowers, heavily covered with crimson and prominent spots; 3–4 ft. high. A white form, var. *album,* is fine.

Sulphur hybrids, having strains of *L. princeps, sulphureum* (*sulphureum* × *regale*) in them; all tall, late-blooming in July or Aug. White trumpets tinted green, brown, or crimson, and with varying degrees of yellow or rose in throats.

Tigrinum. Four–six ft., pink-orange flowers; bloom from July to Sept. Belong in semi-wild place.

Testaceum. A hybrid between *L. candidum* and *L. chalcedonicum.* Pale peach-colored, nodding flowers; 5–7 ft. June.

It will be noted that some of the above hybrids are derived from species of *Lilium* not enumerated in the general list of species. This is inevitable as specialists in lily hybridization often use species unknown except by the experts. — H. M. F.

INSECT PESTS. *See* bulb maggo• pests at BULBS. Use pesticide #1 for chewing pests and aphids. (*See* SPRAYS AND DUSTS.)

DISEASES. When tips of leaves turn brown, it is caused by a disturbance in the bulb or poor soil conditions. Thus sprays will not control this condition. A leafspot• often becomes severe on some varieties of lily grown outdoors. When the first spots are observed, apply pesticide #1 or #11 (*see* SPRAYS AND DUSTS) and repeat 3 or 4 times at 10-day intervals.

Yellow streaks in the foliage indicate mosaic• disease and stunted or "flat" plants indicate another virus disease. Dig and discard bulbs of plants with virus. Bulbs of the Easter lily

should be dipped for 30 minutes in pesticide #5 plus #10 before planting, to prevent the possibility of a basal root rot.

LILY. For the true lily *see* LILIUM. Many other lily-like plants are called lily, or the word occurs as part of their common name.

If you do not know the full common name of these plants, you will find them noted among the following genera:

Agapanthus	Haemanthus
Amaryllis	Hedychium
Anthericum	Hemerocallis
Belamcanda	Hymenocallis
Brodiaea	Kniphofia
Calochortus	Leucocrinum
Clivia	Narcissus
Cooperia	Nymphaea
Doryanthes	Sprekelia
Erythronium	Victoria
Eucharis	Zantedeschia
Fritillaria	Zephyranthes
Gloriosa	

Also the next few entries.

All the cult. plants of which lily is part of the name are also entered in the ENCY-CLOPEDIA under their preferred common names, such as adobe lily, Amazon lily, calla lily, Mariposa lily, etc., and the quickest way to find them is to turn at once to such entries, if you happen to know them. If not, the list of genera above may provide the clue for this most widely used and confusing of vernaculars.

LILY FAMILY. An immense group of very diverse plants, containing such well-known garden subjects as onion, lily, tulip, smilax, hyacinth, bunchflower, yucca, and the dracaenas. For all the garden genera and the characteristics of the family *see* LILIACEAE.

LILY LEEK = *Allium Moly.*

LILY-OF-THE-FIELD = *Sternbergia lutea.* *See also* ANEMONE CORONARIA.

LILY-OF-THE-INCAS. *See* ALSTROEMERIA PELEGRINA.

LILY OF THE NILE. *See* AGAPANTHUS.

LILY-OF-THE-VALLEY. A single species of very fragrant perennial herbs, constituting the genus **Convallaria** (kon-va-lair′-i-a) of the lily family, found wild in Eurasia and in the higher mountains from Va. to S. Car. The only species, **C. majalis,** is cult. throughout the temperate world for its fine, persistent, but not evergreen foliage, but especially for its delicately scented, white, nodding flowers. Leaves all basal, from a horizontal rootstock, the blades oblong-oval, usually forming dense mats. Stalk of the flower cluster arising from the ground, 5–8 in. high, the cluster a loose, often somewhat 1-sided raceme of bell-shaped, white, nodding flowers, the tips of the corolla recurved. Stamens• 6, not protruding. Fruit a red berry about ¼ in. in diameter. The American plant is called *C. montana* by some. The *var.* **fortunei** has

---

• Special articles on the subjects indicated by an asterisk (•) will be found at the words so marked.

larger leaves and flowers. Occasionally a pink-flowered or variegated-leaved sort is offered. (*Convallaria* is from the Latin for a valley.)

CULTURE

The lily-of-the-valley is primarily a shade plant. It can be made to grow in the open, will do fairly well in ground shaded for part of the day, but luxuriates best in places that are under the shade of trees. While very old plantations of it are often seen and they become solid, sod-like masses, the flowers are apt to be few and poor and most of the growth is foliage. The reason is that the plant gets too crowded if let alone for more than three years, when the bed should be dug up and replanted with fresh pips (*see* below).

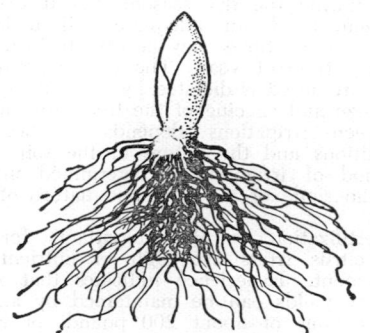

A pip of the lily-of-the-valley ready for planting

The lily-of-the-valley has a horizontal rootstock from which arises a small, upright, detachable portion containing a stout bud and plenty of roots. Commonly called *pips*, these propagative parts of the plant can be stored and are usually offered by dealers in the spring. They are the best material with which to start a bed. The pips should be planted close together, about 1½ in. deep, in good, rich garden soil. Such a bed, top-dressed in the late fall with well-rotted manure, will make a fine mat of foliage within a year or two and will provide plenty of flowers until the rootstocks become crowded.

FORCING. The lily-of-the-valley is widely forced for winter bloom by florists, and this can be done by anyone with a greenhouse. Pips are planted directly in the greenhouse bench in potting mixture* 1 or in pure sand. Keep the bench dark for the first 10–14 days by covering with boards, which should be removed gradually as the pips sprout.

Professional growers use only pips that have been stored for three months at a temperature of about 28°. Such do not need bottom-heat, and will be forced into bloom in about a month from planting time if the greenhouse is kept at about 65°. If you buy the ordinary pips sold by the average

dealer, they will not have been held in cold storage and such pips, to force well, need bottom-heat (which see) of 70°–75°, and a greenhouse temperature of about 65°. In either case, they need plenty of water and, as they come to flowering, as much light as possible. The forcing can, of course, be done at any season of the year only if pips have been held in storage. Otherwise, they must be planted when available, which is usually in Feb.–Mar.

LILY-OF-THE-VALLEY FAMILY. *See* LILIACEAE.

LILY-TURF. *See* OPHIOPOGON and LIRIOPE.

LIMA BEAN = *Phaseolus limensis.* For culture *see* BEAN.

LIMB. 1. The expanded flat part of an individual petal or of a united (*i.e.,* gamopetalous*) corolla; sometimes called a blade. 2. One of the larger branches of a tree.

LIMBER PINE = *Pinus flexilis. See* PINE.

LIME = *Tilia. See* LINDEN.

LIME. There are two true limes, the acid lime (*Citrus aurantifolia*) and the sweet lime (*Citrus Limetta*). Both are grown in the United States, the former giving rise to small but important industries in Florida and California and the latter contributing a rare and interesting, though worthless, horticultural curiosity. In this same category also are to be grouped the so-called Rangpur and Kusaie limes which, though intensely sour and suitable as substitutes for the lime, are in reality mandarins. Mention should also be made of the limequat,* a hybrid of lime and kumquat parentage, which exhibits much of the acidity of the former and some of the hardiness of the latter, though a rather weak grower.

ACID LIME. Two botanical varieties or horticultural races of the acid lime are recognized; the Mexican, West Indian or Key lime and the Tahiti or Persian lime. The former bears smaller fruits, has foliage of lighter color and smaller size, and is decidedly less vigorous and hardy than the latter, which is one of the most beautiful of all citrus trees.

The lime is a tender, evergreen, sub-tropical tree which thrives, unassisted, in tropical and semi-tropical climates, though in sub-tropical regions it requires irrigation. It is the commercial citrus fruit most tender to frost, which restricts its culture to regions of comparative freedom from even light frosts. Temperatures of 28° to 30° are sufficient to cause injury to the West Indian lime and temperatures slightly lower injure the Persian lime. Comparative freedom from wind is required because of the fact that the rind of the fruit is easily injured and bruises result in a scabby condition which lowers the grade. For these reasons the commercial culture of the lime in the United States is limited to Southern Florida and the areas

* Special articles on the subjects indicated by an asterisk (*) will be found at the words so marked.

of mildest winters in Southern California. Even there the frost hazard is often sufficient to result in occasional injury.

Like its relative the lemon, the lime has several more or less overlapping periods of bloom and the result is that fruit ripens almost continuously throughout the year. It also has the ability possessed by other citrus fruits to set and mature the fruits without the necessity of pollination. Such fruits are obviously seedless. As a consequence its culture presents no pollination problem.

SOILS. The lime has a very wide range of soil adaptation, succeeding about equally well on very light soils and moderately heavy soils. It thrives in the hard lime-rock soils of the Florida keys. Heavy and poorly drained soils should be avoided because of the intolerance of the roots to excess moisture and the likelihood of foot-rot and gummosis. It does about equally well under a range of soil reaction from moderately acid to slightly alkaline. Like other citrus trees, however, it is sensitive to even small concentrations of alkali salts, for which reason such soils should be avoided and only irrigation water of good quality be used. Because of its shallow rooting habit deep soils are not required; three to four feet of good soil with adequate drainage will suffice.

The bulk of the West Indian lime production in the United States still comes from the thickets of seedling trees on the Florida keys and this explains the notable variation in size and form of the fruit in markets. The recent plantings, however, are nearly all of superior selections budded on rootstock seedlings, which has always been the practice with Persian lime varieties. The sour or bitter orange (*Citrus Aurantium*) is the rootstock most employed, though the rough lemon (*Citrus Limonia*) is used for lighter soils in Florida. Experience in California indicates that the sour-orange rootstock exerts a moderate dwarfing effect on the trees of both kinds of limes in comparison with the sweet orange (*Citrus sinensis*), grapefruit (*Citrus paradisi*), and rough lemon when used as rootstocks. For heavy soils and regions of high rainfall the sour orange as a rootstock and budding the rootstock seedlings high, 8 to 12 inches, are recommended to avoid gummosis, a disease to which all citrus rootstocks other than sour orange are more or less subject. Nursery trees are propagated by shield-budding seedlings of suitable size, fall or dormant budding being preferred. The trees are usually planted as year-old budlings.

PLANTING. The evergreen nature of the tree and the sensitiveness of its roots to desiccation require that special care be given to the planting operations, particularly in arid regions. In California the practice is almost universal of digging the nursery trees with a 20- to 30-pound ball of earth about the roots, which is held tightly in place by a burlap wrapping. This permits storing the trees under lath until conditions are favorable for planting and insures good results. Lime trees, like other citrus, should not be planted when the soil is cold, which prevents root growth. If balled trees are used and planting properly timed, the trees experience very little setback and start growth almost immediately. The best practice involves heading the trees, usually to a height of 24 to 30 inches, a few weeks before they are dug and balled.

IRRIGATION. In arid regions irrigation is undoubtedly the most important soil management practice. The evergreen nature of the tree, its shallow rooting habit and relatively high water requirement, combine to produce the necessity for irrigation during the dry season; indeed the requirement of an adequate soil moisture supply at all times may necessitate irrigation at any time of year. The total amount of water required is dictated by the climate and the size and spacing of the trees; the period between irrigations depends on weather conditions and the nature of the soil. The method of irrigation is determined mainly by the slope of the land and nature of the soil.

Fertilization is also important, for all the citrus fruits are high in nutrient requirement. Experience indicates that satisfactory yields can be maintained by annual applications of about 200 pounds of nitrogen per acre and that part of it can best be applied in the form of animal manures or leguminous straws which also provide organic matter. Tillage is necessary only to turn under cover crops, weeds, or fertilizers and to facilitate irrigation. Pruning is of minor importance and is confined to the removal of suckers and declined lower limbs and to light thinning of the bearing wood.

The fruit drops when ripe but should be removed by clipping, when the most desirable size is attained, and stored under cool, moist conditions. Within a few weeks it colors and the rind toughens.

There are no named varieties of the West Indian lime. Bearss, a seedless fruit, is the only named variety of the Persian lime. — R. W. H.

PESTS. Pests of limes are in general the same as those of other citrus fruits (*see* ORANGE).

LIME. Because calcium is an absolutely essential constituent of most plants, and because it helps in the availability of many other substances in the soil, some form of lime has been used by farmers since ages before the Christian era. The need for it is just as imperative today, but it is still true that more money is wasted on useless liming, or in actually harmful liming, than ever, largely because the average gardener does not understand its true function nor the form in which lime should be applied.

WHAT LIME DOES. Rain water is generally somewhat acid. It therefore tends to leach

---

* Special articles on the subjects indicated by an asterisk (*) will be found at the words so marked.

out of soil some of the necessary calcium, as well as other soluble materials. If too long continued, this process results in what the farmer calls a sour soil, unfit for clover and for many other crops, but, as we shall see below, often a boon to certain garden plants. If the region is one where there is a natural disintegration of limestone, the loss of lime by leaching is taken care of by the fresh addition of it from the minerals already in the soil which are slowly released. Such an area needs no lime added to it.

But where the basic soil materials cannot replace the leached lime, it is necessary to correct the loss, *but only* if the crop is one actually needing lime, which some do not. Generally speaking, sour soils are unfit for most vegetable or farm crops, but many cult. shrubs and trees are indifferent to moderate deficiencies of lime.

Besides the purely chemical action, lime of the right sort has the peculiar quality of making heavy clay or silt soils more workable. This action is apparently purely physical, for it results in the amalgamation of extremely fine soil particles into somewhat larger units, which allows far better aeration and drainage. On this score alone lime is of the greatest value.

DEFINITIONS. One of the chief wastes in the use of lime comes from the fact that lime is not "just lime." For garden or farm purposes it comes in many forms of greatly different value — all basically derived from limestone, oyster shells, or marl.

1. *Limestone.* The chief source of lime for many growers; useful, however, only when very finely ground. Its objections are its weight, the cost of hauling it from the lime quarry, and the fact that it has less value than hydrated lime which is made from it.

2. *Oyster shells.* Contain about the same amount of beneficial material as ground limestone, but are useful only when ground very fine. The objections are the lack of them except at a few favored places along the seacoast, and the fact that, like ground limestone, they have less value than hydrated lime.

3. *Marl.* This is a mixture of lime, and, usually, fine silts or clays. The mixture often contains uncertain amounts of these three substances, so that marl, unless found locally and at a cheap price, is the least effective way of applying lime.

4. *Chalk.* A poor form of lime. *See* CHALK.

For practical garden and farm use the hydrated lime manufactured from limestone is by far the best material to use, but only if its percentage of calcium oxide is at least 70%. Freshly burned limestone may contain as much as 90% calcium oxide or even more, but it comes in large lumps unfit for use. But hydrated (*i.e.*, burned and slaked) lime is as fine as powder, comes in bags which keep well in a dry place, and is the best for all-round use.

There is no honest objection to hydrated lime (70%), but much trickery has been practiced upon the gardeners and farmers by dealers who offer inferior products under the name of "agricultural lime." Sometimes these are made from an initially poor grade of limestone, and often contain only mere sweepings of white dust, land plaster, and other relatively useless junk. In buying lime it is safer to specify hydrated lime of about 70% calcium oxide content. Some "agricultural lime" meets this specification but much does not.

How to Use Lime

The need for lime can be tested exactly as one tests for soil acidity (for details *see* ACID AND ALKALI SOILS). For most garden crops, except the important exceptions noted below, the soil needs lime if it shows a pH of much below 6.0, usually indicated by the presence of sour dock and other acid-tolerant weeds.

If lime is needed, it should be spread exactly as fertilizer is spread. Ordinarily, a coating enough to whiten the ground thoroughly is sufficient. When hydrated lime is used, spreading is easy (not on a windy day) because the material is as fine as powder and spreads easily either by hand sowing or by a machine for spreading fertilizer.

It should be put on freshly harrowed land or on an area that is to be plowed or harrowed or raked over immediately. More important still is the necessity of spreading it thoroughly, for lime works scarcely at all laterally and a poorly spread coating may leave many acid or sour places in an otherwise limed field.

AMOUNT NEEDED. A very usual application is a "ton of lime to the acre." But such an estimate loses sight of the fact as to what sort of lime is used. Generally speaking, such directions mean ground limestone. Translated into other sorts of lime, such directions mean, for a garden 40 × 70 ft., the following approximate amounts:

100 pounds of ground limestone
78 pounds of hydrated lime
68 pounds of burned lime, in lumps (not recommended)

Such an application should not be repeated more than once in three or four years, unless the tests show that your soil needs more frequent applications.

When Not to Use Lime

Lime is not a fertilizer (which see); therefore, do not add it to the soil of growing crops. Never top-dress growing lawns with it (*see* LAWN). Keep it away from all rhododendrons, azaleas, and other plants of the heath family. Do not put any in the woods soil of the wild garden nor in the bog garden, nor in any other place where acid-tolerant plants are to be grown. (*See* the list of plants at Acid and Alkali Soils.)

Do not add lime in any form to any manure heap, nor to a compost pile if there is manure in it. It does more damage there than anywhere else, for it greatly increases the loss of nitrogen. Never, for the same reason, mix it with any commercial fertilizer. It is sometimes permissible to mix and spread immediately (to save two operations) lime and phosphates, but such a time-saving operation is pure waste with a fertilizer containing nitrogen in any form.

There is no scientific evidence that lime is of any direct benefit to tree fruits, blackberries, gooseberries, currants, raspberries, or strawberries, and it may be positively harmful to many slightly acid potato lands. Moderate applications do have value for most garden plants of the pea family. It is, also, of great value for soils too acid to properly grow Kentucky bluegrass.

limeana, -us, -um (ly-mee-ā′na). Relating to, or from, Lima, Peru; or relating to the lima bean.

LIMEBERRY = *Triphasia trifolia.*

"LIME-HATERS." Plants that are acid-tolerant. They do not "hate" lime, but appear to grow best in soils of a certain degree of acidity. For a list of such *see* Acid and Alkali Soils.

"LIME-LOVING PLANTS." *See* Limestone Plants.

limensis, -e (ly-men′sis). From Lima, Peru.

LIMEQUAT. A hybrid citrus fruit derived from crossing the West Indian lime (*see* Lime) and kumquat. It is more hardy than the common orange, but it is not of much practical value. The fruit is light yellow, more or less oval, nearly 2 in. long, and with a very acid pulp. Its culture is the same as for orange (which see).

LIMESTONE PLANTS. While a considerable number of wild plants are, or are thought to be, confined to regions underlain by limestone, not many garden plants are especially restricted to such regions. The answer is perhaps found in the fact that the great bulk of the common garden plants have been successfully cult. for centuries in a great variety of soils.

There is, too, the question of how much the lime content of the soil is offset by the physical characteristics of it. While much experimental work is still necessary to get at the exact facts, it may be permissible to list most of the cult. species of *Clematis*, possibly *Prunus Mahaleb, Aster Amellus, Anthyllis Vulneraria, Lithodora fruticosa,* and perhaps some of the scillas, as "limestone plants," a designation more common in the literature of gardening than specifically accurate. Another, and perhaps the most certain of all, is the hartstongue fern which appears to be confined, in America,

to limestone ledges. Other garden plants which may be lime-tolerant are *Pellaea, Potentilla fruticosa, Teucrium Marum,* many campanulas, *Daphne, Atropa, Dianthus alpinus,* some acacias, *Paulownia, Eriobotrya, Clerodendron,* and several others.

LIMNANTHACEAE (lim-nan-thay′see-ee). The false mermaid family comprises only two genera of aquatic or marsh herbs of which only *Limnanthes* is cult. *See* this genus for the characters of the family.

LIMNANTHEMUM = *Nymphoides.*

LIMNANTHES (lim-nan′theez). A genus of 7 species of western North American herbs of the family Limnanthaceae, of which **L. douglasi,** the meadow-foam or marsh flower, is cult. in the flower garden. It is a spreading or sprawling annual, 4–8 in. high, and usually branching from the base. Leaves alternate,° compound,° the leaflets arranged feather-fashion and sharply lobed or toothed. Flowers solitary, long-stalked, fragrant, nearly 1 in. wide, white, or yellowish toward the base. Sepals° 3–5, persistent. Petals 3–5, usually notched at the tip. Stamens° twice as many as the petals. Fruit dry. The plant is best treated as a hardy annual (*see* Annuals) and its only requirement is a moist or nearly wet place. (*Limnanthes* is from the Greek for marsh flower, in allusion to its habitat.)

LIMNOCHARIS (lim-nock′a-ris). Tropical American aquatic herbs of the family Butomaceae, comprising only 3 species, of which **L. flava** (sometimes known as *L. emarginata*) is cult. in pools, tubs, or in aquaria for its yellow flowers. Leaves erect, standing 1–2 ft. above the water surface, velvety green, blunt at the tip. Flowers in a stalked cluster (umbel°), the 3 sepals green and persistent, the 3 petals yellow and soon withering. Stamens° many, the outer ones sterile. Fruit a collection of small, splitting pods. The plant is of easy culture in reasonably shallow water and may be propagated by seeds or by the suckers that arise at the base of the flowering stalk. For the plant sometimes offered as *L. humboldti* see Hydrocleis nymphoides. (*Limnocharis* is from the Greek for marsh, in allusion to the habitat.)

LIMODORUM TUBEROSUM = *Calopogon pulchellus.*

LIMONCITO = *Triphasia trifolia.*

Limonia (ly-mō′nǐ-a). An obsolete generic name for certain citrus fruits, especially the lime and lemon.

LIMONIUM (ly-mō′nǐ-um). The sea lavenders or sea pinks comprise a genus of perhaps 200 species of the family Plumbaginaceae, mostly annual or perennial herbs, several of which are widely grown flower garden plants. They have mostly basal, often tufted, leaves. Flowers small, but numerous, in open loose clusters (panicles°) or in

---

* Special articles on the subjects indicated by an asterisk (°) will be found at the words so marked.

branching spikes, prevailingly lavender, rose-pink, or bluish, but sometimes yellow or white. Calyx* often membranous or colored, tubular. Corolla of 5 nearly separate and often clawed* petals. Fruit dry, enclosed by the persistent calyx. (*Limonium* is from the Greek for meadow, perhaps in allusion to the salt marsh habitat of many species.)

While mostly salt marsh plants in the wild state, the cult. sea lavenders are easily grown in the flower garden, preferably in somewhat sandy soils. They are of great use for dried bouquets as the chaffy flowers hold their color for a long time. Some of the more open-clustered sorts are especially fine for the feathery trimmings of flower arrangements, suggesting the baby's-breath. The annuals should be sown where needed, while the perennials are easily increased by division. All bloom in summer or early autumn. Some of the species, especially *L. sinuatum*, are often grown in the cool greenhouse for the florist trade.

There is much confusion in the Latin names of these plants, which are often offered under the name *Statice*. The latter is also used for the thrift (*see* ARMERIA), but many catalogues still list sea lavenders under *Statice* instead of *Limonium*.

bonduelli. An annual or biennial, 15–24 in. high. Leaves oblongish or oval, 4–6 in. long. Flowers yellow, in a branched cluster (panicle*), the branches winged. Algeria.

dumosum. A name of uncertain validity, and the late L. H. Bailey dismisses it with the statement, "Some of the material in the trade is *L. vulgare*."

gmelini. A perennial with the leaves mostly in basal rosettes, differing from *L. vulgare* chiefly in having smaller flowers and shorter leafstalks. Caucasus and Siberia. May.

latifolium. A hairy perennial, 15–24 in. high. Leaves triangular, 4–6 in. long, square cluster much branched, the calyx* white, but the corolla blue. Eurasia. The *var.* album has white flowers, and the *var.* elegantissimum is a finer form with larger flowers.

perezi. Almost shrubby and nearly 3 ft. high. Leaves triangular, 4–6 in. long, square cut at the base, long-stalked. Calyx* bluish-purple, the corolla yellow. Canary Islands. Grown in Calif. and not certainly hardy except in similar climates.

sinuatum. A perennial or biennial, 15–24 in. high. Leaves lyre-like and cut, 6–8 in. long. Flower cluster (panicle*) much branched, the branches 3–5-winged. Calyx* blue, the corolla yellowish white. Mediterranean region. One of the best for the outdoor garden, and often forced by florists.

suworowi. A hardy annual from Turkestan, 6–10 in. high, with a densely crowded cluster of lilac flowers. Summer. A succession of sowings will prolong bloom until frost.

tataricum. A perennial not over 12 in. high. Leaves ovalish, but broader toward the tip, 4–6 in. long. Flower cluster (panicle*) with the branches narrowly winged. Calyx* white, green-veined, the corolla red. Southern Eu. There is a fine dwarf variety. Usually offered as *Statice tatarica*.

vulgare. A perennial, 9–18 in. high. Leaves elliptic or oblongish, 4–6 in. long. Calyx* white, the corolla bluish-lilac. Mediterranean region.

LINACEAE (ly-nay'see-ee). The flax family contains only two genera of garden interest, although 20 genera and over 350 widely distributed species are known. In the cult. genera, *Linum*, which is mostly hardy, is herbaceous, while *Reinwardtia* is a somewhat woody greenhouse plant from India.

Leaves usually alternate,* without marginal teeth in both the cult. genera. Flowers rather showy in both genera, prevailingly yellow or blue, but white or red in some species, always in clusters. In both the cult. genera the fruit is a dry pod (capsule*). *Linum* which yields linen and flax (also flaxseed oil) is the most important genus.

Technical flower characters: Flowers regular. Sepals 5 (rarely 4), usually not united, persistent. Petals opposite the sepals, in *Reinwardtia* somewhat connected at the base into a short tube. Stamens* usually 5, sometimes with 5 additional sterile ones. Ovary superior,* 2–5-celled.

LINANTHUS. See GILIA.

LINARIA (ly-nay'ri-a). Toadflax. A genus of about 125 species of annual or perennial herbs of the figwort family, all from the north temperate zone, a few grown for ornament in the flower garden or rock garden. They are rather slender herbs with opposite* or whorled* leaves, or the upper ones sometimes alternate.* Flowers usually showy, in terminal clusters (spikes or racemes*), the corolla irregular,* with a long tube, and also long-spurred.* Stamens* 4. Fruit a capsule.* (*Linaria* is from the Latin for flax, the leaves of which are like those of some species of toadflax.)

Toadflax is easily grown in most ordinary garden soils. Sow the annual species where wanted, and the perennials are readily increased by division. They may also be grown from seed and should bloom the second season.

aequitriloba = *Cymbalaria aequitriloba*.

alpina. A perennial, rock garden plant, 3–6 in. high, with very narrow leaves. Flowers blue and yellow, the spur about as long as the corolla. Alps. For culture *see* ROCK GARDEN.

Cymbalaria = *Cymbalaria muralis*.

dalmatica. A perennial border plant, 2–4 ft. high, the leaves bluish-green and lance-shaped. Flowers yellow, the straight spur a little shorter than the corolla. Southeastern Eu.

hepaticifolia = *Cymbalaria hepaticifolia*.

maroccana. An annual suited to the rock garden, not over 18 in. high. Leaves very narrow and slender. Flowers red-purple or violet-purple, with a small yellow spot on the lower lip.* Spur about half as long as the corolla. Morocco. For culture *see* ROCK GARDEN.

origanifolia. A perennial, usually less than 12 in. high. Leaves oblongish or broader toward the tip. Flowers pinkish-purple or whitish, with a yellow patch on the lower lip.* Spur shorter than the corolla. Southern Eu. Referred by some to the genus *Chaenorrhinum*.

purpurea. A showy flower garden perennial, 2–3 ft. high. Leaves lance-shaped or narrower. Flowers purple, but the lower lip somewhat

---

* Special articles on the subjects indicated by an asterisk (*) will be found at the words so marked.

white-bearded, the curved spur about equaling the corolla. Southern Eu.

vulgaris. Common toadflax; also called butter-and-eggs. A perennial Eurasian herb, often weedy throughout N.A., usually 12–15 in. high, sometimes double this. Leaves numerous, very narrow. Flowers yellow, the lower lip somewhat orange-bearded. Spur about the same length as the corolla, which is about 1 in. long.

linariifolia, -*us,* -*um* (lin-air-i-i-fol'i-a). With flax-like leaves.

LINDANE. *See* No. 4 at INSECTICIDES.

LINDELOFIA (lin-del-ō'fi-a). Himalayan perennial herbs of the family Boraginaceae, comprising only two species, one of which, **L. longiflora** (sometimes offered as *L. spectabilis*), is grown in the rock garden. It is a leafy-stemmed, hairy herb, 12–18 in. high, with some basal and a few alternate* stem leaves, the upper more or less heart-shaped or stem-clasping. Flowers deep blue, about ¼ in. long, much resembling anchusa, but the stamens* protruding. Fruit a collection of nutlets, with hooked bristles. The plant is tolerant of many kinds of soils, but needs reasonably good drainage and protection from slush and wet feet in winter. (Named for Friedrich von Lindelof, German patron of botany.)

LINDEN. Lime or basswood. A group of ornamental deciduous trees belonging to the genus **Tilia** (till'i-a) of the family Tiliaceae. There are about 30 species native to the north temperate zone. The leaves are alternate,* toothed, usually heart-shaped at the base, and with one side longer than the other. The flowers are small, yellowish-

Leaf and flower cluster of the linden

white, fragrant and borne in long-stalked, drooping clusters; attached to the flower stalk for about half its length is a thin, oblong bract* that constitutes one of the prominent characteristics of this group. Fruit is the size of a small pea, dry and hard.

(*Tilia* is the old Latin name of the linden.)

The lindens are handsome trees of good habit and comparatively rapid growth. They make excellent shade trees and are much used along streets and avenues. Due to the abundant nectar the flowers attract many bees. The wood is light, easily worked and used in interior trim. Although not particular, they prefer a rich, moist soil and are liable to suffer during dry spells. Propagation is by seed, which is best sown soon after it ripens.

T. americana. American linden. Tall tree sometimes to 120 ft. Leaves roundish-ovate, 4–8 in. long, heart-shaped at base, pointed at tip, coarsely toothed, dark green on upper surface, paler beneath with small tufts of hairs in the vein axils.* Flowers 6–15 at each bract.* June. Canada southward to Ala. and eastern Tex. Hardy from zone* 3 southward. Also known as *T. glabra.*

T. argentea = *Tilia tomentosa.*

T. cordata. Small-leaved linden. Shapely tree, 90–100 ft. high. Leaves rounded, 1½–3 in. long, heart-shaped at the base, with a short, tapered tip, toothed, dark green above, paler or whitish on the under surface, with tufts of brown hairs in the vein axils.* Flowers yellowish, fragrant, in late June or early July. Europe. Hardy from zone* 3, possibly zone* 2, southward.

T. euchlora. Tree to 50 ft. or more with somewhat pendulous branches. Leaves about 4 in. long, roundish-ovate and sharply toothed, heart-shaped at the base, with one lobe longer than the other, glossy on upper surface, paler below with tufts of brown hairs in the vein axils.* Flowers 3–7, in pendulous clusters. June. Hybrid origin. Hardy from zone* 3 southward. One of the most attractive lindens.

T. europaea. Common European linden, and a hybrid between *T. cordata* and *T. platyphyllos.* It closely resembles another hybrid, *T. euchlora,* and differs from it mostly in the leaves being dull green on the upper side. *T. europaea* is rare in cult. in this country, mostly being replaced by *T. cordata* and *T. platyphyllos.* Hardy from zone* 3 southward.

T. glabra = *T. americana.*

T. grandifolia = *Tilia platyphyllos.*

T. petiolaris. A tree up to 75 ft. high, closely related to the silver linden (*T. tomentosa*), and differing from it chiefly in having pendent branches. Eurasia. Hardy from zone* 4 southward. July.

T. platyphyllos. Large-leaved linden. A tall, shapely tree to 120 ft. Leaves round-ovate, 3–4 in. long, heart-shaped at base, toothed, dark green above, paler and usually hairy beneath, especially on the veins and midrib. Flowers whitish, in pendent, 3-flowered (rarely more) clusters. Fruit oval, 3–5-ribbed. June. Europe. Hardy from zone* 3 southward; *var.* **rubra.** A form with red branchlets; *var.* **laciniata.** The leaves of this variety are deeply cut into narrow sections.

T. tomentosa. Silver linden, also called white linden. A tree growing 90 ft. or more high, rather pyramidal in habit, with upright branches; young branchlets downy. Leaves 2–5 in. long, rounded, heart-shaped at base or straight across, sharply toothed, occasionally slightly lobed, dark green above, under surface covered with silvery-white down. Flowers whitish, 3–10. July. Eurasia. Hardy from zone* 3 southward.

T. vulgaris = *T. europaea.*

---

* Special articles on the subjects indicated by an asterisk (*) will be found at the words so marked.

LINDEN FAMILY = Tiliaceae.

LINDERA (lin-der′a). A group of 60 species of aromatic shrubs and trees of the laurel family, most of them tropical, but the one below the well-known spicebush of our swamps and woods. Leaves (in ours) without marginal teeth, alternate.* Flowers small, yellow, blooming long before the leaves unfold, unisexual.* Sepals 6, colored. Petals none. Male flowers with 9 stamens.* Fruit fleshy, nearly round, bright red. (*Lindera* was named for J. Linder, a Swedish physician.)

The spicebush is of the easiest culture in most garden soil. If it has any preference it is for partial shade and a moist site. The bush is particularly attractive very early in the spring for its mass of yellow bloom. Sometimes offered as *Benzoin*.

Benzoin. Spicebush; called also spicewood and Benjamin-bush. A shrub 8–15 ft. high. Leaves more or less oblong, but wedge-shaped at the base, 3–5 in. long. Flowers small, crowded in small, nearly stalkless clusters that are about ⅓ in. long. Ont. to Fla. and westward. Mar.–Apr. Hardy from zone* 2 southward. Fall foliage yellow. Also known as *Benzoin aestivale*.

LINEAR. Narrow, long, and with essentially parallel edges, as are many leaves.

linearifolia, -us, -um (lin-ee-ā-rĭ-fō′lĭ-a). Narrow-leaved.

linearis, -e (lin-ee-ā′ris). Linear.*

lineata, -us, -um (lin-ee-ā′ta). Lined or striped.

LING = Heather.

LING KO = *Trapa bicornis*.

LINGON-BERRY = *Vaccinium Vitis-Idaea*.

lingua, -us, -um (ling′gwa). A tongue; or tongue-like.

lingulata, -us, -um (ling-you-lay′ta). Tongue-like.

linifolia, -us, -um (ly-ni-fō′li-a). With flax-like leaves.

LINNAEA (lin-nee′a). Twinflower, One, or perhaps two, species of herb-like, woody, trailing evergreen plants of the honeysuckle family, found throughout the cooler parts of the north temperate zone, but extending north to Alaska and northern Siberia. They have opposite,* stalked, roundish leaves with shallowly scalloped margins. Flowers in pairs, at the end of slender, upright stalks. Corolla more or less bell-shaped, 5-lobed. Stamens* 4. Fruit dry, not splitting, 1-seeded. (Named for Linnaeus.*)

The twinflower requires partial shade, good drainage, and an acid humus of pH 5 (*see* ACID AND ALKALI SOILS), in order to thrive. It is thus suitable only to specially prepared places in the rock garden or wild garden, preferably north of zone* 4. *See* WILD GARDEN.

borealis. Twinflower. Prostrate, its creeping stems slightly hairy. Leaves about 1 in. long, usually minutely hairy-fringed on the margin, and with a few scattered hairs on the upper surface. Flowers fragrant, rose-pink or white, about ⅓ in. long. Fruit yellow. Throughout northern and sub-arctic regions. June–Aug. The native American twinflower is sometimes called *L. borealis* var. *americana*.

LINNAEUS. Perhaps the most famous botanist in the world. While commonly called Linnaeus, he was a Swede whose real name was Karl von Linne, born 1707, died 1778. The great contribution which Linnaeus made was that, for the first time, he worked out a system for naming plants which is still the basis of our modern system. It discarded most of the pre-Linnaean* complexities and substituted for every plant only two names — the first one for its genus, the second to designate its species. That is still the basis for naming all hort. plants, of which Linnaeus grew many in his now world-famous garden at Upsala, to which many make pilgrimages from all over the world.

His system of naming and classifying plants was contained in two of his books, *Species Plantarum*, 1753, and *Genera Plantarum*, 1754. Later he elaborated the plan in many other volumes, but from these two stem all the modern methods of naming plants. *See* PLANT NAMES.

linoides (ly-noy′deez, but *see* OÏDES). Resembling flax (*Linum*).

LINOMA = *Dictyosperma*.

LINOSYRIS (ly-no-sy′ris). Old World perennial herbs of the family Compositae, the only cult. species being *L. vulgaris*, the goldilocks, grown for its numerous heads of late-blooming flowers. It is a smooth herb, 18–24 in. high, with alternate,* narrow leaves about 1 in. long. Flower heads about ½ in. wide, without rays,* pale yellow, and effective only because they are grouped in large, branching clusters (corymbs*). It is easily grown in any garden soil and may be propagated by division of its roots. Called by some *Aster Linosyris*. (*Linosyris* is a combination of *Linum*, flax, and *Osyris*, a non-hort. genus.)

LINSEED OIL. *See* FLAX; also LINUM.

LINUM (ly′num). Flax. Nearly 200 species of rather slender annual or perennial herbs of the family Linaceae, all but one of the cult. species grown only for ornament. The single economic species is the common flax which yields linseed oil and linen. Leaves generally alternate,* stalkless, narrow and without marginal teeth. Flowers in generally terminal clusters (racemes* or cymes*), day-blooming and rather fleeting. Sepals and petals each 5, separate. Stamens* 5, alternating with the petals. Fruit a small, dry capsule.* (*Linum* is the classical name of the flax.)

The ornamental linums are of very simple culture. One of them, the flowering flax (*L. grandiflorum*), is a widely cult. hardy annual. Like other hardy annuals, its seed should be sown where the plants are to

---

* Special articles on the subjects indicated by an asterisk (*) will be found at the words so marked.

grow. The perennial species are propagated by division. The leaves of all species look so much alike as to make repetition of their characters useless for purposes of identification.

alpinum. A perennial 4–6 in. high. Flowers blue. Eu. See BLUE GARDEN.

austriacum. A slender perennial, not over 24 in. high, its leaves thread-thin, about ½ in. long, and faintly dotted. Flowers about ¾ in. wide, bluish-purple. Southern Eu. June–July.

campanulatum. A somewhat woody-based perennial, 10–15 in. high. Leaves narrowly spoon-shaped, with 2 minute glands near the base. Flowers nearly 1½ in. wide, yellow and with orange stripes on the petals. Southern Eu. Summer.

flavum. Golden flax. A perennial, 1–2 ft. high. Flowers about ¾ in. wide, golden-yellow. Eu. Another plant, sometimes offered as *L. flavum*, is likely to be *Reinwardtia indica* (which see).

grandiflorum. Flowering flax. A widely grown hardy annual, 1–2 ft. high. Flowers nearly 1½ in. wide, red or pink or in shades of either. Northern Af. The var. **coccineum** with scarlet flowers, and the var. **rubrum** with bright red flowers are the two best-known forms.

lewisi. Prairie flax. A perennial, 2–3 ft. high. Flowers about 1½ in. wide, blue. Western N.A.

narbonnense. A perennial, 1–2 ft. high. Flowers about 1½ in. wide, sky-blue with a white eye.* Eu.

perenne. A perennial, 1–2 ft. high. Flowers about 1 in. wide, clear sky-blue. Eu. The var. **album** has white flowers.

salsoloides. Perennial, partly evergreen herb, 6–8 in. high. Flowers white with a purple eye.* Southern Eu.

usitatissimum. Common flax, and the source of linseed and linen. An annual herb, 3–4 ft. high. Flowers about ½ in. wide, usually blue, sometimes white. Eu., but often established as an escape in N.A. See FLAX.

LION'S-EAR = *Leonotis Leonurus.*

LION'S-TAIL = *Leonurus Cardiaca;* also *Leonotis Leonurus.*

LIP; LIPPED. That part of an irregular corolla which resembles a protruding lip, as in the snapdragon. The latter has an upper, erect, and 2-lobed lip, and a lower, spreading, and 3-lobed one. Such flowers are called 2-lipped. The lip is a common feature of many flowers, especially in the mint and figwort families, and in many orchids. It is, of course, never present in regular* flowers.

LIPARIS (lip'a-ris). Twayblade. A large genus of orchids, widely distributed and growing in the ground, of secondary hort. interest, but two of the native species grown in the wild garden. They are erect, small, smooth, perennial herbs from a bulbous base, from which arise usually 2, chiefly basal, broad, rather thickish leaves (in ours). Flowers very irregular,* borne in a loose raceme* at the end of a slender stalk, prevailingly yellowish-green, or purplish. Sepals and petals nearly equal, narrow and spreading. Lip* nearly flat. Fruit

a small capsule.* (*Liparis* is from the Greek for fat or shining, in allusion to the leaves.)

lilifolia. Twayblade. Usually about 6 in. high, the leaves ovalish, 3–5 in. long. Flowers 5–15 in the cluster, madder-purple, the lip* more or less wedge-shaped. Eastern U.S. June–July. It should be grown in a shady part of the wild garden in well-drained but good rich woods soil.

loeseli. Twayblade; called, also, fen orchis. Usually about 5 in. high. Leaves more or less elliptic, 2–4 in. long, more or less keeled.* Flowers 3–6 in the cluster, yellowish-green, the lip* oblongish. In bogs, meadows, and moist thickets, N.A. and Eu. June–July. Can only be grown in wet or moist places, but will stand open sunlight.

LIP-FERN. See CHEILANTHES.

LIPPIA (lip'pĭ-a). A large genus of often aromatic herbs or shrubs of the family Verbenaceae, nearly all tropical American, only two of much hort. interest. One is the popular old favorite, the lemon verbena, while the other is a widely used ground cover in Calif. and other warm regions where it often replaces lawn grasses. Leaves opposite* or whorled.* Flowers small, resembling those in *Lantana*, usually in small clusters (heads or spikes). Corolla slightly oblique, 4-lobed, or even 2-lipped.* Stamens* 4. Fruit 2 separate nutlets enclosed by the persistent calyx.* (Named for Dr. Auguste Lippi, Italian botanist.)

The lemon verbena is a favorite florists' plant and should be grown in potting mixture* 4. It may be plunged* outdoors during the summer or used as a porch plant in pots. The first species is often mown like grass in Calif., where it is commonly called carpet grass or fog fruit. It is also a bee plant there. The best way to make a lawn of it is to plant sods of it at intervals. It grows rapidly and will usually smother all weeds, especially if kept mown.

canescens. A creeping, prostrate, rapidly spreading plant (*see* above). Leaves about ⅔ in. long, oblongish. Flowers lilac, but yellow-eyed, the head-like cluster scarcely ½ in. in diameter. S.A. Often offered as *L. repens.*

citriodora. Lemon verbena. Citronalis. A shrub 6–10 ft. high and much grown in greenhouses, usually as a pot plant and kept lower. Leaves noticeably lemon-scented, especially when crushed, more or less lance-shaped, 2–3 in. long. Flowers white, generally in spikes, but the clusters sometimes branched. Chile and the Argentine. It is grown outdoors south of zone* 6, but northward as a greenhouse subject, or a summer bedding plant.

repens = *Lippia canescens.*

LIQUIDAMBAR. See SWEET GUM.

LIQUID MANURE. A mixture of cow or horse manure and water, very useful for feeding pot plants, hanging baskets, house plants, or any others where constant watering tends to leach out plant food. Other manures such as guano or hen manure may be used, but usually they are not so easy to procure as cow or horse manure.

The danger of using liquid manure is that too much will be put on at a time or in

---

* Special articles on the subjects indicated by an asterisk (*) will be found at the words so marked.

too strong concentrations. To avoid this, follow the formulas below, and do not use the solutions more than once in ten days or two weeks. What are constantly referred to as "rich feeders" need far more liquid manure than others. No hard-and-fast rule can be given, but a general one is to feed generously the naturally quick-growing sorts, but give less liquid manure to slower-growing species. Most house plants would benefit by an application not oftener than once a month.

FORMULAS FOR LIQUID MANURES

Cow manure, ½ bushel to 50 gallons of water (or 3 gallons of water to 1 dry quart of manure).

Horse manure, ½ bushel to 40 gallons of water (or 2½ gallons of water to 1 dry quart of manure).

Guano or hen manure, 10 pounds to 50 gallons of water (or 5 gallons of water to 1 pound of manure).

Sheep manure, ½ bushel to 60 gallons of water (or nearly 4 gallons of water to 1 dry quart of manure).

In the case of cow and horse manure, some people prefer the water boiling, upon the theory that it kills many hibernating insects. But most busy gardeners use cold water. In any case, stir the mixture once a day for a week before applying. Use well-rotted horse or cow manure; the others can be used in the usual dried state in which they are sold.

Watering with liquid manure is exactly like ordinary watering, except that care must be taken to keep the solution off the foliage. Most housewives, too, prefer to have the operation done outdoors and the plants brought back after a few hours. Practical greenhouse men use liquid manure as part of their regular routine for many plants.

LIQUID MEASURES. *See* WEIGHTS AND MEASURES, 3.

LIQUORICE = Licorice.

LIRIODENDRON. *See* TULIP-TREE.

LIRIOPE (li-rĭ-ō′pe). Lily-turf. Asiatic, stemless, perennial herbs of the lily family, sometimes grown as ground covers in warm regions, as their thick but grass-like leaves are evergreen and very numerous. They have short, thickish rootstocks, and often spread by stolons* to form thick mats. Flowers in terminal clusters (spikes* or racemes*) at the end of stalks that are about as long as the leaves. Corolla small, white, blue, or violet. Stamens* 6. Unlike most plants of the family, *Liriope* has an inferior ovary. Fruit black and berry-like. (Named for the nymph.)

These plants are usually greenhouse subjects in the North, but can be used for ground cover south of New York. For a more hardy lily-turf *see* OPHIOPOGON. *Liriope*, which is often hardy in favorable places north of Washington, is best grown in the cool greenhouse in potting mixture* 3.

graminifolia. The plant passing as this is usually *Liriope spicata*, the true *L. graminifolia* being apparently unknown in cult.

japonica = *Ophiopogon japonicus*.

Muscari. Blue lily-turf. Leaves nearly 18 in. long, about ½ in. wide. Flowers lilac-purple, the stalk of the flower cluster about as long as the leaves. There are forms with fasciated* flower stalks. The *var.* **variegata** has the leaves yellow-striped. Often confused with *Ophiopogon Jaburan*, which is more hardy.

spicata. Creeping lily-turf. Leaves grass-like, but thicker, about 8 in. long. Flowers pale lilac or nearly white, scarcely ¼ in. long, the cluster lax and open. There is a striped-leaved form.

LITCHI (lee′chee). A single species of Chinese tree of the family Sapindaceae, **L. chinensis,** variously called litchi, litchee, leechee, or lychee, and much cult. in warm regions for its fresh fruit. When this is dried it is the litchi-nut of the shops. It is a round-topped, medium-sized tree with compound leaves, with 2–4 pairs of oblongish, pointed, leathery leaflets, which are shining green above but paler beneath. Flowers small, unisexual* or polygamous,* greenish-white, without petals, and in a large, loose, open cluster (panicle*) often a foot long. Fruit a drupe,* the fleshy aril* of its seed being the edible part of the fruit, which is so handsome that the tree is considered an ornamental by some. (*Litchi* is the Chinese name for the plant.)

LITCHI CULTURE

Because of its susceptibility to cold injury, wherein sustained temperatures much below freezing are fatal, the litchi is sparingly grown in the U.S., and planting is limited to only the most frost-free sections of Fla. and Calif. Of the numerous Chinese varieties, few named ones are grown; most trees in Fla. are the Brewster variety. Bright red fruits, of about 1½ in. diameter and with a thin, tough, warty outer skin, are borne in clusters and ripen over a short season in early summer. The white, pulpy flesh has a pleasing flavor either as a fresh fruit or dried.

The trees thrive best in fertile, loamy soils having an acid reaction. Propagation is commonly by seeds or air layering, but may be accomplished by grafting, inarching, and cuttings. They should be set 30–40 ft. apart each way. — G. D. R.

INSECT PESTS. Several scale insects can be controlled by pesticide #21 sprays. Mites are controlled by pesticide #9 dusts. (*See* SPRAYS AND DUSTS.)

DISEASES. A gill fungus infects roots and trunk and may kill trees quickly. Infection can be avoided by elimination of oak roots from soil before planting.

LITHOCARPUS (li-tho-kar′pus). A large group of ornamental evergreen trees of the oak family. They are Asiatic, with one exception, and can be cultivated only in warm climates. The only cult. species is L. densiflora, the tan oak, sometimes known as tanbark oak and chestnut oak, and is found

---

* Special articles on the subjects indicated by an asterisk (*) will be found at the words so marked.

from southern Ore. to northern Calif., where it is abundant along the coast. Under favorable conditions it grows 75–100 ft. high. Leaves leathery and evergreen, alternate,° toothed, more or less oblong, 3–5 in. long and densely covered on the under surface with matted hairs that eventually disappear. The flowers are in upright catkins, 2–4 in. long, with the male flowers toward the top of the catkin and a few female ones at the base. Fruit an acorn about 1 in. long. Possibly hardy from zone° 5 southward. The bark of this tree is of considerable importance for tanning leather. It likes a loamy soil, reasonably moist, is difficult to transplant, and best propagated by seed. Long known as *Quercus densiflora*. (*Lithocarpus* is Greek for stone fruit, referring to the hard shell of the acorn.)

LITHODORA (lith-o-dō'ra). A small genus of rather shrubby plants of the family Boraginaceae from the Mediterranean region, of secondary garden importance. They are often included in *Lithospermum* (which see) from which they differ only in the shrubby habit. (*Lithodora* is from the Greek for rock-inhabiting, in allusion to the habitat of the leading species.)

Lithodora fruticosa should be grown in the rock garden where it will trail over rocks. It can be propagated by cuttings of old wood. In its native region the plant is tolerant of limestone, but does not appear to need it as grown here. The first species is not much known here, but is common in British rock gardens.

diffusa. A low, prostrate, evergreen undershrub. Leaves narrowly lance-shaped. Flowers about ½ in. long, deep blue but striped with reddish-violet. Southern Eu. Sometimes listed as *Lithospermum prostratum* and *L. diffusum*.

fruticosa. A trailing, woody-stemmed, evergreen or persistent plant with narrow leaves having rolled margins and the under surface white-felty. Flowers blue. Southern Eu. Sometimes confused with *Lithodora diffusa*, and often listed as *Lithospermum fruticosum*.

lithophila, -us, -um (lith-ŏff'i-la). Rock-inhabiting.

LITHOPHRAGMA (lith-o-frag'ma). A small genus of herbs of the family Saxifragaceae, all from western N.A., but only **L. affinis,** the woodland star of Calif., of any garden interest. It is a slender-stemmed, sticky-hairy perennial, 8–15 in. high, with a tuberous rootstock, and chiefly basal, often bronzed, roundish leaves that are bluntly and shallowly lobed. Flowers small, white, in a terminal cluster (raceme°). For details of structure see SAXIFRAGACEAE. The plant is grown in the wild garden or rock garden, often under the name *Tellima affinis*. (*Lithophragma* is from the Greek for rock or fence, in allusion to the rocky habitat of some species.)

LITHOSPERMUM (lith-o-sper'mum). Gromwell; also called puccoon. A large genus of annual or perennial herbs of the family Boraginaceae, all from the north temperate zone, a few of them grown in the border or wild garden, but of secondary hort. importance. Leaves alternate,° without marginal teeth. Flowers yellow or blue (in ours), in leafy or bracted,° 1-sided clusters (spikes° or racemes°), the corolla funnel-shaped or salver-shaped, the throat sometimes crested. Stamens 5. Fruit a collection of small nutlets within the persistent calyx.° (*Lithospermum* is from the Greek for stone and seed, in allusion to the hard nutlets.)

The genus has been much confused as to names, as the list below shows very plainly. Shrubby species are to be looked for at *Lithodora*. The true gromwells are of easy culture in the wild garden or border, and may be raised from seed or increased by division.

angustifolium = *L. incisum.*

canescens. Orange puccoon. A hairy-stemmed or hoary perennial, 12–18 in. high. Leaves oblongish or narrower. Flowers orange-yellow, about ½ in. long, essentially stalkless in the cluster. Eastern N.A., but west to Tex. Sometimes known as alkanet.

diffusum = *Lithodora diffusa.*

fruticosum = *Lithodora fruticosa.*

graminifolium = *Moltkia suffruticosa.*

incisum. Yellow puccoon. A diffusely branched perennial, 1–2 ft. high. Leaves very narrow. Earlier flowers bright yellow and about 1 in. long, the later flowers smaller and pale yellow. Central and western N.A. April–July. Sometimes known as *L. linearifolium* and *L. angustifolium.*

linearifolium = *Lithospermum incisum.*

petraeum = *Moltkia petraea.*

prostratum = *Lithodora diffusa.*

purpureo-coeruleum. A perennial herb with a creeping or procumbent stem which is 12–20 in. long. Leaves lance-shaped. Flowers about ½ in. wide, deep blue. Eu. Spring. For culture see ROCK GARDEN. By some assigned to the genus *Buglossoides.*

LITTLE PICKLES. See OTHONNA.

LITTONIA (lit-tone'i-a). A small genus of climbing vines, of the lily family, from tropical Africa, allied to *Gloriosa*, and to be similarly treated. See GLORIOSA. The only cult. species is **L. modesta,** a slender vine, 2–6 ft. high with bright shining leaves each tipped by a tendril.° Flowers about 2 in. long, bell-shaped, orange, on stalks about 2 in. long borne in the leaf axil.° (*Littonia* was named for S. Litton, a Dublin botanist.) Hardy outdoors along the Gulf Coast.

littoralis, -e (lit-to-ray'lis). Pertaining to the seashore.

littorea, -us, -um (lit-tor'ee-a). Of the seashore or seacoast.

LIVE-FOREVER = *Sedum Telephium.*

LIVE OAK = *Quercus virginiana.* See OAK.

LIVERBERRY = *Disporum lanuginosum.*

LIVERLEAF. See HEPATICA.

LIVERWORT. Applied to two very different plants. One is a flowerless plant known as *Marchantia polymorpha*, common in wet places, especially under greenhouse

---

° Special articles on the subjects indicated by an asterisk (°) will be found at the words so marked.

benches. *See* MARCHANTIA. The other liver-wort is the common hepatica (which see).

livida, -us, -um (liv′i-da). Bluish, or black and blue.

"LIVING FOSSIL." *See* METASEQUOIA.

LIVING-ROCK = *Ariocarpus* and *Roseo-cactus.*

LIVISTONA (liv-i-stō′na). Popular Old World fan palms, one of them widely grown by florists under the name of *Latania bor-bonica,* and perhaps the most cult. of all fan palms in America. Of over 23 species, only two others are occasionally grown outdoors in Calif. or Fla. All have more or less ringed trunks and a large crown of fan-like leaves, the stalks of which are some-times prickly in youth. Otherwise the plants are unarmed. Flower clusters branched, appearing among the crown of leaves. Flow-ers small, perfect,* the stamens* 6. Fruit drupe-like, but the flesh thin, 1-seeded. (Named by Robert Brown in honor of P. Murray of Livistone, near Edinburgh.) For culture *see* PALM.

australis. Australian fan palm. Taller than the next species and not so hardy. It may reach a height of 80 ft. Trunk slender, reddish-brown. Leafstalks spiny, especially on young leaves. Leaves 3–6 ft. wide, divided to the middle or below it into 30–50 segments that do not droop and are once- or twice-cleft at the tip. Fruit nearly round, about ⅝ in. in diameter. Aust. As grown in Fla. it has not proved hardy in zone* 8, but is thoroughly hardy in zone* 9.

chinensis. Chinese fan palm; also called fan palm. In maturity 30–40 ft. high, but much lower as a pot or tub plant in which form it is very widely grown in northern greenhouses. Leaves 3–6 ft. wide, divided ⅓ or ½ the distance to the center into many narrow and distinctly ribbed segments which droop at the tip and are also cleft nearly a foot. Fruit ovalish, about ½ in. long. Central China. Hardy from zone* 8, possibly in protected parts of zone* 7 southward. Commonly sold as *Latania borbonica. See* LATANIA.

rotundifolia. A slender-trunked palm 60–80 ft. high. Leaves 3–5 ft. wide, split into 60–90 narrow but short segments which are cleft at the tip, the leafstalk spiny on young leaves. Fruit nearly round, about ¾ in. in diameter. Malaya. Not hardy outside of zone* 9, and not much known here.

Llavea. A generic name for a Mexican fern, but used as a specific name for *Cu-phea Llavea* from Mex.

LOAM. *See* SOILS.

LOASA (low′a-sa). Tropical American herbs (in ours) of the family Loasaceae, usually provided with stinging hairs and of only secondary garden interest. Of 80 or more species only the two below are cult. Both are annual herbs with lobed or com-pound* leaves. Flowers prevailingly white or yellow, but often of additional colors as noted below, solitary in the leaf axils* or in clusters (leafy racemes*). Petals 5, hooded or spreading and alternating with 5 hooded scales, which are bristly on the back. Stamens* many. Fruit a 3–5-valved capsule.* (*Loasa* is the South American name for some species.)

The two below should be grown as tender annuals. *See* ANNUALS.

tricolor. Not over 2 ft. high. Leaves op-posite,* twice-compound, the leaflets arranged feather-fashion. Flowers yellow, but the hooded scales red and the stamens* white. Chile.

vulcanica. From 1–3 ft. high. Leaves sim-ple,* but parted finger-fashion into 3–5 lobes. Flowers white, but the hooded scales yellow and barred red and white. Ecuador and Colombia.

LOASACEAE (low-a-say′see-ee). A fam-ily of 13 New World genera and about 230 species of herbs (rarely woody plants), three genera of which are of garden inter-est. They are *Caiophora, Loasa,* and *Ment-zelia,* the first two of which have stinging hairs; *Mentzelia,* which is the most impor-tant hort. genus, has merely barbed hairs.

Leaves opposite* in *Loasa* (mostly) and *Caiophora,* but usually alternate* in *Ment-zelia.* Flowers regular,* in various kinds of clusters, often showy in *Mentzelia,* the petals flat or hooded, often mixed with sterile, petal-like stamens. Fruit a dry pod (capsule*) in all the cult. genera.

Technical flower characters: Sepals usually 5, the margins overlapping, usually persistent. Petals usually 5, inserted on the receptacle.* Stamens* numerous, and usually mixed with many sterile, petal-like stamens. Ovary gen-erally inferior,* 1-celled.

lobata, -us, -um (lo-bay′ta). Lobed. *See* LOBE.

LOBE. A part or segment of an organ, especially the *lobes* of a petal or leaf. While there is no technical limit to the degree of division which constitutes a lobe, as usually understood a lobe is from ⅛ to ½ the depth of the whole. If the division extends more than halfway to the center, the organ is better described as divided.

LOBELIA (lo-bee′li-a). Showy-flowered perennial or annual herbs of the family Lobeliaceae, comprising about 300 species, some of the tropical sorts (not cult.) being trees. The garden kinds are popular for the border, some for the wild garden, and one a widely used edging plant. Leaves alternate.* Flowers in terminal, often very beautiful clusters (mostly spikes* or ra-cemes*), which are sometimes leafy, or nearly always bracted.* Corolla irregular,* more or less tubular below, but split to the base, 3 of the lobes forming a lip, the other two erect or turned backward. Stamens* uni-ted by their anthers* into a ring around the style.* Fruit a 2-valved capsule.* (Named for Matthias Lobel, a Flemish fa-ther of modern botany.)

Except where noted, the lobelias are of easy culture in the open border. All ex-cept *L. Erinus* are perennials which may be increased by division of the clumps in fall or spring. The edging lobelia (*L. Eri-*

---

* Special articles on the subjects indicated by an asterisk (*) will be found at the words so marked.

nus) is a tender annual and should be grown as such. *See* ANNUALS.

Cardinalis. Cardinal-flower; also called scarlet lobelia. An erect, stiffish perennial, 2½–5 ft. high. Leaves oblongish, 3–5 in. long, coarsely toothed, nearly stalkless. Flowers bright scarlet, about 1½ in. long. Eastern N.A. July–Sept. It needs a moist, shaded place in the wild garden for best development, but will stand some sun if planted in a moist place.

Cardinal-flower (*Lobelia Cardinalis*), a gorgeous scarlet-flowered perennial, good for moist and partially shady sites.

Erinus. Edging lobelia. A tender annual, and one of the most popular of edging plants. *See* EDGING. It is a partly trailing herb 3–8 in. high, the leaves ovalish or narrower, somewhat broader toward the tip. Flowers ½–¾ in. wide, blue (in the typical form), on very slender stalks. S. Af. The *var.* **alba** has white flowers. The *var.* **compacta** is lower and dense, and is the best form for edging. Other forms or named varieties (over a dozen) have variously colored or double flowers, and some have trailing stems and are useful for hanging baskets.

fulgens. A perennial, hairy herb, 2–3 ft. high. Leaves lance-shaped, usually bronzy. Flowers deep red, nearly 1½ in. long. Mex. Hardy from zone* 5 southward, but even there best mulched over the winter.

laxiflora. A hairy perennial, 3–5 ft. high. Leaves ovalish or narrower, toothed. Flowers about 1½ in. long, red and yellow, the stamens protruding. Mex. A plant for the cool greenhouse, especially for pot culture. Seeds sown in Feb. will produce bloom by autumn.

siphilitica. Blue or great lobelia. A hardy perennial 2–3 ft. high, usually quite smooth. Leaves oblong-oval, tapering both ends, 3–5 in. long. Flowers about 1 in. long, deep blue or bluish-purple, very rarely white. Eastern U.S. A good late-flowering blue plant for the autumn garden.

LOBELIACEAE (lo-bee-li-ā'see-ee). The only four garden genera of the lobelia family are herbs, but some of its 24 genera and over 700 species are shrubs and trees in the tropics. Those of hort. interest are grown for their often showy, always irregular* flowers, some of which are 2-lipped.*

Leaves alternate* or basal, the plants often with an acrid or milky juice. Flowers rarely solitary, more often in various sorts of clusters, chiefly in spikes* and racemes.* Fruit a berry in *Centropogon*, but a dry pod (capsule*) in *Downingia*, *Lobelia*, and *Palmerella*, the only other hort. genera.

Much the most important of these is *Lobelia*, which contains many fine garden plants, and some, like the cardinal-flower, suited to the wild garden.

Technical flower characters: Calyx united, its limb 5-lobed or 5-parted. Corolla irregular,* tubular, and mostly 2-lipped,* but the tube sometimes parted nearly to the base. Stamens five, the anthers often united around the style.* Ovary superior,* 2–5-celled, its stigma* fringed.

LOBELIA FAMILY = Lobeliaceae.

LOBLOLLY BAY = *Gordonia Lasianthus*.

LOBULARIA. *See* SWEET ALYSSUM.

LOCOWEED. Many plants poisonous to stock on the western ranges are called locoweed. The only one of garden interest is *Oxytropis lamberti* (which see).

LOCUST. A small group of North and Central American deciduous trees and shrubs belonging to the genus **Robinia** (rō-bin'ĭ-a) of the pea family. The leaves are alternate* and compound,* the leaflets arranged feather-fashion, with an odd one at the tip. Flowers are pea-shaped, white, pink or purple, and borne in pendulous racemes.* Fruit a flat, many-seeded pod. (Named for J. and V. Robin, herbalists to Henry IV of France.) For the biblical locust, *see* CAROB.

The locusts are ornamental both in leaf and in flower. They do well in soil of moderate quality, often thriving in poor, sandy soil. Propagation is mainly by seed, though some may be multiplied by suckers; certain varieties are grafted. The tree species cast so little shade that grass can be grown under locusts more easily than under most other trees. The suckering of the black locust can often become a nuisance.

R. fertilis. Little, if at all, differing from the next species, and with smaller flowers. N. Car. to Ga. June. Hardy from zone* 3 southward.

R. hispida. Rose acacia, also called pink locust. A spreading shrub, usually 3–4 ft. high. The branches are brittle and covered with red bristles. Leaves composed of 7–13 oval or rounded leaflets about 1 in. long. Flowers rose-colored, in few-flowered clusters. Pods bristly, 2–3 in. long, seldom produced. May or June. Va. to Ala. Hardy from zone* 3 southward. One of the handsomest locusts; often suckers freely.

R. kelseyi. A handsome shrub or small tree growing about 10 ft. high. Leaflets 9–11, oval or narrow-oval, about 1 in. long. Flowers rose-colored, 1 in. across, in 5–8-flowered, bristly stalked clusters. May–June. N. Car. Hardy from zone* 3 southward.

R. neo-mexicana. Thorny locust. Spiny, branched shrub or small tree 25–30 ft. tall. Leaflets 15–25, oval to ovate, 1–1½ in. long, downy beneath when young. June. Colo., Utah,

---

* Special articles on the subjects indicated by an asterisk (*) will be found at the words so marked.

N. Mex. and Ariz. Hardy from most parts of zone* 3 southward.

R. Pseudo-acacia. Black locust, also called yellow locust and false acacia. Tree of 70–80 ft. with furrowed brown bark. Leaves 6–12 in. long, often with two spines at base, leaflets 7–19, oval, 1–2 in. long. Flowers white, fragrant, in many-flowered, pendulous racemes 3–5 in. long. Pods smooth, 3–4 in. long. June. Pa. to Okla. and often naturalized elsewhere in N.A. and also in Eu. Hardy from zone* 3 southward. The wood is strong and resists decay in contact with the soil; *var.* **bessoniana,** a slender-branched form developing a rather ovoid head; *var.* **decaisneana,** handsome, rose-colored flowers; *var.* **umbraculifera** develops a dense, rounded head. There is also a var. known as the shipmast locust, possibly the doubtful form called *var.* **rectissima.** It is a good street tree, resistant to dust, smoke, wind and salt spray; also much liked by bees.

R. viscosa. Clammy locust. Tree to 30 or 40 ft., the young twigs and leaf stems covered with sticky glands. Leaves 3–10 in. long, leaflets 11–25, ovate or oval, downy beneath when young. Flowers pink with a yellow blotch, not fragrant, in many-flowered clusters, 2–3 in. long. Pods about 3 in. long, somewhat sticky. May, June. Pa. to Ala. Hardy from zone* 4, and parts of 3, southward.

Locusta, -us, -um (lo-kus'ta). Latin for locust, but of uncertain application to the corn salad (*Valerianella Locusta olitoria*).

LOCUST FAMILY. *See* LEGUMINOSAE.

LOESS. Wind-deposited, usually very rich soils, covering many states in the central part of the U.S. They vary from fine, silt-like material to soils that are practically similar to rich garden loam.

LOGANBERRY (*Rubus loganobaccus*). This bramble fruit, which has blackberry-like, but red, acid fruit is of uncertain origin. It was found or produced by a Judge J. H. Logan in Calif. in 1881. Whether it is a variety of the western dewberry or a hybrid of that species with the red raspberry is a disputed point, and one which may never be settled.

The plant is a vigorous grower and should be treated as a blackberry except for two points: (1) Its canes are so long and inclined to trail that the plant is best trained to wires, and is commercially so grown. The fence-like wire trellises should be about 6 ft. apart, and the plants spaced 8 ft. apart in the row. (2) Except on the Pacific Coast and in other places with mild winters, the loganberry is nearly sure to winter-kill,* or be killed outright, when the temperature drops to zero. This restricts its commercial cult. to Wash., Ore., Calif. and a few places along the Gulf of Mexico. Elsewhere, even with protection, it is not happy and produces far less fruit. Its pests are the same as those of the raspberry (which see).

A form known as Phenomenal, introduced by Burbank, is favored by some California growers in the region about Los Angeles, who claim it has richer, more raspberry-like fruit than the common loganberry.

LOGANIACEAE (lo-gan-i-ā'see-ee). Of the four cult. genera of this family only *Spigelia,* an American herb, is not woody. All the rest of the garden genera are shrubs, trees, or woody vines. Of its 30 genera and over 400 species many contain dangerous poisons in their juice, notably *Strychnos,* which yields strychnine. The other cult. genera are harmless, and comprise very beautiful shrubs in *Buddleia.* The ever-popular Carolina jasmine is in the genus *Gelsemium.*

Leaves opposite.* Flowers usually showy, always in clusters, these spike-like and very handsome in *Buddleia.* Fruit dry in all the cult. genera, except *Strychnos,* where it is somewhat fleshy.

Technical flower characters: Calyx united, its 4–5 lobes free but overlapping. Corolla more or less tubular or funnel-shaped, its limb 4–5-parted. Stamens alternating with the lobes of the corolla. Ovary superior,* 2-celled.

LOGWOOD = *Haematoxylon campechianum.*

LOISELEURIA (loy-zel-loor'i-a). A single species of prostrate, evergreen shrub of the heath family, **L. procumbens,** the alpine azalea or trailing azalea, which grows in cold regions throughout the north temperate zone. It rarely grows above 6 in. high, its trailing stems several times this length. Leaves opposite,* oval or oblong, about ¼ in. long, very numerous. Flowers in sparse terminal clusters, the corolla bell-shaped, scarcely ¼ in. long, white or pink. Fruit a 2–3-valved capsule, surrounded by the withered calyx. An attractive mat-forming evergreen, suited only to the rock garden from zone* 4 northward, and needing a gritty soil with a pH of about 5.0 (*see* ACID AND ALKALI SOILS). (Named for J. C. A. Loiseleur-Deslongchamps, French botanist.) *See* ROCK GARDEN.

LOLIUM (lo'lĭ-um). Rye grass. A small genus of annual or perennial Eurasian grasses, of little garden interest except as they are grown for meadows, pastures, or for lawns. They have erect or ascending, usually unbranched stems and flat grasslike leaves. Flowering spikes terminal, usually interrupted,* the spikelets flattened, the edge toward the stem. Some of them have short awns.* (*Lolium* is the Latin name of one species.)

They are not cult. for ornament, the seed being sown for pasture or meadow purposes, and as temporary turf in warm regions.

italicum = *Lolium multiflorum.*

multiflorum. Italian rye grass, but called Australian rye grass in Calif. An annual grass 15–30 in. high. Leaves nearly 8 in. long and about ⅓ in. wide. Flowering spikes nearly 1 ft. long, the spikelets awned,* and with 20–30 flowers. Eu., and naturalized in N.A. Sometimes offered as *L. italicum,* and widely used

---

* Special articles on the subjects indicated by an asterisk (*) will be found at the words so marked.

as a winter turf in warm regions, planted over Bermuda grass. *See* LAWN.

perenne. Perennial rye grass; also called English meadow grass. A tufted, perennial grass 15–24 in. high. Leaves almost 5 in. long, about ⅛ in. wide. Spikes about 1 ft. long, the spikelets not awned, and with 5–10 flowers. Eurasia, and naturalized in N.A.

temulentum. Darnel; also called bearded darnel. An annual grass, 2–4 ft. high. Leaves about 10 in. long and ¼ in. wide. Spikes about 1 ft. long, the spikelets only 4–8-flowered, awned. Eu., and naturalized in N.A. Its seeds yield a narcotic poison.

LOMARIA = *Blechnum*.

lomariifolia, -us, -um (lo-mare-i-i-fo′li-a). With leaves like a fern of the discarded genus *Lomaria*, now considered as *Blechnum*.

LOMBARDY POPLAR = *Populus nigra italica*.

LOMENT. A dry fruit, differing from a true legume* (pea) in being constricted between the seeds, the constrictions often being so deep that the loment may break into separable parts. *See* DESMODIUM and HEDYSARUM. Loments are confined to a few genera in the pea family.

Lonchitis (lon-ky′tis). A generic name for a few non-hort. ferns; used as a specific name at *Polystichum Lonchitis*, which is supposed to resemble the genus *Lonchitis*.

LONDON PLANE = *Platanus acerifolia*.

LONDON PRIDE = *Saxifraga umbrosa*.

longa, -us, -um (long′ga). Long.

LONGAN = *Euphoria Longana*.

Longana (long-gan′a). Latinized version of longan. *See* EUPHORIA.

LONG-DAY PLANTS. *See* PHOTOPERIODISM.

LONGEVITY OF SEEDS. *See* Viability at GARDEN TABLES II.

LONGEVITY OF TREES. *See* GARDEN TABLES III.

longiflora, -us, -um (lon-ji-flō′ra). With long flowers.

longifolia, -us, -um (lon-ji-fō′li-a). With long leaves.

longipes (lon′ji-peez). Long-stalked.

longipinnata, -us, -um (lon-ji-pin-nay′ta). Long-pinnate, that is, with long compound* leaves, the leaflets of which are arranged feather-fashion.

longiscapa, -us, -um (lon-ji-skape′a). With a long flowering stalk (scape).

longissima, -us, -um (lon-jiss′i-ma). Longest.

LONGLEAF PINE = *Pinus palustris*. *See* PINE.

LONG MOSS = *Tillandsia usneoides*.

LONG PEPPER = *Capsicum frutescens longum*.

LONGWOOD GARDENS. *See* No. 11 at GARDEN TOURS.

LONICERA (lon-iss′er-ra). The honeysuckles comprise a group of 180 or more species of shrubs and woody climbers in the honeysuckle family. They are found throughout the northern hemisphere in both the Old World and America. Leaves opposite,* usually entire,* rarely evergreen. The flowers are tubular or bell-shaped, equally 5-lobed or more often 2-lipped,* the upper lip composed of four lobes and the lower of one. They are borne in pairs in the leaf axils* or in clusters at the ends of the branches. Fruit a fleshy berry. (Named for Adam Lonitzer, a 16th-century German naturalist.)

Practically all the honeysuckles are worthy of cultivation. The tall forms are fine for shrub borders and general use while certain of the lower ones are adapted to the rock garden. The often showy flowers are produced abundantly and are sometimes sweetly scented. The fruits are white, yellow, orange, red, blue, or black, quite ornamental, and a favorite food for birds. They are of easy cultivation, thriving in almost any place, though a loamy soil, reasonably moist, is best. Propagation is by seeds or cuttings.

bella. An upright shrub growing 9 or 10 ft. high with spreading branches that are a bit hairy when young. Leaves ovate to oblong, 1–2 in. long, sometimes hairy beneath. Flowers white to pink, fading yellow. Fruit red. May–June; fruit July–Aug. Hybrid origin, and considered by some as a form of *L. morrowi*. Hardy from zone* 3 southward. *Var. albida.* Flowers white; *var. rosea.* Flowers rosy-pink.

browni. A hybrid, climbing honeysuckle (*sempervirens* × *hirsuta*), much like the trumpet honeysuckle (*L. sempervirens*) but with the flower more irregular. There are several hort. forms with orange-red or scarlet flowers. Hardy from zone* 3 southward. Summer.

Caprifolium. Common honeysuckle or Italian honeysuckle. A climbing vine sometimes attaining 20 ft. Leaves oval or elliptic, bluish-green beneath, 2–4 in. long, the upper 2 or 3 pairs fused, forming a cup or disk. Flowers in clusters at the ends of the branches, yellowish-white, sometimes tinged purple, about 2 in. long, 2-lipped,* tube slender. Fruit orange. May–June. Eu. and western Asia. Hardy from zone* 3 southward.

chrysantha. An upright shrub of 10–12 ft. The young branches are usually hairy but this character varies. Leaves oval or narrowly oval, pointed, 2–4 in. long. Flowers yellow, about ¾ in. long, tube swollen at base. Fruit red. May–June; fruit Aug.–Sept. Asia and Japan. Hardy from zone* 3 southward.

dioica. Small honeysuckle, sometimes called small woodbine. Shrub with spreading, sometimes twining, branches. Leaves oval or oblong, 2–4 in. long, the under surface conspicuously bloomy, the upper pairs grown together. Flowers in terminal clusters, yellow, sometimes tinged purple, about ¾ in. long, tube swollen at base. Fruit red. May–June; fruit July–Aug. Quebec to Ga. and Mo. Hardy from zone* 2 southward.

flava. Yellow honeysuckle. Spreading, twining vine to 10 ft. Leaves elliptic, to 3 in. long, blue-green on under surface, upper pairs fused to form a disk. Flowers orange-yellow, fragrant, about 1 in. long, tube slender, not swollen at base. May–June. N. Car. to Okla. Hardy from zone* 3 southward. Perhaps the handsomest of the American honeysuckles.

fragrantissima. Shrub growing 8–10 ft. high

---

* Special articles on the subjects indicated by an asterisk (*) will be found at the words so marked.

with spreading, somewhat recurved branches that form a rounded mass. Leaves oval, thick, 1–2 in. long, dark green above, paler beneath, evergreen in mild climates. Flowers creamy-white, very fragrant. Jan.–Mar. China. Hardy from lower part of zone* 3 southward. Valued for its good foliage and early flowers.

gracilipes. An erect shrub, 4–6 ft. high. Leaves short-stalked, broadly ovalish, 1–3 in. long, the margins reddish, bluish-green in youth on the under side. Flowers hanging, solitary, short-stalked, funnel-shaped, about ¾ in. long, pinkish-red. Fruit football-shaped, red. Jap. April–May. Hardy from zone* 4 southward.

halliana = Lonicera japonica halliana.

heckrotti. A low shrub with spreading, sometimes twining branches. Leaves oblong or oval, 1–2½ in. long, whitish beneath. Flowers 1½ in. long in terminal clusters, purple outside, yellow within, tube slender. June. Probably a hybrid. Hardy from zone* 3 southward. An attractive honeysuckle that blooms over a long period.

henryi. A free-growing, half-evergreen vine with slender, climbing or prostrate branches that are covered with stiff hairs. Leaves oblong, 1–4 in. long, pointed at the tip. Flowers borne in the leaf axils,* purple-red, ¾ in. long. Fruit black. China. Hardy from zone* 3 southward. June–Aug.

hildebrantiana. The largest of all climbing honeysuckles, the immense woody stem reaching a height of 60–80 ft. Leaves evergreen, ovalish, 3–6 in. long, 2–4 in. wide. Flowers 4–6 in. long, fragrant, white at first, ultimately orange, nearly 3 in. wide, and borne in a large terminal cluster (raceme*). An extremely showy vine but hardy only in zones* 8 and 9. Burma to southern China. Summer.

hirsuta. Rough woodbine. Twining vine, the young branches covered with stiff hairs. Leaves oval, 2–4 in. long, downy on both sides, especially the lower, the upper pairs fused to form an elliptic disk. Flowers in terminal clusters, bright yellow, 1 in. long, the tube swollen at base. June–July. Quebec to Sask. and Pa. Hardy from zone* 3 southward.

involucrata. Twinberry. Shrub to 3 ft. with upright, slightly angled branches. Leaves elliptic-oval, 2–5 in. long. Flowers about ½ in. long with two large bracts at the base, yellow, tinged with red, borne on upright stalks. Fruit black, shiny. May–June. Quebec to Alaska and in the mountains to Mex. Hardy from zone* 1 southward.

japonica. Japanese honeysuckle. A vigorous, half-evergreen climber growing 20–30 ft.; branches slender, hairy. Leaves ovate to oblong, 1–3 in. long, pointed, usually downy beneath. Flowers white, tinged purple, fading to yellow, sweetly scented, 1–1½ in. long, 2-lipped,* the tube slender. Fruit black. June. Asia. Naturalized in eastern U.S. where it can become a dangerous nuisance, as it is so rampant that if it gets out of control it will smother all other vegetation. Hardy from zone* 3 southward. Var. **aureo-reticulata.** Leaves smaller and veined with yellow, tender; var. **chinensis.** Flowers to 2 in. long, reddish outside; leaves practically hairless except on the veins beneath. Var. **halliana.** Hall's honeysuckle. Flowers white, fading to yellow, not tinged purple.

korolkowi. Spreading, graceful shrub 8–12 ft. tall. Leaves oval to ovate, pointed, about 1 in. long, hairy, especially beneath, bluish-green. Flowers pale rose, ⅔ in. long. Fruit red. May–June; fruit Aug. Hardy from zone* 3 southward. Attractive when in leaf because of its bluish cast. Var. **floribunda.** Flowers

freely; leaves generally broader, not tapered at base. Var. **zabeli,** the zabel honeysuckle, differs only slightly from the type, having somewhat broader leaves, nearly heart-shaped at the base.

maacki. A vigorous, wide-spreading shrub often 10–15 ft. high. Leaves ovate, with long, slender point, 1½–3 in. long, sometimes hairy. Flowers ⅔ in. long, white aging yellow. Fruit red. May–June; fruit Sept.–Oct. Manchuria, Korea. Hardy from zone* 3 southward. One of the handsomest and largest honeysuckles, conspicuous in bloom and with bright red berries in the fall. Var. **podocarpa.** Hardly distinguishable from the type, leaves broader and habit more spreading.

maximowiczi. A shrub 5–8 ft. high, the twigs purplish. Leaves elliptic or ovalish, 1½–4 in. long, smooth and green above, paler and hairy beneath. Flowers about ½ in. long, violet-red. Fruit football-shaped, red, more or less persistent. Korea. May–June. Hardy from zone* 4 southward.

morrowi. An erect shrub, 6–8 ft. high, the twigs hollow. Leaves elliptic or oblongish, 1½–3 in. long, sparingly hairy on the under side. Flowers in pairs at the leaf joints, about 1 in. long, white in youth, yellowish later. Fruit red. Jap., but sometimes an escape in N.A. May–June. Hardy from zone* 2 southward.

nitida. An evergreen or half-evergreen shrub, rather low, though sometimes to 6 ft. with slender branches. Leaves small, thick, glossy, oval to rounded, ¼–½ in. long. Flowers white, fragrant. Fruit purple. May; fruit Sept.–Oct. China. Hardy from zone* 5, and milder parts of 4, southward. Distinguished by its small, glossy leaves.

Periclymenum. Woodbine. Twisted eglantine. A woody climber sometimes reaching 20 ft. Leaves variable, ovate to obovate, 1½–2½ in. long, bluish-green beneath, upper pairs almost stalkless but never fused. Flowers in terminal clusters, yellowish-white, often tinged with red, fragrant, about 2 in. long, tube slender. Fruit red. June–August; fruit Aug.–Sept. Eu., northern Africa, As. Minor. Hardy from zone* 3 southward.

pileata. Low, spreading, evergreen or half-evergreen shrub growing about 1 ft. or so high and having almost horizontal branches. Leaves ovate to oblong, ½–1½ in. long, glossy. Flowers white, fragrant, about ⅓ in. long. Fruit purple. April–May; fruit Oct. China. Hardy from zone* 5 southward. Adapted to use in the rock garden.

ruprechtiana. Shrub of good habit, growing 8–10 ft. high. Leaves ovate to lance-shaped, pointed, 2–4 in. long, pale and downy beneath. Flowers white, turning yellow, ¾ in. long, not fragrant, tube thick, swollen at base. Fruit red or orange. May, June; fruit Aug.–Sept. Manchuria, northern China. Hardy from zone* 3 southward.

sempervirens. Trumpet honeysuckle, also called coral honeysuckle. Climbing vine, evergreen in mild climates. Leaves oval to oblong, 1⅓ in. long, bluish-green beneath, and slightly downy, upper pairs united to form a disk. Flowers in terminal clusters, bright orange or red outside, yellow within, about 2 in. long, corolla lobes of almost equal length. Fruit orange to scarlet. May to Aug. Mass. to Fla., Tex. and Neb. Hardy from zone* 3 southward.

standishi. An upright, rather coarse shrub to 6 or 8 ft. with peeling bark and spreading branches that are bristly hairy when young; partly evergreen in mild climates. Leaves ovate-

---

* Special articles on the subjects indicated by an asterisk (*) will be found at the words so marked.

lanceolate, thick, 2–4 in. long, pointed, bristly hairy beneath, sometimes on upper surface. Flowers creamy-white, fragrant, ½ in. wide. Fruit red. March–April. China. Hardy from zone* 3 southward. Valued for its early flowers; inferior to *L. fragrantissima*.

syringantha. Graceful, spreading shrub 6–9 ft. high. Leaves oblong to oval, ½–1 in. long, smooth. Flowers rosy-lilac, sweetly scented. Fruit red. May–June. Hardy from zone* 3 southward and half-evergreen in zone* 5, or south of it possibly evergreen.

tatarica. Tartarian honeysuckle, also known as garden fly honeysuckle and bush honeysuckle. An upright, vigorous shrub of pleasing habit growing 8–10 ft. high. Leaves oblong-ovate, pointed, 1–2½ in. long, pale beneath. Flowers white to pink, about ¾ in. long, 2-lipped.* Fruit red. May–June; fruit July–Aug. Russia and Siberia. Hardy from zone* 2 southward. The commonest of the bush honeysuckles; ornamental and easily grown. *Var.* **alba.** Flowers white; *var.* **grandiflora rosea.** Flowers rosy-pink, larger; *var.* **rosea.** Flowers rosy-pink outside, paler within.

tellemanniana. A hybrid, climbing honey-suckle (*tragophylla*, a non-hort. species, × *sempervirens*) with the flowers in stalked clusters (heads) of two distinct tiers (whorls*), dark yellow and 2-lipped. A showy vine, hardy from zone* 3 southward. Summer.

thibetica. Low, spreading shrub, forming a rounded mass to 5 ft.; young shoots purplish and downy. Leaves oblong, pointed, ⅓–½ in. long, often in 3's, smooth, above, white-hairy beneath. Flowers about ½ in. across, in pairs, often clustered at the joints, pale or rosy-purple, fragrant. Fruit red. May–June; fruit Aug. and Sept. Western China. Hardy from zone* 3 southward. A good, spreading or sprawling shrub, sometimes confused with *L. syringantha* but distinguished by the hairy under surface of the leaves.

Xylosteum. European fly honeysuckle, bush honeysuckle. A bushy shrub growing about 10 ft. high. Leaves oval to obovate, pointed at tip, rounded or wedge-shaped at base, paler and hairy beneath. Flowers yellow, often tinged red, about ½ in. across, tube swollen at base. Fruit red. May–June; fruit Aug.–Sept. Eurasia. Hardy from zone* 3 southward.

yunnanensis. A twining honeysuckle, not over 15 ft. high. Leaves oblongish, 1½–3½ in. long, the upper pair united at the base, hence nearly perfoliate,* whitish beneath. Flowers yellow, odorless, in a close nearly stalkless, terminal cluster (whorl*). Yunnan. June. Hardy from zone* 6 and in protected sites in zone* 5, southward.

LOOFA. *See* LUFFA.

LOOSESTRIFE. A name applied to several different groups of plants. *See* LYSIMACHIA, LYTHRUM, STEIRONEMA, and DECODON.

LOOSESTRIFE FAMILY = Lythraceae.

LOPEZIA (low-peez'ia). A genus of American herbs or under-shrubs belonging to the family Onagraceae, used chiefly as green-house plants. Leaves small, alternate,* broadly lance-shaped, the margin saw-like. Flowers small, produced in clusters at the ends of the branches. Petals 5, the 2 upper bent upward a little way from their base. At the bend there seems to be a drop of honey, in reality a dry, glossy piece of hard tissue which deceives flies. The real nectaries,*

however, are at the base of the flower. Stamens* 2, one of which is fertile, the other petal-like. Fruit a small, round capsule* which splits into 4 cells containing the seeds. (Named for Thomas Lopez, a Spaniard who wrote on the natural history of the New World.)

Sow seeds in April, ¹⁄₁₆ in. deep, in the cool greenhouse, in fine potting soil.

albiflora. A soft-wooded perennial up to 2 ft. high. Leaves broadly lance-shaped, 1–1½ in. long. Flowers small, produced at the ends of the branches, the petals white, tinged pink near the center. Mexico. Sept.–Oct.

coronata. Crown-of-jewels. Annual and not over 1 ft. high. Flowers lilac, the 2 side petals red at the base. Mexico.

lineata. A shrubby perennial 1–3 ft. high. Stems and leaves slightly hairy, the leaves ovalish, short-stalked. Flowers small, in terminal clusters (racemes*), red. Mexico. Sept.–Nov.

lophantha, -us, -um (lo-fan'tha). Having crested flowers.

LOPHOPHORA (lo-fo-for'ra). A small genus of globe-shaped or top-shaped cacti of southwestern U.S. and adjacent Mex., one of them, *L. williamsi*, the peyote, yielding the famous narcotic known as "mescal buttons." It is a bluish-green cactus about 3 in. in diameter, with 5–13 low ribs, often white-hairy. Flowers pale pinkish-white, nearly 1 in. wide. For cult. *see* CACTI. (*Lophophora* is from the Greek for crest-bearing, in allusion to the white tufts of hair.)

LOPHOSPERMUM SCANDENS = *Maurandia Lophospermum*. The word *lophosperma, -us, -um* (lo-fo-sper'ma) means having tufted or crested seeds.

LOQUAT (*Eriobotrya japonica*). The Chinese loquat, also commonly termed Japan plum and Japanese medlar, is grown in Calif., the Gulf states, and Fla., but seldom fruits north of the citrus areas. The tree withstands temperatures of 10 to 15 degrees without material injury, but the fruit or blossoms, on the tree in midwinter, are damaged by a few degrees of frost. Commercial plantings are few, these mainly in Calif., although trees are frequently seen in yards and garden plantings since the attractive evergreen foliage and symmetrical growth habit make them desirable for ornamental planting even if fruiting is irregular. Fruit ripens from Feb. to May, the dates of maturity depending upon both variety and locality. Borne in large clusters, the fruit varies in shape from spherical to pyriform; in size, from 1 to 3 in. long; and in color, from pale yellow to deep orange. The flesh is firm and juicy with a pleasant, sprightly flavor, and while the fruit usually is eaten out of hand it is also cooked and makes a jelly of superior quality. The sugar content is from 10 to 13% and there is a difference in degrees of acidity among varieties.

A wide range of soils, including sands and clays with either an alkaline or acid reac-

---

* Special articles on the subjects indicated by an asterisk (*) will be found at the words so marked.

tion, are adapted to loquat culture. A regular moisture supply, together with adequate drainage, is desirable, although the tree is quite drought-resistant. Amounts and kinds of fertilizers required will depend on soil type, the more fertile requiring little other than nitrogen, while the more sandy will need a complete mixture to insure greatest thrift and large-sized fruit. Addition of organic materials by mulching, leguminous cover-cropping, or application of stable manures is of benefit. Planting distances are from 12 × 24 ft. to 20 × 20 ft. The closer spacing tends to crowd the trees and is believed by some to increase fruit size. Little pruning is required other than shaping the young tree and later removal of excess branches and dead wood. Thinning of fruit is practiced to some extent to increase size.

The many introduced or locally developed varieties have been divided into two groups — the Japanese and Chinese, the differentiation based on fruit shape, color, size, flavor, and season of maturity. Those of the Japanese grouping are the smaller, juicier, less acid varieties with light-colored flesh (Early Red excepted) and spherical shape. In addition to numerous seedlings, the following are among varieties grown: Advance, Champagne, Thales, Early Red, Tanaka, and Premier. Propagation is by seeds, grafting, shield budding, and occasionally by cuttings. Loquat seedlings are preferred for stocks but quince may be used. — G. D. R.

INSECT PESTS. Few pests have been recorded; they include codling moth, green apple aphid, some scale insects, and general feeders. *See* Insect Pests at APPLE.

LORATE. Tongue- or strap-shaped.

LORDS-AND-LADIES = *Arum maculatum.*

LORETTE PRUNING SYSTEM. *See* PRUNING.

lorifolia, -us, -um (lor-i-fō′li-a). With strap-shaped leaves.

LOROMA = *Archontophoenix cunninghamiana.*

LOROPETALUM (lor-o-pet′a-lum). A single Chinese evergreen shrub of the family Hamamelidaceae, closely related to the witch-hazel, but evergreen. Leaves alternate,* without marginal teeth. Flowers resembling the witch-hazel (*see* HAMAMELIS), but white and much more showy. The only species, **L. chinense,** is a shrub 6–12 ft. high, with ovalish leaves 1–2 in. long. Petals strap-shaped, about 1 in. long. Fruit a woody capsule. The shrub is not much known in cult. and probably not hardy north of zone* 5, although it will stand some frost, if the wood is mature (*see* HARDINESS). Propagated by seeds or it may be grafted upon stock of the witch-hazel. It blooms in April–May. (*Loropetalum* is from the Greek for strap and petal, in allusion to the shape of the petals.)

LOTE BUSH = *Zizyphus obtusifolia.*

lotifolia, -us, -um (lo-ti-fō′lĭ-a). With leaves like those of the genus *Lotus.*

LOTUS. The word *lotus* has many different meanings. The lotus of the lotus-eaters was probably derived from *Zizyphus Lotus,* one of the non-hort. jujubes (*see* ZIZYPHUS). But *lotus* has also been applied to several water lilies (*see* NYMPHAEA and NELUMBO). And Linnaeus applied *lotus* to a group of plants of the pea family. This genus *Lotus* comprises perhaps 140 species of Old World, but largely European, herbs or under-shrubs with compound* leaves, composed of 3–5 leaflets, or sometimes apparently with several simple* leaves. Flowers mostly pea-like, solitary, or in pairs, or in small clusters (umbels*), yellow, white, or purple. Fruit a cylindrical, several-seeded pod (legume*). (The name *Lotus,* as used by Linnaeus for these plants, has no connection with the classical lotus, nor has it any connection with the genus *Diospyros,* where it is a specific name.) For a related plant *see* HOSACKIA.

The only cult. species of the genus *Lotus* are of secondary garden importance, although the bird's-foot trefoil is a foliage plant of wide use. The ornamental species are *L. Jacobaeus* and *L. bertholeti,* neither of which is hardy in the East.

bertholeti. A prostrate shrub, 1–2 ft. high, its foliage silvery. Leaflets 3–7, narrow. Flowers showy, scarlet. Canary and Cape Verde Islands. Can be grown outdoors only in Calif. and similar climates, elsewhere in the cool greenhouse in potting mixture* 3. Often used as a ground cover.

corniculatus. Bird's-foot trefoil; also called ground honeysuckle, baby's-slippers, and bloomfell. A perennial, rather sprawling herb, 1–2 ft. high. Leaflets 3, ovalish, but broadest toward the tip. Flowers yellow or sometimes red-tinged. Eurasia, and occasionally a troublesome weed in the U.S. *See* the list at WEEDS.

Jacobaeus. St. James's-flower or St. James's-pea. A perennial herb, 2–3 ft. high. Leaflets 3–5, very narrow. Flowers black-purple, or yellow, or sometimes both colors on the same plant. Cape Verde Islands. Can be grown outdoors only in Calif. and similar climates.

Tetragonolobus. Winged pea. A prostrate, annual herb grown (but not much here) for its edible pods and seeds. Leaflets 3, oval. Flowers purplish-red. Pods 4-sided. Southern Eu. Considered by some as belonging to *Tetragonolobus,* a genus not here maintained.

LOUISIANA. The state, at the apex of the Mississippi delta, enjoying a mild and equable climate, and exceptionally well watered, lies wholly in zones* 6 and 7. Its state flower is the magnolia.

SOILS. Louisiana belongs to the coastal plain province, rich alluvial plains extending its entire length and constituting the full area of many parishes (counties). Bluff lands, pine flats, pine hills, upland, prairie, wooded lowlands, marsh and coast marsh form the other agricultural soil divisions. The state is traversed by the valleys of the Mississippi, Red, Ouachita, and Sabine rivers, and covered with an intricate network of

---

* Special articles on the subjects indicated by an asterisk (*) will be found at the words so marked.

ARK.

MONROE
Mar. 11 - Nov. 13
247 days
SHREVEPORT
Mar. 6 - Nov. 12
251 days Rainfall 49 in.

ZONE 6

MISS.

ALEXANDRIA
Mar. 11 - Nov. 13
247 days

ZONE 7 HAMMOND
Rainfall 58 in. *Mar. 8 - Nov. 13*
250 days

LAKE CHARLES
Mar. 2 - Nov. 19
262 days NEW ORLEANS
Feb. 18 - Dec. 5
290 days

Gulf of Mexico

PORT EADS
Feb. 8 - Dec. 13
308 days

LOUISIANA

The zones of hardiness crossing Louisiana are those shown on the map located at Zone, which should be consulted for details. The dates are the average latest killing frost in spring and the first one in the fall. The figures below the dates show the average length of the growing season. The rainfall figures (in inches) are for total annual rainfall in the regions so indicated.

large water-basins and bayous. The sandy loam sloping back from the streams is easily cultivated. Much of this recent alluvial soil is of alkaline reaction, whereas the other areas tend to the acid side of the pH* scale. Black, heavier soil is found back from the streams, and the bluff lands of certain northern parishes are yellowish-gray, but very fertile. Swamp reclamation has brought much new fertile soil into use.

FRUITS. As northern Louisiana partakes largely of the continental climate, such fruits as peaches and other stone fruits thrive well there, and at the present time there is a young and progressive peach industry started in the Ruston area. Other fruit crops such as pears and some apples are also grown in northern Louisiana. The fig is the most universally grown fruit and can be found in every parish and practically every home orchard. The proximity of the Gulf of Mexico to the southern part of the state results in a milder temperature, and the satsuma orange can be grown from Baton Rouge on south. Plaquemines Parish is noted for its high-quality oranges, particularly the Washington Navel, satsumas, and sweet oranges. The strawberry is the leading fruit crop in Louisiana and is grown largely in the Hammond area. The pecan is the leading nut fruit. As a commercial nut, tung-oil has developed into a new agricultural enterprise with the center of activity located in Washington Parish. Some interest is shown in blackberries and dew-

berries, primarily in the fresh state and for making preserves. Both of these berries can be grown in almost any parish of the state.

VEGETABLES. Practically all vegetables may be and are grown in the state. Truck farming for winter and early spring markets of the North is a major industry in the southerly regions. Some vegetables in great local favor have not penetrated other markets, such as the mirliton, or vegetable pear. The sweet potato is the leading vegetable crop of the state, located primarily in St. Landry and Lafayette parishes and the surrounding area. This area produces more sweet potatoes than any other section of the United States. Following sweet potatoes such crops as okra, Irish potatoes, snap beans (bush and pole), and winter vegetables, such as shallots, mustard, turnips, and beets, are produced. Tomatoes, eggplant, and bell peppers are grown largely in southern Louisiana, particularly in Plaquemines, St. Bernard, Tangipahoa, and St. James parishes. Watermelon and peas are the best vegetables grown in the northern parishes of the state along with the sweet potato area in Webster and West Carroll. Certain vegetables are produced throughout the year, and fresh vegetables can be found on the market from truck areas and home gardens every day in the year. Sweet potatoes, okra, and snap beans make up the largest canning crops, and there are over 30 plants processing these products, both canned and frozen. Aromatics and condiments are raised for the local cuisine, and some for shipment, notably the peppers. Tabasco is grown largely for condiments, while the cayenne is grown for seasoning and medicinal uses. Tabasco is produced for the world markets in Iberia, St. Martin, and Lafayette parishes. Cotton, corn and oats are found in the northern and central parishes. Perique tobacco is produced in St. James Parish, which is the only place in the world where this variety of tobacco is grown commercially.

FLOWERS. Native flora embrace almost all genera of trees, shrubs, vines, and herbs common to the continent, except alpine and desert species and some of the tropical kinds found on the Florida peninsula. Over twenty species of violet — blue, white, purple, rose-purple — have been reported, and many species of verbena. Many wild iris (over 100 varieties among these), not all of them recognized by the experts, have been described. See Louisiana hybrids under Beardless Group at IRIS. Also there are many species of hibiscus, of the sarracenias, the droseras, and the terrestrial orchids (and some epiphytes*). *Stewartia* and dogwood, swamp lilies and water hyacinth make brilliant display in their places.

The long growing season, however, and brief rest period handicap many plants which are favorites in higher latitudes, such

---

* Special articles on the subjects indicated by an asterisk (*) will be found at the words so marked.

as lilacs and peonies, which, as perennials, can be grown only in the northern part of the state where some severe cold is assured each winter. Many perennial bulbs must be treated as biennials, and the habits of others undergo a change.

Beds of tropical croton, caladium, acalypha, and other foliage plants, however, gain a brilliance and variety of color that is impossible except under this long sunshine. In the southern parishes poinsettias, six to fifteen feet high, usually wave their great scarlet bracts through Christmas, and are never removed from the open. Roses can be brought into bloom for most months of the year; so can dahlias, except for January, and even then perhaps on the Lower Coast, and their roots need be disturbed only for dividing. Many typical tropicals may be left outdoors permanently in parts of the state, with proper covering on approach of frost (carelessness in this is responsible for frequent disappointments). Most bulbs can be, or should be, left in the ground. The creole Easter lily, a form of *Lilium longiflorum*, greatly improved in size and number of blossoms, has been cultivated for generations.

Azaleas, camellias, gardenias, pomegranates, redbuds, crape myrtles, hydrangeas, altheas, night jasmine, are favored shrubs. Most evergreens do well in all sections, and many flowering vines add beauty, most conspicuously the perennial coral vine which is always in blossom from early summer until frost. Chrysanthemums are raised in abundance, and the quantities of this flower used on All-Saints' Day almost surpass belief. A great many varieties of palms add to the tropical aspect of southern parishes (and suffer depredations on Palm Sunday), and a few hardier varieties can be grown throughout the state under selected conditions.

GARDENS. Almost every city or rural household has its flower garden, but gardening in Louisiana has been too easy a task to arouse the combative genius of the average householder. There is at present a strong tendency to landscaping, to specializing, and to scientific methods and study of effects. Gardening possibilities are almost unlimited, and the spread of the garden club movement has aroused new interest in horticultural work. Magnificent gardens always have existed in every part of the state. The most famous one at present is perhaps the Jungle Gardens of Iberia Parish, an old estate renowned for its flowers and birds, and chiefly for its unexcelled collections of camellias and iris. Active garden clubs exist in practically every city and community in the state. This includes clubs for both men and women. Due to interest in this field there is an extensive research program on ornamentals at Louisiana State University, on camellias, native iris, gladioli, daylilies, hibiscus, and chrysanthemums; and in co-operation with the American Rose Society there is a large rose garden on the L.S.U. campus which attracts thousands of visitors each year.

CLIMATE. The climate is greatly modified by the 1500-mile, deeply indented coastline on the Gulf of Mexico, and by the 3097 square miles of water surface included in the 48,506 square miles of inland area. Annual average temperature for northern Louisiana is 65.2°, for southern Louisiana 68.2°. Mean temperature for January ranges from 34.6° at Grand Cane to 49.8° at Burrwood; mean temperature for July, from 95.1° at Antioch to 88.8° at Burrwood. Growing season averages from 209 days at Liberty Hill to 330 at Burrwood. Killing frost is frequently escaped in fall or spring, sometimes both, in southern Louisiana, and is exceedingly rare on the Lower Coast and coastal belt, as also are the extreme high temperatures of summer. Growing season on the Lower Coast is practically 365 days, frost being reported at Burrwood in 12 out of 22 years.

FROST DATA

Town	Average date of last killing frost in spring
Shreveport	Mar. 21
Monroe	Mar. 16
Alexandria	Mar. 16
Hammond	Mar. 11
Lake Charles	Feb. 14
New Orleans	Feb. 4
Port Eads	Jan. 10

Town	Average date of earliest killing frost in fall
Shreveport	Nov. 6
Monroe	Nov. 11
Alexandria	Nov. 6
Hammond	Nov. 16
Lake Charles	Dec. 6
New Orleans	Dec. 11
Port Eads	Dec. 26

Average annual rainfall is 49.63 inches for northern Louisiana, 57.95 for southern Louisiana; ranging from 43.99 inches at Shreveport to 64.75 at Amite. For northern Louisiana greatest precipitation is in December and March, for southern Louisiana in June, July, and August.

The address of the Agricultural Experiment Station which has kindly supplied this information is Baton Rouge 3, La. Garden club activities include many chapters of the Louisiana Garden Club Federation, Box 1106, Baton Rouge 1, La.

LOUSEWORT. *See* PEDICULARIS.

LOVAGE. *See* LEVISTICUM.

LOVE-APPLE. The tomato and *Solanum aculeatissimum.*

LOVE-ENTANGLE = *Sedum acre.*

* Special articles on the subjects indicated by an asterisk (*) will be found at the words so marked.

LOVE-IN-A-MIST = *Nigella damascena.*

LOVE-LIES-BLEEDING = *Amaranthus caudatus.*

LOVE-VINE = *Clematis virginiana.*

LUCERNE = *Medicago sativa.*

lucida, -us, -um (lew'si-da). Bright or shining.

LUCULIA (loo-kew'li-a). Himalayan shrubs of the family Rubiaceae, all the known species occasionally grown for ornament, generally in the cool greenhouse. They deserve to be much better known, for they are very handsome in bloom. They have opposite,* leathery leaves, and large, showy, terminal flower clusters (corymbs*) often nearly 12 in. wide. Corolla salver-shaped, its lobes rounded. Fruit a nearly woody capsule,* the seeds winged. (*Luculia* is probably a Latin version of a native name for them.)

These plants need a cool greenhouse and potting mixture* 3. They are winter-blooming and just before the buds begin to swell they will respond to liberal supplies of liquid manure. Plunge* outdoors in the summer, in partial shade, but bring them back to the cool greenhouse at the end of Aug. Keep the temperature around 50° at night, until they get ready to bloom, when a night temperature of 55° should be provided.

gratissima. A shrub 10–15 ft. high (less as cult.), the leaves oval-oblong, 4–6 in. long. Flowers about 1½ in. wide, pink or rose-pink, the cluster about 6 in. wide. Himalavas.

intermedia. From 8–12 ft. high (less as cult.), the leaves oblongish, 4–6 in. long. Flowers nearly 2 in. wide, reddish, the cluster 6–8 in. wide. Himalayas.

speciosa. Probably not distinct from *L. gratissima* and considered a larger-flowered form of it.

LUCUMA (loo-kew'ma). Tropical American shrubs and trees of the family Sapotaceae, comprising over 60 species, but only *L. nervosa*, the canistel, ti-es, or eggfruit of any hort. interest. It is a tree up to 25 ft. high, grown for its edible fruit in the tropics and only in the warmest parts of zone* 9 in Fla. Leaves alternate,* leathery, without marginal teeth, oblongish, 5–8 in. long. Flowers small, white (for details *see* SAPOTACEAE). Fruit fleshy (a berry), maturing in late summer, roundish, or egg-shaped, 2–4 in. long, orange-yellow, the pasty flesh orange-colored and sweetish. The tree is propagated by seeds and is indifferent as to soil. For a plant sometimes offered as *Lucuma mammosa see* ACHRAS ZAPOTA. (*Lucuma* is the Peruvian name for one of the species.)

LUDWIGIA (lud-wig'i-a). False loosestrife. Swamp or aquatic, often rather weedy, herbs of the family Onagraceae, comprising about 30 species, of which only **L. mulertti** is of hort. interest, although several native species may be dug from the wild. This cult. species is a weak-stemmed

aquatic herb, its stems rooting at the joints. Leaves opposite,* evergreen, without marginal teeth, oblongish or narrowed at the base to a stalk as long as the blade, green above, purple beneath. Flowers yellow (for details *see* ONAGRACEAE). Fruit a capsule, the top of which is crowned with the persistent calyx* lobes. The plant will not survive northern winters, but it is useful in greenhouse pools or in aquaria. (Named for C. G. Ludwig, German botanist.)

LUFFA (luf'fa). A small genus of tropical Old World gourds of the cucumber family grown chiefly for ornament or for their interesting fruits. They are tendril*-bearing, quick-growing, herbaceous, annual vines, with alternate,* 5–7-lobed leaves. Flowers yellowish or whitish, the male and female separate on the same plant. Male flowers in racemes,* the female solitary. Petals 5. Fruit with a dry or papery rind, the interior fibrous. The dried fibrous skeletons of the fruit, which are cucumber-shaped or club-shaped, are common in tropical markets where they are sold as though sponges, usually under the names of dishcloth gourd, vegetable sponge, rag gourd, or loofa. (*Luffa* is a Latinized version of the Arabic name for these gourds.)

The dishcloth gourds need the same culture as cucumbers, but they are even more sensitive to cold. As the vines, with plenty of heat and a rich soil, will grow 10–15 ft. high, they need the support of a trellis or post.

acutangula. Leaves very rough, not as large as in the next, and more angled than lobed. Fruit club-shaped, 9–12 in. long, ridged, the black seeds not margined.

cylindrica. The usual species in cult. and a strong-growing vine. Leaves 5–12 in. long, or nearly as wide and circular, with 3–7 lobes, the margins toothed. Fruit cucumber-shaped, 12–20 in. long, the black seeds margined.

LUNARIA. *See* HONESTY.

LUNGAN = *Euphoria Longana.*

LUNGWORT. *See* PULMONARIA and MERTENSIA.

LUPINE. *See* LUPINUS.

LUPINUS (loo-pine'us). A genus of many species belonging to the pea family. It is found in N.A., S.A., and on the shores of the Mediterranean Sea. All are hardy, and can be divided into three groups: the tree, herbaceous perennial, and annual lupines. The tree lupine is shrubby, growing 4–8 ft. Leaves compound,* finger-shaped, and covered with short, grayish hairs on upper and lower sides. Flowers showy, pea-like, in loose racemes* at the ends of the branches. Fruits, when ripe, are blackish, flattened pods about 3 in. long, containing 5 or 6 kidney-shaped, brown seeds. The perennials and annuals have herbaceous stems varying in height from 1–4 ft. Leaves like the tree group in shape, but sometimes bright green, especially on the upper side. Flowers pea-like, produced

---

* Special articles on the subjects indicated by an asterisk (*) will be found at the words so marked.

A garden lupine

in dense terminal racemes.* Fruits similar to the tree group. (*Lupinus* is from Latin for a wolf, from an ancient superstition that the plants tend to impoverish the soil.)

Propagated from seeds, but the perennials may be divided in early spring. Sow in deeply dug, good garden soil in April–June, ½ in. deep, in permanent position, allowing plenty of space as roots are large. Good drainage is essential to carry plants through the winter. They will transplant, but do much better if let alone. However, as the perennials are sometimes long in germinating, it is advisable to sow them in a seed bed that can be left undisturbed until the following spring. There are many good hybrids of varying hues of blue, pink, yellow, and white. They make good showy border plants. A few species are used for fodder. The tree lupine is adaptable for training on sunny walls or a trellis. Annual varieties are much grown in greenhouses for early spring flowering. For greenhouse cult. sow seed in Aug.–Nov.

Perhaps finer than any of the species listed below are the plants imported from England known as Russell lupines. Developed by George Russell of Yorkshire, after many years of selection and hybridizing, their flowering spikes are from 2½–3½ ft. high, the upper two-thirds of the spike a closely packed cluster of gorgeous bloom. Seeds are difficult to germinate unless nicked with a file, and if left too long in the soil without germination are apt to rot. For this reason it is better to sprout them in pure sand or in potting-mixture* 1.

arboreus. Tree lupine. Stems shrubby, 4–8 ft. high and slightly hairy. Leaves compound,* the leaflets finger-shaped, growing in a circle at the tip of a common stalk, hairy on both upper and lower sides. Flowers sulphur-yellow, fragrant, in loose racemes* at the ends of the branches. Calif. The var. **albus** has white flowers. There is also a purple-flowered form.

cruckshanki = *Lupinus mutabilis cruckshanki*.

densiflorus. Annual, handsome, shrub-like plant, up to 18 in. high. Leaves with both stalk and leaflets hairy. Flowers in closely packed, terminal racemes,* white, yellow, or rose. Calif.

hartwegi. Annual to 3 ft., really a perennial, but grown as an annual, very hairy and somewhat branching. Leaflets 7–9. Flowers blue, partially rose-colored. July–Sept. The *vars.* **albus, coelestinus, roseus,** and **ruber** are color forms. Mex.

mutabilis. Annual to 4 ft. Leaves bright green. Flowers attractive. White with yellow or violet markings on upper petal, fragrant. The *var.* **cruckshanki** has bluish flowers, shaded violet; the *vars.* **roseus** and **versicolor** are color forms. S.A.

nanus. Annual, and not over 15 in. high, often branching from the base. Leaflets 5–7, hairy on both sides. Flowers in loose racemes,* on slender stalks, blue, with purple spots on the upper petal. Pods and seeds small. Particularly good grown in masses. Calif.

perennis. Quaker bonnets; the common wild lupine of eastern N.A., and 1–2 ft. high. Leaves and stem hairy. Flowers blue, varying to white. Prefers a sandy soil and it is difficult to dig from the wild.

polyphyllus. A hardy perennial and a good garden species to 5 ft. high, with stout, herbaceous stems. Leaves large and dark green. Flowers in long racemes.* Pods very woolly. Colors in shades of yellow, white, and blue. The *var.* **moerheimi** is more compact and considered the finest. The *vars.* **albus** and **roseus** are color forms. Western N.A.

subcarnosus. Bluebonnet, and the state flower of Texas. A showy, silky-hairy annual 8–12 in. high. Flowers blue, with a white or yellow spot. Pods about 1½ in. long and silky. Tex., and blooming there early in spring. May.

texensis = *L. subcarnosus*.

lupulina, -us, -um (lup-you-ly′na). Like a hop (*Lupulus*).

Lupulus (lup′you-lus). Literally, a little wolf. As a specific name *Lupulus* was applied to the hop, because it was once called the willow wolf from its climbing so persistently over willow trees.

lurida, -us, -um (lure′ri-da). Pale yellow; also fire-like.

lusitanica, -us, -um (loo-si-tan′i-ka). From Lusitania, an old name for Portugal.

lutea, -us, -um (loo′tee-a). Yellow.

lutescens (loo-tess′senz). Golden or yellowish.

LYCASTE (ly-kas′tee). Tropical American, chiefly tree-perching, very showy orchids, of which over 30 species are known, but only **L. skinneri** much cult. It is a popular greenhouse orchid with oblongish pseudobulbs* 3–5 in. long, bearing 1–3 long leaves which are oblongish, 9–15 in. long, folded like a fan in the bud, sheathing at the base, and much longer than the short stalk of the solitary flower. Flowers pink and white, 5–6 in. wide, waxy, the sepals and petals similar in shape but the petals shorter. Lip* oval, 3-lobed, spotted, but generally red-purple, the middle lobe bent backward. Guatemala. See Tropical Orchid Cultivation at ORCHID for culture. (Named for the daughter of Priam.)

LYCHEE = *Litchi chinensis*.

---

* Special articles on the subjects indicated by an asterisk (*) will be found at the words so marked.

LYCH GATE. For twelve centuries many English country churchyards have been entered through a lych gate. Originally of somber significance, they may be, as the illustration shows, a delightful feature of any garden. They are simply covered gateways to a garden or section of one, serving not only as an architectural feature, but a temporary shelter

LYCH GATE

An attractive and sometimes quite simple entrance to a garden, adapted from English churchyards.

from sun or rain. The simplest lych gates were nothing more than two uprights with a small, often thatched roof over the gateway. But more elaborate ones, like the illustration, are needed if the approach is to a somewhat more elaborate garden. Sometimes there are seats along the inner edges of the paved walkway, and vines clamber over the gate.

LYCHNIS (lick'nis). Catchfly. Campion. A genus of about 40 herbs of the pink family, mostly from the north temperate zone and northward, some old garden favorites cult. for centuries. They are erect plants, annuals or biennials, but mostly perennial and often with sticky hairs. Calyx with 5 teeth. Petals 5, with a claw* at the base, the limb* rounded or sometimes 2-cleft or fringed. Stamens* 10. Fruit a capsule.* For closely related plants, also called catchfly or campion, *see* SILENE. (*Lychnis* is from the Greek for lamp, in allusion to the flame-colored flowers of certain species.)

The campions are of very simple culture in any ordinary garden soil. The perennials may be increased by division, and seed of the annuals sown where wanted. A few are biennials and should be grown as such. *See* BIENNIALS. Mostly summer-blooming, unless otherwise noted. The plants are sometimes offered as *Agrostemma*, and some

of them are also called *Melandrium* and *Viscaria*.

alba. Evening or white campion. A sticky-hairy biennial, or perhaps perennial, 1–2 ft. high. Leaves ovalish or oblong. Flowers about 1 in. wide, night-blooming, fragrant, in a few-flowered cluster (panicle*). Eu., often weedy, and naturalized along the Atlantic seaboard.

alpina. A smooth, tufted perennial 6–9 in. high, the leaves lance-shaped or narrower. Flowers about ⅓ in. wide, in a dense, terminal cluster (head). Arctic and alpine regions of the northern hemisphere, and best suited to the rock garden (which see).

arkwrighti. A hybrid species of garden origin, a perennial resembling *L. haageana*, but with scarlet flowers.

chalcedonica. Scarlet lychnis; also called Maltese or Jerusalem cross and scarlet lightning. A hairy, perennial herb 18–30 in. high, the leaves ovalish or lance-shaped, and usually clasping. Flowers about 1 in. wide, scarlet, in dense, terminal clusters (heads*). Siberia; often an escape* here. The *var.* alba has white flowers; and other color forms and a double-flowered sort are offered.

Coeli-rosa. Rose-of-Heaven. A widely planted garden annual 12–15 in. high, the leaves very narrow. Flowers solitary, terminal, about 1 in. wide, rose-pink. Mediterranean region. It is sometimes sold as *Agrostemma* or as *Silene*. There are forms with red or purple-eyed flowers and one with toothed petals.

coronaria. Mullein pink; also called dusty miller and rose campion. A white-woolly, biennial or perennial herb 18–30 in. high. Leaves ovalish or oblong. Flowers solitary, terminal, about 1 in. wide, crimson. Southern Eu. and often an escape* in the U.S. White and double-flowered forms are offered.

Flos-cuculi. Cuckoo-flower; also called ragged robin. A hairy, perennial herb 12–20 in. high, sticky toward the top. Leaves narrowly lance-shaped, the upper ones smaller and stalkless. Flowers red or pink, in loose clusters (panicles*), the petals with 4 narrow segments. Eurasia; naturalized in the eastern U.S. White and double-flowered forms are offered.

Flos-Jovis. Flower-of-Jove. A white-woolly, perennial herb 12–20 in. high. Leaves ovalish or oblong, more or less clasping. Flowers red or purple, about ½ in. wide, in dense clusters (umbel*-like). Southern Eu., in the mountains.

haageana. A hybrid campion of garden origin, more or less hairy, usually not over 12 in. high. Flowers nearly 2 in. wide, usually in clusters of 2's or 3's, the petals 2-lobed and also with 2 teeth, usually orange-red or crimson.

lagascae = Petrocoptis lagascae.

pyrenaica. A rock garden, perennial species not over 4 in. high, the basal leaves spatula-shaped and about 1½ in. long, the stem leaves heart-shaped. Flowers about ¼ in. wide, solitary and long-stalked, blush-pink. Pyrenees. Also offered as *Petrocoptis pyrenaica*.

Vaccaria = Saponaria Vaccaria.

Viscaria. German catchfly. A perennial herb 5–18 in. high, the stem smooth except beneath the flowers where it is sticky-hairy. Leaves long, narrow, tapering. Flowers red or purple, in interrupted* clusters, the petals somewhat notched. Eurasia. White and also double-flowered varieties are offered.

LYCIUM (liss'i-um). Matrimony-vine. A group of ornamental shrubs of the potato family. Though there are about 100 species in the temperate and sub-tropical re-

---

* Special articles on the subjects indicated by an asterisk (*) will be found at the words so marked.

gions of the world only a few are hardy. Their habit is often loose and the branches are frequently reflexed or arching and spiny. The flowers are small and borne singly or clustered in the leaf axils.* Leaves alternate,* deciduous, small, not toothed. Fruit a berry, usually red. (Greek name for a spiny shrub from Lycias.) Sometimes called box-thorn.

The matrimony-vine, though ornamental, is often rank and coarse in growth and should be used only where it will have plenty of room in which to spread. It is adapted to arbors and fences and is excellent for covering piles of rocks and unsightly objects; planted closely it makes an impenetrable barrier.

Cultivation is simple; they seem to thrive in ordinary soil and prefer good drainage. Propagated by seeds, cuttings, layers, or suckers.

chinense. A vigorous, strong-growing shrub with spreading or arching branches to 12 ft. long. Leaves quite variable in size and shape, usually ovate or lanceolate and about 1 in. long though sometimes to 3 or 4 in. Flowers purple. Fruit orange to scarlet. June–Sept.; fruit Aug.–Sept. Eastern Asia. Hardy from zone* 3 southward. *Var.* **ovatum.** Leaves broader and rhombic in shape, to 4 in. long; fruit larger, blunt at tip.

europaeum. An upright, bushy shrub growing about 6 ft. high, thorny. Leaves gray-green, lanceolate, rounded or pointed at tip. Flowers violet. Fruit red, oval. May; fruit Aug. Southern Eu. Hardy only in mild regions. Usually confused with *L. halimifolium* from which it differs in having a longer, more slender corolla, smaller leaves and in being less hardy.

halimifolium. Washington's bower. Shrub of 8 or 9 ft. with slender, spreading, sometimes spiny branches. Leaves variable, usually oval or narrow, 1½–2 in. long. Flowers dull purple, soon fading, on slender stalks. Fruit oval, red, ⅔ in. long. June–July, and often again in Oct. Southeastern Eu. to western Asia. Hardy from zone* 3 southward.

vulgare = *Lycium halimifolium.*

lycoctonum (ly-cock'to-num). Greek name for the wolfsbane, which was thought to poison wolves. *See Aconitum lycoctonum* at MONKSHOOD.

LYCOPERSICUM. *See* TOMATO.

LYCOPODIACEAE. *See* LYCOPODIUM.

lycopodioides (ly-ko-po-dĭ-oy'deez). Like a club moss.

LYCOPODIUM (ly-ko-pō'di-um). Club moss. Evergreen, moss-like herbs, the only cult. genus of the family **Lycopodiaceae** (ly-ko-po-di-ā'see-ee) or club moss family, a few sometimes cult. in the wild garden, but best known for their much-to-be-deplored use in the making of Christmas wreaths. For the latter purpose there is a wide destruction of the wild plants annually. They have erect or creeping stems and tiny, scale-like, often overlapping leaves which are so numerous as to completely hide the stem. The club mosses are fern allies (which see) and thus produce no flowers. Instead they produce minute spores, often in special,

club-shaped, stalked spikes, or occasionally in the axils* of the upper leaves. (*Lycopodium* is from the Greek for wolf and foot, assumed to be in reference to a fancied resemblance.)

The club mosses, some of which are called ground pine, are of far more historical than hort. interest. The ancestors of some of them were huge trees in the Carboniferous and helped to form the coal measures. Today they have dwindled to a few low herbs suited only to shady places in the wild garden, where they need rich woods soil (not especially acid) and plenty of moisture. Those below can easily be divided, and some of them root at the joints.

clavatum. Running pine; also called ground pine (not related to the true pines). A creeping herb, the stems often 8–9 ft. long, the very leafy branches ascending, but scarcely 3 in. high. Spore*-bearing spikes usually 1–4 in each stalk, each spike pencil-thick and 2–4 in. long. North temperate zone; common in woods in northern N.A.

complanatum. Ground cedar (not a true cedar). Not so long-trailing, the erect branches often divided fan-like. Spore*-bearing spikes 1–4 on each stalk, the spikes 2–5 in. long. North temperate zone and common in woods in northern N.A.

dendroideum = *Lycopodium obscurum.*

obscurum. Stems creeping underground, the ascending branches erect, bushy, almost tree-like, but not over 10 in. high, the scale-like leaves longer than in the other species and not hugging the stem. Spore-bearing spike nearly stalkless. Woods in northern N.A. and As.

LYCORIS (ly-kō'ris). Asiatic, bulbous, amaryllis-like herbs of the family Amaryllidaceae, including perhaps 6 species. They have strap-shaped leaves which develop before the flowers appear. Flowers fragrant, the petals united below into a short tube, the segments crisped, lilac-pink or pink. Style* protruding but the stamens about the length of the petals. The flower cluster is a loose umbel* at the end of a solid stalk (scape*). For culture of the first two species in the greenhouse follow the directions for the plants mentioned at amaryllis. The third species is much more hardy. (Named for the mistress of Mark Antony.)

aurea. Golden spider-lily. Foliage bluish-green, the leaves strap-shaped, about ¾ in. wide, and 12 in. long. Flowers funnel-shaped, erect, golden yellow, nearly 3 in. long. China. Summer. Not hardy north of zone* 7. Some of the plants grown as this may be *L. traubi*, a species not well understood.

radiata. Foliage green, the leaves strap-shaped, about ½ in. wide, and 12–14 in. long. Flowers pink to deep red (white in *var.* **alba**). China. Summer. Not reliably hardy north of zone* 6.

squamigera. Hardy amaryllis. A very showy amaryllis-like bulbous plant, more hardy than the other two, and perfectly safe for outdoor culture from zone* 5 southward, and often above this in sheltered sites and with a winter mulch. Leaves about 1 in. wide and 12 in. long. Flowers fragrant, nearly 3 in. wide, rose-lilac (purple in a hort. var.). Jap. Summer. Sometimes offered as *Amaryllis halli.*

---

* Special articles on the subjects indicated by an asterisk (*) will be found at the words so marked.

lydia, -us, -um (lid′i-a). From Lydia, an ancient country in Asia Minor.

LYGODIUM (ly-gō′di-um). Climbing fern. Vine-like ferns of the family Schizaeaceae, chiefly tropical but one native in the eastern U.S. Of the 40 known species the three below, and perhaps others, are cult. in greenhouses (or outdoors for *L. palmatum* and *L. japonicum*) for their graceful habit and feathery foliage. They have long, climbing or trailing stems, or the stalk of the much-divided frond assuming the aspect and functions of a stem. In the latter case, what look like leaves are actually segments of a many-times compound frond, which may have the ultimate segments arranged finger-fashion or feather-fashion. (*Lygodium* is from the Greek for flexible, in allusion to the slender, pliant stems.)

For the culture of the greenhouse sorts *see* FERNS AND FERN GARDENING.

japonicum. The leading greenhouse lygodium, and a slender plant with much-divided, pale green and soft-textured fronds. Ultimate segments arranged feather-fashion, about 1 in. long, variously toothed. Eastern Asia to Aust. Grown outdoors along the Gulf Coast and often a rampant pest there.

palmatum. Hartford fern, Alice's fern. A hardy, native, climbing or sprawling fern. Fronds nearly round, 4–7-lobed, finger-fashion, the lobes not toothed. Eastern U.S. It should be grown in partly shady places in the fern garden or wild garden, and it needs an acid soil with a pH 4.0–5.0 (*see* ACID AND ALKALI SOILS).

scandens. A greenhouse lygodium, slender but more bushy and not so high-climbing as *L. japonicum*, and the foliage bluish-green. Ultimate segments 1–2 in. long, arranged finger-fashion, sometimes faintly lobed. Eastern As.

LYME GRASS. *See* ELYMUS.

LYON BEAN = *Stizolobium niveum.*

LYONIA (ly-o′nĭ-a). A genus of handsome shrubs of the heath family, comprising about 30 species found in N.A. and eastern As., 3 of them cult. for ornament. They are closely related to *Pieris*, but the latter are evergreens, while only the fetter-bush is evergreen among the lyonias. They have alternate,* short-stalked leaves and small flowers in dense clusters (racemes*) which may be in the leaf axils* or terminal. Corolla white or pinkish, mostly urn-shaped or bell-shaped. Stamens* 10. Fruit a small capsule* opening by terminal pores. (Named for John Lyon, an American botanist.) Sometimes known as *Xolisma.*

The lyonias need a distinctly acid soil, preferably sandy and with a pH of about 5.0 (*see* ACID AND ALKALI SOILS). They should have a permanent mulch of dried leaves and do not like disturbance of their roots. They are chiefly shrubs for the more informal border, the closely related genera *Pieris* and *Leucothoë* furnishing horticulturally more desirable shrubs. Propagated by cuttings.

ligustrina. Swamp andromeda; also called maleberry, he-huckleberry, and privet andro-meda. A spreading shrub 7–10 ft. high. Leaves elliptic or oblongish, 2–3 in. long, nearly without marginal teeth. Flower cluster terminal, leafless, composed of racemes* grouped in a panicle, white. New England to Fla. and westward. May–June. Hardy from zone* 2 southward. Prefers moist sand. Sometimes offered as *Andromeda ligustrina.*

lucida. Fetter-bush. An evergreen shrub 4–6 ft. high. Leaves broadly elliptic, 2–3 in. long, shining. Flowers in a terminal, leafy cluster (raceme*), white or pinkish. Va. to Fla. and La. April–May. Hardy from zone* 6 southward. Sometimes sold as *Pieris lucida* and *Xolisma nitida.*

mariana. Stagger-bush. Wicopy. A shrub 4–6 ft. high. Leaves ovalish or elliptic, 1–2½ in. long, without teeth. Flowers white, nodding, in clusters (racemes*) from the leaf axils,* the clusters a little leafy. R.I. to Fla. and Tex. May–June. Hardy from zone* 3 southward. Sometimes sold as *Pieris mariana.*

LYONOTHAMNUS (ly-o-no-tham′nus). A single evergreen shrub or small tree of the rose family, ornamental but tender. The one species, *L. floribundus*, the Santa Cruz ironwood or Catalina ironwood, is found only on Santa Catalina Island, and is suited only to similar climates. It has opposite,* lanceolate* leaves, 4–8 in. long, and small white flowers in flat, terminal clusters 4–8 in. across. Fruit a woody capsule. Considered difficult to propagate; cuttings of basal sprouts perhaps the best method. The *var.* asplenifolius is a form with deeply lobed leaves, and sometimes develops into a tree of 75 ft. (Named for W. S. Lyon, who sent specimens of this shrub to Asa Gray.)

lyrata, -us, -um (ly-ray′ta). Lyrate.

LYRATE. Lyre-shaped, *i.e.*, having a larger terminal and smaller lateral lobes, some of which are irregularly cut or divided.

LYSICHITUM (ly-sik′i-tum). An evil-smelling, perennial herb of the arum family, *L. americanum*, the yellow skunk-cabbage, found in western N.A. It differs only in technical characters from the common skunk-cabbage (which see) and needs similar conditions. Very early in the season the sheathing spathe* encloses the spadix* but the latter elongates and ultimately protrudes beyond the withered spathe.* (*Lysichitum* is from the Greek for free and cloak, in allusion to the spathe.*) The only other species is Asiatic.

LYSIMACHIA (ly-si-mack′ĭ-a). Loosestrife (for other loosestrifes *see* LYTHRUM, DECODON, and STEIRONEMA). A genus of about 140 species of widely distributed perennial herbs of the family Primulaceae, a few of them grown for ornament, although some are inclined to be weedy. Leaves without marginal teeth, variously arranged. Flowers solitary or in clusters, sometimes in the leaf axils* or often terminal. Corolla more or less bell-shaped or wheel-shaped. Stamens* 5–6. Fruit a 5-valved capsule.* (Named for King Lysimachus.)

The loosestrifes are of secondary gar-

---

* Special articles on the subjects indicated by an asterisk (*) will be found at the words so marked.

den importance and should be grown in reasonably moist sites in the open border. All are erect herbs except *L. Nummularia,* the moneywort, which is a good, creeping ground cover. Most of them bloom in the summer and all of them are easily increased by division in spring or fall.

ciliata = *Steironema ciliatum.*

clethroides. A somewhat hairy herb, 2–3 ft. high. Leaves alternate,* more or less oblong or oval-lance-shaped, tapering at both ends, 3–6 in. long. Flowers about ½ in. wide, white, in narrow, terminal spikes. Eastern As.

Nummularia. Moneywort; also called creeping Charlie and creeping Jennie. A prostrate perennial with trailing stems that root easily at the joints. Leaves opposite,* nearly round, about ¾ in. in diameter. Flowers solitary in the leaf axils, stalked, yellow. Eu., but commonly naturalized in eastern N.A. A good ground cover for moist, partly shady places, but it will also grow in full sunshine. *See* Creepers and Trailers at VINES.

punctata. An erect herb 2–3 ft. high. Leaves 3 or 4 at each whorl,* oval-lance-shaped. Flowers in whorls* in the leaf axils,* the corolla yellow. Eu., but naturalized in the eastern U.S.

vulgaris. Golden loosestrife; also called willow-wort. A thick-set, bushy, erect perennial 3–5 ft. high. Leaves oval or lance-shaped, opposite* or in whorls.* Flower clusters (panicles*) leafy, the corolla yellow. Eurasia, but naturalized in eastern N.A.

LYTHRACEAE (lith-ray'see-ee). The loosestrife family comprises over 22 genera and 500 species of widely distributed herbs, shrubs, and trees, a few of which, like the crape myrtle (*Lagerstroemia*), are of wide garden interest. Among the herbs are *Cuphea, Lythrum,* and *Decodon,* while *Lawsonia* (which yields henna) is, like the crape myrtle, woody.

Leaves generally opposite* (whorled* in some), without marginal teeth, flowers mostly in the leaf axils,* solitary or in clusters, the individual flower stalks usually with 2 bracts.* They are very showy in *Lythrum, Decodon,* and the crape myrtle, less so in *Lawsonia,* where, however, they are very fragrant. In *Cuphea* is the peculiar little cigar-flower, much grown in greenhouses and as a bedding plant. The fruit is a dry pod (capsule*), usually enclosed by the sometimes showy calyx.

Technical flower characters: Flowers regular* or irregular.* Calyx more or less bell-shaped, free from the ovary, mostly 4–6-toothed or lobed, and sometimes with secondary teeth between, sometimes petal-like. Petals 4–6, inserted at the throat of the calyx, sometimes (in the cigar-flower) none. Ovary superior.* Style 1.

LYTHRUM (lith'rum). Loosestrife (for other loosestrifes *see* LYSIMACHIA, DECODON, and STEIRONEMA). A group of annual or perennial herbs of the family Lythraceae, comprising about 30 widely scattered species, the three below often grown in moist places for their showy bloom. They have 4-sided stems and mostly opposite* leaves. Flowers in terminal clusters (spikes* or racemes*) or solitary in the leaf axils,* purple or purplish-pink in those below. Calyx* tubular or cylindric, 8–12-ribbed. Petals 4–6 (in ours). Stamens* 4–12, some longer than the others. Fruit a 2-valved capsule,* enclosed by the calyx.* (*Lythrum* is from the Greek for blood, in allusion to the color of the flowers in some species.)

The ones below are best grown along the edges of pools or streams, although they may be grown in the open border. All are perennials of easy culture so long as the site is moist. They can be increased by division. They bloom in summer.

alatum. Milk willow-herb. An erect perennial 3–4 ft. high, the 4-sided stems narrowly winged. Leaves opposite* or some alternate,* stalkless, oblongish or narrower, about 1 in. long. Flowers solitary in the leaf axils,* purple, scarcely ½ in. wide. N.A.

Salicaria. Purple loosestrife; also called purple willow-herb and red Sally. A wand-like perennial 2–3½ ft. high, the base somewhat woody. Leaves willow-like, 3–4 in. long. Flowers in dense, showy, leafy, terminal spikes, the corolla bright purple and about ¾ in. wide. Eurasia, but commonly naturalized in the marshes of N.A. The *var.* roseum superbum has darker colored and larger flowers and includes the hort. form known as Morden's pink; *var.* tomentosum has white-felty foliage.

virgatum. Related to the last but with smaller flowers in leafy clusters (racemes*). Eurasia, but occasionally naturalized in New England.

M

MAACKIA (mack'i-a). A small group of Asiatic trees of the pea family. Leaves opposite,* compound,* the leaflets arranged feather-fashion, 1½–3 in. long. The white pea-like flowers are borne in upright terminal clusters 4–6 in. long. Fruit a flat pod 2–3 in. long. (Named for R. Maack, a Russian naturalist.)

The maackias are hardy ornamental trees of good habit and with rather showy clusters of white flowers. They are not particular about soil, but like an open, sunny position. They are easily propagated by seeds.

amurensis. Tree of 40–45 ft. Leaves composed of 7–11 elliptic or oval leaflets, 2–3 in. long. Flowers white, in erect clusters (racemes*). Pods about 2 in. long. July or Aug. Manchuria. Hardy from zone* 3 southward.

chinensis. A tree eventually attaining almost 70 ft. Leaflets 11–13, oval to elliptic, 1–3 in. long, downy beneath. Flowers white, in terminal clusters. July–Aug. Central China. Hardy from zone* 3 southward. Very much like the

---

* Special articles on the subjects indicated by an asterisk (*) will be found at the words so marked.

above species but with shorter leaves and narrower, hairy leaflets.

hupehensis = *Maackia chinensis*.

MACADAMIA (mac-a-dam'ĭ-a). Slow-growing Australian trees of the family Proteaceae, only **M. ternifolia**, the Queensland nut, of hort. interest among its 5 known species. It is grown somewhat in zones* 8 and 9, both in Calif. and Fla., and is a tree up to 50 ft. high. Leaves in whorls* of 3 or 4, oblongish or narrower, nearly 12 in. long, bright green, remotely spiny-toothed and suggesting a long holly leaf. Flowers small (for details *see* PROTEACEAE), white, borne in pairs which are grouped in racemes* nearly 12 in. long. Fruit a hard drupe,* its edible seed globe-shaped, about 1 in. in diameter, very hard-shelled, and commonly (though incorrectly) called the nut. It grows very slowly and will not fruit for several years, preferring a moist, fertile soil. It may be increased from seeds, which must be stratified and then brought into the greenhouse and given gentle bottom-heat. Chiefly grown for its edible seeds. (Named for Doctor John Macadam, secretary of the Victoria Philosophical Institute.)

MACARTNEY ROSE = *Rosa bracteata*.

MACEDONIAN PINE = *Pinus Peuce*. See PINE.

MACHAERANTHERA (ma-kee-ran'the-ra). A small genus of herbs of the daisy family, found in western N.A. and closely related to *Aster*. They have alternate, bristly leaves and in the only cult. species rather showy heads of flowers in clusters (panicles*). The Tahoka daisy, the only cult. species, is **M. tanacetifolia**, an annual from S.D. to Mex. and Calif., 1–2 ft. high, the leaves much divided, the segments bristle-tipped. Flower heads nearly 2 in. wide, lavender-blue, the rays slender and pointed. Best grown as a tender annual (*see* ANNUALS) but the seeds should be put in the refrigerator (not deep freeze) for 2 weeks before planting, which is 6 weeks before outdoor planting is safe. (*Machaeranthera* is from the Greek for bristly anthers, in allusion to a technical flower character.)

MACHAEROCEREUS (ma-kee-ro-seer'ee-us). A small genus of erect and bushy or prostrate, very spiny cacti, found in Lower Calif. and Mex. and cult. in desert gardens for ornament. They have usually long, ribbed branches, the central spine of each cluster dagger-like. Flowers day-blooming, not very large, yellow or purple (in ours). Fruit fleshy, edible in the second species, at first spiny, but the spines fall off as the fruit ripens. (*Machaerocereus* is from the Greek for sword or dagger and *Cereus,* in allusion to the dagger-like central spines.)

For culture *see* CACTI.

eruca. A prostrate cactus, its radiating branches dying at one end and growing onward at the other, thus impossible to grow in a pot. Stems 3–7 in. in diameter, densely spiny. Flowers more or less tubular, 4–5 in. long, yellow. Fruit about 2 in. in diameter, globe-shaped.

gummosus. Pitahaya (for others *see* LEMAIREOCEREUS, HYLOCEREUS, and ECHINOCEREUS). More or less bushy and erect, nearly 3 ft. high, sometimes clambering in age. Branches 7–9-ribbed, very spiny, the spines in groups of 15–20. Flowers 4–5 in. long, purple. Fruit scarlet, edible, somewhat acid, widely used as food by the natives. It is not easy to grow in the greenhouse, and flowers there only rarely.

MACLEAYA (mack-lay'a). Showy, perennial, border plants of the poppy family, both the known species grown for ornament, often under the name of *Bocconia*. They are almost shrubby, erect herbs with stalked, alternate,* leaves which are deeply lobed, generally bluish-green or gray, especially beneath. Flowers small but very numerous in long terminal clusters (panicles). Sepals 2, petal-like and cream-colored. Petals none. Stamens* many and showy. Fruit an egg-shaped, stalked, 2-valved capsule.* (Named for Alexander Macleay, colonial secretary in Australia.)

The first species is a handsome, striking plant for the herbaceous border, but it needs plenty of space. They are rich feeders and need a good soil. Easily propagated by division.

cordata. Plume poppy; also called tree celandine. A stout perennial, 4–6 ft. high. Leaves nearly 8 in. wide, white on the under side, about 7-lobed. Flower cluster about 1 ft. long, very showy. Stamens* 24–30. China and Jap. June–July.

microcarpa. Somewhat similar but with the leaves merely hairy on the under side, and with only 8–12 stamens.* Central Asia.

MACLURA (ma-cloor'ra). A single species, **M. pomifera**, the Osage orange, or Bois d'Arc as it is sometimes called, is a spiny tree of about 50 ft., and belongs to the mulberry family, growing naturally from Ark. to Kan. Leaves alternate,* ovate to oblongish, pointed, 1½–4 in. long, shiny above. The trees are dioecious,* the male flowers small, greenish, and borne in pendulous clusters; the female flowers are also greenish but in dense heads. Fruit round, 2–5 in. across, greenish, somewhat suggestive of an orange, but worthless. Sometimes described as *Toxylon*. May, June; fruit Aug., Sept. Hardy from zone* 3 southward.

Although the Osage orange is a tree, it is often trained as a hedge, its spiny branches making an effective barrier. Growing naturally it forms an open-headed tree with spreading branches and furrowed orange-brown bark. The large fruits, though inedible, are odd and interesting. The trees are quite adaptable to ordinary conditions and are usually propagated by seeds. In the prairie states it makes a good windbreak (which see). (Named for W. Maclure, an American geologist.)

MACNAB CYPRESS = *Cupressus macnabiana*.

MACOMBER. See RUTABAGA.

macradena, -us, -um (mak-ra-dee'na). With large glands.

---

* Special articles on the subjects indicated by an asterisk (*) will be found at the words so marked.

macrantha, -us, -um (ma-kran'tha). Large-flowered.

macrobotrys (mak-ro-bō'triss). With a large, grape-like cluster.

macrocanthos (mak-ro-kan'thos). With large spines or thorns.

macrocarpa, -us, -um (mak-ro-kar'pa). Large-fruited. A variant is *macrocarpon.*

macrocephala, -us, -um (mak-ro-sef'fa-la). With large heads.

macromeris, -e (ma-krom'er-is). With many parts, or large ones.

macrophylla, -us, -um (mak-ro-fil'la). Large-leaved.

macropoda, -us, -um (ma-krop'o-da). Large- or stout-stalked.

macrorhiza, -us, -um (mak-ro-ry'za). With large roots or rootstocks.

macrosperma, -us, -um (mak-ro-sper'ma). Large-seeded.

macrostachya, -us, -um (mak-ro-stack'ī-a). With large or long spikes.

macrothyrsa, -us, -um (mack-ro-thyrs'a). With a large thyrse.*

maculata, -us, -um (mak-you-lay'ta). Spotted.

madagascariensis, -e (ma-da-gas-kar-i-en'-sis). From Madagascar, an island off the east coast of Africa.

MADAGASCAR JASMINE = *Stephanotis floribunda.*

MADAGASCAR PERIWINKLE = *Vinca rosea.*

MAD-APPLE. See EGGPLANT.

MADDER = *Rubia tinctorum.*

MADDER FAMILY. A huge family of plants, all but a handful tropical shrubs and trees like coffee, cinchona, the gardenia, and the trees yielding ipecac. Among hardier sorts are the sweet woodruff, bluets, bedstraw, the partridge-berry, and the button-bush. For a complete list of the cult. genera and their characters *see* RUBIACEAE.

MADEIRA-VINE = *Boussingaultia baselloides.*

MADEIRA-VINE FAMILY = Basellaceae.

MADIA (may'dĭ-a). Tarweed. A small genus of sticky-hairy, annual herbs of the family Compositae, all but one of them from western N.A., the remaining, Chilean. They are of secondary garden interest but both are grown on the Pacific Coast. Leaves mostly alternate.* Flower heads yellow, composed of disk* and ray flowers, the latter 3-lobed. (*Madia* is the native Chilean name for the Chilean species.)

The cult. species are heavy-scented annuals, the seed of which should be sown where wanted. The flower heads are not particularly showy and close in full sunshine.

elegans. Not over 24 in. high, the leaves very narrow, 3–5 in. long. Flower heads long-stalked, about ¾ in. wide, generally yellow, but sometimes the head brown-eyed.* Ore. and Calif. to Nev.

sativa. Chilean tarweed. A coarse, stout annual, 3–4 ft. high, the leaves lance-shaped or narrower, 1–2 in. long. Flower heads scarcely ½ in. wide, brownish-yellow, essentially stalkless. Chile; but naturalized in Calif. and Ore.

MADONNA LILY = *Lilium candidum.*

MADRAS THORN = *Pithecolobium dulce.*

MADROÑA = *Arbutus menziesi.*

MADWORT = *Alyssum.*

MAGELLAN BARBERRY = *Berberis buxifolia.*

magellanica, -us, -um (ma-jel-lan'i-ka). From the Straits of Magellan, S.A.

MAGIC TREE = *Cantua buxifolia.*

magnifica, -us, -um (mag-niff'i-ka). Magnificent or showy.

MAGNOLIA (mag-nō'lĭ-a). A genus of North American, West Indian, Mexican, and Asiatic evergreen or deciduous trees or shrubs of the family Magnoliaceae, comprising about 50 species. Leaves alternate,* without marginal teeth, large. Flowers regular, solitary, usually large and showy, commonly white, yellow, rose, or purple, appearing with or before the leaves on the species not evergreen. Petals 6–15. Sepals* 3, often petal-like, the stamens numerous. The fruit is a cone-like brown or scarlet body, the seeds of which when ripe hang by thread-like cords. (Named for Pierre Magnol, a botanist of Montpelier.)

For culture *see* below.

acuminata. Cucumber tree. A large handsome tree, reaching 100 ft. in height. Bark gray-brown, deeply ridged in mature trees. Small branches at first covered with soft hairs, later smooth, red-brown and shining. Leaves 6–10 in. long, somewhat oval or oblong, pointed at the end, soft-hairy and light green beneath. Flowers not showy, 2–3 in. high, cup-shaped. Petals 6. Sepals pointed, much smaller than the petals, soon turning back. Fruit somewhat oval or oblong, 3–4 in. long, becoming pink, or red. *Var.* **cordata** is found in Georgia. The branches are at first upright, then spreading, soft-hairy. Leaves not pointed, and hairy beneath. Flowers smaller than the type, canary yellow in color. Ont. to Ga. and westward. May. Hardy from zone* 4 southward.

campbelli. A large Himalayan tree, but scarcely over 80 ft. high as cult. in the Pacific Northwest and along the Gulf Coast, the only favorable sites for it in the U.S. Leaves ovalish, 6–8 in. long, half as wide, smooth above, but with flattened hairs beneath. Flowers cup-shaped, 6–10 in. wide, pink outside, but red or crimson inside, extraordinarily showy. Feb.–Mar., hence impossible of cult. in frosty regions.

conspicua = *Magnolia denudata.*

cordata = *Magnolia acuminata cordata.*

denudata. Yulan. A tree becoming 50 ft. high, the branches spreading, young growth soft-hairy. Leaves oval, 4–7 in. long, 3–4 in. broad, tapering to the base, rounded at the end with a short point, light green and sparingly soft-hairy beneath. Flowers large, cup-shaped,

---

* Special articles on the subjects indicated by an asterisk (*) will be found at the words so marked.

or broader, 5–6 in. across, white, fragrant. Petals and sepals alike, 9, fleshy. Fruit brownish, cylinder-shaped 3–4 in. long. Central China. April–May. Hardy from zone* 3 southward.

fraseri. Mountain magnolia. A tree growing 50 ft. high with smooth young growth. Leaves broadly oval or narrower, 8–12 in. long, heart-shaped and eared at the base, smooth with a slight bloom* beneath. Flowers creamy-white, fragrant, 9–11 in. across. Petals 6–9, 4 to 5 in. long. Sepals 3, quickly falling. Fruit 4 to 5 in. long, rose-red. Va. to Ga. and Ala. June. Hardy from zone* 3 southward.

glauca = Magnolia virginiana.

grandiflora. Evergreen magnolia; also known as bull bay and big-leaved magnolia. A large evergreen tree of noble proportions, becoming 100 ft. high. The branchlets and buds are rusty-woolly when young. Leaves 5–8 in. long, somewhat oblong in shape, tapering both ways, leathery, shining above and rusty-woolly beneath. Flowers cup-shaped, coming out of great silky-hairy buds, 6–8 in. across, white, fragrant. Petals usually 6, rarely 9–12, fleshy. Sepals 3, petal-like. Fruit 4 in. long, heavy, rusty-woolly. Var. **lanceolata** is more hardy than the typical form and has narrower leaves, is of narrow pyramidal growth, and is sometimes known as var. exoniensis. N. Car. to Fla. and Tex. May–June. Hardy from zone* 5 southward.

Kobus. A hardy tree growing to 30 ft. high, but usually shrubby in cult. Branchlets smooth. Leaf and flower-buds soft-hairy. Leaves broadly oval, 2½ to 4 in. long, abruptly pointed, pale and almost smooth beneath. Flowers blooming in advance of leaves, 4–5 in. across, lily-shaped, white. Petals 6–9, thin with a faint purple line at the base outside. Sepals* 3, small and narrow, soon falling. Fruit 4–5 in. long, dark brown. Var. **borealis** is a pyramidal tree, very hardy, but not blooming freely when young. The leaves are larger than the typical form and the flowers pure creamy-white. Jap. April–May. Hardy from zone* 3 southward, but unsuited to the deep South. For the var. **stellata**, see M. STELLATA.

liliflora. A large spreading shrub, the branchlets smooth except near the tips; buds soft-hairy. Leaves, somewhat oval, 3–7 in. long, light green and soft-hairy beneath when young, narrowing to a short point. Flowers lily-shaped,

slightly fragrant, white inside, purple outside, 8 in. across, on short stout stalks. Petals 6, 3–4 in. long. Sepals 3, shorter than the petals, soon falling. Fruit brown, oblong. China, much cult. in Jap. May–June. Hardy from zone* 4 southward. Var. **nigra** has larger flowers, darker purple outside and light purple inside, appearing partly with the leaves.

loebneri. A hybrid magnolia (Kobus × stellata) resembling the star magnolia (M. stellata) but with larger leaves and flowers. Cult. as for the star magnolia.

macrophylla. Large-leaved cucumber tree. A round-headed tree to 50 ft. high, with stout, spreading branches. Young growth woolly. Leaves very large, oblong to somewhat oval, 1–3 ft. long, soft-hairy and with a slight bloom* beneath. Flowers opening after the leaves, cup-shaped, creamy-white, fragrant, 10–12 in. across. Petals 6, turned backward above the middle, purplish at base. Sepals* shorter than the petals. Fruit nearly round, rose-color when ripe. Ky. to Fla., west to Ark. and La. May–June. Hardy from zone* 4 southward.

obovata. A handsome tree growing up to 100 ft. high. Young growth smooth and purplish. Leaves broadly oval, 1 ft. or more long, blunt-pointed, with the bloom* beneath when young. Flowers opening with the leaves, cup-shaped, 5–7 in. across, white, fragrant. Petals 6–9, leathery. Sepals* similar but shorter. Filaments* and pistils* bright crimson. Fruit 8 in. long, brilliant scarlet. Jap. May–June. Hardy from zone* 3 southward.

parviflora = M. sieboldi.

rustica rubra = M. soulangeana rubra.

salicifolia. A slender tree becoming 30 ft. high. Branchlets and leaf buds smooth, with a slight bloom.* Flower buds densely soft-hairy. Leaves light green above, elliptic or narrower, 3–5 in. long, with a bloom beneath. Flowers blooming before the leaves, about 5 in. across, white or purple at base, fragrant. Petals 6, sometimes 7–13. Sepals narrow, half as long as petals, greenish-white. Fruit 3 in. long, rose-colored. Jap. April–May. Hardy from zone* 3 southward.

sieboldi. A small tree growing 30 ft. high, with young growth covered with flattened soft hairs. Leaves 2–6 in. long, elliptic or broadly oval, bluntly pointed, soft-hairy and with a bloom* beneath. Flowers cup-shaped, fragrant, white, 3–4 in. across. Petals 6. Sepals shorter, pink. Fruit crimson, 1½ in. long. Jap. and Korea. June–July. Hardy from zone* 4 southward. Often called Oyama magnolia.

soulangeana. A large shrub or small tree, a hybrid between M. denudata and M. liliflora. Leaves broadly oval, slightly soft-hairy beneath. Flowers appearing before the leaves, cup-shaped, 6 in. across, purplish, seldom white, scentless or fragrant. Sepals usually petal-like, sometimes small and greenish. It originated in 1820. There are numerous forms among which are var. **alba superba** with pure white flowers, var. **alexandrina** with white flowers tinged purple outside toward the base, var. **lennei** with broader leaves and flowers white inside, rosy-purple on the outside; var. **rubra** has red flowers and is often offered as M. rustica rubra. These forms are among the most popular and handsome of our flowering shrubs. May. Hardy from zone* 2 southward.

stellata. A much-branched spreading shrub or small tree, up to 15 ft. high, the young growth densely soft-hairy. Leaves broadly oval to oblong, 1½–4 in. long, smooth, dark green above, light green beneath. Flowers appearing before the leaves, white, fragrant, 3 in. across.

Magnolia soulangeana, one of the handsomest of spring-flowering trees

Petals and sepals the same, 12–18, narrow, 1½ in. long, spreading and at length turned back. Fruit 2 in. long, red. Jap. March–April. Hardy from zone* 4 southward, but it flowers so early that its bloom is often destroyed by late frosts. Not suited to the deep South. The *var.* rosea has beautiful pale-pink flowers. Some authors have suggested that *M. stellata* is a mere var. of *M. Kobus*, a view not here adopted.

thompsoniana. A hybrid magnolia (*tripetala* × *virginiana*), usually a vigorous shrub, resembling *M. virginiana*, but the leaves longer and paler beneath, and the fragrant white flowers 5–6 in. wide. A very handsome plant. June.

tripetala. Umbrella tree. A tree with spreading branches and open head, growing to 40 ft. high. Leaves oblong to broadly oval, 1–2 ft. long, pointed, pale green and soft-hairy beneath. Flowers appearing with leaves, cup-shaped, white, 10 in. across, of unpleasant, heavy odor. Petals 6–9. Sepals* shorter, soon turning back. Fruit 4 in. long, rose-pink. Pa. to Ala. and west to Ark. and Mo. May–June. Hardy from zone* 3 southward.

virginiana. Sweet bay; also known as beaver-tree, white bay, swamp bay, or swamp laurel. A deciduous* shrub, or half-evergreen tree, growing 60 ft. high in the South and evergreen there, but a shrub northward. Branchlets smooth. Buds soft-hairy. Leaves oblong or elliptic or narrower, pointed or blunt, with a bloom beneath, and at first silky soft-hairy, 3–5 in. long. Flowers appearing with the leaves, rounded, 3 in. across, white, very fragrant. Petals 9–12. Sepals shorter and thinner, spreading. Fruit 2 in. long, red. Mass. to Fla. and Miss., near the coast. May–June. Hardy from zone* 3 southward, and generally a bog plant and preferring acid soils.

Magnolia Culture

Because certain members of the genus produce their flowers before the foliage is developed, a selection of species and varieties may be chosen which will offer flowering color from March until July and, quite often, well into Aug. The fruit ripens in Aug. and Sept. and appears in the form of long, colored, cone-like formations which split longitudinally at maturity, exposing scarlet-colored seeds.

The first species to show flower is *Magnolia stellata* which comes into bloom about the last week of March and is a shrubby plant hardy north of Boston. It is immediately followed by *Magnolia salicifolia, Kobus, denudata, soulangeana,* and *liliflora,* all of which produce their flowers before the development of the leaves. During the second week in June, *Magnolia acuminata, obovata, tripetala, fraseri, sieboldi,* and *macrophylla* come into bloom. The last mentioned is not hardy north of Rochester, N.Y. Among the evergreen species are *Magnolia grandiflora* which is hardy only south of Wilmington, Del., and *Magnolia virginiana* which although hardy nearly throughout the U.S. retains its foliage only in the warmer sections of the country.

Good drainage rather than a rich soil is the prime essential for the successful cultivation of *Magnolia.* However, for best results it is recommended that some natural fertilizer such as well-rotted stable or cow manure be applied about the base of each plant every two or three years. All magnolias have fleshy roots, which makes transplanting a tedious and painstaking operation. Whenever possible they should be left alone and not transplanted. In the North, spring transplanting is better than fall transplanting. Their root system cannot stand injury or drying out and, for this reason, all material should be carefully balled and burlapped when moved. For details *see* Planting.

Pruning of *Magnolia* is not necessary for the production of flowers and with few exceptions this operation may be dispensed with except as required for the occasional removal of dead or diseased wood.

Propagation is accomplished by several methods. The species are most commonly grown from seed which should be sown as soon as it falls from the tree. The hybrids and varieties are veneer-grafted on *Magnolia Kobus,* the work being done in the greenhouse during Jan. Layering is an excellent method for the amateur. Vigorous shoots are selected near the base of the plant and, after having the bark scarred with a knife, are pegged to the ground and covered with a few inches of soil. After one or two seasons these shoots are severed from the plant and set out in good soil. After a few years a vigorous plant will result. Budding is also practiced and is perhaps superior to grafting. *Magnolia Kobus* is used as a stock and the buds are tied from the top down, the opposite of the usual procedure in work of this kind. — D. W.

Insect Pests. Large concave scales often stunt growth and produce mold. Kill them with dormant superior oil sprays applied before budbreak. Two or three late-summer applications of pesticide #21 will kill young scales. These applications will also control a mealybug. (*See* Sprays and Dusts.)

MAGNOLIACEAE (mag-no-li-ā'see-ee). The magnolia family, geologically very ancient, contains some of our most beautiful garden shrubs and trees in its 10 genera and over 100 species, most of which, except *Magnolia, Kadsura,* and *Liriodendron* (*see* Tulip-tree), are tropical.

Leaves alternate,* mostly without marginal teeth, the bud enclosed by the large, sheathing stipules.* Flowers very showy in *Magnolia* and *Liriodendron* (*see* Tulip-tree), less so in *Drimys, Michelia, Illicium, Kadsura,* and *Schisandra,* the only other cult. genera. The fruit is peculiar in most genera, being a cone-like collection of dry fruits, which in *Magnolia* becomes fleshy (often scarlet) with the seeds suspended (for a brief time) on thread-like strings. All have perfect* flowers except *Kadsura,* a woody Asiatic vine with unisexual,* mostly solitary flowers, and berry-like fruit.

Technical flower characters: Sepals and petals often indistinguishable, when obvious the sepals 3, rarely 4, the petals 6 or more. Stamens many, spirally arranged. Ovary of many carpels (*see* Pistil), superior,* 1-celled.

MAGNOLIA FAMILY = Magnoliaceae.

---

* Special articles on the subjects indicated by an asterisk (*) will be found at the words so marked.

MAGNOLIA GARDENS. *See* No. 1 at GARDEN TOURS.

Mahagoni (ma-ha-gō′nee). West Indian vernacular for the mahogany.

MAHALA MAT = *Ceanothus prostratus.*

Mahaleb (ma-hǎ′leb). Original Arabic name for *Prunus Mahaleb,* the mahaleb cherry.

MAHERNIA (ma-her′ni-a). A genus of perhaps 30 species of chiefly South African herbs or under-shrubs of the family Sterculiaceae, only **M. verticillata,** the honey bell, of hort. interest. It is a sprawling shrubby plant, never over 6 in. high, the stems rough. Leaves alternate,* deeply cut into narrow segments. Flowers in pairs, nodding, yellow, fragrant, about ½ in. long. Calyx* bell-shaped, but the corolla of 5 separate, flat petals. Stamens * 5. Fruit a 5-valved capsule.* The honey bell is more widely grown in the cool greenhouse as a basket plant than outdoors where it is hardy only in southern Calif. It blooms in winter and early spring, and is sometimes offered as *M. odorata.* (*Mahernia* is an anagram of *Hermannia.*)

MAHOBERBERIS (ma-ho-ber′ber-is). A bigeneric* hybrid and including only a half-evergreen shrub of the family Berberidaceae, **M. neuberti,** a hybrid between *Mahonia Aquifolium* and *Berberis vulgaris.* It is a shrub growing nearly 6 ft. high, without spines on the branches. Leaves 1–3 in. long, broadly oval to oblong, toothed or spiny, occasionally 3–5 leaflets, all on the same plant. It has not been known to bloom and is of secondary hort. interest. It is sometimes confused with *Berberis ilicifolia.*

MAHOGANY. The true mahogany is *Swietenia Mahagoni* (which see). For other cult. plants sometimes called mahogany *see* EUCALYPTUS and CERCOCARPUS.

MAHOGANY FAMILY = Meliaceae.

MAHOGANY GUM = *Eucalyptus robusta.*

MAHONIA (ma-hō′ni-a). A genus of American and Asian evergreen, thornless shrubs, rarely small trees, comprising about 90 species of the barberry family. Leaves alternate,* compound, the leaflets arranged feather-fashion (pinnate*), or rarely in 3's, spiny, often turning purplish in autumn. Petals 6. Sepals* 9, the flowers yellow, fragrant, in terminal clusters (racemes* or panicles*). Fruit a dark blue berry, usually covered with a bloom, rarely red or whitish. (Named for Bernard M'Mahon, an American horticulturist.)

Mahonias are handsome low-growing evergreens for the shrubbery border and foundation planting. They should be planted in sheltered positions or protected from the wind and sun in winter. Some of the western species do well as far north as Canada where they are protected by a heavy covering of snow all winter. They are increased by seeds and suckers, and by layers and cuttings of half-ripe wood under glass. They are sometimes listed as *Odostemon.*

Aquifolium. Oregon grape. A shrub 3 to 10 ft. high. Leaflets 5–9, shiny, ovalish or oblong in shape, stiff, leathery, the marginal teeth spiny. Flowers yellow, fragrant, in dense, erect terminal clusters (racemes*) 3 in. high. Fruit a small bluish berry, edible. British Columbia to Ore. April–May. Hardy from zone* 3 southward.

bealei. A shrub with stout, upright stems, sometimes 12 ft. high. Leaflets 9–15, round-oval, with a few large teeth on the margins, the end leaflets larger, bluish-green, with a slight bloom beneath, stiff and leathery. Flowers lemon-yellow, fragrant, in close-growing, upright, terminal clusters (racemes*) 6 in. high. Fruit bluish-black. China. March–May. Hardy from zone* 4 southward.

fortunei. A shrub 3–5 ft. high, the leaves compound, with 3–8 pairs of leaflets that are elliptic, 2½–4½ in. long, the margins with 5–10 teeth. Flower clusters (racemes*) 3–5 in. long. China. Hardy from zone* 5 southward. Closely related to *M. bealei.*

japonica. A shrub similar to *M. bealei.* Leaflets ovalish to oblong with a long spine at the end and with 5 or 6 strong spiny teeth on the margin, yellowish-green beneath and not as rigid-leaved as *M. bealei.* Flowers small, yellowish, in drooping, close-growing, terminal clusters. Fruit bluish-black. Jap. Hardy from zone* 4 southward.

lomariifolia. A winter-blooming shrub with the evergreen, compound leaves having 10–20 pairs of leaflets, which are 2–3 in. long and nearly ¾ in. wide, blunt at the base, the margins with 2–6 teeth, the tip almost spine-like. Flower cluster (raceme*) 3–7 in. long. Yunnan. Nov.–Dec. Hardy from zone* 7 southward.

nervosa. Oregon grape; also known as water holly. A shrub 2 ft. high, usually lower. Leaflets 11–19, oval to narrower, leathery, shiny above, pale beneath, with spiny teeth on the margin. Flowers bright yellow, fragrant, in erect terminal clusters 8 in. long. Fruit somewhat oval, dark blue with a bloom,* edible. British Columbia to Calif. May–June. Hardy from zone* 4 southward.

pinnata. California barberry. A shrub up to 12 ft. high. Leaflets 7–13, somewhat oval to narrower, spiny-toothed on the margins, slightly shiny and green beneath. Flowers pale yellow in terminal clusters in the axils* of the leaves. Fruit almost round, purplish-black. Calif. and N. Mex. to Mex. Hardy from zone* 6, and possibly from zone* 5 southward. Thought by some to be a var. of *M. Aquifolium.*

repens. Creeping barberry. A shrub with underground rooting stems, rarely more than 1 ft. high. Leaflets 3–7, roundish-oval, 1½–2½ in. long, dull bluish-green above, with a bloom* below, leathery, and with spiny marginal teeth. Flowers in terminal clusters (racemes*) at the ends of the branches. Fruit small, black, with a bloom.* British Columbia to N. Mex. and Calif. May. Hardy from zone* 3 southward.

trifoliolata. Agarita; also known as algerita. A shrub sometimes 8 ft. high. Leaflets 3, oblong or narrower, with coarse marginal teeth, stiff. Flowers few, in a terminal cluster (raceme*). Fruit red, used in jelly. Occasionally planted in Tex. Tex., N. Mex. and Mex. Not certainly hardy north of zone* 6.

MAHON STOCK = *Malcomia maritima.*

MAIANTHEMUM (may-an′thee-mum). Generally woodland, low, perennial herbs of the lily family, two of them cult. in the wild garden, and suggesting the lily-of-the-valley, but far inferior as hort. subjects. They have

---

* Special articles on the subjects indicated by an asterisk (*) will be found at the words so marked.

creeping rootstocks and a short stem having only 2 or 3 leaves, and terminated by a short raceme of small white flowers. These are 4-parted, have 4 stamens,* and are followed by a somewhat speckled berry. (*Maianthemum* is from the Greek for May and flower, in allusion to their spring blooming.)

They are of easy cult. in the wild garden, preferably in reasonably moist, partly shady places, where they will make large patches in a few years. Both species flower in early spring.

bifolium. Nearly 9 in. high and hairy. Leaves more or less triangular, but deeply heart-shaped at the base, the stalk about 1 in. long. Flower cluster about 1 in. long. Eurasia.

canadense. Wild lily-of-the-valley; also called Mayflower and bead-ruby. Usually about 5 in. high, rarely 7 in., the leaves only 1 or 2 on the stem, very short-stalked. Flowering cluster nearly 2 in. long. Eastern N.A. and west to Man. In New England sometimes called Solomon's-seal.

MAIDEN. A one-year-old, single-stemmed plant, used for budding or grafting in the production of trees or shrubs, often called a whip. *See* Planting at FRUIT CULTURE.

MAIDENHAIR. *See* ADIANTUM.

MAIDENHAIR SPLEENWORT = *Asplenium Trichomanes.*

MAIDENHAIR-TREE = *Ginkgo biloba.*

MAIDENHAIR-VINE = *Muehlenbeckia complexa.*

MAIDEN PINK = *Dianthus deltoides.*

MAIDEN'S-WREATH = *Francoa ramosa.*

MAINE. The state flower and tree is the white pine. The state lies wholly in zones* 2 and 3.

SOIL AND TOPOGRAPHY. Maine lies in a region of comparatively recent glaciation and, perhaps because of this, marked soil variation exists. The "patchy" condition, together with factors related to topography, such as exposure to winds, air and water drainage, slope, etc., and to micro-climates, make the care in selection of sites for vegetable and fruit crops particularly important. Most Maine soils are acid, and with those crops requiring near neutral soils there will be a marked response to lime application. Dolomitic limestone is preferred to overcome the deficiency of magnesium which is quite widespread. The use of commercial fertilizers is essential to produce high crop yields.

VEGETABLE CROPS. Nearly all kinds of vegetables can be grown in the state. Cool-season crops such as members of the cabbage family, lettuce, peas, and root crops are well adapted to the climate and develop superior quality. The warm-season crops, such as melons, watermelons, peppers, eggplant, and lima beans, can be grown satisfactorily in the southern region and where soil and exposure are suitable. It is possible to raise these crops in other areas by careful site selection and the em-

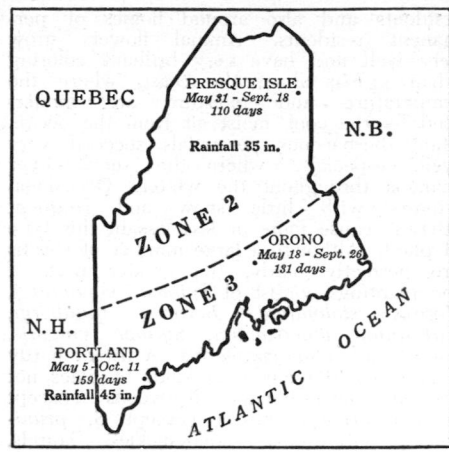

MAINE

The zones of hardiness crossing Maine are those shown on the map located at ZONE, which should be consulted for details. The dates are the average latest killing frost in spring and the first one in the fall. The figures below the dates show the average length of the growing season. Rainfall figures (in inches) are for total annual rainfall in the regions so indicated.

ployment of special cultural techniques to lengthen the growing season.

FRUIT CROPS. It is possible to grow both tree and small fruits in the home garden in most parts of the state.

The small fruits consist primarily of strawberries, raspberries, and high-bush blueberries (limited at present to zone* 3). Other small fruits are grown in home gardens to a limited extent. Currants and gooseberries are prohibited in a large portion of the state in the interests of protection against white pine blister rust. Grapes may be grown in certain parts of the state, again by careful site selection and using those varieties which are hardy and which require a short growing season in which to mature.

Apples comprise the principal tree fruit. Dwarf apple trees perhaps hold the most promise for the home gardener. There is some question as to the hardiness of certain dwarfing rootstocks but they are known to survive in the southern part of the state (zone* 3).

Plums and sour cherries may be grown throughout zone* 3. Sweet cherries and peaches are generally unsuccessful because of winter injury even in the most southerly part of the state. In northern Maine only the most hardy varieties of fruits will succeed. The list of such varieties is very limited, so a wide assortment of fruits in this area is not possible.

ORNAMENTALS. Many beautiful flower gardens are found on the estates of summer

---

* Special articles on the subjects indicated by an asterisk (*) will be found at the words so marked.

residents and also around homes of permanent residents. Annual flowers grow very well and have very brilliant coloring when grown along the coast, where the temperature and moisture are moderated by the cool, moist air from the ocean. Many herbaceous perennials succeed very well, especially where the snow cover remains throughout the winter. Occasional winters with little snow and frequent "thaws" cause more or less loss in this type of plant. Although a large number of shrubs are perfectly hardy, the greater part of the plantings consist of *Spiraea vanhouttei, Cornus stolonifera, Berberis thunbergi, Virburnum americanum, Syringa vulgaris,* and *Philadelphus coronarius.* A list of hardy shrubs would include all kinds of lilacs not grafted, mock-oranges, dogwoods (except the flowering), spireas (except *S. prunifolia*), viburnums, honeysuckles, laurels, rhododendrons, and most shrub evergreens. The American elm, some maples, and evergreens make up the majority of the ornamental trees used. Occasional nut trees are found, but for the most part fail to bear good crops.

MAINE FROST DATA

Town	Average date of last killing frost in spring	Latest-known killing frost	Average date of earliest killing frost in fall	Earliest known killing frost
Presque Isle	May 31	June 29	Sept. 18	Sept. 6
Orono	May 18	June 5	Sept. 26	Sept. 2
Portland	May 5	June 3	Oct. 11	Sept. 11

The average annual rainfall varies between 35 and 45 inches from the northern inland part of the state to the coast regions, respectively. The mean precipitation during growing season for these regions is from 18 to 21 inches, which is ample for most crops. Under certain conditions, some gardeners find irrigation practical. Proximity to the ocean, vast wooded areas, and about 2500 inland lakes all aid in minimizing crop damage by summer temperature extremes and drying winds.

The address of the Agricultural Experiment Station, which has kindly supplied this information about the state, is Orono, Maine. The station is always ready to answer gardening questions.

Garden club activities include clubs of the Garden Club of America, the home office of which is at 598 Madison Avenue, New York 22, N.Y. There are also over 20 clubs affiliated with the Garden Club Federation of Maine.

MAIZE. *See* CORN.

majalis, -e (ma-jay′lis). Literally May-time; usually meaning May-flowering.

major, majus. Greater.

MAJORANA. *See* SWEET MARJORAM.

MAKI = *Podocarpus macrophyllus Maki.*

MALABAR GOURD = *Cucurbita ficifolia.*

malabarica, -us, -um (ma-la-bar′i-ka). From Malabar, India.

MALABAR NIGHTSHADE. *See* BASELLA.

malabathrica, -us, -um (ma-la-bath′ri-ka). From Malabar.

MALACEAE. *See* ROSACEAE.

Malachodendron (ma-lack-o-den′dron). Old name for plants now included in *Stewartia.*

malacoides (ma-la-coy′deez, but *see* OïDES). Soft and tender like a mallow.

MALACOTHRIX (mal′a-ko-thricks). A group of herbs of the family Compositae, all from western N.A. and chiefly perennials, but the only cult. species annuals. The two below are essentially stemless, and have a basal rosette of much-divided leaves. Flower heads (in ours) bright yellow, composed only of ray flowers,* solitary in the first species, but the flowering stalk branched and with several heads in the second. (*Malacothrix* is from the Greek for soft hair, in allusion to the hairy foliage of some species.)

Treat both species as hardy annuals (*see* ANNUALS). They are natural inhabitants of sandy soils.

californica. Not over 12 in. high. Basal rosette of leaves woolly in youth. Leaves divided finger-fashion into narrow, line-like segments. Flower heads about 1¾ in. wide, somewhat dandelion-like. Calif. April–June (in Calif.), later when sown as a hardy annual.

glabrata. Similar to the above and perhaps only a variety of it, differing in the young leaves being smooth from the first, and the flowering stalk usually branched. Ore. to Calif. and Nev.

MALANGA = *Xanthosoma atrovirens.*

MALATHION. *See* #5 at INSECTICIDES.

MALAY JEWEL-VINE = *Derris scandens.*

MALCOLM STOCK = *Malcomia maritima.*

MALCOMIA (mal-cō′mi-a). Commonly called Mahon, Malcolm or Virginia stock. A small genus of low, grayish herbs belonging to the family Cruciferae, or mustard family. Stems branching profusely, making a compact plant. Leaves simple, alternate,* slightly cut. Flowers white, purple, or reddish in a loose cluster at end of branches, the petals 4, long and narrow. Pods usually long and narrow, containing one or two rows of seeds. (Named for William Malcolm, an English horticulturist.) Propagated by seeds. Sow in permanent position, in masses in ordinary garden soil, in early spring, about ¹⁄₁₆ in. deep. The Virginia stock was much used in English cottage gardens in the Victorian era.

flexuosa. The plant so offered is usually *Malcomia maritima.*

littorea. Perennial to 12 in. The whole plant is covered with short, white hairs. Leaves narrow, lance-shaped. Flowers purple. It can be grown as an annual. Mediterranean region.

maritima. The Virginia stock. An annual of

---

* Special articles on the subjects indicated by an asterisk (*) will be found at the words so marked.

spreading habit 6–12 in. high. Leaves simple, ovalish. Flowers reddish to white. The *var.* **alba** is a color form. Mediterranean region.

MALE. See **FEMALE.**

MALE BAMBOO = *Dendrocalamus strictus.*

MALEBERRY = *Lyonia ligustrina.*

MALE FERN = *Dryopteris Filix-mas.*

MALLOW. See **MALVA.** For other plants sometimes called mallow *see* **SPHAERALCEA,** **CORCHORUS, ALTHAEA, HIBISCUS,** and **LAVATERA.**

MALLOW FAMILY = Malvaceae.

MALOPE (ma-lō′pe). A genus of nearly a dozen smooth or hairy annual herbs of the family Malvaceae, found in the Mediterranean region. Leaves alternate, without marginal teeth, occasionally 3-parted. Flowers showy, about 3 in. across, white, violet, or pink, surrounded by three heart-shaped bracts.* (*Malope* is a name used by Pliny for some kind of mallow.)

These plants are easily cultivated in any ordinary garden soil.

grandiflora = *Malope trifida grandiflora.*

trifida. Grows from 2–3 ft. high. Leaves smooth, 3-parted. The flowers grow on stalks, singly, from the axils* of the leaves; they are 2–3 in. across, rose or purple, blooming nearly all summer. Eu. and northern Africa. *Var.* **grandiflora** has larger, deep rosy-red flowers, and is sometimes known as *M. grandiflora. Var.* **rosea** has rose-colored flowers. *See* **ANNUALS.**

MALPIGHIA (mal-pig′i-a). Tropical American shrubs and trees of the family Malpighiaceae, comprising over 40 species, only two of them of much garden interest. They have opposite,* short-stalked leaves, and not particularly showy flowers in short-stalked clusters (cymes* or umbels*) in the leaf axils.* Petals 5, usually not quite equal. Stamens* 10. Fruit a drupe* with 3 stones. (Named for Marcello Malpighi, Italian naturalist.)

Neither species can be grown outdoors north of zone* 9, although they are apparently indifferent as to soils in Fla. The first is occasionally grown for ornament, while *M. glabra* is grown in the tropics, and to some extent in southern Fla., for its acid fruits used in preserves. Propagated by cuttings or by seeds.

coccigera. A West Indian shrub, rarely more than 3 ft. high. Leaves holly-like, spiny-margined, nearly ¾ in. long. Flowers about ½ in. wide, pink, the clusters few-flowered.

glabra. Barbados cherry. A shrub 5–10 ft. high, the leaves ovalish or narrower, 1–3 in. long, spiny, without marginal teeth. Flowers rose-pink. Fruit red, acid, about the size of a cherry, now widely used as a rich source of vitamin C. Southern Tex. to tropical America.

MALPIGHIACEAE (mal-pig-ĭ-ā′see-ee). A family of 55 genera and over 650 species of tropical shrubs, trees or vines, only two genera of which, *Malpighia* and *Thryallis,* are of secondary hort. interest. These are shrubby.

Leaves mostly opposite.* Flowers not particularly showy, in various kinds of clusters, nearly regular,* the petals often fringed or toothed. Fruit usually separating into 3 nut-like segments, which are sometimes winged in *Thryallis* but more or less fleshy in *Malpighia.*

Technical flower characters: Flowers hermaphrodite.* Sepals 5. Petals 5, usually unequal, and with a slender claw.* Stamens 10, some occasionally sterile, usually partly united. Ovary superior.* Styles usually 3.

MALTESE CROSS = *Lychnis chalcedonica.*

MALUS (may′lus). A genus of North American and Eurasian, mostly deciduous, trees or shrubs, of the rose family, rarely with spiny branches, but occasionally with spurs of the wild or escaped species becoming thorn-like. Leaves alternate,* toothed or lobed, folded or rolled in bud, with stipules.* Flowers, usually in advance of foliage, regular, white to pink or carmine, in umbel-like terminal clusters (racemes*). Petals 5, usually rounded, or broadly oval. Stamens* 15–20 or more. Fruit a true pome,* fleshy, often edible. Some of our most beautiful and valuable ornamental trees belong to this genus, as well as important fruit trees. Commonly known as apple; also as crabapple, crab, or crabtree. The cultivated apple is *M. pumila.* For the culture, diseases, and insect pests of the apple and the ornamental species below, *see* **APPLE.** (*Malus* is the ancient Latin name of the apple.) All are early spring-bloomers, and many of them called *Pyrus* (which see). Next to the Japanese flowering cherries, the ornamental crabapples are among the finest of flowering trees. Unfortunately most of them will not thrive in the deep South.

For many hybrids and hort. varieties impossible to include here, see *Ornamental Crab Apples* by A. den Boer, published by Am. Assoc. of Nurserymen, Washington, D.C., 1959.

adstringens. A hybrid crabapple (*baccata* × *pumila*) with pinkish flowers and leaves that are hairy on the under side. Fruit red, yellow, or green. There are several hort. forms such as Martha, Hyslop, and Transcendent.

angustifolia. Southern crabapple. A slender-branched tree growing to 25 ft. high, partially evergreen. Leaves 1–3 in. long, narrowly oblong, toothed or without marginal teeth, smooth and light green beneath. Flowers 1 in. across, pink or rose, fragrant. Fruit 1 in. or less in diameter, nearly round, depressed at both ends, yellow-green. *Var.* **rosea** has deeper rose-colored flowers. N.J. to Fla. and La. Hardy from zone* 4 southward.

arnoldiana. A hybrid derived from crossing *M. floribunda* and *M. baccata.* A large bush or tree, 25 or more ft. high. Leaves 2–4 in. long; at first soft-hairy, then smooth, oblong, sharp-pointed, toothed. Flowers larger or lighter-colored than *floribunda.* Fruit also larger, yellow instead of red. Handsome bush, much used in shrubbery plantations or as a specimen on the lawn. Hardy from zone* 3 southward.

atrosanguinea. Carmine crabapple. A hybrid between *M. halliana* and *M. sieboldi.* A handsome, bushy shrub resembling *M. floribunda.* Leaves smooth, shining, toothed. Flowers rose-

---

* Special articles on the subjects indicated by an asterisk (*) will be found at the words so marked.

purple, not fading to white. Fruit red. Hardy from zone* 4 southward. Often known as *Pyrus atrosanguinea.*

baccata. Siberian crabapple. A round-headed tree, sometimes growing 40 ft. high, with many smooth, slender, wiry branchlets. Leaves 2½–4 in. long, thin, smooth, somewhat oval, toothed, pointed. Flowers white, 1½ in. across. Fruit ¾ in. or less in diameter, yellow or red. Siberia and Manchuria and northern China. Common in cultivation. *Var.* **mandshurica** has soft-hairy leaves, flower stalks and calyx,* fragrant flowers, and larger fruit. *Var.* **niedzwetzkyana** has red bark, wood, leaves, flowers and fruit. Southwest Siberia and Turkestan. *Var.* **jacki** is similar, but has smooth leaves and a smaller, bright-red fruit. Hardy from zone* 2 southward.

brevipes. A small tree, perhaps not distinct from *M. floribunda,* but a lower plant and with smaller, white flowers. Origin unknown.

communis = *Malus pumila.*

coronaria. American crab; often called sweet crabapple or garland crabapple. A twiggy, stiff-branched tree becoming 30 ft. high, foliage becoming quite smooth. Leaves thin, 2–3 in. long, nearly oval, sharp-toothed or sometimes notched. Flowers 1 in. or less across, rose, changing to white. Fruit 1 in. in diameter, flattened at ends. Ont. to Ala. west to Mo. Hardy from zone* 3 southward. Sometimes known as *Pyrus coronaria.*

dawsoniana. A small tree, thought to be a cross between *M. fusca* and *M. pumila.* Leaves somewhat oval, 1½–3½ in. long, toothed, seldom lobed. Flowers 1 in. across, white. Fruit, yellow or green, flushed red. Both flowers and fruit twice as large as *M. fusca.* Hardy from zone* 3 southward. Also known as *Pyrus dawsoniana.*

floribunda. Showy crabapple. A large bush or tree with wide-spreading branches, becoming 25 or more feet high. Leaves dull green, somewhat oval in outline, 2 to 3 in. long, sharp-toothed. Flowers 1¼ in. across, rose or rose-red, fading white. Fruit ⅓ in. in diameter, red. Commonly supposed to be a hybrid between *M. baccata* and *M. sieboldi,* but probably a distinct species introduced from Jap., perhaps of Chinese origin. Hardy from zone* 3 southward. Sometimes known as *Pyrus floribunda.* A hybrid between *M. floribunda* and *M. prunifolia,* with pale pink, semi-double flowers, is often offered as *M. scheideckeri.*

fusca. Oregon crabapple. A shrub or small tree sometimes 30 ft. high. Leaves somewhat oval, 3–4 in. long, sharply toothed, often 3-lobed, at first soft-hairy on both sides, later smooth above. Flowers white, ¾ in. across, 6–12 in a flat-topped cluster. Fruit oblong, ½–¾ in. long, yellow or green, flushed red. Northern Calif. to Alaska. Not often seen in cultivation, but interesting as supposed parent of *M. dawsoniana.* Hardy from zone* 2 southward. Sometimes listed as *Pyrus fusca.*

halliana. A shrub or tree with loose, open head, growing 18 ft. high. Young branchlets soon smooth, purple. Leaves shiny above, 2 to 3 in. long, somewhat long, oval, pointed, toothed, the midrib* purplish. Flowers deep rose, the calyx purple, 1–1½ in. across, on slender, purple stalks. Fruit ⅓ in. in diameter, purplish. Western China. *Var.* **parkmani** is a semidouble-flowered form. It was grown by Francis Parkman, the historian, near Boston. Hardy from zone* 3 southward. Also called *Pyrus halliana.*

hopa and **hoppi.** Trade names for a crabapple reputed to be derived from a cross be-

tween *M. robusta* and *M. baccata niedzwetzkyana.* Widely offered and a handsome, medium-sized tree, with deep purplish-red flowers. Origin unknown.

hupehensis. See P. THEIFERA.

ioensis. Prairie crabapple. A tree growing 30 ft. high, branchlets downy. Leaves somewhat oval or oblong, 2–4 in. long, toothed, occasionally lobed, sharp-pointed, sometimes downy beneath. Flowers 1–2 in. across, white or rose-tinted. Fruit almost round, sometimes angled, greenish, waxy. Bechtel's crab is a double-flowered form. Ind. to Minn., Okla., and Mo. The double-flowered form is very handsome and often cult. as an ornamental. Hardy from zone* 3 southward.

Kaido = *Malus micromalus.*

Malus = *Malus pumila.*

micromalus. Kaido crabapple. A small tree of upright habit, growing 25 ft. high. Leaves almost oblong, 2–4 in. long, narrowing to the base and long-pointed, shiny. Flowers deep pink, 1½ in. across. Fruit nearly red, hollowed at base. Perhaps a hybrid of *M. spectabilis* and *M. baccata.* Hardy from zone* 4 southward.

niedzwetzkyana = *M. baccata niedzwetzkyana.*

nivalis = *Pyrus nivalis.*

prunifolia. A small tree with young growth soft-hairy. Leaves 2–4 in. long, ovalish or elliptic, short-pointed, soft-hairy beneath, later smooth. Flowers about 1½ in. across, white. Fruit 1 in. in diameter, yellow or red, very abundant, and held long on tree. Northeastern As. *Var.* **rinki,** the Ringo crabapple has leaves soft-hairy beneath, flowers pink and calyx* somewhat hairy. Eastern As. Hardy from zone* 3 southward. Sometimes known as *Pyrus prunifolia.*

pumila. The common apple. A round-headed, short-trunked tree growing 45 ft. high. The young branches are downy. Leaves 1¾–4 in. long, elliptic or ovalish, pointed, glossy above, downy beneath, bluntly toothed. Flowers 2 in. across, white and pink, appearing with first foliage. Fruit nearly round, yellow and red. Eu. and As. Cult. since ancient times. The parent of most of our cult. apples. Frequently known as *Pyrus malus* and as *Malus communis.* *Var.* **paradisiaca,** the Paradise apple, is a dwarf form. For apple cult. and best varieties *see* APPLE.

purpurea. A hybrid of *M. baccata niedzwetzkyana* and *M. atrosanguinea.* Young branchlets purple. Leaves when young purple, smaller than *M. pumila niedzwetzkyana,* shining. Flowers with oblong petals. Fruit small. *Var.* **aldenhamensis** is a small tree with leaves somewhat more oval, soft-hairy beneath or nearly smooth, veined and with purple rib. Flowers wine-red, partially double. Fruit deep purple-red. *Var.* **eleyi** has leaves reddish when unfolding, downy beneath, and a purple rib. The flowers are wine-red. Fruit conical-shaped, deep purple-red. Hardy from zone* 4 southward.

robusta. A hybrid crabapple, also called Siberian crab and derived from crossing *M. baccata* and *M. prunifolia.* It has small white or pinkish flowers in great profusion. Fruit nearly round, red or yellow.

sargenti. A low, bushy, much-branched, spiny shrub, 3–5 ft. high. Young growth downy. Leaves 2–3 in. long, ovalish or elliptic, short-pointed, toothed, turning orange and yellow in autumn. Flowers pure white, 1 in. across, 5 or 6 in a cluster, the petals oval, overlapping. Fruit nearly round, ½ in. or less in diameter, dark red with a slight bloom.* Jap. Hardy from zone* 3 southward.

---

* Special articles on the subjects indicated by an asterisk (*) will be found at the words so marked.

scheideckeri. *See* M. FLORIBUNDA.

sieboldi. Toringo crabapple. A shrub with spreading branches, and up to 15 ft. high. Young growth soft-hairy. Leaves 1–2½ in. long, broadly oval, with coarse marginal teeth, or 3- or 5-lobed. Flowers pink or deep rose in bud. Fruit pea-shaped, ⅓ in. in diameter, red or brownish yellow. This is the cult. dwarf mountain form. Jap. *Var.* **arborescens** is a graceful tree growing about 30 ft. high, with larger, less soft-hairy and less deeply lobed leaves than the typical form and with flowers nearly white. This is the common wild form. Hardy from zone* 3 southward. Also known as *Pyrus sieboldi*.

spectabilis. A small ornamental tree up to 25 ft. high. Leaves 2–4 in. long, narrower than those of the common apple, stiff, shiny, short-pointed. Flowers 1½–2 in. across, deep rose-red in bud, fading to blush, semi-double or single. Fruit ¾–1 in. in diameter, yellowish, sour and bitter. China, but not known in the wild. Often listed as *Pyrus spectabilis*. *Var.* **albi-plena** has double white flowers and is one of the handsomest crabapples when in bloom, though the fruit is not showy. A hort. form has double rose-pink flowers. *Var.* **riversi** has larger leaves, and larger double pink flowers. Hardy from zone* 3 southward.

sylvestris = M. *pumila.*

theifera. A small tree about 20 ft. high with stiff, spreading branches. Young growth soft-hairy, soon becoming smooth. Leaves 2–4 in. long, with sharp marginal teeth, pointed. Flowers 3–7 in a cluster, white or pinkish, fragrant. Fruit ⅓ in. across, greenish-yellow with red cheek. China and the Himalayas. Sometimes called *Malus hupehensis* and *Pyrus theifera.* Hardy from zone* 3 southward.

toringoides. A beautiful shrub or small tree, 25 ft. high. Young growth soft-hairy, soon becoming smooth. Leaves, 1–3 in. long, with sharp marginal teeth, often 3-lobed. Flowers 1 in. or less across, 6–12 in a cluster, white or pinkish. Fruit ½ in. in diameter, yellow, usually with red cheek. Western China. Frequently listed as *Pyrus toringoides*. Hardy from zone* 3 southward.

trilobata. A shrub or tree growing to 18 ft. high. Young growth soft-hairy. Leaves 3-lobed, with fine saw teeth on margin, 2–3 in. long, shining, bright green above. Flowers 1 in. across, 6–8 in a cluster, white. Fruit ¾ in. in diameter, longer than broad. Western As. Often known as *Pyrus trilobata*. Hardy from zone* 3 southward.

Zumi. A pyramidal tree, 20 ft. high. Similar to M. *sieboldi arborescens.* Leaves somewhat oval or oblong, 1½–3½ in. long, pointed, with marginal teeth, or lobed. Flowers 1 in. across, pink in bud, but becoming white. Fruit about ½ in. in diameter, round, red. Jap., but considered a hybrid between M. *baccata mandshurica* and M. *sieboldi.* Hardy from zone* 3 southward.

MALVA (mal'va). Mallow. About 30 species of widely distributed herbs of the family Malvaceae, several grown for ornament, but some rather weedy. They have alternate,* usually angled, lobed, or dissected leaves. Flowers mostly in the leaf axils,* solitary or clustered, most of them with 3 or 2 involucre*-like bracts beneath them. Calyx* united, but 5-cleft. Petals 5, with a notch at the tip, mostly pink or white. Fruit a collection of ultimately separable, but at first united, carpels, joined to form a depressed, cheese-shaped cluster. (*Malva* is from the Greek for emollient, in allusion to the mucilaginous juice of some species.)

These mallows are far less satisfactory than those found in the closely related genus *Hisbiscus* (which see). But *Malva* is of easy culture in any ordinary garden soil. The annuals may be sown where needed, as they are hardy annuals (*see* ANNUALS). The perennials are also of very simple cult., and may readily be divided in spring or fall. Besides the ones below there are several others which are mere weeds, although only *M. rotundifolia* is really a serious weed.

alcea. Vervain mallow; called also European mallow. A perennial resembling M. *moschata,* but its leaves only once-parted, each of the 5 parts not again divided. Eu.; sometimes an escape* in N.A.

chinensis = *Malva verticillata.*

crispa. Curled mallow. A rank-growing, unbranched annual, 4–10 ft. high, occasionally much more, the thick, nearly tree-like, stem leafy throughout. Leaves 5–7-lobed, the margins crisped or curled. Flowers scarcely ¼ in. wide, white, in dense clusters in the leaf axils.* Eu., often persisting in old gardens and sometimes an escape.*

moschata. Musk mallow; also called musk rose. A hairy, perennial herb 1–2 ft. high. Stem leaves 5-parted, the divisions cleft or divided into narrow segments. Flowers pink or white, nearly 2 in. wide, mostly confined to the upper leaf axils.* Fruit downy. Eu., but sometimes an escape in N.A. The var. **alba** always has white flowers.

pulchella = *Malva verticillata.*

rotundifolia. The common mallow, often called cheeses from the shape of its fruit. A common, prostrate herb, usually a pest and one of our worst weeds. Eurasia. *See* the list at WEEDS. Sometimes called M. *neglecta.*

verticillata. Curled mallow. An annual or perennial, rather weedy herb, not very different from M. *crispa,* but usually lower and with pink, stalkless flowers. Eurasia. Sometimes known as M. *pulchella* and M. *chinensis.*

MALVACEAE (mal-vay'see-ee). The mallow family is of much garden interest, for it contains many showy herbs, some foods, cotton, and a few shrubs and trees among its 50 genera and perhaps 1200 species, which are scattered all over the world.

Leaves alternate,* the main veins arising from the base of the blade, many of the leaves deeply lobed or cut, sometimes dissected. Flowers showy in many genera, especially in *Althaea* (*see* HOLLYHOCK), *Callirhoë, Hibiscus, Lavatera, Malope, Malvaviscus,* and *Sidalcea.* A common characteristic in most genera is a ring of bracts* just beneath each flower, sometimes very near the calyx.

Among tropical plants are *Abutilon, Hoheria, Lagunaria, Plagianthus,* and *Thespesia,* some of which are grown outdoors in frost-free parts of Calif. and Fla., or in the greenhouse. *Gossypium* is the cotton. *Malva* contains both decorative plants and weeds. *Pavonia* and *Sphaeralcea* complete the genera of garden interest.

---

* Special articles on the subjects indicated by an asterisk (*) will be found at the words so marked.

Technical flower characters: Flowers regular* and hermaphrodite,* usually with 5 petals and 5 sepals, both free, or the sepals sometimes united. Stamens numerous, united to form a tube which surrounds the styles. Ovary superior,* its often separate segments forming a dry fruit, the segments of which fall separately; rarely berry-like.

malvaeflora, -us, -um (mal-vee-flō'ra). With mallow-like flowers.

MALVASTRUM (mal-vas'trum). *See* SPHAERALCEA COCCINEA.

MALVAVISCUS (mal-va-vis'kus). Hairy, tropical American shrubs or shrubby herbs of the family Malvaceae, a few of the dozen species grown for ornament outdoors in zones* 8 and 9, rarely in the greenhouse northward. They have alternate,* more or less heart-shaped, somewhat lobed leaves. Flowers showy, red, somewhat resembling a closed abutilon, because the petals do not spread, and are more or less erect. Below each flower are 7–12 narrow bracts.* Stamens* protruding. Fruit berry-like and sticky at first, ultimately dry and separating into segments. (*Malvaviscus* means sticky mallow, in allusion to the fruit.)

Out of doors in Fla., the Gulf Coast, and in Calif., these plants, sometimes called Turk's-cap, are of easy cult. in a variety of soils. In the greenhouse they need potting mixture* 3 and a warm-temperate house. The Latin names are in some confusion, especially as to the identity of the commonest species in cult.

arboreus. Monacillo. A low shrub, not very different from *M. mollis,* with which it is often confused. It has smaller leaves than *M. mollis* and its leaves are not velvety as in that species. Tropical America. Sometimes sold as an abutilon.

conzatti. A shrub, the leaves more or less heart-shaped or ovalish, not usually lobed, but with rounded marginal teeth. Flowers nearly 2 in. long, red. Mex. and Guatemala. The plant offered as this is usually *M. grandiflorus.*

grandiflorus. A shrub 10–12 ft. high, the ovalish-oblong leaves scarcely lobed, but toothed. Flowers almost 2½ in. long, red. Mex. This is a showy shrub, perhaps more commonly cult. in the far South than any of the other species and blooms from late summer to frost. Also known as *M. penduliflorus.*

mollis. A low shrub, the leaves more or less angled or lobed, the margins wavy or toothed, velvety, especially on the under side. Flowers about 1½ in. long, scarlet. Mex. to northern S.A. Often grown in the South and in northern greenhouses, usually under the name of *M. arboreus.*

MAMEY = *Mammea americana. See also* ACHRAS.

MAMEY FAMILY = Guttiferae.

MAMMEA (mam'mee-a). A small genus of tropical trees of the family Guttiferae, only **M. americana,** the mamey or mammee-apple, of any hort. interest. It is cult. in the tropics for its edible fruit, but only to a very limited extent in the warmest parts of southern Fla. It is a tree 40–60 ft. high, with opposite,* thick, glossy leaves 6–8 in. long.

Flowers white, about 1 in. wide, fragrant (for details *see* GUTTIFERAE). Fruit a drupe,* nearly round, the rind russet, the flesh yellow, sweet in the best varieties, somewhat acid in the poorer ones. The fruit is nearly 6 in. in diameter and contains 1–4 large seeds, by which the plant is propagated. (*Mammea* is derived from mamey, the W.I. name for the cult. species.) For another plant, with a very different fruit, but also called mamey, *see* ACHRAS.

MAMMEE-APPLE = *Mammea americana.*

MAMMILLARIA (mam-mill-ā'rĭ-a). Pincushion cactus. A genus of over 300 species of globe-shaped, depressed, or shortly cylindric cacti, chiefly from the deserts of N.A., a few of them widely cult. in desert gardens and as house plants. The plant body is prominently tubercled instead of ribbed, the tubercles arranged in loose spirals and between them (*i.e.,* in the pits) there is usually a small tuft of hairs, wool, or bristles. At the tip of most tubercles is a collection of spines. Flowers day-blooming, somewhat bell-shaped, not large but often brilliantly colored. Fruit berry-like. The plants are sometimes known as *Neomammillaria.* (*Mammillaria* is in allusion to the nipple-like tubercles.)

Cactus fanciers and specialists are known to grow over 50 species of these popular succulents, but of these only a few are likely to interest the average grower. Many plants, often credited to *Mammillaria* are now credited to other genera. Those admitted to the ENCYCLOPEDIA should be sought at CORYPHANTHA, EPITHELANTHA, ESCOBARIA, PEDIOCACTUS, and STROMBOCACTUS.

For culture *see* CACTI.

bocasana. A clustered, mound-forming cactus, the individuals nearly round and about 1½ in. in diameter. Tubercles roundish, stiff-hairy at their bases. Spines 50 or more in a cluster, silky or hairy, with a central, hooked, brown spine. Flowers tan-colored. Mex.

camptotricha. A clustered cactus, the individuals nearly spherical and about 2 in. in diameter. Tubercles elongated, curved, hairy at the base. Spines only 2–4, bristle-like, twisted, yellowish. Flowers white, about ½ in. long, greenish within. Mex.

carnea. A solitary, cylindric cactus, about 3 in. high, not clump-forming. Tubercles with woolly bases, 4-angled and nearly ½ in. long. The 4 spines are of unequal length. Flowers flesh-pink, about 1 in. long. Mex.

celsiana. A solitary cactus, roundish at first, ultimately cylindric and 4–5 in. high. Tubercles woolly at base, cone-shaped. Spines 24–26 in each cluster, with 4–7 central yellow spines about ½ in. long. Flowers red. Mex.

compressa. Usually growing in small clumps, the plant body more or less cylindric, bluish-green. The pits between the tubercles are woolly. Spines usually 4 to a cluster. Flowers about ½ in. long, pink. Central Mex.

elegans. A depressed-globose cactus, flattened at the top and about 2 in. in diameter. Tubercles egg-shaped, slightly or not at all woolly at their bases. Spines bristle-like, white, 25–30 in a cluster, with 1–3 central spines. Flowers red. Mex.

---

* Special articles on the subjects indicated by an asterisk (*) will be found at the words so marked.

elongata. A clump-forming, erect or prostrate cactus, the individuals nearly 4 in. long and densely spiny. Tubercles without basal hairs or bristles. Spines very numerous, interlacing, and without a group of central spines. Flowers white. Mex.

geminispina. A bright green, somewhat cylindric cactus, woolly between the tubercles and very spiny. Spines 16–24 in each cluster, 2–4 erect, all the rest spreading, all bright-colored but with black tips, hence very striking. Flowers dark red. Central Mex.

gigantea. A usually solitary (rarely in clumps) cactus, globose, about 4 in. high, flattened at the top and much wider than high. Tubercles woolly at the base, long, somewhat angled. Spines in groups of 12, with 4–6 central spines. Flowers greenish-yellow. Mex.

heyderi. A globose cactus, somewhat flattened at the top. Tubercles woolly at the base, cone-shaped. Spines bristle-like, white, 20–22 in a group with a single central brownish spine. Flowers pink. N. Mex. and Tex.

lasiacantha. Plant body not much over 1 in. in diameter, nearly globe-shaped, extremely spiny, the pits between the minute tubercles not woolly. Spines 40–60 at each cluster, hairy, scarcely 1/10 in. long. Flowers nearly 1/2 in. long, pinkish. Western Tex. and northern Mex.

plumosa. Feather-ball. Plant body very small, usually growing in clusters, the whole completely hidden by the mass of short white spines, underneath which is the white wool of the tubercle-pits. Flowers about 1/4 in. long, white. N. Mex. and northern Mex.

rhodantha. Plant body more or less cylindric, nearly 10 in. high, the pits of the roundish tubercles bristly. Spines 15–26 at a cluster, white, 4–6 in the center erect, the rest divergent. Flowers about 1/2 in. wide, rose-pink. Mex.

schiedeana. A clump-forming cactus, the individuals nearly round, about 2 1/2 in. in diameter. Tubercles white-bristly at their bases. Spines white, bristle-like, 30 in a group with 6–8 central spines. Flowers about 1/2 in. long, white. Mex.

sempervivi. A solitary or somewhat clump-forming cactus, the individuals broader at the top than at the base. Tubercles very woolly at the base, angled. Spines 3–7 in a group, often falling out, and with 2 central brown spines about 1/8 in. long. Flowers white, red-striped. Mex.

spinosissima. Plant body more or less cylindric, 9–12 in. long and about 4 in. thick, the tubercles not prominent, the pits bristly. The whole plant is covered with spines, of which there are about 28 at each spine-cluster. Flowers about 1/2 in. long, purplish. Central Mex.

tetracantha. A usually solitary, but sometimes clump-forming cactus, the individuals nearly 3 in. in diameter and spherical. Tubercles woolly at the base, faintly angled. Spines yellowish-white, 4 in a group, with no central spines. Flowers rose-pink. Mex.

mammillaris, -e (mam-mill-ar'is). With nipple-like protuberances.

mammosa, -us, -um (mam-mō'sa). With breasts or nipples.

MAMMOTH CLOVER = *Trifolium pratense serotinum.* See CLOVER.

MAMONCILLO = *Melicocca bijuga.*

MANCA CABALLO = *Homalocephala texensis.*

MANDACARU = *Cereus Jamacaru.*

MANDARIN ORANGE = *Cirus nobilis deliciosa.*

MANDEVILLA (man-de-vil'la). Tropical American, woody vines of the family Apocynaceae, comprising perhaps 50 species, of which **M. suaveolens,** the Chilean jasmine, is the only species of hort. interest. It is a high-climbing, woody vine with opposite,* oblong or heart-shaped leaves, 1–3 in. long, and pale bluish-green beneath. Flowers fragrant, showy, white or pinkish, more or less funnel-shaped, nearly 2 in. wide, mostly in loose clusters (racemes*). Fruit consisting of 2 pods (follicles*). The plant is widely grown as an outdoor subject in the southern U.S. If grown in the greenhouse, it needs a warm-temperate house (*see* GREENHOUSE), and should be planted direct, not in a pot or tub. It needs a peaty, sandy loam, and is propagated by cuttings over bottom-heat. While called Chilean jasmine, it is a native of the Argentine. (Named for Henry J. Mandeville, British minister at Buenos Aires.)

MANDIOCA = *Manihot esculenta.*

MANDRAGORA (man-drag'o-ra). A genus of stemless perennials, belonging to the potato family. They have thick, tuberous roots, divided into 2 leg-like branches, hence the name mandrake. Leaves growing from the tips of the roots, simple,* undivided, but with wavy margins. Flowers purple or violet-blue, cup-shaped, borne in clusters on stems rising between the leaves. Fruit an oblong, juicy berry which contains the seeds. (*Mandragora* was the name used by Hippocrates, said to mean that the plant is hurtful to cattle.) Mandrake in America means the mayapple (*Podophyllum*).

There are many superstitions connected with this plant; some say it is the dudaim mentioned in Genesis. It is related to the belladonna, has poisonous qualities, and is not usually cultivated. One of the legends concerns the Crucifixion.

autumnalis. A small form of the next, with violet flowers and smaller roots and leaves. Southern Eu. and northern Af.

officinarum. Common mandrake. Height about 1 ft., the roots spindle-shaped, often branching. Leaves ovalish, nearly 1 ft. long. Flowers bluish, about 1 in. long. Southern Eu. Also called devil's-apple.

MANDRAKE. Traditionally mandrake is *Mandragora officinarum* (which see), but in America the name is often applied to the mayapple (*Podophyllum peltatum*). See MAYAPPLE.

mandshurica, -us, -um (mand-sure'i-ka). From Manchuria.

MANEB. See FUNGICIDES.

MANETTIA (ma-net'ti-a). Tropical American, woody vines of the family Rubiaceae, two of the 40 known species grown for ornament. Leaves evergreen, opposite* (in ours). Flowers yellow and red (in ours), the corolla more or less tubular, the lobes

---

* Special articles on the subjects indicated by an asterisk (*) will be found at the words so marked.

spreading or slightly recurved. Stamens*
4–5. Fruit a 2-valved, many-seeded capsule.* (Named for Xavier Manetti, a Florentine botanist.)

The two below are often grown as greenhouse vines, as they will clamber over rafters,
trellises, etc. They need a cool greenhouse
and potting mixture* 3, and may be propagated by cuttings over bottom-heat.* Outdoors their cult. must be confined to zones*
8 and 9, and they are grown in Calif. and
Fla.

bicolor. A smooth vine with nearly stalkless, lance-shaped leaves. Flowers solitary,
about ¾ in. long, red below but yellow-tipped,
the lobes of the calyx* more or less erect.
Style* protruding. Brazil.

inflata. Resembling the last, but the stems
hairy and the leaves hairy on the veins beneath. Flowers also similar, but the lobes of
the calyx* recurved, and the style* not protruding. Paraguay and Uruguay.

MANETTI ROSE = *Rosa chinensis manetti.*

MANETTI-VINE = *Boussingaultia baselloides.*

MANFREDA. See Agave virginica.

MANGEL-WURZEL. See Rutabaga.

MANGIFERA. See Mango.

MANGO. Asiatic or Indo-Malayan fruit
trees, comprising the genus Mangifera (man-
jif'fer-ra), of the sumac family, comprising
perhaps 20 species, of which M. indica, the
common mango, is of a world-wide cult.
throughout the tropics, and, as noted below,
to a limited extent in the U.S. It is a splendid, round-headed tree up to 90 ft. high,
with lance-shaped, alternate leaves, 8–14
in. long. Flowers small, pinkish-white,
scarcely ⅓ in. long, usually in terminal clusters (panicles*) and sometimes polygamous.*
Fruit large, fleshy, aromatic (often with a
turpentine odor), drupe*-like, usually red
or yellowish-orange, very juicy, and not long-
keeping. (*Mangifera* is from *mango*, the
original vernacular for the best-known species, and from the Latin to bear, in allusion
to the fruit.) Its young growth is pinkish.

Mango Culture

The mango is among the oldest and most
highly esteemed of cult. fruits, and because
of its excellent quality and widespread usage
has been termed the "apple of the tropics"
and "king of fruits." Native to tropical As.,
it is now found throughout the tropics in
plantings of few to many irregularly planted
trees and is seldom grown in numbers in
regular orchard form. Strictly tropical in requirements, the tree endures but little frost,
and is grown in the U.S. only in southern
Fla. and in a very limited way in Calif.
Although first introduced into Fla. over one
hundred years ago, the past quarter-century
has seen the greatest development in its culture and the fruit is now produced in fair
quantity.

The smooth-skinned, ovoid-pointed fruits,
yellow to red in color, are most attractive

in appearance. Choice grafted varieties are
not to be confused with the more common
"turpentine" sorts. The former are rich,
sweet, and spicy, with flesh of melting texture and free of objectionable fibers; the
latter, although quite edible, have a fibrous
flesh and distinct turpentine flavor. There
is much variation in shape and size of the
fruit, that of common seedlings usually being
small, while better varieties may weigh up
to 3 lbs. or more. Ripe fruits contain from
11 to 19 per cent sugar — in the form of
sucrose, ½ to 1 per cent protein, little or no
starch, and are a source of vitamins A and C.
Served principally as a dessert, the fruit
also may be used in the preparation of
chutneys, sherbets and preserves.

But few of the hundreds of named varieties are grown in Fla. These include for
the most part the Haden, Kent, Keitt, Zill,
Irwin, Edward, Palmer, and Sensation. The
Haden, because of its quality, large size,
attractive color, and free-bearing habit, is
most widely planted. Beginning in May, the
season of maturity extends with a few varieties into late fall.

Although thriving on some of the poorest
of sandy soils, the trees attain their greatest
size on more fertile types. They are symmetrical in growth habit and are planted
extensively for their shade and ornamental
value. The large size in maturity requires
wide spacing for maximum development,
usually not less than 30 × 30 ft. Fertilizers
are of value, but an excess of nitrogen may
stimulate too much vegetative growth at the
expense of fruit production. Bearing age is
reached in 5 to 7 years, and the trees are
exceptionally long-lived.

Propagation is commonly by veneer grafting and budding, and to some extent by
inarching, crown grafting, and by seeds. —
G. D. R.

Insect Pests. Mites and scales are controlled by dormant 1.5% superior oil sprays.
Addition of pesticide #21 increases effectiveness. Summer sprays of pesticide #14 or
currently recommended miticides will stop summer mite infestations. Thrips are controlled
by pesticide #1. (See Sprays and Dusts.)

Diseases. The most serious disease is anthracnose* which spots the foliage and flowers,
and stains and rots the fruit. The disease can
be controlled with pesticide #2 (see Sprays
and Dusts) applied at 7-day intervals during
flowering period and at 14-day intervals after
flowering.

MANGO FAMILY = Anacardiaceae.

MANGO MELON. See Melon.

Mangostana (man-go-stan'a). Latinized
form of mangostan, the Malayan name for
the mangosteen.

MANGOSTEEN. See Garcinia.

manicata, -us, -um (man-i-kay'ta). Long-
sleeved; often applied to flowers with a long,
tubular calyx.*

MANIHOT (man'ĭ-hot). A very large,
chiefly Brazilian genus of herbs, shrubs, and
trees of the family Euphorbiaceae, of far

---

* Special articles on the subjects indicated by an asterisk (*) will be found at the words so marked.

more economic than hort. significance, at least in the U.S. They have alternate,* often lobed or cut, but simple* leaves and a milky juice. In some, especially the herbs, there is an immense starchy root, poisonous in the most important species until treated, but yielding a farina used as a staple food by all Brazilian natives, who call it manioc or mandioca. Elsewhere, and the plant is now grown all over the tropical world, it is called cassava and is the chief source of tapioca. Other species, all trees, produce an inferior sort of rubber. Flowers greenish-yellow, the male and female in different clusters on the same plant, both without petals. (For details see EUPHORBIACEAE.) Fruit a capsule.* (*Manihot* is a native Brazilian name for these plants.)

The only species of any importance in the U.S. is *M. esculenta*, the common cassava, which is grown in Fla. more for stock food than anything else. It is occasionally grown in northern greenhouses, where it needs a warm but dry house. All the species are easily propagated by cuttings over bottom-heat.*

carthaginensis. Yuquilla. A medium-sized tree, the leaves 5–7-lobed, the lobes again parted or divided. Flowers in small clusters (racemes*), the calyx* about ½ in. long. A desert tree ranging from southern Tex. to S.A.; little known in cult.

dulcis. Sweet cassava. A shrubby herb 3–12 ft. high, perhaps not distinct from the next, but its root smaller and not initially poisonous. Brazil. There are several varieties cult. in the tropics, but the plant is little known here.

esculenta. Cassava or tapioca-plant; in Brazil called manioc or mandioca. A woody herb or a shrub, 3–9 ft. high, the leaves 3–7-parted, the lobes narrow, tapering, 4–8 in. long. Flowering cluster a panicle,* the calyx less than ½ in. long. Brazil. The poisonous roots, which may weigh 20 pounds, are rendered wholesome by a process of maceration, pressure to squeeze out some of the juice, and finally heat to drive off the rest. The plant is also known as *M. utilissima.*

utilissima = *Manihot esculenta.*

MANILA GRASS = *Zoysia Matrella.*

MANILA HEMP = *Musa textilis.*

MANILA TAMARIND = *Pithecolobium dulce.*

MANIOC = *Manihot esculenta.*

MANITOBA. The province lies wholly in zone* 1.

SOILS. A wide range of soil types, from light sand to heavy gumbo clay, including acid peat, is to be found. In general, the northern and eastern portion is of granite formation, tending to somewhat acid reaction, whereas the southwestern or prairie section is considered as of limestone formation and is usually neutral or slightly alkaline. The Red River Valley is, to large extent, heavy clay.

GARDENING CENTERS

VEGETABLE GARDENING on an extensive scale is found chiefly near the city of Winni-

peg, and there notably on the silty clay soil near the Red and Assiniboine rivers. The produce of the market gardeners is known widely for its excellent quality. Cauliflower, tomatoes, sweet corn, cabbage, celery, cucumbers, beans, peas, muskmelons, and root crops are grown under auspicious conditions. The canning industry has specialized in peas and beans. There is a growing development in commercial vegetable gardening for local trade near other cities and large towns.

SMALL FRUITS. The culture of small fruits has recently spread over a considerable territory from the Brokenhead River on the east, and Dauphin on the north, to near the Saskatchewan boundary on the west. Raspberries and strawberries are mostly grown. Gooseberries are considered a reliable crop, but there is only moderate market demand for these and currants. It is considered highly desirable to have facilities to water artificially during periods of dry weather.

TREE FRUITS. Apples, plums, and sand cherry (*Prunus besseyi*) hybrids are grown in home gardens as far north as Swan River, but commercial plantations are chiefly in southern Manitoba, near the eastern slope of the Pembina Mountains, but to some extent also on the eastern slope of, or near the eastern side of, the Riding Mountains, and in the Turtle Mountains.

The apples grown are Russian varieties, hardy productions from the Central Experimental Farm, Ottawa, and from the experi-

MANITOBA

The zones of hardiness crossing Manitoba are those shown on the map located at ZONE, which should be consulted for details. The dates are the average latest killing frost in spring and the first one in the fall. The figures below the dates show the average length of the growing season. Rainfall figures (in inches) show (1) the total annual rainfall and (2) the amount falling in the growing season at the places indicated.

---

* Special articles on the subjects indicated by an asterisk (*) will be found at the words so marked.

ment stations of Minnesota and South Dakota, and seedlings of these which have been developed around Morden.

Recommended plum varieties are limited nearly altogether to select natives, and to hybrids which carry some blood of native plums or sand cherries. *Prunus nigra* is found growing in the woodlands as far north as the Duck Mountains, and the sand cherry as far as Hudson Bay Junction.

Cherries are mostly of Russian Morello types and *Prunus tomentosa*. These are planted for home use.

Grapes of eastern early-maturing varieties are ripened successfully in southern areas, but require winter mulching of the vines. The native *Vitis vulpina* is fairly common in the Riding Mountains.

GREENHOUSE CROPS. Tomatoes and cucumbers are grown under glass in some bulk near Winnipeg. However, most Manitoba glass is reserved for growing cut flowers, pot plants, and bedding stock.

ORNAMENTAL TREES AND FLOWERS. The prairies are featured by considerable air movement, and a first consideration of the farm home is tree shelter. Materials mostly used are *Caragana*, green ash, white spruce, box-elder, willow, poplar, and Scotch pine. *See* WINDBREAK.

Ornamental trees in popular favor include native mountain-ash, white birch, Colorado spruce, Swiss stone pine, Amur maple, hackberry, basswood, Russian olive, and Ohio buckeye. Shrubs most used are *Caragana*, lilacs, honeysuckle, spireas, dogwoods, hawthorns, viburnums, elder, sumac, tamarisk, dwarf willows, buffaloberry, *Cotoneaster*, golden currant, flowering plum, Russian almond, and bush roses. The better classes of roses require soil mulch for winter protection. Woody vines in common use are native grape, bittersweet, Virginia creeper, hardy clematis, and climbing honeysuckle.

An extensive list of herbaceous perennials are grown effectively. Those esteemed include peony, iris, delphinium, lilies, *Gypsophila*, *Dianthus*, asters, monkshood, spireas, hollyhock, hardy phlox, sedums, campanulas, daisies, and tulips.

A number of nursery firms catering to the prairie trade are located at different centers.

CLIMATE. Manitoba horticulture is limited by comparatively low winter temperatures and uncertain summer precipitation. These disadvantages are lessened by establishing a shelter belt with snowtrap and a local system of irrigation.

FROST DATA

Town	Average date of last frost of 29° F. or lower	Latest-known killing frost
Winnipeg	May 13	May 27
Brandon	May 21	June 21
Morden	May 17	June 7
Dauphin	May 17	May 23

FROST DATA

Town	Average date of earliest frost of 29°	Earliest-known killing frost
Winnipeg	Sept. 30	Sept. 13
Brandon	Sept. 19	Aug. 28
Morden	Sept. 28	Aug. 26
Dauphin	Sept. 29	Sept. 12

RAINFALL

Town	Total annual precipitation	Total precipitation April 1 to Sept. 30
Winnipeg	20.59	14.28
Brandon	15.47	11.22
Morden	17.65	12.48
Dauphin	16.30	11.22

The above information is supplied by the Dominion Experimental Station, Morden, Manitoba. The station is always ready to answer questions pertaining to gardening.

MANNA ASH = *Fraxinus Ornus*. *See* ASH.

MANNA GUM = *Eucalyptus viminalis*.

MAN-OF-THE-EARTH = *Ipomoea pandurata*.

MANROOT = *Ipomoea pandurata*.

MANURE. Not so long ago a school of chiefly feminine gardeners did not admit the word *manure* into polite hort. discussion. The absurdity of such fastidiousness is now everywhere admitted. For manure is the dung of animals, and as such is very different from any commercial or chemical fertilizer, however carefully prepared. Whether or not, as we shall see presently, it is as rich in plant nutrients as some of the commercial fertilizers, it has been for three thousand years the chief supply of the things that plants need.

There is little use in comparing the relative merits of fertilizers and manure. Their function is different. In the case of fertilizers definite chemicals are put into the soil for a relatively quick and sure return so far as the immediate crop is concerned. That result is fairly certain, other things like good cultivation, the proper climate, and freedom from pests being assumed. But it must never be forgotten that commercial fertilizers add little permanent value to the soils, and it is exactly this thing which most manures accomplish. Soil cannot be indefinitely treated as a laboratory to produce crops and only that percentage of nutrients added to it that chemical analyses show to be the chief needs of the crops. Because manure, or the dung of animals, adds much more than this to the soil, it always will, or should, have an important place in any permanent garden scheme.

Manure is much more than a chemical

* Special articles on the subjects indicated by an asterisk (*) will be found at the words so marked.

analysis of it shows. The processes of digestion, combustion, and final evacuation of the food of the manure-producing animals leave much undigested vegetable matter in the excrement. In the case of bedded animals, like cows and horses, the bedding (usually straw or sphagnum moss or sawdust) is naturally mixed with the excrement, so that what we call manure is a compound of partly decomposed vegetable matter (the bedding) and the nutrients contained in the excrement itself. In fresh manure the strawy material predominates, but in well-rotted manure the straw is much reduced and, by weight or volume, the well-rotted manure is thus far more valuable and consequently much more expensive. It has also been shown that manure contains needed trace elements, which chemical fertilizers do not unless they have been added. *See* TRACE ELEMENTS.

COMPARISON OF COMMON MANURES

While manure is used as a definite crop stimulator, its greatest value is that it not only does this, but adds a large proportion of humus to the soil. The great item of its value in this regard is that while commercial fertilizers add not one scrap to the moisture-holding capacity of a soil, manure adds a great deal. *See* HUMUS.

Apart from this humus content, manures differ in their chemical constituents, and a comparison of the leading sources of manure should be known to all prospective purchasers of it. The U.S. Department of Agriculture has published the following figures:

AVERAGE COMPOSITION OF FRESH MANURES PER TON

Source	Nitrogen	Phosphoric acid	Potash
	lbs.	lbs.	lbs.
Hen	20	16	10
Hen, air-dried	40	30	19
Sheep	20	9	17
Sheep, air-dried	45	20	40
Hog	13	7	10
Horse	11	6	13
Cow	9	6	8
Mixed	10	5	10

HORSE MANURE. The leading source of manure and the most valuable, as it is the quickest to decompose. If not used fresh, a practice which is not advisable in small, hand-worked gardens, because of the straw in fresh manure, it can be stacked in heaps, never more than 4 ft. deep, and allowed to decompose. It will take about 6–8 months of handling to produce well-rotted manure, during which time it should be turned two or three times and kept pretty wet to prevent spontaneous combustion. The wetting or rainfall should not be allowed to leach out the valuable constituents of this farmyard product. It is a common sight, on poorly managed farms, to see coffee-colored water running away from badly constructed or inadequately covered manure piles. Such a procedure is simply wasting the most valuable, because most soluble, constituents of the manure. Lime in any form should never be added to the manure pile.

Horse manure, in intensively cultivated crops, can be spread 3 in. deep and plowed or harrowed into the soil. Commercial growers often use it at the rate of 50 tons per acre. If you purchase it, see that your bids are for cubic yards, not tons, as the latter method of purchase often means paying for water hosed into the pile the day before. Fresh horse manure generates more heat than any other kind, and is the only one useful to put in the pit of a hotbed.

COW MANURE. Slower acting than horse manure but usually less strawy, and it can often be applied directly to the soil without composting. It is especially valuable in making liquid manure (which see). Many growers prefer it for water lilies, and when it is dried and easier to handle than in the fresh state, it is widely used by experienced gardeners for greenhouse potting soil. *See* POTTING MIXTURES.

HOG MANURE. Not widely available, but, as the table shows, it is a valuable source of plant food. Many commercial market gardeners find it profitable, but its foul odor makes it unsuited to most home gardens.

HEN AND POULTRY MANURE. Because of its ease of handling and its richness in plant food, chicken manure is one of the most valuable of all manures for the small garden. If you cannot purchase it and wish to use it from your own poultry (hens, ducks, or turkeys), see that the dropping boards are covered with a thin layer of acid phosphate to which a little dry soil or sand has been added. Clean the boards once a week and allow the mixture to dry a little before using. No lime should be used on the dropping boards. Hen manure is especially valuable because it contains not only nitrogen but large percentages of phosphoric acid and potash. Guano is about as valuable as chicken manure, but must always be purchased. When available, pigeon manure is about the same as any bird manure, all of which must be used with care as they are relatively strong. Do not let them touch roots.

SHEEP MANURE. This, when fresh, will produce nearly as much heat as horse manure. But few gardeners have access to it in this state and it is better to buy it, dry, from dealers. Its value is approximately that of hen manure, so that its use should be dictated by cost and availability.

OTHER MANURES

Besides the more usual sources of manure, there are a few special plant foods, usually classed as manures, although they are not so, strictly speaking.

FISH. The Indians used fish for the cul-

---

* Special articles on the subjects indicated by an asterisk (*) will be found at the words so marked.

tivation of their corn. It is still used along the coast by fishermen who combine fishing and gardening. Used chiefly for its nitrogen and phosphoric acid, fish has only about half, or even less, of these substances than manure. Because of its odor and relatively low value as fertilizer, fish should only be used where it is very cheap. Its use is forbidden in some sections due to the odor when decomposing. The only way to avoid this is to follow the old Indian plan of burying the fish.

SEAWEED. Along the coasts there are many gardeners who use seaweed, wrack, and sometimes salt-marsh ooze for fertilizer or manure. The only value of such material beyond, of course, its humus content, is in the potash it contains. Compared to stable manure it is low in nitrogen and especially in phosphoric acid. If you live near a source of supply, it should be remembered that seaweed is best collected in Jan.–Mar. and plowed under as soon as possible. If stacked for long, it becomes simply a slimy mass with which nothing can be done. Eel-grass, however, can be stacked, as it is not a seaweed and has more fiber. It is, however, of less fertilizing value than seaweed.

The commercial harvesting of the giant kelp of the Pacific Coast is done for the potash extracted from it. Kelp, one of the largest seaweeds in the world, cannot be put on the land directly. *See also* COTTON-SEED MEAL.

SYNTHETIC OR ARTIFICIAL MANURE. During World War I there was, with much reason, a tremendous amount of interest in a discovery made at the Rothamsted Experiment Station in England. It involves the use of straw, leaves, crop remains, grass cuttings, or other refuse vegetable matter. To this certain chemicals are added, under the conditions noted below, and the result is what is widely known as artificial or synthetic manure. The process was patented in England and here under the trade name of Adco.

Since then many American Experiment Stations have published formulas for the production of synthetic manure, which compares very favorably with stable manure. The agricultural experiment stations of N.Y., Pa., Iowa, Wis., and R.I. have all worked on this, well knowing that the passing of the horse and the increasing cost of stable manure make a serious situation for gardeners. The consensus of opinion on the production of artificial manure gives the following directions:

Make a pile of vegetable refuse (*see* above), not over 4–6 ft. high. Make the pile of 6-in. layers which should be tramped or packed down, thoroughly watered, and on which should be sprinkled the salts to be described presently. Keep on packing the 6-in. layers and following the plan until the pile is the desired height, making the top with a central depression to hold all rain water. Do not fail to water each layer

nor to put the salts on it, as the process is only effective when these details have been carefully attended to.

Water the pile with a hose frequently, and if it shows a tendency to heat up, the pile must be forked over. Fermentation, however, is what is desired, and if directions have been followed it should begin within a week. At ordinary summer temperatures (slower in cool weather) the refuse will in three or four months resemble well-rotted horse manure in texture and composition.

In calculating the amount of straw, etc., figure that 1 ton of dry straw will make about 2 tons of synthetic manure, fermentation and the large amount of water explaining the increase. For one ton of dry straw about 150 pounds of salts will be needed, divided as follows: about 70 pounds of ammonium sulphate, 60 pounds of ground limestone, and 20 pounds of superphosphate. Those who do not want to bother with this mixing can use Adco or similar prepared products.

When completed, the synthetic or artificial manure can be used like well-rotted stable manure.

How to Use Manure

There is little danger of using too much manure so long as it is plowed under and the land left without planting for two or three weeks. Manure is so expensive that it is necessary to know how little to use rather than caution one not to use too much.

A generous allowance of well-rotted stable manure is 32 tons to the acre, but half this amount will often produce 80% of the crop that would have developed if the 32 tons had been used. In other words, doubling the manure does not necessarily double the crop, and in fact it very rarely does. Manure being costly, it is better to use it sparingly, and for most gardens 16–20 tons per acre is ample. For small gardens use about 1 ton for an area 30 × 70 ft.

For stable manure much the best plan is to spread it early in the season and plow it under a week or two before planting time. Fresh manure needs a longer period between plowing under and planting time, preferably two or three months.

Guano and the manures from hens, sheep, etc., while higher in plant food than stable manure, contain far less humus. This fact and their cost limit their use to sprinkling between the rows of vegetables and working them into the soil with a hoe or wheel cultivator. They are strong and should not touch the plants nor be sown in the drills unless thoroughly covered with soil.

For those who cannot get manure, there is a very good substitute provided by the use of fertilizers and by what is called green manuring. *See* FERTILIZERS, GREEN MANURING, HUMUS. *See also* LIQUID MANURE.

MANZANITA. *See* ARCTOSTAPHYLOS.

MAPLE. About 120 species of American and Old World, mostly deciduous trees, rarely

---

* Special articles on the subjects indicated by an asterisk (*) will be found at the words so marked.

shrubs, constituting the genus **Acer** (ā'sir) of the family Aceraceae. The leaves are opposite,* simple and lobed, or compound.* The flowers commonly unisexual,* small, in terminal clusters (panicles*) or flat-topped clusters (corymbs*). Fruit a two-winged key (samara*). (*Acer* is the ancient Latin name of the maple.)

Many of the maples are grown as shade trees, also for their ornamental foliage which often assumes brilliant hues in the fall, and for timber. They have a watery juice, in some species used to make syrup and sugar. For culture *see* below.

A. buergerianum. A small tree, the young growth smooth. Leaves 3-lobed, 1–2 in. across, lobes triangular, margins toothed, dark green above, pale beneath. Flowers small, in a compound, soft-hairy, terminal cluster (panicle*). Fruit smooth, the wings parallel. Eastern China and Jap. May. Hardy from zone* 4 southward.

A. campestre. A round-headed tree 30 ft. or less high, the branches slightly corky. Leaves 3–5-lobed, 2–4 in. across, dull green above, soft-hairy beneath, turning yellow in autumn. Flowers greenish, in erect, flat-topped clusters (corymbs*). Fruit usually soft-hairy, the wings spreading horizontally. Eurasia. May. Hardy from zone* 2 southward and heat-tolerant.

A. cappadocicum. A tree 50 ft. high. Leaves 5–7-lobed, heart-shaped at base, 3½–5½ in. across. Flowers pale yellow, small, in smooth, flat-topped clusters (corymbs*). Fruit with wings spreading at a wide angle. Caucasus, western As. to Himalayas. May–June. Hardy from zone* 4 southward.

A. circinatum. Vine maple. Small, round-headed tree 30 ft. high, more usually a wide-spreading shrub with handsome foliage, beginning to color red and orange in late summer and early autumn. Branches smooth, slender. Leaves 7–9-lobed, 4–5 in. across, with marginal teeth. Flowers small, in 6–20 flowered, flat-topped clusters (corymbs*). Petals white, the sepals purple and larger. Fruit with wings spreading almost horizontally. British Columbia to Calif. April–May. Hardy from zone* 3 southward, but poor at low altitudes.

A. dasycarpum = *Acer saccharinum.*

A. Ginnala. A shrub or tree 20 ft. high. Branches smooth and slender. The leaves 3-lobed, 1½–4 in. long, the end lobe usually much longer than the side ones, with marginal teeth, dark green and shiny above, light green beneath. Flowers yellowish-white, fragrant, in compound, terminal clusters (panicles*). Fruit smooth with wings nearly parallel. Central and north China, Manchuria and Jap. May. Hardy from zone* 3 southward.

A. griseum. Paperbark maple. A tree, not over 25 ft. high, its papery, gray, flaking bark resembling that of the paper birch. Leaves compound, the 3 leaflets elliptic or ovalish, 1½–4 in. long, coarsely toothed. Flowers in short-stalked, hairy clusters (racemes*). Fruit hanging, its wings spreading. China. May. Hardy from zone* 5 southward.

A. japonicum. Shrub or small tree. Leaves light green, turning crimson in autumn, smooth, 7–11-lobed, 3–5½ in. across, with marginal teeth or lobes. Flowers purple, in flat-topped clusters (corymbs*). Fruit with wings spreading almost horizontally. Jap. May. Hardy from zone* 4 southward.

A. macrophyllum. Oregon maple. A large, stately tree, growing 100 ft. high. Leaves deeply 3–5-lobed or cut, 1 ft. or more across, dark green, almost leathery, pale green beneath, turning brilliant yellow or orange in fall. Flowers yellow, fragrant, in narrow, hanging compound clusters (panicles*) 5 in. long. Fruit with wings of key spreading at right angle or nearly upright, the nutlet with stiff, yellow hairs. Alaska to Calif. Often planted as a shade tree where native. May. Hardy from zone* 4 southward.

A. Negundo. Box-elder. A quick-growing tree 70 ft. high. Leaves compound,* the 3–5 leaflets arranged feather-fashion (pinnate*), bright green, 2–4 in. long. Flowers before the leaves, yellowish-green, the male in flat-topped clusters (corymbs*), the female in hanging, terminal clusters (racemes*), borne on separate trees. Fruit with wings set at an acute angle and usually incurved. The typical form from New England and Ontario to Minn., Neb., Kan., Tex., and Fla. Very hardy and frequently planted for shelter belts in the Northwest. March–April. Hardy from zone* 1 southward. *Var.* **variegatum** has white-margined leaves.

A. nigrum. Black maple. A native tree, 70–120 ft. high, with furrowed blackish bark. Leaves 3-lobed, 5–7 in. wide, dull above, yellowish-green and softly hairy beneath. Flowers yellow-green. Fruit smooth. Eastern N.A. westward to S.D. Hardy from zone* 2 southward. April.

A. palmatum. Japanese maple. Small, graceful tree to 25 ft., or a shrub. Branchlets smooth and slender. Leaves 5–9-lobed or divided, 2–4 in. across, the lobes with marginal teeth and pointed, smooth, turning bright red in fall. Flowers purple, small, in small, flat-topped clusters (corymbs*). Fruit with wings spreading at an obtuse angle and incurved, the nutlet smooth. Korea and Jap. Introduced about 1820. There are many horticultural varieties, of which the leaves are of many forms and colors. *See* below. Hardy from zone* 3 southward.

A. pensylvanicum. Moosewood; also known as striped maple. A small tree, sometimes 40 ft. high. Branchlets green, striped with white lines, conspicuous in winter. Leaves round to broadly oval, 3-lobed at the tip, 4–7 in. long, the lobes long-pointed, rusty, soft-hairy beneath when young, turning bright yellow in fall. Flowers yellow, in drooping, terminal clusters (racemes*), 7 in. long. Fruit with wings spreading at a wide angle. Cooler parts of eastern N.A. May–June. Hardy from zone* 2 southward, but poor at low altitudes.

A. platanoides. Norway maple. A smooth tree, attaining 100 ft. in height. Leaves 5-lobed, 4–7 in. across, bright green, with marginal teeth, turning yellow in autumn. Flowers greenish-yellow, in erect, many-flowered, stalked, flat-topped clusters (corymbs*). Fruit drooping, with horizontally spreading wings. There are many varieties. Eu. and Caucasus. Long cultivated, and blooming before the leaves unfold. April–May. Hardy from zone* 2 southward. The *var.* **schwedleri**, usually called Schwedler's maple, has handsome red young foliage, which ultimately becomes green. The *var.* **Crimson King** keeps the deep-red color of its foliage throughout the season. The *var.* **globosum** is a lower, round-headed form.

A. Pseudo-platanus. Sycamore maple. A large, vigorously growing tree, sometimes 100 ft. high. Leaves 5-lobed, 3½–6½ in. across, dark green and smooth above, with a slight bloom* beneath. Flowers yellowish-green, in drooping, compound, terminal clusters (panicles*). Fruit with wings spreading at acute

---

* Special articles on the subjects indicated by an asterisk (*) will be found at the words so marked.

or at right angle. Eu. and western As. Cult. for centuries. There are many varieties. May. Hardy from zone° 2 southward.

A. rubrum. Red maple. A large tree attaining a height of 120 ft., valuable as an ornamental tree in parks or as shade tree on the street. Leaves 3–5-lobed, 2–4 in. long, shiny above, with bloom beneath, turning brilliant scarlet and yellow in autumn. Conspicuous red flowers before the leaves. Fruit bright red when young, smooth on a slender stalk, wings of key spreading at a narrow angle. Newfoundland to Fla., west to Minn., Iowa, Okla. and Tex. March–April. Hardy from zone° 1 southward. The *var.* **columnare** has a fastigiate° habit.

A. rufinerve. A medium-sized tree, not over 35 ft. high, its handsome foliage crimson in the autumn. Leaves prevailingly 3-lobed, rarely with 2 small basal lobes in addition, 3–6 in. long, the veins on the under side reddish-hairy in youth. Leafstalk also reddish-hairy. Flowers in an upright, red-hairy cluster (raceme°). Fruit with spreading wings. Jap. May. Hardy from zone° 4 southward.

A. saccharinum. Silver maple. A large tree 120 ft. high. Leaves deeply 5-lobed, 3–6 in. across, lobes long-pointed, and with marginal teeth, bright green above and silvery-white beneath, turning yellow in fall. Flowers short-stalked without petals. Fruit soft-hairy when young, the wings widely spread and sickle-shaped. Eastern N.A. There are several varieties, one of them (*var.* **wieri**), with deeply dissected, narrow leaf lobes, being the popular Wier's cut-leaved maple. Feb.–Mar. Hardy from zone° 2 southward. Branches and twigs brittle.

A. saccharum. Sugar maple. A tall tree, often up to 120 ft., the bark furrowed or shaggy in age. Leaves 3–5-lobed, resembling the Norway maple, but without the milky juice, 4–6½ in. wide. Flowers greenish-yellow, appearing before the leaves unfold. Fruit with widely divergent keys. Eastern N.A., west to Tex. The leading source of maple sugar. April. Hardy from zone° 2 southward. The *var.* **monumentale** has a fastigiate° habit.

A. spicatum. Mountain maple. A shrub, very rarely a tree up to 20 ft. high, the foliage turning from orange to scarlet in autumn. Leaves 3-lobed (rarely 5-lobed), 3–5 in. long, heart-shaped at the base, coarsely and irregularly toothed on the margin. Flowers small, greenish-yellow, in erect, stiffish, hairy clusters (spikes°). Wings of the fruit divergent. Eastern N.A. May. Hardy from zone° 2 southward, but poor at low altitudes.

A. tataricum. A shrub or tree to 20 ft. high. Leaves broadly oval to almost oblong, with marginal teeth, 2–4 in. long, long-pointed, bright green, turning yellow in autumn. Flowers greenish-white, in upright, compound, terminal clusters (panicles°). Fruit bright red, conspicuous in late summer, the wings of the key nearly parallel with the nutlet. Southeastern Eu. and western As. May. Hardy from zone° 2 southward.

Maple Culture

Maples are among the best of our ornamental shade trees, both as garden specimens and as street trees, for there are some that are suitable in almost any kind of ornamental planting, coast to coast. They vary in height from 15 feet to 75 feet or more, and in habit from round and globose to

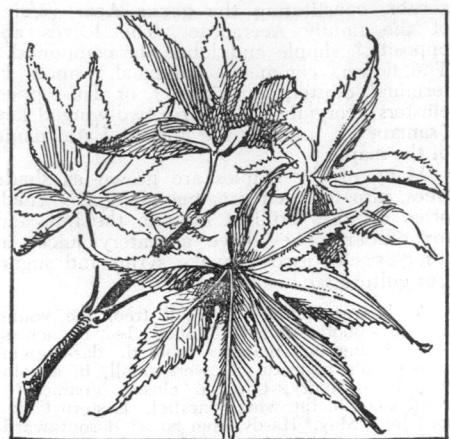

One of the numerous leaf forms of the Japanese maple

fastigiate° and pyramidal. Chiefly used as shade trees, there are some, especially varieties of the Japanese maples, that are used for their colorful red or pale-green foliage, as well as for their low, rounded habit and beautifully cut leaves. There are over 120 kinds of maples being grown in the Arnold Arboretum in Boston, most of them with outstanding autumn color.

Some, like the silver maple (*A. saccharinum*), are not used much because they are weak-wooded, even though they do grow fast. The red maple also has weak wood but is frequently used for naturalizing nonetheless. The box-elder (*A. Negundo*) is actually a weed tree, very fast in growth, very weak-wooded and only of value in the Midwestern states where drought conditions are sufficient to prevent the growing of other trees. The sugar maple, though slower in growth than some of the others, is a perfect tree for displaying fall color of reds, orange, and yellow.

Around modern homes of the ranch type, the smaller maple species are becoming increasingly popular. Species like *A. Ginnala, circinatum, tataricum,* and *campestre* seldom grow over 25 feet tall and hence are just tall enough for the one-story house. The columnar forms of the red, sugar, and Norway maples are becoming increasingly used as street trees for narrow streets. In fact, one form of the Norway maple (*A. platanoides globosum*) is so rounded in habit that it is ideal for planting underneath electric-light wires and never grows tall enough to interfere with them.

All maples have vigorous growth and are easy to transplant. They will grow in any good soil in areas with a sufficient amount of rainfall. Some, especially the Norway maple, are notorious for the fact that their feeding roots are very close to the surface of the soil. This, combined with the low-

---

° Special articles on the subjects indicated by an asterisk (°) will be found at the words so marked.

hanging branches which always give a dense shade, makes it almost impossible to grow plants underneath such trees unless the lower branches are trimmed off and much light is permitted to come in. — D. W.

INSECT PESTS. Leaf feeders of many species can be controlled with pesticide #19 or #1. Early spring sprays of lime sulphur or pesticide #20 will control gall-producing mites. Pesticide #21 or #20 will control aphid species and leafhoppers. Sprays of superior-type oils when dormant will control scales. On sugar maple, which may be injured by oil, use pesticide #21 when young scales appear and repeat 2–3 weeks later. Leopard moth larvae work in branches and should be immediately pruned out. (See INSECT PESTS, and also SPRAYS AND DUSTS.)

DISEASES. Leaf diseases common to many species of maple are anthracnose* and leaf-spot.* These are controlled with pesticide #3 or #5 (see SPRAYS AND DUSTS), applied at bud-break and repeated twice at 10-day intervals. Tar spot is a leaf disease particularly severe on silver maple. The black, tar-like spots on the upper surface of the leaf may be so numerous that much defoliation will occur. Control with a single application of pesticide #3 or #5, early in the spring *before* buds start to open.

Diseases which are present in the trunk or branches are wilt,* canker,* and wood rot.* If leaves on some or all branches wilt suddenly, cut into the wood beneath the bark. A blue-black stain indicates a disease known as Verticillium wilt and is often fatal. The cankers and wood rots should be treated by a reputable tree expert.

Maples, particularly the Norway, are quite subject to girdling roots. The roots which encircle the trunk just below the soil line should be removed or the tree will strangle itself. Leaf scorch* is quite common on many species of maple, but is seen most often on the thin-leaved Japanese red maples.

MAPLE FAMILY = Aceraceae. *See* MAPLE.

MARANTA (ma-ran'ta). Tropical American foliage plants of the family Marantaceae, comprising about 14 species, grown mostly for ornament in the greenhouse, but one cult. in warm countries for its starchy root, the source of arrowroot. Leaves mostly basal, sometimes a few on the fleshy stem, wholly without marginal teeth, always with a more or less sheathing leafstalk. In some species the leaves are beautifully colored, in which case they are grown only for the foliage. Flowers (when produced) in racemes* or panicles,* more or less tubular, but usually enlarged or with a 1-sided swelling at the base, the upper part slightly unequal. Stamens,* or some of them, petal-like. (Named for B. Maranta, Venetian botanist.)

Many plants commonly called *Maranta* by the florists actually belong to the genus *Calathea* (which see), and some plants offered as *Calathea* belong here, especially the plant often offered as *Calathea bicolor.* Both *Maranta* and *Calathea* require the same greenhouse treatment as *Caladium* (which see), although the latter does not belong to the same family as either of the others.

Maranta needs a rich soil and frequent applications of liquid manure.

arundinacea. Arrowroot. A slender, branched herb 2–6 ft. high, grown in tropical regions for its starchy root which yields arrowroot (sometimes called Bermuda arrowroot, but not native there). It is cult. for ornament in the greenhouse mostly in the *var.* **variegata** which has yellow- or white-marked leaves which are oval-oblong, 6–8 in. long, tapering at the tip but rounded at the base. Flowers white. Tropical America, but naturalized in Fla.

bicolor. Not over 1 ft. high, and the leading cult. plant, grown for its handsome foliage. Leaves oblongish or elliptic, wavy-margined, purple beneath, but pale bluish-green above, but with a pale band along the midrib, and dark-blotched between this band and the margins. Brazil. Often, or usually, offered as *Calathea bicolor.*

leuconeura. Not over 1 ft. high, and a handsome foliage plant for the greenhouse. Leaves broadly elliptic, blunt or short-tapering, grayish- or bluish-green above, but with white bands along the veins above, purplish or grayish beneath. Brazil. The *var.* **kerchoveana** has the leaves red-spotted on the under side; and the *var.* **massangeana** has smaller leaves which are rich purple beneath.

MARANTACEAE (ma-ran-tay'see-ee). The arrowroot family is almost wholly tropical, but one of its cult. genera, *Thalia,* extends into the swamps and marshes of the southeastern U.S. The family comprises about 26 genera and possibly 280 species of herbs, most of which have tuberous root-stocks, from one of which, *Maranta,* arrowroot is derived. The other cult. genus is *Calathea,* which, with *Maranta,* furnishes many handsome foliage plants of greenhouse culture.

Leaves without marginal teeth, mostly basal and two-ranked,* usually narrowed into a more or less sheathing leafstalk, often (in hort. varieties) variegated or with a metallic sheen. Flowers (rarely produced in cult. greenhouse plants) very irregular,* not showy, mostly in head-like clusters, the whole surrounded by sheathing bracts.* Fruit dry or a berry. This and several other related families were once included within the Scitamineae (which see).

Technical flower characters: Sepals 3. Petals 3, usually joined to form a tube or one forming a hooded structure. Ovary inferior,* 3-celled. Style and stigma 1 each.

MARCHANTIA (mar-kan'tĭ-a). A curious group of flowerless plants without true leaves, commonly called liverworts, and of little garden interest except as they become naturalized in moist places, as under greenhouse benches or occasionally on wet rocks, and because they can smother seedlings if too profuse. The plant body, which hugs the soil, consists of a leaf-like thallus* 4–5 in. long and about 1 in. wide. From the thallus arise small, stalk-like bodies which bear the sexual organs. M. polymorpha is the commonest of the many known species and is often seen in greenhouses. It is never cult., but appears as if spontaneously.

---

* Special articles on the subjects indicated by an asterisk (*) will be found at the words so marked.

MARCOTTAGE = Layering.

margarita, -us, -um (mar-gar-ree′ta). Pearly in color or texture.

margaritacea, -us, -um (mar-gar-i-tay′-see-a). Pearly in color or texture.

margaritifera, -us, -um (mar-gar-i-tiff′e-ra). Bearing pearls, or as if bearing them.

marginalis, -e (mar-jin-ā′lis). Margined; usually with a different color or texture, as are some leaves.

MARGINAL SHIELD FERN = *Dryopteris marginalis.*

marginata, -us, -um (mar-jin-ā′ta). Margined or striped.

MARGUERITE = *Chrysanthemum frutescens.*

MARIA = *Calophyllum antillanum.*

Mariana, -us, -um (mar-ĭ-ā′na). Named for the Virgin Mary, or for Maryland.

MARICA. *See* NEOMARICA.

MARIHUANA. *See* CANNABIS.

MARIGOLD. The name *marigold* is commonly applied to several different kinds of plants. One is the pot marigold (*see* CALENDULA), which has scentless leaves; another is **Tagetes** (tay-gee′teez), the subject of this article. Still other plants in which marigold is part of their name should be looked for at *Bidens, Dimorphotheca, Mesembryanthemum,* and at MARSH MARIGOLD.

Tagetes, which includes the African and French marigold, is neither French nor African, but comprises a group of about 30 species of tender annual herbs of the family Compositae, all native from N. Mex. to the Argentine. They have strong-scented foliage, the leaves mostly opposite* and usually finely dissected. Flower heads showy, solitary, or clustered. Below each head is a series of involucral bracts,* united into a cup-like base. (*Tagetes* may be named for Tages, an Etruscan god, but this is not certain.)

For culture *see* below.

T. erecta. African marigold (long thought to be native there), better called Aztec or big marigold. An erect, rather bushy herb 18–24 in. high and branched. Leaves finely divided, the segments narrow and toothed. Flower heads 2–4 in. wide, yellow or orange, the rays with a long claw* or even quilled in some forms. The stalk of the head is swollen just below the cluster. Mex.

T. lucida. A sweet-scented marigold from Mex., really a perennial, but grown as a tender annual. It has undivided, nearly stalkless leaves and usually grows only about 1 ft. high. Flower heads scarcely ½ in. wide, in dense clusters, the rays only 2–3 to each head, orange-yellow.

T. patula. French marigold. A much-branched annual, rarely over 1 ft. high, the leaves divided, the segments narrow and toothed. Flower heads about 1½ in. wide, the numerous rays yellow but with red markings. Mex. There are many hort. forms, ranging from pure yellow to nearly pure red, and some are double-flowered. There is also a dwarf variety useful for edging.

T. tenuifolia. An annual, cult. chiefly in the *var.* pumila, which is a dwarf form scarcely 12 in. high, with very small heads of clear yellow flowers. Mex. The variety is an attractive window-box plant.

MARIGOLD CULTURE

Marigolds of the type of *Tagetes lucida* and the African marigold are best suited to the open border, for they are erect, relatively branchy plants without the compact habit of the French marigold. The latter is a valuable bedding plant because of its compact, bushy habit. It also flowers very well from the middle of June until frost.

All marigolds are good for cutting, with the exception of *T. lucida,* which has less showy flowers than the other three. Some people do not like either the French or African marigold as a cut flower because of the strong odor of the foliage. All leaves should be cut from the submerged part of flowering stalks.

French Marigold (*Tagetes patula*). A scented-foliaged, tender annual, with yellow or reddish flowers, found in hort. forms, and widely grown as a summer bedding plant.

These marigolds, for early bloom, are best treated as tender annuals (*see* ANNUALS), and they thrive better if the last shift from the bed where they were raised is into pots. Sometimes the seed is sown directly where wanted, especially that of the African marigold, but this delays bloom far behind those raised from seed indoors and subsequently planted outdoors. They all need summer heat, so should not be put outdoors until cool weather has passed.

marilandica, -us, -um (mar-i-lan′di-ka). From Maryland.

MARINE IVY = *Cissus incisa.*

MARIPOSA LILY = *Calochortus.*

maritima, -us, -um (ma-rit′i-ma). In the sea or on seashores.

---

* Special articles on the subjects indicated by an asterisk (*) will be found at the words so marked.

MARJORAM. The word is applied to two wholly distinct plants. For the common or pot marjoram, sometimes called wild marjoram, see ORIGANUM VULGARE. For the other marjoram see SWEET MARJORAM.

MARL. See LIME.

MARLBERRY = *Ardisia paniculata.*

MARMALADE BOX. See GENIPA AMERICANA.

MARMALADE PLUM = *Achras Zapota.*

marmorata, -us, -um (mar-more-ray'ta). Mottled.

maroccana, -us, -um (ma-rock-kay'na). From Morocco.

MAROON GARDEN. See RED GARDEN.

MARRAM = *Ammophila arenaria.*

MARRUBIUM. See HOREHOUND.

MARSHALLIA (mar-shall'i-a). A small genus of North American plants of the family Compositae, usually tufted,* about 1 ft. high, and the leaves without marginal teeth. Flowers in heads, without rays,* suggesting the scabious. **M. trinervia,** sometimes known as Barbara's-buttons, has a stalk usually leafy halfway up. Flowers purplish, whitish, or pink. Treated as an ordinary outdoor perennial in the border. Va. and southward. *M. grandiflora,* closely related, is also offered. (Named for Moses Marshall, American botanist.)

MARSH FERN = *Dryopteris Thelypteris.*

MARSH FLOWER = *Limnanthes douglasi.*

MARSH MALLOW = *Althaea officinalis.* See HOLLYHOCK. See also HIBISCUS MOSCHEUTOS.

MARSH MARIGOLD. Marsh, or swamp, perennial herbs constituting the genus **Caltha** (kal'tha) of the buttercup family, growing in the north temperate and arctic zones. There are about 20 species. The stem is hollow, the leaves roundish, heart- or kidney-shaped, without teeth. The flowers are 1 to 2 in. across, without petals, but having pink, white or yellow petal-like sepals.* The fruit is a collection of small, dried pods (follicles*). (*Caltha* is the old Latin for marigold and applied by Linnaeus to this genus.)

C. leptosepala. A perennial herb growing 1 ft. high. The leaves oval, 3–4 in. long. Flowers white, tinged blue on the outside, growing singly. In marshes from New Mexico to Alaska.

C. palustris. Cowslip, and the common marsh marigold of N.A.; also called king-cup, May-blob and gools. From 1–2 ft. Leaves 3–6 in. wide. Flowers bright yellow, several together. Growing in marshes or by brooks in eastern U.S. Easily transplanted to the wild garden, or it will grow in rich, moist soil in the border if given partial shade. Increased by division or by seeds.

MARSH TREFOIL = *Menyanthes trifoliata.*

MARSILEA (mar-sill'ee-a). Aquatic or marsh herbs, and the only cult. genus of the family **Marsileaceae** (mar-sill-ee-â'see-ee), the pepperworts, which are flowerless plants classed with the fern allies (which see). They are of little hort. importance, but the two below are often found in aquaria, or, in the case of *M. quadrifolia,* in outdoor pools in the North. They have 4-parted or compound,* cloverlike, floating leaves, which arise from long runners. The spores are borne in small cases near the base of the leafstalk in the second species, but, in the first, on short stalks which bear nothing else. (Named for Giovanni Marsigli, Italian botanist.)

The pepperworts are of very easy culture in aquaria and pools. The first species is not hardy and can only be grown in greenhouse pools or aquaria or outdoors in the far South. But *M. quadrifolia* is naturalized in several places in the U.S. and may completely choke the surface of a pool unless kept in check.

drummondi. Nardoo. An Australian aquatic suitable for aquaria or greenhouse pools, the four leaflets wavy-margined and more or less white-hairy.

quadrifolia. A Eurasian perennial, aquatic herb, naturalized in several places in the U.S. and often a local pest. Leaflets or the 4 cloverlike segments not hairy and not notched.

MARSILEACEAE. See MARSILEA.

Martagon (mar'ta-gon). A specific name derived from the Italian martagone, a kind of turban, and applied to the lily *Lilium Martagon.*

MARTINEZIA (mar-ti-nee'zi-a). A small genus of very spiny, tropical American feather palms, of which only **M. caryotaefolia,** from Colombia, is cult., mostly in the warmest parts of southern Fla. It has a solitary, ringed trunk, 40–60 ft. high (less in cult.), but not usually more than 6 in. thick, and covered with long, needle-like, black spines. Leaves 4–6 ft. long, also spiny, the segments or leaflets 7–12 in. long, each segment broadest toward the tip and there more or less cut or jagged after the fashion of the fish-tail palms. Flowering cluster not over 18 in. long, its sheath (spathe*) very spiny, the male and female flowers separate, but in the same cluster. Fruit yellow, 1-seeded, about ¾ in. long, more or less egg-shaped. In Fla. it grows equally well in shade or open sunlight. (Named for Archbishop B. J. Martinez Compañon, of Peru, who collected plants there.) Sometimes known as *Aiphanes.*

MARTYNIA = *Proboscidea.*

MARTYNIACEAE. See PROBOSCIDEA.

Marum (mar'rum). An old and unexplained name for *Teucrium Marum.*

MARUMI KUMQUAT = *Fortunella japonica.*

MARVEL-OF-PERU = *Mirabilis Jalapa.*

MARYLAND. The black-eyed Susan is the state flower. The state lies mostly in zones* 4 and 5, but zone* 3 just crosses

---

* Special articles on the subjects indicated by an asterisk (*) will be found at the words so marked.

the northern edge of the state, and zone* 6 extends up to the region around Eastville, Va.

In a state like Maryland where the altitude varies from a few feet above sea level to more than 2000 feet, topography becomes an important factor in determining the character of the soil, the facility and economy of cultivation, and in the range of climate.

The state forms a portion of the Atlantic slope and is divided into three important divisions: (1) The Coastal Plain, (2) The Piedmont Plateau, and (3) The Appalachian Region.

The Coastal Plain, comprising nearly half the area of the state, is divided into two sections by the Chesapeake Bay, the eastern portion being known commonly as the Eastern Shore, while the western part is spoken of as Southern Maryland. This region is characterized by broad, level stretches increasing in elevation as it joins the Piedmont Plateau on the west.

The soils of the Coastal Plain are generally sandy in character, although several areas are fine-textured and often poorly drained. The soils of the area are lacking in organic matter which results in their being light in color. Phosphoric acid seems to be the element most needed in the soils of this region, although a complete fertilizer will generally give best returns.

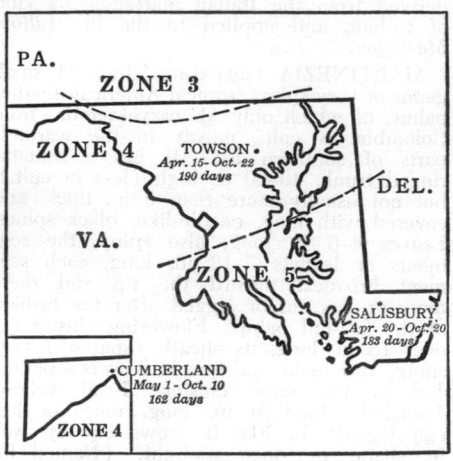

MARYLAND

The zones of hardiness crossing Maryland are those shown on the map located at ZONE, which should be consulted for details. The dates are the average latest killing frost in spring and the first one in the fall. The figures below the dates show the length of the growing season. Rainfall is adequate.

The Piedmont Plateau, extending from the southwest to the northwest, occupies the north-central portion and includes about one fourth of the area of the state. The region is undulating in topography, and the northern highland section has an average elevation of 800 to 900 feet.

The soils for the most part are fine-textured, consisting mainly of brown or yellowish-brown friable* loams. They respond to additional supplies of nitrogen and phosphoric acid and frequently to potash. Because of the rolling character of the land, surface drainage is often excessive and erosion results where soil is improperly handled.

Western Maryland is a part of the Appalachian Region and includes the highest, roughest, and most densely forested, sections of the state. It is divided into the Blue Ridge District on the east, the Greater Appalachian Valley in the center, and the Allegheny Plateau on the west.

The eastern section consists of typically limestone valleys with fine-textured loam soils and with many limestone outcrops. The soils are brown, dark brown, or reddish brown in color and phosphoric acid seems to be the element most needed. Much of the remaining portion of this area is unfit for agricultural crops because of its mountainous character.

In a general way the chief garden centers include the Eastern Shore and the north-central portions of the state.

FRUITS. The apple and the peach are the two leading fruits grown and these represent more than three fourths of the total production of fruit in the state. Approximately half of the apple production is centered in Washington County, with other counties of the Piedmont Plateau contributing the bulk of the remainder. Wicomico and Talbot counties of the Eastern Shore and Anne Arundel County in Southern Maryland are important producing centers.

The commercial production of strawberries is located largely on the Eastern Shore, Somerset, Wicomico, and Worcester counties leading in the production of this fruit.

Washington County leads in the production of peaches. Most of the counties of the Piedmont Plateau and Wicomico in the Coastal Plain comprise important producing areas.

The production of cherries and plums is relatively unimportant and confined mainly to Washington County and the Piedmont Plateau.

Raspberries are grown in heaviest production in the Hagerstown valley. Blackberries and dewberries are grown mostly in Washington and Allegany counties.

POTATO. The white potato is one of the minor crops grown in the state. The early crop which constitutes more than one half the total production is produced almost entirely on the Eastern Shore, with Worcester and Somerset counties contributing the major share of the production. The late crop is more generally distributed with about 70 per cent of the farms reporting some production.

Sweet potatoes are produced mainly on the lighter soils of the Coastal Plains with

Wicomico County furnishing three fourths of the total production.

VEGETABLES. Approximately 120,000 acres are devoted to the production of vegetables. This does not include vegetables produced in home gardens to the value of over $3,000,000. A large variety of types are grown; yet the major portion is concerned with only a relatively few crops. In order of their relative importance the following eleven crops represent 90 per cent of the total value of all vegetables, exclusive of white and sweet potatoes: tomatoes, sweet corn, beans (snap), cantaloupes, spinach, peas, cucumbers, cabbage, asparagus, beans (lima), and watermelons.

The greatest production of sweet corn is in Harford, Baltimore, Carroll, Frederick, and Talbot counties with scattered production in other areas.

Baltimore, Somerset, Carroll, and Wicomico counties furnish three fourths of the total production of snap beans, while the production of lima beans is concentrated mainly in Wicomico, Talbot, Somerset, and Dorchester counties of the Eastern Shore.

Baltimore County furnishes the major portion of the spinach crop. Peas which are grown primarily for canning are produced mainly in Carroll, Caroline, Talbot, Baltimore, and Dorchester counties. Wicomico County produces more than three fourths of the cucumbers grown in the state. Caroline and Dorchester counties are other producing centers. Three fourths of the cabbage is produced in Baltimore County. Most of the asparagus is grown in the Eastern Shore counties, with Kent County leading.

Wicomico County is the largest producer of watermelons, although a considerable acreage is planted also in Dorchester and Caroline counties.

ORNAMENTAL PLANTS. With the exception of the western mountainous section of the state, the climatic conditions are favorable to the development of a wide variety of ornamental trees, shrubs, and flowers.

Characteristic deciduous trees are the elm, red maple, tulip-tree, oaks, wild cherry, black gum, sweet gum, beech, dogwood, redbud, and sassafras. In the mountain section the sugar maple is common.

A characteristic slender, columnar form of the red cedar is common in the lower altitudes. Other common evergreens include the pines, hemlock and the American holly.

Many native shrubs and wild flowers are to be found in many sections although some forms are rapidly disappearing.

In the last decade there has been a notable extension in the number and acreage of nurseries, particularly those devoted to the production of plants for ornamental purposes. The rapid development of garden clubs also indicates a widespread interest in ornamental plants. A feature of the area in general is the overlapping of northern and southern types of plants. This contributes to the wide variety of forms to be met with in the state.

On the Eastern Shore there are many 18th-century manor and plantation houses, some of them with magnificent gardens that are open to the public at specified times. *See* GARDEN TOURS.

CLIMATE. The climate of the state is equable with mild winters and warm summers usually tempered by cool spells originating in more northern latitudes. Spring and autumn are both delightful seasons.

The growing season or frost-free period for the eastern half of the state is remarkably long, averaging 180 days.

The rainfall is generally well distributed and averages 40.93 inches. The amount falling during the growing season is about 28 inches, which is ample.

The address of the Agricultural Experiment Station, which has kindly supplied this information about the state, is College Park, Maryland. The station is always ready to answer gardening questions.

FROST DATA

Av. date of last killing frost in spring	Latest-known killing frost	Av. date of earliest killing frost in fall	Earliest-known killing frost
Cumberland, May 1	May 17	Oct. 10	Sept 6
Towson, April 15	May 12	Oct. 22	Oct. 7
Salisbury, April 20	May 12	Oct. 20	Oct. 8

Garden club activities in the state are extensive. They include clubs of the Garden Club of America, the home office of which is 598 Madison Avenue, New York. There are also over 95 clubs and 37 junior clubs belonging to the Federated Garden Clubs of Maryland.

marylandica, -us, -um (mare-ĭ-lan′di-ka). From Maryland.

Mas. A species name at *Juniperus* and *Cornus*, implying male, or male flowers.

MASCARENE GRASS = *Zoysia tenuifolia*.

MASDEVALLIA (mas-de-vall′ĭ-a). Tropical American, tree-perching orchids (epiphytes*), with grotesque and rather showy flowers, a few of the 150 species cult. in greenhouses, but not widely. They have no pseudobulbs,* the thick, sheathing leaves somewhat swollen at the base. Petals small. Calyx greatly enlarged and thus the most prominent part of the flower. Some of the calyx lobes are often cut into long drooping tails. (Named for Joseph Masdevall, Spanish botanist.)

These orchids, which appear to have no common name, should be grown as epiphytes.* See the section on the culture of greenhouse orchids at ORCHID. The times given are the blooming period in the greenhouse.

bella. Leaves about 7 in. long. Flowers

---

* Special articles on the subjects indicated by an asterisk (*) will be found at the words so marked.

yellow, but brown-spotted, solitary, the stalk about 7 in. high, the tails nearly 4 in. long. Colombia. Jan.–May.

chimaera. Leaves nearly 1 ft. long. Flowers in clusters of 2–6, yellow, but with crimson-purple spots, the tails purple-brown and nearly 1 ft. long. An extremely showy plant from Colombia. Nov.–Feb. The hort. forms of this are chiefly prized for the fantastic shape of the flowers.

coccinea. Leaves about 10 in. long. Flowers generally violet-red, but the petals white, and one of the sepals produced into a long tail. Colombia. March–June. More cult. than the others and known in several hybrid forms.

tovarensis. Leaves about 5 in. long. Flowers white, in clusters of 2–4, the stalks about 5 in. long, the yellow tails about 6 in. long. Venezuela. Nov.–Feb.

MASK-FLOWER. *See* ALONSOA.

MASSACHUSETTS. The trailing arbutus is the state flower. The state lies wholly in zones* 3 and 4. Soils vary widely even in one neighborhood but are mostly friable* loams of varying degrees of fertility. Stones are abundant over much of the state and outcropping ledges and rough topography make 60% or more of the land suitable for forestry only. Much of the agricultural land is productive and well suited to the growing of fruits and vegetables. With unsurpassed markets it furnishes the basis for a sound and continuing agriculture. Massachusetts soils are characteristically acid and liming is necessary for maximum yields of crops that are not acid-tolerant.

GARDENING AND FRUIT-GROWING AREAS. The chief vegetable-gardening center in Massachusetts is west and north of Boston, although definite gardening areas have developed around every city. Crops are much the same in all districts and include asparagus, beans, beets, cabbage, carrots, cauliflower, celery, cucumbers, lettuce, onions, parsnips, peas, peppers, radishes, rhubarb, spinach, sprouting broccoli, tomatoes, squash, and sweet corn.

The greenhouse vegetable industry is nearly all within twenty-five or thirty miles of Boston. The chief greenhouse crops are tomatoes, cucumbers, lettuce, and rhubarb. Mansfield is the location of an intensive greenhouse development, mostly devoted to cucumbers.

Aside from districts centering about the cities, there are more isolated sections on Cape Cod and in the Connecticut Valley which grow specialized vegetable crops, often on a large scale. The principal vegetable crops on Cape Cod are asparagus and rutabagas. In the Connecticut Valley where onions and tobacco are the main crops, asparagus, root crops and other vegetables are grown on an increasing acreage. Both Cape Cod and the Connecticut Valley are within easy trucking distance of Boston and other marketing centers.

Apples are grown for market in almost every part of the state. Good fruit soils and orchard sites are abundant over most of the state. The most intensive district lies in western Middlesex and eastern Worcester counties, where deep, well-drained soils afford splendid conditions for tree growth.

Massachusetts lies on the northern edge of the commercial peach belt and peach-growing is confined to the more favored sites. Destructive spring frosts are much less common than in many districts farther south but the intense cold of midwinter sometimes kills peach fruit buds, and protected sites with good air drainage are almost a necessity for profitable peach production. The industry is scattered and lies mostly in Hampden, southern Worcester, Middlesex, Plymouth, and Bristol counties.

Pear orchards lie mostly in the eastern half of the state but pears are grown, at least for home use, in all parts of the state. Plums are grown widely for home use but not extensively for market.

Strawberries are grown for market more or less around every city. Aside from this there are important producing centers in the Falmouth district on Cape Cod, in Bristol

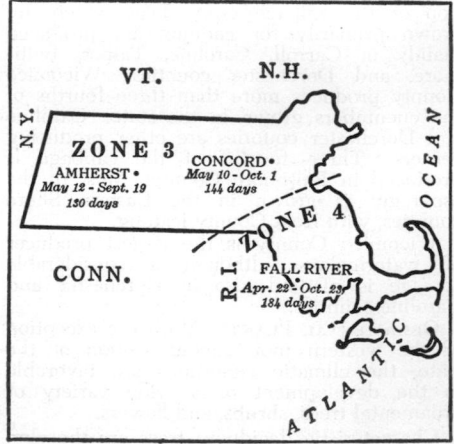

MASSACHUSETTS

The zones of hardiness crossing Massachusetts are those shown on the map located at ZONE, which should be consulted for details. The dates are the average latest killing frost in spring and the first one in the fall. The figures below the dates show the length of the growing season. Rainfall is adequate.

County around Dighton, and a smaller district south of Boston in Abington and Marshfield. Grapes are grown everywhere for home use and there are small commercial vineyards near every city. There are, however, no centers of grape production.

Raspberries are profitable and are widely grown, especially in the eastern half of the state. The nearest approach to a center of production is the New Salem district in eastern Franklin County.

---

* Special articles on the subjects indicated by an asterisk (*) will be found at the words so marked.

CLIMATE. Winters are often severely cold but unbroken by thaws and therefore less trying to plant life than some milder climates. The summers usually afford good growing conditions for northern plants and prolonged drought is rare. The following data is from the records of the United States Weather Bureau:

Town	Average date of last killing frost in spring	Latest-known killing frost
Amherst	May 12	June 8
Concord	May 10	June 21
Fall River	April 22	May 12

Town	Average date of earliest killing frost in fall	Earliest-known killing frost
Amherst	Sept. 19	Aug. 22
Concord	Oct. 1	Sept. 2
Fall River	Oct. 23	Sept. 17

The average total annual precipitation for Massachusetts is 42.72 inches. The average total precipitation for the crop-growing season, April to September inclusive, is 21.10 inches.

The address of the Massachusetts Agricultural Experiment Station, which has supplied this information about the state, is Amherst. The station is always ready to answer gardening questions.

Garden club activities include several clubs of the Garden Club of America, the home office of which is 598 Madison Avenue, New York 22, N.Y. There are also many clubs affiliated with the Garden Club Federation of Massachusetts. See also HORTICULTURAL SOCIETIES.

Mastacanthus (mas-ta-kan'thus). An old, and now obsolete, name for *Caryopteris.*

MASTERWORT = *Heracleum lanatum.* See also ASTRANTIA.

MASTICA. A plastic material for use on greenhouse glass and hotbed sash, in place of putty.

MASTIC-TREE = *Schinus molle.*

MAT BEAN = *Phaseolus aconitifolius.*

MATHIOLA (ma-thy'o-la). Stocks belong to a genus of the mustard family containing 50 species of Old World annuals, perennials, or sub-shrubs, only two species in common cultivation. Leaves alternate,* without marginal teeth, or wavy, or cut into segments. Flowers in terminal clusters (racemes*), lilac, purple, or white, with many variations. Petals 4, with a long claw.* Fruit, a pod. (Named for Peter Andrew Matthioli, 1500–1577, Italian writer on plants.) Sometimes spelled *Matthiola.*

Common garden and florist flowers, grown in ordinary garden soil. For culture, see STOCK.

bicornis. Evening stock. Low-growing annual or biennial herb, much branched. Leaves 1½ to 3 in. long, narrow, with or without marginal teeth. Flowers small, scattered, purple, very fragrant, opening in the evening. Fruit, a two-horned pod. Eurasia.

incana. Stock, also called Brompton stock and gillyflower. They are biennial or perennial herbs, with many intermediate races, growing erect from 1 to 2 ft. Leaves felty, usually oblong, 2½ to 4 in. long. Flowers white, blue, purple or reddish, blush, or yellowish, fragrant, usually double, though some of the single forms are most desirable. Fruit, a pod without horns. Southern Eu. Var. **annua**, the ten-weeks stock, is less woody at the base. It is grown from seeds started in late winter or early spring in the house or greenhouse; usually handled as a half-hardy annual. It makes a fine house plant from seeds started in summer (*see* STOCK).

MATILIJA POPPY = *Romneya coulteri.*

MATRICARIA (ma-tri-cay'rĭ-a). An Old World genus of the Compositae, closely related to *Chrysanthemum,* with which it is often confused. It contains about 40 species of annuals, biennials and perennials. The leaves are finely cut, often strong-scented. Flowers in heads, the disk* flowers yellow, the rays* white, or lacking. They are known as wild camomile, false camomile, or matricary. Some of them are used in the garden, others have been introduced as weeds. The cultural requirements are similar to the hardy species of *Chrysanthemum.* (*Matricaria* is derived from the Latin for mother, in allusion to its use in sickness.)

capensis = *Chrysanthemum Parthenium.*

Chamomilla. German camomile; aslo called sweet false camomile. An annual growing from 1–2 ft. in height, smooth, branched. Leaves finely cut. Flower heads 1 in. across with 10 to 20 ray* flowers. Eu. and northern As. Sometimes an escape* in eastern U.S. Occasionally called simply camomile, but that name properly belongs to *Anthemis nobilis.* See HERB GARDENING.

inodora. Scentless camomile; also called corn mayweed. An annual growing about 2 ft. high, much-branched, the foliage scarcely scented. Leaves much cut. Flower heads 1½ in. across, with 20 to 30 white rays. Eurasia. Also called M. maritima by some, but named *inodora* by Linnaeus.* Var. plenissima has large, double white heads. It is common in gardens, sometimes under the name of Bridal Rose.

parthenoides = *Chrysanthemum Parthenium.*

tchihatchewi. Turfing daisy. A low, carpeting perennial with finely dissected leaves. Flower stalks 8–10 in. high, the heads white, daisy-like, about ¾ in. wide. Asia Minor. When sown thickly it will form a sort of turf, which may be mown to prevent flowering. See Grass Substitutes at LAWN.

MATRICARY. See MATRICARIA.

MATRIMONY-VINE. See LYCIUM.

matronalis, -e (ma-tro-nay'lis). Matronly; sedate; as used for plants it often implies that they are hoary.

Matsudana (mat-su-da'na). From or near Matsuda, Jap.

* Special articles on the subjects indicated by an asterisk (*) will be found at the words so marked.

MATTEUCCIA = *Pteretis*.

MATTHIOLA = *Mathiola*.

MAUL OAK = *Quercus chrysolepis*. *See* OAK.

MAURANDIA (mau-ran′dĭ-a). Mexican perennial, more or less climbing, herbs of the family Scrophulariaceae, three of the 6 known species cult. for their showy, gloxinia-like flowers. They have mostly alternate,* rather angular and usually coarsely toothed leaves. Flowers in the leaf axils,* the corolla showy, slightly irregular, somewhat swollen at the base, the throat bearded in lines. Stamens* 4. Fruit a many-seeded capsule.* (Named for Catharina P. Maurandy of Cartagena, Spain, a student of botany.)

These showy herbs can be grown as perennials in climates like Calif., or occasionally as biennials. But most of them will bloom from seed the first year if treated as tender annuals (*see* ANNUALS). They will also flower in the cool greenhouse during the winter. To get the best results from seed, sow in potting mixture* 3, cover the pot or pan with glass, and keep as near 60° as possible. Greenhouse specimens may also be increased by cuttings taken in January. All those below have also been credited to the genus *Asarina*.

barclaiana. Leaves halberd-shaped, but without marginal teeth, about 1 in. long. Flowers velvety-purple outside, about 1½ in. long, the sticky sepals* long-tapering. A very showy plant from Mex.

erubescens. Foliage sticky-hairy, the leaves more or less triangular, toothed, 3–4 in. long. Flowers nearly 3 in. long, rose-red, the sepals* leafy. Mex. Often grown as *M. scandens*.

lophospermum. Closely related to the last, but the corolla tube is not hairy on the outside as in that species; also the sepals are sharper-pointed than in *M. erubescens*. Mex. Sometimes offered as *Lophospermum scandens*.

mauritanica, -us, -um (mau-ri-tay′ni-ka). From Mauretania, French West Africa.

mauritiana, -us, -um (mau-ri-she-ā′na). From the island of Mauritius.

MAURITIUS HEMP. *See* FURCRAEA GIGANTEA.

Max. A specific name for the soybean (which see).

maxima, -us, -um (macks′i-ma). Large or largest.

MAYAPPLE. Woodland, perennial herbs constituting the genus **Podophyllum** (po-do-fil′lum) of the family Berberidaceae, all but one of the 5 known species Asiatic, the other North American. They have a creeping rootstock from which springs a forked stem. Leaves of two sorts, one solitary, shield-shaped, and with the leafstalk attached to the center of the 3–7-lobed blade, the others in pairs. Flowers cup-shaped, nodding, white or pinkish, waxy, usually short-stalked in the fork of the stem. Petals and sepals colored alike. Fruit a berry. (*Podophyllum* is from the Greek for foot and leaf, in allusion to

the stout leafstalks.) *See* PODOPHYLLACEAE.

These should be grown only in good rich woods soil in shady or partly shady parts of the wild garden. They can easily be propagated by division of the rootstocks, which in the native species are medicinal. *See* MEDICINAL PLANTS.

P. emodi. A little-known plant from the Himalayas, the leaves 3–5-lobed, bronzy in youth. Flowers white or pale pink. Fruit red.

P. peltatum. The common mayapple of eastern N.A., called also Indian apple, Mayflower, and mandrake (for the true mandrake *see* MANDRAGORA). Not over 18 in. high, the leaves nearly 12 in. wide, generally 5–7-lobed, and green. Flowers white, rather unpleasantly scented, nearly 2 in. wide. Fruit yellow, about 1 in. long, edible when fully ripe, otherwise somewhat dangerous. May.

MAY-BLOB = *Caltha palustris*. *See* MARSH MARIGOLD.

MAYFLOWER. Many plants have been so called. Two of the best-known Mayflowers are hepatica and trailing arbutus (see both terms). For other Mayflowers in the ENCYCLOPEDIA *see* MAIANTHEMUM CANADENSE, MAYAPPLE, and CLAYTONIA VIRGINICA. There is no plant to which *Mayflower* should be restricted.

MAYPOP = *Passiflora incarnata*.

Mays. Original Indian name in the Caribbean for corn; now usually spelled maize. *See* CORN.

MAYTEN = *Maytenus Boaria*.

MAYTENUS (may-tee′nus). A large genus of evergreen shrubs and trees of the family Celastraceae, all but a handful from S.A., the rest West Indian, and only **M. Boaria**, the mayten, of any hort. interest. As cult. in Fla., Calif., and similar climates it is a tree not usually over 25 ft., but higher in the wild. Leaves leathery, lance-oval, about 1¼ in. long, alternate,* stalked and toothed. Flowers very small, greenish, polygamous,* clustered in the leaf axils.* Chile. The mayten is a graceful tree with more or less hanging branches. It is sometimes planted as a street tree in the tropics. (*Maytenus* is the Latinized version of the Chilean *mayten*, the native name for these trees.)

MAYWEED = *Anthemis Cotula*. *See* list at WEEDS.

MAZUS (may′zus). A small group of low, prostrate, perennial herbs of the family Schrophulariaceae, three of the six known species grown in the rock garden or as ground covers. All are from Asia, Indo-Malaya, or Australasia. They have alternate* or opposite* leaves, or sometimes only basal ones, all stalked, toothed or cut. Flowers blue or white, sometimes yellow-eyed, in terminal, slightly 1-sided clusters (racemes*). Corolla irregular* and 2-lipped, the upper lip erect and 2-lobed, the larger lower lip 3-lobed and with 2 ridges in the throat. Stamens* 4. Fruit a capsule. (*Mazus* is Greek for teat, in allusion to the ridges on the corolla.)

---

* Special articles on the subjects indicated by an asterisk (*) will be found at the words so marked.

The plants are not difficult to grow and are easily increased by division. *M. Pumilio* is not hardy north of zone° 5 and ·should be mulched even there over the winter. They are good plants for covering bare ground, the species being erect. The first two are evergreen in mild climates.

japonicus. A prostrate perennial, only the flowering branches erect and sometimes 6–9 in. high. Leaves ¾–2 in. long, coarsely but bluntly toothed. Flowers blue, about ⅝ in. long, the ridges on the lower lip brown-spotted, and bearded. Eastern As. Sometimes known as *M. rugosus.* May–June.

Pumilio. A prostrate perennial, the underground stems creeping. Leaves nearly 3 in. long, coarsely toothed or sometimes without teeth. Flowers white or bluish, about ⅓ in. long, sometimes yellow-eyed. Australia. June–July.

reptans. A ground-covering perennial, not over 2 in. high, rooting at the joints. Leaves lance-shaped or elliptic, about 1 in. long and coarsely toothed. Flowers small, in 1-sided profuse clusters, prominently 2-lipped, lavender or purplish-blue. Himalayas(?). June–Aug.

MAZZARD CHERRY. *See* Prunus avium.

McKEE JUNGLE GARDENS. *See* No. 5 at Garden Tours.

Meadia (meed′i-a). The specific name for a shooting star (*Dodecatheon*), named for Richard Mead, an English doctor.

MEADOW-BEAUTY. *See* Rhexia.

MEADOW-BEAUTY FAMILY = Melastomaceae.

MEADOW FESCUE = *Festuca elatior.*

MEADOW-FOAM = *Limnanthes douglasi.*

MEADOW FOXTAIL = *Alopecurus pratensis.*

MEADOW LILY = *Lilium canadense.*

MEADOW PINK = *Dianthus deltoides* and *Habenaria fimbriata.*

MEADOW RUE. *See* Thalictrum.

MEADOW SAFFRON. *See* Colchicum.

MEADOW SALSIFY = *Tragopogon pratensis.*

MEADOWSWEET = *Spiraea alba* and S. *latifolia. See also* Filipendula.

MEADOW VIOLET = *Viola papilionacea.*

MEALY BELLWORT = *Uvularia perfoliata.*

MEALYBUG. Scale insects that live under white, woolly masses, and suck their food from the victim. Mealybugs are everywhere, especially in greenhouses. *See* True Bugs at Insect Pests. *See also* the Insect Pests at many greenhouse plants.

MEANS GRASS = *Sorghum halepense.*

MEASURES. For sizes, volumes, capacity, etc., *see* Weights and Measures. For the number of plants per acre, amount of seed, height of trees, longevity of seed, etc., *see* Garden Tables.

MECONOPSIS (me-kō-nop′sis). A genus of about 45 species of annual or perennial herbs of the poppy family, single-stemmed or branched and with a yellow juice. Leaves alternate,° without marginal teeth, divided or cut, short-stalked or stalkless. Flowers borne singly, or in flat-topped or branching, terminal clusters, yellow, reddish or blue. Petals 4, sometimes 5 to 9. Fruit, a pod (capsule°), oblong or club-shaped. As., N.A., western Eu. (*Meconopsis* is derived from the Greek for poppy-like.)

A number of species of *Meconopsis* are popular in the border and in the rock garden. They are mostly hardy and grow from seed sown in the open in the spring, or they may be started in the house or greenhouse and transplanted. In order to have the annual or biennial sorts blossom the second year the seedlings should be carried on in pots over summer and planted out in the autumn. Most of them, however, do not like the heat and dryness of our hot summers and are hence best grown in partial shade and with ample moisture.

baileyi = *Meconopsis betonicifolia baileyi.*

betonicifolia. A perennial herb growing as high as 6 ft. Leaves 6 in. long, somewhat oval or oblong, with large marginal teeth, or nearly divided to the center, covered with bloom on the under side. Flowers blue-violet or purple, 2 in. across, in broad, flat-topped clusters (cymes°). Tibet and Burma. The var. baileyi differs only in the ovary° being covered with yellowish bristles instead of being smooth, as in the typical form, and in its blue flowers. It is a fine blue-flowered var., but difficult to grow in the East, needing protection from hot winds and applications of liquid manure as it approaches blooming.

cambrica. Welsh poppy. A pale green, slightly hairy, perennial herb growing 2 ft. high, and forming large tufts. Leaves 4–6 in. long, cut feather-fashion (pinnate°), the parts of the leaf with sharp marginal teeth, and having a bloom beneath. Flowers pale yellow, 2 in. across, borne singly, high above the finely cut foliage. Rocky woods and shady places in western Eu.

heterophylla. Wind poppy. A smooth, slender, annual herb, 1 to 2 ft. high. Leaves 4–6 in. long, cut irregularly feather-fashion. Flowers brick-red, with purple center, 2 in. across, satiny in texture, borne singly on slender stalks. An attractive plant from western N.A., by some considered as of the genus *Stylomecon.*

napaulensis. Satin poppy. A perennial from 3 to 6 ft. high, making a mound of attractive foliage, covered with a bloom. Leaves cut feather-fashion (pinnate°), covered with rusty hairs. Flowers pale blue, satiny crinkled, with rounded petals. Central As. Called also *M. wallichi.*

pratti. An annual herb growing 3 ft. high. Leaves 3½–5½ in. long and 1 in. wide. Flowers blue, sometimes tinged with purple, in long terminal clusters (racemes°). China. Called also *M. horridula.*

wallichi = *M. napaulensis.*

MEDEOLA (me-dee′o-la). A perennial woodland herb of the lily family, growing in eastern N.A. There is but one species *M. virginiana*, known as Indian cucumber-root, because of the taste of the edible root. It grows 2 ft. high. The leaves are 3–5 in. long and about 2 in. wide, growing in two widely separated whorls° Flowers small,

---

° Special articles on the subjects indicated by an asterisk (°) will be found at the words so marked.

greenish, nodding, in an umbel,* surrounded by the upper circle of leaves. The fruit is a purple berry. It is found mostly in damp soil and suited mostly for the wild garden. (Named for the sorceress Medea, because of its supposed medicinal virtues.)

media, -us, -um (mee′dĭ-a). Intermediate.

MEDIACID. A soil term for acid soils with a pH of 5.0. For the details *see* ACID AND ALKALI SOILS.

MEDIC. *See* MEDICAGO.

medica (med′ĭ-ka). From the ancient country of Media, now part of Iran.

MEDICAGO (med-i-kā′go). A genus of about 50 species of annual and perennial herbs, rarely shrubs, of the pea family. Leaves alternate, the leaflets arranged feather-fashion, in threes, and toothed. Flowers small, pea-like, yellow or violet, in terminal clusters, or in heads from the axils* of the leaves. The fruit is a spirally twisted, unsplitting pod, smooth or spiny, 1- to few-seeded. Commonly known as medic or hop-clover. Old World plants and naturalized in N.A. (Named from Medice, the Greek name for alfalfa which is supposed to have come from Media.)

Some of the annual species are grown for ornament and are easily propagated from seed in any ordinary garden soil. Other species are important forage and bee plants.

arabica. Spotted medic. A downy, spreading annual. The flowers 3 to 5, yellow. The pods spiny. Eu. naturalized in N.A.

hispida. Bur clover. A nearly smooth annual, similar to *M. arabica*, but pods having a thin, sharp edge, and furrowed. Eurasia, and naturalized in N.A.

lupulina. Black medic; also known as none-such, and one of the plants that passes for shamrock. An annual, deep-rooted herb, much-branched, the branches 2½–3 ft. long. Flowers small, light yellow. The fruit, a nearly smooth pod, becoming black. Eu., widely naturalized. Often confused with clover, but the heads of flowers are smaller. It is of no garden value, but is sometimes used for forage.

sativa. Alfalfa; also known as lucerne, purple medic, Burgundy trefoil, or, in California, as Spanish trefoil. A smooth perennial, from 1 to 3 ft. high, and having a long taproot. The leaflets are small, and have distinct marginal teeth. Flowers purplish, in short terminal clusters (racemes*), from the axils* of the leaves. The pods are slightly downy and twisted. Eurasia, now widely grown for a forage plant, especially in western N.A. It is an important bee plant in Calif. If grown for the first time on a site it needs the right sort of bacteria inoculation. *See* LEGUME INOCULATION.

MEDICINAL PLANTS. The collection and cultivation of plants useful in healing is far older than the growing of ornamentals. Our earliest gardens and botanical writings were by men who studied the wild flora more from the medical than the strictly botanical viewpoint. That interest, well over three thousand years old, has never waned, but the U.S. has been singularly out of the picture so far as the cult. of medicinal plants is concerned.

Not one of the really important plant drugs is grown here. The climate is wholly unsuited to cinchona (quinine) or to the cocaine. And the culture, from the drug standpoint, of the plants that produce opium, henbane, ephedrine, aconite, camphor, and several other standard drugs, has not so far been a commercial success, but *see* EPHEDRA. (The production of opium from *Papaver somniferum* is, of course, illegal in the U.S. *See* POPPY.) The causes of the failure are two-fold.

Cheap labor abroad is available for the exacting cultural demands of these plants. All of them can be and most of them are grown in various parts of the U.S., chiefly as ornamentals or for interest. But some of them have been experimented upon by the U.S. Department of Agriculture, and several are grown by large pharmaceutical firms. It was soon found that merely growing the plant is one thing and getting it to produce a yield of its active constituents is quite another. Still more difficult is doing this more economically than foreign growers who are long practiced in the art. In Mich. there are commercially profitable plantations of digitalis.

There is no doubt that with our diversity of climate and soils, especially in a state like Calif., drug plants like the ones mentioned above can some day be grown upon a commercial basis. But much needs to be known about their cultural demands, especially soil and climatic requirements, before that end will be accomplished.

No one should think of undertaking the culture of such plants without a thorough study of them in the regions where they are known to be productive. All of them have long been in cult., and some varieties are far better than others, and a productive variety under one set of conditions may be worthless in another country, or even in the same one, with different handling.

What, then, can be grown in this country? A few things of value in medicine and pharmacy, mostly plants native in the temperate regions of N.A. It is upon these that any intelligent grower should concentrate. But even in this restricted field there are pitfalls. One must be certain that the plant selected cannot be collected more cheaply from wild plants, because this is still an industry of very considerable proportions in this country and Canada. Before starting the culture of any drug plant, study the current prices in lists of wholesale dealers in them.

Among plants of medicinal value, those apparently most worth cultivating are the following:

†Arnica (*Arnica montana*)
†Cascara sagrada (*Rhamnus purshiana*)
 Castor-oil plant (*Ricinus communis*)
 Goldenseal (*Hydrastis canadensis*)
†Licorice (*Glycyrrhiza glabra*)

* Special articles on the subjects indicated by an asterisk (*) will be found at the words so marked.

Mayapple (*Podophyllum peltatum*)
Senega snakeroot (*Polygala Senega*)
Virginia snakeroot (*Aristolochia Serpentaria*)
Wild ginger (*Asarum canadense*)

Those marked with a dagger (†) are suited only to the specialized, rather dry sections of Calif. and should not be attempted, for drug production, elsewhere. All of them can be grown as ornamentals in many other parts of the country. All are entered elsewhere in the ENCYCLOPEDIA and further information about them should be sought for under their names.

The third plant in the list is a common summer-bedding foliage plant all over the country (*see* CASTOR-OIL PLANT), but the production of oil from its seeds is at present confined to tropical regions. It can, however, be grown for oil in southern Calif., Tex., and in southern Fla. But no one should start such an enterprise without careful study of varieties suited to these regions.

The rest of the plants in the list are native American woodland plants of which the goldenseal is by far the most valuable from the medicinal standpoint. All of them, except cascara sagrada, can be grown under the same conditions as ginseng. *See* GINSENG. The latter is not a real medicinal plant at all, the once very large trade in it being based upon the ignorance and superstition of the Chinese, to whom practically all ginseng was sent. Most of them can also be grown in the shadier parts of the wild garden. *See* WILD GARDEN. This location obviates the need for lath shade as in most ginseng plantations. Cascara sagrada is a shrub the cult. of which should not be undertaken far away from its native region. *See* RHAMNUS PURSHIANA.

Even in this rather meager list of medicinal plants worth growing, there are two things to remember: one is the danger of collected sources producing a cheaper product than you can grow; the other, and much more serious, thing is the fact that only a comparatively small amount of any of them, except goldenseal, is needed. In other words, wholesale production would depress the market for any of them. The growing of medicinal plants is thus a very interesting pastime, but can rarely be a serious hort. operation.

No mention is made here of scores of medicinal plants, mostly weedy herbs, for which there is always a steady market. They are grown or collected on a considerable scale, largely by Italians. But their average price ranges from 3–20 cents per pound (dried), and either growing or collecting them is scarcely a profitable undertaking to any busy gardener.

Many plants grown for their fragrant foliage or flowers, and usually classed as "herbs," also yield medicines; some, like mint, on a considerable scale. These are all treated at the article on HERB GARDENING, and the information about them need not be repeated

here. Some of the old wives' remedies made from such plants were known as simples, but their use is often local and traditional rather than medicinal.

MEDINILLA (med-in-nil′la). A genus of about 100 species of handsome Old World greenhouse shrubs and trees of the family Melastomaceae, two of which are grown for ornament. They have attractive, generally opposite* leaves with 3–9 main veins. Flower clusters very showy in the first species because of the highly colored bracts.* Flowers white or rose, in long, branching clusters (panicles*). Petals 5 (in ours). Stamens 8–10. Fruit a berry crowned by the lobes of the persistent calyx.* (Named for Jose de Medinilla, Governor of the Marianas Islands.)

Plant in potting mixture* 4, provide plenty of water and a warm greenhouse for these showy plants of the tropical forests of southeast Asia, where both the cult. species are native. *M. magnifica* is a very striking plant when in bloom, but is not much grown. Both of them want a good light greenhouse, but protection from the direct rays of the sun.

amabilis = *Medinilla teysmanni.*

magnifica. An evergreen shrub or small tree (about 10–15 ft. as cult.), the stems 4-angled. Leaves ovalish or oblong, nearly 12 in. long. Flowers about 1 in. long, and with striking, pinkish bracts.* Philippines.

teysmanni. Stems 4-angled, the leaves ovalish or oblong, nearly 12 in. long. Flowers about 2 in. long, the cluster erect, about 1 ft. long, and without bracts.* Petals red. East Indies.

mediterranea, *-us,* *-um* (med-ĭ-ter-ray′-nee-a). From the region bordering the Mediterranean Sea.

Medium. A pre-Linnaean* name for certain species of bellflower (*Campanula*). *See also* MEDIA.

MEDLAR. *See* MESPILUS.

megacantha, *-us,* *-um* (meg-a-kan′tha). Large-spined.

megapotamica, *-us,* *-um* (meg-a-po-tam′-i-ca). Of or from a big river.

MEGASEA = *Bergenia.*

megastigma, *-us,* *-um* (meg-a-stig′ma). With a large stigma.*

MEIWA KUMQUAT = *Fortunella crassifolia.*

MELALEUCA (mel-a-lew′ka). Bottlebrush. Tea-tree. A genus of Australian trees and shrubs of the myrtle family, comprising 100 species, closely allied to the genus *Callistemon.* Leaves mostly alternate,* simple. Flowers red, white, or yellow in spikes or heads, the stamens* so much protruding that the flowers resemble a bottlebrush. Fruit a capsule. (*Melaleuca* is from the Greek for black and white, in allusion to the black trunk and white branches of one species.)

These shrubs and trees are freely planted in Calif. and in other warm regions, some

---

* Special articles on the subjects indicated by an asterisk (*) will be found at the words so marked.

as ornamental shrubs, others to fix muddy shores, and others for timber. They grow well in almost any type of soil. They are propagated by cuttings of ripened wood and by seeds. The capsules are gathered in summer and allowed to ripen on sheets of paper or in boxes. They can also be grown in the cool greenhouse in potting mixture* 4.

armillaris. Shrub or small tree, sometimes 30 ft. high. Leaves crowded, very narrow, ¾ in. long, ¹⁄₁₆ in. or less wide, smooth, pointed, and often curved at the tip. Flowers white, the spike-like cluster 2 in. long.

decussata. Large shrub or small tree up to 20 ft. high. Leaves opposite,* small and narrow, ½ in. long and ⅛–⅛ in. wide, sharp-pointed. Flowers lilac, the spikes 1 in. or less long.

ericifolia. A large shrub or small tree. Leaves narrow, ½ in. or less long. Flowers yellowish-white, in spikes 1 in. long. Sterile flowers in nearly round, terminal heads.

hypericifolia. Hillock-tree. Tall, smooth shrub. Leaves mostly opposite,* oblong or narrower, 1½ in. long and ¼ in. wide, blunt or abruptly pointed. Flowers rich red, in dense spikes 2–3 in. long.

Leucadendron. Cajuput tree; also known as punk-tree or paper bush. Large, conspicuous tree, with spongy bark, shredding in wide strips. Leaves 2–4 in. long, ½–¾ in. wide, tapering at both ends. Flowers creamy-white, in terminal spikes 2–6 in. long.

melanoleuca, -us, -um (me-lan-o-loo′ka). Black and white.

melanocarpa, -us, -um (mel-an-o-kar′pa). Black-fruited.

melanoxylon (mel-an-ox′ee-lon). Having black or dark-colored wood.

MELANTHACEAE. See LILIACEAE.

melanthera, -us, -um (mel-an′ther-ra). With black anthers.

MELANTHIUM (mel-an′thĭ-um). Unimportant garden plants of the lily family, found in bogs from N.Y. to Fla. and westward and suited only to the bog garden. Less than half a dozen species are known, of which **M. virginicum,** the bunchflower, is the only one likely to be cult. It is a stout plant with a thickish rootstock and mostly basal leaves in a dense, rosette-like cluster, the leaves narrow and about 12 in. long. Flowering stalk nearly 4½ ft. high, crowned at the top with a large branching cluster (panicle*). Flowers small, greenish-white, often unisexual* or polygamous.* Fruit a 3-valved, many-seeded capsule.* (*Melanthium* is from the Greek for black flower, perhaps in allusion to the dark-colored flowers of some species.)

MELASTOMACEAE (me-las-toe-may′see-ee). The meadow-beauty family comprises, among its cult. genera, chiefly tropical trees and shrubs, except the meadow-beauty (see RHEXIA), which is a native herb in the bogs and marshes of eastern U.S. There are over 150 genera and nearly 4000 species, some of great beauty as to flowers or leaves, often both. Practically all are tropical, the Amazon valley being especially rich in them.

Leaves opposite* (sometimes whorled*), the chief veins often running from the base to tip in strikingly arched curves, sometimes handsomely colored. Flowers often very showy and in magnificent clusters, sometimes also, with brightly colored bracts.* Fruit a berry, or dry, enclosed in the often persistent calyx.

The family furnishes some of our most beautiful greenhouse plants, but they are not much cult. except *Tibouchina, Medinilla, Miconia,* and *Phyllagathis,* all trees or shrubs. Tropical, herbaceous plants, chiefly grown for their strikingly handsome foliage include: *Bertolonia, Sonerila, Heterocentron, Schizocentron* (a vine-like plant with purple flowers), and *Centradenia.* All are occasionally grown outdoors in frost-free, warm regions with plenty of moisture.

Technical flower characters: Flowers regular.* Calyx united into a tube which is 4–5-lobed at the tip, and often joined to the mostly inferior* ovary. Petals 4–5. Stamens* 4–5 or 8–10, sometimes alternating as to length.

Meleagris, -e (mel-ee-ā′gris). Speckled like a guinea-hen.

MELIA (mee′lǐ-a). A genus of Asian or Australian, deciduous or half-evergreen trees of the family Meliaceae. About a score have been described, but only one is in common cult. in this country, **M. Azedarach,** the China-tree, also known as Chinaberry and bead-tree. It has alternate compound leaves, the leaflets arranged feather-fashion (pinnate*) and toothed. Flowers conspicuous, in compound, terminal clusters (panicles*), from the axils* of the leaves, white or purple. It is a mostly deciduous tree of spreading habit, sometimes growing 50 ft. high, with furrowed bark. The fruit is nearly round, yellow, ¾ in. across, hanging on after the leaves fall. Himalayas and China. Cult. since the 16th century and naturalized in all warm-temperate and tropical regions around the world. The *var.* **umbraculiformis,** the Texas umbrella tree, has drooping foliage, on erect, crowded branches which spread from the trunk like spokes, thus giving an umbrella-like effect. It originated before 1860, and is hardy up to zone* 5. (*Melia* is an ancient Greek name for the ash, but given to the genus by Linnaeus.)

MELIACEAE (mee-lǐ-ā′see-ee). The mahogany family is of little garden interest, none at all if it were not for the widely cultivated China-tree (see MELIA). Of the other two cult. genera, *Swietenia* (the mahogany) is tropical and so are most of the species of *Cedrela,* except the hardy *C. sinensis.* The family has over 40 genera and 700 species, nearly all tropical shrubs and trees.

Leaves mostly alternate* and compound,* often very large, the leaflets arranged feather-fashion. Flowers not showy (except in *Melia*), usually in many-branched clusters. Fruit fleshy and colored in *Melia,* a some-

---

* Special articles on the subjects indicated by an asterisk (*) will be found at the words so marked.

what leathery pod (capsule*) in the other cult. genera.

Technical flower characters: Calyx 4–5-cleft, the edges of the lobes overlapping. Petals 4–5, free, or united to the stamens. Stamens* 8–10, usually united into a tube. Ovary superior,* mostly 2–5-celled.

MELIANTHACEAE (mee-lĭ-an-thay'see-ee). A family of African trees and shrubs with only 3 genera and about 17 species, having two cult. genera, *Greyia* and *Melianthus*, grown for ornament in warm regions or, rarely, in greenhouses.

Leaves alternate,* compound* in *Melianthus*, simple* in *Greyia*. Flowers very irregular* in *Melianthus*, but regular* in *Greyia*, borne in terminal clusters (racemes*) in both genera, or the clusters sometimes in the leaf axils.* Fruit a dry pod (capsule*).

Technical flower characters: Flowers hermaphrodite*; by the twisting of flower stalks each flower is inverted. Sepals 4 or 5. Petals 4 or 5, one of them in *Melianthus*, abortive and long-clawed.* Stamens* 4 in *Melianthus*, 10 in *Greyia*. Ovary superior.*

MELIANTHUS (mee-lee-an'thus). Honeybush. Strong-scented, handsome, evergreen, South African shrubs of the family Melianthaceae, rather popular in southern Calif. for outdoor cult. but little grown elsewhere. Of the six known species only **M. major**, which is sometimes called the honey-flower, is of hort. interest. It grows 7–10 ft. high, and has alternate,* compound* leaves which are nearly 1 ft. long. Leaflets arranged feather-fashion, toothed, the stalks winged. Flowers about 1 in. long, reddish-brown (for details *see* MELIANTHACEAE), the showy cluster nearly 1 ft. long. Fruit a papery capsule.* (*Melianthus* is from the Greek for honey and flower, in allusion to the sweet flowers.)

MELICOCCA (mel-i-cock'a). Two tropical American species of trees of the family Sapindaceae, one of them, **M. bijuga**, the genip (also called mamoncillo or Spanish lime), cult. for its fruit in Fla., where it fruits best near Key West, although it is hardy as far north as Palm Beach. It is a tree up to 50 ft. high, the leaves alternate,* compound,* the leaflets only 2 pairs, more or less elliptic and 2–4 in. long, the stalks winged. Flowers fragrant, small, greenish-white, the male and female on different trees, or occasionally polygamous.* Fruit fleshy (a drupe*), about 1 in. in diameter, the flesh yellow, juicy, rather sweet, but well liked. Care must be taken to see that there are ample supplies of both male and female trees, in the absence of which there will be no fruit. Some plantations have failed because this has not been looked after. (*Melicocca* is from the Greek for honey and berry, in allusion to the taste of the fruit.)

MELILOT. *See* MELILOTUS.

MELILOTUS (mel-li-lō'tus). Melilot or sweet clover. Weedy herbs of the pea fam-

ily, comprising about 20 species, all from the Old World, and of no garden interest except as planted for forage, soil improvement, or as bee plants. They are annual, biennial, or perennial herbs with rather sweet-smelling foliage, and have compound* leaves with only 3, essentially stalkless, leaflets. Flowers very small, pea-like, in narrow, spire-like clusters (racemes*) which may be terminal or in the leaf axils.* Fruit a small, egg-shaped pod, with only 1 or 2 seeds, not pea-like and scarcely splitting. (*Melilocca* is from the Greek for honey lotus, in allusion to the fragrance of the foliage and its similarity to the genus *Lotus*.)

The sweet clovers are of very simple requirements and are more often roadside waifs than cult. plants. But any of them are useful as green manure, and the white melilot is much liked by bees. If grown for green manure, for the first time on a particular site, it is a good plan to provide a culture of the bacteria usually associated with their roots. *See* LEGUME INOCULATION.

alba. White melilot; also called Bokhara clover. A Eurasian biennial herb, widely naturalized in the U.S. It grows from 5–8 ft. high and is very bushy. Flowers white. Summer. The *var.* **annua**, the Hubam clover, is used for forage. It matures in a single season.

caerulea = *Trigonella caerulea*.

indica. A Eurasian perennial, not over 3 ft. high, found as an occasional weed over the eastern U.S. but grown as a cover crop on the Pacific Coast. Leaflets wedge-shaped, but slightly notched at the tip. Flowers yellow.

officinalis. Yellow melilot; also called King's clover. Resembling *M. indica*, but the leaflets larger, nearly oval, and not notched. Flowers yellow, larger than in *M. indica*.

MELISSA (me-lis'sa). Lemon-scented Eurasian herbs of the mint family, comprising only 3–4 species, of which only **M. officinalis**, the lemon or bee balm, is in cult. It is an erect perennial, with opposite,* broad, toothed leaves and a square stem. Leaves 1–3 in. long. Flowers irregular,* 2-lipped, not over ½ in. long, white, arranged in small, close clusters in the leaf axils.* It is widely grown for its value in seasoning; for its culture *see* HERB GARDENING. A variegated-leaved form is sometimes grown for ornament in the border. Both bloom in late summer, and the common form is occasionally naturalized in eastern N.A. (*Melissa* is Greek for bee, perhaps in allusion to the shape of the flower or to the sweet odor of the plant.) It may become a pest from self-sown seed, which is very plentiful.

mellifera, -us, -um (mel-lif'er-ra). Honey-bearing.

Melo (mee'lo). Old Latin for melon. *See* CUCUMIS.

MELOCACTUS (me-lo-kak'tus). A genus of tropical American, largely Caribbean cacti, grown for interest rather than ornament, outdoors only in the warmest parts of the U.S. and in greenhouses devoted to succulents. Of the 18 known species only the 3 below are of much hort. interest. The plant body

---

* Special articles on the subjects indicated by an asterisk (*) will be found at the words so marked.

is melon-shaped, globular, or cylindric, or
sometimes like a flattened orange, with 9–20
prominent ribs, upon which are borne clustered spines. Flowers not large or showy,
usually pinkish or red, mostly opening in
the middle of the afternoon, and borne on
a terminal, cushion-like or hairy structure,
often colored and turban-like (hence the
common name of Turk's-cap cactus for one
of them). Fruit fleshy. (*Melocactus* is from
the Latin for melon and *Cactus*, in allusion
to the shape of the plants.) By some considered as belonging to the genus *Cactus*.

For culture *see* CACTI.

communis. Turk's-head or Turk's-cap cactus.
Plant body cylindric or roundish-cylindric, not
over 12 in. high (less as cult.), the terminal,
fez-like, flower-bearing part tawny red. Ribs
10 or 11, the spines needle-like. Flowers about
1½ in. long, red. Jamaica.

intortus. Plant body nearly globular and
nearly 3 ft. high, the terminal, flower-bearing
part a densely woolly head, often 8–9 in.
high. Ribs 14–20, the yellowish-brown spines
about 3 in. long. Flowers about ¾ in. long,
pinkish. W.I.

macrocanthos. Plant body depressed-globu-
lar (*i.e.*, orange-shaped), but 8–11 in. high,
the terminal, flower-bearing part 8–9 in. long.
Spines of 2 sorts, the outer ones of each
cluster needle-like and flattened, the central
ones stouter and erect. Flower pinkish, about
¾ in. long. Curaçao and neighboring islands.

MELON. The term as commonly used
includes the fruits of two distinct genera of
the Cucurbitaceae — *Cucumis Melo*, the
cantaloupe or muskmelon, honeydew, casaba,
and related varieties; and *Citrullus vulgaris*,
the watermelon and citron (*see* WATER-
MELON).

CUCUMIS MELO. A warm-temperate annual, with trailing or climbing, soft, hairy
vines. The fruit varies greatly in the many
cult. forms or botanical varieties. Native
to Persia or As. *Var.* **reticulatus:** Netted or
nutmeg melons. Includes Central American
varieties of cantaloupes and muskmelons.
Fruit with netted skin, shallow sutures* and

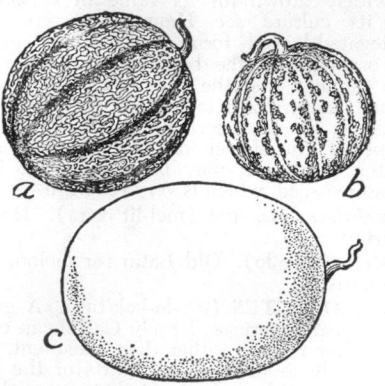

(*a*) Netted or nutmeg melon; (*b*) a European
type of cantaloupe; (*c*) the winter melon, to
which belong the casaba and honeydew melon.

ribs, and flesh varying from light green to
reddish-orange, with a musky odor. *Var.*
cantalupensis: Eu. cantaloupe. Fruits have
hard rinds and are rough, warty, or scaly.
Not grown in N.A., but many varieties of
what are universally but incorrectly called
cantaloupes are grown here, and conforming to this usage they will hereafter be
called cantaloupes or muskmelons, as in the
U.S. the terms are interchangeable. *Var.*

A melon vine. Note the unforked tendrils,*
which are forked in the watermelon.

inodorus: Winter melons. Fruits lack musky
odor, ripen late, and keep well. Skin smooth,
ridged, or corrugated; flesh whitish, light
green, or orange. Here belong the Crenshaw,
Persian, casabas and honeydews. *Var.* **flex-
uosus:** Snake melon. Long, slender, crooked,
non-netted fruits. Inedible. A novelty in
N.A. *Var.* **chito:** Mango melon, vegetable
orange, vine peach. Fruits size and shape
of orange; yellow or greenish; flesh white,
not fragrant, cucumber-like. Used for making preserves and pickles. *Var.* **dudaim:**
Pomegranate melon, Queen Anne's pocket
melon. Small, round, very fragrant, inedible.
Used in U.S. only for ornamental purposes.

The cantaloupe in U.S. originated with
the introduction of the Netted Gem variety
from France in 1881. From this the varieties collectively known as Rocky Ford have
been developed, particularly in the Rocky
Ford district of Colo. Prior to 1895 muskmelons, lacking quality, uniformity, and ability to withstand shipping, were available
locally for only a few weeks each summer:
high-quality melons are now available from
May to October.

CULTURE. For successful culture cantaloupes require a long, warm growing season.
In cool sections of eastern and northern U.S.,
to secure a sufficiently long season, plants
must be started under protection and transplanted to the field when frost danger is past,

---

* Special articles on the subjects indicated by an asterisk (*) will be found at the words so marked.

as in the case of the famous Montreal melon. In Imperial Valley of Calif. the earliest crop is secured by planting in Nov. and Dec. and protecting the individual plants with glassine paper covers or Hotkaps, until frost danger is past. Additional protection is given a small acreage by "brushing" or placing strips of heavy paper along the north side of each row. Hotkaps and brush are removed as early as the season allows.

Melons thrive on any well-drained, friable,* fertile soil: for early crops a light, sandy loam is preferred. Excessive alkali should be avoided. Manures or fertilizers are not generally used for market gardens but in home gardens the use of a forkful of well-rotted manure or a cupful of complete fertilizer applied directly below each hill, is recommended, but neither must touch the roots.

Where irrigation is necessary, *i.e.*, the semi-arid Southwest, melons are grown on raised beds, with a smooth slope, preferably facing south; in regions of summer rainfall, on level ground. Seed is drilled in rows with a seeder or planted in hills by hand just above the water mark on the south slope of the bed. If planted on the level, seed should be planted in rows 6 to 8 ft. apart, and hills 3 to 5 ft. in the row, with 2 or 3 plants per hill. Plant double that number and thin to 2–3 per hill. Seed should be planted 1–1½ in. deep.

When transplanting is necessary, the plants are started in a hotbed or greenhouse. Plant bands or pots are used and the plants set in the field while quite small, without disturbing the root system, as melons and other plants of the cucumber family transplant with difficulty. When seed is planted directly to the field, the soil must be warm and frost danger past; the seed germinates best at about 80° F. and will rot in a cold, damp soil; 6 to 12 days are required for germination. If field conditions are not favorable for germination, the seed may be soaked overnight, germinated on moist cloth or paper, and put in the ground when the root is an inch long.

Edibility of cantaloupes and related melons depends on texture, flavor, and sweetness. During ripening the flesh softens, due to change of pectic substances to soluble form; sugars increase up to the "full slip" stage, then decrease. There is no reserve of starch; sugars decrease after removal from vine and will not increase if picked green. The expressed juice should contain at least 8% soluble solids; high-quality fruits contain 12 to 15%. In certain varieties the fruit stalk is naturally detached at maturity or "slips"; in others, not. Yellowing of the skin and softening of the blossom end of the fruit accompany maturity. Flavor depends on variety and growing conditions.

For the West and Southwest the chief varieties are: Hale's Best (several strains), Perfecto, Hearts of Gold, Emerald Gem (orange flesh); Honey Dew, Honey Ball (green flesh). The Persian, a large, coarse,

orange-fleshed variety, and Golden Beauty casaba, white-fleshed, are shipped from California, as well as the Crenshaw, a recent var. with wrinkled skin and superb, salmon-orange, and very sweet flesh. Most of these vars. cannot be grown in the East, except Hale's Best and Hearts of Gold which do well both in the West and East.

For the home grower in the East the best varieties are: Granite State (developed by the University of New Hampshire); good for short-season areas; Hackensack, Montreal, Honey Rock, Rocky Ford (in several strains) are all green-fleshed, and, some think, superior to all others. Of the orange-fleshed varieties perhaps the finest are: Hearts of Gold, Pride of Wisconsin, Delaware Queen, Delicious, and Hale's Best. Contrary to popular belief the presence of squash or pumpkin vines has no effect whatever on the flavor of adjacent melons, but the seed of such erratic crossing is useless for future planting.

MELONS IN THE GREENHOUSE. This is unnecessary except in short-season regions in the northern states and Canada, and should be attempted only by those who can devote a whole greenhouse to them, for the temperature demands are exacting. The night temperature must not be below 70° and the day temperature 80°–85°. Seed may be planted in potting mixture* 4, to which an extra amount of well-rotted manure should be added. If grown in the bench, the soil need not be over 6 in. deep, or the seed may be planted in boxes of the same depth. Some growers prefer to start the plants in pots and transfer them later to the permanent place. They should be started in small pots and gradually potted-on until they need a 5-in. pot, when they are ready for planting out in the greenhouse.

The vines must be trained to grow as near the glass as possible and, of course, all female flowers must be hand-pollinated, preferably on clear, bright days. As the fruit sets and increases in size, a net must be attached firmly to the roof of the house and the maturing fruit cradled in it; otherwise, the weight of the fruit will tear the vine from its support.

Growing melons so as to get fruit in winter is not easy, because the vines must be kept in active growth, which means plenty of water and frequent applications of liquid manure. Keeping up such a program during the dull or relatively dark days of winter is apt to provoke disease unless the houses are watched very carefully. Keeping the proper atmospheric moisture in the house demands wetting down the floors twice during the night as well as during the day.

The best varieties for forcing (nearly all English) are: 1. (Green-fleshed) Sutton's Ringleader, Perfection, Windsor Castle; 2. (Scarlet-fleshed) Sutton's A-1, Sutton's Scarlet; 3. (White-fleshed) Royal Favorite, Hero of Lockinge.

INSECT PESTS. Control of cucumber beetles and melon aphids is given at CUCUMBER.

---

* Special articles on the subjects indicated by an asterisk (*) will be found at the words so marked.

Because of longer vine life, beetles must be kept down to avoid wilt. Pickleworm and melon worm are both southern pests but occasionally are seen in the North. Control with pesticide #20 sprays. (*See* Sprays and Dusts.)

Diseases. *See* Cucumber.

MELON FAMILY = Cucurbitaceae.

Melongena (mel-on-gee′na). Pre-Linnaean* name for the eggplant or some relatives of it. *See* Solanum.

MELON PEAR = *Solanum muricatum.*

MELON SHRUB = *Solanum muricatum.*

Melopepo (mee-lo-pee′po). A specific name derived from the old names for melon and pumpkin, signifying a melon-like pumpkin. *See* Cucurbita.

MEMORIAL ROSE = *Rosa wichuraiana.*

MENDEL. Gregor Mendel (1822–1884) experimented with garden peas for eight years in an Augustinian cloister garden in Brünn, Czechoslovakia. In 1865 he presented his results and interpretations before the local scientific society, which in 1866 published them. They attracted no attention until 1900, when similar results, obtained independently by several scientists, brought them into prominence, and Mendel soon became known as the father of genetics, or the modern study of heredity, variation, environment, and their interrelations.

Mendel thought of the character differences between true-breeding pea varieties as occurring in pairs — tall *vs.* dwarf varieties, colored *vs.* white-flowered varieties, smooth *vs.* wrinkled-seeded varieties. From experiments and studies on seven pairs of such characters, he arrived at certain conclusions which have become known as Mendel's laws. These are three in number — dominance, segregation, and independent assortment.

Mendel found that when a true-breeding tall variety of pea was crossed with a true-breeding dwarf variety, the offspring (F₁)* were all tall. Because only the tall character appeared, he called it *dominant.** Since the dwarf character was not expressed, though potentially inherited, he called it *recessive* (*see* Dominant). All characters, he thought, were either dominant or recessive, but we know now that, in many cases, both are partially expressed, resulting in characters intermediate between those of the parents. Whichever variety was used as pollen parent, the same results were obtained.

Pollinating any one of these F₁ tall plants with their own pollen (self-pollinated), the seed obtained produced approximately 3 tall plants to 1 dwarf. Self-pollinating these plants, Mendel found the dwarfs produced only dwarfs, whereas the talls were of two kinds — 1 tall out of 3 bred true, while the remaining 2 talls each had offspring approximately three-fourths of which were tall, and one-fourth dwarf. Mendel thought of these characters as being represented in the pollen grains and egg cells. Diagrammatically, the

above described three generations may be shown thus:

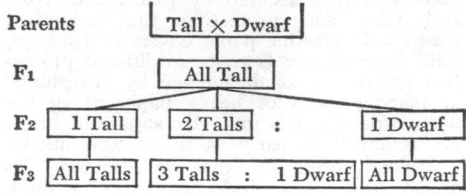

Parents	Tall × Dwarf			
F₁	All Tall			
F₂	1 Tall	2 Talls :		1 Dwarf
F₃	All Talls	3 Talls : 1 Dwarf		All Dwarf

Combining tall and dwarf in an F₁ hybrid, only tall shows. Segregation takes place, and both the grandparental types (tall and dwarf) reappear in a definite, predictable ratio.

The third contribution Mendel made to an understanding of heredity is "independent assortment," which simply means that any two of these pairs of characters previously described, when present in the same F₁ plant, are inherited as though they were associated purely by accident or chance. The result is that a tall, colored-flowered race crossed with a dwarf, white-flowered race would produce only tall, colored-flowered offspring, which when selfed* would give a predictable ratio in this case — 9 tall colored : 3 tall white : 3 dwarf colored: 1 dwarf white — which is only another way of saying (3 talls + 1 dwarf) × (3 colored + 1 white).

Since 1900, experiments testing these laws have been performed on thousands of varieties of hundreds of species of plants involving many different kinds of characters, and although many new so-called laws have been discovered which add complications, Mendel's contributions have been abundantly confirmed. With these aids, plants can be more and more written in terms of formulas, as chemists do with their compounds. In plants such as maize, peas, tomatoes, sweet peas, and others on which research has been very extensive, one can quite definitely predict the result of many crosses, as chemists do when combining compounds.

To plant breeders, an understanding of Mendel's laws saves time, does away with much useless labor, makes desired results more certain and shows the limitations of what can be expected. Such knowledge provides a lighted road as against an unlighted pathway. — O. E. W. *See also* Plant Breeding.

MENISPERMACEAE (men-i-spur-may′-see-ee). The moonseed family, mostly woody vines in 65 genera and over 400 species, is chiefly tropical, but the only two cult. genera, *Cocculus* and *Menispermum*, are hardy over considerable areas of the U.S. They do not have very showy flowers, but are considerably grown for the handsome foliage and bluish-black or red fruit which often hangs in profuse clusters.

Leaves alternate.* In some species of *Menispermum* the leafstalk arises from the

* Special articles on the subjects indicated by an asterisk (*) will be found at the words so marked.

middle of the blade or near it, instead of from the base. Male and female flowers on separate plants, usually in clusters or small bunches in the leaf axils.* Fruit small, fleshy, the stone usually sculptured.

Technical flower characters: Sepals* 6, in two series; or 10. Petals 6 (in our genera), mostly smaller than the sepals. Stamens* 6 or more. Ovary superior.*

MENISPERMUM (men-i-spur'mum). Moonseed. A genus of only 2 species of North American and Asian twining, woody vines of the family Menispermaceae. Leaves alternate,* shield-shaped, 3–7-lobed. Flowers small, white or yellow in terminal clusters (racemes*) or compound terminal clusters (panicles*). Sepals 4–10. Petals 6–9. Fruit a drupe.* (*Menispermum* is from the Greek for moon and seed.)

Moonseed vines have attractive foliage and are suitable for outdoor culture in the North. They are easily grown from seed or cuttings of ripened wood, or the East Asian species spread by suckers. Only the female plants produce fruit.

canadense. Canada moonseed; also called yellow perilla. Climbing to 12 ft. Leaves round-oval, 4–8 in. long, not toothed, occasionally lobed, soft-hairy beneath when young. Fruit black, resembling grapes. Quebec to Ga. and Ark. May–June. Hardy from zone* 3 southward.

dauricum. Twining to 12 ft. Leaves round-oval, 2½–5 in. long, usually toothed, lobed, pointed, smooth, with a bloom beneath. Flowers in slender-stalked, umbel*-like, compound terminal clusters (panicles*). Fruit black, about ⅜ in. across, in dense clusters. Eastern As. June. Hardy from zone* 3 southward.

MENTHA. *See* Mint.

MENTHACEAE = Labiatae.

mentorensis, -e (men-tor-ren'sis). From or originating in Mentor, Ohio.

MENTZELIA (ment-zee'li-a). A genus of the Loasaceae, containing about 60 species of American annual or perennial herbs, shrubs, or trees, usually with barbed but not stinging hairs. Leaves usually alternate,* without marginal teeth, cut into lobes or cleft almost to the center. Flowers white, yellow, or red, often showy, borne singly, or in terminal clusters (racemes*), or in flat-topped clusters (cymes*). Petals usually 5. Stamens* numerous. Fruit a pod (capsule*), opening at the top. (Named for Christian Mentzel, a German botanist.)

A few species are easily cultivated in the flower garden from seeds sown where the plants are to grow.

aurea = *Mentzelia lindleyi.*
decapetala. Prairie lily; also known as gumbo lily. A biennial herb 1 ft. or more high, the leaves much cut. Flowers white or yellow, 3–5 in. across, the stamens protruding, opening toward night, and very fragrant. S.D. to Tex.
laevicaulis. Blazing star. A stout, perennial herb growing from 2 to 3½ ft. Leaves long, narrow, 2 to 8 in. long, the edges wavy, with marginal teeth. Flowers light yellow, 2½ to 4 in. across, the petals pointed. Wyo. to Calif.

lindleyi. An annual, 1 to 4 ft. high, single-stalked, or branched and straggling. Leaves 2 to 3 in. long, coarsely toothed or cleft. Flowers 1½ to 2½ in. across, bright yellow, opening in the evening and closing the following morning, very fragrant. Calif. Sometimes offered as *Bartonia aurea.*

MENYANTHACEAE. *See* Gentianaceae.

MENYANTHES (men-yan'theez). A single cult. species of bog or marsh perennial herbs of the gentian family, found in the cooler parts of the north temperate zone and not uncommon in many parts of N.A. The only species, **M. trifoliata,** the buckbean (also called bogbean and marsh trefoil), is a sprawling, rather fleshy herb with creeping rootstocks and long-stalked, compound* leaves with 3 oblongish leaflets without marginal teeth. The leafstalk is sometimes as long as 10 in. and sheathing at the base. Flowers in terminal, 10–20-flowered, long-stalked clusters (racemes*). Corolla shortly funnel-shaped, about ½ in. long, usually white (rarely purplish), bearded on the inside, blooming from May–July. Fruit a slowly splitting capsule,* nearly ¾ in. long. The plant can be grown only in the bog garden (which see). (*Menyanthes* is from the Greek, perhaps signifying a flower that blooms successively.)

MENZIESIA (men-zee'sĭ-a). A genus of American and Asian small, deciduous shrubs of the heath family comprising about 7 species. Leaves alternate,* without marginal teeth. Flowers in terminal clusters, bell- or urn-shaped. Stamens 5–10, not protruding. Fruit a leathery capsule.* (Named for Archibald Menzies, an English surgeon and naturalist.)

They are of no particular ornamental value, but are very hardy in the North and often planted in the rock garden. They are easily propagated by seeds, by layers, and by cuttings of mature wood under glass. The only cult. species is:

pilosa. Minnie-bush. A shrub sometimes growing 6 ft. high. Leaves twice as long as wide or longer, abruptly sharp-pointed, soft-hairy above and fringed with hairs. Flowers bell-shaped, ¼ in. long, yellowish-white or pinkish, few, drooping. Capsule somewhat oval, covered with glandular* bristles. Pa. to Ga. and Ala. on the mountains. May–June. Hardy from zone* 3 southward. Use soil with a pH of 4–5. For a plant listed as *M. polifolia* see Daboecia cantabrica.

MERATIA = *Chimonanthus.*

MERCURIALIS (mer-cure-ĭ-āl'is). Mediterranean herbs or under-shrubs of the spurge family, of little hort. significance, the only one of garden interest being **M. annua,** the herb mercury, an annual weedy plant once, and sometimes still, grown for its medicinal qualities. It is a sprawling herb, 1–2 ft. high, the leaves opposite,* ovalish or narrower and usually toothed. Male and female flowers on different plants and usually without petals and inconspicuous. Fruit a capsule.* The plant is a native of eastern and

---

* Special articles on the subjects indicated by an asterisk (*) will be found at the words so marked.

northern Af., but is common as a naturalized weed in many parts of the U.S. (Named for Mercury.)

MERCURY. See Mercury at FUNGICIDES.

MERTENSIA (mer-ten′sĭ-a). Bluebells. Lungwort. Showy, mostly shade-enduring, and in ours, perennial herbs of the family Boraginaceae. Of the 40 known species, all from the north temperate zone, many, and the three below, are native in N.A. They often have bluish-green foliage, the leaves alternate,* often dotted. Flowers usually drooping, in terminal, rather loose, somewhat 1-sided clusters (racemes* or cymes*). Corolla more or less funnel-shaped, blue or purplish (in ours), sometimes bearded in the throat. Stamens* 5. Fruit a collection of 4 nutlets. (Named for Franz Carl Mertens, German botanist.)

Besides the three below, a number of native lungworts are apt to be dug from the wild and planted in the wild garden, especially in the Rocky Mountain region, where there are several species. The ones below need partial shade and a moist site for best development, although *M. virginica* can be grown in the open border. As they can be divided only with great difficulty, it is best to raise new plants from seed, which should be sown as soon as harvested. Mertensias die down early in the season.

ciliata. A Rocky Mountain herb with pale or grayish-green foliage; not over 2 ft. high. Leaves ovalish or oblong. Flowers bright blue, about ½–¾ in. long. Spring.

oblongifolia. A perennial, 6–9 in. high, suited only to cool moist sites and not easy to maintain. Leaves spoon-shaped or narrower, 1–2 in. long. Flowers in a somewhat tight cluster, the corolla tube purple, the bell-like apex blue. Western N.A. May–June.

virginica. Virginia cowslip; called also tree or American lungwort and Roanoke bells. A smooth herb up to 2 ft. high, the foliage pale green. Leaves elliptic or oblongish, long-stalked, decurrent* at the base, 3–7 in. long. Flowers about 1 in. long, the tube purplish, but blue when the corolla expands. In rich, moist woods, Ont. to Ala. and westward. April–May. The *var.* **alba** has white flowers, and there is also a pink-flowered hort. form.

MESA OAK = *Quercus engelmanni.* See OAK.

MESCAL BEAN = *Sophora secundiflora.*

MESEMBRYANTHEMUM (me-sem-brĭ-an′thee-mum). Fig-marigold. As originally, and here, understood, the fig-marigolds comprise a huge genus of fleshy-leaved, annual or perennial, mostly desert herbs (rarely shrubby) of the family Aizoaceae. All but a handful of nearly 2000 species are South African, and all the cult. species come from there, although some of them are naturalized escapes* in Calif. Systematic botanists, mostly South Africans, have divided this huge aggregation of plants into many other genera, some of which apply to the species below; notably *Aptenia, Carpanthea, Carpobrotus, Cryophytum, Dorotheanthus, Faucaria,* and *Lampranthus.* While such segre-

gated genera may be essential for a systematic botanical understanding of these plants, they have long been grown by gardeners under the name *Mesembryanthemum,* which is here retained for the cult. species below.

While some non-hort. species have condensed, almost cactus-like and generally leafless plant bodies, closely simulating the desert stones among which they grow, the cult. sorts have usually fleshy leaves, mostly without marginal teeth (some spiny-margined). In a few species the leaves are covered with glittering dots, hence the name ice-plant for some of them. Flowers large and showy, often with a superficial resemblance to a daisy, from the great number of petals and stamens,* mostly white, red, or yellow. Calyx* with 5 rather leafy lobes. Fruit a many-seeded capsule,* but fleshy in one species. (The name is from the Greek for midday-flower, from the opening of the flowers of some species in sunshine and their closing at night and during cloudy weather.)

In growing the plants below it must not be forgotten that nearly all of them are inhabitants of hot, dry deserts and consequently heat is essential to proper development. The annuals can be grown as such (see ANNUALS), provided there is a long, warm, and not too moist growing season. The perennials cannot be grown outdoors north of zone* 7, and even south of this their need for heat and dryness is better provided for in southern Calif. than in Fla. In the former state the plants are popular, and dealers or fanciers have many other species than the ones here noted. To include all those known to be in cult. in the U.S. would be to devote more space to *Mesembryanthemum* than they are worth — at least to most American gardeners. Their greenhouse culture is the same as for any other succulent (which see). See also SAND GARDEN.

aurantiacum. A perennial, much resembling *M. aureum,* but the flowers about 1½ in. wide, orange, and the petals in about 3 series.

aureum. A perennial herb, woody at the base and not over 2 ft. high. Leaves fleshy, more or less bluish-green, 1–2 in. long, narrow and 3-angled. Flowers usually solitary, long-stalked, golden-yellow, about 2 in. wide, the petals in many series.

cordifolium. A perennial 1–2 ft. high, branched, not very fleshy, minutely warty. Leaves more or less heart-shaped, flat, opposite,* usually stalked, scarcely 1 in. long. Flower purple, solitary, not over ½ in. wide, short-stalked. A good window-garden plant.

criniflorum. An interesting and widely grown annual, somewhat resembling *M. lineare,* but with larger, daisy-like flowers, ranging from pink and apricot to buff, tan, and crimson.

crystallinum. Ice-plant; called also sea fig and sea marigold, especially in Calif. The most commonly grown of all the species and an annual (or grown as such). Foliage covered with glistening dots. The plant is prostrate, with alternate,* flat, fleshy leaves that are ovalish, but clasping at the base. Flowers nearly stalkless, white or pale pink, about ¾ in. wide.

* Special articles on the subjects indicated by an asterisk (*) will be found at the words so marked.

Much grown for its glistening foliage, both as a garden annual and as a pot plant. Naturalized along the Calif. coast, and much cult. there. Reported as a pot herb with edible leaves used like spinach.

edule. Hottentot fig. A prostrate or sprawling perennial, with a woody base, sometimes used to cover banks in Calif. Leaves 3–4 in. long, opposite* and joined at the base, 3-sided and fleshy. Flowers yellow, short-stalked, about 3 in. wide, very showy. Fruit fleshy and edible (in Africa). It is sometimes an escape* or even naturalized in Calif.

gramineum = Mesembryanthemum lineare.

lineare. An annual with little or no stem, the branches prostrate, and making a dense clump 6–8 in. wide, the whole plant warty. Leaves 2–3 in. long, opposite and joined at the base. Flowers very numerous, about 1¼ in. wide, solitary on stalks 1–4 in. long, pink with a red center, or white, pink, or red throughout. Should be grown as a flower garden annual. Sometimes sold as M. gramineum or M. tricolor.

spectabile. A rather woody, prostrate perennial, the crowded leaves bluish-green, pointed, 3-angled, nearly 3 in. long. Flowers 2–3 in. wide, purple or magenta, the filaments* white. One of the most widely grown.

tigrinum. An almost stemless perennial, the leaves in opposite pairs, bluish-green, 1–2 in. long and white-dotted, the coarse marginal teeth tapering to fine hairs. Flowers nearly 2 in. wide, yellow. S. Af.

tricolor = Mesembryanthemum lineare.

mesopotamica, -us, -um (me-so-po-tay′-mi-ka). From Mesopotamia.

MESPILUS (mes′pĭ-lus). A genus containing one small, deciduous, Eurasian tree, sometimes thorny, of the rose family, **M. germanica,** the medlar, growing 20 ft. or more high. Leaves oblong or narrower, alternate,* short-tapering, pointed, 3–5 in. long, short-stalked, slightly soft-hairy and dull green above, soft-hairy beneath. Flowers solitary, white or blush, 1½–2 in. across, appearing after the foliage. Stamens* 30–40, the anthers* red. Fruit apple-shaped, open-topped, 12 in. across, edible after frost or when almost rotten; sometimes used in preserves. Propagated by seeds or by grafting on seedling stock, or on pear, quince, or hawthorn. Long cultivated. Var. **gigantea** has much larger fruit, and *var.* **abortiva** is a seedless form with small fruit. (*Mespilus* is the old Latin name for the medlar.)

MESQUITE. A genus of tropical or subtropical thorny trees or shrubs belonging to the pea family, comprising about 25 species, and known as **Prosopis** (pro-soap′is). Stems with or without spines. Leaves twice-compound, leaflets small, not toothed. Flowers not pea-like, greenish, small, in roundish spikes, growing from the axils* of the leaves. Pod very narrow, leathery, not splitting. (*Prosopis* is from the Greek for the butterbur, but the meaning is obscure as related to mesquite.)

The mesquite is usually a thorny shrub, only a few feet high in the desert, where it is of great economic importance as a forage plant throughout the southwestern states.

P. juliflora. Honey locust; mesquite; algaroba. A West Indian species with many pairs of leaflets close together, thin, elliptic to oblong, the ends and base blunt and round. *Var.* **glandulosa** is the common one with more rigid, narrow leaflets. It is an important bee plant in Calif., Tex., N. Mex., southern Calif. and Mex., but otherwise of little hort. significance, outside of the desert garden.

metallica, -us, -um (me-tal′li-ca). With a metallic sheen.

METASEQUOIA (met-a-see-quoy′a). An extraordinarily interesting monotypic genus of coniferous trees, heretofore known only as fossils, variously estimated from 30–50 million years old and reputedly the ancestors of *Sequoia* (which see). In 1946 it was discovered as a living tree near Mo-tao-chi, 70 miles west of Wan Hsien, in the province of Hupeh, Chinà. Seeds were secured and young trees of what has been called "dawn redwood" or "living fossil" are now offered by several nurseries. The only species, **M. glyptostroboides,** a close relative of our Californian *Sequoia,* is a tree quite similar in aspect to our southern cypress (*Taxodium*) and loses its leaves each autumn. Leaves (needles) opposite, arranged in flat sprays, the leaves about ¾ in. long. Cones about ¾ in. long, comprising about 12 scales, the seeds winged. Easily propagated by lateral shoot cuttings, planted in moist sand in Sept. in the greenhouse. They should root within 5 weeks. The tree has proved hardy from zone* 4 southward, and many specimens are now 20–35 ft. high. In its native habitat it is a tree up to 150 ft. It is a rapid-growing tree and sets its persistent cones freely in cult. (*Metasequoia* is from *meta,* akin to, and *Sequoia,* in reference to its relationship to *Sequoia.*)

METCALFE BEAN = Phaseolus metcalfei.

Metel (me′tel). An Arabic name for *Datura Metel.*

METHOXYCHLOR. See No. 4 at INSECTICIDES.

METROSIDEROS (met-tro-sy-deer′os). Iron tree. Ironwood. Very hard-wooded trees of the family Myrtaceae, comprising 30 species, all from Australasia and the Pacific Islands, the only two commonly cult. species from N. Z. They are tall trees with chiefly opposite* leaves and showy red flowers in mostly terminal clusters (cymes*). Calyx more or less turban-shaped. Petals 5. Stamens many, long-protruding, and most conspicuous. Fruit a leathery capsule.* (*Metrosideros* is from the Greek for heart and iron, in allusion to the hard wood.)

Both species, especially the first, are planted in zones* 8 and 9 for ornament. They are not hardy elsewhere, and their cult. is mostly confined to southern Calif. They can be propagated by cuttings.

robusta. Rata. A round-headed tree 60–100 ft. high, less as usually cult. Leaves 1–1½ in. long, smooth, ovalish, or oblong. Flowers dark red, the clusters dense. Fruit about ¼ in. long. In N.Z. the tree starts as an epiphyte.*

---

* Special articles on the subjects indicated by an asterisk (*) will be found at the words so marked.

tomentosa. Lower than the last and much-branched. Leaves 2–4 in. long, broadly oblong, mostly white-felty on the lower surface. Flowers dark red. Fruit about ½ in. long.

MEXICAN. As an adjective *Mexican* is linked to many plants from Mexico or the region once included in it (most of our Southwest and Guatemala). Those that occur in this book and their proper equivalents are:

Mexican apple = *Casimiroa edulis;* Mexican avocado = *Persea americana drymifolia;* Mexican bamboo. See POLYGONUM CUSPIDATUM; Mexican blue palm = *Erythea armata;* Mexican bush sage = *Salvia leucantha;* Mexican coral drops = *Bessera elegans;* Mexican cotton = *Gossypium mexicanum;* Mexican fireplant = *Euphorbia heterophylla;* Mexican firevine = *Senecio confusus;* Mexican ground cherry = *Physalis ixocarpa;* Mexican horned poppy = *Argemone alba;* Mexican ivy = *Cobaea scandens;* Mexican jumping bean. See JUMPING BEAN; Mexican lime, *see* Acid Lime at LIME (the citrus fruit); Mexican orange = *Choisya ternata;* Mexican rubbertree = *Castilla elastica;* Mexican star = *Milla biflora;* Mexican stone pine = *Pinus cembroides* (*see* PINE); Mexican tea = *Chenopodium ambrosioides* (*see* list at WEEDS); Mexican tulip poppy = *Hunnemannia fumariaefolia.*

mexicana, -us, -um (meck-si-kay′na). From Mexico.

MEZEREON = *Daphne Mezereum.*

MEZEREON FAMILY = Thymelaeaceae.

Mezereum (me-zeer′ee-um). Native Persian name for *Daphne Mezereum.*

MICE. See ANIMAL INJURY.

MICHAELMAS DAISY. The name applied to late summer- and fall-blooming, hardy, perennial asters. In Europe, especially in England, these plants are greatly valued for garden adornment and cut flowers, and some specialists in hardy plants list more than 100 named varieties in their catalogues. The majority of these varieties have been derived by selection and hybridization of North American wild asters. The New York aster (*Aster novi-belgi*) is a species most prolific in the production of garden forms — over 80 named varieties being ascribed to this species. Among other native asters which have been developed by European cultivators are: the New England aster (*A. novae-angliae*), *A. cordifolius, A. ericoides,* and a few others.

Varieties of *A. Amellus,* a Eurasian species, are commonly included in lists under the heading of "Michaelmas Daisies." It is doubtful if this species and its derivatives should be included, as their earliness of bloom (August), habit of growth, and type of flowers, single them out from the general appearance of this group.

The fall-blooming asters vary in color from white to almost red, and from pale lavender to deep purple. In size they range from the 6 to 8 inches of Violet Carpet to the

5 ft. of Arizona Sunset. In habit, there are the spreading kinds such as Canterbury Carpet; the low-growing compact varieties, of which Little Red Boy is an example; and those having the pyramidal shape of Mt. Everest.

Doubts have been expressed as to whether any real improvement over wild types has been effected by the hybridization and seedling selection carried out by European growers. A prominent English horticulturist says that in his opinion "almost any of the wild asters, if accorded the cultural treatment given to the garden forms, would equal the beauty of the named varieties." While not subscribing to this statement, nevertheless it must be admitted that most of the wild asters do respond with larger flowers and more vigorous growth when given liberal treatment in the flower garden.

American nurserymen, in general, list only a tenth of the varieties offered in the European trade, and restrict their offerings to the *novae-angliae* and *novi-belgi* groups. Following is a selection from the varieties available in this country:

NOVAE-ANGLIAE VARIETIES:
   Arizona Sunset, 4–5 ft. Salmon-pink.
   Jessie Curtis, 4–5 ft. Flower buds red, open flowers red-purple.
   Survivor, 4 ft. True deep pink.
NOVI-BELGI VARIETIES:
   Blue Skies, 3–4 ft. Light blue.
   Eventide, 3–4 ft. Semi-double, deep violet-blue.
   Peace, 2½–3 ft. Large rosy-mauve.
   Plenty, 2½–3 ft. Semi-double, extra-large, soft blue.
   Violetta, 3 ft. Deep rich blue, semi-double.
   Winston Churchill, 2½–3 ft. Nearest to red of any aster.
OREGON-PACIFIC semi-dwarf and dwarf asters are mostly the originations of Prof. Breithaupt.
Semi-dwarf:
   Little Red Boy, 1½ ft. Bright China rose.
   Persian Rose, about 15 in. First blooms in Aug., continuing until mid-Oct.
   Twilight, 18–20 in. Deep blue, early Aug.
Dwarf:
   Twinkle, 1 ft. Amaranth-rose with white-tipped centers.
   Pacific Amaranth, 10–12 in. Amaranth-purple, mid-Aug. to mid-Oct.
   Pacific Horizon. Similar to the preceding except for flower color, described as "delicate blue."
   Princess Margaret Rose, 12–15 in. Deep pink, compact habit.
   Snowball, 8–10 in. White with golden centers.
   Violet Carpet, 6–8 in. Violet-blue. Sept.–Oct.

CULTIVATION. To get best results with Michaelmas daisies, deep, moist, rich soil

---

* Special articles on the subjects indicated by an asterisk (*) will be found at the words so marked.

must be provided and annual division of clumps practiced. The *novae-angliae* kinds will thrive in wet situations. Some of the best English growers of these plants trench° the ground 3 ft. deep and set out in early spring young plants that were rooted from cuttings made the preceding fall and carried over winter in cold frames. Good success is also obtained by separating the clumps every fall or spring, and planting only the strongest divisions (each of 2 or 3 shoots°) obtained from the outside of the clump. These divisions in the case of the strong varieties should be set 3 feet apart and the smaller kinds 2–3 feet apart. Not more than three or four shoots should be allowed to develop from each clump. To overcome the sparse effect in spring of such wide spacing, they may be interplanted with early-blooming and maturing bulbous plants, such as daffodils. The really dwarf forms should be spaced according to their spread. For example those which grow to 18 inches across should be set 18 inches apart on centers. These, in general, do not require annual division, nor is it necessary to limit the number of shoots in each clump.

Strangely enough many of the improved forms of wild asters have not been very successful under American cultivation. They are subject to mildew, and also to a wilt disease. The beauty of this group and their value in the perennial border, in beds by themselves, and as cut flowers, are such that it is well worth while to make special efforts to grow them. Mildew may be kept under control by the use of sulphur preparations, and it is possible that the wilt disease could be overcome by propagation with short cuttings in fall and rotation of planting situations. — M. F.

MICHAUXIA (me-show′ĭ-a). A small genus of herbs of the family Campanulaceae, all from Asia Minor, the only cult. species being **M. campanuloides**, a perennial herb grown in the border for its rather showy, drooping flowers. It is a stout herb, 3–5 ft. high, with alternate,° lance-shaped, irregularly toothed and bristly leaves. Flowers more or less bell-shaped, about 2 in. long, white, but tinged with purple, the 8–10 lobes of the corolla somewhat recurved. July. While a perennial, it can be raised as a biennial (*see* BIENNIALS), and is more suited to Calif. than to regions with cold, slushy winters. (Named for André Michaux, famous French botanist in America.)

MICHELIA (me-chel′ĭ-a). A genus of Asiatic trees or shrubs of the Magnoliaceae, comprising nearly 50 species. They resemble *Magnolia*, but the flowers come from the axils° of the leaves. Flowers solitary, sepals and petals similar, 9–15, or more. Fruit a long spike of leathery carpels. (Named for P. A. Micheli, a Florentine botanist.)

Michelias are propagated by seed sown immediately when ripe, or stratified, or by ripe-wood cuttings, bearing one or two leaves, started under glass with bottom-heat.° An excellent greenhouse plant for the North, where it needs a cool house and potting mixture° 5.

fuscata. Banana-shrub. A shrub attaining a height of 10–15 ft. Young growth covered with a brownish wool. Leaves elliptic or narrower, smooth in maturity. Flowers 1–1½ in. across, brownish-yellow, edged with light carmine, and having a strong banana fragrance. China. Hardy outdoors from zone° 7 southward, and popular in Calif. and along the Gulf Coast, its odor unpleasant to some.

MICHIGAN. The state flower and tree is the apple, and the state lies wholly in zones° 1, 2, and 3. It is a state rich in natural plant materials, in places of interest to gardeners, and in horticultural tradition. The Wolverine State consists of two peninsulas, the so-called Upper Peninsula and the Lower Peninsula, the latter being the larger of the two and containing most of the population. The state as a whole is approximately 400 miles long and 310 miles wide, with a land area of some 57,000 square miles. A relatively flat, somewhat rolling plain, it rises to about 573 feet above sea level in the southeast, and reaches a maximum altitude of 2023 feet in the Porcupine Mountains of the Upper Peninsula.

CLIMATE. Although climate can be modified with mulches and with protective structures and artificial heat for the growing of garden plants, climate is still the most important single factor which determines what can or cannot grow. The interval between the last killing frost in the spring and the first killing frost in the fall varies from about 70 days in the Upper Peninsula to about 175 days in the southwestern and southeastern corners of the state. The date of the last freeze in the spring ranges from May 1 to June 10, and the first killing frost in the fall may occur as early as late August or as late as October 20, depending on where in Michigan you happen to be. Long-season varieties of plants such as the Concord grape and many varieties of watermelon will therefore not ripen properly above the southern half of the Lower Peninsula.

A second very significant climatic factor is the modifying effect of the Great Lakes, which all but surround the state, particularly Lake Michigan. The prevailing westerly winds carry the air from Lake Michigan, which is cooler in the summer and warmer in the winter than corresponding air over land masses, over a strip of western Michigan, making its winters and summers milder than they would otherwise be. This modifying effect also occurs on the east coast of the Lower Peninsula, but to a lesser degree, because the wind direction is toward the lake rather than from it.

Because the lakes warm up more slowly than land in the spring, they also protect from spring frosts the blossoms of all woody plants growing close to the lakes. This protection is especially valuable with fruiting plants like the strawberry, raspberry, peach, and cherry which tend to bloom very early.

° Special articles on the subjects indicated by an asterisk (°) will be found at the words so marked.

MICHIGAN

The zones of hardiness crossing Michigan are those shown on the map located at ZONE, which should be consulted. The figures show the length of the growing season, in days. For rainfall, *see* text.

Farther inland, these fruits can be grown successfully only on sloping sites which protect them in the spring because slopes prevent cold air from accumulating and killing blossoms on frosty nights.

Minimum winter temperature for specific location is an important limiting factor with many garden crops in Michigan. The less hardy plants such as the peach, black raspberry, tulip-tree, Oregon grape, flowering dogwood, and *Magnolia soulangeana* can be grown successfully only in the southern third of the Lower Peninsula. Here, temperatures rarely fall to −10° F. The northern limit for plants such as these extends farther north along the west coast of the state, on Lake Michigan. The more tender crops, including many varieties of azaleas, cannot be grown in Michigan at all.

As one moves both inland and northward, the minimum winter temperatures drop progressively. During one of the coldest Michigan winters on record, in January, 1912, temperatures of −35° F. were recorded in the north central portion of the Lower Peninsula, and −45°F. in the Upper Peninsula. Such temperatures will kill all but the hardiest species. Only the hardiest varieties of apple, red raspberry, and viburnum, and plants like gooseberry and currant, lilac, sumac, and arborvitae will survive such severe winters. Gooseberries and currants, however, are restricted in this region because of the presence of commercial plantings of white pine.

The Michigan gardener can grow many of the relatively tender woody plants and perennials far beyond their natural northern limits by using winter mulches, windbreaks

of various types, and by utilizing cold frames and hotbeds. In the northern areas, the more tender low-growing species are insulated very effectively from low winter temperatures by the blanket of snow.

The combination of warm days and cool nights which prevails in much of Michigan during the summer makes this state an excellent area for the growing of many garden crops. Sweet corn, tomato, celery, carrot, cauliflower, and muskmelon develop high quality under these conditions, as do the cherry, peach, plum, and apple.

However, no garden will flourish with insufficient water. And unfortunately, the state's 30 to 34 inches of rain are so distributed that many garden crops will not do their best without additional water. The Michigan gardener must therefore be sure that he has a good source of water for the garden during dry periods. If he is unwilling or unable to do a lot of watering, particularly on sandy soils, he should select only the most drought-resistant varieties such as the Robinson strawberry, fescue grasses for the lawn, barberry, sand cherry, and the like. In addition, he should use all the moisture-conserving means at his disposal, summer mulches, and lots of water-holding organic matter such as manure and peat.

SOIL AND THE GARDEN. All of Michigan was glaciated during the last ice age, and as the glaciers receded they scored the earth's surface, leaving water behind in the gouged-out spots, particularly in the western part of the state. Deposits of decaying vegetation accumulated under water, developing into peat bogs and eventually into muck (highly organic soils) as the lakes formed swamps and then dried up completely. Peat and muck make up about one-seventh of the land area of Michigan. These organic soils, which are often quite acid, are excellent for blueberry, cranberry, and Oregon grape, and are well suited for onions, carrots, and celery. Because such soils are often located in a depressed area, they are usually very subject to frost and are therefore hazardous as sites for fruits.

Because of their mode of origin, Michigan soils are usually not uniform in large areas. They range from compact clays, which are hard to handle and drain, to almost pure sands, which are subject to wind and water erosion, very infertile, and very droughty except when close to water. The sandy soils are well suited for any garden crops — most vegetables, strawberry, raspberry, cherry, and peach — provided that ample amounts of fertilizer and water are used. Lawns are more difficult to establish and maintain on these lighter soils, and benefit from heavy applications of peat, manure, and even clay, provided that it is mixed well with the sand before seeding. The fescue grasses are best, and drought-resisting species such as barberry, sand cherry and the wayfaring tree (*Viburnum*) are preferred. The heavier, water-retaining, and more fertile soils are most suitable for Kentucky and Merion bluegrass, apple, pear, plum, and grape, for delphinium, dahlia, peony, and other plants which are deep-rooted.

GARDENS, PARKS, AND SHOWS. The following gardens, parks, and flower shows of Michigan are well worth visiting:

Ann Arbor: Nichols Arboretum and Botanical Garden, University of Michigan.

Augusta: Kellogg Bird Sanctuary and Arboretum.

Detroit: Palmer Park Arboretum; Oak Park; Garden Center, Belle Isle; Spring Flower Show.

Dearborn: Greenfield Village.

East Lansing: Beal-Garfield Botanical Garden; rose, dahlia, gladiolus, annual flower and woody ornamental test gardens, and fruit and vegetable test plots at Michigan State University; campus of Michigan State University.

Hillsdale: Slayton Arboretum and Botanical Garden.

Holland: Tulip festival in May.

Jackson: Ella Sharp Memorial Park.

Lansing: Cooley Gardens; Potter Park.

Ovid: Vaughan Seed Company gladiolus farm.

Tipton: Hidden Lake Gardens.

ORGANIZED GARDEN ACTIVITIES. Many garden clubs are very active in all parts of Michigan, including over 70 clubs affiliated with the Federated Garden Clubs of Michigan. The Michigan Horticultural Society, consisting of many of the outstanding amateur and professional horticulturists in the state, sponsors the Detroit Flower Show. Michigan State University issues a number of attractive folders on various phases of gardening and home landscaping. The University also provides a professional horticulturist who devotes his full time to gardening problems.

MICONIA (my-kō′ni-a). A genus of tropical American shrubs or trees of the family Melastomaceae, comprising nearly 600 species. Leaves opposite,* usually stalked, with or without marginal teeth. Flowers rather small, white, rose, purple, or yellow. Petals 4–8, spreading or turned back. Calyx lobes 4–8, short. Fruit a dry, leathery berry. (Named for D. Micon, Spanish physician.)

Miconias are often grown in the warm-temperate greenhouse for their handsome foliage. They should be given fibrous soil, plenty of water, and shaded from direct sunlight. They are propagated by cuttings of ripened wood over bottom-heat.*

magnifica. A shrub several ft. high when cult. Leaves broadly oval, 2–2½ ft. long, with wavy margins, shining green above, reddish-bronze below, with prominent white or light green veins. Flowers inconspicuous, in compound terminal clusters (panicles*). Mex.

MICRAMPELIS = *Echinocystis.*

micrantha, -us, -um (my-kran′tha). Small-flowered.

MICROBE. *See* BACTERIA.

microcarpa, -us, -um (my-kro-kar′pa). Small-fruited.

microcephala, -us, -um (my-kro-seff′a-la). Small-headed.

MICROCITRUS (my-crow-sit′rus). A genus of 4 Australian, very spiny shrubs, or small trees of the family Rutaceae. Leaves broadly oval, sometimes wedge-shaped. Flowers very small. M. australasica, the finger-lime, is the only cult. species. It is a tree 30–40 ft. high. Young leaves very small, the mature leaves 1–1½ in. long, broadly oval. Fruit yellow, longer than broad, 4 in. long by 1 in. thick, the juice acid. Much hardier than the lemon or lime, otherwise the culture is similar. It has been crossed with *Citrus mitis,* the Calomondin or Panama orange. The young plants are quite ornamental, and likely to be useful for a hedge in warm climates because of the dense, spiny growth. (*Microcitrus* is from the Greek for *small,* and *Citrus.*)

MICRO-CLIMATE. Purely local conditions of shade, topography, exposure to drying winds, and the evaporating power of the air will affect one site in a garden more than another. The sum of such factors, which often dictate success or failure, is often called a micro-climate. As every gardener knows, plants do better in one place than in another, often if separated by only a small distance. One of the things that dictate such differences is the purely local micro-climate which cannot upset major climatic factors (heat and rainfall) but often modifies them locally. Good gardeners have long known this, but the professionals have a term for it — micro-climate.

microdasys (my-kro-dass′iss). A little thickened.

micromalus (my-kro-may′lus). A small apple or crabapple. *See* MALUS.

MICROMERIA (my-kro-meer′ĭ-a). A large genus of herbs of the mint family, mostly from the north temperate zone, a few grown in the rock garden or for their fragrant foliage (*see* FRAGRANCE). They are mostly trailing or prostrate plants with small, opposite* leaves and angled or square stems. Flowers small (none over ¼ in. long), irregular* and 2-lipped, mostly crowded in the leaf axils,* sometimes solitary there, or in terminal spikes. Fruit a collection of tiny nutlets, hidden by the persistent calyx.* (*Micromeria* is derived from *micromeris.**)

The plants are of reasonably easy culture in the rock garden or border, except the first species which is not well suited to regions of cold, wet winters. Best propagated by division of the roots in spring.

chamissonis. Yerba Buena. A Pacific coast trailing perennial, its branches rooting at the tips, hence making close patches. Leaves roundish, nearly 1 in. long, hairy, and wavy on the margins. Flowers mostly solitary, white. Called by some M. douglasi.

piperella. Not over 6 in. high and sprawling

---

* Special articles on the subjects indicated by an asterisk (*) will be found at the words so marked.

or trailing. Leaves smooth, more or less ovalish. Flowers in small clusters, reddish-purple. Southern Eu.

rupestris. A low-growing, dense, heath-like perennial, its prostrate stems turning up at the ends. Leaves like pennyroyal in odor, very numerous and small. Flowers white, but lavender-spotted, blooming from July to frost. Southern Eu. and a fine plant for the rock garden or border.

micromeris, -e (my-kro-mee′ris). Having few or small parts — petals, sepals, etc.

micropetala, -us, -um (my-kro-pet′a-la). With small petals.

microphylla, -us, -um (my-kro-fil′la). Small-leaved.

MIDDLETON PLACE GARDENS. *See* No. 2 at GARDEN TOURS.

MIDRIB. The principal vein or rib of a leaf.

MIGNONETTE. Erect or reclining herbs, sometimes woody at the base, constituting the genus **Reseda** (re-zee′da), family Resedaceae. It contains 50 or 60 species, of which only a few are cultivated. **M. odorata,** the common mignonette, is of the greatest horticultural interest. It has a number of varieties, especially *var.* grandiflora arborea, a large garden form. They are erect or declining herbs, annual or biennial. The leaves are alternate* or clustered. The flowers are small in terminal clusters or spikes, the petals 4 to 7, toothed or cleft. The fruit is a capsule, usually 3–6-horned or angled, and opening at the top when ripe. Mediterranean region and the Red Sea. (*Reseda* is the Latin name of a plant, from the word meaning to heal or assuage.)

Mignonette, although not showy, has such a delightful fragrance that it is extensively grown as a garden flower. The outdoor culture is very simple. The seeds should be sown where the plants are to grow and the seedlings thinned, as mignonette is exceedingly difficult to transplant. A first sowing should be made in late April in the North and another in July to extend the season of bloom. The soil should be rich, and the bed should be in shade part of the day.

For a number of years mignonette has been popular as a cut flower in winter. It is successfully cult. under glass in about the same manner as carnations are treated. Use potting mixture* 4 about 5 in. deep on the benches, over an inch of well-rotted manure. Three sowings of seed are made, one in July, one in August, and one in September, and the soil lightly watered. After the plants have formed a number of true leaves they are thinned to stand a few inches apart. They should be grown in a cool house, the temperature ranging between 45° and 65°. Mignonette must never be allowed to dry out, but never overwatered; water on the foliage will often cause spotting. It should be kept constantly growing. When the flower shoots are well set it is well to apply a mixture of 1 part sheep manure and 2 parts loam, or an application of weak liquid manure water. The side shoots should be pinched back to throw vigor into the central stalks, and the mature plants supported by wire rings. *See* Pinching at TRAINING PLANTS.

Mignonette is grown in pots also, but this is attended with more difficulty. Fill 2½-in. pots with potting mixture* 4, similar to that used in the benches. Plant several seeds in a pot, and after plants have developed three or more leaves, remove all but the sturdiest. Instead of pinching the side shoots as in bench culture, in pot-grown mignonette the center shoot is pinched back, thus developing a bushy, symmetrical growth of side shoots. Never allow plants to become pot-bound, transplanting when necessary until the plants are in 7–8-in. pots. Water carefully and support the mature plants with stakes.

MIGNONETTE FAMILY = Resedaceae.

MIGNONETTE-TREE = *Lawsonia inermis.*

MIGNONETTE-VINE = *Boussingaultia baselloides.*

mikanioides (my-kay-nĭ-oy′deez, but *see* OïDES). Like the climbing hempweed (*Mikania*), a weedy vine scarcely worth cult.

MILDEW. *See* DOWNY MILDEW and POWDERY MILDEW.

milfoil = *Achillea Millefolium.*

miliacea, -us, -um (mil-ĭ-ā′see-a). Relating to millet.

MILKMAIDS = *Cardamine pratensis.*

MILK PURSLANE = *Euphorbia corollata.*

MILK THISTLE = *Silybum Marianum.*

MILK VETCH. *See* ASTRAGALUS.

MILKWEED. Milky-juiced, rather showy, but sometimes rather weedy, perennial herbs constituting the genus Asclepias (as-klee′pĭ-as), of the family Asclepiadaceae, and including over 100 species chiefly from the New World, but a few African. The cult. species are chiefly North American plants for the wild garden, but two of those below are tropical and must be grown in the greenhouse in the North. Leaves opposite* or in whorls,* rarely alternate,* without marginal teeth. Flowers regular,* often showy, especially in the tropical species, usually in close, roundish clusters (umbels*), but sometimes in few-flowered clusters in the leaf axils.* Corolla deeply 5-cleft. Stamens* with the filaments joined in a circle around the style.* (*See* ASCLEPIADACEAE.) Fruit a pair of follicles,* the many seeds with a tuft of hairs, often beautifully silky. (*Asclepias* is the Greek name of these plants, in honor of Asclepios, the god of medicine.)

The native species are of very simple culture in the right kind of site, which is indicated for each. The tropical species, A. curassavica, can only be grown in the greenhouse northward. It is a more showy plant than any of the native species and is often forced by florists. A. mexicana can

---

* Special articles on the subjects indicated by an asterisk (*) will be found at the words so marked.

be grown outdoors in mild sections of the country, but not in the East north of zone° 6.

A. curassavica. Blood-flower. From 2–4 ft. high, the stem smooth or nearly so. Leaves opposite,° oblongish or narrower, 3–5 in. long. Flowers about ¼ in. high, brilliant orange-red. Fruits 1½–4 in. long, essentially smooth. Tropical America, and a weed there, but the showiest of all the milkweeds.

A. incarnata. Swamp or rose milkweed. A stout, rather coarse herb, 3–4 ft. high. Leaves oblongish or narrower, 4–7 in. long, tapering at the tip. Flowers rose-purple, about ¼ in. wide, the cluster ball-like and nearly 3 in thick. In swamps and wet places, eastern N.A. and west to Colo. Summer.

A. mexicana. From 3–5 ft. high, the leaves opposite° or in whorls,° narrowly lance-shaped, 4–6 in. long. Flowers small, greenish-white, sometimes tinged with purple. Ore. to Mex. and not suited to outdoor cult. in the East, north of zone° 6.

A. tuberosa. Butterfly-weed; also called pleurisy-root and orange milkweed. The showiest of all the native milkweeds and thriving in dry, sandy soil in N.A. It is a rough-hairy herb, 1–3 ft. high, erect or sprawling. Leaves coarse, oblong, or lance-oblong, 2–6 in. long, usually short-stalked. Flowers about ¼ in. wide, bright orange, the cluster very showy. Aug.–Sept.

A. verticillata. Whorled milkweed. A slender-stemmed, leafy herb, usually 12–20 in. high. Leaves in whorls° of 3–7, smooth, narrow, the margins slightly rolled. Flowers greenish-white, the clusters rather loose. In dry places, often in the woods, eastern N.A. and westward to New Mex. and Sask.

MILKWEED FAMILY. Besides the true milkweeds, this family includes many herbs, shrubs, and woody vines, nearly all with a milky juice. It also includes some cactus-like succulents belonging to the genus *Stapelia* and others, mostly from South Africa. For a complete list of the hort. genera and the characters of the family *see* ASCLEPIADACEAE.

MILK WILLOW-HERB = *Lythrum alatum.*

MILKWORT. See POLYGALA.

MILKWORT FAMILY = Polygalaceae.

MILLA (mil′la). A single cult. species of bulbous herbs of the lily family found from New Mexico and Arizona to Mexico, and grown for ornament. The only cult. species is **M. biflora,** the Mexican star, often cult. under the name of *Bessera elegans*, for which it is often mistaken, but *see* BESSERA. It has basal, cylindric leaves and fragrant, white flowers nearly 2½ in. wide. The flowers are in a loose cluster of 3–5 blooms at the end of a naked stalk 12–18 in. high. Corolla salver-shaped, its separate segments 3-veined. Stamens° 6. Fruit a stalkless capsule.° (Named for J. Milla, Spanish gardener at the Madrid court.)

The plant can be grown in pots for winter or early-spring bloom. Put several bulbs in a pot, using potting mixture° 3, and grow in a cool greenhouse, allowing about 3 months from planting until bloom is wanted. For outdoor culture treat exactly as with gladiolus

(which see), as the bulbs will not stand outdoors in severe climates. For the plant sometimes advertised as *M. uniflora see* BRODIAEA UNIFLORA.

Millefolia, -us, -um (mil-lee-fō′lĭ-a). Literally "thousand-leaved"; as a specific name usually indicating finely dissected leaves, as in *Achillea Millefolium;* or leaves with many leaflets.

MILLET = *Panicum miliaceum* or *Setaria italica,* the latter usually called foxtail millet. For other plants to which the name millet is sometimes applied, *see* ELEUSINE, PENNISETUM, ECHINOCHLOA, and PANICUM TEXANUM.

MILTONIA (mil-tō′nĭ-a). Very handsome, tree-perching, South American orchids, comprising over 20 species, several of which are in the collections of orchid fanciers, the 2 below more generally grown. They differ only in technical characters from *Odontoglossum* and from *Oncidium.* They have short pseudobulbs° bearing one or two leaves at the top and others sometimes at the base. Flowers 1 to several at the end of a stalk arising from the base of the pseudobulb.° Sepals and petals very similar, but the petals a little broader. Lip large, sometimes 2-toothed, but not lobed, and usually expanded. (Named for Viscount Milton, a patron of horticulture.)

For culture *see* greenhouse orchids at ORCHID.

roezli. Pseudobulbs° oblongish, nearly 2 in. long. Leaf solitary, nearly 1 ft. long, very narrow. Flowers 2–3, the stalk about 6 in. long, each flower 3–5 in. wide, flattish, white, but with a purple blotch or band at the base of each petal, the lip brownish at the base. Colombia. It usually blooms in the winter and again in the spring.

vexillaria. Resembling the last, but with broader leaves and larger flowers which are rose-pink, but the lip streaked with yellow and red. Ecuador and Colombia. Blooms from April–June.

MIMBRE = *Chilopsis linearis.*

MIMOSA (my-mo′sa). An immense genus of mostly tropical American herbs, shrubs, and trees of the pea family, some of the 250 species planted for ornament in the tropics, but only the two below much known in cult. in the U.S. They have alternate,° twice-compound° leaves, the leaflets numerous, usually very small, arranged feather-fashion, and very sensitive in the first species. Flowers not pea-like, small, more or less tubular, in dense, ball-like clusters, and rose-purple or lavender in those below. Stamens protruding. Fruit a flat pod (legume°), ultimately separable into 1-seeded joints. (*Mimosa* is from the Greek for mimic, in allusion to the sensitive collapse of the leaves of some species.) *Mimosa* is incorrectly applied to the silk tree (*Albizzia Julibrissin*).

The first species is one of the most extraordinary plants grown in the greenhouse. It is a roadside weed in the tropics. Upon

---

° Special articles on the subjects indicated by an asterisk (°) will be found at the words so marked.

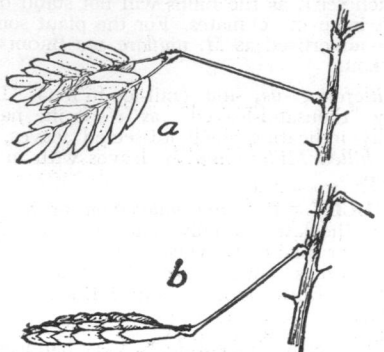

The sensitive plant (*Mimosa pudica*) before (*a*) and after (*b*) the shock to its leaves has caused them to collapse.

the slightest irritation all the leaflets immediately fold up face to face, and the whole leaf collapses, and if the shock is sufficient, all the leaves will do likewise. Much nonsense has been written about the "nerves" of this plant, but the fact remains that its reaction to shock (or cloudy weather) is one of the most remarkable cases of physiological response known in the plant world. It must be grown in a warm greenhouse in potting mixture* 4. The second is a spiny shrub, also chiefly grown in the greenhouse, but cult. outdoors in zones* 8 and 9, especially in southern Calif.

pudica. Sensitive plant; also called humble plant. A low, somewhat woody perennial, more or less hairy and slightly spiny. Leaflets very small, sensitive (*see* above). Flowers rosepurple or lavender, the ball-like clusters longstalked in the leaf axils.* Tropical America, and naturalized in Fla. and along the Gulf.

spegazzini. A spiny shrub, 4–6 ft. high. Leaflets larger than in the last and far less sensitive. Flowers rose-purple, the ball-like clusters dense. Argentina. Grown for ornament in southern Calif. and occasionally in the greenhouse.

MIMOSACEAE. *See* LEGUMINOSAE.

MIMOSA FAMILY. *See* LEGUMINOSAE.

MIMULUS (mim′you-lus). A genus of about 80 declining or erect annual or perennial herbs, or sometimes sub-shrubs, of the figwort family. Plants smooth or hairy, often sticky or clammy. Leaves opposite,* with or without marginal teeth. Flowers showy, 2-lipped,* often spotted, giving the effect of a face (hence the name monkey-flower), growing singly from the axils* of the leaves, or in terminal clusters (racemes*). Fruit an oblong or very narrow pod. Found in North and South America, As., Aust., S. Af. and very numerous in western N.A. These plants are sometimes called *Diplacus*. (The name is derived from the Latin for a little mimic, from the grinning face.)

A few species of monkey-flowers are grown in the garden and in the greenhouse, and some of the large kinds in gardens in California. Those cultivated by florists in the greenhouse are grown from seed sown in January in potting mixture* 3; they are also increased by cuttings and division. In the open they require semi-shade and plenty of water. Though perennials they are generally treated as annuals. *M. luteus*, which often has spotted flowers, is the main source of most of the cult. types.

cardinalis. A perennial, sticky and hairy herb, with weak or erect stems, 1 ft. high. Leaves 4½ in. long with sharp marginal teeth. Flowers red, occasionally yellow, 2-lipped,* 2 in. long, the stamens* protruding. Utah to Ore. and Lower California.

guttatus. A smooth perennial herb, 1½ ft. high. Leaves nearly oval, with small marginal teeth. Flowers yellow, generally with red or brown dots on the throat, 2-lipped, 1½ in. long. Calyx* much swollen in fruit. Alaska to Mex. Easily transplanted, or grown from seed in the wild garden. Thought by some to be a var. of *M. luteus*.

langsdorfi = *Mimulus guttatus*.

lewisi. A perennial, sticky and hairy herb, nearly 2½ ft. high. Leaves oblong, about 2½ in. long, with very fine marginal teeth. Flowers rose-red or rose-purple. Var. alba has white flowers. British Columbia to Calif. and Utah, in mountain meadows, and in shady, moist ground at lower elevations.

luteus. A smooth or slightly downy, perennial herb with a declining stem 8 in. high, larger forms 2 to 4 ft. high. Leaves almost oval, 1 in. or more long, with sharp, marginal teeth. Flowers deep yellow, commonly with dark spots within, 1½ in. long, growing in loose terminal clusters (racemes*). Summer. Alaska to N. Mex.

primuloides. A low, carpeting perennial, 2–4 in. high, the leaves in rosettes which spread by stolons.* Flowers golden yellow, sometimes spotted with reddish or brownish dots, not over ¾ in. long, and generally solitary. It can only be grown in cool, decidedly moist places, imitating its wild habitat in the mountains of northwestern U.S.

ringens. A branching herb 1 to 4 ft. high, perennial from rootstocks. the stems 4-angled. Leaves oblong or narrowly lance-shaped, 3–4 in. long, sharply cut on the margins. Flowers violet, occasionally white. Growing in wet places in eastern N.A. A common native plant, easily established in colonies in the wild garden.

tigrinus. A trade name (without botanical validity) for hybrids between *M. luteus* and *M. guttatus*.

MINER'S LETTUCE = *Montia perfoliata*.

MING TREE. A florists' concoction involving the use of twiggy branches of a Californian manzanita, to which are wired pads of the prostrate alpine buckwheat (*Eriogonum ovalifolium*), all of which are painted green. These dead replicas of living Japanese dwarf trees are also sold under the equally misleading name of Peruvian cypress. *See also* SYNGONANTHUS.

miniata, -us, -um (min-i-ā′ta). Vermilion.

MINIATURE GARDENS. For what are usually, in this country, considered living miniature gardens *see* TERRARIUM. For small models of landscape or garden (all artificial), used in flower shows and as permanent exhibits, *see* MODEL GARDENS.

Miniature gardens, in England, but much less so here, has come to mean the cultivation in boxes or troughs of many dwarf trees, low perennials, rock garden subjects, and other plants that will stand the specialized environment on the window sill, porch, or on a penthouse roof. It requires much skill, a good deal of patience, and is relatively expensive. The plant materials are too extensive to quote here and they are all listed in *Miniature Gardens* by Anne Ashberry (London: C. A. Pearson, Ltd., 1951).

minima, -us, -um (min'i-ma). Smallest.

MINIMACID. A term for slightly acid soils with a pH of about 6.0. For details *see* ACID AND ALKALI SOILS.

MINIMALKALINE. A term for soils that are neutral or slightly alkaline, with a pH of 7.0–8.0. For details *see* ACID AND ALKALI SOILS.

MINNESOTA. The showy lady's-slipper is the state flower. The state, north-centrally located, lies almost wholly in zone* 1. Kandiyohi County, a few miles west of the Twin Cities, is the approximate geographical center of North America, exclusive of Alaska.

The drainage of the state empties into three great systems. The northeastern part drains into the Atlantic Ocean through the Great Lakes and St. Lawrence River system; the northwestern into Hudson Bay through the Red River of the North system; and the remainder of the state, approximately two-thirds, into the Gulf of Mexico through the Mississippi River system.

Recurring glaciations and stream erosion have given Minnesota a diversified topography. Although the altitude varies from 602 to 2230 feet, the greater portion of the state is level or gently rolling without strong reliefs. Nearly 7 per cent is covered by lakes, a great many of them occupying basins among moraine ridges and knolls and on outwash plains.

The native vegetation of the state is also diversified, varying from that of the typical prairie in the western and southwestern parts, through the hardwood forest area bordering the prairie to the coniferous forest area comprising, approximately, the northeastern third of the state.

SOILS. The soils of Minnesota are widely diversified. A small portion of the state's surface is made up of rock outcrops and wind-blown sand which is unsuited to horticulture. Limited areas are covered with stream deposits and large areas by lake deposits, both glacial and modern. Loess* covers an extensive area in southeastern Minnesota. There are about 7,000,000 acres of peat in the state, much of which has been and is being put into production, a considerable portion being devoted to the production of potatoes and vegetable crops. The soils of the remainder of the state are clayey in nature, intermixed with gravelly or sandy moraine and outwash plain

MINNESOTA

The zones of hardiness crossing Minnesota are those shown on the map located at ZONE, which should be consulted for details. The dates are the average lastest killing frost in spring and the first one in the fall. The figures below the dates show the length of the growing season. Rainfall figures (in inches) show (1) the total annual rainfall and (2) the amount falling in the growing season at the places indicated.

deposits. As a general rule, Minnesota soils are fertile and productive.

HORTICULTURE. Horticulture provides both a vocation and an avocation for many people in Minnesota. A profitable vocation is provided for the thousands of fruit growers, market gardeners, truck farmers, potato farmers, food processors, nurserymen, florists, professional gardeners, and merchants who sell horticultural products or supplies. An avocation is provided for the ever-growing number of amateur gardeners who grow ornamentals, fruits, and vegetables to beautify their home grounds and to provide food for their families.

VEGETABLES, including potatoes, are extensively grown for fresh market, for processing, and for home use. Most of the common vegetables do well, especially the cool-season vegetables. In northern Minnesota, only the early-maturing varieties of long-season crops such as tomatoes, sweet corn, and melons should be planted. The vegetables most commonly grown include: asparagus, lima beans, snap beans, beets, broccoli, cabbage, carrots, cauliflower, sweet corn, cucumbers, kohlrabi, lettuce, muskmelons, onions, peas, peppers, potatoes, pumpkins, radish, rhubarb, squash, swiss chard, tomatoes, and watermelons.

FRUITS. The following fruits are commonly grown in Minnesota: apples, crabapples, pears, plums, sour cherries, grapes, raspberries, strawberries, currants, and gooseberries. Of these only the apple, raspberry, and strawberry are important commercially. The climate is too severe for peaches and sweet cherries.

---

* Special articles on the subjects indicated by an asterisk (*) will be found at the words so marked.

Blueberries, although they grow wild in northern Minnesota, are not cultivated to any extent. The most important varieties of fruits are listed. *Apples:* Oriole, Beacon, Wealthy, Fireside, Haralson. *Crabapples:* Chestnut, Whitney, Dolgo. *Pears:* Parker, Mendel. *Plums:* Underwood, Superior, Redglow, Toka, Mount Royal (prune type). *Sour cherries:* Northstar, Meteor. *Grapes:* Red Amber, Bluebell, Beta, Worden. *Raspberries:* Latham, Newburgh. *Strawberries:* Premier, Dunlap, Robinson, Superfection, Red Rich. *Currants:* Red Lake, Cascade. *Gooseberry:* Pixwell. Many of these varieties were developd by the University of Minnesota Agricultural Experiment Station at their Fruit Breeding Farm near Excelsior.

ORNAMENTAL HORTICULTURE. Minnesota has a wealth of native trees, shrubs, and herbaceous flowering plants that add beauty to the natural landscape. Some of these are propagated and used in landscaping. In addition, many introduced species thrive and are widely used. Plants are continually being developed through breeding to meet the requirements of the Minnesota climate.

As a result of the widespread interest in ornamental horticulture, an important florist and nursery industry has developed in the state. Minnesota also provides a ready market for cut flowers, foliage plants, rose plants, and other nursery stock that can be produced more economically in more favorable climates.

The varieties of ornamental plants grown in Minnesota are too numerous to list. The following are a few of the more common types grown.

Evergreen trees: Black Hills, blue, and white spruce; Norway, white, Scotch, ponderosa, and Austrian pine; Douglas fir; Eastern arborvitae; red cedar and juniper.

Deciduous trees: American elm; sugar, red and Norway maples; green ash; American linden; hackberry; European mountain-ash; flowering crabapples; paper birch.

Evergreen shrubs: Mugho pine; Savin, Pfitzers, and Andorra junipers.

Deciduous shrubs: (large) Virginal mockorange; Tartarian and Zabel honeysuckle; red osier and gray dogwoods; flowering plum, *Hydrangea paniculata grandiflora;* buffaloberry; high-bush cranberry, nannyberry and arrowwood viburnums; Chinese and common lilacs. (medium) Hills-of-Snow hydrangea; Rugosa, Harison's Yellow, and Father Hugo's rose; Japanese barberry; Van Houtte spirea; *Cotoneaster acutifolia.* (small) Alpine currant; Lemoine deutzia; burningbush; golden mock-orange; Garland and Anthony Waterer spirea; shrubby cinquefoil; coralberry.

Vines: Engelmann creeper; Boston ivy (protected sites); clematis varieties; bittersweet; trumpet honeysuckle.

Perennial flowers: Tulips, irises, peonies, garden phlox, columbine, hollyhock, chrysanthemums, fall asters, *Hemerocallis,* plantainlilies, lilies, Oriental poppies, veronicas, and monardas.

CLIMATE

Minnesota has a mid-continental climate which is characterized by warm summers and cold winters. Wind directions are very variable and there are no prevailing winds from one direction over long periods of time. The sun never shines with equatorial directness and there are no large mountain ranges or large bodies of water, except Lake Superior, to affect the climate. The rainfall is fairly uniform and the average annual precipitation varies from about 20 inches in the northwestern to about 32 inches in the southeastern part. The mean annual temperature varies from 35° F. in the northeastern to 45° F. in the southeastern.

FROST IN MINNESOTA

Station	Date of last killing frost in the spring	
	Average	Latest
Moorhead	May 10	June 8
Two Harbors	May 19	June 17
Virginia	May 29	June 23
Rochester	May 11	May 30
St. Paul	April 24	May 23
Winona	May 1	May 25
Fergus Falls	May 11	June 6
Morris	May 10	June 7
Worthington	May 14	June 6

Station	Date of first killing frost in the fall	
	Average	Earliest
Moorhead	Sept. 25	Aug. 25
Two Harbors	Sept. 27	Sept. 7
Virginia	Sept. 14	Aug. 16
Rochester	Sept. 27	Aug. 30
St. Paul	Oct. 8	Sept. 18
Winona	Oct. 5	Sept. 10
Fergus Falls	Sept. 24	Sept. 6
Morris	Sept. 27	Sept. 5
Worthington	Sept. 30	Sept. 7

RAINFALL IN MINNESOTA

Station	Average precipitation in inches	
	Annual	(Approximate) During growing season
Moorhead	22.87	12
Two Harbors	26.66	15
Virginia	27.59	14
Rochester	28.43	16
St. Paul	27.17	16
Winona	30.00	20
Fergus Falls	24.00	13
Morris	23.78	12
Worthington	27.43	15

The address of the Minnesota Agricultural Experiment Station, which has kindly supplied this information about the state, is St. Paul 1,

* Special articles on the subjects indicated by an asterisk (*) will be found at the words so marked.

Minnesota. The station is always ready to answer gardening questions.

Garden club activities include clubs of the Garden Club of America, the home office of which is at 598 Madison Avenue, New York 22, N.Y. There are also chapters of the Federated Garden Clubs of Minnesota.

MINNIE-BUSH = *Menziesia pilosa.*

minor, -us (my'nor). Smaller.

MINT. Strong-scented perennials, 25 to (some think) 200 in number, constituting the genus **Mentha** (men'tha) of the family Labiatae. They have square stems and opposite,* undivided, aromatic leaves. Flowers small, purple, pink or white, clustered in the axils* of the leaves, in terminal spikes, or in heads. The fruit is a collection of small, smooth nutlets.* Native in northern Eurasia and Aust., but several are naturalized in N.A. (*Mentha* is derived from the Greek Minthe, a nymph, and from the Latin *menta,* mint.)

These herbs are occasionally grown for ornament, but more frequently for their essential oils, present in all their parts. They are easily grown from seed or propagated by cuttings or by division, and they soon become established and tend to run wild. They should be divided in the spring, and replanted every year or so, as they make crowded clumps if left alone.

M. arvensis. Corn mint; also called field mint and wild pennyroyal. A perennial herb, the stem erect, 2 ft. high and producing runners 2 ft. in length. The leaves are slightly downy, 1 to 2 in. long, rounded at the base. The flowers grow in circles in the axils* of the leaves. This species in various forms is widely distributed. Eurasia and N.A., frequently naturalized. *Var. piperascens,* the Japanese mint, is a larger plant, 3 ft. high, with leaves longer, 1½ to 3 in., narrowed at the base, with sharp marginal teeth. The var. produces much more oil.

M. citrata. Bergamot mint. A smooth, perennial herb, stalk 2 ft. in length, reclining on the ground, much-branched, with underground, rooting stems. The leaves are 2 in. long, broad or narrow, with a pointed tip. The flowers are in the upper axils* of the leaves or in spikes 1 in. long. Eu., naturalized in N.A. Also known as *M. aquatica.*

M. piperita. Peppermint; also known as brandy mint. A perennial herb 1 to 3 ft. high, characterized by its strong, pungent oil, reproducing by underground stems, or by rooting branches. Leaves about 3 in. long, narrow, with marginal teeth. Flowers purple, seldom white, in terminal spikes, nearly 3 in. long. Eu. For culture and uses *see* HERB GARDENING. Much grown commercially in Indiana (which see).

M. Pulegium. Pennyroyal. A perennial herb with prostrate, much-branched stems. Leaves downy, round-oval, with small marginal teeth. Flowers small, bluish-lilac, in circles in the axils* of the leaves. Eurasia. See HEDEOMA.

M. requieni. A small, creeping herb with threadlike stalks and very small, round leaves. Flowers mauve or pale purple, growing in whorls* in the leaf axils.* The plant is peppermint-scented. Corsica. For culture *see* ROCK GARDEN.

M. rotundifolia. Horse mint; also known as apple mint. A downy, occasionally sticky, perennial, reproducing by leafy, underground stems. The latter are sometimes unbranched and at other times branching, and 20 to 30 in. high. Leaves oval, 1–2 in. long. Flowers purple, in dense spikes, 2–4 in. long. Eu., naturalized in N.A.

M. spicata. Spearmint; also known as common garden mint or green mint. A smooth herb 1–2 ft. high, perennial by underground, rooting stems. Leaves 1–2½ in. long, having marginal teeth. The flowers in interrupted* spikes, the central spike higher than the others. Eurasia, extensively naturalized in old gardens in N.A. For culture and uses *see* HERB GARDENING.

MINT-BUSH. See PROSTANTHERA.

MINT FAMILY. A very large group of plants, difficult to identify as to species, but nearly all having the family characters of aromatic herbage, opposite* leaves, and square stems. The flowers are so various that the garden genera are hard to distinguish, as they include, besides the true mint, plants like coleus, rosemary, sage, savory, basil, thyme, and the scarlet salvia. For the complete list of the hort. genera and their differences *see* LABIATAE.

MINT GERANIUM. The costmary. *See* CHRYSANTHEMUM BALSAMITA.

MINUARTIA. *See* ARENARIA.

minuta, -us, -um (my-new'ta). Very small.

MIRABILIS (mi-rǎ'bil-is). Tropical American perennial herbs of the family Nyctaginaceae, one of them, the common four-o'clock, widely grown as a tender annual. Of the 8 known species only this one, and sometimes *M. longiflora,* are of garden interest. They have (in their native region) thickened or tuberous roots and opposite,* generally stalked leaves. Flowers solitary or a few from a calyx*-like involucre,* the true calyx corolla-like, tubular, and variously colored (red, yellow, or white). Petals none. Stamens* 5–6. Fruit a leathery ribbed achene.* (*Mirabilis* is from Latin for wonderful.)

The common four-o'clock and *M. longiflora* are both easily grown as tender annuals (*see* ANNUALS), or if later bloom is desired, they can be sown where wanted. They are so popular that, especially in the four-o'clock, there are many hort. forms, such as compact, dwarf, or even variegated sorts. They are often permanent, either as perennials or by self-sown seed.

Jalapa. Four-o'clock; also called Marvel-of-Peru. A perennial (grown as a tender annual) 14–30 in. high, quick-growing. Leaves ovalish, smooth, the stalk about half the length of the blade. Flowers nearly 1 in. wide, the tube 1–2 in. long, usually solitary in the involucre,* Aug.–Oct. Flowers open late in the afternoon.

longiflora. A sticky-hairy herb 2–3 ft. high, the leaves more or less heart-shaped. Flowers 3 or more in the involucre, fragrant, the tube nearly 5 in. long and white, the expanded limb often rose or violet. Mex. Flowers open after sundown. If desired, the roots of this may be dug in the fall, stored, and planted again in the spring. It is not hardy in the North.

MIRLITON = *Sechium edule.*

---

* Special articles on the subjects indicated by an asterisk (*) will be found at the words so marked.

MISCANTHUS (mis-kan'thus). A genus containing about 6 tall, perennial grasses of the Old World, grown for their decorative effect on the lawn or in the border. The species most commonly grown is M. sinensis, usually called *Eulalia,* and often *M. japonicus.* The leaves are grass-like, 1 in. wide and 2–3 ft. long, with a prominent, whitish, central line, usually growing in heavy clumps. Flowers in beautiful feathery, compound, terminal clusters (panicles*), 2 ft. in length, the whole plant 4 to 10 ft. high. China and Japan, and an occasional escape* in N.A. *Var.* **gracillimus** has even finer leaves. *Var.* **variegatus** has leaves striped white, or yellowish; *var.* **zebrinus**, the zebra-grass, has banded leaves. (*Miscanthus* is from the Greek for a stem and flower, in allusion to the stalked spikelets.)

MISSISSIPPI. The state flower and tree is the evergreen magnolia. The state lies wholly in zones* 5, 6, and 7. The soils of Mississippi can be divided into 10 more or less distinct areas. These are the Delta, Loess,* Gulf Coast, Longleaf Pine, Central Prairie, Shortleaf Pine, Flat Woods, Pontotoc Ridge, Northeast Prairie, and Northeast Highlands.

The Delta area lies between the Mississippi and Yazoo rivers, and is characterized by a relatively flat topography and fertile, alluvial loam and clay loam soils. The Loess* area is a belt 30 to 40 miles wide on the eastern border of the Delta area. The soils are yellow to dark brown, fine-textured and moderately fertile silt loams. The Gulf Coast area is a strip 15 to 20 miles wide on the coast. It consists mostly of level areas of fine silt loam, generally low in organic matter.

The Longleaf Pine area occupies a major portion of the southern part of the state. It is gently rolling and consists of gray, brown and yellow sandy loams, which are open textured, well drained and low in organic matter. They are generally adapted to the growing of horticultural crops when well fertilized.

The Central Prairie is a narrow belt of clay loam soils about 20 miles wide on the northern border of the Longleaf Pine area. The Shortleaf Pine area, of sandy loam soils, lies north of the Central Prairie and east of the Loess area. Rather high ridges between the streams are characteristic features.

The Flat Woods, Pontotoc Ridge, Northeast Prairie, and Northeast Highlands are narrow strips extending north to south and situated in the northeastern portion of the state. The Flat Woods area is mostly flat. The Pontotoc Ridge consists of a series of ridges which form the divide between the Tombigbee and Mississippi rivers' drainage systems. The Northeast Prairie is gently rolling to undulating and the Northeast Highlands is comparatively hilly and rugged. These soils are sandy loams and clay loams.

The principal garden-crop areas are as follows: The tomato, snap bean, green pepper, and cabbage trucking area in the vicinity of Hazlehurst and Crystal Springs and the watermelon section in the vicinity of Lucedale and Mize.

The following fruits are grown throughout Mississippi for home use and local markets, with no large commercial districts: peaches, plums, pears, bunch grapes, muscadine grapes, dewberries, and strawberries.

Apples are best adapted to northeast Mississippi, but are grown throughout the north half of the state for home use. Figs are planted for home use throughout the south half of the state, and sparingly in north Mississippi.

Plantings of named varieties of pecans are most extensive in the coast counties and the Delta. Native trees have been top-worked to named varieties throughout the state, especially in the vicinity of Natchez. *See* PECAN.

There are approximately 100,000 acres of tung-oil trees in the Coast area, mostly in Pearl River County and adjoining counties.

Outstanding native trees are the longleaf pine, live oak, magnolia, sweet gum, black gum, elm, hackberry, pecan, shell-bark hickory, bald cypress, and holly. Ornamental small trees include redbud, dogwood, yaupon, deciduous holly, and fringe-tree. Many species of shrubs and wild flowers are common, such as: wild azalea, callicarpa, iris, mistflower, perennial asters, and violets.

The average annual rainfall is 61.02 inches at Biloxi; 55.21 at Crystal Springs; and 49.93 at Tupelo. During the growing season the rainfall at Biloxi ranges from 2.93 to 6.8 per month with a total of 46.58; at Crystal Springs

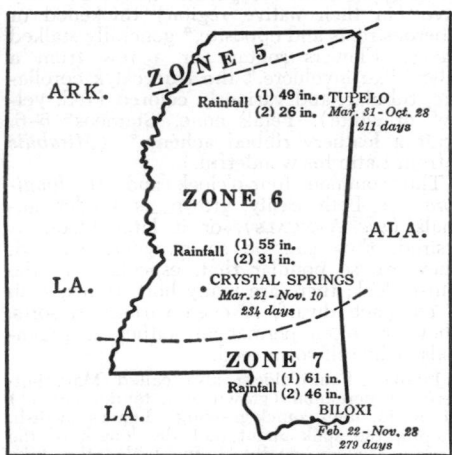

ARK.

ZONE 5

Rainfall (1) 49 in.• TUPELO
(2) 26 in. *Mar. 31 - Oct. 28*
211 days

ZONE 6

Rainfall (1) 55 in.
(2) 31 in.

CRYSTAL SPRINGS
Mar. 21 - Nov. 10
234 days

LA.

ALA.

ZONE 7

Rainfall (1) 61 in.
(2) 46 in.

BILOXI

LA.

Feb. 22 - Nov. 28
279 days

MISSISSIPPI

The zones of hardiness crossing Mississippi are those shown on the map located at ZONE, which should be consulted for details. The dates are the average lastest killing frost in spring and the first one in the fall. The figures below the dates show the length of the growing season. Rainfall figures (in inches) show (1) the total annual rainfall and (2) the amount falling in the growing season at the places indicated.

from 3.11 to 5.81 with a total of 31.30; and at Tupelo from 2.59 to 4.44 with a total of 26.20. In spite of these apparently large amounts of rainfall, droughts may occur at any time during the growing season, due to the fact that the rainfall for an entire month may fall in one or two rains.

The address of the Agricultural Experiment Station which has kindly supplied this information about the state is State College,

CLIMATE

Part of state	Town	Av. date of last killing frost in spring	Latest-known killing frost
North Central	Tupelo Crystal Springs	March 31 March 21	April 17 April 25
South	Biloxi	Feb. 22	March 26

Part of state	Town	Av. date of earliest killing frost in fall	Earliest-known killing frost
North Central	Tupelo Crystal Springs	Oct. 28 Nov. 10	Oct. 11 Oct. 21
South	Biloxi	Nov. 28	Oct. 30

Mississippi. The station is always ready to answer gardening questions.

Garden club activities include over 245 clubs affiliated with the Garden Club of Mississippi, Inc. Near Pass Christian and Gulfport are some of the finest gardens in the south.

mississippiensis, -e (mis-sis-sip-pĭ-en′sis). From the state of Mississippi, or from the Mississippi River region.

MISSOURI. The hawthorn is the state flower and the flowering dogwood the state tree. The state lies wholly in zones* 3 and 4 and is frequently referred to as the "heart of America" because of its central location. It includes an area of 68,727 square miles, or 43,985,280 acres divided into 114 counties. Native vegetation varies from the grassland prairies in the west and northern portions to the forested Ozarks in the south and east. Much tillable land is in the valleys of the Missouri, Grand, and Mississippi rivers and their tributaries.

CLIMATE. The climate and weather variations make for interesting challenges and exasperations to the gardener. Great variations occur from summer to winter and day to day, most of which are unpredictable more than five days in advance. This limits the selection of species and eliminates some of the more choice kinds that are not adaptable to these extremes. In some instances, however, the gardener can overcome the weather whims by careful choice of site and added protection.

Mean monthly temperatures vary from 33°

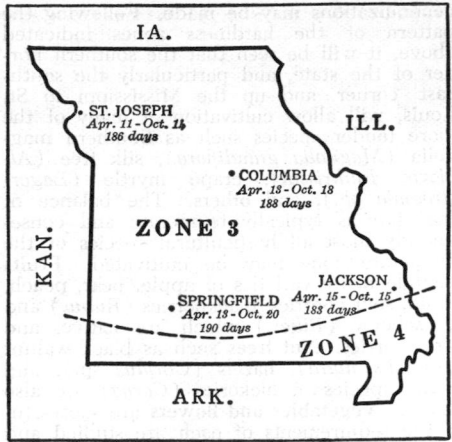

MISSOURI

The zones of hardiness crossing Missouri are those shown on the map located at ZONE, which should be consulted for details. The dates are the average latest killing frost in spring and the first one in the fall. The figures below the dates show the average length of the growing season.

in winter to near 80° in summer with readings ranging from a minimum near 0° to a maximum of 110°. Of greatest significance are the daily fluctuations that may occur in winter of −10° to above freezing and many times without snow cover. These variations are due to the three weather systems (Canadian, Rocky Mountain, and Gulf) that converge on Missouri.

Rainfall averages 40 inches with a gradient from lesser amounts in the northwest to greater in the southeast, but much of it distributed over the more favorable growing months in spring and fall. Supplemental irrigation may be necessary in July and August for maximum crop response.

The growing season averages 185 days for most of the state, but may be considered over 200 days for most gardening practices. Seasonal activities are further extended for many gardening enthusiasts in their hobby greenhouses.

SOIL. All major soil types are found in Missouri, from the rich glacial and river deposits in the north and the wind-blown loess along the rivers, to the eroded hills in the south-central and the weathered sandy loam of the "bootheel" in the southeast. For the most part they all have good basic qualities that can be made very productive with only slight modifications. Soil-testing services are available in nearly every county agent office and at the University for a more complete understanding of the soil and what it might need for certain crops.

SPECIES DISTRIBUTION. A complete listing of all garden species and their distribution in the state is impossible here, but some

* Special articles on the subjects indicated by an asterisk (*) will be found at the words so marked.

generalizations may be made. Following the pattern of the hardiness zones indicated above, it will be seen that the southern border of the state, and particularly the southeast corner and up the Mississippi to St. Louis, will allow cultivation of many of the more tender species such as Southern magnolia (*Magnolia grandiflora*), silk tree (*Albizzia Julibrissin*), crape myrtle (*Lagerstroemia* sp.), and others. The balance of the state is typically temperate and consequently most all horticultural species of the temperate zone may be cultivated. **Fruits** include many varieties of apple, pear, peach, plum, sour cherries, blackberries (*Rubus*) and gooseberry (*Ribes,*) which are native, and strawberries. **Nut trees** such as black walnut (*Juglans nigra*), hazels (*Corylus* sp.), and many species of hickories (*Carya*) are also native. **Vegetables and flowers** are successful if the requirements of each are studied and seasonal care and individual needs are observed in their culture. **Ornamental trees and shrubs,** both deciduous and evergreen, are likewise innumerable in Missouri cultivation. Certain tender southern species are limited to the south part of the state defined above. **Turf grasses** are dominantly Kentucky bluegrass and its improved varieties, but redtop, fescues, orchard grass, perennial rye grass, and Bermuda varieties have certain advantages in site or area location.

PUBLIC GARDENS. Many gardens and collections in Missouri are open most of the year. Missouri Botanical Garden, familiarly known as Shaw's Garden, in St. Louis, has a large conservatory, regular shows, and many acres of outdoor plantings. The Missouri Botanical Garden Arboretum at Gray Summit is as renowned for its outdoor collections as for the orchid collection in its greenhouses. In the Jewel Box located in Forest Park, St. Louis, are to be found seasonal indoor flower displays, and the adjoining garden contains a large rose garden and memorial floral clock. In central Missouri the A. B. Chance Company at Centralia has continued the display garden of the late A. B. Chance for public enjoyment from May to October. The Highway Gardens at the grounds of the Missouri State Fair in Sedalia is a joy to visitors, as are the entire fairgrounds during Fair week. The Kansas City Parks Department has some outstanding plantings, chief of which are in Swope Park and Luce Memorial Park. The latter contains a widely known rose garden as a joint project of the Parks Department and the Kansas City Rose Society. Neosho, in southwest Missouri, has gained national recognition as the "Flower Box City" from its generous use of this form of gardening and ornamentation.

The boulevard and park system of St. Joseph has attracted much comment in this "Pony Express" territory of the state.

Mention of Missouri's well-landscaped highways is unnecessary to the summer traveler. Special attention must be given to the Ten-Miles of Roses from Jackson to Cape Girardeau on Highway U.S. 61, the "Governor's Highway" (U.S. 54) from Jefferson City to Louisiana, and the two Blue Star Highways, U.S. 40 and U.S. 50. Highway travel through the Ozarks in May to see the flowering dogwood (*Cornus florida*) and in October for the fall coloration are semi-annual pilgrimages for thousands of lovers of natural beauty.

HORTICULTURAL ORGANIZATIONS. Active amateur organizations for certain phases of horticulture are: Missouri African Violet Society (several local chapters, also); Missouri Gladiolus Society; St. Louis Horticultural Society; Friends of the Garden (St. Louis); Federated Garden Clubs of Missouri (over 400 local clubs affiliated); National Headquarters for the National Council of State Garden Clubs (St. Louis); Men's Garden Club of America (local chapters); Heart of America Gladiolus Society (Kansas City); Dahlia and Chrysanthemum Societies (Kansas City and St. Joseph); Rose Societies in Kansas City, Springfield, and St. Joseph; Begonia Society and Gloxinia Society (Kansas City); Iris Societies in St. Louis, Mid-Missouri, and Kansas City, and many others.

INSTITUTIONS. Several institutions of horticulture and near-related activities are: The University of Missouri Department of Horticulture at Columbia with its specialists in pomology, floriculture, vegetable-growing, landscape and nursery, food technology, and soil-testing service; Missouri Botanical Garden at St. Louis; State Conservation Nursery at Licking; and Missouri Fruit Experiment Station at Mountain Grove.

MISSOURI BOTANICAL GARDEN. *See* BOTANIC GARDEN.

missouriensis, -e (miz-zur-i-en′sis). From Missouri.

MISSOURI GOURD = *Cucurbita foetidissima.*

MISSOURI PRIMROSE = *Oenothera missouriensis. See* EVENING PRIMROSE.

MIST. Recently the advantages of growing cuttings, young seedlings, and other plants in an atmosphere permeated by a fine mist has been much advocated. To meet the demand for contrivances that would permit a regulated amount of mist to be diffused through the atmosphere, various types of automatic nozzles have been devised, so spaced and timed that the atmosphere is pretty constantly moist. They are, of course, useful only in the confined space of a greenhouse, propagating bench, or other closed space.

The undeniable advantages of certain plants being grown in a constantly moist atmosphere, something comparable to that in a tropical rain-forest, may well outweigh the obvious disadvantages that can come from too much mist, *i.e.,* leaching of nutrients and possible rotting of roots. Mist culture is mostly a professional job for those able to discriminate between its advantages and hazards. *See* the section on rooting softwood cuttings under mist at CUTTINGS.

---

* Special articles on the subjects indicated by an asterisk (*) will be found at the words so marked.

MIST-FLOWER = *Eupatorium coelestinum.*

MISTLETOE. This is not a garden plant and cannot be cultivated, as it is a parasite* on trees, in America, usually upon oaks. The common mistletoe of the eastern U.S. is *Phoradendron flavescens*, found from N.J. to the Gulf. In the West other species, and even genera, furnish mistletoe, but none can be cultivated. The mistletoe of history and legend is *Viscum album*, an Old World parasite unknown in America.

MISTLETOE CACTUS = *Rhipsalis Cassytha.*

MITCHELLA (mit-chel'la). An evergreen, rather woody, prostrate herb of the family Rubiaceae, found in woods over most of the eastern half of N.A. The only cult. species, M. repens, the partridge-berry, also called twinberry, squawberry, and teaberry, is a wild garden plant for shady places and good, rich, woods soil, not especially acid. It has slender stems, not usually over 15 in. long, rooting easily at the joints and making flat patches. Leaves opposite,* nearly round, about ¾ in. wide, green, but sometimes with white lines. Flowers borne in united pairs, at the end of a short stalk. Corolla funnel-shaped, white, about ½ in. long. Fruit a showy, scarlet, berry-like drupe,* usually with 8 nutlets. It is one of the best plants for a winter terrarium, and is often used for a centerpiece decoration, but it does better under a glass, as it does not like the heat and dryness of a room. (Named for John Mitchell, a Virginia botanist.) *See* WILD GARDEN.

MITELLA (my-tell'a). A small genus of North American and Asiatic delicate, perennial, woodland herbs of the family Saxifragaceae, usually having alternate* leaves. M. diphylla, commonly called mitre-wort, bishop's-cap, or fairy-cap, grows about 1½ ft. high. Leaves stalkless, heart-shaped, with marginal teeth, growing in pairs. Flowers small, white, in a terminal cluster 6–8 inches long, the petals deeply cut. Fruit a pod, soon widely splitting. Quebec to S. Car. and Mo. Excellent in the shaded rock garden or in the wild garden. (*Mitella* is the diminutive of *mitra*, a cap, in allusion to the shape of the fruit.)

mitis, -e (my'tis). Mild or gentle.

MITRA = *Astrophytum myriostigma.*

MITREWORT = *Mitella diphylla.* For false mitrewort *see* TIARELLA.

MIXTURE OF SOILS. See POTTING MIXTURES.

MOCCASIN FLOWER = *Cypripedium acaule.*

MOCK CUCUMBER = *Echinocystis lobata.*

MOCK-ORANGE. A genus of North American and Eurasian deciduous shrubs, mostly erect, but with curved or drooping branches, of the family Saxifragaceae, known as Philadelphus (fil-a-del'fus) and comprising about 60 species, having solid white pith, and close or flaky bark. Leaves opposite,* with or without marginal teeth. Flowers white, rarely purple near the base, solitary or in small clusters, often fragrant. Sepals and petals 4. Stamens* numerous. Fruit a capsule* with numerous small seeds. They are variously known as mock-orange or syringa. Mock-orange is also applied to *Laurocerasus caroliniana.* (*Philadelphus* is the name given by Linnaeus, from King Ptolemy Philadelphus, 3d century B.C.)

These shrubs and their numerous hybrids are widely planted in the shrubbery border. They bloom in late spring and are very showy. Pruning should be done immediately after blossoming, for they flower from wood of the previous year. They are propagated from cuttings, seeds, layers, and suckers. Cuttings are usually made from mature wood, but softwood cuttings may be started in frames in summer.

P. coronarius. Common mock-orange; also known as sweet mock-orange, or false syringa. A shrub to 10 ft. high. Bark dark brown and peeling off on last year's growth. Leaves ovalish to oblong, pointed, 1½–4 in. long. Flowers creamy-white, very fragrant, in 5–7-flowered, terminal clusters (racemes*). Eu., southwest As. *Var.* dianthiflorus and *var.* flore-pleno have double flowers. *Var.* aureus. Golden mock-orange. A form with the leaves bright yellow in youth. June. Hardy from zone* 2 southward.

P. cymosus. A hybrid mock-orange, probably derived from a cross between *P. lemoinei* and *P. grandiflorus.* It has peeling bark, and is otherwise very similar to the Lemoine hybrids. Several hort. vars. belong here, notably Bannier, Norma, etc.

P. falconeri. A shrub to 8 ft. high. Leaves ovalish to narrower, 2–3 in. long, slightly hairy on veins beneath, those on young shoots broadly oval and toothed. Flowers 3–7 on slender, smooth stalks or in 7-flowered, flat-topped terminal clusters 1½ in. across, pure white and fragrant. Possibly a hybrid between *P. coronarius* and *P. laxus.* Hardy from zone* 3 southward.

P. gordonianus. A shrub 9–12 ft. high. Bark yellowish-gray, not peeling off. Leaves ovalish to oblong, pointed, coarsely toothed, soft-hairy beneath. Flowers 1½–2 in. across, fragrant, in 7–9- rarely 11-flowered clusters (racemes*). British Columbia to northern Calif. June–July. Hardy from zone* 4 southward.

P. grandiflorus. Closely related to *P. inodorus,* and by some considered merely a var. of it, differing in having somewhat larger leaves and flowers nearly square in cross-section. N. Car. to Fla. and Ala. June. Hardy from zone* 3 southward. Along the Gulf Coast commonly called English dogwood, although it is neither a dogwood nor English.

P. inodorus. A handsome, upright shrub, with arching branches and peeling bark. Leaves ovalish to broader, 3–5 in. long, pointed, occasionally toothed, smooth and shiny. Flowers 1–3, cup-shaped, 1½–2 in. across, not scented. N. Car. to Ga. and Miss. June. Hardy from zone* 4 southward.

P. laxus. A shrub growing 4 ft. high. Young growth smooth. Leaves 2–3 in. long, ovalish to narrower, slightly hairy beneath, sometimes

---

* Special articles on the subjects indicated by an asterisk (*) will be found at the words so marked.

toothed, nearly always without marginal teeth, sharp-pointed, drooping, stiff. Flowers 1–3, scentless, 1½ in. across. Ga. June. Hardy from zone° 5 southward.

P. lemoinei. An upright, spreading shrub, 4–6 ft. high, a hybrid between *P. microphyllus* and *P. coronarius*. Leaves ovalish to narrower, pointed, smooth above, stiff-hairy beneath. Flowers in 3–7-flowered, terminal clusters (racemes°), 1½ in. across, very fragrant. Some of the horticultural forms are Avalanche, Boule d'Argent, Candelabre, Manteau d'Hermine, and Mont Blanc. June. Hardy from zone° 2 southward.

P. lewisi. A shrub growing 6 ft. high, the bark brownish, tardily peeling. Leaves ovalish to oblong, 1–3 in. long, pointed, with or without marginal teeth. Flowers 1–1½ in. across, in 5–9-flowered, terminal clusters (racemes°). Mont. to Wash. and Ore. June–Aug. Hardy from zone° 3 southward. The state flower of Idaho.

P. magdalenae. A shrub up to 12 ft. high, the bark usually peeling. Leaves ovalish to narrower, pointed, with marginal teeth, soft-hairy above, stiff-hairy beneath. Flowers about 1 in. across, scentless, in 7–11-flowered clusters (racemes°). Western China. June. Hardy from zone° 3 southward.

P. microphyllus. A shrub growing to 4 ft. high, the bark brown, peeling. Leaves ovalish to oblong, sharp-pointed, shiny and smooth or stiff-hairy above. Flowers usually solitary, 1 in. across, with a delightful pineapple fragrance. Colo. to N. Mex. and Ariz. June–July. Hardy from zone° 4 southward.

P. nivalis. A hybrid shrub, the brown bark peeling. Leaves ovalish, with marginal teeth, slightly soft-hairy beneath. Flowers 1–1½ in. across, in 5–9-flowered clusters (racemes°). June. Hardy from zone° 2 southward.

P. pekinensis. A shrub growing up to 6 ft. high, the bark brown and peeling. Leaves oblong, or ovalish, smooth except beneath, stalks purplish. Flowers 1–1½ in. across, creamy, fragrant, in 5–9-flowered clusters (racemes°). North China to Korea. June. Hardy from zone° 3 southward.

P. virginalis. Probably a hybrid between *P. lemoinei* and a variety of *P. nivalis*. Bark brown and peeling or gray-brown and slightly peeling. Leaves ovalish, 2½–3 in. long, slightly toothed, soft-hairy above. Flowers semi-double or double, in 3–7-flowered clusters (racemes°). Useful for forcing (which see). Some horticultural forms are Argentine, Glacier, and Virginal.

P. zeyheri. A spreading shrub up to 6 ft. high, the bark brown, and peeling. Leaves ovalish, 3½–4 in. long, taper-pointed, slightly toothed or not, smooth except on veins beneath. Flowers 1½–2 in. across, in 3–5-flowered clusters. Of hybrid origin. June. Hardy from zone° 3 southward.

MOCK PRIVET = *Phillyrea*.

MOCK STRAWBERRY = *Duchesnea indica*.

MODEL GARDENS. For flower-show exhibits and sometimes in the development of an extensive estate, it is often desirable to make a model of the property, showing grading, buildings, planting, and lawn. Such models are far easier to understand than an architect's drawing or specifications, and they can be made most attractive if carefully done to scale and colored in harmony with the finished design.

Because they are gardens in miniature, with no living material in them, various substitutes for trees, shrubs, lawns, etc., have been devised, the handling and placing of which in the model require considerable skill and knowledge.

The foundation must come first and it should be of plasticine or it can be of newspapers boiled to a pulp, to which flour paste or glue is added. While still workable, either of these materials can be moulded to any desired topography, but before they "set," trees, shrubs, or models of buildings must be placed, because after the foundation becomes hard it is difficult to add such features.

Coloring material for tinting soil, plants, stones, buildings, etc., may be ordinary house paint, pastel crayons, Tintex, or aniline dyes. If shiny effects are needed, use enamel paints, or, for dull finish, add turpentine to paints.

To make grass, use freshly mixed plasticine stippled with a stiff-bristled brush, and then colored. Or grass may be made with terry cloth, ratiné, or bath-towel material.

For making paths, green sawdust, sandpaper, Wheatena, Cream of Wheat, or roofing paper, all appropriately colored, will simulate gravel, sand, or paved walks. For walls, use bits of painted laths, cartons, or cardboard.

In making miniature hedges or formal, clipped evergreen plantings like box, use rubber sponge, ordinary sponge, or fine baby sponge, cut and colored in accordance with your plant. Use aniline dyes for ordinary sponge and a water paint for rubber sponge. For low, evergreen edging, use pussy-willow catkins dyed with Tintex.

The most difficult operation is making shrubs and trees that look effective in the model. The trunk and main branches should be dried twigs, roots upside-down (for the crown), broom bristles, twisted wire (usually covered with tire tape, linen, etc.) or pipe-cleaners. This framework must all be shellacked and twisted into shape before any "foliage" is added. Just before the shellac is put on, mineral wool, Brillo, lamb's wool or similar material should be drawn through the shrub or tree to make a base upon which the "foliage" is put. The latter consists of feathery bits of moss, cut-up bits of cotton or linen, raffia, velvet, dyed cereal grits, sawdust, sponge, feathers, or tiny segments of fern fronds, depending on what the nature of the tree may be. Sometimes a whole "tree" can be made from one dried plant or part of it, as an elm tree from goldenrod, or a spruce from ground pine (see LYCOPODIUM).

For flowers it is usually best to use those described at DRIED FLOWERS, coloring them to suit your composition.

To simulate water, use sheets of cellophane or some clear celluloid substitute. Pools can be made by letting into the ground shallow trays covered with cellophane. For foam use shaving soap, and for a meandering stream use silver paper.

Miniature ornaments can be made from

° Special articles on the subjects indicated by an asterisk (°) will be found at the words so marked.

clay, pencil erasers, soap, or even from bread, all colored to your design. Buildings, steps, and other architectural features can be cut from soap, made of cardboard, or of plaster mixed with cotton batting held together with glue. Often kindergarten toys or the ten-cent store will provide many useful accessories.

Model gardens cannot, of course, be made without a good deal of deftness and skill. In addition to the items already mentioned, the following equipment will be found useful: fine brads, sharp knives and scissors, rubber gloves (for aniline dyes), orange sticks, tweezers or forceps, toothpicks, green thread, putty, clay, upholstery needles, and liquid glue.

When made, the models are very fragile and must be packed with the greatest care if it is necessary to ship them. The foundation should be screwed to the bottom of a tight box and all possibly loose structures (fences, buildings, etc.) held in place by tire tape.

modesta, -us, -um (mo-des′ta). Modest.

MODESTO ASH = *Fraxinus velutina.* See ASH.

MOHAWKWEED = *Uvularia perfoliata.*

MOHRODENDRON = *Halesia.*

MOLD. See SOILS. See also Fungi at PLANT DISEASES.

Moldavica (mol-dă′vi-ka). An old generic name for the dragon-heads. See DRACO-CEPHALUM.

MOLES. See ANIMAL INJURY.

MOLINIA (mo-lin′ĭ-a). A small genus of tufted, perennial, Eurasian grasses, one of them, **M. caerulea,** planted for ornament. It is a stiff, smooth grass, 3–5 ft. high, with somewhat stiff, grass-like leaves 6–12 in. long. Flowering cluster (panicle*) 7–15 in. long, its branches mostly erect, bearing the 2–4-flowered, sharp-pointed, greenish or purplish spikelets which are without awns.* Eu., but naturalized in the U.S., and sometimes known as *Aira caerulea.* It is of simple culture in any soil. A lower, variegated-leaved form is sometimes used for edging. (Named for J. Molina, Chilean botanist.)

molleoides (mol-lee-oy′deez, but see OÏDES). Like something softly hairy.

mollis, -e (mol′lis). Softly hairy.

mollissima, -us, -um (mol-lis′i-ma). Very softly hairy.

Mollugo (mol-lew′go). A specific name derived from the genus *Mollugo,* which is of no garden interest.

MOLTKIA (molt′kĭ-a). A genus of Eurasian hairy, perennial herbs of the family Boraginaceae, containing about 8 species, 2 or more of which are used as alpines in the rock garden. It is closely allied to *Lithospermum* and often listed under that name. Leaves alternate,* undivided, hairy or downy. Flowers blue or yellow, somewhat

funnel-shaped, the stamens* protruding, usually growing in terminal or flat-topped clusters (racemes* or cymes*). Fruit a collection of small nutlets. (Named for Count Joachim Gadske Moltke, Denmark.)

graminifolia = *Moltkia suffruticosa.*
petraea. A somewhat woody, perennial herb, growing 6 to 12 in. high. Leaves 1½ in. long, very narrow, covered with a thick, white down. Flowers deep violet-blue, ½ in. long, generally in flat-topped clusters. Eu. Also known as *Lithospermum petraeum.*
suffruticosa. A somewhat woody perennial growing 1½ ft. high. Leaves very narrow, covered with white down beneath. Flowers purple-blue, ½ in. long. Italy. Also known as *Lithospermum graminifolium.*

MOLUCCA BALM = *Molucella laevis.*

MOLUCELLA (mol-lew-sell′a). Two species of aromatic, Old World annual herbs of the mint family, both found in old-fashioned gardens, one widely cult. They have opposite,* stalked, generally toothed leaves. Flowers very small, in whorls* in the leaf axils,* the tiny, irregular, white or pinkish corolla scarcely or not at all exceeding the bristly or prickly calyx.* Fruit a collection of 4 nutlets, nestled in the shell-like, persistent, green calyx* in the first species. (*Molucella* is a diminutive of *Molucca,* but neither plant is known from this East Indian island.)

Both species are best grown as tender annuals (*see* ANNUALS) and are of easy culture.

laevis. Bells of Ireland. Molucca balm; also called shell-flower. A simple* or branching herb 2–3 ft. high. Leaves roundish or heart-shaped, ¾–1½ in. long. Flowers fragrant, very numerous, the calyx with 5 small prickles, but expanding in fruit and the nutlets nestled in it; hence the name, shell-flower. Western As. A common florists' flower, forced in the winter under medium heat, its green, showy calyx very handsome.

spinosa. An annual (or perhaps a biennial) 5–7 ft. high, the stems brownish-red. Leaves ovalish, deeply cut or toothed. Calyx with 8 long prickles or spines. Southern Eu. and Syria.

Moly (mō′lee). An ancient name for some reputedly medicinal plant of great value. See ALLIUM.

Mombin (mom′bin). Tropical American native name for *Spondias Mombin.*

MOMORDICA (mo-more′di-ka). A genus of over 40 species of tropical Asian or African tendril*-bearing vines of the cucumber family, two of them grown for ornament, mostly in warm regions. Both are annuals of quick growth. Leaves alternate,* compound* or deeply divided. Male and female flowers separate, sometimes on different plants or on the same one, both solitary (in ours), yellow or white, stalked, the stalk bearing a prominent bract.* Corolla bell-shaped or more open, parted nearly to the base. Fruit oblongish or globe-shaped, tardily splitting, the seeds with a showy aril* (in some). (*Momordica* is from the Latin to bite, in allusion to the jagged seeds of some species.)

---

* Special articles on the subjects indicated by an asterisk (*) will be found at the words so marked.

Being tropical vines they are best treated, in the North, as tender annuals (*see* AN-NUALS). In the South they make quick growth and will soon cover a porch or screen. The second species is very handsome in fruit.

Balsamina. Balsam apple. A high-climbing, herbaceous vine, the tendrils* unbranched. Leaves 2–4 in. wide, 3–5-lobed, the lobes pointed. Flowers yellow, the center darker, about 1 in. wide in the male flowers, smaller in the female. Fruit egg-shaped, about 2 in. long, slightly warty, orange, its seeds flat, gray or brown, usually scalloped on the edges. Old World tropics.

Charantia. Balsam pear. A taller-growing vine than *M. Balsamina* and with larger, more deeply lobed leaves. Flowers very similar, but the bract* on the flower stalk without teeth. Fruit oblongish or oval, 4–8 in. long, more warty than in the balsam apple, orange-yellow, when split showing the bright scarlet arils* of its seeds. Old World tropics.

monacantha, -us, -um (mo-na-kan'tha). With a single spine or thorn.

MONACILLO = *Malvaviscus arboreus.*

monadelpha, -us, -um (mo-na-dell'fa). Monadelphous.

MONADELPHOUS. Having the stamens* united by their filaments* into a single group, as in many plants of the pea family. *See* LEGUMINOSAE.

monandra, -us, -um (mo-nan'dra). Having one stamen.*

MONANTHES (mo-nan'theez). A genus of the Crassulaceae containing about 10 fleshy, small, perennial, tufted herbs, usually glandular*-hairy. Leaves opposite* or alternate,* nearly always in rosettes. Flowers usually solitary, or in terminal clusters (raceme*) or in flat-topped clusters (cymes*). Petals 6 to 12, with petal-like scales. The species most commonly grown, **M. atlantica**, is a native of the Canary Islands and Morocco. The branches are 1 to 3 in. long, lying on the ground and bearing at the ends rosettes of 20 or more fleshy leaves, each about ⅛ of an inch in length. Flowers golden-yellow, spotted with red on the back, growing on stalks from the ends of the branches. It is also known as *Sedum atlanticum.* For culture *see* SUCCULENTS. (*Monanthes* is from the Greek for solitary and flower, in allusion to the often solitary flower.)

MONARDA (mo-nar'da). A North American genus of the mint family including 17 species of annual or perennial aromatic herbs, some of which are grown for their showy flowers. Leaves opposite* and with marginal teeth. Flowers rather large, white, red, purplish, yellow or mottled, 2-lipped,* often with showy, colored bracts* beneath the flower clusters, which are terminal or in the leaf axils.* They are known as horse mint and bergamot. (Named for Nicolas Monardes, a Spanish botanist and physician.) The monardas are rather coarse plants, but often very brilliant in color. Those of

Oswego Tea or Bee Balm (*Monarda didyma*), a scarlet-flowered native perennial good for moist or dry places.

striking color should be grown in masses along the banks of a stream or in a corner of the woods. They are easily cult., growing readily in any good soil. They spread quickly and should be divided often, spring division being much more successful than fall, as the fall-divided clumps often winter-kill.

citriodora. Lemon mint. An annual herb growing about 1 ft. high. Leaves oblong or narrower, with small marginal teeth. Flowers white or pinkish, not spotted, growing in heads from the axils* of the leaves, or at intervals on a spike. Whole plant delightfully lemon-scented. Ill. to Neb. and Tex. Also called *M. pectinata.*

didyma. Bee balm; also called Oswego tea or red balm. A perennial herb, somewhat hairy, with a sharply 4-angled stem, growing 3 ft. high. Leaves 3 to 6 in. long, slightly longer than oval, pointed. Flowers scarlet, nearly 2 in. long, in terminal clusters, surrounded with red-tinged bracts.* Quebec to Ga. and Tenn. *Var.* **alba** has white flowers; *var.* **rosea**, rose-colored flowers, and there are improved, scarlet forms. *See also* HERB GARDENING.

fistulosa. Wild bergamot. A softly hairy or smooth perennial herb, growing 3 ft. high. Leaves narrowly oval, 4–6 in. long. Flowers lilac to purple, 1½ in. long, growing in terminal clusters, the surrounding bracts* whitish or purplish. Eastern N.A. Easily transplanted to the wild garden, in dry situations, and is sometimes effectively used in combination with perennial phlox in the hardy border. *Var.* **alba** has white flowers. *See* HERB GARDENING.

MONARDELLA (mo-nar-del'la). About 15 species of aromatic, mostly Californian herbs of the mint family, not much known in the garden, but **M. villosa**, the coyote mint, grown for ornament. It is a perennial, 12–18 in. high, the foliage hairy, its leaves more or less oval, about 1 in. long, and opposite.* Flowers purple, pink, or white, about ½ in. long, in dense, terminal, head-like clusters. It differs only in technical characters from *Monarda.* It is of easy culture

* Special articles on the subjects indicated by an asterisk (*) will be found at the words so marked.

in Calif., and can be increased by division in the spring. Eastward its availability is uncertain. (*Monardella* is a diminutive of *Monarda,* which these plants resemble.)

MONDO = *Ophiopogon.*

MONESES (mo-nee′seez). **A genus of** perennial, evergreen herbs of the heath family, growing in N.A. and Eurasia, having only one species, M. **uniflora,** known as one-flowered wintergreen. Stem prostrate, the leaves roundish, toothed, about 1 in. long, clustered near the base of the stem. Flower solitary, on a drooping stalk, 5 or 6 in. long. Corolla white or pink, fragrant, about ¾ in. across, the petals 5, and spreading. Fruit a capsule,* about ¼ in. across. The one-flowered wintergreen grows in moist, cool woodlands, and should only be grown in shady places in the wild garden. (*Moneses* is from the Greek for single delight, alluding to the pretty solitary flower.)

MONEYWORT = *Lysimachia Nummularia.*

monilifera, -us, -um (mo-nil-liff′er-a). Necklace-like.

MONIMIACEAE. See PEUMUS.

MONKEY-COCONUT = *Jubaea spectabilis.*

MONKEY-FLOWER. See MIMULUS.

MONKEY-POD. See SAMANEA SAMAN.

MONKEY-PUZZLE = *Araucaria araucana.*

MONKEY'S-BREAD. See ADANSONIA DIGITATA.

MONKSHOOD. The aconites, or, as some of them are called, the wolfsbanes, are mostly showy perennial herbs comprising the genus **Aconitum** (ak-ko-ny′tum) of the buttercup family. Of over 80 species, nearly all from the north temperate zone, only a handful are of garden interest, and one of them, *A. Napellus,* the common monkshood, yields the drug aconite, of world-wide use as a heart sedative. All are dangerously poisonous (not to the touch). They have usually thickened or even tuberous roots and leaves that are cleft or divided finger-fashion, but not compound.* Flowers very irregular,* mostly in terminal clusters (panicles* or racemes*), prevailingly blue or purple, but white or yellow in some. Sepals* 5, petal-like, one of them large, hood-shaped (hence monkshood) or helmet-like. Petals 2–5, two of them spur-like and contained in the hood, the others small or wanting. Stamens* numerous. Fruit a collection of many-seeded follicles.* (*Aconitum* is the ancient classical name of the monkshood.) None are happy in warm regions.

The monkshoods are showy garden plants (but children should be warned against the poisonous juice). They prefer partial shade and a rich soil, preferably with a pH of 5–6. The taller sorts need staking, as they are somewhat weak-stemmed plants. They are fine plants for late summer and early

autumn gardens, and some of the blue-flowered sorts are particularly valuable for the blue garden (which see). All the cult. kinds are best treated as perennials, and bloom the second or third year from seed. They may also be increased by division, but generally they dislike being moved. Their foliage superficially resembles the closely related larkspurs (*see* DELPHINIUM), but the latter does not have the helmet-shaped flowers of the monkshoods.

A. **Anthora.** Not over 2 ft. high, the divisions of the leaf very narrow. Flowers with the helmet extended into a short beak, pale yellow. Southern Eu. July–Aug.

A. **autumnale.** A Chinese perennial, 4–5 ft. high, the leaves 5-lobed. Flowers generally blue, sometimes whitish or lilac, the helmet nearly closed. There is doubt as to the true identity of the plant usually offered as A. *autumnale,* as it may be a form of A. *fischeri.*

A. **Cammarum.** A perennial, 3–4 ft. high, the lobes of the much-divided leaf blunt. Flowers in a loose cluster, purple, the helmet nearly closed. Hungary. The plant is sometimes offered as A. *exaltatum.*

A. *exaltatum* = *Aconitum Cammarum.*

A. **fischeri.** One of the most popular of the garden monkshoods and from 4–6 ft. high. Leaves 3-lobed, the lobes often notched. Flowers generally blue (rarely white), the helmet extended into a spur-like visor. A very handsome plant from eastern Asia, badly confused as to identity and names, as many gardeners' names appear to be referable to this species. Sept.–Oct.

A. **lycoctonum.** Wolfsbane. A perennial 4–6 ft. high, the leaves with 3–9 broadish segments which are toothed. Flowers yellow or creamy-white, in spikelike racemes.* The upright helmet in constricted below the top. Eurasia.

A. **Napellus.** The common monkshood and the source of the drug aconite, but cult. here for ornament. It is not over 4 ft. high, the leaves twice- or thrice-divided into narrow segments. Flowers blue, the broad helmet with a beak-like visor. Eu. An extremely poisonous plant. There is a white-flowered variety, and the *var.* sparksi, with pale blue flowers, is fine for the blue garden (which see).

A. **uncinatum.** Wild monkshood. A native perennial, weak, partly climbing, but not over 5 ft. high. Leaves 3–5-lobed, the lobes again divided or deeply toothed. Flowers blue. In rich, moist woods, especially along streams, Pa. to Ga. and Ind. Best suited to shady, moist places in the wild garden. June–July.

A. **wilsoni** = A. *fischeri.*

MONK'S PEPPER-TREE = *Vitex Agnus-castus.*

MONOCARP. A plant that blooms and sets seed only once and then dies. Common examples are annuals, biennials, some century plants and a few palms.

MONOCOTYLEDON. A plant having only one cotyledon* or seed leaf. Monocotyledonous plants usually have parallel-veined leaves and the parts of their flowers (petals, stamens, etc.) in threes or multiples of three. Common examples of monocotyledonous plants are grasses, lily, palm, iris, tulip, gladiolus, crocus, and the orchids. *See* DICOTYLEDON.

---

* Special articles on the subjects indicated by an asterisk (*) will be found at the words so marked.

MONOECIOUS (mo-nee′shus). Having the male and female flowers separate, but on the same plant, as in many members of the cucumber family, some palms, and in all the walnuts and oaks. See DIOECIOUS.

monogyna, -us, -um (mo-noj′y-na). Having one pistil.°

monophylla, -us, -um (mo-no-fil′la). Single-leaved; sometimes used for plants with only one leaflet.

monosperma, -us, -um (mo-no-sper′ma). One-seeded.

monspeliensis, -e (mon-spell-i-en′sis). From Montpellier, France.

monspessulana, -us, -um (mon-spess-u-lay′na). From or near Montpellier, France.

MONSTERA (mon-steer′ra). A genus of tropical American aroids, comprising perhaps 30 species, of which **M. deliciosa**, the ceriman, is cult. in northern greenhouses for its remarkable foliage, and in tropical regions and southern Fla. for its fruit. It is a strong-stemmed, climbing plant with many cord-like, aerial roots. Leaves 2–3 ft. long, nearly as broad, much cut into large, rounded lobes, the body of the blade plentifully perforated with oblong or elliptic holes, some of which may be 3–4 in. long. Leafstalk long, stout, sheathing at the base and channeled. Flowers borne on a dense, club-shaped spadix,° which is 8–10 in. long and about 2 in. thick, ultimately developing into a cone-like mass of fleshy, sweet fruits, which are aromatic and flavored somewhat like a mixture of banana and pineapple. For details of its flower structure see ARACEAE. In greenhouses it needs a stout support, potting mixture° 4, plenty of water and a warm, moist greenhouse. Under these conditions it will often fruit in the greenhouse. It will stand no frost. In southern Fla. the fruits are occasionally to be found in the markets, but the plant is chiefly grown for its extraordinary foliage. (*Monstera* is of unknown origin.) The plant is sometimes known as *Philodendron pertusum.*

monstrosa, -us, -um (mon-strō′sa). Large or monstrous.

MONTANA. The state flower is the bitter-root (*Lewisia rediviva*) and the state tree is the ponderosa pine (*Pinus ponderosa*).

The state lies within zones° 1 and 2, but conditions are so varied because of different altitudes that one has to consider the micro-climate in selecting plants.

Gardens, particularly in sections east of the continental divide, benefit immeasurably from properly planned and cared-for shelter-belts. Having a good shelterbelt means growing better tree and small fruits, better vegetables and ornamentals. Most good belts consist of one or two outside rows of shrubs or shrub-like trees such as *Caragana*, Russian olive, and Western red cedar. Taller trees are suggested for the inner rows, including such trees as the green ash, American elm,

Chinese elm, cottonwood, and poplar. White willow makes a good substitute for *Caragana*, Russian olive, and Western red cedar where moisture tends to collect and remain, or where the water table is high. The very inside row can be planted with Colorado spruce, Black Hills spruce, and ponderosa pine.

In-the-row spacing for *Caragana* should be 3 ft. apart, for Russian olive 6 ft. apart, and for large deciduous trees and evergreens 8 ft. apart. Spacing between rows should be 12–16 ft. apart. Five rows are suggested for the average dry-land belt. A three- or four-row planting is suggested for irrigated belts. Between-the-row spacing for irrigated belts can be reduced to 12 ft. Clean cultivation and summer fallow a year in advance of planting new trees is advised, particularly for dry-land plantings.

In Montana spring planting is advised for most nursery stock, including deciduous trees and shrubs and evergreens. Evergreens can be transplanted successfully after new growth has started to mature in August. Little fall planting is advised in this state because of the uncertainties of the fall season and the extreme dessication effect of the dry winter atmosphere and drying winds. Likewise, pruning of trees and shrubs should be done in spring or early summer. Fall-pruned trees may be killed back during winter by dessication and extreme cold.

While the range of ornamental trees and shrubs that can be grown in the zone° 1 area is limited, it is extensive enough so that one can develop good landscape effects and interesting plantings. The range of plant materials is much more extensive in zone° 2. In this zone there are some locations where even the more tender plants can be grown. There is one small area south and west of Billings that has very favorable climatic conditions for growing horticultural crops. This area centers around the towns of Joliet and Bridger and vicinity.

One important garden practice is watering. Reducing the amount of watering around late summer helps new plant growth to better maturity. However, this does not mean plants should go into the winter dry. At about the time trees are showing good maturity — *i.e.*, when leaves are coloring up and beginning to drop — all ornamental plants will benefit from a good thorough watering that will penetrate the soil at least 3 ft. Evergreens and deciduous trees, like birch, that are heavy feeders of moisture are especially in need of this treatment. Evergreens that do not receive sufficient water during the winter months show a condition the next spring or early summer known as "winter burn." Birch trees show inadequate watering by the killing back of new growth. Gardeners should do everything possible to encourage good maturity in their ornamentals before winter sets in. Avoiding overstimulation with nitrogen fertilizers, especially in late summer, is helpful.

° Special articles on the subjects indicated by an asterisk (°) will be found at the words so marked.

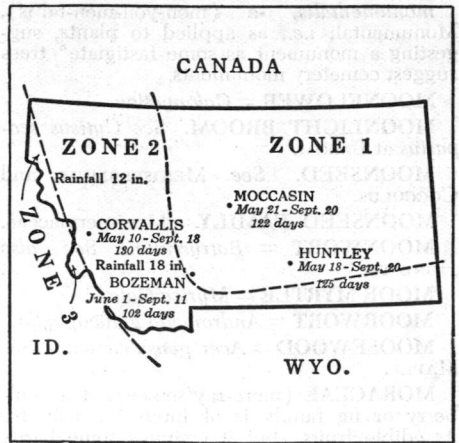

MONTANA

The zones of hardiness crossing Montana are those shown on the map located at ZONE, which should be consulted for details. The dates are the average latest killing frost in spring and the first one in the fall. The figures below the dates show the length of the growing season. Rainfall figures (in inches) are for total annual rainfall in the regions so indicated.

SOILS. Most of the soils in the state have pH readings above 7.0, that is, they are alkaline. These soils contain considerable lime or calcium. As a general rule, no additional lime is needed on such soils. In fact, the problem is just the opposite. Because of the high lime content of the soil, elements like phosphorus and iron, although they may be abundant in such a soil, frequently are tied up in a form not usable by the plant. Consequently, phosphorus is one of the elements very generally needed in fertilizer programs in the state. Evidence for the need of more iron shows up as yellowing between the midribs in the foliage of plants, or in severe cases, the foliage may be completely yellow. This term is known as lime-induced chlorosis or iron chlorosis. Plants that are particularly susceptible to lack of iron in the soil are roses, spirea, mountain-ash, raspberries, strawberries, apples, plums, etc. As a general rule, woody plants in the Rose family have been most susceptible. Even cottonwoods and poplar have shown chlorosis under high lime conditions, and even lawns have shown response to iron feedings.

The iron chelates, especially the forms recommended for alkaline soils, such as Chel 330 and Sequestrene NaFe, have offered good correction. Older correctives such as acid peat moss, sulphur, ferrous sulphate, and aluminum sulphate have been variable in their effectiveness, and in some cases have had adverse toxic effects.

There are a few areas, especially in the mountain sections where acid soils prevail.

These are local, and soil tests would reveal their nature. Generally, nitrogen and phosphorus have been the two major elements lacking in soil in the state. Home gardeners use complete fertilizers such as 4–12–6, etc. Since many of the state's soils are low in organic matter, it is strongly advocated that gardeners use some source of organic matter in their garden fertilizing and soil-building practices. Source of organic matter is well-decayed manures, leaf mold, green manure crops, and composts.

There is evidence of the need for boron in certain soils in the state. Crops like cabbage, cauliflower, turnips, and apples have indicated the need for this element in certain areas. It should not be applied indiscriminately since excess boron can result in serious plant-nutrition problems. The whole problem of boron nutrition should be checked by a specialist and his recommendations followed. Sulphur and zinc deficiencies exist in some soils. Saline soils present a problem in a few areas.

SOME PLACES OF GARDEN INTEREST. Large natural displays of native flowers on the Cooke City road (Bear-tooth Highway) and in Glacier National Park. Best displays in July.

Rose Test Garden, an official garden of the American Rose Society, at Missoula, Montana.

Corvallis, Montana, Horticultural Branch Station. Vegetables, fruits and ornamentals under test. About 450 varieties of iris on display in early summer.

Montana State College Horticulture Department, Bozeman, Montana. About 450 to 500 varieties of iris on test in and around Bozeman. Extensive plantings of ornamental trees, shrubs, and annual and perennial flowers on test. Also work with fruit and vegetables. A breeding and testing program with outdoor and greenhouse chrysanthemums.

Rock garden of Mr. Carl Neufelder at Butte, Montana. An extensive collection of alpine plants. The finest garden of this kind in the state.

Washoe Park, Anaconda, Montana. Bedding and garden flowers featured, and tuberous begonias.

Garden clubs are active in the state in all regions. In 1958 there were 88 clubs with a membership of 2226 belonging to the Montana Federation of State Garden Clubs and the National Council of State Garden Clubs. Women's clubs, home demonstration clubs, and other unaffiliated garden clubs throughout the state carry gardening activities in their programs. Gardening and beautification of home grounds are important projects for the 4-H club members and other young people's groups.

The address of the Agricultural Experiment Station, which has kindly contributed this account of the state, is Bozeman, Montana. They have issued valuable bulletins on lawns, fruits, vegetables, and flowers suitable for the state.

* Special articles on the subjects indicated by an asterisk (*) will be found at the words so marked.

montana, -us, -um (mon-tay'na). Growing on a mountain or in a mountainous region.

MONTANOA (mon-ta-nō'a). Tropical American shrubs and trees of the family Compositae, comprising perhaps 30 species, only those below of garden interest and little known outside of warm regions. The cult. species are shrubby and have opposite* leaves. Flower heads small or medium-sized, composed of both ray and disk flowers, white in those below. (Named for Don Luis Montana, Mexican naturalist.)

They can be grown as greenhouse pot plants, or outdoors as bedding plants in zones* 8 and 9. They need a warm-temperate greenhouse and potting mixture* 3. As they are winter-blooming, they are useful as sub-tropical bedding plants.

bipinnatifida. Not over 8 ft. high, and a strong-growing, erect, shrubby plant. Leaves more or less deeply cut feather-fashion, hairy. Flower heads white, nearly 3 in. wide. Mex.

hibiscifolia. Shrub 10–15 ft. high, the leaves divided finger-fashion nearly to the middle, and 9–12 in. wide. Flower heads about 1½ in. wide, white. Guatemala and Costa Rica. A striking plant with very showy leaves.

MONTBRETIA. *See* Tritonia.

MONTEREY PINE = *Pinus radiata.* See Pine.

montevidensis, -e (mon-te-vi-den'sis). From Montevideo, Uruguay.

MONTEZUMA CYPRESS = *Taxodium mucronatum.*

MONTHLY ROSE. An obsolete term for roses now included among descendants of the tea rose and China rose.

MONTIA (mon'ti-a). A genus of about 18 small, annual or perennial North American herbs of the family Portulacaceae. Leaves usually opposite,* small, smooth, fleshy. Flowers usually very small, nodding, the 3 petals more or less joined, white or pale rose-color. Flowers are solitary or in loose terminal clusters (racemes*). Fruit a 3-seeded pod. (Named for Giuseppe Monti, professor of botany at Bologna.)

These herbs are grown for ornament, one as an interesting salad or pot herb. They are very easily cultivated, for the seed may be sown in spring or summer in the ground where the plants are to stand.

parviflora. A slender green herb, often covered with a bloom.* Leaves basal, spoon-shaped or very narrow. Flowers white or rose. Western N.A.

perfoliata. Winter purslane; also called Indian lettuce, or miner's lettuce. An annual herb, coarse, green, often reddening with age. Basal leaves 1 to 3 in. broad. Flowers small, white, on stalks 1 ft. high, beneath them 2 disk-like stem leaves. Western N.A. Often used as a salad or pot herb, and it has been introduced into many other regions and countries.

monticola, -us, -um (mon-tick'o-la). From mountains.

MONTREAL BOTANICAL GARDEN. *See* Botanic Garden.

monumentalis, -e (mon-you-men-tal'is). Monumental; *i.e.,* as applied to plants, suggesting a monument as some fastigiate* trees suggest cemetery monuments.

MOONFLOWER = *Calonyction.*

MOONLIGHT BROOM. *See Cytisus scoparius* at Broom.

MOONSEED. *See* Menispermum and Cocculus.

MOONSEED FAMILY = Menispermaceae.

MOONWORT = *Botrychium. See also* Honesty.

MOOR MYRTLE = *Myrica Gale.*

MOORWORT = *Andromeda glaucophylla.*

MOOSEWOOD = *Acer pensylvanicum. See* Maple.

MORACEAE (more-ray'see-ee). The mulberry or fig family is of interest chiefly for its edible fruits. but it contains some hardy and tropical trees of ornamental value among its 60 genera and over 2000 species, many of which are tropical. Part, or all, of this family is by some called the Artocarpaceae.

Rubber is derived from *Castilla.* Fruits are found in *Ficus* (figs), *Artocarpus* (breadfruit), and *Morus* (*see* Mulberry). *Maclura* (the Osage orange) and *Broussonetia* are grown for ornament outdoors over most of the U.S. Nearly all genera have milky juice, and all cult. genera are woody plants.

Leaves alternate*; in *Artocarpus* and some species of *Ficus* often much cut or lobed, but simple.* Flowers small and inconspicuous, the male and female ones separate.

The fruit of this family is complicated (*see* Fig). The other genera have fleshy fruit formed from the amalgamation of the ovaries of several flowers, sometimes embedded in the fleshy remains of ripening flower parts other than the ovary. (*See* Syncarp.)

Technical flower characters: Flowers regular,* without much distinction between petals and sepals, which together usually total 4. Ovary superior,* 1–2-celled.

MORAEA (more-ee'a). Also spelled *Morea.* Iris-like, and in ours, South African herbs of the family Iridaceae, comprising over 60 species. They bear corms* or rootstocks and have basal, sword-shaped or narrower, leaves. Flowers almost exactly like *Iris* which this genus replaces in the southern hemisphere. Unlike *Iris, Moraea* is not hardy outdoors in the North, and should be grown in the cool greenhouse with much the same conditions as for *Freesia* (which see). With protection *M. Pavonia* is occasionally hardy as far north as zone* 4. They are unlike *Iris,* also, in that their flowers last only a day; consequently they are poor substitutes for iris when the two can be grown. (Named for Robert Moore, English botanist.) Some species are offered as *Dietes.*

bicolor. Nearly 2 ft. high, its sword-shaped leaves about as long, pale green. Flowering stalk branched, the flowers nearly 2 in. wide, pale yellow, but brown-blotched at the base.

---

* Special articles on the subjects indicated by an asterisk (*) will be found at the words so marked.

glaucopsis. About 2 ft. high, the stem often branched. Leaves very narrow, usually solitary. Flowers fleeting, about 1 in. long, white, with an almost black spot at the base.

iridioides. Leaves in fan-like, basal rosettes, arising from a creeping rootstock. Flowers nearly 3 in. wide, borne on the end of a bracted* stem, white, the claws* streaked or marked with yellow. Can be grown outdoors in Calif., where it blooms from early spring to Nov.

Pavonia. Peacock iris. A corm*-bearing herb with narrow, usually softly hairy leaves. Flowers orange-red, with a dark spot at the base of each petal or segment, without claws.* There are several color forms, as yellow, purple or white, but most of them are dark-spotted at the base of the petals. Often offered as *Pavonia.*

polystachya. A poisonous bulbous plant (not to the touch) with a black corm* about ¾ in. in diameter. Leaves only 3 or 4, strongly ribbed. Flowers lilac, the base of each petal with a yellow blotch, flowering one at a time in a lax cluster (corymb*). S. Af. Its native name is tulp, *i.e.,* a wild tulip.

ramosa. A leafy-stemmed herb, 2–3 ft. high, the stem usually tortuous. Leaves very narrow, about 18 in. long. Flowers numerous in an open cluster (corymb*), yellow, about 1¼ in. long.

MORAINE. *See* ROCK GARDEN.

MORAINE LOCUST = *Gleditsia triacanthos inermis. See* HONEY LOCUST.

MORDEN'S PINK. *See* LYTHRUM SALICARIA.

MOREA = *Moraea.*

MORELLO. *See* CHERRY.

MORETON BAY CHESTNUT = *Castanospermum australe.*

MORETON BAY FIC = *Ficus macrophylla.*

MORETON BAY PINE = *Araucaria cunninghami.*

morifolia, -us, -um (more-i-fō′lĭ-a). Mulberry-leaved.

MORINA (more-ry′na). Asiatic, somewhat thistle-like herbs of the family Dipsacaceae, related to the teasel, but the flowers in whorls, forming interrupted* spikes. Of the 10 known species only **M. longifolia,** sometimes called whorl-flower, is in general cult. It is a Himalayan, hardy perennial, 3–4 ft. high, the foliage usually hairy, thistle-like, but handsome. Leaves nearly 6 in. long, about 1 in. wide. Flowers white, but later pink or red, the corolla tubular and surrounded by the 2-lobed, slightly irregular, spiny calyx.* June–July. It is a stout plant, useful in the border. (Named for Louis Morin, French botanist.)

MORINDA (more-rin′da). Tropical shrubs or trees, rarely vines, of the family Rubiaceae, two of the 60 species grown for ornament in zones* 8 and 9, little known as cult. plants otherwise, except in India. Leaves mostly opposite.* Flowers small, crowded in dense heads, these solitary in the leaf axils* or sometimes clustered. Corolla more or less tubular, white (in ours), and joined to each other at the base. Stamens* mostly 5. Fruit fleshy. (The name is a combination of *Morus* [mulberry] and *indica,* in allusion to the Indian mulberry.)

The plants are of easy culture in a variety of soils in Calif. and Fla., and they are scarcely known elsewhere. The first species yields red and yellow dyes.

citrifolia. Indian mulberry. A small tree with somewhat 4-angled branches. Leaves shining, short-stalked, more or less elliptic, 7–10 in. long. Flower heads solitary, short-stalked, in the leaf axils,* the corolla tube about ½ in. long. Fruit nearly 2 in. long, yellowish. India to Australasia.

Royoc. Wild mulberry; called also yawweed. A West Indian, erect or vine-like shrub, not over 4 ft. high, commonly naturalized in southern Fla. Leaves narrowly oblong, 2–4 in. long. Flowers in heads. Fruit yellow, about 1 in. wide.

MORINGA (more-ring′ga). Tropical Old World trees, and the only genus of the family **Moringaceae** (more-ring-gay′see-ee), of which the only cult. species is **M. oleifera,** the horse-radish tree, so named from its pungent, edible root. It is a small, soft-wooded tree, not over 25 ft. high, with corky bark and thrice-compound,* very feathery leaves. The whole leaf may be 2 ft. long, but its ultimate leaflets are very numerous and small. Flowers white, fragrant, nearly an inch wide, in loose clusters (panicles*) in the leaf axils.* Fruit a 9-ribbed, cylindric pod, often 15 in. long, its seeds 3-angled and winged. The tree is hardy only in zones* 8 and 9, but has become established as an escape* in southern Fla. Its seeds yield ben oil (oil of ben), used for lubricating watches. (*Moringa* is the Latinized version of the Malay name for this tree.)

MORNING-GLORY. *See* IPOMOEA.

MORNING-GLORY FAMILY. All the garden genera are vines, which vary in uses from the showy morning-glory to the sweet potato. Some are pernicious weeds. For the hort. genera *see* CONVOLVULACEAE.

Morsus-ranae (more-sus-ray′nee). Frog's-bit.

motoria, -us, -um (mo-tor′i-a). With moving parts; or moving.

MORUS. *See* MULBERRY.

MOSAIC. Virus diseases which produce a yellowing or chlorosis* on either side of the veins of a leaf. Some mosaic diseases also cause the color in flower petals to "break" or become streaked with green, white, or yellow. The mosaic diseases are spread from diseased plant to healthy plant by insects (usually aphids) and may be transmitted by workers who use tobacco, or by rubbing against the plants with tools.

mosaica, -us, -um (mo-zay′i-ka). With a pattern-like difference in color.

moschata, -us, -um (mos-kay′ta). Musky or musk-scented.

---

* Special articles on the subjects indicated by an asterisk (*) will be found at the words so marked.

Moscheutos (mo-shoo'tos or mos-kew'tos). Pre-Linnaean* name for some mallow. *See* HIBISCUS.

MOSCHOSMA = *Iboza riparia.*

MOSQUITO. Insect nuisance in any garden. They can only breed in standing water and all such should be eliminated as a first step in mosquito control. Area sprays of pesticide #17, #21, or other new materials will control mosquitoes in most areas for parties or special occasions. Regular fogging of these materials will give reasonable control. Fundamental control is to eliminate standing-water breeding spots. Pesticide #17 dusts on water will control larvae of most species but may kill other wildlife, hence, are not practical. (*See* SPRAYS AND DUSTS.) — L. G. M.

MOSQUITO BILLS = *Dodecatheon hendersoni.*

MOSQUITO-PLANT; MOSQUITO-TRAP = *Cynanchum acuminatifolium. See also* CASTOR-OIL PLANT.

MOSS. The true mosses are flowerless plants scarcely cult., except in the wild garden and when used to line hanging baskets. For covering old logs, wet rocks, and moist, shady banks, nothing is finer than moss, which must be collected from the woods. *See also* SPHAGNUM, LYCOPODIUM. For flowering moss *see* PYXIDANTHERA. For Spanish or long moss *see* TILLANDSIA.

MOSS CAMPION = *Silene acaulis* and *S. Schafta.*

MOSS GARDEN. Few mosses are really cult., but they can be made to grow in a terrarium (which see). Collected specimens will often grow for months in the protection from heat and dryness afforded by a terrarium.

MOSS PINK = *Phlox subulata.*

MOSS ROSE = *Rosa centifolia muscosa.*

MOSSY-CUP OAK = *Quercus macrocarpa. See* OAK.

MOSSY STONECROP = *Sedum acre.*

MOTH BEAN = *Phaseolus aconitifolius.*

MOTHER BULB. The old bulb around which bulblets* are formed.

MOTHER-OF-THOUSANDS = *Saxifraga sarmentosa.*

MOTHER-OF-THYME = *Thymus Serpyllum. See* THYME.

MOTHER SPLEENWORT = *Asplenium bulbiferum.*

MOTHERWORT = *Leonurus Cardiaca.*

MOTH MULLEIN = *Verbascum Blattaria.*

MOTH ORCHID. *See* PHALAENOPSIS.

MOULD. Both the disease known as such and the garden soil are often so spelled, but the ENCYCLOPEDIA prefers *mold.*

MOUNTAIN. As an adjective *mountain* has been linked with the names of many plants that grow, or were once thought to grow, upon mountains. Those in the ENCYCLOPEDIA and their proper equivalents are:

Mountain-ash (*see* first main entry below); Mountain avens (*see* DRYAS); Mountain azalea = *Azalea canescens;* Mountain bluet = *Centaurea montana;* Mountain camellia = *Stewartia ovata;* Mountain cranberry = *Vaccinium Vitis-Idaea;* Mountain creeper = *Thunbergia fragrans* and *Porana paniculata;* Mountain currant = *Ribes alpinum;* Mountain ebony = *Bauhinia variegata;* Mountain fetter-bush = *Pieris floribunda;* Mountain fleece = *Polygonum amplexicaule;* Mountain fringe = *Adlumia fungosa;* Mountain heath = *Phyllodoce caerulea;* Mountain hemlock = *Tsuga mertensiana* (*see* HEMLOCK); Mountain holly = *Nemopanthus mucronatus;* Mountain holly fern = *Polystichum Lonchitis;* Mountain laurel = *Kalmia latifolia;* Mountain leatherwood = *Fremontia californica;* Mountain magnolia = *Magnolia fraseri;* Mountain mahogany (*see* CERCOCARPUS); Mountain mint (*see* PYCNANTHEMUM); Mountain maple = *Acer spicatum* (*see* MAPLE); Mountain parsley = *Cryptogramma crispa acrostichoides;* Mountain pine (*see* DACRYDIUM); Mountain queen = *Hesperoyucca whipplei;* Mountain rose = *Antigonon leptopus;* Mountain rose-bay = *Rhododendron catawbiense* (for the common rose-bay *see* R. MAXIMUM); Mountain sage = *Artemisia frigida;* Mountain sandwort = *Arenaria groenlandica;* Mountain saxifrage = *Saxifraga oppositifolia;* Mountain snow = *Euphorbia marginata;* Mountain spinach = *Atriplex hortensis;* Mountain starwort = *Arenaria groenlandica.*

MOUNTAIN-ASH. A genus of Eurasian and North American deciduous trees or shrubs of the rose family called **Sorbus** (sor'bus), comprising perhaps 80 species. Leaves alternate,* simple* or compound,* the leaflets arranged feather-fashion (pinnate*), sharply toothed. Flowers white, many and showy, in terminal, branching, flat-topped, leafy clusters (corymbs*). Petals 5, broad or narrow, clawed.* Stamens* 15–20. Fruit a small, berry-like pome.* (*Sorbus* is the ancient Latin name.)

Most of the species of *Sorbus* may be grown easily even in dry soil. Rare kinds are propagated by grafting on *S. americana* or *S. Aucuparia.* Others increased by seeds or by layers. All the species are sometimes called *Pyrus,* a generic name not here applied to mountain-ash. For pests, *see* APPLE.

S. americana. American mountain-ash. A smooth tree becoming 30 ft. high. Leaflets 13–15, bright green, narrow, taper-pointed, with sharp marginal teeth. Flowers white, ⅕ in. across, in compound terminal clusters (corymbs*). Berries round, bright red. Common in woods, Labrador to Manitoba, south in the mountains to N. Car. and westward. May–June. Hardy from zone* 2 southward. Use soil with pH 4–5.

S. Aria. Whitebeam. A broad-headed tree, sometimes 50 ft. high, remaining a shrub on poor lands. Young growth soft-woolly. Leaflets

* Special articles on the subjects indicated by an asterisk (*) will be found at the words so marked.

elliptic or ovalish, 2–5 in. long, with marginal teeth, sharp-pointed or blunt, usually wedge-shaped, bright green and smooth above, white, soft-woolly beneath, leathery. Flowers in flat-topped terminal clusters (corymbs*), 2–3¼ in. across. Fruit orange-red or scarlet with mealy flesh. Eu. Long cult. May. Hardy from zone* 3 southward.

S. Aucuparia. Rowan tree; also known as European mountain-ash. A tree 50 ft. or more high. Leaflets 9–15, 1–2 in. long, oblong or narrower with a bloom beneath, hairy or smooth. Flowers ⅓ in. across, in compound terminal clusters (corymbs*), 4–6 in. across. Fruit round, bright red. Eu. to western As. and Siberia. Long cult. *Var.* pendula has long, drooping branches. June. Hardy from zone* 2 southward. There are many other hort. forms or varieties, some with cut leaflets, yellow fruit, and one with edible fruit (in preserves).

S. decora. A tree 30 ft. high, or shrubby. Leaves of 11–17 leaflets from 2½–3 in. long, with spreading teeth, smooth and dark green above. Flowers white, ⅓ in. across, in flat-topped terminal clusters (corymbs*). Fruit bright red. Labrador to Minn., southern N.Y. and Vt. May. Hardy from zone* 2 southward.

S. domestica. Service tree. A tree with scaly bark, reaching 60 ft. Leaves with 11–21 leaflets, narrow-oblong, pointed and with sharp marginal teeth, smooth above, woolly-haired beneath. Flowers ½ in. across, in dense, pyramidal terminal clusters, 2½ to 4 in. across. Fruit apple- or pear-shaped, yellowish-green or brownish, tinged with red. Southern Eu., North Africa, western As. May. Hardy from zone* 3 southward.

S. hybrida. A tree attaining 40 ft. Leaves ovalish or longer, 3–5 in. long, with 1–4 pairs of leaflets at the end, the leaflets toothed, and woolly beneath. Flowers ½ in. across in compound, flat-topped, terminal clusters (corymbs*), 2½–4 in. across. Fruit nearly round, red. Of hybrid origin. Scandinavia. May. Hardy from zone* 3 southward.

S. quercifolia = S. thuringiaca.

S. scopulina. A shrubby, western form of S. americana. It rarely reaches over 10 ft. high. Foliage as in S. americana. Berries nearly ¾ in. in diameter. Western N.A. May–June. Hardy from zone* 3 southward.

S. thuringiaca. A hybrid mountain-ash (Aucuparia × Aria), and a tree 20–30 ft. or more. Leaflets 1–3 pairs, bluntish at the tip. It is sometimes confused with S. hybrida to which it is closely related. Not a particularly interesting tree, but carried by many dealers.

S. tianshanica. A small tree, not over 15 ft. high, usually shrubby, the twigs ultimately red-brown and shining. Leaflets 9–15, lance-shaped, narrowed at the tip, 1½–3½ in. long, toothed. Flower cluster loose, 4–9 in. wide, the individual flower about ⅝ in. wide. Fruit nearly round, red. Central Asia. June. Hardy from zone* 5 southward.

MOUNT MORGAN WATTLE = Acacia podalyriaefolia.

moupinensis, -e. From Moupin in Western China.

MOURNING BRIDE = Scabiosa atropurpurea.

MOURNING CYPRESS = Cupressus funebris.

MOURNING IRIS = Iris susiana.

MOUSE-EAR CHICKWEED = Cerastium vulgatum. See list at WEEDS.

MOUSE-EAR HAWKWEED = Hieracium pilosella. See list at WEEDS.

Moutan (moo'tan). The Chinese name of the tree peony.

MOWING. See LAWN.

MOXIEBERRY = Gaultheria hispidula.

MUCKLAND GARDENING. In many sections of the country, especially in the glaciated part of N.A., there are large deposits of muck or peat, popularly supposed to be the most productive soils in the U.S. With proper treatment they may be.

If you have on your property a tract of real swamp or a bog, a simple way to determine whether its draining and reclamation are worth considering is to study the existing wild vegetation. Generally speaking, if the trees are hardwoods like maple, tupelo, black ash, or elm, the muck will probably be productive without too great an initial cost for rectifying it. But if the trees are tamarack, arborvitae, black spruce, or if there are none and the area is covered with large patches of sphagnum moss and typical bog shrubs like *Chamaedaphne calyculata, Andromeda glaucophylla,* or *Ledum,* the venture may be doubtful.

For the successful utilization of muckland is based upon two things: (1) Regulation of its water level; and (2) its acidity or alkalinity, which is roughly indicated by the wild vegetation as outlined above. But the acidity or alkalinity needs closer study than merely observing the native flora.

(1) REGULATION OF WATER LEVEL. All mucklands are accumulations of vegetable matter which grew in, or were supplied with, plentiful amounts of water. In their present untouched state they are usually saturated with far too much water to make gardening possible. Furthermore, the muck may be anywhere from 75% to 90% decayed vegetable matter, which is like a sponge for holding water. Study the levels and see if by ditching or draining it is possible to get the permanent water table about 2½ ft. below the finished ground level. This makes an ideal condition, because the success of muckland gardening depends upon capillarity bringing up from this permanent reservoir of water enough for crop needs. If the water table is too near the surface, the roots will be drowned; if it is too deep, the upper layer of muck will become powder dry and failure will be certain. Of course one could put in an overhead irrigation system (*see* IRRIGATION), but in a properly managed muck scheme no money should be spent on irrigation, for mucklands are used precisely because they have ample supplies of water. For details of draining *see* DRAINING.

(2) ACIDITY OR ALKALINITY. Most failures in muckland gardening have come from neglect of this. To test the muck for acidity or alkalinity, collect samples from many dif-

---

* Special articles on the subjects indicated by an asterisk (*) will be found at the words so marked.

ferent parts of the area and from depths ranging from the surface to 2 ft. down. Take care
that no perspiration from the hands, tobacco
ash, or other alkaline substances get into your
samples, and see that the containers are of
some neutral material — a flower pot is excellent. Then run a series of tests exactly
as described in the article ACID AND ALKALI
SOILS to determine the pH value of your
samples.

If the muck tests from pH 6.0 to 7.5, there
is little that needs to worry you about its
availability, for most crops will grow perfectly within this range, provided you can
manage the water table as outlined above.
But if the muck tests from pH 5.5 down to
4.0 or even 3.8, a serious problem is presented at once. For no ordinary garden
crop will grow in such an acid muck.

Muck soils with a pH of 3.9–5.5 must be
treated, preferably with ground limestone, at
the rate of 9 tons per acre (½₀ of an acre =
33 × 66 ft.), and this treatment must be repeated whenever the acidity shows a tendency
to return, which is likely after the second or
third year. Whether you decide to use such
a site is really a question of whether the
money spent for limestone will be repaid by
the admittedly high yields from good muckland. Some commercial growers use the limestone, but most prefer to seek a more neutral
site.

The third possibility, much more rare than
the other two, is that the muck is definitely
alkaline, that is, it tests from pH 7.5 to 8.5 or
even higher. In such a place aluminum sulphate at the rate of about 8 tons to the acre
(½₀ acre = 66 × 33 ft.) would have to be
applied. Such application is as doubtful a
venture as the application of limestone for the
too acid site.

MUCKLAND CROPS. Assuming proper soil
acidity and water conditions, there are several vegetables that show tremendous yields
on muckland. In order of their especial value

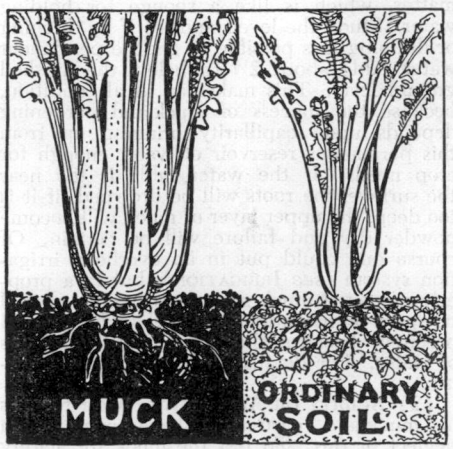

The effect of muckland on celery

for muck soils these are: celery, carrots, onion,
horse-radish, lettuce, Chinese cabbage, potatoes, and spinach. And among flowers, the
common garden aster (*Callistephus*) and the
sweet pea do well on muck.

Plants that require a long, warm growing
season will usually not do well on muck, because it is late in warming up and, in wet
weather, mucks may be cold. Such plants as
beans, melons, eggplants, peppers, and tomatoes should not be planted in muck.

Contrary to popular opinion, muck soils are
not permanently fertile without the addition
of plant food. Because they are so high in
humus, there is little need for stable manure,
and none at all for green manuring. But most
regularly cropped muck soils will repay an application of commercial fertilizer with a 2–8–
10 ratio (*see* FERTILIZERS) at the rate of
about 1½ tons per acre (½₀ of an acre =
66 × 33 ft.). Half this is applied at the time
of spring plowing; the rest is top-dressed in
the rows during the summer. And some
growers, especially on lettuce and spinach,
use nitrate of soda for the second application,
but not more than 400 pounds per acre.

For the use of swamp land, without rectifying the soil, as a site for a wild or swamp
garden *see* SWAMP.

mucosa, -us, -um (mew-kō'sa). Mucilaginous or slimy.

MUCRO. *See* MUCRONATA.

mucronata, -us, -um (mew-kro-nay'-ta).
Having a mucro; *i.e.*, a short, sharp point, as
in many leaves.

mucronulata, -us, -um (mew-kron-u-lay'ta).
Having a slender sharp point.

MUEHLENBECKIA (mew-len-beck'ĭ-a).
Somewhat woody, shrub-like or vine-like
plants of the family Polygonaceae, all from
the south temperate zone, three of the 30
known species grown more as oddities than
for ornament. They have wire-like or flattened, usually greenish, and sometimes leafless
stems. Leaves, when present, alternate,*
small, with sheathing stipules.* Flowers
small and inconspicuous, in small clusters in
the leaf axils.* Petals none, the sepals
chaffy or becoming fleshy in age. Fruit a 3-
angled achene.* (Named for H. G. Meuhlen-
beck, a Swiss physician.)

The muehlenbeckias can be grown outdoors
in Calif. or Fla., but are rather rare in cult.,
except *M. complexa.* In the greenhouse they
need potting mixture* 3 and a cool, dry house.
The first two species are occasionally used for
hanging baskets, as their prostrate or sprawling, wire-like stems are very hardy if they
happen to be neglected. *M. platyclados* is a
curious, essentially leafless, erect shrub. The
plants are sometimes known under the names
of *Calacinum* and *Homalocladium.*

axillaris. A sprawling or prostrate, bushy
plant, its wire-like stems forming a compact
mass, but not over 1 ft. long. Leaves scarcely
¼ in. long. New Zealand. Sometimes known
as *M. nana.*

* Special articles on the subjects indicated by an asterisk (*) will be found at the words so marked.

complexa. Wire-vine; also called maidenhair-vine. A twining, green-stemmed vine with wire-like stems. Leaves nearly circular, about ½ in. in diameter. New Zealand. Often planted in Calif.

nana = *Muehlenbeckia axillaris.*

platyclados. Ribbon-bush; also called centipede-plant. An erect shrub, 6–9 ft. high (half this in cult.), with ribbon-like, jointed, green branches about ½ in. wide, leafless at flowering time and sometimes for months. Leaves (when present) lance-shaped, about 1 in. long. Fruit apparently a red or purplish berry, but this is merely a covering for the achene* within. Solomon Islands.

Mugo (mew′go). A native name in the Alps for the Swiss mountain pine (*Pinus Mugo*).

MUGWORT = *Artemisia vulgaris.*

MULBERRY. These fruit-bearing trees, one of them widely grown in the Far East as food for silkworms, comprise 12 species of the genus **Morus** (more′us) of the family Moraceae, all the cult. species of which are Asiatic except a native American one. They have alternate,* often lobed leaves, and small, greenish flowers in stalked, hanging catkins,* the male and female separate, sometimes on different trees. Petals none, the sepals usually 4. Fruit edible, berry-like, but actually an aggregate* fruit, resembling a blackberry, consisting of a dry fruit (achene*) covered with the fleshy sepals from several flowers. (*Morus* is the old Latin name of the mulberry.)

For culture *see* below.

M. acidosa = *M. australis.*

M. alba. White mulberry. The tree (or a form of it) cult. in eastern Asia for its leaves, the food of silkworms. It is not over 50 ft. high. Leaves broadly oval, 3–5 in. long, usually lobed, and coarsely toothed, bright green above. Fruit insipid, sweetish, nearly 1¾ in. long, usually white, sometimes pinkish-violet. China. Hardy from zone* 1 southward. The *var.* **tatarica,** the Russian mulberry, is smaller, more hardy, and usually has red fruit. The commonly grown weeping mulberry is grown as a standard upon which is grafted a pendulous-branched variety. There are many other varieties of this tree, which has been grown in Eu. since 1596, and for two thousand years before this in China.

M. multicaulis. Perhaps only a variety of the white mulberry, but with larger leaves, and usually only shrub-like in habit. It is of little hort. interest here, but is considered the best mulberry for silkworm culture in China, and was once planted in an attempt to introduce that industry into the U.S. — a failure.

M. rubra. Red or American mulberry. A tree up to 60 ft. high, with scaly, brown bark. Leaves ovalish, softly hairy beneath, 4–6 in. long, sharply toothed and sometimes irregularly lobed. Fruit red or purplish-red, about 1 in. long. Eastern N.A., west to Tex. Not much planted for ornament, but rather common on old properties, where its fruit is eaten by chickens, hogs, and children.

MULBERRY CULTURE

As ornamental trees the mulberries are practically unknown except for the very popular weeping mulberry, one of the most satisfactory weeping trees for the lawn known in this country. Derived from the Russian mulberry, it is extremely hardy. It originated in Carthage, Mo., about 1883. The Russian mulberry (*M. alba tatarica*) is also widely planted in wind-swept, bleak regions as a windbreak, as is the closely related Osage orange.

As fruit trees mulberries suffer from the fact that their fruit is either too sweet or too insipid to have won much favor. Furthermore, the fruit is difficult to keep or ship and is thus rare in the markets. Most mulberry cult. is thus local, for home consumption only. There are, however, several well-known hort. varieties for fruit-bearing mulberries, notably Black English, Downing, Hicks, and New American. Anyone contemplating the planting of mulberries would do well to use one of these varieties rather than the species from which they have been derived, mostly *M. alba* and *M. rubra*. All mulberry fruits are much loved by birds. A recent development is a non-fruiting mulberry derived from vegetatively produced male trees, of interest to those who object to the undeniable litter of mulberry fruit.

There is no trouble about growing mulberry trees, for their soil tolerance is large. Any ordinary farm or garden soil will do. If they are to be planted as an orchard (some are for hog feed), space the trees about 30 ft. apart each way.

For the French mulberry *see* CALLICARPA AMERICANA. For the paper mulberry *see* BROUSSONETIA.

INSECT PESTS. Control red spider mites with pesticide #14. Bagworms can be picked off. *See* SPRUCE and PERSIMMON for fall webworm control. (*See* SPRAYS AND DUSTS.)

DISEASES. Trees may lose entire branches due to a canker* disease. Dead branches should be removed during the fall or winter, making the cuts at least a foot below any visible sign of canker area. In the South, a swelling of the fruit is known as popcorn disease. It is more of an oddity than a real trouble and does not cause serious harm. A mildew* occasionally mars the foliage in southern states. It should be controlled with pesticide #3 (*see* SPRAYS AND DUSTS), starting when first spots are noticed and repeated at 10-day intervals.

MULBERRY FAMILY = Moraceae.

MULCH AND MULCHING. Mulching is a practice that does at once what nature would ultimately do to any piece of ground that was bare. After being prepared by digging or cultivating, nature would produce a crop of something, ranging from green scum to trees, without human assistance.

One theory of mulching is that, by covering the soil in the vicinity of growing plants during the early stages of growth, and especially during warm weather, moisture will be retained in the soil and thus be available to the plants.

The winter use of a mulch has the same idea of retaining moisture. It is much better for plants to freeze wet than dry, and the mulch helps this.

---

* Special articles on the subjects indicated by an asterisk (*) will be found at the words so marked.

DUST MULCH. The process of shallow surface cultivation is known as the dust mulch. This is especially valuable in the cultivation of long rows of either vegetables or flowers on light soil. By forming a layer of dust on the surface, the moisture that ordinarily would rise to the surface and evaporate is checked and the plants are benefited. *See* CULTIVATION.

MULCHING MATERIAL. Leaves, rotted cow and horse manure, straw, salt hay, grass cuttings, peat moss, pine needles, coconut fiber, sawdust, buckwheat hulls, ground corn cobs, burlap, and prepared paper are the principal materials used for mulching purposes.

From the point of view of their initial purpose, that of holding surface moisture, they rank about equally, but they vary considerably

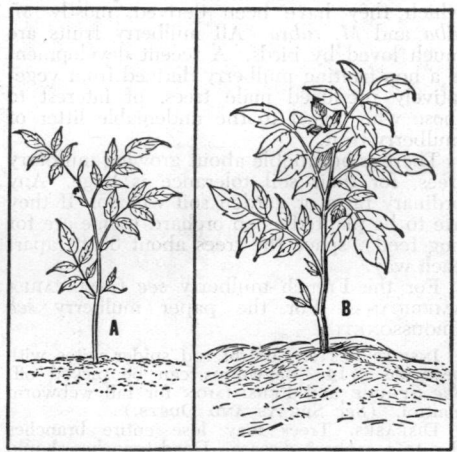

A. A plant without a mulch. *B.* Effects of a good mulch of rotted manure.

as to their desirability. No hard-and-fast rules as to their usage can be laid down that will apply universally. Soil, climate, and the conditions of any vicinity vary so rapidly that what might work out all right in one place fails in another.

Nature's own mulch — leaves when available in quantity, are excellent for mulching rhododendrons, azaleas, evergreens, deciduous shrubs, and all native woodland plants. They are also useful on perennial borders and rock gardens. One objection to them is that they blow away so easily. They can, however, be worked into the soil and thus become available as plant food, but the roots of rhododendrons and azaleas should not be disturbed in working in a leaf mulch. Soft-leaved mulches, such as maple or willow, decay rapidly, but oak leaves decay slowly and often hold water that may freeze. The remedy is to make the mulch deep enough to minimize this difficulty.

Thoroughly rotted cow and horse manure are excellent for mulching ornamental and fruit trees, shrubs and berry bushes, rose and asparagus beds, perennial borders and rock gardens. They also serve the dual purpose of providing plant food.

PLAIN STRAW will serve in place of leaves or rotted manure, when they are not available. It is also specially used for mulching strawberry beds. The principal function in this case is to keep the fruit clean; though it also serves as an aid to the runners.

SAWDUST. This makes a fine mulch, 2–3 in. thick, especially if it is old and derived from pine trees although hardwood sawdust is also valuable. All sawdust has a tendency to withdraw nitrogen from the soil and, to overcome this, mix for each 160 sq. ft. of sawdust mulch, 2 in. thick, about one pound of ammonium nitrate or two pounds of nitrate of soda.

SALT HAY has come into vogue as a general mulch in recent years. As a winter covering it provides a light, yet dense mulch and is largely used by commercial growers of pansies to cover their beds. It has no plant food value and must be raked off and either stored in stacks for future use, used for bedding, or burned.

GRASS CUTTINGS make a temporary mulch during the summer, but disappear quickly under extremes of heat and moisture; also they may, with straw and salt hay, be a fire hazard.

PEAT MOSS has a tendency to form a waterproof covering; thus during a dry spell it sheds much available moisture. This neutralizes its value for conserving moisture, but it is an excellent mulch for all acid-soil plants.

COCONUT FIBER has qualities similar to peat moss.

PINE NEEDLES make a natural mulch for pine trees and could be used for other conifers, but they are too acid for general garden purposes; which means they are fine for all plants of the heath family. In the South many object to them because they harbor chiggers.

BURLAP is used in the germination of seedlings and would do all that mulch paper does. It is rather expensive for this purpose, however.

PAPER MULCH is the most efficient mulch for large-scale planting in rows. It is made up in rolls of various widths and stands up to the weather better than ordinary paper. Originally used on Hawaiian pineapple fields, it is now widely used where none of the above materials are available, and, by some, in preference to all of them. There is no doubt that black mulching paper, spread in the row, conserves much moisture. But caution must be used as to the kind selected, as some have shown a tendency to leach undesirable material into the soil. Only mulching paper guaranteed against this should be used. For smaller-scale paper mulching the material is also sold in squares, provided with a slit in the center for slipping over individual plants. It is relatively quite expensive.

GLASS WOOL. Finely spun glass, commonly called glass wool, is also available for mulch-

Paper mulch, showing the method of laying it, and (*in the inset*) a crop after it has matured with a paper mulch.

ing. Its advantages are complete freedom from vermin, and its non-absorbent quality so that it does not become sodden. It has been tried as a mulch for both outdoor collections, especially in the rock garden, and as a material for growing paper-white narcissus in water, where glass wool replaces pebbles. *See also* VERMICULITE.

MULE-EARS. *See* WYETHIA.

MULE-FAT = *Baccharis viminea.*

MULLEIN. *See* VERBASCUM. For Cretan mullein *see* CELSIA CRETICA.

MULLEIN PINK = *Lychnis coronaria.*

multicaulis, -*e* (mul-ti-cau'lis). Many-stemmed.

multicava, -*us,* -*um* (mul-tĭ-cay'va). Much-hollowed.

multifida, -*us,* -*um* (mul-tiff'i-da). Multifid; *i.e.,* much-divided or parted.

multiflora, -*us,* -*um* (mul-tĭ-flōra). Many- or profusely flowered.

MULTIFLORA BEAN = *Phaseolus coccineus.*

MULTIFLORA ROSE. *See* ROSA MULTIFLORA.

multijuga, -*us,* -*um* (mul-tĭ-jew'ga). In many yokes or pairs; applied to leaflets.

multiplex (mull'ti-plex). Much-folded.

MULTIPLIER ONION = *Allium Cepa aggregatum. See* ONION.

multiradiata, -*us,* -*um* (mul-tĭ-ray-dee-ā'ta). Many-rayed, as are the heads of some daisies; sometimes with many petals, as are the flowers of *Mesembryanthemum.*

multiscapoidea, -*us,* -*um* (mul-ti-skay-poy'-dee-a). With many scapes or stalks.

MUM. Florists' slang for chrysanthemum.

MUME = *Prunus Mume.*

MUNG BEAN = *Phaseolus aureus.*

Mungo (mung'go). Latinized version of *mung,* the name in India of the black gram (*Phaseolus Mungo*).

munita, -*us,* -*um* (mew-ny'ta). Armed or fortified.

muralis, -*e* (mew-ray'lis). Growing on walls.

muricata, -*us,* -*um* (mure-ĭ-kay'ta). Roughened with hard points.

MURRAYA (mur'rie-a). Also spelled *Murraea.* A small genus of aromatic Indo-Malayan shrubs or small trees of the family Rutaceae, sometimes known as *Chalcas.* The only cult. species is M. exotica, the orange jasmine, frequently planted in Fla. and Calif. for its handsome evergreen leaves and beautifully fragrant, white flowers. It is a tree-like shrub 10–12 ft. high with no spines and alternate,* compound* leaves consisting of 3–9 ovalish, shining leaflets, 1–2 in. long. Flowers more or less bell-shaped, about ¾ in. long, the 5 petals pointed. Stamens* 8–10. Fruit an egg-shaped, red berry, usually a little less than ½ in. long. India. A very handsome ornamental, which blooms several times a year. Not hardy north of zone* 8. M. paniculata, of India, is closely related to *M. exotica* and is less desirable, as its flower cluster is more meager. It is sometimes called cosmetic-bark tree because an Indian cosmetic is derived from its bark. (Named for J. A. Murray, an English editor of some of the works of Linnaeus.)

MUSA (mew'sa). Giant herbs chiefly from the Indo-Malayan region and belonging to the family Musaceae, their huge, fleshy, tree-like stems formed of the tightly packed sheaths of the leaf bases. They have usually large rhizomes from which springs the single, trunklike stem which flowers only once and then is replaced by suckers from the base. Leaves very large, without teeth, having a single, stout midrib* from which diverge many parallel, transverse veins along which the leaves split into ribbons in the wind (seldom in the greenhouse). Flower cluster terminal, appearing amongst the crown of leaves. It consists of a long, usually drooping spike composed of colored, tightly overlapping bracts, between each of which is a flower. These are highly irregular* and consist of a tubular calyx which splits down one side, and a single petal. Stamens* 6, one of them sterile and petal-like. Fruit long, berry-like, regularly seedless and sterile in the common banana, but producing seeds in some others. The collection of the fruits forms the familiar "hand" of bananas. (Named for Antonio Musa, physician to the first Emperor of Rome.) Recent studies on the banana and its relatives make it appear that all the Latin names below may be incorrect. The technical proficiency of such studies (still incomplete and continuing), involving determinations of diploid, triploid, and tetraploid variants (*see* CHROMOSOMES), is impressive. It does not, however, warrant the rejection of the Latin

---

* Special articles on the subjects indicated by an asterisk (*) will be found at the words so marked.

names used below, most of them assigned by Linnaeus and hallowed by a couple of centuries of usage. Under such studies, for instance, the Abyssinian banana would belong to *Ensete* and be written *Ensete ventricosum,* a suggestion here rejected. For a technical account of these proposals see the papers of E. E. Cheeseman in *Kew Bulletin* for 1947, 1948, and 1949.

For culture *see* BANANA.

cavendishi. Dwarf, Cavendish, or Chinese banana. Not over 6 ft. high and cult. chiefly for ornament, the stems 5–6 in. thick. Leaves 2–4 ft. long, about half as wide, bluish-green, often colored or spotted when young. Flowering spike drooping, with reddish-brown bracts,* the calyx yellowish-white. Fruits very numerous, often 200 in the cluster, 6-angled, 4–5 in. long, somewhat curved and fragrant, mostly seedless, edible. Southern China. This does not produce the small, edible banana which is a variety of *M. sapientum.* The dwarf banana is widely planted for bedding in warm regions. For cult. *see* BANANA.

Ensete. Abyssinian banana. A huge, tree-like herb, 20–40 ft. high, the stem swollen at the base. Leaves 10–20 ft. long, about 2–3 ft. wide. Flowering spike erect, its bracts* reddish-brown, the flowers whitish. Fruit inedible, dry, 2–3 in. long, bearing a few large black seeds. Abyssinia.

paradisiaca. Plantain. Closely resembling the common banana, but the fruit larger, green when ripe, good only when cooked, and a staple food for millions of poor people in the tropics. The fruit is seedless. India.

sapientum. The common banana. A tree-like, fleshy-stemmed herb 15–30 ft. high. Leaves 5–10 ft. long, 18–24 in. wide. Flowering spike drooping, 3–5 ft. long, its bracts purplish-violet or brownish, the flowers yellowish-white. Fruits usually 100 or less in the whole cluster, yellow when ripe, sweet, and edible without cooking, seedless. India. Cult. for centuries and now found in innumerable varieties. Two of the best-known are the small, red-skinned sort, and another small-fruited kind known as lady-finger banana, with a very thin skin. For culture *see* BANANA.

textilis. Abaca; the plant yielding Manila hemp. Not over 20 ft. high, its leaves scarcely 2 ft. long, their stalks containing the finest cordage fiber in the world (Manila hemp). Flowering spike drooping. Fruit inedible, about 3 in. long, with many black seeds. Philippine Islands, and grown there as a major industry; also in Central America.

MUSACEAE (mew-zay′see-ee). The banana family comprises the largest herbs in the world, often of tree-like stature, but true herbs, except in the extraordinary traveler's-tree of Madagascar (*see* RAVENALA), and in some species of *Strelitzia.* There are only 5 tropical genera and perhaps 80 species found in the family, which, with some others, were once included in the Scitamineae.

Four genera are in cult. *Musa* (the banana and plantain) is a world-wide tropical fruit. *Heliconia, Strelitzia,* and *Ravenala* are grown in greenhouses or tropical regions for their strikingly beautiful flowers, among them the bird-of-paradise flower (*see* STRELITZIA).

Leaves gigantic, without marginal teeth, usually with long, channeled, and sheathing leafstalks (holding much water in the huge, fan-like crown of *Ravenala*). Flowers in clusters from between sheathing bracts* (spathes*) which are often highly colored, hence very showy. Fruit various; a seedless berry in the cult. varieties of the common banana, but with seeds in the other species, a woody capsule in *Ravenala,* often dry or fleshy in the other cult. genera.

Technical flower characters: Sepals 3, free or united. Petals 3; sepals 3. Stamens* 6, one of them abortive or sterile. Ovary inferior,* 3-celled.

musaica, -us, -um (mew-zay′i-ka). Mosaic-like; mottled.

MUSCADINE = *Vitis rotundifolia.*

MUSCARI (mus-cay′ree). Grape-hyacinth. Small bulbous, herbaceous perennials, comprising about 50 species of the lily family, natives of the Mediterranean region, and early spring-flowering. Leaves 4–6, long and narrow, green. Flowers on a leafless stalk, in a terminal raceme,* blue and white, or pink. The individual flower is urn-shaped and drooping, segments of the corolla ending in 6 teeth-like points, or they may be much cut. Stamens* 6. Fruit, a 3-celled capsule. (*Muscari* is from the Latin for musky, in allusion to the musky odor of some of them.) They are occasionally called baby's-breath.

For culture *see* below.

armeniacum. Leaves nearly 15 in. long, about ¼ in. wide, channeled at the base, dark green on the lower surface. Flowers 30–40 in a tight, terminal cluster, blue, but white- or flesh-tipped. Asia Minor. April.

azureum = *Hyacinthus ciliatus.*

botryoides. Bluebells; called also starch hyacinth. Grows to a height of 9 in. Leaves ¼ in. wide. Flowers fragrant, about ¼ in. high, blue, the lower flowers fertile, having both stamens and pistil, the upper flowers sterile. A great garden favorite. Var. **album** (white), and var. **carneum** (pink) are color varieties. Southern Eu.

comosum. Tassel-hyacinth. Leaves 1 in. wide. Flowers blue or violet. Eurasia. Var. **monstrosum,** commonly called the feather-hyacinth, is light mauve, with the corolla lobes much cut and feathered.

conicum. Grows to a height of 6 in. Leaves ¼ in. wide. Flowers violet-blue. Southern Eu.

latifolium. Leaf flat, nearly 1 in. wide, and 12 in. long, only a single leaf to each bulb. Flowers blue, in a terminal, rather loose cluster of 10–20 blooms. Asia Minor.

moschatum. A musk-scented perennial 6–8 in. high. Leaves ½–¾ in. wide. Flowers purplish at first, ultimately yellowish or brownish. Asia Minor.

neglectum. Not over 9 in. high, the leaves very narrow, channeled, scarcely ⅓ in. wide. Flowers dark blue, fragrant, in a dense, terminal cluster (raceme*) with 30–40 blooms. Southern Eu.

paradoxum. Not over 3 leaves to each bulb, the leaves 8–9 in. long, nearly ¾ in. in diameter, terete. Flowers bluish-black, but green inside, in a dense, terminal cluster (raceme*), faintly scented. Caucasus.

GRAPE-HYACINTH CULTURE

The grape-hyacinths are among the spring's most valuable bulbous plants, easy to grow

* Special articles on the subjects indicated by an asterisk (*) will be found at the words so marked.

and making fine spreads of color. They thrive and increase rapidly in sunny situations where the soil is deep and rich and somewhat sandy. Many kinds make a fall growth, and should be planted in September or early October, 3 in. deep and 3 or 4 in. apart in generous quantities. Certain species are very sweet-scented. Among these are *M. conicum* and *M. moschatum.* Planted thickly beneath Japanese flowering cherries, the variety Heavenly Blue makes a lovely show. The feather-hyacinth, *M. comosum monstrosum,* is frequently forced indoors. *M. botryoides* will hold its own and increase when planted in grass. All the species are useful for massing along the edges of shrubbery borders or in colonies between perennials. They do not require frequent lifting and replanting but will look after themselves without attention. The flowering of the different species covers many weeks of the spring, beginning after the snowdrops and scillas have come to an end. Propagated by seeds and offsets. — L. B. W.

muscipula, -us, -um (mus-kip′you-la). A mousetrap or like one. *See* DIONAEA.

muscosa, -us, -um (mus-ko′sa). Moss-like.

MUSHROOM. Of many wild species of edible fungi (*see* FUNGUS) only the common mushroom (*Agaricus campestris*) can be considered as a cultivated plant. By some this is now called *Psalliota campestris,* a suggestion not followed here. The subterranean truffle, perhaps the greatest delicacy in the fungus world, is unknown in America, its collection or cultivation being confined chiefly to southern France.

The common mushroom, which is often spontaneous on lawns and fields, is much safer to grow than to collect. Wild plants, which are not uncommon in August and September, if moisture conditions are right, closely resemble very deadly relatives of the common mushroom. No absolutely safe method can be given to distinguish the edible

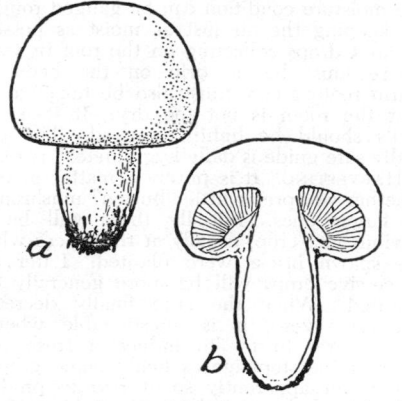

Common mushroom (*Agaricus campestris*). (*a*) The mature plant and (*b*) a cross-section showing its gills.

mushroom from very similar poisonous toad-stools, and none will be attempted here. Amateur attempts to make the distinction result in many deaths every year.

NATURE OF THE PLANT. *Agaricus campestris* is one of the fleshy fungi with a stout stalk and, in maturity, an umbrella-shaped cap or crown. It produces no flowers or seeds but, as in other fungi, is reproduced by spores* — a somewhat technical process of which only one stage is of interest to the grower, as we shall see presently. Like most other fungi it is never green (produces no chlorophyll*) and thus does not manufacture plant food as do all normal green plants. But the mushroom does make a very nutritious and palatable food for us from the material in which it grows — manure. Living upon organic matter and having no green coloring substance in its makeup dictates the sort of place in which the mushroom is best grown. It should be dark, and no better organic matter has been found than stable manure. Darkness, manure, temperature, and moisture are the four essentials of mushroom-growing and they are all important.

The darkness may be secured in any convenient cellar, cave (there are acres of artificial mushroom caves under Paris), quarry, or in a covered pit. Securing darkness is usually easier than providing the other three essentials of mushroom-growing.

MANURE. Well-rotted manure is useless for the mushroom bed. Fresh, hot, steaming horse manure, in which there is plenty of straw, is absolutely necessary to start the process outlined below. Manure where the animals have been bedded with shavings, sphagnum moss, salt hay, or almost any other form of bedding should be rejected, as should the synthetic or artificial kinds. *See* MANURE. No stable manure that has been disinfected or to which fly dope has been added can be used.

Pile up the fresh, straw-laden manure in a heap of sufficient size so that it will not dry out. Small piles of a bushel or two are nearly useless. Preferably the pile should not be less than 4 ft. deep. Wet the pile thoroughly and let it stand for a few days until fermentation starts. Turn the pile over thoroughly after a few days, as the manure must not "burn." Wet it down again and let it stand for a few more days. During the first three turnings of the pile the temperature of the manure will probably be between 130° and 150°, which is satisfactory at this stage.

After each turning and wetting, a process that should be continued for 23–35 days, the temperature of the manure will gradually fall, and nearly all of the foul odor will go. When the temperature at the center of the pile reaches 70°–75°, the manure is ready to be put in the mushroom beds.

MAKING THE BEDS. The manure compost, having reached about 70°, is then put into layers 6–8 in. deep on the benches or ledges upon which the plant will be grown or sometimes on the floor. It should be packed down reasonably but it should not be tamped or rammed down. To save space some growers build benches one above another which, as light is not needed, is a good plan, provided that temperature and moisture conditions can be controlled.

Planting should not begin until the temperature of the manure in the bed has fallen to between 58° and 65°, and the air temperature of the house should be kept at about this. If over 75° air temperature is permitted for 24 hours, failure may result, and if air temperature falls below 50° the crop, while it is not killed, will be much delayed. Once the mushroom bed starts into activity the air temperature of the house must be kept as nearly as possible to 56°–58°. At this stage air temperatures below 50° or above 60° are detrimental or may be fatal.

PLANTING. Mushrooms are started from spawn, which comes in spawn bricks or in cartons. Whichever is used the principle is the same. They both consist of the dried state of a certain stage in the life history of the mushroom which is held in a dormant condition. Planting this material in beds prepared as outlined above provides the opportunity for the plant to complete another stage of its life history — which is the mushroom as we know it. The heat and moisture conditions of the bed and house are such that the plant should begin to grow about 10–15 days after planting.

Pieces of spawn about 2 in. square should be planted in the bed 10 in. apart in both directions. The pieces of "brick" should be pressed into the manure compost not more than 1–2 in. deep. At this stage it is important to see that little or no water is added to the bed. If it is drenched, failure is certain. If air temperature has been properly managed, there should be enough moisture in the manure to permit the spawn brick to grow. If, on the other hand, the manure shows a tendency to dry out, water it very gently with a fine-rose watering pot, using tepid water. On no account use cold water from a hose.

After the spawn has been in the bed 10–15 days, the first sign of activity will be a series of white, thread-like ramifications which will spread in all directions from each piece of spawn. In about 3 weeks from planting the manure should be pretty completely infested with these threads (mycelium, see illustration below). Then the final planting operation should be completed. This consists of covering the whole bed about 1 in. deep with good garden loam, free of stones, fertilizer, weeds, or any residue of insecticides or fungicides. Some growers prefer the virgin soil immediately beneath freshly stripped sod.

SUBSEQUENT CARE. After the beds have been covered with the layer of soil, it will be from 6–7 weeks before the first small mushrooms appear above the surface. If all conditions are right, the bed should then bear continuously for two or three months

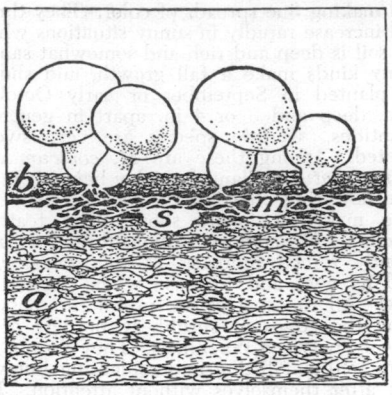

Cross-section of mushroom bed.

a) Six to eight in. of manure.
b) About ¾ in. of good soil.
s) A piece of mushroom spawn.
m) The growth of mushroom mycelium (see text) from which the crop springs.

or even more, after which the "spent" manure should be removed, never again to be used for mushrooms, although it is valuable material to add to the compost pile, or to use as ordinary manure. Being "spent," it is useless, of course, for a hotbed.

During the period of waiting for the mushrooms to appear, and while the bed is in production, the utmost care must be taken about temperature and moisture. The air temperature must be kept as near 56°–58° as possible. The beds must never be allowed to dry out, but they *must not be soaked.* Water the surface layer of soil just enough to keep it moist (not muddy). Use tepid water (rain water is fine) and sprinkle very lightly with a fine-rose watering pot.

The moisture conditions of the air are equally important. If you use a hygrometer,* see that humidity is kept near 70–75 per cent as possible. If you have no instrument, the moisture condition can be gauged roughly by keeping the air just as moist as possible without drops collecting on the roof or walls. There must be no drip on the beds. In warm regions care must also be taken to see that the room is not too dry. If it is, the walls should be lightly sprayed. The only really safe guide is daily hygrometer* reading.

HARVESTING. It is purely a matter of taste whether you prefer little "button" mushrooms, or larger ones. Initially there will be an obvious first crop, usually at the places where the spawn bricks were planted. Later and successive crops will be more generally distributed. When the crop finally decreases to nearly zero, it is questionable whether it is better to try to induce a fresh crop or treat the stoppage as final. Some growers induce an apparently spent bed to produce a final crop by one thorough soaking of the bed with tepid water. But the plan often fails.

---

* Special articles on the subjects indicated by an asterisk (*) will be found at the words so marked.

When the bed is finally cleared of spent manure, the whole house should be thoroughly hosed out, disinfected, dried off, and allowed to rest a few weeks before a fresh lot is started.

OTHER METHODS

This somewhat elaborate technique of mushroom-growing is not the only one, but it is the only sure one for quantity production. Many thoughtful readers are no doubt wondering why the need for darkness, considering that the plant is rightly called *Agaricus campestris,* that the latter word means *of the field,* and that mushrooms are not uncommon on lawns.

Darkness is not necessary for the final stage of the life history of the mushroom, but it is for other phases of it. And conditions of temperature and moisture are better controlled in a dark cellar or cave than in open sunlight. For certain and quantity production there is no doubt about the need for darkness. But if a reasonable amount of failure can be tolerated, one very troublesome operation can be avoided and a crop may still be fairly sure.

When the manure is fresh, before stacking, separate out the straw and mix the pure dung with good garden loam, using ⅔ manure and ⅓ soil. Mix thoroughly and put in the beds immediately. Thereafter the process of planting and subsequent care must follow rigidly the directions given for the more usual method.

Still another short cut, with a higher proportion of failure, is to use a cold frame or hotbed. Fill in with the mixture exactly as outlined for the regular method, but keep the bed covered with a 6-in. layer of straw or mats. Moisture and temperature conditions are hard to control in such a makeshift, but if it is on the north side of the house, and the weather is not too hot, some sort of a crop is fairly sure. Follow, as nearly as possible, the planting directions for the regular method.

The final, most hazardous, but by far the easiest, method is to plant 2-in. squares of spawn brick about 2 in. deep in the lawn. Moisture conditions will often be unfavorable and no crop will result that year. But if the moisture conditions are nearly right, a crop may be expected in late August or early September, and once planted, the chances of several annual crops are not very remote.

Recently it has been suggested by Dr. S. S. Block and George Tsao of the University of Florida that acceptable mushrooms derived from the oyster mushroom (*Pleurotus ostreatus*) can be grown on sawdust, fortified with a nutrient (oatmeal). The idea needs considerable study to get it beyond a laboratory technique.

MUSK MALLOW = *Malva moschata* and *Hibiscus Abelmoschus.*

MUSKMELON. *See* MELON.

MUSK ROSE = *Rosa moschata* and *Malva moschata.*

MUSQUASH-ROOT = *Cicuta maculata.*

MUSTARD. As a plant name *mustard* is applied to many weedy, chiefly annual herbs of the family Cruciferae, some of them serious pests. The true mustards all belong to the genus *Brassica* (which see), especially *B. juncea, B. nigra,* and *B. hirta.* Varieties of the first species are sometimes grown as greens, but the genus *Brassica* contains much more important plants, like the cabbage, cauliflower, brussels sprouts, etc. While all these are finer than the leaf mustard (*B. juncea*), a form of it known as Southern Curled is widely grown for greens.

MUSTARD FAMILY. A huge aggregation of plants, containing, besides the edible cabbage, cauliflower, broccoli, radish, and cress, many garden flowers like the stock, sweet alyssum, candytuft, and honesty. For many other garden genera and a description of the family *see* CRUCIFERAE.

mutabilis, -e (mew-tab'il-is). Changeable, especially as to color.

MUTATION. Simply speaking, any hereditary change in a character not due to crossing — a sport or break. Usually an alteration of a single gene,* in which one kind of gene is changed into another kind — as for example — a gene for green leaves in corn into a gene for yellow leaves, or a blue-flowered chicory gene into one that brings about white flowers. These gene* alterations are largely responsible for character differences between strains, varieties, species, and still larger plant groups.

They are the variations* that the plant breeder looks for in examining thousands of plants of a wild or a cultivated species. They are the off-types of a given variety. In a bed of seedlings, just one often of thousands has crinkled leaves, wavy flower petals, dwarf stature, yellow foliage, marked change in leaf or flower shape, earlier flowering period, increased yield, greater disease resistance, and so on. These are often mutations. By saving them a new variety comes into being.

Mutations occur more commonly among seedlings, but there are many records of bud mutations — variations in which a part of the plant such as a branch is altered so as to yield a different type of fruit, or an everblooming race of flowers. The Starking sport of the Delicious apple, involving an earlier and richer red coloring of the fruit, appeared as a branch of an ordinary Delicious tree. Many other cases of this type in apples have been found, several of which have high commercial value. The New Dawn rose illustrates another valuable bud mutation. The well-known June-flowering Dr. van Fleet climbing rose produced a branch which flowers more or less continuously through the summer and fall. Cuttings from this branch gave rise to New Dawn.

Flower-color bud sports or mutations often arise on dahlias, monthly roses, chrysanthemums, and azaleas. Talisman has given rise to several that are commercially propagated.

* Special articles on the subjects indicated by an asterisk (*) will be found at the words so marked.

Presumably most plant species mutate, but some mutate more often than others. Contrast asparagus and lily-of-the-valley (rare) with corn and dahlias (common). Generally speaking, mutations occur more often among seed-propagated plants than those multiplied by asexual methods, such as cuttings, grafting, budding, tubers, corms, bulbs, etc.

Mutations seemingly occur among all sorts of characters — size, color, stature, flavor, yield, odor, etc. Their appearance is unpredictable. The majority of them will breed true in respect to the altered character on selfing.* Many of them require more coddling than the type from which they arise, although this by no means follows.

Mutants have been experimentally produced through the use of changes in temperature, aging of seed, X rays, and radium. Some of these are new, and many are similar to those occurring naturally. In the latter case, the process is speeded up. In time, such efforts may result in valuable new types, especially among plants that are commonly asexually propagated. — O. E. W. *See also* VARIATION. Radioactive isotopes and colchicine* have also been used to induce mutation.

MUTISIA (mew-tiss′ĭ-a). A genus of evergreen, flowering shrubs, of about 60 species of the tropical Andes, belonging to the family Compositae, few of which are in cultivation and these few mostly climbers. Leaves alternate* and compound,* the leaflets ovalish. The leafstalk is prolonged into a tendril, by which means the plant climbs. Flowers in large heads, composed of both ray* and disk* flowers, the ray flowers purple, rose or yellow. (Named for Joseph C. Mutis, a South American botanist.)

Mutisia can be grown in a cool greenhouse or outside where the temperature does not drop below 40°. Propagation by cuttings of half-ripened shoots in sand under a bell-jar or in a propagating frame in a temperature of 55°–65°, preferably in May or June. As soon as rooted, pot into a compost 3 parts loam, 1 part leaf mold, and 1 part sand. When the plants begin to grow, water freely, and apply liquid manure before flowering. Prune slightly after flowering. They are suitable for training up rafters or trellis. If grown outside, plant in sheltered position in good, rich soil.

Clematis. A good, cool greenhouse climber, the rather woody stem hairy. Leaflets 4–5 pairs, ovalish. Flower heads about 2 in. across, with bright red ray flowers. Peru.

MYCELIUM. *See* the second illustration at MUSHROOM.

MYCOLOGY. The study of fungi. *See* FUNGUS.

MYCORHIZA. The common association of the mycelium of a fungus and the roots of certain plants, notably oaks, beeches, nearly all the heath family, and most orchids. The association is a symbiotic one (*i.e.*, of advantage to both organisms and hence not parasitic) in that the extraordinarily complex chemical action set up by mycorhiza is essential for the food supply of both organisms. It is this that makes the cult. of plants which habitually rely on mycorhiza difficult unless the soil contains them. Most forest soils and some others are impregnated with mycorhiza, which hence play an all-important part in the food supply. The practical hort. significance of this is that all plants needing these conditions, common in many woodland plants, should be planted with as much of their native soil as possible.

MYOPORACEAE (my-o-pore-ray′see-ee). A family of chiefly Australian and Pacific Island shrubs and trees of secondary garden interest. Of its 5 genera and 90 species, only *Myoporum* (chiefly from Australasia and the Pacific Islands) is in cult., mostly in greenhouses.

Leaves alternate,* opposite* or scattered, usually without marginal teeth, sticky in *Myoporum.* Flowers regular* in *Myoporum,* in not particularly showy clusters. Fruit fleshy.

Technical flower characters: Calyx more or less tubular, 5-parted or cut. Corolla tubular or funnel-shaped and regular* in *Myoporum.* Stamens 4, two longer than the others, and with a fifth one sterile. Ovary superior,* 2-celled, or sometimes 2–10-celled.

MYOPORUM (my-o-pore′rum). Somewhat heath-like shrubs or trees, comprising perhaps 25 species, and the only cult. genus of the family Myoporaceae (which see for their characters). Only two are cult. for ornament, mostly in the greenhouse, but outdoors in Calif. and similar climates. (*Myoporum* is from the Greek implying that the leaves are dotted.)

They should be grown in the cool greenhouse in potting mixture* 4. Hardy outdoors only in zones* 8 and 9. Propagated by cuttings.

acuminatum. A shrub with alternate,* resinous-dotted leaves, about 3 in. long, generally narrow or lance-shaped. Flowers white, about ⅓ in. long, nearly bell-shaped, bearded within. Fruit nearly globe-shaped. Aust.

laetum. A shrub or small tree, not over 15 ft. high. Leaves shining, bright green, thickish, generally lance-shaped, 2–4 in. long. Flowers about ½ in. long, white, but with purple spots. N. Z.

myosotidiflora, -us, -um (my-o-so-ti-di-flō′-ra). With flowers like those of the next genus.

MYOSOTIDIUM (my-o-so-tid′ĭ-um). A perennial herb of the Chatham Islands (N. Z.), of only one species of the family Boraginaceae. The only species, **M. Hortensia**, grows to a height of 12–18 in. Leaves broad at the base, narrowing to a point, becoming smaller as they approach the top of the plant, covered with stiff, gray hairs. Flowers dark blue, becoming lighter toward the center, in dense cymes,* the individual flowers ½ in. across. Propagate from seeds, sown in early spring where intended to bloom, ⅛ in. deep in ordinary soil. Treat as an annual. Several sowings may be made dur-

---

* Special articles on the subjects indicated by an asterisk (*) will be found at the words so marked.

ing the summer as it produces flowers from seeds in 8–10 weeks. *See* BLUE GARDEN. The plant is sometimes offered as *M. nobile*. (*Myosotidium* is from the Greek for like forget-me-not, to which this genus is closely related.)

MYOSOTIS. *See* FORGET-ME-NOT.

MYRIAD-LEAF = *Myriophyllum verticilla-tum.*

MYRICA (mir-ĭ'ka). Shrubs or trees, often pleasantly aromatic, belonging to the family Myricaceae, and comprising about 50 species, three of which are cult. in specialized places. They have alternate* leaves and small, greenish, inconspicuous flowers, without sepals or petals, the male and female separate and often on different plants, mostly in catkins.* Fruit fleshy or nut-like, covered with an aromatic wax or resin. (*Myrica* is an old Greek name for some shrub, probably the tamarisk, and of no real significance here.)

The first and last species are admirable shrubs for very dry, sandy soils, as both grow naturally in such places. Both species are commonly called bayberry, but neither is the true bayberry (which see). *Myrica Gale* is a bog shrub and should be grown in the bog garden. All are easily propagated by seeds, especially the first species.

asplenifolia. *See* COMPTONIA PEREGRINA.
carolinensis = *M. pensylvanica.*
cerifera. Wax myrtle; called also bayberry and tallow-shrub. A tall shrub or small tree, never more than 35 ft. high. Leaves evergreen or very persistent, more or less lance-shaped, 1–3 in. long. Fruit grayish-waxy, aromatic. Southern N.J. to Fla. and Ark. Hardy from zone* 4 southward.
Gale. Sweet gale; also called moor or bog myrtle. A bog shrub, not usually over 4 ft. high. Leaves deciduous,* lance-shaped or broadest toward the tip, 1–2½ in. long. Fruit resinous-dotted, in dense catkins. Northern N.A. and northern Eurasia. Hardy from zone* 4 northward. It grows naturally in cool bogs almost to the Arctic Circle, but southward, in the mountains, to N. Car. Useful only in acid sites in the bog garden.
pensylvanica. Bayberry. A shrub 3–8 ft. high, the leaves ultimately falling, but often holding on until early winter. Leaves very aromatic, more or less elliptic or broadest toward the tip, 3–4 in. long. Fruit conspicuously grayish-waxy, very aromatic, and used in making bayberry candles. Eastern N.A., mostly along the coast. Hardy from zone* 2 southward.

MYRICACEAE (mi-ri-cay'see-ee). Commonly called the bayberry family, although the true bayberry (*Pimenta*) does not belong here. The Myricaceae contains only two genera, both of secondary importance as garden shrubs and trees, and both having resinous-dotted, aromatic foliage. One is *Myrica,* containing the bayberry or wax myrtle, the other *Comptonia* or sweet fern.

Leaves alternate.* Male and female flowers on separate twigs or even on separate plants, small, and inconspicuous. Fruit a small, often waxy nut, or fleshy. Both the genera furnish shrubs for more or less specialized conditions (dry sand or bogs).

Technical flower characters: Petals and sepals wanting; the rudimentary flowers in small catkins.* Stamens 2–16. Ovary 1-celled.

MYRICARIA (mi-ri-cay'ri-a). Tamarisk-like shrubs of the family Tamaricaceae, not much known in cult., but **M. germanica,** the German or false tamarisk, a native of Eurasia, grown for ornament. It is somewhat more hardy than the closely related *Tamarix,* from which it is separated only by technical characters. Leaves extremely small and scale-like, practically clothing the wand-like stems which are 4–6 ft. high. Flowers pinkish, very small, but numerous, in dense spire-like clusters (racemes*), which are terminal or in the leaf axils.* Fruit a 3-valved capsule.* May–July. Hardy from zone* 3 southward. (*Myricaria* is derived from *Myrica,* the old Greek name of the tamarisk.)

MYRIOPHYLLUM (mi-ri-o-fill'um). Water-milfoil. Widely dispersed, fresh-water aquatic herbs of the family Haloragidaceae, two of the 40 known species popular plants for pools and aquaria. They have hair-like submerged leaves, but sometimes above-water leaves that are broader, toothed, or sometimes without teeth, especially in some of the native, non-hort. species. Flowers extremely minute, lacking sepals* or petals, or both. Fruit a collection of small nutlets, sometimes roughened on the back and not splitting. (*Myriophyllum* is from the Greek for myriad-leaved, in allusion to the many, fine, thread-like leaves.)

The plants are of the easiest culture in any aquarium, where cuttings may be planted in mud or sand. In large pools, especially southward, they may become a nuisance as they grow quickly and may choke a pool in a season or two.

proserpinacoides. Parrot's-feather. Water feather. An extremely graceful aquatic with a weak stem, about 6 in. of which grows above the water, the rest submerged. Leaves feathery, composed of 10–25 hair-like divisions. Chile and Uruguay. The commonest and best species for aquaria.

verticillatum. Myriad-leaf. Plant nearly all submerged, the underwater leaves in whorls* of 3, the segments hair-like. The above-water leaves (when produced) more or less lance-shaped and deeply cut or divided, but not hair-like. North temperate zone.

myriostigma, -us, -um (mi-ree-o-stig'ma). With many stigmas.*

MYROBALAN PLUM = *Prunus cerasifera* and *Terminalia Catappa.*

MYRRH. *See* MYRRHIS.

MYRRHIS (mir'ris). Myrrh. A hardy, perennial, aromatic herb, of only 1 species belonging to the carrot family and a native of Eu. It is the common myrrh, **M. odorata,** also known as sweet cicely of Eu., but not the myrrh of the Bible. It grows 2–3 ft. high. Leaves compound,* the leaflets lance-

---

* Special articles on the subjects indicated by an asterisk (*) will be found at the words so marked.

shaped, finely divided, having a fern-like appearance, fragrant, and chiefly grown for this. Flowers small, whitish, inconspicuous, produced in compound umbels.* Fruit a capsule about 1 in. long, strongly ribbed. A graceful plant, used in the olden times as a flavoring. Propagated by seeds sown outdoors in ordinary soil ½ in. deep, in open sunny border, in Sept. or Apr., but preferably as soon as seeds are ripe. The roots may be divided in Oct. or Mar. (*Myrrhis* is from the Greek for perfume.)

MYRSINACEAE (myr-sin-a′see-ee). A chiefly tropical family of widely distributed shrubs and trees, comprising about 30 genera and over 500 species. Leaves generally alternate,* glandular-dotted and leathery. Flowers regular, sometimes unisexual, the calyx 4–5-lobed and the united corolla 4–5-lobed. Stamens 5,* usually borne on the petals. Ovary inferior or superior, followed by a one- to many-seeded drupe. The only hort. genera here considered are *Ardisia* and *Myrsine*.

MYRSINE (myr-sy′ne). A genus of over 80 species of shrubs and trees with alternate, leathery leaves, the flowers unisexual (*i.e.*, male and female flowers separate). The only cult. species is **M. africana**, of the Old World tropics, an evergreen, bushy shrub 2–4 ft. high, with inconspicuous pale-brown flowers followed by (in females) a purplish-blue, pea-sized, attractive fruit. Hardy in zones* 8 and 9, possibly in zone* 7. It is essential to have both male and female shrubs. Can be grown in the cool greenhouse in potting mixture* 4.

Myrsinites (mir-sin-eye′teez). A pre-Linnaean* name for several quite different plants. *See* PACHISTIMA, EUPHORBIA.

MYRSIPHYLLUM = *Asparagus asparagoides*.

MYRTACEAE (mir-tay′see-ee). The myrtle, allspice, or guava family, comprising 72 genera and nearly 3000 species of chiefly tropical, aromatic shrubs and trees, is of outstanding interest to gardeners in warm regions, and to many florists. Among the cult. genera are *Eucalyptus, Eugenia, Leptospermum, Melaleuca, Callistemon,* and *Metrosideros,* all, and some very widely, grown for ornament, especially outdoors in Calif. and Fla. and also in greenhouses. *Callistemon* is especially fine as a greenhouse shrub.

Fruit-yielding or economic genera are *Psidium* (*see* GUAVA), *Feijoa, Pimenta* (allspice and the true bayberry), and *Rhodomyrtus*. *Myrtus* contains the classical myrtle, and the other cult., mostly ornamental genera, are: *Agonis, Angophora, Calothamnus,* and *Tristania*.

Leaves mostly opposite* and evergreen, usually without marginal teeth. Flowers often very showy, solitary or in clusters, quite often with a few or many bracts* in the clusters.

Fruit very various, a nut, pod, berry or drupe.*

Technical flower characters: Flowers hermaphrodite* and regular.* Sepals 4 or 5, usually free, but their bases merged with the fleshy receptacle, which is joined to the ovary in most genera. Petals 4–5. Stamens* very numerous, conspicuous and furnishing most of the flower color in some genera (*Callistemon* and *Melaleuca*). Ovary inferior,* 1–many-celled. The fruit is usually surrounded by the persistent calyx-lobes.

myrtifolia, -us, -um (mir-ti-fō′li-a). With leaves like the myrtle (*Myrtus*).

MYRTILLOCACTUS (mir-til-lo-kak′tus). A small genus of chiefly Mexican, very spiny, tree-like cacti, of which **M. geometrizans**, the garambullo, is grown for oddity or interest in desert gardens in the Southwest. It is a much-branched, tree-like plant up to 15 ft. high, the branches about 4 in. thick, 5–6-ribbed and bluish-green. Spines usually 6 at each cluster, the central one erect and dagger-like, the other 5 diverging, and more slender. Flowers not over 1 in. wide, day-blooming, whitish. Fruit about the size of a pea, purplish and edible. For culture *see* CACTI. (*Myrtillocactus* means a myrtle-like cactus, in reference to the fruit, as the habit is very unlike a myrtle.)

MYRTLE. The true myrtle is *Myrtus communis* (which see). But several other plants are occasionally called myrtle. *See* LAGERSTROEMIA, RHODOMYRTUS, ANGOPHORA, VINCA MINOR, LEIOPHYLLUM, MYRICA CERIFERA, and UMBELLULARIA.

MYRTLE FAMILY. An immense family of chiefly tropical shrubs and trees, generally aromatic, and including the guava, eucalyptus, allspice, and the true myrtle (not the creeping myrtle or periwinkle). For a list of all the garden genera and a description of the family *see* MYRTACEAE.

MYRTUS (mir′tus). Myrtle. Tropical or sub-tropical shrubs or trees of the family Myrtaceae, comprising over 100 species, from the Old and New World, only a handful of any garden interest, one of them the classic myrtle of legend and history and widely grown for ornament. They have opposite,* simple leaves without marginal teeth, very aromatic in some species. Flowers white or pink (in ours), solitary in the leaf axils* or in few-flowered clusters, neither large nor showy. Petals 4–5. Stamens* numerous, longer than the petals but not conspicuously protruding. Fruit a berry, crowned with the persistent calyx-lobes. (*Myrtus* is the classical Greek name of the myrtle.)

The first species is widely planted throughout zones* 7, 8, and 9 for its handsome evergreen foliage. Northward it is a common greenhouse pot plant, much grown by florists for decoration. It needs a cool greenhouse and potting mixture* 4. Propagated by cuttings of half-ripened wood under glass; or by seeds. The other two species are little grown.

communis. The true myrtle. An evergreen,

---

* Special articles on the subjects indicated by an asterisk (*) will be found at the words so marked.

aromatic shrub, 3–9 ft. high. Leaves ovalish to lance-shaped, 1–2 in. long, shining green, almost stalkless. Flowers about ⅜ in. wide, white or pinkish. Fruit about ½ in. long, bluish-black, or white in a hort. form. Mediterranean region and western As. The *var.* microphylla has smaller and much more numerous, nearly overlapping leaves; *var.* flore-pleno is double-flowered; *var.* variegata has variegated leaves. There are many other hort. forms differing mostly in stature or leaf-form.

ralphi. A shrub or small tree, not over 15 ft. high. Leaves ovalish, ¾–1 in. long. Flowers pinkish, about ½ in. wide. Fruit about ⅓ in. long, dark red. N. Z.

Ugni. Chilean guava. A shrub or small tree, not over 20 ft. high. Leaves shining green above, whitish beneath, leathery and more or less oval. Flowers rose-pink, and beneath them are 2 persistent bracts.* Fruit about ½ in. in diameter, purplish-red, pleasant-flavored and edible.

N

NABAM. See Fungicides.

NAEGELIA (nay-ge′li-a). A small genus of tropical American herbaceous, tuberous-rooted perennials, of the family Gesneriaceae, often referred to as *Gesneria,* to which they are closely allied, and by some as *Smithiana,* which may be the technically correct name for it. Leaves opposite,* soft, velvety, and heart-shaped. Flowers tubular, red or yellowish-white, in terminal clusters. Fruit a dry capsule.* (Named for Karl von Naegeli, a Munich professor of botany.) Cultivated in greenhouses and propagated by seeds, tubers, or offsets. Sow seeds on surface of well-drained pots of sandy peat in temperature of 75° in March or April. Cuttings of young shoots should be inserted in pots of sandy peat in temperature 75°–85° in spring. Tubers may be divided before starting the plant into growth after resting period. Plant 1 in. deep, singly in 5-in. pots or 1–2 in. apart in larger sizes. Use a potting compost of 2 parts fibrous peat, 1 part loam, 1 part leaf mold, with a little decayed cow manure and silver sand. Water moderately until plants are 3–4 in. high, then water freely. Apply liquid manure once a week when flower buds appear, but after flowering gradually reduce water until foliage dies down, then keep dry during winter months. A good place is under the bench* as they should not be stored in too dry a place.

cinnabarina. Grows to 2 ft. high. Leaves covered with red or purplish hairs. Flowers about 1½ in. long, drooping, tubular, red on upper side, and the throat spotted with white. A fine winter-blooming plant. Mexico.

multiflora. Grows to 1½ ft. Leaves with long hairs, also velvety. Flowers numerous, hanging, white, or cream-colored, the tube narrow. Mexico.

zebrina. Grows to 2 ft. Leaves densely hairy, having distinctly marked veins of purple, red, or dark brown. Flowers red, with yellow spots, 1½ in. long, the tube contracted at the base. Particularly good for fall flowering. Mex.

NAGAMI KUMQUAT = *Fortunella margarita.*

NAIAS (nay′as). A large genus of submerged aquatic plants of the family Naia-

daceae, one of them, N. flexilis, often used as an aquarium plant. It is a slender, weak-stemmed plant with very small unisexual flowers and thread-like leaves. It is found in fresh water throughout the north temperate zone, and is sold by dealers in aquarium plants. (*Naias* is from the Greek for a water nymph.)

NAKED FLOWER. One without petals or sepals* as in the willow and *Myrica.*

NAMA (nay′ma). American herbs or sub-shrubs of the family Hydrophyllaceae, comprising 36 species, of which the only one of garden interest is N. parryi, a native of Calif. It is a shrubby perennial, 3–6 ft. high, the stem ½ in. in diameter. Leaves alternate,* without stalks, dark green, long and narrow. Flowers violet-blue in small lateral clusters, funnel-shaped, about ½ in. long. May–July. Cult. in Calif., but almost unknown elsewhere. (*Nama* is from the Greek for stream or spring, in allusion, possibly, to the moist site of some species.) Sometimes referred to the genus *Eriodictyon.*

nana, -us, -um (nay′na). Small.

NANDIN = *Nandina domestica.*

NANDINA (nan-dy′na). A single species of evergreen shrub of the family Berberidaceae, native in China and Japan, hardy outdoors only from zone* 5 southward. The only species is N. domestica, the nandin, sometimes called sacred or heavenly bamboo, although it has nothing to do with any bamboo. It is an attractive shrub, 6–8 ft. high, with alternate,* twice- or thrice-compound* leaves, the ultimate leaflets narrow, 1–2 in. long and very handsome in their fall red color. Flowers small, white, not showy, but the clusters (panicles*) nearly a foot long and handsome. Sepals* numerous, in series of 3, gradually passing into the white petals. Stamens* as many as the petals. Fruit a red, 2-seeded berry about ½ in. in diameter, very handsome when ripe, and the chief attraction of the plant. The shrub is not particular as to soil, but prefers a reasonably moist site, failing which it should be regularly watered.

---

* Special articles on the subjects indicated by an asterisk (*) will be found at the words so marked.

North of zone* 6 it is often hardy in protected places, where, if the top should be winter-killed, the roots may survive, especially if they are well mulched.* June–July. (*Nandina* is the Latin version of the Japanese name for this shrub.)

NANKEEN (or Nanking) **LILY** = *Lilium testaceum.*

nankinensis, -e (nan-kin-en'sis). From Nanking, China.

NANKING CHERRY = *Prunus tomentosa.*

NANNYBERRY = *Viburnum Lentago.*

napaulensis, -e (na-paul-en'sis). From Nepal.

Napellus (na-pel'lus). Literally a little turnip; as a specific name used to designate small turnip-like roots, as in *Aconitum Napellus. See* MONKSHOOD.

Napobrassica (nay-po-brass'i-ka). Literally, a "turnip-mustard" or a "rape-mustard"; used as a specific name for the rutabaga (*Brassica Napobrassica*).

Napus (nay'pus). A pre-Linnaean* name for the rape (*Brassica Napus*).

narbonnensis, -e (nar-bon-en'sis). From Narbonne, France.

NARCISSUS (nar-sis'sus). Important, chiefly hardy, bulbous plants of the family Amaryllidaceae, comprising about 40 species, most of them European, very widely grown for ornament or fragrance, and including such well-known plants as the daffodil, jonquil, paper-white, the Chinese sacred lily, and the poet's narcissus. All bear bulbs. Leaves generally rush-like or more or less terete in cross-section in the jonquil and its relatives, but flat or nearly so in the common daffodil, basal in all sorts, and usually about the length of the flowering stalk. Flowers prevailingly white or yellow, often nodding. Calyx and corolla not separable as such, but modified in two ways: (1) The flower having a central crown (corona) which is long and tubular (in the trumpet narcissus or daffodil); or (2) the central crown (corona) reduced to a shallow, ring-like cup (as in the jonquil and poet's narcissus). Outside of this central corolla-like organ are the six segments which comprise the petals and sepals. In the group with a long tubular corona there is the typical hose-in-hose* effect of one flower growing within another. Stamens* 6, usually hidden in the crown. Fruit a 3-lobed, many-seeded capsule.* The species have been much hybridized so that those below are somewhat uncertain as to exact botanical identity, although they represent the chief sorts in cult. (*Narcissus* is possibly named for the mythological youth so fond of his own reflection that after long gazing at it he was changed into the flower.) They are sometimes called Lent lilies.

For the garden uses and culture *see* below.

Bulbocodium. The petticoat or hoop-petticoat narcissus (or daffodil). Leaves channeled or nearly round in cross-section, usually longer than the flowering stalk, which is 4–12 in. high. Flowers solitary, yellow or white, the crown longer than the tubular corolla. Southern France and Morocco.

cyclamineus. A little-known species from Portugal, with solitary flowers having a very short tube and recurved, lemon-yellow segments, which are shorter than the orange-yellow crown and strongly turned upward. For culture *see* ROCK GARDEN.

incomparabilis. Leaves flat, about 12 in. long and ¼ in. wide. Flower solitary, the corona about half the length of the tube, wavy-edged. Southern Eu.

Jonquilla. The common jonquil. Leaves nearly 18 in. long, rush-like and nearly terete. Flowers in clusters of 2–6, fragrant, yellow, the tube about 1 in. long, the corona less than half as long as the segments. Southern Eu. and northern Af. Double-flowered forms are known.

johnstoni = *N. Pseudo-narcissus johnstoni.*

juncifolius. A little-known jonquil, its rush-like leaves scarcely 6 in. long. Flowers 1–4 in the cluster, yellow, the tube about ½ in. long, the corona about half the length of the segments, darker yellow and wavy-edged. Double-flowered forms are known.

minor. A yellow trumpet narcissus. Perhaps merely a form of *N. Pseudo-narcissus.* It has yellow flowers, the corona sulphur-yellow, and the whole plant is scarcely more than 5 in. high. The *var.* **minimus** is still smaller, and rarely grows over 3 in. high. Both are rock garden species. *See* ROCK GARDEN for culture.

moschatus. White trumpet narcissus. Perhaps merely a form of *N. Pseudo-narcissus,* but with cream-white flowers, the segments slightly twisted, sulphur-yellow-tinged in youth, ultimately white, the corona as long as the segments and pure white.

odorus. Campernelle jonquil. Leaves about 12 in. long, very narrow or rush-like. Flowers in clusters of 2–4, fragrant, yellow, the tube about ¾ in. long, the wavy or lobed corona about half as long as the segments. Double-flowered forms are offered.

poetaz. *See* Narcissus Culture below.

poeticus. Poet's narcissus. Pheasant's-eye narcissus. Leaves about 18 in. long, and ¼ in. wide, flat and grass-like. Flowers very fragrant, white, the tube about 1 in. long, the corona very shallow, much shorter than the segments, the edges wavy and conspicuously red-margined. Southern Eu. The *var.* **ornatus** is earlier-flowering. Double-flowered forms are also known.

Pseudo-narcissus. The common trumpet narcissus or daffodil. A stout, long-cult. plant now of many forms and coming in innumerable named garden types. Leaves flat, 12–18 in. long, usually just reaching the flowers. Corolla about 2 in. long, typically pale yellow, the segments and corona mostly of a slightly different shade. Corona very long, deeply wavy or even slightly fringed. Eu. There are many forms, some with double flowers. The *var.* **johnstoni** has paler yellow flowers with reflexed segments.

Tazetta. Polyanthus narcissus. Leaves flat, about 18 in. long and nearly ¾ in. wide. Flowers generally white, fragrant, usually in clusters of 4–8, the tube about 1 in. long, the corona much shorter than the segments and usually pale yellow. Eurasia and in the Canary Islands. Long cult. and the origin of many popular hort. forms, but not hardy outdoors in frosty regions, for it is normally autumn-growing.

---

* Special articles on the subjects indicated by an asterisk (*) will be found at the words so marked.

Among the best known is the Paper White narcissus forced on a great scale by florists for winter bloom. As the name indicates, it is pure white. The *var.* **orientalis,** the Chinese sacred lily or joss flower, has white segments and a darker yellow crown about ⅓ the length of the segments. Commonly grown in bowls of pebbles and water in the house. For notes on culture *see* below.

triandrus. Leaves about 12 in. long, rush-like or nearly round in cross-section. Flowers pure white, the tube about ¾ in. long. Corona cuplike, with the margins not crisped or wavy, about half the length of the segments. Southwestern Eu. For culture *see* ROCK GARDEN.

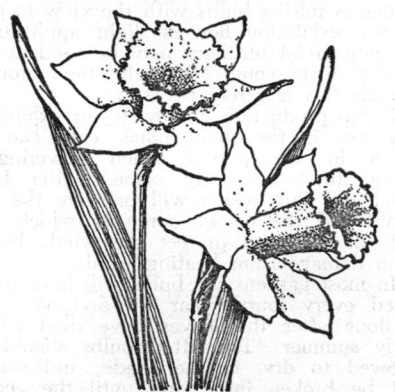

Trumpet narcissus (daffodil)

NARCISSUS CULTURE

KINDS. From the gardener's point of view all narcissus may be divided into two sections — the relatively small group of species and their derivatives that are of value in rock gardens and the front of borders, and the great collection of horticultural forms that have been derived from relatively few species.

The first group contains the small yellow trumpets, *N. minor* and its variety *minimus;* the white trumpets, mostly derived from *N. moschatus;* the hoop-petticoats, forms of *N. Bulbocodium* in white and various yellow tones; *N. cyclamineus,* a trumpet with characteristically reflexed petals; the forms of *N. triandrus,* with fuchsia-like flowers in ivory-white and yellows; and several forms of the true jonquil. For the culture of these, *see* ROCK GARDEN.

The second group consists of the selected and hybrid forms, all of which have come from the several trumpet narcissi, commonly called daffodil, and of *N. poeticus,* together with the hybrids between these and between their innumerable progenies. In the South and on the Pacific Coast, the bunch-flowered *N. Tazetta,* which grows during the winter and blooms in late winter, may be more useful in some parts as the chief element for garden use. In the North, only the hybrids resulting from the *poeticus* × *Tazetta,* once known conveniently

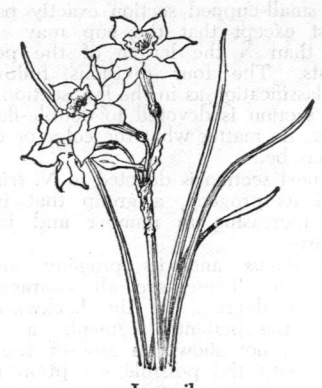

Jonquil

as "Poetaz," may be used to represent this section.

Because hybridization has been carried on through so many generations, narcissus have now come to be classified by a purely arbitrary grouping based on the size of the floral parts and their coloration. The older classification that made an attempt to report the derivation in the original hybrid groups has been abandoned.

The trumpet section, in which the length of the trumpet is equal to or greater than the length of the perianth segments or petals, is divided into three sections, one for pure-yellow flowers, one for bicolors in which the trumpet is yellow and the perianth white, and one for pure-white flowers.

The large-cupped section is made up of the great mass of varieties that are not quite trumpets, and is divided into four sections: (*a*) yellow perianth and colored cup, which may be yellow or yellow stained with other color; (*b*) white perianth, colored cup; (*c*) white perianth, white cup; and (*d*) any not in the above. The latter group includes all varieties of the proper proportions but with other colors in the cup, chiefly to care for the rapidly developing pink and salmon-colored group.

Poet's narcissus

---

* Special articles on the subjects indicated by an asterisk (*) will be found at the words so marked.

The small-cupped section exactly parallels the last except that the cup may not be longer than ¾ the length of the perianth segments. The four divisions follow the same classification as in the last section.

One section is devoted to double-flowered varieties, no matter what the color or dimensions may be.

The next section is devoted to *N. triandrus* and all its progeny, a group that is constantly increasing in number and in ease of culture.

Cyclamineus and its progeny are the next group. These are all characterized, in varying degrees, by the backward carriage of the perianth segments, a character that is not shown in any of the other sections with the possible exception of the Triandrus group.

Jonquilla sets the standard for the next group, and includes not only *Jonquilla* itself but the closely related species. Many of the hybrids of *Jonquilla* and *odorus* are coming to approximate the characters usually found in the small-cupped section.

Tazetta now includes not only the forms of *Tazetta* itself but its various garden hybrids, once known as "Poetaz."

Poeticus. This section includes not only the several wild forms of the species, still grown in gardens, but the numerous garden forms gotten by interbreeding. All are characterized by the glistening white of the perianth, the very flat center or "eye" which may vary from yellow with a red margin to almost pure red, to others in which green color from the throat comes up into the surface. Many are late-flowering and all have a characteristic scent.

The tenth section is given over to "wild forms and hybrids," a rather catch-all group, in which *N. Bulbocodium* will be the most frequent representative.

Section 11 is *the* catch-all into which can be put any not fitting into any of the above sections.

PLANTING. Narcissus are suited to a wide range of climatic conditions, but not all will do equally well in all parts of the country. In the extreme North, it would appear that many of the yellow trumpets and their close progeny do less well, which is also true in the extreme South. In the North, therefore, the small-cupped, *Poeticus*, and *Jonquilla* sections should be tried first. In the extreme South, the small-cupped, *Jonquilla*, *Triandrus*, and *Tazetta* sections should constitute the point of departure, though some of the members of these groups do not flourish.

In planting, bulbs can well be put to the rule-of-thumb depth of one and one-half times the depth of the bulb itself, erring always by planting deeper in case of doubt. In naturalistic plantings where one does not wish to have to replant, to care for natural increase, any oftener than possible, still deeper planting will slow up the rate of increase. On the other hand, if one wants a rapid increase of any kind, shallow planting will produce a quick split-up of the bulb into many small offsets, which can later be replanted at a proper depth to bring them back to flowering size.

No animal manures should be used with narcissus, but only the usual safe commercial fertilizers and humus. Some accidents have been reported where peat moss touched the bulbs. To insure all bulbs, if the base of the bulb is set in sand there is not much danger. No bulbs should be placed where drainage is poor, as that also affects the base of the bulb and induces rot. If one is raising bulbs with the view to producing exhibition flowers, light applications of commercial fertilizer may be used as the shoots first come through the ground, though this is rarely necessary.

If the production of flowers for exhibition purposes is the main issue, care can be given in the period when flowering is about to begin, with some shelter from wind and sun, which will preserve the fine quality of the colors, some of which will fade in sun, and protect the whole bloom from damage from beating winds.

In most gardens the bulbs will have to be lifted every fourth year for division. This is done after the leaves have died off in early summer. The lifted bulbs should be allowed to dry, in the shade, and should not be broken into parts until they come apart easily as damage to the base is serious. Replanting may be done at once, or the bulbs can be stored in a cool, airy place until autumn. They should be examined periodically to see that rot does not appear — something that is most likely to show in white-flowered sorts. All planting should be carried out at whatever date is needful to allow the bulbs to have at least one month for good root development before the soil is cold. The farther north one gardens, the earlier the planting date.

All narcissus may be forced, using potting mixture* 4 with bone meal substituted for cow manure. Many may be grown in bowls of pebbles and water. In all cases, roots must be well developed before the pots are brought to light and the best flowers will come when the temperature of room or greenhouse is kept low, as it would be in the open in spring. For details of forcing *see* BULBS. At the same article will be found the description of how to treat narcissus when naturalized in the lawn. There is no more effective way to mass them unless one has an open woodland at his disposal.

VARIETIES

When it comes to the choice of varieties, the possibilities are almost endless. The usual limiting factor will be the price — which is high in the case of new sorts that exist in limited stocks — and after that, one's personal preferences. The best procedure is to visit any good collection, and as many good exhibitions as possible. Nearly all the varieties offered in trade at present have ex-

* Special articles on the subjects indicated by an asterisk (*) will be found at the words so marked.

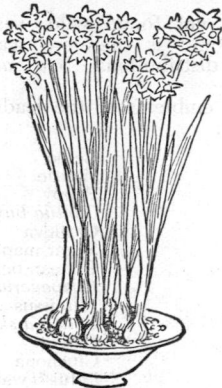

The Chinese sacred lily (*Narcissus tazetta orientalis*), and the popular paper white, can be grown in a bowl of pebbles and water.

cellent health, so that one need pay no attention to older books that suggest some varieties of problematical vigor. Any list will be unsatisfactory in some ways to some readers, and, with the constant offering of new sorts, will be dated almost immediately. The varieties that are named here probably will remain in gardens as long as such old plants as Emperor, Hera, *ornatus*, and their contemporaries. No attempt is made to place them in their sections, all of which can be determined from commercial catalogues. If catalogues note that a variety is late-blooming, it should not be grown in regions where there is very hot weather in the blooming period, unless some control of moisture is possible. The recommended varieties are:

Garron, Hunter's Moon, Content, Effective, Cantatrice, Beersheba, Fortune, Dunkeld, Dervish, Polindra, Red Hackle, Truth, Binkie, Chunking, Market Merry, Blarney, Limerick, Lady Kesteven, Cushendall, Foggy Dew (very late), Cheerfulness, Daphne, Mary Copeland, April Tears, Niveth, Silver Chimes, Beryl, February Gold, Cherie, Trevithian, Lanarth, Golden Perfection, Cragford, Sarchedon, all the *Bulbocodiums*, Rose of Tralee, and Wild Rose. — B. Y. M.

INSECT PESTS. *See* control at BULBS.
DISEASES. The most common troubles with narcissus are rots which are present on the roots and base of bulbs, or on neck of plant between top of bulb and soil line. When leaves emerge in the spring and suddenly wilt and die, examine the neck for small black or brown seed-like objects attached to the neck. Such bulbs and surrounding soil should be removed. Do not buy bulbs with seed-like objects present on or under the husks.
Occasionally leaves will have yellow streaks in them which characterize mosaic* disease. Dig and discard these plants to prevent spread of virus to neighboring plants.

narcissiflora, -us, -um (nar-siss-i-flō'ra). With narcissus-like flowers.

NARDOO = *Marsilea drummondi.*

Nardus (nar'dus). Latin equivalent for the old Asiatic nard, the name for the grass *Cymbopogon Nardus,* and its aromatic oil.

NARTHECIUM (nar-thee'sĭ-um). Called by some *Abama.* Hardy perennial herbs of the lily family, not very common in the bogs and swamps of eastern Asia, Eu., and N.A., and comprising only about 6 species, the following being the only ones of garden interest. Leaves grass-like. The flowering stalk rises from the center of the leaves and is crowned by a raceme* of yellowish-green flowers. Petals 6. Stamens* 6. Fruit a 3-celled capsule,* its seeds with a little tail at each end. (*Narthecium* is from the Greek word *narthecion,* a chest or box, but of uncertain application here.)
Propagated by seeds sown in March or April, or by division of roots in October or March. The plants must be grown in acid soil or boggy peat. Moist beds, borders, or margins of ponds are only tolerably suitable places, as naturally the plants are often found growing in sphagnum moss.

americanum. Bog-asphodel; called also yellow grass. A rare plant confined to the pine-barren bogs of N.J. and Del. Leaves 3–8 in. long, gray-hairy. Pods gray. June–Sept.
californicum. Leaves iris-like, but only about ⅛ in. wide and 4–8 in. long. Flower cluster 3–4 in. long. Pods salmon color. Calif.

NASEBERRY = *Sapota Achras.*

NASTURTIUM. The common garden nasturtium comprises the genus Tropaeolum (tro-pee'o-lum), the only one of the family Tropaeolaceae, with about 65 species of annual or perennial, soft-stemmed herbs, most of which are climbing. They are natives of the cooler parts of S.A. The perennial species have tuberous underground stems but in all other respects resemble the annuals. Leaves alternate,* more or less round, light green, with strongly marked veins radiating from the center from which the stalk arises. Leafstalk fleshy and sensitive, curling round any object with which it comes in contact, enabling the tall kinds to climb as much as 10 ft. Flowers are showy and solitary, growing from the axils* of the leaves, pale yellow, orange, scarlet, crimson or dark red. Sepals 5, joined at the base, 3 prolonged into a spur at the back of the flower. Petals usually 5, broad, suddenly narrowing at the base into a kind of stalk where they join the sepals. Stamens* 8, curving toward the back of the flower. Fruit 3-celled, with 1 seed in each cell. (*Tropaeolum* is from the Greek for trophy, in allusion to the shield-shaped leaves.) *Nasturtium,* as a Latin name, is the correct name for the watercress (which see).
Easily cultivated from seeds or cuttings. Sow seeds where plants are required to bloom, 1 in. deep, in April or they may be sown in pots or boxes in the cool greenhouse and transplanted. Soil should not be

---

* Special articles on the subjects indicated by an asterisk (*) will be found at the words so marked.

too rich or plants will produce lots of foliage and few flowers. Cuttings may be made from the young shoots at any time; they should be about 4 in. in length and inserted in sand, in shady part of the cool greenhouse or cold frame, where they will root in a few days. Cuttings rooted in Sept. make excellent pot plants for flowering in the cool greenhouse and can be used for house window plants. Nasturtiums make excellent coverings for trellis, posts, and rocks. The flowers make very attractive decorations when cut.

T. lobbianum = *Tropaeolum peltophorum.*

T. majus. Common nasturtium or Indian cress, so called because the young flower buds and fruits are used as seasoning. (*See* HERB GARDENING.) Strong-climbing annual, growing to a height 8–12 ft. Leaves round, on long stalks. Flowers 2½ in. across, yellow-orange sometimes striped and spotted with red. The *var.* **nanum** (Tom Thumb) is a dwarf form; *vars.* **atropurpureum** (dark red), **coccineum** (scarlet), and **heinemanni** (chocolate) are color forms. S.A. A beautiful, low-growing, late-flowering, yellow form is known as Golden Gleam.

T. minus. Dwarf nasturtium. Of scrambling habit and smaller than *T. majus.* Flowers 1½ in. or smaller. S.A. *See* HERB GARDENING.

T. peltophorum. A climbing annual, slightly hairy, except under sides of leaves, which are long-stalked. Flowers 1 in. long, and long-spurred, orange-red. S.A.

T. Peregrinum. Canary-bird flower. An annual of tall-climbing habit. Leaves round, but deeply cut into 5 finger-like sections. Flowers pale yellow, 1 in. long. A particularly dainty type used in English cottage gardens. Peru.

NASTURTIUM = Watercress.

NASTURTIUM FAMILY = Tropaeolaceae.

natalensis, -e (nay-tal-en′sis). From Natal, South Africa.

NATAL GRASS = *Tricholaena rosea.*

NATAL ORANGE = *Strychnos spinosa.*

NATAL PLUM = *Carissa grandiflora.*

natans (nay′tanz). Floating.

NATIONAL ARBORETUM. *See* ARBORETUM.

NATIONAL BOTANIC GARDEN. *See* BOTANIC GARDEN.

NATIONAL COUNCIL. Short for National Council of State Garden Club Federations. It is an amalgamation of the garden club federations of over 46 states, comprising 10,905 clubs, with a membership of nearly 400,000. Its central office is 160 Central Park South, New York 19, N.Y. It includes most garden clubs that are not affiliated with the Garden Club of America.

NATIONAL FLOWERS. There is no national floral emblem for the U.S., although many suggestions have been put forward, notably mountain laurel, columbine, flowering dogwood, and rose. Perhaps only the latter is found in some form in every state in the Union, but it is already the national flower of England, and is not peculiarly American, as is the mountain laurel. But the latter is not found wild west of Ohio and Tenn., and is therefore scarcely "national" in distribution. *See also* STATE FLOWERS.

The floral emblems of the leading foreign countries are:

Argentina	Ceibo
Australia	Wattle
Belgium	Poppy
Bolivia	*Cantua buxifolia*
Brazil	Cattleya
Canada	Sugar maple
Chile	Chilean bellflower (*Lapageria rosea*)
China	Narcissus
Costa Rica	*Cattleya skinneri*
Denmark	Clover
Ecuador	Cinchona
Egypt	Lotus (water lily)
England	Rose
France	Fleur-de-lis
Germany	Cornflower
Greece	Violet
Holland	Tulip
Honduras	Rose
India	Lotus (Zizyphus)
Ireland	Shamrock
Italy	Lily
Japan	Chrysanthemum
Mexico	Prickly pear
Newfoundland	Pitcher-plant
New Zealand	Silver fern
Norway	Heather
Persia (Iran)	Rose
Poland	Poppy
Russia	Sunflower
Scotland	Thistle
South Africa	†*Protea cynaroides*
Spain	Pomegranate
Sweden	Twinflower
Switzerland	Edelweiss
Wales	Leek

†*Protea cynaroides* is a non-hort. plant of the family Proteaceae.

NATIVE. Indicating that a plant grows naturally in a particular country, state, or region, and is neither introduced through planting nor naturalized.*

NATIVE FUCHSIA. *See* CORREA.

NATIVE PLANTS. *See* WILD GARDEN.

NATIVE ROSE. *See* BAUERA.

NATURALIZED. The permanent establishment of a foreign plant in a native flora.

NATURALIZING. The planting of bulbs, herbs, shrubs, or trees in quantity in such fashion as to suggest a natural growth; as bulbs can suggest an Alpine meadow, shrubs a thicket, or trees a forest.

NATURAL ORDER. *See* PLANT FAMILY.

NAUTILOCALYX (naw-till′o-kay-lix). A small genus of South American weak-stemmed plants of the family Gesneriaceae, two grown as pot plants in the warm greenhouse. They have opposite leaves, often with a winged leafstalk. Flowers in the leaf axils,* often with 2 or more leafy bracts.* Calyx irregular. Corolla more or less tubular, white or yellow. Fruit a 2-celled capsule.* (*Nautilocalyx* was named for its nautilus-like calyx.)

---

* Special articles on the subjects indicated by an asterisk (*) will be found at the words so marked.

For the cult. of the two below, *see* COLUM-
NEA. Neither do well as house plants.

bullatus. Stem erect, reddish-brown, 1–2
ft. high. Leaves elliptic, 5–9 in. long, dark-
green, hairy, but sometimes bronzy above, the
under surface rose-pink. Flowers yellow, about
1 in. long, 8–10 in the cluster, the corolla
hairy on the outside. Peru (in Amazon region).
Sometimes offered, incorrectly, as *Episcia tessellata.*

lynchi. Related to the above but the leaves
shorter and smooth on the upper surface, except
on the veins. Lower leaf-surface reddish-purple.
Flowers pale yellow, usually in 2's or 3's, about
1½ in. long. A fine foliage plant. Colombia
(?). Sometimes offered, incorrectly, as *Alloplectus lynchi.*

NAVEL ORANGE. A usually seedless orange in which the ovary is abortive and
appears as a small, secondary fruit within
a fruit, mostly just beneath a pointed or
depressed section of the rind. It originated
as a bud-sport* in a monastery garden in
Bahia, Brazil, from whence it was imported into the U.S. in 1870. From it has
come the Washington Navel, one of the most
widely grown varieties in Calif. See
ORANGE.

NAVELWORT = *Cotyledon umbilica.* See
also OMPHALODES.

NEANTHE BELLA. An uncertain name
for *Chamaedorea elegans.*

neapolitana, -us, -um (nee-a-pol-i-tay′na).
From Naples.

NEAPOLITAN VIOLET. The Parma violet. See VIOLA ODORATA.

NEBRASKA. The state flower is the goldenrod, the state tree is the American elm,
and the state lies in zones* 2 and 3. "The
Land of Shallow Waters" was the meaning
of an Indian word from which Nebraska
derived its name. This was an apt description of the many rivers, more miles of
them than in any other state, running eastward across the state to join the Missouri.
The state slopes to the east from an average
elevation of over 4000 feet on the western
border to less than 1000 feet at the southeast corner. This greater elevation gives
the western part of the state more severe
winter temperatures and a growing season 1½ months shorter than the eastern
part. The precipitation varies from approximately 14 inches on the western border to 35 inches at the southeast corner.

SOILS. In the eastern end of the state the
soils are of loessial origin — the pure loess*
of the Missouri River hills often being 50
feet or more in depth. There are also
some evidences of glaciation in this section.
The sandhill area includes most of the territory north of the Platte River in the
central part of the state. Soils of alluvial
nature are found along the Platte and Republican river valleys while in the panhandle section high tablelands are the general rule. The fertility, aside from the
sandhill area, is reasonably good. Acid soils

NEBRASKA

The zones of hardiness crossing Nebraska are
those shown on the map located at ZONE, which
should be consulted for details. The dates are
the average lastest killing frost in spring and
the first one in the fall. The figures below the
dates show the average length of the growing
season. Rainfall figures (in inches) are for total
annual rainfall in the regions so indicated.

are seldom found, but in some areas alkali
is a problem.

The greatest horticultural achievement in
Nebraska has been in tree-planting. Although eastern species of trees, including
elms, oaks, hackberry, Kentucky coffee
tree, honey locust, etc., had pushed westward up some of the river valleys when
the state was settled, the great expanses between the rivers were practically treeless.
A large area of ponderosa pine in northwestern Nebraska, still existing, and other
isolated stands of pine in the western part
of the state, along with Eastern and Western red cedar, were almost the only
serious competition to the endless grasslands.
These treeless plains challenged the early
settlers and Nebraska was soon known as
"The Tree Planters' State." J. Sterling
Morton was responsible for the establishment of Arbor Day. His lovely home at
Nebraska City was given to the state and
is now Arbor Lodge State Park. Large
plantings of many woody and garden plants
adorn the grounds. Millions of trees were
planted each year, especially under the
timber-culture act which required the planting and care of 10 acres with so many
trees to acquire title to a 160-acre homestead. Approximately 33,000,000 trees have
been planted on farms since 1926 under
the Clarke-McNary tree distribution program. The Prairie States Forestry Project, popularly known as the shelterbelt
program, planted more miles of field
shelterbelts in Nebraska than in any other

---

* Special articles on the subjects indicated by an asterisk (*) will be found at the words so marked.

state. Over 4000 miles of shelterbelts, comprising over 45,000,000 trees, were planted. This achievement did much to modify the bleak appearance of central and western Nebraska. Unfortunately, these shelterbelts were often located adjacent to roads and have been unpopular with motorists in winter because of the snowdrifts they create.

Professor Charles E. Bessey of the University of Nebraska early envisioned pine forests growing on the sandhills area of Nebraska. This is one of the most unique areas in the world, and it comprises about one-fourth of the state's area. Lying mostly in the northwestern part of the state, it consists of rolling hills of sand covered with grass and dotted with lakes. Nebraska ranks second only to Minnesota in the number of lakes. The streams from the area are most constant in their flow. The sand absorbs even heavy rains and then releases the water slowly to the streams. Through Dr. Bessey's efforts, the U.S. Forest Service planted and developed an area near Halsey now known as the Nebraska National Forest. A nursery there provides several million evergreen seedlings each year for planting in the plains area.

This emphasis on tree-planting has been a necessary prelude to other phases of horticulture in Nebraska. High average wind velocities combine with high temperatures, bright sunshine, and low relative humidity during the summer to make transpiration rates of plants high. Dry winds in winter dessicate and kill plants. These factors make windbreaks essential for the successful culture of vegetable gardens, home fruit-plantings, flowers, and many shrubs.

The state tree is the American elm, although the cottonwood or Siberian elm is more typical of the state. Shade trees used are principally American elm, pin and bur oak, hackberry, honey locust, maples, green ash, linden, Siberian elm, and cottonwood. Evergreens used are pines, Eastern and Western red cedars, spruces, and Douglas fir.

Sour cherries, plums, and strawberries grow well everywhere in the state. Apples and pears can be grown everywhere, but the more winter-hardy varieties should be planted outside eastern Nebraska. Principal wild fruits harvested are the choke cherry in the south and east, the sand cherry in the central and west, the buffalo-berry in the central, black raspberries in the south-central, and plums in all areas of the state.

Vegetables and flowers typical of other parts of the Midwest are grown, although the more severe climate of western Nebraska confines the growing of some perennials, such as roses, to the hardiest kinds unless special care is used for winter protection. The cooler summer nights of this western area make it especially well adapted for producing the cole vegetables and sweet corn, however. These crops all require irrigation, and recent increases in the state's irrigated acreage, to approximately 2,000,000 acres, have made water available for home plantings as well as for the fields. Wild flowers abound in the sandhills region where the soil has never been disturbed by the plow.

The Agricultural Experiment Station which has kindly supplied this information is at Lincoln, Nebraska, and they will be happy to answer any inquiries on gardening.

nebulosa, -us, -um (neb-you-lō'sa). Indefinite or obscure. Sometimes applied to flowers that make a cloudlike mass.

NECK. The stem-like but thickened extension at the tip of some tuberous roots or bulbs, notably in the onion, rutabaga, and in some amaryllises.

NECKLACE ORCHID=*Coelogyne dayana.*

NECKLACE TREE. *See* Ormosia.

NECROSIS. The death of a plant, or part of it, caused by fungus, virus, or bacterial diseases, or by mechanical injury.

NECTAR; NECTARY. A very sweet substance, chiefly water and sugar, secreted by the nectary of many flowers, and the chief source of honey. Nectaries are usually near the base of a flower, often near the base of a petal or stamen. This forces the insect visitor to get deep down in most flowers in order to reach the nectar. In the process the insect usually becomes dusted with pollen, so that nectar contributes directly to the cross-pollination of flowers. *See* Pollination.

While the nectaries of most flowers are simple glands for secreting nectar, and are usually near the base of the flower, they are often elaborately contrived. In the common toadflax and columbine the nectaries are borne in the ends of the spurs. In the grape they are distinctly swollen receptacles between the base of the stamens, while in the buttercup the nectaries form scales on the petals. Most remarkable of all are the nectaries of orchids, some of which are very beautifully concealed.

A special form of nectary, not borne in the flower, is often found on leafstalks or near the base of them. Such nectar as is secreted by these glands is apparently of no value in ensuring cross-pollination by insects. But in certain tropical trees this non-floral nectar often attracts ants, which actively repel leaf-eating insects. The latter might defoliate the tree if this helpful association of ants and nectar were not in operation.

NECTARINE. A smooth-skinned, hairless peach. Known for over 2000 years, nectarines are also well known in the U.S., and much grown in Calif. Their culture is the same as for the peach (which see). While there are no constant differences, except lack of a fuzzy coat, between the nectarine and peach, the flavor of the former is thought by some to be richer and sweeter than that of the peach. Nectarines, like peaches, have clingstone and freestone° varieties.

The origin and repeated reappearance of nectarines on peach trees and peaches on nectarine trees is one of the most interesting phenomena known in the fruit world. It occurs everywhere, often in the absence of the other tree, and is not due to cross-pollination. Darwin, who studied the problem for years, came to the conclusion that it was caused by bud mutations, or, as some call them, bud-sports. No competent plant breeder or pomologist is willing to hazard even a guess as to the cause of these bud mutations. Much nonsense has been written about them, but the fact remains that their occurrence remains essentially unexplained.

Nectarines, on the whole, do better west of the Rocky Mountains than east of them. The only varieties likely to be met are: Hunter, Kentucky, Red Roman, Sure Crop, and Quetta (sometimes known as Persian). The latter was introduced by the U.S. Department of Agriculture.

NEEDLE CAST. A fungus disease of conifers, not to be confused with common wind burn.° When a fungus infection occurs, a small area near the base of the needle turns brown. Later, the entire needle from the infected point outward will die. In the case of scorch° or wind burn, the needles gradually turn brown, starting at the outer tip.

NEEDLE PALM = *Rhapidophyllum hystrix.*

neglecta, -us, -um (neg-lek'ta). Neglected; often used as a specific name for a garden plant of negligible value.

NEGLECTED ORCHARDS. If long neglected, weedy, ridden by pests, and with pretty old trees in them, most orchards do not pay for renovation. It is quite another matter, however, to try to reinvigorate a favorite tree or even a few of them.

Study the cultural articles on all the leading fruits, especially, of course, the particular one on your own tree. Get rid of weeds, trim out all dead or diseased wood, and then prune according to the directions given at your particular fruit. Top-dress with a good layer of well-rotted manure, and keep up a steady program of spraying for insects and disease.

These operations are all relatively expensive, and with the quick-bearing, small trees of the modern nurseryman so cheap, the renovation is by no means a profitable operation. For old apple-tree renovation *see* APPLE.

Negundo (nee-gun'do). Specific name for the box-elder (*Acer Negundo*) which was once thought to belong to a genus called *Negundo*. See MAPLE.

NEILLIA (nee'li-a). Asiatic, spirea-like shrubs of the rose family, 3 of the 10 known species grown for ornament. They have alternate,° simple leaves, usually lobed, and doubly toothed. Flowers small, but showy, as the cluster (raceme° or panicle°) is often very handsome. Calyx° bell-shaped to tubular, its 5 lobes erect. Petals 5, white or pink. Stamens° 10–30, in 1–3 series. Fruit a small, dry pod, enclosed by the persistent calyx. (Named for Patrick Neill, Scotch botanist.)

These attractive little shrubs are of easy cult. in a variety of soils, and have proved hardy in many regions of long winters and bitter winds. They may be propagated by cuttings of green wood under glass, or by seeds.

sinensis. Not over 6 ft. high, usually about half this. Leaves ovalish or oblong, 1¾–3½ in. long, more or less lobed. Flowers pinkish, nodding, about ¾ in. long, the cluster (raceme°) about 2 in. long. China. May–June. Hardy from zone° 2 southward.

thibetica. Not usually over 5 ft. high, often less. Leaves ovalish, but long-tapering at the tip, 2–3½ in. long, sparingly lobed. Flowers pink, short-stalked, about ¾ in. long, the cluster (raceme°) nearly 3 in. long. China. Hardy from zone° 3, perhaps from zone° 2, southward.

thyrsiflora. Not usually over 4 ft. high, occasionally up to 6 ft. Leaves ovalish, 3-lobed, 1¾–4½ in. long. Flowers white, short-stalked, the cluster terminal, branched, nearly 3 in. long. Himalayas. Aug.–Sept. Hardy from zone° 3 southward.

NELUMBIUM = *Nelumbo.*

NELUMBO (nee-lum'bo). Lotus. A genus of 2 species of strong-growing water plants of the family Nymphaeaceae, one a native to N.A., the other to the Orient. They are chiefly distinguished by their large leaves, growing from 3–6 ft. above the water, the flowers growing even higher than the leaves, sometimes as much as 5 ft. above the water. Flowers at the top of strong, leafless stalks, showy, solitary, cup-shaped, 5–10 in. across, with many petals, closing at night. Fruit a large capsule° with a flat top which when ripe has many openings like a pepper-pot through which the seeds are dispersed. (*Nelumbo* is the old Ceylonese name for the second species.)

They are of easy cultivation, and very attractive for shallow pools in formal gardens, but plenty of space must be allowed for their strong-growing rootstocks. Propagation by division of the rootstocks in May. Plant in shallow tubs, boxes or baskets, in a mixture of turfy loam and cow manure, 2 in. deep, covering the top of the containers with ½ in. clean sand to keep the water clean. Place in water so that the tops of the containers are 8 in. below surface. The water should be in the pool several days before planting, as the plants will fail to grow if water is too cold. After growth commences water may be added a further 6 in. The pool should be in bright sun-

---

° Special articles on the subjects indicated by an asterisk (°) will be found at the words so marked.

light. In Oct. the Oriental variety, which is tender, should have the water drained off and containers, for convenience, gathered together in one part of the pool. Cover them completely with 3 ft. of salt hay or strawy manure, where they can safely be left until the following spring. Where only 1 or 2 plants are in question they can be lifted from the pool and stored in a frostproof place, in which case they must not be allowed to become dry. If the water is deep enough to prevent the rootstocks from freezing, the East Indian lotus can be left out all winter.

lutea. American lotus or water chinquapin. Leaves usually 1–2 ft. above water surface, cupshaped, 1–2 ft. wide. Flowers pale yellow, 1–2 ft. above the surface, 8–10 in. across. Suitable for natural ponds where water is deep enough to prevent freezing of rootstocks in mud during the winter. Eastern N.A. Formerly called *Nelumbium pentaphyllum.*

nelumbo = *N. nucifera.*

nucifera. East Indian lotus, or more commonly called the Egyptian lotus, although not native there. Rootstock long and jointed, with small, scale-like leaves. The true leaves, growing 3–6 ft. above the water, are large and round, the leafstalk being joined to the middle of under side, slightly grayish in color due to a waxy covering. Flowers, which grow higher than the leaves, are 4–10 in. across, pink or rose, and sweet-scented. Petals many, usually in 2 rings. Many varieties in cultivation, varying in color from white to red. The *var.* **pygmaea** is a dwarf form, rosy-pink in color, very suitable for smaller pools. Southern As. to Aust.

NEMATODES (Eelworms). Of the plant-feeders, almost all are microscopic in size. Some produce root or plant galls that are easily visible. Many plant ailments previously diagnosed as poor soils, incorrect nutrition, and a dozen other conditions are caused by nematodes.

Nematode damage is usually characterized by a poor root system. Galls may be produced, as in root-knot, which are fleshy swellings of the root actually containing one or more greatly distended female nematodes whose bodies contain hundreds of eggs. Later, these eggs hatch into young larvae which move elsewhere and reproduce the cycle. Other species either enter the roots entirely and destroy cells or feed from the outside, causing lesions which may be invaded by root-destroying bacteria or fungi. In addition to the root-knot galls, symptoms are reddened lesions on roots, stubby roots, superfluous root-branching, swollen root tips, rotting bulbs, and twisted growth of stems. In any area, damage varies greatly and apparently healthy plants stand next to stunted, unthrifty ones.

Except for root-knot, absolute identification of nematode damage depends on examination of roots under a microscope by skilled technicians. If nematodes are suspected, there is little that can be done to effectively correct the condition on growing plants.

A new class of pesticides known as nematocides is being developed. At present, the temporary soil sterilants such as ethylene dibromide (EDB), dichloropropenes (D-D, Telone and others), Vapam, and methyl bromide are most used. (See FUMIGATION.) These materials are all very plant-toxic and are best used as preplanting soil treatments in fall or early spring on fallow ground. Small packages are available and, if used exactly as recommended on the label, will control nematodes sufficiently to allow for one season's crop. These materials are all toxic to man and must be handled with care. Treatment of certain plants with Nemagon (Fumazone) and VC-13 as soil drenches has produced good results. This type of treatment is in the development stage and no general recommendations can be made at this time. For control of stem and foliar nematodes, use of malathion (*see* SPRAYS AND DUSTS) at double concentration on a regular schedule will give reasonable results.

At present, best advice to gardeners who want to avoid nematodes and their accompanying problems is this:

1. Start with clean plants. If you grow your own from seed, use a sterile medium for starting. Insist on clean plants from your supplier.

2. Do not plant in known infested soils. Fallowing of soils and either submerging or complete drying out will greatly reduce the problem with many species.

3. Water and fertilize plants well. Most infestations can be counteracted by good care.

4. An excellent Farmers' Bulletin of the U.S. Department of Agriculture on the use of the conventional nematode-control materials can be obtained from your county agricultural agent or your state agricultural college. — L. G. M.

NEMESIA (ne-mee'she-a). Tender African annual or perennial herbs or sub-shrubs, comprising 50 species, belonging to the family Scrophulariaceae. The annuals are the only ones of garden interest. Stem square, and grooved. Leaves simple,* lance-shaped, not stalked, in alternating pairs, becoming smaller toward the top. Flowers in terminal clusters. Corolla short and tubular, the expanded limb wide, flat, and 2-lipped, the base of the lower lip forming a small spur, the upper being cut into 4 segments. Colors yellow, brown, crimson, pink, blue, white, often showing 2 colors in one flower. (*Nemesia* was used by Dioscorides for some kind of snapdragon.)

Nemesia makes a very dainty garden plant, especially if planted in masses. It is easily propagated from seed sown in boxes of sandy loam in a cool greenhouse or cold frame in Feb. or early Mar. for flowering in June, July, or Aug. When planting out allow 8 in. between plants. It is essential for them to have an early start so as to make as much growth as possible before

---

* Special articles on the subjects indicated by an asterisk (*) will be found at the words so marked.

summer heat. They are often grown as greenhouse plants. Seeds should be sown the end of Aug. and grown in a cool greenhouse. They will make good pot plants for Feb. and Mar. flowering. They are much improved by pinching. *See* Pinching at TRAINING PLANTS.

strumosa. Grows to a height of 2 ft. Leaves 2–3 in. long. Flowers white, yellow, or purple, deeply marked on the outside. The *var.* **suttoni** is much superior, having larger flowers and a better range of colors, which come very true from seed. *See* BLUE GARDEN.

NEMOPANTHUS (nee-mo-panth′us). A single species of not particularly handsome shrubs of the holly family, much more attractive in fruit than in flower. The only species is **N. mucronatus,** the mountain holly or prick-timber, which is wild in the forests of eastern N.A. It is scarcely over 6–8 ft. high, with alternate,° short-stalked, elliptic leaves, ¾–1¾ in. long. Flowers small, inconspicuous, greenish-white, mostly unisexual,° with mostly 5 sepals and 5 petals. Fruit a dull red drupe° about ¼ in. in diameter. The shrub prefers cool, moist woods and should not be planted in dry, open places. Its foliage turns yellow in autumn. Hardy from zone° 2 southward. (*Nemopanthus* is from the Greek for thread and flower, in allusion to the slender flower stalks.)

NEMOPHILA (nem-off′i-la). A North American genus, comprising 18 species of annual herbs of the family Hydrophyllaceae, a few of much garden interest. Some are climbing, while others are dwarf or trailing plants. All are hairy. Leaves usually much cut, alternate° or opposite.° Flowers showy, growing at the tips of the branches in clusters. Corolla bell-shaped,

blue, white, purple, or spotted. Calyx of 5 spreading sepals° with additional leafy growths alternating, the latter increasing in size when fruiting. Fruit a dry capsule.° (*Nemophila* is from the Greek for grove, and love, in allusion to the plants growing in a shady place.)

Propagation is by seeds sown in ordinary garden soil in early spring in masses where intended to bloom. Position must be partly shady.

aurita. Fiesta-flower. Of scrambling habit, climbing by means of prickles on the stems to a height of 3–6 ft. Leafstalks embracing the stem. Leaves deeply cut. Flowers 1 in. wide, violet, lighter on the outside. In low, shady grounds, Sacramento Valley to San Diego, Calif. Also known as *Pholistoma aurita.*

insignis = *N. menziesi.*

maculata. Five-spot. Grows to a height of 6 in. Leaves lyre-shaped, cut into 5–9 segments, blunt at the tip. Flowers bell-shaped, white, with a purple spot at the base of each petal. Western and central Calif.

menziesi. Baby blue-eyes. Grows to a height of 6 in. Leaves cut into 7–9 segments. Flowers bell-shaped, bright, clear blue, ½–1 in. across. There are white, and also blue and white forms. A garden favorite. Calif. *See* ROCK GARDEN.

nemoralis, -e (nem-o-ray′lis). In groves or woods.

nemorosa, -us, -um (nem-o-rō′sa). Growing in shady woods.

NEOMAMMILLARIA (nee-o-mam-mill-ā′-ri-a) = *Mammillaria.*

NEOMARICA (ne-o-maa′ri-ka). A genus of perhaps a dozen species of showy, tropical, iris-like herbs (family Iridaceae), one of them an old favorite as a house plant. They have fan-like clusters of leaves, and iris-like, fugitive flowers borne on a long, leafy, winged stalk. Fruit a capsule. (*Neomarica* is from *neo,* new, and *Marica,* an old name for these plants.)

Marica has for long been the Latin name for these plants but is now abandoned for technical reasons. There seems to be no authentic common or vernacular name for them, in spite of their long cult. as house plants. Perhaps because of this various names have been manufactured for them such as "apostleflowers," "twelve apostles," "false flag," "walking iris," etc. The species below are not hardy outdoors except in zones° 8 and 9. Their indoor cult. is easy. Use potting mixture° 3 and give them plenty of water as they approach blooming. Propagated by division of their rhizomes.°

gracilis. Not over 18 in. high, the leaves about 1 in. wide. Flowers nearly 2 in. wide, with inner, small, blue segments, and larger outer white ones with brown and yellow markings. Brazil.

northiana. The most common cult. species and larger than the one above. Flowers nearly 4 in. wide, fragrant, the outer segments white, the inner violet, both variegated at the base. Brazil.

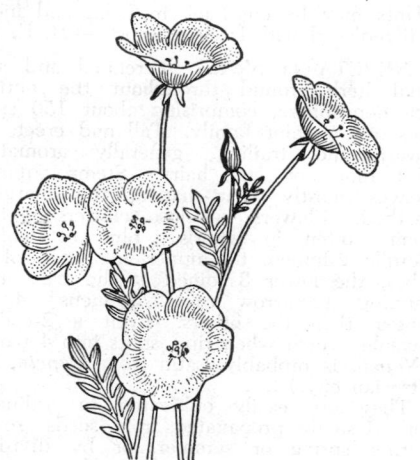

Baby Blue-eyes (*Nemophila menziesi*). Fine Californian annual, preferably for partly shady sites, with a profusion of blue (rarely white) flowers in midsummer.

° Special articles on the subjects indicated by an asterisk (°) will be found at the words so marked.

neo-mexicana, -us, -um (ne-o-mecks-i-kay'-na). From New Mexico.

NEOWASHINGTONIA = *Washingtonia.*

nepalensis, -e (ne-pal-en'sis). From Nepal.

NEPENTHACEAE. *See* NEPENTHES.

NEPENTHES (ne-pen'theez). Pitcher-plant. Climbing, often tree-perching, or bog herbs, sometimes a little woody at the base, and the only genus of the family **Nepenthaceae** (ne-pen-thay'see-ee). Chiefly East Indian, but extending into Madagascar, these Old World pitcher-plants are among the showiest of all insectivorous plants, useful only in the greenhouse, as indicated below. Leaves alternate,* usually longish, but prolonged at the tip into a long tendril* which is terminated by a hollow, pitcher-like, winged structure with a thickened rim, a lid, and, on the inside of the pitcher, several honey glands. Usually the pitchers are suspended (upright) at the end of the long tendril,* and the bottom of the pitcher contains water into which an insect slips and is drowned. *See* INSECTIVOROUS PLANTS. Flowers inconspicuous, the male and female on different plants, without petals, and 3–4 sepals. Male flowers with 4–16 united stamens.* Fruit a leathery capsule,* the seeds tailed. (*Nepenthes* is from the Greek for removing all sorrow, whether because of the often beautifully colored pitchers, or in allusion to assumed narcotic properties is uncertain.)

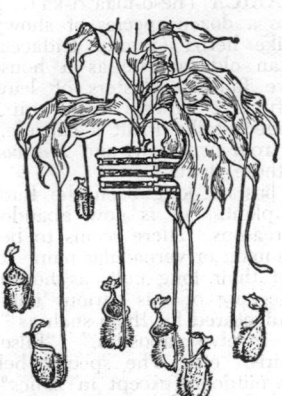

Nepenthes in an orchid basket

The species below are often replaced by named hybrid forms, of which scores were offered when there was a craze for growing these interesting and often beautifully colored plants. Some of these hybrids are also included. Now they are chiefly confined to the larger greenhouse collections, although florists occasionally display them in their windows. For culture *see* below.

domini. A hybrid; the pitchers beautifully mottled with green and purple, the wings fringed.

hookeriana. Pitchers nearly 6 in. long and 3 in. in diameter, green, but purple-marked, their wings broad and double-fringed, or sometimes unfringed. Borneo.

mastersiana. A hybrid; pitchers dark crimson, or greenish-crimson, often purple-spotted, their wings small, sometimes fringed.

phyllamphora. Pitchers nearly 6 in. long, about 1½ in. in diameter, reddish-green or red, their wings narrow and cord-like. East Indies and southern China. Also called *N. mirabilis.*

veitchi. Pitchers almost 8 in. long and 3 in. in diameter, hairy, yellowish-green to reddish, their wings fringed. Borneo.

CULTURE OF NEPENTHES

Nepenthes are grown from seeds or cuttings, requiring at all times heat, moisture, and shade. The hybrids developed in cultivation are generally showier and easier to grow. Seeds germinate in a month or less if sown on the moist surface of fine sphagnum and peat, under a bell-jar in a temperature of 80°–85°. Mature shoot cuttings root readily early in the year, if stuck through empty inverted pots over sphagnum or fiber in a close, moist case, with bottom-heat of 80°. When rooted, pot in equal parts peat-fiber and sphagnum, with a dash of fine charcoal and sharp sand, replacing in the case, for a few days, to encourage a good start. Later, they grow best in orchid baskets suspended from a hothouse roof in a minimum temperature of 65°–70°, using similar compost as before, only coarser.

Syringe daily and water freely when actively growing. Removing the growing point after several leaves have formed gives finer pitchers. Flowering is prevented unless seed is required. Leggy* plants may be cut back in Feb., and inert soil replaced with fresh compost. — H. E. D.

NEPETA (nep'e-ta). Perennial and annual herbs found throughout the northern hemisphere, comprising about 150 species of the mint family. Tall and erect, or dwarf and trailing, generally aromatic, and more or less hairy. Stems square. Leaves mostly heart-shaped, the margins toothed. Flowers in close clusters on the stems, often in whorls,* blue or white. Corolla 2-lipped, the upper composed of 2 lobes, the lower 3 joined at the base and forming a narrow tube. Stamens* 4, 2 longer than the others. Fruit a 2-celled capsule, which when ripe, splits into 4 parts. (*Nepeta* is probably Latin from *Nepete,* an Etrurian city.)

They are easily cultivated in ordinary soil. Usually propagated from seeds, sown during spring or summer, or by division of roots, but sometimes from the runners which creep along the ground.

Cataria. Commonly known as catnip or catmint, owing to its attraction for cats. Perennial, with sturdy, straight stems, growing 2–3

---

* Special articles on the subjects indicated by an asterisk (*) will be found at the words so marked.

ft. high. Leaves grayish-green, heart-shaped, hairy. Flowers white or lilac, ¼ in. long, produced in several clusters toward the tip of the branches. Eurasia, but naturalized in N.A. For another plant attractive to cats, *see* AC-TINIDIA POLYGAMA.

Glecoma = *Glecoma hederacea.*

hederacea = *Glecoma hederacea.*

macrantha = *Dracocephalum sibiricum.*

mussini. A perennial growing to 2 ft., covered with tough, whitish hairs, giving the whole plant a light-gray appearance. Branches many. Leaves lance-shaped, 1–2 in. long, slightly wrinkled. Flowers blue, with dark spots, ½ in. long, in loose clusters forming a long raceme.* A great garden favorite used either as a border or rock plant, or for bedding (which see). Caucasus. Persia. Also liked by cats.

nuda. A perennial, growing to 4 ft. high. Leaves lance-shaped, 2 in. long, light green. Flowers in clusters, white, spotted purple, about ½ in. long. Southern Eu.

ucranica. A perennial growing to 2 ft. high, slightly hairy. Leaves lance-shaped. Flowers blue, small, inconspicuous, in loose clusters. Eastern Eu. and western As.

NEPHROLEPIS (nee-froll'e-pis *or* nephro-lee'pis). Sword fern. An extremely important genus of ferns of the family Polypodiaceae, all tropical or sub-tropical. Only a few of its 35 known species are grown for ornament, one of them having given rise to the Boston fern, easily and deservedly the most popular house fern in the U.S. They grow in the ground, or some are tree-perching (epiphytes*), and have long, not always compound, fronds, which are variously cut, mostly feather-fashion, into many segments. In some forms of the Boston fern the fronds have become extremely fine and feathery. Spore cases on the upper forks of the veins, on the lower side of the segments, more or less kidney-shaped. (*Nephrolepis* is from the Greek for kidney and scale, in allusion to the shape of the spore cases.)

For culture (except the Boston fern) *see* Greenhouse Ferns at FERNS AND FERN GARDENING.

The Boston fern (*Nephrolepis exaltata bostoniensis*) originated, by chance, in a lot of plants of *Nephrolepis exaltata* sent from Philadelphia to Boston about 1894. One of the shipment had more gracefully drooping, somewhat broader fronds, and it grew faster than the common *N. exaltata.* Subsequently it was given the varietal name *bostoniensis,* has been grown by the million, traveled to every country in the world, and is the best of all house ferns. This is partly due to the fact that it endures house conditions better than most ferns, to its fairly quick growth, and also because even with some neglect it will ultimately grow into an immense, bushy fern. If grown on a pedestal, its fronds will often become several feet long (in some varieties).

While the Boston fern will endure house conditions, it responds to decent treatment like any other fern. As it gets larger, repot in potting mixture* 4. During the sum-

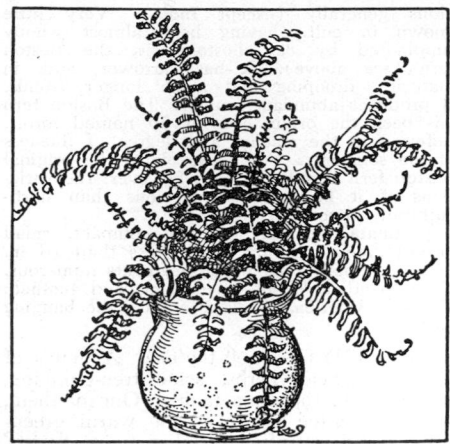

The Boston fern was a chance sport (mutation) originating in Philadelphia.

mer put the plant outdoors, preferably plunged* if the fronds are not too long, or at any rate in the shade.

Because it is a quick-growing, active plant, it needs plenty of water. If possible, plunge the pot in a pail of water whenever the plant gets anywhere near dry. If you cannot tell how dry it is, because the pot is crammed with roots and frond bases, tap the pot smartly with the knuckles. If it gives off a sharp, ringing sound, the plant needs water. If, on the other hand, the tap sounds dead or sodden, there is pretty sure to be enough soil moisture for the present. It will grow in ordinary room temperatures, but it will not stand frost. On many days, if outdoor temperature is above 45°, it can profitably be put outdoors during a rainy day.

While scores of varieties of the Boston fern have been developed since 1900, the most popular is still the common sort, and it appears to be the best for house conditions.

The species of fern are:

acuminata. Fronds nearly 3 ft. long and a third as wide, drooping, the segments narrowly lance-shaped and coarsely toothed. The plant produces many runners. Malaya.

biserrata. Fronds 2–4 ft. long, 6–10 in. wide, the segments thick, the frond stalk scurfy. Segments rather distant. 2–6 in. long, the margins faintly round-toothed, and eared at one side of the base. Malaya. The *var.* **furcans** has the segments forked.

cordifolia. Tuber fern. An erect fern, the rootstocks bearing tubers. Fronds about 24 in. long and 2½ in. wide. Segments about 1½ in. long, numerous or crowded, bright green and sharply toothed. Tropics. There are several varieties in cult., especially a low, compact one, and another with plumy fronds. Some are variegated.

exaltata. Sword fern. Fronds stiff and erect, 3–5 ft. long and nearly 6 in. wide. Segments numerous, close together, 2–3 in. long, obscurely toothed or without teeth. Tropical re-

---

* Special articles on the subjects indicated by an asterisk (*) will be found at the words so marked.

gions generally (except India). Very little known in cult., having been almost wholly supplanted by *var.* **bostoniensis**, the Boston fern (*see* above). It has narrower, and, in maturity, drooping and much longer fronds. It produces abundant runners. The Boston fern has been the origin of over 50 named forms, differing in the amount and degree of fineness of the segments. For house plants the original Boston fern is still the best, however, the variations of it being more ingenious than horticulturally important.

pectinata. Basket fern. A compact, small grayish-green fern, the fronds less than 18 in. long and about 1 in. wide. Segments numerous, close together, about ½ in. long and toothed. Tropical America. A good fern for the hanging basket.

NEPHTHYTIS (neff-thy′tis). A genus of tropical African herbs, some tree-climbing, belonging to the arum family. One of them, N. **afzeli,** often grown in the warm greenhouse, and is often displayed in florists' windows. It has creeping rhizomes,° halberd-shaped leaves (variegated in a hort. form) on long leafstalks. Spathe° green. (*Nephthytis* is from the Egyptian *Nephthya,* a mythological character.) Under the incorrect name of *Nephthytis,* many dealers offer the Chinese evergreen, which belongs to the related genus *Aglaonema* (which see for the Chinese evergreen).

neriifola, -us, -um (neer-ee-i-fō′lĭ-a). With leaves like the oleander (*Nerium*). It is sometimes spelled *nereifolia.*

NERINE (ne-ry′ne). A genus of South African bulbous herbs of the family Amaryllidaceae, two of the 18 known species cult. for their handsome fall and early-winter bloom. Leaves all basal, strap-shaped. Flowers funnel-shaped, in a close terminal cluster (umbel°) on a solid stalk. Corolla with practically no tube, its segments scarcely separable as to petals or sepals, red, often crisped on the margins. Stamens° 6, sometimes protruding, but 3 shorter than the others. Fruit a 3-valved capsule.° (Named after the nereids, or perhaps for one of them, the daughter of Nerius.)

These are best grown, in the North, in pots in the cool greenhouse, where they flower in the late fall, or they may be forced almost any time if the bulbs have been rested for four or five months before planting. Bulbs started in Oct. will bloom at Christmas, if given plenty of water. Use potting mixture° 3. When the plant is through blooming, after which the leaves develop, the water should gradually be reduced, and stopped altogether when the bulbs are resting. During the resting period, the time for which is indicated by the yellowing of the leaves, the pots should be turned on their sides, in the sun, and left there without water until the plants are to be started into growth. In Calif. and similar climates they may be grown outdoors, but from about May to Aug. the bulbs are better lifted and stored in a cool, dry place, and planted again in Sept.

curvifolia. Flowers scarlet, the petals not much crisped. Stamens° scarcely protruding. Leaves (appearing after the bloom) usually 6, about 12 in. long, curved and thick. Not so much grown as the *var.* **fothergili,** which is the best of the nerines for forcing. It is a more robust plant than the type and the cluster bears more flowers.

fothergilli = *Nerine curvifolia fothergilli.*

sarniensis. Guernsey lily (not native there, but grown there after its importation from South Africa). Flowers crimson, about 10 in the cluster. Corolla about 1½ in. long, its segments somewhat crisped, the stamens° protruding. Leaves (appearing after the bloom) about 12 in. long, ¾ in. wide, not curved. There are several varieties, mostly slight variants as to flower color, which ranges from rose-pink to deeper scarlet.

NERIUM. *See* OLEANDER.

NERO'S-CROWN = *Tabernaemontana coronaria.*

NERTERA (ner′ter-ra). Tender, creeping, perennial herbs of the family Rubiaceae, comprising 6 species. Native of the Andes, N.Z., Aust., Hawaii, and Malaya. They have opposite leaves, small axillary flowers and a red berry. (*Nertera* is from the Greek for lowly, in allusion to the habit.)

The only cult. species is propagated by seeds, or by division of the rootstocks. Sow seeds in spring in the greenhouse or cold frame. Plant out in June in cool, shady spots in rich, sandy soil, or grow as a pot plant for greenhouse decoration or house plant. It is used as a ground cover in Calif., if the ground is moist and shady.

granadensis. Bead-plant. Grows to a height of 6–10 in. Stems square. Leaves short-stalked, small, ⅛ in. long, ovalish, leathery. Flowers solitary, inconspicuous, and greenish. Fruit a showy, orange-colored, transparent berry the size of a pea, which persists for months. Tasmania, N. Z., and S. A. Formerly called *N. depressa.*

nervosa, -us, -um (ner-vō′sa). Nerved or veined.

NETTLE. Stinging herbs of no interest to to the gardener, except to uproot them (with gloves on). Those below belong to the genus **Urtica** (ur′ti-ka; ur-ty′ka) of the family Urticaceae. There are over 50 species of nettles, mostly annual or perennial herbs with opposite, stalked, usually toothed leaves, covered, sometimes not very obviously so, with stinging hairs. Flowers small, without petals, greenish, in loose or head-like clusters, the male and female separate, sometimes on different plants. Fruit dry (an achene°), enclosed by the persistent sepals. (*Urtica* is the Latin name of the nettles and is from *urere,* to burn.)

U. dioica. Stinging or great nettle. A very bristly and stinging herb, 15–30 in. high. Leaves ovalish or heart-shaped, deeply toothed, often nearly 5 in. long and 3 in. wide. Flower cluster forked. Eurasia; naturalized in N.A. The thrifty Scotch use the young foliage like spinach.

U. pilulifera. Roman nettle. An annual herb, 1–2 ft. high. Leaves ovalish or heart-

---

° Special articles on the subjects indicated by an asterisk (°) will be found at the words so marked.

shaped, 1–3 in. long. Male flower clusters branched, the female in close heads. Southern Eu.

NETTLE FAMILY = Urticaceae.

NETTLE TREE = *Celtis occidentalis.* See HACKBERRY.

NEUTRAL. A soil term applied to those soils which are neither acid nor alkaline. *See* ACID AND ALKALI SOILS.

NEVADA. Sagebrush is the state flower. The state lies wholly in zones* 3, 4, 5, and 6, which, because of the mountains, turn sharply northward, instead of running east and west as in most of the country.

SOILS. The soils in Nevada are variable. In the western valleys, along the east side of the Sierra Nevada range, the soils are generally composed of decomposed granite and other igneous rocks. They have a fair supply of organic matter and are, on the whole, relatively free from alkali. Soils suitable for gardening are usually readily found.

The soils in the central valleys farther to the east are generally more alkaline, heavier in texture, and lower in organic matter. Here greater care must be exercised in selecting a site for a garden. Farther east toward the headwaters of the Humboldt River the soils, while variable, improve in quality.

The soils of the southern half of the state are nearly always of limestone origin, and are apt to contain harmful amounts of alkali in their native condition. They are normally low in organic matter. Garden soils in this area must be selected with extreme care.

CHIEF GARDENING CENTERS. Reno and Las Vegas are the chief gardening centers. Here hardy vegetables and fruits, including potatoes, tomatoes, peas, beans, sweet corn, squash, carrots, onions, and other common garden vegetables, are grown in great variety for the local market.

Fallon, in the lower Carson Valley, is a center for the growing of cantaloupes. The Mason Valley is noted for its potatoes.

The Moapa Valley in the extreme south has a mild climate and is noted for its early spring vegetables and its summer melons. The vegetables include asparagus, radish, lettuce, spinach, carrots, and green onions. Cantaloupes and watermelons are marketed in July. Many millions of tomato plants are grown for shipment to Utah.

A little farther north the Pahranagat Valley is important as a general gardening area, growing a wide range of vegetables similar to those of the Reno area. The climate is milder than that of Reno and the growing season is longer.

FLOWERS AND SHRUBS. Roses are perhaps the most universally grown of all flowers. They do well nearly everywhere in the state. The tall-bearded iris is also widely grown and thrives in most localities. Many bulbs adapted to a short growing season,

such as narcissus, hyacinths, tulips, and gladioli, are quite satisfactory. The dahlia does well in certain areas, but is not suitable for general use over the state. Most of the short-season annuals can be grown any place in the state where the soil is suitable.

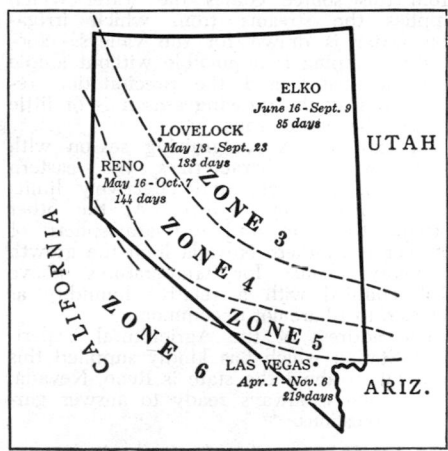

NEVADA

The zones of hardiness crossing Nevada are those shown on the map located at ZONE, which should be consulted for details. The dates are the average latest killing frost in spring and the first one in the fall. The figures below the dates show the average length of the growing season. For rainfall *see* text.

In the extreme south, stocks, larkspur, and snapdragon are favorites.

In the western valleys there is some English ivy; the Virginia creeper is a common vine, growing extremely well. Hops, morning-glory, perennial pea, and, to some extent, sweet peas, are commonly used for climbing vines in the colder zones. Virginia creeper is used to some extent in the extreme South, though the Boston ivy is better. Wild grapes and certain European grapes, as Thompson's seedless and Muscat, are grown in arbors in this area. Oregon grape and *Pyracantha* are grown as ornamentals.

The rainfall over the state is scant, averaging about 9 inches per year. In the

FROST DATES

Town	Average date of last killing frost in spring	Latest-known killing frost	Average date of earliest killing frost in fall	Earliest-known killing frost
Reno	May 16	June 13	Oct. 7	Sept. 13
Lovelock	May 13	July 14	Sept. 23	Aug. 7
Elko	June 16	May 12	Sept. 9	Oct. 4
Las Vegas	April 1		Nov. 6	

* Special articles on the subjects indicated by an asterisk (*) will be found at the words so marked.

valleys where the crops are grown, the rainfall is only about half the average for the state as a whole, and in the extreme south it is still less, averaging about 3½ inches per year at Las Vegas. The heaviest storms are normally received during the winter when deep snows are deposited on the mountains. From this source comes the water which supplies the streams from which irrigation water is drawn for the valleys. Successful cropping is impossible without ample irrigation water, and the precipitation received during the growing season is of little practical benefit to crops.

An extremely short growing season with severe winters characterizes the eastern portion of the state and effectively limits the types of crops grown. At the other extreme the heat and dry atmosphere of summer in southern Nevada limit the growth of many plants; for temperatures above 115° coupled with a relative humidity as low as 8 to 10 are not uncommon.

The address of the Agricultural Experiment Station which has kindly supplied this information about the state is Reno, Nevada. The station is always ready to answer gardening questions.

NEVIUSIA (nev-ĭ-ous′ĭ-a). A single species of shrubs of the rose family, N. alabamensis, the snow wreath, confined to Ala. but hardy up to zone* 3, and sometimes cult. for its white, feathery masses of flowers which bloom in June–July. It is an alternate*-leaved shrub, 3–5 ft. high, with ovalish or oblong, doubly-toothed leaves 1–3 in. long. Flowers without petals, the beautiful white color due to the many stamens,* the flowers nearly 1 in. wide, usually in clusters of 3–8. Fruit a collection of somewhat fleshy achenes.* Toward the upper part of zone* 3 it may need winter protection. (Named for R. D. Nevius, its discoverer.)

NEW BRUNSWICK. For the gardening possibilities in New Brunswick, *see* the articles on the nearly similar regions, at Nova Scotia and Maine.

NEW ENGLAND ASTER = *Aster novae-angliae.*

NEW HAMPSHIRE. The lilac is the state flower, and the state lies wholly in zones* 2 and 3. The important horticultural crops are apples, blueberries, potatoes, vegetables, and specialty crops. Apple production is mostly in the southern half of the state. McIntosh, Red Delicious, and Cortland are the principal varieties grown, McIntosh being the leading one. This variety grows to perfection in New Hampshire, taking on a color and finish that cannot be obtained in the more southerly apple regions. The low-bush blueberry is second in importance in fruit production. They are grown on the hilltops and hillsides in the areas south of Lake Winnepesaukee and in the Temple Mountain and Mt. Monadnock region. Small fruits such as straw-

berries and raspberries are grown only for home use and roadside sales.

Vegetable production is mostly in the Merrimack Valley and near the larger cities in the state. Squash, sweet corn, and cucumbers are the principal crops. Hubbard and butternut squash are the popular varieties and produce high yield. Cucumbers are grown largely for pickles. Other vegetables grown in considerable quantity are cabbage, snap beans, shell beans, celery, peas, carrots, beets, and tomatoes.

The home garden has a real place in the family living. Conditions are favorable for the production of the vegetables mentioned and only a small area is required to supply the vegetable needs of a family. Plant-breeding at the University of New Hampshire has developed a number of vegetables that are adapted to the short growing season, among them Chatham and Victor tomatoes, Black Beauty eggplant, Baby Blue Hubbard squash, Bush Butternut squash, New Hampshire Midget watermelon, and Granite State muskmelon.

Potatoes are grown in all sections of the state, but the culture of this crop finds its highest development in northern New Hampshire in Coos County. In this region potatoes are usually planted about June 1. The first killing frost often occurs as early as Sept. 1–10 thus making potatoes a 90- to 100-day crop. The rich soil and cool climate, together with the use of green-manure crops and a liberal application of high-analysis commercial fertilizers, make it possible to produce yields of 400 to 500 bushels per acre. The high yield in the 300-bushel Potato Club for 1957 was 734 bushels per acre.

It has been shown experimentally that certified potatoes (potatoes free from virus diseases) outyield home-grown potatoes for seed by many bushels. Since it is almost necessary to grow certified potatoes for seed in 100 days or less the northern New Hampshire country provides ideal conditions for the production of this crop. Specialty crops also represent an important part of horticulture in New Hampshire.

As for flowers, quality again is the important factor, rather than quantity. Certain flowers, like asters, gladiolus, and roses, are shipped to the New York markets and command a premium price because of the intensity and the freshness of the flower color. The glare of the sun is tempered by the relatively high humidity of the atmosphere, thus preventing the burning out or fading of the more delicate shades.

Large numbers of summer residents are attracted to the state by its mountains, lakes, and seashore. Many of them have built estates of considerable size, and the landscaping of these and many of the summer hotels and golf clubs is extremely attractive.

The average date of the last killing frost in the spring is May 11 for the southern part of the state, and June 1 in the

* Special articles on the subjects indicated by an asterisk (*) will be found at the words so marked.

extreme north. In the autumn the first killing frost may be expected about Sept. 5 in the extreme north and about Oct. 1 in the vicinity of Concord. All figures, of course, are much changed at elevations along the Presidential Range, where the frost-free period is sometimes not over 60 days. Rainfall is adequate over all the state, averaging 40–45 in. per year.

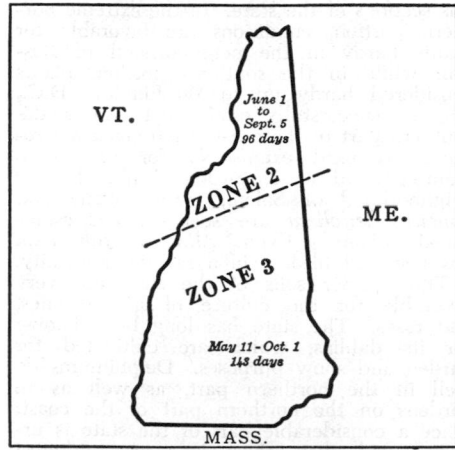

NEW HAMPSHIRE

The zones of hardiness crossing New Hampshire are those shown on the map located at ZONE, which should be consulted for details. The dates are the average latest killing frost in spring and the first one in the fall. The figures below the dates show the average length of the growing season.

The address of the Agricultural Experiment Station which has kindly supplied this information about the state is Durham, N.H. The station is always ready to answer garden questions.

Garden club activities include 38 clubs of the New Hampshire Federation of Garden Clubs, which celebrated its twenty-fifth anniversary during 1958. This group has a membership of 2500 people. It has affiliation with the National Council of State Garden Clubs, Inc., which has offices in New York City and a permanent home at the Missouri Botanical Gardens, with a total membership of over 400,000. There are New Hampshire branches of the American Rock Garden Society, Herb Society, Rose Society, Iris Society, etc. The Garden Club of America, whose office is at 598 Madison Avenue, New York 22, N.Y., also operates in the state.

NEW JERSEY. The violet is the state flower. The state lies wholly in zones* 3, 4, and 5.

SOILS. The soils of the state are of wide range of texture and fertility. The state has been divided into 5 soil zones, the borders of which run practically parallel and in a NE–SW direction. Soil zone 1, in the northwest corner of the state, is bounded by a line from the New York state line near Quarryville to the Delaware River above Belvidere. The land is hilly and mountainous and the soils are typically relatively heavy. Soil zone 2 is bounded on the southeast by a line from Cresskill to the Delaware River between Phillipsburg and Frenchtown. This, too, is a rolling, hilly and mountainous section where the soils are predominantly heavy loams, well drained, of granitic derivation in the highlands, while limestone soils occupy the valleys. In this region are many lakes of glacial formation and large areas of muck soils. Soil zone 3 is bounded on the southeast by a line from

NEW JERSEY

The zones of hardiness crossing New Jersey are those shown on the map located at ZONE, which should be consulted for details. The dates are the average latest killing frost in spring and the first one in the fall. The figures below the dates show the average length of the growing season.

Perth Amboy to the Delaware River at a point just above Trenton. This is the Piedmont section, gently rolling country with low, stony ridges. On the ridges is a rather heavy soil derived from the dense traprock; but the prevailing soils are the red soils derived from red shale and sandstone. The first two and the northern half of the third zone are glaciated. The fourth soil zone is bounded by a line from Raritan Bay. This is the heavy coastal plain belt, containing very sandy loams and light sands. In this belt are the pine barrens and much bog land.

CHIEF GARDENING CENTERS. New Jersey has long been known as the Garden State, because, lying as it does between two of the largest markets in the country, New York and Philadelphia, its soil resources have been

---

* Special articles on the subjects indicated by an asterisk (*) will be found at the words so marked.

devoted to the production of vegetable and other horticultural crops for these markets, as well as for its own citizens.

VEGETABLES

Because of the topography and the fairly open nature of the soil, a section in the northeastern part of the state (Hudson and parts of Passaic, Bergen, and Morris counties) is adapted to the growing of early-spring truck crops, such as spinach, lettuce, early beets, carrots, and so on. In the northwestern part are large muck areas devoted to the culture chiefly of lettuce, onions, and celery. A considerable area in soil zones 2 and 3 is devoted to late truck, such as late sweet corn and cabbage. In Monmouth County is an area devoted to general vegetable crops, especially asparagus. Soil in zone 4 is particularly favorable for the production of potatoes and the southern half to tomatoes. In middle soil zone 4 are large acreages of early sweet corn. Sweet potatoes are grown extensively in the southern part of soil zone 5, as well as large quantities of peppers and other truck.

FRUITS

Apples are grown to some extent in soil zones 1 and 2, where conditions are favorable for winter apples, such as Baldwin, Greening and Stayman. Another apple district is located in soil zone 4 in the neighborhood of Freehold, and summer apples are grown extensively in the middle part of soil zone 4 in Burlington, Camden and Gloucester counties. Peaches are most extensively grown in the southern and southwestern section. Bush fruits and strawberries are the chief fruit of parts of Atlantic and Cumberland counties; while cranberries and cultivated blueberries occupy bogs and drained bogs in Atlantic, Burlington and Ocean counties.

ORNAMENTAL HORTICULTURE

The whole of the northeastern section of the state (Hudson, Bergen, Passaic, Essex, Union, and parts of Somerset, Middlesex and Monmouth counties) is very thickly populated because of its proximity to New York City, and the same is true to a lesser extent of parts of Burlington, Camden, and Gloucester counties in relation to Philadelphia. In consequence of this large suburban population and the nearness of these two metropolitan markets, New Jersey has always been among the leading states in the production of nursery and florists' products.

NATIVE PLANTS. The great laurel (*Rhododendron maximum*) is abundant in the northern part of the state and to some extent on the ridges along the Delaware River, as far south as Burlington County. Mountain laurel is plentiful in the southern part of the state. American holly is found on the coastal plain section. Oaks of various species are standard trees in all parts of the state. Sugar and red maple and white ash contribute to autumnal effect. Sycamores are found near streams, and red gum or sweet gum is abundant in the south-central part. The pine barren area has a peculiar flora of its own.

CULTIVATED PLANTS. Because of the variation in topography and climate, a very wide range of plants can be grown in the various sections of the state. In the extreme northern portion, conditions are favorable for plants hardy in the neighborhood of Boston; while in the southern portion, plants considered hardy up to Washington, D.C., may be successfully established. Along the southern part of the coast, *Hydrangea macrophylla* is used extensively for foundation plantings and as a garden shrub. In the neighborhood of Salem, crape myrtle and *Poncirus trifoliata* are seen as well-established plants. Even *Albizzia Julibrissin* has been established in a favorable locality.

The heavier soils of the state are very favorable for the culture of iris, peonies, and roses. The state has long been known for its dahlias, which are cultivated for garden and show purposes. Delphiniums do well in the northern part, as well as in gardens on the northern part of the coast. Since a considerable part of the state is urban or suburban, there is a great interest in home gardens and, in consequence, a very wide range of herbaceous material is grown, both annual and perennial.

Conditions are very favorable in certain sections for alpine and rock gardening. Along the seacoast, especially the upper section, very successful gardens are cultivated under great difficulties, such as soil texture and the salty breezes.

CLIMATE

Because of the form and geographical location of the state, a difference of more than a month in season is observed in a study of the frost data:

FROST DATA

	Eleva-tion	Average date of last killing frost in spring	Latest-known killing frost
Cape May	17	April 5	April 22
Vineland	109	April 21	May 22
New Brunswick	110	April 21	May 17
Charlotteburg	719	May 12	June 21

	Eleva-tion	Average date of earliest killing frost in fall	Earliest-known killing frost
Cape May	17	Nov. 10	Oct. 22
Vineland	109	Oct. 20	Sept. 22
New Brunswick	110	Oct. 19	Sept. 22
Charlotteburg	719	Sept. 26	Sept. 11

* Special articles on the subjects indicated by an asterisk (*) will be found at the words so marked.

RAINFALL

	Elevation	Av. annual rainfall	Average rainfall in growing season
Cape May	17	40.30	23.43 (Apr. to Oct.)
Vineland	109	45.08	26.68 (Apr. to Oct.)
New Brunswick	110	46.52	28.73 (Apr. to Oct.)
Charlotteburg	719	49.57	22.08 (May to Sept.)

The address of the Agricultural Experiment Station is New Brunswick, N.J. The station is always ready to answer gardening questions.

NEW JERSEY TEA = *Ceanothus americanus.*

NEW MEXICO. The state flower is the *Yucca* or Spanish bayonet. The state lies in zones* 4, 5, 6, and 7.

Soil, water, and climatic conditions vary greatly from one area to another in New Mexico. A large portion of the state is occupied by mountains. Mountain ranges in the south are arid and support little vegetation. The northern ranges are high in altitude and support heavy growth of

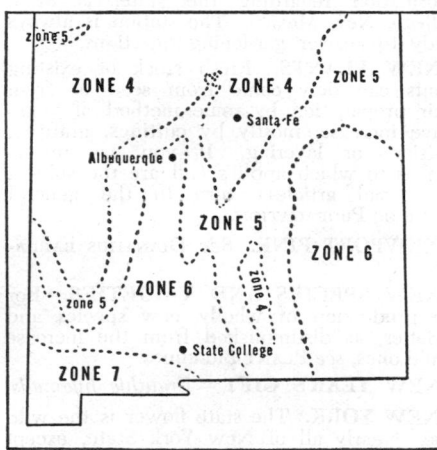

NEW MEXICO

The zones of hardiness crossing New Mexico are those shown on the map located at Zone, which should be consulted for details. For rainfall, which is critical, and very locally distributed, and for the length of the growing season, *see* the text.

pine, spruce, fir, forage grasses, and other plants. In the western half of the state, river valleys provide water for irrigation and rich agricultural lands. These valleys support a major portion of the population. From the Pecos River valley to the eastern border of the state, grassed plains support large numbers of livestock. In the Pecos River valley and in De Baca, Quay,

Curry, Roosevelt, and Lea counties irrigation is practiced to grow field and horticultural crops. Annual rainfall in some parts of Roosevelt, Curry, Quay, Union, Harding, and Colfax counties is high enough for non-irrigated production of many crops. Non-irrigated crop production is also possible in some of the higher valleys of north-central New Mexico.

The soils in the river valleys, on the whole, are deep but variable in texture due to the shifting of the river channels over the years. Heavy clay soils and light sandy soils often are present within short distances of each other. All soils, with the exception of a few small areas in the northern mountain valleys, are alkaline in nature. Low areas along the rivers often become excessively high in alkaline salts and plant growth is retarded. Provision of drainage channels and over-irrigation to leach these salts from the soil can restore productivity to these "white alkali" soils. "Black alkali," a condition caused by excess sodium salts concentration in the soil, also occurs. Adequate drainage, the application of gypsum or other calcium compounds, and leaching are used to lower the sodium level in these soils.

Along the edges of the valleys, between the mountains and the river plain, are areas in which soils of extremely low fertility occur. These soils are often coarse sand or gravel. They are of importance to the gardener since many of the state's urban areas have developed on these soil types.

Soils in the eastern plains area are fertile, but often shallow and underlaid by rock or caliche* layers. Shallow-rooted plants can do well on these soils, while deep-rooted plants grow poorly unless efforts are made to penetrate and break up these rock or caliche layers.

The climate of New Mexico is characterized by a high percentage of clear days, low relative humidity, infrequent periods of high winds, and wide temperature differences between day and night. The frost-free period varies from over 225 days in the extreme southwest corner of the state to less than 100 days in the high mountain areas. The low humidity reduces damage to plants from fungus and bacterial disease, although infrequent rainy periods can bring about losses in localized areas. In the eastern half of the state sharp temperature drops due to cold weather moving across the Great Plains from Canada and the north-central states often result in severe cold-weather damage. In southern New Mexico summer heat damage to many ornamentals is quite common.

The growing of flowers, vegetables, ornamentals, and lawns in New Mexico is very rewarding if their culture is adjusted to fit the soil, water, and climatic conditions of the area. Many of the common fertilizer materials of the East and South, such as lime and bone meal, have little use here due to the prevalence of alkaline

* Special articles on the subjects indicated by an asterisk (*) will be found at the words so marked.

soils. Most of the acid-tolerant plants such as hydrangea, holly, azalea, and rhododendron are practically unknown.

In zone* 7 and the southern portion of zone* 6 many perennial plants of questionable winter hardiness can be grown. *Vinifera* grapes, pomegranate, Japanese privet, wax privet, Texas ranger (*Leucophyllum texanum*), silverberry, and *Pittosporum Tobira* are a few which can be grown with some degree of success only in this area of the state. In zone* 7 and all of zone* 6, the common plants include the pecan, hackberry, Russian olive, ashes, honey and black locusts, Osage orange, apple, peach, mulberry, sycamore, cottonwoods, poplars, willows, and elms of the deciduous shade trees; deodar cedar, Arizona cypress, juniper, piñon pine, and Alleppo pine of the evergreen trees; abelia, flowering almond, artemisia, barberry, buddleia, caragana, caryopteris, quince, desert willow, forsythia, althaea, jasmine, crape myrtle, California and amur privet, honeysuckle, mock-orange, spirea symphoricarpos, lilac, and chaste tree of the deciduous shrubs; barberry, cotoneaster, euonymus, Spanish broom, mahonia, nandina, photinia, and pyracantha of the broad-leaved evergreens; and juniper and arborvitae of the coniferous evergreens. The prevailing lawn grass is Bermuda although bluegrass and other cool-season grasses are commonly grown in the northern area of zone* 6 and in special situations in southern zone* 6 and zone* 7. Hardy cool-season vegetables and flowers are grown in the fall, winter, or spring in both zones with tender, heat-tolerant vegetable and flower types furnishing summer production.

In zone* 5 most of the ornamentals listed for northern zone* 6 do well except those which lack sufficient winter hardiness. Sycamore, soapberry, abelia, crape myrtle, pomegranate, euonymus, photinia and some species of pyracantha do not do well in zone* 5. Kentucky bluegrass is the prevailing lawn type with other cool-season grasses being used frequently. Hardy, cool-season vegetables and flowers do well even for summer production. Only special, short-season varieties of the tender, heat-tolerant vegetables do well. Tender flowers are commonly used for summer color.

In zone* 4, the number of satisfactory ornamental flower and vegetable types is further reduced. Most of the deciduous trees, pines and junipers, and deciduous shrubs of zone* 5 do well in zone* 4. Only mahonia of the broad-leaved evergreens, however, can consistently withstand the winter temperatures. The bluegrasses and hardy, cool-season vegetables and flowers do well in zone* 4 but the growing season is insufficient for most of the tender types.

In New Mexico, as in all arid regions, lack of vegetative growth has resulted in low organic-matter levels in the soil. Since decomposition of organic matter is a primary source of soil nitrogen, most New Mexico soils are low in this element. For this reason, liberal applications of organic matter and the use of commercial nitrogen fertilizers are practiced with success by gardeners in the state.

FROST DATES

Town	Average date of last killing frost in spring	Latest-known killing frost	Average date of earliest killing frost in fall	Earliest-known killing frost
Albuquerque	April 14	May 1	Oct. 26	Sept. 17
Santa Fe	April 23	May 18	Oct. 19	Sept. 25
State College	April 9	May 8	Oct. 26	Oct. 1

The average annual precipitation is about 15 inches, but varies from less than 6 inches at the lower elevations in northwestern New Mexico to more than 34 inches near the tops of some of the higher mountains. About two thirds of it generally falls during the growing season.

The address of the Agricultural Experiment Station, which has kindly supplied this information regarding the state, is State College, New Mexico. The station is always ready to answer gardening questions.

NEW PLANTS. Fresh stock of existing plants can only come from seed or from their propagation by some method of vegetative increase, mostly by cuttings, grafting, division, or layering. If you are uncertain as to which applies (all are the subject of special articles) turn to the general article on PROPAGATION.

NEWPORT PINK. *See* DIANTHUS BARBATUS.

NEW SPECIES AND VARIETIES. For the production of wholly new species and varieties, as distinguished from the increase of old ones, *see* PLANT BREEDING.

NEW YEAR'S GIFT = *Eranthis hyemalis.*

NEW YORK. The state flower is the wild rose. Nearly all of New York State, except Long Island, lies wholly within zones* 2 and 3. Long Island and Staten Island are on the northern edge of zone* 4, which also includes most of the City of New York. Most of the horticultural crops common to the temperate zone are grown successfully within the borders of the state. This does not mean that all of these crops can be grown successfully in all parts of the state. In some regions the growing season is too short for many long-season, heat-demanding plants, such as melons, lima beans, eggplant and peppers, and the winters are too cold for tree fruits.

New York is outstanding in the beauty of its home surroundings, whether they are large private estates, or small urban, suburban or rural homes. Climatic conditions are such that herbaceous and woody ornamental plants, native over wide areas,

---

* Special articles on the subjects indicated by an asterisk (*) will be found at the words so marked.

NEW YORK

The zones of hardiness crossing New York are those shown on the map located at ZONE, which should be consulted for details. The dates are the average latest killing frost in spring and the first one in the fall. The figures below the dates show the average length of the growing season.

grow freely, and in the southern sections of the state many species that are native to the South survive normal winters. There is, however, a comparatively small area where acid-soil plants, such as azaleas, rhododendrons, and others, find naturally favorable conditions for growth. Such areas are in the Adirondack and Catskill mountains, along the Hudson River, and extending some distance along the northern shore of Long Island Sound.

SOILS

The soils of New York cover a wide range of classes, including clay, clay loam, silty-clay loam, silt loam, gravelly silt loam, loam, sandy loam, fine sandy loam, fine sand, and organic or muck soil. All of the mineral soils are used for a wide range of crops, including fruits, vegetables, and ornamental plants. The organic soils that are under cultivation are used mainly for the production of celery, onions, lettuce, potatoes, carrots, and a few other vegetables. Such soils are considered almost ideal for celery, lettuce, and onions, and a large part of the acreage of these crops grown in New York is produced on muck soil. *See* MUCK-LAND GARDENING.

CHIEF HORTICULTURAL CENTERS

The fruit sections of New York State may be designated as the Ontario and Erie lake plains, comprising the northern part of the territory embraced by the counties of Oswego, Wayne, Monroe, Orleans, Niagara, Erie, and Chautauqua; the Finger Lakes,

including parts of Genesee, Ontario, Steuben, Schuyler, Yates, Tompkins, Seneca, Cayuga, and Onondaga counties; the Hudson Valley, including the river slopes and the adjacent uplands of the more important counties of Albany, Rensselaer, Columbia, Greene, Ulster, Dutchess, Orange, and Rockland, and the Champlain Valley, comprising a more or less narrow belt along the main waterway in Clinton, Essex, Warren, Saratoga, and Washington counties. Saratoga and Washington counties are in the Hudson Valley drainage basin, but in the matter of varieties and development they belong rather in the Champlain Valley group.

The distribution of plantings and the segregation of most of the orchards in the above areas have been the result of experience and the survival of the fittest. It will be noted that the fruit areas are characterized by the proximity of large bodies of water, such bodies of water having a moderating influence on the climate of the surrounding land, reducing losses from winter-killing and from frost injury in late spring and early fall.

Apples are an important crop in all of the above sections. The lake plain section has nearly half the total number of apple trees in the state, the Hudson Valley and the Finger Lakes about a fifth each, and the Champlain Valley and other counties the remaining fraction. Apples are the only commercial fruit grown in the Champlain Valley.

Peaches are largely confined to the lake plains and the lower Hudson Valley. Over half of all the peach trees are found in the former section and over a quarter in the latter. Over two-thirds of the cherry trees are found on the Ontario and Erie lake plain.

Over half of the pear trees are likewise to be found along the two Great Lakes and about a fourth in the Hudson Valley.

The Erie shore is the predominating grape section, containing approximately three-fourths of the total number of vines. Grapes are also of importance in the Finger Lakes region and the Hudson Valley.

Small fruits are of some importance in all three sections.

Vegetables are grown for home use and, to some extent, for market, in practically all of the agricultural regions of the state. The principal commercial, vegetable-producing areas are on Long Island and in Erie, Chautauqua, Niagara, Genesee, Orleans, Monroe, Ontario, Livingston, Wayne, Onondaga, Madison, Oneida, Oswego, and Albany counties. This production includes intensive market gardening around the important cities of New York, Albany, Schenectady, Syracuse, Rochester, and Buffalo, as well as more specialized types of vegetable-growing in various areas.

One of the specialized types of production is the growing of celery, lettuce, onions, carrots and other special crops on the muck soils in Genesee, Orleans, Monroe, Livingston, Wayne, Onondaga, Oswego, Madison, and Orange counties. Another type is the growing of cauliflower in Suffolk, Delaware, and Erie counties and the production of cabbage as a general farm crop in Ontario, Monroe, Orleans, Niagara, Wayne, Onondaga, and Cortland counties.

The growing of flowers and other ornamental plants is widespread. Commercially the cut-flower industry is most important in the southeastern section, especially on Long Island, but in the vicinity of all important cities cut flowers and potted plants are grown for sale. The principal kinds of cut flowers grown are roses, carnations, chrysanthemums, snapdragons, sweet peas, and calendulas. More and more interest is manifested in the growing of flowers out of doors for sale, and cloth houses are in rather wide use. The improved quality of the flowers grown in cloth houses makes the growing of asters, gladioli, snapdragons, sweet peas and others of similar nature for cut-flower sales remunerative during the summer. Soil and climatic conditions in some sections, particularly on Long Island, are especially favorable for the production of bulbs.

The growing of nursery products is fairly widespread, but the most important areas of production of ornamental woody plants are in the north-central section.

In both rural and suburban sections there is increasing interest in home beautification by the use of native plant materials. There is a growing appreciation of the beauty and appropriateness in the use of such native trees as beech, birch, and maples in the deciduous group and hemlock, cedars, pines, and spruces in evergreens. Native shrubs, such as viburnums and similar types, are generally planted, not only about homes but around public properties, such as school buildings, libraries, churches, and in village squares. Wild flower gardens are also popular where areas suited for their growth are available.

CLIMATE

New York State has a great diversity of climate due to difference in latitude, in altitude, and in distance and direction from large bodies of water. In general, the average annual temperature decreases about one degree F. for each degree of latitude. New York State lies between 41° and 45° north latitude. Altitude is more important than latitude, since for every rise of 300 feet there is an average decrease in temperature of about one degree F. The land surface in New York ranges from sea level to more than 5000 feet. The elevated sections also have a higher rainfall than do the lower areas. Land heats and cools faster than does water, therefore temperatures over water areas are more uniform than those over land areas,

and, in general, regions near large bodies of water are not subject to sudden changes in temperature that are experienced farther inland. The climate of the regions lying along the Great Lakes and near the Atlantic Ocean is influenced greatly by the proximity of these bodies of water. These regions have a longer growing season, and a larger percentage of sunshine for the growing season than any other portion of the state.

The average date of the last killing frost in spring and the first killing frost in fall for several locations in the state is given in the following table:

FROST DATES

Station	Last killing frost in spring	
	Average	Latest
Albany	April 24	May 30
Binghamton	May 4	May 29
Buffalo	April 28	May 23
Canton	May 6	June 2
Cutchogue, L.I.	April 20	May 12
Ithaca	May 4	June 9
Jamestown	May 14	June 20
New York City	April 11	April 30
Rochester	April 27	May 27
Setauket, L.I.	April 13	April 26
Syracuse	April 23	May 5

Station	First killing frost in fall	
	Average	Earliest
Albany	Oct. 15	Sept. 15
Binghamton	Oct. 8	Sept. 14
Buffalo	Oct. 22	Oct. 3
Canton	Sept. 29	Sept. 11
Cutchogue, L.I.	Oct. 29	Oct. 4
Ithaca	Oct. 9	Sept. 11
Jamestown	Oct. 6	Sept. 15
New York City	Nov. 6	Oct. 15
Rochester	Oct. 22	Sept. 14
Setauket, L.I.	Nov. 9	Oct. 21
Syracuse	Oct. 22	Sept. 21

The average length of the growing season varies from 90 days in portions of the Adirondack Mountains to 200 days on the western end of Long Island. In the regions along Lake Erie and Lake Ontario the growing season varies from about 170 to 180 days and decreases eastward and southward from the lakes. Likewise, the length of the growing season decreases northward and westward from the Atlantic Ocean.

The mean sunshine, expressed in percentage of the possible sunshine, for the growing season, varies from 50 to 62, the regions of greatest sunshine being along the shore of Lake Ontario and near the Atlantic Ocean. The percentage of sunshine decreases eastward and southward from Lake Ontario and northward and westward from the ocean. The region of lowest sunshine, 50 to 54 per cent, embraces the area bounded by a line from the southwest corner of Steuben County on the west diagonally across the state to Warren and Washington counties and then southwestward through Albany, Greene, Ulster, and Sullivan counties.

There is a wide variation in the annual and growing-season (April–August) precipitation in New York State. The average annual precipitation varies from less than 30 to more than 50 inches, and the growing-season rainfall from less than 12 to more than 20 inches. In general, the regions of heaviest precipitation are: (1) the Adirondack Mountains and surrounding areas, including most or all of Madison, Oneida, Lewis, Herkimer, and Hamilton counties and parts of Fulton, Montgomery, and Otsego counties; (2) southeastern New York south and east of a line running through Columbia, Greene, and Sullivan counties; (3) Chautauqua and Cattaraugus counties.

The address of the Agricultural Experiment Station which has kindly supplied this information about the state is Cornell University Agricultural Experiment Station, Ithaca, New York. There is also another important station at Geneva, N.Y., which has specialized in fruits. Both stations are always willing to answer gardening questions.

Garden club activities are more extensive than in any other state. There are several clubs of the Garden Club of America, the home office of which is at 598 Madison Avenue, New York 22, N.Y. In addition there are over 200 clubs affiliated with the Federated Garden Clubs of New York State, Inc. *See also* HORTICULTURAL SOCIETIES, BOTANIC GARDEN, and ARBORETUM.

NEW YORK ASTER = *Aster novi-belgi.*

NEW YORK BOTANICAL GARDEN. *See* BOTANIC GARDEN.

NEW ZEALAND BUR = *Acaena microphylla.*

NEW ZEALAND FLAX = *Phormium tenax.*

NEW ZEALAND ICE-PLANT = NEW ZEALAND SPINACH.

NEW ZEALAND SPINACH. A good hot-weather substitute for spinach, belonging to the genus **Tetragonia** (tet-ra-gō′nĭ-a) of the family Aizoaceae. Of tne 20 known species, mostly from the southern hemisphere and eastern Asia, only **T. expansa,** the New Zealand spinach, is of interest to the gardener. It is a stout, annual herb with prostrate, thickish stems often several feet long. Leaves alternate,° more or less triangular or ovalish-triangular, 2–4 in. long, thickish, somewhat glistening with minute dots (hence its other name of New Zealand ice-plant). Flowers very small, 1 or 2 in the leaf axils, yellowish-green, without petals. Fruit dry, small, more or less 4-angled, top-shaped and horned. (*Tetragonia* is from the Greek for four-angled, in reference to the fruit.)

New Zealand spinach can be grown whenever or wherever the heat is too great for ordinary spinach. Usually the plant

sprawls so much that it makes large round patches, so that planting in hills is more satisfactory than in rows. The seed germinates slowly and it is best to soak the seed for a few hours in very hot water before planting. The hills should be 3–4 ft. apart. Sow 3 seeds at each hill, thinning them to a single plant later. Some growers prefer to start plants in the hotbed and transplant outdoors when warm weather has arrived. While the plant is commonly called New Zealand spinach and is native there, it is also native in Jap., Aust., and S.A. The young new leaves are far better than old ones; the latter sometimes become strong-tasting. Harvest the upper leaves and tips of the shoots.

NEW ZEALAND WINEBERRY = *Aristotelia racemosa.*

NICANDRA (ny-kan′dra). Strong-growing annual herbs from Peru, comprising 2 species of the family Solanaceae, one of garden interest. It has escaped° from cultivation and become naturalized in tropical America. (It was named for Nikander, an ancient poet of Colophon.)

Propagated by seeds, sown ⅛ in. deep in pots or boxes of light soil in temperatures 55°–65° in March. Transplant the seedlings, 3 ft. apart, outdoors, in May, in ordinary soil. Seeds may also be sown outdoors in April, transplanting the seedlings in June.

Physalodes. Apple-of-Peru. A strong, spreading, annual herb, growing to a height of 4 ft. Leaves alternate,° ovalish, the margins toothed. Flowers solitary, tubular, blue, 1–2 in. across and on curving stalks. Fruit, a 3–5-celled, many-seeded berry enclosed in an inflated calyx. Occasionally offered under the name "shoofly."

NICOTIANA (ni-ko-she-ā′na). Herbaceous annuals and perennials, occasionally shrubby or tree-like, mostly tropical and comprising 45 species of the potato family, all American except for one found in Aust. They grow 2–20 ft. high, and have mostly large, soft leaves, the whole plant more or less covered with short, sticky hairs. Stems branching, sometimes fasciated.° Leaves alternate,° simple, the juice having narcotic or poisonous properties. Flowers in clusters at the ends of the branches, sweet-scented, mostly opening from 5 P.M. to 8 A.M. but remaining open on sunless days, white, greenish-yellow or purple. Calyx° of 5 partly united, green sepals. Corolla tubular or funnel-shaped. Stamens° 5. Fruit, a dry capsule,° 2–4-celled, containing numerous and exceptionally minute seeds. (Named for Jean Nicot who introduced tobacco to the French Court.)

Plants are easily grown from seeds, sown under glass in shallow boxes of finely sifted sandy soil in early spring. Sow seeds on the surface of soil, and press down with a small flat board, water with a fine spray and stand boxes in the shady part of cool

---

° Special articles on the subjects indicated by an asterisk (°) will be found at the words so marked.

greenhouse or cold frame. When germinated move to a sunny position, and as soon as large enough transplant into small pots or boxes, transplanting to the garden as soon as danger of frost is over. They grow well in ordinary garden soil, but lime and potash are beneficial. They must have a warm, sunny position and be kept well supplied with water during hot, dry weather. Apply small quantity of fertilizer every 10 days when plants are in flower. Perennial species are usually treated as annuals, as they flower freely from seed the same year. Except for one species which yields tobacco, nicotianas are very useful border plants, both for their fragrance and their long flowering period, which begins in July and continues until frost. They are sometimes grown as pot plants, in 6–8-in. pots.

affinis = *Nicotiana alata grandiflora*.

alata. Tender perennial, growing to 5 ft., erect and slender. Leaves to 4 in. long, not stalked, the tip blunt or pointed. Flowers fragrant, in a loose raceme,* the tube white within, violet without, the limb yellowish-green, 2 in. across. Brazil, Uruguay, Paraguay. The *var.* **grandiflora**, jasmine tobacco, has much larger flowers, the tube being more open and white. It often seeds itself and is treated as an annual. *See* ANNUALS.

glauca. Tree tobacco. Tree-like, and sometimes 20 ft. high, the foliage blue-green, not hairy. Leaves long-stalked, heart-shaped, or ovalish. Flowers in loose, terminal, bracted clusters. Calyx tubular, its 5 teeth-like lobes slightly hairy. Corolla yellow, 1½ in. long, constricted, its lobes oval. S.A., but naturalized in Tex. and Calif. Grown for its stately habit and blue-green foliage.

sanderae. A hybrid annual of bushy habit, growing to 3 ft. Leaves spoon-shaped to 1 ft. long, short-stalked. Flowers to 3 in. long, the tube greenish-yellow, tinted rose, becoming carmine-rose as it expands, its lobes pointed. Originated by Sander and Sons, St. Albans, Eng.

suaveolens. An Australian, densely hairy annual, 1–2 ft. high, the upper foliage smooth. Flowers night-fragrant, about 2 in. long, nodding, white inside, purplish-green outside, borne in terminal clusters (racemes*).

sylvestris. Herbaceous perennial growing to 5 ft. Leaves not stalked, broad, spoon-shaped, wrinkled, partly clasping the stem. Flowers drooping, in clusters. Calyx short, slightly swollen, its lobes pointed. Corolla white, night-fragrant, the tube 3–3½ in. long. Argentina.

Tabacum. Tobacco. Herbaceous annual growing to 6 ft. and covered with short, sticky hairs. Leaves thin, not stalked, partly clasping the stem, 1 ft. or more long, broadly lance-shaped. Flowers stalked, in bracted clusters (racemes*). Corolla 2 in. long, the tube white, whitish, rose, or purplish-red, its lobes pointed. Grown as an agricultural product but it is a striking garden plant. Tropical America. *See* TOBACCO.

NICOTINE. A poisonous alkaloid derived from tobacco and once widely used as an insecticide. In its crude form it is an oily, yellowish liquid, and is so used after dilution with water. It also comes in dried form suitable for dusting. Newer materials have largely replaced nicotine.

Jasmine Tobacco (*Nicotiana alata grandiflora*). A beautifully night-fragrant, white-flowered perennial, 3–5 ft. high, somewhat tender northward.

NIDULARIUM (nid-you-lay′rĭ-um). Showy, Brazilian, tree-perching plants of the family Bromeliaceae, comprising perhaps 30 species, of which the two below are grown in the greenhouse for the handsome foliage and brilliantly bracted* flowers. The ones below have practically no stems and a dense basal rosette* of broad-based, but otherwise strap-shaped, often spiny-toothed leaves. Flower cluster almost stalkless, nestled in the center of the leaf rosette, but just beneath it a cluster of brilliantly colored, leaf-like bracts,* joined into a sort of involucre.* Corolla, in ours, whitish, more or less tubular. Sepals* not united. Fruit a berry. (*Nidularium* is from the Latin for nest, in allusion to the nest-like position of the flower cluster.)

Should be grown in pots or orchid baskets with a mixture composed of ⅓ potting mixture* 3 and ⅔ chopped fern fiber or coir. They need a warm, moist greenhouse with a night temperature of about 65°, and plenty of water during their active growing season (Mar.–Aug.). During the winter they need much less water, often a light sprinkling of the foliage being sufficient. Propagated by the usually frequent suckers which arise below the rosette of leaves.

amazonicum = *Canistrum amazonicum*.

fulgens. Leaves about 12 in. long and nearly 2 in. wide, mostly spotted with dark green. Flowers white, but the bracts beneath the dense head-like cluster, brilliant scarlet. The plant is sometimes offered as *N. pictum*.

innocenti. Leaves about 12 in. long, scarcely over 1 in. wide, green but tinted red or brown. Flowers white, the bracts beneath the dense head-like cluster, red.

pictum = *Nidularium fulgens*.

Nidus (ny′dus). Latin for a nest. *See* ASPLENIUM NIDUS.

---

* Special articles on the subjects indicated by an asterisk (*) will be found at the words so marked.

NIEREMBERGIA (near-em-berg'ĭ-a or -ber'jĭ-a). Cup-flower. Tropical American perennial herbs or under-shrubs of the potato family, comprising about 25 species, of which 4 are grown for their attractive tubular flowers. They are inclined to sprawl or creep, and have alternate* somewhat scattered leaves without marginal teeth. Flowers white or pale blue, mostly near the ends of the twigs. Calyx more or less bell-shaped, 5-parted. Corolla long-tubed, the 5-lobed limb abruptly expanded, yellow in the throat in ours. Stamens* 5, protruding, one shorter than the others. Fruit a 2-valved capsule.* (Named for J. E. Nieremberg, a Jesuit professor of natural history at Madrid.)

While these plants are hardy or very nearly so up to zone* 4, it is safer to dig them up for the winter and plunge* in a cold frame. They may also be grown in the cool greenhouse where *N. frutescens* will bloom almost continuously. They can be propagated by seeds, by cuttings in the fall (wintered in the greenhouse), or by division of the rooting stems of *N. rivularis*.

caerulea. The hardiest of all the cup-flowers and a perennial 6–9 in. high, but better treated as a tender annual. Leaves very narrow, scarcely ¾ in. long. Flowers about 1 in. wide, blue but yellow in the throat, numerous. Argentina. Aug.–Sept. Reported as hardy (?) in Ontario.

frutescens. A well-known one in cult. and more erect than sprawling, often 1–3 ft. high. Leaves very narrow, usually about 1 in. long, scattered. Flowers nearly 1 in. wide, white, or lilac- or blue-tinted, the limb of the corolla saucer-shaped. Chile. Can be grown in the border or in the greenhouse. Forms are offered with purple or with larger flowers.

gracilis. More or less sprawling and not over 6–8 in. high. Leaves very narrow, scarcely ½ in. long, the upper ones a little hairy. Flowers white, but purple-tinged or veined toward the center, the limb somewhat convex. Argentina.

hippomanica = *N. caerulea*.

rivularis. Whitecup. Creeping and rooting at the joints, forming a dense mat. Leaves oblongish, nearly 1 in. long, stalked. Flowers cream-white, sometimes rose- or blue-tinged, the bell-shaped limb 1–2 in. wide. Argentina. Perhaps the best-known of the four. For cult. *see* Rock Garden.

NIGELLA (ny-jell'a). Herbaceous annuals, comprising about 16 species, mostly natives of the Mediterranean region, belonging to the buttercup family. Stems erect, branching. Leaves alternate,* often of lace-like appearance, owing to their being finely divided in thread-like segments. Flowers blue or white, produced at the ends of the branching stems, each flower enclosed by much-branched, thread-like bracts* growing from the base. Petals 5–8, notched. Stamens* indefinite in number. Pistils* usually 5–10, separated at the top, but united at the base. Fruit an inflated capsule, containing many hard black seeds which are dispersed through openings at the top. The seeds were at one time used as pepper.

(*Nigella* is from the Greek for black, in reference to the black seeds.)

Sow seeds ⅛ in. deep, where required to bloom, in ordinary soil, in sunny beds or borders. Plants do not require much attention except to thin out to 8 in. apart.

damascena. Love-in-a-mist; also called devil-in-the-bush. Height 8–10 in., much branched. Leaves lace-like, bright green. Flowers light blue or white, 1½ in. across, set in the midst of thread-like bracts. Fruit, a globe-shaped capsule.* Southern Eu. *See* Blue Garden.

sativa. Fennel-flower. Height 1 ft., branching. Leaves lance-shaped, not cut. Flowers blue, solitary, not enclosed in lace-like bracts. Fruit an inflated capsule. Seeds sometimes used for seasoning. Mediterranean region. *See* Herb Gardening.

niger (ny'jer). Black.

NIGGER-TOES. *See* Bertholletia excelsa.

NIGHT-BLOOMING CEREUS. As now understood, none of the plants known as night-blooming cereus belong to the genus *Cereus*. For the three best-known ones, all called night-blooming cereus, *see* Hylocereus undatus, Selenicereus pteranthus, and Nyctocereus serpentinus. The first is the most widely cult. of the three. All are at their best after midnight. *See also* Trichocereus and Epiphyllum oxypetalum, which is widely grown and flowered as a house plant.

NIGHT-BLOOMING FLOWERS. *See* Nocturnal Flowers.

NIGHT GARDENS. *See* Lighting.

NIGHT JASMINE = *Nyctanthes Arbor-tristis* and *Cestrum nocturnum*.

NIGHT PHLOX = *Zaluzianskia*.

NIGHTSHADE. *See* Solanum. *See also* Basella.

NIGHTSHADE FAMILY = Solanaceae.

NIGHT SOIL. Human excrement, forbidden here, but widely used as manure in China and some other countries.

nigra, -us, -um (ny'gra). Black.

nigricans (ny'gri-kanz). Black.

nigrofructa, -us, -um (ny-gro-fruck'ta). Black-fruited.

NIKAU PALM = *Rhopalostylis sapida*.

NIKKO FIR = *Abies homolepis*. *See* Fir.

Nil. Arabic vernacular for a morning-glory. *See* Ipomoea Nil.

NINEBARK. *See* Physocarpus.

NIOBE. *See* Plantain-lily.

"NIPPON BELLS." *See* Shortia.

NIPPON CHRYSANTHEMUM OR DAISY = *Chrysanthemum nipponicum*.

nipponica, -us, -um (nip-pon'i-ka). From Japan.

NITELLA (ny-tell'a). A large genus of submerged aquatics, belonging to the algae,* one of them N. flexilis, a stonewort, used in aquaria. It has green, brittle stems, no flowers, and whorls of slender green leaves.

---

* Special articles on the subjects indicated by an asterisk (*) will be found at the words so marked.

It is sold by dealers in aquarium plants, and it will readily cling to pebbles or sand in the bottom of the tank. (*Nitella* is from the Latin for splendor, which scarcely characterizes these plants.)

nitens (ny'tenz). Shining.

nitida, -us, -um (nĭ'tĭ-da). Shining.

NITROGEN. One of the essentials for plant growth. For the sources of it and its use as an ingredient of fertilizers *see* FERTILIZERS. For the role of nitrogen in the chemical composition of plants *see* PLANT FOODS.

nivalis, -e (niv-vay'lis). Snowy; *i.e.*, white.

nivea, -us, -um (niv'e-a). Snowy; *i.e.*, white.

nivosa, -us, -um (niv-vō'sa). Snowy; *i.e.*, white.

nobilis, -e (nō'bil-lis). Famous or renowned; sometimes, also, noble.

nocturna, -us, -um (nock-tur'na). Night-blooming.

NOCTURNAL FLOWERS. While most flowers bloom in daytime, and many close at night, there are an appreciable number that bloom at night and are apt to be closed or nearly so in bright sunshine.

By far the greatest number of these night-blooming flowers are tropical. They are often white, sometimes very fragrant, and the presumption is (not always verified) that they are pollinated only by night-flying insects, mostly moths. The most spectacular of these nocturnal flowers is, of course, the night-blooming cereus, the blooms of which are nearly 12 in. long, extremely fragrant, and usually come to perfection after midnight. They mostly open only once and then wither. But several other tropical flowers bloom for several nights, notably the night jasmines (*see* NYCTANTHES and CESTRUM). Many other tropical plants do this, but they are not usually cult. plants.

Among hardy garden flowers that bloom at night, or at least do not begin to bloom until toward or after sunset, perhaps the outstanding belong to the genus *Nicotiana*. Also night-blooming are the evening primroses. A brief list of other plants mostly blooming at night would include the following, all of which are entered in the ENCYCLOPEDIA under the names given below:

Agave virginica	Mathiola bicornis
Akebia quinata	Mirabilis
Brunfelsia americana	Nymphaea (some
Cooperia	tropical sorts)
Gladiolus tristis	Petunia axillaris
Daylily (*Hemerocallis*	Saponaria
thunbergi)	Schizopetalon walkeri
Hesperis	Silene noctiflora
Lonicera heckrotti	Yucca (some species)
Lychnis alba	Zaluzianskya

While all of these may flower in the day, especially toward evening, their finest flowering is always at night, and their greatest fragrance comes long after sundown. Any of them may flower during the day if the weather is overcast.

NODDING LILAC = *Syringa reflexa*. See LILAC.

NODDING TRILLIUM = *Trillium cernuum*.

NODE. The place at which a leaf, bud, or other organ (sometimes the branch of a flower cluster) joins the stem to which it is attached; a joint. The space between such joints is sometimes, but incorrectly, called a node. Properly, it is an internode.

NODULE. *See* TUBERCLE.

nodulosa, -us, -um (nod-you-lō'sa). Tubercled. *See* TUBERCLE.

NOISETTE ROSE = *Rosa noisettiana*.

NOLANA (no-lay'na). Prostrate perennial herbs, grown as annuals, comprising about 57 species of the family Nolanaceae, and natives of Chile and Peru. Stem angular, sometimes spotted and streaked, smooth or sticky, the much-branched ends turning upward. Leaves usually in pairs, spoon-shaped. Flowers bell-shaped, solitary, stalked, borne in the axils* of the leaves, blue or purple, rarely white or rose. Stamens* 5. (Nolana is from the Latin for a little bell, in reference to the shape of the flower.)

Suitable for rock gardens or barren hillsides, as they like light sandy soil and sunny position. They can also be utilized for hanging baskets. Propagate by seeds, sown in patches in April, thinning out to 4 in. apart. They are not much in cultivation, the Chilean bellflower being the best-known.

atriplicifolia. Chilean bellflower. Stems spotted and streaked with purple on the upper side, spreading from the root, and about 1 ft. long. Leaves spoon-shaped, fleshy. Flowers blue with white and yellow throat, 2 in. across. The *var.* **violacea** has violet flowers.

lanceolata. Whole plant covered with white hairs. Leaves lance-shaped, 4–6 in. long. Flowers deep blue, with the throat spotted creamy-white, 2 in. across.

paradoxa = *Nolana atriplicifolia*.

prostrata. Resembles *N. atriplicifolia*, but the flowers are smaller, and with a purple-veined throat. Peru. It may be only a form of the first species.

NOLANACEAE (no-lan-ā'see-ee). A small family of South American herbs or undershrubs, containing only 2 genera and about 63 species, of which *Nolana* is the only one of hort. interest. *See* NOLANA.

NOMENCLATURE. *See* PLANT NAMES.

NONE-SO-PRETTY = *Silene Armeria*.

NONESUCH = *Medicago lupulina*.

nonscripta, -us, -um (non-scrip'ta). Undesignated or undescribed.

NOODLE-GOURD. *See* VEGETABLE SPAGHETTI.

NOODLE-PLANT. A trade name for a small decorative gourd.*

NOOTKA CYPRESS = *Chamaecyparis nootkatensis*.

---

* Special articles on the subjects indicated by an asterisk (*) will be found at the words so marked.

nootkatensis, -e (noot-ka-ten'sis). From Nootka, near Vancouver.

NOPAL = *Opuntia lindheimeri,* but *see also* NOPALEA.

NOPALEA (no-pay'lee-a). Six species of *Opuntia*-like, Mexican cacti, one of which, N. **cochenillifera,** the cochineal plant, was once the most important economic cactus in cult., now grown mostly for interest or ornament. Upon it fed the cochineal insect, the source of a famous dye, now largely replaced by synthetic products. It is a tree-like, branched cactus, 10–15 ft. high. Joints fleshy and leaf-like, oblongish, 15–20 in. long, and generally spineless. Unlike most other cacti, there are often produced small, nearly terete leaves, which soon drop off, and may often be wanting. Flowers scarlet, about 2 in. long. Fruit a red, juicy, edible berry, nearly 2¼ in. long. The cochineal plant can only be grown in frostless regions, or northward in the greenhouse. *See* CACTI. For centuries the plant and its insect were very important commercially, and were known to the Aztecs long before the Spanish conquest. They called it nopal, of which *Nopalea* is the Latin version.

NOPALXOCHIA. *See* EPIPHYLLUM.

NORDMANN FIR = *Abies nordmanniana. See* FIR.

NORFOLK BOTANIC GARDEN. *See* No. 20 at GARDEN TOURS.

NORFOLK ISLAND PINE = *Araucaria excelsa.*

NORTH CAROLINA. The dogwood is the state flower. The state lies wholly in zones* 5 and 6. The production of horticultural crops and the development of horticultural industries in North Carolina are closely identified with the climate and soil of the four natural subdivisions of the state commonly known as the Coastal Plain, Sandhill, Piedmont, and Mountain sections.

The Coastal Plain includes a belt bordering on the Atlantic Ocean and extending about 150 miles westward to the Piedmont and Sandhill sections. This area is characterized by soils of a light, sandy texture, mostly underlaid with clay, varying from coarse sands to sandy loams and fine, sandy loams. These soils warm up quickly, are easily cultivated, and are therefore valuable for vegetable-growing. The winter and early spring temperatures are usually very mild, making this region especially adapted to the production of early vegetable crops for shipment to northern markets. The city of Wilmington lies in the center of the most intensive truck-growing area of the state. The winter temperature at Wilmington seldom goes below 20° F. under normal conditions.

The most important truck crop grown in the Coastal Plain is the early Irish potato. Other vegetable crops that are grown more or less generally throughout the area

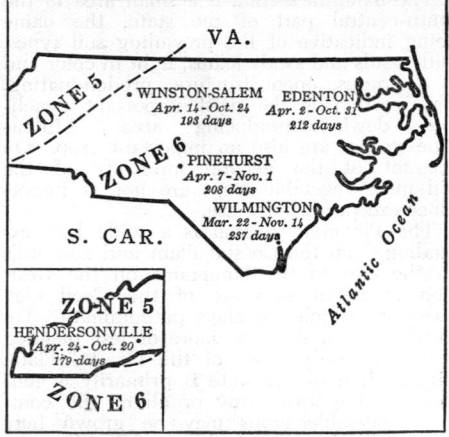

NORTH CAROLINA

The zones of hardiness crossing North Carolina are those shown on the map located at ZONE, which should be consulted for details. The dates are the average latest killing frost in spring and the first one in the fall. The figures below the dates show the average length of the growing season.

are sweet potatoes, snap beans, lima beans, peas, tomatoes, squash, cucumbers, watermelons, cantaloupes, mustard, kale, cabbage, collards, turnips, peppers, onions, okra, beets, carrots, radishes, and corn. In the Wilmington area the chief market crops are lettuce, cucumbers, string beans, lima beans, peas, early turnips, cabbage, spinach, radishes, sprouting broccoli, beets, and carrots. Here the growing season is so long that it is often possible to grow three different crops successively on the same piece of land during one season.

In the vicinity of Wilmington a considerable acreage is now being devoted to the growing of bulbs — narcissus, Dutch iris, tulips, and gladiolus. These flowers come into bloom so early in the spring that the shipment of cut flowers has become an important item as a side line of the bulb industry. This section of the state is also noted for its great variety of native evergreens, trees, and flowers, chief among which are pines, cypress, holly, yaupon, inkberry, a cherry laurel, leucothoë, dogwood, fringe-tree, tulip-tree, live oak, magnolia, sweet bay, smilax, Spanish moss, and the rare Venus's-flytrap. Gardenias, camellias, and the more tender *indica* azaleas can be successfully grown along with the more hardy shrubbery.

Strawberries, blueberries, dewberries, figs, Muscadine grapes and, to a lesser extent, peaches, are the fruit crops grown commercially in the Coastal Plain. However, adapted varieties of practically all the common fruits can be grown for home use.

* Special articles on the subjects indicated by an asterisk (*) will be found at the words so marked.

The Sandhill section is a small area in the south-central part of the state, the name being indicative of the prevailing soil types, with sands and sandy loams, light in color and of a porous, open structure, predominating. This section is the most important peach- and dewberry-producing area. Muscadine grapes are also an important crop. On account of the general infertility of the soil most vegetable crops are not of importance except for home use.

The Piedmont section is a wide belt extending from the Coastal Plain and Sandhills on the east to the Mountains on the west. The Piedmont soils are of the Cecil clay series, in which the clays predominate. Toward the east they are more or less blended with the sandy types of the Coastal Plain. This section of the state is primarily a general farming area. Any or all of the common vegetable crops may be grown here for home use and near-by markets, but the section cannot generally compete with the Coastal Plain section in the production of truck crops for market. The season is somewhat later and the soils heavier and therefore harder to work.

The Piedmont is well adapted to the growing of fruits, chief of which are apples, peaches, grapes, pears, and red raspberries along the western edge of the area. Strawberries, blackberries, plums, and cherries may also be grown. Of the native shrubs, flowering dogwood, the various haws, crabapples, viburnums, and redbud are distinctive of this area. Here also are the hardwood forests.

The Mountain section of North Carolina includes approximately the western one-sixth of the state, extending from the edge of the Blue Ridge on the east to the Great Smoky range on the west. The soils of this area are mostly clay loams and sandy loams of the Porter series. This area is of great horticultural importance. The Irish potato, for seed purposes and eating, is the most important truck crop. Cabbage, snap beans, dry beans, lima beans, onions, rhubarb, sweet corn, tomatoes, turnips, rutabagas, celery, spinach, lettuce, beets, and carrots thrive in this section.

The leading fruit of the Mountain section is the apple. Pears, peaches, plums, cherries, raspberries, blackberries, strawberries, and grapes are grown to a lesser extent.

The native shrubs and trees are characteristic of the section. Here we find hemlock, balsam, white pine, chestnut, sourwood, cucumber tree, sugar maple, black walnut, serviceberry, hardy azaleas, rhododendron, mountain laurel, leucothoë, galax, trailing arbutus, wintergreen, ginseng, goldenseal, and many kinds of ferns. Dahlias and other flowers reach perfection in the mountains.

CLIMATE

The climate of North Carolina varies greatly from the Coast, where it is tempered by the Gulf Stream, to the Mountains where the high altitudes give a climate comparable to the New England states.

The following table gives frost data for various points in the state:

Name of Town	Average date of last killing frost in spring	Latest-known killing frost
Wilmington	March 22	May 1
Edenton	April 2	April 26
Pinehurst	April 7	April 26
Winston-Salem	April 14	May 15
Hendersonville	April 24	

Name of Town	Average date of earliest killing frost in fall	Earliest-known killing frost
Wilmington	Nov. 14	Oct. 16
Edenton	Oct. 31	Oct. 12
Pinehurst	Nov. 1	Oct. 12
Winston-Salem	Oct. 24	Oct. 2
Hendersonville	Oct. 20	

The average length of the growing season from the above table is 237 days for Wilmington, located on the Coast, 193 days for Winston-Salem, in the Piedmont, and 179 days for Hendersonville, in the Mountains. In the higher altitudes of the Mountain area the growing season is somewhat shorter.

A word should be said about thermal belts. They are belts, more or less indefinite in width, where the minimum temperatures average higher than at either base or summit of the ridge, free from the frost of the valley and from the freezes of the higher levels. Within this belt foliage is often fresh and green when that above and below has been killed by frost. A number of these thermal belts are found in the North Carolina mountains and are of great importance to the fruitgrower.

The annual rainfall of the state will average approximately 50 inches for the Coastal area, 47 inches for the Piedmont and 54 inches for the Mountains. One station, Highlands, in the Mountain area, has an average annual rainfall of approximately 80 inches.

The address of the Agricultural Experiment Station which has kindly supplied the information about the state is State College Station, Raleigh, N. Car. The station is always ready to answer gardening questions.

Garden club activities include clubs of the Garden Club of America, the home office of which is 598 Madison Avenue, New York 22, N.Y. There are also over 60 clubs affiliated with the Garden Club of North Carolina.

NORTH DAKOTA. The state flower is the wild rose, the state tree the swamp ash, and the state lies wholly in zone* 1.

SOILS. The soils of North Dakota are contained in three major physiographic areas: the Red River Valley, the till plain, and the Missouri Plateau.

---

* Special articles on the subjects indicated by an asterisk (*) will be found at the words so marked.

The Red River Valley occupies the bed of glacial Lake Agassiz and extends from South Dakota to the Canadian border in a belt about 30 miles wide. Sandy loam soils occupy beaches and stream deltas on the west side of the valley. The soils of the lake plain are silt loams, silty clay loams, and clays. Most of the clay soils (Fargo series) occur in the south half of the valley, and silt loam and silty clay loams (Bearden and Overly series) are most common in the northern half.

The till plain lies between the Red River Valley and the Missouri River. This area is bisected by a belt of terminal and end moraines. The Barnes, Aastad, and Hamerly soils lie east of the moraines and the Williams soils west of the moraines. Most of the soils have developed in glacial till and are usually loam-textured. In areas of glacial meltwater deposits, sandy loam and silt loam textures are also found.

The soils of the Missouri Plateau have developed in materials from shale, siltstone, and sandstone. The Morton series is most common and usually has silt-loam texture, while the Vebar series is mostly fine sandy loam.

CLIMATE. The climate of North Dakota is typified by comparatively cool summers. This coupled with a long day-length (16 hours of sunlight in midsummer) are environmental reasons why North Dakota can produce good, high-quality horticultural crops under conditions of a relatively short growing season. Moisture is a limiting factor but most of the rainfall is received during the growing season, with the heaviest concentration in May and June. Precipitation during the growing season ranges from about 16 inches in the east to about 10 inches in the west. Efficient crop use is made of this limited moisture because of an interaction of climatic factors. Although the evaporation rate is high during the summer months, this is offset by the long day-length period and the cooler summer temperatures, particularly during the night. This interaction effect allows for maximum growth. The effect of the long midsummer days, coupled with the efficient moisture use, results in extremely rapid plant growth which allows certain crop varieties to reach maturity in a shorter time in this area than it would take them to mature in an area farther south.

Generally there is a difference of about five degrees in average summer temperature between the southern and northern parts of the state. The southern portion of the state is about two weeks earlier in the spring than the northern portion, and the first killing frost comes about ten days later than that in the northern portion. This enables the growers in the south to have a growing season of about three weeks longer duration. The longest frost-free season is found in the extreme southeast portion of the state and along the Missouri River.

Variations in climate are common throughout the state. Fargo, Bismarck, Devil's Lake, Langdon, Dickinson, and Williston are towns selected representing these variations.

FROST DATA

Town	Av. date of last killing frost in spring	Av. date of first killing frost in fall	Av. length of frost-free season (days)
Fargo	May 12	Sept. 26	137
Bismarck	May 10	Sept. 22	135
Devil's Lake	May 15	Sept. 22	130
Langdon	May 28	Sept. 12	107
Dickinson	May 19	Sept. 14	118
Williston	May 14	Sept. 23	132

Not only are there considerable variations in the state, but the annual variation in a particular area is also large. For example, at Fargo, frost has occurred as late as June 10 in the spring and as early in the fall as August 29. Because of this variation, considerable care must be exercised with the more tender horticultural crops. Light frosts, that do not fall under the classification of killing frosts, are detrimental to these tender plants. To be critical of seeding or transplanting periods, dates later than the average date of the last killing frost in the spring are recommended. For example, at Fargo the date for transplanting tomatoes, one of the major garden crops, is during the last week of May, usually not earlier than May 25. Not only can light frosts be a problem but the cold nights which are quite prevalent

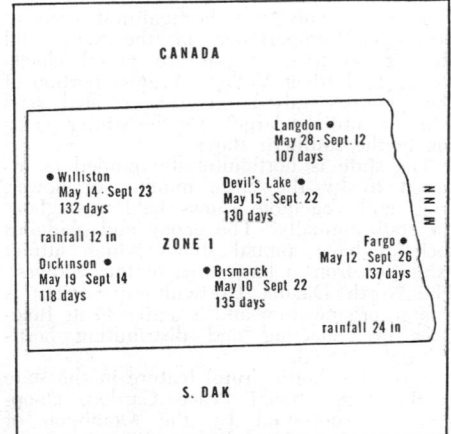

NORTH DAKOTA

The zones of hardiness crossing North Dakota are those shown on the map located at ZONE, which should be consulted for details. The dates are the average latest killing frost in spring and the first one in the fall. The figures below the dates show the average length of the growing season. Rainfall figures (in inches) are for total annual rainfall in the regions so indicated.

---

* Special articles on the subjects indicated by an asterisk (*) will be found at the words so marked.

in May and early June will tend to slow up normal development. Thus the gardener will have to have a good knowledge of the hardiness of the crop before he plants.

Market gardening is most prevalent around the larger towns such as Fargo, Grand Forks, Jamestown, and Bismarck. Gardening in these areas is largely for the local market. Home gardens are very common in the towns and on the farms. Tomatoes, beans, potatoes, radishes, lettuce, peas, sweet corn, squash, and cucumbers are the more common vegetables grown. Small fruits such as raspberries, strawberries, currants, and gooseberries are also common. Of the tree fruits, apples and plums predominate. These tree fruits are usually grown on hardy understocks for better winter survival.

Another phase of horticulture that is as important as the home garden is home production of ornamentals, both annual and perennial. The ideal summer conditions are conducive to excellent growth, and vivid expressions of the various colors are usual for these flowers. Peonies and gladiolus are well adapted to the area, as are the hybrid lilies. Transplanted geraniums and petunias are two annual types that remain showy throughout the summer.

The principal native ornamental trees are elm, box-elder, poplar, bur oak, and willows among the deciduous trees, and bull pine and red cedar among the evergreens. Some of the more colorful shrub plants, not necessarily native to the area, are lilac, dogwood, honeysuckle, and cotoneaster. All these are hardy in the area and are used extensively in landscaping.

There is only one horticultural crop of commercial importance in the state and that is potatoes. These are raised chiefly in the Red River Valley. A good portion of the potatoes raised are for certified seed which is utilized largely for the winter planting in the southern states.

The state is horticulturally minded as attested to by the large number of flower, fruit, and vegetable shows held throughout the state annually. The peony and gladiolus societies have annual shows which attract exhibitors from a large area of the Midwest. The North Dakota Horticultural Society is a large organization and is active in its functions of collecting and distributing horticultural material.

A notable horticultural feature in the state is the International Peace Garden, co-operatively sponsored by the Dominion of Canada and the United States. This garden is located in the Turtle Mountain area. It is approximately 2400 acres in area.

With the proper selection of varieties and use of good cultural practices it is possible to raise satisfactorily nearly all kinds of vegetables, and most kinds of fruits and flowers, for home ornamentation and use. It is best, however, to grow varieties adapted to the area. Determinate* tomato varieties, for example, will perform much better than the indeterminate* type. Early-maturing sweet corn is better adapted than the longer-season types. Recommendations as to varieties and the best cultural methods may be obtained from the North Dakota Agricultural Experiment Station at Fargo, which has kindly supplied this information about the state.

NORTHERN BEDSTRAW = *Galium boreale.*

NORTHERN RED CURRANT = *Ribes rubrum.*

NORTHERN WHITE CEDAR = *Thuja occidentalis.*

NORTHERN WHITE PINE = *Pinus Strobus. See* PINE.

NORWAY MAPLE = *Acer platanoides. See* MAPLE.

NORWAY PINE = *Pinus resinosa. See* PINE.

NORWAY POPLAR. *See* POPULUS BALSAMIFERA.

NORWAY SPRUCE = *Picea Abies. See* SPRUCE.

NOSEBLEED = *Trillium sessile.*

novae-angliae (no-vee-ang'li-ee). From New England.

NOVA SCOTIA. The climate of Nova Scotia is favorable for the growth of all the principal garden crops. In general the last spring frost is not later than the 24th of May and there is rarely fall-frost injury until the latter part of September. The seeding of tender vegetables such as corn and beans is usual around the 20th of May, at which time the soil has warmed up sufficiently for good germination. It is possible to mature early-maturing field beans and corn. The planting of tomatoes, eggplants, and peppers started under glass is general the last week in May and early in June, and in the more favored sections, with favorable soil, early kinds will mature practically a full crop. The province lies within zones* 2 and 3.

The summers usually are fairly dry, and in some years the precipitation may not be sufficient for continued vigorous growth on light, sandy soils. The autumns are generally ideal, although in some years the precipitation is greater than required, and unusual rains in September and October may hamper crop harvesting. Because of the maritime situation the air is high in humidity, and for this reason the rainfall requirement is not so great as that of more inland locations. The average mean summer temperature is around 63°, and rarely does the highest day temperature exceed 83°. The winter is not low in temperature and a drop to below zero is of short duration and happens only a few times during the winter.

The soil is a sandy loam for the most part, and such soils are available for gardening on almost any farm. The market for gar-

---

* Special articles on the subjects indicated by an asterisk (*) will be found at the words so marked.

den produce is limited because of the small population. Market gardeners are located adjacent to all the large centers of population, and can fully supply the market during the growing period for the staple vegetable crops. Vegetables such as root crops, cabbage, pumpkins, squash, and potatoes are stored on the farms in various sections and shipped to markets in the winter when prices are better.

There has been considerable trade in the rutabaga from Nova Scotia to New England markets in the past. Certified potatoes for seed purposes are grown quite extensively for the West Indies market, but this trade is limited.

From the foregoing it will be noted that no country offers better opportunity for the general culture of most vegetable crops, and their culture is general on all farms. Asparagus of excellent quality is produced. Celery of excellent quality is readily grown. Sweet peppers and eggplants have been mentioned previously. Spinach, lettuce, and peas are of the excellent quality possible only under moderate climatic conditions.

NOVA SCOTIA

The zones of hardiness crossing Nova Scotia are those shown on the map located at ZONE, which should be consulted for details. The dates are the average latest killing frost in spring and the first one in the fall. The figures below the dates show the average length of the growing season.

A climate suitable for vegetable crops is also suitable for all small fruits, of which strawberry and raspberry are the most important. Apples, plums, pears, and cherries are extensively grown, and in very protected situations peach trees of early sorts mature fruit. Grapes are perfectly hardy, but the summer temperature and length of season make maturity difficult, except of early varieties such as Moyer.

Needless to say, a climate suitable for fruits and vegetables is also excellent for both annual and perennial flowering plants. The tender annuals are started under glass and transplanted the last of May. Many of the hardy annuals are handled this way also and give earlier bloom. The various perennials, such as iris, peony, columbine, delphinium, and similar plants, grow to perfection. The dahlia does exceptionally well and the canna is readily grown. All bulb plants, including lilies and gladioli, do well. The leading ornamental shrubs grow and bloom to perfection.

With canning plants offering an outlet for surplus crops at paying prices, more attention is given to special canning crops such as peas, beans, beets, carrots, asparagus, corn, and tomatoes. These canneries also greatly increase the small-fruit plantings through being able to use all such surplus crops.

noveboracensis, -e (no-ve-bor-ra-sen′sis) From New York.

NOVELTIES. The procession of horticultural novelties is endless. In the last few years thousands of new varieties or forms of existing species have been put forward — flowers, fruits, vegetables, and ornamental shrubs and trees. How many exist five or ten years after their launching?

The desire to produce them is laudable, for progress in horticulture can only come from those willing to breed, select, and ultimately disseminate novelties of promise. Reputable dealers, and all the national societies devoted to special plants (dahlia, rose, sweet pea, iris, gladiolus, etc.) have for years tried to set up standards as to just what a novelty should be. In part they have been successful, but hosts of plants put out as novelties are mere trivial variations of existing plants. Such "novelties" are not worth the time to grow them, and emphatically the gardening public should be put on its guard against them.

Guarding against fraud is perhaps more difficult in the field of hort. than in any other. The number of existing forms of plants is so huge that no one person, nor even a group of specially interested judges, can be absolutely sure that the proposed novelty is really new — let alone know the future value of it.

Perhaps the most significant event in this much-debated field is the plan of having novelties of worth registered and patented at the U.S. Patent Office. *See* PLANT PATENTS. Of the hundreds that apply for such registration, many are rejected. That is a pretty fair criterion of the worth of many plants offered for registration as novelties.

For the average gardener or visitor to the larger flower shows where novelties are yearly offered in profusion, the attitude should be a keen appreciation of the effort to launch them, tempered with a rea-

---

* Special articles on the subjects indicated by an asterisk (*) will be found at the words so marked.

sonable degree of skepticism for the often extravagant claims. At first the novelties are always expensive. And a good rule to follow might be this: If you are impatient and experimental and rich, try all that interest you. But if your gardening budget is limited, wait and watch. Real novelties of worth survive the fanfare of their launching, just as the Shirley poppy and Boston fern have done. And some day they will be as cheap.

novi-belgi (no-vi-bel′ji). From New Netherlands; *i.e.,* New York.

nucifera, -us, -um (new-sif′fer-ra). Nut-bearing.

nuda, -us, -um (new′da). Naked.

nudicaulis, -e (new-di-cau′lis). Naked-stemmed.

nudiflora, -us, -um (new-di-flō′ra). Naked-flowered.

nuécensis, -e (new-a-sen′sis). From the Nueces River region of Texas.

Nummularia, -us, -um (num-mew-lair′-i-a). Coin-like; *i.e.,* round and thin.

nummularifolia, -us, -um (num-mew-lair-i-fo′lee-a). With coin-shaped leaves.

nummularioides (num-mew-lair-i-oy′deez). Like the moneywort.

NUPHAR (noo′far). Often known as *Nymphozanthus.* Coarse aquatic plants of the family Nymphaeaceae, comprising about 25 species of which the best-known is the common spatterdock (often called yellow pond lily or cow lily) and known to science as **N. advena.** Leaves large, thick, nearly 12 in. long, more or less ovalish, some submerged, others floating and some on erect stalks above the surface. Flowers yellow, never fully opened, more or less globe-shaped, about 2½ in. thick, standing above the surface, and much less attractive than in the closely related water lilies. Its culture is easy in any pool, and it often chokes them with its coarse, profuse foliage. Eastern U.S. (*Nuphar* is probably from *nenufar,* an Arabic name for some water lily.)

NURSERY. An establishment where young plants are propagated and grown until they are ready for permanent planting. Few private owners have room for a nursery, but many would profit from having one. For in no other way can new stocks be obtained so easily and cheaply.

For most of us a nursery is a commercial establishment, and for purposes of the U.S. Census a nursery is defined so as to exclude bulb growers, growers of flowers and fruits under glass, and seed-raisers. This pretty closely coincides with the general idea that a nursery is a place for propagating and growing herbs, shrubs, trees, and vines.

NUT. Technically, a nut is a hard, bony, one-celled fruit that does not split. A typical example is an acorn, or a hazelnut.

Horticulturally, the term *nut* is more inclusive, and includes almond, pecan, hickory-nut, coconut, peanut, and the Brazil-nut, all of which are technically seeds borne in a fruit that is not a nut at all. For nuts in the hort. sense *see* NUTS AND NUT CULTURE.

nutans (new′tanz). Nodding.

nutkana, -us, -um (noot-kay′na). From or near Nootka Sound, British Columbia.

NUTLET. A small nut (in the technical sense of nut*).

NUTMEG. The Moluccan spice tree producing this (and mace) is not known to be in outdoor cult. in the U.S. For the California nutmeg *see* TORREYA CALIFORNICA.

NUTMEG GERANIUM = *Pelargonium odoratissimum.*

NUTMEG MELON. See MELON.

NUT PINE = *Pinus cembroides edulis.* See PINE.

NUTRIENT SOLUTIONS. See SOILLESS GARDENING.

NUTS AND NUT CULTURE. The food value of nuts is so high and their use is so much on the increase that the production of them has become an important business in the U.S. Nut-growing is possibly not a garden operation at all and should thus be excluded from a book devoted to gardening. For, as a serious crop, they are mainly grown on land unsuited to gardening. Nuts are ideal crops for rough hillsides, or to replace second-growth or poor forests, and in such places the cost of the preparation of the land need be no more than for any forestry project. There are, however, nut crops that need as much care as any fruit orchard, and, especially in Calif., the production of them is a highly organized hort. operation.

Some of the major nut-producing plants, their best varieties, and how to grow them, are dealt with in detail in special articles in the ENCYCLOPEDIA. For an account of them *see:*

†Almond	Hickory
Butternut (*see*	†Litchi
Walnut)	†Peanut
Chestnut	†Pecan
†Coconut	Pignut (*see*
Filbert (*see* HAZEL)	HICKORY)
Hazelnut (*see* HAZEL)	†Walnut

Note: Those with a † are best suited to the warmer sections of the country. The rest are hardy, in some of their varieties, over most of the U.S.

While the above list includes the more important plants cult. in this country for their nuts (in the hort. sense), there are many other plants in the ENCYCLOPEDIA which yield edible products to which the term nut is generally applied. In the list below, some of these plants may be of interest to those seeking new or little-known sources of food, or oils, or industrial applications of plant products. A few of them

---

* Special articles on the subjects indicated by an asterisk (*) will be found at the words so marked.

are already important in highly specialized fields. Those suited only to warm or tropical sections of the country are marked with a †. Because some of them may be known only by their technical or common name both are included, the one in black-face type being the entry word which should be sought for additional information about them.

†**Areca Catechu.** Betelnut.
Beech. *Fagus.*
†**Betelnut. Areca Catechu.**
†**Cashew. Anacardium occidentale.**
Chinquapin (*Castanea*). **Chestnut.**
Chufa. Cyperus esculentus.
Cobnut (*Corylus*). **Hazel.**
†**Cohune. Attalea Cohune.**
Earthnut. Cyperus esculentus.
Groundnut. Apios americana.
Groundnut. Peanut.
†**Kolanut. Cola acuminata.**
†**Physic-nut. Jatropha Curcas.**
†**Pistachio. Pistacia vera.**
†**Tung-oil tree.** *Aleurites fordi.*
Water chestnut. Trapa natans.

Nux-vomica (nucks-vom'i-ka). A specific name meaning the vomiting nut, or one that causes it. *See* STRYCHNOS.

NYCTAGINACEAE (nick-ta-ji-nay'see-ee). The four-o'clock family has only three genera of garden interest, but they include the beautiful *Bougainvillaea* of the tropics, the popular four-o'clock (*Mirabilis*) of all old-fashioned gardens, and the genus *Abronia*, often called sand verbena on the Pacific Coast, where they are very popular.

The 30 genera and over 300 species, predominantly tropical American, are mostly shrubs and trees (a few herbs) with simple* leaves having no marginal teeth. Flowers without petals, but usually (especially in *Bougainvillaea*) very showy, from the profusion of colored bracts* which may be separate or united. In the four-o'clock the calyx is tubular and petal-like. Fruit small, dry (an achene*), grooved or winged. The magnificent *Bougainvillaea* is perhaps the most showy vine in cult., but suited only to the warmer regions of Fla. and Calif. The family is sometimes called Allioniaceae.

Technical flower characters: Flowers regular,* usually hermaphrodite.* Colored bracts present and showy, usually below the petal-like, often tubular calyx. Petals none. Stamens* 1–many. Ovary superior.* Style 1.

NYCTANTHES (nick-tan'theez). A single species of jasmine-like tree of the olive family, a native of India, and cult. in zones* 8 and 9, or in greenhouses northward, for its very fragrant, night-blooming flowers. The only species is **N. Arbor-tristis** the night jasmine, called, also, the hursinghar, tree-of-sadness, and sad tree. It is a shrub (or small tree in India) with opposite,* ovalish, short-stalked, roughish leaves and

4-angled twigs. Flowers in a close head, the latter grouped in branched clusters (cymes*). Corolla white, its tube orange. Fruit a nearly round capsule,* about ¾ in. long. It needs a warm-temperate greenhouse and potting mixture* 4 if grown under glass. In Fla. it thrives on a variety of soils. Propagated by cuttings of half-ripened wood over bottom-heat. (*Nyctanthes* is from the Greek for night flower, in allusion to its nocturnal blooming.)

NYCTOCEREUS (nick-to-seer'ee-us). A small group of mostly Mexican or Central American climbing cacti, with magnificent, fragrant, night-blooming flowers, one of them commonly called night-blooming cereus (they once belonged to the genus *Cereus*). They are at first erect, but ultimately climb 6–8 ft. high. The branch-like stems are many-ribbed and the spines are numerous. Flowers white, the outer segments bract-like and spiny. Fruit red, berry-like, black-seeded. (*Nyctocereus* is from the Greek for night and *Cereus*, in allusion to the nocturnal bloom.)

For culture *see* CACTI. For other cacti known as night-blooming cereus *see* HYLOCEREUS, SELENICEREUS and EPIPHYLLUM.

guatemalensis. Not so well known as the next, but very similar. The chief differences are that the plant is shorter and that its branches (without support) are apt to root at the downward-curving tip. Guatemala.

serpentinus. One of the plants commonly cult. as night-blooming cereus. Stems ultimately 6–8 ft. high, the ribs low and the branches somewhat weak. Ribs 10–13. Flowers about 6 in. long. Mex.

NYMPH. The immature state of certain insects. They occasionally do some damage. *See* INSECT PESTS.

NYMPHAEA (nim-fee'a). Water lily or pond lily, also called nymphea. A genus of herbaceous water plants of about 40 species distributed through tropical and temperate regions of the world, and belonging to the water lily family (Nymphaeaceae). They have beautiful showy flowers in various shades of white, red, pink, yellow, and blue, some species opening only at night but the majority during the day. The underwater perennial rootstocks are usually thick and fleshy, sometimes tuberous, and are embedded in the mud. They grow horizontally or erect, and from them the leaves and flowers are produced. Leaves roundish, green on the upper side, sometimes purplish on under side, floating, or growing 3–4 in. above the water when crowded. Leafstalk long, thick and flexible, composed of loosely packed tissue, having small air cavities which help the leaves to float. Flowers solitary, on long, cord-like stalks, the calyx of four or more long, green sepals* which completely enclose the petals when flower is closed. When open they lie flat on the water, exposing the petals and stamens,* or in some species the flowers stand out of the

---

* Special articles on the subjects indicated by an asterisk (*) will be found at the words so marked.

The flowers of hardy water lilies usually lie afloat, while the tender sorts often stand out of the water.

water. Petals many, arranged in a closely packed spiral, though apparently on the same level, giving the flower a cup-like appearance. Stamens* many, with yellow or purplish anthers.* Ovary many-chambered, many-seeded, splitting when the seeds are ripe. (Named for *Nympha,* a Greek and Roman nature goddess.) Sometimes known as *Castalia.*

For culture and a discussion of the many beautiful hybrids *see* WATER GARDEN.

alba. European white water lily. Strong and hardy. Leaves crowded on the rootstocks, roundish, 4–12 in. across, red when very young. Flowers white, 4–5 in. across, open most of the day. Petals broad and ovalish. Seeds small. Eu. and northern Af. *Var.* **candidissima** has yellow leaves when young and pure white flowers. It is the first to bloom in spring, continuing until early fall.

caerulea. Blue lotus of Egypt, also called Egyptian lotus. Tropical. Leaves ovalish, the under surface green with dark purple splotches, 12–16 in. across. Flowers 3–6 in. across. Sepals marked with black lines and dots. Petals light blue, dull white at the base. Flowers freely but is not showy. Egypt and central Af.

capensis. Cape Blue water lily. Sub-tropical. Leaves ovalish, 12–16 in. across. Flowers rich sky-blue, 6–8 in. across. Sepals green outside, whitish inside. Petals blue, white at the base. A very beautiful species. S. Af. The *var.* **zanzibariensis** has somewhat smaller leaves and larger flowers of deep blue, 6–12 in. across. Sepals green outside, deep purplish-blue within, and on the margins. The forms *zanzibariensis azurea* and *rosea* are color forms.

colorata. A tropical African water lily, the leaves 6 in. wide, green above, purple beneath. Flowers 3–4 in. wide, the petals pale violet-blue, light yellow at the base. Stamens* purple, but yellow at the base.

flavovirens. Tropical. Leaves shield-shaped, 15–17 in. across, the under side pure green. Flowers white, 6–8 in. across. Sepals pure green. Petals pointed. Mexico. Sometimes known as *N. gracilis.*

gracilis = *Nymphaea flavovirens.*

Lotus. Egyptian white lotus. Tropical. Leaves 12–20 in. across, dark green on upper side, brownish on under side. Flowers 5–10 in. across, white with the outer petals pinkish. Sepals green. Opens at night until nearly noon next day. Egypt.

marliacea. A series of hardy hybrids, many of which are yellow.

mexicana. Yellow water lily. Sub-tropical. Rootstock erect and tuberous. Leaves oval, 4–8 in. across, green but blotched brown on the upper side, crimson-brown, with black spots on the under side. Flowers 4 in. across, standing above water. Petals canary-yellow, gradually getting smaller toward the center and merging into the stamens. Fla. to Mexico. Also called *N. flava.*

odorata. White water lily; toad lily and our common white water lily of N.A. Hardy. Leaves 3–10 in. across, roundish, leathery, thick, purplish-red when young, dark green above, purplish-red beneath. Flowers white, fragrant, 3–5 in. across, opening in early morning and until noon. Sepals green, tinged with reddish-brown. Petals broadly lance-shaped. Stamens yellow, numerous, the outermost becoming petal-like and white. Eastern N.A. The hardy *var.* **rosea,** found at Cape Cod, is pink-flowered; the *var.* **gigantea** is tropical, and has pure white flowers, 4–7 in. across; the *var.* **minor** is hardy, and has smaller leaves and flowers, 2¼–3¼ in. across, the sepals definitely purple, and is a shy bloomer; the *var.* **sulphurea** is a hort. form, the leaves 4–6 in. across, like *odorata,* but blotched with brown, the flowers pale yellow, 4–5 in. across, open in the morning.

ovalifolia. Tropical. Leaves 10 in. long and 6 in. wide, having brown blotches above, but plain green beneath. Flowers deep blue, closed in dull weather. Tropical Af.

pygmaea = *Nymphaea tetragona.*

tetragona. Hardy. It is the smallest species in cultivation and has been much used for hybridization. Leaves reddish-brown beneath, 3–4 in. across. Flowers white, 1½–2½ in. across, opening only in the afternoon. Grows readily from seed and is a shy bloomer. Siberia to Japan, and in northeastern N.A.

tuberosa. Hardy. The rootstocks have tubers, 1–3 in. long, that easily become detached. Leaves green, the leafstalks with longitudinal brown stripes. Flowers 4–9 in. across, pure white, the sepals green, opening in the morning. N.A. The *var.* **richardsoni** has more petals and is ball-like when fully open.

NYMPHAEACEAE (nim-fee-ā'see-ee). The water lily family, all aquatic plants, comprises about 8 genera and perhaps 55 species, widely distributed, especially in the tropics. Besides the common water lily (*see* Nymphaea) it includes the showy plants known as lotus (*see* Nelumbo) and the magnificent *Victoria,* the largest water lily in the world, which grows in S.A. Less important cult. genera are *Brasenia* and *Nuphar.* All of these except *Brasenia* have broad, sometimes immense, leaves and extremely showy flowers. The remaining cult. genus *Cabomba,* an aquarium plant, has finely dissected submerged leaves and minute flowers. It and *Brasenia* are sometimes considered as constituting a separate family, the Cabombaceae (then called the fanwort or water shield family), but not here kept separate.

Most of the water lily family have thick rootstocks which creep in the mud and from which arise long-stalked leaves and flowers, some floating, others erect above the water surface. In many of them the floral parts are very numerous and the transition from green sepals to colored petals, and to often sterile, petal-like stamens is very gradual. Fruit various: of separate carpels in *Cabomba* and *Brasenia;* berry-like in *Nymphaea, Victoria,* and *Nuphar;* but in *Nelumbo* there is a fleshy, pitted receptacle that stands far above the water, its pits containing the large seeds. For the culture of all these *see* Water Garden.

NYMPHEA = *Nymphaea.*

NYMPHOIDES (nim-foy'deez, but *see* Oïdes). Widely distributed, floating aquatic plants of the family Gentianaceae, three of the 20 known species grown in pools or tubs for their attractive yellow or white flowers. Leaves alternate,* floating, more or less ovalish or heart-shaped at the base. Flowers borne in the leaf axils,* sometimes stalked. Calyx*

5-parted. Corolla somewhat wheel-shaped, its deeply 5-parted lobes often fringed. Stamens* 5. Fruit a capsule.* (*Nymphoides* means nymphaea-like; *i.e.,* like a water lily.) Also called *Limnanthemum.*

The cult. is the same as for water lily. *See* Water Garden. All bloom in midsummer.

cordatum. Floating heart. Leaves about 2 in. wide, ovalish or roundish, purple beneath. Flowers white, about ½ in. wide, in small clusters (umbels*) in which are occasional small tubers. N.A. and perfectly hardy over the winter. Also called *N. lacunosum.*

indicum. Water snowflake. Leaves nearly round, 2–6 in. in diameter, with a deep split at the base, the margin otherwise entire.* Flowers about ¾ in. wide, in short-stalked umbels,* white, but yellowish toward the center. Tropical regions. Not hardy northward, and suited to greenhouse or warm-region pools. There is a form with dark yellow or golden flowers.

lacunosum = *N. cordatum.*

peltatum. Leaves nearly round, about 4 in. wide, the stalk attached to the middle of the blade. Flowers yellow, about 1 in. wide, very numerous and showy. Eurasia, sparingly naturalized in the eastern U.S. and perfectly hardy up to zone* 4. A very handsome aquatic, but spreading rapidly and often hard to hold in check.

NYMPHOZANTHUS (nim-fo-zan'thus) = *Nuphar.*

NYSSA (nis'sa). A small genus of North American and Asiatic trees of the dogwood family, two (both American) cult. for ornament, especially for their fine autumnal foliage. They are generally known as tupelo or sour gum, and *N. sylvatica* has perhaps the most distinctive branching of any native tree. Leaves alternate,* practically or wholly without marginal teeth. Flowers small, greenish, not showy, borne in small, head-like clusters, unisexual* or polygamous.* Fruit an oblong, 1-seeded drupe,* black-purple in both those below. (*Nyssa* is from the Greek for a nymph, in allusion to the moist or swampy site of the native species.) Credited by some to the Nyssaceae.

Both species are hard to transplant and still more difficult to dig from the wild. Nursery-grown trees, properly root-pruned and delivered with a ball and burlap, are the safest. Or they may be raised from seed, but it must be fresh and stratified at once. Both will do best in low, moist sites.

aquatica. Tupelo gum; also called bay poplar, cotton gum, and sour gum. A swamp tree 70–100 ft. high, not much cult. Leaves slightly toothed, oblongish, 5–7 in. long, green above, paler beneath. Fruit usually solitary, about 1 in. long. Southern Ill., Mo., and Va. to Fla. and Tex. Hardy from zone* 5, possibly from zone* 4 southward. Also called *N. uniflora.*

sylvatica. Sour gum; called, also, pepperidge, black gum, and tupelo. A tree 60–90 ft. high, its branches horizontal but drooping very gradually and gracefully at the ends. Leaves 3–5 in.

* Special articles on the subjects indicated by an asterisk (*) will be found at the words so marked.

long, somewhat broader toward the pointed tip, mostly without any marginal teeth. Fruit usually in clusters of 1–3, about ⅔ in. long. Eastern N.A., but more common along the coast southward than northward. Hardy from zone* 3

southward. In the autumn its foliage turns first a dull, brick red, later a brilliant scarlet. One of the finest native trees for moist sites.

NYSSACEAE. See CORNACEAE.

O

OAK. The finest hardwood timber trees in the temperate world, and also furnishing many species of great beauty for planting on lawns, parks, street, or for the home woodlot. All oaks, as here restricted, belong to the genus **Quercus** (kwer′kus) of the family Fagaceae. The genus comprises perhaps 200 species, nearly all from the north temperate zone, a few outliers in mountainous regions in the tropics. By far the larger number are evergreen, especially the Asiatic species, and the group as a whole just misses being evergreen in N.A., where many species have leaves, usually withered, that persist over most of the winter. In the list below, however, only those whose leaves stay green through the winter are designated as evergreen. All others are deciduous.*

Leaves alternate,* stalked, variously lobed, toothed or divided in most species, but unlobed and without teeth in a few. In those that are lobed or toothed, about a third have the lobes or teeth bristle-pointed (the black oak group) but the rest have no bristles on the lobes or teeth (the white oak group); but this character does not hold in the evergreen species. Flowers unisexual,* but on the same tree, the male in drooping catkins,* the female in short spikes, or solitary, both without petals. Most of them flower very early in the spring. Fruit a true nut (the acorn) set in a cup-like involucre,* which may surround the nut only at the base, or partly or completely cover it; the cup sometimes fringed. In some species the acorns are edible and others furnish large quantities of food for hogs. (*Quercus* is the classical Latin name for the oak.)

For other trees sometimes called oak, or where oak is part of the name *see* CASUARINA, GREVILLEA, LITHOCARPUS, and RHUS. For a weedy herb known as Jerusalem oak *see* CHENOPODIUM BOTRYS.

For the culture and uses of the true oaks *see* below. Over 60 species are known to be cult. of which the following are most likely to be met.

Q. acuta. Japanese evergreen oak. A small evergreen tree. Leaves not lobed, and without teeth, sometimes wavy-margined. Acorn-cup hairy. Jap. Usually hardy from zone* 5 southward; thriving along the Gulf Coast.

Q. agrifolia. California live oak; called, also, Coast live oak and encina. Evergreen tree 60–90 ft. high, often shrubby in cult. Leaves with wavy-bristle-pointed teeth, generally ellip-

Leaves of the black oak group (*left*) and the white oak group (*right*)

tic, 2–3 in. long. Cup of the acorn hairy. Calif. Hardy only from zone* 6 southward.

Q. alba. White oak. A magnificent round-headed tree (in the open) 60–100 ft. high. Leaves broadest toward the tip, bluntly 5–9-lobed, the lobes not bristle-tipped. Cup of the acorn only ¼ its length. Eastern N.A. Hardy from zone* 2 southward. Probably the largest of all the native oaks, old specimens being over 20 ft. in circumference.

Q. bicolor. Swamp white oak. Not over 70 ft. high, usually less. Leaves somewhat broader toward the tip, 4–6 in. long, coarsely toothed or lobed nearly to the middle, the lobes not bristle-tipped, whitish beneath. Cup of the acorn about ⅓ the length of the nut. Eastern N.A. Hardy from zone* 2 southward.

Q. borealis. See QUERCUS RUBRA.

Q. Cerris. Turkey oak. A tree up to 100 ft. high, less as cult. here. Leaves oblongish, 3–5 in. long, with 4–9 pairs of sharp-pointed lobes, which are without teeth. Cup of the acorn roughish, covering about ½ of the nut. Eurasia. Hardy from zone* 4 southward.

Q. chrysolepis. Cañon live oak; also called maul oak. An evergreen tree 50–80 ft. high. Leaves elliptic, 2–4 in. long, the margins rolled or toothed, but not lobed, white-felty beneath. Cup of the acorn felty, only about ¼ the depth of the nut. Ore. to Lower Calif. Hardy from zone* 6 southward.

Q. coccinea. Scarlet oak. An upright, more or less cylindric tree 50–80 ft. high. Leaves oblongish, 4–6 in. long, shining green, sharply and deeply 7–9-lobed, the lobes bristle-tipped.

---

* Special articles on the subjects indicated by an asterisk (*) will be found at the words so marked.

Cup about ⅓ the length of the nut. Eastern N.A. Hardy from zone* 2 southward. Turns brilliant scarlet in the fall.

Q. densiflora = *Lithocarpus densiflora.*

Q. dumosa. California scrub oak. An evergreen shrub not over 8 ft. high. Leaves scarcely 1 in. long, without lobes, but often spiny-toothed, green above, paler beneath. Cup about ½ the length of the acorn. Calif. Hardy from zone* 6 southward.

Q. engelmanni. Evergreen white oak; also called mesa oak. An evergreen tree 40–60 ft. high. Leaves oblongish, 1–2 in. long, not lobed, but sometimes toothed. Cup of the acorn about ½ its length. Southern Calif. Probably not hardy in the East.

Q. hemisphaerica = *Quercus laurifolia.*

Q. Ilex. Holm oak. An evergreen tree 40–60 ft. high, with prickly holly-like leaves 2–3 in. long, and yellow-felty beneath. Cup of the acorn about ½ its length. Southern Eu. Hardy from zone* 6 southward.

Q. ilicifolia. Scrub oak. Much resembling *Q. prinoides,* but with sharper, bristle-tipped lobes to the leaves. Eastern U.S. Very hardy everywhere and good for dry, sandy soils.

Q. imbricaria. Shingle or laurel oak. A tree 40–60 ft. high. Leaves oblongish, 4–6 in. long, without lobes, teeth or bristles. Cup of the acorn a little less than half its length. N.J. to Tenn. and westward. Hardy from zone* 3 southward.

Q. laurifolia. Laurel oak. Darlington oak. A half-evergreen tree 40–60 ft. high. Leaves oblongish, 4–6 in. long, unlobed or sometimes faintly lobed, without teeth or bristles. Cup only ¼ the length of the acorn. N.J. to Fla. and La. Hardy from zone* 4 southward. Also called *Q. hemisphaerica,* which some consider the correct name for the Darlington oak.

Q. lobata. Valley or California white oak. A tree up to 100 ft. Leaves about 2½ in. long, with 7–11 blunt lobes, gray-felty beneath, the lobes not bristle-tipped. Cup about ⅓ the length of the acorn. Calif. Hardy from zone* 6 southward.

Q. lyrata. Over-cup oak. Swamp post oak. A gray-barked tree 70–90 ft. high, the young twigs hairy. Leaves oblongish or ovalish, narrowed at the base, deeply cut into 6–8 lobes, the whole leaf 6–9 in. long. Cup almost completely covering the ovoid acorn, the fringe of the cup ragged. Southeastern U.S. Hardy from zone* 4 southward.

Q. macrocarpa. Bur oak; also called mossy-cup oak. A tree up to 100 ft. Leaves 7–10 in. long, deeply lobed, the terminal lobe larger than the others, none of them bristle-tipped. Cup about ½ the length of the acorn and conspicuously fringed. Eastern N.A. and west to Tex. Hardy from zone* 2 southward.

Q. montana = *Quercus Prinus.*

Q. nigra. Water oak. Not over 80 ft. high. Leaves bluish-green, about 3 in. long, without lobes or 3-lobed at the tip. Cup about ⅓ the length of the acorn. Del. to Fla. and Tex. Hardy from zone* 4 southward and semi-evergreen along the Gulf Coast.

Q. palustris. Pin oak. Not over 80–90 ft., usually less in cult., the branches conspicuously horizontal. Leaves more or less elliptic, 4–5 in. long, sharply and deeply 5–9-lobed, shining green, the lobes bristle-tipped. Cup scarcely ⅓ the length of the acorn. Eastern N.A. Hardy from zone* 3 southward and a valuable street or lawn tree. *See below.*

Q. Phellos. Willow oak. Not over 60 ft. high. Leaves narrowly oblong, 4–5 in. long, without teeth, lobes or bristles. Cup about ¼ the length of the acorn. Long Island, N.Y., to Fla. and Tex. Hardy from zone* 4 southward.

Q. prinoides. Scrub oak. A shrubby oak, usually not over 6 ft. high, often less. Leaves oblong, 3–5 in. long, bluntly toothed but not bristle-tipped. Acorns small, the cup about ½ the length of the nut. Me. to Ala. and Tex. Hardy from zone* 2 southward.

Q. Prinus. Chestnut oak; also called rock chestnut oak. A tree up to 100 ft. high. Leaves chestnut-like but not bristle-tipped, yellowish-green above, 5–7 in. long. Cup about ⅓ the length of the acorn. Eastern N.A. Hardy from zone* 2 southward. Long mistaken for *Q. montana.*

Q. Robur. English or British oak. A round-headed tree, not over 80 ft. high. Leaves 3–5 in. long, broadest toward the tip, with 6–14 rounded lobes, without bristles. Cup about ⅓ the length of the acorn. Eurasia and northern Af. Hardy from zone* 3 southward. Many hort. forms are known, mostly in Eu.; one, the *var.* **fastigiata,** has a columnar habit. Others have variegated or even dark purple foliage.

Q. rubra. Red oak. Botanists consider that there are two forms of this native oak. The more northerly one, called *Q. borealis,* has leaves pale green on the under side. For the more southerly form, they retain the name *Q. rubra,* and this tree is "tawny or grayish pubescent beneath." Most gardeners consider them all as *Q. rubra,* the red oak. It is a tall, relatively quick-growing oak with 3–11 (usually 5–7) sharp-pointed lobes that are bristle-tipped. Acorn-cup from ⅛ (in the southern) to ⅓ (in northern) the length of the nut. Hardy from zone* 3 southward, for the northern form, which is the better of the two and widely planted for ornament. The southern form is hardy from zone* 4 southward and is not so widely known. Creating still greater uncertainty as to the correct name for the red oak, is the recent suggestion that the name *Quercus rubra* be abandoned, and that the "correct" name for the red oak is *Quercus borealis maxima.*

Q. stellata. Post oak. A round-headed tree, sometimes 100 ft. high, usually about half this. Leaves lobed lyre-fashion, leathery and roughish, 6–8 in. long, the lobes blunt and rounded, without bristles. Cup of the acorn from ⅓ to ½ the length of the nut. Mass. to Fla. and westward, especially common along the edges of the salt marshes and even on the dunes, where it becomes a picturesque, wind-wrenched, bushy tree. Hardy from zone* 3 southward.

Q. Suber. Cork oak. Its bark, harvested every 10–15 years, is the source of cork (mostly in Spain and Portugal). A tree not over 40 ft. high, its outer bark thick and corky. Leaves evergreen, ovalish, or oblong, without lobes but coarsely toothed, green above, gray-felty beneath. Cup about ⅓–½ the length of the acorn. Southern Eu. and northern Af. Hardy from zone* 6 southward. Many trees are now producing commercial cork in Calif.

Q. velutina. Black or yellow oak; called, also, quercitron. A columnar tree 100–125 ft. high, its inner bark conspicuously yellow-orange. Leaves 7–9 in. long, ovalish or oblong, 7–9-lobed, the lobes sharp-pointed and bristle-tipped. Cup of the acorn ½ or more the length of the nut. Ont. to Fla. and west to Tex. Hardy from zone* 3 southward.

Q. virginiana. Live oak. An evergreen tree, usually round-headed and not over 70 ft. high,

---

* Special articles on the subjects indicated by an asterisk (*) will be found at the words so marked.

often draped with the Spanish moss in the southern part of its range. Leaves elliptic or oblong, 3–5 in. long, without lobes, very rarely toothed, and with no bristles, green above, white-felty beneath. Acorn-cup felty, about ¼ the length of the nut. Va. to Fla. and Mex. Hardy from zone * 6 southward.

Oak Culture

The oak is one of the largest hard-wooded groups of deciduous trees hardy in the temperate sections of the U.S. Although somewhat slow-growing when compared to many other trees, it develops at a sufficient rate to permit good size in plantings of moderate age and its longevity is surpassed by no other ornamental tree. Both deciduous and evergreen types are in cultivation but only the former are hardy throughout the colder parts of the country.

The value of the oak in ornamental work lies in its massive, shapely habit and beautiful, lustrous, green foliage. In some of the forms, such as *Quercus macrocarpa* and *Prinus*, the foliage coloring is further enhanced by a silvery sheen on the under side of the leaves. Although all of the oaks are beautiful in autumn, *Quercus coccinea* and *palustris* are especially planted for their autumn effect. Their leaves turn a beautiful scarlet during October and, in the species *coccinea*, remain on the tree until spring. *Quercus prinoides* and *ilicifolia* are shrubby and form effective plantings when used in quantity in light soil. *Quercus Ilex* and *Suber* are both evergreen and are commonly cultivated in Europe. In this country, they are hardy chiefly in Calif. and in the South. Among the native evergreen species are: *Quercus virginiana*, from the Southeast; and *chrysolepis* and *agrifolia*, from California. *Quercus palustris* is often grown as a street tree because of its pyramidal habit and rapid growth.

The oaks like a rich deep soil, without hardpan.* Some of the species, among them *Quercus rubra, stellata, coccinea,* and *imbricaria,* prefer a light, sandy loam. *Quercus bicolor, nigra, alba,* and *Phellos* will do best in a heavy, damp clay.

Some care is necessary in transplanting certain species of the oak. *Quercus alba,* the white oak, is not easily moved except while young, and where large specimens are desired, the red, black, or pin oaks will transplant more easily. Oaks are excurrent trees; that is, they have a single main trunk extending their entire length. For this reason, pruning operations during transplanting should be restricted, if possible, to heading back the lateral branches and preserving the main stem. This will prevent the formation of several main branches and a stubby head which generally result when the original single leader is damaged or removed.

Propagation is usually by seed which is planted in the fall immediately after it is gathered. If planting at this time is impossible, the seed should be stratified in damp sand or moss until spring. Sprouting may occur while in storage but no harm will be done if the seed is not permitted to dry out after planting. The number of hybrid oaks is innumerable and many varieties are known. Few, however, are commonly grown. Propagation of the hybrids and varieties is by grafting in the greenhouse during Jan. Cleft and tongue grafts are used with *Quercus rubra* or *velutina* for stock in the black oak group and *Q. Robur* for the white oak group. In Europe, some of the evergreen forms are increased by layering and cuttings, but such methods are seldom employed in this country. — D. W

INSECT PESTS. Oval yellow egg masses of gypsy moth may be removed in winter in the infested New England area. However, pesticide #19 or #17 sprays will control caterpillars of this and many other species. Control scales by pruning and dormant miscible oils. Gall insects on leaves and twigs are best ignored except for gouty oak gall which should be pruned out and prunings destroyed in fall. (*See* Sprays and Dusts.)

DISEASES. The most important disease of oak is wilt.* It was first recognized and named in 1940, although some reports indicate that it may have been present at the turn of the century. This fungus disease is most serious in Midwestern states, although it has been found as far east as New York, Pennsylvania, and Maryland. While some species die more quickly than others, all infected trees will die. The general symptoms are dulling and upward curling of leaves, followed by browning and then death of the tree within several months to several years. The sapwood, just beneath the bark, turns brown or black. The disease spreads to adjacent trees of the same species by passing through roots which are naturally grafted or fused. No other natural transmission of the disease is known. Control consists of removing all diseased trees as well as all oak within 50 feet of the diseased specimens.

Following a rainy spring, anthracnose* may be serious on members of the white oak group, causing light-tan leaf spotting and partial defoliation. Members of the black or red oak groups remain relatively free from anthracnose. The blacks and reds, however, do get a disease known as oak blister or leaf curl. Light green blisters appear on the upper surface. Both the anthracnose and the leaf blister or curl may be controlled with a single application of pesticide #8 (*see* Sprays and Dusts), just before leaf buds open in the spring.

A number of canker* diseases may affect the trunk or branches and various wood rots attack the trunk and roots. Treatment of these troubles usually requires the services of a tree expert.

OAK APPLE. The galls found on some oak trees caused by various insects. They do little harm.

OAKESIA and **OAKESIELLA.** *See* Uvularia sessilifolia.

OAK FAMILY = Fagaceae.

OAK FERN = *Dryopteris disjuncta.*

OAK-LEAVED GERANIUM = *Pelargonium quercifolium.*

OAT. *See* Avena.

---

* Special articles on the subjects indicated by an asterisk (*) will be found at the words so marked.

OAT GRASS. *See* ARRHENATHERUM.

Obassia (o-bas'si-a). Native Japanese name for *Styrax Obassia.*

obconica, -us, -um (ob-kon'i-ka). Inverted cone-shaped.

OBEDIENT PLANT = *Dracocephalum virginianum.*

obesa, -us, -um (o-be'sa). Fat.

oblata, -us, -um (ob-lay'ta). Oblate; *i.e.,* flattened at the ends. Also named for the Oblate Fathers.

obliqua, -us, -um (ob-ly'kwa). Oblique or lop-sided.

OBLONG. A common descriptive term in botanical literature and throughout this book. Technically an oblong is a rectangle with parallel edges, two of which are longer than the other two. In plants, especially in leaves, to which the term is mostly applied, a perfect oblong is so rare as to be almost unknown. Hence, *oblong* and *oblongish* are here used as indications of approximate outline rather than as precise terms.

oblonga, -us, -um (ob-long'ga). Oblong.*

oblongifolia, -us, -um (ob-long-i-fō'li-a). With oblong leaves.

obovata, -us, -um (ob-o-vay'ta). Obovate; *i.e.,* ovate, but with the broad end upward.

obscura, -us, -um (ob-skure'ra). Hidden or obscured.

obtusa, -us, -um (ob-tew'sa). Obtuse.*

obtusata, -us, -um (ob-tew-say'ta). Bluntish.

OBTUSE. With a blunt or dull tip, as in many leaves and fruits.

obtusifolia, -us, -um (ob-tew-si-fō'lĭ-a). Blunt-leaved.

OCA. *See* OXALIS.

occidentalis, -e (ok-si-den-tay'lis). Western.

OCHNA (ok'na). Tropical Old World shrubs and trees, and the only cult. genus of the family **Ochnaceae** (ok-nay'see-ee) which comprises 16 other genera and over 250 species. The only cult. plant is **O. multiflora** of tropical Af. which is grown for ornament in southern Calif., rarely in greenhouses. It is a shrub 3–5 ft. high with alternate,* leathery, oblongish leaves 3–5 in. long, toothed and with prominent veins. Flowers regular, yellow, the calyx of 5 separate, petal-like sepals; petals 5, slightly twisted. Fruit fleshy (a drupe*). Propagated by cuttings of partly ripened wood, in late summer. (*Ochna* is from the Greek for a pear tree, in allusion to the pear-like leaves.)

ochnacea, -us, -um (ok-nay'see-a). Resembling the genus *Ochna.*

OCHNACEAE. *See* OCHNA.

ochroleuca, -us, -um (o-crow-lew'ka). Yellowish-white.

OCIMUM (os'si-mum). Aromatic annual or perennial herbs, rarely shrubs, of the mint family, comprising over 60 widely distributed species, of which one is cult. for its fragrant foliage. Leaves opposite.* Flowers small, irregular,* crowded in whorls* which are grouped in branching clusters (often racemes*). Corolla very small, usually not exceeding the toothed calyx,* the lobes or teeth recurved in fruit. (*Ocimum* is from the Greek for an aromatic plant, possibly for the basil.)

The basil (*O. Basilicum*) is the only one of much hort. importance. For its varieties and culture *see* HERB GARDENING.

Basilicum. Basil; also called sweet basil. A much-branched annual (or often grown as such) 1–2 ft. high. Leaves purplish, oval, 1–2 in. long. Flowers white- or purplish-tinged, about ¼ in. long. Tropical Old World and the Pacific Islands. *See* HERB GARDENING.

"OCONEE BELLS." *See* SHORTIA.

OCOTILLO = *Fouquieria splendens.*

octandra, -us, -um (ok-tan'dra). Having eight stamens.

octopetala, -us, -um (ok-to-pet'a-la). Having eight petals.

oculirosea, -us, -um (o-kew-ly-rō'zee-a). Crimson-eyed.

ocymoides (o-sy-moy'deez, but *see* OÏDES). Resembling a plant of the genus *Ocimum* (which see).

odessana, -us, -um (o-des-say'na). From Odessa, in the Ukraine.

ODONTIODA (o-don-ti-o'da). A little-known group of bigeneric* orchids. They include crosses between the genus *Odontoglossum,* which is fairly well known in cult., and *Cochlioda,* a genus scarcely known except to orchid fanciers, who are the only people interested in *Odontioda.*

ODONTOGLOSSUM (o-don-to-gloss'um). A large genus of tree-perching (epiphytic*), tropical American orchids, 4 of its 100 species cult. in the greenhouse for their odd, showy flowers. They have short, rather broad pseudobulbs* which bear 1–3 leaves. From the base of the pseudobulb* arises a slender, long-stalked flower cluster (panicle* or raceme*). Petals and sepals generally similar, the petals sometimes a little broader. Lip* lobed, the middle one with a fleshy crest near the base, the two side lobes smaller and erect. (*Odontoglossum* is from the Greek for tooth and tongue, in allusion to the teethlike crest on the central lobe of the lip.)

Besides the species below there are many others, and numerous hybrids, but they are known mostly only to orchid fanciers. The odontoglossums need a relatively cool greenhouse because they grow far up on tropical mountains. For general culture *see* Tropical Orchid Cultivation at ORCHID.

* Special articles on the subjects indicated by an asterisk (*) will be found at the words so marked.

citrosmum = *Odontoglossum pendulum.*

crispum. Leaves 12–16 in. long, 2–3 from each pseudobulb. Flowers nearly 3 in. wide, the cluster with 8–20 blooms, white, but brown-spotted, the lip wavy-margined, the throat yellow. Colombian Andes. There are many hort. vars.

grande. Leaves about 12 in. long and 3 in. wide, usually 2 to each pseudobulb. Flowers nearly 5 in. wide, yellow but brown-spotted, the lip wavy. The flowers are mostly in clusters of 3–6. Guatemala.

pendulum. Leaves about 12 in. long and 3 in. wide. Flowers about 3 in. wide, white or rose-pink, the lip rose-colored. The cluster is a many-flowered raceme* nearly 16 in. long. Mex. Sometimes known as *O. citrosmum.*

pulchellum. Pseudobulb with 2–3 leaves that are dark green, very narrow, and about 12 in. long. Flower cluster 12–15 in. long, 8–10-flowered and handsome. Flowers fragrant, about 1 in. wide, white, with purple dots on the base of the lip, which is yellow. Mex. and Central America. Winter-blooming (in the greenhouse).

ODONTONEMA (o-don-to-nee′ma). Tropical American herbs or shrubs of the family Acanthaceae, **O. strictum,** the only one of its 30 species likely to be much found in cult. It is an erect shrub 4–6 ft. high with opposite,* oblongish leaves 4–6 in. long and without marginal teeth. Flowers crimson, about 1 in. long, borne in a terminal, small-bracted* spike-like cluster. Corolla nearly regular, 5-lobed. Stamens* 4, two of them sterile. Fruit a capsule.* It can be grown outdoors only in zones* 8 and 9, where it is rather widely planted for ornament. Its greenhouse cult. is the same as for *Jacobinia* (which see). (*Odontonema* is from the Greek for thread and tooth, in allusion to the toothed filaments* of the stamens.*)

ODONTONIA (o-don-tō′ni-a). A group of bigeneric* orchids, resulting from the crossing of *Odontoglossum* and *Miltonia.* They are little known except to orchid fanciers.

ODOR. For plants fragrant in the garden *see* FRAGRANCE. For those cult. chiefly as a source of perfume *see* PERFUME PLANTS.

odora, -us, -um (o-do′ra). Fragrant.

odorata, -us, -um (o-do-ray′ta). Fragrant.

odoratissima, -us, -um (o-do-ra-tiss′i-ma). Most fragrant.

odorifera, -us, -um (o-do-rif′fer-ra). Having or bearing fragrance.

ODOSTEMON = *Mahonia.*

OEDEMA. This trouble, sometimes spelled edema, is the result of an improper water balance in the plant and is not associated with a disease organism. Small corky areas develop on under side of leaves when the soil is too wet and humidity is high. Geranium, cabbage, tomato, *Taxus,* and others suffer from oedema.

OENOTHERA. *See* EVENING PRIMROSE.

officinalis, -e (off-fi-si-nay′lis). Producing, or thought to produce, a medicine.

officinarum (off-fi-si-nay′rum). Of the apothecaries.

OFFSCAPE. A little-used term among landscape architects for the region in the offing; distant from the immediate landscape.

OFFSET. A short lateral shoot, arising at or near the base of a plant, usually rooting and thus producing a new plant. It is common in the houseleek, some crinums, and

Offsets (on the short stems) of the houseleek

in many agaves, and provides one of the easiest methods of propagation. *See also* RUNNER, STOLON.

OHIO. The carnation is the state flower, the buckeye the state tree. The state lies wholly in zones* 3 and 4.

SOILS. The soils in the western half of Ohio developed from limestone materials and have a reaction much more favorable for the growth of horticultural crops than the soils of eastern Ohio which developed from sandstone and shales and are as a rule distinctly acid.

As a result of the favorable reaction, these western Ohio soils developed an organic matter content of approximately 10 per cent. These black soils conserve moisture, retain their desirable physical state more easily, and supply more fertilizing materials upon decay than do the light-colored soils in the eastern half of the state which contain an average of only 2 per cent organic matter.

The fifty thousand acres of muck scattered throughout the northern part of the state are used largely for vegetable production. *See* MUCKLAND GARDENING.

CHIEF VEGETABLE-GROWING CENTERS. The largest acreages of vegetables are grown in the vicinities of the four largest cities, *i.e.,* Cleveland, Cincinnati, Toledo, and Columbus. Onions, potatoes, carrots, beets, turnips, celery, and parsnips are grown extensively on the muck in Hardin, Stark,

* Special articles on the subjects indicated by an asterisk (*) will be found at the words so marked.

Summit, Mohoning, Wayne, and Lorain counties. Early tomatoes, cabbage, cucumbers, and sweet corn are grown for trucking in Washington and Lawrence counties. Tomatoes and sweet corn for canning are grown in the central and western portions of the state. Cabbage for kraut is grown in the north-central counties of Huron, Lorain, and Erie.

WOODY ORNAMENTAL TREES AND SHRUBS. Ohio is well adapted to the production of nursery stock. Nurserymen are licensed in the state but about half of them are growers of bulbs, berry plants, or fruit trees only. Many acres of land are devoted to nursery production in the state, the largest centers being in Lake, Hamilton, Cuyahoga, Miami, Montgomery, and Clark counties.

The nurserymen devoted to the production of woody ornamentals grow a wide range of plant materials. The northeastern section is especially fortunate in that the climate is comparatively cool and moist. Some of the evergreens, such as the firs and hemlocks, are not entirely satisfactory in the southern part of the state, but here many of the more tender broad-leaved evergreens can be grown and used to good advantage. With few exceptions, the deciduous ornamental plants can be produced advantageously in Ohio.

FLOWERS. The majority of annual and perennial flowers are hardy and satisfactory throughout Ohio. Those normally considered half-hardy or tender may usually be grown along the Ohio River without any difficulty. The production of perennial plants commercially is largely confined to the nursery producing section but they are especially grown in the Lake County territory.

The florist industry is one of the largest in the country due to the large industrial centers scattered throughout the state. Large amounts of glass are found around Cleveland, Cincinnati, Akron, Youngstown, and other large cities. Many small wholesale ranges are scattered through the rural areas of the northern half of the state. Many of these specialize in certain crops such as geranium, hydrangeas, and cyclamen.

The amateur gardener's interest in flowers extends into practically every county, urban and rural areas alike.

FRUIT. The fruit district of major importance in Ohio is on favorable sites in the counties bordering Lake Erie, including Ottawa, Erie, Sandusky, Lorain, Huron, Cuyahoga, Lake, Geauga, and Ashtabula counties. This region also embraces the commercial grape-growing district of Ohio and in addition, a considerable quantity of grapes are produced on the islands of Lake Erie, where the climate is favorable for the ripening of Catawba and Delaware varieties. The sour cherry industry centers around Clyde in Sandusky County.

OHIO

The zones of hardiness crossing Ohio are those shown on the map located at ZONE, which should be consulted for details. The dates are the average latest killing frost in spring and the first one in the fall. The figures below the dates show the average length of the growing season.

Apples, peaches, plums, pears, and small fruits are widely grown on favorable sites throughout this district. A considerable planting of apples is found in the Columbiana-Mahoning district of eastern Ohio. On favorable sites in southeastern Ohio — in Lawrence, Jackson, Gallia and Washington counties — a considerable acreage of apples is found and in this region Rome Beauty is the predominating variety. A large number of apple orchards are found on favorable sites throughout the state, particularly in localities where local marketing can be developed. Scattered counties with important fruit interests are Clermont, Ross, Fairfield, and Licking. Strawberries are grown rather widely over the state for local marketing. Black raspberries are produced in considerable quantity around Lucasville in Scioto County; around Clyde in Sandusky County, and throughout the northern and eastern Ohio fruit belt. There is a scattered planting of peaches on favorable sites throughout the fruit counties of Ohio, with a trend toward location of orchards on sites that permit local marketing.

CLIMATE. The average length of the crop-growing season is 190 days near Lake Erie and in the southwestern part of the state. The average length of the growing season is 160 days for the north-central portion of the state, 150 days for the northeastern tier of counties and from 160 to 190 days for the south-central counties. The average dates for frosts in Cleveland, Cincinnati, and Columbus are shown in the following table:

---

* Special articles on the subjects indicated by an asterisk (*) will be found at the words so marked.

Town	Av. date of last killing frost in spring	Latest-known killing frost	Av. date of earliest killing frost in fall	Earliest-known killing frost
Cleveland	April 16	May 21	Nov. 4	Oct. 2
Columbus	April 18	May 17	Oct. 19	Sept. 21
Cincinnati	April 9	April 26	Oct. 23	Sept. 30

RAINFALL. The average rainfall is about 34 inches in northern, 35 inches in central, and 39 inches in southern Ohio. The percentage of possible sunshine is 49 at Cleveland, 54 at Columbus, and 57 at Cincinnati. The prevailing winds are from the southwest although in the Cleveland area the winds come from the southeast almost as frequently.

The average rainfall is about 4.4 inches for May, 5.3 inches for June, 5.9 inches for July, 4.9 inches for August, 3.5 inches for September, and 2.1 inches for October.

The address of the Agricultural Experiment Station which has kindly supplied this information about the state is Wooster, Ohio. The station is always ready to answer gardening questions.

Garden club activities in Ohio, due to the high development of ornamental hort., are extensive. The Garden Club of America, whose home office is at 598 Madison Avenue, New York 22, N.Y., has clubs in Cincinnati, Cleveland, Dayton, and other places. There are also many clubs of the Garden Club of Ohio and of the Ohio Association of Garden Clubs.

OHIO BUCKEYE = *Aesculus glabra*. See HORSE-CHESTNUT.

OÏDES. A very common Greek suffix in the botanical and hort. names of plants meaning *like* or *resembling*. It is commonly, but not properly, pronounced oy'-deez (exactly as in toy'deez). The Trojans correctly called it o-eye'deez, a three-syllable effort which is apparently beyond the patience of most gardeners. *Oides* occurs in such words as *ulmoides* (elm-like), *betuloides* (birch-like), *cerastioides* (chickweed-like), and many others.

OIL OF BEN. See MORINGA OLEIFERA.

OIL SPRAYS. See No. 7 at INSECTICIDES.

OKLAHOMA. The mistletoe is the state flower, the redbud the state tree. The state lies wholly in zones* 4, 5, and 6.

SOILS. About 80 per cent of the surface soils in Oklahoma are fine sandy loams with friable* sandy clay or compact clay subsoils. Enough clay occurs in some soils to produce an unfavorable physical condition. The depth of the surface soil is a very important factor in determining plant adaptation. Most of the soils in the eastern half of the state are deficient in phosphorus. About 30 per cent of the soils in this area are very acid. The majority of Oklahoma soils are deficient in organic matter. Fertilizers such as 10–20–10 or 5–10–5

(*see* FERTILIZERS), which are used on garden soils, may also be applied to areas where flowers or shrubs are grown. The rate of application should be about one to two pounds for every 100 square feet of soil.

FRUITS AND NUTS. Fruits and nuts produced in Oklahoma are pecans, apples, strawberries, peaches, blackberries and dewberries, grapes, pears, cherries, plums, walnuts. Considerable quantities of pecans are annually harvested each year, the most important producing counties being Okmulgee, Okfuskee, Lincoln, Carter, Jefferson, Garvin and Love. Pecans are found growing wild along the streams in practically all sections except the northwestern ⅓ of the state, being much more abundant in areas from the south-central to the northeastern corner of the state.

Apples, as well as other fruits, are produced in many different sections of the state. As a rule, the producing areas are rather scattered, the greatest concentration for apples being found in the following counties: Cherokee, Adair, Delaware, Pottawatomie, Seminole, Cleveland, Tulsa, and Okfuskee.

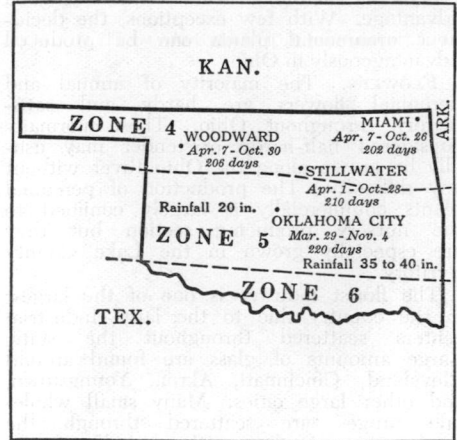

OKLAHOMA

The zones of hardiness crossing Oklahoma are those shown on the map located at ZONE, which should be consulted for details. The dates are the average latest killing frost in spring and the first one in the fall. The figures below the dates show the average length of the growing season. Rainfall figures (in inches) are for total annual rainfall in the regions so indicated.

In the western part of the state there are some very interesting orchards which are located in the sandy type of sub-irrigated soil usually found along the rivers and streams in Major, Dewey, and Woodward counties. Some of the best apples produced in the state are grown in that area, usu-

* Special articles on the subjects indicated by an asterisk (*) will be found at the words so marked.

ally in rather isolated orchards. The most profitable phase of apple-orcharding in Oklahoma is probably the production of early-ripening varieties.

Strawberries, especially the Blakemore, are produced for market in most of the eastern counties of Oklahoma, particularly those located in the northern tier of eastern counties. The following counties have a large acreage of strawberries: Adair, Sequoyah, Delaware, Cherokee, Ottawa, Craig, Muskogee, LeFlore, and Tulsa.

Peaches have in the past been planted in practically all sections of Oklahoma. However, due to late spring frosts the orchards are being discontinued in many of the older sections of the state, and production is increasing in the southeastern section of the state where crops are not so frequently lost. At the present time some of the most important counties are Logan, Tulsa, LeFlore, Grady, McCurtain, Beckham, and Cherokee.

Blackberries, especially the Lawton, and dewberries are produced in all parts of Oklahoma. They are widely grown, being produced for commercial purposes in rather an intensive way in the following counties: Pottawatomie, Major, Caddo, Oklahoma, Grady, Stephens, Hughes, and Cleveland.

Many different varieties of grapes succeed in Oklahoma, some varieties being used in one section of the state, others in another. The most important grape counties are Oklahoma, Tulsa, Beckham, Stephens, Dewey, and Caddo.

Other fruits are produced more or less uniformly over the state in scattered tracts of small areas.

VEGETABLES. The vegetable crops are produced in large quantities in Oklahoma, many sections of the state being especially well suited to the production of some of the leading types. The following vegetables are produced in Oklahoma: early potatoes, sweet potatoes, watermelons, tomatoes, cantaloupes, onions, beans, sweet corn, cabbage, radishes, and spinach.

ORNAMENTALS. While greenhouses are found in most parts of Oklahoma the industry has centered around Ardmore, Muskogee, Oklahoma City, and Tulsa, producing the usual greenhouse crops. Major production in recent years has changed from the cut-flower crops, such as roses and carnations, to the flowering pot plants such as year-round pot chrysanthemums, azaleas, poinsettias, hydrangeas, lilies, and others. In addition, year-round production of cut chrysanthemums is popular, and to some extent minor cut-flower crops and spring bedding and vegetable plants. In 1956 there were approximately 1,825,000 square ft. of greenhouse area in the state.

Nurseries of ornamentals are found predominantly in these sections of the state. Conditions are much more suitable and favorable in the eastern and southern parts of the state for the production of nursery stock.

CLIMATE. The accompanying tables indicate the range of Oklahoma weather conditions. In a general way the eastern part of the state receives approximately 35 to 40 inches of rainfall, while the central portion of the state receives about 30 inches of rainfall. The western portion of the state receives approximately 20 inches of rainfall. The detailed figures, which show an ample annual supply, except at Kenton, are:

Town	Yearly rainfall in inches
Oklahoma City	31.1
Woodward	24.7
Kenton	17.6
Muskogee	39.5
Idabel	43.7
Stillwater	33.6
Miami	43.5

FROST DATA

Town	Average date of last killing frost in spring	Date of latest-known frost in spring
Oklahoma City	March 29	April 30
Woodward	April 7	May 8
Kenton	April 23	May 15
Muskogee	March 26	....
Idabel	March 26	....
Stillwater	April 1	May 1
Miami	April 7	April 22

Town	Average date of killing frost in fall	Date of earliest-known frost in fall
Oklahoma City	Nov. 4	Oct. 7
Woodward	Oct. 30	Sept. 26
Kenton	Oct. 19	Sept. 27
Muskogee	Nov. 4	....
Idabel	Nov. 10	....
Stillwater	Oct. 28	Oct. 8
Miami	Oct. 26	Oct. 10

Garden club activities in the state include about 600 clubs affiliated with the Oklahoma Association of Garden Clubs.

The City of Tulsa has a fine Garden Center on a nine-acre site adjacent to Woodward Park and the Municipal Rose Garden. It includes the Garden Center Building with an auditorium, greenhouses, horticultural library and a staff.

The Department of Horticulture at Oklahoma State University, which is at Stillwater, has kindly supplied this information and is always glad to answer garden questions.

OKRA (*Hibiscus esculentus*). A tall, annual Old World herb cultivated for the peculiar, mucilaginous taste of its immature pods, commonly called gumbo.

It is primarily a tropical crop, but can

* Special articles on the subjects indicated by an asterisk (*) will be found at the words so marked.

be grown here where cucumbers or tomatoes are hardy. To produce the best crop, however, it wants much summer heat and therefore does better south of zone* 6 than north of it.

The plant is a tall, rank grower, and the rows should not be less than 4–5 ft. apart. The seeds should not be sown until the ground is definitely warm. Sow the seeds 1 in. deep and space them every few inches, but thin out the seedlings so that the plants will be at least 2 ft. apart as they mature. Some dwarf, but not so prolific, varieties can be planted closer than this.

Okra is successful on a variety of soils in the South, where it is chiefly grown, and it requires no other attention than cultivation to keep down weeds. Like any other crop it grows better on good land than on poor soil, but too heavily fertilized soils may produce more herbage than pods.

The best varieties are: Perkins Spineless, White Velvet, Clemson Spineless, and Louisiana Green Velvet. It is important to pick the pods while young and tender, and to allow ripening only in those pods to be saved for seed. Old pods are unfit for food. It takes about an ounce of seed for 75 ft. of row.

INSECT PESTS. Loopers may be controlled with arsenicals or pesticide #1. (See SPRAYS AND DUSTS.)

DISEASES. A wilt* disease known as Verticillium attacks okra as well as many other plants in the garden. Do not plant okra, tomato, strawberry, or chrysanthemum in an area where okra has died from wilt disease.

Plants with pale green streaks in the leaves have mosaic* disease and should be destroyed to prevent transmission of the virus to neighboring plants.

OLD-FASHIONED FLOWERS. The flowers common in cultivation two hundred years ago are sometimes called old-fashioned flowers, but with little real reason. Many of our best-known garden flowers have been cult. for over two thousand years, among them the rose, chrysanthemum, peony, hollyhock, narcissus, lily, marigold, foxglove, and many flowering shrubs and trees.

But old-fashioned flowers do seem to mean, in America at least, those that were cult. in the pre-Revolutionary gardens of our ancestors. Among them were the hollyhock, pansy, marigold, foxglove, lily-of-the-valley, some lilies, tulip, narcissus, iris, Virginia stock, and candytuft. Much remains to be done on the definite date of introduction of many common flowers into America. The gardens at the Williamsburg Restoration in Va. have the finest collection of pre-Revolutionary flowers.

OLD MAN = Artemisia Abrotanum.

OLD-MAN-AND-WOMAN = Sempervivum tectorum. See HOUSELEEK.

OLD-MAN CACTUS = Cephalocereus senilis.

OLD-MAN'S-BEARD = Chionanthus virginicus. See also CLEMATIS VITALBA and C. VIRGINIANA.

OLD WOMAN = Artemisia stelleriana.

OLD WOOD. Ripened wood suitable for making hardwood cuttings.

OLEA. See OLIVE.

OLEACEAE (o-lee-ā'see-ee). The olive, ash or lilac family comprises one of the more important groups of garden shrubs and trees, for it includes Fraxinus (see ASH), Forsythia, Ligustrum (see PRIVET), Jasminum, and Syringa (see LILAC), all of outstanding importance in the garden. There are only 20 genera and perhaps 500 species in the family, which is widely distributed over the earth. The most important genus is Olea (see OLIVE), and the other hort. genera, besides those above, most of them ornamental, are Abeliophyllum, Chionanthus, Fontanesia, Forestiera, Nyctanthes, Osmanthus, and Phillyrea. The family is sometimes called Jasminaceae.

Leaves prevailingly opposite,* mostly without marginal teeth, evergreen in several genera (olive, Osmanthus, Osmarea, Phillyrea, and several privets). Flowers extremely handsome and showy in the lilac, Jasminum, Forsythia, Chionanthus and some other genera, but small and inconspicuous in the olive and ash which has (usually) no petals. Fruit a true drupe* in the olive, dry and winged (a samara*) in the ash, and a fleshy or dryish berry in several other genera.

Technical flower characters: Flowers regular,* prevailingly hermaphrodite,* usually borne in profuse clusters. Calyx 4-lobed or none. Corolla tubular and 4-lobed, or of four separate petals or none. Stamens* usually 2. Ovary superior,* mostly 2-celled.

OLEANDER. Widely cult. ornamental evergreen shrubs or small trees comprising the genus Nerium (neer'i-um) of the family Apocynaceae, all of them with a dangerously poisonous juice. They are sometimes called rose-bay. Leaves opposite* or more usually in whorls* of 3, rather thick and leathery, without teeth. Flowers in showy terminal clusters (cymes*). Corolla funnel-shaped, its limb bell-shaped, and with 5 fringed or broad teeth, slightly twisted to the right. Stamens not protruding. Fruit a cluster of 2 long, cylindrical follicles.* (Nerium is the Greek name of the oleander.) For the yellow oleander see THEVETIA NEREIFOLIA.

For outdoor culture and varieties see below. Of the three known species, N. Oleander is by far the commonest in cult., but it is usually without any fragrance. The other cult. species, N. indicum, has beautifully vanilla-scented flowers. Neither is certainly hardy outdoors north of zone* 7 and anyone trying to grow them in zone* 6 should protect them over the winter.

As tubbed plants for northern summers the oleander is nearly as popular as the laurel. See LAURUS, as the winter care of oleanders, in the North, is the same as for the laurel or bay tree. Oleanders also

---

* Special articles on the subjects indicated by an asterisk (*) will be found at the words so marked.

make good pot plants for the house, but children should be warned against their poisonous juice. Plunge* the pots outdoors from June to Sept., inclusive, in full sunshine. House plants will be most likely to flower from March to May, and during the dark winter months do not keep them too moist. About March 1 increase the amount and frequency of watering and put them in a sunny window.

N. indicum. Sweet oleander. Usually not over 8 ft. high, the leaves narrowly lance-shaped, 6–10 in. long, the margins rolled. Corolla sweet-scented, pink or white, about 2 in. wide, often double in hort. forms. Persia to Jap.

N. Oleander. Common oleander; also called rose-bay. A shrub or small tree 8–25 ft. high, leaves narrowly oblong, 4–8 in. long, dark green above, paler, and with a prominent midrib beneath. Flowers white, red, pink, or purple, about 2½ in. wide, often double in hort. forms. Southern Eu. and northern Af., but cult. throughout the tropical and sub-tropical world and often naturalized there. Its juice and fruits are poisonous. For its many varieties *see* below.

Outdoor Oleander Culture

Oleanders are propagated from cuttings, hardwood or softwood. In the lower South, hardwood cuttings, cut about 8 inches long, are planted in open ground. Softwood cuttings are taken in the summer and usually handled in a greenhouse. Cuttings root readily when placed in bottles of water, which should be changed at intervals to keep it fresh.

Oleanders grow readily in a variety of soils. For best results these should be moist, well drained, and furnished with a goodly supply of organic matter. They are well adapted for town and city planting in the South. Full sunshine is best. They are not affected by drying winds, smoke, salt spray, and soot.

In gardens, oleanders are suitable for the shrubbery border, for making screens, and for planting against bare walls of large buildings. Frequently they are grown along roads and walks. Grown in tubs or pots, they make good house plants and are frequently grown in greenhouses. When in flower in spring and summer they are very decorative and even when out of bloom they are attractive evergreen specimens.

Oleanders are commonly grown as shrubs with numerous stems. When they become too dense they should be thinned. They stand pruning well. If they become straggly and open they may be cut back severely, even within a few inches of the ground. The stems may be reduced to one and the shrub grown as a tree. From time to time, as additional stems or trunks appear, they should be cut out.

Varieties

As already indicated, color usually runs through the gamut of white, pink, and red.

There are single and double sorts in these colors. They differ in their resistance to low temperatures; Cardinal, a brilliant red, so far as observed, is the hardiest of all. There is a light-yellow variety. Mostly they are designated by color, but a few have been given varietal horticultural names:

Brilliant   Single, rose-red.
Jannock   Single, large flowers, bright red.
Mrs. Roeding Double, salmon-pink.
Mrs. Swanson Double, soft pink.
Sister Agnes   Single, pure white. — H. H. H.

OLEARIA (o-lee-ā′rĭ-a). Tree aster or daisy tree. Mostly Australasian shrubs and trees of the family Compositae, with aster-like flowers. Of the 100 or more known species, over 20 are in occasional cult. in Calif., of which the three below are by far the best-known. Leaves mostly alternate, nearly always white-felty beneath. Flower heads aster-like, the ray flowers in a single row, white or violet (in ours). The heads are usually grouped in clusters (corymbs* or panicles*), but sometimes solitary. (*Olearia* is derived from *Olea*, because of the olive-like foliage of some species.)

The outdoor cult. of olearias is mostly confined to Calif., and of the three below *O. haasti* is the most hardy. Propagated by cuttings of half-ripened wood or by seeds.

forsteri = *Olearia paniculata.*

haasti. A bushy shrub 6–8 ft. high. Leaves oblongish, about 1 in. long, without marginal teeth. Flower heads white, about ½ in. wide, in long-stalked clusters (corymbs*). N. Z. The hardiest species, but not safe above zone* 7 or possibly 6.

paniculata. A shrub or small tree 15–20 ft. high. Leaves oblongish or ovalish, 2–3 in. long, the margins wavy. Flower heads white, about ⅓ in. wide, in a branched cluster (corymb*). N. Z. Suited only to zones* 7 and 8. Sometimes known as *O. forsteri.*

stellulata. A shrub, not over 5 ft. high. Leaves oblongish or narrower, 2–3 in. long, wavy-toothed. Flower heads violet, showy, mostly in branched clusters (panicles*). Australia. Suited only to zones* 7 and 8.

OLEASTER = *Elaeagnus angustifolia.*

OLEASTER FAMILY = Elaeagnaceae.

oleifera, -us, -um (o-le-if′fer-ra). Oil-bearing or oily.

oleracea, -us, -um (o-ler-ā′sĭ-a). Of the vegetable garden; used in cooking.

OLERICULTURE. See Vegetable Gardening.

olitoria, -us, -um (o-li-tō′rĭ-a). Pertaining to the vegetable garden or to vegetable gardeners.

OLIVE. Evergreen shrubs and trees of the Old World comprising the genus **Olea** (ŏ′lee-a) of the ash family, one of its 50 known species cult. for centuries for its fruit (the olive). It is a tree 25–70 ft. high (usually less as cult. in Calif.), with opposite* leaves having no marginal teeth. Flowers small, white (*see* below). Fruit a true drupe* (the common olive is the only edible

* Special articles on the subjects indicated by an asterisk (*) will be found at the words so marked.

one). (*Olea* is the classical Latin name of the olive.)

O. europaea. The common olive. Branches thornless (but a wild thorny variety is known). Leaves elliptic or oblongish, 1–3 in. long, green above, silvery and somewhat scurfy beneath. Flowers fragrant, in clusters (panicles*) shorter than the leaves. For fruit *see* below. Native throughout the Mediterranean region, but only in the hottest parts of it. For hardiness *see* below.

For the false olive *see* ELAEODENDRON. For the Russian olive *see* ELAEAGNUS ANGUSTIFOLIA. For the tea olive *see* OSMANTHUS.

OLIVE CULTURE

The olive was brought to N.A. from Spain, and to Calif. from Mex. by the Mission fathers. It is a hardy sub-tropical evergreen of high heat requirement, the commercial culture of which in this country is limited to the Pacific Southwest. Remarkably resistant to heat and drought, for satisfactory bearing it requires moderate water supply. Northward distribution is limited by cold, as the tree suffers injury at 15°, the fruit at 28°. It succeeds in Gulf Coast states, but high atmospheric humidity prevents setting of the fruit. Because of late blooming and the amount of heat necessary to mature it, the fruit requires a long, hot, growing season. It does not ripen until late fall even in the hottest regions. Commercial culture is restricted, therefore, to interior valleys of Calif. and warmer portions of Ariz. Principal climatic hazards in its culture are early fall frosts, before harvest, and desert winds during blooming and fruit-setting period.

The olive tree is remarkably tenacious of life and one of the longest-lived and most beautiful of all fruit trees. In Calif. some of the original trees are still in existence; in the Mediterranean region trees are known many centuries old (*see* Age of Trees at GARDEN TABLES III). Under favorable conditions it attains great size. Most varieties exhibit a tendency toward alternate bearing, and two large crops are rarely produced in succession. Most varieties appear self-fruitful to a reasonably satisfactory degree, though in occasional seasons advantages of cross-pollination are evident.

The flowers are small and inconspicuous, and extremely numerous; many of them are imperfect, however. Borne only on growth of the previous season. Pollen produced in abundance. Fruit small, rarely exceeding 2 in. in length and 1¼ in. in diameter; and the form ranges from apple-shaped to football-shaped. When fully ripe the color ranges from reddish-purple to black. Ripening season extends from Oct. to Dec. 15. In some varieties, when pickled, the flesh separates readily from the seed, in others not. The principal constituent of the fruit is oil; when extracted and clarified, known as olive oil. It occurs

in seed and flesh, though the latter gives the best quality. Fresh fruit never edible because of bitter principle contained in the flesh, which gives a most unpleasant taste. This substance is removed in most processing or pickling treatments. Range in oil content varies from 15 to 30 per cent of fresh weight.

The olive propagates readily from cuttings, either hardwood or softwood tip cuttings.

The tree has a wide range of soil adaptation, but requires good drainage. It has no special cultural requirements, but the high premium paid for large-sized fruit makes important those practices which promote attainment of this objective. Among these are irrigation, pruning, and fruit-thinning. Moderately severe pruning increases the size of the fruit, but at expense of both size of crop and tree. Fruit-thinning not only increases the fruit size but also materially assists in overcoming the alternate bearing tendency. Evidence indicates that this fruit responds to fertilization and that nitrogen is the element which increases yields.

Increase in yield is usually associated with smaller size of fruit, and the yield is unquestionably restricted by shading. It is necessary, therefore, to provide proper spacing or to regulate the size of trees by pruning.

Fruit for pickling is harvested by hand and must be handled carefully for high quality. It is usually picked to color, and several pickings are required because of unevenness in ripening. It is best picked in baskets or buckets, the latter sometimes containing water to prevent bruising.

While grown abroad primarily for extraction of the oil, in this country the industry is based entirely on pickling or processing the fruit, oil extraction providing merely an outlet for fruit of small size or inferior grade. The American oil, however, equals the best imported product. There are several pickling processes, the principal being the Calif. ripe-olive process, which turns out a uniform dark-colored fruit with a rich, nutty flavor and high food value. Succession of lye treatments and washings removes the bitterness, and aeration provides uniform dark color necessary for standardization of product.

The fruit is then canned in light brine and sterilized at 240° F. for one hour. It is one of the safest of all canned products. Small quantities are pickled green, some by the method just described and some by lactic-acid process employed for the imported product. Some fruit is also processed by curing in heavy brine or ground rock salt, without lye.

Practically all the commercial production is located in Calif. A major fruit as grown in the Mediterranean basin, where Spain and Italy are the principal countries.

The major varieties in Calif., and their

---

* Special articles on the subjects indicated by an asterisk (*) will be found at the words so marked.

countries of origin, are as follows: Mission, Manzanillo, Sevillano (Spain), and Ascolano (Italy). Sevillano and Ascolano, are large-fruited varieties, sometimes called Queen olives. — R. W. H.

INSECT PESTS. Scale insects such as black scale may be controlled by oil sprays in summer at 1.5–2% strength. Do not apply when temperatures are over 90° F. Addition of pesticide #21 will increase kill. During post-bloom period, oleander and parlatoria scales can be controlled. Use heavy pesticide #17 spray to keep out borers on stubs in spring. (See SPRAYS AND DUSTS.)

DISEASES. Knots or swellings often appear as the result of a bacterial disease. Although not usually fatal to the part of the tree affected, these knots should be removed.

A rot of the trunk or roots, known as shoestring root rot, may weaken some trees. Black, brittle "shoestrings" are present just under the bark or on the surface near the soil line. Diseased trees usually decline and slowly die.

OLIVE FAMILY. Shrubs and trees, many of them of great garden importance, are found in the olive or ash family. Among them are the olive, privet, lilac, jasmine, ash, and *Forsythia*. For a complete list of the commonly cult. genera and the characters of the family *see* OLEACEAE.

OLIVERANTHUS (ol-i-ver-ran'thus). A Mexican perennial herb, the only one of the genus, and belonging to the family Crassulaceae. The only species, **O. elegans**, is an erect herb to 20 in. high. Leaves fleshy, broad at the tip, narrowing to the base, crowded near the tip of the stems. Flowers 1–2 at the ends of branches, bright red, tipped with yellow, 1 in. long. Petals free nearly to the base. Pistils* 5, separate. It is sometimes offered as *Cotyledon elegans* or *Echeveria harmsi*, which some consider the correct name for it. (Named for the late G. W. Oliver of the U.S. Dept. of Agriculture.)

It is an attractive summer-flowering plant, not hardy north of Washington, D.C. It does well in sandy soil, in sunny positions, and is suitable for rock gardens or borders. Propagated from seeds and by stem and leaf cuttings.

oliviformis, -e (ol-iv-i-for'mis). Olive-shaped.

olympica, -us, -um (o-lim'pi-ka). From or near Mount Olympus, Greece.

Omorika (o-more-ree'ka). Serbian vernacular for the spruce *Picea Omorika*.

OMPHALODES (om-făl-lō'dez). Navel-wort. Low annual or perennial herbs, comprising about 25 species, closely allied to *Cynoglossum* of the forget-me-not family, which they resemble, and natives of Eu. and As. Stems smooth or slightly hairy. Basal leaves long-stalked, lance-shaped or heart-shaped, the stem leaves smaller, fewer, and alternate.* Flowers blue, sometimes pinkish, arranged in loose, one-sided racemes.* Calyx joined halfway down. Corolla united to form a short tube, usually white, but with vein-like markings radiating from the center, giving it a star-like appearance. Stamens* 5, not protruding. Fruit 4-celled, when ripe splitting into 4 separate parts, each containing one or more seeds. (*Omphalodes* is from the Greek for navel-shaped, in allusion to the seeds.)

The annual species should be sown where required to flower, in ordinary garden soil, in moist, half-shady position. Sow the seeds ⅛ in. deep. Seeds sown in spring will flower the same season, and if sown in Sept. will flower in early spring. Hardy. Perennial species require the same treatment, but seeds should be sown in spring. They may also be propagated by division of roots in Sept. or April. All grow best in a cool, partially shaded position, where the soil is neutral or slightly alkaline. *Omphalodes* is not much in cultivation, but is sometimes used as ground cover or in the rock garden.

cappadocica. A perennial, 6–10 in. high. Leaves usually heart-shaped, with prominent veins, and soft-silky hairs, the lower leaves stalked. Flowers bright, clear blue, with markings at the throat. One of the best for shady spots in the rock garden. Spring. Asia Minor.

linifolia. Annual, up to 1 ft., the foliage light green. Lower leaves wedge-shaped, the upper spear-like, with slightly hairy margins. Flowers white, the corolla tube twice as long as the calyx.* The *var.* **caerulescens** is a color form, having blue flowers. This species can be grown on dry or stony ground. Spring or summer. Spain and Portugal.

verna. Creeping forget-me-not. A perennial, growing to 8 in. high, the main stems prostrate, but with erect, flowering stems. Leaves ovalish, the lower ones long-stalked. Leaves on flowering stems short-stalked and spear-like. All are pointed. Flowers borne in pairs, in loose racemes,* the individual flowers about ½ in. across. Often used as a ground cover. Spring. Eu.

ONAGRACEAE (o-na-gray'see-ee). The evening primrose family, sometimes called the fuchsia family, includes many herbs with showy flowers, a few tropical genera, and one or two aquatic or mud-inhabiting herbs. There are over 30 genera and about 600 species, most common in the temperate parts of the New World.

From the garden standpoint *Fuchsia* is perhaps the best-known plant. It is prevailingly tropical American and needs greenhouse culture. The other tropical genera are *Jussiaea* (treated as a tender annual) and *Lopezia* (Mexican herbs or shrubs). All the other cult. genera are herbs, often with very fine bloom, and easily grown outdoors over most of the U.S., the exception being *Zauschneria*, which is native in Calif. The herbaceous genera of relatively easy culture are: *Clarkia, Epilobium, Eucharidium, Gaura, Godetia,* and *Oenothera* (*see* EVENING PRIMROSE). *Ludwigia* and *Trapa,* like *Jussiaea,* are aquatic or mud-inhabiting.

Leaves alternate* or opposite.* Flowers usually showy and regular,* but appearing irregular in *Fuchsia,* sometimes solitary, more often in handsome clusters. Fruit a

---

* Special articles on the subjects indicated by an asterisk (*) will be found at the words so marked.

dry pod (capsule*), often with silky-haired seeds in some genera, fleshy and berry-like in others.

Technical flower characters: Calyx 2–6 (typically 4)-lobed, its tube joined to the inferior* ovary. Petals 4, mostly clawed.* Stamens 4 or 8, inserted on the throat of the calyx tube. Ovary 2–4-celled.

ONCIDIUM (on-sid'i-um). Very beautiful, tropical American, tree-perching (epiphytic*) orchids, comprising over 500 species and many hort. varieties, of which a great number are grown by orchid specialists, but few are in general cult. They have small pseudobulbs* from which arise 1 or 2 leaves that are usually long, narrow, and without teeth. Flowers very numerous, the long, slender, branched cluster very handsome. Corolla very irregular,* although the sepals are usually uniform, but sometimes two of them are united or partly so. Petals similar to the remaining sepal. Lip various, often beautifully colored, spreading at nearly right angles to the column, its crest swollen or tubercled. (*Oncidium* is from the Greek for tubercle, in allusion to the swollen crest of the lip.)

For culture *see* the article ORCHID (greenhouse species).

ampliatum. Leaves only 2, arising from a rounded, compressed, and wrinkled pseudobulb 2–4 in. wide, purple-blotched. Leaves 8–12 in. long, 2–3 in. wide, leathery. Flowers about 1 in. wide, with small, yellow, red-blotched sepals, yellow petals and lip. Tropical America.

flexuosum. Pseudobulb with one or two leaves which are 8–10 in. long. Flowering stalk 2–3 ft. long, branched, forming showy cluster (panicle*). Flowers about 1 in. wide, yellow, but reddish-brown and spotted near the base. Tropical S.A.

ornithorynchum. Leaves only two, 8–10 in. long. Flowering stalk drooping, 12–18 in. long, branched into a many-flowered cluster (panicle*). Flowers about ¾ in. wide, heliotrope-scented, pale purple or lilac, the lip yellow-crested. Mex. and Central America.

Papilio. Butterfly-orchid. Leaf only 1, usually red-mottled, about 8 in. long and 2 in. wide. Flower nearly 3½ in. wide, solitary but blooming in succession, on a slender stalk nearly 3 ft. long. Petals and sepals narrow, brown but yellow-spotted. Lip yellow but brown-margined. Venezuela. Blooming most of the year in the greenhouse.

sphacelatum. Leaves 2–3 at each pseudobulb, nearly 24 in. long. Flowering cluster (panicle*) loosely branched, 3–5 ft. long. Flowers about 1 in. wide, prevailingly yellow, brown-spotted, the lip darker yellow with a red band near the tip. Mex. to Central America.

splendidum. A showy orchid thought by some to be a variety of the closely related *O. tigrinum* (a usually non-hort. species). It has 1–2 leaves at each pseudobulb, the leaves 10–12 in. long, keeled on the back. Flowering stalk 24–40 in. long, loosely branched into an open cluster (panicle*). Flowers yellow, blotched or barred with red-brown, 2–3 in. wide. Guatemala.

varicosum. The commonest species in cult. and often seen in florists' windows. Leaves 2, nearly 9 in. long and very narrow, but tough. Flowers about 1 in. wide, very numerous in a long, slender, branched, usually drooping clus-

ter nearly 5 ft. long. Sepals and petals greenish-yellow, but spotted with red-brown. Lip, the only really showy part of the bloom, golden-yellow, its crest toothed or tubercled, sometimes blotched with red-brown. Brazil. Blooming Oct.–Jan. in the greenhouse. The *var.* rogersi has flowers (mostly the lip) nearly 2 in. wide, yellow, but with showy red bars.

ONE-FLOWERED WINTERGREEN = *Moneses uniflora.*

ONION (*Allium Cepa*). The underground bulb of this pungent, strong-smelling plant has been extremely popular for many centuries. Today there are two main types that interest the gardener. They are the young, green or white, bunching sorts eaten fresh and before the mature bulb has formed. The other and much more widely grown sort develops a large, coated bulb with a papery skin. These are used fresh (rarely, for they are pretty strong), or more often boiled or fried. Certain varieties of them can be easily stored for considerable periods.

VARIETIES. *For bunching and eating green:* Egyptian or Tree. Beltsville Bunching. Also any var. from sets (*see* below). *For mature bulbs:* Danvers, in several strains. Ebenezer. Yellow Globe. Yellow Bermuda (a poor keeper). Prizetaker (a good keeper). The Yellow Bermuda is one of the mildest for slicing and eating fresh.

SOILS AND FERTILIZERS. Onions require a rich, well-drained soil, but any good vegetable-garden soil will be satisfactory so long as it is not too stony. The bulbs need a loose, friable* soil in which to expand. To be sure it is rich enough use a pound of well-rotted manure to each square foot of soil and in addition use 4–5 pounds of a fertilizer with a 4–8–10 ratio (*see* FERTILIZERS) to each 100 square ft. (approximately a ton to the acre). Stable manure should always be used if it is the only enrichment the onion soil will have.

The soil must be moist, as the plant will not thrive in dry sites. It is grown successfully in nearly all but the desert states, but it thrives best in the comparatively cool North. Commercial production in Fla. and Calif. is based upon using their comparatively cool winter and early spring months. *See also* MUCKLAND GARDENING.

METHOD OF STARTING. There are three ways of raising onions: by seeds, by sets, and by the multipliers or potato-onions that often develop among the flower clusters.

For most home gardeners raising onions from seed is a tedious failure more often than a success. Seedling plants, raised by the expert dealers, are inexpensive and far easier to handle. These seedlings are one of the most satisfactory methods of starting an onion patch.

Onion sets are also very inexpensive in the amounts needed by the average household. The "set" consists of a small, dried, immature bulblet* which has been raised from seed the previous year and picked

---

* Special articles on the subjects indicated by an asterisk (*) will be found at the words so marked.

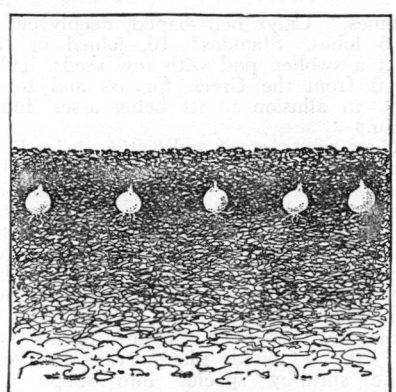

Cross-section of an onion bed, showing the sets
planted about 2 in. apart and 2 in. deep.

when young. These immature bulblets will
each produce a mature onion during the
season. Sets are used almost exclusively for
the bunching type of spring onion eaten
fresh. They are also used by many for mature onions, because of the ease of planting
and from the fact that while seedlings may
wilt, the young sets scarcely ever fail.

The third method of starting is peculiar.
Many plants of the genus *Allium* (onion and
its relatives) occasionally produce bulbils*
among the flower cluster. These are not
true bulbs like the sets, but an aerial,
bulb-like organ from which a new plant will
grow. Because of this curious character
such plants are often called multiplier- or
potato-onions. They may be bought at the
dealers and their use is largely confined to
the onions to be bunched and eaten fresh.

Whichever method is used, it is of the
greatest importance to secure true stock,
authentic as to variety and from a most
reliable dealer. Cheap stock, especially in
sets, will very likely end in relatively costly
failure.

PLANTING. We may safely disregard
growing onions from seed. It is so troublesome that many large commercial growers
prefer to buy seedlings ready to plant, or
sets.

If sets are used, they may be planted
about 10 days before it is safe to put out
seedlings. Sets should be planted, one to a
hole, about 2 in. deep. Or you can plant
them in a 2-in. drill. In either case, the
space between bulblets should be 4 in. for
the onions you expect to grow to maturity,
and 1½ in. for the bunching type, which will
soon be pulled out. Keep the rows 15 in.
apart (more if motor cultivator is to be
used).

If seedling plants, instead of sets, are used,
they should be planted upon the same intervals as those already given for sets. Plants
may be set out whenever reasonably warm
weather has arrived. A fair criterion
for your neighborhood is when the common
lilac has just passed out of bloom.

Some growers, especially those using the
easily stored sets, will plant a succession of
onions so as to ensure a crop until frosty
weather arrives. But it should be remembered that mature onions take from 120
to 160 days to develop, so that successional
sowings will very likely have to be harvested before maturity or as bunching
onions.

CULTIVATION. The onion is, in spite of its
bulb, a shallow-rooted crop, and its bulbs are
very easily injured by implements. It is
necessary to cultivate enough to keep down
weeds and conserve moisture, but the cultivator or hoe should not go more than an
inch or two below the surface, and no
bulbs must be disturbed. On small patches
the scuffle hoe is much the safest tool to use.
Keep the soil pulverized at all times.

If chicken manure is available, sow between the rows, about a month after the
plants have been set out, enough of it to
make a thin covering of the center of the
space between the rows. Gently and shallowly work it into the soil. Its high nitrogen
content makes poultry manure an exceedingly valuable fertilizer for onions. Some
growers use two applications of it about
five weeks apart. It must not touch the
plants.

HARVESTING. There are few crops where
you can plan with such exactitude for your
needs as with onions grown from sets.
Plant only as many as your present or winter needs demand. When the tops turn
yellow and begin to wilt it is time to pull up
the bulbs. Some, not mature, but perfectly
satisfactory for immediate use, can be harvested before this. But for those you expect to store, it is better to allow them to
come to full maturity.

The tops should be cut off the pulled onions
about an inch above the bulb and the bulbs
spread out on the barn floor or upon
racks to dry off thoroughly the surface
moisture. This will take from 10–14 days.
A sane guide as to their proper curing is
that the neck or cut-off stem is no longer
green and plump but more or less shriveled.
When this stage is reached, onions may
safely be stored, preferably in airy crates
or net sacks, in a cool, well-ventilated, dry
room.

For the preferred position and sequence
of onions in your garden *see* KITCHEN
GARDEN. For the sea onion *see* URGINEA
MARITIMA and SCILLA VERNA.

INSECT PESTS. In summer, thrips can be
stopped by application of pesticide #1 or #21.
Dry years present the worst problem. Maggot
attack is best stopped by combination seed treatment. After emergence of seedlings or after sets
begin to grow, apply pesticide #21 or #1 at
weekly intervals for 4 to 6 weeks. (*See* SPRAYS
AND DUSTS.)

DISEASES. If the smut* disease causes black,
powdery eruptions on the onions, use specially
treated seeds in subsequent years. Pelleted
seeds may be obtained which have both a
fungicide and insecticide as a seed treatment.
If leaves become scorched,* blasted, or cov-

---

* Special articles on the subjects indicated by an asterisk (*) will be found at the words so marked.

ered with mildew,* apply pesticide #11 (*see* SPRAYS AND DUSTS) at weekly intervals.

To prevent rotting during storage, select firm, clean onions and store in a relatively dry area where they will not freeze.

Onites (o-ny'teez). An old generic name for a section of the genus *Majorana*.

ONOBRYCHIS (o-no-bry'kiss). Perennial Eurasian herbs or spiny shrubs, comprising about 80 species of the pea family. Leaves compound,* the leaflets entire,* lance-shaped, opposite,* the main leafstalk ending in a leaflet. Flowers pea-like, deep rose to light pink, in racemes* or spikes. Calyx of 5 sepals, sometimes prickly and jointed at the base. Stamens* 10, 9 joined by their stalks, 1 free. Fruit a pod which does not split. (*Onobrychis* is from the Greek for food of asses, in allusion to the use for forage.)

Cultivated generally for its fodder value, especially in Europe, but occasionally used in the flower border, and planted in masses. Propagated from seeds sown in spring or summer for flowering the following year. Sow seeds ½ in. deep where intended to bloom in ordinary soil. They will grow in poor or sandy soil.

Caput-galli. Height 1 ft. Leaflets small. Flowers flesh-colored. Pods hard and dry. Mediterranean region.

viciaefolia. Sainfoin or Saintfoin, also called holy clover. It usually grows to a height of 2 ft. Leaflets many, ovalish, 1 in. long, slightly hairy on the under side, light green on the upper. Flowers pale pink or white. Pods curved on the lower edge, with teeth-like margins, sometimes prickly. This is the species used for fodder. Eu. and northern As.

ONOCLEA (o-no-klee'a). A single species of hardy, rather coarse ferns of the family Polypodiaceae, common in moist thickets and meadows nearly throughout N.A., Eu., and As., and sometimes grown in such sites in the fern or wild garden. The only species, **O. sensibilis,** is the sensitive fern, so called because its leaflets are supposed to, and sometimes do, fold up slightly when picked. Its foliage fronds are 2–4 ft. high, more or less triangular-oval, leafy, twice-compound,* its ultimate segments oblongish, slightly lobed or unlobed. The spores are borne on special spore-bearing fronds which are about 2½ ft. high, twice-compound, the ultimate segments rolled into berry-like or bead-like bodies. For culture *see* FERNS AND FERN GARDENING. (*Onoclea* is of no application here, being originally applied to a borage by Dioscorides.) For the plant often offered as *O. Struthiopteris, see* PTERETIS STRUTHIOPTERIS.

ONONIS (o-no'nis). Restharrow. Hardy, herbaceous perennials and deciduous* shrubs, comprising 70 species, belonging to the pea family, chiefly natives of Eu. and northern Af. Leaves compound,* but usually with only 3 clover-like leaflets. Flowers butterfly-shaped, yellow, purple or light pink, rarely white, solitary or 2–3 in short racemes.* Calyx bell-shaped, deeply cut into 5 lobes. Stamens* 10, joined or free. Fruit a swollen pod with few seeds. (*Ononis* is from the Greek for ass and to delight, in allusion to its being asses' fodder in Eu.)

They are easy of cultivation in ordinary garden soil. Propagated by seeds or division. Sow seeds ¹⁄₁₆ in. deep in semishady position, outdoors in April or in boxes in cool greenhouse or cold frame in March. As soon as large enough plant out where intended to bloom, in sunny banks or borders or in the rock or wild garden. Flower stems should be cut down in Oct., and the plants mulched with manure during winter. Lift and divide plants every 4–5 years. Prune shrubby species into shape after flowering.

arvensis = *Ononis spinosa.*

fruticosa. A shrub 2–3 ft. high, the young twigs sticky-hairy, ultimately smooth. Leaflets practically stalkless, oblong to ovalish, about 1 in. long, grayish-green and irregularly toothed. Flowers rose-pink or white streaked with red, about 1 in. long, the stalk of the cluster (panicle*) sticky-hairy. Southern Eu. and N. Af. Summer. Hardy from zone* 5 southward.

rotundifolia. Attractive shrubby plant, growing to 18 in. high. Leaflets 3, ovalish, with teeth-like margins. Flowers bright rose, 2 or 3 together, produced on short stalks in the axils* of the leaves. Upper petal shaded deeper rose. Southern Eu.

spinosa. A European perennial, not over 2 ft. high, occasionally thorny, and a little shrubby. Leaflets 3, oblongish, with a wedge-shaped base. Flowers usually solitary, rose-pink. July. Called by some *O. procurrens.*

ONOPORDUM (o-no-por'dum). Coarse-growing, annual or biennial, European spiny herbs, comprising 20 species of the family Compositae, generally grayish in color. Stems ridged and ragged. Leaves large, as long as 1 ft., alternate,* the veins radiating from the midrib, the margins prickly spined. Leaf blade much decurrent,* thus giving the ragged appearance to the stem. Flower heads borne in a cup-shaped ring of prickly or cobwebby bracts,* solitary or in clusters, generally in globe-shaped heads, purple or white. (*Onopordum* is an old Greek name derived from ass and to consume, in allusion to its being asses' fodder.)

They are not much in cultivation, but suitable for a sunny position where plants can be given a dark background. Propagated by seeds, sown ⅛ in. deep in sunny position in April. When large enough plant out in well-drained, sunny borders, singly or in groups of 3, allowing plenty of space.

Acanthium. Scotch thistle or cotton thistle, but sometimes sold as Robert Bruce. Biennial, and 3–9 ft. high. Lower leaves as much as 1 ft. long, silver-white, and spiny. Flower heads pale purple, cobwebby, generally solitary, to 2 in. across, globe-shaped. Eu.

bracteatum. Tall, cottony, much-branched biennial. Lower leaves broadly lance-shaped, with shallow lobes and tipped with stout, yellow spines. Upper leaves much smaller. Flower

---

* Special articles on the subjects indicated by an asterisk (*) will be found at the words so marked.

heads large and globe-shaped, the ring of bracts round the head curving outward. Mediterranean region.

tauricum. White and hairy, growing to 6 ft. high. Leaves narrow and long, the margins wavy and spiny. Flower heads in clusters, purple. Southern Eu.

ONOSMA (o-nos′ma). Little-known Eurasian herbs of the family Boraginaceae, comprising over 80 species of which few are cult., and only **O. stellulatum** likely to be seen here. It is a hairy, perennial herb 6–8 in. high, with alternate,* very narrow leaves. Flowers yellow, tubular, nodding, about 1 in. long, borne in 1-sided, forked clusters (cymes*). In this country less known than the *var.* **tauricum** (sometimes offered as *O. tauricum*) which has the leaf margins rolled and larger flowers, which bloom all summer, while *O. stellulatum* blooms only in June. The plant needs a light, open, sunny exposure, preferably with somewhat sandy soil. It is sometimes grown in the rock garden. (*Onosma* is from the Greek for ass and scent, in allusion to the fancied resemblance in the odor of some species to that animal.)

ONTARIO AND QUEBEC. These two provinces lie wholly within zones* 1, 2, and 3. The mildest areas are the Essex and Niagara peninsulas in Ontario which are sheltered by Lake Erie. The climate, and consequently the horticultural materials and practices, varies greatly from Harrow and St. Catharines where temperature seldom drops below 0° F. to Kapuskasing, Ontario, and Normandin, Quebec, where the temperature often reaches −40° F.

Soils vary as much as the climate, though not with it — from wind-blown sands to mucks and from heavy clay to muskeg. Glacial lake soils are common in central and southwestern Ontario. Glacial limestone soils, podsols,* and brown forest soils are also common to both provinces.

Commercial horticulture — fruit-growing, truck farming, canning crops, greenhouses, and nurseries — is concentrated in the milder regions as is the population, but home gardening, particularly with ornamental material, is carried on generally and has increased greatly in popularity in the past ten to fifteen years.

The following tables give information of interest from seven weather stations in different areas:

FROST DATA

Location	Average date of last killing frost in spring	Latest recorded frost
Harrow	May 11	May 25
Kapuskasing	June 14	July 20
Montreal	May 1	May 20
Normandin	June 4	June 18
Ottawa	May 6	May 29
St. Catharines	May 11	May 27
Toronto	May 6	May 22

FROST DATA

Location	Average date earliest killing frost	Earliest recorded fall frost
Harrow	Oct. 11	Sept. 26
Kapuskasing	Sept. 5	Aug. 1
Montreal	Oct. 15	Sept. 29
Normandin	Sept. 14	Aug. 30
Ottawa	Sept. 30	Sept. 3
St. Catharines	Oct. 21	Oct. 8
Toronto	Oct. 12	Sept. 23

RAINFALL

Location	Total annual precipitation	Precipitation during growing season
Harrow	23.72	10.26
Kapuskasing	27.54	18.03
Montreal	40.67	17.22
Normandin	32.41	16.61
Ottawa	34.34	15.80
St. Catharines	27.94	12.47
Toronto	32.33	14.27

VEGETABLE AND SMALL FRUIT AREAS. These are found near all the larger cities in the south and central areas, particularly on muck soils south of Montreal and north of Toronto, and on sandy soils near Ottawa, Toronto, and London. The largest developments for canning and shipping are in the Holland marsh area north of Toronto, in Lambton County, and in the Essex and Niagara peninsulas.

FRUIT CROPS. The recommended kinds vary with the climate. In the Niagara and Essex peninsulas where the influence of the Great Lakes is felt, cherries, grapes, peaches, and plums are grown extensively. Apples, pears, raspberries, and strawberries are much more generally distributed throughout the counties bordering Lake Ontario and in the St. Lawrence Valley.

GREENHOUSES AND NURSERIES. These produce florists' crops and woody plant material and are largely concentrated in the triangle bounded by Toronto, Windsor, and Niagara with a smaller area south of Montreal. The largest greenhouse concentrations are at Brampton and Port Dover for florist crops, and at Leamington for out-of-season vegetables.

EDUCATION. Degrees in horticulture are offered at the Ontario Agricultural College, Guelph, Ontario, and at Macdonald College, Ste. Anne de Bellevue, Quebec. More elementary horticultural training in connection with degrees in agriculture is offered at The Oka Institute, La Trappe, Quebec, the Agricultural College, Ste. Anne de la Pocatière, Quebec, or in diploma courses at the Ontario School of Agriculture at Kemptville and Ridgetown, Ontario. Horticultural training of a more practical nature can be secured at the schools of apprentice gardeners maintained by the Montreal Botanic Gardens in Montreal or the Niagara Parks Commission, Niagara Falls, Ontario.

---

* Special articles on the subjects indicated by an asterisk (*) will be found at the words so marked.

HORTICULTURAL SOCIETIES. Membership is drawn largely from amateur gardeners, as with American garden clubs. The societies are greatly encouraged and to some extent subsidized by the two provincial departments of agriculture. The Ontario Horticultural Association is made up of some 200 societies with total membership of 40,-000; the Quebec Horticultural Federation is made up of 40 societies with a membership of 6000.

Rainfall (1) 40 in (2) 17 in.
QUEBEC
Rainfall (1) 34 in. (2) 15 in.
MONTREAL May 1 Oct. 15 167 days
OTTAWA May 6 - Sept. 30 147 days
Lake Huron
TORONTO May 6 - Oct. 12 159 days
Rainfall (1) 23 in. (2) 10 in.
I Ontario
ST CATHARINES May 11 Oct. 21 163 days
HARROW May 11 - Oct. 11 153 days
Erie
UNITED STATES

ONTARIO AND QUEBEC

The zones of hardiness crossing Ontario and Quebec are those shown on the map located at ZONE, which should be consulted for details. The dates are the average latest killing frost in spring and the first one in the fall. The figures below the dates show the average length of the growing season. Rainfall figures (in inches) show (1) the total annual rainfall and (2) the amount falling in the growing season at the places indicated.

PLANT MATERIAL. Naturally this varies in the different climatic zones. In the Essex and Niagara peninsulas, hybrid tea roses can be grown without protection. Azaleas, laburnum, magnolia, and tulip-trees can also be grown if they are sheltered from prevailing winter winds. In the North, however, only the hardiest trees and shrubs such as ash, birch, caragana, elm, lilac, poplar, soft maples, spruce, and Tartarian honeysuckle will survive.

Suitable lists of plants for the different areas can best be obtained from bulletins on various phases of horticulture published by the Canada Department of Agriculture, Ottawa, Ontario, or by the provincial Department of Agriculture, Toronto, Ontario, or Quebec, Quebec.

PUBLIC GARDENS AND PARKS. These are scattered generally throughout all the populated areas. Even some of the most northerly communities such as Arvida and Noranda in Quebec and Kapuskasing and Temiskaming in Ontario have attractive parks with interesting displays, particularly of annual flowers which thrive in the long hours of daylight during the short summer.

At Quebec, the fondness of the French for "parterre" bedding brightens the historic Plains of Abraham as well as the grounds surrounding public buildings.

Montreal has several excellent parks as well as a very fine botanic garden in the east end of the city which is very well planned. The large greenhouses contain a wealth of tropical and "stove" plants. The outside plantings are arranged as a series of gardens for medicinal plants, herbs, economic plants, roses, phlox, etc. A large arboretum and rock gardens are also being developed. One of the main activities is the encouragement of children's gardens. At the College of Notre Dame in the suburb of St. Laurent there is a very interesting rock garden on the side of the "mountain." Many fine private gardens in the City of Montreal and suburbs show interesting hillside treatments. At the west end of the island of Montreal three spots of garden interest are: The well-laid-out grounds of Macdonald College, which is the faculty of agriculture of McGill University, full of interesting mature trees and shrubs; the Morgan Arboretum, a new development where native trees are being grown in blocks of considerable size rather than as specimens, and one of the best private rock gardens in the country, belonging to Mr. Cleveland Morgan.

In Ottawa, the national capital, the Federal District Commission maintains many miles of beautifully planted driveways through the city and into the Gatineau Hills in Quebec where there are large recreation parks. The display of daffodils in Rockcliffe Park and three quarters of a million tulips along the driveways attract many tourists in May.

The gardens of the Central Experimental Farm and Dominion Arboretum are also located here. In the former there are extensive variety test gardens of crab-apples, daylilies, iris, lilacs, peonies, phlox, roses, and other plants as well as experimental work pertaining to their culture. The arboretum contains a very large collection of trees and shrubs sufficiently hardy to grow where −20° F. is fairly common in winter.

Toronto's chief horticultural spots are the grounds around the provincial Parliament buildings and those of the Canadian National Exhibition. There is a wealth of beautiful private gardens and suburban estates, the owners of which are glad to receive interested visitors, but which are not regularly open to the public.

The parks board of the City of Hamilton has made the most of a good climate and attractive natural setting. There is a very fine collection of conifers and herbaceous material in Gage and McMasters parks.

* Special articles on the subjects indicated by an asterisk (*) will be found at the words so marked.

The recently established Royal Botanic Garden has control over large tracts of varied terrain which it is rapidly developing into areas of great beauty. The Spring Garden which contains large collections of *Iris* and *Hemerocallis* and the Rock Garden made in an old gravel pit are its two most notable features to date.

The Niagara Parks Commission has developed a beautiful system of driveways and parks for some 20 miles on the Canadian side of the Niagara River. The highlights of interest are Victoria Park where there are many trees and shrubs not hardy enough to grow elsewhere in eastern Canada. The Oakes Garden Theatre is outstanding in garden design. The largest floral clock in the country is at the powerhouse of the Hydroelectric Power Commission.

A little farther north there are parks in London, the Shakespeare Garden in the excellent Avonbank Park at Stratford, and the estate of the late H. J. Sims at Kitchener which has the largest private collection of trees and shrubs. Guelph is the home of the Ontario Agricultural College, the oldest school of its kind in Canada, with a campus full of interesting mature trees and shrubs. Guelph has attractive parks, and interesting water gardens are located at the Ontario Reformatory.

Everywhere there is a keen interest in gardens which provides recreation for people who work and pleasure for those who observe.

ONYCHIUM (ō-nick′ĭ-um). A small genus of widely distributed ferns of the family Polypodiaceae, of which the only cult. species is **O. japonicum**, a little fern admirably suited to the conservatory or for centerpieces on the table; known as claw-fern or carrot fern. Fronds very graceful and fragile, thrice- or even more compound,* the ultimate segments oblongish, about ½ in. long, toothed or divided, the divisions again toothed; the foliage of great delicacy. For culture *see* FERNS AND FERN GARDENING. (*Onychium* is from the Greek for claw, in allusion to the shape of the lobes of the ultimate frond segments.)

opaca, -us, -um (o-pay′ka). Opaque or pale.

OPEN-POLLINATED. Varieties resulting from pollination that is not controlled as contrasted with hybrids in which pollination is controlled. *See* CROSSING.

OPHIOGLOSSACEAE (o-fĭ-o-gloss-ā′-see-e). The adder's-tongue family comprises a small group of ferns of little garden interest except, possibly, in the rock garden or wild garden. Of the 4 genera and 90 species, two are in cult.—*Botrychium* and *Ophioglossum.*

They are delicate ferns having simple* leaves without marginal teeth in *Ophioglossum,* but compound* or dissected ones in *Botrychium.* The spores* are borne on a separate, leaf-like organ, often branched, and not on the back of ordinary fronds as in most forms. *See* both genera for further notes on these little-grown plants.

ophioglossoides (o-fĭ-o-glos-soy′deez, but *see* OÏDES). Resembling the adder's-tongue (*Ophioglossum*).

OPHIOGLOSSUM (o-fĭ-o-gloss′um). Adder's-tongue fern. A genus of about 30 species of small, widely distributed ferns of the family Ophioglossaceae, only one, **O. vulgatum,** the common adder's-tongue of Eurasia and N.A., occasionally planted in the fern or wild garden. It bears two sorts of fronds. The foliage fronds are usually solitary, erect, narrowly ovalish, about 12 in. long without teeth, lobes, or divisions, the blade a little shorter than the stalk. Fertile fronds, which bear the spores,* are about 2 in. long, the stalk 8–10 in. long. The plant grows mostly in moist meadows or thickets and has little decorative value. (*Ophioglossum* is from the Greek for serpent and tongue, in allusion to the shape of the foliage fronds.)

OPHIOPOGON (o-fĭ-o-pō′gon). Lily-turf. Useful ground-covering plants of the lily family, sometimes known by the name *Mondo.* All of the few species are natives of eastern Asia and are hardy up to the edge of zone* 3. They prefer moist, shady banks and make admirable plants for ground cover under trees. Leaves all basal, grass-like, but much thicker, growing in such masses as to suggest turf. Flowers small, nodding, usually borne in small clusters that do not exceed the foliage. Corolla small, not over ¼ in. long, and, unlike nearly all plants of the lily family, with an inferior* ovary. Fruit berry-like. (*Ophiopogon* is from the Greek for snake and beard, in somewhat fanciful allusion to the shape of the flower cluster.)

There is also another plant known as lily-turf. *See* LIRIOPE. From the latter *Ophiopogon* differs only in technical characters, but the two species below are generally more hardy than *Liriope* and more widely used for ground cover under shade. They are evergreen, almost sodforming plants, easily increased by division.

Jaburan. Jaburan. Leaves up to 15 in. long, usually less, and arising from a mass of cord-like roots. Flowers white, about ½ in. long. Fruit violet-blue, oblong. Jap. The *var.* **variegatus** has white-striped leaves.

japonicus. The best as a sod-farming ground cover, the leaves dark green, 8–10 in. high and arising from underground stolons,* the roots bearing small tubers. Flowers light lilac, about ¼ in. long. Fruit pea-sized, blue. Eastern As.

ophiuroides (o-fĭ-your-roy′deez, but *see* OÏDES). Like a plant of the genus *Ophiurus,* which is scarcely of garden interest.

OPIUM POPPY = *Papaver somniferum. See* POPPY.

OPLISMENUS (o-plis′me-nus). Tropical or sub-tropical, mostly weak or sprawling, sometimes climbing grasses, comprising 15 species, of which **O. compositus,** the basket

---

* Special articles on the subjects indicated by an asterisk (*) will be found at the words so marked.

grass, is often cult. for ornament, often under the name *O. hirtellus*. It is a perennial from tropical Africa and America, not hardy northward, and has prostrate, weak stems that root at the joints. Leaves flat, 2–4 in. long, ½–1 in. wide, sheathed at the clasping base, usually velvety beneath. Flower cluster of alternate* and somewhat distant racemes,* the spikelets awned.* The plant is often used for edgings in the South, and for hanging baskets or grown under the greenhouse bench in the North, often in the *var.* vittatus, which has white- and pink-striped leaves. (*Oplismenus* is from the Greek for awned,* in allusion to the awned* spikelets.)

OPLOPANAX (op-lo-pay′nacks). Three species of horribly prickly but ornamental shrubs of the family Araliaceae, some native in eastern As., but **O. horridus,** the devil's-club, from Alaska to Calif. It is a bushy shrub 6–10 ft. high, spiny throughout, with large, alternate,* long-stalked, deeply 5–7-lobed leaves that are roundish in general outline, nearly 10 in. wide and prickly both sides. Flowers small, greenish-white (for details *see* Araliaceae), crowded in small umbels,* which are grouped in a large, terminal, branched cluster (panicle*). Fruit fleshy, scarlet, about ⅓ in. long. A handsome shrub with fine foliage and showy fruit; hardy from zone* 4 southward and of easy culture, although it prefers moist sites in proximity to the sea. (*Oplopanax* is from the Greek for weapon in allusion to its prickles, and *Panax*, which see.) The plant is sometimes sold as *Fatsia horrida*.

OPPOSITE. Having the point of attachment, as of leaves, twigs, etc., precisely opposite each other; not alternate. *See* Alternate.

oppositifolia, -us, -um (op-pos-i-ti-fō′li-a). Opposite*-leaved.

OPULASTER = *Physocarpus*.

opulifolia, -us, -um (op-you-li-fō′li-a). With leaves like the guelder rose.

opuloides (op-you-loy′deez, but *see* Oïdes). Like the guelder rose, an old name for which was *Opulus*. *See* Viburnum Opulus Sterile.

Opulus (op′you-lus). An interesting specific name. *Opulus* is the same as *Populus* (the poplars). But Linnaeus,* without apparent reason, used *Opulus* as a specific name for a *Viburnum*, which has nothing to do with a poplar. *See* Viburnum Opulus.

OPUNTIA (o-pun′ti-a; also o-pun′she-a). Prickly pear, some of them also called tuna and cholla. A very large genus of cacti, spread from New England to Tierra del Fuego and comprising over 265 species, of which over 40 are grown in the collections of various cactus specialists, but only those below in even general cult. The group is in much confusion as to its naming, perhaps due to its diverse habit and the fact that many species have been described before the flowers or fruit were known, and many of these turned out to be well-known species when flowers and fruit were finally secured. As now understood, *Opuntia*, so far as cult. specimens are concerned, is of two general types: (1) Those with flat or broad joints (which include some of those called tuna) and (2) those with cylindrical or roundish joints (which include some of those known as cholla). The habit of the genus also varies widely. Some are prostrate or clambering plants without a trunk, while others, mostly tropical, are tree-like, but not so high as some other tree-like cacti. Flowers usually solitary, not clustered, often yellow, but pink and white flowers are also found. Fruit usually a juicy berry, edible in some. The spines of *Opuntia* vary from several in a cluster to none at all, the spineless species once much exploited as cattle feed, but less grown for that purpose today. (*Opuntia* is of obscure origin as applied to these cacti. It may be derived from a town in Greece, *Opus*, but the cacti are practically all American, and occur in Greece only as introduced plants.)

For general culture *see* Cacti. Those marked with a † are generally hardy up to the limits of zone* 4, or even into zone* 3, under favorable conditions. The rest are wonderful plants for succulent gardens in the Southwest, but must be grown northward only in greenhouses. The opuntias, besides the spines, generally have glochids* on the joints and the fruits. In the edible sorts the glochids* must be cut off the fruits or they may choke whoever eats them.

Opuntia is one of the worst group of cacti to handle, for besides the spines, they have cushion-like masses of short, barbed hairs from which the spines and flowers arise.

basilaris. Not over 4 ft. long, erect or more usually prostrate, with flat joints that are broadly oval, 6–9 in. long and generally spineless. Flowers nearly 3 in. wide, purple or white. Western U.S. and northern Mex.

brasiliensis. A branching prickly pear, 8–12 ft. high, the stems cylindric but the joints flat, terminal, and almost leaf-like, not very spiny. Flowers about 2 in. long, yellow. Tropical S.A.

†compressa. The common and only wild prickly pear of the northeastern U.S. Joints flat, oblong or ovalish, 3–5 in. long, the whole plant prostrate. Spines 1–2 at each cluster, often lacking. Flowers yellow, 2–3 in. wide. New England and Ontario to Ala. and Mo. Long known as *O. vulgaris* and more recently as *O. humifusa*. Called Barbary fig in N. Af. where it was introduced.

cylindrica. A tall cactus up to 10 ft. high, and branched. Joints cylindric, blunt at the tip, with short white spines or sometimes with none. Flowers about 1 in. long, scarlet. Peru and Ecuador.

engelmanni. A flat-jointed cactus, sometimes bushy in Mex., but without a definite trunk. Joints oblongish to nearly round, usually 6–8 in. long, but sometimes as much as 1 ft. long.

---

* Special articles on the subjects indicated by an asterisk (*) will be found at the words so marked.

Spines 3–4 at each cluster (10 in old plants), or sometimes none in young joints. Flowers yellow, often 3–4 in. wide. Fruit red, about 2 in. long. Tex. and Ariz. to Mex.

erinacea. A flat-jointed prickly pear, mostly low and spreading. Joints very spiny, oval or oblong, 3–5 in. long. Flowers yellow or yellowish-red. Southwestern U.S.

Ficus-indica. Indian fig. A flat-jointed cactus, bushy or tree-like and sometimes 15 ft. high. Joints oblongish, 15–25 in. long, and usually spineless. Flowers yellow, nearly 4 in. wide. Fruit juicy, red, edible, 2–3½ in. long, pear-shaped. Probably central Mex., but cult. throughout the tropical world, the markets of which nearly always have Indian figs for sale.

†fragilis. A low, clump-forming cactus, the fragile joints flattish or even globular, easily detached. Spines 5–7 in each group, brownish. Flowers about 2 in. wide, yellow. Western N.A.

glomerata. A low, clustered cactus, its globular or cylindric joints tubercled, not over 2 in. wide or long, often spineless, or with papery, thin, flat spines 3–4 in. long. Flowers light yellow, about 1½ in. wide. Argentina.

†imbricata. A shrubby cactus, often 8–12 ft. high, the joints about 1 in. in diameter, much tubercled* and covered with sheathed spines. Flowers about 2 in. long, purple. Southwestern U.S. and adjacent Mex.

leptocaulis. Tasajillo. A bushy or tree-like cactus, the trunk 2–3 in. in diameter. Joints cylindric. Spines slender, solitary on young joints, but 2–3 in a cluster on old plants. Flowers about ¾ in. wide, greenish-yellow. Southwestern U.S. and adjacent Mex.

lindheimeri. Nopal; also called cacanapa. A tree-like, flat-jointed cactus, 8–12 ft. high and with a trunk, or sometimes merely spreading. Joints ovalish or broader, sometimes nearly circular and 8–10 in. in diameter, bluish-green. Spines 1–6 in each cluster. Flowers yellow or red about 3 in. wide. Fruit purple, pear-shaped, about 2 in. long. La. to Tex. and Mex.

megacantha. Tuna. A tree-like cactus, 10–15 ft. high, and with an obvious trunk. Joints flat, oblongish or wider, 14–24 in. long. Spines white, 1–5 in a cluster. Flowers yellow or orange, nearly 3 in. wide. Fruit pear-shaped, red, about 3 in. long and edible. Mex. and much cult. there for its juicy fruit, which is the chief tuna in the market.

microdasys. A sprawling prickly pear, the flat joints oblong or nearly round, 4–6 in. long and essentially spineless. Flowers yellowish-red, about 1½ in. long. N. Mex.

monacantha. This and its *var.* **variegata** have considerable currency in the trade, but are often only *O. compressa.*

phaeacantha. A low, nearly prostrate, flat-jointed cactus. Joints 4–6 in. long, less than half as wide. Spines 1–4 in each cluster. Flowers about 2 in. wide, yellow. Fruit about 1½ in. long, contracted at the base. Tex. and Ariz. to N. Mex. and Mex.

†polyacantha. A low, nearly prostrate, flat-jointed cactus, the joints nearly circular and about 3½ in. wide. Spines 5–9 in each cluster. Flowers about 2 in. wide, pale yellow on the inside, but reddish-tinged on the outside. N. Dak. to Wash., south to Tex. and Ariz. Probably hardy up to zone* 2.

rufida. Perhaps merely a var. of *O. microdasys*, but with an erect stem, 3–5 in. high, and its nearly round, flat joints about 10 in. wide. Flowers about 2 in. long, yellow or orange. Tex. and adjacent Mex.

schickendantzi. A shrubby, much-branched

cactus, 5–7 ft. high, its joints somewhat cylindric or partly flattened, grayish-green, faintly tubercled. Spines about ¾ in. long, one or two in each group. Flowers nearly 2 in. wide, yellow. Argentina.

schotti. A prostrate cactus, rooting freely and, in the wild, forming patches 8–10 ft. wide. Joints cylindric or club-shaped, much tubercled,* 2–3 in. long and about ¾ in. in diameter. Spines with whitish wool at their base. Flowers about 1½ in. long, yellow. Tex. and adjacent Mex.

Tuna. Tuna. A low, prostrate, flat-jointed prickly pear, the joints oblongish, 3–6 in. long. Spines yellow, 2–6 in a cluster. Flowers about 2 in. wide, yellow but tinged with red. Fruit red, pear-shaped, about 1½ in. long. Jamaica, and the leading tuna in the W.I., where it is cult. for its edible fruits.

vulgaris = *Opuntia compressa.*

ORACH = *Atriplex hortensis.* It is also sometimes applied to *A. patula*, for which *see* Orach in the list at WEEDS.

ORANGE. For the true orange *see* the next entry. For various other plants to which the name of orange is sometimes applied *see* CHOISYA, CITROPSIS, STRYCHNOS, LAUROCERASUS CAROLINIANA. *See also* MOCK-ORANGE and MACLURA.

ORANGE. The orange is much the most important of all the citrus fruits and its culture provides major fruit-growing industries in both Florida and California. There are two principal species: the sweet or common orange (*Citrus sinensis*), the production of which comprises the industries mentioned, and the sour or Seville orange (*Citrus Aurantium*), which is used in this country primarily as a rootstock. The mandarins (including the tangerine), which belong to the species *C. nobilis*, are often incorrectly referred to as oranges. Likewise, the fruit of the species *C. Bergamia* is commonly called the bergamot orange, though it is actually a close relative of the lemon.

SWEET ORANGE. The sweet orange, like other citrus fruits, is a tender, subtropical evergreen, which is subject to injury by frost. It is much hardier than the lime, however, and considerably more so than the lemon, though less hardy than the sour orange. Temperatures of 25 to 26 degrees cause injury to the fruit and young growth and at 20 degrees severe tree injury occurs. Unlike the lime and lemon, the orange requires a high total amount of heat to ripen the fruit, though the variation in amount of heat necessary for different varieties is notable. This gives rise to early-ripening, midseason, and late-ripening varieties. In regions of cool summers and mild winters such as the coastal area of southern California, varieties of high-heat requirement (late-maturing), such as Valencia, ripen in the summer of the year following bloom, a season when they experience no competition with oranges from other states. This explains the apparent ever-bearing characteristic of this variety: at the period of bloom the

---

* Special articles on the subjects indicated by an asterisk (*) will be found at the words so marked.

crop of the previous season is approaching maturity; at other seasons the trees regularly carry the crops of two succeeding blooms. In regions of hot summers, however, varieties of lower heat requirement, such as Hamlin, Parson, and Washington Navel, ripen in the fall or winter of the year of bloom and hence carry but one crop of fruit. A proper combination of varieties and climatic zones, therefore, permits a marked extension of the ripening season. In California one early and one late variety, grown in three climatic zones differing in amount of heat, provide an all-year ripening season; this situation seems not to occur elsewhere.

The orange thrives in tropical climates, but the color and quality are poor. Its commercial culture is restricted to semitropical and sub-tropical regions; in the latter, irrigation is required to supplement the rainfall. Sudden heat waves during the fruit-setting period in early summer are likely to cause excessive shedding of the young fruits, known as "June drop"; the navel* varieties are especially affected. Desiccating winds accentuate loss from this cause. Comparative freedom from wind, or wind protection, is required for satisfactory yields and quality, though the orange is less sensitive to this factor than either the lime or lemon.

The sweet orange has a much wider range of climatic adaptation than the lime and lemon, but its commercial culture in the United States is limited to central and south Florida, the lower Rio Grande Valley of Texas, and areas of mild winters in Arizona and California.

The orange, like other citrus fruits, does not require pollination for fruit-setting, and hence there is no pollination problem in its culture. Unpollinated fruits are seedless, which is a desirable commercial character. The fruits vary greatly in seediness, depending on variety and the opportunity for pollination. Three classes are recognized — seedless, commercially seedless, and seedy. The first class, represented by Washington Navel, is seedless when planted in solid blocks, because it produces virtually no functional pollen; in mixed blocks, where pollination occurs, it rarely produces seeds because it normally has few or no functional ovules. The commercially seedless varieties — Valencia, Hamlin, Enterprise and others — produce viable pollen in abundance, but have few functional ovules.* The seedy varieties have many functional ovules* and plenty of viable pollen.

The orange fruit exhibits a pronounced tendency to doubling, and this frequently results in the production of a navel, a small, rudimentary secondary fruit embedded in the apical end of the primary fruit. Many varieties exhibit this phenomenon occasionally, some frequently, a few regularly. The latter are known as navel oranges; one of these, the Washington Navel, is an important commercial variety. A few varieties, known as blood oranges, regularly have the juice red-colored and exhibit a reddish blush on the rind. This coloration is not constant, however; in some localities and seasons it is much more pronounced than in others.

PROPAGATION. The orange, like other citrus fruits, is propagated by budding on seedling rootstocks. The seed is planted shallowly in seedbeds, usually under partial shade provided by lath, as early in spring as the soil becomes warm enough, usually March or April. The seedlings remain there until a year later, when they are transplanted to nursery rows. They usually attain suitable size for budding by the end of the second growing season. The trees are usually planted as year-old budlings, though they may be allowed to grow in the nursery another year. The rootstocks most used are the sweet orange itself and the rough lemon. The trifoliate orange (*Poncirus trifoliata*) commonly, though not always, dwarfs sweet orange varieties. Rough lemon (*Citrus Limonia*), a vigorous, disease-resistant kind of lemon (*see* LEMON) is used only where other rootstocks do not thrive. It should be avoided where possible because of its effects on the quality of the fruit; the color is paler, the rind thicker, the juice and acid content lower, and the fruit tends to drop from the trees when full maturity is attained.

PLANTING. The evergreen nature of the tree and the sensitiveness of the roots to injury from desiccation require that special care be used in handling and planting nursery trees, particularly in arid regions. In California the use of balled nursery trees is almost universal; in Florida the high atmospheric humidity favors planting the trees bare-rooted. The trees should not be planted when the soil is cold, for citrus roots have a high temperature requirement for growth. Late spring is the preferred time for planting in California; in Florida, early spring or fall. The best practice involves heading back the trees a few weeks before they are dug. In arid regions newly planted trees require frequent but light irrigation and should be protected against sunscald* by whitewashing or wrapping. For the first two or three winters they should be protected against frost.

SOILS. Like other citrus trees, the orange has a wide range of soil adaptation and succeeds almost equally well on light and moderately heavy soils. It is sensitive to both high lime content and excess moisture, for which reason such soils sould be avoided. Excellent drainage is a requirement and reduces the likelihood of root diseases. A soil reaction from moderately acid to slightly alkaline seems to give equally satisfactory results. Like other citrus trees, however, the orange is sensitive to even small concentrations of alkali salts and only

---

* Special articles on the subjects indicated by an asterisk (*) will be found at the words so marked.

soils free from alkali, and irrigation water of good quality, should be used. Because of its shallow rooting habit deep soils are not required; three to four feet of good soil, adequately drained, will suffice.

IRRIGATION. In arid regions irrigation is the soil-management practice of greatest importance. An adequate soil-moisture supply must be maintained at all times, for the tree is evergreen and active to some degree throughout the year. In hot climates this may require 10 to 15 irrigations; in the cool coastal belt of southern California 3 or 4 may suffice. The total amount of water required depends upon the climate and the size and spacing of the trees; the period between irrigations depends on weather conditions and the water-storing capacity of the soil in the rooting zone.

The maintenance of satisfactory yields requires regular and heavy fertilization. Nitrogen has been demonstrated to give results. An adequate fertilization program in California consists of about 200 pounds of nitrogen per acre per year and 3 tons dry weight of decomposable organic matter. Approximately half the nitrogen is supplied in chemical form and the balance in bulky organic form — 10 tons of dairy manure, or its equivalent in bean straw, alfalfa hay, or similar substances. Somewhat less total nitrogen is used in Florida, where complete fertilizers are applied two or three times per year. For the most part tillage operations are employed to turn under weeds or fertilizers, and to facilitate irrigation. Pruning is of very minor importance and is confined to the opening up of the trees for better penetration of light and to the removal of dead or dying branches.

When ripe the fruit should be clipped from the tree; this tends to prevent decay.

Valencia, a commercially seedless, late-ripening sort of wide range of climatic adaptation, is the most important variety. Washington Navel, early-ripening and seedless, is next in importance and is grown in California and Arizona. It is restricted in climatic range and produces low yields of poor-quality fruit in semi-tropical climates. Parson and Hamlin are important varieties in Florida, and Pineapple, Homosossa, and Jaffa are the principal mid-season varieties — R. W. H.

INSECT PESTS. Armored scales are the most serious pest. Summer sprays of 1.3 to 1.5% superior summer oils give over 90% control, particularly when most scales are young. Two scalicide sprays per year are best. Several mite species cause trouble. Lime sulphur 2–100 in winter is good for rust mite and six-spotted mite. Red mite is controlled by Ovex. Mealybugs, whitefly, plant bugs, and aphids are controlled by pesticide #21. Treat trunks with pesticide #15 to keep out ants. (See SPRAYS AND DUSTS.)

DISEASES. There is such a long list of both serious diseases and slight disorders of orange and other citrus fruits that interested growers should contact their state agricultural experiment stations for bulletins on citrus diseases and their control. Among the more common diseases which may be controlled with pesticides are scab* and melanose. Scab produces brown, wart-like, corky areas on fruit, leaves, and twigs. Melanose causes small, hard, brown spots giving the fruit, leaf, and twig an appearance and feel of sandpaper. For scab control, use pesticide #3 (see SPRAYS AND DUSTS) just before the spring flush of growth and repeat when ⅔ of the petals have fallen. A single application of the same pesticide within 1 to 3 weeks after fruit-set will control the melanose disease. In some areas, pesticide #11 is now being used instead of the copper. However, the copper will control not only the scab and melanose, but also helps to control Spanish moss, lichens, greasy spot, algal spot, and a copper-deficiency disorder known as exanthema.

A number of fungi cause root and foot rots. Orange and other citrus should not be planted soon after land is cleared of oak or Australian pine because roots of these trees may carry one of the fungi and result in infection of the citrus crop. Some of the foot rots may be treated by excavating soil around base of trees, cutting out as much diseased wood as possible, and then mounding soil to a depth of 1 foot around base of diseased tree. Keep soil moist to induce new root formation from base of the trunk. Foot rot is less serious if soil is fairly acid. In California, one type of root rot has been controlled with soil injections of carbon disulphide.

A number of virus diseases have caused serious loss in various areas where orange and other citrus crops are grown. Psorosis or scaly-bark disease causes a mosaic* type of pattern in leaves and produces wrinkled, scaly, or pocked bark. Another virus disease, Tristeza or quick decline, may cause death of trees. This disease affects only trees on sour orange and grapefruit rootstock. Some trees may continue to live for 25 years after infection, but the crop is greatly reduced. Cut out the virus-diseased trees and use disease-free stock for replanting.

ORANGEBERRY = *Triphasia trifolia.*

ORANGE CONEFLOWER = *Rudbeckia fulgida.*

ORANGE-EYE BUTTERFLY-BUSH = *Buddleia davidi.*

ORANGE GARDEN. See YELLOW GARDEN.

ORANGE GUM = *Angophora lanceolata.*

ORANGE HAWKWEED = *Hieracium aurantiacum.* See list at WEEDS.

ORANGE JASMINE = *Murraya exotica.*

ORANGE LILY = *Lilium croceum.*

ORANGE MILKWEED = *Asclepias tuberosa.* See MILKWEED.

ORANGE MILKWORT = *Polygala lutea.*

ORANGE PUCCOON = *Lithospermum canescens.*

ORANGEROOT = *Hydrastis canadensis.* See GOLDENSEAL.

ORANGE SUNFLOWER = *Heliopsis scabra.*

orbiculata, -us, -um (or-bick-you-lay′ta). Round.

ORCHARD. See FRUIT CULTURE.

ORCHARD GRASS = *Dactylis glomerata.*

---

* Special articles on the subjects indicated by an asterisk (*) will be found at the words so marked.

ORCHID. There are thousands of species of orchids, of which many hundreds are in cult. For a complete list of all the genera of orchids in the ENCYCLOPEDIA, *see* ORCHIDACEAE, at which entry will also be found an account of their flower structure.

Here we are concerned only with their uses as garden or greenhouse plants, and as such they are culturally divided into two groups: (1) those that are hardy outdoors and grow mostly in the ground (terrestrial orchids), and (2) tropical orchids suited only to the greenhouse in the North or to lath houses in frost-free regions. Some kinds among the latter can also be grown in the house and put outdoors in the summer.

Hardy Orchid Cultivation

The terrestrial orchids are beautiful and are well worth cultivation in the rock garden or wild garden, or in the bog. Most of the species are easily grown if proper attention is given to their requirements and they will thrive if a few important details are followed in reference to their culture. Usually they are transplanted at the wrong season, that is, just as the flowers are opening. This method is to be condemned, as then the plant is developing the roots for the following year, and if injury results from the lifting, the plant dies. (*Cypripedium acaule* is a good example of this.) The correct method is to mark the plants when in flower, allowing them to develop until September or October. By this time the roots or tubers will have matured, and the risk of transplanting will have been reduced to the minimum, providing the plant is taken up with a ball of soil attached to the roots.

The next problem is the one of soil, and too much emphasis cannot be laid on the importance of proper soil conditions for the plant. Nearly all the native orchids require a soil with an acid base, and most prefer a soil of a fibrous loam or peaty character with ample moisture throughout the entire season. *See* ACID AND ALKALI SOILS.

The woodland plants do best if given the protection and partial shade of vegetation such as trees or shrubs. Up to the present very little has been accomplished relative to the raising of native orchids from seed and their propagation has been neglected. Most of the plants are purchased from the many dealers in native plant material, they being collected by thousands from the wild.

Some of the hardy orchids inhabit bogs, some are at home on sandy plains, while others prefer the companionship of the meadow grasses where the soil is cool and moist. It is therefore essential to take into consideration their native habitat when they are to be transplanted into the garden. The conditions under which they grow are very important if the best results are to be achieved.

Protection during winter is another factor of importance. This can best be accomplish-

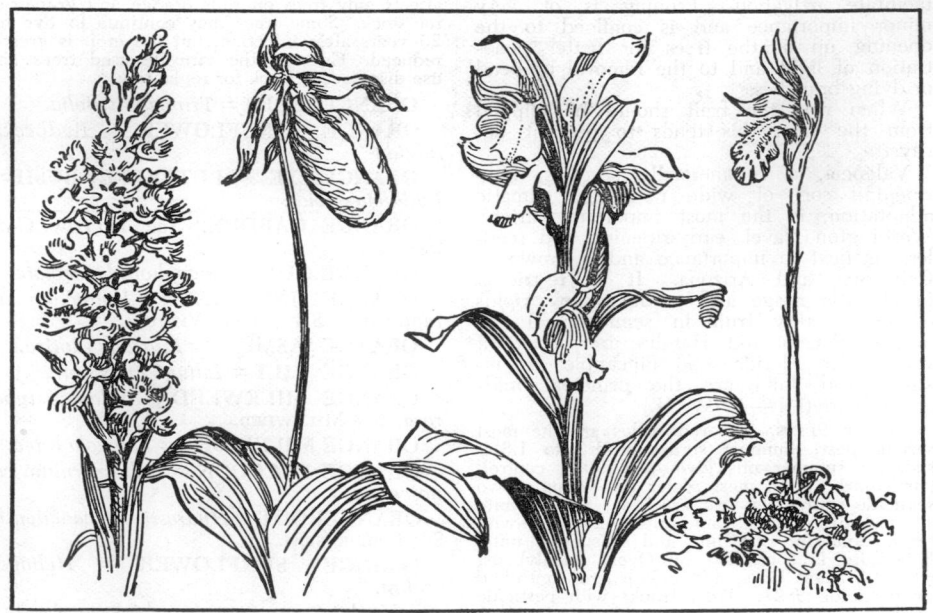

FOUR TYPES OF HARDY ORCHIDS

(*Left to right*) fringed orchis (*Habenaria*), lady's-slipper (*Cypripedium acaule*), showy orchis (*Orchis spectabilis*), and arethusa (*Arethusa bulbosa*).

* Special articles on the subjects indicated by an asterisk (*) will be found at the words so marked.

GREENHOUSE ORCHIDS
(A) Dendrobium; (B) Oncidium; (C) Odontoglossum; (D) Cattleya

ed, after freezing weather sets in, by covering the plants with a mulch of leaves to the depth of about four inches, or two inches of peat moss may be used.

KINDS TO GROW. The species designated by a dagger are bog orchids; for culture *see* BOG GARDENING. Other species are humus plants of the woods and should be grown in accordance with the suggestions made above. A few are dealt with in more detail at the article on WILD GARDEN.

†*Arethusa bulbosa*	Dragon's-mouth
†*Calopogon pulchellus*	Swamp pink
Cypripedium acaule (*see* WILD GARDEN)	Moccasin flower
†*Cypripedium arietinum*	Ram's-head lady's-slipper
†*Cypripedium Calceolus parviflorum*	Small lady's-slipper
Cypripedium Calceolus pubescens (*see* WILD GARDEN)	Large yellow lady's-slipper
Cypripedium reginae	Showy lady's-slipper
†*Habenaria Blephariglottis*	White fringed orchis
†*Habenaria ciliaris*	Yellow fringed orchis
Habenaria fimbriata	Purple fringed orchis
†*Habenaria psycodes*	Pink fringed orchis
Orchis rotundifolia	Showy orchid
Orchis spectabilis	Shin-plasters
†*Pogonia ophioglossoides*	Rose pogonia

Other hardy orchids, not quite so showy as those above, will be found at APLECTRUM, GOODYERA, and LIPARIS.

TROPICAL ORCHID CULTIVATION

By far the larger part of the world's orchid population is indigenous to the tropics. The two chief centers of distribution are Asia and South and Central America. There are six major cultivated groups of orchids and each of these groups has its own particular cultural requirements.

CATTLEYA TRIBE. The genus *Cattleya*, its allies and hybrids represent the most important orchid group. They are the standard florists' orchid and are more widely grown and hybridized than any other. The Cattleyas and their relatives are native to South and Central America, where they grow from 3000 to 6000 ft. elevation. Culturally they like temperatures of about 75°–85° F. during the day and from 55°–65° F. at night. Cattleyas like abundant light (2500–4000 foot-candles of light intensity). A well-grown plant which is receiving optimum light should have hard, leathery leaves which are greenish-yellow in color. Watering should consist of a morning sprinkle or spray over the foliage and pot (providing the sun is out) and a biweekly soaking that thoroughly saturates the pot; 60–70% humidity is considered ideal.

HOME CULTURE OF CATTLEYA. Many orchids can be successfully grown in the home. Cattleyas easily adapt themselves to room culture, and many amateurs have been successfully growing and flowering them on window sills year after year. The chief difficulties encountered in the home culture of any orchid are low humidity, improper light and, frequently, too high a night temperature. Cattleyas grown in the home are usually placed over a pan or tray

---

* Special articles on the subjects indicated by an asterisk (*) will be found at the words so marked.

which is filled with moist gravel. This increases the humidity around the plants and helps prevent excessive desiccation. An east or south window usually gives proper light, and night temperature of 70° F. in the home during the winter months usually results in a 60°–65° F. temperature for plants which are kept near the window. In summer, from May to September, many home growers have found that their plants benefit from being suspended beneath trees in the garden. Here they should receive, if possible, some early morning sun as well as late afternoon sun, and be in the shade during the hottest part of the day. Under garden conditions, Cattleyas can be watered thoroughly almost every day and fertilized once a month with any standard commercial fertilizer used at half the concentration recommended for house plants.

CYMBIDIUM TRIBE. Cymbidiums are native to Asia where they grow on mountain slopes, from India to Burma, at 5000 to 8000 ft. elevation. These beautiful orchids are carried on long, graceful sprays and are frequently a mixture of contrasting soft and bright colors. Cymbidiums like a cool climate where the night temperatures are 50°–55° F. and day temperatures stay below 85° F. They like a higher light intensity than the Cattleyas and demand frequent waterings and bimonthly fertilizing. If Cymbidiums are to be grown with Cattleyas, the greenhouse should have a night temperature of 50°–55° F. with optimum light conditions for Cattleyas being maintained. Cymbidiums cannot be recommended for home culture as their light and temperature requirements cannot be satisfied in the average home. In some frost-free sub-tropical areas of the United States, however, Cymbidiums can be grown out of doors in open garden beds the year round, but do not flower well if heat is too great.

CYPRIPEDIUM TRIBE. This tribe includes the oldest members of the orchid family. They are singularly different from all other orchids as their lip is present in the form of a pouch or shoe. All the tropical Cypripediums (botanically often called *Paphiopedilum*) require somewhat more shade than Cattleyas. They like 1500–2500 F.C. of light. Inasmuch as the Cypripediums have no water-storage organs (pseudobulbs) they should always be kept moist and never allowed to become excessively dry. The mottled-leaved group of Cypripediums will grow well at *Cattleya* temperatures as they are considered "warm-growing." Those without the mottled leaves, however, are considered "cool" growers, and do best at temperatures given for Cymbidiums. Most of the Cypripediums grow beautifully in average homes. An east window is usually preferred and many growers set their plants outside under a shady tree in the warm season

of the year. This is especially beneficial in areas where the summers are unusually hot. Many homes are now air-conditioned, and of course, under these conditions Cypripediums should remain indoors the year round. It should also be mentioned, in passing, that the tropical Cypripediums have some of the longest-lasting flowers in the orchid family. It is not unusual for a flower to stay in good condition for six weeks.

VANDA TRIBE. Many new and beautiful *Vanda* hybrids have been created, principally by breeders in the Hawaiian Islands. *Vanda* flowers vary tremendously in color so that anyone can find some pleasing shades. These plants are sun-loving and like high humidity and an open, loose potting medium. They should, therefore, be placed in a warm, sunny spot and preferably grown in baskets. They will benefit from a monthly feeding of any weak organic or inorganic fertilizer and often are quite tall.

Phalaenopsis: The beautiful moth orchid

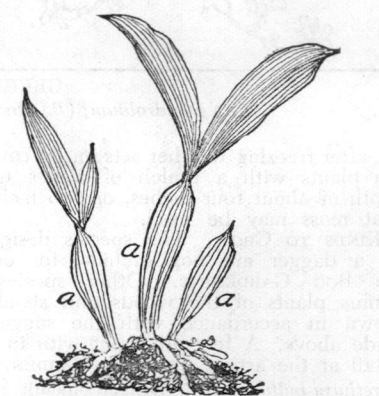

A tropical orchid with its pseudobulbs (*a*)

with its white or pink flowers is a universal favorite. These plants are rather demanding, requiring a constant high night temperature of 65°–70° F., a well-shaded spot of 1000–1500 F.C., and a potting medium that is constantly moist. Like the Vandas, *Phalaenopsis* benefits from frequent fertilizing. In general, members of this tribe cannot be recommended for home culture, although many of the Vandas grow and flower well in the garden during the summer months under conditions prescribed for Cattleyas.

ODONTOGLOSSUM TRIBE. This is one of the largest tribes in the orchid family and one that is always popular with the hobbyist. It contains three important genera; *Oncidium, Miltonia,* and *Odontoglossum,* all of which are indigenous to South and Central America. Many of the plants in this group are "cool-growing," requiring night temperatures of 50° F. or below. Nevertheless many of them can be successfully grown along with Cattleyas in the average greenhouse. Varying degrees of success have been reported by people attempting to grow these plants in their homes. A good rule of thumb for home culture would be, if you are having success with a *Cattleya* or two and maybe a *Cypripedium*, try growing a plant from the *Odontoglossum* group, preferably an *Oncidium*, as they adapt easily and are extremely showy when flowering.

DENDROBIUM TRIBE. This large Asian tribe contains some 900 species, and of course, many man-made hybrids. The warm-growing, evergreen Dendrobiums have long cane-like stems and produce lovely arching or pendent sprays of flowers of varying colors. These Dendrobiums require plenty of light, water, and air. They also seem to prefer small pots and frequent fertilizing. In general they grow well in the greenhouse with Cattleyas. The "cool" Dendrobiums are semi-deciduous in nature, dropping a portion of their leaves annually. They are kept cool (50° F. at night), and sparingly watered from November through January. During this dry, cool period they form many flower buds along their stems (canes). After these flower buds are formed, resumption of normal watering and higher temperatures of 58°–66° F. at night will result in flowering within several weeks. Most members of this tribe cannot be recommended for anyone other than an experienced home culturist as their flowers seldom open in a close stuffy atmosphere.

POTTING AND DIVIDING

Any successful orchid-grower must sooner or later tackle the problem of potting and dividing his plants. This is done when the plant outgrows its container or the potting materials decompose. The ideal time to re-pot any orchid is when the new growth is just beginning to send out its new roots. All tropical orchids are classified as epiphytes* or semi-epiphytes, that is, plants that grow on trees or in rotting vegetable material. Consequently, they will not grow in soil. The task of re-potting has been greatly simplified by the recent introduction of a new potting medium called fir bark. Traditionally most orchids were grown in a fibrous root of the *Osmunda* fern (orchid peat) which had to be packed firmly and accurately around the newly potted plant. This procedure is very time-consuming and precise. In general, most growers have abandoned *Osmunda* in favor of fir bark. Dividing an orchid plant is relatively simple. After removing the plant from the container, saw or cut it into convenient pieces with three or more pseudobulbs each (*see* illustration on opposite page), following the natural lines of division. Each new section is placed in a pot and then the pot is filled with moistened fir bark around the plant. Be sure to keep the plant upright with one hand and to allow enough room for future growth. Do not press the bark too firmly and be sure and stake the plant securely. If the rhizome is setting level on top of the bark, your job is finished; otherwise, start all over again. Newly potted plants should not be watered excessively until a new root system is well established; they do however, benefit from frequent, light syringing. One word of caution: never allow fir bark to become excessively dry, as it will not readily take up water again.

DANGER SIGNALS. Orchids are among the world's toughest plants. They can live for long periods under adverse conditions and still flower abundantly. Nevertheless, it is necessary that every orchid-grower be familiar with some of the common danger signals which sick orchids display. When a plant displays one or more of these characteristics it is time for you to act, as the plant is not happy in its environment.

CONDITION	CAUSE	REMEDY
1. Wrinkled, thin, and flabby leaves	Usually improper watering	More or less water
2. Yellow leaves	Excessive light	Shade plant
3. Smaller new growths	Not enough water	Increase watering frequency
4. Soft growths, very green foliage (usually poor or no flowers)	Insufficient light	Increase light intensity

MONTHLY CALENDAR OF ORCHID BLOOMS

January
Cattleya trianae
Coelogyne cristata
February
Cymbidium insigne
Cattleya aurantiaca
March
Cattleya mossiae
Dendrobium nobile
April
Oncidium ampliatum
May
Diacrium bicornutum
Epidendrum atropurpureum
June
Cattleya warscewiczi
Cypripedium callosum
July
Epidendrum nemorale
August
Cattleya dowiana
Oncidium flexuosum
September
Odontoglossum pendulum
Vanda tricolor
October
Odontoglossum grande
Cattleya labiata
November
Cattleya bowringiana
Dendrobium Phalaenopsis
December
Cattleya percivaliana

For descriptions of these and other

---

* Special articles on the subjects indicated by an asterisk (*) will be found at the words so marked.

orchids mentioned in this article, *see* the different genera (in the body of the book). — R. J. G.

The present address of the American Orchid Society is Botanical Museum, Harvard University, Cambridge 38, Mass.

DISEASES. Various leafspots* and anthracnose* may spot or discolor leaves and a rust* may cause orange, powdery material to form on the lower surface of the leaf. If water drops on a flower, a gray mold* or flower spot may result. These troubles are not usually too serious.

When light or dark streaks develop parallel with the veins, it indicates mosaic* or other virus diseases and plants should be destroyed.

Occasionally the base of the pseudobulb will turn black and rot. Cut off the diseased portion at least one inch below the rotted area and let

Potting an orchid in fir bark or bark of redwood. Most tree-perching sorts are best grown in these wooden cribs (orchid baskets).

the plant dry for a few days following the cutting before replacing in the orchid fiber or other growing medium.

ORCHIDACEAE (or-kid-day'see-ee). The orchid family probably has the most spectacularly beautiful flowers in the world. It is an enormous group of perhaps 500 genera and over 15,000 species, possibly many more, scattered all over the world, but most frequent and most showy in the tropics. All are herbs, varying from the relatively large epiphytes* of the tropical forest to tiny plants growing in the ground in temperate regions, where many of them are bog plants. Most tropical genera grow attached to trees (*see* EPIPHYTES), while most temperate-region genera grow in the ground, usually in forest humus or in bogs, a few in meadows, and some in dry, sandy woods. *See* ORCHID for directions as to how to grow both groups.

The tropical orchids often have leaves with a swollen base (a pseudobulb) which stores water over the dry season, and from which the blade often falls away in droughts. Temperate genera do not have pseudobulbs. In all genera there are no marginal teeth. They may have thickened,

thread-like, or bulbous roots, or fleshy, brittle ones, but in all genera there is a bacterial relationship between the roots and the plant food absorbed by them. In many tropical genera the air roots of the epiphytes are covered with a whitish film that absorbs atmospheric moisture (*see* VELAMEN).

The flowers of orchids present extreme specialization to insect fertilization (Darwin devoted two volumes to it). They also present extreme difficulty in separating the different genera, even considering only the small number in cult. The typical orchid flower is highly irregular* and composed of 3 outer segments (sepals*), usually similar, and often not showy. There are three inner segments (petals), two of which may be more or less alike, but the third forms a lip or spur of infinite variety of shape and color in the different genera. Sometimes the spur may be a foot long (*see* ANGRAECUM). Again there is no spur, but the lip is bag-like, twisted, or contorted. The stamens and pistil are joined into a single organ (the gynandrium), sometimes called the column. The structure, shape, and contents of this gynandrium are of endless variety.

The leading cultivated genera of orchids are easily divided (but difficult to distinguish) upon the basis of their habitat. They form two groups.

1. TROPICAL GENERA OF GREENHOUSE CULTURE.
   (*a*) The leading and most showy are: *Calanthe, Cattleya* ("the" florist orchid), *Coelogyne, Cymbidium, Cypripedium* (also temperate), *Dendrobium, Diacrium, Epidendrum, Laelia, Lycaste, Odontoglossum, Oncidium, Phaius, Sobralia, Stanhopea,* and *Vanda.*
   (*b*) Secondary tropical orchid genera, often very beautiful, but less grown: *Aerides, Angraecum, Brassavola, Gomesa, Miltonia, Phalaenopsis, Peristeria, Renanthera,* and *Zygopetalum.*

There are a few other tropical cult. genera, among them vanilla, almost the only orchid of economic importance.

2. TEMPERATE GENERA MOSTLY GROWN IN THE GROUND, often in rich woods humus or in bog gardens.
   Aplectrum, Arethusa, Calopogon, Calypso, Cypripedium (some tropical), *Epipactis, Goodyera, Habenaria, Liparis, Orchis, Pogonia,* and *Spiranthes.*

See all these genera for further notes on them.

ORCHID BASKET. A crib-like basket, usually square and about 4–5 in. deep. Its sides and bottom are made of stout slats about ½ in. square, and usually there is a space of about ½ in. between the slats. Such a basket will not hold soil, but it is

---

* Special articles on the subjects indicated by an asterisk (*) will be found at the words so marked.

admirable for holding orchids or other air plants potted chiefly in fiber or fir bark, or the bark of redwood. *See* illustration at ORCHID.

ORCHID FAMILY = Orchidaceae.

ORCHID JUNGLE. *See* No. 18 at GARDEN TOURS.

ORCHID TREE = *Bauhinia variegata.*

orchioides (or-kĭ-oy′deez, but *see* OÏDES). Orchid-like.

ORCHIS (or′kiss). Woodland, hardy orchids, comprising over 80 widely distributed species of which the two native ones are cult. in the wild garden. They have tuberous roots, mostly basal leaves, and not especially showy flowers in terminal clusters (racemes*). Flowers very irregular, magenta or white, and magenta-spotted (in ours). Sepals similar, free or united, usually larger than the petals. Lip turned downward, generally spurred below. (*Orchis* is Greek for testicle, in allusion to the rounded tubers of some species.)

They require rich woods soil and the partial shade of the wild garden. *See* WILD GARDEN.

rotundifolia. Shin-plasters. Leaf solitary, nearly circular, 6–7 in. long, almost as wide. Flowers magenta, the stalk of the cluster naked. Lip white, but magenta-spotted, 3-lobed. Quebec to N.Y. and westward, mostly in the mountains. June–July.

spectabilis. Showy or gray orchis. Flowering stalk nearly 12 in. high, the cluster bracted.* Leaves 2, basal, shining, oblongish, 3–7 in. long, 2–4 in. wide. Flower purple-magenta, the petals and sepals united to form a hood. Lip white, but violet-blotched. Eastern N.A. May–June.

ORDER. *See* PLANT FAMILY.

oregana, -us, -um (o-ree-gay′na). From Oregon.

OREGANO. A trade name for various herbs of European origin, used as condiments. A good many of such mixtures contain *Origanum vulgare* (which see).

OREGON. As part of a name, *Oregon* has been applied to many plants native to Oregon or to the region near it. The hort. species so named and found in this book are:

Oregon cedar = *Chamaecyparis lawsoniana;* **Oregon cluster.** A variety of hop (which see); **Oregon crabapple** = *Malus fusca;* **Oregon grape** = *Mahonia Aquifolium* and *M. nervosa;* **Oregon laurel** = *Arbutus menziesi;* **Oregon maple** = *Acer macrophyllum* (*see* MAPLE).

OREGON. The Oregon grape is the state flower, the Douglas fir the state tree. The state lies wholly in zones* 3, 4, 5, and 6, which, due to the proximity of the mountains and the ocean, extend generally north and south instead of east and west as they do over half of the United States.

CLIMATE. Oregon has an extremely wide range of climatic conditions, due largely to the influence of elevation, mountain chains, ocean currents, and large bodies of water.

Winter temperatures as low as 54° below zero have been recorded in the Blue Mountain section of eastern Oregon, yet there are locations in the state where frost seldom occurs. The growing season in Oregon varies from as short as 30 days at very high altitudes to as long as 245 days in certain favored localities. Obviously these wide extremes have a pronounced influence on the state's horticultural geography.

East of the Cascade Mountains the high plateau areas normally experience rigorous winters, early and late frosts, and comparatively low precipitation, both in summer and winter. Horticulture in eastern Oregon thrives only in sheltered valleys that lie at fairly low altitudes and where irrigation is the common practice. In the regions west of the Cascade Mountains the climate is generally mild with heavy winter precipitation and long, fairly dry summers. The coastal areas of the state generally experience mild winters, very heavy rainfall during winter, and summers that are cool but comparatively dry.

In western Oregon, as well as in eastern Oregon, irrigation during the dry summer months is usually required to obtain maximum performance from plants.

SOILS. Oregon has a wide variety of soils, ranging in texture from almost pure sand and gravel to heavy types such as the "adobe" soils of southern Oregon which may contain as much as 60 to 70 per cent clay. As a rule, the soils of Oregon that lie east of the Cascade Mountains are alkaline in reaction while those of the more humid areas west of the Cascade Mountains are inclined to be acid, with the exception of those in the extreme southern portion which may be somewhat alkaline.

The soils considered to be the best for vegetable crops in western Oregon are usually found among the series classified as Chehalis, Newberg, Columbia, Peat (Beaver Dam), Willamette, Sifton, and Coquile. In southern Oregon the Neal and Columbia series are considered best for vegetable crops while Wind River, Milton, Onyx, and Columbia are considered best in eastern Oregon.

Among the best of the fruit soils in western Oregon are the Aiken, Olympic, Willamette, Powell, Chehalis, and Newberg. In southern Oregon, Columbia, Kerby, Corning, Medford, and Meyer series are among the best. In eastern Oregon, the Underwood, Columbia, Wind River, Milton, Catherin, and Alicel are all good fruit soils. Regardless of classification, however, a good fruit soil in Oregon must be well drained and must have sufficient depth to accommodate root development.

ORNAMENTAL GARDENING. Oregon is noted for the broad diversity of its ornamental horticulture. This is possible because of the wide range of climate, soil, and topo-

---

* Special articles on the subjects indicated by an asterisk (*) will be found at the words so marked.

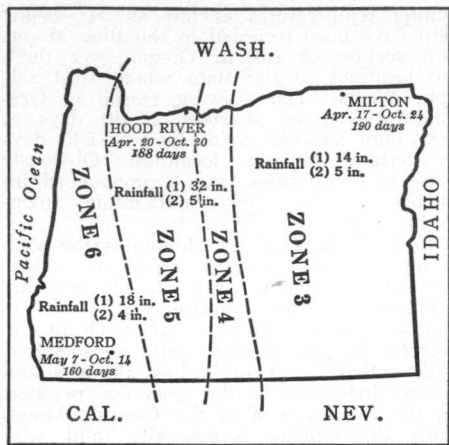

WASH.

*MILTON
Apr. 17 - Oct. 24
190 days

|HOOD RIVER
Apr. 20 - Oct. 20
188 days

Rainfall (1) 14 in.
(2) 5 in.

Rainfall (1) 32 in.
(2) 5 in.

ZONE 6

ZONE 5

ZONE 4

ZONE 3

Pacific Ocean

IDAHO

Rainfall (1) 18 in.
(2) 4 in.

MEDFORD
May 7 - Oct. 14
160 days

CAL.   NEV.

OREGON

The zones of hardiness crossing Oregon are those shown on the map located at ZONE, which should be consulted for details. The dates are the average latest killing frost in spring and the first one in the fall. The figures below the dates show the average length of the growing season. Rainfall figures (in inches) show (1) the total annual rainfall and (2) the amount falling in the growing season at the places indicated.

graphical features. In the portions of the state that experience rigorous winters, ornamental gardening is pretty much confined to the hardy herbaceous perennials, summer annuals, the hardy conifers, and deciduous trees and shrubs. On the other hand, the list of plant materials available for the mild portions of the state includes practically all of the hardy herbaceous perennials, summer annuals, bulbous and tuberous plants, conifers, deciduous trees and shrubs, as well as a wide array of broad-leaved evergreens. The coastal counties are especially well adapted to many of the garden annual and perennial flowers. Commercial growing of English holly is carried on in the areas of the state that experience mild winters and comparatively cool summers. The nursery industry, which centers largely in the vicinity of Portland, is a major horticultural enterprise.

VEGETABLE GARDENING. While vegetable gardening in some form is carried on in practically all parts of Oregon, the most intensified vegetable areas are the Willamette Valley, comprising nine counties which border on the Willamette River in western Oregon, the Milton-Freewater area in the northeastern portion of the state, the Ontario section in extreme eastern Oregon, the Umpqua Valley of western Oregon, and the Rogue River Valley of southern Oregon. Other areas where vegetables are produced in some quantity

are Hermiston, The Dalles, and the coastal counties. Some of the coastal counties are especially well adapted to the cool-weather crops. Deschutes County in central Oregon and Klamath County in southern Oregon are extensively engaged in the growing of potatoes.

Oregon's vegetable enterprise breaks down into three categories as follows: (1) production for processing, which involves principally canning, freezing, and dehydration; (2) production for the fresh market, and (3) production for home consumption. Production for processing, which is of major importance in the state, includes such crops as green beans, peas, carrots, sweet corn, pumpkins, and beets.

Vegetable production for the fresh market centers largely around the city of Portland where no less than 32 different vegetables are grown. In addition to the Portland area, Milton-Freewater produces tomatoes and asparagus for the early fresh market. The Tualatin Valley and Ontario produce dry onions and Hermiston, the Umpqua Valley, and the Rogue River Valley produce melons and cantaloupes. Head lettuce for out-of-state shipment is also grown in the vicinity of Ontario.

The home vegetable garden has long been an important factor in the horticulture of Oregon. Most farmers, and many urban dwellers as well, engage in this enterprise. The nature of the home vegetable garden in Oregon naturally varies with the climate of the particular region and with the wishes and desires of the owner. In the coastal areas the home vegetable garden is usually confined to the cool-climate crops while in the warmer sections of the state one finds most of the temperate-zone vegetables including tomatoes, watermelons, cantaloupes, sweet potatoes, eggplant, ground cherries, and peanuts. Gardening during the winter months is fairly common in the areas of the state that experience mild winters. In such gardens one usually finds vegetables such as cauliflower, cabbage, Brussels sprouts, celery, turnips, and broccoli. In the areas of Oregon where early and late frosts are common, vegetable gardening is naturally restricted to crops that are capable of withstanding frost, at least to some degree, and to crops that are quick-maturing.

FRUIT-GROWING. While fruit-growing in Oregon is confined largely to a few favored regions, the homeowner usually finds a number of fruits that will thrive in his area. The Willamette Valley is particularly noted for the large assortment of fruit crops it can produce reasonably well. In this area the homeowner may grow such tree fruits as apples, pears, quinces, sweet cherries, sour cherries, peaches, nectarines, plums, prunes, filberts, and English walnuts and he may grow to a high degree of perfection such small fruits as strawberries, trailing blackberries of many

* Special articles on the subjects indicated by an asterisk (*) will be found at the words so marked.

types, upright blackberries, dewberries, red raspberries, black raspberries, highbush blueberries, gooseberries, and currants.

In southern Oregon, particularly in the Rogue River Valley and the Grants Pass area, the homeowner can grow practically all of the fruits that thrive in the Willamette Valley, but in addition he can grow apricots and some varieties of the European or *vinifera*-type grapes. The Rogue River Valley is recognized for the excellence of its pears and peaches. In the coastal areas the fruit list is more restricted, although some varieties of apples and pears do fairly well as do most of the small fruits, including cranberries if one is so fortunate as to have access to a small plot of bog soil.

In the areas of eastern Oregon, however, one may encounter some difficulty if he attempts fruit-growing at high altitudes where growing conditions are generally unfavorable. The exceptions to this are the sheltered valleys that lie at comparatively low altitudes. Some of these valleys are unusually well adapted to fruit-growing. The Hood River Valley, for example, is noted for its apples, pears, cherries, and strawberries. The Milton-Freewater area is very well adapted to apples, prunes, cherries, peaches, and some small fruits. The Dalles is recognized for its cherries, apricots, and peaches, but also produces other fruits reasonably well, including some of the varieties of European grapes. Hermiston, Ontario, Grand Ronde Valley, and Eagle Valley are other districts of eastern Oregon well adapted to a number of the deciduous fruits.

Garden club activities continue at an accelerated pace in Oregon. The number of active units in the Oregon Federation of Garden Clubs now exceeds 300. This is a ten-fold increase during the past twenty-year period.

While Oregon can boast of many fine state parks intended for the accommodation of visitors and tourists, the state as a whole does not have many outstanding gardens of purely horticultural interest. Two such gardens, however, are worthy of mention. One is the International Rose Test Garden located in Washington Park in Portland and the other is Lambert Gardens, also located in Portland.

The address of the Agricultural Experiment Station, which has kindly supplied this information, is at Corvallis, Ore. The station is always glad to answer garden questions.

oregona, *-us*, *-um* (o-re-go′na). From Oregon.

OREGON GRAPE = *Mahonia Aquifolium.*

orellana, *-us*, *-um* (o-rel-lay′na). Named for a branch of the Amazon River.

organensis, *-e* (or-gan-en′sis). From the Organ Mountains, Brazil.

ORGANIC GARDENING. A term for a very old concept in the proper management of the land. It involves the addition and preservation of humus, the use of animal manure instead of chemical fertilizers, and of course the making of a compost pile. In accomplishing these most desirable objects the gardener will do well to read the following in this book: MANURE. COMPOST PILE. HUMUS. GREEN MANURING.

There is no question that manure, compost, and heavy mulching (6–8 in. thick) of hay, grass clippings, etc., will produce good crops of vegetables and flowers, especially on soils naturally deficient in moisture-holding capacity or in plant food, or in both. Such response to good hort. practice should not delude the grower into assuming that plants so grown are immune to pest attack or have significantly higher food value.

ORGAN-PIPE CACTUS = *Pachycereus marginatus.*

orgyalis, *-e* (or-jee-ā′lis). About six feet long.

ORIENTAL ARBORVITAE = *Thuja orientalis.*

orientalis, *-e* (or-ee-en-tay′lis). From the Orient; eastern.

ORIENTAL PLANE = *Platanus orientalis.*

ORIENTAL POPPY = *Papaver orientalis.* See POPPY.

origanifolia, *-us*, *-um* (or-rig-gan-i-fō′li-a). With marjoram-like leaves.

ORIGANO = Oregano.

origanoides (or-rig-ga-noy′deez, but *see* OÏDES). Like a marjoram (*Origanum*).

ORIGANUM (or-rig′a-num). A small genus of Eurasian perennial herbs of the mint family, of which the only cult. species is **O. vulgare**, the pot or wild marjoram, sometimes called winter-sweet. (It is not the sweet marjoram.) The pot marjoram is a hardy perennial herb with aromatic foliage and creeping or horizontal rootstocks. Leaves opposite,* broadly oval, about 1 in. long. Flowers small, irregular,* 2-lipped, purplish-pink, borne in spike-like clusters. The plant is often naturalized in N.A. The *var.* prismaticum is reputed to be more hardy than the type. It is one of the ingredients of imported oregano. For its culture and uses *see* HERB GARDENING. For a plant sometimes offered as *O. majorana, see* SWEET MARJORAM. (*Origanum* is thought to be the old Greek name for the plant and means delight of the mountains.)

ORIGIN OF CULTIVATED PLANTS. All cultivated plants must, of course, have originated from wild ancestors. Sometimes, in fact most often, the process of passing from a weedy ancestor to a definitely cultivated plant is lost in the past. Reconstructing such histories is one of the most fascinating of the many problems of the historical botanist, but little space can be given to it here. From such studies, however, the gar-

---

* Special articles on the subjects indicated by an asterisk (*) will be found at the words so marked.

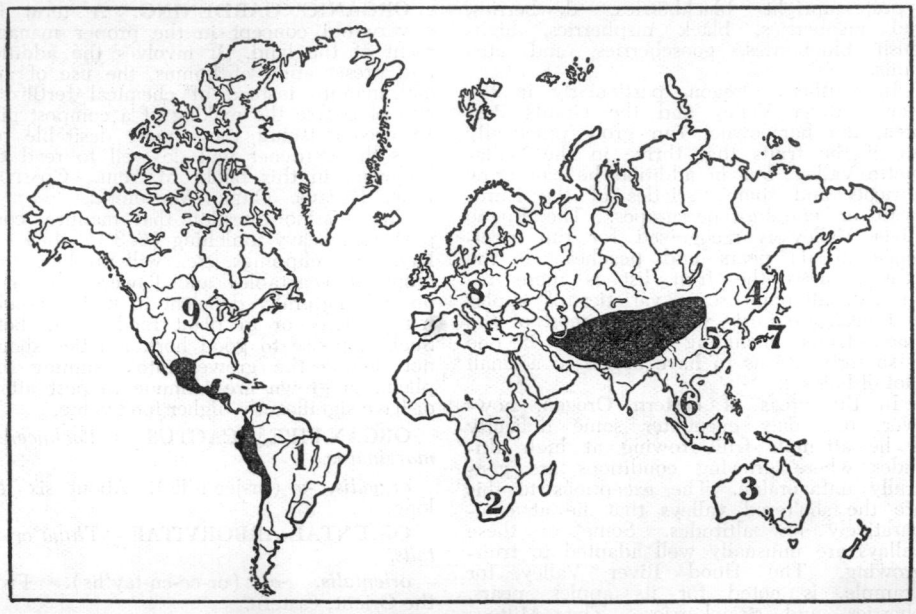

ORIGIN OF SOME CULTIVATED PLANTS

The black area in Mexico and southward is the region where the Aztecs grew Indian corn, tobacco, guava, vanilla, dahlia, marigold, cosmos, and many other New World plants. The black area in northwestern S.A. gave us the potato, quinine, cocaine, and many Peruvian, Bolivian, and Chilean ornamentals. The black area in central Asia gave us the common Old World vegetables and fruits listed in the article below and many garden flowers. The figures on the map show the approximate origin of the following:

1. Chocolate, lima bean, Pará rubber, peanut, tomato, sweet potato, many orchids and palms.
2. Garden geranium, gladiolus, freesia, and many Cape bulbs (which see).
3. *Eucalyptus, Banksia,* and many other plants popular in Calif. originated in Aust. and neighboring islands. (*See* AUSTRALIAN.)
4. Ginkgo, many chrysanthemums, and a great variety of trees and shrubs came from various parts of China. (*See* CHINESE.)
5. Most citrus fruits.
6. Sugar, ginger, nutmeg, rice, and banana, and, to the eastward, the coconut palm, many palms and orchids.
7. Many ornamental garden plants. (*See* JAPANESE.)
8. Europe is far less important in the origin of cult. plants than the other regions mentioned. (*See* EUROPEAN.)
9. Among ornamental plants, temperate N.A. has given us sunflower, many bulbous plants, besides shrubs and trees. For lists *see* AMERICAN, CANADA, INDIAN, CALIFORNIA, etc.

dener may glean much of historical interest. It is not perhaps of much practical importance to the average gardener to know where his chief crop plants have come from, but it adds much of cultural and educational interest. So much is this true that a brief record of some of the facts of the origin of cultivated plants is worth recording here.

All scientists are pretty well agreed that there have been two main regions responsible for the origination of most of our commonly cultivated plants — Asia and Asia Minor in the Old World, and the region from central Mexico to Chile in the New.

Let us take the American one first. It is hard now to realize what the voyage of

Columbus was to mean to the history of cultivated plants. In 1492 the Old World had never heard of the potato, sweet potato, corn, peanut, tobacco, pineapple, chocolate, guava, cinchona, rubber, cocaine, string bean, lima bean, tomato, dahlia, cosmos, marigold, upland cotton, or vanilla, every one of which was well known to the Aztecs or the Incas, but not often to both of them. Besides these and many more, there are whole families of plants, some of them enormous, that are wholly American, and were unknown before the Spanish conquest. The two most notable are the pineapple family with about 1000 species and the cactus family with over 1200.

Perhaps 2000 years before Columbus arrived, some of these purely American

* Special articles on the subjects indicated by an asterisk (*) will be found at the words so marked.

plants had already split up into any number of horticultural forms, notably corn, chocolate, tobacco, and potato, around which an immensely rich and varied civilization had grown up in Mexico and Peru. So highly developed had these people become that the Spanish conquerors were astounded. Such a degree of culture was, and always must be, built upon the basis of a stable agriculture. But, before Columbus, that agriculture did not include one major cereal (except corn), few of our common vegetables, no sugar, coffee, or tea and others to be mentioned presently.

The Old World had existed for nearly 1500 years without American plants, and probably for countless centuries before that. Most commonly grown European vegetables have been in cultivation over 2000 years, some much longer. But few of them are really European in origin, any more than most of the people appear to be. Sometimes a wild ancestor of a commonly cult. vegetable will be a European plant, but the origin of the vegetable as a cult. crop is more often Asiatic.

Somewhere in the vast reaches of central Asia which stretch from Pamir to China, there must have been a primitive agriculture for a very long period. For somewhere in this region it appears certain that the following plants became real cultivated plants for the first time:

Apple	Cucumber	Pear
Artichoke	Endive	Plum
Asparagus	Lettuce	Quince
Barley	Oats	Radish
Beet	Onion	Rhubarb
Cabbage	Parsley	Rye
Carrot	Pea	Turnip
Celery	Peach	Wheat
Cherry		

While this is an impressive list, it is mostly of plants of the temperate zone and is by no means complete. And it does not include such flowers as peony, hollyhock, narcissus, chrysanthemum, foxglove, or dozens of others — all from the Old World. And if the tropical and sub-tropical Old World is counted, as it should be, we must add the coconut palm, banana, sugar cane, date, all citrus fruits, tea, coffee, the watermelon, and most of the important drug plants except cocaine and quinine.

In purely ornamental plants eastern Asia is also outstanding for the greatest concentration of species in the barberry, oak, rhododendron, fir, spruce, pine, azalea, and flowering cherries. Far more than in the New World, these Asiatic primitive people seem to have originated many varieties of ornamental plants. The Incas and the Aztecs spent more effort on creating varieties of corn, tobacco, chocolate, and the potato.

ORIGIN OF NEW PLANTS. *See* Propagation.

ORIGIN OF NEW SPECIES AND VARIETIES. *See* Plant Breeding.

ORIXA (o-rick′sa). A genus of deciduous shrubs of the family Rutaceae, the foliage aromatic when crushed. The only species is **O. japonica** of eastern Asia, a shrub 6–9 ft. high, its young twigs hairy. Leaves alternate,* oblongish, 2½–5 in. long, short-stalked, finely round-toothed on the margin, bright green. Male and female flowers on separate shrubs, greenish, followed by a greenish-brown, dry fruit, with black seeds. Spring-flowering and not showy. Hardy from zone* 5 southward. (*Orixa* is derived from the Japanese name for this shrub.)

ORMOSIA (or-mo′sĭ-a). Little-known tropical trees of the pea family, comprising over 20 species of which only **O. monosperma,** the necklace tree, appears to be cult. It is hardy only in zone* 9, or possibly in zone* 8, and is a large tree with compound* leaves. Leaflets arranged feather-fashion, usually of 5 pairs and an odd one at the end. They are oblongish, 3–4 in. long. Flowers pea-like, blue, about ¾ in. long, in large, showy clusters (panicles*) which are rusty-hairy. Fruit a 1-seeded, leathery pod (legume*), not over 1½ in. long, the seeds scarlet, with a black patch. (*Ormosia* is from the Greek for necklace, in allusion to the use of the seeds for making necklaces.)

ORNAMENTAL FRUITS. *See* the list at Autumn Garden.

ORNAMENTALS. A common garden term for plants cult. mostly for their showy flowers or fruits. Common examples are trees (which see), shrubs (for the showy ones *see* Flowering Shrubs) and, of course, annual and perennial garden flowers. In catalogues the term *ornamentals* is used in contrast to plants useful for food, spices, timber, etc.

ornata, -us, -um (or-nay′ta). Ornamental or ornate.

ORNITHOGALUM (or-ni-thog′a-lum). Hardy or tender bulbous herbs of the lily family, comprising about 100 species, the hardy ones natives of Europe and western Asia, the tender species of Africa. Bulbs rather small. Leaves narrow or broad, tapering to a point at the tip. Flowers in clusters (racemes*) on leafless stems, sometimes as high as 3 ft. Individual flowers stalked, and with a small, leafy bract. Petals 6, separate, spreading, white, yellow, or orange-red. Stamens* 6. Fruit a dry, 3-valved capsule.* (*Ornithogalum* is from the Greek for bird and milk, in allusion to the egglike color of some species.) In S. Af., and sometimes here, *O. thyrsoides* is called chinkerichee, especially the *var. aureum.*

The outdoor species are generally used for wild gardens, as the bulbs increase so quickly as to become a nuisance in beds or borders. Propagate by offsets* removed from old bulbs when dormant. They require no attention. The tender species may be grown as border plants in the South or in cool greenhouses or sunny windows in temperate regions. They should

---

* Special articles on the subjects indicated by an asterisk (*) will be found at the words so marked.

be planted in a compost of 2 parts sandy loam, 1 part leaf mold and sand. Plant the bulbs Sept.–Feb., 1 in. deep, in pots, bowls or boxes with good drainage. Water moderately when growth begins, freely when in full growth, gradually withholding water when foliage begins to turn yellow. Apply liquid manure when flower buds appear. Bulbs can be dried and stored for use the following year.

arabicum. Bulb oval. Leaves 5–8, pale green, 1–1½ ft. long, ¾ in. wide. Flower stem 1–2 ft. Flowers 6–12, white, 1 in. long, with prominent black pistils.* Makes good pot plant. Mediterranean region.

nutans. Star-of-Bethlehem. Bulbs oval, 1 in. in diameter, producing offsets freely. Leaves pale green, 1–1½ ft. long, ¼–½ in. wide. Flower stalks 8–12 in. long. Flowers 3–12, white inside, green outside, with a white margin, nodding. This species can be used for naturalizing. Asia Minor.

thyrsoides. Bulbs globe-shaped, 1½ in. thick. Leaves 5–6, 1–2 in. wide, 6–12 in. long, the margins slightly hairy. Flower stems 6–18 in. long. Flowers 12–30 in a dense raceme,* white or yellow. South Africa. Not hardy north of zone* 6. The *var.* **aureum**, with golden-yellow flowers, is often known here as chinkerichee.

umbellatum. Star-of-Bethlehem; also called summer snowflake and Sleepy Dick. Bulbs round, 1 in. thick. Leaves 6–12 in. long, ¼–½ in. wide, veined or spotted white. Flowering stem 6–8 in. long. Flowers 12–20 in the cluster, star-like, white, the 3 outer segments having green margins. Common in American gardens. Mediterranean region, widely naturalized in eastern N.A. and often an invasive pest.

ornithorhynca, -us, -um (or-nith-o-rink′a). Like a bird's beak.

Ornus (or′nus). An ancient name for the flowering ash.

ORONTIUM (or-ron′she-um). Golden club, also called floating arum and water dock. Hardy water plant of northeastern U.S., the only species being **O. aquaticum**, of the arum family. It is a strong-growing aquatic plant, found in shallow pools and ponds or sides of slow-moving streams, and of little garden importance, but sometimes used in the bog or wild garden. Rootstocks thick and fleshy. Leafstalks 10–20 in. long. Leaves floating or erect, depending on the depth of the water, 2–5 in. wide, 6–12 in. long. Leaf blade with no central midrib, but strongly marked with numerous parallel veins. Flowers arranged in a closely packed cluster (the spadix*), which is long, yellow, and cylindrical; the spathe* small and inconspicuous. See ARACEAE. (*Orontium* was adopted from the Greek by Linnaeus, but is of uncertain application to this plant.)

OROXYLON (or-rox′i-lon). A single species of Indo-Malayan tree of the family Bignoniaceae. **O. indicum**, the Indian trumpet-flower, cult. for ornament in Calif. and Fla., and hardy only in zones* 8 and 9. It is a tree up to 40 ft. high with very striking foliage. Leaves 2–4 ft. wide, thrice-com-

pound, its leaflets very numerous, ovalish, 4–5 in. long, without teeth, glossy-green. Flowers bell-shaped, about 3 in. wide, white or purplish, its fine lobes crisped. Stamens* 5, slightly protruding. Fruit a slender, flattened pod, 2–3 ft. long, about 2½ in. wide. The tree needs a rich soil, plenty of moisture, and may be propagated by seeds or by cuttings over bottom-heat.* (*Oroxylon* is from the Greek for mountain tree, although the plant grows also in lowlands.)

ORPINE = *Sedum Telephium.*

ORPINE FAMILY. A very large group of mostly succulent plants suited to dry places. Besides the orpine, it includes the stonecrops, houseleeks, and many other plants with thick leaves or stems. For a list of the garden genera *see* CRASSULACEAE.

ORTET. A term for the original plant of a clone.*

ORTHOCARPUS (or-tho-kar′pus). A genus of 30 species of New World annual or perennial herbs of the family Scrophulariaceae, generally called owl's-clover in Calif., where some species are native. The only plant of garden interest is **O. purpurascens**, the escobita, which is an annual scarcely 12 in. high. Leaves alternate,* much cut into thread-like segments, the upper ones bract*-like, colored, and among the flower clusters. The latter are usually spikes and very showy, nearly 4 in. long. Flowers irregular, 2-lipped,* about 1 in. long, purple or crimson, the lower lip white but with yellow or purple streaks. Bracts* in the flower cluster tipped with red. The escobita can be treated as a hardy annual. See ANNUALS. (*Orthocarpus* is from the Greek for erect fruit, in allusion to the upright, small pods.*)

ORYZA. See RICE.

OSAGE ORANGE. See MACLURA.

OSIER WILLOW = *Salix viminalis.* See WILLOW.

OSMANTHUS (oz-man′thus). Tea olive; also called sweet olive (not a true olive). Evergreen shrubs or small trees of the olive family, all but one of the 10 known species Asiatic or Polynesian, but the devilwood (*O. americanus*) a native of the southeastern U.S. Leaves opposite,* spiny-toothed or with no teeth. Flowers often very fragrant, not showy, usually unisexual or polygamous,* and borne in terminal clusters (cymes* or panicles*), or these sometimes in the leaf axils.* Calyx* short and 4-lobed. Corolla tubular, but short, 4-lobed at the summit. Stamens* mostly 2, not protruding. Fruit fleshy, egg-shaped, a drupe* with a single stone. (*Osmanthus* is from the Greek for fragrance and flower, in allusion to the most fragrant species, *O. fragrans.*)

The tea olives, especially *O. fragrans*, are very popular shrubs in the warmer sections of the country, where they are grown in a variety of soils. Occasionally

---

* Special articles on the subjects indicated by an asterisk (*) will be found at the words so marked.

they are grown under glass in the North and need a cool greenhouse and potting mixture* 4. Propagated by late-summer cuttings of half-ripe wood, rooted under glass, more rarely by seeds which are scarce and take nearly two years to germinate.

americanus. Devilwood. A tree 20–40 ft. high. Leaves elliptic or narrower, 4–6 in. long, without marginal teeth, shining green above. Flowers fragrant, greenish. Va. to Fla. and Miss. Hardy from zone* 6 southward. May.

Aquifolium = Osmanthus ilicifolius.

armatus. A shrub 6–10 ft. high, related to O. ilicifolius, but the leaves only remotely spiny-margined. Flowers fragrant, not over ⅓ in. long, with a slender stalk. Western China. Sept.–Oct. Hardy from zone* 6 southward.

delavayi. A shrub 6–10 ft. high, the shoots downy. Leaves evergreen, leathery, ½–1 in. long, short-stalked and finely toothed on the margin. Flowers white, in sparse clusters from the leaf axils,* or terminal. Fruit nearly round, bluish-black. China. April. Hardy from zone* 6 southward. Also called Siphonosmanthus delavayi.

forresti. A shrub 10–20 ft. high, the oblongish leaves 4–9 in. long, spiny-toothed or toothless, with 10–16 conspicuous veins on the under side. Flowers fragrant, white, about ⅓ in. long. Fruit football-shaped, about ½ in. long, bluish-purple. China. Sept. Hardy from zone* 6 southward.

fortunei. A fragrant, hybrid shrub, 4–6 ft. high, derived by crossing O. fragrans and O. ilicifolius. Leaves ovalish, 3–4 in. long, spiny-toothed on the margin. Sept. Hardy from zone* 5 southward. Resembles the English holly.

fragrans. The most common in cult., and a shrub or small tree sometimes up to 25 ft. high. Leaves ovalish or oblong, 2–4 in. long, slightly toothed or without any teeth. Flowers white, very fragrant, the corolla divided nearly to the base. Southeastern As. Hardy from zone* 6 southward, but also grown in northern greenhouses. April. It is sometimes offered as Olea fragrans.

ilicifolius. A shrub 15–20 ft. high. Leaves oblong to ovalish, 1½–2½ in. long, the margins with a few spiny teeth. Flowers fragrant, white, the corolla divided almost to the base. Jap. Hardy from zone* 5 southward. June–July. There are several hort. forms, mostly with variegated, golden, or purplish foliage. Var. **myrtifolius** has leaves without the spiny-toothed margin. The plant makes a good hedge subject where hardy. See HEDGES. Called by some O. heterophyllus.

myrtifolius = O. ilicifolius myrtifolius.

OSMAREA (os-mare′i-a). A bigeneric* hybrid derived from crossing Osmanthus delavayi and Phillyrea decora. **O. burkwoodi,** the only species, is an evergreen shrub with opposite, short-stalked elliptic or oblong leaves 1–2 in. long, the margins finely toothed, but not spiny. Flowers small, fragrant, white, in small clusters in the leaf axils,* or the clusters terminal. April–May. Hardy from zone* 5 southward. Its cult. is easy in any good garden soil. (Osmarea is an attempt to combine Osmanthus and Phillyrea.)

OSMARONIA (oz-ma-rō′nĭ-a). A single species of shrub of the rose family found on the Pacific Coast from British Columbia to Calif. and cult. for ornament. The only species, **O. cerasiformis,** the osoberry, is an upright shrub 10–15 ft. high, its branches erect. Leaves alternate,* stalked, oblongish, 2–4 in. long, without marginal teeth. Male and female flowers on different plants, sometimes polygamous,* greenish-white, fragrant, mostly in short clusters (racemes*), the individual flower stalks with two bractlets. Petals oblongish. Stamens* 15, five shorter than the other 10. Fruit a collection of small, bluish-black drupes,* about ½ in. long. The plant blooms in April–May, and prefers partial shade and a moist site. Propagated by fresh or stratified seeds or by suckers. (Osmaronia is of doubtful origin.)

OSMOSIS. A process in physiological chemistry by which solutions of different density, separated by a permeable membrane, tend to become of the same density. Water and a solution of sugar and water, separated by such a membrane, will, in a few hours, have a common density. For physical and chemical reasons the flow or osmosis is mostly from the less dense to the denser solution. It is upon this theory, and with some added physiological factors, that the microscopic membrane found in all root hairs permits absorption by the root of soluble plant food in the soil. Also the pressure set up by this osmotic process is the cause, at least in part, of the ascent of sap, commonly called root pressure.

OSMUNDA (oz-mun′da). Coarse, stiffish, easily grown ferns, the only cult. genus of the family **Osmundaceae** (oz-mun-day′see-ee), all those below mostly from the north temperate zone, but a few others tropical. They have erect fronds that are cut, divided, compound,* or twice-compound,* usually in large basal clusters. The foliage fronds are usually different from the spore*-bearing ones, but in other species some of the leaf segments are modified to bear spores.* (Named for Osmunder, a Saxon name for the god Thor.)

For culture see FERNS AND FERN GARDENING. Much of the orchid peat formerly used for potting orchids is derived from the fibrous roots, etc., of the first two species, much collected for this purpose, and often called osmunda fiber.

cinnamomea. Cinnamon fern. Foliage fronds taller than the spore*-bearing ones, the stalks rusty-woolly. Blades deeply cut or divided into narrowly lance-shaped segments, the ultimate divisions also deeply cut, but the frond not compound.* Spore-bearing frond similar, but smaller, brownish, contracted and soon withering. In wet, low woods or thickets, N.A., Eurasia, and southward to Brazil.

claytoniana. Interrupted fern; also called Clayton fern. An upright fern, the fronds 2–4 ft. high, sometimes even more. Fronds deeply divided, but not compound,* the divisions with many deeply cleft segments. Most of the outer leaves are exclusively foliage fronds, but some of the inner leaves have, toward the center of the frond, a few divisions that are brownish and wholly spore*-bearing. In wet or moist places, eastern N.A., also in eastern As.

---

* Special articles on the subjects indicated by an asterisk (*) will be found at the words so marked.

regalis. Royal fern. Fronds long-stalked, twice-compound,* the ultimate segments somewhat distant, oblongish, 2–3 in. long, without teeth or divisions. Some of the main divisions of the compound leaf are wholly spore-bearing, brown, and much narrower than the foliage segments. Throughout the U.S. in moist places, usually in the open, but widely distributed in tropical America, Eurasia, and Af.

OSMUNDACEAE. See OSMUNDA.

OSMUNDINE = Osmunda fiber (see OSMUNDA). Its use as orchid peat is now replaced by fir bark. See Potting and Dividing at ORCHID.

OSOBERRY = Osmaronia cerasiformis.

OSTERDAMIA = Zoysia.

OSTRICH FERN. See PTERETIS.

OSTROWSKIA (os-trow'ski-a). A single perennial species of central Asiatic herbs of the family Campanulaceae. The only species, **O. magnifica,** is a tall herb resembling a giant bellflower (Platycodon), to which it is closely related, differing in having whorled* leaves. The plant grows 4–6 ft. high. Leaves ovalish, 4–6 in. long, toothed. Flowers blue, nearly 3½ in. wide, in a sparse, terminal cluster, usually not more than 4–5 blooms in all, but very showy. The plant is apt to die out in a year or two, and it needs winter protection north of zone* 5. Propagated by division or by cuttings of young shoots. (Named for N. Ostrowski, a Russian patron of botany.)

OSTRYA (os'tri-a). Hop-hornbeam. A genus of 7 species of American or Eurasian hard-wooded trees of the birch family, **O. virginiana,** the American hophornbeam (also called ironwood and leverwood), cult. for ornament and native in eastern N.A. It is a moderately ornamental tree, usually about 30 ft. high, but often taller in the wild. Leaves alternate,* ovalish, 3–5 in. long, sharply and double-toothed. Male and female flowers separate, on the same tree, greenish and inconspicuous, the female clusters ultimately forming bladdery, fruiting bracts, between which are the nutlets. The tree is closely related to Carpinus (see HORNBEAM). The fruiting cluster is hoplike and the most attractive feature of the hop-hornbeam, as its flowers bear neither petals nor sepals. Hardy from zone* 2 southward. (Ostrya is an old Greek name for some tree with hardwood, but not for this one.)

OSWEGO TEA = Monarda didyma.

OTAHEITE APPLE = Spondias cytherea.

OTAHEITE GOOSEBERRY = Phyllanthus acidus.

OTAHEITE ORANGE = Citrus taitensis.

Otaksa (o-tak'sa). Japanese name for the hortensia (Hydrangea macrophylla Otaksa).

OTHAKE SPHACELATA = Polypteris hookeriana.

OTHONNA (o-thon'na). South African succulent shrubs or herbs of the family Compositae, comprising over 80 species, of which **O. crassifolia** (also known as O. capensis) is often grown in greenhouses or in hanging baskets. It is a drooping or trailing perennial herb with alternate,* fleshy or pulpy, cylindrical leaves nearly 1 in. long (hence sometimes called "little pickles"). Flower heads solitary, bright yellow, about ½ in. wide, at the ends of slender stalks 3–6 in. long, thus standing far above the essentially prostrate foliage. They bloom only in sunlight. The plant is a rampant grower in any well-drained soil, preferably potting mixture* 3. It needs a cool greenhouse, and, as a basket plant, will stand considerable neglect. (Othonna is a Greek name of no known application to this genus.)

OUR LADY'S THISTLE = Cnicus benedictus.

OUR LORD'S CANDLE = Hesperoyucca whipplei.

OUTDOOR LIVING. See PLANNING THE HOME GROUNDS.

OUVIRANDRA. See APONOGETON.

OVAL. Broadly elliptic; usually about 1½ times as long as broad and rounded at the ends. The term is often confused with ovate (which see).

OVAL FLOWER BED. For the number of plants needed for an oval flower bed see GARDEN TABLES IV.

ovalifolia, -us, -um (o-val-i-fō'li-a). Oval-leaved.

ovalis, -e (o-vay'lis). Oval.

OVAL KUMQUAT = Fortunella margarita.

OVARY. The usually swollen base of a pistil, containing one or more ovules, which, after fertilization, become the seeds. In most flowering plants the ovary and/or its attendant parts become the fruit. See FLOWER, FERTILIZATION.

ovata, -us, -um (o-vay'ta). Ovate (which see).

OVATE. Egg-shaped in outline with the broader end downward, usually applied to surfaces. The technical distinction between ovate and oval is clear enough, but it often breaks down in hort. and botanical descriptions, because leaves, to which it is mostly applied, may well be ovate or oval on the same plant. In such cases the common term is oval, although many leaves so designated are slightly egg-shaped.

OVER-POTTING. A common fault of amateur growers, which results in plants being grown in pots too big for them. For details see POTTING.

ovifera, -us, -um (o-vif'fer-ra). Ovule-bearing; literally egg-bearing.

ovina, -us, -um (o-vy'na). Relating to sheep; woolly or sheep-like. In plant names it also signifies sheep fodder.

---

* Special articles on the subjects indicated by an asterisk (*) will be found at the words so marked.

OVOID. Egg-shaped (ovate); usually applied to solids.

OVULE. The usually minute body (often numerous) within the ovary,* which becomes the seed, after the ovule had been fertilized. In the pine and its relatives the ovule is naked (see GYMNOSPERM). See FERTILIZATION.

OWL'S-CLOVER. See ORTHOCARPUS.

OWL'S-CROWN = *Gnaphalium sylvaticum.*

OWN-ROOT. A common term in hort. and applied to those plants that are budded or grafted upon roots of the same or closely related species or varieties. Own-root roses are preferred by some growers, while many lilacs are grown upon privet stock, and such would not be own-root plants.

OXALIDACEAE (ox-al-i-day'see-ee). The wood sorrel family does not mean much in the gardening world, but two of its 9 genera, *Oxalis* and *Averrhoa*, are grown for ornament. The family comprises about 900 species. *Oxalis*, while partly weedy, contains some beautiful herbs for the wild garden (the wood sorrel) as well as some greenhouse species. *Averrhoa* comprises tropical evergreen trees with edible fruit and can be grown outdoors only in zones* 8 or 9.

Leaves compound,* the leaflets arranged finger-fashion in *Oxalis*, but feather-fashion in *Averrhoa*. Flowers not very showy (but fine in some species of *Oxalis*), usually in clusters. Fruit a dry pod (capsule*) in *Oxalis*, but fleshy and edible in *Averrhoa*.

Technical flower characters: Flowers regular* and hermaphrodite.* Sepals 5. Petals 5, sometimes slightly united at the base. Stamens* 10. Ovary superior,* 5-celled, the styles separate.

OXALIS (ox'a-lis; *also* ok-sal'is). Wood sorrel. A very large and interesting group of sour-juiced herbs, the chief genus of the family Oxalidaceae, producing somewhat woody climbing plants in the Andes, edible tubers in Mexico, some beautiful wild flowers in our woods, and several rather weedy, yellow-flowered roadside weeds. Of the over 800 species, which are most abundant in the Andes and South Africa, only a few are of any hort. interest. All have compound,* clover-like leaves, the leaflets always arranged finger-fashion, folding up at night or in dark, weather (hence described as "going to sleep"). Flowers solitary, or more often in few-flowered clusters, white, pink, red, or yellow. Sepals and petals 5 each. Stamens* 10, 5 longer than the others. Fruit a capsule.* (*Oxalis* is from the Greek for sour, in allusion to the sour juice of most species.)

The species of *Oxalis* come from such widely different regions that no general cultural directions will apply. See the different species for notes on culture. All are low herbs (3–6 in.) except *O. ortgiesi*. Some non-hort. species produce the widely eaten oca of the Andes (tuberous roots). For the blue oxalis *see* PAROCHETUS.

Acetosella. Common wood sorrel; called, also, sleeping beauty and sheep sorrel. It is also one of the plants known as shamrock.* A woodland, stemless, perennial herb. Leaflets 3, notched. Flower solitary, about ¾ in. wide, at the end of a short stalk. Petals white, but pink-veined, blunt, but not notched. Northern Eu. and N.A. A June-blooming plant needing rich woods soil and shade. Suitable for the wild garden. Some prefer the name of *O. montana* for the American form of this common wood sorrel.

adenophylla. A perennial herb with tuberous roots. Leaflets 12–22, notched, about ½ in. long, bluish-green. Flowers pink, but veined with deeper pink. Chile. A winter-blooming greenhouse plant. Grow in potting mixture* 3, in a cool greenhouse, and when through flowering the tubers should be lifted and stored in a cool, dark place, and planted again in the autumn.

bowiei. A perennial herb with a thickened rootstock and scaly bulbotubers. Leaflets 3, notched. Flowers nearly 2 in. wide, rose-purple, blooming late in summer and in the autumn. South Africa. It is not hardy over the winter and its tubers should be grown exactly as are gladioli (which see).

brasiliensis. A perennial, from a small bulb, 3–5 in. high. Leaflets 3, almost round, notched at the tip, green. Flower solitary, about 1 in. long, magenta-red, but yellow in the throat, the petals slightly notched. Brazil. Grow as in *O. adenophylla*. Thrifty outdoors along the Gulf Coast.

cernua. Bermuda buttercup (neither native in Bermuda nor a buttercup, but naturalized there). A bulbous, South African herb with 3 notched leaflets. Flowers yellow, about 1½ in. wide, nodding. Hardy in the Far South, but in the North to be treated the same as *O. adenophylla*.

corniculata. The common yellow wood sorrel of our roadsides. A perennial herb, the leaflets 3, notched. Flowers about ½ in. long, yellow, in few-flowered clusters. Eu., but widely naturalized in N.A. More a weed than a garden plant.

deppei. A perennial, 4–8 in. high. Leaflets 4, minutely toothed on the margin, nearly round, about 1 in. long, blunt at the tip. Flowers in a long-stalked cluster (umbel*) exceeding the leaves, red or purplish-violet, the petals slightly notched. Mex. There is also a white-flowered var. Tubers edible (in Mex.). Grow as in *O. adenophylla*.

enneaphylla. A perennial herb with tuberous roots. Leaflets 9–20, notched, bluish-green. Flower solitary, white, but purple-veined. Falkland Islands. To be grown as in *O. adenophylla*.

hirta. An erect or trailing perennial, the stem 8–15 in. long. Leaflets 3, hairy, nearly spoon-shaped, not notched, and about ⅜ in. long. Flowers solitary, long-stalked, funnel-shaped, purplish-violet, yellow in the throat. S. Af. Grow as in *O. bowiei*.

lasiandra. A perennial from many small scaly bulbs. Leaflets 5–10, usually 8, tongue-shaped, slightly notched at the tip, red-blotched beneath. Flowers in a tight cluster (umbel*), the petals rounded, not notched, red. Mex.

lobata. A low, stemless perennial, scarcely 4 in. high. Leaflets 3, deeply notched at the tip, generally oblongish, hairy, sometimes lobed, about ⅓ in. long, sometimes black-spotted. Flowers solitary, yellow, often dotted and veined red. Chile. Hardy outdoors from zone* 5 southward.

---

* Special articles on the subjects indicated by an asterisk (*) will be found at the words so marked.

ortgiesi. A leafy-stemmed perennial herb, 12–18 in. high. Leaflets 3, cut fishtail-fashion at the tip. Flowers yellow, but veined darker yellow, usually in long-stalked clusters (cymes*) from the leaf axils.* Peruvian Andes. To be grown as in O. adenophylla.

rosea = Generally, as offered, Oxalis rubra.

rubra. A perennial herb, the leaflets 3, notched. Flowers in a cluster (umbel*) which is higher than the leaves. Petals rose-pink, but darker-veined, sometimes lilac or even white. Brazil. Sometimes grown in the window garden or in the greenhouse, or outdoors far southward. Should be handled as in O. adenophylla.

valdiviensis. A perennial herb with a bulbous root. Leaflets 3, notched. Flowers in long-stalked clusters (umbels*), the petals bright yellow, but brown-striped within. Chile. While this is a true perennial, it will bloom from seed in a single season if treated as a tender annual. See ANNUALS.

violacea. Violet or purple wood sorrel. A perennial, woodland herb. Leaflets 3, notched at the tip. Flowers several in a cluster, the stalk of which arises from the ground. Petals rose-purple, rarely pinkish-white. In rich woods, Que. to Fla. and west to the Rocky Mountains. Culture is the same as for O. Acetosella.

OXERA (ok'ser-ra). Australian shrubs or woody vines of the family Verbenaceae, only O. pulchella of the 15 known species likely to be cult. here. It is a woody vine grown for ornament in southern Calif. and scarcely hardy elsewhere. Leaves opposite,* oblongish, 3–5 in. long, without marginal teeth. Flowers white, trumpet-shaped, about 2 in. long, in forked clusters (cymes*). Calyx* showy, greenish-yellow. Corolla 4-lobed. Stamens protruding. Fruit fleshy. A very handsome climber, useful also in the warm-temperate greenhouse, although little known here. (Oxera is derived from the Greek for sour and sap, as the sap is acrid.)

OXEYE. See BUPHTHALMUM and HELIOPSIS.

OXEYE CAMOMILE = Anthemis tinctoria.

OXEYE DAISY = Chrysanthemum Leucanthemum.

OXLIP = Primula elatior.

Oxyacantha. An old generic name for some species of Crataegus.

OXYCOCCUS. See VACCINIUM.

OXYDENDRUM (ok-si-den'drum). A single species of beautifully white-flowered trees of the family Ericaceae, found wild from Pa. to Fla. and La. and cult. for ornament up to the limits of zone* 3. The only species, O. arboreum, the sourwood or sorrel-tree, is 30–50 ft. high. Leaves alternate,* stalked, bitter-tasting, oblongish, 6–8 in. long, brilliantly scarlet in the fall. Flowers small, not over ⅓ in. long, in drooping clusters (racemes*) 8–10 in. long, very handsome in midsummer and fragrant. Fruit a gray-hairy capsule.* While the tree is hardy north of its wild range, it is of slow growth, and few cult. specimens reach the dimensions given. (Oxydendrum is from the Greek for sour and tree, in allusion to the acid foliage.)

oxyphylla, -us, -um (ox-i-fill'a). With sharp leaves.

OXYTROPIS (ox-it'ro-pis). Perennial herbs and shrubs comprising about 230 species of the pea family, mostly natives of Asia, but about 18 species found in the Rocky Mountains. They are not of much garden interest, but occasionally used in the rock garden. (Oxytropis is from the Greek for sharp and a keel, in allusion to the shape of the flower.)

Easily propagated by seeds or division, the only cult. species prefers a dry, sandy loam, in a sunny position.

lamberti. Locoweed, so called because it poisons sheep and cattle. A tufted perennial with strong taproot. Height to 1½ ft. Leaves compound,* the leaflets 7–14 pairs and covered with silky hairs on the under side. Flowers on leafless stalks, twice as high as the leaves, pea-like, arranged in short, dense spikes, usually purple or violet. Fruit a leathery pod, covered with silky hairs. There are hort. color forms. Great Plains from Canada to New Mex.

OYAMA MAGNOLIA = Magnolia sieboldi.

OYSTER PLANT. A name applied to several plants, but commonly and most correctly to Tragopogon porrifolius, the salsify (which see). For the Spanish oyster plant see SCOLYMUS. The name oyster plant is also applied to Rhoeo discolor (which see), and the name of vegetable oyster is applied to the common oyster plant (Tragopogon porrifolius).

OYSTER SHELLS. See LIME.

P

P₁, P₂, See F₁, F₂, F₃.

pabularis, -e (pab-you-lay'ris). Suitable for pasture; fodder.

PACHISTIMA (pa-kiss'ti-ma). A genus of the staff-tree family (Celastraceae) comprising two North American species. They are low evergreen shrubs, with small opposite* leaves and inconspicuous flowers that are borne in the leaf axils.* (Pachistima is from the Greek for thick stigma.)

They are fairly ornamental, forming neat evergreen tufts, and adapted to the rock garden or borders of low evergreen plantings. They prefer a sandy, somewhat peaty soil, but are not particular so long as the situation is well drained. Propagated by seeds, cuttings, or layers. The name is sometimes spelled Pachystima.

canbyi. Rat-stripper. Low shrub growing about 1 ft. high, with trailing, rooting branches.

* Special articles on the subjects indicated by an asterisk (*) will be found at the words so marked.

Leaves ½ to 1 in. long, linear or narrowly oblong, toothed toward the tip, the margins turned under. Flowers tiny, reddish, on slender stems from the leaf axils.* May. Open rocky slopes of the mountains in Va. and W. Va. to Ky. and Ohio. Hardy from zone* 3 southward.

Myrsinites. Spreading shrub with stiff branches, sometimes to 2 ft. high. Leaves narrow-oblong or elliptic, ⅓–1¼ in. long, toothed toward the tip, the margin slightly turned under. Flowers white to reddish. May to Aug. In the woods from British Columbia to Calif. and N. Mex.

PACHYCEREUS (pack-i-seer'ee-us). Mostly Mexican tree-like or columnar cacti, comprising perhaps 10 species which differ from *Cereus* only in technical characters. They have tall, deeply ribbed stems, and are definitely trunk-like and woody at the base, often branched at the top. Flowers day-blooming, not very showy, often scaly or spiny on the outside. Fruit bur-like, dry. (*Pachycereus* is from the Greek for thick and *Cereus,* in allusion to the huge stems.)

The three below are suited only to tropical desert gardens, and are too big for greenhouse culture northward. *See* CACTI.

marginatus. Organ-pipe cactus. Stems not usually branched, 15–20 ft. high, 5–7-ribbed, the ribs white-cushioned along the ridge. Spines 5–8 at each cluster, one central and erect, the others spreading, none over ¾ in. long. Flowers about 1½ in. long, funnel-shaped, brownish-purple. Mex. Also known as *Lemaireocereus marginatus.*

pecten-aboriginum. Hairbrush cactus. A stout cactus, the trunk 6 ft. long and 12 in. in diameter, crowned with many erect, ribbed branches up to 30 ft. high. Ribs 10–11. Spines in clusters of 8–12, one or two central and erect, the others spreading, usually ½ in. long or less. Flowers about 2 in. long, white inside, but purplish outside. Fruits bur-like, used by the Indians as combs, hence *pecten-aboriginum.* Mex.

pringlei. A huge, columnar cactus, 20–30 ft. high, with a woody trunk, often with upright, many-ribbed branches. Spines 20 or even more at each cluster, black-tipped, often wanting on old branches. Flowers about 3 in. long, white. Fruit felty and bristly. Lower Calif.

pachyphylla, *-us,* *-um* (pack-i-fill'a). Thick-leaved.

PACHYPHYTUM (pack-i-fy'tum). Little-grown Mexican succulent plants of the family Crassulaceae, **P. compactum** sometimes found in greenhouses or in desert gardens in frost-free regions. It is a bluish-green herb, 8–12 in. high, with very thick leaves borne in rosettes on the stem. Leaves broadest above the middle. Flowering stalk curved at first, ultimately erect, and bearing a 1-sided cluster (raceme*) of red flowers. Mex. For culture *see* SUCCULENTS. (*Pachyphytum* is from the Greek for thick plant, in allusion to the thick leaves.)

PACHYRHIZUS. *See* YAM BEAN.

PACHYSANDRA (pack-i-san'dra). Low-growing perennial herbs or sub-shrubs comprising 5 species of the family Buxaceae and natives of N.A. and eastern As. Stems fleshy.

Leaves alternate,* simple, spoon-shaped, the upper half with teeth-like margins. Flowers greenish-white, in spikes, the lower flowers fertile, having 4 sepals and a pistil,* the upper having 4 sepals, 4 stamens* and a rudimentary pistil,* and not fertile. Fruit a small, whitish, oval berry. (*Pachysandra* is from the Greek for thick and men, in allusion to the stamens.)

Pachysandra can be grown readily in ordinary soil, making admirable ground cover for either shady or sunny positions, particularly useful under large trees or on steep banks. *P. terminalis* is especially useful for this purpose. Easily propagated by cuttings taken in July or Aug., planted in a mixture of ½ sand and ½ soil, in a cold frame which should be well watered and shaded until cuttings are rooted. For making a quick ground covering they should be planted 8–12 in. apart.

procumbens. Allegheny spurge. Evergreen in the South, deciduous* in the North. Stems trailing at first and then becoming erect. Leaves alternate,* ovalish, dingy green, 2–4 in. long. Flowers white or purplish in spikes produced from the leaf-bearing stems. Grown mostly for its early spring flowers. Ky. to Fla. and La.

terminalis. Japanese spurge. Growing to 1 ft., the stems beneath the surface of the soil sending out underground runners or stolons,* hence its quick-spreading habit. Leaves thick, dark, glossy-green, spoon-shaped, alternate. Flowers white in terminal spikes, 3–4 in. long. Jap. One of the best evergreen ground covers for partly shady places.

INSECT PESTS. For control of scales, *see* EUONYMUS. For leaf rollers use pesticide #21 (*see* SPRAYS AND DUSTS).

DISEASES. In any bed of pachysandra, but particularly following weakening by scale insects, a canker* disease may kill many plants. Both the upright and the underground stem will have brown areas which will feel like sandpaper due to the mass of fungus on the stem. Clean out as much diseased material as possible and use pesticide #5 (*see* SPRAYS AND DUSTS) as soon as new growth starts in the spring. Repeat twice at 10-day intervals.

PACHYSTACHYS (pack-i-stack'is; *also* pack-iss'tack-is). Tropical American shrubs comprising 6 species of the family Acanthaceae, the one below the only plant of hort. interest. They differ only in technical characters from *Jacobinia.* (*Pachystachys* is from the Greek for thick spike, in allusion to their dense flower clusters.)

Grown chiefly as a greenhouse plant, sometimes grown outdoors in the southern states. Propagated from cuttings of young shoots in early spring. If grown as pot plants, potting mixture* 5 should be used.

coccinea. Also known as *Jacobinia coccinea,* and *Odontonema strictum,* to which it is closely allied. Grows to 9 ft. Leaves simple, ovalish, to 8 in. long, margins sometimes wavy. Flowers in dense terminal heads, scarlet, 2 in. long. Calyx of 5 sepals. Corolla tubular, widely 2-lipped. Stamens* 4. Fruit a 2-celled, many-seeded capsule. S.A.

PACHYSTIMA = *Pachistima.*

pacifica, *-us,* *-um* (pa-siff'i-ka). From the

* Special articles on the subjects indicated by an asterisk (*) will be found at the words so marked.

Pacific, usually from the islands of the Pacific; sometimes from our Pacific Coast.

PACIFIC DOGWOOD = *Cornus nuttalli.*

PACKING. Cut Flowers. The container should either be a shallow box of light wood or cardboard only deep enough to hold one layer of flowers or, if deeper, be fitted with trays, each to hold one layer of flowers.

The boxes must be lined with oiled paper or plastic (polyethylene) and these must be arranged in such a way as to fold over the top to prevent side drying. Wet paper must be packed around the stems to prevent their drying out, and to provide humid atmosphere. There must be sufficient space between the lid and the flowers to prevent heating. If on a regular flower route, it may be sufficient to have paper packing over the stems to make a tight lid contact, but it is far safer to lace the flower stems to the bottom of the box by means of a packing needle and string. Orchids, camellias, and gardenias are kept apart by means of cotton batting or paper excelsior to prevent mechanical injury — in the case of orchids it is imperative to sew the stems to the bottom of the box. Flowers should be in water overnight before packing.

Potted Plants. Plants may be packed upright one layer deep or horizontally in several layers. The plants must be wet at the roots, the plants firmly staked and tied. Cover the top of the soil with damp moss and tie on firmly to prevent the shaking out of the plant; sometimes banding with paper is necessary. Moist moss or excelsior must be between the pots and over the bottom of the crate. It is advisable to cleat in the pots by passing over them inch strips of wood and nailing to the sides.

Horizontal packing is by tiers at both ends of the crate. The pots are laid on their sides and cleated in front. Ventilation is provided through the sides.

Nursery stock is balled in moist moss and packed in open or tight crates or sown up in bagging.

PAEONIA. See Peony.

PAEONIACEAE. See Ranunculaceae.

PAGODA TREE = *Sophora japonica.*

PAINTBRUSH. The orange hawkweed; see No. 29 at Weeds and Weeding. For Flora's-paintbrush see Emilia.

PAINTED-CUP. See Castilleja.

PAINTED DAISY = *Chrysanthemum coccineum.*

PAINTED LADY. See Chrysanthemum coccineum, Phaseolus coccineus, and Phlox paniculata.

PAINTED-LEAF = *Euphorbia pulcherrima.*

PAINTED-TONGUE = *Salpiglossis sinuata.*

PAINTED TRILLIUM = *Trillium undulatum.*

PAK-CHOI = *Brassica chinensis.*

palaestina, -us, -um (pal-ees-ty'na). From Palestine.

PALAQUIUM (pa-lay'kwee-um). Indo-Malayan, milky-juiced trees of the family Sapotaceae, of far more economic than hort. interest, as one of them, **P. Gutta,** is the gutta-percha tree, which is occasionally cult. for interest in zone* 9. It is hardy nowhere else in the U.S. Not over 40 ft. high. Leaves alternate,* leathery, ovalish, 3–4 in. long, rusty beneath. Flowers small, white, in short-stalked clusters in the leaf axils.* Corolla scarcely ⅓ in. long. Fruit a small, egg-shaped berry. (*Palaquium* is Latinized version of a Philippine Island vernacular for one of the species.)

PALE CORYDALIS = *Corydalis sempervirens.*

PALE LAUREL = *Kalmia polifolia.*

PALIURUS (pal-i-your'us). A small genus of Eurasian, usually spiny shrubs or small trees of the family Rhamnaceae, **P. Spina-Cristi,** the Christ's-thorn or Jerusalem thorn, cult. more for legendary interest than ornament. By some it is supposed to be the plant from which the Crown of Thorns was made. It is a shrub or small tree 10–20 ft. high, with both hooked and straight spines. Leaves alternate,* ovalish, 1–1½ in. long, prominently 3-veined and finely toothed on the margin. Flowers very small, greenish-yellow, in small clusters (cymes*). Fruit nearly 1 in. in diameter, brownish-yellow, leathery. Southern Eu. to northern China. June–July. Hardy from zone* 5 southward. It is easily grown in open, sunny places, preferably in well-drained soil. (*Paliurus* is the old Greek name for these plants.)

pallens (pal'lenz). Pale.

pallida, -us, -um (pal'lid-a). Pale.

pallidiflora, -us, -um (pal-lid-i-flaw'ra). Pale-flowered.

PALM. Decorative foliage plants, widely grown both in greenhouses and outdoors in suitable climates for their striking habit and beautiful leaves. As usually cult. their flowers and fruits are of secondary interest and are often not produced at all. As hort. subjects they lend themselves to all sorts of fine groupings, both outdoors as in Calif. and Fla., and as florists' pot or tub plants for indoor ornament.

There is no need to repeat here the kinds and characters of all the palms entered in the Encyclopedia. A complete list of the genera and an account of the characters of the family will be found at the next entry, Palmaceae.

Of the 45 genera which appear to represent the leading palms in cult. in the U.S. many are little known or rarely grown and will not be dealt with here. The ones below have been selected because of their availability, their ability to stand cultivation, and their decorative value. The list includes the most important palm genera in cult. here, and

* Special articles on the subjects indicated by an asterisk (*) will be found at the words so marked.

Coconut palms in Florida

all are entered in their proper alphabetical sequence. Those with a † are also widely grown by florists for indoor decoration, and usually make good house plants, or are used as tubbed specimens for porches or patios.

FAN PALMS (*i.e.*, the leaves palmate*)

†Chamaerops	Serenoa
Coccothrinax	Thrinax
†Livistona	Trachycarpus
Rhapidophyllum	Washingtonia
Sabal	

FEATHER PALMS (*i.e.*, the leaves pinnate*)

Actinophloeus	†Hedyscepe
Archontophoenix	†Howea
†Arecastrum	†Phoenix
Caryota	Pseudophoenix
†Chamaedorea	Roystonea
†Chrysalidocarpus	†Syagrus
Cocos	

There are, also, especially attractive palms to be found in the genera *Ceroxylon, Erythea, Jubaea,* and *Latania,* but most of them are more cult. outdoors than in the greenhouse. Of the few palms native in the U.S. only *Sabal* and *Washingtonia* are outstanding hort. subjects, the first being commonly planted from N. Car. to the Gulf, while *Washingtonia* is a valuable Californian native plant, widely grown there for avenue planting and as a specimen on the lawn. In Fla. another native palm, *Pseudophoenix sargenti,* is widely planted for ornament, while *Serenoa,* also a native, is less popular. Other native palms for outdoor cult. will be found in the genera *Thrinax* and *Coccothrinax.*

Within the U.S. the coconut palm is of no economic importance. It is somewhat planted in Fla. but only for ornament. Its real home is in the Old World tropics and the commercial exploitation of it is chiefly in regions warmer than any part of the U.S. (*see* COCONUT). The only cult. palm of real economic importance in the U.S. is the date palm (*Phoenix dactylifera*). See DATE. There are also valuable decorative palms in the genus *Phoenix,* especially *P. canariensis* which is widely planted in Calif. for ornament. This and *P. reclinata* are commonly planted along the Gulf Coast.

While the outdoor cult. of most palms must be limited to frost-free regions, there are certain of them that will stand occasional frosts, and such relatively hardy palms are much planted. The chief genera containing such plants are *Brahea, Chamaedorea, Chamaerops, Coccothrinax, Erythea, Jubaea, Latania, Livistona, Sabal, Serenoa, Trachycarpus,* and *Washingtonia. Sabal,* particularly, contains species hardy as far north as the coast of N. Car., and the only palm native in Eu., *Chamaerops humilis,* is perhaps the hardiest of all palms. Not one of these, however, is really hardy north of zone* 6 in the East.

INDOOR CULTURE. Outdoors any of the palms cult. in the U.S. will ultimately produce a trunk, flowers, and fruit, but as cult. in the greenhouse or as house plants, they rarely, if ever, do so. In other words, practically all palms in the greenhouse are cult. only in the juvenile state. Of these the feather palms in the genera *Chrysalidocarpus, Howea, Phoenix,* and *Syagrus* are by far the most important. For many people these constitute all the palms they ever see because these contain the palms one sees in the florists' windows. And of these, two species of *Howea,* commonly called *Kentia,* are probably the most widely cult. palms in America.

For the culture of *Chrysalidocarpus* (and of *Areca* and *Arenga*) *see* CHRYSALIDOCARPUS. For the culture of many other genera, which require less heat than *Chrysalidocarpus,* the best greenhouse temperature is 55°–60° at night, and about 10° warmer during the day. Use potting mixture* 4 and be careful not to use too large a pot. A common fault among householders is to over-pot palms, thus reducing their chances of continuous growth and inviting too great an accumulation of water in the pot. This results in slacking of growth and often leads to yellowing of the foliage.

The ideal should be to keep all potted palms on the edge of being pot-bound.* Water them freely during their most active growing season (April–Oct.), but reduce the amount of water during the winter when most palms are merely marking time. This is especially true of house palms, which due to relative darkness are practically dormant. Such plants need only just enough water to keep from drying out. After all danger of frost is past, all house palms are better plunged* outdoors, in the shade, and then they should be watered liberally, every third week with liquid manure (which see).

---

* Special articles on the subjects indicated by an asterisk (*) will be found at the words so marked.

In the greenhouse most of the commonly cult. palms need the glass shaded, either by paint or by roller shades, as most palms will burn badly if exposed to the sun through clear glass.

For those who may not know the different genera of palms the list below may be useful in identifying any particular one known only by its common name. It includes most of the common cult. palms of the U.S. and all will be found at their proper generic names in the body of this book. To save space the word palm is omitted in the list, but it applies to most of them; *i.e.*, Betel = Betel palm.

A mature specimen of the dwarf fan palm (*Chamaerops humilis*), one of the hardiest of all palms

African hair = *Chamaerops*
African oil = *Elaeis*
Areca = usually *Chrysalidocarpus*
Australian fan = *Livistona*
Betel = *Areca*
Bitter-stem = *Hyophorbe*
Bluestem = *Sabal*
Bottle = *Hyophorbe*
Buccaneer = *Pseudophoenix*
Cabbage = *Sabal, Roystonea, Pseudophoenix*
California fan = *Washingtonia*
Cane = *Chrysalidocarpus*
Chinese fan = *Livistona*
Cluster = *Actinophloeus*
Coconut = *Cocos*
Cohune = *Attalea*
Coquito = *Jubaea*
Curly = *Howea*
Date = *Phoenix*
European fan = *Chamaerops*
Everglade = *Paurotis*
Fiji fan = *Pritchardia*
Fish-tail = *Caryota*
Flat = *Howea*
Fountain = *Livistona*
Gachipaes = *Guilielma*

Gomuti = *Arenga*
Ground rattan = *Rhapis*
Guadalupe = *Erythea*
Hemp = *Trachycarpus*
Hog cabbage = *Pseudophoenix*
Jaggery = *Arenga, Caryota*
Kentia = *Howea*
Kittul = *Caryota*
Mexican blue = *Erythea*
Monkey-coconut = *Jubaea*
Needle = *Rhapidophyllum*
Nikau = *Rhopalostylis*
Palma dulce = *Brahea*
Palmetto = *Sabal, Thrinax, Coccothrinax*
Palmiste = *Roystonea*
Panama-hat = *Carludovica* (not a palm)
Pejibaye = *Guilielma*
Pignut = *Hyophorbe*
Pindo = *Butia*
Plumy coconut = *Arecastrum*
Porcupine = *Rhapidophyllum*
Queen = *Arecastrum*
Raffia = *Raphia*
Royal = *Roystonea*
Sabal = *Sabal*
Sago = *Cycas* (not a plam)
Sargent = *Pseudophoenix*
Saw-cabbage = *Paurotis*
Saw palmetto = *Serenoa* and *Paurotis*
Silvertop palmetto = *Coccothrinax*
Spindle = *Hyophorbe*
Sugar = *Arenga*
Thatch = *Coccothrinax, Thrinax*
Toddy = *Caryota*
Totai = *Acrocomia Totai*
Umbrella = *Hedyscepe*
Wax = *Ceroxylon*
Wild date = *Phoenix*
Windmill = *Trachycarpus*
Wine = *Caryota, Jubaea*

INSECT PESTS. Various scales and mealybugs attack in greenhouses. Control with superior-type oil sprays. *See also* COCONUT.

PALMACEAE (pal-may'see-ee). The palm family, sometimes called the Arecaceae, are the most distinctive and noble foliage plants of the tropics. They range from stemless plants of pot culture to the magnificent royal palm (*Roystonea*) which, in many tropical cities, notably in Rio de Janeiro, makes imposing avenues of feathery foliage. While their hort. uses are extensive their economic importance is still greater, notably the coconut (*Cocos*), the date (*Phoenix*), and the African oil palm (*Elaeis*). Many other palms are of wide use in the arts and industries for fiber, food, drugs, resins, wood, etc., and are also cult. for ornament. Among these are species of *Arenga, Butia, Caryota* (the fish-tail palms), and *Raphia* (raffia).

The great mass of its 150 genera and more than 1200 species are real denizens of the tropics, but some of the cult. genera will stand considerable frost (*see* PALM).

All the palm family are easily (but not technically) divided into two groups by their leaves — the feather palms, with pinnate (*i.e.*, arranged feather-fashion) leaflets, and the

---

* Special articles on the subjects indicated by an asterisk (*) will be found at the words so marked.

fan palms, with palmate (*i.e.*, arranged fin-ger-fashion) leaflets or segments to the other-wise undivided leaf. In both sorts the leaf is usually long-stalked.

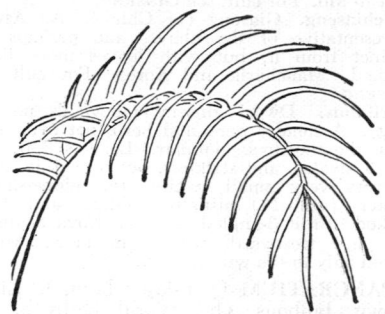

Leaf of a feather palm

The fan palms in the remaining hort. gen-era (not including those already mentioned) are: *Brahea, Chamaerops, Coccothrinax, Ery-thea, Latania, Livistona* (the chief fan palm of the florists), *Pritchardia, Rhapidophyllum, Rhapis, Sabal, Serenoa, Thrinax, Trachycar-pus,* and *Washingtonia.* All the rest of the cult. genera (not including those already mentioned) are feather palms of which the outstanding genera for decorative use by florists are: *Arecastrum, Chrysalidocarpus, Howea* (usually called *Kentia*), *Syagrus,* and some (not the date) species of *Phoenix.*

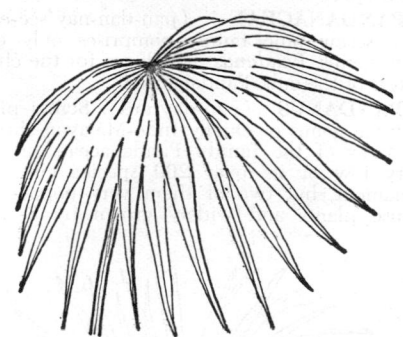

Leaf of a fan palm

Most palms have a single trunk with a crown of leaves at the top. Some of these leaves are of huge size (65 ft. long) in their native regions, but much smaller in cult. Large-leaved feather palms among the cult. genera include species of *Archonoto-phoenix, Attalea, Dictyosperma, Raphia, Guil-ielma, Hedyscepe, Jubaea,* and *Rhopalostylis.* Some palm trunks are very spiny, as in certain species of *Acrocomia,* while other genera have a peculiar bottle-neck swelling of the trunk, as in *Hyophorbe.* The rattan palms (*Calamus*), scarcely in cult. in Amer-ica, are climbing vines with stems, in Ceylon, hundreds of feet long.

Because of their beauty and decorative value there is no limit to the number of palm genera that may be in cult. in America. Some special collections (*see* the Montgomery collection in Fla. at ARBORETUM) have a tremendous variety. But for most gardeners in Fla. or Calif., or the Gulf Coast between them, the genera so far mentioned and the few to follow constitute the chief plants of interest in the palm family. The remain-ing genera (all feather palms) are: *Actino-phloeus, Areca, Chamaedorea, Ceroxylon, Martinezia, Paurotis, Ptychosperma,* and *Pseudophoenix.*

The individual flowers of the palms are small and inconspicuous, but the cluster in which they are normally crowded is often large and handsome. Typically this unopened cluster is enclosed between sheathing bracts* (a spathe*) from which it issues at bloom-ing time. The spathe may be persistent, woody, and boat-shaped in some genera. Flowers perfect* or unisexual,* with 3 petals and 3 sepals, or the 6 indistinguishable as either, generally greenish or yellowish. Sta-mens usually 6, but many more in some genera, notably *Howea.* Ovary superior,* 3-celled. Fruit various, often a very hard nut or fleshy (*see* Cocos).

Because few greenhouse palms ever pro-duce either flowers or a trunk their exact identification is most difficult. The technical characters in this family are mostly in the flowers and fruit, neither of which is norm-ally produced until the plant has grown a trunk. For cult. and hort. uses *see* PALM.

PALMA CHRISTI = *Ricinus communis.* See CASTOR-OIL PLANT.

PALMA DULCE = *Brahea dulcis.*

PALMA SAMANDOCA = *Samuela carne-rosana.*

palmata, -us, -um (pal-may′ta). Palmate.*

PALMATE. With leaflets, or with the lobes or veins of a simple leaf, radiating

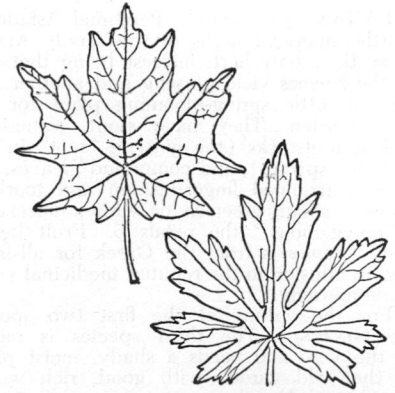

Palmate leaves, showing the palmate arrangement of veins (*left*) and leaf lobes (*right*).

* Special articles on the subjects indicated by an asterisk (*) will be found at the words so marked.

from one point. *Digitate* and *palmate* are often used interchangeably, *digitate* being more often applied to leaflets, as in the horse-chestnut, and *palmate* to the lobes or veins of a simple leaf, as in a maple. *See* PINNATE.

PALMERELLA (pal-mer-rel′la). A small genus of perennial herbs of the family Lobeliaceae, found in Mex. and southern Calif., **P. debilis** cult. in the border for ornament, but of uncertain hardiness in the North. It is a slender herb, 1–2 ft. high, with alternate,* narrow leaves, 2–3 in. long, and without marginal teeth. Flowers tubular, about ¾ in. long, the tube white, the 2-lipped* limb bluish, the cluster a terminal raceme.* Fruit a capsule. (Named for Dr. Edward Palmer, American botanist.)

PALMETTE VERRIER. A method of training fruit trees. *See* TRAINED FRUIT TREES.

PALMETTO (pal-met′to). A variant of the Spanish *palmito*, a little palm. *See* SABAL. For the saw or scrub palmetto *see* SERENOA. For the silvertop palmetto *see* THRINAX and COCCOTHRINAX. For the cabbage palmetto *see* SABAL.

PALM FAMILY = Palmaceae.

PALM GRASS = *Setaria palmifolia.*

palmifolia, -us, -um (pal-mi-fō′li-a). With palm-like leaves.

PALMISTE = *Roystonea oleracea.*

PALO-VERDE = *Cercidium torreyanum* and *Parkinsonia aculeata.*

palustris, -e (pa-lus′tris). Growing in a marsh.

PAMPAS GRASS. *See* CORTADERIA.

PAN. *See* FLOWER POTS. *See* also HARDPAN.

PANAMA-HAT PLANT = *Carludovica palmata.*

PANAMA ORANGE = *Citrus mitis.*

PANAMA RHUBARB. *See* RHUBARB.

PANAMIGA = *Pilea pubescens.*

PANAX (pay′nacks). Perennial Asiatic or North American herbs of the family Araliaceae, their only hort. interest being that two of the species yield ginseng and another is a delicate little spring-blooming plant for the wild garden. They have stout, sometimes forked rootstocks (the ginseng "root" in the first two species), and compound* leaves, the leaflets arranged finger-fashion and toothed. Flowers small, greenish or white, unisexual* or polygamous,* the petals 5. Fruit berrylike. (*Panax* is from the Greek for all-healing, in allusion to the reputed medicinal value of the ginseng.)

For the culture of the first two species *see* GINSENG. The third species is native in the U.S. and needs a shady, moist place in the wild garden with good, rich woods (not too acid) soil.

quinquefolius. Ginseng (of America). A smooth herb 10–18 in. high, the rootstock spindle-shaped and often forked. Leaflets 5, oblongish, 3–5 in. long, thin and sharply toothed. Flower cluster (umbel*) solitary. Fruit red, about ½ in. in diameter. June. Quebec to N.Y. and southward in the mountains to Ga., west to Mo. For cult. *see* GINSENG.

Schinseng. Ginseng (of China). An Asiatic representative of the above, and perhaps not distinct from it, but with leaves more finely toothed. Manchuria and Korea. For cult. *see* GINSENG.

trifolius. Dwarf ginseng (it yields no ginseng). A slender perennial herb, not over 4 in. high, the rootstock globular. Leaflets 3–5, usually 3, ovalish and stalkless, not over 1 in. long. Flowers very small, white, the globe-shaped cluster (umbel*) usually solitary and long-stalked. Fruit 3-angled, yellow. Nova Scotia to Ga. and westward, mostly in moist woods. Suited only to the wild garden.

PANCRATIUM (pan-kray′shĭ-um). Little-known, bulbous, Old World herbs of the family Amaryllidaceae, with mostly narrow, strap-shaped, basal leaves. Of the 14 known species only the sea daffodil, **P. maritimum** of the Mediterranean region, is likely to be much cult. It has a globe-shaped bulb which tapers into a neck,* from which arise the bluish-green leaves that are about 2 ft. long. Flowers white, lily-like, fragrant, 5–10 in a terminal cluster (umbel*) on a stout, solid, somewhat flattened stalk. Fruit a 3-valved capsule.* The culture of *P. maritimum* is the same as for amaryllis (which see). For the plant sometimes offered as *P. calathinum, see Hymenocallis calathina* at SPIDER-LILY. (*Pancratium* is from the Greek for all-powerful, in reference to reputed medicinal value of some species.)

PANDANACEAE (pan-dan-nay′see-ee). The screw pine family comprises only one hort. genus, *Pandanus,* which see for the characters of the cult. Pandanaceae.

PANDANUS (pan-day′nus). Screw pine. A large genus of chiefly Indo-Malayan shrubs or trees of the family Pandanaceae, only a very few of its over 200 species cult. for ornament, but two of them very popular as house plants and widely grown by florists.

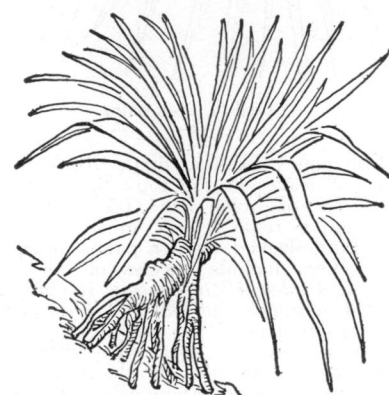

A mature pandanus, with its prop roots

---

* Special articles on the subjects indicated by an asterisk (*) will be found at the words so marked.

In maturity they have a distinct trunk, but as cult. for pot plants this is rarely developed. Many large, tubbed specimens in greenhouses and outdoor plants in the South develop considerable trunks, but in the tropics these plants may well be 30–60 ft. high in some species and palm-like in the huge, terminal crown of leaves which in most species, especially in maturity, are conspicuously spirally arranged. In some species there are large prop roots, especially in old specimens. Flowers (rare in cult. specimens) without petals or sepals, the naked pistils* and stamens* separate and scattered over the cluster (mostly heads* or spikes*). Fruit aggregate,* often ball-like or cone-like, and heavy. (*Pandanus* is a Latinized version of a Malayan name for some species.)

The cult. screw pines, especially *P. veitchi,* are very good house plants. For perfect growth, however, they need a tropical greenhouse, plenty of moisture, and are best grown in potting mixture* 3. In the greenhouse their culture is very much the same as for palms, and they do best when the glass is partly shaded. For the household management of *P. veitchi,* one of the most widely grown of florists' plants, *see* HOUSE PLANTS.

pygmaeus. A small screw pine, the trunk, if produced, not over 2 ft. high. Leaves 1–2 ft. long, scarcely ⅛ in. wide, spiny on the margins and on the midrib below. Madagascar.

sanderi. Possibly only a form of *P. veitchi,* but the leaves narrower and golden-banded instead of silver-banded. It is also a more densely tufted plant than *P. veitchi.* Timor, East Indies.

utilis. In the tropics up to 60 ft. high, its prop roots often arising 15–20 ft. from the ground. Leaves bluish-green, 1–3 ft. long, about 3 in. wide, its spines red. An immense, striking, very spiny Madagascan plant, commonly planted outdoors in frost-free regions, and sometimes in greenhouses.

veitchi. A very popular pot or house plant, the leaves 2–3 ft. long, about 2½ in. wide (less in young plants), usually arching, prominently white or silver-banded, spiny-margined. Probably from Polynesia, but its identity, as well as that of the related *P. sanderi,* is still in doubt.

PANDORANA = *Pandorea.*

PANDOREA (pan-door'ee-a). Tropical Old World, showy, woody vines of the family Bignoniaceae, three of the 16 known species grown for ornament in zones* 8 and 9. They have opposite,* compound,* evergreen leaves, the leaflets arranged feather-fashion, with an odd one at the end. Tendrils* none. Flowers pink or white, the corolla funnel-shaped. Stamens* 4, not protruding. Fruit an oblong pod, its seeds winged. (*Pandorea* and *pandorana* are both derived from Pandora, the sister of Prometheus.)

The pandoreas are not much grown in the U.S. They need an open, sunny site, rich, well-drained soil, and may be propagated from greenwood cuttings under glass. Not hardy north of zone* 7.

jasminoides. Bower plant. Leaflets 5–9, practically stalkless, ovalish or narrower, 1–2 in. long. Flowers white, or pinkish in the throat, 1½–2 in. long, the lobes of the corolla scalloped.

Australia. Sometimes known as *Tecoma jasminoides.*

pandorana. Wonga-wonga. Leaflets 3–9, elliptic or ovalish, 1–2½ in. long. Flowers white or yellowish-white, but violet-spotted in the throat, not over ¾ in. long, but showy from the profuse clusters. Australia. Also offered as *Tecoma australis.*

ricasoliana. Leaflets 7–10, short-stalked, ovalish, about 1 in. long. Flowers about 2 in. long, pink but red-striped. Pod 10–12 in. long. South Africa. Sometimes offered as *Tecoma* or *Podranea ricasoliana.*

pandurata, -us, -um (pan-dure-ray'ta). Fiddle-shaped.

PANIC GRASS. *See* PANICUM.

PANICLE. A loose, open flower cluster which blooms from the center or bottom toward the edges or top of it. The main stalk (axis) is never terminated by a flower. Strictly, a panicle is a compound raceme.* Typical examples are the oat, the Adam's-needle, the olive, and the catalpa. Flower clusters in which the inflorescence is a panicle are said to be paniculate or panicled.

Panicle

paniculata, -us, -um (pan-ick-kew-lay'ta). Panicled. *See* PANICLE.

PANICUM (pan'i-kum). Panic grass. A large genus of over 500 species of annual or perennial grasses found in all parts of the world, but mostly in the tropics. They are of creeping or erect habit, and vary considerably in height and the size of the leaves. The flowers are usually in light feathery clusters, in which the upper flowers are fertile and the lower flowers rarely so. (*Panicum* is from an old Latin name for Italian millet.)

A few of these grasses are grown for grain or fodder and occasionally for ornament (*see* DRIED FLOWERS). Propagated from seeds, but the perennials may be divided. Annuals can be used in the garden. Sow in patches ⅛ in. deep, in early spring, thinning plants out when 1 in. high to 3 in. apart. Perennials may be divided in Oct.

maximum. Guinea grass. Perennial, growing to 8 ft., in bunches. Stems stout. Leaves

---

* Special articles on the subjects indicated by an asterisk (*) will be found at the words so marked.

to 2 ft. long, ½ in. wide with light central vein. The flower clusters, 1–2 ft., are arranged in spreading whorls, the clusters shiny. Used for forage in the South. Africa.

miliaceum. Millet. Broomcorn millet. Annual, 3–4 ft. high. Leaves to 10 in. long, 1 in. wide, soft. Flower clusters of drooping habit, about 1 ft. long, the stalks slender and crowded. The smooth, shiny seed is almost white. Cultivated from earliest times for fodder and grain. East Indies.

purpurascens. Pará grass. Strong-growing perennial, which has both creeping and erect stems, the creeping ones rooting in the soil at every joint and spreading 10–20 ft., the erect stems growing to 10 ft. Leaves to 1½ ft. long and ½ in. wide, rough edge, more or less hairy. Flower clusters 8–12 in. long. Used as forage in the tropics.

texanum. Texas millet. Colorado grass. Annual, to 3 ft., of creeping habit and softly hairy. Stems stout, to 4 ft. high. Leaves 6–8 in. long, about ¾ in. wide. Flowers in one-sided, crowded clusters. It is not much cultivated. Tex.

virgatum. Switch grass. Strong perennial, to 6 ft. high. Leaves 12–15 in. long, ½ in. wide, with rough margins. Flower clusters to 18 in. long, the stalks spreading. Sometimes grown as an ornamental grass. Me. to Central America.

pannosa, -us, -um (pan-nō′sa). Tattered.

PANSY (*Viola tricolor hortensis*). Pansies are universal favorites, their adaptability to the large and small gardens making them one of the most useful plants in cult. They may be planted as edging plants, or in masses of mixed or separate colors, in the flower border or in beds. Used as a ground cover between roses or tulips they make a beautiful display from midwinter (in the South) to early summer, some excellent color combinations being made this way. Planting between tulips should be done early in Oct.; tulips should, however, be planted first, then the pansies 8 in. apart. They will then make a complete carpet the following spring, without injury to the bulbs which will grow up through them.

VARIETIES. There are many excellent varieties on the market, some of the best for size and substance being of American origin, Ore., N.J., Mass., Pa., and Ohio having produced some of the finest strains. It is wise to procure seeds from specialists as home-saved seeds soon degenerate. Unusual strains are Mastodon, strong-growing, with large flowers, beautifully marked and shaded in many colors (Ore.); Ullswater Blue, large flower of cornflower blue with blue-black center (Eng.); Crimson Queen, wallflower red with dark center. Clear white and yellow forms may be obtained, but pansies are generally admired for their color variations or their waved or frilled petals.

Winter-flowering varieties, where only very slight frosts occur, will bloom outside all winter. These can be grown in a cold frame or cool greenhouse. A strong strain with flower stalk to 10 in. and large flowers, for greenhouse cult., has also been distributed with great success.

SOILS. Pansies do well in good rich garden soil, but prefer cool, moist conditions, their roots never being allowed to become dry at any time. They are best raised from seed every year as the old plants become straggling and the flowers small, often dying completely during the hot summer months. Not allowing seeds to form prolongs the flowering considerably. They are very hardy and will withstand 15° or more, but in northern localities should have a light covering of salt hay or strawy manure from late fall until early spring.

The new crop of seeds is usually obtainable early in Aug. and this is the best time for sowing. If plants are required to bloom the same fall, seed should be sown in July. Prepare a cold frame or seedbed outdoors by digging and well pulverizing soil, leveling with rake and making surface very fine, water thoroughly and allow surface to dry until soil will not cling to the fingers. Then sow seeds thinly, ⅛ in. deep, in rows. This is easily done by making slight depressions with back of iron rake or with a pointed stick. After sowing they should be watered with a fine spray and shaded from strong sunlight until germinated, when the shading should be gradually reduced. This may be done by removing shades from 4 P.M.– 10 A.M., thus shading only during the hottest part of the day. Never allow the seeds to become dry. As soon as large enough, transplant to nursery bed or permanent position as the plants must not be allowed to become crowded in the seedbed. Seeds may also be sown in Sept. or early Oct. in a cold frame, but must then remain there during winter, transplanting in the spring.

Pansies root easily from cuttings made from the side shoots of young growth, which are produced after the flowering season. The cuttings should be put in a cold frame in ½ sand, ½ soil, keeping sashlights closed, and shaded from strong sunlight for 4 weeks, then admitting light and air gradually. For the closely related Johnny-jump-up, *see* VIOLA.

DISEASES. When pansy crops are grown continuously in the same soil, a root rot or wilt* disease may gradually build up. Plantings should be rotated every couple of years.

A spotting of leaves and stems may be controlled with pesticide #5 (*see* SPRAYS AND DUSTS) applied at 10-day intervals during the spring. Just before plants are covered with straw in the fall, a single application of the same pesticide should be made.

PAPAVER. See POPPY.

PAPAVERACEAE (pap-pa-ver-ray′see-ee). The poppy or bloodroot family contains a few genera of outstanding garden interest. The chief favorite is *Papaver* (*see* POPPY), but in California it may well be *Platystemon* (*see* CREAMCUPS), or the California poppy (*Eschscholtzia*), or the beautiful Matilija poppy (*Romneya*). *Sanguinaria* (*see* BLOODROOT) is a wild garden favorite in the East; *Stylophorum* somewhat less so.

The family contains about 25 genera and over 450 species of herbs (rarely shrubs) that are most common in the north temperate zone.

---

* Special articles on the subjects indicated by an asterisk (*) will be found at the words so marked.

Argemone and *Hunnemannia,* however, are largely Mexican, and *Dendromecon* is a Californian shrub. The other cult. genera are *Eomecon, Glaucium, Macleaya,* and *Meconopsis,* while *Chelidonium* is somewhat weedy. Most of these plants have a milky juice or colored juice, and alternate* or basal leaves, which are often lobed or divided.

The flowers in most genera are extremely showy, but often wither rapidly when picked, and in some genera the petals fall naturally within a day or two. Fruit a dry pod (capsule*), the juice of the unripe pod of *Papaver somniferum* yielding opium.

Technical flower characters: Flowers regular* and hermaphrodite.* Sepals usually 2, soon falling. Petals 4–6, the margins overlapping, soon falling in many genera, and wrinkled in some. Stamens* many. Ovary superior.* Style* short or none.

PAPAW = *Carica Papaya* and *Asimina triloba.*

Papaya (pap-py′ya). Tropical American vernacular for the papaw. *See* CARICA.

PAPERBARK = *Melaleuca Leucadendron.*

PAPERBARK MAPLE = *Acer griseum.* See MAPLE.

PAPER BIRCH = *Betula papyrifera.* See BIRCH.

PAPER BUSH = *Edgeworthia papyrifera* and *Melaleuca Leucadendron.*

PAPER MULBERRY = *Broussonetia papyrifera.*

PAPER PLANT = *Cyperus Papyrus.*

PAPER TREE = *Edgeworthia papyrifera.*

PAPER WHITE. *See* NARCISSUS TAZETTA.

PAPHIOPEDILUM. *See* CYPRIPEDIUM.

Papilio (pap-pill′i-o). A butterfly. *See* ONCIDIUM.

PAPILIONACEAE. *See* LEGUMINOSAE.

PAPILIONACEOUS. Having pea-like flowers. For a description and picture of them *see* LEGUMINOSAE.

PAPOOSE-ROOT = *Caulophyllum thalictroides.*

PAPPUS. *See* COMPOSITAE.

papyracea, -us, -um (pap-i-ray′see-a). Papery.

papyrifera, -us, -um (pap-i-rif′fer-ra). Paper-bearing.

PAPYRUS = *Cyperus Papyrus.*

PARADISE. A dwarf variety of apple (*Malus pumila paradisiaca*), used for grafting stock of dwarf apple trees. *See* APPLE.

PARADISEA (par-a-di′see-a). St. Bruno's-lily. Herbaceous, hardy perennials of only one species, belonging to the family Liliaceae and a native of the Pyrenees, Apennines, Alps and Juras. (Named for Giovanni Paradisi of Modena, Italy.)

It is of easy cultivation either from seeds or division. Seeds may be sown in spring in

a cool greenhouse or cold frame, and transplanted to partially shaded border of soil rich in leaf mold and decayed cow manure.

Liliastrum. Leaves basal, about 12 in. long, narrow. Flowers, 2–10, borne on slender, leafless stem, 12–18 in. high, in loose racemes, the corolla fragrant, white, funnel-shaped, and about 2 in. long. May–June.

PARADISE FLOWER = *Solanum wendlandi.*

paradisi, paradisiaca, -us, -um (par-a-di-si-ā′ka). Of parks or gardens.

paradoxa, -us, -um (par-a-dock′sa). Strange or paradoxical.

PARAFFIN. A substitute for grafting wax, but care must be used not to put it on when hot enough to cause injury. It has been advocated especially in grafting nut trees, and is widely used by nurserymen to prevent too rapid drying out of small shrubs, especially roses, while in transit. Ordinary paraffin used as in fruit-preserving will do, but it must be cooled off before being applied to grafts.

PARÁ GRASS = *Panicum purpurascens.*

PARÁ NUT = *Bertholletia excelsa.*

PARÁ RUBBER-TREE = *Hevea brasiliensis.*

PARASITE. A plant that steals all its food from another, to which it is attached. No true parasites can therefore be garden plants, although many tree-perching orchids, aroids, ferns, and plants of the pineapple family are often incorrectly called parasites. Actually, they are epiphytes (which see). Parasites are most frequent among the fungi. *See* PLANT DISEASES, MISTLETOE.

PARASOL TREE = *Firmiana simplex.*

pardalina, -us, -um (par-da-ly′na). Spotted like a leopard.

PARIS DAISY = *Chrysanthemum frutescens.*

PARKINSONIA (par-kin-sō′nǐ-a). Tropical, usually spiny, shrubs or trees of the pea family, only one of the 5 known species likely to be met. It is the Jerusalem thorn or ratama (or retama), sometimes called the horse bean, and known to science as **P. aculeata,** and probably a native of tropical America. It is grown in zone* 6 and southward for ornament, and is a tree up to 30 ft., its spines nearly 1 in. long. Leaves thrice-compound,* the ultimate leaflets very numerous, scarcely ¼ in. long, but the whole leaf nearly 12 in. long and drooping. Flowers not pea-like, yellow, fragrant, in clusters 4–6 in. long. Petals 5,* some larger than the others. Fruit a legume,* constricted between the seeds, nearly 5 in. long. The tree, which in the young state makes a good hedge plant, is much grown from Charleston, S. Car., to Fla. and in Calif. (Named for John Parkinson, herbalist.) Often called palo-verde along the Gulf Coast.

PARMA VIOLET. *See* VIOLA ODORATA.

PARMENTIERA (par-men-tǐ-ee′ra). A

---

* Special articles on the subjects indicated by an asterisk (*) will be found at the words so marked.

small genus of tropical American shrubs or trees of the family Bignoniaceae, comprising only two species, one of which, **P. cerifera,** the candle tree from Panama, is planted for ornament in the warmest parts of Fla. (zone* 9). It is a medium-sized, spiny tree with compound* leaves, the 3 leaflets broadest toward the tip, and 1–2 in. long. Flowers funnel-shaped, but slightly irregular, about 3 in. long, white, but with a conspicuous, brownish calyx.* Fruit a hanging, candle-like, smooth, yellowish-white pod, nearly 3–4 ft. long. A striking tree in fruit, but little known in cult. (Named for A. A. Parmentier, French horticulturist.)

PARNASSIA (par-nass′i-a). Grass-of-Parnassus. Low-growing herbaceous perennials comprising about 30 species of the family Saxifragaceae, found in wet or damp and shady places throughout the northern hemisphere. Growing from 6 in. to 2 ft. high, they have a graceful, showy appearance. Leaves basal, with long stalks, the blades smooth, ovalish or kidney-shaped and green. The flower stalk bears 1 stalkless leaf. Flowers solitary, white or yellow, strongly veined with green. Calyx* of 5 sepals, joined at the base, green. Corolla of 5 petals. Fertile stamens 5, alternating with the petals. Ovary 1-celled, many-seeded. (*Parnassia* was named from Mt. Parnassus.)

Not of much garden interest except for cool, very damp, shady places, such as the sides of bogs, lakes or rivers. Propagated by seeds or division. Seeds should be sown in moist, boggy peat in shady position outdoors in fall or spring.

californica. A Californian representative of a European plant. Height to 16 in. Leaves ovalish, kidney-shaped at base, 1–2 in. long. Leaf on flower stalk above the middle. Flowers 1½ in. across. Mountains of Calif.

caroliniana = *P. glauca.*

fimbriata. Height to 1 ft. Leaves kidney-shaped, 1–1½ in. long. Leaf on flower stalk partly clasping at middle. Petals fringed. Western N.A.

glauca. Height 1–2 ft. Leaves ovalish, sometimes heart-shaped at base, 1–2 in. long. Leaf on flower stalk clasping, below the middle. Flowers 1½ in. across. This species is the most suitable for cultivation. Swamps and bogs, eastern N.A. Formerly called *P. caroliniana.*

PARNASSIACEAE. See SAXIFRAGACEAE.

PAROCHETUS (par-o-key′tus). Attractive herbaceous perennial of trailing habit, of only one species, belonging to the pea family, and a native of the mountains of Asia and East Africa. (*Parochetus* is derived from the Greek for near and a brook, in allusion to its wild habitat.)

communis. Shamrock-pea. Grows 2–3 in. high, the root-like stems creeping. Leaves compound*; leaflets 3, similar to the shamrock, except that they are marked deeply at the base with a brown crescent and have no stalk. Flowers produced in the leaf axils,* pea-shaped, upper petal cobalt blue, 2 side petals pink. Fruit a pod, 1 in. long. Propagated by seed sown 1⁄16 in. deep in light, sandy soil in March or April, or by division of plants in March. Plant

out in ordinary garden soil in margins of sunny borders or rockeries. They can also be used for hanging baskets.

PARROT BEAK = *Clianthus puniceus.*

PARROTIA (par-rō′ti-a). A single cult. species of shrub or small tree of the family Hamamelidaceae, **P. persica,** a native of Persia, and with foliage resembling the witch-hazel. It is not over 20 ft. high, the leaves alternate,* ovalish or oblong, 3–4 in. long, coarsely toothed toward the tip, turning scarlet, orange, or yellow in the fall, and long-persistent. Flowers in dense heads nearly ½ in. in diameter, blooming before the leaves unfold, the head surrounded by brown-hairy bracts.* Petals none. Fruit an egg-shaped, beaked capsule.* March–April. Hardy from zone* 3 southward. (Named for F. W. Parrot, German naturalist.)

PARROT'S-BILL = *Clianthus puniceus.*

PARROT'S-FEATHER = *Myriophyllum proserpinacoides.*

PARSLEY. This best-known plant for garnishing is the only cult. species of the genus **Petroselinum** (pet-ro-se-ly′num) of the carrot family, which comprises only 6 species of European herbs. The common parsley, **P. crispum,** is a biennial or soon-failing perennial which should be planted every other year or so to secure a steady supply, though it will sometimes persist without replanting. It is a much-branched herb, 10–15 in. high, the leaves thrice-compound,* the ultimate segments wedge-shaped, and with crisped margins in one of the commonest hort. forms. Flowers very small, greenish-yellow, in compound umbels* (for details see UMBELLIFERAE). Fruits ribbed, about 1⁄8 in. long. The common parsley is best raised from seed, which, however, is of slow and uncertain germination. The latter can be hastened by soaking the seeds in warm water for a few hours before planting. For family needs only a small patch is required and this can often be started from the roots that are frequently on parsley as purchased from the store. Simply cut off the leaves and plant the roots. Such roots, planted in pots kept on the kitchen window-sill, will yield a crop of leaves through the winter, as will well-mulched plants outdoors. The diseases and pests of parsley and their control are the same as for celery (which see). For culture and uses of parsley see HERB GARDENING. The best vars. are Moss Curled and Double Curled. The *var.* **radicatum,** the turnip-rooted or Hamburg parsley, is a form grown mostly in Eu. for its parsnip-like, much-thickened root. (*Petroselinum* is from the Greek for rock parsley.)

PARSLEY FERN = *Cryptogramma crispa var. acrostichoides.*

PARSNIP. The common garden parsnip is the only cult. species of the genus **Pastinaca** (pas-ti-nay′ka), (family Umbelliferae), which comprises about a dozen species of Eurasian biennial or perennial herbs. **P.**

---

* Special articles on the subjects indicated by an asterisk (*) will be found at the words so marked.

sativa, the cult. parsnip, is a strong-scented, robust biennial with a much-thickened tap-root, often 10–18 in. long and 3½ in. in diameter at the apex. Stems 3–5 ft. high (at flowering time), branching, grooved, and becoming hollow with age. Leaves twice-compound,* the leaflets coarse, ovalish or oblong, usually toothed or lobed or both. Flowers small, greenish-yellow, in a large, compound umbel* (for details *see* UMBELLIFERAE). Fruit flattened, ribbed, the margins winged. (*Pastinaca* is from the Latin for food, in allusion to the edible root.) Also called *Peucedanum sativum.*

PARSNIP CULTURE

As a root crop parsnips require a deep, rich, but not too heavy soil. Stony land or those soils with too much clay or silt are not suited to growing good parsnips. Sandy, but rich, soils produce the best roots.

Seed should be sown as early in the spring as the ground can be worked, as a full season is required for growth, and in any case the parsnip is primarily a fall and winter vegetable. Rows should be about 14 in. apart (more if a tractor or horse cultivator is to be used), and the drills need be no more than ½ in. deep. The seed germinates slowly and poorly so that plenty of seed should be sown to allow the plants to be thinned to about 4½ in. apart. Because germination is so slow it is a good plan to sow radishes in the same drill; they will come up and mark the row long before the parsnips are up. This also allows for one or two cultivations of the soil before the parsnips have germinated.

More than almost any other vegetable parsnips are improved by cold, or even by freezing. They may be harvested all through the fall and some may be left in the ground all winter. But they should be mulched to prevent alternate thawing and freezing, which soon spoils the roots, and to facilitate digging. If it is desired to dig them all up in the late fall, the dug roots can be buried or put in a cold but frost-free pit.

A variety known as the turnip parsnip is only rarely grown in this country, but is comparatively well liked in Eu. It has a turnip-shaped root.

While some people object to the strong taste of parsnips, they are among the most nutritious of the root crops, and their flavor is always better after prolonged cold weather. The plant is thus unsuited to the warmer parts of the country. The best varieties of the common parsnip are Hollow Crown and Model.

INSECT PESTS. *See* CELERY and CARROT.

PARSNIP FAMILY = Umbelliferae.

PARTED. Cleft or divided nearly, but not quite, to the base; applied mostly to leaves, more rarely to petals.

PARTERRE. *See* BEDDING.

PARTHENIUM (par-thee′nĭ-um). New World herbs or under-shrubs of the family Compositae, of more economic than garden

interest. The only cult. species, **P. argentatum,** the guayule, a native of the southwestern U.S. and adjacent Mex., was once widely and is still somewhat cult. for the pustules of rubber found in its tissue, but guayule is of less economic interest than formerly. It is a much-branched, desert under-shrub, 2–3 ft. high, with alternate,* narrow, silvery leaves 1–2 in. long. Flower heads not over ¼ in. wide, the tiny ray flowers white. The plant has little decorative value, and for commercial cult. the plants are raised from seed and planted in rows 2–3 ft. apart, set out in March. No one should contemplate such a planting with commercial exploitation in mind, for over 30 million dollars have been lost in guayule. It was well known to the Aztecs, but has been largely supplanted by plantation rubber from the East. During World War II the U.S. Department of Agriculture revived its cult. during the shortage of plantation rubber (*Hevea*). (*Parthenium* is an old Greek name for a plant with white ray flowers and has been variously applied. It is a specific name at *Chrysanthemum.*)

parthenioides (par-thee-ni-oy′deez, but *see* OĪDES). Like a plant of the genus *Parthenium.*

PARTHENOCARPY. The production of fruit without pollination and fertilization.

PARTHENOCISSUS (par-thenn-o-sis′sus). All the members of this genus, which is in the grape family and sometimes called *Psedera,* are woody climbers from eastern Asia and N.A. They are grown chiefly for their good foliage and the fact that most of them cling firmly to walls and trees by means of disk-tipped tendrils.* The leaves are alternate* and composed of 3–5 leaflets. Flowers small, inconspicuous, in clusters opposite the leaves. Fruit small, dark blue or almost black. (*Parthenocissus* is from the Greek meaning virgin ivy.)

These vines are widely used on brick, stone or wooden surfaces where they cling firmly and form a dense cover. They are adapted to city conditions and some forms assume brilliant colors in the fall. They are not particular about soil, but grow more vigorously in a fairly moist loam. They may be propagated by seeds, cuttings, or layers.

henryana. A handsome but tender species whose leaflets are 1½–3 in. long, narrowly ovate or sometimes broader above the middle, toothed only toward the tip, velvety or bronze above with silvery markings, and reddish beneath. Flowers in slender panicles* 3–6 in. long. Fruit blue. July. China. Possibly hardy from zone* 5 southward. Also known as *Ampelopsis henryana.*

quinquefolia. This species, commonly called Virginia creeper, woodbine, or American ivy, is a vigorous, tall-growing vine. Leaflets 5, elliptic to oblong, 2–5 in. long, pointed, toothed. Flowers inconspicuous. Fruit blue-black, bloomy. July. Nova Scotia to Mexico. Hardy from zone* 2 southward. Also known as *Ampelopsis quinquefolia.* Leaves become scarlet in the fall; *var.* **engelmanni,** the Engelmann creeper, is a form with small leaves; *var.*

---

* Special articles on the subjects indicated by an asterisk (*) will be found at the words so marked.

hirsuta, young growth usually hairy and red when young, leaves hairy beneath; *var.* **saint-pauli,** leaflets oblong-obovate with spreading teeth, the young growth hairy; short rootlets sometimes appear on the branches.

tricuspidata. Boston ivy or Japanese ivy. Climbs high and clings firmly. Leaves either of 3 leaflets or simple* and 3-lobed, to 10 in. long, usually shiny on both sides. Flowers inconspicuous. Fruit blue-black, bloomy. July. Japan and China. Hardy from zone* 3 southward. Also known as *Ampelopsis tricuspidata.* Hardy and ornamental; foliage colors well in the fall; *var.* **lowi,** a form with leaves ¾–1½ in. long, simple or with 3 leaflets; of slower and more restrained growth, not dense; *var.* **purpurea,** leaves purple; *var.* **veitchi,** smaller leaves, purple when young.

vitacea. This species does not have the adhesive disks on the tendrils and is usually low and rambling. Leaflets 5, elliptic to oblong, 2–5 in. long, toothed. Flowers yellowish, inconspicuous. Fruit blue-black, bloomy. June. Hardy from zone* 2 southward. Also known as *P. inserta* and perhaps only a var. of *P. quinquefolia.* N.A.

PARTRIDGE-BERRY. See MITCHELLA.

parviflora, -us, -um (par-vi-flow′ra). Small-flowered.

parvifolia, -us, -um (par-vi-fō′li̇-a). Small-leaved.

PASPALUM (pas′pa-lum). Annual or perennial grasses comprising about 250 species of the grass family, found throughout temperate and warmer regions of the world, but mostly in America. The flowering spikelets are arranged in 1-sided racemes.* (*Paspalum* is from the old Greek name for millet.)

These grasses are not of much garden interest, although their other uses are diverse. A few are grown for ornament, while 1 species is sometimes used for lawns in place of Bermuda grass, and yet another is grown for its fodder value in Argentina.

dilatatum. A coarse-growing perennial, up to 5 ft. high. Leaves to 1 ft. long, and ½ in. wide. Flowers in loose, 1-sided clusters to 5 in. long. Argentina, but naturalized in the southern states.

racemosum. An annual of creeping habit, with stems to 3 ft. high. Leaves 5 in. long, about 1 in. wide. Flowers numerous in clusters 6 in. long. Colombia and Peru.

PASQUE-FLOWER. Very beautiful perennials, distinguished from the windflowers by long, plumy fruits. Often considered as a separate genus (*Pulsatilla*), but here considered as of the genus *Anemone* (which see). Among the pasque-flowers are *Anemone alpina, A. halleri, A. patens, A. Pulsatilla,* and *A. vernalis.*

PASSIFLORA (pass-i-flow′ra). The passion-flowers are tendril*-climbing vines, and comprise the only cult. genus of the family Passifloraceae (pass-i-flow-ray′see-ee). All but a few of the 400 species are natives of the New World, and several are cult. for ornament, while a few tropical sorts yield edible fruits like the granadilla. Leaves alternate,* stalked, lobed, or undivided. Flowers often showy, regular, the 3–5 sepals often petal-like, and sometimes tubular. Petals 3–5, or sometimes none. Within the flower is a usually fringed, often differently colored corona* or crown composed of many free filaments, or sometimes tubular and fringed at the top. Stamens* mostly 5, the filaments* united. Fruit a berry, edible in some. (*Passiflora* is Latin for passion-flower, in allusion to the flowers suggesting the Crucifixion.)

Some of the passion-flowers are handsome, stem-climbing vines (*see* VINES), but useful only from zone* 7 southward, and some of them are really suited only to the warmest regions of the country.

The granadilla and related species which yield widely used tropical fruits are scarcely known outside extreme southern Calif. and Fla., and are not commercially grown in the U.S., as the fruits are too perishable to ship. They make delicious soft drinks and sherbets in tropical countries, and jam and marmalade are also made from them.

The most widely grown of the ornamental sorts is the maypop or wild passion-flower (*P. incarnata*), which is native from Va. to Tex. It is a strong-growing vine, which dies down each winter. Few of the others will stand any frost. All have rather striking flowers.

alato-caerulea. A hybrid passion-flower with 3-lobed leaves. Flowers nearly 4 in. wide, fragrant, white outside, pink inside, the crown purple, blue and white. Fruit not edible.

caerulea. Leaves 5-lobed, the lobes narrow. Flowers nearly 4 in. wide, fragrant, pink, but the crown white and purple. Fruit about 1½ in. long, yellow. Brazil. There are forms with even larger flowers, and one known as Constance Elliott has white flowers.

edulis. Purple granadilla. Leaves deeply 3-lobed, the lobes toothed. Flowers about 2 in. wide, white, the crown white and purple. Fruit edible, dark purple, nearly 3 in. long. Much grown in the tropics for the fruit. Brazil.

incarnata. Maypop or wild passion-flower. The hardiest of the lot. Leaves 3-lobed, the lobes toothed. Flowers 1½–2 in. wide, white, the crown purplish-pink. Fruit edible, yellow, about 1½ in. long. Md. to Fla. and Tex.

laurifolia. Yellow granadilla; also called water lemon and Jamaica honeysuckle. Leaves unlobed. Flowers nearly 4 in. wide, white but red-spotted, the crown white and violet. Fruit edible, yellow, 2–3 in. long. Tropical America.

manicata. Leaves 3-lobed, the lobes ovalish and toothed. Flowers almost 4 in. wide, scarlet, the crown blue. Fruit yellowish-green, not edible. Northwestern S.A. Cult. for its extremely showy flowers. It climbs to the tops of trees in southern Calif.

mollissima. Leaves 3-lobed, the lobes toothed, and the leaf hairy on the under surface. Flowers about 3 in. wide, rose-pink, the tube of the calyx* nearly 5 in. long. Fruit yellow, not edible. Andes.

quadrangularis. Granadilla or giant granadilla. The leading passion-flower cult. for its fruit which is greenish-yellow, edible, and nearly 10 in. long. It is a strong-growing vine with winged stems and unlobed leaves. Flowers fragrant, about 3 in. wide, white, the crown purple and white. Tropical America. Often cult. also for ornament. There is a variegated-leaved variety.

---

* Special articles on the subjects indicated by an asterisk (*) will be found at the words so marked.

trifasciata. A slender Peruvian vine with angled and striped stems. Leaves 3-lobed, 2½–5 in. long, nearly as wide, mottled with white or greenish-yellow along the veins. Flowers 1–1½ in. wide, yellowish-white. Needs greenhouse cult.

PASSIFLORACEAE. *See* PASSIFLORA.

PASSION-FLOWER. *See* PASSIFLORA.

PASTINACA. *See* PARSNIP.

PASTURE ROSE = *Rosa carolina.*

patagonica, -us, -um (pat-a-gon′i-ka). From Patagonia.

Patagua (pa-taw′gwa). Native name in Chile for *Crinodendron Patagua.*

patens (pay′tenz). Spreading.

PATENTS. *See* PLANT PATENTS.

PATHOGEN. An organism, usually microscopic, causing disease in plants. The pathogen may be carried by wind, water, animals, or insects. (*See* PLANT DISEASES and VECTOR.)

PATHOLOGY. *See* PLANT DISEASES.

PATHS AND PAVING. The number, arrangement, length and width of walks in a garden will obviously depend on its plan. If the walks must be narrow, 18 in. is a sufficient width to enable one person to walk comfortably. For two persons a width of about 4 ft. 9 in. is necessary.

Garden paths are usually made of grass, flags, slates, bricks, gravel, or pebbles.

Flagstone paving

Where the traffic is not sufficient to wear bare spaces, grass walks in gardens may be attractive, economical to make, and not difficult to maintain. Stepping stones, so popular nowadays, were probably used to take up the wear and tear of feet-abrading spaces in the grass, and the transition was not very far to a pavement of flagstones, squared or irregular, with grass or other dwarf plants growing between them. Grass walks through meadows are common in England and may be used here, especially where grass is allowed to grow in order to permit naturalized spring bulbs to ripen.

FLAGS. If flags or slates are laid with mortar joints the best practice is to set them on a bed of concrete 4 in. thick laid over a bed of sand, gravel or cinders 6 in. deep, so that the thickness of the walk construction is 11 to 12 in. or more. The flags (or slates), whether of rectangular or irregular shapes, should be cut so that their joints, although they may not be quite even, do not have the wide variations permissible in flags laid in the ground with grass or other plants between. Such flags, laid flush with the general surface, are the most generally useful and popular and the least expensive. Considerable variety in the size and shape of the stones adds to the interest of the pattern; but no stone small enough to rock when trodden on should be laid. For a list of plants suitable to grow in chinks in the paving *see* PAVEMENT PLANTING.

Spaces between stones may be very varied in form and width, according to the stones available, and these should not be broken or trimmed more than is really necessary. Skill and patience are necessary to set stones of different thickness on a firm bed with a true upper surface.

If stepping stones only are required, they may be set with their centers 2 ft. 3 in. or less apart. If the flags are rectangular they may be of different sizes, the openings between to be 2–4 in. wide. Concrete* slabs may be used, cast either in the ground or not. It is quite practicable to make a good-looking surface of concrete by using a cinder aggregate and floating off some of the surface cement, and even by adding fine gravel or pebbles. But to produce a good piece of work of this class requires a skilled and interested workman willing to make experiments.

BRICKS. Bricks may be laid in mortar with a foundation as described for flags. Or they may be laid dry, *i.e.*, on a bed of sand or cinders 4 in. or more deep, with or without sand between the joints. A very wide sand joint between bricks (as much as ½ in.) is sometimes desirable, and it is even practicable, by mixing some soil with the sand joint, to grow small plants such as arenarias between or, in shady, damp places, moss. Bricks laid in mortar may be set flat or on edge, but bricks laid dry are better on edge. For garden walks they should be of a good quality dark red and not too smooth. Bricks are usually laid in walks in rows at right angles to the line of the walk or in a herringbone pattern. In a narrow walk this pattern may be used to advantage with the bricks parallel and at right angles to the walk line. Other and more complex patterns may be worked out by those preferring them.

There are also walks made in "crazy" patterns of bricks or any pieces of stone that can be arranged to make a surface reasonably easy to walk on. Construction is the same as for bricks or flags laid in mortar. The design must depend on the designer and his materials, and it is advisable to piece together an experimental pattern before starting to lay it in mortar.

Stepping stones let into the sod

GRAVEL. Gravel walks (of mixed sand and pebbles) are useful in districts where there are gravels with natural binders. They may be laid 2–3 in. deep, or more, on a broken stone or cinder foundation or on the bare ground. In the latter case, the gravel should be deep enough to prevent the growth of weeds, at least 4 in. or more.

PEBBLE SURFACE. Pebble-surface walks are made of reinforced pebble concrete on a bed of sand or cinders having the surface so manipulated that the close-set pebbles are exposed. While the mortar is still wet, it is treated with a chemical which prevents the surface mortar from setting, so that it can be brushed off, leaving the surface of the stones exposed. It is not advisable to attempt the construction of this kind of walk without the aid of a professional.

Various kinds of oil-bound aggregate walks with specially treated surfaces are found, and anyone interested should consult an expert or one of the companies furnishing the materials. — H. A. C.

Patientia (pay-tee-en'shi-a). Latin for patience; applied to the herb patience (*Rumex Patientia*) by Linnaeus.

PATIO GARDENS. See PLANNING THE HOME GROUNDS.

PATTYPAN. See CUCURBITA PEPO MELO-PEPO.

patula, -us, -um (pat'you-la). Spreading.

pauciflora, -us, -um (pau-si-flow'ra). Few-flowered.

paucifolia, -us, -um (pau-si-fō'li-a). Few-leaved; also, sometimes, small-leaved.

PAULLINIA (paul-lin'i-a). A large genus of tropical American and African woody vines of the family Sapindaceae, only **P. thalctri-folia** of the 140 known species of any hort. interest. While a Brazilian vine of considerable size, it is grown as a greenhouse pot plant and should be kept pinched back to induce plenty of stocky growth and foliage, for which the plant is chiefly grown. Leaves thrice-compound,* 4–9 in. long, the ultimate segments small, bronze-tinted, the whole leaf very feathery and fern-like. Flowers very small, pink, with 4 petals and 4 sepals, mostly unisexual,* and borne in small clusters (corymbs*). Fruit a somewhat fleshy, 3-valved capsule.* A related, non-hort. species yields the famous Brazilian tonic, guaraná. *P. thalictrifolia* needs a tropical greenhouse, plenty of moisture, and should be grown in potting mixture* 4. (Variously credited as named for Simon Paulli, a Danish botanist, or for C. F. Paullini, German botanist.)

PAULOWNIA (paul-ō'ni-a). A small group of deciduous Chinese trees of the fig-wort family (Scrophulariaceae). They are ornamental and vigorous, but only the one below is much grown. The leaves are opposite* and variable in size and shape, usually entire,* but sometimes lobed, suggesting the catalpa. The flowers fragrant, tubular, resembling the foxglove, white to violet and borne in terminal clusters (panicles*), before the leaves. Fruit an ovoid, pointed capsule* containing a great many small, winged seeds. (Named for Princess Anna Paulowna of the Netherlands.)

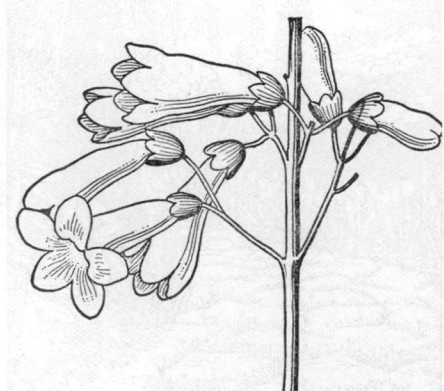

Empress Tree (*Paulownia tomentosa*). A showy quick-growing tree, its pale violet flowers blooming before or with the unfolding of the leaves.

The paulownias are handsome trees when in bloom, making good lawn specimens, but not long-lived. The flower buds are exposed during winter, and north of Philadelphia they often fail to develop, due to frost injury. Plants are sometimes cut to the ground in the spring so that vigorous, large-leaved shoots will be thrown up. They seem to prefer a rich, loamy soil and sheltered situation. Propagation is by seeds, or by stem

* Special articles on the subjects indicated by an asterisk (*) will be found at the words so marked.

or root cuttings. Growth is very rapid in youth, but due to a deep taproot they are difficult to transplant, which should be done only in early spring.

imperialis = *Paulownia tomentosa*.

tomentosa. Empress tree. Tree of 30–50 ft. with thick, stiff branches, rather open in habit and becoming round-topped. Leaves hairy, more or less ovate, entire* or lobed, varying in size from 5–10 in. on ordinary growth, to 2 ft. or more on vigorous shoots. Flowers pale violet, about 2 in. long. May or June. China. Hardy from milder parts of zone* 3 southward. Escaped from cultivation in the eastern states from N.Y. to Ga.; *var.* **lanata,** leaves more densely hairy beneath; *var.* **pallida,** flowers whitish-violet.

PAUROTIS (pau-rote'is). A fan palm of southern Fla., the Bahamas, and Cuba, useful only in zone* 9. Trunks slender, usually in clusters of 6–8, without prickles. Leaves long-stalked, the stalks spiny. Flowers small, 2 or 3 together, or often only 1. Fruit a black drupe. (Name from the Greek referring to the few spathes of the inflorescence.)

wrighti. Everglade palm, called, also, saw cabbage palm and saw palmetto. Handsome palm often 20 ft. high when full grown, the stems in colonies. Leaves green both sides, the blade 2½ ft. wide and cut nearly halfway down into many divisions which are themselves split. Leafstalk 5 ft. long, its prickles upward-curving. Fruit about ¼ in. in diameter. This palm, also known as *Serenoa arborescens* and *Acoelorraphe wrighti*, is little known outside of Fla.

PAVEMENT PLANTING. In the spaces between random flagstones it is possible, and often attractive, to scatter low, prostrate plants. Among the best of these, rarely more than 2–3 inches high, are succulents to be found in the genus *Sedum* (mostly white or yellow); in the prostrate forms of *Veronica* (mostly blue); *Lobelia Erinus* (blue and an annual); and in the genus *Mentha* (*see* MINT). Still others are the thrifts, candytufts, thymes and gold-dust (*Alyssum saxatile compactum*) which is higher and resistant to the heat and sun of most pavements. The soil between the flags should be reasonably good topsoil, not the sand on which flags are usually laid. *See* PATHS AND PAVING.

Pavia (pay'vi-a). A specific name derived from the genus *Pavia*, once used for the buckeye and its relatives. *See* HORSE-CHESTNUT.

PAVONIA (pa-vō'ni-a). Evergreen herbs or shrubs, comprising about 150 species of the family Malvaceae, found in the warm and tropical regions of the world. They grow sometimes as high as 20 ft. Leaves alternate,* sometimes cut. Flowers yellow, pink, or purple, solitary or in clusters, usually having conspicuous bracts* in united pairs. (Named for J. Pavon, part author of a book on Peruvian and Chilean flora.) For a very different, bulbous plant sometimes known as *Pavonia*, see MORAEA PAVONIA.

They are not of much garden interest, except for a few species, which are used as hothouse plants in the North and grown outdoors in warmer climates. Propagated by seeds or cuttings in early spring, using potting mixture* 4.

hastata. Shrubby perennial, growing to 6 ft. high. Leaves halberd-shaped, the margins toothed. Flowers solitary, pink with a dark spot at base of the petals, about 1 in. long. S.A.

multiflora. Shrubby perennial. Leaves alternate,* lance-shaped, 6–10 in. long, and narrow, the margins toothed. Bracts* 1½ in. long, narrow and pointed, whorled, covered with red hairs. Flowers purple, 1½ in. long, in terminal clusters. Stamens* 2½ in. long. Brazil.

spinifex. Shrub to 20 ft. Stems slender, sparsely branched. Leaves ovalish, slightly hairy on both sides. Flowers yellow, 1 in. long, solitary. Tropical America; naturalized in southern U.S.

Pavonina, -us, -um (pa-vo-ny'na). Like a peacock.

PAWPAW = Papaw.

PEA. For the common garden pea *see* the next main entry. There are many other plants to which the name *pea* has been applied, or where it is part of their name. Those in the ENCYCLOPEDIA and their proper equivalents are:

Asparagus pea = *Psophocarpus tetragonolobus;* **Black pea** (*see* LATHYRUS); **Butterfly pea** (*see* CENTROSEMA and CLITORIA); **Chick-pea** (*see* CICER); **Glory-pea** (*see* CLIANTHUS); **Pigeon pea** = *Cajanus Cajan;* **Rosary pea** = *Abrus precatorius;* **Sweet pea** = *Lathyrus odoratus* (*see* SWEET PEA); **Winged pea** = *Lotus tetragonolobus.*

There are also many others, some of them of minor importance. *See also* the genera LATHYRUS, PISUM, VIGNA, and DOLICHOS.

PEA. The garden pea is the most important species of the genus **Pisum** (py'sum) which belongs to the Leguminosae or pea family.

The genus comprises six or seven annual or perennial herbs, mostly native in the Mediterranean region and western Asia, only the following of any garden importance. It has compound* leaves, the leaflets arranged feather-fashion,* and the main leafstalk always ends in a branched tendril.* At the base of the main leafstalk are two prominent, leaf-like organs (much-developed stipules*). The flowers are typically pea-like (for a description *see* LEGUMINOSAE). The fruit is the well-known pea pod, a legume,* the seeds of which furnish the common pea. In one variety (*see* below) the pod is also eaten. (*Pisum* is the classical name of the pea.) The only cult. species is:

P. sativum. Here belongs the tall-growing pea, which needs brush for support. It grows from 3–6 feet high, has smooth foliage and oval or oblong leaflets about 1½ in. long. The stipules (*see* above) are mostly larger than the leaflets. Flowers usually white. Pod 2–4 in. long, the seeds wrinkled or smooth. The plant has several varieties: (1) *var.* **arvense,** the field pea, with pinkish-purple flowers. Grown only for forage and of no garden interest; (2) *var.* **humile,** the early dwarf pea (the common

---

* Special articles on the subjects indicated by an asterisk (*) will be found at the words so marked.

low sort of the garden), which grows only from 8–24 in. high and has shorter pods than the tall type; (3) *var.* **macrocarpon,** the edible-podded or sugar pea. This has soft pods with little or none of the papery lining common in the other sorts. The pods, as well as the seeds, are used (mostly in Europe). This variety is little known in America.

PEA CULTURE

Tall sorts = *Pisum sativum*

Dwarf sorts = *Pisum sativum humile*

The garden pea combines two features of great value. It is not only very nutritious and rich in Vitamins A, B, and C, but provides many advantages of a green vegetable. Hence its first-rate importance as a garden crop. Unfortunately for the home gardener, it is a cool-season plant, or an all-season crop for only the coolest climates, as in zones* 1 and 2, or for high altitudes elsewhere. Occasionally, in proximity to cool sea water, as along the coast of Maine and the Maritime Provinces, it can also be grown all through the growing season.

Elsewhere peas must be grown between the time when the ground is workable and the heat of summer, which they will not tolerate. Some growers try to utilize the coolness of autumn by making late sowings, but such crops are rarely satisfactory. For most of the home gardeners the pea must be a spring crop. Its all-year-round presence in the markets is due to the great value of the crop and the fact that somewhere in such a large country there is always a period of a few cool weeks in which to grow them. The tall sorts mature in 60–80 days, the low or bushy types in about 55 days.

SOILS AND FERTILIZERS. Any good garden soil will grow peas. If it has been manured the autumn previous, that is a help. If manuring is left until just before planting, it is essential that only well-rotted manure be used, as fresh manure is dangerous for this crop. Although the pea is a legume, and consequently absorbs nitrogen from the air (see LEGUMINOSAE), it does not begin doing so until some time after germination. It is consequently of advantage to use a commercial fertilizer with a ratio of 4–8–8 (see FERTILIZERS), at the rate of 500 pounds to the acre (about 2 pounds per 100-ft. row).

If the manure or fertilizer is thoroughly plowed in and the soil raked smooth, planting may begin.

PLANTING PEAS. Almost no garden crop is so easy to start as peas. Seed of the low sorts should be planted just as early as the ground can be worked. You need not wait for the last erratic late frost. Choose a time approximating the average day when the last frost in your region may be expected (see the name of your state for frost dates). Plant on that day or even a little before it. Planted pea seeds are not injured by the surface soil being touched by frost, and the earliest possible planting date is always the best. Sowing pea seed should be practically the first spring activity in the vegetable garden.

The tall varieties are better planted about 10 days later than the low sorts.

For the first plantings of low varieties make the drills about 2 in. deep (in a light, sandy soil) or 1 in. deep if the soil is heavy and has much clay in it. Later plantings should be in drills about twice this depth, but only half filled at first. As the plants grow, the trench is gradually filled up. The object of this deeper drill, for later plantings, is to secure greater coolness and moisture for the roots of plants that will have to face greater heat.

In planting low varieties the seed should be scattered rather freely in the drill, certainly not less than an inch apart, and some very competent growers prefer less space between the seeds. As the plants come up they may be thinned so that the final plants will be 2–3 in. apart. If left at the one-inch intervals, the plants will be too crowded. It takes about 1 pound of seed for 100 ft. of row for the dwarf varieties. Rows should be 18 in. apart.

Tall varieties are planted somewhat differently. The rows should be about 30–36 in. apart and the seeds are planted in double rows. Make two parallel drills about 6 in. apart (or one trench 6 in. wide) and about 4 in. deep. Plant the seeds about 2½ in. apart (closer if expense does not matter) in each drill, or on the outer edges of the 6-in. trench if this method is easier. Cover the seeds with only enough soil to half fill the drills or trench, putting in the rest of the soil as the plants come up.

The object of this double row, with 6 in. between the plants, is that the space between will be occupied by the brush or wire needed for the support of these tall varieties. It should be set before the seed is covered (see below). Use a pound or pound and a half of seed for each double row of 100 ft., but see that the ultimate stand is spaced (by thinning) about 4 in. apart.

CULTIVATION. Peas need only sufficient cultivation to keep down weeds. If your garden is a reasonably well-kept one, the space between the double-rowed tall sorts should be fairly free of weeds, due to the growth of the pea plants. If not, hand weeding is the only remedy.

VARIETIES. Most low varieties have smooth seeds and shorter pods, and are less desirable as to yield and flavor than the usually wrinkle-seeded, larger-podded tall sorts. The great merit of the low sorts is their quicker maturity, and the freedom from the bother of supports. According to their classes, the home grower will find most satisfaction in using the following varieties:

LOW or BUSH PEAS (needing no support).
　Early: Little Marvel, Greater Progress.
　Late: Alderman, Giant Stride, Stratagem, Asgrow 40.
　TALL PEAS (for later planting and needing support). Alderman Improved Tele-

---

* Special articles on the subjects indicated by an asterisk (*) will be found at the words so marked.

phone, Dark-podded Telephone, Lincoln.

EDIBLE-PODDED.

Mammoth Melting Sugar (tall), Dwarf Gray Sugar (low).

SUPPORTS FOR TALL VARIETIES. These should be placed at planting time. Twiggy brush (with the bark on) is perhaps the best, but not always available. It should be about 4–5 ft. high after the stems are sunk in the ground enough to make it a stout support. It should also be close enough together so that no wandering tendril will fail to find a support.

Many prefer to use ordinary chicken wire 4–5 ft. high. Stretch it as tightly as possible between stout posts at each end of the row. Then tie it to dahlia stakes set at 6-foot intervals for greater stiffening. The advantage of the wire is that, after cleaning, it may be rolled up, posts and all, and stored for next season, whereas the brush is not so easy to manage once the pea season is over.

HARVESTING AND YIELDS. It is easy to see when peas are ready for picking. The younger they are, the better. And, for the home gardener, they should never be picked more than an hour or two before they are cooked.

Yields vary greatly, depending on the variety used, the soil, and especially upon the amount of heat that is encountered by later sowings. Some put in several sowings of the dwarf sorts at 10-day intervals. But some of the later lots may be overtaken by the heat and yield little or nothing. Only one planting of the tall sorts is advisable unless your summers are consistently cool.

For the average family of 5, the yield from 2 pounds of pea seed, split about half between tall and low varieties, should be ample. If only low varieties are used, gambling on several succession plantings at 10-day intervals will give you an ample supply until heat ends the pea season.

For the preferred position and sequence of peas in your garden *see* KITCHEN GARDEN.

INSECT PESTS. Green aphids can ruin the crop. Spray or dust thoroughly with pesticide #21 or nicotine. (*See* SPRAYS AND DUSTS.)

DISEASES. Continuous planting of peas in the same area may result in a build-up of one of the fungi causing root rot. Plant peas in another area when soil becomes too infected to secure a good crop.

The presence of aphids on the plants may result in transmission of mosaic* virus disease which causes white blotches in the leaves and results in poor yields. It is better not to raise peas adjacent to an over-wintering legume* such as alfalfa.

Occasionally leaves and pods will have black circular spots caused by one of the fungi or a bacterium. These diseases are not usually serious unless extended rains or foggy weather keep leaves wet.

Failure of plants to emerge from the ground indicates damping-off* which may be controlled with one of the combination seed treatments available for all legumes.

In our experience, more peas in the home garden are lost to birds than to all the diseases combined.

PEACH (*Amygdalus Persica*). This is a medium-sized tree useful for the home grounds because it needs less space than some of the larger fruit trees. It has been grown in China for over 3000 years. It can be planted 20 feet apart, each way, and is fairly tolerant of a variety of soils, so long as they are not too wet. The tree will not thrive if its "feet are in the water." More than almost any other fruit tree it thrives in sandy or stony loams, and there is good evidence that fertilizers or manure may provide lush growth of leaves and twigs, often at the expense of fruit production. For the average home grower any light sandy loam that will grow vegetables will be good for peaches.

The tree is short-lived (10–20 years) and highly intolerant of bitter cold, and late frosts often kill its blossoms and the fruit crop of that year. Such late spring frosts do not, however, do the tree any harm; they simply stop all or a good part of the fruit crop that season.

This sensitiveness to winter cold and the occasional loss of the fruit from late spring frosts make it most important to choose only the varieties suited to your climate. There are some regions where cultivation of the peach is impossible, generally because they are too cold. But like most fruit trees, the peach does need a winter chilling. Some regions in the southern part of the coastal plain are too warm and moist for most varieties of it, not only because they do not provide winter chilling sufficient for healthy growth, but also because warm humid summers promote some dangerous peach diseases.

The ideal site is thus one with a well-drained soil, good summer heat (with little humidity), reasonably mild winters, and an absence of erratic and unpredictable frosts when the tree is in bloom. This is not so easy, for the peach is one of the earliest of all the common fruit trees to bloom — often as soon as April 15 near New York, and earlier than this farther south. Proximity to large bodies of water is a help, as they ameliorate winter cold, and often prevent late frosts from doing appreciable damage. The shores of Lake Erie and Lake Ontario are good peach areas, as are Long Island and southern New Jersey, while much of central New York State is somewhat hazardous, except near the Finger Lakes.

All peach varieties are divided into clingstone and freestone, the latter being best for eating out of hand, while clingstone is preferred by commercial canners. The flesh of the fruit clings to the stone, and such varieties scarcely need to concern the home grower, except for the fact that some of these clingstone varieties are hardier and more productive than freestone kinds. All the varieties below are freestone unless designated otherwise.

---

* Special articles on the subjects indicated by an asterisk (*) will be found at the words so marked.

VARIETIES

Choosing peach varieties is rather difficult. There are hundreds of them, the climatic requirements are elastic, and their season of fruiting varies. Also different growers have preferences as to yellow or white-fleshed sorts. There are, too, a bewildering number of "new" peaches, widely advertised "novelties," and the legitimate production of new sorts by reliable hybridists. From this mass the following will provide a choice of well-tested varieties that should cover the wants of any home gardener who lives within the area where peach-growing is wise and safe.

ANGEL. Not a very good sort, but standing the heat of northern Florida. Fruit with white flesh, but reddish near the pit, ripening June 15–July 1 in Florida.

ARP. Clingstone. A very early variety with fine yellow flesh, originating in Texas but of great climatic adaptability.

BELLE. Universally called, except by the experts, Belle of Georgia and probably the finest-tasting white-fleshed peach in existence; midseason. Also available in dwarf form.

CARMAN. Almost clingstone. A white-fleshed peach of wide adaptability, an early ripener, and pleasantly mild, although it is considered a trifle tart by some. Also available in dwarf form.

CHAMPION. A white-fleshed peach of very superior flavor, but the fruits are apt to be small on poor soils. The taste is as fine as in Belle; midseason. Also available in dwarf form.

EARLY CRAWFORD. Early to midseason. A superior yellow-fleshed peach, with almost unsurpassed flavor. Its only fault is a tendency to unproductiveness in some seasons. Also available in dwarf form.

ELBERTA. The most widely grown peach in America and one of the distinctly poorer varieties. Its great virtues are the gorgeous reddish-orange skin, juicy yellow flesh, and fine keeping qualities when shipped. But even when allowed to ripen on the tree its fruit is, according to the late U. P. Hedrick, "scarcely edible by those who know good peaches"! Not recommended for the home grower, although nearly 90 per cent of all store peaches are of this variety. Also available in dwarf form.

GOLDEN JUBILEE. A fine yellow-fleshed variety, maturing in midseason, the fruit large, and bruising easily. Tree productive and vigorous. Also available in dwarf form.

GREENSBORO. A white-fleshed, very early peach, of chief use because of its adaptability to the cooler parts of the range of peach culture.

HALEHAVEN. Midseason. A fine, yellow-fleshed variety, with a vigorous, productive tree, and considerable climatic adaptability. Also available in dwarf form.

HALL YELLOW. An early, yellow-fleshed peach, with an agreeable flavor. Suited only to areas of summer heat and humidity.

HONEY. Midseason, its creamy-white flesh aromatic, rich, and sweet. It was a direct importation from China, via France, and brought a spicy tang to peach blood.

J. H. HALE. Self-sterile* and must be interplanted with other varieties. Midseason, the flesh yellow, of better flavor than most commercial varieties, and the fruit larger than almost any other. Also available in dwarf form.

MARIGOLD. Clingstone. Medium-sized, yellow-fleshed fruit, maturing in midseason. Quality good and the tree vigorous.

MAYFLOWER. Clingstone. A medium-sized fruit with greenish-white flesh, maturing very early, and with only slightly acid juice.

MIKADO. Self-sterile* and must be interplanted with other varieties. Similar to Marigold, but freestone and maturing among the earliest of all yellow-fleshed varieties — about five days earlier than Marigold.

ORIOLE. Midseason, the yellow-fleshed fruit not so large as Elberta, but of much better flavor. Tree hardy and productive.

SOUTH HAVEN. A fine, very late peach, often not ripening until mid-September. Fruit medium-sized, yellow-fleshed, juicy, and sweet.

SOUTHLAND. A variety developed by the U.S. Department of Agriculture in 1946 and now widely spread in the South. Flesh yellow, the skin light blush. Suitable for home garden, but also keeps well.

PLANTING. At planting time, the peach tree should be one year old from the bud, vigorous but not succulent from overgrowth, well rooted and free from crown gall. Peach trees in America are practically always budded on seedlings grown from the pits of wild peaches — at least such was the case until recent years when cannery pits have been substituted by some for the wild pits. Planting distances depend upon the suitability of the soil for the peach and on the variety. On poor soils trees may be set as close as 18 ft. apart each way, but on rich soils 20, 22, and even 24 ft. are distances none too great. Different varieties vary greatly in the size of trees, some being very compact growers and others wide-spreading, factors affecting distances.

When the trees are set they should be headed back to about 24 in. and either pruned to a whip or left with three or four scaffold branches evenly spaced, the lowest one a foot or thereabouts from the ground. The crotches should not be too acute, as later the tree will split. The peach does not stand transplanting well, and this cutting back to a whip or to stubs of branches should be done to prevent excessive transpiration.*

PRUNING. Subsequent pruning and training resolve themselves into two rather distinct problems: To increase the vigor of the tree; and to train the tree to a form that will make orchard operations easy and give a maximum amount of fruit-bearing wood.

---

* Special articles on the subjects indicated by an asterisk (*) will be found at the words so marked.

At best the peach is a short-lived tree, 20 years in an orchard being a long span of life, and most growers want a short life and a productive one for their trees, say 16 or 18 years, and prune to secure this objective. This means a greater amount of pruning for the peach than for any other tree fruit. In general, this rule should guide peach pruners: Varieties weak in growth must be pruned severely; strong-growing sorts are pruned rather lightly.

CARE OF PEACH TREES. Assuming that you started with a one- or two-year-old whip and that you have pruned it in accordance with the above directions, when can you expect fruit? In most varieties there should be some by the second year, quite a lot more the third, and a full crop thereafter. Which brings us to an essential of peach culture.

Left to itself nearly any peach tree will bear so much fruit that its branches will break off with the weight of it, or the fruits will be so crowded as to stunt their growth. The remedy is thinning out the fruit. There will, in any case, occur what the professionals call "June drop," which is a natural shedding of a small amount of immature fruit. But this is not enough.

Just after June drop, deliberately pick off enough unripe fruit so that no peach is nearer than 5 to 6 inches to any other. This will lessen the load on the branches, not exhaust the tree, and increase the size of the individual fruit. It also obviates the propping up of branches which one often sees in orchards where they have neglected to thin the fruit in June.

WEST OF THE ROCKY MOUNTAINS

Peaches may be grown successfully in many areas west of the Rocky Mountains where there is available water and the winter temperatures do not become too cold nor late spring frosts occur too frequently. In the southern part of this region, such as for example in southern California, the winters may be too mild to enable most varieties to bloom properly the following spring. Peaches, in common with other deciduous fruits, require a certain amount of winter chilling of their buds to enable them to open properly in the spring. The amount of chilling varies with the variety. Varieties with low chilling requirements are needed for areas with mild winters. While the quality of the fruits of the peach tree seems to be rather definitely influenced by climatic conditions, peaches of excellent quality can be grown in many areas of rather diverse climates when the above limitations are considered.

The home gardener will find a wider range of areas suitable for peach-growing in this region than will the commercial orchardist since he is not restricted by the need for a profit or of meeting certain market grades in the fruit. The home gardener, for example, will often find it desirable to grow peach trees in areas where the occurrence of spring frosts is too frequent for a successful commercial enterprise.

The young trees are propagated by budding on seedlings grown from seeds obtained from local dry yards or canners. The nurseryman sells them as one-year-old trees or as June-budded trees. The latter are trees which have been budded in the early summer following the spring in which the seeds have been planted. These trees are smaller than the one-year-old trees at the time of buying but will produce as good a tree as those bought at one year of age.

Peach trees will show a definite response to a lack of available water in the size of the tree and the size and quality of the fruit. This fact needs to be kept in mind when planting peach trees west of the Rocky Mountains since a large part of this area has a deficiency of summer rainfall. The manner of adding irrigation water is of little importance. It is important, however, that the tree have available water in the root zone during the growing season. If only a few trees are to be planted, basins can be thrown up around them by hand, and they can be watered by means of a hose or a pipe. Or water may be added by a sprinkler if the ground is level enough. If very many trees are to be planted, it will be found advisable to use some type of irrigation system. This should be decided upon and the ground leveled and prepared prior to the planting of the trees. *See* IRRIGATION.

In these states, peach trees may be planted in the winter or early spring. In the sections where the winters are quite mild, the trees may be planted any time during the period when the young trees are dormant. A common practice is to wait until after there has been sufficient winter rainfall to moisten the ground thoroughly before planting. In the sections where considerable freezing occurs during the winter, it will be advisable to delay the planting until spring.

After planting, the trees should be headed back to 24 to 30 inches. In most cases, the side branches which have developed in the nursery will not be desirably located for permanent scaffold branches, so it will be necessary to remove them. These should be cut back, leaving a stub about a quarter of an inch long. Whitewashing to prevent sunscald during the first summer is desirable. Pruning at the end of the first summer should consist in the selection of three branches for the permanent scaffolds. These should be at different levels on the trunk, 6 or 8 inches apart and equally spaced around the trunk. All other branches should be removed and the permanent scaffolds lightly headed back. At the end of the second summer, the secondary scaffolds, 5 to 7 in number, should be selected and all other branches removed. Pruning the bearing peach tree consists in removing objectionable branches, and sufficiently heavy cutting to maintain a desirable balance between new growth and the crop borne by the tree.

---

* Special articles on the subjects indicated by an asterisk (*) will be found at the words so marked.

Some form of cultivation is generally practiced for the successful production of good trees and fruit. The frequency of cultivation, however, may vary widely and will depend almost entirely upon the availability of water. If there is an abundance of water, the only cultivations may be those required to incorporate the cover crop, either of weeds or one that has been planted, into the soil. If there is not an abundance of water, more frequent cultivations are necessary to remove the competition of the weeds for the moisture supply.

VARIETIES. Three distinct groups of varieties which serve three different uses are grown in these states. The canning industry uses, almost exclusively, clingstone varieties which are firm-fleshed, of a golden-yellow color, of a good symmetrical size and shape, and ripen uniformly throughout. They are picked when the flesh has reached its full yellow color, but before softening has begun. Varieties used for canning, in order of ripening are: Vivian, Fortuna, Cortez, Paloro, Peak, Johnson, Gaume, Carolyn, Sims, Halford, Corona.

A variety that is suitable for drying should preferably be a freestone* with a small pit, the flesh should be sweet in taste, of a clear yellow color with no red at the pit, of a firm texture, and have a low drying ratio. For drying, the fruit is allowed to become fully mature before picking. After removal of the pit, the halves are placed on trays, with the cut surface up, exposed to fumes of burning sulphur for three to four hours and then either dried in the sun or in a dehydrating plant. Two varieties, the Muir and Lovell, are the chief ones used for drying, although the Elberta is dried in smaller amounts.

Varieties grown for fresh fruit in areas with sufficient winter chilling are in general the same as those already listed for the region east of the Rocky Mountains. In addition the following varieties are among those with low chilling requirements which have been developed by breeding programs for areas with mild winters. They are listed in their order of ripening.

VENTURA. A yellow-fleshed freestone with a red blush. The fruit is slightly flattened and almost without a pointed tip. The flavor is sub-acid. The trees are vigorous and upright. It has a low chilling requirement.

BONITA. An attractive light-yellow peach with a deep-red blush. It has a dark-pink seed cavity with fingers of pink extending into the flesh. The flavor is sweet with an occasional touch of bitterness. The tree is vigorous and upright. It has a low chilling requirement.

SUNGLOW. Fruit is medium large, golden-yellow with a red blush; flesh is light yellow with a medium-pink seed cavity; it is smooth in texture, juicy, and rich-flavored. The tree is vigorous and upright. It has a medium chilling requirement.

ANZA. Fruit is attractive, yellow-fleshed, firm, sweet, and juicy; flesh is of good texture and quality. The tree is rather upright and only moderately vigorous. It has a chilling requirement slightly less than J. H. Hale.

HERMOSA. Fruit is white-fleshed with skin color ranging from pink to solid red; the flavor is sweet and mild. The tree is of fair vigor with a rather spreading type of growth; it has large conspicuous flowers. It is a heavy bearer, coming into production early. It has a low chilling requirement.

RUBIDOUX. The fruit is greenish-yellow with a dull red blush; flesh is light yellow and the deep red of the seed cavity extends into the flesh; it is sweet and well flavored. The tree is vigorous and moderately spreading. It has a low to medium chilling requirement.

The foregoing varieties are all freestones and cover a maturity range of approximately six weeks. They are especially suited for gardeners who live in areas whose winters are too mild to adequately satisfy the chilling requirements of the standard, conventional varieties. — L. D. D.

INSECT PESTS. Curculio snout beetles and their larvae deform young fruit and cause it to drop. Control of the beetle is essential at the time the shucks* are splitting on the young peach fruit. If scale insects become a problem, apply a dormant oil spray (see SPRAYS AND DUSTS). Oriental fruit moth is a problem in some areas along the eastern seacoast. Special sprays of DDT at regular strength in early July will aid in control of this pest. Application for control of curculio will aid in fruit-moth suppression. Peach tree borers must be controlled every year. Apply DDT at 6 times normal concentration in early July and again in August to tree trunks up to the first crotch to kill moths and young borers.

DISEASES. Leaf curl* is a fungus disease causing the leaves to curl and turn pink or red and drop prematurely. Pesticide #5 (see SPRAYS AND DUSTS) should be applied once, anytime between leaf-drop in the fall and before bud-break in the spring.

Brown rot causes blight* of flowers and a rot of ripe fruit. Pesticide #1, #2 or #9 should be applied at 4- to 5-day intervals from the time buds are pink until petals fall, and at 2-week intervals afterwards.

Peach scab* is a fungus disease causing freckles or small spots on the surface of fruit. The spray schedule used for brown-rot control will usually control the scab also.

Another spot of fruit is caused by a bacterium. This disease may be quite serious in some seasons, resulting not only in many small, rather deep craters in flesh of the peach, but also a leafspot* which results in severe leaf fall. There is no really satisfactory control for this disease other than planting of resistant varieties which will grow in your particular area.

A number of virus diseases known as yellows,* little peach, phony peach, and others, are spread by insects and usually result in complete loss of fruit production and death of the tree. Trees suspected of having one of the virus diseases and having abnormal leaf yellowing, small leaves, small, late, or abnormally early-ripening fruit, should be destroyed.

Commercial orchardists may apply a dozen or more sprays each year, utilizing 5 or more different chemicals. For a plant hobbyist with

* Special articles on the subjects indicated by an asterisk (*) will be found at the words so marked.

just a few trees, the following program is suggested.

PEACH SPRAY PROGRAM

Time	Material
1. Dormant spray, before buds show any green.	Pesticide #5
2. When flower shows first pink, and repeat in 5 days.	" #1, #2, or #9
3. When shucks* split, and repeat in 10 days and 20 days.	" #1 or #23
4. As fruit starts to color, and repeat one week later.	" #1, #2, or #9

For pesticides, *see* SPRAYS AND DUSTS. For control of borer and Oriental fruit moth in the East, *see* text above.

PEACH BELLS = *Campanula persicifolia.*

PEACH FAMILY. See ROSACEAE.

PEACH-LEAVED WILLOW = *Salix amygdaloides.* See WILLOW.

PEACOCK-FLOWER = *Delonix regia; see also* ADENANTHERA.

PEACOCK IRIS = *Moraea Pavonia.*

PEA FAMILY. Perhaps the most important family of plants to the gardener because it includes pea, bean, clover, vetch, peanut, soybean, and many other crop plants. Among ornamental favorites are acacia, wisteria, genista, broom, lupine, gorse, locust, laburnum, and the redbud. And it also yields many drugs, such as licorice, and some poisons. For its many cult. genera, and a description of its flowers and fruits, *see* LEGUMINOSAE.

PEANUT. Brazil is the native home of the peanut, which belongs to the genus **Arachis** (ă′ra-kis) of the pea family. Of the 7 known species only the common peanut, **A. hypogaea**, sometimes called goober or groundnut, is cult., but this species is of wide economic importance. It is an annual herb 12–18 in. high, with alternate,* compound* leaves, its 4 ovalish leaflets 1½–2½ in. long, without marginal teeth. Flowers of two kinds: one set showy, yellow, pea-like, and sterile; the others, also yellow, but fertile and on recurved stalks which touch the ground, penetrate it, carrying the fertilized ovary beneath the surface where it ripens (the peanut). Unlike nearly all other fruits of the pea family, this one does not split. Seeds oily and nutritious. (*Arachis* is from the Greek for some pea-like plant, but of very uncertain application to the peanut.)

PEANUT CULTURE

As an interesting, annual, economic plant the peanut can be grown anywhere in the U.S. below zone* 3, but it needs far more heat to ripen its underground fruit than it usually finds north of zone* 5. Consequently, its commercial cult. is confined to the warmer parts of the country and from zone* 6 southward is its preferred climatic region in the U.S. It is widely grown in most tropical countries.

In zones* 3 and 4 an occasional long hot summer will permit fruit to ripen, but in the North generally the peanut is mostly an interesting curiosity because of its extraordinary fruiting habits.

In its own climatic region the seeds, removed from the pod if the latter is hard to split, are sown in drills about 30 in. apart, the plants to be spaced 8–10 in. apart in the row. Do not sow them until warm weather is assured, because the plant does not like coolness and is killed outright by frost.

Warm, sandy loams are the best for the peanut, and its commercial culture, which is more a large-scale agricultural operation than a hort. one, is confined to such soils. Like any other crop it needs to be cult. to keep down weeds and conserve soil moisture. But the plant will stand much heat and considerable drought.

There are two general types of peanut grown. One is the runner peanut in which the vine-like plant is apt to sprawl, consequently needing more space than the second form known as the bunch peanut. In the latter the plant is bushier and essentially erect. The bunch peanut is mostly grown by those who harvest the tops for forage. For the runner peanut the spacing should be more than that given above, which is for the bunch type.

Harvesting is like that of any root crop — the peanuts must be dug or plowed out when ripe. Usually the whole plant is plowed out and, with the peanuts attached, stacked on frames off the ground for curing and drying. They should be stacked in such a way that the nuts are covered by the foliage while curing, as the peanut will discolor if exposed to the weather while curing.

INSECT PESTS. Control leafhoppers by pesticide #1 or #17. Corn earworm and other leaf feeders are killed by pesticide #17. Soil treatments control wireworms and white grubs. See No. 4 at INSECTICIDES. (*See also* SPRAYS AND DUSTS.)

DISEASES. If plants wilt and die as a result of root rot, or if southern blight produces black seed-like objects at the base of plants, do not grow peanuts in this area for at least 3 years. Use a grass or cereal crop for a period before returning with peanuts.

To prevent loss of seedlings from damping-off,* treat the seed with one of the commercial seed treatments recommended by your state agricultural experiment stations.

If leafspot* appears, dust plants with pesticide #3 or #9 (*see* SPRAYS AND DUSTS) and repeat 3 times at 10-day intervals.

PEANUT FAMILY. See LEGUMINOSAE.

PEAR. For the common pear *see* the next main entry. For other plants to which the name *pear* is also applied *see* PSIDIUM (for alligator pear), MOMORDICA (for balsam pear), OPUNTIA (for prickly pear), and SECHIUM (for vegetable pear).

PEAR. Because the pear is more suited to the Pacific Coast than to the East, the

---

* Special articles on the subjects indicated by an asterisk (*) will be found at the words so marked.

chief cultural notes on this fruit will be grouped under the first section of this article.

On the Pacific Coast

With few exceptions, pear varieties of high quality grown in America are of European origin. These sorts belong to the species *Pyrus communis* or European pear. The Japanese cultivate many varieties of *Pyrus pyrifolia* or Japanese pear, not pleasing to the occidental taste, because of the number of stone* cells in the flesh. Hybrids between these species, which are intermediate in quality, are grown to a certain extent in all parts of America. *P. pyrifolia* strains, either pure or hybrid, tend to resist pear blight, undoubtedly the greatest single factor limiting the growth and production of pears. *See* below.

Pears are grown successfully under many conditions. Warm, dry summers apparently favor high quality, especially in certain varieties. Although some pears are as sensitive to cold as peaches, winters should be chilly enough to break the "rest period." In general, pears will withstand about the same winter temperatures as the rather tender Baldwin apple. The pear blooms relatively late and so can be planted more widely than almonds, apricots, and peaches; frosty locations, however, should be avoided. Artificial heating of pear orchards is economically questionable. Windy locations should be avoided, as fruit often scars, even if not blown from the tree.

Soils. A well-drained, deep clay loam is probably best for pears, although they are grown on many soils. Adequate moisture should be available, either from rainfall, or from irrigation.* Most orchards are clean cultivated, although many, especially in Wash., have a permanent cover crop such as alfalfa. Pear trees grown in sod or in soils low in fertility may benefit from the application of nitrogenous fertilizers. If the ground is clean cultivated, barnyard manure is perhaps the best source of additional fertility. At all events, the effect of the addition of fertilizers should be determined first on a few trees before treatment of the whole plantation. Excessive vegetative growth, especially in bearing trees, whether induced by fertilization or irrigation, is undesirable: it encourages development of pear blight.

Although pear trees are long-lived and may eventually reach great size, this fruit will do well when the trees are planted relatively close. Many old orchards are as close as 16 × 16 ft. When grown as dwarfs (on quince roots), 12 × 12 ft. is a good spacing; possibly the most popular distance is 20 × 20 ft. for standard trees.

The most common root for pears is the French (*P. communis*). Though it suckers rather badly and is susceptible to pear blight and pear root aphis, it is adaptable to various soil conditions, vigorous, long-lived, and partially resistant to oak fungus; and produces splendid fruit.

The Japanese root (*P. pyrifolia*), widespread on the Pacific Coast, especially in Calif., is resistant to pear root aphis, but only partially resistant to pear blight. After 20 years' experience, Calif. orchardists have concluded — as did South African growers 30 or more years ago — that this root is highly unsatisfactory. It is poorly adapted to soils having high moisture or lime content. After 12 to 15 years, the trees often stop growth. Probably the most serious drawback, however, is the "Black End" or "Hard End" affecting much of the crop. Often the calyx end is hard and black, or merely hard. The fruit is ruined for fresh consumption, canning, and drying. There is apparently no causal organism, nor any correlation with soil, climate, or culture condition. This disease has never appeared on quince stock, and but rarely on French-rooted trees.

With quince (*Cydonia oblonga*), sometimes used as a dwarfing stock for pears, double-working is often necessary. Hardy is universally satisfactory as the intermediate variety. Several plantings of Bartletts in Calif. now 75 years old were thus propagated. The resultant fruit is excellent. With good soil and culture, the trees are only semi-dwarfs. The quince root is particularly well adapted to moist, heavy soils.

Planting. Usually a one-year-old whip, 4 to 6 feet high, with a caliper of ½ inch at the base, is planted and immediately headed to about 30 inches. This planting is generally done in the spring when the soil is moist and before the young tree has started root or top activity. Whitewash the entire tree at planting to prevent sunscald.* Some growers prefer the use of tree protectors for this purpose. At the end of the first summer, three branches are selected so that a good spacing up and down the trunk is secured, all others are removed. This spacing is more important than balancing the growth around the stem, since the next season's

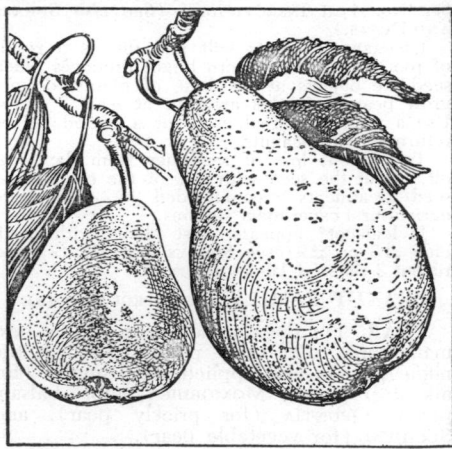

Bartlett (*right*) and Seckel (*left*) pears

* Special articles on the subjects indicated by an asterisk (*) will be found at the words so marked.

shoots take care of this problem. The distance between the origin of the branches on the trunk never changes during the life of the tree. If possible, space these main scaffolds° 6 to 8 in. apart and head back moderately to encourage the appearance of secondary scaffolds during the second summer. At the end of the second season in the orchard, the new shoots are thinned out and a few (4–5) saved and lightly headed. Follow the same procedure during the next few years, heading only where a new branch is desired and thinning out superfluous shoots. After the tree comes into bearing, the pruning given will necessarily vary with the variety and growing conditions. Maximum crops and abundant replacement wood do not go hand in hand. The crop should be limited by removal of the wood sufficient to induce a new shoot growth of from 12 to 18 inches over the periphery of the tree. Pruning for size of fruit is often profitably supplemented by thinning the fruit. In windy locations, this practice is often desirable to prevent scarring of the fruit.

The pear is well adapted to espalier and cordon training, and is thus grown in many European fruit gardens. These methods of handling should more often be used by the amateur fruitgrower in this country, and the pear tree lends itself particularly well to these practices. See TRAINED FRUIT TREES.

Cross-pollination is needed by most pear varieties, including Bartlett, except in especially favorable locations, such as the interior valley pear sections of Calif. Any two pear varieties that blossom at the same time will successfully cross-pollinate each other. Efficient pollinations may be secured with the minimum number of pollinators by planting these as every third tree in every third row. This gives one tree in nine to the pollinating sort.

PICKING. Pears ripen to better quality off the tree. Unless picked early, they develop more stone° cells and a coarser texture. Whether for shipping, canning, or drying, therefore, they are not harvested tree-ripe. Pears may be stored at temperatures down to 32° F., but thereafter should be ripened at above 60° F.

Pears for drying — ripened, halved, with calyx and stem removed — are exposed on trays to the fumes of burning sulphur from 6 to 24 hours, and then placed in the sun to dry. After a day or so, the trays are stacked and the drying slowly completed. About 5 pounds fresh make 1 pound dry.

VARIETIES. Most of the varieties of pears raised in the United States, either by the amateur or commercial grower, are of European origin. A definite effort was made, particularly in Belgium and France, for more than a century (1730–1850) to secure improved varieties. Many of our better varieties thus originated. Little attention has been given to systematic pear breeding in America, and the general prevalence of pear blight has undoubtedly killed many natural seedlings. Many of the better pear varieties now

growing in this country originated as chance seedlings. A few of the best varieties will be discussed in the approximate order of their ripening. Those marked with a † are suited to the East. See below.

† BARTLETT. This is the most important variety in the U.S. Of English origin, it is known, except in U.S., as the Williams Bon Chretien. Trees large and productive. Fruit large to very large, clear yellow, often with blush. Excellent quality. Best flavor and texture developed when grown where summer temperatures are high. Suitable for dessert, canning, and drying. Susceptible to pear blight. Season, September in N.Y.; last of June to September in western U.S.

BEURRE HARDY. A French variety, originated about 1850. Makes satisfactory union with quince root. Trees grow to large size and produce heavy crops. Fruit large, greenish-yellow under a light russet. Very good quality. A popular variety on the English market. Somewhat less susceptible to pear blight than Bartlett.

† KIEFFER. An American hybrid between a European variety and a Japanese. Trees vigorous, reaching good size, productive.

Kieffer (*right*) and Beurre Bosc (*left*) pears

Fruit large to very large, rough, blushed with brownish red. Flesh granular, often gritty, juicy, below medium quality. Because of partial resistance to pear blight, widely grown in warm, humid sections in southeastern U.S. and Mississippi Valley.

† SECKEL. Of Penn. origin. Tree vigorous, productive. Fruit very small, yellowish-brown, often lightly russeted; sweet and of best quality. An excellent sort for the home garden. More resistant to pear blight than most varieties.

† BEURRE D'ANJOU. This old French variety is vigorous. The trees reach large size and are irregular in productivity. Fruit large, greenish to yellow; very good in quality. Unless well grown, fruit often subject

---

° Special articles on the subjects indicated by an asterisk (°) will be found at the words so marked.

to internal breakdown known as "Anjou spot." Trees are moderately susceptible to pear blight.

† BEURRE BOSC. A Belgian variety of great vigor, but straggly growth, especially as a young tree. Of medium productivity. Fruit large to very large with long, tapering neck; greenish-yellow, often overlaid with very heavy russet. When well grown, of highest quality, especially on heavy soils. Trees are very susceptible to pear blight and stony pit.

DOYENNE DU COMICE. A French variety of good vigor. Irregular to shy in productivity. Fruit large, yellow with faint reddish-brown russet. Quality, the best. Moderately susceptible to pear blight.

† WINTER NELIS. An old Belgian variety, slow in growth, but eventually reaching great size. Trees difficult to train when young, due to twisting habit of growth. Fruit small to medium, yellow-green, often completely overlaid with russet; very good in quality; an excellent storage variety. The most resistant of the European varieties to pear blight. — W. P. T.

EAST OF THE ROCKY MOUNTAINS

The pear reaches perfection in few places east of the Rocky Mountains for the reason that the climate in this great region is uncongenial to it. Pears are at their best only in equable climates and do not endure well the sudden and extreme variations in weather to which all parts of North America excepting the Pacific states are subject. In the region under consideration, commercial pear culture is confined to favorable localities between the Atlantic and the Great Lakes. A few varieties, hybrids with the Japanese pear, can with difficulty be grown in the Gulf states and the states of the plains.

The reasons given above, and the further one that of all fruits the varieties of this one are most variable in quality, keep the fruit from being a favorite with those who grow fruits for home use. Gardeners do not like to grow varieties that should produce fruits of high quality and then harvest a crop indifferent in flavor, color, and texture because of some slight uncongeniality in soil or climate.

On the other hand, those who love choicely good fruits find the charm of individuality more marked in the pear than in any of its orchard associates. The fruits of varieties of pears are, perhaps, more varied in size, shape, texture, and flavor than those of any other hardy tree fruit. The length of season is longer than that of any other fruit, excepting the apple. For these reasons the pear is the fruit of fruits for connoisseurs. A splendid collection can be grown, given favorable soil, a fairly equable climate, careful attention to culture, and drastic treatment of pear blight which everywhere in America is a scourge. *See* below. For the cordon and other specially trained trees, *see* TRAINED FRUIT TREES.

The pear, under the limitations named, can be grown in most soils and locations where the apple succeeds. It likes a rather heavier soil than the apple and can be planted on clays too heavy for the apple. The items of culture — cultivation, pruning, fertilization — are much the same as for the apple, or in eastern America nearly the same as those set forth in the longer article on pear-growing on the Pacific Coast. *See* above.

Perhaps the need of cross-pollination in eastern pear-growing needs especial emphasis, since in this great region many varieties are grown, some of which are wholly self-sterile. Mixed plantings of two compatible varieties blooming at the same time, set in blocks of two or three rows, are generally required to ensure a set of fruit.

The following varieties for the East are named in order of ripening:

TYSON. Fruit yellow, small, choicely good. Tree large, very vigorous, productive, blight-resistant. Zones* 2 and 3 and southward east of the Great Lakes.

CLAPP FAVORITE. Fruit yellow with bright blush, symmetrical, quality fair, softens at center quickly. Tree large, vigorous, fairly productive, very susceptible to blight. Zones* 2 and 3 and southward east of the Great Lakes.

BARTLETT. For description *see* above. All parts of zones* 2 and 3 and southward where pears can be grown.

GORHAM. Fruit yellow, large, Bartlett type and flavor but ripens 2 weeks later. Tree like that of Bartlett but blight-resistant. Succeeds wherever Bartlett is grown.

SECKEL. For description *see* above. Zones* 2 and 3 and southward in all parts where pears are grown.

CAYUGA. A seedling of Seckel with much larger fruits which otherwise are similar. Tree similar with the same adaptations.

BEURRE BOSC. For description *see* above. Favored localities in zones* 2 and 3 and southward east of the Great Lakes.

BEURRE D'ANJOU. For description *see* above. Zones* 2 and 3 and southward where pears can be grown.

WINTER NELIS. For description *see* above. Succeeds only in very favorable localities in zones* 2 and 3.

INSECT PESTS. *See* APPLE for codling moth control. Early season applications of pesticide #1 (*see* SPRAYS AND DUSTS) will control psylla, a jumping plant louse, thrips which injure buds, and leaf-destroying sawfly larvae or slugs. Dormant oil sprays will control bluster mites which darken and deform foliage.

DISEASES. Unfortunately the better varieties of pear, such as Bartlett, Bosc, and Anjou, cannot be grown successfully in many areas, due to fireblight* disease. In some states the research workers have had some control of this bacterial disease by using two or three sprays during the blooming period. One of the antibiotic* materials known as streptomycin has been the material giving some disease control. Contact your local county agricultural agent or state experiment station for details for your area. Although some control may be obtained with pruning out diseased wood and cankers* of the disease, it

---

* Special articles on the subjects indicated by an asterisk (*) will be found at the words so marked.

often works so rapidly that trees are almost completely killed.

Some varieties of pear will defoliate prematurely each year as a result of scab. This fungus disease not only causes leafspot* but a black spotting of the fruit. Use pesticide #11 (*see* SPRAYS AND DUSTS) when flower buds first show color and repeat before flowers open and again at petal-fall.

PEAR FAMILY. *See* ROSACEAE.

PEAR HAW = *Crataegus uniflora.*

PEARL ACACIA = *Acacia podalyriaefolia.*

PEARL BUSH = *Exochorda racemosa.*

PEARL MILLET = *Pennisetum glaucum.*

PEARLWORT. *See* SAGINA.

PEARLY EVERLASTING = *Anaphalis margaritacea.*

PEAR TOMATO = *Lycopersicum esculentum pyriforme.* See TOMATO.

PEA SHRUB. *See* CARAGANA.

PEAT. A word of widely different significations in hort. Peat, in the technical sense, consists of the partially or wholly decomposed remains of plants; in other words, peat is the first stage in the process of the formation of coal. Old but unconsolidated peat is really muck, and its hort. use is discussed at MUCKLAND GARDENING.

Long before peat has reached the muck stage of decomposition its uses to the gardener are various, depending upon its origin and its stage of rotting. The only partially decomposed roots and rootstocks of many ferns are gathered for what is known as orchid peat, because it is used for potting up orchids. For that use *see* the culture of greenhouse orchids at ORCHID. It is now being replaced by fir bark.

When the peat is wholly of upland origin, derived from the partial or complete decomposition of the leaves, twigs, or trunks of trees and shrubs, it is usually called leaf mold or humus and may be very acid or almost neutral. Acid peat is usually brownish, what the foresters call raw, and in this state is very valuable for plants of the heath family and for certain wild flowers, but not for all. *See* ACID AND ALKALI SOILS. *See also* HUMUS. Much later, as the woodland peat becomes older and nearly black, it usually loses its acidity, and in this stage it is typical rich woods soil, of the greatest use in the wild garden.

By far the largest amount of peat, outside of that derived from the forest floor, is derived from bog mosses of the genus *Sphagnum.* In its fresh-growing state sphagnum moss is intensely acid. And even when partially decomposed, sphagnum peat is still so acid that it is the best material for use in the bog garden. Much later (perhaps 200–500 years) it is in the process of becoming muck which may or may not be acid, depending on conditions of decomposition. There is also much peat derived from the decomposition of sedges, particularly in

Ohio and Mich. It is not strongly acid. *See* MUCKLAND GARDENING.

The value of peat, like any other humus, is largely its great water-holding capacity. In woods soil and in the bog it provides an ideal environment for microscopic organisms upon which many wild plants depend, at least in part, for getting their food.

"PEAT-LOVERS." A common, but misleading term in hort. literature. Some plants *grow* in peat, especially acid peat, not because they "love" such sites, but becuase they must. To call such plants peat-lovers is more picturesque than truthful. Actually they are acid-tolerant plants. For a list of them *see* the list at ACID AND ALKALI SOILS.

PEAT MOSS. A popular mulch prepared from the peat of ancient sphagnum bogs and from sedge peat. *See* MULCH AND MULCHING, and SPHAGNUM.

PEA TREE = *Caragana;* also *Agati grandiflora.*

PECAN (*Carya Pecan*). Millions of pecan trees are wild or have been planted in the southern states and up the Mississippi and its tributaries as far north as Iowa. The pecan is now grown far beyond the wild range of the original species, which covered the region from Iowa and Ind. to Ala., Tex. and Mex. Today there are over 70 million bearing trees, most of them wild. Thomas Jefferson brought the first pecan trees from the Mississippi Valley to Va. and gave George Washington some of them. He planted them March 25, 1775, and three of them are still at Mount Vernon.

The wild population of pecan trees is very erratic as to the size of the nut and yields, and the tree rarely comes true from seed. These two facts have made it necessary to bud or graft really fine varieties upon existing trees. And thousands of relatively old trees have been thus top-worked. But millions of seedlings are raised every year, not to be allowed to grow until bearing age, for the crop may be worthless. The year-old seedlings are simply used as stock upon which fine varieties are budded. *See* BUDDING.

Most non-commercial growers will not care to bother with the somewhat elaborate technique of top-working old trees, or to wait for the slow process of budding. It is far better to purchase trees from a reliable dealer, and of the variety suited to your region. Pecan varieties, more than in most nut trees, are extremely important, as some are suited only to special conditions or regions.

VARIETIES. While the pecan will stand many degrees of frost, and some varieties have stood temperatures as low as 20° below zero, the tree is primarily a southern one. And, while some varieties will stand winter cold, they need a lot of summer heat to produce good nuts. The northern limit of pecan culture is about zone* 4 and in this region the following varieties are the best:

---

* Special articles on the subjects indicated by an asterisk (*) will be found at the words so marked.

Busseron, Butterick, Green River, Indiana, Niblack, and Posey. Not all dealers will have all these varieties, but most of them are available, at least from a few dealers.

South of zone* 4, especially in the lowlands of the Mississippi, other and better pecan varieties are available. The tree is also cult. throughout the southern states, far outside its wild range, and certain varieties seem best adapted to these areas while some do better in the drainage area of the lower Mississippi. For the latter region, the real center of wild distribution, the best varieties are: Stuart, Schley, Van Deman, and Curtis. In the East, that is, from N. Car. to Fla. and Ala., the best varieties are: Bradley, Curtis, Moneymaker, President, and Stuart, and in eastern Tex. the same varieties are also suitable.

More than 100 named varieties of pecan are in the trade, but many of them are relatively useless because of poor yield, thick shells, or climatic restrictions. Those selected above have stood the test of the comparatively few years since pecan varieties have been even partially standardized. Many others of promise are constantly coming forward. The prospective planter will do well to visit the nursery where such are offered and get a complete history of the parent tree. It is useless to plant seeds of it, and only guaranteed budded or grafted trees should be accepted. There are now hundreds of thousands of relatively useless pecan trees throughout the South, due to the ignoring of these simple essentials.

PLANTING. The young pecan tree has a deep (3–4 ft.), stout taproot. It *must* be carefully handled, for upon the taproot will depend its chance of successful transplanting. During the first year few or maybe no lateral roots will develop, so it is important to dig a deep hole and see that the taproot has good soil, well packed in. Also it must be remembered that the mature tree will have a root spread twice as great as its spread of branches, which means that, for orchard planting, pecan trees must be at least 80 ft. apart each way, or within 25 years their root systems will be touching.

The rooting habits of the pecan have an important bearing upon its cultivation. Once the young tree is established it begins sending out in all directions many long, lateral roots. These are all in the upper layers of the soil, many of them scarcely 12 in. below the surface, and sometimes only 6 in. If cultivation is to be done, and it should be in all extensive plantings, it must be with a shallow cultivator, not with the plow. Cultivation is most beneficial to keep down weeds which otherwise would rob such shallow-rooted trees too much. To avoid the trouble of cultivation some growers keep the pecan orchard in sod or weeds, but it is not a good plan.

YIELDS. Mature pecan trees yield from 100–600 pounds of nuts a year. But it takes many years for the trees to get to such a prolific stage of bearing, and few ever reach the higher figure. Some top-worked trees

have been very good yielders. One of them, in Mississippi, the whole top of which was changed to the variety Stuart, had the following record:

	Pounds of nuts			Pounds of nuts
1st year	5	7th year		75
2nd "	20	8th "		110
3rd "	20	9th "		210
4th "	35	10th "		240
5th "	60	11th "		250
6th "	100	12th "		350

This was, of course, a mature but undesirable tree when its top was grafted with Stuart cions. Young budded or grafted trees would not reach such bearing for many years. Perhaps a fair average for young trees would be 6–20 pounds in ten years after planting. Crop failure often comes when heavy rain coincides with the production of pollen, hence interfering with wind pollination.

INSECT PESTS. The hickory shuckworm which destroys shucks* and prevents normal development is a bad pest. Reduce attack by tilling under dropped nuts. Case-bearing caterpillars are controlled in spray schedule below. Long-snouted weevils appear in late season. Control damage by schedule below. Heavier than normal sprays of pesticide #17 (*see* SPRAYS AND DUSTS) may be needed. Jarring trees weekly in late summer and catching weevils on sheets and destroying them, is effective on home trees. Aphids are easily controlled by pesticide #21 or #20. Several stinkbugs attack ripening fruit and produce black spots on kernels. Control is best on regular schedule. For scale and apple tree borer control, *see* APPLE. If buds and nuts are attacked in very early season, control this curculio damage by pesticide #20 when buds first show green.

DISEASES. Scab is the most common disease of pecan. The small black spots on leaves, twigs, and fruit appear at first to be of little importance, but as spots increase in size and number they cause severe loss. To reduce scab infection, knock old leaf-stems and nut husks from the tree before new growth begins in the spring. Rake and burn fallen leaves, or disk ground to cover them. Following the spray program will give good results.

Downy spot produces frosty-appearing areas on the lower surface of leaves. Vein-spot disease turns the mid-vein of leaves a dark brown. Two different fungi produce dark leaf-spots.* In the scab spray program, these diseases will be controlled.

The following spray program will control the common insects and diseases of pecan.

PECAN SPRAY PROGRAM

Time	Material
1. At bud-break.	Pesticide #3
2. First leaves half grown.	" #3
3. Tips of nuts turn brown.	" #11, and #17 or #21
4. Three to four weeks later.	" #11, and #17 or #21
5. Three to four weeks later.	" #11, and #17 or #21
6. Three to four weeks later.	" #11 and #17

For pesticides, *see* SPRAYS AND DUSTS.

---

* Special articles on the subjects indicated by an asterisk (*) will be found at the words so marked.

pecten-aboriginum (peck-ten-ab-o-rij′i-num). Native's comb. *See* PACHYCEREUS.

pectinata, -us, -um (peck-ti-nay′ta). Comb-like.

PEDALIACEAE. *See* SESAMUM.

pedata, -us, -um (pe-day′ta). Pedate (which see).

PEDATE. Palmate,* with the lateral or side lobes cleft or divided; usually applied to leaves.

PEDICEL. *See* PEDUNCLE.

PEDICULARIS (pe-dick-you-lay′ris). Wood-betony. Lousewort. A large genus of annual or perennial herbs, comprising about 300 species of the family Scrophulariaceae, scattered throughout the northern hemisphere, but a few found in S.A. Mostly erect, 3 in.–3 ft. high. Leaves alternate* or whorled, or sometimes in opposite pairs, generally finely cut into many segments. Flowers purplish, red, rose or white, borne in the axils of bracts* in a terminal raceme.* Corolla 2-lipped, tubular. Stamens* 4, 2 long and 2 short. Fruit a capsule*; seeds few. (*Pedicularis* is from the Latin for louse, in allusion to the supposed effect on sheep eating it.)

Propagated by seeds and division. Sometimes difficult to grow owing to its being partially parasitic on roots of other plants, therefore not a favorite, and suited mostly to the wild garden.

canadensis. Herbaceous, hairy perennial, growing to 18 in. high. Leaves 5 in. long, segmented. Flowers yellow, often tinged red, ¾ in. long. Fruit 3 times as long as the persistent calyx.* April–June. Eastern N.A., in the woods.

lanceolata. Smooth, herbaceous perennial to 3 ft. high. Leaves to 5 in. long, slightly segmented. Flowers yellow, ¾ in. long. Fruit when ripe same length as calyx. Sept.–Oct. Ont. to Tenn. and westward.

PEDILANTHUS (ped-i-lan′thus). Tropical American, cactus-like, succulent plants of the spurge family, comprising over 30 species, only one of which is much cult. It is the redbird cactus, also called slipper-flower and Jew bush, and known to science as P. tithymaloides. It is a shrubby plant 4–6 ft. high, with fleshy, milky-juiced, zigzag stems, with ovalish leaves 2–4 in. long, keeled on the midrib beneath, and toothed. Flowers minute, bright red, in dense clusters (cymes*), the colored involucre spurred (hence slipper-flower). Fruit a capsule, about ¼ in. long. It is native from Fla. to Venezuela, and is often grown in the greenhouse northward. For its indoor cult. *see* SUCCULENTS. (*Pedilanthus* is from the Greek for slipper-flower.) Its juice is caustic, irritant, and emetic.

PEDIOCACTUS (ped-i-o-kak′tus). A single species of globe-shaped or orange-shaped cactus, P. simpsoni, the snowball cactus, so called because in the young state the plant is densely covered with white wool, most of which is lost in age. The plant body is about 6 in. thick, tubercled, and densely spiny. Spines 15–20 in a cluster, needle-like, 5–7 of

the center ones erect and stouter than the diverging lateral spines. Flowers pinkish, about 1 in. long, funnel-shaped, and borne among tufts of white wool at the top of the plant. Fruit dry. It is one of the hardier species of cacti, being native from Kan. to Wash. and N. Mex. For culture *see* CACTI. It does not take kindly to transfer from the wild. (*Pediocactus* is from the Greek for plain and *Cactus,* in allusion to its growing on the Great Plains.)

PEDUNCLE. The stalk of a solitary flower, or the main stalk of a flower cluster. Each of the flowers in a cluster may have its own individual stalk, which is then properly called a pedicel.

peduncularis, -e (pe-dunk-you-lar′is). Having a stalk or peduncle.*

pedunculata, -us, -um (pe-dunk-you-lay′-ta). Having a stalk or peduncle.*

PEEGEE. An abbreviation, and often the trade vernacular, for *Hydrangea paniculata grandiflora,* sometimes written in the catalogues *Hydrangea p. g.*

PEENTO. A Chinese variety or race of rather tender peaches having flattish fruit. In the U.S. they are grown only in sub-tropical parts of the Gulf states, mostly as a valuable rootstock for grafting.

PEEPUL = *Ficus religiosa.*

PEJIBAYE = *Guilielma Gasipaes.*

pekinensis, -e (pee-kin-en′sis). From Pekin (now Peiping), China.

PELARGONIUM (pee-lar-gō′ni-um). Garden geranium. Stork's-bill geranium. A large genus of South African tender perennial herbs and shrubs of the family Geraniaceae, their habits being very diverse in the different species, of which there are over 250. Stems strong-growing or trailing, herbaceous or woody. Leaves alternate,* stalked, simple, entire* and roundish, or much cut and often fern-like, some deeply marked on the upper side, smooth or hairy, a few fragrant. Flowers in umbel-like clusters growing on a leafless stalk from the axils* of the leaves. Individual flowers showy, varying from pure white, pink, crimson and bright scarlet in color, irregular. Calyx* of 5 sepals joined at the base. Petals 5. Stamens* 10. Ovary 5-celled, splitting into 5 sections when ripe, each containing 1 seed. (*Pelargonium* is from the Greek for a stork, in allusion to the shape of the fruit.) The validity of many of the names below is in considerable doubt, as the nomenclature of this genus is in much confusion.

capitatum. A rose-scented sub-shrub, 1–2 ft. high, the stems hairy, rather weak and apt to sprawl. Leaves long-stalked, about 1½ in. wide, 3-lobed, but heart-shaped at the base, the lobes toothed. Flowers in dense clusters, rose or rose-purple. S. Af.

crispum. Growing to 3 ft. with erect, thin, woody-wiry stems, having many upright branches, slightly hairy. Leaves alternate,* in 2 rows, short-stalked, small, roundish, 3-lobed, margins crinkled, lemon-scented. Umbels 1–3-

---

* Special articles on the subjects indicated by an asterisk (*) will be found at the words so marked.

flowered. Flowers pink, 2 upper petals lined deeper pink, 3 lower petals long and narrow.

denticulatum. Weak-growing, erect, to 1 ft. high. Leaves with long, finger-like lobes, the lobes deeply toothed, flat, smooth on the upper side, rough-hairy on the under side, and with balsamic odor. Umbels 3–4-flowered, with short, hairy stalks. Flowers lilac-rose or purple, 2 upper petals 2-lobed with dark markings.

domesticum. Show geranium. Fancy geranium. Lady Washington geranium. These common names are perhaps not properly associated with the true *domesticum* but have been classed under this species. Growing to 2 ft., of straggling habit. Stems soft, fleshy and hairy when young, lower part becoming hard and woody in age. Leaves 2–4 in. across, roundish, slightly lobed, toothed. Umbels few- to many-flowered. Flowers large, white, pink, or red, 2 upper petals usually blotched darker.

echinatum. Cactus geranium. Not over 20 in. high, the fleshy stem clothed with hooked, soft prickles (remains of the stipules*). Leaves about 1–1½ in. wide, 5–7-lobed, the lobes toothed, green above, white-felty beneath. Flowers white with one petal red-spotted, but sometimes all red-purple. S. Af.

fragrans. Erect habit, growing to 1 ft., lower branches woody. Leaves numerous, roundish, hairy, margins wrinkled, lower leaves long-stalked, upper leaves without stalks. Umbels 4–8-flowered. Flowers whitish with pink veins. Closely allied to *odoratissimum.*

graveolens. Rose geranium. Growing to 3 ft., woody. Leaves roundish in outline, 5–7-lobed, lobes toothed, fragrant. Umbels 5–10-flowered, flowers rose-pink. *See* HERB GARDENING.

hortorum. Fish geranium. Growing 1–6 ft. high, the stems strong and fleshy. Leaves 3–5 in. across, roundish, generally having a deep horseshoe-shaped marking or zone on the upper side, the margins scalloped. The plant has a faint, fish-like odor. Umbels many-flowered. Flowers red, salmon-pink, or white.

odoratissimum. Nutmeg geranium. The apple geranium is probably a variety. Stems erect, at first weak and spreading, up to 18 in. high. Leaves small, roundish, covered with soft, short hairs, hence grayish, the margins scalloped. Nutmeg-scented. Umbels 5–10-flowered. Flowers white, 2 upper petals veined deep pink.

peltatum. Ivy geranium. Stems trailing to 4 ft. long, fleshy when young, becoming woody below in age, angled at the joints. Leaves ivy-shaped, 5-pointed, bright glossy-green. Umbels 5–7-flowered. Flowers white to deep rose, upper petals having dark markings.

quercifolium. Oak-leaved geranium. An aromatic, much-branched sub-shrub, 2–4 ft. high. Leaves cut feather-fashion, the lobes wavy-margined and sharp-toothed, the whole leaf 2–4 in. wide. Flowers purple with darker markings and a dark spot on the upper petal, usually in sparse clusters (umbels*). S. Af.

tomentosum. Peppermint geranium. A shrubby plant, peppermint-scented, 3–5 ft. high, the foliage and stems covered with white hairs. Leaves velvety, 3–5-lobed, 3–4 in. wide, the lobes with very small teeth. Flowers in a 4–20-flowered cluster (corymb*), generally white, but the larger upper petal reddish at the base.

GARDEN GERANIUM CULTURE

Gardeners for convenience divide the pelargoniums into 4 groups, each differing in its method of culture, and each having its own particular use in the greenhouse or garden. They are all known as geraniums both by gardeners and the general public, although botanically they are not geraniums, but this name has been in use so long that it is doubtful if it will be discontinued. All are tender and can only be grown outside all year round in frost-free localities. Most pelargoniums in cultivation are hort. varieties.

GROUP 1. This type, known as the Show or Fancy pelargoniums (Lady Washington geranium), have the largest individual flowers of the genus. They make very showy pot plants either for cool greenhouse or house plants, in a sunny window. Propagated from cuttings of firm shoots 3–4 in. long in July, inserted in a mixture of ½ sand, ½ soil in 2-in. pots, watering well after planting. They should then be placed in a cold frame or greenhouse in an airy position and shaded from strong sun.

As soon as rooted pot into 4-in. pots in potting mixture* 3, keeping plants near the glass to promote sturdy growth. When 6 in. long pinch out tip of shoots to make plant branch, more flowers being obtained by this method. In early Jan. re-pot into 6-in. pots, keeping in a cool, airy place, and water sparingly during winter months. Temperature should be 45°–60°. Water well from March–June, and when flower buds appear give small quantity of a general fertilizer once a week until first flowers open.

After flowering prune back to within 4 in. of the base, stand plants outdoors in full sun until new shoots appear, then take out of pots and remove most of the old soil. Re-pot into smaller pots, placing them under glass in Sept. Large specimens can be made by pruning old plants less, using 5-in. pots when re-potting and potting on into 7- or 8-in. pots. Good drainage and firm potting are essential. *See* POTTING.

GROUP 2. This type, known as Zonal or Fish geraniums, is the one so much used at one time for garden and window-box decoration and is still one of the best for continuous bloom from early summer to late fall. Included in this group are the variegated forms with white and green leaves, others with gold and bronze-shaded leaves, used for edging or color contrasts. Propagated from cuttings 3–5 in. long of young, short-jointed shoots in early Sept., avoiding sappy growths. Insert in mixture of 2 parts soil and 1 part sand, placing 5 round the edge of 5-in. pot. Water and stand in shady position outside or in cool greenhouse for 2 weeks, by which time a callus* will have formed.

They must then be moved to a sunny position in greenhouse or cold frame. When well rooted pot singly into 3-in. pots, using potting mixture* 3. Re-pot in Feb. or early March into 5-in. pots in which they should remain until planted out in the garden toward the end of May. Plants grow best when pots are standing on a bed of coal ashes or fine gravel with sufficient space between for air

---

* Special articles on the subjects indicated by an asterisk (*) will be found at the words so marked.

to circulate freely. Water sparingly during winter or stems will develop stem rot and die. Temperature should be 45°–60°. Flower buds should be picked off until April.

This type grows well in ordinary garden soil, if not too rich in nitrogen, which makes the plants develop fleshy stems and leaves, but few flowers. Plant in light, sunny position, never in complete shade. In frost-free localities they may be grown outside all year, plants often growing 6–8 ft. when trained on a trellis or wall.

GROUP 3. This type, known as Ivy-leaved geraniums, having weak stems, ivy-shaped leaves, and many flowers, is admirably adapted for hanging baskets, ornamental vases or for window-box planting. Large specimens can be made by growing several in a large box or tub and training on wires to any desired shape. They may also be planted in beds 1 ft. apart and allowed to trail over

An easy method of rooting a cutting of garden geranium

the ground, forming a good ground cover with many flowers. Propagate the same as Fish geraniums, except in the young stages smaller pots may be used. When grown close together, in winter, each plant should be staked, when plants are about 8 in. high.

GROUP 4. This type, known as scented-leaved geraniums, are general favorites, due to their varied fragrance. There are over 200 varieties in cult., the best-known being the lemon, rose, cinnamon, nutmeg, and apple. Grown entirely for their leaves, they make good window plants, or may be grown outside in summer, when they will grow rapidly. Their stems are useful and fragrant decorations. Propagate as for Fish geranium.

For the average amateur an easy method of wintering these tender geraniums is to lift the plants in fall, shake off nearly all soil from the roots, and hang them upside down in a cool cellar (no furnace heat). In mid-May, cut back the withered stems to 6–8 inches and

plant outdoors, repeating the initial procedure. They will sprout new leaves and shoots and bloom in a short time. All garden geraniums root easily in moist sand if a slip 4–6 inches long, with most leaves removed, is inserted 1–2 inches deep, covered with a bell-jar and kept moist.

INSECT PESTS. Control leaf feeders with pesticide #1. (*See* SPRAYS AND DUSTS.) To control slugs (snails) use slug baits (*see* at INSECTICIDES).

DISEASES. In the garden or greenhouse the leaves may become spotted or blighted* after invasion by several fungi and one bacterium. The fungus diseases are controlled by using pesticide #5 or #11 (*see* SPRAYS AND DUSTS), at 10-day intervals and by keeping old blossoms and dead leaves removed from the plants.

When cuttings are taken from stock plants, set cuttings in clean sand or rooting medium and drench once with pesticide #5 to help prevent rot of base of cuttings. In the greenhouse, do not set a new crop of potted plants on a bench where poinsettia or pelargonium were growing the previous season unless the bench is first drenched with pesticide #5. This will help to prevent a black root-rot common to both types of plant.

If leaves wilt, starting at the bottom and progressing upward, and if inside of stem is brown, it indicates a bacterial wilt* disease. Discard plants and sterilize soil with steam (*see* SOIL STERILIZATION). If leaves curl and have ring-spot* symptoms, discard plants because virus disease is present. The soil need not be sterilized for control of the virus.

Small corky spots on lower surface of leaves and on stems are indications of oedema.* Since this is not a disease, but rather the result of wet soil and high humidity, there is no serious aspect to the trouble.

PELECYPHORA (pell-e-siff′o-ra). A single species of low, tubercled, Mexican cactus, **P. aselliformis**, the hatchet-cactus, sometimes cult. in desert gardens or in greenhouses northward. The plant body is cylindric, not over 4 in. high, about 2 in. in diameter, its strongly flattened tubercles arranged in prominent spirals, each tubercle crowned with a solitary spine. Flowers about 1 in. wide, bell-shaped, purple, or the outer segments whitish. For culture *see* CACTI. (*Pelecyphora* is from the Greek for hatchet-bearing, in allusion to the fancied resemblance of the flattened tubercles to a hatchet.)

Pelegrina (pell-i-gry′na). Native name in Chile for *Alstroemeria Pelegrina*.

PELICAN-FLOWER = *Aristolochia grandiflora*.

PELLAEA (pell-ee′a). Cliff brake. A large, widely distributed genus of ferns of the family Polypodiaceae, comprising 85 species, a few grown in the greenhouse or outdoors for ornament. They are mostly rock-inhabiting ferns, most of them inhabiting limestone. Fronds simply compound,* or in some species twice- or thrice-compound,* the stalks sometimes brown-hairy and chaffy, but usually polished and dark-colored. Spore* cases oblongish or circular, usually near tips of free veins, and often covered by the rolled edge

---

* Special articles on the subjects indicated by an asterisk (*) will be found at the words so marked.

of the segment. (*Pellaea* is from the Greek for dusky, in allusion to the usually dark frond stalks.)

The last two species are not hardy in the North and should be grown in the cool greenhouse. *P. atropurpurea*, a native plant, can be grown in the fern garden, preferably on a dry limestone wall. For cult. and propagation *see* FERNS AND FERN GARDENING.

atropurpurea. A hardy fern, not over 1 ft. high, the fronds tough, leathery, only oncecompound,* the stalks dark purple and polished. Segments of the frond about 2 in. long and ⅜ in. wide. Eastern N.A. A plant for the hardy fern garden.

densa = *Cheilanthes densa*.

rotundifolia. Fronds not over 1 ft. long, once-compound,* the stalks shaggy and brownhairy. Ultimate segments alternate, oblongish or rounder, the terminal one arrow-shaped, all faintly angled or toothed, or the margins entire. New Zealand. A greenhouse fern.

viridis. Fronds nearly 2 ft. long, the brown, shining stalk rather stiff and stout. Fronds twice- or thrice-compound,* each main division again compound, the ultimate segments varying from narrow to broad or even oval or arrowshaped. Africa. A greenhouse fern.

PELLIONIA (pell-i-o′ni-a). A genus of 15 species of often creeping herbs, or some a little shrubby, all from tropical As. or the Pacific islands. The cult. species have ornamental foliage, small unisexual, green flowers. Although belonging to the Urticaceae the foliage is without stinging hairs and *Pellionia* is closely related to *Pilea*. Both those below are greenhouse plants and should be grown as with pileas. (*Pellionia* was named for A. M. J. A. Pellion, a ship's officer on Freycinet's journey around the world.)

daveauana = *P. repens*.

pulchra. A fleshy-stemmed, creeping perennial, the stems purplish. Leaves alternate, oblique, the veins blackish on the upper side, purplish on the under side. Indo-China.

repens. A soft, thick-stemmed, creeping perennial with small, alternate leaves that are ½–2 in. long, the blades bronzy green, violettinged or with a central band of bright green. Flowers green and inconspicuous. Indo-Malaya. A handsome foliage plant. Usually offered as *P. daveauana*.

PELLUCID. Having the tissue transparent, as in many water plants.

PELTANDRA (pel-tan′dra). Arrow-arum. North American bog or water herbs of the arum family, one of the two known species occasionally cult. in the bog garden or along the edges of pools. It is the green arrowarum, sometimes called poison arum and known to science as *P. virginica*. Leaves large, coarse, arrow-shaped, the stout, sheathing stalk about 3 times as long as the blade. Spathe* elongated, ultimately leathery and partly enclosing the green, berry-like fruit when ripe. Flowers minute, the male above the female, completely covering the spadix (*see* ARACEAE). There is no difficulty about growing arrow-arum in any wet place, and it will grow well nowhere else, but it can be very invasive. (*Peltandra* is from the Greek

for disks and flowers, in allusion to a technical character of the male flowers.)

peltata, -us, -um (pell-tay′ta). Peltate.*

PELTATE. Having the stalk attached away from the margin of a leaf blade, and

Peltate leaf

often in the center of it. Peltate leaves are apt to be shield-shaped, as in the common garden nasturtium and in the water shield (*Brasenia schreberi*).

PELTIPHYLLUM (pell-ti-fill′um). A monotypic genus of herbs of the saxifrage family, closely allied to *Saxifraga* and differing from it only in technical characters. The only species, **P. peltatum,** the umbrella plant, from wet banks in Ore. and Calif., is much larger than the cult. saxifrages, being a perennial 3–4 ft. high with very large, basal, long-stalked leaves. Leafstalk 2–3 ft. long, the leaves, nearly round, 5–7 in. wide, cut into 9–15 toothed lobes, the leafstalk attached to the middle of the leaf (peltate*). Flowers about ½ in. wide, pinkish-white, very numerous in terminal clusters (corymbs*), appearing before the leaves. Not certainly hardy in the East except in cool, moist sites without bitter winters. (*Peltiphyllum* is from *peltata* and *phylla*, *i.e.*, a peltate* leaf.) The plant is sometimes offered as *Saxifraga peltata*.

PELTOPHORUM (pell-toff′o-rum). A genus of tropical trees of the pea family, only one of the 6 species, **P. pterocarpum,** of hort. interest. It is an Indo-Malayan, quick-growing tree, up to 50 ft. high, planted for ornament in Fla. and throughout the tropics. It has twice-compound,* rusty-hairy leaves, the ultimate leaflets about ¾ in. long, and in 10–20 pairs. Flowers yellow, fragrant, not pea-like, the 5 petals nearly equal. Pod flattish, not splitting. The tree is hardy only in zone* 9, and resembles the royal poinciana except for the yellow flowers. (*Peltophorum* is from the Greek for shield-bearing, in allusion to the shape of the stigma.*) Sometimes offered as *P. ferrugineum* or *P. inerme*.

pendula, -us, -um (pen′dew-la). Hanging.

---

* Special articles on the subjects indicated by an asterisk (*) will be found at the words so marked.

penduliflora, -us, -um (pen-dew-li-flow'ra). With hanging flowers.

PENIOCEREUS (pen-i-o-seer'ee-us). A single species of cactus from western Tex., Ariz., and Mex., **P. greggi**, the deerhorn cactus, cult. in desert gardens for its curious habit, and showy, nocturnal, white flowers. It has a huge, turnip-like root, nearly 2 ft. in diameter, from which arise angled, leafless stems, 6–10 ft. long and about 1 in. in diameter, erect or sprawling. Spines small, black, 6–11 in a cluster, the central one or two erect, the rest divergent. Flowers nearly 8 in. long, white, but reddish on the outside. For culture *see* CACTI. There is one other species from Lower Calif. (*Peniocereus* is from the Greek for phalloid and *Cereus*, in allusion to the shape of the branches.)

pennata, -us, -um (pen-nay'ta). Same as *pinnata*.

PENNISETUM (pen-i-see'tum). A genus of 50 species of chiefly tropical grasses, some economic, and a handful grown for ornament in the border. They are annual or perennial grasses with erect stems (tall in the pearl millet) and grass-like leaves, sometimes colored in the hort. forms. Flowering cluster a spikelike panicle,* the spikelets having beneath them bristles, sometimes plumed, which are often longer than the spikelets. Fruit a grain in the pearl millet and edible. (*Pennisetum* is from the Greek for feather and bristle, in allusion to the often plumed bristles of some species.)

The pearl millet (*P. glaucum*) is a tropical annual, grown in the tropics for its grain which is used as food. In the U.S. it is suited only to the South and is little grown except for forage. *P. alopecuroides* and *P. ruppeli* are ornamental, hardy perennials grown in the border for ornament. They are of easy cult. and may be increased by division.

alopecuroides. A slender-stemmed grass, 2–4 ft. high, hairy as far up as the spike. Leaves bright green. Flowering spike 2–6 in. long, silvery, the anthers* purplish. Bristles of the spikelet long and conspicuous. China. Sometimes known as *P. japonicum*.

americanum = Pennisetum glaucum.

glaucum. Pearl millet, also known as Indian and African millet. A tall, annual, tropical grass of unknown origin, the stems stout, 6–10 ft. high. Leaves 2–3 ft. long, rough on the edges and on the veins. Flowering spike cat-tail-like, 12–18 in. long, with a leaf-like, spreading bract.* Spikelets with plumed bristles. Fruit an egg-shaped, bluish or whitish grain about ⅛ in. long, which usually bursts the enclosing envelope. Occasionally known as *P. americanum*, but probably not American.

japonicum = Pennisetum alopecuroides.

ruppeli. Fountain grass, and the leading ornamental species. A gracefully arching perennial grass 3–4 ft. high. Leaves many, 15–20 in. long, about ⅛ in. wide, sometimes with the margins rolled, green (or variously colored in the hort. forms). Spikes 6–10 in. long, curved or nodding, the bristles of the spikelets about 1 in. long. In the most popular cult. forms the spikes and foliage may be rose-

purple, or, in the *var.* cupreum, coppery. A handsome ornamental grass native in Abyssinia, but hardy over most of the country.

PENNSYLVANIA. The state lies wholly in zones* 3 and 4. Its state flower is the mountain laurel, the state tree the hemlock.

SOILS. Pennsylvania soils vary widely in every possible manner, with the result that the state contains some of the best and considerable areas of the poorer soils in northeastern United States. Soils not adapted for growing any specific class of plants are under a severe handicap. It should be recognized, however, that a particular soil, unsuited for

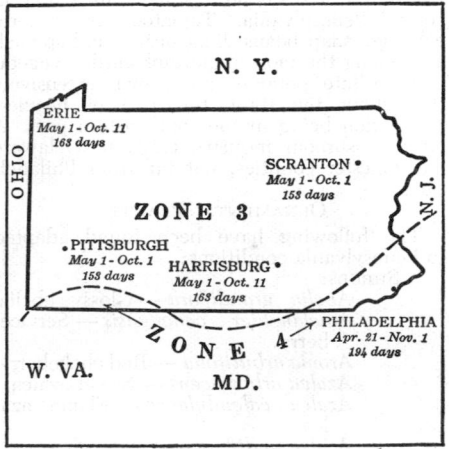

PENNSYLVANIA

The zones of hardiness crossing Pennsylvania are those shown on the map located at ZONE, which should be consulted for details. The dates are the average latest killing frost in spring and the first one in the fall. The figures below the dates show the average length of the growing season.

the commercial production of any given crop, may often be successfully utilized in an amateur way, where the gardener is not dependent for revenue on the produce, and where he feels it worth while in results obtained to go to more trouble and expense to make artificially an area suitable for his purposes than could ever be justified commercially.

CHIEF GARDENING CENTERS. These are in general located in and about the larger cities of the state and in the more densely populated counties surrounding the cities of Pittsburgh, Philadelphia, Scranton, and Harrisburg.

MAIN FRUIT AND VEGETABLE AREAS. The principal fruit crops in Pennsylvania are the apple and the peach. While some orchards are found in most of the counties of the state, the area of greatest concentration is in Adams County near Gettysburg. Other orchards are scattered through south-central Pennsylvania and in eastern Pennsylvania in the Lehigh

* Special articles on the subjects indicated by an asterisk (*) will be found at the words so marked.

Valley. A concentrated fruit and vegetable industry is located near the shores of Lake Erie. Here grapes are the major crop, which is used for making grape juice. Other small fruits, peaches, and sour cherries are also grown here.

Canning crops are produced most abundantly in south-central and central Pennsylvania, although canneries are now found in many parts of the state. Tomatoes, sweet corn, and peas are among the principal vegetables grown for canning. Market garden areas occur throughout the state, being largest in southeastern Pennsylvania; they are also concentrated near other large cities, such as Pittsburgh, and in the Susquehanna Valley in central Pennsylvania. Tomatoes, sweet corn, cabbage, snap beans, lima beans, and spinach are among the more important garden vegetables. White potatoes are grown extensively throughout the state, the area of heaviest production being in the southeastern part. A large mushroom industry exists in Delaware and Chester counties, not far from Philadelphia.

Ornamental Plants

The following have been found adapted to Pennsylvania conditions:

Shrubs:

Abelia grandiflora — Glossy abelia.
Amelanchier canadensis — Serviceberry.
Aronia arbutifolia — Red chokeberry.
Azalea arborescens — Sweet azalea.
Azalea calendulacea — Flame azalea.
Azalea nudiflora — Pinxter-flower.
Azalea viscosa — Swamp honeysuckle.
Berberis thunbergi — Japanese barberry.
Berberis thunbergi minor — Box barberry.
Buxus sempervirens — Common box.
Chaenomeles lagenaria — Flowering quince.
Cornus alba sibirica — Siberian dogwood.
Cornus florida — Flowering dogwood.
Cornus Mas — Cornelian cherry.
Cornus stolonifera — Red osier dogwood.
Daphne Cneorum — Rose daphne.
Deutzia gracilis — Slender deutzia.
Euonymus alata — Winged spindletree.
Euonymus fortunei vegeta — Evergreen bittersweet.
Forsythia intermedia — Golden bell.
Forsythia suspensa — Weeping golden bell.
Hibiscus syriacus — Rose-of-Sharon.
Hydrangea arborescens grandiflora — Hydrangea.
Hypericum prolificum — Shrubby St. John's-wort.
Ilex verticillata — Winterberry.
Kalmia latifolia — Mountain laurel.

Kolkwitzia amabilis — Beauty-bush.
Laburnum anagyroides — Goldenchain.
Ligustrum amurense — Amur River privet.
Ligustrum obtusifolium regelianum — Regel's privet.
Ligustrum vulgare — Common privet.
Lonicera fragrantissima — Winter honeysuckle.
Lonicera japonica halliana — Hall's honeysuckle.
Lonicera maacki — Amur honeysuckle.
Lonicera tatarica — Tartarian honeysuckle.
Myrica pensylvanica — Bayberry.
Pachysandra terminalis — Japanese spurge.
Philadelphus lemoinei — Lemoine mock-orange.
Philadelphus virginalis — Virginal mock-orange.
Rhododendron maximum — Rosebay rhododendron.
Rhodotypos scandens — Jetbead.
Spiraea Bumalda — Anthony Waterer spirea.
Spiraea prunifolia plena — Bridal wreath.
Spiraea thunbergi — Thunberg spirea.
Spiraea vanhouttei — Vanhoutte spirea.
Stephanandra incisa — Cut-leaf stephanandra.
Symphoricarpos chenaulti — Snowberry.
Syringa amurensis japonica — Japanese tree lilac.
Syringa chinensis — Chinese lilac.
Syringa persica — Persian lilac.
Syringa villosus — Late lilac.
Syringa vulgaris — Common lilac.
Viburnum burkwoodi — Burkwood viburnum.
Viburnum cassinoides — Withe-rod.
Virburnum dentatum — Arrow-wood.
Viburnum dilatatum — Linden viburnum.
Viburnum Opulus — European cranberry bush.
Viburnum prunifolium — Black haw.
Viburnum sieboldi — Siebold viburnum.
Viburnum tomentosum — Doublefile viburnum.
Viburnum tomentosum sterile — Japanese snowball.
Vinca minor — Periwinkle.
Weigela florida — Weigela.

Deciduous Trees:

Acer Ginnala — Amur maple.
Acer palmatum — Japanese maple.
Acer platanoides — Norway maple.
Acer saccharum — Sugar maple.
Aesculus octandra — Yellow buckeye.

---

* Special articles on the subjects indicated by an asterisk (*) will be found at the words so marked.

Ailanthus glandulosa — Tree-of-Heaven.
Betula pendula — Weeping birch.
Catalpa speciosa — Northern catalpa.
Cercidiphyllum japonicum — Katsura tree.
Cercis canadensis — American redbud.
Cercis chinensis — Asiatic redbud.
Cladrastris lutea — Yellow-wood.
Crataegus Crus-galli — Cockspur thorn.
Crataegus Oxyacantha — English hawthorn.
Crataegus Phaenopyrum — Washington thorn.
Elaeagnus angustifolia — Russian olive.
Fagus grandifolia — American beech.
Fagus sylvatica — European beech.
Fraxinus americana — White ash.
Ginkgo biloba — Ginkgo or maidenhair-tree.
Gleditsia triacanthos — Honey locust.
Gymnocladus dioica — Kentucky coffee-tree.
Halesia carolina — Silver-bell tree.
Koelreuteria paniculata — Golden-rain tree.
Liquidambar Styraciflua — Sweet gum.
Liriodendron Tulipifera — Tulip-tree.
Magnolia acuminata — Cucumber tree.
Magnolia soulangeana — Soulange magnolia.
Malus atrosanguinea — Carmine crabapple.
Malus floribunda — Japanese flowering crabapple.
Malus hopa — Hopa crabapple.
Malus ioensis plena — Bechtel's crab-apple.
Malus sargenti — Sargent's crabapple.
Platanus acerifolia — London plane.
Prunus sargenti — Sargent's cherry.
Prunus Padus — European bird cherry.
Quercus borealis — Red Oak.
Quercus palustris — Pin oak.
Salix babylonica — Weeping willow.
Sorbus Aucuparia — European mountain-ash.
Tilia americana — American linden.
Tilia europaea — European linden.
Ulmus americana — American elm.

CONIFEROUS EVERGREENS:
Abies concolor — White fir.
Abies veitchi.
Chamaecyparis obtusa — Hinoki cypress.
Chamaecyparis pisifera plumosa.
Juniperus chinensis pfitzeriana.
Juniperus communis depressa — Prostrate juniper.
Juniperus communis hibernica — Irish juniper.
Juniperus horizontalis douglasi — Waukegan juniper.
Juniperus Sabina tamariscifolia.
Juniperus squamata meyeri.
Juniperus virginiana — Red cedar.
Juniperus virginiana glauca.
Larix decidua — European larch.
Picea engelmanni — Engelmann's spruce.
Picea pungens kosteri — Koster's blue spruce.
Pinus resinosa — Red pine.
Pseudotsuga taxifolia — Douglas fir.
Taxus baccata repandens.
Taxus cuspidata — Japanese yew.
Taxus cuspidata capitata.
Taxus cuspidata nana.
Thuja occidentalis — Arborvitae.
Tsuga canadensis — Hemlock.

ANNUALS AND PERENNIALS: Practically all the annual and perennial garden flowers of temperate regions grow in the state.

FROST DATES

Town	Average date of last killing frost in spring	Date when chance of killing frost in spring falls to 10 per cent
Philadelphia	Apr. 21	May 1
Pittsburgh	May 1	May 21
Erie	May 1	May 21
Scranton	May 1	May 21
Harrisburg	May 1	May 21

Town	Average date of earliest killing frost in fall	Date when chance of killing frost in fall rises to 10 per cent
Philadelphia	Nov. 1	Oct. 11
Pittsburgh	Oct. 1	Sept. 21
Erie	Oct. 11	Sept. 21
Scranton	Oct. 1	Sept. 21
Harrisburg	Oct. 11	Oct. 1

The above dates are for the Weather Bureau Stations only. Because of local topography or some other reason, wide variations in the frost dates, hence the length of the growing season, frequently occur in neighboring areas.

RAINFALL

The average total annual precipitation for Pennsylvania varies only slightly with the locality from 36 to somewhat over 40 inches. The rainfall during the growing season from May to September, inclusive, is from 16½ to 18½ inches on the average. However, for any given month from year to year, the total may fluctuate widely. Irrigation where practicable is of value at some period in nearly every year and is often practical in an amateur garden when it is not possible commercially.

The address of the Pennsylvania Agricultural Experiment Station which has supplied this information about the state is University

---

* Special articles on the subjects indicated by an asterisk (*) will be found at the words so marked.

Park, Pennsylvania. The station is always ready to answer gardening questions. Help in answering your problems may be secured through the county agricultural agent who is located at each county seat. His advice is free.

Garden club activities include several clubs of the Garden Club of America, the home office of which is 598 Madison Avenue, New York 22, N.Y. There are also clubs affiliated with the Garden Club Federation of Pennsylvania.

PENNY-CRESS = *Thlaspi*.

PENNYROYAL = *Mentha Pulegium*. See MINT.

PENNYWORT = *Cotyledon umbilica*.

PENSTEMON = *Pentstemon*.

pensylvanica, -us, -um (pen-sil-vay'ni-ka). From Pennsylvania.

pentagona, -us, -um (pen-tag'o-na). Five-angled.

pentagyna, -us, -um (pen-ta-jy'na). With five pistils.*

pentalopha, -us, -um (pen-ta-low'fa). Five-ridged.

pentandra, -us, -um (pen-tan'dra). With five stamens.*

pentantha, -us, -um (pen-tan'tha). Five-flowered.

pentaphylla, -us, -um (pen-ta-fil'la). Five-leaved; or often, with five leaflets.

PENTAS (pen'tas). Chiefly African herbs or under-shrubs of the family Rubiaceae, P. **lanceolata** the only one of the 30 known species of hort. interest. It is a somewhat woody herb 1–2 ft. high, with opposite,* ovalish leaves 4–6 in. long. Flowers tubular, about 1 in. long, pale purple, hairy in the throat, usually stalkless, or nearly so, in a close cluster (cyme* or corymb*). Stamens* usually 5. Fruit dry. This is an attractive greenhouse plant for the North or may be used as a bedding subject in the Far South. It needs a tropical greenhouse and potting mixture* 5 in the North, and can be propagated by cuttings of partly ripened wood over bottomheat.* It is sometimes offered as *P. carnea*, and comes also in white and in red flowers. (*Pentas* is from the Greek for five, in allusion to most of the floral parts being in fives.)

PENTHOUSE GARDEN. See PLANNING THE HOME GROUNDS.

PENTSTEMON (pent-ste'mon). Beardtongue. A large genus of perennial herbs (rarely shrubs) of the family Scrophulariaceae, one of them Asiatic, all the rest of the 300 species North American, chiefly from the western U.S. They have opposite* or whorled* leaves, and showy, 2-lipped,* tubular flowers, mostly in terminal clusters (racemes* or panicles*) that bloom in summer. Calyx* 5-parted. Corolla with the lower lip 3-lobed, the upper lip 2-lobed. Stamens 5, 4 of them fertile, the fifth sterile and often bearded. Fruit a capsule. (*Pent-

stemon* is from the Greek for 5 stamens,* which the genus has, although one is sterile.)

The beardtongues include attractive border plants, some rock garden species, and a few of uncertain hardiness in the eastern states north of zone*4, especially in the case of those species native along the Pacific Coast. The cult. of the species grown chiefly in the rock garden will be found at ROCK GARDEN. The others, all perennials, will often flower rather quickly from seed, some the first year, especially forms known as *P. gloxinioides*. Generally, the beardtongues can be grown in full sunshine, but they tend to die out in a year or so if kept there. Most of them do better if given a light mulch in winter, especially those from the Pacific Coast. Many of the species are important bee plants in the West. The recently organized American Pentstemon Society welcomes those interested in these plants. The secretary is Mrs. E. M. Babb, 215 Lambert Street, Portland, Me.

acuminatus. St. Joseph's-wand. Stems smooth, bluish-green, 1–2 ft. high. Leaves ovalish, 2–3 in. long, without teeth. Flowers about ¾ in. long, blue, the sterile stamen* bearded. Wash. and Ore.

alpinus. Stems smooth, not over 1 ft. high. Leaves lance-shaped, 2–4 in. long, without teeth. Flowers about 1 in. long, bluish-purple, the sterile stamen* not bearded. Rocky Mountains. For cult. *see* ROCK GARDEN.

angustifolius. Stems smooth, bluish-green, not over 12 in. high. Leaves lance-shaped or narrower, 1½–2½ in. long, without teeth. Flowers about ¾ in. long, blue, the sterile stamen* bearded. Prairies from S. Dak. to Mont. and N. Mex. Sometimes known as *P. caeruleus*.

antirrhinoides. A shrub, 3–6 ft. high, not hardy eastward. Leaves oblongish or narrower, about ½ in. long. Flowers about ⅝ in. long, yellow, the sterile stamen* bearded. Southern Calif., and not certainly hardy except in similar climates.

barbatus. A stout perennial 4–6 ft. high, the stems smooth. Leaves narrow. Flowers about 1 in. long, red, the lower lip* bearded, the sterile stamen* not bearded. Utah to Mex. A good pink hort. form is Pink Beauty.

caeruleus = *Pentstemon angustifolius*.

centranthifolius. Scarlet bugler. Stems 2–3 ft. high, bluish-green. Leaves thick, ovalish or narrower, 1½–2½ in. long without teeth. Flowers about 1 in. long, red, the sterile stamen* not bearded. Calif. to Ariz.

Cobaea. A hairy-stemmed perennial 1–2 ft. high. Leaves oblong or wider, 3–5 in. long, toothed. Flowers nearly 2 in. long, purplish, not much 2-lipped, the sterile stamen* bearded. Prairies, Neb. to Tex.

cordifolius. A shrub, half erect or climbing, the stem hairy. Leaves oval, 1–2 in. long, toothed. Flowers about 1 in. long, scarlet, the sterile stamen* bearded. Southern Calif. and not hardy in colder regions.

crandalli. A slightly hairy, more or less prostrate perennial, not over 8 in. high. Leaves oblongish or narrower, not over ¾ in. long. Flowers about 1 in. long, blue, the sterile stamen* bearded. Mountains of Colo.

davidsoni. An alpine, rock-garden, mat-forming, prostrate perennial, not over 2 in. high. Leaves ovalish, about ⅓ in. long, with-

---

* Special articles on the subjects indicated by an asterisk (*) will be found at the words so marked.

out marginal teeth. Flowers about 1¼ in. long, lilac or purple, the sterile stamen* bearded. Pacific Coast.

diffusus. A bushy, hairy perennial 1–2 ft. high. Leaves ovalish or narrower, 1½–2½ in. long, deeply toothed. Flowers blue or purple, about ¾ in. long, the sterile stamen* bearded. British Columbia to Ore.

Digitalis. Foxglove beardtongue. A nearly smooth herb, 3–5 ft. high. Leaves ovalish or narrower, 4–6 in. long, toothed. Flowers about 1 in. long, white (rarely pink), the tube dilated, the sterile stamen* bearded. Quebec to Ala. west to S. Dak. and Tex.

fruticosus. A shrub or tough, woody herb, 3–4 ft. high, the leaves spoon-shaped, about 1 in. long and toothed on the margin. Flowers purple, about 1 in. long, the sterile stamen* smooth. Western N.A.

glaber. A smooth-stemmed perennial, 1–2 ft. high. Leaves oblongish, or broadest toward the tip, 4–6 in. long, without teeth. Flowers about 1 in. long, blue or purple, the sterile stamen* not bearded but somewhat hairy. N. Dak. to Wyo. For cult. *see* ROCK GARDEN.

gloxinioides. A race or group of garden hybrids thought to be derived from crossing *P. hartwegi* and *P. Cobaea.* They are found in many colors and will generally bloom the first year from seed.

grandiflorus. A stout, upright perennial, 4–6 ft. high, the stems smooth. Leaves ovalish or broader toward the tip, 1½–2½ in. long. Flowers lavender-blue, about 2 in. long, the sterile stamen* bearded. Prairies, Ill., N. Dak. and Wyo.

hartwegi. Not over 4 ft. high, the stems nearly smooth, purplish. Leaves ovalish or narrower, without teeth. Flowers very showy, the clusters drooping, the corolla nearly 2 in. long, slightly curved, brilliant scarlet. Colder parts of Mex. and uncertainly hardy northward, even with winter mulch.

heterophyllus. A smooth shrub 3–5 ft. high. Leaves lance-shaped or narrower, 1½–2½ in. long, without teeth. Flowers about 1½ in. long, purple, the sterile stamen* smooth. Calif. For cult. *see* ROCK GARDEN.

hirsutus. A sticky-hairy perennial, 2–3 ft. high. Leaves oblongish or narrower, 3–4½ in. long, toothed. Flowers purple or violet, about 1 in. long, the sterile stamen* and the throat densely bearded. Quebec to Va. and Tex.

laetus. A hairy perennial about 12 in. high, the leaves nearly 3 in. long, lance-shaped or narrower, the margins toothless. Flowers about 1 in. long, bluish-purple or blue, white-marked, in branched clusters (racemes*); the sterile stamen* smooth. Western U.S.

laevigatus. A nearly smooth perennial, 2–3 ft. high. Leaves oblongish or narrower, 4–6 in. long, toothed. Flowers about 1 in. long, purple, the sterile stamen* bearded. N..J to Fla. and westward.

menziesi. A woody-based perennial, 4–6 ft. high, the leaves oblong or ovalish, not over ¾ in. long. Flowers violet-blue or purple, about 1 in. long, the sterile stamen* bearded. May. British Columbia to Ore.

nitidus. Perhaps not specifically distinct from *P. acuminatus,* but differing in its bluish-green foliage and narrower leaves. Flowers blue, about ¾ in. long, the sterile stamen* bearded. Western N.A.

ovatus. A hairy-stemmed perennial, 2–4 ft. high. Leaves broadly oval, 2–3 in. long. Flowers about ¾ in. long, first blue then purple,

the sterile stamen* bearded. Ore. to British Columbia.

rattani. Not over 18 in. high. Leaves oblong or triangular-oval, 1½–2¼ in. long, toothed. Flowers about 1 in. long, lavender, the sterile stamen* not bearded but slightly hairy. Calif.

rupicolus. A shrubby, rock garden plant, not over 5 in. high, the stems hairy. Leaves ovalish or nearly round, bluish-green, not over ½ in. long. Flowers about 1½ in. long, crimson, the sterile stamen* smooth. Wash. For cult. *see* ROCK GARDEN.

scouleri. A woody herb or sub-shrub, 10–18 in. high. Leaves lance-shaped, about 2 in. long, sparingly and minutely toothed. Flowers nearly 2 in. long, lilac or rose-purple, the sterile stamen* smooth. Pacific Coast.

spectabilis. A smooth, bluish-green perennial, 4–6 ft. high. Leaves ovalish or narrower, 2–3½ in. long, toothed. Flowers rose-purple or lilac, about 1 in. long, the sterile stamen* smooth. Ariz. and Calif.

torreyi. Perhaps not more than a variety of *P. barbatus,* but with scarlet flowers and the lower lip not bearded. Colo. to northern Mex.

unilateralis. Not over 2 ft. high, the stems smooth. Leaves narrowly lance-shaped or broadest toward the tip, 3–4 in. long. Flowers about ¾ in. long, blue, the sterile stamen* smooth, the flower cluster 1-sided. Wyo. to Utah. For cult. *see* ROCK GARDEN.

wilcoxi. A smooth erect perennial, 2–4 ft. high, the leaves ovalish, 2–3 in. long, and without marginal teeth. Flowers about ¾ in. long, blue or pink, the sterile stamen* bearded. Northwestern U.S.

PEONY. These outstandingly beautiful garden flowers are all derived from perennial herbs (one woody) of the genus **Paeonia** (pee-ō′ni-a) of the buttercup family, which comprises about 33, chiefly Asiatic, species. Of these the 6 below, with their varieties and derivative hybrids, make up most of the garden peonies of today, although other species are to be found in the collections of fanciers and are used chiefly in making new crosses. All are erect herbs from tuberous or thickened roots, the leaves large, some basal, others on the stem, all compound,* sometimes thrice-compound* or with dissected segments. Flowers large, showy, usually solitary and terminal, rarely a few in a cluster, variously colored (*see* below). Sepals 5. Petals 5–10, but much more numerous in some of the hort. varieties (especially the double-flowered types). Stamens numerous, some of them sterile and petal-like. Fruit a collection of dried pods (follicles*), the seeds fleshy. (Named, or thought to be, for a Greek god of healing, Paeon.)

For culture *see* below. All are spring-blooming.

P. albiflora. The chief source of the Chinese or common peony (*see* below). Root a collection of narrow tubers. Stems erect, unbranched and with one flower, or branched and with 2–5 flowers, usually 2–3½ ft. high. Leaves twice-compound,* the ultimate segments often red-veined, not lobed or dissected, usually oblongish or narrower. Flower stalk long, stout, often bracted.* Petals 8, or much more in

---

* Special articles on the subjects indicated by an asterisk (*) will be found at the words so marked.

some hort. sorts. Stamens* golden-yellow. Fruit usually smooth. Jap., China, and Siberia. Called by some *P. lactiflora*. The *var*. **festiva** has large, white, double flowers. The *var*. **sinensis** has double, very large, crimson flowers. The latter is sometimes offered as *P. sinensis*.

P. lutea. A somewhat shrubby perennial, 2–3 ft. high. Leaves compound, the ultimate segments oblongish, cut or lobed. Flowers nearly 4 in. wide, golden-yellow. Fruit smooth. China.

P. mlokosewitschi. A perennial from the Caucasus, not over 2½ ft. high, the leaves twice-divided, the veins and margins red. Flowers nearly 5 in. wide, yellow. Of chief interest as one of the parents of several hybrid peonies. June.

P. Moutan = *Paeonia suffruticosa*.

P. officinalis. Not over 3 ft. high. Leaves twice-compound,* the oblongish ultimate segments lobed. Flowers nearly 4 in. wide, crimson, white, or yellowish. Fruits white-felty. Southern Eu. and western As. For its varieties *see* below.

P. sinensis = *Paeonia albiflora sinensis*.

P. suffruticosa. Japanese tree peony. A much-branched shrubby plant 4–6 ft. high, often less as cult. Leaves twice-compound,* the ultimate segments 3–5-lobed and pale beneath. Flowers sometimes 12 in. wide, rose-red or white. Fruit densely hairy. China. There are many color forms and varieties (*see* below). Hardy up to zone* 4, and in favorable places to zone* 3.

P. tenuifola. Not over 18 in. high, and with creeping rootstocks. Leaves thrice-compound,* the ultimate segments narrow and fern-like. Flowers 3–4 in. wide, crimson or purple. Fruit hairy. Southeastern Eu. and western As.

VARIETIES

CHINESE, OR ALBIFLORA PEONIES are the descendants of *Paeonia albiflora* (also known as *P. sinensis*), which may probably still be found growing wild in northeastern Asia. The Chinese long ago took the wild plant from its native countryside into their gardens and cultivated it for many centuries until the original small, single flowers in white or mauve-pink were developed into semi-doubles and full doubles in white, pink, and even red; so that when Chinese peonies were first brought to Europe, about 1800, more than a hundred distinct varieties already existed in the gardens of China. We seem to be justified in regarding all varieties in this great group as simply mutations from the original wild plant, without the addition of any other species. These are the common peonies of our gardens.

Chinese peonies soon became popular in Europe and from there came over to America; for 150 years horticulturists have busied themselves with raising plants from seed for the purpose of getting new and improved varieties. These June-blooming peonies are so well suited to the American climate that they have become one of our most widely grown garden plants. Thousands of new varieties have been raised and put on the market, either as cut flowers or for the garden, and the stream shows no signs of abating.

TYPES OF BLOOM among the common peony group consist of (1) singles, (2) "Japanese" and (3) doubles. The singles have only one or two rows of petals, with the true pollen-bearing stamens in the center. Those of the so-called "Japanese" type also have one or two rows of petals, but the central stamens are petaloid* — short or long, flat or twisted, white, yellow, pink, red, or striped, but with no pollen, or very little. The doubles display a still further transformation, in which the stamens have become completely altered into true petals so that the differentiation between outer petals and inner petals is lost.

In compiling the following list of varieties of the common peony, the list of *Most Popular Peonies,* published in 1957 by the American Peony Society, was consulted. Under type and color, the varieties are arranged roughly in the order of blooming.

DOUBLES: *White:* Festiva Maxima, Le Cygne, Kelway's Glorious, Baroness Schroeder, Elsa Sass, Victory. *Blush:* Alice Harding, Frances Willard, Solange. *Light Pink:* Mrs. Franklin D. Roosevelt, Thérèse, Moonstone, Minuet, Hansina Brand, Myrtle Gentry, Nick Shaylor. *Deep Pink:* M. Jules Elie, Walter Faxon, Mrs. Livingston Farrand, Sarah Bernhardt, Blanche King. *Red:* Richard Carvel, Kansas, Félix Crousse, Longfellow, Mary Brand, Matilda Lewis (dark), M. Martin Cahuzac (dark), Karl Rosenfield, Philippe Rivoire (dark), Tempest (dark), Ruth Elizabeth.

"JAPANESE" TYPE (beautiful and much to be recommended): *White:* Isani Gidui. *Pink:* Ama No Sode, Westerner, Tamate Boku, Nippon Gold. *Red:* Hari-ai-nin, Mikado, Charm, Nippon Beauty, Nippon Brilliant.

SINGLES: *White or Blush:* Le Jour, Pico, Krinkled White. *Pink:* Sea-Shell. *Red:* Arcturus, Imperial Red, President Lincoln.

"ANEMONE TYPE" as a term has now rather gone out of use, and varieties such as Laura Dessert and Primevère, once listed, are now usually classed as doubles.

OFFICINALIS PEONIES are derived from a European species (*P. officinalis*) which has been in cultivation for several centuries and which through mutations has yielded a few varieties, some of them double. The single variety *lobata* (sometimes referred to as *peregrina*), and especially *lobata* Sunbeam, is worth growing for its vivid red, but generally speaking, the *officinalis* peonies, as May-blooming garden plants, have been superseded by the tree peonies and by the new hybrids.

HYBRID PEONIES are the new peonies of this century, for only recently has the attention of breeders turned toward the almost unexplored possibilities in crosses between the various species of *Paeonia*. The hybrid tree peonies will be discussed later. In the herbaceous, Lemoine in France introduced in 1905–09 a few lovely hybrids of *P. Wittmanniana* crossed with the Chinese peonies.

---

* Special articles on the subjects indicated by an asterisk (*) will be found at the words so marked.

In America, beginning about 1915–20, several hybridists began independently to cross the albifloras with the many forms of *P. officinalis,* including *lobata.* To Edward Auten, Jr., the late Lyman Glasscock, and the late A. P. Saunders we owe the large majority of a very superb new race of hybrids. Dr. Saunders has in addition produced hybrids from other species, among them *P. coriacea, P. emodi, P. macrophylla,* and *P. mlokosewitschi,* the only truly yellow herbaceous species. (Aside from *P. mlokosewitschi* these species are little known except to specialists. — EDITOR) The new hybrids have greatly extended the color range of our herbaceous peonies, especially in brilliant new pinks and reds, but also in lavenders and ivory yellows; many of them are May-blooming. Several well-known kinds, mostly singles, are listed below (by color and then roughly in order of blooming). *White:* Windflower, Chalice, Garden Peace, White Innocence. *Ivory-yellow:* Lady Gay, Starlight, Claire de Lune, Moonrise. *Pink* (salmon, coral, cherry): Firelight, May Dawn, Salmon Glow, May Delight, Janice, Lovely Rose, Nathalie, Laura Magnuson. *Red* (singles and doubles): Red Charm, Flame, Rose Marie, John Harvard, Chocolate Soldier, Alexander Woollcott, Carina, and Cardinal's Robe.

TREE PEONIES are descendants of the wild plant, *P. suffruticosa,* native to western China. This plant makes a permanent woody growth above ground, whereas the herbaceous kinds die back to the ground in autumn. It was the Chinese who took *P. suffruticosa,* as they did *P. albiflora,* from its native habitat into their gardens many centuries ago, cultivated it, and developed it into our modern tree peony; but the Japanese commercialized it, hence the name "Japanese tree peony" by which it is usually known. It is called by the Chinese the "King of Flowers," and it is in truth not only the grandest of all the peonies, but one of the most beautiful of all garden plants. The single and semi-double forms are generally preferred by connoisseurs to the more lumpy-appearing doubles.

The tree peony, after suffering from undeserved neglect in America during the past 40 years, is now apparently coming into its own, and there are now a number of nurseries offering fine kinds. Tree peonies bloom in May, and come in white, blush, all shades of pink and red (including some splendid cherries and scarlets), and on into crimson and darkest maroon, as well as magenta, purple, and lilac-rose. There are indeed many hundreds of names, and those of any one color differ a little from one another, and all are so splendid that the purchaser is counseled to take the advice of any highly-recommended nursery. Certainly almost any white or light pink is sure to be beautiful. These names, while not offered with any idea that they are the best, may serve as suggestions. Listed by approximate color, and then alphabetically, all are single or semi-double. *White:* Gessekai, Renkaku, Tama sudare, Yaso okina. *Pale and light pink:* Howzan, Shin ten shi, Tama fuyo, Yae zakura. *Deep and bright pink:* Hatsu hinode, Kagura jishi, Shu ja kumon. *Red:* Hinode sekai, Impumon. *Deep purple-maroon:* Kokamon, Rimpo, Suma no ichi, Ubatama.

A very remarkable new race of hybrids has been produced by crossing the tree peony with the wild yellow *P. lutea.* Begun by Lemoine, this work was carried on by A. F. Saunders. These lutea hybrids range in color from palest yellow through gold, tea-rose, apricot, to crimson and deep mahogany-red. Among the best of these are: Souvenir de Maxime Cornu, Alice Harding, and Chromatella among the French doubles, and Argosy, Silver Sails, Age of Gold, Harvest, Renown, and Black Pirate among the American kinds, chiefly single or semi-double.

CULTURE AND CARE

Set herbaceous peonies, only in autumn, so that the buds or eyes are no deeper than 2 inches below ground level (higher in warm climates). The ground should be well prepared in advance. If new plants must be set in ground that formerly contained peonies, the soil should be very thoroughly turned over and re-enriched. A hole 2 feet wide and 2 feet deep is a minimum. All peonies like full or almost full sunlight, free air circulation, and plenty of water, but *good drainage* is an essential. In fall, cut back all stalks of herbaceous peonies to the ground, remove, and destroy. Disease may be harbored by too heavy mulches or other surface debris, by continued or undrained moisture, or continued warmth. Healthful measures are: sunlight, circulating air, good drainage, and good feeding. Bone meal (one handful per plant in spring and fall) is safe and beneficial. Manure should be well aged and should never come in contact with roots or stems. Use commercial fertilizers very sparingly, if at all. Tree peonies and lutea hybrids like the same treatment, except that half-shade will protect the delicate blooms. These are usually grafted plants. Today, deep planting is recommended. The cion* (top part), whether or not it has made any "own roots," may be buried halfway, or even more.

PEONIES FROM SEED. Peonies are easily raised from seed. Sow in autumn in the open, either in a frame or well-prepared bed. Some will germinate the following spring, but most the spring after that. Bloom may appear in the third year or later. A plant six or seven years old may begin to show its permanent qualities, such as doubleness, etc. Only species seedlings will come true; seedlings of hybrids or of "developed" kinds, such as the albifloras or the tree peonies, will be unlike the parent plant in color and form. The hope of producing new varieties distinct from or superior to those already in existence lies in an

---

* Special articles on the subjects indicated by an asterisk (*) will be found at the words so marked.

immense mass production of seedlings, or in careful intercrossing between parents selected for highest quality, or in actual hybridization, using the species or some of the new hybrids of known fertility.

PROPAGATION of herbaceous peonies is fairly easy but it is slow, which accounts for the fact that some varieties remain rather expensive for quite a number of years. Any mature plant, with five or more stems, may be lifted in the fall, the long roots cut back to six inches or less, and the clump washed clean with a hose. It may then be cut up into pieces, each of which should consist of at least one bud or "eye" with a well-attached piece of root. (Eyes with very little root will probably grow, but "blind" roots, without eyes, will not. Only *P. officinalis* and some of its hybrids are exceptions to this rule.) These divisions are then planted, and in several years, when they have matured, the process of propagation may be repeated.

Propagation of tree peonies and their hybrids is best done by grafting upon herbaceous peony roots, preferably the albifloras. Practically all commercial stocks are done in this way. In any case *P. officinalis* roots should not be used, for they make buds on root fragments, resulting in undesirable suckers.

The American Peony Society exists to further public interest in and knowledge of the peony. It publishes a quarterly bulletin and organizes an annual peony exhibit. The Society's small comprehensive *Handbook* is available from the secretary, Mr. George W. Peyton, Box 1, Rapidan, Virginia. — S. S.

DISEASES. The most common disease of peony is flower blight* which is most serious during prolonged wet spells. Just as buds are ready to open, use pesticide #11 (*see* SPRAYS AND DUSTS) and repeat at 5-day intervals during the blooming period.

If all leaves in a clump suddenly wilt and die, inspect the soil at the base of the leafstalks for small brown or black seed-like objects. These indicate a wilt* disease and the clump should be dug, all top growth discarded, and the roots set in another location.

If leaves have mosaic* or ring-spot* symptoms it is best to discard the entire clump, since some of these virus diseases will live from year to year in the plant.

There are a number of minor leafspots* and blights but these are not usually serious enough to warrant use of pesticides.

PEPEROMIA (pep-er-ō′mi-a). A huge genus of tropical, often fleshy herbs of the family Piperaceae, only those below of the 500 known species in general cult. They are chiefly Brazilian, stemless herbs very widely grown as foliage plants by florists. Leaves thick, fleshy, ovalish, without teeth, the thick, red stalk often attached away from the margin (peltate*). Flowers minute, crowded on a dense, slender, usually curving spike. For details *see* PIPERACEAE. These very popular little plants require a tropical greenhouse, plenty of moisture, and benefit from fortnightly applications of liquid ma-

nure. They root easily from cuttings (or even from cut leaves) in sand over bottom-heat. While they are plants of the moist Brazilian forests, they are also good pot plants for the living room. *See* HOUSE PLANTS. (*Peperomia* is from the Greek for pepper-like, in allusion to its close relationship to the true pepper.)

argyreia. The most commonly cult. species and an excellent house plant. It is a stemless herb, 4–6 in. high, the white-marked, ovalish, red-stalked, basal leaves 3–5 in. long, the stalk attached away from the margin (peltate*). Flowers minute, crowded on a dense, slender, usually curving spike. Brazil. Usually offered under the incorrect names of *P. sandersi* or *P. sandersi argyreia.*

obtusifolia. A partially prostrate or decumbent herb, the stems wrinkled, reddish, and rooting at the joints. Leaves oblongish, 3–5 in. long, slightly notched at the tip, eared at the base, the margins reddish. Flowers minute, on red-stalked spikes. Tropical America.

sandersi, and *var.* **argyreia** = *P. argyreia.*

DISEASES. The base of peperomia and the lower leaves where they touch the soil may turn black and rot. Watering plants from the bottom will help to prevent this disease.

Plants which show symptoms of ring-spot* virus should be destroyed and no propagating material should be taken from them.

PEPINO = *Solanum muricatum.*

Pepo (peep′o). Pre-Linnaean* name for the pumpkin. It is also the modern botanical name for the specialized type of berry found in most plants of the cucumber family. It is a fleshy fruit that does not split and usually has a hard rind. Common examples are the watermelon, melon, pumpkin, and the gourds.

PEPPER. For the true pepper (the spice) *see* PIPER. For the red, Cayenne, green, and other fleshy-fruited peppers *see* CAPSICUM.

PEPPER-BUSH = *Leucothoë racemosa.* For the sweet pepper-bush *see* CLETHRA.

PEPPER FAMILY = Piperaceae.

PEPPER-GRASS. See LEPIDIUM.

PEPPERIDGE = *Nyssa sylvatica.*

PEPPERMINT = *Mentha piperita.* See MINT.

PEPPERMINT GERANIUM = *Pelargonium tomentosum.*

PEPPERMINT GUM = *Eucalyptus amygdalina.*

PEPPER-ROOT. See DENTARIA.

PEPPER-TREE. The tree that produces ordinary pepper (the spice) is *Piper nigrum* (which see). For the plant commonly called pepper-tree in Calif. and elsewhere *see* SCHINUS MOLLE.

PEPPER-VINE = *Ampelopsis arborea.*

PEPPERWORT. See MARSILEA.

PERAMIUM = *Goodyera.*

peregrina, -us, -um (pe-re-gry′na). Foreign or exotic.

PERENNIAL. Lasting through more than

---

two seasons' growth, often much more. Perennial is usually applied, especially by gardeners, only to herbs, but all woody plants are, of course, perennial in their growth. For the uses of perennial herbs in the garden *see* PERENNIALS. *See also* ANNUAL, BIENNIAL.

PERENNIAL CANDYTUFT = *Iberis sempervirens*. *See* CANDYTUFT.

PERENNIAL HONESTY = *Lunaria rediviva*. *See* HONESTY.

PERENNIAL PEA = *Lathyrus latifolius*.

PERENNIAL PHLOX = *Phlox paniculata*.

PERENNIAL RYE GRASS = *Lolium perenne*.

PERENNIALS. A perennial is a nearly ever-living plant. It forms the background of all gardens in temperate climates. It is the encouragement of the beginning gardener; it is the stay of the advanced one. Its growth, generous and fine, means that it may be divided and shared, thus giving it a true social value; and its beauty for gardens great or humble is undisputed. William Robinson and Miss Jekyll have earned the undying homage of all good gardeners, the one for his re-introducing of perennials into gardens, the other for her pictures of high beauty in their use.

LIST. A partial list of the more important perennials follows:

Alyssum, arabis, hardy aster in variety, astilbe, aubrieta, avens, betony, bluebells, boltonia, bugle, bugloss, campanula in variety, campion, candytuft, cerastium, Christmas rose, chrysanthemum in variety, cinquefoil, clematis, coreopsis, evening primrose, gaillardia, gas-plant, globeflower, globe thistle, gypsophila, incarvillea, iris in variety, larkspur in variety, lily in variety, mallow, nepeta, pea, pentstemon, peony in variety, pink, plantain-lily, plume poppy, polemonium, poppy, rock cress, St. John's-wort, sneezeweed, speedwell, spiderwort, sunflower, thermopsis, thrift, torch lily, valerian, wild indigo, wormwood in variety, yarrow and yucca.

But what a poor substitute for description are the words "in variety" here. This list tells nothing of the loveliness of the newer hardy asters, it gives no hint of the pearl-like buds of wormwood, *Artemisia vulgaris lactiflora*, of the soft effect of *Artemisia* Silver King, so useful as a "between plant" in the border. Such alyssums as Silver Queen (*A. saxatile*), such candytufts as Queen of Italy, such irises as those from the early *I. pumila* to the latest Japanese varieties, with the great range of beautiful flowers between — all come to mind as the generic names are written. Delphiniums are in marvelous colors today, of many types and even of many heights. Among larkspurs, *Delphinium grandiflorum* is one of the best of all perennials, 2–4 ft. high and of a pure cobalt blue. And the tall kinds are now so familiar as to need no heralding. From lily-of-the-valley and *Lilium tenuifolium*, which is perhaps the smallest of all lilies, to *L. regale*, *L. specio-*

sum and the great *L. auratum*, this family is now widely spread over the gardens of the world.

PROPAGATION

The simplest ways of raising perennials in one's own garden are from seed, by division, and by root cuttings. There is no such interesting gardening as this; there is none so economical. We sow in July a few lines of a precious variety of delphinium from some foreign source or from our own good plant; we almost forget the existence of the row of seedlings; suddenly in the following year a rarely lovely spire of blue shows itself on a two-foot plant, and we remember that in this place last summer we carefully put in seed. For seeding, the earth should be of good quality and finely worked, and if the soil is heavy, mix sand with it. Partial shade is a help to quick germination.

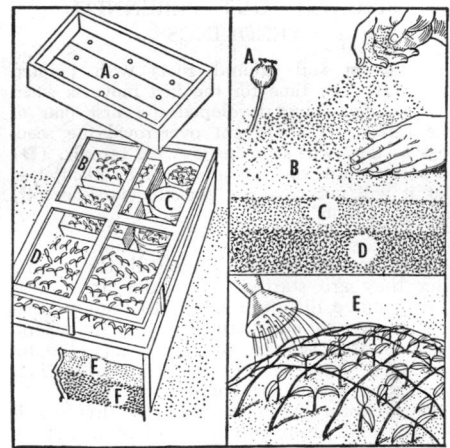

RAISING PERENNIALS FROM SEED

At the left: A flat (*A*) and the young seedlings in flats or pots (*B, C,* and *D*) in a hotbed. Note the depth of soil (*E*) and manure (*F*) in the hotbed. Electric cables often replace manure. (*See* COLD FRAME.)

At the right: planting poppy seeds directly where they are shed (*A*). Sow them broadcast (*B*), give very shallow covering of soil and press in firmly with the hands or a board. The upper layer of soil (*C*) should be finely pulverized, and the soil thoroughly spaded below this (*D*). Cover the seedbed with brush (*E*) and water very gently every other day.

Sow the seed thinly in the row, cover to about three times its own thickness, and firm the earth down with a board. If the weather is dry after sowing in the open border or bed, sprinkle every other day. Keep weeds down after the seedlings are large enough so that weeding will not disturb their roots, and cultivate when the plants are strong enough to bear this. In a northern climate,

---

* Special articles on the subjects indicated by an asterisk (*) will be found at the words so marked.

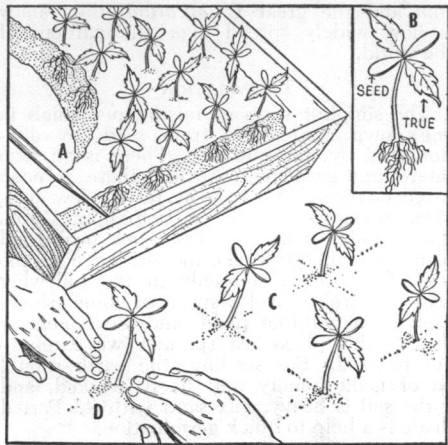

PRICKING OUT PERENNIAL SEEDLINGS

(A) Loosen soil around roots with pointed stick. (B) The time for the first move is when the seedlings have developed the first pair of true leaves. (C) Do not overcrowd the seedlings as they will soon be growing rapidly. (D) Be sure to firm the soil around each plantlet so that it will not have air pockets (*i.e.*, no soil) around its roots.

do not transplant seedlings till the spring after they are started; in milder areas it is well to move little perennials to their permanent places in early autumn, say mid-Sept. Such is the variety of American climates and soils, however, that minute directions cannot be given for this procedure.

Propagation by cuttings or by dividing is a quick and interesting method of increasing the stock of perennials. Nothing is more pleasing than to see how quickly a row of two-inch-long cuttings of roots of the hardy phlox, *Phlox suffruticosa*, set in rows in a seedbed in Sept., will send up leaflets. Take up a root with a sharp knife or scissors, cut any or all of the rootlets into two-inch lengths, and plant them in well-prepared ground in an upright position, with the top about half an inch below the surface. Growth will soon start. Oriental poppies, arabis, Japanese anemone and gypsophila, and *Anchusa azurea*, may also be increased in this manner. German iris and the other tall bearded irises and hybrids should be taken up very soon after blooming, say in July, the earth shaken from their rootstocks and these pulled gently apart, leaving at least three rootlets to every rhizome. They may be cut apart with a sharp knife or spade, but pulling is better. *Arabis alpina* (the double-flowered form), so much finer than the single variety, may be increased by taking cuttings of the young growth in June and growing them in sand.

Most gardeners divide perennials at the end of three years, as they begin to show signs of straggling or thinning out. In the colder climates dividing is much better done in spring than in autumn, but it should take place early, when the leaves are not more than two in. high. In the case of Michaelmas daisies or hardy asters which increase tremendously in favorable seasons, the whole root should be lifted, and the ring of plantlets surrounding the old central root should be the only parts used. In hardy phloxes the plant may be cut with a sharp spade into as many small sections as desired. To divide herbaceous peonies (the tree peony cannot be divided), lift and wash the root and separate the sections with a sharp knife.

CARE AND CULTIVATION

Set perennials in well-spaded and well-manured ground. As a rule perennial plants stay in one position for a long time, only the quickly spreading ones, such as Michaelmas daisies, dracocephalum and the like, needing an annual thinning out; therefore an especially well-prepared soil is the great thing toward success. Most plants prefer full sun, though the plantain-lilies and certain lilies, such as *Lilium regale*, will do well in half-shade. The application of a good commercial fertilizer is advised when plants are in bud, or bone meal in the early stage of growth. Frequent cultivating, especially in dry weather, will enormously improve the plants and their bloom. With these precautions, and with a light mulch of leaves or hay (sometimes held down by cornstalks) for the first winter, perennials should become the most valuable additions to the flower border, because the most striking and permanent.

The cutting back of perennial plants is an important part of their care. Michaelmas daisies may be kept at almost any desired height by cutting them judiciously in June. Peonies will send forth magnificent blooms if only one bud is allowed to one stem. Delphiniums, of course, have a second bloom if cut back after the first one. The persistence of hollyhock plants is greatly encouraged if they are cut back hard after blooming, though now and then a special stalk may be reserved for seed. Such low-growing subjects as the hardy alyssums and the dwarf veronicas should be cut back hard after flowering and well fertilized to give strength for next year's bloom.

WINTER PROTECTION

It is often forgotten that the real danger to perennial plants does not come in winter but in spring, with its alternate freezing and thawing. For that reason, with plants that must be protected, leaves should not be closely packed around their roots or crowns; some light framework, such as evergreen boughs or tree branches, should first be placed over the plants and the leaves laid upon these, thus keeping the plants beneath dry. No covering should be done until the ground is frozen.

The longevity of perennials is touched

---

* Special articles on the subjects indicated by an asterisk (*) will be found at the words so marked.

upon constantly in garden writing, but few records seem to have been kept. There is known, however, a plant of dictamnus which has lived in a New England garden through four generations. The perennials observed as hardy in northeastern N.Y., after the rigors of two unusually severe winters, are: peonies, iris, pinks, certain campanulas, *Pentstemon glaber,* iberis, arabis, delphinium, phloxes in variety, lily-of-the-valley, veronica, lilies, such as *Lilium candidum, regale,* and *elegans,* also *Nepeta, Thalictrum, Platycodon, Heuchera, Sidalcea, Anchusa,* columbine, *Armeria, Thermopsis, Hemerocallis,* and sedum.

GROUPING

A vast and most pleasurable aspect of this subject is the grouping of perennials, but it can be only lightly touched upon here. As to variety of perennials in one border, it is safe to say that all may be used together, provided that enough gray-leaved plants such as *Stachys lanata* and *Cerastium tomentosum* for the front of the border, *Eryngium amethystinum* and the ornamental thistles, and such plants as *Aruncus sylvester,* boltonia, hardy asters, *Artemisia vulgaris lactiflora,* and thalictrums, are placed among other flowers of brighter colors. These plants, of more or less subdued color, harmonize the other hues, and the result may be as beautiful as an old Persian rug. For contrasts in color, either in planting or for cutting — and nothing is so fine as the right tall tulip or the right perennial in flower before a shrub which has proved itself a beautiful companion — there are these one or two suggestions: *Iris variegata,* Sachem below the lilac (*Syringa sweginzowi superba*); iris Monsignor or Archevêque with *Veronica latifolia,* Royal Blue nearby; tree peony Argosy near a Persian Yellow Rose, *Tripterygium* fronted by a damask rose, or golden-leaved privet with a foreground of the hardy alyssum Basket-of-Gold, will illumine even a shaded border in early spring. *Elsholtzia stauntoni* is charming in early Sept. with dwarf hardy asters below its racemes of lavender.

A good juxtaposition of perennials for July would be *Thalictrum glaucum* with a tall delphinium nearby, such as Isla, the new beauty from England, or some of the light blue Lyondel delphiniums, or *Clematis recta* and *Salvia nemorosa* below all these. This results in a nice picture of pale yellow, light blue, cream-white and deep violet flowers in one and the same spot. *Iris sibirica* Perry's Blue — the bluest of irises — with one of the new varieties of daylilies below it, or again, the same iris beside a blooming plant of peony Thérèse, make two excellent combinations. Rose Frau Karl Druschki, one of the hardiest of the family, with *Salvia farinacea* below and around it makes a picture worth creating, though the salvia is hardy only in the warmer parts of the country. *Lilium elegans,* its orange-red blooms against masses of common elder, delphinium (larkspur) near the rich pink of clematis Ville de Lyon grown against a wall, these complement each other unusually well. Endless is the variety in placing, lovely are the pictures that ensue when the perennial plant is part of a good composition in gardens. — L. Y. K.

If it were possible to pick the twenty leading genera from which to select the most popular garden perennials they would probably be found among the following. All of them have special articles on them where the different species and their culture should be sought. Some of these genera also contain annuals* (which see):

Achillea	Gypsophila
Alyssum	Heuchera
Anemone	Lilium
Aquilegia (*see* COLUMBINE)	Lupinus
Aster (not the China aster)	Paeonia (*see* PEONY)
Campanula	Papaver (*see* POPPY)
Chrysanthemum	Pentstemon
Delphinium	Phlox
Dianthus	Primula
Digitalis (*see* FOXGLOVE)	Veronica

perennis, -e (per-en'nis). Perennial.*

PERESKIA (per-res'ki-a). Tropical American, tree-like, shrubby or vine-like cacti, unlike all others in bearing true, flat, alternate* leaves. Of the 20 known species the two below have long been grown for their fruit or for ornament, especially in the tropics. They have woody, branching stems which are spiny. Spines in pairs, without sheaths and without the cushion of barbed bristles found in the closely related genus *Opuntia.* Flowers in small clusters (in ours), the stamens* numerous. Fruit fleshy, juicy, often edible. (Named for N. Claude Fabry de Peiresc, French scientist.)

For cult. *see* CACTI. They can only be grown in frost-free regions, and are not generally grown in the greenhouse.

aculeata. Barbados gooseberry; also called lemon vine and blade-apple. Ultimately a woody vine 10–20 ft. long, at first shrubby and erect. Leaves oblongish, 2–3 in. long, short-stalked. Spines usually 2 to a cluster, curved. Flowers about 1½ in. wide, fragrant, white, yellowish or pink, mostly in clusters (corymb* or panicle*). Fruit about ¾ in. in diameter, yellow. Tropical America. There is a variety with crimson, yellow, and green leaves.

Bleo. A shrub or tree 10–20 ft. high, the trunk often 4 in. thick and spiny. Leaves oblongish, 3–6 in. long. Spines solitary, straight. Flowers 1½–2 in. wide, rose-purple. Fruit pear-shaped, 1–2 in. long. Brazil. Often cult. under the name *P. grandifolia.*

grandifolia. Usually the plant cult. as this is *P. Bleo.*

PERFECT. As to flowers, those that bear both male (stamens*) and female (pistils*) organs of reproduction. *See* COMPLETE and ESSENTIAL ORGANS.

perfoliata, -us, -um (per-fo-li-ā'ta). Perfoliate; *i.e.,* with the stem passing through the leaf, as in some honeysuckles.

---

* Special articles on the subjects indicated by an asterisk (*) will be found at the words so marked.

perforata, -us, -um (per-fore-ray′ta). Perforated, *i.e.*, with holes.

PERFUME PLANTS. The cultivation of plants from which volatile and aromatic oils are commercially extracted is not to be undertaken lightly by anyone, for it is very much in the same category as the cultivation of medicinal plants. In other words, the risks are great and the production of these oils abroad is an old, established art.

Comparatively few plants are used in the art of perfumery on a scale to make their cult. worth while, for many very sweet-smelling flowers are useless when it comes to holding their odor long enough to be worth cult. for perfumery. For the leading sorts *see* FRAGRANCE. *See also* CANANGA.

Plants actually used in perfumery, such as the rose, violet, and lavender, are all but unknown in this country as commercial sources of their beautiful odors. The cult. of them for this purpose is practically confined to southern Eu. and Asia Minor.

Of the plants containing volatile oils in sufficient strength to be worth extracting, only the following are of possible significance in the U.S.

Peppermint	Tansy	Lavender
Spearmint	Wormseed	Rosemary
Wormwood	Rose geranium	Thyme

Of these the rose geranium, which yields an oil indispensable in perfume manufacture, is by far the most important, but the chief source of it, commercially, is still Turkey and northern Africa. And this illustrates as well as any other on the list the difficulty of growing such plants here in competition with old and practiced growers.

Climate, soil, the time of harvesting, and special strains or varieties of these plants, all make it a decidedly expert business to grow any of them for the perfume trade. The quality and quantity of the oil vary from season to season, and especially from youth to age of the plant. Most of them appear to be at their most fragrant stage about the time of blooming.

The extraction of the oil is a highly technical chemical problem needing expert training. All of which means that growing perfume plants may be a very pleasant, fragrant pastime for the gardener, but except, possibly, in Calif. it cannot be considered much else. The sole exception is, of course, the large-scale extraction of peppermint and spearmint oil in Mich. and Wash., but neither are real perfume plants.

While the commercial extraction of perfumes is thus a rather technical process, anyone may experiment in homemade perfume making by following the directions below: Put at the bottom of a stone jar a layer of cotton batting about 1 in. thick, thoroughly soaked in pure olive oil. Upon the oil-soaked cotton place a thin layer of whatever flower you desire, preferably picked early in the morning of the day you begin the operation. Pull off all green parts of the flower (calyx*

or bracts*), and if the petals are thick, detach them. Over the layer of flowers sprinkle a little common salt. Repeat the process until the jar is filled with alternate layers of oil-soaked cotton and salt-sprinkled petals — all well pressed down. Then tie a piece of oiled paper over the jar and put it in the sun for two days.

This is usually long enough for nearly all the fragrance of the flowers to have passed into the oil-soaked cotton. Put the latter into a clean cheesecloth bag and squeeze out all the oil that you can into stoppered bottles. Such a mixture will make a surprisingly delightful homemade perfume.

PERGOLA. *See* STRUCTURES.

pergracilis, -e (per-gras′il-is). Very slender.

PERIANTH. Collective term for the calyx* and corolla,* especially when they are more or less indistinguishable, as in many lilies and other monocotyledons.*

PERICARP. The ripened wall of the ovary,* usually much modified in the mature fruit; sometimes fleshy, or even bony as in nuts.

Periclymenum (pe-ri-cly′men-um). Pre-Linnaean* name for the woodbine (*Lonicera Periclymenum*).

PERIGYNOUS. Having the calyx,* stamens,* etc., inserted around the ovary and not below it. A common example is the apple blossom, which has an inferior* ovary, the stamens,* calyx,* etc., being inserted around it, hence *perigynous.*

PERILLA (per-rill′a). A small genus of tender, herbaceous annuals of the mint family, natives of eastern Asia. Leaves green, or dark reddish-brown, in opposite* pairs, inversely heart-shaped. Flowers small, in pairs, borne in the axils* of bracts in terminal racemes.* (Origin of name obscure.)

They are suitable for beds or borders where color contrasts are required. Propagated by seeds or cuttings. Seeds should be sown under glass in Feb. or Mar. in a temperature of about 60°, in finely sifted, sandy soil, ⅛ in. deep. Transplant to pots or boxes in potting mixture* 2, and transfer outdoors at the end of May. Cuttings may be made in Aug. and kept through the winter in a warm greenhouse, from which cuttings may be taken again in spring for planting out in May. It frequently self-sows in warmer parts of the country.

frutescens. Leaves green on both sides, occasionally marked reddish-brown, opposite, slightly wrinkled, inversely heart-shaped, the margins slightly toothed, 3–6 in. long. Flowers 3–8 in a raceme,* the corolla white, sometimes tinged red, and small. India and Jap. The *var.* **crispa** is the form generally cult. in gardens, its leaves of dark reddish-brown with bronzy sheen being particularly handsome. This variety rarely grows more than 2 ft. high, and is often called beefsteak plant.

nankinensis = *Perilla frutescens crispa.*

PERIPLOCA (per-ip′lo-ka). Silk vine. A small genus of Old World milky-juiced,

---

* Special articles on the subjects indicated by an asterisk (*) will be found at the words so marked.

woody vines of the milkweed family, one of them, **P. graeca**, of southern Eu. and western As., a stem-climbing vine grown for ornament from zone* 5 southward. It may climb up 25–40 ft. high, and has opposite,* oblongish, stalked leaves, 2–4½ in. long, without marginal teeth, dark shining green above, paler beneath. Flowers about 1 in. wide, greenish-brown, in long-stalked terminal clusters (cymes*), the corolla wheel-shaped, its lobes oblong, softly hairy and spreading. Fruit a collection of narrow, smooth pods (follicles*) 3–5 in. long. It is easily propagated by seeds or by layering, and is inclined to be invasive. (*Periploca* is from the Greek for twine and about, in reference to the twining habit.)

PERISTERIA (pe-ri-ster'i-a). Tropical American orchids, the genus mostly South American, with evergreen foliage and large pseudobulbs.* The only cult. species, of the 10 known, is **P. elata**, a remarkable, waxy-flowered orchid from Panama, variously called Holy Ghost flower, dove flower, and dove orchid. It has 3–5 large, plaited leaves to each pseudobulb,* the blade nearly 3 ft. long and about 6 in. wide. Flowering spike nearly 5 ft. high, composed of 12–25 flowers that are about 2 in. wide, fragrant, white, but the lip* spotted with red inside, the whole flower cup-shaped and very beautiful. July–Aug. For cult. *see* the section on greenhouse orchids at ORCHID. (*Peristeria* is Greek for dove, in allusion to the shape of the flower.)

PERISTROPHE (per-i-strō'fe). A genus of 15 species of chiefly tropical, Old World herbs or under-shrubs of the family Acanthaceae, two of them somewhat grown in the greenhouse for ornament. Leaves opposite,* without marginal teeth. Flowers in few-flowered clusters, each surrounded by a series of bracts* which are longer than the 5-lobed calyx. Corolla irregular,* the tube expanded, the limb 2-lipped,* the lower lip 3-lobed or 3-toothed. Stamens* 2. Fruit a capsule.* (*Peristrophe* is from the Greek for belted around, in allusion to the involucre*-like bracts beneath the flowers.)

They should be grown in the warm-temperate greenhouse in potting mixture* 4, and need plenty of moisture, but not too moist air. Easily propagated by cuttings, but the first species is usually grown as an annual.

angustifolia. Probably an annual and usually grown as such, much-branched, weak but ultimately erect. Leaves lance-shaped, 2–3 in. long, tapering both ends. Flowers red, the bracts* hairy-margined. Java. Chiefly grown in the *var.* **aureo-variegata,** which has yellow-variegated leaves.

speciosa. An erect or spreading, somewhat woody under-shrub, 2–3 ft. high, the stems more or less swollen at the joints. Leaves ovalish or elliptic, 4–5 in. long. Flowers violet-purple, about 2 in. wide and long, the stamens* protruding beyond the lower lip. India.

PERIWINKLE = *Vinca minor.*

PERLITE. A white, glass-like, silica de-

rivative, about ⅒ the weight of sand, useful as a cutting medium but without any nutrients. *See* VERMICULITE.

PERMANGANATE OF POTASSIUM. Once widely used to get rid of earthworms, but now replaced by chlordane. *See* EARTHWORMS.

PERNETTYA (per-net'ti-a). Evergreen shrubs of the heath family, ranging from Mex. to Tierra del Fuego, only **P. mucronata** of its 25 known species of hort. interest. It is a low, much-branched shrub, not over 2 ft. high. Leaves alternate,* short-stalked, ovalish, about ¾ in. long, usually bristly-toothed. Flowers about ¼ in. long, solitary, nodding, the corolla urn-shaped, white or pinkish. Fruit a many-seeded red berry, but lilac in the *var.* **lilacina;** bright red in the *var.* **coccinea;** and white in the *var.* **alba.** May–June. Chile. Grown chiefly for the attractive, winter-persisting fruit. Hardy from zone* 5 southward, and preferring a moist, sunny, rather acid soil; suited only to the Pacific Coast. (Named for A. J. Pernetty, who wrote *A Voyage to the Falkland Islands.*)

PEROVSKIA. Russian sage. A small, central Asian genus of salvia-like herbs or under-shrubs, belonging to the mint family (*see* LABIATAE) one of them, **P. atriplicifolia,** grown for ornament. It is a shrubby plant 3–5 ft. high, the foliage with a sage-like odor when bruised. Leaves nearly lance-shaped or broader, coarsely toothed, 1½–4 in. long. Flowers blue, in scattered and widely spaced whorls at the tip, blooming in Sept. The plant is not quite hardy in the North, but new shoots appear if it has been winter-killed. It prefers open sunny places and can be propagated by summer cuttings which root easily, preferably under glass in the North. (*Perovskia* was named for Vasili A. Perovski, a Russian governor of Orenberg, a former province in the Volga region.)

perpusilla, *-us*, *-um* (per-pew-sil'la). Very small.

PERSEA (per'see-a). Tropical or subtropical trees and shrubs, usually aromatic, belonging to the family Lauraceae, all but one of the 50 known species American, the other from the islands of Canary, Madeira, or Azores. The chief hort. species is *P. americana*, the avocado; the other two cult. species are grown for ornament. Leaves alternate,* without marginal teeth. Flowers small, greenish, the petals and sepals similar, usually totaling 6. Stamens* 12. Fruit a drupe (large in the avocado). (*Persea* is an ancient name for some Persian or Egyptian tree, and of no known application to these.)

For the culture and varieties of the avocado *see* AVOCADO. The other two species are grown for their evergreen, ornamental foliage which suggests the true laurel (*Laurus*). They can be propagated by seeds or cuttings.

americana. Avocado; also called alligator pear. A tree, usually 40–60 ft. high (less in cult. varieties) and much-branched. Leaves ovalish or elliptic, 4–8 in. long. Flowers in dense, terminal clusters, greenish, very small. Fruit pear-shaped, or nearly round, 3–6 in. long, green at first, but yellowish in maturity, the yellow, oily flesh of delicious flavor. Seed 1, large. Tropical America. The *var.* drymifolia, with anise-scented foliage and thinnerskinned fruit, is the Mexican avocado. For the cult. of both kinds *see* Avocado.

Borbonia. Red bay; also called bull bay. An evergreen tree 30–40 ft. high. Leaves oblongish or a little narrower, 4–6 in. long, faintly bluish-green. Fruit about ½ in. long, blue or blue-black, red-stalked. In low places, Del. to Fla. Hardy from zone 5 southward. Not much planted, but an ornamental tree, especially in the winter with its red-stalked fruit.

indica. A small, evergreen tree, with oblong, leathery leaves, 4–6 in. long. Flowers very small, in few-flowered clusters in the leaf axils.* Fruit about ¾ in. long, scarcely fleshy. Azores, Madeira, and Canary Islands. Hardy only in zones* 8 and 9, and planted for its fine evergreen foliage in Fla. and Calif.

PERSIAN BUTTERCUP = *Ranunculus asiaticus.* See Buttercup.

PERSIAN LILAC = *Syringa persica.* See Lilac.

PERSIAN LIME. *See* Acid Lime at Lime (the citrus fruit).

PERSIAN MELON. *See* Melon.

PERSIAN WALNUT = *Juglans regia.* See Walnut.

persica, -us, -um (per'si-ka). From Persia.

Persicaria (per-si-cay'ri-a). A now obsolete generic name for plants here included in *Polygonum. See* the lady's-thumb at Weeds.

persicifolia, -us, -um (per-si-si-fō'li-a). With peach-like leaves.

PERSIMMON. The persimmon belongs to the large, chiefly tropical and sub-tropical genus Diospyros (dy'os-py'ros) of the ebony family. Although this genus includes about 200 species, only 4 can be considered hardy. The leaves are usually alternate* and entire. The male and female flowers are borne on separate trees, the males white. Fruit a large, fleshy berry containing 1–10 flat seeds; the calyx continues to grow after the corolla has fallen and is conspicuous at the base of the fruit. (*Diospyros* is from the Greek for Jove's grain, in allusion to the edible fruit.)

The persimmons are of some ornamental value, having glossy leaves of good color, and though the flowers are hardly noticeable, the orange or yellow fruits are quite decorative. The Japanese persimmon, *D. Kaki,* is cultivated in the southern states and Calif., and its large fruits are of commercial importance.

For cultivation *see* below.

D. Kaki. Japanese persimmon. Deciduous tree attaining 40 ft. or more. Leaves more or less oval, 2–6 in. long or longer, glossy above, somewhat downy beneath. Flowers yellowish. Fruit 3 in. long, orange, variable in size and color. June. China, and early introduced into Jap., hence the common but not strictly correct name of Japanese persimmon. Hardy from zone* 5 southward.

D. Lotus. Date plum. Deciduous tree of about 40 ft. Leaves oval, tapered at ends, 2–5 in. long, glossy above, hairy on veins beneath. Flowers reddish or greenish. Fruit globular, about ¾ in. long, yellow or purplish, variable in size and shape. June. Fruit in Nov. Himalayas, China, and Asia Minor. Hardy from zone* 3 southward.

D. virginiana. The common persimmon, sometimes called American persimmon, is a tree of 50 ft., occasionally to 100 ft., with somewhat pendulous branches and thick bark that is deeply cut into squares or rectangles. Leaves oval to ovate, pointed at tip, broader and more rounded at base than in *D. Lotus,* glossy above, paler beneath and often hairy along midrib. Flowers yellowish-white, bellshaped, with 4 lobes, male flowers in 3's, female flowers solitary. Fruit globular, to 1½ in., orange. May–June. Conn. to Tex. and north to Kan. Hardy from zone* 3 southward.

PERSIMMON CULTURE

There are two principal kinds: American (*Diospyros virginiana*) and Japanese (*D. Kaki*), the latter the chief persimmon of commerce. *Diospyros Lotus,* a small-fruited Old World species, is employed as rootstock for grafting.

AMERICAN PERSIMMON. A warm-temperate, deciduous fruit found wild in the eastern states; can be grown as far north as R.I. and the Great Lakes. Small tree in the open, but under forest conditions often much larger. The sexes usually separated, requiring male trees for satisfactory bearing. Fruit 1–2 in. diameter, round, yellow to yellowishred, until ripe highly astringent. Astringency is usually lost during ripening, but this is not dependent upon the action of frost. Ripening season Aug. to Dec. Propagated by whip-grafting or budding young seedlings. Large trees may be cleft-grafted. Transplanting young trees is difficult because of long taproot, although the tree has a wide range of soil adaptation and no special cultural requirement. Wild trees sucker* freely. Bestknown good varieties: Early Golden, Miller, Ruby.

JAPANESE PERSIMMON. A hardy, subtropical, deciduous fruit of Chinese origin, but introduced into this country from Jap. Withstands 10° F., but usually injured at 0°. It has a wide range of climatic adaptation. Calif. and from Texas across the Gulf Coast and up the Atlantic seaboard as far north as Long Island, N.Y. The quality is best in regions of moderate summer heat and freedom from wind. Moderately small, spreading tree.

The principal varieties bear only female flowers and ordinarily do not require pollination, the fruit being parthenocarpic* and seedless. If pollinated, seedy fruits result; in some varieties seed formation causes dark coloration of the flesh, in others not. Some varieties bear flowers of both sexes, and fruit is then normally seedy. Still others bear male flowers sporadically. Perfect flow-

* Special articles on the subjects indicated by an asterisk (*) will be found at the words so marked.

ers are occasionally found. It is safest, though usually unnecessary, to plant both male and female varieties.

Fruit small to large (3–4 in. long, 4–5 in. diameter), tomato-shaped to conical, yellow to red. Ripening season Sept. to Dec. With exception of the Fuyu variety, the immature fruits are astringent. Astringency disappears in dark-fleshed fruits before softening, in others with softening. It can be removed by freezing, prolonged immersion in warm water, or subjection to alcoholic fumes, smoke, carbon dioxide or ethylene. This last is practiced commercially in Calif.

Propagated by whip-grafting or budding on seedlings of the American, Japanese or *Lotus* species, the two former preferred in Calif. It has a wide range of soil adaptation and no special cultural requirements.

Commercial culture of the Japanese persimmon is important in China and Jap.; but in this country, it is confined mainly to Calif., Fla. and Tex.

Principal commercial varieties: Hachiya (outstanding), Tanenashi, Hyakume, Triumph, Tamopan, and Fuyu. — R. W. H.

PERSIMMON FAMILY = Ebenaceae.

PERSISTENT. Hanging on, even though withered, as do some oak leaves and many fruits. *See* EVERGREEN.

persoluta, -us, -um (per-so-lew′ta). A garland, or garland-like.

perulata, -us, -um (per-you-lay′ta). Pocket-like.

peruviana, -us, -um (pe-roo-vi-ā′na). From Peru.

PERUVIAN BARK. *See* CINCHONA.

PERUVIAN CYPRESS. *See* MING TREE.

PERUVIAN DAFFODIL. *See* SPIDER-LILY.

PERUVIAN LILY. *See* ALSTROEMERIA.

PERUVIAN MASTIC = *Schinus molle.*

pestifer (pes′ti-fer). A pest; pestiferous.

PESTS. For the main garden pests *see* INSECT PESTS, PLANT DISEASES, ANIMAL INJURY, and Bird Nuisances at BIRDS.

PETAL. One of the usually colored segments of a flower, distinct and separate in some, but united and forming a gamopetalous* corolla in others.

PETALOID. Petal-like in color or texture, as are some sepals and sterile stamens.*

PETALOSTEMON (pet-a-los-tee′mon). Also spelled *Petalostemum.* Prairie clover. American, mostly western, perennial herbs comprising about 40 species of the pea family. Leaves compound,* the leaflets unequal, lance-shaped, the margins rolled on the upper edge when young. Flowers pea-like in short or long spikes, white, purple, or violet. Fruit a short pod (legume). (*Petalostemon* is from the Greek for petal and stamen, in allusion to the way in which these are joined.)

Petalostemons are not much in cultivation, but may be used in the rock or wild gardens, as their low, bushy habit is attractive.

candidum. White tassel-flower. Grows to 2 ft. high, the stems erect and smooth. Leaves compound,* the leaflets 5–9, lance-shaped, about 1 in. long. Flowers white, growing in the axils* of awl-shaped bracts,* in slender spikes to 4 in. long. Seed pods hairy. Midwestern states.

decumbens. Slightly hairy, the stems erect or trailing, 1–2 ft. long. Leaves compound,* the leaflets 5–7, lance-shaped, ¾ in. long. Flowers pink, the short, thick spikes about ¾ in. long. Ark. to Tex.

purpureum. Red tassel-flower. Smooth or slightly hairy, growing up to 3 ft. high. Leaves compound,* short-stalked, the leaflets 3–5, spear-shaped, ¾ in. long. Flowers violet or purple, the dense clusters about 2 in. long. Central N.A.

PETASITES (pet-a-sy′teez). Butterbur. Hardy perennial herbs comprising about a dozen species of the daisy family (Compositae), found throughout the northern hemisphere. They have thick, fleshy rootstocks from which grow numerous underground runners, spreading rapidly. Leaves appearing in early spring after the flowers, basal, large, covered with matted, wool-like hairs on the under side. Flowers white-purple, in heads, borne on a stalk which has numerous, scale-like bracts.* Calyx of individual flowers is represented by a ring of hairs to which the seeds are attached. The seeds may be carried by the wind for considerable distances. (*Petasites* is from the Greek for a broad-brimmed hat, in allusion to the large, broad leaves.)

They are of little garden interest, but useful covering for stony or unsightly banks where more choice plants will not grow. Easily propagated from seeds or division of roots.

fragrans. Winter heliotrope. Sweet coltsfoot. Evergreen, growing 6–12 in. high. Leaves roundish, smooth and green on the upper side, fine-matted with hairs on the under side, the margins toothed. Flower heads small, fragrant, dirty-white to purple, blooming in early spring. Mediterranean region.

japonicus. Grows to 6 ft. high. Leaves roundish, 3–4 ft. across, with wavy margins. Flower heads several, borne at the top of a common flowering stalk, arranged in an upright cluster. A showy plant for moist places. Island of Sachalin.

petiolata, -us, -um (pet-i-o-lay′ta). Having a petiole (leafstalk).

PETIOLE. A leafstalk. Sometimes the stalk is winged, as in the orange, when it is called a winged petiole.

petraea, -us, -um (pe-tree′a). Rock-inhabiting.

PETREA (pe′tre-a). A genus of 30 species of tropical American shrubs or woody vines of the family Verbenaceae, P. volubilis, the purple wreath or queen's-wreath, much grown for ornament in Fla. in zone* 9, and also in the greenhouse. It is a handsome woody vine, often growing 15–20 ft. high. Leaves evergreen, opposite,* leathery, more or less

---

* Special articles on the subjects indicated by an asterisk (*) will be found at the words so marked.

oblong, 3–6 in. long, usually wavy-margined. Flowers light violet, in terminal clusters (racemes*) that may be 8 in. long. Calyx tubular, its blunt, colored lobes much longer than the tube. Corolla funnel-shaped. Fruit a 2-celled drupe,* completely hidden by the persistent, colored, and showy calyx. The plant is often grown in the warm-temperate greenhouse, preferably planted out. Its profuse bloom in early spring is most attractive. In Fla. it can only be grown in absolutely frost-free regions. There is also a choice white-flowered var. (Named for Lord Robert James Petre, a patron of botany.)

PETROCOPTIS (pet-ro-cop′tis). A small genus of herbaceous perennials, found in the Pyrenees, belonging to the pink family, comprising only 3 species. Leaves basal, narrow, in clusters or rosettes. Flowers pale pink-rose, in branching clusters. They are closely related to *Lychnis*. (*Petrocoptis* is from the Greek for cleft and rock, in allusion to their rooting in the clefts of rocks.)

A charming little plant for the rock garden, easily propagated from seeds sown in spring in the cold frame, transplanting later to ordinary garden soil.

Lagascae. Grows 2–4 in. high. Leaves smooth, shiny, lance-shaped. Leaves on flowering stem arranged in 2 rows. Flowers pale rose, with white center, ¾ in. across. Seeds woolly. Also known as *Lychnis Lagascae*.

PETROSELINUM. See PARSLEY.

PE-TSAI = *Brassica pekinensis*. For cult. see CHINESE CABBAGE.

PETTICOAT NARCISSUS = *Narcissus Bulbocodium*.

PETUNIA (pe-too′ni-a). An important group of garden flowers, the petunias comprising the genus *Petunia* which has about a dozen species of annual or perhaps perennial, weak, straggling, clammy or sticky herbs, nearly all from the Argentine. They have soft, flabby leaves, without marginal teeth, alternate* below but the upper ones opposite.* Flowers variously colored (see below), the corolla funnel-shaped, its limb often slightly irregular* or even obscurely 2-lipped.* Stamens* 5, 4 in pairs, the odd one smaller, rudimentary, and sterile. (*Petunia* is a Latinized version of a South American vernacular for tobacco, to which they are allied.)

For culture see below.

axillaris. A white-flowered ancestor of the garden petunia, about 18 in. high, the flowers dull white, about 2 in. long, nocturnally fragrant. Argentina. Not much cult. now, but often seen persisting in old gardens.

hybrida. Common garden petunia. A sticky-hairy annual, derived from crossing the first and last species. It has a weak, but usually erect stem, 8–18 in. high. Leaves variable. Flowers (depending on the strain) from 2–4½ in. wide, sometimes fringed, double, or crisped and ranging from white to red-purple, often striped, barred, or otherwise marked. For cult. and hort. varieties see below.

violacea. Stems very weak and slender, sticky-hairy. Leaves ovalish, short-stalked, those near the flowers in pairs. Flowers about 1½ in. long, violet or rose-red, the limb of the corolla slightly unequal. Argentina.

PETUNIA CULTURE

The garden petunias (*Petunia hybrida*) are very popular tender annuals, widely used for bedding, window boxes, pot plants, or for the border. They are all best treated as tender annuals, the seed started indoors or in the greenhouse 7–8 weeks before the plants are to be put outdoors. This should not be done until warm weather is settled. Nearly all the strains are summer bloomers and will stand no frost. For the details of handling tender annuals see ANNUALS. Those who do not wish to start the plants indoors can sow seed (after warm weather has come), but such plants will be delayed in flowering.

Unfortunately, petunias, while often self-sown in some of the strains, are quite likely to revert to a wild type, so that self-sown seedlings are pretty sure to deteriorate, which means that for the finest types fresh seed from a reliable dealer should be started every year.

A large-flowered, fringed type of modern petunia, one of the best tender annuals for seaside planting.

The petunia has been much hybridized and now comes in many colors, notably white, pink, blue, red, some self-colored, others edged with white, some with a varicolored eye,* many with a star-like center and one, at least, green-edged.

As to form, the flowers are either single and funnel-shaped (the usual sort) or, in some of the finer strains, ruffled, doubled, or crisped. All the latter are unstable when it comes to raising them from seed, but may be increased by cuttings wintered in the greenhouse. While petunias, as grown here, are treated as tender annuals, their wild ancestors were most probably perennials.

For different purposes the petunia has been

---

* Special articles on the subjects indicated by an asterisk (*) will be found at the words so marked.

bred into at least two types of habit. The relatively dwarf, bushy types, such as Rosy Morn, Apple Blossom, Copper Red, Heavenly Blue, or Violet Queen are best for bedding. For window boxes those sometimes called balcony petunias, which have weaker and almost trailing stems, are most useful. One of the best is Balcony Blue. Other fine varieties are Exquisite, Pink Beauty, Black Prince, and Pride of Portland. *See* PINK GARDEN.

Peuce (pew'see). Greek name for the Macedonian pine.

PEUMUS (pe-you'mus). A single species of Chilean evergreen trees, and the only cult. genus of the family Monimiaceae (mo-nim-i-ä'see-ee), which comprises about 30 genera of tropical trees with opposite* leaves, rather small, inconspicuous flowers with many stamens, and dry or fleshy fruits. The only cult. species is **P. Boldus**, the boldo, which is cult. in Calif. for its evergreen, fragrant foliage. It is about 20 ft. high, the leaves leathery, warty, rough, more or less ovalish. Male and female flowers on different trees, neither showy, white, and grouped in small clusters (panicles*). Fruit a collection of 2–5 small, stalked, edible drupes.* While a valuable economic tree (wood, charcoal, fruit, dyes, and medicine) in Chile, it is little known here outside of Calif., where it is cult. only for ornament. (*Peumus* is the Chilean name for it.)

PEYOTE = *Lophophora williamsi.*

P.G. Same as peegee.

pH. A symbol for the hydrogen ion concentration (acidity and alkalinity) of soil solutions. For the details *see* ACID AND ALKALI SOILS.

PHACELIA (fa-see'li-a). American herbaceous annuals, or occasionally perennials, found mostly in the northwestern states, comprising about 130 species of the family Hydrophyllaceae. Leaves simple or compound,* alternate,* fleshy, sometimes hairy, the veins prominent on the under side. Flowers blue, purple or white, arranged in rolled one-sided racemes,* the raceme unrolling as the flowers open. Individual flowers on short stalks. Calyx* of 5 narrow sepals, widening toward the apex, but joined at the base. Corolla bell-shaped, the petals 5, sometimes having sterile anther* lobes between the petals, at the top of the tube. Stamens* 5, conspicuous. Fruit a dry pod (capsule*). (*Phacelia* is from the Greek for a bundle, in allusion to the flowers.)

Phacelias are important bee plants and easily cult. (*see* ANNUALS). They require open, sunny positions and are best planted in masses.

campanularia. Californian bluebell. Annual, to 8 in. high, the stem and leaves fleshy, leafstalk reddish, and grooved on the upper side. Leaves simple, ovalish and wrinkled, the margins bluntly lobed, the upper surface covered with short hairs that are like velvet to the touch. Flowers in one-sided racemes,* deep blue, bell-shaped, marked with 5 white, sterile anther-lobes between the petals. Deserts of southern Calif.

grandiflora = *Phacelia Whitlavia.*

tanacetifolia. Fiddleneck. An erect annual, 2–3 ft. high, the leaves divided into fine segments, tansy-like, hairy. Flowers blue, small, numerous in slender, curved spikes. Calif. Seeds can be sown ⅛ in. deep, where wanted, in the spring.

viscida. An annual, not over 2 ft. high. Leaves ovalish and toothed. Flowers deep blue, the center purple or whitish. Calif. Sometimes offered as *Eutoca.*

Whitlavia. Californian bluebell. Annual, to 1½ ft. high, loosely branching, hairy. Leaves ovalish, the margins toothed. Flowers blue or purple, bell-shaped, in one-sided racemes,* the tube of corolla 1 in. long, the lobes spreading. Southern Calif. The *var.* gloxinioides has white flowers with blue center, while *var.* alba has entirely white flowers.

phaeacantha, -us, -um (fee-a-kan'tha). Dark-spined.

PHAEDRANTHUS (fee-dran'thus). A single Mexican species of showy woody vines of the family Bignoniaceae, **P. buccinatorius,** the clarin, widely grown there for ornament, but suited here only to the warm-temperate greenhouse. It is an extremely handsome, evergreen vine with opposite,* compound* leaves, the leaflets 2, the terminal one usually replaced by a branched tendril. Flowers in drooping terminal clusters (racemes*), the corolla tubular or funnel-shaped, nearly 4 in. long, bright red, but yellow at the base. This vine, sometimes known as *Bignonia buccinatoria,* is cult. in Calif. in most of zone* 8 and all of zone* 9. In the greenhouse it should be planted out. (*Phaedranthus* is from the Greek for splendid flower, in allusion to the showy bloom.)

phaenopyra, -us, -um (fee-no-py'ra). Literally, with spiny pears; *i.e.,* fruit.

PHAIUS (fay'i-us). Sometimes spelled *Phajus.* Very showy, large, Old World tropical orchids, some terrestrial, the rest tree-perching (epiphytes*), comprising 30 species, of which the two below, especially *P. grandifolius,* are often cult. in the greenhouse for their showy bloom. Both the cult. species bear pseudobulbs,* from which spring 2–6 large, sometimes spotted leaves. The flowering stalk is leafless but sheathed, often 3–4 ft. long, and bears a cluster (raceme*) of 7–20 flowers. Sepals and petals nearly alike, free, usually spreading. Lip* usually swollen, sometimes spurred behind, 3-lobed. (*Phaius* is from the Greek for swarthy, in allusion to the dark-colored flowers of some species.)

For culture *see* section on greenhouse orchids at ORCHID.

flavus. Leaves 2–3 at each pseudobulb,* yellow-spotted, 15–24 in. long. Flower cluster with 7–10 blooms, the flowers about 3 in. wide, yellow, but the tip of the lip brownish-yellow and wavy. Malaya. Blooming in April–May in the greenhouse.

grandifolius. The common species in cult. Leaves 4–6 at each pseudobulb,* 2–3 ft. long, green. Flower cluster with 12–18 blooms, the flowers 3–4 in. wide, silvery-white outside,

---

* Special articles on the subjects indicated by an asterisk (*) will be found at the words so marked.

yellowish-brown within, the lip purple, margined with yellowish-brown. China and Aust. Thought by some to be P. tankervilliae.

PHALAENOPSIS (fal-ee-nop'sis). Moth orchid. Indo-Malayan tree-perching (epiphytic*) orchids comprising over 50 species and many hort. hybrids, and including some of the finest of cult. greenhouse orchids. They have leafy stems, no pseudobulbs,* the leaves oblong, thick, and leathery, sometimes mottled. Flower clusters drooping (panicles*), the flowers generally white, but often tinged rose or purple. Sepals spreading, almost equal, usually shorter than the petals. Lip* variously shaped, but not spurred, sometimes marked or with appendages at the tip. (Phalaenopsis is from the Greek for moth-like, in allusion to the flowers.)

For culture see Tropical Orchid Cultivation at ORCHID.

amabilis. A widely grown and very popular greenhouse orchid. Leaves oblongish, 7–15 in. long, pale green. Flowers 3–5 in. wide, pure but dull white, stained with yellow blotches, the lip with a few purple spots. Philippine Islands and Malaya. Oct.–Dec. There are many forms or varieties known to orchid fanciers, most of them with variously colored lips.

Aphrodite. Possibly a distinct species, but considered mostly as a variety of P. amabilis. It has smaller flowers and the lip* is darker-colored at the base. Philippine Islands. Sometimes known as P. sanderiana.

stuartiana. Leaves mottled when young, 8–12 in. long, nearly 5 in. wide. Flower cluster drooping, the flowers about 2 in. wide, generally white but spotted with reddish-brown, the lip* yellow and similarly spotted. Philippine Islands. Nov.–Feb.

PHALARIS (fal'ar-ris). Ornamental and seed-yielding grasses found in the north temperate zone, cult. for the sometimes variegated foliage and one of them a source of bird seed. They are annual or perennial grasses with flat, grass-like leaves, comprising about 20 species. Flower cluster terminal, usually a narrow spike or panicle,* its spikelets flattened but not awned.* (Phalaris is an old Greek name for some of the species.)

The first species is a perennial and a popular border plant, especially in the striped-leaved variety. It is of easy culture in any ordinary garden soil and may be increased by division of the clumps. The canary grass is an annual, the seed of which should be sown where wanted.

arundinacea. Reed canary grass. A stout perennial grass, 4–6 ft. high. Leaves about 12 in. long and ¾ in. wide. Flowering cluster (panicle*) nearly 8 in. long, dense, its branches erect. North temperate zone. Much more widely grown is the var. picta, known as ribbon-grass or gardener's-garters. It has white-and-yellow-striped leaves, and is sometimes known as P. variegata.

canariensis. Canary grass. An annual, 18–24 in. high. Leaves about 6 in. long and ¼ in. wide. Flowering cluster (spike) more or less egg-shaped, about 1½ in. long, its ripe seeds, for which it is grown, shining and straw-

colored and a favorite feed for birds. Eu., but naturalized in the U.S.

variegata = Phalaris arundinacea picta.

PHANEROGAM. Any plant producing flowers and seeds in the ordinary garden sense of those terms. It includes all garden plants except those mentioned at CRYPTOGAM, and is a botanical rather than a hort. term. Flowering plants are thus said to be phanerogamous; i.e., having the reproductive organs manifest. See CRYPTOGAM.

PHASEOLUS (fa-see'o-lus). Bean. A genus of 200 species of annual or perennial, mostly tropical herbs of the family Leguminosae, of outstanding garden importance because it contains the string or snap bean, the lima bean, the scarlet runner, and several others used in warm regions for food or forage. They are chiefly twining plants (bushy in some dwarf hort. sorts), with compound* leaves, mostly with 3 leaflets. Flowers pea-like, but the keel coiled, variously colored. Fruit a somewhat flattened or cylindrical pod (legume*), edible in the string bean, but grown for the highly nutritious seeds in the lima bean and many others. (Phaseolus is the Latin name of the bean.)

While a few of the beans, like the scarlet runner, are grown for ornament, the most important are the string bean and lima bean, grown for food. For their culture see BEAN.

Most of the others are forage plants, or grown for their seeds in warm countries, and not much planted in the U.S.

aconitifolius. Mat bean; also called moth bean. A low, more or less trailing annual. Leaflets 3, cut or divided into 3–5 narrow segments. Flowers yellow. Pod nearly cylindrical, 1–2 in. long, its seeds gray, sometimes black-mottled. India (?). Much cult. in India for edible seeds and for forage, but little known in the U.S.

acutifolius latifolius. Tepary bean. An annual, twining when robust but bushy on poor soils. Leaflets ovalish or narrower, pointed, 2–3 in. long, without marginal teeth. Flowers white or light violet, about ⅓ in. long. Pod beaked, flattened, 2–3 in. long. Seeds yellow, brown, white or bluish-black. Mex. and Ariz. It is a drought-resistant food plant suited to dry regions.

angularis. Adzuki bean. Annual and bushy, 1–2½ ft. high. Leaflets 2–3½ in. long, sometimes shallowly lobed. Flowers yellow. Pod 2½–5 in. long, cylindric, its seeds variously colored, the pod usually constricted between them. As. Much grown there for food and somewhat cult. in this country.

aureus. Mung bean; also called gram, and green or golden gram. Resembling the black gram (P. Mungo) but the seeds not usually blackish, the pod short-hairy, and usually taller than the black gram. India (?), and much cult. there for food, also in the Philippines, Jap., etc., but not much grown here.

calcaratus. Rice bean. Weakly climbing annual, 3–6 ft. high. Leaflets broadly oval, 2½–3½ in. long, usually pointed, very rarely 3-lobed. Flowers yellow. Pod usually curved, 3–5 in. long, short-beaked, the seeds red, black, brown, or straw-colored. Asia, and cult. there for food (seeds), but little known in the U.S.

* Special articles on the subjects indicated by an asterisk (*) will be found at the words so marked.

Caracalla. Snail-flower; also called cork-screw-flower. A tender, perennial vine, 10–20 ft. high, cult., but rarely for ornament in the greenhouse or outdoors in Calif. Leaflets oval-ish, pointed. Flowers fragrant, yellowish or purplish, the keel shaped like a snail's shell. Tropics, probably of the Old World.

coccineus. Scarlet runner; also called *multi-flora* or flowering bean, and painted lady. A tall-growing vine, actually a perennial, but grown as an annual for ornament. Leaflets broadly oval. Flowers scarlet, showy. Pod nearly 1 ft. long, its seeds nearly 1 in. wide. Tropical America. The scarlet runner is grown for ornament, but it is probably the original of the beans grown by the Aztecs. A modern *var.* albus, called the White Dutch runner, or Dutch case-knife bean, has white flowers and is grown for its edible seeds. Both it and the scarlet runner should be grown the same as pole beans. *See* BEAN. There is also a dwarf, bushy form of the White Dutch runner.

limensis. Lima bean. A tropical American perennial herb, grown as an annual in the North, its stems climbing. Leaflets broadly oval, sharp-pointed. Flowers yellowish-white. Pods 3–5 in. long, about 1 in. wide, flattened, the seeds flat, ½–¾ in. long. The *var.* limeanus is the bush or dwarf lima bean. For the culture of both *see* BEAN.

metcalfei. Metcalfe bean. A perennial herb of the southwestern U.S. and adjacent Mex. and grown there mostly for forage. It has long, trailing stems and a large, fleshy root. Leaflets oblongish or broader, 2–3 in. long, blunt. Flowers reddish-purple. Pod flat, 1½–2½ in. long, slightly curved, the seeds brownish-black.

multiflorus = *Phaseolus coccineus.*

Mungo. Black gram; also called urd and gram. A hairy, spreading annual, 1–3 ft. high. Leaflets ovalish, 2–4 in. long, sharp-pointed. Flowers scarcely ¼ in. long, yellow. Pod nearly terete, 1½–2 in. long, covered with long hairs, the short beak hooked. Seeds black, but with a white spot. India(?), and grown there for food. Not much known in the U.S.

vulgaris. The common string bean; called also kidney bean (England), haricot (France), and usually snap bean here (the wax, butter, and stringless beans are forms of it). A tall, twining annual, the stem hairy. Leaflets broadly oval, pointed, 4–6 in. long, not lobed. Flowers yellowish-white (rarely purplish), ½–¾ in. long. Pod slender, slightly curved, 4–8 in. long (longer in some English forms), its beak curved. Seeds oblongish, of many colors in numerous hort. forms. Probably tropical American. The *var.* humilis is the common bush or dwarf bean. An interesting form is the pinto bean, with mottled seeds, and grown for them in the southwestern U.S. For culture and varieties *see* BEAN.

PHEASANT'S-EYE = *Adonis annua.*

PHEASANT'S-EYE NARCISSUS = *Narcissus poeticus.*

Phegopteris (fee-gop'ter-is). An old generic name for certain ferns here placed in *Dryopteris.*

PHELLODENDRON (fell-o-den'dron). Cork-tree. A genus of 8 or 9 species of deciduous, Asiatic trees of the rue family. Leaves opposite,* compound,* with leaflets arranged feather-fashion. Leafstalks swollen at the base, and concealing the buds. Male and female flowers are borne in terminal clusters on separate trees; they are greenish-yellow, small and inconspicuous. Fruit black, berry-like. (*Phellodendron* is the Greek name for a cork-tree, but not the one producing cork, for which *see* OAK.)

The cork-trees are of rapid growth when young, developing into shapely, round-headed trees. They make good lawn specimens. The foliage is dark green, decorative and turns yellow in the fall; although the flowers are not showy they are followed by clusters of black fruits that hang on the tree for several months and are interesting in winter. Both leaves and fruit are strongly aromatic when crushed. The trees will grow in almost any soil and may be propagated by seeds.

amurense. Amur cork-tree. Tree of 40–50 ft. with gray, deeply fissured, corky bark. Leaves 10–15 in. long with 5–13 ovate or oval leaflets, 2–4 in. long. Flowers yellow-green, small, in clusters 2–3 in. across. Fruit black, berry-like. June. Northern China, Manchuria. Hardy from zone* 2 southward.

chinense. Tree growing 20–35 ft. high with thin, slightly fissured, brown bark. Leaves to 15 in. long, with 7–13 leaflets 3–5 in. long, hairy beneath. Flowers yellowish-green in compact, hairy clusters that are higher than broad. Fruit black. June. China. Hardy from zone* 2 southward.

Phellos (fell'os). An old name for a group of oaks that includes the willow oak (*Quercus Phellos*). *See* OAK.

PHENOLOGY. An absorbingly interesting science having to do with the relation of climate to the periodic response to it, and, in the garden, best manifested in the time of flowering and fruiting.

Herbs, shrubs, and trees come into flower with enough regularity so that their blooming is often rather accurately predictable. The annual progression of bloom in the garden is well enough known to make a rough timetable of plants in flowers for every month of the year. The details of that are not repeated here for they will be found under each month, in simple form, at EVERBLOOMING GARDEN.

All gardeners should keep yearly records for at least a few woody plants and herbs. Such tabulations from different parts of the country would be very valuable if correlated with weather data, especially temperature. But contrary to popular opinion, it is not always temperature that dictates the time of blooming. Recent studies on the length of the day (*i.e.,* the number of hours of sunshine per day) indicate that illumination even more than temperature is a determining factor in phenology. In any given locality the blooming of some plants, but not all, comes with such regularity that its occurrence seems more certainly connected with the length of the day (a constant factor) than it is with temperature, which is always erratic. Phenology is well worth study by any thoughtful gardener. *See* PHOTOPERIODISM.

PHENOMENAL BERRY. A form of the loganberry (which see).

---

* Special articles on the subjects indicated by an asterisk (*) will be found at the words so marked.

PHENYL MERCURY. *See* FUNGICIDES.

philadelphica, -us, -um (fill-a-del'fi-ka). From Philadelphia.

PHILADELPHUS. *See* MOCK-ORANGE.

philippinensis, -e (fill-i-pin-en'sis). From the Philippine Islands.

PHILLYREA (fill-i-ree'a). Mock privet. Four species of evergreen shrubs or small trees of the olive family, native to the region about the Mediterranean. The opposite° leaves are toothed or entire.° Flowers 4-lobed, small and white or greenish, in axillary clusters; male and female on separate plants. Fruit globular or oval, black. (*Phillyrea* is the ancient Greek name for these plants.)

The phillyreas have rather ornamental foliage and are useful in mixed evergreen plantings. They are dependably hardy only in the southern states and on the Pacific Coast, where they seem to prefer a sunny situation and to thrive in soil of average quality. Propagation is by seeds or summer cuttings.

angustifolia. A dense evergreen shrub, growing about 10 ft. high. Leaves linear, to 2½ in. long and about ⅜ in. wide, tapered at both ends, usually entire.° Flowers white, fragrant. Fruit black, round or oval, ¼ in. wide. May–June. Southern Eu. and northern Africa. Hardy from parts of zone° 5 southward.

decora. An upright shrub, 6–9 ft. high, with spreading branches. Leaves oblongish or narrower, 2½–5 in. long, mostly without marginal teeth, yellowish-green on under side. Flowers white, small, in dense clusters (racemes°). Fruit black, football-shaped. Western As. April–May. Hardy from zone° 5 southward. One of the parents of the bigeneric° hybrid *Osmarea.*

latifolia. Shrub or occasionally a small tree to 30 ft. high. Leaves 1–2½ in. long, variable in shape, usually ovate or rounded ovate, toothed. Flowers dull white, in small clusters. Fruit blue-black, rounded or oval, ¼ in. long. May–June. Southern Eu., Asia Minor. Hardy from milder parts of zone° 5 southward.

vilmoriniana = *P. decora.*

phillyreoides (fill-i-re-oy'deez, but *see* OÏDES). Like a plant of the genus *Phillyrea* (which see).

PHILODENDRON (fill-o-den'dron). Handsome, tropical American foliage plants of the family Araceae, often grown in greenhouses for ornament, more rarely outdoors in zone° 9. They often climb many feet in the tropics and some are tree-perching. Most of them need support as grown in the greenhouse. Of over 200 species only the few below are of general hort. interest, but scores are known to fanciers. They have (in maturity) rather woody stems and thick, fleshy, very variable leaves with sheathing, usually channeled, leafstalks. Flowers minute, unisexual° (*see* ARACEAE), crowded on a spadix° which rarely exceeds the boat-shaped, often colored spathe.° Fruit fleshy. (*Philodendron* is from the Greek for tree-loving, in allusion to their nearly universal habit of climbing up trees.)

As cult. greenhouse plants the philodendrons need a warm, moist house and potting mixture° 3, to which about ⅓ its bulk of orchid peat or fir bark has been added. They grow rapidly and need plenty of space. During the bright sunny months the glass should be shaded. Propagated by cuttings or division of the woody stems. Some of them are popular as house plants, especially *P. cordatum.* The identification of the species is difficult on account of the many hybrids and hort. forms.

cordatum. A useful house plant which can be grown in water or soil. It is a trailing plant from Brazil with oblong leaves, 12–15 in. long, 2–5 in. wide, heart-shaped at the base and the basal lobes about 4 in. long. Spathe° 2–3 in. long.

devansayeanum. Not high-climbing, the stem short and thick. Leaves ovalish or heart-shaped or nearly round, reddish in youth, long-pointed at the tip, 12–20 in. long, the stalk purplish in youth, round in cross-section. Spathe° nearly 6 in. long, the tube white, the limb red-margined. Peru.

dubium. An extremely dubious name, common in the trade, for a *Philodendron* otherwise unknown.

giganteum. High-climbing, often with hanging, whip-like roots. Leaves 2–3 ft. long, the stalk 3–4 ft. long, the blade ovalish or heart-shaped, sharp at the tip, deeply split near the base. Spathe° 6–10 in. long, the tube purplish, the limb yellowish-green. W.I.

hastatum. A trade name (unknown botanically) for an aroid described as from Brazil, with "green, fleshy, arrow-shaped leaves and a gorgeous inflorescence with tubular pale green spathe°, red inside." Origin unknown.

lindeni = *Philodendron verrucosum.*

panduriforme. A climbing aroid, the lower leaves oblong, the upper fiddle-shaped, the terminal ones arrow-shaped. Spathe° yellowish-white, rolled inward. Brazil.

pertusum = *Monstera deliciosa.*

Selloum. An aroid with a stout, almost tree-like stem from which thick roots arise. Leaves ovalish or oblong, lobed, long-stalked, the blades 18–28 in. long. Spathe° hooded at the top, green but white-bordered on the outside, whitish inside. Brazil.

verrucosum. Stems swollen at the joints, angled, grayish-green. Leaves oval or heart-shaped, pointed at the tip, deeply split at the base, green but pale-lined above, pale green but salmon-lined beneath, the stalks red, both bristly and hairy. Spathe° purplish. Central and South America.

PHLEBODIUM AUREUM = *Polypodium aureum.*

PHLEUM (flee'um). Perennial grasses, comprising 10 species of the grass family, found throughout the temperate regions of the world. They are of no garden interest, but one species is valuable agriculturally, being extensively grown for hay, but it does not make good permanent pasture. (*Phleum* is from the Greek for a kind of reed.)

pratense. Timothy. Herd's grass. Grows to 5 ft. high, but varies according to conditions under which it is grown. Leaves 12 in. long, ¼ in. wide. Flowers in cylindrical spikes 3–6 in. long. Eurasia; naturalized in N.A.

° Special articles on the subjects indicated by an asterisk (°) will be found at the words so marked.

PHLOMIS (flō'mis). Jerusalem sage. Strong-growing perennial herbs or sub-shrubs, comprising about 70 species of the mint family, found in the Mediterranean region and as far east as China. A few species are grown in wild gardens for the large flowers. Stems coarse, and square, 1½–6 ft. high. Leaves large, ovalish or heart-shaped, opposite.* Flowers yellow, purple, or white, in whorls in the axils.* Corolla 2-lipped, the upper lip* hairy. Stamens* 4, 2 long and 2 short. Fruit 2-celled, when ripe splitting into 4 parts, each containing a seed. All of them are more or less woolly. (*Phlomis* is an old Greek name for the mullein and of no application here.)

Easily propagated by seeds, cuttings, or division of tubers.

alpina. Perennial, growing to 1½ ft. high. Leaves heart-shaped, about 8 in. long, and 6 in. across. Flowers numerous, in whorls.* Siberia.

fruticosa. Jerusalem sage. A many-branched sub-shrub, 2–4 ft. high, and covered with yellowish, matted hairs. Leaves ovalish, to 4 in. long, wrinkled. Flowers yellow, numerous in whorls.* Southern Eu.

tuberosa. Herbaceous perennial with thick tuberous roots. Stems 4–6 ft. high, smooth or slightly hairy. Leaves heart-shaped, 6–8 in. long. Flowers purple, in 30–40 flowered whorls.* Southern Eu. and As.

PHLOX (flocks). Perennial and annual, usually hardy herbs, comprising about 50 species of the family Polemoniaceae, found mostly in N.A., but a few Asiatic. Growing from a few inches to 4 ft. high, some are strong and erect, others trailing. Stems sometimes becoming slightly woody at base. Leaves lance-shaped, opposite,* and in pairs, or alternate,* smooth or slightly hairy. Flowers in terminal, loose or closely packed clusters. Individual flowers showy, ranging in color from pure white to bright red, pale lilac or purple, usually having a conspicuous eye-like marking at the opening of the corolla tube. Calyx of 5 sepals united halfway down. Corolla of 5 united petals, forming a short, narrow tube, the lobes opening salver-wise. Stamens* 5, usually enclosed in the corolla tube. Fruit a 3-celled capsule,* usually only 1 seed in each cell maturing. (*Phlox* is from the Greek for flame, in allusion to the flowers.)

Phloxes are general garden favorites for the border or rock garden and should be grown in full sun. Their easy culture and long flowering periods make them particularly useful. Propagated from seeds, cuttings, and division of roots. Annuals are grown from seeds sown in early spring in cool greenhouse or cold frame, or they may be sown a little later outdoors where required to bloom. Sow ⅛ in. deep, in well-pulverized soil. If sown in greenhouse or cold frame they must be transplanted when 2 in. high where required to bloom, and set 8 in. apart. They may be grown as pot plants.

Perennials are usually grown from cut-tings or division of roots to enable the gardener to keep the true plant. They should be taken up and divided every 3 years. Cuttings for the spring-flowering, trailing species should be made July–Aug., from the tips of young shoots, 2–3 in. long. Insert in ½ sand and ½ soil, in well-shaded cold frame, keeping sashlights closed during day and opened slightly at night for 3–4 weeks. When rooted, sashlights should be removed. Old plants after flowering may be trimmed back and roots divided and replanted. Cuttings for the tall, summer-flowering species should be made in Sept. or as soon as young growths appear in early spring. Follow the same culture as the trailing types, using a cool greenhouse in the fall if more convenient. They grow well in any ordinary garden soil, but better results will be obtained by using rich soil and watering well during dry periods. Division of roots may be made in early spring.

adsurgens. A rock garden, evergreen perennial with nearly prostrate stems about 12 in. long. Leaves ovalish or elliptic, glossy, about 1 in. long. Flowers pink or whitish, about 1 in. wide, in a lax cluster (corymb*). N. Calif. to Ore. Useful only in acid, well-drained sites in the rock garden, and doubtfully hardy in the East. May.

amoena. Spreading perennial to 1 ft. high. Leaves numerous, broadly lance-shaped, 2 in. long. Flowers purplish-pink, ¾ in. across, in close terminal clusters. Spring. See ROCK GARDEN. N. Car. to Fla. and westward. Sometimes known as *P. procumbens*, which is the reputed correct name for the usually cult. plant.

arendsi. A hybrid perennial, growing to 2 ft. Leaves broadly lance-shaped, to 4 in. long. Flowers lavender or mauve, 1 in. across, in large, loose clusters. June–July.

argillacea = *Phlox pilosa*.

bifida. Sand phlox. Resembling *P. subulata*, but with the tips of the petals more deeply notched. Sandy or rocky places in central U.S. April–May and flowering about a fortnight earlier than *P. subulata*.

carolina. Early perennial phlox. Growing to 3 ft. high. Stems slightly woody at the base. Leaves broadly lance-shaped, thick, 3–5 in. long. Flowers purple, sometimes rose or white, ¾ in. across, in loose clusters. Mostly cult. in hort. forms. June–July. Often offered as *P. suffruticosa*, and some forms of it approach *P. ovata*.

decussata = *P. paniculata*.

diffusa. A spreading perennial, growing to 4 in. high. Leaves lance-shaped, ½ in. long. Flowers white, ½ in. long, solitary. British Columbia to Calif.

divaricata. Blue phlox. Wild Sweet William. Erect perennial, growing to 18 in., with creeping, flowerless stems which root, thus increasing the size of the plant rapidly. Leaves broadly lance-shaped, 2 in. long. Flowers mauve, to 1 in. across, in loose clusters. Spring. Eastern N.A. The *var.* **alba** (white) and **laphami** (violet-blue) are color forms.

douglasi. Perennial, and spreading to 10 in. wide. Leaves spear-like, ½ in. long. Flowers solitary, small, white or lavender. Western N.A. For culture see ROCK GARDEN.

drummondi. Annual phlox. Drummond phlox. Texan pride. Erect annual growing to

---

* Special articles on the subjects indicated by an asterisk (*) will be found at the words so marked.

1½ ft. Leaves broadly lance-shaped, to 3 in. long. Flowers ranging from white to purple, also buff, 1 in. across, in umbel-like clusters. Tex. The *var.* **cuspidata** has fringed petals, while the *var.* **stellaris**, the star phlox, has star-shaped flowers, the petals being deeply cut and pointed. May–Aug.

glaberrima. A smooth (rarely slightly hairy) perennial, 2–4 ft. high, the stem often leafless below. Leaves lance-shaped or narrower, 2–4 in. long. Flowers about ¾ in. wide, red-purple to white in a loose (rarely tight) cluster (corymb*). Central and southern U.S. May–June.

maculata. Wild Sweet William. Erect perennial, growing 3 ft. high, the stems purple-spotted. Leaves lance-shaped, 3–5 in. long. Flowers pink or purple, ½ in. across, in loose racemes.* June–July. Eastern N.A.

nivalis. Camla or trailing phlox. A low prostrate perennial phlox, resembling *P. subulata*, and called by some *P. hentzi*. Leaves not over ¾ in. long. Flowers white or pink, about 1 in. wide. Va. to Fla. and Tex. May.

ovata. A perennial, growing to 2 ft. high, spreading at first, then becoming erect. Leaves broadly lance-shaped, 1–2 in. long. Flowers purple, 1 in. across, in small, loose clusters. May–June. Pa. to Ala. and westward. Sometimes known as *P. carolina*, a wild plant closely related to *P. ovata*, but by some considered a separate species.

paniculata. Garden phlox. Perennial phlox. Strong stems, growing to 4 ft. high. Leaves broadly lance-shaped, thin, 3½–5 in. long, with prominent veins. Flowers varying in color, 1 in. across, in large, spreading clusters. Varieties of this species are much cult. July–Aug. Eastern U.S.

Here belong many popular garden forms. Of the scores of valid sorts a fair selection might include Africa (carmine, with red "eye"), Antonin Mercier (lilac, with white eye), B. Compte (purple), Blue Boy (bluish, no true blues in *Phlox paniculata*), Border Queen (low and pink), Charles Curtis (red), Enchantress (salmon-pink, with dark eye), Fiancée (white), George Stipp (salmon-pink, with lighter eye), Harvest Fire (salmon-orange), Lilian (light pink), Mary Louise (white), Rhinelander (salmon-pink, with red eye), Widar (reddish violet, with white eye).

pilosa. Prairie phlox. Slender, erect perennial, up to 18 in. high. Leaves lance-shaped, narrow, 2–3 in. long. Flowers varying in color from white to purple, ¾ in. across in small clusters. June. Eastern N.A. Also offered as *P. argillacea*.

procumbens. See PHLOX AMOENA.

reptans = *Phlox stolonifera*.

stolonifera. Perennial, growing to 1 ft. high, with creeping, flowerless stems which root and cause the plant to increase. Leaves broadly lance-shaped, 2–3 in. long, covered with short hairs. Flowers purple or violet, ¾ in. across, in dense clusters. For culture *see* ROCK GARDEN. June. Pa. to Ga. and westward.

subulata. Ground pink. Moss pink. Flowering moss. Evergreen, creeping perennial forming a dense mat, growing to a height of 6 in. Leaves crowded, needle-like, ½ in. long. Flowers bright purple, pink, or white, ¾ in. across, in dense clusters. Especially useful in the rock garden. See ROCK GARDEN. May. N.Y. to Tenn. and westward. The varieties E. T. Wilson (bluish), and Vivid (pink) are the best in their respective colors.

suffruticosa. See PHLOX CAROLINA.

DISEASES. The most common complaint of phlox-growers is that of a drying of the lower leaves resulting in a spindly plant with little foliage. The cause of this trouble is not known but is considered to be the result of dry or poorly fertilized soil. No pesticide will remedy this condition, even though it is commonly called "blight."

A powdery mildew* similar to that which attacks rose may be controlled with applications of pesticide #9 (*see* SPRAYS AND DUSTS) used at 10-day intervals, starting as soon as first mildew is noted.

Various leafspot* diseases may mar the foliage and rust* may appear in western areas. These troubles are not usually serious enough to warrant use of pesticides, but growers will get good results with pesticide #1 or #11 used at 10-day intervals.

PHLOX FAMILY = Polemoniaceae.

phoenicea, -us, -um (fe-ni'see-a). From Phoenicia.

phoenicolasia, -us, -um (fee-nick-o-lay'-zi-a). Purple-haired.

PHOENIX (fee'nix). An important genus of feather palms, including the date and several others widely grown for ornament. There are scarcely a dozen known African and Asiatic species, at least five of which are of hort. importance. Spineless, except for the spine-like lower segments on the leaves of some species. Trunk not usually tall (as cult.), nor woody, often consisting merely of the woody bases of old leaves. Leaflets or segments long and narrow, the midrib replaced by a ridge, along each side of which are two prominent veins. Male and female flowers on different plants, rarely blooming in cult. (except on the date palm). Flowers small, yellowish, borne on long, drooping, branched stalks. Stamens* 6. Fruit a fleshy drupe,* its seed with a single groove. (*Phoenix* is an old Greek name for the date.)

For the cult. of the ornamental species (all but the date) *see* PALM. See also DATE.

canariensis. A handsome, ornamental palm 50–60 ft. high in the wild, much less as cult. Leaves 15–20 ft. long, the leaflets or segments very numerous, standing at different angles from the main leafstalk, narrow, long-pointed, the lower ones spiny. Fruiting cluster often drooping, 3–8 ft. long, the fruit egg-shaped or roundish, yellowish-red. Canary Islands. A deservedly popular palm, more hardy than many others and widely planted throughout zones* 8 and 9, sometimes even hardy in protected places in zone* 7. Much used for avenue planting in Calif.

dactylifera. Date or date palm. A tall palm, usually producing suckers at the base. Leaves erect when young and stiffish, drooping in age, the segments or leaflets 12–18 in. long, bluish-green, the lower ones spiny. Fruit oblongish, 1–3 in. long, the pulp sweet. Western Asia or northern Africa, but exact home uncertain. It has been cult. for perhaps 4000 years. For culture and varieties *see* DATE.

reclinata. Trunks usually several in a clump, 10–20 ft. high. Leaves cottony beneath when young, losing it in age. Leaflets recurved at the tip, often in pairs or 3's, not over 12 in. long, the lower ones replaced by long spines. Fruit about ¾ in. long, brown or reddish.

---

* Special articles on the subjects indicated by an asterisk (*) will be found at the words so marked.

Africa. Widely planted for ornament, but not so hardy as *P. canariensis*.

roebelini. A dwarf, very slender-leaved palm, not over 4–6 ft. high, and widely used as a very desirable pot plant, or outdoors in zones* 8 and 9. Stems usually several, sometimes with a swollen base. Leaves very graceful, drooping, the segments very narrow, rather soft, generally opposite,* a few of the lower ones replaced by weak spines. Fruiting cluster scarcely 12 in. long, the fruit about ½ in. long. Cochin-China.

sylvestris. Wild date. Trunk up to 50 ft. high (less as cult.), solitary. Leaves drooping, bluish-green or even grayish, the leaflets or segments very numerous, rigid, borne in small groups and at divers angles from the main leafstalk. Fruit about 1 in. long, oblongish, orange-yellow. India. Commonly planted in Calif. and about as hardy as *P. canariensis*.

PHOENIX-TREE = *Firmiana simplex*.

PHORADENDRON. See Mistletoe.

PHORMIUM (for′mi-um). A genus of only two species of large perennial herbs of the lily family, grown for ornament in Fla. and Calif., but for the valuable fiber of one of them in N. Z., where they are native. They have basal, distichous,* very tough, long and sword-shaped leaves, without marginal teeth or spines. Flowering stalk usually exceeding the leaves, the upper part with alternate* and bracted* branches upon which the flowers are borne. Flowers red or yellow, 1–2 in. long, tubular, somewhat curved, the 6 stamens* protruding. Fruit a 3-celled capsule. (*Phormium* is from the Greek for basket, in allusion to the fiber of the leading species.)

They can be grown outdoors only in zones* 8 and 9, where their culture presents no difficulties. Seeds sown in early spring will germinate in time for plants to be set out that year, or they may be increased by dividing the roots. Their fine long foliage, especially when planted in clumps, is a striking object on any lawn or in the border, but in the latter place they need plenty of space.

colensoi. Leaves 5–7 ft. long, about 2 in. wide, and not so rigid as in *P. tenax*. Flowers nearly 1½ in. long, yellow. N. Z. Sometimes offered as *P. cookianum*.

cookianum = *Phormium colensoi*.

tenax. New Zealand flax; also called flax lily. An important cordage fiber plant in N. Z., but cult. here for its striking leaves which may be 15 ft. high, about 5 in. wide, very tough and leathery, usually red-margined and shreddy at the tip. Flowers about 2 in. long, dull red, the whole cluster well above the foliage. The *var.* variegatum has white- and yellow-striped leaves. There are also forms with reddish-purple, and with white-striped leaves.

PHOTINIA (fō-tin′i-a). Most of the species of *Photinia*, comprising about 40 species, which belong to the rose family and come from northern Asia, are ornamental. They are deciduous or evergreen shrubs or trees with alternate,* often leathery leaves. The flowers are white, have 5 petals, and are borne in clusters (corymbs* or panicles*). Fruit round or oval (a pome*),

red, about ¼ in. long. (*Photinia* is from the Greek for shining, in allusion to the glossy leaves.)

The photinias are excellent ornamental shrubs; the deciduous species have attractive white flowers and red fruits and the leaves turn red and scarlet in the fall, while the evergreen species have, in addition, handsome, shiny foliage. They like a sunny place in well-drained, loamy soil. Propagation is by seeds and cuttings.

arbutifolia. See Toyon.

glabra. Evergreen shrub 8–10 ft. high. Leaves elliptic to oblong-obovate, 2–3½ in. long, wedge-shaped at base, finely toothed. Flowers white, in clusters (panicles*) 2–4 in. across. Fruit red. May–July. Jap. Hardy from zone* 5 southward.

serrulata. An evergreen shrub or sometimes a small tree of 30–40 ft. Leaves oblong, shiny, reddish when young, finely toothed, 4–8 in. long. Flowers white in clusters 4–6 in. across. Fruit red. May–July. China. Hardy from zone* 5 southward. A very handsome shrub.

villosa. Deciduous shrub or small tree to 15 ft. Leaves obovate to oblong-obovate, 1–3 in. long, pointed at tip, finely toothed, hairy beneath. Flowers white, in clusters 1–2 in. across, stems warty. Fruit red. June. Jap., China and Korea. Hardy from zone* 3 southward.

PHOTOPERIODISM. The response of plants to the length of the day, especially as it affects their blooming. Generally, in the temperate zones, there will be from 12–16 hours of possible daylight during the growing season, and most plants from such regions demand that much light for normal flowering. Such plants are called long-day plants, and comprise most garden flowers.

Within the tropics or sub-tropics, however, the length of the day may be only about 10 hours of daylight, and plants from such regions are designated short-day plants. They often will not flower if brought to a long-day region, or will delay flowering until the waning daylight promotes it. The chrysanthemum is a typical example of a short-day plant — hence its fall flowering.

Since photoperiodism has been better understood, many growers upset its action by electric illumination or by shading. That is why some long-day plants can be successfully forced into bloom in a greenhouse at almost any time, by simply controlling the length of the day. See Chrysanthemum. Many plants, however, appear to be indifferent as to the length of the day.

PHOTOSYNTHESIS. As the etymology of the word suggests, photosynthesis is an activity of plants carried on in the light. It is incomparably the most important function of all leaves, for it is the name for the process by which they manufacture starch and sugar, a feat which the chemists have never yet duplicated.

Upon photosynthesis depend all other activities of plant life. It involves the action of

---

* Special articles on the subjects indicated by an asterisk (*) will be found at the words so marked.

the presence of food brought from the sunlight upon the green coloring substance (chlorophyll) in all leaves. This action, in roots, water, and certain gases, results in the manufacture of starch, then sugar. For the details of the process *see* PLANT FOODS.

PHRAGMIPEDIUM. *See* CYPRIPEDIUM.

PHRAGMITES (frag-my'teez). Tall, perennial, mostly marsh grasses, natives in the north temperate zone and in S.A., one of the three known species cult. for its handsome foliage and its beautifully plumed fruiting cluster. The only cult. species, **P. communis** (sometimes called *P. maxima*), the common reed grass, is a striking plant, 10–15 ft. high. Leaves 12–20 in. long and about 2 in. wide. Flower cluster terminal, 6–12 in. long, much branched, its spikelets, especially in fruit, beautifully silky from its many soft hairs. While growing naturally in marshes it is readily cult. in ordinary garden soil, preferably somewhat moist. Its plumy panicles make fine winter decorations. Eurasia and N.A. There is also a variegated leaved form. (*Phragmites* is from the Greek for hedge-like, in allusion to its hedge-like growth along ditches.)

Phu (fu). Arabic name for *Valeriana Phu.*

PHYGELIUS (fy-jee'li-us). South African, rather small, smooth shrubs of the family Scrophulariaceae, comprising only two species, one of them, **P. capensis**, the Cape fuchsia (not a real fuchsia) grown for ornament. It is not over 4 ft. high, has a 4-angled stem, and usually opposite,* ovalish or narrower, toothed leaves, 3–5 in. long. Flowers scarlet, drooping, in terminal clusters (panicles*), 9–18 in. long. Corolla tubular, a little curved, about 2 in. long, the five lobes almost equal, the four stamens protruding. Fruit a capsule.* The Cape fuchsia can be grown in the cool greenhouse northward, in potting mixture* 4, or it may be grown outdoors from zone* 6 southward, and perhaps in protected parts of zone* 5. Propagated by seeds or from autumn-taken cuttings. (*Phygelius* is from the Greek for sun flight, in allusion to its supposed need for shade.)

PHYGON. *See* Dichlone at FUNGICIDES.

PHYLLAGATHIS (fill-ag'a-this). About 6 species of mostly Indo-Malayan or tropical Chinese, greenhouse shrubby plants of the family Melastomaceae, only **P. rotundifolia** of Sumatra of hort. interest. It is a shrubby plant, 1–2 ft. high, with a 4-angled stem and large, showy, opposite,* ovalish leaves, 5–7 in. long, faintly toothed, green and plaited above, metallic and blue- or purplish-red beneath. Flowers rose-red, about ½ in. wide, crowded in a dense, head-like, short-stalked cluster, beneath which are 5–6 purple bracts. A showy, handsome plant for the tropical greenhouse, needing high temperatures from spring to autumn and plenty of moisture. Use potting mixture* 3. Propagated by cuttings, taken in early spring, over bottom-heat.* (*Phyllagathis* is from the Greek, and probably refers to the bracts* beneath the flower cluster.)

phyllamphora, -us, -um (fil-am'for-a). A specific name applied to a species of *Nepenthes* and meaning a cavity leaf; *i.e.,* a pitcher. *See* NEPENTHES.

PHYLLANTHUS (fill-an'thus). A genus of 500 species of mostly trees and shrubs (a few non-hort. species are herbs) of the spurge family, widely distributed over the earth, but chiefly tropical. The only plant of hort. significance is **P. acidus**, the Otaheite gooseberry, star gooseberry or gooseberry-tree, a native of India and Madagascar, naturalized in Fla. It is a tree up to 20 ft. high, grown in Fla. for its acid fruit used for preserving. Branches scarred with the remains of deciduous, leaf-bearing branchlets. Leaves alternate,* but distichous,* ovalish, 2–3 in. long. Flowers small, red, without petals, crowded in small clusters (panicles*), these sometimes in the leaf axils.* Fruit a berry, angled, about ⅝ in. long. Propagated by seeds or by cuttings. For the plant sometimes known as *P. nivosus see* BREYNIA NIVOSA. (*Phyllanthus* is from the Greek for leaf-flower, some non-hort. species bearing their flowers on apparent leaves.)

PHYLLITIS (fill-eye'tis). A small genus of rather leathery-fronded, hardy ferns of the family Polypodiaceae, one of them, **P. Scolopendrium**, the hartstongue fern, occasionally grown in the outdoor fern garden. It is a widely scattered evergreen fern found in Eu. and at a few sporadic localities in N.A., most of them limestone regions. Fronds undivided, strap-shaped, 7–18 in. long, without lobes or teeth, but sometimes wavy-margined. Spore* cases long, usually in pairs and standing at nearly right angles to the midrib, numerous. Suited only to the outdoor fern garden and apparently, in America, a limestone plant. In Eu., and among fern specialists here, there are many forms with divided, crisped, dwarf, or crested fronds. (*Phyllitis* is from the Greek for leaf, and is also the old Greek name for the hartstongue fern.) Some prefer to call the American plant *var. americana.*

PHYLLOCACTUS. *See* EPIPHYLLUM and ZYGOCACTUS.

PHYLLODIUM (plural phyllodia). An expanded, leaf-like leafstalk. While leaf-like, there is no true leaf blade. Phyllodia, among cult. plants, are chiefly confined to certain species of *Acacia* (which see); also called phyllode.

PHYLLODOCE (fill-od'o-see). A small group of low, evergreen shrubs, of the heath family (Ericaceae), found in N.A. and northern Eurasia. The leaves are al-

---

* Special articles on the subjects indicated by an asterisk (*) will be found at the words so marked.

ternate* and linear, the margins often rolled under. Flowers urn-shaped or bell-shaped on slender, nodding stems. Fruit a dry, 5-celled capsule.* (*Phyllodoce* — a sea nymph.)

These attractive little shrubs are adapted to the rock garden, but somewhat difficult to grow. They like a cool, moist, shaded place and peaty soil. Propagation is by seed, cuttings, and layers.

breweri. Dwarf evergreen shrub of tufted habit, growing about 1 ft. high. Leaves linear, ½–¾ in. long, the margin rolled under. Flowers saucer-shaped, ½ in. long, 5-lobed, purplish-rose, on slender stalks forming a terminal cluster, but growing from the leaf axil.* May. Calif. Hardy from zone* 4 southward.

caerulea. Mountain heath. A low, much-branched, evergreen shrub, growing about 6 in. high. Leaves linear, ¼–½ in. long, finely toothed. Flowers urn-shaped, ⅓ in. long, bluish-purple, borne singly or clustered, on nodding stalks. June–Aug. Northern N.A. and Eurasia. Hardy from zone* 1 southward.

empetriformis. A rather dense and tufted shrub, growing 6–9 in. high. Leaves ¼–½ in. long, narrow. Flowers bell-shaped, reddish-purple, ¼ in. long on slender stalks. April–May. British Columbia to Calif. Hardy from zone* 3 southward. Probably the most adaptable of the group.

glanduliflora. Related to *P. caerulea*, but about twice as high, and the flowers sulphur-yellow. Alaska to Mont. and Ore. For cult. *see* WILD GARDEN.

PHYLLOSTACHYS (fill-o-stack′is). Bamboo-like, Asiatic woody-stemmed grasses, generally more hardy than the true bamboos. Of the 25 known species several are grown for ornament. They have moderately tall, hollow, flattened or grooved stems and creeping rootstocks. Leaves grass-like, but relatively broad, short-stalked, and usually checkered. Flowering cluster a terminal, mostly leafy panicle,* the spikelets with protruding stamens,* and plumy stigmas.* (*Phyllostachys* is from the Greek for leaf and spike, in allusion to the leafy inflorescence.) Many of the species die after flowering, but maintain themselves by many suckers which arise from the creeping rootstocks.

For culture *see* GRASSES. For related and other bamboo-like grasses *see* BAMBOO.

aurea. Golden bamboo. Erect, yellow-stemmed grass, 9–15 ft. high, the upper leaf-joints distant and with a swollen band beneath them. Leaves 2½–5½ in. long, about ¾ in. wide, the sheath bristly, dark green above, bluish-gray beneath. China and Jap. Hardy from zone* 5 southward.

aureosulcata. A showy and relatively hardy bamboo, 10–25 ft. high, with creeping rootstocks and hence soon making large clumps. Stems ridged, the depression between the ridges yellow. Leaves 5–7 in. long, smooth above but densely hairy on the lower surface. China. Hardy from zone* 5 southward.

bambusoides. See P. RETICULATA.

nigra. Leafy-stemmed, and very woody grass, 15–20 ft. high, the stems green at first, later black, the stems white-banded just below each joint. Leaves 2½–5 in. long, about ¾ in.

wide, minutely toothed on the margin (*i.e.*, a cutting edge), bluish-green below. China and Jap. Hardy from zone* 5 southward.

reticulata. Timber bamboo. Upright, often 25 ft. high, sometimes as much as 90 ft., more or less bloomy below the leaf joints. Leaves 4–6½ in. long, about 1¾ in. wide, bluish-green below, the sheaths bristly. China. Hardy from zone* 5 southward. By some the plant cult. as this is considered as *P. bambusoides*.

PHYMOSIA = *Sphaeralcea*.

PHYSALIS (fiss′a-lis). Husk tomato. Ground cherry. Annual or perennial herbs, found throughout warm and temperate regions, but mostly American, comprising about 100 species and belonging to the family Solanaceae. Leaves alternate,* ovalish, or heart-shaped. Flowers 1–2, produced in the axils* of the leaves, inconspicuous, blue, or whitish-yellow. Calyx* after fertilization has taken place becomes inflated and colored, enclosing the round, yellow or green, 2-celled, sometimes sticky berry containing the seeds. (*Physalis* is from the Greek for bladder, in allusion to the inflated calyx.)

Mostly grown for the ornamental calyx* which becomes pale yellow to deep orange in the fall. When cut these will keep for weeks in the house. A few are grown for their edible fruits. Easily propagated by seeds or division of the roots, but usually treated as tender annuals. Sow seeds in early spring in cool greenhouse or cold frame in sandy soil. As soon as large enough to plant out transfer to permanent position, planting 1 ft. apart. They will grow in ordinary garden soil, but prefer open, sunny position. Division of roots may be made in early spring. For the edible fruit of some tropical American species the name jamberry has been suggested.

Alkekengi. Winter cherry. Chinese lantern-plant. Strawberry tomato. Hardy perennial, growing to 2 ft. high, with long, creeping, underground stems that quickly increase size of plant. Leaves ovalish, 2–3 in. long, the margins hairy. Flowers whitish. Fruit a small red berry, enclosed in large, orange-red inflated calyx.* Southeastern Eu. to Jap.

edulis = *Physalis ixocarpa*.

francheti = *Physalis Alkekengi*.

ixocarpa. Tomatillo. Mexican ground cherry. Tender annual, growing 3–4 ft. high. Leaves ovalish, 2–3 in. long, the margins toothed. Flowers ¾ in. across, yellow, with 5 blackish spots in the throat. Fruit a bluish, sticky berry enclosed in an inflated calyx which has purple veins. Mex.

peruviana. Cape gooseberry. Tender perennial, growing 1–3 ft. high. Leaves heart-shaped, covered with soft hairs. Flowers pale yellow, ½ in. long, the throat purple. Fruit an edible, yellow berry, enclosed in a long-pointed calyx.* Tropics.

pruinosa. Strawberry tomato. Strong-growing hardy annual, dwarf, with angular, erect and spreading stems, covered with gray hairs. Leaves ovalish, 3–4 in. long, coarsely toothed. Flowers dull yellow. Fruit an edible, greenish-yellow berry, enclosed in a large, hairy calyx. N.A.

Physalodes (fiss-a-low′deez). An old ge-

---

* Special articles on the subjects indicated by an asterisk (*) will be found at the words so marked.

neric name for the apple-of-Peru, now included in *Nicandra*.

PHYSIC-NUT = *Jatropha Curcas.*

PHYSOCARPUS (fy-so-kar′pus). Ninebark. Attractive, white-flowered, spirealike shrubs of the rose family, all the 12 species North American except a single Asiatic one. They have shreddy or peeling bark, and alternate,* stalked, toothed, and often 3-lobed leaves. Flowers small, white in the cult. species, crowded in dense terminal clusters (corymbs*), the sepals and petals 5 each. Stamens* 20–40. Fruit a collection of inflated follicles,* the seeds shining and yellowish. (*Physocarpus* is from the Greek for bladder and fruit, in allusion to the inflated follicles.*)

The ninebarks (sometimes known as *Opulaster*) are of easy culture in any ordinary garden soil. Their flowers, while small, are attractive from the profusion of their clusters. Propagated by seeds or cuttings. Both species flower in June.

monogynus. Not over 3 ft. high, the leaves broadly kidney-shaped, rather deeply 3–5-lobed. Flower clusters sparse, white, but sometimes pinkish. Fruits 2 to a cluster, hairy and united to about the middle. Western U.S. Hardy from zone* 3 southward.

opulifolius. An erect or arching shrub 5–8 ft. high. Leaves ovalish or rounded, 2½–3½ in. long. Flower cluster profuse, nearly 2 in. wide, the individual flowers scarcely ¼ in. wide. Fruits usually 5 to a cluster, smooth. Eastern N.A. Hardy from zone* 2 southward.

PHYSOSTEGIA = *Dracocephalum virginianum.*

PHYTEUMA (fi-tew′ma). Rampion; also called horned rampion. Eurasian perennial herbs of the family Campanulaceae, comprising about 40 species, the few cult. ones mostly suited to the rock garden. They are upright herbs with basal and alternate* stem leaves, some of them narrow enough to be grass-like. Flowers in dense terminal clusters (mostly head-like), prevailingly blue, but sometimes whitish. Corolla not opening very much, sometimes its 5 narrow segments remaining closed. Flower buds long, curved and horn-like. Fruit a capsule,* crowned by the persistent calyx-lobes. (*Phyteuma* is an old Greek name for any plant, but of no significance as applied to these.)

For culture *see* ROCK GARDEN.

hemisphaericum. Not over 6 in. high and tufted. Leaves very narrow, without marginal teeth. Flowers blue, rarely whitish, in dense, ovalish, head-like clusters. Alps.

orbiculare. A perennial, 8–18 in. high, the basal leaves somewhat heart-shaped, the stem leaves narrower, or almost linear. Flowers blue or purple, crowded in a head-like cluster. Central Eu. Summer.

scheuchzeri. Erect and 10–18 in. high. Leaves oblongish or narrower, toothed. Flowers in a dense, globe-shaped cluster about 1 in. thick, violet-blue, below it a series of narrow, long bracts.* Southern Eu.

spicatum. Erect and 2–4 ft. high. Basal leaves long-stalked, the stem leaves ovalish to much narrower, toothed. Flower clusters dense, in oblong spikes, the flowers white but green-tipped. Eu.

PHYTOLACCA (fy-to-lak′ka). Pokeweed or pokeberry. Mostly tropical trees and shrubs, a few perennial herbs of the temperate zone, belonging to the family Phytolaccaceae, comprising 35 species, and of very diverse hort. interest. They have alternate,* simple* leaves without marginal teeth. Male and female flowers on separate plants in *P. dioica,* but the flowers perfect* in the common poke. Flowers small, in terminal clusters (racemes*), without petals, the 4–5-parted calyx corolla-like. Fruit a usually staining berry, edible in some species. (*Phytolacca* is from the Greek for plant and the French or Italian for *lac,* in allusion to the staining berries.)

For cultural notes *see* each species.

americana. Poke or pokeweed; also called scoke and inkberry. A dangerous, strong-smelling, weedy herb 6–10 ft. high, common as a wild plant in eastern N.A., especially in wet places and among coastal sand dunes. Its root, which resembles horse-radish, is violently, perhaps even deadly, poisonous. Leaves oblong-oval, 6–9 in. long, often red-veined or red-stalked. Flowers white. Fruit a blackish-red berry. Not much cult., although a handsome plant. All children should be warned about its dangerous roots, although the young foliage is used by some, after much boiling.

decandra = *Phytolacca americana.*

dioica. Umbra. An evergreen, handsome tree, much grown for ornament in southern Calif. and similar climates (not hardy elsewhere). Leaves elliptic or ovalish, its midrib projecting beyond the tip. Flowers white. It is a tree of very rapid growth and specimens scarcely 50 ft. high may (in Calif.) have a trunk diameter of 6 ft.

PHYTOLACCACEAE (fy-toe-lak-kay′-see-ee). The pokeweed family is of secondary garden interest. Of its 16 genera and perhaps 100 species of herbs, shrubs, and trees, only *Phytolacca* and *Rivina,* mostly tropical, are of the least garden significance. The former, largely weedy, contains one quick-growing tree that is cult. outdoors in Fla. and southern Calif., while *Rivina* is fairly common as a greenhouse plant.

Leaves alternate,* without marginal teeth. Flowers in racemes,* either terminal or in the axils* of the leaves, not very showy and without petals. Fruit a fleshy berry in both the cult. genera.

Technical flower characters: Flowers regular* and hermaphrodite.* Calyx more or less tubular, 4–5-parted at the top, petal-like. Petals none. Stamens* 4 and alternate with the calyx lobes in *Rivina,* more numerous in *Phytolacca.* Ovary superior.*

PIAROPUS = *Eichhornia.* See WATER HYACINTH.

PICEA. See SPRUCE.

PICH = *Calliandra portoricensis.*

PICKERELWEED. *See* PONTEDERIA.

---

* Special articles on the subjects indicated by an asterisk (*) will be found at the words so marked.

PICKERELWEED FAMILY = Pontederia-ceae.

PICOTEE. *See* CARNATION.

picta, -us, -um (pick'ta). Painted; *i.e.,* often variegated.

picturata, -us, -um (pick-ture-ray'ta). Variegated.

PIE-PLANT. *See* RHUBARB.

PIERATES CRUZE GARDENS. *See* No. 10 at GARDEN TOURS.

PIERIS (py-ear'is). Valuable, broad-leaved evergreen shrubs or small trees of the heath family, very widely planted for ornament, comprising only 8 species from N.A. and eastern As., two of which are the chief hort. species. They have generally alternate,* stalked, toothed leaves. Flowers in terminal clusters (narrow panicles*), the buds very obvious all the winter previous to blooming. Corolla white, urn-shaped, its 5 lobes short. Stamens* 10. Fruit a dry capsule.* (Named for the Muse.)

The uses of *Pieris* in the garden are many. They are fine for gateway plantings, as accent plants in the shrubbery, and for the rock garden. They should be grown in peaty, somewhat sandy and moderately acid soils (*see* ACID AND ALKALI SOILS) and should be kept mulched with leaves. They are slow-growing, rather expensive, but very handsome shrubs, propagated by seeds or by layers.

floribunda. Mountain fetter-bush. An erect shrub, 3–4 ft. high. Leaves elliptic or ovalish, 1½–3½ in. long, pointed, minutely hairy on the margin. Flowers nodding, the cluster upright, 2–4½ in. long. Va. to Ga. April–May. Hardy from zone* 4 southward, and in sheltered places in zone* 3. Sometimes known as *Andromeda floribunda.* It is a useful plant for forcing (which see), but difficult to move when old.

japonica. A splendid evergreen shrub 3–8 ft. high, or even more in age. Leaves oblongish, 1½–3½ in. long, dark shiny green. Flower clusters hanging, 3–5 in. long, the corolla about ⅜–⅝ in. long. Jap. Apr.–May. Hardy from zone* 4 southward. Often sold as *Andromeda japonica.*

lucida = *Lyonia lucida.*

mariana = *Lyonia mariana.*

taiwanensis. An evergreen shrub, 4–6 ft. high, its leaves broadly lance-shaped, 2–5 in. long. Flowers in a dense cluster (a panicled* raceme*), the individual flowers nodding and about ⅓ in. long. Formosa. April–May. Hardy from zone* 6 southward.

PIGEONBERRY = *Duranta repens* and *Cornus alternifolia.*

PIGEON GRAPE = *Vitis aestivalis.*

PIGEON PEA = *Cajanus Cajan.*

"PIGGY-BACK PLANT" = *Tolmiea menziesi.*

PIGNUT. Various inferior hickory-nuts are classed as pignuts, but they are scarcely worth cultivating. For the hickories worth attention *see* HICKORY.

PIGNUT PALM. *See* HYOPHORBE.

PIGWEED = *Chenopodium album. See* the list at WEEDS.

PILEA (py'lee-a). Also known as *Adicea.* American annual or perennial herbs, mostly tropical, comprising about 500 species, and belonging to the family Urticaceae. Stems fleshy, much-branched and spreading. Leaves opposite,* small, fleshy, and ovalish. Flowers greenish, inconspicuous, produced in small clusters in the axils* of the leaves. In some plants the flowers have stamens* only, in others pistils* only, while some have both stamens* and pistil.* Fruit, which does not split, 1-celled, 1-seeded. (*Pilea* is from the Latin for cap, in allusion to the flowers.)

Two species are cult. in the greenhouse, one for the neat, fern-like habit and the interesting manner in which the pollen is discharged explosively when dry, the other being the panamiga. It is this which explains the common name of artillery-plant for the first species. They are easy of cult., and propagated by cuttings inserted in sharp sand, in a temperature of 65°. As soon as rooted they should be put in 2-in. pots in potting mixture* 2. Re-pot when necessary, in 5-in. pots, and use potting mixture* 3. They should be watered plentifully at all times.

involucrata = *P. pubescens.*

microphylla. Artillery-plant. Annual, of spreading habit, to 1 ft. high. Leaves small, fleshy, broadly lance-shaped, about ¼ in. long. Flowers bear both stamens* and pistil.* Tropical America.

pubescens. Panamiga. A low-growing foliage plant, recently introduced into cult. Leaves ovalish, 2–3 in. long, brownish-green, toothed and velvety. Flowers minute, greenish, in a flat cluster (cyme*). A good house plant, needing partial shade, plenty of water, and easily rooting in sand or vermiculite.

muscosa = *Pilea microphylla.*

serpyllifolia = *Pilea microphylla.*

pileata, -us, -um (py-lee-ā'ta). Having a cap.

PILOCEREUS = *Cephalocereus.*

pilosa, -us, -um (py-low'sa). Pilose; *i.e.,* hairy, with long, soft hairs.

Pilosella (py-low-sell'a). Pre-Linnaean* name for the mouse-ear hawkweed. *See* the list at WEEDS.

PILOTWEED = *Silphium laciniatum.*

pilularis, -e (pill-you-lay'ris). Globule-like, or bearing minute globules.

pilulifera, -us, -um (pill-you-lif'fer-a). Globule-bearing.

PIMELEA (py-mee'lee-a). Rice-flower. Tender Aust. and N.Z. shrubs comprising about 100 species of the family Thymelaeaceae. Leaves opposite* and crowded on the stem, rolled when young, ovalish. Flowers showy, small, white or pink, in heads or clusters surrounded by reddish bracts.* Fruit like a tiny plum. (*Pimelea* is from the Greek for fat, in allusion to the oily seeds.)

The one below is grown as a cool-greenhouse plant. Propagated by seeds or cuttings. Seeds should be sown ⅛ in. deep, in light, sandy soil in temperature 55°–65°, Feb.–May. Cuttings of young shoots, 2–3 in.

---

* Special articles on the subjects indicated by an asterisk (*) will be found at the words so marked.

long, should be inserted in 1 part peat, 2 parts sharp sand, in temperature 55°–65° in March or April. Transplant when rooted to 2-in. pots and potting mixture* 2. As the plants increase in size, re-pot firmly, in 5-in. pots and use potting mixture* 3. After flowering trim back and re-pot. Shoots should be pinched back to induce bushy growth. Plants should be grown in humid atmosphere and shaded from the sun in summer months. They are subject to red spider if conditions are too dry.

decussata = *Pimelea ferruginea.*
ferruginea. Much-branched shrub, 2–3 ft. high. Leaves ovalish, about ½ in. long. Flowers rose-pink, in round heads surrounded by colored bracts,* the cluster about 1 in. wide. Western Aust.

PIMENTA (pi-men′ta). Aromatic, tropical American trees of the family Myrtaceae, two of the five known species of far more economic than ornamental value. They have opposite,* leathery, usually thick leaves. Flowers small, white (in ours), in compact clusters (cymes*), the petals and sepals separate. Fruit a fleshy, berry-like drupe.* The genus differs only in technical ovary characters from the closely related *Eugenia.* (*Pimenta* is the Latinized version of the Spanish pimento, which is now the English name for the fruit of *P. officinalis,* and should not be confused with pimiento.)
Both species can only be grown in zone* 9 as they will stand no frost. *P. officinalis* is somewhat grown in Fla. but only for ornament, as the production of allspice has not been found profitable.

acris. The true bayberry; also called bay rum tree and wild clove. A very aromatic tree, 30–45 ft. high, its fragrant oil yielding bay rum. Leaves elliptic or broadest toward the tip, 4–6 in. long. Flowers small, white. Fruit about ⅓ in. long, dark brown. W.I. and in northern S.A. Scarcely known in cult. in the U.S.
officinalis. Allspice; also called pimento. An aromatic tree 20–40 ft. high. Leaves oblongish, 5–7 in. long. Flowers small, white. Fruit about ¼ in. long, dark brown. W.I. and Central America. Its dried fruits are the pimento (not pimiento, for which *see* CAPSICUM) or allspice.

PIMENTO = *Pimenta officinalis.* Sometimes, incorrectly, pimento is mistaken for pimiento (which see).

PIMIENTO. The fruits of certain peppers of the genus *Capsicum* (which see).

PIMPERNEL = *Anagallis.*

PIMPINELLA. See ANISE.

pimpinellifolia, -us, -um (pim-pi-nel-li-fō′-li-a). With anise-like leaves.

PINACEAE (py-nay′see-ee). The pine, fir, or spruce family might properly be called also the larch, cedar, or hemlock family. It contains in its 33 genera and over 250 species the greatest group of ornamental evergreen shrubs and trees in the world, most of them suited to outdoor culture in all parts of the U.S. with adequate rainfall (*see* individual genera for details).

The trees are commonly called conifers, because of their coniferous (cone-bearing) type of flower and fruit (*see* below). Many of the genera are resinous and aromatic, and their timber, or turpentine, or gums are of great economic importance.

A few genera are wholly tropical or sub-tropical so far as their cult. species are concerned. *Agathis, Araucaria, Callitris, Cunninghamia* (one species nearly hardy northward), *Fitzroya,* and *Keteleeria* are grown outdoors only in southern, relatively frost-free regions, or in greenhouses. *Araucaria excelsa* (the Norfolk Island pine) is a very common plant in florists' windows.

By far the most important hort. genera, however, are those of wide outdoor cultivation for their beautiful evergreen foliage, and of these the pines, spruces, firs, umbrella pine, and hemlock are the most important. *See* these terms and *Thuja, Chamaecyparis,* and *Juniperus* for the really important plants of chief hort. interest. The larch (*Larix*), *Pseudolarix, Metasequoia,* and *Taxodium* are not evergreen, but included here for their cone-bearing habit. They shed their leaves in the fall, unlike the other, truly evergreen, cult. genera.

A group of perhaps secondary garden interest in America comprises the genera *Cedrus, Cupressus, Libocedrus,* and *Thujopsis.* Many beautiful trees are found in them, such as the incense cedar and the funereal cypress of the Old World, but they are more widely cult. in Europe than here. The two remaining cult. genera are noteworthy. *Sequoia* contains the famous big tree of Calif. and the redwood, while forests of *Pseudotsuga* (the Douglas fir) are one of the great timber assets of Washington and Oregon. Both these genera, especially *Pseudotsuga,* are also widely cult. for ornament.

Leaves generally evergreen, more or less needle-like or awl-shaped in the pines, spruces, firs, hemlock, larch, *Pseudolarix, Cedrus,* and a few other genera, but scale-like and pressed tightly into twig-like or fan-shaped clusters in *Juniperus* (mostly), *Thuja, Thujopsis, Chamaecyparis, Cryptomeria, Cupressus,* and *Libocedrus.* Some of these genera are included in the families Cupressaceae and Taxodiaceae which are not here kept separate from the pine family.

The flowers and fruit of the Pinaceae differ from most other garden plants. There is no flower in the garden sense of that term. Instead there are naked male and female organs of reproduction borne above or below but always between small, often woody scales. It is the conical aggregation of these scales of the female flowers that results in the cone, best typified by the common pine cone. Sometimes the conescales are prickle-tipped, and in some pines the cone is enormous, while in *Sequoia* and the hemlock the cones are small. In some

---

* Special articles on the subjects indicated by an asterisk (*) will be found at the words so marked.

genera the cone is scarcely recognized as such, notably in the berry-like fruits of the juniper. (*See also* TAXACEAE.)

In most genera the male and female flowers are on different twigs and in some on different trees, but the female cone, which ultimately bears the seed, is the only permanent one. The male flowers produce much pollen (almost cloud-like masses in the pines), always wind-borne.

Between mature scales of the female cone the naked, often winged seed develops. Upon sprouting it sends up more than two seed leaves or cotyledons, and the plants are thus said to be polycotyledons — almost unique in the plant world, which otherwise has only one or two seed leaves.

PINCH OFF. *See* PRUNING. *See also* DIS-BUDDING.

PIN-CLOVER = *Erodium cicutarium.*

PINCUSHION. *See* SCABIOSA.

PINCUSHION CACTUS. *See* MAMMIL-LARIA and CORYPHANTHA.

PINCUSHION-FLOWER = *Hakea laurina.*

PINDO PALM = *Butia capitata.*

PINE. For the true pine *see* the next main entry. Many other plants have been called pine, or the word is part of their name. For those found in this ENCYCLO-PEDIA *see* AGATHIS, ARAUCARIA, CALLITRIS, CASUARINA, DACRYDIUM, LYCOPODIUM, PAN-DANUS, and SCIADOPITYS.

PINE. Magnificent evergreen trees, con-stituting the genus **Pinus** (py'nus) of the family Pinaceae, of outstanding value both for timber and as widely cult. ornamentals. There are about 80 known species, nearly all from the north temperate zone, a few outliers in the Mex., and the W.I. and in Malaya. In nearly all pines the trunk is (without injury) continuous, and has whorls* or tiers of branches, seldom with sporadic branches outside the whorl. Leaves (the permanent ones) needle-like, borne in sheathed clusters of 2–5, very rarely solitary, the sheaths parchment-like or pellucid and only enclosing the bases of the leaves. There are, in addition, small, scale-like leaves, which soon fall and are rarely noticed. Male flowers consisting of naked, catkin-like or cone-like masses of anthers* which produce much pollen (dust-like clouds of it in some species). Female flowers consisting of naked ovules between the bases of woody scales, the collection of the latter forming the familiar pine cone. Scales of the cone, in some species, tipped with a recurved prickle. Seeds, edible in some species, usually winged. The trees are all wind-pollinated. (*Pinus* is the old Latin name for the pine.)

There are probably over 50 species of pine in cult. in different parts of the U.S., many of them known only to specialists in these evergreens. The ones in the list below have been selected because of their availability, their ease of culture, or their

beauty in the landscape. Many valuable tim-ber trees have been omitted because their culture is largely a forestry project out-side the scope of this book. Even among those admitted, only some are of outstand-ing hort. importance and these especially desirable species are marked with a †. Only the characters of the leaves and cones are of significance in determining the identity of the different pines, and all other characters are omitted below.

Big-cone pine (*Pinus coulteri*), a handsome Californian evergreen

Because of the arrangement of pine needles in bundles of usually 2, 3, or 5 in each sheath, the different species are often spoken of as two-leaved, three-leaved, or five-leaved pines. Only the latter group, often generally called white pine, is subject to blister rust (*see* Diseases below).

For culture of the pines *see* below.

† = Especially desirable hort. species.

P. aristata. Hickory pine. Bristle-cone pine. A much-branched tree seldom over 40 ft. high, the whitish twigs resinous. Needles 5, often covered with whitish resin, 1–3 in. long. Cones cylindric, 2–4½ in. long, the scales tipped with a slender, curved spine. Southwestern U.S. Hardy from zone* 5 southward; often shrubby as cult.

P. austriaca = *Pinus nigra.*

P. banksiana. Jack pine; also called scrub or gray pine. A shrubby tree, rarely more than 60 ft., usually less. Leaves 2 in. long, stiff, twisted, 2 in each sheath. Cones oblongish, 1–2 in. long. Northeastern N.A. west to Alberta. Hardy from zone* 2 southward. Sometimes known as *P. divaricata,* and useful for northern dune planting.

P. canariensis. A tree up to 100 ft. in the wild, much less as cult. Needles 3, bluish-green when young, pale green in age, nearly 12 in. long, slender and graceful. Cones short-stalked, cylindric, 6–9 in. long, about 3 in. wide, solitary or in small clusters. Canary Islands. Hardy from zone* 7 southward.

P. caribaea. Cuban pine. A tree 70–100 ft. high. Needles 2–3 in a cluster, ½–¾ in. long,

---

* Special articles on the subjects indicated by an asterisk (*) will be found at the words so marked.

in crowded clusters, dark, glossy green. Cones 4–5 in. long, the scales prickle-tipped, the seeds black. Southeastern U.S. and Caribbean area. Hardy from zone* 7 southward.

†**P. Cembra.** Swiss stone pine. A slow-growing tree 40–75 ft. high. Leaves 4–5 in. long, 5 in each sheath. Cones more or less egg-shaped, about 3½ in. long, the seeds edible. Eurasia. Hardy from zone* 3 southward.

P. cembroides. Mexican stone pine, there called piñon. A low tree, not usually over 25 ft. high. Leaves about 2 in. long, 2 or 3 in each sheath. Cones nearly globular, about 2 in. long, seeds edible. Ariz. to Mex. The *var.* **edulis,** the nut pine, is a hardier form found from Wyo. to N. Mex. The species is hardy from zone* 6 southward, while *var.* edulis is hardy as far north as zone* 4 and perhaps beyond. The *var.* **monophylla** has only 1 needle to a sheath.

P. contorta. Shore pine. Beach pine. A round-headed, rather densely-branched tree, not over 30 ft. high as cult., usually less. Needles 2, stiff, rigid and twisted, 1–3 in. long. Cones stalkless, ovoid, oblique, not over 3 in. long, the scales tipped by a slender prickle. Western N.A. Hardy from zone* 6 southward.

P. coulteri. Coulter pine; also called big-cone pine. A magnificent forest tree, up to 75 ft. high. Leaves stiffish, 8–12 in. long, bluish-green, 3 in each sheath. Cone cylindric, drooping, nearly 14 in. long and 4 in. thick. Calif. Hardy from zone* 4 southward.

†**P. densiflora.** Japanese red pine. A round-headed tree up to 90 ft. high. Leaves bluish-green, 3–5 in. long, 2 in each sheath. Cones oblongish, about 2 in. long. There are several hort. forms with white- or yellowish-tipped leaves, and the *var.* **umbraculifera,** the tanyosho, is a dwarf form with an umbrella-shaped head. Jap. Hardy from zone* 3 southward.

P. divaricata = *Pinus banksiana.*

P. edulis = *Pinus cembroides edulis.*

P. excelsa = *P. griffithi.*

P. flexilis. Limber pine; also called white pine (in the West). Not over 70 ft. high, usually half that. Leaves stiff, dark green, 2–3 in. long, 5 in each sheath. Cones egg-shaped, 4–6 in. long. Western N.A. Hardy from zone* 4 southward.

†**P. griffithi.** Himalayan pine. A tree 70–150 ft., the bark grayish-green. Needles in clusters of 5, drooping, from 5–8 in. long, slender, bluish-green, the margins minutely toothed (hence rough). Cones pendulous, 7–12 in. long, cylindric, resinous, the seeds tiny. Himalayas. Hardy from zone* 4 southward. Also called *P. wallichiana* and *P. excelsa.*

†**P. halepensis.** Aleppo pine. A round-headed, open tree up to 60 ft. high. Leaves light green, 3–4 in. long, 2, or rarely 3, in each sheath. Cones egg-shaped or conical, about 3 in. long. Mediterranean region. Hardy from zone* 6 southward, and considerably planted in Ariz. for ornament.

†**P. jeffreyi.** Jeffrey pine. An immense forest tree, up to 180 ft. high. Leaves 5–8 in. long, pale bluish-green, 3 in each sheath. Cones conical or egg-shaped, 9–12 in. long. Ore. to Calif. Hardy from zone* 4 southward.

P. koraiensis. Korean pine. A pyramidal tree 50–80 ft. high. Leaves dark green, 3–4 in. long, 5 in each sheath. Cones oblongish, 4–6 in. long. Korea and Jap. Hardy from zone* 3 (in sheltered places) and zone* 4 southward.

P. Laricio = *Pinus nigra.*

P. montana = *Pinus Mugo.*

†**P. Mugo.** Swiss mountain pine. Shrubby or nearly prostrate, rarely a tree up to 25 ft.

Leaves numerous, bright green, 1½–2 in. long, 2 in each sheath. Cones egg-shaped, about 2 in. long. Southern Eu., but high up in the Alps. Hardy from zone* 2 southward. An extremely valuable evergreen for low, massed plantings. There are many varieties, especially the commonest form which is a prostrate shrub, the *var.* **mughus.** It is a very popular, shrubby, almost prostrate form.

†**P. nigra.** Austrian pine. A pyramidal tree up to 90 ft. high. Leaves dark green, 4–6½ in. long, 2 in each sheath. Cones egg-shaped or conical, about 3 in. long. Southern and central Eu. and in Asia Minor. Hardy from zone* 3 southward. Long known as *P. austriaca* and *P. Laricio,* it is one of the most widely cult. pines in the country, and, with *P. thunbergi,* the best for city conditions. There are also many hort. varieties, one of them being *var.* **calabrica,** the Corsican pine, which forms a narrower crown than the typical species.

†**P. palustris.** Longleaf pine. An important timber pine from the southeastern U.S., usually 90–120 ft. high, with light orange-brown bark. Needles in 3's, dark green, very handsome, 15–25 in. long on young trees, somewhat less on older ones. Cones cylindric, 6–8 in. long, the scales with a recurved prickle at the tip. A splendid lawn tree, but certainly hardy only from zone* 6 southward.

P. parviflora. Japanese white pine. In the cult. state, usually a grafted tree, low, and with wide-spreading branches. Leaves about 1 in. long, twisted, 5 in each sheath, usually crowded near the ends of the twigs, thus appearing in dense, small tufts. Cones egg-shaped, 2–3 in. long. Jap. Hardy from zone* 3 southward.

†**Peuce.** Macedonian pine. A slow-growing pyramidal tree, 40–60 ft. high, usually less as cult., with grayish-brown bark. Needles 5, minutely toothed, 3–5 in. long. Cones yellowish, short-stalked, cylindric, 5–8 in. long, the scales not prickle-tipped. Balkans. Hardy from zone* 4 southward.

P. Pinea. Italian stone pine. A tree up to 80 ft. high. Leaves bright green, stiff, 6–8 in. long, 2 in each sheath. Cones egg-shaped, nearly 5 in. long. Southern Eu. and northern Af., there cult. for its edible seeds. Hardy from zone* 6 southward.

†**P. ponderosa.** Western yellow pine; also called bull, yellow, or ponderosa pine. A magnificent timber pine, often 150 ft. high, less important as a cult. tree. Leaves dark green, 8–11 in. long, 3 in each sheath. Cones oblongish, nearly 6 in. long. British Columbia to Tex. and Mex. Hardy from zone* 4 southward. The *var.* **scopulorum,** the Rocky Mountain yellow pine, is a lower tree, hardy as far north as zone* 3. Both are more planted in the western states than eastward.

P. pungens. Table Mountain pine. Prickly pine. Poverty pine. A fairly unimportant native timber tree, not over 30–40 ft. high. Needles 2 or 3, rigid and twisted, 2–3½ in. long, bluish-green. Cones more or less football-shaped, 2½–4½ in. long, the scales tipped with a stiff, hooked prickle. Uplands, N.J. to Ga. Closely related to and almost as worthless as the pitch pine.

P. radiata. Monterey pine. An irregular-headed, extraordinarily picturesque tree, confined to the coast of southern Calif. and not certainly hardy elsewhere. Leaves bright green, 4–6 in. long, 3 in each sheath.

†**P. resinosa.** Red or Norway pine, the latter name said to originate from Norway, Me., where the tree is common. A very valuable, quick-

---

* Special articles on the subjects indicated by an asterisk (*) will be found at the words so marked.

growing tree, useful for timber or in ornamental plantings. It makes a pyramidal tree up to 100 ft. high. Leaves glossy-green, 4–6 in. long, 2 in each sheath. Cones egg-shaped or conical, about 2 in. long. Newfoundland to Pa. and west to Minn. Hardy from zone* 1 southward.

P. rigida. Pitch pine. A scraggly, often picturesque tree, worthless for timber, firewood, and most hort. uses, but an excellent tree for exposed, wind-swept dunes along the Atlantic Coast. Leaves dark green, stiff, 4–5 in. long, 3 in each sheath. New Brunswick to Ga. and inland to Ky. Hardy from zone* 2 southward.

P. sabiniana. Digger pine. A medium-sized, crooked-branched, round-headed tree, not usually over 45 ft. Needles 3, 12–18 in. long, rather weak and bluish-green. Cones stalked, recurved, football-shaped, 8–14 in. long, the scales sharp-pointed and tipped with a hooked prickle. Calif. Hardy from zone* 5 southward.

†**P. Strobus.** White pine; also called northern white pine and (in Eng.) the Weymouth pine. One of the outstanding timber pines of N.A. and perhaps the most beautiful of all the eastern species, often reaching 150 ft. in maturity. Leaves soft, bluish-green, 4–5 in. long, 5 in each sheath. Cones cylindric, 4–6 in. long. Eastern N.A. Hardy from zone* 2 southward. There are many hort. forms of this most popular pine, some with variegated foliage, others dwarf, and one with a columnar, erect habit (fastigiate).

†**P. sylvestris.** Scotch pine. In age an irregular, round-topped tree up to 75 ft., the bark cinnamon-brown. Leaves stiff, twisted, bluish-green, 2–3 in. long, 2 in each sheath. Cones egg-shaped or conical, about 2 in. long. Eurasia. Hardy from zone* 2 southward. There are many hort. forms with variously colored foliage (white, golden, yellow, variegated) and one with pendulous branches. There is also a columnar form (*var.* **fastigiata**).

†**P. thunbergi.** Japanese black pine. Perhaps only a form of the Austrian pine, but with somewhat shorter, darker-colored leaves, that are rarely over 4 in. long, 2 in each sheath. Cones not over 3 in. long. Jap. Hardy from zone* 3 southward, and far quicker-growing than the Austrian pine which it bids fair to replace as one of the most satisfactory of cult. pines from the Old World, especially in exposed, wind-swept places along the seacoast.

PINE CULTURE

Contrary to popular belief, the pine does not require a really rich soil and, for the most part, will do quite well in a rather light soil. Drainage is by far the most important consideration, for few pines will succeed in wet soil. Exposure and winter sun are great enemies of the pine. In the summer a drying wind will do far greater damage than dry soil, for this group of plants are so constituted that their roots reach far into the earth and exact from it whatever moisture there may be present. The leaves cannot withstand dry, scorching wind resulting in excessive transpiration which, in severe cases, browns the foliage. A warm winter's sun, such as may be received from a direct southern exposure, often causes a similar effect. Late in winter it is not uncommon for the sun's heat to become quite intense during the middle of the day, although the temperature at night may be at the lowest point of the year. This alternate changing of temperature causes an expansion and contraction of the cellular structure of the leaves which damages the tissues and causes the well-known browning of the foliage. The best cure for these conditions is to arrange the plant in a sheltered location. A northern slope is excellent for most conifers because it removes the danger of sun-scorching and, to a large extent, the effect of our westerly drying winds.

The roots of the pine cannot stand exposure to the air and, for this reason, it is necessary to remove them with a ball of earth when transplanting. The pine is one of the few conifers which forms a more or less distinct taproot and, hence, it becomes a considerable task to move large specimens, although it is by no means an impossibility. Commercial growers make a practice of systematic root pruning to prevent undue taproot development and to encourage the growth of fibrous roots.

White pine (*Pinus Strobus*), of eastern North America, one of our finest evergreens

Pruning the pine for shape and form is a painstaking task and must be carefully planned. If a plant becomes misshapen or unbalanced do not use a cutting instrument unless the malformation is very pronounced, in which case it is probably too late to practice corrective pruning. Select those branches which are too long or unsymmetrical and examine the tip. Except during the early summer months, there will be seen a cluster of buds which will develop during the coming season. If the branch is too long, pick out the center bud. This operation will stop terminal growth for one year and the remaining buds will develop lateral branches of considerable vigor. Dead or diseased parts are, of course, removed in the customary way.

Propagation is accomplished by seed and

---

* Special articles on the subjects indicated by an asterisk (*) will be found at the words so marked.

grafting. The species are raised from seed planted in the spring after all danger of frost has passed. The varieties and forms are veneer-grafted. Seedlings of a hardy species closely related to the variety are used as stock. The forms of the five-needled group are grafted on white pine seedlings, while the pines having less than five needles to a cluster employ seedlings of the Scotch or Austrian pine. — D. W.

INSECT PESTS. Control white pine weevil by spraying shoots (only) with 1% pesticide #17 (see SPRAYS AND DUSTS) before new growth starts in spring. Usually only small trees need protection. Shoot moths attack growing tips and may be controlled by conventional pesticide #17 sprays (twice at two-week intervals) as new growth elongates. Spray tips only. Stop sawfly larvae with arsenicals. Pine needle scale may be controlled by sprays of dormant oil or pesticide #21 in later spring as new scales appear. To combat borers, fertilize, and prune out dead branches.

DISEASES. White pine blister rust° is the best-known and most destructive disease of young white pines. Cankers° occur on the stem and branches, characterized at certain times by the production of masses of orange fungus growth. Death of branches or entire trees will result. Currants and gooseberries should be eliminated for a distance of 900 feet from white pine stands in areas where the blister rust is present. See GOOSEBERRY. Other rust diseases affect other kinds of pine. A disease known as the pine-oak rust has oak as an alternate host, and the infections on two- and three-needle pines result in large galls° on branches or trunk.

A needle cast° often causes loss of needles on mature trees or even death of seedling plants of the two- and three-needle pines. Soon after a small black area appears about the middle or in the lower third of the needle, the outer portion then turns brown. Spraying with pesticide #3 (see SPRAYS AND DUSTS) is necessary in nursery stock in some areas of the country. Start applications as soon as new growth starts in the spring and repeat 3 times. Do not confuse needle cast with common scorch° or wind burn° which causes a gradual browning of needles, starting at the tip. This condition is most common during a dry summer or may occur during the winter, particularly if trees are in an exposed location.

A blight° of growing tips of two- and three-needle pines is caused by a fungus. Prune out diseased tips and use pesticide #3 at bud-break and repeat when new growth is 2 inches and again when 6 inches long.

Pinea (py-nee′a). Latin for pine cone.

PINEAPPLE. The common pineapple comprises a single species of the genus *Ananas* (a-nă′nas) of the family Bromeliaceae, perhaps originally from the Amazon Valley, but certainly confined to tropical America, known as A. comosus, often called A. sativus.

Its wild ancestor is unknown, and at the time of the Conquest the Indians had developed several varieties. Besides being a delicious fruit, it is botanically an extraordinarily interesting one. What we call the fruit (the ordinary pineapple) is actually a syncarp,° composed partly of the thickened, very fleshy stalk of the inflores-

cence (the juicy part of the mature fruit) and the sterile ovaries which form berries (the angular segments embedded in the fruit). No other cult. fruit has the stem passing through it, as in the pineapple — a stem prolonged beyond the top of the fruit and bearing the familiar tuft of scaly leaves. This crown of leaves, if detached, will grow into a new plant.

Leaves sword-shaped, spiny-margined, borne in a dense basal rosette, from the center of which rises the flowering, bracted, and leafy stalk, bearing at the top a tuft of leaves (these subsequently form the crown of the fruit). The flowering stalk is 2–4 ft. high. Flowers stalkless, violet or reddish, completely sterile in the common cult. varieties, but functional in the wild plant, where the coalescence of parts forming the fruit (see above) is not so complete, and the "fruit" may be more open, bear flowers, and subsequently true

A young pineapple fruit; for development see text.

berries, which are abortive and buried in the flesh of the cult. pineapple. The plant suckers freely from the base (i.e., forms ratoons°). It is never epiphytic°. (*Ananas* is the Latinized version of the South American vernacular for the plant.) A variegated-leaved form is sometimes grown for ornament.

While *Ananas comosus* is usually considered to be the only species, some authorities recognize 4 others. But the plant has been so long cult. (before the Spanish conquest) that these species may well be mere forms of A. comosus.

PINEAPPLE CULTURE

The pineapple, originating in tropical America, has become common in most tropical countries and, either fresh or canned, is known and highly prized as a dessert fruit nearly everywhere. Since the time when Fla. ceased to be a factor in production, America's supply has been almost wholly from the West Indian and

° Special articles on the subjects indicated by an asterisk (°) will be found at the words so marked.

Hawaiian Islands. Southern Fla. at one time had some 5000 acres producing over 1,000,000 crates annually, but, due to soil depletion, nematode attack and other factors, the industry has gradually declined to a production of only a few thousand crates. Within recent years the acreage has again slightly increased. The plants cannot be grown elsewhere in the U.S. on account of their temperature requirements.

Porous, thoroughly drained soils are required. In Fla., two types are planted, the deep "scrub pine" or "hickory scrub" sands and flatwoods pine-land. The former, though quite sandy and requiring rather heavy fertilization, has comprised the major part of the acreage. Fertilizers are used in annual amounts ranging from 1 to 2 tons per acre, in 3 or 4 applications; the formulae approximate a 4–6–6 ratio for younger plants and 5–5–10 for the fruiting crop (see FERTILIZERS). Plants are grown for the most part in open fields, but slat sheds, about 7 ft. high and giving half-shade, are used to some extent — mainly for the Smooth Cayenne variety on flatwood soils. Plants are commonly set 22 × 22 in. in 6-row beds and to a lesser extent 10 × 12 in. in 2-row beds with wide spacing between. According to spacing, 8 to 12 thousand plants are set to the acre. Planting is usually in Aug. or early Sept.

Propagation is mostly by slips (stem suckers), although ratoons* (basal suckers) and the crowns (fruit tufts) are sometimes used. Old plantings are perpetuated by allowing the ratoons* from the matured plant to develop in place. Seeds are seldom planted except in the effort to develop new varieties. Slips are set in the soil 2–4 in. and suckers somewhat deeper. Fruit is matured in the second year after setting the slips, and annually thereafter in the old planting which may continue to produce satisfactorily for several years. The main season of fruit maturity is from May into July. At no stage of growth does the fruit contain more than a trace of starch, so that plant-ripened fruits, containing more sugar, are nearly always superior in flavor to those picked partially immature. Ripe fruit contains from 8 to 15 per cent sugar and is a source of vitamins A, B, and C.

Varieties grown include mainly the Red Spanish, a few Smooth Cayenne, and Abachi and a few others in negligible quantity. — G. D. R.

INSECT PESTS. Mealybugs, attended and fostered by ants, do direct injury and spread disease. The use of insect-free stock and measures to reduce ant numbers aids in controlling them. Pesticide #21 (see SPRAYS AND DUSTS) is effective for mealybug control. Dusting with pesticide #9 has been used with good results in control of pineapple mites.

PINEAPPLE CACTUS = *Coryphantha robustispina.*

PINEAPPLE FAMILY = Bromeliaceae.

PINEAPPLE-FLOWER = *Eucomis comosa.*

PINEAPPLE GUAVA = *Feijoa sellowiana.*

PINEAPPLE SQUASH. A type of smooth-skinned summer squash. See SQUASH.

PINE-BARREN BEAUTY = *Pyxidanthera barbulata.*

PINE FAMILY. Evergreen, cone-bearing trees and shrubs of first-rate timber and hort. importance. The most important groups are the pines, spruces, firs, cypress, cedar (see these terms), and many others. For the other cult. genera and a description of the family see PINACEAE. See also EVERGREENS and TAXACEAE.

PINETUM. A collection of pines and, usually, other conifers.

PIN-EYED. A tubular flower in which the protruding stigmas* are visible in the throat of the corolla, but the stamens* are hidden within it. If the anthers* are visible but the stigmas* hidden within the tube, the flower is said to be thrum-eyed.

PINGUICULA (pin-gwick′you-la). Butterwort. Insectivorous herbs, comprising over 40 species of the family Lentibulariaceae, found in damp places throughout the northern hemisphere and in S.A. They often grow in sphagnum moss. Leaves basal, generally in rosettes, fleshy, the upper side covered with a greasy secretion to which small insects adhere. Flowers white, purple or yellow, solitary, on leafless stalks 6–12 in. high. Corolla 2-lipped,* and long-spurred* at the base. Fruit a capsule.* (Named from the Latin *pinguis* for fat, in allusion to the leaves.)

Pinguiculas are not of much garden importance, but are sometimes grown for their novelty. Propagated by seeds or division of plants. Seeds should be sown on the surface of shallow pans, filled with equal parts of chopped sphagnum moss, peat and sand, and be kept moist in a temperature of 55°–65° under a bell-jar. March–April. They should be transplanted into pans filled with equal parts of fibrous peat and sphagnum moss with broken crocks at the bottom. These pans should be stood in saucers of water on inverted pots covered with bell-jar and stood in shade. Bell-jar should be removed ½ hour each day. Divisions of plants may be made in spring.

grandiflora. Grows to 8 in. high. Leaves basal, ovalish, 2–3 in. long, in rosettes, pale green in color. Flowers violet, 1 in. long, ¾ in. across, the lobes wavy. Western Eu.

vulgaris. Common bog violet or butterwort. Sheepweed. Grows to 6 in. high. Leaves basal, in rosettes, ovalish, to 2 in. long. Flowers violet-blue, ½ in. long and broad. Northern hemisphere. See INSECTIVOROUS PLANTS.

Pinguin (pin′gwin). West Indian native name for *Bromelia Pinguin.*

PINK. As a general term *pink* is best restricted to plants of the genus *Dianthus* (which see). But it is widely used for many other plants, especially in the related genera *Silene* and *Lychnis,* and for still others from

---

* Special articles on the subjects indicated by an asterisk (*) will be found at the words so marked.

which it should perhaps be excluded. But popular usage has applied *pink* to plants in the genera *Helonias, Limonium, Lobelia, Phlox,* and *Spigelia* (*see* these genera).

PINK CALLA LILY = *Zantedeschia rehmanni. See* CALLA LILY.

PINK CORYDALIS = *Corydalis sempervirens.*

PINK FAMILY. A very large family of plants, all herbs having opposite* leaves and swollen joints, and usually with handsome flowers. Besides the carnation and pink, it contains the baby's-breath, catchfly, chickweeds, and the bouncing bet. *See* CARYOPHYLLACEAE.

PINK FRINGED ORCHIS = *Habenaria psycodes.*

PINK FRITILLARY = *Fritillaria pluriflora.*

PINK GARDEN. In borders or gardens composed chiefly of pink, blush, rose-colored or carmine flowers, the inclusion of numerous plants having gray foliage is helpful in bringing about a pleasant effect, and as foils a few white flowers, as well as those of pale yellow or lavender coloring, may be introduced. Stone walls make a good background for flowers in this color scale, or such features as are made of wood as trelliswork, fences, gates, arbors, or seats may be painted silver-gray, pure white, or Prussian blue.

SHRUBS OR SMALL TREES TO BE USED AS BACKGROUND OR ACCENTS

SPRING-FLOWERING. *Azalea nudiflora* 5–8 ft., *A. schlippenbachi* 5–8 ft., *A. vaseyi* 5–10 ft.; *Cornus florida rubra* to 20 ft.; *Crataegus Oxyacantha plena* 15 ft.; *Kolkwitzia amabilis* 5–6 ft.; *Malus floribunda* 15–20 ft., *M. halliana* 15–20 ft., *M. ioensis* (Bechtel's Crab) 10–15 ft.; *Prunus glandulosa rosea* (Flowering Almond) 4–5 ft.; *Amygdalus Persica* (double-flowering Peach) to 20 ft.; *Prunus sieboldi, P. subhirtella* to 20 ft., *P. triloba* 6 ft.; *Rhododendron carolinianum* 3–6 ft.; many hybrid rhododendrons, blush to deep pink, 3–8 ft.; *Viburnum carlesi* 3–5 ft.; *Deutzia rosea* 1–3 ft., *D. scabra* (pink form) 6–10 ft.

SUMMER-FLOWERING: *Hibiscus syriacus* to 12 ft.; *Kalmia latifolia* 4–8 ft.; *Robinia hispida* 6–7 ft.; *Rosa blanda* 3–6 ft., *R. nitida* 1–2 ft., *R. spinosissima* Stanwell Perpetual 5–6 ft.; *Weigela florida* 6 ft.; *Tamarix africana* to 10 ft.

AUTUMN-FLOWERING: *Lespedeza thunbergi* to 10 ft.; *Spirea Bumalda* Anthony Waterer 2 ft.

TALL PLANTS FOR USE IN BACKGROUND

SUMMER-FLOWERING: *Althaea rosea* (Hollyhock) double and single, blush to carmine; *Boltonia latisquama;* dahlias; *Lavatera trimestris splendens* (annual).

AUTUMN-FLOWERING: *Aster novae-angliae* (pink form); *Cosmos,* pink form (annual); dahlias, blush to carmine.

PLANTS OF MEDIUM HEIGHT

SPRING-FLOWERING: *Aquilegia* pink vars.; *Centranthus ruber; Dicentra eximia, D. spectabilis; Pulmonaria saccharata.*

SUMMER-FLOWERING: *Antirrhinum,* blush to carmine (annual); *Callistephus,* annual asters, blush to carmine; *Astilbe davidi* vars. America, Gloria, Gruno, Meta Immink, Queen Alexandra, Rose Pearl, *A. japonica; Boltonia latisquama nana; Centaurea Cyanus,* pink form; *Chrysanthemum coccineum* (pyrethrum) blush to carmine; *Clarkia elegans* Salmon King; *Dianthus barbatus; Gladiolus* pale to deep pink and rose; *Gypsophila elegans carminea; Iris* (pink forms); larkspur (annual) blush to carmine; *Lilium speciosum rubrum; Lupinus polyphyllus moerheimi; Malva Alcea, M. moschata; Monarda didyma; Papaver* (annual) single and double, blush to cherry; *Papaver orientale* vars. Mrs. Perry, Queen Alexandra, Victoria Louise; *Paeonia* (double and single pink vars.); *Pentstemon barbatus* Pink Beauty; *Phlox paniculata* vars. Annie Cook, Elizabeth Campbell, Enchantress, Johnson's Favorite, Jules Sandeau (dwarf), Mme. Paul Dutrie, Painted Lady, Peachblow, Rheinlander; *Potentilla nepalensis willmottiae; Sidalcea malvaeflora* Rosy Gem; stocks (annual); *Veronica spicata rosea; Zinnia* (annual) blush to carmine.

LOW-GROWING PLANTS FOR FOREGROUND

SPRING-FLOWERING: *Aster alpinus ruber; Aubrieta,* rose vars.; *Armeria maritima laucheana, A. plantaginea; Bellis perennis* (pink); *Crucianella stylosa; Hyacinthus orientalis* (bulb); *Myosotis,* pink forms; *Papaver nudicaule* Coonara Pink; *Phlox amoena, P. subulata* (pink); *Saponaria ocymoides; Scilla hispanica* Rosalind, *S. nonscripta* Blush Queen (bulbs); *Tulipa clusiana,* tulips, many vars. early, Cottage, Darwin, etc. (bulbs).

SUMMER-FLOWERING: *Antirrhinum* (annual) dwarf forms, blush to carmine; *Dianthus caesius, D. deltoides,* hybrid pink vars., *D. chinensis* (pink form); *Iberis umbellata* (annual) blush to rose; *Petunia* (annual) vars. Exquisite, Pink Beauty, Pride of Portland, Rosy Morn; *Phlox drummondi* (annual) blush to rose; *Silene pendula rosea* (annual), *S. Schafta; Tunica Saxifraga; Verbena* Miss Willmott.

CLIMBERS

Clematis montana rubens (spring); *Convolvulus* (annual pink); roses, many climbing and pillar varieties (summer); sweet peas (spring). — L. B. W.

PINK LADY'S-SLIPPER = *Cypripedium acaule.*

PINK LOCUST = *Robinia hispida,* and *R. Pseudo-acacia decaisneana. See* LOCUST.

PINKROOT = *Spigelia marilandica.*

PINKSTER-FLOWER = *Azalea nudiflora.*

PINK VINE = *Antigonon leptopus.*

PIN-MONEY GARDENING. Favorably situated gardeners (*i.e.,* on well-traveled

---

* Special articles on the subjects indicated by an asterisk (*) will be found at the words so marked.

highways) can often turn an honest penny and a quick one by selling seasonal flowers. Without erecting an elaborate roadside stand (essential if the business grows), it is quite possible and often surprisingly lucrative to offer cut flowers for sale.

To keep flowers fresh it is essential to have plenty of containers for water, to keep the flowers out of the sun and wind, and not to cut more blooms than can be sold each day. If there is no tree shade it would be better to erect some sort of a temporary shelter over the selling table or counter.

If traffic is heavy and you are likely to have brisk trade it is necessary to grow the plants mentioned below in greater quantities than the average garden is likely to provide. For most small stands, and all large ones, it is better to grow plants in rows, exactly as one plants vegetables. Perennials can be left in the rows permanently. All annuals should be sown in succession so as to provide continuous bloom. *See* ANNUALS. *See also* BULBS.

Local prices in the florist shops will be the best guide as to the price to charge. Prices fluctuate widely, depending on the season, locality, and most of all on the available supply from professional sources.

As to the kinds of flowers to offer, the list might be legion. Perhaps a good selection for the beginning amateur should include, by season, the following bulbs and perennials:

Early Spring: Bulbs such as crocus, snow-drop, snowflake, grape-hyacinth, narcissus, and squill.

Spring: Bulbs such as tulips and hyacinth. Flowers such as tall bearded iris, peony, columbine, pink, coral bells, lily-of-the-valley.

Early Summer: Lily, daylily, Japanese iris, lupines, larkspur, bellflower, foxglove.

Summer: Gladiolus, China aster (*Callistephus*), Shasta daisy, lily, phlox, sneezewort, Stokes aster, red-hot poker, early chrysanthemum, pentstemon, montbretia.

Fall: Chrysanthemum, Michaelmas daisy, *Sedum spectabile,* native asters and goldenrod, autumn crocus, winter daffodil, tuberose.

No bloom of shrubs or trees is listed, for most gardeners do not have enough of these to warrant mutilation by cutting. The exception is that an old lilac hedge may be improved by a reasonable annual cutting (preferably in late bud) and fragrant lilac is always in brisk demand.

All the plants in the above list are of easy culture and the details of how to grow them should be sought at the appropriate entries.

If you decide to confine the sale to annuals a good selection might include: cornflower, African daisy, coreopsis, Cape marigold, garden balsam, summer cypress, marigold, ten-weeks stock, zinnia, jasmine tobacco, sweet scabious, blue lace-flower, and cosmos. *See* ANNUALS.

Vegetables, of course, can be included, but local stores usually supply the needs of most country communities.

PINNA (plural pinnae). One of the ultimate divisions or leaflets of a compound* leaf which is pinnate (which see). *Pinna* is most often applied to fern fronds.

pinnata, -us, -um (pin-nay'ta). Pinnate.*

PINNATE. With leaflets, or with the veins of a simple* leaf, arranged as are the segments of a bird's feather, *i.e.,* opposite or alternate from each other along a common

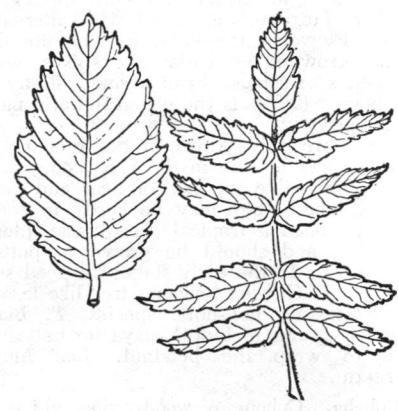

Leaves, showing pinnate veining (*left*) and pinnate arrangement of leaflets (*right*)

axis, not radiating from one point. Compound leaves which are pinnate are thus, and often in this book, said to have their leaflets arranged feather-fashion. *See* PALMATE.

PINNATIFID. Cut or divided (but not compound*), as in the segments of a bird's feather. *See* PINNATE.

pinnatifida, -us, -um (pin-nat-i-fid'a). Pinnatifid.

PINNULE. The smallest division of a compound leaf or fern frond; a diminutive of pinna (which see).

PIN OAK = *Quercus palustris. See* OAK.

PIÑON = *Pinus cembroides. See* PINE.

Pinsapo (peen-sap'o). Spanish vernacular for the Spanish fir.

PINTO BEAN. A variety or form of the common string bean (*Phaseolus vulgaris*) with mottled seeds. It is grown chiefly in the southwestern states, both for its seeds and for the herbage used as forage.

PINUS. *See* PINE.

PINXTER-FLOWER = Pinkster-flower. *See* AZALEA NUDIFLORA.

PINYON = Piñon. *See Pinus cembroides* at PINE.

PIP. The raised crown or individual root-stock* of a plant, as distinguished from a mass of rootstocks. Pips are sometimes valu-

---

* Special articles on the subjects indicated by an asterisk (*) will be found at the words so marked.

able for propagation purposes, especially in the lily-of-the-valley (which see for an illustration of a pip), and are found occasionally in other plants. *Pip* is also colloquial for a small seed.

PIPER (py′per). A huge genus of mostly tropical herbs, shrubs, woody vines or even trees of the family Piperaceae, very largely aromatic and of little hort. but much economic interest. Of over 600 species only the three below are likely to be found in cult., the first two (cubeb and pepper) grown here mostly for interest, the last an ornamental greenhouse climber. All the cult. species are climbers (in youth at least) with alternate* leaves. Flowers extremely simple, minute, unisexual, crowded on catkin-like spikes, without petals or sepals. Fruit a small, fleshy, or dry berry. (*Piper* is the classical Latin name for pepper.)

These are only grown in the greenhouse, their outdoor culture in the U.S. being practically impossible for lack of heat and moisture, although they may be hardy in zone* 9. They need a tropical greenhouse, plenty of water, and should be grown in potting mixture* 4. In the early stages all need support, but *P. Cubeba* becomes tree-like in age. An interesting non-hort. species, *P. Betle*, is widely grown in Indo-Malaya for its leaves, used to wrap the betelnut. See ARECA CATECHU.

Cubeba. Cubeb. A woody vine, ultimately treelike. Leaves elliptic or ovalish, or narrower, pointed at the tip, unequally heart-shaped at the base. Fruit nearly ¼ in. in diameter, brownish, yielding the cubebs of commerce. East Indies.

nigrum. The true pepper (but see CAPSICUM). A woody vine, with aerial roots. Leaves broadly oval or nearly round, unequally heart-shaped at the base. Fruit about ¼ in. in diameter, yellowish-red when ripe. The dried whole fruit yields black pepper, but when the outer shell is taken off, the resulting product is white pepper. East Indies.

ornatum. An ornamental greenhouse climber grown for its handsome foliage. Leaves ovalish or nearly round, 2½–5 in. long, the upper side at first pink-spotted, ultimately white-spotted, the stalk attached to or near the middle of the leaf blade. Celebes.

PIPERACEAE (py-per-ray′see-ee). The pepper family is only of value because it contains the plant yielding common black pepper (*see* PIPER), a very different plant from the kitchen garden pepper (*Capsicum*). The family also includes the genus *Peperomia* which contains foliage plants of greenhouse culture that are widely grown for ornament. The family comprises 9 genera, and perhaps 1200 species, nearly all tropical. Most of them are herbs or shrubs with jointed stems.

Leaves alternate* (rarely opposite* in *Peperomia*), often thick or fleshy and usually minutely, but distinctly spotted with small dots, always without marginal teeth. Flowers minute, without petals, crowded on slender, usually pencil-thick spikes. Fruit berry-like,

often aromatic, in *Piper* yielding both pepper and cubeb.

Technical flower characters: Sepals and petals none, the flowers unisexual* in *Piper*, hermaphrodite* in *Peperomia*, regular* in both. Stamens (in the cult. genera) 1–4. Ovary superior,* 1-celled and with a single ovule.

piperascens (py-per-ras′senz). Like peppermint.

piperella (py-per-rel′a). A little pepper-tree, or like one.

piperita, -us, -um (py-per-ry′ta). Pepper-like, or like the pepper-tree (*Piper nigrum*).

PIPEVINE = *Aristolochia durior.*

PIPSISSEWA = *Chimaphila umbellata.*

PIQUERIA (py-queer′i-a). Also known as *Stevia*. Tropical American herbaceous and shrubby perennials, comprising about 20 species, and belonging to the family Compositae, only one of garden interest. Leaves opposite,* toothed, broadly lance-shaped, with short stalks. Flowers fragrant, white, in small heads arranged in clusters growing from the axils* of the leaves. (Named for A. Piquer, a Spanish botanist of the 18th century.)

Easily propagated from seeds or cuttings and they require little attention. Seeds should be sown in light, sandy soil in cool greenhouse in Mar., or cuttings made in Feb. or Mar. inserted in sand. When rooted, pot in 2-in. pots in potting mixture* 3. Pots should be transferred outdoors when danger of frost is over, plunged* in beds of coal ashes, where they can remain until early Oct. They should then be removed to greenhouse for Dec. flowering. Plants may be used in the garden in frost-free localities, but they are of a straggling habit and should be kept staked and tied.

trinervia. Called by nurserymen *Stevia serrata.* Perennial, growing to 3 ft. high. Leaves broadly lance-shaped, toothed, and with prominent veins on the under side. Flower heads arranged in clusters, white, fragrant. Useful for cutting in winter. Central America. The *var.* variegata has leaves with broad white edges and is sometimes used as a bedding plant for color effects.

pisifera, -us, -um (py-sif′fer-a). Literally, pea-bearing; as a specific name it usually indicates plants bearing merely small, pea-like fruits.

PISTACHE, PISTACHIO. See PISTACIA.

PISTACIA (pis-tash′i-a). Aromatic shrubs or trees of the family Anacardiaceae, most of the 9 species Eurasian, but one from the Canary Islands and another from Calif. and Mex. Only the two below are of hort. interest, one of them being grown for its seeds which yield pistache. They have alternate,* compound* leaves, the leaflets arranged feather-fashion, in ours without an odd one at the end. Male and female flowers on separate plants, small, inconspicuous, without petals, and mostly in lateral clusters (panicles*). Fruit a dry drupe, its seeds, in *P. vera*, the pistachio nut of commerce. (*Pistacia* is the Latin name of the pistachio.)

---

* Special articles on the subjects indicated by an asterisk (*) will be found at the words so marked.

The second species can only be grown outdoors in regions suited to the olive, which fact confines its cult. mostly to Calif. The first is planted mostly for ornament or for grafting stock for *P. vera*, which is often grown upon it. The pistachio should be planted about 25 ft. apart each way, and for every 20 female trees it is necessary to interplant 4 male trees to be sure of pollination.* Propagated mostly by budding or grafting, especially for *P. vera*.

chinensis. Chinese pistachio. A tree up to 60 ft. high, not evergreen. Leaflets in 5–6 pairs, more or less lance-shaped. Fruit flattened, about ¼ in. long, scarlet at first, ultimately purplish. China. Grown for ornament, and as grafting stock for the next, in Calif. and Fla., its foliage handsomely colored in the autumn. Hardy from zone* 5 southward.

vera. Pistachio. Not over 30 ft. high. Leaflets in 1–5 pairs, generally oval, but tapering at the base. Fruit oblong or egg-shaped, red and wrinkled, about 1 in. long, the kernel of its stone rich, oily, green or yellowish-green and the source of pistache. Mediterranean region and the Orient. Hardy only in zones* 8 and 9, but unsuited to this region in Fla. because of excess moisture. It is somewhat grown commercially in Calif.

PISTIA (piss'ti-a). A single, free-floating aquatic plant of the family Araceae, found in nearly all tropical countries and also Fla. and Tex., and widely used in aquaria or in pools. It will stand no frost, and should have a water temperature 70°–75°. The only species is **P. Stratiotes**, the water lettuce, which has a rosette of roundish or ovalish, thick, spongy leaves, 2½–5½ in. long, from the floating mass of which hang (beneath the surface) many feathery, hair-like roots. Flowers extremely minute, in the axils* of the leaves (*see* ARACEAE). Fruit fleshy, minute. (*Pistia* is said to be from the Greek for liquid, in allusion to the aquatic habit.)

PISTIL. The complete female organ of reproduction in flowers. The typical pistil consists of a usually swollen base (the ovary) containing the ovules (which will become seeds after fertilization), a shank-like stalk (the style), and a club-shaped or variously divided tip (the stigma). Upon the latter, pollen is deposited and begins the process ending in fertilization (which see).

A pistil may have only one chamber or several, and in the latter case is called a compound pistil. Whether of one or more chambers or cells, a pistil is technically considered to be a much-modified leaf, rolled to form the chamber. Such a leaf is known as a carpellary leaf and a 1-celled pistil is then also properly called a carpel. When the ovary is several-celled (*i.e.*, a compound pistil), it is conceived as being formed of several carpellary leaves, and thus to be (theoretically) composed of several carpels. That such a concept of a pistil is more than a theory is proved by those fruits which split into component and often separable carpels, as in *Magnolia*, the Trochodendraceae, *Brachychi-*

ton, *Zanthoxylum,* and in many plants of the mallow family.

PISTILLATE. Bearing only pistils.* *See* FEMALE.

PISUM. *See* PEA.

PIT. A very useful adjunct in any garden of more than simple requirements, because pits make the best winter storage for tubbed hortensia hydrangeas, bay trees, oleanders, orange trees, and a lot of other tubbed plants that need freedom from severe frosts, but no winter heat. *See* illustration at HYDRANGEA.

The best type of pit should be nearly all below ground, at least 6–8 ft. deep (more if taller plants are to be wintered) and preferably with brick or concrete walls and a dirt floor. The walls may extend above the general ground level a few inches, but more than this invites too much exposure to cold.

The roof should have just enough pitch to allow rain to drain off. If the pit is of any size, the roof should be of removable shutters, the size of a hotbed sash, and of solid wood if there must be no light in the pit during winter. Otherwise hotbed sash can be used. The shutters should overhang the pit walls enough to keep rain from draining into the pit, which should be dry all winter.

Some elaborate pits are made with steps down into them. But this is not necessary and may let in too much cold. The theory of a pit is that the tubs are put far below the level of frost penetration, and with proper covering (extra mats may be needed in zero weather), they make snug quarters for plants needing this sort of winter care.

PITAHAYA. The name in Spanish America for many cacti with edible fruit. Those in this ENCYCLOPEDIA will be found at *Machaerocereus gummosus, Lemaireocereus thurberi, Hylocereus undatus,* and *Echinocereus polyacanthus.*

PITANGA = *Eugenia uniflora.*

PITCHER-PLANT. Insectivorous plants with their leaves modified into variously shaped, pitcher-like organs. For the common pitcher-plant of eastern N.A. *see* the next entry. For other pitcher-plants *see* NEPENTHES and DARLINGTONIA.

PITCHER-PLANT. Several insectivorous genera are called pitcher-plants, but by far the most common is **Sarracenia** (sar-ra-see'-ni-a), a genus of herbaceous perennials, comprising 10 North American species belonging to the family Sarraceniaceae. This interesting group of plants consists of both hardy and tender species found only in bogs or wet places where the soil consists of sandy peat, or sphagnum moss. All have creeping underground stems. Leaves basal, pitcher-like, or tubular, with a lid at the top. Some are pale green, often blotched purplish-red, or white, with conspicuous veins that also vary in color. Insects are attracted by nectar. For the method of catching insects and for other carnivorous plants *see* INSECTIVOROUS PLANTS. Flowers solitary, on leaf-

---

* Special articles on the subjects indicated by an asterisk (*) will be found at the words so marked.

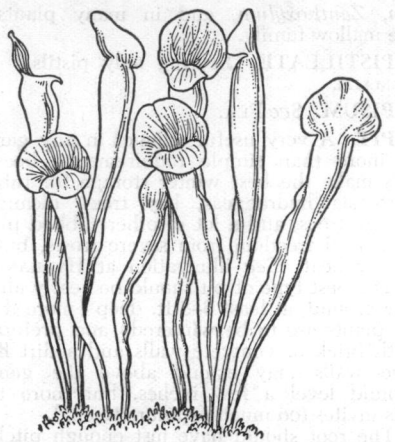

Trumpets (*Sarracenia flava*). A showy pitcher-plant from the southeastern U.S. with yellow and red "pitchers" (leaves); to be grown in wet sphagnum moss.

less stalks, nodding, yellow, purplish-green or crimson. Calyx* of 5 sepals which are often colored. Stamens* numerous. Pistil with an umbrella-like stigma.* Fruit a capsule.* (Named for Dr. D. Sarrasin, physician and naturalist of Quebec.)

Not much in cult. except in botanic gardens. Propagated by seeds or division of rootstocks in March or April. They must be grown in acid peat or sphagnum.* *See also* DARLINGTONIA and NEPENTHES.

S. drummondi. Tender perennial. Leaves to 4 ft. high, upright, green, deeply purplish-veined. Lid ovalish, nearly erect, with a wavy margin. Flowers purplish, 2–4 in. across. One of the most showy of the species. Bogs, Ga., Fla., and Ala.

S. flava. Trumpets. Yellow pitcher-plant. Trumpet-leaf. Tender perennial. Leaves to 3 ft., yellow-green with crimson throat, sometimes entirely crimson, with prominent veins. Lid bent over the opening. Flowers yellow, 2–4 in. across. Va. to Fla.

S. purpurea. Common pitcher-plant. Side-saddle-flower. Huntsman's-cup. Indian pitcher. Hardy perennial. Leaves to 1 ft. long, green or dark purple. Lid almost upright. Flowers purplish, to 2 in. across. Labrador to Fla. and the Rocky Mountains. The floral emblem of Newfoundland.

S. rubra. Pitchers long, slender, winged, 10–18 in. long, the lid ovalish, erect, somewhat bent. Pitcher reddish, paler at the summit, purple-streaked. Flowers fragrant, red, nearly 2 in. wide, solitary. Bogs, N. Car. to Fla. May.

PITCHER-PLANT FAMILY = Sarraceniaceae.

PITCH PINE = *Pinus rigida.* See PINE.

PITHECELLOBIUM = *Pithecolobium.*

PITHECOLOBIUM (pi-thee-ko-lō′bi-um). A genus of over a hundred tropical trees and shrubs of the pea family, a few cult. for ornament in zone* 9 or the most protected sites in zone* 8. They have alternate,*

twice-compound* leaves, and white flowers in globe-shaped, acacia-like heads, or in dense spikes in some non-hort. species. Corolla not pea-like, its stamens much-protruded. Fruit a flattish pod (legume*), variously twisted or coiled. (*Pithecolobium* is from the Greek for monkey and earring, in allusion to the coiled pods.) Sometimes spelled *Pithecellobium.*

dulce. Guamachil (sometimes spelled huamuchil); called also Manila tamarind and Madras thorn. A tree up to 50 ft. high, the leafstalks often with a pair of thorns to replace the stipules.* Leaflets very numerous, blunt, oblongish, about 1 in. long, very one-sided. Flower clusters finely hairy, the white, globe-shaped flower clusters about ¾ in. in diameter. Pods 5–6 in. long, spirally twisted, its black seeds shining. Mex., but early taken to the eastern tropics and long thought to be native in the Philippines. It needs staking in its early stages as growth is rapid and sometimes unsymmetrical without support. Widely used as an avenue tree in Fla.

Saman = *Samanea Saman.*

Unguis-cati. Cat's-claw; also called Florida cat's-claw and black bead. A spiny shrub or small tree, not over 15 ft. high. It resembles the first species, the flower clusters are smooth, the heads greenish-yellow and the red, spirally twisted pods 2–4 in. long. Fla., the W.I., and northern S.A.

PITTOSPORACEAE (pit-toss-spor-ray′see-ee). The tobira family, largely Australian, includes four genera of garden interest. *Hymenosporum, Pittosporum,* and *Bursaria* include shrubs and trees, while *Sollya* is a beautiful, flowering, woody, almost climbing shrub often grown as a vine. There are 10 genera and over 150 species in the family. All the cult. genera can be grown outdoors only in warm regions. *Pittosporum* and *Sollya* are not uncommon greenhouse plants, especially the former, which is the only cult. genus that is found also, outside Australia.

Leaves alternate,* often leathery or thick. Flowers rather showy, especially in *Pittosporum* and *Sollya,* nearly always regular,* and in various sorts of clusters. Fruit (in the cult. genera) a dry pod (capsule*), but berry-like in some (non-hort.) genera.

Technical flower characters: Sepals* 5. Petals 5, clawed, the claws* sometimes united at the base. Stamens* 5. Ovary superior.* Style 1.

PITTOSPORUM (pit-toss′por-um). Australian laurel. Chiefly Australasian evergreen shrubs and trees of the family Pittosporaceae, comprising over 100 species, of which several are grown for ornament in zones* 8 and 9, especially in southern Calif., and one in the greenhouse. They have alternate, or on young twigs apparently whorled* leaves, wavy-margined and faintly toothed or without teeth. Flowers in clusters or solitary, usually terminal, but sometimes in the leaf axils.* Sepals* 5, usually distinct. Petals 5, mostly clawed and more or less joined at the base, free above. Fruit a capsule,* its seeds sticky. (*Pittosporum* is from the Greek for resinous and seed, in allusion to the sticky seeds.)

The Australian laurels and the related genus *Hymenosporum* cannot be grown outdoors

---

* Special articles on the subjects indicated by an asterisk (*) will be found at the words so marked.

with safety north of zone* 8, but they are very popular shrubs and trees in Calif., Fla., and along the Gulf Coast. They are of easy culture in a variety of soils and are propagated by seeds, by cuttings of half-ripened wood or by grafting on *P. undulatum,* all preferably in a cool greenhouse. *P. Tobira* and a variegated-leaved form of it are often grown as pot plants in the cool greenhouse. It needs potting mixture* 4 and is a handsome plant.

crassifolium. Karo. A shrub or small tree, not over 25 ft. high. Leaves 2–3 in. long, ovalish or broader toward the tip, shining green above, white-felty beneath. Flower clusters terminal, the corolla red, about ½ in. wide. Fruit about 1¼ in. long, densely hairy. N. Z.

eugenioides. Tarata. A tree up to 40 ft. high. Leaves 2–4 in. long, wavy-margined, elliptic but pointed. Flower clusters (compound umbels*) terminal, the corolla about ¼ in. long, yellowish and fragrant. N. Z. There is also a variegated-leaved variety.

phillyraeoides. Butter-bush. A small tree (up to 20 ft.), the branches drooping. Leaves 3–4 in. long, lance-shaped or narrower. Flowers yellow, about ⅓ in. long, solitary or in small clusters in the leaf axils.* Fruit about ½ in. long, yellow. Aust.

rhombifolium. Diamond-leaf laurel. A tree 60–80 ft., usually less in cult. Leaves 3–4 in. long, ovalish or diamond-shaped, rather coarsely toothed above the middle. Flowers in terminal clusters (corymbs*), the corolla white, about ¼ in. long. Aust.

tenuifolium. Tawhiwhi or black mapau. A tree 20–30 ft. high. Leaves 1½–2½ in. long, oblongish, wavy-margined. Flowers solitary or in small clusters in the leaf axils,* the corolla dark purple, about ½ in. long. N. Z. There is also a variegated-leaved form.

Tobira. Tobira. A shrub 6–15 ft. high, useful for hedges in Calif. and Fla., and often grown as a pot plant in greenhouses. Leaves thick and leathery, ovalish but blunt toward the tip, 3–4 in. long. Flower clusters terminal, the corolla fragrant, greenish-white, about ½ in. long. Fruit densely hairy, about ½ in. long. China and Jap. The *var.* variegatum has white-marked leaves. Both are hardier than any other *Pittosporum,* have lemon-scented foliage and brittle twigs.

undulatum. Victorian box; also called cheese-wood. A tree 30–40 ft. high. Leaves oblongish or narrower, 4–6 in. long, wavy-margined, tapering at the tip, shining green. Flower clusters terminal, the corolla fragrant, white, about ½ in. long. Fruit about ½ in. long. Aust.

viridiflorum. A shrub 15–20 ft. high. Leaves leathery, shining green, more or less ovalish, 2–3 in. long, the margins rolled. Flower clusters dense, terminal. Corolla yellowish-green, about ¼ in. long. Fruit about ¼ in. long. South Africa.

PITYROGRAMMA (pi-ti-ro-gram′a). Gold fern. Silver fern. Known to gardeners as *Gymnogramma.* American, mostly tropical, evergreen ferns comprising about 90 species belonging to the family Polypodiaceae. Some have creeping underground stems. Fronds dark green, twice-compound,* the ultimate segments broad at the base, narrowing at the tip, cut or dissected. Spore* cases on under side of fronds, on the veins. Leafstalk and

under side of fronds covered with white or yellow powdery substance. (*Pityrogramma* is from the Greek for bran-like, in allusion to the powder on the fronds.)

Easily grown in the greenhouse, in temperatures not below 55°. They are commonly used as house plants. Propagated by spores sown on the surface of fine, sandy peat under a bell-jar in temperature 75°–85° at any time. Division of the plants may be made in Feb. They should be grown in potting mixture* 4.

sulphurea. Jamaica gold fern. Leafstalks shorter than the leaves. Leaves to 1 ft. long, 5 in. wide. Under side covered with pale yellow, powder-like substance. Leaflets much cut. West Indies.

triangularis. California gold fern. Leafstalks to 1 ft. Leaves 7 in. long, to 6 in. wide. Under side covered with deep yellow, powder-like substance, occasionally white. Calif. to British Columbia.

PLAGIANTHUS (pla-ji-an′thus). Australasian trees or shrubs, comprising about 12 species of the family Malvaceae. Hardy only in sheltered places from zone* 7 southward. The cult. species are trees to 60 ft. high, or shrubs to 12 ft. Leaves simple, alternate.* Flowers white, with 5 petals; some having stamens* and pistil,* others stamens only or pistil only. (*Plagianthus* is from the Greek for oblique flower.)

Only the following two grown in southern Calif.

betulinus. Ribbonwood. Growing to 60 ft. with trunk to 3 ft. across. Leaves 1–3 in. long, ovalish, coarsely toothed. Flowers small, yellowish-white, in loose axillary clusters. N. Z.

pulchellus. Shrub 9–12 ft. Leaves lance-shaped, 1–3 in. long, coarsely toothed. Flowers white, small, in long, loose clusters, growing from the axils* of the leaves. Aust.

plana, -us, -um (play′na). Flat.

PLANE. See PLATANUS.

PLANERA JAPONICA = *Zelkova serrata.*

PLANE TREE. See PLATANUS.

PLANE TREE FAMILY = Platanaceae. See PLATANUS.

planifolia, -us, -um (play-ni-fō′li-a). Flat-leaved.

PLANNING THE HOME GROUNDS. *Editorial Note:* The article below has been prepared for this edition by Mr. Garrett Eckbo, Am. Soc. Landscape Architects, South Pasadena, California. In it he has used parts of articles in our last edition contributed by Ralph E. Griswold, Bryan L. Lynch, Armistead Fitzhugh, and Harold A. Caparn, together with various shorter notes taken from earlier editions.

While any home which does not cover its lot completely will leave some ground space around it for landscape development, to most of us the phrase "home grounds" implies property of a scale sufficient to allow some freedom of choice in development. This we might call a suburban scale, a lot of

---

* Special articles on the subjects indicated by an asterisk (*) will be found at the words so marked.

perhaps 100 × 200 feet. Such space allows the articulation of some or all of the following: terraces and patios for outdoor living, service and gardening areas, game or swimming areas, show gardens of various sorts, private park space with grass and trees, off-street parking for cars, and so on. Larger properties become farms or estates; smaller are forced to concentrate on one of the above aspects, usually outdoor living or gardening. The planning and design of home grounds are part of a larger field known as landscape architecture.

LANDSCAPE ARCHITECTURE is the conscious design process through which considerable portions of the landscape in which we live are developed, adjusted, or adapted to provide us with maximum livability and convenience. It may cover not only gardens but larger elements such as parks and playgrounds, schools and colleges, hospitals and other institutions, industrial and commercial developments, neighborhood and community areas.

While all of the landscape we see, wherever we are, is one picture and one design problem, most of it is shaped by many disconnected decisions made by different people at different times. Many of these decisions, including those most influential, give little or no thought to conscious design objectives. Without such thought the physical quality of the landscape is unpredictable. The function of landscape architecture as a conscious discipline is to make such quality predictable and controllable.

Landscape architecture as a process is open to participation by anyone with adequate talent and understanding. However the development of these capabilities usually requires so much training and experience that the field is generally considered professional. About fifteen colleges and universities in the United States give professional training. Use of the term "landscape architect" is now limited by state licensing laws in California and Louisiana, and other states are expected to pass similar laws soon. These place landscape architects on the same professional level as architects and engineers. The American Society of Landscape Architects functions to set standards for professional practice throughout the country. A landscape architect practicing professionally charges for his services directly, and does not make money from the sale of materials or labor. This is essential to his objectivity in selecting materials or procedures for his clients.

This general article gives only the main features of good planning. There is no substitute for knowledge and judgment, and conditions differ widely over the country. So does the ability of people to cope with the practical and financial implications of planning even a simple garden. For all but the simplest the beginner would do well to call in the services of a trained professional. He will avoid many mistakes.

In order to meet the needs of the greatest number of readers practical applications of landscape architecture have been treated under the following special articles:

For garden structures such as gazebo, pavilion, pergola, summer house, etc., *see* STRUCTURES.

For night illumination of the garden, *see* LIGHTING.

For special features in the garden, *see* ARBORS, BANKS, BOWLING GREEN, DRIVES, EDGING, FENCES, GATES AND GATEWAYS, HEDGES, JAPANESE GARDENS, PATHS AND PAVING, SERVICE YARD, STEPS, WALLS AND WALL GARDENING, and WATER.

DESIGN. Landscape design begins with the study of the ground. Study means thought plus observation. Even the flattest piece of ground devoid of trees or any natural element of interest is bound to have some suggestion for the beginning of a design. Whether the ground is a rectangular lot in the heart of a city or a country estate of many acres, the nucleus of a plan is there. Perhaps this nucleus is only a limited view, a particular orientation with the sun, or a condition of the soil. It may even be a suggestion that comes from the surrounding territory.

This inevitable suggestion that comes from the most nondescript plot of ground is called the potential design. Look for it; it is there. And from the recognition of this potential design come all the variety and originality which make landscape design so fascinating. The clever person will detect this natural individuality and develop from it a plan which expresses the character of his particular site.

The purpose in studying natural conditions is to design sympathetically, not destructively. Having studied sympathetically, the designer will naturally make no change where he cannot improve. Such changing and improving to create new beauty is the essence of landscape design, to which artists have directed their talents for many centuries. These changes, when skillfully done according to a well-composed plan, should produce an effect more beautiful than the natural condition.

There are a very few simple basic rules for creating landscape beauty which will produce results according to the artistic ability of the designer.

Regard the entire property as the complete picture. Within this picture such elements as the house and other buildings, garden areas, service areas, walks, and drives must be arranged. No one of these elements should be thought of in detail until they have all been logically related in an organized plan. Plan-organization in its preliminary stages is a process of trial and error, in which the various elements are shifted about until they fit the natural conditions and the proposed use. In this process the house is the controlling element.

There is no arbitrary rule about locating a house unless dictated by deed or building restrictions. It should command the most desirable views and exposure to the sun for the best rooms.

* Special articles on the subjects indicated by an asterisk (*) will be found at the words so marked.

Location on the lot should conserve the greatest possible and most desirable space on the living side of the house. Where the lot is wide enough to allow anything but a central location the house should be pushed as close to the property line as possible on the service side, leaving only enough space to present a satisfactory appearance to the next neighbor.

Distance back from the street, unless controlled by restrictions, should be a minimum necessary to present an attractive picture. This frontage is rarely desirable or usable area in this motor age. Any area on the street side is wasted as far as private use is concerned, and contributes very little to the rapidly passing public to whom a small area, if properly developed, can appear just as attractive as twice the space.

When an approximate house location is determined, the garden, lawn, service, drive, and walk areas should be blocked out roughly. Adjustments have to be made until they all fit logically together with the proportional amount of space required by each. In this adjustment ideas for better arrangements develop until the whole scheme seems to work perfectly.

To make a plan work perfectly it must first of all have unity, meaning it must tie together. If walks, buildings, walls, or terraces break up the plan so that one part does not have a logical relation to the others, the lack of unity will create an unpleasant sensation and always be disturbing. Simplicity of arrangement with the fewest possible divisions of area produces the greatest unity. For instance, a garden projected out into the middle of a lawn will break up the lawn into small areas which amount to nothing and destroy the quiet beauty of the area. The same garden placed at one side of the lawn could be arranged to preserve the unity of the whole scheme without sacrificing the garden. And so with walks; if they cut up the plan in unpleasant shapes they detract from the unity and are annoying to look at, while they should be arranged to bind the plan together with agreeable lines.

Quite as important as unity in design is harmony, which means consistency. A gazing globe or sundial stuck out in the middle of the front lawn is obviously out of harmony and inconsistent with its purpose. Not all questions of harmony are as obvious as this illustration. To be successful all materials used in landscape design should harmonize with each other in color, texture, and shape. A picket fence harmonizes with a Colonial frame house, while an elaborate brick wall, beautiful in itself, would be completely out of harmony. A simple test of the harmony of any element in design is whether or not it is conspicuous or whether it seems to take its place in relation to the complete scheme. Plants, color, or architectural features which call attention to themselves, without any relation to other plants, color, or architectural features are out of harmony and do not belong.

Harmony in the size of things is called good proportion and all design is basically a matter of proportion. It is the relative size or proportion of the elements of a design which controls its beauty. A walk ten feet wide leading up to a modest cottage is out of proportion and would be ridiculous. Many equally ridiculous mistakes in proportion escape the designer merely because they are not so easily recognized.

A formal garden

Naturally, proportion varies with the effect desired and the size of one feature may be exaggerated to create a special effect. A sense of proportion is a matter of instinct or training and no rules can be made to take the place of such a sense. Questions of proportion can, however, be checked by comparing the size of elements in a proposed design to similar elements in a design which has already proved pleasing.

The entire outdoor surroundings of our living area are in a sense gardens. When grounds are considered in this sense the open lawns, terraces, utility areas, and pleasure gardens are all a part of the garden. Considering any detached area as the garden, independent of the rest of the property, and beautifying this area, leaving the other areas unattractive, is wasting an opportunity. It is quite as important that utility areas as well as those devoted to pleasure be made attractive. Someone must spend much of his time around the garage, the laundry yard, or vegetable garden. Such areas can be quite as attractive as the pleasure areas if they are given equal thought in planning. If garden art occupied the same relation to complete living today that it did in past ages, gardening would no longer be considered a privilege of the fortunate nor a leisure pastime; it would be considered an essential normal activity of good living.

To distinguish the area generally referred to

An informal setting well suited to the development of a wild garden

as the "garden" from the garden conceived as a complete grounds, the term "pleasure garden" should be used. Compared to the other areas the pleasure garden is free from utility requirements and devoted entirely to enjoyment. *See* Garden Room.

There should be an agreeable merging of the interior plan of the house with the pleasure garden. This transition can be accomplished best by projecting vistas into the garden from the window or door openings. If the garden plan relates to the views from the interior rooms it serves the double purpose of providing a pleasant outlook as well as its own garden interest. *See* Vista.

Houses are inevitably geometric and, therefore, formal in shape. Gardens connected with the house must harmonize with its architectural lines.

In working out from the house into the garden the dominant architectural lines should be projected into the garden plan and the architectural materials and general character of the garden should harmonize with the house. As the garden design recedes further from the influence of the house it may gradually become less architectural. If the house has a picturesque character with a rambling park and informal materials it naturally requires less architectural treatment in the garden areas.

After the skeleton lines of the garden have been determined in relation to the house plan the development of the design on these basic lines depends on the intended use. If the garden is to serve primarily as a picture to be seen from the house it must be visualized like a painting. If it is to be used for outdoor living and entertainment it will require shade, paving, and open lawn in preference to flowers. If the objective is the growing of flowers for cutting or color effect, trees and lawn will be minimized. Perhaps the garden must serve all of these functions to some extent.

It is not necessary to determine too arbitrarily just what the use of the garden shall be, but it is essential to anticipate exactly how the uses are to be unified in the design. Nothing but confusion can result from failure to plan for definite use. The available area, the natural shape of the ground, existing trees and means of access by steps and paths usually suggest the general scheme.

Not until the proposed scheme is fairly well visualized as to size, shape, and general character should questions of detail be considered. Width and detailed shape of paths, height of walls, location and shape of pools or other architectural ornaments should not be the controlling features in the design but should gradually evolve as the major elements of the plan progress. Details of planting, color schemes, and sculptural ornament should also be controlled by, rather than control, the general scheme.

The formation of a perfect snowflake is typical of the process by which garden design should evolve. From the center or controlling idea the design expands uniformly toward its ultimate shape, with major radiating lines gradually breaking up into more intricate patterns, but always according to a perfectly unified scheme in which every element contributes its proportional value to the completed design. Such a process prevents distortion of any one unit and avoids inconsistencies of function, scale, proportion, color, or pattern.

Country Estate. This is a complete residential unit on one to many acres of land, separated from immediate contact with city or suburb. Land of an acre or more tends to become either a farm or an estate. Farm use is primarily productive, as a means of livelihood, while the estate is oriented toward pleasure, relaxation, good living, and escape from the pressures of urban life. These two ideas are not incompatible: good living can be had on a farm, and an estate can be productive. However, the elements which do not produce either income or subsistence tend to dominate the estate, which is supported by income from other sources. On the other hand, few farms can afford estate-type amenities. These may include long private drives, garages, stables, cottages for gardener and chauffeur, extensive areas of pleasure garden and park landscape, cutting and vegetable gardens, tennis courts, swimming pools, and facilities for special types of livestock.

The design of the country estate must be based on the principles of approach outlined above. However, their application takes on much more expanded, enriched, and complicated forms and patterns. Estate planning includes larger and richer architectural and topographical elements, more and more complex functional elements and technical problems, broader relationships to the surrounding landscape, and greater demands for pleasure and aesthetic experience. Historically, country estates and their forerunners, palace gardens, have been considered the peak products of landscape architecture and the most important examples for instruction in professional schools.

Until the 1930's the great Renaissance gardens of Italy and France and the great private parks of England were most influential in American landscape thinking. Since then suburban-scale home grounds, modern art and architecture, the Mediterranean patio and the Oriental garden have become strong influences. However the demand for estate-scale living and show, and the broad design thinking needed to meet it, have by no means vanished from the American scene.

The scale and complexity of development problems presented by any property of an acre or more makes mandatory careful and complete advance planning of both physical arrangements and economic budgets for construction, installation, *and* maintenance. Physical planning must recognize and provide for all possible elements, even if they are only tentative or several years away. Visual, functional, technical, and economic relations between the public and approach areas, service and work areas, private living spaces, and general living, pleasure garden, and landscape areas must be worked out with great care. Careful planning for future maintenance problems will have definite influence on the plan. Water supply, drainage patterns, sewage disposal, and fire protection are all dominant planning considerations in such isolated residential units. Entrance drives, parking and turning spaces for cars have engineering problems not found on smaller properties. Service or garage court must be convenient without being visible from the main approach. The gardener's cottage and greenhouse should be close to the vegetable and flower gardens, and all of these may be part of the pleasure garden complex. Ample storage facilities for maintenance equipment and materials, roots, potted plants, furniture, etc., must be provided. The main house and gardens must be carefully oriented in relation to views, sun, and wind. Stables must be located so that winds will carry odors away. Thorough soil surveys and analyses, and complete soil conditioning programs as needed, are fundamental to the development of good plantings. Permanent tree and shrub patterns, carefully selected, spaced, and installed, will work with structures and topography to create the primary space organization of the estate. The kinds selected should be easily adaptable to the local soil and climate, and to the expected maintenance procedures.

SMALL GARDENS. On properties of one-eighth of an acre (the 50 × 100-foot lot) or less, space restrictions are such that few of the amenities of suburban or country living can be enjoyed. Few houses on small lots are designed to make the most of the available space. As a result there is tremendous waste of livable land area and potential privacy. Integrated design of house and garden together at the same time is more important on small properties than on large,

and happens less often. The great potential of the small lot for intimate, convenient, urbanized living, with maximum privacy and spatial richness, is seldom achieved.

In order to make the most of small residential properties it is important to minimize the space devoted to public approach, drive, and service activities, maximize the space devoted to general private living, and place the living and dining quarters and bedrooms in such a relation to this private space that they can function as completely integrated indoor-outdoor units. Then you will have made the most of the land available to you. Thereafter choice can be made as to whether the space is to be used primarily for gardening, for recreation such as small private swimming pool, or for general outdoor living. It will be difficult on small property to concentrate adequately on more than one of these uses, although portions of the others may be introduced at small and secondary scale.

CITY GARDENS. The most extreme problem in small-garden design is found in our older cities, particularly those most highly industrialized and motorized. Lots as narrow as sixteen feet, surrounded by connected buildings two or more stories high; sour soil, poor drainage, little sunlight, air filled with soot, fumes and smog — all of these place a major strain on the imagination of the designer and the skill of the gardener. The former will tend to concentrate on structural elements for the creation of garden spaces, while the latter concentrates on producing better growth from smaller plant beds. Integration of the efforts of these two can produce delightful gardens in the midst of the city.

Great visual pleasure and outdoor living amenity can be developed with simple, light, elegant structural controls. Floor most of the garden with brick, stone, or concrete in simple rectangular patterns. Leave only a few beds, at or near the sides, for carefully placed trees, shrubs, or flowers. These beds can be raised as much as a foot with wood or masonry curbs, for better soil and drainage. Enclose the garden with wood or masonry walls six to eight feet high where needed, and paint them white or light neutral tones if the garden is dark. Use light wood or metal treillage frames to support vines or make a pattern against these walls or those of surrounding buildings. Use treillage and vines also for higher screening at the sides or overhead. Such screens can be used to control sun, wind, and vision from outside.

When the basic structural framework is established the careful incorporation of a few trees, shrubs, and vines, and flower beds can create a fairyland quality in the city garden. Success of such planting depends chiefly on the condition of the soil, with sunlight and water as the other essential controls. For plant materials suited to city gardens, *see* BACKYARD GARDEN and SHADY GARDEN.

PENTHOUSE GARDEN. A very special problem among city gardens is the rooftop or penthouse garden. This has its origin in the

---

* Special articles on the subjects indicated by an asterisk (*) will be found at the words so marked.

zoning laws which require setbacks in the upper stories of tall buildings, thus providing terraces on which man can exercise his gardening ingenuity. In planning for the garden, however, it is wiser to content oneself with creating the illusion of a garden, by using only a minimum of city-proof plants in a pleasant setting of good architectural backgrounds and accents.

One of the chief reasons for choosing architectural rather than horticultural treatment for the penthouse garden is the presence of conditions inimical to the growth of plants. The handicaps of insufficient soil, high winds, lack of moisture, and constant deposit of soot and dirt on the leaves make it difficult for even the hardiest plants to survive. These difficulties can be overcome to a certain extent by installing windbreaks of glass or lattice fences, where building restrictions permit, by artificial irrigation systems, and in the case of new buildings, by constructing the building so as to permit the additional load of topsoil, two to three feet deep, properly drained, over the terrace area. Without these rather expensive and often impracticable aids to horticulture, the penthouse gardener has the alternative of resigning himself either to the exclusive use of privet, ailanthus, and wisteria, or to the annual replacement of all his plant material.

With the windbreak, irrigation, and proper soil depth it is possible to enlarge greatly the planting list. One can then grow Japanese flowering cherries (*Prunus subhirtella* is the best), flowering crabapples (*Malus floribunda, coronaria, theifera, sieboldi*), lilacs, forsythia, Rose-of-Sharon (*Hibiscus syriacus*), *Pieris japonica*, hawthorns (*Crataegus Phaenopyrum, Crus-galli, intricata, Oxyacantha*), and others of the hardier flowering shrubs and trees. In general, it is better to choose plants with smooth, even shiny leaves, rather than those with rough, hairy ones, as the soot and dirt are more easily removed.

Flower bloom in the penthouse garden is restricted to very few disease-resistant perennials and annuals. Iris, peonies, chrysanthemums, among the perennials, and petunias, lobelia, lantana, zinnias and French marigolds, among the annuals, make the list of successful plants on the roof. Provision should be made for a foot of well-enriched soil, at least a half day's sun and daily, thorough watering. All soil should be fertilized with bone meal and shredded cow manure, or a well-balanced commercial fertilizer every year. The flowers should be grown either below the parapet wall or with a windbreak of hedge or trellis behind them. The high, persistent wind on most terraces will snap off stems and dry up the leaves almost immediately unless the plants are well sheltered.

The most satisfactory blooms in the penthouse garden are the spring-flowering bulbs. Tulips, narcissus, and hyacinths, planted in the fall, give a mass of color in April and May. The bulbs should be renewed each fall for full success, and the soil refertilized before planting them. A covering of peat moss and evergreen boughs for the winter is advisable over all bulb plantings.

Aside from the difficulty of making plants live and thrive, the architectural treatment is advisable from purely aesthetic standpoints. In the first place the flat planes of the house walls, the parapet, and the adjoining buildings are made into a more harmonious whole by utilizing them in the decorative scheme, and combining them with allied or identical shapes and materials. The house walls may be covered by perspective trellis in interesting pattern, with an occasional vine tracery against it. Where it is desirable to block out part of a neighboring building or to frame an interesting view of the skyline, the parapet wall (usually rather ugly, with its copper flashing and heavy coping) may be concealed by trelliswork extended to the necessary height and designed to reveal or obliterate neighboring objects. Where the terrace extends around two sides of the penthouse, an illusion of distance and spaciousness is gained by an open arch or gateway through which one catches a glimpse of the garden beyond.

The use of running water in a city garden does much to make it enticing and interesting. A simple wall fountain, with a shallow basin below, is possible at a very little expense. An old lead cistern or a shallow stone pool basin may be made into a mirror pool with a figure or a fountain jet for accent opposite a door or window. Where the terrace construction makes piping difficult or prohibitively expensive a small pipe run from the hose connection can be concealed behind the planting and will be ample for the small amount of water needed for a pool supply.

In making the penthouse garden the wisest initial expenditure is for suitable, well-designed, permanent, architectural background and accent, with provision for protection from wind and dirt, adequate water supply and rich soil. With these basic elements provided and an allowance for refurnishing the planting each year, the penthouse garden, whether a tiny terrace outside the living room or a great expanse of gardens and allées surrounding a large penthouse, may be a source of enjoyment and outdoor activity throughout the year, with an expenditure in keeping with the size of the property and the tastes of the owner.

FURNITURE AND ORNAMENT

Furniture on the penthouse terrace must be of a sturdy type to withstand the constant exposure to weather conditions. In many of the European terraces this has been planned for at the time the building is erected, and tables and benches of concrete are made as an integral part of the structure. It should also be made of a material heavy enough to be wind-resistant. Stone and iron benches are the most practical if not the most comfortable penthouse furniture, and can be kept clean in city conditions where

---

* Special articles on the subjects indicated by an asterisk (*) will be found at the words so marked.

PENTHOUSE GARDEN ON A ROOF MADE FOR IT

See text for the management of roof gardens where such a weight of soil and water is impossible.

soot is prevalent by turning the hose on them. But when comfort is desired, iron, with wooden-slatted backs and seats, or wooden furniture forms a good compromise. Terrace furniture of a less formal nature, of iron laced with rawhide, or seats slung with awning material make for a greater degree of informality and are suitable if a casual outdoor living room is desired. Stick-willow chaises and chairs, with cushions covered with water-resistant material, add to the comfort and livable quality of the terrace.

As many penthouse terraces are lived on in summer, and looked at in winter, it is desirable to furnish them with permanent decorations such as trellises and iron wall brackets which support vines or contain pots for plants. These should be made to conform to the general architectural character of the building itself. In many instances fences and gates are necessary for the insurance of privacy and protection. These, if made of grilled iron, can be designed to harmonize with the wall brackets and trellises that are in use. Wood fences are also a desirable medium, although frequently discouraged because of fire laws.

Pots of all varieties are definite terrace ornaments, but should be made of material heavy enough to have a wind resistance, such as concrete, iron, lead, and other metals. Pots of flowers add color and charm to a terrace and have the advantage of being easily moved so that the effect of flower planting can be placed wherever a touch of color is needed according to season. These potted plants can also be brought into the house when the cold days come so that an investment in plant material is not lost.

For protection against rain and sun the terrace awning is an important feature. Awnings may be of the type that are regulated by a roller device and when closed are protected by an overhanging guard. What are perhaps more satisfactory are those supported by structural piping over which the awning is permanently stretched. As a preventive against fire hazard there is available a fireproof awning material which is impervious even to a lighted cigarette thrown from an upper window or to sparks blown from adjacent chimneys.

Perhaps one of the most interesting and neglected features in terrace decoration is the use of sculpture. Sculptured figures are a delight to the eye in wind and rain, and also when weighted with snow. These figures should be selected with great care, both for the quality of design and from the point of view of proper scale. They should be placed at some focal point which fits in with the general landscaping scheme of the terrace or where they can be equally enjoyed when looked at from the room adjoining the terrace itself. It is important that sculpture, particularly if placed on a parapet, be securely attached to its base so there may be no fear of any danger of its falling on passers-by.

* Special articles on the subjects indicated by an asterisk (*) will be found at the words so marked.

The more formal and decorative type of sculpture seems to fit in well with the average architectural rigidity that surrounds it. Carved stone, bronzes and lead, and if the terrace is lavish and formal, possibly marble, are the best mediums for figures that perform this decorative function.

OUTDOOR LIVING. In the past twenty years, beginning in California but now spreading throughout the country, there has been a great development of interest in making use of the garden spaces around the house to expand its livability, comfort, and convenience. This has meant recognition that house and lot are one design problem, not two; that the grounds are useful for much more than gardening activities; and that outdoor space can be designed for use and enjoyment by non-gardeners as well as gardeners.

Expansion of the livability of the house implies expansion of comparable elements: ground surfacing adequate to use; enclosure adequate to privacy and intimate scale; shelter adequate for local climate control; furnishing and enrichment with special detail adequate for comfort, pleasure, and delight.

Outdoor living has been traditional for thousands of years in mild climates around the world. The *patio garden* which is the typical product of this tradition represents the most complete and intimate integration of indoor and outdoor living space. *Courtyard gardens* represent the adaptation of this concept of intimate integration to more extreme northerly climates. *Terraces* provide comparable outdoor space for houses of the more traditional northern box form, which is less easily integrated with the garden spaces around it. *Garden rooms* may provide special and delightful spaces for outdoor living, taking advantage of special landscape or topographical situations, for those who do not require direct connections with the house.

An area of special interest is the Japanese house and garden, which represents a degree of integration comparable to patio gardens, though different in concept. Although these are thought of as being relevant to California and Hawaii in the United States, they did in reality develop in a climate nearly as severe as that of our eastern states. The lessons of Japanese house and garden design are more directly relevant to the eastern United States than to the West. They prove that it is possible to have lovely intimate gardens as part of one's year-round daily living even in extreme northeastern climates. Modern technology can easily solve the problem of the wintertime discomfort of the traditional Japanese house. See JAPANESE GARDENS.

PATIO AND COURTYARD GARDENS are intimately related to the house, which surrounds them on at least two sides. They are therefore usually small; they may use up the entire outdoor space on a small city lot, or they may be a small fraction of the grounds of a larger suburban or country property.

In either case they are primarily rooms for outdoor living. The floor is mostly paved to provide space for furniture, with planting reduced to small beds. The enclosure, if not provided by the house itself, is usually best created by structural walls. These function immediately and are more reliable than planted enclosures, especially for small spaces. Built-in seats may be incorporated in the wall construction to conserve the open space of the patio. If it leads into adjacent garden space the enclosure need not be so high as to block vision.

Shelter from sun, wind, or overhead view may be provided by arbor, pergola, or awning construction or by one or more trees of a type which will not outgrow the space. The entire patio or courtyard design must have the refinement and livable intimacy in detail that we expect in a living room. Enrichment of the patio is provided by carefully selected furnishing; by flowering plants or specimens selected for fragrance, texture, structure, or silhouette, in beds in the paving or in pots or tubs on it; by rocks and pebbles of interesting form, color, and texture; by water in small basins, fountains, or channels; and by art work in tile, mosaic, fresco, or sculpture. The relatively small size of these outdoor rooms requires very careful selection and refinement in materials and detail. They should be more imaginative and picturesque than the rooms which they adjoin. In spite of historical precedent the patio or court will feel larger and more spacious if the center is kept open. If this center is sunken, with two or three steps leading down into it, the appearance of size and interest is increased.

Historically the patio is a product of mild or hot dry climates around the world, particularly the Latin Mediterranean and South American countries. The courtyard is a product of the temperate, humid, cold-winter climates of Europe and North America. However, it is dangerous to concern ourselves with such precedents to the point of imitation or reproduction. Our design forms must spring from our own problems, resources, and needs. The heat and drought which produced the patio, with its paving, enclosure, shade, trickle of water, and restricted greenery, are similar to the climate of the southwestern United States — but our patios need not look like their historical precedents. Likewise the fact that European courtyards were Gothic, Romanesque Renaissance, or Baroque does not mean that courtyards in the northern U.S. must look like them. These influences combined with those of modern technology and art and Oriental design philosophy can produce contemporary American patios and courtyards as livable and beautiful in their time and place as any historical example.

Grass in a hot, dry climate is a luxury, and seldom looks well, but the ground may be covered instead with a paving of black and white pebbles, tiles, cobblestones, or flags. Colored pebbles, in harmonizing tints, also may be skillfully combined with architectural

---

* Special articles on the subjects indicated by an asterisk (*) will be found at the words so marked.

details. They come in a variety of colors such as Belgian black, red and yellow verona, emerald and oak-leaf green, mother-of-pearl, jet black, and pure white. Pebbles used in the making of paths should be set in cement, never left loose to roll under foot, while those used for conventionalized designs are kept in position in the beds by means of steel or wood curbings. If preferred, a ground cover may be clipped close, to resemble grass. Pansies, violets, myrtle, portulaca, sedums, crassula, dwarf cotoneaster, or English ivy, are all desirable plants for this purpose.

Space for soil beds is usually totally absent or very limited. This introduced the custom of placing plants in individual containers at strategic points. If flowering plants are used they can be shifted around for different color effects and are easily replaced with fresh ones when the blossoms fail. A vivid effect can be obtained by the use of annuals such as the larkspur, African marigolds, candytuft, nigella, *Phlox drummondi*, nasturtium, blue salvia, verbena, and certain of the California wild flowers, such as lupines, godetias, clarkia, nemophila, cream-cups, and California poppies in shades of pink, rose, cream, and the original golden-yellow. The beds might be edged with spring bulbs, such as *Tulipa clusiana* and *T. kaufmanniana,* or freesias, crocus, and scilla.

Another good planting scheme is to place a shrub or small tree in the center of each bed and cover the ground with low-growing foliage plants, or even a ground cover of English ivy, creeping juniper, or some other shade-tolerant plant. For a four-bed planting, two shrubs of one kind and two of another might be placed diagonally across from each other; a variety of the Indian hawthorn, *Raphiolepis delacouri,* with pale pink blossoms, is especially recommended in combination with camellias, or streptosolen, with its wealth of small, trumpet-shaped flowers of reddish-yellow. Gardenias and rosebushes, unpruned, especially tea-roses and small-sized wild lilacs (*Ceanothus*), are also good in conjunction with each other. The tamarisk is one of the most beautiful as well as one of the most useful shrubs for this purpose. Against soft-toned plaster walls it resembles a mist of green and rose, with its feathery leaves and flowers, withstands salt spray, and makes an excellent windbreak. For general utility purposes *Pittosporum Tobira,* with small, fragrant, white blossoms resembling daphne, is generally satisfactory. It blooms in winter when flowers are scarce, has beautiful rich foliage and prunes well. The beds are edged, as a rule, with tile or brick, although box may be preferred. Garden paths may be of pebbles, tile, hard-trodden earth, or stepping stones.

A well, pool, or fountain is made of cement, tiles, generally Talavera or maiolica, or of painted wood lined with tile in a contrasting color, and the shape and size are optional with the whim of the owner. Aquatics are sometimes planted directly in the pool, and potted plants in gay tile or clay containers are grouped around the curbing or set upon the ledge. Tropical water lilies in shades of rose, cerise, pink, yellow, and white, both the day- and night-blooming sorts, may be used in the large pools, but the tendency in the smaller ones is to leave the surface of the water clear. Tiny little pools are often sunk at the intersections of paths, with a rim of polychrome tile rising a few inches above the surface. The water spouts up from the center and falls back into the pool itself.

Other pools are built high on pedestals which may stand two or even three or more feet above the ground, the water overflowing from the basin being carried off in shallow-tiled or cement channels. The walls which surround the wells are usually two and a half to three feet high and either circular, six- or eight-sided. They are made of whitewashed brick, tiles, or painted wood, usually with a maiolica rim made all in one piece, known as "brocales." Wall fountains are set into niches or built into tiled panels, occasionally directly into the garden wall itself.

Next to tiles the most characteristic feature of any patio garden is the potted plants. They are used as accents, to outline a pool or the beds and borders of walks; they encircle the well-tops, stand singly on stairways, hang from the balconies around the patio, and grace the *balcóns* above the street; they are placed casually against a green bit of shrubbery, march across the rooftops in serried ranks, and stand in close formation on the pavement tiles — in other words, wherever there is a level spot or a niche in the garden walls. Aside from the purely decorative, their most useful purpose is as fillers-in. One can move them about and compose a brilliant garden today and a cool green one for tomorrow. Color schemes may be built around the flower pots, such as pale blue patio walls, clothed with espalier orange trees, black-and-white-tiled flooring, and blue-and-white-tiled pots filled with orange zinnias. Tree ferns with delicate fronds like lace, dwarf palms, heliotrope, azaleas, calla lilies, tuberoses, myrtle, rose geranium, and bamboo and papyrus are grown in pots for a variety of purposes.

The COURTYARD GARDEN, mostly for regions climatically unfit for patios, is protected and sheltered from the winds and permits of an entirely different type of planting than an open garden somewhat removed from the house or in a patio. It is invariably small in area, and all available space must be used to the greatest advantage. Materials should be choice evergreens such as *Buxus sempervirens, Taxus cuspidata,* or *Ilex crenata,* which can be controlled in their growth and should take the place of the more rampant-growing deciduous shrubs. The walls surrounding the court are as important a part of the garden as the horizontal area

* Special articles on the subjects indicated by an asterisk (*) will be found at the words so marked.

An attractive, but somewhat expensive, type of courtyard garden. For simpler and less expensive treatments *see* BACKYARD GARDEN.

and should be treated as part of the ornamental scheme. Espaliered fruit trees, *Hedera Helix, Euonymus fortunei,* or pillar roses and wisteria are more suitable than rank-growing vines.

Courts are invariably shaded on one side or the other part of the day, which is part of their charm, and the plant materials must be selected to thrive in this shade. At best the plant materials are merely a background in a courtyard and should not be crowded. Large paved areas are necessary to provide space for furniture, and the remaining ground space should be covered with hardy ground covers such as *Hedera Helix, Pachysandra terminalis,* or *Vinca minor.* This ground cover may be made more interesting by interplanting *Narcissus* and *Scilla,* which will poke up through the ground cover in the spring. During the summer lilies thrive under these same conditions, and a mass effect of *Lilium testaceum,* followed by *Lilium regale* and then *Lilium speciosum* will give continued interest.

Where the courtyard is sufficiently open to allow ample sunlight for perennials they may take the place of the ground cover and those plants which thrive only under shaded conditions. If the garden is to be used only in summer use annuals; for yellow, dwarf marigolds; for white, small, single bedding petunias; for blue, *Ageratum* or *Lobelia;* for purple, blue petunias or heliotrope; for pink or red, either petunias or geraniums.

If windows open onto the courtyard, color may be added by window boxes filled with fuchsias, lantanas, or petunias. Where space does not permit of bedding plants use ornamental pots of geraniums, *Hibiscus,* or Shasta daisy. In cases where most of the court is taken up by paving, set standard heliotrope, geraniums, lantanas or fuchsias, also *Agapanthus* or tuberous-rooted begonias, around in informal groups to break up the severity of the paving.

Nothing is more ornamental or pleasant in a courtyard garden than a small pool or fountain surrounded by a few potted plants. The water has a cooling effect and adds life and interest to the court. Such fountains must be proportionate in size to the court, but have infinite possibilities for variation in design. If the pool is raised 15 in. from the surrounding walk level, with the coping 12 to 15 inches wide, it is just the right height to serve as a seat.

Large, picturesque trees like apple or hawthorn should be included incidentally in the plan of the court to offset the severity of its architectural surroundings. Use mature rhododendrons, tubbed oleanders, *Pieris japonica, Azalea yedoensis poukhanensis,* or mature *Taxus cuspidata.* There is already sufficient architectural interest in the surrounding walls without repeating similar architectural forms in the planting. Compact, formal-shaped evergreens like *Juniperus communis hibernica, Juniperus chinensis globosa,* or *Juniperus chinensis pyramidalis* may accentuate entrances to the courtyard, but this type of compact emphatic form, either in upright, spiky effects or low, clipped, globular forms like *Thuja occidentalis globosa,* should be used sparingly. Plants which require large space for maturity, like the pines and spruces, have no place in

* Special articles on the subjects indicated by an asterisk (*) will be found at the words so marked.

the courtyard. *Pyracantha, Taxus, Buxus,* or *Ilex* which can be controlled are preferable in this sort of work.

TERRACES AND GARDEN ROOMS. The typical terrace is a paved area against one wall of a house, making an extension for the indoor living space and a connection between the house and the garden beyond. A garden room, on the other hand, is a space not directly connected with the house, perhaps some distance away from it, which is developed for livability, use, and comfort because of some special natural feature, or a need of the owner. It should be born in mind that discussion of categories such as "patio," "courtyard," "terrace," and "garden room" does not mean that there are only four types of outdoor living spaces, and that what you do must conform to one of them. On the contrary these are only examples of the variety of design problems and solutions, and this variety is unlimited and should not be categorized. The charm and fascination of garden design lies precisely in the endless possibilities for individualized design produced by the multiple combinations of people, land, architecture, climate and materials. — G. E.

For details of terraces and garden rooms, *see* both these terms.

PLANT. It is impossible to define *plant* in terms only of the use of the word in hort. Plants range in size from bacteria to kelp, a seaweed often several hundred feet long; and it includes thousands of algae and fungi of no interest to the gardener. *Plant* in the hort. sense includes the flowering plants and the ferns, all of which belong to various families (*see* PLANT FAMILY). *See also* FERNS AND FERN GARDENING.

For the various parts of individual plants, *see* the articles at ROOT, STEM, LEAF, FLOWER, FRUIT, and SEED.

PLANTAGO. *See* Plantain in the list at WEEDS.

plantaginea, -us, -um (plan-ta-gin'i-a). Plantain-like.

Plantago-aquatica (plan-tay-go-a-kwat'i-ka). A specific name derived from an old genus, *Plantago-aquatica,* not used here for water plantain (*Alisma Plantago-aquatica*).

PLANTAIN. The true plantain is *Musa paradisiaca,* a world-wide tropical vegetable. *See* MUSA. But the word *plantain* is also applied to weeds of the genus *Plantago. See* the list at WEEDS. For the other plants to which the name plantain is sometimes applied *see* ALISMA, ERIGERON, GOODYERA, and HELICONIA.

PLANTAIN-LILY. Perennial, widely cult. garden herbs of the genus **Hosta** (hos'ta) of the lily family, often known under the names of *Funkia* and *Niobe.* Of the 10 known species, all from China and Jap., most are in common cult., especially those below. They are tufted plants, grown both for their handsome, conspicuously ribbed, basal leaves, and their white, lilac, or blue

A plantain-lily

flowers in terminal clusters (spikes or racemes*) terminating a usually bracted stalk that arises from the leaves. Flowers tubular, usually expanded at the summit, the six lobes not distinguishable as petals and sepals, all petal-like. Stamens 6. Fruit an elongated capsule,* rarely produced in some species. (Named for N. T. Host, Austrian botanist.)

Plantain-lilies are of the easiest culture and are common in old-fashioned gardens, especially under partial shade and in moist sites. They will, however, grow perfectly in the open border and are readily increased by spring or fall division of the clumps. They are sometimes known as daylily, but the latter name is better restricted to the related genus *Hemerocallis* (*see* DAYLILY).

H. caerulea. Leaves broadly oval, narrowed to a winged stalk, the blade 4–9 in. long, the foliage standing 18–24 in. high. Flowering cluster slightly taller, pale or deep blue, the corolla 1½–2 in. long. By some called *H. ventricosa.* Summer. A lower form with later, white flowers has had the unverifiable name of *minor alba* attached to it.

H. decorata. Not very different from the better-known *H. undulata,* but the leaves blunt at the tip, and with darker-lilac, drooping flowers, nearly 2 in. long. Jap. Summer.

H. fortunei. Leaves 4–5 in. long, oval-heart-shaped, pale bluish-green. Flowering cluster much exceeding the foliage, the corolla about 1½ in. long, pale purple or white. June–July.

H. glauca = *H. sieboldiana.*

H. japonica = *Hosta lancifolia.*

H. lancifolia. Leaves oval-lance-shaped or narrower, tapering both ends, the blade 4–6 in. long, the stalk much longer. Flowering stalk 18–24 in. high, the corolla 1½–2 in. long, pale lavender or lilac. Summer. The *var. albo-marginata* has white-margined leaves; and the *var. tardiflora* blooms in autumn, and by some is considered a separate species. Sometimes known as *H. japonica.*

H. minor alba. *See* H. CAERULEA.

H. ovata = *H. caerulea.*

H. plantaginea. Leaves very strongly ribbed, oval-heart-shaped, 6–10 in. long, 4–6 in. wide, long-stalked. Flowering stalk 18–24 in. high,

* Special articles on the subjects indicated by an asterisk (*) will be found at the words so marked.

the corolla white, fragrant, 4–5 in. long. Aug.–Oct. One of the most common in old gardens, and sometimes known as *H. subcordata.*

H. sieboldiana. Leaves oval-heart-shaped, 6–10 in. long, the leafstalk so long as to overtop the flowering stalk. Flowers thus half-hidden by the foliage, numerous, pale lilac, 2–2½ in. long. June–July. Called by some *H. glauca.*

H. subcordata = *Hosta plantaginea.*

H. undulata. The tallest of all the cult, species, the flowering stalk often 3 ft. high. Leaves broadly ovalish, sometimes heart-shaped at the base, 6–8 in. long, the stalk a little longer. Corolla about 2 in. long, funnel-shaped, pale lavender, the flowers numerous. June–July, but usually following *H. sieboldiana* and *H. fortunei.*

H. variegata = *H. undulata.*

H. ventricosa. A name suggested by some for *H. caerulea.*

PLANT BREEDING. This is an old practice, but a real understanding of its principles is very new. Three primary proceedings are involved — selection,* inbreeding,* and hybridization or crossing.* Selection is the simplest and the oldest. Far back beyond historic records man noted wild plants of a species better than the average, just as today small boys often know about special persimmon, papaw, or wild plum trees. Primitive man, having noted these more desirable representatives, next transferred them to his home surroundings, either by transplantation, conscious or accidental planting of their seeds, or by offshoots. Pride and appreciation in his discovery eventually led to further selection, through choice of superior seedlings.

This illustrates both selection and a kind of crude, unconscious inbreeding, through relative isolation. Selection* and inbreeding* are still just as simple in everyday practice, except for the greater understanding many of us have as to what we are doing, and consequent refinement in methods. Now we plant bushels of seed, and hunt for these variations. Now we protect these highly desirable variants with various devices that prevent them from making misalliances, and we realize that it is worth our while to take special care of them and their offspring — even at times the weakest — rather than let them struggle and compete in unfavorable environments with their less desirable wild types.

The third plant-breeding practice is hybridization or crossing.* Natural crossing has undoubtedly given man — even primitive man — many of his most desirable types of cultivated plants, and until very recently he has been practically unconscious of this fact. Corn and bread wheat are both now suspected to have arisen in this fashion. Probably the same thing is true of potatoes, bananas, tomatoes, and tobacco. Natural hybrids are by no means uncommon even in the wild. The collection of many types, varieties, and species, in nurseries, test gardens, arboretums, botanic gardens, and estate and palace surroundings has undoubtedly greatly facilitated natural hybrid production, and this went on before historic records began, even as it does today among relatively primitive peoples.

Many of our best varieties of plums, apples, berries, flowers, and other cultivated plants have originated as chance seedlings, but with an observer standing by, so to speak, who saved them for posterity. These chance seedlings very often represented some type of hybrid, and from their progeny, through selection, inbreeding and further crossing, have come still more desirable types, of which Golden Bantam sweet corn and the Early Rose potato are examples.

Conscious plant hybridization, in which the worker has some idea of what he was doing, is a little over 200 years old, while scientific hybridization is very much younger. In the former one crosses varieties having desirable characters that are to be combined, and grows the progeny of the cross, hoping to find among it the type with, or approaching, the desired combination. In many cases, he does; in many others, he does not, in which case he tries again, if he is persistent. No particular attention is paid to the ancestry of the parents, and no great precautions are taken to labeling or prevention of contamination from undesirable pollen. The actual parentage is often more or less a guess, especially as regards the pollen parent. Again, seeds of known hybrids of such plants as irises and roses and apples are planted, the progeny grown, and selection practiced.

Little knowledge of the fundamental principles of variation* and inheritance are necessary in this method of plant breeding, but one needs to be thoroughly familiar with the nature and kinds of material, and as persistent and enthusiastic as an artist. This method often wastes time and produces discouragement because of failure in attempting the impossible. The varieties produced by this method, which last, are largely chance combinations, "winning numbers in a living lottery." For every individual saved, thousands are destroyed.

The scientific method often provides shortcuts by decreasing the time element, lessening the amount of work involved, sustaining enthusiasm by pointing out the road and the limitations of what can and cannot be done. Through its use in some cases, and this will be increasingly true, one can definitely calculate the difficulties and possibilities of obtaining the desired type. In other words one can come near to making a new desired type to order, by shuffling the available characters through crossing, selection, re-crossing, and again selecting. This has been done in obtaining disease-resistant beans and wheat, and more desirable types of tobacco and sweet corn. — O. E. W. *See also* MUTATION and MENDEL.

PLANT DISEASES. The causes of diseases in plants are analogous to those which produce maladies in the human or animal bodies. Some are non-infectious and not

---

* Special articles on the subjects indicated by an asterisk (*) will be found at the words so marked.

caused by pathogens.* They are sometimes referred to as *physiogenic troubles* to contrast them with *pathogenic diseases* which are infectious and are caused by pathogens. If we compare them with human ills, we would say that a *physiogenic trouble* of a plant is analogous to sunburn, frostbite, malnutrition, or food poisoning in a human. The *pathogenic diseases* of plants are analogous to measles, smallpox, or malaria in a human.

PHYSIOGENIC TROUBLES. Some of the physiogenic troubles of plants are chlorosis,* leaf scorch,* oedema,* scald,* and wind burn.* Plants may also be injured or killed by toxic chemicals in the soil or improper chemicals on the foliage. In sour soil, *Taxus* and many grasses are yellow and grow poorly while azalea, *Rhododendron,* and pin oak are dark green and prosper. In sweet soil the situations are reversed.

When a gardener inspects a "sick" plant to diagnose the cause of the illness, he should first consider all the possibilities of physiogenic troubles. Is soil too wet or dry, too hot or cold, too sweet or sour? Is there enough or too much fertilizer? Has oil, salt, gas, weed killer, termite-proofing chemical, or other poisonous material been spilled or injected into the soil. Improper chemicals for termite-proofing may injure a tree 50 feet from the treated building if the tree roots extend into the area treated. Has the tree or bush been transplanted or has a soil-fill of as little as 12 inches been placed over the root area within the past few years? Can you associate the sudden death of a tree or a 50-foot diameter circle of plants with a recent lightning storm?

Plants which grow poorly or die if planted within the root area of a black walnut tree are azalea, *Rhododendron,* potato, tomato, pepper, blackberry, raspberry, etc. Does the trunk of a large old tree go straight into the ground, instead of having a nice buttress at the base? Dig down for a foot or so and inspect for and remove girdling roots. Before running out to buy a spray or dust to put on your sick plant, explore all possibilities of physiogenic troubles. In our experience, more plants are ill with physiogenic troubles than are sick with pathogenic diseases.

PATHOGENIC DISEASES. The pathogenic diseases of plants are caused by some of the fungi,* bacteria,* and viruses.*

FUNGI are found everywhere and frequently are of vital importance to man's well-being. A large number of the species, however, are important enemies to cultivated crops. There probably is no plant in the universe that is not susceptible to some one of this immense group of lower plants. Among the diseases caused by fungi are anthracnose,* black knot,* black spot,* blight,* canker,* damping-off,* downy mildew,* some galls,* gray mold,* some leaf blights,* some leafspots,* needle cast,* powdery mildew,* rust,* smut.* some wilts,* and some yellows.* The life history of the fungi which cause these diseases may be rather complicated and must be studied carefully by the grower if intelligent control measures are to be applied. The body of the fungus usually consists of thread-like wefts which resemble cobwebs. Various types of fruit bodies arise from these threads and serve as a means of identification to the specialist who deals with such lower forms. The important point to the grower is that many of the fungi have two types of fruiting, sexual and asexual. The one type may enable the parasite to live through the winter or during unfavorable weather periods, while the other aids in rapid reproduction and infection when the crop is growing. In nearly all cases the control recommendations are based on a knowledge of these two stages.

BACTERIA. The life history of a bacterium is quite simple. It reproduces by growing smaller in the middle until finally the cell divides into two. This division continues at an extremely rapid rate when environmental conditions are favorable. It may live in a dormant stage on or in plant seeds, plant refuse, hibernating insects, or soil during the winter, and then be splashed or carried to susceptible crops when the weather is optimum for its entrance into the plant parts. Among the diseases caused by bacteria, are, crown gall,* fireblight,* some galls,* some leaf blights* and leafspots,* some rots, and some scabs,* slime flux* and some wilts.*

VIRUS DISEASES. Nearly all plants seem to be susceptible to some virus. The principal symptoms of the affected host are mottling, variegation, rolling of leaves, yellowing, distortion, and dwarfing. Because of the symptoms the names generally applied to such diseases are: leaf curl,* mosaic,* ring spot,* spotted wilt,* streak,* and yellows.* Sometimes characteristic symptoms are caused by the combining of two or more viruses in the same host.

Each virus usually is specific for a given host* or a narrow group of hosts, although in some cases, as in aster yellows and curly top of beet, the viruses affect an extremely large number of plants. Since the virus cannot be cultured, it must be classified by the symptoms it causes on the plant, the length of time it will remain alive in expressed sap, the amount of heat required to make it inactive, the plants it will infect, and the insects which act as carriers. In most cases it gains entrance into the plant when sucking insects, which transmit it, are feeding. Aphids and leafhoppers are common vectors.* as the insect carriers are named. In certain cases, as in bean mosaic, it is carried in the seed, or in the tubers, as in the potato.

DISSEMINATION OF FUNGI, BACTERIA, AND VIRUSES. The means by which all the disease-producing organisms are disseminated also is important in any control program. For instance, if a parasite can be kept from a country or any localized area, the cost of protecting each plant or eradicating the invading organism can be eliminated. Conse-

* Special articles on the subjects indicated by an asterisk (*) will be found at the words so marked.

quently the grower should be much interested in the manner in which these lower plant forms are spread from one field to another.

Wind is one of the important agents in spore dissemination. Luckily, many spores are so dried by the air currents which carry them that they are not viable when they finally land on their favorite host. Rust spores,* among others, however, may be carried long distances by prevailing winds and probably account for unexpected epidemics that arise seemingly from nowhere.

The chief method of dissemination from one plant to another is by the splashing of rain. A raindrop may land on a spore mass which includes thousands of individuals. This drop may then be washed into a puddle, the water of which in turn is splashed into a distant puddle, and so on throughout the field. During rainstorms rivulets of water flow from an infested field to a neighboring one, thereby infesting soil that may never have grown a diseased crop. Flooding, too, disseminates organisms that otherwise might have been confined to a small area. Shallow wells and ponds from which water is drawn for greenhouses are breeding places for some of the fungi that kill seedling plants or cause rots on recently potted cuttings.

Contaminated soil is an important source for later infection of plants. A field that has grown one diseased crop may retain the parasite for one year or possibly for many years. If such contaminated soil is carted into the greenhouse, or is left clinging to roots of seedlings that are transplanted, the harmful organism may be spread into many fields. In a similar way plants imported from other countries may have clinging to their roots soil that harbors parasites which have never before been introduced into the country. Some soils when wet are sticky, so that when a drove of animals walk through a contaminated field during a rainy day, they may convey enough infested mud to adjoining fields to cause a serious outbreak of some plant disease the following season.

It is a common practice to drop undesirable plant parts in the garden where the crop is grown or toss them into a heap for humus the following year. If such trash is not thoroughly composted, disease-producing organisms may remain alive in the affected plant tissue and serve as a source of infection when the same or a related crop is grown there again. It seems fitting, also, to throw rotted plant parts onto the manure pile, but the practice becomes dangerous if the manure is spread over the fields for fertilizer, and susceptible plants grown on this same soil. The presence of the manure may stimulate the growth of the fungus as well as that of the plant, as in the case of corn smut.

Every grower has learned to his sorrow that plant parasites may be transmitted in seeds, bulbs, tubers, cuttings, and other living plant parts. Many of our most obnoxious pests were introduced into this country in this manner. Such transmission is so common that the careful grower is ever attempting to find sources of seeds or other propagating plant parts that are free from fungi, bacteria, and viruses.

Insects are responsible for the spread of many diseases. Plant lice and leafhoppers are generally associated with virus transmission. In some cases, such as the bacterial wilt of the cucumber, melon, squash, etc., bacteria cannot overwinter except in the presence of beetles. The spores of many fungi may cling to bodies of migrating insects, and thus be carried long distances. Higher animals may also serve as carriers.

Environmental Influences

No control measures of plant diseases are wholly adequate if environmental conditions have not been taken into consideration. The organisms which cause diseases are affected favorably or adversely by much moisture or little moisture in the air or soil, high or low temperatures, amount of sunlight, type of soil, acidity or alkalinity of the soil, humus content of the soil, and sometimes even by the kind and quantity of the fertilizer.

Soil Moisture in excess may be as harmful, so far as plant diseases are concerned, as heavily moisture-laden air. It is a general observation that late-blight rot of potatoes is common in wet soil. Nearly all kinds of root rots are increased by water-holding soil. The trouble can be avoided either by changing the crops to different types of soil, or by soil drainage. Tile drainage tends to remove heavy rainfalls quickly and so restore the aerated condition of the soil necessary to the health of roots. Soil moisture sometimes can be decreased by frequent cultivation or stirring of the surface layer. This is practiced in seedbeds where various fungi that cause damping-off* live in the very topmost soil.

Temperature is closely related to the severity of attack by many parasites. In the field the temperatures cannot be governed but the time of planting may sometimes be altered to such an extent that the crop is not subjected to the temperature favorable for the parasite. Several of the pathogens on peas thrive best in warm soil. Therefore if the crop is planted very early, the dry, hot weather of midsummer is avoided. Similarly, early potatoes may avoid late blight because they mature before the arrival of cool nights in the autumn.

A quick way to warm a soil is to drain it well, for it takes much more of the sun's energy to heat water than it does dry soil. It is for this reason that some parasites are found only in wet soils.

In greenhouses where the temperature may be raised or lowered almost at will, it is possible to protect the plants by growing them in a temperature unsuitable for the growth of the pathogens.* Raising the night temperature reduces the ravages of white rust of radish, the anthracnose of lettuce, and gray

---

* Special articles on the subjects indicated by an asterisk (*) will be found at the words so marked.

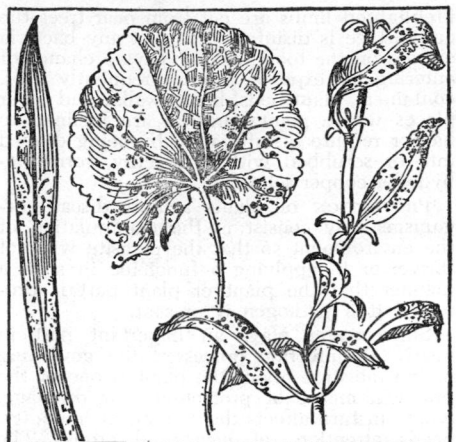

Rust symptoms on leaves of carnation (*left*), hollyhock (*center*) and snapdragon (*right*). For control *see* the disease notes at each crop.

mold rot of many plants. Lowering the temperatures hinders the growth of still other parasites.

SOIL ACIDITY. Modifying the acidity or alkalinity of the soil will aid in the control of some diseases. Clubroot* of cabbage and other crucifers can be reduced if hydrated lime is added to the soil, a few weeks before planting, to raise the reaction to slightly above neutral. On the other hand, scab of potato may be reduced by adding sulphur to acidify the soil. (*See* ACID AND ALKALI SOILS.)

STORAGE. The most obvious application of lowering temperatures to protect plant parts is cold storage. All kinds of perishable plants can be kept for months if the temperature is lowered sufficiently to stop completely the development of pathogens.* Each crop may require a slightly different temperature for best results. The watery mold rot of celery is kept in check only when the storage is maintained at slightly below 32° F. Potato tubers acquire a sweetish taste if held much below 37° F., while sweet potatoes and squashes can be kept well at still higher temperatures. In order to insure further the keeping qualities of the crops placed in cold storage, they should not be subjected to high temperatures between harvesting and storage; they should be placed in clean containers, and the storage-room walls and floors should be washed with a fungicide to remove the refuse from previously contaminated crops.

PLANT DISEASE CONTROL MEASURES

EXCLUSION. Diseases of plants may be controlled by preventing the introduction of disease into uninvaded areas. Exclusion may be effected by intercepting the pathogen* en route to the uninvaded area; by eliminating the pathogen* from the carrier before admitting the latter to the area; or by pro-

hibiting the introduction of natural carriers of the parasites from known or suspected centers of distribution. (*See* QUARANTINES.)

ERADICATION is the removal, elimination, or destruction of the pathogen in certain areas where it already is established. The removal of diseased plants from among the healthy is a very common method of eradication. It is known as *roguing*, and is applicable to all stages in plant growth. Many of the virus diseases can in part at least be controlled in this manner. It is almost the only way in which woodlots can be kept free from affected timber. When cankers or twig blights are present, it usually is not necessary to remove the entire tree, for the trouble can successfully be combated merely by the removal of the affected parts, that is, by *pruning*. This applies generally to shade and fruit trees.

The removal of infested plant refuse is a type of eradication by elimination which might be employed advantageously more often than it is at present. It consists primarily in the collection and removal of fallen parts of plants which are infested with pathogens.* Fallen leaves, fruits, and twigs often harbor the pathogen or serve for its saprophytic development just where it will be in the best position for inoculation of new growth the next season. Raking and burning, removal and composting, or burying are some of the ways of getting rid of dangerous debris, and therefore of eliminating the parasites which have been harbored there. For the same reason, it may be necessary to remove and sterilize (*see* SOIL STERILIZATION) soil in greenhouse benches or in cold frames.

Another means of elimination is the extirpation of weeds or other plants that act as hosts* for the same parasites that affect any given cultivated group. A long list of such examples might be given. Some rather common diseases which are controlled, either completely or in part, in this manner are: cucumber and tomato mosaic, the virus of which remains active during the winter in the roots of such perennial plants as milkweed, ground cherry, pokeweed, and catnip. Many of the rusts have alternate hosts and when one of these hosts is eradicated the rust disappears. Among these are the white pine blister rust whose alternate hosts are the currant and gooseberry, the apple rust, which spends part of its life on the cedar tree, and to a lesser degree, the black rust of cereals, one stage of which requires the common barberry* for reproduction. On farms where care is taken to keep out all wild mustard and related weeds, clubroot of cabbage can be controlled more successfully.

Cultivation helps in eradication of the parasite in at least two ways. The stirring of the soil tends to dry the surface and make it unfavorable for the growth of the molds and bacteria that so frequently are present near the base of susceptible plant stems. Thus young seedlings may sometimes be protected from damping-off* molds by keeping the sur-

* Special articles on the subjects indicated by an asterisk (*) will be found at the words so marked.

face soil well stirred. The more common effect of cultivation, however, is to turn under diseased plant refuse so deeply that the parasite cannot get an opportunity of causing infection, at least until the crop is mature enough to withstand the injury.

If the old apple leaves, bearing the winter stage of scab, or cherry leaves carrying the leafspot fungus, are turned under deeply, much of the early spring inoculum is destroyed. Most of the leafspots or blights on cultivated crops are reduced in intensity if the previous affected crop is plowed under. Summer cultivation, also, may destroy weed hosts.

Nearly every grower knows the importance of crop rotation, but seldom practices it sufficiently. When a dangerous fungus or bacterium once becomes established in a field, there is almost no way in which it can be eradicated unless it can be starved out by growing plants which are immune to the organism. In the corn-wheat country one of the common pathogens affects both crops, so that it is necessary to have in the rotation hay or other crops which are not affected by the fungus. The black-leg fungus of cabbage lives as long as three years in the soil, thus requiring at least a four-year rotation with other crops to starve it out completely. Nearly every cultivated plant is affected by one or more parasites which get into soil and require rotation of crops for their eradication. It is true, however, that some fungi, especially those that cause wilts, may remain alive so long that crop rotation cannot be depended upon to reduce the amount of inoculum. Furthermore some crops cannot well occur in the same rotation with others. For instance, cabbage, susceptible to clubroot, requires soil with plenty of lime, while potatoes cannot be grown in such soil for fear of being disfigured by common scab. Similarly, strawberries and watermelons require a fairly acid soil for best growth while alfalfa would not thrive under such conditions.

DISINFECTION AND DISINFESTATION. These are both of extreme importance in the eradication of plant pathogens. The term disinfection usually is applied to the killing of a parasite after it once has established a relationship with the host, while disinfestation is the killing of organisms that may be clinging to any host parts. Thus in the case of powdery mildew of plants, the talcum-like growth of the fungus on the upper side of the leaf has been made before sulphur is applied to kill the fungus. In the loose smuts of wheat and barley or in black-leg of cabbage, the fungus threads grow into the seed. When the seeds are disinfected with hot water the fungi gradually are killed. Potato tubers have clinging to them black, tar-like specks, the resting bodies of one of the common parasites of the potato. When the tubers are dipped into mercury solutions the fungus is killed before it establishes a feeding relation with the host; therefore, the dipping is considered disinfestation. When fireblighted limbs are cut from pear trees the cut surface is disinfested so that any bacteria carried on the tools will not have a chance of entering on the exposed tissue. Frequently tools, containers, plant beds, board walks, and other places where plant parasites are inclined to harbor require disinfestation by being dipped into or scrubbed with a mercury, formaldehyde, or copper solution.

PROTECTION of plants against disease organisms may consist in the manipulation of the environment so that the parasite will not thrive, or in applying a fungicide in such a manner that the plant or plant part is protected if a pathogen is present.

Since water plays an important part in nearly all infection processes, the governing of the moisture about the plant is one of the practical means of protection. Air drainage, which in turn affects the amount of humidity, needs attention for nearly all crops. The movement of the air through the crop tends to hasten evaporation and removes the moist air from the vicinity of the plants. In humid regions where rains, dews, and fogs are of frequent occurrence, it is necessary in disease control that free water on the plants should be evaporated quickly. Air drainage is accomplished by the selection of a location for planting where air currents are not retarded.

Hillside plants have in most cases a natural air drainage, for cool air tends to flow downward. Low places in a field, high, thick hedgerows, the presence of high weeds, plants crowded too closely together, and poorly pruned trees all tend to hinder air currents, so that dew or rain may stand in droplets on the leaves for a few hours longer than would be true otherwise and thus permit parasites to gain an entrance into the host.

In greenhouses, plants can sometimes be kept dry and infection avoided by applying all the water to the soil through sub-irrigating pipes or tile.

Although the methods described above are all methods of protection, the use of protective fungicides is the most commonly recognized method. (*See* SPRAYS AND DUSTS, SPRAYING AND DUSTING, and FUNGICIDES.)

If wounds of any considerable size on woody parts of trees are left exposed, rots may set in before a protective callus has time to form. Consequently, wound dressings are used on flat wound surfaces, or in cavities made in the removal of diseased wood from trunks or limbs. These act as barriers in preventing the invasion of numerous wood-destroying fungi.

The important diseases of the leading plants in the ENCYCLOPEDIA and their control follow the culture of them at each entry. — S. H. D.

PLANT FAMILY. A family of plants is a group of related genera (*see* GENUS), united by the botanists because they all have a family resemblance, although quite distinct one from another.

A simple illustration is the poppy family, known to science as the Papaveraceae, a family name composed of *Papaver* (the poppy) and *aceae** (belonging to). The poppy family comprises about 25 genera, of which over a dozen are garden plants, among them the poppy itself, the California poppy, the prickly poppy, etc. (for the list of them *see* PAPAVERACEAE). These genera of the poppy family are included within it because of similar flower or fruit structures, which are also the basis for the identity and scope of all the other plant families.

Some plant families have such a strong family likeness that even the uninitiated will at once pick out plants belonging to them — such, for instance, as the grass family (Gramineae), daisy family (Compositae), pea family (Leguminosae), mint family (Labiatae), or the lily family (Liliaceae). But other plant families, based upon more technical characters, will only be recognized by the expert.

While the grouping of plants into families is essential for purposes of systematic classification, few gardeners take as much notice of what family their favorites belong to as they should. Because of this, and to give the users of this book a quick method of tracing related plants, all of the families of cultivated plants are entered and described in the ENCYCLOPEDIA at their proper alphabetical position, and at each family is a list of all the cult. genera in it. And at every genus the name of the family is always mentioned. This double entry of all generic and family names makes comparison and cross-referencing as simple as it can be.

There are 191 families of cult. plants included in the book, and space forbids repeating a list of them here. From the hort. standpoint the twenty most important are:

Gramineae (grass family)
Liliaceae (lily family)
Iridaceae (iris family)
Palmaceae (palm family)
Orchidaceae (orchid family)
Fagaceae (beech family)
Caryophyllaceae (pink family)
Ranunculaceae (buttercup family)
Cruciferae (mustard family)
Rosaceae (rose family)
Leguminosae (pea family)
Rutaceae (rue family)
Euphorbiaceae (spurge family)
Malvaceae (mallow family)
Myrtaceae (myrtle family)
Umbelliferae (carrot family)
Ericaceae (heath family)
Labiatae (mint family)
Compositae (daisy family)

Some confusion exists in older books, and in some modern ones in England, between the words *family* and *order*. In modern botany and hort. there need not be, for a family is what has been outlined above, while an order is a group of families — a botanical classification which has no place in a book like this. But for many years *order* and *na-*

tural order were used loosely to designate what is now called a plant family; hence the confusion. *See also* GENUS and SPECIES.

PLANT FOODS. There are but two sources for the food of most garden plants, the air and the soil. From the former they absorb various gases, the use of which will be apparent presently, while from the soil plants absorb water and various substances carried in solution in water. The sole exceptions to these general statements are certain tropical tree-perching plants which absorb moisture from the air (no other plants do), and the peculiar insectivorous plants which are the only ones to digest directly nitrogenous materials. *See* INSECTIVOROUS PLANTS. *See also* FOLIAR FEEDING.

For simplicity it will be convenient to separate the discussion of plant foods into those derived from the air and those from the soil. We should not forget that the plant makes no such distinction. What happens in an ordinary leaf on a sunny day is actually a perfect balance of chemical and physical factors, whether from the air or soil. The source of the materials, while very different, is of little significance to the leaf which can carry on its function only by combining all materials including light.

FROM THE AIR. An ordinary green leaf, with its cells distended with water from the roots (*i.e.*, turgid), stands out with its blade surrounded by air and its surface exposed to sunlight. Ordinary air is roughly composed of 78% nitrogen, 20% oxygen, 1% argon, and only about .03 of 1% carbon dioxide. But it is the latter that is of incomparably the greatest importance to the leaf. Through its pores it absorbs the air with the minute fraction of carbon dioxide, the latter being absorbed by the cells of chlorophyll (the green coloring matter of leaves).

By a process not yet thoroughly understood, this chlorophyll, in the presence of water, carbon dioxide, and sunlight, transforms the first two into starch — the first end product of the whole process. Nothing else in the world has this power of manufacturing starch, which is soon, however, in most plants changed to various kinds of sugars.

FROM THE SOIL. The process outlined above can only be carried on when there is a regular supply of water and the substances soluble in water. These are absorbed by the roots and travel through the stem, leafstalk midrib, the finest ramifications of the veins, and finally to the individual cells of chlorophyll. What reaches the chlorophyll is never pure water, but water containing the various plant foods found in the soil. These are phosphorus, potash, and nitrogen (often in the form of ammonia or nitrates), and a few other substances of minor importance. The plant's need of the major three substances from the soil is imperative, a point well illustrated by burning a plant and analyzing the ash.

These two sources — air and soil — comprise the basic raw materials of all plant foods. What the plant does with them, such as mak-

---

* Special articles on the subjects indicated by an asterisk (*) will be found at the words so marked.

ing woods, gums, resins, seeds, and piling up huge reservoirs of starch and sugar (potato and sugar cane), comes more within the scope of plant physiology than hort. For the gardener the whole process, while of tremendous interest, is of practical import only to see that the plant is supplied with raw food materials. Nature takes care of the air source without any thought. Food from the soil, however, is another matter. For the two chief adjuncts of soil food *see* FERTI-LIZERS, MANURE.

PLANTING. This entry has to do with the operation of planting in the sense that one plants a shrub, tree, or herb. It does not include planting *en masse*, which is really a problem of design. Nor does it deal with the planting of seeds of vegetables or annuals. For these *see* SEEDS AND SEEDAGE, and the separate articles on the culture of the different vegetables. *See also* ANNUALS.

Planting as a hort. operation involves two main things, the plant and the soil, as well as many minor ones, such as the weather and watering. Before taking up either in detail it is well to consider some general facts about the plant and the soil in which you propose to put it.

In any planting operation the shock of moving a living organism from one place to another should never be forgotten. The moment you dig up a rooted plant, whether herb, shrub, or tree, you break, for a briefer or longer time, the continuity of its food and water supply. Hence, as general principle number one, never make this period of transition from one home to another a moment longer than it must be. Even with the greatest care and the least possible loss of time, there is still a large element of shock in any planting operation, and to reduce this, general rule number two is practiced by all skillful gardeners. It is to reduce by about ¼–⅓ the top of the planted specimen of all woody plants except evergreens. In other words cut back drastically all such plants at the time of planting. Such pruning reduces by ¼ or ⅓ the number of leaves for the first season after planting and by so much reduces the water requirements of the newly planted specimen. This may seem drastic, but long experience has proved it the only safe rule. It cannot always be followed with herbs because at planting time they usually have no tops, and in any case they suffer less than do woody plants from shock.

It may be objected that some woody plants, such as privet, spirea, willow, forsythia, and quite a few others, are moved with great ease and begin almost at once to grow in their new home. While this is partly true of such plants, it is not so generally true that the average planter can afford to ignore either of the main principles outlined above. To follow them usually means at least 90% of success, while to ignore them, even for easily transplanted specimens, may mean failure.

BALL AND BURLAP (usually abbreviated to B & B in the catalogues). Most evergreens, azaleas, rhododendrons, magnolias, box, sour gums, some oaks, and most of the broad-leaved evergreens are far more difficult to plant than the average run of nursery stock. In other words, they resent the breaking of the continuity of their food and water supply so much that special planting methods are necessary to overcome this hazard.

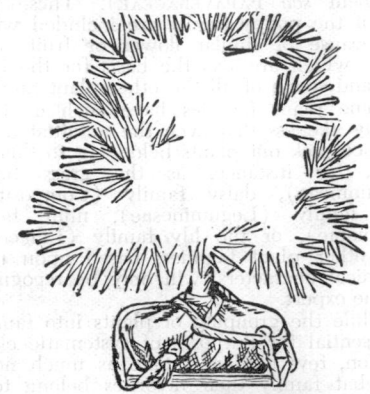

An evergreen showing the ball and burlap method of protecting its roots while awaiting planting.

All competent nurserymen dig such plants with a ball of soil in which (because of root pruning) there are many small feeding roots. The ball of soil is immediately tied up, pudding-fashion, in tightly roped or sewn burlap or canvas. This keeps the roots in constant contact with the soil and the bagging or canvas is not taken off until planting time. For most small plants burlap is used, and as it rots quickly, it can usually be left on and planted with the ball, especially if it is slit in one or two places just before planting. Canvas, which is used for all larger plants, is often a somewhat elaborately stitched affair for which a renting charge is made. It should, therefore, and also because it rots too slowly, be removed at the last moment before planting, and returned to the nurseryman, together with a board platform to which all good-sized ball and burlap trees will be roped.

The object of the ball and burlap method is to keep the roots free from wind and dry air. If the specimens arrive before you are ready to plant, put them under a tree or in a cool shed, and water the balls thoroughly until you are ready to plant them.

The best season for planting ball and burlap plants is early in the spring, and from Aug. 15–Sept. 15 over all the country north of zone 5. South of this their planting season is less important, but they should never be put into cold, wet soil just before frosty weather, as they need a period of a few weeks, in the fall, to get a fresh start.

THE SOIL

In any sort of planting it is of the greatest importance to see that the soil is suitable. We

---

* Special articles on the subjects indicated by an asterisk (*) will be found at the words so marked.

need not repeat here the differences in the value of topsoil and subsoil, nor discuss the relative merits of clay, loam, sandy loams, etc. All these details you will find at SOILS and the cross-references originating there. And if you need to enrich the soil *see* FERTILIZERS and MANURE for the details of these operations.

But a few general soil directions should not be forgotten. If the planting operation is a small one, or expense no object, dig the holes for the plant and cart away all the subsoil, replacing it with good topsoil. Of course separate the subsoil and the topsoil when digging the hole, retaining the latter for planting.

If the planting operation is a large one, or the expense of hauling in enough topsoil is prohibitive, follow this procedure: Dig a hole the desired size, separating the excavated soil into three piles: (1) the best topsoil; (2) the best of the subsoil; and (3) the worst of the subsoil. In planting put some of the topsoil in the bottom of the hole and the rest around the roots of the plant. Then fill in with the best of the subsoil and put the worst of the subsoil at the top. Large-scale plantings, managed this way at no cost for fresh topsoil, and well mulched with manure for a season or two, will often not have 5% of failure.

The only objection to such a method is that the plants will not grow quite so fast nor so well for the first year or so as they would in good topsoil, which should always be used if it is available.

Sometimes the soil is underlaid by an impervious belt of hardpan or by rocky ledges. Such a site would make planting impossible if it were not for dynamite (which see). *See also* HARDPAN.

PLANTING

In digging holes for any planting it is essential to make them deep and wide enough to amply take care of the roots, or ball if the specimen is a ball and burlap plant. No specific depths or widths can be given, for plants vary so much. But a general rule should be to make the hole about ⅓ deeper and wider than the spread of roots on the new plant. This will allow ample space.

It is quite useless to put the roots at the bottom of a hole on the freshly exposed subsoil. Fill in the hole with enough topsoil to bring it up to the desired height. The final depth of the partly filled hole is determined by the old soil line on the stem of the specimen to be planted. Most shrubs and trees should be set at their old level, but a few, like box and privet, should be set a trifle deeper.

In filling in with topsoil, before the specimen is planted, do not merely throw the soil in and smooth it off. Jump in the hole several times until the topsoil is well packed down, and on this firmed-down layer place the roots of the plant. If the soil under the roots is not well tamped, settling will inevitably leave air pockets in which feeding roots will dry out, and if there are enough of such air holes the plant will be what the gardeners call "hanged," *i.e.*, killed or crippled, even though planted, for lack of its feeding roots being in contact with the soil. So important is this that many gardeners, especially in England, follow the process of

PUDDLING (sometimes called mudding). Because it was well known that it is not the large roots that matter most in a planting operation, but the small feeding roots, the

Puddling

puddling method was devised centuries ago. Its object is to coat all the roots with a thin film of wet soil just before planting. They are dipped in a slimy mixture of good fine loam and water and then planted. This insures closer contact of the fine feeding roots than is possible without it, even with the greatest care in filling the hole. There is no doubt that puddling, especially in dry weather, is a beneficial method. Its objections are that it is a troublesome, messy job, and on large-scale plantings often too much so to be worth it.

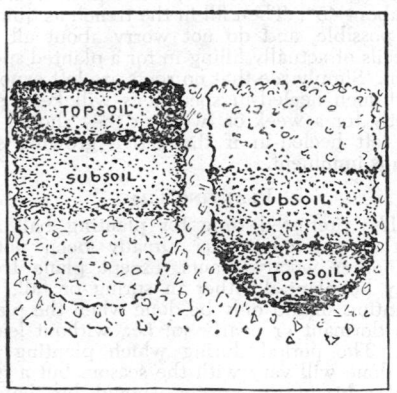

Putting topsoil (*right*) where it will do most good. At the left the natural layers of topsoil and subsoil. For details *see* text.

* Special articles on the subjects indicated by an asterisk (*) will be found at the words so marked.

Roots. In all woody plants it will be found that there are some large roots and many smaller ones. At planting time the larger ones are of the least importance. If any are broken or bruised, cut them off, making a clean diagonal cut with a knife or pruning shears. Such cut roots will almost certainly put out a lot of fine feeding roots, which is exactly what the newly planted specimen most needs. Even if there are no broken or injured roots, it is a good plan to cut off the ends of the largest roots just to induce the production of feeding roots. *See* Root.

All being now ready, the hole properly filled, the roots cared for, and the specimen cut back as outlined above, the final planting should be done. It is by far the quickest of the whole series of operations. See that the specimen is straight and gradually fill in the soil, using the feet or a rammer so that the top-soil will be thoroughly packed around the roots. In other words, leave no air pockets.

Do not at first fill the hole quite up to the general ground level, but about 2 in. below it. Such a shallow well will hold water whether from rain or the hose and for the first year such a depression, while unsightly, is of benefit to the plant. You can, however, avoid its necessity if you are willing to water your newly planted shrubs and trees whenever they need it.

Remember, also, that for all trees, a good stout pole should be set in the hole *before* it is filled up. Place the specimen in the hole, then drive down the pole so as to injure no roots, and deep enough to make a firm support. The pole should be about 4 in. from the trunk, and extend up at least 6 ft. above ground after being driven down. To this pole wire the young tree, not girdling the tree in the process. Cut up pieces of old hose and loop this loosely around the trunk. Run stout wire through the hose (and hence around the trunk) and secure its ends firmly to the pole about 18 in. below the top of the latter. From or near the first branches of the tree, if no pole is used, stretch three tight guy wires fastened to stakes driven firmly in the ground, each of the stakes from 4–5 ft. from the trunk. Leave staking on the tree for the first two years, and if guy wires are used see that they are kept tight. Without these the wind will so loosen the feeding roots that successful tree planting is sometimes long delayed, and the tree may die if shaken too violently by the wind. Most shrubs will not need staking.

MULCHING. Most shrub and tree plantings will be benefited by a mulch of manure put on just after planting. For the details of this *see* MULCH AND MULCHING. For special plants like rhododendron, azalea, and broad-leaved evergreens the mulch should be of leaves. For details *see* these three entries.

HEELING-IN

It is often impossible to plant shrubs and trees the moment they arrive. If they are packed in sphagnum moss or if the bundle of roots is tied up in burlap (not balled and burlapped, *see* above), and you intend to plant them in a day or so, simply put them in a cool shed or under a tree and wet them down.

All nursery stock, except ball and burlap plants, will come without any soil on the roots, however they are packed. If planting is to

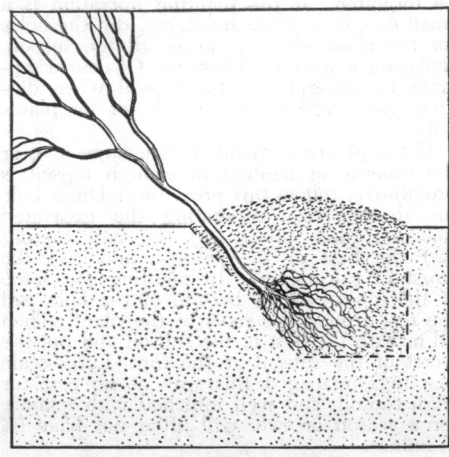

HEELING-IN

Temporary device for protecting dormant plants before permanent planting. Cover the roots, set in a trench, to prevent their drying.

be done soon, simply follow the procedure in the paragraph above.

If there is to be more delay, unpack the plants and heel them in, a practice universal with all experienced gardeners. Heeling-in simply consists in temporary planting. Dig a trench long enough to take care of your shipment, and deep enough to cover completely all roots when the trench is filled. Pack the plants as closely together as possible without injuring the roots, and tip the tops at an angle of about 45°. Then fill in the trench as quickly as possible, and do not worry about all the details of actually filling in for a planted specimen. Simply see that no roots are left exposed and such heeled-in specimens will keep perfectly for a week or two, but they should not be left heeled-in if the active growing season is imminent.

PLANTING TIME

The preferred time for planting ball and burlap specimens has already been noted. All other woody plants, except plane trees, may be planted either in spring or fall, but planting should only be done when the plants are dormant or nearly so; *i.e.*, without leaves on. The period during which planting can be done will vary with the season, but a general rule, in the spring, should be that all woody plants should be in the ground about a week before they would normally leaf out. In order to prolong the planting season, many nurserymen dig their stock and keep it in a cool (sometimes refrigerated), dark place. Such treatment naturally retards development and prolongs the planting season. In the fall there is no trouble about this. *See* AUTUMN PLANTING. Plane trees (*Platanus*) should be planted only in the spring, as should most magnolias.

HERBACEOUS PLANTING

The planting of herbs is much less troublesome than the details outlined above, chiefly because they are shallow-rooted. Because of this they rarely extend their roots below the layer of topsoil, and the operation of planting them is comparatively easy. Some gardeners prefer to reduce the roots of herbaceous plants, as shown in the illustration.

MOVING HERBACEOUS PERENNIALS

(A) Insert spading fork deeply so as not to cut roots. (B) Lift out carefully and cut back the top and any broken or very long roots. (C) The plant in its new site: (1) Firm the soil with foot or spade handle; (2) water it plentifully; (3) see that the roots are well spread; (4) be sure the soil around and just below the roots is good topsoil, enriched with well-rotted manure if possible; (5) if the subsoil is clay or hardpan, remove it and fill in with coarse gravel for better drainage.

The only caution is to see that they are firmly planted so that there will be no air pockets about their roots. And in the case of fleshy-rooted herbs especial care must be used to prevent their heaving. In fact, this heaving, caused by the alternate thawing and freezing of the soil, is often a source of a lot of trouble. The only remedy is deep, firm planting or a mulch. *See* HEAVING.

There remain two other sorts of planting, both the subject of special entries. For the spring and fall planting of bulbs *see* BULBS. For the planting of greenhouse material in pots or tubs *see* POTTING.

PLANTING TABLES. *See* GARDEN TABLES I.

PLANT NAMES. Unhappily for all gardeners and botanists, plants are cursed with two sets of names, the Latin ones of science, and the vernacular names of common speech.

Because the latter are much better known than technical Latin names, a special effort has been made to include in this book as many valid common names as possible. About 4730 common names are entered, far less than the 9191 species and varieties. Many cult. plants have no common name, and for such none have been entered, their Latin name having to suffice and being far preferable to so-called common names manufactured by the bookish. The really valid common names of plants come from the people to the books, not the other way around. But many well-known plants have several, and in some cases, alas, dozens of vernacular names. Those that are obscure, or too local, or purely colloquial have had to be excluded. But the 4730 that are entered have wide usage behind them in some part of the country. The ENCYCLOPEDIA contains more valid common names than any other garden publication, and a word here may help the reader to find them. As in any other encyclopedia, they are entered in strict alphabetical sequence. Look for red oak, **New England** aster, **white** spruce, **black** oak, **pink** lady's-slipper, etc., under the bold-face word, not under oak or spruce or lady's-slipper or aster. You will, of course, find them under oak or spruce or lady's-slipper or aster, but much more quickly and directly (*i.e.*, referred to the exact species) by going to the first word of names that contain two. For all others the strictly alphabetical entry needs no explanation.

LATIN NAMES. While common names are better known than technical ones, the Latin names are far more precise and comprise the only universal method of plant naming (nomenclature). In the vast majority of cases, garden plants have only two names, thus: *Dianthus deltoides*. The first name tells us that the plant belongs to the genus *Dianthus*, the pinks, while *deltoides* tells us that it is the maiden pink. The first name is thus the generic name and is applied to all other plants in the genus *Dianthus*, while *deltoides* is a specific name applied only to this particular species of *Dianthus*.

In some cases it becomes necessary to designate still further a plant which already has a generic and specific name. This third name, also in Latin, is a *varietal* one (*i.e.*, it designates a particular variety of a species). Such varietal names appear as the third of a trio thus: *Dianthus deltoides glaucus*, which tells us that this is a variety (hence the abbreviation *var.*) of the maiden pink, with bluish-green foliage.

Recent suggestions that hort. varieties such as Baby Rambler, Blue Dawn, Snow Queen, and thousands of others, should be designated as **cultivars** have not been adopted for this edition. *See* CULTIVAR. For most gardeners such names designate a *variety*, in spite of the fact that technically they are no doubt true *cultivars*. See VARIETY.

Most species names, like *deltoides* above, are always written without a capital letter, while the generic name always has an initial capital letter. Hence *Dianthus deltoides* is correct but *dianthus Deltoides* would not be. There are, however, exceptions to this general rule, and the reader may wonder why *Pentstemon Digitalis, Lobelia Cardinalis, Chrysobalanus Icaco*, and scores of other specific names are written with an initial capital letter. The answer is that according to the rules of botanical nomenclature, specific names derived from an old generic name (*i.e., Digitalis* or *Cardinalis*) must be written with the capital initial letter. Also certain vernacular or common names such as *Icaco* must also have an initial capital letter. There are other reasons, too long to be enumerated here, why certain specific names are capitalized, and throughout this book some specific names are capitalized, while the bulk of them are not.

Because specific and true varietal names are in Latin (usually derived from Greek) and their meanings may be unknown to many owners of the ENCYCLOPEDIA, nearly all such names used in this book have been entered at their proper alphabetical place, pronounced and defined. Over 2280 such specific and varietal names are entered, the only ones omitted being those based on the names of persons and hence obvious; *i.e., grayi, wilsoni, thunbergi*. See also SPECIES, GENUS, VARIETY.

SYNONYMS. Because many authors in widely scattered parts of the world and of many degrees of competence have had a hand in christening plants with Latin names, it happens pretty frequently that a plant acquires several, to the permanent confusion of everyone. Unfortunately, the literature of botany and hort. is strewn with thousands of these invalid Latin names, for, of course, a plant should have only one that is really valid. All others are invalid or untenable and may be grouped here under the general term of *synonyms* (there are several technical interpretations of the term). In most books synonyms, which are more confusing to the amateur than almost any other feature of nomenclature, follow the valid name, always in parentheses. A typical illustration is:

Plumeria rubra (*P. acuminata*).

This indicates to the initiated that *P. acuminata* is, for some reason, an untenable name for *P. rubra;* in other words, a synonym of it. The obvious question is, Why not omit all reference to the untenable *P. acuminata* and thus avoid future confusion? The answer is that while technically invalid it may have been once widely current in any number of books or other printed records, especially nurserymen's catalogues.

Wherever synonyms have had sufficiently wide usage to demand notice they have been entered in the ENCYCLOPEDIA, but not in the technical way above cited, because few of our readers may understand its significance. Instead all synonyms are added separately, under some such phrase as "known also as —", "sometimes offered as — ."

PLANT PATENTS. On May 23, 1930, certain amendments to the general patent laws were adopted constituting what is generally known as the "Plant Patent Act," despite the fact that it is wholly supplementary to the laws relating to mechanical processes and gadgets.

Over 1880 plant patents have been granted, predominantly to roses. Other subjects patented are carnations, chrysanthemums, freesias, fruits, especially the peach, and many ornamentals.

The life of a plant patent is seventeen years, during which time the owner may legally defend against infringement. He may sell or lease the patent plants or propagating rights, or he may even refuse to permit the introduction of the plant. He may make licenses of any sort, or arrange for a royalty.

His patent rests on a claim of novelty in color, form, habit, hardiness, or any other distinction established to the satisfaction of the Patent Office authorities. He may patent a new seedling, or the variation from an existing variety called a "sport." Plant patents are of use only to professional breeders of new vars. which have reputed merit. Such plants are usually more expensive than the vars. from which they have been derived, and the public should weigh this increased cost against the reputed advantages of the patented plant.

PLANT PATHOLOGY. See PLANT DISEASES.

PLANTS FOR SPECIAL PURPOSES. All plants are grown for ornament or for utility. For the former *see* the many articles on seasonal or color gardens, the lists at ANNUALS and PERENNIALS, SHRUBS, TREES, and VINES. For plants grown for utility *see* KITCHEN GARDEN, FRUIT CULTURE. For an over-all picture of the subject *see* WHY AN ENCYCLOPEDIA? in the Introduction to this book.

PLANTS PER ACRE. For the number needed at different intervals from 1×1 in. to 100×100 ft., *see* GARDEN TABLES I.

PLASH. See PLEACH.

PLATANACEAE. See PLATANUS.

platanifolia, -us, -um (pla-tan-i-fō'li-a). With leaves like the plane tree (*Platanus*).

platanoides (pla-ta-noy'deez, but *see* OïDES). Like a plane tree (*Platanus*).

platantha, -us, -um (pla-tan'tha). With broad leaves.

PLATANUS (plă'ta-nus). Plane, plane tree, or buttonball tree. Valuable forest trees, one a hybrid and perhaps the best all-round street tree, and the only genus of the family **Platanaceae** (pla-ta-nay'see-ee), and comprising about 10 species from N.A. and Eurasia.

---

* Special articles on the subjects indicated by an asterisk (*) will be found at the words so marked.

They have large, long-stalked, alternate* leaves, lobed and veined finger-fashion. Flowers small, inconspicuous, in dense, ball-like, stalked clusters, the male and female separate on the same tree. The female clusters mature into a persistent, ball-like mass (a syncarp*) of small nutlets, the fruiting cluster conspicuous most of the winter in the London plane. The outer bark of all species peels off in large plates, exposing the much lighter inner bark. (*Platanus* is the classical Greek name for the plane tree.) One of the leading arias in Handel's opera *Serse* is *Ombra mai Fù*, an ode to a plane tree. This soprano aria is the familiar "and preposterous arrangement now known as Handel's Largo." (Philip Hale.)

The first species, the London plane, is a hybrid between the second and third species. It is the most widely planted street tree in London, Paris, and most American cities in the temperate region. It stands abuse, smoke, dust, and windy streets better than any other tree. The second species, the American buttonwood or sycamore, while probably the largest deciduous tree (in girth) in the U.S., does not take so kindly to city cult. The third species is scarcely, or not at all, known in cult. in America, but commonly listed — all the nurserymen's trees being actually *P. acerifolia*. The fourth species is useful only in southern Calif. and similar climates.

The London plane, the only important cult. one, should not be planted in the autumn north of zone* 5. Otherwise, its culture is easy.

acerifolia. London plane. A tall, widely spreading tree up to 140 ft. Leaves 3–5-lobed, cut off at the tip, 5–9 in. wide. Fruiting clusters in groups of 2–5, bristly, about 1 in. in diameter, winter-persisting. A hybrid between *P. occidentalis* and *P. orientalis*. Hardy from zone* 3 southward. Perhaps the best of all street trees.

occidentalis. Buttonwood; also called sycamore (but not the true sycamore of the Bible which is a non-hort. species of *Ficus*, *F. Sycomorus*). A very large forest tree, the trunk with an immense girth in maturity. Leaves 5–9 in. wide, commonly 3-lobed, but sometimes 5-lobed. Ball-like fruiting clusters solitary, rarely 2, about 1½ in. in diameter, not bristly. Eastern N.A., reaching its greatest known girth (42 ft. 3 in.) in bottom-lands near Worthington, Ind. Hardy from zone* 3 southward, and a good tree for country planting, but not for city streets.

orientalis. Oriental plane. Not so tall as the other two. Leaves 5–7-lobed, 4½–8 in. wide. Ball-like fruiting heads in clusters of 2–6, about 1 in. in diameter, bristly. Eurasia, and cult. there, but rare or unknown in cult. in America. Hardy from zone* 6 southward. All plants offered as this in the U.S. are sure to be *P. acerifolia*.

racemosa. A large tree, up to 120 ft., much planted as a shade tree in southern Calif. Leaves deeply 3-lobed, 6–9 in. wide, the margins often remotely toothed. Fruiting heads 2–7, nearly stalkless. Southern Calif. and adjacent Mex. Hardy from zone* 7 southward, but only in dry regions.

INSECT PESTS. Lacebugs yellow foliage in summer. Control with pesticide #21 (*see* SPRAYS AND DUSTS) when seen.

DISEASES. During a rainy spring the buttonwood or sycamore may be completely defoliated as a result of anthracnose* disease. The London plane is much more resistant and only a few twigs and leaves may be killed. A single application of pesticide #8 (*see* SPRAYS AND DUSTS), just as buds start to break in the spring, will give good control.

In some sections of mid-Atlantic states a disease known as plane tree canker is fatal to London plane tree. Many thousands have been killed in eastern Pennsylvania and New Jersey. The only known means of transmission of the disease is through pruning operations or mechanical injuries.

platycentra, -us, -um (plat-i-sen'tra). With a broad center.

platyceras (plat-i-see'ras). Having broad horns.

PLATYCERIUM (plat-i-seer'i-um). Also known as *Alcicornium*. Staghorn or elkhorn fern. A genus of 7 species of large, strong-growing ferns found growing on branches or trunks of trees, or on wet rocks, in tropical Af., As., and Aust., and belonging to the family Polypodiaceae. They have two kinds of fronds; one sterile, large, round, and plate-like, enclosing the roots and clasping the support on which it grows. The base of this frond is thick, as this is where the plant stores its water; the outer portion thin and membranous, wavy in outline. The other kind of frond is 1–6 ft. long, narrow at the base, widening out and branching into lobes like a stag's horn. These lobes droop, the under sides being partially covered with large, brown patches where the spores* are produced. The plant gets part of its moisture from the air but also by catching the rain. The roots are embedded in humus formed by the decaying sterile leaves and sometimes penetrate the bark of the tree on which the plant is growing. (*Platycerium* is from the Greek for broad horn, in allusion to the leaves.)

Generally cult. in greenhouse, in temperature not less than 60°. Propagated by spores or division of plants, usually the latter. Pieces of plant are wired onto a piece of wood hung on the side of a damp greenhouse. Shade and dampness essential.

bifurcatum. Grayish-green, the fertile fronds, 2 or 3 together, hairy, drooping, 1–3 ft., branching into 6–8 narrow lobes with brown patches (spores) on under side extending to the tips. Sterile leaves have wavy margins. Aust. and Polynesia.

Stemmaria. Grayish-green. Fertile fronds drooping, to 3 ft. long, covered with short, white hairs on the under side. Lobes 4, spore patches not extending to the tips. West tropical Af.

willincki. Grayish-green, thinly covered with small, branching hairs when young. Fertile fronds growing 3 together, to 3 ft. long, branching into two about ⅔ of their length, one branch continuing entire and narrow, the other branching into numerous lobes all bearing spore patches nearly to the tips. Java.

---

* Special articles on the subjects indicated by an asterisk (*) will be found at the words so marked.

platyclados (plat-i-clay′dos). With broad branches.

PLATYCODON (plat-i-kō′don). A single, showy, perennial herb of the bellflower family from Eastern As., P. grandiflorum, commonly called balloon-flower, and widely cult. for ornament. It is an erect herb, 18–30 in. high, the leaves alternate,* ovalish or narrower, 2–3 in. long. Flowers usually solitary, long-stalked, broadly bell-shaped or deeply saucer-shaped, 2–3 in. long, dark blue (or pale or white in some hort. forms). Fruit a 5-celled capsule, splitting at the top. There are dwarf (*var.* mariesi) forms, and one with the 10 lobes of the corolla making it appear star-like (*var.* japonicum). There are also double and semi-double flowered forms. A handsome border plant, summer-blooming, and of easy cult. in most garden soils. Increased by division in spring. (*Platycodon* is from the Greek for broad bell, in allusion to the shape of the corolla.)

platyneuron (plat-i-new′ron). With broad nerves or veins.

platypetala, -us, -um (plat-i-pet′a-la). With broad petals.

platyphylla, -us, -um (plat-i-fill′a). Broad-leaved. Sometimes written *platyphyllos.*

PLATYSTEMON. *See* CREAM-CUPS.

PLEACH. A method of pruning and training plants to produce a hedge-like wall. The trees, or shrubs are planted about 4–5 ft. apart, and most of the front and back branches are removed. The side branches are more or less interwoven and slightly slit at the base

Pleached trees

(pleached, also called plashed), and as the tree grows, the narrow hedge-like effect is very striking. A pleached allée can be an imposing feature in any garden, but it takes time and patience to produce it. One of the finest pleached allées in the world is at the Schönbrunn Palace, Vienna, made of the London plane.

PLEIOBLASTUS. *See* ARUNDINARIA and BAMBUSA.

pleioneura, -us, -um (ply-o-new′ra). Many-veined.

plena, -us, -um (plee′na). Double; usually double-flowered.

pleniflora, -us, -um (plen-i-flow′ra). Double-flowered.

plenissima, -us, -um (plen-iss′i-ma). Most doubled.

PLEURISY-ROOT = *Asclepias tuberosa.* *See* MILKWEED.

plicata, -us, -um (ply-kay′ta). Plaited or folded in plaits.

PLOWING. One of the oldest agricultural operations in the world, having for its object the turning over of soil needed for planting, but it is scarcely a hort. operation. *See,* however, GREEN MANURING and SOIL OPERATIONS.

PLUM. For the common plum see the next main entry. For other genera to which the name is also applied, or in which *plum* is part of the name, *see* ACHRAS, CARISSA, CHRYSOBALANUS, COCCOLOBIS, DIOSPYROS (at PERSIMMON), FLACOURTIA, and SPONDIAS. *See also* PRUNUS.

PLUM. More than almost any other fruit tree, plums are apt to be self-sterile,* especially the Japanese varieties. This means that they must scarcely ever be planted alone, and the home grower who does not have room for at least two different varieties had better leave plums out of his fruit garden. Some plums are self-fertile,* especially the European varieties, and in the list of recommended varieties those that are self-sterile* will be so designated. All others are self-fertile.* It is especially important in those that are self-sterile to see to it that the variety selected for cross-fertilization belongs to the same *group* of plums — otherwise there will be no fruit.

Plums, so far as commonly cultivated, are naturally divided into four groups, three of which comprise most of the worth-while varieties. These are:

EUROPEAN PLUMS, often called domesticas, the best-known varieties of which are the green gage (Reine Claude) and its relatives. But many others have dark skins. All varieties are freestone, and generally pointed. Most cultivated plums are in this group.

DAMSON PLUMS, sometimes called insititias, considered by some as a mere variety of the European plum, but the fruits are all clingstone, seldom more than an inch in diameter, and generally round.

JAPANESE PLUMS are nearly all self-sterile,* but they have a wider range of climatic adaptability than others, and are valued especially for resistance to some plum pests. Their original home was China. Fruit round or conical, pointed, generally clingstone, and considered inferior to the European sorts.

NATIVE AMERICAN PLUMS. These comprise varieties that have originated from the wild plums of the United States, or have been crossed with Japanese varieties. Some of them have fine flavor, but their great virtue is that they can be grown in parts of the country where plum culture would otherwise be impossible. Scarcely known in the eastern states.

The origin of these different groups rather complicates plum culture, besides the necessity of interplanting only with trees of the same group where self-sterility occurs. Their original native habitat dictates the size of the trees, the shape of the fruit, its flavor and especially the ability of the tree to stand what is frankly the unsuitable climate of eastern and coastal North America for many desirable plums. Of these some occur within the European group of plums, and all of these, while thriving in California, do not like the extremes of heat and cold found elsewhere. That is why they are mostly confined to areas near Lakes Erie and Ontario, do well in Nova Scotia, and in the Finger Lakes region of New York and along the Great Lakes. Proximity to large bodies of water helps to temper climatic extremes.

Proximity to the eastern seacoast is, however, an entirely different matter, particularly in the South, for humidity is generally unfavorable, especially as some plum pests thrive so well as to make plum culture almost impossible. It is completely so over large sections of the South, except for a few special varieties. Hence, in no other group of fruits is it more important to know and study your local conditions.

In the lists below, each recommended variety will not only have its preference for climatic zones* indicated, but also the group to which it belongs on account of the necessity of choosing another variety within its own group (and only such) to provide foreign pollen in case the variety is self-sterile.*

Plums differ also in their soil preferences. Most varieties within the European and Damson groups grow best on heavy loams, and an admixture of clay will do no harm. But the Japanese varieties do better on light sandy loams, while the native American kinds are tolerant of a variety of soils.

Next to the peach, the plum is the earliest flowering of our fruit trees and hence most likely to be blasted by an erratic spring frost. Such a hazard can be combated by planting the trees on a north-facing slope if this is possible, as that may retard the opening of flower buds beyond the period of such frosts.

Plums, like peaches, tend to set more fruit than it is wise to let them carry to maturity. They, too, are subject to "June-drop" of fruit, but this is not enough, and immature fruits should be picked off in late June so that no fruit is nearer to any other (when full grown) than 2½ to 4 inches — depending on the variety. The damsons should be spaced at the smaller interval.

Although everyone would like to have a few plum trees in the fruit garden, it is generally a difficult matter to grow them along the Atlantic Coast. It is no accident that practically all the plums grown in New York State come only from counties bordering Lake Ontario, Lake Erie, the Finger Lakes, and the upper part of the Hudson Valley, near Albany. Anywhere else there is either too severe winter cold or too much humidity in the summer.

High humidity favors the growth of parasitic fungi that have decimated commercial plum cultures on the coastal plain. Although the home grower has remedies for the control of these pests, they are relatively troublesome and expensive. A good many amateurs, therefore, decide to abandon plum culture in regions that no expert can recommend. This is not necessary if you will take the trouble to combat these difficulties. *See* below.

VARIETIES

(The zones* indicated for the different varieties only show the severity of winter cold. These numbers cannot show the factor of summer humidity which is so critical in plum culture. *See* above.)

EUROPEAN

*Often called Domesticas. All are self-fertile.**

ARCHDUKE, zones* 3 and 4. A late plum, the fruit nearly round, reddish-purple at first, becoming dark blue.

ARCTIC, zones* 2 and 3. A midseason plum, nearly round, dark purple or black; one of the hardiest to winter cold, often called Moore's Arctic. Also available in dwarf form.

BRADSHAW, zones* 3 and 4. A midseason, ovalish fruit, dark purple, covered with a bloom. The tree is relatively free of serious fungous pests. Also available in dwarf form.

GRAND DUKE, zones* 3 and 4. Late-fruiting variety, and one of the largest of European plums. Fruit elongate-oval, nearly 2 inches long, purple, and with a bloom.

GREEN GAGE. *See* Reine Claude, below.

IMPERIAL EPINEUSE, zones* 3 and 4. Fruit purplish-red, very sweet and of delicious flavor; midseason to late.

ITALIAN PRUNE†, zones* 3 and 4. Sometimes listed as Fellenberg. A splendid variety for culinary use, the fruit purple-black. Also available in dwarf form.

REINE CLAUDE, zones* 3 and 4. This is *the* green gage plum, although the fruit is actually yellow. It was so called by an English gardener who worked for a family named Gage. They imported a lot of plums from a monastery in France in the eighteenth century, all of which were labeled except one. To this the gardener applied the name Green Gage, and so it has been called ever since. It was actually the variety Reine Claude, named for Queen Claude when brought from Italy to France about 1500. Also available in dwarf form.

STANLEY, zone* 3. Fruit deep blue, with

†This and many other plums are sun-dried on the Pacific Coast to make prunes. This cannot be done in the East without artificial heat, and great care is required to produce satisfactory results. *See* PRUNE.

---

* Special articles on the subjects indicated by an asterisk (*) will be found at the words so marked.

a bloom, nearly 2 inches long and of fine flavor; midseason. Also available in dwarf form.

WASHINGTON, zone* 3. Fruit light yellow, ovalish, rather sweet; midseason.

DAMSONS
Both self-fertile

FRENCH, zone* 3. The best of the damson varieties, the fruit purple-black, with a bloom. Not so productive as Shropshire, but the fruit larger and of better quality.

SHROPSHIRE, zones* 3 and 4. Similar to the above, but with somewhat inferior flavor. Its chief virtues are its tremendous production of fruit and ability to stand more winter cold. Also available as a dwarf tree.

JAPANESE PLUMS

All are clingstone fruits and all are self-sterile* and must be interplanted with varieties that are also in this group.

ABUNDANCE, zones* 3 and 4. Fruit red, with a bloom and matures early. Its best flavor is ensured by picking it a day or so before it is ripe and allowing it to ripen at room temperature. Also available as dwarf tree.

BEAUTY, zones* 3, 4, and 5. Fruit deep red, the flesh also tinged with red, more or less conical; midseason. Tree large and productive.

BURBANK, zones* 3, 4, and 5. An early plum, nearly round in outline, the skin red, the flesh reddish and of good quality. Also available in dwarf form.

FORMOSA, zones* 3, 4, and 5. One of the largest fruits among the Japanese plums, oval, the skin yellowish-red, the flesh pale yellow; midseason. Also available in dwarf form.

RED JUNE, zones* 3 and 4. An early plum, the fruit roundish-oval to heart-shaped, pointed, bright red, and with a bloom. Also available as a dwarf tree.

NATIVE AMERICAN PLUMS

These are mostly derived from wild plums or have been crossed with other sorts, often with Japanese plums. All the fruits in those below are in some shade of red, and all of the group are self-sterile* and must be interplanted with related varieties of the native group. In the catalogues they are sometimes called *native*, *American*, or *hybrid* plums. All are freestone, except those mentioned as clingstone. None of them provide as good fruit as the European group, but they can be grown in parts of the country where most European plums will not thrive.

AMERICA, zone* 2 southward. An early or midseason plum, roundish-oval, and with a bloom.

GOLDEN, zone* 3 southward. One of the showiest of all red plums, nearly round and quite large, but the flavor is inferior to some other native sorts; early.

DE SOTO, zones* 2 and 3. A midseason plum, nearly spherical or ovalish, and about 1½ inches in diameter; nearly clingstone.

SURPRISE, zones* 2 and 3. Clingstone, deep red and of fine flavor; midseason.

POTTAWATTOMIE, zone* 2 southward. Clingstone, early plum, the fruit currant-red. Tree dwarf and apt to straggle.

WILD GOOSE, zones* 3 and 4. Fruit red and with a bloom, round-oval and slightly pointed. One of the best of the native plums; midseason.

WOLF, zone* 2 southward. Fruit dull red, roundish, small, but of fine flavor; midseason.

There are two dozen plum varieties scattered among the four groups in the above lists, and the home grower may well wonder which to choose. Because of the diversity of their habitats and their preference for specialized places, it is impossible to reduce the number of recommended varieties.

If, however, you have room for only a few trees, it is better to choose from the European and Damson groups, for they are all self-fertile.* But if you live within the area where plums are risky, the native American sorts are safer.

CULTIVATION. In common with all fruits, plums do best under tillage — sod-mulch culture should be the exception, never the rule. Tillage consists of plowing in the spring, followed by frequent cultivation until late July when a cover crop of clover, oats, barley, buckwheat, or other succulent crop should be planted to be plowed in late autumn or

Plums cult. under sod (*right*) and under cultivated soil (*left*). A tree under sod produced 65 pounds of fruit, while a tree of the same variety with soil cultivation yielded 83 pounds.

early spring. It may be assumed that if the trees are vigorous and bearing well, fertilizers are not needed. When the foliage is light in color, the growth scant, and the fruits small, nitrate of soda might be tried at the rate of 3 to 5 pounds per tree. In garden culture, where most often trees are kept in

---

* Special articles on the subjects indicated by an asterisk (*) will be found at the words so marked.

sod, the grass should be cut and used as a mulch supplemented by manure or straw. Trees so grown nearly always respond to nitrate of soda or its equivalent in some other fertilizer.

PRUNING. Usually plum trees are trained about a central leader, but some Japanese varieties do well trained to the vase shape. Superfluous branches, those that cross, and one making an acute crotch should be cut out. Pruning should humor the natural growths of the exceedingly variable plum. The Japanese sorts usually require heavy pruning; domesticas and damsons, comparatively little; native sorts much, to train the scraggling wayward growths.

Plums may be spaced 18 feet apart each way for the damson, native American, and the Japanese sorts; but the European varieties should be at least 20 feet apart on reasonably good soils, and on richer soils they should be at least 22 or 24 feet apart. *See also* Dwarf Fruit Trees at DWARFING.

BEACH PLUM. There is one native plum (*Prunus maritima*) that is a garden subject in the region where it is native. It is the beach plum, which grows wild from New Brunswick to Delaware, almost exclusively in coastal dunes, the downs at Montauk, Long Island, and among rocky pastures near the sea in New England.

It is a low or medium-sized shrub with a profusion of white flowers, followed by dark-purple fruit which has a musky or guava-like flavor that makes it very popular for beach plum jelly. Attempts to improve this wildling are practically confined to Cape Cod, where the plant is very common. It can scarcely be recommended as a garden plant unless you have sandy dunes available.

WEST OF THE ROCKY MOUNTAINS

Plums afford a wide variety of fruit and tree types for the gardener. One or more species is adapted to almost every area of the West except the more extreme conditions of the high desert and hot, low, desert elevations of the Southwest. Both ornamental and edible forms are useful in the garden. The edible plums belong mainly to three species, the Japanese plum (*Prunus salicina*), European plum (*Prunus domestica*), and the damson plum (*Prunus domestica insititia*). However, varieties of many of our native plums of the Midwest and East are known and are adapted to wide areas west of the Rockies. These are less generally available to the gardener and are often quite susceptible to certain diseases which make them less favorable for garden subjects. The highest-quality plums are among the three species mentioned.

The European plum is hardiest and therefore best adapted to the more rigorous northern areas of the western district. They have also the advantage of blooming later, thereby escaping some of the frost hazards which usually prevail at the time the Japanese plums bloom. Damson plums are as hardy

as European plums, but bear small, tart fruit which is useful mainly for jams and jellies. *Prunus cerasifera* (myrobalan plum) and *P. blireiana* are species with many ornamental forms. The fruit of some of these is edible but not of high quality. Prunes are a special class of European plum (*see* PRUNE).

Plums will do well in portions of Idaho, the eastern-valley fruit districts of Washington and Oregon and throughout the Central and coastal valleys of northern California up to elevations of approximately 2500 feet. In southern California both European and Japanese varieties are grown at elevations of approximately 3000 to 4000 feet. A few varieties have been selected which will do well in the mild winter areas of southern California.

CULTURE. The cultural requirements of plums follow closely those described for tree fruits in general. (*See* FRUIT CULTURE WEST OF THE ROCKY MOUNTAINS.) This applies particularly to the soil, irrigation, and fertilization of trees.

Fruit thinning is important in the case of the Japanese plum because this species tends to set exceedingly heavy crops which result in reduced fruit-tree vigor and production of small, unattractive fruit. The European varieties, on the other hand, do not set so heavily but often need to be thinned. Damson plums are generally not thinned, even under conditions of heavy sets. Certain cultural operations differ somewhat from the practice followed for other fruit species, and differ between plum species; these are discussed below.

PRUNING. Plum trees are usually headed at a height of 18 to 24 inches at the time of planting and trained to 3 to 5 main branches during the succeeding years. Each of these branches will in turn give rise to secondary branches. Subsequent training consists primarily of thinning out the shoots following each year's growth, and heading back the branches at the height it is desired to hold the tree. Varieties of upright growing habit are pruned by cutting to outside branches; the reverse situation obtains if the variety tends to spread unduly. All plums bear on spurs and the problem of replacing fruiting wood is therefore not an important consideration in pruning.

Japanese plums grow vigorously and most varieties branch freely. They therefore require rather heavy pruning to space branches adequately and for penetration of light through the trees. They are also pruned somewhat more severely than other plum species to aid in reducing fruit-set, as this is so often excessive. European and damson plums do not branch as freely as the Japanese and hence require less severe pruning. Otherwise pruning practices are essentially the same. Ornamental plums generally follow the growth habit of the Japanese species most closely, and may be pruned similarly.

VARIETIES. A large number of Japanese

---

* Special articles on the subjects indicated by an asterisk (*) will be found at the words so marked.

plum varieties are available for the garden. In order of ripening, the following are high-quality, attractive kinds affording a succession of fruit from early June to fall: Beauty, Formosa, Santa Rosa, Redheart, Wickson, Mariposa, Satsuma, Duarte, Red Ace, Inca, Late Santa Rosa, and Kelsey. Not all of these are favored for commercial production but all are highly desirable for garden use. Other varieties may be found in nurseries and the above list is not intended to be exclusive. Among those named varieties are yellow and red to purplish-red varieties. Some have yellow or amberish flesh while others, like Mariposa, Duarte, and Red Ace, are so-called blood plums; that is, the flesh is red at maturity. The Japanese varieties are characterized by large size and heart shape.

European plums for the garden include the varieties Tragedy, Anita, Emilie, Late Tragedy, Pond, Italian, Green Gage, Standard, and President. This is far from being an inclusive list, for hundreds of varieties are known. These varieties, given in order of ripening, afford a succession of fruit from early July to fall. European plums are usually dark red or blue in color although, among those listed above, Pond is pinkish-red and Green Gage is greenish or yellow. The flesh color of all is greenish to yellowish. In the Northwest the Italian (Fellenberg) is by far the most popular European plum grown. Certain varieties of European plums not listed above are grown for the production of prunes. (*See* Prune.)

Damson plums available at nurseries are usually sold as blue or white Damson. Shropshire and Frogmore are the best-known damson plums. The varieties are small, nearly round, and quite tart when mature. They are used primarily in the making of jams and jellies, for which they are highly desired.

Species of native plums are usually not widely distributed among nurseries. Varieties may be locally known and grown and can be recommended for the garden wherever they are available. Generally the fruit is smaller than that of the species listed above (except the damsons), softer, and not often of as good quality. The ornamental plums are grown for their red foliage or for the beautiful double pink flowers. Foliage color is usually best in cooler climates. In warm districts the red of the emerging spring foliage soon fades.

POLLINATION. Many varieties of plums, both of the European and Japanese species, are unfruitful when pollinated with their own pollen. A few varieties are intersterile. To insure satisfactory yields provision should be made for cross-pollination. The Japanese plums Beauty, Santa Rosa, and Late Santa Rosa are partially self-fruitful, and because of the excessive setting habits of this species, provision for pollination is often not necessary. However, in the Northwest it has been found helpful in the production of annual crops even of these varieties. Combina-

tions of Japanese varieties named above which are intersterile are: Beauty and Kelsey, Beauty and Formosa, Duarte and Kelsey, Inca and Mariposa, and Kelsey and Santa Rosa. All other combinations should be interfruitful when planted in the garden. Mariposa and Inca, because of their early blooming habits, tend to precede the other varieties named in time of bloom. For this reason they should not be relied upon to provide pollination for the other varieties. All of the European varieties listed above are self-sterile except for Green Gage which is partially self-fruitful. However, in the case of the European plums any combination of the varieties named will produce adequate crops. The damson plums are self-fruitful and need no provision for pollination.

European and Japanese plums are so distinct in their botanical relationship that cross-pollination between varieties belonging to these two species does not occur.

It should be remembered that bees are essential to the successful cross-pollination of fruit trees. Bees range over a rather wide area so that in most regions of the West, wild as well as domestic hive bees will afford the necessary bee activity for successful cross-pollination. However, in highly developed urban districts lack of bees may constitute a barrier to successful culture of varieties requiring cross-pollination.

HARVESTING. The proper time to harvest plums is usually indicated by changes in color and (or) softening of the fruit. The fruit of a single variety is usually harvested in two or three pickings over a period of about 10 days, the fruit produced on the upper and outside portions of the tree ripening first. Some varieties hold well on the tree for days or even weeks after the time they are sweet and flavorful to the taste. They may be harvested at any time during this period for table use. In general early varieties soften rapidly and must be harvested as they ripen, whereas late-maturing varieties more commonly have the characteristics of holding in edible condition on the tree. This characteristic is more marked for some varieties than for others, even within a given seasonal period.

Early-maturing Japanese varieties will normally not store well for long periods but may be held in ripe condition in a refrigerator for a week or more. Late-maturing varieties, on the other hand, may be held for considerable periods either in a refrigerator or in a cool basement. In the latter case they should be picked firm-ripe rather than fully tree-ripe before storing.

It is more difficult to determine the proper time to harvest European plums than is the case with Japanese plums. Many varieties color highly long before they are edible. The best criterion is probably taste. As the plums sweeten and become flavorful they are ready for harvest. In the case of the European plums it is generally best to harvest them before they become soft on the tree. They

---

* Special articles on the subjects indicated by an asterisk (*) will be found at the words so marked.

may be ripened at a moderate temperature, as in a basement, and will attain maximum flavor as they then soften. The later-maturing varieties especially may be held in cool storage, some for a considerable period of time. For this purpose they should be spread out in a single layer to prevent the spread of rots which may attack some individual fruits.

Damson plums should be harvested slightly before they normally soften on the trees. As the upper and outermost fruits start to soften, the remainder may be taken in one picking and used for the making of jams and jellies.

Native varieties generally ripen rapidly with marked color changes and softening as they mature. They should be picked at this time and used before deterioration. They do not store well but may be kept for a few days in the refrigerator. — C. O. H.

INSECT PESTS. Control scales by dormant oils. Curculio attacks shortly after the fruit appear and may be controlled by arsenicals or pesticide #18 (see SPRAYS AND DUSTS) or #1. Control aphids with pesticide #21.

DISEASES. Same as for the cherry (which see).

plumaria, -us, -um (ploo-may'ri-a). Plumed.

PLUMBAGINACEAE (plum-ba-ji-nay'see-ee). The plumbago family contains among its 10 genera and 400 widely distributed species many plants that have long been favorites among gardeners. Chief among them is *Armeria* (the thrift) and *Acantholimon* which is a favorite among rock gardeners. *Limonium* contains both the sea lavender of our salt marshes and other garden plants widely used for dry bouquets. *Ceratostigma* and *Plumbago*, partly shrubby, are plants of warmer climates.

Plants apparently stemless and with basal leaves in a rosette* in *Armeria*, *Acantholimon*, and *Limonium*, but with obvious stems and alternate* leaves in the other cult. genera. Flowers usually rather showy and regular,* in dense button-like clusters in *Armeria* and *Acantholimon*, more open and spreading in the other genera. Fruit dry, usually enclosed by the persistent calyx.

Technical flower characters: Flowers hermaphrodite.* Calyx tubular or funnel-shaped, 5-toothed, bracted* at the base, sometimes colored. Corolla tubular or of 5 partly united petals. Stamens* 5. Ovary superior, 1-celled.

plumbaginoides (plum-ba-ji-noy'deez, but *see* OÏDES). Resembling a plant of the genus *Plumbago* (which see).

PLUMBAGO (plum-bay'go). Leadwort. A genus comprising about 12 species of subshrubs or herbs, sometimes climbing or trailing, mostly perennial, of the family Plumbaginaceae, and natives of southern Eu., Af., As. and tropical America. Stems slender. Leaves alternate,* simple, not cut, broadly lance-shaped. Flowers in terminal spikes or clusters, blue, white or red. Individual flower has calyx of 5 sepals sometimes colored. Co-

rolla long, narrow, tubular, with 5 lobes which open saucer-like. (*Plumbago* is from the Latin for lead, as some species were thought to be a remedy for lead poisoning.)

Grown mostly in a cool greenhouse, but may be used in the garden in summer months. They make excellent pot plants. Propagated by seeds or cuttings. Seeds should be sown on the surface of sandy peat, slightly covered with sand, in temperature 65°–75° in Feb. or Mar. Cuttings may be made of young side shoots, 2–3 in. long, inserted in equal parts of sand and peat in propagating frame or under bell-jar in Feb. or Aug. When rooted transplant to potting mixture* 1, finally to potting mixture* 3. If old flowering shoots are cut back, the plants will bloom all summer. They should be allowed to become partially dry through Dec.–Jan., when plants may be cut back, old soil shaken out and re-potted. They should then be kept in a temperature of 65°, when they will soon start into growth.

capensis. Tender shrub of spreading habit, growing to 8 ft. or more. Leaves alternate, lance-shaped, smooth and thin in texture, 2–3 in. long. Flowers in terminal clusters, azure-blue. Corolla tubular, narrow, to 1½ in. long. Petals 5, spreading saucer-like, ¾ in. across. S. Af. The **var. alba** is a white form. This species most general in cult.

indica = P. rosea.

Larpentiae = *Ceratostigma plumbaginoides*.

rosea. An East Indian tropical perennial, often sprawling or climbing, but not over 30 in. high. Leaves ovalish, 3–4 in. long, their short stalks clasping the stem. Flowers about 1 in. long, rose- or purplish-red, in spiky clusters. The **var. coccinea** has more brightly colored and larger flowers. The plant is by some called *Plumbago indica*.

scandens. Toothwort. Tender shrub of spreading habit, rarely vine-like. Leaves broadly lance-shaped, to 5 in. long. Flowers white, the corolla tube ½–¾ in. long. Tropical America.

PLUMBAGO FAMILY = Plumbaginaceae.

PLUMCOT. A hybrid between the plum and apricot, of more scientific than hort. importance. It was originated by Burbank in 1901. Little is heard of it today, although two hort. varieties of it are offered by a few nurseries. The original was named Rutland plumcot by Burbank, and the only other one is a variety called Apex. The fruit is fuzzy-skinned like an apricot, but the flesh is deep red and slightly acid. Little is known of its culture, but it has been grown in Calif., N.Y., and N.J., and thus appears to have a wide climatic tolerance. The fruit is of no commercial importance.

PLUME GRASS. See ERIANTHUS.

PLUMELESS THISTLE. See CARDUUS.

PLUME POPPY = *Macleaya cordata*.

PLUMERIA (ploo-meer'i-a), also spelled *Plumiera*. Frangipani or temple tree. Tropical American, very handsome shrubs and trees of the family Apocynaceae, widely cult. in zone* 9 for their showy, funnel-shaped, fragrant flowers. They have a milky juice,

---

* Special articles on the subjects indicated by an asterisk (*) will be found at the words so marked.

thick, fleshy branches, and alternate* leaves which are feather-veined but also have a prominent marginal vein, without marginal teeth. Flowers in terminal, stalked clusters (cymes*), each flower with bracts* beneath it which soon fall. Corolla lobes slightly twisted, the slender tube long. Stamens* 5. Fruit a pair of leathery pods (follicles*). (Named for Charles Plumier, French botanist.)

Of the 50 known species of *Plumeria*, only three are in common cult. and of these *P. rubra* is the best-known. They flower mostly when leafless, but occasional flowers are produced over a period of several months. The plants are popular in southern Fla., especially the first and last species. They are propagated by cuttings in early spring.

acuminata = *P. rubra*.

acutifolia. *See* P. RUBRA.

alba. A tree up to 35 ft. high. Leaves lance-shaped or narrower, 7–10 in. long, not over ½ in. wide, the margins rolled, the under surface white-hairy. Flowers white, about 1 in. wide, the lobes of the corolla about as long as the tube. W.I.

emarginata. A tree, usually less than 20 ft. high. Leaves ovalish, 5–7 in. long, 2–3 in. wide, slightly notched at the tip, hairy on the under side. Flowers white, the corolla lobes rounded and about 1 in. long. Cuba.

rubra. Red jasmine. A shrubby tree, not over 15 ft. high. Leaves oblongish or broadest toward the tip, 12–16 in. long, 3–4 in. wide, pointed. Flowers very fragrant, pink or reddish-purple, about 2 in. long, the blunt lobes of the corolla longer than the tube. Mex. to Venezuela. The *var.* acutifolia has white or rose-white flowers with a yellow center.

PLUM FAMILY. *See* ROSACEAE.

PLUMIERA = *Plumeria*.

plumosa, -us, -um (ploo-mō′sa). Plumose; *i.e.*, plumed, usually feathery or with fine, silky hairs.

PLUM TOMATO. *See* TOMATO.

PLUMY COCONUT = *Arecastrum romanzoffianum.*

PLUM-YEW. *See* CEPHALOTAXUS.

PLUNGE. To bury the flower pot in which a plant is growing up to its rim in the soil outdoors or in ashes or sand or moss on the greenhouse bench. Many tender plants are plunged outdoors in the summer, and do far better than if the pot were standing on the surface. The advantages of plunging are that the plant does not dry out as much as if the pot were exposed and that while getting this benefit of growing in the ground, it can still be lifted in the fall without the shock of transplanting or re-potting.

Plunging is a very common hort. operation, especially useful to gardeners forced to leave house plants neglected for a time. If plunged they will often survive without watering for considerable periods, provided they are grown in common, not glazed pots and plunged in the shade. The plants most often plunged are chrysanthemums, calla lily,

A plant plunged outdoors for the summer

some alpine plants, *Maranta*, many ferns, camellias, and any other pot plant.

pluriflora, -us, -um (plur-i-flow′ra). Many-flowered.

Pneumonanthe (new-mo-nan′thee). A specific name derived from the genus *Pneumonanthe*, which is scarcely of hort. interest. *See* GENTIANA.

POA (pō′a). Annual and perennial grasses found throughout the temperate and cold regions, comprising about 200 species. They have no decorative value, but are very useful for lawn mixtures or for permanent pastures. (*Poa* is an old Greek name for grass.)

For culture and uses *see* LAWN.

compressa. Canada bluegrass. Wire grass. Perennial, growing to 2 ft., with creeping rootstocks. Leaves bluish-green, to 4 in. long, and ⅛ in. wide. Flowers in short, loose clusters. Useful on poor soils and in shady places. Eu., but naturalized in N.A.

nemoralis. Wood meadow grass. Coarse perennial, to 3 ft. high, but with spreading habit. Leaves to 5 in. long, ⅛ in. wide. Flowers in long, narrow clusters. Used in shady places for pasture and lawn. Eurasia.

pratensis. Kentucky bluegrass. June grass. Perennial to 3 ft. with creeping rootstocks. Stems spreading, hairy at base. Leaves 4–7 in. long, ¼ in. wide. Flowers in pyramidal clusters to 8 in. long. Best lawn or pasture grass, and much used in lawn-grass mixtures. Eurasia, and naturalized in N.A. *See* LAWN.

trivialis. Perennial to 3 ft. Stems spreading at the base. Leaves to 7 in. long, ¼ in. wide. Flowers in loose clusters 6 in. long. Good for shade mixtures for lawn or pasture (*see* LAWN). Eu., naturalized in N.A.

POACEAE = Gramineae.

POD. Technically, any dry fruit that splits open, as a pea pod. But *pod* and *seed pod* have long lost any technical significance among gardeners, to whom a pod is pretty much any dry fruit that contains seeds.

Podagraria (po-da-gray′ri-a). Greek for foot and chain; *i.e.*, the gout. *See* AEGOPODIUM.

PODALYRIA (pō-da-lir′i-a). South African

---

* Special articles on the subjects indicated by an asterisk (*) will be found at the words so marked.

evergreen shrubs comprising about 20 species, belonging to the pea family. Leaves alternate,* simple,* ovalish, to 2 in. long. Flowers pea-like, solitary, or in 2–3 flowered clusters, produced in the axils* of the leaves, purple, pink or white. Fruit a roundish pod, covered with silky hairs. (Named for Podalyrius, son of Aesculapius.)

Propagated from seeds sown under glass in early spring and later grown in potting mixture* 3. They are grown outdoors in the southern states, and in Calif.

calyptrata. Shrub to 6 ft. Leaves 1–2 in. long, 1 in. wide, hairy on both sides. Flowers pink.

sericea. Grows 4–6 ft. high, but of spreading habit. Whole plant covered with soft, silvery hairs. Leaves broadly lance-shaped. Flowers purple.

podalyriaefolia, -us, -um (po-da-lir-i-ee-fō'-li-a). Having leaves like a plant of the genus *Podalyria*.

podocarpa, -us, -um (po-do-kar'pa). Having stalked fruits.

PODOCARPUS (po-do-kar'pus). Handsome evergreen trees or shrubs of the family Taxaceae, mostly from the southern hemisphere (one Asiatic) and chiefly from the mountainous parts of it. Of the 65 known species only a few are in cult. in the U.S., mostly in Calif., the Gulf Coast and Fla., and they are doubtfully hardy elsewhere. Leaves alternate,* mostly narrow or ovalish, but not scale-like or needle-like, and not suggesting the foliage of a coniferous evergreen. Male and female flowers on different plants, the male flowers consisting of naked, catkin-like masses of anthers,* the female consisting of a solitary, naked ovule between 1 or 2 small bracts. Fruit fleshy-stalked, mostly plum-like, or berry-like. (*Podocarpus* is from the Greek for foot and fruit, in allusion to the prominent stalk to the fruit.) In the South commonly, but incorrectly, called Japanese yew.

The four below grow in a variety of soils and present no difficulties beyond the fact that they will not stand severe frosts. Any area north of zone* 6 is dangerous except possibly for *P. alpinus* which is hardier than the others. Occasionally *P. elongatus* is grown in the cool greenhouse as a foliage plant. It needs potting mixture* 4, to which a little acid peat should be added.

alpinus. A densely branched shrub or small tree, not over 15 ft. high. Leaves narrow, about ½ in. long, blunt, dull green above, but paler beneath. Fruit egg-shaped, about ⅛ in. thick, red. Aust. and Tasmania.

andinus. A tree 15–30 ft. high, densely branched. Leaves practically stalkless, about 1 in. long, narrow, green above, but with 2 whitish bands beneath. Fruit egg-shaped, yellowish-white, about 1 in. long. Chile.

elongatus. African yellow-wood. A tree up to 70 ft. high in the wild, much less as cult. and mostly prized in Calif. for its young state, and as a foliage plant. Leaves narrow, 2–3 in. long, pointed and rather thin. Fruit globe-shaped, about ⅓ in. in diameter. Mountains of South Africa and tropical Africa.

macrophyllus. Much the commonest in cult. in the U.S., and a tree 40–60 ft. high. Leaves lance-shaped, 3–4 in. long, dark green above, paler beneath. Fruit egg-shaped, about ½ in. long, greenish-purple, the fleshy stalk purple. Jap. A dependable and useful house plant, while young, and kept in a tub or large flower pot. The var. **Maki,** the maki of the Japanese, is usually only a shrub and has smaller, more crowded leaves. China. Less hardy than the typical *P. macrophyllus.*

PODOLEPIS (pō-doll'e-pis). Australian annual or perennial herbs, comprising about 16 species, found in the family Compositae. Leaves alternate,* long and narrow, covered with short, cotton-like hairs when young. Flowers in terminal heads, yellow, pink, or purple. The flower head is surrounded by a ring of numerous, overlapping, thin, transparent bracts,* usually colored. (*Podolepis* is from the Greek for foot and scale, in reference to the bracts.)

In cult. *Podolepis* is usually a half-hardy annual. Propagated by seeds, sown in sandy soil, ⅛ in. deep, in temperature of 55°–65°, under glass. Transplant to porous soil and sunny position outdoors at the end of May. They may also be sown outdoors at the end of April. When transplanting, space 4 in. apart. Suitable for the rock garden. They can also be used as pot plants, using potting mixture* 4.

aristata. Annual, growing to 1 ft. high. Leaves long and narrow, partly clasping the stem. Flower heads solitary, yellow, 1 in. across, surrounded by a whorl of numerous, thin, transparent bracts.*

PODOPHYLLACEAE. A family maintained by some to include the following in this book, here credited to the indicated families: *Diphylleia* and mayapple (Berberidaceae) and goldenseal (Ranunculaceae).

PODOPHYLLUM. *See* MAYAPPLE.

PODRANEA. *See* PANDOREA RISCASOLIANA.

PODSOL. White or gray, somewhat ashy soil, found in many regions, its color and texture due to the weathering of organic matter, mostly the litter of the forest. Many podsols ultimately become good garden soils.

POET'S NARCISSUS = *Narcissus poeticus.*

POGONIA (po-go'ni-a). Beautiful, mostly bog-inhabiting orchids of the north temperate zone, the only North American species, **P. ophioglossoides,** the rose pogonia, adder's-mouth, or snakemouth, being also the only cult. one. It is a 3-leaved bog plant, usually with a single, long-stalked basal leaf, and one or two essentially stalkless stem leaves, 1–3 in. long, and oblongish. Flower solitary, fragrant, nodding, pale rose-purple, with a single bract beneath it. Petals and sepals nearly equal, about 1 in. long. The hanging lip* is beautifully crested and fringed. Eastern N.A. Suited only to the bog garden, and a pH of 4–5. June–July. (*Pogonia* is from the Greek for bearded, in allusion to the lip.*)

POGONIRIS. *See* IRIS.

---

* Special articles on the subjects indicated by an asterisk (*) will be found at the words so marked.

POINCIANA (poin-si-ā'na). Showy tropical trees or shrubs of the pea family, widely cult. for ornament in warm regions, but in the U.S. their outdoor cult. must be confined to zones* 9 or 8, the most favorable parts of zone* 7 (but *see* P. GILLIESI). Both the commonly cult. species are shrubs with alternate,* twice-compound* leaves, the very numerous leaflets arranged in pairs, feather-fashion, and without an odd one at the end. Flowers not pea-like, the 5 broad, separate, showy petals slightly unequal. Stamens* 10, distinct and protruding. Fruit a narrow, flattened pod (legume*). (Named for M. de Poinci, a governor of the French W.I.) For the tree known as the royal poinciana, probably the most showy of all cult. trees, *see* DELONIX.

The two below are cult. throughout most of Fla., the Gulf states, and in Calif. While not as spectacular as the royal poinciana (*see* DELONIX), they are extremely handsome shrubs. Propagated by seeds, which are best soaked in warm water for several hours, as they germinate with difficulty. Later they should be grown along in pots, but may be planted out when a foot or two high. They grow well in a great variety of soils.

gilliesi. Bird-of-paradise bush. A shrub or small tree, the branches straggling and sticky-hairy. Leaflets very numerous and small, the foliage thus graceful and feathery. Flowers yellow, the bright red stamens* protruding 4–5 in. and very showy. Pods 3–4 in. long. S.A. Reported as hardy, with protection, up to the middle of zone* 5. Sometimes offered as *Caesalpinia gilliesi.*

pulcherrima. Barbados pride; also called Barbados flower-fence and dwarf poinciana. A prickly shrub 6–10 ft. high. Leaflets very numerous, ½–¾ in. long. Flowers orange-yellow, the bright red stamens protruding 2–2½ in. long. Pods about 4 in. long. Tropical regions and widely cult. there, often under the name of *Caesalpinia pulcherrima.*

regia = *Delonix regia.*

POINSETTIA (poin-set'ti-a). Tropical American herbs or shrubby plants of the spurge family, two of them widely grown for their gorgeously colored bracts* (often mistaken for flowers). They have a milky juice and alternate,* often lobed, thin leaves. Flowers small, colored, but not very conspicuous because of the brilliantly colored bracts beneath the small, nearly stalkless cluster. The plants of this old genus are now considered as of the genus *Euphorbia* (which see).

For the culture of the common poinsettia of the florists, which is *Euphorbia pulcherrima* and its varieties, *see* below.

POINSETTIA CULTURE

This showy plant has become a symbol of Yuletide. In southern California and in much of tropical America, it grows luxuriantly out of doors. The typical species has scarlet bracts* beneath the rather uninteresting greenish-yellow flowers. The double variety is very distinct, having a double series of bracts. There is also a variety with pink bracts and still another with white ones. Some varieties have oak-like leaves, while others have egg-shaped leaves.

Poinsettia is grown in pots singly, or several in one pot. Late-rooted plants are adapted for making an attractive basket if, around early September, a number, established in small-sized pots, can be worked out through the wires of the basket.

Store away in January in a temperature of 50° minimum and keep dry until May, when they may be stood in a temperature of 60° and given water. They may be rooted from the end of June until early September. It is important that the cuttings do not wilt. When taken from the parent plant, prepare for insertion in the propagating bench by cutting below a node* and removing unnecessary leaves. Have water handy to submerge them, thus reducing transpiration.*

Dibble them tightly into sand that has been pounded firmly into the bench, in a house in which the atmosphere is moist and not inclined to airiness. Water thoroughly when inserted and soak every morning thereafter. Spraying the foliage in the late afternoon should be avoided to forestall the appearance of fungus diseases. The glass should have a permanent shading, and on very hot and bright days a further shading of cheesecloth or paper should be used. In from two to three weeks these cuttings will have made sufficient roots to be potted into 2½-in. pots in potting mixture* 1. Shade a few days until the roots have gotten a hold of the soil. Later re-pot in potting mixture* 3 as the demand arises. After the pots are filled with roots, feed twice a week with weak liquid manure. This will be particularly useful when the bracts are being formed, but cease feeding when the actual flowers begin to show.

For bench growing, plant in potting mixture* 3, about August 15, those that are established, in 4-inch pots.

Poinsettias are sun-loving plants and never form their bracts well if at all shaded when full grown. Grow as near the glass as possible and during the summer months the ventilators should always be open. When fall approaches guard against the temperature dropping below 60° and avoid drafts or a too dry condition at the roots, which would result in a losing of foliage. The management of gift plants in the house is quite difficult, for no ordinary room approximates the conditions outlined above. One poinsettia expert writes of gift plants "you are smart if you discard them" after the inevitable shedding of foliage due to room temperature and lack of humidity.

INSECT PESTS. Control scales with oil sprays or pesticide #21 (*see* SPRAYS AND DUSTS) before bracts appear.

DISEASES. Cuttings may drop over as a result of a fungus rot at the soil line. Place cuttings in sterilized sand and soil (*see* SOIL

---

* Special articles on the subjects indicated by an asterisk (*) will be found at the words so marked.

STERILIZATION) and if the soil line rot does occur, drench with pesticide #10 (*see* SPRAYS AND DUSTS).

Cuttings or mature plants may have yellow leaves and slits in the stems. If slits have a watery or mucilaginous exudation, the plants have a bacterial canker* disease. Discard all such plants.

POINSETTIA FAMILY = Euphorbiaceae.

POINT REYES LILAC = *Ceanothus gloriosus.*

POISON ARUM = *Peltandra virginica.*

POISON BAIT. This is used in the control of two sorts of pests. For the bait for insects *see* No. 9 at INSECTICIDES. For the poison bait used against animal nuisances *see* ANIMAL INJURY.

POISON BULB = *Crinum asiaticum.*

POISON BUSH. See SWAINSONA.

POISON HAW = *Viburnum molle.*

POISON HEMLOCK. Two horticulturally unimportant Eurasian biennial herbs comprising the genus **Conium** (ko-ny'um; also kō'-ni-um) of the carrot family, the only cult. species, **C. maculatum** (sometimes called "winter fern"), a dangerously poisonous plant, and the hemlock that killed Socrates. It is a rank-growing herb, 2–4 ft. high, with finely cut, twice-compound* leaves, the ultimate segments toothed or cut. Flowers minute, white, in many small clusters (umbels*) which are grouped in a compound umbel. Fruit small, flattened, 5-ribbed. It is of no garden interest, but children should be taught to know and avoid it. (*Conium* is the ancient Greek name for it.) For a related, somewhat similar, and also poisonous plant *see* CICUTA.

POISON IVY. The common poison ivy is *Rhus radicans*, or *R. Toxicodendron* as it was formerly called, and is one of the few native plants that are poisonous by contact. For the difference between poison ivy and Virginia creeper, sometimes confused with it, *see* the picture below. A similar Pacific

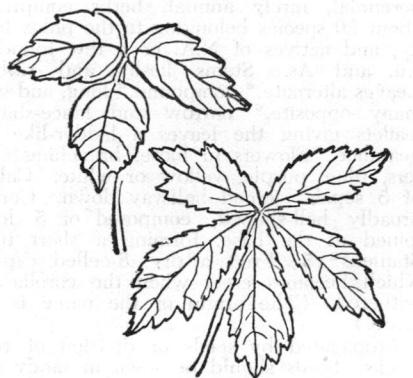

Poison ivy (*upper left*) and the Virginia creeper (*lower right*), the leaves of which confuse many.

Coast species, also poisonous, is *Rhus diversiloba*, often called poison oak in the west. The plants differ also in their fruit, the poison ivy having small, white, berry-like fruits, while those of the Virginia creeper are black or blackish-purple.

The irritating, non-volatile oil which is secreted upon the leaves of the poison ivy is the cause of the painful, itching skin eruption. If you know you have touched its foliage and can take steps within a few minutes, the best home remedy is to smear the affected part with a paste made of the cheapest laundry soap available. If this is impossible and the skin irritation has already begun, it is advisable to consult a physician at once. While the skin irritation may be no more than a nuisance, it can become serious, and in rare cases fatal. For the eradication of it *see* Poison Ivy in the list at WEEDS. A related plant is the poison sumac (*Rhus Vernix*) of the swamps of eastern N.A. It is a tall shrub with reddish twigs, 7–13 leaflets and white fruits resembling those of poison ivy. It is even more poisonous than poison ivy and the remedies for it are the same as those given above. Various ointments, face creams, etc., impregnated with different chemicals have been suggested as preventives. Conflicting reports of their efficacy make definite recommendations hazardous. For the injection method of prevention see your physician.

POISON OAK = *Rhus diversiloba.* See POISON IVY.

POISONOUS PLANTS. Fortunately, not many garden plants are dangerously poisonous. Of course any medicinal plant may be poisonous if a considerable amount of it is eaten, and in fact many relatively harmless plants can cause trouble if taken in too large quantities. The only caution needed for such plants is a little common sense and moderation, but no amount of either will save one from the effects of really poisonous plants.

Of the common garden plants or weeds listed in the ENCYCLOPEDIA, only the following are really serious. They may be divided into those poisonous by contact, and those which are poisonous only when eaten. For a description of them turn to the names in the list below.

CONTACT POISONS

POISON IVY and POISON SUMAC. There are at least three poisonous species of *Rhus: radicans, diversiloba,* and *Vernix.* See POISON IVY.

CYPRIPEDIUM. The pink lady's-slipper is occasionally somewhat poisonous.

PRIMULA. One greenhouse species is very irritating to some people. It is *Primula obconica.*

URTICA. The nettles have more nuisance value than actually poisonous qualities. The stinging sensation which they cause is usually not lasting.

---

* Special articles on the subjects indicated by an asterisk (*) will be found at the words so marked.

POISONOUS ONLY IF EATEN

This group contains all the really serious poisons, some of them deadly. They will be found, with descriptions of their leaves, flowers, and fruit, in the body of the ENCYCLOPEDIA under the names in boldface type in the list below. If there is the least suspicion that any of them have been eaten by children, who are apt to do much casual nibbling, send for a physician at once. The poisonous part of each is in parentheses.

Aconitum Napellus. **Monkshood** (all parts very dangerous).

Arum maculatum. Lords-and-ladies (all parts dangerous).

Atropa Belladonna. Belladonna (all parts deadly).

Cicuta maculata. Water hemlock (all parts dangerous).

Conium maculatum. **Poison hemlock** (all parts deadly).

Datura Stramonium. Jimsonweed (all parts deadly).

Delphinium. Most of the larkspurs (foliage).

Digitalis. **Foxglove** (foliage dangerous).

Euphorbia pulcherrima. Poinsettia (juice dangerous).

Gelsemium sempervirens. Carolina jasmine (juice dangerously poisonous).

Helleborus niger. Christmas rose (root a violent heart poison).

Hyoscyamus niger. Henbane (the juice is deadly).

Kalmia. Both the native laurels (foliage).

Laburnum anagyroides. Golden chain (seeds dangerous).

Nerium Oleander. **Oleander** (all parts very dangerous).

Pedilanthus tithymaloides. Redbird cactus (juice caustic, irritant and emetic).

Phytolacca americana. Poke (root and seeds dangerous).

Prunus serotina. Wild black cherry (wilted foliage very dangerous). Also the related *P. virginiana.*

Rhododendron. All species (foliage).

Ricinus communis. **Castor-oil plant** (seeds deadly).

Solanum nigrum. Deadly nightshade (wilted foliage deadly).

Strychnos Nux-vomica. Strychnine (juice deadly).

Taxus baccata. Yew (leaves dangerous, but the aril* eaten by some).

These do not exhaust all the poisonous garden plants, but the list includes the worst of them. There are also several very deadly toadstools. See MUSHROOM.

WHAT TO DO. Amateur doctoring for such serious poisons is worse than folly because prompt, expert care may save life. Some of the narcotics may give little indication that their baleful effects have already begun; they cause the so-called "sleep of death." The moment the patient shows the least symptoms (pain, headache, vomiting, drowsiness, or convulsions), send for a doctor at once, and if possible, show him a specimen of the plant causing the trouble.

While some authorities give what are called "home remedies" for various poisonous plants, they are omitted from this book because of the danger from the unskilled use of them. The antidotes to really serious poisons are as dangerous as the poisonous plant itself, and should be given only by a physician.

POISON SUMAC = *Rhus Vernix.* See POISON IVY.

POKE, POKEBERRY. See PHYTOLACCA.

POKER-PLANT. See KNIPHOFIA.

POKEWEED. See PHYTOLACCA.

POKEWEED FAMILY = Phytolaccaceae.

POLECAT-WEED. See SKUNK-CABBAGE.

POLEMONIACEAE (pole-ee-mo-ni-ā'-see-ee). The phlox family needs no introduction to most gardeners, and would need none at all if it did not contain several other less-known plants among its 15 genera and over 270 species which, while widely distributed, are most common in N.A. Besides *Phlox,* which is perhaps more widely grown than any other garden flower, the following genera are all hardy: *Collomia, Gilia,* and *Polemonium.* The only other cult. genera are *Cobaea,* a tendril-climbing vine, and *Cantua,* which is an aromatic shrub. Both are greenhouse plants, the former widely grown as a quick-blooming annual.

Leaves alternate* or opposite,* simple* or compound.* Flowers, especially in the hort. forms of *Phlox,* very showy and profuse, nearly always in clusters, often in corymbs.* Fruit a dry pod (capsule*).

Technical flower characters: Flowers regular* and hermaphrodite.* Calyx often bell-shaped, its lobes 5. Corolla tubular or funnel-shaped, its lobes or teeth 5. Stamens* 5, alternating with the lobes of the corolla and attached to it. Ovary superior,* usually 3-celled, its style 1, but usually 3-branched.

POLEMONIUM (pō-lee-mō'ni-um). Hardy perennial, rarely annual, herbs comprising about 20 species belonging to the phlox family, and natives of N.A. or a few found in Eu. and As. Stems fleshy, and ribbed. Leaves alternate,* compound,* long, and with many opposite,* narrow and lance-shaped leaflets giving the leaves a ladder-like appearance. Flowers in loose, branching clusters, blue, purple, yellow or white. Calyx* of 5 sepals* joined halfway down. Corolla broadly bell-shaped, composed of 5 lobes joined at the base, forming a short tube. Stamens* 5. Fruit a dry, 3-celled capsule which becomes erect when the corolla has withered. (The origin of the name is obscure.)

Propagated by seeds or division of rootstocks. Seeds should be sown in sandy soil, in a cold frame or cool greenhouse in early spring, and transplanted to permanent position as soon as large enough to handle. They will grow in ordinary garden soil. Plant 9–12

---

* Special articles on the subjects indicated by an asterisk (*) will be found at the words so marked.

in. apart. Division of rootstocks, with the exception of *P. caeruleum*, should be made in March or April, for *P. caeruleum* in Sept. or Oct.

caeruleum. Greek valerian. Jacob's ladder. Charity. Strong-growing, to 3 ft. Leaves crowded at the base, and longer than the stem leaves. Leaflets many. Flowers blue, 1 in. across, drooping, in large clusters. A good border plant. Eu. The *var.* **album** has white flowers.

carneum. Loosely branching, to 2 ft. Leaflets to 1½ in. long, broadly lance-shaped. Flowers in clusters, salmon-pink, fading to purple, 1½ in. across. Calif. and Ore.

confertum. Skunkweed. An evil-smelling perennial, 6–8 in. high, the compound leaf with 15–20 pairs of nearly round leaflets.* Flowers about 1 in. long, violet or bluish-violet. N. Mex. to Wyo. in the mountains.

humile = *P. pulcherrimum*, or in trade catalogues, *P. richardsoni*.

pulchellum = *P. pulcherrimum*.

pulcherrimum. A perennial, not over 12 in. high, the stems clustered and clammy. Leaflets 15–27 in the basal leaves, but fewer in the stem leaves. Leaflets ovalish. Flowers violet-blue, yellow or whitish at the throat. Western N.A. Sometimes offered as *P. humile*.

reptans. Bluebell. American abscess-root. Growing to 1 ft., of spreading habit, not creeping. Leaflets broadly lance-shaped. Flowers light blue, to ¾ in. long, in loose clusters. N.A.

richardsoni. Low-growing, to 9 in. high, with creeping, underground stems. Leaflets small and ovalish. Flowers blue or purple, ½ in. across, in clusters. Suitable for the rock garden and blue garden (*see* BLUE GARDEN). Arctic regions. Sometimes known as *P. humile*.

POLIANTHES. See TUBEROSE.

polifolia, -us, -um (po-li-fō'li-a). With the whitish leaves of the poly (*Teucrium Polium*), a European herb of no garden interest.

polita, -us, -um (po-ly'ta). Polished.

POLLARD. A tree so pruned that all its main branches are cut back to the trunk. Pollarding is a brutal sort of pruning, sometimes practiced to induce a dense, globe-like mass of foliage. It probably originated for the production of osiers, which are very plentiful on willow trees that have been pollarded. *See Salix viminalis* at WILLOW.

POLLEN. The male element in the process which culminates in the fertilization of the ovule in all flowering plants. It is borne by the anther* and is usually a mass of yellow, dust-like or sticky particles, the pollen grains. Each pollen grain, if deposited upon a receptive stigma,* may result in the fertilization of an ovule. For some interesting figures on the viability of pollen, *see* CROSSING. *See also* POLLINATION and FERTILIZATION.

POLLEN TUBE. See FERTILIZATION.

POLLINATION. The act or process by which pollen is transferred from an anther* to a stigma.* It is the first step in fertilization, but far from the completed impregnation of the ovule. *See* FERTILIZATION.

The main agents in pollination are insects, which carry from flower to flower a considerable cargo of pollen. Often the visit of the insect is not for the pollen but for nectar,* which it uses in the making of honey. But in the process of getting the nectar most insects get pollen-dusted, which means that they are ready to act as pollen carriers. Another very usual method of pollination is by the wind, which carries the pollen of all grasses, sedges, pines, and most catkin-bearing trees. Among aquatic plants, the water, especially in submerged species, acts as a pollen carrier. In the tropics bats and snails also carry pollen. The last, and from the

Bees and butterflies are the most common agencies of pollination, but wind, water, snails, and bats are also pollinators.

breeding standpoint, the most important method is artificial pollination. Upon the ability of the plant breeder to accomplish this depends the making of hybrids or crossing. For the details of artificial pollination *see* CROSSING. *See also* BEES AND BEE PLANTS.

polyacantha, -us, -um (pol-i-a-kan'tha). Many-spined.

polyandra, -us, -um (pol-i-an'dra). With many stamens.

polyantha, -us, -um (pol-i-an'tha). With many flowers.

polyanthemos (pol-i-an'thee-mos). Many-flowered.

POLYANTHUS = *Primula polyantha*.

POLYANTHUS NARCISSUS = *Narcissus Tazetta*.

POLYBRID. A term proposed for hybrids resulting from crosses between species, hybrids, or genera, which are not clonal and hence variable. It is a term not in general use.

polycarpa, -us, -um (pol-i-kar'pa). With several carpels (*see* PISTIL).

POLYCOTYLEDON. A plant sprouting with more than two seed leaves (cotyledons), as

---

* Special articles on the subjects indicated by an asterisk (*) will be found at the words so marked.

the pine and its relatives. Most garden plants have one seed leaf (monocotyledonous) or two seed leaves (dicotyledonous).

POLYGALA (pol-lig′a-la). Milkwort. A large genus of hardy or tender, annual and perennial herbs or sub-shrubs, a few tree-like, comprising over 500 species of the family Polygalaceae, found throughout the world, about 40 species in N.A. Leaves alternate,* lance-shaped. Flowers in terminal clusters, or spikes, in some species showy. Colors various. Calyx* of 5 sepals,* 3 small, 2 large, sometimes colored. Petals 4–5. Fruit a 2-celled capsule, sometimes winged. (Polygala is from the Greek for much milk, in reference to a superstition that some species increased the supply of cow's milk.)

The tropical species are unusual in cult. Propagate by cuttings taken in spring. Cuttings should be inserted in sandy peat in temperature of 55°–65°, under a bell-jar in shady position. When rooted pot into potting mixture* 2, potting on in potting mixture* 3. After final potting water freely and stand outdoors in summer months. The tender one below can also be grown outdoors in the southern states and in Calif. Hardy species are propagated by seeds and cuttings. Seeds may be sown in fall or early spring in sandy soil in a cold frame and transplanted to permanent position as soon as large enough to handle. Cuttings should be made in Sept., inserted in sandy peat in a cool greenhouse or cold frame.

Chamaebuxus. Bastard box. A low, evergreen, creeping sub-shrub, about 8 in. high, fit only for the rock garden, with alternate, elliptic or narrower, almost box-like leaves 1–1½ in. long. Flowers in pairs or solitary, yellowish-white, but with red spot. Central Eu. April–May. Hardy from zone* 4 southward.

dalmaisiana. Tender hybrid shrub, 3–6 ft. high. Leaves ovalish, to 1 in. long, not stalked. Flowers in terminal racemes,* purplish-red, the lower petal whitish. Long flowering period. Considered by some as a form of *P. myrtifolia,* a species otherwise little grown in this country.

lutea. Orange milkwort. A very showy hardy annual. Flowers yellow, in dense terminal cluster. Suited only to the bog garden (which see). L.I. to Tex. near the coast. Summer.

paucifolia. Flowering wintergreen. Fringed milkwort. Gay-wings. Trailing perennial 3–6 in. high. Lower leaves small and scale-like, upper leaves clustered, ovalish, 1½ in. long. Flowers reddish-purple, sometimes white, in 1–4 flowered clusters. Corolla conspicuously fringed. New Brunswick to Ga. and westward in rich woods, and suited only to the wild garden, with a pH of 4–5. May.

Senega. Seneca or Senega snakeroot. Perennial, 1–1½ ft. high. Leaves lance-shaped, to 2 in. long. Flowers small, greenish-white in terminal spikes. Eastern N.A. June. Roots used medicinally. Needs a soil with a pH of 4–5. See MEDICINAL PLANTS.

vayredae. Resembling *P. Chamaebuxus,* but lower, with smaller leaves and with purplish flowers with yellow spot. Spain. May. Hardy from zone * 5 southward.

POLYGALACEAE (pol-lig-a-lay′see-ee).

The milkwort family comprises about 12 genera and 1000 species of herbs, shrubs, and trees, some of them found nearly throughout the world, but wanting in N.Z. and a few other places. The only cult. genus is *Polygala,* which see for the characters of the garden Polygalaceae.

polygama, -us, -um (pol-lig′a-ma). Polygamous; *i.e.,* with both perfect* and imperfect flowers. See HERMAPHRODITE.

POLYGAMOUS. See POLYGAMA.

POLYGONACEAE (pol-lig-o-nay′see-ee). The buckwheat or rhubarb family is important because of these two plants, rather than for its genera of plants with showy flowers. Among its perhaps 30 genera and over 900 species of herbs, shrubs, vines, and trees, of very wide distribution, only a handful are grown for ornament. Of these *Antigonon,* which is a showy tropical vine, is easily first. *Eriogonum* comes perhaps second, and comprises many herbs from the western U.S. *Polygonum,* except for a few species, is largely weedy, and *Rumex* (the dock) is chiefly a pest (*see* the list at WEEDS).

The two economic genera are *Rheum* (*see* RHUBARB) and *Fagopyrum* (*see* BUCKWHEAT). The only other cult. genera are tropical. They are *Muehlenbeckia* and *Coccolobis,* both shrubs or trees of slight garden interest.

Most of the plants have jointed stems. Leaves simple,* but very various as to arrangement and shape, their stalks, however, always surrounded by a split, membranous, or chaffy sheath near the base. True flowers scarcely showy, without petals, but often grouped in relatively handsome clusters, the color of which is due to bracts* or wing-like structures in the flower. Fruit small, dry (an achene*), sometimes surrounded by remains of the flower, occasionally fleshy, or prominently winged.

Technical flower characters: Flowers mostly hermaphrodite.* Sepals 2–6, sometimes united and colored, but scarcely petal-like, often merely chaffy. Petals none. Stamens* 2–9. Ovary superior,* usually 1-celled.

POLYGONATUM. See SOLOMON'S-SEAL.

POLYGONUM (pol-lig′o-num). Smartweed. Knotweed. Erect, trailing or climbing, annual or perennial herbs, the climbing species sometimes woody, comprising about 150 species of the family Polygonaceae. They are found throughout the world, their habits being very diverse. Stems angled, swollen at the joints where leaf base clasps the stem, sometimes spotted or streaked brown. Leaves alternate* and simple. Flowers small, in terminal spikes or loose racemes. Calyx of 5 sepals generally colored pink or white. Corolla absent. Stamens* 3–9. Fruit dry, triangular, 1-celled, 1-seeded. (*Polygonum* is from the Greek for many-jointed, in allusion to the stems.)

Easy of cult., but only a few species worth it, these generally being climbers which are grown for their foliage and flowers.

All are useful bee plants. Propagated by seeds, cuttings and division of rootstocks. Annuals are propagated from seed (*see* AN-NUALS). Perennials may be propagated from seeds sown in cool greenhouse or cold frame in early spring, transplanting to permanent positions as soon as large enough to handle. Cuttings of the woody species may be made by taking pieces of the hard wood about 8 in. in length, in Dec. Insert them in sand to ½ their length in a cold frame, where they should be left until the following April, when callus will have formed. They may then be planted in permanent position in ordinary garden soil in sun or shade. Perennial rootstocks may be divided in March or April. Perennials should be given manure annually.

affine. Hardy perennial with creeping rootstock. Leaves basal, lance-shaped, brownish in color, 6 in. or more long, margins finely toothed. Flowering stalk to 1½ ft. Flowers in dense spikes, 2–3 in. long, bright rose in color. Fall. For cult. *see* ROCK GARDEN. High Himalayas.

amplexicaule. Mountain fleece. Hardy perennial, with spreading rootstock, which is also woody. Stems green, growing to 3 ft. Leaves ovalish, margins wavy. Upper leaves clasping the stem, lower leaves short-stalked. Flowers in terminal spikes, to 6 in. long, rose or white. July. Good border plant. High Himalayas. *Var.* **rubrum** has fleecy red flowers in profusion in Sept.

auberti. Silver-lace vine. Fleece-vine. Chinese fleece-vine. Lace-vine. Hardy, twining, woody perennial with slender stems growing to 25 ft. Leaves to 2½ in. long, alternate, broadly lance-shaped. Flowers greenish-white, fragrant, in long, erect or drooping clusters, growing from the axils* of the leaves near top of plant. Aug. Excellent for pergola or trellis (*see* VINES). Western China and Tibet.

aviculare. Knotweed. *See* list at WEEDS.

baldschuanicum. Similar to *P. auberti*, but with larger rose-colored flowers, in numerous, dense clusters. Aug. Bokhara.

Convolvulus. Black bindweed. *See* list at WEEDS.

cuspidatum. Mexican bamboo, although it is neither Mexican nor a bamboo. Strong-growing, hardy perennial, to 8 ft. high. Leaves roundish, and sharply pointed, base of leaf clasping stem, to 5 in. long. Flowers small, greenish-white, numerous, in loose clusters growing from the axils* of the leaves. Late summer and early fall. A handsome and quick-growing plant, useful as a screen, but so rampant that, without rigid control, it readily becomes a pest very difficult to eradicate. Jap. Often offered as *P. sieboldi* or *P. zuccarini*, and a red-flowered form is also offered. The *var.* **compactum** is a dwarf form about 2 ft. high.

orientale. Prince's-feather. Annual growing to 6 ft. high, hairy, much-branched. Leaves ovalish, 6–10 in. long, base of leaf clasping the stem. Flowers pink or rose, in branching spikes, to 3 in. long. Flowers clustered on the spikes. Fall. As. and Aust., naturalized in N.A.

Persicaria. Lady's-thumb. Annual to 2 ft. Leaves lance-shaped, with dark brown spot near the middle. Flowers pink, sometimes greenish, in dense spikes 2 in. long. Summer. A garden weed (*see* list at WEEDS). Eu., naturalized in America.

Reynoutria. A rather coarse perennial ground cover, 4–6 in. high, but the stems 8–15

in. long and sometimes partially erect, grooved, and purple-spotted. Leaves short-stalked, broadly ovalish, about 3½ in. long, the margins wavy. Flowers minute, numerous, in spiky, showy clusters from the leaf joints, pink or white. Jap. Aug.–Sept. Will stand heat, drought and indifferent soil.

sieboldi = *Polygonum cuspidatum.*
zuccarini = *Polygonum cuspidatum.*

polylopha, *-us*, *-um* (pol-i-lō′fa). Much-crested or much-tufted.

polymorpha, *-us*, *-um* (pol-i-mor′fa). Many- or variously formed.

POLYPETALOUS. With separate petals. *See* the illustration at GAMOPETALOUS.

polyphylla, *-us*, *-um* (pol-i-fil′la). Many-leaved.

POLYPLOID. *See* CHROMOSOME.

POLYPODIACEAE (pol-i-po-di-ā′see-ee). The polypody family comprises most of the common ferns of cult., both hardy and tropical. For the others (largely tree ferns and a few unimportant genera) *see* CYATHEACEAE, OPHIOGLOSSACEAE, OSMUNDACEAE, and SCHIZAEACEAE.

The ferns have simple or much-dissected, or compound leaves, usually called fronds, of the greatest diversity of shape, but widely cult. because of their beauty. For the hort. uses and culture of ferns *see* FERNS AND FERN GARDENING. All the ferns agree in having their young leaves start in a crosier-like coil, which in some tropical genera is very large and striking, often being clothed with a shaggy or velvety sheath. Scarcely any have a distinct trunk, as do the tree ferns, but some are woody at the base and many have very stout rootstocks.*

The family is a huge one, comprising in its 170 genera and over 7000 species perhaps three-quarters of all known forms, which in former geological periods were far more numerous than now. None produce flowers. For a description of the organs that replace flowers and for the function of the dust-like spores found on the back of many fern fronds *see* FERNS AND FERN GARDENING.

Because the characters that differentiate the ferns are wholly technical (residing in the microscopic spores* and how they are borne) the following cult. genera are grouped mostly upon how they are grown. Some of the genera are in more than one group due to the great diversity of geographical range in which they grow.

1. **Fern genera mostly for the outdoor fern garden or for the wild garden.**
   Adiantum, Asplenium, Athyrium, Camptosorus, Cheilanthes, Cryptogramma, Cystopteris, Dennstaedtia, Dryopteris, Onoclea, Pellaea, Phyllitis, Polypodium, Polystichum, Pteridium, Pteretis, Woodsia, and *Woodwardia.*

2. **Fern genera in which some or all of the species require greenhouse culture, some needing much heat and moisture.**
   Adiantum, Asplenium, Blechnum, Coniogramme, Cyclophorus, Cyrtomium,

---

* Special articles on the subjects indicated by an asterisk (*) will be found at the words so marked.

Davallia, Doodia, Dryopteris, Elapho-glossum, Nephrolepis, Onychium, Pityro-gramma, Platycerium, Polypodium, Po-lystichum, and *Pteris.*

3. **Fern genera containing the most widely grown greenhouse species.**

Used as decorative plants by florists, for centerpieces, window boxes, house plants, etc.

Adiantum, Cyrtomium, Davallia (for hanging baskets and fern balls), *Doodia, Nephrolepis* (includes the Boston fern), *Odontosoria, Onychium, Pityrogramma,* and *Pteris.*

Groups 2 and 3 can, of course, be grown outdoors in many parts of the South.

From these three groups and from the cultural notes at FERNS AND FERN GARDENING, the enthusiast can make a selection to suit his fern needs. See also each of the genera for description of the species and for further notes.

polypodioides (pol-i-po-di-oy′deez, but *see* OÏDES). Resembling a polypody.

POLYPODIUM (pol-i-pō′di-um). Polypody. A genus of over 1000 species of ferns of the family Polypodiaceae, scattered all over the world, and of such diverse habit that some are hardy ferns of our woodlands, some tropical tree-perchers (epiphytes*), and one is commonly called the resurrection fern. Nearly all have a creeping rootstock (rhizome) from which the frond stalks arise, and upon which they leave a scar when falling off. While the genus is very large, only a handful are in cult. and none is of first-class hort. importance. They have simple or compound* fronds upon the back of which are the conspicuous, round, naked spore* cases. (*Polypodium* is from the Greek for many feet, in allusion to the often branched rhizome.*)

The first and second species are greenhouse ferns, the hare's-foot polypody being rather widely cult. as it is a good house plant. For their culture *see* FERNS AND FERN GARDENING. The common polypody (*P. vulgare*) is useful only in the outdoor fern garden, preferably in the shade and in a moderately acid soil.

aureum. Hare's-foot fern; also called golden polypody. A stout, rather coarse fern 2–4 ft. high, its copious rootstock brown and scaly and very apt to creep out of the pot in which it is grown. Fronds long-stalked, the blade simple,* oblong, 12–18 in. long, the margins deeply cut on the lower half of the frond, the segments 6–12 in. long and about 1 in. wide, the whole frond green or deep bluish-green. Tropical America, and the source of several hort. forms, some of them prominently bluish-green. There are also crested or fringed or wavy-leaved forms (*P. mandaianum*), probably originating as mutations. Often offered as *Phlebodium aureum.*

polypodioides. Resurrection fern. A drought-resistant fern, mostly growing on trees, and the most abundant of all epiphytic* ferns in Fla. Fronds 5–7 in. long, 1–2 in. wide, cut into oblong segments, evergreen. In the dry season the fronds are coiled so that the plant is a mere ball of apparently dead leaves, but in moist conditions opening and continuing growth — hence its name of resurrection fern. (For an account of a still more extraordinary resurrection plant *see* ANASTATICA.) Southeastern U.S. southward to tropical America.

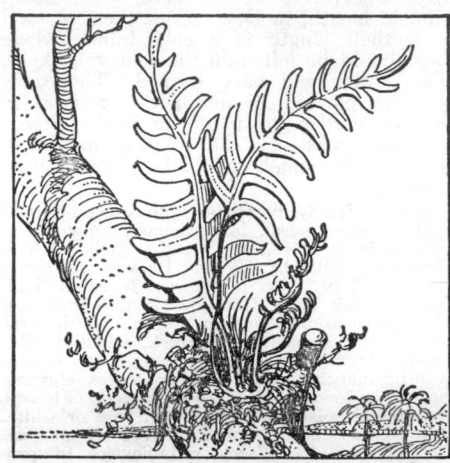

The resurrection fern (*Polypodium polypodioides*) in its growing state. When dry it curls up into a ball-like mass.

vulgare. The common polypody of European woodlands; also called wall fern. A very common fern (the North American form sometimes designated as *P. virginianum*) with fronds practically evergreen, 1–2 ft. long, 3–5 in. wide, deeply cut into segments that are 1½–2 in. wide, the segments near the middle of the frond longer than the lower ones. Eurasia. N.A., and common on banks, rocky ledges, or even on trees in the South. Of easy culture in woods soil, preferably with pH 4–5.

POLYPODY. See POLYPODIUM.

POLYPODY FAMILY = Polypodiaceae.

POLYPTERIS (pol-lip′ter-is). North American herbs comprising 4 species belonging to the family Compositae, of erect branching habit, to 4 ft. high. Leaves alternate,* simple. Flowers purplish, rose or pale pink, in loose, clustered heads. Heads surrounded by 2 whorls of bracts,* generally colored at the tips. Ray flowers showy. Fruit 4-sided. (*Polypteris* is from the Greek for many-winged, in allusion to the pappus.)

Not of much garden importance, only *P. hookeriana* in cult. It is a hardy annual (*see* ANNUALS). *Polypteris* likes sandy soil and sunny positions.

hookeriana. Also known as *Othake sphacelata.* Strong-growing annual, to 4 ft. high, slightly hairy and sticky. Leaves lance-shaped, to 4 in. long. Flower heads 1 in. or more across. Ray florets reddish, deeply divided into 3 segments, to ½ in. long. Whorls of bracts tipped purple. Neb. to Tex.

* Special articles on the subjects indicated by an asterisk (*) will be found at the words so marked.

POLYSCIAS (pol-lis′i-as). A large genus of about 70 species of tender, showy shrubs and trees of the family Araliaceae, with handsome foliage. They are natives of tropical Af., India, and the Pacific Islands. Leaves compound,* variable in shape and color. Flowers inconspicuous, whitish-green in clustered umbels*; rarely seen in cult. Fruit small, berry-like. (*Polyscias* is from the Greek for many and shade, in reference to the abundant foliage and shade.)

Chiefly grown as greenhouse foliage plants, although grown outdoors in the South. They need potting mixture* 5, a warm, moist greenhouse and plenty of water. The color of the foliage is best produced under partial shade. Most of what the florists call aralias belong here.

balfouriana. Densely branched, spreading tree to 25 ft. Stem grayish-green. Leaves long-stalked, swollen and clasping at the base. Leaflets generally 3, roundish, to 4 in. across, coarsely toothed, sometimes white at the margins. New Caledonia.

filicifolia. Strong-growing shrub, to 8 ft. Leaves varied in form. Leaflets to 1 ft. long, many, sometimes deeply cut into many segments, or entire,* even on the same plant. Pacific Islands.

fruticosa. Shrub to 8 ft. Leaves with 3 or more leaflets, ovalish or lance-shaped, to 4 in. long, toothed, and deeply cut. India. The *var.* **plumosa** has small and very narrow leaflets.

guilfoylei. A small tree growing to 20 ft. Leaflets ovalish, remotely toothed, to 5 in. long, often blotched white on the margin. Polynesia. The *var.* **laciniata** has leaflets with white margins, cut into long teeth. In the *var.* **victoriae** the leaflets are divided into many segments.

polystachya, -us, -um (pol-i-stack′i-a). With many spikes.

POLYSTICHUM (pol-lis′ti-kum). Hardy ferns, comprising over 200 species, belonging to the family Polypodiaceae, and found throughout the temperate regions. Underground stem, sometimes short and thick, or thin and creeping. Leaves usually evergreen, compound, the leaflets entire or cut into many segments. Spore cases in round patches, in rows on the veins on the under side of the fronds. (*Polystichum* is from the Greek for many rows, in allusion to the spores.)

Some of the species are also known as *Aspidium.* A few make good house plants, but all can be grown in damp, shady places in gardens or woods. They are easily cult., the chief requirements being plenty of water and a moderately acid soil. Propagated from spores,* but a few by division of rootstocks. Spores should be sown in pans on the surface of a mixture of peat moss, sand, and loam, then covered with bell-jar and shaded, keeping damp at all times. As soon as large enough to handle, plants should be pricked off into pans, using a mixture of equal parts of sand, loam, peat, and leaf mold. Finally, use potting mixture* 5. Division of rootstocks may be made in early spring. This is also the best time for making new plantings.

acrostichoides. Also known as *Dryopteris acrostichoides.* Dagger fern. Christmas fern. A hardy, evergreen fern, the fronds to 2 ft. long, in dense clusters growing from the crown of the stem. Fertile leaves, that is, those bearing spores, have shorter leaflets than the sterile leaves. Leaflets lance-shaped, 1–2 in. long, slightly toothed. Suitable for house plant. Eastern N.A.

aculeatum. A tufted, more or less scaly-stemmed fern, its fronds 1–3 ft. long, 6–12 in. wide, the ultimate segments lance-shaped below, the upper ones unequal-sided and more or less ovalish. A tough, hardy fern, common in temperate regions of the Old World.

brauni. Prickly shield fern. Rootstock thick, growing obliquely. Leaves to 2 ft., forming a ring around crown of stem. Leafstalks covered with hair-like scales. Leaflets in pairs, narrow and pointed, the margins toothed. Leaves die down in fall. N.A. and Eu.

falcatum = *Cyrtomium falcatum.*

Lonchitis. Mountain holly fern. Hardy, evergreen, the fronds nearly 2 ft. long, stiff and leathery. Leaflets lance-shaped, to 1½ in. long. N.A., Eu. and As.

munitum. Giant holly fern. Hardy, evergreen, the leafstalks to 1 ft. long, covered with chaffy scales. Leaves to 3½ ft. long, the leaflets long and narrow, sharply toothed, sometimes cut into segments. Western N.A.

POMACEAE. *See* ROSACEAE.

POMADERRIS (pō-ma-der′ris). Victorian hazel. Tender shrubs and trees, found in Aust., N.Z., and the South Pacific Islands, comprising about 22 species, belonging to the family Rhamnaceae. Leaves alternate,* simple.* Flowers in loose clusters, growing from the axils* of the leaves, near the ends of the branches. Individual flowers numerous, small. Calyx greenish-white. Corolla none. Fruit, a small 3-celled capsule.* (*Pomaderris* is from the Greek for lid and skin, in allusion to the capsule covering.)

Only one species in cult., grown in the southern states and Calif. for ornament. Propagated by cuttings of half-ripened shoots in July inserted in a mixture of sandy peat under glass.

apetala. Tainui. A small tree to 20 ft. Leaves ovalish, 3–4 in. long, with white-woolly hairs on the under side, brownish on the veins. Flowers greenish-white, in long, loose clusters, 3–7 in. long. Aust. and N.Z.

POMARIUM. An old name for a fruit orchard.

POMATO. A true chimera,* produced by grafting tomato cions on potato stock, and more of a scientific curiosity than a hort. subject. It has fragrant, tomato-like, juicy fruit, used as is the tomato. *See* CHIMERA. It was originally called potomato, and the grafts were made either way. In those in which tomato was the stock and the potato the cion, it was thought that the resulting plant would produce potatoes under ground and tomatoes in the air — an illusory hope. It has also been called topato.

POME. Typically, the fruit of an apple, pear, quince, hawthorn, and related plants. It is technically a fleshy fruit without a

---

* Special articles on the subjects indicated by an asterisk (*) will be found at the words so marked.

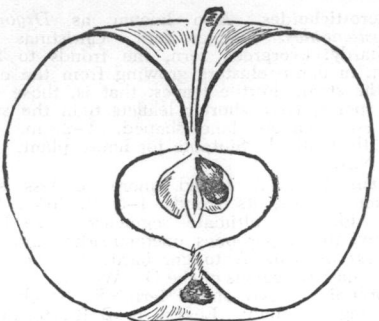

Cross-section of an apple (pome).
For details *see* text.

stone, but having several seeds, usually within a papery or bony chamber at the center, which is all that remains of the ripened ovary. The fleshy, juicy part of a pome is mostly the much-enlarged receptacle.*

POMEGRANATE. A delicious but little-known fruit in the U.S., and thought by some to be insipid here, but prized for centuries abroad. It is derived from the only cult. species of the genus **Punica** (pew'ni-ka) of the family Punicaceae. The common pomegranate is **P. Granatum,** an Asiatic shrub or small tree, 10–20 ft. high, and hardy outdoors only in zone* 5 and southward. It often has spiny-tipped branches and opposite,* short-stalked, oblongish or oval-oblong, shining leaves, 1½–3 in. long. Flowers in small clusters of 1–5, at the ends of short shoots borne in the leaf axils.* Calyx leathery, partly tubular, the 5–7 lobes persistent on the fruit. Corolla of 5–7 separate, wrinkled, orange-red petals, the flowers about 1¼ in. wide. Stamens* numerous. Fruit a fleshy, several-chambered, brownish-yellow, white, pink, or red berry, orange-sized, the juicy flesh crimson and slightly acid. (*Punica* is the old name for Carthage, the pomegranate having once been called the apple of Carthage.)

POMEGRANATE CULTURE

The pomegranate, one of the oldest of cultivated fruits and well known to Theophrastus, is not much grown in the U.S., where its outdoor cult. is confined to zone 5 and southward. It is, however, perfectly hardy in southern Md. on the Eastern Shore. Calif. and Fla. are best suited to it, but in the latter state it is chiefly grown for home use or for ornament.

The trees, if grown for the best fruit, should be set 15–20 ft. apart each way, and the numerous shoots from the base should be cut out in order to make the plant more compact and tree-like. It will grow well in a great variety of soils, and where not grown for fruit, makes an extremely attractive hedge, as its flowering period may last

several weeks (April–May), and the showy fruit ripens in July–Aug.

The easiest method of propagation is to use the numerous shoots that spring up around all pomegranate trees.

If fruit is the desired aim, the best varieties are Wonderful, Sweet, Acid, and Dwarf. If the plant is grown mostly for ornament, and it is very decorative, the best varieties are Double Dwarf, Double Acid, Double Red, and several other double-flowered sorts that do not produce edible fruit. Some of these decorative forms, and even the fruiting pomegranate, are occasionally grown in the cool greenhouse for ornament. They are then kept pruned and make handsome plants for pot or tub. Use potting mixture* 4.

POMEGRANATE FAMILY = Punicaceae.

POMEGRANATE MELON. *See* MELON.

POMELO = *Citrus paradisi. See* GRAPE-FRUIT.

pomeridiana, -us, -um (po-mer-id-i-ā'na). Flowering in the afternoon.

POMICULTURE = Fruit culture.

POMME BLANCHE = *Psoralea esculenta.*

POMOLOGY. Fruit culture; and especially the study of various varieties of fruit.

POMPELMOUS = *Citrus maxima.*

POMPON. A hort. term for button-like heads of flowers, much smaller and usually more compact than the ordinary flower heads of the plant. Pompons are found among varieties of chrysanthemum and dahlia, and in a few other groups. *See* CHRYSANTHEMUM, DAHLIA.

PONCIRUS (pon-sy'rus). A single, spiny, deciduous* species of Chinese trees of the family Rutaceae and the hardiest of all the citrus fruits, although its fruit is inedible. The only species is **P. trifoliata** (sometimes known as *Citrus trifoliata*), the hardy or trifoliate orange, grown for ornament from zone* 4 southward, where it forms impenetrable, defensive hedges. It is also used as grafting stock for the more tender citrus fruits. The tree, sometimes called the trifoliate orange, is rarely over 20 ft. high, its spines mostly about ¾ in. long. Leaves alternate,* compound,* its 3 leaflets oval or oblong, 2–3 in. long, the stalk winged. Flowers white, usually fragrant, nearly 2 in. wide, flattish, the 5 petals oblongish and longer than the sepals. Stamens* 8–10. Fruit orange-like, but scarcely over 2 in. in diameter, its flesh dryish, very acid, but fragrant. (*Poncirus* is from the French *poncire,* for a kind of citron.)

POND-APPLE = *Annona glabra.*

POND CYPRESS. *See* TAXODIUM DISTICHUM.

ponderosa, -us, -um (pon-der-rō'sa). Heavy or massive.

PONDEROSA LEMON. *See* LEMON.

PONDEROSA PINE = *Pinus ponderosa. See* PINE.

* Special articles on the subjects indicated by an asterisk (*) will be found at the words so marked.

POND LILY. *See* NYMPHAEA.

PONGAMIA (pon-gay'mi-a). A genus of only one species of trees of the pea family, found in tropical As. and Aust. and cult. in southern Fla. and Calif. for ornament. The only species is **P. pinnata,** the Kurum oil tree, or Poonga oil tree, which grows up to 40 ft. Leaves compound,* bright green, leathery, strongly aromatic. Leaflets 5–7, in pairs, ovalish. Flowers pea-shaped, reddish-pink to white, in loose racemes 5 in. long growing from the axils* of the leaves. Fruit a short pod, to 2 in. long and 1 in. wide, woody and flat, its one seed containing a thick, reddish-brown oil. (*Pongamia* is a Latinized version of a Malayan name for the tree.)

PONTEDERIA (pon-te-deer'i-a). Pickerelweed. American hardy perennial aquatic herbs of 5 species of the family Pontederiaceae. They have strong-growing rootstocks, creeping horizontally in the mud of shallow pools. Leaves long-stalked. Flowers blue, in spikes. Individual flowers funnel-shaped, 2-lipped,* both the upper and lower lips being divided into 3 lobes. Blooms profusely but fades quickly. (Named for G. Pontedera, an Italian botanist.) Useful for shallow pools, edges of ponds, slow-moving streams, and for the bog garden. Propagated by division of rootstocks in early spring.

cordata. Pickerelweed; called also alligator wampee. Grows to 4 ft., usually in clumps. Leaves roundish, arrowhead-shaped at base, to 10 in. long, and 6 in. wide. Base of leafstalk sheathed. Flowers in spikes, blue, with 2 yellow or white spots on the upper lip. There is also a narrow-leaved form. Eastern N.A.

PONTEDERIACEAE (pon-te-deer-i-ā'-see-ee). The pickerelweed family includes only two cult. genera, *Pontederia,* the pickerelweed, and *Eichhornia* (*see* WATER HYACINTH). Both are aquatic, the first native in America and very showy in pools with its midsummer bloom. The water hyacinth, often a pest in tropical rivers, is a beautiful floating plant suitable for greenhouse pools or for outdoor culture in the summer. The family comprises only 8 genera and perhaps 25 species, found throughout the world except Eu.

Leaves spongy and floating in *Eichhornia,* erect and narrow or heart-shaped in *Pontederia.* Flowers irregular,* crowded in spikes, very showy in both genera. Fruit dry, a 1-seeded utricle* in *Pontederia,* and a dry pod (capsule*) surrounded by the withered flower parts in *Eichhornia.*

Technical flower characters: Flowers with the six segments colored alike, hence not easily separable into sepals or petals, more or less funnel-shaped, but irregular.* Stamens* 3 or 6, often long-protruding, of unequal length. Ovary superior,* 3-celled.

pontica, -us, -um (pon'ti-ka). From Pontus, an old name for a region south of the Black Sea in Asia Minor.

POOLROOT = *Eupatorium aromaticum.*

POONGA OIL TREE = *Pongamia pinnata.*

POOR-MAN'S MANURE. *See* SNOW.

POOR-MAN'S-ORCHID. *See* SCHIZANTHUS.

POOR-MAN'S-WEATHERGLASS. The scarlet pimpernel. *See* the list at WEEDS.

POOR-ROBIN'S-PLANTAIN = *Erigeron pulchellus.*

POPCORN = *Zea Mays everta. See* CORN.

POPINAC = *Acacia farnesiana.* For the white popinac *see* LEUCAENA GLAUCA.

POPLAR. For the true poplars *see* POPULUS. For another tree sometimes called poplar *see* TULIP-TREE.

POPPLE. *See* POPULUS.

POPPY. For the true poppies (*Papaver*), *see* the next main entry. Many other plants also have *poppy* as part of their names. Those in this book are: *Argemone, Dendromecon, Eomecon, Eschscholtzia, Glaucium, Hunnemannia, Hydrocleis, Macleaya, Meconopsis,* and *Romneya.*

POPPY. The true poppies all belong to the genus **Papaver** (pap'a-ver), and comprise about 100 species of annual or perennial herbs of the family Papaveraceae, found mostly in the temperate regions of Eu. and As. and a few in western N.A. They vary in height from 6 in. to 4 ft. Leaves basal, generally many and usually deeply segmented and hairy. Flowers solitary, on a long, flowering stalk, when in bud nodding but straightening as the flower opens. Calyx* of 2 sepals,* which fall when the petals open. Corolla of 5 petals, vividly colored red, violet, yellow, or white, sometimes blotched at the base. Stamens* numerous. Fruit a capsule,* 4–20-celled, with numerous minute seeds. The capsule is covered with a shield-like cap, underneath which small pores are formed, through which the seeds are dispersed. Any part of the plant if cut or broken exudes a milky substance. (*Papaver* is the classical Latin name of the poppy.)

For culture *see* below.

P. alpinum. Alpine poppy. Hardy perennial, with short stem, 1–2 in. above the ground from which the numerous leaves and flower stalks are produced. Leaves 4–6 in. long, grayish-green, cut into 2–3 deep lobes, which are again cut into many segments. Flowers on stalks to 10 in. high, white or yellow, fragrant. Fruit an oblong capsule. Alps.

P. bracteatum. Hardy perennial, growing to 3 ft. high, the whole plant covered with stiffish hairs. Leaves to 1 ft. long, and 4 in. across, segmented almost to midrib, the lobes opposite and toothed. Flower stalk with leafy, toothed bracts.* Flowers red. Mediterranean region.

P. californicum. An annual, 12–24 in. high, the branches erect. Leaves divided or parted feather-fashion, 2–3 in. long, the lower ones stalked, the upper stalkless. Flowers about 2 in. wide, the stalk long and hairy. Petals red, but green or blackish-green at the base. Calif. Summer.

P. glaucum. Tulip poppy. Annual, growing to 2 ft. Stem leaves bluish-green, cut into

* Special articles on the subjects indicated by an asterisk (*) will be found at the words so marked.

deep lobes which are opposite each other. Flowers cup-shaped, scarlet, inside marked at the base. This species produces numerous flowers. Syria. Perisa.

P. nudicaule. Iceland poppy. Hardy perennial to 1 ft. high. Leaves smooth or hairy, cut into equal lobes. Flowering stalk to 15 in. high, hairy. Flowers 1–2 in. across, sweet-scented, the colors ranging through white, red, yellow, and orange. Arctic regions. A good pink hort. form is Coonara Pink.

P. orientale. Oriental poppy. Strong-growing, hardy perennial, 3–4 ft. high, with stout, deeply growing rootstocks. The whole plant is covered with stiffish hairs. Leaves to 18 in. long, segmented almost to midrib, the lobes being opposite and sharply toothed. Flowering stalks have leafy, segmented bracts,* which get smaller toward the top. Flowers showy, to 6 in. across, scarlet, the petals marked at the base purplish-black. Mediterranean region. There are many fine hort. forms, among the red ones being Beauty of Livermore, Goliath, Olympia, and Taplow Scarlet.

P. pavoninum. Annual to 1 ft., hairy. Leaves lobed and sharply toothed. Flowers scarlet, to 1 in. across. Petals have a dark spot at base. Turkestan and Afghanistan.

P. pilosum. Perennial to 3 ft. Leaves irregularly segmented, covered with soft hairs. Flowering stalk branched. Flowers brick-red to orange, about 2 in. across. Mt. Olympus in Asia Minor.

P. Rhoeas. Corn poppy. Annual to 3 ft. Stems branching and wiry. Leaves irregularly lobed, sometimes entire, deep green in color. Flowers red, deep purple, scarlet, or occasionally white, 2 in. across. Eu. and As., naturalized in N.A. The Shirley poppy was originated from this species by the Rev. W. Wilks at Shirley, Eng., and has become a great garden favorite. The common corn poppy is the one immortalized in Flanders during World War I.

P. somniferum. Opium poppy (*see* HERB GARDENING). Strong-growing annual, 3–4 ft. high. Leaves grayish-green, coarsely lobed and toothed. Stem leaves clasping. Flowers white, pink, red, or purple, 3–4 in. across. Greece and Orient. It is the juice of the unripe pod which yields opium, but not commercially in the U.S., where its production is illegal. *See* MEDICINAL PLANTS.

POPPY CULTURE

Most poppies are of easy culture. They need (1) light loam or sandy soil containing humus, (2) sun, (3) ample room for development.

Annual poppies dislike transplanting. Seed of these should be sown in autumn unless the winters are exceptionally severe, in which case sow seed in early spring. Seed of perennials and biennials may be sown under glass or in cold frames, transplanted to small pots of potting mixture* 2, and planted in the early spring, with as little disturbance as possible, in the permanent locations. Cover all poppy seed very lightly. Annual poppies will grow in poor soil, but if given a better soil will pay for it with increased size and greater beauty. Perennial poppies will flourish in rich loam with good drainage.

The brilliant red Oriental poppy of the Mediterranean region (*P. orientale*) is a most satisfactory large plant for the peren-

nial border. It should be staked before the bloom matures and should remain undisturbed for several years to develop its full beauty. Mulch* in autumn with old manure and dig this in in spring. The plant makes an autumn growth. The easiest method of propagation is to dig up the long taproot, when dormant in August, cut it into small pieces and start these in light, sandy loam. Some of the newer hybrid Oriental poppies are superior to the type and come in rich orange, pink, salmon, and claret shades, and in white.

The Iceland poppy, a beautiful hardy perennial from the Far North

The yellow and orange Iceland poppy (*P. nudicaule*), from Arctic regions, is one of the best smaller perennial poppies. It requires light soil and perfect drainage. Without this it will rot off at the collar and die, often when at its best. It blooms the first year from seed and often self-sows freely. There are many interesting hybrid Iceland poppies in shades of pure pink, as well as stronger strains with larger flowers and long stems.

Papaver pilosum is somewhat similar to *P. nudicaule*, a perennial, self-sows freely, and thrives in light soil. It has long-stemmed flowers about the size of the Iceland poppy, generally in shades of orange or brick-red.

The alpine poppy (*P. alpinum*) is a most satisfactory rock garden poppy. It likes good drainage and light, gritty soil, and seeds freely. The flowers, on stems a few inches high above gray cut foliage, are of white, orange, and shades of pink. The modern varieties of alpine poppy are especially good. Although a perennial it is satisfactory when treated as an annual.

Many poppies, whether annual or perennial, are apt to stop flowering by midsummer, but the perennials will often make new foliage in the fall.

---

* Special articles on the subjects indicated by an asterisk (*) will be found at the words so marked.

The opium poppy (*P. somniferum*) and the Shirley poppy, tall annuals, both need plenty of room in which to grow. If the plants are not thinned, results will be poor. Both these poppies will flourish in either sandy soil or loam. The opium poppy has smooth, gray foliage, large flowers, double or single, and grows several ft. tall. There are two main strains, one with fringed (the so-called carnation poppies) and the other with unfringed petals. The colors run through all shades of purple, crimson, red, and pink, to white. The Shirley poppy, developed from the common scarlet, black-centered corn poppy of Eurasia (*P. Rhoeas*), has single flowers in shades of scarlet, pink and salmon, and white, all without the black center of the original type. When given plenty of room the Shirley poppy will make a plant two or three ft. across, with many flowers of great beauty.

The tulip poppy (*P. glaucum*) of Syria and Persia is an annual, or in mild climates, a biennial. It thrives in loose, gravelly soil and is a branching plant with gray foliage and single, cup-shaped, scarlet flowers.

POPPY ANEMONE = *Anemone coronaria*.

POPPY FAMILY. A medium-sized family of chiefly herbaceous plants, including, besides the poppy, the California poppy, bloodroot, cream-cups, and the tree poppy. For the cult. genera and a description of the family *see* PAPAVERACEAE.

POPPY MALLOW. See CALLIRHOË.

populifolia, -us, -um (pop-you-li-fō'li-a). With leaves like a poplar (*Populus*).

populnea, -us, -um (pop-pull'nee-a). Poplarlike.

POPULUS (pop'you-lus). Poplar; some of them also called cottonwood, aspen, and popple. A genus of quick-growing, softwooded trees of the willow family, comprising about 30 species from the north temperate zone (a few in warmer parts of northern Africa). They have alternate,* stalked, usually ovalish leaves. In some species (the quaking aspens) the leafstalk is compressed or slightly twisted or both, causing the leaves to shiver or quake in the slightest wind. Male and female flowers on separate trees, both in hanging catkins which bloom before the leaves unfold (in ours), the individual flowers minute, without petals or sepals. Fruit often silky, the small 2–4-valved pod ripening before the leaves are fully grown. (*Populus* is the classical Latin name of the poplar.)

For culture *see* below. All of them bloom early in the spring. Many recent hybrids or clones* have been developed for reforestation and pulpwood, but they are scarcely hort. trees.

alba. White, or silver-leaved poplar; abele. From 30–70 ft. high, or even more. Leaves not quaking, 3–5 in. long, lobed or cut fingerfashion, prominently white beneath. Eurasia. Hardy from zone* 2 southward. The *var.*

nivea has leaves still whiter beneath; *var.* **pyramidalis** is a valuable accent plant with a columnar habit. The latter variety is sometimes known as *P. bolleana.*

balsamifera. Balsam poplar. Tacamahac. A stout tree up to 90 ft. high. Leaves not quaking, 5–7 in. long, somewhat rounded at the base. Eastern N.A. and hardy everywhere. The tree has had many names in the past, among them *P. monilifera.*

berolinensis. A very hardy poplar of hybrid origin, admirably suited for cult. in the northern prairie states and for windbreaks.* It is a columnar tree, resembling the Lombardy poplar, but much hardier. It has yellowish-gray, hairy twigs and angularly ovalish, long-pointed leaves. Hardy from zone* 1 southward.

bolleana = *Populus alba pyramidalis.*

canadensis. Often called Carolina poplar, but not native there and thought to be a French hybrid (in 1750) between *P. balsamifera* and *P. nigra;* only male trees are known. A tall tree, 50–90 ft. high. Leaves quaking, ovalish or triangular, 3–4 in. long, usually broad-based and minutely hairy on the margins. The *var.* **eugenei,** Carolina poplar, has a narrowly pyramidal habit. *See* culture below. There are also several other habit varieties, one of them fastigiate. Hardy from zone* 2 southward.

candicans. Balm-of-Gilead; also balsam poplar. A tree up to 90 ft. high; only female trees are known. Leaves not quaking, broadly oval or triangular, broad but heart-shaped at the base, coarsely blunt-toothed, 4–6½ in. long, whitish and hairy beneath. Buds sticky. Of unknown, but possibly of hybrid, origin, and considered by some to be a clone.* Hardy from zone* 3 southward.

deltoides. Cottonwood. A tree up to 90 ft. Leaves quaking, 5–7 in. long, somewhat heart-shaped at the base. It is a short-lived tree, its center soon rotting. Eastern N.A. Hardy from zone* 2 southward. Not to be used for permanent planting.

eugenei = *Populus canadensis eugenei.*

grandidentata. Large-toothed aspen. A somewhat weedy tree, 40–60 ft. high. Leaves quaking, 3–4 in. long, coarsely toothed, at first whitish beneath, later smooth. Eastern N.A. Hardy from zone* 2 southward.

maximowiczi. A quick-growing vigorous tree, 50–90 ft. high, with spreading branches and deep-fissured gray bark on old trunks. Leaves ovalish, elliptic or sometimes nearly round, 3–5 in. long, the tip pointed and twisted, whitish on the under side. Male catkins 2–8 in. long, the fruiting ones 8–12 in. long. Jap. Hardy from zone* 4 southward.

monilifera = *Populus balsamifera.*

nigra. Black poplar. A wide-spreading tree, 40–90 ft. high. Leaves quaking, broadly triangular-oval, or wedge-shaped, 3–4 in. long, nearly as wide, finely blunt-toothed. Eurasia. Hardy throughout the country, but much less planted than the *var.* **italica,** the Lombardy poplar, with a columnar fastigiate habit. Many consider *P. alba pyramidalis* a tree superior to the Lombardy poplar, which has been perhaps overplanted in the U.S.

simoni. A narrow-headed tree, 20–36 ft. high. Leaves not quaking, ovalish or squarish, 3–5 in. long, white or pale green beneath. China. Hardy from zone* 2 southward. There are also fastigiate and weeping varieties available.

tremula. European aspen. A round-headed tree rarely up to 90 ft. high, usually less than half this, the twigs a little sticky. Leaves quaking, thin, roundish or ovalish, 2–3 in. long,

* Special articles on the subjects indicated by an asterisk (*) will be found at the words so marked.

the teeth large. Eurasia and northern Africa. Hardy throughout.

tremuloides. Quaking aspen. A tree up to 90 ft. high. Leaves quaking, ovalish or nearly round, broad at the base, finely toothed, the teeth glandular. N.A. and hardy throughout. The *var.* pendula has drooping branches.

POPLAR CULTURE

The hardiness and fast growth of the poplar make it a valuable economic tree. It has been used as an ornamental, but because of vigorous growth, weak wood, and voracious roots, it should be kept out of most gardens and planted only in poor sites. It will thrive under almost all conditions, but prefers a damp soil and lowland. When compared with other trees of similar size and habit, it is short-lived, and, wherever possible, its use should be restricted to situations where other materials will not succeed. In this way, the present overplanting and stereotyped use of this group will be lessened. In many localities, the poplar is employed for street planting. This cannot be recommended because of its relatively short life, brittle branches, and vagrant root system, which often causes trouble by growing into sanitary and drainage systems.

Lombardy poplars. *See also* POPULUS ALBA PYRAMIDALIS.

Populus alba pyramidalis, known also as *Populus bolleana,* is an excellent form of upright habit and is commonly used for windbreaks.* It is less formal and more graceful than the more common Lombardy poplar (*Populus nigra italica*). Where a large, somewhat spreading tree is desired, the Carolina poplar (*Populus canadensis eugenei*) is most desirable. *Populus balsamifera* and several fast-growing hybrids are now being grown in large numbers for reforestation purposes. The white poplar (*P. alba*) is commonly planted in many Midwestern areas, where other trees will not

grow for lack of sufficient rainfall. The fast growth of the poplar prevents soil erosion and its timber is available in a short time for pulpwood.

Propagation by hardwood cuttings is the usual method. The cuttings are taken in the fall and buried over winter in sand. Because the group hybridizes freely, seed is not commonly used. The several weeping forms are grafted six to eight feet high on standards. For this work, *Populus grandidentata* is most often used. — D. W.

DISEASES. Various canker* diseases may cause eruptions in the bark of branches or main trunk. If just a few cankers are present, the diseased portions should be removed, making the pruning cuts several inches below the cankered area. Spraying with pesticides is of no value.

In some areas during some growing seasons, a rust* disease may cause many orange pustules on the leaf surface. During years when the disease is serious there may be considerable leaf drop. Although no experimental work has been done on control of poplar rust, the use of pesticide #5 or #11 (*see* SPRAYS AND DUSTS) would probably lessen the severity of the disease if sprays were applied early in the spring.

PORANA (por-ray'na). A genus of 15 species of tropical Old World twining herbs of the family Convolvulaceae, one of them, **P. paniculata,** the mountain creeper or horsetail creeper, occasionally grown for ornament in zones* 8 and 9, mostly in Fla. It is a tall-climbing (30 ft.), herbaceous vine, with alternate,* ovalish or heart-shaped leaves, 4–6 in. long, and white-hairy beneath. Flowers resembling the morning-glory, but small, not over ⅓ in. wide, white, in profuse clusters (panicles*). India. Sometimes known as "white corallita" in Fla., but that name is better applied to *Antigonon.* (*Porana* is the native name for these plants.)

PORCUPINE PALM = *Rhapidophyllum hystrix.*

Porphyrio (por-fear'i-o). Named for the purple gallinules of Europe, because of their purple color. *See* GENTIANA PORPHYRIO.

porrifolia, -us, -um (por-ri-fō'li-a). With leek-like leaves.

Porrum (por'rum). Latin for the leek.

PORTIA TREE = *Thespesia populnea.*

PORT ORFORD CEDAR = *Chamaecyparis lawsoniana.*

portoricensis, -e (por-to-ri-sen'sis). From Puerto Rico.

PORTUGUESE CYPRESS = *Cupressus lusitanica.*

PORTUGUESE LAUREL = *Laurocerasus lusitanica.*

PORTULACA (por-tew-lăk'a). Purslane. Low-growing, mostly trailing annual or perennial herbs, comprising about 100 species of the family Portulacaceae, and found in tropical and temperate regions. Stems soft and fleshy, often reddish in color. Leaves alternate,* small, thick, entire, often spoon-shaped, 1–2 in. long. Flowers usually ter-

---

* Special articles on the subjects indicated by an asterisk (*) will be found at the words so marked.

minal, opening only in full sunlight, sometimes inconspicuous, sometimes showy. Calyx* of 5 sepals.* Corolla of 5 petals, in varying colors. Stamens* numerous. Fruit a small capsule,* containing many seeds, splitting transversely. (*Portulaca* is the Latin name of the purslane.) Only 1 species of garden importance. Propagated by seeds sown in June where required to bloom in sunny places, or by bits of the stem inserted in the soil.

grandiflora. Rose moss. Garden portulaca. Sun moss. Wax pink. Trailing, prostrate, annual, much-branched and fleshy. Leaves simple, spoon-shaped, to 1 in. long. Flowers terminal, showy, 1 in. across, ranging in color from white, pink, yellow, red, or purple. Suitable for dry, sunny rockeries, dry banks, or border edges. Brazil.

oleracea. Purslane. Pussley. Trailing annual with reddish, fleshy stems, the joints of which produce roots when in contact with the soil. Leaves thick and fleshy, spoon-shaped, to 2 in. long. Flowers small, bright yellow. Persistent garden weed. *See* list at WEEDS. A hort. *var.* is **sativa,** with thicker, mostly erect stems, used by some as "greens," mostly in Eu.

PORTULACACEAE (por-tew-lă-kay'see-ee). The purslane family, notorious because it contains the pestiferous "pussley," also comprises several very beautiful garden plants among its 16 genera and 500 species. They are mostly herbs, but some tropical genera are shrubby, especially the African *Portulacaria*, a greenhouse plant with fleshy leaves. All the family have a tendency toward thick or fleshy leaves.

The most popular of the garden genera is *Portulaca*, in spite of its weedy members. Some of the garden forms are among the gayest-colored of all flowers. *Montia* is sometimes grown as a salad. *Calandrinia* comprises a few rather important species with quick-fading flowers. *Claytonia* (the spring beauty) is chiefly for the wild garden. *Talinum* and *Lewisia* (largely for the rock garden species) are somewhat widely cult.

Leaves alternate* or opposite,* always without marginal teeth. Flowers regular, showy in some genera, but quickly fading in most, and opening only in sunlight in a few. Fruit mostly a dry, 3-valved pod (capsule*).

Technical flower characters: Sepals* 2. Petals 4 or 5, sometimes slightly united at the base, often notched at the tip. Stamens* of an indefinite number. Ovary superior,* except in *Portulaca*.

PORTULACARIA (por-tew-lak-cay'ri-a). Fleshy-leaved, little-known, South African shrubs or small trees of the family Portulacaceae, **P. afra,** the purslane tree, grown in Calif. for interest more than ornament, and also in the cool greenhouse northward. It is a stout-stemmed, soft-wooded tree, 8–12 ft. high, with opposite, very fleshy, blunt leaves mostly less than ½ in. long. Flowers pink, scarcely ⅒ in. wide, clustered (panicled*) in the upper leaf axils.* Fruit dry, 3-winged, scarcely or only tardily splitting.

The tree should be grown as a succulent (which see). it will not stand much frost. (*Portulacaria* means similar to *Portulaca*.)

portulacea, -us, -um (por-tew-lay'see-a). From *Portulaca*, the old Latin name of the purslane; hence any thick-leaved plant.

POSOQUERIA (po-so-queer'i-a). Tropical American shrubs or small trees, comprising about 15 species of the family Rubiaceae. Leaves simple,* opposite,* leathery, ovalish, the stipules* (leafy growths at the base of the leafstalks) 2, large. Flowers in terminal clusters, fragrant, white, pink or red. Calyx* of 5 sepals.* Corolla 5-lobed, tubular. Stamens* 5, showy. Fruit a large, fleshy berry. (*Posoqueria* is derived from a native name for these trees in Guiana.)

Not much cult., except as a tropical greenhouse plant, but grown outdoors in southern Fla. Propagated by cuttings.

latifolia. Tree to 20 ft. Leaves dark green, shiny, 8–10 in. long. Flowers to 6 in. long, white, tubular, the lobes opening salver-like. Fruit a yellow, globe-shaped berry 2 in. across. Mex to S.A.

POSSUM HAW = *Ilex decidua*. *See* HOLLY and VIBURNUM NUDUM.

POST OAK = *Quercus stellata*. *See* OAK.

POTASH. For its use in fertilizers *see* FERTILIZERS. As part of the food of plants *see* PLANT FOODS.

POTATO. For the culture of the common potato *see* the next main entry. *See also* DIOSCOREA, SWEET POTATO, APIOS, ALLIUM CEPA AGGREGATUM, and SOLANUM JASMINOIDES, for other plants sometimes called potato.

POTATO (*Solanum tuberosum*). This upland Andean plant has become the staple vegetable crop of the temperate world within the last 150 years. Its high starch content and food value make it a most important garden plant, but one not to be undertaken if your garden is too small for the space potatoes need. *See* KITCHEN GARDEN for plan and details.

The earliest Spanish chronicler of the potato told us that it originally grew far up in the Andes, where the Incas valued it highly. It is a region where it freezes, at least a little, during every month in the year. Potatoes have never gotten over their fondness for that ancient coolness, and that is why their culture is limited, or should be, to regions having a long cool spring for the early varieties, and a reasonably cool summer for the later sorts, which are usually stored for winter use.

The best potato regions are in the North, especially Maine and the states along the Great Lakes. Enormous yields are harvested on eastern Long Island, where proximity to cool sea water makes a very favorable environment. Thousands of acres are planted within a few hundred feet of the ocean, just behind the dunes. Similarly favored localities are rare, but the potato is planted suc-

---

* Special articles on the subjects indicated by an asterisk (*) will be found at the words so marked.

cessfully all over the U.S. by utilizing the coolest season for the early varieties. Late potatoes are not successful in regions of great summer heat.

The commercial production of early potatoes follows the waning winter from Florida northward in the East. In California, where crops are very heavy, they utilize the relatively brief cool season of favored localities with great success. Of course all mountain states can grow it easily, the elevation bringing just the conditions potatoes need.

SOILS AND FERTILIZERS. Most good garden soils are suitable for potatoes. Many indications, especially in the soils of Long Island, point to a somewhat acid soil being the most favorable. And soils with a pH value of 5 or 6 are often very prolific (*see* ACID AND ALKALI SOILS for details of making the tests and controlling the soil acidity). Other regions produce good crops with a normal, nearly neutral soil.

The soil, however, must be very rich, and not too stony to permit proper tuber development. Fresh stable manure is to be avoided, and even well-rotted stable manure had better be plowed under the autumn before spring planting. If manure is used, allow 15–20 tons per acre (10 wheelbarrow loads for a 100-ft. row). Most commercial growers rely upon special potato mixtures (available at all dealers) of commercial fertilizers. These are drilled into the trenches in which the plants will grow, at the rate of 3000 pounds per acre (about 12 pounds per 100-ft. row). If commercial fertilizer is used, it is imperative that none of it touches the planted "seed" (*see* below).

PLANTING. The ordinary seed of the potato, resulting from its blossom, is never used (except for breeding experiments). Potatoes are propagated and universally grown by cutting up an ordinary potato tuber, allowing one or two "eyes" (really buds of the underground stem) to each piece. Cut the pieces so that there will be as much flesh as possible for the eyes, as the plant will live on this stored food while sprouting.

It is essential, in view of the disastrous diseases to which the potato is subject (*see* below), that only certified, disease-free tubers (commonly called seed) be purchased from a thoroughly reliable dealer. They cost a little more, but their use may prevent failure. After the tubers have been cut, it is well to allow them to callus* slightly before planting. They will do this naturally if spread thinly in a cool, dry place for 24 hours. Some growers dust them over with fine, powdery soil.

Make the trenches or drills about 5 in. deep, and put a piece of cut potato tuber every 12–14 in. The rows should be 2 ft. apart for the early varieties and 2½–3 ft. apart for the late sorts. Cover the tubers thoroughly. They will take nearly three weeks to sprout above ground.

The date for planting is important. All the early varieties should be planted at least 10 days or two weeks before the date of the average last killing frost in your region (*see* the name of your state for frost data). Even considerable frost after planting will not harm the buried seed, and an early start is essential if heat and disease are to be avoided.

Late varieties (*see* below) are planted about 6 weeks after the early sorts. Except in the most favorable regions, with long, cool summers, their use is to be avoided by most home gardeners. Their diseases and harvesting are very difficult problems over much of the country. They are, however, as in Maine, eastern Long Island, Michigan, and Idaho, grown (mostly commercially) with great success.

It takes about 5–8 pounds of tubers (depending on their size and the frequency of their "eyes") to plant 100 ft. of row, the final yield of which should be about a bushel. Commercial yields average 400–550 bushels per acre on Long Island and in Maine, much less over most of the country. A single favorable Long Island acre has yielded over 900 bushels. The American record appears to be 1145 bushels, on a high-altitude Colorado farm.

CULTIVATION. Clean, frequent cultivation is essential, especially in the early stages. No weeds and a dust mulch should be the rule for the first few weeks. As the plants get bushy it will be more difficult to culti-

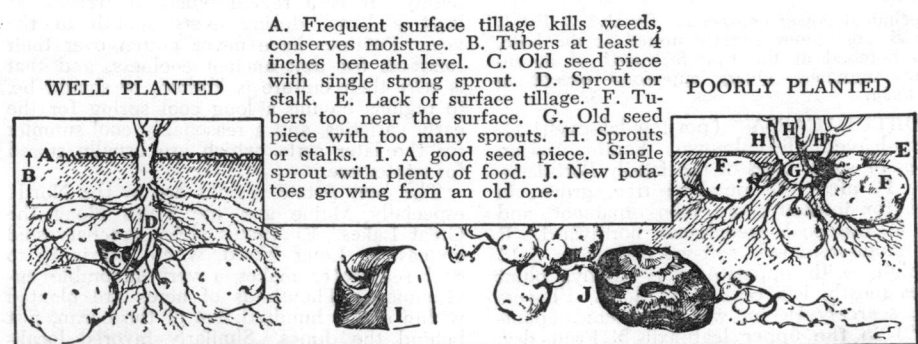

WELL PLANTED　　　**POORLY PLANTED**

A. Frequent surface tillage kills weeds, conserves moisture. B. Tubers at least 4 inches beneath level. C. Old seed piece with single strong sprout. D. Sprout or stalk. E. Lack of surface tillage. F. Tubers too near the surface. G. Old seed piece with too many sprouts. H. Sprouts or stalks. I. A good seed piece. Single sprout with plenty of food. J. New potatoes growing from an old one.

* Special articles on the subjects indicated by an asterisk (*) will be found at the words so marked.

vate, but it must be kept up until the tops show signs of withering, as they always do when the tubers are approaching maturity. *See* CULTIVATION.

It is, of course, necessary to cultivate with sufficient care so as not to disturb the tubers, which, as the crop approaches harvesting, will occupy much more space than the original width of the trench. At the last or next to the last cultivation, the soil should be hoed, or plowed, over the plants on both sides so as to make a ridge or mound about 10 in. high, through which the tops will keep on growing until the end.

HARVESTING. When the tops have finally withered, potatoes may be dug. The early varieties can be left in the ground for a short period after they are ready to dig, if the weather is not too warm and wet.

The late varieties are quite safe to leave in the ground for 4–6 weeks after the tops have withered, and some growers risk leaving early potatoes for considerable periods.

After digging, the potatoes must only be dried enough to remove soil moisture and loose soil (a few hours in the sun is enough). They must then be stored in a cool, perfectly dark place. For winter storage of the late varieties the best temperature is about 37°. If light strikes the stored tubers, they will become green, and possibly poisonous. If the temperature is too high (room temperature), they will sprout.

VARIETIES: For early potatoes the best varieties are Cobbler, Bliss, Triumph, and Cherokee.

For late potatoes use Katahdin, Kennebec, Chippewa, Sebago, White Rose (in Calif.), Russet Burbank (also called Netted Gem) in the West, and Russet Rural.

The so-called Idaho potato, a variety unknown to the experts, but widely publicized, is Russet Burbank, a late potato.

INSECT PESTS. Wireworms may attack tubers in soil. Pre-treat ground as for Japanese beetle. Flea beetles, Colorado potato beetle, blister beetles, and many foliage feeders can be controlled with pesticide #19 or #1 (*see* SPRAYS AND DUSTS). Use a regular schedule. Corn borers attack vines. Control with pesticide #17. Big tomato hornworms can be controlled by TDE sprays or dusts. Tuber moth, a pest in the South, is controlled by applications of pesticide #17 or #1 in late season. Storage houses should be clean, and spray of pesticide #17 on walls will help. *See* SPRAYS AND DUSTS. For aphids, use pesticide #21.

DISEASES. Early blight* is a fungus disease which causes target-like dead areas on the leaves. The spots first appear on older leaves and if not controlled may result in defoliation of all but the new growing tips. Late blight may appear at any time when temperatures are low and plants are wet for a considerable period. Black spots, similar to oil smudges, appear on leaves and stems and when the disease is severe may cause a dark discoloration and rot of tubers. Both early and late blight are controlled with pesticide #7 or #11 (*see* SPRAYS AND DUSTS) applied at 10-day intervals, starting when plants are 6 inches high.

Scab* is a disease attacking only the tubers, making them rough and corky. The disease is worst in sweet or alkaline soils. If previous attempts to raise potatoes have resulted in scab, the gardener should broadcast sulphur and disk it in before planting. Use sulphur at the rate of 100–300 pounds per acre (about 1 pound per 200 square feet). Virus diseases such as mosaic,* leaf curl,* and many others may reduce yields. Because these diseases increase rapidly when growers save their own seed potatoes, it is advisable to secure certified seed for planting each year.

POTATO BEAN = *Apios americana.*

POTATO FAMILY. A huge family of plants of outstanding hort. importance, containing foods, drugs, poisons, narcotics, and some garden flowers. It comprises herbs, shrubs, vines, and trees from all over the world, and includes the potato, tomato, pepper (not the common black pepper), tobacco, petunia, matrimony-vine, henbane, and many others. For an account of them *see* SOLANACEAE.

POTATO-LEAVED TOMATO = *Lycopersicum esculentum grandifolium.* See TOMATO.

POTATO ONION = *Allium Cepa aggregatum.* See ONION.

POTATO VINE = *Solanum jasminoides* (not the true potato).

POT-BOUND. A plant growing in a pot or tub, with the roots so closely packed that there seems little room for further growth. Some plants, however, bloom best when pot-bound, and many others grow more thriftily under such conditions, notably the palms. *See* POTTING.

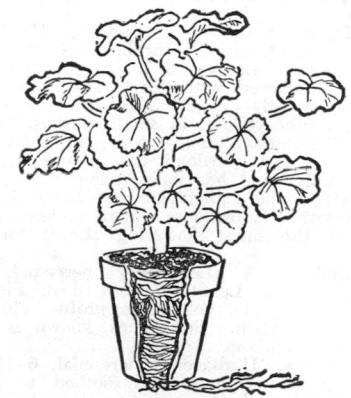

A pot-bound plant which needs repotting. For details *see* POTTING.

POTENTILLA (pō-ten-till′a). Cinquefoil. Perennial, rarely annual herbs, or small shrubs, comprising over 300 species of the rose family, found in temperate and arctic regions mostly in the North. Stems creeping or erect, the creeping species rooting at the joints. Leaves compound.* Leaflets 3 or

---

* Special articles on the subjects indicated by an asterisk (*) will be found at the words so marked.

many, more or less hairy. Flowers in numerous small, loose clusters, yellow, white, or red. Calyx* of 5 sepals,* joined at the base, forming a cup. Corolla of 5 petals growing on the calyx rim. Stamens* numerous. Fruits several, dry, one-seeded. (*Potentilla* is the diminutive of Latin *potens*, powerful, in allusion to supposed medicinal properties.)

Only a few of the perennials are in general cult. Among the hybrids are very good double-flowered varieties, and Gibson's Scarlet is a good red-flowered form. Easily propagated by seeds or division of rootstocks. Seeds should be sown in sandy soil, ⅛ in. deep, in shallow pans, in temperatures 55°–65° in cool greenhouse or cold frame in early spring. Seedlings may be transplanted outdoors as soon as large enough to handle, in ordinary garden soil. Rootstocks may be divided in Sept. or Mar. and Apr. Herbaceous potentillas should be lifted and divided every 3 years. Shrubby species may be propagated from cuttings of half-ripened wood in Sept. and Oct.

argyrophylla. Herbaceous perennial. Stem to 18 in. Leaves compound*; basal leaves long-stalked. Leaflets 3, coarsely and sharply toothed, the under side covered with matted, whitish hairs. Flowers in loose, long-stalked clusters, yellow, 1 in. across. Commonly cult. and a good border plant. June–Aug. Himalayas.

atrosanguinea. Similar to *P. argyrophylla*, but with larger leaves and dark purple or red flowers. Himalayas.

fragiformis. A hairy perennial, 5–8 in. high, the leaves parted into 3 coarsely toothed segments (or leaflets). Flowers about ¾ in. wide, yellow, in rather sparse clusters. Siberia. Summer.

fruticosa. Shrubby cinquefoil. Hardhack. Small, much-branched shrub, 1–4 ft. high. Leaves small. Leaflets 3–7, lance-shaped to 1 in. long, covered with short, silky hairs, the margins slightly rolled. Flowers numerous, showy, bright yellow, in small clusters. June–Aug. Tolerates a limey soil. Eu., As. and N.A. The *var. purdomi* has smaller leaflets, is less hairy and has pale yellow flowers. In *var. veitchi* the leaflets are not hairy; flowers creamy-white. *P. fruticosa* and its varieties make some of the finest flowering shrubs for the garden.

glandulosa. A sticky-hairy perennial, not over 2 ft. high. Leaflets 7–9, toothed. Flowers about ½ in. wide, yellow, in profuse clusters. S. Dak. to Calif. Sometimes known as *Drymocallis glandulosa*.

grandiflora. Herbaceous perennial, 6–15 in. high. Leaflets 3, hairy and toothed, to 1 in. long. Flowers showy, golden-yellow, to 1 in. across, in branching few-flowered clusters. July–Aug. Good border plant. Eu.

hybrida. A group of hybrid cinquefoils derived from crossing *P. argyrophylla* and *P. nepalensis*. They are showy garden plants with generally purple flowers. June.

multifida. Herbaceous, spreading plant, to 4 in. high. Leaflets deeply cut into narrow segments, with short, white hairs on the under side. Flowers small, yellow, 2–3 in a cluster. For cult. *see* ROCK GARDEN. Eu.

nepalensis. Strong-growing, herbaceous perennial to 2 ft. Basal leaves to 12 in. long. Leaflets of stem leaves 2–3 in. long, toothed, green on both sides, slightly hairy. Flowers showy, rose-red, to 1 in. across, long-stalked, in branching clusters. July–Aug. For cult. *see* ROCK GARDEN. Himalayas. The *var. willmottiae* is a dwarf free-flowering form, with magenta-rose flowers.

nitida. An alpine, mat-forming, prostrate perennial, fit only for the rock garden, the whole plant not over 1½–2 in. high. Leaves divided into 3 tiny segments, silvery on both sides. Flowers solitary, essentially stalkless, about 1 in. wide, pink or white. Alps. Summer.

pyrenaica. Strong-growing, herbaceous perennial, 4–12 in. high. Leaflets 5. Stem leaflets small, to ¾ in. long, finely toothed toward the tip. Flowers golden-yellow, to 1 in. across, in loose clusters. July–Aug. Pyrenees.

russelliana. A hybrid cinquefoil derived from crossing *P. nepalensis* and an unknown species. It has scarlet flowers. June–July.

tonguei = *Potentilla tormentillo-formosa*.

tormentillo-formosa. A prostrate cinquefoil with trailing stems, the tips erect and 8–10 in. high. Leaflets 3–5, coarsely toothed. Flowers yellow with a red center. Of hybrid origin, and much cult.

tridentata. Three-toothed cinquefoil. Herbaceous perennial, growing to 1 ft. Leaves mostly basal. Leaflets 3, dark shiny green on upper side, with 3 teeth at the tip. Flowers small, white, in loose clusters. July–Aug. For cult. *see* ROCK GARDEN. Eastern N.A.

POTERIUM (po-teer'i-um). Southern European under-shrubs, comprising only 1 species of the family Rosaceae, *P. spinosum*. It may be propagated from seeds sown in the spring or from cuttings of half-ripened shoots in late summer. It is a small, deciduous, spiny under-shrub with compound* leaves. Leaflets small, 7–15, hairy. Flowers in short spikes of 2 kinds, sterile and fertile, small. Calyx of 5 sepals, greenish, petals none. Fruit red, berry-like. Not of much hort. interest. (*Poterium* is the Greek name for some plant, but not certainly for this one.) Hardy from zone* 5 southward.

For the plant known as *P. canadense, see* SANGUISORBA CANADENSIS. For *P. Sanguisorba, see* SANGUISORBA MINOR.

POT HERBS. A somewhat general name for any herbs cooked in a pot, as spinach, kale, collards, chard, etc. For a more specialized use of certain herbs used in seasoning, and sometimes called pot herbs, *see* HERB GARDENING.

POTHOS = *Scindapsus*, so far as hort. species are concerned.

POT MARIGOLD = *Calendula officinalis*.

POT MARJORAM = *Origanum vulgare*.

POTOMATO = Pomato.

POT PLANTS. Those that commonly come, or are grown in, flower pots, usually started in the greenhouse or hotbed. Common examples are calceolarias, begonias, Easter lilies, etc. The term is largely confined to trade circles.

POTPOURRI. Of the many ways of making potpourri, the most usual are the dry and the moist. As the latter method is very

---

* Special articles on the subjects indicated by an asterisk (*) will be found at the words so marked.

tedious and perhaps no better, only the dry method will be noted.

Take two quarts of rose petals and buds — of course, the sweet-smelling varieties only should be used. Put them on sheets of paper in an airy room to dry, which should take about twenty-four hours. Sprinkle with a thin layer of table salt (some people prefer to add a little benzoic acid to the salt). Add sweet geranium or lemon verbena leaves, a few bay leaves, lavender, heliotrope, mignonette, jasmine, garden pinks, carnations, sweet violets, orange or lemon blossoms, any sweet-smelling herb, such as rosemary, basil, marjoram, anise, etc. A bit of cedar leaf and some balsam needles can be added, but always keep in mind that roses must predominate. The leaves should be dried before mixing with the rose petals.

As you add the other flowers to the rose petals, add more salt. When all the flowers are thoroughly dry, add a spice mixture made of one-quarter ounce each of powdered cloves, mace, cinnamon, and allspice; one-eighth ounce each of crushed coriander, cardamon seeds, powdered gum storax, and powdered gum benzoin; and one ounce of violet sachet powder. Mix the flowers thoroughly with the spice mixture, then dampen with a bit of brandy. A drop or so of attar of rose will enhance the fragrance. Leave the potpourri in a tightly covered crockery jar for some weeks, stirring occasionally. When ready for use, put in bowls, to give a delicious scent to the rooms.

If powdered storax and benzoin are not easily procurable, use a small amount of gum storax and tincture of benzoin, and rub in the various spices until dry.

POTS. *See* FLOWER POTS.

POTSHERDS. A very old term, spanning from the Book of Job to the modern gardener, for broken pottery. In modern hort. it nearly always indicates merely broken flower pots or crocks used for drainage. Potsherds are put over the hole in the bottom of a pot to keep water from washing out the soil and to allow air to get into it.

POTTING. The practice of supplying, within a flower pot or tub, the room for root development as the needs of the plant demand. Clean flower pots should always be used, as the tender roots do not freely circulate around the pot if they have to contend with remnants of soil left over by a previous occupant. Also the plants will not readily slip out of a dirty pot when they must be re-potted. Proper drainage is of the utmost importance to ensure healthy plants. A piece of broken pot or crock, as it is popularly called, should be placed over the hole and sufficient rough material, such as the refuse from sifted soil, be placed over this according to size of pot used. Pots above 6 in. may have 3 or 4 in. of drainage, the smaller sizes less.

Many experienced gardeners soak flower pots in water before using as such soaked pots do not absorb moisture from the soil.

Potting mixtures* are fully discussed at another entry, but where much potting is done a compost heap is of greatest importance. This should be made of top sod taken from a rich pasture and stacked up for future use as follows: Place two feet of sod with the grass side down, on this put 8 in. of cow or barnyard manure and continue to build this up to any size or height, finishing with a layer of manure. To use, cut a slice from the front of the stack all the way down. This will give you a good rich loam to put under the potting bench for general use, to which can be added the necessary sand, peat, leaf mold, or fertilizer to produce any of the described potting mixture formulas.

Provided the proper mixture is used and the soil is in the right condition, neither too wet nor too dry, a plant should be potted firmly, but as a general rule soft-wooded plants, like cinerarias, primulas, calceolarias, geraniums, etc., do not require such hard potting, and the soil can be pressed in quite firmly with the fingers. But hard-wooded plants, like azaleas, camellias, ericas, boronias, genistas, rhododendrons, chorizemas, acacias, etc., should be hard-potted by the use of a potting stick, usually a piece of broom handle 18 in. long and wedge-shaped on one end. Never court disaster by using a cracked pot, as it always breaks at the wrong time.

How to Pot a Plant Properly

Put the plant in the center of the pot in which has been previously placed the necessary soil mixture — to about half full.

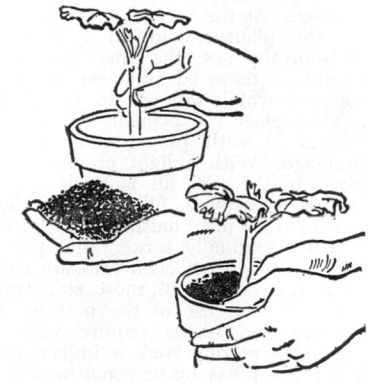

The correct steps in a potting operation. Be sure the soil is firmed about the roots, and that the drainage hole at the bottom is covered by crocks or gravel.

Do not depress the roots, but rather build up a small mound and place the plant on top. In this position the roots will fall downward, and when the pot has been filled

* Special articles on the subjects indicated by an asterisk (*) will be found at the words so marked.

with soil and pressed down firmly the roots will be in a natural position. This refers more particularly to plants being potted for the first time. When potting vigorous-growing plants, such as *Pandanus, Areca, Livistona,* or *Phoenix,* a generous pruning of the roots is necessary as these plants have such a strong root system that they may raise the plant out of the pot. This treatment also permits keeping the plant in a pot most suitable to its size.

A small shift, *i.e.,* to only a slightly larger pot, is always advisable, and very firm potting is necessary. Keep the soil as level as

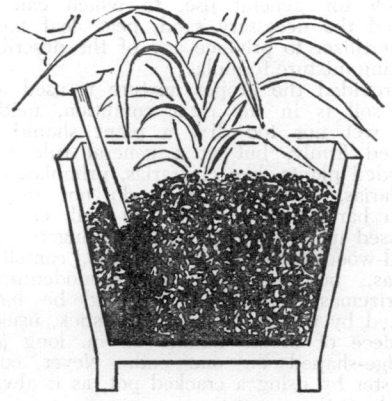

For larger specimens it is best to use a potting stick. It ensures the soil being well packed around the roots.

possible, finishing 1 in. below the rim of the pot to allow for proper watering. The process of potting is simple if a few rules are observed. At the second and subsequent pottings the plant should be carefully removed from the pot, the edge around the ball should be removed and also any drainage material which adheres to the ball of earth. Then place the plant in the new pot, filled about ⅛ with proper soil, including free drainage. With a light pressure center it upright in the pot, fill in with soil and press firmly all around, filling to just below the rim of the pot, finishing as level as possible. By gradually turning the pot and using the thumbs a sufficient pressure can be given for the potting of most soft-wooded plants without the use of the potting stick, but hard-wooded plants require very firm potting, and a potting stick is indispensable.

When a plant has become pot-bound, *i.e.,* the pot entirely filled with roots, a condition which is sometimes necessary to induce flowering, no harm will result if attention is given to feeding at this time. But unless relieved by potting-on, in the case of foliage plants and palms, the plant becomes hard and stunted and will eventually turn yellow and lose its foliage. At this stage the roots should be reduced by chopping about ⅓ of

the ball and the remaining roots loosened out with a pointed stick. Use a pot one size larger than the old one, pot firmly, and keep in a close atmosphere until root action begins.

The roots of palms may be cut down without injury to the plant, so that a reduced size of pot can be used. There is always danger of overpotting, which should

Reduce the root system of a pot-bound plant before re-potting. For details *see* text.

be carefully guarded against. A plant that is not doing well will often respond by being put into a smaller pot.

The time for potting plants must largely be decided by their condition. The best time is after the plant has just started into growth, or just before growth is completed. In the first case the growing plant is full of energy and able to stimulate the newly disturbed roots into immediate activity. In the second case, the ripening process being nearly completed, the tendency is for the plant to increase its root action and store up the vital energies contributed by sun and air for the maturing of the plant. So this time is ideal for shifting plants, but the operation should not be delayed until too near maturity, or root action will become dormant and inactive and take hold of the new soil too slowly.

Considerable judgment must be used in the class of plants to be potted, and the purpose for which they are grown. Some soft-wooded plants may need potting once a month, while hard-wooded plants may only need potting once in two years. Foliage plants whose objective is fine foliage should be shifted to larger pots and be potted oftener than flowering plants where matured growth is the basis of perfect flowering.

The condition of the roots is the best indication of the needs of the plant. When the roots reach the side of the pot and hunt around for food, then is the time to give it additional space, but so long as the roots are not freely developed on the outside of the ball there is sufficient room for further growth without re-potting. Potting must be entirely controlled by the condition

* Special articles on the subjects indicated by an asterisk (*) will be found at the words so marked.

of the roots, and frequent systematic potting will prevent the plants from becoming pot-bound.

After potting foliage plants a genial temperature should be maintained, moderation in watering, and a closer atmosphere with gentle syringing of the foliage. All these assist in getting root action started. Plants usually respond quickly to this treatment, but it may be necessary to give slight shade for a few days.

Never pot a plant when it is dry. The new soil will absorb all the water, and the old ball of soil will not get sufficient for the need of the plant, which will eventually turn yellow and growth will be retarded. A good plan is to water the plants the day before you are to handle them. On the other hand if the soil is too wet it is apt to fall away from the plant and so damage the roots. A good gardeners' test for soil of the proper moisture content is to squeeze it in the hand and if it forms a close ball it is too damp, but if it just retains the form of the hand it is right for potting. Never use the finely sifted soil for potting, but when the compost is being mixed break up all lumps of soil and manure with the back of the spade, removing all stones. After it has been turned over a few times it will be fine enough for all ordinary potting. Always endeavor to pot the plant as firmly as the old ball, and be sure the new soil is evenly packed down, leaving no empty spaces, so that the roots can take hold of the new soil quickly. It will be impossible to pot hard-wooded plants hard enough without the use of a potting stick to ram the soil well down, even in the small sizes, and it is essential that only sound pots be used or they will not stand the hard potting. *See also* FLOWER POTS.

POTTING MIXTURES. Nearly all plants grown in pots, tubs, or window boxes, have rather definite soil requirements. These may vary with the age of the plant, its ancestral home, and many other things. Fortunately, most of these requirements can be reduced to the six standard potting mixtures, the preparation and uses of which are listed below. Throughout the ENCYCLOPEDIA the preferred potting mixture for all potted plants, and for many others, is indicated by the numbers one to six. The mixtures were decided upon by consultations between the Editor, Montague Free, G. H. Pring, B. Y. Morrison, H. E. Downer, and the late W. H. Judd. These mixtures should be prepared in accordance with the following:

POTTING MIXTURE 1. For potting up rooted cuttings taken from sand.

2 Parts sharp sand
1 Part loam
1 Part leaf mold (or peat moss for acid-tolerant plants)

POTTING MIXTURE 2. For transplanted seedlings and for cuttings when moved from Mixture No. 1.

1 Part sharp sand
1 Part loam
1 Part leaf mold

POTTING MIXTURE 3. For general potting, especially for such plants as the garden geranium (*Pelargonium*), fuchsias, chrysanthemums, *Sansevieria, Pandanus,* palms, etc.

1 Part sharp sand
2 Parts loam
1 Part leaf mold (or humus)
½ Part dried cow manure
1 Five-inch flower pot full of bone meal to each bushel of the mixture

POTTING MIXTURE 4. For plants requiring more humus than in Mixture No. 3, such as begonias, many ferns, primulas, etc.

2 Parts sharp sand
2 Parts loam
2 Parts leaf mold (or humus)
½ Part dried cow manure
1 Five-inch flower pot full of bone meal to each bushel of the mixture

POTTING MIXTURE 5. For potting many hard-wooded plants such as azaleas, ericas, *Daphne,* and certain ferns.

2 Parts sharp sand
2 Parts loam
2 Parts peat moss
1 Part leaf mold (or humus)
⅓ Part dried cow manure

POTTING MIXTURE 6. For most cacti and succulents.

2 Parts sharp sand
2 Parts loam
1 Part broken flower pots (or soft brick broken into small pieces)
½ Part leaf mold (or humus)
1 Five-inch flower pot full of bone meal
1 Five-inch flower pot full of ground limestone

to each bushel of the mixture.

POTTING-ON. The gradual increase of the size of the flower pot to take care of increased root development. Potting-on requires several shifts or re-potting operations. For details *see* POTTING.

poukhanensis, -e (poo-ka-nen'sis). From Poukhan, Korea.

POVERTY PINE = *Pinus pungens. See* PINE.

POWDERY MILDEW. A disease caused by a specific group of fungi and not to be confused with downy mildew.* The powdery mildew produces a white, powdery growth, usually on the upper surface of the leaf. During early stages of infection the white fungus growth may be rubbed off and the leaf will still be green beneath the mildew spot. The disease may result in stunted growth, but rarely kills much of the plant even though the fungus envelops entire shoots. Such shoots should be removed because the disease can overwinter in the buds and start new infections early the following spring. This mildew is spread by wind-blown spores* and may be controlled with regular applications of sulphur or Karathane.

* Special articles on the subjects indicated by an asterisk (*) will be found at the words so marked.

(*See* FUNGICIDES and SPRAYS AND DUSTS.)

praealta, -us, -um (pree-al'ta). Very tall.

praecox (pree'cocks). Very early.

praestans (pree'stanz). Excellent or distinguished.

PRAIRIE. As an adjective *prairie* has been used as part of the name of many plants of plains and prairies, mostly from the central part of N.A. Those in the ENCYCLOPEDIA and their proper equivalents are: Prairie button snakeroot = *Liatris pycnostachya;* Prairie clover (*see* PETALOSTEMON); Prairie coneflower = *Ratibida columnaris;* Prairie crabapple = *Malus ioensis;* Prairie flax = *Linum lewisi;* Prairie gentian = *Eustoma russellianum;* Prairie lily = *Mentzelia decapetala* (*see also* COOPERIA); Prairie mallow = *Sphaeralcea coccinea;* Prairie phlox = *Phlox pilosa;* Prairie pine = *Liatris spicata;* Prairie pointer = *Dodecatheon Meadia;* Prairie rose = *Rosa setigera;* Prairie smoke = *Geum triflorum;* Prairie wakerobin = *Trillium recurvatum.*

pratensis, -e (pra-ten'sis). Growing in meadows.

pravissima, -us, -um (pra-viss'i-ma). Very crooked.

precatorius (pre-ka-tor'i-us). One who prays; hence applied to plants yielding seeds used as rosaries. *See* ABRUS.

PRE-LINNAEAN. As applied to Latin plant names, pre-Linnaean indicates the existence of the name before the publication by Linnaeus of his *Species Plantarum* in 1753. Many pre-Linnaean names were adopted by Linnaeus and are in common use today, especially as specific names. A few examples (the pre-Linnaean name in boldface) are: *Campanula* **Medium,** *Cardiospermum* **Halicacabum,** *Hibiscus* **Moscheutos,** and *Leonotis* **Leonurus.** *See* LINNAEUS.

PRESERVING MELON = *Citrullus vulgaris citroides.* See WATERMELON.

PRETTY-FACE = *Brodiaea ixioides.*

PRICKING-OUT. See SEEDS AND SEEDAGE.

PRICKLE. See SPINE.

PRICKLY ASH. See ZANTHOXYLUM.

PRICKLY COMFREY = *Symphytum asperum.*

PRICKLY LETTUCE = *Lactuca Scariola.* See list at WEEDS.

PRICKLY PEAR. See OPUNTIA.

PRICKLY PHLOX = *Gilia californica.*

PRICKLY PINE = *Pinus pungens.* See PINE.

PRICKLY POPPY. See ARGEMONE.

PRICKLY SHIELD FERN = *Polystichum brauni.*

PRICKLY THATCH = *Thrinax microcarpa.*

PRICKLY THRIFT = *Acantholimon.*

PRICK-TIMBER = *Euonymus europaeus* and *Nemopanthus mucronatus.*

PRIDE-OF-CALIFORNIA = *Lathyrus splendens.*

PRIDE-OF-INDIA = *Koelreuteria paniculata.*

PRIDE-OF-ROCHESTER. See DEUTZIA SCABRA.

PRIM = *Ligustrum vulgare.* See PRIVET.

PRIMROSE. For the true primrose *see* PRIMULA. For other plants to which the name primrose is often applied *see:* ARNEBIA CORNUTA, EVENING PRIMROSE, and STREPTOCARPUS.

PRIMROSE FAMILY = Primulaceae.

PRIMROSE JASMINE = *Jasminum mesnyi.*

PRIMROSE WILLOW. See JUSSIAEA.

PRIMULA (prim'you-la). Primrose. A large genus of over 500 species of low-growing, herbaceous perennials and a few biennials, of the family Primulaceae, chiefly natives of the northern hemisphere, and found mostly in alpine and cool localities. Stem short, or none. Leaves crowded, stalked, long and narrow, or roundish or tufted, the midrib generally prominent on the under side. Flowers on leafless stalks, sometimes with leafy bracts,* solitary, or in loose umbels,* or whorled in tiers, or in rounded heads. Flowers in various shades of yellow, white, red, blue, pink, and purple. Calyx* of 5 sepals,* joined halfway, usually slightly inflated, generally pale green. Corolla of 5 lobes, tubular at the base, opening salverwise. Stamens* 5, not protruding. In some species the stamens are prominent at the opening of the corolla tube (thrum-eyed) and in others the pinheaded stigma* is conspicuous (pin-eyed*). Fruit a dry, many-seeded capsule. (*Primula* is a diminutive of *primus,* first, in allusion to the spring bloom.)

For culture *see* below.

acaulis = Primula vulgaris.

aurantiaca. Not over 10 in. high. Leaves broadly lance-shaped, narrowed to a winged stalk, 6–8 in. long, the margins minutely toothed. Flowers about ½ in. long, reddish orange, arranged in interrupted clusters (umbels*). China. July. A hardy species.

Auricula. Auricula. Hardy perennial, to 8 in. high. Leaves basal, 2–4 in. long, thick and fleshy, ovalish, grayish-green, smooth, or white-powdery, toothed. Flowers varied in color, but usually with a conspicuous eye, in many-flowered umbels. April–May. Alps. Suitable for rock garden (*see* ROCK GARDEN), beds or borders.

beesiana. Strong-growing perennial, to 2 ft. high. Leaves basal, to 6 in. long, narrow, wrinkled, irregularly toothed. Flowers rose-red, with a yellow eye, in several whorls on each stalk. June. China. Good bog garden plant.

bulleyana. Strong-growing perennial, to 2½ ft. high. Leaves broadly lance-shaped, thin, margins sharply toothed. Flowers deep yellow, in several whorls* on each stalk, with small leafy bracts* under each whorl.* June. Suit-

---

* Special articles on the subjects indicated by an asterisk (*) will be found at the words so marked.

able for bog garden and rock garden (*see* ROCK GARDEN). China.

cachemeriana or **cashmeriana.** *See* P. DENTICULATA.

capitata. Stiff-growing perennial, to 19 in. high. Leaves basal, broadly lance-shaped, 3–5 in. long, grayish on under side, margins finely toothed. Flowers lavender, in a dense, many-flowered, rounded head. April–May. Suitable for rock garden, beds or borders. Himalayas.

chionantha. A hardy perennial, 12–18 in. high, the lance-shaped or oblong leaves 7–10 in. long, narrowed into a winged stalk, yellow-mealy beneath. Flowers fragrant, nearly 1 in. wide, white, in interrupted clusters (umbels°). Yunnan. May–June. Needs moist, partly shaded site.

clusiana. A low perennial from the Austrian Alps, not over 7 in. high, the pointed glossy leaves 2–3 in. long and forming basal rosettes. Flowers white-eyed, but carmine-lilac, 2–6 in an umbel.° A crevice plant for rock gardens.

cortusoides. Hardy perennial, to 1 ft. high. Leaves basal, ovalish, heart-shaped at the base, 2–4 in. long, slightly hairy and lobed. Flowers rose-color, in loose, many-flowered umbels.° May–June. Suitable for rock garden (which see for cult.). Siberia.

denticulata. Hardy perennial, 10–15 in. high. Leaves basal, broadly lance-shaped, 2–5 in. long, thin, usually white-powdery. Flowers lilac, in dense clusters. Flower clusters surrounded by small, leafy bracts.° May. Himalayas. The *var.* **cachemiriana** (or **cachmeriana**) has more powdery leaves and flowers of rich purple, with a yellow center. Both suitable for the rock garden. *See* ROCK GARDEN, also GRAY AND LAVENDER GARDEN.

elatior. Oxlip. Hardy perennial, to 8 in. high. Leaves basal, ovalish, 2–4 in. long, wrinkled, slightly hairy on under side, midrib prominent on under side. Flowers yellow, showy, in many-flowered umbels.° April–May. Suitable for rock garden, border, or naturalizing. Eu. and western As.

farinosa. Bird's-eye primrose. Strong-growing perennial, to 1 ft. high. Leaves basal, broadly lance-shaped, 4–6 in. long, white-powdery on the under side. Flowers lilac, with yellow throat and eye, small, in many-flowered umbels.° May–June. Suitable for rock garden and border. Alpine regions of Eu. and As.

florindae. Strong-growing perennial, to 4 ft. high. Leaves basal, ovalish, with heart-shaped base, 8 in. or more long, with reddish-brown stalk. Flowers sulphur-yellow, drooping, in loose, many-flowered, mealy clusters. June–July. Suitable for the bog garden. Tibet. Not hardy in severe climates.

forbesi. Baby primrose. Slender-growing, tender perennial, to 15 in. high. Leaves basal, ovalish, with heart-shaped base, 1–2 in. long, slightly white-hairy. Flowers lilac or rose in several whorls on each stalk. Feb.–Apr. Grown in greenhouse. China and Burma.

frondosa. Dwarf-growing perennial, to 5 in. high. Leaves basal, small, thin, spoon-shaped, usually white-powdery on under side, the margins slightly toothed. Flowers, lilac, in many-flowered umbels.° April–May. Suitable for rock garden or border. Balkans.

helodoxa. Not distantly related to *P. aurantiaca*, but taller (15–24 in. high) and with yellow flowers. Yunnan and Burma. Not as hardy as *P. aurantiaca*, and needing protection, or even a cool greenhouse northward.

japonica. Strong-growing perennial, to 2 ft. high. Leaves broadly lance-shaped, 4–6 in.

long, thin, the margins slightly toothed. Flowers purple, pink, or white, glistening, in several whorls on each stalk. There are small, green, leafy bracts° under each whorl. June–July. Suitable for rock garden. Many hort. color forms. Japan.

juliae. Not over 3 in. high and to be grown only in the rock garden. Leaves nearly round, heart-shaped at the base. Flowers nearly 1 in. wide, red or rose-red, on slender stalks about 2 in. high. There are white-flowered and crisped-leaves vars. Caucasus.

malacoides. Fairy primrose. Tender perennial, to 1½ ft. high. Leaves basal, numerous, with long, slender stalks, the blade ovalish, with heart-shaped base, thin, slightly hairy, the margins deeply lobed and toothed. Flowers lilac or pink, small, in several whorls on each stalk. Jan.–Apr. Grown in greenhouse. China.

marginata. A low perennial from the Eu. Alps with mealy foliage and not over 5 in. high. Leaves silvery-margined, oblong, about 4 in. long. Flowers in profuse umbels,° the corolla about 1 in. wide and purple-red. A rock garden species. May.

obconica. Tender perennial, to 1 ft. high. Leaves basal, stalked, ovalish, to 4 in. long, slightly covered with short, sharply pointed hairs, which when handled by some people cause a poisonous irritation. Flowers lilac or pink, in many-flowered umbels.° Jan.–Apr. Grown in greenhouse. China. Many good hort. forms.

parryi. Nearly 12 in. high, the oblongish leaves 6–8 in. long and narrowed into winged stalks. Umbels° profuse, the corolla about 1 in. wide, yellow-eyed but purple. Rocky Mountains. Summer.

polyantha. Polyanthus. A group of garden, hybrid primroses, probably derived from the oxlip, cowslip, and the English primrose. They average about 1 ft. high and their leaves are narrowed into winged stalks. They are found in many colors and the cluster is usually profuse. May. The most easily grown of all primroses.

pubescens. A group name for many hybrids that usually have *P. Auricula* as one of the parents. Most of them have whitish flowers with a red "eye."

pulverulenta. Hardy, strong-growing perennial, to 3 ft. high. Leaves basal, broadly lance-shaped, to 16 in. long, thin, margins irregularly toothed. Flowers purple, with orange eye, in several whorls on each stalk. There are small leafy bracts below each whorl. Flower stalks silvery. May–July. Suitable for the bog garden. China.

secundiflora. A perennial, usually not over 8 in. high, the leaves oblongish, 2–3 in. long, covered with yellow meal (farina), in youth, on the under side. Flowers in 1-sided clusters (umbels°), purple-violet or darker, each flower about ¾ in. wide. Western China. May–June. A hardy species.

sieboldi. A Japanese hardy primula, 6–8 in. high, the leaves oblongish, stalked, coarsely toothed or even lobed, heart-shaped at the base, 3–4 in. long. Flowers in crowded clusters (umbels°), nearly 2 in. wide, white, pink, or purple, usually with a different colored "eye." May–June. There are several variously colored hort. forms. Prefers moist sites.

sikkimensis. Hardy, strong-growing perennial, 1–2 ft. high. Leaves basal, narrow, 4–5 in. long, wrinkled, margins sharply toothed. Flowers yellow, slightly drooping, in many-flowered umbels.° Calyx powdery. Small, leafy bracts surround the umbels.° May–June. Suitable for

° Special articles on the subjects indicated by an asterisk (°) will be found at the words so marked.

the bog garden. Himalayas. Not hardy in severe climates.

sinensis. Chinese primrose. Tender perennial, to 10 in. high. Whole plant covered with short hairs. Stem 1–4 in. high, slightly woody. Leaves crowded on the stem, fleshy, stalked, roundish, lobed, the margins toothed, prominently veined on the under side. Flowers large, in several colors, with conspicuous eye, in large umbels.* Jan.–Apr. Grown in greenhouse. China. The *var.* **stellata,** the star primrose, has smaller star-shaped flowers.

spectabilis. A low, rock garden perennial from the Eu. Alps, not over 4 in. high. Leaves shiny, stiff, oblongish, 3–4 in. long. Flowers about 1 in. wide, purplish-red, in few-flowered umbels.* Summer.

stellata = *Primula sinensis stellata.*

veitchi. A Chinese perennial up to 12 in. high, the leaves nearly round, about 4 in. wide, long-stalked and silvery on the under side. Flower clusters profuse, rose-colored, often one umbel* arising from a lower one. Called, also, *P. polyneura.*

veris. Cowslip (*see* Herb Gardening). Hardy perennial to 8 in. high. Leaves basal, wrinkled, broadly lance-shaped, 3–4 in. long, slightly hairy on under side. Flowers yellow, with orange eye, fragrant, in nodding umbels.* Calyx pale green, slightly inflated. May. Suitable for rock garden, border, or naturalizing. Eurasia. There are double-flowered forms.

viscosa. A sticky perennial, 6–8 in. high, its foliage evil-smelling. Leaves ovalish or narrower, 5–7 in. long, narrowed at the base, irregularly toothed, especially toward the tip. Flowers fragrant, violet or rose-lilac, about ½ in. wide. Pyrenees and Alps. May–June.

vulgaris. English primrose. Hardy perennial, to 6 in. high. Leaves basal, broadly lance-shaped, 3–5 in. long, wrinkled, the margins crinkled. Flowers numerous, or solitary, on slender, slightly hairy stalks, usually yellow. April–May. Suitable for the rock garden (*see* Rock Garden), border, or for naturalizing. Eu. Often called *P. acaulis.* There are many color forms, the *var.* **caerulea** being suitable for the blue garden. There are double-flowered and hose-in-hose* forms. *See* Blue Garden.

wulfeniana. A tufted, low perennial, not over 2 in. high and best suited to the rock garden. Leaves ovalish or narrower, 1–2 in. long, shining, the toothless margin cartilaginous. Flowers about 1 in. wide, deep rose, the throat white. Alps. April–May. Not for open border.

Primula Culture

The hardy species of *Primula,* with their early spring to early summer blooming period, deserve a place in every garden. The conditions under which the various species grow being so diverse, even the smallest garden will provide conditions suitable for one or more species. All require shade during the summer months. Some of the places in which they may be grown are the rock garden where they do not overrun other plants; the bog garden, which provides a splendid location for many of the showy, strong-growing species which when once established are not harmed if the roots are completely under water during the winter. In such a position they will often naturalize themselves, but only in regions of mild winters.

Flower beds and borders are suitable for the shorter species. The naturalizing of *P. vulgaris, P. veris,* and *P. elatior* under deciduous trees or in the grass is particularly beautiful in the early spring. These three species demand cool, moist positions.

Propagated by seeds or division. Seeds are best sown as soon as ripe, Sept.–Oct., in a cool greenhouse or cold frame or they may be sown in early spring. Soil should be finely sifted and composed of 1 part loam, 1 part leaf mold, and ½ part sand. Seeds should be sown ⅛ in. deep, watered and shaded from the sun. If seeds are sown in the fall they should be carried through the winter in cool greenhouse or cold frame and transplanted as soon as danger of frost is over, to permanent positions. Leaf mold added to the soil where permanent plantings are made is beneficial. The hardy primulas are best not covered in winter except while young.

The cowslip (*Primula veris*)

The tender species of *Primula* make admirable pot plants grown in the cool greenhouse for winter flowering. They are generally treated as annuals. Propagated by seeds or division. Seeds should be sown in March or April, ¹⁄₁₆ in. deep, in well-drained pans. Soil should be the same as for the hardy species. Pans must be covered with glass until seeds have germinated to prevent drying out, and be kept in temperature of 55°–65°. When the plants have 3 leaves, they should be transplanted 2 in. apart in the same mixture. When large enough pot into 3-in. pots, using potting mixture* 4. As plants increase in size they should be transplanted into larger pots as necessary, using the same mixture.

They should be kept in a cold frame during the summer months, shaded from sunlight, keeping the sash lights on, but allowing plenty of air. This may be accomplished by resting the sash lights on

4- or 5-in. flower pots. Good drainage is essential, but the plants must never be allowed to become dry. On returning plants to cool greenhouse they should be kept in a temperature of 45°–55°. These tender primulas make good house plants, and if kept in a cool room will last for many months.

Double varieties do not produce seeds and are propagated by division of rootstocks or cuttings in early spring.

Contrary to popular belief, primulas do not set up a skin irritation, with the exception of *P. obconica,* and then not always so. See POISONOUS PLANTS. For rock garden conditions suitable for primulas, see ROCK GARDEN.

The American Primrose Society welcomes those interested in *Primula.* Its present address is 3616 N.E. Bellevue-Redmond Road, Kirkland, Wash.

DISEASES. Primulas are susceptible to two fungus diseases, gray mold* and leafspot.* Application of fungicides is not usually necessary, but if either becomes severe, control with pesticide #1 or #11 (*see* SPRAYS AND DUSTS), applied at 10-day intervals.

If plants are weak and flower poorly, examine the roots for swellings or nodules which indicate the presence of root knot nematode.* Do not try to raise primulas in this area in following years.

PRIMULACEAE (prim-you-lay′see-ee). The primrose family, all herbs, comprises 24 genera and over 1000 widely distributed species, most abundant in the north temperate zone, and contains many old garden favorites. Of these the chief is easily *Primula,* comprising not only the primrose and cowslip, but several greenhouse plants of wide cult. and many rock garden species. *Cyclamen,* a favorite pot plant, mostly needs greenhouse culture, but nearly all the rest of the family are plants of the open border, the rock garden, or the wild garden, while a few are marsh or semi-aquatic species. *Anagallis* is largely weedy.

Trientalis and *Dodecatheon* are most suited to the wild garden. *Androsace, Soldanella,* and *Douglasia* are chiefly for the rock garden, while *Lysimachia* (which includes creeping Charlie) and *Steironema* are of easy cult. in the open border.

The leaves are alternate* or opposite,* or even whorled,* and in many genera in a basal rosette. Flowers regular,* solitary or in various sorts of clusters (often in umbels*), very showy in *Cyclamen,* although the flower is solitary. Fruit a dry pod (capsule*) splitting into 5 or 10 segments.

Technical flower characters: Calyx more or less tubular or bell-shaped. Corolla funnel-shaped, or tubular and abruptly expanded above, mostly 5-lobed. Stamens 5, opposite the corolla lobes and borne on them. Ovary generally superior,* 1-celled, with many ovules. Style and stigma 1.

primulina, -us, -um (prim-you-ly′na). Primrose-colored.

primuloides (prim-you-loy′deez, but *see* OïDES). Like a primrose (*Primula*).

PRINCE'S-FEATHER = *Polygonum orientale,* and *Amaranthus hybridus hypochondriacus.*

PRINCE'S-PINE = *Chimaphila umbellata.*

prinoides (pry-noy′deez, but *see* OïDES). Like a plant of the obsolete genus *Prinos,* which included plants now classed among the hollies.

PRINSEPIA (prin-see′pi-a). A small genus of spiny Asiatic shrubs of the rose family, only **P. sinensis** in cult. and grown for its bloom and fruit. It is an attractive, arching shrub, 4–6 ft. high, its spines slender but sharp, about ¾ in. long. Leaves alternate,* oval-lance-shaped, long-pointed, 2–3 in. long, bright green and minutely hairy on the essentially entire* margin. Flowers yellow, about ½ in. wide, in clusters of 1–4. Petals 5, nearly round. Stamens* 10. Fruit purplish, about ⅓ in. long (a drupe*), its stones slightly sculptured. March–April. Hardy from zone* 3 southward. Propagated by seeds sown when ripe or by cuttings of green wood under glass. Manchuria. (Named for James Prinsep, a meteorologist.)

Prinus (pry′nus). *Prinus* is an old generic name for certain oaks and is used as a specific name for the chestnut oak. *See* OAK.

prismatica, -us, -um (priz-mat′i-ka). Prismlike.

PRITCHARDIA (prit-chard′i-a). Erect, spineless, Pacific Island fan palms, comprising half a dozen species, of which **P. pacifica,** the Fiji fan palm, is planted in Fla. for ornament, but is hardy only in zone* 9. It has a smooth trunk, 15–30 ft. high, with a crown of handsome, fan-shaped leaves at the top. Leaves 3–4 ft. wide, green both sides, cut rather shallowly into about 90 narrow, stiffish segments, which are long-pointed. Leafstalk about 3 ft. long, spineless. Flowers small, greenish, the cluster shorter than the leaves. Fruit about ½ in. in diameter, globe-shaped. (Named for W. T. Pritchard, British consul in Polynesia.) Also known as *Eupritchardia.*

PRIVET. Best known as hedge plants, privet comprises many other species of the genus **Ligustrum** (ly-gus′trum) of the olive family. Of the 50 known species, all from the Old World, those below are of chief hort. interest. They are shrubs, or rarely trees, with opposite,* generally ovalish, often persistent or evergreen, or half-evergreen leaves, without marginal teeth. Flowers small, white, sometimes malodorous, mostly in terminal clusters (panicles*), often not produced on clipped hedge specimens. Corolla short-tubular, its 4-lobed limb* spreading. Stamens* 2. Fruit a small, berry-like drupe,* usually black or bluish, 1–4-seeded. (*Ligustrum* is the classical Latin name of the privet.)

---

* Special articles on the subjects indicated by an asterisk (*) will be found at the words so marked.

For culture and uses *see* below. All those not specified as persistent, half-evergreen, or evergreen, drop their leaves in the autumn. Practically all are without autumnal color.

L. acuminatum. A shrub 4–6 ft. high, its branches upright. Leaves 2–3 in. long, more or less wedge-shaped at the base, hairy on the midrib beneath. Flower clusters nearly 2 in. long, the stamens* protruding. Jap. June. Hardy from zone* 3 southward. The *var.* **macrocarpum** is more stiffly erect and has larger fruit.

L. amurense. Amur privet. A shrub 10–15 ft. high, its branches erect. Leaves half-evergreen, 1¾–2½ in. long, hairy on the midrib beneath. Flower cluster almost 2 in. long, the corolla with a longer tube than lobes. Northern China. June–July. Hardy from zone* 3 southward. Resembles the California privet (*L. ovalifolium*), but is hardier, and not so suited for hedges.

L. coriaceum = *Ligustrum japonicum rotundifolium.*

L. Ibolium. Ibolium privet. A hybrid derived from crossing *L. ovalifolium* with *L. obtusifolium,* and a useful, but not much grown, hedge plant. It is an upright shrub, hardier than the California privet (*L. ovalifolium*), the leaves hairy on the midrib beneath. Flower cluster slightly and softly hairy. Aug. Hardy from zone* 4 southward.

L. Ibota. A rare and little-known privet, long mistaken for *L. obtusifolium* (the true ibota privet). It is a shrub 4–6 ft. high, the branches spreading. Leaves 1–2 in. long, hairy on the midrib beneath. Flower clusters head-like, 4–8-flowered, scarcely over ½ in. long. Jap. June. Hardy from zone* 3 southward, but one of the least decorative of the privets.

L. indicum. An evergreen shrub or small tree, the twigs hairy. Leaves oblong or oval-oblong, pointed, 2–5 in. long, hairy on the under side. Flower clusters broad, furnished with stalked bracts.* Himalayas. July–Aug. Hardy from zone* 7 southward, and used for hedges in Calif.

L. japonicum. Wax privet. An evergreen shrub 7–10 ft. high. Leaves oblong-oval, leathery, 3–4 in. long, smooth. Flower clusters 4–6 in. long, the tube of the corolla only slightly longer than the lobes. Jap. and Korea. July–Sept. Hardy from zone* 5 southward. A useful hedge plant. The *var.* **rotundifolium** (sometimes offered as *L. coriaceum*) is a lower, more compact shrub, with lustrous, dark green, more numerous leaves. A reputed hybrid between this var. and the next species is the Suwannee River *Ligustrum,* thought to be more hardy than either of its assumed parents, perhaps up to zone* 4.

L. lucidum. An evergreen shrub or even a small tree, up to 30 ft. high. Leaves pointed, 4–6 in. long, shining and smooth. Flower cluster nearly 10 in. long, the tube and lobes of the corolla about of equal length. Jap. and China. Aug.–Sept. Hardy from zone* 5 southward. Occasionally planted as a street tree, especially in central and northern Fla. and in Tex. and Calif.

L. massalongianum. An evergreen shrub, not over 3 ft. high. Leaves narrowly lance-shaped, 2–3 in. long, smooth. Flower cluster 2½–3½ in. long, slightly hairy. Himalayas. July–Aug. Hardy from zone* 6 southward.

L. nepalense = *L. indicum.*

L. obtusifolium. Ibota privet (but *see L. Ibota*). A spreading or arching shrub, 6–10 ft. high. Leaves elliptic or oblongish, 1½–

2½ in. long, hairy beneath. Flower clusters nodding, not over 1½ in. long, the corolla tube thrice longer than its lobes. Jap. July. Hardy from zone* 3 southward and long known, incorrectly, as *L. Ibota.* A widely cult. shrub with profuse flowers and black, slightly bloomy fruit. The *var.* **regelianum,** Regel's privet, is lower and has horizontally spreading branches.

L. ovalifolium. California privet, really a native of Jap., and less used in Calif. for hedges than in the East. A compact, half-evergreen shrub, 5–20 ft. high, easily the most widely used hedge plant in the U.S. Leaves 2–2½ in. long, shining, without any hairs. Flower cluster 3–4 in. long, the corolla tube longer than its lobes. July. Surely hardy from zone* 4 southward, but in zone* 3 sometimes killed to the ground or outright by severe winters. There are many hort. forms, mostly with variegated or variously margined leaves, marked either with yellow or white. The common green form is the best for hedges.

L. quihoui. A Chinese privet, 4–6 ft. high, the branches spreading and somewhat rigid. Leaves elliptic or oblongish, 1–2½ in. long. Flower cluster hairy, the spikes in a branched cluster 5–8 in. long. Aug.–Sept. Hardy from zone* 6 southward.

L. sinense. A Chinese privet up to 12 ft. high, the branches spreading. Leaves elliptic or oblongish, 1½–3 in. long, hairy on the veins beneath. Flowers in a loose, hairy, branching cluster (panicle*) 3–5 in. long. July. Hardy from zone* 6 southward, and escaping along the Gulf Coast where it is nearly evergreen.

L. vulgare. Common privet or prim. Next to *L. ovalifolium* the most widely grown of all hedge privets, because it is hardier than *L. ovalifolium,* but its leaves are not half-evergreen over most of the country, sometimes so southward. It is a shrub 6–15 ft. high. Leaves oblong-oval, 1¾–2½ in. long. Flower cluster not over 2 in. long, the corolla tube shorter than or about the length of its lobes. Eu. and northern Af., sometimes naturalized in the U.S. July. Hardy from zone* 3 southward. There are many hort. forms, with golden, variegated, white-margined or otherwise marked foliage. There is also a variety with yellow fruit.

PRIVET CULTURE

No shrubs grow so easily as privet, and many professional gardeners scorn the whole group as being decidedly weedy shrubs. One of the most famous of them wrote, "the meanest of all mean shrubs, but popular beyond all others, its weed-like facility of increase making it dear to those to whom something growing with a fungus-like rapidity is a treasure." There is also what he calls their "vile and sickly odor."

While the fact of rapidity of growth and malodorous flowers is true, it remains that the privets contain some ornamental shrubs, particularly among the really evergreen species. Of these the best are *Ligustrum japonicum, L. lucidum, L. massalongianum* and *L. indicum,* none of them, unfortunately, hardy in the North.

For hedge plants the outstanding one is the California privet (*L. ovalifolium*), followed closely by *L. vulgare,* and as fair substitutes, *L. Ibolium* and *L. amurense.* For their use as hedge plants *see* HEDGES. The rest of the species are moderately dec-

---

* Special articles on the subjects indicated by an asterisk (*) will be found at the words so marked.

orative shrubs for the border, their chief attraction being their fruits.

Most of the commonly grown privets will stand more smoke, dust, wind, and even sea spray than any other shrubs. In other words, they are of the easiest culture in a variety of soils and in the most unfavorable sites. All of them are easily increased from slips rooted in moist sand, and the hedge species will often root in any garden soil. Most of them are also easily raised from seed.

INSECT PESTS. Control scales with dormant oils. Mites and aphids will be controlled by pesticide #1 or #21. (See SPRAYS AND DUSTS.) Pesticide #17 damages privet.

DISEASES. Anthracnose may seriously damage common privet. Small cankers on the twigs or larger lesions on the lower stem and roots lead to death of twigs and sometimes whole plants. Eradication by removal and burning of affected parts is the best control known. California privet is immune to this disease but very susceptible to winter injury.

PRIVET ANDROMEDA = *Lyonia ligustrina.*

PROBOSCIDEA (pro-bos-sid'i-a). Curiously fruited annual (in ours), clammy or sticky herbs, and the only cult. genus of the family **Martyniaceae** (mar-tin-i-ā'see-ee), which comprises 2 other genera and about 10 species, all from the tropics or sub-tropics. The only cult. species is P. **louisianica** (often known as *P. louisiana* or *Martynia louisianica* or as *P. jussieui*), the unicorn-plant or devil's-claw; also called proboscis-flower. It is a sprawling annual, with alternate* or nearly alternate, roundish-oval, thick, soft leaves that are 7–10 in. wide, and heart-shaped at the base. Flowers bell-shaped or funnel-shaped, the limb slightly 2-lipped,* yellowish-purple, in few-flowered clusters in the axils. Corolla about 1½ in. long. Stamens* 4, joined by the anthers.* Fruit a hanging, woody, curved and beaked capsule,* the body of which is about 3 in. long. Beak splitting when dry and forming 2 hooked appendages, nearly 3 in. long. In the South the young and still green fruits are used like pickling cucumbers. The plant is a tender annual needing the same conditions for culture as the tomato (which see), but should be set at least 5 ft. apart each way. The plant is native in the southeastern U.S. (*Proboscidea* is from the Greek for snout, in allusion to the long-beaked fruit.)

PROBOSCIS-FLOWER = *Proboscidea louisianica.*

procera, -us, -um (pro'ser-ra). Tall.

procumbens (pro-kum'benz). Procumbent; *i.e.,* trailing, but not rooting. See RUNNER.

procurrens (pro-cur'renz). Creeping or extended.

PROLIFERATION. The horticulturally useful attribute of many plants to produce offsets,* bulbils,* or other vegetative means of propagation. Proliferous organs and the tendency of some plants to proliferation are

of the greatest value to the gardener who uses such parts to increase his stock, notably in the houseleek (offsets), some onions (bulbils), and in begonia (a proliferating leaf).

Quite often the ability to produce a new plant on an existing growing one furnishes the most interesting cases of proliferation. Sometimes a new plant will sprout directly from a growing leaf, as in *Asplenium bulbiferum.* And in at least one case a whole new crop of young plants will start from the leaf margin, as in the air plant (see BRYOPHYLLUM PINNATUM). While proliferation can be induced by an injury, as in making a leaf cutting of begonia, the causes of natural proliferations are wholly unknown.

prolifica, -us, -um (pro-liff'i-ka). Prolific, as to flowers or fruit.

PROPAGATING FRAME. An ingenious, practical, and simple apparatus for germination of seedlings or rooting of cuttings has been devised by the Office of Foreign Plant and Seed Introduction of the U.S. Department of Agriculture. It consists of a box 6 ft. long, 3 ft. high, and 3 ft. wide, the front comprising two doors hinged at the top. It can be made of wood or fiberboard. One foot above the bottom a board is fastened in the center of the box, to which two 40-watt fluorescent tubes are attached, facing downward.

In the bottom place flats or trays containing sand or vermiculite* in which seeds are planted or cuttings inserted. There is no glass, for the artificial light replaces sunlight. The principle upon which it works is thus akin to a Wardian case or terrarium.* An initial watering of the sand or vermiculite* is all that is necessary. These propagating frames can be put in the cellar or storeroom, plugged into an electric socket, and allowed to run until seeds have sprouted or cuttings struck root. If ordinary room temperature is much below 70° F. there must be bottom heat (an ordinary electric bulb or two placed under the trays or flats) and in this case a basal apron should be provided to keep in the heat.

For rooting cuttings a white or pink fluorescent tube (not a daylight tube) is preferable. For seedlings a tube with blue-violet rays has proved most satisfactory. The device is a boon to those without greenhouse or hotbed equipment as it can be set up anywhere in the house where it is warm enough.

PROPAGATION. The increase of new plants from existing ones. For the origin of really new plants (*i.e.,* new species and varieties) see PLANT BREEDING. It is unnecessary to repeat here the best method of propagating the different plants in this book, for at every entry the preferred method has been mentioned. Here we are concerned chiefly with the principles of propagation and with guiding the gardener to the proper articles where the details will be found.

The propagation of plants falls into two very different categories: (1) Those raised

---

* Special articles on the subjects indicated by an asterisk (*) will be found at the words so marked.

from seeds or spores,* the production of both of which involves sexual union, hence called sexual reproduction; (2) those propagated vegetatively, in ways to be discussed presently, without the intervention of sexual union, hence called asexual reproduction or vegetative propagation.

SEEDS AND SPORES. How these are produced will be found at FERTILIZATION (for seeds) and at FERNS AND FERN GARDENING (for spores). At the latter entry also there is a description of how young ferns are raised from spores.

Raising new plants from seed, still the commonest form of propagation, is treated in detail at SEEDS AND SEEDAGE, and need not be repeated here.

VEGETATIVE PROPAGATION. Some plants will not come true from seed; others, like the banana, pineapple, and the navel orange, ordinarily have no seeds; and for many others the increase of new plants is much quicker and easier without using seeds. The Greeks knew this well, and Theophrastus wrote a description of the making of cuttings.

Whatever method is used it involves two different principles. One is the ability of plants to send out roots from an injured (i.e., a cut) surface, and sometimes without any cutting; the other is the ability of the tissue of related plants to weld and grow as one when properly united.

In the first category the gardener finds the ability to root from a cut surface of the greatest use. In hundreds of plants he makes a cutting or slip which when inserted in the proper medium will ultimately produce roots and a new plant. For the details of this extremely common method of vegetative propagation see CUTTINGS.

In the second category, the gardener, instead of detaching the injured (i.e., cut) member, leaves it on the parent plant. When properly handled and covered with soil this will root, after which it is detached and grows into a new plant. Some, in fact many, plants will root at the joints without injury so long as the stem is covered with soil. In any case propagation by this method usually involves laying a stem down so it can be covered with soil, hence the operation is known as LAYERING, which see for the details.

In both cuttings and layering the production of new roots is the object sought. But in the remaining forms of vegetative propagation very different tactics are followed. Both of them are based upon the ability of properly joined tissue to weld or grow together. But mere welding would be of no value if the piece brought to the union did not contain one or more buds which would ultimately flourish. It is upon the ability of detached buds, or of a single one, to grow, once the welding process is accomplished, that the remaining methods are based. One of them, because it uses only a single bud, is known as BUDDING; the other, using several buds, is known as GRAFTING. For the details

and management of both see BUDDING, GRAFTING.

Budding, grafting, and layering, while not exclusively so, are largely means of propagating woody plants. Cuttings may be made of both woody and herbaceous plants. But the last method of propagation, by division or separation of the existing clump, is used practically always upon herbaceous perennials. For the details of this see DIVISION. See also OFFSETS, RUNNER.

PROPHET-FLOWER = *Arnebia Echioides.*

PROP ROOT. A root that acts as a prop or support. Prop roots originate from stems, but ultimately penetrate the soil, serving both as anchors and food gatherers. Corn produces them (see CORN), and many other plants do also. The most notable are the screw pines (see PANDANUS) which, in the tropics, may produce prop roots far up the trunk. These diverge from it, ultimately penetrate the soil many feet from the trunk, and make large, stem-like prop roots.

proserpinacoides (pro-ser-pin-a-koy'deez, but see OïDES). Resembling a plant of the genus *Proserpinaca*, which does not contain cult. plants. See MYRIOPHYLLUM.

PROSOPIS. See MESQUITE.

PROSTANTHERA (pros-tan'ther-a). Mintbush. Tender Australian shrubs or small trees, comprising about 40 species, belonging to the mint family. Leaves simple,* opposite,* ovalish or lance-shaped, scented. Flowers in whorls or terminal clusters, white, red, or purple. Calyx* of 5 sepals, joined halfway down. Corolla broadly tubular, dividing into 2 lips.* Stamens* 4, in pairs, 2 long, and 2 short. Fruit 2-celled when young, when ripe splitting into 4, each part containing 1 seed. (*Prostanthera* is from the Greek for add to and anther, in reference to a technical feature of the anthers.)

Grown in the greenhouse, but can be grown outside in the southern states and in Calif. Propagated from cuttings of young shoots taken in the early spring. When grown as a pot plant use potting mixture* 5.

nivea. Handsome shrub 3–6 ft. high, and of shiny appearance. Stems slender and much-branched. Leaves simple,* small, narrow, to 1½ in. long, entire, margins slightly rolled. Flowers in axillary whorls,* pure white or tinged blue.

rotundifolia. Shrub 3–7 ft. high. Leaves small, ovalish, to ½ in. long, the margins entire or slightly cut into rounded teeth. Flowers purplish-blue, ½ in. long, in terminal clusters (racemes*).

prostrata, -us, -um (pros-tray'ta). Lying flat; prostrate.

PROSTRATE JUNIPER = *Juniperus communis depressa.*

PROSTRATE PIGWEED = *Amaranthus blitoides.* See list at WEEDS.

PROTEACEAE (pro-tee-ā'see-ee). The Australian Oak family is very large, comprising over 50 genera and perhaps 1100

---

* Special articles on the subjects indicated by an asterisk (*) will be found at the words so marked.

species of trees and shrubs, mostly Australian, but found also in South Africa, Asia, and South America. The genera are ornamental shrubs and trees, grown outdoors in southern Calif. and Fla., or in greenhouses where some of them are rather widely grown, especially *Leucadendron* (the silver tree), *Banksia, Hakea,* and *Grevillea.* The other cult. genera are *Macadamia,* with an edible nut (the Queensland nut), and the very showy *Embothrium.*

Leaves alternate* or scattered (whorled* in some), sometimes tiny and awl-shaped or needle-like, always without marginal teeth, expanded and very silvery in *Leucadendron.* Flowers usually in dense clusters, without petals, male and female on different plants in *Leucadendron.* Fruit various, usually a nut, capsule,* or drupe.*

Technical flower characters: Sepals 4, united or more or less tubular. Petals none. Stamens* 4, opposite the sepals, and borne on them. Ovary superior,* the style 1 and undivided.

PROTECTING PLANTS. Most people infer that winter protection of plants is an effort to keep the plants warm by wrapping them up, just as we clothe ourselves in a fur coat during the winter. This, however, leaves out of consideration the fact that a plant has no body warmth which might be preserved by a warm covering, and that within a few hours it will be just as cold as if it had no protection. A plant which dies from the effect of frost at a temperature near the freezing point — as, for instance, most tropical plants — cannot be kept alive outdoors with any amount of covering. Only artificial heat in a greenhouse or room will sustain it over the winter.

Those who reason this far not infrequently reach the conclusion that there is therefore no sense in covering plants at all; that either they are hardy and need no covering or they are not hardy and covering will not save them, hence they are better not raised at all. This, however, is as much a mistake as it is an illusion that we cover plants in order to keep them warm.

For what reason then do we cover them? This question cannot be answered without explaining that hardiness is by no means only the ability to withstand low temperatures. It includes also the capacity to stop and start growth at the most opportune time in fall and spring, and to resist effectively the fatal loss of moisture which may be caused when the winter sun or drying winds act upon the frozen twigs, buds, or evergreen leaves.

Hardiness further implies the ability to remain dormant, or at rest, during prolonged warm spells in the latter part of the winter; and to send the roots down deeply enough to reach beyond the destructive influence of violent fluctuations of temperature which are frequent in the upper, exposed layers of the soil.

If these facts are understood, it is easy to understand also in what manner a covering may assist a plant in its struggle against the hardships imposed upon it by the winter; and this understanding, again, will help us to apply the covering most effectively.

How to Apply a Winter Covering

A heavy covering, applied with the wrong notion that it has to keep the plant warm, may easily smother and kill an otherwise hardy plant. At any rate, it will do more harm than good. A light covering, on the other hand, which simply protects the plant against the drying effect of sun or wind,

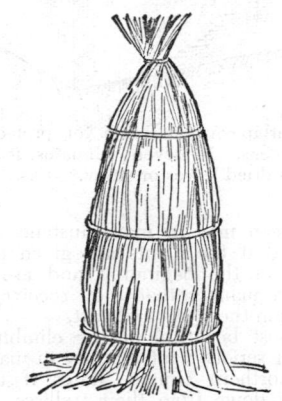

This plant is not tied up to keep it warm.
For reasons *see* text.

or which, if applied to the ground around the plant, will prevent violent fluctuations of temperature and preserve the moisture content of the soil, may be the deciding factor between life and death.

A covering of the ground around the plant — called mulch by the gardener, and consisting of leaves or straw or well-decayed manure — if applied after a heavy freezing, and especially if accompanied by shading of the upper parts of the plant, will also serve to prevent certain plants from starting into growth during warm spells in February or early March. This early growth usually suffers serious injury from later frosts. Such covering, then, actually serves to keep the plant cool instead of warm. *See* MULCH.

Plants Which Need Protection

A covering, which mainly consists in shading, either in the form of burlap, stretched on a wire frame over the whole plant — as generally practiced with boxwood — or in the form of a screen, made from laths, straw mats or burlap and set up in particular on the east and south sides of the plant, can be recommended for most broad-leaved evergreens and for many conifers, if they have been planted in an exposed place. This same type of plant will also be greatly benefited by a mulch of leaves or well-decayed manure applied in the fall. The necessity for

---

* Special articles on the subjects indicated by an asterisk (*) will be found at the words so marked.

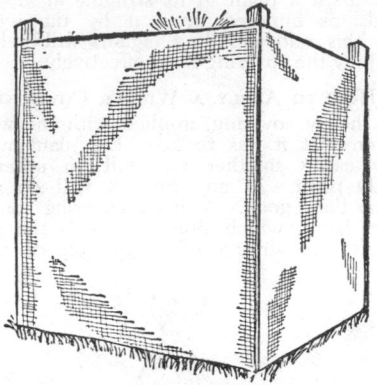

Useful burlap-covered frame for protecting box or evergreens. In severe climates it is often filled with dried leaves or straw.

a sun-screen may in many instances be circumvented if the plants are given the right exposure in the beginning and are located in such a manner that they receive natural shelter from the south and east.

The most beautiful of the climbing roses will suffer serious winter injury in many parts of the northern United States if they are not taken down from their trellises, bundled up with straw, and covered with soil. The hybrid tea roses need protection only to their crown, which is achieved by heaping soil over them to a height of about one foot.

Most rock garden plants are benefited by a dressing of stone chips, which will prevent moisture from stagnating at their crowns. Since in their native haunts these plants usually are accustomed to a snow covering, which with us they frequently do not get, we have to provide for many of them a protection which in some manner will take the place of the missing snow. Pine branches have been found to be most effective for this purpose, since they will shed moisture quickly and will never pack down tightly. All moisture-holding litter must be avoided on alpine plants.

Sunscald* of trunks or frost-splitting of recently planted trees may be prevented by wrapping the trunks in burlap during the winter months. For the methods of fighting cold in orchards see FROST AND FROST CONTROL.

SPRING FROSTS

Often an untimely late frost will apparently kill some freshly started seedlings. A good method is to sprinkle such lightly before sunrise, which will often save them. Such a plan is only effective after light frosts in late spring, and sprinkling while the temperature is below freezing will do more harm than good.

If you anticipate a late spring frost, you may reduce the loss of heat through radia-

tion from the ground by covering the garden at sundown with cheesecloth, or even better, by paper pegged down. And in the case of individual plants, a paper bag slipped over them will do the job. There are also several waxed paper or plastic coverings for such emergencies, and they may be used many times.

Some recent and very careful experiments with various kinds of individual plant protectors (used for transplanted seedlings of tomato, melon, etc.) show that the various devices sold by the dealers are effective in the following order: waxed paper, glassene, and cel-o-glass, all of which saved the plants under them, while of unprotected plants in the same row 92% were killed by frost. — H. T. See HARDINESS.

PROTHALLUS. A stage in the reproduction of ferns. See Spores and Reproduction at FERNS AND FERN GARDENING.

PROTOPLASM. The living cell tissue of all plants and animals, and assuming many forms. See CHLOROPHYLL for one of the most important.

PROVENCE ROSE = *Rosa gallica.*

pruinata, -us, -um (pru-i-nay′ta). Same as *pruinosa.*

pruinosa, -us, -um (pru-i-nō′sa). Pruinose; *i.e.,* with a whitish, hoary bloom.*

PRUNACEAE. See ROSACEAE.

PRUNE. Prunes are merely certain varieties of the European plum (*Prunus domestica*) which, on account of their high sugar content, can be successfully sun-dried. These plums may be used fresh as dessert fruit, their use not being limited to the production of prunes. Belonging to the hardy European plum species prunes may be grown over wide areas of the West (*see* PLUM). In California the French (Prune d'Agen) is the leading variety. Minor varieties are Robe de Sergeant, Imperial, and Sugar. In the Northwest the Italian (Fellenberg) prune is grown almost exclusively. The latter variety is used fresh and canned.

The culture of prunes is essentially the same as that discussed for the dessert varieties of European plums. Pruning is usually less severe than that given to dessert plums, and the trees are often allowed to attain greater size. Thinning is usually omitted in the case of plums grown to produce commercial prunes, but under conditions of excessive set a better product and more attractive fruit is obtained if thinning is practiced. Excessive crops often cause severe dieback of branches.

Harvesting is quite different from the harvesting of dessert plums. The fruit is allowed to become ripe on the tree, at which time it either drops naturally, as in the coastal areas of California, or is shaken from the tree by jarring the limbs. The fruit is then picked up from the ground, dipped in hot water or a hot lye solution (1 lb. to 20

* Special articles on the subjects indicated by an asterisk (*) will be found at the words so marked.

gallons water) and then spread on trays in the sun to dry.

Drying is done by placing the fruit in a single layer on trays exposed to the sun. The trays are left spread for a period of 4 to 5 days up to 2 weeks, depending upon the temperature and amount of sunlight during the drying period. Low humidities favor rapid drying. The fruit should be covered or moved under cover during rains which could cause rotting and molding when the fruit is drying. After the preliminary drying in the sun, the trays of fruit should be stacked, the top tray being covered, and drying in open continued until the prunes attain a leathery texture. As large and small prunes dry at different rates, the prunes then are bulked in a box and the moisture allowed to equalize. They may then be stored under cool conditions until used. Storing in closed jars is preferred to prevent infestations of dried-fruit insects. — **C. O. H.**

PRUNELLA (pru-nell'a). Low-growing, hardy, perennial herbs, comprising 6 species of the mint family, and natives of Eu. and As. Stems square. Leaves simple,° opposite,° the veins prominent on the under side, margins generally toothed. Flowers purple or violet-blue, in dense heads or spikes. Calyx° of 5 sepals° joined halfway down, enclosing the ripened fruit. It closes and points upward in dry weather but opens and stands horizontally in damp weather. Corolla short and tubular, 2-lipped.° Stamens° 4, in pairs, 2 long, and 2 short. Fruit 2-celled when young, but splitting into 4 parts when ripe, each part containing 1 seed. (*Prunella* is believed to be from a German word for the quinsy, for which these plants were considered a specific.)

Not much in cult., as most species are garden weeds, but can be used for damp and shady places in the rock or wild garden. Easily propagated from seeds or division of rootstocks. Seeds should be sown in early spring, in cool greenhouse or cold frame, and transplanted to permanent positions as soon as large enough to handle. Seeds may be sown outdoors in April, when division of rootstocks also may be made.

grandiflora. Hardy perennial, to 9 in. high. Leaves ovalish, margins toothed or entire. Flowers purplish-blue, 1 in. long. June—July. Suitable for the blue garden (*see* BLUE GARDEN). Eu. There are several hort. color forms.

incisa = *Prunella vulgaris*, probably the *var. laciniata*.

vulgaris. Self-heal. Heal-all (*see also* the list at WEEDS). Hardy perennial, to 2 ft. high, of spreading habit. Leaves ovalish to lance-shaped, to 4 in. long, margins toothed or entire. Flowers violet, ½ in. long. June—Oct. Eu.; naturalized in N.A. The *var.* laciniata has cut leaves, and is considered by some as a separate species, *P. laciniata*.

prunifolia, -us, -um (pru-ni-fō'li-a). With cherry-like leaves.

PRUNING. The practice of cutting or trimming existing growth on woody plants for the benefit of that left on the tree, shrub, or vine, done mostly to promote flower and fruit production, or to make the plant more shapely.

FRUIT TREES

The object of pruning, which in horticultural parlance means to cut or trim, is manifold. With fruit trees, while in the young state, it is done to shape the trees according to one's desires, that is to say, by proper and careful pruning one lays the foundation of a tree, whether it is to be a standard, bush, espalier, or any other type of tree. As a rule, the gardener buys his fruit trees when their form is already established, from the nurseryman who has done the preliminary pruning. From that time on, the purpose of pruning is to keep the trees shapely and to make them fruitful. Left to their own devices after planting, young fruit trees will more or less run wild and make much useless wood before reaching the fruiting stage, which in itself naturally steadies future growth.

If one aspires to grow his own fruit trees from the start, he must either bud or graft the desired varieties on the proper rootstocks, or buy one-year-old trees known as whips, which are upright stems with practically no branches. If to be grown on as a standard° or half-standard, the young tree must be allowed to run upward to the desired height before it is topped to make it branch. Standards have usually a six-foot stem or trunk, half-standards three to four feet. Any shoots that appear on the lower part of the stem should be cut away clean, but until the top is removed and the desired branches are definitely under way, the stem should not be trimmed too closely, as all the leaves possible are needed to stimulate root growth. Bush trees usually have a short leg, and the one-year-old whips should therefore be cut back to the desired point, and the succeeding shoots carried forward as branches. Trained types of trees are similarly treated at the start and afterward dealt with as described in the entry on TRAINED FRUIT TREES.

The groundwork of the tree secured, the pruning that follows is to encourage fruitfulness, as well as to keep the tree shapely. Whether the tree has one or two stems only, as in cordons, or six or more main branches, as in a bush, it is natural for such stems or branches to push forth lateral growths, particularly from the upper portions. These branchlets or laterals theoretically are the fruiting parts of the tree. Whatever the type of tree, the stems or branches must be encouraged to branch from the base up. The cordon stem or the branches of a bush tree may in the first year grow a yard, and if this growth is permitted to stand unpruned, the following spring it will probably push laterals from the upper eyes, the lower ones remaining dormant, resulting in after years in a tree with blank spaces. As a rule, it is good policy to cut back all main stem growths made the previous year about

° Special articles on the subjects indicated by an asterisk (°) will be found at the words so marked.

one-third; that is, when a tree is in the making, no matter what its shape, the leaders should be so cut back early in the spring to induce the emission of laterals fairly close together. This cutting back one-third should be done each year until the tree has attained the size and height wanted, by which time it should be fruiting; after that, all the leaders should be cut back entirely every season, the vigor of the tree being maintained by the laterals it makes, and feeding. These remarks, in the main, relate to apples and pears. Cherries and plums are apt to make fruiting laterals and spurs rather more readily, and as a rule they are kept to standard or bush forms. When once they start fruiting, little pruning is needed, except in the way of removing wild shoots that threaten to spoil the shape of the tree. Plums respond well to espalier training if they are to be grown on a wall. Peaches, usually grown in bush form, require but moderate pruning after they attain fruiting size, the removal of shoots that tend to crowd being all that is necessary.

WHEN TO PRUNE. In the small or moderate-sized garden, apples and pears are the most valuable fruits because they can be kept within any desired limits, especially when on dwarfing stocks. In the orchard, where large trees are permissible, the customary time for pruning is during the late fall or even in the winter when the weather is fairly mild. If summer pruning is done at all, the usual plan, if the trees are of bush type, is to cut back the strongest laterals halfway, completing the pruning during the winter. For the home garden, and even in orchards where the trees have been kept to a low stature, we favor the Lorette system of pruning, a system devised by a noted French specialist for pears, but which is also applicable to apples and to some extent to other fruits. *See* TRAINED FRUIT TREES.

One of the great failings of stereotyped fruit pruning is that it encourages much useless growth. We have seen garden trees pruned year after year with sedulous care, yet the desired fruit has been sparse or entirely absent; particularly is this the case if trained trees are not on dwarfing stocks. It should be understood that apples and pears produce their fruits on spurs or short laterals, not direct from the trunks or branches. As stated, the main stems or branches persistently produce laterals every season, and the natural reaction to cutting away these laterals is the production of still more wood. A tree naturally will settle down to fruiting in due time if left alone, but the gardener, unlike the orchardist, wants small trees to fruit, and if he follows the usual winter pruning custom he is apt to be disappointed.

The Lorette system, in effect, is quite technical and requires intense study, but one can follow the general principles quite readily. Instead of the usual pruning practice, which is to cut back all laterals during the winter to the last bud or two, as well as the leaders if the tree has reached full size, Lorette pruning entails all summer and no winter pruning, and the heading back of the leaders in early April. Scientific study has shown that the fruit buds are formed

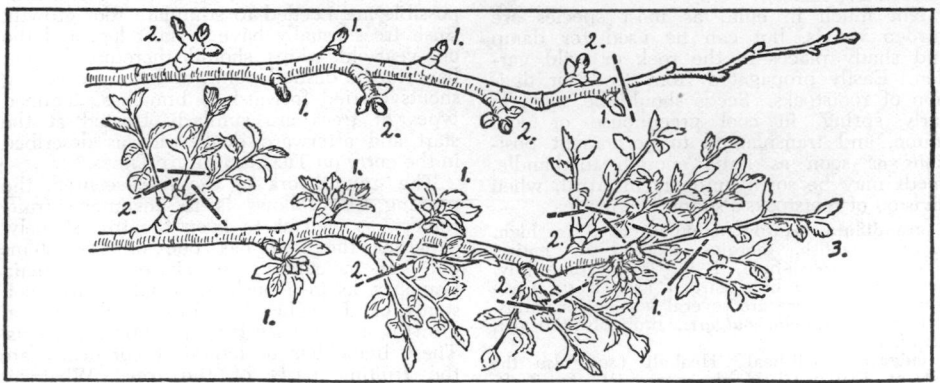

LORETTE SYSTEM OF PRUNING
(As Illustrated by the Apple)

The upper, dormant branch shows at (1) the natural fruit spurs and at (2) the growth buds of sterile shoots to be pruned in June (see below). Note the long terminal leader which should be cut back to the point indicated early in April.
The lower figure is the same branch in June, before pruning. (1) The natural fruit spurs showing fruits just beginning to set. (2) The sterile spurs with their new growth, which should be cut back as indicated when 12 inches long (usually in June) to induce formation of fruit buds for next season. At (3) is shown the leader which should be allowed to grow during this season, but cut back next April as shown in the upper figure.

* Special articles on the subjects indicated by an asterisk (*) will be found at the words so marked.

by the end of June or thereabouts, at least in Europe. It is, therefore, useless to assume that winter pruning can bring about fruit buds. There are instances where obvious fruit buds have in the spring changed to growth buds and vice versa, but in a general way it is definitely known that fruit buds are set during the middle of the year, and if they are not there in embryo no winter pruning will create them; in fact, the only effect of such pruning is to make the eyes left push forth more strong growths, and so on *ad infinitum. See* TRAINED FRUIT TREES.

The modern summer pruning entails the removal of all laterals above 12 inches in length at the end of June or thereabouts, sharp pruning shears being used so that the shoots are cut clean back to the base, leaving only the basal cluster of leaves where the dormant, invisible eyes are situated. During the balance of the summer, the remaining laterals, when they lengthen out, are so cut back, whether they emanate from the spurs or from the branch itself. Those that do not reach 12 inches may be cut back in late fall unless they carry plump-looking buds at the tips. It is quite common for shoots six inches or so in length to bear fruit buds at the tips, some varieties of apples being essentially tip bearers. As a rule, however, it is good policy to keep the spurs fairly short. Spurs are short, stubby branchlets that should each carry one or more clusters of fruit buds. Some varieties make natural spurs fairly freely, especially after they have started fruiting, but in the main, artificial spurs have to be encouraged by pruning as outlined.

Contrary to what one might expect, the hard cutting-back of the laterals during the summer does not encourage all the basal eyes to start into growth. A few may, and they can be cut back in late fall. The old-time summer system of pruning the laterals half back, on the other hand, excites quite a mass of new growths. The leaders, that is, the top growths of cordons or the branches of other types of trees, must, however, be allowed to run through the season untouched and either be cut out entirely or partly back at the beginning of April, according to whether the tree has reached its full size or is in the making. The Lorette system can be practiced on any apple or pear, and if, under the usual winter pruning system or no pruning at all, the tree has fruited sparsely or well, it will be found advantageous. For the home gardener, summer pruning is infinitely more comfortable and the operator is better able to see what he is doing.

Reverting to the term *spurs*, these, as stated, are the fruit-bearing branchlets. Natural spurs may extend only an inch or two from the main branch. Artificial spurs, induced by repeated pruning, may extend much farther, especially on old trees that have been fruiting over a long period. These artificial spurs perforce carry growth eyes and produce laterals each season. A tree

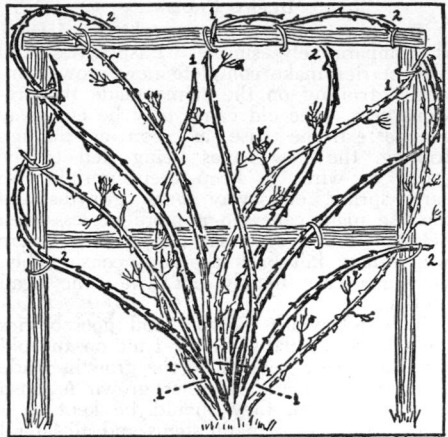

CORRECT PRUNING OF RAMBLER ROSE

(1) Cut back to the base growths that have flowered when bloom is finished; (2) retain the new shoots which will produce flowers the following year.

must produce a requisite amount of foliage to ensure healthiness, and only by producing laterals can it make the necessary leaves. Summer pruning as outlined does not of course denude the tree of foliage beyond the safety margin, but it does check some of the food supply to the roots, and after pruning it is, therefore, good policy then to give the trees a good dressing of fertilizer and water if conditions are dry. The reason for not heading back the leading growth or growths is that these keep the sap active so that the roots are not entirely robbed of support. Left to carry on the major part of the work, these leaders usually grow quite vigorously. As stated, the heading back must not be done until early April when the trees are preparing to make new growths.

THINNING. When fruit trees, particularly apples, pears, and peaches, have reached full bearing, it is desirable to disbud if the trees appear to be carrying too many fruits over a given area. It may look well to see a branch laden heavily, and an apple or pear may set several fruits on each spur, but if the spurs are six inches or so apart it is too much to expect choice, large fruits if several hang on each spur. It is sometimes desirable to remove some of the flower clusters when they are overabundant, but ordinarily the thinning out can best be done as soon as the fruitlets are set. Too heavy a set of fruit allowed to remain invariably means a light or no crop the following year. It is often assumed that fruit trees have to have blank years. Such is not the case, but if overtaxed one season, they are apt to be barren the following year, especially if not well fed. This applies equally to peaches and plums, as well as to apples and pears.

---

* Special articles on the subjects indicated by an asterisk (*) will be found at the words so marked.

Berry Fruits

The pruning of most other kinds of fruits is comparatively simple. Raspberries and blackberries make complete new growth annually, fruiting on the stems made the previous year. The old canes may be cut away at the extreme base as soon as through fruiting, the new canes being tied to the stakes or wires to keep them upright. In early spring, cut away weak growths and top the main canes to a more or less even height, from five to six feet; but a severe winter may kill back the tops considerably, in which case merely cut away the dead portion.

Red and white currants and gooseberries are pruned similarly. They fruit on the old wood as a rule, seldom on the growths made the previous year. Whether grown in bush or cordon form, they should be kept to a definite number of main stems and all lateral growths cut back within half an inch every season. All shoots appearing from the base should be cut away entirely, unless needed to replace main stems that have become weakened by age or borers. To permit sun and air to reach the main branches, cut back the longest laterals halfway during July, and complete the pruning after the foliage has dropped. Black currants are not spur fruiters. They fruit on both old and new wood and need only have the oldest stems cut away after fruiting.

Grapevines can be pruned in varying degrees according to the position they occupy. For the different systems used for the *vinifera* and common varieties *see* Grape.

Ornamental Trees and Shrubs

The pruning of trees and shrubs is for two purposes: to keep them shapely, and, in the case of flowering subjects, to encourage better quality blooms. Young trees, whether for shade purposes or for ornamental use, have all undergone more or less pruning and trimming at the hands of the nurseryman, and, aside from the removal of lower branches to give more stem length as they increase the heads, they require only occasional attention to prevent crowding. Flowering trees of all kinds, too, require but a moderate amount of trimming or pruning, mainly to keep them shapely, as when once they reach flowering age pruning has but little influence upon flower production, and only in exceptional instances is it necessary to disbud. As a rule, the more flowers an ornamental tree bears, the more it is appreciated, whether it be a dogwood, *Magnolia*, flowering crab, cherry, or plum. Some ornamental trees, such as the cherry, crab and plum, flower largely on natural spurs; the redbud (*Cercis canadensis*) blooms directly on the branches and stems, while the *Magnolia* and sundry others flower on the points of the previous year's growth.

Flowering shrubs come under two headings, those that flower in the spring, and those that bloom any time after June. The

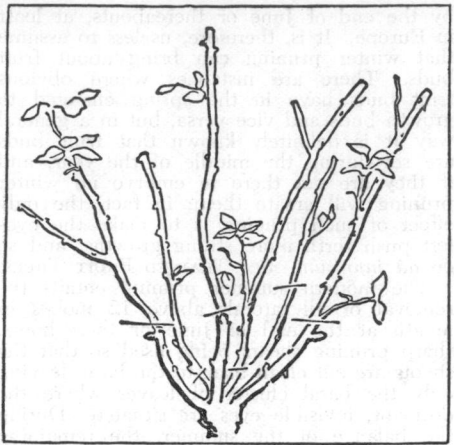

DORMANT ROSEBUSH IN APRIL

Prune where the cuts are shown, leaving not more than 3–6 buds on strong shoots, and cutting weak shoots to the base.

late bloomers, when pruning is necessary, must be subjected to the knife only in winter or early spring. For the most part they flower largely on the wood made the same season. By trimming or pruning in the spring, new wood that will duly flower is encouraged. Spring-bloomers, on the other hand, largely flower on the wood made the previous season. To prune any time after the leaves fall would mean the removal of much flowering wood. Immediately after flowering is finished is the time to prune or trim spring-flowering shrubs.

Examples of spring-flowering shrubs, to be pruned after flowering, are: *Azalea, Cercis,* dogwood, *Diervilla, Kalmia, Kerria, Leucothoë, Philadelphus, Pieris, Rhododendron, Rhodotypos, Spiraea, Syringa* (lilac), and *Viburnum.* Late-flowering shrubs, to be pruned while dormant, are: *Buddleia, Clethra alnifolia, Caryopteris, Hibiscus syriacus, Hydrangea,* and *Vitex.* Of these, *Buddleia, Caryopteris,* and *Vitex* are often cut back to the ground each season in any case, especially where they are doubtfully hardy.

It should be understood that the pruning of shrubs is mainly for the purpose of keeping them shapely and within bounds. They should not be trimmed like a privet hedge, and if they are naturally tall growers it must not be assumed that constant trimming will keep them dwarf, except at the expense of flowering. The habit of each shrub must be studied. If naturally prone to sending up new growths from the base, cut away old wood near the ground line. Shrubs with a branching habit should be pruned less vigorously, but at the same time sufficiently to prevent overcrowding of the growths. All deciduous trees and shrubs should be well cut back or pruned at planting time. Dam-

---

* Special articles on the subjects indicated by an asterisk (*) will be found at the words so marked.

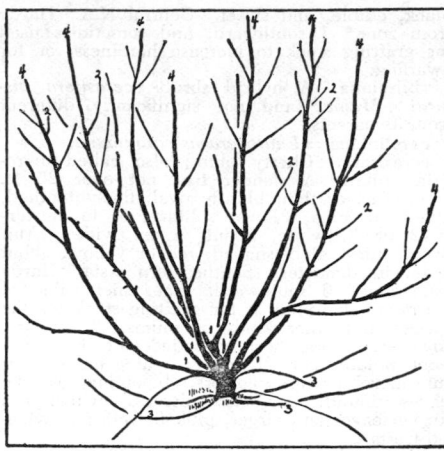

PRUNING CURRANT OR GOOSEBERRY BUSHES

(1) Fruiting main stems, to be retained; (2) lateral branches, to be cut back halfway at the end of June; (3) basal shoots, to be removed at any time; (4) the leaders, to be headed back each fall to keep the bushes about 4 ft. high.

aged and long, straggly roots should also be trimmed off clean. See Root Pruning.

Shearing is a form of pruning practiced on hedges to keep them dense and compact. In northern climates the last shearing should be done sometime in July, otherwise the growths made later will not have time to ripen, and severe damage may be done by hard freezing. The shearing of coniferous evergreens at no time is to be recommended unless formal-shaped trees are desired. To encourage growths and keep them shapely, junipers, *Thuja*, etc., may be pruned any time between May and July, the work being done with the knife or sharp pruning shears, otherwise known as secateurs. Short lengths of growth only should be removed. If the size is to be kept to definite limits, the leader must be stopped and the side branches frequently gone over. Conifers cannot be cut hard back like deciduous subjects, as the old wood lacks power to make new growth.

PERENNIALS AND ANNUALS

The term pruning is not applicable to herbaceous perennials and annuals, but both can be benefited by disbudding or disshooting. Perennials, such as *Phlox, Helenium, Aster, Artemisia vulgaris, Delphinium,* etc., after the first season are apt to produce too many stems for the area the roots occupy, and if all are allowed to remain the flower clusters will be curtailed in size, however well the plants are fed. Exhibition flowers of this class are usually grown on single-stemmed plants specially propagated, but in the garden roots up to three or four years old will give superb results if in May the gardener goes over his plants and removes all but the strongest shoots. Two or three are enough for *Delphinium* and not more than six for the others. With *Delphinium* the shoots should be cut out low; in other cases it is often possible to pull out the weak growths. Annuals, such as China asters, African marigolds, zinnias, etc., by disbudding, can be made to produce larger and finer flowers. These plants usually branch naturally after the center flower bud starts to develop. The side branches in turn develop a bud and make laterals. By pinching out the surplus laterals the leading flowers are much benefited.

Dahlias, if well grown, also require disshooting and disbudding. If a *Dahlia* plant with one stem has the top pinched out when it is 12 inches or so tall, it will send out several laterals, each of which will duly produce a cluster of three buds. The best of the three only is retained, assuming a fine large flower is wanted. In the meantime, several stems will start pushing forth laterals at the upper leaf joints. These are duly nipped out, only those at the base being allowed to develop. Thus, if a plant originally has six stems, six to 12 more will take their places after the flowers are cut, and unless unduly late or frost comes early, these will likewise flower. Constant disshooting and the removal of portions of foliage are necessary if high-class flowers are desired.

Outdoor chrysanthemums of the Pompon class require no disshooting, and disbudding, unless rigorously done, is not worth while. Large-flowered sorts, however, whether outdoors or under glass, must not be allowed to have more than two or three stems and only one flower bud on each stem is permissible. All side shoots that develop after the flower bud shows must be removed. — T. A. W. *See also* Root Pruning.

PRUNING SAW and SHEARS. See No. 10 at Tools and Implements.

PRUNUS (proo'nus). A large and immensely important genus of shrubs and trees of the rose family, nearly all from the north temperate zone, a few reaching to the Andes. It comprises over 200 species and includes all the plums, cherries, and apricots, and some consider it as including still other closely related plants like the peach and almond (including the flowering almond), here kept separate in the genus *Amygdalus* (which see). A few evergreen species, considered by some as belonging to *Prunus,* are here assigned to *Laurocerasus* (the cherry laurels).

Besides the outstanding importance of the fruit trees in *Prunus,* it contains all the Japanese flowering cherries (*see* below) and many other superb flowering shrubs and trees, the fruit of which is generally inedible and often wanting.

All, or nearly all, deciduous trees and shrubs with alternate,* never compound*

* Special articles on the subjects indicated by an asterisk (*) will be found at the words so marked.

leaves which are nearly always sharply toothed. Flowers in clusters (corymbs* or racemes), or sometimes few or only one, white, pink, or red (in some hort. forms), typically with 5 sepals, 5 petals, and many stamens. In some of the hort. forms there is much doubling of the petals and sometimes no functional stamens and no fruit. The latter is typically a drupe,* that is, a fleshy fruit with a single stone, hence often called stone fruits. The stone is generally flattish and grooved in the plums, but round and ungrooved in the cherries. (*Prunus* is the classical Latin name of the plum tree.)

For culture of the important edible species *see* CHERRY, PLUM, and APRICOT. *See also* PEACH and ALMOND for the culture of trees sometimes included in *Prunus*. For the ornamental, flowering species *see* below. Those especially desirable for their bloom or foliage, and usually grown for no other purpose, are marked with a dagger (†). All bloom early in the spring, some before the leaves expand.

americana. Wild or yellow plum. A native American tree 20–30 ft. high, usually less as cult. Leaves willow-like, 3–4 in. long, about 1 in. wide. Flowers white, 2–5 in a cluster, about 1 in. wide. Fruit about 1 in. in diameter, mostly yellow, sometimes red. Eastern N.A. Hardy from zone* 3 southward.

Amygdalus = *Amygdalus communis.*

angustifolia. Chickasaw plum. A native American twiggy shrub or small tree, usually not over 12 ft. high. Leaves trough-like, lance-shaped, 1–3½ in. long. Flowers 2–4 in a cluster, white, about ⅝ in. wide. Fruit nearly round, about ½ in. in diameter, red or yellow. Southeastern U.S. Hardy from zone* 4 southward. The *var.* watsoni, the sand plum, from Kansas and vicinity, is a low bush with zigzag twigs.

Armeniaca. Apricot. A tree 15–25 ft. high. Leaves roundish or heart-shaped, hairy on the veins beneath, 2–4½ in. long. Flowers solitary, about 1 in. wide, blooming before the leaves unfold, white or pink. Fruit smooth-skinned (in maturity), nearly stalkless, about 1¾ in. in diameter. Western Asia. For culture and varieties *see* APRICOT. Its flowers are so attractive that it is sometimes cult. for ornament. Hardy from zone* 5 southward, but its blossoms often killed by late spring frosts, except in the region of commercial cult., *i.e.*, Calif.

avium. The common sweet cherry. A tall tree with birch-like outer bark. Leaves oblongish or broader toward the tip, 2½–6 in. long. Flowers white, 3–6 in a cluster (umbel*). Fruit nearly globe-shaped, stalked. Eurasia, and of very ancient culture. Hardy from zone* 3 southward, or north of this for many hort. varieties. It is often an escape, and is then sometimes known as the Mazzard cherry, used mostly as grafting stock. The *var.* duracina is a hard-fleshed cherry (*see* CHERRY); *var.* juliana is the heart cherry; and the *var.* regalis is the Duke cherry. The Duke cherry is called by some *P. effusus.* For culture and best varieties *see* CHERRY.

besseyi. Sand cherry. Hansen bush cherry. A low shrub with often prostrate stems. Leaves elliptic or ovalish, 1–2½ in. long. Flowers 2–4 in a cluster, white, about ⅓ in. wide. Fruit nearly round, about ½ in. in diameter,

black, edible, and sweet. Central N.A. Hardy from zone* 1 southward, and sometimes used for grafting stock to increase hardiness, or for dwarfing.

†blireiana. A hybrid shrub (*cerasifera pissardi* × *Mume*) and not significantly different from its parents.

caroliniana = *Laurocerasus caroliniana.*

cerasifera. Cherry plum; also called myrobalan plum. A slender tree not over 25 ft. high. Leaves thin, bluntly oval, finely toothed, 1½–2 in. long. Flower solitary, or in clusters of 2 or 3, white, about ¾ in. wide. Fruit sweet, juicy, globe-shaped, red or yellow, about 1 in. in diameter. Southeastern Asia. Hardy from zone* 3 southward. The chief value of the myrobalan plum is for grafting stock for the apricot and other kinds of plums. There are, however, several hort. varieties cult. for ornament, notably *var.* divaricata, which has smaller but more profuse flowers, blooming as the leaves unfold; and *var.* pissardi, which has purple leaves and larger, pink flowers and wine-red fruits.

Cerasus. Sour cherry. A round-headed tree not over 35 ft. high, inclined to sucker from the base. Leaves elliptic-oval, rather stiff, pointed, 2–3½ in. long, doubly toothed. Flowers white, about 1 in. wide, in profuse clusters. Fruit sour, scarcely ¾ in. in diameter, red. Eurasia. Hardy from zone* 3 southward. For culture and best varieties *see* CHERRY.

†cistena. A hybrid shrub or small tree (*pumila* × *cerasifera pissardi*) and not differing significantly from *P. pumila.*

communis = *Amygdalus communis.*

†dasycarpa. Purple apricot. A very showy small tree, never over 25 ft. high, the twigs purplish. Leaves elliptic-oval, 1½–2½ in. long, long-pointed, finely toothed, hairy on the veins beneath. Flowers white, about 1 in. wide, very numerous and blooming before the leaves expand. Fruit (rarely produced) dark purple, hairy, acid, nearly globe-shaped, about 1½ in. in diameter. Thought to be a hybrid between the apricot and cherry plum; unknown as a wild tree. Hardy from zone* 3 southward.

†davidiana = *Amygdalus davidiana.*

domestica. Common plum. A round-headed tree, not usually over 25–30 ft. high. Leaves elliptic or broadest toward the tip, 2¼–4½ in. long, the margins coarsely but bluntly toothed. Flowers greenish-white, about ¾ in. wide, the clusters sparse, but very numerous and blooming before the leaves expand. Fruit, from long cult. and many hybrid races, various, but typically oblongish or egg-shaped, bluish-black, sweet, and with a free stone (clingstone in some hort. forms). Eurasia. Hardy, in some of its forms, nearly throughout the country. The *var.* insititia, the damson plum or bullace, considered by some as a separate species (*P. insititia*), has larger, pure white flowers and a clingstone fruit. For culture and best varieties of both the common plum and damson, *see* PLUM.

effusus. *See* PRUNUS AVIUM REGALIS.

†glandulosa. Flowering almond (but it is not a true almond, for which *see* AMYGDALUS COMMUNIS). A very showy shrub, and not over 5 ft. high. Leaves ovalish-oblong, or narrower, 1½–4 in. long. Flowers very numerous, but in clusters of 1 or 2, blooming before the leaves unfold, white or pinkish, about ¾ in. wide. China and Jap. Hardy from zone* 3 southward. There are several hort. varieties, among the best being *var.* rosea with pink flowers; *var.* sinensis with double pink flowers; and *var.* albo-plena with double white flowers.

---

* Special articles on the subjects indicated by an asterisk (*) will be found at the words so marked.

Few of the varieties produce fruit, but in the typical form it is red and about ⅓ in. in diameter.

hortulana. Hortulan plum. A native American plum, and the basis of several cult. varieties (*see* PLUM). A tree not over 30 ft. high. Leaves oblong-oval or elliptic, long-pointed, 3½–5½ in. long. Flowers 2–4 in each cluster, white, about ½ in. wide. Fruit (in the wild form) about 1 in. in diameter, reddish-yellow. Del. to Tenn., Iowa, and Okla. Hardy from zone* 3 southward. For culture and best varieties *see* PLUM.

†**ilicifolia.** Islay; also called evergreen cherry. A handsome, evergreen shrub or small tree, native from San Francisco to southern Calif. and Lower Calif., not over 30 ft., usually much less as cult. Leaves hollylike, 1–2 in. long, spiny-toothed. Flowers white, about ⅓ in. wide, in finger-shaped clusters (racemes*). Fruit red or black, about ⅔ in. in diameter, the flesh edible but scanty. Hardy from zone* 7 southward; unhappy in the East.

†**incisa.** An early-flowering shrub, rarely a small tree, never over 30 ft., usually much less as cult. Unfolding leaves purplish, ovalish, 1–3 in. long, hairy above and on the veins beneath, doubly toothed. Flowers 1–3 in a cluster, but numerous and nodding, white or pinkish. Fruit football-shaped, about ⅝ in. long, blackish-purple. Jap. April. Hardy from zone* 5 southward.

insititia = *Prunus domestica insititia.*

japonica. A shrub 3–5 ft. high, closely related to the flowering almond (*P. glandulosa*) and often confused with it. If it differs, *P. japonica* has more finely toothed leaves and has somewhat more of pink or white flowers. Central As. Hardy from zone* 3 southward.

†**lannesiana.** Japanese flowering cherry; or often called simply flowering cherry. A tree, not over 30 ft. high, the twigs smooth. Leaves oval or oval-oblong, 2½–5 in. long, sharply and doubly toothed, the teeth bristly. Flowers 2–5 in a cluster, pink in the typical form, but white, red, or double-flowered in many of the hort. forms, fragrant, usually in a raceme*-like, leafy-bracted* cluster. Fruit (often wanting) small, black, shining. Jap. Hardy from zone* 4 southward. This is often considered merely a var. of *P. serrulata.* For its culture and varieties *see* below.

†**Laurocerasus** = *Laurocerasus officinalis.*

†**lusitanica** = *Laurocerasus lusitanica.*

†**lyoni.** An evergreen tree, 20–30 ft. high, from the islands off the coast of southern Calif., but widely grown in warm regions in Calif. and not much elsewhere. Leaves ovalish or narrower, without marginal teeth on mature leaves. Flowers about ¼ in. wide, in clusters (racemes*) from the leaf joints, white. Fruit about 1 in. wide, dark purple. Perhaps only a form of *P. ilicifolia.*

Mahaleb. Mahaleb or St. Lucie cherry. A Eurasian tree of no value for its fruit, but widely used for grafting stock for better cherries. It is a loose-headed tree, with the young twigs hairy. Leaves broadly oval or roundish, 1¼–2½ in. long, bluntly round-toothed. Flowers in finger-shaped clusters (racemes*), 6–10 in a cluster, white and fragrant. Fruit about ¼ in. in diameter, black. Hardy from zone* 3 southward. For its use as grafting stock *see* CHERRY.

maritima. Beach plum. A native American shrub found on coastal dunes and rocky shores from New Brunswick to Del., not over 6 ft. high, the lower branches often decumbent. Leaves ovalish or elliptic, 2–3½ in. long, sharply toothed, often riddled by leaf miners. Flowers pure white, about ¾ in. wide, in clusters of 2–3, but very numerous. Fruit globe-shaped, dull purple or blackish, bloomy, its flesh delicious, suggesting the guava in flavor. Hardy from zone* 3 southward, and often cult. on Cape Cod, where improved vars. have been developed. *See* PLUM.

Mume. Japanese apricot. A small tree or shrub with slender green branches and broadly oval leaves, 1½–3½ in. long, sharply toothed and usually hairy on both sides. Flowers light pink, fragrant, and extremely prolific. Fruit nearly spherical, about 1½ in. in diameter, greenish-yellow, scarcely edible except in various Japanese vars. little known here. China and Japan. There are many hort. vars. grown mostly for profuse, very early bloom. Some of these are called "flowering plums."

†**nana.** Dwarf Russian almond (not a true almond, for which *see* AMYGDALUS COMMUNIS). A shrub scarcely over 4½ ft. high, cult. for ornament. Leaves lance-shaped or broader toward the tip, 1½–3 in. long, sharply toothed. Flowers in clusters of 1–3, rosy-red, about ¾ in. wide. Fruit hairy-skinned, egg-shaped, about ¾ in. long. Eurasia. Hardy from zone* 3 southward. Sometimes, and probably more correctly, known as *Amygdalus nana*, as its affinity appears to be with that genus rather than with *Prunus.* There are several hort. varieties, some with white or pink flowers. The plant is by some called *P. tenella.*

nigra. Canada or red plum. A native American, narrow-headed tree, rarely over 30 ft. high. Leaves generally elliptic, 3–5 in. long, coarsely and doubly, but bluntly toothed. Flowers 3–4 in a cluster, white but fading pink, about 1 in. wide. Fruit ellipsoid, about 1½ in. long, red or yellowish-red. Quebec to Ga. and westward and northwestward. Hardy from zone* 1 southward. It is the parent or origin of several cult. fruit trees. For culture and varieties *see* PLUM.

Padus. Bird cherry; also called European bird cherry. A tree up to 40 ft. high, not especially decorative and of no fruit value. Leaves elliptic or oblongish, 3–5½ in. long, sharply toothed, grayish beneath. Flowers fragrant, white, about ½ in. wide, in finger-shaped, hanging clusters (racemes*). Fruit black, about ½ in. in diameter. Eurasia. Hardy from zone* 2 southward.

pensylvanica. Wild red cherry. A native American tree, not over 30 ft. high, sometimes shrubby. Leaves oblongish or lance-oblong, 3–5½ in. long, sharply but finely toothed, the tip prolonged. Flowers 2–5 in a cluster (umbel*-like), white, about ¾ in. wide. Fruit globe-shaped, about ⅓ in. in diameter, red. Throughout most of northern N.A. Hardy from zone* 2 northward.

Persica = *Amygdalus Persica.*

pissardi = *P. cerasifera pissardi.*

†**pumila.** Sand cherry. An attractive, white-flowered American shrub, sometimes 6 ft. high, usually lower, and the old branches decumbent. Leaves narrow, but broadest toward the tip, 2–3 in. long, finely toothed. Flowers white, 2–3 in a cluster, very numerous, about ½ in. wide. Fruit purple-black, about ⅓ in. in diameter. Shores of the Great Lakes, especially on the dunes. Hardy from zone* 1 southward.

salicina. Japanese plum. An important source of many fruit trees (*see* PLUM). Not over 25 ft. high. Leaves oblong or elliptic, but somewhat broader toward the tip, 2½–4½ in. long, doubly toothed, the tip prolonged. Flowers mostly 3 in a cluster, white, about ¾ in.

---

* Special articles on the subjects indicated by an asterisk (*) will be found at the words so marked.

long, yellow or reddish, sometimes pointed at the tip. China, but early introduced into Jap. Hardy from zone° 3 southward. For culture and varieties see PLUM.

†**sargenti.** An extremely handsome tree, 50–75 ft. high, the smooth bark brown. Leaves elliptic or broader, 3–5½ in. long, colored purple when unfolding, sharply toothed. Flowers rose-pink, nearly 1½ in. wide, in stalkless clusters (umbels°) of 2–4, but very numerous. Fruit nearly round, about ½ in. in diameter, purplish-black. Jap. April–May. Hardy from zone° 4 southward.

serotina. Wild black cherry; also called choke cherry. An important American timber tree in parts of its range, elsewhere very weedy and widely planted by birds along fence-rows. In maturity, and in the forest, up to 90 ft. high, less as usually seen. Leaves oblongish, or narrower, 2½–5½ in. long, its numerous marginal teeth incurved. Flowers white, fragrant, sometimes unpleasantly so, about ½ in. wide, in long, hanging, finger-shaped clusters, blooming long after the leaves expand. Fruit round, about ⅓ in. in diameter, ultimately black, sour. Throughout eastern N.A. and hardy everywhere. The juice of its wilted foliage is dangerously poisonous.

†**serrulata.** Flowering cherry. Japanese flowering cherry. Typically, a tree up to 30 ft. high, much smaller in some of the numerous hort. varieties. Leaves ovalish or narrower, 2¾–5½ in. long, long-pointed, toothed or doubly toothed, the teeth short-bristly. Flowers typically white, 3–5 in a cluster (raceme°-like), the cluster with a few leafy bracts.° Fruit (often wanting) black. Jap., China, and Korea. The most commonly cult. variety is white and double-flowered. For this and many others see below. Hardy from zone° 3 southward.

†**sieboldi.** Resembling *P. serrulata*, but the twigs and under side of the leaves softly hairy. Unknown as a wild tree, but long cult. in Jap., where it is one of the flowering cherries. Hardy from zone° 3 southward, but not much known in the U.S.

spinosa. Sloe. Blackthorn (for an American plant known as black thorn see CRATAEGUS UNIFLORA). A thorny shrub or small tree, freely suckering at the base, usually less than 12 ft. high. Leaves numerous, small, scarcely over 1½ in. long. Flowers 1 to a cluster, but very numerous, blooming before the leaves unfold, white, about ⅔ in. wide. Fruit nearly round, about ¾ in. in diameter, bluish-black and with a bloom, but the flesh reddish, tart, and used to flavor sloe gin. Eurasia. Hardy from zone° 3 southward. The source of most Irish blackthorn walking-sticks.

†**subhirtella.** Rosebud cherry. A very showy Japanese tree, 20–30 ft. high, rarely shrubby. Leaves ovalish or oblong-oval, 1½–3 in. long, often doubly toothed, hairy on the veins beneath. Flowers 2–5 in a cluster, but very numerous, nearly 1 in. wide, light pink, the petals notched. Fruit about ⅓ in. in diameter, black. Jap. Hardy from zone° 3 southward. A particularly fine form is the *var.* **pendula,** with gracefully hanging branches, and more cult. than the typical form. The *var.* **autumnalis** is fall-flowering.

tenella. See PRUNUS NANA.

tomentosa. Nanking cherry. A shrub or small tree (cherry), not over 10 ft. high, cult. chiefly for ornament. Leaves numerous, rather crowded, more or less elliptic, 2½–3½ in. long, unequally toothed. Flowers 1–2 in a cluster, white or pinkish-white, about 1 in.

wide. Fruit nearly round, about ¾ in. in diameter, red and edible. China. Hardy from zone° 1 southward.

†**triloba.** Flowering almond. Usually a shrub, rarely a tree up to 10 ft. high. Leaves broadly oval, sometimes 3-lobed, coarsely double-toothed, 1½–2½ in. long, a little hairy beneath. Flowers 1 or 2 in an essentially stalkless cluster, pinkish, nearly 1½ in. wide, appearing before the leaves expand. Fruit hairy, red, about ½ in. in diameter, often lacking. China. Hardy from zone° 3 southward, but most cult. in the *var.* **flore-pleno,** a double-flowered pink shrub of great beauty. The flowering almond has been so long known to gardeners as *P. triloba* that it seems best to retain that name here, although its hairy fruit and other characters reveal the fact that it belongs with the almond and peach and technically should bear the name *Amygdalus.*

virginiana. Choke cherry. A shrub-like counterpart of *P. serotina*, rarely over 10 ft. high, still more rarely tree-like and 20 ft. high. The simplest way to distinguish its foliage from *P. serotina* is by the divaricate marginal teeth, which in *P. serotina* are incurved. Fruit dark purple-black, sour. Throughout northern N.A. and hardy everywhere. Of little decorative value, but children should be warned against the dangerously poisonous juice of its wilted leaves.

†**yedoensis.** Flowering cherry. Japanese flowering cherry. A very showy tree up to 40 ft. high, the young twigs slightly hairy. Leaves elliptic or broader toward the tip, 2½–5½ in. long, strongly double-toothed. Flowers 5–6 in a cluster (short and raceme°-like), white or pink, faintly fragrant. Fruit round and black, often wanting. Unknown as a wild tree, but long cult. in Jap. and supposed to have originated there by crossing *P. subhirtella* and *P. lannesiana.* Hardy from zone° 3 southward, and widely cult. in some of the many named Japanese forms (see below).

ORNAMENTALS

The shrubs and trees grouped under the general names of flowering cherry, Japanese flowering cherry, flowering plum, flowering apricot, and flowering almond are among the most decorative plants in cult. Most of the species from which such plants have been derived are marked with a dagger (†) in the above enumeration. But there are innumerable named forms, especially among the Japanese flowering cherries, nearly all derived from *Prunus lannesiana, P. serrulata,* and *P. yedoensis,* although other species could with equal justice be called Japanese flowering cherries, notably *P. sieboldi* and *P. subhirtella,* the latter usually called the rosebud cherry.

JAPANESE FLOWERING CHERRIES. The Japanese, who have grown these plants for centuries, have assigned hundreds of Japanese vernacular names to them, but most such names are more a source of confusion here than a help in identifying them. The following Japanese named forms, however, are widely grown under their Japanese varietal names. Some of the best are: Higan-sakura (also a fall-flowering form of it); Shidare-higan-sakura (a weeping form of Higan-sakura); Somei yoshino-sakura (derived from *P. yedoensis*); Fujisan-sakura (white-flowered); Asahi-Botan (a dwarf variety suitable

---

° Special articles on the subjects indicated by an asterisk (°) will be found at the words so marked.

for the rock garden); Amanogawa (resembling a Lombardy poplar in habit, flowers rose-pink); Naden (derived from *P. sieboldi;* a good shade tree); Kofugen (similar to Naden, but flowers deeper pink); and Shirofugen (resembling Kofugen, but flowers ultimately white). Kwanzan is one of the best double-flowered sorts, with deep rose-pink bloom. Two other varieties, without Japanese names, are Paul Wohlert (semi-dwarf with deep pink flowers) and Ruth Wohlert (with double, deep-pink flowers).

A Japanese flowering cherry tree and its blossom

The culture of these ornamentals presents no greater difficulties than are found among the fruit trees. *See* PLUM, CHERRY, APRICOT, PEACH, and ALMOND, the two last belonging to the genus *Amygdalus*, but closely related. All appear to favor well-drained soils and open sunlight. The shrubs do not need much space, but the tree-like, Japanese flowering cherries should be planted at least 20–25 ft. apart each way. Their magnificent bloom in early spring is helped by a good winter mulch of well-rotted manure. The finest collection in the country is that at the Tidal Basin, Washington, D.C., presented by the City of Tokyo in 1912. They usually bloom during the first two weeks in April.

For the pests of the ornamental species of *Prunus, see* those mentioned at CHERRY, PLUM, APRICOT, and PEACH.

prurita, -us, -um (pru-ry′ta). Itching; or causing it.

PSALLIOTA. *See* MUSHROOM.

PSEDERA = *Parthenocissus.*

Pseudacorus (sood-ak′o-rus). False sweet flag. *See* IRIS.

PSEUDERANTHEMUM (soo-der-ran′-thee-mum). A large genus of widely distributed tropical plants of the family Acanthaceae, a few grown in the greenhouse for their sometimes colored foliage or for their variously colored flowers. They are shrubby or herbaceous plants with opposite* leaves, having no marginal teeth (in ours), but the margins wavy in one of the cult. species. Flowers white or purplish in those below, the corolla tubular, its 5 lobes very nearly regular, sometimes 2 of them smaller than the other 3. Stamens* 4, 2 of them infertile. Fruit a stalked, oblong capsule.* (*Pseuderanthemum* is from the Greek for false and *Eranthemum,* a closely related genus.)

The culture is the same as for *Eranthemum* (which see).

atropurpureum. A smooth-stemmed shrub, 3–4 ft. high. Leaves broadly oval, 3–6 in. long, purple or pinkish-purple, usually blotched (rarely green or yellow-spotted). Flowers white, but with rose-purple center and spots, or purplish throughout, the corolla tube short, the lobes spreading and about 1½ in. wide. Polynesia.

bicolor. A smooth-stemmed shrub, 2–3 ft. high. Leaves narrowly ovalish, 4–8 in. long, tapering both ends, dark green. Flowers stalkless, in spikes which arise in the leaf axils.* Corolla with a slender tube, the limb salvershaped, about 1½ in. long, white, but the lower lobes purple-spotted. Polynesia (?).

reticulatum. A smooth-stemmed shrub, 2–3 ft. high, the branches angled. Leaves oval-lance-shaped, 6–10 in. long, tapering at the tip, the margins wavy, dark green but the veins golden. Flowers short-stalked in small clusters (panicles*), the corolla tubular, white, but the throat purple and one of the lobes purple-spotted. The tube is about ½ in. long, the expanded lobes about 1½ in. wide. New Hebrides.

Pseudo-acacia (soo-do-a-kā′sha). False acacia.

pseudo-armeria (soo-do-ar-meer′i-a). Resembling a thrift (*Armeria*); hence, a false thrift.

PSEUDOBULB. The swollen, stem-like, often grooved base of many orchids. It usually stores water and food upon which the plant thrives during the dry season. Pseudobulbs usually bear one or more leaves at the top, and the flowering stalk from the base or top. *See* ORCHID.

pseudocactus (soo-do-kak′tus). False cactus, or like a cactus.

Pseudo-camellia (soo-do-ka-mee′li-a). Like a camellia; a false camellia.

Pseudo-capsicum (soo-do-kap′si-kum). Pre-Linnaean* name for the Jerusalem cherry, meaning false pepper.

PSEUDOLARIX (soo-do-lar′ricks). Golden larch. A single species of Chinese, cone-bearing trees of the pine family, resembling the true larch in dropping its leaves in the fall. The only species, P. amabilis (often known as *P. kaempferi*), is a popular ornamental tree, 60–100 ft. high or more (in the wild), its branches in tiers. Leaves narrow, line-like, 1¼–2¾ in. long, scattered on long shoots, but clustered or whorled on the short, lateral spurs, turning bright golden-

---

* Special articles on the subjects indicated by an asterisk (*) will be found at the words so marked.

yellow in autumn. Male and female flowers separate on the same plant, the male flowers catkin-like, the female flowers solitary and consisting only of a naked ovule between the scales of the cone. Mature cone egg-shaped, reddish-brown, 2¾–3½ in. long, its woody scales notched at the tip. The golden larch is of simple culture in most garden soils, except those derived from limestone which should be avoided. (*Pseudolarix* is from the Greek for false and *Larix,* the closely related true larches.)

PSEUDOPHOENIX (soo-do-fee′nicks). One or perhaps more species of West Indian feather palms, the only cult. species **P. sargenti,** also a native of a few keys in Fla., and much cult. there from Miami southward. It is known as hog cabbage palm, buccaneer palm, and in Miami as the Sargent palm. It does not grow over 25 ft. high, the trunk about 12 in. in diameter, and usually bulged near the middle. Leaves in a terminal crown, the leaf about 4–6 ft. long, the larger leaflets or segments 16–18 in. long, less than this toward the top and bottom of the leaf. Fruits cherry-like, about ¾ in. in diameter, orange-red. It grows well in the sandy soils of Fla., and is often used as a substitute for the royal palm, although it is far less decorative than the latter. (*Pseudophoenix* is from the Greek for false and *Phoenix,* the date.)

Pseudo-platanus (soo-do-plat′a-nus). Literally, a false plane tree (*Platanus*); used as a specific name for the sycamore maple (which see).

PSEUDOSASA. *See* ARUNDINARIA.

PSEUDOTSUGA (soo-do-soo′ga). Magnificent evergreen trees of the pine family, comprising 6 species from western N.A. and eastern As. The only commonly cult. species is **P. taxifolia,** the Douglas or red fir, which is one of the most valuable timber trees of the Northwest, reaching a height of nearly 300 ft. and trunk diameters of 10–12 ft. This, the typical form of the coast ranges from British Columbia to Calif., is not a satisfactory evergreen in the eastern states, but a form of it from the Rocky Mountains does well in the East and should be specified when ordering. Leaves spirally arranged, straight, rarely curved, line-like, about ¾ in. long, with 2 pale bands beneath. Cones egg-shaped, 2½–4½ in. long, hanging, the scales rounded and concave. Seeds 2 under each scale. The Rocky Mountain form is hardy from zone° 4, southward; it grows more slowly than the timber tree of the Northwest. Of the several hort. varieties, two of the best are *var.* **fastigiata,** a pyramidal form, the branches upright; and *var.* **glauca** with bluish-green foliage, and also known in a form with pendulous branches. The Douglas fir was long, and is still sometimes known by the name *P. douglasi;* more recently it has been suggested to call it *P. menziesi,* not here adopted. (*Pseudotsuga*

is from the Greek for false and *Tsuga,* the hemlock, to which it is closely related.)

PSIDIUM. *See* GUAVA

PSORALEA (so-ray′lee-a). Scurfy pea. Indian turnip. Tropical and sub-tropical herbs, shrubs, or sub-shrubs, comprising about 150 species (about 30 of which are North American), belonging to the pea family. They are annuals, biennials, or perennials, usually marked with transparent black spots, and strongly fragrant. Roots sometimes tuberous. Leaves compound,° the leaflets ovalish or lance-shaped. Flowers in clusters or spikes, terminal, or growing from the axils° of the leaves. Individual flowers pea-like, blue, purplish or white, the keel darker. Fruit a short, 1-seeded pod. (*Psoralea* is from the Greek for warty, in reference to the spots.)

Not of much garden importance, but the shrubby species cult. as greenhouse plants. The herbaceous species may be propagated by division of the roots in early spring.

cuspidata. Herbaceous perennial, growing to 2 ft. high, the roots tuberous. Leaflets 5, ovalish. Flowers blue, in dense spikes. May–June. S. D. to Tex.

esculenta. Indian breadroot. Pomme blanche. Herbaceous perennial, to 1½ ft. high, with edible, tuberous roots. Leaflets 5, ovalish. Flowers bluish, in dense spikes. May–July. Prairies, east of the Rocky Mountains.

PSYCHOTRIA (sy-kō′tri-a). An enormous group of tropical shrubs and trees of the family Rubiaceae, related to coffee, but only a handful of the 500 known species in cult. for ornament. The one most likely to be met is **P. capensis,** the wild coffee, which is cult. in southern Fla. and not hardy elsewhere. It is an evergreen shrub or small tree, with ovalish, shining, opposite° leaves, a little broader toward the tip, 3–5 in. long. Flowers yellow, very small, tubular, in branched clusters (corymbs°), the ends of the branches each with an ultimate umbel°-like cluster. Fruit black, shining, fleshy (a drupe°). Its cultural requirements are the same as for *Ixora* (which see). South Africa. (*Psychotria* is from the Greek for life-preserving, in allusion to the medicinal properties of some non-hort. species.)

psycodes (sy-kō′deez). Fragrant.

Ptarmica (tar′mi-ka). Greek for sneeze-producing. See ACHILLEA.

ptarmicoides (tar-mi-koy′deez, but *see* OÏDES). Resembling the sneezewort (*Achillea Ptarmica*).

PTELEA (tee′lee-a). Perhaps 3 species of North American shrubs or small trees of the family Rutaceae, of secondary hort. interest, although **P. trifoliata,** the hop-tree or wafer ash, is planted for ornament. It is a coarse shrub or small tree, not over 20 ft. high, with strong-smelling foliage. Leaves alternate,° compound,° the 3 leaflets elliptic or oblong, essentially stalkless, 2–4½ in. long, usually faintly dotted. Flowers greenish-white, about ⅛ in. wide, inconspicuous.

° Special articles on the subjects indicated by an asterisk (°) will be found at the words so marked.

(For details *see* RUTACEAE.) Fruit a dry, notched, veiny samara* about ¾ in. long, nearly round, its 2 seeds plump. Que. to Fla. and westward. Hardy from zone* 2 southward and of easy cult. if grown in a moist, partly shady place. Propagated by autumn-sown seeds. (*Ptelea* is the Greek name for the elm tree and of uncertain application to the hop-tree.)

pterantha, -us, -um (ter-ran'tha). With winged flowers.

PTERETIS (ter-ree'tis). A small genus of Eurasian and North American hardy ferns of the family Polypodiaceae, two of them occasionally cult. in the outdoor fern garden. They have twice-compound foliage fronds which are borne in a circle that surrounds the fertile or spore-bearing fronds. The latter have the ultimate segments contracted and pod-like, and surround the spore* cases. Both those below are rather bold, coarse ferns suited to shady places. (*Pteretis* means *Pteris*-like.) The plants are sometimes known as *Matteuccia*.

For culture *see* FERNS AND FERN GARDENING.

pensylvanica. The ostrich fern of N.A. A tall, robust fern, the foliage fronds 6–10 ft. long (stalks 8–14 in. long), broadly lance-shaped, the ultimate segments usually with a rolled margin, narrow and deeply cut. Spore*-bearing, *i.e.*, fertile, fronds shorter, the pod-like segments almost necklace-like, brown. Eastern N.A. Often offered under the name of the next species, or as *P. nodulosa*.

Struthiopteris. The ostrich fern of Eu. Similar, but the foliage fronds 3–5 ft. long, the stalk 3–5 in. long. Eu. Often offered as *Onoclea Struthiopteris*.

PTERIDIUM. See BRAKE.

pteridoides (ter-ri-doy'deez, but *see* OÏDES). Resembling a fern of the genus *Pteris*.

PTERIS (teer'is). Mostly tropical ferns of the family Polypodiaceae, probably comprising over 250 species, a few of which are very commonly grown in greenhouses and for fern dishes under the name of brake, although the true brake or bracken is *Pteridium* (*see* BRAKE). They have once- or twice-compound* fronds, the ultimate segments of which have usually rolled margins beneath which are the spore* cases. The foliage of all the cult. species is very feathery, but lasting, and they are hence good plants for the home. (*Pteris* is from the Greek for wing, in reference to the feathery fronds.)

For culture *see* Greenhouse Ferns at FERNS AND FERN GARDENING. The two best-known and most useful are the forms of *P. cretica* and *P. serrulata*.

cretica. A widely distributed tropical and sub-tropical fern, its fronds not over 12 in. high, the stalks slender and straw-colored. Fronds once-compound,* the ultimate segments about ¼ in. wide, the lowermost often deeply cut. Commonly grown for fern dishes and centerpieces, especially in some of the crested or much-divided hort. forms.

ensiformis. A slender fern, the foliage fronds erect, 15–20 in. high, once-compound, the ultimate segments about ¼ in. wide. Spore*-bearing fronds shorter, but the segments nearly ⅜ in. wide. Indo-Malaya and Aust.

multifida = *Pteris serrulata*.

quadriaurita. A tropical, somewhat coarse fern, its fronds 2–3 ft. long and half as wide. Ultimate segments (pinnules*) scarcely ¼ in. wide and without teeth. Mostly grown, and chiefly by florists, in the *var.* argyraea which has the margins white-bordered.

serrulata. A slender fern, widely grown for fern dishes and centerpieces, the fronds nearly 18 in. high and 12 in. wide in maturity, usually half this as cult. Fronds once-compound,* the ultimate segments long and very narrow, the main stalk winged. Some of the lower segments are 2–3-forked. China and Jap. There are many crested, dwarf, or variegated hort. varieties. The plant is sometimes offered as *P. multifida*, which some consider the correct name for it.

wimsetti = A crested form of *P. cretica*.

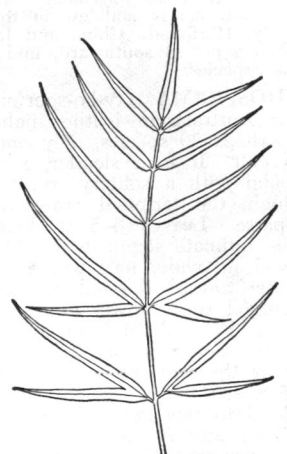

A narrow-fronded fern (*Pteris cretica*) widely used in fern dishes or for centerpieces. Some forms are crested.*

PTEROCARYA (teer-o-kar'i-a). Wing-nut. Horticulturally unimportant Asiatic trees of the family Juglandaceae, comprising 8 species, of which **P. stenoptera** is cult. for ornament. It is a tree up to 100 ft. high (in the wild), with alternate,* compound* leaves, the leaflets arranged feather-fashion and with an odd one at the end, the main stalk winged. Leaflets 11–23, oblongish, 3–4 in. long. Male and female flowers separate on the same tree, both in catkins. Fruit an oblong, winged, 1-seeded nutlet, arranged in racemes, 8–14 in. long. China. Hardy from zone* 4 southward, and propagated by seeds or by layers. *P. fraxinifolia*, from Persia, has no wings on the leafstalk, and prefers moist sites. (*Pterocarya* is from the Greek for wing and *Carya*, the hickory, in allusion to the winged nut.)

* Special articles on the subjects indicated by an asterisk (*) will be found at the words so marked.

PTEROSTYRAX (teer-ro-sty'racks). Three species of Asiatic shrubs or trees of the family Styracaceae, two of them cult. for ornament. They have alternate,* stalked leaves and fragrant white flowers in large clusters (panicles*). Petals 5, separate. Stamens* 10. Fruit an oblongish, dry drupe,* ribbed or winged. (*Pterostyrax* is from the Greek for wing and *Styrax,* a closely related genus.)

The two below prefer a reasonably moist site. The second species should be better known, for it is handsome during June when its fragrant, hanging clusters of flowers are in bloom. Propagated by seeds or by layers.

corymbosa. A shrub or small tree, the leaves elliptic or ovalish, 3–5 in. long, finely toothed, the teeth bristly. Flower cluster (a corymbose panicle*) 3–5 in. long, the stamens* unequal. Fruit densely hairy, 5-winged. Jap. and China. Hardy from zone* 3 southward.

hispida. Epaulette-tree. A tree up to 45 ft. high, the leaves oblongish, 5–7 in. long, minutely toothed, the teeth not bristly. Flower cluster hanging, 7–10 in. long, the flowers white, fragrant, nearly stalkless in the cluster. Fruit bristly, 10-ribbed. China and Jap. June. Hardy from zone* 3 southward, and the most widely cult. species.

PTYCHOSPERMA (ty-ko-sper'ma). East Indian or Australasian feather palms, comprising perhaps 20 species, only one, **P. elegans,** in cult. It is a slender, ringed, unarmed palm with a solitary trunk not over 20 ft. high, the terminal crown of leaves rather sparse. Leaves 3–5 ft. long, bright green, the ultimate segments 18–24 in. long and 1⅓–3 in. wide, narrowed at the base but broader toward the oblique, cut-off, or deeply jagged tip. Flower cluster not over 20 in. long. Fruit about ¾ in. long. Eastern Aust. Cult. outdoors and hardy only in zone* 9 or the warmest parts of zone* 8. For culture *see* PALM. Several other plants are credited to this genus but belong elsewhere. They are: *P. alexandrae* = *Archontophoenix alexandrae; P. macarthuri* = *Actinophloeus macarthuri.* Most plants offered as *Balaka seemanni* belong here. (*Ptychosperma* is from the Greek for folded seed, in allusion to a technical character of the seed.)

pubens (pew'benz). Downy or sparsely soft-hairy.

puberula, -*us,* -*um* (pew-ber'you-la). Somewhat hairy.

pubescens (pew-bes'senz). Pubescent.*

PUBESCENT. Covered with soft hairs.

PUCCOON. *See* LITHOSPERMUM.

PUDDING-PIPE TREE = *Cassia Fistula.*

PUDDLING. *See* PLANTING.

pudica, -*us,* -*um* (pew'di-ka). Bashful or retiring.

PUERARIA (poo-er-ray'ri-a). A genus of Asiatic and East Indian rapid-growing vines of the pea family, **P. thunbergiana,** the kudsu-vine of China and Jap., often cult. for ornament. It is a somewhat woody,

hairy-stemmed vine, often climbing to a great height, not certainly hardy north of zone* 5, and often killed to the ground south of this, but growing again from its thick, starch-yielding root. Leaves compound,* the 3 leaflets broadly oval or nearly round, 3–6 in. long, hairy, with a small point. Flowers pea-like, purple, about ⅝ in. in diameter, fragrant, in dense, upright clusters (racemes*) nearly 10 in long. Pod (legume*) hairy, flat, oblongish, 1¾–4 in. long. The vine (sometimes known as *P. hirsuta* and *P. lobata*) is a quick grower and useful for making a dense shade over arbors. More useful for temporary than permanent planting, but widely grown in the South, chiefly as a valuable forage crop, but often a weedy pest in southern gardens. Propagated by division or by seeds. (Named for M. N. Puerari, Swiss botanist.)

PUERTO RICAN ROYAL PALM = *Roystonea borinquena.*

pugioniformis, -*e* (pew-ji-o-ni-for'mis). Dagger-shaped.

PUKA = *Griselinia lucida.*

pulchella, -*us,* -*um* (pull-kell'a). Beautiful, or merely pretty.

pulcher (pull'care). Beautiful.

pulcherrima, -*us,* -*um* (pull-ker'ri-ma). Most beautiful.

pulla, -*us,* -*um* (pull'a). Nearly black.

pulloides (pull-oy'deez). Approaching blackness.

PULMONARIA (pul-mo-nay'ri-a). Lungwort. Low-growing perennial herbs, comprising about 10 species of the family Boraginaceae, and natives of Eu. They have creeping rootstocks, and are more or less hairy. Basal leaves long-stalked, broadly lance-shaped, sometimes mottled. Upper leaves few and alternate.* Flowers blue or purplish, in terminal, coiled clusters, which straighten as the flowers open. Calyx of 5 sepals.* Corolla funnel-shaped, sometimes with a hairy throat. Stamens* 5, not protruding. Fruit 2-celled when young, splitting into 4 parts when ripe, each part containing 1 seed. (*Pulmonaria* is from the Latin for lung, in allusion to the plants being a supposed remedy for diseases of the lungs.)

Pulmonarias make useful spring-flowering, border plants. Easily cult. in ordinary garden soil. Propagated by division of roots in Sept., or early spring, or by seeds sown in a cold frame or outdoor seedbed in early spring. They may be transplanted to permanent positions as soon as large enough to handle.

angustifolia. Grows 6–12 in. high. Leaves lance-shaped. Flowers blue. April–May. Useful border plant. The *vars.* **alba, aurea,** and **azurea** are hort. forms.

officinalis. Grows 6–12 in. high. Basal leaves with long stalks, tufted, lance-shaped, mottled, and covered with coarse hairs. Flowers purplish-red, in terminal, branching clusters.

saccharata. Bethlehem sage. Grows to 1½ ft. high. Basal leaves broadly lance-shaped,

---

* Special articles on the subjects indicated by an asterisk (*) will be **found at the words** so marked.

mottled, white. Flowers white or reddish-purple, in terminal clusters. April–May. Prefers shade.

PULQUE AGAVE = *Agave atrovirens.*

PULSATILLA (pul-sa-till′a). Pasque-flower. Anemone-like herbs of the buttercup family, now included in the genus *Anemone* (which see).

PULSE CROPS. *See* LEGUMES.

pulverulenta, -us, -um (pull-ver-you-len′ta). Dusty or powdered.

pulvinata, -us, -um (pull-vi-nay′ta). Like a cushion.

pumila, -us, -um (pew′mi-la). Small.

pumilio (pew-mill′i-o). Small or dwarf.

PUMMELO = *Citrus maxima.*

PUMPKIN. The common field pumpkin, which is too sprawling for the average garden, is derived mostly from *Cucurbita Pepo* (which includes the common sort), *C. maxima* (which includes very large squashes that often pass as pumpkins), and *C. moschata* (large-fruited varieties of squash that also pass as pumpkins). For the technical differences between these *see* CUCURBITA.

The common sort of pumpkin often develops huge fruits which differ from the closely related winter squashes in not keeping over the winter and in being usually orange in color and furrowed. But all the plants in this series have been much hybridized so that their exact identity is often in doubt.

From the garden standpoint all are grown in the same way. They are plants of tropical origin and must be grown only in our warmest season. Two or three seeds can be planted about 2 in. deep, in hills that are at least 6 ft. apart each way, or they may be interplanted with corn as most farmers do. They will stand any amount of heat, but are retarded by cool weather. In other words, do not plant them until the ground is really warm.

For those who want especially large fruits a good plan is to sow pumpkin seeds on hills made over the spent manure from a mushroom bed or from a hotbed. The plants are rich feeders, but if grown in manure the rank excess of vine should be pinched back or more foliage will be produced than fruit. One of the best varieties for pumpkin pie is Small Sugar. Other desirable vars. are Connecticut Field and Winter Luxury.

Some people prefer the bushy sorts, but they do not produce such large fruits as the normal, widely sprawling, prostrate vines. If you live in zone[*] 3 or north of it, pumpkin seeds are best planted in paper pots in the hotbed or greenhouse and transplanted to the open ground when warm weather arrives. Otherwise, they may not finish fruit-ripening before the first frost.

INSECT PESTS. *See* SQUASH.

DISEASES. *See* CUCUMBER.

punctata, -us, -um (punk-tay′ta). Punctate; *i.e.*, dotted or spotted.

punctilobula, -us, -um (punk-ti-lob′you-la). With dotted or spotted lobes.

pungens (pun′jenz). Pungent.[*]

PUNGENT. Sharp-pointed; also with a sharp or acrid taste.

PUNICA. *See* POMEGRANATE.

PUNICACEAE (pew-ni-kay′see-ee). The pomegranate family consists only of the genus *Punica*, which comprises only 2 species. One of them is *P. Granatum*, the pomegranate, while the other is a little-known plant from the island of Socotra. For a description of *P. Granatum see* POMEGRANATE.

punicea, -us, -um (pew-niss′ee-a). Purplish-red.

PUNK-TREE = *Melaleuca Leucadendron.*

PUPA (plural pupae). An intermediate, usually inactive stage in the life history of many insects. While most insect pests do little damage during the pupal stage, that period is often the best one in which to destroy them. The cocoon of the butterfly is a common example of the condition of an insect while it is still a pupa. *See* INSECT PESTS.

PURGING-NUT = *Jatropha Curcas.*

PURPLE. As an adjective *purple* is used as part of the name of many plants that are of interest to the gardener. Those in this book, and their proper equivalents, are:

Purple apricot = *Prunus dasycarpa;* Purple beech = *Fagus sylvatica atropunicea* (*see* BEECH); Purple boneset = *Eupatorium purpureum;* Purple cestrum = *Cestrum purpureum;* Purple chokeberry = *Aronia prunifolia;* Purple coneflower (*see* ECHINACEA); Purple coral-pea = *Hardenbergia monophylla;* Purple daisy = *Echinacea angustifolia;* Purple foxglove = *Digitalis purpurea* (*see* FOXGLOVE); Purple fringed orchis = *Habenaria fimbriata;* Purple granadilla = *Passiflora edulis;* Purple loosestrife = *Lythrum Salicaria;* Purple medic = *Medicago sativa;* Purple mombin = *Spondias purpurea;* Purple mullein = *Verbascum phoenicum;* Purple ragwort = *Senecio elegans;* Purple rock cress (*see* AUBRIETA); Purple trillium = *Trillium erectum;* Purple willow-herb = *Lythrum Salicaria;* Purple wood sorrel = *Oxalis violacea;* Purple wreath = *Petrea volubilis.*

purpurascens (pur-pure-ras′senz). Purplish.

purpurea, -us, -um (pur-pure′ee-a). Purple.

purpureo-coerulea, -us, -um (pur-pure-ee-o-see-roo′lee-a). Purplish-blue.

PURSHIA (pur′shi-a). A single species of straggling, western American shrubs of the rose family, *P. tridentata*, the antelope-brush, is grown for ornament. It is a silvery-foliaged shrub, 4–6 ft. high, with alternate,[*] very small, stiff, narrow leaves that are ¼–⅝ in. long and 3-toothed at the tip. Flowers yellow, solitary, about ½ in. wide, the 5 petals thin, not showy. Stamens[*] about 25. Fruit a hairy achene,[*] longer than the persistent calyx. Rocky Mountain region to Ore. and

---

[*] Special articles on the subjects indicated by an asterisk (*) will be found at the words so marked.

Calif. May. Hardy from zone* 4 southward. The *var.* **glandulosa** has even smaller and sticky leaves, is little known in cult., and not so hardy as the typical form. (Named for F. T. Pursh, a German botanist who traveled in, and wrote much about the plants of N.A.)

PURSLANE = *Portulaca.* See *also* the list at WEEDS. For the winter purslane *see* MONTIA.

PURSLANE FAMILY = Portulacaceae.

PURSLANE TREE = *Portulacaria afra.*

PUSCHKINIA (push-kin′i-a). A small genus of spring-blooming, bulbous herbs of the lily family, comprising two species, one of which, **P. scilloides,** the striped squill, is cult. for ornament (for culture *see* below). It has basal leaves, about 12 in. long and 1 in. wide, and small, striped, bluish, bell-shaped flowers, about ½ in. long in a terminal cluster (raceme*) at the end of the flowering stalk, not very showy. Asia Minor. (Named for Count A. A. M. Pushkin, Russian chemist.)

PUSCHKINIA CULTURE

The striped squill is not a showy garden ornament, but it very distinctly has its uses. These small cousins of *Scilla,* with their pale striped bells gathered in dense trusses on the slender 4 to 6 in. stems, are capable of making a modest but charming display. Planted in close colonies on a sunny plain in the rock garden, with a foreground of pink *Arabis,* they show to advantage. If used in a border it should be in large numbers if they are to be effective, and they should not be placed in competition with coarse growths. They bloom in early April. The bulbs are quite hardy as far north as Canada. They should be planted 3 in. deep and 3 in. apart in September or early October. A sandy, nourishing soil is the best for them, and they thrive equally well in sun or half shade. The bulbs need not be disturbed for several years, unless flowering is falling off, when they may be dug up after the foliage has fully ripened, and replanted in fresh soil. The bulblets may then be detached from the old bulbs for purposes of propagation. — L. B. W.

pusilla, -us, -um (pew-sill′a). Very small or dwarf.

PUSSLEY = Purslane. *See* the list at WEEDS.

PUSSYTOES = *Antennaria.*

PUSSY WILLOW. *See* WILLOW.

PUTTYROOT = *Aplectrum hyemale.*

PUYA (pew′ya). Mostly Chilean desert plants of the family Bromeliaceae, comprising over 80 species of spiny, rather large herbs, two or three occasionally grown in the cool greenhouse. They inhabit cool, dry, stony slopes of the upper Andes and, while herbs, have stout, somewhat woody stems in maturity. Leaves in a dense rosette, spiny-tipped and spiny-margined, stiff, long, and narrow. Flowers blue or greenish-yellow in those below, in terminal spikes or racemes,* the cluster bracted.* Flower segments mostly free. Fruit a somewhat fleshy, 6-valved capsule.* Often dying after fruiting and propagated by stolons.* (*Puya* is the Chilean vernacular of some of the species.)

For culture *see* SUCCULENTS.

alpestris. Nearly stemless, the leaves 18–24 in. long, about 1 in. wide, pale on the under side. Flowers blue, about 1½ in. long, with a metallic sheen, the anthers* orange. Flower cluster much-branched. Chile.

chilensis. With a distinct, stout stem, 3–5 ft. high. Leaves nearly 4 ft. long, very narrow, bluish-green. Flowers greenish-yellow, about 2 in. long, the cluster branching. Chile.

PYCNANTHEMUM (pick-nan′thee-mum). Mountain mint. North American hardy, herbaceous perennials, comprising about 20 species of the mint family. Leaves fragrant, simple,* entire, opposite,* smooth or hairy. Flowers white or purple, small, in many-flowered whorls, with numerous bracts,* forming small terminal heads. Calyx of 5 sepals.* Corolla 2-lipped. Stamens 4, in pairs, 2 long and 2 short. Fruit 2-celled when young, splitting into 4 parts when ripe. (*Pycnanthemum* is from the Greek for dense and blossom, in allusion to the dense flower heads.)

They are not of much garden importance, but are grown as border plants for their fragrant foliage. Easily propagated from seeds, which may be sown in a cold frame or outdoor seedbed in early spring. They may be transplanted to permanent positions as soon as large enough to handle, in ordinary garden soil.

flexuosum. Slender-growing herb, to 2½ ft. high. Leaves narrow, 1–2 in. long. Flowers white, in small, crowded heads. Fields, southeastern U.S.

incanum. Grows to 3 ft. high. Leaves to 3 in. long, and 1½ in. wide, covered with white hairs on the under side. Flowers white, in loose clusters, 1½ in. across. Eastern U.S.

virginianum. Strong-growing, to 3 ft. high. Leaves to 2 in. long, lance-shaped. Flowers lilac-white, in small, dense heads. Eastern U.S.

pycnocarpon (pick-no-kar′pon). With densely crowded or many fruits.

pycnostachya, -us, -um (pick-no-stack′i-a). Thick-spiked.

pygmaea, -us, -um (pig-mee′a). Small.

PYRACANTHA (py-ra-kan′tha). Firethorn. A small genus of Asiatic evergreen, thorny shrubs of the rose family, most of the species cult. for their fine foliage and ornamental fruits. They have alternate,* short-stalked leaves, and small, white flowers in branched clusters (compound corymbs*). Petals 5, nearly round. Stamens* 20, the anthers* yellow. Fruit fleshy (a pome*), red or orange, usually crowned with the persistent calyx. (*Pyracantha* is from the Greek for fire and thorn, in allusion to the thorny twigs and showy fruit.)

---

* Special articles on the subjects indicated by an asterisk (*) will be found at the words so marked.

The fire-thorns are closely related to *Cotoneaster* and need the same general culture. But several of them are not hardy everywhere, and the notes on hardiness should be studied carefully. For the best method of propagation *see* Softwood Cuttings at CUTTINGS.

angustifolia. A shrub 8–12 ft. high, its branches sometimes prostrate. Leaves narrowly oblong, or wedge-shaped at the base, sometimes notched at the tip, 1½–2 in. long, ashy beneath. Flower cluster densely felty. Fruit orange or brick-red, about ⅓ in. in diameter. China. May. Hardy from zone* 6 southward.

atalantioides. An evergreen shrub, 10–15 ft. high, its handsome elliptic or oblongish leaves 1–4 in. long, pale beneath, without teeth or with finely wavy-margined teeth. Flowers numerous in profuse clusters (corymbs*), white. Fruit about ½ in. thick, scarlet or crimson, winter-persistent. China. May–June. Hardy from zone* 5 southward. Some of the material offered as *P. gibbsi* belongs here.

coccinea. Everlasting thorn. The best-known species in cult., and a shrub 12–20 ft. high. Leaves ovalish, 1–1½ in. long, toothed, ultimately without hairs. Flower cluster hairy. Fruit bright red, about ⅓ in. in diameter. Eurasia. May. Hardy from zone* 4 southward. The *var.* lalandi has the leaves less deeply toothed, and bears orange-red fruit. It is hardier and more vigorous than the typical form. *Var.* aurea has yellow fruit. All do well when trained against a wall, especially the *var.* lalandi. *See* VINES. Also called *Cotoneaster Pyracantha.*

crenato-serrata. A handsome shrub, 5–9 ft. high, its young twigs rusty-hairy. Leaves broadest toward the tip, 1–3 in. long, the margins wavy, but not toothed. Flowers about ½ in. wide, the clusters 1½–2½ in. wide. Fruit nearly round, about ½ in. thick, brick-red. China. May–June. Hardy from zone* 5 southward. Some of the material offered as *P. gibbsi* and as *P. yunnanensis* belongs here.

crenulata. A small tree, more often a shrub, its young twigs rusty-hairy. Leaves oblongish, bristle-tipped, 1–3 in. long, with finely-toothed and wavy margin. Flowers nearly ¾ in. wide, in loose and rather sparse clusters. Fruit nearly round, about ½ in. thick, orange-red. Himalayas. May–June. Hardy from zone* 6 southward. Not so freely fruiting as *P. crenato-serrata.* The *var.* rogersiana, from southwestern China, has somewhat larger, red-orange fruit.

formosana = *Pyracantha koidzumi.*

gibbsi. A confused name in the trade, some of the plants so offered being *P. atalantioides,* others *P. crenato-serrata.*

koidzumi. A shrub, the leaves mostly clustered at the ends of the twigs. Leaves oblongish, or broader toward the tip, about 1 in. long, without marginal teeth, hairy and pale on the lower side. Flower cluster nearly without hairs. Formosa. Hardy from zone* 7 (?) southward. Sometimes known as *P. formosana.*

yunnanensis = *P. crenato-serrata.*

INSECT PESTS. For lace bugs *see* RHODODENDRON.

DISEASES. Scab* on fire-thorn will cause black spotting of leaves and blackening and dropping of fruit. Use pesticide #5 (*see* SPRAYS AND DUSTS) just as new growth begins and treat twice more at 10-day intervals.

pyramidalis, -e (pir-ra-mi-day′lis). Like a pyramid.

pyrenaica, -us, -um (py-re-nay′i-ka). From the Pyrenees.

PYRETHRUM. A very old garden name, and also once a generic name, but of confused application. As now understood, the common garden pyrethrum is *Chrysanthemum coccineum* (which see). Most plants once credited to the genus *Pyrethrum* are now included in *Chrysanthemum* or *Matricaria.*

PYRETHRUM INSECTICIDES. A short residual but excellent contact insect-killer of low toxicity to man. Available as dust or spray. *See* INSECTICIDES.

pyrifolia, -us, -um (py-ri-fō′li-a). With pear-like leaves.

pyriformis, -e (py-ri-for′mis). Pyriform; *i.e.,* pear-shaped.

PYROLA (pī′ro-la). Shinleaf. Hardy, low-growing perennials of the northern hemisphere, comprising about 40 species of the family Ericaceae. Rootstocks spreading. Basal leaves in clusters, evergreen, roundish. Flowers nodding, whitish, green, or purplish, solitary or in terminal racemes,* on a stalk having scale-like bracts.* (*Pyrola* is a diminutive of *Pyrus,* the pear, in allusion to supposed resemblance of leaves.)

Pyrolas are not of any garden importance, and can be used only in the wild garden. They are not easy of cult. as they do not like being transplanted and are near to being saprophytes.* They thrive best in sandy peat or in rich woods soil, in a shady position.

americana. Consumption-weed. Indian lettuce. Canker lettuce. Strong-growing, to 12 in. high. Basal leaves roundish, to 2 in. long, with leafstalk longer than the thick, dark, glossy, green leaf blade. Flowers numerous, white, waxy, sweet-scented, in loose terminal racemes. Aug. Eastern N.A. Considered as the American form of the Eurasian *P. rotundifolia,* by some.

elliptica. Lesser wintergreen. Grows 8–10 in. high. Leaves ovalish, with leafstalk shorter than the thin, dull, olive-green leaf blade. Flowers greenish-white, waxy, fragrant, in loose 5–10-flowered clusters. June–July. N.A.

rotundifolia. This is probably the Eurasian form of our native *Pyrola americana* (which see).

PYROLACEAE. *See* ERICACEAE.

PYROSTEGIA (py-ro-stee′gi-a). Extremely showy, South American tendril*-bearing, woody vines of the family Bignoniaceae, comprising about 20 species, of which *P. ignea,* the flame-vine of Brazil, is cult. for ornament outdoors in zone* 9 and the most protected part of zone* 8. It is a quick-growing, high-climbing, evergreen vine, its tendrils 3-forked and clinging to stone or wood. Leaves compound,* the 2–3 leaflets ovalish, 1 in. long, pointed at the tip. Flowers in dense clusters, tubular, nearly 3 in. long, reddish-orange, slightly 2-lipped,* the lobes of the corolla turned backward, and white-margined with hairs. Fruit a long, slender pod, 8–12 in. In Fla. it blooms pro-

---

* Special articles on the subjects indicated by an asterisk (*) will be found at the words so marked.

fusely for several weeks in midwinter, and often again in summer, but more sparsely, and is considered to be, next to *Bougainvillaea,* the finest vine in cult. there. (*Pyrostegia* is from the Greek for fire and roof, in allusion to the color of the flowers.) Often known as *Bignonia venusta.*

PYRUS (py′rus). Pear. An Old World genus of trees (rarely shrubs) of the rose family, of outstanding hort. importance because it contains the pear and a few other, mostly ornamental, plants, or trees used as stock for pear grafting. There are about 20 known species, of which only 4 are in common cult., and of these the fruit tree is far the most important. They have alternate,* stalked leaves and white flowers in umbel-like clusters which bloom with or before the expanding of the leaves. Petals 5, nearly round, but narrowed to a claw.* Stamens* 20–30, the anthers red or dark-colored. Fruit a pear-shaped pome,* technically differing from the closely related apple only in the possession of stone or grit cells in the flesh. (*See* STONE CELLS.) (*Pyrus* is the classical Latin name [spelled *Piris*] of the pear tree.)

For the cult. of the pear and the trees related to it *see* PEAR.

For the many other plants once, and sometimes still, credited to *Pyrus see* below.

calleryana. A Chinese tree, showy when in bloom, but of chief interest as possible grafting stock for the common pear. Leaves ovalish or broader, 1½–3½ in. long, bluntly toothed. Flowers nearly 1 in. wide. Fruit nearly globe-shaped, brown-spotted, ⅓–½ in. in diameter. April. Hardy from zone* 3 southward.

communis. Common pear tree. A broad-headed, sometimes long-lived tree, up to 45 ft. high, rarely somewhat higher. Leaves roundish or ovalish, a little wedge-shaped at the base, rather hard-textured, 1–3½ in. long. Flowers nearly 1 in. wide, appearing with the leaves. Fruit pear-shaped, but very variable in the cult. sorts. Eurasia. April. Hardy from zone* 3 southward, and in some hort. forms hardy to zone* 2. For culture and best varieties *see* PEAR. Old and escaped trees are sometimes a little spiny.

nivalis. Snow pear. A small, often white-felty tree with ovalish, pointed leaves, 2½–3¾ in. long, wedge-shaped at the base. Flowers showy, nearly 1½ in. wide. Fruit nearly globe-shaped, 1–2 in. in diameter. Eastern Eu. and Asia Minor. April. Hardy from zone* 3 southward. Somewhat planted for ornament and its fruit used for making pear cider. Also known as *Malus nivalis.*

pyrifolia. Japanese pear; also called sand pear. A Chinese tree (long cult. in Jap.) with oval-oblong, pointed leaves 3–5½ in. long, sharply bristly toothed. Flowers about 1½ in. wide, appearing with or just before the leaves. Fruit apple-shaped, brownish, the flesh hard. April. Hardy from zone* 2 southward, and the origin of many cult. varieties, the Kieffer among them. For the place that Japanese pears have made in American fruit culture *see* PEAR. Formerly known as *Pyrus serotina.*

PYRUS AND ITS ALLIES

The ancient Greeks and Romans distinguished two distinct genera to include the apples and pears. To the first they gave the name *Malus,* and to the pears, *Pyrus.* In modern times some botanists have included all these plants in *Pyrus,* a proceeding not followed here; others have included some in *Malus,* others in *Aronia* and in still other genera. The confusion in naming is thus very great. The four species listed above are the ones here considered as properly assigned to the genus *Pyrus.*

But many other plants will be found in various catalogues, books, experiment station bulletins, etc., under the name *Pyrus.* So far as these are in the ENCYCLOPEDIA, they should be looked for as indicated below:

Pyrus americana = Sorbus americana. *See* MOUNTAIN-ASH.
Pyrus arbutifolia = Aronia arbutifolia.
Pyrus Aria = Sorbus Aria. *See* MOUNTAIN-ASH.
Pyrus atropurpurea = Aronia prunifolia.
Pyrus atrosanguinea = Malus atrosanguinea.
Pyrus Aucuparia = Sorbus Aucuparia. *See* MOUNTAIN-ASH.
Pyrus coronaria = Malus coronaria.
Pyrus dawsoniana = Malus dawsoniana.
Pyrus decora = Sorbus decora. *See* MOUNTAIN-ASH.
Pyrus floribunda = Malus floribunda.
Pyrus fusca = Malus fusca.
Pyrus halliana = Malus halliana.
Pyrus ioensis = Malus ioensis.
Pyrus kaido = Malus micromalus.
Pyrus malus = Malus pumila.
Pyrus melanocarpa = Aronia melanocarpa.
Pyrus micromalus = Malus micromalus.
Pyrus nigra = Aronia melanocarpa.
Pyrus prunifolia = Malus prunifolia.
Pyrus purpurea = Malus purpurea.
Pyrus sargenti = Malus sargenti.
Pyrus sieboldi = Malus sieboldi.
Pyrus spectabilis = Malus spectabilis.
Pyrus toringoides = Malus toringoides.
Pyrus trilobata = Malus trilobata.
Pyrus Zumi = Malus Zumi.

PYXIDANTHERA (pix-i-dan′ther-ra). A small genus of evergreen, cushion-forming, prostrate plants of the family Diapensiaceae, commonly called pyxie, pine-barren beauty or flowering moss. The only cult. species is **P. barbulata.** It grows in moist, sandy, somewhat acid soils, from the pine-barrens of N.J. to S. Car., and is only suited to such sites in the rock garden or wild garden. Leaves alternate,* crowded, very narrow, scarcely ¼ in. long. Flowers not clustered, very numerous, but actually solitary, white or pinkish, bell-shaped, scarcely ⅛ in. wide. Fruit a tiny, globe-shaped capsule.* April. An attractive, evergreen, trailing plant for specialized sites, but unsuited to the ordinary garden. (*Pyxidanthera* is from the Greek for a small box and anther,* in allusion to the lid-like opening of the latter.) There is another species in N. Car.

PYXIE = *Pyxidanthera barbulata.*

PYXIE FAMILY = Diapensiaceae.

---

* Special articles on the subjects indicated by an asterisk (*) will be found at the words so marked.

Q

QUACK GRASS = *Agropyron repens.* *See* list at WEEDS.

quadrangularis, -e (kwad-rang-you-lar′is). Four-angled.

quadrangulata, -us, -um (kwad-rang-you-lay′ta). Four-angled.

quadriaurita, -us, -um (kwad-ri-or-ree′ta). Four-eared, or lobed.

quadricolor (kwad-rick′o-lor). Four-colored.

quadrifida, -us, -um (kwad-riff′i-da). Cut into four segments.

quadrifolia, -us, -um (kwad-ri-fō′li-a). Four-leaved, or with four leaflets.

QUAIL-BRUSH = *Atriplex breweri.*

QUAKE GRASS = *Bromus brizaeformis.*

QUAKER BONNETS = *Lupinus perennis.*

QUAKER LADIES = *Houstonia caerulea.*

QUAKING ASPEN = *Populus tremuloides.*

QUAKING GRASS. See BRIZA.

Quamash (kwa′mash). Probably the original, and Indian, form of camas. *See* CAMASSIA QUAMASH.

QUAMASIA = *Camassia.*

QUAMOCLIT (kwam′o-klit). Star-glory. Tropical American annual or perennial vines, comprising about 12 species of the family Convolvulaceae, with tall-growing, climbing stems. Leaves alternate,* simple or compound.* Flower clusters in the axils* of the leaves, long-stalked, sometimes branching. Individual flowers red or yellow, the corolla salver-shaped. Fruit a dry capsule.* (*Quamoclit* is of uncertain origin.)

They are useful climbers, as they can be grown as annuals and used as a covering for trellises or screens. Easily propagated from seeds sown in a cool greenhouse or cold frame in early spring. They may be transplanted to permanent position as soon as danger of frost is over. Mostly planted in the southern states, and in Calif.

coccinea. Star ipomoea. An annual vine growing to 10 ft. high. Leaves simple,* heart-shaped, 4–6 in. long, sometimes angularly lobed. Flowers about 1½ in. long, scarlet, but with a yellow throat. Tropical America; naturalized in the southern states. Sometimes known as *Ipomoea coccinea.*

lobata. Strong-growing perennial, growing 15–20 ft. high. Leaves heart-shaped, to 3 in. across, divided into 3 lobes. Flowers on opening crimson, fading to pale yellow, to ¾ in. wide, with a short tube. Stamens* prominent. July–Sept. Mex.

pennata. Cypress-vine. Annual, growing to 20 ft. high. Leaves compound.* Leaflets opposite, many, and thread-like. Flowers scarlet,

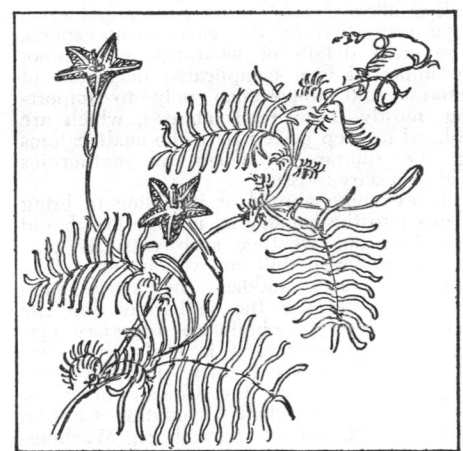

Cypress vine (*Quamoclit pennata*)

funnel-shaped, to 1½ in. long. Tropical America, but naturalized in the southern states, and widely planted in Calif.

sloteri. Cardinal climber. A hybrid vine derived from crossing *Q. coccinea* and *Q. pennata.* It has leaves deeply lobed, the segments 7–15, and scarcely ½ in. wide. Flowers nearly 2 in. long, scarlet without, but the throat white. July–Sept.

QUANTITY OF SEED. For the amount of seed needed for different crops and different-sized gardens *see* GARDEN TABLES I.

QUARANTINES. In November of 1918 the U.S. Department of Agriculture, after several public hearings, passed a plant quarantine act which provided that on and after June 1, 1919, certain restrictions would be enforced regarding the entry of plant material from foreign countries into the U.S. The purpose of the act was to protect the existing plants in this country from infestation by insect and plant disease pests that had not already been introduced. Its great objective was the preservation of many agricultural crops, and also ornamentals, from the ravages of foreign pests.

The main feature of the quarantine so far as ornamental plants are concerned was the exclusion from the country of all ball and burlap nursery stock. The soil by which such material is surrounded is reasonably sure to carry spores* or dormant states of insect pests, and when the stock is unpacked and grown, the pests are sure to spread, and many times have become very serious. Such restrictions stopped the importation of azaleas, rhododendrons, box, evergreens, many broad-leaved ever-

* Special articles on the subjects indicated by an asterisk (*) will be found at the words so marked.

greens, and all other shrubs and trees whose roots must be surrounded by soil or sphagnum moss while in transit. The quarantine also provided for the exclusion of many other plants, or propagative parts of them, because of specific dangers. And for some plants importation, while permitted, is allowed only under permit and upon rigid inspection by the government experts. The exact details of what can and cannot be imported is a complicated document of interest and importance only to importing, mostly commercial interests, which are obliged to keep posted as to the modifications of the quarantine which the authorities find necessary to issue.

Those going abroad or intending to bring plants into the country by importation should first find out whether such entry is permitted, under permit or without one. The rules, to meet sudden emergencies, are changed whenever the authorities see the need. Unless you obtain the necessary permission and permits, it is likely that your stock will be refused entry. For the latest regulations write to the Chief, Bureau of Entomology and Plant Quarantine Control, U.S. Department of Agriculture, Washington, D.C.

In addition to these government regulations, nearly every state has special or local quarantines. They change frequently and if you contemplate moving plant material from one state to another it is wise to write to the experiment stations of both states for the latest regulations. *See* the name of your state for the address of the experiment station.

QUEBEC. *See* ONTARIO.

QUEEN ANNE'S-LACE. *See* CARROT.

QUEEN ANNE'S POCKET MELON = Pomegranate melon. *See* MELON.

QUEEN-CUP = *Clintonia uniflora.*

QUEEN-OF-THE-MEADOW = *Filipendula Ulmaria* and *Spiraea salicifolia.*

QUEEN-OF-THE-NIGHT = *Cestrum nocturnum.*

QUEEN-OF-THE-PRAIRIE = *Filipendula rubra.*

QUEEN OLIVE. Large-fruited olives derived from the varieties Sevillano and Ascolano. *See* OLIVE.

QUEEN PALM = *Arecastrum romanzoffianum.*

QUEEN'S-FLOWER = *Lagerstroemia speciosa.*

QUEENSLAND NUT = *Macadamia ternifolia.*

QUEEN'S-WREATH = *Petrea volubilis.*

QUEEN VICTORIA ARBORVITAE = *Thuja occidentalis alba.*

QUENOUILLE TRAINING. A French system of pruning and tying to produce, in ornamental shrubs and trees, a nearly perfect cone-shaped outline. It is little known

Quenouille training

in the U.S., and involves patient and laborious tying down of lower branches and pruning of upper ones. For training fruit trees *see* TRAINED FRUIT TREES.

quercifolia, -us, -um (kwer-si-fō'li-a). With leaves like the oak (*Quercus*).

QUERCITRON = *Quercus velutina.* See OAK.

QUERCUS. *See* OAK.

QUICKLIME. Burned and slaked lime, which see.

QUILLAJA (quill-ā'ya). A small genus of South American evergreen trees of the rose family, comprising only 3 or 4 species, of which **Q. Saponaria**, the soapbark tree, is occasionally cult. in zones* 8 and 9, especially in Calif., for ornament. It is a tree up to 60 ft. high, with alternate,* shining, ovalish, toothed leaves 1½–2 in. long. Flowers white, unisexual,* polygamous* or the sexes on different trees in rare instances, usually in terminal, sparse clusters. Petals 5, small. Stamens* 10. Fruit a collection of 5 leathery follicles,* united by their bases. Chile. Little known outside of southern Calif., but interesting because of its saponaceous (*i.e.*, lathering) bark. Propagated by cuttings under glass. (*Quillaja* is from the Chilean vernacular *quillai,* meaning to wash, in allusion to the saponaceous bark.)

QUINA. *See* CINCHONA.

quinata, -us, -um (kwi-nay'ta). In fives.

QUINCE. A single species of medium-sized trees, constituting the genus **Cydonia** (sy-dō'ni-a) of the rose family, the common quince being **C. oblonga** (sometimes called *C. vulgaris*), a native of Persia and Turkestan, and cult. since before the Christian era, but not much in the U.S. Usually not over 25 ft. high, the leaves alternate,* stalked, without marginal teeth, oval or oblong, 2½–4 in. long, densely soft-hairy beneath. Flowers white or light pink, solitary at the ends of leafy shoots. Sepals* 5, ultimately turned backward. Petals 5. Stamens* 20. Fruit a many-seeded pome,* of

---

* Special articles on the subjects indicated by an asterisk (*) will be found at the words so marked.

a peculiar, almost guava-like flavor when cooked (useless otherwise), pear-shaped, yellow, and slightly hairy. (*Cydonia* is the Latin name of the quince.) For the plant known as *C. japonica see* CHAENOMELES, which also includes all the showy shrubs and trees known as flowering quince.

QUINCE CULTURE

Closely related to the apple and pear, the quince is like neither, for it has a spicy, aromatic flavor unlike its better-known relatives. Because the fruit is inedible without cooking, it is little grown, although those who know it deplore this neglect, because its flavor is like no other temperate-zone fruit.

The tree is medium-sized, should be planted about 20 feet apart each way, but most home gardeners will need only a single tree. It should begin to bear 3 or 4 years after planting, and last about 30 years. The fruit is more or less pear-shaped, very hard and gritty when green, but delicious when stewed. Its aroma is so strong and distinctive that fresh fruit should not be stored with apples or pears. It is easier to store than either the apple or pear.

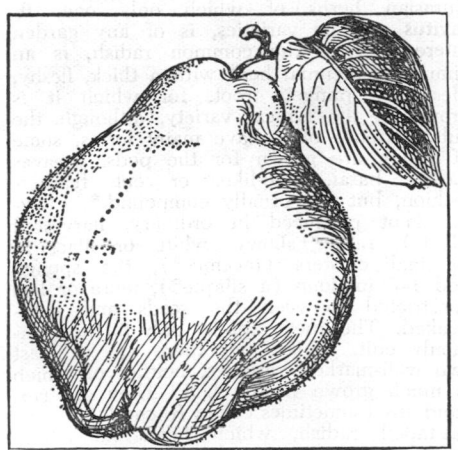

Quince fruit and foliage

The quince prefers a heavy, almost clayey soil and can be grown wherever apples thrive. It is inclined to be shallow-rooted, so deep cultivation is risky. Ordinarily it can be grown as a lawn or field specimen, as the flowers are showy.

Of the few varieties offered by nurserymen one called Orange is the best, followed by Champion. Both can be had as dwarfs if you cannot spare space for a standard quince tree.

The quince may well be left to grow in its natural shape with little pruning to train the tree. The habit of growth is crooked and scraggly and some heading-back is required to correct these natural tendencies. Interfering and superfluous branches should be removed. The trees bear year in and year out and sometimes overbear, in which case pruning may be used to thin the crop and stimulate greater growth. Pruning should be done only in winter or early spring.

The quince fruit has a delicate skin which shows bruises easily, to the great detriment of the clear golden color. The fruits must, therefore, be handled with much care in picking and storing.

The Angers quince, a French variety, is largely used as a rootstock for dwarfing pear trees. *See* Dwarf Fruit Trees at DWARFING.

QUINCE FAMILY. *See* ROSACEAE.

QUINCUNX. An old method of spacing orchard trees to save space by planting them alternately in the row.

QUININE. *See* CINCHONA.

QUININE BUSH = *Garrya elliptica.*

QUININE TREE. *See* CINCHONA.

quinquefolia, -us, -um (kwin-kwe-fō′li-a). With 5 leaves or 5 leaflets.

quinquenervis (kwin-kwe-ner′vis). Five-veined.

QUISQUALIS (kwis-kwā′lis). A small genus of woody vines of the family Combretaceae, the only cult. species being **Q. indica,** the Rangoon creeper from Indo-Malaya and the Philippines, which is grown for ornament in southern Fla. (hardy outdoors, nowhere else). It is a quick-growing vine, without tendrils, having oblong, stalked, abruptly pointed, opposite* leaves, 3–5 in. long. Flowers showy, blooming all summer (in Fla.), the long-tubed calyx green, the fragrant corolla white, changing to pink or red. Fruit a dry, leathery, 5-angled capsule,* not over 1 in. long. Propagated by seeds or cuttings over bottom-heat.* (*Quisqualis* means, literally, who or what for, and was coined by its author as a joke as he did not know what the plant was.)

QUIXOTE-PLANT = *Hesperoyucca whipplei.*

---

* Special articles on the subjects indicated by an asterisk (*) will be found at the words so marked.

R

RABBITS. *See* ANIMAL INJURY.

RABBITEYE BLUEBERRY. A tall-growing high-bush blueberry (*Vaccinium*) from the southern states. *See* BLUEBERRY.

RABBIT'S-TAIL GRASS = *Lagurus ovatus.*

RACCOON GRAPE = *Vitis vulpina.*

RACE. *See* VARIETY.

RACEME. An elongated flower cluster, blooming from the bottom upward, with a single main stalk, from which arise the

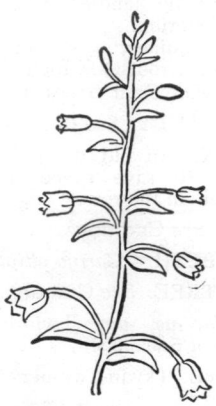

Raceme

stalks of the individual flowers. The main stalk is never terminated by a flower, and when branched, the cluster is known as a compound raceme. Typical examples are the currant, mustard, honey locust, fireweed, squill, and lily-of-the-valley. *See* PANICLE and SPIKE.

racemiflora, -us, -um (ra-see-mi-flow′ra). Having flowers in racemes.*

racemosa, -us, -um (ra-see-mō′sa). *See* RACEME.

RACHIS (ray′kiss). The main stalk of a flower cluster or the main leafstalk of a compound* leaf.

radiata, -us, -um (ray-di-ā′ta). Radiate; *i.e.*, rayed, often having spreading rays or petals. *See* COMPOSITAE.

RADICAL. Having to do with root; as *radical* leaves are basal or root leaves.

radicans (rad′i-kanz). Rooting, especially along the stem.

radicata, -us, -um (rad-i-kay′ta). Rooted; often strongly rooted.

RADICHETTA. An Italian salad plant, also called Italian dandelion, said to be an annual form of the chicory (*Cichorium Intybus*), with radical, dandelion-like leaves. It is sown ¼ in. deep, thinly in early spring, in rows 12–18 in. apart, the seedlings thinned out to 6 in. apart. Also known as asparagus chicory and sprouting chicory. Harvest the leaves when young.

RADICLE. The first young root put forth from a seed; or, among gardeners, a similar initial root put forth from a tuber* or rootstock.*

RADICULA. A much-abused generic name variously applied to several different plants. For an incorrect garden application of it *see* HORSE-RADISH.

RADIOACTIVE FERTILIZER. *See* FERTILIZERS and FOLIAR FEEDING.

RADISH. This is the easiest of all vegetables to raise, and all the cult. varieties of it belong to the genus **Raphanus** (raf′an-us) of the mustard family, comprising about 6 Eurasian herbs of which only one, R. **savitus** and its varieties, is of any garden interest. This, the common radish, is an annual or biennial herb with a thick, fleshy, pleasantly pungent root, for which it is grown in the typical variety, although the cult. varieties of it have many forms, some of which are grown for the pods. Leaves mostly basal, lyre-like, or cut feather-fashion, but not usually compound.* Flowers (not produced in ordinary, harvested plants), rather showy, white or lilac, in terminal clusters (racemes*), the spongy pod 1–3 in. long (a silique*), more or less constricted between the seeds and long-beaked. The above applies only to the commonly cult. radish, but there are at least two well-marked varieties, neither of which is much grown in the U.S. They are *var.* **caudatus** (sometimes called *R. caudatus*), the rat-tailed radish, which bears no edible root, but a long, curved, often twisted pod, 8–12 in. long, used as are common radishes; and *var.* **longipinnatus**, the Chinese radish, which has leaves 1–2 ft. long, with 8–12 leaflets, and bears long, durable and hard roots, which are usually cooked. It is sometimes known as the winter radish and is little known here. The Japanese call it daikon. The typical species, *R. savitus*, is a cultigen,* unknown in the wild, and may be derived from *R. Raphanistrum*, a European herb now widely distributed in N.A. as a naturalized weed. (*Raphanus* is the classical Latin name of the radish.)

RADISH CULTURE

The common radish will germinate in 4–5 days and, if grown properly, will

---

* Special articles on the subjects indicated by an asterisk (*) will be found at the words so marked.

have useful roots ready to harvest in 28–40 days. If it takes longer than this, the roots will be spongy, acrid, or woody — hence, useless. The secret of getting crisp, delicious radishes is quick growth. For this they need a rich soil in good tilth* and free of stones. Sow the seeds about ⅓ in. deep in drills not over 8–12 in. apart. Small, quick-growing roots (the only kind worth harvesting) can be secured by early planting, preferably sifting out the largest seeds and rejecting the smaller ones.

Some of the varieties offered by seedsmen are especially adapted to forcing in the hotbed or greenhouse, but the common sorts are better for outdoor cult. Of these the best are Early Scarlet Globe, White Icicle (long), and Cavalier. Generally, they do better in the cool spring and fall months than in the summer, for which season special varieties have been developed. All through the spring a succession should be sown every 10 days. Keep in mind that an old radish is a worthless one and begin harvesting as soon as possible. They *must* be quickly grown and, of course, kept thoroughly cultivated. If quickly grown neither insect pests nor diseases are serious.

RADISH FAMILY = Cruciferae.

Radula. A once-used generic name for a section of *Haworthia.*

RAFFIA = *Raphia Ruffia.* It is the split leaf segments of this palm, now often replaced by various sorts of "paper string," which florists and nurserymen use for tying. It is more resistant to weather than any of the new artificial tying strings, mostly made of paper. Consequently, raffia is still the favorite tying material for grafting, budding, and many other hort. operations. While tough and lasting, raffia does not cut tissues as would string.

RAG. The white, stringy, central cord, the partitions, and the inner, white skin investing the orange and other citrus fruits. The amount of rag in the different varieties is a criterion of their value, as fruits with too much rag are inferior.

RAGGED ROBIN = *Lychnis Flos-cuculi.*

RAGGED SAILOR = *Centaurea Cyanus.*

RAG GOURD. See LUFFA.

RAGWEED = *Ambrosia artemisiifolia.* See list at WEEDS.

RAGWORT. See SENECIO.

RAINBOW CACTUS = *Echinocereus rigidissimus.*

RAINFALL. Few statistics issued by the Weather Bureau are of more importance than those on rainfall, which includes both rain and melted snow in all annual summaries.

Rainfall is the only practical source of soil moisture and the amount of rainfall thus dictates what can be grown in any particular region. From the crest of the Alleghenies to the Atlantic the annual rainfall varies from 35–50 in. per year, which is ample for the growth of heavy forest, and for practically all garden crops. Summer droughts may retard or even ruin shallow-rooted garden plants, but generally, the rainfall is adequate for most garden needs.

From the Alleghenies westward there is a gradual reduction of rainfall. In the Great Plains states it falls to such a figure that forest is no longer possible and is replaced by grassland. The cult. of many evergreens and broad-leaved evergreens in such a region is impossible or very difficult. Still farther west, and throughout the region from western Tex. to southern Calif., there is not enough rainfall for even grassland to survive, and we have instead the desert or semi-desert of the cactus country. Such regions may have fertile soil, but without irrigation (which see) they are useless for most garden plants.

In the extreme northwestern coastal region there is the heaviest rainfall in the U.S., resulting in the magnificent coniferous forests of British Columbia, Wash., Ore., and northern Calif., and making of this region a place as favorable for gardening as England.

So important are these rainfall figures, especially the amount that falls in the growing season, that they have been included in the account of each state and Canadian province. See the name of your state or province for the significant rainfall data of your locality. *See also* DRIP.

Many experienced gardeners always water greenhouse plants with rain water rather than tap water. The various chemical and bacteriological safeguards which municipal water systems must set up, do things to tap water which are not found in pure rain water. Hence the frequency of the old-fashioned rain barrel in some very extensive greenhouse ranges.

RAIN LILY. See COOPERIA.

RAIN TREE = *Samanea Saman.*

RAISIN. The dried, sweet fruit of certain varieties of grapes. For the best varieties of grapes for raisin-making and the conditions necessary to produce them *see vinifera* varieties at GRAPE. For the Japanese raisin tree *see* HOVENIA DULCIS.

RAKING. The smoothing and pulverizing of soil before seeding. There is no better tool for it than the common steel-toothed rake, the teeth of which should be kept sharpened. As in cultivating or hoeing, the only instruction necessary is to so arrange your work that you never have to walk over raked soil. Where the area is too large (*i.e.*, half an acre or more), hand raking is too expensive and a harrow should be used (*see* HARROWING). But for the final touches only raking will put the soil in the finest shape, especially if the

---

* Special articles on the subjects indicated by an asterisk (*) will be found at the words so marked.

To make soil friable* there is no
substitute for raking.

ground is being prepared for a lawn
(which see). *See also* SOIL OPERATIONS.

RAMET. A term to designate an individual plant of a clone.*

RAMIE. *See* BOEHMERIA NIVEA.

RAMONDA (ray-mon'da); also spelled
Ramondia. Delicate little perennial herbs
from the mountains of Eu. and among the
only hardy representatives of the family
Gesneriaceae (for the others *see* HABER-
LEA). Of the 3 known species, the two below are grown for ornament, mostly in
rock gardens where their culture requires considerable care. They are nearly
stemless herbs, covered with reddish, soft
hairs. Leaves chiefly basal. Flowers typically purple or bluish-lavender (white in
a hort. form), flat-bell-shaped, almost without a tube, and borne sparsely at the end
of a leafless stalk. Fruit an oblong, rather
pointed capsule.* (Named for L. F. E. von
Ramond de Carbonnières, French botanist.)
For culture *see* ROCK GARDEN.

nathaliae. Low herb with oval, wavy-
toothed, hairy leaves. Flowers lavender-blue,
but yellow-eyed, the corolla 4-lobed. Serbia
and Bulgaria.
myconi. Not over 3 in. high, the ovalish
leaves hairy and deeply toothed. Flowers purple, about 1 in. wide, the corolla 5-lobed.
Called by some *R. pyrenaica.* Pyrenees. There
is also a white-flowered hort. form.

RAMONTCHI = *Flacourtia indica.*

ramosa, -us, -um (ra-mō'sa). Branched.

ramosissima, -us, -um (ra-mo-siss'i-ma).
Much-branched.

RAMPION. *See* PHYTEUMA.

RAM'S-HEAD LADY'S-SLIPPER = *Cypripedium arietinum.*

RANCHO SANTA ANA. *See* BOTANIC
GARDEN.

RANGOON CREEPER = *Quisqualis indica.*

RANUNCULACEAE (ra-nun-kew-lay'see-
ee). The buttercup or crowfoot family,
often, and with equal reason, called the
peony or hepatica family, is horticulturally
important as well as being a large natural
group of herbs (a few are vines). There
are about 40 genera and perhaps 1500
known species, nearly all of which come
from the cooler parts of the north temperate zone.

By far the most important garden genus
is Paeonia (*see* PEONY) for which a separate family, the Paeoniaceae, has been suggested on technical grounds. *Delphinium,
Anemone, Aquilegia* (*see* COLUMBINE), *Clematis,* and *Aconitum* (*see* MONKSHOOD) are
extremely popular garden plants, some of
them with very showy flowers. Some of the
genera are of comparatively easy cult., but
see each of them for further notes.

A perhaps secondary group of garden
genera, some of which, however, are very
old garden favorites are: *Adonis, Eranthis, Helleborus, Nigella, Trollius,* and
Trautvetteria. More suited to the wild
garden and nothing like so showy are:
Actaea, Anemonella, Caltha (*see* MARSH
MARIGOLD), *Cimicifuga, Coptis, Hepatica,
Hydrastis* (*see* GOLDENSEAL), *Isopyrum,*
and *Xanthorhiza* which is somewhat shrubby.
For *Ranunculus see* BUTTERCUP, and for the
meadow rue *see* THALICTRUM.

Leaves alternate* or opposite,* but basal
in many genera, usually divided or even
compound,* but undivided in some. Flowers very various. In the peony they are
larger than in any other genera in the
family, in some hort., double-flowered
forms often 5 in. across, or more. In all
the rest of the garden genera the flowers
are smaller, but sometimes, as in *Delphinium,* in spectacular clusters. In two genera
the flowers are very irregular* and more
or less spurred* (*see* DELPHINIUM and
MONKSHOOD). They are spurred,* but
regular, in *Aquilegia* (*see* COLUMBINE).
All the rest of the cult. genera have regular*
flowers but some, like *Hepatica* and *Thalictrum,* lack petals.

Most of the garden plants are perennials,
but most *Clematis* and *Xanthorhiza* are
woody plants. The fruit is dry and in most
genera made up of separable follicles* or
achenes,* but berry-like in *Actaea* and in
some other genera.

Technical flower characters: Sepals 3–15,
sometimes petal-like, in other genera hooded
and irregular. Petals 3–5, sometimes lacking,
and in a few genera prominently spurred or
hooded. Stamens* many. Ovary superior.*

ranunculoides (ra-nun-kew-loy'deez). Like
a buttercup.

RANUNCULUS. *See* BUTTERCUP.

Rapa (ray'pa). Classical name of the turnip.

rapacea, -us, -um (ra-pay'see-a). Rape-
like or turnip-like.

RAPE = *Brassica Napus.*

RAPHANUS. *See* RADISH.

---

* Special articles on the subjects indicated by an asterisk (*) will be found at the words so marked.

RAPHIA (ray'fi-a). Chiefly tropical African or Madagascan feather palms of no hort. interest except for **R. Ruffia** which yields raffia, a very widely used tying fiber. The raffia palm is practically unknown in cult. in the U.S. outside of the collections of a few specialists, but it could be grown in southern Fla. It has a trunk 25–30 ft. high, crowned with perhaps the largest known leaves in the world. These stand straight upward, are often 65 ft. long, the stalks about 10–15 ft. long. There are a tremendous number of leaflets which are stiffish, 2–5 ft. long, and grayish beneath. It is from them that raffia is harvested. Fruit oblongish, beaked, 1–2 in. long. Tropical Af., but chiefly Madagascar, where most raffia fiber comes from. (*Raphia* is from the Greek for needle, in allusion to the short, sharp beak of the fruit.)

RAPHIOLEPIS (ra-fi-ol'e-pis). Asiatic handsome, evergreen shrubs of the rose family, comprising only half a dozen species of which two are widely planted for ornament from zone* 7 southward, more rarely in the cool greenhouse northward. They have alternate,* thick, fleshy, short-stalked leaves and white or pink flowers in rather showy terminal clusters (panicles* or racemes*). Petals 5. Stamens* 15–20. Fruit a bluish-black or purplish-black, generally round pome* with 1–2 seeds. (*Raphiolepis* is from the Greek for needle and scale, in allusion to the scale-like bracts* in the flower cluster.)

All the species are popular in Calif. and along the Gulf Coast, where they can be grown in a variety of soils. While they will stand some frost they cannot be grown safely north of zone* 7, and do best south of this. If grown in the greenhouse, use potting mixture* 5 and keep in the cool house. Propagated by seeds or by cuttings of ripe wood, under glass.

delacouri. A hybrid between the second and third species, but having toothed leaves and pink flowers. It forms a compact, showy shrub, often used in southern patios.

indica. Indian hawthorn. Not over 5 ft. high. Leaves oblongish, or narrower, 2–3 in. long, bluntly toothed. Flowers pinkish-white, about ½ in. wide, the clusters loose and without hairs. Southern China. The *var.* **rosea** is a reputedly new var. with darker pink flowers.

umbellata. Yeddo hawthorn. A shrub, often low and spreading, but occasionally 8–10 ft. high. Leaves very thick, 2–3 in. long, slightly toothed, the margins rolled. Flowers white, about ¾ in. wide, fragrant, the clusters dense and hairy. Jap. The *var.* **ovata** has broader leaves without marginal teeth.

rapunculoides (ra-pun-kew-loy'deez, but *see* OïDES). Resembling a *Rapunculus*, an obsolete name for some bellflowers.

RARERIPE = Ratheripe.

rariflora, -us, -um (rare-ri-flow'ra). With a few, or with loosely clustered, flowers.

RASPBERRY. Four groups of raspberries, each with many varieties, are grown in North America. These are, in order of introduction to cultivation: the European red raspberry, derived from the wild red raspberry of Europe; the American red raspberry, the cultivated form of the American wild red raspberry; the black raspberry, or blackcap, also a cultivated native; and the purple-cane raspberries, hybrids between varieties of the two reds and the black raspberry. The culture of these four groups differs only in minor details, possibly most in method of propagation. All belong to the genus *Rubus,* which see.

Red raspberries are propagated from suckers that spring up from the roots of fruiting plants. These suckers may be set in the field as they are taken from the mother plants, or they may be grown for a year in nursery rows, a procedure not often warranted. Black and purple raspberries are propagated by tipping. Late in the summer, the snake-like tips of canes which have dropped to the ground develop roots. Under cultivation, the tips are buried to prevent whipping by the wind. By the following spring roots have formed and the tipped plants are set in the field or for a season in the nursery row.

SOILS. Raspberries are not choosers as to soil but seem to be most at home, especially the reds, in warm, sandy loams, while the blacks and purples take to heavier, moister loams and even to clays. Some variety may be found for any good garden soil. In soils too moist the plants "run to wood" and bear little fruit so that good drainage is imperative. A soil on which potatoes grow well is ideal for the reds; one on which corn grows well, for the blacks and purples. Whether soils are acid or alkaline matters little to raspberries — lime applied to raspberry soils is wasted; so, for the most part, are commercial fertilizers, but organic matter from stable manure or cover crops is a prime requisite.

Climate plays an important part in the selection of sites. Raspberries are tender to both cold and heat and withstand either extreme rather less well than, say, the apple. The blacks are more easily hurt by cold and less easily by heat than the reds. European reds are tender, alike, in American winters and summers. Varieties of all four groups vary in what they will stand from climate. All like climates tempered in winter and summer by bodies of water.

CULTURE. Raspberries of any of the four types are grown either in hills or solid rows. Red raspberries are set 5 × 5 ft. in the hill system; black and purple need a little more room and are often set 6 × 6 ft. apart. In the hedgerow system, the rows for reds are 6 or 7 ft. apart and plants in the row 2 or 3 ft. apart. Blacks and purples need at least a foot greater distance each way.

---

* Special articles on the subjects indicated by an asterisk (*) will be found at the words so marked.

Spring is the time to plant. Before planting, the canes should be cut back to 4 to 6 in. Cultivation should be begun as soon as the ground can be worked in the spring and continued until after picking, when a cover crop should be sown.

Raspberry canes are biennial and the fruiting canes should be cut out as soon as the crop is harvested. Black and purple varieties naturally run to long, sprawling

The dotted lines show how much terminal growth should be pruned from bearing raspberry canes.

canes difficult to manage. To prevent this, the shoots should be pinched in June when they have reached the desired height; red raspberries should not be so pinched. Spring pruning of red raspberries consists in cutting back the fruiting canes to a height of 4 or 5 ft., depending on the vigor of the variety; weak canes should be removed. At the spring pruning lateral branches on the black and purple types should be shortened to 6 or 8 in. Spindling canes bear little fruit and rob stronger ones; thin these out, leaving 5 or 6 strong canes to each plant.

Raspberries are tender fruits and require careful handling. The fruit should be picked every other day during the height of the season and always when berries are free from moisture. Overripe berries spoil quickly. Picking should be done in the cool of the morning and the berries should be kept in a cool place until consumed.

VARIETIES. The three groups are described in order of ripening. Red varieties may be grown in zones* 1, 2, and 3; black and purple varieties, in zones* 2, 3, and 4.

RED-FRUITED VARIETIES

CHIEF. An early variety, resistant to disease; fruit is rather small, but firm and of good quality.

LATHAM. An old and very popular sort, with larger fruit than Chief, but the plants are less resistant to disease in some localities.

JUNE. Has large fruit that keeps better than most, is very early, and comparatively free from disease.

RANERE. Sometimes called St. Regis. A valuable sort because it is later-fruiting than June, and in favorable sites may also fruit again later in the summer. Fruit not so good as Latham or June.

CUTHBERT. Has bright red, medium-sized fruit of good quality. Moderately susceptible to disease.

NEWBURGH. A vigorous grower with large firm fruit; nearly immune to disease.

VAN FLEET. Only a moderately good bearer, and the fruit does not compare with June, Latham, or Newburgh, but valuable as it will grow in warm regions, which are unfit for most red raspberries.

PURPLE-FRUITED VARIETIES

COLUMBIAN. Fruit large, late, dark-purple to blackish, of good quality, and profusely borne. Plants susceptible to disease.

SHAFFER. Perhaps not superior to Columbian, but more productive, suitable especially for canning, and less susceptible to disease.

SODUS. Resembling Columbian, but even more productive. Fruit more acid than Columbian, and not of such good quality. It is almost free of disease.

BLACK-FRUITED VARIETIES

CUMBERLAND. A midseason variety with a large berry of good quality; quite subject to disease.

PLUM FARMER. Fruit large, with a bloom, and of the best quality. Somewhat subject to disease in some localities, but nearly immune in central New York State.

BLACK PEARL. Not unlike Plum Farmer, the fruit, however, glossy; the plant nearly immune to disease.

NAPLES. Fruit large, glossy, rather late, mildly acid; the plant nearly immune to disease.

EUROPEAN RED RASPBERRIES

Berries of the European reds are better in quality than those of the American, but the plants are less hardy. Gardeners might grow Lloyd George for its splendid fruits.

LLOYD GEORGE. Berries dark red, very large, excellent quality, early. Plants medium in productiveness, vigor, and healthfulness.

INSECT PESTS. Fruitworms and their adult beetles can be controlled by pesticide #21 (*see* SPRAYS AND DUSTS) beginning near blossome time. Red-necked cane borer grubs should be pruned out in early spring. Just before blossoming a strong application of pesticide #17 will help control adult beetles. Canes

* Special articles on the subjects indicated by an asterisk (*) will be found at the words so marked.

with a row of holes drilled in side have been attacked by tree cricket for egg-laying. Prune out eggs in spring. Later on the young may be controlled by pesticide #21. Jumping plant lice and aphids may attack leaves. Control these and mites with pesticide #21. A borer working around crowns often kills plants in the East. Control by spraying with double-strength pesticide #17 plus summer oil or plus pesticide #21 in late summer and again in early fall.

DISEASES. The most serious troubles of raspberry are the virus diseases such as mosaic* and leaf curl.* All plants with symptoms of virus disease should be destroyed and aphids, which transmit the virus, should be controlled.

Anthracnose* causes a spotting of leaves and stems and spur blight* results in dark canker-like areas on the stems. Both diseases may be controlled by a single application of pesticide #4 (see SPRAYS AND DUSTS) when buds are just breaking dormancy in the spring, followed by applications of pesticide #2 or #5 when new growth is 6 inches and again when 12 inches long.

The bacterial disease, crown gall,* may reduce size of plants when numerous galls are present on the roots or lower part of the stems. Remove and destroy these plants.

RASPBERRY FAMILY. *See* ROSACEAE.

RATA = *Metrosideros robusta.*

RATAMA = *Parkinsonia aculeata.*

RATHERIPE. Maturing earlier than the rest of the fruit on a tree; sometimes called rareripe. Neither term is in much use in this country, but will be heard in England.

RATIBIDA. Coneflower. A genus of North American, somewhat weedy, perennial herbs of the family Compositae, occasionally grown in the flower border. Leaves alternate,* more or less divided finger-fashion. Flower heads solitary, the rays* yellow and showy, the tubular disk* flowers brownish and on a rounded or arched disk.* The genus is sometimes known as *Lepachys.* (*Ratibida* is of unknown origin.)

Both the plants below are of the easiest cult. in any ordinary garden soil. They are not particularly choice garden subjects, but are sometimes dug from the wild in their native region. Propagated by division.

columnaris. Prairie coneflower. A rough-hairy, perennial herb, 1½–2½ ft. high, its leaf segments narrow and line-like. Flower heads nearly 2 in. wide, yellow, the disk* very prominent and columnar. Central U.S. south to Mex. Summer. The *var.* **pulcherrima** has brownish-purple rays.* There is also a double-flowered form, more showy than the typical plant.

pinnata. Often up to 5 ft., the stem rough-hairy. Segments of the leaf lance-shaped, the leaf 3–5 in. long. Flower heads nearly 5 in. wide, yellow, sunflower-like, but the disk* oblong. Eastern N.A. Summer. A coarse but showy plant.

RATOON. A basal sucker used for propagation in the pineapple, sugar cane, and banana. Other plants produce ratoons,

Ratoon of pineapple

which, because they already have roots, make useful material for propagating plants that ordinarily do not set seeds. The term is more commonly heard in the tropics, and is also used as a verb, as to *ratoon* a pineapple field; *i.e.,* propagate by using ratoons.

RAT-POISON PLANT = *Hamelia erecta.*

RATS. *See* ANIMAL INJURY.

RAT-STRIPPER = *Pachistima canbyi.*

RAT-TAIL CACTUS = *Aporocactus flagelliformis.*

RAT-TAILED RADISH = *Raphanus sativus caudatus. See* RADISH.

RATTAN. The plants yielding rattan belong to the genus *Calamus,* which, in Ceylon, are climbing palms with stems several hundred feet long. They are scarcely known in cult. here. For a cult. palm called ground rattan *see* RHAPIS EXCELSA.

RATTLEBOX. *See* CROTALARIA.

RATTLE-BUSH = *Baptisia australis.*

RATTLESNAKE FERN = *Botrychium virginianum.*

RATTLESNAKE MASTER. A name applied to several North American plants thought to have some efficacy against the poison of rattlesnakes. Those found here are: *Eryngium yuccifolium, Agave virginica, Liatris scariosa* and *L. squarrosa,* and *Habenaria ciliaris.*

RATTLESNAKE PLANTAIN = *Goodyera pubescens.*

RAVENALA (ra-ven-nay′la). Extraordinary banana-like plants of the family Musaceae, one Brazilian, the other the famous traveler's-tree of Madagascar, R. madagascariensis, often cult. for its very striking habit in regions where the banana is hardy. In maturity it has a stout, palm-like trunk, 20–40 ft. high, crowned with a tuft of immense, banana-like leaves so arranged (*i.e.,* two-ranked) that the foliage stands in one plane like a gigantic fan. Leaves 20–30 ft. long, the channeled, sheathing stalks hold-

* Special articles on the subjects indicated by an asterisk (*) will be found at the words so marked.

The traveler's-tree of Madagascar

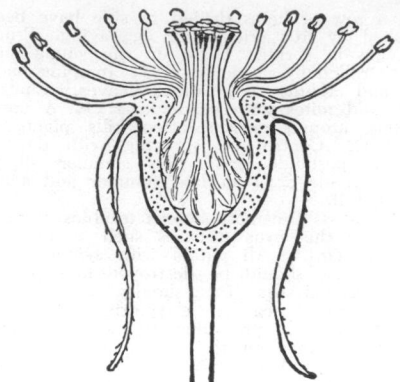

Cross-section of the receptacle (dotted) of a rose flower. It ultimately forms the rose hip.

ing much water at the point of insertion. For flower characters *see* MUSACEAE. The fruit is quite unlike the closely related banana in being a 3-celled, woody capsule.* In southern Fla. (it is hardy nowhere else in the U.S.) the leaves are, like the banana, often torn by the wind, but with little or no damage. Fla. plants do not usually reach the dimensions given above, but plants up to 30 ft. high are not uncommon. (*Ravenala* is a Latinized version of the Madagascan name for the tree.)

RAVENNA GRASS = *Erianthus Ravennae.*

RAY. Loosely, any narrow, spreading petal, or the outer and sometimes sterile flowers in an umbel.* Correctly, a ray is one of the flat, marginal flowers in a head of the aster, sunflower, daisy, etc., as distinguished from the central disk flowers. See COMPOSITAE.

RECEPTACLE. A term of several meanings in botany and hort., although all of them originate in the basic fact that a receptacle is the much-modified stem-end upon which a flower is borne; an alternative term for it is *torus.*

It takes many forms to which special terms are applied. In some plants of the rose family the receptacle and part of the united calyx are fused into what is known as the hypanthium, which later provides most of the fleshy, juicy part of apple and pear fruits. Most, or perhaps all, of a rose hip is the enlarged receptacle. In other families it is often mistaken for a true fruit (*i.e.,* a ripened ovary), especially in the fleshy "fruits" of *Elaeagnus* and some plants of the Trochodendraceae. Perhaps the most familiar receptacle is the strawberry, the fleshy part of which is all receptacle, the only real fruits being what

are commonly called the seeds embedded in the surface.

The disk, upon which is inserted the head of flowers in the Compositae or daisy family, is another familiar example of a receptacle.

RECESSIVE. See DOMINANT.

RECHSTEINERIA. See CORYTHOLOMA.

reclinata, -us, -um (reck-li-nay'ta). Reclinate; *i.e.,* bent backward.

recta, -us, -um (reck'ta). Upright or straight.

recurva, -us, -um (re-ker'va). Recurved; *i.e.,* bent downward.

recurvata, -us, -um (re-ker-vay'ta). *See* RECURVA.

RED. As part of a name, *red* is applied to many garden plants and things. Those that are found in this book and their proper equivalents are:

Red ash = *Fraxinus pensylvanica* (*see* ASH); **Red balm** = *Monarda didyma;* **Red baneberry** = *Actaea rubra;* **Red bay** = *Persea Borbonia;* **Red beech** = *Fagus grandifolia* (*see* BEECH); **Red-berried elder** = *Sambucus racemosa* (*see* ELDER); **Redberry** = *Heteromeles arbutifolia* (*see* TOYON); **Red birch** in the East, *Betula nigra,* in the West, *Betula fontinalis* (*see* BIRCH); **Redbird cactus** = *Pedilanthus tithymaloides;* **Red box** = *Eucalyptus polyanthemos;* **Red buckeye** = *Aesculus Pavia* (*see* HORSE-CHESTNUT); **Redbud** (*see* first main entry below); **Red cabbage** = *Brassica oleracea capitata* (for culture *see* CABBAGE); **Red calla lily** = *Zantedeschia rehmanni* (*see* CALLA LILY); **Red cedar** in the East, *Juniperus virginiana,* in the West, *J. scopulorum* (also applied to *Thuja plicata*); **Red chokeberry** = *Aronia arbutifolia;* **Red clover** = *Trifolium pratense* (*see* CLOVER); **Red cluster pepper** = *Capsicum frutescens fasciculatum;* **Red cohosh** = *Actaea rubra;* **Red dead nettle** = *Lamium purpureum;* **Red dogwood** = *Cornus*

* Special articles on the subjects indicated by an asterisk (*) will be found at the words so marked.

florida rubra, also *C. sanguinea;* Red elder = *Sambucus pubens* (*see* ELDER); Red false mallow = *Sphaeralcea coccinea;* Red fescue = *Festuca rubra;* Red fir = *Pseudotsuga taxifolia;* Red garden (*see* second main entry below); Red gum = *Eucalyptus rostrata;* Red haw = *Crataegus mollis;* Redheart = *Ceanothus spinosus;* Red horse-chestnut = *Aesculus carnea* (*see* HORSE-CHESTNUT); Red-hot poker = *Kniphofia Uvaria;* Red ironbark = *Eucalyptus Sideroxylon;* Red jasmine = *Plumeria rubra;* Red kowhai = *Clianthus puniceus;* Red larkspur = *Delphinium nudicaule;* Red mahogany = *Eucalyptus resinifera;* Red maids = *Calandrinia ciliata menziesi;* Red maple = *Acer rubrum* (*see* MAPLE); Red mombin = *Spondias purpurea;* Red mulberry = *Morus rubra* (*see* MULBERRY); Red oak (*see* Quercus rubra at OAK); Red osier = *Cornus stolonifera;* Red pepper (*see* CAPSICUM); Red pine = *Pinus resinosa* (*see* PINE); Red plum = *Prunus nigra;* Red raspberry = *Rubus idaeus strigosus;* Red ribbons = *Eucharidium concinnum;* Redroot = *Lachnanthes tinctoria;* Redroot = *Ceanothus americanus;* Redroot = *Sanguinaria canadensis* (*see* BLOODROOT); Red sage = *Lantana Camara;* Red Sally = *Lythrum Salicaria;* Red sandalwood = *Adenanthera pavonina;* Red shanks = *Geranium robertianum;* Red sorrel = *Hibiscus Sabdariffa* (the roselle); Red spruce = *Picea rubens* (*see* SPRUCE); Red tassel-flower = *Petalostemon purpureum;* Redtop = *Agrostis stolonifera;* Red trilium = *Trillium sessile;* Red turtlehead = *Chelone lyoni;* Red valerian = *Centranthus ruber;* Redwood = *Sequoia sempervirens;* Red whortleberry = *Vaccinium Vitis-Idaea.*

REDBUD. Very attractive shrubs or small trees constituting the genus **Cercis** (sir'sis) of the pea family, three of the 7 known species often grown for their showy flowers, which bloom in early spring, mostly before the leaves expand. Unlike most plants of the pea family, the leaves are not compound,* but simple and usually roundish or heart-shaped, stalked, and with the veins arranged finger-fashion. Flowers small, but usually numerous, pealike or nearly so, rose-pink or rose-purple in the cult. sorts. Stamens* 10, not united. Fruit (a legume*) flat, thin, and narrowly winged, its seeds flattened. (*Cercis* is the ancient Greek name for the European species.) The redbud is often known as Judas-tree.

They are of easy cult. in open, rather sandy loams, but do not like heavy, moist sites, and are hard to move when mature. They may be propagated by seeds, by layers, or by greenwood cuttings, preferably under glass, except for the layers. Their very early bloom, usually about peach-blossom time, makes them useful for color in the shrubbery while most plants are still dormant.

C. canadensis. American redbud. A small,

round-headed tree, not usually over 30 ft. high, mostly half this. Leaves broadly oval or nearly round, heart-shaped at the base, 3–5½ in. long, pointed at the tip. Flowers about ½ in. long, rosy-pink, in clusters of 4–8, but the clusters very numerous. Pod about 3 in. long. N.Y. and Ont. to Fla. and Tex. Hardy from zone* 3 southward. There is also a white, and a double-flowered form.

C. chinensis. Asiatic redbud. Much resembling the last, but with leaves more deeply heart-shaped at the base, larger and more numerous, rosy-purple flowers and slightly longer pods. Central China. A finer cult. shrub or small tree than the American redbud, but not quite so hardy, and doubtfully safe north of zone* 4.

As cult. this is more apt to be shrubby than tree-like, and flowers when younger than does *C. canadensis.* It is sometimes offered as *C. japonica.*

C. japonica = *Cercis chinensis.*

C. Siliquastrum. A tree up to 30 ft. high, usually less as cult. Leaves rounded or notched at the tip, generally roundish, 3½–5½ in. long. Flowers rose-purple, nearly ¾ in. long, in clusters of 3–6. Pods nearly 4 in. long. Eurasia. Not certainly hardy above zone* 5 or the most protected parts of zone* 4. There is also a white-flowered form.

DISEASES. Branches in mature plants will suddenly display wilted, then brown leaves as a result of canker.* Prune out the branch, cutting at least 6 inches below the sunken cankered area. Although some branches may die each year, new suckers or branches soon take their place and entire plants are not usually lost.

RED GARDEN. Pure red or scarlet flowers are not uncommon, but a garden or border planted solely with them would be crude and garish, unless relieved by the use of many white flowers and white accessories. A softening influence is furnished by the introduction of flowers of blue-gray coloring. Dark red and maroon are admirable in toning down the sharp scarlets. Example: Maroon Sweet William used with *Lychnis chalcedonica.* In a red garden the brilliant autumn coloration of certain shrubs and trees may be made use of, if desired, as well as such as have conspicuous red berries. *See* AUTUMN FOLIAGE.

SHRUBS AND SMALL TREES

Chaenomeles japonica (Japanese flowering quince), 6 ft., spring; *Ribes sanguineum,* 8 ft., spring; *Weigela* Eva Rathke, 8 ft., June; *Rhododendron* vars.; Rose vars. June.

TALL PLANTS FOR USE IN BACKGROUND

SUMMER AND AUTUMN FLOWERING: *Althaea rosea* (Hollyhock), red and maroon; *Dahlia* vars.; *Gladiolus,* Dr. F. E. Bennett, Pfitzer's Triumph, Aflame, etc.; *Helenium autumnale rubrum; Lilium bulbiferum; L. chalcedonicum, L. superbum, L. tigrinum; Lychnis chalcedonica; Pentstemon torreyi; Phlox* Africa, Goliath, Firebrand, Debs, Coquelicot, etc.; *Salvia splendens* vars. (annual); *Kniphofia Uvaria grandiflora; Zinnia* vars. (annual).

---

* Special articles on the subjects indicated by an asterisk (*) will be found at the words so marked.

PLANTS OF MEDIUM HEIGHT

SPRING FLOWERING: *Aquilegia canadensis, A. skinneri; Brevoortia Ida-Maia* (bulb); *Fritillaria imperialis* vars., *F. recurva* (bulbs); *Tulipa eichleri, T. fosteriana, T. gesneriana, T. greigi, T. ingens, T. praestans, T. sprengeri;* also Darwin, Cottage, and Breeder tulips in red varieties (bulbs). See TULIPA.

SUMMER AND AUTUMN FLOWERING: *Alonsoa warscewiczi* (annual); *Antirrhinum* vars.; Balsam (annual); Carnation, hardy border strains; *Centranthus ruber; Clarkia* Vesuvius; *Delphinium nudicaule; Gaillardia* Burgundy; *Geum chiloense* Mrs. Bradshaw; *Heuchera; Lilium canadense, L. elegans* vars., *L. philadelphicum; Linum grandiflorum; Lobelia Cardinalis, L. fulgens; Lychnis haageana; Monarda didyma; Tritonia* James Coey, Lord Nelson, Princess, etc.; *Papaver* annual vars., *P. orientale* Beauty of Livermore, Goliath, Olympia, Taplow Scarlet; *Paeonia officinalis rubra, P. tenuifolia,* and red-flowered hort. forms. See PEONY; *Physalis alkekengi; Potentilla* Gibson's Scarlet.

LOW-GROWING PLANTS

SPRING, SUMMER, AND AUTUMN FLOWERING: *Antirrhinum,* dwarf (annual); *Dianthus cruentus; Dianthus* annual vars.; *Eschscholtzia* Geisha (annual); *Helianthemum* red vars.; *Primula* red vars.; *Silene virginica; Tulipa linifolia, T. montana; Verbena* Etna, Spectrum Red (annual); *Zinnia* dwarf vars.

CLIMBERS

Clematis texensis; Lonicera sempervirens; Nasturtiums (annual); Rose, climbing, redflowering vars. See ROSE; Scarlet Runner Beans (annual); Sweet Peas (annual); *Campsis grandiflora* (30 ft., tender north of zone* 5); *C. radicans,* 20 ft., *see* TRUMPETCREEPER; Cypress vine.

TENDER BEDDING PLANTS

Begonias (tuberous-rooted); Geraniums; Cannas, Fuchsias. — L. B. W.

rediviva, *-us,* *-um* (re-di-vi′va). Restored to life; freshened.

REDWOOD = *Sequoia sempervirens.*

REED = *Arundo Donax.*

REED CANARY GRASS = *Phalaris arundinacea.*

REED GRASS = *Phragmites communis.*

REED MACE = *Typha latifolia.* See CATTAIL.

reflexa, *-us,* *-um* (ree-fleck′sa). Reflexed; *i.e.,* bent downward.

refracta, *-us,* *-um* (ree-frak′ta). Broken.

REFRIGERATION. See STORAGE.

regalis, *-e* (ree-gay′lis). Royal.

REGEL'S PRIVET = *Ligustrum obtusifolium regelianum.* See PRIVET.

regia, *-us,* *-um* (ree′ji-a). Royal.

reginae (ree-jy′nee). Pertaining to a queen.

REGULAR FLOWER. One that is essentially symmetrical, because its petals or other organs are of uniform size, not twisted,

A regular (*i.e.,* symmetrical) flower

and regularly arranged. Most flowers are regular, but many, as the snapdragon, salvia, azalea, and all the peas and orchids, are not. Instead they have irregular* (*i.e.,* unsymmetrical) flowers, which are often 1-sided, 2-lipped,* twisted, or, in the orchids, of fantastic irregularity. See IRREGULAR FLOWER.

REHMANNIA (ray-man′i-a). Showy, Asiatic, somewhat sticky, perennial herbs of the family Scrophulariaceae, two of the half-dozen known species grown for ornament, outdoors from zone* 7 southward, elsewhere in the cool greenhouse. They have tall, sparsely leaved stems, which usually branch from the base, and alternate,* oblongish, coarsely toothed or lobed leaves. Flowers irregular* 2 in. or more long, 2-lipped,* the front lobe 3-cleft, the other lobe 2-cleft. Stamens* 4, not protruding. Fruit a broad, many-seeded capsule,* surrounded and half-hidden by the bell-shaped calyx.* (Named for Joseph Rehmann, Russian physician.)

These very showy herbs may be grown in most garden soils or in potting mixture* 3 in the cool greenhouse. If raised from seed they will bloom the second year and may then be propagated by cuttings.

angulata. Not over 3 ft. high. Leaves with numerous sharp teeth, or with a few toothed lobes. Flowers red, the upper lip* scarlet-margined, the lower lip orange-dotted. Corolla about 2 in. long. China. The *var.* **tigrina** has spotted flowers; *var.* **tricolor** has purple flowers which later become violet-rose, the whitish throat purple-spotted.

elata. Nearly 6 ft. high, the leaves few-lobed, the lobes not toothed. Flowers 2–3 in. long, generally rosy-purple, but the yellow throat red-dotted. China.

---

* Special articles on the subjects indicated by an asterisk (*) will be found at the words so marked.

REINECKIA (ry-neck'i-a). A single species of Asiatic herbs of the lily family, **R. carnea** of China and Japan, with creeping underground stems and somewhat grass-like, but fleshy, basal leaves, 12–18 in. long and less than ½ in. wide. Flowers small, almost stalkless, flesh-colored, borne in small, short clusters (racemes*) which are much exceeded by the leaves. Corolla bell-shaped, its lobes recurved. Fruit a small, nearly globe-shaped berry. The foliage closely resembles *Ophiopogon* and *Liriope,* but these do not have the pink flowers of *Reineckia* and bear capsular fruits instead of a berry. (Named for J. Reinecke, a German gardener.)

REINWARDTIA (rine-wardt'i-a). Two East Indian under-shrubs of the family Linaceae, one of them, **R. indica,** the yellow flax, grown in the warm-temperate greenhouse or outdoors in zones* 7, 8, and 9 for ornament. Not over 4 ft. high, and best kept compact by frequent pinching. Leaves alternate,* without marginal teeth, more or less elliptic, with a sharp tip. Flowers yellow, 1–2 in. wide, solitary or in few-flowered, close clusters, the 5 petals (somewhat united below) soon falling. Fruit a round, 6–8-valved capsule.* Use potting mixture* 3. Often grown under the name *R. trigyna,* which some consider the correct name for it, or *Linum flavum.* (Named for K. G. K. Reinwardt, Dutch scientist.)

REJUVENATION. The restoration of vigor to old or neglected orchard trees. For a discussion of its desirability and methods *see* NEGLECTED ORCHARDS.

religiosa, -us, -um (re-li-ji-ō'sa). Sacred or religious.

REMONTANT. Having a second blooming season, as do many roses, some delphiniums, and various other plants. In some of them it is induced by cutting back, or by extra feeding, after the first crop of bloom.

REMONTANT ROSE. A hybrid perpetual rose. *See* ROSA BORBONIANA.

RENANTHERA (re-nan'ther-ra). Indo-Malayan tree-perching orchids, comprising about 10 species, but only **R. imschootiana** of much interest to most growers. It is a leafy-stemmed orchid, about 12 in. high, without pseudobulbs,* the oblongish leaves about 3 in. long and 1 in. wide. Flowers red and yellow, nearly 2 in. wide, borne in a drooping, branched, red-stalked cluster, 12–18 in. long, usually in Feb.–April in the greenhouse. Petals and sepals nearly similar, but the petals a little shorter than one of the sepals. Lip* small, scarlet, its crest yellow. For culture *see* the section on greenhouse orchids at ORCHID. (*Renanthera* is from the Greek for kidney-shaped and anther,* in reference to a technical anther character of another species.)

RENEALMIA NUTANS = *Alpinia speciosa.*

reniformis, -e (re-ni-for'mis). Reniform; *i.e.,* kidney-shaped.

RENOVATE. To prune, usually gradually, all the old wood from a shrub, thus inducing new, fresh growths. In this sense *see* PRUNING. Renovate is also used to describe the process of rejuvenating worn-out or neglected orchard trees. In this sense *see* NEGLECTED ORCHARDS. One can also renovate worn-out lawns or borders.

repandens (ree-pan'denz). Wavy-margined.

repens (ree'penz). Creeping.

reptans (rep'tanz). Creeping.

RESCUE GRASS = *Bromus catharticus.*

RESEARCH. In the sense of original investigation, few gardeners have time, patience or training for research. But it is research, by those equipped to carry it on, that has affected many of the plants and all the garden operations in this book. Fundamental research is carried on in all experiment stations (*see* the name of your state for the nearest one), by the U.S. Dept. of Agriculture, at all botanic gardens and at many schools of hort. *See* GARDEN SCHOOLS.

RESEDA. *See* MIGNONETTE.

RESEDACEAE (res-e-day'see-ee). The mignonette family comprises 6 genera and over 70 species of herbs of the Mediterranean region, the only one of garden interest being the mignonette. The cult. plants are annual or biennial herbs with alternate leaves and very fragrant, irregular flowers. Fruit a capsule.* For culture and description of species *see* MIGNONETTE.

resinifera, -us, -um (rez-i-niff'e-ra). Resin-bearing.

resinosa, -us, -um (rez-i-nō'sa). Resinous.

RESTHARROW. *See* ONONIS.

RESTING PLANTS. Plants are said to be resting when they are in a quiescent period, and fail to develop growth, even though provided with heat and moisture and subjected to good cultural treatment. We speak of the resting period of plants, in the fall of the year, when the trees and shrubs complete their annual growth and, in the case of the deciduous ones, lose their leaves after bud development has taken place. They become inactive so far as is revealed by their exterior conditions. Such plants then go into their rest period, and under natural conditions remain at rest for periods of weeks or months.

In temperate climates these periods of quiescence, to a marked degree, coincide with the winter cycle. From this it is easy to assume that the rest period has been brought about in response to temperature conditions. But in plant material growing in the tropics we find a similar condition, and the various trees and plants go through a period of growth and quiescence.

When woody plants such as roses, lilac, *Prunus,* etc., are brought into the forcing house, they show little activity for a time, a longer or shorter period elapsing before growth is noticeable. This varies to a large extent with the species of plant and its treatment

---

* Special articles on the subjects indicated by an asterisk (*) will be found at the words so marked.

before being transferred to the forcing house. Many species, after having been subjected to frost respond to forcing treatment quite readily. As an example take lily-of-the-valley; the new crop pips are worthless to the forcer unless they have been subjected to chilling by frost or to cold-storage treatment. This treatment also is favorable to the forcing of lilacs, roses, etc. As is indicated this quiescence is an internal factor and not a factor related to temperature and other external conditions.

It has been shown that treatment with chemical vapors such as ether or chloroform would break this dormant period and permit the buds to develop normally. Not only ether and chloroform but a number of other chemicals, including ethyl bromide, ethyl iodide, carbon tetrachloride, etc., could be successfully used in breaking the rest periods of plants.

As an example of resting, let us take the grapevine *Vitis vinifera* as grown under glass, after the crop has ripened and the bunches of fruit have been cut. The ventilators of the house are kept open, night and day, allowing an abundance of air to circulate among the vines. Waterings are gradually reduced and full sun is allowed to reach the plants. In the course of very few weeks the vines will enter the quiescent stage. This period is known to the horticulturist as the resting period, preceding as it does the period of activity or growth. While many experiments have been conducted to influence the continuity of growth in plants, these have not been successful.

Take again plants growing in the tropics. The orchid *Cattleya trianae*, for example, in order to produce flowers, is required to pass through a quiescent period. Nearly all epiphytic* orchids are subject to a period of rest, growth taking place during the rainy season, while their resting period occurs during the dry season. This prepares the plants for the blossoming period and at the same time prevents them from making weak and puny growths which would take place if nature attempted to keep them in a period of activity throughout the year.

Success with forcing the various bulbous plants such as hyacinths, tulips, narcissus, amaryllis, gloxinias, nerines, and the like, is more dependent on the resting period, which is the ripening period of the bulbs, than for the good cultural treatment the bulbs are subject to when being forced.

It seems apparent then that this law of nature is exacting. It requires that a plant go through a period of rest and dormancy in order to prepare it for the mission it has to fulfill; namely, to grow, flower, and fruit. *See* HARDINESS.

RESURRECTION FERN; RESURRECTION PLANTS. At least three different plants in general cult. have the ability to assume, during a dry period, the appearance of death, mostly by coiling up their foliage into a dense, brownish mass. But they retain the ability to renew growth when water is available, and may repeat this alternate dormancy and growth many times. By far the most famous resurrection plant is *Anastatica hierochuntica* (which see). For the resurrection fern *see* POLYPODIUM POLYPODIOIDES. For the third resurrection plant *see* SELAGINELLA LEPIDOPHYLLA.

RETAMA = *Parkinsonia aculeata*.

RETARDING. Retarding the growth in plants has been practiced by growers for many years. We may speak of it as the direct antithesis of forcing (which see), and it should in no way be confused with resting, the functions of resting and retarding being quite distinct operations.

Growers of azaleas and Easter lilies well know the value of retarding. In fact, it would not be possible to time and bring into flower large houses of Easter lilies for Easter Day were it not for the fact that the plants can be forced and retarded at the will of the grower. Sunny or sunless days as well as the earliness or lateness of Easter Day are important factors to consider in lily forcing. The bulbs of lilies do not develop growth simultaneously; therefore, the ones making more rapid growth would have to be retarded in some manner while those slow to start would need encouragement by being forced at a higher temperature. With azaleas, as the natural period of flowering arrives, the buds begin to swell and soon burst into flower unless in some way or other their growth is retarded. If the Easter festival is late many of the early and free-flowering varieties are apt to be at their best several days or weeks in advance of the festival.

On many private estates and commercial establishments, sheds, houses, and deep pits are to be seen. These structures are largely used for retarding purposes.

RETARDING HOUSE

A particularly useful structure from a practical standpoint for retarding plants is one built in the manner of an even-span greenhouse with a rather low roof running east and west. The roof is shingled, save for ventilators (sash 3×4 feet) placed at intervals on the north side of the house. No other light is available. The house is benched in similar manner to a greenhouse. This structure proves an ideal house in which to retard the flowering period of plants or to hold them when in flower for several days before being marketed. Azaleas, hydrangeas, cherries, lilacs, astilbe, lilies, bulbs, and various other plant material are kept in an inactive condition. The plants are watered as occasion requires, and the house is held at a temperature of 40° to 42° F. at night, an abundant amount of air being administered throughout the day. Humidity is controlled by moistening the sand under the benches with water. In the case of some species of plants the dormancy is extended for several weeks.

COLD STORAGE. In the case of *Lilium longi-*

---

* Special articles on the subjects indicated by an asterisk (*) will be found at the words so marked.

florum and its varieties, used so much for cut-flower work by the florist, the bulbs on their receipt from Japan or other countries are placed in cold storage to retard growth. They are taken out in numbers as required and forced. Lilies may be had the full cycle of the year by this method of retarding growth.

PITS. The cold pit is much used for the purpose of retarding plant growth. It is virtually a deep hotbed frame with or without sash but without any heat. It can also be used to carry bedding plants through the winter and shrubs and bulbs for forcing. When used as a retarding medium the glass is shaded with whiting and gasoline, or lath screens are placed over the glass; sometimes cheesecloth is all that is needed to give the necessary shade in mild regions. *See* PIT.

COOL GREENHOUSE. Half-span greenhouses having a northern aspect may function as retarding houses for many native or exotic flowering plants. By vigilant attention regarding air, shading, and watering this structure is capable of retarding plant material for a great length of time.

An example of nature's retardation is best exemplified in what is known as a late spring. The cold weather and low temperatures are the factors involved. The principles governing the holding of plant materials in a state of retardation beyond their natural period of lethargy are largely those of temperature, shade, and moisture.

reticulata, -us, -um (re-tick-you-lay'ta). Reticulated; *i.e.*, netted, especially netted-veined.

RETINISPORA. *See* CHAMAECYPARIS. It is sometimes spelled *Retinospora.*

retorta, -us, -um (ree-tor'ta). Twisted backward.

retusa, -us, -um (ree-too'sa). Notched.

REVERSION. The assumed tendency of some cult. plants to revert to an ancestral type.

REVIVING WILTED FLOWERS. *See* WILTING.

revoluta, -us, -um (rev-o-lew'ta). Revolute; *i.e.*, rolled backward or downward; applied especially to leaf margins so rolled.

REX BEGONIA. *See* BEGONIA REX.

Reynoutria. A name for a section of the genus *Polygonum.*

RHAMNACEAE (ram-nay'see-ee). The buckthorn family is of secondary garden importance in spite of its 45 genera and over 600 species. All are trees, shrubs, or woody vines, rather spiny in *Paliurus, Colletia,* and *Zizyphus* (which yields the jujube), and more showy in *Ceanothus* than in the few other cult. genera. *Rhamnus,* of little or no decorative value, is chiefly grown for its medicinal qualities (cascara sagrada, etc.). *Berchemia* is a woody vine. *Hovenia* is Asiatic and hardy from zone* 4 southward, while *Pomaderris* is Australasian and more tender.

Leaves mostly alternate,* and simple. Flowers regular* usually small, whitish or greenish, of little decorative value except in some species of *Ceanothus,* and mostly in clusters. Fruit dry and winged in some genera, in others fleshy.

Technical flower characters: Sepals 5, the margins touching, rarely 4. Petals 4 or 5 (wanting in some species of *Rhamnus*). Stamens* 4 or 5, opposite the petals. Ovary inferior* or superior,* mostly 2–3-celled. Styles* 2–4.

rhamnoides (ram-noy'deez, but *see* OÏDES). Like a buckthorn (*Rhamnus*).

RHAMNUS (ram'nus). Buckthorn. A large group of horticulturally unimportant, but medicinally significant, shrubs or trees of the family Rhamnaceae, most of the 100 known species from the north temperate zone, a few from Brazil and South Africa. The cult. species are chiefly shrubs, often somewhat thorny, with alternate* or opposite* leaves. Flowers small, greenish, unisexual* or polygamous, often without petals and never showy. Fruit a nearly round drupe. (*Rhamnus* is the old Greek name for the buckthorn.)

The buckthorns have no decorative value as flowering shrubs or trees. *Rhamnus purshiana* is the only source of cascara sagrada and is cult. for that purpose on the Pacific Coast (*see* MEDICINAL PLANTS). Also in Calif. *R. californica,* an evergreen, is a relatively important bee plant. The others, sometimes cult. for ornament, are indifferent hort. subjects, with no very special soil requirements, except that most of them prefer moist to dry sites. Some, like *R. caroliniana,* have red fruits for a time, but most of them ultimately are black-fruited.

Alaternus. An evergreen shrub, 10–15 ft. high, the leaves elliptic or ovalish, 1–3 in. long, remotely or not at all toothed, shining dark green above, paler beneath. Flowers inconspicuous, yellowish-green, followed by a small black fruit. Mediterranean region. March. Hardy from zone* 6 southward.

californica. Coffeeberry. An evergreen shrub, 4–6 ft. high. Leaves oblongish, 1½–2½ in. long, finely toothed. Flowers small, greenish, in umbels.* Fruit red, ultimately black. May–July. Ore. to Calif. Not hardy north of zone* 5; planted as a bee plant in Calif.

caroliniana. Yellow bush. Indian cherry. A shrub, or even a small tree up to 25 ft. high. Leaves elliptic or oblongish, 4–6 in. long, without marginal teeth or very finely toothed. Flowers in small umbels, not showy. Fruit red at first, ultimately black, about ⅜ in. in diameter. Southeastern U.S., west to Tex. and Neb. May–June. Hardy from zone* 4 southward.

cathartica. Common buckthorn. A shrub, 10–25 ft. high, the twigs often thorny. Leaves ovalish, 2–3 in. long. Male and female flowers on different plants. Fruit black. Eurasia, but often escaped* in the eastern U.S. May–June. Long cult., sometimes under the names of hart's-thorn, waythorn or rhineberry, and useful in the informal shrubbery or as an informal hedge plant. Hardy everywhere.

davurica. A stout, spreading shrub or small

* Special articles on the subjects indicated by an asterisk (*) will be found at the words so marked.

tree, 8–20 ft. high, with sometimes spiny twigs. Leaves elliptic or oblongish, 2–4½ in. long, the margins wavy-toothed, the blades green above but grayish beneath. Flowers and fruit as in *R. cathartica*. Eastern Asia. Hardy from zone* 2 southward.

Frangula. Alder buckthorn. A shrub or small tree, not over 18 ft. high. Leaves ovalish, or broadest toward the tip, 1½–2½ in. long. Flowers in clusters (umbels*) of 2–10. Fruit red at first, ultimately black. Eurasia and northern Af., naturalized sporadically in the U.S. May–July. Hardy everywhere. One of the best from the hort. standpoint because of its lustrous leaves that turn bright yellow in autumn. The *var.* aspleniifolia has much narrower and wavy-margined leaves, the foliage hence feathery.

purshiana. Cascara sagrada; also called bearberry, chittamwood and shittimwood. A tall shrub, or occasionally a tree to 40 ft. high. Leaves elliptic to oblongish, 6–8 in. long, finely toothed. Flowers in small, hairy clusters (umbels*). Fruit purplish-black. British Columbia to northern Calif. and Mont. May–June. Hardy from zone* 5 southward. *See* MEDICINAL PLANTS. The dried bark yields the drug.

RHAPIDOPHYLLUM (ra-pid-do-fill'um). A single species of low, spiny fan palms, R. hystrix, the needle or porcupine palm and sometimes called blue palmetto. It is found in low, moist places from the coastal plain of S. Car. to Fla. and Miss. It is a nearly stemless palm, the base horribly armed with the needles of the leaf-sheaths, the needles 7–15 in. long. Leaves 2½–3½ ft. wide, cut into many stiff, narrow, prominently ribbed segments, which are 2-toothed or cut at the tip, and about 1½ in. wide. Flowering and fruiting cluster smothered in the leaf-sheaths and needles near the base of the plant. Fruit somewhat fleshy, egg-shaped, about 1 in. long. In Fla. it grows in dense, low masses. (*Rhapidophyllum* is from the Greek for leaf and *Rhapis*, in allusion to the leaves being like those of *Rhapis*.)

RHAPIS (ray'pis). A small genus of Asiatic somewhat reed-like, low, mostly tufted fan palms, two of the 5 known species very widely grown as tub palms for indoor decoration and for patios, also outdoors in zones* 8 and 9. They are usually several-stemmed and fibrous, and have fan-like, much-parted leaves on slender, unarmed stalks. Male and female flowers on different plants, the calyx and corolla 3-toothed. Stamens* 6, in the male flowers, replaced by 6 infertile stamens* in the female ones. Fruit 1-seeded and berry-like. (*Rhapis* is from the Greek for needle, in allusion to the narrow leaf segments.)

For culture and uses *see* PALM.

excelsa. Ground rattan. Stems thin, several or numerous, conspicuously fibrous, 5–6 ft. high. Leaves fan-shaped, sometimes with 3–7 segments, usually with 10, green both sides, notched at the tip, the stalks flattened and somewhat fibrous at the base. China (?). Long grown as R. *flabelliformis,* and widely cult. for ornament by florists.

humilis. A lower palm than *R. excelsa,* and practically stemless. Leaves fan-like, the segments mostly 9 or more, some of them spreading or pointing backwards. China.

Rhaponticum (ray-pon'ti-kum). Literally, the sour rhubarb; the name *Rhaponticum* derived from the Pontic rha or rhubarb.

RHEA = *Boehmeria nivea.*

RHEUM. See RHUBARB.

RHEUMATISM-ROOT = *Jeffersonia diphylla* and *Chimaphila maculata.*

RHEXIA (rex'i-a). Meadow-beauty. Pretty little North American perennial herbs, of the family Melastomaceae, which is otherwise largely tropical and woody. Of the 15 known species only the two below are of any hort. interest. They are attractive little wild flowers, suited only to the bog garden, and needing acid (*see* ACID AND ALKALI SOILS), preferably moist, sand. Leaves essentially stalkless, opposite,* rather prominently 3–5-veined. Calyx* 4-lobed, bell-shaped at the base. Petals 4, oblique, rather showy, purplish in those below. Stamens* 8. Fruit a 4-valved capsule.* (*Rhexia* is from the Greek for breaking, and of no known application here.)

Suited only to the bog garden (which see).

mariana. A slender, hairy-stemmed plant, 1–2 ft. high. Leaves narrowly oblong, 1–1½ in. long. Flowers about 1 in. wide, pale purple, the clusters (cymes*) few-flowered. In pine-barren bogs. Eastern U.S., west to Ky. June–Sept.

virginica. Deer grass; also called handsome Harry. A nearly smooth-stemmed herb, 9–15 in. high, the stem angled. Leaves ovalish, 1½–2 in. long, the margins hairy-fringed. Flowers nearly 1½ in. wide, purple, in few-flowered clusters (cymes*). In sandy bogs along the coast, eastern N.A. July–Sept.

RHINEBERRY = *Rhamnus cathartica.*

RHIPSALIDOPSIS. See SCHLUMBERGERA.

RHIPSALIS (rip'sa-lis). Willow cactus; also called mistletoe cactus (they strongly resemble mistletoe). A curious genus of mostly tree-perching (epiphytic*) cacti, comprising over 60 species scattered from Fla. to the Argentine. They are leafless cacti, the slender, usually rope-like stems provided with hairs, bristles, or wool, but no spines. Branches cylindric or often flattened. Flowers small, not showy, stalkless on the edges of the branches. Fruit mistletoe-like. (*Rhipsalis* is from the Greek for wickerwork, in allusion to the mass of branches which usually grow much mixed up together.)

Rhipsalis and the closely related *Hatiora,* while true cacti, do not inhabit deserts. They grow mostly on trees in tropical forests and should be grown in orchid baskets in the warm-temperate greenhouse, preferably suspended from the roof. Use ½ potting mixture* 6 and ½ orchid peat. They are chiefly grown for their interesting mistletoe-like aspect, and have otherwise little or no decorative value.

Cassytha (sometimes spelled *Cassutha*). The common mistletoe cactus. A much-branched plant, the stems cylindric, pencil-thick, usually 3–4 ft. long (sometimes 10 ft. in Brazil), the branchlets about 1 ft. long. Flowers scarcely ¼ in. wide. Fruit very like that

of the mistletoe. Common throughout tropical America, and naturalized in the Old World tropics. Called by some *R. baccifera.*
salicornioides = *Hatiora salicornioides.*

RHIZOME. A rootstock.*

rhizophylla, -us, -um (ry-zo-fill′a). A specific name meaning, literally, root-leaved; usually applied to plants in which the leaves are all basal.

rhodantha, -us, -um (ro-dan′tha). With flowers like a rose.

RHODANTHE. *See* HELIPTERUM MANGLESI.

RHODE ISLAND. The state flower is the violet, the state tree the maple, and the state lies wholly in zone* 4.

Soil and climatic variations within the smallest state are much greater than would be expected in an area of much greater size.

SOILS. The soils of Rhode Island have been subjected to extreme glaciation and relatively few areas of any one soil are found. Prominent soil types include Gloucester stony loam, Merrimac stony loam, and Warwick sandy loam. Bernardston loam is found in the Newport area. There are no true clays, but a few fine silts. Many areas used for homes have shallow, poorly drained soils or the other extreme — those which are light and droughty. The natural soil reaction is very acid with a pH of 4.5 not uncommon. The organic matter level is relatively low and both the heavy and light soils respond to liberal applications. Soil fertility is usually low and a complete fertilizer is required for good results.

CLIMATE. Due to the influence of the ocean and large bay areas extending into the center of the state, very great differences in both summer and winter temperatures are found within a few miles. Under special conditions, winter temperature lows may differ as much as 25°. Thus, peaches are seldom winter-killed in the Bay area, but may not be a safe crop in the northern part of the state. Growing season, the period between average last spring frost and first fall frost, varies from 120 to 223 days as indicated below.

Block Island	223 days
Providence	200 days
Portsmouth	192 days
Greenville	171 days
Kingston (Hill)	167 days
Slocum	145 days
Kingston (Plains)	136 days
Wood River Junction	120 days

The two readings at Kingston demonstrate the influence of elevation, a phenomenon common to most areas.

The ocean influences average spring and fall temperatures, as well as the extremes. When 32° F. was registered at Providence, the following readings were secured at other stations:

	Spring	Fall
Block Island	34.2	38.3
Kingston (Plains)	28.2	26.5
Kingston (Hill)	32.4	26.0
Slocum	31.4	26.0
Wood River Junction	27.6	24.0
Greenville	32.3	27.0
Portsmouth	30.0	30.3

From the above data, one can readily understand a difference of a week to 10 days in the blooming time of common plants.

Precipitation is fairly well distributed and for the state averages about 42 inches per year with a variation of about 9 inches. In general, areas close to sea level have less rain than those farther inland and at higher elevations. The prevalence of fog in the coastal sections compensates, to some extent, for lack of rainfall. However, for assurance of maximum growth, intensive crops will require irrigation most seasons.

HORTICULTURAL CROPS. An intensive fruit industry is located north and west of Providence. Apples are the principal crop, with peaches in second place. A few pears are grown, but almost no plums or cherries, although all do well. Small fruits, including fox grapes, strawberries, raspberries, most brambles, and blueberries, are well adapted and are grown to a limited extent throughout the state. Cranberries do well on suitable sites. Apricots, nectarines, *vinifera* grapes, boysenberry, etc., do not ordinarily do well.

Most vegetables do well in both commercial and home gardens. Melons may need to be started under protection and should be on light, early soils. Variety selection is important for watermelons. Conditions are especially favorable for asparagus, tomatoes, beans, peppers, squash, cabbage, broccoli, sweet corn, and Irish potatoes. Commercial production is for local fresh markets only; there is no processing industry.

FLORICULTURE. Both indoor and outdoor flowers are widely grown. Carnations, chrysanthemums, roses, snapdragons, and miscellaneous pot plants are grown in greenhouses. Outdoor commercial crops include gladioli, asters, and shade chrysanthemums. Hybrid tea roses are normally winter-hardy and widely planted.

Nurseries are of increasing importance with a sizable industry, especially on Newport island, shipping stock considerable distances out of state. The relatively temperate climate and high humidity make the growing of ornamental evergreens especially successful. A good-sized nursery in Little Compton has developed and grows especially winter-hardy roses. Near the Great Swamp in Washington County, a sizable nursery specializes in rhododendrons. Interest in azaleas is increasing.

Native plants, including rhododendrons, azaleas, laurel, shadblow, and dogwood make a beautiful display at the appropriate time of the year. Many exotic specimens may be found, especially on estates in Bristol, Narragansett, and Newport.

* Special articles on the subjects indicated by an asterisk (*) will be found at the words so marked.

Points of special interest to gardeners include Roger Williams Park in Providence, especially the spring tulip and fall chrysanthemum displays; the Brownell Rose Gardens in Little Compton; the Greene Herb Gardens at Greene; the laurel display on Ministerial Road, South Kingstown; and some of the Providence and Newport private gardens open to the public on occasion. Westerly has a small, but very well-kept park. The Newport Horticultural Society and the Rhode Island Horticultural Society are active in the area. The University of Rhode Island's Department of Horticulture maintains a trial rose garden and both annual and perennial gardens to which the public is welcome. A Palm Sunday Show at the University greenhouses is a very popular event. The Rhode Island Federation of Garden Clubs and the Garden Club of America both operate within the state. The address of the Agricultural Experiment Station, which has kindly supplied this information about the state is Kingston, R.I.

RHODE ISLAND BENT = *Agrostis capillaris.*

RHODODENDRON (ro-do-den'dron). A very large genus of evergreen or deciduous shrubs, rarely trees, of the family Ericaceae, chiefly from the north temperate zone, a few on the high mountains of the Old World tropics, but none in Mex. Considered by some authorities as including *Rhododendron* proper, *Azalea,* and *Rhodora;* the two latter are here kept separate because of the long tendency of gardeners to separate them from *Rhododendron.* See AZALEA and RHODORA.

The rhododendrons, as here limited, are chiefly evergreens (many azaleas and rhodora are deciduous), with alternate* leaves, which are mostly stalked, always without marginal teeth. Flowers very showy, mostly tubular or funnel-shaped, the 5-lobed limb slightly irregular.* Stamens* 5-10. Fruit a capsule.* (*Rhododendron* is from the Greek for rose and tree, and is the old Greek name for the oleander, but applied by Linnaeus to these plants.)

For culture *see* below.

While gardening practice keeps *Azalea, Rhodora,* and *Rhododendron* separate, there are no technical characters that warrant such separation. Because of this all the names of *Rhododendron* species (taken in its broad sense) admitted to this book are listed below. Those belonging to *Azalea* or *Rhodora* are cross-referenced to those genera and descriptions, and culture of them should be sought there. All those described here are considered true rhododendrons in the garden sense. Their cult. in hot, dry regions is unsatisfactory or impossible.

altaclarense. A hybrid shrub, closely related to *R. catawbiense,* but with deep-crimson flowers, and not so hardy as *R. catawbiense.*

amoenum = *Azalea obtusa amoena.*

arborescens = *Azalea arborescens.*

arboreum. A tall evergreen shrub, 18–30 ft. high. Leaves nearly 7 in. long, white-felty or rusty beneath. Flowers about 1¼ in. wide, red, pink, or white, bell-shaped, sometimes spotted. Himalayas. March–May. Hardy from zone* 6 southward.

augustini. An evergreen shrub, 10–18 ft. high, the twigs scaly and hairy. Leaves oblongish or narrower, 1½–3½ in. long, scaly beneath and with the midrib bristly. Flowers blue or pale blue, about 1½–3 in. wide, rarely more than 3–4 in the cluster. China. April–May. Hardy from zone* 6 southward.

barbatum. Evergreen shrub or tree, 15–40 ft., with peeling gray bark. Leaves oblongish, 4–8 in. long, narrowed at the tip. Flowers crimson, the closely packed truss 4–5 in. wide. Himalayas. May. Suited chiefly to northern Ore. and Wash.

calendulaceum = *Azalea calendulacea.*

californicum = *R. macrophyllum.*

campylocarpum. A bushy evergreen shrub, 4–8 ft. high, the elliptic leaves 2–4 in. long, rounded or heart-shaped at the base, grayish-blue beneath. Flowers yellow, in a loose cluster, the anthers* red. Himalayas. May. Suited chiefly to northern Ore. and Wash.

canadense = *Rhodora canadensis.*

canescens = *Azalea canescens.*

carolinianum. Carolina rhododendron. An evergreen shrub, 4–6 ft. high. Leaves 2–3 in. long, rusty and scaly beneath. Flowers bell-shaped, nearly 1½ in. wide, pale rose-purple to whitish. Mountains of N. Car. May–June. Hardy from zone* 3 southward. Used as a tubbed or potted plant for penthouse gardens, as well as for the border. An extremely handsome plant.

catawbiense. Mountain rose-bay. A magnificent evergreen shrub 12–18 in. high. Leaves 3–5 in. long, shining green above, paler beneath. Flowers bell-shaped, nearly 2½ in. wide, lilac-purple. Mountains from Va. to Ga. May–June. Hardy from zone* 3 southward. The parent of many of the finest hort. forms of rhododendron. *See* below.

caucasicum. A dwarf evergreen shrub, never over 2 ft. high. Leaves 2–4 in. long, brownish beneath. Flowers narrowly bell-shaped, nearly 2 in. wide, white. Caucasus. May. Hardy from zone* 4 southward, but rare in cult. Of chief interest as one of the parents of hybrid rhododendrons. *See* below.

ciliatum. A widely spreading evergreen shrub, 4–8 ft. high, the foliage, twigs, and flower stalks bristly. Leaves elliptic, scaly on the under side and about 3 in. long. Flowers red at first, ultimately pink or white, in clusters of 3–5. Himalayas. April–May. Hardy from zone* 6 southward.

cinnabarinum. An evergreen shrub, 6–8 ft. high. Leaves ovalish, 2–4 in. long, gray-green above, paler and scaly beneath. Flowers in a drooping cluster, the corolla tubular, about 1½ in. long, red. Himalayas. May–June. Suited chiefly to northern Ore. and Wash.

dauricum = *Rhododendron mucronulatum.*

decorum. An evergreen shrub, 6–10 ft. high, the oblong leaves 4–6 in. long, bluish-green beneath. Flowers 8–10 in the cluster, the corolla funnel-shaped, pink or white. China. May–June. Hardy from zone* 5 southward.

deleiense. Plants offered as this are likely to be *R. tephropeplum.*

fargesi. An evergreen shrub or small tree, 8–20 ft. high, the elliptic leaves 2–4 in. long, grayish-green beneath. Flowers 6–10 in the cluster, the corolla about 2½ in. wide, white or rose and red-spotted. China. May–June. Hardy from zone* 5 southward.

ferrugineum. A low evergreen shrub, not

* Special articles on the subjects indicated by an asterisk (*) will be found at the words so marked.

Rhododendron carolinianum, a fine evergreen shrub of the Carolina mountains, with pale rose-purple or whitish flowers. For cult. *see* text.

over 3 ft. high. Leaves 1–2 in. long, shining green above, rusty and scaly beneath. Flowers funnel-shaped, about ½ in. wide, pink or carmine. Central European mountains. July–Aug. Hardy from zone* 4 southward. For cult. *see* ROCK GARDEN.

fortunei. An evergreen shrub, 8–12 ft. high, the twigs smooth. Leaves oblongish, 6–10 in. long, pale green above, bluish-green beneath. Flowers pinkish, fragrant, 3–4½ in. wide, showy because of being clustered in racemes.* China. May–June. Hardy from zone* 5 southward.

gandavense = *Azalea gandavensis.*

griersonianum. An evergreen shrub, 6–10 ft. high, its twigs and leafstalks sticky and bristly. Leaves lance-shaped, woolly on the under side. Flowers trumpet-shaped, about 2½ in. wide, scarlet, the lobes toward the base downy. China. June. Hardy from zone* 5 southward.

griffithianum. An evergreen shrub, 6–8 ft. high. Leaves 8–12 in. long. Flowers fragrant, bell-shaped, nearly 3 in. wide, pure white. Himalayas. Little known in cult. but one of the parents of many fine hardy, hybrid forms.

hinodegiri = *Azalea obtusa hinodegiri.*

hippophaeoides. An evergreen shrub, scarcely 3 ft. high, the oblongish leaves 1–2 in. long, densely scaly on both sides. Flowers bluish-purple, only about 1½ in. wide, broadly bell-shaped. China. April–May. Hardy from zone* 5 southward.

hirsutum. An evergreen shrub, 1–3 ft. high, its twigs scaly and bristly. Leaves elliptic or oblongish, 1–2 in. long, dark green above, somewhat scaly beneath, wavy-margined. Flowers as in R. *ferrugineum.* European mountains. June. Hardy from zone* 4 southward and one of the few to tolerate limy soils.

impeditum. A low evergreen shrub, 1–3 ft. high with densely scaly foliage. Leaves elliptic, not over ¾ in. long, rusty beneath. Flowers solitary or 2, bluish-purple, about ¾ in. wide. China. May–June. Hardy from zone* 6 southward.

indicum. See AZALEA INDICA.

japonicum = *Azalea japonica.*

kaempferi = *Azalea obtusa kaempferi.*

keiskei. An erect or procumbent evergreen shrub, if erect 4–8 ft. high, usually procumbent as cult. Leaves ovalish, 2–4 in. long, scaly beneath. Flowers 3–6 in the cluster, the corolla bell-shaped, pale yellow. Jap. May–June. Hardy from zone* 5 southward.

laetivirens. A hybrid, evergreen, low-spreading shrub, not over 3 ft. high. Leaves narrowly elliptic, 2–5 in. long, bright green. Flowers about 1½ in. wide, rose-pink. June. Hardy from zone* 5 southward.

lapponicum. A beautiful little alpine evergreen shrub, 6–12 in. high. Leaves scarcely ¾ in. long, rusty and scaly beneath. Flowers bell-shaped, about ½ in. long, rose-purple. Arctic and alpine regions of the northern hemisphere. June–July. Hardy from zone* 4 far northward, but suited only to the rock garden (which see).

ledifolium = *Azalea mucronata.*

leucaspis. An evergreen shrub, 2–3 ft. high, the elliptic leaves 1–2 in. long, bluish-gray and scaly beneath. Flowers solitary (rarely in 2's or 3's), the corolla more or less flat, nearly 2 in. wide, white. Tibet. March. Suited only to protected sites in northern Ore. and Wash.

macranthum = *Azalea macrantha.*

macrophyllum. An evergreen shrub, 6–10 ft. high. Leaves 4–6 in. long. Flowers nearly 2½ in. wide, rose-purple but brown-spotted. British Columbia to Calif. May–June. Hardy from zone* 5 southward. Also known as R. *californicum.* The state flower of Washington.

maximum. Great laurel. Rose-bay. A splendid evergreen shrub, rarely a tree, 10–25 ft. high, or even more. Leaves 7–10 in. long, densely hairy beneath. Flowers bell-shaped, about 1½ in. wide, rose-pink but green-spotted. Eastern N.A. June–July. Hardy from zone* 3 southward. A very handsome evergreen shrub, but its showy flowers much hidden by the foliage. *See* below.

micranthum. An evergreen shrub 3–5 ft. high, its elliptic leaves ¾–1½ in. long, scaly on the under side. Flowers very small, white, densely crowded in a cluster (raceme*) which is only 1½ in. long. China and Korea. May–June. Hardy from zone* 4 southward.

minus. An evergreen, usually straggling shrub, 4–5 ft. high or sometimes more. Leaves 2–4 in. long, scaly on the under side. Flowers funnel-shaped, about 1¼ in. wide. S. Car. to Ga. and Ala. June–July. Hardy from zone* 4 southward.

molle = *Azalea mollis.*

morelianum. A hybrid evergreen shrub, 6–10 ft. high, closely related to R. *catawbiense,* and differing from it chiefly in having lilac-violet flowers (instead of lilac-purple). May–June. Hardy from zone* 3 southward.

mucronatum = *Azalea mucronata.*

mucronulatum. Not over 6 ft. high, the branches upright. Leaves deciduous* or half evergreen, narrowly lance-shaped, 1–3 in. long, somewhat scaly. Flowers slightly hairy without, funnel-shaped or bell-shaped, about 1½ in. wide, rosy-purple, appearing before the leaves unfold. Eastern As. Sometimes offered as *Azalea daurica.* A profuse bloomer with handsome yellow-bronze autumnal foliage.

nudiflorum = *Azalea nudiflora.*

obtusum = *Azalea obtusa.*

occidentale = *Azalea occidentalis.*

ponticum. An evergreen shrub, 6–10 ft. high. Leaves 4–6 in. long, pale on the under side. Flowers narrowly bell-shaped, nearly 2 in. wide, purple but brown-spotted. Spain, Portugal, and Asia Minor. May–June. Hardy from zone* 4 (with protection) southward. Little grown as a species, but one of the parents of many fine varieties.

poukhanense = Azalea yedoensis poukhanensis.

praecox. A hybrid evergreen or partially evergreen shrub (perhaps better grouped with Azalea), 3–5 ft. high, the elliptic leaves 1–4 in. long, a little hairy on the margin, rusty beneath. Flowers sparse, about 2 in. wide, rose-purple. April. Hardy from zone* 4 southward.

pubescens. An evergreen shrub, 4–6 ft. high, the twigs, leaves and calyx* densely hairy. Leaves narrow, about ¾ in. long, and scattered rather sparsely on the twigs. Flowers 2 or 3, mostly in terminal clusters, the corolla pink or white, tubular. China. May. Hardy from zone* 5 southward.

racemosum. An evergreen shrub, 3–5 ft. high and perhaps better grouped with Azalea. Leaves elliptic or broader, ¾–2 in. long, smooth above, bluish-green and scaly beneath. Flowers about 1 in. wide, pink, in clusters of 3–6 at the leaf joints. China. April–May. Hardy from zone* 5, possibly in sheltered places from zone* 4, southward.

roseum. See AZALEA NUDIFLORA.

schlippenbachi = Azalea schlippenbachi.

smirnovi. An evergreen shrub, 12–18 ft. high. Leaves 4–6 in. long, densely brown-hairy beneath. Flowers narrowly bell-shaped, nearly 3 in. wide. Caucasus. May. Hardy from zone* 3 southward. An interesting, but somewhat straggling shrub, one of the parents in some hybrid forms.

tephropeplum. An evergreen shrub, 3–4 ft. high, the twigs scaly. Leaves oblongish, 1–2 in. long, about ¾ in. wide, sharp-pointed at the tip. Flowers 3–5 in a cluster, the corolla bell-shaped, pink or crimson, the stigma* crimson. Tibet and Burma. May. Suited chiefly to northern Ore. and Wash.

ungerni. An evergreen shrub, 15–20 ft. high. Leaves 4–6 in. long, densely brown-hairy beneath. Flowers broadly bell-shaped, nearly 2 in. wide, pinkish-white. Caucasus. May. Hardy from zone* 3 southward. It is one of the parents of many fine hybrids.

vaseyi = Azalea vaseyi.

viscosum = Azalea viscosa.

williamsianum. A low evergreen shrub, usually not over 3 ft. high, the twigs sticky. Leaves nearly round or broadly oval, 1–3 in. long. Flowers pale pink, about 2½ in. wide, solitary or in 2's. China. May–June. Hardy from zone* 5 southward.

yedoense = Azalea yedoensis.

yodogavum = Azalea yedoensis.

yunnanense. A partially or half-evergreen shrub, 6–8 ft. high and more or less globe-shaped. Leaves thin, narrow-elliptic, 1½–3 in. long. Flowers 2–4 in the cluster, the corolla funnel-shaped, about 1½ in. long, white or pink, crimson-spotted. China. May. Hardy from zone* 6 southward. A fine shrub with profuse bloom.

RHODODENDRON CULTURE

Rhododendrons are probably the most magnificent of flowering evergreen shrubs that the northern gardener can have. Those in gardens in this country are mostly hybrids, derived chiefly from crossing the American R. catawbiense with the tender Oriental R. arboreum, as well as some garden hybrids. A few have blood of the European R. cau-casicum and some others are hybrids of R. smirnovi and of R. griffithianum. All are plants requiring acid soil, rich in humus, and abundantly supplied with moisture, especially during the growing season which usually follows flowering. Although sunlight is essential to full flowering, the plants will grow in shade and, in all cases, some shade should be provided as protection from the early morning sunlight during winter. (General cultural notes as for Azalea, which see, remembering particularly the constant need of a deep, well-rotted, acid humus mulch.*)

Native rhododendrons in this country are mountain plants, with the dwarf R. carolinianum and R. minus and the taller R. catawbiense and R. maximum as the conspicuous plants in many parts of the Appalachians, and R. macrophyllum from California to British Columbia on the Pacific Coast. Although the first two are commonly referred to as dwarf, in nature they may reach a height of five or six feet. In cultivation they are much more likely to make a more spreading plant with lesser stature. They have small leaves of fine dark-green color that cover the rather twiggy growth of the bushes. The flowers come in crowded heads, usually white with greenish dots on the upper lobes in R. minus, and pale pink in R. carolinianum. Because of this more delicate growth and smaller foliage, these plants make excellent contrast with the more robust R. catawbiense and R. maximum.

In R. catawbiense the typical flower color is lilac-purple, but there is considerable variation toward rose-purples, and albinos are known and cultivated. Possibly this has been of more value as a parent than for itself, for from it have come the gorgeous hybrids such as Mrs. C. S. Sargent, Kettledrum, Gomer Waterer, Amphion, Parson's Gloriosum, and the like. In R. maximum the chief value is in the growth and the foliage, for the flowers are often hidden by the young growths that surround them, as they do not open until all the other native species have finished their blooming. As they are essentially white, sometimes pink-tinted, the floral display is not comparable to that of some other sorts. The foliage, however, is superb enough to warrant use of the plant for foliage alone.

On the Pacific Coast the native species somewhat resembles R. catawbiense both in habit and in flower.

Europe contributes the rather tender lavender R. ponticum, once largely used for stocks in grafted rhododendrons, the pinkish or yellowish-white caucasicum, rose-colored smirnovi, and more rarely the pink and white ungerni to the large shrubbery. All of these save the first are hardy and tolerant of both summer heat and winter cold.

The real home of the rhododendron, however, is the Orient, with the greatest number of species and forms in China. In these forms there is the greatest diversity of stature, habit, and color, from the many low, thicket-forming species of the high mountain ranges in China to the tall, tree-like species of

---

* Special articles on the subjects indicated by an asterisk (*) will be found at the words so marked.

Burma. From such trials as have been made, cold does not seem to be the sole determining factor. Apparently light has much to do with success, for many species seem to suffer most if they do not have long periods of gray weather and abundant moisture in the air. These are conditions that are somewhat difficult to supply in cultivation and limit the general use to seacoast regions where fogs contribute to their happiness.

Like azaleas, rhododendrons are easily raised from seed, although the tall species come more slowly to flowering. Propagation is also possible by layers and piece-root grafts in winter, as well as the usual grafting methods. — B. Y. M.

Two methods of propagation have been widely used. The first, mostly useful to commercial growers, requires a special outdoor propagating frame. The second needs a propagating frame in a greenhouse. The outdoor propagation depends upon a device like an ordinary cold frame but with an essentially watertight board bottom. In this is put three layers of the following: Bottom layer is 1 part spent mushroom manure to 3 parts granulated peat moss; middle layer is equal parts of sedge peat and sand; top layer is pure sand. At the start, before compression and watering, the lower layer is about 3½ in. deep, the middle layer about 1 in. thick and the upper layer of sand about 2½ in. thick. No peat should be more acid than pH 5.0 (see ACID AND ALKALI SOILS).

Cuttings of young growth, made in Aug. or early Sept., without a heel,* and only permitting three leaves (all others should be trimmed away) are planted 2 × 2 in. apart, or closer if the var. is small-leaved, and set deep enough so that leafstalks are just touching the sand. Sprinkle them with enough water to keep the upper layer moist, which will be true once the lower layers have soaked up enough water to permit capillarity to work. Once this condition is reached, watering once a week until frost will usually be sufficient. In the winter water should be added, if necessary, only when the rooting medium has thawed out. Cuttings will root in the late fall or following spring if proper conditions are maintained. This means that no direct sunlight must ever hit the sash covering the frame. Otherwise ventilation, and hence more watering, will be necessary.

The other method of propagating rhododendrons is by leaf cuttings. Only leaves with an axillary bud (see AXIL) are taken, with a sufficient heel* to include the bud. The cuttings are put in a propagating frame in the greenhouse filled with a mixture of 2 parts peat moss and 3 parts sand, over bottom-heat of 70–75° F. Thereafter they should be handled as are any others rooted in the greenhouse. See CUTTINGS.

The named forms of rhododendrons are legion, practically all of them of hybrid origin. Not all of them are worth the expense and time for long trials. In the list below are named forms, which, over a period of many years, have been a magnificent success. They were selected from over two hundred varieties, tested for two decades at the estate of the late Lowell M. Palmer, Esq., at Stamford, Conn., not far from Long Island Sound. All proved perfectly hardy there.

Album elegans	Maximum Wellsianum
Album grandiflorum	Maxwell T. Masters
Atrosanguineum	Mirandum
Bacchus	Mrs. Charles Sargent
Bluebell	Mrs. Harry Ingersoll
Boule de Neige	Mrs. John Clutton
Caractacus	Mrs. J. P. Lade
Charles Dickens	Mrs. Milner
Delicatissimum	Mrs. R. G. Shaw
Edward S. Rand	Mrs. R. S. Holford
Everestianum	Mrs. Shuttleworth
F. D. Godman	Mrs. S. Simpson
Giganteum	Old Port
Guido	Picturatum
Hamlet	Purity
Hannibal	Purpureum elegans
Henrietta Sargent	Purpureum
H. H. Hunnewell	grandiflorum
H. W. Sargent	Ralph Sanders
James Bateman	Roseum elegans
James Macintosh	Scipio
James Nasmyth	Sefton
Kettledrum	Sherwoodianum
King of the Purples	Silvio
Lady Armstrong	Sir Thomas Seabright
Madame Carvalho	

The list includes 50 varieties which may be considered among the most satisfactory of all rhododendrons. As to their culture at Stamford, Mr. Palmer left the following notes: "They do not like lime, nor do they like a heavy clay soil. Most important of all they do not want disturbance of their roots, so mulch them with leaves, and do not take the leaves off in the spring. Merely add to the mulch each autumn enough leaves to replace those lost through decay or by the wind. The leaf-mulch should be eight to ten inches thick."

As to shade, many rhododendrons grow naturally under complete or partial shade of a forest canopy. If that is not available, one may still plant rhododendrons, but shade should be provided for the first three years. A simple method is to make slat screens, the slats being one and a quarter inches apart. Put the screens on posts so that they are about three feet above the tops of the plants. These should be left out continually, but after the second summer remove alternate slats which will let through twice the amount of light. One more summer's protection, with this increased amount of sunshine, and the plants are ready to grow without protection, except for a winter covering of evergreen boughs, or if these are not available, dried cornstalks will do. If neither is to be had, the lath screen may be put back. Some protected places need no winter covering, but it is safer to put it on anywhere north and east of New York City.

INSECT PESTS. Control lace bugs with pesticide #21 (see SPRAYS AND DUSTS) when they appear. Borers, chiefly a caterpillar, can be stopped by applying 3 or 4 double-strength

---

* Special articles on the subjects indicated by an asterisk (*) will be found at the words so marked.

applications of pesticide #17 to branches (only) at 3-week intervals beginning in late spring. Prune out and destroy infested areas. Termites will attack older plants. Use conventional pesticide #15 soil treatments.

DISEASES. Wilt* is the most serious disease of rhododendron. Small plants may be killed quickly. Large plants die branch by branch. Red streaks in the wood, just beneath the bark at the soil line, indicate the wilt disease. Remove diseased plants and do not place rhododendron back in this area.

Various fungi cause leafspots.* Spray with pesticide #5 (see SPRAYS AND DUSTS) when new leaves appear in spring and repeat twice at 10-day intervals. The pinkster gall (see AZALEA) is occasionally a problem on rhododendron.

RHODOMYRTUS (ro-do-mir′tus). Tropical Australian, Asiatic, or East Indian shrubs and trees of the family Myrtaceae, **R. tomentosa**, the hill gooseberry or downy myrtle, grown in nearly frost-free regions for its berry, used for jam. It is a shrub 3–5 ft. high, with opposite,* short-stalked, blunt, more or less elliptic leaves 1–2½ in. long. Flowers 1–3 in each cluster, rose-pink, about ¾ in. wide, the 5 petals densely hairy on the outside. Fruit a globe-shaped, purplish berry about ½ in. in diameter. Tropical Asia and the Philippines. In Fla. it can be grown up to zone* 8 on a variety of soils and will stand an occasional frost. Propagated by seeds. (*Rhodomyrtus* is from the Greek for rose myrtle, in allusion to the myrtle-like, rose-pink flowers.)

rhodopensis, -e (ro-do-pen′sis). From Rhodope, Bulgaria.

rhodopeum (ro-dō-pee′um). From or near the Rhodope Mountains, Bulgaria.

RHODORA (ro-doe′ra). A small genus of azalea-like shrubs of the heath family, the only cult. species being the beautiful **R. canadensis**, the rhodora immortalized in Emerson's poem. It is a shrub 2–3 ft. high, with alternate,* dark green, deciduous leaves, 1½–2 in. long, without marginal teeth, gray-hairy beneath. Flowers irregular,* 2-lipped, very showy, about 2 in. wide, rose-purple. Newfoundland to N.J. and Pa., mostly in the mountains. March–April. Flowering before the leaves expand. Hardy from zone* 4 northward. Its cult. is the same as for *Azalea* (which see). (*Rhodora* is from the Greek for a rose, in allusion to the rose-purple flowers.)

RHODOTYPOS (ro-do-ty′pos). A single species of hardy, Asiatic shrubs of the rose family, **R. scandens**, variously known as jetbead, white kerria, and corchorus. It is a handsome shrub, 4–6 ft. high, with opposite,* short-stalked, doubly toothed leaves which are more or less oblongish, 3–4 in. long. Flowers pure white, nearly 2 in. wide, the 4 petals suggesting a single rose. Sepals* 4, toothed, alternating with 4 small bracts.* Fruit a collection of 4 shining, black, dry drupes set in the persistent calyx. China and Jap. Hardy from zone* 3 southward and widely grown both for attractive flowers and fruit. May.

Of easy cult. in any ordinary garden soil and propagated by seeds or cuttings. Sometimes known as *R. kerrioides* and *R. tetrapetala*. (*Rhodotypos* is from the Greek for rose and type, in allusion to the flowers resembling a single rose.)

Rhoeas (ree′as). The Latin name of the corn poppy (*Papaver Rhoeas*). See POPPY.

RHOEO (ree′o). A single species of Nicaraguan fleshy, short-stemmed perennial herbs of the family Commelinaceae, **R. discolor**, sometimes known as oyster plant or boat lily. It has densely overlapping, narrow leaves, nearly 12 in. long, purplish on the under side, the bases sheathing. Flowers white, the sepals 3 and the petals 3, the latter soon withering, the flowers borne in a dense umbel* which is enclosed by 2 boat-shaped bracts.* Also called *R. spathacea*. The common form in cult. is the *var.* **vittatus**, which has the leaves purple both sides, but yellow-striped above. The plant is naturalized in Fla. and is occasionally grown in sub-tropical gardens, more often as a pot plant in the warm-temperate greenhouse. It needs potting mixture* 4 and plenty of moisture. (The origin of *Rhoeo* is unknown.)

RHCICISSUS. See CISSUS CAPENSIS.

RHOMBIC. Having the shape of a rhombus, an equilateral parallelogram with oblique angles.

rhombifolia, -us, -um (rom-bi-fō′li-a). With rhombic leaves.

rhomboidea, -us, -um (rom-boy′dee-a). Rhombic.

RHOPALOSTYLIS (ro-pal-o-sty′lis). A few feather palms from N.Z. and vicinity, one of them, **R. sapida**, the nikau palm, cult. for ornament in southern Calif. It is the only native palm of N.Z., grows up to 25 ft. high, with an unarmed trunk up to 8 in. in diameter. Leaves very handsome, more or less erect, 6–8 ft. long, the segments or leaflets very numerous, 2–3 ft. long, 1–2 in. wide, the stalk with a sheathing base. Flower cluster from just below the leaf crown, 12–15 in. long, the fruit red, egg-shaped, about ½ in. long. Scarcely known outside of Calif. Sometimes offered as *R. baueri*. (*Rhopalostylis* is from the Greek for club and style, in allusion to the club-shaped style.*)

RHUBARB. A group of deep-rooted, perennial, acid-juiced herbs constituting the genus Rheum (ree′um) which comprises perhaps 30 species of stout, Asiatic herbs of the family Polygonaceae. They have basal, long-stalked leaves, which are divided or veined finger-fashion, the leafstalks channeled or sheathed. Flowers small, greenish-white, or reddish at the end of a stout central stalk which bears numerous flowers in dense, panicled clusters. Fruit a strongly winged achene.* (*Rheum* is from the old Greek word for rhubarb.)

For the culture of the common garden rhubarb *see* below. The only other cult. species, *R. palmatum*, is mostly grown for its striking

* Special articles on the subjects indicated by an asterisk (*) will be found at the words so marked.

foliage. It is easy to grow in any rich garden soil and is a handsome, hardy foliage plant.

R. palmatum. Resembling the common rhubarb, but the leaves deeply lobed. Northeastern As. Chiefly grown in the *var.* atrosanguineum, which has reddish flower clusters; and the *var.* tanguticum, which has longer leaves, not so deeply lobed.

R. Rhaponticum. Common garden rhubarb; also called pie-plant, and wine plant. A stout perennial herb, cult. for its pleasantly acid, wholesome leafstalks which are 12–30 in. long, green or red. Leaf blade roundish, not lobed, about 18 in. wide, often wavy-margined. Flowering stalk 4–6 ft. high, hollow. Siberia.

RHUBARB CULTURE

One of the most permanent crops in the vegetable garden is rhubarb. It must, like asparagus, be put in a position so that annual plowing or harrowing will not disturb it, and once established it should not be moved. If the directions given below are followed, a row of rhubarb will continue to bear for many years. Good vars. are McDonald, Victoria, and Valentine. Ten or fifteen roots will be enough for a small family, but twice that many are needed if the family is large, or more frequent cuttings are wanted, or if it is to be used for wine making.

SOIL PREPARATION. Rhubarb will grow in most ordinary garden soil, but to get the best results it is necessary to do much more than

Rhubarb plants should be allowed to develop fully in the summer.

merely plant the roots in such a soil. The chief value of the crop is the length and succulence of the leafstalks, both of which qualities demand quick growth in the early spring.

To be sure of getting such a growth it is better to dig a trench about 1 ft. wide and 2½ ft. or even 3 ft. deep. Save all the topsoil from the excavation, but cart away all the subsoil. Fill in the trench with old, well-rotted cow manure up to within 1 ft. of the top. Pack the manure well, filling in enough to bring the level of manure 1 ft. below finished grade after all shrinkage or settling. Then use

enough topsoil to cover the manure about 8 in. deep, the topsoil level then being 4 in. below the general soil level. Pack down the topsoil well, adding enough to make it 4 in. below finished grade when settled.

At this stage of preparation you have a rich, deep trench, filled in as directed, and ready for planting. The stout rhubarb roots should be planted 4–5 ft. apart in the trench, covered with the final 4 in. of topsoil, and well firmed in the soil. If more than one row is needed, make them 4–5 ft. apart.

In such a trench rhubarb will grow well. It must be kept cultivated, both to conserve moisture and to keep down weeds. During the first season after planting, no stalks should be cut, but cutting, or rather pulling, the stalks may begin the second season and continue every spring.

Even after the harvesting is over for the season, the plant must be well taken care of, for it is during the summer that it is storing in its roots the food that will make next year's stalks. Every fall the plants should be mulched with strawy manure, which should be dug in early in the spring.

If you want rhubarb during the winter and have the proper sort of cellar, it can be forced by following the directions given at CELLAR GARDENING.

The so-called Panama rhubarb is a variety of the common sort with longer, nearly stringless, sweet stalks, grown in Calif. and other warm regions.

INSECT PESTS. Wingless, large, brown snout beetles and their larvae can be kept away from plants by clearing plant growth away from base and treating soil liberally with 5% pesticide #15 powder (*see* SPRAYS AND DUSTS) twice in spring.

DISEASES. A fungus may occasionally cause spotting at the base of leaves and eventual wilting of plants may result. Remove badly wilted plants and start clean, healthy plants in a new area.

RHUBARB FAMILY = Polygonaceae.

RHUS (rus). Sumac. A large genus of shrubs and trees of the family Anacardiaceae, the 150 species scattered very widely. Among them are several plants, notably the poison ivy and poison sumac, which are the only serious contact poisons in our native flora, but they are not garden plants. *See* POISON IVY for a description of them and for remedies. The juice of a related, non-hort., Asiatic tree, still more poisonous, yields lacquer.

The cult. sumacs, none of which are poisonous, are shrubs or small trees with usually compound* leaves, the leaflets arranged feather-fashion and with an odd one at the end; simple-leaved in *R. ovata* and *R. integrifolia.* Flowers small, greenish, perfect or polygamous,* the petals, sepals, and stamens* each 5. Fruit a small drupe, clustered, red and hairy in all the cult. sumacs, but smooth and white or gray in the poisonous but not cult. poison ivy and its relatives. (*Rhus* is from the old Greek name for the sumac.)

* Special articles on the subjects indicated by an asterisk (*) will be found at the words so marked.

The cult. sumacs are of little decorative value until the autumn, when their foliage turns a more brilliant red than almost any other shrubs or trees. Their fruits are also handsome. They are easily grown in any garden soil, or even in dry sand or on rocky hillsides, and may be readily raised from seed.

americana = *Cotinus obovatus.*
aromatica. Fragrant sumac. A sprawling shrub 18–36 in. high. Leaflets 3, ovalish, 2–3 in. long, coarsely toothed, the foliage aromatic. Flowers greenish-yellow, borne in small spikes and blooming before the leaves expand. Eastern N.A. March–April. Hardy from zone* 2 southward. Also known as *R. canadensis.*
copallina. Dwarf sumac. A shrub or small tree, 7–15 ft. high. Leaflets 9–21, oblong or narrower, not toothed, 3–4 in. long, the main leafstalk conspicuously winged. Flowers greenish, in a dense, terminal, branched cluster. Eastern U.S., especially common in dry, sandy soils. July–Aug. Hardy from zone* 3 southward, and will stand smoke, sand, or even cinders.
cotinoides = *Cotinus obovatus.*
Cotinus = *Cotinus Coggygria.*
diversiloba. A Pacific Coast relative of the poison ivy (which see).
glabra. Smooth sumac. A shrub or small tree 8–20 ft. high, wholly without hairs. Leaflets 11–31, oblongish or narrower, 4–5 in. long, toothed. Flowers green, in a dense terminal cluster (panicle*). N.A. June–July. Hardy from zone* 2 southward. It has showy, red-hairy fruits.
hirta = *Rhus typhina.*
integrifolia. Sourberry. A shrub or small tree from southern Calif. and hardy only in similar climates, with evergreen foliage and simple* leaves, without teeth or with a few. Flowers pinkish-white in hairy clusters, followed by deep red and hairy fruits.
ovata. Sugar bush. An evergreen shrub from the desert regions of southwestern U.S. and little grown elsewhere. It is a smooth shrub, 6–10 ft. high with simple,* ovalish leaves, 1–3 in. long. Flowers greenish-white, in short, dense clusters (spikes*). Fruit hairy, dark red.
radicans. *See* POISON IVY.
Toxicodendron. *See* POISON IVY.
trilobata. Squaw-bush; also called lemonade sumac. Somewhat resembling *R. aromatica,* but the foliage ill-scented and smaller. Leaflets 3, ovalish, coarsely toothed, ¾–1¼ in. long. Flowers greenish, in small spikes blooming before the leaves expand. Ill. and Tex. to the Pacific Coast. March–April. Hardy from zone* 3 southward. Not so showy as *R. aromatica* and more upright.
typhina. Staghorn sumac. A shrub or small tree, 10–30 ft. high, the twigs densely brown-hairy. Leaflets 11–31, oblong-lance-shaped, 4–5 in. long, toothed. Flowers greenish in a large, terminal cluster (panicle*). Northern N.A. June–July. Hardy from zone* 3 southward. The *var. laciniata* has the leaflets attractively and finely cut into narrow segments. The staghorn sumac is by far the best from the hort. standpoint, as both its showy fruiting cluster and gorgeous autumnal foliage are most attractive. It was long known as *R. hirta.*
Vernix = Poison sumac. *See* POISON IVY.

rhytidophylla, -us, -um (rit-i-do-fill′a). With wrinkled leaves.

RIB. Any vein or nerve in a leaf. The main one is the midrib.*
RIBBON-BUSH = *Muehlenbeckia platyclados.*
RIBBON-GRASS = *Phalaris arundinacea picta.*
RIBBON PLANT. *See* CHLOROPHYTUM.
RIBBONWOOD. *See* HOHERIA and PLAGIANTHUS.

RIBES (ry′beez). A large genus of sometimes prickly shrubs, mostly from temperate regions, belonging to the family Saxifragaceae, and of first-rate hort. importance because it includes the currant, gooseberry, and several related shrubs grown for ornament. There are over 140 species, but beyond the few below most of them are not in general cult., except in a few collections of specialists. Leaves alternate,* simple,* but usually lobed finger-fashion. Flowers prevailingly greenish, yellowish, or reddish, the sepals usually colored and larger than the petals, which are sometimes very small or lacking. Stamens* 5. Fruit a true, juicy berry, bristly in the gooseberry. The individual flower stalks are jointed in the currants, but not jointed in the gooseberries, for which some retain the name *Grossularia;* the gooseberries are also usually spiny, the currants without spines. (*Ribes* is a Latinized version of an Arabic name for a plant with an acid juice.)

For the culture and uses of the fruit species *see* GOOSEBERRY, also CURRANT. The other, ornamental species are of easy culture and may be propagated by layering, cuttings, or by seeds. All bloom early in the spring and fruit in midsummer. The genus provides an alternate host for white pine blister rust, especially the common gooseberry and the black currant. Neither may be planted near any of the white pines. *See* GOOSEBERRY.

alpinum. Mountain currant. Alpine currant. An ornamental shrub, 5–8 ft. high. Lobes of the leaf toothed. Flowers in upright clusters (racemes*) greenish-yellow, the male and female on different plants. Fruit scarlet, smooth. Eu. Hardy from zone* 5 southward.
aureum. Golden or flowering currant. A widely cult., showy, unarmed shrub, 4–6 ft. high. Lobes of the leaf only slightly toothed. Flowers yellow, fragrant, in drooping clusters (racemes*), ultimately reddish. Fruit purplish-brown, smooth. Western N.A. Hardy everywhere. Often confused with *R. odoratum* (which see).
gordonianum. A hybrid between the buffalo currant (*R. odoratum*) and the flowering currant (*R. sanguineum*). It resembles the former, but has yellow flowers which turn red, and are somewhat sticky. Hardy from zone* 4 southward. Popular as an ornamental currant.
Grossularia. The garden or English gooseberry. A spiny shrub, 3–4 ft. high, the twigs bristly. Lobes of the leaf blunt-toothed. Flowers in clusters of only 1 or 2, green. Fruit acid, generally bristly, or at least glandular*-hairy, typically green, but yellow or even red in some forms. Eurasia and northern Af. Hardy from zone* 6 northward. For culture and varieties *see* GOOSEBERRY.

---

* Special articles on the subjects indicated by an asterisk (*) will be found at the words so marked.

nigrum. Black currant; also called European black currant. An unarmed shrub, 4–6 ft. high. Lobes of the leaf irregularly toothed. Flowers greenish-white, the clusters (racemes*) drooping. Fruit black, smooth, of fine flavor. Eurasia. Hardy from zone* 6 northward. There are many varieties, some of them, with the species, the source of the garden black currants. In all of them the bruised foliage has a heavy odor. For culture and varieties *see* CURRANT.

odoratum. Buffalo currant. An ornamental, unarmed shrub, 4–6 ft. high. Lobes of the leaf coarsely toothed. Flowers yellow, fragrant, the clusters showy and drooping. Fruit black, smooth, edible, especially in a variety known as Crandall which is sometimes grown for the fruit. Central U.S. Hardy from zone* 6 northward. One of the finest ornamental currants and closely related to *R. aureum* with which it is often confused. The only constant difference is that *R. odoratum* has sepals less than half as long as the tube of the calyx, and its young twigs are definitely pubescent, while *R. aureum* has nearly smooth young twigs and sepals more than half as long as the tube of the calyx.

rubrum. Northern red currant. An unarmed shrub, 4–6 ft. high. Lobes of the leaf toothed. Flowers greenish-brown, the clusters drooping. Fruit red, edible. Eurasia. Hardy from zone* 6 northward; scarcely cult. in America, but commonly so in northern Eu.

sanguineum. Flowering currant. A very ornamental and widely cult., unarmed shrub, 8–10 ft. high. Lobes of the leaf irregularly toothed. Flowers red, the sticky, drooping, many-flowered clusters (racemes*) very showy. Fruit bluish-black, with a bloom. Northwestern N.A. Hardy from zone* 6 northward. An extremely popular bush, useful for the red garden, but found in many hort. forms, some with pink, white, deep red, or with double flowers.

sativum. Common garden currant. An unarmed shrub, 3–5 ft. high. Lobes of the leaf toothed. Flowers greenish-purple, the profuse clusters (racemes*) drooping. Fruit normally red, smooth, juicy. Western Eu. Hardy from zone* 6 northward. For culture and varieties *see* CURRANT.

RICCIA (rick′si-a). A large genus of very simple, free-floating aquatic plants of no interest to the gardener, except for one or two that are used on the surface of aquaria. They are minute, flowerless plants, without differentiation of stem and leaf, microscopic sexual organs, and usually grow in masses on the water surface, hence looking like green scum. They resemble *Lemna,* which, however, is a flowering plant.

RICE. A widely grown cereal grass, and the only cult. species of the genus Oryza (o-ry′za), which compromises about 6 species of chiefly marsh grasses from the East Indies. The common rice is **O. sativa,** next to wheat the most important cereal in the world and probably the staple food of more people than rely upon wheat. Typically, it is a water-inhabiting grass, 3–4 ft. high, with smooth, angled stems mostly hidden in the long leaf-sheaths. Leaves grass-like, flat, 6–12 in. long, about ½ in. wide, roughish. Flowering cluster terminal, branched (a pan-icle*), usually curved to one side, the spikelets flat and ribbed. Fruit the familiar rice grain, normally yellowish, but white when polished. There are cult. varieties with red grains, and several adapted to upland cultivation. (*Oryza* is a Latinized version of Arabian name for rice.) Its cult. is purely an agricultural operation and hence omitted here. For wild rice *see* ZIZANIA.

RICE BEAN = *Phaseolus calcaratus.*

RICE-FLOWER. See PIMELEA.

RICE-PAPER TREE = *Tetrapanax papyriferus.*

RICHARDIA. An old name for the calla lily (which see).

RICH-MAN'S CABBAGE. See CAULIFLOWER.

RICHWEED = *Collinsonia canadensis* and *Eupatorium rugosum.*

ricinifolia, -us, -um (ri-sin-i-fō′li-a). With leaves like the castor-oil plant (*Ricinus*).

RICINUS. See CASTOR-OIL PLANT.

rigens (ry′jenz). Stiff or rigid.

rigida, -us, -um (ri′ji-da). Stiff or rigid.

rigidissima, -us, -um (ri-ji-diss′i-ma). Very stiff or rigid.

RIMU = *Dacrydium cupressinum.*

RING. To girdle a tree; *i.e.,* remove a complete circle of its outer bark and cambium, usually resulting in the death of the tree. See BARK.

ringens (rin′jenz). Ringent; *i.e.,* gaping; used mostly to describe certain 2-lipped corollas. See MIMULUS.

RINGO CRABAPPLE = *Malus prunifolia rinki.*

RING SPOT. The term applied to those virus diseases and a few fungus diseases which produce yellow rings on the leaves of plants. (*See* CHLOROSIS.) The virus ring spot disease overwinters in perennial plants such as dahlia and chrysanthemum or on the winter-annual chickweed. In the spring the virus is transmitted to annual plants such as tomato, pepper, sweet pea, etc., by thrips.* All plants with ring spot symptoms should be destroyed.

riparia, -us, -um (ry-pay′ri-a). Of riverbanks.

RIPE. As usually understood a fruit is ripe when it is ready to eat. Properly, however, *ripe* signifies that the fruit has matured to the point where its seeds are ready for germination.

A common hort. use of *ripe* describes the condition of the wood of a cutting, cion, etc., indicating that they are in fit condition for propagation. Ripe wood is thus wood that will root well or, in grafting, is ready for a perfect union.

Ritro (rit′ro). Native name in southern Eu. for *Echinops Ritro.*

rivalis, -e (ry-val′is). Growing in or near brooks.

---

* Special articles on the subjects indicated by an asterisk (*) will be found at the words so marked.

RIVER ASH = *Fraxinus pensylvanica.* See ASH.

RIVERBANK GRAPE = *Vitis vulpina.*

RIVER BIRCH = *Betula nigra.* See BIRCH.

RIVER SUNFLOWER = *Helianthus decapetalus.* See SUNFLOWER.

RIVINA (ri-vy'na). Weak-stemmed, tropical American perennial herbs of the family Phytolaccaceae, one of the three known species, R. humilis, the bloodberry or rougeplant, grown for ornament. It is a spreading herb, 1–3 ft. high, with alternate,* ovalish leaves, 2–4 in. long and without marginal teeth. Flowers small, white or pinkish, without petals, the 4-parted calyx petal-like. The clusters are erect or weak racemes,* far more attractive in fruit than in flower. Fruit a yellow, orange, or usually a red berry. The plant, sometimes known as *R. aurantiaca,* is common throughout Fla. and the Gulf states and is also cult. there. It is also grown, but not commonly, in the warm-temperature greenhouse northward. Use potting mixture* 4. (Named for A. Q. Rivinus, a German botanist.)

rivularis, -e (riv-you-lar'is). Growing in or near brooks.

ROADSIDE IMPROVEMENT. One of the best activities of garden clubs has been the improvement and preservation of roadsides. It is still true, however, that thousands of miles of American highways remain painfully hideous. Hot dog stands, gas stations, and billboards still disfigure miles of what should be restful and pleasant highways. The elimination of the billboards and the restriction of the two other causes of disfigurement are best illustrated by the superb parkways radiating from some of our larger cities, notably those in Westchester and Long Island, near New York. Such parkways are the best of all solutions of highway beautification problems. They are so costly, however, that only public money makes them possible.

The local garden club can, on a small scale and often very inexpensively, adopt the principle of parkway development for a country road. Its activities should take two main channels: (1) Encouraging better-looking and adequately planted gas stations and refreshment stands, and (2) planting of bare spots along the edges of the roads.

(1) The vested right of anyone to set up a stand or gas station, however hideous, cannot be legally denied. But the garden club often can and should offer to advise or even help in planting the surroundings of such. They can perhaps appoint a committee to pass on the plans for such structures. No compulsion need be exercised, but it does lie in the club's power to encourage and patronize owners who co-operate in such a scheme for roadside improvement. Most of the large oil companies already maintain good-looking gas stations. But the local dealers' stations and the refreshment stands remain a problem. Without legal compulsion,

the garden club and civic improvement societies are often the only agencies that can deal with this purely local problem. And prizes and patronage are more potent arguments for co-operation than anything else.

(2) Roadside Planting. In many places the widening or straightening of roads leaves ugly scars, which, left to themselves, become mere thickets or patches of weeds. Permanent planting of shrubs and trees, and even seeding level places to lawn is advised. But the latter should be done only if there is adequate provision for permanent care, without which such plantings become weedy thickets in a few years.

Masses of shrubbery or trees, however, especially on country roads, can be planted with the expectation of their needing little subsequent care beyond spraying. While it is sometimes desirable to plant the sorts native in the region, there is nothing against the use of any shrub or tree material that is hardy and suitable. The fetish that foreign plants are "unnatural" and out of place has worn a bit thin, because the inherent artificiality of all roads makes the use of native or exotic plants equally welcome in beautifying them. See TREES, STREET TREES, FLOWERING SHRUBS.

Unless there is adequate provision for permanent care, it is unwise to use ordinary perennials, although on really woodland roadsides it is often possible to make attractive displays of native wild flowers and hardy ferns. See WILD GARDEN, FERNS AND FERN GARDENING.

ROANOKE BELLS = *Mertensia virginica.*

ROBERT BRUCE. See ONOPORDUM ACANTHIUM.

ROBINIA. See LOCUST.

ROBIN'S-PLANTAIN = *Erigeron pulchellus.*

Robur (rō'bur). Old name for the oak of England. See *Quercus Robur* at OAK.

robusta, -us, -um (ro-bus'ta). Stout or robust.

robustispina, -us, -um (ro-bus-ti-spy'na). Stout-spined.

ROCAMBOLE. The pointed bulbs of a garlic-like plant (*Allium Scorodoprasum*) used as is garlic, for flavoring. It is not much cult. in the U.S.

ROCHEA (rō'she-a). South African succulent herbs or under-shrubs of the family Crassulaceae, R. coccinea a popular florists' plant grown for its showy red bloom. It has usually several stems, 12–18 in. high with many opposite,* simple, fleshy, ovalish leaves about 1 in. long and so numerous as to be overlapping. Flowers tubular, nearly 2 in. long, brilliant scarlet, fragrant, crowded in a dense, terminal, head-like cluster, somewhat resembling a phlox. The limb of the corolla is expanded, and about ½ in. wide. Fruit dry. A good pot plant, useful for house decoration, as its bloom is lasting. For cult. *see*

---

* Special articles on the subjects indicated by an asterisk (*) will be found at the words so marked.

SUCCULENTS. It is sometimes sold as *Crassula coccinea*. (Named for François de la Roche, French botanist.)

ROCHESTER, N.Y. See ARBORETUM and GARDEN TOURS.

ROCK ASTER = *Aster alpinus*.

ROCK BRAKE. See CRYPTOGRAMMA.

ROCK CHESTNUT OAK = *Quercus Prinus*. See OAK.

ROCK CRESS = *Arabis*.

ROCK ELM = *Ulmus thomasi*. See ELM.

ROCKERY. A passé term for a rock garden.

ROCKET. See HESPERIS.

ROCKET CANDYTUFT = *Iberis amara*. See CANDYTUFT.

ROCKET LARKSPUR = *Delphinium Ajacis*.

ROCKET SALAD = *Eruca sativa*.

ROCKFOIL. See SAXIFRAGA.

ROCK GARDEN. Rock gardens furnished with alpine and saxatile* plants are a comparatively recent development in horticulture. Alpine plants, according to Paxton, have been grown in England since the 16th century, but in those early days they were grown as pot plants in cold frames, or planted out in the flower border, and not in rock gardens.

The use of rockwork in gardens was introduced to the western world toward the close of the 17th century — the idea coming from China and Japan. Unfortunately the motive that inspired the Chinese and Japanese in the construction of their rockwork was not imported with the practice and the result was that in many European gardens grottoes, cascades, caves, and rockeries consisting of meaningless jumbles of rocks interspersed with soil were erected. Examples of a good idea gone wrong are still in evidence in so-called rock gardens that are nothing more than rock piles planted with unsuitable material.

Apparently it was not until about the middle of the 19th century that it occurred to anyone that alpine plants and rockwork could be in any way connected. Nowadays it is so obviously an ideal combination that it seems unbelievable that the connection should have been missed for so long. F. Dawtrey Drewitt in his book *The Romance of the Apothecaries' Garden at Chelsea* states that a rock garden was constructed there in 1772 for the growth of alpine plants, but whether Mr. Drewitt just assumed that alpines were grown in it or whether he has real evidence on this point does not appear. The rock garden had its inception in the fact that Sir Joseph Banks, on his return from Iceland in 1772, brought with him a quantity of lava which was supplemented by forty tons of stone from the Tower of London. Later, someone donated a quantity of flints and chalk. Brain coral, bricks, and conch shells also had a place in this rock garden. Many of the early rock gardens exhibited a similar lack of perception, on the part of the builders, of the desirability of a certain amount of unity, and the importance of avoiding incongruities in rock garden construction. Even in the famous rock garden of the Royal Botanic Gardens at Kew, as late as 1910, broken masonry and portions of brick piers could be seen substituting for rocks.

During the past forty years or so, considerable progress has been made in the art of rock garden construction, so that today in this country, as well as in Europe, where rock gardening is most highly developed, rock gardens may be seen which are artistically correct and well adapted to the cultivation of alpine and rock plants.

THEORY OF ROCK GARDENS

It is correct to assume that the ideal rock garden is one capable of supporting a healthy growth of alpine and rock plants. In order to display them in an appropriate setting, and to provide proper cultural conditions, in part at least, approximating those under which they grow in nature, a rock garden is necessary.

Apart from their value in providing a picturesque and natural setting, the rocks in a rock garden have several distinctly utilitarian functions to perform. They help to keep the ground cool; they conduct moisture to the roots of the plants and prevent, in part, its loss by evaporation. As many alpine plants grow in situations where the soil is constantly moistened, during the growing season, with ice or snow water, the importance of providing a cool root run is immediately obvious. The rocks serve to give shade and shelter and aid in promoting the efficient drainage which is so necessary. Also they hold up the soil, making it possible to provide a variety of contours in the garden.

One of the difficulties in growing alpine plants under lowland conditions is the great difference in the length of the growing season compared with what they experience when growing wild. In the vicinity of New York the growing season (between the last frost of spring and the first frost of autumn) is 210 days; whereas in their natural habitats the growing season is about half this length. For the length of the growing season in your region *see* the frost dates at the name of your state or province.

As long ago as 1857 Dr. Regel, in a paper on the Swiss alpine flora and the culture of alpine plants, advanced the theory that alpine plants require a much poorer soil under cultivation than they do when they are growing under natural conditions. The reason given is that when alpines are planted in poor soil it slows up their rate of growth and in a measure compensates for the long growing season they experience under lowland conditions. Whether or not Dr. Regel's theory is tenable it is generally agreed that

---

* Special articles on the subjects indicated by an asterisk (*) will be found at the words so marked.

an overrich soil is not good for alpine and rock plants under cultivation. In the first place it is likely to stimulate their growth so that they no longer possess the characteristic compactness of habit which is one of their charms. Another disadvantage of a rich soil and consequent lushness of growth is that the plants are likely to "damp off" during the hot, humid periods in summer, or die from the effects of the winter.

TYPES OF ROCK GARDENS

The forms that rock gardens take are many and varied, ranging from the many-pocketed erection made solely for the purpose of growing a large collection of alpine and rock-inhabiting plants, to the type designed purely as a landscape feature, in which the plants are merely incidental decorative material. The ideal garden lies between these extremes and consists of a construction in which the rocks are arranged artistically — usually with some relation to what one might find in nature, and placed in such a way that a reasonably large collection of plants may be cultivated.

A type that is satisfactory when the general surroundings permit of its construction is in the form of a winding ravine. Such a garden affords every conceivable aspect, a desideratum when dealing with the more capricious alpines.

Then there is the mound type formed by building up above the surrounding level over a central core made up largely of drainage material. This kind of a garden, because it quickly dries out, is more likely to be satisfactory in sections which have considerable rainfall evenly distributed throughout the growing season.

Some rock gardens consist of a series of raised rocky beds from one to three feet in height with winding walks between. Such construction is good when the main object in view is the cultivation of a collection.

A sloping bank may afford opportunity for the construction of an interesting rock garden and in some instances a rock garden has been effectively used in place of the usual turf of a terrace slope.

Some purely formal types of rock garden are in existence and are quite appropriate if the home is formal in architecture and the garden has to be placed near it. In such cases the garden may consist of raised beds supported by almost vertical stone walls laid up without cement and planted. (See WALLS AND WALL GARDENING.) Walks of flagstone of random sizes with rock plants growing in the crevices between the stones form an appropriate concomitant.

When the garden supplements existing rocky outcrops it is important that the new construction should be in harmony with them. These outcrops may appear to be ideal as a nucleus for rock garden construction (and sometimes they really are), but appearances are often deceptive and the soil pockets in the vicinity of the rocks may be too shallow to admit of the cultivation of the plants it is desired to grow.

In order to be correct and to avoid a jar-

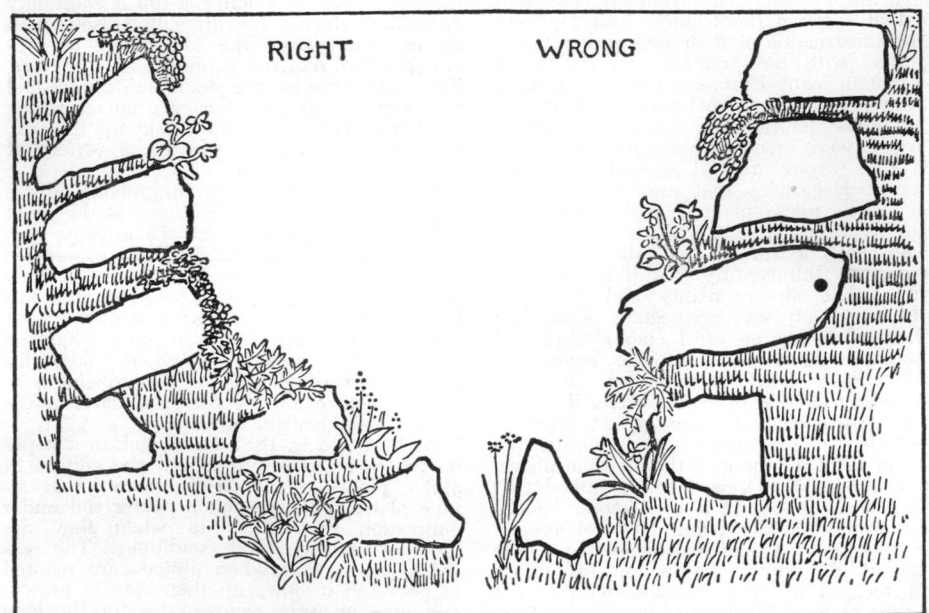

THE RIGHT AND WRONG WAYS TO BUILD A ROCK GARDEN
The rocks should always be placed so that moisture runs into, not out of, the garden.

* Special articles on the subjects indicated by an asterisk (*) will be found at the words so marked.

ring note the rock garden must be in harmonious relation with its surroundings. If the architecture of the house is formal and it is necessary to place the rock garden in its proximity it is a mistake to attempt a replica of wild mountain scenery.

When the house and surroundings are informal, more especially if the plot has sharp contours, the rock garden that partly imitates and partly idealizes nature should be constructed.

If the plot and general environment present a level surface a rock garden that rises much above the general level looks like an excrescence and entirely out of place. When it is desired to make a rock garden under such conditions it is a good plan partially to screen it with a shrub planting which will also serve as a background for the rock garden. Diversity of contour in a garden of this kind may be obtained by excavating a winding walk and using the soil thus obtained to provide height along the sides.

Miniature Gardens in Stone Troughs and Sinks

Miniature gardens planted with alpines and rock plants in cattle or horse troughs and in old-fashioned stone sinks assumed the proportions of a fad during the 1930's, especially in England. So great was the demand that the countryside was thoroughly ransacked, as were builders' yards, so troughs became as scarce as hens' teeth. This resulted in the construction of artificial troughs and sinks made of concrete. These have the advantage of being made any convenient size. They may range from $15 \times 9 \times 6$ inches deep (inside measurements) to $30 \times 15 \times 10$ inches or larger. The sides and bottom should be two inches thick for the small sizes, up to three inches for the larger ones. These last will need to be reinforced by one-inch-mesh wire netting. When constructing the forms, provision should be made for several holes, ½ to 1 inch across, in the bottom.

Here are some factors that need consideration. The smaller of the two containers described above has 810 cubic inches and the weight of the soil is approximately 35 lbs. The concrete will weigh approximately 50 lbs., giving a total of 85 lbs. — which is plenty for one person to handle. The permanent location should be decided before soil is filled in the boxes; also the height above the ground.

When planting those species that are subject to decay at the crown it is desirable to allow a space sufficient to accommodate a 1-inch layer of stone chips. This can be done by filling the trough with soil loosely to the brim, striking it off level, and then pressing it down to one inch below the rim.

In the case of lime-tolerant plants use oyster shells or broken limestone (¼- to ½-inch pieces); and for "lime-haters," use granite or sandstone chips. These can be bought at most seed or feed stores, or garden centers.

It is desirable to limit each container to plants that require the same cultural conditions — sun or shade; acidity or alkalinity of the soil, the same amount of watering, etc.

What, if anything, is gained by growing plants in sinks and troughs? It gives the grower a better chance to grow finicky plants; by raising them on piers it is possible to bring the plants nearer to eye level, which is desirable in the case of tiny alpines; because it eliminates much of the squatting and bending over, it is a boon to those who suffer from creaking knees and aching backs; and the specialist has a chance to provide the right conditions for his pet plants.

Site and Aspect

As a general rule the site of the rock garden should be in the open, not subjected to the drip from trees or to competition from their roots. *See* Drip.

Preferably the subsoil should be of a porous nature, permitting the rapid drainage of surplus moisture. This is true despite the fact that some alpines thrive in boggy situations.

No matter what the aspect of the garden may be, some rock plants can be found that will thrive in it. But, in order to provide varied cultural conditions for a large collection of plants it is well to have many aspects. When the bulk of the collection is to be made up of alpine plants the garden should face, in the main, north or northeast. Although many of our choicest alpines are exposed to blazing sunshine in their native haunts they appreciate a little shade during the hottest part of the day when grown in lowland regions of the temperate zone. This shade can be provided by the conformation of the rock garden and by large individual rocks.

The Kind of Rock to Use

As a general rule the stone available locally should be used even though it may not be ideal for the purpose. By using local stone there is less danger of constructing a garden that looks incongruous in its setting. The use of imported rocks may result in a better-looking garden *per se*, but if it introduces a jarring note into the general surroundings it is artistically inadmissible. The use of alien material may be permissible when it is possible to construct and screen the rock garden so that it can only be seen as a unit and not in relation to surrounding topography.

Weather-worn limestone of irregular shapes is perhaps the most pleasing material for construction and the easiest to work with. But weathered rocks of almost any kind can be used to advantage, provided they are angular and blocky in form, of a neutral color, and of pleasing appearance. Stratified rocks, when they are not too thin, permit the construction of picturesque effects in the

---

way of ledges, cliffs, and bold promontories.

The kind of rock that is commonly known as "tufa," because of its porosity, cavities, and lime content is admirable from the standpoint of providing ideal cultural conditions for certain groups of lime-tolerant rock plants, but its color and general appearance are against its extended use.

Other things being equal, rocks that are sufficiently porous to absorb considerable moisture, but sufficiently dense so that they do not crumble when exposed to the weather are to be preferred.

Glacial boulders may be used in rock garden construction if they are of varied size and not too spherical in outline. They should be used sparingly, and the general idea in mind when making the garden should be the simulation of a boulder-strewn slope, such as one might be expected to find on a terminal moraine.

The worst kind of rocks to work with are small, spherical boulders. If these are the only kind available it would be well to give up the idea of a rock garden. But if they are used it should be with the sole idea of making it possible to grow alpines and rock plants in such a manner that they will hide most of the rocks.

Only in exceptional cases should more than one kind of rock be used in the rock garden. It has many times been said, and it is worth repeating here, that a rock garden is a rock garden, and not a collection of geological specimens.

Water in the Rock Garden

Although ornamental water in the form of a cascade, brook, or pool is not absolutely necessary, it does add movement, interest, and attractiveness to the rock garden. Furthermore, in its immediate vicinity it affords opportunity to provide special cultural conditions for certain groups of plants. It should not, however, be introduced unless it can be done convincingly with a natural appearance. A "spring," whose source is the city water main, gushing from the top of a hill, does not look quite right. *See* Water.

Grading

Having decided on the location and knowing the kind and amount of rock available, the next step is to remove the topsoil from the area that is to be the rock garden. This topsoil with the modifications to be described below is the medium in which the rock plants will be planted. For convenience in handling later on, part of the topsoil should be placed on the walk and part on the outskirts of the rock garden.

Once the topsoil is removed, the subsoil should be shaped so that its contours roughly conform to the configuration the rock garden is to assume. If the garden is being built on sloping ground, it will probably be desirable to dig into the bank at strategic points and use the excavated soil

to heighten nearby areas to obtain more rugged effects.

When the site of the rock garden is level the best plan is to make a valley by digging out the area where the walk is to be and use the excavated material to gain height on the sides. In gardens made in this way it usually is necessary to provide a drain or drains at the lowest points to carry off surface water, otherwise after a rainstorm the walks may be knee-deep in water.

Drainage

When the subsoil has been graded the next step is to provide ample drainage. If the subsoil is naturally gravelly and porous no artificial drainage will be necessary, but if it is impervious to moisture, provision must be made to carry excess water quickly away from the roots of the alpines. This should be done even though drainage is not so important in most parts of this country as it is in rainy England.

It has been found that a 12-inch layer of coarse coal ashes, underneath the rock garden soil, works admirably. Preferably, ashes should be used with the dust sifted out, and which have been exposed to the weather for six months or more so that injurious compounds have had an opportunity to leach out. If ashes are not available, brickbats, small rocks, or similar material can be substituted.

Soil

The nature of the climate has an important bearing on whether one should lean toward porosity or retentiveness in making up a soil mixture. In a rainy section extreme porosity is desirable, but in a region where long periods of drought are experienced a more retentive soil is preferred. In either case, if the more capricious alpines are to be attempted, the soil surface should be mulched with stone chips or fine gravel. This prevents moisture from collecting around the crowns of the plants — which is likely to be fatal in wet climates — and conserves the soil moisture in dry ones.

The soil used should not be rich. It should be porous so that excess water may rapidly drain away and at the same time be capable of holding sufficient water so that the plants do not suffer from drought. If the topsoil is a fairly good garden loam the above requirements may be achieved by making up a mixture of three parts loam, two parts crushed stone ($\frac{1}{8}$ to $\frac{3}{8}$ inches), one part sand and two parts humus. This humus may be leaf mold, swamp muck that has been kept high, and fairly dry, for two years, or granulated peat moss. The latter is all the better if it has been exposed to the weather for a year or two before being used. If it is acid it should be neutralized by the addition of lime before using it. About $\frac{1}{2}$ lb. of ground limestone to a bushel of humus will be near the amount required. By using the above mixture as a base soil it is possible, by the

---

addition of crushed limestone, acid peat, or sand in special sections of the rock garden, to provide the right soil conditions for plants tolerant of lime, acid, and sand respectively.

The importance of soil reaction in respect to acidity and alkalinity probably has been overestimated. Among alpine and rock plants some, such as *Arenaria groenlandica, Empetrum nigrum,* and *Loiseleuria procumbens,* are definitely intolerant of lime. On the other hand, some species such as *Campanula, Daphne,* and most species of *Dianthus* delight in a limy soil. But most alpine and rock plants are reasonably tolerant and will thrive in a soil with a reaction between pH 6 and pH 7.5, provided that it is porous. *See* ACID AND ALKALI SOILS.

MORAINE OR SCREE

Along about 1908 began the advocacy of moraine or scree gardens as an aid in growing intractable high alpines. A moraine or scree in rock gardener's parlance consists of a bed of stones, two feet or more deep, with or without a small proportion of soil and humus, and watered either from above or below. One conception of a moraine is of a watertight basin two feet deep and of any convenient length and breadth filled with a mixture made up of 5 parts crushed stone (½ in. and smaller), 1 part sand, and 1 part sifted leaf mold. Water is supplied during the growing season through a pipe at the upper end and the surplus drawn off by an outlet at the other end *1 ft. below the surface.* Another outlet is necessary at the bottom of the basin to drain off all water during the winter. The theory back of this practice is that there is a constant supply of cool water running through the rooting medium, thus supplying the moisture and cool root-run that high alpines delight in; while comparatively dry conditions are provided during the winter when the plants are at rest.

Many growers prefer not to bother with sub-irrigation in the moraine and rely on rainfall or occasional overhead watering. In the rock garden of the Brooklyn Botanic Garden a moraine of this type with the soil mixture described above has been fairly successful; such plants as *Silene acaulis, Geranium argenteum,* and some of the encrusted saxifrages taking very kindly to this treatment.

Almost indefinite changes can be made in the character of the stony mixture. It may be of limestone, sandstone, or granite, with varying portions of sand and humus. An experimenter in Ireland using dozens of different mixtures found that pure limestone chips, including the dust just as it came from the crusher, gave best results, whereas a neighbor 5 miles distant found that limestone and soil, 3 to 1, was the most satisfactory mixture.

In order to give an air of verisimilitude to the moraine it might be well to construct it so that it seems to be pouring out from between two rocks on a slope and broadening out, more or less fan-shaped, toward the base. A few flattish rocks placed here and there will serve as stepping stones and help mitigate the gravel-walk appearance that is inevitable.

CONSTRUCTING THE ROCK GARDEN

Before starting the actual work of putting the rocks in place it is a helpful procedure to study rock arrangements as they occur in nature, not necessarily with a view to finding something that may be copied, but to get the right spirit so that a garden may be made which is an idealization of Nature's work, but not too far removed from it.

Having shaped up the subsoil and placed the drainage material, about ¾ of the prepared soil should be spread over the site, reserving the remainder for filling behind and between the rocks as they are put in position. Try to provide soil 2 ft. deep in the planting areas.

Except when the rocks are quite small, tools will be necessary as an aid in moving them. One of the most useful is a two-wheel truck such as that used by longshoremen. With one of these, and two planks on which to run it, quite large rocks may be moved with ease. Crowbars to use as levers and some chunky blocks of wood (which are lighter to handle than stones of similar size) to serve as fulcra are also necessary. Iron pipes from 2 to 4 inches in diameter and about 3 feet long form suitable rollers should their use be required. When the construction is extensive and very large rocks are to be handled, the aid of a derrick may be necessary.

Starting from the lowest point, place each rock on its broadest base, making sure that the soil beneath it is packed firmly. Sometimes it will be desirable to dig out soil to make room for a rock and sometimes a rock may stand free and the space behind it be filled from the soil held in reserve. In general from ⅔ to ¾ of the rock should be hidden by the soil it is holding in place.

Where the slope is gentle the rocks should be used sparingly, providing wide, sloping shelves on which the plants may be grown. Concentrate the rocks where the grade is steepest, in some places leaving little more than a crevice for the reception of the plants.

The rocks should tilt toward the soil so that rain may be conducted to the roots of the plants.

When stratified rocks are used, place them so that the stratification lines lie in one plane. As a general rule the strata should be slightly off horizontal. If placed vertically and the rocks are of a crumbling nature the effects of weather may cause them to disintegrate more rapidly than is desirable. Of course if neighboring rock formations exhibit vertical strata the rock garden should be made to correspond.

If the rocks are too small to gain the desired

---

* Special articles on the subjects indicated by an asterisk (*) will be found at the words so marked.

height when used singly it is sometimes possible by careful matching to place several rocks together, giving the appearance, when planted, of a single fissured rock.

WALKS

Walks in the rock garden may be of turf, gravel, or flat stones. Turf walks, although pleasing in appearance and suggesting alpine meadows, present a problem in upkeep owing to the difficulty of mowing in proximity to rocks. The invasion of the planting areas by grass stolons* is also a disadvantage. The best way to overcome these difficulties is to place a barrier between the lawn and the edge of the garden. This can be a 6-inch-wide strip of metal — aluminum or rust-resistant steel. This should be driven into the soil far enough from the rocks to permit the use of a 1-wheel lawn-edge trimmer. Remove one inch of topsoil on the garden side and replace it with stone chips or some similar covering to discourage weeds.

Gravel walks are permissible in gardens where there is considerable traffic, provided their color harmonizes with the general surroundings; but for most rock gardens flat rocks interplanted with dwarf carpeting plants are to be preferred. In small gardens where the traffic is light these walks may take the form of irregular stepping stones with plants between. *See* PAVEMENT PLANTING.

Whichever kind of walk is chosen ample under-drainage must be provided so that there is no standing water during rainy periods.

PLANTING

Rock plants may be set out in early fall or spring. In general in an established rock garden, hardy, early-blooming subjects should be planted in the fall. As most of the nurserymen specializing in rock garden plants grow a good proportion of their stock in pots it is possible to obtain material that may be planted at any time during the growing season without checking growth.

When planting, the soil should be packed firmly about the roots, taking care to leave no air spaces. When crevices between rocks are to be planted it is better to do so as the work of construction proceeds, since it is a difficult and tedious task properly to spread out the roots and pack the soil around them in existing crevices. A natural appearance should be aimed at in planting the rock garden. Avoid setting the plants in straight lines.

As a general rule all the plants of one variety should be grouped together rather than to spot them all over the rock garden. It may be desirable to depart from this practice when it is necessary to find the right cultural conditions for a species that is known to be difficult.

Although the alpine plant enthusiast as a rule pays little attention to grouping plants with reference to their color values, being quite content with a kaleidoscope so long as his plants are healthy, those who find pleasure in harmonizing color schemes have plenty of scope for their efforts in planting the rock garden.

GENERAL CARE

In the spring as soon as the frost is out of the ground and the winter covering has been removed it is necessary to look carefully over the garden and restore to earth any roots that have been heaved out by the action of frost. It is good at this time to apply a mulch of equal parts of stone chips and leaf mold. Prostrate plants such as mountain avens seem to benefit greatly from a mulch of this kind worked among their prostrate stems.

It is important to ensure that the plants do not suffer from lack of moisture during spring. A drought in May when the plants are actively growing may injure them.

A careful watch must be kept at all times for weeds. As it is seldom possible to use a hoe, weeding in the rock garden is largely a matter of finger and thumb work, with a hand fork or small cultivator to help remove the stubborn weeds, and to loosen the surface soil. In connection with weeding it should be remembered that the most beautiful plant may become a weed if it is growing in the wrong place, therefore keep a close watch on the more exuberant rock plants so that they may be restrained should they show signs of overwhelming weaker, choicer material.

WATERING

Most alpines and rock plants require abundant water when they are actively growing. Some authorities recommend subirrigation by means of perforated water pipes, but this is expensive to install and quite likely to get out of order. The simplest way to water the rock garden is by means of sprinklers throwing a fine spray. These should be left in one position long enough to soak the ground thoroughly. Some plants such as the silvery-leaved milfoils and some of the more difficult high alpines are likely to suffer from too much overhead watering. These should be segregated and water supplied by pouring water into a short length of porous drain tile, or even an ordinary flower pot, permanently sunk in the ground beside them. A method of applying water that may solve the problem of watering the rock garden as a whole, as well as those plants which object to overmuch water on their leaves, is by means of portable, perforated, flexible pipes, or cloth hose from which the water may drip or ooze upon the ground in the vicinity of the plants.

WINTER PROTECTION

In sections of the country where the rock garden is covered with a thick layer of snow all winter there is no need to worry about winter protection. It is in those regions where frost and thaw alternate that protection is needed — not to keep the plants warm, but to keep the ground frozen, to shade the plants from late winter sunshine, and prevent

---

* Special articles on the subjects indicated by an asterisk (*) will be found at the words so marked.

them from starting into premature growth which may suffer from late frosts.

The kind of covering used must be light and of such a nature that it will not mat down into a soggy mass as a result of exposure to rain. Evergreen boughs such as fir or pine are the best possible covering. Salt hay or oak leaves may be used if evergreen boughs are not available. In localities where considerable rain is experienced during the winter it may be necessary to protect from overhead moisture, by placing over them a pane of glass on suitable supports, such plants as the silvery-leaved milfoils (*Achillea*) and any woolly-leaved high alpines. The covering should not be put on until the ground has been frozen sufficiently to stop all growth for the season.

PROPAGATION

BY SEEDS. The seeds of most rock plants germinate readily if planted in a cool greenhouse in March. Some kinds apparently need a period of after-ripening at low temperatures to ensure a good stand. Seeds of this nature may be planted in the fall and left out of doors. A plan that is followed successfully in England and one that would probably be equally successful here is to plant the seeds in late fall or early winter and place the seed pots or flats in a cold frame which is filled with snow as soon as it is available. When the snow has melted, the seeds are brought into a slightly heated greenhouse when germination usually is prompt. Those kinds which mature their seeds early may be planted as soon as they are ripe.

BY CUTTINGS AND DIVISION. Plants of garden origin such as *Phlox subulata* varieties or hybrids, and species which seldom set seeds should be propagated vegetatively. Cuttings of young shoots from 1 to 3 inches long may be made and inserted in sand in a shaded cold frame in July and August.

Species which bloom and make their growth early in the spring may be taken up and divided in late summer. Those which start into growth and bloom late in the season may be divided in spring. The divisions should be planted in soil that is somewhat more porous than that in which the parent plant is growing and kept watered and shaded until new roots are formed. In the case of many alpine and rock plants procumbent shoots are produced which root as they grow. These may be dug up for propagation purposes without disturbing the parent plant.

WHERE ROCK GARDENS MAY BE MADE.

If we except mountainous regions, the place in North America where rock gardens are likely to be most successful (in the sense of being able to grow without too much trouble the alpine plants that are considered ideal rock garden material) are Oregon, Washington, and British Columbia. Many rock gardens, furnished with a large proportion of alpine plants, are in existence in the eastern states from Philadelphia northward. There is considerable interest in rock gardening in many of the southern states, and in the high-lying sections there is no reason why some at least of the alpine plants should not be grown. In the Middle West, particularly in Ohio, where there is a successful Rock Garden Society, rock gardening is in great favor and fair collections of the more tolerant alpines are grown.

The cultivation of most high alpines is certain to be attended with almost insuperable difficulties except in regions having a low summer temperature and a growing season of 140 days or less.

But rock gardens can be made and furnished with other than what we normally think of as rock garden material. If anyone is fortunate enough to possess a wooded, rocky ravine on his property, there is offered an opportunity to develop it as a charming wild flower garden by planting our native woodland flowers.

In some of the northeastern states rocky outcrops are common which could be converted into pleasing landscape features by a judicious planting of such subjects as dwarf junipers and cotoneasters.

Unfortunately, the human race is prone to want "what is not," and garden makers, instead of making full use of natural features, seem to prefer to blast out the rocks and make a level greensward if they are in a rocky region, and import rocks at great expense to make a rock garden if they live on the great plains.

Rock gardens should not be attempted in rockless regions, more especially if the climate is such that it does not admit of the cultivation of alpine plants. But there are many parts of the country where picturesque rock formations abound, and these may appropriately be embellished with whatever plant material is available.

PLANTS FOR THE ROCK GARDEN

Sufficient has already been said to indicate that the preferred plants for the rock garden are alpines or other plants which exhibit a similar dwarf or compact habit of growth.

In general, species which thrive as well in flower border or shrubbery as they do in the rock garden should be used with reluctance and looked upon as mere fillers, tolerated only until more suitable material is obtainable.

Bedding plants, such as begonia, pelargonium, petunia, heliotrope, and lantana, are absolutely taboo. Annuals should be used very sparingly, resolutely avoiding commonplace varieties, such as portulaca and sweet alyssum. The chief use of annuals in the rock garden is to cover bare ground left by dying down of early spring bulbs.

Dwarf evergreens may be planted with discretion to give accent and provide some variety in height. If properly chosen and placed, they look in keeping with the rest of the plants. Evergreens are occasionally of value to hide errors in construction.

The importance of carefully choosing the

* Special articles on the subjects indicated by an asterisk (*) will be found at the words so marked.

Crevice plants for the rock garden: *Saxifraga macnabiana* (foreground) and candytuft

plants for the rock garden cannot be over-emphasized. If the wrong material is used, the rock garden loses its air of distinction and becomes merely a flower garden in which there are rocks.

The following plants, except where noted, will grow in the soil mixture previously described without overmuch coddling.

Except where otherwise indicated, the plants should be grown in open, sunny situations. Light shade during the hottest part of the day is desirable in regions having high temperatures, except for those kinds whose indicated preference is for hot, dry situations.

Those recommended for beginners are marked with a dagger (†).

Achillea ageratifolia. Gray, toothed foliage. Daisy-like flowers on 8-in. stems.

A. clavenae. Silvery leaves, flowers as above on 4-in. stems.

†A. tomentosa. Green, woolly leaves, flowers yellow on 8-in. stems.

The achilleas mentioned above thrive best in sunny situations and rather poor, stony soil.

Aethionema coridifolium. Sometimes sold as *Iberis jucunda*. Blue-gray, glaucous foliage smothered with dense heads of pink flowers 4 in. in height.

A. grandiflorum. Makes a graceful bush, 12 in. high, with loose spikes of pink flowers.

A. pulchellum. Drooping, and much-branched. Flowers rose-pink. About 8 in. high.

Aethionema is a much-hybridized genus. Exceptionally good forms should be propagated by cuttings of young shoots in summer. As they tend to be short-lived under cultivation, a few should be propagated every year. They require a sunny spot and well-drained soil mixed with crushed limestone.

†Alchemilla alpina. Grown for its beautiful foliage; shining green above, and silvery with silken hairs below. The flowers are dowdy and should not be allowed to form.

†Alyssum alpestre. Prostrate, with hoary foliage; yellow flowers produced over a long period in spring.

A. argenteum. Grayish leaves, golden-yellow flowers, 18 in. high.

†A. saxatile. Its myriads of yellow flowers, surmounting the hoary leaves, are showy. It is a sprawly plant about 1 ft. high.

Androsace carnea. Tufts of green foliage, heads of pink flowers on 2–3 in. stems.

Increase the amount of humus and stone chips for the above. Light shade during the hottest part of the days is desirable.

A. lanuginosa. Makes long, trailing shoots with silvery leaves. Umbels of rose-lilac flowers in succession in late summer. Splendid when seen draping dark-colored rocks.

†A. sarmentosa. Foliage in rosettes. Plant spreads by runners similar to those of strawberry. Flowers in pink umbels* on 6-in. stems. Does well in moraine, but will grow in normal rock garden soil.

†Anemone Pulsatilla. Often sold under the name of *Pulsatilla vulgaris*. It has large, rich purple flowers, with masses of golden stamens.* Each flower is surrounded by a lacy ruff cf gray-green, hairy bracts.* Its achenes* with long, feathery styles prolong its attractiveness after the blossoms have fallen. It is more in keeping with the rest of the rock garden plants if grown in poor soil with plenty of crushed limestone — in rich soils it grows too lush.

A. sylvestris. Flowers white on 8-in. stems. This species needs a cool, moist, shady spot and plenty of humus in the soil.

†Aquilegia alpina. Flowers large, of deep, clear blue, with golden stamens, on 18-in. stems.

†A. canadensis. Flowers cinnabar-red and yellow. Height from one to two ft. or more, dependent on soil. Plant in poor, rocky soil for best results. It becomes coarse and weedy-looking in rich soil.

†A. caerulea. Flowers lavender-blue and white on one- to two-ft. stems.

†A. flabellata nana. Quite dwarf — about 9 in. Flowers white, leaves glaucous.

Aquilegias will grow in full sun, but seem to prefer partial shade.

†Arabis albida. Gray, woolly leaves and 8-in. spikes of white flowers. The double-flowered form is unobjectionable, and indeed preferable, because of its long blooming period. This species is often sold under the name *A. alpina*.

A. aubrietioides. Grayish, hairy leaves in close tufts, surmounted by 6-in. spikes of pink flowers. Not very permanent.

A. kellereri. Makes a mat of silvery foliage closely hugging the ground. Heads of small white flowers. Plant in moraine or very gritty soil.

Arenaria balearica. When happy, covers

* Special articles on the subjects indicated by an asterisk (*) will be found at the words so marked.

soil and rocks with a ¼-in. carpet of bright green, studded in spring with pure white flowers, on 2-in. stems. It needs a cool, moist, well-drained spot and porous rocks over which to spread. Although sometimes a troublesome weed in English rock gardens, it is difficult to establish here.

†**A. grandiflora.** Green, pointed leaves. Flowers pure white on 6-in. stems.

A. montana. A trailing species with grayish leaves, and large white flowers. In England it may ramble happily through the walls (of brick laid without mortar) of a cold frame.

†**Aster alpinus.** Daisy-like, purple flowers on 8-in. stems. There are many forms, including a white one — not so good, but the variety known as *specious* is very good indeed.

†**Aubrieta.** This genus forms one of the stand-bys in European gardens. When exposed to the hot sun of American gardens the flowering period is considerably shortened. Good varieties are: Bridesmaid, soft pink; Lavender Queen, Crimson King; Dr. Mules, dark purple; Moerheimi, gray foliage and pale pink flowers. These varieties must be propagated by cuttings or division to keep them true to type. Many American nurserymen raise them from seed and offer under color only.

Campanula bellardi. A variable plant with quivering, bell-shaped flowers on slender 4-in. stems. It has a habit of flowering itself to death. Plant in moraine or very gritty soil. Sometimes called *C. pusilla.*

†**C. carpatica.** A strong and "easy to grow" kind. The foot-long stems tend to flop and may smother any choice plants in their vicinity.

There are many forms ranging in color from white to deep blue.

C. excisa. Violet-blue, narrow, bell-shaped flowers. Grow it in moraine or gritty soil from lime.

C. garganica has a central tuft of leaves and spreading, prostrate branches. The flowers are flat and starry, ranging in color from white to slaty-blue.

†**C. portenschlagiana.** One of the easiest of the dwarf campanulas. It has violet-blue flowers and grows 4–5 in. high.

Campanula is a genus that contains a large number of species suitable for rock gardens. Space does not permit mention of the dozens of fine species available.

Cymbalaria aequitriloba. A trailer built along the lines of the Kenilworth ivy but much smaller in all its parts. Farrer calls it "a Tiny Tim of extraordinary charm." Fine for crevices.

Dianthus alpinus. Perhaps the best of all the mountain pinks. It forms a mat of glossy, green foliage, surmounted by rose-pink flowers the size of a 50-cent piece, 3-in. stems. It needs ample drainage with

a liberal supply of limestone chips in the soil.

†**D. gratianopolitanus.** Bluish foliage, and fringed, pink flowers delightfully fragrant. Often called *D. caesius.*

†**D. deltoides.** Forms dense mats of green foliage and small, deep-pink blooms abundantly produced.

D. neglectus. Grassy tufts of foliage, pink flowers with a satiny-buff reverse, on 5-in. stems. Good for the moraine.

Almost any of the dwarf dianthuses look well in the rock garden. The commoner kinds should be prevented from seeding, for otherwise there is certain to be a crop of self-sown seedlings which are likely to run out choicer plants.

†**Dicentra eximia.** Fern-like foliage and racemes of rose-pink flowers.

Dodecatheon radicatum. A shooting star from the West, which in May sends up a flower stem of about 14 in. surmounted by a cluster of pale lilac-rose flowers. Needs light shade, a moist situation, and loamy soil.

Douglasia vitaliana. (Sometimes sold as *Androsace.*) Forms flat mats of narrow, greenish-gray leaves, at blooming time almost completely hidden by the clear, citron-yellow flowers. It should receive moraine treatment.

Draba aizoides. Forms dense tufts of spiny-looking rosettes with yellow flowers on stems 2–3 in. high.

D. olympica. Similar, with golden-yellow flowers 4 in. high.

The drabas are well adapted for crevice planting — preferably in limestone.

Dryas octopetala. A prostrate shrub, its branches clothed with evergreen, tiny, oak-like leaves. The flowers are creamy-white, on 2–3-in. stems, looking something like those of *Anemone sylvestris.* It should be top-dressed in spring with a half-and-half mixture of leaf mold and stone chips.

†**Epilobium nummularifolium.** A carpeting plant 1 in. high with tiny, round, bronzy leaves. The flowers are insignificant. It is a valuable plant to cover the ground where spring-flowering bulbs are planted.

Erinus alpinus. A tufted plant with 3–4-in. stems of rosy-purple flowers. It is a biennial or short-lived perennial. Plant in partial shade. Suitable for crevices. There is a form with carmine flowers, and one that is white.

†**Genista sagittalis.** A dwarf shrub which makes a mat of trailing branches with erect, curiously winged twigs, surmounted by yellow pea-like blossoms. It needs a hot, dry situation.

Gentiana acaulis is divided by some into five or more distinct species. The segregate known as *G. gentianella* is the one most amenable to cultivation. It requires a deep, rich, well-drained soil and abundance of crushed limestone. The flowers are enormous, of true gentian blue, aris-

---

* Special articles on the subjects indicated by an asterisk (*) will be found at the words so marked.

ing, stemless, from a tuft 1 in. high of green foliage. It blooms in May.

†**G. septemfida.** This species and its many forms are among the most tolerant of the worth-while gentians. It grows happily in well-drained but rather moist soil, in sun or partial shade. In August it produces clusters of flowers of soft, clear blue, on rather weak 8-in. stems.

This genus contains some of the most valued of alpine plants. The most desirable species are ofttimes difficult of cultivation, while the dowdy, weedy kinds, as usual, will thrive anywhere.

Gypsophila cerastioides. A dwarf (2–3 in.), tufted* plant with white flowers, marked with purple lines. It comes from the Himalayas.

†**G. repens.** A trailing species with gray-green foliage, and airy sprays of white, or rose-tinted, small flowers.

†**Helianthemum nummularium.** Sometimes sold as *H. vulgare* and *H. Chamaecistus.* There are many garden varieties offered under such names as: *grandiflorum, cupreum, tomentosum, venustum, roseum, stamineum, macranthum,* etc.; all of which are good rock garden plants in sections where the winters are not too severe. Helianthemums are shrubs of more or less prostrate habit, some with gray and some with green foliage. The individual flowers are fleeting, but are produced in succession over a long period. The color range includes white, yellow, pink, copper, and crimson. They require a well-drained soil, well limed; and a sunny situation. When flowering is over the plants should be lightly sheared to promote a more compact habit. North of Philadelphia the bushes should be protected by covering with evergreen boughs. We are convinced that a poor sandy soil is necessary to help them survive in regions where the winters are really cold. It is a good plan to root cuttings of young shoots in midsummer and carry them over winter in a cold frame, as a measure of insurance against winter losses, and to replace specimens that have grown too large or become worn out. They may readily be raised from seeds but the seedlings are likely to be variable.

Hypericum (*see* St. John's-wort).

H. polyphyllum. Makes a tuft of slender shoots 6 in. long clothed with small bluish-gray leaves and topped with golden flowers.

H. reptans. One of the loveliest. It makes a trailing mat of vivid green with large golden flowers in succession throughout the summer. It comes from Sikkim and sometimes winter-kills* in the vicinity of New York.

Iberis (*see* Candytuft).

†**I. sempervirens.** A sprawling evergreen shrub, showy when its white flowers are displayed in May. Admirable for draping over large rocks. Should be lightly sheared after blooming.

†**Iris cristata.** A dwarf, with creeping rhizomes. The leaves are pale green, about 6 in. long. Flowers of pale blue on 3–4 in. stems. There is a white form that is desirable. *I. cristata* does best in partial shade.

I. gracilipes. Forms a tuft of narrow, curving leaves, and pinkish-lavender flowers on graceful stems. Give it a gritty soil, with lots of humus, and partial shade.

I. tectorum. Rather large for the small rock garden. Strong clumps of leaves with bright lilac flowers on 18-in. stems. Plant in well-drained soil, in sun.

†**Leontopodium alpinum** (*see* Edelweiss). This easily grown plant is reputed to be responsible for many Alpine tragedies, when climbers have lost their footing in the endeavor to pluck its flowers. Its bracts, which look like gray flannel, are said to become white when planted in a soil that is rich in lime. It will grow in any well-drained soil.

Mentha (*see* Mint).

†**M. requieni.** A tiny creeper which closely hugs the ground. The leaves are small, orbicular, and emit an aromatic fragrance when bruised. The flowers are almost microscopic, violet in color, produced in late June. A good carpeting plant for a moist spot.

†**Nierembergia rivularis.** A low-growing plant, spreading by underground stems. The flowers, almost 2 in. in diameter, 2–3 in. high, white, with a yellow throat, are produced from June until the fall. This

Edelweiss (*Leontopodium alpinum*) in a congenial setting

sometimes fails to survive the winter out of doors in the vicinity of New York. To be on the safe side, portions should be dug up and kept in the cold frame over the winter.

Pentstemon glaber. Glaucous, bluish leaves;

---

* Special articles on the subjects indicated by an asterisk (*) will be found at the words so marked.

flower spikes 1–2 ft. with large, bright blue or purplish flowers.

P. heterophyllus. Green leaves, lance-shaped and linear. Flowers on slender stems 2 ft. or more high. Opalescent, pink, and rose-purple.

P. rupicolus. A dwarf (3–6 in.), creeping species from the Cascade Range. Small, blue-green, leathery leaves. Comparatively large red flowers. Needs gritty soil and shade during the hottest part of the day.

P. unilateralis. Glaucous, bluish-green leaves; flower stems up to 2 ft. with the blue flowers arranged mostly on one side.

There are many other species of *Pentstemon* suitable for rock garden planting. In general they require gritty soil, and object to moisture during winter. Many of them are not long-lived under cultivation and it is a good plan to propagate a few every year so as to have vigorous young plants coming along to replace those that succumb to the effects of winter.

Phlox adsurgens. A westerner with prostrate stems and glossy leaves. The flowers are large, varying from white to deep pink or a combination of these colors. Good drainage and partial shade.

†**P. amoena.** A low, spreading plant with rosy flowers on 6–8-in. stems in early spring.

†**P. divaricata.** Flowers blue in cluster on 12–18-in. stems. The varieties *laphami* and "Perry's variety" have a longer blooming season. They should be grown in light shade, in soil well supplied with humus; not a true rock garden plant.

P. douglasi. Forms a small tuft of narrow, pointed leaves, with lilac or white flowers. It is not easy to grow. In wet regions a well-drained, gritty soil and protection from moisture during winter are probably desirable.

†**P. stolonifera.** Makes a trailing mat of light green foliage, spreading by means of reddish runners which root as they grow. Flowers purple in loose, sparse clusters on 6–12-in. stems. Partial shade.

†**P. subulata.** A well-known and easily grown species. The color of the flowers in some forms is rather overwhelming. The varieties: *lilacina*, pale lilac; *alba*, white; and Vivid, salmon pink, are unobjectionable.

Phyteuma hemisphaericum. Tufts of grassy foliage, tiny blue flowers in almost globular heads on 3–6-in. stems.

P. scheuchzeri. Heads of blue flowers on 1-ft., slender, bare stems.

Polygonum affine. A trailing species from the Himalayas with evergreen, attractive foliage which assumes bronzy tints in the fall. The deep-pink flowers are produced from August to Oct. in dense spikes on 6-in. stems.

†**Potentilla nepalensis.** A species from the Himalayas growing about 2 ft. high, with rose-crimson flowers produced from July to the fall. Its variety *willmottiae* is dwarfer.

†**P. tridentata.** An evergreen about 6 in. high with deep-green leathery leaves, and small white flowers in summer. Sun or shade.

†**Primula Auricula.** Thick, mealy leaves, and yellow flowers, with a ring of meal in the throats. Plant in partial shade and mix crushed limestone in the soil. A very variable species.

P. bulleyana. A strong-growing species, with leaves like those of Cos lettuce, and red-gold flowers in candelabra tiers on 2-ft. stems in July. Needs a rich, damp, deep soil and light shade; not a true rock garden plant.

†**P. denticulata.** Rosettes of strong foliage and rounded heads of soft lilac flowers on 10-in. stems in early spring. Damp, well-drained soil in sun or light shade.

P. frondosa. Crinkly leaves, gray with meal on the under sides. Pink flowers in loose heads on 3–4-in. stems. Partial shade.

†**P. japonica.** A "lettuce-leaved" type with tiers of flowers, on 2-ft. stems. The color varies from white to magenta. The deep-crimson forms are most desirable.

If the soil is really wet they grow well in full sun; otherwise they should be planted in partial shade; not a true rock garden plant.

Primula is one of the largest alpine genera. Hundreds of species are suitable for rock gardens, but unfortunately many of them are difficult under cultivation.

Ramonda nathaliae. Rosettes of glossy green; flowers lavender-blue with four-lobed corolla.

R. myconi. Rosettes dull green, with many rufous hairs; flowers purple, corolla with five lobes. Also called *R. pyrenaica.*

The ramondas are among the choicest alpine plants. They should be planted in rock crevices, facing north in deep, peaty soil, with the rosettes flat against the rocks so that no water may lodge in the centers of them.

†**Saponaria ocymoides.** A trailing species with myriads of pink flowers. Valuable for draping rocks in full sun. Needs a well-drained soil.

†**Saxifraga Aizoon.** A species, with lime-encrusted leaves, which runs into dozens of varieties, with white, pink-spotted, or yellowish flowers and silvery leaves.

Plant in gritty soil on a north slope or in shade of large rocks.

S. apiculata. This forms a cushion made up of innumerable tiny rosettes of evergreen, strap-shaped leaves. The flowers, of primrose yellow, are in loose heads on 3–4-in. stems. Shade during hottest part of day. Moraine soil with ⅓ humus; plenty of water in early spring.

S. cochlearis. One of the "encrusted" group, with rosettes of reflexed, silvery leaves, and 6–8-in. sprays of pure white blossoms.

---

* Special articles on the subjects indicated by an asterisk (*) will be found at the words so marked.

Plant on north side of large rock in deep soil mixed with crushed limestone.

†S. decipiens. A variable species, with many garden hybrids. Flowers of the type are white — the hybrids vary from white to crimson. It is one of the "mossy" saxifrages. This group requires a deep, gritty soil with ⅓ humus and partial shade. Small stones should be laid on the soil about the plants to conserve moisture and keep the ground cool. Keep a stock of young plants coming along — propagating them by taking off rosettes in Aug. and inserting them in sand and humus in a shaded cold frame.

†S. hosti. When happy, forms cushions made up of rosettes of silvery, encrusted leaves. The flowers are white on 12–18-in. stems.

†S. macnabiana. It has a 12–18-in. panicle* of white flowers, speckled with crimson dots. One of the easiest of this group to grow. See illust., page 1030.

S. moschata. A dwarf, spreading "mossy" with many varieties ranging in color from creamy-white to red.

S. oppositifolia. Makes prostrate mats of tiny foliage with flowers that, in many varieties, tend toward magenta in color. In the vicinity of New York it is difficult to grow it beyond the seedling stage. It needs cool conditions, a stony soil and lots of water in spring.

There are hundreds of species and varieties of Saxifraga suitable for rock gardens. Such species as S. hosti and Aizoon run into scores of varieties and hybrids. With the increasing interest in rock gardening in America, and more knowledge concerning their culture in our varied climate, considerably more than the sixty or so varieties now offered by some specialists may be expected to be listed in their catalogues.

†Sedum acre. Dwarf, fleshy, bright green leaves and golden flowers. Should be used with discretion as it is potentially a pernicious weed, because any portion of the plant that is broken off and left lying on the ground is liable to form a new colony.

†S. album. Evergreen ground cover with tiny sausage-like leaves and pure white flowers in July.

†S. dasyphyllum. One of the most delightful sedums. Compact clusters of almost globular, blue-gray leaves on 2–3-in. stems. It has loose heads of white or rose-tinted flowers. Will thrive in a shallow soil.

†S. reflexum. Mats of narrow, fleshy leaves, with 8-in. stems surmounted by heads of yellow flowers in July.

†S. sarmentosum. Too vigorous and invasive a grower for the small garden. Trailing shoots, clothed with fleshy, green leaves. The flowers are yellow. Will grow in part shade.

†S. sexangulare. Stems 2–3 in. high, densely clothed with narrow, cylindrical leaves. Flowers yellow.

†S. spurium. A trailing evergreen with flat leaves and pinkish flowers. The deeply colored var. coccineum is preferable.

Sempervivum (see HOUSELEEK).

†S. arachnoideum. The small rosettes are covered with woolly strands. Attractive at all times and especially so when displaying its starry red flowers on 6–8-in. stems. The size attained by this and other species is determined largely by the character of the soil in which they are growing. In poor, stony soil the rosettes are small, and increase in size if planted in rich, porous earth.

†S. calcareum. Bluish-green rosettes 2 in. in diameter — each leaf tipped with reddish-brown. Flowers light red on stems up to 1 ft. A distinct species.

†S. fauconnetti. A small edition of S. arachnoideum but not so cobwebby. In poor soils the rosettes may be not more than ⅛ in. in diameter.

†S. soboliferum. Globular rosettes with numerous pill-like offsets* attached by short, slender threads which break and allow the offsets to roll away and form colonies.

Silene acaulis. Forms dense cushions of tightly packed rosettes of tiny, pointed leaves. Collected plants from the Italian Alps may have the foliage almost completely hidden by the rose-pink flowers but it is a shy bloomer under cultivation. Plant in moraine.

†S. alpestris. Low, dense masses of shining green foliage and myriads of pure white flowers on branching stems 6 in. high. A grand plant for sun or partial shade.

†S. Schafta. Leafy tufts, with rose-pink flowers produced over a long period in late summer and early fall.

†Thymus Serpyllum. A useful, fragrant ground cover for sunny situations, especially in limy soils. The flowers vary in color from white to rose-purple on erect stems a few inches high. A distinct form known as var. lanuginosus with gray, woolly leaves is desirable.

†Tunica Saxifraga. A tufted* plant with airy foliage on thin, wiry stems which are surmounted by tiny, pink, dianthus-like flowers. It is in bloom from May to Nov. and is especially valuable in poor soils in hot, dry situations.

†Veronica gentianoides. A strong-growing kind with low, leafy tufts of glossy green foliage and foot-high spires of large, pale blue flowers. Does best in fairly good soil.

†V. incana. Has silvery-gray leaves and 8–12-in. spikes of small violet-blue flowers. Worth growing for foliage alone. Dryish, well-drained soil.

†V. pectinata. Prostrate mats of hoary, deeply toothed leaves. There is a rose-colored form and one that has blue flowers. Grows well in partial shade.

---

* Special articles on the subjects indicated by an asterisk (*) will be found at the words so marked.

†**V. repens.** A creeper barely 1 in. high with small, egg-shaped, glossy leaves. Pale blue, almost white flowers, arising just above the foliage. A delightful, tolerant plant which, however, prefers partial shade and moist soil.

†**V. spicata.** A variable species, in general appearance similar to *V. incana,* but with green leaves.

†**V. latifolia.** Grows rather too large (20 in.) for the small rock garden. It is a handsome, lush-looking plant with profuse spikes of large, rich blue flowers. There is a form commonly sold as *rupestris* (probably referable to *V. latifolia dubia*) which is preferable for rock garden planting. This forms low mats with spikes of flowers 3–4 in. high which may be almost any color from white to rose and deep blue.

†**Viola cornuta.** An alpine pansy of which there are many garden varieties. The flowers of pale violet are produced throughout the summer. The *var.* George Wermig has deep-violet flowers and the *var.* alba has pure white flowers. Rich, well-drained soil and partial shade.

Bulbs, Corms, and Tubers. Many of the smaller-growing bulbs, which are difficult to accommodate in the flower border, find ideal quarters in the rock garden, and may with propriety be used there. *Colchicum, Crocus, Erythronium,* etc., contain alpine representatives. Following is a list of kinds which are not difficult to grow.

Chionodoxa luciliae
C. sardensis
　Beautiful and easy; among the first flowers of spring.
Colchicum autumnale
C. speciosum
　Valuable for their fall blooms. The foliage, which appears in spring, is coarse and unattractive.
Crocus (spring-flowering)
　C. biflorus
　C. susianus
Crocus (autumn-flowering)
　C. speciosus, and varieties. These are the showiest of the fall crocuses.
　C. zonatus
　　Fall-blooming crocuses should be planted as soon as the corms are obtainable in Aug. or Sept. They are valuable because they bloom at a time when rock garden flowers are scarce.
Eranthis hyemalis
Erythronium americanum
　E. johnsoni
　E. revolutum
　　Erythroniums should be planted in shade in well-drained soil, rich in humus.
Fritillaria meleagris. The curious, checkered, pendent flowers are interesting and beautiful.
Galanthus nivalis. *See* Snowdrop.
G. elwesi

Valuable for giving early bloom in partially shaded places.
Leucojum vernum. *See* Snowflake.
Lilium. The small lilies, such as *L. tenuifolium,* may be used to advantage.
Muscari botryoides
　M. botryoides album
　Muscari Heavenly Blue
Narcissus Bulbocodium
　N. cyclamineus
　N. minor
　N. minor minimus. This grows only 3 in. high.
　N. triandrus and varieties.
　　The above are all good rock garden plants. Strong-growing varieties of *Narcissus* should be kept to the flower border or naturalized.
Scilla sibirica. When planted in masses provides sheets of deep blue color.
Sternbergia lutea. Bright yellow goblet-like flowers in Sept. Needs a well-drained, sunny, sheltered spot.
Tulipa. Most of the small wild tulips may be used in the rock garden. The following are desirable species:
　T. clusiana
　T. Dasystemon
　T. kaufmanniana
　T. linifolia

Dwarf Trees and Shrubs
Evergreen:
　Arctostaphylos Uva-ursi. Trailer, 4–5 in.; sandy soil.
　Berberis candidula
　Chamaecyparis obtusa compacta
　Cotoneaster dammeri. Prostrate habit.
　Daphne Cneorum
　Erica carnea
　Euonymus fortunei minimus. Low, sprawly climber.
　Hedera Helix conglomerata. A dwarf, semi-upright form of English ivy.
　Juniperus excelsa stricta. Upright.
　J. horizontalis douglasi. Trailing.
　J. squamata meyeri. Spreading.
　Picea glauca conica. *See* Spruce.
　Pieris floribunda. Peaty soil.
　Pinus Mugo. *See* Pine.
　Rhododendron ferrugineum
　Thuja occidentalis ellwangeriana
　T. orientalis sieboldi
　Vaccinium Vitis-Idaea. Peaty soil.
Deciduous:
　Cotoneaster adpressa
　C. horizontalis. For large rock gardens.
Annuals
　Androsace lactiflora
　Ionopsidium acaule
　Linaria maroccana
　Mesembryanthemum lineare
　Nemophila menziesi
　Sanvitalia procumbens
　Sedum caeruleum
　S. hispanicum

All of the plants in the lists will be found at their proper entries elsewhere in this book, and should be sought there for additional information. The American Rock Garden

---

* Special articles on the subjects indicated by an asterisk (*) will be found at the words so marked.

Society welcomes members interested in the growing of these charming plants of the mountains and rocky ledges. It may be addressed at 238 Sheridan Ave., Hohokus, N.J. — M. F.

ROCK GOLDENROD = *Solidago canadensis*. See GOLDENROD.

ROCK JASMINE = *Androsace*.

ROCK PINK = *Talinum calycinum*.

ROCK PURSLANE. See CALANDRINIA.

ROCKROSE. See CISTUS.

ROCKROSE FAMILY = Cistaceae.

ROCK SAXIFRAGE = *Saxifraga virginiensis*.

ROCK SPEEDWELL = *Veronica fruticans*.

ROCK SPIREA = *Holodiscus*.

ROCK SPRAY = *Cotoneaster microphylla*.

ROCKY MOUNTAIN BEE-PLANT = *Cleome serrulata*.

ROCKY MOUNTAIN FIR = *Abies lasiocarpa*. See FIR.

ROCKY MOUNTAIN FLOWERING RASPBERRY = *Rubus deliciosus*.

ROCKY MOUNTAIN RED CEDAR = *Juniperus scopulorum*.

ROCKY MOUNTAIN YELLOW PINE = *Pinus ponderosa scopulorum*. See PINE.

RODGERSIA (rod-jer'si-a). Hardy herbaceous perennials comprising about 5 species of the family Saxifragaceae and natives of China and Japan. They have spreading rootstocks which are thick and black. Leaves long-stalked, large, alternate,* simple or compound,* bronze-green in color. Leaves of some species are cut into finger-like segments, while others have leaflets in pairs. Flowers small, numerous, greenish-white in large, showy, terminal clusters to 1 ft. long, similar to *Astilbe*. Calyx of 5 sepals, usually greenish-white. Corolla usually absent. Stamens* 10. Fruit a dry capsule. (Named for Admiral John Rodgers, U.S.N.)

These strong-growing plants, with their feathery flower clusters make good plants for the half-shade border where they must be allowed plenty of space. Though considered hardy in the northern states they are benefited by a light covering in the winter. They require plenty of water and prefer peaty soil. Propagated by division of the rootstocks in March or April.

podophylla. Strong-growing plant to 5 ft. high, with scaly rootstocks. Leaves large, divided into 3 finger-like lobes with toothed margins. Flowers small, yellowish-white, in terminal clusters, 1 ft. long. China.

tabularis. Grows to 3 ft. Leaves long-stalked, roundish, the margins being deeply cut into teeth-like segments. Flowers white, numerous, in terminal clusters. China.

ROGUE, ROGUING. In a population of normal plants there are often a few non-typical ones. Usually, as *rogue* has come to be used, these are inferior or diseased or stunted or otherwise undesirable. Getting rid of them is called *roguing*, a very common practice among plant breeders, pathologists, and done every day by ordinary gardeners. It is a process of selection by elimination.

ROHDEA (rō'dee-a). Tender perennials comprising only one species, but of many varieties, from Japan and China, belonging to the family Liliaceae. Much interest is shown in these plants in China and Japan, where they are cult. extensively. They make useful house plants if kept in a cool position. The only species is **R. japonica**, with a long and round rootstock. Leaves basal, green, leathery, upright, 18–30 in. long, and 3 in. wide, 9–12 arranged in a rosette. Flowers on a short, thick, leafless stalk, in short dense spikes, hidden by the leaves. Fruit a berry, with red pulp, usually 1-seeded. (Named for Michael Rohde, physician and botanist of Bremen.) Grown chiefly as a foliage plant, as its flower cluster is inconspicuous and resembles an aroid.*

ROLLING. For lawn rolling *see* LAWNS.

ROMAINE LETTUCE = *Lactuca sativa longifolia*. For culture *see* LETTUCE.

ROMAN GARDEN. From the Greeks the Romans inherited a tradition of gardening that ultimately produced the most ornate and sumptuous gardens in the world. Even as early as the Caesars there were immense public gardens in Rome, and every palace and the homes of the rich were embellished with gardens the like of which will perhaps never be seen again.

Some part of these ancient gardens is preserved to this day in spite of hordes of barbarians who burned palaces and trampled over gardens already hundreds of years old. To these, Pliny who built several, and wrote letters describing them, is almost our only guide. Gardens do not survive neglect, but their permanent features persist. So much was made of stonework, balustrades, bridges, statues, fountains, and pools that these are almost our only hint of the design of these elaborate and highly ornate gardens of the ancient Romans.

The plant material used in the first and second century A.D. — long before plant exploration became common — was very limited. The Romans had the incomparable cypress, the fig, flowering cherries, olive, pomegranate, pine, cedar, oak, a few shrubs, hedges, much topiary* work, and a liberal use of water, both for coolness and irrigation.

Fifteen hundred years later, notably in the gardens of the Medici and other wealthy families, we see the final flowering of the art of gardening in Italy, particularly in Rome, Florence, and Tivoli. Raphael, Leonardo da Vinci, and a host of landscape architects worked for years to create lasting pictures of beauty and splendor. Many of these world-famous gardens are still well kept up and open to the public — those in Rome or vicinity including the Forum, the Vatican, Villa Medici, Villa d'Este, Villa Aldobrandini, Villa Falconeri, and many others.

---

* Special articles on the subjects indicated by an asterisk (*) will be found at the words so marked.

In the U.S., the reproduction of such gardens is next to impossible. The enormously elaborate palaces, for which such gardens were fitting embellishment, are no longer being built, and the few that were made years ago are now mostly put to other uses. But entrancing bits of such gardens can be made here, notably in California, where climate permits the cultivation of most of the shrubs and trees upon which the beauty of Roman gardens chiefly depends.

Such reproductions of bits of Roman gardens are obviously beyond the scope or training of the amateur gardener. Steps, bridges, pools, statues, balustrades, and other permanent adornments need designs by an expert, preferably an Italian landscape architect.

The plant materials that one can use are those listed above for the ancient gardens of Rome plus a wealth of material that was not available even to the Medici. Hedges of yew, rosemary, box, and various species of evergreen *Berberis* would be useful. *See* particularly the plants listed at Sub-tropical Garden. *See also* Hedges.

Beyond the use of shrubs and trees, the Roman gardens were lavish in the use of perennial ground-covers. *See* Ground Covers. Also there was elaborate use of parterre bedding plants. *See* Bedding. Thus, though it is possible to create artistic reproductions of parts of a Roman garden, they are expensive to build, and almost prohibitive in their maintenance cost.

ROMAN HYACINTH = *Hyacinthus orientalis albulus.*

ROMAN NETTLE = *Urtica pilulifera. See* Nettle.

ROMAN WORMWOOD = *Artemisia pontica.*

ROMANZOFFIA (ro-man-zoff'i-a). A small genus of low, perennial herbs of the family Hydrophyllaceae, found in western N.A., one of them, R. sitchensis, providing an attractive white-flowered plant for edging. It is scarcely over 6 in. high, the rootstock bearing small tubers. Leaves mostly basal, roundish or heart-shaped. Flowers small, white, borne in a small terminal cluster (raceme*) at the end of a stalk which arises from the ground. Easily grown in any ordinary garden soil and propagated by division of the rootstocks. (Named for Count Nicholas Romanzoff, a Russian nobleman.)

ROMERO = *Trichostema lanatum. See* Bluecurls.

ROMNEYA (rom'nee-a). Tender perennial herbs or sub-shrubs, comprising 2 species from Calif. and Mex., belonging to the poppy family. They grow to 8 ft. high, have spreading rootstocks and branching stems. Leaves in pairs, stalked, broadly lance-shaped, deeply lobed, to 4 in. long. Flowers solitary, at the ends of the branches, white, to 6 in. across. Calyx of 3 sepals. Corolla of 6 petals, all alike. Stamens* numerous. Fruit a many-seeded capsule.* (Named for T. Rom-

ney Robinson, who discovered the species below.)

Romneyas make beautiful garden plants, but are difficult to establish, unless grown in pots and transplanted without too much disturbance of the roots. They are sometimes grown as greenhouse plants in the northern states. May be propagated by seeds, which are best sown as soon as ripe. Seeds should be sown on the surface of a mixture of fine sandy peat in well-drained pans under a bell-jar in a temperature of 55°–60°. As soon as large enough to handle they should be transplanted into separate pots containing a similar mixture. Roots should be disturbed as little as possible. When well established they may be transplanted to permanent positions in sunny, well-drained borders, which have been treated with peat and sand. To move well-established plants, cut well down.

coulteri. Matilija poppy. California tree poppy. Grows to 8 ft., much-branched above. Leaves thin, paper-like. Flowers white, to 6 in. across, solitary. Calif. and Mex.

RONDELETIA (ron-de-lee'shi-a). A genus of over 80 species of tropical American evergreen shrubs and trees of the family Rubiaceae, the two below (and perhaps others) grown for ornament. They have generally opposite* leaves, rarely in whorls of 3. Flowers tubular, the limb 5-lobed (in ours), showy, crowded in dense clusters mostly from the leaf axils.* Stamens* 4–5. Fruit a many-seeded capsule.* (Named for William Rondelet, French naturalist.)

The rondeletias are handsome shrubs, well-liked in zones* 8 and 9 for their profusion of orange or red or pink flowers, and handsome foliage. They grow well outdoors in a variety of soils and may be propagated by cuttings of half-ripened wood. They are also to be grown northward in the warm-temperate greenhouse (*see* Greenhouse), in potting mixture* 5.

cordata. A shrub, 5–7 ft. high. Leaves oblongish or ovalish, 3–5 in. long, practically without hairs. Flowers pink or rose-red, about ¼ in. wide, hairy on the outside, the throat yellow-bearded. Guatemala.

odorata. A shrub 4–6 ft. high. Leaves ovalish or oblong, 1–2 in. long, the margins rolled. Flowers about ½ in. wide, orange-red, but yellow-throated. Panama and Cuba. The best-known of the rondeletias and sometimes offered as R. speciosa.

speciosa = *Rondeletia odorata.*

ROOF GARDEN. The modern development of gardens on the roof, or on terraces, has come mostly in cities where the height of buildings has forced "set-backs" every ten stories or so. The use of such terraces and the roof itself as a garden site has been widely adopted in most large cities. For the details of planting, design, maintenance, etc., of such gardens *see* Penthouse Garden at Planning the Home Grounds.

ROOF HOUSELEEK = *Sempervivum tectorum. See* Houseleek.

ROOF IRIS = *Iris tectorum.*

---

* Special articles on the subjects indicated by an asterisk (*) will be found at the words so marked.

ROOT. The organ that gathers most of the food of the plant from the soil, and, in epiphytes,* some from the air (*see also* VELAMEN). From the gardening standpoint, the root is the underground food-gathering organ, but technically, and also practically, it is much more. A proper understanding of its function and structure may avoid many common garden mistakes, especially in dealing with woody plants.

A much-magnified root showing the root hairs, which are the real food gatherers.

Practically all the larger, easily seen ramifications of roots are functionally inactive as food gatherers. They are of greatest use, however, as conductors of the food gathered by parts of the root system not so easily seen, and as anchors. The food gatherers are the tiny root hairs or tips, most of which are provided with a relatively hardened root cap. The latter more easily penetrates the soil than the root hair itself, but it is the root hair that functions as the actual absorber of plant food.

It is for this reason that nurserymen root prune woody plants. By reducing the amount of mere conducting roots (the larger ones) they force the plant to produce a greater number of root hairs. This relatively compact mass of small roots, with their much greater profusion of food-gathering root hairs, greatly eases the shock of transplanting woody plants. For tuber and tuberous root *see* TUBER. Tree roots, especially those near the surface, often rob gardens of much water and plant food.

ROOT-BOUND = Pot-bound.

ROOT CROPS. Among the common root crops, all the subjects of special articles, are carrot, turnip, parsnip, onion, beet, potato, and sweet potato. The term thus includes underground crops other than those derived from true roots, because the potato is a tuber, and the onion a bulb. Popular usage, however, will continue to call these underground crops *root* crops, whether true roots or not. Other less known root crops are salsify* and skirret.

ROOT GALL. An abnormal swelling on the roots of plants usually caused by disease or nematodes. There are many plants, especially in the pea family, that bear tubercles or nodules that may be mistaken for root galls. But tubercles or nodules of this sort are beneficial.

ROOT-HARDY. Hardy only because the root survives. Many plants, killed to the ground every year, survive because their roots only are hardy. *See* HARDINESS.

ROOT NODULE. *See* ROOT TUBERCLE.

ROOT PRESSURE. *See* OSMOSIS.

ROOT-PROMOTING CHEMICALS. *See* HORMONES.

ROOT PRUNING. Root pruning scarcely needs explanation, and in the garden it is rarely necessary to practice it, except where ornamental trees have become too rapacious by invading flower borders or the vegetable garden. The maple, for example, is apt to send out masses of fibrous roots fairly close to the surface, and assuming these roots get beyond the legitimate bounds, the gardener, in defense of his cherished plants, must from time to time put a check upon their ramifications, especially if the offending tree happens to be in a neighboring garden or lot. By digging a trench 18 or 24 inches deep, six or more feet from the tree, any thong-like roots from which the fibrous mass is produced may be cut and the unwanted fibers afterwards taken out. To stop further invasions a corrugated iron or cement barrier may be set in the trench.

Root pruning of fruit trees to make them fruitful is an old-time practice, and where an established tree of some size is not responsive to fair treatment except in the way of making wild and useless wood, it may be assumed that the tree has more roots than are good for it. As a rule such a tree has a tap or central root and none too many

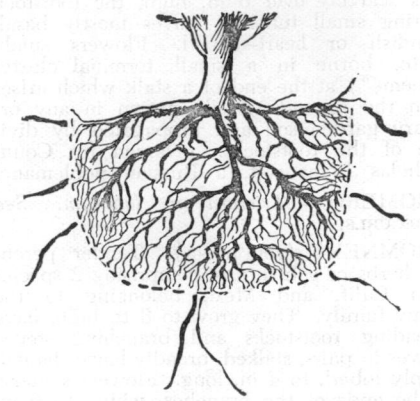

Root pruning. The roots beyond the dotted line should be cut off to promote the growth of feeding roots near the stem.

* Special articles on the subjects indicated by an asterisk (*) will be found at the words so marked.

fibrous roots near the surface. By carefully excavating around the tree one can find whether there are any large anchor roots. The severing of these should be accomplished so that the cut surface is uppermost, but with large trees this should not be done close to the tree. Do not damage any thin or fibrous roots. Failure to find any fair-sized roots around the tree is almost a sure indication that a wild taproot must be got at and severed. This work should be done in the late fall. The arduous task of root pruning is not recommended unless the tree is worth the effort, as the Lorette system of pruning (*see* PRUNING) will in a season or two make the tree see the error of its ways.

Root pruning of ornamental trees and shrubs is a more common and truly essential practice in nurseries, inasmuch as all the stock grown is for future sales. Anyone who has attempted to lift cedars, dogwoods, and other trees from the wild will have noted that the roots are disproportionate to their size compared with well-grown nursery stock of the same size. Indeed, there is but a slim chance of wildings above two or three feet surviving. The reason is that wildings have stood from the seed stage in one spot undisturbed, and consequently have made a few heavy roots rather than a mass of fibrous ones. The nursery stock, raised from seed, cutting or graft, is encouraged to make fibrous roots by the process of lining out in the field. A year or two later the young plants are lifted and set farther apart, and before they reach specimen size they may be shifted several times, or if set wider apart in the first place to avoid transplanting, they are treated to a root-pruning process by means of a machine, the blade of which passes beneath them at a certain depth and severs all delving roots. This lifting or root-pruning process is carried on with both evergreen and deciduous material until of specimen size. Deciduous trees cannot profitably be lifted and transplanted after they reach a large size, and they become a liability unless they can be taken up with a ball of soil by special machines. Temperamental deciduous trees, like magnolias and dogwoods, must also be lifted with a ball after they are three or four years old, and all evergreens, both coniferous and broad-leaved, after the lining-out stage are invariably lifted with a ball. The more shifts such plants undergo, the more matted is the root ball. *See* Ball and Burlap at PLANTING.

In the garden, most evergreens, even after being established some years, still retain the matted ball of roots and may be shifted with such if the facilities for moving such heavy weights are available. Deciduous shrubs of movable size can be prepared for transplanting to a new spot by forcing a sharp spade around and fairly close to the stems. Done during summer, this will encourage more fibrous roots and make shifting in the fall rather easier. Moving very large speci-

mens, however, is not a practical proposition for the gardener, while it is practically useless to attempt shifting large magnolias. — T. A. W.

ROOTSTOCK. The word has two distinct meanings to the gardener. Most fruit culturists and those interested in grafting use *rootstock* as the term for the underground *stock* upon which a desirable variety has been grafted.

Much more commonly, a rootstock is the usually swollen, but more or less elongated underground stem of a perennial herb, common examples being the rootstocks of the iris and Solomon's-seal. Botanists usually call a rootstock a rhizome, and so do many gardeners.

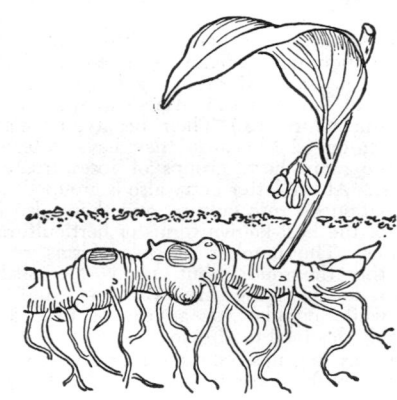

A rootstock is an underground stem provided with eyes (buds) for next season's growth, and with roots for food gathering.

Because a rootstock is usually an underground organ, many people mistakenly call it a root. But it is a storage organ and not a food gatherer, and therefore not a root. Most rootstocks have quite obvious roots attached to them.

The practical garden advantage of a rootstock is great. Most of them can be easily divided in the spring or fall, thus serving as the easiest method of propagation. This is possible because all rootstocks (being modified stems) bear buds from which the new plant will sprout. Roots bear no buds so that divided roots will usually not produce new plants.

All underground stems are not rootstocks. *See* BULB, CORM, and TUBER.

ROOT TUBERCLE. On the roots of certain plants there are small swellings caused by the action of certain nitrogen-fixing bacteria. On all plants other than legumes these swellings are properly called root nodules. On leguminous plants such swellings, which have an important function in capturing free nitrogen from the air, are called root tubercles.

For their practical significance *see* LEGUME INOCULATION.

ROPE BARK = *Dirca palustris.*

ROQUETTE = *Eruca sativa.*

RORIPA (ror'ri-pa). An old and untenable name for two garden plants, now considered as belonging to other genera. One is the horse-radish (*Armoracia rusticana*). See HORSE-RADISH. The other is the watercress (*Nasturtium officinale*). See WATERCRESS.

ROSA (rō'za). Rose. A genus of shrubs or vines, comprising all the true roses, and typifying the family Rosaceae. According to the usual concept of them there may be 200 true species of roses, but one authority has credited to Eurasia alone over 4000 species. In any case, the differences between species, even the few below, are mainly technical, and it seems better here to direct attention only to their more obvious characters. They have been selected from over 75 species known to be cult. in America, with two things in mind: (1) Their beauty, or ease of cult.; or (2) because they have entered into the main hort. groups of roses treated at ROSE. At the latter entry also is grouped all information on rose culture, and there also is a list of the best-known forms or horticultural varieties. The number of these forms runs into the thousands, but many are little known today, some are worthless, and a few, while popular for a year or two, are probably destined to oblivion.

Rosa, as a genus, comprises prickly shrubs or vines with alternate,* compound* leaves, the leaflets arranged feather-fashion, and always with an odd one at the end. The prickles may be hooked or straight. Flowers solitary or in small clusters, typically with 5 petals in wild, single roses, but much doubled in most of the hort. forms, nearly always fragrant. Stamens* numerous. Pistils* numerous, enclosed at the base in a cup-shaped receptacle,* which enlarges in fruit, becomes fleshy and berry-like (the familiar rose hip) and encloses the true fruits which are bony achenes.* (*Rosa* is the old Latin name of the rose.)

For culture *see* ROSE. All the species below have single flowers unless otherwise noted. They represent wild species of roses from which, with others, all the beautiful horticultural forms have been derived, mostly by a complicated history of breeding and selection. Some of them are not hardy in the North, although their hort. descendants are often perfectly so, due to selection or breeding. Wherever possible the hort. forms which have originated from any of the species are noted, although the parentage of some of our finest cult. varieties is in much confusion. Even the wild species below are known to hybridize naturally. Mostly May or June flowering, unless otherwise noted.

alba. Thought to be a natural hybrid between *R. gallica* and *R. canina*, 4–6 ft. high, the prickles hooked. Leaflets usually 5, broadly elliptic, 2–2½ in. long. Flowers semi-double to double, about 3 in. wide, pinkish. The unusually fragrant *var.* suaveolens is little known here but is a source of attar of roses in southern Eu., for which it is much cult.

arvensis. A trailing rose with scattered prickles. Leaflets generally 7, ovalish, 1–1½ in. long. Flowers about 1½ in. wide, white, not fragrant, in small clusters. Eu. June–July. Hardy from zone* 3 southward. The *var.* ayreshirea, the Ayreshire rose, is a more vigorous plant. Double-flowered plants, sometimes classed as Ayreshire roses, are hybrids.

banksiae. Banks or Lady Banks' rose. A beautiful, climbing, evergreen rose, often 15–40 ft. high, with a few hooked prickles or none. Leaflets 3–5 (rarely 7), elliptic-oval, 1½–2½ in. long. Flowers in profuse clusters (umbels*), a little fragrant and white or yellow, not over 1 in. wide. China. June–Aug. Hardy from zone* 6 southward.

blanda. A native rose, 4–6 ft. high, its slender stems mostly without prickles, but often bristly. Leaflets 5–7 (rarely 9), elliptic-oblong, 1½–2½ in. long. Flowers pink, about 2 in. wide, usually solitary, but sometimes in few-flowered clusters. Eastern N.A. Hardy from zone* 2 southward.

borboniana. Bourbon rose. A famous hybrid rose, derived from crossing a recurrent form of *R. damascena* with the China rose, and with successive crossing with *R. chinensis* hybrids and other roses, resulting in the Hybrid Perpetual class. It is an upright shrub with prickly and bristly stems. Leaflets 7, ovalish or narrower. Flowers rose-pink, double or nearly so, about 3 in. wide. July–Sept. Hardy, at least in some of its forms, from zone* 3 southward.

bracteata. Macartney rose. A trailing or partly climbing evergreen rose, with stout, hooked prickles. Leaflets 5–9, elliptic or broader toward the tip, 1½–2 in. long, shining above. Flower solitary, white, about 3 in. wide, beneath it a series of conspicuously toothed bracts.* China, but naturalized from Va. to Fla. and Tex. Aug. Hardy from zone* 6 southward. Midsummer to fall.

brunoni. Himalayan musk rose. A partially climbing rose with stout, short, hooked prickles. Leaflets 5–7, elliptic or oblongish, 2–2½ in. long. Flowers white, very fragrant, nearly 2 in. wide, in many-flowered clusters (corymbs*). Himalayas. June–July. Hardy from zone* 6 southward. Often mistaken for, and offered as, the true musk rose (*R. moschata*).

canina. Dog rose. A shrubby rose 6–9 ft. high, the stems arching, and furnished with stout hooked prickles. Leaflets 5–7, ovalish or elliptic, 1–1½ in. long. Flowers nearly 2 in. wide, white or pink, solitary or in few-flowered clusters. Eu. Hardy from zone* 4 southward. The plant much used for propagating stock.

carolina. Pasture rose. A native rose, the erect stems not usually over 3 ft. high, bristly and with slender, straight prickles. Leaflets 5 (rarely 7), ½–1¼ in. long. Flowers usually solitary, rose-pink, about 2 in. wide. Eastern U.S. June–July. Hardy from zone* 3 southward. One of the best of our native roses and good for the shrub border.

cathayensis = *R. multiflora cathayensis.*

centifolia. Cabbage rose. Hundred-leaved rose. An upright rose, 4–6 ft. high, with creeping rootstocks, the stems both prickly and bristly. Leaflets mostly 5, hairy both sides, 1½–2 in. long. Flowers double, nearly 3 in. wide, solitary, nodding, pink and fragrant. Caucasus. June–July. Hardy from zone* 3 south-

---

* Special articles on the subjects indicated by an asterisk (*) will be found at the words so marked.

ward. A very old rose, known since ancient times, and found in many varieties. One of them is the *var.* muscosa, the moss rose, which has the flower stalk and calyx* sticky and mossy.

cherokeensis = *Rosa laevigata.*

chinensis. China rose; also called the Bengal rose. An upright, partly evergreen rose, not over 3 ft. high, the stems with a few, somewhat hooked prickles, occasionally unarmed. Leaflets 3–5, broadly oval, 2–2½ in. long, shining green above, paler below. Flowers usually solitary, rarely long-stalked, about 2 in. wide, crimson to pink or even white. China. July–Oct. Hardy from zone* 6 southward. An important species because it is the origin of many hort. forms. The *var.* **manetti**, the Manetti rose (by some considered a variety of *R. noisettiana*) has been widely used as stock for many tea roses. The *var.* **minima**, the fairy rose, is a dwarf shrub, rarely over 18 in. high with small, single or double, rose-red flowers. From this and other plants has come the Baby Rambler. The *var.* **semperflorens**, the Chinese monthly rose, has usually solitary, crimson or deep-pink flowers. The *var.* **viridiflora**, the green rose, has its petals and sepals transformed into green sepal-like leaves.

cinnamomea. Cinnamon rose. An erect shrub 4–6 ft. high, with short, hooked prickles, or unarmed. Leaflets 5–7, elliptic or oblongish, 1–1½ in. long, densely hairy beneath. Flowers about 2 in. wide, fragrant, purplish-red, solitary or only a few in the cluster. Eurasia, occasionally an escape* in the eastern U.S. Hardy from zone* 3 southward.

damascena. Damask rose. An erect shrub, 5–7 ft. high, the stems with hooked prickles and sometimes also bristly. Leaflets 5 (rarely 7), ovalish or oblong, 2–2½ in. long. Flowers double, pink or red, fragrant, mostly in loose clusters (corymbs*). Asia Minor (?). June–July. Hardy from zone* 4 southward. Cult. in Eu. as a source of attar of roses. *See* HERB GARDENING. The *var.* **versicolor**, the York and Lancaster Rose, has white-striped, semi-double flowers, or some white and some pink flowers on the same plant.

Eglanteria. The eglantine or sweetbrier. A much-branched shrub, 5–8 ft. high, with pleasantly aromatic foliage, the stems bristly and with strongly hooked prickles. Leaflets 5–7, nearly round or broadly oval, about 1 in. long, sticky. Flowers nearly 2 in. wide, pink, generally solitary. Eu., commonly naturalized in the U.S. Hardy throughout. Long known as *R. rubiginosa.*

fendleri. *See* ROSA WOODSI.

foetida. Austrian brier. An erect or arching shrub, 7–10 ft. high, the stems with straight prickles. Leaflets 5–9, broadly ovalish, 1–1½ in. long. Flowers nearly 3 in. wide, deep yellow, unpleasantly scented. Western As. Hardy from zone* 3 southward, but not an easy rose to grow. The *var.* **bicolor**, the Austrian copper brier, has the flowers orange-scarlet or coppery inside. The *var.* **persiana**, the Persian Yellow. has double, yellow flowers.

gallica. Provence or French rose. An upright shrub, 3–4 ft. high, the rootstock creeping, the stems densely prickly and bristly. Leaflets 3–5, broadly elliptic, 2–2½ in. long. Flowers nearly 3 in. wide, solitary, pink, or crimson. Eurasia. Hardy from zone* 3 southward. *See* HERB GARDENING. The *var.* **officinalis**, the apothecary's rose, has usually double flowers, and is found in old gardens.

harisoni. Harison's yellow rose. A hybrid rose (*foetida* × *spinosissima*) resembling the Austrian brier but with paler yellow flowers.

It stands bitter winters and is widely grown in cool regions.

hugonis. Hugo rose, often called Father Hugo's rose. A handsome, free-flowering shrub, 6–8 ft. high, the branches drooping, beset with flattened, straight prickles and bristles. Leaflets 5–13, ovalish or elliptic, ½–¾ in. long. Flowers solitary, about 2 in. wide, yellow. China. Hardy from zone* 3 southward and one of the best single, yellow roses in cult. It is one of the few roses that thrive in poor soil and should not be manured.

laevigata. Cherokee rose. A Chinese rose, widely naturalized in the southern states. It is an evergreen, climbing rose, often 15 ft. high, with scattered, hooked prickles. Leaflets 3 (rarely 5), elliptic-oval, 1¾–2½ in. long, shining. Flowers nearly 3½ in. wide, white, fragrant, and solitary. Hardy from zone* 7 southward. It is the origin of a much more hardy, very popular climbing rose known as Silver Moon. It is the state flower of Ga.

lucida = *Rosa virginiana.*

moyesi. A Chinese rose, 7–10 ft. high, with 7–13 leaflets which are about 1½ in. long. Flowers dark red, about 2 in. wide, usually solitary or sometimes two together. Fruit nearly 2 in. long, showy, orange-red. Hardy from zone* 3 southward. June.

moschata. Musk rose. An arching or partly climbing rose with straight or slightly curved prickles. Leaflets 5–7, oblongish, 1½–2 in. long. Flowers musk-scented, white, nearly 2 in. wide, in usually 7-flowered clusters (corymbs*). Mediterranean region. Hardy from zone* 6 southward, but not much grown, most of the plants under the name of *R. moschata* being *R. brunoni.*

multiflora. Multiflora rose. A climbing or trailing rose with stout, hooked prickles. Leaflets 5–9, generally oblongish, 1–1½ in. long. Flowers about ¾ in. wide, fragrant, often double, in many-flowered clusters (panicles* or corymbs*). Jap. and Korea. July–Aug. Hardy from zone* 3 southward. With the var. *cathayensis*, the source of many important climbing or prostrate hort. varieties, and possibly entering into the variety known as Crimson Rambler. The *var.* **cathayensis** is a form with more flexible growth, with pink or rose-colored flowers. China. June–July. Hardy from zone* 3 southward.

nitida. A low native rose, rarely over 18 in. high, the stems densely bristly and with slender, straight prickles. Leaflets 7–9, oblongish, about 1 in. long, shining. Flowers generally solitary, about 2 in. wide, rose-pink. Newfoundland to Conn. Hardy from zone* 2 southward.

noisettiana. Noisette rose, also called Champney rose. A widely grown hybrid rose derived from crossing *R. chinensis* with *R. moschata.* It is an erect shrub 7–10 ft. high, the prickles hooked and reddish. Leaflets 5–7, oblong to ovalish. Flowers white, pink, red, or yellow in many-flowered clusters (corymbs*). Hardy from zone* 6 southward. A climbing form of it is the well-known Maréchal Niel rose, with yellow flowers.

nutkana. A native American rose, 3–5 ft. high, the dark brown, upright stems with large, straight prickles. Leaflets 5–9, broadly elliptic, 1½–2 in. long. Flowers solitary, nearly 2 in. wide, mostly rose-pink. Alaska to Wyo., Idaho, and Calif. June–July.

odorata. Tea rose. An evergreen, tea-scented, partially climbing rose with hooked prickles. Leaflets 5–7, ovalish or oblong, 2–3 in. long, shining above. Flowers solitary or

---

* Special articles on the subjects indicated by an asterisk (*) will be found at the words so marked.

2 or 3 in a cluster, nearly 3 in. wide, usually double, white, pink, or yellow. China. June–Oct. Hardy from zone° 6 southward. Little cult. in its original form, but entering widely into many hort. forms.

palustris. Swamp rose. A native rose, the upright stems 4–6 ft. high, often reddish, armed with straight prickles and bristles. Leaflets mostly 7, narrowly oblong, 1½–2 in. long. Flowers about 2 in. wide, pink, in few-flowered clusters (corymbs°). Eastern N.A. June–Aug. Hardy from zone° 2 southward.

polyantha. An old and obsolete name for plants now included in *R. multiflora.*

rubiginosa = *Rosa Eglanteria.*

rubrifolia. An erect shrub, 4–6 ft. high, its twigs purplish and with a bloom, the prickles few and small. Leaflets 7–9, more or less elliptic, 1–2½ in. long, green or reddish-tinged, toothed. Flowers not showy, red, 1½–2½ in. wide. Fruit nearly round, smooth and red, about ⅝ in. in diameter. Eu. June–July. Hardy from zone° 2 southward.

rugosa. An upright shrub, 4–6 ft. high, ultimately making large patches (10–20 ft. in diameter). Stems densely bristly and prickly, the prickles straight. Leaflets 5–9, more or less elliptic, 1½–2 in. long, very rough and veiny on the upper surface, shining. Flowers usually solitary, nearly 3½ in. wide, red or white. Jap. and China. July–Aug. Hardy from zone° 3 southward, and rather commonly escaped, especially near the seashore in the eastern U.S. There are many hort. varieties, some with double flowers.

sempervirens. An evergreen in mild climates, climbing or trailing with scattered-hooked prickles. Leaflets 5–7, ovalish or narrower, 1½–2 in. long, shining. Flowers almost 2 in. wide, fragrant, white, mostly in few-flowered clusters (corymbs°). Mediterranean region. June–July. Hardy from zone° 5 southward.

setigera. Prairie rose. A climbing or arching rose, often 15 ft. high, the prickles scattered and hooked. Leaflets 3 (rarely 5), ovalish or oblong, 3–4 in. long. Flowers about 2 in. wide, rose-pink, but fading to whitish, mostly in few-flowered clusters (corymbs°), Eastern U.S., but west to Neb. and Tex. June–Aug. Hardy from zone° 3 southward. It is the most vigorous of all native American roses.

spinosissima. Scotch rose; also called Burnet rose. An erect shrub, 2–3 ft. high, the stems densely covered with straight prickles and bristles. Leaflets mostly 7–9 (rarely 5 or 11), roundish, ½–¾ in. long. Flowers solitary, but numerous, about 2 in. wide, pink, white, or yellow. Eurasia. Hardy from zone° 3 southward. There are many varieties and forms of this long-cult. rose. The *var.* **altaica** is more vigorous and less spiny than the typical plant; white-flowered.

virginiana. A native rose, 4–5 ft. high, its prickles often hooked. Leaflets 7–9, elliptic, dark shining green above, the marginal teeth pointing upward. Flowers pink, solitary or a few, 2–3 in. wide, their stalks covered with sticky hairs. Fruit red, about ½ in. in diameter. Eastern N.A. June–July. Hardy from zone° 2 southward. Autumnal foliage red. Often offered as *Rosa lucida.*

watsoniana. An arching or runner-bearing rose, of little hort. value except for its habit. Leaflets 3–5, narrow, without teeth but with wavy margins. Flowers white or pink, very small, scarcely ½ in. wide, but in profuse clusters (corymbs°). Fruit red, pea-sized, usually seedless. Known only as a cult. plant

from Jap., and possibly originating as a sport of *R. multiflora.* June. Hardy from zone° 5 southward.

wichuraiana. Memorial rose. A prostrate or trailing, half-evergreen rose, the strong prickles hooked. Leaflets 7–9, roundish, blunt, shining, ¾–1 in. long. Flowers nearly 2 in. wide, white, fragrant, mostly in clusters (corymbs°). Eastern Asia. July–Oct. Hardy from zone° 3 southward. The origin of many valuable roses useful for covering walls and banks, among them the old favorites Dorothy Perkins, Dr. Walter Van Fleet, and many fine modern varieties.

woodsi. A prickly native shrub, 4–6 ft. high. Leaflets 5–7, oblongish, ½–1½ in. long, bluish-green and toothed. Flowers pink or sometimes white, usually only 1–3, and about 1½–2½ in. wide, red. Central N.A. June–July. Hardy from zone° 2 southward. The *var.* **fendleri,** often offered as *R. fendleri,* is lower and its leafstalks are sticky. It extends westward and southward to British Columbia and Mex., but is not superior to the typical *R. woodsi.*

xanthina. An Asiatic shrub related to *R. hugonis,* but with double or semi-double yellow flowers as usually cult., although the wild form is single-flowered. China and Korea. Hardy from zone° 3 southward.

The above enumeration of species roses has been greatly helped by the advice of Mr. Roy E. Shepherd. As every gardener knows, the various horticultural forms derived from some of the above species are far finer than any of the wild species, and for an account of these forms and their culture *see* the article on ROSE, also by Mr. Shepherd.

rosacea, -us, -um (ro-zay'see-a). Rose-like.

ROSACEAE (ro-zay'see-ee). The rose family is one of the two or three most important plant families to the gardener. It is often called the strawberry, raspberry, or spirea family, but besides these it includes many other genera of outstanding value to the flower enthusiast, the fruit culturist, and to the grower of some of our most decorative shrubs and trees.

As here considered the rose family is a tremendous aggregation of herbs, shrubs, and trees, comprising about 100 genera and well over 3000 species of very wide distribution. They have not always been considered as of one big family, but as three. The segregation of these three families (here considered as tribes) has considerable cogency, as will be seen from the tabulation below. In order to aid the student all the genera of the Rosaceae will be numbered in accordance with that tabulation.

1. Rose tribe or rose family proper (the Rosaceae in the old restricted sense). Fruit not like the plum or apple, usually dry, but *see* STRAWBERRY.

2. Apple tribe or family, often called the pear or quince family (the Malaceae or Pomaceae). Here are grouped the fleshy-fruited, largely edible genera typified by the apple, *i.e.,* with the fruit a pome,° and an inferior° ovary.

° Special articles on the subjects indicated by an asterisk (°) will be found at the words so marked.

3. Peach tribe or family, often called the plum, almond, or cherry family (the Amygdalaceae, also called the Drupaceae or Prunaceae). Here are grouped the fleshy-fruited, largely edible genera typified by the peach or plum or cherry, *i.e.*, with the fruit a drupe* and with a superior* ovary. Quite generally called the stone fruits.

While many gardeners will disregard these distinctions, they have much hort. basis, and still more botanical significance. Because of this all the genera below will be indicated by number as to their proper tribe in accordance with the above tabulation.

The garden genera of the whole rose family may be grouped, culturally, as follows:

I. GROWN PRIMARILY FOR FRUIT.
   Amygdalus (3), *Chrysobalanus* (3), *Cydonia* (2) (*see* QUINCE), *Eriobotrya* (2), *Fragaria* (1) (*see* STRAWBERRY), *Malus* (2), *Prunus* (3), *Pyrus* (2), *Rubus* (1).

II. TROPICAL OR SUB-TROPICAL GENERA grown for ornament, outdoors mostly from zone* 7 southward, elsewhere in greenhouses.
   Heteromeles (2) (*see* TOYON), *Quillaja* (1), *Laurocerasus* (3) (some hardy), *Lyonothamnus* (1), and *Raphiolepis*, (2)

III. ORNAMENTAL SHRUBS, TREES, AND VINES of outdoor culture over a good part of the country (but *see* individual genera for specific details). A few genera also contain herbs.
   Acaena (1), *Adenostoma* (1), *Amelanchier* (2), *Aronia* (2), *Cercocarpus* (1), *Chaenomeles* (2), *Cotoneaster* (2), *Crataegus* (2), *Exochorda* (1), *Holodiscus* (1), *Mespilus* (2), *Kerria* (1), *Neviusia* (1), *Osmaronia* (3), *Photinia* (2), *Physocarpus* (1), *Prinsepia* (3), *Prunus* (3), *Purshia* (1), *Pyracantha* (2), *Rhodotypos* (1), *Rosa* (1), *Sorbaria* (1), *Sorbus* (2) (*see* MOUNTAIN-ASH), *Spiraea* (1), *Stephanandra* (1) and *Stranvaesia* (2).

IV. ANNUAL OR PERENNIAL HERBS FOR THE BORDER, ROCK GARDEN or wild garden, of outdoor culture over most of the country (but *see* individual genera for specific details). A few genera also contain woody plants.
   Alchemilla (1), *Aruncus* (1), *Dalibarda* (1), *Dryas* (1), *Duchesnea* (1), *Filipendula* (1), *Geum* (1), *Gillenia* (1), *Potentilla* (1), *Poterium* (1), *Sanguisorba* (1) and *Waldsteinia* (1).

Among these lists are such outstanding fruits as the pear, apple, quince, plum, peach, almond, apricot, strawberry, blackberry, raspberry. *See* these terms for the culture and hort. varieties of each.

By far the most important decorative material will be found in Group III (the ornamental shrubs and trees), which includes such old favorites as the rose, spirea, hawthorn, shadbush, flowering quince and all the splendid flowering cherries, and many other fine shrubs and trees. The herbaceous plants (Group IV) are much less important, some of the genera being suited only to the wild garden.

Leaves alternate,* compound* in several genera (*Rosa, Rubus,* etc.) but often simple.* For the fruits *see* tabulation above. The flowers of the Rosaceae have typically 4–5 sepals and petals, but these are inserted on the edges of a hypanthium (*see* RECEPTACLE). This is of various shapes. In the rose it forms the rose hip, and in the blackberry it is the cone-shaped structure that is left on the bush when the fruit is picked. Stamens* usually numerous. Ovary superior* or inferior.*

ROSA MONTANA = *Antigonon leptopus.*

ROSARIUM. An old name for a rose garden.

ROSARY PEA = *Abrus precatorius.*
   Rosa-sinensis (ro-za-sy-nen'sis). Rose-of-China. See HIBISCUS.

ROSA SOLIS = *Drosera rotundifolia.*

ROSE. The perforated end of the spout of a watering pot, which permits a fine spray to be delivered on seedlings, etc.

ROSE. For the culture and varieties of the garden rose *see* the next main entry. The word *rose,* however, has been applied to many other plants. Among the most important, and their proper equivalents, are:
   Bridal Rose = *Matricaria inodora plenissima.*
   California Rose = *Convolvulus japonicus.*
   Christmas Rose = *Helleborus niger.*
   Confederate Rose = *Hibiscus mutabilis.*
   Cotton Rose = *Hibiscus mutabilis.*
   Guelder Rose = *Viburnum Opulus sterile.*
   Japanese Rose = *Kerria japonica* (double-flowered).
   Native Rose. See BAUERA.
   Rose-apple = *Eugenia Jambos.*
   Rose-bay. See RHODODENDRON and OLEANDER.
   Rose Mallow = *Hibiscus Moscheutos.*
   Rose Milkweed = *Asclepias tuberosa.* See MILKWEED.
   Rose Moss = *Portulaca grandiflora.*
   Rose-of-China = *Hibiscus Rosa-sinensis.*
   Rose-of-Heaven = *Lychnis Coeli-rosa.*
   Rose-of-Jericho = *Anastatica hierochuntica.*
   Rose-of-Sharon = *Hibiscus Syriacus.*
   Rose Pink. See SABATIA.
   Rose Pogonia = *Pogonia ophioglossoides.*
   Rockrose = *Cistus.*
   Sun-rose = *Helianthemum.*
   Tuberose. See TUBEROSE.

ROSE. The many beautiful roses that we enjoy today have evolved, through mutation and both natural and artificial hybridization, from primitive, mostly five-petaled native roses of the wastelands of the northern hemisphere.

Several rose classes that were once considered the ultimate in perfection have been superseded by supposedly superior types. But the old types still remain in the gardens

---

* Special articles on the subjects indicated by an asterisk (*) will be found at the words so marked.

of rose hobbyists or in the neglected yards of old homesteads. Among these are the Albas, Bourbons, Chinas, Centifolias, Damasks, Gallicas, Mosses, Noisettes, and Teas (not the Hybrid Teas). Approaching oblivion are three comparatively modern types; the Hybrid Perpetuals, Polyanthas, and Ramblers. Today's favorites are the Hybrid Teas, Floribundas, Grandifloras, Large-flowered Recurrent Climbers, and the Miniature Roses.

The interest in the replaced classes is so little that we will deal with them but briefly and many will be grouped together. Availability is a factor in suggesting the varieties grouped under each class.

The Albas, Centifolias (the Cabbage Rose), Damasks, Gallicas, and Mosses are, for the most part, but once-blooming — a sturdy and hardy shrub type that require but little care and can compete favorably with other shrubs. They deserve retention primarily for this purpose and their historical value, although several of them bear very beautiful and fragrant flowers. As these roses thrive best on their own roots and commercially produced plants are usually budded onto a foreign understock there is a decided advantage in planting them so that the bud-union is four or five inches below the surface of the soil. If this is done they will eventually develop their own roots. Moderate to heavy fertilization in the spring and following the June bloom, and the removal of older wood occasionally, renews the plant and encourages maximum flower production.

The following brief description of each class may be supplemented by reference to the parent species which appear under Rosa.

ALBAS. Forms of *R. alba* or hybrids in which the characteristics of this species rose are pronounced. Fairly vigorous, non-recurrent shrubs bearing semi-double to double flowers in shades of light pink or white.

CENTIFOLIAS. Varieties or hybrids of *R. centifolia*, the Cabbage or Hundred-leaved rose of our ancestors. Mostly hardy and semi-vigorous once-blooming shrubs, producing extremely double and fragrant flowers. The majority are shades of pink although the color range is from white to light carmine.

DAMASKS. Hybrids of *R. damascena*. Moderately vigorous and hardy shrubs that bear very fragrant, usually pink flowers of varying petalage. A few varieties have a tendency to repeat in the fall but they are characteristically once-blooming.

GALLICAS. Varieties and hybrids of *R. gallica*, producing pink, red, purple, or variegated flowers on compact upright shrubs of moderate growth. None repeat.

MOSSES. Distinguished from the Centifolias, which they otherwise resemble and from which they were derived, by a moss-like growth on the buds and flower stems.

BOURBONS. Descendants of the original *R. borboniana*. Blossoms are large, well formed, of distinct and intermediate tones of white, pink, red, or purple.

NOISETTES. The original *R. noisettiana* was a hybrid of *R. moschata* and a form of *R. chinensis*. Later forms were obtained by crossing the original with the Tea roses. The name is generally restricted to the climbing forms. Typically cluster-flowering and recurrent but not hardy.

RUGOSAS. Forms or hybrids of *R. rugosa* that produce blossoms of various colors and are of varying degrees of hardiness and recurrence. Mostly shrub types.

TEAS. Derived from *R. odorata* (the tea-scented rose), mostly through crosses with members of the Noisette family. Blossoms are characteristically drooping, of soft pink or yellow, and the plants are very recurrent but not adapted to culture in the North.

CHINAS. Derivatives or forms of *R. chinensis*, the first "perpetual-flowering" rose to reach the Western world. Bushes are of moderate growth and produce small to medium-sized, almost scentless flowers in small open clusters, almost continuously throughout the growing season. They are generally more hardy than the Hybrid Teas.

HYBRID TEAS. Originally crosses between the Hybrid Perpetuals and the Teas but the color range has been increased by the introduction of *R. foetida* blood.

HYBRID PERPETUALS. One of the immediate ancestors of the Hybrid Teas but differ generally from that class in their greater vigor, laxer growth, more abundant foliage, less recurrence, and large globular flowers.

POLYANTHAS. Originated as hybrids of *R. multiflora* and *R. chinensis* but not at present confined to roses of this parentage.

Under each class are listed some preferred varieties, together with their stature, color, and other significant data.

ALBAS

CELESTIAL. Double; pale pink to light blush; 5 to 6 ft.

MAIDEN'S BLUSH. Soft blush; 6 to 8 ft. Double.

CENTIFOLIAS

TOUR DE MALAKOFF. Soft lilac-mauve; 7 ft., double.

VARIEGATA DE BOLOGNA. Double; white with purple stripes; 4 to 5 ft.

DAMASKS

CELSIANA. Double; pale pink; 4 to 5 ft.

GLOIRE DE GUILAN. Semi-double; pale pink; 4 to 5 ft.

LEDA. Double; pale blush-pink; 4 to 5 ft. Sometimes repeats.

MME. HARDY. Double; white; 4 to 6 ft.

GALLICAS

BELLE DES JARDINS. Double; violet-red with white stripes; 6 to 8 ft.

CARDINAL DE RICHELIEU. Double; dark rich violet; 6 to 8 ft.

* Special articles on the subjects indicated by an asterisk (*) will be found at the words so marked.

MOSSES

CRESTED MOSS. Double; deep pink; 4 to 5 ft.
DEUIL DE PAUL FONTAINE. Double; purple-red; 3 to 4 ft. Sometimes repeats.
SALET. Double; deep pink; 4 to 5 ft. Repeats.

BOURBONS

The Bourbon class is slightly recurrent and moderately vigorous and hardy but its members are not sufficiently rugged to withstand continued neglect and the flowers are generally inferior to those of the Hybrid Perpetual class of which it was a parent. Culture is basically the same as that suggested for the preceding, though deep planting is not as essential. All of the following are double-flowered:

COMMANDANT BEAUREPAIRE. Pink striped with darker tones; 4 to 5 ft.
COUPE DE HEBE. Delicate pink; 4 to 6 ft.
LA REINE VICTORIA. Rosy pink; 6 to 7 ft.
SOUVENIR DE LA MALMAISON. Flesh-pink; 4 to 5 ft.

The Noisettes, Teas, and Chinas range from moderately to extremely recurrent but the first two deserve retention only in regions having mild winter temperatures. The Chinas are somewhat more hardy than the average Hybrid Tea and surpass all of them in individual blossom production. The color range and petalage is considerably less, however. The Noisettes are mostly in the climbing or pillar category and the Teas are of bush or bedding type, although there are a few derivatives of extremely vigorous growth. The cultural requirements of these classes is approximately the same as that suggested for the modern types of roses. Pruning should be moderate as they bloom best on wood produced during the preceding season. The blossoms of the following suggested varieties are either semi-double or double.

NOISETTES

BEAUTY OF GLAZENWOOD. Brilliant shades of yellow, orange, and red; 12 to 15 ft.
LAMARQUE. White; 10 to 14 ft.

TEAS

BARONNE HENRIETTE SNOY. Peach-pink-shaded cream; 3 to 4 ft.
CATHERINE MERMET. Pale pink; 3 to 4 ft.
DUCHESSE DE BRABANT. Pink; 5 to 6 ft.
GLOIRE DE DIJON. Creamy white, tinted amber and blush; 15 to 20 ft.

CHINAS

LOUIS PHILIPPE. Scarlet red; 4 to 5 ft.
OLD BLUSH. Light pink; 4 to 5 ft.

Previous to the development of the Hybrid Tea class, the Hybrid Perpetuals surpassed all others in popularity and at one time there were more than 3000 named varieties. It is regrettable that so few of them are now available as they constituted a very valuable class of sturdy, semi-hardy roses that produced large well-formed flowers in practically every color except yellow. Although most members were not dependably recurrent, many could be induced to repeat if properly fertilized and pruned. Authorities disagree somewhat as to the proper pruning procedures but the consensus of opinion is to remove all except last year's wood in early spring and shorten this to about three feet. Bloom recurrence is also encouraged by removing the spent blooms. They also require ample fertilization in the spring and following the June bloom. All bear double flowers and reach a height of about five feet.

BARONNE PREVOST. Soft lilac-rose.
DUKE OF EDINBURGH. Scarlet-crimson.
FERDINAND PICHARD. Pale pink with red stripes.
GEORGE ARENDS. Pink.
GLOIRE LYONNAISE. White.
MRS. JOHN LAING. Pink.

The Polyantha roses were never extremely popular but they did satisfy the desire for a dwarf to semi-dwarf, extremely floriferous, and quite hardy bedding rose of cluster-flowering type. Their descendants, the Floribundas, have practically replaced them in favor as the individual flowers are larger and of better form. As the value of the Polyanthas depends mostly on the quantity rather than the quality of the individual flowers, pruning should be limited to the removal of dead and extremely old stems and the shaping and thinning out of the plants. Moderate fertilization is advised. The following representative varieties average about 18 inches in height.

CAMEO. Semi-double; shell-pink and salmon.
CECILE BRUNNER. Double; light pink on a yellow base.
CRIMSON ROSETTE. Double; red.
MARGO KOSTER. Double; light orange.
ORANGE TRIUMPH. Double; scarlet-orange.
PINK ROSETTE. Double; soft pink.

More restricted gardening areas and the demand for recurrent blooming types that bear larger and better-formed flowers contributed to the demise of the once popular ramblers. They still possess some value, however, where growing space is unlimited and a thick impenetrable hedge or screen is desired. The small cluster-flowering types, such as Dorothy Perkins, Crimson Rambler, and Chevy Chase, bloom more profusely if all second-year wood is removed immediately after blooming. The large-flowered types represented by Dr. W. Van Fleet, Dr. Huey, Silver Moon, etc., require only the removal of unproductive wood and that which is four or five years of age or older. The lateral branches which bore blooms the previous season may be cut back to 2 or 3 eyes if the desire for maximum bloom production justifies the labor required. The best of those still sold by growers are:

DR. HUEY. Small, semi-double crimson-maroon blossoms, produced singly or in cluster. Moderately vigorous.

---

* Special articles on the subjects indicated by an asterisk (*) will be found at the words so marked.

Dr. W. Van Fleet. Large, double, well-formed pink blossoms. Extremely vigorous to 20 ft.

Mme. Gregoire Staechlin. Semi-double, ruffled, delicate pink flowers; 12 to 15 ft.

Little need be said concerning the value or the popularity of the Hybrid Tea class. They are presently obtainable in practically every desirable color except blue, and leading hybridists predict that we may soon have varieties of that color. Unfortunately most varieties are susceptible to disease and require winter protection throughout a major portion of our country. Their desirable attributes, however, overshadow their deficiencies and they will probably continue to be our preferred class for many years. The highest rated varieties are classed according to color.

Red: Crimson Glory, Charlotte Armstrong, Chrysler Imperial, Tallyho, Rubaiyat.

Pink: First Love, Picture, Radiance, Curly Pink, Show Girl.

Yellow: Eclipse, Lowell Thomas, Golden Dawn, McGredy's Yellow, Soeur Thérèse.

White: Pedralbes, McGredy's Ivory, Blanche Mallerin, Mme. Jules Bouche, Frau Karl Druschki.

Blends: Peace, Tiffany, Helen Traubel, Good News, Mme. Henri Guillot.

Single Hybrid Teas: Dainty Bess (pink), Golden Wings (yellow).

The Floribunda class was founded by crossing varieties of the Hybrid Tea and the Polyantha classes and has attained considerable popularity during recent years as a bedding or hedge rose. It has already superseded the Polyanthas in favor and may eventually become a rival of the Hybrid Teas. The color range is exceptionally wide; most varieties bear well-formed flowers in small to large clusters; they are very floriferous and

are slightly more hardy and disease-resistant than the Hybrid Teas. Procurable varieties are so numerous that it is difficult to compile a brief list. The following however have received the highest ratings by the American Rose Society.

Red: Spartan, Red Pinocchio, Eutin, Frensham, Donald Prior.

Pink: Betty Prior, The Fairy, Pink Bountiful, Rosenelfe, Else Poulsen.

Yellow: Goldilocks, Marionette, King Boreas

White: Dagmar Spath, Summer Snow, Irene of Denmark.

Blends: Fashion, Vogue, Ma Perkins, Masquerade.

The Grandifloras are more vigorous than either parent (the Hybrid Teas and the Floribundas) and produce larger, well-formed blossoms in small clusters, or individually, throughout the summer. They rival some of the semi-climbers in stature but, unfortunately, are but little, if any, hardier than the Hybrid Teas. Their future is assured in moderate climates but is questionable where the winters are severe. Further cross-breeding with the Hybrid Teas in an effort to improve blossom size and color range may gradually merge this class with the parent Hybrid Tea class. The present outstanding varieties are:

Buccaneer (yellow)
Carrousel (dark red)
June Bride (white)
Montezuma (light red)
Queen Elizabeth (pink)
Roundelay (dark red)

Although nurserymen report that the present trend is toward bush or bedding-type roses rather than climbers there is still a considerable demand for not-too-vigorous climbing or pillar roses that produce well-formed flowers recurrently. In this category

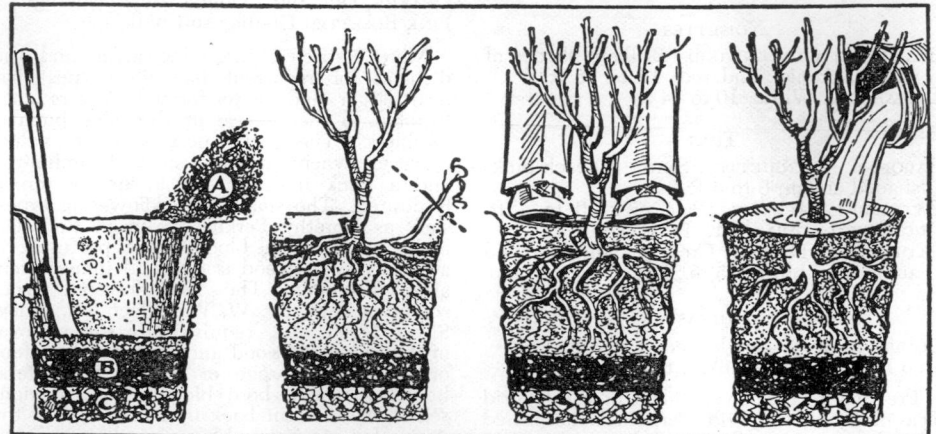

FOUR STEPS IN CORRECT ROSE PLANTING

A = Topsoil, B = Manure, C = Drainage material. From left to right: Dig an ample hole and use good topsoil for planting. See that all roots are well spread out and covered, cutting off old ones (as shown by dotted line). Be sure to firm the soil thoroughly around the roots and, finally, water the plant.

* Special articles on the subjects indicated by an asterisk (*) will be found at the words so marked.

are a few hardy and semi-hardy varieties and many of the not dependably hardy climbing sports of the Hybrid Teas. The latter require adequate winter protection in the North and, if frozen to the ground, will not bloom the following season. Pruning should be confined to the removal of dead and extremely old wood. The following are recommended (Cl. = Climbing):

Red: Cl. Etoile de Hollande, Cl. Crimson Glory, Blaze.

Pink: New Dawn, Cl. Picture, Blossomtime.

Yellow: Golden Showers, High Noon.

White: White Dawn.

Blends: Cl. Peace, Dream Girl.

The right way to cut a rose (*left*) and the result of it (*right*) which is to produce more flowers.

The so-called Miniature roses are becoming increasingly popular with many rose lovers as they are suitable for edging and rock garden use as well as for pot and flower box culture in or out of doors. They are mostly derivatives of *R. chinensis minima,* the fairy rose, an old Chinese dwarf rose, and range in height from about 3 inches to slightly more than a foot. Their stature alone does not entirely justify their classification as they possess other determining characteristics; the well-formed buds and closely spaced foliage are extremely small, the canes are thin, the plants are very free-flowering and are surprisingly hardy. In fact, in most parts of our country, an inverted flower pot provides adequate winter protection. They root readily from cuttings and this is the accepted method of propagation as they lose their miniature status when budded onto a vigorous understock. Heavy fertilization will also contribute to the same result. A few climbing forms that may grow to five feet, although they retain their class characteristics, have recently been developed. Extremely old wood on both the bush and climbing types should be thinned out occasionally. The following varieties are presently available:

DIAN. Soft red, double flowers; 12 in.

OAKINGTON RUBY. Double red; 12 in.

JACKIE. Double, yellow; 12 in.

CANDLEFLAME. Single; red, yellow, and orange shades; 12 in.

PINK CAMEO. Double rose-pink flowers. Climbing to 5 ft.

CLIMBING JACKIE. Similar to Jackie but grows to 3 or 4 ft.

The species, or native wild roses, deserve more recognition than they have received in the past as they may be used to advantage in the border and for naturalizing. They require but little care and produce an enormous crop of flowers (usually 5-petaled) each year. In most instances the flowers are followed by brightly colored seed hips (fruits) which prolong their season of attractiveness, provide feed for the birds, and are good subjects for flower and foliage arrangements. It is regrettable that but few of them are obtainable from growers. The best of those that are obtainable are *R. hugonis, R. spinosissima altaica, R. wichuraiana,* and *R. multiflora.* The latter is a popular understock for other less vigorous roses and is used extensively for pasture fences and institutional and highway planting. Descriptions of these and other desirable species will be found under ROSA.

There are several shrub-type roses, not previously mentioned, that have considerable merit. The most important of these are hybrids of the species *R. rugosa* that range from 2 to 8 feet in stature, are of varying degrees of hardiness and recurrence, and are obtainable in many colors.

AGNES. Double, pale amber, hardy, non-recurrent. Six feet.

AUTUMN BOUQUET. Well-formed, double, pink. Recurrent. Not dependably hardy; 4 to 5 ft.

BLANC DOUBLE DE COUBERT. Double, white; non-recurrent, hardy; 5 to 6 ft.

F. J. GROOTENDORST. Carnation-like red flowers; recurrent, hardy; 4 to 5 ft.

HON. LADY LINDSAY. Double, two-toned pink; recurrent, not dependably hardy; 3 ft.

PINK GROOTENDORST. A pink-flowering form of F. J. Grootendorst.

SARA VAN FLEET. Semi-double, rose-pink; hardy, recurrent; 7 to 8 ft.

SIR THOMAS LIPTON. Double white; hardy, recurrent; 6 to 8 ft.

VANGUARD. Well-formed, double, orange-scarlet. Sometimes hardy and recurrent; 6 to 10 ft.

CULTURE

The prevalent and erroneous idea that rose culture is highly specialized gardening, requiring considerable labor, expense, and experience has kept many persons from pursuing it. The culture of roses may be somewhat more complicated than that of some other plants but the results justify the slight additional effort. There is no reason why you cannot succeed if you possess a satisfactory location and are willing to apply a reasonable amount of common sense and effort to their culture. Incidentally, any soil that is adequately drained and will grow vegetables, flowers, or a weed crop will produce roses. The location should receive at least six hours of sunlight daily and contain no living tree roots that might compete with the roses for food and moisture. A few basic rules and recommendations follow.

(1) Purchase plants from a reputable dealer as cheap roses are rarely a bargain and require as much, if not more, care than good ones. Price alone should not be the controlling factor, as many of the older and therefore less costly varieties are superior to some of the recently introduced patented ones. The fact that they have remained popular for years is proof that they possess merit. They have survived the onrush of numerous highly publicized varieties, many of which have since been forgotten. Dormant two-year-old field-grown plants represent the best value, although potted roses may be used to fill late-season vacancies in the rose bed. The roses sold in elaborately decorated cartons do not receive the after-packaging care they require and many of the roots are sacrificed to fit the container.

(2) The excessive drying of roots and tops before planting handicaps the future performance of the plant and may even prove fatal. Every precaution should be taken to prevent the drying influence of sun and wind. If roses are shriveled on arrival the entire plant may be buried for a day or two in damp soil to restore normal plumpness. When planting must be postponed for an extended period of time a similar procedure should be followed but, in this instance, the plants should remain buried until you are prepared to plant them.

(3) Although most nurseries now ship plants properly pruned for planting, it is advisable to cut tops back to about 12 inches above the crown and remove all heavily damaged or broken roots and canes and all small twiggy growth. The understock stub (usually about an inch long) is dead tissue and should be cut back flush with the main stem. This stub protrudes above the area where the green-wooded top joins the brown-colored main stem and roots. Do not mutilate the roots as their development is comparatively slow and the preservation and retention of as large a root system as possible contributes to future normal growth.

(4) Dig a hole sufficiently large to accommodate the roots without crowding, coiling, or crossing, and deep enough so that the bud-union will be at proper depth. Where the severity of the climate justifies winter protection, the union should be an inch or so below the surface of the soil. In more moderate areas it may be level with, or slightly above, the surface.

(5) Spread the roots out in all directions and slightly downward. Then cover them with an inch or two of loose (not lumpy) soil and fill the balance of the hole with water. The water will eliminate air pockets as it seeps away and this procedure is much better than tamping the soil, which frequently causes it to become too compact and may damage the roots as well as sink the plant too deeply.

(6) Then fill the hole with soil and scatter a small handful of commercial fertilizer around each plant. Fertilizer should not be mixed with the soil at planting time. When applied on the surface its descent is so gradual that it does not reach the roots until they have developed sufficiently to receive it.

(7) The next step is to mound soil to the top of the stems. When roses are planted in the fall this mound provides winter protection and in spring planting it retains moisture in the stems until the roots have become established. In the latter event it should be removed in about ten days or two weeks, preferably on a cloudy day or in late afternoon. Burlap, heavy paper, boxes, or baskets are acceptable substitutes for shading spring-planted roses but, for winter protection, there is no substitute for soil.

(8) After the mounds have been removed the application of a mulch to the surface of the bed has many advantages. It eliminates considerable labor by reducing the weed population, retains moisture, prevents the puddling effect of rain, gradually builds up the organic content of the soil, and keeps it several degrees cooler during the hot summer months. The beginner may consider the latter virtue relatively unimportant but he will soon discover that a reduced soil temperature will encourage blossom production. Roses are cool-weather plants and definitely dislike warm soil. The cost and availability of the various mulching materials in your locality should determine the type you use. Those that pack tightly and shed water are not recommended. Those that retain moisture for long periods should not contact the canes or crown as this may induce the development of certain diseases. Most mulching materials absorb soil nitrogen as they decompose but release it during the latter stages of decomposition. When mulches of this type are used it is advantageous to add extra nitrogen during the early stages of decomposing.

(9) Remove all tags or labels that may girdle or otherwise injure the stems and substitute other markers with which to identify the varieties. It is easy to forget names and they become increasingly important as your interest in roses develops.

(10) If you live in an area where winter protection is required, all bush-type roses that are susceptible to winter injury should be protected with a mound of earth in early fall. The ambition of the grower will determine the height of the mound, but bear in mind that more wood will survive the winter under a mound of generous proportions. A mound 5 or 6 inches high, after settling, may be considered of minimum size. Although the

---

* Special articles on the subjects indicated by an asterisk (*) will be found at the words so marked.

mound may be applied while the weather is still pleasant and the plants are in bloom, the tops should not be cut back until later. In fact there are some advantages in retaining all wood except the extremely long canes until spring. Considerable injury may result to new growth if the mounds are not removed before the buds begin to swell in the spring. In northern Ohio this operation is best performed in mid-March. Severely cold weather does not occur after that time and the plants are not injured by light freezes. The protection of climbing roses is dependent on their degree of hardiness in the area in which they are grown. Those requiring protection may be laid on the ground and covered with soil or wrapped, on their supports, with burlap or building paper. In semi-mild areas, tree roses will usually survive if the tops and trunks are similarly wrapped. They are not adapted to climates where the winters are severe but may live if one side of the root system is unearthed and the entire plant is laid on the ground and covered with soil.

(11) The proper fertilization of established plants presents somewhat of a problem but most growers use three applications of commercial fertilizer each year. The first is applied as early spring growth begins, the second immediately following the June bloom, and the third about a month and a half later. The amount applied at each feeding should be in proportion to the size of the plant as a large plant requires more food than a small one. For example, and as a basis, each feeding of the average Hybrid Tea rose consists of a handful of fertilizer distributed evenly around the plant and worked into the soil. It is impossible to suggest the proper fertilizer for any individual garden as the types and basic fertility of soils differ greatly. All of the three major elements are usually required, however. A 4-12-4 or a 5-10-5 analysis is adequate under most conditions although one containing a greater proportion of nitrogen may be better for the first two feedings. This is particularly true if the beds are mulched with a nitrogen-absorbing material. Incidentally, roses require a considerable amount of water if they are to grow and bloom properly. An occasional heavy soaking of the rose beds will pay dividends.

(12) Pruning is best performed in two stages and the first of these is best undertaken before growth begins in the spring. This consists of removing all dead and unrequired wood and the general shaping of the plant. As the actual extent of winter injury may not be discernible until growth begins, a second pruning back to healthy, uninjured wood is often necessary. At this time all wood should be cut back to the point where the bark is hard and green and the pith is white or cream-colored. In some instances the bark may be green but the pith is brown. This denotes that the cane has suffered some winter injury and will die when the weather becomes hot and the demand for food in-

creases. Although winter injury dictates the extent of pruning in some localities it is always advisable to retain as much wood as possible. This wood constitutes the framework on which new growth is produced, and blossom production corresponds with leaf area. It is interesting to note that approximately six healthy leaves are required to manufacture sufficient food to produce an average blossom. It is therefore apparent that a plant lacking framework on which to bear leaves cannot be extremely floriferous. This fact should also be remembered when cutting blooms and the stem should be as short as practical.

The proper procedure is illustrated although the stem might be even one leaf shorter than shown. In pruning, all cuts should be made just above a bud and those on canes larger than lead-pencil size should be coated with shellac, tree-wound dressing, caulking compound, floral (modeling) clay, or any other practical material that does not contain turpentine. The proper method of pruning climbers, shrubs, and the older type of roses is discussed under their class groupings. Quite frequently the beginner is reluctant to attempt pruning as he fears that, due to lack of experience, he may seriously injure his roses. There is nothing complicated, mysterious, or technical about the task and even the authorities disagree as to the extent. In fact no phase of rose-growing permits greater leeway. The beginner may use his own initiative and will rarely, if ever, seriously injure his plants if he pursues the policy of retaining as much good wood as possible and removes only the dead, diseased, and extremely old wood. Of course extremely rampant growth should be cut back to improve the form of the plant. — R. E. S.

The present address of the American Rose Society is 4048 Roselea Place, Columbus 14, Ohio.

INSECT PESTS. Dormant oil sprays control scales of several species. Regular applications of pesticide #19 or #1 (see SPRAYS AND DUSTS) control leaf feeders of many species. Destroy stem borers by pruning out. Aphids and mites are controlled by pesticide #1 or #21.

Under glass, aerosols of many types will control mites, aphids, and leaf feeders. Follow precautions on container. Follow a regular application schedule. Pesticide #1 mixtures will control other pests.

DISEASES. The most common disease of rose is black spot.* Irregular black areas blotch the leaves, after which leaves yellow and drop. Plants may become almost denuded and few flowers then develop. Use pesticide #1 or #5 (see SPRAYS AND DUSTS) applied at 10-day intervals, starting when new growth is about 6 inches long.

Powdery mildew* causes severe curling of leaves on susceptible varieties. Weekly applications of pesticide #6 or #9 should start as soon as first mildew is noticed.

Several canker* diseases produce brown or purple areas on the canes, after which all growth above the canker will die. Prune out cankered canes, making the cut at least 2 inches below the canker. The pesticides used

* Special articles on the subjects indicated by an asterisk (*) will be found at the words so marked.

for black spot will help to prevent canker diseases.

If plants appear weak, examine the stem at the soil line and the roots near the crown of the plant for crown gall.* Remove such plants and try to get all such galls out of the soil area before planting another rosebush.

rosea, -us, -um (ro'zee-a). Rose-colored.

ROSE ACACIA = *Robinia hispida.* See Locust.

ROSE-APPLE = *Eugenia Jambos.*

ROSE-BAY. A name applied to at least four very different plants. The two most important are the oleander and the *Rhododendron maximum.* See also Epilobium angustifolium and Tabernaemontana coronaria.

ROSEBUD CHERRY = *Prunus subhirtella.*

ROSE CAMPION = *Lychnis coronaria.*

ROSE-COLORED GARDEN. See Pink Garden.

ROSE FAMILY. Rose relatives are legion, including herbs, shrubs, and trees. Few are as showy, individually, as the rose itself, but among the many garden groups are spirea, pearl bush, jetbead, ninebark, hawthorns, the mountain-ash, and all the showy flowering cherries and crabapples. Besides these ornamentals, the rose family contains such important fruits as the strawberry, blackberry, raspberry, peach, plum, apple, pear, and quince. For a complete list of the many genera *see* Rosaceae.

ROSE GARDENS. There are hundreds of public and private rose gardens — far too many to enumerate here. For a list of them write to American Rose Society, 4048 Roselea Place, Columbus 14, Ohio.

ROSE GERANIUM = *Pelargonium graveolens.*

ROSE HIP. The much-enlarged, fleshy, berry-like receptacle* of the rose. It is not technically a fruit although commonly called so. Actually, it encloses the true fruits of the rose, which are bony achenes.* See Rosa.

ROSELLE = *Hibiscus Sabdariffa.*

ROSE MALLOW. See Hibiscus Moscheutos.

ROSEMARY. Hardy perennial evergreen shrubs, comprising the genus **Rosmarinus** (rosma-ry'nus) which has only one species, a native of the Mediterranean region, and belonging to the mint family. These shrubs are general garden favorites, owing to their strongly scented leaves and flowers. The only species is R. officinalis. It grows up to 6 ft., and is of upright habit, much-branched. Leaves small, lance-shaped, to 1 in. long, grayish-green on the upper side, covered with short white hairs on under side. Flowers light blue, in clusters growing from the axils* of the leaves. Calyx of 5 sepals. Corolla tubular, 2-lipped,* upper lip consisting of 2 lobes, lower lip of 3 lobes. Stamens* 4, in pairs, 2 long, 2 short. Fruit 2-celled when young, splitting into 4 parts when ripe. Mediterranean region.

Propagated from cuttings. Cuttings should be made in Sept. of young shoots about 6 in. long, which should be inserted in a mixture of ½ sand and ½ soil, in a cool greenhouse or cold frame. After rooting they should be planted in potting mixture* 2, and left in cold frame during winter months. See Herb Gardening. In the northern states they require sheltered positions. They make good hedge plants in the southern states. (*Rosmarinus* is from the Latin for sea-dew, in allusion to its being found on the sea cliffs of southern France.)

ROSEMARY FAMILY = Labiatae.

ROSEMARY WILLOW = *Salix Elaeagnos.* See Willow.

ROSE MILKWEED = *Asclepias tuberosa.* See Milkweed.

ROSE MOSS = *Portulaca grandiflora.*

ROSEOCACTUS (rose-e-o-kak'tus). A small genus of low, half-buried cacti, closely related to *Ariocarpus* (which see), grown more for interest than beauty. The chief cult. species is R. fissuratus, one of the living-rocks.* It has a nearly spherical, much-tubercled* plant body with a depression at the top. Flowers 1–2 in. wide, usually pink. Tex. and adjacent Mex. For cult. *see* Cacti. (*Roseocactus* is named for J. N. Rose and cactus.)

ROSE-OF-CHINA = *Hibiscus Rosa-sinensis.*

ROSE-OF-HEAVEN = *Lychnis Coeli-rosa.*

ROSE-OF-JERICHO = *Anastatica hierochuntica.*

ROSE-OF-SHARON = *Hibiscus syriacus;* also *Hypericum calycinum.* See St. John's-wort at Saint.

roseo-picta, -us, -um (ro-zee-o-pick'ta). Rose-blotched or rose-marked.

ROSE PINK. See Sabatia.

ROSE POGONIA = *Pogonia ophioglossoides.*

ROSETTE. A usually radiating cluster of basal leaves, common in many herbs, especially plants like the houseleek and in most saxi-

A terminal rosette (*above*) is not so common as the basal rosette found in houseleek and many other plants.

---

* Special articles on the subjects indicated by an asterisk (*) will be found at the words so marked.

frages. Rosettes are common also as the first-year stage of many biennials. While rosettes are usually basal, they are sometimes terminal, as in the sago palm (*Cycas revoluta*), and in many other plants.

ROSETUM. A rose garden.

ROSINWEED. See SILPHIUM. See also CHRYSOPSIS VILLOSA.

ROSMARINUS. See ROSEMARY.

rostrata, -us, -um (ros-tray'ta). Beaked.

ROSY MILFOIL = *Achillea Millefolium roseum.*

ROTATE. Applied to flowers which have a very short tube and a flat, expanded, more or less wheel-shaped limb.* A typically rotate corolla is the moneywort or creeping Charlie; also in many flowers of the genus *Solanum* (potato, etc.).

ROTATION OF BLOOM. A continuous succession of plants in bloom is perhaps more desired than almost anything else in the garden. A list of plants, arranged by the months in which they flower, will be found at EVERBLOOMING GARDEN. From such a list anyone can plan a garden for a continuous rotation of bloom.

ROTATION OF CROPS. An agricultural and horticultural practice of very ancient use, based upon the fact that too long occupancy of one site by a single crop is neither good for it nor for the soil in which it grows.

Such a plan, which should operate over a period of years to be effective, should be so arranged that the same kind of crop never occupies the same soil for two successive years. The advantages of this are that overwintered diseases or insect pests will not have the same crop upon which to feed. Also soils are at least thought to get "tired" of one-crop occupancy. Whether or not they really do so is a disputed point among the experts. In any case, rotation can do no harm, and for centuries it has been most beneficial by actual test.

It is usually impossible to follow any rotation scheme in ornamental plantings, except, of course, for annuals and bulbs, which should be rotated if possible. But in the vegetable garden rotation is to be strongly recommended. For details of several rotation schemes see KITCHEN GARDEN.

ROTENONE. See No. 3 at INSECTICIDES.

ROTTEN WOOD. See WOOD ROT.

ROTUND. Circular; orbicular.

rotundifolia, -us, -um (ro-tun-di-fō'li-a). Round-leaved.

ROTUNDIFOLIA GRAPES. Another name for Muscadine grapes, derived from *Vitis rotundifolia* (which see).

ROUEN LILAC = *Syringa chinensis.* See LILAC.

ROUGE-PLANT = *Rivina humilis.*

ROUGH LEMON. See LEMON.

ROUGH WOODBINE = *Lonicera hirsuta.*

ROUND KUMQUAT = *Fortunella japonica.*

ROUND TANKS. For contents *see* WEIGHTS AND MEASURES, 5.

ROWAN TREE = *Sorbus Aucuparia.* See MOUNTAIN-ASH.

ROYAL BOTANICAL GARDENS. See BOTANIC GARDEN.

ROYAL FERN = *Osmunda regalis.*

ROYAL HORTICULTURAL SOCIETY. See HORTICULTURAL SOCIETIES.

ROYAL LILY = *Lilium regale.*

ROYAL PALM. See ROYSTONEA.

ROYAL POINCIANA = *Delonix regia.*

ROYAL WATER LILY = *Victoria regia.*

Royoc (roy'yock). Tropical American vernacular name of *Morinda Royoc.*

ROYSTONEA (roy-stone'ee-a). Royal palm. Magnificent feather palms from tropical America (one extending into extreme southern Fla.), planted throughout the tropical world. Three of the 6 known species are planted for ornament in Fla., but only in zone* 9 or the southernmost part of zone* 8. Some tropical cities, notably Rio de Janeiro, have magnificent avenues of these royal palms, most of which are native in the West Indies.

Royal palm

They are tall, single-stemmed, unarmed palms, the trunks sometimes bulging, crowned with an immense tuft of large, gracefully drooping leaves, the stalk of which is usually concave or convex in cross-section. Male and female flowers separate in the same cluster, which arises just below the crown of leaves. Fruit scarcely over ½ in. in diameter, generally roundish and bluish. (Named for General Roy Stone, American engineer in Puerto Rico.)

The royal palms are scarcely known in greenhouses and they have never been successfully grown outdoors in Calif. In Fla. by far the most commonly planted and hardiest is *R. regia.* Taller and more tender is *R. oleracea,* suited only to zone* 9. Also very tender is the Puerto Rican *R. borinquena.* It is lower than the other two but does better on light sandy soils than either of the other royal palms.

borinquena. Puerto Rican royal palm. Not usually over 35 ft. high as cult., the trunk swollen about ¾ of the way to the top, tapering above and below the swelling. Leaves about 10 ft. long, its many segments or leaflets about 2–2½ ft. long, 2 in. wide, tapering to a fine point. Fruit egg-shaped or roundish, yellowish-brown. Puerto Rico and St. Croix.

oleracea. Barbados royal palm; also called palmiste and cabbage palm. A slender-stemmed palm, sometimes 120 ft. high, the swelling of the trunk near the base. Leaves 10–15 ft. long, more or less ascending at first, ultimately drooping. Fruit oblong-roundish, the cluster hanging far below the leaves. W.I. A magnificent avenue palm.

regia. Cuban royal palm. Usually not over 70 ft. high, the trunk swelling near the middle or just above it, tapering above and below the swelling. Leaves 10–15 ft. long, usually drooping from the first, and generally covering the flower and fruit cluster. Fruit nearly round, scarcely ½ in. in diameter. Cuba, Panama, and perhaps elsewhere in tropical America; also native on some of the Fla. Keys and in the Everglades. Widely planted in southern Fla.

RUBBER-PLANT. The common rubber-plant of the florists, and a good house plant is *Ficus elastica* (which see). It produces India rubber, but true rubber is derived from *Hevea brasiliensis* (which see).

RUBBER-TREE = *Hevea brasiliensis.*

RUBBER-VINE. *See* CRYPTOSTEGIA GRANDIFLORA.

RUBBISH. Rubbish may be placed roughly into two classes — combustible and non-combustible. The former includes organic matter such as leaves, grass, weeds, branches from shrubs and trees, mulch, and paper; the latter, inorganic matter such as stones, metallic objects, glass, and vegetable refuse that is not readily dried.

Leaves from deciduous trees and lawn clippings may be used as mulch* or put into the compost* heap and permitted to rot. With the addition of Adco, a clean, odorless manure may be secured in three to four months. It would be well, however, not to include in this vegetable manure any weeds whose seed is partially or fully matured, as germination may not be totally destroyed by rotting. *See* Synthetic Manure at MANURE. However, some part of the vegetable refuse is unfit for the compost heap, vegetable manure, or for mulching and must be disposed of in some other manner, preferably by incineration.

Of the two methods of incineration, the open fire with its ever-present "fire hazard," and the small portable incinerator, the latter is to be preferred. Large branches of trees or shrubs and flower stalks such as hollyhocks,

dahlias, delphiniums, and other refuse too bulky to be placed in the portable incinerator are best destroyed in small open fires. It is better to do this on a windless day. The fire should be placed at an adequate distance from trees or shrubs, so that any change in the air current would not cause scorching of the branches or foliage. Small fires to which refuse may be added from time to time are to be preferred to large fires that may easily get beyond control and do irreparable injury to the surrounding vegetation.

All other rubbish of mineral or vegetable origin that cannot be destroyed by incineration must be disposed of by hauling to the public dump, or, if in small quantities, by burial in a pit or trench. In the case of metallic objects the disintegration after burial will be hastened if they are first put into the incinerator to burn off the protective coating.

rubella, -us, -um (roo-bell'a). Reddish.

rubens (roo'benz). Red.

ruber (roo'ber). Red.

rubescens (roo-bess'senz). Becoming reddish.

RUBIA (roo'bi-a). Perennial herbs of about 40 species of the family Rubiaceae, found distributed throughout the temperate and tropical regions of the world. Leaves generally in whorls* of 4–8, narrowly lance-shaped, sometimes stalked, smooth or covered with prickly hairs. Flowers small, greenish-yellow or white, in terminal clusters, or in the leaf axils.* Fruit a small berry. *R. tinctorum* has red, fleshy roots. (*Rubia* is from the Latin for red.) These plants are not of much garden importance, although *R. tinctorum* is grown for its dye, which is obtained by grinding the roots.

tinctorum. Common madder. Growing to 4 ft., of spreading habit. Leaves in whorls of 4–6, lance-shaped, 2–4 in. long, with prickly hairs on midrib and margins. Flowers greenish-yellow, small, in branching clusters. Southern Eu. and As.

RUBIACEAE (roo-bi-ā'see-ee). The madder or coffee family while a very large one (400 genera and 7000 species) is more important commercially than from the garden standpoint. It includes herbs, shrubs, and trees, most of them tropical, and a few of world-wide importance, like *Coffea* and *Cinchona* (quinine). Only a handful are suited to outdoor culture in frosty regions. Of these, herbs (sometimes slightly woody) are found in *Asperula, Galium, Houstonia, Mitchella,* and *Rubia,* while the only generally hardy, woody plant is *Cephalanthus* (*see* BUTTONBUSH).

All the rest of the cult. genera are shrubs, vines, or trees of tropical or sub-tropical regions to be grown outdoors only in frost-free parts of the country or in greenhouses. These tender genera, mostly of secondary garden importance, are *Bouvardia, Coprosma* (some nearly hardy), *Hamelia, Hoffmannia* (a greenhouse foliage plant), *Ixora, Luculia,*

---

* Special articles on the subjects indicated by an asterisk (*) will be found at the words so marked.

Manettia (vines), *Morinda* (includes the Indian mulberry), *Nertera* (tender ground cover), *Pentas* (nearly herbaceous), *Posoqueria, Psychotria, Rondeletia,* and *Serissa,* which is, however, hardy from zone* 5 southward. Two other tropical genera are far more important. One is *Gardenia* which includes the florists' flower of that name, the other is *Genipa* with edible fruit (the genipap).

Leaves opposite* (or whorled* in a few genera), usually without marginal teeth. Flowers mostly regular, very showy in some of the tropical genera (*Ixora, Hamelia*) and attractive in *Cephalanthus,* mostly in various sorts of clusters, but in pairs in *Mitchella.* Fruit fleshy or dry.

Technical flower characters: Calyx* more or less united, 2–6-cleft or parted. Corolla united, 4–6-lobed, the edges of the lobes touching (not overlapping). Stamens* 4–6, borne on the corolla. Ovary inferior,* mostly 2-celled, the style* 1.

rubioides (roo-bi-oy'deez, but *see* OïDES). Resembling the madder (*Rubia*).

rubra, -us, -um (roo'bra). Red.

rubrifolia, -us, -um (roo-bri-fo'li-a). Red-leaved.

rubrofructa, -us, -um (roo-bro-fruck'ta). Red-fruited.

RUBUS (roo'bus). An immense genus of shrubby, usually prickly plants of the rose family, including all the wild brambles, the cult. blackberry, dewberry, and raspberry, and a few others grown for ornament. Nearly all the 400 reputedly different species are from the north temperate zone, but a few outliers are found on tropical mountains, in the southern hemisphere, and a small group of species extends to or beyond the Arctic Circle. They are erect or trailing plants, many of them with biennial canes (*i.e.,* leafy the first year, but flowering and fruiting the second year and then dying). The first-year canes, bearing only leaves, are known as turions. Some species bear perennial canes.

Leaves alternate,* simple and lobed, or more usually compound* and the leaflets arranged finger-fashion (rarely feather-fashion). Flowers prevailingly white, but purplish-pink in a few, the 5 petals often rounded, sometimes small or even wanting. Stamens* numerous. Fruit (in ours) a collection of small, sometimes dryish drupelets,* the "berry" (*i.e.,* the edible part) of two sorts: (1) In the blackberry and dewberry the mass of fleshy drupelets (commonly called seeds) adheres to the fleshy receptacle* which is part of the "berry" and eaten with it; (2) in the raspberry (including the blackcap) the mass of drupelets,* or what is incorrectly called the berry, parts from the receptacle* when picked, and the "fruit" is hollow. In other words we eat the receptacle* in blackberries, but leave it on the plant in the raspberry. The loganberry, of hybrid origin, is usually considered as having fruits of the blackberry type, although one

of its parents is a raspberry. (*Rubus* is the old Latin name of the brambles.)

Perhaps no genus of plants, except *Crataegus,* is in such a chaotic condition as to Latin names and identities as the brambles. While there are supposed to be 400–500 species, some authorities recognize nearly twice this number. In addition, there are hundreds of natural and induced hybrids. All that can be done here is to list a few of the more important species that appear to or may be involved in the production of the four major fruit crops, and a few others grown for ornament or interest. The major fruit crops, all the subjects of separate articles which should be consulted for varieties and culture, are: BLACKBERRY, DEWBERRY, RASPBERRY, and LOGANBERRY. The species involved in the production of the common cult. blackberry are omitted from the list below because they are unknown. It seems to have been derived from a group of North American species or hybrids of wild brambles. While over 60 species of *Rubus* are recorded as being cult. in the U.S., the inclusion of all of them here does not seem to be warranted, nor have we included the scores of wild brambles.

Turion as used below means a first-year cane bearing leaves only. Plants bearing perennial canes are noted as perennials.

deliciosus. Boulder raspberry. Rocky Mountain flowering raspberry. A perennial, shrubby plant, the stems without prickles or bristles. Leaves simple,* roundish, shallowly 5–7-angled, irregularly toothed, about 2 in. wide. Flowers white, nearly 2 in. wide. Fruit (a raspberry) dark reddish-purple, worthless. Colo. May. Hardy from zone* 4 southward. Grown for ornament.

flagellaris. Dewberry. A trailing blackberry, the very prickly, but not sticky stems rooting at the tip. Leaflets 3–5, ovalish or triangular, toothed. Flowers white, not numerous, in a forking cluster. Fruit (a blackberry) nearly round or oblongish, black. Eastern N.A., west to Minn. and Ark. May–June. Hardy from zone* 3 southward, but seldom grown in the wild form here noted. For the cult. and varieties of the common dewberry, apparently derived from this species, and notes on hardiness *see* DEWBERRY. *See also* RUBUS TRIVIALIS.

hispidus. Swamp dewberry. A perennial, prostrate, vine-like plant, with 3 leaflets, no prickles, but bristly stems. Leaflets partly evergreen, toothed, blunt. Flowers small, white, few and inconspicuous. Fruit (a blackberry) sour and relatively worthless. Eastern N.A., west to Wis. and Mo. May. Hardy everywhere. Planted only for ground cover in moist, shady places.

idaeus. European raspberry. An erect, shrubby plant with biennial prickly or bristly stems. Leaflets 3 (5 on the turions), toothed, gray-white. Flowers white and small. Fruit (raspberry) conical or thimble-shaped, mostly red. Eurasia. Scarcely known here, but the source of some cult. red raspberries. The *var.* **strigosus,** a closely related form from N.A. and eastern As., has fruit which is flatter or hemispherical and is the source of most of the red raspberry varieties. *See* RASPBERRY.

illecebrosus. Strawberry-raspberry; also called balloon-berry. An arching, very prickly

---

* Special articles on the subjects indicated by an asterisk (*) will be found at the words so marked.

plant, its stems practically herbaceous, about 4 ft. high and forming patches. Leaflets 5–9, narrow, long-pointed, 3–4 in. long. Flowers white, about 1 in. wide, fragrant. Fruit (a raspberry) scarlet, large, but insipid or sour, sometimes used cooked. Jap. July–Sept. Hardy from zone* 3 southward. Planted for ornament.

laciniatus. Cutleaf or evergreen blackberry. An arching or trailing blackberry, its perennial canes prickly or ultimately smooth. Leaflets 3–5, evergreen or nearly so, cut into fine, toothed segments. Flowers white or pinkish, in branched clusters (panicles*). Fruit (a blackberry) small, nearly round, black and sweet. Eu., but naturalized on the Pacific Coast. June–July. Hardy from zone* 4 southward. Grown mostly for ornament, although it may be the part origin of some cult. blackberries.

loganobaccus. Loganberry. A vigorous blackberry-like, prickly plant, the canes bluish-green, somewhat vine-like. Leaflets 3 (5 on turions), ovalish or wider, toothed, gray-felty beneath. Flowers white, nearly 2 in. wide, sometimes double. Fruit nearly 1¼ in. long, acid, red. For origin and culture *see* LOGAN-BERRY (which also includes a variety known as Phenomenal).

occidentalis. Blackcap raspberry. Thimble-berry. An erect, prickly plant, the stems very bluish or even bluish-purple, ultimately arching over and rooting at the tip, hence making impenetrable thickets unless controlled. Leaflets 3, ovalish but tapering, doubly toothed, conspicuously white-felty beneath. Flowers whitish, small, in dense, prickly clusters. Fruit (a black raspberry) black, but with a slight bloom. Eastern N.A., west to N. D. and Colo. May–June. Hardy from zone* 2 southward. The source of several hort. varieties. Its cult. is the same as for raspberry (which see).

Flowering raspberry (*Rubus odoratus*)

odoratus. Flowering raspberry. A showy shrub with perennial, bristly or sticky, but not prickly stems, 4–6 ft. high, the bark shreddy. Leaves simple,* broadly heart-shaped, 4–8 in. wide, generally 5-lobed, irregularly toothed, green and hairy both sides. Flowers purplish or rose-purple, nearly 2 in. wide, showy. Fruit (a raspberry) red, dryish, and worthless. Eastern N.A., west to Mich. and Tenn. June–Aug.

Hardy from zone* 2 southward. Planted for ornament, but best suited to partial shade in the informal shrub border, as it ultimately makes large patches.

phoenicolasius. Wineberry. An upright, shrubby plant, the canes arching and ultimately rooting at the tip, densely covered with red, sticky hairs and a few weak, straight prickles. Leaflets mostly 3, purple-veined, white-felty beneath. Flowers small, pinkish or white, the calyx large and red-bristly. Fruit (a raspberry) red, small, edible, but insipid. Jap. and China, often running wild from old gardens in eastern N.A. July–Aug. Hardy from zone* 3 southward. Rather ornamental, but making impenetrable thickets if let alone.

procerus. Himalaya-berry (not from the Himalayas). A woody, perennial-stemmed, creeping or clambering blackberry, the stems 20–30 ft. long and very prickly. Leaflets 3–5, densely white-felty beneath, partly persistent, doubly toothed. Flowers white, the clusters white-felty. Fruit (a blackberry) thimble-shaped. Eu. Introduced into the U.S. about 1890 and somewhat grown for fruit in Calif. It needs trellis or fence-like support and the general cult. methods followed for dewberry (which see).

trivialis. Southern dewberry. A creeping or trailing blackberry, the stems very prickly and often with sticky bristles. Leaflets partly evergreen, 3–5, narrowly oblongish, toothed, smooth. Flowers white or pinkish, in long clusters (panicles*). Fruit (a blackberry) oblong, black. Md. to Fla. and Tex. April–May. For the cult. and varieties *see* DEWBERRY. Other plants are involved in the production of the cult. dewberry, notably *R. flagellaris*.

RUBY GRASS = *Tricholaena rosea.*

RUDBECKIA (rood-beck'i-a). Coneflower. North American hardy perennial, annual or biennial herbs, comprising about 25 species, of the family Compositae. Leaves usually alternate,* simple or compound,* in some species much cut and lance-shaped, the veins prominent, the margins deeply toothed toward the tip. Flowers in terminal or axillary heads, generally yellow, in most species the disk florets* being brown or black. Fruit dry, 1-celled, 1-seeded. (Named for two Professors Rudbeck, father and son.)

Rudbeckias are useful border plants, easily cult. Propagated by seeds or division of root-stocks. Seeds should be sown thinly, ⅛ in. deep, in early spring in the cool greenhouse or cold frame or later in outdoor seedbed. They may be transplanted to permanent positions as soon as large enough to handle. Division of rootstocks may be made in March or April. One of the most popular of all perennials is the Golden Glow, a variety of *R. laciniata*, which is of very easy culture.

bicolor. Thimble-flower. Annual, 1–2 ft. high, covered with short, stiff hairs. Leaves lance-shaped, to 2 in. long, not cut. Flowers in heads, ray florets* yellow, sometimes purplish-black at base, disk florets black. Pine woods of southern states. The *var.* **superba**, the Erfurt coneflower, has larger flowers, the ray florets being purplish-brown at base.

fulgida. Orange coneflower. Perennial, to 2 ft. high. Leaves broadly lance-shaped, to 4 in. long, more or less hairy on both sides. Flowers in heads 1½ in. across, ray florets

* Special articles on the subjects indicated by an asterisk (*) will be found at the words so marked.

golden-yellow with orange base, disk florets purplish-black. N.J. to Va. and Ind.

hirta. Black-eyed Susan. Annual or biennial, growing 1–3 ft. high, covered with short, stiff hairs. Leaves broadly lance-shaped to 5 in. long, margins toothed. Flowers in heads 3–4 in. across, ray florets* golden-yellow, disk florets purplish-brown. Eastern U.S.

laciniata. Perennial to 12 ft. high. Leaves smooth, deeply cut into 3–5 lobes, the lobes broadly lance-shaped, deeply toothed toward the tip. Flowers in heads 4 in. across, ray florets yellow, drooping, disk florets greenish-yellow. Eastern to midwestern N.A. The *var.* **hortensia,** the Golden Glow, has double flowers, and is so popular that it is anathema to some.

maxima. Perennial to 9 ft. high. Leaves grayish-green, ovalish, to 1 ft. long, stem-clasping at base. Flowers in heads 5–6 in. across, ray florets yellow, drooping, disk florets brownish. Southern U.S. July–Aug.

newmani = *Rudbeckia speciosa.*

purpurea = *Echinacea purpurea.*

speciosa. Perennial to 3 ft. high. Leaves broadly lance-shaped, to 6 in. long, margins toothed. Flowers in heads 3–4 in. across, ray florets yellow, sometimes with an orange base, the disk florets brownish-purple. N.Y. to Ga. and Mo. Sometimes known as *R. newmani.*

subtomentosa. Sweet coneflower. Perennial to 6 ft. high, the whole plant covered with grayish hairs. Leaves ovalish, sometimes 3-lobed, to 5 in. long, margins toothed. Flowers in heads; ray florets* yellow, sometimes dark at base, disk florets dull brown. Midwestern states.

triloba. Brown-eyed Susan. Biennial to 5 ft. high. Leaves bright green, thin, lower ones 3-lobed, margins toothed. Flowers in heads 2–2½ in. across, ray florets deep yellow with orange or brown base, the disk florets brownish-black. Southeastern U.S.

rudis, -e (roo'dis). Wild, not cultivated; the word means, literally, of the rubbish pile.

RUE. Aromatic perennial herbs or undershrubs, comprising the genus **Ruta** (roo'ta) of the family Rutaceae, all the 40 known species from Eurasia or the Canary Islands. The common rue, R. graveolens, is usually the only one in cult. It is an evergreen under-shrub or woody herb, with twice-compound,* alternate,* leaves, the ultimate leaflets small. Flowers dull yellow, about ½ in. wide, in a terminal cluster (a loose cyme*). Petals 5, concave, fringed on the margin. Stamens* 8–10. Fruit a 4–5-lobed capsule.* Southern Eu. Cult. for centuries, and once called herb of grace because it was associated with repentance. For cult. *see* HERB GARDENING. The moist foliage is an irritant to some, especially in the heat of summer. (*Ruta* is the old Latin name of the rue.) For meadow rue *see* THALICTRUM.

RUE ANEMONE = *Anemonella thalictroides.*

RUE FAMILY. Tropical or warm-region trees, like the bael and all the citrus fruits, comprise most of the cult. plants in the rue family. But some trees or under-shrubs or even herbs of cooler regions are found in the family, such as the rue itself, the gas-plant, the prickly ash, and the genus PHELLODEN-DRON. For a complete list of the cult. genera *see* RUTACEAE.

RUELLIA (roo-ell'i-a). Tender and hardy perennial herbs or under-shrubs, comprising about 350 species, belonging to the family Acanthaceae, and found throughout the world. Leaves simple, opposite.* Flowers solitary, or in clusters, generally in blue or purple shades, sometimes white or red. Calyx* of 5 sepals,* joined at the base. Corolla of 5 lobes, funnel-shaped or salver-shaped. Stamens* 4, in pairs, 2 long, 2 short. Fruit a capsule,* which explodes when seeds are ripe. Seeds possess surface hairs which, when wet, swell and stick to the ground. (Named for Jean de la Ruelle, French botanist.)

They are not much in cultivation, but a few species are grown as warm-greenhouse plants in the northern states or in the open garden in the South. *Ruellia humilis,* though hardy and attractive, is rarely seen. Propagated by cuttings or seeds. Cuttings of young shoots should be made in late spring or early summer, in a temperature of 75°–85°.

amoena. Perennial from 1–2 ft. high. Leaves broadly lance-shaped, to 5 in. long, margins wavy. Flowers bright red, 1 in. long, in long-stalked, axillary clusters. S.A.

ciliosa = *H. humilis.*

devosiana. Sometimes known as *Pellionia.* Low-growing, tender perennial, to 18 in. high. Leaves roundish, to 2 in. long, with white veins on the upper side, and the under surface purple. Flowers small, solitary, white, veined lilac-blue, to 1¾ in. long. This species makes a good greenhouse plant for the hanging basket. Brazil.

humilis. Hardy herbaceous perennial, from 1–2½ ft. high. Leaves broadly lance-shaped. Flowers blue, fleeting, nearly 2 in. long, in loose clusters. Central U.S. Often known as *R. ciliosa.*

makoyana. A Brazilian relative of *R. devosiana,* grown mostly for its foliage, which is greenish-violet above and purple beneath.

rufa, -us, -um (roo'fa). Red.

Ruffia. Tropical African name for the palm yielding raffia. See RAPHIA.

rufida, -us, -um (roo'fi-da). Reddish.

rufinerve, -is (roo-fi-ner've). With rusty veins or with rusty hairs on the veins.

rugosa, -us, -um (roo-gō'sa). Rugose; *i.e.,* rough.

RUMEX (roo'mecks). Dock or sorrel. Perennial herbs comprising about 150 species of the family Polygonaceae, found throughout the world. They have strong roots with simple, basal, or stem leaves. Flowers in long, branching clusters, small, usually greenish-white. Flowers on same plant are sometimes of 2 kinds, some bearing stamens* only, others pistils* only. Calyx* of 6 sepals. Corolla absent. Stamens* 6. Fruit a 3-sided capsule, often winged. (*Rumex* is the Latin for sorrel.)

They are not much in cultivation, as most species are garden weeds. A few, however, are grown for their leaves, which are edible,

---

* Special articles on the subjects indicated by an asterisk (*) will be found at the words so marked.

and a few for decoration. Easily propagated from seeds, which may be sown outdoors in early spring.

abyssinicus. Spinach-rhubarb. Strong-growing perennial to 9 ft. high. Leaves arrowshaped to lance-shaped, to 7 in. long. Flowers of 2 kinds, stamens only or pistil only. Leaves sometimes used as spinach and leafstalks as rhubarb. Abyssinia.

Acetosa. Sorrel. Erect-growing perennial to 3 ft. high. Stems ridged. Basal leaves ovalish, arrow-shaped at base, thin, light green in color, to 5 in. long. Stem leaves narrowing to a sharp point. Flowers of 2 kinds, stamens only, or pistil only. Leaves used as "greens." Eu. and As., naturalized in N.A. The *var.* Large Belleville is the form generally cult.

Acetosella = Sheep's-sorrel. *See* list at WEEDS.

crispus = Curled dock. *See* list at WEEDS.

hymenosepalus. Canaigre. Perennial to 3 ft. high, with clustered tuberous roots, from which tannin is obtained. Leaves broadly lance-shaped, to 1 ft. long. Flowers in clusters 1 ft. or more long. Okla. to Calif.

Patientia. Herb patience. Spinach-dock. Strong-growing perennial to 6 ft. high. Basal leaves 8–10 in. long, tapering both ends, margins wavy. Stem leaves broadly lance-shaped. Flowers in branching clusters, 2 ft. long. Basal leaves excellent for "greens" if used in spring. Eu., naturalized in N.A.

RUNNEL. A tree that has been pollarded. *See* POLLARD.

RUNNER. A weak, usually prostrate shoot that roots at the joints, as in the strawberry. Runners afford a very easy method of propagation in those plants that produce them; all that is necessary for propagation is to detach the rooted joints. *See also* STOLON and PROCUMBENS.

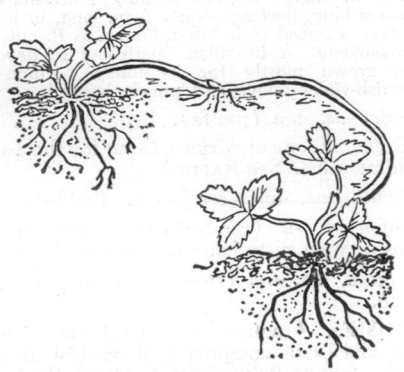

Runner of the strawberry

RUNNER PEANUT. *See* PEANUT.

RUNNING BIRCH = *Gaultheria hispidula.*

RUNNING MYRTLE = *Vinca minor.*

RUNNING PINE = *Lycopodium clavatum.*

RUNNING STRAWBERRY-BUSH = *Euonymus obovatus.*

rupestris, -e (roo-pes′tris). Rock-inhabiting.

rupicola, -us, -um (roo-pick′o-la). Growing on ledges or cliffs.

RUPTUREWORT. *See* HERNIARIA.

ruscifolia, -us, -um (rus-ki-fō′li-a). Having leaves like the butcher's-broom (*Ruscus*).

RUSCUS (rus′kus). A small genus of low shrubs belonging to the lily family, found from Madeira to the Caucasus, one of them, R. aculeatus, the butcher's-broom or Jew's-myrtle, widely cult. for its foliage which is often colored for winter decoration (*see* DRIED FLOWERS). It is a prickly, stiff, evergreen shrub, 2–3 ft. high, without obvious leaves but with leaf-like branches (cladophylls*) that are ovalish, ¾–1¼ in. long, thick, and leathery, and prickle-tipped. Male and female flowers on different plants, small, greenish, inconspicuous, borne in the middle of the leaf-like branches. Fruit a bright red (rarely yellow) berry about ⅜ in. in diameter. Very widely grown by florists for the Christmas trade, and dyed red. Useful for winter decoration, as the leaf-like branches do not fall as would true leaves. Also grown outdoors from zone* 7 southward. Eu. If grown outdoors (it is popular in Calif.), it is important to get both male and female plants or there will be no fruit. In the greenhouse it needs potting mixture* 4 and a cool house. (*Ruscus* is the old Latin name of this plant.)

RUSH. *See* JUNCUS. For flowering Rush *see* BUTOMUS.

RUSSELIA (rus-see′li-a). Tender, tropical American shrubs, comprising about 20 species of the family Scrophulariaceae. Stems much-branched and slender, often pendulous. Leaves opposite* or in whorls,* small, sometimes scale-like. Flowers showy, red, in branching clusters, the individual flower growing from scale-like bracts.* Calyx* of 5 sepals joined at the base. Corolla tubular, opening into 2 lips,* upper lip 2-lobed, lower lip 3-lobed. Stamens* 4, in pairs. Fruit a dry, many-seeded capsule.* (Named for Alexander Russell.)

Russelias make good warm-greenhouse plants, but may be grown outdoors in the South. Easily propagated by cuttings. Cuttings should be made in spring and inserted in clean sand in a temperature of 75°. When rooted they may be transplanted into small pots using potting mixture* 2. In final potting, use potting mixture* 3.

equisetiformis. Fountain-plant. Coral plant. Shrubby, much-branched plant, growing to 4 ft. high. Branches slender and smooth, square, drooping. Leaves small, bract*-like toward the top, broadly lance-shaped, the margins toothed. Flowers in clusters, 1–2 flowered. Mex., naturalized in Fla.

juncea = R. *equisetiformis.*

sarmentosa. Resembling R. *equisetiformis,* but with no scale-like leaves, and the flower clusters more profuse. Mex.

RUSSIAN ALMOND = *Prunus nana.*

RUSSIAN MULBERRY = *Morus alba tatarica.* See MULBERRY.

* Special articles on the subjects indicated by an asterisk (*) will be found at the words so marked.

RUSSIAN OLIVE = *Elaeagnus angustifolia.*

RUSSIAN SAGE. See Perovskia.

RUSSIAN THISTLE = *Salsola pestifer.* See the list at Weeds.

RUSSIAN TURNIP = Rutabaga.

RUSSIAN WORMWOOD = *Artemisia sacrorum.*

RUST. This term applies to plant diseases caused by different fungi, each specific to a small group of plants. A rust disease does not indicate that the leaf is brown and rust-colored, but rather that it has rusty brown or orange powdery pustules on the leaf. Many gardeners reier to leaf scorch* as "rust," but this is not the correct name.

Many rust diseases require alternate hosts (two unrelated plants) to continue the cycle of the disease. A typical example is cedar-apple rust in which spores* of the fungus infect the cedar or juniper in the late summer and pass the winter in those plants. In the spring, galls* form on the cedar and produce spores which blow to the apple, hawthorn, or quince tree where they cause infections resulting in rust spots on leaves and fruit. These spots in turn form spores which then infect the cedar. Other examples of rusts requiring alternate hosts are white pine and currant or gooseberry rust, wheat and barberry rust, ash and marsh-grass rust.

Some rust diseases do not require alternate or different hosts but continue to cause infection on other plants of the same type. Examples requiring only one host are hollyhock, carnation, snapdragon, asparagus, and bean.

Not all rust diseases can be controlled with chemicals but where fungicides* are of value the ferbam and zineb materials have proven most helpful (*see* Sprays and Dusts). — S. H. D.

rustica, -us, -um (russ'ti-ka). Wild or rural.

rusticana, -us, -um (rus-ti-kay'na). Relating to the country.

RUSTY GUM = *Angophora lanceolata.*

RUTA. See Rue.

RUTABAGA (*Brassica Napobrassica*). Rutabagas, also called Macomber and Winter turnips, are very similar to but hardier than the common turnips, although they do not resemble them in appearance, having smooth, shiny foliage of a bluish green and a tuber with a long, leafy neck.* They require longer to mature than turnips, and to secure heavy crops of large roots for stock-feeding the seed should be sown in the North from June 15 to July 1, in rows two to two and a half feet apart. They make one of the best winter feeds available for sheep. One ounce of seed will sow four hundred feet of drill; one to two pounds of seed are required per acre when sown in drills; and four to five pounds per acre if sown broadcast. The plants should be spaced about one foot apart. They will reach their full growth by

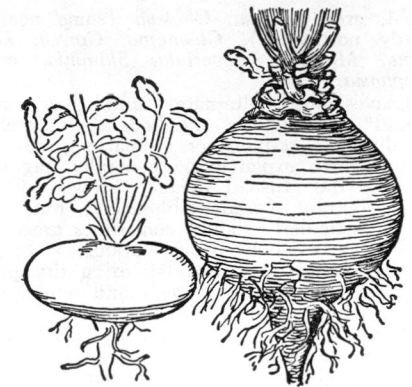

Common turnip (*left*) and the rutabaga (*right*). The latter is often called yellow turnip.

October and should be harvested after a frost but not allowed to freeze, as this would interfere with their keeping qualities.

They are splendid for table use and as they are a late-season crop are highly valued. They have firmer flesh than turnips and can be stored in the cellar in moist sand or in pits for use during the winter and well into the spring. For table use, seed should be sown about July 15 or even later in the season. Those late-planted rutabagas will be of better quality, although not so large. The soil should be rich and moist.

For fall home use, seeds may be sown two or three weeks earlier than for those for storing purposes. Good varieties for table use are Improved Purple-top, Improved Long Island, American Purple-top, and Laurentian.

A large-rooted, yellow-fleshed var., mostly an agricultural crop, grown for cattle feed, is known as Swede, Swedish turnip, Russian turnip, or mangel-wurzel.

RUTACEAE (roo-tay'see-ee). The rue or citrus family comprises a few unimportant genera of little cultural value, and a group of perhaps the most important fruit trees in the country (orange, grapefruit, lime, lemon, etc.) — the citrus fruits. The family is a large one (140 genera and about 1500 species), mostly tropical, but the following shrubs and trees, mostly Eurasian or North American, are cult. outdoors in most of the U.S.: *Evodia, Phellodendron, Poncirus* (a hardy, inedible orange), *Ptelea,* and *Zanthoxylum; Ruta* and *Dictamnus,* largely herbaceous, are plants for the open border.

The rest of the cult. genera are all tropical or sub-tropical and are grown outdoors only in essentially frost-free parts of the country, or in greenhouses. Of these, *Citrus* and its related or pertinent genera (*Citropsis, Fortunella,* and *Microcitrus*) are by far the most important, because of their fruit, but edible fruit are also found in *Casimiroa.* Other cult. genera, grown mostly for orna-

---

* Special articles on the subjects indicated by an asterisk (*) will be found at the words so marked.

ment, are: *Boronia, Choisya* (some nearly hardy northward), *Cleonema, Correa, Diosma, Murraya, Severinia, Skimmia,* and *Triphasia.*

Leaves mostly alternate,* simple* or compound* (in *Citrus, Phellodendron,* etc.), usually with resinous or aromatic glands in them, which explains the generally fragrant odor of the crushed foliage. Flowers often very fragrant (orange blossom), but not often particularly showy, sometimes greenish and inconspicuous. Fruit various, a berry in the orange and its relatives, a dry pod (capsule*) in several genera and sometimes with a winged fruit (*Ptelea*).

Technical flower characters: Flowers mostly regular*; dioecious* in *Phellodendron* and *Zanthoxylum.* Sepals* 4–5, often partly united. Petals 4–5, sometimes none. Stamens* 8–10. Ovary superior.

Ruta-muraria (roo-ta-mu-rare'i-a). A wall rue.

ruthenica, -us, -um (roo-thenn'i-ka). From Russia.

RUTLAND BEAUTY. *See* Hedge Bindweed (No. 17) in the list at Weeds.

RYE. An important agricultural grass, one of 3 Eurasian species of the genus **Secale** (see-kay'le), but of interest to the gardener only in the form known as winter rye which is a useful plant for green manuring (which see). It is a form of the common rye, **S. cereale,** an important grain in the making of rye bread and whiskey. Rye is an annual grass 3–5 ft. high, its erect, slender stems bluish-green. Leaves grass-like, rather soft, 12–18 in. long, about ½ in. wide. Flower cluster a close-set, terminal spike, long and much-awned,* the spikelets on a tiny zigzag stalk. Fruit the familiar grain of rye, oblongish, about ⅓ in. long and minutely grooved. The common rye is unknown as a wild plant, but is probably a cultigen* derived from one of the European species. (*Secale* is an old Roman name for some cereal, but not certainly of this one.) For wild rye *see* Elymus.

RYE GRASS. *See* Lolium.

S

SABAL (say'bal). Palmetto. New World fan palms, comprising about 20 species, a few native in the southeastern U.S. and much planted there for ornament. They

The palmetto (*Sabal Palmetto*) is one of the commonest wild and cult. palms in the southeastern states.

have moderately tall trunks in S. *blackburniana* and S. *Palmetto,* but none in S. *minor* and in several other (non-hort.) species where the trunk is buried or altogether

lacking. Leaves fan-like, but only in S. *minor* with the stalk ending at the blade. In the other two the leafstalk appears as though continued through the blade. Flower cluster from among the leaves, branched, usually drooping, the flowers small, greenish-white. Sepals and petals 3 each. Stamens* 6. Fruit a roundish or pear-shaped, dark-colored drupe.* (*Sabal* may be derived from a native name for a South American species.)

Sabal is one of the hardiest genera of palms, the common S. *Palmetto* being native from N. Car. to Fla., mostly along the coast. They are of the easiest cult. and thrive on the sandy soils of the coastal plain. S. *Palmetto* is not certainly hardy north of the coastal region of N. Car., and the other two are not safe north of the limits of zone* 8 or 7. All the cult. species were once included in the genus *Inodes.*

blackburniana. Bermuda palmetto. A stout palm, the trunk sometimes 35 ft. high, usually shedding the old leaf bases. Leaves 5–9 ft. wide, green both sides but checkered beneath, cut nearly halfway by its many segments which are 1–2 in. wide, usually with a single, stout fiber at each cleft. Flower cluster large, and much-branched. Fruit nearly round, about ½ in. in diameter, black. Bermuda. Not hardy north of zone* 8.

glabra = *Sabal minor.*

minor. Dwarf palmetto; also called bluestem. An apparently stemless palm, the leafstalks arising from the ground. Leaves bluish-green or pale green, stiffish, the central segments divided about half the depth of the blade, the others more deeply cleft. Flower cluster

---

* Special articles on the subjects indicated by an asterisk (*) will be found at the words so marked.

about as long as the leaves, much-branched. Fruit round, about ⅓ in. in diameter. N. Car. to Fla. and Tex., and preferring moist sites. Not particularly showy. Hardy up to zone* 7.

Palmetto. The common palmetto of the southeastern states, often called cabbage palmetto. In maturity its trunk may be 70–90 ft. high, and is usually clothed with the persistent leaf bases, but ultimately bare of them below. Leaves not very numerous in the terminal crown, green, 5–8 ft. or more wide, conspicuously fibrous. Central segments cleft more than halfway to the center, the other segments more deeply cleft, all the tips curving or drooping. Flower cluster much-branched, usually longer than the leaves, hence hanging below the withered but persistent leaves. Fruit round, black, nearly ½ in. in diameter. N. Car. to Fla., mostly near the coast.

SABATIA (sab-bay′she-a). American centaury; also called sea pink and rose pink. A genus of 20 species of annual or biennial, mostly weak herbs of the gentian family, found in eastern N.A. and of little hort. interest except for **S. dodecandra.** It is a pretty little salt-marsh herb, 7–15 in. high, the leaves narrowly lance-shaped or even line-like. Flowers pink (rarely white), the corolla with a very short tube, its limb expanded into 9–12 rather showy, rounded lobes. Stamens* 4–12, the anthers* coiled. Fruit a small, egg-shaped or roundish capsule.* Useful only in seaside gardens in moist, salty sand or in salt marshes. Conn. to Fla., along the coast. July–Sept. (Named for L. Sabbati, an Italian botanist.)

Sabdariffa (sab-da-riff′a). Turkish vernacular name for the roselle (*Hibiscus Sabdariffa*).

Sabina (sa-by′na). An old generic name (derived from the Sabines) for certain plants now included in *Juniperus.*

sabiniana, -us, -um (say-bin-i-an′a). Like the savin (*Juniperus Sabina*).

SABRE BEAN = *Canavalia gladiata.*

SACASIL = *Wilcoxia poselgeri.*

saccharata, -us, -um (sack-a-ray′ta). Sugary or sweet.

saccharifera, -us, -um (sack-a-riff′er-a). Bearing sugar.

saccharina, -us, -um (sack-a-ry′na). Sweetish.

saccharoides (sack-a-roy′deez, but *see* OÏDES). Like sugar or the sugar cane (*Saccharum*).

SACCHARUM (sack-kar′rum). Woodystemmed, tall grasses, chiefly East Indian, of no garden interest, but **S. officinarum,** the sugar cane, of world-wide economic importance. It is a solid-stemmed plant 10–15 ft. high, the stem green or purplish, conspicuously ringed, its juice the source of sugar. Leaves very like common corn but longer, and with rough or cutting edges. Flower cluster terminal, usually a branching panicle 15–30 in. long, the branches plume-like but drooping, rarely produced except in the tropics and often infertile there. Probably

a cultigen,* as sugar was cult. centuries before it was known in Eu. or America (early 16th century). Most of the profitable varieties need more heat than is found in the U.S., but some sorts are grown in La. and Fla. (*Saccharum* is an old Greek word for sugar, and is used also as a specific name for the sugar maple.)

SACRED BAMBOO = *Nandina domestica.*

sacrorum (sack-ror′rum). Sacred.

SAD TREE = *Nyctanthes Arbor-tristis.*

SAFFLOWER = *Carthamus tinctorius.*

SAFFRON CROCUS = *Crocus sativus,* often called simply saffron, which it yields. For the false saffron *see* CARTHAMUS TINCTORIUS.

SAGE. For the common sage *see* SALVIA. For other plants to which the name sage is sometimes applied *see* PULMONARIA SACCHARATA, PHLOMIS FRUTICOSA and AUDIBERTIA.

SAGEBRUSH. See ARTEMISIA TRIDENTATA.

SAGINA (sa-jy′na). Pearlwort. Slender annual or perennial herbs, often tufted* or matted, belonging to the pink family, all the dozen known species from the north temperate zone. The only one of much garden interest is **S. subulata,** a Corsican perennial evergreen herb, grown in the rock garden or border for its prostrate, moss-like foliage and profusion of tiny white flowers. It is a tufted plant with very small but numerous leaves. Flowers very small, the petals 5. Stamens* 5. Fruit a tiny, 5-valved capsule. Of easy culture and readily propagated by division. (*Sagina* is an old Greek name for spurry, a weedy, non-hort. plant also found in this genus.)

sagittalis, -e (sa-ji-tay′lis). Arrowhead-shaped or arrow-like.

SAGITTARIA (sa-jit-tair′i-a). Arrowhead. Hardy and tender perennial aquatic or marsh herbs, comprising about 30 species of the family Alismaceae, found in temperate and tropical regions throughout the world, except Af. and Aust. They are of erect habit, or a few with submerged leaves. Rootstocks thick and tuber-like. Underwater leaves ribbon-like, the floating leaves ovalish, those growing above the surface of the water, arrow-shaped. Flowers in whorls,* on leafless stalks, of 2 kinds, usually on the same plant. Male flowers above the female ones, or in some cases perfect* flowers are produced, having both stamens* and pistils* in the same flower. Sepals* 3, small, greenish-white. Petals 3, white or spotted. Stamens* and pistils* numerous. (*Sagittaria* is from the Latin for arrow, in allusion to the arrow-shaped leaves.)

Sagittarias are useful for shallow water, bogs, or aquariums. Easily cult. but subject to aphis. Propagated by seeds sown ¼ in. deep in rich soil in boxes placed in shallow water, or by division of the tuber-like roots in March or April.

engelmanniana. Grows to 18 in. high.

* Special articles on the subjects indicated by an asterisk (*) will be found at the words so marked.

Leaves arrow-shaped, 6–8 in. long. Flowers white, to 1 in. across. Mass. to S. Car.

graminea. An erect aquatic with narrowly elliptic leaves above the water, or submerged and with the leaves narrower. Flowers white, in clusters of 2–12, always above water, and not showy. Good for the aquarium. Eastern N.A., in swamps or shallow water.

latifolia. Common arrowhead. Wapatoo. Grows to 4 ft. high. Leaves arrow-shaped, variable in width. Flowers pure white, to 1½ in. across. N.A. Its edible roots were the tule potatoes of the Indians in Oregon.

montevidensis. Giant arrowhead. Tender. Growing to 6 ft. high. Leaves arrow-shaped, lobes at the base of leaf as long as the blade. Flowers 2 in. or more across, with brownish spot at the base of the petals. S.A., naturalized in southern U.S.

natans. The plant offered as this is variously credited to Eurasia and to S. Car. It is a floating aquatic with narrow leaves and tiny white flowers, also floating. Of quite uncertain status.

sagittifolia. Grows to 4 ft. high. Leaves arrow-shaped, variable in width. Flowers white, about 1 in. across, spotted purple at the base of the petals. This species produces underground tubers which are edible. Eurasia. The *var.* **flore-pleno** with double flowers is the form usually cult.

sagittata, -us, -um (sa-ji-tay′ta). Sagitate; *i.e.,* arrowhead-shaped.

sagittifolia, -us, -um (sa-ji-ti-fō′li-a). With arrowhead-shaped leaves.

SAGO PALM. See CYCAS REVOLUTA.

SAGO PALM FAMILY = Cycadaceae.

SAGUARO; SAHUARO = *Carnegiea gigantea.*

SAILOR CAPS = *Dodecatheon hendersoni.*

SAINFOIN = *Onobrychis viciaefolia.*

SAINT. Many plants were named for the saints during the Middle Ages, long before Latin names were invented for them. Those in this book and their proper equivalents are: **St. Andrew's-cross** = *Ascyrum hypericoides;* **St. Augustine grass** = *Stenotaphrum secundatum;* **St. Barbara** (*see* BARBAREA); **St. Bernard's-lily** = *Anthericum Liliago;* **St. Brigid** (*see* ANEMONE CORONARIA): **St. Bruno's-lily** = *Paradisea Liliastrum;* **St. Dabeoc's-heath** = *Daboecia cantabrica;* **Saintfoin** = *Onobrychis viciaefolia;* **St. James's-flower** = *Lotus Jacobaeus;* **St. James's-lily** = *Sprekelia formosissima;* **St. James's-pea** = *Lotus Jacobaeus;* **St. John's-bread** = *Ceratonia siliqua* (*see* CAROB); **St. John's-wort** (*see* first main entry below); **St. John's-wort family** = Hypericaceae; **St. Joseph's-wand** = *Pentstemon acuminatus;* **St. Lucie cherry** = *Prunus Mahaleb;* **St. Patrick's cabbage** = *Saxifraga umbrosa* **Saintpaulia** (*see* second main entry below); **St. Peter's pence** = Honesty; **St. Thomas tree** = *Bauhinia tomentosa.*

SAINT JOHN'S-WORT. The St. John's-worts comprise a useful group of herbs or under-shrubs constituting the genus **Hypericum** (hy-per′i-kum) of the family Hypericaceae. While most of the 300 known species, nearly all from the north temperate zone, are somewhat weedy, those below are popular for the border or rock garden. Some are occasionally known as tutsan. Leaves generally opposite,* mostly resinous-dotted, without marginal teeth or lobes. Flower yellow (in ours), in clusters (cymes*), or solitary. Petals 5, somewhat oblique. Stamens* many, usually conspicuous. Fruit a capsule* (in ours). (*Hypericum* is an old Greek plant name of uncertain application here, perhaps meaning under, or among, the heather.)

The St. John's-worts are of simple culture, except for the rock garden species which are discussed at ROCK GARDEN. Some, as indicated below, do better in partial shade. They may be propagated by division or by seeds.

H. aureum = *H. frondosum.*

H. bucklei. An under-shrub, not over 12 in. high, the stems 4-angled, decumbent or ascending. Leaves elliptic or broader toward the tip, ½–¾ in. long. Flowers few, nearly 2 in. wide. N. Car. to Ga. June–July. Hardy from zone* 4 southward. Suitable as ground cover or for the rock garden.

H. calycinum. Rose-of-Sharon. Aaron's-beard. An evergreen under-shrub, not over 12 in. high. Leaves oblongish, 3–4 in. long, pale beneath. Flowers few or solitary, about 2 in. wide. Southeastern Eu. and Asia Minor. July–Sept. Hardy from zone* 4 southward. A good ground cover in shady places and for sandy soils. *See* SAND GARDEN.

H. Coris. An evergreen under-shrub, not over 12 in. high. Leaves very narrow, about 1 in. long, in whorls* of 4–6. Flowers about ¾ in. wide, in clusters (cymes*). Southern Eu. July–Aug. Hardy from zone* 5 southward.

H. densiflorum. An evergreen shrub, 4–6 ft. high, the branches 2-angled. Leaves narrowly oblong, 1–2 in. long. Flowers in dense clusters (cymes*), not over ½ in. wide. L.I. to Fla., west to Mo. and Tex. July–Sept. Hardy from zone* 4 southward.

H. fragile. A low shrub, scarcely 9 in. high and suited mostly to the rock garden. Leaves slightly bluish-green, ovalish, scarcely ¼ in. long. Flowers nearly 1 in. wide, pale gold, in terminal clusters (cymes*). Greece. Summer.

H. frondosum. Shrub, not over 3 ft. high, the bark reddish and peeling. Leaves oblongish, bluish-green, 2–3 in. long. Flowers nearly 2 in. wide, solitary or few. Southeastern U.S. July–Aug. Hardy from zone* 4 southward. Also called *H. aureum.*

H. kalmianum. An evergreen under-shrub, 2–3 ft. high, the stems 4-angled. Leaves narrowly oblong, 1½–2½ in. long. Flowers few, about 1 in. long. Quebec to Ill. Aug. Hardy from zone* 3 southward.

H. moserianum. Gold-flower. A hybrid under-shrub, not over 2 ft. high, the stems reddish; one of the best cult. species. Leaves ovalish, 1–2 in. long. Flowers nearly 2½ in. wide, solitary or in few-flowered cymes.* The *var.* **tricolor** has white-variegated leaves edged with red. Both are hardy from zone* 5 southward and bloom in midsummer.

H. olympicum. An under-shrub, not over 12 in. high. Leaves oblongish or narrower, 1–1½ in. long. Flowers nearly 2½ in. wide, in terminal clusters (cymes*). Southeastern Eu. and Asia Minor. Hardy from zone* 6 southward.

---

* Special articles on the subjects indicated by an asterisk (*) will be found at the words so marked.

H. patulum. An evergreen shrub, 2–3 ft. high. Leaves ovalish or oblong, 1½–2½ in. long. Flowers about 2 in. wide, solitary or in sparse clusters (cymes*). Jap. July–Sept. Eastern As. Hardy from zone* 5 southward. The *var.* **henryi,** from China, is a more vigorous, larger-flowered plant, hardy up to zone* 4 and possibly zone* 3.

H. polyphyllum. A perennial herb with ascending stems, not over 12 in. high. Leaves elliptic or narrower, not over ⅓ in. long. Flowers nearly 2 in. wide, in terminal clusters (cymes*). Armenia. For culture *see* ROCK GARDEN.

H. prolificum. Bush broom. An evergreen shrub, 4–5 ft. high, the branches 2-edged, the bark peeling. Leaves oblongish or narrower, 2–3 in. long. Flowers about ¾ in. wide, in terminal clusters (cymes*). N.Y. to Iowa and southward. July–Sept. Hardy from zone* 4, possibly from zone* 3 southward.

H. repens. A prostrate, perennial herb. Leaves oblongish or much narrower, scarcely ½ in. long. Flowers about 1 in. wide, in terminal clusters (cymes*). Southeastern Eu. and Asia Minor. Not certainly hardy north of zone* 5.

H. reptans. A prostrate shrub, rooting at the joints. Leaves oblongish or elliptic, about ½ in. long. Flowers solitary, about 1 in. wide. Himalayas. For culture *see* ROCK GARDEN. Not certainly hardy north of zone* 5.

H. rhodopeum. A low perennial or subshrub not over 6 in. high, and a vigorous grower. Leaves oblong, spotted, about ½ in. long and stalkless. Flowers bright yellow, nearly 1½ in. wide, in few-flowered clusters (cymes*), the petals black-dotted near the margin. Asia Minor. Spring. Not hardy north of zone* 6.

SAINTPAULIA (saint-paul'i-a). Very beautiful, tropical African, essentially stemless herbs of the family Gesneriaceae, 4 of the possibly 11 known species often grown for their handsome flowers. They are hairy plants with long-stalked basal leaves which form an open rosette. Flowers very showy, generally violet, in long-stalked, few-flowered clusters (cymes*). Corolla with a short tube, its lobes beautifully 2-lipped.* Fertile stamens* 2; also there are 2 infertile ones. Fruit a 2-valved, oblong or globose capsule,* (Named for Baron Walter von Saint Paul, who discovered the fourth species.)

The great popularity of African violets in the last 15 years has made necessary a more extensive account of these plants than has appeared in earlier editions. To most lovers of house plants the cultivated forms are of far more interest than the species from which they have been derived. For the cult. and vars. of the African violet see the section following the enumeration of the species immediately below.

The four readily available species admitted here are less than half of the eleven recognized by H. E. Moore, Jr., in his recent treatment of the genus (*African Violets, Gloxinias and Their Relatives,* Macmillan, 1957). Part of such restriction is due to the unavailability of these rare species, and some of it to taxonomic refinements beyond the competence and perhaps the patience of most gardeners. There are, for instance, only three species recognized in the recently issued *Dictionary of Gardening* (2nd edition, 1956) by the Royal Horticultural Society, London.

confusa. A rather confused species to which the incorrect name of *S. diplotricha* has been applied. It does not differ materially from *S. ionantha,* the distinguishing characters being given as "leaves thin, with appressed hairs (thicker, with erect or spreading hairs in *S. ionantha*), and with a cylindrical instead of a nearly globose capsule." Usambara Mountains, Tanganyika.

diplotricha. Plants long grown under this name are now referable to *S. confusa.* The true *S. diplotricha* is known only in the collections of botanic gardens and a few fanciers. It differs from *S. ionantha* by having "hairs on the leaves of different lengths" (same length and conspicuous in *S. ionantha*). There is scarcely any other significant difference between these two species. Usambara Mountains, Tanganyika.

grotei. A trailing African violet, useful for hanging baskets. Leaves long-stalked, the stalks 5–10 inches long, the blades roundish, coarsely toothed, heart-shaped at the base, 1–3½ in. long, covered with long and short hairs. Flowers 2–4, shorter-stalked than the leaves, bluish-violet. Capsule cylindrical, about one inch long. Usambara Mountains, Tanganyika.

ionantha. The original of the African or Usambara violets, and an essentially stemless plant, with a basal rosette of nearly round leaves on hairy stalks 1½–2½ in. long. Leaf blade shallowly toothed, 1½–3 in. long, green above, darker or even purplish beneath, covered with hairs of equal length. Flowers 2–8, violet in the wild form (but *see* below), about 1 in. wide. Capsule nearly globose. Tanga, near Zanzibar. Tanganyika. Most of the hort. forms are derived from this species (*see* below).

kewensis = *S. ionantha.*

tongwensis. Not very different from *S. ionantha,* and said to differ chiefly in having the leaves pale beneath, somewhat elliptic, and by having purple flowers. It also differs in

African Violet (*Saintpaulia ionantha*), an African perennial, very popular as a house plant and found in innumerable varieties. For a list *see* text.

---

* Special articles on the subjects indicated by an asterisk (*) will be found at the words so marked.

producing a definite stem up to 6 in. in length. Mt. Tongwe, Tanganyika.

CULTURE

African violets (they are, of course, not violets) make one of the most satisfactory of all house plants. Blooming nearly all the year (according to var.), needing little space, and the average temperature and humidity of a living room suiting them reasonably well, it is no wonder that there are hundreds of vars. (some think thousands!) and that in the last twenty years the African Violet Society has accumulated a huge membership.

The plants have a few cult. necessities which must be observed, based largely upon the kind of ancestral home they inhabit — *i.e.*, tropical elevations in Africa. Without unduly discouraging the enthusiast with a lot of technical details, a few rules based on them make for success, and failure to observe them usually means unsatisfactory plants.

1. TEMPERATURE. Not over 85° nor less than 60° at night.
2. HUMIDITY. No living room is humid enough. Therefore place the pots on wet sand or gravel, but do not allow the pots to stand in water; raise them an inch above the wet substratum.
3. LIGHT. No direct sunlight through the window (except in Dec., Jan., and Feb.). A north window is fine, or a south window shaded by plastic or glass fiber curtains.
4. SOIL. Perfect drainage is essential. Soil should be ⅓ good loam, ⅓ chopped peat or sphagnum moss, ⅓ clean sand. Sterilize the soil to prevent infestation.
5. FERTILIZER. Water with weak liquid manure every other week. If this is not available use water-soluble fertilizers, being careful to follow the directions on the container.
6. WATER. Never let the plants dry out, but do not overwater (*i.e.*, fill up all the air spaces in the soil). Use water at room temperature, and rain water is generally better than tap water if the latter is too alkaline. A little less than a cupful a day, depending on temperature and humidity, is usually sufficient.
7. POTS. Small flower pots (3½–4 in. in diameter) are better than larger ones. If the plant gets too many crowns, divide them and re-pot.
8. PROPAGATION. Division is easiest. But leaf cuttings are also easily made. Choose a thrifty leaf, cut it from the stem, leaving part (or none) of the leafstalk. Put the leaf blade (or leafstalk if you saved it) in moist sand or vermiculite (or in a tumbler of water) and put the cuttings in a warm place. When roots develop put in a 2-in. pot with the above soil mixture.
9. FAILURE TO BLOOM. Not uncommon and usually due to easily corrected errors, such as improper temperature, too little or too much water, overcrowding of the plant in the pot.
10. VARIETIES. Next to impossible to recommend many that will be valid in a few years. There are currently hundreds, their differences often imaginary and their availability sometimes confined to a few specialists. The following list of 25 has been culled from the latest and "best" 100 chosen by vote of the African Violet Society. But it is also restricted to those that are not only in that list but in several earlier ones, which means that they have stood the test of history — a rather brief one as cult. varieties go. Listed alphabetically they are (double-flowered vars. marked D):

†Bicolor (bicolor)
Black Magic (blue) D
†Blue Boy (blue)
Blue Warrior (blue)
California Dark Plum (red)
Double Margaret (purple) D
Double Neptune (blue) D
Double Orchid Sunset (orchid) D
Du Pont Lavender Pink (orchid)
Edith Cavell (orchid) Fringed
Gorgeous (orchid)
Innocence (white)
†Mentor Boy (blue)
†Neptune (purple)
Pink Cheer (pink)
Purity (white) D
Purple Knight (purple)
Sailor's Delight (blue) D
Sea Girl (blue) D
Sir Lancelot (bicolor)
Snow Girl (white)
Snow Prince (white)
Sunrise (orchid)
Violet Beauty (bicolor)
White Madonna (white) D

Such is the ephemeral nature of African violet varieties that of the above rather meager list of 25, only four were in existence as long ago as 1947. These are marked with a dagger (†). In addition there are a few varieties of so-called miniatures that are about half normal size.

The African Violet Society issues a quarterly journal, *African Violet Magazine*. The present address of the society is P.O. Box 1326, Knoxville, Tenn.

INSECT PESTS. Control of almost invisible cyclamen mites which deform plants is necessary. (*See* CYCLAMEN.)

DISEASES. Gray mold* may cause a rot of leaves and crown of plant, particularly if crowns are wet and dead leaves or flower parts are allowed to remain on the plant. Pesticide #5 (*see* SPRAYS AND DUSTS) should be applied at 10-day intervals if the disease becomes serious. Proper cultural conditions, however, will do more for the plants in preventing gray mold.

A powdery mildew* will occcasionally cause curling of leaves with typical white, powdery blotching. Remove infected leaves and use pesticide #6 or #9 at weekly intervals.

* Special articles on the subjects indicated by an asterisk (*) will be found at the words so marked.

SALAD BURNET = *Sanguisorba minor.*

SALAD CHERVIL. *See* ANTHRISCUS.

SALAD PLANTS. In its original sense a salad plant was one in which the leaves were eaten raw. Of these probably the most universally popular is lettuce. In varying combinations with cucumbers, tomatoes, onions, and sweet peppers it forms the year-round salad dish. Unfortunately for the home gardener, it does not stand heat well. But other salad plants may be substituted, or combined with each other.

Corn or field salad is one of the earliest of all the raw salad materials. Fall-sown plants are hardy and in much demand for winter use. Both leaves and stems are chopped together, with the outer stalks of celery added, for a green salad. Endive is popular for autumn and winter use. It should not be cut before frost, as frost improves the flavor. The heart portion makes the best salad. French endive or Witloof chicory is a European delicacy now in common use in this country. *See* CELLAR GARDENING. The large, tender, white sprouts thrown out by the roots are the parts used. Chinese cabbage, also called celery cabbage, makes a good salad. The large midribs of the leaves are white, crisp, and very tender, with a delicate flavor.

Finnochio or Florence fennel is in general appearance and use much like celery, although the top is different. The enlarged leafstalk blanches easily, is crisp and tender, and the heart is used for salads. Celeriac or knob celery may be used either raw or cooked. If cooked it is usually sliced and served with French dressing. The blanched main stalks only of cardoon are used for salad, answering the same purpose as celery. Jerusalem artichokes are sliced and served raw, with dressing, or baked potatoes.

Leek, blanched and pulled young, is sliced and used alone as a salad or as garnishing. Double curled chervil, like parsley, is chopped fine and used with other raw salad materials. The chopped leaves of chives are a good seasoning for green salads. The seeds are used to season cooked salads. Cress and watercress are excellent as garnishings or eaten alone with a dressing. Dandelions are eaten raw or cooked, while mustard may be used like lettuce or with other salads. For the culture of these plants *see* the special articles devoted to them. *See also* HERB GARDENING.

SALAL = *Gaultheria Shallon.*

SALICACEAE (say-li-kay'see-ee). The willow family comprises only Salix (*see* WILLOW) and the poplars (*see* POPULUS), which together total about 330 species. Except for the weeping willow and Lombardy poplar, they are mostly trees and shrubs of secondary garden importance, most of them being rather short-lived. But the willows are often useful bushes along water courses or pond edges, and the osiers are used for basketmaking.

Leaves always alternate* and undivided.

Flowers in catkins* (the pussy willow is an example), appearing with or before the leaves unfold, the male and female catkins on different trees. Fruit a small, splitting pod (capsule*), the seeds surrounded by silky tufts.

Technical flower characters: Flowers minute, each flower (in the catkin) in the axil* of a minute bract.* Sepals and petals none. Stamens* 2–many. Ovary 1-celled.

Salicaria, -us, -um (sal-i-care'i-a). Resembling a willow.

salicariaefolia, -us, -um (sal-i-care-i-eye-fō'li-a). With leaves like *Salicaria,* an old name for plants now included in *Lythrum,* which have willow-like leaves.

SALICETUM. A growing collection of willows.

salicifolia, -us, -um (sal-i-si-fō'li-a). With willow-like leaves.

salicornioides (sal-i-kor-ni-oy'deez, but *see* OÏDES). Resembling a plant of the genus *Salicornia,* which are salt-marsh herbs of no garden interest.

saligna, -us, -um (sa-lig'na). Willow-like.

SALIX. *See* WILLOW.

SALLOW = *Salix Caprea. See* WILLOW.

SALOMONIA = *Polygonatum. See* SOLOMON'S-SEAL.

SALPIGLOSSIS (sal-pi-gloss'is). Chilean half-hardy annual or perennial herbs, comprising about 8 species, of the family Solanaceae, mostly covered with short, sticky hairs. Leaves alternate,* broadly lance-shaped, the margins wavy or slightly cut. Flowers in loose terminal clusters growing from the axils* of small, leafy bracts.* Individual flowers large, showy, varying in color through purple, blue, brown, yellow, and cream, all having a velvety appearance and generally veined with gold. Calyx* of 5 sepals, joined ¾ of their length. Corolla funnel-shaped, widely open at the throat, the 5 lobes notched. Stamens* 5, 2 long, 2 short, and 1 sterile. Fruit a 2-celled capsule. (*Salpiglossis* is from the Greek for tube and tongue, in allusion to the form of the corolla.)

These plants are beautiful for the garden, and make useful cut flowers. They can also be grown in the greenhouse for April flowering. Easily cult. as tender annuals. *See* ANNUALS. Salpiglossis must be sown early in Feb. in cool greenhouse or in Mar. in cold frame so as to enable them to make good growth before planting out after warm weather arrives. For greenhouse culture they should be sown Aug.–Sept.

grandiflora = *Salpiglossis sinuata.*
sinuata. Painted-tongue. Half-hardy annual, growing to 3 ft. high, and of branching habit. Leaves broadly lance-shaped, margins bluntly toothed. Flowers large, funnel-shaped, with wide, open throat, in various colors. Chile.

SALSIFY (*Tragopogon porrifolius*). As now utilized in the U.S., salsify is one of the secondary root crops, less known than it should

---

* Special articles on the subjects indicated by an asterisk (*) will be found at the words so marked.

be. It has a delicious flavor and, in the main, can be grown somewhat like parsnips. In the markets it is often called oyster plant or vegetable oyster. For a related plant known as black salsify, with a similar, but black-

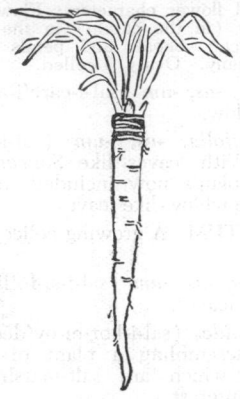

Salsify

skinned root, *see* Scorzonera. For another closely related plant, usually called Spanish oyster-plant, *see* Scolymus.

Salsify is an all-season crop and needs even a longer growing season than the parsnip to produce good roots, which are long, tapering, and white-skinned. Consequently, it cannot be grown where there is a short growing season, and north of zone* 3 it may not mature before frost. It is comparatively hardy and seed can be sown as soon as the ground is workable in the spring. Sow the seeds in drills about ½ in. deep and keep the rows about 12 in. apart (twice this if motor or horse cultivation is to be used).

The soil must be deeply dug or plowed, at least a foot of pulverized or friable* loam being necessary for proper root development. It does best on somewhat sandy loams, and if the soil is heavy (*i.e.*, too much clay or silt) it should be lightened by the addition of sand, or better yet by liberal applications of well-rotted stable manure. The plant is a rich feeder and responds well to manure, or if this is lacking, to a good all-round fertilizer with a 5–8–5 ratio (*see* Fertilizers). Coarse, fresh, and rough manure should not be used as it is apt to make the roots rough and prongy.

Most families will find a 50-ft. row of salsify enough. The plants should stand, after thinning, about 4 in. apart in the rows, and they should be regularly cultivated (*see* Cultivation), but, as in other root crops, care must be used not to injure the roots. Plants may be harvested as needed in the fall, and the roots may be left in the ground all winter if the row is mulched (*see* Mulch), and dug as wanted. Or, if the winters are too severe for this, the roots may be dug in the fall and stored (*see* Storage). The best variety is Sandwich Island.

SALSOLA PESTIFER = Russian thistle. *See* the list at Weeds.

salsoloides (sal-so-loy'deez, but *see* Oïdes). Resembling a plant of the weedy genus *Salsola* for which *see* Russian Thistle in the list at Weeds.

SALT. In any concentration such as sea water, salt is not tolerated by most garden plants, and only by a few salt-tolerant wild plants found along sea beaches, salt meadows, etc. Salt has no place in the garden except that some use it lightly to top-dress asparagus.

SALTBUSH. *See* Atriplex.

SALT CEDAR = *Tamarix gallica.*

SALT HAY. For those living near coastal marshes salt hay is valuable material for winter mulching. It does not pack down so much as ordinary hay or straw.

SALT PLANTS. *See* Seaside Gardens.

SALT TREE = *Tamarix aphylla* and *Halimodendron Halodendron.*

saluensis, -e (sal-u-en'sis). From or near the Salween River in Yunnan. *See* Camellia saluensis.

SALVER-SHAPED. As applied to flowers, salver-shaped means having a slender tube and an abruptly expanded limb,* as in phlox.

SALVIA (sal'vi-a). Sage. Annual, biennial, or perennial herbs, under-shrubs, or shrubs, comprising about 700 species, belonging to the mint family, and distributed throughout the tropical and temperate world. Stems usually square. Leaves in pairs, opposite,* simple, ovalish or lance-shaped, sometimes hairy, the margins toothed or deeply cut into segments, smaller toward the top. Flowers in whorls,* the clusters 2- to many-flowered, growing from the axils* of small, leafy bracts and arranged in terminal spikes or racemes.* Colors varying from scarlet, purple, blue to white and pale yellow. Calyx 5-lobed, joined about halfway down. Corolla 2-lipped,* 3 lobes in the lower lip and 2 in the upper lip. Stamens* 4, in pairs, 2 long, 2 short. Fruit 2-celled when young, splitting into 4 parts when ripe. (*Salvia* is from the Latin to be healthy, in reference to the medicinal properties of some species.)

Salvias are grown for their flowers and for their leaves, the leaves of some species being used for seasoning. Easily propagated from seeds, division of rootstocks, or by cuttings. Seeds should be sown in the early spring in the cool greenhouse or cold frame and transplanted to permanent positions as soon as large enough to handle. Tender species may not be planted out until danger of frost is over. Division of rootstocks should be made in Sept. or Mar.–Apr. Cuttings should be made in Sept. or early spring. Salvias require open, sunny positions and plenty of water in dry weather. Many of the cult. and wild species are important bee plants.

argentea. Silver sage. Half-hardy biennial growing to 4 ft. high, covered with white-woolly hairs. Basal leaves broadly ovalish, 6–8

---

* Special articles on the subjects indicated by an asterisk (*) will be found at the words so marked.

in. long, cut into lobes. Flowers in interrupted, 6–10-flowered whorls.* Individual flower showy, upper lip longer than lower, whitish-yellow or purplish. Mediterranean region. June.

azurea. Perennial growing 4–5 ft. high. Leaves green, smooth, lance-shaped, slightly toothed. Flowers blue or white in interrupted, 6-flowered whorls.* Calyx slightly hairy. Central U.S. Aug. The *var.* offered as **grandiflora** is *Salvia pitcheri.*

coccinea. Texas sage. Perennial to 2 ft. high, slightly woody at base, covered with short, soft hairs. Leaves ovalish, 2–3 in. long, margins toothed. Flowers scarlet, to 1 in. long, in 6–10-flowered whorls. S. Car. to Fla. and Tex., and tropical America. July to frost.

farinacea. Perennial to 3 ft. high, covered with whitish, short hairs, and mealy. Leaves stalked, lance-shaped, to 4 in. long, bluntly toothed. Flowers 1 in. long, in many-whorled* racemes, violet-blue. Flower stalks sometimes bluish. Tex. *See* BLUE GARDEN. Good for cutting. Summer.

glutinosa. An erect, sticky-hairy, Eurasian perennial, 2–3 ft. high. Leaves oblongish, heart-shaped at the base, 6–8 in. long, the upper ones smaller. Flowers about 1½ in. long, pale yellow, in a loose cluster (raceme*). July.

grandiflora. *See* AUDIBERTIA.

greggi. A woody perennial or sub-shrub, 2–3 ft. high, the leaves oblong, without marginal teeth, only about ¾ in. long, spotted with glands. Flowers scarlet or red, about 1 in. long, in a 6–8-flowered cluster (raceme*); a hort. form is white. Southwestern U.S. and adjacent Mex. Not hardy northward.

haematodes. A hairy biennial, 2–3 ft. high, the leaves mostly in a basal rosette, their stalks flattish. Leaves ovalish, with a heart-shaped base, 7–9 in. long, about 6 in. wide. Flowers violet-blue, in whorls,* the clusters arranged in a large panicle.* Greece. Summer.

jurisici. A hairy perennial, 8–15 in. high, the lower leaves long-stalked and wavy-margined, the upper cut into narrow segments about 4 in. long. Flowers bluish-purple, scarcely ½ in. long, in interrupted clusters (racemes* or whorls*). Serbia. June.

leucantha. Mexican bush sage. Small-growing shrub to 2 ft. high. Leaves lance-shaped, to 6 in. long, covered with white-woolly hairs on the under side, the margins toothed. Flowers white, ¾ in. long, in whorled* racemes. Calyx showy, covered with short, lavender hairs. Mexico. June. Not hardy in severe climates.

mellifera = *Audibertia stachyoides.*

nemorosa. Violet sage. Strong-growing, much-branched perennial, growing to 3 ft. high. Leaves lance-shaped, to 4 in. long, wrinkled, hairy on the under side, margins toothed. Flowers purplish-violet, to ½ in. long, in whorled, slender spikes to 16 in. long. Eu. and western As. Also known as *S. superba.* The *var.* **alba** is smaller, and has shorter spikes of white flowers.

officinalis. Garden sage. *See* HERB GARDENING. Hardy under-shrub, growing to 2 ft. high. Branches and leaves covered with short, white hairs. Leaves stalked, broadly lance-shaped, 2–3 in. long, wrinkled, slightly toothed. Used for seasoning. Flowers purplish-blue or white, in many-flowered whorls, in short racemes. Mediterranean region. If planted close enough it can be clipped to make a low hedge.

patens. Half-hardy perennial, growing to 2½ ft. high and covered with short, sticky hairs. Leaves stalked, arrow-shaped, margins toothed. Flowers gentian-blue, 2 in. long, in

pairs, in widely spaced racemes.* *See* BLUE GARDEN. Mountains of Mexico. Summer.

pitcheri. Half-hardy perennial, growing 4–5 ft. high and covered with short, grayish hairs. Leaves lance-shaped, slightly toothed. Flowers deep violet-blue or white, 1 in. long, in many-flowered whorls,* in long racemes. Midwestern states. Aug.–Sept. Often offered as *S. azurea grandiflora.* Some of the offered plants may, according to some, be *S. blepharophylla* which comes from Mex.

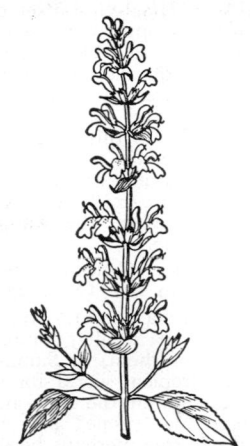

Garden Sage (*Salvia officinalis*). A fragrant perennial used for seasoning, its showy purple-blue flowers also very fragrant.

polystachya. *See* AUDIBERTIA.

pratensis. Hardy perennial, growing to 3 ft. high. Leaves ovalish or heart-shaped, wrinkled, slightly spotted with red, the margins toothed. Flowers bright bluish-purple, 1 in. long, in interrupted,* whorled* racemes. Eu. Summer.

sclarea. Clary. Clear-eye. Hardy biennial, growing to 3 ft. high. Leaves broadly ovalish, to 9 in. long, covered with grayish hairs, the margins toothed. Bracts* thin, colored, white at the base, rose at the tip. Flowers bluish-white, 1 in. long in loose, whorled* racemes. Southern Eu. Aug. *See* HERB GARDENING.

splendens. Scarlet sage. Tender shrub, growing to 8 ft. high, but when grown as an annual, usually not over 3 ft. Leaves stalked, bright green, wrinkled, ovalish, to 3½ in. long, the margins toothed. Bracts* colored. Flowers scarlet, 1½ in. long, in whorled* racemes. Calyx scarlet. Brazil. Summer. This is the common red salvia so widely used for summer bedding. For this purpose it must be grown as a tender annual. *See* ANNUALS. There are also rose-colored and whitish forms.

stachyoides. *See* AUDIBERTIA.

SALVIA FAMILY = Labiatae.

SALVINIA (sal-vin′i-a). Free-floating, small, aquatic plants of the family Salviniaceae, one of them, **S. auriculata,** of tropical America, a popular aquarium plant and useful for greenhouse pools or in the open in the South. It will stand no frost. It is a fern ally, hence producing no flowers and reproduced by spores.* The plant grows usually in masses on

---

* Special articles on the subjects indicated by an asterisk (*) will be found at the words so marked.

the surface of the water and consists of nearly round leaf-like fronds, about ⅜ in. wide, from which are suspended hair-like, feathery, and very graceful roots (beneath the surface). The under side of the fronds is usually pimply or hairy. The plant is sometimes known as *S. natans,* but the true *S. natans* is a hardy, non-cult. species with oblong fronds. (Named for Antonio M. Salvini, Italian professor.)

SALVINIACEAE (sal-vin-i-ā'see-ee). A small family of free-floating, very small aquatic plants, its two genera, *Azolla* and *Salvinia,* both grown for aquaria and in greenhouse pools. They are extremely simple plants (fern allies), without flowers or seeds, and reproduced by spores.* For this process *see* FERNS AND FERN GARDENING.

The leaves of *Salvinia* are about ½ in. long and not cut, while *Azolla* grows in moss-like, feathery masses on the water and has much-divided foliage.

Saman (sam'an). Central American vernacular for the rain tree (*Samanea Saman*).

SAMANEA (sa-mā'nee-a). Tropical American trees of the pea family, comprising over 30 species, one of them, **S. Saman,** planted throughout the tropical world for shade and ornament, but cult. in the U.S. only in extreme southern Fla. (zone* 9). It is commonly called rain tree, perhaps because its innumerable leaflets fold at night and at the approach of cloudy or rainy weather. Much nonsense has been written about its "causing" rain. Other names for it are saman (or zaman) and, in Hawaii, monkey-pod. It is a flat-topped tree, usually 40–70 ft. high, but the canopy often 100 ft. wide. Leaves thrice- or twice-compound,* the ultimate leaflets very numerous, roundish, and about 2 in. long. Flowers yellowish, acacia-like, packed in dense ball-shaped clusters, from which the numerous light crimson stamens* protrude thrice the length of the corolla. Fruit a straight, thickish pod, 6–8 in. long, which does not split, its seeds surrounded by a pulp. The plant is sometimes known as *Pithecolobium Saman,* but in *Pithecolobium* the pods are usually twisted or curved. (*Samanea* is derived from saman.)

SAMARA. A one-seeded fruit which does not split, and is provided with a more or less membranous wing. Common examples are found in the fruits of ash, maple, and elm. Often known as key fruits, especially in the maple.

Sambac (sam'bac). Native name in India for *Jasminum Sambac.*

sambucina, -us, -um (sam-bew-sy'na). Elder-like.

SAMBUCUS. *See* ELDER.

SAMUELA (sam-you-el'a). Date yucca. Yucca-like plants of the lily family, comprising only a few species from the southwestern U.S. and Mex., two of them cult. for interest or ornament in desert gardens but not hardy north of zone* 7. They have stout, tree-

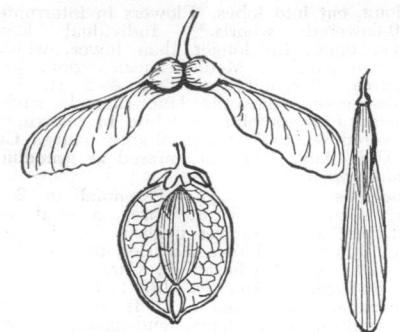

Samaras of maple (*above*), elm (*lower left*), and the ash

like trunks, crowned with a mass of narrow, sword-shaped, sharp-pointed leaves, the margins of which bear conspicuous fibers. Flowers white, more or less tubular, but widely expanded above, generally larger and more showy than in *Yucca.* The cluster (a large panicle*) is borne at the end of a long stalk. Fruit a capsule.* (Named for Sam F. Trelease, American botanist.)

The two below are considerably planted in western Tex., N. Mex., Ariz. and southern Calif., the first species especially. In Mex. the natives use the pulp of the trunk for stock feed. Both the flowers and fruit are eaten by the Mexicans.

carnerosana. Palma samandoca. Trunk 10–18 ft. high, usually unbranched. Leaves 12–18 in. long, 2–3 in. wide. Flowers nearly 4 in. wide, the tube about 1 in. long. Fruit 2–3 in. long. Mex.

faxoniana. Trunk 9–15 ft. high, often branched near the top. Leaves 3–4 ft. long, 2–3 in. wide. Flowers almost 4 in. wide, the tube usually less than ½ in. wide. Fruit 2–3 in. long. Western Tex.

SANCHEZIA (san-key'zi-a). Tropical South American perennial herbs or shrubs, comprising about 11 species, of the family Acanthaceae. Leaves simple, opposite,* large, ovalish shiny green, sometimes striped white or yellow. Flowers orange, red, or purple, tubular, in terminal clusters. Calyx 5-lobed, joined at the base. Corolla with 5 lobes, rounded at the top, tubular below. Stamens* 2 perfect, 2 sterile, inserted on the corolla tube. Fruit a 2-celled capsule,* with usually 4 seeds in each cell. (Named for Josef Sanchez, Spanish professor.)

Not much in cultivation, but grown in the tropical greenhouse in the North or outdoors in the southern states. Propagated by cuttings of young shoots, inserted in sand under a bell-jar, from March–July, in a temperature of 60°–70°. For greenhouse cult. use potting mixture* 5.

nobilis. Shrub growing to 5 ft. high, its stems square. Leaves broadly lance-shaped, to 1 ft. long. Flowers yellow, 2 in. long, growing from the axils* of bright red bracts,* in loose clusters. Rim of corolla rolled under. Stamens* prominent. Ecuador. The *var.* **glaucophylla**

---

* Special articles on the subjects indicated by an asterisk (*) will be found at the words so marked.

has yellow or white markings along the leaf veins.

SAND. The best material to lighten up heavy soils (*i.e.*, those with too much clay or silt), and for the cutting bench. Sharp sand is rather coarse, has no loam or silt in it and is best for hort. purposes. The value of sand is that there is nothing in it to decay, and when coarse (*i.e.*, sharp) it allows better aeration than any other rooting medium.

Ordinary builders' sand fills all hort. requirements and is the only sort to be used in the mixing of concrete or cement. If for the latter purpose, or for the rooting of cuttings, it is necessary to avoid sea sand as it usually contains too much salt for either purpose. Sand from the back of the dunes may sometimes be used, but it is safer to soak a quart of it in 2 quarts of distilled water for an hour and taste the extract. If it is brackish, the sand should be avoided. For technical definition, and the size of the particles in sand *see* SOILS. For the growing of plants in sand and water *see* SOILLESS GARDENING.

SANDALWOOD. The true sandalwood (*Santalum album*) is a partially parasitic tree from India, unknown in cult. in the U.S. For red sandalwood *see* ADENANTHERA PAVONINA.

SAND BINDER. Along the coast it is often necessary to stop shifting dunes from inundating the garden. In New Zealand and France millions of acres of pasture and farm land have been rescued from such a fate.

In the U.S., and nearly throughout the world, the best plant for this purpose is the marram grass. *See* AMMOPHILA for description and details of planting this grass. When marram has completed the first step in transforming a shifting dune to a stable one, other herbs and finally shrubs and trees can complete the process.

For later details of planting, once the sand has stopped being wind-blown, *see* the plants mentioned at SAND GARDEN.

SANDBOX-TREE. *See* HURA.

SANDBUR = *Cenchrus tribuloides*. *See* list at WEEDS.

SAND CHERRY = *Prunus besseyi* and *P. pumila*.

SAND CLOVER = *Anthyllis Vulneraria*.

SAND GARDEN. In many sections of the country there are sandy areas that seem unpromising from the garden standpoint. Not many of the finer hort. plants will grow in pure sand, or if they do, it is only just to survive.

Assuming that your sandy area is not made up of shifting dunes (if it is *see* SAND BINDER), and that it is not salty (if it is *see* SEASIDE GARDENS), the problem is one of selecting plants that will grow in pure sand, and tolerate the often intense midday heat of the sand during the summer. Temperatures of the upper inch of the sand on a clear day may be as high as 120°, even in regions otherwise comparatively cool. Desert sands in the Southwest are much hotter. Not many plants, wild or cult., will stand such conditions. But some will, notably the cacti (which see), and a few others listed below. All are entered at their proper places elsewhere in the ENCYCLOPEDIA. Notes on their hardiness will be found at these entries and will not be repeated here. All those below will grow without more water than rainfall, if in a region where the annual rainfall is 30 in. or more. *See* the name of your state for rainfall figures. For places with more heat and less rainfall than 20–25 in. it is better to use species mentioned at DESERT GARDEN.

LOW PLANTS. One of the best sand plants is the bearberry (*Arctostaphylos Uva-ursi*), which is really a prostrate woody vine. Two others, especially suited to intense heat and the white sands of the pine barren regions, are *Eupatorium hyssopifolium* and *Euphorbia corollata*. Among other genera which contain sand-tolerant herbs or low shrubs the most useful are:

Aralia nudicaulis (wild sarsaparilla)
Arenaria (sandwort)
Artemisia stelleriana (dusty miller)
Asclepias tuberosa (milkweed)
Atriplex (orach)
Calluna (heather)
Cerastium (chickweed)
Chrysopsis (golden aster)
Desmodium canadense (bush trefoil)
Eupatorium (boneset)
Euphorbia (spurge)
Hypericum (*see* ST. JOHN'S-WORT)
Lathyrus (beach pea)
Liatris (button snakeroot)
Mesembryanthemum (fig-marigold)

TALLER SHRUBS AND TREES. There are fewer woody plants able to withstand the conditions in pure sand. By far the best are:

Myrica pensylvanica
Prunus maritima
Prunus pumila
Rhus copallina
Salix tristis
Sophora viciifolia
Ulex (*see* FURZE)

Besides these the vines found among the wild species of *Smilax* and the Virginia creeper (*Parthenocissus*) all do well in pure sand. So will the pitch pine (*Pinus rigida*) and the Jack pine (*P. banksiana*), and especially *P. thunbergi*, among coniferous trees.

There are many other native plants suited to the sand garden. Most of them are not considered hort. subjects and so cannot be had from the dealers. The only way to get them is by digging from the wild. It will be found that this is no easy task, as many sand plants have deep taproots,* sometimes 3 ft. long, although the top may be only a small herb. Quite often too, as in *Arenaria* and *Euphorbia*, the taproot is very brittle, so that digging it out uninjured is a slow job. *See also* DESERT GARDEN. For the growing of plants in sand and water *see* SOILLESS GARDENING.

---

* Special articles on the subjects indicated by an asterisk (*) will be found at the words so marked.

SAND LILY = *Leucocrinum montanum.*

SAND MYRTLE = *Leiophyllum buxifolium.*

SAND PEAR = *Pyrus pyrifolia.*

SAND PHLOX = *Phlox bifida.*

SAND PLUM = *Prunus angustifolia watsoni.*

SAND VERBENA = *Abronia.*

sandwicensis, -e (sand-wi-sen'sis). From the Sandwich (Hawaiian) Islands.

SANDWORT = *Arenaria.*

sanguinale, -is (san-gwi-nay'le). Blood-red.

SANGUINARIA. See BLOODROOT.

sanguinea, -us, -um (san-gwin'ee-a). Blood-red.

SANGUISORBA (san-gwi-sor'ba). Burnet. Hardy perennial herbs of the north temperate regions, comprising about 35 species, belonging to the rose family. Leaves alternate,* compound.* Flowers small, crowded in short spikes at the top of long flowering stalks. Flowers may be male (stamens* only) or female (pistil* only) or both. Calyx of 4 sepals, petal-like, spreading. Corolla absent. Stamens many. Fruit 1-celled, 1-seeded, enclosed in the dry, persistent calyx. (*Sanguisorba* is from the Latin for blood, and drink up, in allusion to supposed styptic properties.)

Not much in cultivation but grown in the border, or for their leaves which are used for flavoring. Easily cult. Propagated by seeds sown in early spring or by division of rootstocks in Sept., Mar. or Apr.

canadensis. Also known as *Poterium canadense.* Strong-growing perennial to 6 ft. high. Leaves compound, leaflets 5–17, opposite,* broadly lance-shaped, to 3 in. long, margins toothed. Flowers white, numerous, in spikes to 6 in. long. Eastern N.A.

minor. Salad burnet. Toper's-plant. Hardy perennial, growing to 2 ft. high. Leaves compound, leaflets 7–19, opposite, ovalish, ¾ in. long, deeply toothed. Flowers greenish, in short spikes, ½ in. long. Leaves edible. See HERB GARDENING. Eurasia, naturalized in N.A. Sometimes offered as *Poterium Sanguisorba.*

obtusa. Japanese burnet. A vigorous perennial, 2½–4 ft. high, the leaves mostly basal, long-stalked, 6–8 in. long. Leaflets 5–17, oblongish, about 2 in. long, blunt, toothed on the margin. Flowers red, small, but showy in numerous short spikes, the stamens* protruding. Jap. July–Aug. Often offered as *Poterium obtusum.*

SANITATION. As a hort. term sanitation means the destruction or deep plowing-under of diseased plants so that future healthy ones may escape infection. It also means the eradication of growing plants infected with insects or diseases for which there is no known remedy. The destruction (preferably burning) of such plants may be painful but it is often necessary to prevent infestation of the remainder.

SAN SEBASTIAN = *Cattleya skinneri.*

SANSEVIERIA (san-se-veer'i-a). Bowstring hemp; also called snake plant and leop-

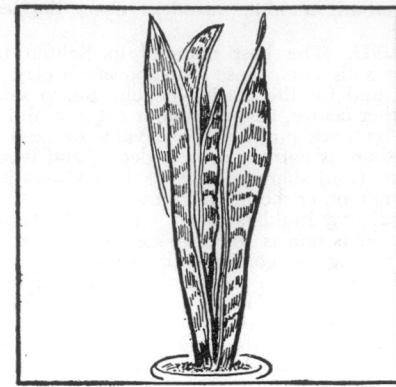

Sansevieria thyrsiflora, the common snake plant.

ard lily, especially in the florists' shops. Tender, herbaceous perennials, comprising about 54 species of the lily family, natives of Af. and India. They have short, thick rootstocks, with thick, erect, basal leaves, which may be flat or concave. Leaves long and narrow, often variegated, or mottled. Flowers on leafless stalks, in a long, cylindrical raceme or spike, white or pale yellow in color, showy, but often wanting in cult. Individual flowers, tubular, with 3 petal-like sepals, and 3 petals. Stamens* 6. Fruit a 3-celled capsule.* (Named for Raimond de Sangro, Prince of Sanseviero.)

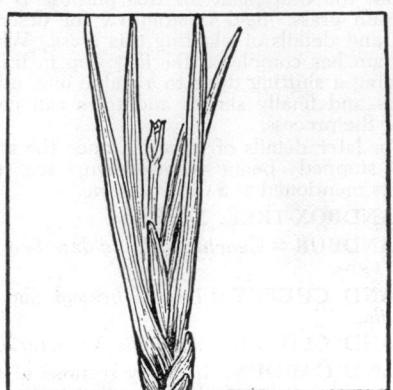

Sansevieria cylindrica, a bowstring hemp less commonly cult.

These plants are easily cult. and make excellent house plants (which see), as they do not require much sunlight. Often grown outdoors in the southern states. Propagated by division of the rootstocks in early spring, or leaves may be cut into pieces about 3 in. long and inserted in sand, in a temperature of 55°–60°, when a new rootstock will form. Some of the broad-leaved species have been tried in Fla. as a source of fiber.

* Special articles on the subjects indicated by an asterisk (*) will be found at the words so marked.

cylindrica. Leaves to 5 ft. long, cylindric, thick, often banded across with light, grayish-green. Flower stalks shorter than the leaves, the flowers white, sometimes tinged pink, numerous, in a raceme to 1 ft. long. Tropical Af., especially in the deserts of Abyssinia.

guineensis = Sansevieria thyrsiflora.

laurenti = Sansevieria trifasciata laurenti.

thyrsiflora. Leaves 1½ ft. long, 3½ in. wide, flattish, banded across with pale green, the margins yellow. Flowers greenish-white, fragrant, 1½ in. long, the cluster 10–12 in. high. S. Af. This is the common snake plant of the shops and stands more abuse as a house plant than almost any other. If given reasonably good care it often blooms in Aug. in the living room.

trifasciata laurenti. Similar to S. zeylanica, but with yellow-striped leaves. Belgian Congo.

zeylanica. Leaves to 2½ ft. long, and 1 in. wide, concave, banded across with pale green, and lined on the back. Flowers white, 1½ in. long, in spikes. Ceylon. The leaves are sometimes nearly cylindrical.

SANTA ANA CAÑON. See BOTANIC GARDEN.

SANTA CRUZ IRONWOOD = Lyonothamnus floribundus.

SANTA CRUZ WATER LILY = Victoria cruziana.

SANTA MARIA TREE = Calophyllum antillanum.

SANTA MARTA = Heliocereus speciosus.

SANTOLINA (san-to-ly′na). Evergreen, aromatic under-shrubs of the family Compositae, most of the 8 species from the Mediterranean region. They have alternate, finely divided leaves, and solitary, globe-shaped, yellow flower heads, all without ray* flowers. The first species is reported as hardy at Boston, but it and the last two are more safely wintered over in the cold frame. Propagated by cuttings in spring. (Santolina is from an old name, Santum linum, of S. virens.)

Chamaecyparissus. Lavender cotton. A silvery-gray, evergreen woody perennial or sub-shrub, 1–2 ft. high. Leaves cut into very narrow segments. Flower heads solitary, terminal, the stalk about 6 in. long. Southern Eu. Summer. Hardy up to zone* 5, and above with a mulch.

incana = S. Chamaecyparissus.

neapolitana. An evergreen sub-shrub, 2–3 ft. high, the foliage white-felty. Leaves dissected into thread-thin segments, scarcely ¼ in. long. Flower heads bright yellow, about ¾ in. thick, on a slender stalk 5–6 in. long. Southern Italy. Summer.

rosmarinifolia = S. neapolitana.

virens. An evergreen, somewhat woody perennial, 10–18 in. high, the foliage smooth and dark green. Leaves very narrow, nearly 2 in. long, the margins toothed. Flower heads solitary, about ½ in. in diameter, on stout stalks that are 6–10 in. high. Southern Eu. July. Once called holy flax.

SANVITALIA (san-vi-tal′i-a). North American tender, herbaceous annuals, comprising about 4 species, belonging to the family Compositae. Leaves simple, opposite,* ovalish. Flowers in small terminal heads. Ray florets* yellow or white, the disk florets

brown or purplish-black. Fruit dry, 1-celled, 1-seeded. (Sanvitalia was named for a noble Italian family, the Sanvitali.)

Sanvitalias are easily cult. They prefer light, open soil in full sun. Propagated by seeds sown in early spring in a cold frame, or where wanted after warm weather has arrived.

procumbens. Trailing annual, growing about 6 in. high, covered with short hairs. Stems much-branched. Leaves ovalish, about 1 in. long. Flower heads numerous, to 1 in. across. Ray florets yellow, disk florets purplish-black. Mex. See ROCK GARDEN.

SANWA MILLET = Echinochloa crus-galli frumentacea.

SAP. Popularly, the juice of plants. But sap comprises crude sap, an upward stream which carries soluble salts absorbed by the roots, and elaborated sap, which is the result of what has happened to crude sap in the leaves. It is the elaborated sap, usually a downward stream, which contains sugar (as sugar cane, sugar maple, some palms, etc.). From the elaborated sap also the plant manufactures the highly complex gums, oils, resins, and often milky juice (latex). It is from the coagulated latex we get rubber, gutta-percha, chicle, and many other products. Technically, latex is not sap, although commonly so called. Some of the gums produced from elaborated sap are useful to trees in sealing wounds.

sapida, -us, -um (sap′i-da). Of pleasing taste.

sapienta, -us, -um (say-pee-en′ta). Pertaining to wise men; or to authors.

SAPINDACEAE (sap-in-day′see-ee). The soapberry family means little to the average northern gardener. Although it comprises about 100 species of shrubs and trees, most of them are tropical and only Sapindus (some species), Xanthoceras, and Koelreuteria are much grown outdoors in the North. The latter is somewhat extensively grown for ornament. The family is also called Dodonaeaceae.

In the tropics (less so in Fla. and southern Calif.) the family is much more important because of its fruit: Blighia (the akee), Euphoria (the longan), Litchi (the litchi), and Melicocca are the chief genera with useful fruit. The remaining cult. genera, grown mostly for ornament in frost-free regions or in greenhouses, are: Cardiospermum (a summer annual vine), Dodonaea, and Paullinia.

Leaves alternate,* undivided or compound,* with or without an odd leaflet at the end, sometimes thrice-compound. Flowers nearly regular, never very showy, nearly always in clusters (cymes* or panicles*), mostly unisexual.* Fruit various; dry or fleshy, a drupe,* nut, or sometimes winged.

Technical flower characters: Sepals 4–5. Petals 4–5, or wanting, usually with scales or hairs at the base. Stamens* 8 or 10, in two distinct series. Ovary superior,* mostly 3-celled.

SAPINDUS (sa-pin′dus). Soapberry. Chiefly

tropical American trees, comprising about 15
species of the family Sapindaceae, of secondary hort. importance, but the two below
native in Fla. and planted for interest or ornament. They have alternate,* compound*
leaves, the leaflets arranged feather-fashion,
and with an odd one at the end. Flowers very
small, greenish or whitish, inconspicuous,
borne in a large terminal cluster (panicle*).
Petals 4–5. Stamens* 8–10. Fruit a fleshy
or somewhat leathery berry, the pulp easily
lathering like soap, the seeds bony and black.
(*Sapindus* is partly Latin for soap, combined
with *Indian*, in allusion to the Indians' use of
the berries for soap.)

Sapindus marginatus drops its leaves during
the winter, although it is considered as a satisfactory shade tree in Fla., in spite of the lack
of showy flowers. S. *Saponaria* is evergreen.
They grow well in dry, sandy soil. Propagated by seeds.

marginatus. A tree up to 30 ft. high. Leaflets 7–13, stalked, narrowly oblong, pointed
both ends, 4–5 in. long. Fruit inverted egg-
shaped, yellow, about 1 in. long, keeled on
the back, ripening in late summer. The pulp
is reported to have about 30% of saponin.
Fla. and tropical America. Hardy in zones* 8
and 9, perhaps in the southern part of zone* 7.

Saponaria. Not over 30 ft. high. Leaflets
7–9 in. long, elliptic or oblong, 2½–3½ in.
long, evergreen. Fruit nearly round, about ⅝
in. in diameter, orange-brown, ripening in early
summer or spring. Southern Fla. to the W.I.
and tropical America. Hardy only in zone* 9.

SAPIUM (say'pi-um). A genus of 100
species of poisonous-juiced tropical trees of the
spurge family, only one cult. This is S. sebiferum, the Chinese tallow-tree, also called
vegetable tallow, a native of southern China
and Jap. and naturalized from S. Car. to Fla.
and La. It grows up to 50 ft. high (less as
cult. here), and has alternate* ovalish or
angled leaves 1–3 in. long, slenderly long-
stalked, the stalks ultimately red. Flowers not
showy, without petals (*see* EUPHORBIACEAE),
in terminal spikes, 2–4 in. long. Fruit a 3-lobed
capsule,* about ½ in. wide, the seeds white.
It is for the latter that the plant is grown in
many regions, the waxy covering yielding a
tallow-like substance used for soap and candles. In the U.S. cult. for ornament, but not
hardy north of zone* 7. It is somewhat
poplar-like and grows in a variety of soils.
Propagated by seeds or cuttings, or sometimes
by grafting. (*Sapium* is the old Latin name
for the genus.) Autumn color brilliant.

SAPODILLA = *Sapota Achras.*

SAPODILLA FAMILY = Sapotaceae.

SAPONARIA (sap-o-nair'i-a). Hardy annual or perennial herbs, comprising about
50 species, belonging to the pink family, and
found in the north temperate zone, but chiefly
in the Mediterranean region. Leaves simple,
opposite,* more or less lance-shaped, smooth
or hairy. Flowers showy, in loosely branched
clusters, pink or white in color. Calyx 5-lobed,
tubular. Corolla of 5 petals, alternating with
the sepals. Stamens* 5. Fruit a dry, 2–3-

celled capsule.* (*Saponaria* is from the Latin
for soap, the bruised leaves and stem of some
species forming a lather in water.)

Saponarias make useful plants both for the
border and rock garden. Easily propagated
by seeds, division of the rootstocks or by
cuttings. Seeds should be sown in early
spring, ⅛ in. deep, in a mixture of sandy
loam, in a cool greenhouse or cold frame.
Division of the rootstocks may be made in
Sept., Mar. or Apr. Cuttings of young shoots
taken in Aug.–Sept. should be inserted in a
mixture of half sand and half soil, and shaded
from sun until rooted.

caespitosa. A low, tufted* perennial,
scarcely 3 in. high, the tiny, narrow leaves
mostly basal, sharp-pointed. Flowers rose-pink,
in tight clusters (nearly umbels*), the petals
notched. Pyrenees. June–July. Best suited to
the rock garden.

ocymoides. Trailing, much-branched perennial, growing to 9 in. high and covered with
soft hairs. Leaves broadly lance-shaped. Flowers bright pink, in loose clusters. Calyx purple.
Suitable for rock or pink garden. Central and
southern Eu. May–Aug. There is a white-
flowered variety.

officinalis. Bouncing Bet. Soapwort. Strong-
growing perennial, to 3 ft. high, not much-
branched. Leaves broadly lance-shaped to 3
in. long. Flowers pink or white, about 1 in.
long, in dense clusters. Western As., naturalized
in N.A. May–Sept., mostly blooming at night.
The *var.* flore-pleno, with double flowers, is
the form usually grown. Both are useful border
plants.

Vaccaria. Cowherb or cockle. Also known
as *Lychnis Vaccaria*, and by some as *Vaccaria
segetalis*. Annual, growing to 3 ft. high. Leaves
smooth, broadly lance-shaped. Flowers deep
pink, ¾ in. across, in loose clusters. Eu.,
naturalized in N.A., and often a weed in the
fields, although a desirable garden plant. There
is a white-flowered form.

SAPOTA (sa-pō'ta). A single species of
densely foliaged, tropical American trees of the
family Sapotaceae, commonly called sapodilla
or naseberry, and known to science as Sapota
Achras (sometimes called *Achras Zapota*,
but *Achras* includes the sapote or marmalade-
tree). The sapodilla, hardy only in zone*9,
is very widely grown throughout the tropical
world for its fruit, but even more important
is the milky latex harvested in Yucatan and
neighboring regions for chicle used in chewing gum, hence often called chicle-tree. Not
over 60 ft. high, its alternate,* leathery,
oblongish, evergreen leaves 4–6 in. long, without marginal teeth. Flowers solitary in the
leaf axils, short-stalked, white, about ½ in.
wide, or less. Sepals* hairy on the outside,
usually 6, in 2 series. Corolla urn-shaped.
Stamens* 6, alternating with 6 sterile, petal-
like stamens. Fruit an apple-shaped berry,
russet and scurfy on the outside, the flesh
yellowish, granular, sweet, and delicious.
Seeds 1–several, black. Can only be safely
grown in extreme southern Fla. Fruit ripening is scattered through most of the year.
Propagated by shield budding in May, or by
grafting. Seeds may also be sown, but the
results are uncertain. (*Sapota* is a native

---

* Special articles on the subjects indicated by an asterisk (*) will be found at the words so marked.

name in tropical America for this and several related trees.)

SAPOTACEAE (sa-pō-tay'see-ee). The sapodilla family scarcely touches the northern garden except for the genus *Bumelia,* shrubby plants of the southeastern U.S. and southward. All the rest of the 30 genera and over 400 species are tropical shrubs and trees, mostly with a milky juice. In one of them, *Sapota,* the coagulated milky latex yields chewing gum, and in another, *Palaquium,* it yields gutta-percha.

Some genera furnish tropical fruits little known in the North: *Achras* (marmalade plum), *Chrysophyllum* (*see* STAR-APPLE), and *Lucuma,* the canistel.

Leaves alternate,* without marginal teeth, often rather thick and leathery. Flowers never very showy, often solitary or a few clustered in the leaf axils.* Fruit a berry, often edible.

Technical flower characters: Sepals 4–6, separate, and mostly in two series. Corolla united, its lobes with small appendages or slightly fringed. Stamens* as many as the lobes of the corolla, and opposite them, often with some sterile. Ovary superior.*

SAPOTE = *Achras Zapota.* For the white sapote *see* CASIMIROA EDULIS.

SAPROPHYTE. A plant that lives on the dead remains of other plants, as do the Indian pipe and a few other wild flowers. Naturally such plants can be cultivated only with rare success. They get their food with the aid of various microscopic organisms of decay (fungi and bacteria), which help to decompose the material upon which saprophytes live. This means that the few cult. saprophytes which can be grown thrive only in woods soil impregnated with the organisms upon which they rely for getting their food. *See also* PARASITE. The whole subject of saprophytism, while of absorbing interest to the botanist, really lies outside the scope of gardening.

SARATOGA HORTICULTURAL FOUNDATION. A non-profit hort. institution founded at Saratoga, Calif., in 1951, devoted to the orgination and dispersal of varieties of desirable shrubs and trees suitable for the western U.S.

SARCOCOCCA (sar-ko-kok'a). A small group of Asiatic and Malayan evergreen shrubs of the family Buxaceae, closely related to the box, but with alternate* and longer leaves. Two of the 6 known species are planted for ornament, but they are not certainly hardy north of zone* 5. Leaves stalked, without marginal teeth, rather leathery. Flowers small, whitish, without petals, the male and female separate on the same plant. Fruit a black or dark red, fleshy, berry-like drupe* with 1 or 2 seeds. (*Sarcococca* is from the Greek for fleshy and berry, in allusion to the fruit.)

Their culture is the same as for box (which see). Propagated by seeds.

hookeriana. A shrub 4–6 ft. high. Leaves lance-shaped or oblong, 2–3 in. long, pointed at the tip, wedge-shaped at the base. Fruit nearly round, about ⅓ in. in diameter, black. Himalayas. Sept.–Feb. Valued in Ore. and Wash. as a source of evergreen foliage, for which it is now cult. The *var.* humilis is half the height of the type and is a good ground cover in shady places south of zone* 5.

ruscifolia. A shrub 4–6 ft. high in the wild, usually less as grown here and a useful ground cover for partially shady sites. Leaves ovalish or elliptic-oval, 2–3 in. long, shining green above. Flowers white, fragrant. China. Sept.–Feb. A useful dish-garden plant in its young stages.

sardensis, -e (sar-den'sis). From Sardinia.

SARGENT PALM = *Pseudophoenix sargenti.*

SARGENT'S WEEPING HEMLOCK = *Tsuga canadensis pendula.* See HEMLOCK.

sarmatica, -us, -um (sar-mat'i-ka). From Sarmatia, an obsolete name for the region north of the Black Sea; also for Poland.

sarmentosa, -us, -um (sar-men-tō'sa). Sarmentose; *i.e.,* bearing runners.

sarniensis, -e (sar-ni-en'sis). From the Channel Island of Guernsey.

SARRACENIA. See PITCHER-PLANT.

SARRACENIACEAE (sar-ra-see-ni-ā'-see-ee). The pitcher-plant family is of chief interest because of its insect-catching, and its ability to digest them. *See also* NEPENTHES, DROSERACEAE, and UTRICULARIA.

There are only two cult. genera in this group of insectivorous plants. *Sarracenia* (*see* PITCHER-PLANT) and *Darlingtonia,* the California pitcher-plant, are both cult. as curiosities, and the former has some species with very handsomely colored pitchers.

Leaves mostly in a basal rosette. They are modified so that they are more or less shaped like a bent pitcher, hold considerable water, and the inside of the pitcher is slippery or so furnished with hairs that the insect can get in but not out. Both genera are bog plants, and both have more or less of a lid or flap to the pitcher.

Technical flower characters: Petals and sepals 5. Stamens* many. Ovary superior.* Fruit a capsule.*

SARSAPARILLA. The true sarsaparilla (various tropical American species of *Smilax*) is not a cult. plant in the U.S. For the wild sarsaparilla *see* ARALIA NUDICAULIS.

SASA. See ARUNDINARIA and BAMBUSA.

SASKATCHEWAN. For the garden possibilities of this province *see* the accounts of the generally similar conditions in MANITOBA, MONTANA, and NORTH DAKOTA.

SASSAFRAS (sass'a-frass). Three species of deciduous trees of the family Lauraceae, two of them Asiatic or Formosan, the third, **S. albidum,** long known as *S. variifolium,* the common sassafras of eastern U.S. It is usually a small, slender tree, but specimens up to 100 ft. high, and a girth of over 12 ft., are known on Gardiner's Island, L.I. Leaves alternate,* without teeth, but often irregu-

---

* Special articles on the subjects indicated by an asterisk (*) will be found at the words so marked.

larly and lopsidedly lobed, or regularly 3-lobed, the lobes rounded, or some leaves (even on the same twig) unlobed, generally ovalish, 3–5 in. long. Flowers often unisexual, yellow (*see* LAURACEAE), usually in racemes* that bloom before the leaves unfold, delightfully fragrant. Fruit bluish-black, with a bloom, on fleshy, bright red stalks. While it grows in a wide variety of soils it is not of the easiest cult. Almost no native tree has such gorgeous scarlet foliage in the fall. April–May. (*Sassafras* is from the Spanish *salsafras*, in reference to the medicinal value of its root bark.)

SASSAFRAS FAMILY = Lauraceae.

SATIN-FLOWER. *See* HONESTY, SISYRINCHIUM and GODETIA GRANDIFLORA.

SATINLEAF = *Chrysophyllum oliviforme.* *See* STAR-APPLE.

SATINPOD. *See* HONESTY.

SATIN POPPY = *Meconopsis napaulensis.*

sativa, -us, -um (sa-ty'va). Cultivated.

SATSUMA ORANGE = *Citrus nobilis Unshiu.*

SATUREIA. *See* SAVORY.

saturejoides (sat-ur-e-oi'deez). Savory-like.

SAUSAGE-TREE = *Kigelia pinnata.*

SAVIN = *Juniperus Sabina.*

SAVORY. The summer and winter savory are fragrant herbs, which, with others, constitute the genus **Satureia** (sat-you-ree'a) of the mint family. The name is sometimes spelled *Satureja.* They are hardy annual, or perennial, aromatic herbs or small shrubs, comprising about 100 species distributed through the warm regions of the world. Stems usually square. Leaves opposite,* ovalish or lance-shaped, the margins sometimes toothed. Flowers pink, white, or purplish, in whorls,* in axillary or terminal racemes.* Calyx 5-lobed, usually tubular. Corolla a narrow tube opening into 2 lips, upper lip 2-lobed and flat, the lower lip 3-lobed and widely flaring. Stamens 4, in pairs, 2 long, 2 short. Fruit 2-celled when young, splitting into 4 parts when ripe, each containing a seed. (*Satureia* is the old Latin name for the savory.)

Grown chiefly for their leaves which are used for flavoring. Sometimes grown in the border for their flowers. Easily cult. in ordinary garden soil. Propagated by seeds, division of rootstocks, or by cuttings. Seeds should be sown ⅛ in. deep, outdoors, in early spring. Division of rootstocks may be made in Sept. or early spring. Cuttings of young shoots may be made in spring; they should be inserted in a mixture of ½ sand and ½ soil, in a cold frame, and kept shaded until rooted.

alpina. Alpine savory. Much-branched perennial, shrubby at the base, growing to 6 in. high. Leaves small, ovalish, ½ in. long, slightly toothed. Flowers purple. Whorls* 4–6-flowered, in terminal spikes. Mediterranean region. Sometimes offered as *Calamintha alpina,* and as *Acinos alpinus.*

hortensis. Summer savory. *See* HERB GARDENING. Annual, growing to 18 in. high. Leaves lance-shaped, 1½ in. long. Flowers pink, lavender or white, in loose whorls,* in spikes. Eu., naturalized in the U.S.

montana. Winter savory. Small shrub, growing to 15 in. high. Leaves rigid, lance-shaped, to 1 in. long. Flowers white or purplish, in loose whorls,* in spikes. Eu. and N. Af. *See* HERB GARDENING.

SAWARA CYPRESS = *Chamaecyparis pisifera.*

SAW CABBAGE-PALM = *Paurotis wrighti.*

SAW FERN = *Blechnum serrulatum.*

SAWDUST. *See* MULCH AND MULCHING.

SAW PALMETTO = *Serenoa repens* and *Paurotis wrighti.*

SAXATILE. Inhabiting rocks, or growing in rocky places.

saxatilis, -e (sack-at'i-lis). Saxatile.*

SAXIFRAGA (sacks-iff'ra-ga). Saxifrage. Rockfoil. Annual or biennial, but mostly perennial, herbs, comprising about 300 species of the family Saxifragaceae, found chiefly in the temperate regions of Europe and America. They are of very diverse habit, but usually low-growing, spreading or creeping, the rootstocks spreading by offsets* or runners.* Leaves thick and fleshy or soft and moss-like, sometimes arranged in a rosette, the shapes of the leaves varying from roundish or spoon-shaped to ovalish. Margins generally toothed, often encrusted as with lime, hence silvery. Flowers pink, white, purple, or yellow, in clusters. Calyx* of 5 sepals, spreading. Corolla of 5 or more petals. Stamens* 10 or more. Fruit a 2-celled capsule,* many-seeded. (*Saxifraga* is from the Latin for stone and to break, in allusion to supposed medicinal remedy for gallstones.)

Saxifragas and the genus *Bergenia* make useful plants for the rock garden or border, as they seldom run over the other plants. The foliage changes color with the seasons and so gives great variety. The alpine species can be planted in the clefts of rocks. For best results in growing saxifragas, plant in positions shaded from midday sun, in gritty soil with lime. Easily propagated from seeds, division of the rootstocks, or by runners and bulblets,* the latter being found in some species. Seeds should be sown ⅛ in. deep, in sandy soil, in a cool greenhouse or cold frame, in early spring. As soon as large enough to handle, they should be pricked off into pans until well established, when they may be transferred to permanent positions. Division of the rootstocks, runners, and bulblets* may be made in spring or summer. *See* ROCK GARDEN.

aizoides. A shallow-rooted, mat-forming perennial, 6–9 in. high. Leaves chiefly basal, crowded, narrow, about ¾ in. long, without

---

* Special articles on the subjects indicated by an asterisk (*) will be found at the words so marked.

teeth, but sometimes faintly hairy on the margin. Flowers orange-yellow, about ½ in. wide, seldom more than one to each branch of the cluster. Arctic and alpine regions of the northern hemisphere. June–July. Best suited to the rock garden in cool regions.

Aizoon. Strong-growing perennial, to 20 in. high. Leaves basal, in dense rosettes, narrowly spoon-shaped, 1¼ in. long. Margins toothed and encrusted. Flowers in clusters, creamy-white, with purple markings, ½ in. across. Alpine N.A., Eu. and As. Summer. The *var.* **baldensis** has short, thick, gray leaves, with whitish flowers. The *var.* **brevifolia** has white flowers. The *var.* **flavescens** has clear yellow flowers. The *var.* **lagaveana** is a dwarf form with silvery-gray leaves and reddish stems, the flowers creamy-white, wax-like. The *var.* **pectinata** has silver-margined leaves, with white flowers spotted with red. All good for border or rock garden (which see).

altissima. Strong-growing perennial, to 2 ft. high. Leaves basal, thick, to 4 in. long, rounded at the apex. Margins toothed, the teeth tough. Flowers white, but marked with purple to ½ in. across, in clusters. Flower stalks slightly hairy. Tyrol. Summer. Considered by some as only a var. of *S. hosti.*

andrewsi. A hybrid between *S. Aizoon* and a European species. It grows up to 6 in. high. Flowers white, marked red. Useful rock garden plant.

apiculata. A hybrid saxifrage, and a dwarf perennial, to 3½ in. high, forming a dense mat. Leaves inversely spoon-shaped, with small, open pores round the margins. Flowers yellow, in small, loose clusters. For cult. *see* Rock Garden.

borisi. A small, hybrid perennial, not over 3 in. high, with basal rosettes of gray-green leaves. Flower stalks red-hairy, the flowers yellow, conspicuous. Hort. origin. May–June.

burseriana. A densely tufted* or cushion-like perennial, 2–4 in. high, the silvery-gray, spiny leaves in many-leaved basal rosettes. Flowers usually solitary, nearly 1 in. wide, ultimately white but red in bud. Eu. May–June. There are several fine vars. with larger flowers, smaller stature, red-stalked flowers, or with yellow flowers.

caespitosa. Dwarf perennial, strong-growing,

Three saxifrages: (*A*) *Saxifraga sarmentosa*; (*B*) *S. Aizoon*; (*C*) *S. oppositifolia*

to 6 in. high, and of tufted* habit. Leaves deep green, 3-lobed, about ½ in. long. Flowers white, to ½ in. across, in loose clusters. Northern N.A. and Eurasia. Spring.

cartilaginea. Perennial, to 9 in. high. Leaves in rosettes, narrow, to 1 in. long, the margins with tough teeth. Flowers white, rose, or purple, to ½ in. across. Asia Minor.

cochlearis. Perennial, to 9 in. high, growing in thick tufts.* Leaves narrowly spoon-shaped, to 1 in. long, the margins with tough teeth. Flowers white, to ¾ in. across, in loose clusters. Alps. Spring. For cult. *see* Rock Garden.

cordifolia = *Bergenia cordifolia.*
crassifolia = *Bergenia crassifolia.*
cuneifolia. Perennial, to 1 ft. high. Leaves broadly lance-shaped, to 1½ in. long, in rosettes. Margins toothed at the apex. Flowers white, yellow at the base, ¼ in. across, in loose clusters. Eu. Summer.

decipiens. Perennial, 6–12 in. high, growing in dense tufts.* Leaves wedge-shaped, cut into 3–5 narrow lobes. Flowers white, to ½ in. across. There are many hort. varieties with larger or differently colored flowers. Eu. Spring. For cult. *see* Rock Garden.

elizabethae. A hybrid saxifrage, and a dwarf perennial, 2–3 in. high, growing in small, cushion-like tufts.* Leaves in rosettes, deep green. Flowers yellow, large, in 3–5-flowered clusters. Summer.

hosti. Strong-growing perennial, to 2 ft. high. Leaves in rosettes, about 4 in. long, rounded at the tip. Margins wavy and encrusted as with lime. Eu. Spring. For cult. *see* Rock Garden.

lantoscana = *Saxifraga lingulata lantoscana.*
ligulata = *Bergenia ligulata.*
lingulata. Perennial, to 1 ft. high, growing in tufts.* Leaves narrow and spoon-shaped, to 3 in. long. Margins rolled under and encrusted. Flowers white, ½ in. across, in loose, many-flowered clusters. Pyrenees. Summer. The *var.* **lantoscana** has shorter and blunted leaves.

longifolia. A short-lived perennial, treated by some as a biennial, with a densely leafy, sticky-hairy stem, 10–25 in. high. Basal rosettes of leaves 3–6 in. wide. Stem leaves linear or narrowly spoon-shaped, 2–3 in. long. Flowers extremely numerous, about ½ in. wide, in many-flowered clusters (panicles*), white. Pyrenees. July–Aug. There are several fine vars.

macnabiana. A hybrid saxifrage growing to 18 in. high. Leaves basal, in rosettes, 2–3 in. long. Margins toothed and encrusted. Flowers white, spotted purple, in long loose-branching clusters. Summer. For cult. *see* Rock Garden.

marginata. A densely tufted* perennial, often forming cushions or mats, not over 4 in. high. Leaves mostly in a basal rosette, the lower part of each blade hairy on the margin, but cartilaginous toward the tip. Flowers about ½ in. wide, in a loose cluster (corymb*), the stalks black-hairy and sticky. Italy. June–July.

moschata. Perennial, to 5 in. high, growing in tufts.* Leaves narrow, sometimes cut in 2–3 lobes. Flowers greenish-yellow, occasionally purple or white. Eu. Spring. For cult. *see* Rock Garden.

oppositifolia. Mountain saxifrage. Perennial, to 2 in., spreading and forming dense mats. Leaves ovalish, ¾ in. long, slightly hairy. Flowers rose or purple, ½ in. across, in small, loose clusters. Eurasia and northern N.A. For cult. *see* Rock Garden.

---

* Special articles on the subjects indicated by an asterisk (*) will be found at the words so marked.

peltata = *Peltiphyllum peltatum.*

sarmentosa. Strawberry geranium. Aaron's-beard. Beefsteak saxifrage. Mother-of-thousands. Trailing perennial, growing to 2 ft. long, sending out runners like the strawberry. Leaves basal, long-stalked, roundish, heart-shaped at base, to 4 in. across, hairy, dark green, marked with white on upper side and reddish on under side. Margins coarsely toothed. Flowers white, ¾ in. across, in loose racemes. Useful basket or pot plant for the house. Eastern As. Summer. Also known as *S. stolonifera.*

umbrosa. London pride. St. Patrick's cabbage. Perennial, growing to 1 ft. Leaves basal, in rosettes, thick, ovalish, to 2½ in. long, often reddish on the under side. Margins with tough teeth. Flower stalks reddish. Flowers small, white, with numerous pink spots, in loose-branching clusters. Often used for an edging plant in Eng. Eu. Early summer.

virginiensis. Early saxifrage. Rock saxifrage. Perennial, growing to 1 ft. high. Leaves basal, in rosettes, ovalish, to 3 in. long, the margins toothed. Flowers white, about ¾ in. across. Eastern N.A. May.

SAXIFRAGACEAE (sacks-i-fray-gay′see-ee). The saxifrage family is a large and important one to gardeners, to fruit-growers and especially to lovers of its many decorative shrubs. While it is a large and natural family (about 80 genera and perhaps 1050 species), many botanists have split it into several smaller families, not here considered as such. For reference they are listed here:

> Hydrangeaceae or hydrangea family
> Grossulariaceae or gooseberry family
> Escalloniaceae
> Iteaceae
> Parnassiaceae

As here treated, all these are considered as one big family, the Saxifragaceae, which contains many genera of wide cult. The only important fruit is found in *Ribes* (currant and gooseberry).

The most important decorative shrubs are in the genera *Deutzia, Philadelphus* (*see* MOCK-ORANGE), and *Hydrangea,* but other woody genera yielding fine decorative shrubs, trees, or woody vines are: *Decumaria, Schizophragma, Carpenteria,* and *Itea,* all of which are more or less hardy in the North. *Bauera* and *Escallonia* are more tender and sometimes grown in the cool greenhouse or outdoors in warmer regions southward.

In perennial, or rarely annual, herbs for the open border, wild garden, or rock garden the family is very rich. Those mostly suited to the open border are *Heuchera* (also for the wild garden, and one or two for the greenhouse), *Bergenia, Astilbe, Jamesia,* and *Rodgersia.* The wild garden genera are best exemplified by *Boykinia, Heuchera, Mitella, Tanakaea, Tellima,* and *Tiarella,* while those most suited to rock gardens are *Peltiphyllum, Saxifraga, Tolmiea,* and *Lithophragma.* The only two remaining cult. genera are *Francoa,* a somewhat tender herb from Chile, and *Parnassia,* which are largely bog plants.

Leaves various, often in a basal rosette* in the herbs, but alternate* or opposite* in the trees and shrubs. Flowers regular,* very showy and profuse in many of the shrub genera (*Deutzia, Philadelphus,* and *Hydrangea,* especially), smaller but most attractive in many of the rock garden saxifrages and in some wild garden plants. Fruit dry in most genera, but a berry in *Ribes* and some others.

Technical flower characters: Sepals and petals 4 or 5. Stamens* 4 or 5, or 8 or 10. Ovary inferior* or superior,* of 2–5 segments which are usually wholly or partly united, but sometimes separate.

SAXIFRAGE. *See* SAXIFRAGA.

SAXIFRAGE FAMILY = Saxifragaceae.

SAXIFRAGE PINK = *Tunica Saxifraga.*

scaber (skay′ber). Rough.

scaberrima, -us, -um (skay-ber′ri-ma). Very rough.

SCABIOSA (skay′bi-ō′sa). Scabious. Pincushion. Hardy annual or perennial herbs, comprising about 80 species of the family Dipsacaceae, found mostly in the temperate regions. Leaves simple, opposite,* ovalish or lance-shaped, often lobed or deeply cut. Flowering stalk long. Flowers in terminal heads, surrounded by 2 rows of small, leafy bracts,* blue, purple, brownish-black, reddish-brown, pink, cream, or white. Calyx represented by bristles. Corolla tubular, sometimes 2-lipped,* with lower lip greatly extended. Stamens 4. Fruit a 1-celled capsule* which does not split. (*Scabiosa* is from the Latin for itch, in allusion to the medicinal use of some species.)

Scabiosas make good garden plants, the flowering period being long. Easily cult. in ordinary garden soil. Propagated by seeds or division of rootstocks. Seeds should be sown in a cold frame as early as possible in spring. Perennial species sometimes flower the first year. Division of rootstocks should be made in March or April. Established plants should be taken up every 3 years and the soil well dug with manure before replanting.

atropurpurea. Sweet scabious. Mourning bride. A tender annual growing 2–3 ft. high and of branching habit. Basal leaves broadly lance-shaped, cut in lyre-shaped lobes. Margins coarsely toothed. Flowers dark purple, pink, or white, the heads to 2 in. across. Eu. The *var.* **candidissima** has white flowers which are sometimes double. The *var.* **grandiflora** has larger flower heads.

caucasica. Hardy perennial, growing to 2½ ft. high. Basal leaves narrowly lance-shaped, entire.* Stem leaves lance-shaped, cut into narrow segments. Flowers in flattish heads, light blue, to 2–3 in. across. The *var.* **alba** has white flowers. The *var.* **magnifica** has large, deep lavender-blue flowers. *See* GRAY AND LAVENDER GARDEN. Caucasus, in the mountains.

Columbaria. A perennial, 1–2 ft. high, the basal leaves broadly ovalish and toothed, the stem leaves dissected into narrow segments. Flower heads blue or bluish-purple, solitary, about 1¼ in. thick, on slender stalks. Eurasia and Af. Summer.

fischeri. A much-branched perennial, 10–20 in. high. Leaves much dissected into linear, narrow segments. Flower heads about 2½

---

* Special articles on the subjects indicated by an asterisk (*) will be found at the words so marked.

in. wide, violet-blue, on stiff stalks. Siberia. July to frost.

graminifolia. A perennial, 6–12 in. high, with silvery foliage. Leaves not dissected, but narrow and without marginal teeth. Flower heads flattish, about 1½ in. wide, pale blue or mauve, the rays notched. Eu. A mat-forming plant best suited to the rock garden.

japonica. Perennial, of tufted habit, growing to 2 ft. high. Leaves broadly lance-shaped, divided into many narrow lobes. Flowers violet-blue, in heads to 2 in. across. Jap. *See* GRAY AND LAVENDER GARDEN.

lucida. A rock garden perennial, 7–10 in. high, the silvery leaves oval to oblong, cut into fine segments. Flowers in dense heads, rosy-lilac, the heads about 1½ in. wide. Central Eu. in the mountains. Summer.

ochroleuca. A perennial, 12–20 in. high, the foliage whitish-hairy. Lower leaves lyre-shaped, long-stalked. Upper leaves divided feather-fashion into narrow segments. Flower heads bright yellow, long-stalked. Eurasia. July to frost.

scabiosaefolia, -us, -um (skay-bi-o-si-fō′li-a). Having leaves like the scabious (*Scabiosa*).

SCABIOUS. *See* SCABIOSA. For the shepherd's-scabious *see* JASIONE PERENNIS.

scabra, -us, -um (skay′bra). Rough.

SCABROUS. Rough to the touch, as are many leaves.

SCAFFOLD. The lateral branching caused by initial pruning of fruit trees to produce the desired shape and branching of the canopy. *See* PRUNING.

SCALD. This term applies to a type of injury resulting from intense sunlight on tender growth of plants. If the top of a tree, such as beech, is pruned out, the upper surface of the then exposed branches will scald. In the northern hemisphere the south side of the trunk of recently transplanted trees will scald. Fruit, such as tomato, pepper, eggplant, and apple, may scald on the side facing the sun. Scald is usually evidenced by brownish, irregular spots.

SCALE. A small, often dry, leaf or bract.*

SCALE INSECTS. Very troublesome garden pests, the young of which suck the juices of plants. For a description of scale insects *see* True Bugs at INSECT PESTS. Various sorts of scale insects attack important hort. plants. Some of the most important are (1) San Jose scale (*see* illustration), (2) oyster-shell scale, (3) black scale, mostly on citrus trees in Calif., (4) terrapin scale, and (5) scurfy scale. All are minute sucking insects which firmly attach themselves to the bark, often on twigs and young branches. The control for those attacking outdoor plants is an oil spray or lime-sulphur spray applied just before growth starts in the spring. Commercially prepared mixable oils and lime-sulphur sprays are effective if directions on the container are carefully followed. In the greenhouse, use of pesticide #21 (*see* SPRAYS AND DUSTS) or other phosphate insecticide on plant material will control young stages and sometimes the adults.

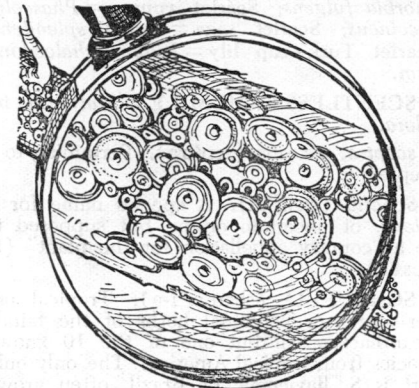

San Jose scale, one of the most destructive of the scale insects, shown (magnified) as it occurs on twigs.

SCALLION. A young onion, the base somewhat swollen, but without a true bulb, or pulled before the bulb develops. Scallions are grown for bunching and eating green. *See* ONION for culture. *Scallion* is also sometimes used for the leek and for shallot (*see* both terms).

SCALLOP SQUASH. *See* CUCURBITA PEPO MELOPEPO.

SCAMMONY = *Ipomoea pandurata.*

scandens (skan′denz). Climbing.

SCAPE. A flower stalk, usually leafless, that arises at the ground. Scapes often, however, bear small scales or bracts.* Scapose plants are common in the garden, such as tulip, bloodroot, most primroses, and many others.

SCARBOROUGH LILY = *Vallota speciosa.*

Scariola (scare-i-ō′la). An old generic name for the prickly lettuce and its relatives now included in *Lactuca*. *See* Prickly Lettuce in the list at WEEDS.

scariosa, -us, -um (scare-i-ō′sa). Scarious; *i.e.*, with leaf-like, usually small bracts or other organs, which are thin, nearly transparent, or membranous, and not green.

SCARLET. As an adjective *scarlet* is linked with the names of many plants or objects in the garden. Those in this book and their proper equivalents are:

Scarlet bloom = *Eucalyptus ficifolia;* **Scarlet bugler** = *Pentstemon centranthifolius;* **Scarlet-bush** = *Hamelia erecta;* **Scarlet clematis** = *Clematis texensis;* **Scarlet eggplant** = *Solanum integrifolium;* **Scarlet-flowered gum** = *Eucalyptus ficifolia;* **Scarlet fritillary** = *Fritillaria recurva;* **Scarlet garden** (*see* RED GARDEN); **Scarlet larkspur** = *Delphinium cardinale;* **Scarlet lightning** = *Lychnis chalcedonica,* also *Centranthus ruber;* **Scarlet lobelia** = *Lobelia Cardinalis;* **Scarlet lychnis** = *Lychnis chalcedonica;* **Scarlet oak** = *Quercus coccinea* (*see* OAK); **Scarlet pimpernel** = *Anagallis arvensis* (*see* list at WEEDS); **Scarlet plume** = *Eu-*

---

* Special articles on the subjects indicated by an asterisk (*) will be found at the words so marked.

phorbia fulgens; Scarlet runner = *Phaseolus coccineus;* Scarlet sage = *Salvia splendens;* Scarlet Turk's-cap lily = *Lilium chalcedonicum.*

SCENTLESS CAMOMILE = *Matricaria inodora.*

sceptra, -us, -um (sep′tra). Pertaining to a scepter.

Schafta (shaff′ta). A species name for a *Silene;* of uncertain origin, but supposed to be a "country appellation for the plant" (in Russia).

SCHAUERIA (shau-er′i-a). Tropical under-shrubs or perennial herbs of the family Acanthaceae, all but one of the 10 known species from tropical America. The only cult. sort is S. *flavicoma,* of Brazil, often grown in the warm-temperate greenhouse for its showy, yellow flowers. It is a woody under-shrub, 2–4 ft. high. Leaves opposite,* without marginal teeth, ovalish or oval-lance-shaped, 4–6 in. long, broad at the base, but tapering at the tip. Flowers about 1½ in. long, light yellow, in a dense, close, head-like cluster. Corolla tubular below, but 2-lipped,* the lower lip with 3 segments. Fruit a slender-stalked capsule. It needs plenty of moisture and should be grown in potting mixture* 4. (Named for J. C. Schauer, a German professor.)

SCHEFFLERA (sheff-leer′a). A genus of over 150 species of shrubs and trees of the family Araliaceae, widely distributed in mostly Old World tropics. They have usually compound leaves, the leaflets arranged finger-fashion, and mostly long-stalked. Flowers minute, in large, showy clusters (compound panicles*), but seldom in cult. One of them, S. *actinophylla* of Australia, has recently become deservedly popular as a house plant. It is a tree 20–30 ft. high (much less as cult.) with 6–8 leathery, glossy-green elliptic leaflets, 6–8 in. long, without marginal teeth. Flower cluster (when produced) up to 18 in. long. It stands room conditions very well, even partly darkened places, and is easily propagated by air layering. Needs potting mixture* 4. (Named in honor of J. C. Scheffler of Danzig.) Often called umbrella tree or Australian umbrella tree, and thought by some to belong to the genus *Brassaia.*

Schinseng (shin′seng). The Chinese name for the plants known to us as ginseng.

SCHINUS (sky′nus). Chiefly South American resinous trees of the family Anacardiaceae, comprising perhaps 15 species, the two below much grown for ornament in Calif. and Fla., usually under the name pepper-tree, although neither is a true pepper. (*See* PIPER and CAPSICUM.) They have alternate,* and in ours compound* leaves, the leaflets stalkless and with an odd one at the end. Male and female flowers on different trees, small, white, in branched clusters (panicles*). Petals 5. Stamens 10. Fruit a

berry-like, reddish drupe.* (*Schinus* is Greek for the true mastic-tree, which these resemble in being resinous.)

The first species is one of the most popular shade trees in Calif., being hardy from San Francisco southward, except in the mountains. As part of its attractiveness is the fruit, care must be taken to ensure this by planting both male and female trees. The other species is more commonly planted in Fla. where S. *molle* does not do so well. Both grow in a variety of soils, and are of simple cult., but S. *molle* is often attacked by scale and should be carefully sprayed. (*See* SCALE INSECTS.) Both are easily raised from seed.

molle. Pepper-tree; also called California pepper-tree (not native there), Peruvian mastic-tree, or simply mastic-tree. An evergreen tree, 20–30 ft. high, its branches gracefully drooping. Leaflets numerous, narrowly lance-shaped, toothed or sometimes without teeth. Flowers in a much-branched terminal cluster, yellowish-white. Fruit rose-red, about ¼ in. wide, persisting most of the winter. Peru, but widely planted throughout the tropical world. *Molle* is not Latin (*see* MOLLIS), but from the Peruvian vernacular *Mulli.*

terebinthifolius. Brazilian pepper-tree. Christmasberry tree. An evergreen, small tree or shrub, its branches not drooping. Leaflets 5–9, about 2 in. long, dark green above. Flowers in a denser cluster than in S. *molle.* Fruit bright red, smaller than in S. *molle.* Brazil. Hardy in zones* 8 and 9, and especially popular in Fla. where its bright red berries persist over the winter months.

SCHISANDRA (sky-zan′dra). Also spelled *Schizandra.* Aromatic woody vines of the family Magnoliaceae, all its 24 species Asiatic except for one (non-hort.) in the south-eastern U.S. The only commonly cult. species is S. *chinensis,* a high-climbing vine with the male and female flowers on different plants so that both sexes must be planted to ensure fruit. Leaves alternate,* ovalish or broader toward the tip, 3–4 in. long. Flowers white or pink, about ½ in. wide, in few-flowered, stalked clusters in the leaf axils.* Sepals and petals alike, totaling 7–12. Stamens* 5–15. Fruit a collection of berry-like, ripened carpels, in a spike-like, drooping mass. China and Jap. May–June. Hardy from zone* 3 southward, and very attractive in fruit (Aug.–Sept.). Easily propagated by seeds or layers. (*Schisandra* is from the Greek for cleave and man [stamen], in allusion to the cleft anthers* of one species.)

SCHISMATOGLOTTIS (skiz-mat-o-glott′-is). Tender perennial herbs from the Malay Archipelago, comprising about 75 species of the family Araceae. Rootstocks thick and branching, sometimes showing above the ground. Leaves lance-shaped, heart-shaped, or arrowhead-shaped, often variegated. Flowers in a spike on a long leafless stalk enclosed in a large green or colored spathe,* similar to Jack-in-the-pulpit. Flowers of 2 kinds, male (stamens only) on the upper portion, and female (pistil only) on the lower

---

* Special articles on the subjects indicated by an asterisk (*) will be found at the words so marked.

portion. Fruit a small berry. (*Schismatoglottis* is from the Greek for falling tongue, in allusion to the spathe.*)

These plants are grown mostly for their leaves, and can only be grown where a temperature of about 70° is available through the winter. Sometimes used as house plants. Propagated by cuttings of pieces of the stem about 2 in. long, inserted in sandy soil under a bell-jar, in a temperature of 75°–85° in early spring. For pot culture use potting mixture* 4.

picta. Leafstalk to 1 ft. long. Leaves ovalish, heart-shaped at base, to 8 in. long, and 5 in. wide, light green, marked with white spots. Spathe* enclosing the spadix,* greenish-yellow, 2½ in. long. Java. A handsome, but very tender, foliage plant.

schistosa, -us, -um (shiss-tō'sa). Easily cleaved or divided.

SCHIZAEA (sky'zee'a). A genus of about 25 chiefly tropical species of very small ferns of the family Schizaeaceae, only **S. pusilla**, the curly-grass, likely to be cult. and then only in moist sand or sphagnum moss with a strongly acid reaction. (*See* ACID AND ALKALI SOILS.) Localized in bogs in Nova Scotia, Newfoundland, and the pine-barrens of N.J., the curly-grass looks more like a tiny grass than a fern. Fronds of two sorts, the spore*-bearing ones slightly longer than the sterile fronds, not over 5 in. high, both narrow, hair-like, or grass-like, slightly twisted. The fertile fronds are minutely divided, feather-fashion toward the summit, the tiny segments bearing the spores.* Of no decorative value, but sometimes grown for interest. (*Schizaea* is from the Greek for cleft, in allusion to the cleft fronds of some species.)

SCHIZAEACEAE (sky-zee-ā'see-ee). A small and horticulturally unimportant family of ferns, comprising only 4 genera and about 160 species, nearly all tropical. The only cult. genera are *Schizaea*, a very small and unfern-like bog plant of northeastern N. A., and *Lygodium* which includes climbing ferns (both hardy and greenhouse) somewhat grown for ornament. *See* both these genera for further details.

SCHIZANDRA = *Schisandra.*

SCHIZANTHUS (sky-zan'thus). Fringe-flower. Butterfly-flower; also called poor-man's-orchid. Chilean half-hardy, brittle annuals, comprising about 11 species of the family Solanaceae. Leaves alternate,* broadly lance-shaped, usually cut into many fern-like, light green segments. Flowers showy, in terminal, loose, many-flowered clusters, of many colors. Corolla margins usually of contrasting colors or shades, with streaks and spots of another color or shade at the base. Calyx* 5-lobed, joined at the base. Corolla a short tube opening widely into 2 lips,* the upper 2-lobed, the lower 3-lobed. Stamens* 2, prominent. Fruit a small, 2-celled capsule.* (*Schizanthus* is from the Greek for split and flower, in allusion to the corolla.)

Fringe-flowers are best grown as pot plants in the cool greenhouse for winter or spring flowering, but make very attractive garden plants where the temperature is moderate. Propagated by seeds. For winter flowering, seeds should be sown Aug.–Sept. ⅛ in. deep, in sandy soil, in temperature of 60°–70°. When large enough to handle, plants should be pricked off into pans, using potting mixture* 2, then moved into 3-in. pots, and use potting mixture* 4, continuing with this mixture when re-potting into larger pots until final potting. Throughout their growing period they should be kept in a temperature of 45°–55°. For a method of improving the bloom *see* Pinching at TRAINING PLANTS.

For the garden, seeds should be sown ⅛ in. deep, in sandy soil, in cool greenhouse or cold frame in Feb. or Mar., in a temperature of 50°–60°, following the same procedure as for greenhouse culture, planting out in the garden as soon as danger of frost is over.

grahami. Strong-growing, to 5 ft. high. Flowers lilac or rose, the middle of the upper lip* marked orange or yellow.

pinnatus. Strong-growing, to 4 ft. high. Flowers 1½ in. across, lower lip lilac or purplish, upper lip usually paler, lower part of upper lip marked yellow which is again spotted or marked purple toward the base. The colors vary considerably. Stamens* prominent.

retusus. Grows to 2½ ft. high. Flowers to 1¾ in. across, usually deep rose, the upper lip* marked orange, except for the margin.

wisetonensis. Hybrid between *S. pinnatus* and *S. grahami.* Growing to 4 ft. high. Flowers white, blue, pink or brownish, the middle of the upper lip* streaked yellow. The most widely grown species and having many fine, colored vars.

SCHIZOBASOPSIS (sky-zo-ba-zop'sis). Also known as *Bowiea.* South African bulbous plants of the lily family, comprising only one species, **S. volubilis**, which is a perennial with a thick underground bulb about 5 in. across which produces offsets.* The center of the bulb sends up each year a long, twining, much-branched, green stem, with a few scale-like leaves that quickly drop off. Flowers greenish-white. It is an interesting plant for the greenhouse or may be grown outdoors in the South. It requires a dry atmosphere and should be grown in potting mixture* 6. Propagated by seeds or division of the bulb. Bulbs should be dried off during the summer months and re-potted in Oct. when they should be kept well watered. The plant is one of the most perfectly adapted drought-resistant species known. Its large bulb has been known to put forth an annual growth while stored on a museum shelf for four consecutive years. (*Schizobasopsis* is from the Greek meaning like the genus *Schizobasis,* which is of no hort. interest.)

SCHIZOCARP. A dry fruit, really a compound fruit composed of several 1-seeded fruits which do not split themselves, but split from each other. Many plants in the mallow family bear schizocarps.

SCHIZOCENTRON (sky-zo-sen'tron). Mex-

---

* Special articles on the subjects indicated by an asterisk (*) will be found at the words so marked.

ican creeping perennial herbs of the family Melastomaceae, comprising only one species, **S. elegans** (also known as *Heterocentron elegans*). It is a much-branched, creeping perennial, which roots at the joints, forming thick mats. Leaves stalked, small, ovalish, to ½ in. long. Flowers solitary, on short, slender stalks, purple, 1 in. across. Much grown as a basket plant in the greenhouse. Propagated by seeds or cuttings, and grown in potting mixture* 3. (*Schizocentron* is from the Greek for split and spur, in allusion to a technical character of the anthers.*)

SCHIZOCODON (sky-zo-kō'don). Japanese hardy evergreen shrubs, comprising 1–2 species of the family Diapensiaceae, and growing only a few inches high. Leaves basal, stalked, roundish-heart-shaped at base, sometimes bronzy, leathery, the margins wavy and coarsely toothed. Flowers deep rose, pink, or white, 4–6 borne on leafless stalks, nodding. Calyx of 5 sepals. Corolla funnel-shaped and fringed. Stamens* 5. Fruit a 3-celled capsule. (*Schizocodon* is from the Greek for cut and bell, in allusion to the fringed corolla.)

These plants are rarely seen in gardens, but make useful rock garden plants in partially shaded positions. Propagated by division of roots in April. They should be grown in equal parts of sandy peat and leaf mold and watered freely in dry weather. They should be protected during winter.

macrophyllus = *S. soldanelloides.*

soldanelloides. Fringed galax. Fringe-bell. Tufted* plant growing only a few inches high. Leaves basal, stalked, roundish, leathery, the margins coarsely toothed. Flowers to 1 in., nodding, deep rose, shading to white at edges. Early spring. Considered by some as belonging to *Shortia.*

SCHIZONOTUS. *See* HOLODISCUS and SORBARIA.

SCHIZOPETALON (sky-zo-pet′a-lon). Chilean half-hardy annuals, comprising about 5 species of the family Cruciferae, of erect habit, growing 1 ft. or more high. Leaves alternate,* ovalish, the margins wavy or deeply cut into lobes. Flowers white or purple, almond-scented, in long racemes, each flower stalk in the axil* of a leafy bract. Calyx of 4 sepals. Corolla of 4 petals, fringed. Stamens* 6, 2 short, 4 long. Fruit a 2-celled capsule.* (*Schizopetalon* is from the Greek for cut and petals, in allusion to the fringed petals.)

These plants are grown in the cool greenhouse, or as tender annuals in the border, for their fragrant, mostly night-blooming, white flowers. Propagated by seeds. *See* ANNUALS.

walkeri. Growing to 1 ft. high, of weak habit. Leaves ovalish, 4–5 in. long, rough, margins wavy and cut. Flowers white, almond-scented, night-fragrant, in terminal racemes.

SCHIZOPHRAGMA (sky-zo-frag′ma). Asiatic woody vines of the family Saxifragaceae, only **S. hydrangeoides** of the three known species likely to be cult. It much resembles *Hydrangea petiolaris* and is often mistaken for that plant. It is a high-climbing vine, often 30 ft. long, with opposite,* nearly round leaves, 3–4 in. wide, pale on the under side and toothed. Flowers white, in loose, terminal, more or less flat-topped clusters (corymbs*). Central flowers fertile, small, composed of 4–5 sepals, 4–5 petals, and 10 stamens.* Outer marginal flowers showy, sterile, consisting of only 1 large white sepal. (*Hydrangea petiolaris* has several sepals in its sterile marginal flowers.) Jap. July. Hardy from zone* 3 southward. The vine climbs by aerial rootlets, but it needs support or it will trail on the ground and do poorly. Propagated by seeds or by layers. (*Schizophragma* is from the Greek to cleave and wall, in allusion to the splitting of its capsules.*)

SCHIZOSTYLIS (sky-zo-sty′lis). South African tender perennial herbs, comprising 2 species, belonging to the Iris family. Rootstocks thick and fleshy. Leaves narrow, sword-shaped. Flowers red, borne at the top of stalk about 1 ft. long, enclosed in a large membranous bract (spathe*). Fruit a 3-celled capsule. (*Schizostylis* is from the Greek for to cut and style, in allusion to the thread-like segments of the style.)

Much cult. in the greenhouse for late-autumn flowering, and outdoors in mild climates. Propagated by division of the rootstocks in early spring. They require plenty of water during growing period.

coccinea. Crimson flag. Kafir lily. Growing 1–2 ft. high. Leaves 18 in. long and narrow. Flowers red, to 2 in. across, the tube straight and about 1 in. long.

SCHLUMBERGERA (shlum-ber-ger′a). A small genus of Brazilian cacti, related to *Zygocactus* (which see), one of them **S. gaertneri,** the Easter cactus, a favorite house plant. Stems upright, the branches drooping and furnished with oblongish, flattish joints, 2–3½ in. long; the joints with beard-like, yellowish-brown bristles. Flowers scarlet, about 2½ in. long, followed by a red fruit. Some prefer to call the Easter cactus *Rhipsalidopsis gaertneri,* and the closely related Christmas cactus *Schlumbergera truncata,* neither proposal here adopted. *See* ZYGOCACTUS. Its cult. is the same as for *Zygocactus.* (Named for Frederick Schlumberger, a Belgian horticulturist.) For **S. bridgesi,** see ZYGOCACTUS.

schoenantha, -us, -um (skee-nan′tha). With a reed-like flower.

schoenoprasa, -us, -um (skee-no-pray′za). Rush-like or reed-like.

SCHOLAR-TREE. *See* SOPHORA JAPONICA.

SCHOTIA (shot′i-a). An unimportant genus of African shrubs or small trees of the pea family, but the two below grown in Fla. and similar climates for ornament. Leaves alternate,* compound,* the leaflets arranged feather-fashion, without an odd one at the end. Flowers not pea-like, the 5 petals slightly unequal, and sometimes shorter than

---

* Special articles on the subjects indicated by an asterisk (*) will be found at the words so marked.

the colored calyx.* Stamens* 10, nearly free. Fruit an oblongish pod (legume*). (Named for Richard Schot, who traveled with Jacquin when the latter was exploring in America.)

Both those below are grown on a variety of soils in Fla. and southern Calif. Their rather large clusters (panicles*) of pink or red flowers, in early spring, are handsome.

brachypetala. A small tree, not over 20 ft. high. Leaflets 8–10, oblongish. Flowers crimson, most of the color coming from the calyx, which exceeds the small petals. South Africa.

latifolia. Kaffir-bean tree. A tree 20–30 ft. high. Leaflets 4–8, ovalish or roundish, 1–2½ in. long, the main leafstalk narrowly winged. Flowers pinkish, the clusters much-branched, the petals longer than the calyx.* South Africa.

SCIADOPITYS. See UMBRELLA PINE.

SCILLA (sill'a). Squill. A large genus of bulbous herbs of the lily family, most of the 100 known species from the temperate regions of Eurasia, and several cult. for their cheery, mostly early spring bloom. Leaves narrow, almost grass-like in some species, basal, usually appearing with the bloom. Flowers small, blue, white, or purple, bell-shaped, in a terminal cluster (raceme*) at the end of a naked stalk which arises from the leaf cluster. Corolla segments 6, not actually joined but apparently so. Stamens* 6. Fruit a 3-lobed or 3-angled capsule.* (*Scilla* is the old Latin and Greek name for these plants.) *See also* URGINEA. The second and third species are by some considered as of the genus *Endymion*. The attempt to force squills in the greenhouse, as can easily be done with hyacinth and tulip, usually ends in failure. For outdoor culture *see* below.

amoena. Star hyacinth. Not over 6 in. high, the leaves nearly ¾ in. wide. Flowers blue or whitish, nearly ¾ in. wide, usually only 4–6 in the cluster. Central Eu.

campanulata = *Scilla hispanica.*

hispanica. Spanish bluebell. Spanish jacinth. At least 12 in. high, sometimes more, the leaves nearly 1 in. wide. Flowers blue, nearly 1 in. wide, and a fine plant for the blue garden (which see) in the typical form. Clusters 12–15-flowered. Spain and Portugal. The *var.* **alba** has white flowers. A good pink-flowered form is the variety Rosalind. *See* PINK GARDEN. Other fine hort. forms are Blue King, Blue Queen, Excelsior, La Grandesse, and Rose Queen. *Scilla hispanica* is sometimes called *S. campanulata.*

nonscripta. The common bluebells of England, also called wood hyacinth. Not over 1 ft. high, the leaves about ½ in. wide. Flowers fragrant, blue, in 6–12-flowered clusters, the corolla more or less cylindric, about ½ in. wide. Eu. Often known as *S. nutans,* and a fine plant for the blue garden (which see). Blush Queen is a good pink-flowered hort. variety. *See* PINK GARDEN.

nutans = *Scilla nonscripta.*

peruviana. Cuban lily. A showy squill from the Mediterranean region, but mistakenly named as from Peru. Leaves nearly 1 in. wide. Flowers purple or reddish (white in a hort. variety), about ½ in. long, in handsome clusters of 50 or more flowers.

sibirica. Siberian squill. About 4–6 in. high, the leaves about ½ in. wide. Flowers nodding, deep blue, about ½ in. wide, rarely more than 3–5 to a cluster. *See* BLUE GARDEN. Eurasia. A good, early-flowering bulb for the rock garden.

verna. Sea onion. Not over 6 in. high. Leaves nearly ¾ in. wide. Flowers about ½ in. wide, blue, fragrant, the clusters (racemes*) branched. Western Eu.

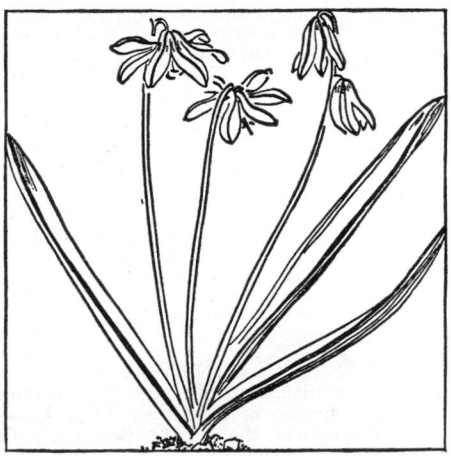

Scilla sibirica

SQUILL CULTURE

Scillas are easily grown and increase rapidly in rich, sandy soil, preferably in partial shade. The low-growing early kinds, such as *S. sibirica,* should be planted in hundreds or thousands beneath spring-flowering, deciduous shrub and trees, at the edge of woodland or in the rock garden. *S. sibirica* will thrive under evergreen trees where little else will survive. The tall, late-blooming bluebell type, forms of *S. nonscripta* and *S. hispanica,* are fine in wide plantations in open woodlands or set along the edges of fern borders. They also make good carpet plants for beds of May tulips. Plant from September through October, setting the bulbs three times their own depth in the soil and 3 or 4 inches apart. The different species flower from March well into May. They are easily increased by bulblets* from the older bulbs taken in autumn. An occasional top-dressing of old manure or good soil is beneficial in the fall. — L. B. W.

scilloides (sill-loy'deez, but *see* OïDES). Like a squill (*Scilla*).

SCINDAPSUS (sin-dap'sus). Ivy arum. Also known as *Pothos.* Tender, climbing, perennial herbs, comprising about 20 species of the family Araceae, natives of the East Indies and Malaya. They have small roots on their stems, similar to the English ivy, by means of which they climb. Leaves simple, roundish, or heart-shaped, 6–18 in. long, usu-

---

* Special articles on the subjects indicated by an asterisk (*) will be found at the words so marked.

ally variegated and lobed. Flowers in spikes enclosed in a spathe.* For details *see* ARACEAE. Fruit a berry. (*Scindapsus* is an old Greek name for some other plant.) The second species is rather widely cultivated, and should be grown in the warm greenhouse. Propagated by rootstocks in Feb. or Mar. Soil should be composed of equal parts of rough peat, sphagnum* moss, charcoal, and coarse sand.

aureus. Hunter's robe. Colombo agent. Devil's-ivy. Tall, climbing plant. Leaves ovalish or broadly lance-shaped, to 18 in. long and 12 in. wide, sometimes lobed, marked pale yellow. Flowers in spikes enclosed in a spathe.* Solomon Islands. The *var.* wilcoxi has the variegations of the leaf more sharply defined than in the type.

pictus. Growing to 40 ft. high. Leaves ovalish to 6 in. long and 3 in. wide, one side of the blade larger than the other, bright green, with darker green spots. Flowers in spikes enclosed in a white spathe,* about 3 in. long. East Indies. The *var.* argyraeus, the silver vine, has heart-shaped leaves marked with silvery-white spots on the upper side. It is the usual form in cult.

SCION = Cion.

SCIRPUS (skir′pus). Bulrush. Aquatic, or marsh, perennial, grass-like herbs, comprising about 200 species of the family Cyperaceae, found throughout the world. Rootstocks fibrous, fleshy, or tuberous. Leaves grass-like, in 3 rows, sheathing the stem, the margins finely toothed. Flowers numerous, in club-like spikes or terminal clusters. See CYPERACEAE. (*Scirpus* is from the Latin for bulrush.) For the "bulrush" of Moses, *see* CYPERUS PAPYRUS.

A few species only in cultivation, generally grown for ornament in the bog or water garden. Sometimes used for thatching houses in Eu. Propagated by seeds or division of rootstocks.

cernuus. Also known as *Isolepis gracilis*. Densely tufted plant, with thin, fibrous roots. Stems to 1 ft. high, round, slender, and drooping. Leaves scale-like at the base of the stem. Flowers in small spikes. Eu. This species makes attractive pot plants if kept in a damp condition.

tabernaemontani. Strong-growing plant to 2 ft. or more high. Leaves few, sheathing the base of the stem. Flowers in terminal clusters of small spikes. Eu. There is a variety with white-banded stems.

tuberosus = *Eleocharis tuberosa*.

SCITAMINEAE. An old, and with some a still current, name for a large group of plants here considered as belonging to the families Cannaceae, Marantaceae, Musaceae, and Zingiberaceae. *See* these families.

Sclarea (sklair-ee′a). A pre-Linnaean* name for the clary, in allusion to its bright flowers. *See* SALVIA SCLAREA.

SCLERANTHUS ANNUUS = Knawel, which see in the list at WEEDS.

SCLEROCACTUS (skleer-o-kak′tus). Two species of globe-like, very spiny cacti from the southwestern U.S., one of them, S. whip-

plei, cult. in the desert garden, or in the greenhouse. The plant body is nearly globe-shaped, about 3 in. wide, occasionally nearly cylindric and 4–6 in. long. There are 13–15 ribs, each furnished with clusters of spines. Spine-clusters with usually 4 central, sometimes hooked spines, and 7–11 divaricate spines which are not hooked. Flowers about 1½ in. wide, purple or lavender. Fruit scaly and fibrous. Colo., Utah, and northern Ariz. (*Sclerocactus* is from the Greek for hard or tough, and *Cactus*, apparently in allusion to the spines.)

SCOKE = *Phytolacca americana*.

Scolopendrium (sko-lo-pen′dri-um). An old generic name for the hartstongue fern. *See* PHYLLITIS.

SCOLYMUS (skoll′i-mus). Annual, biennial or perennial herbs, comprising 3 or 4 species of the family Compositae, found in the Mediterranean region. They are strong-growing and have a thick, sometimes edible, taproot.* Stems much-branched. Leaves alternate,* much-cut, with spiny margins. Flowers in heads, ray and disk florets all long, yellow. Fruit 1-celled, 1-seeded. (*Scolymus* is the old Greek name for the species below.)

Not much in cultivation, but S. *hispanicus* is grown for its roots which are similar in flavor to the oyster plant. Propagated by seeds sown where required to mature, ⅛ in. deep, thinning out to 12 in. apart.

hispanicus. Spanish oyster plant. Golden thistle. Strong-growing biennial, to 2½ ft. high. Root to 1 ft. long and 1 in. thick. Stems much-branched. Leaves lobed, the margins spiny and thistle-like. Flowers in small heads, yellow. S. Eu. For a related, also edible plant, *see* SALSIFY.

scoparia, -us, -um (sko-pair′i-a). Broom-like.

scopulina, -us, -um (skop-u-ly′na). Twiggy.

scopulorum (skop-you-lor′um). Of the rocks; sometimes used as a specific name for plants from the Rocky Mountains.

SCORCH. A symptom of some plant trouble caused by hot weather, insufficient water, girdling roots, etc. Leaves of broad-leaved plants typically have browning between the veins and around the edge of the leaves. The conifers start turning brown at the tip of the needles and the discoloration gradually progresses down the needle. Plants which have been moved recently and those in more exposed locations usually scorch first.

There are a number of plastic-like materials on the market which can be mixed with water and sprayed on plants to prevent water loss from the leaves and thus help prevent scorch.

scorodoprasa, -us, -um (score-ro-do-pray′-sa). Resembling garlic.

SCORPIOID. Coiled, and with the flower cluster usually 1-sided, as in many forget-me-nots; coiled like a scorpion's tail.

* Special articles on the subjects indicated by an asterisk (*) will be found at the words so marked.

scorpioides (score-pi-oy′deez, but *see* OïDES). Scorpion-like; *i.e.*, scorpioid.*

SCORPION GRASS. See FORGET-ME-NOT.

SCORPION SENNA = *Coronilla Emerus*.

SCORZONERA (skor-zo-neer′ra). A genus of over 100 species of chiefly perennial Old World herbs of the family Compositae, only one, **S. hispanica**, the black salsify, of any garden interest. It is a secondary root vegetable, the foliage also sometimes used for salad. It is a perennial herb, 15–24 in. high, with a deep, tapering, white-fleshed, but black-skinned root, used as is common salsify, and thought to be superior to it by some. Stems much-branched. Leaves alternate,* clasping, more or less lance-shaped, or narrower, often dissected or lobed. Flower heads solitary, long-stalked, yellow (lavender in common salsify). Eu. The plant, introduced into England in 1576, is little known in the U.S. and is grown much like common salsify (which see), but is more difficult to raise. While a true perennial it is raised as an annual or biennial, the seeds being sown only after the ground is warm. (*Scorzonera* is from an old French word for serpent, the black salsify being a reputed cure for snake bites.)

SCOTCH. As an adjective *Scotch* has been applied to several things of garden interest. Those in this book and the proper citations to where they are noted in detail are:
Scotch broom = *Cytisus scoparius* (*see* BROOM); **Scotch crocus** = *Crocus biflorus;* **Scotch curlies** = Scotch kale (*see* KALE); **Scotch heath** = *Erica cinerea;* **Scotch kale** (*see* KALE); **Scotch marigold** = *Calendula officinalis;* **Scotch pine** = *Pinus sylvestris* (*see* PINE); **Scotch pink** = *Dianthus plumarius;* **Scotch rose** = *Rosa spinosissima;* **Scotch soot** (*see* SOOT); **Scotch thistle** = *Onopordum Acanthium*.

SCOURING RUSH = *Equisetum hyemale*.

SCREE. See Moraine at ROCK GARDEN.

SCREEN PLANTING. If the area to be screened and the space available for screen planting are small, as on a city or suburban lot, the most effective planting screen may be a high hedge (*see* HEDGES). On larger spaces the screen should be a mass planting of conifers or mixed conifers and deciduous trees. Conifers have the advantage of making an effective screen at all seasons of the year, and pines, with their rounded tops, make a more solid mass to the limit of their height than spiry-topped firs or spruces. See EVERGREENS. If the screen is to serve as a windbreak, a very important question in many localities, and especially near the seashore, blue spruce and Austrian pines are favorites and, in some localities, the Japanese black pine has proved to have remarkable resisting power to ocean winds. In similar conditions it is likely that *Cryptomeria* would be a good windbreak if its cost did not prohibit its use in sufficient quantities.

In many localities windbreaks are necessary to protect houses, orchards, or crops. Deciduous trees make good windbreaks where there is room to plant enough of them, more especially as a windbreak, to be efficient, is not necessarily tight. Two rows of trees staggered in any convenient alignment and 15 ft. or more apart, depending on the growth of trees and time allowed for the windbreak to become effective, may serve, but it would be better to plant more rows, especially as the trees protect each other from the winds. Trees native to the region are usually desirable as being acclimated. Windbreaks* should not be planted so as to interfere with a normal circulation of air. *See* TREES.

SCREW PINE. See PANDANUS.

SCROPHULARIA (skroff-you-lair′i-a). Figwort. Annual or perennial herbs, comprising about 150 species of the family Scrophulariaceae, found throughout the northern hemisphere, generally in damp places. They are of erect habit, growing from 2–10 ft. high, usually strong-smelling. Leaves generally opposite,* simple, ovalish, the margins toothed. Flowers small, greenish-yellow or purple, in loose, terminal branching clusters. Calyx of 5 sepals. Corolla tubular, slightly irregular. Stamens* 2 long, 2 short, and 1 sterile (staminode*). Fruit a 2-celled capsule,* the seeds dispersed through pores. (*Scrophularia* was named from its supposed use in the cure of scrofula.) Not generally cult. as they are regarded as weeds or wild garden plants. Propagated by seeds or division of roots.

aquatica. Strong-growing perennial, to 4 ft. high, with square stems. Leaves smooth, shiny, ovalish but heart-shaped at base. Flowers purple, in loose-branching clusters, to 2 ft. long. Wet places, Eu. and western As.

lanceolata. Strong-growing perennial, to 6 ft. high, covered with fine hairs. Leaves broadly lance-shaped, short-stalked. Margins toothed. Flowers green or purplish, in long branching clusters. Northeastern N.A.

leporella = *Scrophularia lanceolata*.

marilandica. Perennial, growing to 8 ft. high, the stems smooth and grooved. Leaves broadly lance-shaped, about 5 in. long, with thin stalks. Flowers greenish-purple, ¾ in. long, in long branching clusters. Eastern N.A.

SCROPHULARIACEAE (skroff-you-lair-i-ā′see-ee). The figwort, snapdragon, or foxglove family (175 genera and over 4000 species) contains many hardy garden plants, a few shrubs and trees, and several plants extensively grown for ornament in greenhouses. It contains no fruits or vegetables, but many are poisonous (not to the touch), and a few yield valuable medicines, notably *Digitalis* (*see* FOXGLOVE).

Among its more notable, mostly herbaceous, genera for the outdoor garden are: *Antirrhinum* (*see* SNAPDRAGON), which is also forced, *Alonsoa, Celsia, Chelone, Collinsia, Digitalis* (*see* FOXGLOVE), *Erinus, Leucophyllum, Linaria, Nemesia* (tender annuals), *Mimulus, Pentstemon, Scrophularia, Synthy-*

---

* Special articles on the subjects indicated by an asterisk (*) will be found at the words so marked.

ris, Torenia (tender annuals), *Verbascum* (some weedy), *Veronica* (includes, also, tender shrubs from New Zealand), *Veronicastrum, Wulfenia,* and *Zaluzianskya.* Another group of herbs of somewhat difficult culture comprises *Castilleja, Orthocarpus,* and *Pedicularis.*

The leading genera for greenhouse culture (or for frost-free regions outdoors) are: *Angelonia, Calceolaria* (a popular florists' flower), *Cymbalaria* (the Kenilworth ivy), *Diascia* (also outdoors), *Isoplexis, Maurandia, Phygelius, Rehmannia, Russelia,* and *Veronica* (the tender New Zealand shrubs).

The only other cult. genera are *Mazus,* which are low, mat-forming herbs, and *Paulownia,* the only hardy tree of the family in the North.

Leaves opposite,* alternate* or whorled. Flowers mostly irregular,* often notably so, and 2-lipped,* usually very showy, and mostly in clusters, rarely solitary. Many of the cult. genera are extremely handsome, especially the foxglove, *Calceolaria,* snapdragon, and a number of greenhouse plants. Fruit nearly always a dry pod (capsule*), usually many-seeded.

Technical flower characters: Flowers hermaphrodite.* Calyx more or less tubular. 4–5-toothed or divided. Corolla united, its 4–5 lobes nearly equal in a few genera, but notably 2-lipped in many others; nearly always more or less irregular.* Stamens* 4, two shorter than the others. Ovary superior,* mostly 2-celled.

SCRUB OAK = *Quercus ilicifolia, Q. prinoides,* and *Q. dumosa.* See Oak.

SCRUB PALMETTO = *Serenoa repens.*

SCRUB PINE = *Pinus banksiana.* See Pine.

SCUM. The green scum which frequently disfigures the surface of pools or ponds is caused by microscopic algae (*see* Alga), uncounted millions of which constitute the floating scum. Several chemicals will destroy them, but the danger is considerable of destroying goldfish or desirable aquatic plants, unless the chemicals are used in minute concentrations.

Copper sulphate (blue vitriol) is the best, but it must be used with care. The algae are peculiarly sensitive to it and will disappear if a cotton bag containing copper sulphate (a dangerous poison) is dragged through the water. If at all possible, estimate the number of gallons of water to be treated (a gallon is 231 cubic inches, which is approximately a cylinder 7 in. in diameter and 6 in. high).

In using copper sulphate, put the fresh crystals in a cotton bag and tow it in a boat, making several criss-cross passages through the scum-infested water. Note, from the table below, the minute concentrations of copper sulphate that will be effective for the scum. Increasing the concentration may kill fish or valuable plants, neither of which will be in the least injured if the table is followed carefully.

Gallons of water	Drams of copper sulphate needed (16 drams = 1 ounce)
555	1/10
1,110	1/5
2,777	1/2
5,555	1
11,110	2
55,550	5
88,880	16 (*i.e.,* 1 oz.)

While it is difficult to estimate the number of gallons in irregularly shaped pools, and pools of irregular depths, the following table may serve as a guide:

Size of square pools, in feet	Depth 3 ft. Gallons	4 ft. Gallons	5 ft. Gallons
6 × 6	807	1077	1346
8 × 8	1436	1914	2393
10 × 10	2244	2992	3740
12 × 12	3231	4308	5385

SCUPPERNONG = *Vitis rotundifolia.*

SCURFY PEA. See Psoralea.

SCURVY-GRASS. See Cochlearia; also Barbarea verna.

SCUTCH GRASS = *Cynodon Dactylon.*

SCUTELLARIA (skew-te-lair'i-a). Skullcap. Annual or perennial herbs or small shrubs, comprising about 220 species of the mint family, found throughout the world, but chiefly in the temperate regions. Leaves opposite,* simple, sometimes cut into lobes. Margins often toothed. Flowers blue, violet, scarlet, or yellow, 2-lipped,* growing in the axils* of bracts, and arranged in spikes. Calyx bell-shaped, 5-lobed. Corolla tubular, opening into 2 lips. Stamens 4, in pairs, 2 long, 2 short. Fruit 2-celled when young, splitting into 4 nutlets when ripe. (*Scutellaria* is from the Latin for dish, in allusion to the calyx.)

Not generally cult., but grown in the border or rock garden. Propagated by seeds or division of rootstocks. Seeds should be sown in early spring, in sandy soil, 1/8 in. deep, in a cool greenhouse or cold frame, and transplanted to permanent positions as soon as large enough to handle. Division of the rootstocks should be made in March or April.

alpina. Spreading perennial, about 10 in. high, with creeping stems that root at the joints. Leaves small, ovalish, to 1 in. long, slightly toothed. Flowers white and purple, 1 in. long, in thick, terminal racemes.* Eurasia.

baicalensis. Spreading perennial, to 1 ft. high. Leaves lance-shaped. Flowers blue, in racemes.* Eastern As. The *var.* **coelestina** has large, bright blue flowers, 1 in. long.

SCYTHIAN LAMB = *Cibotium Barometz.*

SEA BUCKTHORN = *Hippophaë rhamnoides.*

SEA CAMPION = *Silene maritima.*

SEACOAST GARDENS. See Seaside Gardens.

SEA DAFFODIL = *Pancratium maritimum.*

SEA DAHLIA = *Coreopsis maritima.*

* Special articles on the subjects indicated by an asterisk (*) will be found at the words so marked.

SEA FIG = *Mesembryanthemum crystallinum*.

SEAFORTHIA ELEGANS. *See* ARCHONTOPHOENIX CUNNINGHAMIANA.

SEA GRAPE = *Coccolobis uvifera*.

SEA HOLLY. *See* ERYNGIUM.

SEA HOLLYHOCK = *Hibiscus Moscheutos*.

SEA-ISLAND COTTON = *Gossypium barbadense*.

SEA-KALE (*Crambe maritima*). A little-known vegetable in the U.S., the young, blanched shoots of which are used like asparagus. It is a seacoast perennial from Eu., and with proper care should yield an annual crop for 6–10 years, when the plants should be renewed.

Like rhubarb, it should be put in a part of the garden where it will not be disturbed by spring plowing, as it does not like to be moved once it becomes established. The plants should be at least 3–4 ft. apart each way, as after the cutting season they have a wide spread due to their conspicuous, bluish-green leaves.

Sea-kale

The season for sea-kale is very early in the spring, as the young shoots appear above ground long before the leaves expand. They must be blanched before cutting, and the easiest way to accomplish this is by heaping loose earth over the shoots as they appear. Some growers prefer to cover the shoots with boxes or flower pots, with a cork in the hole in the bottom of the pot. All light must be excluded or blanching will not be complete and the stalks are apt to be tough. (*See* BLANCHING.) Properly grown and blanched sea-kale is delicious. The shoots, which are the young leafstalks, should be about 12 in. high when cut.

The plant needs a deep, rich, heavily manured soil and a reasonable degree of moisture. Its handling is very much the same as for rhubarb (which see). While seeds of it are offered by most dealers, the quickest way to propagate it is by root cuttings.

Strong root cuttings, planted in the spring, if given good cultivation, should be ready for harvesting the following spring. Plants raised from seed, which is easily done if they are handled like early cabbage (which see), will not produce plants fit for cutting short of three years.

The cutting season for sea-kale must stop once the leaves begin to expand. When this happens, the soil used for blanching should be smoothed off and the plant allowed to grow as it will, which means there will be a mass of tough, long, cabbage-like leaves and a cluster of white flowers up to 3 ft. high. During this stage the plant needs no attention beyond cultivation to keep down the weeds and to conserve moisture. Do not cut the foliage down until fall, when the plants should be given a light mulch of strawy manure. The summer growth is important, as upon it depends the growth of the following spring. *See also* KALE.

SEA LAVENDER. *See* LIMONIUM.

SEALWORT = *Polygonatum biflorum*. *See* SOLOMON'S-SEAL.

SEA LYME GRASS = *Elymus arenarius*.

SEA MARIGOLD = *Mesembryanthemum crystallinum*.

SEA ONION = *Urginea maritima* and *Scilla verna*.

SEA PINK. *See* SABATIA, ARMERIA, and LIMONIUM.

SEA POPPY = *Glaucium*.

SEA PURSLANE = *Atriplex hortensis*.

SEASIDE DAISY = *Erigeron glaucus*.

SEASIDE GARDENS. Gardening near the sea, to be successful, requires taking into consideration four important factors — wind, sand, salt spray, and salt fog.

If flowers other than typical salt, shore, or strand plants are desired, windbreaks of evergreen shrubs and hardy growth should be used as a protective barrier. Shade trees, shrubs, buildings, and even natural slopes will, to some extent, protect the plants from intense light and heat. The sandy, porous soil should be mixed with heavier earth, and well-rotted manure added, in order that they may obtain proper nourishment and moisture. If a lawn is desired, a special mixture of "Seashore" lawn grass, composed of deep-rooting varieties, must be used. *See* LAWN. Ordinary lawn grass will not thrive in sandy soil. Four inches of good garden soil, above a two-inch layer of heavy clay, will keep the lawn in good condition. Perennials, such as hollyhocks, foxgloves, Canterbury bells, iris, Oriental poppies, delphiniums, phlox and peonies, do well in mixed beds or borders. Annuals may be used as fillers-in or to provide brilliancy of color. Cornflowers, nasturtiums, petunias, and portulaca, all of which are sun-loving and drought-resistant plants, do well near the shore without protection or special bedding. Roses, hydrangeas, and other shrubs may be grown if well protected from high winds and salt spray.

---

* Special articles on the subjects indicated by an asterisk (*) will be found at the words so marked.

Chief consideration in this article, however, is given to such planting materials as are suited to seashore gardens, without the necessity of preparing special soils and planting conditions.

EASTERN ATLANTIC COAST. Plants must fit both soil and environment, so that each type of seacoast — sand dunes, coastal strip, or brackish marshes, will require a different floral planting, with the exception of such flowers as thrive in more than one kind of soil.

Beach grass makes an excellent sand binder for the dunes and coastal strips, as does also sea lyme grass. Holly, black oak, beach plum, wild cherry, California privet, tamarisk, Jack

Making a garden near the sea must begin with a protecting plantation to shut off high winds and salt spray.

pine, with its twisted, wind-blown branches, and Japanese black pine may be used for hedges and windbreaks, on dunes or beach. Pitch pine may be planted as a hedge or mixed with Jack pine as a forest. One of the best of all trees, almost on the dunes, is the London plane. Flowering or fruiting shrubs for the shore are *Cornus baileyi*, bayberry, the common barberry, elderberry, groundsel bush, tamarisk, Scotch broom, *Rosa rugosa*, and sumac. Farther back may be planted high-bush blueberry, sweet pepperbush, arrow-wood, and wild roses. If the coastal strip is low and moist, white swamp honeysuckle may be planted where it has some protection. Other moist-ground plants with a fair resistance to salt spray and fog are pin oaks, red maple, virburnum, and witch-hazel. Mugo pines do well in practically all soil conditions along the shore and are easily naturalized.

Among herbs the sandworts are useful for dry, sandy spots where, if allowed to spread, they will form thick mats closely covered in spring and summer with small, white blossoms. Dusty miller thrives on sand and

gravel alike. Sea pinks (*Armeria*) or sea lavender (*Limonium*), in shades of white, yellow, rose, lavender, and blue, require the usual culture for annuals and perennials. But they make excellent cut flowers and may be dried for use with everlastings. In the East, sand verbenas must be treated as annuals, doing best near the shore when sown in the open. Both the yellow and pink may be used. Sea poppies (*Glaucium*), with their golden or orange blossoms, grow wild in a few places in the eastern coastal section.

Brackish marshes are lovely with plantings of Turk's-cap lilies, seaside goldenrod, rose mallow, and blue chicory. Bracken and marsh ferns require plenty of moisture and not too much salt. Hardy buckthorn may be planted along the edge of a marsh.

PACIFIC COAST. Due to the difference in climatic conditions, many plants are available for naturalization on the seacoasts of the Pacific that are too tender to stand the rigors of an eastern winter. Likewise hedges for protection are desirable, but not absolutely essential. Privet, *Rosa rugosa* (also hardy eastward), the common barberry, sea buckthorn, and many native shrubs may be used as hedges. The beach grass makes an excellent soil binder. Sand verbenas, beach pea (*Lathyrus littoralis*), seaside daisy or beach aster, cerastiums, native sedums, and California wild flowers of many sorts, planted as annuals, may be used as sand plants. *Coreopsis maritima*, the sea dahlia, also likes sandy places. A creeping rock spray (*Cotoneaster horizontalis*) is beautiful when covering a rocky coast. Sea campion (*Silene maritima*) is a hardy perennial which gives best results when used in the rock garden or border. *Mesembryanthemum*, the ice-plant, is commonly naturalized along the shores of southern California, but may be grown as an annual farther north.

SUB-TROPICAL. This includes the south Atlantic Coast, the Gulf shore region, and southern California. Among the many trees and shrubs for seaside gardens are seaside mahoe, *Ficus aurea*, *Pittosporum Tobira*, coconut palm and silver palmetto, the sea grape, the sea urchin, and the caiuput- or punk-tree, which is one of the most easily naturalized. Good hedge material is the coco plum, the hardy orange (*Poncirus trifoliata*), the Australian pines (*Casuarina*), and in California, especially for windbreaks and ornament, *Atriplex breweri* and *Lavatera assurgentiflora*. A fine, southern rose mallow (*Hibiscus grandiflorus*) is a good plant for the coastal lowlands, while centipede-grass will quickly cover the sandy places with thick, matlike growth. This requires no cutting. The sea dahlia likes a sandy spot, while the sea holly is an excellent border plant. *See* the body of the ENCYCLOPEDIA for cultural notes and hardiness of the plants suited for seaside gardens. *See also* SAND GARDEN.

SEASIDE GOLDENROD = *Solidago sempervirens*. See GOLDENROD.

SEASIDE MAHOE = *Thespesia populnea*.

SEASIDE PAINTED-CUP = *Castilleja latifolia.*

SEASIDE PLUM = *Coccolobis uvifera.*

SEASONAL GARDENS. Planning the flower garden so that most of the bloom will come at definite seasons is necessary for those who spend more time in the country during one season than another. For the convenience of such seasonal gardeners, the more important plants flowering at each season have been grouped under the headings SPRING GARDEN, SUMMER GARDEN, AUTUMN GARDEN, and WINTER GARDEN. *See* these special articles, or, if you want particular data for any one month, *see* EVERBLOOMING GARDEN.

SEASONAL WORK. *See* GARDEN CALENDAR.

SEA SQUILL = *Urginea maritima.*

SEA URCHIN = *Hakea laurina.*

SEA URCHIN CACTUS = *Echinopsis.*

SEAWEED. For its use as manure *see* MANURE.

SEA WORMWOOD = *Artemisia canadensis.*

SEBESTEN = *Cordia Sebestena.*

Sebestena (seb-es-tee'na). An Arabic name for an evil-smelling plant.

sebifera, -us, -um (seb-biff'er-ra). Tallow-bearing.

SECALE. *See* RYE.

SECATEURS. *See* No. 10 at TOOLS AND IMPLEMENTS.

SECHIUM (seek'i-um). A single, rather important species of tendril-bearing, perennial, tropical American vines of the family Cucurbitaceae, known to science as **S. edule**, but widely grown for its edible fruit or young root tubers under a variety of names, of which the chief are chayote and huisquil. Other names for it are chuchu, Christophine, cahiota, vegetable pear, and, in La., mirliton. It is a quick-growing vine with herbaceous stems, and alternate,* broadly triangular or ovalish leaves, 7–10 in. long, and shallowly lobed. Flowers small, whitish, unisexual* (for details *see* CUCURBITACEAE), the male flowers in clusters, the female solitary or two, in the leaf axils.* Fruit generally pear-shaped, furrowed, green or white, 3–4 in. long, fleshy, enclosing a single seed, 1–2 in. long. (*Sechium* is from a W.I. vernacular name for the plant.)

CHAYOTE CULTURE

The plant can be grown as a perennial, which it really is, if the ground does not freeze more than an inch or two. This confines its cult. as a perennial mostly to zones* 7, 8, and 9. It may be grown as an annual farther north, but it needs heat and a long growing season and may not mature fruit if planted too far north.

It is a scrambling vine for which a support must be provided, and the plants should not be closer than 10 ft. apart each way. Sometimes it produces only male or only female flowers, so it is safer to have several vines together rather than one, which may turn out to be of one sex only, although this is not usual.

If planted in good rich soil, each vine will produce from 50–100 fruits in a single season. They are mostly used boiled, like squash, and are very popular throughout the tropics. Where the plant is really perennial, and there is continuous growth, as in the tropics, the large tuber produces smaller ones which are harvested and used like potatoes.

The chayote may be started from seed, the whole 1-seeded fruit usually being planted, the stem end being left slightly exposed. Plant the fruit where the vine is to stand if in the region where chayote may be left out all the year.

secunda, -us, -um (see-kun'da). Secund; *i.e.*, one-sided; applied to flower clusters, or sometimes to leaves, when the flowers or leaves are arranged only on one side of the stalk.

secundata, -us, -um (see-kun-day'ta). *See* SECUNDA.

secundiflora, -us, -um (see-kun-di-flow'ra). With a 1-sided flower cluster.

SEDGE. *See* CAREX.

SEDGE FAMILY = Cyperaceae.

SEDUM (see'dum). Stonecrop. Low-growing, annual or perennial, fleshy herbs, chiefly perennial, comprising about 500 species, belonging to the family Crassulaceae, found through the temperate and colder regions of the northern hemisphere. They are diverse in habit, some creeping, with the stems rooting at the joints or trailing, some tufted,* others in rosettes, while still others are upright. Leaves alternate,* or opposite* or in whorls.* Margins sometimes cut. Flowers white, yellow, pink, red, or blue in terminal clusters. Calyx of 4–5 sepals. Corolla of 4–8 petals. Stamens* double the number of petals. Fruits of 4–5, 1-celled follicles,* each with several seeds. (*Sedum* is from the Latin to sit, in allusion to the way they grow on rocks and walls.)

Sedums and the related genus *Gormania* are particularly adapted to the rock garden, but a few species can be used in the flower border. Easily cult. in ordinary garden soil. Good drainage is essential with most species, as they do not thrive in wet positions during winter. Propagated by seeds, division of roots, cuttings, and leaves. Seeds should be sown ⅛ in. deep, in sandy soil, in the cool greenhouse or cold frame in early spring. Division of the roots should be made in Sept., Mar. or Apr. Cuttings may be made during spring and summer. These should be inserted in sandy soil in cold frame or cool greenhouse. It is not necessary to shade from sun except for the species having thin leaves.

acre. Wall pepper. Mossy stonecrop. Golden moss. Gold-dust. Love-entangle. Low, evergreen, creeping perennial, to 5 in. high, forming a carpet. Leaves alternate, small, triangular to ⅛ in. long, fleshy, crowded on the stem. Flowers bright yellow in terminal clusters. Especially suitable for dry places. Eu.

---

* Special articles on the subjects indicated by an asterisk (*) will be found at the words so marked.

and As. June. The *var.* aureum is a weaker plant, the leaves of which are yellow in the spring. *See* ROCK GARDEN.

adolphi. A fleshy, usually sprawling, evergreen perennial, sometimes bushy. Leaves lance-shaped or broader, about 1½ in. long, yellowish-green and red-margined. Flowers starlike, about ¾ in. wide, in a dense, branched cluster. Mex. Mar.–Apr. Not hardy outdoors.

Aizoon. Strong-growing perennial, to 18 in. high. Rootstocks thick and tuberous. Stems upright, not branched. Leaves alternate,* broadly lance-shaped, to 3 in. long. Margins sharply toothed. Flowers yellow to orange, to ½ in. across, in terminal branching clusters. Siberia and Jap. June–Aug.

alberti. A creeping evergreen perennial, scarcely 2 in. high. Leaves narrowly linear, about ½ in. long. Flowers about ½ in. wide, white. Sinkiang. June.

album. Worm-grass. Creeping evergreen, to 8 in. high. Leaves alternate,* fleshy, cylindrical, to ½ in. long. Flowers white, to ¼ in. across, in terminal branching clusters. Mediterranean region. July. The *var.* murale has purplish leaves and pale pink flowers. *See* ROCK GARDEN.

Anacampseros. Not over 6 in. high, generally procumbent, and with half-evergreen foliage. Leaves alternate,* roundish, gray-green, about 1 in. long. Flowers about ¼ in. wide, pale violet or purplish. Southern Eu. July.

anglicum. Creeping evergreen, forming a carpet, to 2 in. high. Leaves alternate,* fleshy, cylindrical, to ¼ in. long. Flowers white, to ½ in. across. Western Eu. Summer.

arboreum. *See* CRASSULA ARGENTEA.

atlanticum. *See* MONANTHES ATLANTICA.

bifolia. Leaves usually only two, 4–8 in. long, less than ½ in. wide, concave on upper surface, faintly hooded at the tip. Flowers blue (red or white in hort. vars.) in a triangular cluster (raceme*). Southern Eu. Mar.–Apr.

caeruleum. Annual, to 4 in. high. Leaves alternate,* fleshy, ovalish, to ¾ in. long. Flowers blue, marked white at base, to ¼ in. across. Mediterranean region. Summer. *See* ROCK GARDEN.

cauticolum. Not very different from *S. sieboldi,* and distinguished, if at all, by its opposite leaves and more lax, early, flower cluster. Jap. Sept.

crassipes. An unbranched, erect, smooth perennial, 6–12 in. high. Leaves numerous, alternately arranged, about ½ in. long, narrow, toothed in the upper third. Flowers about ½ in. wide, greenish-white, densely crowded in a flat-topped cluster that is 1–1½ in. wide. Eastern As. June.

dasyphyllum. Tufted* evergreen, with slender branches, to 2 in. high. Leaves opposite,* fleshy, cylindrical, to ⅛ in. long. Flowers flesh-color, tinged yellow at the base, ¼ in. across. Eu. and northern Af. June. For cult. *see* ROCK GARDEN.

douglasi. An unbranched evergreen perennial, 6–12 in. high. Leaves numerous, crowded, alternately arranged, very narrow, almost terete,* about ¾ in. long, sometimes red-tinged. Flowers stalkless, about ½ in. wide, yellow, in a lax cluster. Western N.A. June–July.

ellacombianum. Related to *S. Aizoon,* but without the thickened rootstock. It is an unbranched arching perennial, 4–7 in. high. Leaves in a flattened cluster, green, with wavy margins. Flowers about ⅜ in. wide, yellow, in a close, flat cluster. Jap. Aug.–Sept.

ewersi. An unbranched, bluish-green perennial, 6–12 in. high. Leaves oppositely arranged, stalkless, and the stem appearing to pass through the roundish leaves, which are about ¾ in. wide. Flowers about ½ in. wide, purple-pink, in a dense convex cluster (cyme*). Western Himalayas to Mongolia. Aug.–Sept.

fosterianum = *Sedum rupestre fosterianum.*

guatemalense. A creeping or procumbent perennial, rooting at the joints and not hardy in frosty regions. Leaves narrow, cylindrical, about ½ in. long. Flowers about ⅛ in. wide, yellowish-red. Guatemala. May–June.

glaucum = *Sedum hispanicum minus.*

hispanicum. Perennial, but treated as an annual, and growing to 6 in. high. Leaves grayish-green, becoming reddish, crowded on the stem, to ½ in. long. Flowers flesh-pink, to ½ in. across. Southern Eu. and western As. The *var.* minus has bluish foliage. July. For cult. *see* ROCK GARDEN.

kamtschaticum. Erect perennial, growing to 9 in. high. Leaves alternate* or opposite,* ovalish, to 2 in. long, the margins toothed. Flowers orange-yellow, to ¾ in. across. Northeastern As. July–Aug.

lydium. Creeping evergreen, to 3 in. high. Leaves crowded on the stem, fleshy, cylindrical, to ¼ in. long. Flowers white, ¼ in. across. Asia Minor. June.

maximowiczi = *Sedum Aizoon.*

middendorffianum. Perennial, of tufted* habit, to 1 ft. high. Leaves alternate,* lance-shaped, to 1½ in. long, the margins toothed. Flowers yellow, to ¾ in. across. Siberia and Manchuria. June–July.

morganianum. A trailing, pendent plant with many stems and densely clothed with whitish-green, incurved, nearly cylindrical leaves that are about 1 in. long. Flowers red, in a terminal cluster (corymb*). Mex. Not hardy outdoors in frosty regions, but as its stems may droop 2–3 ft., a useful plant for hanging baskets in the cool greenhouse.

nevi. A tufted* perennial not over 4 in. high. Leaves paddle-shaped, about ½ in. long. Flowers about ½ in. wide, white, but the anthers* purple. Va. to Ill. and southward. June.

obtusatum = *Gormania obtusata.*

oppositifolium = *Sedum spurium.*

oreganum = *Gormania oregana.*

pachyphyllum. An evergreen perennial, 3–4 in. high, with fleshy stems that sometimes root at the joints. Leaves red-tipped, blunt, cylindrical, about 1 in. long, pointed upward. Flowers showy, about ½ in. wide, yellow, in a close cluster (cyme*) that is nearly 2 in. wide. Mex. Not hardy outdoors in frosty regions.

pratensis. Leaves 3–6, narrowly strap-shaped, 6–12 in. long, smooth and narrowed both ends. Flowers blue, about ⅕ in. long, in a dense 12–30-flowered cluster (raceme*). Yugoslavia. May.

pruinatum. Evergreen, of spreading habit, to 6 in. high. Leaves grayish-green, alternate* narrow, fleshy, to ¾ in. long. Flowers pale yellow, to ¾ in. across. Portugal. Summer.

pulchellum. Widow's-cross. Flowering moss. Evergreen, growing to 1 ft. high. Leaves crowded on the stems, fleshy, narrow, cylindrical, to ¾ in. long. Flowers purplish, to ½ in. across. Southeastern U.S. June–July.

purdyi. A Californian perennial, 3–4 in. high, the oblonglike leaves about 1 in. long and borne in a flat rosette. Flowers white, about ½ in. wide, grouped in a dense cluster

---

* Special articles on the subjects indicated by an asterisk (*) will be found at the words so marked.

(cyme*). Leaves are credited with proliferation (which see).

reflexum. Yellow stonecrop. Creeping evergreen, forming a carpet. Leaves crowded on the stem, fleshy, narrow, cylindrical, to ½ in. long. Flower stalks to 1 ft. Flowers golden-yellow, to ½ in. across. Eu. Summer. For cult. *see* Rock Garden.

rupestre. Creeping evergreen, forming a carpet. Leaves crowded on the stem, gray-green, narrow, to ¾ in. long. Flowers golden-yellow, to ½ in. across. Eu. Summer. The *var.* **forsterianum** has dark green leaves.

Three common sedums. At the left, *Sedum Telephium;* below, *S. acre;* at the right, *S. pulchellum.*

sarmentosum. Trailing evergreen. Leaves in whorls* of 3, broadly lance-shaped, to 1 in. long. Flowers bright yellow, to ½ in. across. Northern China and Jap. Summer. For cult. *see* Rock Garden; but it can become an invasive weed.

sexangulare. Creeping evergreen, to 4 in. high, forming a carpet. Leaves crowded on the stem, arranged in a spiral, narrow, to ¼ in. across. Eu. Summer. For cult. *see* Rock Garden.

sieboldi. Trailing perennial, to 1 ft. high. Leaves in whorls* of 3, grayish-green, reddish toward the margin, roundish, to 1 in. across. Flowers pink, to ½ in. across. Jap. Late fall, and a handsome plant. *See* Autumn Garden.

spathulifolium. An evergreen perennial, 3–4 in. high, the foliage bluish-green, but often red-tinged. Leaves spoon-shaped, flat, about 1 in. long, in a terminal rosette, those on the flowering shoots oblongish and stalkless. Flowers about ½ in. wide, yellow, in a leafy, flat-topped cluster (cyme*). Western N.A. May–June. There are several vars., one of them with purplish foliage offered as *var.* **purpureum.**

spectabile. Strong-growing perennial, to 2 ft. high. Leaves in whorls of 3, grayish-green, ovalish. Margins of upper part toothed. Flowers pink, to ½ in. across. Jap. and central China. Aug.–Sept. *See* Autumn Garden.

spurium. Strong-growing, creeping evergreen, to 6 in. high. Leaves opposite,* ovalish, 1 in. or more long. Flowers pale pink, to ½ in. across. Caucasus and southwest As. Summer. For cult. *see* Rock Garden. Often called *S. stoloniferum.*

stahli. Evergreen, growing to 8 in. high, slightly hairy. Leaves opposite,* roundish, to ½ in. across. Flowers yellow, to ½ in. across. Mex. Summer and fall.

stoloniferum. *See* Sedum spurium.

Telephium. Orpine. Live-forever. Strong-growing perennial, to 18 in. high. Leaves ovalish, to 3 in. long, the margins toothed. Flowers reddish-purple. Eurasia. Late summer.

ternatum. A native, creeping perennial, the flowering stalks 3–4 in. high. Leaves of lower stems in 3's, the blades oblongish, about ¾ in. long, narrowed at the base. Upper leaves narrower and scattered. Flowers white, ½ in. wide, in a leafy cluster (cyme*). Eastern U.S., mostly in moist rocky places. May–June.

watsoni = *Gormania watsoni.*

weinbergi. *See* Graptopetalum.

SEED. The ripened, fertilized ovule* of a flower, usually in some sort of a fruit (which see), but naked in the pines and related plants. The essential part of a seed is the embryo.* For raising plants from seed *see* Seeds and Seedage.

SEEDAGE. *See* Seeds and Seedage.

SEEDBED. *See* Seeds and Seedage.

SEED COLLECTING. Saving seed from favorite plants or from especially good strains is often desirable, but should be undertaken with an understanding of its potentialities. Many garden flowers will not come true from home-grown seed collections, this being especially true of horticultural varieties among annuals and certain perennials. Most shrub and tree seeds, on the other hand, are reasonably sure to come true to type, and so will some vegetables. But in the latter there is the constant danger of foreign

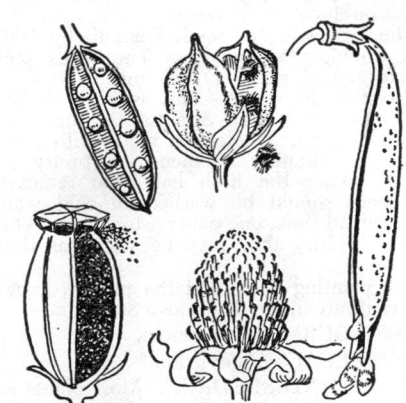

Seed pods of sweet pea (*right*), iris (*upper center*), rose-of-Sharon (*upper left*), poppy (*lower left*), and the fruiting head of zinnia (*lower center*).

pollen* adulterating the population. Only trial and error can tell you which seeds are worth saving and which will probably bring disappointment.

If seeds are to be saved, select the healthiest and finest blooms and allow only these

---

* Special articles on the subjects indicated by an asterisk (*) will be found at the words so marked.

to set seeds. All other flowers on the plant should be pinched off, thus throwing to those that will produce seed all the nourishment possible.

When the fruit is ripe, it should be harvested and brought into a warm, dry place, ready for pulling and cleaning the seed.

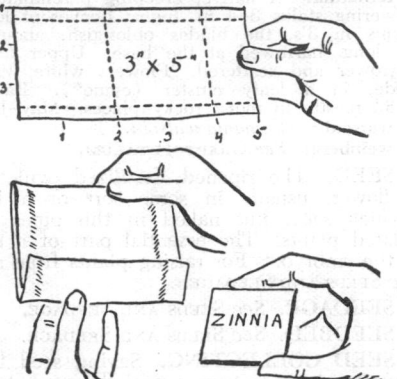

A simple, home-made seed packet, easily made from a piece of paper 3 × 5 in.

This should be done as soon after the fruit will easily release its seeds as possible. The seeds should then be stored in paper packets, or in stoppered bottles if they are to be kept for a long time, and it should be remembered that vermin are fond of most seeds. If paper packets are used, they had better be stored in tin boxes.

The harvesting of seeds from fleshy fruits is a troublesome business. The seeds must be cleaned of pulp or flesh mechanically or by soaking in water. This is often a long and messy job, but essential if the seeds are to be kept. Uncleaned seeds with fleshy parts still clinging to them are pretty apt to rot. After the flesh has been removed, the seeds should be washed in cold water and spread out on papers to dry. When thoroughly dry they may be stored as those above.

For planting seed, and the process known as stratification, *see* SEEDS AND SEEDAGE.

SEED-GERM. *See* EMBRYO.

SEED LEAF. A cotyledon.*

SEEDS AND SEEDAGE. Most plants are raised from seed in spite of many other methods of propagation (which see). The reasons for this are that no other means of increasing one's stock is so easy, and that seeds, because most of them will endure a reasonably long period of dormancy, can be stored and used as wanted, while most cuttings and other methods of vegetative reproduction must be fitted to the seasonal demands of such operations.

While seeds can be kept, they cannot be kept indefinitely and still retain the power to sprout. Much work has been done on the viability of seeds after storage for briefer or longer periods. It is unnecessary to repeat this data here, for it will be found at GARDEN TABLES II. Nor are we here concerned with the number or percentage of average germination of the different sorts of seeds. Few of them have 100% germination chances, and in planting it is always best to allow enough extra seed to take up the inevitable failure of a certain percentage of nearly all varieties to sprout. *See* GARDEN TABLES II.

Nor is it necessary to repeat here the details of the amount of seed needed per acre or for 100 ft. of row in the vegetable garden. All such data will be found at GARDEN TABLES I, where, also, will be found further statistical information on the number of seeds to an ounce or pound.

Here we are concerned with seeds chiefly as they provide the easiest method of increasing or propagating plants — in other words, with their power to germinate. For a simple device for sprouting seeds in the house, *see* PROPAGATING FRAME.

GERMINATION

Most seeds need moisture and darkness in order to sprout, and ordinary soil provides the easiest method of supplying both. But there are times when moisture can be too great or when, because of the fineness of the soil particles, the circulation of air through them is retarded. In ordinary garden soil the conditions seem nearly perfect for the germination of most seeds, especially when these are not too small. But there are certain seeds that will not sprout without much more attention than merely planting them. These are described in detail below.

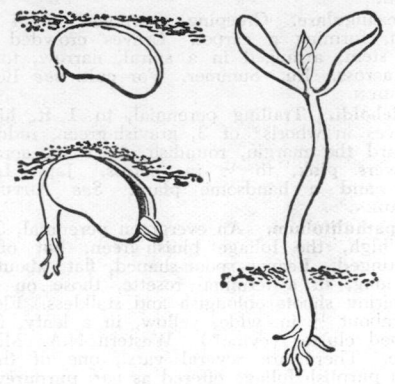

Germination of a bean seed, the final stage being the production of the first pair of leaves (*at right*).

From the practical gardening standpoint we must distinguish among at least three main methods of managing seeds: (1) Those that grow where planted, as do most vegetable and annual flower seeds; (2) those

---

* Special articles on the subjects indicated by an asterisk (*) will be found at the words so marked.

that are planted with the expectation that their seedlings will be several times transplanted before being finally planted; and (3) those seeds that must be stratified.

(1) SEEDS PLANTED WHERE THEY ARE TO STAY. This applies to nearly all the common vegetables and to the seeds of those flower garden annuals which are sown where needed — in other words, the hardy annuals. Tender annuals (see ANNUALS) come under the second category, i.e., those that will be several times transplanted before final planting, and their handling will be described under (2).

For those sown where needed the chief thing to remember is the *depth* to plant. Very fine and small seeds must never be sown with more than a thin layer of soil over them — barely covered, in fact. A good plan is to see that the upper layer of soil for such seeds is finely pulverized, then scatter the seeds, and merely rake them in very gently. Such a method will leave some seeds only partly covered, some shallowly covered, and some not covered at all. Then lightly tamp the soil with the back of a spade or board and this will firm the seeds in the soil (even the uncovered ones) enough so that they will germinate.

These fine seeds are hard to manage as to their early water needs, especially before and just after germination. Being so shallowly planted, they are very likely to become dried out, and to prevent this they should be watered with a very gentle, fine spray, preferably in the late afternoon. A heavy downpour, or water from a hose, will, of course, wash them out. But a fine spray from a fine-rose watering can or syringe will be just what they need.

For the usual run of more ordinary and larger seeds there is much less trouble about the depth to plant them. A fair general rule is to plant them 2–3 times as deep as their own diameter, whether in drills* or sown broadcast. Variations from this rule are noted in certain cases at the description of the different plants needing special depths in this book. Another general caution in the usual handling of seeds is to plant them somewhat more shallowly in heavy (i.e., clay) soils and a little deeper in sandy ones, the obvious reasons being that the sandy soils are drier and heavy soils moister, and the ideal condition we are seeking is just the medium amount of moisture necessary for germination.

The germination of most such generally handled seeds will ordinarily occur in a few days, and in the case of very tardy ones in from 2–3 weeks. For some vegetable seeds that are both small and slow to sprout it is a good plan to plant a quickly germinating seed (like radish) with the slow one in the same drill.* The radishes will mark the row (for purposes of cultivation*) long before the tardy seeds are up. Several such cases are noted in the articles on the culture of special vegetables.

(2) SEEDLINGS THAT NEED TRANSPLANT-

Sifting soil for fine seeds and a method of sowing those too small to be handled with the fingers.

ING. While the usual run of vegetable and annual flower seeds are sown where wanted and therefore come under the methods described under (1), there are many others that are sown with the understanding that their seedlings must be several times transplanted before being put in their final location. The chief plants needing such attention are:

Tender Annuals (see ANNUALS).
Vegetable Plants, such as tomatoes, peppers, the cabbage tribe, celery, and many others noted in the special articles on the culture of vegetables. *See also* KITCHEN GARDEN.
Flower Garden Perennials.
Many Greenhouse Plants.
Many Shrubs and some Trees.

While the details of handling such a miscellaneous lot of seeds will naturally vary, the main fact that applies to all of them is that the seeds are started in flats, pots, or boxes, or in a specially prepared seedbed. After germination they are several times transplanted, and for the details of this *see* the section below on the management of seedlings.

For large-scale operations a seedbed is prepared, usually in the hotbed or cold frame, or under a lath screen outdoors, or sometimes in a propagating bench in the greenhouse. And in some cases the latter must be supplied with bottom-heat (which see), but seeds needing this are noted at their proper entries throughout the ENCYCLOPEDIA. For all others, the seeds, whether planted in seedbeds or in boxes, pans, or flats, need the following general conditions.

The reason for their special requirements is that they germinate with difficulty or that immediately after germination they are unfit to cope with the conditions they will finally meet as growing plants. It does not matter, in their initial management, which cause prevents their handling, as in (1), because their treatment is the same. They *must* be pro-

---

* Special articles on the subjects indicated by an asterisk (*) will be found at the words so marked.

vided with special soil, with moisture, and usually with shade, until they have germinated, all of which are difficult to control in the open.

Ordinary garden soils such as are all right for the seeds discussed at (1) are of no use for the seeds here under consideration. For them a mixture of good garden loam and sand mixed half and half is what is needed, or in the case of greenhouse plants potting mixture* 2 is a good substitute for many of them. Whichever is used, the principle is the same. It is that such seeds need more moisture than plant food in order to germinate. And soils without sand in them, while holding moisture satisfactorily, may rot the seeds before allowing them to germinate. But with a liberal mixture of sand, and with proper watering, the seeds can be kept moist without the danger of rotting. In certain cases, noted in the body of this book, chopped-up osmunda* fiber, coir, or sphagnum* moss may be mixed with the sand or even replace it. But for most seeds under consideration in this section, sand should make up about ½ of the material in which they are planted. Many experienced growers germinate "difficult" seeds in vermiculite or shredded sphagnum* moss.

The depth to plant these seeds is the same as discussed under (1), but the conditions of moisture and the necessity for shade are very different. As for most home gardeners such seeds will be planted in pots, pans, flats, or boxes, it is necessary to point out that these must be provided with perfect drainage, so that while plenty of water can be used, it will never stagnate at the bottom of the container. The only way to be sure of this is to fill ½ or ¼ of the pot or box with pieces of broken flower pots or crocks, and in the case of flats to put a layer of sphagnum moss about ¾ in. thick under the soil.

While water is a prime necessity, it is usually inadvisable to keep up a steady and sometimes harmful excess of watering. To avoid the necessity of this and still keep the seed pans or boxes moist, it is usually better to shade them. Depending on the scale of your operations this may be accomplished by lath screens, by cheesecloth, paper, or in the greenhouse propagating bench by shading the glass.

The object in all cases is the same: to preserve a moist atmosphere just over the soil in which your seeds are planted. Sometimes a sheet of ground glass over a flower pot is all that is necessary, or several flats may be put in a cold frame and cheesecloth frames made to replace glass sash. Or in the nursery seedbed, a light brush screen, put about 5 in. above the soil, will give the same result, or a lath screen may be used. The danger in all such methods of shading is that too much moisture will accumulate, which is just as fatal as to let the seedbed or containers dry out. Specific directions for the daily maintenance of proper moisture

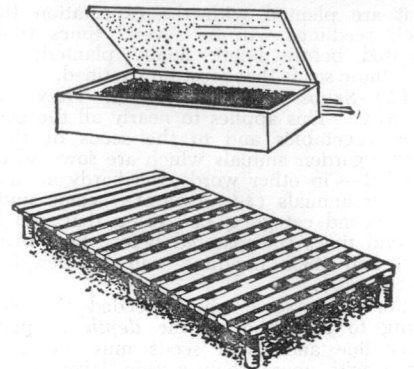

A glass cover (raised) for a seed box, and a lath shade for a seedbed. Both are used to keep the air and soil moist.

conditions are impossible to describe. The thing to keep in mind is that shade and moisture (and of course watering) must be so regulated that the seeds are never without sufficient moisture, that they get enough fresh air (but no drying wind), but that stagnation of soil moisture or air does not invite the condition known as damping-off (which see).

Some growers, in order to avoid these difficulties, never water their seeds directly at all. They plant them in the usual way in a flower pot which is set in a larger flower pot. The space between the inner and outer pot is packed with sphagnum* moss and this is watered freely and regularly. The inner pot (it must not be glazed) absorbs what moisture is needed from the sphagnum and keeps its seeds in just the right condition of moisture, provided the whole contrivance is covered with a sheet of ground glass until the seeds have sprouted.

Seedlings in an inner pot which is surrounded by wet sphagnum* moss from which they absorb enough moisture to avoid direct watering of the seedlings.

* Special articles on the subjects indicated by an asterisk (*) will be found at the words so marked.

When the seeds have germinated they must be grown along for a longer or shorter period, depending on the variety, and are then ready for, and in fact demand, special handling. *See* the section below upon the management of seedlings.

A few seeds, in spite of every care, will not germinate within a reasonable time, say 1–6 weeks. They have such slow germination that the grower is apt to think they have died. This may be so, but it is better to carry such pans or flats along for 10–15 months (even 2 years in extreme cases) before throwing their contents away. Such notoriously slow germinations are noted at their proper entries in the body of the book, so you will be on your guard in such cases.

There are, too, a few seeds, also noted specially at their proper entries, which will not germinate without soaking in warm water, or filing their husks, or soaking in acids, or planting in specially acid soils, but such are the exceptions. Much more common are those that come under the third method of handling seeds.

(3) STRATIFIED SEEDS. The stratification of seeds is an attempt to imitate the natural conditions of those trees and shrubs which drop their seeds in late summer but which do not germinate them until the following or even the second spring. Many trees naturally do this, especially nut trees, while others, like most evergreens, sprout their seeds as soon as dropped.

Those that retard germination for 6 or for 18 months (*i.e.*, the first or second spring after falling) are naturally kept from drying out and dying, and in the process nature does three things to them. Merely by letting the litter of the forest floor cover them they are kept in the dark, kept from drying out, and throughout most parts of the country they are more or less frozen, although the experts are undecided whether actual freezing is a necessity or not. There is no doubt that such seeds need a prolonged chilling even if not frozen.

The nursery practice of imitating these conditions is known as stratification. It consists of planting such seeds as soon as harvested in boxes of pure sand, often in wire cages if rodents are a pest, and then burying the boxes about 6 in. deep, in the shade, preferably on a well-drained slope. If the region is a reasonably moist one, the stratified seeds need no further attention until they are taken up and planted according to the directions given at (2).

All seeds needing stratification are so indicated in the body of the ENCYCLOPEDIA, and should be handled as described above. Some very small ones may be placed between layers of cheesecloth buried in sand to facilitate finding them in the spring. Or some prefer to put fine seeds in bags of mosquito wire before burying. But most stratified seeds are big and easily sifted out of the sand when needed.

Before considering the management of seedlings, it is necessary to point to two special sorts of seedage described elsewhere. One is the seeding of lawns, which will be found at LAWN. The other is the reproduction of fern spores.* The latter are not true seeds, but their handling approximates the methods mentioned at (2). For the details *see* FERNS AND FERN GARDENING.

MANAGEMENT OF SEEDLINGS

Much depends upon the careful growth of a tiny seedling as soon as it is germinated and commences life on its own account. All through its early stages it is subject to the dangers incident to life in nature, and we must care for these tender seedlings so that we may reap the benefits to be derived from the germination methods described above.

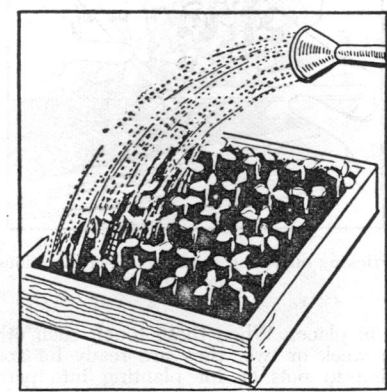

Water pricked-off seedlings very gently, with as fine a spray as possible.

Seedlings are nature's own way of propagation, and most plants have the power of reproduction by seed, but many kinds under cultivation require considerable care to bring the seedlings to maturity. Attention must be given the seedling as soon as germination

Stratified seeds

---

* Special articles on the subjects indicated by an asterisk (*) will be found at the words so marked.

takes place, as neglect at this stage means ruin.

As soon as the seedling makes its second leaf it must have attention or it will become weak and spindly, and while perhaps too small to handle with the fingers, a pointed stick may be used to transfer the young plants to flats, which is generally known as pricking off or pricking out. Flats should be made about 3 in. deep, 14 in. wide, and 24 in. long. This is a good size to handle, and will accommodate 42 plants spaced 2 × 3 in. If 12-in. ends are used and 3-in. stock, it will leave openings in the bottom, just wide enough for perfect drainage. The soil for flats should be reasonably fine and sifted only to remove stones and large lumps, and be a little lighter than the plants will ultimately need.

Drainage can be assured by covering the bottom of the flat with strawy manure which also acts as a stimulant when the young roots reach it. Or sphagnum* moss may be used for the lowest layer. Assuming the proper soil has been prepared, the flat properly drained, filled, pressed down around the outer edge and leveled off, not too dry or too wet, it is ready to receive the plants.

With a pointed stick dig out a small batch of seedlings, separate them and transfer to the flat individually, gently pressing each

Pricking off young seedlings. For directions *see* text.

one in place. When these touch each other, in a week or two, they are ready for transferring to pots or for planting into permanent quarters. Some seed germinates very slowly and the seedlings appear at irregular intervals. In such cases the seedlings should be pricked off several in a pot as they appear.

The greatest menace to raising seedlings is their tendency to damping-off after they appear. This is caused by insufficient air and the right conditions of heat and moisture to encourage the growth of a fungus which spreads with alarming rapidity. If not

checked damping-off will eventually spread over the whole seedbed and destroy every seedling. For the control of this *see* Damping-off.

After the seedlings are pricked off they should be given a good watering to settle the soil around the plants, shaded from direct sunlight for a few days, and kept in a closer and warmer atmosphere. Little water will be required until growth commences, and great care is needed to prevent a saturated condition of the soil which would cause it to become sour. But a light sprinkling for a few days will freshen them up and not wet the soil too much. After the seedlings have recovered from their slight check they may be allowed plenty of light and air, and strong, sturdy plants will result. If the plants are allowed to remain in the flats too long, they ripen up and start flowering, and at the best become drawn, leggy,* and weak, so as soon as ready they should be planted out or potted on (*see* Potting-on) as the case demands.

A few seeds with very hard coats are slow to germinate. Those garden plants where delayed germination is helped by special techniques are mentioned at the plants involved, especially at CALONYCTION, IPOMOEA, and SWEET PEA.

segeta, -us, -um (se-get′a). Growing in cornfields.

SEGMENT. One of the divisions of a leaf, petal, or sepal. Segments are not properly parts of a compound leaf, although leaflets are quite generally called segments. *See* LEAFLET.

SEGREGATION. Hybridization or crossing brings together two characters belonging to different strains, races, varieties, species, etc. It creates new combinations at once of already existing characters, and these first-generation hybrids can be propagated by various asexual* methods such as cuttings, grafts, etc. But the new combinations are relatively few if one stops at the F_1* generation — only one per cross in many cases. If these F_1's* are selfed or backcrossed on the recessive parent, many more new combinations are obtained, amounting to hundreds if the original parents were distinct in a larger number of characters and genes.*

This is what segregation brings about. In other words, when the hybrid plant produces its reproductive cells, segregation separates the character determiners brought together by crossing, and produces an opportunity for many new combinations and rearrangements of characters to take place. Thus, in a cross between some tall yellow and certain white four-o'clock races, the immediate offspring would be all tall light yellow, which is new and could be asexually propagated, but by selfing this hybrid, six kinds would be obtained — tall yellow, dwarf white, tall white, dwarf yellow, tall light yellow and dwarf light yellow — four of them new, and all could be propagated by root division. This is a very simple illustration of what

---

* Special articles on the subjects indicated by an asterisk (*) will be found at the words so marked.

occurs in practice, since the forms crossed often have many hereditary qualities that one does not notice or are not expressed, except through hybridization. Thus two white-flowered races of sweet peas produce colored-flowered offspring; two dwarf types of corn produce talls; certain self-colored bean varieties produce mottled progeny; some four-o'clock species hybrids are more cold-resistant than either parent. — O. E. W.

Seguine (se-gwin'e). Tropical American vernacular for the dumb cane (*Dieffenbachia Seguine*).

SELAGINELLA (see-laj-i-nell'a). Annual or perennial herbs of fern-like habit, and related to the ferns, comprising about 500 species of the family Selaginellaceae. They are distributed mostly through tropical regions, generally in damp places in forests, but sometimes in desert places. They are of diverse habits — some small and creeping, others erect, while still others are climbing. Leaves small, scale-like, in various shades of green, sometimes with metallic shadings. They are crowded on the stems, opposite* in pairs, one being smaller than the other, the smaller pressed against the stem, so giving an alternate* appearance. They do not bear flowers, but the tips of the shoots bear scale-like leaves of equal size, in the axils* of which the spores* are produced. (*Selaginella* is from the Latin *selago*, an old name of a club moss.)

These plants are usually grown in the greenhouse. They make useful pot plants for table decoration. Easily cult. in potting mixture* 4. Shade and plenty of water are essential. Propagated by pieces of the plant which can be inserted in permanent pans or pots, as they do not need transplanting. Several pieces will quickly cover a pan. They can be used for covering unsightly places under greenhouse benches.

kraussiana. Creeping, moss-like perennial, with stems that root at the joints. Leaves bright green. Azores to S. Af. Excellent for pans or pots, and the most commonly grown sort, often as if spontaneous under greenhouse benches.

lepidophylla. Resurrection plant. Desert perennial, growing to 4 in. high, in dense tufts.* Stems curling inward when dry, giving plant a ball-like appearance. *See* ANASTATICA. Leaves ovalish, one side of blade larger than the other, green, paler on the under side. Tex. to S.A.

rupestris. Perennial, of tufted* habit, growing 4–5 in. high. Stems much-branched. Leaves white-tipped. In damp places, eastern N.A.

SELAGINELLACEAE (see-laj-i-nel-lay'-see-ee). A family of flowerless, moss-like plants, the only genus of which is *Selaginella*, which see for the characters of the family.

SELECTION. Many wild plant species are genetic mixtures (the sum of many strains) and the same statement is true of many cultivated varieties and strains. This is especially true of plants such as corn and sugar beets which are commonly cross-fertilized, and much less true of self-fertilized

plants such as peas, beans, and sweet peas. Cross-fertilized plants represent more hybridity than self-fertilized types. In sugar beets the thrip insect is the cross-pollinator. In corn, it is the wind.

Wild sugar beets contain 7 to 14% sugar. By saving seed only from the sweetest beets for two generations, Vilmorin obtained types with 21% sugar. This illustrates selection. What Vilmorin did was simply to separate out by selection high-sugar strains. The genes* for these were already in the wild species. No new ones were produced by selection. Once the desired result is attained through selection, the strain or variety remains thus, barring mutation* and providing crossing is prevented. Selection among self-fertilized plants is less apt to produce results. In the past selection has probably been the largest factor in producing new, desirable types, and every observant gardener practices it today. — O. E. W. *See* PLANT BREEDING, MUTATION.

SELENICEREUS (se-len-i-seer'e-us). Beautiful night-blooming, mostly climbing or trailing cacti, comprising about 16 species found from Tex. to the Argentine, one of them widely grown in the greenhouse or outdoors in the Far South as a night-bloom-

A night-blooming cereus (*Selenicereus pteranthus*)

ing cereus. They have ribbed or angled stems with many aerial* roots which help them to climb. Spines few and small. Flowers white, usually very large, the outside scaly and often with tufts of hair, the outer segments often greenish or brownish. Fruit berry-like, but covered at first with bristles, hairs, and spines. (*Selenicereus* is named for the moon goddess and *Cereus*.)

For culture *see* CACTI.

grandiflorus. Stems stoutish, 7–8-ribbed or the ribs fewer. Spines needle-like, usually mixed with white hairs. Flowers about 7 in. long, white, but salmon-colored on the outside, fragrant. Cuba and Jamaica.

macdonaldiae. An extremely showy cactus with creeping stems that are 5-angled when

---

* Special articles on the subjects indicated by an asterisk (*) will be found at the words so marked.

young, but ultimately nearly terete,* about ½ in. thick, the spines few and short. Flowers reddish-yellow on the outside, 10–14 in. long, the numerous petals white; not fragrant. Uruguay and Argentina.

pteranthus. Night-blooming cereus. Stems 1–2 in. thick, rather strongly 4–6-angled, the spines 1–4 at each cluster. Flowers 10–12 in. long, remarkably sweet-smelling, white. Mex. Widely grown in greenhouses and frequently used in hybridizing with S. *grandiflorus* and with *Heliocereus speciosus. See also* HYLO-CEREUS and NYCTOCEREUS.

SELENIPEDIUM. *See* CYPRIPEDIUM.

SELFED. *See* SELF-POLLINATION.

SELF-FERTILIZATION. The fertilization of an ovule by its own pollen; often called close fertilization. *See* FERTILIZATION. *See also* CLEISTOGAMOUS FLOWERS.

SELF-HEAL = *Prunella vulgaris. See also* the list at WEEDS.

SELF-POLLINATION. The process by which a flower is pollinated by its own pollen, or, more broadly, by pollen from any other flower on the same plant. Such a flower is said to be selfed. *See* CROSSING.

SELF-STERILITY. In the flowering plants, the inability of normal pollen from any given plant to fertilize its own flowers. This occurs in over 100 different species involving 50 plant families. It is more frequent in some families than in others. Among these are the rosaceous fruits — sweet cherries, plums, almonds, apples, pears, and Japanese quince. It is also a striking phenomenon among hippeastrums, gladioli, avocados, carnations, poppies, cabbage, rye, Cornelian cherries, and muscadine grapes.

Many of the plants mentioned are asexually propagated and very often planted without considering this aspect. They flower profusely, look healthy, but fail to set fruit. This is especially true of small home-garden plantings of the rosaceous fruits. Not all varieties of economic plants nor of a given species behave thus. Many are self-fertile, but in those varieties in which it does occur, it is emphatically hereditary, and interplanting with suitable varieties is the only practical remedy. *See* CROSS-STERILITY; *see also* Self-fertile and Self-sterile at FRUIT CULTURE. — O. E. W.

SEMIAQUILEGIA. *See Aquilegia ecalcarata* at COLUMBINE.

SEMIARUNDINARIA. *See* ARUNDINARIA.

semidecandra, -us, -um (sem-i-de-kan'-dra). With five stamens.

semperaurescens (sem-per-or-res'senz). Always golden.

semperflorens (sem-per-flow'renz). Ever-or continuously flowering.

sempervirens (sem-per-vy'renz). Ever or always green.

sempervivi (sem-per-vee-vee). Like a houseleek.

sempervivoides (sem-per-vi-voy'deez). Like a houseleek.

SEMPERVIVUM. *See* HOUSELEEK.

SENECA GRASS = *Hierochloë odorata.*

SENECA SNAKEROOT = Senega snakeroot (*Polygala Senega*). *See* SENEGA.

SENECIO (sen-ee'si-o). Groundsel. Ragwort. Annual, biennial, or perennial herbs, shrubs or small trees, and a few climbers, comprising over 1200 species of the family Compositae, found throughout the world. Leaves alternate* or basal. This genus being among the largest and therefore having diverse habits is difficult to define, the chief difference being in the rings of bracts which surround the head. These do not overlap each other, and the lower bracts are scale-like, giving a calyx-like appearance to the upper ring of bracts.* The flower heads are generally yellow, but sometimes purple, red, blue, or white, solitary or in clusters. The heads are often showy, composed of ray* and disk florets,* but the ray florets are sometimes absent. (*Senecio* is from the Latin for old man, in supposed allusion to the pappus.)

Comparatively few of these species are in cultivation, but a few are used for the border. The chief hort. species is S. *cruentus*, the cineraria of the florists, and a useful decorative plant for the house.

Some of the species below are occasionally credited to the genus *Cineraria. See* that entry for an explanation of its varied use. Some are also known as *Kleinia*, a genus not here maintained.

aureus. Golden ragwort. Strong-growing, hardy herbaceous perennial, to 2 ft. high, sometimes slightly hairy. Basal leaves stalked, ovalish, heart-shaped at base, to 6 in. long, purplish on the under side. Margins toothed. Stem leaves smaller, cut into lobes almost to midrib. Flowers yellow, in heads to ¾ in. across in many-headed, branching clusters. Eastern N.A. June–July.

Cineraria. Dusty miller. Hardy, branching, herbaceous perennial, growing to 2½ ft. high, covered with long, white, matted hairs. Leaves alternate,* thick, cut into narrow, rounded lobes. Flowers yellow or cream, in heads to ½ in. across, in small terminal clusters. Mediterranean region.

clivorum = *Ligularia clivorum.*

confusus. Mexican fire-vine. A tender, attractive herbaceous vine, 6–8 ft. high, with a smooth stem. Leaves ivy-like, about 2 in. long, rather fleshy and thick. Flower heads about ½ in. thick, in terminal clusters, the rays orange, ultimately orange-red. Mex. Cult. outdoors in Fla. and along the Gulf Coast, but not hardy northward.

cruentus. Low-growing, herbaceous perennial, sometimes covered with white-woolly hairs. Leaves alternate,* large, long-stalked, ovalish or heart-shaped. Margins wavy and toothed. Flowers in heads, in clusters. Canary Islands. This species is the parent of the cineraria of the florists. For cult. *see* CINERARIA.

Doronicum. Leopard's-bane. Hardy, herbaceous perennial to 2½ ft. high, slightly hairy. Leaves alternate,* with thick, fleshy stalks and veins, broadly lance-shaped, to 7 in. long. Margins sometimes toothed. Flowers showy,*

* Special articles on the subjects indicated by an asterisk (*) will be found at the words so marked.

orange or yellow, in heads 2½ in. across, 2–3 heads on each stalk. Bracts surrounding heads black-tipped. Useful border plant for spring-flowering. Southern Eu.

elegans. Purple ragwort. Tender annual, growing to 2 ft. high, covered with sticky hairs. Leaves broadly lance-shaped, to 3 in. long, either lobed or toothed. Flowers in heads, disk florets yellow, ray florets purple or red. Heads in loose branching clusters. S. Af. Can be grown in the border or as a cool greenhouse plant. *See* ANNUALS.

Jacobaea. Tansy ragwort. Perennial, growing to 4 ft. high. Basal leaves to 8 in. long, cut into lyre-shaped lobes, stalked. Stem leaves broadly lance-shaped, to 6 in. long, cut into 2–3 lobes. Flowers yellow, in heads ½ in. across, numerous, in branching clusters. Eu., naturalized in N.A. Useful border plant. Can be used for cutting.

kaempferi = *Ligularia kaempferi.*

mikanioides. German ivy. Tender, herbaceous, climbing perennial, smooth and shiny. Stems woody at base. Leaves alternate,* fleshy, bright green, ovalish, cut into 4–5 pointed lobes. Flowers yellow, in small heads, in few-headed clusters, of disk florets only. S. Af. Suitable for window boxes, and a good house plant.

pulcher. Strong-growing perennial, to 4 ft. high, covered with long, fine, white hairs. Leaves lance-shaped, to 10 in. long, slightly lobed, with rounded teeth. Flowers in heads to 3 in. across, ray florets reddish-purple, disk florets yellow. Uruguay and Argentina. Hardy if grown in well-drained soil.

purshianus. A densely hairy perennial, 5–8 in. high. Leaves chiefly basal, broadly spoon-shaped, nearly 2 in. long. Flower heads about ¾ in. wide, in a lax cluster (cyme*), the rays bright yellow. Western N.A. Summer.

scandens. Climbing perennial, with woody stems, hairy when young. Leaves gray-green, ovalish or broadly lance-shaped, often lobed at the base, covered with short hairs. Flowers yellow, in heads, in loose, branching clusters. China.

succulentus. A low, succulent, South African shrub with fleshy stems and clustered, thick leaves which are cylindrical, about 1¼ in. long and bluish-green. Flowers yellow, the heads about ½ in. wide, in few-flowered clusters (corymbs*). South Africa. Also known as *Kleinia repens.*

Senega (sen′e-ga). Latinized form of Seneca, and now perpetuated in Senega snakeroot, first known as a medicinal plant by the Seneca Indians.

SENEGA SNAKEROOT = *Polygala Senega.*

senilis, -e (sen′i-lis). Senile; usually old and white-haired.

SENNA. *See* CASSIA. For other plants sometimes called senna *see* COLUTEA and CORONILLA EMERUS.

SENNA FAMILY. *See* LEGUMINOSAE.

sensibilis, -e (sen-sib′i-lis). Sensitive.

SENSITIVE FERN = *Onoclea sensibilis.*

SENSITIVE PLANT = *Mimosa pudica.*

senticosa, -us, -um (sen-ti-ko′sa). Thorny.

SENTINEL FIR = *Abies alba pyramidalis.* *See* FIR.

SEPAL. One of the separate parts of a calyx (which see).

SEPARATION. *See* DIVISION.

Sepium (see′pi-um). Found along hedges or fences.

septemfida, -us, -um (sep-tem-fid′a). Cut into seven segments.

septiceps (sep′ti-seps). Seven-headed.

SEPTUM. A partition within an organ, especially a fruit, as the *septum* in honesty (which see).

sepulcralis, -e (se-pul-crah′lis). Having to do with a tomb.

SEQUOIA (see-kwoy′ya). Magnificent relics of a once widely distributed genus of coniferous trees of the pine family. Today there are only two species localized in Calif. and remnants of an ancient group which have been found as fossils in many parts of

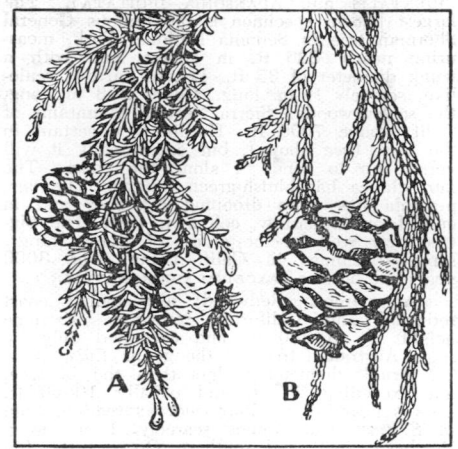

Foliage and cones of the redwood (A), and the giant sequoia (B)

the world. The survivors include only the giant sequoia or big-tree and the California redwood, both gigantic evergreens. Leaves small, decurrent,* mostly 2-ranked, narrow, more or less hugging the twigs in the big-tree. The trees are without flowers in the ordinary sense of that term, the male flowers consisting of bunches of spirally arranged stamens* in clusters in the leaf axils,* the female in cone-like clusters with 5–7 naked ovules between the cone scales. The ovules and cones ultimately ripen into a small, woody cone with 5–7 winged seeds at each cone scale. (Named for Sequoiah, a Georgia Indian and the inventor of the Cherokee alphabet.) The technical characters used to support the transfer of the big-tree to the proposed genus Sequoiadendron do not seem to warrant the change. For the finest appreciation of the giant sequoia see *The Forest Giant,* by Adrien Le Corbeau, translated by T. E. Lawrence.

---

* Special articles on the subjects indicated by an asterisk (*) will be found at the words so marked.

Neither the big-tree nor the California redwood takes kindly to cult. in the East. Climatic conditions in their native habitat are practically impossible to imitate in the East. The big-tree grows high up in the Sierras, while the California redwood is found between the coast range and the Pacific in northern Calif. and southern Ore., a region of high rainfall and much fog. In fact the present distribution of the redwood and that of the fog are almost identical. In the East the only places approximating this are near the sea and along the shores of Lake Erie or Lake Ontario. At Rochester, N.Y., there was once a sequoia over 50 ft. high, but even this is a pygmy compared to the growth of sequoias in their native environment. A few other giant sequoias have been grown in the East. *See also* METASEQUOIA.

gigantea. Giant sequoia or big-tree. The largest coniferous tree in the world (for deciduous trees of huge girth *see* PLATANUS OCCIDENTALIS and ADANSONIA DIGITATA). The largest known specimen is the famous General Sherman tree in Sequoia National Park, measuring nearly 320 ft. in height, and with a trunk diameter of 35 ft. Leaves narrow, scale-like, scarcely ½ in. long. Cones 2–3 in. long, the scales woody. Sierra Nevada Mountains of Calif. above 7000 ft. Hardiness uncertain in the East (*see* above), but occasionally it will persist up to zone° 4 along the coast. The *var.* glauca has bluish-green foliage. The *var.* **pendula** has more drooping branches and in cult. forms a narrow, columnar tree. The big-tree may well be the oldest of living things, some specimens in Calif. being over 3000 years old, but *see* TAXODIUM MUCRONATUM.

sempervirens. Redwood; also called coast redwood and California redwood. Extreme height up to 340 ft. and exceeded only by some Australian trees of the genus *Eucalyptus.* The trunk diameter is less than the big-tree, not exceeding 28 ft. and usually 10–20 ft. Leaves nearly 1 in. long, more spreading than in *S. gigantea.* Cones scarcely 1 in. long. Northern Calif. and southern Ore. in the fog belt. Scarcely adapted to the East, but making magnificent forests in its own region, far more extensive than the big-tree, and an important source of valuable timber. For hardiness notes see above; it is certainly not hardy in the East above zone° 5. The *var.* glauca has bluish-green foliage. There is also a form with pendulous branches. The burls of the redwood are often sold by florists. They make interesting growths when put in water. *See* BURL.

SERBIAN SPRUCE = *Picea Omorika.* See SPRUCE.

SERENOA (ser-en-ō′a). A single species of small, horticulturally rather unimportant fan palms found from S. Car. to Fla. and Tex., sometimes cult. for ornament, but very common throughout its range. The only species is S. repens, the scrub or saw palmetto, which is usually nearly stemless and forms large patches. Leafstalks prickly, the blades fan-shaped, 2–2½ ft. wide, divided or cleft to or below the middle into about 20 rather stiff segments which are 2-toothed at the tip. Flower clusters usually longer than the leafstalks, branched, the flowers perfect.° Fruit

½–¾ in. long, egg-shaped or roundish, black, 1-seeded. The plant is of easy culture in many types of soil and spreads rapidly. It generally has creeping stems, but some are erect and several feet high. For the plant sometimes called S. *arborescens see* PAUROTIS WRIGHTI. (Named for Sereno Watson, American botanist.)

sericea, -us, -um (ser-riss′ee-a). Silky.

sericofera, -us, -um (ser-i-kō′fer-a). Silky or bearing silk.

SERINGERA = *Hevea brasiliensis.*

SERISSA (se-riss′a). A single species of Japanese shrubs of the family Rubiaceae, **S. foetida,** often cult. for ornament in the cool greenhouse or outdoors from zone° 5 southward. It is a low shrub, 15–24 in. high with opposite,° nearly stalkless, ovalish leaves, nearly ½ in. long and evil-smelling when bruised. Flowers white, about ⅜ in. long, in rather floriferous clusters, or solitary, on small flowering twigs. Corolla funnel-shaped, its 4–6 lobes bluntly 3-lobed. Corolla tube hairy on the inside. Fruit a nearly round drupe.° (Serissa is a Latinized form of the native name for the plant.) Dwarf forms of it are useful in the dish garden (which see).

serotina, -us, -um (ser-rot′i-na). Tardily flowering or fruiting.

Serpentaria (ser-pen-tair′i-a). An old and now obsolete name for certain species of *Aristolochia* (which see).

SERPENT GOURD = *Trichosanthes Anguina.*

serpentina, -us, -um (ser-pen-ty′na). Snake-like.

serpyllifolia, -us, -um (sir-pill-i-fō′li-a). Having leaves like the thyme, an ancient name for which was *Serpyllum.*

Serpyllum (sir-pill′um). An obsolete generic name for one of the thymes.

serrata, -us, -um (sir-ray′ta). Serrate.°

SERRATE. Having teeth like those of a saw.

serratifolia, -us, -um (sir-rat-i-fō′li-a). Having serrate° leaves.

serrulata, -us, -um (sir-roo-lay′ta). Serrulate; *i.e.,* having minute, saw-like teeth.

SERVICEBERRY = *Amelanchier.*

SERVICE TREE = *Sorbus domestica.* See MOUNTAIN-ASH.

SERVICE YARD. There are few places, even quite small ones, where it is not of advantage to provide a screened or sheltered place in which to wash the car, dry clothes, keep the ash and garbage cans, and perhaps a tool box. Often it is possible to combine such a service yard with the garage and at the same time provide space in which to turn a car. The latter is the most space-demanding.

If a two- or three-car garage and the necessary space for turning the cars is to be provided, the total area cannot be less

---

° Special articles on the subjects indicated by an asterisk (°) will be found at the words so marked.

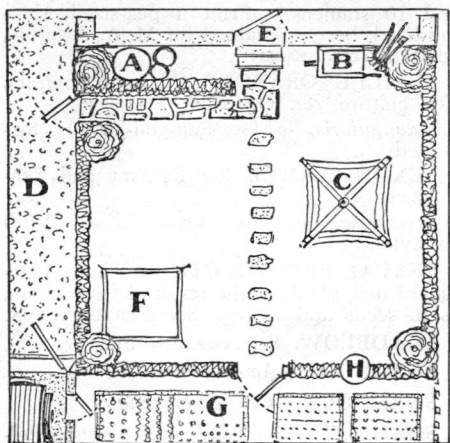

**A PRACTICAL AND ATTRACTIVE
SERVICE YARD**

(A) Ash and garbage cans, well screened. (B) Wheelbarrow, tools, etc. (but *see* TOOL HOUSE). (C) Clothes reel. (D) Drive to garage. (E) Entrance from kitchen door. (F) Children's wading pool. (G) Garden. (H) Hedge surrounding the yard.

than 40 × 40 ft. and for comfort had better be more than this. Sometimes it is necessary to save space by combining the needed area for cars with that necessary for drying clothes. If this is done, clothes poles are, of course, impossible, and a single-pole, 4–5-arm drier must be used. These are set in a socket flush with the ground and can be folded up and removed when not needed.

Whichever type of service yard your needs demand, it is essential that such activities be screened from the house and from other parts of the garden; the higher and thicker the screen, the better. If your space must be limited you may not have room for the necessary depth of planting to make the most desirable type of screen. The best and most costly screen planting would be evergreens, but very satisfactory screens can be made of deciduous shrubs and trees. For the necessary space and the preferred plants for either type of screen *see* SCREEN PLANTING.

If the space available will not permit of screen planting, the next best thing to do is to plant a stout hedge around the service yard. For the space needed for this, the planting and the best hedge plants, *see* HEDGES.

Upon the assumption that you are still too cramped to permit the use of a hedge, the final solution for hiding the service yard is a trellis with some large-leaved or dense-growing vines over it. For the details of these *see* TRELLIS and VINES.

Where it is possible to keep the service yard proper separate from the garage and

turning space, there arises the question of whether lawn or pavement is the best floor for a service yard. Unless there is much traffic through the service yard, it is cooler and far more attractive to keep it in lawn. But if this is impossible, it may be paved, at least along the lines of clothes-hanging. See PATHS AND PAVING. The latter plan also has winter advantages, because when such paths are kept clear of snow, pavement takes little damage from alternate freezing and thawing. But a much-used grass track around the clothes lines may become a muddy path.

SESAL VEGETAL. *See* BLIGHIA SAPIDA.

SESAME = *Sesamum indicum.*

SESAMUM (ses'a-mum). Tropical African and Asian herbs of the family **Pedaliaceae** (ped-al-i-ā'see-ee) which includes 13 other genera and perhaps 50 species of herbs or shrubs, all from the Old World and all of them with generally opposite,* usually somewhat slimy leaves. The only cult. species of *Sesamum* is S. *indicum* (long known as S. *orientale*), the sesame, the seeds of which are the benne (or benny) of commerce, known in Africa as sim-sim, and used as food and for their oil. The plant is a rough-hairy herb, 1–2 ft. high, with oblongish or narrower leaves, 3–5 in. long, the lower often 3-parted, the upper sometimes alternate.* Flowers about 1 in. long, white or pink, solitary in the leaf axils.* Corolla tubular, its limb 2-lipped,* the upper lip 2-lobed and shorter than the 3-lobed under lip.* Fruit an oblongish capsule.* Little grown in the U.S. and suited only to zones* 8 or 9, but can be grown as an annual northward. The commercial production of benne is chiefly African and Indian. (*Sesamum* is the Greek version of the Arabic name for the sesame.)

SESBANIA (sez-ban'i-a). Widely distributed tropical herbs or shrubs of the pea family, comprising perhaps 30 species, of which only S. **exaltata**, native in the central U.S., and southward to tropical America, is of garden interest. It is a coarse annual, 8–12 ft. high, grown chiefly as a cover crop or for green manure in its native region and in Calif. Leaves compound,* the leaflets arranged feather-fashion, without an odd one at the end, usually about ¾ in. long. Flowers showy, pea-like, yellow but purple-spotted, mostly in clusters (racemes*) that are 3–4 in. long. Fruit a flattish pod (legume*) 7–9 in. long. It is only used as an annual, warm-country cover crop sown in early spring, and is sometimes known as S. *macrocarpa.* For the plant occasionally called S. *punicea see* DAUBENTONIA PUNICEA. For S. *grandiflora see* AGATI GRANDIFLORA. (*Sesbania* is the Latinized version of the Arabian name for a related species.)

sesquipedalis, -e (ses-kwi-pe-day'lis). Literally, one and one-half a foot's length; *i.e.,* 18 in.

SESSILE. Stalkless.

---

* Special articles on the subjects indicated by an asterisk (*) will be found at the words so marked.

sessilifolia, -us, -um (ses-sil-i-fō′li-a). With stalkless leaves.

sessilis, -e (ses′si-lis). Stalkless.

SET. A common but rather indefinite garden term used in several senses, as a verb usually implying that an ovule has been fertilized and the ovary is on the way to producing a fruit; as in the phrase — a tree has *set* fruit.

Used as a noun *set* means some small propagative part of a plant, the most common application being to an onion *set*, which, in the plural are small bulblets* used for the planting of onions. See ONION.

SETARIA (see-tair′i-a). Chiefly agricultural, warm-country, annual or perennial grasses, comprising about 75 species, only two of them here admitted, and one of these chiefly a forage or fodder grass. They have grass-like leaves and a large, spike-like terminal cluster (panicle*), each spikelet having beneath it a long bristle which persists after the spikelet has fallen. Fruit an edible grain in the first species. (*Setaria* is from the Latin for bristle.) They are sometimes known under the name *Chaetochloa*.

The first species and its several varieties is only of agricultural interest and is grown as an annual grass. The second, grown for ornament, is found in greenhouses and sometimes is spontaneous there. Its chief value is the handsome foliage.

italica. Foxtail millet. An annual grass 3–5 ft. high, mostly unbranched. Leaves grass-like, rough, about ¾ in. wide, the basal sheath fringed with hairs. Flowering cluster 2–10 in. long, about 1¼ in. thick, the bristles green, purplish, or brown. Cult. for forage or hay. Probably a cultigen.* The *var.* nigrofructa, Hungarian grass, has nearly black grains; *var.* rubrofructa, Siberian or Turkestan millet, has the grain reddish-orange; and the *var.* stramineofructa, the German or Golden Wonder millet, has large spikes and yellow grains.

palmifolia. Palm grass. A slender, perennial grass, 4–6 ft. high. Leaves grass-like, but nearly 1 in. wide at the middle and tapering to a fine point at the tip, the sheathing base strongly hairy on the margins. Flower cluster 8–12 in. long, not usually continuous. East Indies. There is also a form with variegated leaves, usually in stripes.

setigera, -us, -um (see-tij′er-a). Bristly.

setispina, -us, -um (see-ti-spy′na). With bristly spines.

setosa, -us, -um (see-tō′sa). Bristly.

SEVEN-BARKS = *Hydrangea arborescens.*

SEVEN-STARS = *Ariocarpus retusus.*

SEVEN-TOP TURNIP = *Brassica Rapa septiceps.*

SEVERINIA (sev-er-in′i-a). A single species of spiny shrubs or small trees of the rue family, **S. buxifolia** of southern China and Formosa, grown for ornament or for hedges south of zone* 7. It has simple,* alternate* leaves, ovalish, about 1 in. long, somewhat resembling box, but with a spine on each side of the buds. Flowers solitary or few in the leaf axils,* white and small, with 5 petals

and 10 stamens.* Fruit a pea-sized, shining black berry. (Named for M. A. Severino, an Italian professor.)

SEVILLE ORANGE = *Citrus Aurantium.* For culture *see* ORANGE.

sexangularis, -e (sex-ang-you-lar′is). Six-angled.

SEX IN PLANTS. See FEMALE and FERTILIZATION.

sexstylosa, -us, -um (sex-sty-lō′sa). With six styles.*

SEXUAL REPRODUCTION. The production of new plants as the result of fertilization, as in seeds and spores. *See* FERTILIZATION.

SHADBLOW. *See* AMELANCHIER.

SHADBUSH = *Amelanchier.*

SHADDOCK = *Citrus maxima.*

SHADE. The ability of some plants to tolerate shade, the necessity for shade in certain specialized gardens, the need for shading seedlings, and the erection of lath screens to provide shade — all are different phases of the response of plants to light, and what we must do to meet that response. It seems best here to separate the different ways in which shade is a garden factor as follows. All the subjects below are treated as special articles under the headings or cross-references noted below:

Shaded Lawn. *See* LAWN for grasses suited for shade.

Shade Plants. For those that are shade-enduring *see* SHADY GARDEN. *See also* WILD GARDEN.

Shade Trees. *See* TREES.

Shading. *See* the article SHADING for the best methods of providing shade for the plants that need it.

SHADING. There are several reasons for shading outdoor plants. Seedbeds in the open must be given some shade. Seedlings newly transplanted must be protected from hot sun and wind. Shades are used to prevent burning of tender plants which must be watered in full sun. Large plants which have been moved must be shaded until established in the new quarters. Flowers grown for cutting purposes, which fade in strong light, must be shaded at certain times. Shade is sometimes necessary to regulate the flowering time of plants intended for flower-show exhibit.

Shades are for temporary use and must be portable. Plants needing constant shade should be planted in permanently shady outdoor places, or in the shade of a pergola, lath house or greenhouse. The simplest way to shade a single small plant is an inverted flower pot. This can be used only temporarily and under constant inspection, as it admits insufficient light and air and is a harbor for slugs and wood lice. An ideal portable shade for seedbeds and transplanted seedlings is made of laths nailed 2 in. apart across a flat square or oblong frame of light wood mounted on four strong but slender legs tall enough to hold the frame above the level of the plants.

---

* Special articles on the subjects indicated by an asterisk (*) will be found at the words so marked.

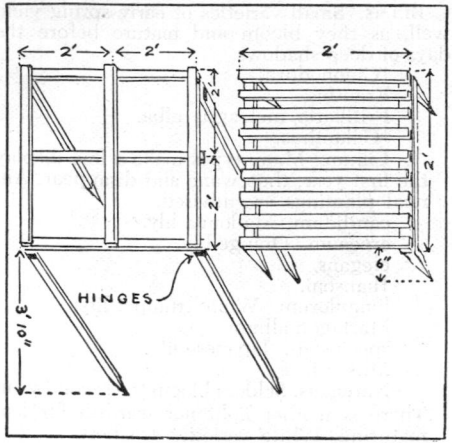

SHADING

At the right, a practical, movable lath shade for plants, or small areas. At the left, a wooden frame for taller plants. It can be covered with cheesecloth or burlap. The hinged legs allow it to be folded up and easily stored.

Handy sizes for this type of shade are 2 ft. × 2 ft. and 4 ft. × 18 in. Several small shades, which can be placed close together, are better than one large one which is clumsy to handle. If denser shade is needed, sacking or newspapers can be laid on top of the laths.

For taller plants a light wooden frame 4 ft. × 4 ft. square, strengthened by two narrow cross-strips and covered with heavy cheesecloth or light unbleached muslin is very satisfactory. It is supported by four legs, 1 in. × 1 in. × 3 ft. 10 in. These are pointed at the bottom and hinged at the top to the corners of the square frame, like a card table. This type of shade, giving protection, with plenty of light and air, is particularly good for flowers in the cutting garden and for shade-loving plants during a period of intense heat.

A satisfactory device for shading late-sown sweet peas and all tall flowers grown in rows is as follows. Make a temporary frame by setting firm stakes at the four corners of the row and others at 3-ft. intervals down both sides, and screw a metal eye into the top of each corner stake. Take a strip of heavy cheesecloth or light unbleached muslin the length of the row, tack each end of it to a stick (preferably round) and screw a hook fitting the eyelets on the corner stakes into each end of each stick. This cloth can then be stretched along the top of the temporary frame, hooked to the corner stakes and supported by the side stakes. It will be needed only during the hottest part of the day and can easily be unrolled and rolled up. A stitched hem along each side will strengthen the cloth. If the exposure is windy, strings should also be attached every 3 ft. to tie into additional eyelets screwed into the side stakes. If permanent shelter is necessary, as well as temporary shade, a strip of cloth can also be stretched vertically along the exposed side of the row and tacked to the stakes to hold it in position. Various modern plastics have made some of these shading devices seem old-fashioned, but they are more lasting than plastics.

Espaliered fruit trees and vines trained against a wall or fence can be protected from a dangerously hot sun by strips of unbleached muslin tacked to round poles and dropped from the top of the fence or wall in the manner of window shades.

SHADOW BOX. A shadow box is an individual box or container which permits exhibitors at flower shows greater scope in arrangements, backgrounds, and colors without conflicting with other compositions. The boxes are made of wood with space approximately two feet seven inches high, two feet wide, and ten inches deep. These should be placed about two feet from the wall. Architects' cloth is stretched across the front of the frame, which is hinged to make it easier to stage the exhibit. In the large boxes the light, preferably 60–100 watts and adjustable as to height, should hang at the back about

Shadow box

six or eight inches from the the floor. In small boxes concealed lights are often placed at the front edge to allow proper lighting. The chief drawback to shadow boxes is the heat caused by the electric lighting. Fragile blossoms only last one day and must be replaced if the show is of longer duration.

SHADY GARDEN. To the theory that a garden is necessarily composed of flower beds, many a tree was once sacrificed to provide needed light and sun for massed bloom, and corners full of potential serenity and repose were neglected as garden areas. As realization awoke that flowers were but incidentals in the plan, the green garden was evolved, form and texture taking precedence of color. Next came the discovery that only a modicum of sun was needed for many species, so waste dark spots were reclaimed, and the

* Special articles on the subjects indicated by an asterisk (*) will be found at the words so marked.

garden of shade took its place among other specialized developments.

Success lies not only in using suitable materials, but in following certain tenets, many of them suggested by Nature herself. Provide good drainage, as soil stagnation comes easily in dusky places. Lighten heavy earths with sand. Delay spring housecleaning and let it be scant. Many of the plants resent poking, make late appearances, and in order to have any semblance of luxuriance, should be allowed to bring forth their seedlings when and where it strikes their fancy. The shady garden is an excellent spot for seed germination, especially those needing many months and an interim of cold for fulfillment. An abundance of water is necessary at all times, and a mulch to conserve the dampness. Evaporation will not be great, especially under trees, but they rob soil moisture quickly. As conditioning fertilizers are better than quick stimulants, a high proportion of phosphorus is needed, especially bone meal or superphosphates. Lime well areas not demanding acid soils, and enrich with pulverized sheep manure. While dogmatic statements are unwise, the following notes are pertinent.

Seldom replace a failure with the same plant; it is usually waste effort. Expect no masses of bloom, but enjoy each flower for its own beauty. White varieties of any plant group do best. When a plant self-sows and colonizes its tribe, it is an indication that the location is to its liking. Accept it, whether it is a favorite or not. The shady garden is seldom one of early frosts, but it is one of early coolness. Many inmates, both bulbs and plants become biennial in bloom, requiring two seasons instead of one for recuperation.

There are various degrees of shade. The solitude of some country spot where the sun is excluded merely by trees or occasional buildings, with a fair circulation of untainted air, presents fewer obstacles than a hemmed-in city or suburban section, where the atmosphere is laden with dust or fumes, and the tree drip, always pernicious to many plants, becomes deadly from factory or chimney deposits.

Shade-tolerant Plants

All species in these lists are described under their proper entries elsewhere in this book, to which reference should be made for a description of them and for notes on their hardiness. Those marked with a dagger (†) are especially adapted to the shade condition found in cities. The others are more suited to the ordinary country atmosphere and to the shade of trees. Those with a double dagger (††) will stand the dense shade and drip of maple trees.

ANNUALS. Expect little, and disappointment will be less keen. Start seeds in heat; transplant seedlings.

Ageratum	Nicotiana
Alyssum	Petunia
Calendula	Zinnia

BULBS. Small varieties of early spring yield well, as they bloom and mature before the days of deep shadows.

†Chionodoxa.
Eranthis.
Fritillaria meleagris alba.
†Galanthus.
Lilium. Many types make a fine display the first year, then wane and disappear. Annual plantings are advised.
   candidum. Madonna lily.
   croceum. Orange lily.
   elegans.
   †hansoni.
   longiflorum. White-trumpet lily.
   Martagon album.
   speciosum. Japanese lily.
Muscari.
Narcissus. Seldom bloom the second year. There is neither light nor warmth for leaf maturing. White varieties are best.
†Scilla. Plant among lilies-of-the-valley.
Tulips. Yield bloom, but the stems are weak. Cottage varieties most satisfactory. None permanent, treat as annuals.

EVERGREENS. Coniferous and broad-leaved evergreens.
  Background.
  ††Rhododendron.
  ††Taxus cuspidata. Japanese yew.
    Tsuga canadensis. Hemlock.
    Tsuga caroliniana. Spruce pine.
  Medium.
    Azalea.
  ††Euonymus fortunei.
    Leucothöe catesbaei.
  ††Taxus canadensis. Ground hemlock.
GROUND COVERS. The following will be found useful, but there are others, some doing well in partial shade. See GROUND COVERS.
    Ajuga reptans. Bugle.
  †Hedera Helix. English ivy. Put in young plants closely together.
    Lonicera japonica halliana, pegged down.
    Lycopodium obscurum.
    Lysimachia Nummularia. Moneywort.
  †Glechoma hederacea. Ground-ivy.
  ††Pachysandra terminalis.
  †Vinca minor. Periwinkle.
PERENNIALS.
  Tall.
    Aconitum. In variety. Few flowers, foliage good.
  ††Cimicifuga racemosa. Black snakeroot.
    Delphinium. Needs good staking. Flowers few, color good.
  ††Eupatorium rugosum. White snakeroot.
  †Thalictrum. All varieties.
  Medium.
  ††Astilbe japonica.
    Campanula persicifolia. Peach bells.
  †Dicentra. All varieties.
  ††Hosta. All varieties.
  ††Mertensia virginica. Virginia cowslip.
  ††Myrrhis odorata.
    Paeonia. Single.

---

* Special articles on the subjects indicated by an asterisk (*) will be found at the words so marked.

Phlox divaricata. Blue phlox.
†Tradescantia virginiana. Spiderwort.
Low.
†Astilbe simplicifolia.
†Convallaria majalis. Lily-of-the-valley.
Corydalis. All varieties.
Geranium ibericum.
Heuchera sanguinea. Coral bells.
Iris pumila.
Oenothera fruticosa youngi.
†Polemonium reptans. Bluebell.
Primula vulgaris. English primrose.
††Tiarella cordifolia. Foam flower.

SHRUBS. Abundant foliage is all that can be depended upon. If blooms come they are the more appreciated for their fickleness. The best species or variety for shade growing is given. Heights will differ in shade from those attained in sun.
Background.
††Amelanchier canadensis.
Crataegus crus-galli.
†Forsythia suspensa. Weeping golden bell.
††Hamamelis virginiana. Witch-hazel.
††Hydrangea arborescens. Wild hydrangea.
††Hydrangea paniculata.
Lonicera fragrantissima.
Syringa. Lilac.
Medium.
Kerria japonica.
Kolkwitzia amabilis. Beauty-bush.
†Ligustrum amurense.
Lonicera henryi.
†Rubus odoratus. Flowering raspberry.
Spiraea japonica.
Spiraea vanhouttei.
Stephanandra incisa.
Viburnum acerifolium. Dockmackie.
Low.
††Xanthorhiza simplicissima. Yellow-root.

TREES. Two of value to the shady garden both in foliage form and habit of growth.
Koelreuteria.
††Ailanthus. Difficult to start, but the best of all trees for city backyards with little sun. Plant a small seedling, or a sucker.*

VINES. Good foliage but few flowers are all that can be expected. Three-year roots should be bought with a surplus of vigor to spend in becoming established.
††Actinidia. All species.
Aristolochia durior. Dutchman's-pipe.
††Celastrus scandens. Bittersweet.
†Humulus japonicus. Called an annual. but springing up from the roots each year, in perennial fashion.
Lonicera japonica.
†Polygonum auberti. Silver-lace vine.
Pueraria thunbergiana.
Wistaria. If the runners are pegged down it makes a good ground cover.
Cobaea scandens.
Echinocystis lobata. Wild balsam apple. Self-sows, thus becoming persistent. These last two are annuals. *See also* VINES.

WILD FLOWERS AND FERNS. Many of these are adapted through their natural habits to shade conditions. *See* WILD GARDEN. *See also* FERNS AND FERN GARDENING.

In the city when plants are under trees, the oil and soot deposits on the tree leaves are washed down upon them and form an added menace to the naturally obnoxious drip. The plant foliage becomes coated, transpiration is checked, and the plant slowly suffocates. In small gardens it is possible to keep the large-leaved types such as rhododendrons sponged off with soap and water, and others well and continuously washed off with the hose spray. The conifers are especially grateful for this treatment. *See* DRIP. — H. M. C.

SHAGBARK HICKORY = *Carya ovata* and *C. laciniosa. See* HICKORY.

SHAKESPEARE GARDEN. A garden designed to include the furniture, statuary, and other features of gardens in Shakespeare's time, but also, and most important, to grow in such a setting all the plants mentioned by him in the plays or other poetry. Not all of these can be grown outdoors but many can and lists of them are available in various works on Shakespeare. Most Shakespearean gardens are in public parks and can be seen at Central Park, New York City; Toledo, Alliance, and Cleveland, Ohio; Bridgeport, Conn.; Portland, Ore.; Cedarbrook Park, Plainfield, N.J.; Convent, N.J.; Golden Gate Park, San Francisco, Calif.; University of Pennsylvania, Philadelphia, Pa., and in some other cities.

Shallon (shall'on). Original Indian vernacular for the salal (*Gaultheria Shallon*).

SHALLOT (*Allium ascalonicum*). An onion-like plant, often called eschallot, and grown for the small, pointed, grayish bulbs, sometimes called cloves.* These are the separable parts of the parent bulb and are used for cooking or for flavoring and are considerably milder than onions. They are more popular in Eu. than here.

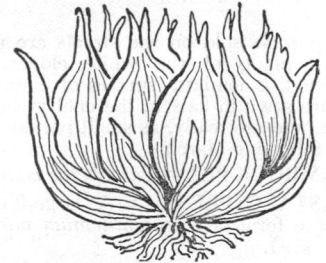

Shallot, showing the cloves*

Shallot is grown by planting the small bulbs just as onion sets are planted (*see* ONION), and their subsequent care and cultivation are the same. But unlike the onion, the maturing bulb of shallot separates into sections (cloves) which are harvested in the fall and will keep, when dried as are onions, for several months.

* Special articles on the subjects indicated by an asterisk (*) will be found at the words so marked.

The young leaves of shallot are sometimes harvested as are those of bunching onions and usually pass for onions in this state. Also young onion bulbs are sometimes sold as shallots, but the latter can usually be told by their grayish color, and by the fact that they are pointed and more or less angular. The shallot is sometimes called cibol, but that name is better restricted to the Welsh onion (*Allium fistulosum*). The insect pests of shallot are the same as for the onion.

SHALLU = *Sorghum vulgare roxburghi.*

SHAMROCK. In different seasons and in different regions at least three cult. plants pass as "shamrock." The most common and perhaps the true shamrock, if there is one, is the common white clover (*Trifolium repens*). Another plant often sold as shamrock is the hop clover (*Medicago lupulina*). The third is a wood sorrel (*Oxalis Acetosella*). Which is the true shamrock might be left to the Irish, if they agreed, but they do not. In the U.S.

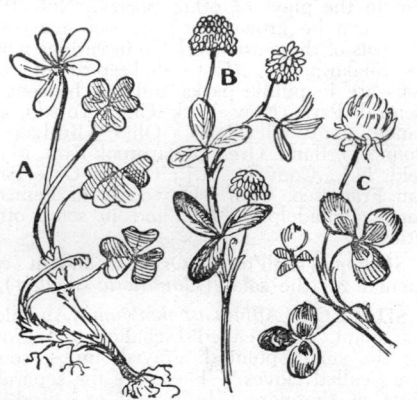

Three plants that pass as shamrock: (*A*) *Oxalis Acetosella*; (*B*) *Medicago lupulina*; (*C*) *Trifolium repens.*

the shamrocks sold on the streets are usually seedling plants of the white clover or of *T. dubium*, a non-hort. species of clover. The seeds are sown in flats in the cool greenhouse in Sept. and are ready, as small potted plants, by the following March.

SHAMROCK PEA = *Parochetus communis.*

SHASTA CYPRESS = A large-flowered, handsome form of *Chrysanthemum maximum* (which see).

SHAWNEE SALAD = *Hydrophyllum virginianum.*

SHEATH. Any tubular or sheathing organ, often leaflike or membranous, which surrounds the base of a stalk or helps to form one. Sheaths are common in the grasses, in some plants of the family Polygonaceae and on many flower stalks. Some bracts* are sheathing, notably in the palms, and the sheathing leaf bases of the banana make up its stem.

SHEEPBERRY = *Viburnum Lentago.*

SHEEP-LAUREL = *Kalmia angustifolia.*

SHEEP'S-BIT = *Jasione perennis.*

SHEEP'S-FESCUE = *Festuca ovina.*

SHEEP SORREL = *Oxalis Acetosella.*

SHEEP'S-SORREL = *Rumex Acetosella.* See list at WEEDS.

SHEEPWEED = *Pinguicula vulgaris.*

SHELLBARK HICKORY = *Carya ovata* and *C. laciniosa. See* HICKORY.

SHELL-FLOWER = *Chelone glabra, Molucella laevis,* and *Alpinia speciosa.*

SHELTER TREES. See WINDBREAK.

SHE-OAK. See CASUARINA.

SHEPHERDIA (shep-her′di-a). Three species of very hardy North American shrubs of the family Elaeagnaceae, two of them in rather common cult., the third evergreen and known mostly in the wild. They are spreading shrubs, one of them prickly, with opposite,* stalked leaves, and inconspicuous, small, yellowish flowers, the male and female on different plants. Petals none. Calyx* or sepals* petal-like. Stamens* 8. Fruit fleshy, drupe-like, really a dry fruit enclosed by the fleshy calyx, edible in the first species. The genus was once and is sometimes still called *Lepargyrea.* (Named for John Shepherd, a curator of the Liverpool Botanic Garden.)

Both species are among the hardiest shrubs in cult., being perfectly at home far up into zone* 1. They will stand dry, wind-swept sites, stony soils, and much abuse, especially the first species, which is sometimes planted for hedges in places where no other hedge plant will survive. Easily propagated from seed. If fruit is wanted, both sexes must be planted.

argentea. Buffaloberry; also called wild oleaster and silverleaf. A spiny or thorny shrub or small tree, 10–18 ft. high, the foliage silvery both sides. Leaves oblongish, ½–2½ in. long, more or less wedge-shaped at the base. Fruit egg-shaped, yellowish or red, about ⅓ in. long, sour, but prized for jellies. Central N.A. far northward. April–May.

canadensis. Buffaloberry. Not over 8 ft. high and without spines or thorns. Leaves elliptic or ovalish, ¾–1½ in. long, green above, silvery beneath. Fruit egg-shaped, yellowish-red, about ⅓ in. long, nearly tasteless. Throughout northern N.A. and northward to Alaska. April–May.

SHEPHERD'S-PURSE = *Capsella Bursa-pastoris.* See list at WEEDS.

SHEPHERD'S-SCABIOUS = *Jasione perennis.*

SHERWOOD GARDENS. See No. 13 at GARDEN TOURS.

SHEUGH. An old term for heeling-in, which see at PLANTING.

SHIELD FERN. See DRYOPTERIS.

SHINGLE OAK = *Quercus imbricaria.* See OAK.

---

* Special articles on the subjects indicated by an asterisk (*) will be found at the words so marked.

SHINLEAF. See PYROLA.

SHINLEAF FAMILY. See ERICACEAE.

SHIN-PLASTERS = *Orchis rotundifolia.*

SHIPMAST LOCUST. See *Robinia Pseudoacacia* at LOCUST.

SHIRLEY POPPY. See *Papaver Rhoeas* at POPPY.

SHITTIMWOOD. A name applied to two cult. plants. See BUMELIA LANUGINOSA, which is perhaps better called chittamwood. See also RHAMNUS PURSHIANA.

SHOEBLACK PLANT = *Hibiscus Rosasinensis.*

SHOOFLY = *Baptisia tinctoria.* See also NICANDRA PHYSALODES.

SHOOT. Any growth, usually lateral, from a bud, which diverges from a main axis or stem. A shoot may, and often does, produce both flowers and leaves, but many leafy shoots do not produce flowers until the second season.

SHOOTING STAR. See DODECATHEON.

SHORE PINE = *Pinus contorta.* See PINE.

SHORE PLANTS. See SEASIDE GARDENS.

SHORT-DAY PLANTS. See PHOTOPERIODISM.

SHORTIA (short'i-a). Low-growing evergreen herbs, comprising 2 species of the family Diapensiaceae, and natives of the mountains of N. Car., S. Car., and Jap. They have creeping, underground stems, and basal, roundish, or heart-shaped, shining green, stalked leaves, the margins wavy. Flowers white, solitary, on leafless stalks to 8 in. high. Calyx* of 5 sepals surrounded by a few scaly bracts.* Corolla of 5 petals, bell-shaped. Stamens* 5, growing on the petals, alternating with 5 sterile stamens. Fruit a

Shortia galacifolia, a rare perennial from the Carolina mountains needing shade and a peaty soil. Flowers waxy, white, and usually blooming in May. Not suited to open places.

3-celled capsule. (Named for Dr. Charles W. Short, Kentucky botanist.)

The American plant below is especially adapted for the rock garden but must be grown in shade, in soil composed of sandy peat and leaf mold. It is difficult to establish, so should not be moved more than necessary. Propagated by division in April. It and the second species have no valid common names, and the first has long been simply called shortia. Names, however, have been manufactured for them by the bookish, and "Oconee Bells" for the American plant and "Nippon Bells" for the Japanese one, have a certain currency.

californica = *Baeria coronaria.*

galacifolia. Leaves basal, long-stalked, roundish, sometimes heart-shaped at base, the margins wavy. Flowering stalk slender, to 8 in. high. Flowers white, to 1 in. across, nodding. Mountains of N. Car. and S. Car.

soldanelloides = *Schizocodon soldanelloides.*

uniflora. Resembling *S. galacifolia,* and perhaps not distinct from it, but differing in its more deeply heart-shaped, wavy-margined leaves. Jap.

SHOW GERANIUM = *Pelargonium domesticum.*

SHOWY CRABAPPLE = *Malus floribunda.*

SHOWY LADY'S-SLIPPER = *Cypripedium reginae.*

SHOWY ORCHIS = *Orchis spectabilis.*

SHOWY PRIMROSE = *Oenothera speciosa.* See EVENING PRIMROSE.

SHRIMP PLANT = *Beloperone guttata.*

SHRUB. The distinction between a tree and shrub is difficult to make and breaks down in many commonly cult. plants. Generally a shrub is a low, woody plant that has several stems instead of a single trunk, as most trees have. But quite a few trees bear several trunks or branch rather low down and are hence shrub-like, while some shrubs tend to have only one main stem and are then tree-like.

For garden purposes shrubs are of infinite variety. There is no need to repeat here all those found in this book. Those that are particularly showy will be found listed at FLOWERING SHRUBS. Some beautiful evergreen sorts are noted at BROAD-LEAVED EVERGREENS. See also AZALEA, RHODODENDRON. For the uses and care of shrubs see Shrub Border at BORDER. See also PRUNING.

SHRUB. A common name for *Calycanthus.*

SHRUBBERY. A shrub border or a planting of shrubs. See BORDER.

SHRUBBY ALTHAEA = *Hibiscus syriacus.*

SHRUBBY BITTERSWEET = *Celastrus scandens.*

SHRUBBY CINQUEFOIL = *Potentilla fruticosa.*

SHRUBBY FERN = *Comptonia peregrina.*

SHRUB YELLOWROOT = *Xanthorhiza simplicissima.*

SHUCK. The outer husk of a fruit, as in

---

* Special articles on the subjects indicated by an asterisk (*) will be found at the words so marked.

the hickory, or the husks of corn. A more unusual use for *shuck* is a specialized one. In the flowers of the peach and cherry the calyx* becomes gradually drier and is ultimately pushed off by the expanding fruit. Such a shed calyx is known as a shuck.

SIBERIAN CRABAPPLE = *Malus baccata* and *M. robusta.*

SIBERIAN ELM = *Ulmus pumila.* See ELM.

SIBERIAN IRIS. *See* IRIS ORIENTALIS and I. SIBIRICA.

SIBERIAN LARKSPUR = *Delphinium grandiflorum.*

SIBERIAN MILLET = *Setaria italica rubrofructa.*

SIBERIAN SQUILL = *Scilla sibirica.*

SIBERIAN TEA = *Bergenia crassifolia.*

SIBERIAN WALLFLOWER = *Erysimum asperum.*

sibirica, -us, -um (sy-bir'i-ka). From Siberia.

SICANA (si-kay'na). Tropical American tendril*-bearing, fleshy-stemmed vines of the family Cucurbitaceae, comprising only three species, one of them, **S. odorifera**, the cassabanana or curuba, grown for its fragrant, ornamental fruit which is also edible. It is a perennial, high-climbing vine (to 40 ft.), with angled stems and branched tendrils.* Leaves alternate,* nearly round, 7–12 in. wide, conspicuously lobed, heart-shaped at the base, the margins shallowly angled or wavy-toothed. Flowers yellowish, the male and female separate, but on the same plant. Male flowers about ½ in. long. Female flowers about 2 in. long. Fruit very fragrant, cylindric or oblong, 15–24 in. long, orangered. Brazil(?). It can only be grown, as a perennial, in regions of strong summer heat, from the southern edge of zone* 7 southward. Elsewhere it can be started as a tender annual, and will make a quick growth, but may not flower or fruit northward. (*Sicana* is the Peruvian name for it.)

siceraria (siss-er-rare'i-a). Of or pertaining to cider (or an intoxicating drink); applied to *Lagenaria siceraria,* hence a "gourd for cider drinking."

SICKLE THORN = *Asparagus falcatus.*

sicula, -us, -um (sick'you-la). A little dagger.

SIDALCEA (sy-dall'see-a). False mallow. Annual or perennial herbs, comprising about 30 species of the family Malvaceae, natives of western N.A. Leaves alternate,* simple,* cut into finger-like lobes. Flowers purple, pink, or white, in terminal spikes. Calyx* of 5 sepals. Corolla of 5 petals. Stamens* in groups united by their filaments.* Fruits kidney-shaped, several, united at first, ultimately separable. (*Sidalcea* is a compounded word derived from *Sida* and *Alcea,* both of which are non-hort. genera.)

Sidalceas make good border plants, and only the perennial species are in cult. Easily propagated by seeds or division of roots. Seed should be sown in a cold frame in ordinary garden soil in early spring. They may be transplanted as soon as large enough to handle. Division of roots may be made in Sept., Mar., or Apr. Plants should be lifted every 3 years and soil well manured before replanting. They are sometimes rather short-lived and behave more like biennials than perennials.

candida. Perennial, growing to 3 ft. high, the foliage bright shining green. Lower leaves roundish, heart-shaped at base. Margins deeply cut, with rounded lobes. Upper leaves cut into 5–7 finger-like lobes. Flowers white, to ¾ in. across, in terminal spikes. Rocky Mountains.

malvaeflora. Wild hollyhock. Checkerbloom. Erect-growing perennial to 2 ft. high. Lower leaves bluntly lobed. Upper leaves cut into narrow segments. Flowers rose, to 1½ in. across, in many-flowered spikes. Calif. A good pink form is Rosy Gem. *See* PINK GARDEN.

parviflora. Strong-growing perennial, to 4 ft. high, the foliage bright green, slightly hairy. Leaves cut into finger-like segments. Flowers rose, to ½ in. across, in long, slender spikes. S. Calif.

SIDE OATS. *See* AVENA SATIVA.

Sideroxylon (si-der-rock'si-lon). A specific name derived from the genus *Sideroxylon* which is scarcely of hort. interest; it means hard wood. *See* EUCALYPTUS.

SIDESADDLE-FLOWER = *Sarracenia purpurea.* *See* PITCHER-PLANT.

SIERRA LILY = *Lilium parvum.*

SIERRA SHOOTING STAR = *Dodecatheon jeffreyi.*

SIEVE. Sifting soil through a screen or riddle is old garden practice to eliminate stones, roots, and often grubs. A small, circular sieve with a wire mesh with holes not over ¼ in. in diameter, is a useful tool. Larger ones, used by contractors to sift sand, are needed if much soil is to be sifted.

SIGHTSEEING. *See* GARDEN TOURS.

SIGHTWORT = *Chelidonium majus.*

sikkimensis, -e (sick-kim-en'sis). From Sikkim, India.

silaifolia, -us, -um (si-lay-i-fō'li-a). With leaves like a plant of the genus *Silaus,* a group of weedy herbs of no interest to hort.

SILENE (sy-lee'ne). Catchfly. Campion. Tender and hardy, annual, biennial, or perennial herbs, comprising about 500 species, belonging to the pink family, and distributed throughout the world. They are of erect, tufted or spreading habit, and the stems or calyx are sometimes sticky. Leaves opposite,* simple, without teeth. Flowers solitary or in loose-branching clusters, white, pink, or red. Calyx tubular, its 5 lobes teeth-like. Corolla of 5 separate petals. Stamens* 10. Fruit a capsule.* (*Silene* is from the Greek for saliva, in reference to the sticky stems of some species.)

Silenes are useful rock garden or border

---

* Special articles on the subjects indicated by an asterisk (*) will be found at the words so marked.

plants, although not many of the species are in cultivation. Easily propagated from seeds, by division, or by cuttings. The seeds of the annual species may be sown in the fall or spring. Seeds should be sown ⅛ in. deep, where plants are required to bloom. Seeds of perennial species should be sown ⅛ in. deep, in the cold frame, in early spring. They may be transplanted when large enough to handle. Division of plants may be made in Sept., Mar., or Apr. Cuttings of young shoots may be taken in July, and inserted in sandy soil in a cold frame, shading from sun until rooted. Perennials once established should not be moved but may be top-dressed each year with a mixture of soil and manure.

acaulis. Cushion pink. Moss campion. Tufted* perennial, to 2 in. high. Leaves lance-shaped, ½ in. long. Flowers purplish-red, solitary, ½ in. across. Eu. and N.A. June–Aug. For cult. see ROCK GARDEN.

alpestris. Alpine catchfly. Spreading perennial, to 6 in. high, with sticky stems. Leaves lance-shaped. Flowers satiny-white, ½ in. across, in loose clusters. Mountains of Eu. Summer. It is best grown in the moraine. See ROCK GARDEN. Also called *Heliosperma alpestre*. The var. **flore-pleno** has double flowers.

Armeria. Sweet William catchfly. None-so-pretty. Erect, glaucous, green annual, growing to 2 ft. high. Leaves broadly lance-shaped, to 3 in. long. Flowers light or deep pink, to ½ in. across, in terminal clusters. Southern Eu., naturalized in U.S. Summer.

caroliniana. Wild pink. A slender, unbranched, native perennial, 5–12 in. high, usually a little sticky. Leaves broadly lance-shaped, 2½–5 in. long, short-stalked. Flowers white or pink, about ¾ in. wide, in a sparse, terminal cluster, the petals not notched. In dry woods, eastern N.A. May. A closely related plant, *S. wherryi*, differs only in technical characters and is found in the central U.S.

compacta. Bright green biennial, growing to 2 ft. high. Leaves ovalish, to 2 in. long. Flowers pink, in densely clustered heads, to 3 in. across. Heads surrounded by a ring of leafy bracts.* Eastern Eu. and Asia Minor. June.

fortunei. Perennial, growing to 3 ft. high, the lower part of the stem woody. Leaves narrowly lance-shaped. Flowers white or pink, to ½ in. across, in short clusters. Calyx tube 1 in. long. Petals 2-lobed. China. Sept.

hookeri. Low-growing perennial, to 5 in. high. Leaves ovalish, to 2 in. long. Flowers white or pink, solitary, to 2 in. across, with fringed petals. Calif. and Ore.

maritima. Sea campion. Perennial, growing to 1 ft. high, grayish-green. Leaves broadly lance-shaped. Flowers white, ¼ in. across, in 1–4-flowered clusters. Calyx inflated. Petals lobed. Eu. June.

noctiflora. Erect annual, growing to 2 ft. high. Leaves lance-shaped. Flowers pale pink, opening at night, in small clusters. Petals 2-lobed. Eu.

orientalis = *Silene compacta*.

pendula. Spreading annual, growing to 10 in. high, covered with soft hairs. Leaves broadly lance-shaped. Flowers flesh-pink, to ½ in. across, in loose-branching, hanging clusters. Petals 2-lobed. Mediterranean region. The *var.* **rosea** has rose-colored flowers. See PINK GARDEN.

Saxifraga. Tufted perennial of shrubby habit, growing to 10 in. high. Leaves narrowly lance-shaped. Flowers greenish white, solitary, or in 2–5-flowered clusters. Petals 2-lobed. Eu. and Asia Minor.

Schafta. Moss campion. Perennial, of spreading habit, growing to 6 in. high, covered with short, soft hairs. Leaves small, lance-shaped, in rosettes. Flowers rose or purple, 1–2 flowers on each stalk. Petals notched. Caucasus. For culture see ROCK GARDEN.

stellata. Starry campion. A robust, unbranched native perennial, 7–20 in. high, the stem hairy. Leaves stalkless, ovalish or broadly lance-shaped, 3–6 in. long, pointed at the tip. Flowers white, about ¾ in. wide, star-like, the petals deeply notched. Eastern U.S. July.

virginica. Fire-pink. Indian pink. A showy, native perennial, 6–10 in. high. Leaves thin, oblongish or spatula-shaped. Flowers few, in a loose cluster (cyme*), the petals deep crimson, 2-cleft. In sandy and rocky woods, eastern N.A. June–Aug.

wherryi. Probably a geographical race of *S. caroliniana* (which see) and not significantly different from it.

SILICLE. See SILIQUE.

siliqua, -us, -um (sil-li′kwa). A silique.*

Siliquastrum (sil-li-kwas′trum). Bearing a silique* or a fruit like it.

SILIQUE. The dry, pod-like fruit of plants of the mustard family. It splits down both seams, leaving a parchment-like center. The term silique is properly restricted to those that are long and slender, as in the mustards. When, as in honesty and the shepherd's-

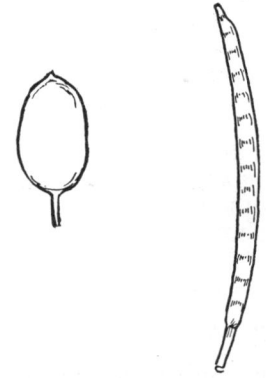

Silique (*right*) and a silicle (*left*)

purse, fruit is short or nearly roundish, it is called a silicle. See CRUCIFERAE.

SILK-COTTON TREE. See CEIBA.

SILK-COTTON TREE FAMILY = Bombacaceae.

SILK-OAK = *Grevillea robusta*.

SILK-TASSEL TREE = *Garrya elliptica*.

SILK TREE = *Albizzia Julibrissin*.

SILK VINE. See PERIPLOCA.

SILKWEED = *Asclepias*. See MILKWEED.

---

* Special articles on the subjects indicated by an asterisk (*) will be found at the words so marked.

SILKY. Covered with fine silky hairs, as are the leaves, and sometimes other parts, of many plants.

SILKY CAMELLIA = *Stewartia Malachodendron.*

SILKY CORNEL = *Cornus Amomum.*

SILPHIUM (sill'fi-um). Rosinweed. Hardy herbaceous perennials, comprising about 12 species of the family Compositae, natives of N.A. They are tall, strong and coarse herbs, the leaves opposite,* alternate* or in whorls,* the blades sometimes encircling the stem and holding water. Leaf margins sometimes lobed or toothed. Flower heads usually yellow, similar to the sunflower. Bracts* surrounding the head, leaf-like. Ray florets fertile, disk florets sterile. (*Silphium* is a Greek name for some resinous plant, but not of these, although adopted by Linnaeus for them.)

Easily cult., growing well in full sun. Propagated by seeds or division of roots. Seeds should be sown ¼ in. deep, in good garden soil, in cold frame or outdoor seedbed, in spring or early summer. Division of roots may be made in Sept., Mar., or Apr.

laciniatum. Compass-plant. Pilotweed. Growing to 12 ft. high, the stems and leaves covered with short, stiff hairs. Leaves broadly lance-shaped, to 1 ft. long, cut in 1–2 lance-shaped lobes. Upper leaves clasping the stem. Flower heads to 5 in. across. Midwestern states. July–Sept.

perfoliatum. Cup-plant. Indian cup. Growing to 8 ft. high, with square stems. Leaves ovalish, to 1 ft. long. Upper leaves clasping the stem. Flower heads to 3 in. across. Eastern N.A. July–Sept.

SILT. See SOILS.

SILVER BEET = Swiss chard. See BEET.

SILVER-BELL TREE. See HALESIA.

SILVERBERRY = *Elaeagnus commutata.*

SILVER FERN. See PITYROGRAMMA.

SILVER FIR = *Abies alba.* See FIR.

SILVER-LACE VINE = *Polygonum auberti.*

SILVERLEAF = *Shepherdia argentea.*

SILVER-LEAVED POPLAR = *Populus alba.*

SILVER LINDEN = *Tilia tomentosa.* See LINDEN.

SILVER MAPLE = *Acer saccharinum.* See MAPLE.

SILVER MORNING-GLORY. *Argyreia splendens.*

SILVER-ROD = *Solidago bicolor.* See GOLDENROD.

SILVER SAGE = *Salvia argentea.*

SILVER SHILLING = Honesty.

SILVERTOP PALMETTO = *Coccothrinax argentea* and *Thrinax microcarpa.*

SILVER TREE = *Leucadendron argenteum.*

SILVER-TRUMPET TREE = *Tabebuia argentea.*

SILVER VINE = *Scindapsus pictus argyraeus* and *Actinidia polygama.*

SILVER VINE FAMILY = Dilleniaceae.

SILVER WATTLE = *Acacia decurrens dealbata.*

SILVERWEED = *Thalictrum dioicum.*

SILVERY. Covered with silvery hairs or scales, as are the leaves of many of the plants in the list of "silver" entries above this one. Other genera in which there are plants with a silvery sheen will be found at *Santolina, Potentilla, Helianthemum.*

SILVERY SPLEENWORT = *Athyrium thelypteroides.*

SILVICULTURE. The growing of trees, *en masse,* for timber, firewood, or other use, as distinguished from the growing of trees for ornament. Silviculture is thus scarcely a garden operation, but *see* FORESTRY.

SILYBUM (sil-ly'bum). Annual or biennial herbs, comprising only 2 species of the family Compositae, natives of Eu., Af., and As. Leaves alternate,* with white spots and veins on the upper side, the margins lobed and spiny. Flower heads purplish, solitary and nodding. Bracts* surrounding the head, many, forming a globe-shaped receptacle for it. (*Silybum* is an old Greek name applied by Dioscorides to thistle-like plants.)

Grown as an ornamental plant for the silvery leaves. Also grown as a vegetable, roots, leaves, and flower heads being edible. Easily cult. Propagated from seeds. Seeds should be sown ⅛ in. deep, in ordinary garden soil where required to mature. If sown early they will bloom the first year.

Marianum. Lady's-thistle. Milk thistle. Holy thistle. Annual, sometimes biennial, growing to 4 ft. high. Leaves to 2½ ft. long, glossy, the margins wavy and spiny. Flower heads purplish-red, to 2½ in. across. Bracts* surrounding heads curved and spiny. Mediterranean region, naturalized in Calif.

SIMAROUBACEAE (sy-mar-roo-bay'see-ee). A family of over 30 genera of chiefly tropical shrubs and trees with alternate,* compound* leaves, the leaflets arranged feather-fashion. They have mostly small flowers, sometimes unisexual* and drupe-like fruit. The only genus of cult. interest is *Ailanthus,* which see for further particulars of the family Simaroubaceae.

SIMLING. See SQUASH.

SIMPLE. In a leaf, having only one blade to the main leafstalk; not compound.* For the sense in which a flower cluster is said to be simple, *see* INFLORESCENCE.

As a noun, *simple* is used for a medicinal herb or the medicine made from it, but this use of simple is disappearing with the passing of much old medical lore regarding the supposed or real medicinal virtue of many plants, always, in the old days, called simples.

simplex (sim'plecks). Unbranched.

simplicifolia, -us, -um (sim-pliss-i-fō'li-a). With simple,* not compound* leaves.

simplicissima, -us, -um (sim-pli-siss'-si-ma). Very much unbranched.

---

* Special articles on the subjects indicated by an asterisk (*) will be found at the words so marked.

SIM-SIM = *Sesamum indicum.*

sinensis, -e (sy-nen'sis). From China.

SINGLE FLOWERS. See DOUBLE FLOWERS.

SINNINGIA. See GLOXINIA.

sino-ornata, -us, -um (si-no-or-nay'ta). Literally, a Chinese ornamental; applied as a specific name to a showy Chinese gentian.

sinuata, -us, -um (sin-you-ā'ta). Sinuate; i.e., wavy-margined.

SINUS. Any recess or depression between two lobes; as the sinus of an oak leaf, or the usually sharper sinus of a maple leaf.

siphilitica, -us, -um (siff-i-lit'i-ca). Reputedly useful as a medicine for syphilis.

Sipho (sy'fo). A tube or pipe.

SIPHONOSMANTHUS (sy-fon-os-man'-thus) = *Osmanthus delavayi.*

SIRIS = *Albizzia Lebbek.*

SISAL = *Agave sisalana.*

sisalana, -us, -um (sy-sa-lā'na). From Sisal, an abandoned seaport on the coast of Yucatan. See AGAVE SISALANA.

Sisarum (sy-sair'rum). Greek name for some plant with an edible root, of uncertain application as applied to *Sium Sisarum.*

Sissoo (sis'soo). East Indian vernacular name for *Dalbergia Sissoo* (which see).

SISYRINCHIUM (sis-i-rink'i-um). Blue-eyed grass. Low-growing, American half-hardy or hardy perennial herbs, comprising about 75 species of the iris family, of grass-like habit, and with short rootstocks. Leaves erect, long and narrow, parallel-veined, pale green, or bluish-green, mostly shorter than the flowering stalk. Flowers reddish-purple, blue or yellow, in terminal umbels* enclosed in 1–2 bracts* (spathe*). Calyx of 3 colored sepals, the corolla of 3 petals, alternating with the sepals, widely open. Stamens* 3. Fruit a 3-celled capsule.* (*Sisyrinchium* is an old Greek name, at one time applied to another plant.) Sometimes known as satin-flower.

Not usually cult., but they make attractive flower border plants if planted in clumps, especially in damp places. They can also be used for naturalizing in the wild garden. Easily cult. Propagated by seeds or division of roots. Seeds should be sown ⅛ in. deep, in a cold frame in early spring. They may be transplanted as soon as large enough to handle. Division of roots should be made in Aug. or Sept.

angustifolium. Hardy perennial, growing to 1 ft. high. Leaves narrow, pale bluish-green. Flowering stalk flat and twisted. Flowers deep blue, with a 6-pointed white, star-like center, accented with golden-yellow, in 3–4-flowered umbels.* N.A. May–Aug. See BLUE GARDEN.

californicum. Golden-eyed grass. Half-hardy perennial, growing to 1 ft. or more. Leaves many, erect, to 10 in. high, and ½ in. wide. Flowering stalks flat, and winged. Flowers bright yellow with brown markings, in 3–6-flowered umbels.* Ore. to Calif.

douglasi. Spring bell. Hardy perennial, to 1 ft. high. Leaves short, sheathing the stem.

Flowers reddish-purple, sometimes white, in 3–4-flowered umbels.* Western N.A. March. See WINTER GARDEN. Apt to be short-lived.

grandiflorum = *S. douglasi.*

sitchensis, -e (sit-chen'sis). From Sitka, Alaska.

SITE. While few gardeners can choose what might be considered a perfect site, there are a few things about site and exposure that are worth consideration. The purely aesthetic aspect of site, such as the utilization of distant scenes or vistas, the planting-out of the objectionable objects, or the screening-out of the noise and dust of the street — these are part of landscape design.

Here we are concerned mostly with site as it affects planting, and thoughtful gardeners will do well to study their site thoroughly before making any plans. The two most important things about a site are its exposure and topography.

A site exposed to bitter winds, or to the still more trying winds from the South in March and April, should be avoided for evergreens, if possible. Such a site should be protected by dense screen planting. Another site which is difficult to control is one exposed to steady sea breezes. But some very fine gardens have been made directly back of the dunes by molding the sand and planting dense groves of the London plane or the Japanese black pine. Such an ambitious changing of the fundamentals of a site is not always possible. But what every gardener can do is to consider site as pretty much fixed by local topography and plant with relation to his site.

Such common-sense procedure involves the planting of things out of the direct wind, if possible. It avoids the lowest places for the most tender of the woody plants, because of cold-air drainage to such places. And it sees that every advantage is taken of topography, soil condition, and water supply, rather than the reverse. See MICRO-CLIMATE.

SITFAST = *Ranunculus repens.* See Creeping Buttercup in the list at WEEDS.

SITKA COLUMBINE = *Aquilegia formosa.* See COLUMBINE.

SITKA CYPRESS = *Chamaecyparis nootkatensis.*

SITKA SPRUCE = *Picea sitchensis.* See SPRUCE.

SIUM (si'um). A genus of 10 species of perennial herbs of the family Umbelliferae, mostly from the north temperate zone, only S. Sisarum, the skirret, of any garden interest, and a root crop of secondary importance. It is a tuberous-rooted, perennial herb, 1–3 ft. high, with compound* leaves, the leaflets arranged feather-fashion, usually in 1–3 pairs, narrow and toothed. Flowers very small, white, in a terminal, much-divided, compound umbel.* Fruit flattened, dry, 3-ribbed on the face and ribbed on either edge. The roots, which are used like salsify, need most of the season for development. Seeds should be sown in drills in the spring (or late fall

---

* Special articles on the subjects indicated by an asterisk (*) will be found at the words so marked.

southward). Germination is slow and poor and allowance should be made for this and for the fact that the plants will have to be thinned to 8 in. apart in the row. The roots may be harvested in the fall or left in the ground all winter. In the latter case a light mulch of straw or leaves will facilitate digging. The skirret came from eastern As., and is little known here. (*Sium* is an ancient Greek name for a marsh plant, most of the genus growing in such places.)

SKEWERWOOD = *Euonymus atropurpureus.*

SKIMMIA (skim′i-a). Somewhat tender Asiatic evergreen shrubs of the family Rutaceae, two of the 9 known species grown for ornament. They have alternate,* short-stalked, dotted leaves, without marginal teeth, decidedly aromatic when crushed. Flowers small, white, some of them perfect,* others polygamous,* and in the first species the sexes on different plants. The male flowers are larger than the others, very fragrant, and borne in larger clusters (panicles *). Female flowers usually with 4–5 sterile stamens.* Fruit red, berry-like, but actually a drupe* with 2–5 stones. (*Skimmia* is the Latin version of a Japanese native name for some species.)

The skimmias are handsome evergreen shrubs, occasionally grown in the cool greenhouse northward where they should be given potting mixture* 4 and preferably plunged* during the summer. Their chief value is for outdoor plantings in the South, as indicated below. In the first species care must be taken to plant both male and female shrubs if the attractively colored fruits are desired. Propagated by seeds or by cuttings over bottom-heat.*

fortunei = *Skimmia reevesiana.*

japonica. A low, densely branching shrub, 3–5 ft. high, or often less. Leaves more or less crowded at the ends of the twigs, elliptic or oblongish, 3–5 in. long, yellowish-green. Male and female flowers usually on different plants, yellowish-white, about ⅓ in. wide. Fruit nearly round, about ⅓ in. thick, bright red. Jap. April–May. Hardy from zone* 6 (with protection) or from zone* 7 southward.

reevesiana. Similar to *S. japonica*, but about half as high, and with narrower and shorter leaves. Flowers generally perfect* or polygamous,* whitish. Fruit inverted egg-shaped, dull crimson. China. April–May. Hardy from zone* 5 southward. Sometimes known as *S. fortunei.*

SKIRRET = *Sium Sisarum.*

SKULLCAP. See Scutellaria.

SKUNK-CABBAGE. A single species of foul-smelling marsh herbs constituting the genus **Symplocarpus** (sim-plo-kar′pus) of the family Araceae, common in wet places in eastern N.A. and of little garden interest, except as occasionally transferred to shady, wet places in the wild garden. The only species, **S. foetidus**, the common skunk-cabbage, also called swamp cabbage and polecat-weed, is a coarse herb with a very large, deep root. Leaves large, handsome, nearly round, the blades 8–12 in. in diameter, all basal, long-stalked, and appearing after the flowers. The latter appear in late Feb. or Mar. in a closed, beautifully colored, sheath-like spathe,* within which is the club-shaped spadix* (*see* Araceae for details). Fruit an aggregate of brownish-green, berry-like units. The plant is also known as *Spathyema.* For a Pacific Coast skunk-cabbage *see* Lysichitum. (*Symplocarpus* is from the Greek for connection and fruit, in allusion to the coalescence of the ovaries into an aggregate fruit.)

SKUNK SPRUCE = *Picea glauca.* See Spruce.

SKUNKWEED = *Polemonium confertum.*

SKY-FLOWER = *Duranta repens* and *Thunbergia grandiflora.*

SKYROCKET = *Gilia aggregata.*

SLATY GUM = *Eucalyptus tereticornis.*

SLEEK-LEAF = *Leiophyllum buxifolium.*

SLEEPING BEAUTY = *Oxalis Acetosella.*

SLEEPY DICK = *Ornithogalum umbellatum.*

SLENDER BLUE FLAG = *Iris prismatica.*

SLIME FLUX. A diseased condition of certain trees that results in the oozing of a semi-fluid exudation, which, unlike gum, does not harden. Its cause is obscure and not really understood. Healthy conditions and manuring to ensure good growth may be insurance against it, but no real control is known.

SLIME MOLDS. These molds are common in gardens, greenhouses, and on lawns. They do not harm the plant on which they attach themselves, since their source of nourishment is decaying organic matter in the soil. At times the slime molds appear as irregular masses of yellow or white slimy material. A few days later the mass turns gray or black as it forms spores.* It is commonly found in patches on the lawn where it produces "gray pearls" on the leaf blades. Break up the mass with a rake, or wash off with water.

SLIP. A cutting. See Cuttings. The word slip is also applied, occasionally, to the ratoons* of the pineapple.

SLIPPER-FLOWER = *Pedilanthus tithymaloides.*

SLIPPERWORT. See Calceolaria.

SLIPPERY ELM. In the East, *Ulmus rubra* (*see* Elm). In the West, *Fremontia californica.*

SLOE = *Prunus spinosa.* The fruit is used to flavor sloe gin; its wood is the blackthorn.

SMALLER YELLOW LADY'S-SLIPPER. See Cypripedium Calceolus.

SMALL FRUITS. See Bush Fruits.

SMALL HONEYSUCKLE = *Lonicera dioica.*

SMALL-LEAVED LINDEN = *Tilia cordata.* See Linden.

---

* Special articles on the subjects indicated by an asterisk (*) will be found at the words so marked.

SMALL PLACE. *See* Planning the Home Grounds.

SMALL SOLOMON'S-SEAL = *Polygonatum biflorum. See* Solomon's-seal.

SMALL WOODBINE = *Lonicera dioica.*

SMARTWEED. *See* Polygonum.

SMILACEAE. *See* Liliaceae.

SMILACINA (smy-la-see′na). False Solomon's-seal. Perennial herbs, comprising about 20 species of the lily family, natives of North America and temperate Asia, with thick rootstocks. Leaves simple,* alternate,* broadly lance-shaped, with parallel veins. Flowers greenish-white in racemes* or terminal branching clusters, sometimes fragrant. Calyx of 3 colored sepals. Corolla of 3 petals alternating with the sepals. Stamens* 6 in 2 whorls.* Fruit a 3-celled berry. (*Smilacina* is a diminutive of *Smilax,* to which these plants are related.)

Not much in cultivation, but can be used in the hardy border or wild garden. Easily propagated by division of roots. They can be raised from seed, but period before flowering time would be several years.

racemosa. Wild spikenard. Treacleberry. Growing to 3 ft. high. Leaves alternate,* ovalish, to 6 in. long. Flowers greenish-white in terminal, branching clusters, to 4 in. long. Fruit a pinkish-red berry. Shaded places, N.A.

stellata. Starry Solomon's-seal. Growing to 20 in. high. Leaves broadly lance-shaped, to 5 in. long, clasping the stem. Flowers greenish-white in short racemes.* N.A.

SMILAX (1). The term has two distinct hort. meanings. The common smilax of the florists, widely used for decoration, is usually *Asparagus asparagoides,* the culture of which is discussed at Smilax (2). But *Smilax,* as a genus of plants, comprises the common catbriers or greenbriers, and they are the plants here considered. The genus *Smilax,* which belongs to the lily family, comprises over 300 species of herbaceous or woody, usually prickly vines, widely distributed in both tropical and temperate regions. All climb by tendrils,* borne in pairs in the leaf axils.* The lower leaves are reduced to scales, but the upper ones produce proper blades, which are without marginal teeth, but sometimes slightly lobed, with 3–9 main veins, and sometimes blotched with white. Male and female flowers always on separate plants, small, greenish-yellow or white, mostly in small, stalked umbels* in the leaf axils.* Sepals and petals totaling 6, alike, soon falling. Male flowers with 6 stamens.* Fruit a small berry. (*Smilax* is the ancient Greek name for these vines.)

The plants of the genus *Smilax* are of the easiest culture, and the only real difficulty is to prevent them from making impenetrable, prickly thickets as they always do in the wild. For such a purpose they are surpassed by almost no other cult. plants. Elsewhere they easily become a nuisance. They grow in all sorts of soils, but most often in sandy, poor ones. Only a very few are cult. Some tropical species yield sarsaparilla.

herbacea. Carrion-flower. Stems not prickly or only slightly so, usually dying down at the end of the season. Leaves not evergreen, ovalish to narrower, 3–5 in. long, generally heart-shaped at the base. Fruit bluish-black, in rather handsome, long-stalked umbels.* Eastern N.A. May.

laurifolia. A high-climbing, very prickly vine, the prickles straight. Leaves evergreen, thick and leathery, oblongish, 2½–5 in. long, 3-veined, dark green above, paler beneath. Fruit black, usually produced the second season. N.J. to Fla. and westward. July–Aug. Hardy from zone* 4 southward.

rotundifolia. Common catbrier; also called horse brier. A green-stemmed, wiry vine, prickly, but the prickles never at the joints. Leaves nearly round, shining, green both sides, more or less heart-shaped at the base, 2–4½ in. wide. Fruit bluish-black. Eastern N.A. June. Often a prickly nuisance on estates, and difficult to eradicate, as it has numerous, long-creeping rootstocks.

The last two species are highly inflammable and a fire hazard.

SMILAX (2) (*Asparagus asparagoides*). Smilax is propagated from seeds. Seeds should be sown thinly in flats during the month of February. When the plants are from 2

Above, the smilax of the florists (*Asparagus asparagoides*); below, the common catbrier (*Smilax rotundifolia*).

to 3 inches high, prick off into 2¼-in. pots in a soil composed of 3 parts loam, 1 part well-decayed cow manure. In early May the plants should be shifted into 4-inch pots, and by the middle of June they will be ready for benching. *See* Bench.

Grow in a well-drained, solid bed containing a soil the texture of a rose soil. Plant at a distance of 10 × 7 in. In training, place a wire close to the soil near the plant and a wire parallel to this near the roof of the greenhouse, and at each plant run up a string of silkaline. Keep the bed cultivated and train the new growths as they develop. Smilax, when established, makes rapid

---

* Special articles on the subjects indicated by an asterisk (*) will be found at the words so marked.

growth; therefore, liberal waterings are necessary. Syringe to keep down red spider and fumigate with tobacco occasionally to destroy aphids. Water sparingly after cutting until new growth appears, then top-dress with a good, rich soil. A temperature of 60°–65° gives best results. The house should be shaded during the early spring and summer. It thrives outdoors along the Gulf Coast.

SMILING WAKEROBIN = *Trillium undulatum*.

SMITHIANTHA. See NAEGELIA.

SMOKE. For most city gardeners and for many suburban ones smoke is a serious cause of failure or at least the explanation for poor and stunted plants. Smoke is of different sorts and degrees of harmfulness to plants. The worst of all are the industrial smokes from smelters and gas works, which are usually fatal if long continued. They definitely poison the air and prevent the normal interchange of gases in leaves, as described in the article PLANT FOODS.

Ordinary chimney smoke, mostly from soft coal or anthracite, while harmful, is chiefly so from the sooty deposit left on leaves, especially in foggy weather. Still more likely to stick to foliage is the smoke from oil-burning furnaces, and perhaps from your own. In this connection, it pays to study weather charts for the prevailing direction of the wind, and try to keep your choicer plantings to windward of this menace.

The smoke deposit derived from these non-industrial chimneys can, in small gardens, be removed by frequent syringing, or even sponging off of the leaves of broad-leaved plants. But such a task becomes too much of a steady chore, and if there is no escape from the smoke it is better to choose relatively smoke-resistant plants.

SMOKE-ENDURING SHRUBS, VINES, AND TREES

After many years of experiment the plants most likely to endure smoke have been found to be the following. For a description of each, turn to the names listed, and in the body of the ENCYCLOPEDIA OF GARDENING will be found notes on their general culture and hardiness. Especially fine smoke-endurers are marked with a dagger (†).

Acanthopanax sieboldianus
†Ailanthus altissima
Aralia spinosa
Aucuba japonica
Berberis thunbergi
†Campsis radicans
†Catalpa bignonioides
Chaenomeles japonica
Cornus Mas
Cornus sanguinea
†Deutzia scabra
†Elaeagnus multiflora
Elder (*Sambucus canadensis*)
Forsythia (most species)
†Hibiscus syriacus

†Hydrangea paniculata
†Lonicera tatarica
†Lycium halimifolium
Mock-orange (*Philadelphus coronarius*)
Mulberry (*Morus alba*)
Physocarpus opulifolius
†Platanus acerifolia
†Privet (most species)
†Rhamnus cathartica
Rhodotypos scandens
†Rhus copallina
†Spiraea vanhouttei
†Symphoricarpos (all species)
Viburnum Opulus

From such a collection it is possible to choose plants for a border screen that may strain out a lot of the deposit from smoke fumes. Behind such a protective planting it is often feasible to grow a fairly good garden, but only if most of the smoke can be sifted out by these smoke-enduring species.

SMOKE-TREE. See COTINUS.

SMOKING BEAN TREE. See CATALPA.

SMOOTH ALDER = *Alnus rugosa*. See ALDER.

SMOOTH-LEAVED ELM = *Ulmus carpinifolia*. See ELM.

SMOOTH SUMAC = *Rhus glabra*.

SMOOTH WINTERBERRY = *Ilex laevigata*. See HOLLY.

SMOTHER CROP. Sometimes fallow land, or a lawn being plowed up for reseeding, or a part of the vegetable garden, will suddenly become invaded by a crop of noxious weeds. The quickest way to stop this, if it is not desired to keep the land cultivated, is to plant a smother crop. As the name implies, the crop, if properly planted, will smother out the weeds.

If the invaders are mostly low weeds, Dutch clover, buckwheat, and particularly soybeans are as good smother crops as any. They must be sown broadcast, and very thickly, as the object is to get as thick and dense a stand as possible. If the weeds are higher, it is better to use oats or rye as the smother crop. When they have accomplished their purpose, smother crops should be plowed under (with the remains of the weeds). In the case of the grains, they will have to be harvested when ripe and only the stubble turned under. Smother crops are more often used on farms, but they may be equally useful in the garden on a smaller scale.

SMUDGES. It was long thought that smoky fires, so managed that they covered the orchard with a pall of smoke, were the best method of frost control. It is now known that the application of direct heat, smokeless or nearly so, is by far the most effective. See FROST.

SMUT. A type of fungus disease which usually produces a mass of gray or black spores* on the diseased portion of the plant. The cells under the black spores are killed, which makes it differ from slime mold.* The

---

* Special articles on the subjects indicated by an asterisk (*) will be found at the words so marked.

smut disease most encountered by the gardener is one which attacks corn and produces a gray, leathery mass on the ear or tassel. This mass eventually breaks open to release the black spores.

SNAIL-FLOWER = *Phaseolus Caracalla.*

SNAILSEED. *See* Cocculus.

SNAKE EGGPLANT. *See* Solanum Melongena serpentinum.

SNAKE GOURD = *Trichosanthes Anguina.*

SNAKE GRASS = *Tradescantia virginiana.* *See* Spiderwort.

SNAKE-HEAD = *Chelone glabra.*

SNAKE LILY = *Brodiaea volubilis.*

SNAKE MELON. *See* Melon.

SNAKEMOUTH = *Pogonia ophioglossoides.*

SNAKE PALM = *Hydrosme rivieri.*

SNAKE PLANT. *See* Sansevieria.

SNAKEROOT. More than 20 different plants have had the name snakeroot applied to them. Two of the best-known, among cult. plants, will be found at *Cimicifuga* and *Asclepiadora decumbens.* For other plants to which the name snakeroot is sometimes, or in part, applied, *see* Aristolochia, Eryngium, Eupatorium, Liatris, Polygala.

SNAKES. All the harmless sorts, such as garter snakes or black snakes, do the garden no harm and some good, for they feed upon insects, mice, moles, etc. Destruction of snakes, except the poisonous sorts, is hence absurd in spite of popular aversion to them.

SNAKE'S-HEAD = *Fritillaria Meleagris.*

SNAKE'S-HEAD IRIS = *Hermodactylus tuberosus.*

SNAP BEAN. The string bean (*Phaseolus vulgaris*). For culture *see* Bean.

SNAPDRAGON. Very popular garden and florists' flowers, all belonging to the genus **Antirrhinum** (an-tir-ry'num) of the family Scrophulariaceae, comprising over 30 species. They are hardy, herbaceous perennials or annuals, and natives of the northern hemisphere. Erect, climbing, or of spreading habit, sometimes covered with short, sticky hairs. Leaves alternate,* lance-shaped or ovalish, with heart-shaped base, sometimes bluntly lobed. Flowers solitary or in long terminal racemes,* the individual flower growing from the axil* of a small, leafy bract,* white, yellow, pink, red, or purple. Calyx* of 5 sepals. Corolla tubular, pouched, forming a mouth, the upper lip* 2-lobed, the lower lip 3-lobed, the lips turning outward. Stamens* 5, 4 fertile growing inside the corolla tube, 1 sterile. Fruit a dry, 2-celled capsule,* many-seeded. Seeds dispersed through pores. (*Antirrhinum* is from the Greek for like a nose, in allusion to the shape of the flower.)

For culture *see* below.

A. Asarina. Perennial, of spreading habit, covered with short, sticky hairs. Leaves oval-

ish, heart-shaped at base, cut into 5 rounded lobes. Flowers solitary, white or pale pink, to 1½ in. long. Southwestern Eu. Also called *Asarina procumbens.*

A. coulterianum. Chaparral snapdragon. Bright green, erect or climbing annual, to 3 ft. high. Leaves ovalish, to 1½ in. long. Flowers purple to white, with yellow hairs in throat of corolla, ½ in. long, in racemes. Calif.

A. majus. Common snapdragon, also called toad's-mouth. Bright green perennial, growing to 3 ft. high. Leaves lance-shaped, to 3 in. long. Flowers reddish-purple, sometimes white, to 1½ in. long, in long terminal racemes.* Mediterranean region. There are many hort. color forms in this species. *See* below.

Snapdragon Culture

Snapdragons are among the finest flowering plants for the garden. The hort. varieties which have been derived from the species *A. majus* can be obtained in so many colors from pure white through various shades of yellow, pink, orange, flame, red, and purple, that planted in masses they make a great show for the most humble gardener.

Snapdragon

They are divided roughly into 3 groups, the dwarf, growing to 9 in., the intermediate, growing to 20 in., and the tall, growing to 4 ft. All three have their place in the flower border or colored gardens, while the dwarf and intermediate can be used to advantage for bedding. They can also be grown for cut flowers in the greenhouse or outdoors, the tall-growing usually being used for the greenhouse.

The flowering period of the snapdragons can be extended by sowing seeds at different periods and by keeping the seed pods picked off. They are easily cult., but thrive best when grown under cool conditions. Propagated by seeds or cuttings.

For outdoor culture, seeds should be sown in light, sandy soil 1/16 in. deep, in a cold frame or in flats in a cool greenhouse in

---

* Special articles on the subjects indicated by an asterisk (*) will be found at the words so marked.

Aug. or Sept. As soon as large enough to handle they should be pricked off into a cold frame, continuing in light, sandy soil, about 3 in. apart, where they should be allowed to stand through the winter. They must be protected from hard frost, and this can be done by covering the sash with mats or old straw or hay. Air must be admitted every day when the temperature is above freezing. They must not be allowed to become dry.

In the spring the sash should be taken off every day and gradually left open at night so as to harden the plants off. They will stand a little frost if this treatment is given gradually. After this, they should be planted out where required to flower as early as possible so as to get well established before the hot weather. Seeds may also be sown in Jan. or Feb. in pans in cool greenhouse, pricked off into flats, and then removed to cold frame for hardening, before planting out in the garden. These plants will bloom a little later. In localities where there is not more than 15° of frost, they may be entirely grown out of doors.

For greenhouse culture, for winter- and spring-flowering, seeds should be sown from June–Aug. in pans in the coolest part of the greenhouse or in a cold frame, where they should be shaded from the sun until they have germinated. They should then be pricked off into flats and placed in the cold frame.

When 4 in. high they should be potted into 4-in. pots, using potting mixture* 3, still keeping them in the cold frame. After 2 weeks the tips should be pinched back to make them bushy. They may remain in these pots until a bench* has been prepared from Sept.–Jan., according to the time when they are required to flower. For instance, if sown in June and benched in Sept. they should flower the end of Dec. Benches should not be less than 4 in. deep; 6 in. is better. Soil for the bench should be old pasture loam and cow manure which has been lying for 6 months, and should be well mixed before filling the bench.*

Seedlings should be planted 10 in. apart and watered thoroughly to settle the soil round the roots. They should then be kept rather on the dry side until strong growth begins, in temperature of 45° at night and 55°–60° during the day. Four to six of the strongest shoots should be selected for flowering and all others pinched out. As the flowering stems grow, all side shoots must be pinched off. When plants are about 15 in. high, a light dressing of artificial manure should be given every week until the first flower opens.

Cuttings are only taken when it is desired to keep a particular variety or color, as plants do not always come true from seed. Cuttings root readily if inserted in sand and shaded from sun at any time.

Ants are very partial to snapdragon seeds, which are very small, and unless precautions are taken will carry them all away. To prevent this the seed pans should be placed on inverted pots in saucers of water, so making it impossible for the ants to reach the newly sown seeds. After germination the ants will not do any harm.

INSECT PESTS. Common greenhouse pests, such as aphids, leaf tiers, whiteflies, mites, and thrips, attack snapdragon (see CHRYSANTHEMUM, CARNATION, and BEGONIA). A black stink bug injures flowers outdoors (see tarnished plant bug at DAHLIA).

DISEASES. The most common disease of snapdragon is rust.* When plants are about 4 inches high, use pesticide #5 or #11 (see SPRAYS AND DUSTS), applied at 10-day intervals. Many varieties of snapdragon are now available which are rust-resistant, and should be used if gardeners do not wish to apply pesticides.

Leafspot* and blight* occasionally cause defoliation or death of plants if spots become numerous on the stem. The same pesticide as used for rust will prevent these two troubles.

In many areas a wilt* disease may cause death of entire plants. The disease is caused by the same organism which weakens chrysanthemums. Less common on snapdragon is another type of wilt disease known as southern wilt. The stem appears white and dry near the soil line. If small, black, seed-like objects are found inside the stem or around the plant at the soil line, it indicates this wilt disease. Destroy infected plants of both wilt diseases, and do not replant snaps in this area.

The foliage of snapdragon often becomes crinkled as a result of powdery mildew.* Use pesticide #9 at weekly intervals for control.

SNAPDRAGON FAMILY = Scrophulariaceae.

SNAPWEED. *See* IMPATIENS.

SNEEZEWEED. *See* HELENIUM.

SNEEZEWORT = *Achillea Ptarmica*.

SNOW. The white blanket of snow is a valuable protection to all perennial crops, but it is effective generally only from zone* 3 northward, as south of this, snow cover is either erratic or lacking altogether. The places of greatest snowfall in the U.S. are in the coast ranges in Ore., Wash., and northern Calif., where an annual accumulation of 8–10 ft. is not uncommon.

Besides its value as a winter protection to the plants it covers, snow is also of great value to plowed land. Hence comes its name of "poor-man's manure." It does not, of course, add any more plant food than rain does, but on many soils its accumulation and gradual thawing do help the physical texture of the soil.

SNOWBALL = *Viburnum Opulus sterile*. See also V. TOMENTOSUM STERILE.

SNOWBALL CACTUS = *Pediocactus simpsoni*.

SNOW-BELL = *Styrax americana*.

SNOWBERRY = *Symphoricarpos albus*. For the creeping snowberry *see* GAULTHERIA HISPIDULA.

SNOW BUSH = *Breynia nivosa*.

SNOWDRIFT = Sweet Alyssum.

---

* Special articles on the subjects indicated by an asterisk (*) will be found at the words so marked.

SNOWDROP. Pretty little spring-blooming bulbous herbs, comprising the genus **Galanthus** (ga-lan'thus) of the family Amaryllidaceae, all Eurasian, and 3 of the 10 known species cult. for their handsome, very early bloom. They have small bulbs, a solid flowering stalk, and only 2–3 narrow, basal leaves. Flowers solitary at the end of the stalk, usually nodding, the outer segments white, the inner green or greenish, without a tube. Stamens* 6. Fruit a 3-valved capsule.* (*Galanthus* is from the Greek for milk and flower, in allusion to the white bloom.) They are sometimes called Candlemas bells.

For culture *see* below.

G. byzantinus. Leaves broader than in the other 2 species, bluish-green, the margins recurved. Flowers about ¾ in. long, oblongish, the inner segments green, the outer white. Southeastern Eu. Jan.–Mar.

G. elwesi. Giant snowdrop. Flowering stalk 10–18 in. high, the leaves about 7 in. long, ¾ in. wide, very bluish-green. Flowers nearly 1¼ in. long, the inner segments partly green, the outer white. Asia Minor. Dec.–Apr.

G. nivalis. Common snowdrop. Flowering stalk 7–12 in. high, the leaves 6–8 in. long and not over ¼ in. wide. Flowers fragrant, about ¾ in. long, the inner segments partly green, the outer white. Eu. and southwestern As. Jan.–Apr. There is also a double-flowered form.

Snowdrop Culture

The flowering of the different snowdrop species covers many weeks of the early year. They are the first flowers to make their appearance and as such are very welcome. Most of the kinds flourish in light, rich soil beneath deciduous trees and shrubs, and in such positions the rotting leaves supply all the nourishment they require. But *G. elwesi* prefers a sunny situation and sandier soil, and a mulch of well-decayed manure may be given every other autumn.

Snowdrops should be planted in hundreds or thousands to make an effective display. If happy they increase freely and may be left undisturbed for years to form large, close colonies. It is of prime importance to get the bulbs planted early, in August if possible, certainly in September. Set them 3 in. deep and 3 in. apart. They may be combined with winter aconites, chionodoxas, snowflakes, *Scilla sibirica*, the early *Crocus* species, *Hyacinthus azureus*, and Christmas roses. Pussy willow bushes set about with snowdrops and Christmas roses provide the earliest garden picture of the year. — L. B. W.

SNOWDROP TREE. *See* HALESIA.

SNOWDROP WINDFLOWER. *See* ANEMONE SYLVESTRIS.

SNOWFLAKE. Spring- or autumn-flowering bulbous herbs, comprising the genus **Leucojum** (lew-kō'jum) of the family Amaryllidaceae, three of the 10 known species often cult. in the flower garden. All are natives in Eu. They have small bulbs and a hollow flower stalk which usually exceeds the basal, narrow leaves. The leaves appear with the spring-flowering species, but after the bloom in the fall-flowering sorts. Flowers not tubular, mostly nodding, the inner and outer segments alike, but often differently colored, generally white and tinged with red or green. Stamens* 6. Fruit a 3-valved capsule,* its seeds nearly globe-shaped. (*Leucojum* is from the Greek for white violet, probably in allusion to the violet-like odor of its flowers.) For the water snowflake *see* NYMPHOIDES INDICUM.

For culture *see* below.

L. aestivum. Flowering stalk 9–12 in. high, the leaves as long or a little longer, and about ½ in. wide. Flowers in clusters of 2–8, each flower about ¾ in. long, white, but green-tipped, on a slender, individual stalk. Eu. Late spring. Gravetye Giant is an especially fine hort. form.

L. autumnale. Flowering stalk 7–9 in. long, the shorter, thread-like leaves appearing after the fall bloom. Flowers 1–3 together, on slender, drooping, individual stalks, the corolla about ½ in. long, white, but red-tinged. Southern Eu. and northern Af. Fall.

L. vernum. Flowering stalk 9–12 in. high, the leaves a little less and about ½ in. wide. Flowers solitary, fragrant, white, but green-tipped, nodding, about ¾ in. long. Central Eu. Early spring.

Snowflake Culture

The snowflakes are perfectly hardy and flourish in rich garden soil of a somewhat sandy character. Planted in bold clumps between shrubs, in borders of ferns, or in the rock garden they are very effective. Once planted, 4 or 5 in. deep and about 4 in. apart, they need not be disturbed for years. They are easily propagated by bulblets,* which may be detached after the leaves have withered. The finest of the genus is Gravetye Giant, a form of *L. aestivum*. Its large blossoms are very showy and quite fragrant. Grouped with *Chionodoxa luciliae* it makes a cheerful early picture. — L. B. W.

SNOW-IN-SUMMER = *Cerastium tomentosum.*

SNOW-ON-THE-MOUNTAIN = *Euphorbia marginata.*

SNOW PEAR = *Pyrus nivalis.*

SNOW POPPY = *Eomecon chionanthum.*

SNOW TRAP. *See* WINDBREAK.

SNOW TRILLIUM = *Trillium nivale.*

SNOW WREATH = *Neviusia alabamensis.*

SOAPBARK TREE = *Quillaja Saponaria.*

SOAPBERRY. *See* SAPINDUS.

SOAPBERRY FAMILY = Sapindaceae.

SOAP PLANT = *Chlorogalum pomeridianum.*

SOAPWORT. *See* SAPONARIA.

SOBOLE. A sucker arising from the ground, often developing into a stem as important as the main one, especially in some palms which are then said to be soboliferous. Such plants appear to grow in clumps, but may be only a single one with several soboles.

---

* Special articles on the subjects indicated by an asterisk (*) will be found at the words so marked.

SOBRALIA (so-bray′li-a). Reed-like, leafy, stemmed, tropical American orchids with very showy flowers. They grow in the ground and comprise perhaps 60 species, of which **S. macrantha**, of Mex. and Guatemala, is by far the most popular in cult., although others are known in collections of fanciers. It has leafy stems 6–7 ft. high, the leaves tapering, 6–9 in. long, strongly veined, somewhat folded like the leaves of a fan. Flowers several, in a short terminal cluster (raceme*), generally short-lived. Flowers very irregular,* 5–6 in. wide, the petals and sepals spreading, pinkish-purple, the lip large, wavy-margined, deep purple. An extremely showy plant in bloom (May–July in the greenhouse), but the flowers not good for cutting, as they do not last. For culture *see* Tropical Orchid Cultivation at ORCHID. (Named for a Spanish botanist, D. F. M. Sobral, otherwise unknown.)

socotrana, -us, -um (so-ko-tray′na). From the island of Socotra, in the Indian Ocean.

SOD. *See* TURF.

SODIUM SELENATE. A suggested insecticide, used by some commercial growers of greenhouse flowers for the control of aphids, red spider, and mites. Its basis is selenium, a dangerous poison, and for crops that are edible its use is not without hazard. Also, concentrations greater than those advised by the experts, especially on soil in greenhouse benches, may kill all the plants one wishes to protect. Sodium selenate is for the use of professional growers who understand its dangers. — L. G. M.

SOFT RUSH = *Juncus effusus.*

SOFT SCALE. A scale insect with a very soft body. They are sometimes very destructive. One of the worst is the terrapin scale (which see).

SOIL BLOCK. A compressed "brick" of soil, containing seeds or rooted cuttings, which can be planted without disturbance of the roots.

SOIL. The source of all food which the plant does not get from the atmosphere, and the only food supply which can be controlled or at least ameliorated by the gardener; but *see* FOLIAR FEEDING. Since it is the basic material in which most plants are rooted, the soil has been much studied by the experts — its physical make-up, its chemical composition, and its greatly varying response to fertilizers, manure, and lime. Such a body of information is essential to the soil scientists, and much of what they have discovered is now translated into the common practice of the farmer and gardener. Not all of it, however, for there are still two diametrically opposed views of the proper management of soils. The first considers it as a medium to which commercial fertilizers can be added to produce a crop, without too much regard for the future. That, unhappily, has been a too common practice in the U.S., resulting in our yields

per acre, except for field corn, being the lowest in the world. The other concept, and the one here recommended, is to constantly build up the fertility, moisture-holding capacity, and hence the humus content of the soil. Special articles in this book deal with this so there is no need to repeat details here. *See*, especially, HUMUS, GREEN MANURING, COMPOST PILE, MANURE, and ORGANIC GARDENING. Following this procedure results in permanent enrichment of the soil, which is obligatory in many land leases in Europe, and is of paramount importance to the farmer and gardener.

For the latter there are two phases of soil that should be considered: (1) What it is, what kinds of soil there are, and their chemical make-up. All of this basic information is grouped under the general article SOILS (or at the articles cross-referenced from there). (2) What we do *with* soils, a topic which has for its scope the common garden skills such as plowing, digging, and the like. These are all summarized at the article SOIL OPERATIONS (or at the special cultural articles cross-referenced from it).

There still remains the much-debated question of soil acidity and alkalinity. All the information on this is at the entry ACID AND ALKALI SOILS.

The subject of soils is so important that we summarize here all the leading articles on it in this book. They will be found in the body of the book as they are listed below:

Soils (general, including kinds and texture).

Soil Moisture (general). *See also* special articles on IRRIGATION, MUCKLAND GARDENING.

Soil Management.

Soil Operations (general). *See also* special articles on CULTIVATION, DIGGING, HARROWING, HOEING, PLANTING, RAKING.

Fertility (brief). *See also* the articles on FERTILIZERS, MANURE, LIME.

Acid and Alkali Soils.

SOIL ACIDITY. *See* ACID AND ALKALI SOILS.

SOIL BINDERS. On banks too steep for turf, or in places where loose soil invites erosion, it is often desirable to plant herbs, shrubs, or even trees to cover the ground and hold the soils. In most gardens such places can be planted with the plants mentioned at GROUND COVERS and BANKS.

SOIL CONDITIONERS. Soils that contain too much clay are sticky, and will not crumble if dropped from the hand after being pressed into a lump. Everyone knows such soils; if the clay content is too high they are next to useless. The reason for this is that they contain colloidal material, which, as the etymology of *colloid* implies, means that they are something like glue. The soil, of course, does not contain real glue, but it is a glue-like property which holds the all but microscopic clay particles so tightly together that little aeration is possible, the moisture-holding capacity is too high — in other words, the soil is a sticky, wet mess in the spring and a sun-cracked nuisance in the summer.

The correcting of such a deficiency must have as its first objective the reduction of the effectiveness of the colloidal material in the clay. For a thousand years farmers have used lime for this, as in addition to reducing the acidity of soils (a purely chemical action) it has the capacity to unite microscopic clay particles into larger units. Such a remarkable property of lime ensures better aeration, reduces the colloidal action, and decreases the moisture-holding capacity of clay soils. Unfortunately this action is neither very strong nor prolonged.

Until recently such liming of farm and garden clay soils has been almost routine practice. The only other recourse is the mixing of plentiful amounts of organic matter (manure, compost, cover crop, etc. *See* these terms) into the soil. On a small scale, in most gardens, and if the soil is not impossibly clayey, this combination of liming and organic matter will make the soil manageable.

Where organic matter is not available, as in many home gardens, still another remedy is to add enough ordinary sand to lighten the soil. This must, of course, be thoroughly mixed with the clay soil, and since sand is all but inert it adds nothing to the fertility of the mixture, which the compost or manure certainly do.

Hence the origin of *soil conditioners*, a fairly new term in garden literature, but the need for which is as old as gardening. They use no lime, no compost or cover crops, and rely for their reputed action on chemical discoveries that have been made since 1950.

The basis of the reputable ones (some of the more bizarre have had restraining orders clamped down on them by the Federal Trade Commission) is that certain chemicals (*i.e.*, synthetic polyelectrolytes) have the reputed capacity to amalgamate both clay and silt particles in the soil, and hence do for them what lime and organic matter did, and do it more effectively. Such a concept quite naturally aroused tremendous interest, a good measure of skepticism, and downright unbelief by traditional gardeners.

Most of the experiment stations tested the leading varieties of soil conditioners, and enthusiasm — not unmixed with rather blatant advertising — ran high for the first year or two. Then reports of a somewhat more restrained tempo began to be repeated. The burden of them is that while certain of these products did have the effects claimed for them (a truly remarkable discovery), they were not always effective and, except for small areas, their cost is fantastic.

Furthermore, except for their effects upon the physical texture of soils, they add no plant food, nor do they provide an adequate environment for soil organisms (fungi and bacteria) upon which so much of soil fertility depends. Also, some of them might be explosive if mixed with ammonium nitrate, a common fertilizer ingredient. All that has been said above applies only to the reputable soil conditioners put out by responsible manufacturers.

Similar or imitative products, of which there are several, should be purchased only after weighing the above statements, and using a reasonable amount of purchaser's caution. Some of their advertising plays upon the eager gardener who will do or spend anything to "improve the soil," and is not always equipped to appraise the blatant claims.

To summarize the soil conditioner situation:

1. If your soil is in reasonably good tilth you need none. Most good garden loams do not need them.
2. If you have soil with too much clay or silt in it and you cannot add lime or organic matter, a reputable soil conditioner may be the answer, especially if your area is small (*i.e.*, less than 200 sq. ft.), since the expense is considerable.
3. If you use a soil conditioner follow the instructions on the container *with great care*. Too much of any of them may injure or kill plants.
4. Do not expect soil conditioners to last indefinitely; neither will lime or manure.
5. They must be raked or spaded into the ground, since surface spreading is useless.
6. Some soil conditioners are used diluted with water. If so used, follow dilution directions with great care. One such preparation is currently advertised at $9.95 per gallon (enough for 1000 sq. ft.!).
7. Soil conditioners do not add trace elements to the soil; compost and manure often do.
8. Soil conditioners are of little or no use on peat or muck soils.
9. Soil conditioners are no substitute for summer mulching. They may help to create a dust mulch by making heavy soils more friable. *See* Dust Mulch at MULCH AND MULCHING.
10. Soil conditioners will have little or no effect upon the natural fertility of your soil, *i.e.*, its nutritive ingredients.

The advantage of soil conditioners is unquestioned if their use and limitations are understood. As in the case of "magic" fertilizers, however, irresponsible and reckless dealers have put out a number of products for which there is no justification.

SOIL IMPROVEMENT. *See* GREEN MANURING.

SOIL INOCULATION. *See* LEGUME INOCULATION.

SOILLESS GARDENING. Growing plants in nutrient solutions has been a common procedure in laboratories for over a hundred years. No soil is used, the nutrient solutions are carefully controlled, and the plants are kept upright by wire frames or rooted in some sterile medium.

* Special articles on the subjects indicated by an asterisk (*) will be found at the words so marked.

So usual is this method that the scientific fraternity was not a little amazed to see a rush of publicity and a host of new terms applied to this almost routine procedure.

Many new terms were coined for it, such as *hydroponics, tank farming, water culture, chemical gardening, tray agriculture,* and no doubt others. Some were put out in good faith, but others were the result of publicity that ruins scientific progress as well as deceiving the public. Sifting fact from fiction seems to indicate what should be clearly understood before anyone attempts to grow plants in water instead of soil. These are:

1. Most plants, under proper conditions, *can* be grown in water, to which balanced rations of nutrient solutions must be regularly added.
2. Such water culture, except in rare instances, will not produce any better or larger yields than plants grown in soil.
3. Water culture solves the difficulty that some city dwellers have in never getting any really decent garden soil. Also some commercial growers, due to disease troubles, are glad to use water culture.
4. In a country with no scarcity of soil, such as the United States, water culture on any real agricultural scale is manifestly unnecessary. Where soil is scarce and water cheap, as in Holland, soilless gardening is perhaps justified.
5. Soilless gardening is no magic trick. It still needs common sense to grow plants and some knowledge that besides nutrient solutions plants require light and air, reasonable freedom from disease, and proper temperatures.

How to Start

Notwithstanding the handicaps and limitations there will always be gardeners who will want to grow plants in water instead of soil. To do so requires a brief study of the chemicals necessary to make the nutrient solutions. In the articles on FERTILIZERS and PLANT FOODS it is stated that the three principal food constituents of soils are phosphorus, nitrogen, and potash. But there are many other substances found in nearly all soils which plants demand, but only in minute quantities. Because some of these are so dilute, they are spoken of as *trace elements* (which see), while the more usual constituents are, for purposes of soilless gardening, known as *culture solutions.*

Culture solutions must contain more elements than ordinary fertilizer mixtures, because we must supply the other things found in adequate amounts in nearly all soils.

The forms in which these must be supplied and the accuracy necessary for their proper mixture will no doubt drive many water culturists to buying ready-prepared chemical mixtures in dried form, of which there are many on the market. But most growers will want to mix their own, both for safety and cheapness.

Nutrient Solutions

A general, all-purpose culture solution can be prepared in small quantities by purchasing four chemicals that can be had at any drugstore and in many florists' shops. If bought at the latter, it is essential to specify the grade of chemicals sold in drugstores and not the grade of chemical fertilizer for which an entirely different formula is necessary.

The formula (using drugstore chemicals) should be prepared as follows:

Culture Solution

Dissolve separately, each in a pint or more of tap water:

Monobasic potassium phosphate, 1¼ teaspoonfuls (or exactly 5.9 grams)

Calcium nitrate, 4 teaspoonfuls (or exactly 20.1 grams)

Magnesium sulphate, 1½ teaspoonfuls (or exactly 10.7 grams)

Ammonium sulphate, ½ teaspoonful (or exactly 1.7 grams)

Thoroughly dissolve the salts and then pour each into a container to which enough water is added to make exactly five gallons. This culture solution may be stored for a week or two, but it is better to mix fresh lots from time to time.

Trace Elements

The making of the culture solution alone does not mean that one is ready to grow plants in it. They need the trace elements, and unfortunately the latter cannot be mixed permanently with the culture solution, but must be added just before the latter is used. Otherwise trace element solutions and culture solutions must be kept strictly apart. The trace element solution may be prepared as follows:

In a pint of water dissolve

Ferrous sulphate, ½ teaspoonful (or exactly 2.5 grams)

Boric acid, ¼ teaspoonful (or exactly 1.4 grams)

Magnesium sulphate, ¼ teaspoonful (or exactly 0.9 gram)

Zinc sulphate, ¼ teaspoonful (or exactly 1.1 grams)

It is absolutely essential to add to the culture solution the above trace element solution in the following proportions:

Culture solution — 5 gallons

Trace element solution — 2 teaspoonfuls, to be added only when culture solution is to be actually used. (Never add trace element solution to *stored* culture solution.)

The above procedure has produced successful plants under water-culture methods for some years. Even the comparatively simple solutions here proposed may seem too burdensome to many, and the alternative is to purchase ready-mixed chemicals to which only water is added according to the directions on the box.

---

* Special articles on the subjects indicated by an asterisk (*) will be found at the words so marked.

How to Grow the Plants

The principle of soilless gardening is quite simple. Some method must be devised of keeping roots in the nutrient solution (culture solution + trace element solution), allowing some air space above the latter, and anchoring the plant upright. The simplest of all is to fill a small tank, vase, or milk bottle seven-eighths

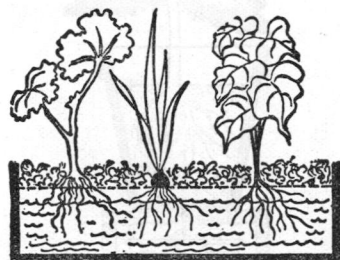

Plants in a small tank. Upper layer of excelsior to keep them erect; below, an air space, and the tank about seven-eighths full of nutrient solution.

full of the nutrient solution and suspend the plant so that the roots are in the water while the upright stem is held by a wire frame or even a clip. (*See* illustration.) This can be accomplished by a piece of wire netting (which must be painted with asphalt paint, as no rust should be allowed to drip into the nutrient solution) tied over the neck of the bottle or vase. Seedlings of sufficient size or small potted plants can be held in place easily by wedging with bits of excelsior or glass wool. The only important thing to remember is that their roots must be immersed in the nutrient solution.

It must here be emphasized that if plants once grown in soil are to be changed to water culture, *all soil particles* must carefully be removed or they will contaminate the nutrient solution.

If larger containers are used, of wood, metal, or cement, there must be no ordinary paint used, no caulking material except tar, and cement tanks must be painted with asphalt paint. These precautions are necessary because the nutrient solutions may be ruined by leaching out the soluable elements from ordinary lead paints, from exposed nail heads, from zinc or galvanized tanks, and especially from cement.

On a Larger Scale

Many enthusiasts may wish to grow more plants than are possible in a single vase. In this case tanks of any convenient size can be made or purchased, in which may be grown a variety of ornamental plants and vegetables. For this purpose a wire netting of convenient mesh must be stretched over the container as shown in the illustrations. If the tank is too long to prevent the netting from sagging in the center, one or more cross-strips

of wood or metal can be employed to solve this difficulty.

Because most plants need more support than the aperture of the netting, most growers use also a layer of excelsior through which the stems pass, thus insuring that the plants stand

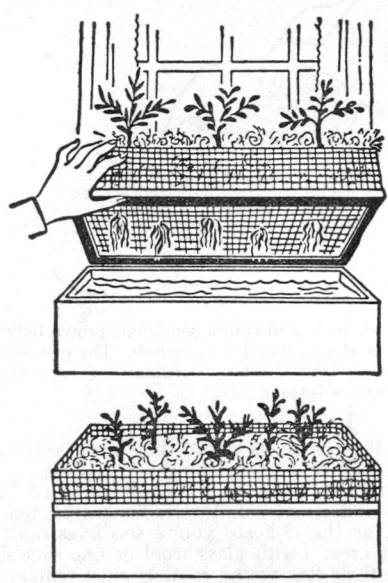

Plants held erect with excelsior. The lower figure shows the normal position of the wire tray holding the excelsior. In the upper figure the tray is tilted to show the roots which would normally be immersed in the nutrient solution.

upright. If the plants — tomatoes, for instance — ultimately produce tall stems, these must be tied to wire frames, or the plants will topple. The admitted nuisance of this, without the professional equipment of a commercial greenhouse, is so great that many soilless gardeners have adopted a substitute — sand.

Sand or Gravel Culture

This is exactly the same as water culture except that pure sand (no sea sand unless thoroughly washed) is used. Fine gravel is also used in some commercial operations. Fill the container three-quarters full of sand in which the plants are rooted exactly as though grown in soil. Sufficient nutrient solutions are then poured in to keep the sand saturated. This procedure avoids most of the difficulty of keeping water-culture plants in an erect position.

Raising Seedlings

Most seeds can be germinated between moist sheets of blotting paper, and this principle is utilized to germinate seedlings by the soilless-garden technique. Nutrient solutions should be only about half or three-quarters

---

* Special articles on the subjects indicated by an asterisk (*) will be found at the words so marked.

strength for this and the container must be kept full enough to maintain actual contact with the cheesecloth upon which the seedlings are germinated. (*See* illustration.)

Pan of seeds and young seedlings, grown between sheets of paraffined cheesecloth. The cheesecloth must be kept moist by constant contact with the nutrient solution.

After the seeds sprout they must be thinned out exactly as in pricking off seedlings. (*See* SEEDS AND SEEDAGE.) The difficulty of doing this under water culture is far greater than in soil, as the delicate young seedlings must be kept erect (with glass wool or fine excelsior) and their fine young rootlets must remain immersed in the nutrient solution below.

When the seedlings are a week or two old, the nutrient solution should be gradually brought up to full strength, and as the stems increase in length and roots get more sturdy, the level of the nutrient solution must be lowered enough to keep an air space between the water level and the top of the container. To keep this water level at a uniform height is essential, and requires constant watchfulness, especially at ordinary room temperatures.

"WATERING"

It seems useless to speak of "watering" plants that are growing in water, and in the ordinary sense it is. But nutrient solutions evaporate fast enough so that they must be constantly renewed, and their constituents of plant food may easily become exhausted by root absorption.

To overcome this, it is advisable to add fresh nutrient solution to keep it at a uniform height, no matter what the loss from absorption, evaporation, or seepage (as in some wooden tanks). In addition to this, it is advisable to drain off *all* the nutrient solution once in ten days or a fortnight and add a fresh mixture of nutrient solution. If pure water culture (not sand culture) is being practiced, this is easily done by siphoning off the old nutrient solutions.

If you are using the sand method of water culture, described above, the old nutrient solution cannot so easily be drained off, so that it

Sand culture method. An ordinary flower pot (painted on outside) three-quarters full of sand saturated with nutrient solution. The drainage hole at bottom can be partially closed with a cork if desired, except when the sand is to be cleaned.

is better to wash such sand by running pure tap water through it. A hole in the bottom of the container, through which tap water drains off during this cleaning period, is wholly or partly corked up when the fresh nutrient solution is permeating the sand.

PLANTS FOR SOILLESS GARDENING

Almost any decorative plant suitable for house culture and many vegetables can be grown in water. The chief limitation is the very practical one of providing support for tall-growing varieties, and the size of the container needed for the growth and maturity of most vegetables. It is this that has made soilless gardening principally a fad, or, in the case of the commercial grower, a necessity with which the average amateur is never faced. It was, however, used on a large scale in some Pacific islands, with little or no soil, to grow fresh vegetables for our forces in World War II; also on the islands of Curaçao and Aruba which have little soil.

SOIL MANAGEMENT. The year-by-year management of cultivated soils requires a little thought and planning. For more than two thousand years it has been known that continuous cropping of any one area will ultimately deplete its fertility unless something is done to overcome the annual loss of plant food. And even more disastrous is the continued use of one kind of crop upon the same land.

To overcome these difficulties two things are obvious but are quite often ignored. One is to fertilize the soil; the other is to practice a rotation of crops. The latter is the better plan.

* Special articles on the subjects indicated by an asterisk (*) will be found at the words so marked.

This means so planning your garden that exactly the same crop does not occupy exactly the same piece of land in two successive years. This is impossible, of course, in permanent ornamental plantings, but it can be easily accomplished in the vegetable garden. Several suggestions for such rotations will be found in the section Rotation of Crops at KITCHEN GARDEN. It can often be done in the flower garden, especially with annuals and biennials, and when replanning the perennial border it is well to keep the rotation principle in mind.

The reasons for rotation are not thoroughly understood. It appears to be a highly complex adjustment as between soil fertility, the phenomenon known as "sick soils" (*i.e.*, tired of one crop), and the more obvious fact that insects and diseases are left without their favorite food if the crop is elsewhere. So many destructive organisms winter-over in the soil that changing crops is one of the best ways to starve out such pests.

SOIL MIXTURES. For the natural mixtures of soils as they occur in the garden *see* SOILS. For the mixtures suitable for potting and window boxes *see* POTTING MIXTURES.

SOIL MOISTURE. The only source of soil moisture is rainfall, but what the physicists call "free water" (*i.e.*, not held by the soil particles) is of little or no use to plants, except aquatics. In other words, the only soil moisture of any use to the gardener is that known as *capillary* water, a film of which surrounds each soil particle. By capillarity such soil moisture is constantly rising from the permanent ground water and most of it is either used by the plant or is lost by evaporation.

Two things are indicated by this fact — increase if possible the water-holding capacity of your soil, and try to stop or retard its evaporation from the surface. The latter is best accomplished by creating a dust mulch upon the surface, the details of which will be found at CULTIVATION. Another way to conserve soil moisture is by a mulch, the details for which will be found at MULCH AND MULCHING.

Increasing the moisture-holding capacity of garden soils is often necessary and sometimes imperative. Ordinary garden soils vary greatly in their capacity to hold water, the light (*i.e.*, sandy and gravelly) ones holding too little, and some heavy clay and silt soils holding too much. The latter condition can be relieved by adding sand to small areas and often later to large ones. *See* LIME.

But light, sandy soils need particular attention when it comes to their moisture-holding capacity, especially in view of the ease with which they lose water during summer droughts. The reason they do so is because the coarseness of their soil particles allows too much space for air and too little opportunity for the retention of capillary water.

The remedy for this condition is the addition of humus, the moisture-holding capacity of which is far higher than any mineral soil. There are two ways of getting humus into soils deficient in it. The first and most expensive is by direct addition of commercial humus. For details of this *see* HUMUS. The second, slower, but much less expensive method is to grow crops upon the soil and plow them under. For this method *see* GREEN MANURING.

SOIL OPERATIONS. The operations necessary for the proper preparation of garden soils are governed by several factors, the most important of which are: the type of soil under consideration (its physical and mechanical condition); the purpose for, or the object of its preparation; and the size of the plot to be prepared. These factors govern the proper methods of procedure, and the selection of suitable implements to be employed. All the main sections below are also the subjects of special articles, where the details of the various soil operations should be sought. Here they are merely summarized.

For all gardening purposes a well-drained, deep, fertile topsoil is essential. This soil should contain a liberal amount of available plant food; it must warm readily; be rich in humus; be porous and friable,* yet absorbent and retentive of moisture for the best growth and development of plant life.

Where space permits, tractor or horse-drawn implements may be used in the preparation of the soil, though, in some instances, especially the home grounds or gardens, space is limited and hand tillage must be resorted to.

DRAINING

Proper drainage should receive first consideration, for plants will not thrive in wet, soggy soils. Sandy or gravelly soils seldom require artificial drainage, therefore we are more concerned with the heavy soils, or those having clay or "hardpan" subsoils. Drainage, where necessary, may be accomplished by providing furrows or open ditches, covered ditches, by tiling, subsoiling, or by deep wells. The method must be governed by the requirements of the individual case. *See* DRAINING.

Good drainage ensures better germination of seeds; more vigorous growth; earlier maturity and greater productivity by improving the mechanical and physical condition of the soil; encourages bacterial development, making plant food more easily and quickly available; aids in warming the soil; makes it more porous, thus keeping it in a sweet and friable* condition; and makes it more absorbent and retentive of moisture. Weed seeds do not germinate as readily, for they require an abundance of moisture, and insect pests are not so liable to harbor in well-drained soils. Also all soil operations are more efficiently and economically facilitated.

PLOWING

Proper drainage having been provided, turning the soil, either by plowing or digging

---

* Special articles on the subjects indicated by an asterisk (*) will be found at the words so marked.

(spading), is the next consideration. The object is to stir the soil; to incorporate or work into it humus or organic matter, either in the form of stable manure or green cover crops; to loosen or aerate it, thereby increasing the chemical action of bacteria,* which is very essential to proper plant growth and development; to turn under trash, etc. Plowing or turning the soil, especially when humus in some form has been turned under, increases its moisture-holding capacity and encourages stronger and deeper root development.

DIGGING

Digging or spading is another method of turning the soil and must be resorted to where space is limited. Though the method differs, the object of and the results secured are practically identical with plowing. Hand digging must be practiced where flower and shrub beds or borders, or other small areas, are to be spaded or turned. *See* DIGGING.

HARROWING AND RAKING

Preparation of the soil after plowing is best done by harrowing or raking, which pulverizes the clods, and levels and firms the seedbed. The fine surface soil thus formed acts as a blanket, preventing the escape of soil moisture through cracks.

Frequent harrowing ventilates the soil; kills vast numbers of weed seedlings; aids capillary attraction or the movement of soil fluids; hastens the decomposition of manurial or vegetable matter, thus making plant food more readily available; increases bacterial development, and encourages deep, vigorous root growth. It also kills or checks insect pests, especially grubs and cutworms.

We must resort to hand raking where space is limited or where an exceptionally fine seedbed is desired, as in the building of lawns, flower beds, etc., and also in their maintenance. The object of or results secured by raking are identical with harrowing, excepting that a more exacting finish and a finer surface are obtained. In the preparation of the soil, harrowing or raking should be done after every rain, but never when the ground is wet or sticky.

ROLLING

The seedbed should be firmed by rolling after the surface has been well pulverized. Horse- or tractor-drawn roller may be used, space permitting; otherwise, hand-rolling must be resorted to.

Rolling prevents the rapid escape of soil moisture; reveals inequalities of the surface; firms the seedbed; assures quicker and better germination; and allows soil fluids to be brought up by capillary attraction which would otherwise be lost to growing plants.

Injury to crops and lawns caused by heaving or frost action can be overcome or partially corrected by rolling lightly early in spring, thereby pressing the raised plant roots back into the soil.

CULTIVATION

Though ideas and methods of cult. vary greatly, an understanding of certain conditions is necessary to apply them properly.

Cultivation should be practiced often and thoroughly during the early part of the growing season, to keep down weeds; to prevent excessive evaporation of soil moisture by forming a dust mulch; to stimulate the capillary movement of air and moisture in the soil, necessary to the life of the bacteria which make plant food available.

Many types of cultivators are in use — tractor- or horse-drawn where space permits, and hand cultivators for limited areas. Proper selection depends upon local conditions. *See* CULTIVATION.

HOEING

The garden hoe is most suitable where space is limited, and for most purposes — to cult. flowers or shrubs, etc.; between plants in the row; to furrow out rows for seeding or planting; to eradicate weeds; to loosen the soil, etc. The object of hoeing and the benefits derived are almost identical with cult. in most soil operations. *See* HOEING.

TOP-DRESSING

Top-dressing, as generally understood by the average person, applies to the fertilization of lawns. It is just as beneficial for flowers and vegetables, trees or shrubs, etc. The materials used as top-dressing may be in the form of compost, peat moss, manure, bone meal, tankage, or commercial fertilizers.

The purpose is to supply an immediate source of available plant food to growing plants and, in most instances, organic matter as well.

Top-dressing aids in the absorption and retention of moisture; the suppression of weeds; the development of soil bacteria; and aids capillary movement. It also increases the yield and improves the quality of plants or crops so treated. *See* TOP-DRESSING.

TRENCHING

Trenching, practiced where surface soils are very poor, or where a very deep, fertile soil is required, consists of mixing or working manure into the soil to a depth of 18 in., applying the manure as the earth is being turned, after first having removed some of the soil from the trench to the required depth, to facilitate mixing.

Another method is to remove the soil entirely from the space to be trenched to a depth of 12 to 18 in., then put 6 in. of well-rotted manure in the bottom of the trench and fill in with good topsoil.

Trenching, which is laborious, promotes deep vigorous root growth; prevents injury by drought; and assures an abundant supply of plant food for many years. *See* TRENCHING.

HEAVING

Heaving of the soil, caused by frost action, is more severe in moist soils, especially in soil

---

* Special articles on the subjects indicated by an asterisk (*) will be found at the words so marked.

depressions, where water stands. It tears the fibrous roots of the plants, causing them to winter-kill. Severe heaving may be overcome by providing proper soil drainage, and the injury to plants lessened by applying a mulch, either in the form of manure, peat moss, marsh hay, straw, leaves, or evergreen boughs. The injury to lawns and other crops may be lessened or corrected by rolling in the early spring, when the surface of the soil is dry. See HEAVING.

SOILS. The soil is a mixture of weathering rock and organic matter which covers the earth in a thin layer. It is a medium from which all plants and animals draw, directly or indirectly, a large part of their sustenance. The soil is the home of the plant roots and the storehouse of the mineral elements and water.

The term soil, as used here, includes both the topsoil or surface soil and the subsoil down to the parent material. The soil is composed of solids, liquids, and gases. The solid portion of most soils is composed of minerals and organic matter, both in all stages of decomposition. In all except the organic soils (mucks and peats) the mineral part predominates. The spaces between the soil particles are normally occupied by air and water, the proportion of each depending on the character of the soil and the conditions under which it is functioning. As the water increases the air decreases and vice versa. A representative silt-loam soil, when in good condition for plant growth, contains approximately 50% solid matter and 50% pore space. At optimum moisture about half of the pore space is occupied by water and half is filled by air. The 50% solid matter represents roughly 45% mineral and 5% organic matter, by volume.

ORIGIN OF SOILS

Mineral soils are formed from the breakdown of rocks at the earth's surface by mechanical disintegration and by chemical action. The kind of rock (limestone, granite, sandstone, and shale) determines to a large extent the character of the soil. Mechanical disintegration of the rock material is brought about by erosion, by differential expansion of the minerals, by frost action, and by plants and animals. Chemical decomposition is hastened by the action of water, oxygen, and carbon dioxide. Some, for instance, known as lateritic soils are so called because of the iron oxide in them which makes them a characteristic reddish color. In humid sub-tropical and tropical climates, chemical soil weathering is intense and continuous. Biological activity also goes on rapidly under these conditions and the organic matter is quickly reduced to carbon dioxide and other simple substances.

Organic soils (see HUMUS and MUCKLAND GARDENING) are formed from the remains of plants and animals, deposited under water. Drainage waters and other transporting agencies bring in mineral matter which subsequently becomes incorporated with the organic materials.

Mineral soils (the solid part) vary in organic matter content from a trace to 12 to 15%. So-called organic soils contain from 20 to 90 or 95% of organic matter. Representative types of organic soils contain 70 to 80% of organic matter.

SURFACE SOIL AND SUBSOIL

The term **surface soil** or topsoil is applied to the upper or surface layer. In cultivated soils the term refers to the portion that is modified by tillage and by the decomposition of organic matter. In other cases, where the color of the upper portion is modified by accumulation of organic matter, the term is applied to the full depth of the color horizon.

The **subsoil** is the layer immediately beneath the surface soil. In many cultivated mineral soils the subsoil is lighter in color than is the surface soil and, if composed of the same material, is always more compact.

CLASSIFICATION OF SOILS

Soils are classified in various ways and with many divisions, but only the soil type and the soil class (textural grade) will be considered here.

SOIL TYPE. A soil which, throughout the extent of its occurrence, has relatively uniform profile characteristics, represents a **soil type.** A name unmodified may refer to the dominant or **key** type of the series. Any particular soil of a series is designated by its textural name, as **sandy loam, clay, clay loam,** etc. To this is added the series name. The type name is, therefore, made up of two parts, the first designating the series and the second the individual within the group. Examples are Dunkirk clay loam, Norfolk sandy loam, and Carrington silt loam. The first word in each of these type names designates the series and the others the textural grade or class. All of them taken together are the name of the soil type.

SOIL CLASS (Textural Grade). The **soil class** or **textural grade** is a classification based on texture alone. **Texture** is the term used to indicate the coarseness or fineness of the soil. The textural composition is determined by a mechanical analysis, which is a laboratory process. The system used by the United States Department of Agriculture separates the soil into seven sizes as shown below.

UNITED STATES DEPARTMENT OF AGRICULTURE CLASSIFICATION OF SOIL PARTICLES

Name of soil	Size in millimeters (1 millimeter = 0.397 inch)
Fine gravel	2 to 1
Coarse sand	1 to 0.5
Medium sand	0.5 to 0.25
Fine sand	0.25 to 0.10
Very fine sand	0.10 to 0.05
Silt	0.05 to 0.005
Clay	0.005 and below

* Special articles on the subjects indicated by an asterisk (*) will be found at the words so marked.

Soils are divided into three groups determined by the proportion of the several sizes as given in the table. These three groups, **sandy soils, loamy soils,** and **clayey soils,** are separated into classes as follows:

Sandy soils	Loamy soils	Clayey soils
Gravelly sands	Coarse sandy	Gravelly clays
Coarse sands	loams	Sandy clays
Medium sands	Medium sandy	Clays
Fine sands	loams	Heavy clays
Very fine sands	Fine sandy loams	
	Very fine sandy	
	loams	
	Silt loams	
	Silty clay loams	
	Clay loams	

SANDY SOILS. A **sandy soil** is loose and single-grained. The individual grains can be seen and felt readily. If squeezed in the hand when dry, it will fall apart when the pressure is released. When moist a sandy soil can be formed into a ball, but it will crumble readily when touched. Soils classed as sandy contain less than 15% of silt and clay. The different classes of sandy soils are separated on the basis of the proportion of the various sand separates making up the soil. **Coarse sands** contain 35% or more of fine gravel and coarse sand, and less than 50% of fine sand or very fine sand. **Medium sands** contain 35% or more of fine gravel, coarse and medium sand, and less than 50% of fine or very fine sand. **Fine sands** contain 50% or more of fine and very fine sand, while **very fine sands** contain 50% or more of very fine sand. Sandy soils are known as "early soils" because they dry out early in the spring and warm up earlier than other soils. They are naturally infertile soils since they are leached readily. They are considered valuable for very early crops which do not require a long season. The sands are not retentive of moisture, and are not, therefore, suitable for long-season crops, or those that are grown during the drier part of the season, unless they are irrigated. The moisture-holding capacity of sands can be increased by the addition of organic matter in the form of manure and soil-improving crops. *See* MANURE and GREEN MANURING.

SANDY LOAMS. A **sandy-loam soil** is one that contains much sand, but which has enough silt and clay to make it hold together somewhat. The individual grains of sand can be seen and felt. If sandy loam is squeezed when moist it will form a cast that will bear careful handling without breaking. These soils contain from 20 to 50% of silt and clay. The four classes of sandy loams are separated on the basis of the percentage of the various separates as follows: **Coarse sandy loams** 45% or more of fine gravel and coarse sand; **medium sandy loams** 25% or more of fine gravel, coarse sand and medium sand, and less than 35% of very fine sands; **fine sandy loams** 50% or more of fine sand, or less than 25% of fine gravel, coarse and medium sand; **very fine sandy loams** 35% or more of very fine sand.

Sandy loams are more retentive of moisture and of nutrients than are the sands and are considered better for general garden purposes. They are not as early as are the sands, but are earlier than the silts, silt loams, clays and clay loams. They are considered almost ideal soils where earliness is of prime consideration. Both the sands and sandy loams may be worked soon after rains or after irrigation and this is a great advantage in early preparation of the soil and in keeping weeds under control by cultivation.

LOAM SOILS. A **loam** is a soil having a relatively even mixture of the different grades of sand and of silt and clay. It is mellow, has a somewhat gritty feel, and is plastic when moist. If squeezed in the hand when dry it will form a cast that will hold together when handled carefully, while a cast made of moist loam can be handled freely without breaking. Loams contain less than 20% of clay, from 30 to 50% of silt and from 30 to 50% of sand. Such soils are more retentive of moisture and nutrients than are the sands and sandy loams and are considered good for general purposes.

SILT LOAMS. **Silt loams** contain less than 20% of clay, 50% or more of silt, and less than 50% of sand. These soils have a moderate percentage of clay, with half or more of soil made up of the size called "silt." When dry silt loam breaks up it is cloddy or lumpy, but the lumps can be readily broken down, and when pulverized it feels smooth and soft. When wet it runs together, and when either dry or wet it will form a cast when squeezed.

CLAY LOAMS. This group contains from 20 to 30% of clay. A soil in this group that contains less than 30% silt and from 50 to 80% sand is called a **sandy clay loam;** one with from 20 to 50% silt and from 20 to 50% sand is known as **clay loam,** while one containing from 50 to 80% of silt and less than 30% sand is known as **silty clay loam.** A clay loam is fine textured and usually breaks up into clods and lumps that are hard when dry. The moist soil is plastic and will form a cast that will stand much handling without breaking. When the moist soil is pressed between the thumb and fingers it will form a thin ribbon which will break readily. Clay loams are more retentive of moisture than the soils of coarser texture, but they are difficult to prepare and are not as good for early crops. The physical condition is improved by freezing and thawing, by the addition of organic matter and to some extent by liming. *See* LIME.

CLAYS. These contain 30% or more of clay. **Sandy clay soils** contain from 30 to 50% of clay, less than 20% silt, and from 50 to 70% sand; **clay soils** contain 30% or more of clay, less than 50% silt, and less than 50% sand; **silty clay soil** contains from 30 to 50% of clay, from 50 to 70% silt, and less than 20% sand. A clay soil is fine-textured and usually forms hard lumps when dry. It is plastic and sticky when wet. When the wet soil is pinched between the thumb and fingers it will form a

---

long, flexible ribbon. In general, heavy clays are not well suited to gardening, but they can be improved as mentioned for clay loams. Clay and clay loams both puddle badly if plowed, harrowed, or cultivated when wet. Well-drained clay and clay loams are very productive when properly managed.

Rich versus Poor Soil

In general, a **rich** or **fertile** soil is one that contains an abundance of organic matter. The organic matter is the most active portion of the soil. Through the action of bacteria and fungi the tissues of the organic matter are broken down to humus, and, in this process, organic acids are set free, which act on the mineral portion of the soil. Thus a soil well supplied with organic matter is likely to be richer in available nutrients than are similar soils low in organic matter.

A **poor** or **infertile** soil is one that is deficient in organic matter and in available nutrients. If a soil is well supplied with organic matter it is not likely to be deficient in available nutrients. Coarse-textured soils deficient in organic matter are low in water-holding capacity and for this reason are unproductive unless irrigated, even though nutrients are supplied in abundance. A soil may be well supplied with organic matter and yet be unproductive. Lack of drainage, consequently lack of aeration; an excess of compounds that are toxic to plants; or lack of some minor element, such as iron, zinc, copper or manganese, may render a soil unproductive when it is well supplied with organic matter and the common nutrients. A soil may be unproductive for certain crops when it contains parasitic organisms that attack those crops. Many areas, infested with nematodes that cause root knot, for example, are unproductive as far as the crops seriously attacked are concerned. Soils so affected are sometimes called "sick soils," but the term may be applied to soils that are unproductive because of the presence of substances that are toxic to plants. *See also* Manure, Fertilizers, and Soil Conditioners. — H. C. T.

SOIL STERILIZATION. Soil sterilizing is recommended for prevention of damping-off* and control of many fungus diseases which cause root rot of larger plants. Sterilizing with steam is the best method. After soil has reached a temperature of 180° F., maintain that temperature for 30 minutes. Home gardeners who do not have facilities for steam sterilizing can do a similar job by placing a large potato on the soil in a shallow pan and putting it in the oven. When the potato is baked, the soil is sterilized. *See* Fumigation for chemical methods of control.

SOIL TESTING. For acid and alkali tests *see* Acid and Alkali Soils. For testing for fertility *see* Fertility.

SOIL WASHING. See Erosion.

SOJA MAX = *Glycine Max. See* Soybean.

SOLANACEAE (so-la-nay'see-ee). The potato family, often called the tobacco or tomato family, is easily one of the leading hort. groups of plants, for it includes vegetables of world-wide cultivation, narcotics, drugs, tobacco, and many garden flowers. There are over 80 genera and perhaps 3000 species, most abundant in the tropics, but common, also, in temperate regions.

Vegetables dominate the leading cult. genera. *Solanum* includes the potato and the eggplant, as well as many tropical shrubs and trees. For *Lycopersicum see* Tomato. The common garden peppers (both green and red) are found in *Capsicum*.

Tobacco (*see* Nicotiana) comes second in importance among the cult. genera, followed by *Atropa*, which yields belladonna.

The genera cultivated mostly for ornament are readily divided into tropical sorts needing greenhouse protection and genera hardy outdoors over most of the country. The leading tropical genera are: *Brunfelsia, Cestrum, Cyphomandra, Fabiana, Schizanthus* (also for outdoor cult.), *Solanum* (many species), *Solandra*, and *Streptosolen*. Many of these are grown outdoors in the South or in Calif.

There are, also, several important genera of garden plants, all perennials or tender annuals, and some very widely grown for ornament. They are *Browallia, Nicandra, Nierembergia, Petunia, Physalis*, and *Salpiglossis*. The only other genera of garden interest are *Lycium* (shrubs), *Datura* (tropical trees and weeds), and *Mandragora* (the true mandrake). Many of the plants contain poisonous alkaloids, some deadly. *See* Hyoscyamus.

Leaves alternate.* Flowers regular,* or rarely irregular,* solitary in a few, but mostly in various sorts of clusters, showy in some genera, especially in *Datura, Nicotiana*, and *Petunia*. Fruit a dry pod (capsule*) or a berry, sometimes surrounded by a brightly colored, persistent and bladdery calyx (*see* Physalis).

Technical flower characters: Flowers hermaphrodite.* Calyx 5-lobed, sometimes persistent. Corolla usually with a short tube, but expanded upward into a flattish, wheel-shaped flower. Stamens* 5, alternate with the corolla lobes, often connected by the anthers. Ovary superior,* usually 2-celled, with many ovules.

SOLANDRA (so-lan'dra). Tropical American woody, climbing plants, comprising about 4 species of the potato family. Leaves alternate,* ovalish and leathery. Flowers large, solitary, greenish-white or yellow. Calyx tubular, 5-lobed. Corolla funnel-shaped, its limb 5-lobed. Stamens* 5. Fruit a 2-celled berry. (Named for Daniel C. Solander, Swedish naturalist.)

The second species is much grown in the greenhouse where the temperature does not drop below 50°, or outdoors in zones* 8 and 9. Propagated by cuttings, inserted in a mixture of sand and peat and then grown in potting mixture* 3. As these plants are winter-flowering they require plenty of water from Oct.–Apr., but should not be given much water during the summer, to ensure the wood being well ripened.

---

* Special articles on the subjects indicated by an asterisk (*) will be found at the words so marked.

grandiflora. Climbing to 30 ft. high. Leaves simple, alternate,* ovalish, to 5 in. long, thick and bright green. Flowers solitary, fragrant, yellowish-white. Calyx 2–3 in. long. Corolla 6–7 in. long. W.I. Popular in Calif. for outdoor cult.

guttata. Chalice vine. Of shrubby habit, more or less climbing, growing to 20 ft. high, and covered with short downy hairs. Leaves ovalish, to 6 in. long, hairy on the under side. Flowers fragrant, solitary, white, turning yellow with age, marked purple, to 9 in. long. Mex. The plants offered as this may be S. hartwegi, a closely related species, with yellow flowers.

solanina, -us, -um (so-la-ny'na). Potato-like.

SOLANUM (so-lay'num). A huge genus of herbs, shrubs, vines, and sometimes trees, typifying the family Solanaceae, comprising over 2000 species, and of nearly world-wide distribution, but overwhelmingly tropical. Some of them are of outstanding garden importance, for the genus includes the potato and eggplant; others are decorative plants for the greenhouse or outdoor culture in the South; some are pernicious weeds. The common name of the whole genus is nightshade.

Leaves alternate,* the juice of the wilted leaves deadly in some species, suspect in most others. Flowers often borne in the leaf axils* or near them, often solitary or in few-flowered clusters. Calyx* united. Corolla regular, shallowly bell-shaped or wheel-shaped (rotate), the 5 stamens* usually inserted on its throat. Fruit a berry, edible in some species, deadly poisonous in others. (*Solanum* is thought to be from the Latin for quieting, perhaps in allusion to the dangerously narcotic properties of some species.)

The genus is so variable that it is impossible to give general cultural directions. For the culture of the two most important garden crops see POTATO and EGGPLANT. The cult. of the others is noted at each species. Over 40 kinds are in cult. in the U.S., but the following are most likely to be met.

aculeatissimum. Love-apple. Usually grown as a tender annual, 1–3 ft. high, the stems branched and prickly. Leaves prickly, lobed, ovalish. Flowers small, nodding, white. Fruit red, tomato-like, about 1½ in. thick, popular in dried winter decorations. Tropics.

auriculatum. A beautiful, velvety, unarmed shrub, 12–18 ft. high. Leaves ovalish or oblong, 5–8 in. long, without marginal teeth, often bearing smaller, roundish leaves in the axils.* Flowers bluish-white or violet, about ½ in. wide, mostly in small clusters (corymbs*). Fruit about ¾ in. thick. Tropical Asia and America. Suited only to zones* 8 (with protection) and 9. A very handsome shrub. Also called S. *mauritianum*.

Capsicastrum. False Jerusalem cherry. An unarmed shrub, not over 2 ft. high, and generally resembling the true Jerusalem cherry (S. *Pseudo-capsicum*), but with grayish foliage and less persistent fruit. Brazil. Its culture is the same as for S. *Pseudo-capsicum*.

carolinense. Horse nettle. A perennial and pernicious weedy herb, both the leaves and stem armed with yellow, straight prickles. Flowers violet or white. Berries orange-yellow.

Eastern N.A., and west to Tex. A troublesome weed. See Horse nettle in the list at WEEDS.

Dulcamara. The traditional bittersweet (for the plant so called in America see CELASTRUS); also called withywind and climbing nightshade. A scrambling, vine-like herb, often climbing up to 8 ft. high, more often prostrate or nearly so. Leaves 2–4 in. long, ovalish-oblong, but sometimes lobed at the base. Flowers in loose clusters, the corolla violet, but green-spotted, about ½ in. wide. Fruit scarlet, about ½ in. thick. Eurasia, but commonly naturalized in N.A. Scarcely cult., but all should be warned against its dangerously poisonous berries and the juice of its wilted leaves.

esculentum = *Lycopersicum esculentum*. See TOMATO.

giganteum. A tree-like or shrub-like biennial, 10–20 ft. high, the stem prickly. Leaves 6–8 in. long, oblongish, beautifully silky white beneath. Flowers blue or light violet, about ½ in. wide and borne in profuse showy clusters. Fruit globe-shaped, about ¼ in. in diameter, red. India. Hardy only in zones* 8 and 9. Called, in Calif., African holly, although it is neither African nor a holly.

integrifolium. Scarlet or tomato eggplant (not the true eggplant). A hairy and prickly annual herb, 2–3 ft. high, grown for its ornamental fruit. Leaves oblong-ovalish, shallowly lobed, 6–8 in. long. Flowers about ¾ in. wide, white, in sparse clusters. Fruit furrowed, nearly round, scarlet or yellow, about 2 in. thick. Af. It should be grown as a tender annual. See ANNUALS.

jasminoides. Potato vine (not the true potato). A very handsome, tender, woody vine, 8–10 ft. long, smooth and without prickles. Leaves ovalish or narrower, 2–3 in. long, simple,* or the lower ones with a tendency to be compound.* Flowers showy, about 1 in. wide, white, but blue-tinged, star-like, in handsome, branched clusters. Brazil. Hardy only in comparatively frost-free regions, but a popular ornamental in Fla. and Calif.

Lycopersicum = *Lycopersicum esculentum*. See TOMATO.

Melongena. A hairy, perennial herb or under-shrub from tropical Africa and Asia, scarcely known in cult. except for the *var.* esculentum, the eggplant, which is grown as an annual in the U.S. It is a stout herb 2–4 ft. high, the angled or lobed leaves 10–15 in. long. Flowers violet-purple, nearly 2 in. wide, usually nodding. Fruit a large berry, usually dark purple and shining, but sometimes white, yellow, or striped, 6–10 in. long. For cult. see EGGPLANT. There is a dwarf variety with smooth leaves and smaller fruit. The *var.* serpentinum, the snake eggplant, has nearly cylindrical fruit about 1 in. thick and a foot long, coiled or curved at the tip.

muricatum. Pepino. Melon pear. Melon shrub. A little-known perennial herb or under-shrub, 2–3 ft. high, grown in warm regions for its edible fruit. Foliage spiny. Leaves oblongish or narrower, 4–6 in. long, the margins sometimes wavy. Flowers about ¾ in. wide, bright blue. Fruit egg-shaped, 4–6 in. long, yellow, but marked with purple. Peru.

nigrum. Black or deadly nightshade. A weedy very variable annual herb, found in some of its forms throughout the temperate and tropical zones, 1–2 ft. high, its foliage clammy. Leaves ovalish-lance-shaped, 3–5 in. long, often somewhat angled. Flowers about ½ in. wide, white, mostly in sparse, drooping clusters. Fruit black (in the wild form), about ¼ in. thick. The juice of the wilted leaves

---

* Special articles on the subjects indicated by an asterisk (*) will be found at the words so marked.

Solanum jasminoides

is dangerously poisonous. The fruit, in some improved garden forms, known as garden huckleberry, sunberry, and wonderberry, is used for making pies. It has been suggested, perhaps correctly, that the garden huckleberry be designated as *Solanum intrusum* and the wonderberry or sunberry be called *Solanum burbanki.* The unripe fruit is poisonous in some wild forms. The plant is easily grown, as an annual, in any garden soil.

Solanum Pseudo-capsicum

Pseudo-capsicum. Jerusalem cherry. A popular greenhouse pot plant, much grown by florists for its persistent, scarlet or yellow fruits, which are globe-shaped and about ½ in. in diameter. It is an unarmed shrub, 2–4 ft. high, with oblongish, wavy-margined leaves 3–4 in. long, and shining green, at least above. Flowers about ½ in. wide, white. Old World. Both this and S. *Capsicastrum* should be grown in potting mixture* 4 in the warm-temperate greenhouse, and may be propagated by seeds or cuttings.

seaforthianum. A smooth, unarmed, woody vine, 8–10 ft. long. Leaves generally compound,* nearly 7 in. long, the leaflets of unequal size. Flowers about 1 in. wide, starlike, blue or purple, in small clusters (cymes*). Fruit pea-size, scarlet. Tropical America, and hardy only in zone* 9, or possibly protected parts of zone* 8.

tuberosum. Potato; also called white or Irish potato. A weak, unarmed, but sticky herb with edible tubers. Leaves compound,* the leaflets of irregular size. Flowers about 1 in. wide, white, lavender, or pinkish-lavender. Fruit globe-shaped, about ¾ in. thick, yellowish or green, often not produced in the cult. varieties. Originally a native of the high Andes of old Peru (modern Ecuador, Peru, Bolivia, and northern Chile), in a region "where it freezes a little every month of the year," according to the first chronicler of the potato, Pedro de Cieza de Leon (1538). For culture and varieties *see* POTATO.

wendlandi. Costa Rica nightshade; also called paradise-flower. A climbing, prickly shrub, but not hairy. Leaves compound,* the terminal leaflet larger than the others, or sometimes the upper leaves simple.* Flowers showy, about 2 in. wide, lilac-blue, in handsome, branched clusters. Costa Rica. Hardy only in zone* 9, and possibly in protected parts of zone 8, and a popular ornamental in Fla.

SOLDANELLA (sol-da-nell′a). Low-growing, hardy, perennial herbs, comprising perhaps 10 species of the family Primulaceae, natives of the mountains of Eu. They have short rootstocks, and basal, long-stalked leaves, roundish and with a heart-shaped base. Flowering stalk slender, 6–15 in. high. Flowers solitary or in umbels,* blue, violet, or rose, to ¾ in. across. Calyx of 5 sepals. Corolla tubular, opening salverwise. Stamens 5.* Fruit a 5-celled capsule.* (*Soldanella* is from the Latin for a small coin, in reference to the shape of the leaves.)

Soldanellas are often seen in American gardens, but they are a bit difficult to establish. They are suitable for the rock garden or border. Propagated by seeds or division of roots. Seeds should be sown in March or April in pans, ¹⁄₁₆ in. deep, in a mixture of sandy loam and peat. Pans should be placed in the cold frame and shaded from the sun. As soon as plants are large enough to handle they should be pricked off into the cold frame and still shaded from the sun. When large enough, plant in permanent positions in damp, shady places, using same mixture of soil throughout.

alpina. Grows to 6 in. high. Leaves roundish, to 1½ in. across. Flowers pale blue, in 1–3-flowered umbels.* Blooms in early spring. Most suited to the rock garden (which see).

montana. An alpine perennial, 10–15 in. high, the long-stalked, mostly basal leaves nearly orbicular, about 2½ in. in diameter, the stalk sticky-hairy. Flowers about ¾ in. wide, blue, the petals eroded, the cluster (an umbel*) rather sparse. Mountains of southern Eu. April–May. Suited only to the rock garden.

soldanelloides (sol-dan-nel-loy′deez, but *see* OÏDES). Like a plant of the genus *Soldanella* (which see).

---

* Special articles on the subjects indicated by an asterisk (*) will be found at the words so marked.

SOLDIER'S-PLUME = *Habenaria psycodes*.

SOLIDAGO. See GOLDENROD.

SOLIDASTER (solid-as'ter). A hybrid genus resulting from the crossing of *Aster ptarmicoides* and some unknown species of goldenrod, originated at Lyon, France, about 1910. The only species **S. luteus** (often offered here as *Aster hybridus luteus* or *Asterago*) is a perennial herb 18–26 in. high with narrow, remotely toothed leaves 3–4 in. long. Flowers small, in a much-branched cluster, the ray* flowers light yellow, the disk* flowers darker yellow. Cult. as in the perennial species of *Aster*. (*Solidaster* is a combination of *Aster* and *Solidago*.)

SOLID BULB. A corm.*

SOLITARY. Borne singly, but not necessarily alone. Many flowers and fruits are described as being solitary, *i.e.*, one to a single main stalk, and thus not part of a cluster. But such solitary flowers may be borne on a shrub or tree in great profusion, as in the sloe (*see* PRUNUS SPINOSA).

SOLLYA (soll'ya). Australian evergreen twining shrubs, comprising about 3 species of the family Pittosporaceae. Leaves alternate.* Flowers blue, nodding, in loose, terminal, few-flowered clusters. Calyx of 5 sepals. Corolla spreading, of 5 petals. Stamens* 5. Fruit a 2-celled capsule. (Named for Richard Horsman Solly, English naturalist.)

Sollyas are cult. in the greenhouse or outdoors in the South, and widely so in Calif. Seeds should be sown ⅛ in. deep, in light, sandy soil, in the cool greenhouse, in early spring. Cuttings of young shoots may be taken in March or April and inserted in sand in a temperature of 65°–75°. Both seedlings and cuttings when rooted should be potted into potting mixture* 1, and later into No. 3.

heterophylla. Australian bluebell creeper. Grows to 6 ft. high or more, with slender, twining stems. Leaves narrowly lance-shaped, to 2 in. long, light green on the under side. Flowers blue, about ½ in. long, in terminal clusters. Western Aust. Grown extensively in Calif.

SOLOMON'S LILY = *Arum palaestinum*.

SOLOMON'S-SEAL. Generally hardy, herbaceous perennials, often growing in moist places, and constituting the genus Polygonatum (po-lig-o-nay'tum) of the lily family. There are about 25 species distributed throughout the northern hemisphere. Rootstocks thick and branching, about 2 in. below the surface of the soil, and from them the aerial stems are produced each spring, dying down in the fall. Stems erect at first, then slightly bending. Leaves on the upper part of the stem only, in 2 rows, alternate,* simple, broadly lance-shaped or ovalish, parallel-veined. Flowers white or greenish-white, in hanging, 1–many-flowered clusters growing from the axils* of the leaves. Flower tubular, 6-lobed. Stamens* 6. Fruit a 3-celled berry. (*Polygonatum* is from the Greek for many knees, in allusion to the many joints of the rootstocks.) Sometimes known as *Salomonia*.

These plants are useful in the damp or half-shady places in the garden. Easily cultivated in ordinary garden soil. Propagated by division of rootstocks in Oct., Mar., or Apr. Rootstocks should be planted about 2 in. below the surface of the soil. The species *P. multiflorum* is sometimes grown as a pot plant in the cool greenhouse for early spring flowering. For false Solomon's-seal, *see* SMILACINA. In New England Solomon's-seal is sometimes applied to *Maianthemum canadense*.

P. biflorum. Grows to 3 ft. high. Leaves broadly lance-shaped, to 4 in. long, slightly hairy on the under side. Flowers greenish-white, ½ in. long, in 1–4-flowered umbels.* Eastern N.A. May. A form is designated by some as *P. pubescens*.

P. canaliculatum. Strong-growing, to 8 ft. high. Leaves ovalish, to 6 in. long, bright green. Flowers ¾ in. long, in 1–8-flowered umbels. N.A. June. Often called *P. commutatum*.

P. multiflorum. Grows to 3 ft. high. Leaves broadly lance-shaped, bright green. Flowers greenish-white, ¾ in. long, in 2–8-flowered umbels.* Eurasia.

SOLOMON'S-SEAL FAMILY. See LILIACEAE.

somaliensis, -e. From Somaliland.

somnifera, -us, -um (som-niff'er-a). Causing sleep.

SONCHUS OLERACEUS = Sow thistle, which see in the list at WEEDS.

SONERILA (sohn-er-rill'a). Tender perennial herbs, or small shrubs, comprising about 75 species of the family Melastomaceae, natives of India, and the Malay Archipelago. Leaves opposite,* generally ovalish, with purplish veins, variously spotted on the upper side, often scarlet or purplish on the under side. Flowers usually rose, sometimes purple, in spikes or racemes.* Calyx of 3 sepals. Corolla of 3 petals. Stamens 3. Fruit a 3-celled capsule. (*Sonerila* is a Latinized version of a native name for some species in India.)

Sonerilas are of garden interest as greenhouse plants, where they are grown for their ornamental foliage. Difficult of cultivation, as they require a temperature not below 75°, shade, and atmospheric moisture. Plants do not like water on their leaves. Propagated by seeds and cuttings. Seeds may be sown and cuttings taken from Jan.–May. Soil should be composed of equal parts of fibrous peat, sphagnum moss, charcoal, and sand. Good drainage essential.

margaritacea. Grows to 12 in. high. Leaves broadly lance-shaped, with pearl-white spots in rows on upper side. Under side purplish. Flowers rose. Java. Summer. There are several forms with variously colored leaves.

songarica, -us, -um (son-gar'i-ka). From Songchin, Korea.

SOOT. This smutty, black nuisance in most large cities is detrimental to the growth

---

* Special articles on the subjects indicated by an asterisk (*) will be found at the words so marked.

of plants and is one of the greatest hazards of city gardens. *See* SMOKE.

Much old, and chiefly English, garden literature abounds with references to the value of soot as a fertilizer, and soot still has its adherents today, even in America. Its older advocates were perhaps justified, for it does contain small quantities of plant nutrients, which were worth considering in the days when standard fertilizer mixtures were unavailable. At the present time soot has no place in the garden.

A possible exception is Scotch soot, a kind derived from the burning of peat. As peat fuel is little known in the U.S., Scotch soot is scarce, unless imported in bags. In any case, it is really a form of wood ashes, and not so high in potash as the latter. *See* ASH AND ASHES.

SOOT DEW. *See* SOOTY MOLD.

SOOTY MOLD. A common "disease" of trees with aphids* or scale* insects present on them, or on shrubs and flowers under trees which are infested with these insects. The sooty-mold fungus does not parasitize a plant, but merely grows in the honeydew or droppings from sucking insects. It will be noted that the sooty mold is predominantly on the upper surface of the leaves. Sprays with fungicides will not control it. Eradicate the insect pests with proper spray materials.

SOPHORA (so-for'ra). Handsome, profusely flowering shrubs or trees of the pea family, most of the 20 known species Asiatic, but a few in N.A. Leaves compound,* the leaflets arranged feather-fashion, with an odd one at the tip. Flowers pea-like, usually in showy clusters (panicles* or racemes*). Fruit a stalked pod (legume*) constricted between the seeds, splitting very slowly if at all. (*Sophora* is the Latin version of an Arabian vernacular for a tree with pea-like leaves.)

They do well on a variety of soils and can be propagated by green-wood cuttings or by layering. Seeds germinate very slowly.

davidi = *Sophora viciifolia.*

japonica. Pagoda tree; also called Japanese pagoda tree and Chinese scholar tree. A spreading, round-headed tree, 40–60 ft. high, sometimes more. Leaflets 7–17, stalked, oval-ish or narrower, 1–2 in. long. Flowers about ½ in. long, yellowish-white, the clusters (panicles*) loose, 12–15 in. long, very showy. Pods 2–3 in. long. China and Korea. July–Sept. Hardy from zone* 3 southward. The *var.* **pendula** is a very picturesque form with drooping branches.

secundiflora. Mescal bean. An evergreen shrub or small tree, the shining leaflets 1½–2½ in. long. Flowers fragrant, about 1 in. long, violet-blue, the terminal cluster (raceme*) nearly 4 in. long. Pod 6–8 in. long. Tex. and N. Mex. to northern Mex. Not hardy north of zone* 7.

viciifolia. A shrub 6–8 ft. high. Leaflets 13–19, elliptic, nearly ½ in. long, slightly notched at the tip. Flowers about ⅝ in. long, bluish-violet or paler, in clusters (racemes*) with 8–12 flowers. Pods 1½–2 in. long. China.

June. Hardy from zone* 3 southward. Useful for dry, sandy places Often offered as *S. davidi,* which some consider its correct name.

SOPHROCATLAELIA. A trigeneric* hybrid derived from crossing the orchid genera *Sophronitis, Cattleya,* and *Laelia,* and known only to orchid specialists.

SOPHRONITIS (so-fro-ny'tis). Tender Brazilian orchids, comprising about 8 species. They are small plants growing on the branches of trees or pieces of wood, with thick, fleshy rootstocks and small, bulb-like stems, at the top of which grow 1–2 narrow leaves. Flowers showy, rosy-red with yellow, scarlet, or violet markings, solitary or in short terminal racemes.* Sepals and petals similar to each other except 1, which forms the lip* which has 1 center wide lobe, and 2 smaller erect side lobes. (*Sophronitis* is from the Greek for modest, in allusion to the pretty flowers.)

Grown in the greenhouse in a moist atmosphere, in shade, preferably in shallow pans with good drainage, osmunda* fiber and charcoal. Keep a winter temperature of 55°–65° and a summer temperature of 65°–80°. They require little water during winter months. *See* ORCHID.

coccinea. Leaves narrow, to 3 in. long. Flowers solitary, bright scarlet, to 4 in. across, lip marked yellow at the base. Also, and perhaps correctly, known as *S. grandiflora.*

SORBARIA (sor-bair'i-a). False spirea. Tender or hardy, Asiatic deciduous shrubs, similar to *Spiraea,* comprising about 8 species, and belonging to the rose family. Leaves alternate,* compound,* the leaflets in odd numbers, lance-shaped with toothed margins. Flowers white, small, numerous, in large branching clusters. Calyx* of 5 sepals. Corolla of 5 petals. Stamens* many. Pistils 5, joined at the base. (*Sorbaria* is derived from *Sorbus,* in allusion to the resemblance of the leaves.)

These plants are grown for their clusters of white flowers. Useful for the shrubbery or wild garden. They should not be associated with choice low-growing shrubs, as they spread rapidly. Easily propagated by seeds, hardwood or root cuttings. They are sometimes known as *Schizonotus.*

aitchisoni. Also known as *Spiraea aitchisoni.* Strong-growing, to 10 ft. high. Stems not much branched. Leaves large, leaflets 15–21, lance-shaped, bright green. Flowers white, in branching erect clusters, to 10 in. long. Western As. July–Aug. Hardy from zone* 4 southward.

arborea. Grows to 18 ft. Leaflets 13–17, lance-shaped, to ½ in. wide, hairy on the under side. Flowers white, in loose branching clusters, to 1 ft. long. China. The *var.* **glabrata** has bright, shining green leaflets. July–Aug. Hardy from zone* 4 southward.

sorbifolia. Also known as *Spiraea sorbifolia.* Hardy shrub, to 6 ft. high. Leaflets 13–21, lance-shaped, sometimes hairy on the under side. Flowers white, in dense, erect, branching clusters. Northern As. June–July. Hardy from zone* 1 southward.

SORBARONIA. A bigeneric* hybrid de-

---

* Special articles on the subjects indicated by an asterisk (*) will be found at the words so marked.

rived from crossing plants of the genera *Sorbus* and *Aronia*. Several such crosses are known, but they are of little garden interest.

sorbifolia, -us, -um (sor-bi-fō'li-a). With leaves like mountain-ash (*Sorbus*).

SORBOPYRUS. A bigeneric* hybrid derived from crossing plants of the genera *Sorbus* and *Pyrus*. They are not much grown in the U.S., but two such crosses have long been cult. in Eu.

SORBUS. *See* MOUNTAIN-ASH.

SORGHO = *Sorghum vulgare saccharatum*.

SORGHUM (sor'gum). Coarse Old World grasses, perhaps of only two species, but so long cult. for grain, syrup, brooms, and for forage that the varieties are many and the identity of the species most uncertain. They are tall, annual or perennial, quick-growing grasses with broad leaves and usually a very large terminal cluster (panicle*), the fruits of some of which have been important food plants for centuries. In others the branches of the panicle are commercially harvested for brooms. They have been assigned at different times to the genera *Andropogon* and *Holcus*. (*Sorghum* is from the Italian name for the plant.)

halepense. Johnson grass; called also Means grass and Aleppo grass. A stout, perennial forage grass of great value in warm regions, and much grown in the South, but prone to become a weedy nuisance in gardens. Stems up to 6 ft., leafy, the leaves 2 ft. long and 1 in. wide. Flowering clusters (panicle*) nearly 2 ft. long, its branches spreading. Mediterranean region, but naturalized and weedy in the southern states.

sudanense. Sudan grass. Very like *S. halepense*, but an annual, and somewhat used for forage in the southern U.S. It can only be grown in warm regions. Africa.

vulgare. Sorghum. A stout annual grass, its pithy stem up to 12 ft. high and yielding in one variety a rich syrup. Leaves 2 ft. long and about 2 in. wide. Flowering cluster very variable as developed over the centuries in the widely different varieties listed below. Tropical Af. (probably). For culture of the typical form *see* below. It is called *S. bicolor* by some. Its most important varieties are:

var. **caffrorum.** Kafir. Taller and stouter than the type, producing no syrup, but grown for the edible grain of which there are white, red, and black forms. Called, erroneously, kafir corn (it has nothing to do with corn). A tall form of it is known as African millet.

var. **caudatum.** Feterita. More slender, but 6–14 ft. high. Flowering cluster (panicle*) narrow, ultimately producing a nutritious, broadly elliptic, white, yellow, or red grain.

var. **drummondi.** Chicken-corn. Not over 6 ft. high, the flowering cluster (panicle*) pyramidal, 12–16 in. long, the ultimate grain oval, orange-yellow. Commonly grown in the South for chicken feed.

var. **Durra.** Durra. An age-old cereal grain along the Nile, but little grown here. Flowering cluster (panicle*) compact, ovalish, more or less recurved, the grain nearly globe-shaped. A form of it is known as Jerusalem corn.

var. **roxburghi.** Shallu. A grain sorghum in India, but little known in the U.S. The stem is as tall as the type and somewhat waxy. Flowering cluster (panicle*) oblongish, dense, its branches erect. Grain elliptic.

var. **saccharatum.** Sorgho; also called sweet sorghum or sugar sorghum. The most important of all the varieties, because its rich, sweet sap is a commerical source of syrup. Its foliage also furnishes fodder. It grows 6–12 ft. high, and has a usually erect flowering cluster (panicle*), but sometimes it is recurved. It produces no edible grain.

var. **technicum.** Broomcorn. A stout grass 10–15 ft. high, grown for the very stiff branches of its large flowering cluster (panicle*). These rigid, stiff, slightly twisted branches may be 18–30 in. long in the largest sorts, and 12–20 in. in the smaller varieties. Both are commercially harvested for the making of brooms.

SORGHUM CULTURE

The sorghums are very stout, corn-like grasses, of more commercial than hort. interest. Their culture is mostly a large-scale agricultural operation, although their plumy tassels are handsome.

From a practical standpoint the varieties listed above may be divided into three groups: (1) Those grown for the sweet juice, and often generally called sugar sorghums or sorgho. They yield a widely marketed, honey-like syrup; (2) the broom corns, grown commercially for the bristle-like branches of the inflorescence, used in the making of whisk brooms; and (3) forage grasses of which the best-known is Johnson grass, sometimes a pernicious weed.

All the sorghums should be grown in regions of long, hot summers, preferably south of zone* 4, although some varieties will fruit north of this. They should be grown like field corn, but the rows should be 6–8 ft. apart, as several varieties are as tall as sugar cane (8–15 ft.).

They thrive on the sandy soils of the coastal plain region of southeastern U.S., but will also grow in the richer loams of ordinary garden soil. Like corn they need cultivating to keep down weeds.

SORREL. *See* RUMEX. For Jamaica sorrel *see* HIBISCUS SABDARIFFA. For wood sorrel *see* OXALIS.

SORREL-TREE = *Oxydendrum arboreum*.

SORUS (plural *sori*). The collection of spore cases under or in which are the spores* of ferns. The sori usually occur on the under side of fern fronds, and resemble small fruiting bodies, hence sometimes called (incorrectly) fruit dots. For the reproduction of ferns *see* FERNS AND FERN GARDENING.

SOTOL. *See* DASYLIRION.

SOURBERRY = *Rhus integrifolia*.

SOUR CHERRY = *Prunus Cerasus*.

SOUR GUM. In the North, *Nyssa sylvatica*; in the South, *N. aquatica*. *See* NYSSA.

---

* Special articles on the subjects indicated by an asterisk (*) will be found at the words so marked.

SOUR ORANGE = *Citrus Aurantium.* For culture *see* ORANGE.

SOUR SOIL. *See* SOILS; LIME.

SOURSOP = *Annona muricata.*

SOURWOOD = *Oxydendrum arboreum.*

SOUTH AFRICAN PLANTS. Within recent years many South African plants not generally in cult. have become popular in American gardens. They fall into four main categories: (1) Succulents; (2) Bulbous plants; (3) Annual and perennial herbs; and (4) Shrubs and trees. *See* the various genera mentioned below for special cultural directions or notes on related species. Not all of them can be grown outdoors in the North.

(1) SUCCULENTS. The desert regions of South Africa offer even a wider choice of succulents than is found among the cacti, an American group of plants unknown in South Africa. Among the leading Cape succulents are plants of the genus *Euphorbia*, some of which greatly resemble our tree-like cacti.

Other succulent plants, mostly belonging to the lily, milkweed, or orpine family, will be found at the following genera:

Cotyledon	Aloe
Crassula	Haworthia
Rochea	Gasteria
Portulacaria	Senecio
Schizobasopsis	Stapelia
Mesembryanthemum	Huerniopsis

Also from South Africa comes the plant commonly called asparagus fern (*see* ASPARAGUS), which, although not a succulent, has its leaf area reduced in response to semi-desert conditions. *See also* SUCCULENTS.

(2) BULBOUS PLANTS. Scarcely any region in the world has yielded so many valuable garden bulbs as South Africa. Among the most valuable are *Gladiolus* and many relatives of it in the iris and lily families. The following genera are either exclusively South African or contain species from that country.

Lachenalia	Watsonia
Crinum	Clivia
Brunsvigia	Gloriosa
Moraea	Ixia
Freesia	Haemanthus
Sparaxis	Antholyza
Acidanthera	Dierama
Lapeyrousia	Schizostylis

Very different from any of these is the beautiful *Zantedeschia rehmanni,* which is closely related to the common calla lily of the florists' shops. For this and related species *see* CALLA LILY.

(3) ANNUALS AND PERENNIALS. While many American gardeners will not care to go to the trouble of raising South African succulents, and some may not care to grow many of the bulbous plants, anyone can grow the annuals or perennials, not a few of which will bloom from seed the first year.

While most South African annuals are tender and thus need to be started under glass some weeks before they can be put out-doors, many of them may be sown where wanted.

All the genera below are noted in the body of this book and whether they are to be treated as tender or hardy annuals is noted at each entry. If you don't know the difference in the culture of hardy and tender sorts *see* ANNUALS.

The following genera contain some of the most beautiful South African wild flowers and are to be had as seeds from many dealers. Some are a little woody, and others are usually grown only in the greenhouse.

Arctotis	Charieis
Felicia	Dimorphotheca
Gazania	Gerbera
Heliophila	Nemesia
Ursinia	Venidium
Anchusa	Streptocarpus
Pelargonium	Zaluzianskia

(4) SHRUBS AND TREES. Nearly all woody plants from South Africa are plants of greenhouse culture in the northern states, but are popular for outdoor culture from zone* 8 southward. The list of shrubs, trees, and vines from the Cape is far too long to cite here. Notable among the genera containing South African species grown in American gardens are:

Erica	Acacia
Leucadendron	Phygelius
Tecomaria	Podocarpus
Podalyria	

Of these, by far the most important, as hort. subjects, are the South African heaths (*see* ERICA), and these are widely grown both in the greenhouse and outdoors.

SOUTH CAROLINA. The Carolina jasmine is the state flower, the cabbage palmetto the state tree. The state lies wholly in zones* 6 and 7.

In the upper half or the Piedmont section of the state the soil is largely clay loams and in the lower half or Coastal Plain section sands and sandy loams predominate. Both types of soils vary greatly in fertility and in adaptability to various crops.

In the upper Coastal Plain an area crosses the state in a line with Hamlet, North Carolina, and Augusta, Georgia, about thirty-five miles in width, which is known as the Sandhills, and there the soil is largely coarse to fine sandy. The extreme northwestern corner of the state is mountainous, the Piedmont section is gently to steeply rolling while the Coastal Plain is gently rolling to flat.

All deciduous fruits can be grown in some part of the state and in the southeastern corner even Satsuma and round oranges as well as a few grapefruit trees are grown in home orchards.

The main fruit areas are in Spartanburg, Greenville, and Laurens counties in the Piedmont section. Peaches, apples, and grapes are the principal fruits grown. In the Coastal Plain Chesterfield, Richland, and Saluda counties grow peaches and dewberries. Horry County grows most of the

---

* Special articles on the subjects indicated by an asterisk (*) will be found at the words so marked.

SOUTH CAROLINA

The zones of hardiness crossing South Carolina
are those shown on the map located at ZONE,
which should be consulted for details. The
dates are the average latest killing frost in
spring and the first one in the fall. The figures
below the dates show the average length of
the growing season.

strawberries, although they can be grown
throughout the state. Peaches are adapted to
all parts except the lower Coastal Plain and
certain varieties of grapes can be grown in
all counties. The Muscadine grapes are
largely grown in the Coastal Plain and
Labrusca and other American species in the
Piedmont. Pecans are best adapted to the
middle Coastal Plain, although they are
grown throughout the state.

Vegetable production is largely centered in
the Coastal Plain. The main crops grown are
asparagus, lima and snap beans, beets, cabbage, cantaloupes, cucumbers, lettuce, peas,
peppers, Irish potatoes, sweet potatoes,
spinach, squash, tomatoes, and watermelons.
Charleston and Beaufort counties are the
chief commercial areas for Irish potatoes,
cabbage, string beans, tomatoes, beets, carrots, etc.; Hampton, Allendale, Bamberg, and
Barnwell counties, watermelons; Barnwell,
Allendale, Charleston, and Orangeburg counties, cucumbers; Barnwell, Saluda, Edge-
field, and Aiken counties, asparagus; Barnwell, Bamberg, Allendale counties, cantaloupes
and cucumbers; Florence, Orangeburg, and
Williamsburg counties, peas.

On account of high temperatures during
July and August few vegetables are grown
during those months except in the extreme
northwestern part. It is the usual practice
to grow two crops each year of many vegetables in most of the state, while some crops,
such as cabbage and lettuce, in the Coastal
Plain are grown throughout the winter. The
gardener anywhere in South Carolina can
truly have a "year round" garden whether

it be vegetables or flowers and flowering
shrubs.

Market gardening is most developed around
the cities and larger towns, Charleston, Columbia, Greenville, Spartanburg, Florence,
Sumter, and Anderson.

Many varieties and species of flowers,
ornamental trees, and shrubs are adapted to
the entire state, a complete list of which
would be too lengthy for this article. The
following are the chief flowers and ornamental plants.

ORNAMENTAL PLANTS FOR SOUTH
CAROLINA GARDENS

Gardening in South Carolina varies considerably from the mild winter climate of the
coastal counties to the higher elevations in
the western part of the state. For instance,
in Charleston County plants such as geranium, ferns, several species of palms, *Plumbago capensis, Beloperone guttata,* and *Bignonia chamberlayni* survive the winters. Annuals and biennials such as pansy, English
daisy, *Myosotis, Calendula,* stocks, and snapdragons are planted in late October and
early November for February, March, and
April blooming. Only the most heat-resistant
annuals such as zinnia, marigold, verbena,
and petunias are satisfactory for summer
flowering. Some of the most reliable perennials for the coastal section are *Hemerocallis,
Stokesia,* Shasta daisy, *Iris sibirica,* and
Phlox divaricata. Peonies and *Delphinium*
are not satisfactory. Bulbs and tubers such
as *Narcissus, Lycoris, Amaryllis, Canna,* lilies,
Ranunculus, Anemone, Zephyranthes, and
Dutch iris are planted extensively.

The somewhat cooler summers and winters
with temperatures below freezing in the
western half of South Carolina provide better growing conditions for the usual summer annuals and the popular perennials.
Annuals such as marigold, *Zinnia, Salvia,
Scabiosa, Petunia, Verbena,* nasturtium, aster,
Dianthus, Vinca rosea, and dwarf dahlia
and snapdragons are grown from seed sown
usually in March and early April. Seed of
alyssum, poppies, larkspur, annual phlox, and
Nemophila is sown in October. Sweet peas
are planted in November for April and May
flowering.

Among the perennials grown in western
South Carolina are *Alyssum saxatile, Anthemis, Dianthus, Dicentra, Chrysanthemum,*
several species of *Iris, Hemerocallis, Phlox
paniculata, Eupatorium,* peony, *Aquilegia,
Tritoma,* and hardy aster. All of the bulbs
and tubers grown in coastal South Carolina
are used, with the addition of tulips.

South Carolina provides ideal growing conditions for most of the broad-leaved evergreen shrubs such as *Abelia, Aucuba, Berberis, Eurya, Daphne, Euonymus, Gardenia,
Feijoa,* many species and varieties of *Ilex,
Ligustrum, Mahonia, Pyracantha, Camellia,*
and *Azalea.*

Deciduous flowering shrubs commonly
grown are flowering quince, pearl-bush, *For-*

* Special articles on the subjects indicated by an asterisk (*) will be found at the words so marked.

sythia, *Hydrangea, Spiraea, Kolkwitzia*, althea, *Lonicera, Weigela, Deutzia*, and *Philadelphus.*

In small flowering trees dogwood, redbud, crabapple and crape myrtles are well adapted to South Carolina conditions. For shade trees several species of oak, maple, tulip poplar, and mimosa (*Albizzia Julibrissin*) are popular.

Near Charleston are found the famous Magnolia, Middleton, and Cypress gardens. All three feature *Camellia japonica* and azaleas. In Orangeburg, the city park known as Edisto Gardens is noted for its azaleas and American Rose Society test garden. Kalmia Gardens at Hartsville features an extensive collection of ornamental plants. The Swan Lake Gardens of Sumter are noted for Japanese iris.

CLIMATE

The number of growing days per year varies from 221 in the northwest corner of the state to 294 at Charleston.

Town	Average date of last killing frost in spring	Latest-known killing frost
Charleston	Feb. 20	Apr. 2
Columbia	Mar. 17	Apr. 17
Greenville	Mar. 30	Apr. 21

Town	Average date of earliest killing frost in fall	Earliest-known killing frost
Charleston	Dec. 11	Nov. 8
Columbia	Nov. 18	Oct. 30
Greenville	Nov. 6	Oct. 10

The yearly rainfall for the whole state has averaged 47.74 inches for the past 70 years. The rainfall is well distributed throughout the year, although November, December, and January average slightly less precipitation than the other months. Occasionally very heavy rains occur in a few hours in small areas. The average number of clear days is 175; partly cloudy days, 95; and cloudy days, 95.

There are now about fourteen thousand (14,000) members in the Garden Club of South Carolina which is affiliated with the National Council of Garden Clubs. There are also many garden clubs not federated, men's garden clubs, the South Carolina Camellia Society, the South Carolina Rose Society, the South Carolina Iris Society, and the South Carolina Hemerocallis Society.

The address of the Agricultural Experiment Station which has kindly supplied this information about South Carolina is Clemson. The station is always ready to answer gardening questions.

SOUTH DAKOTA. The pasque-flower is the state flower, the cottonwood the state tree. The state lies wholly in zones* 1, 2, and 3. The variation in the vegetative growth from south to north is typical of the change in latitude. The change in type of vegetation from east to west is much more marked. In the eastern border of the state the vegetation is characteristic of the northern prairie. Westward it gradually changes to one of Great Plains character. Along the western edge of the state the Rocky Mountain type of vegetation is found.

SOILS. The soils east of the Missouri River are of glacial origin and consist largely of glacial till types. West of the Missouri River the soil is of sedimentary origin and consists of several different types.

CHIEF GARDENING CENTERS. The possibilities of horticulture in South Dakota are somewhat difficult, due to cold and frequently open winters, protracted drought periods during the growing season, and the drying southwest winds. However, if suitable sites

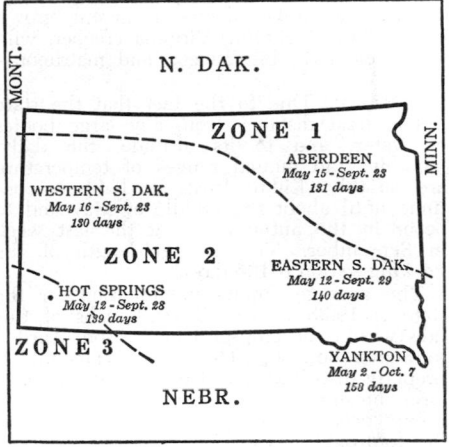

SOUTH DAKOTA

The zones of hardiness crossing South Dakota are those shown on the map located at ZONE, which should be consulted for details. The dates are the average latest killing frost in spring and the first one in the fall. The figures below the dates show the average length of the growing season. Annual rainfall is about 20 in. per year.

and soils are chosen, hardy kinds and varieties selected, and the plants given proper care, the home gardener should be successful in growing fruits, vegetables, flowers, and ornamental plants. The commercial horticultural sections of the state are located in the southeastern and Black Hills regions. Horticultural enterprises are carried on in home gardens over the entire state.

MAIN FRUIT AND VEGETABLE AREAS. The principal fruit crops are the apple, plum, currant, gooseberry, and red raspberry. The principal vegetable crops are the potato, melons and other vine crops, cabbage, onion,

* Special articles on the subjects indicated by an asterisk (*) will be found at the words so marked.

tomato, sweet corn, pea, bean, carrot, beet, asparagus, and rhubarb.

FLOWERS, ORNAMENTAL TREES, AND SHRUBS. The principal perennial flowers are the peony, iris, hollyhock, larkspur, daisy, and many others. There are over one hundred native species of shrubs, namely: *Mahonia,* hazel, currant, spirea, juneberry, choke cherry, lead plant, prickly ash, burningbush, shrubby cinquefoil, sumac, buffaloberry, dogwood, *Viburnum* and *Symphoricarpos* species. There are nearly as many native species of trees, namely: American elm, green ash, box-elder, basswood, bur oak, hackberry, black walnut, black cherry, canoe birch, hawthorn, honey locust, silver maple, willow, poplar, cottonwood, Black Hills spruce and pine, red cedar, and juniper. There are many exotic species of trees and shrubs that are adapted to the state, among them Colorado spruce, white fir, Austrian pine, Chinese elm, *Caragana,* Russian olive, lilac, honeysuckle, *Cotoneaster,* and barberry. There are a number of vines commonly grown in the state, including Virginia creeper, wild grape, clematis, bittersweet, and matrimonyvine.

CLIMATE. Due to the fact that the state lies a great distance from any large bodies of water, and to its altitude, the daily, monthly, and annual ranges of temperature are variable. Killing frosts are liable to continue until about the middle of May and to occur in the autumn during the last week in September. The average length of the growing season is 135 days.

The average annual precipitation for the state is 19.98 inches. Three-fourths of this falls within the crop-growing season, April 1 to September 30. The normal amount, if properly distributed, will produce good crops. Drought sufficient to reduce crop production occurs occasionally, but a real crop failure due to drought is rare.

	Average date of last killing frost in spring	Latest-known killing frost
Yankton	May 2	May 24
Aberdeen	May 15	June 21
Hot Springs	May 12	June 7
Western S. D. (Av. of 42 sta.)	May 16	June 7
Eastern S. D. (Av. of 47 sta.)	May 12	June 8

	Average date of earliest killing frost in fall	Earliest-known killing frost
Yankton	Oct. 7	Sept. 14
Aberdeen	Sept. 23	Aug. 20
Hot Springs	Sept. 28	Sept. 6
Western S. D. (Av. of 42 sta.)	Sept. 23	Sept. 2
Eastern S. D. (Av. of 47 sta.)	Sept. 29	Sept. 4

There are over 50 garden clubs affiliated with the South Dakota State Federation of Garden Clubs; the present address is Highmore, South Dakota.

The address of the Agricultural Experiment Station which has kindly supplied this information about the state is Brookings, South Dakota. The station is always ready to answer gardening questions.

SOUTHERN CANE = *Arundinaria gigantea.*

SOUTHERN CRABAPPLE = *Malus angustifolia.*

SOUTHERN CYPRESS = *Taxodium distichum.*

SOUTHERN DEWBERRY = *Rubus trivialis.*

SOUTHERN SMILAX. *See* SMILAX (2).

SOUTHERN WHITE CEDAR = *Chamaecyparis thyoides.*

SOUTHERNWOOD = *Artemisia Abrotanum.*

SOW THISTLE = *Sonchus oleraceus. See* list at WEEDS.

SOYBEAN. Of over 40 species of the genus **Glycine** (gly-sy'ne), only **G. Max,** the soybean, is of any hort. importance. Like the rest of the species it is a native of the Old World and is more of a farm than garden crop. It is the mainstay of the agriculture of Manchuria, in which country and in Jap. it is native. It is an erect, bushy annual, 3–6 ft. high, with alternate* compound leaves composed of 3 ovalish leaflets 3–6 in. long and without marginal teeth. Flowers pea-like but inconspicuous, white or purplish. Pods (legumes*) short-stalked, drooping, 2–3 in. long, about ½ in. wide, hairy and brownish. Seeds globe-shaped, variously colored in the many varieties now in cult. (*Glycine* is from the Greek for some plant with edible parts, but not certainly this one.) The plant was long known as *Soja Max.*

SOYBEAN CULTURE

While soybeans have been grown as a food crop in China and Jap. for thousands of years, their use in the U.S. is chiefly as forage, for green manuring and for its seeds. The plant is an annual requiring a warm summer for maturity, but it will also stand considerable drought, and is thus admirably adapted to some of the prairie states and is widely grown there, sometimes under irrigation. It is a fine smother crop if sown broadcast, especially on land to be made into a lawn.

SPADING. *See* DIGGING.

SPADIX. The thick, usually fleshy and crowded spike of flowers in members of the arum family and in a few other plants. A common example is the central "Jack" (spadix) in the Jack-in-the-pulpit, surrounded by the pulpit, which is a spathe. *See* ARACEAE. Spathes may be of many shapes and are found in other plants than

---

* Special articles on the subjects indicated by an asterisk (*) will be found at the words so marked.

the aroids.* In some palms the spathe may be several feet long, boat-shaped, and woody.

SPAGHETTI-PLANT. A trade (usually hawker's) name for a small decorative gourd. *See* GOURDS.

SPANISH BAYONET = *Yucca aloifolia* and *Y. filamentosa.*

SPANISH BLUEBELL = *Scilla hispanica.*

SPANISH BROOM = *Spartium junceum* and *Genista hispanica.* For related plants *see* BROOM.

SPANISH BUTTONS = *Centaurea nigra.*

SPANISH CEDAR = *Cedrela odorata.*

SPANISH CHESTNUT = *Castanea sativa.* See CHESTNUT.

SPANISH DAGGER = *Yucca aloifolia* and *Y. gloriosa.*

SPANISH FIR = *Abies Pinsapo.* See FIR.

SPANISH GARDEN. The type of gardening introduced into America by the Spaniards and really based upon the art of the Moors. Its outstanding characteristic is the use of the patio, and the necessity of making gardens in regions of intense heat, bright sunshine, and deficient rainfall.

Many beautiful gardens of this type are to be found in N. Mex., Ariz., Calif., Fla., and, most of all, in Latin America.

SPANISH HEATH = *Erica australis.*

SPANISH IRIS. See IRIS XYPHIUM.

SPANISH JACINTH = *Scilla hispanica.*

SPANISH JASMINE = *Jasminum grandiflorum.*

SPANISH LICORICE = *Glycyrrhiza glabra.* See LICORICE.

SPANISH LIME = *Melicocca bijuga.*

SPANISH MOSS = *Tillandsia usneoides.*

SPANISH NEEDLE = Beggar-ticks, which see in the list at WEEDS.

SPANISH ONION. See ALLIUM FISTULOSUM.

SPANISH OYSTER PLANT = *Scolymus hispanicus.*

SPANISH PLUM = *Spondias purpurea.*

SPANISH TREFOIL = *Medicago sativa.*

SPARAXIS (spa-racks'is). Wand-flower. Harlequin flower. South African perennial herbs with bulbous corms, comprising about 6 species, belonging to the iris family. Spring-flowering plants, closely allied to *Ixia.* Leaves basal, narrow, sword-shaped, with parallel veins. Flowers yellow, rose, red, or purple, often tinged brown, in short spikes, each flower enclosed in a cut or fringed spathe.* Calyx* of 3 colored sepals. Corolla of 3 petals alternating with the sepals. Stamens* 3. Fruit a 3-celled capsule.* (*Sparaxis* is from the Greek for torn, in allusion to the torn spathe.*) For cult. *see* IXIA.

grandiflora. Leaves narrow, to 1 ft. long. Flowering stalk to 1 ft. high. Flowers yellow, or purple, 1 in. or more long, solitary or in few-flowered spikes.

pulcherrima = *Dierama pulcherrima.*

tricolor. Growing to 18 in. high, similar to *S. grandiflora,* except that flowers are variable in color, usually having 3 distinct colors, but the throat always bright yellow.

SPARMANNIA (spar-man'i-a). Tender African shrubs or small trees, comprising about 5 species of the family Tiliaceae, usually covered with erect, soft, silky hairs. Leaves alternate,* heart-shaped, toothed, or sometimes lobed. Flowers white, in numerous terminal clusters (umbels*). Calyx* of 4 sepals. Corolla of 4 petals. Stamens* many. Fruit a prickly capsule.* (Named for Andreas Sparmann, Swedish naturalist.)

Sparmannias are very attractive and showy, even after the flowering period. They can be grown outdoors in frost-free localities, and make good greenhouse pot plants for winter flowering. Propagated by cuttings. Cuttings of the tips of young shoots, taken in early spring, will flower the following winter. They should be grown in potting mixture* 3. They like plenty of light and air at all times. After flowering they may be cut back, re-potted, and grown on for flowering the next year.

africana. Growing to 20 ft. high. Leaves to 9 in. long, heart-shaped at base, cut into 5–7 lobes, the margins toothed. Flowers white, to 1½ in. across, with prominent yellow stamens.* Fruit spiny, ½ in. across. The *var.* **flore-pleno** has double flowers.

SPARTIUM (spar'shi-um). A single species of essentially leafless shrubs of the pea family, **S. junceum,** the Spanish or weaver's broom, often grown for its profusion of yellow bloom. It has grooved, rush-like stems, 6–8 ft. high, with alternate,* simple* leaves (when produced). Flowers fragrant, pea-like, yellow, about 1 in. long, mostly in terminal clusters (racemes*) that may be 15 in. long, hence very showy. Fruit a flattened pod (legume*), about 4 in. long and hairy. A handsome shrub in bloom, otherwise of indifferent aspect. Southern Eu. May–Sept. (or all year in Calif.). Hardy from zone* 6, possibly from zone* 5 (with protection), and southward. Much planted in Calif. on a variety of soils. Propagated by cutting or by seeds. (*Spartium* is from the ancient Greek name for the plant.) *See* BROOM and GENISTA for closely related plants.

SPATHE. A leaf-like or often colored bract* which surrounds or encloses a flower cluster. A common example is the "pulpit" which surrounds and hoods the spadix* in the Jack-in-the-pulpit. *See* ARACEAE. But many other plants than the aroids* bear spathes, which surround or are just below the flower clusters in most of the iris family, many palms, the banana, and in some plants of the lily and amaryllis families. Sometimes a spathe may be papery or membranous, but in many palms it is hard, woody, and boat-shaped.

SPATHIPHYLLUM (spath-i-fill'um). Tropical American perennial herbs, comprising about 27 species of the family Araceae, having thick rootstocks and basal leaves. Leafstalks to 2½ ft. long, sheathing at the base. Leaves large, broadly lance-shaped, thin, with strong-marked midrib. Flowers in a spadix,* enclosed in a large leafy bract (spathe*) similar to Jack-in-the-pulpit. Flowers of 2 kinds, male (stamens* only) on the upper part of the spadix, and female (pistil* only) on the lower part. (*Spathiphyllum* is from the Greek for leaf and spathe, in allusion to the leaf-like spathe.*) They are not much in cultivation, but sometimes grown in the warm greenhouse for their foliage. Propagated by division of the rootstocks. They should be grown in potting mixture* 4.

floribundum. Leafstalk to 6 in. long. Leaves lance-shaped, to 6 in. long, and 2½ in. wide, one half of the leaf blade larger than the other, dark green on upper side, paler green on under side. Flowers greenish-yellow, enclosed in a white spathe* 2½ in. long. Colombia.

patini. Leafstalk to 1 ft. long. Leaves lance-shaped, to 10 in. long, and 2½ in. wide. Flowers enclosed in a whitish spathe*, which is about 3 in. long. Colombia.

SPATHODEA (spath-ō′dee-a). Tropical African evergreen trees, comprising about 3 species of the family Bignoniaceae, growing 20–70 ft. high. Leaves compound,* bright green. Leaflets unequal in number, sometimes only 3, the margins without teeth. Flowers scarlet, in loose terminal clusters. Calyx of 5 sepals, joined together, but splitting on one side to the base, exposing the corolla. Corolla large, bell-shaped, its limb 5-lobed. Stamens* 4, in pairs, 2 long, 2 short. Fruit a woody capsule to 8 in. long. (*Spathodea* is from the Greek for spathe*-like, in allusion to the shape of the calyx.*)

Spathodeas are only grown in sub-tropical or tropical areas, as they do not flower until they become large trees. Propagated by seeds or cuttings.

campanulata. Large evergreen tree, growing to 70 ft. Leaves compound, to 1½ ft. long, bright green. Leaflets 9–19, lance-shaped, to 4 in. long, slightly hairy on the under side when young. Flowers scarlet, to 4 in. long, in many-flowered, loose, terminal clusters. Calyx tough and leathery. A popular, quick-growing, very handsome tree, considerably planted in the warmer parts of Fla., where it is called African tulip-tree.

spathulata, -us, -um (spath-you-lay′ta). Spatulate; *i.e.*, spoon-shaped.

spathulifolia, -us, -um (spath-u-ly-fo′li-a). With spoon-shaped leaves.

SPATHYEMA. See SKUNK-CABBAGE.

SPATTERDOCK = *Nuphar advena.*

SPATULATE. Spoon-shaped.

SPAWN. See MUSHROOM.

SPEAR. A young shoot; as of asparagus.

SPEARFLOWER = *Ardisia.*

SPEAR LILY. See DORYANTHES.

SPEARMINT = *Mentha spicata.* See MINT.

SPECIAL COLOR GARDENS. *See* COLOR GARDENING.

SPECIES (plural species). A group of individual plants more like each other than anything else and all belonging to a single genus.* Sometimes the genus has only one species in it, as the giant cactus is the only species in the genus *Carnegiea,* the bloodroot the only species in the genus *Sanguinaria,* the castor-oil plant the only one in *Ricinus,* and so on.

Such species are easily recognized by everyone, for they have no relatives with which they may be confused. Genera containing only one species (usually called monotypic genera) are, however, comparatively rare. Much the most usual case is presented by genera like *Aster, Rosa, Solanum, Rhododendron,* or *Chrysanthemum.* They may contain anywhere from two to over one thousand species, and it is in such cases, by far the most numerous in this book, that the validity and usefulness of *species* is evident.

For grouped around each species (as a concept) are a lot of individual plants more like each other than like any similar group or species in that genus. To recognize and delimit this category of individuals, botanists, and perforce gardeners, have applied to each species a *specific* name.

These species names, of which there are over 2200 in this book, are all defined and pronounced at their proper alphabetic entries (*see* EGLANTERIA, CANINA, MOSCHATA for those used in *Rosa* below), unless they happen to be derived from people's names such as *grayi, wendlandiana, wilsoni,* and hence of obvious origin and meaning.

Species names are usually, but not always, supposed to indicate some feature of the particular plant. Hence *alba* for white, *rubra* for red, *canadensis* for from Canada, etc. The meaning of such species names will be found throughout the book, as many of them have not only an interesting history but actually help to describe the plant. Some species names are misleading, however, because the person who christened a particular plant may have mistaken its origin or have been mixed up as to its true identity. The species name cannot be changed, however, once the plant is properly christened, which accounts for occasional names that are confusing. All such have been noted wherever they occur.

Throughout botanical and hort. literature this specific or species name (always in Latin or Greek), in italics, follows the name of the genus, which tells us at once that it not only belongs to that genus but is a specified and limited part of it. To illustrate:

Rosa is the genus name of all the roses, and *Rosa* contains many species. Each of them has its own specific name such as,

Rosa Eglanteria for the sweetbrier.
Rosa canina for the dog rose.
Rosa moschata for the musk rose.

In each case the second name is the spe-

---

* Special articles on the subjects indicated by an asterisk (*) will be found at the words so marked.

cies or specific name and must always be used if one needs to specify exactly to which of many members of the genus *Rosa* the particular plant belongs. For the reason why certain specific names have an initial capital letter, as in *Eglanteria, see* PLANT NAMES. Often, in this book and throughout hort. literature, you will find *Rosa* (or of course other generic names) written out in full when first used, but abbreviated afterwards. This is done merely to save space; and the three species of rose mentioned above would then be written

> *Rosa Eglanteria, R. canina,* and *R. moschata*

> not

> *Rosa Eglanteria, Rosa canina,* and *Rosa moschata.*

Throughout this book, also to save useless repetition, even the initial *R.* is omitted, once the genus name is clearly stated, as at *Rosa* and all the other genera in the book. *See* ROSA where the species are listed alphabetically (without the abbreviation *R.*). *See also* GENUS, PLANT NAMES, VARIETY.

speciosa, -us, -um (spee-si-ō′sa). Showy.

speciosissima, -us, -um (spee-si-o-siss′i-ma). Very showy.

SPECKLED ALDER = *Alnus incana. See* ALDER.

spectabilis, -e (speck-tab′i-lis). Remarkably showy.

SPECULARIA (speck-you-lair′i-a). Hardy annual herbs, comprising about 12 species of the family Campanulaceae, found in the northern hemisphere, with one in Australia. They are low-growing, erect, or of spreading habit, the leaves alternate,* lance-shaped, the margins sometimes toothed. Flowers blue, purple or white, in 1–3-flowered clusters, growing from the axils* of the leaves. Calyx tubular Corolla widely open to ¾ in. across, its limb 5-lobed. Stamens* 5. Fruit a 3-celled capsule. (*Specularia* is from *Speculum-Veneris,* which see.)

Useful annual for the border or rock garden. Easily cult. Seeds may be sown in fall or early spring where required to bloom, or may be sown in a cold frame and transplanted.

Speculum-Veneris. Also known as *Campanula Speculum.* Venus's-looking-glass. Growing to 15 in. high, and of erect habit. Leaves broadly lance-shaped, to 1½ in. long, the margins toothed. Flowers deep blue, or white, to ¾ in. across, in 1–3-flowered clusters. Sepals curved. Mediterranean region.

speculata, -us, -um (speck-u-lay′ta). Like a looking-glass.

Speculum-Veneris (speck-you-lum-ven′er-is). The looking-glass of Venus. *See* SPECULARIA.

SPEEDWELL. *See* VERONICA. *See also* the list at WEEDS.

SPERGON. *See* Chloranil at FUNGICIDES.

SPERGULA ARVENSIS = Spurry. *See* the list at WEEDS.

sphacelata, -us, -um (sfa-see-lay′ta). Withered or diseased.

SPHAERALCEA (sfee-ral′see-a). Globe mallow. Shrubs or perennial herbs, comprising about 65 species of the family Malvaceae, mostly natives of tropical and sub-tropical America, but a few found in South Africa. Leaves alternate,* lance-shaped or roundish and lobed, the margins sometimes toothed. Flowers large and showy, lilac, pink, or red, solitary or in clusters, terminal or growing from the axils* of the leaves, with 3 small, scale-like bracts* beneath each flower. Calyx* of 5 sepals. Corolla of 5 petals. Stamens* many. Fruits many, growing in a ring at the top of the disk-like receptacle.* (*Sphaeralcea* is from the Greek for globe, and *Alcea,* which see.) They are sometimes offered as *Phymosia* and *Malvastrum.* Sometimes cult. in the warm greenhouse or grown outdoors in the South. Propagated by seeds or cuttings made from the tips of young shoots. The last two are not hardy in the North.

coccinea. Red false mallow or prairie mallow. A woody-based, perennial herb, 8–12 in. high, usually silvery-hairy, with the alternate* leaves parted into narrow segments. Flowers brick-red, about 1 in. wide, mostly in close, terminal clusters (racemes*). It is practically a weed in central N.A., but is grown in the flower garden, where it is of very easy cult.; propagated by division. Often offered as a *Malvastrum.*

rosea. Shrub, growing to 12 ft. high. Leaves roundish and lobed. Flowers rose, in clusters. Bracts* on flower stalks united at the base. Guatemala.

umbellata. Shrub, growing to 15 ft. high. Leaves roundish, slightly cut into 7 lobes. Flowers scarlet, to 2 in. across, in axillary clusters, the petals white-marked at the base. Mex.

vitifolia = *Sphaeralcea rosea.*

sphaerocarpa, -us, -um (sfeer-o-kar′pa). Round-fruited.

sphaerocephala, -us, -um (sfeer-o-seff′a-la). Round-headed.

SPHAGNUM (sfag′num). A large group of generally bog mosses, mostly with pale or ashy foliage and of little cult. importance, but widely used for packing plants and for other purposes; chopped up it is a useful medium on a seedbed.

Dried sphagnum, which comes in large bales, has many uses, for its ability to hold water makes it a good medium for rooting plants which are air-layered. *See* LAYERING.

Coming mostly from bogs, sphagnum is generally acid, often very much so. It is consequently of the greatest use in the bog garden, where some orchids and insectivorous plants grow better in wet sphagnum than in anything else.

Commercial preparations of sphagnum, baked to kill weeds, and with the acid removed and sometimes mixed with dried cow manure, are extremely useful forms of humus (which see).

SPHENOGYNE. *See* URSINIA.

---

* Special articles on the subjects indicated by an asterisk (*) will be found at the words so marked.

spicc, -us, -um (spy'ka). A spike (or ear) of grain.

Spicant (spy'kant). Spiked or spike-like.

spicata, -us, -um (spy-kay'ta). Spiked; or having flowers in a spike.*

SPICEBERRY = *Gaultheria procumbens.*

SPICEBUSH. In the East, *Lindera Benzoin;* in Calif., *Calycanthus occidentalis.*

SPICE TREE = *Umbellularia californica.*

SPICEWOOD = *Lindera Benzoin.*

spiculifolia, -us, -um (spick-you-li-fō'li-a). Having sharp-pointed leaves.

SPIDERFLOWER = *Cleome spinosa,* but *see also* TIBOUCHINA.

SPIDER-LILY. Rather showy, chiefly tropical American bulbous herbs, comprising the genus **Hymenocallis** (hy-men-o-kall'is) of the family Amaryllidaceae. Of the 40 known species only four are of much cult. interest, although there are wild species, found from S. Car. to Fla., which are sometimes transferred to grounds in their own region. They have narrow, strap-shaped, basal leaves and few-flowered clusters (umbels*) of white flowers at the end of a stout, solid stalk. Corolla white, cylindric and united below, broadening at the top and with narrow segments. Stamens* 6, their filaments* much broadened and united at the base into a white, cup-like structure which is very conspicuous. Fruit a 3-valved capsule. (*Hymenocallis* is from the Greek for beautiful membrane, in allusion to the cup-like base of the stamens.*) Also called Peruvian daffodil.

The spider-lilies are popular plants for outdoor culture in tropical gardens. In the North they need greenhouse care and should be planted in large pots or small tubs, as their bulbs become large in age. Use potting mixture* 4 and grow in the warm-temperate house. *Hymenocallis caribaea* blooms in the winter, and its bulbs should be rested in the summer (*see* RESTING PLANTS). *H. calathina* is a summer bloomer and should be rested during the winter. The plants are closely related to *Pancratium,* of which they are considered American representatives by some.

H. calathina. Basket-flower. Bulb with a long, stout neck* from which arise the 6–8 leaves which are nearly 2 ft. long and 2 in. wide, two-ranked. Flowers nearly 8 in. long, tubular for about half this length, the segments narrow. The cup-like base of the stamens nearly 2 in. wide, fringed, the stamens protruding beyond it about ½ in. Peruvian and Bolivian Andes. Often offered under the names *Pancratium calathinum* and *Ismene calathina.* Often grown outdoors as far north as zone* 5, where it should be lifted over the winter.

H. caribaea. Bulb with little or no neck. Leaves 12–20, usually 2–3 ft. long, nearly 3 in. wide, not 2-ranked. Flowers fragrant, about 6 in. long, tubular for about half this length. Cup-like base of the stamens about 1 in. wide, the stamens protruding beyond it nearly 2 in. Fla. and W.I.

H. festalis. A hybrid spider-lily, about 18 in. high, the flowers white. One of its parents

is *H. calathina* and it has little advantage over that species.

H. occidentalis. Leaves bluish-green, 12–18 in. long and about 1½ in. wide, tapering at both ends. Flowers white, the segments 4–5 in. long, the cup-like crown about half this. Flowers borne in a lax cluster at the summit of a naked, stout stalk. Southeastern U.S. in rich swamps. Aug.

SPIDER ORCHID. See BRASSIA.

SPIDER PLANT. See CHLOROPHYTUM ELATUM.

SPIDERWORT. Rather weak-stemmed watery-juiced, perennial herbs constituting the genus **Tradescantia** (tray-des-kan'ti-a) of the family Commelinaceae, all the 100 known species American, and mostly tropical. Three are occasionally cult. in the hardy border, and one is an extremely popular greenhouse plant for hanging baskets — the wandering Jew (for another plant so called *see* ZEBRINA PENDULA). Leaves (in ours) long and narrow, or ovalish and stalkless, without marginal teeth. Flowers white or bluish-purple, or even pinkish, rather ephemeral. Sepals 3, often green or colored. Petals 3, separate. Stamens* 6. Fruit a 3-valved capsule.* (Named for John Tradescant, gardener to Charles I.) The plants are sometimes known as widow's-tear.

The hardy spiderworts (*H. bracteata* and *H. virginiana*) are of easy cult. in most garden soils, preferring some moisture and partial shade to open, dry sites. They can easily be divided in the spring, or detached joints of their stems will usually root in any sandy soil. The wandering Jew also roots easily from cuttings or even broken bits of stem. It is common in greenhouses and often runs wild under the benches. It is a useful plant for hanging baskets, where, because of its drooping habit, it soon covers the sides of the basket.

T. bracteata. A hardy perennial, not over 12 in. high. Leaves narrowly lance-shaped, 6–8 in. long. Flowers blue or purplish-blue, the 2 bracts* beneath them wider than the leaves and boat-shaped. Central U.S. June–Aug.

T. brevicaulis. An uncertain name for a plant assigned by some to *H. virginiana* or to the native non-hort. species *T. longipes.* A common name in the trade.

T. dracaenoides = *Spironema fragrans,* usually. The true *T. dracaenoides,* rare or little known in cult., is a Mexican plant with tuberous roots, hairy-margined leaves, and rose-pink flowers.

T. fluminensis. Wandering Jew. A prostrate or trailing plant, the leaves ovalish, 2–2½ in. long, pointed both ends, essentially stalkless. Flowers white. S.A., but naturalized in warm sections of the U.S. A very common plant in greenhouses, widely used for hanging baskets, and useful as a house plant, as it will grow in almost any soil so long as it is kept moist. The *var.* **variegata** has white-striped leaves and is even more common in cult. than the normal green form. There are also yellow-marked varieties. *See also* ZEBRINA PENDULA.

T. virginiana. Common spiderwort, sometimes called snake grass. A hardy perennial, 2–3 ft. high. Leaves 12–15 in. long, scarcely 1 in. wide, often channeled. Flowers violet-

---

* Special articles on the subjects indicated by an asterisk (*) will be found at the words so marked.

purple or bluish. Eastern U.S., west to Ark. May–Aug. The *var.* **alba** has white flowers.

T. zebrina = *Zebrina pendula.*

SPIDERWORT FAMILY = Commelina-ceae.

SPIGELIA (spy-gee′li-a). Tender or hardy American annual or perennial herbs, comprising about 50 species of the family Loganiaceae. Leaves opposite,* ovalish or broadly lance-shaped, thin. Flowers red, yellow, or purple, in one-sided, branching clusters. Calyx* narrowly tubular. Corolla tubular, its limb 5-lobed. Stamens* 5, growing on the corolla tube. Fruit a 2-celled, flattish capsule. (Named for Adrian von der Spigel, Dutch botanist.)

These plants are not much in cultivation, a few species grown in the greenhouse, and the one below as a border plant. Propagated by division of roots in March or April. Soil should be deeply dug, and a little leaf mold added to it. They prefer half-shady positions and plenty of water in hot weather.

marilandica. Pinkroot. Worm-grass. Starbloom. Hardy perennial, growing to 2 ft. high. Leaves ovalish, to 4 in. long. Flowers tubular, red with yellow throat, to 2 in. long in terminal one-sided clusters. Md. to Fla. and westward. Summer. It yields a remedy for intestinal worms.

SPIKE. A raceme*-like cluster in which the individual flowers are stalkless or nearly so (they are stalked in a raceme*). Common examples of a spike are found in the true pepper (*see* PIPER), the prince's-feather (*Polygonum orientale*), the mignonette, and in the hyssop.

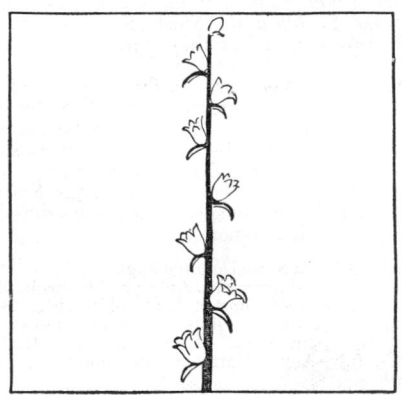

Spike

SPIKED ALDER = *Clethra alnifolia.*

SPIKE GRASS. See UNIOLA.

SPIKE HEATH = *Bruckenthalia spiculifolia.*

SPIKELET. A small spike,* especially one of the small spikes which make up the inflorescence of the grasses.

SPIKENARD = *Aralia racemosa.*

SPINACH. The garden spinach is one of only 3 or 4 species of Asiatic annual herbs constituting the genus **Spinacia** (spin-ach′i-a), of which **S. oleracea** is the common spinach. They belong to the goosefoot family (Chenopodiaceae). Leaves alternate,* mostly basal or nearly so, ovalish, or ovalish-oblong, or in some cult. varieties roundish, usually crinkly margined. The stem leaves (not usually produced on harvested plants) are smaller and narrower. Flowers small, unisexual* (for details *see* CHENOPODIACEAE). Fruit a utricle,* surrounded by a small, prickly, capsule-like body (commonly but incorrectly called the seed). There is also a variety, little known, where the fruit is invested with a covering that is not spiny. (*Spinacia* is from the Latin for spine, in allusion to the husk of the fruit.) *See also* NEW ZEALAND SPINACH.

SPINACH CULTURE

Spinach is a cool-season annual, grown as a pot herb or for greens. No spinach will stand extreme summer heat without bolting* seed stalks. For this reason the seed must be sown early in the spring or late in the summer, to avoid the danger of the crop maturing in July or August. For spring and summer use, sow as early as the ground can be worked, and make successive plantings every two weeks until May 15. The leaves will be ready for use four or five weeks after sowing; however, it should not be used much later than the middle of June. For autumn use, sow seeds about August 1. The spinach will grow very large and can be cut from the first of September until the ground freezes.

To winter-over, and have extra early spring spinach, seed should be sown in early September. Although the plants are hardy in well-drained soil as far north as New York, and probably considerably farther north, it is best to give a winter protection of straw or leaves. Uncover gradually in the spring when danger of severe freezing is past. For home use during the winter, seed may be sown in the hotbed, or young plants transplanted to frames in the fall and covered to secure good green leaves.

The best results are obtained with spinach which is grown on soil containing an abundance of plant food, especially nitrogen. The ground cannot be too rich and the pH should preferably be between 8.0 and 6.0, but not less than 6.0. (*See* ACID AND ALKALI SOILS.) Nitrate of soda or ammonium sulphate in solution should be applied as a fertilizer. Two or more applications should be made; a sprayer, used as an applicator, provides for even distribution. About one ounce of nitrate of soda to two gallons of water makes a full-strength solution. Ammonium sulphate is slower to take effect upon the plants but contains more nitrogen than nitrate of soda and the effect is longer lasting.

For home consumption seed should be sown in drills about twelve inches apart and covered to a depth of not more than one inch. If grown for commercial purposes the rows should be at least two feet apart, to allow

---

* Special articles on the subjects indicated by an asterisk (*) will be found at the words so marked.

proper cultivation by power tillage. One ounce of seed will sow one hundred feet of drill.

Certain types of spinach, such as Savoy, are excellent for both market and home use as are Long Standing Bloomsdale Savoy, King of Denmark, and Early Hybrid Virginia. For fall sowing, Virginia Blight Resistant Savoy; for canning, medium-sized Thickleaf; and for wintering-over, Eskimo, which is hardy and stands cold well.

INSECT PESTS. Control yellow-necked blue flea beetle with pesticide #1 or #21 (*see* SPRAYS AND DUSTS). Aphids are killed by pesticide #21. Keep out pigweed since leaf miners and other pests migrate over to spinach. Weekly applications of pesticide #21 will control leaf miners.

DISEASES. In some areas a considerable loss in stand may result from damping-off.* Seed treatment, with one of the many commercial preparations, will prevent the heavy losses at time of seed germination.

Downy mildew* or blue mold will coat the lower surface of leaves during some growing seasons. As soon as disease is noticed, apply pesticide #7 or #11 (*see* SPRAYS AND DUSTS) at weekly intervals until plants near time for harvest.

The virus yellows* may reduce stand, particularly if aphids are numerous. Plant yellows-resistant varieties such as Virginia Savoy or keep aphids under control.

SPINACH-BEET = Swiss chard. *See* BEET.

SPINACH-DOCK = *Rumex Patientia.*

SPINACH FAMILY = Chenopodiaceae.

SPINACH-RHUBARB = *Rumex abyssinicus.*

Spina-Christi (spy-na-kriss'ti). Christ's-thorn. *See* PALIURUS.

SPINACIA. *See* SPINACH.

SPINDLE PALM = *Hyophorbe verschaffelti.*

SPINDLE-TREE. *See* EUONYMUS.

SPINDLING. Inclined to produce more stalk and foliage than flowers or fruit. It may be caused by too rich a soil, or by crowding. It is often caused, in greenhouses, by growing plants too far from the glass. A more common garden term for spindling is leggy.*

SPINE. A strong, often woody, very sharp-pointed body arising from the wood or other tissue, but not usually from a bud. A weak or slender spine is usually called a prickle, such as those commonly found on the rose or blackberry. But the spine is more often applied to the armature of plants like the cacti. *See* THORN.

SPINESCENT. Somewhat spiny.

SPINIFEX (spin'i-fecks). Spiny or prickly.

SPINK = *Dianthus deltoides.*

spinosa, -us, -um (spy-nō'sa). Spiny.

spinosissima, -us, -um (spy-no-siss'i-ma). Very or most spiny.

spinulosa, -us, -um (spin-you-lō'sa). Weakly spiny.

SPIRAEA (spy-ree'a). Spirea (the pre-ferred spelling for the common name; *see* SPIREA for other plants so called). An important and valuable genus of handsome flowering shrubs of the rose family, comprising nearly 100 species, mostly from the north temperate zone, but a few southward to Mex. and the Himalayas. All are deciduous* shrubs with alternate,* mostly toothed or lobed leaves, rarely altogether without teeth, nearly always stalked. Flower clusters usually showy, mostly of umbel-like racemes,* sometimes of panicles* or corymbs.* Individual flowers small, prevailingly white or pinkish-purple, the sepals and petals 5 each. Stamens* 15–60. Fruit a dry pod (follicle*), splitting along the inner seam. (*Spiraea* is from the Greek for a wreath or garland, for which some species were probably used.)

Of the 100 known species, and many hybrids, over 55 are known to be in cult. in the U.S., but only a selection of the best of them can be included here. Fortunately, the garden spireas are of the simplest culture, as they thrive in a variety of soils and under all sorts of exposures. Of course they repay attention as do any other flowering shrubs, but they thrive with less attention than many others. If they have a preference, it is for open sunshine and a reasonably moist site.

Such is the popularity of spireas that they are perhaps more widely planted than any other flowering shrubs, especially the early-blooming sorts like S. *arguta,* S. *vanhouttei,* S. *prunifolia,* S. *crenata,* and S. *trilobata,* some of which include the sorts commonly called Bridal Wreath. Scarcely less popular are the later-blooming forms like S. *Bumalda,* S. *japonica,* S. *salicifolia,* S. *tomentosa,* and the especially popular S. *billiardi.* Most of these require little pruning, unless they happen to winter-kill.

Most of them are easily propagated by seeds, sown when ripe or stratified, or by cuttings of green wood in the greenhouse, and many of them can be easily layered as some tend to arch over and root at the tips.

As will be seen below, the genus *Spiraea* once included many species now considered to belong to other genera.

aitchisoni = *Sorbaria aitchisoni.*

alba. Meadowsweet. An upright shrub, 4–6 ft. high. Leaves short-stalked, oblongish, 1–2½ in. long. Flowers white in leafy, pyramidal clusters (panicles*). Fruit smooth. Eastern N.A. July–Aug. Hardy from zone* 3 southward.

albiflora. A shrub closely related to S. *japonica* and differing from it chiefly in having white flowers. Jap. June–July. Hardy from zone* 4 southward. The trade name for this is usually S. *japonica alba.*

arguta. Garland spirea. A hybrid shrub derived from crossing S. *thunbergi* with another hybrid. It resembles S. *thunbergi* but is a little taller, more vigorous, and much more freely flowering. May. Perhaps the most profusely blooming of all white-flowered early spireas.

Aruncus = *Aruncus sylvester.*

astilboides = *Astilbe astilboides.*

billiardi. A very popular hybrid spirea, 4–6

---

* Special articles on the subjects indicated by an asterisk (*) will be found at the words so marked.

ft. high, derived from crossing *S. douglasi* with
S. salicifolia. Leaves oblongish, 2–3½ in. long,
often doubly toothed, but without teeth toward
the base, grayish beneath. Flowers bright rose-
red, in narrow, dense clusters (panicles*).
Fruits smooth. July–Aug. Hardy from zone*
3 southward.
 blumei. The plant usually offered as this
is *S. trilobata*, the true *S. blumei* being rare
in cult.
 bullata. An upright, compact shrub, 9–15
in. high, the twigs rusty-hairy. Leaves ½–1
in. long, roundish, strongly puckered. Flowers
tiny, scarlet, many, in a cluster that is 2–3
in. wide, and these so profuse as to cover
the plant. Jap. July. Hardy from zone* 5
southward.
 Bumalda. A very widely cult. and popular
spirea, derived from crossing *S. japonica* and
another Japanese species not much known in
cult. By some considered as a variety of *S.
japonica*, or "may be a hybrid between *S.
albiflora* and *S. japonica*," and because of this
uncertainty here retained as *S. Bumalda*. Not
over 2 ft. high, the twigs striped. Leaves ovalish or lance-shaped, doubly toothed. Flowers
white to dark pink. July. Not much grown
in the typical form, as the *var. froebeli*, a
taller plant with bright crimson flowers, is more
likely to be in the nurseries. So is the *var.*
Anthony Waterer, perhaps the most popular
of all late-flowering spireas. It is more compact than the typical species, has narrower
leaves, and bright crimson flowers. Other vars.
are offered, usually of uncertain identity.
Among them are *var. crispa* and *var. normani*,
the latter originating in the garden of T. R.
Norman at Painesville, Ohio. Both may not
be significantly different from Anthony Waterer.
All bloom in late June or July and are hardy
from zone* 3 southward.
 callosa = *Spiraea japonica*.
 camtschatica = *Filipendula camtschatica*.
 cantoniensis. An arching shrub, not over
5 ft. high. Leaves somewhat angularly oblongish, wedge-shaped at the base, 1–2½ in. long,
pale beneath, deeply toothed. Flowers white,
in dense, smooth clusters (umbels*). China
and Jap. June. Hardy from zone* 4 southward.
Known also as *S. reevesiana*.
 crenata. A slender shrub scarcely over 3
ft. high. Leaves oblongish or narrower, wedge-
shaped at the base, ¾–1¾ in. long, distinctly
3-veined. Flowers white in dense, slightly hairy
clusters (umbels*). Eurasia. May. Hardy from
zone* 3 southward.
 douglasi. A beautiful Pacific Coast spirea,
5–8 ft. high, its twigs reddish, hairy, and
striped. Leaves narrowly oblong, 1½–4 in.
long, white-felty beneath, unequally toothed
toward the tip. Flowers deep rose-red, in
showy, densely hairy clusters (panicles*) which
may be 4–7 in. long. British Columbia to
Calif. July–Aug. Hardy from zone* 4 southward.
 Filipendula = *Filipendula hexapetala*.
 fortunei = *Spiraea japonica fortunei*.
 froebeli = *Spiraea Bumalda froebeli*.
 japonica. An upright shrub, 4–6 ft. high.
Leaves ovalish or oblong, wedge-shaped at the
base, ¾–2¾ in. long, hairy on the veins
beneath. Flowers pink, in much-branched,
rather loose clusters (corymbs*). Jap. June–
July. Hardy from zone* 3 southward. The
var. **fortunei** is somewhat taller, has leaves
smooth beneath, and incurved, doubly toothed
leaf teeth. It is found in China. The *var.*
macrophylla has much larger and puckered
leaves but smaller flower clusters. It is of

hort. origin. For the plant offered as *S. japonica
alba, see* Spiraea albiflora. Plants offered
as *S. callosa* are *S. japonica*.

Spiraea vanhouttei (above), one of the bridal
wreaths. Below, the Anthony Waterer variety
of *S. Bumalda*.

 latifolia. Meadowsweet. An upright shrub
3–7 ft. high, the twigs reddish-brown and
angled. Leaves broadly elliptic, pointed both
ends, 1½–3 in. long, coarsely toothed. Flowers white or pinkish, in broadly pyramidal
clusters (panicles*). Northeastern N.A. June–
Aug. Hardy from zone* 3 northward.
 macrothyrsa. Related to *S. billiardi*, and
also a hybrid. It has dense clusters (panicles*)
of pink flowers, the branches of the cluster
almost horizontal. July–Aug. Hardy from zone*
3 southward.
 margaritae. A handsome, hybrid spirea, 3–5
ft. high, the twigs purple-brown. Leaves narrowly elliptic, or somewhat broader, abruptly
pointed at the tip, wedge-shaped at the base,
2–3½ in. long, coarsely and doubly toothed.
Flowers bright pink in large, leafy, slightly
hairy clusters (corymbs*). July, and also, less
profusely, in late Aug.–Sept. Hardy from zone*
3 southward.
 opulifolia = *Physocarpus opulifolius*.
 prunifolia. Bridal wreath (a name also applied to *S. vanhouttei*). Not much cult. in
the typical, wild form, but in the *var.* **plena**,
one of the most widely cult. of all spireas.
It is a slender shrub, 4–6 ft. high, with arching, somewhat angled branches. Leaves elliptic
or elliptic-oblong, pointed both ends, ¾–2 in.
long, finely toothed. Flowers pure white, double, very numerous, but in 3–6-flowered, nearly
stalkless clusters (umbels*). Eastern As. April–
May. Hardy from zone* 3 southward.
 reevesiana = *Spiraea cantoniensis*.
 salicifolia. Queen-of-the-meadow; also called
bridewort. A rather stiffly erect shrub, 4–6
ft. high, the twigs slightly angled and yellowish-
brown. Leaves oblongish or narrower, pointed
at both ends, 2–3½ in. long, sharply and closely
toothed. Flowers rose-pink, in slender, pyramidal, hairy clusters (panicles*). Eurasia.
June–July. Hardy from zone* 2 southward.
 sorbifolia = *Sorbaria sorbifolia*.
 thunbergi. A handsome, twiggy spirea, 3–5

---

* Special articles on the subjects indicated by an asterisk (*) will be found at the words so marked.

ft. high, its foliage orange-scarlet in the fall. Leaves narrowly lance-shaped, ¾–1¾ in. long, sharply toothed, bright green. Flowers pure white, very numerous, but in 3–5-flowered, nearly stalkless clusters (umbels*). China and Jap. April–May. Hardy from zone* 3 southward.

tomentosa. Hardhack; also called steeplebush. A stiff, upright shrub, its branches brownfelty. Leaves ovalish, 1½–2½ in. long, unequally toothed, densely gray or brownish-felty beneath. Flowers rose-purple, in narrow, densely brown-felty, spire-like clusters (panicles*). Fruit hairy. Eastern N.A. July–Sept. Hardy from zone* 2 southward.

trichocarpa. An erect shrub, 4–6 ft., the branches spreading. Leaves oblongish, 1–2 in. long, pointed at the tip, few-toothed. Flowers white, very numerous, in a branched, hairy cluster (umbel*-like). Fruits hairy. Korea. June. Hardy from zone* 3 southward. Some of the plants passing as Bridal Wreath may belong here.

trilobata. A shrub much resembling the far more popular *S. vanhouttei,* but smaller in all its parts, and the leaves somewhat blunter. As. May–June. Hardy from zone* 3 southward. Some of the plants offered as *S. blumei* belong to this species.

ulmaria = *Filipendula Ulmaria.*

vanhouttei. Bridal wreath. By far the most commonly cult. spirea in America, and standing smoke and city conditions better than most. It is a hybrid between *S. cantoniensis* and *S. trilobata,* and is a slender shrub 4–6 ft. high, with beautifully arching branches. Leaves somewhat angularly ovalish, pointed at the tip, ¾–1¾ in. long, pale beneath. Flowers pure white, very numerous, in many-flowered clusters (umbels*). May–June. Hardy from zone* 3 southward. A good spirea for forcing (which see).

spiralis, -e (spy-ral'is). A spiral; or spirally arranged.

SPIRANTHES (spy-ran'theez). A genus of about 25 species of delicate, terrestrial orchids, mostly from the north temperate zone, about 10 of them scattered in meadows or bogs over N.A. They are small plants with clustered rather fleshy roots, bracted* flowering stalks and chiefly basal, narrow, almost grass-like leaves. Flowers very small, irregular,* white, arranged in spirals from the twisting of the main flower stalk. They are of little hort. importance except for **S. cernua,** the ladies'-tresses, one of the largest-flowering of the American species. It is a meadow plant, usually hidden among grass or other herbs in the wild, 7–18 in. high. Leaves very narrow, about the height of the flower stalk, without marginal teeth. Flowers about ¼ in. long, turned downward, the spiral cluster (spike*) 3–5 in. long. Other native species are likely to be transferred to the wild garden where they need moist, meadow-like conditions or the sphagnum of the bog garden. All were once called *Ibidium.* (*Spiranthes* is from the Greek for coil or curl, in allusion to the spirally twisted flowering stalk.)

SPIRE. An old, and now unusual, term for a shoot or sprig; also, as a verb, to become spindling.

SPIREA. Properly, spirea is the preferred

common name of shrubs belonging to the genus *Spiraea.* But spirea is much used for other plants which resemble *Spiraea.* The common potted spirea of the florists may be *Aruncus sylvester,* an *Astilbe,* or a *Filipendula.* Other plants to which the name spirea is applied will be found at *Caryopteris* and *Sorbaria.*

SPIREA FAMILY. *See* ROSACEAE.

SPIRONEMA (spy-ro-nee'ma). A single species of Mexican weak-stemmed herbs of the family Commelinaceae, **S. fragrans,** usually grown under the name *Tradescantia dracaenoides,* and called also *Callisia fragrans.* It is a greenhouse plant for the hanging basket, with trailing stems 1–2 ft. long, and transparent foliage. Leaves oblong or narrower, sheathing at the base, pointed at the tip, prominently parallel-veined. Flowers waxywhite, fragrant, the petals diaphanous, the sepals green. Stamens* 6. (*Spironema* is from the Greek for spiral thread, in allusion to the stalks of the anthers.*)

SPIT. A spade, or a single spadeful of soil. Spit is also, but rarely, used as a verb, meaning to dig.

SPITTLE INSECTS. Small sucking insects that live on low-growing plants and in summer produce masses of whitish, frothy material in which they live. These are usually known as cuckoo spittle or frog spittle, because many believe such white masses are made by frogs, toads, etc. Spittle insects are not usually harmful and "frog spittle" does no damage to most plants.

SPLEENWORT. *See* ASPLENIUM and ATHYRIUM.

splendens (splen'denz). Splendid or showy.

splendida, -us, -um (splen'di-da). Splendid or showy.

SPONDIAS (spon'di-as). Tropical fruit trees of the sumac family, grown for their fleshy, edible fruits, which are usually called ciruela, and are little esteemed in the U.S. Leaves alternate,* compound,* the leaflets arranged feather-fashion, with an odd one at the end. Flowers small, often polygamous,* mostly in branched clusters (panicles* or racemes*). For details *see* ANACARDIACEAE. Fruit a fleshy drupe, its single large stone covered with many spines which penetrate the fleshy, yellow pulp and make separation of it difficult. (*Spondias* is an old Greek name for a plum-like fruit, in allusion to the fleshy drupes.*)

The first species and *S. Mombin* are somewhat grown in zone* 9 in Fla., and are hardy nowhere else. Less known is *S. purpurea,* the purple mombin, which is also very tender. All are of simple culture on a variety of soils, so long as the region is frost-free. Easily propagated by seeds.

cytherea. Otaheite apple; also called vi-apple and ambarella. A tree up to 60 ft. high. Leaflets 11–13, oblongish, slightly toothed or without teeth, about 3 in. long. Flowers whit-

* Special articles on the subjects indicated by an asterisk (*) will be found at the words so marked.

ish. Fruit resembling a large yellow plum, 2–3 in. long, the flesh acid or sweetish, not highly regarded and used mostly for preserves. It ripens in winter in Fla. Society Islands. Called by some *S. dulcis*.

 lutea — *Spondias Mombin.*

 Mombin. Yellow mombin; also called hog plum. A very common tree throughout tropical America and elsewhere, and cult. in extreme southern Fla.; often up to 60 ft. high. Leaflets 7–17, ovalish or narrower, 3–4 in. long, essentially without teeth. Flowers purplish-green. Fruit egg-shaped, 1–1½ in. long, yellow, sweetish or slightly acid, ripening in late summer and considered inferior to *S. purpurea*. Tropical regions generally. Also known as *S. lutea*.

 purpurea. Purple or red mombin; also called Spanish plum. A tree scarcely over 30 ft. high. Leaflets 7–23, oblongish, about 1 in. long. Flowers greenish. Fruit yellowish-red or red at maturity, 1–2 in. long, its flesh highly prized in tropical America, either raw or cooked, but little known in Fla. Tropical America.

SPONGE TREE = *Acacia farnesiana.*

SPORE. The microscopic organ upon which ferns, mosses, lichens, fungi, and algae depend for reproduction. Spores are far smaller than even the smallest seeds, contain no embryo, and are functionally very different. But in the reproductive processes of the flowerless plants they replace seeds. For the germination and subsequent life history of the only spores of garden interest *see* FERNS AND FERN GARDENING. Many spores also provide a quick and easy method of spreading disease. *See* PLANT DISEASES.

SPORT. *See* MUTATION.

SPOTTED CALLA LILY = *Zantedeschia albo-maculata. See* CALLA LILY.

SPOTTED COWBANE = *Cicuta maculata.*

SPOTTED MEDIC = *Medicago arabica.*

SPOTTED SPURGE = *Euphorbia maculata. See* list at WEEDS.

SPOTTED WINTERGREEN = *Chimaphila maculata.* The plant is also called rheumatism-root and dragon's-tongue; it may be a partial saprophyte.*

SPRAYING AND DUSTING. For additional information *see* FUNGICIDES, INSECTICIDES, INSECT PESTS, and FUMIGATION. The aim of spraying or dusting is usually to place a light, uniform coating of pesticide over the plant surface, for maximum effectiveness, minimum plant injury, and minimum cost.

 Dusting is more expensive than spraying, cannot be carried out if winds are high, and is less effective since dusts work off foliage easier than dried spray residues. With dusts, more pesticide can be put on a leaf and more plant injury caused.

 Sprays can be applied when winds are higher, are cheaper than dusts, and give a more lasting residue. However, it takes longer to mix up sprays, and they cannot be effectively used if foliage is wet whereas dusts adhere readily to dew-dampened plants.

 The object of spraying is to apply as much spray mixture per unit of leaf surface as can

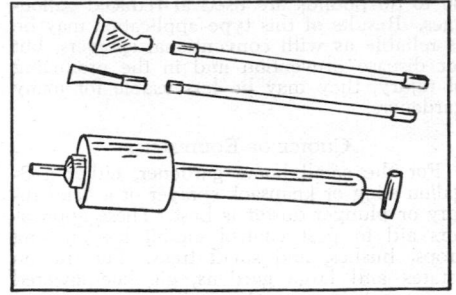

A small plunger duster

be applied before "run-off" occurs. Fine particles are desirable. In dusting, a light cloud of the pesticide, enveloping the plant, is best.

 Due to the different character of various plants, the amount of spray or dust applied per acre of plants or per tree is not constant. On a tomato field in early season, 30 gallons of spray or 15 pounds of dust may be enough. In late season, the amount of spray required may be 150 gallons or 60 pounds of dust. The gardener's judgment is best policy.

 Recently, use of concentrated sprayers which inject a finely divided mist in an air blast and push the pesticide into trees or across crop rows has become common. Concentrates of four to eight times or greater have been used

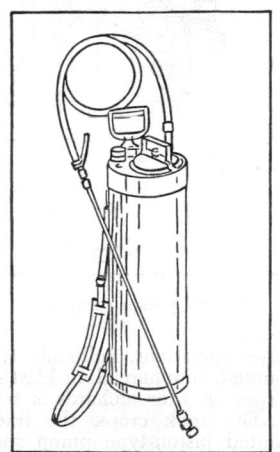

A small sling-type hand sprayer

at appropriately reduced gallonages. These "mist blowers" require exacting care in application and may produce plant injury to a greater degree than the conventional or "dilute" applications.

 For row crops, low-gallonage sprays have been adopted in many areas. Instead of the standard pressure of 200–400 pounds per square inch in "dilute" sprays, pressures of

---

* Special articles on the subjects indicated by an asterisk (*) will be found at the words so marked.

40 to 80 pounds are used at reduced gallonages. Results of this type application may be as reliable as with conventional sprayers, but for disease prevention and in the producing of injury, they may be less usable for many gardeners.

CHOICE OF EQUIPMENT

For the small home gardener, either a 3-gallon sling or knapsack sprayer or a hand rotary or plunger duster is best. These applicators aid in pest control on all low-growing crops, bushes, and small trees. For use on estates and large gardens, gasoline-powered equipment is mandatory. Small sprayers of 25–35 gallon capacity, capable of producing pressure of 150–200 or more pounds per square inch, are most useful. These sprayers have a piston-type pump, which is more satisfactory than the nylon-roller pumps of low-gallonage sprayers. These sprayers are mounted on wheels and are easily moved by hand about the yard in small orchards or in gardens.

Attachments to garden hoses, known as hose proportioner sprayers, are quite effective and readily purchased. With normal water pressures and by virtue of Venturi action, garden hoses can be effectively transformed into sprayers. For city homes and smaller gardens, the hose proportioner apparatuses are very effective.

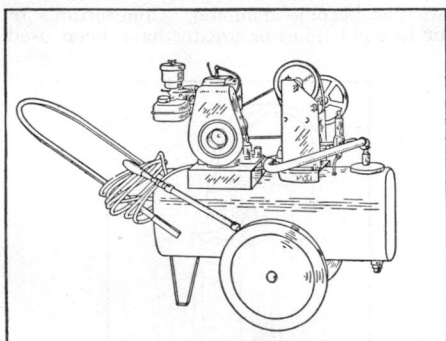

A small power sprayer

For larger operations, full-scale truck- or tractor-mounted, commercial air-blast or high-gallonage sprayers (for orchards or trees) are advisable. On truck crops, the tractor- or trailer-mounted piston-type pump spray rigs are best.

Some small portable dusters powered by lightweight gasoline motors are now for sale. These dusters have good application for grape arbors, areas of truck crops up to an acre or two in size, and about estate plantings.

Power dusters which are mounted on and powered by tractors (with power take-off), or are on trailers with a gasoline motor, find best use on larger acreages of row crops.

Fog machines of various types which produce insecticidal fogs are most applicable for

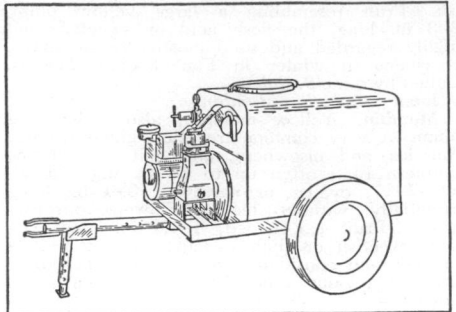

A large power sprayer, tractor- or truck-drawn

temporary cleaning of gnats, mosquitoes, and the like from areas or buildings. The amount of residue applied to plant surface by fog machines is not sufficient to control most insect pests.

CARE OF EQUIPMENT

Most modern insect or disease chemicals are relatively non-corrosive to sprayers or dusters. However, a certain amount of maintenance is necessary. For best available information on your sprayer or duster, refer to the manufacturer's manual for directions. Specific instructions for before use, after use, before fall storage and pre-spring use are given. — S. H. D. and L. G. M.

SPRAY INJURY AND RESIDUE. Using too heavy dosages of chemical often injures fruit or foliage. Follow directions carefully. Poor drying conditions, soft foliage, and low or extremely high temperatures promote injury. Do not expect washing to remove residues of synthetic hydrocarbons. For use on food crops, all chemicals now have an interval between last application and harvest. Best advice is to read the label and follow directions. — L. G. M. and S. H. D.

SPRAYS AND DUSTS. Most insect pests of plants may be controlled with one or more chemicals known as insecticides* and many of the plant diseases caused by fungi may be prevented with one or more chemicals known as fungicides.* In general we refer to these chemicals which control insect and disease pests as pesticides. For each of the pests there is usually one pesticide which is more efficient than the others. Commercial orchardists and vegetable-growers, as well as florists, nurserymen, and professional gardeners and tree experts, use perhaps 20 or more different pesticides. The amateur gardener who wishes to have his property as free from pests as possible must follow the footsteps of the professional or commercial grower.

For the person who has the garden as a hobby and would like to spend more time with the plants than with the selection of the best pesticide, we recommend the use of general-purpose mixtures whenever possible.

* Special articles on the subjects indicated by an asterisk (*) will be found at the words so marked.

PESTICIDE (Fungicides)	SPRAYING		DUSTING
	3 Gals.	50 Gals.	
1. General-purpose mixture	Manufacturer's recommendation		
2. captan, 50% W.P.	1 oz.	1 lb.	5%
2a. captan, 50% W.P.	½ oz.	½ lb.	—
3. copper	Manufacturer's recommendation		
4. dinitro	Manufacturer's recommendation		
5. ferbam, 76% W.P.	1 oz.	1 lb.	7%
5a. ferbam, 75% W.P.	½ oz.	½ lb.	—
6. Karathane	¼ oz.	¼ lb.	—
7. maneb, 80% W.P.	1 oz.	1 lb.	—
8. phenyl mercury, 10%	½ oz.	½ pint	—
8a. phenyl mercury, 10%	¼ oz.	¼ pint	—
9. sulphur	Manufacturer's recommendation		
10. Terraclor, 75% W.P.	1½ oz.	1½ lb.	—
11. zineb, 65% W.P.	1 oz.	1 lb.	5%
12. corrosive sublimate	(See instructions at FUNGICIDES)		

PESTICIDE (Insecticides)			
13. aldrin	Manufacturer's recommendation		2.5%
14. aramite	"	"	3 %
15. chlordane	"	"	5 %
16. heptachlor	"	"	2.5%
17. DDT	"	"	5 %
18. dieldrin	"	"	1.5%
19. lead arsenate	"	"	—
20. lindane	"	"	1 %
21. malathion	"	"	4 %
22. metaldehyde	"	"	15 %
23. methoxychlor	"	"	5 %
24. nicotine sulphate	"	"	—
25. perthane	"	"	5 %
26. pyrethrins	"	"	0.1%
27. rotenone	"	"	1 %
28. summer oil a	"	"	—
29. dormant oil a	"	"	—

W.P. = wettable powder
a = superior-type self-emulsifying oils

These consist of a mixture of several insecticides and fungicides selected for their broad scope. Some pesticide manufacturers go one step further and prepare three general-purpose mixtures: one for fruit, one for vegetables, and one for flowers. It is up to the gardener — how thorough a job do you want to do in pest control?

Unfortunately, not all chemicals can be put in general-purpose combinations. In this group are the summer and dormant oils, dinitro, mercury, and others. For this reason the gardener will find that he may not have the option to use a general-purpose mixture, but must use a specific pesticide for control of some pests.

PESTICIDES. Before you purchase a pesticide, read the article on SPRAYING AND DUSTING. The equipment you use will determine whether you purchase a wettable powder or emulsion for use in a sprayer or a material formulated for dusting in a "duster."

After purchasing the pesticide, read the label on the package. The United States Department of Agriculture and the Pure Food and Drug laws require accuracy on the label. If instructions are followed and use is made of precautions set forth on the label, the results will be good and you will face no danger from use of the pesticide.

Some pesticides, such as copper, dinitro, sulphur, etc., are available in such a wide range of concentrations that exact amounts cannot be given in the table above. Use materials at the manufacturer's recommendation when no specific dosage is given in the table.

Some materials are not available for use in dusting equipment, either because they are liquids or are materials which are not stable for long periods when formulated as a dust. — L. G. M. and S. H. D.

SPREADER. Any oil emulsion, soap, or other substance added to an insecticide or fungicide, which spreads the desired ingredients over the foliage more effectively than they could be distributed without the spreader. The term is also used as an equivalent of filler in fertilizers.

SPREADING DOGBANE = *Apocynum androsaemifolium*.

SPREKELIA (spreck-kee′li-a). Tender Mexican or Guatemalan bulbous herbs of the family Amaryllidaceae, comprising only 1 species, *S. formosissima*, the St. James's-lily or Jacobean lily. It is also known as *Amaryllis formosissima*. Bulb ovalish. Leaves few, narrow, thick, to 1 ft. long. Flowers solitary, on a leafless stalk, to 1 ft. high, which appears before the leaves. Flower about 4 in. long, enclosed in a membranous spathe.* Calyx of 3 sepals, bright red, cylinder-like. Corolla of 3 petals, narrow and erect, bright red, alternating with the sepals. Stamens 6. Fruit a 3-celled capsule.* For cult. see AMARYLLIS. (Named for J. H. von Sprekel-

* Special articles on the subjects indicated by an asterisk (*) will be found at the words so marked.

son, who introduced the genus to Linnaeus.)

SPRIG. A young shoot.

SPRIG BUDDING. An erroneous term for a form of grafting (which see).

SPRING. As an adjective *spring* has been applied to many garden plants or operations. Those that occur in this book and their proper equivalents are:

Spring beauty (*see* CLAYTONIA); Spring bell = *Sisyrinchium douglasi;* Spring garden (*see* second main entry below); Spring heath = *Erica carnea;* Spring lily = *Erythronium albidum;* Spring meadow saffron = *Bulbocodium vernum;* Spring onion = *Allium fistulosum;* Spring planting (*see* third main entry below); Spring starflower = *Brodiaea uniflora;* Spring vetch = *Vicia sativa;* Spring vetchling = *Lathyrus vernus.*

SPRING FROST. See PROTECTING PLANTS.

SPRING GARDEN. It is not always possible or desirable to devote a special area of the grounds to a single season. There are times however, when it is both practicable and advantageous to do this. A garden planted wholly with spring-flowering bulbs, shrubs, and hardy plants may be a charming feature, especially if it is possible to so place it that it need be on view only when in its prime. Or in cases where the owner later removes to another locality for the summer months there is every reason to devote the entire planting space to early-flowering subjects.

One of the advantages of a sequestered spring garden is that in it the taste for bulbs may be freely indulged, without provision being made to hide their subsequent untidy dying off. Lovely and informal spring gardens are contrived in light woodland, where bulbous things thrive exceedingly, or a wide irregular border may be laid out against a bank of early-flowering shrubs and evergreens. Again a spring garden may be enclosed in a hedge of evergreens or some flowering shrub, such as hawthorn or Japanese quince, or by espaliered fruit trees on a wall of brick, stone, or stucco.

The plan of such a garden would probably be in the form of a pattern of little beds, perhaps edged with dwarf box, with a straight border following the line of the enclosure, and some formal feature, such as a sundial, a wellhead or bit of statuary, used as a focal point. The planting of such a garden will necessarily be somewhat formal, the beds filled with evenly spaced bulbs floored over with a ground cover of *Arabis,* English daisies, violas, wallflowers or forget-me-nots, but the outer border may be more unconventional and permit the use of shrubs and a few flowering trees, underplanted with irregular groups and drifts of bulbs and hardy plants in harmonious color relation.

If the spring garden is in a wood or along a bank of shrubs, its planting may be wholly informal, and in the case of the border, if it runs from sun into shade, the range of available material will be greatly increased.

The furnishings of any spring garden will largely consist of bulbous things and shrubs, but a judicious intermingling of certain hardy plants that qualify for admission by reason of their forehanded blossoming, or because of the beauty of their young foliage, brings about a fuller and more interesting effect. The happiest results are secured if the planting is done in long, irregular drifts of a single kind of plant or bulb, rather than in small groups, which are apt to appear spotty and restless. The plants and bulbs should be selected and placed with due consideration for a pleasing color harmony with each other and with the flowering trees and shrubs also made use of. If space permits, the pewter-gray trunks of beech trees, and groups of white-stemmed birches and red-stemmed dogwoods enhance the early spring scene. Trees and shrubs with conspicuous catkins are also valuable and, in the shaded sections, the uncurling fronds of ferns add much interest.

A choice of material for a spring garden would include species and varieties of the following:

BULBS: *Brodiaea; Calochortus; Camassia; Chionodoxa; Eranthis; Erythronium; Fritillaria; Galanthus; Hyacinthus ciliatus; H. amethystinus; Iris reticulata; Leucojum; Muscari; Narcissus; Ornithogalum; Puschkinia; Scilla; Trillium; Tulipa; Uvularia;* and *Zygadenus.*

HARDY PLANTS: *Adonis amurensis,* A. *vernalis* (yellow); *Ajuga reptans metallica crispa* (foliage); *Alyssum saxatile citrinum* (yellow); *Anemone quinquefolia* (white); *Aquilegia* (foliage); *Arabis albida* (white or rose, single or double); *Asarum* (foliage); *Aubrieta* vars. (purple, lavender, rose); *Bellis* (pink, rose, white); Bloodroot (white); *Brunnera macrophylla* (blue); *Erysimum asperum* (orange); *Claytonia virginica* (pink and white); *Clintonia* (greenish-white); *Corydalis cheilanthifolia* (yellow), C. *lutea* (yellow); Cowslips (yellow); *Dicentra eximia* (rose), D. *spectabilis* (pink); *Dianthus plumarius* (foliage); *Doronicum* (yellow); *Epimedium* (foliage); *Euphorbia epithymoides* (yellow); Ferns (foliage); *Festuca ovina glauca* (foliage); *Geranium ibericum* (violet); *Helleborus orientalis* (rose, cream, greenish); *Hepatica* (blue, white, pink); *Heuchera* (foliage), *Iberis* (white, mauve); *Iris pumila* vars. (blue, violet, white, yellow), I. *cristata* (lavender); Lavender Cotton (foliage); Lily-of-the-valley (white); *Mertensia virginica* (blue); *Phlox divaricata* (lavender), P. *amoena* (pink), P. *subulata* (lavender, white, pink); *Polemonium caeruleum* (blue), P. *reptans* (blue); Polyanthus primroses (yellow, white, orange, etc.); *Polygonatum canaliculatum* (cream); *Primula vulgaris* vars. (yellow, white, rose, blue), P. *denticulata* (mauve, white); *Pulmonaria angustifolia* (blue), P. *saccharata* (blue); *Bergenia ligulata* (pink); *Smilacina racemosa* (white); *Thalictrum glaucum* (foliage); *Viola blanda* (white), V. *cornuta* vars. (lavender, rose, purple, yellow, white), V.

---

* Special articles on the subjects indicated by an asterisk (*) will be found at the words so marked.

gracilis (purple), *V. odorata* (mauve, white, purple); Wallflowers (yellow, orange, brown).

SHRUBS AND TREES: *Berberis* vars.; *Corylopsis* vars.; *Cercis canadensis*, *C. Siliquastrum;* Japanese Flowering Cherry; Crabapples (*Malus baccuta*, *M. coronaria*, *M. floribunda*, *M. halliana*, *M. ioensis*, *M. sargenti*, *M. theifera*); *Daphne Cneorum*, *D. Mezereum;* Dogwoods (*Cornus florida*, *C. Kousa*, *C. Mas*, *C. nuttalli*); Ericas; Flowering Almond; *Forsythia;* Hawthorns; Japanese Quince; Kalmias; *Kolkwitzia amabilis; Laburnum;* Lilacs; *Lonicera;* Magnolias; Peach, double-flowering vars.; *Philadelphus* vars.; *Pieris floribunda*, *P. japonica; Prunus cerasifera pissardi*, *P. tomentosa*, *P. triloba; Azalea obtusa amoena*, *A. obtusa kaempferi; Rhododendron ferrugineum; Rhodora canadensis; Azalea yedoensis poukhanensis; Ribes* (Flowering Currant); *Spiraea; Viburnum carlesi.*

CLIMBERS: *Akebia quinata; Clematis montana* and var. *rubens; Jasminum nudiflorum;* Wisterias, white and purple vars.

The culture of these spring garden plants, and the hardiness of them (most are perfectly hardy over much of the country), will not be repeated here. All the plants in the lists are entered in the ENCYCLOPEDIA at their proper alphabetical places, and should be sought there by anyone planning a spring garden. — L. B. W.

SPRING PLANTING. There is every advantage in getting as much planting done in the spring as possible, except one. That is the onrush of spring itself. The daily march of increasing sunshine, longer days and greater heat, all contribute to making the spring planting season a hectic one for most gardeners, but of great value to the plants.

Of course the planting of vegetable and flower seeds can be varied a little, one way or the other, by circumstances other than the march of spring. Such variations merely mean earlier or later crops. The preferred or proper time for sowing such seeds will not be repeated here, for it is stated at the cultural notes on all the more important crops, whether flowers or vegetables.

The chief difficulty about spring planting lies in those crops which, because they are fast coming out of winter dormancy, *must* be planted before it is too late. This applies to all woody plants, whether fruit trees, ornamental shrubs, trees, or vines, and to the division of many perennial herbs.

The advantages of planting these in the spring are obvious. If you complete the job in time (*i.e.*, before they have leaved out), such plants get a full season's growth before they enter their first winter after transplanting. But sometimes, due to other imperative spring work (for which *see* the spring months at GARDEN CALENDAR), it is simply impossible to complete planting before it is too late. Except for plane trees, and a few others noted at their proper entries, this need not disturb the gardener. For most woody plants can just as well be planted in the fall,

which, because of a waning season, is a far more leisurely planting time. *See* AUTUMN PLANTING.

Plane trees and magnolias should only be planted in the spring. Evergreens* and broad-leaved evergreens (which see) may be planted in the spring, but if that is impossible, their second planting period over much of the country should be between Aug. 15 and Sept. 15. For the actual details of planting shrubs, trees, vines, or perennial herbs *see* PLANTING. If you are equipped so that you can retard the normal growth of nursery stock, you can, of course, greatly prolong the spring planting season. For the details of this *see* RETARDING. *See also* SEEDS AND SEEDAGE.

SPROUTING BROCCOLI = *Brassica oleracea italica*. For culture *see* BROCCOLI.

SPROUTING CHICORY. *See* RADICHETTA.

SPROUTS. Short for Brussels sprouts (which see).

SPRUCE. Usually majestic, sometimes gigantic evergreen trees, comprising the genus **Picea** (py-see′a, py′see-a) of the pine family, of first-rate hort. importance, also widely used for timber and in the making of paper pulp. Only 40 species of spruce are known, all from the northern hemisphere, and generally from the cooler and moister parts of it. They have (without injury and ignoring some dwarf hort. forms) a single, unbranched trunk, with tiers or whorls of branches, and often the outline of the tree is almost exactly the shape of a candle flame. Leaves small, very numerous, needle-like, each on a tiny foot-like cushion or stalk, from which it falls away very readily when dry. The leaves are rarely flat, generally being somewhat 4-sided in cross-section. Flowers, in the garden sense, none, being composed in the male flowers only of naked anthers,* and in the female of naked ovules between the scales of what is ultimately the cone. The latter are mostly drooping in fruit, the scales becoming somewhat woody, but not really woody or prickly as in many pines. Seeds 2 under each scale, the seeds winged. (*Picea* is the classical Latin name of the spruce.)

For culture and uses *see* below. Some people confuse the spruces with the firs, but this is not necessary if a few facts are kept in mind:

SPRUCE (*Picea*)

Leaves generally 4-sided.

Leaves easily falling (leaving a spur-like attachment on the twig), hence a poor tree for Christmas greens.

Cones generally drooping.

FIR (*Abies*)

Leaves flat.

Leaves persistent even when dead (and leaving no spur-like attachment when falling), hence the best of all trees for Christmas greens.

Cones always erect.

---

* Special articles on the subjects indicated by an asterisk (*) will be found at the words so marked.

Over 30 species and scores of hort. varieties are known to be in cult. in the U.S. Those below have been selected as the most representative, readily available, and generally hardy of the cult. spruces.

P. Abies. Norway spruce, and probably the most widely cult. evergreen tree in America. A pyramidal tree up to 150 ft. high, the mature bark reddish-brown, the branches pendulous at the end. Leaves about ¾ in. long, shining, dark green. Cones 5–7 in. long. Eu. Hardy from zone* 2 southward. Many hort. forms of the typical tree (which is sometimes known as *P. excelsa*) have been developed for special purposes. Some differ in habit or stature, others in the color of the young or mature foliage. The leading ones are:

var. argentea. Leaves variegated with white.

var. aurea. Leaves, or the young ones, golden-yellow.

var. compacta. A low, dense, nearly globe-shaped dwarf; also in variegated form.

var. conica. A low, dwarf form with conical habit.

var. gregoryana. A dwarf form, not over 2 ft. high, its branchlets crowded and pale.

var. maxwelli. A dwarf, flattish form, not over 2 ft. high, the branchlets short and thick; very dense.

var. nana. A dwarf, 1–2 ft. high, with orange-yellow foliage.

var. pendula. Medium-sized plant with hanging branches.

var. procumbens. Prostrate form with bright yellow twigs.

var. pygmaea. Dwarf, dense, not over 1 ft. high.

P. ajanensis = *Picea jezoensis*.

P. alba = *Picea glauca*.

P. albertiana. Considered by some as the correct name of the Alberta spruce, here treated at *Picea glauca* var. *albertiana*.

P. alcockiana = *Picea bicolor*.

P. asperata. Dragon spruce. A tall tree, up to 75 ft., much less as cult., the bark gray-brown, peeling off in flakes, the twigs hairy and yellowish, or sometimes smooth. Leaves ½–¾ in. long, densely crowded, sharp-pointed and stiff. Cones 3–5 in. long, purplish in youth. Western China. Hardy from zone* 2 southward and useful as one of the few spruces that will stand exposure to salt spray.

P. bicolor. Alcock spruce. A pyramidal evergreen, up to 75 ft. high, the bark grayish-brown. Leaves about ¾ in. long, with 2 white bands on the upper side. Cones cylindric, 3–4 in. long. Jap. Hardy from zone* 3 southward. Sometimes known as *P. alcockiana*.

P. canadensis = *Picea glauca*.

P. engelmanni. Engelmann's spruce. A splendid evergreen tree up to 150 ft. high, its whorls* of branches numerous and rather close. Leaves nearly 1 in. long, bluish-green, slightly curved, and a little flattish. Cones 2–3 in. long. British Columbia to Ore., Ariz., and N. Mex. Hardy from zone* 1 southward. One of the finest and hardiest of the cult. spruces. The *var.* argentea has silvery leaves; *var.* glauca, blue leaves; and the *var.* fendleri has drooping branchlets and slightly longer leaves.

P. excelsa = *Picea Abies*.

P. glauca. White or skunk spruce. A tree nearly 100 ft. high, the branches ascending, but the branchlets drooping. Leaves about ¾ in. long, bluish-green. Cones cylindric, 1½–2 in. long. Northern N.A. Hardy from zone* 1 southward, and a very handsome tree. The

var. albertiana, the Alberta spruce, has shorter cones and more crowded leaves. It is especially suited to states like Minn. and Iowa, where, as well as in neighboring states, it is preferred to the typical form. The *var.* caerulea has the leaves still more blue-green. The *var.* conica is a dwarf, conical form, useful as an accent plant or for the rock garden. *Var.* densata, the Black Hills Spruce, is a slow-growing var. from S. D., with more compact habit and with the leaves lighter bluish-green. *Picea glauca* has been, at different times, called also *P. alba* and *P. canadensis*.

P. jezoensis. Yeddo spruce. A tree up to 150 ft. high, the bark grayish and scaly. Leaves more or less flattened, nearly ¾ in. long, dark green beneath, silvery above. Cones 2½–3½ in. long. Northern As. and Jap. Hardy from zone* 3 southward.

P. koyamai. A pyramidal spruce, 40–60 ft. high, the bark grayish-brown, the twigs reddish-brown. Leaves ¼–⅝ in. long, curved or straight, with 2 white bands on upper surface. Cones oblongish, 2–4 in. long, green at first, ultimately brown. Korea and Jap. Hardy from zone* 3 southward.

P. mariana. Black spruce. A native spruce, usually not over 50 ft. high, and often growing in bogs. Leaves scarcely ¾ in. long, dull green. Cones ¾–1½ in. long. Throughout northern N.A. and south to Va. Hardy from zone* 1 southward, but suited only to boggy sites.

P. Omorika. Serbian spruce. An evergreen tree up to 100 ft. high, the branches ascending. Leaves somewhat flattened, scarcely ½ in. long, dark green beneath, but with 2 white bands above. Cones 2–2½ in. long. Southern Eu. Hardy from zone* 3 southward and a very satisfactory spruce for the eastern states.

P. orientalis. A magnificent evergreen, sometimes reaching 180 ft. in height, but much less in cult., the branches ascending, but the branchlets often drooping. Leaves glossy green, scarcely ½ in. long. Cones 2–3½ in. long. Caucasus and Asia Minor. Hardy from zone* 3 southward, but of rather slow growth.

P. polita. Tigertail spruce. An evergreen tree up to 120 ft. high, the bark gray and rough. Leaves very stiff, spreading, prickly, nearly 1 in. long, dark, glossy green. Cones 4–5 in. long. Jap. Hardy from zone* 3 southward.

P. pungens. Blue spruce; also called Colorado blue spruce. A beautiful American evergreen tree, often 140 ft. high in the wild, less as cult., the whorls of branches rather remote. Leaves rigid, stiff, prickle-pointed, nearly 1¼ in. long, bluish-green. Cones 3–4 in. long. Rocky Mountain region. Hardy from zone* 1 southward. Much cult., but still more so in the *var.* kosteriana, Koster's blue spruce, which is one of the most popular of all blue spruces for lawn planting. It differs from the typical tree in having still more bluish foliage, and in the pendulous branches. The *var.* compacta is a low, dense form with twiggy branchlets. There are also several other color forms, one with green leaves.

P. rubens. Red spruce. A forest tree found from maritime Canada to the mountains of N. Car. and the chief source of paper pulp in the Northeast. It is rarely cult. but found in many woodlots. It has 4-angled, green needles about ½ in. long. Cones not over 2 in. long, reddish brown. Hardy from zone* 2 southward, but only in the highlands.

P. sitchensis. Sitka spruce. A magnificent tree, sometimes up to 180 ft. high, less as

---

* Special articles on the subjects indicated by an asterisk (*) will be found at the words so marked.

cult., the branches horizontal, but forming a majestic, pyramidal tree. Leaves somewhat flattish, prickle-tipped, nearly 1 in. long, dark, glossy green below, silvery above. Cones 3–4 in. long. Alaska to Calif. Hardy from zone* 4 southward, but not in the East, as it demands more summer moisture than is found along the Atlantic seaboard.

SPRUCE CULTURE

The spruce is without doubt the most versatile of our cultivated conifers, and offers a wide selection of material, ranging in size from small shrubby plants to huge forest specimens. The dwarf forms are particularly adapted to foundation plantings and several of the really diminutive varieties of the Norway and Oriental spruce may be well employed in the rock garden. Because of its dense habit, the spruce lends itself admirably to protective plantings such as hedges and windbreaks. Whether the hedge be for purposes of protection or purely ornamental, there is an excellent choice of materials. *Picea polita*, the tigertail spruce, so called because of its sharp needles, has long been planted as a protective barrier and, as such, equals the effectiveness of a barbed entanglement. For the ornamental hedge there is a selection of narrow, upright forms ranging in height from less than fifteen inches to more than twenty feet. Spruce hedges should be much wider at the base than at the top, otherwise lower branches will die for lack of light. *See* the illustration at HEDGES.

Like all of the conifers, the spruce must be carefully transplanted. The roots react quickly to drying out and, hence, should always be moved with a ball. The root system of this group lies close to the surface and spreads horizontally. The absence of a distinct taproot facilitates moving, although this operation will be easier if root pruning is practiced to stimulate short fibrous growth.

Specimen plantings of the spruce seldom require pruning other than the occasional removal of dead or diseased wood. The habit of growth is dense, and the general outline sufficiently symmetrical so that little or no pruning for form is required. Where some corrective shaping is desired, it is best to disbud rather than use the knife. Disbudding consists of the removal of the terminal bud on those branches which are growing out of place or are developing too fast and thus giving the specimen a thin, lanky appearance. In the case of hedges, a knife or shears may be employed in order to obtain a dense growth within exact limits. All pruning work should be done in August.

The spruce, like most conifers, is not overparticular as regards soil, although it will do best in a light, sandy loam. Its requirements for moisture are far more exacting and it will thrive neither in a really dry soil nor in a poorly drained one. A well-drained, cool, deep soil should be provided. Few conifers are more susceptible to exposure than the spruce, and drying winds and strong winter sun must be avoided. Because it does not

Foliage and cones of Norway spruce (*below*) and the Colorado blue spruce (*above*)

mind partial shade, it is often possible to secure protection from the elements without resorting to planting on northern slopes, the most common method of natural protection. It is unsuited to coastal regions in the South.

Propagation is accomplished by seed, grafting, and cuttings. The species are grown mostly from seed sown late in spring and carefully watered and shaded during the first year to prevent damping-off.* Most of the forms are propagated by veneer grafting on *Picea Abies* in the greenhouse during Jan. The well-known Koster's blue spruce is now grafted in large numbers on potted seedlings of *Picea pungens* during Aug. It is safe to say that any spruce can be grown from cuttings, although varieties of *Picea Abies* and *P. glauca* root easier than most of the others. Cuttings are made from hardwood taken with a heel* and set in washed sand during Dec. They are kept under glass at a temperature of seventy degrees for at least six weeks, after which time root action will generally have commenced. After two or three months they are taken from the sand and potted in a light, rich soil. They are generally set out in the propagating beds late in the spring. — D. W.

INSECT PESTS. *See* budworms and sawfly larvae at FIR. Cut off galls and destroy by late summer. Spray tips of branches in fall, or in spring before new growth starts, with pesticide #20 (*see* SPRAYS AND DUSTS). Control overwintering mites by carefully applied oil sprays in dormant season or by miticides such as pesticide #14 or Kelthane in summer. Pick bagworms or spray with arsenicals or pesticide #1 as young develop in late spring.

DISEASES. The most common and serious disease of spruce is canker,* which may kill large branches. From the cankered area, pitch or resin will exude and drop to lower branches. When the pitch hardens, it turns bluish-white. No pesticide has proven of value for control of the canker disease. Prune out all diseased

---

* Special articles on the subjects indicated by an asterisk (*) will be found at the words so marked.

branches, cutting the branch where it originates from the main trunk. Do pruning during the winter or at a time when the needles are dry.

A number of rust * diseases attack needles of spruce, producing orange pustules, and often resulting in needle drop. Another rust disease occasionally causes a witches'-broom.* These brooms should be removed from the tree.

SPRUCE FAMILY = Pinaceae.

SPRUCE PINE = *Tsuga caroliniana.* See HEMLOCK.

SPRUE. Poor, thin, unsatisfactory asparagus.

SPUR. A tubular, hollow prolongation in certain flowers, as in the columbine, caused by the coalescence of petals or sepals, ordinarily secreting nectar.

Spur is also used to designate any short, stubby shoot, as in some fruit trees where the spur bears the flowers. A spur, in this sense, is often of importance in pruning. *See* When to Prune at PRUNING.

SPURGE. *See* EUPHORBIA. For the Allegheny and Japanese spurge *see* PACHYSANDRA.

SPURGE FAMILY. A very large family of plants, including herbs, shrubs, and trees, among them snow-on-the-mountain, the poinsettia, the castor-oil plant, the crown-of-thorns, the rubber-tree of Brazil, and all the showy garden crotons. For a description of the family and a list of the cult. genera, *see* EUPHORBIACEAE.

SPURGE LAUREL = *Daphne Laureola.*
spuria, -us, -um (spure'i-a). False.

SPUR PEPPER = *Capsicum frutescens.*

SPURRY = *Spergula arvensis. See* list at WEEDS.

squalida, -us, -um (skwal'i-da). Squalid; often evil-smelling.

squamata, -us, -um (skwam-may'ta). With scale-like, very small leaves or bracts.*

squamigera, -us, -um (skwam-mij'er-a). Scaly.

squamosa, -us, -um (skwam-ō'sa). Scaly.

SQUARE FLOWER BED. For the number of plants needed *see* GARDEN TABLES IV.

SQUARE TANKS. For contents *see* WEIGHTS AND MEASURES, 5.

squarrosa, -us, -um (skwa-rō'sa). Squarrose; *i.e.,* with spreading or recurved tips.

SQUASH. The botanical identity of the various garden and farm plants that go under the name of squash and pumpkin is discussed at *Cucurbita,* to which all of them belong. For practical purposes it does not matter what their origin may be, and in fact it is often unknown. Here we are concerned only with the garden types of squashes and how to grow them.

The common garden squashes (some of them are in reality pumpkins, which see) are best divided into two main types, depending on the use of their fruits — summer squashes and winter squashes. Color of the rind does not always indicate ripeness, and in the summer squashes the rind should be soft enough to prick with the thumbnail before picking.

SUMMER SQUASHES. These comprise several forms, but they all agree in having fruits that are used soon after harvesting and generally the fruits do not, or are not, kept through part of the late fall and winter, as are the winter squashes.

Of the summer squashes there are two well-marked forms or types — the crookneck, usually called summer crookneck squash, and the pineapple, Pattypan, or scallop squashes. In the summer crookneck squash the outer skin is much puckered or furrowed, in addition to the crooked neck of the fruit, and the flesh is yellow. The Pattypan or scallop squashes are not crooknecked, the outer skin is smooth, and the flesh is generally greenish or greenish-yellow. The latter (*i.e.,* white, flat, and scalloped-edged squashes) are commonly called simling, really cymling, throughout the South. While the ancestral types of all these were probably vine-like, the modern varieties are without tendrils,* or very few, and because they are compact, bushy plants are usually called bush squashes (or pumpkins, for some of them belong to the pumpkin affinity). Among the bush squashes there are sorts whose fruits are smooth, suggesting a cucumber. The fruits are harvested while immature and much used by those of Italian extraction. A popular var. of these is zucchini, the fruits of which are dark green (when picked) and not over 6–8 in. long, but best picked when quite young.

AUTUMN AND WINTER SQUASHES. These are also divided into those that have a crooked neck, as in the winter crookneck squash, and those varieties that are smooth-skinned. Some of the latter produce huge fruits, nearly all yellow, which pass for pumpkins. An old and well-known variety of these winter squashes is the Hubbard. Here, also, belong the variety known as Boston Marrow, Vegetable Marrow, and the forms known as Turban squash or "squash-within-a-squash" (*see* CUCURBITA MAXIMA TURBANIFORMIS). Of these winter squashes modern vars. include the Acorn, Butternut, Buttercup, and Blue Hubbard. Most of these store easily.

CULTURE

Whatever type of squash is grown, they must be treated as extremely tender annuals, especially the winter and autumn varieties, which in some northern regions will ripen their fruits uncertainly, due to lack of heat and a short growing season. There is generally, except in the coldest regions, no difficulty about raising summer squashes, but all sorts repay quick growth and plenty of heat.

If you have space and prefer to grow the vine-like forms, the hills should be at least 8 × 8 ft. apart, but if space requirements make the bush forms imperative — and they

* Special articles on the subjects indicated by an asterisk (*) will be found at the words so marked.

are far easier to grow, cultivate, and harvest — the hills can be about 30 in. apart each way.

It is useless to put squashes in a heavy, wet soil, for they grow too slowly in such places. It is better to select a warm, sandy loam upon which they thrive if it can be made rich enough. Since they are spaced so far apart, there is no use in a program of general soil enrichment for squashes, but every reason for concentrating the fertilizer or manure under the hills. A good plan is to dig out about 2 ft. of indifferent soil and fill in with a half-and-half mixture of sandy loam and well-rotted manure. Or if this is lacking, mix about 1 pound of a good commercial fertilizer with the soil.

For the summer squashes of the bush type, unless your soil warms up very slowly, the seeds should be planted directly in the hills, 4–5 seeds to a hill, which should ultimately be thinned to 2 or 3 plants to a hill, depending upon their vigor and the ravages of the cutworms.

If your season is short or the soil slow to warm up, the seeds can be started in the hotbed, sown in paper pots or old strawberry baskets about 1 month (no longer) before outdoor planting is possible. When really warm weather has come, 3–4 seedlings should be planted at each hill. The objection to starting plants ahead of time is that they are apt to prematurely flower and fruit soon after transplanting — usually with a single flower or fruit. If they do so, and if you want more and later fruit, the premature flower should be pinched off as soon as it forms.

For the winter squashes or for any that have long, sprawling vines, it is better to start them in the hotbed, as outlined above, if you live in a region with a short growing season. Otherwise, some of the late fruits will be caught by frost before maturity. In any case, the vine-like ones should be watched to see that all the growth does not run to vine and leaf at the expense of fruit. This is especially likely in rich soils or in ones that get extra top-dressings of fertilizer.

If you are out for a record-sized fruit (and many of the large kinds of winter squash habitually pass as pumpkins), the top-dressing with fertilizer is a good plan. The only caution is to keep such vines well pinched back, and also to pinch off all but one, or at most two, fruits. Also top-dressing should not include nitrate of soda, but a mixture of fertilizers containing more phosphoric acid and potash than nitrogen (*see* FERTILIZERS). *See also* PUMPKIN.

INSECT PESTS. Grayish-brown squash bugs are controlled, particularly as young, by pesticide #1 or #18 (*see* SPRAYS AND DUSTS). The squash borer, a caterpillar (especially on *C. maxima* varieties), is controlled by pesticide #20 or #27, applied as vines begin to run and repeated 2–3 times. Kill borers in stem by knife.

Young plants can be protected from cucumber beetles and ladybird beetles by meth-

oxychlor or pesticide #27. Pesticide #20 controls aphids.

DISEASES. *See* CUCUMBER.

SQUASH FAMILY = Cucurbitaceae.

SQUAWBERRY — *Mitchella repens.*

SQUAW-BUSH = *Rhus trilobata.*

SQUAW-ROOT = *Caulophyllum thalictroides.*

SQUAW WATERWEED = *Baccharis pilularis.*

SQUILL. *See* SCILLA. *See also* URGINEA.

SQUINANCY = *Asperula cynanchica.*

SQUIRREL-CORN = *Dicentra canadensis.*

SQUIRREL'S-EAR = *Goodyera repens.*

SQUIRREL'S-FOOT FERN = *Davallia bullata.*

SQUIRREL'S-TAIL GRASS = *Hordeum jubatum.*

SQUIRTING CUCUMBER. *See* ECBALLIUM.

ST. The abbreviation for Saint (which see for all names beginning with St.).

stachyoides (stack-i-oy′deez, but *see* OÏDES). Like a betony ot the genus *Stachys.*

STACHYS (stack′iss). Betony. Woundwort. Annual or perennial herbs, comprising about 200 species of the mint family, distributed throughout the world, but chiefly in the temperate zones, and mostly in damp or wet places. Generally they have fibrous roots and erect stems, but S. *sieboldi* has tuberous, edible roots. Leaves opposite,* smooth or hairy, ovalish or broadly lance-shaped, the margins entire* or toothed. Leaves on the upper part of the stem reduced to leafy bracts.* Flowers purple, scarlet, yellow, or white, in 2–many-flowered whorls,* arranged in terminal spikes. Calyx joined about ¾ of its length. Corolla tubular, opening into 2 lips.* Stamens* 4, in pairs, 2 long, 2 short. Fruit 2-celled, splitting into 4 parts when ripe. (*Stachys* is a Greek name used by Dioscorides for another genus.) Sometimes offered as *Betonica.*

A few species are useful in the flower border and one in the kitchen garden. Easily cult. in ordinary garden soil. Propagated by seeds sown in early spring or by division of roots in Sept., Mar., or Apr. The edible species S. *sieboldi*, the Chinese artichoke, is the one grown as a vegetable. Tubers should be planted in April, 4–6 in. deep, in rows 18 in. apart. They may be dug as required in the fall.

Betonica = S. *officinalis.*

ciliata. Perennial, growing to 6 ft. high, slightly hairy. Leaves ovalish to 6 in. long, the margins toothed. Flowers reddish-purple, to 1 in. long, in terminal, whorled* spikes, to 8 in. long. British Columbia to Ore.

corsica. Annual, and of sprawling habit, covered with short, soft hairs. Leaves bluntly ovalish, to ½ in. long, with rounded teeth. Flowers pinkish-white, to ¾ in. long, in distant 2–4-flowered whorls.* Mediterranean region.

grandiflora. Hardy perennial, growing to 3

* Special articles on the subjects indicated by an asterisk (*) will be found at the words so marked.

ft. high, slightly hairy. Leaves ovalish, heart-shaped at the base, with rounded teeth. Lower leaves long-stalked. Flowers violet, showy, to 1 in. long, in 20–30-flowered whorls.* Also offered as *Betonica grandiflora.* Asia Minor. The *var.* **superba** has bright mauve-purple or white flowers.

lanata. Lamb's-ears. Hardy perennial, growing to 1½ ft. high, covered with soft, white, woolly hairs. Leaves large, 4–8 in. long, broadly lance-shaped, the margins entire.* Flowers small, purple, in densely flowered whorls.* Caucasus and Persia. Often seen in English cottage gardens. Also known as *S. olympica.*

officinalis. Wood betony. An erect, rather coarse perennial, 10–20 in. high. Leaves oblong to ovalish, blunt at the tip, 2–4 in. long, with irregularly wavy margin. Flowers about ½ in. long, in dense clusters (whorls*) arranged in an interrupted spike 1–3 in. long. Eurasia. June–July. Usually offered as *S. Betonica.*

sieboldi. Chinese or Japanese artichoke. Chorogi. Knotroot. Erect, slightly hairy perennial, growing to 18 in. high, producing numerous small, white, edible tubers underground. Leaves broadly lance-shaped. Flowers small, white or pink in small spikes. China and Jap. For cult. *see* above.

STAFF-TREE. See CELASTRUS.

STAFF-TREE FAMILY = Celastraceae.

STAG BUSH = *Viburnum prunifolium.*

STAGGER-BUSH = *Lyonia mariana.*

STAGHORN FERN. See PLATYCERIUM.

STAGHORN SUMAC = *Rhus typhina.*

STAKES AND STAKING. Plants are staked for protection from wind and storm and to preserve their symmetry and beauty. Only experience, which often comes too late to prevent damage, will convince the amateur grower of the necessity of staking. It is especially needed by weak-stemmed and

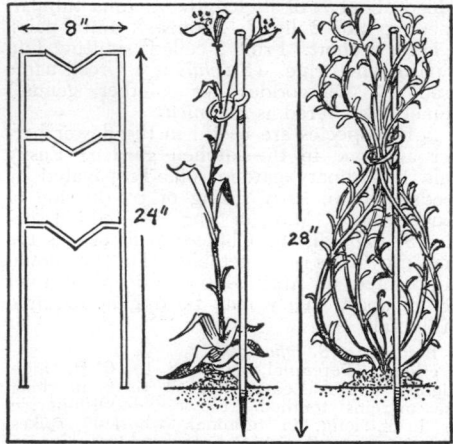

STAKES AND STAKING

At the left, a simple wire contrivance for staking annuals. Use two of them connected by 2 or 3 crosswires. In the center, the right way to stake a larger plant. At the right, a wrong but common method of staking.

top-heavy plants; tall plants surmounted by tall leafless flowering stems; tall plants in isolated positions; plants which have been disbudded, thus losing the natural support of the side branches; flowers which are grown for cutting, especially when a long stalk is desired. Specific kinds generally needing staking are the taller snapdragons, delphiniums, dahlias, lilies, chrysanthemums, the taller campanulas, climbing plants. Many plants such as Michaelmas daisies will, if the center growth is pinched out, take on a lower, bushier form and make their own support. The shelter of a fence or house wall will take the place of staking with hollyhocks.

The essentials of staking are: (1) sinking the stakes firmly, for weak staking is useless; (2) staking before the need is apparent; (3) staking inconspicuously. Early staking is concealed by the later growth of the plant, especially if the stakes are placed as near as possible to its center and the tying done carefully. This is particularly true of bushy plants with soft outlines, such as peonies and gypsophila, which do not need such tall stakes as chimney bellflowers, for instance. If plants, especially annuals and climbers, remain unstaked too long, no amount of skill can hide the mistake.

Stakes can be made and painted at home or bought ready-made. Home-made ones are often more satisfactory. Stakes should be a little shorter than the final height of the plant. For annuals, light bamboo canes or #4 wire stakes are best. For shrubs with heavy stems use 2 in. × 2 in. lumber in short lengths which will support the lower part of the stem where bending is most likely. Iron rods are also good for this purpose. Between these two extremes are a number of stake sizes. For chrysanthemums use ⅞ × ⅞ in. thick and 2 to 3 ft. long. For dahlias and delphiniums use slightly thicker stakes, 4½ to 5½ ft. long. All wood stakes should be pointed at the foot.

Plants with many stalks of heavy-headed flowers, such as peonies, need either many stakes or an encircling wire to which the upper parts of the flower stems are tied. Or separate wire supports made of two uprights connected by two or three crosspieces can be set round the plant. Both these devices are on the market. For plants needing slight restraint but not firm tying, use an upright with a loop of wire attached. Secure the wire to the upright with a twist, curve the two ends round the flower stem and hook them together.

For tying use a soft string which will not cut, green or natural-color raffia or green silk-aline thread. In tying, first fasten the string or raffia firmly to the stake, then pass it round the flower stem, tying firmly enough to prevent friction, but not so tightly as to check the growth. The knot should be on the inner side, where it shows least. Use plenty of stakes. Never economize by trying to control a plant of several stems with one stake.

* Special articles on the subjects indicated by an asterisk (*) will be found at the words so marked.

All wooden and wire stakes should be thoroughly cleaned and dried each autumn, painted and put away until the next season. Dull green is the most satisfactory color. The underground section of the stake, which is apt to deteriorate first, should be treated with at least three coats of paint and a coat of tar or creosote.

For sweet peas, low climbers with tendrils,° gypsophila, and carnations, branching twigs are better than stakes. The twigs cannot be used year after year, as can wooden and wire stakes, but they are cheap, easy to procure and inconspicuous, and preserve the natural beauty of the plant.

STALK. Loosely, the stem of any organ, but *stem* is a term better restricted to the main axis or stalk of a plant. The term *stalk* has several specialized meanings when used accurately. Thus a leafstalk is properly a petiole°; a flower stalk may be a peduncle,° pedicel,° or a scape°; the stalk of an anther is properly called a filament (*see* STAMEN); while the stalk of a fern frond is usually called a stipe.

STAMEN. The male organ in a flower. The typical stamen consists of a shank-like stalk (the filament) and, at the summit, a small bulbous or oblongish organ (the anther), which secretes and discharges the male pollinating substance (the pollen). The latter is the familiar and usually yellow "dust" found in flowers. *See* FLOWER for the position and insertion of stamens. Some flowers bear infertile stamens. *See* STAMINODE.

STAMINATE. Bearing only stamens. *See* FEMALE.

STAMINODE. A functionless, sterile or infertile stamen. They often resemble a true stamen but produce no pollen. Some staminodes, however, are petal-like and showy, as in the canna and some peonies. The technical term is staminodium.

STANDARD. 1. A tree or shrub which by grafting or training is restricted to a single, tree-like stem, usually shorter than normal, and in which all growth is concentrated in a

A standard (1)

terminal crown of foliage. Standards are popular in formal plantings, because their height and often umbrella-shaped form is fixed. Some standards have weeping branches which have been grafted at the desired height, as in the weeping mulberry. Among other plants often grown as standards are forms of catalpa, rose, and several fruit trees.

2. The upper, broad, and usually erect petal of a pea flower; called also a banner or vexillum. The term is also applied to the three erect petals of an iris flower to distinguish them from the three drooping ones known as "falls."

STANDARD CATALPA = *Catalpa bignonioides nana.*

STANDING CYPRESS = *Kochia scoparia trichophila,* also *Gilia rubra.*

STANHOPEA (stan-hope′ee-a). Tropical American orchids, comprising about 50 species, mostly tree-perching (epiphytes°), with thick branching stems and pseudobulbs,° which are sheathed with thin scales, each bearing one large leathery leaf. Flowers borne on leafless, drooping stalks which emerge from the under side of the plant. Flowers large, scented, mostly yellow, variously spotted with purple or red, to 7 in. across, in racemes.° Sepals and petals curved, similar to each other, excepting one, which forms the lip,° which is pouched or boat-shaped, with the middle part of the lobe fleshy and horn-shaped on either side. Fruit a 3-celled capsule. (Named for the Earl of Stanhope, of the Medico-Botanical Society of London.)

For cult. *see* ORCHID (greenhouse species).

tigrina. Flowers scented, large, to 7 in. across, in 2–4-flowered hanging racemes.° Sepals and petals yellow, marked purplish-blue, the lip white at tip. Mex. Aug.–Nov. Also known, perhaps correctly, as *S. hernandezi.*

wardi. Leaves large, leathery. Flowers 6–10, in hanging racemes, to 16 in. long. Sepals and petals orange-yellow, spotted with purple, inside of lip° dark purple and velvety. Guatemala to Venezuela. July–Sept.

STANLEYA (stan′lee-a). Perennial herbs, comprising about 10 species of the mustard family, natives of northwestern N.A. Leaves alternate,° bluish-green, the margins sometimes lobed. Flowers yellow, in long terminal racemes.° Calyx of 4 sepals, narrow. Corolla of 4 petals, also narrow, alternating with the sepals. Stamens° 6, 4 long, 2 short. Fruit a long capsule.° (Named for Edward Stanley, Earl of Derby.)

Easily cult., the one below making a useful border plant. Propagated by seeds or division of the roots. Seeds should be sown ⅛ in. deep, in sandy soil, in a temperature of 50°–60° in the cool greenhouse, or cold frame in early spring. They should be gradually hardened off and planted in a sunny position. Division of the roots may be made in Sept., Mar. or Apr.

pinnata. Growing to 5 ft. high. Leaves varying from ovalish to lance-shaped. Lower leaves usually cut into segments, under leaves

---

° Special articles on the subjects indicated by an asterisk (°) will be found at the words so marked.

entire.* Flowers golden-yellow, in long, terminal racemes.* Western U.S.

stans (stanz). Upright; erect.

STANLEY PARK. *See* No. 7 at GARDEN TOURS.

STAPELIA (sta-pee'li-a). Carrion-flower. South African cactus-like, desert plants, comprising over 100 species of the milkweed family. They are low-growing plants with thick, fleshy, green or colored stems which are 4-sided and grooved, sometimes with protuberances. There are no real leaves, which are represented by scales, spines, or bristles. Flowers large with very unpleasant odor, curiously marked and barred with dull red, yellow, or purple, growing from the angles of the stem. Calyx* of 5 sepals. Corolla of 5 petals, fleshy, spreading and variously colored, sometimes marbled or barred. The petals bear at the base 2 rows of outgrowths which are also colored, forming a crown or corona, the outer row petal-like, the inner scale-like. Fruit 2-celled. (Named for J. B. Van Stapel, Dutch physician.)

Stapelias are usually seen in botanic gardens, or specialists' collections of succulents, though a few species are grown in the greenhouse for their curious flowers. For cult. *see* SUCCULENTS. Perhaps two dozen other species are in cult. in America, mostly in desert gardens in Calif.

gigantea. Growing to 9 in. high. Stems dull green. Flowers to 18 in. across, salver-shaped, hairy, purple and light brown, marked with crimson lines. Summer.

grandiflora. Stems nearly 12 in. long, green, velvety with the angles notched. Flowers nearly 6 in. wide, purplish brown, covered, especially along the edges, with whitish or purplish hairs, otherwise unmarked. Often grown as a pot plant from Va. southward.

hirsuta. Stems not over 8–9 in. long, with compressed angles. Flowers 3–5 in. wide, cream-colored, wrinkled, with transverse bands of purple, the center with white and purplish hairs, the petals slightly recurved at the tip.

variegata. Growing to 6 in. high. Stems green, often tinted purple. Flowers 1–5, growing at the base of the stem, to 3 in. across, under surface green, upper surface wrinkled and ridged, greenish-yellow, with dark purplish-brown spots.

STAPHYLEA (staf-i-lee'a). Bladder-nut. Shrubs or small trees comprising the only commonly cult. genus of the family **Staphyleaceae** (staf-i-lee-ā'see-ee) which includes 4 other genera and perhaps 25 species, all from the north temperate zone. The bladder-nuts, of which 15 species are known, but only the two below much cult., are small trees, or, as grown, more often shrubs with opposite,* compound* leaves, the leaflets arranged finger-fashion, with an odd one at the end. Flowers white, or greenish-white, not very showy, arranged in a terminal cluster (panicle*). Sepals,* petals,* and stamens,* each 5. Fruit an inflated, membranous, usually 3-sided capsule,* the seeds bony (hence the name bladder-pod). The plants are more showy in fruit than in flower. (*Staphylea*

is from the Greek for cluster, in allusion to the branching of the flower cluster.)

One of the cult. species is from N.A., the other from the Caucasus. Both prefer partial shade and a reasonably moist, rich soil. There is little use of planting either on rocky or sandy, wind-swept slopes. Easily propagated by sowing fresh seed (or it may be stratified), or by cuttings.

colchica. Usually a shrub 8–12 ft. high. Leaflets 5 (or 3 on flowering twigs), oval-oblong, 2–3½ in. long, sharply toothed. Flower cluster 2–3 in. long, erect or a little pendulous. Flowers about ⅝ in. long. Fruit much inflated, 1½–3½ in. long. Caucasus. May–June. Hardy from zone * 3 southward.

trifolia. A shrub or small tree, 8–14 ft. high. Leaflets 3, elliptic or ovalish, sharply, unequally, but somewhat irregularly finely toothed, 1½–3½ in. long. Flower cluster nodding, about 2 in. long, the flowers scarcely ½ in. long. Fruit 1½–3 in. long. Eastern N.A. May. Hardy from zone* 2 southward.

STAR ACACIA = *Acacia verticillata.*

STAR ANISE = *Illicium verum.*

STAR-APPLE. Tropical ornamental or fruit trees comprising the genus Chrysophyllum (kriss-o-fil'lum) of the family Sapotaceae, most of the 60 species from tropical America. They mostly have a milky juice and alternate,* leathery leaves, often golden-hairy on the under side, without marginal teeth, and with many transverse, lateral, parallel veins. Flowers small, inconspicuous, usually in nearly stalkless clusters. For details *see* SAPOTACEAE. Fruit a globe-shaped or oblongish berry, edible in some species. (*Chrysophyllum* is from the Greek for golden leaf, in allusion to the golden hairs on the under side of many of the leaves.)

The first species is grown chiefly for its fruit, although the under side of the foliage is very handsome. The satinleaf, as its name implies, has still more handsomely colored foliage, but is grown only for ornament. Neither species can be grown with safety north of zone* 8, which confines their cult. to the warmest parts of Fla. There they do well on a variety of sandy soils, which, however, should be manured if too poor in plant food. They are medium-sized trees and need not be spaced more than 25–30 ft. apart.

C. Cainito. The common star-apple; called also cainito. A tree 25–30 ft. high, occasionally more. Leaves oval-oblong, 3–5 in. long, deep green above, golden and felty beneath. Fruit apple-shaped, 2–4 in. thick, smooth, greenish-purple, the flesh white and sweet when ripe. The cross-section of the fruit suggests a star (hence star-apple) in the arrangement of its seeds. Fruit ripening in late spring or early summer, and rarely seen in the North. Tropical America. Not safe north of zone* 8.

C. oliviforme. Satinleaf. A small, round-headed tree, rather compactly branched, the coppery under surface of the leaves very showy. Leaves ovalish or elliptic, 2–3½ in. long, deep green above. Fruit ovalish, scarcely ¾ in. long, deep purple, usually found at most seasons, due to the irregular flowering period. Fla. Bahamas and the W.I. Hardy as far

---

* Special articles on the subjects indicated by an asterisk (*) will be found at the words so marked.

north as protected parts of zone* 8. Grown only for ornament.

STAR-BLOOM = *Spigelia marilandica.*

STAR CACTUS. *See* ASTROPHYTUM.

STARCH. The first, and incomparably the most important, food manufactured in the green leaves of plants and never yet produced synthetically. It is made from a combination of sunshine, gases from the air, water and plant foods from the soil, worked upon by the green coloring matter of the leaves (chlorophyll*). For details of this process *see* PLANT FOODS. The starch in potatoes, rice, corn, etc., is not manufactured in the seeds or tubers, but in the leaves, and simply stored in other parts of the plant for future use.

STARCH HYACINTH = *Muscari botryoides.*

STARFLOWER = *Trientalis borealis.* For the spring starflower *see* BRODIAEA UNIFLORA.

STAR-GLORY = *Quamoclit.*

STAR GOOSEBERRY = *Phyllanthus acidus.*

STAR-GRASS. *See* ALETRIS FARINOSA and HYPOXIS.

STAR HYACINTH = *Scilla amoena.*

STAR IPOMOEA = *Quamoclit coccinea.*

STAR JASMINE = *Trachelospermum jasminoides.*

STAR LILY = *Leucocrinum montanum* and *Lilium concolor.*

STAR-OF-BETHLEHEM = *Ornithogalum umbellatum* and *O. nutans.*

STAR-OF-JERUSALEM = *Tragopogon pratensis.*

STAR-OF-TEXAS = *Xanthisma texanum.*

STAR PHLOX = *Phlox drummondi stellaris.*

STAR PINE = *Araucaria excelsa.*

STAR PRIMROSE = *Primula sinensis stellata.*

STARRY CAMPION = *Silene stellata.*

STARRY GRASSWORT = *Cerastium arvense.*

STARRY SOLOMON'S-SEAL = *Smilacina stellata.*

STARTER SOLUTIONS. Many gardeners have wondered if newly transplanted annuals, seedlings, or vegetable plants could not be given a boost. To overcome the shock of transplanting, most gardeners rely upon copious watering and, where available, liquid manure. Since the advent of the high-formula fertilizers, mentioned at FOLIAR FEEDING, there is a better and far more effective method.

The high-formula fertilizers mentioned at FOLIAR FEEDING are all designed to be immediately soluble in water, which ordinary dry fertilizers, especially the phosphates, are not. They are made to be gradually released so that there will be a sustained yield of nutrients as the plant develops. In the case of newly transplanted material, ordinary dry fertilizers may be too slow.

For such a contingency the entirely soluble high-formula fertilizers are ideal. By following the directions on the box, all that is necessary is adding the proper amount of water. For most crops 1 oz. (2 level tbs.) to a gallon of water will be sufficient. For small plants about 1 pt. or a little less of such a solution, applied at the time of transplanting, will give good results. Use a watering can, unless you have extensive plantings, for which there is an automatic device.

The use of these starter solutions is practised by some commercial growers for seedlings, cuttings, or newly potted plants. The packages come in 1–5-lb. containers, sizes practical for the average gardener. The solutions are, of course, relatively expensive, and when sold in tablet form (often with rather lurid claims and no formula) the cost is far too high. But the legitimate use of these concentrated fertilizers as starter solutions is a reasonably new and desirable improvement over old methods.

STAR VIOLET = *Houstonia serpyllifolia.*

STARWORT. *See* STELLARIA and ASTER.

STATE FLOWERS. The different states of the Union have floral emblems, sometimes chosen by the legislature, sometimes by vote of the school children, or by suggestions from garden clubs. In many cases, as will be seen from the list below, the plant is not native in the state that chose it.

STATE FLOWERS

Alabama. Goldenrod
Alaska. Forget-me-not
Arizona. Giant cactus
Arkansas. Apple blossom
California. California poppy
Colorado. Columbine
Connecticut. Mountain laurel
Delaware. Peach blossom
District of Columbia. American beauty rose
Florida. Orange blossom
Georgia. Cherokee rose
Hawaii. Hibiscus
Idaho. Mock-orange
Illinois. Violet
Indiana. Zinnia
Iowa. Wild rose
Kansas. Sunflower
Kentucky. Goldenrod
Louisiana. Magnolia
Maine. White pine
Maryland. Black-eyed Susan
Massachusetts. Trailing arbutus
Michigan. Apple blossom
Minnesota. Showy lady's-slipper
Mississippi. Magnolia
Missouri. Hawthorn
Montana. Bitter-root
Nebraska. Goldenrod
Nevada. Sagebrush
New Hampshire. Lilac
New Jersey. Violet

---

* Special articles on the subjects indicated by an asterisk (*) will be found at the words so marked.

New Mexico. Spanish bayonet
New York. Rose
North Carolina. Dogwood
North Dakota. Wild rose
Ohio. Carnation
Oklahoma. Mistletoe
Oregon. Oregon grape
Pennsylvania. Mountain laurel
Puerto Rico. Poinsettia
Rhode Island. Violet
South Carolina. Carolina jasmine
South Dakota. Pasque-flower
Tennessee. Iris
Texas. Bluebonnet
Utah. Globe tulip
Vermont. Red clover
Virginia. Flowering dogwood
Washington. *Rhododendron macrophyllum*
West Virginia. Great laurel
Wisconsin. Violet
Wyoming. Painted-cup

All of these plants are in this book, mostly entered under the Latin name of the genera to which they belong. They are also entered under the common names given in the above list and should be sought in the body of the book if the Latin name is wanted for these state flowers. *See also* NATIONAL FLOWERS and STATE TREES.

STATE TREES. Some of the states have chosen, by legislative action or by less official means, a state tree. Those so chosen are the following. Where a state is omitted it means that no tree has yet been selected.

Arkansas	Pine
California	Redwood
Colorado	Colorado blue spruce
Delaware	American holly
Florida	Cabbage palmetto
Georgia	Live oak
Hawaii	Coconut palm
Illinois	Oak
Indiana	Tulip-tree
Maine	White pine
Michigan	Apple
Mississippi	Evergreen magnolia
Nebraska	American elm
North Dakota	Swamp ash
Ohio	Buckeye
Oklahoma	Redbud
Oregon	Douglas fir
Pennsylvania	Hemlock
Rhode Island	Maple
South Carolina	Cabbage palmetto
South Dakota	Cottonwood
Tennessee	Red cedar
Texas	Pecan
Utah	Colorado blue spruce
Vermont	Sugar maple
Virginia	Flowering dogwood

All of these will be found in this book at their proper entries, cross-referenced to the Latin names of the trees.

STATICE. *See* ARMERIA; for the plant offered as *Statice tatarica, see* LIMONIUM TATARICUM.

STATISTICS. *See* GARDEN TABLES; also WEIGHTS AND MEASURES.

STAUNTONIA (staun-tō'ni-a). A small, little-known genus of Asiatic woody vines of the family Lardizabalaceae, with evergreen leaves. The only cult. species, S. **hexaphylla**, is a tall-growing vine, sometimes reaching 40 ft. in height, with alternate,* compound* leaves, the 3–7 leaflets arranged finger-fashion, more or less oval, and 3–4 in. long, pale green beneath. Male and female flowers separate, but on the same plant, white but tinged with violet, about ¾ in. wide, fragrant, borne in small clusters (racemes*) in the leaf axils.* Stamens* 6, more or less connected. Petals none, the 6 sepals petal-like. Fruit fleshy and berry-like. Jap. and Korea. May–June. Hardy from zone* 6 southward, and best grown in partial shade and rich, moist soils. Propagated by green-wood cuttings under glass. (Named for Sir G. L. Staunton, Irish explorer in China.)

Stechados = Lavandula Stoechas.

STECKLING. A term for a slip or cutting; also a *steckling,* in sugar-beet regions, is a late-planted sugar beet, grown for seed production but not for its root.

STEEPLEBUSH = *Spiraea tomentosa.*

STEIRONEMA (sty-ro-nee'ma). Loosestrife. North American perennial herbs, comprising about 6 species, of the family Primulaceae. Leaves usually opposite,* sometimes in whorls,* lance-shaped. Flowers yellow, solitary or clustered, growing from the axils* of the leaves. Calyx of 5 sepals. Corolla of 5 petals, each petal curling inward enclosing a stamen,* giving the flower a wheel-like appearance. Alternating with the petals are 5 sterile stamens (staminodes*). Fruit a dry capsule. (*Steironema* is from the Greek for sterile threads, in allusion to the staminodes.*) For other plants called loosestrife, *see* LYSIMACHIA and LYTHRUM.

They are not much in cultivation, but can be used in damp or shady places in the flower border or wild garden. Propagated by division of roots in Sept. or early spring.

ciliatum. Fringed loosestrife. Also known as *Lysimachia ciliata.* Strong-growing, to 4 ft. high, not much branched. Leaves opposite,* broadly lance-shaped, to 6 in. long. Flowers yellow, to 1 in. across. Moist places in U.S., naturalized in Eu. July.

STELLARIA (stell-lair'i-a). Starwort. Chickweed. Stitchwort. Annual or perennial herbs, comprising about 100 species, of the pink family, distributed throughout the world, chiefly in the temperate regions, and rather weedy. They are of spreading, tufted or scrambling habit, the stems weak and much-branched. Leaves opposite,* lance-shaped, sometimes hairy. Flowers small, generally white, in loose branching clusters. Calyx* of 5 sepals. Corolla of 5 petals, spreading, star-like. Stamens* 5–10. Fruit a dry capsule.* (*Stellaria* is from the Latin for star, in allusion to the shape of the flower.)

These plants are mostly garden weeds, the

---

* Special articles on the subjects indicated by an asterisk (*) will be found at the words so marked.

only cult. species, *S. Holostea*, being the most showy. It may be used in the wild garden or for covering dry banks. Propagated by seeds.

Holostea. Greater stichwort. Easter-bell. Also known as *Alsine Holostea*. Hardy perennial, with creeping rootstocks, and of scrambling habit, to 2 ft. high. Leaves lance-shaped, to 3 in. long, slightly hairy. Flowers white, showy, to ¾ in. across, numerous, in loose, branching terminal clusters. Calyx slightly hairy. Eurasia, naturalized in N.A.

media. Chickweed. *See* list at WEEDS.

stellaris, -e (stell-lar′is). Star-like.

stellata, -us, -um (stell-lay′ta). Star-like.

stellulata, -us, -um (stell-you-lay′ta). Somewhat, or a little, star-like.

STEM. The main axis of a plant, usually called the trunk in a tree, but mostly called the stem in shrubs or woody vines. In herbs the stem is sometimes known (loosely) as the stalk, but the latter term has, properly, a more restricted meaning. *See* STALK.

While most stems are aerial, *i.e.*, above ground, there are many underground stems, which are commonly but incorrectly called roots. Actually they are rootstocks (which see), and often valuable propagative material for the gardener because they bear buds (which roots never do), from which new plants may arise. *See also* BULB.

The stems of woody plants differ from those of herbs in bearing buds which will survive the winter above ground. But the stems of all but a handful of herbs die down to the ground each winter. This fundamental difference in habit dictates our methods of propagating plants. *See* PROPAGATION.

While most stems are woody or herbaceous, there are a few families or genera of plants that bear most unusual stems. Some, as in the cacti, and in certain cactus-like spurges, function as do leaves, but are often much swollen and store large amounts of water. *See* CACTI, SUCCULENTS. Others are essentially leafless, or quite so, and such plants have green, wire-like, or flat leaf-like stems. *See* ACACIA, MUEHLENBECKIA, RUSCUS, and ASPARAGUS.

STEM CLIMBER. *See* VINES.

STEMMARIA (stem-mair′i-a). An old generic name for certain ferns now included in *Platycerium* (which see).

STENANTHIUM (sten-an′thi-um). A perennial herb with bulbous rootstocks, of the family Liliaceae, of the U.S. and Mex. Leaves mostly growing at the base of the stem. Flowers greenish-white, often nodding, in loose or pyramidal clusters. Calyx* of 3 colored sepals, united at the base, forming a short top-shaped tube. Corolla of 3 petals alternating with the sepals attached to the short tube. Stamens* 6. Fruit a 3-celled capsule.* (*Stenanthium* is from the Greek for narrow flower, in allusion to the sepals and petals.)

It is of little garden importance, but occa-sionally grown in the wild garden, where it needs a distinctly acid soil of pH 4–5.

gramineum. Feather-fleece. Growing to 5 ft. high. Leaves to 1 ft. long, and ¾ in. wide, the upper ones reduced to bracts.* Flowers greenish-white, to ¾ in. across, numerous in pyramidal clusters to 2 ft. long. Southeastern U.S. Long known as *S. robustum*.

STENOLOBIUM (sten-o-lō′bi-um). A small genus of tropical American shrubs and trees of the family Bignoniaceae, **S. Stans**, the yellow elder, a very popular ornamental throughout zones* 8 and 9, and hardy even in protected parts of zone* 7. It is a large shrub or tree, scarcely over 20 ft. high, with opposite,* compound* leaves, the leaflets borne feather-fashion. Leaflets 5–13, lance-oval, 3–4 in. long, pointed at the tip, the margins toothed. Flowers showy, yellow, the corolla more or less funnel-shaped, about 2 in. long, the inside of the tube hairy toward the base. Fruit a narrow capsule,* 6–8 in. long. Of easy cult. and a deservedly popular ornamental, as its cluster of late-blooming flowers is borne in profusion. It is quick-growing, more often shrubby in the U.S. but a tree in the tropics. Other names for it are *Tecoma Stans* and *Bignonia Stans*. (*Stenolobium* is from the Greek for narrow lobes, in allusion to the narrow fruit.)

stenopetala, -us, -um (sten-o-pet′a-la). With narrow petals.

stenophylla, -us, -um (sten-o-fill′a). Narrow-leaved.

stenoptera, -us, -um (sten-op′ter-ra). Narrow-winged.

STENOTAPHRUM (sten-o-taff′rum). Tropical, or sub-tropical, perennial creeping grasses of no hort. importance except that one of the three known species, **S. secunda-tum**, is the St. Augustine grass, widely used for lawns in the South where better lawn grasses will not thrive. *See* LAWN. It is a creeping grass, rooting at the joints, the leafy stems 3–12 in. high. Leaves grass-like, but short and flattish, blunt, rarely over 3 in. long. Flower spike stiff, terminal, 2–5 in. long, the spikelets borne in sunken pits on one side of the stalk of the spikelet. S. Car. to Tex. and throughout tropical America. A form with white-striped leaves is used in hanging baskets. (*Stenotaphrum* is from the Greek for narrow trench, in allusion to the pits in which the spikelets are borne.)

STEPHANANDRA (steff-a-nan′dra). Asiatic shrubs of the rose family, two of the four known species grown for ornament, although their spirea-like flowers are rather unimpressive. Leaves alternate,* more or less lobed and toothed. Flowers small, white, in terminal clusters (panicles* or corymbs*). Calyx* cup-shaped, its lobes 5. Petals 5, about the length of the calyx lobes. Stamens* 10–20. Fruit an oblique, scarcely splitting, dry pod (follicle*), with 1–2 shining seeds. (*Stephanandra* is from the Greek for crown and man, in allusion to the crown of rather persistent stamens.*)

---

* Special articles on the subjects indicated by an asterisk (*) will be found at the words so marked.

Stephanandras are of easy culture in ordinary garden soils, but are not much grown because the closely related genus *Spiraea* provides far finer hort. material. They are easily propagated by seeds, cuttings or by division.

flexuosa = *Stephanandra incisa.*

incisa. An arching shrub 5–8 ft. high, the stems often drooping. Leaves ovalish, long-pointed, 2–2½ in. long, lobed almost to the middle, the lobes toothed. Flowers greenish-white, the stamens* 10. Jap. and Korea. June. Hardy from zone* 4 southward, possibly in zone* 3 with protection. Foliage reddish-purple in the fall. Sometimes offered as *S. flexuosa.*

Tanakae. Not over 6 ft. high. Leaves 2–4 in. long, shallowly 3-lobed or deeply toothed, the teeth also toothed. Flowers white, the stamens* 15–20. Jap. June–July. Hardy from zone* 4 southward, probably in zone* 3 with protection. Foliage yellow, orange, or scarlet in the fall.

STEPHANOTIS (steff-a-no′tis). Twining woody vines, comprising about 15 species of the family Asclepiadaceae, natives of Madagascar and the Malay Archipelago. Leaves opposite, thick and leathery. Flowers showy, large, white, in umbel*-like clusters growing from the axils* of the leaves. Calyx* of 5 sepals. Corolla of 5 lobes, opening salver-wise, the tube to 2 in. long, swollen at the base and sometimes at the throat. There is a small crown at the opening of the corolla tube. (*Stephanotis* is from the Greek for crown and ear, in allusion to the crown.)

Only *S. floribunda* is in general cultivation, and it makes one of the best greenhouse climbers or specimen plants. It should be grown in a winter temperature of 55°–65° and in summer at 70°–90°. Propagated by cuttings made from half-ripened shoots. Shoots should be inserted in a mixture of ½ sand and ½ peat in individual pots in March, and placed in a confined, moist position, shaded from sun, until rooted. When pots are filled with roots they should be re-potted into potting mixture* 5, shaded from sun, given plenty of water, and be syringed daily, as they are subject to mealy-bugs. They should be cut back occasionally to obtain several leads. These plants require shade and air through summer, but in the fall should be given less water until Feb., and a temperature of 55°–65°. They should be cut back and re-potted every year.

floribunda. Madagascar jasmine. Wax flower. Stems twining. Leaves ovalish, thick and leathery, to 4 in. long. Flowers waxy-white, fragrant, in umbel-like clusters in the leaf axils.* Madagascar. *See* VINES. It is grown outdoors in Fla. and southern Calif.

STEPPING STONES. *See* PATHS AND PAVING.

STEPS. Steps are devices for making easier the passage on foot from one level to another. Therefore, no matter what the height of the ascent or the size of the building above, they must always be adapted to the human scale, by which is meant that they must be convenient for climbing both by children and grownups. Since their height and

A simple, built-up set of curved steps

depth or width of tread can vary only within narrow limits, a dignified or imposing effect can only be obtained by increasing their length.

Outdoor steps should generally be less steep than indoor steps. Space within a building is usually so valuable that it cannot be spared to make steps of the easiest ascent. Steps of wooden stairs in the average house are likely to be about 8 in. high and 10 in. deep, with a projecting nose increasing the width of tread to about 11 in. But a garden step of these dimensions will be neither comfortable to climb nor pleasant to look at, and since the quality of restfulness is indispensable to the well-designed garden, the proportions of the steps, which are usually conspicuous objects, are of much importance. For a 12-in.-wide step the height of the riser should not exceed 6 in., and this is a good general proportion for small garden steps and adjusts itself well to a bank of about 1 vertical: 2 horizontal.

Outdoor steps are frequently made of wider treads than 12 in. and when they are, the risers are usually lower. Thus a height or riser of 5 in. with a tread width of 14 in. or 15 in. makes a step pleasant both to look at and to climb, and many steps are found of still lower rises and wider treads.

The aesthetic value of garden steps is great. They express human uses and their strong horizontal and vertical lines are a good foil to the plant forms around them. A flight of a few steps may, of itself, often be just the constructed thing needed to accent and vitalize the plan of a simple garden, formal or informal.

To anyone asking, When, where and how should garden steps be used? the answer might be made, Wherever they are necessary. That is to say, whenever and wherever it is felt to be better to pass from one level to another by a sudden transition rather than by a continuous slope. This, of course, is predicated on a good plan or layout in which all the lines have been laid down simply and constructively and the different

* Special articles on the subjects indicated by an asterisk (*) will be found at the words so marked.

Solid stone steps with iron railings

Stone steps with parapet

levels foreseen. In such cases, steps will fall into their natural places on the plan: they will be put, in fact, where they will do most good. Not infrequently it is desirable to interrupt an easy grade by two or three steps, or even by a single step, making the grades still more easy; but such steps should be placed only where it is felt that, for some reason, a line of separation is appropriate. Such steps may be made either in narrow lawns or paved walks. Steps should be of the width of the walk which they terminate, side walls (if any) being outside of the walk lines.

Steps are usually straight (rectilinear) in all dimensions, but curved steps, either con-

vex or concave, are common. In fact steps may be made to fit almost any desired lines. There are many effective flights of convex garden steps, especially in England, each step being of longer diameter than the one above it. Such steps should give on a wider open space below than the walk above them, so as to provide for the radiation or distribution of the traffic instead of confining it within the width of the walk.

As to materials and construction of steps, there are masonry steps of stone, brick, or concrete which are likely to be part of a terrace wall or other structure. It is not possible within the limits of this article to go into details of construction of such steps, but

STEPS IN A NATURALISTIC SETTING IN FRANKLIN PARK, BOSTON

* Special articles on the subjects indicated by an asterisk (*) will be found at the words so marked.

it might be said that it should correspond with that of the wall or other structure of which they are part, their foundations or supports being laid below frost line.

But the most generally useful garden steps are those made of local materials, of stones that will split naturally into flat slabs, such as slate or bluestone, or, in fact, of any stones with one flat side. If flagstones with at least one straight edge are obtainable, these can be laid on other flagstones or bricks to make steps of the required height, while underneath should be a layer of broken stone or cinders 12 in. or more thick to make a good bed. The bottom of this bed should be horizontal or, better still, with a slight pitch forward to avoid sliding: this is in order to drain water away from under the steps. Stones for the treads should be large and heavy enough not to be easily displaced. Stones of each step should overlap those of the step below, say, an inch or more.

A formal flight of garden steps with a balustrade

In many districts where there are no laminated or easily splittable stones there are water-worn stones with one flat side which can be made into practicable and attractive steps especially appropriate in natural or naturalistic compositions. But the building of these requires a good deal of ingenuity and patience, and it is not often that one can find a workman able to build such steps satisfactorily. It would be better for the garden owner to make them himself, with only the aid of the hired man. He is likely to get a thrill out of his work far exceeding that of some more expensive amusements. The general construction of such steps is similar in principle to that of flagstone steps described above. Useful tools to have around are a small and larger crowbar and a pick and shovel.

GRASS STEPS. An attractive alternative for any of those suggested above is a flight of grass steps. They cannot be used, of course, in places where there is much traffic, for the grass will not stand concentrated wear and tear. But as infrequently used steps they are very charming, especially in secluded, partially shaded gardens. Make the steps broad and with shallow risers. Cut the earth very evenly and see that there is adequate topsoil. They must be turfed with the finest quality of turf, carefully laid and watered for the first few weeks. For details see TURF. — H. A. C.

STERCULIA (ster-kew′li-a). A large genus of tropical trees of the family Sterculiaceae, only S. foetida of hort. interest, and this little known outside of extreme southern Fla., perhaps because it is hardy nowhere else. It is a smooth-barked tree, 40–60 ft. high, the branches inclined to be in tiers (whorled*). Leaves alternate,* compound,* the leaflets arranged finger-fashion, Leaflets 5–9, oblongish or narrower, pointed, 5–9 in. long. Flowers blooming with the unfolding of the leaves, purplish-red, decidedly bad-smelling, and borne in clusters (panicles*) in the leaf axils.* Flowers unisexual* or polygamous,* the 5 sepals petal-like, the petals lacking. Fruit a collection of 5 woody carpels, 3–4 in. long, green outside but bright red within, the seeds large, hard and black. Somewhat grown for ornament in Fla. and propagated by seeds or cuttings of green wood. For other trees, sometimes offered as Sterculia, see BRACHYCHITON and FIRMIANA SIMPLEX. (Sterculia is from the Latin for manure, in allusion to the unpleasant odor of some species.)

STERCULIACEAE (ster-kew-li-ā′see-ee). The chocolate family (50 genera and 750 species) is almost exclusively tropical and of more interest in commerce than as the source of garden plants. Mostly trees and shrubs, the outstanding economic genera are Theobroma (chocolate) and Cola (the kola nut), neither of which is much cult. outside of tropical plantations.

Ornamental tender plants are found in Dombeya, Brachychiton, Firmiana, and Sterculia, some of which become trees if planted outdoors in frost-free areas. Fremontia and Thomasia (one a ground cover) are grown in Calif., rarely in greenhouses, while Mahernia is herbaceous and furnishes an attractive greenhouse herb for hanging baskets.

Leaves alternate,* simple,* or if compound, the leaflets arranged finger-fashion. Flowers nearly always clustered, relatively showy and with petals in some genera (Dombeya, Theobroma, Mahernia, etc.), but without petals and relatively inconspicuous in Firmiana and Cola. Fruit dry, often a capsule,* nearly always splitting.

Technical flower characters: Flowers perfect* or unisexual.* Calyx tubular or bell-shaped, deeply 5-parted or cleft. Petals 5 or none. Stamens* 5 or more, and in two series, some sterile, the fertile ones united into a tube. Ovary superior,* 2-celled.

sterilis, -e (ster′ri-lis). Having no flowers or infertile ones.

STERILITY. The inability to produce normal living offspring. Varietal crosses are generally fertile; species hybrids are often sterile, and not infrequently fertile or partially so,

* Special articles on the subjects indicated by an asterisk (*) will be found at the words so marked.

especially if the hybrid is back-crossed to one of the parents. Crosses between genera are usually sterile. (*See* Crossing, also Self-sterility.) — O. E. W.

STERILITY OF FRUIT TREES. Unproductive fruit trees are often a problem to the home grower, but rarely so to the professional orchardist, because he avoids as many of the causes of it as possible. The failure to set fruit, or to set satisfactory amounts of it, may be due to three main causes:

(1) The flowers of certain fruit trees are sterile to their own pollen. In such cases it is essential to interplant other closely related varieties or forms, thus ensuring a supply of pollen that will effectively fertilize the ovules. There is no need to repeat the details of what fruits require this sort of planting, nor the varieties needed for interplanting, because all such cases are noted in the special cultural articles on the different fruits. *See* the one you are having difficulty with.

(2) Improper culture and pruning will also cause trees to fail. Most orchard fruits do not require applications of fertilizer or manure, except in limited amounts and at special times. Too rich a soil will provoke more wood and foliage than fruit. *See* the directions regarding soils and fertilizers at the cultural articles on all the main fruit crops.

Another common cause of fruit failure is incorrect pruning. This is covered in detail at the main fruit articles, and for the general principles of pruning fruit trees *see* Pruning.

(3) In many early-flowering fruit trees there is the constant hazard of an untimely frost while they are in full flower. This, while it kills the blossoms in some tender sorts, practically stops insect visitors to all flowers and thus prevents pollination* even in those blossoms that survive the cold. There is, of course, no remedy for this unless you live in a region where orchard heating is possible (*see* Frost). For the small home grower, in the East, this is impossible. Then close proximity to a large body of water or the choosing of the most favorable site on the property is the only insurance one can provide against untimely frosts. *See* the general article on Fruit Culture.

STERLING FOREST GARDENS. See No. 22 at Garden Tours.

STERNBERGIA (stern-ber'ji-a). Winter daffodil. A genus of Eurasian bulbous herbs of the family Amaryllidaceae, one of them, **S. lutea,** the winter daffodil or lily-of-the-field, an attractive fall-blooming plant for the border or rock garden. Leaves basal, 8–12 in. long, about ¾ in. wide, without teeth, appearing with the flowers and usually persisting over the winter. Flowers yellow, fragrant, with a very short tube and erect, veined, oblongish segments, not over 1½ in. long. The flowers are solitary, rarely 2, at the end of a stalk 4–7 in. high. Stamens* 6. Southern Eu. and Asia Minor. For culture *see* below. (Named for Count Caspar Sternberg, a botanist.)

Winter Daffodil Culture

There are not many yellow-flowered bulbous plants blooming in the autumn, so the winter daffodil, aside from its other attractions, has a special color value. The dark green, strap-shaped leaves make their appearance in late August, and the glowing, orange-yellow, crocus-like blooms follow by the middle of September. The flowers, like the leaves, are of strong texture and will endure weather that would spoil the appearance of crocuses and colchicums.

Several flowers are produced by each bulb, carried on a stout stem to a height of from 4 to 7 in. The bulbs should be put in the ground as early in August as they may be procured and set about four inches deep. A gritty, nourishing soil suits them best and a sheltered position against a south-facing wall, or in a warm nook in the rock garden where they will receive a good baking.

Seed is not always formed in this climate, but the bulbs increase readily by bulblets.* Frequent lifting and replanting is not recommended, but if they are not flowering well the bulbs may be lifted and replanted in fresh soil after the foliage has quite died away. The foliage usually persists over the winter, withering away in early spring. They are hardy as far north as zone* 4 and may be wintered in well-drained soil in sheltered places in zone* 3. Where they flower together, lavender-flowered *Crocus speciosus* makes a good companion for groups of *Sternbergia.* — L. B. W.

STEVIA (stee'vi-a). A very large genus of New World herbs of the family Compositae, none of which appear to be garden plants, although the name *Stevia* has also been applied to some rather commonly cult. plants. All the latter belong to the genus *Piqueria,* which see for garden plants offered as *Stevia.*

STEWARTIA (stew-art'i-a). Also spelled *Stuartia.* Showy, white-flowered shrubs or trees of the family Theaceae, comprising 8 species found in the southeastern U.S. or eastern Asia, 5 of them cult. for ornament. Leaves alternate,* short-stalked, toothed. Flowers solitary, mostly in the leaf axils,* more or less cup-shaped, usually with one or two bracts* below the calyx* which is made up of 5 (rarely 6) sepals.* Petals 5 (rarely 6), roundish, finely round-toothed or wavy, blunt, silky on the outside. Stamens* numerous. Fruit a woody, 5-celled capsule.* (Named for John Stuart, Earl of Bute, a patron of botany.) Sometimes known as *Malachodendron.*

All the shrubs below need partial shade and a moist, rich loam partly mixed with moderately acid peat. They may be propagated by seeds or by layers, or by cuttings of half-ripened wood taken in Aug. or Sept. and kept under glass.

koreana. A tree 20–30 ft. high, the bark brown and flaky. Leaves elliptic, 3–5 in. long, narrow-pointed at the tip, rounded at the base, sparingly toothed. Flowers nearly 4 in. wide, in the axils* of the lower leaves, the white

---

* Special articles on the subjects indicated by an asterisk (*) will be found at the words so marked.

petals spreading. Fruit beaked, about ¾ in. long. Korea. July–Aug. Hardy from zone* 5 southward. Thought by some to be identical with the last species.

Malachodendron. Silky camellia. A shrub 8–12 ft. high, the twigs hairy. Leaves elliptic-oblong, 2½–4½ in. long, pointed at the tip, finely toothed and hairy on the margin. Flowers nearly 4 in. wide, white, but the anthers* bluish-purple. Fruit about ⅝ in. wide. Va. to Fla. and Ark. June–Aug. Hardy from zone* 5 southward.

monadelpha. A tree up to 75 ft. high in the wild, much less as cult., with softly hairy twigs. Leaves 2–3 in. long, oblongish or elliptic, faintly toothed on the margin. Flowers solitary, 1½–2½ in. wide, short-stalked, white. Jap. July–Aug. Hardy from zone* 6 southward.

ovata. Mountain camellia. A shrub 10–15 ft. high, the twigs smooth. Leaves ovalish or oblong, 2½–5½ in. long, remotely toothed. Flowers nearly 3 in. wide, white, but the anthers* orange. Fruit about ¾ in. long. Mostly in the mountains, N. Car. and Tenn. to Ga. July–Aug. Hardy from zone* 3 southward. The *var.* **grandiflora** has still larger and more handsome flowers with purple stamens.* Autumn foliage orange-scarlet.

pentagyna = *S. ovata.*

Pseudo-camellia. A large shrub or small tree, rarely more than 25 ft. as cult., much more in the wild, the red bark peeling in large flakes. Leaves more or less elliptic, 2–4 in. long, pointed, rather thick and turning brilliant crimson in autumn. Flowers solitary, 2–3 in. wide, cup-shaped, white. Jap. July–Aug. Hardy from zone* 5 southward. Closely allied to *S. koreana.*

STICK. *See* Bud Stick.

STICK-TIGHT = *Bidens.*

STICKY LEAVES. Some leaves are normally sticky because they are covered with glandular* hairs. For generally smooth leaves that become sticky in warm weather *see* Honeydew.

STIGMA. The termination of the style* and ovary,* and the organ that receives the pollen at pollination. Stigmas may be forked or minutely globe-shaped, but they are usually sticky enough for pollen to adhere to them. *See* Flower.

STINGING NETTLE = *Urtica dioica. See* Nettle.

STINKING CEDAR = *Torreya taxifolia.*

STINKING CLOVER = *Cleome serrulata.*

STINKING GLADWIN = *Iris foetidissima.*

STINKWEED = *Ailanthus altissima.*

STIPA (sty′pa). Feather-grass. Perennial grasses comprising about 100 species, and distributed throughout the world, except in the colder regions. Leaves narrow, grass-like, the margins rolled. Flowers borne in loose branching clusters, each spikelet bearing a long feathery awn,* from 1½ in. to 1 ft. long. (*Stipa* is from the Greek for stipe, in allusion to the awns.)

Cult. for their feathery appearance, as they may be cut and dried for ornament. Propagated by seeds or division of roots, they may be grown in ordinary garden soil. The long

awns of some species are dangerous to sheep and cattle.

elegantissima. Grows to 3 ft. high. Spikelets in loose branching clusters, to 8 in. long. Awns* feathery, to 1¼ in. long. Flower stalks hairy. Aust.

pennata. Growing in tufts to 3 ft. high. Spikelets in dense clusters. Awns* to 1 ft. long, the lower part smooth and twisted, the upper part feathery. Good ornamental species. Eu. and As.

STIPE. The stalk of a fern frond; more rarely, the stalk of an ovary. Such a stalked ovary, and the subsequent fruit, are said to be stipitate.

stipulata, -us, -um (stip-you-lay′ta). Having stipules,* often prominent ones.

STIPULE. One of the small, leaf-like or membranous organs found at the base of many leafstalks, usually in pairs. They may be conspicuous, as in the pea, inconspicuous as in many shrubs, or ephemeral when they drop off as soon as the leaf expands. In some plants the stipules are replaced by thorns as in *Pithecolobium dulce.*

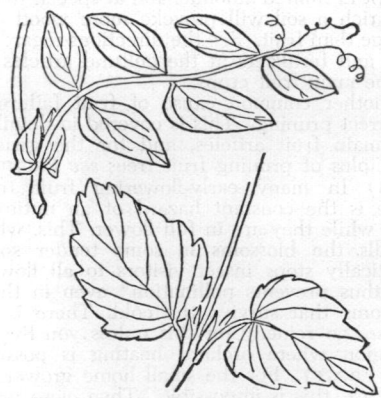

Stipules of the pea (*above*) and of a viburnum (*below*)

STITCHWORT. *See* Stellaria.

STIZOLOBIUM (sty-zo-lō′bi-um). Velvet bean. Annual, chiefly Old World tropical vines of the pea family, those below introduced into Fla. for ornament, but mostly as forage plants for regions too hot for good forage grasses. They are very strong-growing vines with alternate,* compound* leaves composed of 3 leaflets. Flowers showy, pea-like, white or deep purple, mostly in few-flowered clusters (racemes*). Fruit a heavy, ridged, hairy pod (legume*), with large, nearly round or oblongish seeds. (*Stizolobium* is from the Greek for stinging pods, in allusion to the stinging hairs found on the pods of some species.)

The velvet beans are coarse vines which will sprawl and completely cover the ground. If grown for ornament, and they grow very quickly, they must be given the support of a

---

* Special articles on the subjects indicated by an asterisk (*) will be found at the words so marked.

trellis or arbor. Sow the seeds only in warm, sandy soils, and in regions with much heat, a long growing season and no frost.

deeringianum. Florida velvet bean. A native of Indo-Malaya, but introduced into Fla. Vines very vigorous, sometimes 50 ft. long. Leaflets angled-ovalish, 2–6 in. long. Flowers purple, very showy, the cluster drooping, composed of 5–30 blooms, each about 1½ in. long. Pods black-hairy, the hairs irritating to the skin. Seeds variously marbled or speckled, generally black, brown, and whitish.

Hasjoo. Yokohama bean. Not over 20 ft. long, the ovalish leaflets 4–5 in. long. Flowers dark purple, about 1½ in. long, the clusters (racemes*) 4–6 in. long. Pods 3–4½ in. long, white-hairy, the seeds ashy. Jap.(?).

niveum. Lyon bean. Leaflets wavy-sur-surfaced. Flowers white, the clusters showy, long-stalked, 1–2 ft. long. Pods 4–5 in. long, curved both ends, white-hairy, the seeds flattish. Southern As. and in the Philippines.

pruritum. Cowage; also called cowitch. A tropical vine little known in the U.S., but sometimes grown in southern Fla. Flowers brownish-purple. Pods reddish or blackish, nearly straight, bristly, 3–4 in. long, the seeds spotted, oblongish, used as cattle feed. The bristles on the pod are extremely irritating. Tropics.

STOCK. In a grafting or budding operation that part of a plant which is to receive the bud or cion (which see). Professionals usually refer to the operation of getting the stock ready for its cion or bud as "dressing" the stock. For the details of this *see* GRAFTING, BUDDING. Stock is also a nursery term for a plant from which propagating material is derived.

STOCK (*Mathiola incana*). The several varieties of stocks include Brompton, Intermediate, Queen, and others, but the Ten-weeks fills every want and this variety is used generally either for the greenhouse or outdoors. It is not much subject to disease or destructive insects and makes a desirable plant for all to grow. Easily raised from seed, it makes a gorgeous show of color, many beautiful shades being now available in pastel colors.

Seed may be sown in Feb. or Mar. for outdoor use, and for greenhouse cultivation at any time, remembering that it takes 14 wks. to get them into flower. Seed should be sown in pans in any good soil not too finely sifted, free drainage being essential; to ward against damping-off,* the seed should be sown thinly, covered lightly with soil, and watered sparingly, and this caution should be observed throughout the life of the plant, as stocks resent overwatering.

Prick off into flats 3 in. apart when large enough to handle, and from these into pots for growing on, or into permanent benches or beds. It is important that the plants receive no check at any time, as upon this depends success or failure; this is chiefly the cause of an abnormal crop of single flowers. Beautiful spikes will be produced if all side shoots are carefully pinched out as they appear, and the large individual blooms may be used singly for design work. If a branching spike is preferred, the center should be pinched once, when the plants are 4 in. high, and the side shoots allowed to develop; these will make nice sprays for cut flowers.

Stocks require an even temperature of 50° and plenty of air at all times to keep the plants sturdy. Good plants can be grown in 5-in. and 6-in. pots and when they become filled with roots, applications of liquid manure once a week will prove beneficial. Plant in beds or benches 6 in. apart, 8 in. between the rows. There are many good strains of seed on the market, but it pays to save one's own seed. Select a single flower of good color, grow to a single spike, and allow it to develop its flowers fully. When a number of seed pods have formed, pinch out the end of the spike and allow the seeds to ripen naturally, save all the perfect seeds, and these will produce 90% double flowers. The seed may be kept several years in airtight containers, and still the germination will be 100%.

INSECT PESTS. Some cabbage and general leaf feeders attack stock. Control with pesticide #1 (*see* SPRAYS AND DUSTS).

DISEASES. Damping-off* is common on stock when seeds are sown in unsterilized soil (*see* SOIL STERILIZATION). Plants which are injured but do not die in the seedling stage may later have a condition known as wire stem. Slow-growing plants, if removed from the soil, will have a long, dark main root with little or no formation of small feeding roots. Prior to seeding or transplanting, the soil should be treated by spraying or drenching with pesticide #10 (*see* SPRAYS AND DUSTS).

If mosaic* virus disease is present, destroy the diseased plants and control aphids which transmit the virus to other plants.

Occasionally the southern wilt disease as described under SNAPDRAGON will kill stock plants. There is no pesticide which has proven itself, but the use of pesticide #10 should be helpful.

stoechadifolia, -us, -um (stee-kad-i-fō′li-a). With leaves like the stechados (*Lavandula Stoechas*); which was once assigned to the obsolete genus *Stoechas.*

Stoechas (stee′kas). See STOECHADIFOLIA.

STOKESIA (sto-key′zi-a or stokes′i-a). American hardy perennial herbs of only 1 species, belonging to the family Compositae. Stems purplish, covered with white matted hairs. Leaves alternate.* Flower heads 1–4 in. across, solitary or several on a branching stalk. Flower heads surrounded by several rings of bracts,* the outermost bracts leaf-like with spine-like teeth, the inner bracts scale-like, sheathing the flowers. Flowers lavender-blue or purplish blue. Ray florets* large, flattening into 5 lobes. Disk florets tubular, getting smaller toward the center. (Named for Jonathan Stokes, M.D., English botanist.)

Stokesia makes a good garden plant. Easily cult. in ordinary garden soil, which must be well drained, as it will not stand too much water at the roots during winter months. Propagated by seeds or division of roots. Seeds should be sown ⅛ in. deep in sandy soil in May in cold frame or outdoor seedbed.

---

* Special articles on the subjects indicated by an asterisk (*) will be found at the words so marked.

When large enough to handle they should be transplanted into nursery beds outdoors, transplanting to permanent positions the following spring. Division of roots should be made in early spring.

laevis. Stokes aster. Stems purplish, covered with white-woolly hairs. Leaves lance-shaped to 10 in. long. Flowers lavender-blue, in heads 2–4 in. across. S. Car. to La. The *var.* alba has white flowers; the *var.* rosea has pink flowers. The plant is sometimes sold as S. *cyanea.*

STOKES ASTER = *Stokesia laevis.*

STOLON. A horizontal stem, just above or beneath the soil, from the tip of which a new plant arises; also a bent shoot that takes root. Stolons are common in the blackberry and in some native azaleas and in many grasses. *See* RUNNER.

stolonifera, -us, -um (stow-lo-niff'er-ra). Bearing stolons.*

STOMA (plural *stomata*). A pore-like opening in the surface of a leaf, through which it takes in gases and discharges other gases and water vapor.

STONE CELLS. The minute gritty cells found in the flesh of the pear; often called grit cells. In some varieties the number and size of the stone cells make the fruit too gritty for pleasant eating.

STONE CRESS = *Aethionema.*

STONECROP. *See* SEDUM.

STONECROP FAMILY = Crassulaceae.

STONE FRUITS. Any fruit having a stone, specifically the plums and cherries; a drupe.

STONE PINE. Several cult. trees are so called, notably *Pinus Cembra* and *P. Pinea,* both European, and *P. cembroides* and *P. cembroides edulis* of the western U.S. and adjacent Mex. The American stone pines are often called nut pines or piñons. *See* PINE.

STONEROOT = *Collinsonia canadensis.*

STONEWORT = *Nitella.*

STOOL. The stump or base, or parent plant, which gives rise to various propagative organs, such as shoots for layering, rootstocks for division, bulbs, buds, etc. A plant is sometimes said to *stool* freely when it produces a crop of such organs. Sometimes stooling is induced as in layering.

STOOL LAYERING = Mound layering. *See* LAYERING.

STOPPING. To stop terminal growth by pinching off shoots, disbudding or pruning. *See* DISBUDDING, PRUNING.

STORAGE. Storage facilities are divided into four classes — a vegetable room especially built for the purpose, a cellar, an outdoor pit or trench, and the quick-freezing method. An abundance of vegetables may be stored by one of these methods for use in winter. It is easier and cheaper to store vegetables than to can them, and the quality is better.

Home storage now includes all methods. The conditions under which vegetables may be stored successfully are: crops of good quality, proper stage of maturity, right degree of temperature, and correct amount of moisture. The proper stage of maturity depends entirely upon the crop. Cabbage, onions, squash, pumpkins, and potatoes should be fully matured when stored; beets, carrots, parsnips, and turnips should be young and tender, as otherwise they become tough and woody. Beets, carrots, parsnips, turnips, and celery require cool, moist conditions; potatoes and cabbage need more moisture, as in too dry an atmosphere they tend to excessive shrinkage; onions and dried beans keep best in a cool, dry atmosphere, while squash, pumpkins, and sweet potatoes have better keeping qualities in a warm, dry place. The best keeping temperature for all vegetables except potatoes is just above freezing.

If space is available, the best way to keep vegetables for winter use is to build a special room with a dirt floor. If a corner of the cellar is used, the floor will probably be of concrete, in which case it should be wet down frequently. Size will depend upon the needs of the family, but a space six by eight feet usually will be ample. Two sides only need be partitioned, using the house walls as the other two, with a window to provide ventilation. Hinge the sash at the top so that it can be kept hooked open except in freezing weather.

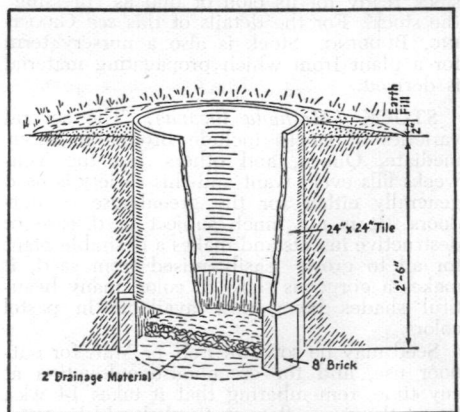

A simple and inexpensive storage device of tile drainpipe 24 × 24 in. sunk in the ground with a wooden or metal top.

Screening is necessary to prevent the entry of flies and vermin, and burlap or sacking may be used over the window to darken the room. Cover each side of the studding with building paper and matched boards. This will leave an air space of approximately four inches between the walls, so that heat from the furnace will not affect the room temperature. The entrance door should fit tightly. Pieces of board should be laid loose on the floor along the wall, and slatted crates for potatoes set on these to allow circulation of air beneath. Tiering the crates will save space. Shelves

---

* Special articles on the subjects indicated by an asterisk (*) will be found at the words so marked.

should be built along the walls to hold canned products and fruits. Beneath the shelves may be built storage bins for vegetables. Many of the root crops keep best when placed on the dirt floor, covered with moist soil, and dug as needed. Cabbage should be put on the shelves, so that air can freely circulate around it. Onions keep well in crates. Parsnips may be left in the garden all winter or stored, but not buried. Storage rooms may also be made under outbuildings or by excavating in banks. Any cellar without a furnace makes an excellent storage space.

Outdoor storage pits or trenches, although not so easy of access in freezing weather, may be used to bury root crops, potatoes, and cabbage. The easiest way is to dig a shallow pit, 10 to 12 inches deep, and line it with leaves, straw or hay to a depth of eight inches. If the pit is located on a slight elevation, a ditch may be dug around it to facilitate drainage. Place the vegetables in the storage pit in a conical heap, and cover with a layer of leaves, straw or hay. Cover with soil to hold the material in place. Before freezing weather put on more soil, and extend a tuft of straw through the top of the pile for ventilation. Several small pits are better than one large one. A more permanent and better storage device, suggested by the Dept. of Agriculture at the University of Indiana, is of drain tile and its construction is shown in the illustration. Celery keeps better in a trench than any other way. It should be taken from the ground before freezing, the plants placed close together, and the trench covered with boards nailed together in the shape of a trough and inverted over it, and the whole covered with litter and soil.

QUICK FREEZING. The storage of meat and vegetables for home use has been revolutionized by the sub-zero deep freezer for preserving perishables until needed. It has limitations, however, as far as the storage of vegetables is concerned, even if they have been well grown. Those not suited to the quick-freezing method include lettuce, tomatoes, celery, cucumbers, and some others that are usually eaten raw. But excellent results are reasonably certain with spinach, parsnip, rhubarb, muskmelon, snap beans, peas, lima beans, beets, carrots, cabbage and cauliflower, both kinds of broccoli, asparagus, kale, and winter squash.

STORAX. *See* STYRAX.

STORAX FAMILY = Styracaceae.

STORK'S-BILL. *See* PELARGONIUM and ERODIUM.

STOVE. An old hort. term for a warm, moist greenhouse. The plants grown in such a temperature were called stove plants. The modern equivalent for a stove house is the tropical house. *See* GREENHOUSE.

STRAIN. A not easily definable category of plants within a variety (which see). The word *strain* is most often used to indicate a group of plants, in a variety, with some character insufficient to make them worth describing as a distinct variety, but different enough to be entitled to some designation. There may thus be a tall, weak, strong, or sickly strain of a particular variety. *Strain*, as a hort. term, is not much used, and seldom with precision.

straminea, -us, -um (stra-min'e-a). Straw-colored.

stramineofructa, -us, -um (stra-min-ee-o-fruk'ta). With straw-colored fruit.

Stramonium (stra-mō'ni-um). An obsolete generic name for plants now included in the genus *Datura*.

STRAND PLANTS. *See* SEASIDE GARDENS.

STRANVAESIA (stran-vee'zi-a). Asiatic evergreen shrubs and trees of the rose family, comprising only 4 or 5 species, of which S. *davidiana*, of western China, is cult. for ornament. It is a broad-leaved evergreen shrub, 15–20 ft. high, with alternate,* oblongish leaves 3–4 in. long, pointed at the tip and wedge-shaped at the base, without marginal teeth. Flowers white, in a terminal, profuse cluster (corymb*), nearly 4 in. wide, the calyx* turban-shaped and 5-toothed. Petals 5. Stamens* about 20. Fruit fleshy, nearly globe-shaped, about ⅓ in. wide, scarlet. June. Hardy from zone* 5 southward. Propagated by hardwood cuttings (*see* CUTTINGS). The *var.* undulata has wavy-margined leaves. (Named for William Fox-Strangways, English botanist.)

STRAP-LEAVED TURNIP = *Brassica Rapa lorifolia*.

STRATIFY, STRATIFICATION. *See* SEEDS AND SEEDAGE.

STRATIOTES (stra-ti-ō'tees). European aquatic perennial herbs of only one species of the family Hydrocharitaceae. This is S. *aloides*, the water-soldier or water-aloe. Rootstocks short and thick. Leaves sword-shaped, fleshy and stiff, the margins sharply toothed. Flowering stalk 5–6 in. high, bearing at its summit a 2-leaved sheath, enclosing several white male flowers, or 1 white female flower. Fruit 6-celled, with many seeds. These plants rise to the surface before flowering and then after flowering sink to the bottom. Easily propagated by the division of the rootstocks in early spring. (*Stratiotes* is from the Greek for soldier, in allusion to the sword-shaped leaves. It is also a specific name at *Pistia*.)

STRAWBERRY. Perennial herbs comprising perhaps 35 species and constituting the genus **Fragaria** (fra-gair'i-a) of the rose family. They are essentially stemless plants except for the long runners,* and are chiefly found in the north temperate zone, but in the western part of the New World some extend southward to Patagonia and one of these, *F. chiloensis*, has entered largely into the making of the cult. strawberry. Leaves compound,* the leaflets 3. Flowers generally white (rarely reddish), in few-flowered clusters at the end of a slender stalk that arises from the ground. In some forms the flowers are unisexual.* Calyx* 5-toothed, the lobes spreading and

---

* Special articles on the subjects indicated by an asterisk (*) will be found at the words so marked.

forming the hull of the strawberry. Petals 5, mostly broad and rounded. Stamens* many. Fruit (in ordinary sense) the much-enlarged, juicy, very fleshy and delicious receptacle,* in which or upon the surface of which are embedded the true fruits which are small achenes,* commonly but incorrectly called the seeds. (*Fragaria* is from the Latin for fragrance, in allusion to the pleasantly aromatic fruit.) "Fruit" as used below means the ripened receptacle.* All flower in early spring.

For culture and varieties *see* below. The four species appear to be the ones most involved in the production of the cult. strawberry, which is the result of long years of breeding, mostly in France, upon plants of American origin. For the barren strawberry *see* WALD-STEINIA FRAGARIOIDES; for the mock or Indian strawberry *see* DUCHESNEA INDICA.

F. chiloensis. A low, bushy plant, its runners* usually forming after fruit is set. Leaves green and glossy above, pale bluish-white beneath, the leaflets broadly wedge-shaped, toothed. Flowers about ¾ in. wide, inclined to droop, standing below the foliage. Fruit firm, large, dark red, the hull* large. Alaska to Patagonia.

F. moschata. Hautbois strawberry. Resembling *F. vesca*, but taller, more hairy, the hull* of the fruit strongly bent backward. Fruit musky, dull red. Eu. More known abroad than here, but it has entered into some cult. varieties.

F. vesca. A sparsely hairy herb 9–12 in. high, the leaves thin and light green. Flower cluster forking, about the same height as the leaves, the leaflets of which are angularly wedge-shaped. Flowers about ½ in. wide, perfect,* standing above the foliage. Fruit small, hemispheric or slightly elongated, the hull* widely spreading. Eu. and possibly (in a form of it) in N.A. Very widely used in strawberry breeding, most of the late fruiting sorts (everbearing) having blood of *F. vesca* in them.

F. virginiana. The common wild strawberry of eastern N.A. A low herb, 4–8 in. high, making runners* from the start. Leaves thin, light green both sides, the leaflets wedge-shaped and toothed. Flower clusters long-stalked, usually erect, and standing below the foliage. Flowers about ¾ in. wide, perfect.* Fruit small, but very sweet, its small hull* spreading. Eastern N.A. It is rarely cult., but has entered into some modern hort. varieties of the strawberry.

STRAWBERRY CULTURE

Few strawberries of today live up to their Latin name of *Fragaria* which Linnaeus gave them over two hundred years ago (1753). He knew the common wood strawberry of Europe, which had already been cultivated for three hundred years, and the common strawberry of eastern North America which he christened *Fragaria virginiana*. Both these wild strawberries were and still are deliciously fragrant.

Earlier, there was introduced into France another American strawberry, found first in Chile and named *Fragaria chiloense*, but subsequently known to grow along the Paci-fic Coast from Alaska to Patagonia. From these three sorts have come the hundreds of varieties known here today, many of their ancestors being produced by French hybridists. The French were so enthusiastic about the garden possibilities of the Chilean sort that to this day their word for strawberry is *fraisier*, taken from the name of Captain Frazier, the young French officer who first brought the plant from Chile to France in 1712.

Before this the only strawberries in cultivation were variants of the common wild strawberries so that the fruit as we know it today is a fairly modern one — many of the others in this book having been cultivated for two thousand years and some of them much longer.

In the course of the breeding which has produced the modern strawberry, we have enormously increased the size, juiciness, and keeping qualities of the berry, but lost some of its fragrance. And somewhere along the line of its brief history the strawberry has lost, in some varieties, its normal sex life. These plants are self-sterile, not because they are infertile to their own pollen, but for the much more serious reason that some varieties produce no male flowers (anthers and pollen) at all and hence depend upon other varieties that do. Such self-sterile varieties must be interplanted with normal-flowered sorts, generally at the rate of 3 normal-flowered sorts to 10 self-sterile kinds, or there will be no fruit.

The varieties listed below will not need this treatment but some good local varieties, offered by nurserymen, are self-sterile and should be so designated by the dealer. If you purchase any varieties other than those listed below, be sure to ask whether or not they are self-fertile. Often purely local varieties unknown beyond the range of their immediate use, and too numerous to list here, are excellent. The only catch is to be sure they are self-fertile.

The strawberry is, as grown, a biennial herb that produces many runners, which root at the joints and upon which we depend for the propagation of new plants. These are needed constantly, because the newly set out plants do not or should not produce any fruit the first year, an abundant crop the second year, and a dwindling one or none at all the third. The home grower will be wise to purchase a few plants each year, unless he has the time and space to propagate new plants from the runners that will be freely produced during the life of the "mother" plant, *i.e.*, the one which he has set out and which will produce fruit only in the second season.

Purchased plants will or should have a few leaves, all but two or three of which should be pinched off before planting. It is well, also, to shear off about one quarter of the root mass at the lower end. The plants must be kept moist if there is any interval between their arrival from the nursery and actual planting. They will grow in any good garden

---

* Special articles on the subjects indicated by an asterisk (*) will be found at the words so marked.

soil — slightly acid, if possible — which preferably should have been cultivated for a year or two and *must be kept free of weeds.* If weedy, the runners and the weeds will soon make an inextricable mat which makes cultivation difficult or impossible. The area between the rows must also be free of weeds, or mulching with straw will be equally impossible, and this is a desirable feature of all good strawberry culture.

Two methods of handling strawberries are available to the home grower — in hills or rows. If you have room for only a few plants they are best isolated in hills (*i.e.,* isolated patches), so that cultivation can go on all around them. If your planting is more extensive it is probably better to grow them in rows. Hills should be about 12 inches apart each way, with one plant in each hill. Rows ought to be at least 30 inches apart, and the plants set about 12 inches apart in the rows. If, as will often happen, the newly set plants bear a few flowers the first season, they should all be picked off, because no fruit should be allowed to mature until the second season.

In planting, see that the new plants are set at the same level as they were when in the nursery — not buried too deep, or with their roots exposed because of too shallow planting. In regions of frost, plants not set deep enough are often frost-heaved and will then die if not immediately replanted.

STRAWBERRY

At the left, an old plant not worth saving. At the right, a vigorous young plant upon which successful growers depend for new stock.

Being a true herb, the strawberry has a much wider geographical range than the fruits that have woody stems, so that there are few regions, except the deserts, where some variety cannot be grown, at least by the home planter. Commercially, they are limited by such factors as keeping quality, which do not affect the home grower.

VARIETIES

Some of the varieties are everbearing, the significance of which will be noted presently. While strawberries are widely distributed, they do not like extremely cold winters, and only a few varieties are suited to zones* 1 and 2.

BELT. *See* William Belt.

BLAKEMORE. Early ripening, with a medium-sized, somewhat tart berry, good for preserving.

CATSKILL. Late-ripening or midseason variety, the berries large, of good quality. Does better in the northern part of the country.

CHESAPEAKE. Late variety, the fruit large, scarlet, firm, and of very good quality.

DORSETT. An early variety, the berries large, lighter in color than some, very juicy and sweet. Apt to flower early and may be caught by late frosts in the northern part of the country.

DUNLAP. Valuable as one of the few varieties suited to cool regions. Berries medium-sized, red, and excellent for preserving.

FAIRFAX. An early variety and an old favorite. Fruit dark red, sweet, and does not keep well, so should not be left on the plant when ripe. Many consider this the finest strawberry in cultivation.

GEM. Everbearing. Useful mostly for late summer and fall fruit; is on the tart side. Useless for spring fruit.

HOWARD 17. This is often incorrectly listed in the catalogues as Premier, but by whatever name, it is one of the best strawberries for the home grower, for productiveness, and for its medium-large berries. The latter are better in the northern than in the southern part of its range.

KLONDIKE. Useful in regions of great heat. Berry slightly acid, the quality only fair, although it is one of the chief varieties to reach the New York market in February–March.

KLONMORE. Useful in the South in a narrow belt about 100 miles north of the Gulf of Mexico. Fruit not up to other varieties.

MASTODON. Everbearing. Unlike most everbearing varieties, this also produces berries in the spring, and although many fail to do so in the autumn, it usually fruits also in fall. Berries of fair quality, somewhat acid.

POCAHONTAS. Flavor tart and good; berries large, red, juicy, ripening about a week later than Blakemore. Originated by U.S. Department of Agriculture. Best from zone* 5 southward.

PREMIER. *See* Howard 17.

PROGRESSIVE. Everbearing. Useful chiefly because it is one of the few everbearing types fit for the North. Fruit conical, dark glossy red, mild and only slightly acid.

ROCKHILL. Everbearing, but often failing to produce fall fruit. Berries similar to Progressive and perhaps not superior, but the plant is very hardy to cold.

SPARKLE. Late-fruiting and one of the best varieties for the home grower. Berries

---

* Special articles on the subjects indicated by an asterisk (*) will be found at the words so marked.

medium to large, very attractive as to looks and flavor. It was originated by scientists at New Jersey Agricultural Experiment Station at New Brunswick.

STELEMASTER. Immune to red stele. Not unlike Blakemore.

SURECROP. Immune to red stele. A var. recently developed by U.S. Department of Agriculture.

TEMPLE. Midseason variety, equal to Sparkle in quality, and originated at Maryland Agricultural Experiment Station at College Park.

WILLIAM BELT. A late-fruiting variety, often listed in the catalogues as Belt. Fruit early to midseason, large, apt to be irregular in shape, deep red, juicy; for the northern home grower, but it does not like drought.

Some of the varieties are marked *everbearing*. The term is really a misnomer, for no strawberry is actually everbearing. The plant is normally spring-flowering, and May and June the usual time of fruit-ripening, depending on the season and your locality. A few aberrant plants have in the past shown a tendency to prolong fruiting into summer and even into the autumn, often at the expense of spring fruiting. Over the years several varieties with this tendency have been isolated, and those who want to have strawberries in the late summer and fall will always choose such varieties, perhaps not knowing that they do not compare with spring-fruiting kinds.

CARE OF THE STRAWBERRY

Once your so-called "mother plants" have been set out as early in the spring as the ground can be worked, you must cultivate your plants and watch for the development of new leaves. Each plant will at first have only two or three, if you followed the directions given earlier, but by one month from planting time it should have 6–7 leaves, and in two months about a dozen. Also in two months it will send out its first runner, of which it may well produce nearly a dozen before the end of the summer. Unless you intend to propagate from these long, prostrate runners, they should all be cut off, in order to produce the greatest crop of leaves possible this first season. If all runners are cut off, the plant may well produce 60–80 leaves, but half this number or less if the runners are left on.

The importance of getting a good crop of leaves the first season is realized only when it is known that, from near the base of leafstalks, the plant matures the buds that will produce flowers and fruit next season. Hence, the value of cutting off all runners if you want maximum yields next year. For those who grow their plants in rows it is often advisable to leave one or two runners on the mother plant. These may be used to propagate the young plants that inevitably root from the tips or joints of all runners. Such a procedure is to be recommended if you use the matted row method. This permits enough runners to root so that your original row of spaced mother plants becomes a matted row of constantly renewed new ones. From such a row all plants that have fruited should be dug out. The matted row method is preferred by many home growers, although it needs constant attention to remove old plants, keep the mat free of weeds, and especially to prevent too many runners from rooting, which will ultimately make the row too crowded.

Because the strawberry is really a biennial, the mother plant should be destroyed as soon as it has finished fruiting. If you want to propagate your own plants separately, take the cut-off runners to a separate bed, and so get the young plants ready for spring planting the next year.

As cautioned earlier, cut off all flowers that bloom the first year. Your plants at this stage will hence be denuded of all flowers and runners and in prime shape to produce (hidden) fruit buds for next year's crop. They will go through the winter in the South without protection, but in zones* 2 and 3, some protection must be provided.

Wheat, rye, or barley straw make the best winter mulch for strawberries, put on about 4 inches deep. In zones* 2 and 3 it should go on about October 20. It need not go on until Thanksgiving in zone* 4. In some sections snow cover may be all the plants need for protection from winter cold, but it is not always safe to rely on this.

In the spring, as soon as frosts are no longer expected, pull the straw from the crowns of the plants and leave it in the row between them. Add some more if the mulch around and between the plants is too skimpy. There should be enough to keep the fruit from getting mud-spattered when it is "teeming." You cannot, of course, cultivate the mulched row.

The subsequent management of a strawberry bed is really a matter of your own choice. Some professional growers plow under all plants that have fruited, well knowing that if left for a third year the yield will be poor or none. In other words they put out fresh stock each year, so that they always have a crop of (a) freshly set out plants that will not bloom until next year, and (b) a current bearing crop, which will be destroyed after fruiting.

The amateur grower, without space or time to propagate his own, unless he uses the matted row method already mentioned, will likely buy fresh plants each year from a reliable nursery. You can judge the number of plants you will need by the fact that a single plant (counting its runner-progeny) may produce a quart of berries. This means that a matted row of strawberries should produce about 2 quarts of berries for each 3 feet of row. Isolated plants in hills will yield more than this, but there is, of course, the loss of space needed for cultivation all around the individual hills. The hill method will always

---

* Special articles on the subjects indicated by an asterisk (*) will be found at the words so marked.

produce the largest and finest fruit, but not so many berries as the row culture.

INSECT PESTS. Several species of grubs attacking roots may be controlled by application of pesticide #15, #16 or #13 (see SPRAYS AND DUSTS) to soil, at rate recommended on package, before planting. Cultivate chemicals into soil. Leaf rollers may be controlled when they appear (best when small) by TDE or pesticide #21. Observe proper precautions on label. Either of these materials and pesticide #20 will control snout beetles that attack and nip off blossoms in spring. Pesticide #20 controls spittlebugs.

Other leaf feeders and sawflies succumb to pesticide #1. Root- and foliage-feeding aphids are kept down by pesticide #21 or #20. Aphids carrying yellows disease require 2 aphid sprays in early spring and 2 in early fall for control.

DISEASES. The most serious disease of strawberry is red stele. Large areas in a bed, particularly where water collects following a heavy rain, may be completely killed. The central core or stele of the main roots will be bright red. There are several strains of the fungus,* some of which are more virulent than others. In those areas where the more virulent fungus strains are present, only the strawberry varieties Stelemaster and Surecrop may be grown.

A wilt* disease (see CHRYSANTHEMUM) may cause a gradual decline of plants. Lower leaves turn brown and a great reduction in crop may result. It is best not to plant strawberries in soil where tomatoes have been raised during recent years, because the disease may be more prevalent.

Several leafspot* diseases cause red or gray spots on leaves and on stems and berry caps. Use pesticide #8A (see SPRAYS AND DUSTS) just as plants break dormancy in the spring. If gray mold* appears on the fruit, use pesticide #2 at 7-day intervals.

STRAWBERRY BEGONIA = Strawberry geranium.

STRAWBERRY-BLITE = *Chenopodium capitatum*. See the list at WEEDS.

STRAWBERRY-BUSH = *Euonymus americanus* and *E. atropurpureus*.

STRAWBERRY FAMILY = Rosaceae.

STRAWBERRY GERANIUM = *Saxifraga sarmentosa*.

STRAWBERRY GUAVA = *Psidium cattleianum*. See GUAVA.

STRAWBERRY PEAR. See HYLOCEREUS UNDATUS.

STRAWBERRY-RASPBERRY = *Rubus illecebrosus*.

STRAWBERRY-SHRUB = *Calycanthus*.

STRAWBERRY-SHRUB FAMILY = Calycanthaceae.

STRAWBERRY TOMATO. See PHYSALIS.

STRAWBERRY TREE = *Arbutus Unedo*.

STRAWFLOWER. The common everlasting known as strawflower is *Helichrysum bracteatum* (which see). For another plant so called see UVULARIA GRANDIFLORA.

STREAK. The term applied to those virus diseases which produce brown or black streaks along the stem or leaves of the plant. Virus streak in tomato may be caused by a single virus or by a combination of two different virus diseases. Because tobacco virus may be transmitted to tomato by hands of smokers, those people working with tomato should wash hands before working with the plants and should not smoke while handling plants.

STREET TREES. Public thoroughfares are generally surrounded by poor soil conditions and, in most cases, cover most of the available planting area with a layer of asphalt or concrete, which is an almost perfect insulator against air and moisture. Hence, every possible aid must be given in the planting of street trees. They should not be set in a hole just large enough to receive the roots but in pits, excavated to a depth of three feet and measuring six feet square, from which the soil has been removed, broken up, and some good fertilizer added. These are filled to the proper depth and the tree planted, taking care that it is set straight and the soil well tramped about the roots. Pits of this size will be suitable for standard nursery stock which measures from nine to twelve feet in height. For details see PLANTING.

Young trees should be protected by iron guards, about eight feet high, made in two sections so that they may be removed. Leave them in place for about three years until the tree is established. In cases where young specimens lean, due to settling or mechanical injury, they should be supplied with guy wires, fastened about the trunk by means of sections of rubber hose passed over the wires to prevent cutting the bark. Where there is but a small space between the curb and sidewalk, or where the street and sidewalk completely surround the tree, iron gratings, three feet square and made in two sections, so they may be removed, should be placed around the base of the tree. This permits all of the space about the tree to be available for use and, at the same time, allows for moisture, ventilation, and cultivation. Also, young trees should be protected from the rather persistent attention of dogs by a loose collar of tin extending up the trunk high enough to spare the lower bark from constant wetting.

Safety is the first essential in the pruning of street trees and calls for the immediate removal of all dead and diseased trees or branches which might be a source of danger to the public. For much the same reason, the form and shape of street trees should be such that they will not hinder or endanger traffic. The trunk should be kept clean for a distance of at least twelve feet from the ground. Branches should clear sidewalks by ten feet and those over streets should be so pruned as to permit a clearance of at least fifteen feet.

Branches should never completely cover the street or adjacent properties. Avenues which are entirely shaded are damp and

---

* Special articles on the subjects indicated by an asterisk (*) will be found at the words so marked.

poorly aired. The same is true when street trees overshade private property as well as often damaging roofs and chimneys by sweeping against them and clogging gutters or drains with leaves. When pruning street trees, the whole planting, rather than the individual specimen, should be considered. Only in this way is it possible to obtain symmetry. In many instances, the removal of lateral branches will stimulate top growth which should be trimmed back occasionally to prevent a lanky appearance.

Spraying requires both curative and preventive treatment. Those trees which have chronic diseases or infestations should be sprayed regularly. The appearance of a new pest calls for immediate action. Most of the common diseases and insects and their proper treatment will be found in the description of the various species.

VARIETIES

The problem of selecting proper types of trees for avenue ornamentation should be carefully considered before such projects are undertaken. Gasoline fumes, smoke, and dust have forced the discontinuance of much ma-

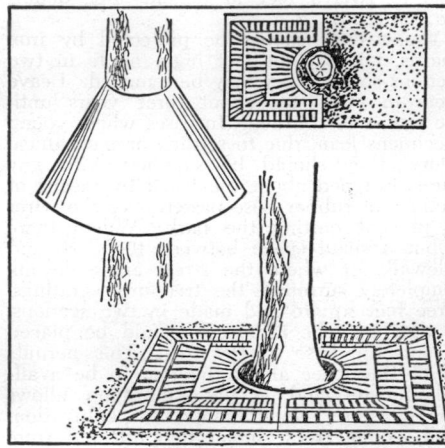

TREE GUARDS

At the left, a practical sheet-metal guard to keep animals from climbing tree trunks. At the right, a fine type of grating for street trees, removable, and allowing air and water to reach the soil.

terial which is well adapted in type of growth to street planting. In general public thoroughfares may be divided into three classes: wide streets, narrow streets, and parkways. In really congested districts where smoke and dust are rampant there is little choice, and the tree-of-Heaven, *Ailanthus altissima,* or the London plane, *Platanus acerifolia,* will probably have to be used.

Wide avenues in residential districts are best planted with large trees such as: the American elm (*Ulmus americana*), the Chinese elm (*Ulmus parvifolia*), the sugar maple (*Acer saccharum*), scarlet oak (*Quercus coccinea*), red oak (*Quercus rubra*), the willow oak (*Quercus Phellos*), white oak (*Quercus alba*), wych elm (*Ulmus glabra*), also *Tilia europaea, T. cordata,* and *T. euchlora.* In good soil, *Magnolia acuminata* may be used.

There are not many suitable planting materials for narrow streets and, if those mentioned above are used, an excessive amount of pruning is necessary to prevent undue shade. Narrow-growing trees are most desirable and, while plenty of such habit are in cultivation, comparatively few will withstand the hardships of roadside planting. Probably the easiest to obtain are the Norway maple (*Acer platanoides*), the pin oak (*Quercus palustris*), and the maidenhair-tree (*Ginkgo biloba*). The city of Rochester, New York, maintains its own nursery for the propagation of special street trees and is growing particularly erect or fastigiate* forms of the American elm, American linden, and Norway maple for this work.

The parkway allows the greatest possibilities in street planting. The sides may be planted with any of the materials already mentioned, provided full sunlight may be permitted to reach the center area. This may then be planted with some form of flowering tree. Magnolias are well suited for this purpose, as are the flowering crabapples.

The proper distance to space street trees varies greatly according to the material used. In general 60 to 75 ft. is proper for the larger species on wide streets with 40 ft. as a minimum for narrow-growing forms on smaller thoroughfares.

In general flowering or heavy-fruiting trees are not desirable for street work because they require good soil and plenty of nourishment for proper growth, conditions which are noticeably absent in most cases. Also their flowers and fruit clutter the street and are a nuisance. Trees which have vigorous root systems should not be employed, as they get into sewers and water mains, causing damage. The following, although sometimes used, cannot be recommended for this work: box-elder (*Acer Negundo*), silver maple (*Acer saccharinum*), willows, poplars, birches, *Ulmus pumila, Catalpa, Gleditsia triacanthos, Platanus occidentalis,* and the horsechestnut (*Aesculus Hippocastanum*). Conifers are seldom a success in avenue ornamentation. *See also* TREES, TREE SURGERY. — D. W.

STRELITZIA (stre-lit′zi-a). Tender South African perennials, comprising about 5 species of the family Musaceae, with thick, underground, woody rootstocks, which in some species grow above the ground and become tree-like. Leaves large, banana-like, long-stalked. Flowering stalks terminal or growing from the axils* of the leaves, bearing 1–2 large, boat-shaped bracts* which are sometimes colored, enclosing the showy

---

* Special articles on the subjects indicated by an asterisk (*) will be found at the words so marked.

flowers. Calyx* of 3 colored sepals, not joined, keel-shaped. Corolla of 3 petals, 2 joined and tongue-shaped, generally blue, the odd petal white or yellow, and standing erect. (Named for the wife of King George III, Charlotte Sophia, of the Mecklenburg-Strelitz family.)

In wide cultivation, and grown in the warm greenhouse for house or porch decoration. They can be grown outdoors where the temperature does not drop below 50°. Propagated by suckers or division of the rootstocks in spring. They can be grown in potting mixture* 4, in a winter temperature of 55°–65° and summer of 65°–90°. They prefer full sun all the year and plenty of water during summer months.

nicolai. Growing to 18 ft. high or more and with a woody stem. Leafstalks deeply grooved on the upper side. Leaves to 4 ft. long and 2 ft. wide. Bracts* purplish, boat-shaped, to 15 in. or more long, enclosing the white, blue-tongued flowers.

reginae. Bird-of-paradise flower. Growing to 3 ft., with underground, woody rootstocks, but no trunk. Leaves basal, to 1½ ft. long, and 6 in. wide, stiff, with strong leafstalks. Bracts boat-shaped, purplish, to 8 in. long, enclosing the orange-yellow flowers, which have a blue tongue. Widely grown and often in florists' windows.

STREPTANTHERA (strep-tan'the-ra). A small genus of bulbous herbs from S. Af., family Iridaceae, allied to *Ixia* and distinguished from it only by technical characters. They are low herbs with sword-shaped leaves, mostly basal and arranged in fan-like clusters. Flowers solitary, or a few, growing in a spathe* at the end of a slender stalk. Petals 6, joined at the base into a short tube, to which the stamens* are attached. Both the species below should be grown as is *Ixia* (which see). (*Streptanthera* is from *streptos*, twisted, and anther,* in allusion to the attachment of the anthers.)

cuprea. Not over 9 in. high, the leaves weak, slender, pointed, 2–4 in. long, about ⅓ in. wide. Flowers 2 or 3, the tube purple, the segments copper-colored, but purplish and yellow-spotted toward the base. June.

elegans. About 9 in. high, the leaves blunt, but with a short, weak, spine-like tip, the leaves arranged in a fan-like, flat cluster. Flowers pinkish-white, but the center blackish and yellow-spotted, the tubular base purple. June.

STREPTOCARPUS (strep-to-kar'pus). Cape primrose. Tender perennial herbs, comprising about 80 species of the family Gesneriaceae, natives of South Africa and Madagascar. They are low-growing plants, producing 1 or several spreading, basal leaves or sometimes with a short stem and opposite* leaves. Flowering stalks growing from the axils* of the leaves, bearing 1–several, pale purple, blue, or reddish flowers. Calyx* of 5 sepals. Corolla 5-lobed, tubular, opening obliquely into 2 lips,* upper of 2 lobes, lower of 3, the throat sometimes hairy and veined with another color. Stamens* 2. Fruit a many-seeded capsule.* (*Streptocar-*

pus is from the Greek for twisted and fruit, in allusion to the fruit.)

These are showy plants which can be grown for house decoration, and need a warm-temperate greenhouse. Easily propagated from seeds, which should be sown ¹⁄₁₆ in. deep in a mixture of equal parts of finely sifted sand, leaf mold, and loam in pans, in a temperature of 55°–65° in Feb. or Mar. They should be kept in a moist, shady position. As soon as large enough to handle they should be pricked off into pans 2 in. apart in a similar mixture, later potting into potting mixture* 4. They prefer cool, moist conditions at all times, a temperature of 40°–50° in winter and of 55°–65° in summer.

hybridus. Leaves 2–3, dark green, ovalish, from 6–12 in. long, wrinkled, covered with soft hairs, the margins wavy. Flowering stalks several, each bearing 6–8 flowers in a cluster. Flowers bright purple, the throat striped dark brown. Corolla tube to 2 in. long. Of hybrid origin and a rather loose designation for many cult. forms.

STREPTOPUS (strep'to-pus). Twisted stalk. Hardy perennial herbs, comprising about 6 species of the lily family and natives of the temperate regions of the northern hemisphere. They have creeping rootstocks which are much-branched. Stems 2½–3 ft. high, hairy, and slightly branched. Leaves alternate, ovalish or lance-shaped, usually clasping the stem, parallel-veined. Flowers bell-shaped, nodding, pink or greenish-white, growing 1–2 on a short twisted stalk from the axils* of the leaves. Calyx* of 3 colored sepals. Corolla of 3 petals alternating with the sepals. Stamens* 6. Fruit a berry. (*Streptopus* is from the Greek for twisted stalk, in allusion to the twisted flower stalks.)

They are not of much garden importance, sometimes grown in the wild garden. Propagated by division of the rootstocks. They prefer damp, shady places, and acid soils of pH 4–5.

amplexifolius. Growing to 3 ft. high. Leaves clasping the stem, ovalish, 3–6 in. long, bright green on under side. Flowers greenish-white, ½ in. long, 2 on a twisted stalk, growing from the axils* of the leaves. Berry red. N.A.

roseus. Growing to 2½ ft. high. Leaves partly clasping the stem, broadly lance-shaped, to 4 in. long. Flowers purplish-pink, ½ in. across, usually 1 flower growing from the axils of the leaves. Berry red. Eastern N.A.

STREPTOSOLEN (strep-to-so'len). Tender perennial shrubs of the family Solanaceae and natives of Colombia and Ecuador. The only species is S. jamesoni (also known as *Browallia jamesoni*) and is of sprawling habit, growing to 6 ft. Leaves alternate,* small, ovalish, wrinkled, slightly hairy, short-stalked. Flowers orange-red, short-stalked in terminal, umbel*-like clusters. Calyx tubular. Corolla tubular, opening salverwise, to ¾ in. across. Tube to 1¼ in. long and twisted. Stamens 4, in pairs, 2 long, and 2 short, growing on the calyx tube. Fruit a capsule.*

---

* Special articles on the subjects indicated by an asterisk (*) will be found at the words so marked.

Mostly grown as greenhouse plants for house decoration, but excellent for the flower border where they can be lifted and taken care of in the greenhouse during the winter in a temperature of 50°–60°. They can of course be grown entirely outdoors in the extreme South and in Calif., where they are very beautiful when trained on a wall. Propagated by cuttings of the young shoots inserted in sand in early spring. When large enough to handle they should be potted into potting mixture* 1 and later into No. 3. They need staking and pinching and can be trained into any shape. (*Streptosolen* is from the Greek for twisted and tube, in allusion to the twisted corolla tube.)

striata, -us, -um (stry-ā′ta). Striped.

stricta, -us, -um (strick′ta). Strict; *i.e.,* rigid and upright, with few or no branches.

STRIKE. To root cuttings successfully; as in the phrase "to strike cuttings of carnations."

STRING BEAN = *Phaseolus vulgaris.* For culture *see* BEAN.

STRINGLESS BEAN. A very young string bean, or a relatively stringless variety of string beans, with little or no "string" along the seams of the pod. *See* BEAN.

STRINGY-BARK. *See* EUCALYPTUS.

STRIPED MAPLE = *Acer pensylvanicum. See* MAPLE.

STROBILANTHES (stro-bi-lan′theez). Perennial herbs or shrubs, comprising about 300 species of the family Acanthaceae, natives of Asia and tropical Africa. Leaves opposite.* Flowers blue, violet, or white, solitary or in clusters, terminal or growing from the axils* of the leaves. Calyx of 5 sepals. Corolla irregular,* tubular, widely opening. Stamens* 2–4. Fruit a capsule.* (*Strobilanthes* is from the Greek for cone and flower, in allusion to the flower cluster, which is cone-like.)

Of considerable garden importance, and grown in the warm greenhouse for their ornamental foliage. They are difficult to cultivate, as they require a constant warm temperature, moist conditions, and syringing daily. Propagated by cuttings of young shoots in Feb. or Mar.

dyerianus. A hairy shrub. Leaves broadly lance-shaped, to 8 in. long, iridescent on the upper side and purplish-blue. Flowers light blue, 1½ in. long, in terminal clusters. Burma.

isophyllus. A low-growing, bushy shrub. Leaves lance-shaped, to 4 in. long, the margins toothed. Flowers blue and white, to 1 in. long, growing in clusters from the axils* of the leaves. India.

STROBILE. Loosely, a small cone; specifically, the cone-like mass of scales and their fruits found in trees like the birch or in the fruits of the hop. *See* CONE.

Strobus (strow′bus). A generic name once applied to certain of the 5-leaved pines and

Strobile of the hop

now left as the specific name of the white pine (*Pinus Strobus*). *See* PINE.

STROMBOCACTUS (strom-bo-kak′tus). A cult. species of Mexican cacti, S. disciformis, cult. for interest or ornament in desert gardens in frostless regions or in the succulent house in the North. It is a top-shaped or nearly round, almost spineless cactus, not over 2 in. in diameter. The plant body is ribbed and tubercled, but the tubercles are not on the ribs and in youth have 1–4 needle-like white spines which fall off as the plant gets old. Flowers about ¾ in. long, white or pink, but red on the outside, and scaly, the scales with paper margins. For cult. *see* CACTI. (*Strombocactus* is from the Greek for top and *Cactus,* in allusion to the top-shaped plant body.)

STRONG. As applied to soils *strong* means that they are productive or fertile. The term has greater validity among dirt gardeners and farmers than among the soil scientists; hence its wide and often cogent use.

STROPHOLIRION CALIFORNICUM = *Brodiaea volubilis.*

STRUCTURES. Since the early days of garden history, structures such as summer houses, garden pavilions, gazebos, pergolas, and tool houses have been built, for the comfort of having such places has always been apparent. The need has been filled in many ways, from the classic temple of the Roman and eighteenth-century gardens to the humble, rustic tool house.

The gazebo is of Dutch origin and is a characteristic feature of old Dutch gardens. Built of brick or stone, gazebos were placed where the passing coach or boat could be easily seen. In the long summer evenings the men still bring their pipes to them and the women their sewing for a few hours of conversation and repose.

The pergola was originally designed to offer a shaded passageway from one building to another, or from one garden feature to another, and it is always at its best when serving this purpose. In modern parlance, however, any structure which has an open,

Gazebo

vine-clad roof goes by that name. *See* ARBORS.

The pergola has always been an important feature of Italian garden design and is capable of great elaboration. In Spain, too, the pergola is much used, but is usually of simple construction — rough beams supported by rustic posts, left natural in color or painted black or blue. Where wood is scarce, the posts may be of concrete, brick, or stone, left exposed or whitewashed. These posts may well rest on a low wall.

Vines should not be allowed to grow too thickly over a pergola, but should clothe it scantily, to reveal its proportions. Two or three different kinds of vines may be grown on the same pergola if they are kept pruned or planted sufficiently far apart.

Garden structures serve a useful or an ornamental purpose and may preferably serve both. They should be considered as architectural features or ornaments, and should not be dotted about the grounds without reference to their surroundings and without regard to the general scheme. In fact, no feature of a garden can be considered as a thing apart, but all must be made to harmonize and fit naturally and inevitably into its proper place and be in keeping with its surroundings. The success of a garden structure depends more often on skill in placing than on form or material.

Such structures may dominate a view of the surrounding country or the color of an adjacent garden. They may terminate a garden path or allée or a cut through a wood. They may be arranged so that it is convenient to serve refreshments in them while enjoying the sight of a game of tennis and may also be useful to store the various "sporting goods" during bad weather. They may merely be quiet places in which to rest or read, away from the life of the house, or conversely they may be used as places in which to play noisy games so that the house itself may be more quiet. They may be filled with furniture and utensils for first lessons in housewifery, which will be the

better learned under such pleasant conditions. They may shelter an object of value, as a spring or a statue.

Often, however, the primary reason for building a garden structure is that the designer feels the aesthetic need of an architectural object in a particular place — perhaps to close a vista or strengthen the corner of a garden wall, and even the humble tool house may be successfully, if skillfully, used in this way.

Not many tool houses are as good-looking or as well placed as this one. *See* TOOL HOUSE.

In a landscape composition, the form of a structure should be considered not only in relation to its surroundings but also in relation to the other buildings in the same picture. In cases where it is near the main house or residence, or closely related by being a part of a formal scheme, it should have similar architectural treatment. It may repeat the architectural style or at least be made harmonious by the use of the same building material or the same color.

Summer house

* Special articles on the subjects indicated by an asterisk (*) will be found at the words so marked.

The question of the relative scale between the two is also important, as the house may tend to dwarf the garden structure and overpower it. French garden designers of the eighteenth century realized this in their latticework shelters, which, though frankly temporary pieces of stage scenery, were nevertheless sufficiently important as to be in scale with the adjacent château.

Where a garden structure is placed in a remote part of the grounds and has no definite relationship to the main house, it should become a part of its wilder surroundings. Here shade or shelter is the primary consideration. The roof may be thatched, the supporting posts left rough or even with the bark on; the whole partly concealed by vines in order to obtain that rough and rustic look so charming in the right place. It may closely fit the ground and have an irregular shape. The gray-green of its painted woodwork may harmonize with the color of the surrounding foliage or its stonework may blend with the outcrop of stone appearing near it. It may be entirely or partly hidden by planting or reduced to comparative insignificance by one or more large, overhanging trees. As it grows old, it will always assume greater harmony with its surroundings.

The interior fittings of a garden structure will depend on circumstances, which should be well studied before the structure is built. As it is essential that the inside be clean in order to be attractive, only materials which are easily cleaned should be used. All these buildings should be convenient and efficient as well as beautiful. Fitness to local conditions and a simple form, obviously expressing a practical need, tend to make a building less expressive of man's fancy, more expressive of his necessity, and so less incongruous with its surroundings. — R. L. F., Jr., and G. E.

strumosa, -us, -um (strew-mō'sa). With cushion-like swellings.

STRYCHNINE. *See* STRYCHNOS NUX-VOMICA.

STRYCHNOS (strick'nos). A genus of 70 species of tropical shrubs and trees of the family Loganiaceae, some yielding valuable medicine, others arrow poisons more dangerous than any known, while *S. spinosa* yields an edible fruit. The two below are grown in extreme southern Fla. and are hardy nowhere else in the U.S. Leaves opposite.* Flowers small, yellowish-white, mostly in terminal, sometimes much-branched clusters (cymes*). For details of flower structure *see* LOGANIACEAE. Fruit fleshy and berry-like. (*Strychnos* is an old Greek name for a kind of nightshade, applied by Linnaeus to these plants, perhaps because so many of them are poisonous.)

Nux-vomica. Strychnine. A medium-sized tree, not over 40 ft. high. Leaves ovalish, 2½–3½ in. long. Flower clusters (cymes*) nearly 2 in. wide. Fruit berry-like, about 1½ in. in diameter, its many seeds the source of strychnine. India.

spinosa. Natal orange. A spiny shrub 7–10 ft. high, the spines about ¾ in. long. Leaves roundish, about 2 in. long, with 5 main veins. Flower clusters branched (a compound cyme*). Fruit yellow, berry-like, nearly 4 in. in diameter, its pulp sweet and edible. Central and South Africa.

STUARTIA = *Stewartia.*

STYLE. The shank-like connection beween the ovary and the stigma. *See* FLOWER.

STYLOMECON. *See* MECONOPSIS HETEROPHYLLA.

STYLOPHORUM (sty-loff'o-rum). Hardy perennial herbs comprising 3 species of the poppy family, one a native of North America and 2 of China. They have thick rootstocks, yellow sap, and mostly basal leaves generally deeply cut almost to the midrib into several lobes. Flowers yellow or red, solitary or in clusters. Calyx* of 2 sepals. Corolla of 4 petals. Stamens* many. Fruit a capsule.* (*Stylophorum* is from the Greek for style, in allusion to the persistent style.)

Not generally cult., but grown in the wild garden. Propagated by seeds or division of the rootstocks in early spring, but it is often invasive and must be controlled rather than propagated. They prefer moist, rich, loose soil and partial shade.

diphyllum. Celandine poppy. Growing to 1½ ft. high, with 2 leaves at top of flowering stalk. Leaves light green, deeply cut into lobes. Flowers deep yellow, to 2 in. across, in 2–5-flowered clusters. Capsules 1 in. long. Western Pa. to Wis. and Tenn. April–May.

stylosa, -us, -um (sty-lō'sa). With a prominent style.*

STYRACACEAE (sty-ra-kay'see-ee). The storax family provides only three genera of hort. interest, *Halesia, Styrax,* and *Pterostyrax,* all trees or shrubs and mostly hardy over much of the country. There are, in the whole family, perhaps 110 species in seven genera which are widely distributed in the New World, Asia, and southern Europe.

Halesia is an ornamental tree with profuse, bell-shaped flowers, and is much cult. Flowers white in all the cult. genera. Leaves alternate* and simple.* Fruit dry or fleshy.

Technical flower characters: Flowers perfect* and regular.* Calyx more or less united, its 4 or 5 segments cleft or lobed. Corolla generally bell-shaped, but of 4–8 petals, partly or wholly united at the base. Stamens* 4–8, or 8–16. Ovary superior* in *Styrax,* inferior in the two other cult. genera.

Styraciflua (sty-ra-see-flew'a). Gum-producing, as is the tree producing gum-benzoin (*i.e., Styrax Benzoin,* a non-hort. Indo-Malayan tree).

STYRAX (sty'racks). Storax. A genus of ornamental shrubs and trees of the family Styracaceae, most of the 100 known species being found in tropical or warm regions, but the three below hardy in the temperate zone. Leaves alternate,* short-stalked, remotely and finely toothed (in ours). Flow-

---

* Special articles on the subjects indicated by an asterisk (*) will be found at the words so marked.

ers white, mostly in terminal clusters (racemes°), the calyx bell-shaped and slightly 5-toothed, usually persistent. Corolla united only at the base, the 5 lobes appearing as if 5 separate petals. Stamens° mostly 10. Fruit a rather dry drupe.° (*Styrax* is the old Greek name for one of the species.)

The plants below are handsome shrubs or small trees, thriving best in open sunlight and in a light, well-drained soil. Propagation is by seeds or by layers, but cuttings are difficult to strike. There are several native species in the southern states which may be transferred to grounds.

americana. Snow-bell. A branched shrub, 6–9 ft. high. Leaves elliptic to ovalish, pointed both ends, finely toothed, 1½–3½ in. long, short-stalked. Flowers white, about ¾ in. long, in loose, lax clusters (racemes°), or solitary at the leaf joints. Southeastern U.S. May–June. Hardy from zone° 4 southward.

japonica. A shrub or small tree, 20–30 ft. high, often less as cult. Leaves broadly elliptic or oblongish, 2–3 in. long, pointed. Flowers about ½ in. long, fragrant, long-stalked, the few-flowered clusters drooping. Fruit egg-shaped, about ½ in. long. China and Jap. June–July. Hardy from zone° 3 southward. A very showy and desirable shrub, well suited to the lawn.

Obassia. A shrub or small tree, 20–30 ft. high, usually less as cult. Leaves nearly round, or broadly oval, 3½–8 in. long, or even more on the main shoots, hairy on the under side. Flowers nearly 1 in. long, fragrant, in many-flowered clusters (racemes°) that may be 6–8 in. long, but are usually half hidden by the foliage. Fruit egg-shaped, nearly ¾ in. long. Jap. May–June. Hardy from zone° 3 southward.

suaveolens (swah-vee-ō'lenz). Pleasing.

suavis, -e (swah'vis). Agreeable.

subacaulis, -e (sub-a-kaul'is). Nearly stemless.

subalpina, -us, -um (sub-al-py'na). Nearly alpine.

subcarnosa, -us, -um (sub-kar-nō'sa). Somewhat fleshy.

subcaulescens (sub-kau-less'enz). With short or no stem; nearly acaulescent.°

subcoerulea, -us, -um (sub-see-roo'lee-a). Almost dark blue.

subcordata, -us, -um (sub-kor-day'ta). Nearly heart-shaped.

subdivaricata, -us, -um (sub-dy-var-i-kay'-ta). Somewhat divergent.

Suber (soo'ber). An old name for the cork oak (*Quercus Suber*). See OAK.

suberosa, -us, -um (sub-e-roe'sa). Somewhat jagged.

subhirtella, -us, -um (sub-hir-tell'a). Slightly hairy.

SUB-IRRIGATION. See WATERING.

subsessilis, -e (sub-sess'i-lis). Nearly stalkless.

SUB-SHRUB. A partly woody plant, half-shrubby, as are some plants in *Artemisia, Chrysanthemum, Pachysandra,* etc.

SUBSOIL. See SOILS.

SUBSPECIES. A somewhat technical designation for a race or form, especially a geographical race, of a species. It is more used by botanists than gardeners, for whom a sub-species is practically the same as a variety (which see).

SUBTEND. To stand close to, and just beneath; as many bracts° subtend the flowers, or clusters, just above them.

subtomentosa, -us, -um (sub-to-men-tō'sa). Almost tomentose; *i.e.,* covered with a soft, felt-like hairiness.

SUB-TROPICAL GARDEN. As the name implies, a sub-tropical region is one that borders on the tropics in climatic environment, but is not truly tropical because of the lower temperature means in winter and the occurrence of frosts of varying intensity at irregular intervals. In the U.S., the sub-tropical areas may be said to be confined to the warmer parts of Fla. and Calif., together with limited protected areas on the Gulf Coast that may be included for a few of the hardiest plants of tropical type.

In sub-tropical regions an opportunity is offered the gardener to create landscape effects that approach the tropical and to use to advantage a wide range of plants not adapted to cooler climates. Broad-leaved evergreen shrubs, palms, bamboos, and flowering trees predominate and combine to lend a "tropical atmosphere." Instead of a bleak winter landscape of defoliated plants and an occasional conifer, the whole is distinctively full-foliaged and of a summery green the year round. A succession of flowering seasons provides a profusion of blossoms in every month, and the invitation into the garden extends its appeal at all seasons. Differences between the sub-tropical and tropical garden are mainly in magnitude of plant variety and may not be so great as between the typical northern garden and the sub-tropical.

Plants of the tropics are predominantly evergreen, and though complete defoliation for relatively short periods occurs with some, the period of leaf fall usually is coincident with the putting out of new foliage. Summer and winter seasons have little influence; moisture relations, rather than temperature, commonly determine the periods of growth and dormancy. Tropical gardens have no minimum temperature restrictions and consequently have access to the whole of the tropical world for variety; sub-tropical ones are confined to the hardier tropical species.

Plants adapted and now grown in sub-tropical gardens are legion. Presumably because of differences in rainfall, humidity, and soils, they differ in variety between Fla. and Calif. A few of the commonly planted genera and species, exclusive of numerous herbaceous types, include:

° Special articles on the subjects indicated by an asterisk (°) will be found at the words so marked.

SHRUBS

Abelia grandiflora
Acacia
Acalypha
Azalea
Breynia nivosa
Buddleia
Callistemon
Camellia japonica
Carissa
Cestrum
Clerodendron
Codiaeum
Cotoneaster
Dombeya wallichi
Duranta repens
Escallonia spp.
Eugenia spp.
Euphorbia
    pulcherrima
Hibiscus
    Rosa-sinensis
Ixora coccinea
Jasminum
Lagerstroemia
Ligustrum
    (evergreen
    species)
Malvaviscus
    arboreus
Nandina domestica
Nerium Oleander
Pittosporum
Plumbago capensis
Poinciana
    pulcherrima
Pyracantha
Tabernaemontana
Viburnum spp.

TREES

Acacia
Albizzia
Araucaria
Bamboos, in variety
Bauhinia, in variety
Callistemon
Cassia
Casuarina
Cinnamomum
Citrus
Dalbergia Sissoo
Delonix regia
Eriobotrya japonica
Eucalyptus
Ficus
Grevillea
Ilex
Jacaranda acutifolia
Mangifera indica
Melaleuca
    Leucadendron
Melia Azedarach
Musa
Palms, in variety
Parkinsonia aculeata
Pithecolobium dulce
Plumeria
Podocarpus
Quercus
Ravenala
    madagascariensis
Schinus
Spathodea
    campanulata
Stenolobium Stans
Tabebuia
Tamarindus indica
Terminalia

VINES

Allamanda cathartica
Antigonon leptopus
Asparagus spp.
Beaumontia grandiflora
Bougainvillaea
Clerodendron thomsonae
Cryptostegia
Ficus pumila
Gelsemium sempervirens
Jasminum
Lonicera
Monstera deliciosa
Passiflora
Pereskia
Petrea volubilis
Porana paniculata
Pyrostegia ignea
Scindapsus aureus
Solandra guttata
Solanum
Tecomaria capensis
Thunbergia
Trachelospermum
    jasminoides

All of these plants are entered at their proper alphabetical place in the ENCYCLOPEDIA OF GARDENING, and should be sought there for details of culture. See also PALM, BAMBOO. The design of a sub-tropical garden follows the main principles of good planning, as in any other garden.

For the proper sequence of garden operations in the sub-tropical garden, which differ from those in cooler regions, see GARDEN CALENDAR. — G. D. R.

subulata, -us, -um (sub-you-lay′ta). Awl-shaped.

SUB-WATER. To water by sub-irrigation. *See* WATERING and WICK WATERING.

SUCCESSION CROPPING. The planting of one crop immediately after the harvesting of another, on the same land, and in the same growing season. It is mostly practiced in the vegetable garden, and, with inter-cropping, provides a valuable method of getting the utmost return from the available space. For the details of succession cropping and inter-cropping *see* KITCHEN GARDEN.

SUCCORY. *See* CICHORIUM INTYBUS.

succulenta, -us, -um (suck-you-len′ta). With thick, fleshy leaves or stems.

SUCCULENTS. In nearly every country there is some region with deficient or periodic rainfall, where totally unrelated plants have been forced to adopt some mechanism to survive the dry season. The outstanding example, in the New World, is furnished by the cactus family, where leaves are usually lacking, and the plant body is green and functions as do leaves, in addition to storing large quantities of water. While the cacti are true succulents, they form such a distinct group that their culture and kinds are usually, and in this book, kept separate from all other succulents. *See* CACTI.

Before discussing the different sorts of succulents it will be well to define the term,

Three common types of succulents belonging to the genera *Stapelia* (*right*), *Aloe* (*lower left*), and *Haworthia* (*above*).

which is confusing to many and has a slightly misleading origin. Succulent is from the Latin *succus*, meaning juice. But if succulent, as a garden term, covered only those fleshy or juicy plants like cacti or the cactus-like spurges, it would be far more limited than usage has made it. For under the term suc-

* Special articles on the subjects indicated by an asterisk (*) will be found at the words so marked.

culent we include, rather loosely it must be admitted, two distinct classes of plants that have quite different ways of overcoming a deficiency of water. The only hort. reason for calling them all succulents is that their culture is approximately the same.

The two main groups of plants that are classed as succulents are those that store water and those that have become adapted to the lack of it, without special storage facilities. In the first group are the cacti and cactus-like spurges (as well as many others to be discussed presently). In these the very fleshy stems or leaves store considerable water upon which the plant draws during the dry season. Such plants are perhaps properly called succulents.

In the second group there are no special water-storage organs. But by reduction of leaf area, or actual leaflessness, or a varnished leaf surface, or ashy-gray foliage, or by other devices, the plants have so reduced their water requirements that they survive the long drought (lasting for years in some Peruvian deserts) just as well as those succulents that store water. This second group of succulents should perhaps not be called so, for they are what the botanist calls xerophytes. But the botanical term, among gardeners, is not likely to replace the word succulent for these drought-resistant plants, although it would make for greater accuracy if it did so. There are also some groups of succulents, like the agaves, that come under both categories. Generally speaking, however, it is possible to separate these two main groups of succulents into those that store water and those that get along without doing so; in other words, into the water-storing and drought-resistant succulents.

WATER-STORING SUCCULENTS

Here belong the cacti (which see), all the cactus-like spurges (see EUPHORBIA), and many other plants with fleshy leaves or stems or both. Among the most common are those from the desert regions of South Africa and elsewhere, found in the genera *Gasteria, Haworthia, Aloe, Mesembryanthemum, Stapelia, Huernia, Huerniopsis, Echeveria, Crassula, Adromischus, Cotyledon, Sempervivum* (see HOUSELEEK), *Rochea, Sedum,* and *Pachyphytum* (see all these genera). There are also scattered succulents in various other genera and families, especially in the genus *Senecio,* and in the families Portulacaceae, Dioscoreaceae, Amaryllidaceae, and Liliaceae (see these entries).

Such plants are grown more for interest or oddity than for beauty, as many of them have grotesque plant forms. There are, however, very gorgeous flower colors in some of them, notably *Mesembryanthemum, Echeveria, Rochea, Kalanchoe, Sempervivum,* and *Pachyphytum.* In others the flowers are inconspicuous, and in *Stapelia, Huernia,* and *Huerniopsis* they are showy but disgusting, because of their foul, carrion-scented odor.

Not a few foliage plants are also found among these fleshy-leaved succulents. Especially in *Echeveria* and *Sedum* the carpet-bedding enthusiast will find many plants of low growth, colored leaves, and compact habit, well suited to this type of planting.

Overwhelmingly these water-storing succulents come from regions of intense summer heat, and equally intense dryness. Many of them will stand no frost and are consequently confined, so far as outdoor cult. is concerned, to the desert or semi-desert regions in southern Calif., Ariz., N. Mex., and western Tex. See DESERT GARDEN. See also CACTI. Their indoor culture will be discussed presently.

But some of the succulents will stand hard freezing so long as this is not interspersed with slush and moisture at their roots, which few or no succulents will stand. That is why only a handful of them can be grown in the northeastern states — mostly sedums, houseleeks, and a very few cacti.

DROUGHT-RESISTANT SUCCULENTS

This group includes very different plants from the water-storing succulents, because they have, without special storage facilities, become habituated to long periods of dryness. Some, like the South American genera *Dyckia, Hechtia,* and *Puya,* all belonging to the pineapple family, have been known to grow for years without a single recorded rainfall. Naturally such plants may be said to exist rather than to grow, but grow they do, very slowly, and mostly when they do get a brief period of moisture.

Better known plants in these drought-resistant succulents will be found in the genera *Dasylirion, Yucca, Agave* (which also includes some fleshy-leaved species), *Fouquieria, Hesperaloe, Hesperoyucca, Samuela,* and *Furcraea.* Nearly all these have leathery or coarse foliage, some are very spiny, and generally their flowers are far less showy than in the water-storing succulents. But in some of these genera the flower cluster is very striking, notably in *Yucca,* and in *Agave* which includes the century plants.

These drought-resistant succulents, of which only some species of *Yucca* will stand wet, slushy winters, do not lend themselves to so many uses as the water-storing kinds. They are often tall, some have palm-like trunks, while others have immense basal rosettes of spiny-margined leaves. In other words, they need space and are more useful for accent plants or for the rear of desert gardens than the generally lower, fleshy-leaved types, most of which are grown in pots.

CULTURE

The culture of both types of succulents is properly based upon a study of the conditions under which they grow naturally. While temperature may, as in some upland Peruvian or Mexican deserts, fall far below freezing, the plants survive this easily if their roots are not rotted by slush or water. The whole secret in growing them is to see that this does not happen.

---

* Special articles on the subjects indicated by an asterisk (*) will be found at the words so marked.

In desert gardens in the Southwest, sandy or gritty soils are easy to find, and in fact most of the local cacti will be found in such soils. The drainage is perfect and no stagnant water ever collects about the roots. These soil and moisture conditions are ideal, if, as nearly always happens, there is intense sunlight and great summer heat. All but a handful of succulents will thrive in such an environment.

When rains do come, the plants make a fair growth, but it is based upon the fact that while water is available, the plants are never bogged in it. They must, when the rain comes, or when you water them, get ample supplies of moisture, but all excess must drain away. And this can only be secured by a sandy or gritty soil.

In the greenhouse or in the home, very different conditions confront the succulent. There is far less sunshine, the plant grows much more slowly and there is grave danger from overwatering, especially in the winter in the comparative darkness of the living room. The first necessity is to see that your succulents, most of which will necessarily be pot plants of the fleshy-leaved type, get the proper soil conditions.

This is best approximated by potting mixture* 6, and the pot should have at least ¼ of its depth filled with broken flower pots, upon which the soil should be put. The lightness of the mixture and the ample drainage at the bottom will take care of any excess water.

There is one final caution for all soils used for succulents. They are peculiarly apt to harbor nematodes and, because the plants are inactive for so long a period, to accumulate trouble due to stagnation of water, this in spite of every care to secure proper drainage in the pots. To reduce these hazards many seasoned growers sterilize all soils for succulents. For the details of this see Soil Sterilization.

The atmosphere in the greenhouse must be kept dry and airy; this is far more important than the temperature, although the latter should be around 55°–60° in the winter and 65°–75° in the summer. If possible, it is better to put the succulents outdoors in the summer, and if this is done, the pots should be plunged* in sand or ashes, in full sunshine.

Water requirements are much greater in the summer than in the dark days of winter. During the latter period the plants should be watered only enough to keep them from drying out — usually once a week is sufficient. If the plants are in the living room, they should be put as near the windows as possible, and turned regularly, for the best results, and watering will require more careful watching. More household succulents are lost from overwatering in the winter than from any other cause.

Poorly grown succulents have a pale and anemic appearance, which is especially likely to be the case when they are grown under glass or in dense shade. Expert growers have two methods for bringing out all the bright leaf colors. The first relates to plants grown in the sun and outdoors in the summer. Gradually stop watering them in the early fall and do not take the plants in until cold weather has really arrived. The second hint is for greenhouse cult. In preparing the plants for Christmas or Easter, diminish the heat until the houses are near the freezing point, at the same time withholding the water. A few days of this treatment will suffice. These suggestions do not apply to cacti.

PROPAGATION

Many succulents, such as *Echeveria*, may be grown from single leaves, provided they are not watered, but are placed on top of dry sand. Nearly all other succulents may be grown from cuttings. These should be allowed to form a callus* or at least the wound should be dried over before planting. Then insert in dry sand and keep without water until growth or shriveling begins. Cuttings while rooting demand plenty of air and light. Some succulents can be propagated like geraniums.

Some of the more desirable aloes are hard to propagate. They may not perfect seed nor produce offshoots. Cutting the stem only causes it to rot and only the head can then be saved. In this case, a hot iron applied to the growing point will frequently cause development of shoots. Some agaves produce bulbils* instead of flowers. These are simply inserted in sand or, if roots have already formed, planted in potting mixture* 3.

Succulent species which have large seeds may be planted in potting mixture* 1 with an overlay of not too fine charcoal. Many of the succulents in the genera *Echeveria* and *Sempervivum* bear seed as fine as dust. These must be pressed firmly down on the surface of finely screened potting mixture* 1, and then sprinkled with a small amount of sifted charcoal dust, but not enough to form a covering layer. The pot is then immersed until evidence of moisture barely shows on the surface of the soil. Cover the pot with glass. Look twice a day for damping-off* which appears as a patch of fine, white, silky threads. Succulent seedlings are subject to this fungus. See DAMPING-OFF. It is good practice to keep a sprayer at hand, but it should have no rubber bulb to deteriorate.

Succulent plants frequently breed abnormal forms. Some of these, especially the crested or cockscombed forms, are highly prized by collectors. In these the stem tends to become fan-shaped, with a line of reduced leaves at the top. Globular growths form masses ranging from caterpillar-shape to those having the appearance of the human brain. As in the cacti, there is also a mania for producing bizarre plants by grafting, especially in forms of *Euphorbia lactea*.

Anyone interested in succulents or cacti is welcome to membership in the Cactus and

* Special articles on the subjects indicated by an asterisk (*) will be found at the words so marked.

Succulent Society (which publishes a journal). Its present address is 132 West Union Street, Pasadena, Calif.

SUCKER. A secondary shoot arising from the lower part of the trunk or from the ground, and usually growing at the expense of the plant producing it. Some plants sucker

Suckers (*below*) and water sprouts (*above*) often steal much food from a tree.

very freely and the growth of the suckers is so rampant as to suggest their other name of thieves.

Suckers that are produced higher up, on large branches or on the trunk, are usually called water sprouts. As in the basal suckers they should be removed, except where they have been induced, as in pollarding. *See also* SOBOLE.

SUCKING-DISK. An adhesive enlargement at the tip of some tendrils.* It aids vines, like certain species of *Parthenocissus*, to cling to walls.

sudanensis, -e (soo-dan-en'sis). From the Sudan.

SUDAN GRASS = *Sorghum sudanense*.

suecica, -us, -um (swee'si-ka). From Sweden.

suffruticosa, -us, -um (suf-frew-ti-kō'sa). Suffruticose, *i.e.*, a little shrubby. Mostly applied to herbs that are woody at the base.

SUGAR-APPLE = *Annona squamosa*.

SUGAR BEET. *See* BEET.

SUGARBERRY = *Celtis laevigata*. *See* HACKBERRY.

SUGAR BUSH = *Rhus ovata*.

SUGAR CANE. The fact that *Saccharum officinarum* (which see) is a tropical crop explains why the culture of sugar cane is a tropical agricultural operation of huge dimensions, and lies outside the scope of this book.

SUGAR CORN = Sweet corn. *See* CORN.

SUGAR GUM = *Eucalyptus cladocalyx*.

SUGAR-LOAF = *Clematis douglasi*.

SUGAR MAPLE = *Acer saccharum*. *See* MAPLE.

SUGAR PALM = *Arenga saccharifera*.

SUGAR PEA = *Pisum sativum macrocarpon*. *See* PEA.

SUGAR SORGHUM = *Sorghum vulgare saccharatum*.

SUGI = *Cryptomeria japonica*.

SULCATE. Grooved.

SULLA CLOVER = *Hedysarum coronarium*.

sulphurea, -us, -um (sul-fure'e-a). Yellow.

SULPHUR-FLOWER = *Eriogonum umbellatum*.

SUMAC. *See* RHUS.

SUMAC FAMILY. A family of woody plants, including shrubs, trees, and vines, and containing such unlike plants as the poison ivy, smoke-tree, pistache, and the mango. For the cult. genera *see* ANACARDIACEAE.

SUMMER BEDDING. The planting of tender ornamentals in flower beds during the summer, very widely done in public parks and in many private gardens. The only objection to it is the expense, as many plants used for summer bedding demand a greenhouse for winter care. Among such are palms, caladiums, crotons, dracaenas, and any other tropical shrubs or trees used in such a scheme. Many of the latter may be plunged* in the bed.

People without greenhouse equipment can, however, find a wide range of plants suitable for summer bedding. Most of the tender annuals (*see* ANNUALS) can be so used. So can the castor-oil plant, cannas, the elephant-ear, or other summer-blooming plants whose rootstocks or bulbs are stored over the winter.

SUMMER CROOKNECK SQUASH = *Cucurbita Pepo Melopepo*. For culture *see* SQUASH.

SUMMER CYPRESS = *Kochia scoparia trichophila*.

SUMMER FIR = *Artemisia sacrorum viride*.

SUMMER GARDEN. There is no difficulty in maintaining a full-flowered garden during June, July, and August. The difficulty lies, rather, in avoiding monotony in the type of flowers used, the too frequent appearance of members of the daisy family (the Compositae) and the summer-flowering phloxes, with their wheel-like regularity of form. Also during this prodigal period, color is apt to get out of hand, with the result that the borders appear hot and restless.

Points to be aimed at in the summer garden are a pleasing arrangement of colors, employing to this end a good many flowers of cool tones, dim blues, lavenders, and numerous plants with gray foliage; the maintenance of a fresh, well-filled appearance by the use of such plants as have fine, lasting foliage — and neatness. The summer bor-

---

* Special articles on the subjects indicated by an asterisk (*) will be found at the words so marked.

ders should appear trim, prosperous and well cared for. The plants should be firmly and inconspicuously staked and relieved of all spent blossoms and seed pods; the paths should be neatly raked and the grass cut short; borders and paths should be kept free of weeds and all climbers rigidly trained and fastened up.

During the summer season there are fewer flowering trees and shrubs than are available earlier in the season, but on the other hand there are a far greater number of annuals and perennials, as well as lilies, gladioli, dahlias, tritonias, and tuberoses. In selecting plants for the summer garden it is wise to employ a preponderance of those having a long season of bloom. There is no need to repeat here the list of herbaceous plants in bloom during June, July, and August, for the important ones are mentioned at EVERBLOOM-ING GARDEN, and their period of bloom specified. *See also* the special articles devoted to ANNUALS, BIENNIALS, and PERENNIALS.

SUMMER-FLOWERING SHRUBS

After the rush of spring bloom it is often difficult to maintain color in the shrub border, which is apt to become rather drab by midsummer. The list below, if followed carefully, will provide bloom in the shrub border from June until early Sept. All the plants mentioned will be found elsewhere in the ENCYCLOPEDIA, and should be sought there for additional notes on culture and hardiness.

Abelia chinensis, 4–6 ft. pink, Aug.; *Amorpha canescens,* 3 ft. blue, June; *A. fruticosa,* 10 ft. blue, July; *Buddleia davidi,* 6 ft. purple, Aug.; *Callicarpa japonica,* 5 ft. pink, July; *Calluna vulgaris,* 15 in. white, rose-carmine, Aug.; *Caragana arborescens,* 10 ft. yellow, June; *Ceanothus americanus,* 3 ft. white, July; *Cephalanthus occidentalis,* 5 ft. white, July; *Chionanthus virginicus,* 15 ft. white, June; *Cladrastis lutea,* 50 ft. white, June; *Clethra alnifolia,* 6 ft. white, Aug.; *Cornus Kousa,* 15 ft. white, June; *Deutzia* vars. 2–10 ft. white-pink, June; *Diervilla Lonicera,* 4 ft. yellow, June; *Genista tinctoria plena,* 3–4 ft. yellow, July; *Hibiscus syriacus,* 10 ft. white, mauve, rose, purple, Aug.; *Holodiscus discolor,* 12 ft. creamy-white, July; *Hydrangea arborescens grandiflora,* 10 ft. white, June–July; *H. paniculata,* 12 ft. white, Aug.; *Hypericum calycinum,* 1 ft. yellow, summer; *H. densiflorum,* 6 ft. yellow, July; *H. aureum,* 4 ft. yellow, Aug.; *H. patulum,* 3 ft. yellow, summer; *Itea virginica,* 10 ft. white, July; *Kalmia angustifolia,* 3 ft. rose-purple, June; *K. latifolia,* to 8 ft. white or pink, June; *Kerria japonica,* 4–6 ft. double or single, yellow, June; *Laburnum anagyroides,* 30 ft. yellow, June; *Lonicera maacki,* 15 ft. white-cream, June; *L. tatarica,* 8 ft. pink or white, June; *Lespedeza bicolor,* 8 ft. purple-rose, July–Aug.; *Lycium chinense,* 10 ft. purple, July; *Oxydendrum arboreum,* 10 ft. white, summer; *Philadelphus* vars. 3–10

ft. white, early June; *Potentilla fruticosa,* 4 ft. yellow, summer; *Rhododendron* vars. 3–8 ft. all colors, June–July; *Rhodotypos scandens,* 5 ft. white, June; *Robinia hispida,* 8 ft. pink, June; *Rhus copallina,* 8 ft. greenish, July; *Rosa,* many vars. 3–8 ft. pink, white, red, June; *Rubus odoratus,* 4–6 ft. rose-purple, June–July; *Sambucus canadensis,* 8 ft. white, July; *Sophora viciifolia,* 6–8 ft. bluish-violet, June; *Spiraea Bumalda,* 2 ft. crimson, Aug.; S. Anthony Waterer, 3 ft. crimson, July; *S. salicifolia,* 6 ft. pink, July; *S. tomentosa,* 4–6 ft. rose-purple, July; *Stewartia ovata,* 12 ft. white, July; *Syringa Josikaea,* 12 ft. violet, June; *S. reflexa,* 10–12 ft. soft pink, June; *S. sweginzowi superba,* 8–15 ft. rose-pink, June; *S. villosa,* 10–12 ft. bright rose, June; *Tamarix gallica,* 8–10 ft. pinkish, June–July; *T. pentandra,* 15 ft. pink, Aug.; *Viburnum,* many species, white, early summer; *Vitex Agnus-castus,* 8–10 ft. violet or white, summer; *V. Negundo,* 10–15 ft. lavender, August. — L. B. W.

SUMMER GRAPE = *Vitis aestivalis.*

SUMMER HOUSE. *See* STRUCTURES.

SUMMER HYACINTH = *Galtonia candicans.*

SUMMER LILAC. *See* BUDDLEIA DAVIDI.

SUMMER PRUNING. *See* the Lorette system of pruning at PRUNING.

SUMMER SAVORY = *Satureia hortensis.* *See* SAVORY.

SUMMER SNOWFLAKE = *Ornithogalum umbellatum.*

SUMMER-SWEET = *Clethra alnifolia.*

SUNBERRY. *See* SOLANUM NIGRUM.

SUNBURN. A burning or singeing of foliage in the greenhouse, due to concentration of the sun's rays; usually caused by imperfections in the glass. The obvious remedy is to provide temporary shade, or to get modern, clear glass. *See* GREENHOUSE.

SUNDEW. *See* DROSERA.

SUNDEW FAMILY = Droseraceae.

SUNDIALS. While the purely ornamental features of sundials come within the range of garden furniture and ornament, their ability to tell time needs a little study. Unless considerable care is used in setting them, their variation from true time may be appreciable.

The first necessity is to have the plane of the sundial absolutely flat, and its base set on concrete or stone, so that there will be no settling. Determine its flatness with a spirit level.

The next step is to determine, precisely, when it is noon in your garden, not noon by radio time or by calling up the telephone company. Both the latter will give you standard time, which may be very different from the time in your garden.

Much the simplest way to find when it is noon for you is to set the sundial temporarily on its bed and see when its gnomon (the shadow-casting part) throws no shadow on

---

Armillary sphere

the dial except a mere slit straight north. At this moment (actually about 2 minutes) the shadow of the gnomon is exactly on a north–south axis, and it is noon.

The sundial can then be cemented in place. Do not think, however, that merely because it indicates noon in your garden that your sundial will be a perfect timepiece. For reasons of space it cannot be explained in detail here, but the sundial will only be exactly correct about 4 times a year, approximately Dec. 25, Apr. 16, June 15, and Sept. 1, and even then it is only correct for sun time. An absolutely accurate sundial can be constructed only if especially made for your precise latitude and longitude. The usual commercial types are accurate only with the limitations outlined.

It will not, of course, register daylight-saving time, and only in a very few places will it exactly register standard time, namely, if you happen to be on the time meridian for the particular time belt in which you live. These are the 75th meridian for Eastern Standard Time, the 90th for Central, the 105th for Mountain, and the 120th for Pacific

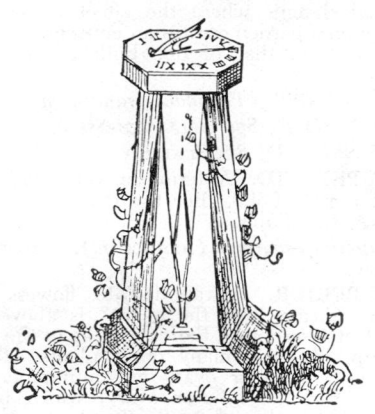

Sundial

Standard Time. If you live east or west of these degrees of longitude, your sundial will be earlier or later than the standard time for your region.

But if you live exactly on the line your sundial will register both sun and standard time with the limitations noted above which are due to the earth's inclination and the shape of its orbit.

Armillary spheres, such as shown in the illustration, are modern and much simplified replicas of the ancient armillary sphere used by the Greeks to tell the arrival of the equinoxes and other astronomical phenomena. Originally there were highly complex contrivances of rings. As garden ornaments they are more interesting historically than useful instruments for time-telling.

SUNDROPS. *See* EVENING PRIMROSE.

SUNFLOWER. Rather coarse, hardy, annual or perennial herbs, comprising the genus **Helianthus** (he-li-an′thus) which contains about 60 species of the family Compositae, found mostly in N.A. They are very diverse in size and character, as they readily hybridize in their natural surroundings, and are therefore difficult to define. The perennial species have varied rootstocks, some thick, woody, and compact, some thick, woody, and spreading, others tuberous. Leaves alternate,* sometimes opposite* above, the margins usually coarsely toothed. Flowers in terminal heads, from 3–12 in. across, the ray florets* yellow, the disk florets yellow, brown, or purple. (*Helianthus* is from the Greek for sun and a flower.)

For culture *see* below.

H. angustifolius. Swamp sunflower. Perennial, growing to 7 ft. high, covered with stiff hairs. Leaves lance-shaped, to 7 in. long. Flower heads 2–3 in. across, solitary, or 2 or 3, yellow, the disk florets purple. Swamps, N.Y. to Fla. and west to Tex. Aug.–Oct.

H. annuus. Common sunflower. Annual, growing to 12 ft. high. Leaves ovalish, to 1 ft. long, hairy on both sides, the margins toothed. Flowers in heads to 1 ft. across, yellow, the disk florets* purplish-brown. Blooms July–Sept. Minn. to Wash. and Calif. The dwarf small-flowered forms are known as Cut-and-come-again.

H. cucumerifolius = *Helianthus debilis.*

H. debilis. Much-branched annual, growing to 4 ft. high, the stems covered with stiff hairs and sometimes marked purple and white. Leaves ovalish or triangular, to 4 in. long, the margins toothed. Flower heads solitary, to 3 in. across, yellow, the disk florets* purplish-brown. Fla. to Tex. July–Sept.

H. decapetalus. River sunflower. Perennial, growing to 5 ft. high. Leaves thin, broadly lance-shaped, to 8 in. long, hairy on the under side. Flower heads many, 2–3 in. across, yellow, the disk florets yellowish. Moist places, Quebec to Ga. and west to Mo. July–Sept.

H. giganteus. Giant, Tall or Wild sunflower, also called Indian potato. Strong-growing perennial, to 12 ft. high, with stiff, hairy stems. Leaves lance-shaped, to 6 in. long, covered with short, stiff hairs, the margins toothed. Flower heads several, to 3 in. across, yellow, the disk florets yellowish. Moist places, eastern N.A. Aug.–Oct.

* Special articles on the subjects indicated by an asterisk (*) will be found at the words so **marked.**

H. laetiflorus. Strong-growing perennial, to 8 ft. high, covered with stiff hairs. Leaves broadly lance-shaped, to 1 ft. long, the margins toothed. Flower heads solitary, or 2 or 3, to 3 in. across, yellow, the disk florets purplish-brown. Dry places, N.A. Aug.–Oct. Known also as *H. scaberrimus.*

H. maximiliani. Strong-growing, branching perennial, to 12 ft. high. Leaves lance-shaped, to 7 in. long, covered with rough hairs on both sides, the margins often toothed. Flower heads many, to 3 in. across, yellow, the disk florets yellowish. Dry plains, midwestern states. Aug.–Oct.

H. mollis. Strong-growing perennial, to 5 ft. high, covered with soft white hairs. Leaves broadly lance-shaped, to 5 in. long, the margins toothed. Flower heads solitary, or few, to 3 in. across, yellow, the disk florets yellowish. Dry places, midwestern states south to Fla. Summer.

H. multiflorus. A trade name for a form of *H. decapetalus.*

H. orgyalis = *H. salicifolius.*

H. rigidus = *H. laetiflorus.*

H. salicifolius. Strong-growing perennial, to 10 ft. high. Leaves lance-shaped, to 16 in. long, drooping, covered with stiff hairs, the margins sometimes slightly toothed. Flower heads many, to 2 in. across, yellow, the disk florets purplish-brown. Dry places, lower midwestern states. Sept.–Oct. Known also as *H. orgyalis.*

H. scaberrimus = *H. laetiflorus.*

H. tuberosus. Jerusalem artichoke. Canada potato. Girasole. Strong-growing perennial, to 12 ft. high, with edible tuberous rootstocks. Leaves ovalish, to 8 in. long, covered with stiff hairs above and soft hairs beneath. Flower heads several, to 3½ in. across, yellow, the disk florets yellowish. N.A. Widely cult. for its edible tubers and one of the few plants cult. by the North American Indians. It is neither an artichoke nor does it come from Jerusalem.

SUNFLOWER CULTURE

Sunflowers are grown both for ornament and use, some species making very effective border plants or shrubbery plantings, while others are used commercially. The common sunflower, *H. annuus*, is the most useful; the dwarf small-flowered forms, commonly called Cut-and-come-again, are useful for the border and for cutting. The tall-growing forms are cult. for their seeds, especially in Russia. These seeds are eaten raw, used in poultry mixtures and as a parrot food. When dried and crushed, valuable oil is extracted, the finest of which is equal to olive oil, while the cruder forms are used for lighting. woolen dressing, soap- and candlemaking. Oil cake made from this oil is used for fattening cattle.

These tall-growing forms are often grown in the cottage gardens of England, where wagers are made in the local inns as to which villager can grow the largest head, which, in this species, turn with the sun from east to west. There are several hort. forms with red or chestnut-colored ray florets,* with double flowers, and one with variegated leaves.

Helianthus debilis is very free-flowering and makes a good cut flower. *H. tuberosus*, Jerusalem artichoke, is widely grown for its potato-like tubers, and it may become a pest if not controlled.

Sunflowers are easily cult. They prefer moist, rich, deeply dug soil and are propagated by seeds or division of the rootstocks. For ordinary garden use, seeds should be sown where required to bloom, ½ in. deep, 1 ft. or more apart, according to the species, in early spring, or they may be sown in a cool greenhouse or cold frame in March and transplanted outdoors for early flowering. Strong supports should be provided for the tall-growing forms. Flower heads should be cut as soon as they are faded to ensure a longer flowering period. In commercial growing the annual form is cult. like corn, earthing up when 6 in. high to prevent stems from blowing down.

Perennial species, although they grow readily from seeds, are usually propagated by the division of the rootstocks in early spring.

In the Jerusalem artichoke, the tubers should be planted about 6 in. deep and 1 ft. apart in rows about 3 ft. wide. They should be taken up in the late fall and stored, like potatoes. Care should be taken in digging to take out every tuber or they become a pest in the garden.

INSECT PESTS. Sunflower moth larvae damage seeds on the plant. Dust flower heads with pesticide #17 when flowers first appear and repeat once or twice at weekly intervals. (See SPRAYS AND DUSTS.) Pesticide #21 would do less damage to beneficial insects. Stalk borers enter stems in spring from overwintering quarters on weeds. Cleanup and cultivation about plants reduces this trouble. Spring applications of any insecticide to stems will keep them down. Leafhoppers and aphids are controlled by pesticide #21.

DISEASES. Although a number of diseases may attack sunflower, the only ones usually encountered in the gardens are leafspot* and occasionally one of the leaf rust* diseases. Use of fungicides is not usually warranted, but gardeners anxious for clean plants may apply pesticide #1 or #5 (see SPRAYS AND DUSTS) at 10-day intervals.

SUNKEN GARDEN. The lowest and usually central part of a garden built on different levels. Sunken gardens are most used in formal designs where the effect of looking *down* on a garden creates an entirely different appeal from that of one built on a single level.

SUN MOSS = *Portulaca grandiflora.*

SUN-ROSE. See HELIANTHEMUM.

SUNSCALD. See SCALD.

SUPERACID. A term for very acid soils with a pH of 4.0. For the details *see* ACID AND ALKALI SOILS.

superba, -us, -um (soo-per'ba). Superb or showy.

SUPERIOR. As applied to flowers this term indicates that the ovary* is above the point of insertion of the calyx,* as in the buttercup, lily, and many other plants. Those having a superior ovary far outnumber the plants with an inferior ovary, which is inserted below the calyx.* See INFERIOR.

---

* Special articles on the subjects indicated by an asterisk (*) will be found at the words so marked.

supina, -us, -um (soo-py'na). Lying on its back.

SUPPLEJACK = *Berchemia scandens.*

SURINAM CHERRY = *Eugenia uniflora.*

susiana, -us, -um (soo-zi-ā'na). From Shushan, a Biblical but now extinct city of Persia. *See* Crocus and Iris.

suspensa, -us, -um (sus-pen'sa). Hung or suspended.

SUTURE. The line or seam that joins the valves of a fruit, or the similar line or seam down which the fruit splits, as in a pea pod. *Suture* is also applied to the furrow-like depression in some melon fruits which do not split.

SUWARRO = *Carnegiea gigantea.*

SWAINSONA (swain-sō'na). Darling pea. Poison bush. Australian herbs or under-shrubs of the pea family, comprising over 50 species, two grown for ornament in the cool greenhouse or outdoors in zones* 8 and 9. They have alternate,* compound* leaves, the leaflets arranged feather-fashion, with an odd one at the end. Flowers rather showy, pea-like, mostly in long-stalked clusters (racemes*) in the leaf axils.* Fruit a much-inflated pod (legume*), usually leathery or membranous. (Named for Isaac Swainson, English horticulturist.)

The first species is an old favorite in northern greenhouses, where it should be grown in potting mixture* 4 and kept in the cool house. It is not so commonly grown outdoors in Fla. and Calif. as its handsome flowers warrant. Propagated by cuttings. In Aust. some species are serious cattle poisons.

galegiflora. A smooth shrub or under-shrub, not over 3 ft. high, its branches apt to sprawl or be partly climbing. Leaflets 11–21, oblongish, about ¾ in. long, blunt or notched at the tip. Flowers red, about ¾ in. long, the cluster usually longer than the leaves. Pod 1–2 in. long, stalked. It blooms nearly throughout the year, and is sometimes called winter sweet pea. There are varieties with white flowers (*var.* **albiflora**), with rose-pink flowers (*var.* **rosea**), and with rose-violet flowers (*var.* **violacea**).

greyana. An under-shrub or woody perennial, 2–3 ft. high, the young foliage white-felty, but losing it later. Leaflets 11–21, oblongish, ¾–1½ in. long, blunt or notched at the tip. Flowers about 1 in. wide, pink, in erect, stalked clusters (racemes*). Pod stalked, inflated, 1½–2 in. long.

SWAMP. A wooded wet area usually unsuited for gardening, but sometimes capable of development for a wild garden, where swamp, but not bog, plants may be grown.

The essential difference between a bog and swamp is what determines the suitability of the latter for plants that will not thrive in the acid soils of most bogs. The typical swamp usually has fairly good drainage through it, and its soil or water will rarely show more acidity than a pH of 6.0 or 6.5. Most bogs are much more acid than this. *See* Acid and Alkali Soils for details of making these tests.

Having determined that the area is actually a swamp, that its tree canopy will provide shade, and that its high and low water levels, one is ready to plan its development. If the place is too wet to walk through, it had better be left alone, because there are only two ways of making it available. The first is to lower the water level, which may be expensive or impossible. The other is to construct raised paths through it. The latter plan is probably the easiest in any case and can be done with cheap fill, such as cinders, cellar excavations, or old road material.

The lines of such paths should be as winding and informal as possible. Such a track as cows might make through a swamp would usually be an excellent guide for the future path.

Many wild flowers, ferns, shrubs, and even trees will be perfectly at home in a swamp of this sort. Of course all native material found growing in swamps in the vicinity may be used. Other plants suitable for such places will be found in the genera *Trillium, Arisaema, Lilium, Polemonium, Viola, Myosotis, Cimicifuga, Actaea,* and *Lobelia.* Others are marked with a dagger in the next entry, and still others will be found among the plants mentioned at Wild Garden. *See also* Muckland Gardening.

SWAMP. As an adjective *swamp* has been linked to the names of many cult. plants, some of which grow, not in swamps, but in marshes, bogs, or even in the salt marshes. In other words, those below, while commonly called swamp pink, swamp honeysuckle, etc., may merely be plants of wet places, often too acid to be candidates for a swamp garden. Those in the Encyclopedia and their proper equivalents are listed below. Those that may be classed as true swamp plants are marked with a dagger (†).

Swamp andromeda = *Lyonia ligustrina;* †Swamp ash = *Fraxinus pensylvanica lanceolata* (*see* Ash); Swamp bay = *Magnolia virginiana;* †Swamp cabbage, *see* Skunk-cabbage; †Swamp dewberry = *Rubus hispidus;* Swamp honeysuckle = *Azalea viscosa;* Swamp laurel = *Magnolia virginiana;* Swamp laurel = *Kalmia polifolia;* †Swamp lily = *Crinum americanum;* Swamp locust = *Gleditsia aquatica* (*see* Honey Locust); Swamp loosestrife = *Decodon verticillatus;* Swamp mahogany = *Eucalyptus robusta;* Swamp mallow = *Hibiscus Moscheutos;* †Swamp milkweed = *Asclepias incarnata* (*see* Milkweed); Swamp pink = *Calopogon pulchellus* and *Helonias bullata;* †Swamp privet = *Forestiera acuminata;* Swamp reclamation (*see* Muckland Gardening); †Swamp rose = *Rosa palustris;* †Swamp spleenwort = *Athyrium pycnocarpon;* †Swamp sunflower = *Helianthus angustifolius* (*see* Sunflower); †Swamp tickseed = *Coreopsis rosea;* Swamp white honeysuckle = *Azalea viscosa;* Swamp white oak = *Quercus bicolor* (*see* Oak).

SWAN RIVER DAISY = *Brachycome iberidifolia.*

---

* Special articles on the subjects indicated by an asterisk (*) will be found at the words so marked.

SWAN RIVER EVERLASTING = *Helipterum manglesi*.

SWEDE = *Brassica Napobrassica*. For cult. *see* RUTABAGA.

SWEDISH CLOVER = *Trifolium hybridum*. See CLOVER.

SWEDISH JUNIPER = *Juniperus communis suecica*.

SWEDISH TURNIP = *Brassica Napobrassica*. For cult. *see* RUTABAGA.

SWEET ALISON = Sweet alyssum.

SWEET ALYSSUM. The ever-popular sweet alyssum is the only cult. species of a small group of Mediterranean herbs constituting the genus **Lobularia** (lob-you-lair′i-a) of the mustard family. The only cult. species is **L. maritima**, also known as snowdrift. It grows to 1 ft. high, and is much-branched and spreading. Leaves alternate,* small, lance-shaped to 1½ in. long. Flowers pungent, numerous, small, white, lilac or purple, in terminal racemes.* Calyx* of 4 sepals. Corolla of 4 petals. Stamens* 6, 4 long, 2 short. Fruit a 2-celled capsule. There are several hort. forms, some being more compact with larger flowers, some having double flowers, while others have variegated leaves. Grown as an annual and usually used for edging. Easily cult. Propagated by seeds, sown ⅛ in. deep in ordinary garden soil in a cool greenhouse or cold frame, in March or April. They should be pricked off into boxes and planted outdoors 6 in. apart, when danger of frost is over. They may be sown thinly where required to bloom, in April or May. Sometimes offered as *Koniga*. (*Lobularia* is from the Latin for a little lobe, perhaps in reference to the forked hairs of some species.) Also known as sweet Alison.

SWEET BASIL = *Ocimum Basilicum*.

SWEET BAY = *Magnolia virginiana*. See also LAURUS.

SWEETBELLS = *Leucothoë racemosa*.

SWEET BIRCH = *Betula lenta*. See BIRCH.

SWEETBRIER = *Rosa Eglanteria*.

SWEET BUCKEYE = *Aesculus octandra*. See HORSE-CHESTNUT.

SWEET-BUSH = *Comptonia peregrina*.

SWEET CASSAVA = *Manihot dulcis*.

SWEET CHERRY = *Prunus avium*. For cult. *see* CHERRY.

SWEET CICELY. See MYRRHIS ODORATA.

SWEET CLOVER. See MELILOTUS.

SWEET COLTSFOOT = *Petasites fragrans*.

SWEET CONEFLOWER = *Rudbeckia subtomentosa*.

SWEET CORN. See CORN.

SWEET CRABAPPLE = *Malus coronaria*.

SWEET FALSE CAMOMILE = *Matricaria Chamomilla*.

SWEET FENNEL = *Foeniculum vulgare dulce*. See FENNEL.

SWEET-FERN. See COMPTONIA.

SWEET FLAG = *Acorus Calamus*.

SWEET GALE = *Myrica Gale*.

SWEET GUM. Few trees turn such a gorgeous color as the native sweet gum, which is the only commonly cult. species of the genus **Liquidambar** (liquid-am′bar) of the family Hamamelidaceae. Only 3 other species are known, all of them Asiatic. Our native sweet gum, L. Styraciflua, is a tree up to 120 ft. high, its twigs and young branches corky-winged. Leaves alternate,* star-like, stalked, much resembling a maple, the 3–7 lobes toothed. Flowers small, inconspicuous, mostly unisexual,* and in dense, globe-shaped clusters. Petals none. Fruit a globe-shaped collection of shining, brown capsules,* each tipped with a spine, the whole head, which may be 1¼ in. in diameter, thus prickly. An extremely handsome tree, its foliage brilliant scarlet in the fall. Conn. to Fla., Mo., Ill., and south to Mex. May. It prefers moist, rich soils and is hardy from zone* 3 southward. Propagated by seeds which, even if stratified, do not usually germinate for two years. (*Liquidambar* is from the Latin for liquid and Arabic for amber, in allusion to the fragrant resin of an Asiatic species.)

DISEASES. The sweet gum is relatively free from serious diseases. A condition in the mid-Atlantic states, which has been termed "sweet gum blight," has resulted in death of many trees. Although it may later be proven to be a true disease, this writer believes it is merely a condition resulting from climatic and environmental changes. It is most prevalent along streets, in new home developments, near grade changes, and where water tables have been changed. – S. H. D.

SWEET HERBS. Fragrant herbs used for condiments or for seasoning, sometimes sweet but often bitter or so considered by many. For the distinction between sweet and bitter herbs, their culture and uses, *see* HERB GARDENING.

SWEETLEAF = *Symplocos tinctoria*.

SWEET LEMON. See LEMON.

SWEET LIME. See LIME (the citrus fruit).

SWEET MARJORAM. Old-fashioned, very fragrant perennial herbs or under-shrubs comprising the genus **Majorana** (ma-jor-ray′na) of the mint family. The only commonly cult. species is the ordinary sweet marjoram, **M. hortensis**, sometimes called the annual marjoram because it is often grown as an annual. It has opposite,* stalked, elliptic leaves, about ½ in. long and without marginal teeth. Flowers small, purplish or whitish, crowded in dense, white-hairy whorls* which are grouped in spikes. Corolla 2-lipped,* not much protruding beyond the oblique calyx.* Eu. For uses and culture *see* HERB GARDENING. The plant is sometimes known as *Origanum majorana*. See ORIGANUM. A related plant, **M. Onites**, is also offered. It differs from *M. hortensis* chiefly in having stalkless leaves and somewhat larger flowers. It is a perennial from Eastern Eu. and western As. (*Majorana* is perhaps derived from an Old French word, *majoraine,* but of uncertain application to this plant.)

SWEET MOCK-ORANGE = *Philadelphus coronarius.* See Mock-orange.

SWEET OLEANDER = *Nerium indicum.* See Oleander.

SWEET OLIVE. See Osmanthus.

SWEET ORANGE = *Citrus sinensis.* For cult. *see* Orange.

SWEET PEA. The sweet pea, *Lathyrus odoratus,* is perhaps the most highly developed of all annuals. Its culture affords pleasure to millions; the production of seeds is an important industry, while as a commercial cut flower it is one of the most popular of crops. The sweet pea was first introduced into England from Sicily in 1700, but not until some 150 years later was it seriously taken in hand by Henry Eckford who raised and introduced more than 200 varieties. To celebrate its 200th year in England, a great show was held in London in 1900, and large annual sweet-pea shows have been held in London ever since. In 1904 Countess Spencer, a wavy-petaled sport of Eckford's Prima Donna, was introduced, and caused such a furore that within a few years the smooth-petaled varieties became obsolete. From the time Eckford began his work to the present time there are records of more than 3000 varieties, but not more than 300 are now in cultivation.

Early in the 20th century, too, the first early-flowering varieties appeared. These were later crossed with the waved Spencers. Their origin and development are entirely American. The early-flowering varieties are not important for outdoor culture; their principal value is that, under glass in a temperature of 50°, they can be flowered from September until the end of June. The late-flowering sorts, when grown under glass, cannot be made to flower before early spring. Outdoors, the early-flowering kinds do not grow so vigorously, and they bloom but little earlier than the ordinary sorts.

Sweet peas are essentially cool weather plants, and they quickly fade away if the temperature persists for long above 75°. In the sea-cooled areas of New England and the Pacific Northwest, sweet peas can be grown successfully throughout the summer. In the central states from coast to coast, high-class sweet peas cannot be grown after mid-June, except at high elevations. In some of the southern states sweet peas can be had for a longer period than farther north, as the plants can make earlier growth and flower in May. In southern California sweet peas can be flowered still earlier and it is in the neighborhood of Los Angeles that at least two-thirds of the world's sweet-pea seeds are produced. But while there are sections of

the United States where it is almost impossible to get a worth-while crop of sweet-pea flowers because winter lingers late and summer comes with a rush, there are few places where it is too cool for this delightful annual.

It follows that in most parts of the United States the need for an early start is highly important. The plants must be well established before hot weather arrives, but if the heat is extreme and persistent, nothing will keep the plants growing vigorously, though it is possible to carry the plants through July and even later if a cheesecloth shading is erected over the plants. *See* Cloth.

While in some seasons it is possible to make a sowing outdoors in the fall, this operation is hazardous. The seed should be sown 2 in. deep in rows in mid-November in the Atlantic states, so that the seeds will germinate but not appear above ground. When hard freezing starts, cover well with salt hay or other litter and remove when growth starts in early spring. Thin out if necessary, and provide support as soon as the plants are 3 or 4 in. tall. A safer plan is to sow the seeds in early October in a cold frame. Give all the ventilation possible until hard frost sets in, then heavily cover the frame with mats. Uncover when winter is departing and, as soon as the ground is workable, carefully set the plants outdoors 4 to 6 in. apart.

The best plan for most sections is to sow in February indoors or in a greenhouse in flats of fairly sandy soil. The white-seeded kinds, which are liable to rot, should have pure sand as a covering; the seeds should not be covered more than ½ in. Water sparingly and place in a temperature of about 60°. As soon as they appear expose to full light and drop the temperature to about 50°. When 2 or 3 in. tall, pot into 2¼-in. pots, singly, and as soon as possible shift to a protected frame. Pinch out the tops when four or five sets of leaves have been made, and plant out, after thorough hardening, in well-prepared soil.

In some sections, even in the neighborhood of New York, if the season proves rather cool, it is possible to grow a respectable crop of sweet peas by sowing where they are to flower, in late March or early April. The soil, however, should be prepared in the fall so that it can settle. This is essential, as sweet peas like firm ground. Sow the seed 2 in. deep and cover with sandy soil.

Mention has been made of the tendency of white seeds to rot. Most white and cream varieties have white seeds, while lavender sorts usually have mottled seeds; these also are rather more weakly than the dark seeds which indicate varieties possessing a red tint. Very dark seeds are apt to be very hard and slow-germinating. It is a good practice to soak all dark seeds in water before sowing, and plant after they have swelled. Any seeds that have not swelled after 24 hours should be "nicked" with a file, but not near the germ, or given a sulphuric-acid bath.

---

* Special articles on the subjects indicated by an asterisk (*) will be found at the words so marked.

From three to five minutes in pure acid is usually sufficient, and the seeds should then be well washed under the faucet before sowing.

To grow good sweet peas the entire plot, or at least rows 2 ft. wide, should be double dug, the whole depth of soil receiving a good dressing of well-rotted manure as well as a moderate application of some good fertilizer. Sweet peas are great feeders and must have nourishment and plenty of moisture.

There are two methods of culture or training, natural and exhibition. The former gives quantities of fair-sized flowers on medium stems. All the laterals are allowed to remain, except that it is sometimes advantageous to cut back the leading growths when they harden, and allow the younger growths to carry on. When once the vines become woody, short-stemmed flowers are certain. Exhibition or cordon growing means fewer but giant flowers, sometimes as many as five and six, on stems 18 in. or more in length. This system is not, however, worth while unless climatic or other conditions permit the plants to grow well into summer, as the finest flowers cannot be obtained until the plants attain a height of 4 ft. or more. The plants should be planted 9 in. or so apart and allowed to carry two or three main growths. All side shoots or laterals that appear in the leaf axils* must be pinched out, leaving only the flower buds that likewise appear in the leaf axils.* So treated, the plants, if conditions permit, grow 8 ft. or more, but can be kept down to a reasonable height by training. Exhibition plants need constant attention and much tying, especially if bamboo stakes are used for supports. To ensure continuous flowering no seed pods should be allowed to develop.

For general purposes, there is no better support for sweet peas than hazel or other twiggy branches, flat trimmed, and pushed firmly into the ground on both sides of the plants. On no account should the young plants be allowed to stand without support after planting, as boisterous winds may damage them. Ordinary large-mesh chicken wire, fastened to strong posts, makes a good support, and for preference this should be on both sides of the rows, as the plants are better able to climb between a double support.

Among the finest varieties are: Spencers, which flower rather early and do not stand the heat (in all colors but yellow); Cuthbertsons, reputedly able to stand summer heat; so-called Giants (taller than the type); Early Flowering; Multiflora (reputedly with 5–6 flowers in a cluster). For fragrance choose Ambition (lavender-lilac), Cheers (pink), Fragrance (cream), Kames (white), Light Blue (blue), and Myra (salmon).

The culture of sweet peas under glass is comparatively simple. The plants are best grown in well-prepared beds, but in a small way they can be successfully flowered in 10-in. pots. For winter flowering sow the seed early in August in 3-in. pots, thinning to two or three when well started. Shift into flower pots or plant out without disturbing the roots. For early-spring flowering sow in November and shift before the roots become pot-bound. Keep cool at all times; never run the night temperature above 50°, and 45° is sufficient. Ventilate freely and fumigate or spray regularly. — T. A. W.

INSECT PESTS. See aphid at PEA, leaf tier at CHRYSANTHEMUM, red spider at ROSE, and sawbugs at CINERARIA. See nematodes and garden centipede at INSECT PESTS.

DISEASES. Sweet peas are subject to several root-rot diseases if grown year after year in the same soil, or in soil where garden peas or beans have been raised.

The virus disease mosaic* may cause streaks in foliage and stunting of plants. The disease is more likely to be severe if aphids are numerous.

If powdery mildew* becomes a problem, apply pesticide #9 (see SPRAYS AND DUSTS) at weekly intervals.

SWEET PEPPER = *Capsicum frutescens grossum.*

SWEET PEPPERBUSH = *Clethra alnifolia.*

SWEET PITAHAYA = *Lemaireocereus thurberi.*

SWEET POTATO (*Ipomoea Batatas*). Originally a tropical American morning-glory, the modern sweet potato is distinctly a warm-season crop or one for regions where there is continuous heat. It is grown commercially only in the South, but good crops may be secured in the East, as far north as southern New Jersey. Generally speaking, it should not be attempted above zone* 5 in the East, although occasional crops can be secured on western Long Island. In the Far West only southern and central Calif., Ariz., N. Mex., and southern and eastern Tex. are really suited to it. Good crops, however, are harvested in southern Ill.

The stems are very long, trailing vines which, as the crop matures, will completely cover the ground between the rows. Because of this, spacing and cultivation must be carefully arranged as in the subsequent directions.

SOILS AND FERTILIZERS. Sweet potatoes do best on very sandy, warm soils. They will not tolerate clay or muck soils, but good crops can often be raised on sandy loams. If the soil is too rich in nitrogen, most of the growth will be vine instead of the desired root. Some growers, because of this, use no fertilizer for sweet potatoes, especially if they follow other crops that were adequately fertilized the year before. An application of a commercial fertilizer with a ratio of 2–8–10 (see FERTILIZERS) at the rate of 4–5 pounds per 100-ft. row should be used if none was used the year previous.

VARIETIES. If you are on or near the northern limits of sweet-potato culture by all means use Big-stem Jersey. It is a mealy, relatively dry-rooted sort that stands up better than the moist-fleshed kinds which can

---

* Special articles on the subjects indicated by an asterisk (*) will be found at the words so marked.

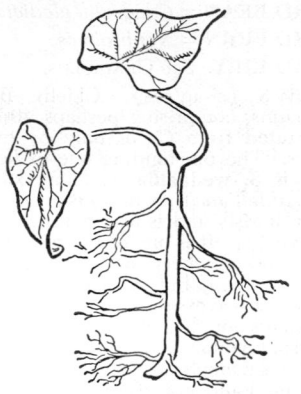

A draw of the sweet potato, and the most convenient way of starting a plantation.

only be grown farther south. Other relatively hardy sorts for the northern part of the sweet-potato region are Yellow Jersey (yellow-skinned) and Red Jersey (red-skinned).

For the moist-fleshed varieties, suited to farther south, the best selection should include: Yellow Belmont, Pumpkin, Puerto Rico and Nancy Hall. Puerto Rico is less inclined to sprawl than the others.

In Calif. Prolific and Priestly, besides those mentioned, are also used.

PLANTING. The home grower (and many commercial ones) rarely raise sweet-potato plants from "seed." Actually the plant does not flower or set true seed as cultivated anywhere in the United States, except, possibly, near Key West. Plants are raised by specialists who utilize the habit of the sweet potato to throw off from its swollen root a shoot that develops from adventitious* buds. These slips or "draws," as they are called, are then separated from the old root and grown along until ready for planting outdoors. The whole process requires so much care and skillful handling that most growers are glad to use the plentiful supplies of such slips that the dealers offer at planting time.

The slips should not be set out before June 20 in southern N.J., but earlier farther southward (March 1 in La., April 1 in Los Angeles). The plant does not want merely absence of coolness; it needs more heat than almost any other garden crop. A soil temperature of 70°–80° is ideal. At a soil temperature of 60° the plant will often stop growth — at 50° it will die if that temperature is maintained.

For the northern varieties make the rows 30 in. apart and plant the slips 15 in. apart in the row. For the southern (mostly moist-fleshed) varieties the rows should be 4–5 ft. apart, and the slips set 20–24 in. apart. In both sorts a cupful of water should be poured over each planted slip.

CULTIVATION. This will be possible only in the early stages of growth because of the great spread of the vines. Do it often and thoroughly or weeds will be a serious problem when cultivation is no longer possible. Cultivation for the conservation of moisture is not very necessary, for the plant will stand dryness more than most vegetables. The period of cultivation may be increased by lifting the vines to prevent their rooting at the joints.

HARVESTING AND SUBSEQUENT CARE. It will take all the growing season for the roots to become big enough for harvesting. There is no surface indication (as in ordinary potatoes) when this time has arrived. When you think it has, dig up a plant and see. By so doing the home grower can harvest part of his crop and leave the rest for subsequent diggings.

If more than temporary needs are harvested, or if an early frost arrives, the sweet-potato grower must act quickly. The vines go black at the slightest touch of frost. If left in place, their juice will pass down into the root and ruin the crop. Cut frost-touched vines at once, leaving the potatoes in the ground for more leisurely digging.

When they are dug, or you have a surplus of roots from unfrosted vines, do not let the roots stand in the sun for more than an hour or two, and they must never be left on the surface of the ground overnight. They must be handled with extreme care, and all injured or cut roots used at once or thrown away. No crop rots quicker than sweet potatoes.

If the harvest is to be kept (as in nearly all commercial production), the roots must be cured at once. This is accomplished by placing them, uninjured, on frames or open-slat trays. Put the trays in a room (often specially constructed) in which the temperature can be kept between 80° and 86°. The heat (preferably applied at the bottom) will drive off much moisture. This must pass out of the room by proper ventilation, not condense on the walls and run down. Continue the process for 10 days or two weeks, after which the temperature is dropped to 55° and held there until the sweet potatoes are used.

Fresh sweet potatoes, without this curing, will last only a brief period without rotting, although their keeping period may, on a small scale, be lengthened by burying them in moist sand.

In the South, the vine, or its root, is sometimes, but incorrectly, called a yam, which is a very different plant. (See DIOSCOREA.)

INSECT PESTS. In the South, a weevil attacks roots. Start with clean slips, dip in pesticide #19 (see SPRAYS AND DUSTS), 1 lb. to 10 gals., before planting and dust in the field with pesticide #17 or #15.

Tortoise-shell beetle and flea beetles can be controlled by pesticide #1 or arsenicals. Treat soil with pesticide #15, #13, or #16 as recommended on label for wireworms and white grubs.

DISEASES. A number of diseases attack sweet potato in the propagation bed, the new "slips," the plants in the field, or the tubers in storage. If a general program for disease

* Special articles on the subjects indicated by an asterisk (*) will be found at the words so marked.

control is followed, the best results will be obtained.

Select clean potatoes and dip in a suspension of 1 pound of captan in 5 gallons of water. In the area where potatoes are to be bedded, mix 3 pounds of superphosphate and 1 pound of ferbam in each 100 square feet of bed surface, and water in. When sprouts and slips are taken from the potatoes, dip them in the same captan mixture as described above, and plant in the field.

In some areas of the country, virus diseases may be serious enough on some varieties to cause serious losses. A mosaic* or yellow dwarf disease reduces size of plants to a point where no potatoes are produced.

SWEET SCABIOUS = *Scabiosa atropurpurea.*

SWEET-SCENTED SHRUB = *Calycanthus.*

SWEET-SHRUB = *Calycanthus.*

SWEETSOP = *Annona squamosa.*

SWEET SORGHUM = *Sorghum vulgare saccharatum.*

SWEET SPIRE = *Itea virginica.*

SWEET SULTAN = *Centaurea moschata.* See also CNICUS BENEDICTUS.

SWEET VERNAL GRASS = *Anthoxanthum odoratum.*

SWEET VIOLET = *Viola odorata.*

SWEET WHITE VIOLET = *Viola blanda.*

SWEET WILLIAM = *Dianthus barbatus.* For the wild Sweet William see PHLOX DIVARICATA.

SWEET WILLIAM CATCHFLY = *Silene Armeria.*

SWEET WOODRUFF = *Asperula odorata.*

SWEET WORMWOOD = *Artemisia annua.*

SWEET YARROW = *Achillea Ageratum.*

SWERTIA. See FRASERA.

SWIETENIA (swy-tee′ni-a). Tropical American trees of the family Meliaceae, of no hort. interest except that one of the three known species, **S. Mahagoni,** the mahogany, is planted for interest or shade in extreme southern Fla. It is the traditional mahogany (there are many African and Philippine Island substitutes) and is a large evergreen tree with hard wood, which becomes redbrown in age. Leaves alternate,* compound,* the 4–8 leaflets arranged feather-fashion, without an odd one at the end. Leaflets leathery, without teeth, 2–4 in. long. Flowers small, inconspicuous, whitish, in clusters (panicles*). Fruit a 5-valved woody capsule,* 3–4 in. long, its winged seeds nearly 2 in. long. (Named for Gerard van Swieten, Dutch botanist and physician.)

SWISS CHARD. See BEET.

SWISS MOUNTAIN PINE = *Pinus Mugo.* See PINE.

SWISS STONE PINE = *Pinus Cembra.* See PINE.

SWITCH GRASS = *Panicum virgatum.*

SWORD BEAN = *Canavalia gladiata.*

SWORD FERN = *Nephrolepis.*

SWORD LILY. See GLADIOLUS.

SYAGRUS (si-ag′rus). Chiefly Brazilian feather palms, comprising perhaps 40 species, and separated from *Cocos* only by technical characters. The outstanding one of hort. significance is **S. weddellianus** (long known as *Cocos weddelliana*), which is very widely grown by florists and is also planted outdoors in southern Fla. It is one of the most delicate, graceful, and feathery of all palms, never over 6–7 ft. high, but with a slender trunk. The drooping leaves usually touch the ground, the segments or leaflets long and narrow. In the usual young state (*i.e.,* a florists' pot plant) the segments are scarcely ¼ in. wide and 4–6 in. long, gracefully drooping. Fruit oblongish or roundish, about ½ in. long, rarely or never produced in greenhouse specimens. Rio de Janeiro. For greenhouse cult. *see* PALM. In Fla. it is prized for outdoor planting, but is safe only in zone* 9, where it makes a very graceful lawn specimen. (*Syagrus* is from the Latin for wild pig, and a name for some sort of palm, but not this one.)

SYCAMORE. The traditional sycamore and the one mentioned in the Bible is *Ficus Sycomorus,* a tree not usually cult. For the tree called sycamore in the U.S. *see* PLATANUS OCCIDENTALIS.

SYCAMORE MAPLE = *Acer Pseudo-platanus.* See MAPLE.

SYDNEY GOLDEN WATTLE = *Acacia longifolia.*

sylvatica, *-us,* *-um* (sill-vat′i-ka). Wood-inhabiting; *i.e.,* a forest plant.

sylvester (sill-ves′ter). Growing in forests.

sylvestris, *-e* (sill-ves′triss). Growing in forests.

SYMMETRICAL. See REGULAR FLOWER.

SYMPHORICARPOS (sim-for-i-kar′pos). Ornamental, hardy shrubs of the honeysuckle family, more showy in fruit than in flower. All but one Chinese species are American, and of the 16 known kinds, all of those below are in pretty frequent cult. here. Leaves opposite,* short-stalked, usually without teeth or lobes. Flowers small, not very showy, mostly in small clusters which are terminal or in the leaf axils.* Corolla not over ⅓ in. long (in ours), bell-shaped or tubular, the limb* 4–5-lobed. Stamens* 4–5. Fruit a rather showy, 2-seeded berry, usually borne in pairs or small clusters. (*Symphoricarpos* is from the Greek for bearing together and fruit, in allusion to the clustered fruits.)

These are excellent shrubs for partly shady places or for the open; they are far more smoke-resistant than many other ornamental plants and thus excellent for city planting. They will also grow in a great variety of soils. Easily propagated by seeds, cuttings,

---

* Special articles on the subjects indicated by an asterisk (*) will be found at the words so marked.

by division, or by detaching the numerous suckers.*

albus. Snowberry. Waxberry. Not over 3 ft. high, the branches slender and upright. Leaves ovalish or oblong, 1–2 in. long, blunt. Flowers pinkish. Fruit white. Throughout northern N.A. June–Aug. Hardy from zone* 2 southward. Well liked by bees. The *var.* laevigatus is nearly twice as tall, and has larger leaves. This is the form most common in cult., usually under the name *S. racemosus.*

chenaulti. A hybrid shrub derived from crossing *S. orbiculatus* with a Mexican species. It is 5–7 ft. high, the leaves hairy beneath. Flowers pinkish. Fruit red, but white-dotted. Hardy from zone* 3 southward and handsome in fruit.

mollis. Partly prostrate or decumbent* shrub, the twigs somewhat velvety. Leaves nearly round, ¾–2 in. wide, hairy both sides. Flowers pinkish, or white. Fruit white. British Columbia to Calif. June–July. Hardy from zone* 3 southward.

occidentalis. Wolfberry; also called buckbrush. Not over 5 ft. high, the branches rather stiff and erect. Leaves ovalish, 2–3 in. long, gray-hairy beneath. Flowers pinkish. Fruit white. British Columbia and Colo. east to Mich. and Kan., probably far northward. June–July. Hardy everywhere.

orbiculatus. Indian currant. Coralberry. A shrub 5–7 ft. high, the branches erect. Leaves elliptic or ovalish, 1½–2½ in. long, pale and hairy beneath. Flowers white. Fruit reddish-purple, plentiful. Pa. to Ga. and westward to S. D. and Tex. July. Hardy from zone* 3 southward, and very attractive in the fall from the profusion of fruit and the long-persistent crimson foliage. *Var.* **leucocarpus** has greenish-yellow flowers and white fruit. It thrives in poor soil and in partial shade. There is also a variegated-leaved form. The plant is often sold as *S. vulgaris.*

racemosus = *Symphoricarpos albus laevigatus.*

vulgaris = *Symphoricarpos orbiculatus.*

SYMPHYANDRA (sim-fi-an′dra). Hardy biennial or perennial herbs, comprising about 8 species of the family Campanulaceae, natives of eastern Eu. and western As. Leaves mostly basal, usually heart-shaped, hairy, and long-stalked. Stem leaves alternate,* few and smaller. Flowers white or yellowish, large, in terminal clusters (racemes*). Calyx of 5 sepals. Corolla bell-shaped. Stamens* 5, joined by their anthers,* forming a tube around the style, for this reason differing from *Campanula.* Fruit a 3-celled capsule.* (*Symphyandra* is from the Greek for anthers grown together.) For culture *see* CAMPANULA.

hofmanni. Hairy perennial, growing to 2 ft. high, with drooping branches. Leaves broadly lance-shaped, to 7 in. long, heart-shaped at base. Margins with small and large teeth. Flowers white, bell-shaped, 1½ in. long and wide, in terminal leafy clusters. Corolla hairy on the inside. Bosnia. July.

pendula. Dwarf, hairy perennial, growing to 1 ft. high. Leaves heart-shaped, the lower long-stalked, the margins coarsely toothed. Flowers yellowish, bell-shaped, to 1¼ in. long, in terminal racemes.* Caucasus.

SYMPHYTUM (sim-fy′tum). Comfrey. Hardy perennial herbs, comprising about 20 species, belonging to the forget-me-not family (Boraginaceae), and natives of Eu., northern Af., and western As. Coarse-growing with thick rootstocks, sometimes tuberous. Stem and leaves covered with bristly hairs. Basal leaves large, the stem leaves alternate* or opposite.* Flowers yellowish, blue, white, rose, or purple, in terminal, 1-sided, branching clusters. Calyx of 5 sepals, hairy on the outside. Corolla tubular. Stamens* 5. Fruit 2-celled, splitting into 4 when ripe. (*Symphytum* is from the Greek meaning to grow together, in allusion to the assumed healing properties.)

The comfrey is grown in the border and is a bit weedy. Propagated by seeds or division of the rootstocks.

asperrimum = *Symphytum asperum.*

asperum. Prickly comfrey. Growing to 5 ft. high. Leaves ovalish, covered on both sides with stiff, bristly hairs, stalked, the stalks winged. Flowers rose, turning blue, about ½ in. long, in terminal, 1-sided clusters. Sometimes used as forage. Russia to Persia.

officinale. Growing to 3 ft. high and much-branched. Leaves broadly lance-shaped, covered with stiff, bristly hairs. Flowers yellowish, rose or white, in terminal, 1-sided clusters. Eu. and As., naturalized in N.A. The *var.* **variegatum** has leaves with creamy-white margins.

SYMPLOCACEAE (sim-plo-kay′see-ee). A family of shrubs or trees comprising only one genus, *Symplocos,* which see for a description of the only cult. species in the Symplocaceae.

SYMPLOCARPUS. See SKUNK-CABBAGE.

SYMPLOCOS (sim-plō′kos). A large genus of 280 species of trees and shrubs found in most tropical and warm regions (except Af.), at least one in the southeastern U.S. They constitute the family Symplocaceae, and two of them are cult. for ornament, although they are of secondary garden importance. Leaves alternate,* evergreen in some species. Flowers usually small and inconspicuous, but pleasantly fragrant, mostly in stalked or nearly stalkless clusters. Calyx* 5-lobed. Corolla 5–10-lobed, or (in ours) with as many nearly distinct petals. Stamens* 15 or more, often in bunches and fastened to the corolla. Fruit (in ours) an orange or blue drupe,* its stone 1–5-seeded. (*Symplocos* is from the Greek for connected, in allusion to the often united stamens.*)

The two below are difficult to propagate, as the seeds are slow to germinate. Also propagated by cuttings of green wood under glass.

paniculata. A shrub or small tree, 20–35 ft. high. Leaves short-stalked, oblongish, 2–3 in. long, the margins finely toothed. Flowers fragrant, white, the clusters 2–3 in. long. Corolla about ⅓ in. long. Fruit about ½ in. long, bright blue. Jap., China, southward to the Himalayas. May–June. Hardy from zone* 3 southward.

tinctoria. Sweetleaf; also called horse sugar in the South. A shrub or small tree 15–24 ft. high, the foliage half-evergreen or evergreen in the deep South. Leaves elliptic to oblongish,

---

* Special articles on the subjects indicated by an asterisk (*) will be found at the words so marked.

thickish, 4–6 in. long, obscurely toothed or with no teeth. Flowers yellowish, fragrant, in dense, nearly stalkless clusters. Corolla about ⅔ in. wide. Fruit about ⅓ in. long, orange or brown. Del. to Fla. and Texas. May. Hardy from zone* 5 southward.

SYNADENIUM (sin-a-dee′ni-um). Fleshy-stemmed African shrubs of the family Euphorbiaceae, the only one of hort. interest being **S. granti,** the African milk-bush. It is an erect shrub, 8–12 ft. high, the branches thick, fleshy, and with a milky juice (probably poisonous). Leaves alternate,* thick and fleshy, broadest toward the tip, 4–5 in. long. Flower clusters red. For details *see* EUPHORBIACEAE. The milk-bush is cult. as an interesting succulent in tropical regions, but it is scarcely hardy outside of zone* 9. If grown in the greenhouse *see* the cultural notes at SUCCULENTS. (*Synadenium* is from the Greek for united, in allusion to a technical character in the involucral glands.)

SYNCARP. A collective fruit (*see* FRUIT). The term is more botanical than horticultural, although syncarps occur in plants like the mulberry, pineapple, and *Annona.* Perhaps the best-known one is the special sort of syncarp found in the fig (which see). All syncarps are the products of the ovaries of several flowers.

SYNDESMON = *Anemonella.*

SYNGONANTHUS (sin-go-nan′thus). Chiefly Brazilian or African herbs of no garden interest except that two of them are widely imported in the dried state as delicate, very small, and beautiful everlastings. The two species are S. *niveus* and S. *elegans,* both natives of southern Brazil.

They have small, button-like heads of chaffy flowers and are conspicuous in florists' windows from their wide use as trimming for miniature trees and other stylistic decorations. *See* MING TREE. The small clusters of *Syngonanthus* are wired onto the miniature tree and provide its "bloom." Some of these trees have been so skillfully covered with these Brazilian everlastings as to suggest a dried, dwarfed tree with its own bloom. *Syngonanthus* belongs to the family Eriocaulaceae, otherwise unknown in cult.

SYNONYMS. Latin plant names that are obsolete or incorrect. *See* PLANT NAMES.

SYNTHETIC MANURE. *See* Artificial Manure at MANURE.

SYNTHYRIS (sin-thy′riss). Hardy perennial herbs, comprising about 15 species, belonging to the snapdragon family (Scrophulariaceae), natives of N.A. and Eu. They are low-growing plants, with thick rootstocks and basal leaves. Leaves smooth or hairy, variously shaped, sometimes deeply cut, long-stalked, the margins toothed. Flowers white, blue, or reddish, in spikes or racemes.* Calyx of 4 sepals. Corolla shortly tubular, 4-lobed or sometimes undivided. Stamens* 2. Fruit a 2-celled capsule.* (*Synthyris* is from the Greek for together, and a little door or valve, in allusion to the fruit.)

They are not of much garden importance, but are sometimes used in the border. Propagated by seeds or divisions of the rootstocks.

lanuginosa. An arctic-alpine, low, white-hairy perennial, useful only in the rock garden, and with woody base. Leaves twice or thrice cut, the segments toothed. Flower stalks exceeding the foliage, the cluster a spiky raceme,* ¾–2 in. long. Flowers pink or bluish-violet. Mountains of Olympic Peninsula, Wash. June.

pinnatifida. Perhaps not in cult. The *var.* **lanuginosa** is now considered as *Synthris lanuginosa.*

reniformis. Growing to 9 in. high. Leaves basal, long-stalked, roundish or kidney-shaped, to 2 in. across, bright, shiny green, the margins deeply toothed. Flowers bluish-purple, ¼ in. long, numerous, in racemes* to 5 in. long. Calif. to Wash.

rotundifolia. Low-growing, to 5 in. high. Leaves basal, stalked, ovalish, heart-shaped at the base, to 2 in. long, slightly hairy, the margins with 2 rows of teeth. Flowers white, small, in few-flowered racemes.* Ore.

stellata. An erect perennial, 7–15 in. high, the smooth leaves divided finger-fashion into 15 doubly toothed lobes. Flower cluster a raceme* 5–7 in. long, usually with 3 or 4 pairs of doubly toothed bracts* beneath the cluster. Flowers blue, about ¾ in. long. Ore. April–May.

syriaca, -us, -um (si-ri-ā′ka). From Syria.

SYRINGA. One of the most confusing names in hort. literature. The genus *Syringa* comprises the lilacs, but the common name syringa is widely used for the shrubs better known as mock-orange. *See* LILAC, MOCK-ORANGE.

syringantha, -us, -um (sir-ing-gan′tha). With lilac-like flowers.

SYSTEMIC INSECTICIDES. *See* No. 6 at INSECTICIDES.

---

* Special articles on the subjects indicated by an asterisk (*) will be found at the words so marked.

T

Tabacum (ta-back'um). Latinized form of the original Indian word for tobacco.

TABEBUIA (ta-be-bew'i-a). A genus of over 60 species of timber trees of tropical America, of the family Bignoniaceae, of which a few have been introduced into zones* 8 and 9 in Fla. as ornamentals. They have handsome winter-blooming flowers in showy clusters. Leaves in those below compound, the leaflets arranged finger-fashion, and without marginal teeth. Flowers in panicles,* funnel-shaped. Stamens* 4. Fruit a long catalpa-like pod (capsule*), seldom setting seed in cult. (*Tabebuia* is derived from the Brazilian vernacular for some species.)

Some of the species are called white cedar and there are many Spanish and Portuguese vernaculars for the valuable timbers of some species. Of the dozen or so introduced into Fla. within comparatively recent times only the two below are likely to interest the average gardener.

argentea. Silver-trumpet tree. An evergreen tree, not over 25 ft. high, its bark soft, corky and whitish. Leaves with 5–7 oblong, silvery leaflets, 4–6 in. long. Flowers yellow, about 2½ in. long, in a showy cluster. Paraguay. March–April, often followed by a new crop of leaves. Often vine-like in youth, ultimately erect.

pallida. White cedar. An evergreen tree, 60 ft. high in the wild, less as cult. in Fla. Leaves with 3–5 elliptic leaflets, 4–6 in. long, persisting through the winter but often renewed after the bloom has passed. Flowers usually pink, sometimes white and pink-veined, in extremely showy terminal clusters (panicles*), the corolla* 2½–3 in. long. Central and northern S.A.; W.I. There is still some confusion as to the identity of this tree in Fla., as another tree passing as *T. pallida* is deciduous.*

TABERNAEMONTANA (ta-ber-nee-montan'a). A genus of about 160 species of tropical shrubs and trees of the family Apocynaceae, two of them planted for ornament in zones* 8 and 9, possibly safe in protected parts of zone* 7. They have opposite* leaves, without marginal teeth, and terminal clusters (cymes*) of rather handsome white or yellow flowers. Calyx* 5-parted. Corolla salver-shaped, its tube cylindrical, the lobes somewhat twisted to the left. Stamens* 5. Fruit a collection of 2 pods (follicles*) or fleshy. (Named for J. T. Tabernaemontanus, German botanist and physician, who is also commemorated by species named for him in *Scirpus* and *Amsonia*.)

The first species is a very popular plant for sub-tropical gardens. It should be planted in rich, sandy loam, not too dry, and preferably in the open. It is not easy to trans-

plant, and potted specimens, derived from cuttings, are best grown along until a foot or two high and then planted with as little disturbance of the roots as possible. Young plants, freshly set out in Sept.–Oct., must be protected from frost (if in zones* 8 or 7), by banking with sand or soil for the first winter. Later they will usually stand without this protection. Propagated by cuttings.

coronaria. Crape jasmine; also called East Indian rose-bay, Adam's-apple, and Nero's-crown. A beautifully fragrant shrub 5–8 ft. high. Leaves shining green, oblongish, 3–5 in. long. Flowers white, 1½–2 in. wide, the lobes crisped. India and cult. throughout the tropical and sub-tropical world, especially in the double-flowered form. Also known as *Ervatamia coronaria*.

grandiflora. A shrub, 4–6 ft. high. Leaves oblongish, 3–5 in. long, pointed at the tip. Flowers yellow, not fragrant, about 1½ in. wide. Central and northern South America. Not much known in cult., but occasionally grown in southern Fla.

TABLE MOUNTAIN PINE = *Pinus pungens*. See PINE.

tabularis, -e (tab-you-lar'is). Flattened like a table.

TACAMAHAC. See POPULUS BALSAMIFERA.

TAGETES. See MARIGOLD.

TAHITI LIME. See Acid Lime at LIME (the citrus fruit).

TAHITI ORANGE = *Citrus taitensis*.

TAHOKA DAISY = *Machaeranthera tanacetifolia*.

TAIL-FLOWER = *Anthurium*.

TAIL-GRAPE = *Artabotrys*.

TAINUI = *Pomaderris apetala*.

taitensis, -e (ty-ten'sis). From Tahiti, one of the Society Islands in the south Pacific.

taiwanensis, -e (ty-wan-nen'sis). From Taiwan (Formosa).

TALINUM (ta-ly'num). Rather fleshy-leaved, perennial herbs of the family Portulacaceae, comprising about 50 species, and of secondary hort. interest except for **T. calycinum**, the rock pink, a native from Ill. to Neb. south to Mex., and occasionally grown in the rock garden. It is an erect plant, 6–12 in. high, from a thick rootstock. Leaves cylindrical, mostly clustered at the base, about 2 in. long, the leaf base broadened. Flowers pink, fugitive, about 1 in. wide, in a loose, terminal, few-flowered cluster (cyme*). Petals, sepals, and stamens* usually 5 each. Fruit a 3-valved, nearly globe-shaped capsule.* The plant prefers a gritty or sandy soil, blooms in June, and repays a light, strawy mulch in winter. (*Talinum*

---

* Special articles on the subjects indicated by an asterisk (*) will be found at the words so marked.

is thought to be derived from a Senegal name for another species.)

TALL BEARDED IRIS. *See* Iris.

TALL COREOPSIS = *Coreopsis tripteris.*

TALL FESCUE = *Festuca elatior.*

TALL MEADOW OAT = *Arrhenatherum elatius.*

TALL MEADOW RUE = *Thalictrum polygamum.*

TALL OAT GRASS = *Arrhenatherum elatius.*

TALL SUNFLOWER = *Helianthus giganteus. See* Sunflower.

TALLOW SHRUB = *Myrica cerifera.*

TALLOW-TREE. *See* Sapium.

TAMARACK = *Larix laricina. See* Larch.

TAMARICACEAE (tam-a-ri-kay′see-ee). The tamarisk family comprises only 4 genera and about 100 species of curious, salt-resistant shrubs and trees, two of which, *Tamarix* and *Myricaria,* are of hort. interest, especially to seashore gardeners. They are apparently leafless, cedar-like, arching shrubs which actually have innumerable scale-like, tiny leaves pressed flat against the twigs, which, especially the smaller ones, fall with the leaves.

Flowers very small, prevailingly pinkish, stalkless, in small spikes, these grouped in a terminal, branching cluster, and in the mass, quite attractive. Fruit a small pod (capsule*). Some species of *Tamarix,* especially *T. gallica,* are widely grown for ornament. Some species make excellent sand binders.

Technical flower characters: Flowers extremely small, regular* and perfect. Sepals 4 or 5. Stamens* 4 or more. Ovary superior,* 1-celled.

TAMARIND = *Tamarindus indica.* For the Manila tamarind *see* Pithecolobium dulce.

TAMARIND FAMILY. *See* Leguminosae.

TAMARINDUS (tam-a-rin′dus). A single species of very widely cult. trees, **T. indica,** the tamarind, belonging to the pea family. Its edible fruit, long thought to come from India, resulted in its being named as from that country, although it is probably native in tropical Africa. Cult. in the U.S. only in zone* 9, as it will not stand the occasional frosts of zone* 8, and has never been a success in Calif. It is an immense round-headed tree, casting an extremely dense shade. Leaves alternate,* compound,* the leaflets arranged feather-fashion, without an odd one at the end, small, numerous, about ⅝ in. long, more or less oblong. Flowers yellow, irregular,* but not pea-like, in terminal clusters (racemes*). Calyx tubular, 4-lobed, colored. Petals 5, the 3 upper overlapping, the 2 lower much reduced and hidden within the tube-like collection of stamens.* Fruit a pod which does not split,

3–8 in. long, somewhat constricted between its large seeds which are embedded in a brownish pulp. It is the latter for which the tree is grown, for it is of pleasing acid flavor, although its sugar content may be over 20%. Grown throughout the tropical world, and in Fla., more often for shade with us than for the pods. It thrives on the sandy soils of southern Fla., and is best propagated by the shield budding of desirable varieties on the stock of the common sorts. (*Tamarindus* is from the Arabic for Indian date, the plant or its fruit once having been so called.)

tamariscifolia, -us, -um (tam-a-riss-i-fō′-li-a). With leaves like a tamarisk.

TAMARISK. *See* Tamarix.

TAMARISK FAMILY = Tamaricaceae.

TAMARIX (tam′a-ricks). The tamarisks comprise an interesting group of shrubs and trees of the family Tamaricaceae, all the perhaps 60 species from Eurasia or Asia Minor, and many of them salt-tolerant plants of semi-desert places, and growing naturally in pure sand. They have very slender branches, and the twigs, which are completely covered by the small, scale-like leaves, are shed with the leaves in the fall. The leaves are very small, hug the twigs, and are scarcely more than 1/16 in. long. Flowers very small, mostly crowded in dense racemes* which are grouped in terminal clusters (panicles*). Fruit a minute capsule.* (*Tamarix* is the old Latin name of these plants.)

The tamarisks are very feathery, slender plants providing a foliage character unlike most plants in cult. They appear superficially leafless because the scale-like leaves are so closely pressed against the twigs, suggesting *Casuarina* or heaths or some forms of juniper in this respect. But the foliage effect is finer with the tamarisks than in either *Casuarina* or the junipers. Because most species are salt- and sand-tolerant, they make excellent plants for the seaside garden, their slender branches swaying easily in the wind, and the plants not having, along the coast, the wind-wrenched appearance of stiffer-wooded plants. Cuttings root very easily in moist sand. Some of the species, in Calif., are useful bee plants.

africana. A shrub 6–10 ft. high. Flower clusters about 3 in. long, borne along the sides of last season's twigs. Mediterranean region. May. Hardy from zone* 6 southward, but little known in cult., and most plants offered as this are *T. parviflora.*

aphylla. Athel tree. Salt tree. A tree or large shrub, 20–30 ft. high, the twigs jointed, usually covered with the persistent, scale-like leaves and the plant thus appearing evergreen. Flowers minute, pink, in terminal clusters (panicles*). Western As. and northern Af., especially in alkali and desert regions. Hardy from zone* 7 southward and useful in seaside gardens and as a windbreak.

articulata = *T. aphylla.*

gallica. Salt cedar; also called French tamarisk. A shrub or small tree 15–25 ft. high,

---

* Special articles on the subjects indicated by an asterisk (*) will be found at the words so marked.

the foliage bluish. Flowers white or pinkish. Mediterranean region. July–Aug. Hardy from zone* 3 southward, and the best-known species in cult., suitable for a variety of soils.

hispida. Kashgar tamarisk. Not over 4–5 ft. high, the twigs somewhat hairy. Flowers pink, the dense racemes* in a terminal cluster (panicle*). East of the Caspian Sea. Aug.–Sept. Hardy from zone* 5 southward.

odessana. A shrub 4–6 ft. high, the slender branches upright. Flowers pink, the slender racemes* about 1½ in. long. Caspian region. July–Sept. Hardy from zone* 3 southward.

parviflora. Somewhat resembling *T. pentandra*, but the flower clusters (racemes*) lateral and on last year's twigs. It is a shrub or small tree, 10–15 ft. high, the twigs purple. Flowers light pink, the clusters 1–2 in. long. Southeastern Eu. April–May. Hardy from zone* 4 southward.

pentandra. A shrub, 10–15 ft. high, the foliage purplish. Flowers pink or rose-pink, mostly in dense racemes,* which are grouped in a large terminal cluster (panicle*). Eurasia. Aug.–Sept. Hardy from zone* 3 southward, and one of the most widely grown species.

TAMPALA. A hort. var. of *Amaranthus tricolor* (which see) with edible foliage, used as in spinach. It is a warm-season crop of which seeds should be sown ¼ in. deep and the plants thinned to be 18 in. apart each way. Harvesting begins when plants are 8 in. high, when the leaves are most tender, or the leaves of taller plants may be cut as needed. Its flavor is liked by some, but others report it as inferior to Swiss chard or New Zealand spinach.

tanacetifolia, -us, -um (tan-a-see-ti-fo'li-a). With tansy-like leaves.

TANACETUM (tan-a-see'tum). Tansy. Very strong-scented, rather weedy herbs of the family Compositae, all the 50 known species from the north temperate zone, and only **T. vulgare**, the common tansy, of any garden interest. It is a rank-growing herb, 2–3 ft. high, with alternate, much-dissected leaves. Flower heads small, button-like (hence its other name of bitter-buttons), yellow, exclusively of disk* flowers, the heads in a flat-topped cluster (cyme*). The *var.* **crispum** has more finely divided and crisped leaves. Eu. Common as a roadside weed over much of eastern U.S. For cult. and uses *see* HERB GARDENING. (*Tanacetum* is from the Greek for immortality, but of uncertain application here.)

TANAKAEA (tan-a-ki'e-a). A genus of only one species of evergreen herbs of the family Saxifragaceae, found in Jap. and cult. for its foliage and greenish-white, petalless flowers. The only species, **T. radicans**, is an evergreen, perennial herb, 6–8 in. high, with long-stalked, ovalish leaves 6–8 in. long, in a basal rosette, the margins toothed and bristly. Flowers very small, the sexes separate, in a small cluster. It needs partial shade and a sandy, moderately acid soil. Not widely cult. (Named for Yoshio Tanaka, Japanese botanist.)

TANBARK OAK = *Lithocarpus densiflora.*

TAN BAY = *Gordonia Lasianthus.*

TANGELO. A citrus fruit derived from crossing the tangerine known as Dancy with a grapefruit variety known as Bowen, in 1897. The tangelo is like neither of its parents, being a pear-shaped, thin-skinned, rather acid, juicy citrus fruit with an orange-colored pulp. Of considerable interest to amateur growers in the Southwest, especially the *var.* Mineola and some others. Tangelo is also of interest to the breeders of citrus fruits. *See* CITRUS.

TANGERINE = *Citrus nobilis deliciosa.*

TANGLEBERRY = *Gaylussacia frondosa.* See HUCKLEBERRY.

tangutica, -us, -um (tan-gew'ti-ka). From or near Tangut, Tibet.

TANIA = *Xanthosoma sagittaefolium.*

TANKAGE. See Nitrogen at FERTILIZERS.

TANK GARDENING. See SOILLESS GARDENING.

TANKS. For contents of tanks *see* WEIGHTS AND MEASURES, 5.

TAN OAK = *Lithocarpus densiflora.*

TANSY. See TANACETUM.

TANSY RAGWORT = *Senecio Jacobaea.*

TANYOSHO = *Pinus densiflora umbraculifera.* See PINE.

TAPE-GRASS = *Vallisneria spiralis.* See EEL-GRASS.

TAPIOCA-PLANT = *Manihot esculenta.*

TAPROOT. The main, central root of a plant, which usually goes straight down and is larger and stouter than the lateral roots. Plants with a deep taproot are harder to transplant than others, for they often lack

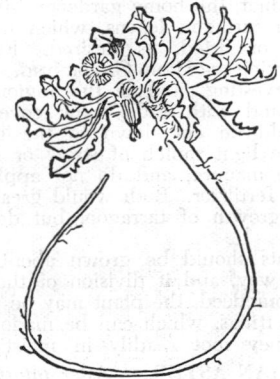

The dandelion is difficult to eradicate because of its taproot. Some trees also bear taproots and they are usually hard to transplant. *See* HICKORY.

the many small feeding roots found on the lateral root systems of most plants. While taproot is more often a characteristic of herbs, some trees, especially in the young

---

* Special articles on the subjects indicated by an asterisk (*) will be found at the words so marked.

stages, develop large taproots, as in the hickories. Such trees are notoriously difficult to move.

TARATA = *Pittosporum eugenioides.*

TARA VINE = *Actinidia arguta.*

TARAXACUM. See DANDELION.

tardiflora, -us, -um (tar-di-flow'ra). Late-flowering.

TARE = *Vicia sativa.*

TARO = *Colocasia esculenta.*

TARRAGON (*Artemisia Dracunculus*). A little known, very pleasantly flavored peren-nial herb, far more popular in Eu. than here. The French, particularly, grow it com-mercially as a source of an aromatic, pungent flavoring extract, which is widely used in flavoring pickles and in the making of tarra-gon vinegar. It is also the flavoring extract which gives the piquant and delightful tang to Dubonnet.

Tarragon is a perennial herb found wild from the Caspian Sea to Siberia, and is closely related to wormwood (*Artemisia Ab-sinthium*). As tarragon rarely, if ever, pro-duces seeds, the plant must be propagated by division of its roots, preferably in early spring. The plant will grow in any ordinary garden soil. As it is not a particularly decora-tive member of the genus *Artemisia*, its cult. really should be restricted to an attempt to produce its essential oil. This is rarely, if ever, done commercially in America, most of our importations of tarragon coming from southern France. It is also known as estragon.

By restricting its cult. to regions where summer rainfall is not too great, there is no reason why a supply of tarragon leaves cannot be harvested in late Aug. and Sept. While they will not be so aromatic as the French product, the home gardener will have a supply of tarragon leaves, which may be used fresh or dried, as desired. For the details of drying see HERB GARDENING.

After harvesting, and if the region is a cold one, and with little snow cover, the plants should be cut down to the ground and given a light mulch of straw or leaves. Do not use manure, and do not apply any commercial fertilizer. Both would greatly in-crease the growth of tarragon, but decrease its flavor.

The plants should be grown about 1 ft. apart each way, and if division of the roots cannot be practiced, the plant may be propa-gated by cuttings, which can be made when desired. They root readily in moist sand.

TARTARIAN ASTER = *Aster tataricus.*

TARTARIAN BUCKWHEAT = *Fagopy-rum tataricum.* See BUCKWHEAT.

TARTARIAN DOGWOOD = *Cornus alba.*

TARTARIAN HONEYSUCKLE = *Loni-cera tatarica.*

TARWEED. See MADIA. See also GRIN-DELIA.

TASAJILLO = *Opuntia leptocaulis.*

TASMANIAN STRINGY-BARK = *Euca-lyptus obliqua.*

TASSEL-FLOWER = *Amaranthus cauda-tus* and *Emilia sagittata.*

TASSEL-HYACINTH = *Muscari como-sum.*

TASSEL-TREE = *Garrya elliptica.*

tatarica, -us, -um (ta-tar'i-ka). From Cen-tral Asia, once called Tartary.

taurica, -us, -um (tau'ri-ka). From the ancient country of Tauris, now Tabriz.

TAWHIWHI = *Pittosporum tenuifolium.*

TAXACEAE (tacks-ā'see-ee). The yew family, next to the Pinaceae (which see), furnishes the most valuable evergreens for the hardy garden, and a few trees or shrubs for the greenhouse or for outdoor, frost-free regions. Of the 11 known genera at least five are in cult., but of the 100 widely distributed species of trees and shrubs, only a dozen or so are of any garden interest.

Taxus, the yew, with only a few species but many hort. varieties, is by far the most important genus. Its rich, lustrous, evergreen foliage is matched by few other plants. Other relatively hardy genera are *Torreya* and *Cephalotaxus,* but see these genera for exact notes on their hardiness. *Podocarpus* and *Dacrydium* can only be grown in rela-tively frost-free regions or in the cool green-house. The leaves are flat and relatively broad in some genera (*Podocarpus*), but needle-like or awl-shaped in *Taxus,* which unlike most of the genera is not resinous.

The only obvious difference between this family and the Pinaceae is that the former produces cones, while the fruit of the yew family is fleshy, part of the flesh being due to an aril.°

taxifolia, -us, -um (tacks-i-fo'li-a). With yew-like leaves.

TAXODIACEAE. See PINACEAE.

TAXODIUM (tacks-ō'di-um). Three mag-nificent evergreen or deciduous trees of the pine family, one Mexican, the other two from the southeastern U.S., often, and in fact, usually called cypress in the U.S., but not the traditional cypress. They have light brown, scaly bark and bear two sorts of branchlets, the upper ones persistent, the lower ones on the shoot deciduous.° Leaves alternate,° flat, line-like, spreading. Male and female flowers separate, but on the same tree, the male flowers consisting of only 6–8 stamens, mostly in drooping clusters (panicles°). Female flowers ultimately pro-ducing a scaly, short-stalked cone, its seeds 3-angled and 3-winged. (*Taxodium* is from the Greek meaning *Taxus*-like.)

The first species is the bald cypress, and a valuable timber tree, as well as being most decorative. While its natural habitat is in the cypress swamps, it will grow on ordi-nary soils, and even on dry sites in the Midwest. The second species is not hardy

---

° Special articles on the subjects indicated by an asterisk (°) will be found at the words so marked.

in the North, and is rarely grown even in southern Calif. or Fla.

distichum. Bald cypress; southern cypress. A deciduous* tree up to 150 ft. high, its trunk decidedly tapering, often buttressed at the base (in the wild), and in its native swamps producing the "cypress knees" which are woody projections of the roots, 4–6 ft. high and about a foot thick, which are thrust above the water. Leaves light green, about ¾ in. long, very numerous, the foliage graceful and feathery, orange in the autumn just before leaf-fall. Cones about 1 in. long. Del. to Fla. west to Ark. and La. Hardy from zone* 3 southward, but always a small tree northward. A closely related tree, *T. ascendens*, the pond cypress, with less spreading leaves and rather upright branches, is sometimes cult.

mucronatum. Montezuma cypress; known in Mex. as ahuehuete. A magnificent evergreen tree, as famous in Aztec history as the oak in England. One of them, in the garden of Montezuma, and another in the churchyard at El Tule, were large trees at the time of the Conquest and are still standing. The tree is lower than our bald cypress, but its crown far wider, one of the oldest being about 120 ft. high, its crown somewhat wider, and with a trunk diameter of over 50 ft. Leaves about ½ in. long, some of them often deciduous. Cones 1½–1¾ in. long. Central Mex. to Guatemala. Hardy only in zones* 8 and 9, and little grown outside of Mex., but occasionally planted in Fla. and southern Calif. It may be the oldest living thing in America, considered even older than the big-tree (*Sequoia gigantea*) by some authorities.

TAXUS (tacks′us). Yew. Beautiful, slow-growing evergreen shrubs and trees of the family Taxaceae, comprising perhaps 8 closely related species, but considered by some as merely forms of a single species which is found over much of the north temperate zone. They have, in age, scaly, reddish-brown bark, and spirally arranged, 2-ranked, typically dark green, narrow leaves, the foliage not resinous or aromatic as in so many conifers. Leaves with 2 yellowish or grayish-green bands on the under side. Male and female flowers on different plants, without sepals or petals, only the female producing the scarlet or brownish, berry-like fruit (a modified cone). The juice of the foliage is dangerously poisonous, but the aril* enclosing the seed is eaten by some. *See* POISONOUS PLANTS. (*Taxus* is the classical Latin name of the yew.)

For culture *see* EVERGREENS. The yews have been cult. since the days of the Greeks, especially *T. baccata*, the English yew. In its tree form this species is a very slow-growing plant, and is consequently rarely grown here. Its shrubby cult. varieties, and the Japanese yew (*T. cuspidata*), are better for evergreen plantings, their fine dark foliage and comparative freedom from disease making these shrubby yews among the most widely popular of all evergreens. Some of them, as noted below, are fine hedge plants and will stand the necessary shearing. Of course, like any other evergreen hedge plant, yews are expensive. For the details of setting out hedge plants *see* HEDGES.

baccata. English yew. A tree (in Eu.) up to 60 ft. high and with a broad, round head. Leaves 1–1¼ in. long, gradually tapering to a slender point. Fruit berry-like, olive-brown, just under ½ in. long. Eurasia and northern Af. Hardy from zone* 4 southward, but not happy in regions of dry, hot summers. This is the typical tree form rarely grown in the U.S., the following hort. varieties being much more useful hort. subjects.

var. **adpressa.** Low shrub or small tree, its leaves scarcely ½ in. long, and not spreading. Comes in several color forms (*i.e.*, foliage golden), and in erect or columnar forms, suited for hedge plants.

var. **argentea** = *var. variegata.*

var. **aurea.** Leaves yellow. Not much grown, and less desirable than some other varieties.

var. **repandens.** A beautiful, low, nearly prostrate form, with wide-spreading branches and bluish-green foliage. This is the hardiest of all the varieties of the English yew.

var. **stricta.** Irish yew. A very handsome columnar form with upright branches, the leaves spirally arranged, and of a fine dark green color. A good accent plant. There are also variegated and golden-foliaged forms. It is less hardy than the typical form.

var. **variegata** (also called *var. argentea*). A shrubby form with whitish-variegated foliage.

var. **washingtoni.** A wide-spreading, shrubby form with golden-yellow foliage.

Besides those listed above, there are perhaps 30 other hort. forms or varieties of this widely planted evergreen. Most of them are minor variations in habit or the color of the foliage.

brevifolia. The plants usually offered as this are *Taxus cuspidata nana*, the true *T. brevifolia* of western N.A. being rare in cult.

canadensis. Ground hemlock. A native American, straggling or half-prostrate, evergreen shrub, rarely over 3 ft. high. Leaves about 1 in. long, dark green, tapering suddenly to a minute, prickle-like point. Berry-like fruit scarlet. N.A. Hardy from zone* 2 southward. Less desirable than the other three species, but useful as a ground cover under the shade of forest trees, especially evergreens. Not suited to open, windswept places. The *var.* **stricta**, while still procumbent, has erect branches.

cuspidata. Japanese yew. The most important horticulturally of all the yews, and the best for hedges. It is far more hardy than the English yew and faster-growing. A tree up to 40 ft. high, much more often a bushy shrub as cult. Leaves about 1 in. long, suddenly tapering to a short, dark green point. Berry-like fruit scarlet. Eastern As. Hardy from zone* 3, and possibly zone* 2, southward. Sometimes sold as *T. sieboldi*. The *var.* **capitata**, widely advertised, is apparently a seedling form of *T. cuspidata*. The *var.* **nana** (often offered as *T. brevifolia*) is a fine, shrubby form. The *var.* **densa** is a compact form scarcely over 3 ft. tall.

intermedia. A trade name for *T. media.*

media. A hybrid yew, derived from crossing the English and Japanese yews, and intermediate in characteristics. The older branchlets are reddish-green. Hardy from zone* 4 southward. The *var.* **hatfieldi** is a shrubby, conical plant with spreading branchlets. The *var.* **hicksi** is nearly fastigiate.* There are many other named forms, as Kelsey, with more spreading branches and Hunnewell, a somewhat more rapid grower, also of spreading habit.

sieboldi = *Taxus cuspidata.*

---

* Special articles on the subjects indicated by an asterisk (*) will be found at the words so marked.

INSECT PESTS. Control mealybugs with pesticide #21 (*see* SPRAYS AND DUSTS). Roots and stems at ground level are attacked by a white legless grub of the black vine weevil. Unthrifty plants are often victims of this grub. Adults hide by day, appearing in late spring and feeding on needles near ground level, chewing the margin of a needle toward the terminal portion. Treat soil under plant with pesticide #15, #16, or #19. (*See* SPRAYS AND DUSTS.)

DISEASES. The yew is relatively free from serious diseases. Contrary to popular opinion, it is a plant which prefers sweet soil or limed soil for rich green foliage. When growing in soil adapted to azalea, rhododendron, etc., it is often pale yellow.

The bark of yew is quite tender and susceptible to injury. When snow sliding from a roof, or breakage from ice storms, results in scuffing even a small section of the bark, the twig or branch will die.

The plant can stand dry soil well, but will not tolerate poorly drained or wet soil. If plants deteriorate and much inside needle-death occurs, examine the root system. If deep roots are dead and only the surface roots are alive, wet feet is the problem. Plants at corners of buildings where rainspouts flood water on the soil are usually the first sites to show trouble.

If yew is planted in an area soon after oak trees or an apple orchard have been removed, the plants may be injured or killed by the shoestring root rot. Black, brittle "shoestrings" attached to the bark near the soil line indicate the root rot.

taygetea (tay-ge-tee'a). From or near Taygetus, Greece.

Tazetta (ta-zet'ta). A small cup; applied to the short crown of *Narcissus Tazetta*.

TEA. For the true tea plant *see* Thea. But *tea* has been applied to many other cult. plants, or is a part of their name. Those in this book and their proper equivalents are:

Appalachian tea = *Viburnum cassinoides*; Crystal tea = *Ledum palustre*; Labrador tea = *Ledum groenlandicum*; Mexican tea = *Chenopodium ambrosioides*; New Jersey tea = *Ceanothus americanus*; Oswego tea = *Monarda didyma*. See also the next few entries.

TEABERRY = *Gaultheria procumbens* and *Mitchella repens*.

TEA FAMILY = Theaceae.

TEA-OF-HEAVEN = *Hydrangea serrata*.

TEA OLIVE. See OSMANTHUS.

TEA ROSE = *Rosa odorata*. For the garden forms of the tea rose *see* ROSE.

TEASEL. See DIPSACUS.

TEASEL FAMILY = Dipsacaceae.

TEASEL GOURD = *Cucumis dipsaceus*.

TEA-TREE. See MELALEUCA and LEPTOSPERMUM.

technica, -us, -um (teck'ni-ka). Specialized or technical.

TECOMA. A tropical genus of shrubs or trees of no garden interest, except that the name *Tecoma* was long applied to the common trumpet-creeper (which see), now in-cluded in the genus *Campsis*. *Tecoma* has also been applied to several other garden plants now included in other genera. For:

Tecoma australis *see* Pandorea pandorana.

Tecoma capensis *see* Tecomaria capensis.

Tecoma grandiflora *see* Trumpet-creeper (*Campsis chinensis*).

Tecoma jasminoides *see* Pandorea jasminoides.

Tecoma radicans *see* Trumpet-creeper (*Campsis radicans*).

Tecoma ricasoliana *see* Pandorea ricasoliana.

Tecoma Stans *see* Stenolobium Stans.

TECOMARIA (teck-o-mair'i-a). A small genus of woody vines or scrambling shrubs of the family Bignoniaceae, grown for ornament. Several are tropical American, but the only cult. one, T. capensis, the Cape honeysuckle, is from South Africa. It can be grown as a vine, or pruned as a scrambling shrub. It is an evergreen plant with opposite,* compound* leaves, the 7-9 leaflets toothed, ovalish, ¾-2 in. long. Flowers orange-red or scarlet, in showy, terminal stalked clusters (racemes*), blooming over most of the year. Corolla slightly irregular, about 2 in. long, funnel-shaped, the upper lip* slightly notched. Stamens* 4, protruding. Fruit a narrow capsule,* about 1½ in. long. It grows profusely in the sandy soils of Fla. and should be propagated by seeds or cuttings. Not certainly hardy north of zones* 8 and 9, but possibly in protected places in zone* 7. A very handsome plant, having also a yellow-flowered form. (*Tecomaria*, derived from *Tecoma*, means resembling that genus.)

tectora, -us, -um (teck-tor'ra). Pertaining to a house roof.

TEFF. An important cereal in Abyssinia. See ERAGROSTIS ABYSSINICA.

TELANTHERA = *Alternanthera*.

TELEGRAPH PLANT = *Desmodium motorium*.

Telephium (tell-ee'fi-um). An old name, of uncertain application, perhaps derived from Telephus of Greek mythology. It is now used for the specific name of *Sedum Telephium* (which see).

TELLIMA (tel-ly'ma). Perhaps 12 species of hairy, perennial herbs of the family Saxifragaceae, from western N.A., one of them, T. grandiflora, the fringe-cups or false alumroot, cult. for ornament. It is a slender herb, 1-2 ft. high, resembling *Mitella*. Leaves chiefly basal, stalked, roundish or heart-shaped, and toothed, about 4 in. wide. Flowers nodding, greenish at first, ultimately pink or reddish, the calyx* inflated, more or less bell-shaped. Corolla of fringed petals. Calif. to Alaska. Suited only to the wild garden and needing shade and woods soil. (*Tellima* is an anagram of *Mitella*.) For the plant sometimes sold as T. *affinis see* LITHOPHRAGMA AFFINIS.

---

* Special articles on the subjects indicated by an asterisk (*) will be found at the words so marked.

tellimoides (tel-li-moy′deez, but *see* Oïdes). Like a plant of the genus *Tellima*.

TEMPERATE HOUSE. A cool greenhouse. *See* Greenhouse.

TEMPERATURE. The total amount of heat and cold determines the wild flora of a region more than any other feature of the climate. This is also true for cult. plants. There are times when minor frosts can be held in check over limited areas (*see* Frost), but generally speaking heat and cold cannot be controlled, and upon the amount of each most gardening and farming must be based.

The wide-scale and long-continuing operation of a factor like low temperatures, for instance, dictates the hardiness of most cult. plants. And upon their response to this the country has been divided into 9 zones* of hardiness. For the details of this and a map *see* Zone. *See also* Hardiness.

The occurrence of killing frosts in spring and autumn, while not such a drastic factor as either extreme heat or cold, does control many hort. operations. And the figures for spring and autumn killing frosts have been tabulated for all the states. See the name of your state for the details of these frost dates.

It would have been still more desirable to include here the figures for effective temperatures, perhaps the most important of all hort. criteria of temperature. But such figures are lacking, although they could be gleaned from weather bureau records if one had the time to do so. As understood by the experts, effective temperatures are those that are effective for plant growth. Between the freezing point and the amount when the plant begins to respond to increased heat, there is an accumulation of heat units of no use to most plants — in other words, ineffective temperatures.

But at about 40°, plant activity does begin to stir, and barley, one of the hardiest of all cereals, will just germinate. The figure of about 40° has thus come to be the base upon which statistics of effective temperatures have been built. And 40° means that, during the day, the hourly maxima and hourly minima, divided by two, give the absolute mean temperature of 40°. And the effective temperatures are the accumulated degrees of that above this base. Such a figure for the growing season at New York totals 5232°, for New Haven, Conn., 4540°, and for Block Island, R.I., 4444°. In other words, that many degrees of temperature, effective for plant growth, accumulated above the base of 40°. Similar figures from deserts and mountains would be extremely valuable, both to gardeners and foresters.

Another temperature factor of garden importance is the incidence of absolute maximal and absolute minimal temperatures. Even brief periods of intense cold or heat are of greater significance than comfortable average temperatures within which most plants grow perfectly well, assuming that rainfall or irrigations are adequate.

In the U.S. the absolute minimum and maximum temperatures are listed below for a few significant places:

	Absolute Minimum Temperatures	Absolute Maximum Temperatures
Boston	−17°	104°
New York	−14°	101°
Detroit	−20°	105°
Chicago	−30°	105°
Northern Montana	−60°	105°
Northern Idaho	−50°	100°
Seattle	10°	90°
San Francisco	20°	98°
Los Angeles	25°	105°
Northern Texas	0	100°
Southern Texas	10°	110°
New Orleans	10°	100°
Key West	41°	95°

Higher and lower temperatures than these have been recorded, as 65° below zero at Bismarck, N. D., and 115° at Yuma, Ariz. These figures, taken from the *Atlas of American Agriculture*, Part II (Climate, Section B, Temperature, Sunshine and Wind), published by the U.S. Weather Bureau, may change somewhat in the future, but most of them are based on 60 years of temperature records.

TEMPLE TREE. *See* Plumeria.

temulenta, -us, -um (tem-you-len′ta). Unsteady or drunken.

tenax (tee′nacks). Strong or tenacious.

TENDER. *See* Hardiness. *See also* Subtropical Garden.

TENDER ANNUAL. *See* Annuals.

TENDRIL. A slender prolongation of the stem or leaf, of the greatest use to climbing plants, because tendrils cling to a support.

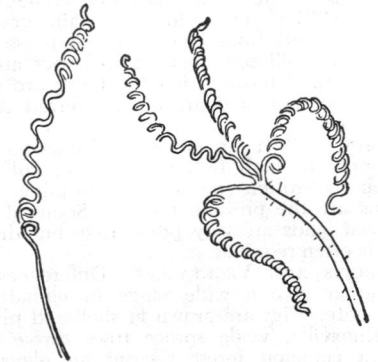

A simple and a branched tendril

Many vines have thread-like, herbaceous tendrils, most of which are highly sensitive to irritation. Much nonsense has been written about tendrils "seeking" a support. They consciously "seek" nothing, but their movements are none the less remarkable, as Darwin found after years of study. Some coil clockwise, others counterclockwise. In some tropical vines tendrils are horribly prickly, while in others, as in *Antigonon*, the tendril is merely a slender tip of the inflorescence. Familiar examples of tendrils may be seen in the grape, pea, and many relatives of the trumpet-creeper.

tenella, -us, -um (te-nell'a). Slender or tender.

TENNESSEE. The iris is the state flower and the red cedar the state tree. The state lies wholly in zones° 4, 5, and 6. It is ribbon-like in shape, extending over 400 miles from its eastern extreme to the western, and is less than 120 miles wide at its widest point. Areas of varying elevation extend in general from the north to the south and have important influences on the climate, soil type, and products of each section of the state.

East Tennessee is mountainous and variable in soil type. A given soil formation tends to extend parallel to the mountain ranges. While the soils of this area are fairly fertile, erosion is a serious problem on all cultivated upland.

Middle Tennessee is divided from the eastern section by a large area of higher elevation known as the Cumberland Plateau, where the soils are usually derived from sandstone and shale. These soils are low in fertility and require large applications of mineral fertilizers to produce satisfactory crops.

The central-basin area is comparable to the Blue-Grass sections of Kentucky. The soils were derived from limestone and are high in natural fertility.

Another plateau or "Highland rim" extends entirely around the central basin and extends over into west Tennessee. The soils of the "Rim" fall into two main groups, those derived from limestone and those derived from siliceous rock. The former are of good natural fertility, but the latter are usually very poor, and are often referred to as the "Barrens."

Large soil areas of west Tennessee are naturally of high fertility but have suffered much by erosion and one-crop farming. Silt loams are the prevailing types. Some of the alluvial lands are very productive, but drainage is often required.

FRUITS AND VEGETABLES. Differences in elevation give a wide range in climate in this state. Figs are grown in sheltered places in Knoxville, while spruce trees thrive and are a common forest tree at an elevation of 5000 feet in the Smoky Mountains nearby. These variations in elevation furnish a certain amount of frost protection on the higher sites and largely account for the success of many apple and peach orchards in east Tennessee. The commercial peach section extends from Clinton and Harriman in the north to Sale Creek near Chattanooga on the south. Peach production varies greatly from year to year, but averages second in value among the fruits shipped out of the state.

The great vegetable district of this state is in Gibson and five or six nearby counties of west Tennessee. Tomatoes, both for shipping north and for canning, lead among the truck crops. Milan, Humboldt, Gibson, Fruit-

TENNESSEE

The zones of hardiness crossing Tennessee are those shown on the map located at ZONE, which should be consulted for details. The dates are the average latest killing frost in spring and the first one in the fall. The figures below the dates show the average length of the growing season. Rainfall is adequate.

land and Trenton are the larger shipping points.

Sweet potatoes thrive in all parts of the state and are prominent in the diet of the people. Production varies from year to year, but usually ranks second to tomatoes in value. Weakley County in the northwestern part ships out the largest tonnage. The adjoining counties of Henry, Gibson, and Carroll rank next in sweet-potato production in the order named.

Early cabbage to ship to northern markets varies greatly in production from year to year, but usually ranks third among the vegetable crops. Gibson County is the center of cabbage production, with the towns of Humboldt, Gibson, and Medina the more important shipping points.

Irish or white potatoes are a small crop in this state compared with sweet potatoes. Much of the spring crop and all the fall crop are used locally. In addition, large quantities of potatoes are shipped in to supply the local markets during the winter season. Columbia and Decherd in middle Tennessee are the more important shipping points.

The snap bean is usually one of the more

° Special articles on the subjects indicated by an asterisk (°) will be found at the words so marked.

important of the minor vegetable crops. In addition to production for home consumption, from 50 to over 125 carloads are shipped out annually. The center for exporting is in Weakley, Gibson, and Haywood counties of west Tennessee.

Strawberries lead among the fruit crops of Tennessee. From 1000 to over 2000 carloads are shipped out annually in addition to local consumption. About half of this tonnage is shipped from west Tennessee. Humboldt, Ripley, and Jackson are the larger shipping towns. The east Tennessee district centers around Rhea County, with Dayton, Evensville, and Spring City as the larger shipping points. The middle Tennessee district lies largely in Sumner County, with Portland, Mitchellville, and Westmoreland as shipping points.

Other fruits such as apples, plums, pears, cherries, and raspberries are produced in small quantities and mostly for local consumption. Considerable quantities of these fruits are shipped or trucked into the state from other districts.

ORNAMENTALS. Tennessee is noted for its many kinds of flowers and ornamental trees and shrubs. Plant life furnishes one of the main attractions in the Smoky Mountains National Park, which lies partly within the state on its eastern border. Rhododendron, laurel, and the flame azalea attract tourists from long distances. Dogwood and redbud are the most attractive of the widely distributed, native flowering shrubs. Roses, both hybrid tea and climbing, are the most popular of the cultivated flowers. Many annuals, as cosmos and zinnias, will reseed themselves from year to year. Jasmine, forsythia, and the various spireas are popular spring-blooming cultivated shrubs. Crape myrtle, abelia, and hibiscus bloom in profusion during the late summer. Various hollies, cedars, euonymus, cherry laurels, junipers, and arborvitae are popular among evergreen shrubs.

CLIMATE. Elevation, both actual and above sea level, markedly influences the climate of many parts of Tennessee. Spring frosts occasionally destroy the first strawberry blossoms where air drainage is not good. Raspberries and rhubarb are more easily grown on the higher elevations where temperatures are lower and the rainfall more evenly distributed throughout the year.

KILLING FROSTS IN TENNESSEE

Town	Average date of last killing frost in the spring	Latest-known killing frost
Knoxville, in east Tennessee	April 2	April 26
Cedar Hill, in middle Tennessee	April 9	April 26
Milan, in west Tennessee	April 6	April 26

Town	Average date of earliest killing frost in the fall	Earliest-known killing frost
Knoxville, in east Tennessee	Oct. 29	Oct. 1
Cedar Hill, in middle Tennessee	Oct. 25	Oct. 9
Milan, in west Tennessee	Oct. 26	Oct. 9

The frost records of Knoxville as reported in the table were taken in the valley and are not comparable to those which could be taken on high elevations. The Cedar Hill records were taken near the Sumner County strawberry district and are fairly representative of that section. The Milan station is located in the West Tennessee trucking district.

Rainfall tends to vary with elevation and is especially heavy on the Cumberland Plateau. It averages less as a rule in May and in September and October than in other months, but is otherwise fairly evenly distributed. The Chattanooga station reports 32.68 inches of rainfall as their record low while the high record is 72.37 inches. This is a variation between years of nearly 40 inches while the average annual rainfall was 50.99 inches. The plateau section near Crossville averaged over 5 inches more of rainfall per year, and it was more evenly distributed both from season to season and within a given year.

The address of the Tennessee Agricultural Experiment Station, which has kindly supplied this information about the state, is Knoxville. The Station is always ready to answer gardening questions.

Garden club activities in the state include clubs of the Garden Club of America, the home office of which is 598 Madison Avenue, New York 22, N.Y. There are also many clubs affiliated with the Tennessee Garden Club.

TENNIS. A lawn game, the standard court for which is 36 × 78 ft.

tenuifolia, -us, -um (ten-you-i-fō′li-a). Having slender or narrow leaves.

TEN-WEEKS STOCK = *Mathiola incana annua.* For cult. *see* STOCK.

TEOSINTE = *Euchlaena mexicana.*

TEPAL. A segment of a flower where there is little difference between sepals and petals, as in some water lilies, most kinds of *Amaryllis,* and in a few magnolias.

TEPARY BEAN = *Phaseolus acutifolius latifolius.*

tephropepla, -us, -um (teff-ro-pep′la). With an ashy exterior (*i.e.,* shawl or coat).

TEPHROSIA (teff-rose′i-a). Ashy-leaved perennial herbs, or, in the tropics, shrubs, of the pea family, comprising over 170 species, mostly from the warmer parts of the world and of moderate hort. interest. They have alternate,* compound* leaves,

* Special articles on the subjects indicated by an asterisk (*) will be found at the words so marked.

the leaflets arranged feather-fashion and with an odd one at the end. Flowers pea-like, white or yellowish-pink (in ours), mostly in racemes.* Pod (legume*) narrow and flattish. (*Tephrosia* is from the Greek for ashy or hoary, in allusion to the foliage.) The plants are often known as *Cracca.*

The first species is a tropical shrub planted for a windbreak in extreme southern Fla., and hardy nowhere else. The goat's-rue is a pretty little native plant suited only to dry, open, somewhat sandy places in the wild garden.

candida. A shrub, 8–10 ft. high, the foliage silky-hairy. Leaflets about 2 in. long. Flowers white, about 1 in. long. Pods 3–4 in. long. India.

virginiana. Goat's-rue; also called catgut and wild sweet pea. A showy-flowered perennial herb, 1–2 ft. high. Leaflets 17–29, narrow, about 1 in. long, silky-hairy. Flowers yellowish-pink, about 1 in. long. Pods 1½–2 in. long. In open places, N.A. June–July. It is a source of rotenone, but not in commercial quantities.

TEQUILA MESCAL = *Agave tequilana.*

tequilana, -us, -um (te-key-lay'na). From Tequila, Mexico.

terebinthifolia, -us, -um (te-re-bin-thi-fō'-li-a). With leaves like the terebinth, a European tree scarcely known in cult. here.

teres (ter'ez). Terete.

TERETE. Round in cross-section, often not quite perfectly so, as in many leaves.

tereticornis, -e (te-ree-ti-kor'nis). With round or terete horns.

TERMINAL. As used in hort. *terminal* has no special meaning other than the common one; *i.e.,* at the end, not lateral. Many flower clusters are so designated to distinguish them from those borne in the leaf axils,* which are hence never terminal.

TERMINALIA (ter-mi-nall'i-a). Chiefly Asiatic, tropical, and very handsome shade trees of the family Combretaceae, comprising over 100 species, some of which yield valuable products (gums, resins, myrobalans, tanning extracts, etc.), but only one in common cult. for ornament. This is the Indian almond, sometimes called tropical almond, and known to science as **T. Catappa,** one of the most widely planted street trees in the tropics, and much used for that purpose in Fla. But as it is hardy only in zone* 9, it is little grown in Calif. It is a tree up to 80 ft. high, with smooth, brownish-gray bark. Leaves alternate,* ovalish, 6–12 in. long, without teeth, but slightly eared toward the base, leathery, and glossy-green. Flowers small and inconspicuous, often unisexual* (for details *see* COMBRETACEAE). Fruit a dryish drupe,* greenish or reddish, angled, about 2 in. long, its seeds almond-like and edible. Malaya. Grows well in a variety of soils, and casts a denser shade than most tropical street trees. While the leaves turn a handsome copper-red before falling, the tree is never quite bare. (*Terminalia* is from

the Latin for terminal, in allusion to the leaves often being borne toward the end of the shoot.)

TERMINALIACEAE = Combretaceae.

terminalis, -e (ter-mi-nall'is). Terminal.*

TERMITES. These destructive insects, commonly called white ants, attack any wood that is in direct contact with the ground. Fence posts and construction timber which touches bare earth should be creosoted, which will repel termites. Wherever possible put some stone or metallic base between timbers and the ground. If wood is once attacked only a professional exterminator can get rid of the pest, which is much more common in the tropics than in temperate climates.

TERNARY = Ternate.*

ternata, -us, -um (ter-nay'ta). Ternate.*

TERNATE. Borne in threes, as are the leaflets in many compound leaves, notably in clover.

ternatea, -us, -um (ter-nay'te-a). From the island of Ternate in the East Indies.

ternifolia, -us, -um (ter-ni-fō'li-a). Three-leaved; or sometimes with ternate* leaflets.

TERRACE. In modern usage *terrace,* as applied to gardening or to garden design, means three things. For terrace gardening as applied to apartment or roof gardening *see* Penthouse Garden at PLANNING THE HOME GROUNDS. For terraces on the ground see the next entry. For *terrace* as applied to the slope between two levels *see* BANKS.

A house terrace (on a sloping plot) serves as a semi-architectural setting for the house. At the right, a sunken terrace, serving as an outdoor living room.

TERRACES. The house terrace forms an architectural base for the house, its clearly defined boundaries providing the necessary transition between the strictly architectural

---

* Special articles on the subjects indicated by an asterisk (*) will be found at the words so marked.

mass and lines of the house and the natural forms of the surrounding landscape. A terrace provides a space for use as an outdoor living room as well as serving to co-ordinate divergent lines of access to the house.

Its size and proportions depend upon the mass of the house and the limits imposed by adjacent topography or other existing features, and should be related to the view which it commands. A broad terrace is restful and lends dignity to a large house. A small house calls for a terrace proportionately small and intimate in scale. Similarly, an extensive view suggests a large terrace, but it should not be so broad as to cut off part of the view from the house. Where there is no view, other factors control the design.

The question of use is of primary importance. If the owners entertain extensively, the terrace should be given ample proportions and should have convenient arrangements for service facilities. Its usefulness will be increased if it can be attractively illuminated at night. A large terrace of this type should be given a dignified, simple treatment. It is desirable to have a restful expanse of turf, unbroken save by one or two well-placed shade trees, and enclosed by an appropriate wall or balustrade or dwarf hedge. Where considerable use is to be made of certain parts of the terrace these areas should be paved with suitable material. A small house usually demands a more intimate terrace treatment.

If it commands an attractive view it is advisable to keep the terrace simple in order to avoid confusion of interests. Otherwise the terrace itself may be made the center of interest. In a small area it is more practical to use brick or flagstone paving than to attempt to maintain turf. Where they will not interfere with general use, soil pockets for plant material may be provided for in the paving. The terrace may be treated as a garden, with beds for shrubs or flowers surrounding the paved area. If space is limited, espaliered shrubs and potted plants would be more practical and equally effective. Further interest may be added by the introduction of such features as a fountain or pool, also certain unusual wall or paving treatments as well as treillage.* Trees for terrace planting should bear proportional relationship to the size of the terrace. For instance, a dogwood might be suitable for a small terrace and an elm tree in scale with a more ample area.

Being higher than the adjacent ground, the terrace usually requires some form of retaining wall. In an informal scheme a turf bank or dry stone wall may be adequate if suitably planted. More pretentious schemes require stone or brick masonry in harmony with the architecture of the house. Steps* and stairways usually add a definite interest to the terrace design. Where appropriate, sculptural features and jardinieres as well as certain architectural embellishments such as a niche or pavilion may supplement the simpler fundamentals of the design. All decorative features, however, should be in keeping with the life and character of the place as a whole. The terrace should be maintained as a functional unit, contributing toward the co-ordination of the more restricted life within the house and the greater freedom of out-of-doors. — A. F.

TERRACLOR. *See* FUNGICIDES.

TERRAPIN SCALE. A destructive soft scale, with a reddish-brown, shiny body about ⅛ in. in diameter. Its control will be found at the chief fruit trees that it attacks.

TERRARIUM. A terrarium is a transparent container, tightly fitted with an adjustable glass cover, in which plants are grown in earth instead of water. It is known also as a

The Wardian case is the oldest type of terrarium.

fernery, Wardian case, bottle garden, crystal garden, and glass garden. Terrariums may be bought in any number of sizes and shapes, or made at home by fitting pieces of glass, cut to the proper size, to a planting pan. The edges may be bound together with silk adhesive binding. Glass aquariums, fish globes, cracker and candy jars — in fact, any glass receptacle with a tight-fitting top — can be used. The tight cover is to prevent the loss of interior humidity, as the terrarium actually answers the purpose of a miniature greenhouse.

The uses of the terrarium are many: for house decoration, plant propagation, nature study, scientific observation, centerpiece, and table garden. Experiment with different sizes, shapes, and planting materials will produce many odd and beautiful results. The size of the case will limit definitely the choice of the materials, but of more importance are the requirements of the plants. Woodland plantings of lichens, moss, trailing arbutus, violets, anemones, partridge-berries, trilliums, bloodroot, and wood ferns are desired by many as winter house decorations. But steam-heated living rooms, with temperatures of 70° to 75°, are much too warm for these cool-temperature plants. These natural woodland plantings can be had, of course, if the temperature can be kept low enough, or the plants replaced easily from time to time. If moss is used, place it face down in the container, so that

* Special articles on the subjects indicated by an asterisk (*) will be found at the words so marked.

A bottle garden is a modern and probably ephemeral variant of the terrarium requiring much deftness in planting.

a fresh green carpet will be visible from the outside. Then arrange your woodland plants and fill in around their roots with rich loam and more moss. Natural scenes may be copied from the woods, using stones for large boulders, a lichen-covered stick for a log, and a seedling evergreen for a tree. Colorful effects are obtained by the addition of bits of tree-growing fungi, twigs with incrusted growing plants, and low-growing flowering plants to force into bloom. Artificial furnishings should be used with discretion.

Sand and large pebbles may be used instead of moss as the drainage layer, with a little charcoal for sweetening. Above this spread an inch or more of topsoil.

Tropical plants with their wealth of color and love of heat and moisture are ideally suited to terrarium culture. Some satisfactory kinds include Chinese evergreen, *Saintpaulia*, small-leaved begonias, rex begonias, croton, peperomia, *Dracaena sanderiana*, creeping fig, selaginella, *Helxine, Pilea, Maranta*, small-leaved ferns as the maidenhair and *Pellaea viridis*. For a terrarium that will be kept in a cool room or sun porch, the following plants may grow better than those strictly tropical ones mentioned above: small-leaved or dwarf English ivy, young plants of boxwood, variegated-leaf forms of euonymus, *Acorus, Pteris, Pittosporum, Primula*, and *Saxifraga sarmentosa*. In all cases select small or young plants as they are in better proportions for an attractive terrarium.

Terrariums require very little care. Watering must be done in moderation, perhaps once in ten days, unless the rooms are excessively hot. No water must be left standing around the roots, or the soil will become sour and soggy. If mold appears, increase the ventilation and it will disappear. If the lid fits very tightly, and the terrarium is given plenty of water, it may safely be left for a number of weeks without attention, as the moisture will condense on the cool glass and drip back into the garden. — C. B. L.

TERRESTRIAL. Growing in the soil, not in the air as do epiphytes.*

tessellata, -us, -um (tes-sell-lay'ta). With a dice-like pattern.

testacea, -us, -um (tes-tay'see-a). Brick-colored; also light brown.

TESTING SOILS. There are three ways of testing soils, so far as their garden uses are concerned. The first is to determine the acidity or alkalinity of them. For the details of this *see* ACID AND ALKALI SOILS.

The second is to get some idea of their fertility. While growing crops upon them is the best method of determining this, those in a hurry will find a shorter (but not so satisfactory) method described in FERTILITY.

The mechanical constituents of your garden soil require attention, but its analysis is a job for a soil scientist. You can, however, determine its gross features by reading the article at SOILS. And its moisture-holding capacity, which is one of the most important things about all garden soils, is discussed at some length at HUMUS.

testudo (tes-too'do). A tortoise. *See* DEAMIA.

tetracantha, -us, -um (tet-ra-kan'tha). With four spines.

tetragona, -us, -um (tet-trag'o-na). Four-angled.

TETRAGONIA. *See* NEW ZEALAND SPINACH.

tetragonoloba, -us, -um (tet-tra-go-nol'-o-ba). With a 4-angled pod.

Tetralix (tet-tray'licks). Pre-Linnaean* name for *Erica Tetralix*.

TETRAPANAX (tet-tra-pay'nacks). A single Formosan species of shrubs or small trees of the family Araliaceae, generally known as the rice-paper tree, and to science as **T. papyriferus** (but long called *Aralia papyrifera* and *Fatsia papyrifera*). It is a shrub or small tree, without spines, the young foliage more or less white-hairy. Leaves alternate, large, heart-shaped or ovalish, deeply 5–7-lobed, the margins toothed, the blade nearly 12 in. wide. Flowers greenish, in numerous small globe-shaped heads (umbels*), these arranged in a large woolly cluster (panicle*); fall-blooming. Sepals, petals, and stamens* 4 each (5 in the closely related *Fatsia*). Fruit a small, globe-shaped berry. An extremely handsome plant for the shrubbery, but its large leaves, which are very striking, and spreading habit need considerable space. Propagated by seeds or cuttings. The plant is not certainly hardy north of zone* 6, and should have a wind-sheltered, preferably half-shady place. It is widely grown in Formosa as a source of rice-paper. (*Tetrapanax* is from the Greek for four and *Panax*, in allusion to the parts of the flowers being in fours.)

TETRAPLOID. *See* CHROMOSOME.

tetraptera, -us, -um (tet-trap'ter-a). Four-winged.

---

* Special articles on the subjects indicated by an asterisk (*) will be found at the words so marked.

TETTERWORT = *Sanguinaria canadensis.*
See BLOODROOT.

TEUCRIUM (too'kri-um). Germander.
Perennial herbs or under-shrubs of the mint
family, comprising about 100 species, the few
below grown for ornament or fragrance. They
have opposite* leaves, which become smaller
and bract*-like near the flower clusters. Flowers in small whorls,* which are arranged in
terminal clusters (mostly racemes* or
spikes*). Corolla 2-lipped,* the lower lip
much larger than the upper. Stamens* 4,
conspicuously protruding. Fruit a collection of
4 small nutlets. (Named for King Teucer,
first king of Troy; a species name at *Veronica.*)

The cult. germanders are partly herbaceous
and hardy over most of the country, but two
of them, *T. Chamaedrys* and *T. Marum,* are
under-shrubs and not generally hardy north
of zone* 6, although with protection they
are grown north of this. Propagated by division or by seeds, and of simple cult. in most
garden soils, although *T. Marum* appears to
be lime-tolerant.

canadense. Wood sage. A native, perennial
herb, 12–30 in. high. Leaves lance-shaped or
ovalish, 3–5 in. long, toothed, hairy on the
under side. Flowers purple or paler, about
¾ in. long, the spike 5–7 in. long. Eastern
N.A. Summer.

Chamaedrys. A prostrate or procumbent
under-shrub. Leaves ovalish, about ¾ in. long,
toothed and hairy. Flowers red-purple or rose,
usually spotted with red and white, about ¾
in. long, the spikes loose. Eu. A good bedding
or edging plant blooming in late summer, but
see above for hardiness. Often called wall germander.

fruticans. Tree germander. An evergreen,
bushy herb, 2–5 ft. high, the branches forked.
Leaves oval, blunt, about 1 in. long, the margins rolled, brown-hairy on the under side.
Flowers in a sparse cluster (racemes*), blue.
Southern Eu. Summer. For the cool greenhouse or outdoors from zone* 7 southward.

Marum. A small, white-felty shrub, not very
showy but with pleasantly scented foliage. *See*
FRAGRANCE. Leaves ovalish, scarcely ⅓ in.
long, without teeth. Flowers purplish, mostly
less than ½ in. long, the clusters (spikes*)
about 1½ in. long. Mediterranean region.
Summer. Grown mostly for its fragrant foliage.
For hardiness *see* above.

orientale. A perennial herb not over 1 ft.
high. Leaves 1½–2 in. long, cut feather-
fashion into narrow segments. Flowers about
½ in. long, violet or blue. Western As.

texana, -us, -um (teck-say'na). From
Texas.

TEXAN PRIDE = *Phlox drummondi.*

TEXAS. The state flower is the bluebonnet, the state tree the pecan. The state lies
wholly in zones* 4, 5, 6, and 7. It ranks
high in the commercial production of fall,
winter, and early spring vegetables. Leading
summer vegetables are watermelon and sweet
potatoes. Most fruits, including apples, berries, peaches, figs, and citrus, are grown commercially in some part of the state. It is
unique in combining such diverse geographic
conditions within its boundaries. In the eastern part the timber belt is not greatly different from the southeastern states. The Gulf
Coastal plain is quite distinct from this. The
Lower Rio Grande Valley is sub-tropical.
The Edwards plateau in the central western
portion is sub-humid. The plains in the Panhandle occasionally experience zero weather.
The extreme western portion is semi-arid and
almost mountainous in character.

TEXAS

The zones of hardiness crossing Texas are those
shown on the map located at ZONE, which
should be consulted for details. The dates are
the average latest killing frost in spring and
the first one in the fall. The figures below
the dates show the average length of the growing season. Rainfall figures (in inches) are
for total annual rainfall in the regions so indicated.

SOILS. The surface soils of the timber
country are sandy loams and may be underlain either with a crumbly clay subsoil or a
dense clay subsoil. The soils of the coastal
plain may be either light or heavy; they are
quite fertile and are inclined to be wet. The
productive soils of the Rio Grande plain are
similar to the coastal plain in character. Irrigation is necessary for fruit and vegetable
production in this region. The soils of the
large central area, including the Edwards
plateau and the Panhandle, are calcareous in
nature. An extensive black-land strip occurs
in the eastern portion. The fruit and vegetable developments are, in general, on the
lighter soil types and those of alluvial origin.

CHIEF GARDENING CENTERS. The Fort
Worth–Dallas area, the Houston–Galveston
area, and the San Antonio area are among
the important horticultural centers. This is
due to the market for local produce and to a

* Special articles on the subjects indicated by an asterisk (*) will be found at the words so marked.

very evident interest in ornamental gardening. The farmers' markets are an important feature of the distributing system. The extensive parks contribute much to a better apprecia- tion of landscape art. Tyler, in Smith County, should be mentioned as the center of an extensive rose industry.

FRUIT AREAS. Citrus-growing in the Lower Rio Grande Valley has developed with amaz- ing rapidity within the last few years. Em- phasis is upon grapefruit because of its high quality. Plums for the early market are grown in east Texas. Peaches are grown at scattered points over a vast area, covering approximately the northeastern quarter of the state. The Galveston–Houston region grows the most strawberries. There is also some production in the northeastern corner of the state and in the Winter Garden below Uvalde. Figures place Smith County first in the entire country in blackberry and dew- berry production. Pecans are grown chiefly on bottom land in the central and eastern portions. Much of the yield comes from na- tive trees. Figs are particularly well adapted to the Gulf Coast east of the Colorado River. Production depends almost entirely upon mar- ket conditions.

VEGETABLE AREAS. According to the last census Texas ranks first in area devoted to many vegetables grown for out-of-state mar- kets. While individual plantings of early tomatoes are not large in Texas, this crop is grown over a wider area than any vegetable except Irish and sweet potatoes, and water- melons. The region around Palestine is the most important in east Texas, but the high plains of west Texas produce late summer tomatoes. The largest sweet-potato acreage is found in the northeast corner of the state. Onion production is concentrated in the La- redo and Corpus Christi districts, in the Winter Garden, in Collin County north of Dallas, and in west Texas. Seed production is a recent development. While watermelons are grown pretty much all over the state, the heaviest production is to the south of San Antonio. Brooks County, just north of the Lower Valley, is also a heavy producer.

ORNAMENTALS. Texas has a great deal of native material of ornamental value. The annuals and perennials are very numerous both as to number of species and especially as to number of individuals, since they liter- ally cover the countryside with bloom in the spring. Perhaps the most noted of these is the Texas bluebonnet (*Lupinus subcarnosus*). Other flowers which paint the landscape are the brilliant red Indian blanket, *Rudbeckia, Oenothera,* and *Verbena,* to mention but a few. The bluebell (*Eustoma*) is conspicuous for the size of its flowers. The cacti provide more variety of both form and color than any other single group. The agaves, yuccas, and related types are characteristic of the South- west. Dry-land ferns are found in the hills of southwest Texas.

In the eastern timber belt the trees and shrubs are for the most part the same as those found farther east. They include the red cedar, the pines, which form the basis for a lumber industry, the broad-leaved evergreens, such as the magnolia, live oak, and American holly, and many deciduous trees, such as sweet gum and tulip-tree. Yaupon (*Ilex vomitoria*) is perhaps the best native ever- green shrub. When established it is drought- resistant and hardy. Agarita (*Mahonia tri- foliolata*) provides exceptionally interesting foliage. Selected individuals of both of these shrubs have very attractive berries. Decidu- ous shrubs with attractive fruits are the coral- berry (*Symphoricarpos orbiculatus*) and the French mulberry (*Callicarpa americana*).

Farther west in the range country the shrubs occupy a dominant position, not only in the landscape but in the lives of the people. "When the Bloom Is on the Sage" is much more than a song. The leading spirits of the "Brush" are the acacias, huisache, and many others, such as *Mimosa* and mesquite. Many of these brilliant-flowered shrubs are still called by their Mexican names.

CLIMATE. There is an immense range in climatic conditions within the state, which intimately affects the gardening activities of the various regions. The Lower Rio Grande Valley is sub-tropical; the Panhandle, which frequently has sub-zero weather in the winter, is very different. Similarly, the annual rain- fall is much greater in the eastern than in the western part of the state. Important factors in gardening here, as elsewhere, are the soil, the available water, and variations in the temperature. More can be done to ameliorate the first two than is possible in the case of the latter. The extent of cold damage in the winter is largely dependent upon the extent of the preceding warm per- iod. Plants that are easily seduced by a week or two of balmy weather must be placed on the north side of a building or some place where the winter growth will be discouraged. While the mild winters permit large acreages of the hardier vegetables and citrus in the southern areas, the peach-growers in the northern part are dependent upon the winter cold to break the dormancy of their trees for a full crop. In the fertile irrigated valleys the disadvantage of light rainfall is partially offset by the small amount of disease present as a result of the low humidity.

The isotherms roughly parallel the coast except in the western part of the state. The following table gives some idea of the situa- tion with respect to the growing season.

TEXAS FROST DATA

Town	Average date of last killing frost in spring	Latest-known killing frost
Brownsville	Feb. 15	Mar. 8
Eagle Pass	Feb. 27	Apr. 5
Beaumont	Feb. 28	Apr. 3
Tyler	Mar. 16	Apr. 25
Lubbock	Apr. 9	May 7

* Special articles on the subjects indicated by an asterisk (*) will be found at the words so marked.

TEXAS FROST DATA

Town	Average date of earliest killing frost in fall	Earliest-known killing frost
Brownsville	Dec. 10	Nov. 14
Eagle Pass	Nov. 26	Oct. 20
Beaumont	Nov. 23	Oct. 29
Tyler	Nov. 18	Oct. 20
Lubbock	Nov. 2	Oct. 19

The greatest rainfall occurs in the eastern portion, decreasing farther west. This ranges from something over 50 inches in the southeast corner to 10 inches at El Paso. The eastern half of the state receives between 30 and 50 inches of rainfall annually. Just west of this is a sub-humid region receiving between 15 and 30 inches. It includes the Panhandle and extends a little east of south to the coast. The country west of a line extending from the southeast corner of New Mexico to Laredo is, in general, semi-arid with arid portions. Most horticultural crops, including apples, pears, and a variety of vegetables, are grown under irrigation in this region. *See* IRRIGATION.

The address of the Agricultural Experiment Station, which has kindly supplied this information about the state, is College Station, and its staff is always ready to answer gardening questions.

Garden club activities include clubs affiliated with the Garden Club of America, the home office of which is 598 Madison Avenue, New York 22, N.Y. There are also over 80 clubs affiliated with the Texas Federation of Garden Clubs.

TEXAS BLUEBONNET = *Lupinus subcarnosus.*

TEXAS BUCKTHORN OR JUJUBE = *Zizyphus obtusifolia.*

TEXAS MILLET = *Panicum texanum.*

TEXAS PLUME = *Gilia rubra.*

TEXAS RANGER = *Leucophyllum texanum.*

TEXAS SAGE = *Salvia coccinea.*

TEXAS STAR = *Xanthisma texanum.*

TEXAS UMBRELLA TREE = *Melia Azedarach umbraculiformis.*

texensis, -e (tecks-en′sis). From Texas.

textilis, -e (tecks′till-is). Woven; or useful for weaving textiles.

THALIA (thay′li-a). Canna-like swamp or aquatic perennial herbs of the family Marantaceae, comprising about 7 species from the warmer parts of America, one of them, **T. dealbata,** the water canna, often grown for ornament. It grows wild from S. Car. to Fla., but north of this it had better be grown in a greenhouse pool, or at least not allowed to freeze. It is a white-powdery, stemless herb, the slender leafstalks nearly 2 ft. long, the blade ovalish, 16–24 in. long, more or less heart-shaped at the base, and

without teeth. Flowers dull violet, borne in spikes at the end of a hollow stalk 4–5 ft. high. Corolla very irregular,* and some of the sterile stamens* petal-like. It does best in wet soil or in shallow water. A related species, **T. divaricata** from Fla., differing in only minor characters, but with narrower leaves, is a recent introduction to cult. (Named for Johann Thal, German naturalist.)

thalictrifolia, -us, -um (tha-lick-tri-fō′li-a). With leaves like the meadow rue.

thalictroides (tha-lick-troy′deez, but *see* OÏDES). Like a meadow rue.

THALICTRUM (tha-lick′trum). Meadow rue. A large genus of graceful perennial herbs of the buttercup family, most of the 120 species found in the temperate zone, and a few of them cult. for ornament. They have basal or alternate* leaves which are twice- or thrice-compound,* the ultimate leaflets of many species suggesting those of the maidenhair ferns. Flowers small, but handsome because of the usually large, terminal, often branching clusters (panicles* or racemes*). Petals none. Sepals sometimes colored and petal-like. Stamens* numerous and often providing most of the color. In many species the flowers are unisexual* or even dioecious (the male and female on different plants). Fruit a collection of small, ribbed or grooved achenes.* (*Thalictrum* is an old Greek name.)

The European and Asiatic species below are far better garden plants than the native American sorts, most of which grow in moist meadows and are best suited to low, sunny places in the wild garden. All are of easy cult. and may be divided in the spring. While over 20 species are in cult. in the U.S., those below are among the best. Most of them, except *T. dipterocarpum,* bloom in early summer.

adiantifolium. A name for some of the many forms of *T. minus.*

aquilegifolium. A branching herb 2–3 ft. high. Ultimate leaflets nearly round or oblongish, broadly few-toothed toward the tip. Male and female flowers on separate plants, the male flowers the more showy from the numerous pinkish-purple stamens,* which are longer than the white sepals. Eurasia. A handsome plant for the herbaceous border; known in several color forms, as white, dark purple, and orange.

dioicum. Early meadow rue; also called silverweed. A native woodland plant, 1–2 ft. high. Ultimate leaflets roundish, bluntly 5–9-lobed. Male and female flowers on separate plants, the greenish-yellow stamens longer than the similarly colored sepals. Eastern N. A. Plant in low, open places in the wild garden.

dipterocarpum. A showy Chinese plant, 1–2 ft. high, the roundish, notched, ultimate leaflets bluish-green on the under side. Flowers nodding, the cluster much-branched, the pale rose or lilac-lavender sepals nearly as long as the stamens. Western China. Late summer. *See* GRAY AND LAVENDER GARDEN.

glaucum. A bluish-green perennial, 3–4 ft. high. Ultimate leaflets ovalish, 3-lobed, and the lobes toothed. Flower clusters (panicles*) dense, the flowers yellow, the stamens longer

---

* Special articles on the subjects indicated by an asterisk (*) will be found at the words so marked.

than the sepals. Southern Eu. Also known as *T. speciosissimum.*

kiusianum. A very small meadow rue, rarely more than 4–5 in. high, and a compact perennial suitable for pot cult., or for outdoors in mild climates. Leaflets broadly ovalish, purple above, toothed on the margin. Flowers purplish, the stamens* much protruded. Jap. May–June. Used by the Japanese in pans which contain their dwarfed trees.

minus. A low border plant 8–18 in. high, the ultimate leaflets very small, roundish and 3-lobed. Flowers greenish-yellow, drooping, in small, loose clusters. Eurasia and northern Af.

polygamum. Tall meadow rue. A branching, native meadow plant 6–8 ft. high. Ultimate leaflets roundish or oblongish, 3-lobed. Flowers small, but very numerous, in a large, branched, terminal cluster, the stamens and white sepals of about equal length. Eastern N.A. Suited to low, open places in the wild garden.

rochebrunianum. A perennial 2–3 ft. high, the stem smooth. Leaves divided into segments suggesting the maidenhair fern, smooth both sides, the margins 3-toothed toward the tip. Flowers purple, in a sparse, pyramidal cluster (panicle*), sometimes pale purple. Jap. It needs partial shade and a reasonably acid soil (pH 6).

THALLUS. The plant body of the algae, mosses, lichens, and a few fungi, which, unlike that of flowering plants, has no true stem, leaves, or root. For the structure known as prothallus *see* Spores and Reproduction at FERNS AND FERN GARDENING.

Thapsus (thap′sus). An old name for the mullein (*Verbascum Thapsus*).

THATCH PALM = *Coccothrinax argentea.*

THAWS AND THAWING. Alternate thawing and freezing in late winter and early spring is usually more damaging than low temperatures. While no one can control this condition, there are things one can do in the garden to ward off its worst effects.

These are twofold. Perhaps the most serious is the opportunity it provides for susceptible woody plants to start into inopportune growth, which is often disastrous if followed by a hard freeze. It is also a particularly trying time for all broad-leaved evergreens and conifers, because a sudden warm spell puts a sudden demand for water upon the roots which they may not, and often cannot, meet. This impetuous water requirement, induced by a few warm, unseasonable days, kills or "burns," as the gardeners say, more plants than wintry blasts. To overcome the worst effects of thawing and freezing, it is necessary to understand just what hardiness is and what plant protection may do. Neither subject will be discussed here for both are fully covered at the articles HARDINESS and PROTECTING PLANTS.

The other effect of thawing and freezing is upon the soil, which in most reasonably moist soils results in heaving. Nothing can be more disastrous to shallow-rooted perennial herbs, or to the lawn. For the first *see* HEAVING. For the heaving of lawns and what to do for it *see* Rolling at LAWN.

THEA (tee′a). Asiatic, mostly evergreen shrubs and trees of the family Theaceae, comprising about 14 species, only one of hort. significance, **T. sinensis,** the tea plant, grown more for interest than ornament, as no tea is produced commercially in the U.S. It is a shrub or small tree, never over 30 ft. high, and as cult. usually a small shrub. It has alternate,* leathery, more or less elliptic leaves (the source of tea), 2–5 in. long, and shallowly toothed. Flowers white, about 1½ in. wide, fragrant, nodding, solitary or in 2–4-flowered clusters. Sepals 5–7. Petals 5, partly united at the base. Stamens numerous in 2 series. Fruit a woody capsule.* India and China. The tea plant is somewhat grown in the U.S., and needs the same cultural care as the closely related genus *Camellia* (which see). There were a few enthusiasts, notably in S. Car., who started the commercial growing of tea, but it has never been much more than an interesting experiment in the U.S. For the plant often advertised as *Thea japonica see* CAMELLIA JAPONICA. (*Thea* is the Latinized version of the Chinese name for tea.)

THEACEAE (tee-ā′see-ee). The tea family, besides the shrub yielding tea (*see* THEA), contains a few other genera of shrubs and trees of considerable garden interest. The family comprises only 16 genera and about 200 species, mostly from warm or tropical regions.

Of these *Camellia* is easily the most important. Requiring greenhouse culture is *Eurya* (evergreen), although both genera can be grown outdoors in regions where the oleander will stand the winter. Two cult. genera with interesting American species are *Stewartia* and *Gordonia,* both with relatively showy flowers.

Leaves simple,* alternate,* usually leathery and often evergreen. Flowers solitary or a few together, often (*Stewartia, Gordonia,* and especially *Camellia*) strikingly handsome. Fruit usually a dry, splitting pod (capsule*), but sometimes fleshy or dry and not splitting.

Technical flower characters: Flowers hermaphrodite.* Sepals 5–7, separate or united at the base, often with 2 bracts* below. Petals mostly 5, separate or united at the base (doubled in some hort. varieties of *Camellia*). Stamens* many (seldom 5), usually more or less joined at the base and joined often to the base of the petals. Ovary superior,* 2–10-celled.

theifera, -us, -um (tee-iff′er-ra). Tea-bearing; often merely tea-like or with the fragrance of tea.

THELESPERMA (thell-e-sper′ma). Coreopsis-like, and in ours, annual herbs of the family Compositae, comprising about 10 species, of which **T. burridgeanum,** from Tex., is a hardy flower-garden annual. It has been called, at times, *Coreopsis atrosanguinea, Thelesperma hybridum,* and *Cosmidium burridgeanum.* It is a hardy annual (*see* ANNUALS) which should be sown where wanted

---

* Special articles on the subjects indicated by an asterisk (*) will be found at the words so marked.

and a branching herb 12–18 in. high. Leaves alternate* and opposite,* much-divided into thread-like segments. Flower heads about 1½ in. wide, long-stalked, the ray* flowers reddish-brown or orange, the margins yellow. It differs only in technical characters from *Coreopsis*, and needs an open, sunny place. Aug.–Sept. (*Thelesperma* is from the Greek for wart and seed in allusion to the warty achenes* of some species.)

THELOCACTUS (thell-o-kak'tus). Medium-sized, more or less globe-shaped cacti from Tex. and adjacent Mex., comprising about a dozen species, of which **T. bicolor**, closely related to *Echinocactus*, is cult. for ornament or interest in desert gardens in the Southwest, and in the succulent greenhouse northward. The plant body is globe-shaped or conical, about 3½ in. in diameter, usually with 8 low ribs. Spines very numerous, colored, 9–18 divaricating ones in a cluster, in the center of which are 4 stouter and erectish spines. Flowers pinkish-purple, nearly 2 in. long. For culture *see* CACTI. (*Thelocactus* is from the Greek for nipple and *Cactus*, in allusion to the nipple-like tubercles on the ribs.)

THELYPTERIS = *Dryopteris*.

Thelypteroides (thell-lip-ter-roy'deez, but *see* OÏDES). Like a fern of the genus *Thelypteris*, here included within *Dryopteris*.

THEOBROMA (thee-o-brō'ma). A small, but commercially very important genus of tropical American shrubs and trees of the family Sterculiaceae. The chief species is **T. Cacao**, the chocolate tree, and in the tropics widely cult. as the source of chocolate and cocoa. It is an evergreen tree, 20–25 ft. high, with alternate,* leathery, oblongish leaves, 8–12 in. long and, without marginal teeth. Flowers small, yellowish, borne mostly on the bark of the larger branches and the trunk (for structure *see* STERCULIACEAE). Fruit a large, woody, ribbed, reddish-brown capsule,* filled with a whitish, rather evil-smelling paste in which are imbedded the seeds (the cacao beans of commerce). These are about the size of a lima bean and the source of both chocolate and cocoa. The plant can only be grown in zone* 9, and nowhere in the U.S. is there heat and moisture enough to make chocolate plantations profitable. (*Theobroma* is Greek for food of the gods, which the Aztecs and Mayans called it.) The name for the tree and its seeds in most tropical countries is cacao.

THERMOMETER. The only caution regarding thermometers, which are necessary for the mushroom bed, cold frames, hotbeds, and greenhouses, is to remember that in all these places there is much moisture at times. This means condensation on the thermometers, which, in consequence, had better be of glass and wood, or all glass, but not of metal, or of only rustless metal.

THERMOPSIS (ther-mop'sis). A genus of about 20 species of North American and Asiatic, rather showy-flowered, perennial herbs of the pea family, at least two of them grown in the herbaceous border for ornament. Leaves alternate,* compound,* with 3 leaflets. Flowers yellow (in ours), pea-like, in chiefly terminal, erect clusters (racemes*). Fruit an oblongish, straight or curved pod (legume*), flattened or inflated. (*Thermopsis* is from the Greek for lupine-like, in allusion to their resemblance to lupines.) Most of them have large, leaf-like, sometimes clasping stipules.*

Of simple culture in most garden soils, but doing better in light, well-drained soils than in heavy ones. They have deep roots and are more drought-resistant than most garden plants. Propagated by spring division of the rootstocks, or by seeds. But the seed should be sown when fresh, and is rather slow to germinate.

caroliniana. Aaron's-rod. A stout, smooth-stemmed, mostly unbranched herb 3–5 ft. high. Leaflets oblongish, silky-hairy beneath. Flower cluster 8–12 in. long, rather stiffly erect. Pod hoary, about 2 in. long. N. Car. to Ga. June–July.

mollis. Bush pea. An erect, branched, hairy herb, 2–3 ft. high. Leaflets oblongish, 1–2 in. long. Flower cluster (raceme*) terminal, 6–9 in. long. Pod 2–4 in. long, somewhat curved at the tip. Va. to Ga. and Ala. June–July.

THESPESIA (thess-pee'zi-a). Tropical Old World trees (rarely shrubs or herbs) of the mallow family, comprising about 10 species. The only one of hort. interest is **T. populnea**, the bendy tree, also called Portia tree and seaside mahoe, much planted in seaside gardens in Fla., the Gulf Coast, and in Calif., and not hardy elsewhere in the U.S. It is a dense-canopied tree, 30–50 ft. high, with alternate,* long-stalked, ovalish or heart-shaped leaves, which are 2½–4½ in. long and poplar like. Flowers bell-shaped, showy, yellow, changing to purple, 2–3 in. wide, mostly in the leaf axils.* Calyx* 5-parted. Petals 5. Fruit a woody, 5-valved capsule* which often does not split. Tropics of As., Af., and Pacific Islands, widely planted and naturalized in Fla., where it blooms in late spring or early summer, although in the tropics it may bloom continuously. Does well in sandy soils. Propagated by seed. (*Thespesia* is from the Greek for divine, as the tree was often planted around temples.)

THEVETIA (thev-vee'shi-a). A genus of tropical American shrubs or small trees of the family Apocynaceae, one of the ten species commonly cult. in zones* 8 and 9 under the name of yellow oleander and known to science as **T. nereifolia**. It is an evergreen shrub or small tree with oleander-like foliage, and showy, yellow, fragrant flowers. Leaves alternate,* leathery, about 4 in. long and ¼ in. wide, the margins rolled. Flowers in a terminal, stalked cluster (cyme*), the corolla funnel-shaped, 2–3 in. long, the limb slightly twisted and longer than the tube. Fruit fleshy, black, about 1 in. wide, triangular (a drupe*), the flesh rather thin. A very popular ornamental for sub-tropical gardens, needing,

* Special articles on the subjects indicated by an asterisk (*) will be found at the words so marked.

in the young state, to be protected from occasional frosts by heaping up earth or sand around the base of the plant. It grows well in the sandy soils of the South and may be propagated by cuttings. (Named for André Thevet, French monk who explored Brazil and first took tobacco seed to Europe.)

thibetica, -us, -um (ti-bet'i-ka). From Tibet.

THIEF. A somewhat fanciful, but not inappropriate name for a sucker.*

THIMBLEBERRY = *Rubus occidentalis.*

THIMBLE-FLOWER = *Rudbeckia bicolor.*

THINNING. A common hort. operation having two objects. One involves the sacrificing of the plants or flowers removed for the benefit of the ones left behind. It is an operation widely practiced both in flower and fruit production where excellence rather than quantity is desired. For the details of this in fruit cult. *see* Thinning at PRUNING. In flowers, it is usually done by pinching out buds, and all commercial growers practice it. See DISBUDDING.

Thinning in another sense is equally important. It involves the pulling out of certain seedlings in a row for the sake of those left. Wherever this is necessary, it has been mentioned in the cultural articles throughout the ENCYCLOPEDIA. Where the thinned seedlings are to be saved and replanted, as in many young vegetable plants and flowers, the operation is usually known as pricking-out. *See* the Management of Seedlings at SEEDS AND SEEDAGE.

THIN SOIL. A poor, shallow soil, deficient in humus or plant food or both. *See* SOILS.

THIRAM. See FUNGICIDES.

THISTLE. Usually prickly-leaved herbs of the genera *Cirsium* or *Carduus.* See both genera. But many other plants have been called thistle, or the word is part of their names. For those in this book *see* CNICUS, ECHINOPS, ONOPORDUM, SALSOLA (*see* Russian thistle in the list at WEEDS), SCOLYMUS, and SILYBUM.

THISTLE FAMILY. See COMPOSITAE.

THLASPI (thl-as'pi). Penny-cress. **A** genus of over 60 species of annual, biennial or perennial, widely distributed herbs of the mustard family. They have mostly basal leaves, but some have a few stem-clasping leaves. Flowers mostly in racemes,* rather small, followed by a tiny, flat, narrowly winged pod. The only cult. species likely to interest the average gardener is **T. alpestre**, a smooth perennial, 8–12 in. high, with chiefly basal leaves, without teeth, stalked and narrowed both ends. Flowers white or reddish-tinged, sometimes violet. Eu. Summer. It is a short-lived perennial, best treated as a biennial. (*Thlaspi* is the classical name of some cress.)

THOMASIA (toe-mass'i-a). A genus of 28 species of Australian, rather low, evergreen shrubs of the family Sterculiaceae, the

two below grown for ornament in southern Calif., but otherwise little known in the U.S. They have alternate* leaves and white or purple flowers in terminal clusters (racemes*). Calyx of 5 sepals, more or less petal-like, and partly united. Petals none. Stamens* 5, or sometimes with 5 extra, sterile ones. Fruit a capsule.* (Named for the brothers Thomas, who collected Swiss plants.)

The first species is grown as a ground cover in southern Calif. Propagated by cuttings of side shoots rooted under a bell-jar in sand. Neither is over 3 ft. high.

purpurea. Leaves oblong or narrower, about ¾ in. long, hairy on the under side, less so above. Flowers purplish, the clusters longer than the leaves.

rugosa. Leaves heart-shaped or ovalish, lobed, 2–3 in. long and wrinkled, densely hairy or felty beneath, only slightly hairy above. Flowers white.

THORN. As a common name *thorn* is properly applied to the hawthorns, for which *see* CRATAEGUS. But it has also been applied to many other plants, or is part of their name. Those in this book and their proper equivalents are:

Blackthorn = *Prunus spinosa;* **Box-thorn** = *Lycium;* **Buckthorn** = *Rhamnus;* **Christ's-thorn** = *Paliurus Spina-Christi;* **Jerusalem thorn** = *Paliurus Spina-Christi* and *Parkinsonia aculeata;* **Kangaroo thorn** = *Acacia armata.*

THORN. A woody spine and nearly always a modified branch, as proved by the nearly universal origin in a bud (*see* SPINE).

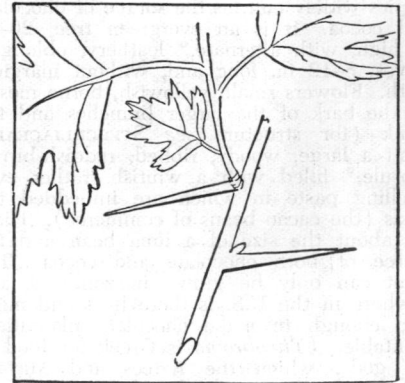

A true thorn

Technically, a rose does not have thorns but prickles, while true thorns are found on such plants as the hawthorn and honey locust (*Gleditsia*).

THORNAPPLE = *Datura Stramonium.* See also CRATAEGUS.

THORNY LOCUST = *Robinia neo-mexicana.* See LOCUST.

THOROUGHWORT. See EUPATORIUM.

---

* Special articles on the subjects indicated by an asterisk (*) will be found at the words so marked.

THOUSAND-FLOWERED ASTER. *See* BOLTONIA.

THOUSAND-HEADED CABBAGE = Brussels sprouts.

THREE-THORNED ACACIA = *Gleditsia triacanthos.* See HONEY LOCUST.

THREE-TOOTHED CINQUEFOIL = *Potentilla tridentata.*

THRIFT. *See* ARMERIA. For the prickly thrift *see* ACANTHOLIMON.

THRINAX (thry′nacks). A small genus of unarmed fan palms of southern Fla., the W.I., and Central America, a few of which are occasionally dug from the wild in extreme southern Fla., but one of them, **T. microcarpa,** the silvertop palmetto (also called prickly thatch and brittle thatch), quite widely planted for ornament. It is 20–30 ft. high, the fan-like leaves nearly 2 ft. wide, and densely silvery on the under side, but pale green above, divided into many deeply cleft, pointed and stiffish segments. Flower cluster from among the leaves, not long, the perfect* flowers borne on short, thick stalks. Fruit white-fleshed, scarcely ⅓ in. in diameter. The palm grows well on sandy soils, but is not certainly hardy north of zone* 9. For the palm sometimes called *Thrinax argentea see* COCCOTHRINAX ARGENTEA. (*Thrinax* is Greek for a fan, in allusion to the fan-like leaves.)

THROAT. The opening to the tubular part of a corolla, usually at the point where the limb* and tube meet.

THROATWORT = *Trachelium caeruleum.*

THRUM-EYED. *See* PIN-EYED.

THRYALLIS (thry-all′is). Horticulturally desirable shrubs of the family Malpighiaceae, some 15 species being scattered from Tex. and Calif. to Brazil. Only one of them, **T. glauca** (sometimes mistakenly called *T. brasiliensis*), is occasionally cult. for ornament from zone* 7 southward. It is a shrub 3–5 ft. high, with bluish-green foliage, the leaves opposite,* without marginal teeth, more or less oblong, 1–2 in. long. Flowers yellow, about ¾ in. wide, borne in slender-stalked clusters (for details *see* MALPIGHIACEAE). Fruit a 3-valved capsule.* A handsome cult. shrub, sometimes grown under glass. Use potting mixture* 4 and keep in the warm-temperate greenhouse. It is a native of Mex. and the W.I. (*Thryallis* is an old Greek name for some plant, but adopted by Linnaeus for this genus.)

THUJA (thew′ya). Arborvitae. Extremely valuable, evergreen, hort. and timber trees of the pine family, found in N.A. and eastern As., comprising only 6 species but with innumerable hort. varieties, most of which are low or at least not tree-like. The wild trees are magnificent forest evergreens and widely cut for timber, especially in the Pacific Northwest. They usually form a pyramidal head. Twigs densely covered with the tiny, scale-like leaves, and standing in flat, fan-like sprays or fronds, the leaves completely covering the twigs. Flowers none, in the usual garden sense, being represented by 6–12 stamens* in the male flower, the female flowers ultimately forming an egg-shaped or oblongish cone with its scales green, but brown when ripe, keeled, and not resembling the familiar pine cone. (*Thuja* is the old Greek name for them, and is sometimes spelled *Thuya.*)

The hort. forms of *T. occidentalis* and *T. orientalis* are among the most widely planted evergreens in the country. As will be seen below, they come in a large variety of shapes and colors. The low or dwarf or bushy kinds are very widely used for foundation planting, for evergreen groups at gateways, and for specimens on the lawn.

Wherever arborvitae grows naturally there is coolness and moisture, and the cult. species will always do best in such regions. But

Various outlines of the American arborvitae: Tree form (*left*), and the globular and columnar dwarf hort. forms at the right.

there are millions of them cult. in city courtyards, for accent plants, in window boxes (dwarf forms), and wherever a handsome evergreen is needed for winter decoration.

While many thousands of *Thuja* are annually set out in cities, the plants do not like wind, dust, or smoke, and few of them survive such an environment for more than a season or two. Away from these conditions, and in places without too much summer heat and too little rain, the arborvitae is one of the finest cult. evergreens. They do especially well along the coast from L.I. to Canada, and in the Pacific Northwest, but indifferently in the central U.S. where their cult. is at least hazardous. For their culture and propagation *see* EVERGREENS. Of the six known species three are grown quite generally in the U.S.

dolabrata = *Thujopsis dolabrata.*

---

* Special articles on the subjects indicated by an asterisk (*) will be found at the words so marked.

occidentalis. The American arborvitae; called also white cedar and northern white cedar. A medium-sized evergreen tree, rarely over 60 ft. high, the trunk buttressed at the base, the bark reddish-brown and furrowed. Leaves dark green or golden-green, the frond-like, fan-shaped, leaf-clothed twigs very handsome. Cones oblong, about ½ in. long, green at first, ultimately brownish, angled. N.A. Hardy from zone* 2 southward, but not in the warm, dry parts of the coastal plain. The common tree form, described above, is rather rare in cult., but has been the origin of innumerable hort. varieties, all of them much lower, shrubby or even dwarf. There are also many forms with variously colored foliage. Of the many varieties in cult. (perhaps over 100) the leading and most horticulturally useful are:

var. **alba.** Queen Victoria arborvitae. Tips of the young foliage white.

var. **boothi.** A low, compact form with larger leaves than some of the others.

var. **columbia.** Foliage variegated with silver; a shrubby form.

var. **compacta.** A form with dense, low habit.

var. **douglasi aurea.** Foliage bronzy-yellow.

var. **douglasi pyramidalis.** A low form with pyramidal habit and handsome fern-like twigs.

var. **ellwangeriana.** A low shrub with juvenile * and adult leaves.

var. **ellwangeriana aurea.** Similar to the one above, but the foliage yellow.

var. **fastigiata.** A columnar shrub, the branches short and upright. A good accent plant.

var. **globosa.** A very common form in cult., with a nearly perfect dome-shaped habit; useful for accent plants.

var. **hoveyi.** A dwarf form with a globe-shaped head of bright green foliage.

var. **lutea.** George Peabody arborvitae. A moderate-sized, shrubby form, of pyramidal habit and bright yellow foliage.

var. **umbraculifera.** A dwarf form with an umbrella-shaped outline.

var. **variegata.** A shrubby form with white-variegated foliage.

var. **vervaeneana.** A small, dense-foliaged form with bronzy leaves.

orientalis. Oriental arborvitae. A rather low, bushy tree, often branching near the base, the bark reddish-brown and scaly. Leaves all alike, the frond-like foliage bright green. Cones egg-shaped, about 1 in. long, rather fleshy and bluish in youth. China and Korea. Hardy from zone* 4 southward, and sometimes sold as *Biota.* It does better in the South than *T. occidentalis.* Its leading hort. varieties are:

var. **aurea-compacta.** A low, compact form with yellow foliage, especially in spring, gradually becoming green.

var. **aurea-nana.** A dwarf form with yellow, spring foliage, ultimately becoming green.

var. **compacta.** A dwarf and compact form.

var. **elegantissima.** A compact form, the foliage in early spring bright yellow.

var. **semperaurescens.** A shrubby form, the leaves more or less permanently golden.

plicata. Western red cedar; also called red cedar and giant arborvitae. A magnificent forest evergreen, and an extremely valuable timber tree, reaching up to 200 ft. high — never in cult. anything like this. Leaves bright green, but white-marked below. Cones oblong, about ¾ in. long. An extremely ornamental tree, native from Alaska to northern Calif. and Mont., mostly in regions of copious rainfall and fog. Hardy in the East only in zones* 3, 4, and 5,

and precariously so if winter winds are bitter and summer droughts too protracted. Its leading hort. varieties are:

var. **atrovirens.** Foliage dark green.

var. **aurea.** Leaves yellowish.

var. **fastigiata.** A columnar form with erect branches.

var. **pendula.** A form with drooping branches.

standishi. A medium-sized evergreen tree, 30–40 ft. high, with shreddy, reddish bark. Leaves minute, yellowish-green above, bluish-green beneath. Cones oblong, about ½ in. long, green at first, brown later. A fine evergreen with pyramidal crown and spreading branches. Jap. Hardy from zone* 4 southward.

THUJOPSIS (thew-yop′sis). A single species of Japanese evergreen trees of the pine family, **T. dolabrata,** the false or Hiba arborvitae, often grown for ornament. It resembles, and is closely related to, the true arborvitae (*Thuja*), differing in having woody, instead of somewhat herbaceous, cone scales. It is a tree up to 50 ft. high, the foliage in flat, frond-like sprays, the leaves glossy above, but with a broad white band beneath. Cones egg-shaped, scarcely ½ in. long, the scales flat and woody. For culture *see* EVERGREENS. Hardy from zone* 4 southward, but only in regions of adequate summer moisture. It does not do well, or fails, in regions of summer heat and dryness. There are dwarf and variegated-leaved forms. Sometimes known as *Thuja dolabrata.* (*Thujopsis* is from the Greek, meaning like *Thuja.*)

THUNBERGIA (thune-ber′ji-a). Mostly Asiatic or African, tender, woody or herbaceous vines or shrubs of the family Acanthaceae, comprising about 100 species, those below grown for ornament. Leaves opposite,* often arrow-shaped at the base. Flowers showy, solitary in the leaf axils,* variously colored, and below them 2 or more leafy bracts.* Corolla funnel-shaped or bell-shaped, sometimes curved, the limb regular* or nearly so, not 2-lipped.* Fruit a beaked capsule.* (Named for Carl Peter Thunberg, noted Swedish botanical author, a traveler in Jap. and S. Af., and a student of Linnaeus.*) Sometimes called clock-vine.

These are popular vines in Calif. and the South, and are commonly grown in the warm greenhouse northward. Use potting mixture* 3. or plant directly in the soil if possible. They are fairly rampant vines and will cover trellises or porches in a short time. Some of the species are more hardy than others, as noted below. Propagated by cuttings or by layering.

alata. Black-eyed Susan. An herbaceous vine, actually a perennial, but it will bloom from seed in one year if the growing season is long. Leaves ovalish or triangular, toothed, 2–3 in. long, the stalk winged. Flowers long-stalked, solitary, about 1½ in. long, white or orange-yellow, but purple-throated. Tropical Africa. Midsummer and later. *See* VINES.

erecta. A shrubby, vine-like plant, not usually over 6 ft. high. Leaves ovalish, 2–3 in. long, the marginal teeth few or none. Flowers

---

* Special articles on the subjects indicated by an asterisk (*) will be found at the words so marked.

nearly 2½ in. long, bluish-purple, the tube white. Tropical Africa. Not hardy north of zone* 8.

fragrans. Mountain creeper. An evergreen, woody vine, somewhat resembling *T. grandiflora*, but more delicate in growth. Flowers pure white, about 1½ in. long, the tube slender, the limb flaring. India. Not certainly hardy north of zone* 9, possibly in zone* 8 with protection.

gibsoni. A perennial, herbaceous vine, the ovalish leaves 2–3 in. long, and with winged stalks. Flowers about 1¾ in. long, orange, solitary and long-stalked, the stalks hairy. Tropical Africa. In Calif. it may be grown as a biennial or annual if the growing season is long.

grandiflora. Sky-flower. The best-known of the genus and a handsome, evergreen, woody vine. Leaves ovalish, 6–8 in. long, rough, 3-veined, the margins angularly toothed. Flowers blue (rarely white), nearly 3 in. long, in drooping clusters (racemes*), very showy. Corolla distinctly, but not deeply, 2-lipped.* India. Aug.–Dec. A rapidly growing, handsome, evergreen creeper, much planted in Fla. and Calif. Hardy from protected parts of zone* 7 southward.

thuringiaca, -us, -um (thur-in-gee-a′ca). From the region around Weimar, Thuringia, Germany.

THURLOW'S WEEPING WILLOW = *Salix elegantissima.* See WILLOW.

THUYA = *Thuja.*

THYME. Pleasantly aromatic woody perennials, or under-shrubs of the mint family, comprising the genus **Thymus** (ty′mus) which contains perhaps 100 species, most of them from the Mediterranean region. Two are widely grown for ornament or for their fragrant herbage, used as seasoning. They are erect or nearly prostrate plants with small, opposite* leaves without marginal teeth, diminishing in the flower cluster to tiny, leaf-like bracts.* Flowers lilac or purplish (in ours), small, mostly clustered in few-flowered whorls,* these distant, or the clusters in the leaf axils.* Calyx tubular, but 2-lipped.* Corolla usually half hidden by the calyx, slightly 2-lipped. Fruit a collection of 4 smooth nutlets. (*Thymus* is an old Greek name for some fragrant plant, perhaps savory or these.)

For the culture of the first 4 species *see* ROCK GARDEN. For the culture and use as seasoning of *T. vulgaris see* HERB GARDENING.

T. azoricus = *Thymus Serpyllum.*

T. citriodorus. A lemon-scented herb of uncertain status, probably related to *T. vulgaris* and thought by some to be of hybrid origin.

T. Herba-barona. A low, woody perennial, 2–5 in. high and generally procumbent, the foliage caraway-scented. Leaves tiny, ovalish or oblong, not over ⅓ in. long, half as wide, glandular,* finely hairy on the margin. Flowers tiny, purplish, in close clusters (heads*). Corsica and Sardinia. Summer. *Herba-barona* is the Corsican vernacular for this herb, which needs open sunshine and a well-drained site.

T. nitidus. A tiny woody perennial or subshrub, not over 4 in. high, and suited only

to the rock garden in a well-drained site. Leaves scarcely ⅓ in. long, less than ⅙ in. wide, very glandular*-dotted beneath. Flowers minute, pale lilac. Sicily. June.

T. Serpyllum. Mother-of-thyme. Creeping thyme. A much-branched, rather woody, prostrate or tufted herb, the stems wiry and rooting at the joints. Leaves short-stalked, more or less elliptic, scarcely ½ in. long. Flowers small, purplish, scarcely protruding beyond the calyx. Eurasia and northern Africa. Summer. For cult. *see* ROCK GARDEN. Of the many hort. varieties of this old-time favorite the best are:

var. **angustifolius.** Has narrow, almost linear leaves.

var. **aureus.** Foliage variegated with yellow.

var. **coccineus.** Taller than the type, the flowers crimson.

var. **lanuginosus.** Woolly thyme. Whole plant gray-hairy.

var. **splendens.** Flowers red.

var. **vulgaris.** Lemon thyme. With smaller, lemon-scented leaves. Sometimes known as *T. Serpyllum citriodorus.*

T. vulgaris. Common thyme. An erect, woody herb, 6–8 in. high, the stems white-hairy. Leaves nearly stalkless, ovalish or narrower, scarcely ½ in. long, the margins rolled. Flowers scarcely ¼ in. long, lilac or purplish. Southern Eu. June. For culture and use *see* HERB GARDENING.

THYMELAEACEAE (ty-me-lee-ā′see-ee). The mezereon family, sometimes called Daphnaceae, is much larger than its hort. importance indicates. Of its 40 genera and over 500 species of shrubs and trees, only a handful are of garden interest. Most of them have tough, acrid bark, especially *Dirca* (the leatherwood) of eastern N.A., which is sometimes cult.

The other cult. genera are *Edgeworthia, Pimelea,* and *Daphne,* of which the last is much the most important because it furnishes several attractive (sometimes evergreen) low shrubs for the rock garden, border, or greenhouse. The other two genera are mostly tender northward.

Leaves mostly alternate,* but opposite in a few. Flowers small, but often attractively clustered in heads, panicles,* or spikes,* mostly without petals. Fruit various, fleshy in *Daphne* and *Dirca;* nut-like or dry in some others.

Technical flower characters: Flower regular* and hermaphrodite.* Calyx-tube or receptacle* often petal-like, the sepals 4–5 (sometimes 6), also petal-like. Petals none or reduced to mere scales. Stamens* mostly 4–5. Ovary superior,* 1-celled or rarely 2-celled.

thymifolia, -us, -um (ty-mi-fō′li-a). With leaves like thyme.

THYMUS. See THYME.

thyoides (thee-oy′deez, but *see* OÏDES). Like the arborvitae (*Thuja*).

THYRSE. A rather dense flower cluster, usually considered as a compound panicle.* It is technically an inflorescence which is branched, the main branch never ending in a flower, but the other branches always ending in one. Common examples are the lilac

---

* Special articles on the subjects indicated by an asterisk (*) will be found at the words so marked.

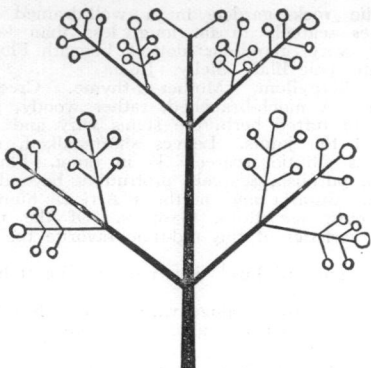

A thyrse (diagrammatic)

and horse-chestnut, and the cluster is much denser than the diagrammatic illustration.

thyrsiflora, -us, -um (thir-si-flow'ra). Bearing flowers in a thyrse.*

thyrsoides (thir-soy'deez, but *see* OïDES). Like a thyrse.*

TI = *Cordyline australis.*

tianshanica, -us, -um (te-an-shan'i-ca). From Tien Shan, in Kirgiz, central Asia.

TIARELLA (ty-a-rell'a). A small group of chiefly woodland perennial herbs of the family Saxifragaceae, found in N.A. and eastern As., and suited to the wild garden. The only commonly cult. species is **T. cordifolia,** the false mitrewort or foam flower, sometimes called the coolwort. It is a beautiful native wild flower with chiefly basal, broadly heart-shaped leaves, 3–4 in. wide, the margins lobed and toothed. Flowers small, white, in a dense, finger-shaped cluster (raceme*) at the end of a slender stem about 8 in. high. Petals 5, with a claw.* Stamens* 10. Fruit a small, membranous, 2-valved capsule.* Eastern N.A., mostly in rich woods, and needing similar conditions in the wild garden, but not difficult to grow. Some prefer to distinguish a form of *T. cordifolia,* from the southeastern U.S., as *T. wherryi,* which is reputed to be a stouter plant with more slender flower clusters. The *var.* **major** is larger and has salmon-pink or red flowers. (*Tiarella* is a Greek diminutive for turban, in allusion to the shape of the pistil.)

tibetica, -us, -um (ti-bet'i-ka). From Tibet.

TIBOUCHINA (ti-boo-ky'na). Spiderflower. Glory-bush. Chiefly Brazilian, bristly or hairy shrubs of the family Melastomaceae, comprising over 200 species, only one of which, **T. semidecandra,** is of much hort. interest, and grown outdoors in sub-tropical gardens, or in the North in the warm-temperate greenhouse. It is a handsome, hairy shrub, 4–6 ft. high, with opposite,* densely hairy, ovalish-oblong leaves, 2–4 in. long, pale beneath, and with 3–7 main veins. Flowers showy, 3–5 in. wide, solitary or in few-flowered, terminal clusters, beneath them 2 nearly round bracts.* Petals 5, violet or reddish-purple. Stamens* 10, of unequal length, some of them sticky-hairy. Fruit a 5-valved capsule,* surrounded by the calyx* tube. Not hardy outdoors north of zone* 8, perhaps in the warmest parts of zone* 7. Sometimes used as a showy summer bedding plant in the North. In the greenhouse use potting mixture* 4. (*Tibouchina* is a Latinized version of the name for some species in the Guianas.)

TICK CLOVER. See DESMODIUM.

TICKSEED = *Coreopsis* and *Bidens.*

TICK TREFOIL. See DESMODIUM.

TIDY-TIPS = *Layia elegans.*

TI-ES = *Lucuma nervosa.*

TIGERFLOWER. See TIGRIDIA.

TIGER LILY = *Lilium tigrinum.*

TIGERTAIL SPRUCE = *Picea polita.* See SPRUCE.

TIGRIDIA (ty-grid'i-a). Tigerflower. Flower-of-Tigris. Showy, tender, bulbous herbs of the iris family, the dozen or so species scattered from Mex. to Chile. One of them, **T. Pavonia,** is grown for ornament, although its large, handsome flowers are rather fugitive. The bulb (actually a corm*) is about 1½ in. in diameter, very starchy, and a favorite food of certain Mexican Indians. Leaves basal, stiffish, more or less sword-shaped, 12–18 in. long. Flowers 3–5 in. wide, red, but with conspicuous spots, generally cup-shaped, and growing from between leaf-like spathes* which are 3–5 in. long. Petals and sepals scarcely distinguishable as such, but the inner segments shorter than the outer, the narrow claw* purple or yellow. Fruit a capsule.* The plant is cult. in several varieties, one of them, the *var.* **conchiflora,** having bright yellow flowers. Others with lavender or white flowers are also known. The plants should be grown like *Gladiolus* (which see), as their bulbs will not stand severe frosts. (*Tigridia* is the Latin for tiger, in allusion to the markings on the flowers.)

tigrina, -us, -um (ty-gry'na). Colored or marked like a tiger.

TILIA. See LINDEN.

TILIACEAE (tilly-ā'see-ee). The cult. genera of the linden or jute family well represent its diversity as to habit and distribution. Of its 40 genera and 400 species, some are herbs, some hardy trees (the lindens), while most are purely tropical plants.

Only four genera are of hort. interest. By far the most important is *Tilia* (*see* LINDEN), also called basswood and lime, which yields some of our finest shade trees. *Corchorus,* an herb, which yields jute, is grown in warm regions. *Sparmannia* contains one African, greenhouse, white-flowered shrub, while *Entelea* is from New Zealand and is planted outdoors in Calif., as is *Sparmannia.*

The bark is usually fibrous and often mucilaginous. Leaves simple* and alternate.*

---

* Special articles on the subjects indicated by an asterisk (*) will be found at the words so marked.

Flowers regular, very fragrant and bee-visited in the lindens, always in clusters. Fruit various; in the linden, the stalk of the fruit and flower cluster arises from the middle of a leaf-like appendage.

Technical flower characters: Sepals 5 (rarely 4 or 3), usually soon falling. Petals 5, or less (in the cult. genera). Stamens* many, free, or united in bunches of 5–10, often a few infertile. Ovary superior,* 2–10-celled.

TILLAGE. *See* CULTIVATION.

TILLANDSIA (till-and′zi-a). A genus of nearly 400 species of chiefly tree-perching (epiphytic*) plants of the family Bromeliaceae, nearly all from tropical America, but a few entering the U.S., and one of them, the Spanish or long moss, a familiar sight throughout the southeastern U.S. They are of very various habit, sometimes stemless and with a basal rosette of narrow leaves, sometimes, as in the Spanish moss, with long-trailing, thread-like stems and very narrow, thread-like leaves. In some species the basal rosette, by the flaring of the leaf bases and their overlapping edges, makes a cup-like cavity which holds water. The leaves of many species are colored or grayish and usually scurfy. Flowers showy in some species, but very small and inconspicuous in the Spanish moss. *See* BROMELIACEAE. Fruit a capsule.* (Named for Elias Tillands, Swedish physician and botanist.)

The tillandsias and the related genus *Guzmania* are nearly all epiphytes,* and consequently light-demanding plants. They must be grown in the warm-temperate or tropical greenhouse in the North, and potted up, if at all, in a mixture of peat fiber or orchid peat. Many of them will grow perfectly if the plant is wired by its roots to a board upon which some orchid peat is fastened. Such boards may be hung from the greenhouse roof or nailed, as high as possible, to a greenhouse wall. They need frequent watering in the spring and summer, but should be allowed to become partially dormant, by reducing their water, during the dark winter months. The Spanish moss needs no attention other than to throw strands of it over the branch of a tree. It absorbs most of its food directly from the atmosphere.

In the collections of fanciers there are many other species than those below, but the three here listed are the only ones commonly grown.

fasciculata. A stiffish plant with a basal rosette of gray-green, narrow leaves 12–18 in. long. Flowers blue, the spike 4–6 in. long, borne mostly in branched clusters which are bracted, the bracts* greenish, but red-tinged. Fla. to Central America and the W.I.

lindeneana. A showy plant with a basal rosette of leaves, which are about 12 in. long and ¾ in. wide. Flowers in large spikes, bluish-purple. Bracts* on the flowering stalks carmine-red. Ecuador and Peru.

usneoides. Spanish or long moss (not a true moss). An extraordinary, lichen-like plant which drapes trees, especially live oaks and cypresses, from Va. southward. Stems and leaves long and thread-like, gray, the dense festoons often hanging over 20 ft. from the branches over which they are hung. Flowers extremely small, yellowish-green. Va. to Fla. and Tex., also in tropical America. It adds, to garden pictures in the South, an extraordinarily weird and misty note, suggesting in the distance a dense fog.

TILTH. That condition of the soil in which it is fit to produce good crops; most often used in the phrase that such a soil is in good *tilth.* There is, however, no precise definition of tilth. As ordinarily understood by gardeners, it means a soil that, having been plowed (or dug) and harrowed (or raked), is sufficiently workable or friable* so that seeds or plants may be planted with ease, and there is a reasonable expectation that they will grow. But the etymology of the word implies that it should be restricted to the cultivation of the soil after the crop is planted. In this sense tilth is the same as cultivation (which see).

TIME OF FLOWERING. For the factors that control the time of flowering *see* PHENOLOGY. *See also* EVERBLOOMING GARDEN.

TIMOTHY = *Phleum pratense.*

tinctoria, -us, -um (tink-tor′i-a). Used by dyers, or for dyeing; hence, usually, handsomely colored.

TINKERS′-WEED = *Triosteum perfoliatum.*

Tinus (ty′nus). Pre-Linnaean * name for the laurustinus (*Viburnum Tinus*).

TIPU = The native name of *Tipuana Tipu.*

TIPUANA (tip-u-ā′na). As here restricted, a genus of ornamental timber trees of S.A., comprising only the tipu, which is widely planted for ornament in Calif. It belongs to the pea family, has compound leaves, an unarmed stem, and showy golden-orange pea-like flowers. The only species is the tipu, **T. Tipu,** a tree often reaching 60 ft. in Calif., low-branching and tent-like in outline. Leaflets 11–21, about 1½ in. long, notched at the tip. Flowers in immense branched clusters (panicles*), persisting for weeks and very showy. Bolivia and Argentina. July (in Calif.). Hardy only in zones* 8 and 9. (*Tipuana* is derived from the native vernacular *tipu.*)

TIRED SOIL. A term scarcely sanctioned by the soil scientists, but of considerable cogency among practical gardeners to indicate a soil exhausted of nourishment for a particular crop. It usually implies that a crop has been grown for too long a period in one spot, and the obvious remedy is to move it. *See* ROTATION OF CROPS.

TISSWOOD = *Halesia monticola.*

titana, -us, -um (ty-tay′na). Huge. *Titanum* is also an old generic name used at *Amorphophallus.*

TITHONIA (ti-thō′ni-a). Tall, sunflower-like shrubs or woody perennial herbs of the family Compositae, found in Mex., Central America, and the W.I. Only one species, **T. rotundifolia** (sometimes known as *T. speciosa*), is of any garden interest, and its cult.

---

* Special articles on the subjects indicated by an asterisk (*) will be found at the words so marked.

is confined to zones* 8 and 9. It is a shrub or woody herb, 4–6 ft. high, with alternate,* broadly ovalish leaves 7–10 in. long, 3-lobed or coarsely round-toothed. Flower heads nearly 3 in. wide, the ray and disk flowers orange-yellow and resembling a sunflower. It is widely cult. here, and also grown in Mex. (Named for Tithonus, a mythological character.)

tithymaloides (ti-thi-ma-loy′deez, but *see* Oïdes). Like a spurge of the genus *Tithymalus* which is of no hort. interest, and is often included in *Euphorbia*. See Pedilanthus.

TI TREE = *Cordyline australis.*

TOAD. A frog-like, perfectly harmless, mostly land-inhabiting animal, common in many gardens and a most welcome visitor. They do not cause warts, but do feed on many injurious insects, slugs, and worms.

TOADFLAX. See Linaria.

TOAD LILY = *Fritillaria Meleagris, Tricyrtis hirta,* and *Nymphaea odorata.*

TOAD'S-MOUTH. See Snapdragon.

TOBACCO (*Nicotiana Tabacum;* for the plant called Indian tobacco *see* Lobelia inflata). The commercial production of tobacco lies quite outside the scope of this book, for many of the most valuable varieties cannot be grown in the U.S. But in spite of being a tender tropical annual, several varieties are grown on a large scale in Va. and southward, and others in Pa., Conn., and even in Canada. All such cult. is based upon the raising of plants under glass, in anticipation of maturing them in the warm growing season outdoors.

TOBACCO FAMILY = Solanaceae.

Tobira (toe-by′ra). Japanese vernacular name for *Pittosporum Tobira.*

TOBIRA FAMILY = Pittosporaceae.

TODDY PALM = *Caryota urens.*

TOLMIEA (toll′me-a). A single species of perennial herbs of the family Saxifragaceae, **T. menziesi,** a somewhat sticky-hairy herb, native from Alaska to Calif. and closely related to *Tiarella.* It differs from the latter in having only 2 or 3 stamens.* Leaves chiefly basal, heart-shaped, more or less lobed or bluntly round-toothed. Stem leaves (when present) 2–4, alternate.* Flowers greenish, the petals very narrow, the terminal cluster (raceme*) 8–15 in. long. Fruit a capsule.* It needs shade and woods soil and is suited only to the wild garden or rock garden. Easily propagated from the runners which are produced freely in summer, and from the young plantlet which arises at the junction of the leaf blade and its stalk; hence sometimes called "piggy-back plant." (Named for Dr. W. F. Tolmie, a surgeon of the Hudson's Bay Company.)

TOLPIS (toll′pis). A genus of about 15 species of small annual and perennial herbs of the family Compositae, chiefly from the Mediterranean region, one of them, **T. barbata,** grown as a hardy annual (*see* Annuals) in the flower garden. It is a slender herb 8–12 in. high, with a milky juice, and basal, lance-shaped, remotely toothed leaves. Flowers yellow, in small heads, not over ½ in. wide, and composed only of ray* flowers, not particularly showy. Beneath the head is a series of thread-like bracts,* some of which are also on the upper part of the flowering stalk. The plant flowers from midsummer to frost, and is sometimes listed as *Crepis barbata.* (*Tolpis* is of unknown origin.)

TOMATILLO = *Physalis ixocarpa.*

TOMATO. The garden tomato and its relatives all belong to the genus **Lycopersicum** (ly-ko-per′si-kum). This is a group of 10 or 12 species of South American herbs, mostly with strong-smelling foliage, belonging to the potato family (*see* Solanaceae). Only the two below are of any garden interest.

Lycopersicum (sometimes written *Lycopersicon*) has compound* leaves (the leaflets sometimes curly), or merely deeply divided leaves, and the foliage is often sticky (glandular). It is closely related to the genus *Solanum* (which see), but wholly lacks the prickles often found in that genus. Flowers yellow, the corolla shallowly bell-shaped or wheel-shaped. Fruit a pulpy berry. (*Lycopersicum* is Greek for wolf peach, perhaps in allusion to its once being thought poisonous.) The only two hort. species are:

L. esculentum. The type from which the common tomato has been derived. It is a spreading, hairy, strong-smelling herb, 3–6 ft. high. Leaves compound, often with smaller leaflets interspersed with larger ones. Flowers 3–7, usually nodding. Fruit red or yellow, 2–3 in. in diameter, the sides more or less grooved. This plant (known also as *Solanum esculentum*) is scarcely grown in cult., but from it the following varieties have been derived:

var. **cerasiforme,** the cherry tomato. The fruit about ¾ in. in diameter, red or yellow, nearly round. Oblong-fruited forms are often called plum tomato.

var. **commune,** the common garden tomato. Its leaflets are scarcely curled. Fruit (very large in some cult. forms) nearly round, but flattened at the ends, the sides not much (or not at all) grooved or furrowed.

var. **grandifolium,** the large-leaved or potato-leaved tomato. This plant has usually 5 rather large leaflets, without teeth or lobes, and few or no smaller scattered leaflets.

var. **pyriforme,** the pear tomato, has pear-shaped fruit, usually about 1½ in. long.

L. pimpinellifolium. Currant tomato. A weak, almost smooth herb, with little odor, many flowers (10–25), and small red fruit suggesting currants. A curiosity from Peru and little grown.

Of these species and varieties, much the most important is the tomato.

Tomato Culture (*Lycopersicum esculentum commune*)

The tomato is perhaps more tender than any other garden plant in such general cult.

---

* Special articles on the subjects indicated by an asterisk (*) will be found at the words so marked.

It is blackened by the least touch of frost, and will grow well only where there is plenty of heat.

The foliage of it is also extraordinarily sensitive to manufactured gas. Concentrations of gas too small to be detected chemically (1–1,000,000 parts of air) will injure or kill tomato leaves, and potted plants are used as gas indicators by some florists who suspect, but could not otherwise prove, that gas is seeping into their greenhouses. Natural gas does not contain ethylene which is the chief offender in manufactured illuminating gas. *See* GAS INJURY.

The outdoor culture of the tomato (once and sometimes still called love-apple) is based upon treating it as a tender annual, plants of which are raised under glass in anticipation of being later put outdoors. Many commercial growers and some home gardeners (in their anxiety to get the earliest possible yields) put the plants outdoors before they really should, and rely upon various devices to protect them from the cold (*see* below).

VARIETIES. Tomato varieties are divided into two groups, early and general season. The former (the only ones possible for zones* 1, 2, and the upper part of zone*3) are grown for the quickness of development; the latter for the supply that should last until frost.

Early: Victor, Fireball, Valiant, Early Hybrid, Sioux, Moreton Hybrid.

Midseason and late: Stokerdale, Marglobe, Rutgers, Manalucie, Long Red.

Many other varieties are offered. Some, like Ponderosa and Beefsteak, yield immense fruit. But they and several others are open to the objection that the fruit is apt to split or show cracks as it matures.

RAISING TOMATO PLANTS. While many home gardeners will prefer to buy potted plants offered by dealers at the time they should be planted out, there is little need to do this, for tomatoes are among the easiest of vegetables to raise from seed. In your calculations for the early varieties, allow 7–8 weeks from the time of sowing seed to the proper date in your locality for setting the plants in the garden (*see* below). *See* DETERMINATE.

Plant the seeds in flats or boxes in a greenhouse where the temperature does not fall much below 70°. If you have no greenhouse, the boxes may be set in the kitchen window, but if there is a gas stove, put the boxes in the bathroom window (assuming the latter is at ordinary room temperature). The usually dry air of a living room is decidedly less favorable.

The seed should be sown in fine, not too rich soil, about ¼ inch deep, either in tiny drills or broadcast as you prefer. Keep the soil moist but not wet. When the seedlings are about 2½ in. high, prick them out and replant on 2 × 2 in. intervals and allow them to grow until they are 4 or 5 in. high. For details *see* SEEDS AND SEEDAGE.

The seedlings are then replanted in individual containers — discarded paper drinking cups, old berry boxes, tomato cans (with a hole in the bottom), or 3-in. flower pots. At this time also must begin the process of gradually checking their growth so that they will be fit to meet the outdoor temperature. The best method is to transfer the pots from the house or greenhouse to the cold frame or hotbed, keeping the temperature at first around 60°, later around 55°. This will check, but not stop their growth and so harden-off the plants.

Tomato plants which have not followed this routine become spindling and weak — wholly unsuited for planting in the garden. If you purchase plants from dealers, see that they are stocky, have been hardened-off, and are generally no more than 8–12 in. high. If your own plants show signs of becoming higher than this, pinch them back to keep them stocky.

General season plants (which are set out three weeks after the early ones) are grown in the same way, but may usually be started in a hotbed or cold frame. These are also, by some, merely thinned to secure stockiness. They are less likely to meet cool nights than the early sorts and there is less need for the routine of hardening them off.

OUTDOOR PLANTING. Left to itself a tomato plant is weak and sprawling. Commercial growers let them sprawl and there is no doubt the yield is heavier when so grown. If you decide to adopt this method, the plants must be set at least 4 ft. apart each way.

The alternative is to tie each plant to a 4-ft. (above ground) stake and pinch off many superfluous leaves. Many home growers prefer this to save space. If you adopt it, set the plants 2½ ft. apart each way. Still another method is to use two stakes fastened to a barrel hoop over which the plant sprawls or is tied.

The date of planting outdoors is of the greatest importance for the early varieties. The plants need heat, both as to air temperature and soil temperature. You, on the other hand, want to set out the plants at the earliest safe date, or even a bit earlier.

In your locality a fair criterion is when the average daily temperature (maximum and minimum divided by two) is at least 60°. Many commercial growers plant earlier than this, well knowing that unprotected plants will be seriously checked by cool night temperatures. To overcome this they cover the plants every night (and on cool days) with one of a number of paper, cardboard, or cellophane plant protectors. Some (in the haste to get early tomatoes) even use these protectors to keep out frost. But the latter is a hazardous business, the likelihood of a killing frost proving you are starting too early. *See* PROTECTING PLANTS.

For most home gardeners the best method is to wait until protectors are no longer necessary.

CULTIVATION AND SOILS. Tomatoes need

---

* Special articles on the subjects indicated by an asterisk (*) will be found at the words so marked.

constant cultivation to keep down weeds and conserve soil moisture, upon which they draw heavily. This is especially true in the early stages of the plants allowed to sprawl. Later these cannot be cultivated without injury to the tender, rather brittle stems.

The home grower should keep on pinching off the extra amount of foliage which staked plants are sure to develop. Pinch off enough leaves so that the sun can easily reach the developing fruit. Staked plants, well grown, ought to produce 8–12 tomatoes per plant (more in some of the general season varieties); unstaked plants from 12–20. These figures make calculation of the number of plants you need reasonably easy. But cold, rainy weather in midsummer would greatly decrease the yield, so it is safer to plant more than seems advisable from statistical evidence. Fruits harvested green just before frost will ripen if left on a sunny window sill.

Any good garden soil will grow tomatoes. Experience has shown that too much (especially nitrogenous) fertilizer or manure close to the plants makes them more likely to produce leafage than fruit. If you are prepared to pinch off the excess leaves, they may be fertilized as for any other rich-feeding crop. Occasionally tomato leaves will curl without any specific disease or insect being responsible. Usually it is caused by lack of humus in the soil, or by too severe pruning, or even by tying them upright to a stake. All of these change the moisture conditions (*i.e.*, light and sunshine) of the plant and it is this that generally causes leaf curl. Ordinarily it is not important.

TOMATOES IN WINTER. The all-year market supply is based upon utilizing the comparatively warm winters of the Far South or sections of Calif. But northern gardeners with a greenhouse or conservatory may have home-grown tomatoes from November to March. These plants are started from seed 10 weeks before the plants are set in the greenhouse bench, and handled as outdoor seedlings to ensure stockiness, but of course are not hardened off. Plant them at 3½-ft. intervals. Keep the night temperature around 60°, the day temperature 65°–70°.

Greenhouse plants are usually grown (by pinching) to a single erect stem tied at intervals to a wire stretched to the roof. When they are in flower they must be pollinated, as this will not be taken care of by insects as in outdoor plants. To pollinate, choose a warm, sunny day and have the air in the house reasonably dry. Gently shake the plants when the pollen is in condition to fall. Usually this jarring will distribute enough. But if you are not certain, use a camel's-hair brush (*see* CROSSING).

For the preferred position and sequence of your outdoor tomato plants *see* KITCHEN GARDEN.

INSECT PESTS. For cutworm, *see* CABBAGE. Arsenicals or TDE will control the young of large hornworms. Remove by hand picking. In late season, TDE may be needed for fruitworm (corn earworm). Aphids of several species yield to pesticide #21 (*see* SPRAYS AND DUSTS) applications.

DISEASES. Of the many diseases and troubles with tomato, the more common are readily controlled. Early blight is a fungus disease causing target-like spots on foliage and may result in defoliation. Late blight produces black spots on leaf and stem, and rough, black areas on the fruit. Anthracnose° causes small target-like spots on fruit. To control these diseases apply pesticide #1, #7, or #11 (*see* SPRAYS AND DUSTS) at 10-day intervals, starting 6 weeks after plants are set in the field.

If tomato is grown in the same area during consecutive years, plants may die as a result of a wilt° disease which attacks the roots. Break open the stem, and if brown streaks are present just under the "bark" of the stem, it indicates the fusarium wilt disease. Use resistant varieties such as Manalucie, Manatee, Kokimo, or others adapted to your locality and recommended by your state agricultural experiment station.

A number of virus diseases, such as mosaic,° spotted wilt,° and leaf curl,° attack tomato. Because some of the virus diseases are carried in tobacco, it is best not to smoke while handling the plants.

Large, sunken black areas at the flower end of the fruit are known as blossom-end rot. This trouble is caused by improper water relationships and thus cannot be controlled with a pesticide. Similarly, a white scald° on the cheek of the fruit indicates sunburn and cannot be controlled by a spray.

TOMATO EGGPLANT = *Solanum integrifolium.*

TOMATO FAMILY = Solanaceae.

tomentella, -us, -um (to-men-tell′a). Almost tomentose.

tomentosa, -us, -um (toe-men-toe′sa). Tomentose; *i.e.*, densely covered with matted, flat hairs. Leaves and stems so clothed have a felt-like appearance.

TONGUE-FERN = *Cyclophorus lingua.*

TOOL HOUSE. In any garden beyond the smallest, some sort of a tool house is much the best solution of the problem of what to do with the tools and implements listed in the next article.

A tool house may be as attractive as the one shown in the picture at STRUCTURES, but more often it must be a simple affair of wood, preferably hidden from the garden proper by planting, or if space does not permit a thick screen of shrubs and trees, the tool house should be covered with vines. *See* VINES.

The interior of the house should have floor space for roller, lawn mower, wheelbarrow, or other large equipment, and it should have several shelves for storing boxes or baskets, and if it has running water and a sink, it will often save the kitchen from much rough washing of vegetables, trimming of flowers, and other jobs better done in the garden.

If possible, the floor should be of cement and there should be pegs or nails on the

---

° Special articles on the subjects indicated by an asterisk (°) will be found at the words so marked.

walls for hanging up everything possible. Because vermin are hard to control in such places, all seeds, bulbs, or tubers should be kept in tin boxes while waiting for planting day. But remember that the house will have no heat, and tender bulbs should not be left out over the winter in regions of severe cold.

One of the best tool houses known has not only plenty of pegs or nails for hanging things up, but overhead crossbeams so arranged that stakes, poles, and other bulky material can be put up there for the winter. In some busy planting seasons the floor of the tool house may be the most convenient place to do many jobs, and the aim should consequently be to keep it as clear as possible.

TOOLS AND IMPLEMENTS. Gardeners are divided between those who loosen reluctant weeds with a broken dinner knife and the more gadget-minded who find in the shops and garden centers a welter of power-driven machines and so-called "garden accessories." Of these there are hundreds, and every garden center, county fair, and most country hardware stores exhibit all and more than the average gardener ever wants or has room to store.

Some of the best gardeners in the country use only a few tools, leaving to others the exploration of the items mentioned above. If we confine our recommendations to the essentials these would have to include only the following (ignoring spraying equipment, which is treated at SPRAYING AND DUSTING):

1. A spade or pointed-nosed shovel. *See* DIGGING.
2. A digging fork; useful for moving perennials whose roots may be cut too severely by a spade; also for manure. *See* DIGGING.
3. A hoe, perhaps both kinds, *i.e.*, the ordinary draw hoe and a scuffle hoe. *See* HOEING.
4. Rakes. A steel-toothed one for soil, and a wooden-tined or bamboo rake for leaves or lawn raking. *See* RAKING.
5. A wheelbarrow; indispensable unless the garden is quite small.
6. A wheel cultivator; necessary only if there are reasonably long rows of vegetables or flowers. The ordinary kind (and far the cheapest) you push yourself, but there are, for larger gardens, many motor-driven garden cultivators. *See* CULTIVATION.
7. Small hand tools:
   a. A dibber; useful for making holes for seedlings, unless you use a pointed stick.
   b. A trowel (preferably all steel); indispensable for planting bulbs or perennials.
   c. Small hand cultivator with 3-/ or 4-pronged teeth.
   d. An asparagus knife; for harvesting asparagus and fine for cutting perennial weeds below the ground level. *See* ASPARAGUS.

8. Watering pot. Essential for watering seedlings (with a fine spray), or, by removal of the rose,* to deliver a stream of water on shrubs or herbs needing a good soaking.
9. A hose (with an adjustable nozzle). Fifty feet is enough for a small garden; 100 ft. for a larger one. More than this is a nuisance to move and bulky to store. With the hose, if in a region of summer droughts, you need enough lawn sprinklers to water the lawn. *See* LAWN for details.
10. Pruning and shearing. There are four essentials:
    a. A good pair of pruning shears; an especially sharp kind known as secateurs for finer pruning.
    b. A pruning saw with double-edged teeth for small branches.
    c. A stouter saw with coarse teeth for larger branches.
    d. Hedge shears, for hedge clipping.
11. Lawn mower. *See* LAWN.

The total, under these headings, comprises only a few items and this may seem a meager equipment for the modern gadgeteer. But with them the gardener can accomplish most ordinary garden operations. All the tools like spades, hoes, forks, or rakes also come in lighter weight and with shorter handles for feminine gardeners who find the standard tools a bit wearing.

Ingenuity could expand the list, but for the beginner the above comprises all that are needed. And many very fine gardens (not commercial establishments) have been made without the use of much else. If there should be other needs (rare in most small places) the list might be expanded by the following:

a. Stout mason's line for keeping alignment of rows in the vegetable garden.
b. Mattock, for loosening tough sod, small stones, and for cutting roots.
c. Pick. For loosening larger stones and densely packed soil.
d. Axe.
e. Sharp knife, especially for grafting and budding.

For kneeling pads, gloves, clothes, baskets, colored cord, thermometers, rain gauges, floral carts, root feeders and dozens of other "garden accessories," the size of your purse and nearness to a shop are the only limiting factors.

TOON, TOONA. *See* CEDRELA TOONA.

TOOTHACHE TREE. *See* ZANTHOXYLUM.

TOOTHWORT = *Plumbago scandens.* *See also* DENTARIA.

· **TOPATO.** *See* POMATO.

TOP-DRESS. As the name implies, top-dressing is the application of a dressing of manure, fertilizer, humus, or the proceeds of the compost* pile to crops without plow-

---

* Special articles on the subjects indicated by an asterisk (*) will be found at the words so marked.

ing. In the garden the material that is used for top-dressing would, or should, be raked in. And in top-dressing a lawn the fertilizer or manure or humus would usually be better distributed if the lawn is thoroughly raked with a steel rake. *See* LAWN.

The great advantage of top-dressing is that the material used for it can be scattered or sown, depending on its consistency, without any disturbance of the crop in place, and to its very decided advantage. Care should be used in top-dressing a border or vegetable garden not to get raw fertilizer or manure on the plants. Spread or scatter it carefully between the rows.

To the amateur top-dressing may seem very like mulching.* But the latter is often, especially in the growing season, for the purpose of conserving moisture or to keep down weeds, neither of which is accomplished by top-dressing. While it is true that a winter mulch of manure may feed the plant, this is not the primary function of a mulch, while top-dressing is purely this or the improvement of the physical condition of the soil.

Materials for top-dressing and the amount used will vary with the crop. On lawns some form of non-acid, weed-free humus (which see) is often of the greatest benefit. It should be scattered about 1 in. thick and raked in. If a commercial fertilizer is indicated, this should be sown like grass seed (no thicker), preferably before a rain.

For the flowers and vegetable garden a good material for top-dressing would be:

2 parts of thoroughly rotted material from the compost* pile.

1 part well-rotted stable manure.

1 part of leaf mold or commercial humus.

The three ingredients should be thoroughly mixed, all lumps broken up, and spread when reasonably dry to ensure an even distribution. Generally such a mixture should not be applied more than ¾ in. thick, and worked into the soil with a rake or cultivator.

Top-dressing is especially valuable on sandy soil, or for crops which are rich feeders or where speed, as in lettuce-growing, is particularly desirable. It is also very beneficial for pot plants where constant watering is apt to leach out much food.

For special sorts of top-dressing, such as those needed for the azaleas and rhododendrons (which are really permanent mulches), for the rock garden, and where commercial fertilizers are used, *see* AZALEA, ROCK GARDEN, FERTILIZERS. *See also* MULCH AND MULCHING.

TOPEPO. A little-known tomato-like vegetable, assumed to be a hybrid between the red pepper and the tomato. It is of no garden significance.

TOPER'S-PLANT = *Sanguisorba minor.*

TOPIARY. Topiary work is the clipping and training of shrubs into ornamental or grotesque figures — which they really are depends upon whether you think topiary work artistic or not. Ever since the days of the Romans, who were expert topiarists, there has always been a prejudice against it, one English writer describing topiary as a "monument of perverted taste." It is undeniably effective only when held within rigid limits and it often has not been. To see an English countryside peppered up with vegetative foxes, birds, children, and all sorts of grotesque geometrical figures is not artistic, but it does show a high degree of hort. skill. Topiary is far more common there than here, and only in a few of the oldest and finest estates is topiary work in America likely to be seen. Legitimate use of topiary, mostly purely architectural, is to be seen at the Alhambra in Granada and in some of the Italian gardens at Florence and Rome.

The basic material, in the North, is usually privet, but far finer effects may be secured from yew or arborvitae, if you live in the region where they are thoroughly hardy. *See* THUJA and TAXUS. *See also* HEDGES for the initial care of privet.

TOP ONION = *Allium Cepa viviparum.*

TOP-WORK. To make over the top of a shrub or tree by substituting better varieties for the existing one. It is usually done

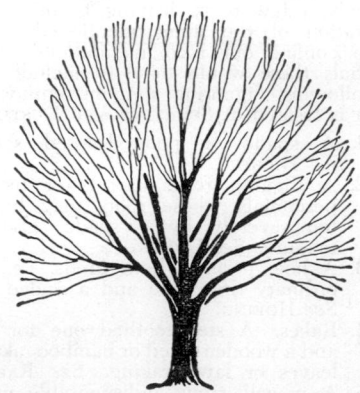

A top-worked tree, the heavy lines showing the original stock, the light lines the new growth resulting from the budding or grafting. Such wholesale top-working takes a few years to complete.

by grafting or budding the desirable varieties upon the existing stock. For the details *see* GRAFTING. *See also* BUDDING.

TORCH LILY. *See* KNIPHOFIA and DORYANTHES EXCELSA.

TORCH TREE FAMILY. The Fouquieriaceae. *See* FOUQUIERIA.

TORENIA (tor-ren'i-a). African and Asiatic perennial or annual herbs of the family Scrophulariaceae, comprising over 40 species, of which **T. fournieri**, from Cochin-China, is a flower-garden plant grown as a tender annual (*see* ANNUALS). It is a much-

* Special articles on the subjects indicated by an asterisk (*) will be found at the words so marked.

branched herb, 10–12 in. high, with a 4-angled stem, and opposite,* ovalish, toothed, stalked leaves, 1½–2 in. long. Flowers blue, or blue-violet and yellow, in stout, stalked clusters in the leaf axils,* or terminal. Corolla 2-lipped,* the upper lip* faintly 2-lobed, the lower lip 3-lobed, the central lobe blotched yellow at the base. Fruit an oblong capsule.* A useful and attractive annual, good for the border, for the rock garden, for edging, and for hanging baskets. There is also an albino form, and the plant blooms readily in the shade. The *var.* **compacta**, the blue wing flower, is a lower form particularly suited for edging (which see). A related species, *T. flava*, with yellow and purple flowers, a native of eastern As., is sometimes seen in rare collections. It should be grown also as a tender annual. (Named for Olaf Toren, Swedish clergyman and botanist.)

TORINGO CRABAPPLE = *Malus sieboldi.*

toringoides (tor-ring-goy′deez, but *see* Oïdes). Resembling the toringo crabapple.

tormentillo-formosa. Like a plant of the obsolete genus *Tormentilla*, now included in *Potentilla*.

TORREYA (tor′ree-a). Six species of Asiatic or eastern North American evergreen trees of the family Taxaceae, three of them grown for ornament. They are handsome trees with fissured bark and the branches in whorled* tiers. Leaves 2-ranked, narrow, stiff, and almost prickle-tipped, with two white or brownish bands beneath. Flowers in the garden sense none, being represented by a collection of 6–8 groups of 4 stamens* each in the male flowers, and stalkless ovules in the female flowers followed by drupe*-like, slightly fleshy fruit. The male and female flowers usually on separate plants. (Named for John Torrey, American botanist.) Also known as *Tumion.*

These plants are closely related to the yews (*Taxus*), being chiefly distinguished by the drupe-like fruit. For cult. *see* Evergreens.

californica. California nutmeg. A tree up to 60 or even 75 ft. high, the bark gray-brown, the branches drooping. Leaves line-like, 2–2½ in. long, shining green. Fruit egg-shaped or oblongish, about 1¼ in. long, light green, but streaked with purple. Calif. March–May. Hardy from zone* 6 southward, occasionally dropping its leaves near the northern edge of its cultural range.

nucifera. A Japanese tree up to 75 ft. high, less as cult. Leaves lance-shaped, ¾–1¼ in. long, dark, shining green above. Fruit stalkless, oblongish, about 1¼ in. long, green, but faintly streaked with purple. May. Hardy from zone* 3 southward.

taxifolia. Stinking cedar. An evergreen tree not over 45 ft. high, usually half that. Leaves narrow, line-like, almost spine-tipped, about 1¼ in. long, dark, shining green above, of decidedly unpleasant odor when bruised. Fruit inverted egg-shaped, about 1¼ in. long, purple. Fla. Hardy from zone* 6 southward, possibly in protected parts of zone* 5.

tortuosa, -us, -um (tor-tew-ō′sa). Tortuose.*

TORTUOSE = Flexuous; *i.e.,* more or less twisting or zigzag.

TORUS. *See* Receptacle.

Totai (toe′ty, also toe-tah′ee). A South American vernacular name for the palm *Acrocomia Totai.*

TOUCH-ME-NOT. *See* Impatiens.

TOURS. *See* Garden Tours.

tovarensis, -e (toe-var-ren′sis). From Tovar, Colombia.

TOWNSENDIA (town-zen′di-a). Western North American perennial (or biennial) herbs of the family Compositae, comprising 20 species, the two below mostly taken from the wild for the informal border or rock garden. They have alternate,* narrow leaves without marginal teeth, and solitary, but usually numerous aster-like heads composed of both ray* and disk* flowers. (Named for David Townsend, Pennsylvania botanist.)

The two below are chiefly Rocky Mountain plants suited to the rock garden, where the first species flowers earlier than almost any other plant of the daisy family. They need a gritty soil, and in the East may not be hardy, for while they can stand any amount of cold, summer heat and moisture do not agree with them.

exscapa. Easter daisy. A practically stemless perennial, the stalkless flower heads nestled in a rosette of very narrow leaves. Flower head with white or purplish rays. Rocky Mountain regions. Feb.–Apr. (in Colo.).

grandiflora. A spreading perennial (sometimes biennial) 9–15 in. high, usually branched. Leaves narrow, line-like. Flower heads about 1 in. wide, blue or violet. Western Neb., Colo., and N. Mex., but not so high in the mountains as the last. Summer.

Toxicodendron (tock-si-ko-den′dron). An old, and now obsolete generic name for the poison ivy and its relatives. *See* Rhus.

TOXYLON = *Maclura.*

TOYON. A single species of beautiful evergreen shrubs from California and Lower California, constituting the genus **Heteromeles** (het-er-om′e-leez) of the rose family. It is an important bee plant, called also (in Calif.) the Christmasberry, redberry, and California holly, and known to science as **H. arbutifolia.** It is a shrub up to 15 ft. high, occasionally tree-like, with alternate,* thick, leathery, oblongish, sharply toothed and abruptly pointed leaves, 2–4 in. long. Flowers white, scarcely ¼ in. wide, in dense clusters (panicles*) 2–3 in. high. Petals 5. Stamens* 10. Fruit bright red (rarely yellow), oblongish, about ¼ in. long, persistent and decorative. Summer. Not hardy north of zone* 7, but widely planted in Calif. for ornament, and much used for Christmas decorations. Propagated by seeds or by layers or cuttings. (*Heteromeles* is from the Greek for different apple, in allusion to the fruit being unlike related genera with apple-like fruit.) It is sometimes offered as *Photinia.*

---

* Special articles on the subjects indicated by an asterisk (*) will be found at the words so marked.

TRACE ELEMENTS. While fertilizers, manure, and lime supply the major needs for plant growth in the form of available nitrogen, phosphoric acid, potash, and lime, most soils contain also adequate amounts of other chemicals upon which plants also depend for proper nourishment. These are found in such minute quantities that the term *trace elements* has been applied to them. The chief ones (deficient in some soils) are iron (*see* IRON CHELATES), manganese, copper, zinc, boron, and molybdenum. From a practical garden standpoint these can generally be ignored, but in some cases minute amounts of these trace elements are added to fertilizers, especially in some boron-deficient soils in the Northwest. Most farm manure contains them. *See also* SOILLESS GARDENING.

TRACHELIUM (tra-kee′li-um). Widely grown perennial herbs of the family Campanulaceae, comprising about half a dozen species from the Mediterranean region, one of which, **T. caeruleum**, the throatwort, is cult. for ornament. It is a biennial or short-lived perennial, 12–30 in. high, with alternate,* ovalish, unequally toothed leaves, 2–3 in. long. Flowers blue (rarely white), in a dense terminal cluster (cyme*). Corolla tubular, about ⅓ in. long, its limb 5-lobed, the lobes narrow. Fruit an angled capsule.* Southern Eu. Summer. Not hardy in the North, where it may be treated as a greenhouse annual, or cuttings may be made of old plants. (*Trachelium* is from the Greek for neck, in allusion to its supposed value for throat trouble.) The genus is closely related to *Campanula*, one of which is called *Campanula Trachelium*, but the true bellflowers are finer garden plants than the cult. species of *Trachelium*.

TRACHELOSPERMUM (tra-kell-o-sper′-mum). Indo-Malayan or Chinese, mostly showy-flowered, woody vines of the family Apocynaceae, one of them **T. jasminoides**, the star or Confederate jasmine, widely grown for ornament from zone* 6 southward, and also a favorite greenhouse plant in the North. It is a high-climbing vine, without tendrils* or aerial roots, which climbs by twining and is rather slow-growing. Leaves evergreen, opposite,* ovalish, short-stalked, narrowed both ends, 2–3 in. long, without marginal teeth. Flowers white, star-like, about ¾ in. wide, most beautifully fragrant, grouped in rather sparse, long-stalked clusters (cymes*). Corolla short-tubed, its oblong lobes twisted to the left. Fruit consisting of 2 long, slender pods (follicles*), which are round in cross-section. The plant, a long-time favorite throughout the South, will grow in a variety of soils, but is slow in getting established. In the greenhouse it should be planted in a tub (using potting mixture* 4), where, by clipping, it can be made into a handsome, bushy plant 3–4 ft. high. It needs a warm-temperate house and moisture during spring and summer, but a cooler house and less water in the winter. Southern China. Blooming outdoors in April–May. **T. asiaticum** of Jap. and Korea, a recently introduced species, has broader leaves and yellowish-white, also fragrant, flowers. It is not quite so hardy as the Confederate jasmine. (*Trachelospermum* is from the Greek for neck and seed, in allusion to the seed having a neck.)

TRACHYCARPUS (tra-kee-kar′pus). Rather low-growing Asiatic fan palms, among the hardiest known, and generally not thriving in the tropics, nor does the only cult. species do well in zone* 9 in Fla. In zone* 8, and over the warmest parts of zone* 7, the one below is perfectly hardy and has been known to stand temperatures of 20°, thus hardy up the coast to Va., and nearly throughout the Pacific Coast. Of the half-dozen or so known species, only **T. fortunei**, the hemp or windmill palm, is commonly cult., but this is widely planted outdoors, and tubbed specimens are much used for patios, porches, and for indoor decoration northward. As cult. it is a low, slow-growing palm, the trunk rarely over 10 ft. high (40 ft. in the wild), and densely clothed with the remains of the old leaf sheaths. Leaves nearly round, fan-like, stiffish, 2–4 ft. wide, divided nearly to the middle into many narrow, pointed segments, the leafstalk roughish. Flower cluster among the crown of leaves, short, the flowers unisexual* or polygamous* (*see* PALMACEAE). Fruit drupe*-like, pea-sized, bluish. Burma, Indo-China, perhaps in Jap. (*Trachycarpus* is from the Greek for rough and fruit, in allusion to the lobed fruit of some species.) The plant is often known as *T. excelsa*, and is just as often offered as *Chamaerops* (which see).

TRACHYMENE (tra-kee-mee′ne). Chiefly Australian annual or perennial herbs of the carrot family, comprising over 25 species, one of which, **T. caerulea**, the blue laceflower, is a very popular flower garden and greenhouse annual. It is grown for its beautiful flowers which strongly suggest a pale blue or lavender edition of the common wild carrot or Queen Anne's-lace (*see* CARROT). It is an erect, but weak-stemmed plant, 18–30 in. high, with twice- or thrice-compound leaves, the ultimate segments narrow, and cut into 3 narrow lobes. Flowers minute, but numerous and borne in a flat umbel,* 2–3 in. wide. Fruit flat (*see* UMBELLIFERAE). The blue lace-flower can be grown as a tender annual, or the seed can be sown directly where wanted (*see* ANNUALS). It is not particular as to soil, but flowers better if the plants are a bit crowded. Commonly grown also in the cool greenhouse, where flowers may be had almost throughout the year by planting a succession of seed. It is commonly grown by florists. (*Trachymene* is from the Greek for rough membrane, in allusion to the fruit of some species.) It is often offered as *Didiscus*.

---

* Special articles on the subjects indicated by an asterisk (*) will be found at the words so marked.

trachypleura, -us, -um (tra-kee-ploor′ra). With rough ribs or veins.

TRADESCANTIA. *See* SPIDERWORT.

TRAGOPOGON (tra-go-pō′gon). Goatsbeard. Rather coarse, taprooted, biennial or perennial Old World herbs of the family Compositae, comprising nearly 40 species, of which only two are of garden interest, one a root vegetable, the other a weedy plant, sometimes cult. for ornament. They are milky-juiced herbs, with narrow, grass-like, sometimes keeled leaves, the base often clasping. Flower heads solitary, large, yellow or purple, all the flowers strap-shaped, with no disk florets.* Fruit a longish, bristly achene.* (*Tragopogon* is Greek for a goat′s beard.)

The first species is cult. only for its edible taproot* (*see* SALSIFY). The second, often a mere weed, is a hardy biennial seldom cult. for ornament and scarcely worth growing.

porrifolius. Salsify; also called oyster plant and vegetable oyster. A biennial with a deep, white-skinned, edible taproot, the stem 3–4 ft. high. Leaves keeled, the base clasping. Flower heads violet or violet-purple, blooming before noon, and usually closing then. Southern Eu. For cult. *see* SALSIFY.

pratensis. Meadow salsify; also called Star-of-Jerusalem. A biennial, weedy herb, 2–3 ft. high, somewhat resembling *T. porrifolius* but the flower head yellow. Eu., but naturalized as a weed in most of N.A., rarely cult. for ornament.

TRAILING ARBUTUS. Very fragrant-flowered, creeping or prostrate woody herbs (strictly they are shrubs), comprising the genus **Epigaea** (ep-i-jee′a) of the heath family, with one Japanese species, and one, **E. repens,** the Mayflower (also called ground laurel and winter pink), perhaps our most fragrant wild flower. It is an evergreen plant of rather difficult culture, suited only to the specialized conditions in the wild garden. Leaves alternate,* stalked, ovalish or oblongish, ¾–2½ in. long, minutely hairy on the margin, green all winter, but replaced by new leaves after the plant blooms. Flowers white or pinkish, about ½ in. long, very fragrant, the corolla with 5 spreading lobes. Stamens* 10, not protruding. Sometimes male and female flowers are separate and on different plants. Fruit a small capsule,* which becomes berry-like after it splits. Seeds extremely minute, often lacking. Eastern N.A. but westward to Mich. and Saskatchewan, mostly in dry woods. April–May. Hardy everywhere, but not easy to grow. For cult. *see* WILD GARDEN. (*Epigaea* is from the Greek for upon the earth, in allusion to its prostrate habit.)

TRAILING AZALEA = *Loiseleuria procumbens.*

TRAILING-BEGONIA = *Cissus discolor.*

TRAILING FIRE = *Gilia rubra.*

TRAILING FUCHSIA = *Fuchsia procumbens.*

TRAILING PHLOX = *Phlox nivalis.*

TRAILING PLANTS. *See* VINES.

TRAINED FRUIT TREES. Anyone who has wandered through France is astounded at the profusion, productivity, and beauty of trained fruit trees, most of which are pear and apple trees. In Normandy it seems as though every farmhouse and barn has fastened to it a magnificently trained fruit tree, and in April this makes an unforgettable picture of loveliness. If one adds to this mile after mile of trees trained as cordons in the fields, it is no wonder the French became the greatest growers of fine pears in the world.

So completely French is the whole concept of trained fruit trees that we have inherited their terms for them, and these need definition:

Espalier: French for an epaulet or shoulder strap, in allusion to the fact that the branches of such trees are trained to be more or less at right angles to the main stem. There are many modifications of the espalier, one the Palmette Verrier (French), another the Fan, which, with the Gridiron, is British.

Cordon: French for cord or rope, in allusion to the fact that such trees are trained along parallel wires and look like leafy ropes. This is the type grown mostly in the open, and often they are trained so that the wires are a foot or two apart and stretch from post to post much as in the Kniffen system for grape-growing here. *See* GRAPE.

All such trained fruit trees, which are a fraction of the size of standards, are grafted on dwarfing understocks, just as are dwarf and semi-dwarf fruit trees. But, in addition to dwarfing, the French orchardists have developed a technique of bending young growth in the proper manner so that the food supply is partially cut off, and this helps in training the tree into the almost architecturally symmetrical forms shown in the illustrations.

The European reason for such trees was twofold. As all branches or twigs are cut off, except those in a single plane, the trees could be trained flat against a south-facing wall, to capture the heat absorbed by brick or stone, as this was often needed to ripen the fruit. Such is never the case here, and in fact espaliers should almost never be put on a south wall because the heat would be too intense for most fruits. The other reason was to increase fruit production in a limited space. That is perfectly possible only by an intensive and continuous system of summer pruning which will be dealt with presently. Without it espaliers and cordons are merely interesting examples of training fruit trees into flat architectural patterns.

It is this that made trained fruit trees in this country an expensive horticultural fad, and it is still not much beyond this, except for a few growers willing to take the time and patience to conquer the rudiments of French perfection. There the method of

---

* Special articles on the subjects indicated by an asterisk (*) will be found at the words so marked.

pruning and manuring trained trees produces so much, and such superior fruit, that the plants must be anchored firmly to wall or wire or they would collapse with the weight.

Their great use in the home garden is that they take practically no space. In flower, especially if pruned in the way to be outlined presently, they make strikingly beautiful and unusual pictures. Their fruit depends upon the variety chosen, but it is often superior to the same variety grown as a standard or even as a dwarf. To cover a wall with trained fruit trees or line a drive or path with a triple-tiered cordon of apples or pears is, while expensive, an interesting and unusual method of producing fruit where there is perhaps no room for a semi-dwarf or even a dwarf.

But no one should attempt to grow them who is not willing to give them almost constant attention, particularly through the summer. Unlike most fruit trees they need rich soil and an annual application of stable manure. The soil around them should be kept cultivated, and the easiest way of applying the manure is to mulch the plants in the fall with a 3-inch layer of well-rotted manure, and dig it in the following spring. The whole theory of feeding trained fruit trees is to encourage the utmost vigor and then, by drastic pruning, force this added strength into fruit production. The plants are grown on dwarfing stocks, their limit of growth is rigidly controlled, and what would be a lush growth of branches, twigs, and leaves in such an overfed standard tree, produces more fruit in a small area than any known method of orchard practice.

The size of trained fruit trees is usually fixed by the nurseryman who trains them. Ordinarily they should be kept to this size by cutting off terminal buds or twigs so that there shall be no increase in length of arms or branches. Most specimens offered by the dealers, no matter how complex their branching, will be from 5 to 8 feet in height for erect forms like the Palmette Verrier or espalier, and from 7 to 10 feet long for the cordon types.

If you decide to increase the height or length of your trained fruit tree it can be done by allowing terminal twigs to grow that should otherwise be cut off. Unless this is done with a good deal of skill and patience, you may well lose the symmetry of your specimen, and hence the chief charm of trained fruit trees.

The ultimate production of blossoms and later of fruit is so tremendous that in April such trees seem to be clothed with a white sheet of bloom, hiding most twigs and branches, and looking for all the world like the most extravagant picture in the catalogues. Such plenty, however, can only be secured by meticulous pruning.

PRUNING TRAINED FRUIT TREES

The ordinary winter pruning of fruit trees, which is usually followed for standards, semi-dwarfs, or dwarfs, will not do for trained trees. In ordinary trees the fruit is borne mostly at the periphery of the plant, but the object is to make practically *all* branches of the trained tree fruit-producing branches.

Horizontal cordon

To accomplish this needs careful study. The tree, as it arrives from the nursery, will have a number of main branches from which, during the first season, other twigs, leaves, and blossoms will spring. Observe them closely, and learn to distinguish the sorts of buds from which leaves, twigs, and blossoms actually arise. Do no pruning the first growing season, as the dealer will deliver the plant properly pruned for that season.

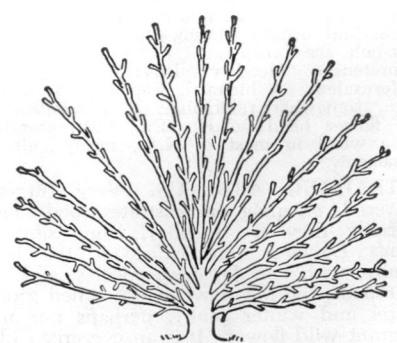

Fan-trained fruit tree

You will notice that blossoms and fruit are almost never produced by leafy twigs, but come from stubby spurs on older wood (*i.e.*, not the current season's growth). It is the object of pruning, not only to take advantage of this fact, but to force the production of such fruiting spurs by removing current growths that produce none. There is, however, some danger in removing too many leafy twigs for a very good reason that owners of trained fruit trees should understand.

All trees, especially these trained dwarfs, have only two sources of food. One is the nutriment from their roots, and the other is the food manufactured by the green coloring matter (chlorophyll) in all leaves. This leaf-manufactured food is so important to trees that without it they would die. This leaf food is drained by downward-moving sap to the roots, which cannot function without it.

It is the nice understanding of the amount of safe summer pruning, in order to maintain food balance, which has resulted in the method outlined below. It was devised years ago by Louis Lorette, and has ever since, and with some modifications, been called the Lorette system of pruning. He was perhaps the most skillful orchardist in France, and practically all French fruit-growers, but few here, have used it. There is an illustration of the Lorette system at PRUNING. Labor costs here make it impracticable commercially, but any amateur can follow it if he practices patience and care.

length, but still do no cutting of *terminal* twigs, *i.e.,* those that increase the length of any main branch.

These terminal shoots should be pruned back to the point where they originated, but not until the following April. If you decide to increase the size of your espalier, these terminal shoots should be cut back only so much as to give you the desired increase in height for espaliers, or in length for cordons.

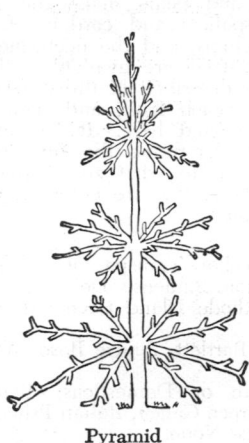

Pyramid

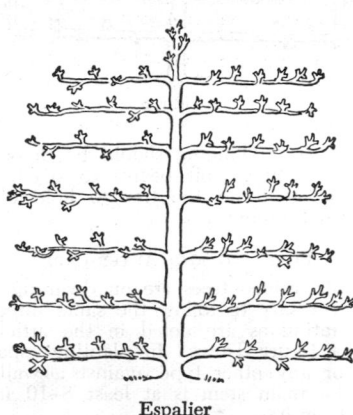

Espalier

The first pruning of lateral leafy shoots should be done about mid-June. Many of them will by that time be 12–15 inches long, or more on some varieties. Cut these, and only these, back to the branch from which they sprang, but be careful to leave the pair of leaves (or it may be a tuft of them) usually found on the branch at the point of emergence of the cut twig. This preliminary cut is cardinal to the whole scheme, for near this basal pair or tuft of leaves there is, or may be, an incipient fruiting spur from which fruit may be expected next year. It will, however, be most unlikely to develop, unless you remove the leafy twig which will otherwise rob the spur of so much food that it may be suppressed. It is, of course, of the utmost importance that you do not injure any *mature fruiting* spur that may also be at the base of the cut twig.

At this stage your plant will be denuded of all leafy twigs that were 12–15 inches long, but you must allow *all shorter twigs to grow on*; also you must leave all terminal leafy shoots alone. This is for the maintenance of the balance between root food and leaf food, mentioned above.

During the rest of the summer keep on removing all leafy shoots, except the terminal ones, from whatever source, when they reach a length of 12–15 inches, but not before. At the end of the summer cut off all leafy twigs that have not reached that

The theory behind this constant summer pruning, which should be done with care and very sharp clipping shears, is that each leafy twig has at its base one or more incipient fruiting spurs that may be forced into growth by diversion to them of food that would be otherwise going to the leafy shoot. You may not force these fruiting spurs out the second year, and it may be the third or fourth, but ultimately you will have your trained fruit tree with far more blossoms than leaves, for which you will be leaving only the young growths (4–8 inches). Some French orchards appear to have almost no leaves, so drastic is this summer pruning, although they must, of course, have enough to keep the tree healthy.

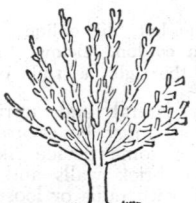

Bush form of training fruit trees

Trained fruit trees, due to this pruning system, are likely to produce too much fruit. It is necessary, especially on young trees, to thin them out so that there is a little air space between each mature fruit. This will greatly increase the size of those left

---

* Special articles on the subjects indicated by an asterisk (*) will be found at the words so marked.

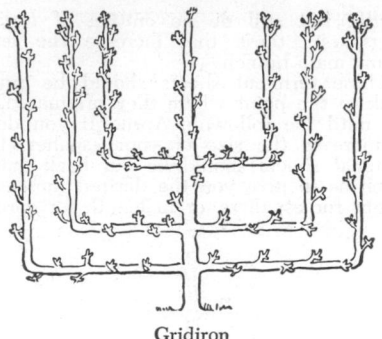

Gridiron

on the tree. Thinning should be done soon after the young fruit begins to swell. Also it is not good for the tree to hold all the fruit it will produce.

PLANTING AND AFTER-CARE

As all trained trees are on dwarfing stock it is necessary to follow the same directions for planting as are noted in the article on DWARF FRUIT TREES. In planting espaliers, fans, or any other type against a wall, see that the main stem is at least 8–10 inches away from it.

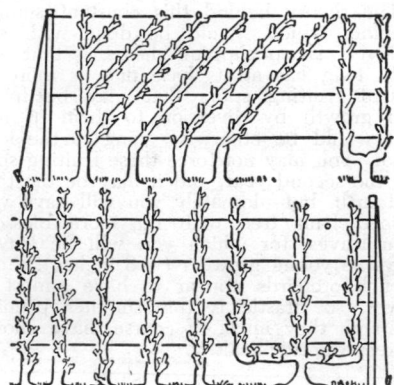

Above, at the left, the oblique cordon; at the right, a twin cordon. Below, the upright cordon; and at the right, a triple cordon.

All main lateral and upright branches against a wall must be securely tied to it. Ring bolts or some device like them must be sunk into brick walls and the branches tied to these with raffia or loose-fitting string. Old leather shoelaces are fine for tying. Leave the tie loose enough so that it will not bind any stem. If you have shingle or clapboard it is better to erect a trellis upon which to tie your tree.

Cordons need stretched wires. For single cordons the wire can be 15–18 inches above the ground. For double cordons a second wire must be strung 15 inches above the

lower one, and so on up to about four wires. Not many cordons will be more than four tiers high. Each must be securely tied to its wire, usually at intervals of 2 feet — less if there is much wind.

VARIETIES OF TRAINED FRUIT TREES

Not all varieties of fruit are to be found in espaliers, cordons, etc. Before ordering any of them it is wise to study the space you have to fit and the form and symmetry of the available types (*see* the illustrations).

Apples and pears make the most satisfactory espaliers and cordons, followed by peaches, plums, and the nectarine. The following varieties are available, all of which have been described at the different articles devoted to each fruit, and such notes will not be repeated here. It is, however, important to determine the question of self-sterility* and to what zone* the variety is suited. These, too, are noted at the articles on each fruit.

APPLES
Early: Yellow Transparent, Gravenstein.
Midseason: Fameuse, Delicious.
Late: Rhode Island Greening, Winesap.
PEARS
Seckel, Bartlett, Beurre Bosc, Winter Nelis.
PLUMS
European or Domesticas: Reine Claude (Green Gage), Italian Prune.
Damsons: None.
Japanese: Abundance.
American or hybrid: None.
PEACHES
Elberta, Champion, J. H. Hale, Golden Jubilee.
NECTARINES
Sure Crop.

TRAINING PLANTS. The term *training*, as applied to plants, is indicative of the fact that the cultivator can control the habit of his plants more or less as he sees fit, but in the main, training is confined to subjects of long-lived character. It can, however, be practiced on some herbs by pinching.

PINCHING. Some annual flowering plants are to some extent so trained. Many, notably *Schizanthus*, mignonette, *Calendula*, etc., are apt to run to flower without branching if the point of the leading growth is not nipped out after they reach 16 in. or so in height. Pinching out the tip induces branching, and by repeated pinching of the succeeding growths it is possible to develop huge specimens of *Schizanthus* or *Nemesia*.

Pinching naturally delays flowering, but when such plants are grown in pots, under glass, it enables the grower to time the flowering when wanted. The greenhouse carnation, if not pinched after the rooted cutting is 6 in. tall, will run up to flower during early summer and few or no blooms will be secured during winter. By successive pinches up to July or August, many shoots that will flower from October on are secured. Marguerites, fuchsias, geraniums (*Pelargon-*

ium), and similar soft and semi-hard-wooded plants grown in pots, especially when desired as large specimens more than one year old, are repeatedly pinched during the growing season, and in some cases the shoots are tied to wire framework to develop formal designs.

Some varieties of chrysanthemums are similarly trained by repeated pinching and tying in various shapes such as domes, pyramids, boats, airplanes, and so forth. The so-called Japanese cascade type of chrysanthemum, easily raised from seed, can in one season be grown to form, when in bloom, a veritable cascade, with branches hanging downward several feet and bearing many hundreds of small, single flowers. Large-flowered varieties, particularly one known as Felton, have been trained in circular form with a spread of 16 ft. and bearing up to 600 or more flowers. Infinite skill and patience and ample greenhouse space are necessary to obtain such specimens. The vogue for these phenomena of culture was more general 40 or 50 years ago than it is today.

The general principles of training by pinching are simple. At the base of every leaf on the stem is one or more dormant-growth buds or eyes. Some of these will naturally develop into side branches or laterals, but the removal of the top of a main stem encourages these dormant buds to grow sooner than they otherwise would. If the tips of these side growths are again pinched, still more shoots will develop. In most cases the first pinch is done when a young plant has six or eight leaf joints, but when a tree-shaped or standard fuchsia, geranium, lantana, or marguerite is desired, the leading shoot is encouraged to go upward until it reaches 3 ft. or more in height, all side shoots being removed as soon as they appear. When a clear stem of the desired height is attained, the point is nipped out, and all succeeding shoots that appear are similarly pinched when they have four to eight leaves until a tree-like head is secured. Careful staking at all times is necessary.

Various climbing plants are trained into globes or other designs by pinching and tying. The English ivy is quite commonly trained over a wire framework when grown in pots or tubs, such specimens being used for outdoor decoration during the summer months. Another system of training entails the use of shears as well as tying the growths onto the framework, this being termed topiary work. It is confined mostly to hardy evergreens and is a long and tedious process. *See* TOPIARY. — T. A. W.

transilvanica, -us, -um (tran-sil-van′i-ca). From Transylvania, Roumania.

TRANSPIRATION. The normal escape of water vapor through the pores of the leaf. It directly affects growth and wilting and the plant regulates the rate of transpiration according to its water requirements and the weather. It differs in this regulatory control from the purely mechanical process of evaporation with which many confuse it. Water evaporates from the soil or a pond, but is *transpired* by leaves, the latter being a highly complicated physiological process.

TRANSPLANTING. Moving plants from one place to another requires the same care as, and does not really differ from, the operation of planting (which see). *See also* Moving Trees at TREES.

TRANSVAAL DAISY = *Gerbera jamesoni.*

TRAPA (trap′a). A genus of about 8 species of aquatic herbs, the only genus of the family **Hydrocaryaceae**, all from the warmer parts of the Old World, one of them, **T. natans,** the water chestnut, grown for ornament in pools or aquaria, but also yielding an edible fruit for which it is cult., mostly in China. It is a beautiful floating aquatic with opposite,* much-dissected, submerged leaves, and clustered, floating ones, which are borne in rosette-like clusters, and have roundish, toothed blades, often beautifully variegated or mottled, and spongy, buoyant leafstalks. Flowers very small and inconspicuous, followed by the 4-pronged, fleshy, but ultimately nut-like fruit which is nearly 2 in. long, and delicious when young. Eurasia, but somewhat naturalized in the eastern U.S. and perfectly hardy. Its seeds fall to the bottom in autumn and sprout in the spring. Another water chestnut, known to the Chinese as Ling Ko, and to science as *Trapa bicornis,* is somewhat similar, but has 2 instead of 4 prongs to the fruits. It is common in Chinese markets and sometimes cult. (*Trapa* is from the Greek for a 4-pronged instrument of war, in allusion to the 4-pronged fruit.) The plant is also called water caltrop and Jesuit's-nut. For the Chinese water chestnut *see* ELEOCHARIS TUBEROSA.

TRAUTVETTERIA (traut-vet-teer′i-a). Rather coarse perennial herbs of the buttercup family, comprising one Asiatic species and another from the southeastern U.S., **T. carolinensis,** the false bugbane, grown in the shady, moist parts of the wild garden. It is a stout, branching plant, 2–3 ft. high, with basal, long-stalked leaves, 6–8 in. wide, deeply 7–11-lobed, the lobes pointed and sharply toothed. Flowers scarcely ¼ in. wide, without petals, but 3–5 concave, whitish sepals which soon fall. Stamens* numerous. Fruit a head-like collection of small follicles.* The plant is closely related to *Thalictrum,* although of very different habit. (Named for E. R. von Trautvetter, Russian botanist.)

TRAVELER'S-JOY = *Clematis Vitalba.*

TRAVELER'S TREE. *See* RAVENALA.

TRAY GARDENING. *See* SOILLESS GARDENING. *See also* Miniature Gardens at ROCK GARDEN.

TREACLEBERRY = *Smilacina racemosa.*

TREBIZOND DATE = *Elaeagnus angustifolia.*

---

* Special articles on the subjects indicated by an asterisk (*) will be found at the words so marked.

TREE. It is impossible to draw a technical definition of a tree. As ordinarily understood it is a woody plant, of some considerable size, with a single stem or trunk. But some palms have several trunks. And many shrubs have only a single stem, and others are taller than many plants that are unmistakable trees. See SHRUB.

Trees as part of the landscape are of far more importance than the attempt to draw sharp distinctions between them and shrubs. For their supreme importance in design and the making of permanent pictures of beauty see TREES.

TREE ASTER. See OLEARIA.

TREE AZALEA = Azalea arborescens.

TREEBINE. See CISSUS.

TREE CELANDINE = Macleaya cordata.

TREE COLLECTIONS. See ARBORETUM.

TREE COTTON. In America, Gossypium barbadense; in the Old World, G. arboreum.

TREE CYPRESS = Gilia rubra.

TREE DAHLIA = Dahlia imperialis.

TREE FERN. See CYATHEA and ALSOPHILA. For other tree-like ferns see also CIBOTIUM and DICKSONIA.

TREE GERMANDER = Teucrium fruticans.

TREE GUARDS. See STREET TREES.

TREE HEATH = Erica arborea.

TREE HEIGHT. See GARDEN TABLES III.

TREE LUNGWORT=Mertensia virginica.

TREE MALLOW. See LAVATERA.

TREE MOVING. See Moving Trees at TREES.

TREE MYRTLE = Ceanothus arboreus.

TREE-OF-HEAVEN = Ailanthus altissima.

TREE-OF-SADNESS = Nyctanthes Arbortristis.

TREE PEONY = Paeonia suffruticosa. See PEONY.

TREE-PERCHING. See EPIPHYTES.

TREE POPPY = Dendromecon rigidum.

TREE RINGS. See ANNUAL RINGS.

TREES. No garden of permanent value is possible without trees. They furnish the most lasting material not only for shade and ornament, but as definite elements in any garden design. Their form and outline, their branching, the winter effects of those with distinctive bark character or colored fruits and, above all, the evergreens* contribute to the garden picture what nothing else can. And this quite apart from their more utilitarian uses as screens, windbreaks, or for street planting. The latter features are dealt with elsewhere (see SCREEN PLANTING, STREET TREES, and WINDBREAKS); here we are concerned only with the ornamental value of trees in the garden. This is very different from the culture of trees for forest purposes, or as a supply for firewood, an art or science generally known as silviculture, and in this book mentioned only briefly (for it is not a garden project) at FORESTRY.

Like many other divisions of horticulture, the growing of trees for ornament has a special name, dear to the pedantic, but not so well liked by the public — arboriculture. From the root arbor, a tree, came the now widely observed Arbor Day, first established in Nebraska in 1872. Special effort is made to plant trees on this day, usually as a community enterprise for school children, and a very useful activity for any garden club.

TREES IN THE LANDSCAPE

While trees are an indispensable feature of any garden, many people think that because they are big and permanent they must be costly. Fortunately there are ample facts and figures to disprove such an illusion. Over a period of years, and taking into account their initial cost and the expense of planting them, they cost far less than a lawn, flower border, vegetable garden or almost any other garden feature. The reason is that over a long period of years the upkeep expense for trees (including proper spraying, pruning, and feeding, where necessary) is very slight, while most other forms of gardening require constant attention. The lack of it will soon ruin most gardens, but many long-neglected places still have splendid trees upon them which need only a minimum of attention when such an abandoned estate or farm property is again transformed into a garden. In other words trees will stand years of neglect, but a garden becomes a wilderness in two seasons without care.

This economic feature of trees vs. other forms of gardening should not be ignored by those by whom steady maintenance expense must be considered. A good grouping of trees, a lawn, and the house, and one has the cheapest, and by no means the least desirable of landscape effects. And, as we shall see presently, such a scheme need not be without color, winter and summer, even if, from motives of economy, shrubs, borders, and beds are omitted. And trees will give a stately dignity to such a place that no riot of midsummer color can approach.

KINDS TO PLANT

Throughout this book there are described at their proper alphabetical entries all the trees admitted into the book — several hundred species. Their inclusion was based upon their availability (through the ordinary trade channels, i.e., nursery catalogues), their beauty, or their special adaptability on account of soils, climate, showy flowers, fruits, and especially upon their value for shade and as permanent features of all good gardens.

It is obviously impossible to treat them all here, and it would be useless repetition of notes on their hardiness, period of flowering, propagation, etc., and other details which should be sought at the different tree entries. But from them it is desirable to mention

---

* Special articles on the subjects indicated by an asterisk (*) will be found at the words so marked.

here those of outstanding use, and these can be grouped into five general classes: (1) Hardy trees grown mostly for shade; (2) Trees grown mostly for flowers; (3) Trees grown mostly for showy fruits, often winter-persistent, or for colored bark; (4) Trees for sub-tropical regions like Fla., the Gulf Coast, and southern Calif.; and (5) Trees for the prairies.

(1) SHADE TREES. These are the main features of any tree planting, and generally speaking they are the sorts which drop their leaves each fall (deciduous*). The kinds and culture of the evergreen or coniferous trees, which are rarely planted for shade, are treated at EVERGREENS. They are chiefly used as specimen plants, for decorative groups, accent plants, but not for shade, except a few pines and the hemlock.

Among the generally hardy shade trees those of most permanent value, all the sub-jects of special articles which should be sought for details, are: OAK, BEECH, LINDEN, ELM, and MAPLE, each of them containing a few or many different kinds. These are, generally speaking, trees of relatively slow growth, but of lasting value in any garden. Other long-lived trees, some of them of great beauty, will be found at *Liquidambar* (sweet gum), *Nyssa* (sour gum), *Platanus* (plane tree or sycamore), Tulip-tree (*Lirio-dendron*, also with beautiful flowers), Horse-chestnut (*Aesculus*, also grown for flowers), Hornbean (*Carpinus*), and *Sassafras*, which also has delightfully fragrant flowers. Less can be said for the Honey Locust, and of secondary importance among the permanent species are trees which will be found at *Broussonetia*, Hackberry, *Koelreuteria, Mack-ia, Maclura,* Mulberry, *Ostrya, Phelloden-dron, Planera,* and *Zanthoxylum.*

No one should plant any of the above with an expectation of quick results, although some of the oaks and the tulip-tree are not so slow-growing as others in this group which are selected for permanent value. *See also* GINKGO.

There are places where quicker-growing trees are demanded and some gardeners are so impatient that they will plant nothing else. A few are listed here, but they should be used with the distinct understanding that they are not long-lived, and that whatever effect you get from them should be rein-forced by planting among them some of those listed above.

Relatively quick-growing trees will be found at BIRCH, POPLAR, WILLOW, ASH, and AILANTHUS, the latter especially good for city conditions (for others *see* SMOKE). Others will be found among the next group.

(2) FLOWERING TREES. While all trees must, of course, have flowers of some sort, there are a few that are far more showy or even spectacular than the common run of shade trees. They are planted primarily for their flowers, and generally speaking they are not as long-lived as the more permanent type of shade trees. All those listed below

should be sought in the body of the EN-CYCLOPEDIA for additional notes upon cul-ture, hardiness, and time of flowering, as these details cannot be repeated here. The most desirable flowering trees will be found at:

> Ash (only *Fraxinus Ornus*)
> Catalpa (catalpa)
> Cladrastis (yellow-wood)
> Cornus (flowering dogwood)
> Crataegus (hawthorn)
> Halesia (snowdrop tree)
> Horse-chestnut (*Aesculus*)
> Laburnum (golden chain)
> Locust (*Robinia*)
> Magnolia (magnolia)
> Malus (flowering crabapples)
> Mountain-ash (*Sorbus*)
> Oxydendrum (sourwood)
> Paulownia (paulownia)
> Prunus (Japanese flowering
>   cherries and others)
> Redbud (*Cercis*)
> Sophora (Japanese pagoda tree)
> Styrax (storax)
> Tulip-tree (*Liriodendron*)

To these, of course, should be added the incomparably fine blossom of the fruit trees in the rose family, notably apple, pear, peach, plum, cherry, apricot, and almond, the last two only in climatically favorable places. *See* each of these fruits for varieties and culture.

(3) TREES WITH SHOWY FRUITS (or with colored bark). Late autumn and winter effects, especially if those below are massed with evergreens, can be secured by using trees in this group. They are all described in detail elsewhere in this book, and additional notes on culture and hardiness should be sought for at the names listed below:

> Beech (handsome pearl-gray bark)
> Birch (white-barked species)
> Cotinus (plumy fruits)
> Crataegus (showy fruits)
> Honey Locust (large flat pods)
> Maple (some with colored bark)
> Mountain-ash (colored fruits)
> Oak (several with long-persistent, au-tumnal colored leaves)
> Platanus (peeling bark and persistent fruits)
> Willow (several with yellow twigs)

Those seeking such effects should also con-sult the list of shrubs and trees with striking autumnal foliage at AUTUMN FOLIAGE. There are, too, many other trees with handsome fruits, such as *Ailanthus* (female trees only), but often these are less conspicuous than those listed above because the leaves are still on while they are in fruit.

(4) SUB-TROPICAL TREES. In frostless or relatively frostless regions, many other trees than those so far mentioned can be grown. As pretty complete lists of such are found elsewhere, they will not be repeated here. *See* SUB-TROPICAL GARDEN, CALI-FORNIA, NEW MEXICO, LOUISIANA, and

---

* Special articles on the subjects indicated by an asterisk (*) will be found at the words so marked.

TEXAS. In this region, also, can be grown some of the tall bamboos and many palms. *See* BAMBOO, PALM.

(5) TREES FOR THE PRAIRIES. From the western edge of the naturally forested area of the U.S. to the eastern escarpment of the Rocky Mountains is a vast tract that is unsuited to many of the trees so far mentioned. There is, in the first place, too little rainfall, too much wind, and often extremely cold winter temperatures. The combination of these and the annual prairie fires of the old days made or kept this huge grassland bare of trees, except in the river valleys.

It is no better suited to most trees today. Evergreens, especially, find such conditions particularly trying, and many other fine forest trees of eastern N.A. and eastern Asia do not thrive in this region. Those that do, therefore, are of outstanding importance in the prairie and plains states. The trees which have best stood these conditions are the following:

Ailanthus (tree-of-heaven)
Ash (only *Fraxinus pensylvanica lanceolata*)
Catalpa (catalpa)
Elm (only *Ulmus parvifolia* and *U. pumila*)
Hackberry (*Celtis occidentalis*)
Honey Locust (*Gleditsia*)
Maclura (Osage orange)
Maple (only *Acer Negundo*, less surely *A. saccharinum* and *A. platanoides*)
Mulberry (only *Morus alba* and its varieties)
Platanus (the London plane, and less surely *P. occidentalis*)
Poplar (several species, *see* POPLAR).
Willow (only *Salix nigra,* and some native species)

Even these trees will need far more care than if grown in more favorable places, especially when young and if in an unprotected (*i.e.,* wind-swept) place. For such sites it is better, before serious tree-planting, to consider the possibility of making a windbreak (which see).

PLANTING AND CARE

The planting of ornamental trees which are meant to be permanent features of the garden should be done with care. It is, after all, done but once, and it is far better to see that both the plant itself and the soil in which it is to go get the needed attention. The details of planting trees and shrubs have all been carefully described elsewhere, and need not be repeated here. *See* PLANTING. The only further caution is to see, until the tree is thoroughly established, that it does not suffer for water, at least during the first year or two. After that it should need no water beyond rainfall, assuming you have picked the right sort of a tree for your locality. *See* the lists above.

Subsequent care is divided into two main categories:
(1) Fighting Pests and (2) Pruning and Injury.

(1) Insect pests and plant diseases are so various and the number of trees so many that no general directions are possible. Throughout this book, the contributing editors in charge of diseases and insect pests have inserted notes on their control at the end of each article on important crops — trees among the rest. If you have disease or insect trouble turn first to the name of your tree in this book, where you will find what to do. It is also advisable to read the general articles on INSECT PESTS, PLANT DISEASES, and SPRAYING AND DUSTING. For the few animal pests that injure trees *see* ANIMAL INJURY.

(2) Pruning and Injury. Shade trees do not usually need pruning beyond the initial cutting-back at planting time, as do many fruit trees and shrubs. The exception to this statement, sometimes seen in old trees, is where two branches rub against each other. One of these, whichever is the easier to remove, should be cut off as near the trunk or branch to which it is attached as possible. For details of this, and for other injuries or wounds, *see* the next article, TREE SURGERY. At that entry, also, will be found what to do when a change of grade may endanger existing trees.

MOVING TREES

Moving very large trees is obviously outside the skill and equipment of the average home gardener, as it is generally, also, outside the scope of even pretentious estates. For any tree with a trunk diameter of 5 in. or more, moving it is then a job for a professional who provides his own equipment, and if he is competent and reliable will guarantee the result. Naturally such experience and service is expensive, and even the very rich will not move many big trees unless there is adequate reason.

Trees of less than 5 in. in diameter can be moved by the careful and intelligent amateur, with a few men and great care. Generally a tree of this size has been growing for a considerable time in one place and its root system is widely ramified. Merely to dig up such a tree and replant in another site is inviting disaster, because its feeding roots are at the ends of its main roots and most of them will be lost, no matter how carefully dug.

If such a tree is to be moved, you should make up your mind at least a year before the move is to be made. Then dig a trench about 3 ft. deep and 18 in. wide completely around the tree, and at about 5 ft. from the trunk. Remove from this circular trench all the soil and cut with an axe or heavy pruning shears all roots that pass through and beyond the trench. This should be done in March or April and the trench filled with a mixture of ½ good garden loam and ½ well-rotted cow or horse manure, thoroughly mixed. If the following growing season is dry, see that the trench of fresh soil is thoroughly watered.

The effect of this operation is to force the tree to produce a lot of new young feeding

---

* Special articles on the subjects indicated by an asterisk (*) will be found at the words so marked.

roots either in the trench or even nearer the trunk. In other words you have been root pruning your tree, exactly as any competent nurseryman does small ones every two years or so, well knowing that such a procedure will greatly help the tree when final moving time arrives.

For you that will be the following March or April. Start digging (with a digging fork, not a spade), and carefully uncover all the roots possible, keeping the uncovered ones tied up in wet bagging if the operation lasts more than a few hours. If in digging you come to downward-pointing large roots that cannot be easily removed, do not hesitate to cut them off, leaving a nice smooth-cut end, which will often, and in fact usually, put out a lot of fresh young feeding roots in the new site.

Great care must be used in this digging operation, both to prevent destruction of as few roots as possible, and, when the tree is finally tipped down and put on a truck, to see that the bark is not rubbed or injured. There must be an ample supply of bagging, old quilts, or plenty of straw to prevent this.

Before actual planting, which is the same as for small trees, only on a larger scale, tip the tree down and thoroughly head it back — which means that about ¼ or ½ of all final twigs and small branches should be removed by pruning. This sounds drastic, but to neglect it will greatly promote failure. You put upon the tree without the heading-back the same burden of water requirements as in its old site, and ask it to ignore the shock of removal. And make no mistake — the move is a shock, which it is your business to lessen as much as possible. For planting operation *see* PLANTING.

When the hole is filled up and the tree started on its new venture, give it a thorough soaking and see that it is carefully guyed by wires. While young trees need only 3 guy wires, it is better to use 4 or even 5 on a large tree. Even with heading-back it will have a large crown of foliage, and no sudden gust from summer showers, nor a steady gale must be allowed to move the trunk in the least. Keep the guy wires tight and see that they don't girdle the trunk or branches, as noted at PLANTING. For the first winter or two it will also pay to give your tree a heavy mulch* of well-rotted manure.

The operation above described is quite possible for most trees that drop their leaves, and do not need to have their roots in soil while being moved. But some deciduous trees, and all evergreens and broad-leaved evergreens cannot be moved in this way. They can only be safely moved by the ball and burlap method described at PLANTING. Among deciduous* trees which should be moved only with the ball and burlap method are magnolias, tulip-tree, sour gum, and the white oak. And all evergreens must be so cared for. The weight of soil to be moved, the risks involved, and the much greater cost of the operation make moving trees of this sort an undertaking to be considered

very carefully. It is primarily a job for professionals. *See* Ball and Burlap at PLANTING.

TREE FEEDING

Transplanted trees, and even those long established, repay an application of plant food once every few years. A general rule is to allow 3 lbs. of a 4–8–4 fertilizer for each inch of trunk diameter. The fertilizer should be divided so that it will half fill holes driven by a crowbar 18 in. deep and spaced 18 in. apart at the outer edge of branch extension. Draw a circle on the ground around the periphery of its crown and make enough holes so that they are about 18 in. apart. After half filling each hole with fertilizer (or manure if available) fill up the hole with good top-soil. Trees may also be mulched with manure in the fall, digging in the manure in the spring, but the fertilizer method avoids odor and flies.

MOUNT VERNON

Before leaving the general subject of trees, it may be worth recording how much our greatest country gentleman was interested in them. His diary is full of notes on those he planted, many of which are still growing at Mount Vernon. Among the trees which General Washington planted, or were already on the property during his lifetime, and are alive today, are:

Ash	Linden
Beech	Magnolia
Box	Mountain-ash
Buckeye	Mulberry
Kentucky Coffee-tree	Pear
American Elm	Pecan
Hemlock	Redbud
American Holly	Red and Sugar Maple
Honey Locust	Tulip-tree
Horse-chestnut	

All but three are native American trees which he planted, or were on the place, between 1783 and 1785, just after the ending of the war and before he became the first President. There are now over 50 specimens at Mount Vernon which were either planted by Washington or mentioned in his diary. In addition he tried 25 other species, some tender exotics, all of which have since died, one being the mahogany! For other collections of trees in this country *see* ARBORETUM.

For statistics on trees, their height, rate of growth, number of seeds per pound, etc., *see* GARDEN TABLES II and III. *See also* DRIP, SMOKE, and SHADE.

TREE SURGERY. Under this general term the garden public has come to group many things in the after-care of trees, whether it involves "surgery" or not. Originally the tree surgeons were developed because the butchery of street trees by public service employees called for trained men and better methods. As the service has now grown, it is of far wider usefulness, and many reliable firms offer complete protection

* Special articles on the subjects indicated by an asterisk (*) will be found at the words so marked.

to existing trees, involving necessary pruning, spraying, feeding where necessary, and most of all the repair of old injuries and those caused by sudden and very destructive ice storms. Many public utility companies now employ tree surgeons for clearing wires or poles of interfering branches.

As in the case of big-tree moving, the tree surgeons, by training and equipment, can do many things which are either impossible for the home gardener to do himself, or are so dangerous that it is far better to let the trained man do them. In all large trees there are times when cat-like agility at considerable heights is necessary, the risks considerable, and the chances of skimped work pretty certain if the operator is not thoroughly at home in the air.

But all owners should understand what is being done, the need for it, and the principles upon which competent and reliable firms do the work. As in any other lucrative business there are many fakers and downright crooks who, merely because they call themselves "tree surgeons," filch the public. A comprehensive program for the after-care tree demands attention to the following details: (1) Pruning, (2) Repair of injury, (3) Spraying, (4) Feeding when necessary, and (5) Saving trees from changes of grade.

(1) PRUNING. Shade trees do not need pruning as do many fruit trees and shrubs. Beyond the initial cutting-back or heading-in at planting time, they may be left to follow their natural development, and will in a few

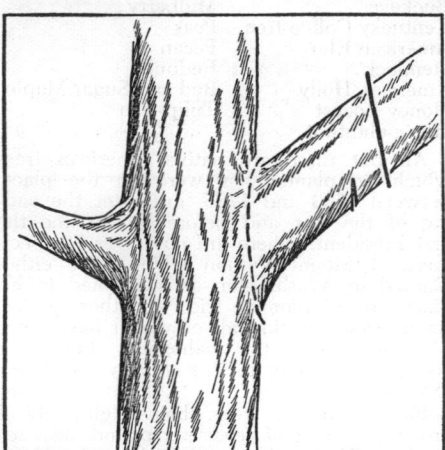

Pruning an old branch. Start by a small undercut. Then saw off the branch, leaving a stub which must be finally cut as shown by the dotted line, as close to the trunk as possible.

years assume the normal shape of canopy peculiar to each. There are many reasons for not interfering with this process.

But in any garden there are times when trees should be pruned because of overhang-

ing branches, interference with buildings, clearance for driveways, diseased branches, and other causes. Most of such pruning can be done by the owner unless the branches to be pruned are very heavy and high up, in which case a professional is by far the best solution.

In removing branches the thing to keep in mind is that trees do everything in their power to repair damage and heal over cut ends. The thing to do is to aid the tree in this process of self-preservation and not hinder it, and an understanding of wound response is all that is necessary.

Trees have an outer, mostly dead bark, and an inner, usually green layer known as cambium (*see* BARK). This cambium layer, usually very thin and just beneath the outer bark, is active and growing every day. As soon as there is an injury (a pruned branch is an injury to the tree) the cambium layer will start at once to grow around all edges of the wound and will, if not prevented, cover the whole wound in a few years with a protective coating that will completely seal the wound, and will later turn into outer bark.

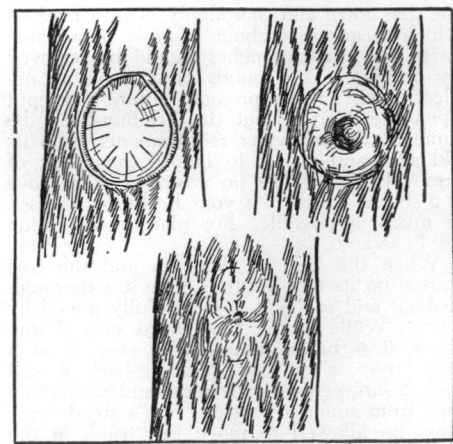

The three stages in the healing process when limbs are properly removed, as shown in the illustration at the left. Upper left, the cambium starting to cover the wound; upper right, nearly covering it; the final stage is the bark-like covering of the wound. This process cannot be completed if a stub is left.

But what if the cambium layer cannot complete its job because there is a stump left of the pruned branch? The cambium cannot grow up and around a stub of this sort, and is forced to stop where it strikes the base of the stub. There is then left a fast-dying (or perhaps dead) stub of an old branch, through which organisms of decay and insect pests can easily get past the protective guard which the cambium layer has been prevented from completing. Of course the

---

* Special articles on the subjects indicated by an asterisk (*) will be found at the words so marked.

remedy is to leave no stumps, as the illustrations show.

Nearly always, in removing a large branch, it is unwise to make the cut as close to the trunk as possible at first. For, as the saw is finishing its work, the weight of the branch will almost certainly tear loose the remnant of uncut wood, and along with it a section of the bark of the trunk, leaving a large gaping wound. The remedy here is to make the first cut at least a foot from the trunk, having previously undercut it as shown in the illustrations. And then, when the weight of the pruned branch is no longer a danger, make a second and final cut as close as possible. *See* the illustrations.

(2) REPAIR OF INJURY. Many injuries are simply of the sort caused by gales in summer or ice storms in winter. This usually means many torn branches which must be cleaned up and their stumps pruned in accordance with the details mentioned just above.

Other injuries, however, call for different methods. Some of the commonest, especially in old trees, are cavities, often of years' standing, filled with punk instead of good wood, and a definite menace to the tree. When these are very large, and near the base of the trunk, they may have so weakened the tree that it is no longer safe to leave. If the tree is in this condition it is wiser to call in professional advice as to whether it can be saved, or whether it is safer to take it down forthwith.

But long before trees reach this stage of decay the watchful gardener should have prevented it. Most decay is caused by fungi which have invaded the sapwood or heartwood through what looked like minor injuries, or through the holes left by borers (*see* WOOD ROT). The moment such a cavity is noted it should be cleaned out completely, even cutting out some of the uncontaminated wood. In other words we should try to make the cavity as sterile of the organisms of decay as the dentist does with a decayed tooth. If the tree cavity is large it will have to be filled, and that is much better done by a professional who comes with the proper tools for thoroughly cleaning and disinfecting the wound, and skillful advice as to whether a composition or cement filling is wisest.

The principle upon which such work must be done is that all decayed material must be removed. It is sometimes half or nearly hidden by the tree's attempt to heal over the cavity, in which case the abortive healing attempt and the rotten wood behind it must both be cut away. The next step, once having gotten down to clean living wood, is to waterproof it with shellac or tar, this protecting application also covering the cambium layer, for it is this layer, given the proper chance, which will finally make the seal over your filling. The final step is to put in the composition or cement filling so that it will be just scantily flush with the cambium layer.

If it extends much beyond the cambium layer it will be impossible for the latter to climb over the filling. But if the filling is just below the cambium layer (about $\frac{1}{16}$ or $\frac{1}{8}$ in.), the latter will soon grow over the edge of your filler and the seal will be then perfect. Any partial seal by cambium is useless, because water and decay organisms will otherwise get inside the cavity and in a few years the trouble will be simply worse. Study the illustrations carefully, whether you are merely filling a small cavity, which any careful operator can repair, or are checking up on a professional hired for a more serious job. No part of tree surgery is so fraught with danger, and crookedness, as repairing old cavities. It really needs the expert operator of a thoroughly reliable firm.

There are two types of filling material for tree cavities: concrete or an elastic cement often called composition filler, and now sold under a variety of trade names. For very large cavities, especially near the base of a tree, and where extra strength is desirable, concrete is the better material. Its disadvantages are that it does not contract and expand at the same rate as the wood of the tree, and consequently it is more difficult to make a perfect seal with it. Some professional operators use concrete inside and elastic cement for the final outside layer of the filler. The elastic cement is by far the best for all small cavities and even for larger ones if high up. It contracts and expands with the wood of the tree and the cambium layer grows more quickly over it than it does over cement.

Still another type of actual or prospective injury is the splitting at the fork of two large branches. The old and wholly wrong method was to chain or wire the two branches and in doing so girdle* both. This inevitably killed both branches by cutting off the proper flow

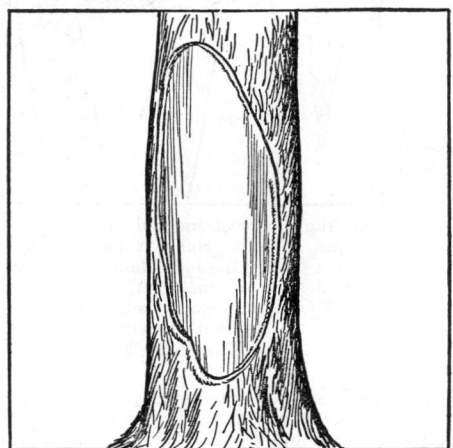

An old, deep wound properly filled and already beginning to seal around the edges of the filler. For details *see* text.

of sap. The modern method, as shown in the illustration, is to use chain or bolts so attached that they give perfect support but do no damage.

(3) SPRAYING. Most reliable tree surgeons offer a complete spraying service, both for insect pests and plant diseases. They have power outfits that do the job more thoroughly than the average home gardener can ever do, and the use of such a service is advised for all large trees.

But for small ones you can do your own by following the directions at SPRAYING AND DUSTING, and by reading the general articles on INSECT PESTS and PLANT DISEASES. Of course blind spraying is as useless as the casual use of any other garden operation. Study the notes on insect pests and plant diseases appended to the account of your particular tree in the body of this book and follow the control methods recommended there.

(4) FEEDING TREES. While most trees do not need any special feeding, especially those in an ordinary garden, some old ones, and those surrounded by pavement, do. For the former the best plan is to dig the soil lightly (with a digging fork, not a spade) as far away from the trunk as the spread of the branches. Do not rake the dug soil, but cover it with a 3-in. layer of old, well-rotted manure. The response is almost immediate.

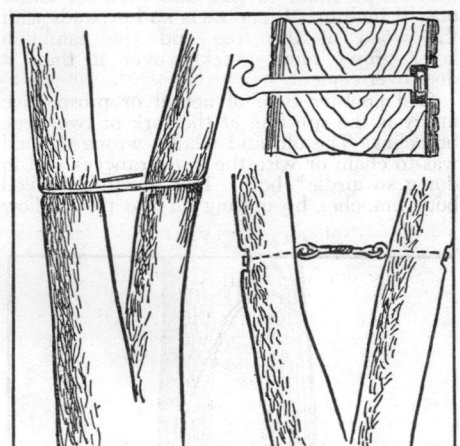

At the left, the incorrect method of supporting weak branches. At the right, a tree properly secured by a bolt through both branches. Above, the details of the bolt, the nut of which should be countersunk below the cambium (see BARK) so that it will be covered eventually, just as cut-off branches are.

One record of such an operation on a Long Island estate showed that a very old and large red oak, upon which a millionaire lavished a bargeload of manure every other year, increased its girth by seven inches in ten years. The tree otherwise was slowing down its activities and getting ready to die,

perhaps a century hence. Few will care to feed trees on this scale, but a manure mulch* for old trees, or young ones, does stimulate growth.

For trees surrounded by pavement, or worse still by concrete, the only remedy is to punch holes in the pavement at about 6-ft. intervals, sink pipes down to the roots and regularly pour liquid manure down the pipes. Trees do not usually need such an expensive method of feeding unless they have been growing for years under such conditions. If possible the pavement should be removed enough to put a small grating around the trunk, which allows at least some air and water to get into the soil.

If it is impossible to provide gratings, the pipe method of feeding and watering trees is, while expensive to install and maintain, a very practical method of saving trees that might otherwise be slowly killed for lack of air and nourishment. The pipes should be flush with the pavement and be provided with a trap cover to keep out refuse. Water can be poured in every other week, and liquid manure (which see) every third week to the great advantage of such smothered trees. And this brings us to another frequent cause of tree troubles.

(5) CHANGE OF GRADE. To grow well, the roots of trees should be the normal distance below the surface common to each species. But it often happens that grading operations must be carried on and result in either burying the tree from one to several feet, or uncovering a lot of roots when the surrounding grade is lowered. Either contingency may be fatal if not corrected.

For trees likely to be buried a dry well of loose stone should be built up to the new grade. Such a well will allow air and water to get down where the roots are, and trees may live for years in such a well, which should preferably be 8–10 ft. in diameter, and as deep as necessary.

For trees whose roots are to be uncovered by a lower grade, the only remedy is to build a tight wall all around the tree, of the necessary height and as far from the trunk as conditions permit. Leave the old soil in place, but cut off all roots that extend beyond the line of the retaining wall to be built. The wall may be made of concrete or of brick, and the final effect is of a tree growing in a walled bed. This is not such a desirable method as in the case of a tree set in a dry well, but it often saves a tree whose roots would otherwise certainly dry out. Trees with these retaining walls should be well mulched with manure for the first year or two, and see that they get plenty of water. When the shock of having lost old roots is over, and the tree has made a new crop of feeding roots in the walled bed, it may well live for years. But the change of grade for such trees should not be more than 2–3 ft. In the case of buried trees protected by dry wells, the grade may be raised as much as 8–10 ft. and the tree still live. For tree guards see STREET TREES.

---

* Special articles on the subjects indicated by an asterisk (*) will be found at the words so marked.

TREE TOBACCO = *Nicotiana glauca.*

TREE TOMATO = *Cyphomandra betacea.*

TREE YUCCA = *Yucca brevifolia.*

TREFOIL. For the bird's-foot trefoil *see* LOTUS CORNICULATUS. For the tick trefoil *see* DESMODIUM.

TREILLAGE 1. A latticework, trellis, or grill for vines. *See* TRELLISES.

2. The wires to which espaliers or other trained fruit trees are fastened.

TRELLISES. Trellises are a form of ornamental slat fence used primarily as a screen. They are usually light wood structures which may or may not support vines. This is one of the earliest known types of garden fence, originally made by weaving together light flexible branches of osier or bamboo. After tools made possible the shaping of wood into thin flat slats the diagonal pattern of woven branches still persisted even though the wood was held in place by nails or pegs.

Trellises were used also to support grapes on the walls of buildings and garden walls, to speed the ripening of the fruit and conserve space. The original practical function of such trellises has been turned to ornamental

Lattice trellis, good for a screen or for support for vines

use in modern times and trellises are often used to support purely ornamental vines on the walls of buildings. This type of trellis should be simple in design, conform to the structural lines of the house, and not compete with the basic architecture. It should be painted the same color as the house, allowing the vines to create a pattern of green over the walls. Lath screen is an alternative term for trellis.

Treillage is a term adopted from the French for a highly ornamental type of trellis greatly admired in eighteenth-century French gardening. Elaborate garden structures were built entirely of treillage which was extremely fragile and perishable. In some cases this treillage was appliqued on walls and masonry buildings. Except for highly stylized

A wall trellis should be firmly secure and is most effective when least evident.

gardens this type of garden ornament has gone out of use in modern gardening.

Grille is a term more often applied to ornamental metal barriers than to wood, although wooden grilles are sometimes used in protected places. Grillework is distinguished from trelliswork by its individually shaped members which are carved in some ornamental design instead of having the identical forms of a trellis. — R. E. G.

tremula, -us, -um (trem′you-la). Quivering; tremulous.

tremuloides (trem-you-loy′deez, but *see* OÏDES.) Resembling the quaking aspen.

TRENCHING. A laborious method of bringing to the surface unused soil and burying soil two seasons in succession. Long popular in England, trenching is not so much in vogue here, perhaps because it is the most costly of soil operations if labor for it must be hired.

It has some advantages, but only if there is sufficient depth of good soil so that in bringing to the surface the unused soil we do not merely bring subsoil where it is not wanted. One of the undoubted advantages is that the soil is better aerated than it will be by plowing, and that if long-continued, one gets deeper, better root development, because the usable soil is made deeper than by any other method of digging.

The operation is simple enough. Dig a trench 10–20 in. deep (*i.e.*, two spades' depth) and 1 ft. wide, putting all the soil in the wheelbarrow and dumping it at the opposite ends from which you start. Just behind the *open* trench take out about half as much soil (5–8 in.) from a 1-ft. strip and throw it in the bottom of the first trench, which should have been loosened, and enriched with a layer of manure. Then take the lower level of soil from the second trench and use it to make the top layer of the first. Keep on doing this until you reach the last trench, which will be filled with the soil you wheeled there for the purpose.

* Special articles on the subjects indicated by an asterisk (*) will be found at the words so marked.

Bastard trenching, a modification of the above, is done by making the initial and all subsequent trenches 2 ft. wide. The soil in each operation is separated into three instead of two layers and manure is put between layers as it is put back. In this case there are three trenches open all the time, and as in ordinary trenching no surface soil is left at the surface. Trench number 1 gets part of its soil from trench 2 and part from trench 3, and so on to the end.

Neither method is likely to find favor with those who can have the garden plowed yearly. But in small gardens it can be profitably employed. In fact, if careful to bring up only about 1 in. of subsoil at each annual trenching, you will ultimately have a far deeper, finer soil than even a subsoil plowing can give. The only real objection to trenching is the labor.

triacanthophora, *-us*, *-um* (try-a-kan-thoff'-o-ra). Bearing three spines.

triacanthos (try-a-kan'thoss). With three spines.

triandra, *-us*, *-um* (try-an'dra). With three stamens.

triangularis, *-e* (try-ang-you-lar'is). Three-angled.

tribuloides (trib-you-loy'deez, but *see* OÏDES). Resembling the genus *Tribulus*, which contains the sandbur. *See* Sandbur in the list at WEEDS.

trichocalyx (try-ko-kay'licks). With a hairy calyx.*

trichocarpa, *-us*, *-um* (try-ko-kar'pa). Hairy-fruited.

TRICHOCEREUS (try-ko-seer'i-ous). A large genus of columnar or trailing cacti, mostly from S.A., a few cult. for ornament and for their fragrant, night-blooming, very large white flowers, although they are not usually called night-blooming cereus, to which they are closely related. *See* NIGHT-BLOOMING CEREUS. They are ribbed cacti, usually spiny, but some nearly spineless, and often with tufts of hairs at the pits on the ribs. For cult. *see* CACTI. (*Trichocereus* is from *tricho*, hair, and *Cereus*, to which they are related.) There are many other species cult. in the collections of fanciers.

pachanoi. A branched cactus, 12–18 ft. high, the branches upward-pointing, and 6–8-ribbed. Spines few or none; if present, not over ½ in. long. Flowers extremely fragrant, night-blooming, about 10 in. long, white, but the outside reddish-brown. Ecuador.

spachianus. Not over 3 ft. high and branching from the base, the branches upward-pointing, the plant thus almost fastigiate.* Ribs of the branches 10–15, white-woolly at the pits on the ribs. Spines 8–10 in each group, brown and bristle-like, with a single central spine. Flowers white, fragrant, night-blooming, about 8 in. long. Argentina.

TRICHOLAENA (try-ko-lee'na). Chiefly tropical Old World grasses, comprising about 15 species, of which T. rosea, the Natal or ruby grass, is the only one of hort. signi-

ficance. It is grown in the South, but not widely, both as forage and for ornament. Grown as an annual, although a perennial plant, it is a handsome grass, 3–4 ft. high, the grass-like leaves 5–8 in. long and about ¼ in. wide. Flowering spikelets softly hairy, arranged in a shining, branched, pink or reddish-brown, terminal cluster (panicle*) nearly 12 in. long and very attractive. South Africa. (*Tricholaena* is from the Greek for hair mantle, in allusion to the softly hairy spikelets.)

Trichomanes (try-ko-man'eez). A specific named derived from the genus *Trichomanes*, which is scarcely of garden interest. *See* ASPLENIUM.

TRICHOME. A hair or hair-like bristle.

trichophylla, *-us*, *-um* (try-ko-fill'a). Hairy-leaved; or with hair-like leaves.

trichosantha, *-us*, *-um* (try-ko-san'tha). With hairy flowers.

TRICHOSANTHES (try-ko-san'theez). Indo-Malayan herbaceous vines of the cucumber family, comprising about 50 species, one of them T. Anguina, the serpent or snake gourd, and sometimes known as the club gourd. It is a tall-growing annual vine (needing support or it will sprawl) with angled, hairy stems and branched tendrils.* Leaves alternate,* broadly angled or lobed, or sometimes unlobed, 5–9 in. long, the margins with weak-prickled, remote teeth. Flowers unisexual,* sometimes on different plants, long-stalked, 2–3 in. wide, white, the corolla more or less cup-shaped, the limb fringed. Fruit 1–5 ft. long, greenish-white, cucumber-like (and used as food in India), very various as to shape, always slender and tapering, but sometimes curved, coiled, or club-shaped and grown for these curious fruits in the U.S. It is one of the oddest of the ornamental gourds (which see). (*Trichosanthes* is from the Greek for hair and flower, in allusion to the fringed corolla lobes.) Sometimes offered as T. *colubrina*.

TRICHOSPORUM = *Aeschynanthes*.

TRICHOSTEMA. See BLUECURLS.

trichotoma, *-us*, *-um* (try-kot'o-ma). Thrice-forked.

tricolor (try'color). Three-colored.

tricostata, *-us*, *-um* (try-kos-tay'ta). Three-ribbed.

TRICUSPIDARIA. *See* CRINODENDRON.

tricuspidata, *-us*, *-um* (try-kus-pi-day'ta). With three sharp, stiff points.

TRICYRTIS (try-sir'tis). Half-hardy perennial herbs, comprising about 9 species of the lily family, natives of Japan and Formosa. They have short, thick rootstocks, usually spreading. Leaves alternate,* simple, ovalish, not stalked, clasping the stem. Flowers solitary, or in small clusters, stalked, terminal or growing in the axils* of the leaves, large, bell-shaped, whitish or purplish and spotted, star-like when fully open. Calyx* of 3 colored sepals. Corolla of 3 petals, alternating with the

---

* Special articles on the subjects indicated by an asterisk (*) will be found at the words so marked.

sepals. Stamens* 6. Fruit a 3-celled capsule.*
(*Tricyrtis* is from the Greek for 3 cavities,
in allusion to the 3 nectar-bearing sacs at the
base of the sepals.)

Tricyrtis make useful garden plants, and are
sometimes grown in pots in the cool greenhouse. Propagated by division of the rootstocks. They may be grown like lilies except
that they should be gradually dried off in the
fall and be kept dry through the winter. When
grown outdoors in the North they should be
lifted for hard frost and stored.

hirta. Toad lily. Hairy perennial growing
to 3 ft. high. Leaves alternate,* ovalish, to
6 in. long. Flowers 1 in. long, whitish, spotted
with purple and black on the inside, growing
in small clusters in the axils* of the leaves.
Jap. *See* AUTUMN GARDEN.

macropoda. Growing to 3 ft. Leaves alternate,* broadly lance-shaped, slightly hairy on
the under side. Flowers in terminal clusters,
pale purple, with small purple spots on the
inside, bell-shaped, ¾ in. long. Jap. and China.
There is a yellow-flowered form.

tridentata, *-us,* *-um* (try-den-tay′ta).
Three-toothed.

TRIENTALIS (try-en-tay′lis). Hardy perennial herbs, comprising 2 species of the family
Primulaceae, one Eurasian, the other in N.A.
They have creeping rootstocks with slender
stems to 9 in. high. Leaves 5–9 in a whorl* at
the top of the stem. Flowers white or pink,
generally 2, with thread-like stalks growing
from the center of the leaves. Calyx* of 5–9
sepals. Corolla of 5–9 petals, wheel-shaped.
Stamens* 5–9. Fruit a capsule.* (*Trientalis*
is from the Greek for ⅓ of a ft., in allusion to
the height.)

These plants are not generally cult., but are
interesting for the wild garden or moist, shady
places in the rock garden. Propagated from
seeds or division of the rootstocks. Seeds
should be sown in April, ⅛ in. deep, in light,
sandy soil in cool greenhouse or cold frame.
They may be transplanted to permanent positions when large enough to handle. They
must be shaded from midday sun at all times.
Division of rootstocks may be made in Nov. or
early spring.

americana = *Trientalis borealis.*
borealis. Starflower. Chickweed wintergreen. Grows 6–9 in. high. Leaves 5–9 in
a whorl at top of stem, lance-shaped, pointed
each end, to 4 in. long, bright green, thin
and shiny. Flowers 2, white, star-shaped, ½
in. across, growing on thin, thread-like stalks
2 in. long. Labrador to Va. and westward.
June.

trifasciata, *-us,* *-um* (try-fas-i-ā′ta). In
three bunches or clusters.

trifida, *-us,* *-um* (triff′i-da). Thrice-cut or
parted.

triflora, *-us,* *-um* (try-flow′ra). Three-flow-
ered.

trifolia, *-us,* *-um* (try-fō′li-a). Three-
leaved; less correctly, with three leaflets.

trifoliata, *-us,* *-um* (try-fō-li-ā′ta). Three-
leaved; often with three leaflets.

TRIFOLIATE ORANGE = *Poncirus trifoliata.*

trifoliolata, *-us,* *-um* (try-fo-li-o-lay′ta).
With three leaflets.

TRIFOLIUM. *See* CLOVER.

TRIGENERIC HYBRID. A hybrid derived
from crossing plants in three different genera.
While such hybrids are rare there are some
among the orchids. *See* BRASSOCATTLAELIA,
BRASSOLAELIOCATTLEYA, and SOPHROCAT-
LAELIA.

trigona, *-us,* *-um* (trig′o-na). Triangular.

TRIGONELLA (try-go-nell′a). Annual or
perennial herbs comprising about 75 species
of the pea family, natives of Eu., As., Aust.,
and tropical Af. Leaves compound,* the leaflets 3, usually with the midrib ending in teeth.
Flowers pea-like, yellow, blue or white, solitary or in umbel*-like clusters or in short,
many-flowered racemes.* Fruit a pod
(legume*) with long point or beak. (*Trigonella* is from the Latin for a little triangle,
believed in allusion to the flowers.)

These plants are not much in cultivation,
but the annual species are grown in the sunny
border. Propagated from seeds. Seeds should
be sown ¼ in. deep in April, in patches where
required to bloom. They should be thinned to
about 3 in. apart.

caerulea. Blue melilot. Annual, growing to
2 ft. high. Leaflets 3, lance-shaped. Flowers
blue and white in long-stalked clusters. Pods
short, with a long beak. Eu. Also offered as
Melilotus caerulea.

Foenum-Graecum. Fenugreek. Annual to 2
ft. high, the stems not branched. Leaflets 3,
ovalish. Flowers whitish, the calyx covered
with soft hairs. Pods sickle-shaped, twice as
long as the beak. South Eu. and As.

trigyna, *-us,* *-um* (try-gy′na). With three
pistils.

TRILISA (tri-liss′a). American perennial
herbs, comprising 2 species of the family Compositae, closely allied to *Liatris.* Roots thin
and fibrous. Stems erect, sometimes covered
with sticky hairs. Leaves alternate,* simple,
the margins sometimes toothed. Flowers rose-
purple, the heads of disk flowers only
and borne in loose-branching clusters. Flower
heads surrounded by 2–3 rows of bracts.*
(*Trilisa* is an anagram of *Liatris.*)

These plants are of easy cultivation, and
suitable for the flower border. Propagated by
seeds or division of the roots. Seeds should
be sown ⅛ in. deep, in spring in cold frame or
outside seedbed, in ordinary garden soil. They
may be transplanted as soon as large enough
to handle. Division of the roots should be
made in early spring.

odoratissima. Carolina vanilla. Vanilla-leaf.
Strong-growing, smooth perennial to 3 ft. high.
Leaves lance-shaped or spoon-shaped, to 10 in.
long, vanilla-scented when crushed, the margins
sometimes toothed. Flowers rose-purple, in
heads, in loose-branching clusters. N. Car. to
Fla. and La.

TRILLIUM (trill′i-um). Wakerobin.
Hardy perennial herbs, comprising about 25
species, belonging to the lily family, and na-

---

* Special articles on the subjects indicated by an asterisk (*) will be found at the words so marked.

tives of N.A. and As. They have thick, short rootstocks from which arise each spring the flowering stalks, bearing at the base scale-like sheathing leaves. The three true leaves are arranged in a whorl* at the top of the stalk. Leaves simple, ovalish, smooth, parallel-veined. Flowers pink, white, greenish-white, purplish or yellow, solitary, short-stalked, growing from the center of the whorl of leaves. Calyx of 3 green sepals. Corolla of 3 spreading petals, alternating with the sepals. Stamens* 6. Fruit a 3-celled berry. (*Trillium* is from the Latin for triple, in allusion to the leaves and flower parts being in threes.)

The trilliums are early spring-flowering plants, easily cult. and are admirably adapted for the wild garden, some of the species being suitable for boggy places. Propagated by seeds or division of the roots. Seeds should be sown in well-drained boxes or pans filled with sandy, rather acid peat, placed in shade in cold frame. As soon as large enough to handle they should be planted out in shady places in similar soil. Division of the roots may be made in Nov. or early spring. They are not generally successful on the Coastal Plain or in the South, except in the mountains.

cernuum. Nodding trillium. Ground lily. Jew's-harp. Grows 1–1½ ft. high. Leaves 3, in a whorl at the top of the stem, not stalked, ovalish, to 5 in. long. Flowers white or pinkish, on short recurved stalks, often hidden by the leaves. Petals wavy, to ¾ in. long. Newfoundland to Ga. and westward.

chloropetalum. The Pacific Coast color forms of *T. sessile* are so named by some. *See* T. SESSILE.

erectum. Purple trillium. Birthroot. Bethroot. Strong-growing, 12–15 in. high. Leaves 3, in a whorl at the top of the stem, ovalish, to 7 in. long, abruptly pointed. Flowers on stalks 4 in. long, white to pink, straw-colored or brownish-purple, unpleasantly scented. Petals to 1½ in. long. Green flies are greatly attracted by this species. Quebec to N. Car. and west to Tex.

Great White Trillium (*Trillium grandiflorum*). The finest of the native trilliums for the wild garden, with white, waxy flowers in May.

erythrocarpum = *Trillium undulatum.*

grandiflorum. Great white trillium. Trinity lily. Strong-growing, to 1½ ft. Leaves in a whorl at the top of the stem, ovalish, to 6 in. long. Flowers erect, on stalks 3 in. long, waxy-white, fading to pink. Petals 1½–2 in. long, curving backwards. Quebec to N. Car. and Minn. and one of the finest for the wild garden.

luteum. *See* T. VIRIDE LUTEUM.

nivale. Snow trillium. Not over 8 in. high, the ovalish, blunt leaves 1½–2 in. long. Flowers scarcely over 1 in. long, white, the stalk erect or drooping, and about 1 in. long. A woodland plant from Pa. and Ky. to Minn. and Iowa. March–May.

ovatum. Coast trillium. Growing to 1½ ft. high. Leaves 3, in a whorl* at the top of the stem, ovalish to 6 in. long. Flowers erect, on stalks 3 in. long, white fading to rose. Petals narrower than in *T. grandiflorum*, to 2 in. long. British Columbia to Calif.

recurvatum. Prairie wakerobin. A woodland perennial, the terminal leaves distinctly stalked, ovalish or nearly round, purple-mottled, 2–4 in. long. Flowers nearly 1½ in. long, brown-purple, practically stalkless, the pointed petals erect. Central U.S. April–May. Suited only to woodsy soil in the wild garden.

rivale. A perennial, 2–10 in. high, the terminal leaves stalked, 1–3 in. long, ovalish but heart-shaped at the base, the leafstalk 1–1½ in. long. Flowers white, purple-dotted, about 1½ in. long, the petals pointed. Flower stalk 1–3 in. long. Ore. and Calif. April–May. Not of easy cult. in the East, needing rich woods soil and freedom from late spring frosts.

sessile. Red trillium. Nosebleed. Bloody butchers. Grows to 1 ft. high. Leaves 3 in a whorl* at the top of the stem, ovalish, often blotched with lighter and darker green. Flowers erect, not stalked, purple or green. Petals narrow, to 2 in. long. N.Y. to Ga. and westward. Color forms of this species are found in Calif. and Ore., and are often called *T. chloropetalum.* For the yellow trillium offered as *T. sessile luteum see* T. VIRIDE LUTEUM.

stylosum. Slender-growing plant to 1½ ft. high. Leaves 3, growing in a whorl* at the top of the stem, ovalish. Flowers pink, on drooping stalks, to 2 in. long. Petals to 2 in. long. N. Car. to Ga. and Ala.

undulatum. Painted trillium. Smiling wakerobin. Grows to 1½ ft. high. Leaves 3, growing in a whorl* at the top of the stem, ovalish, tapering to a sharp point. Flowers white, on stalks to 2 in. long. Petals 1½ in. long, marked with a crimson V. This is one of the most beautiful of the species. Quebec to Ga. and Wis. Sometimes offered as *T. erythrocarpum.*

viride luteum. Yellow trillium. A badly mixed-up species, variously offered as *T. luteum* and *T. sessile luteum,* and our only yellow-flowered wakerobin. It is a perennial, 9–15 in. high, with usually mottled, stalkless leaves that vary from narrow to nearly round, 4–6 in. long, abruptly pointed at the tip. Flowers lemon-scented, yellow or greenish-yellow, stalkless, about 1½ in. long. In rich woods, central U.S. May. Fit only for the wild garden. The true *T. viride* appears not to be in cult.

triloba, -us, -um (try-low'ba, *also* trill'o-ba). Three-lobed.

trilobata, -us, -um (try-low-bay'ta). Three-lobed.

trimestris, -e (try-mes'tris). Pertaining to three months.

---

* Special articles on the subjects indicated by an asterisk (*) will be found at the words so marked.

trinervia, -us, -um (try-ner'vi-a). Three-veined.

TRINITY LILY = *Trillium grandiflorum.*

TRINOMIAL. See VARIETY.

Trionum (try-ō'num). A specific name for a species of *Hibiscus,* of uncertain origin, but perhaps from its three-lobed leaves.

TRIOSTEUM (try-os'te-um). Horse gentian. Feverwort. A small genus of horti-culturally unimportant perennial herbs of the family Caprifoliaceae, mostly from N.A. but a few from eastern Asia. They are rather rank-growing herbs with opposite,* stalkless, usually fiddle-shaped leaves, in the axils* of which are the not very attractive, nearly stalk-less flowers. Calyx tubular, its 5 lobes narrow and persistent. Corolla tubular or bell-shaped, its limbs somwhat oblique. Stamens* 5. Fruit a rather leathery capsule.* (*Triosteum* is a contraction of a Greek word for three bony seeds, in allusion to the usually 3 seeds.)

The horse gentians are not worth growing in the perennial border, but are sometimes cult. in more informal parts of the wild garden. The only cult. species is easily grown in a variety of soils, and found wild along the edges of woods or in thickets. It is a coarse, almost weedy plant. Easily propagated by division.

perfoliatum. Horse gentian; also called horse ginseng, wild ipecac, and tinkers'-weed. Erect, 3–4 ft. high. Leaves joined at the base, the stem passing through them. Flowers about ⅝ in. long, dull purplish-brown. Fruit orange-yellow. Eastern U.S. June–July.

tripartita, -us, -um (try-par'ti-ta). Three-parted.

TRIPHASIA (try-fay'zi-a). A single, fragrant species of tropical Asiatic spiny shrubs of the family Rutaceae, **T. trifolia,** not distantly related to *Citrus.* It is variously called limeberry, bergamot lime, orangeberry, and limoncito, and is widely cult. throughout the tropical and sub-tropical world for ornament. Leaves compound,* the leaflets 3, round-toothed, about 1½ in. long. Spines short, stiff, forked. Flowers resembling an orange blossom, about 1 in. wide, very fragrant. Fruit red, about ½ in. in diameter, fragrant, its pulp spicy, but little used as a fruit. The plant is slightly more hardy than the orange and is sometimes used as a hedge plant in zones* 8 and 9, possibly safe over much of zone* 7. (*Triphasia* is from the Greek for triple, in allusion to the 3 leaflets, 3 sepals, and 3 petals.)

triphylla, -us, -um (try-fill'a). With three leaves; less correctly, with three leaflets.

TRIPLET LILY. See BRODIAEA.

TRIPLOID. See CHROMOSOME.

TRIPTERIS (trip'ter-is). A genus of herbs of the daisy family of no hort. interest, but the word sometimes used as a specific name, meaning 3-winged.

TRIPTERYGIUM (trip-ter-rij'i-um). Hardy, eastern Asiatic, deciduous shrubs, comprising about 3 species of the family Celastra-ceae. They are of straggling habit with flexible, reddish stems, growing to 6 ft. or more. Leaves shiny, bright green, alternate,* stalked. Flowers fragrant, small, white or greenish-white, in terminal branching clusters, to 10 in. long. Calyx* of 5 sepals. Corolla of 5 petals. Stamens* 5. Fruit 3-sided and winged, 1-seeded. (*Tripterygium* is from the Greek for three and wing, in allusion to the fruit.)

These shrubs are not much in cultivation. Propagated from seeds in ordinary garden soil.

regeli. Handsome shrub, growing to 6 ft., with warty, scrambling, reddish-brown branches. Leaves stalked, bright green, ovalish, 3–6 in. long, the margins toothed. Flowers greenish-white, ⅓ in. across, in terminal branching clusters to 8 in. long. Fruit ½ in. long, broadly winged. Manchuria, Korea and Jap. July–Aug. Hardy from zone* 3 southward.

triquinata, -us, -um (try-quin-a'ta). Having 3 groups of 5 leaflets.

tristachya, -us, -um (try-stack'i-a). Three-spiked.

TRISTANIA (tris-tay'ni-a). Chiefly Australasian trees and shrubs of the family Myrtaceae, only **T. conferta,** the Brisbane box, much cult., although there are 25 other species known. It is, as cult. in Calif., a medium-sized tree somewhat resembling a eucalyptus, with alternate,* ovalish or narrower leaves, 3–6 in. long, which are often grouped at the ends of the twigs. Flowers about ¾ in. wide, white, mostly in small clusters (cymes*) in the leaf axils.* Calyx turban-shaped. Petals 5, wide-spreading. Stamens numerous, usually grouped in clusters. Fruit a capsule* more or less enclosed by the persistent calyx. Aust. The tree is cult. in Calif., but scarcely known elsewhere, although it is very attractive in flower. Not certainly hardy north of zone* 8 or the warmest parts of zone* 7. Propagated by seeds or by cuttings of half-ripened wood. (Named for Jules M. C. Tristan, French botanist.)

tristis, -e (triss'tis). Sad, bitter, or dull.

TRITELEIA = *Brodiaea.*

TRITERNATE. Thrice-compound* and with each main division having three leaflets or ultimate segments.

TRITICUM (trit'i-kum). Wheat. Annual or biennial grasses of no garden interest, but **T. aestivum** (sometimes called *T. sativum*) the source of flour and hence, next to rice, the most important cereal grass in the world. Cult. since antiquity, wheat is now unknown as a wild plant and even its original home is in doubt, but it appears to have been somewhere in western Asia. Modern wheat is a cultigen* and an annual grass about 4 ft. high, its flat, grass-like leaves 12–16 in. long, and about ½ in. wide. Flower spikes terminal, about 4 in. long, awned in some varieties, but without an awn* in others. Fruit a caryopsis* (the wheat grain) about ¼ in. long, grooved. Included in the above are the common winter and spring wheats. There are many other varieties for special purposes, macaroni among

---

* Special articles on the subjects indicated by an asterisk (*) will be found at the words so marked.

them, but these belong to agriculture and not to gardening. (*Triticum* is the classical Latin name of wheat.)

TRITOMA. See KNIPHOFIA.

TRITONIA (try-tō'ni-a). Blazing star. Handsome South African bulbous plants of the iris family, known to many gardeners as montbretias, and cult. like the closely related gladiolus. Of the 50 known species only the three below are in common cult. and they are showy, summer-blooming plants with short stems, narrow, sword-shaped leaves, and growing from fibrous or sheathed corms.* Flowering spike 2–3 ft. high, its spathe*-like bracts often 3-toothed. From between these bracts the tubular or bell-shaped corolla emerges, its lobes nearly regular. Fruit a membranous capsule.* (*Tritonia* is explained by its author as referring to a weathercock, in allusion to the variable direction of the stamens* of some species.)

The culture of montbretias is the same as for gladiolus (which see). They should be planted 3–4 in. deep, and about 5 in. apart each way. Among the many named hort. forms, all derived from the second species, are James Coey, Lord Nelson, and Princess, handsome red varieties. See RED GARDEN. The second and third species are, by some, credited to the genus *Crocosmia*).

crocata. A few-leaved, slender, mostly unbranched plant. Flowers nearly 2 in. wide, yellowish-brown or orange-red, in few-flowered, 1-sided clusters (racemes*). There are also light red, scarlet, and purple forms.

crocosmaeflora. The common montbretia of the garden, derived from crossing the next species with *Crocosmia aurea* (which see). It is a much-branched plant, 3–4 in. high, its sword-shaped leaves several to many. Flowers about 2 in. wide, orange-crimson in the typical form, in a long, loose, more or less 2-ranked (distichous*) cluster, the tube of the corolla curved. There are many color forms of this most popular flower garden plant. The original cross which produced this favorite was not made until about 1880.

pottsi. A few- or several-leaved, branching herb, 2–4 ft. high. Flowers about 1 in. long, funnel-shaped, the tube twice as long as the slightly unequal limb. Corolla yellow but tinged with red. Transvaal and Natal. One of the parents of the common montbretia (*T. crocosmaeflora*).

trivialis, -e (triv-i-ā'lis). Ordinary; common or trivial.

TROCHODENDRACEAE (tro-ko-dendray'see-ee). A family of trees or shrubs, three genera of which, *Cercidiphyllum, Trochodendron,* and *Euptelea,* are Asiatic, and somewhat cult. for ornament.

Leaves alternate* in *Euptelea,* opposite* or nearly so in *Cercidiphyllum.* Flowers small, appearing before the leaves in both genera, perfect* in *Euptelea,* but with male and female flowers on separate plants in the other genus. Fruit winged in *Euptelea,* a dry pod in *Cercidiphyllum,* which has very handsome autumnal foliage, and in *Trochodendron.*

Technical flower characters: Petals and sepals none in *Euptelea* or in *Cercidiphyllum.* Sta-

mens* many and usually providing the only color to the flower (sometimes red). Ovary of separate carpels (see PISTIL), sometimes partly immersed in the fleshy receptacle.*

TROCHODENDRON (tro-ko-den'dron). A genus of only one species, **T. aralioides** of eastern As., cult. for ornament. In the wild a tree up to 60 ft. high, but as cult. usually a spreading shrub. It has aromatic bark, alternate or clustered, long-stalked leaves that are elliptic or egg-shaped, with rounded marginal teeth. Flowers in a terminal cluster (raceme*), without petals or sepals, but conspicuous because of the numerous spreading stamens.* Fruit a cluster of 5–10 pods (follicles*). Of easy cult. if treated as the closely related magnolia. June. Hardy from zone* 6 southward. (*Trochodendron* is from the Greek for wheel and tree in reference to the widely spreading stamens.*)

trojana, -us, -um (tro-jay'na). Relating to Troy.

TROLLIUS (trol'i-us). Globeflower. Hardy perennial herbs, comprising about 18 species of the family Ranunculaceae, found in damp places throughout the temperate regions of the northern hemisphere. Rootstocks thick and spreading. Leaves dark green or bronzy-green, deeply cut into lobes, each lobe coarsely toothed. Flowers showy, whitish, orange, yellow or purple, usually solitary at the ends of the branches. Calyx* of 5–15 large, colored, petal-like sepals. Corolla of 5–15 inconspicuous petals. Stamens* many. Fruit a collection of 1-celled, 1-seeded follicles.* (*Trollius* is from the old German word *trol,* round, in allusion to the ball-like flowers.)

Trollius is easily cult. and thrives best in moist, half-shady places. Suitable for the sunken garden and edges of water gardens, though they may be used in the flower border if given similar conditions. Propagated by seeds or division of rootstocks. Seeds should be sown ⅛ in. deep in a moist, shady seedbed, outdoors, in Sept. or Apr. They may be transplanted as soon as large enough to handle. Division of rootstocks may be made in Oct. or early spring.

albiflorus. Considered by some, and here, as merely a Pacific Coast white-flowered form of the common yellow globeflower (*Trollius laxus*) of the eastern U.S., and probably not distinct from it.

asiaticus. Asiatic globeflower. Strong-growing plant, to 2 ft. or more high. Leaves bronze-green, finely lobed, and cut. Flowers solitary, with 10 orange-colored spreading sepals and 10 orange, short, narrow petals. Siberia.

europaeus. European globeflower. Strong-growing, to 2 ft. high, much-branched. Basal leaves on short stalks. Leaves dark green, 5-lobed, cut and coarsely toothed. Flowers 1–2, at the ends of the branches, globular, 2 in. across. Sepals 10–15, lemon-yellow, incurved. Petals lemon-yellow, shorter than the sepals, spoon-shaped. Eu.

laxus. American globeflower. Weak-growing plant to 2 ft. high. Leaves stalked, cut into 5–7 lobes, which are again cut and toothed. Flowers generally solitary, 1–2 in. across. Sepals 5–7, yellowish-green, spreading. Petals

---

* Special articles on the subjects indicated by an asterisk (*) will be found at the words so marked.

5–15, short and narrow. Wet places, Conn. to Pa. and Mich. May.

ledebouri. Golden queen. Strong-growing plant, to 2 ft. high. Leaves deeply lobed, each lobe being again cut and toothed. Flowers yellow, with 5 spreading sepals, and 10–12 short petals. Siberia.

pumilus. Low-growing, to 1 ft. high. Leaves small, 1–2 in. across, cut into 5 lobes, each lobe again cut into 3 segments. Flowers solitary, 1 in. across, yellow. Sepals 5–6, spreading and notched. Petals 10–12, short. High Himalayas.

TROPAEOLACEAE (tro-pee-o-lay′see-ee). A restricted family of chiefly climbing herbs found in the upper elevations of the Andes and Mex., comprising only one genus, *Tropaeolum*. See NASTURTIUM.

TROPAEOLUM. See NASTURTIUM.

TROPICAL ALMOND = *Terminalia Catappa.*

TROPICAL GARDEN. There are, strictly speaking, no true tropical gardens in the U.S., the only place where such a garden might be even possible being near Key West, Fla. For the gardens loosely called tropical, *see* SUB-TROPICAL GARDEN.

TROPICAL LILAC = *Duranta repens.*

TROUT FLOWER; TROUT LILY. See ERYTHRONIUM.

TROWEL. See No. 7 at TOOLS AND IMPLEMENTS.

TRUE ALOE = *Aloe vera.*

TRUFFLE. An underground fungus, perhaps the greatest delicacy of the mushroom world, and neither cult. nor wild in the U.S. or in England. Truffle culture is confined to certain districts in France where dogs and pigs are trained to help harvest them. They grow mostly in association with the roots of young oak trees, thousands of acres of which are planted in France for the purpose. The truffle "spawn" is sown in deep trenches. It often fails and much of the truffle industry is merely harvesting wild plants.

TRUMPET-CREEPER. Very handsome, rampant-growing, woody vines comprising the genus **Campsis** (kamp′sis) of the family Bignoniaceae, all the species cult. for ornament, especially the native one. They are tall-growing vines, without tendrils,° but climbing by aerial rootlets. Leaves opposite,° compound,° the leaflets arranged feather-fashion with an odd one at the end. Flowers showy, orange or scarlet, in terminal clusters (cymes° or panicles°), the calyx tubular or somewhat bell-shaped, the corolla funnel-shaped, its spreading limb oblique, the flowers thus slightly irregular. Stamens° 4, curved. Fruit a long, stalked capsule, its many seeds flattened and with 2 wings. (*Campsis* is from the Greek for curved, in allusion to the curved stamens.°)

Handsome vines, especially the second, which climbs higher than the Asiatic species, but does not flower until older than *C. grandiflora.* They grow easily in a variety of soils, but do best in open places with fertile soil, especially the American species which thrives very well over chicken houses and other outbuildings. All may be propagated very readily by seed, layers, or by cuttings.

C. chinensis = *C. grandiflora.*

C. grandiflora. Chinese trumpet-creeper. Not so high-climbing as the next species and with fewer aerial rootlets. Leaflets 7–9, more or less ovalish, 1½–2½ in. long. Flowers nearly 3 in. wide, scarlet, the tube about half the length of the flower. China. Aug.–Sept. Hardy from zone° 5 southward. Long known as *Tecoma grandiflora* and *Bignonia grandiflora.* A hybrid between this and *C. radicans*, known as *C. hybrida*, is a little more hardy than *C. grandiflora* and nearly as showy.

C. hybrida. See CAMPSIS GRANDIFLORA (above).

C. radicans. Trumpet-creeper; also known as trumpet-vine. A stout, woody vine, often climbing to 30 ft. high, the aerial rootlets numerous. Leaflets 9–11, elliptic or ovalish, 1½–2½ in. long, hairy on the midrib beneath. Flowers orange-scarlet, about 2 in. wide, the tube thrice as long as the expanded part of the corolla. Pa. to Mo., Fla., and Tex. July–Sept. Hardy from zone° 3 southward, and an excellent vine for smoke-ridden cities as well as for the country. It clings firmly to tree trunks or rough walls, and is nearly as showy as the Chinese species. It is sometimes called trumpet-honeysuckle, a name better applied to *Lonicera sempervirens.* Long known as *Tecoma radicans*, and *Bignonia radicans.* The plant is invasive and next to impossible to eradicate.

C. tagliabuana. Also a hybrid between *C. grandiflora* and *C. radicans*, and more handsome and hardier than either. The flowers are tawny-orange, nearly 1 in. long, in loose clusters (panicles°). Mostly offered under the varietal name of Mme. Galen. July–Oct.

TRUMPET-CREEPER FAMILY. A large and diverse group of plants, comprising such unlike garden subjects as the trumpet-creeper, catalpa, and the calabash. For the many genera and their garden uses *see* BIGNONIACEAE.

TRUMPET-FLOWER. Several plants are so called. Those in this book are: the cross-vine (*Bignonia capreolata*); trumpet-honeysuckle (*see* below); almost any plant in the genus *Datura*; yellow elder (*Stenolobium Stans*); and the yellow oleander (*Thevetia nereifolia*).

TRUMPET-HONEYSUCKLE = *Lonicera sempervirens.* But *see* Campsis radicans at TRUMPET-CREEPER.

TRUMPET-LEAF = *Sarracenia flava.* See PITCHER-PLANT.

TRUMPET-LILY = *Lilium longiflorum.*

TRUMPET NARCISSUS = *Narcissus Pseudo-narcissus.*

TRUMPETS = *Sarracenia flava.* See PITCHER-PLANT.

TRUMPET-VINE = *Campsis radicans.* See TRUMPET-CREEPER.

truncata, -us, -um (trun-kay′ta). Truncate; *i.e.*, cut squarely off.

° Special articles on the subjects indicated by an asterisk (°) will be found at the words so marked.

TRUSS. A common garden term, without technical significance, for a more or less compact flower cluster at the end of a stalk, as in the lilac.

TSUGA. *See* HEMLOCK.

tsus-simensis, -e (sus-sy-men'sis). From the Japanese island of Tsus-sima.

TUBE. The usually narrow, cylindric, or funnel-shaped part of a united calyx or corolla.

TUBER. A swollen, mostly underground stem which bears buds as in the potato. Tubers are often confused with a tuberous (*i.e.,* swollen) root, such as those of the

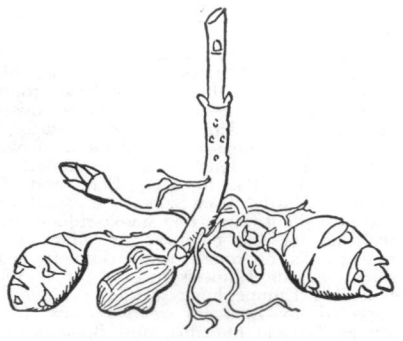

Tuber of the Jerusalem artichoke, showing the eyes (buds)

dahlia, but the latter are true roots just as is the sweet potato, while true tubers are always modified stems. While most tubers are underground, some are borne in the air. *See* DIOSCOREA.

Tuberaria (too-ber-rair'i-a). An old generic name for plants here included in *Helianthemum.*

TUBERCLE. A small tuber. The word is also applied to the pea-like nodules on the roots of most legumes, and to the rounded, knob-like outgrowths on the ridge or face of many cacti.

TUBER CROPS. *See* ROOT CROPS.

tuberculosa, -us, -um (too-ber-kew-lō'sa). Tuberculate; *i.e.,* bearing tubercles (which see).

TUBER FERN = *Nephrolepis cordifolia.*

tuberosa, -us, -um (too-ber-rō'sa). Bearing tubers; or merely tuberous.*

TUBEROSE. The common garden tuberose is the only cult. species of the genus **Polianthes** (po-li-anth'eez) of the family Amaryllidaceae. They are tender, tuberous, perennial herbs, comprising about 12 species, all natives of Mex. The only cult. species, **P. tuberosa,** the common tuberose, however, has not been found wild. It grows to 3½ ft. high and has basal leaves 1–1½ ft. long and ½ in. wide, bright green, reddish at base. Stem leaves clasping the stem, smaller.

Flowers waxy-white, extremely fragrant, in short terminal racemes.* Calyx* of 3 white sepals. Corolla of 3 white petals. Stamens* 6. Fruit a 3-celled capsule.* (*Polianthes* is probably from the Greek for white, shining flowers, in allusion to the waxy-white corolla.) Widely cult. in France for the perfume trade.

The tuberose is easily cult. and propagated by offsets* of the tubers. Offsets should be planted as soon as danger of frost is over or may be started in the cool greenhouse. They should be planted about 2 in. deep and 4 in. apart in rich garden soil. These will not flower the first year so the tubers must be taken up and stored in a dry, frost-free place during winter, and planted 3 in. deep and 6 in. apart the following year, when they will bloom in Oct. Tubers must show signs of life to be worth planting. The double-flowered forms are the ones usually cult.

TUBEROUS. Having a swollen root, usually known as a tuberous root, as in the dahlia; but also applied to true tubers (which see).

TUB GARDENING. An easy method of growing flowers and certain fruits and vegetables for home consumption is by planting them in barrels. Many persons with limited space may thus have pleasures which would otherwise be denied them. Trailing plants such as petunias, nasturtiums, oxalis, and Kenilworth ivy should be used in connec-

If you have no other space, tub gardening is an alternative. Strawberries or flowers may be so grown.

tion with small annuals to secure decorative effects. Plants may be bought from florists or raised from seeds sown in flats. Dewberries, strawberries, and tomatoes, when grown in barrels, ripen two weeks or more before those raised in the garden.

Strawberries are ideal fruit for this form of gardening. The berries are easily protected from birds, kept clean, and they ripen evenly. The holes for the plants

* Special articles on the subjects indicated by an asterisk (*) will be found at the words so marked.

should not be over 4 in. in diameter and 12 in. apart from center to center, staggered, which gives a diagonal spacing of 13½ in. A full-sized barrel will thus accommodate 15 plants on the sides and 3 on the top. Through center of barrel run three boards about 4 in. in width, fastened together in the shape of a triangle. Bore holes down the length of these to aerate the soil, which without ventilation might become sour; close these apertures loosely with hay or excelsior. Water given by means of a sprinkling can must be distributed evenly over the surface soil. Five or six small holes bored in the bottom of the barrel will allow drainage of any superfluous water. Set in a sheltered location on bricks 3 in. from the ground.

tubiflora, -us, -um (too-bi-flow′ra). Having tubular flowers.

TUBS. For all greenhouse or conservatory plants too big for a 12-in. flower pot a wooden tub is essential. They may be of any size, round or square, and should have handles for lifting. Very large tubs should have hooks or rings near the top through which an iron pipe may be inserted. The pipe will allow several men to work at once in lifting heavy tubs.

All tubs are best made of cypress and painted outside but not in. Unless, as in small ones, they have short legs, they should be set on bricks or blocks of wood, not flat on the ground or greenhouse floor. Large, square tubs should be made so that one panel or board near the bottom can be unscrewed to allow examination of the roots and soil. All tubs must be provided with several holes in the bottom to permit of perfect drainage. *See* POTTING.

tubulosa, -us, -um (too-bew-lō′sa). Having tubes.

TUFA; TUFF. A porous, pitted, volcanic rock used in making rock gardens, but it should be used with caution. *See* Kind of Rock at ROCK GARDEN.

TUFTED. Growing in more or less dense tufts or clusters. No single-stemmed plant can ever be tufted, but many plants with several stems, such as some grasses, saxifrages, sedums, etc., are always tufted. When congestion of stems becomes such as to make the plant into a tight, ball-like cushion, such densely tufted specimens are called cushion plants. They are common in dry or alpine situations, the cushion-like habit helping to reduce transpiration.*

TUFTED PANSY. *See* VIOLA CORNUTA.

TUFT TREE = *Cordyline australis*.

TULBAGHIA (tull-bag′i-a). A genus of about 20 species of South African bulbous herbs of the lily family, the one below being almost the only species grown in the U.S. They are related to *Agapanthus* (which see) and need similar cult. **T. violacea** is a stout herb, 15–25 in. high. Leaves 6–10, garlic-scented, 8–12 in. long and about ¼ in. wide. Flowers urn-shaped, purplish-violet, about ¾ in. long, crowded in a terminal cluster (um-

bel*) at the end of a stout stalk 15–25 in. high. S. Af. March. Hardy outdoors only in frostless regions. (*Tulbaghia* was named for Ryk Tulbagh, once Dutch governor at S. Af.)

TULE POTATO. *See* SAGITTARIA LATIFOLIA.

TULIP. For the common tulip *see* TULIPA. For the globe tulip *see* CALOCHORTUS.

TULIPA (too′li-pa). Tulip. Bulbous herbs of the lily family, comprising perhaps 100 species and several thousand horticultural forms, the latter including all the common garden tulips. The wild forms all come from the Old World, from an area stretching from the Mediterranean region to Jap. Bulb generally pointed, the stem single (rarely branched in some species), the leaves mostly basal, but a few on the stem in some tall sorts, generally thick, bluish-green, without teeth. Flowers usually solitary, chiefly erect, bell-shaped or saucer-shaped, the petals and sepals indistinguishable as such, totaling 6 (except in double-flowered forms). Stamens* 6. Fruit a many-seeded capsule.* (*Tulipa* is a Latinized version of an Arabic word for a turban, in allusion to the shape of the flower.)

Tulips are divided into two main divisions — the "species" tulips, derived from wild species and generally breeding true, and the common garden tulips which are the result of centuries of breeding, mostly upon the two species *Tulipa suaveolens* and *T. gesneriana*. Most garden tulips do not breed true and are propagated by their bulbs.

In the discussion of the tulips of hort. significance it will simplify matters to first dispose of the "species" sorts, and then take up the common garden tulips. As the proper method of planting has already been described at BULBS, it will not be repeated here. All are planted in the late fall — Oct.–Nov.

Nearly 40 different species of *Tulipa* have, at times, been grown in the U.S., but of these the selection below will be found the most generally useful. They are nothing like so much grown as the common garden sorts to be discussed at the end of the "species" tulips.

acuminata. Turkish tulip. Related to *T. gesneriana*, hence to garden tulips, *i.e.*, hort. varieties. It is 12–18 in. high, the leaves narrow and irregularly curving. Flowers yellow with red lines, the segments narrow-pointed and 3–4 in. long. Turkey. April.

aucheriana. Leaves mostly near the ground, usually 2–5, strap-shaped and 4–5 in. long. Flowers about 2 in. wide, star-like, pink but with brownish blotch, the inner petals striped green or brown on the back. Persia and Syria. Spring.

australis. Leaves usually 2–5, strap-shaped, channeled, 2–4 in. long. Flower fragrant, solitary, rarely 2, at the end of a stalk 6–10 in. long. Petals yellow, but reddish on the outside, pointed at the tip, about 2 in. long. Southern France and Algeria. April.

batalini. A low tulip, not over 5–6 in. high, the very narrow leaves grass-like. Flowers yellow, blotched gray-yellow, the petals blunt, but

---

* Special articles on the subjects indicated by an asterisk (*) will be found at the words so marked.

sometimes notched at the tip. Bokhara. May. Closely related to *T. linifolia.*

biflora. Leaves bluish-green, very narrow, about 5 in. high, usually bearing only 2 or 3 leaves. Flowers 1–4, about 1 in. long, their stalk not over 3 in. high. Petals opening flat, white, with a yellow blotch near the base, the outer petals green and red on the back. Asia Minor. March. The *var.* turkestanica has broader leaves and 4–5 flowers. It is often offered as *T. turkestanica.*

chrysantha = *Tulipa stellata chrysantha.*

clusiana. Not over 15 in. high, the bulb hairy and small. Leaves narrow. Flowers fragrant, small, the base purple, the pointed tips white or yellowish, the outside striped pinkish-red, hence sometimes called candy-stick tulip. Southern Eu. and Persia.

Dasystemon. Not over 5 in. high, the flowers small, usually several, yellow, but the petals edged with white, and greenish on the back. Turkestan. For culture *see* ROCK GARDEN. Often offered as *T. tarda.*

eichleri. A low plant, 6–12 in. high, the leaves broad but long-tapering. Flowers bluish-black at the base, scarlet above, the petals blunt but with a minute point. Southwestern Asia. For culture *see* ROCK GARDEN.

fosteriana. A stout plant with broad leaves. Flower large, bright crimson, but darker at the base. Turkestan. *See* ROCK GARDEN.

gesneriana. The probable origin of most of the common garden tulips (*see* below). From 12–24 in. high, the leaves broad and ample. Flowers now very variable as to shape, color, and markings (*see* below). Armenia and Persia.

greigi. A low tulip, 6–9 in. high, with rather broad, wavy-margined, dark leaves, usually with reddish dots in rows. Flowers orange-red, the base darker and yellow-margined, the petals minutely pointed. Turkestan.

hageri. A low tulip, the 4–5 smooth, strap-shaped leaves, 6–8 in. long and about ½ in. wide. Flowers 1–4, on a stalk not over 6 in. high, bell-shaped. Inner petals copper or reddish, with a greenish blotch, the outer petals yellow and green, all about 2 in. long. Asia Minor and Greece. April.

humilis. Leaves only 2–4, not over 4 in. long, somewhat bluish-green. Flowers 1 or 2, about 2 in. long, reddish-green on the outside, but with a yellow blotch on the inside, the petals narrow and sharp. Outer petals whitish, brown- or purple-stained. Persia. March.

ingens. Not over 10 in. high, the hairy leaves broad. Flowers vermilion-red, but darker at the base, the petals blunt but with a minute point. Bokhara.

kaufmanniana. Water lily tulip. A showy tulip, 5–10 in. high, the leaves broad but abruptly tapering. Flowers spreading, white or pale yellow, with a yellow center that is red-marked. Turkestan.

kopalowskiana. Leaves flat, 6–8 in. long, about 1 in. wide, bluish-green, not more than 2–4 leaves to each bulb. Flowers 1 or 2, on a 6-in. stalk, the petals spreading and pointed both ends, yellow, but reddish outside, not blotched. Turkestan. April.

linifolia. A low tulip, 5–10 in. high, with narrow, grass-like leaves. Flowers crimson, the base bluish, the petals pointed. Bokhara.

marjoletti. A relatively tall tulip, 18–24 in. high, and thought to be derived from *T. gesneriana,* or from one of its derivatives among the garden tulips. The plants distributed under the name of *T. marjoletti* bear yellowish flowers with the petals purple-margined. Savoy.

maximowiczi. Not significantly different from *T. linifolia* (which see). Bokhara. Spring.

montana. Not over 8 in. high, the leaves bluish-green and long-tapering. Flowers about 2 in. wide, dark crimson, but paler outside, the outer petals pointed. Persia and Afghanistan. Called also *T. wilsoniana.* For culture *see* ROCK GARDEN.

Orphanidea. A medium-sized tulip, the narrow, folded leaves 8–12 in. long. Flower solitary, star-like, the petals nearly 2 in. long, orange-brown, but purple- and green-stained on the outside. Petals sharp-pointed. Turkey and Greece. April.

ostrowskiana. Leaves 2–4, erect, 8–12 in. long, about 1 in. wide. Flower solitary, scarlet, cup-shaped, the segments nearly 2 in. long, green-blotched. Flower stalk about 8 in. high. Turkestan. Spring.

praecox. A stout-stemmed tulip, 12–20 in. high, the bluish-green leaves broadly ovalish, 8–12 in. long, about 3 in. wide. Flower solitary, about 2½ in. long, dull red, blotched green, the blotch yellow-margined. Petals spreading, bent downward at the long-pointed tip. Italy. April.

praestans. A medium-sized tulip, usually 12–18 in. high, the leaves broad and short-tapering. Flowers light red, the petals blunt but with a minute point. Bokhara.

pulchella. Leaves only 2–3, strap-shaped and 4–6 in. long, slightly channeled and smooth. Flowers cup-shaped, but opening flat, about 1½ in. long, solitary or few, reddish purple, blotched with a white-margined, deep blue stain. Outer petals gray or green. Asia Minor. March. Violet Queen is the var. usually offered.

retroflexa. An old group of garden origin, with yellow flowers.

sprengeri. Medium-sized, mostly 8–15 in. high, the pointed leaves long and narrow. Flowers orange-red, the base darker and the petals almost prickle-tipped. Armenia.

stellata. A medium-sized tulip, 6–8 in. high, the 2–5 leaves somewhat wavy, narrow, about 8 in. long and ⅛ in. wide. Flower star-like, flat, about 1½ in. wide, white but yellow-blotched. Afghanistan and N.W. India. April. The *var.* chrysantha (usually offered as *T. chrysantha*) has pure yellow flowers, red-tinged on the back.

suaveolens. Mostly 4–8 in. high and very early flowering. Leaves broad. Flowers fragrant, bright yellow, the petals pointed. Southern Eu.

sylvestris. A weak-stemmed tulip, 8–12 in. high, the 4–5 leaves strap-shaped, channeled, 8–10 in. long and about ⅛ in. wide. Flowers fragrant, usually only 1 or 2, yellow but green and red on the outside. Eu., western As. and N. Af. April–May.

tarda. By some considered the correct name for the plants offered as *Tulipa Dasystemon.*

turkestanica = *Tulipa biflora turkestanica.*

wilsoniana = *Tulipa montana.*

These "species" tulips, sometimes referred to as botanical tulips, are not usually grown in quantity as are the garden tulips, but mostly planted in groups in the border or rock garden. They are fine plants for special color gardens, especially for borders or gardens in which red predominates. Their season of bloom stretches from early April to late May so their color is often the most reliable material to use for such effects at this early season. *See* RED GARDEN. Many of them are also much at home in the rock

---

* Special articles on the subjects indicated by an asterisk (*) will be found at the words so marked.

garden, where their early bloom is most welcome. *See* ROCK GARDEN.

GARDEN TULIPS

The Turks were the first to become interested in tulips and when they overran Europe, the tulip went with them. Since then, the Dutch have been the great breeders of tulips, nearly all of which have been derived from innumerable crosses between *T. gesneriana* and *T. suaveolens*, until recent years when attention has been turned to species never used before, notably *T. kaufmanniana* and the brilliant but difficult *T. greigi*. *T. fosteriana* is also coming into more general use in breeding and it is only reasonable to expect that still others of the wild tulips will be employed in the near future. The gardener, therefore, has at his disposal not only the wild species themselves, many of them of extreme beauty, but others to fit any scheme of color, blooming dates, heights, and usefulness that he may conceive. He will discover also that many of the distinctions once of use, and so noted in older books, are no longer as definite. There are now offered yellow Darwins, a color once thought limited only to Cottage types, and many others that no longer fit precisely into the old categories. This is the inevitable fate of any plant that has been worked over by man through many years. The gardener will also discover that some of the modern varieties are of easier culture than their ancestors, and he will be faced more acutely with the problem as to whether or not he wishes to treat the tulip as an annual bedding plant to be discarded after blooming — the most practical treatment in many gardens.

The main groups remain:

    Early Tulips
    Breeder Tulips
    Cottage Tulips
    Darwin Tulips

but the following are almost runners-up in popular esteem:

    Lily-flowering Tulips
    Triumph Tulips
    Mendel Tulips
    Parrot Tulips
    Kaufmanniana Tulips
    Fosteriana Tulips

Double-flowered clones* are available in nearly all groups and have their own particular charms, especially in flower arrangements of period character.

1. Early-Flowered Tulips. These now embrace practically every color, and any selection is no more than the expression of personal preference. The modern inclusion of dark reds, brownish tints, excellent whites, and pale yellows puts them in the first class. It should be remembered that they are very early (with hyacinths), usually short-stemmed, and have as companions some of the new Kaufmanniana hybrids. Apricot Yellow, Couleur Cardinal, DeWet (scarlet), Diana (white), Ibis (rose-pink), Mon Trésor (yel-

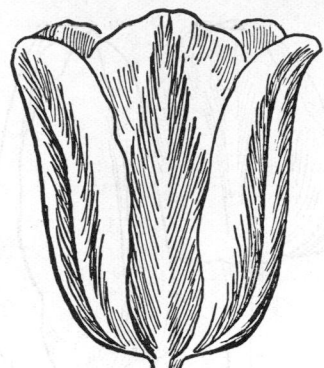

Early tulip

low), Princess Irene (salmon to orange), Van der Neer (plum purple), and Yellow Prince (canary yellow, sometimes flushed scarlet) make a fair coverage of possible sorts.

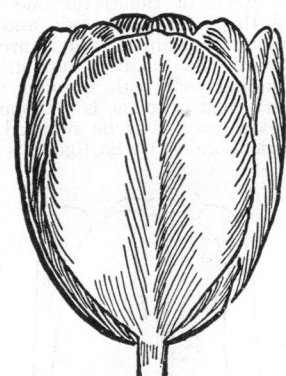

Breeder tulip

2. Breeder Tulips. Tall-stemmed, May-flowering tulips with rounded or square-topped flowers, resembling the Darwins except in color range. This includes purples, bronze, copper, and dull reds, often with a suffusion of yellow. Essentially they are muted colors that are best used with contrasting flowers of pure color. There are some varieties with a contrasting color along the edges or flamed through the center of each petal.

3. Cottage Tulips. Tall-stemmed, May-flowering tulips, usually self-colored, usually with pointed petals, but in more recent years, in some clones,* with rounded petals as in the Darwins. The group is particularly rich in pure yellows, from palest ivory to deep orange, and in very clear pinks. Many of the best varieties are very old. Belle Jaune (dark yellow), Carrara (white), G. W. Leak (geranium-scarlet), John Ruskin (apricot-rose), Mrs. Moon (canary yellow), Queen of Spain (cream, flushed pink),

* Special articles on the subjects indicated by an asterisk (*) will be found at the words so marked.

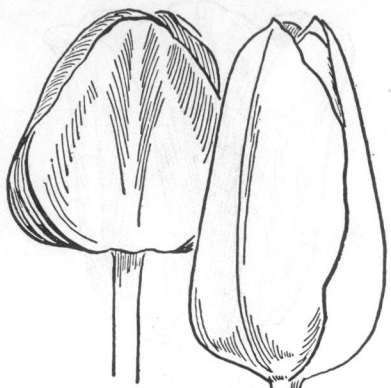

Two types of Cottage tulips

Zomerschoon (salmon-red), a very old and lovely sort.

4. Darwin Tulips. In this section there is almost an excess of riches for one's choice. Nearly all the colors are pure and strong, except among the blues, which are mostly somewhat gray in tonality but still lovely colors, blending well with Breeder varieties. No matter what choice is recommended, others equally good will be omitted. After-glow (apricot-orange), Bartigon, (scarlet),

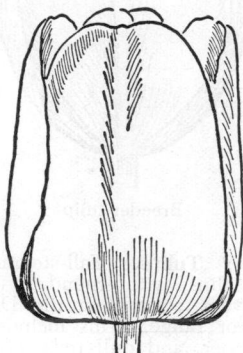

Darwin tulip

Farncombe Sanders (geranium-scarlet), Golden Age (buttercup-yellow), La Tulipe Noire (very dark maroon), Niphetos (lemon-yellow), Pride of Zwanenburg (salmon-pink), Rev. Rollo Meyer (purplish black), The Bishop (deep violet), White City. One should also look at such new breaks as Ossi Oswalda, in which, over a white ground, cherry-red is flushed in varying amounts, a pattern that usually puts this sort among the Cottage tulips of the vintage of Picotee. Again, one might look at the new small group of hybrids between Darwins and *T. fosteriana* that are chiefly in very brilliant reds, and must be used with the same care

that is used for Oriental poppies later in the garden.

5. Lily-flowered Tulips. This is a growing group mostly developed from old Retro-flexa, a clone* that had pointed and strongly reflexed segments, of pure yellow, and Pico-tee, white with pink edges that widened as the flower aged. Varieties are now available in all the usual colors except the darkest purple-reds, maroons, and lavenders. Captain Fryatt (ruby-violet), Ellen Willmott, which used to be a Cottage Tulip (primrose-yellow), Marcellina (salmon-pink), Philemon (white), Picotee (white, edged with pink), and Yellow Marvel (dark yellow) will serve as an introduction to this section.

6. Mendel Tulips. This is a race of tulips that are useful for the interval between the Early and the Darwin tulips, not as tall as the Darwins, but taller than the Early varieties. They are valued chiefly for the colors between white and crimson, with not much in the yellow range.

7. Triumph Tulips. These, like the Mendel tulips, are a garden race, developed apparently in the hope of still further bridging the gap in the flowering seasons between Early and May-flowering tulips. They flower just after the Mendel tulips, are somewhat taller as a group, and again appear to lack the yellow and similar colors, depending on white to pink to deep red for color range. Many have more than one color to the petal, either as a marginal flush of contrasting color or a flame of distinct color through the center of the petal.

8. Parrot Tulips. These are sports from other tulips and as a group are distinguished chiefly by the fringed margins of the segments and often by picturesque unevenness of the surfaces. The color range is wide and includes all colors, with the recent introduction of a good white. It should be noted that the flowers often may have a flake or two of green in the total color, and it should be remembered that frequently the stems are weak so that the heavy heads bear them down. The greatest charm comes when the blooms are cut. From them have come the **Fringed Tulips** which resemble them except that the margins have a definite margin of fringe, often of a distinct hue from that of the petal.

9. Kaufmanniana Tulips. The species itself is a somewhat variable one, essentially yellow with a rose-to-pink color pattern of the three outer segments, and varying amounts of pattern inside at the base of the segments. It is one of the more permanent species under garden culture. In the races offered under this head, one suspects that part are no more than seedling developments of the species itself, with different hues of yellow on the base and different degrees of markings inside and out. The remainder are hybrids with *T. greigi*, a gorgeous but difficult wild tulip with brilliant deep-orange, almost scarlet flowers, and foliage spotted with lines of brown dots. These are transmitted in many of the seedlings, and the gorgeous color as well. In this group, as in many others the choice should be left to the gardener.

10. Fosteriana Tulips. *Tulipa fosteriana* itself is a brilliant wild tulip worthy of a place in any garden. Its offspring, with the exception of White Emperor, are as yet all in the same color range as the species, chiefly brilliant reds, tending toward orange rather than crimson. There is great variation in stem heights, so care should be used in placement. The colors are all strong, so care in association with other plants in bloom at the same time is also necessary.

Beside these 10 well-marked groups of tulips there are several groups, with no great number of clones* in each group, that may well be watched, and there remain the several groups of broken tulips that are best known perhaps from old flower prints, forms that one either likes or dislikes, depending largely on whether or not one likes striped and flamed flowers. These were the wonderful tulips of the days of the "tulipomania" (which see), but they have rather fallen out of favor.

Tulips all like deep, rich soil, neutral to slightly alkaline, a situation that is well drained and sunny, since the flowers open widest in sunshine. They inherit from the wild ancestors a certain impatience with continued summer rains or watering, so in garden practice one either lifts and stores the bulbs for replanting or discards them for new bulbs each year. No animal manures should touch the bulbs, and good commercial fertilizers are best. The depth of the bulb should be that recommended in each catalogue from which orders are placed, remembering that in case of doubt, plant a little deeper. Of all bulbs, tulips may be delayed in planting a little later than any others, though this is not recommended. Spacing should be carefully arranged in order to allow ample root run, and good bulbs should always be purchased as that will insure uniformity in stem heights.

All of the above classes should be planted in late Oct. or Nov., as should the spring-blooming *species* of *Tulipa* mentioned in the list preceding this account of garden tulips. — B. Y. M. *See also* BULBS.

The address of the National Tulip Society is 226 Edgewood Avenue, Westfield, N.J.

INSECT PESTS. *See* BULBS.

DISEASES. The most common disease of tulip is known as fire and is similar to gray mold.* The spotting of leaves and flowers may be prevented by using pesticide #1, #5, or #11 (*see* SPRAYS AND DUSTS). Apply when leaves are 4 inches high and repeat weekly until flowers open. When digging or planting the bulbs, discard any which have black, seed-like objects clustered on the surface, or just beneath the husk of the bulb.

Occasionally a virus disease, mosaic,* causes flowers to "break" in color and produce white or green streaks in the petals. Discard bulbs of these plants.

TULIP DROPPER. An unusual condition in tulips whereby a vegetative shoot grows downward from the bulb and produces a new bulb below the old one. Droppers are occasionally found also in other bulbous plants.

tulipifera, -us, -um (too-lip-iff′er-a). Bearing tulip-like flowers. *Tulipifera* is also an obsolete generic name for the tulip-tree.

TULIPOMANIA. A mania, amounting to hysteria, for the raising and breeding of tulips which swept over Holland in the early 17th century. Gambling and speculation in tulip bulbs reached such a pass that the Dutch government stopped it after $10,000 was paid for a single bulb about 1630.

TULIP ORCHID = *Cattleya citrina.*

TULIP POPLAR = *Liriodendron Tulipifera.* See TULIP-TREE.

TULIP POPPY = *Papaver glaucum.* See POPPY.

TULIP-TREE. A magnificent North American forest tree of the genus **Liriodendron** (lir-i-o-den′dron), belonging to the magnolia family. There are only 2 species, one in the New World, the other in central China. The native tulip-tree, **L. Tulipifera,** also known as whitewood, yellow poplar, and tulip poplar, is a columnar or broadly pyramidal tree up to 150 ft. high, without branches on the lower part of the trunk if in the forest, but often low-branched in the open. Leaves alternate,* broadly oval, or saddle-shaped, the tip very blunt and deeply notched, 3–5½ in. long, stalked. Over each leaf bud are 2 conspicuous stipules* which are long-persistent. Flowers terminal, solitary, showy, tulip- or lily-like, about 2½ in. wide, the 6 petals greenish-white but with an orange band at the base. Sepals 3. Stamens* numerous. Fruit a cone-like mass of long-persistent carpels (*see* PISTIL). Tulip-trees make magnificent lawn specimens, and prefer rich, reasonably moist sites. They are moved with considerable difficulty and only young trees (balled and burlapped, *see* PLANTING) should be tried, and planted only in the spring. Propagated by stratified seeds, or by grafting. Eastern N.A. from Ont. to Fla., Miss., and Wis. June. Hardy from zone* 3 southward. The *var.* **pyramidalis** is a narrowly pyramidal form. (*Liriodendron* is from the Greek for lily and tree, in allusion to the shape of the flowers.) For a tree called tulip-tree in Aust. *see* LAGUNARIA PATERSONI and for one so called in Fla. *see* SPATHODEA CAMPANULATA.

TULP = *Moraea polystachya.*

TUMION = *Torreya.*

Tuna (too′na). Tropical American name for several edible prickly pears. *See* OPUNTIA.

TUNG-OIL TREE. Valuable, economic trees of the spurge family, chiefly from tropical parts of Asia, and constituting the genus **Aleurites** (al-your-i′teez), which besides the one below contains only 5 other species, some of them long cult. in China and Jap. The only one cult. in the U.S. is

---

* Special articles on the subjects indicated by an asterisk (*) will be found at the words so marked.

A. fordi, the tung-oil or China wood-oil tree. Leaves alternate,* ovalish and sometimes 3-lobed, 3–5 in. long. Flowers unisexual,* not showy, mostly in terminal clusters (for details *see* EUPHORBIACEAE). Fruit 2–3 in. in diameter, a smooth drupe.* (*Aleurites* is from the Greek for flour, in allusion to the mealy appearance of some species.)

CULTURE

There are over 100,000 acres devoted to the tung-tree, although its requirements are exacting. It is not satisfactory in the warmer parts of Fla., as it needs a period of winter chilling. Its early flowering and the danger of these flowers being killed by early frosts is great. Its most favorable sites are found in a belt scarcely 75 miles wide, along the Gulf Coast, the northern part of Fla., and extreme southern and southwestern Ga. This hort. industry is based upon importations made by explorers of the U.S. Department of Agriculture.

Tung-oil (China wood-oil) is the oil expressed from the seed of the tung-oil (*Aleurites fordi*) and another Asiatic tree not cult. here. This oil has been used for centuries in China, the native habitat of the trees, and is imported into the U.S. in amounts exceeding 100 million pounds annually. It has numerous uses but is utilized chiefly in the manufacture of varnishes and high-grade paints and in insulating and waterproofing compounds.

In America, only the tung-oil tree (*A. fordi*) is grown commercially. The tree grows rapidly, attaining a mature size in about 10 years, and begins fruiting at an early age. Maturing in late Sept. and Oct., the apple-like fruits fall to the ground and harvesting consists merely in picking them up. They are allowed to dry and are then ready for oil expression, but may be kept for several months without deterioration. Oil extraction is wholly a mechanical process, the hulls being removed by a decorticator and oil expressed from the ground seed by an expeller. Air-dried seeds contain approximately ⅓ their weight in oil.

Although planted on a wide range of soils, including sands, clays, and loams, the preference tends toward loamy types, mostly somewhat acid, about pH 5–6. Thorough drainage is essential and fertilizers are required. Fertilizer kind and quantity will depend on the soils on which planted; usually nitrogen is applied at first, followed with complete mixtures on bearing trees. Leguminous summer cover crops, chiefly the crotalarias, are extensively planted. Pruning requirements are limited to shaping the development of the young tree and later removal of dead wood. Thorough and regular cultivation of young trees is practiced, amounts decreasing with attainment of maturity in the planting.

Propagation is by seeds and budding. Seeds are planted in Feb. and require about 60 days for germination. Seedlings attain a height of 3 to 5 ft. in one season and are of sufficient size and preferred age for transplanting that winter. Planting distances are from 12½ × 30 ft. to 30 × 30 ft. Varieties are mainly based on whether fruits are borne singly or in clusters; the latter yields larger crops and is preferred. Pests and diseases are of little consequence and no spraying has been required. Three scale insects, 2 diseases, and root-knot have been reported. The last seriously affects young seedlings, but not older trees, on nematode-infested soils, and is overcome by planting seeds on newly cleared lands. — G. D. R.

TUNICA (too'ni-ka). Hardy annual or perennial herbs, comprising about 30 species of the family Caryophyllaceae, natives of Eurasia, grown for ornament. They are low-growing plants of tufted and spreading habit. Leaves alternate, small, lance-shaped, about ½ in. long. Flowers pale pink, lilac, or white, in terminal-branching clusters. Calyx of 5 sepals. Corolla of 5 petals. Stamens* 10. Fruit a capsule.* (*Tunica* is from the Latin for a tunic, in allusion to the close-fitting calyx.*)

The saxifrage pink is easily cult. in any ordinary garden soil. Propagated by seeds or division of roots. Seeds should be sown ¹⁄₁₆ in. deep in early spring in cold frame or outdoor seedbed in ordinary garden soil. As soon as large enough to handle they may be planted out in permanent positions. Division of roots may be made in early spring.

Saxifraga. Saxifrage pink; also tunic flower and coat flower. Hardy perennial, growing to 10 in. high, of tufted* and spreading habit. Stems thin and wiry. Leaves small, lance-shaped, to ½ in. long. Flowers pink or lilac, in terminal-branching clusters. Petals deeply notched. Eu. There are several hort. color forms, and one is double-flowered. July to frost.

TUNICATED BULB. *See* BULB.

TUNIC FLOWER = *Tunica Saxifraga.*

TUNKA = *Benincasa hispida.*

tuolumnensis, -e (too-o-loom-nen'sis). From or near Tuolumne County, Calif.

TUPELO, TUPELO GUM = *Nyssa sylvatica.*

TURBAN BUTTERCUP = *Ranunculus asiaticus.* See BUTTERCUP.

turbaniformis, -e (tur-ban-i-for'mis). Turban-shaped.

TURBAN SQUASH = *Cucurbita maxima turbaniformis.* For culture *see* SQUASH.

turbinata, -us, -um (tur-bi-nay'ta). Top-shaped.

TURF. Good turf is the final reward for having made a good lawn, kept it fresh and green and reasonably free from weeds. *See* LAWN.

Such a reward is the finest possible source of sods for repairing lawns, laying along the edges of roads or paths, for steep banks, or for making the attractive grass steps.

Sods should be cut about 12 in. wide and 15 in. long and either used at once, or

---

* Special articles on the subjects indicated by an asterisk (*) will be found at the words so marked.

stacked face to face, in the shade. In no case should they be kept stacked for more than two days, or the grass will become yellowish or whitish, and if left too long killed outright.

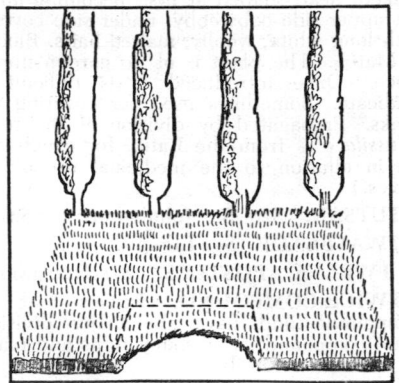

When turf edges are injured, cut the piece as shown by dotted line.

In laying turf there are only two important things to remember. (1) Prepare the soil where it is going, just as carefully as if seeding down a lawn, but enough below finished grade to take care of the thickness of the sods (2–3 in.). (2) In laying the sods see that their edges touch as closely as possible and if there are broken corners fill in with good topsoil, after which the sod should be thoroughly tamped down with a rammer. Merely patting it with the back of a spade is not enough. It must be firmly packed down on the fresh soil and then well watered.

If the turfing is on a very steep bank or on the rim of a grass step, the sods had better be pegged down (wooden meat skewers will do), until the roots have gotten firm hold.

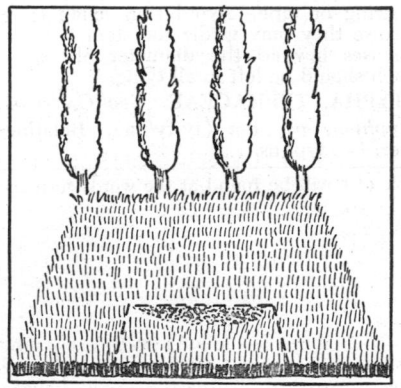

Reverse the broken sod, making a clean edge, and do the re-seeding or re-sodding away from the edge.

Fresh sod on steep banks may otherwise be washed away in a downpour.

If large areas are to be sodded, which, of course, is the quickest way to get a lawn, the freshly laid sod, instead of being rammed, may be thoroughly sprinkled and then rolled with a roller. All holes should be filled with soil or with the mixture of soil and grass seed mentioned in the section on repairing lawns at LAWN. Old or broken sods are, of course, the finest sort of material for the compost° pile.

TURFING DAISY = *Matricaria tchihat-chewi.*

turgida, -us, -um (tur'gi-da). Turgid, *i.e.,* inflated or full; used mostly of plant cells which are swollen because distended with water.

TURION. A shoot developing from the underground bud of a rootstock. Turions are often scaly, but as applied to blackberries and raspberries turions may not be scaly. They are merely young canes which flower and fruit the second year and then die down. *Turion* is also used for the resting winter shoot of some aquatics, as in the frog's-bit.

TURKESTAN MILLET = *Setaria italica rubrofructa.*

TURKEY-BEARD. See XEROPHYLLUM.

TURKEY-CORN = *Dicentra canadensis.*

TURKEY OAK = *Quercus Cerris.* See OAK.

TURKISH HAZEL = *Corylus Colurna.* See HAZEL.

TURKISH TULIP = *Tulipa acuminata.*

TURK'S-CAP or TURK'S-HEAD CACTUS = *Melocactus communis.*

TURK'S-CAP LILY. See LILIUM CHALCEDONICUM, L. MARTAGON, and L. SUPERBUM.

TURMERIC. See CURCUMA LONGA.

TURNIP (*Brassica Rapa*). As commonly understood in America, the turnip is a flattish, rooted, white-fleshed plant, the foliage of which is hairy. But often called turnip is the much larger-rooted, yellow-fleshed plant with bluish-green, smooth foliage. The latter is properly the rutabaga and its culture and varieties should be sought at RUTABAGA, although it is often called yellow turnip. It has a more elongated root with a neck.° See illustration at RUTABAGA. For the Indian turnip *see* ARISAEMA TRIPHYLLUM.

Seeds sown about the last week in July or early in Aug. will provide a crop when they are most wanted in the late fall and winter. The plant is a biennial and if left in the ground all winter will bloom and set seed the following spring.

The seeds should be sown in drills about ¾ in. deep and thickly enough so that the plants can be thinned to 5–6 in. apart. For hoeing or a wheel cultivator, keep the rows about 15 in. apart, but 24–30 in. if power or horse machines are to be used.

The plant does best in a loose friable° loam, and the product is much better if quickly grown. While it is primarily a late fall and winter vegetable, very early varieties have been developed which may be sown as soon as the ground can be worked in the spring. Such can be harvested in the early summer, and should be, because if left in the ground they will go to flower and the roots are then soon useless.

Cultivate as for any other root crop, being careful not to injure young roots with tools. The plant responds to rich soil, but top-dressing with nitrate of soda should be avoided. If necessary, use any well-balanced fertilizer (*see* FERTILIZERS), working it in between the rows about 5 weeks after the seed is planted. The turnip is a cool-season plant and does not like hot, dry regions. The best vars. are Purple-top White Globe, Yellow Globe, Shogoin (for greens), and Seven Top (for greens in the South).

INSECT PESTS. Control flea beetles on tops with pesticide #1 or arsenicals (*see* SPRAYS AND DUSTS). Do not contaminate greens with insecticides closer to harvest than indicated on label. Aphids can be controlled with pesticide #21 if applications are made promptly upon first signs of injury before leaves roll. Cabbage maggot and other species attack turnips in spring and fall. Applications of pesticide #15 dust over the row at weekly intervals when roots begin to enlarge will prevent this damage. To control vegetable weevil, use pesticide #15 dust over the rows.

DISEASES. *See* CABBAGE.

TURNIP CABBAGE. A name applied both to the kohlrabi and the rutabaga. *See* both vegetables.

TURNIP-PARSNIP. *See* PARSNIP.

TURNIP-ROOTED CABBAGE. *See* KOHLRABI.

TURNIP-ROOTED CELERY = Celeriac. *See* CELERY.

TURNIP-ROOTED CHERVIL = *Chaerophyllum bulbosum*.

TURNIP-ROOTED PARSLEY. *See* PARSLEY.

TURTLEHEAD = *Chelone glabra*.

TUSSIE-MUSSIE. An Old English word for a nosegay.

TUSSILAGO (tuss-i-lay′go). Perennial herbs of only 1 species of the family Compositae, and a native of Eurasia. The only species, **T. Farfara**, is the coltsfoot; also called clayweed and coughwort. Rootstocks

thick, and spreading entirely underground. Flowering stem appearing before the leaves, 1–1½ ft. high, covered with scaly bracts.* Flowers bright yellow in solitary flat heads, ½–¾ in. across, each head surrounded by a single row of bracts.* Leaves basal, long-stalked, heart-shaped at first, becoming angular, upper side cobwebby, under side covered with long white, woolly, matted hairs. Blooms in March. The plant is of no garden importance. Once introduced it is difficult to eradicate. Sometimes used for covering dry banks. Propagated by division of the roots. (*Tussilago* is from the Latin, for cough and go, in allusion to the medicinal use of the leaves.)

TUTSAN. *See* St. John's-wort at SAINT.

TWAYBLADE. *See* LIPARIS.

"TWELVE APOSTLES." *See* NEOMARICA.

TWICE-COMPOUND. Leaves that are compound* and have the major divisions again compound, as in many ferns and plants of the carrot family.

TWINBERRY = *Mitchella repens* and *Lonicera involucrata*.

TWINFLOWER. *See* LINNAEA.

TWINING PLANTS. *See* VINES.

TWIN-LEAF = *Jeffersonia diphylla*.

TWIN SISTERS = *Linnaea borealis*.

TWIN-SPUR = *Diascia barberae*.

TWISTED EGLANTINE = *Lonicera Periclymenum*.

TWISTED HEATH = *Erica cinerea*.

TWISTED STALK. *See* STREPTOPUS.

TWO-LIPPED. *See* LIP.

TWO-RANKED. *See* DISTICHOUS.

TYING. Fastening plants to a stake, wall, or trellis should be done so that there is no constriction of the stem, even when increased girth comes with subsequent growth. The best tying materials are soft string, tape, or raffia, the last not as durable as string or tape. Avoid thin string or wire because they may girdle the stem if its girth increases beyond the diameter of the loop which should be left in all tying.

TYPHA, TYPHACEAE. *See* CAT-TAIL.

typhina, *-us*, *-um* (ty-fy′na). Relating to fever; *i.e.*, typhus.

---

* Special articles on the subjects indicated by an asterisk (*) will be found at the words so marked.

U

ucranica, -us, -um (you-kray'ni-ka). From the Ukraine.

UDO. See Aralia cordata.

Ugni (ug'ni). An obsolete generic name for the Chilean guava (*Myrtus Ugni*).

ULE = *Castilla elastica.*

ULEX. See Furze.

uliginosa, -us, -um (you-li-ji-nō'sa). Of wet or marshy places.

ULMACEAE (ul-may'see-ee). The elm family has only 15 genera and about 160 species, nearly all trees, some of the cult. sorts being among our most valuable shade trees. Three genera are in cult. *Ulmus* (see Elm) is by far the most important. *Celtis* (see Hackberry) is quite secondary and *Zelkova* (Asiatic trees and shrubs) is chiefly of botanical interest.

Trees with a watery juice, differing in this respect from the closely related, milky-juiced Moraceae. Leaves alternate,* prevailingly lopsided (inequilateral) at the base. Flowers inconspicuous, without petals, the male and female ones sometimes separate, but on the same tree, often appearing before the leaves unfold. Fruit winged in the elm — nut-like or fleshy in other genera.

Technical flower characters: Calyx of 4–5, rarely more or fewer, sepals which are usually more or less united. Petals none. Stamens* 4–5, rarely twice as many. Ovary superior,* 1-celled.

ULMARIA. See Filipendula.

ulmifolia, -us, -um (ul-mi-fo'li-a). With elm-like leaves.

ulmoides (ul-moy'deez, but see Oïdes). Like an elm (*Ulmus*).

ULMUS. See Elm.

UMBEL. A flower cluster in which all the individual flower stalks arise at one point,

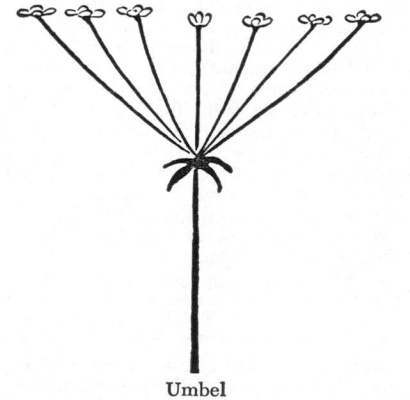

Umbel

the cluster being flat-topped or ball-like, depending on the length of the individual stalks. Umbels are found throughout the carrot family (hence called Umbelliferae), also among the onions and in some of its relatives and in a few milkweeds. In some plants the smaller umbels are themselves grouped in a large umbel which is then said to be a compound umbel.

umbellata, -us, -um (um-bel-lay'ta). Umbellate; i.e., bearing umbels.*

UMBELLIFERAE (um-bel-lif'fer-ee). The carrot, celery, or parsnip family is far more important for its herbs, condiments, or vegetables than for ornamental garden plants. It is by some called Ammiaceae, or Apiaceae.

The family is a huge one (300 genera and probably 3000 species), easily recognized from its prevailingly compound leaves and the arrangement of its flowers in an umbel.* Sometimes the umbel is twice- or thrice-compound, and in a few genera the whole cluster is very large. Each individual flower (often wrongly called a "ray") of the umbel is very small. In *Eryngium* the flowers are in heads. The characters separating the genera reside in the peculiar, usually aromatic fruit (often called "seed") of this family, and are wholly technical.

From the gardening standpoint the cult. genera may be easily divided upon their use, as follows:

1. Furnishing vegetables:
   Apium (see Celery), *Arracacia, Chaerophyllum, Daucus* (see Carrot), *Pastinaca* (see Parsnip).
2. Furnishing seasonings, condiments, garnishes and herbs:
   Anethum (see Dill), *Anthriscus, Angelica, Carum* (see Caraway), *Coriandrum* (see Coriander), *Cuminum, Ferula, Foeniculum* (see Fennel), *Levisticum, Petroselinum* (see Parsley), *Pimpinella* (see Anise). In this connection see also Herb Gardening.
3. Garden flowers for the less important parts of the open border or wild garden, none very showy:
   Aegopodium, Astrantia, Cicuta, Conium (juice deadly poisonous), *Eryngium* (most showy of this group), *Heracleum,* and *Sium.*

There are only two other cult. genera; *Myrrhis,* which is the sweet cicely of Eu., and the Australian *Trachymene,* which is the beautiful little blue lace-flower of the florists' shops.

The stems of many of these plants are hollow, and the leafstalk is often sheath-like or expanded as in the edible celery. The

* Special articles on the subjects indicated by an asterisk (*) will be found at the words so marked.

whole umbel° (*see* above) often has a series of bracts° beneath each subdivision of the whole cluster. This is a very characteristic feature of some genera, and is found in nearly every genus.

Technical flower characters: Flowers regular,° sometimes the outer ones in the umbel sterile and ray-like. Sepals very small or none. Petals 5. Stamens° 5, alternate with the petals and inserted on a ring-like disk. Ovary inferior,° 2-celled. Styles 2. Fruit consisting of 2 ribbed or winged, 1-seeded carpels which separate at the base, but are attached at the top, often provided internally with (aromatic) oil tubes.

UMBELLULARIA (um-bel-you-lair′i-a). A single species of aromatic, evergreen trees, known as the California laurel, spice tree, bay tree, or balm-of-heaven, and to science as **U. californica**, of the family Lauraceae. It is a handsome medium-sized tree, rarely over 25 ft. high, with alternate,° short-stalked, ovalish or oblongish leaves, 3–5 in. long and without marginal teeth. Flowers perfect, yellowish-green, in dense clusters (umbels°) which are ¾ in. thick. Calyx and corolla indistinguishable as such, soon falling. Stamens° many. Fruit a fleshy, egg-shaped, yellowish-green drupe° about 1 in. long. Calif. to Ore. Jan.–May. Hardy along the Pacific Coast and in the East from zone° 6 southward. It prefers reasonably moist soils and is propagated by seeds. In Oregon known as myrtle or myrtlewood. (*Umbellularia* is Latin for a little umbel, in allusion to the flower clusters.)

UMBILICUS = *Cotyledon.*

UMBONATE. With a rounded or bluntish, boss-like projection, arising from an otherwise smooth surface. Umbos are not often found in plants, but a common example is the fruit of the lemon. The cone-scales of some trees in the pine family are also umbonate.

UMBRA = *Phytolacca dioica.*

umbraculifera, -us, -um (um-brack-you-liff′er-a). Umbrella-bearing, hence, umbrella-like.

umbraculiformis, -e (um-brack-you-ly-for′mis). Umbrella-shaped.

UMBRELLA CATALPA = *Catalpa bignonioides nana.*

UMBRELLA LEAF = *Diphylleia cymosa.*

UMBRELLA PALM = *Hedyscepe canterburyana.*

UMBRELLA PINE. A single species of Japanese evergreen trees of the pine family, constituting the genus **Sciadopitys** (sy-a-dop′-i-tis), widely planted for ornament. The only species, **S. verticillata**, is, in Jap., a tree up to 120 ft. high, but much less as cult. here. It is a beautiful evergreen with nearly smooth bark and horizontal branches. Leaves of two sorts, some short and scale-like, the others very handsome, dark glossy-green, and growing in umbrella-like whorls of 15–35 leaves. These are narrow, line-like, nearly 6 in. long, rather soft-textured, furrowed, and with 2 light bands beneath. These are technically

cladophylls° and not true leaves, but appearing so. Flowers none in the garden sense, consisting only of bunches of stamens,° and the female flowers only of naked ovules° between scales. Fruit a woody cone, 3–5 in. long. The umbrella pine is a very handsome, but slow-growing tree, hardy from zone° 4 southward, and does best in places not too dry and windy. For culture *see* EVERGREENS. (*Sciadopitys* is from the Greek for umbrella and pine, in allusion to the leaf arrangement.)

UMBRELLA PLANT = *Cyperus alternifolius* and *Peltiphyllum peltatum.*

UMBRELLA TREE = *Magnolia tripetala* and *Schefflera actinophylla.* For the Texas umbrella tree *see* MELIA AZEDARACH UMBRACULIFORMIS.

umbrosa, -us, -um (um-brō′sa). Shade-enduring.

UMKOKOLO = *Dovyalis Caffra.*

uncinata, -us, -um (un-si-nay′ta). Having a hooked tip.

undata, -us, -um (un-day′ta). Wavy.

UNDER-SHRUB. A low shrub, or sometimes (incorrectly) a stout herb that is woody at the base. An *under-shrub* may be planted under larger ones. The term is not synonymous with sub-shrub.

UNDER-STOCK = Stock.

undulata, -us, -um (un-dew-lay′ta). Undulate; *i.e.,* wavy or wavy-margined.

Unedo (you-nee′do). Classical name of the strawberry tree (*Arbutus Unedo*).

unguicularis, -e (un-gwi-kew-lar′is). With a narrowed base or shank (*i.e.,* clawed°).

Unguis-cati (un-gwis-kat′i). A cat's claw.

UNICORN-PLANT. See PROBOSCIDEA.

UNICORN-ROOT = *Veltheimia viridifolia.*

uniflora, -us, -um (you-ni-flow′ra). One-flowered.

unilateralis, -e (you-ni-lat-er-ral′is). One-sided.

UNIOLA (you-ny′o-la). Spike grass. American perennial grasses, comprising 9 or 10 species, the one below a good ornamental grass. It is a strong-growing plant, 4–5 ft. high. Leaves grass-like, about 9 in. long and 1 in. wide, clasping the stem. Flower spikes in flat, terminal, loose-branching clusters. (*Uniola* is an ancient Latin name for an unknown plant and of little significance here.)

U. latifolia is cult. for the showy ornamental spikes which can be cut and dried in Aug. for house decoration. Easily cult. Propagated by seeds or division of roots. Seeds should be sown ⅛ in. deep in open border where required to bloom. They prefer sandy soil. Division of roots may be made in Oct. or early spring.

latifolia. Flower spikes on slender, drooping stalks, the clusters graceful, about 8 in. long, the stalks very slender. One of the best native ornamental grasses. N.J. to Fla. and Tex.

unioloides (you-ni-o-loy′deez, but *see* OïDES). Like a grass of the genus *Uniola.*

° Special articles on the subjects indicated by an asterisk (°) will be found at the words so marked.

UNION. The proper uniting of a stock and cion* in a grafting operation. *See* GRAFTING.

UNISEXUAL. As to flowers, of one sex only; that is, bearing only stamens in one flower and pistils in another. *See also* MONOECIOUS, DIOECIOUS, and PERFECT.

UNSHIU. Japanese name of the Satsuma orange.

UPLAND COTTON = *Gossypium hirsutum.*

UPLAND CRESS. *See* BARBAREA and LEPIDIUM SATIVUM.

URBINIA (ur-bin'i-a). *See* ECHEVERIA AGAVOIDES.

URCEOLATE. Urn-shaped; mostly used to describe a corolla.

URD = *Phaseolus Mungo.*

UREA. *See* Nitrogen at FERTILIZERS.

urens (your'enz). Stinging or burning.

URGINEA (ur-gin'e-a). Half-hardy bulbous perennials, comprising about 75 species, belonging to the lily family, and natives of the Mediterranean region, India, and S. Af. Bulbs large and scaly. Leaves basal, long and narrow. Leafless flowering stalk appearing before the leaves. Flowers whitish, yellowish or pink, small, growing in the axils* of bracts* or in terminal racemes.* Calyx of 3 colored sepals. Corolla of 3 petals, alternating with the sepals. Stamens* 6. Fruit a 3-sided capsule,* many-seeded. (*Urginea* was named from an Arabian tribe in Algeria known as Ben Urgin.)

These bulbs are cult. for ornament. The bulbs of *U. maritima* are gathered in their wild state for their drug properties, and also contain a large amount of sugar, for which reason they are sometimes used for making whiskey in Sicily.

maritima. Sea onion. Sea squill. Bulbs 4–6 in. thick. Leaves to 1½ ft. long and 4 in. wide, lance-shaped, fleshy, shiny green. Flowers numerous, whitish, ½ in. long in a raceme to 1½ ft. long. Flowering stalk leafless, to 5 ft. long. Canary Islands to Syria and S. Af. It is closely related to, and should be grown as, *Scilla,* which see.

URSINIA (ur-sin'i-a). Annual or perennial herbs or sub-shrubs, comprising about 60 species of the family Compositae, and natives of S. Af. Leaves alternate,* usually deeply cut into narrow lobes, the margins toothed. Flowers in solitary heads, daisy-like. Ray* florets orange or yellow, sometimes purplish-brown at base, the disk florets dark bluish-purple or brown. (Named for John Ursinus of Regensburg, 17th century botanical author.) Sometimes spelled *Ursinea.*

Ursinias make showy garden plants, but only the tender annual species are cult. and they will stand a considerable period of drought, especially *U. anethoides. See* ANNUALS. They may also be grown in the greenhouse as pot plants for early spring flowering, in which case seeds should be sown in Jan.

anethoides. Also known as *Sphenogyne anethoides.* Annual, growing to 1 ft. high, of bushy habit. Leaves deeply cut into narrow lobes. Flowering stalk thin and wiry. Flowers in numerous, solitary heads. Ray florets orange, purple at base; the disk florets* purple.

pulchra. Also known as *Sphenogyne speciosa.* Bushy annual, growing to 2 ft. high. Leaves deeply cut into lobes, each lobe again cut. Flowering stalks bearing small lobed leaves. Flowers in solitary heads about 2 in. across. Ray florets* yellow or orange, marked purple at the base. Disk florets purple.

URTICA. *See* NETTLE.

URTICACEAE (ur-ti-kay'see-ee). The nettle family is of secondary hort. significance, although it has over 50 genera and perhaps 1500 species, largely tropical. The only cult. genera, *Boehmeria* (a tree-like, woody herb, yielding ramie), *Helxine* (a moss-like, prostrate herb of greenhouse or terrarium* culture), *Pellionia,* and *Pilea,* have no stinging hairs, but the nettle (*Urtica*), largely weedy, has them. Many of the non-hort. tropical trees have violently stinging hairs on the leaves and twigs.

Leaves opposite* or alternate.* Flowers always greenish and inconspicuous, in all the cult. genera, unisexual,* in various sorts of clusters. Fruit dry, 1-seeded (an achene*), sometimes surrounded by the fleshy calyx.

Technical flower characters: Male flowers with the calyx 4–5-parted. Female flowers with a tubular, or 3–5-parted calyx. Petals none. Stamens* 4–5. Ovary superior,* 1-celled.

urticaefolia, -us, -um (ur-ti-kee-fō'li-a). Having nettle-like leaves.

USAMBARA VIOLET = *Saintpaulia ionantha.*

usitatissima, -us, -um (you-si-ta-tiss'i-ma). Most useful.

usneoides (uz-nee-oy'deez, but *see* OÏDES). Resembling a lichen of the genus *Usnea. See* TILLANDSIA.

UTAH. The globe tulip is the state flower, the Colorado blue spruce the state tree, and the state lies wholly in zones* 3 and 4.

Many soil types occur in the state of Utah. Since most of the garden areas lie immediately west of the Wasatch Mountains, the garden soils are predominantly sandy loams to clay loams. They are almost entirely shore-line or river deposits. Immediately adjacent to the mountains the soils contain considerable sharp rock and much organic matter; consequently, they are gravelly and very black in color. The larger deltas that have been built by the Bear, Weber, and Provo river systems consist of relatively fine-textured sands, underlain and interspersed with more or less heavy clays. Many of the best agricultural soils occur where these sandy areas merge with the clay areas. Beyond these margins in one direction the soils become quite sandy in some places, while in the opposite direction they may be too heavy for garden purposes. Production of vegetables extends to the heavier soils in the valleys.

FRUITS. The chief fruits are peaches, apples, apricots, and pears. Sweet and sour cherries are produced on a smaller scale.

---

* Special articles on the subjects indicated by an asterisk (*) will be found at the words so marked.

In the southwest corner of the state, Washington County, is an area known as "Dixie." Here are produced some figs, pomegranates, walnuts, pecans, and European or *vinifera* grapes. The principal stone-fruit areas are located on the gravelly loam soils of the old Lake Bonneville terraces and on the gravelly deltas at the foot of the Wasatch Mountains in Salt Lake and Utah valleys. Peaches and sweet cherries are also grown in the Dixie area. The most important fruit-growing counties are Box Elder, Weber, Davis, Salt Lake, Utah, and Washington. Less important areas are located in Cache, Grand, Rich, and Emery counties. The chief areas for apples and pears are Utah, Salt Lake, Weber, and Washington counties. These pome fruits occupy the heavier soils and are usually situated farther from the mountains than the stone fruits. Peaches, apples, sweet cherries, pears, and some apricots are shipped out of the state as fresh fruits; and in addition, apricots, sweet and sour cherries, and some apples are canned.

Small fruits are grown in the same area as stone fruits with the addition of Rich County. They are grown mostly for local markets. Strawberries are more important than raspberries by a 2:1 ratio.

VEGETABLES. Vegetable production occupies an important position in the agriculture of the state. The Irish potato is the most important single crop. The center of production is shifting from the more populous counties near Great Salt Lake to counties in the southwestern part of the state where land values are not so high. The following counties are listed in order of importance for potato production: Iron, Beaver, Sevier, Weber, Washington, Piute, Davis, Utah, Box Elder, and Cache.

Approximately half of the farms report growing vegetable gardens for home use. This garden production represents an important enterprise in the state. While some home gardens and small market gardens are located in all counties of the state, Utah, Davis, Box Elder, Weber, Salt Lake, and Cache counties are the most important vegetable-growing counties and are listed in the order of their relative importance.

The production of vegetables for canning and freezing is important. Since canning crops are grown almost entirely on a contract basis, this industry affords the most certain source of cash income. Tomatoes, peas, sweet corn, snap beans, and cabbage are the major vegetable crops grown for canning and freezing. The cool mountain valleys in Cache, Box Elder, Weber, Sanpete, and Wasatch counties produce peas, sweet corn, and cabbage of the highest quality. These crops are also grown in Utah, Salt Lake, and Davis counties. Tomatoes and snap beans are grown primarily in Davis, Box Elder, Weber, Utah, and Salt Lake counties, with an important acreage of snap beans also in Cache County.

Onions, celery, cantaloupes, cabbage, and carrots are grown for exporting from the state. The areas of production are similar to those of canning crops, with the addition of Emery County where cantaloupes are grown and Iron and Sevier counties for the production of carrots. The soils and climate of various parts of Utah are admirably adapted to growing many high-quality fruits and vegetables. The chief limitation is that the supply of irrigation water is inadequate in certain areas.

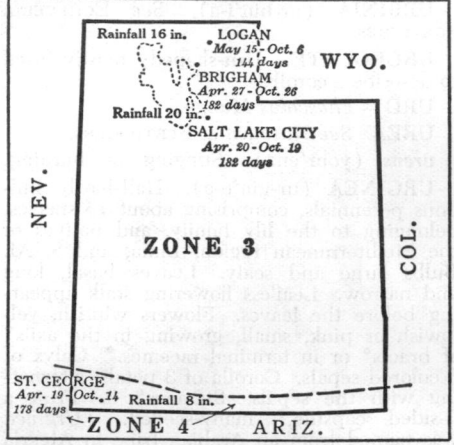

UTAH

The zones of hardiness crossing Utah are those shown on the map located at ZONE, which should be consulted for details. The dates are the average latest killing frost in spring and the first one in the fall. The figures below the dates show the average length of the growing season. Rainfall figures (in inches) are for total rainfall in the regions so indicated.

FROST AND RAINFALL DATA

Place	Average date of last killing frost in spring	Latest-known killing frost in spring
Logan	May 15	June 17
Brigham	Apr. 27	About May 15
Farmington	May 10	June 16
Salt Lake City	Apr. 20	June 18
Provo	May 24	June 17
St. George	Apr. 19	May 20

Place	Average date of earliest killing frost in fall	Earliest-known killing frost in fall
Logan	Oct. 6	Sept. 13
Brigham	Oct. 26	About Oct. 1
Farmington	Sept. 30	Sept. 8
Salt Lake City	Oct. 19	Sept. 22
Provo	Sept. 21	Aug. 31
St. George	Oct. 14	Sept. 13

* Special articles on the subjects indicated by an asterisk (*) will be found at the words so marked.

Month	Average precipitation by months in inches		
	Logan	Brigham	Farm-ington
January	1.75	2.17	2.01
February	1.37	2.25	1.37
March	1.98	2.33	2.52
April	1.66	1.50	2.15
May	2.27	2.28	2.49
June	0.93	1.32	1.06
July	0.62	0.85	0.56
August	0.68	0.46	0.79
September	1.25	1.15	1.05
October	1.38	1.42	1.61
November	1.28	1.67	1.44
December	1.00	1.28	2.04
Total annual	16.17	17.80	19.98

Month	Average precipitation by months in inches		
	Salt Lake City	Provo	St. George
January	1.32	1.55	1.04
February	1.48	1.69	0.98
March	2.06	1.71	1.76
April	2.08	1.44	0.44
May	2.01	1.63	0.37
June	0.88	0.78	0.10
July	0.58	0.66	0.74
August	0.75	0.65	0.74
September	0.94	0.90	0.69
October	1.44	1.29	0.59
November	1.35	1.13	0.52
December	1.37	1.46	0.89
Total annual	16.20	14.58	8.23

The address of the Agricultural Experiment Station which has kindly supplied this information about the state is Logan, Utah. The staff is always glad to answer gardening questions.

Garden club activities include several clubs affiliated with the Utah Associated Garden Clubs which was organized in 1934.

utilis, -e (you'ti-lis). Useful.

utilissima, -us, -um (you-til-liss'i-ma). Most useful.

UTRICLE. A small, often bladdery, 1-seeded fruit that does not split. It is found throughout the goosefoots (Chenopodiaceae) and the Amaranthaceae, the most familiar example being the fruit of the beet.

UTRICULARIA (you-trick-you-lair'i-a). A very large genus (by some considered several) of mostly aquatic or bog herbs, more interesting for their insectivorous habit than as hort. subjects. Of over 300 species, belonging to the family Lentibulariaceae, many tropical species are epiphytes,* and some live in the water found in the pitcher-like rosettes formed by certain plants of the pineapple family. Some of the tropical species are almost orchid-like, in their showy flowers, but are very rare in cult. All the temperate zone species grow in pools, in bogs, or on wet shores. Of these only **U. vulgaris**, the common bladderwort, is of any general hort. interest and it is grown as an aquarium plant. It has finely dissected floating or submerged leaves, about ¾ in. long and provided with numerous, small, insect-catching bladders. *See* INSECTIVOROUS PLANTS. Flowers yellow, about ½ in. long, very irregular,* borne in a few-flowered cluster (raceme*) which stands above the water 5–7 in. (For flower structure *see* LENTIBULARIACEAE.) The bladderwort is a good aquarium plant, a native of the north temperate zone, and some authorities consider the American plant different from the Eurasian form. It is perfectly hardy, and is propagated naturally by seeds and winter buds. (*Utricularia* is Latin for a little bladder, in allusion to the small, insect-catching bladders.)

utriculata, -us, -um (you-trick-you-lay'ta). Having a small, bladdery, 1-seeded fruit.

Uvaria (you-vair'i-a). Resembling a bunch of grapes.

Uva-ursi (you-va-ur'si). Latin for grape and bear; *i.e.*, the "bear's grape," now called bearberry. *See* ARCTOSTAPHYLOS and WILLOW.

uvifera, -us, -um (you-viff'er-a). Grape-bearing; or bearing fruits in a grape-like cluster.

UVULARIA (you-vew-lair'i-a). Bellwort. North American hardy perennial herbs, comprising about 5 species, belonging to the lily family (Liliaceae). They have thick, creeping rootstocks, the alternate leaves not stalked, sometimes clasping the stem, lance-shaped, light green, parallel-veined. Flowers yellow, bell-shaped, or tubular, drooping, solitary, at the ends of the branches. Calyx of 3 colored sepals. Corolla of 3 petals alternating with the sepals. Stamens* 6. Fruit a 3-celled capsule.* (*Uvularia* is from the Latin for palate, in allusion to the hanging flowers.)

These spring-flowering plants are not usually cult., but if grown in light, peaty soil and shade make useful plants for the border or wild garden. They are useful for planting against a north wall. Propagated by division in Oct.

grandiflora. Strawflower. Cornflower. Wood daffodil. Strong-growing, hardy perennial to 1½ ft. high. Stem forked. Leaves not stalked, clasping the stem, lance-shaped, to 5 in. long, dark green, covered with fine white hairs on the under side. Flowers yellow, bell-shaped, to 1½ in. long, drooping at the ends of the branches. Quebec to Ga. and Okla. April–May.

perfoliata. Mealy bellwort. Mohawkweed. Slender perennial to 1½ ft. high. Stem forked. Leaves not stalked, clasping the stem, broadly lance-shaped, to 5 in. long, dark green. Flowers pale yellow, bell-shaped, 1 in. long, drooping at the ends of the branches. Ont. to Fla. and Miss.

sessilifolia. Wild oats. Also known as *Oakesia sessilifolia* or *Oakesiella sessilifolia*. Perennial to 1 ft. high. Leaves lance-shaped, to 3 in. long, deep green, covered with fine hairs on the under side. Flowers greenish-yellow, tube-shaped, to 1¼ in. long, drooping at the ends of the branches. Eastern N.A.

---

* Special articles on the subjects indicated by an asterisk (*) will be found at the words so marked.

V

Vaccaria (vak-kair′i-a). An obsolete generic name for certain cult. plants here included in *Saponaria* (which see).

VACCINIACEAE. See Ericaceae.

VACCINIUM (vak-sin′i-um). A very large genus of erect or prostrate shrubs of the family Ericaceae (by some considered as of the separate family Vacciniaceae), one grown for ornament, but of chief hort. interest because it contains both the blueberry and cranberry. Of over 150 species, which range from the Arctic Circle to the summits of tropical mountains, only those below are of garden interest, and all are of special growth requirements, as noted below. Leaves alternate,* short-stalked, often minutely hairy on the margins. Flowers generally small, not showy, urn-shaped in the blueberries, but deeply 4-parted and with recurved corolla-lobes in the cranberry. Stamens* 8 or 10. Fruit a true, many-seeded berry, crowned with the often persistent lobes of the calyx.* (*Vaccinium* is the Latin name for the whortleberry or the blueberry.)

The blueberries need special cultural requirements which are described in detail at Blueberry. The cranberry, needing special conditions such as are found in natural cranberry bogs, can only be grown where these conditions occur naturally or can be controlled. See Cranberry. The chief remaining species of hort. interest is V. *Vitis-Idaea*, an evergreen, prostrate plant, the culture of which is described at Wild Garden. No plant of the genus *Vaccinium* can be grown under ordinary garden conditions, as they need acid soils ranging from pH 4.0–5.0 (*see* Acid and Alkali Soils). Some confuse the true blueberries with the huckleberries. For the distinctions *see* Blueberry.

Several other wild species of *Vaccinium*, all of the blueberry type, may occasionally be transferred to the garden, but they are scarcely hort. subjects. The identity of many of the wild and cult. species of blueberry is in much doubt as some are diploids,* tetraploids,* etc.

angustifolium. Low-bush blueberry. A deciduous shrub, 12–18 in. high, the narrowly elliptic leaves about 1 in. long. Flowers about ¼ in. long, urn-shaped, white and often with reddish lines. Fruit blue-black, with a bloom, about ¼ in. in diameter. Eastern N.A. April–May. Hardy from zone* 2 southward. Stands heat and dryness.

corymbosum. High-bush blueberry. A spreading, bushy shrub, 8–12 ft. high, the young twigs yellowish-green and warty. Leaves ovalish or elliptic, 2–3 in. long. Flowers about ⅓ in. long, urn-shaped, white or pinkish. Fruit bluish-black, with a bloom. Eastern N.A., mostly in the swamps or bogs. May. Hardy from zone* 2 southward. There are several closely related wild species which are sometimes gathered for *V. corymbosum*. For culture *see* Blueberry.

macrocarpon. Cranberry. Similar to V. *Oxycoccus*, but with blunt leaves, longer stems, and the fruit nearly ¾ in. in diameter. Northern N.A. June–July. Hardy from zone* 2 to 5, and the commercial source of cranberry. For culture and varieties *see* Cranberry. Sometimes known as *Oxycoccus macrocarpus*.

ovatum. Florist's "huckleberry." An evergreen shrub, 7–12 ft. high, with hairy twigs, and very leafy. Leaves brilliant green above, a little paler beneath, oblong or ovalish, ¾–3 in. long, faintly toothed. Flowers bell-shaped, white or pink, about ¼ in. long. Fruit black. Pacific Coast, British Columbia to central Calif. April–May. Its harvested twigs comprise the leading foliage accessory of the florists, to such an extent that the shrub is threatened with extinction.

Oxycoccus. A wild, small-fruited cranberry, and a prostrate, creeping vine with very slender stems. Leaves pointed, evergreen, about ⅓ in. long, bluish-green beneath. Flowers pinkish, about ¼ in. long, deeply 4-parted, and borne in small terminal clusters. Fruit bright red, about ⅓ in. in diameter. Arctic and colder regions of the north temperate zone. May–June. Hardy from zone* 4 northward. Not a commercial cranberry, but the fruits harvested from the wild and used for preserves or jellies.

virgatum. Blueberry. A shrub somewhat resembling V. *corymbosum*, but with the corolla more cylindric, and with black fruit having only a slight bloom. Southern Va. to Fla. and La. April–May. Hardy from zone* 6 southward. Of chief interest as the source of some of the improved strains of blueberry cult. in Fla. See Blueberry. Called by some V. *marianum* or V. *atrococcum*.

Vitis-Idaea. Cowberry; also called red whortleberry, foxberry and lingon-berry. A prostrate, evergreen plant, the rootstocks creeping, but the stems erect, 4–9 in. high. Leaves ovalish, shining green, about 1 in. long. Flowers bell-shaped or urn-shaped, about ¼ in. long, pink, and grouped in nodding clusters (racemes *). Cooler parts of Eurasia and N.A.

vagans (vay′ganz). Wandering or vagrant.

VAGNERA = *Smilacina*.

valdiviensis, -e (val-di-vi-en′sis). From Valdivia, an old name for Chile.

VALERIAN. For the true valerian *see* Valeriana. For other plants to which the name valerian is sometimes applied *see* Centranthus, Fedia, and Polemonium.

VALERIANA (va-leer-i-ā′na). Tender and hardy perennial herbs, under-shrubs, or shrubs, comprising about 200 species of the family Valerianaceae, found distributed mostly in the temperate and colder regions of the northern hemisphere and the tropical

---

* Special articles on the subjects indicated by an asterisk (*) will be found at the words so marked.

and warm regions of the southern hemisphere. Rootstocks thick, spreading, and strong-scented. Stem leaves opposite,* lance-shaped, sometimes cut into lobes, the margins sometimes toothed. Flowers small, white or rose, in compact roundish clusters at the ends of the branches. Calyx not conspicuous at first, but later it develops 5–15 hairy appendages. Corolla narrowly tubular, to ½ in. long, opening into 5 distinct lobes. Stamens* 3. Fruit 3-celled, each cell 1-seeded. (*Valeriana* is probably named for the Emperor Valerianus.)

Valerianas make good border plants and are easily cult. and only the herbaceous species are grown. Propagated by seeds or division of the rootstocks. Seeds should be sown ⅟₁₆ in. deep, in light sandy soil, in sunny positions in cold frame or outdoor seedbed. They may be transplanted as soon as large enough to handle. Division of the rootstocks may be made in Oct. or early spring.

coccinea = *Centranthus ruber*.
officinalis. Common valerian. Garden heliotrope. Cherry pie. Strong-growing perennial herb, 2–5 ft. high. Rootstocks thick and spreading. Leaves broadly lance-shaped, the upper leaves cut into 7–10 pairs of lance-shaped, sometimes toothed segments. Flowers pink, white or lavender, fragrant, in compact roundish clusters at the ends of the branches. The roots of this species are used medicinally. Eu. and northern As., naturalized in N.A.
Phu. Cretan spikenard. Stout-growing perennial, to 3 ft. high. Basal leaves long-stalked, sometimes toothed at the base. Stem leaves divided into 3–4 pairs of lance-shaped segments. Flowers white or flesh-pink, in compact, roundish clusters at the ends of the branches. Caucasus.
rubra = *Centranthus ruber*.

VALERIANAVCEAE (va-leer-i-a-nay'scc-ee). The valerian family comprises 11 genera and about 325 species of chiefly herbs, most abundant in the north temperate zone. Four genera are in cult. for ornament, or as in *Valerianella*, the corn salad, for food.

The other cult. genera are ornamentals. *Centranthus* contains the familiar red valerian, *Fedia* is the African valerian, while *Valeriana* includes the garden heliotrope (not *Heliotropium*).

Leaves opposite.* Flowers small, usually unisexual,* sometimes irregular, and attractively clustered (cymes* or heads*). Fruit small, dry, not splitting, achene*-like, often crowned with the remains of the calyx.

Technical flower characters: Calyx tubular, 5-parted or lobed. Corolla more or less tubular, 5-lobed, sometimes irregular* and spurred* or swollen at the base. Stamens 1–3, rarely 4, borne on the corolla. Ovary inferior,* 1–3-celled, two of the cells empty, the third with a single ovule.

VALERIANELLA (va-leer-i-a-nell'a). Annual herbs comprising about 60 species of the family Valerianaceae, found distributed throughout the temperate regions of the northern hemisphere, mostly in the Mediterranean region. Basal leaves spoon-shaped or roundish, in a rosette. Stem leaves toothed, sometimes deeply cut. Flowers small, white, pale blue or pink, in dense roundish clusters at the ends of the branches. Calyx not conspicuous, but later producing 1–4 appendages. Corolla of 5 spreading lobes. Stamens* usually 3. Fruit 3-celled, each cell 1-seeded. (*Valerianella* is a diminutive of *Valeriana*.)

Valerianellas are usually cult. for their leaves, which are used for salads. Propagated by seeds, which should be sown ½ in. deep, in drills 8 in. apart in ordinary garden soil, from Apr. to Sept. They should be thinned out to 3 in. apart. See SALAD PLANTS.

eriocarpa. Italian corn salad. Leaves to 5 in. long, spoon-shaped, slightly hairy, the margins toothed at the base. Flowers pale blue, in dense round clusters at the ends of the branches. Southern Eu. Best species for warm localities.
Locusta. The typical form of the species is rarely grown, although it is sometimes a weed in the eastern states. The *var.* olitoria, the corn salad, field salad or lambs'-lettuce is the common garden sort. It grows to 1 ft. high. Leaves spoon-shaped, in a dense rosette, the veins prominent. Flowers light blue, in roundish terminal clusters. Eu. and the Orient. A round-leaved variety is grown extensively for the Paris market.

valida, -us, -um (val'i-da). Strong.

VALLEY WHITE OAK = *Quercus lobata.* See OAK.

VALLISNERIA. See EEL-GRASS.

VALLOTA. (val-low'ta). South African bulbous herbs of only one species of the family Amaryllidaceae, **V. speciosa**, the Scarborough lily. It has large bulbs and basal leaves to 2 ft. long and 1 in. wide, appearing at the same time as the flowering stalk, dying down in the autumn. Flowering stalks leafless, stout, hollow, flattish, to 3 ft. Flowers scarlet, funnel-shaped, to 3 in. across, in terminal umbels.* Calyx of 3 colored sepals. Corolla of 3 petals alternating with the sepals. Stamens* 6. Fruit a 3-celled capsule.* (Named for Pierre Vallot, French botanist.) For culture *see* AMARYLLIS.

VALVE. The units or separable parts of a splitting pod. Familiar examples are the two valves of a pea pod or the three valves of an iris pod.

VANCOUVERIA (van-koo-veer'ia). Low-growing, evergreen under-shrubs or woody herbs, comprising 3 species belonging to the barberry family, and natives of the woods of northwestern America. Rootstocks thick and creeping. Leaves alternate,* compound,* the leaflets 3, ovalish, bright glossy-green. Flowers small, white or yellow, in drooping terminal clusters. Calyx of 6 small, colored sepals, bending outward. Corolla of 6 small, narrow petals. Stamens* 6. Fruit 1-celled. (Named for Captain George Vancouver, commander of the *Discovery*, who landed at Vancouver in 1791.)

The cult. species makes an excellent ground cover and can also be used in the border. It

---

* Special articles on the subjects indicated by an asterisk (*) will be found at the words so marked.

will not stand strong sun, although easily cult. except in the East where summers are too hot for it. Propagated by division of the rootstocks. It requires a deep rich soil.

hexandra. Grows to 18 in. high. Leaves compound.° Leaflets 3, ovalish, to 1½ in. long, glossy. Flowers white, to ½ in. long. Woods, British Columbia to northern Calif.

VANDA (van'da). Large-flowered tree-perching orchids, comprising perhaps 50 species found in India, the Malay Islands, China, and New Guinea. They have aerial° roots growing from the stems, and are varied in habit, some being dwarf and erect, covered with numerous leaves arranged in two rows on the stem, while others are taller and of straggling habit, branching and climbing round other plants. Leaves long and narrow, flat or fleshy and grooved, the tip sometimes slightly cut. Flowers showy in various colors, in racemes° growing from the axils° of the leaves. Calyx of 3 colored, spreading sepals. Corolla of 3 petals alternating with the sepals, 2 similar to the sepals and 1 forming a 3-lobed lip,° the middle lobe spreading, the side lobes small and erect. Fruit a 3-celled capsule. (*Vanda* is a native Indian name for some species.)

These handsome orchids are general favorites. Propagated by cuttings. Cuttings should be made of pieces of the tops of the stem cut below 3 or 4 of the aerial roots. They are best grown in orchid baskets. Compost must be composed of live sphagnum° moss, interspersed with large pieces of charcoal. They should be suspended from the roof of a greenhouse in a winter night temperature of 60°–70° and summer of 70°–85°. They should be shaded from midday sun from Feb.–Nov. They require a humid atmosphere at all times, but ventilation should be given whenever weather conditions permit. These plants are subject to scale, which can be kept in check by frequent syringing or spongings with soapy sprays.

caerulea. Erect plant, growing to 2 ft. high. Leaves opposite,° to 10 in. long and 1 in. wide. Flowers light blue, to 4 in. across, in 7–13-flowered racemes° on a flowering stalk to 1½ ft., drooping at the tip. Himalayas.

teres. A climbing or straggling orchid, the round stems 3–8 ft. long and needing support. Leaves opposite,° strap-shaped, 6–8 in. long. Flowers about 4 in. wide, the cluster (raceme°) nearly 12 in. long and showy. Sepals° and petals rose-purple, the lip° smoky-yellow, red-banded. Southeastern As. May–Aug. There are many vars. offered with variously colored flowers.

tricolor. Strong-growing erect plant to 3 ft. high. Leaves many, growing in 2 rows, to 18 in. long and 1½ in. wide. Flowers 2 in. across, in 8–10-flowered racemes° on flowering stalk to 1 ft. long. Petals and sepals wavy, yellow, marked with brown spots. Lip° light purple, veined purple with white side lobes. Java. The *var.* suavis has white sepals and petals marked purple, with the lip° marked purple at the base.

VANILLA (va-nill'a). Nearly 70 species

of tropical, climbing orchids, of no hort. interest save for the Mexican **V. planifolia,** widely cult. in the tropics for its fruit which is the source of vanilla. It is a tall-climbing, fleshy-stemmed vine with oblong, thick, fleshy leaves, 6–8 in. long and about 2 in. wide. Flowers greenish-yellow, about 3 in. wide, grouped in a raceme.° Sepals and petals narrow, the lip° trumpet-shaped, shorter than the petals, its lobes somewhat scalloped. Fruit a slender, bean-like pod. The vanilla was well known to the Aztecs who cultivated the plant for its fragrant, aromatic pods. Its commercial production (much reduced since the production of synthetic vanillin) is now chiefly centered in Mexico, in islands of the Indian Ocean, and in Tahiti. A vanilla vine will, when mature, bear 40–50 vanilla beans a year for years. The plant is occasionally grown in greenhouses, but rarely sets pods, as it needs artificial pollination. (*Vanilla* is the Spanish word for a little sheath or pod.) The plant was long known as *V. fragrans,* and is now found through much of tropical America. For the plant known as Carolina vanilla *see* TRILISA ODORATISSIMA.

VANILLA GRASS = *Hierochloë odorata.*

VANILLA-LEAF = *Trilisa odoratissima.*

VAN TOL. A valuable, grafted variety of the English holly which is reasonably sure to set fruit. *See Ilex aquifolium* at HOLLY.

VAR. The abbreviation for variety (which see).

varia, -us, -um (vair'i-a). Variable.

variabilis, -e (vare-i-ab'i-lis). Somewhat variable.

VARIATION. Differences between plants, or variations, are brought about, genetically speaking, in three different ways. (1) Differences due to changes in environment,° heredity° remaining unchanged — environment being such phenomena as soil, temperature, moisture, and a host of other things external to the plant itself. Commonly these produce changes in size, shape, color, and many other characters. A certain primrose species has white flowers at one temperature and red ones at another and one may see both these flower colors on the same plant at the same time in such an experiment. Many flowers are pink in one soil type and blue in another, as occurs in certain varieties of hydrangea. Some characters are less sensitive to change than others, but it is difficult to generalize on this subject. Height in sorghum and corn is sensitive to both soil and moisture, while height in peas is much less so.

(2) Differences due to changes in heredity, the environment remaining unchanged, are, as regards the plant as a whole, of two sorts — (*a*) mutations° and allied phenomena — in which something hereditarily new has been produced (double flowers from single-flowered plants), and (*b*) new combinations of old character-determiners, producing at times new associations of old characters, such as dwarf yellow four-o'clocks from crosses between tall

---

° Special articles on the subjects indicated by an asterisk (°) will be found at the words so marked.

yellow and dwarf white varieties; or at other times new characters, as exemplified by dwarf light-yellow four-o'clocks from this same type of cross.

(3) Heredity* and environment* may both change, from a formerly recognized state, at the same time or during the same season, so that one might secure a dwarf (environmental) white (hereditary) oat from a tall black variety. — O. E. W.

varicosa, -us, -um (vair-i-kō'sa). Irregularly swollen.

variegata, -us, -um (vair-i-e-gay'ta). Variegated.*

VARIEGATED. Having marks, stripes, or blotches of some color other than the basic ground-color, which is usually green. Variegated leaves are rare among wild plants but pretty common in hort. forms, especially in privet, holly, *Vinca*, many evergreens, and in a host of ornamental foliage plants.

While, generally speaking, the ground-color of variegated leaves is green, there are many very showy foliage plants, especially among the begonias and caladiums, where it is red, orange, yellow, or almost any other color. Some authorities would restrict the term variegation to those instances where the ground-color is green, but there does not seem sufficient evidence for this. Variegation, as used throughout this book, means exactly what it says in the first sentence of this definition. *See also* CHLOROSIS.

VARIETY. Scarcely any term in botany or hort. is so variable in its meaning as *variety*. Strictly, from the botanical standpoint, the word denotes a group or class of plants, within a species, which have constant characters that separate them slightly from the typical form and from other possible varieties found within that species. An illustration:

Rosa chinensis is the China rose, and a good species. But contained within that species are four groups or classes of rose, all differing from the typical *R. chinensis*, but not enough to make them entitled to species names. To these four groups are attached what are called *varietal* names. In other, and strictly correct, words, each is a *variety* of the China rose. Throughout this book a true variety is indicated by *var.*, which is merely the abbreviation for the word variety. The varieties of the China rose thus appear as

var. manetti. The manetti rose.

var. minima. The fairy rose.

var. semperflorens. The Chinese monthly rose.

var. viridiflora. The green rose. *See Rosa chinensis* at ROSA.

Not all cult. species have as many varieties as the China rose, but some have many more, as in corn, sorghum, heather, and several others. The thing to keep in mind throughout this book is that wherever the abbreviation *var.* appears it means variety used in this technical sense, as well as in another to be noted presently.

Most unfortunately, however, the word has several other meanings, neither precise nor adhered to by gardeners. In this looser and very general use of *variety*, the word applies to any race, strain, or named horticultural form which is obviously different from the species to which it belongs. In such a sense it is commonly used to describe a red-flowered form of a white species, or a sour-juiced race of a sweet-juiced species. Most hort. named forms, like American Beauty rose, are varieties in this sense.

This technical and popular use of *variety* for two quite different categories of plants (*i.e.*, true botanical varieties and named horticultural forms) is unfortunate but so universal that the Editor hesitates to adopt the suggestion of some to call named horticultural forms by the comparatively unknown term of *cultivar*. To inflict this concept upon the garden public would subject it to a quite unnecessary burden. The word *variety* is universal while *cultivar* seems to have greater popularity with the pedants than the public. *Cultivar* has thus been rejected for this edition, as it was in the monumental *Dictionary of Gardening*, in 4 volumes and a supplement, issued by the Royal Horticultural Society, London, in 1956. *See also* PLANT NAMES; CULTIVAR.

While the usual method of indicating a variety is as shown above (*i.e.*, *Rosa chinensis* var. *manetti*, etc.), there are many times when convenience or lack of space (as in lists) makes it necessary to omit the abbreviation *var.* In such cases, the name appears as *Rosa chinensis manetti* — a three-combination name known as a trinomial.

VARIETY HYBRID. *See* CROSS-BREED.

variifolia, -us, -um (var-i-i-fō'li-a). With various or variable leaves.

VARNISH-TREE = *Koelreuteria paniculata*.

VEGECULTURE. Vegetable gardening.

vegeta, -us, -um (vej'e-ta). Vigorous; a luxuriant grower.

VEGETABLE. Scarcely needing a definition but often demanding one in the courts, where there is confusion as between the word fruit* and vegetable. No popular definition that is precise can be given of either word. Watermelon is considered a fruit in some sections but a vegetable in others. So are rhubarb and several other plants.

For a list of what everyone understands to be the leading vegetables *see* KITCHEN GARDEN.

VEGETABLE BRAIN. *See* BLIGHIA SAPIDA.

VEGETABLE GARDENING. As the name implies, this is merely the raising of vegetables. The pedantic call it olericulture or vegeculture, while those who do it for profit know it as truck gardening or market gardening. From these purely commercial activities the home gardener may learn much. Their meth-

---

* Special articles on the subjects indicated by an asterisk (*) will be found at the words so marked.

ods, wherever applicable, will be found at the article KITCHEN GARDEN. Vegetables first enter the house through the kitchen. That is why the garden from which they come is properly called a kitchen garden. Thus, for the main details of raising vegetables *see* KITCHEN GARDEN. For the culture of individual crops, *see* CABBAGE, ONION, PEA, POTATO, etc.

VEGETABLE GOLD = *Crocus sativus*.

VEGETABLE MARROW. A variety of squash (which see); *see also* BLIGHIA SAPIDA.

VEGETABLE ORANGE = Mango melon. See MELON.

VEGETABLE OYSTER = *Tragopogon porrifolius.* For culture *see* SALSIFY.

VEGETABLE PEACH OR PEAR = *Sechium edule.*

VEGETABLE SILK. *See* BEAUMONTIA GRANDIFLORA.

VEGETABLE SPAGHETTI. A vegetable marrow (*see* SQUASH), the cooked fruit of which separates into spaghetti-like strings.

VEGETABLE SPONGE. *See* LUFFA.

VEGETABLE TALLOW = *Sapium sebiferum.*

VEGETATIVE REPRODUCTION. Propagation without sex. *See* PROPAGATION.

VEINS. *See* VENATION.

VELAMEN. The white or greenish outer covering of the aerial roots of some tree-perching orchids, and a few other epiphytes.* It has the unusual faculty of condensing and absorbing atmospheric moisture. Almost no other plants can do this, but it is an extremely useful capacity for an epiphyte* in a tropical forest.

VELTHEIMIA (vel-thym'i-a). A small genus of South African bulbous herbs of the lily family, suitable only for greenhouse culture, or outdoors in frostless regions. They have chiefly basal, strap-shaped leaves which more or less sheath the stem. Flowers tubular, the 6 lobes of the corolla short. Stamens* 6. Fruit a 3-chambered pod (capsule*). The only cult. species of interest here is the unicorn-root, **V. viridifolia**, which has brilliantly green (as though varnished) strap-shaped leaves, 8–12 in. long and about 3 in. wide and wavy-margined. Flowers reddish or yellowish, green-spotted, about 1 in. long, in a large, many-flowered cluster (raceme*) 4–6 in. long. The plants need potting mixture* 3, a cool greenhouse, and a resting period when the leaves wither after the bloom passes. (*Veltheimia* was named for A. F. von Veltheim, German patron of botany.)

velutina, -us, -um (vel-loo'ti-na). Velvety.

VELVET BEAN. *See* STIZOLOBIUM.

VELVET BENT = *Agrostis canina*.

VELVET PLANT = *Verbascum Thapsus* and *Gynura aurantiaca.*

VENATION. The arrangement of the veins, usually in leaves, but many petals and not a few fruits have veins. The way veins are arranged in leaves is of prime importance in the classification of plants. In monocotyledons the veins are usually parallel, while most dicotyledonous plants have netted-veined leaves. See MONOCOTYLEDON, DICOTYLEDON.

VENIDIUM (ve-nid'i-um). South African annual or perennial herbs, comprising about 18 species of the family Compositae. Leaves alternate,* deeply cut, stalked, grayish-green, of cobwebby appearance when young. Flowers in solitary heads 4–5 in. across, daisy-like. Ray florets* yellow or orange, sometimes with purple band at the base. Disk florets purplish-black. (Origin of name uncertain.)

Venidiums make showy plants for the border and are sometimes grown as pot plants in the greenhouse. They make excellent cut flowers, opening in the morning and closing at night in the same manner as when growing on the plant. Usually treated as tender annuals. Propagated by seeds. Seeds should be sown in April, ⅛ in. deep, in light sandy soil in greenhouse or cold frame, or later they may be sown outdoors where needed, in full sun. Care should be taken not to overwater at any time as plants are subject to stem rot.

decurrens. Perennial, of branching habit, growing to 2 ft. high. Leaves stalked, generally lyre-shaped, grayish, covered with soft hairs. Flowers in solitary heads, to 2½ in. across. Ray florets golden-yellow. Disk florets* purplish-black.

fastuosum. Annual, growing 2–3 ft. high. Leaves lyre-shaped, grayish, cobwebby when young. Flowers in solitary heads, 4–5 in. across. Ray florets bright orange with purplish band at the base. Disk florets purplish-black. It will stand 3–5° of frost in Calif., but often does not do well in the East, especially if watered too freely.

VENTRAL. The front, inside, or upper side of an organ. *See* DORSAL.

ventricosa, -us, -um (ven-tri-kō'sa). Ventricose; *i.e.*, unequally swollen, as are some flowers or fruits.

VENUS'S-FLYTRAP = *Dionaea muscipula.*

VENUS'S-HAIR = *Adiantum Capillus-Veneris.*

VENUS'S-LOOKING-GLASS = *Specularia Speculum-Veneris.*

venusta, -us, -um (ve-nus'ta). Charming.

vera, -us, -um (ver'ra). True.

VERATRUM (ver-rah'trum). False hellebore. Hardy perennial herbs, comprising about 45 species belonging to the lily family, found throughout the northern hemisphere. Rootstocks thick and highly poisonous. Leaves alternate,* clasping the stem, large, parallel-veined. Flowers greenish-white or purplish, in terminal branching clusters. Calyx of 3 colored sepals. Corolla of 3 petals alternating with the sepals. Stamens * 6. Fruit a 3-celled capsule. (*Veratrum* is an old name for hellebore.) The similarity of the large leaves of the first species to those of *Gentiana lutea*

---

* Special articles on the subjects indicated by an asterisk (*) will be found at the words so marked.

has had fatal consequences to those confusing the two plants. *See* GENTIANA LUTEA.

These plants are not generally cult. for ornament but are sometimes grown in the shady border or wild garden. Easily cult. Propagated by seeds or division of the rootstocks. They prefer damp and shady places. Both species are cult. for the extraction of veratrine, a valuable medicine.

album. European white hellebore. Hardy perennial, growing to 4 ft. high. Rootstock thick and fleshy. Leaves to 1 ft. long, and 5–6 in. wide, stiff, clasping the stem. Flowers in terminal clusters to 2 ft. long, greenish outside, white inside. Petals wavy and toothed. Eu. and northern As.

viride. White or green hellebore. American white hellebore. Indian poke. Strong-growing plant to 8 ft. high. Leaves clasping the stem, to 1 ft. long and 6 in. wide, narrowing toward the tip. Flowers greenish-yellow, hairy, to 1 in. across in terminal branching clusters, to 2 ft. long. Eastern N.A., and very common in swampy woods.

VERBASCUM (ver-bas′kum). Mullein. Hardy biennial or perennial herbs comprising about 250 species of the family Scrophulariaceae, found mostly in the Mediterranean region but naturalized throughout the northern hemisphere. Basal leaves large. Stem leaves alternate* and smaller, generally grayish-green and velvety, being often covered with soft hairs. Flowers yellow, tawny-red, or purple, sometimes white, numerous in showy spikes or racemes.* Calyx of 5 sepals. Corolla of 5 spreading lobes. Stamens* 5, the filaments being covered with showy hairs. Fruit a 2-celled capsule.* (*Verbascum* is an old Latin name used by Pliny for these plants.)

Verbascums are suitable for the large border, edges of shrubberies or the wild garden. Usually treated as biennials. Easily propagated by seeds. Seeds should be sown ⅛ in. deep in light, sandy soil in April or May in cold frame or outdoor seedbed. They may be transplanted as soon as large enough to handle. These plants do not like wet, cold soil.

Blattaria. Moth mullein. Strong-growing biennial to 6 ft. high. Leaves smooth, dark green, ovalish, to 2½ in. long, the margins toothed or cut. Flowers in a long, loose raceme,* white or yellow, marked purple at the base with lilac hairs on the stamen filaments. Eu. and northern As.; naturalized in N.A.

chaixi. Biennial, growing to 3 ft. high, and covered with white-woolly hairs. Leaves ovalish, to 6 in. long, coarsely toothed. Flowers yellow, with purple hairs on the stamen filaments, borne in a raceme with small, side, flower-bearing branches. Southern Eu.

olympicum. Biennial, growing 3–6 ft. high and covered with white-woolly hairs. Leaves ovalish, to 1 ft. long. Flowering stalk thick. Flowers bright yellow, with white-woolly hairs on the stamen filaments, arranged in bunched clusters in the axils* of leafy bracts in a raceme. Greece.

phoeniceum. Purple mullein. Biennial, growing to 5 ft. high. Leaves basal, in a rosette, ovalish, wrinkled, dark green on the upper side, covered with short hairs on the under side, the margins with rounded teeth. Flowers reddish-purple, with purplish-woolly hairs on the stamen filaments, borne in a slender, sometimes branched raceme. S.E. Eu. and As.

Thapsus. Common mullein. Velvet plant. Candlewick. Flannel-leaf. Strong-growing biennial, to 6 ft. high and covered with felty, yellowish hairs. Basal leaves large, to 1 ft. long. Stem leaves smaller, clasping the stem. Flowers yellow, to 1 in. across, in bunched clusters arranged in a spike. Eurasia. Usually considered a weed, and widely so naturalized in N.A.

VERBENA (ver-bee′na). Vervain. Tender or hardy annual or perennial herbs, comprising about 270 species of the family Verbenaceae, natives of America with the exception of 1 species found in Eurasia. Leaves generally opposite,* usually lobed or toothed. Flowers in various shades of white, lilac, red, and purple, small, sometimes stalked, in terminal spikes* or terminal, roundish clusters. Calyx tubular, 5-toothed. Corolla tubular, opening salverwise, its lobes 5, the tube long and narrow. Stamens* 4, in pairs. Fruit 4-celled which when ripe separates into 4 parts, each part containing 1 seed. (*Verbena* is the ancient Latin name of the European vervain.) For the lemon verbena *see* LIPPIA CITRIODORA, for the sand verbena *see* ABRONIA.

Verbenas are useful garden plants for the border and are sometimes grown in the greenhouse as pot plants for house decoration. Usually only the perennial species are grown but they are best treated as tender annuals (*see* ANNUALS). Propagated by seeds or cuttings. Seeds should be sown in March, ⅛ in. deep, in light sandy soil, in cool greenhouse or cold frame and pricked off into boxes or small pots as soon as large enough to handle. They may be transplanted to permanent positions as soon as danger of frost is over. Cuttings are usually made only when it is desired to retain a particular color. To do this plants should be cut down in early Sept. when young shoots will form. Cuttings may then be made from these shoots which should be rooted under glass and kept in cool greenhouse through the winter.

bipinnatifida. A more or less prostrate or decumbent perennial, often rooting at the joints, but best grown as an annual. Leaves finely divided, the divisions themselves cut or cleft. Flowers small, pink, violet, or lavender, in a terminal, open cluster (raceme *). Dry prairies, central U.S. and adjacent Mex.

canadensis. A perennial with creeping rootstocks, the branches growing to 18 in. high, and covered with stiff hairs. Leaves ovalish, to 4 in. long, often cut into 3 lobes. Flowers reddish-purple, lilac, or white, to ⅔ in. across, stalked, in terminal heads. Va. and south and west to Colo.

erinoides. May be *Verbena laciniata* or *Verbena pulchella*.

hastata. Blue vervain. Hardy erect perennial, with square stems, growing 4–5 ft. high. Leaves lance-shaped, to 6 in. long, the margins toothed. Flowers blue, small, in slender spikes. Eastern N.A. *See* BLUE GARDEN.

hortensis. Garden verbena. Tender trailing perennial, growing to 1 ft. high. Leaves broadly lance-shaped, 2–4 in. long, the margins bluntly toothed. Flowers fragrant, pink, red, yellow, or

---

* Special articles on the subjects indicated by an asterisk (*) will be found at the words so marked.

white, in terminal compact clusters. Of hybrid origin and known also as *V. hybrida*. Among the hort. forms of this old garden favorite are Miss Willmott (*see* PINK GARDEN), and Etna and Spectrum Red (*see* RED GARDEN).

laciniata. Tender perennial, of spreading habit, the stems hairy and rooting, the branches erect. Leaves ovalish, deeply cut into 3 lobes, each lobe cut into narrow segments. Flowers lilac, in short, dense, head-like clusters. Argentina and Chile.

pulchella. Perennial, of spreading habit, the stem somewhat woody at the base, hairy and rooting. Branches erect, to 20 in. high. Leaves ovalish, cut into narrow lobes. Flowers blue or lilac, in terminal dense clusters. Southern S.A.

rigida. An erect perennial, 12–20 in. high, with rhizomes * and a 4-angled stem. Leaves oblongish or narrower, 2–3 in. long, toothed. Flowers purplish-blue, the dense spikes 1–2½ in. long. Brazil and Argentina. They will flower in four months from seeding. Often offered as *V. venosa*.

venosa = *Verbena rigida.*

VERBENACEAE (ver-be-nay'see-ee). The vervain or verbena family includes many old garden favorites among its 90 genera and nearly 3000 species. It is largely tropical or sub-tropical, although some cult. genera such as *Verbena* and *Callicarpa* are mostly hardy. Some of the most attractive shrubby genera are not quite hardy over extreme winters, especially *Lippia, Vitex,* and *Caryopteris.*

Clerodendron (one or two hardy), *Duranta, Holmskioldia, Lantana, Petrea* (a woody vine), and *Oxera* (also a vine) are generally tropical. They require greenhouse culture or outdoor sites in southern Fla. and southern Calif. (zones* 8 and 9).

Vitex, Caryopteris, and *Callicarpa* are easily, and deservedly, the most popular hort. genera. All are profuse bloomers.

Leaves prevailingly opposite,* simple* or compound.* Flowers usually irregular* and often 2-lipped,* very ornamental in most of the cult. genera. Fruit nearly always fleshy, none edible.

Technical flower characters: Calyx* united, mostly 4–5-toothed. Corolla tubular or funnel-shaped, its 4–5 lobes irregular* or two-lipped in most genera (nearly regular in *Verbena*). Stamens* generally 4, two shorter than the others. Ovary superior.*

VERBESINA (ver-be-sy'na). American annual or perennial herbs and shrubs, the shrubby species tropical, comprising about 60 species of the family Compositae. Leaves opposite* or alternate, often running down the stem (decurrent*). Flower heads solitary, or in clusters. Ray florets* usually absent. Disk florets yellow, orange, or white. (*Verbesina* is believed to be a meaningless alteration of *Verbena.*)

These plants are of only slight garden importance, although they are used in the wild garden. Propagated by seeds or cuttings.

encelioides. Golden crown-beard. Annual, growing to 3 ft. high. Leaves alternate, ovalish, to 4 in. long, pale green on the under side, the margins toothed. Flowers in solitary heads 2 in. across. Ray florets* golden-yellow. Cent. U.S. south to Mex.

veris (ver'is). True.

VERMICULITE. A mica-like mineral, much lighter than sand and useful as a mulch. It is easier to remove when not needed than sand. Vermiculite can also be used as a medium in which to start seeds, root cuttings, and for the propagation of lilies from bulb scales. It has no plant food in it, but is sterile, weed- and insect-free. *See also* PERLITE.

VERMONT. Red clover is the state flower, the sugar maple the state tree. The state lies in zones* 2 and 3.

SOILS. There are many and variable soil types in Vermont. The loams predominate, but one may find all gradations from coarse sand to fine clay. Most Vermont soils have been developed from the debris deposited by the glacier thousands of years ago. The parent materials which have given rise to our soils are also diverse. They consist of:

glacial till — a mixture of rocks, sand, gravel, silt, and clay.

alluvial deposits — silts and sands deposited by rivers and streams.

sands and gravels — from sorting by water or winds in the distant past.

heavy silts or clays — deposited in former lake beds.

FRUITS AND VEGETABLES. The main fruit and vegetable areas are in the Champlain Valley and in the lower Connecticut River Valley. The leading apple variety is McIntosh which can be grown to perfection under the state's normal climatic conditions. Other varieties include Northern Spy, Delicious, and Cortland. The largest orchards are around 300 acres, but there are many around 200 acres. Approximately 3000 acres of land with around 100,000 trees make up the commercial apple enterprise. There are practically no home orchard plantings that consist of more than a tree or two.

Raspberries and strawberries can also be grown to perfection in the state although at present the local demand is not being met. Latham is still the leading variety of red raspberry, followed by Marcy, Indian Summer, and Viking. Catskill has become the leading strawberry variety although Howard 17 is still extensively grown. Fairland and Robinson strawberry varieties probably rank next in acreage.

All the cool-season vegetable crops may be grown throughout the summer and they do exceptionally well when given proper care. Warm-season vegetable crops, such as watermelon, okra, some varieties of tomato, pepper, eggplant, and cantaloupe, are not too successfully grown. However, short-season varieties of most of these crops have been developed for home garden plantings.

The Irish potato is still the major vegetable crop. Katahdin and Green Mountain are the chief varieties both for table stock and certified-seed sale. Sweet corn and snap beans are grown for commercial canneries.

---

* Special articles on the subjects indicated by an asterisk (*) will be found at the words so marked.

CLIMATE. The general climatic factors in Vermont are wind, sunshine, length of growing period, and rainfall. The winds over most of the state are moderate, and destructive gales of large extent are few. The average hourly velocity of wind in Burlington over a 25-year period is 10.8 miles per hour. The highest velocity on record for a five-minute period was 50 miles. The peak velocity recorded is 72 m.p.h. for a very short period. The prevailing wind was from the south.

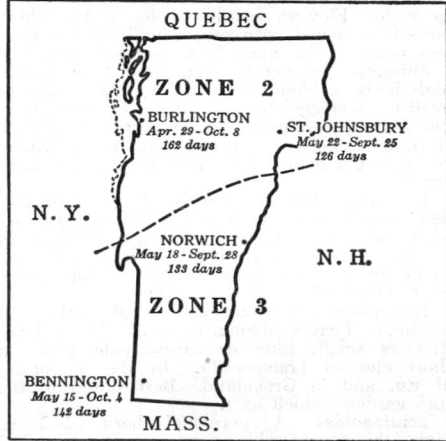

QUEBEC

ZONE 2

BURLINGTON
Apr. 29 - Oct. 8
162 days

• ST. JOHNSBURY
May 22 - Sept. 25
126 days

N. Y.

NORWICH •
May 18 - Sept. 28
133 days

N. H.

ZONE 3

BENNINGTON •
May 15 - Oct. 4
142 days

MASS.

VERMONT

The zones of hardiness crossing Vermont are those shown on the map located at ZONE, which should be consulted for details. The dates are the average latest killing frost in spring and the first one in the fall. The figures below the dates show the average length of the growing season.

Vermont receives about 48% of possible sunshine. The highest monthly average in Burlington is 59% in July, and the lowest is 22% in December.

The humidity is not excessive. It is lowest from April to June, inclusive. Fogs are not frequent, the average number of foggy days in Burlington being eleven per year. An all-day fog is rare. There are more foggy days in the valleys than in the upland sections. Thunderstorms are frequent but not destructive. The average annual number at Burlington is twenty-seven.

CLIMATIC SUMMARY

	No. Frost-free days	Total rainfall (inches)	Growing season (May–Oct.) rainfall (inches)
Burlington	162	32.28	17.09
St. Johnsbury	126	34.68	15.40
Bennington	142	37.71	18.91
Norwich	133	33.78	16.64

As a rule, the rainfall is well distributed throughout the year. Nevertheless, more and more fruit and vegetable growers have been investing in portable irrigation equipment to prevent loss of crops to drought and to afford some protection from late spring frosts.

The address of the Agricultural Experiment Station which has kindly supplied this information about the state is Burlington. The station is always glad to answer gardening questions.

Garden club activities include clubs of the Garden Club of America, the home office of which is 598 Madison Avenue, New York 22, N.Y., and several chapters of the Federated Garden Clubs of Vermont.

verna, -us, -um (ver′na). Spring.

vernalis, -e (ver-nal′is). Having to do with spring; *i.e.*, spring-blooming.

VERNATION. The arrangement of leaves in a bud. Botanists have many special terms for the different methods of folding, curling, twisting, or coiling of young leaves in an unopened bud, but they are scarcely garden terms.

VERNONIA (ver-no′ni-a). Ironweed. Perennial herbs, shrubs, or trees, comprising about 500 species of the family Compositae, distributed throughout the world, the shrubs and trees tropical. Leaves alternate,° simple, lance-shaped, sometimes hairy, the margins toothed. Flowers in heads, in terminal clusters, composed of disk florets° only, purple, pink or white. Flower heads surrounded by numerous overlapping bracts,° their tips sometimes bristle-like. (Named for William Vernon, English botanist.)

A few herbaceous species are cult. for use in the back of the border or wild garden for their autumn flowers. Easily cult. Propagated by division of the rootstocks in early spring. They prefer damp, deep, rich soil.

altissima. Strong-growing perennial, 5–9 ft. high. Leaves deep green, lance-shaped, to 1 ft. long, the margins finely toothed. Flowers purple, in heads ½ in. across. Heads in loose, terminal clusters. N.Y. to Fla. and La. See AUTUMN GARDEN.

crinita. Strong-growing perennial 2–10 ft. high. Leaves narrowly lance-shaped, to 1 ft. long, sometimes covered with hairs, the margins finely toothed. Flowers purple, in heads 1 in. across. Bracts° surrounding the heads green, sometimes tipped red. Mo. to Okla. See GRAY AND LAVENDER GARDEN.

noveboracensis. Perennial, growing 3–7 ft. high. Leaves lance-shaped, to 10 in. long, dark green, the margins finely toothed. Flowers deep purple, in heads ½ in. across, the heads in terminal clusters. Bracts° surrounding the heads bristle-tipped. Mass. to Ga. and Miss.

VERONICA (ver-on′i-ka). Speedwell. A genus of over 250 species of rather unlike plants of the family Scrophulariaceae, some of them hardy herbs for the border or rock garden, but many of them shrubs or small trees, chiefly from New Zealand, and cult. here outdoors only in zones° 7, 8, and 9,

---

° Special articles on the subjects indicated by an asterisk (°) will be found at the words so marked.

especially in Calif., where they are very popular. Some authorities (with a good deal of reason) consider these New Zealand plants as a separate genus, to which the name *Hebe* is applied. But they have for so long been retained as of the genus *Veronica*, and are so generally still known by that name, that they are here included within it. Stem leaves opposite,* (rarely alternate* or whorled*), the upper nearly always alternate.* Flowers mostly in terminal clusters (spikes or racemes*), but these sometimes in the axils* of the leaves. Calyx* united, mostly 4-parted. Corolla almost or completely regular,* mostly with a short tube and a spreading, 4–5-lobed limb. Stamens* 2. Fruit a 2-grooved capsule.* (Named for Saint Veronica.)

Culturally, the two sections of *Veronica* must be treated very differently. The herbs are attractive garden plants for the border or rock garden, nearly all perennials and of easy culture under most ordinary garden conditions. Some are attractively flowering, prostrate plants good for ground cover or for edging. All the herbs should be increased by division, which should be done after flowering, and the plants reset in good rich soil.

The shrubby species from New Zealand grow well in a variety of soils in Calif., where some of them can be clipped into informal hedges. They may be propagated by cuttings of mature wood in fall, most of which will bloom the following season. Some, like *V. traversi,* are occasionally grown in northern greenhouses, where they need a temperate house and potting mixture* 4. All these New Zealand species in the list below (species of *Hebe* to those who maintain that genus) are marked with a dagger (†).

allioni. A mat-forming, rock garden perennial, with a creeping stem rooting at the joints. Leaves short-stalked, about ¼ in. long, leathery. Flowers violet, small, crowded in dense spikes about 2 in. long. Alps. Summer.

amethystina = *Veronica spuria.*

†**amplexicaulis.** A partly prostrate or decumbent shrub, 1–3 ft. high. Leaves very numerous, overlapping, about 1 in. long, without teeth, bluish-green. Flowers white, about ¼ in. long, in spikes about 1 in. long. N.Z.

†**andersoni.** A hybrid veronica, and a much-branched shrub 5–8 ft. high. Leaves 4–5 in. long. Flowers very small, but showy from the handsome clusters (racemes*) which are 4–6 in. long. Corolla white, but violet-tipped. The *var.* **variegata** has the leaves blotched creamy-white. N.Z.

armena. A low, tufted,* rock garden perennial, 3–4 in. high, the leaves much cut into fine segments which are about ¼ in. long. Flowers blue, in a sparse cluster (raceme*). Armenia. Early summer.

austriaca. A perennial herb, 1–2 ft. high, the leaves cut feather-fashion into oblong or narrower segments, downy. Flowers blue, in showy, terminal clusters (racemes*). Eurasia. *See* Blue Garden.

brachysiphon. *See* V. traversi.

†**buxifolia.** A shrub, 3–5 ft. high, with very numerous, overlapping, small, stiff leaves, scarcely ⅓ in. long. Flowers about ⅓ in. long, the clusters (spikes*) about 1 in. long. N.Z.

Chamaedrys. Bird's-eye. An erect perennial, 12–18 in. high, with ovalish leaves, heart-shaped at the base, distinctly toothed. Flowers blue, about ¼ in. long, arranged in a dense, terminal, showy spike 4–6 in. long. Eurasia, and commonly naturalized in eastern N.A. May–June. Perhaps only a form of *V. latifolia.*

†**cupressoides.** A stiffish shrub, its twigs covered by scale-like leaves which in maturity are scarcely ⅒ in. long, but large (¼ in.) on young twigs. Flowers pale purple, about ⅙ in. long, in head-like clusters. N.Z.

decussata = *Veronica elliptica.*

†**elliptica.** A much-branched shrub, 15–20 ft. high. Leaves about 1¼ in. long, and half as wide. Flowers nearly ⅔ in. wide, white, but often veined with purple or blue, the clusters nearly 2 in. long. N.Z. and southern S.A.

filiformis. A mat-forming annual or perennial herb, seldom over 2 in. high. Leaves ovalish, scarcely ¼ in. long. Flowers light blue, drooping, appearing in April. Caucasus. It is a quick-growing plant, good for a ground cover, but a naturalized lawn weed in the eastern U.S.

fruticans. Rock speedwell. A low, rock garden, woody, much-branched perennial, 3–5 in. high, the leaves almost toothless, ovalish, about ⅓ in. long. Flowers blue, with a red eye, small, in a sparse terminal spike. Eu. July–Sept. Often offered as *V. saxatilis.*

fruticulosa. A woody perennial herb, 4–6 in. high. Leaves oblongish, nearly ½ in. long. Flowers small, blue or rarely pale pink, in short clusters (racemes*). In the mountains of Eu. and in Greenland. Best suited to the rock garden (which see).

gentianoides. A perennial herb, 1–2 ft. high, the leaves oblongish or narrower, 2–3 in. long. Flowers blue, veined with darker blue, in rather showy, loose, terminal clusters (racemes*). Southeastern Eu. and As. Minor. ture *see* Rock Garden.

†**hulkeana.** A shrub. 2–3 ft. high, the ovalish, toothed leaves 1½–2 in. long. Flowers about ¼ in. long, white, in a showy, terminal cluster (panicle*) nearly 1 ft. long. N.Z.

incana. A white-hairy herb, mostly 8 in. high or less, occasionally up to 18 in. high. Leaves oblongish, toothed, 2–3 in. long. Flowers blue, the clusters (racemes*) nearly 6 in. long. Eurasia. A good edging plant. For culture *see* Rock Garden.

latifolia, also known as *V. Teucrium,* but either name is in some doubt. Germander speedwell, and the best-known of all the herbaceous species. It is 12–18 in. high, the leaves oblongish or narrower, coarsely toothed. Flowers generally blue, but sometimes white or pinkish. Eurasia. It is a fine border plant, especially the form known as Royal Blue. The *var.* **prostrata** is a nearly prostrate form useful for ground cover. The *var.* **dubia,** a low form popular for the rock garden, is of uncertain identity.

longifolia. A perennial herb, 1–2 ft. high. Leaves oblongish or tapering, toothed, 3–4 in. long. Flowers lilac-blue in dense, terminal clusters (racemes*). Eurasia, naturalized in N.A. Also known as *V. maritima.* The *var.* **subsessilis** has deeper blue flowers and nearly stalkless leaves. *See* Blue Garden.

maritima = *V. longifolia.*

officinalis. A prostrate, perennial, weedy herb with oblongish leaves and pale blue flowers. Eurasia and N.A. *See* Speedwell in the list at Weeds.

pectinata. A prostrate, white-hairy perennial with ovalish or oblong, coarsely toothed leaves.

* Special articles on the subjects indicated by an asterisk (*) will be found at the words so marked.

Flowers deep blue, white-eyed, in profuse clusters (racemes*). Asia Minor. The *var.* **rosea** has rose-pink flowers. For culture *see* ROCK GARDEN.

repens. A moss-like, prostrate perennial, the leaves about ½ in. long and shining. Flowers small, rose-pink or bluish, the clusters few-flowered. Corsica and Spain. There is also a white-flowered form. *See* ROCK GARDEN.

rupestris. *See* VERONICA LATIFOLIA DUBIA.

saturejoides. A low, rock garden perennial, mat-forming from a woody base, not over 3 in. high. Leaves crowded, oblong, about ¼ in. long. Flowers dark blue, crowded in a dense terminal cluster (raceme*). Yugoslavia. May.

saxatilis = *Veronica fruticans.*

†**speciosa.** An evergreen shrub, 3–5 ft. high, the twigs angled. Leaves oblongish, 2–4 in. long, about half as wide, hairy on the upper side along the midrib. Flowers bluish-purple or reddish-purple, small, crowded in terminal clusters (racemes*) that are about 3½ in. long. N.Z. Grown in the cool greenhouse or outdoors from zone* 7 southward.

spicata. Cat's-tail speedwell. A perennial, 15–24 in. high. Leaves lance-shaped, toothed, 1½–2 in. long. Flowers blue, the clusters (racemes*) dense. Eurasia. *See* BLUE GARDEN. The *var.* **rosea** has pink flowers. *See* PINK GARDEN. There is also a white-flowered form.

spuria. Bastard speedwell. A perennial, 12–20 in. high, covered with dense hairs. Leaves line-like, scarcely 1 in. long. Flowers blue, the clusters branched (panicled racemes). Eurasia. *See* BLUE GARDEN.

subsessilis = *Veronica longifolia subsessilis.*

Teucrium. *See* V. LATIFOLIA.

†**traversi.** A thrifty but small, much-branched shrub. Leaves about 1 in. long, scarcely ⅓ in. wide. Flowers white, about ¼ in. long, the cluster (raceme*) 2–3 in. long. N. Z. The most widely grown of the shrubby N.Z. plants, and credited by some to *V. brachysiphon.*

trehani. A common name in the trade, most of the material so offered being *Veronica latifolia dubia* or *V. latifolia prostrata.*

virginica = *Veronicastrum.*

VERONICASTRUM (ver-on-i-cas′trum). A small genus, closely related to *Veronica,* comprising only two species, the only cult. one being **V. virginicum,** culver′s-root; also called blackroot. A native American perennial herb, 4–6 ft. high. Leaves lance-shaped, 4–6 in. long, mostly in whorls. Flowers scarcely ⅛ in. long, in a loose terminal cluster, 6–9 in. long. Eastern N.A. but west to Manitoba. Summer. Suited to the more informal part of the wild garden. Known also as *Leptandra virginica* and *Veronica virginica.* (*Veronicastrum* is from *Veronica* and *astrum,* meaning false.)

verrucosa, *-us,* *-um* (ver-roo-kō′sa). Warty.

verruculosa, *-us,* *-um* (ver-rook-you-lō′sa). Slightly warty.

versicolor (ver-sick′o-lor). Variously colored.

verticillaris, *-e* (ver-ti-sill-air′is). Verticillate (*see* VERTICILLATA).

verticillata, *-us,* *-um* (ver-ti-sill-lay′ta). Verticillate; *i.e.,* arranged in circles around the stem, as in many lilies. *See* WHORL.

VERVAIN. *See* VERBENA.

VERVAIN MALLOW = *Malva Alcea.*

vesca, *-us,* *-um* (ves′ka). Weak and feeble.

VESICARIA (ves-i-care′i-a). Low-growing annual or perennial herbs, comprising about 5 species of the mustard family, natives of central Eu. and the Mediterranean region. Leaves alternate,* crowded at the base, simple, sometimes covered with soft hairs, the margins often deeply cut or toothed. Flowers large, yellow or purple, in racemes. Calyx of 4 sepals. Corolla of 4 petals. Stamens* 6, 4 long, 2 short. Fruit a 2-celled, inflated pod. (*Vesicaria* is from the Latin for bladder, in allusion to the pods.)

Not much in cult., the species below being the one generally grown. It should be treated as a hardy annual. Propagated by seeds sown in early spring where required to bloom.

utriculata. Bladder-pod. Perennial, but grown as an annual; of branching habit, slightly woody at the base, and growing to 18 in. high. Lower leaves ovalish, crowded on the stem. Upper leaves lance-shaped. Flowers yellow, in racemes.* Mediterranean region. Grown mostly for its pods. Considered by some as of the genus *Alyssoides.*

VESPERTINE. Flowering toward dusk.

vestita, *-us,* *-um* (ves-ty′ta). Clothed or covered, often with hairs, scales, etc.

VETCH. *See* VICIA. For other plants occasionally called vetch *see* ANTHYLLIS, ASTRAGALUS, and CORONILLA.

VETCHLING. *See* LATHYRUS.

VETIVER = *Vetiveria zizanioides.*

VETIVERIA (vet-i-veer′i-a). Tropical perennial grasses of only 1 species, and a native of the East Indies, but naturalized in the southern states and scarcely known elsewhere. (*Vetiveria* is the native Tamil name for this grass.)

Vetiver is important in the East, the roots being used for centuries for perfumery and medicinal purposes. Propagated by division of the rootstocks.

zizanioides. Vetiver. Khus-khus. Strong-growing perennial, to 8 ft. high, with thick, aromatic rootstocks. Leaves to 3 ft. long and ⅓ in. wide, clasping the stem, the margins saw-like. Flowers in pairs in short spikes arranged in a raceme a foot long. Also known as *Anatherum.*

VETKOUSIE. *See* MESEMBRYANTHEMUM POMERIDIANUM.

vexillaria, *-us,* *-um* (veck-sill-ar′i-a). Relating to the standard (a petal). *See* STANDARD, 2.

VEXILLUM. *See* STANDARD, 2.

VIABILITY OF SEED. *See* GARDEN TABLES II for the usual length of time for seeds to keep the power of germinating.

VI-APPLE = *Spondias cytherea.*

VIBURNUM (vy-bur′num). A large and valuable genus of shrubs and small trees of

---

* Special articles on the subjects indicated by an asterisk (*) will be found at the words so marked.

the honeysuckle family, many of the 150 known species cult. for ornament. They are chiefly deciduous shrubs of the north temperate zone, with opposite leaves and small, generally white flowers in showy, terminal clusters (panicles* or cymes*). Calyx with 5 very small teeth. Corolla bell-shaped or wheel-shaped, or even tubular. Stamens* 5. Fruit a 1-seeded, fleshy drupe,* often colored handsomely, persistent, and a favorite food of birds. (*Viburnum* is the classical Latin name of *V. Lantana,* the wayfaring-tree.)

The viburnums are generally of the easiest culture and consequently widely popular. Their attractive flower clusters, especially in some sorts known as snowball, and their often showy fruits make them very attractive shrubs. As the list of species indicates, they are found in a variety of heights, and their flowering period stretches over a considerable period. All of them have fine autumnal color in their foliage except *V. odoratissimum, V. Tinus, V. rhytidophyllum,* and *V. suspensum,* which are evergreen. Propagated by stratified seeds, cuttings, or by layering. All are white-flowered unless otherwise mentioned. Some of them are known as haw. Some of the species resemble *Cornus* (which see for the differences).

acerifolium. Dockmackie. Not over 5–6 ft. high. Leaves maple-like, 3-lobed, and coarsely toothed. Flower clusters long-stalked, about 3 in. wide. Fruit black-purple. May–June. Eastern N.A. Hardy from zone* 3 southward. Needs a soil of pH 4–5.

alnifolium. Hobblebush; also called American wayfaring-tree and witch-hobble. A spreading shrub 6–10 ft. high. Leaves nearly round, nearly 7 in. wide, irregularly toothed. Flower cluster flat-topped, nearly 5 in. wide, the marginal flowers nearly 1 in. wide and sterile. Fruit purplish-black. Eastern N.A. May–June. Hardy from zone* 2 southward.

americanum = *V. trilobum.*

betulifolium. A deciduous* shrub, 8–12 ft. high, the twigs purplish. Leaves ovalish or elliptic-oblong, 2–5 in. long, coarsely toothed, hairy in the axils* of the veins beneath. Flowers white, in a short-stalked, loose cluster (cyme*). Fruit nearly round, about ¼ in. wide, red and showy. China. June–July. Hardy from zone* 4 southward.

burkwoodi. A hybrid shrub, originated by A. Burkwood of Kingston-on-Thames, England, often reaching a height of 6–8 ft. Leaves half-evergreen, glossy above but hairy beneath, and with brown veins. Flowers fragrant, white, the cluster nearly 3 in. wide. Hardy from zone* 4 southward.

carlcephalum. A hybrid deciduous shrub (*carlesi* × *macrocephalum*) with the habit and foliage of *V. carlesi.* Flowers very fragrant, white. Considered by some as a superior plant to *V. carlesi,* but not in England, where it originated. April–May. Hardy from zone* 4 southward.

carlesi. A shrub 3–5 ft. high. Leaves ovalish, 2–3½ in. long, hairy both sides. Flowers fragrant, white or pinkish, the clusters (cymes*) dense. Fruit bluish-black. Korea. April–May. Hardy from zone* 3 southward. It is a useful

shrub for forcing, especially because of its handsome, fragrant flowers. *See* FORCING.

cassinoides. Witherod. Appalachian tea. A shrub 8–12 ft. high. Leaves ovalish, 3–4 in. long, finely toothed. Flowers in short-stalked clusters (cymes*). Fruit bluish-black. Eastern N.A. June–July. Hardy from zone* 2 southward.

"chenaulti." A trade name (of no botanical validity) for a shrub of unknown origin and identity.

davidi. An evergreen, compact shrub, not usually over 3 ft. high, the twigs warty. Leaves more or less elliptic, 2½–6 in. long, 3-veined, sometimes faintly toothed on the margin. Flowers dirty white, very small, packed in a flat cluster (corymb*) 2–3 in. wide. Fruit nearly round, ¼ in. long, blue. China. June. Hardy from zone* 6 southward.

dentatum. Arrow-wood. A shrub 10–15 ft. high. Leaves ovalish or round, 2–3 in. long, coarsely toothed. Flowers in long-stalked clusters (cymes*), which are about 3 in. wide. Fruit bluish-black. Eastern U.S. May–June. Hardy from zone* 2 southward. This and *V. cassinoides* are both good, if informal, hedge plants.

dilatatum. A shrub 6–10 ft. high. Leaves nearly round, about 4½ in. wide, hairy both sides and coarsely toothed. Flower clusters about 5 in. wide. Fruit scarlet. Jap. May–June. Hardy from zone* 3 southward, and an attractive shrub in the fall as the fruit is long-persistent.

fragrans. A deciduous* shrub, 5–9 ft. high, flowering before the leaves unfold, the twigs brown. Leaves elliptic, 2–4 in. long, pointed both ends, hairy on the veins beneath, the veins sunken. Flowers pinkish in bud, white when opened, small, fragrant, in loose clusters (panicles*) 1½–3 in. wide. Fruit football-shaped, blue, about ¼ in. long. China. April–May. Hardy from zone* 5 southward.

japonicum. An evergreen shrub, 4–6 ft. high, the foliage a dark, lustrous green. Leaves broadly oval, somewhat angled, 3–6 in. long, remotely toothed above the middle, sharp-pointed at the tip. Flowers white, small, very fragrant, crowded in a dense rounded cluster (cyme*), 3–4 in. wide. Fruit flattened-football-shaped, nearly ½ in. long, red. Jap. June. Hardy from zone* 6 southward.

juddi. A hybrid shrub related to *V. carlesi,* differing in a slightly wider flower cluster, pink in the bud but ultimately white and very fragrant. April–May. Hardy from zone* 4 southward.

Lantana. Wayfaring-tree. A tree-like shrub, 10–15 ft. high. Leaves ovalish, 3–5 in. long, hairy both sides, coarsely toothed. Flower clusters nearly 4 in. wide. Fruit red, but later turning black. Eurasia, but naturalized in the eastern U.S. June–July. Hardy from zone* 3 southward.

Lentago. Nannyberry. Sheepberry. A shrub, but more often tree-like, 20–30 ft. high. Leaves ovalish, 3–4 in. long, finely toothed. Flower clusters nearly 5 in. wide, stalkless. Fruit bluish-black, with a slight bloom. N.A. May–June. Hardy from zone* 2 southward.

macrocephalum. Chinese snowball. A deciduous or half-evergreen shrub, 7–12 ft. high, the twigs scurfy and hairy. Leaves elliptic or oblong, 2–5 in. long, rounded at the base, finely toothed, hairy beneath. Flowers white, in large globe-like clusters 4–7 in. thick, very showy. Most cult. in the *var.* **sterile,** which has the marginal flowers of its flat cluster much

---

* Special articles on the subjects indicated by an asterisk (*) will be found at the words so marked.

enlarged and sterile. China. May–June. Hardy from zone* 5 southward.

molle. Poison haw. A shrub 8–12 ft. high. Leaves nearly round, 3–5 in. long, coarsely toothed, and heart-shaped at the base. Flower clusters long-stalked, about 3 in. wide. Fruit bluish-black. Central U.S. June. Hardy from zone* 3 southward.

nudum. Possum haw. A native viburnum, deciduous, and growing 6–12 ft. high, the twigs a little scurfy. Leaves elliptic or broader, 2–5 in. long, faintly toothed, scurfy both sides when young. Flowers small, white or yellowish-white, stalked, in loose clusters (cymes*) that are 3–5 in. wide. Fruit nearly round, blue-black, about ⅜ in. long. Conn. to Fla. and Tex., mostly near the coast. June–July. Hardy from zone* 3 southward.

odoratissimum. A handsome evergreen shrub, 7–10 ft. high. Leaves ovalish, 4–6 in. long, practically without teeth, shining green above. Flowers fragrant, the clusters (panicles*) about 4 in. high. Fruit red, later black. India to Jap. May–June. Hardy from zone* 6 southward.

Opulus. Cranberry tree. A shrub 8–12 ft. high, useful in cities as it stands smoke very well. Leaves maple-like, 3–5-lobed, about 3½ in. wide, hairy on the under side. Flower clusters nearly 4 in. wide, stalked, the outer flowers nearly ¾ in. wide and sterile. Fruit red. Eurasia and northern Af. May–June. Hardy from zone* 2 southward. The var. **nanum** is a dwarf form with smaller leaves and is a good accent plant. The var. **sterile,** the common snowball or Guelder rose, is by far the most common in cult. Its ball-like flower clusters are wholly made up of sterile flowers. The plant is sometimes offered as *V. Opulus roseum.* It is useful for forcing (which see).

prunifolium. Black haw; also known as stag bush. A shrub or small tree 10–15 ft. high. Leaves broadly ovalish, 2–3 in. long, finely toothed. Flower clusters nearly 4 in. wide, stalkless. Fruit bluish-black, with a slight bloom. Conn. to Fla. and westward. April–May. Hardy from zone* 3 southward.

pubescens. A shrub 5–8 ft. high, the twigs hairy and grayish-brown. Leaves oval or roundish, 2½–5 in. long, coarsely toothed. Flowers white in a slender cluster (cyme*) 3–5 in. wide. Fruit blue-black, about ⅜ in. long. Eastern N.A. July. Hardy from zone* 2 southward. Some call this *V. rafinesquianum.*

rhytidophyllum. An evergreen shrub 7–10 ft. high. Leaves ovalish or oblong, 5–7 in. long, nearly without marginal teeth, wrinkled above, grayish or yellowish beneath, with felty hairs. Flowers yellowish-white, the clusters nearly 8 in. wide. Fruit red, later black. China. June. Hardy from zone* 4 southward.

sargenti. Resembling *Viburnum Opulus,* but with darker bark, thicker and sometimes larger leaves, and larger sterile flowers. Northeastern As. Hardy from zone* 5 southward.

setigerum. A deciduous shrub 7–12 ft. high, the twigs smooth. Leaves stalked, ovalish or oblong, 3–5½ in. long, faintly toothed or toothless, hairy on the veins beneath. Flowers about ¼ in. wide, white, in a 5-rayed cluster (cyme*) about 2 in. wide. Calyx* purple. China. May–June. Hardy from zone* 5 southward, perhaps in zone* 4 (in sheltered sites).

sieboldi. A shrub 8–10 ft. high. Leaves generally ovalish or broader toward the tip, 4–6 in. long, coarsely toothed, hairy beneath, of unpleasant odor when crushed. Flower cluster (panicle*) about 4 in. high. Fruit pink,

later bluish-black. Jap. May–June. Hardy from zone* 3 southward.

suspensum. An evergreen shrub 4–6 ft. high. Leaves ovalish, 3–4 in. long, toothed toward the tip. Flower cluster dense (a panicle*), pinkish, about 1½ in. wide. Fruit red, or black when mature. Ryukyu Islands, near Hong Kong. Hardy from zone* 6 southward.

theiferum = *Viburnum setigerum.*

Tinus. Laurustinus. A handsome evergreen shrub 7–10 ft. high. Leaves oblongish or broader, 2–3 in. long, without marginal teeth, dark green. Flower clusters about 3 in. wide, often faintly pinkish. Fruit black. Mediterranean region. July–Aug. Hardy from protected parts of zone* 6 southward. Long in cult. and a beautiful evergreen shrub, also known in several hort. forms, one with variegated leaves. Flowers unpleasantly scented.

tomentosum. A shrub 7–10 ft. high. Leaves ovalish, 3–4 in. long, hairy on the under side and toothed. Flower cluster long-stalked, more or less flat-topped, nearly 4 in. wide, the marginal flowers sterile and about 1 in. wide. Fruit red, ultimately bluish-black. China and Jap. May–June. Hardy from zone* 3 southward. The var. **sterile,** the Japanese snowball, has a large ball-shaped flower cluster wholly of sterile flowers. It is often offered as *V. tomentosum plicatum,* and is a useful shrub for forcing.

trilobum. Cranberry bush; also called high cranberry. A shrub 8–12 ft. high. Leaves broadly oval, 3-lobed and toothed, 3–5 in. long. Flower cluster short-stalked, nearly 4 in. wide, the marginal flowers sterile, and larger than the others. Fruit scarlet. Northern N.A. May–June. Fruit ripening in late July and persistent over most of the winter. Hardy from zone* 4 northward. Closely related to *V. Opulus* and perhaps not really separable, but the leaves of *trilobum* are smooth on the under side. The plant is sometimes known as *V. americanum.*

wrighti. A sturdy, upright shrub, 7–9 ft. high, the leaves nearly round, coarsely toothed and generally smooth. Flowers white, in a short-stalked cluster (cyme*) nearly 4 in. wide. Fruit red, showy, especially when the autumnal foliage turns red. Jap. May–June.

VICIA (viss'i-a). Vetch. Annual or perennial herbs, comprising about 200 species, belonging to the pea family, found distributed throughout the northern hemisphere and S.A. They are mostly hardy, climbing plants, a few erect. Leaves alternate,* compound, stalked, with 2 small leaf-like appendages (stipules*) at the base. Leaflets usually in 1–12 pairs, ovalish or lance-shaped, in the climbing species the end leaflet modified into a tendril* by means of which the plant climbs. Flowers blue, violet, yellowish, or white, pea-like, usually small, in short racemes* growing from the axils* of the leaves. Stamens* 10, 9 joined by their filaments* and 1 free. Fruit a flat pod (legume*), sometimes white-woolly within. (*Vicia* is the classical Latin name of the vetch.)

For cultivation *see* below.

Cracca. Cow vetch. Climbing perennial, to 5 ft. high. Leaflets lance-shaped, in 9–12 pairs. Flowers violet-purple, sometimes white, ½ in. long, in many-flowered, 1-sided racemes.* Fruit to 1 in. long. A most showy species. Eurasia and N.A.

Ervilia. Ervil. Bitter vetch. Erect, slightly

---

* Special articles on the subjects indicated by an asterisk (*) will be found at the words so marked.

hairy annual, growing to 2 ft. high. Leaflets lance-shaped, in 8–12 pairs, tendril* absent. Flowers rose-color, in 2–4-flowered racemes.* Fruit yellowish, to 1 in. long. Eu.

Faba. Broad bean. Horse bean. Strong-growing, erect, hardy annual growing to 5 ft. high, or more. Stipules* at the base of the leafstalk marked with a black spot. Leaflets ovalish, in 2–6 pairs, not always opposite, tendril* absent. Flowers in short racemes, white with purplish-black spot on the 2 side petals. Fruit a pod, sometimes 6–12 in. long, with a white-woolly lining in which the seeds are embedded. Seeds edible. Cult. from the earliest times in Eu. but scarcely known here. Northern Af. and southwestern As.

sativa. Common vetch. Spring vetch. Tare. Half-hardy, slightly hairy annual or biennial, growing 2–3 ft. high, of climbing habit. Leaflets lance-shaped, in 3–7 pairs. Flowers purplish, usually in a 2-flowered raceme.* Fruits to 3 in. long. Grown for forage, also as green manure (*see* cult. below). Eu.; naturalized in N.A.

villosa. Winter vetch. Hardy, hairy annual or biennial of climbing habit. Leaflets narrowly lance-shaped, in 5–10 pairs. Flowers violet-blue, numerous, in long, 1-sided racemes,* very showy. Fruit an inch long. Eurasia.

VETCH CULTURE

The common and winter vetches and their varieties are used as cover crops in orchards, but more often for their value as a green manure and for forage. Plowing in green vetch crops is very beneficial to the soil, the green part forming humus, which helps to hold moisture in the soil, while their nitrogen-fixing root tubercles add nitrogen to the soil (*see* LEGUMINOSAE). Seed should be sown broadcast, then harrowed and raked. The crop may be plowed under in about 3 months. It is sometimes cut and used as green fodder.

The cow vetch (*V. Cracca*) can be used as an ornamental climber. Propagated by seeds sown in early spring.

INSECT PESTS. Cutworms and corn earworms can be controlled by pesticide #17 (*see* SPRAYS AND DUSTS) or arsenicals. Pesticide #20 will control pea aphids and larvae of alfalfa weevil which feed on the plant in the East. Seed is attacked by one or more species of weevils. Pesticide #20 dust applied after flowers drop will kill weevils and prevent damage.

viciaefolia, -us, -um (vis-i-ee-fo′li-a). With vetch-like foliage. The name is sometimes spelled *viciifolia*.

VICTORIA (vick-tor′i-a). A remarkable genus of South American aquatic plants of the family Nymphaeaceae, two of the three known species cult. for ornament, and the largest water lilies in the world. They have thick rootstocks and long-stalked, huge, floating leaves, the margins turned up at the edges, the leaf thus appearing like a large, shallow, circular, floating pan, beautifully colored and veined; hence the name water platter, which is often applied to them. The stalks of the leaves and flowers and the under side of the leaves covered with stout, usually reddish prickles. Flowers

Victoria, the largest water lily in the world. In the foreground, some ordinary water lilies to show the size of *Victoria*.

floating, 7–18 in. wide, fragrant, white as they open toward evening, becoming pink or red the second day, after which they wither. Petals 50 or more, the stamens* thrice as numerous. Fruit berrylike. (Named for Queen Victoria.)

Of the two species below, *V. cruziana* is the chief one in cult. and is to be attempted only if you can give it the conditions described at WATER GARDEN, otherwise, it cannot be forced into bloom in the North. *Victoria regia*, a more spectacular plant, is found in the hot, steaming lagoons of the Amazon and the neighboring regions and is rare in cult. outside the tropics.

cruziana. Santa Cruz water lily, or water platter. Floating leaves 2–5 ft. wide, the upturned margins 6–8 in. high, the under side of the blade densely hairy, the radiating veins very large and conspicuous. Flowers deep pink or red the second day, the sepals with prickles only at the base. Paraguay.

regia. Royal water lily, or water platter. Floating leaves 3–6 ft. across, the upturned margin 2–4 in. high, the under side of the blade only slightly hairy. Flowers turning dull crimson the second day, the sepals prickly throughout. Amazon River and British Guiana. More difficult to cult. than *V. cruziana* as it needs greater heat. Also called *V. amazonica*.

trickeri = *V. cruziana*.

VICTORIAN BOX = *Pittosporum undulatum*.

VICTORIAN HAZEL = *Pomaderris*.

VIGNA (vig′na). Rather showy, chiefly tropical vines of the pea family, comprising 60 species and cult. mostly as cover crops or for green manuring or forage in the South, where they are sown as annuals, like beans, to which they are closely related. They are herbaceous vines with compound* leaves, having 3 leaflets. Flowers mostly in pairs at the ends of long stalks, pea-like, the pods

---

* Special articles on the subjects indicated by an asterisk (*) will be found at the words so marked.

(legumes*) long and cylindric. (Named for Dominicus Vigna, Italian scientist.) The species, if planted for the first time, need a culture of the proper sort of bacteria. *See* LEGUME INOCULATION.

Catjang. Catjang. Strong-growing, long-stemmed vine, much resembling *V. sesquipedalis*, but its erect pods 3–5 in. long. Tropics, and not so much cult. as the other two. Considered by some as *V. cylindrica*.

sesquipedalis. Asparagus bean. Yard-long bean. A trailing, long-stemmed vine, the leaflets angularly ovalish, 3–5 in. long. Flowers yellow or violet, nearly 1 in. long, usually 2, but sometimes 3, at the end of a long stalk. Pod (legume*) 1–3 ft. long, hanging or often flat on the ground, fleshy and flabby when young. Asia, but widely cult. throughout the tropics and in the southern U.S.

sinensis. Cowpea. Resembling *V. sesquipedalis*, but bushy, the hanging pods 8–12 in. long, not flabby when young. Asia (?). Grown in warm regions for green manure and for forage.

villosa, -us, -um (vil-lō′sa). Villous; *i.e.*, softly hairy.

villosula, -us, -um (vil-lō′su-la). Somewhat softly hairy.

viminalis, -e (vim-i-nay′lis). Osier-like; *i.e.*, willow-like.

viminea, -us, -um (vim-i-nee′a). Twiggy; like a wickerwork of osiers.

VINCA (vin′ka). Evergreen, erect or trailing perennial herbs or under-shrubs, comprising perhaps 8 species of the family Apocynaceae, natives of the Mediterranean region, tropical America, India, and Madagascar. Leaves opposite,* simple, ovalish, shining green, leathery. Flowers blue, pink, or white, salver-shaped, solitary, stalked, growing in the axils* of the leaves. Calyx small, with 5 lobes. Corolla tubular, its 5 lobes slightly twisted to the left. Stamens* 5, growing on the corolla. Fruit 1-celled, 6–8-seeded. (*Vinca* is the name used by Pliny for the periwinkle.)

The species commonly cult. are *Vinca major* and *Vinca minor*. The latter is a trailing evergreen plant, quite hardy, makes excellent ground cover under trees, and is good covering for shady banks. *Vinca major* is widely used for window boxes and commonly sold by florists. Both are easily cult. and propagated chiefly by cuttings or division.

Cuttings of young shoots may also be made during the summer months. They should be inserted in a mixture of ½ sand and ½ soil in a cold frame, kept well watered and shaded from sun. The sash should be kept closed except for an hour each day until rooted, when they may be planted out in ordinary garden soil in a shady position. Tips should be pinched to make plants bushy.

Vinca rosea is used for bedding purposes and for pot plants, and is usually treated as a tender annual. Propagated by seeds sown ⅛ in. deep in pans in Feb. or Mar. under glass in a temperature of 60°–70°. As soon as large enough to handle, they should be potted into 3-in. pots, using potting mixture * 3, and be kept under glass until danger of frost is over. If kept through the winter, cuttings may be taken in early spring.

major. A trailing evergreen, the stems thin and wiry. Leaves opposite, simple, ovalish, heart-shaped at base, shiny dark green. Flowers blue, 1–2 in. across. Eu. The most widely grown form is *var.* variegata, much used in window boxes. Not hardy in the North, but often a ground cover in the South.

minor. Periwinkle. Creeping myrtle. Running myrtle. Trailing, hardy evergreen, the stems thin and wiry. Leaves opposite, broadly lance-shaped, to 2 in. long, shiny dark green. Flowers light blue, ¾ in. across. Eu., naturalized in the U.S. There are several hort. color forms. One of the best ground covers for shady places except in the South.

rosea. Madagascar periwinkle. Tender, erect, ever-blooming perennial, growing to 2 ft., mostly grown as a tender annual. Leaves opposite, lance-shaped, prominently veined. Flowers showy, pink or white, often with reddish eye, 1½ in. across. Madagascar. Also called *Catharanthus roseus.*

VINCETOXICUM ACUMINATUM = *Cynanchum acuminatifolium.*

VINE. The vine of antiquity and history is always the grape. *See* GRAPE for culture and VITIS for the wild species of grape. *Vine* as a general hort. term includes all woody or herbaceous plants that creep, climb, or trail, as distinguished from those that stand without support. For their garden uses *see* VINES.

VINE-BOWER = *Clematis Viticella.*

VINE CACTUS = *Fouquieria splendens.*

VINE FAMILY = Vitaceae.

VINEGARWEED = *Trichostema lanceolatum.* *See* BLUECURLS.

VINE MAPLE = *Acer circinatum.* *See* MAPLE.

VINE PEACH = Mango melon. *See* MELON.

VINES. Under this term the gardener includes all plants, whether woody or herbaceous, that require some support for their proper development. While some climb by tendrils,* others are self-twiners, while still others need to be tied or nailed to the structure they are to cover. Some have sucking disks that help them to cling to their support, as shown in the illustration on page 1267.

By whatever method grown, all the vines of garden interest may be grouped into six classes:

1. WALL-TOP TUMBLERS. This includes familiar favorites suitable for planting on retaining walls, to drape and veil an old ruin, or sprawl gracefully over unsightly objects and tumble about outcroppings of stone and rocky elevations.

2. CREEPERS AND TRAILERS. These re-

---

* Special articles on the subjects indicated by an asterisk (*) will be found at the words so marked.

semble carpets, but the growth takes root at frequent intervals and establishes separate colonies of plants quite independent of the parent group. They resemble ground covers, often sprawling about as undergrowth in woods and natural plantings. *See also* GROUND COVERS.

3. TWINING PLANTS AND STEM CLIMBERS. Here belong plants that support themselves by the spiral action of leaf or stem and climb upon anything near them.

4. WOODY VINES. The grape and many others with tendrils* or sucking disks, upon which they depend for support.

5. ANNUAL VINES. Includes many tender perennials treated as annuals. They are valuable as quick summer fillers and of great decorative value.

6. SOUTHERN AND GREENHOUSE VINES. Many good plants are put to walls and fences in a mixed and careless manner, hence losing their true character and crowding each other out of recognition. Some of these vines have nearly tropical luxuriance and are most valuable in hiding unsightly objects, covering ruins, or traveling to great heights on dead trees. These lusty growers should be kept away from buildings which would otherwise require constant cleaning.

From the six groups of vines below, the gardener can pick nearly everything he needs in the way of herbaceous or woody vines. Remember that every one has additional information at its generic name in the ENCYCLOPEDIA. Turn to these entries for special notes on hardiness or culture, too extensive to duplicate here.

The Dutchman's-pipe has handsome leaves for covering a porch or arbor.

1. WALL-TOP TUMBLERS

These generally need no special fastening and will cling without tying. The plants listed here are very effective in the situations already mentioned, namely, straight bare walls and ruins, which then take on variety and color which they previously lacked.

Rosa wichuraiana. Memorial rose. This is either a creeper or may be used to grow over walls.

Forsythia suspensa. The most graceful of the early golden bells if left unpruned. It is scarcely a vine, but becomes vine-like on steep banks.

Clematis Vitalba and *C. paniculata* are two profuse, white-flowered favorites. *See also* CLEMATIS.

Clematis montana. Well known for its pure white garlands festooning over old ruins, trees, and fences. The *var.* **rubens** is considered one of the most successful to grow. *See also* CLEMATIS.

Lycium chinense and the English ivy will succeed if the wall is shady.

Parthenocissus vitacea is most suitable as a tumbler because it does not cling to supports, and has the most brilliant autumn coloring.

Celastrus scandens. The bittersweet has a poor reputation in a confined area, but for wilderness beauty on poor soil it has no equal. In the autumn it exposes its orange and scarlet fruits.

Ampelopsis japonica yields a decorative berry that changes from white to purple and blue; from zone* 5 southward.

Vitis coignetiae is the most ornamental and healthy of the ornamental grapevines.

Rosa setigera. The prairie rose, if planted in good soil and in an open position, will provide two show seasons, first, in late June with its great wealth of clear pink single flowers. In autumn and winter it is covered with orange-scarlet fruit which provides winter food for birds.

2. CREEPERS AND TRAILERS

This group are mostly prostrate vines or trailers. Perhaps the best known and most easily grown are:

Lysimachia Nummularia. Yellow flowers in summer; prostrate.

Lonicera japonica aureo-reticulata. This is the smallest of all the Japanese honeysuckles; sprawling.

Vinca minor. Periwinkle. Prefers shade. Flowers usually blue; common also as a ground cover.

Hedera Helix. English ivy. Prefers shade. Protect from direct sun after sharp frost; will also cover walls.

Cotoneaster. The genus provides many prostrate vines for covering rocks or banks and all bear attractive fruits. *See* COTONEASTER.

Coronilla varia. Crown vetch. Pink, pealike flowers and feathery foliage; prostrate or sprawling.

Lantana montevidensis. Beautiful, nearly prostrate or trailing shrub with mauve flowers all summer. Useful only from zone* 6 southward.

Saponaria ocymoides. Lavender-flowered or pink-flowered prostrate herb. Prefers moisture, but good drainage.

---

* Special articles on the subjects indicated by an asterisk (*) will be found at the words so marked.

Creeping vines such as English ivy and periwinkle do well under the shade of trees, but the ivy will also climb if it has a chance.

3. TWINING PLANTS AND STEM CLIMBERS

Actinidia arguta. Tara vine. Woody; foliage glossy, with red stalks. Flowers brownish-white.

Actinidia chinensis. Yangtao. Even finer than *A. arguta*, but more tender. Leaf-veins covered with reddish hairs.

Akebia quinata. Flowers purplish-brown, fragrant.

Aristolochia durior. Dutchman's-pipe. Large-leaved, handsome woody vine with yellow-brown flowers.

Celastrus orbiculatus. Resembles the native bittersweet, but it harbors an infective scale that may infest neighboring *Euonymus*.

Decumaria barbara. Hydrangea-like, white-flowered vine, safe only from zone* 5 southward.

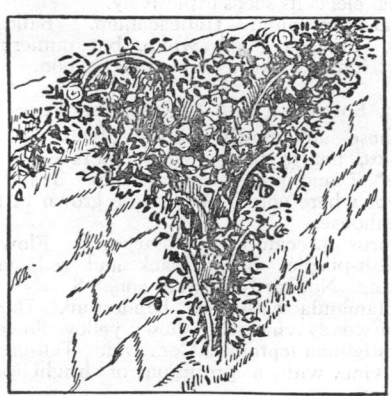

A climbing rose grown against a wall

Eccremocarpus scaber. Showy Chilean vine with orange-red flowers. Not hardy northward except as an annual. *See* ECCREMOCARPUS.

Humulus Lupulus. Hop. Covers almost anything with its profuse foliage in a single season. Flowers inconspicuous. *See* HOP for other species.

Lathyrus grandiflorus. Everlasting pea. Pink and white flowers resembling the sweet pea, but our plant is a perennial.

Menispermum canadense. Canada moonseed. Woody vine with white and yellow flowers.

Passiflora incarnata. Beautiful vine with white and purple flowers in midsummer. Not hardy northward.

Periploca graeca. Silk vine. Flowers greenish-brown. Hardy from zone* 5 southward.

Polygonum auberti. Silver-lace vine. Profuse summer-blooming, white-flowered vine.

Lonicera. Among the climbing honeysuckles the best evergreen ones are *L. japonica*, *L. henryi*, and *L. sempervirens*. The best deciduous climbing honeysuckle is *L. Periclymenum*. Of the native or hybrid species *L. heckrotti* will bloom from June to frost and *L. flava* has yellow flowers. For other species *see* LONICERA.

Among the most showy of all vines, usually needing a trellis or wall for proper support, are the various forms of the climbing roses. *See* ROSE.

4. WOODY VINES LIKE THE GRAPE AND OTHERS WITH TENDRILS* OR SUCKING DISKS*

For this group provide wire for safe attachment, especially as they get older and their large woody stems become heavy.

Vitis. The most ornamental species of grape, easily grown, is *V. coignetiae*. *See* VITIS.

Euonymus fortunei. An evergreen, red-berried creeper, with fine leathery foliage. Suitable for walls.

Wistaria sinensis is the commonest of the cult. wisterias. It is a fine woody vine with an almost tropical cast of foliage. Some

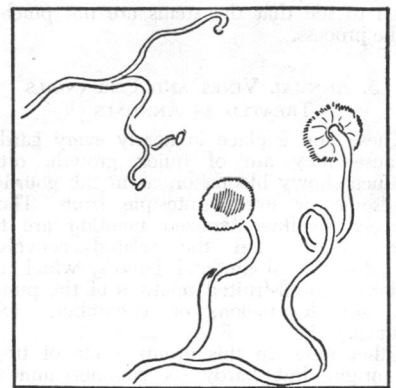

The sucking disks (*enlarged*) at the ends of Boston ivy tendrils which help it to cling to walls.

* Special articles on the subjects indicated by an asterisk (*) will be found at the words so marked.

plants do not always flower. To help them bloom, the vine should be pruned at least three times during spring and summer. After August 1 the new growth can be left for the next spring's pruning. For other fine species *see* WISTARIA.

Hydrangea petiolaris. Climbing hydrangea. A woody vine from Japan which sticks to wood or brick with considerable firmness.

Parthenocissus quinquefolia, the Virginia creeper, and *P. tricuspidata,* the Boston ivy, will both cling to buildings easily and provide brilliant autumnal color. *P. tricuspidata lowi,* a small-leaved form of the Boston ivy, has young foliage which is purplish.

Pyracantha coccinea lalandi. A white-flowered, orange-fruited shrub that does well trained on a wall.

Schizophragma hydrangeoides. A Japanese woody vine somewhat resembling *Hydrangea petiolaris* and more difficult to grow. Scarcely hardy north of zone* 4.

Another group of woody vines, especially suited for limited wall spaces and hardy only in Calif. and other warm regions, comprise the following:

Azara microphylla. A Chilean shrub easily trained on a wall, with greenish flowers and orange fruit.

Jasminum humile. Italian jasmine. Its weak branches are almost vine-like and can be trained on a wall. Flowers yellow.

Ficus pumila. Climbing fig. A slender vine with numerous small leaves. Will completely cover small brick or cement walls, and cling safely in the early stages. Older and larger leaves will not cling, and the plant must be tied to a support.

Many wall-climbing vines, even if they have the sucking disks of the Boston ivy, are best secured by staples driven into the mortar between bricks or stones, when the vines are old and the stems heavy. They may be fastened to the staple by wires run through old pieces of hose, and care must be taken to see that the stems are not pinched in the process.

5. ANNUAL VINES AND PERENNIALS TREATED AS ANNUALS

These find a place in nearly every garden because they are of quick growth, often produce showy bloom, or, as in the gourds,* handsome or even grotesque fruit. Those scarcely needing itemized mention are the morning-glory and the related convolvulus, also the ornamental gourds, which are curious colored-fruited relatives of the pumpkin, squash, melon, or cucumber. (*See* GOURDS.)

Other vines in this group, some of tropical origin but hardy as summer annuals, are:

Quamoclit lobata and *Q. coccinea.* Crimson-flowered herbaceous vines from tropical America. Very showy and quick-growing.

A quick-growing, tropical, annual vine is *Cobaea scandens.*

Tropaeolum. Any of the tall-growing hort. varieties of nasturtium*; also *T. peregrinum,* the Canary-bird flower.

Humulus japonicus. Japanese relative of the common hop. Useful only for foliage. *See* HOP.

Thunbergia alata. Showy, orange-yellow flowers in midsummer. *See* THUNBERGIA for other species.

Echinocystis lobata. Wild balsam apple. A native climber with lobed leaves and profuse white flowers.

Cobaea scandens. Very handsome Mexican vine, usually treated as an annual, with large violet or greenish-purple flowers.

Dolichos Lablab. Hyacinth bean. Showy purple or white flowers, pea-like pods, and large leaflets.

Ecballium Elaterium. Squirting cucumber. Yellow-flowered vine with peculiar fruit which ejects its seeds explosively.

Cardiospermum Halicacabum. Balloon-vine. Flowers small, white, but numerous. Fruit inflated like a miniature balloon.

6. SOUTHERN AND GREENHOUSE VINES

These are mostly woody plants of the tropics, not to be grown outdoors north of zone* 7 and preferably in zones* 8 and 9, except where noted. All can be grown in the greenhouse.

Abrus precatorius. Rosary-pea. Flowers reddish-purple. Seeds black and red, very striking. Not hardy north of zone* 8.

Allamanda cathartica hendersoni. Handsome woody vine with showy yellow flowers.

Antigonon leptopus. Coral vine. Tall-growing vine with a profusion of bright pink flowers.

Aristolochia elegans. Calico-flower. Tropical relative of the Dutchman's-pipe with flowers 3 in. across.

Bignonia capreolata. Cross-vine. Related to the common trumpet-creeper. Hardy to zone* 4.

Bougainvillaea (*see* that genus). These

---

are among the finest and most showy of all tropical vines, often growing 50–60 ft. in height.

Clerodendron thomsonae. Bag-flower. A West African woody vine with very showy white and red flowers.

Clianthus dampieri. Glory-pea. Low-growing vine or weak shrub with scarlet, purple-blotched flowers.

Doxantha Unguis-cati. Cat's-claw. Tropical American woody vine with bright yellow flowers and spiny, claw-like tendrils.

Gloriosa superba. Tuberous-rooted, tropical, herbaceous vine with red and yellow flowers.

Hoya carnosa. Wax-plant. Thick-leaved, low-growing vine with white and pink flowers.

Jasminum grandiflorum. Spanish jasmine. Fragrant white flowers. A shrub to 20 ft. with weak, vine-like branches.

Lapageria rosea. Chilean bellflower. Showy rose-colored flowers nearly 4 in. long. There is a white-flowered hort. variety.

Stephanotis floribunda. Madagascar jasmine. A woody vine with white, fragrant, waxy flowers.

Tecomaria capensis. Cape honeysuckle. Very showy relative of the native trumpet-creeper, with red, orange, or scarlet flowers.

Thunbergia grandiflora. Sky-flower. A woody vine from India with blue flowers.

Trachelospermum jasminoides. Star jasmine. A fragrant, white-flowered vine common throughout the South and hardy to zone* 6.

No account of garden vines would be complete without mention of *Clematis*. But there are so many species and varieties of these handsome plants that there is no space to repeat an account of them here. *See* CLEMATIS. — D. W.

vinifera, -us, -um (vy-niff′er-a). Wine- or grape-bearing. The *vinifera* grapes are *Vitis vinifera*, the leading sorts used for making wine. *See* GRAPE.

VIOLA (vy-ō′la). Violet. Hardy perennial, and a few annual herbs, comprising about 500 species of the family Violaceae, found distributed throughout the temperate regions of the world, and including the violet and the pansy. They are low-growing plants, generally of tufted* habit, some species producing runners. Leaves basal or growing on the stems. Basal leaves simple, heart-shaped or ovalish, sometimes cut into finger-like lobes, slightly wrinkled, stalked, the stalks grooved, the margins coarsely toothed. Stem leaves alternate,* simple, ovalish, usually stalked, the margins with rounded teeth. Two stipules* (leafy appendages) at base of the stem leaves are usually cut into 3 lobes. Flowers stalked, solitary, sometimes nodding, violet, blue, reddish-purple, lilac, yellow, or white. Calyx of 5 sepals. Corolla of 5 petals, 4 arranged in pairs, each pair differing, the lower petal spurred.* Stamens 5, with an orange, shield-shaped appendage at the top of each anther. Fruit a 3-celled, many-seeded capsule. Some species have two kinds of flowers, non-fertile, the showy spring flowers, and fertile, the summer flowers, which are completely closed, never open and are self-fertilizing (cleistogamous*). (*Viola* is the classical Latin name of the violet.)

For culture *see* below. All bloom early in the spring, except some of the hort. varieties, which bloom later.

blanda. Sweet white violet. Low-growing, tufted perennial. Leaves basal, ovalish, slightly hairy on the upper side, stalked. Flowers white, solitary. Petals narrow and reflexed. Quebec to Ga. and westward.

canadensis. Canada violet. Tufted perennial, growing 1 ft. or more. Leaves broadly heart-shaped, stalked, the margins toothed. Flowers white with yellow eye, tinged purple on the outside. Canada and northern U.S.

cornuta. Horned violet. Bedding pansy. Tufted pansy. Tufted perennial with branching stems. Leaves alternate, ovalish, slightly wrinkled, stalked, the margins with rounded teeth. Stipules (leafy appendages) at the base of the leaves, triangular, cut into 3 or more segments. Flowers violet, solitary, stalked. Spain and the Pyrenees. There are many color forms in cult. See ROCK GARDEN.

cucullata. Blue violet. Strong-growing, tufted* perennial to 6 in. high. Leaves basal, broadly heart-shaped, stalked, the margins coarsely toothed. Flowers violet, with white or greenish eye, solitary. Eastern N.A.

florariensis. A hybrid violet (*cornuta* × *tricolor*), originating at Correvon's garden, Floraire, near Geneva. Being a cross between the horned violet and the wild form of the pansy it combines features of both parents. Flowers yellow and purple, much longer-lasting than the pansy.

gracilis. Hairy perennial of straggling habit, growing to 1 ft. high. Leaves simple, alternate, ovalish, slightly toothed. Stipules* (leafy appendages) at the base of the leaves, deeply cut into segments. Flowers violet, long-spurred. (*See* GRAY AND LAVENDER GARDEN.) Macedonia and Asia Minor.

jooi. A low violet with creeping rootstocks, not over 2–3 in. high. Leaves ovalish, long-stalked, heart-shaped at the base, with rounded teeth; about 1½ in. wide. Flowers fragrant, pinkish, purple-streaked, nearly ¾ in. wide. Southeastern Eu. May and often later.

lutea. A leafy-stemmed, pansy-like violet, 3–6 in. high, with creeping rootstocks. Leaves ovalish, rounded at the base, the upper leaves much narrower and pointed at the base, all wavy-toothed. Flowers about 1 in. long, yellow or violet or sometimes both colors. Eu. May. Thought to be one of the ancestors of the garden pansy.

odorata. Sweet violet. Florists' violet. Garden violet. Tufted perennial, producing long runners which root at the joints. Leaves basal, broadly heart-shaped and stalked, the margins with rounded teeth. Flowers deep violet or white, sweet-scented, the spur short. Eu., Af., and As. The hort. *var.* **alba** is a white form. The *var.* **pallida plena**, the Neapolitan violet, is pale lavender and with double flowers. A hort. variety, Marie Louise, a double-flowered, reddish-purple, very fragrant plant, can be substituted here for the Parma violet, a form of the Neapolitan violet, which is apparently not in cult. in the U.S.

pallens. A native violet, stemless, but with

---

* Special articles on the subjects indicated by an asterisk (*) will be found at the words so marked.

a creeping rootstock, and not over 3–5 in. high, the flowers slightly higher than the foliage. Leaves heart-shaped, yellowish-green, 1–4 in. long. Flowers not fragrant, white, the lower petals purple-streaked. N.A., often in moist places. April–May.

papilionacea. Meadow violet. A native stemless violet, with a stout, branching rootstock. Leaves long-stalked, shallowly heart-shaped, rather coarse and 3–6 in. wide. Flowers longstalked, blue, with a lighter center, about ½ in. long. N.A. April–May.

pedata. Bird's-foot violet. Perennial of tufted* habit, with short, thick crown. Leaves basal, cut into lobes shaped like a bird's foot, the lobes cut and toothed near the tip. Flowers usually with 2 upper petals dark violet and 3 lower soft lilac. Eastern and Midwestern states, especially in dry, open places. April–May. There is also a variety with narrower leaf lobes and more showy flowers than the type. *See* WILD GARDEN.

pendunculata. Golden violet. Grass pansy. A Californian violet with a stem 6–12 in. high. Leaves ovalish to triangular, nearly 2 in. wide, blunt at the base. Flowers yellow, brownstreaked, nearly 1 in. long and showy. Flowering in winter in Calif., dormant in summer, and difficult to grow elsewhere.

priceana. Confederate violet. A plant resembling V. *papilionacea* a wild violet, but with the larger, much paler, whitish-blue flowers strongly veined with dark blue stripes. Ky. to Ga. and westward. Long known in cult. in the South, very vigorous and perhaps the most satisfactory and showy of all our wild violets.

pubescens. Yellow violet. A softly hairy, branching herb, 8–12 in. high, most of the leaves near the top, kidney-shaped and with finely toothed margins. Flowers generally solitary or few, yellow. In rich woods, eastern N.A. April–May. Other yellow violets are occasionally dug from the wild.

rotundifolia. A native violet of rich woods, especially under conifers, with a stout, jagged rootstock. Leaves in maturity lying flat on the ground, ovalish, but deeply heart-shaped at the base, in summer 4–6 in. long, much less in spring, rather thick and coarse. Flowers yellow, the lower petals brown-veined. Cooler parts of eastern N.A. May. A wild garden plant needing woodsy, acid soil and deep shade. Not suited to open warm sites.

striata. A leafy-stemmed native violet, 4–15 in. high, the leaves heart-shaped, long-stalked, arising among eroded stipules.* Flowers fragrant, ivory-white but veined brown-purple. U.S. May. Prefers moist and partially shady sites in the wild garden.

tricolor hortensis. Pansy. Heartsease. Johnnyjump-up. Short-lived perennial of straggling habit, growing to 1 ft. or more. Stems branching and usually square. Basal leaves heartshaped, the stem leaves alternate, ovalish or lance-shaped, the margins toothed. Stipules* (leafy appendages) at the base of the leaves, large, cut into small segments near the base. Flowers 3-colored, blue, white, and yellow, solitary, stalked, growing in the axils of the leaves. They differ from the other violas in that the corolla is flattish and roundish and the petals overlap. For cult. *see* PANSY.

VIOLA CULTURE

Violas are among the most popular and useful spring- and summer-flowering plants.

The hort. varieties that are similar to the pansy in appearance and commonly called tufted pansies or horned violets are used extensively for bedding purposes, in fact fulfill the uses of the pansy, as they withstand the summer heat better and have a longer flowering period. Among the best are:

Arkwright Ruby.	Wallflower-red with dark central markings.
Yellow Queen.	Large, deep yellow.
Avalanche.	White.
Blue Butterfly.	Blue.

The smaller flowering violas, with violet-type flowers, are the kind mostly used for the rock garden or edges of the border.

Jersey Gem. Blue.	Lutea splendens. Yellow.
Apricot.	White Perfection.
Mauve Queen.	

Violas are easily cult., but for best results should have partially shaded positions in rich, moist soil. Propagated by seeds, division of rootstocks, and cuttings. Seeds should be sown in boxes, ⅛ in. deep, in cold frame or cool greenhouse in Sept. or early spring. If sown in the fall they must be transplanted to cold frame and kept there during winter; if sown in spring they may be transplanted to permanent positions as soon as large enough to handle. Divisions of rootstocks may be made in Sept. or early spring. Cuttings of young shoots 2–3 in. long may be made in Sept. They should be inserted in sandy soil in a cold frame, shaded from sun. Sash should be kept closed except for an hour each day until rooted. They must be left in the cold frame during the winter, admitting air whenever possible.

The native violets are usually distinguished from violas by having basal leaves, although some, like V. *canadensis* and V. *pubescens*, have stem leaves. They are used extensively for naturalizing in the wild garden. The best species are:

V. *priceana*.	Pale, streaked violet.
V. *pedata*.	Violet-mauve.
V. *cucullata*.	Violet.
V. *canadensis*.	White with purple.

There are also many other wild species which may be transferred to the garden.

These are propagated by seeds and runners. Seeds should be sown ⅛ in. deep, in boxes, and be placed outdoors or in open cold frame in the fall. Exposure to the weather is necessary, as freezing assists germination of the seed. Runners, which some of them produce freely, may be separated from the parent plant as soon as rooted.

Varieties of *Viola odorata*, the sweet or florists' violet, are grown for flowering during the cool months, and sold by the florists under various names. They should be planted in early spring in deep, rich soil outdoors, in semi-shady position, and be kept well watered.

They should be removed to cold frame or cool greenhouse in Sept. If grown in cold

---

* Special articles on the subjects indicated by an asterisk (*) will be found at the words so marked.

frame they must be protected from frost. Winter greenhouse temperature should be 35°–50°. If given heat, the atmosphere must be kept moist or plants will be attacked by red spider. Fertilizer should be given occasionally. Hardy strains of *V.' odorata* can be grown outdoors, but they are not so fragrant as true *V. odorata*.

INSECT PESTS. Red spider can be controlled as at CARNATION. For aphid control, use pesticide #1 or #21 (*see* SPRAYS AND DUSTS).

DISEASES. *See* PANSY.

violacea, -us, -um (vy-o-lay'see-a). Violet-colored.

VIOLACEAE (vy-o-lay'see-ee). The violet family comprises some 16 genera and 800 species of herbs, or in the tropics, shrubs and even trees, of which the only cult. genus is *Viola,* which includes the violets and the pansy. *See* VIOLA.

VIOLET. *See* VIOLA. For other plants to which the name violet is sometimes applied *see* ERYTHRONIUM, HESPERIS, and SAINTPAULIA.

VIOLET IRIS = *Iris verna.*

VIOLET SAGE = *Salvia nemorosa.*

VIOLET WOOD SORREL = *Oxalis violacea.*

VIPER'S-BUGLOSS. *See* ECHIUM.

VIRENS (vy'renz). Green.

virgata, -us, -um (vir-gay'ta). Wand-like; also twiggy.

virginalis, -e (vir-ji-nal'is). Virginal; *i.e.,* white.

VIRGINIA. The flowering dogwood is the state flower and the state tree. The state lies wholly in zones° 4, 5, and 6.

SOILS. The natural regions of the state embrace the coastal plain, the piedmont plateau and the limestone valleys, and each of these regions has its own particular types of soil. The limestone valleys lie between the Blue Ridge Mountains on the southeast and the Allegheny Mountains on the northwest.

Only the well-drained soils of the coastal plain now have horticultural possibilities for truck farming and for floriculture, and they include the following series of soils: Norfolk, Moyock, Onslow, Craven, Kalmia, Rustin, and Sassafras. These soils are all derived from a parent material of unconsolidated sands and clays of marine deposit and they vary in topography from smooth to rolling. In the piedmont plateau region the soils of greatest horticultural possibilities are derived from granite and basic rocks. Among the soils of granitic origin, the most extensive are Cecil fine sandy loam and Appling fine sandy loam; and the principal difference between these two types is that the subsoil of Appling is lighter in color than that of Cecil. Davidson loam or clay loam is derived from diorites or other basic rock and is known locally as red land and is one of the most productive soils in this region.

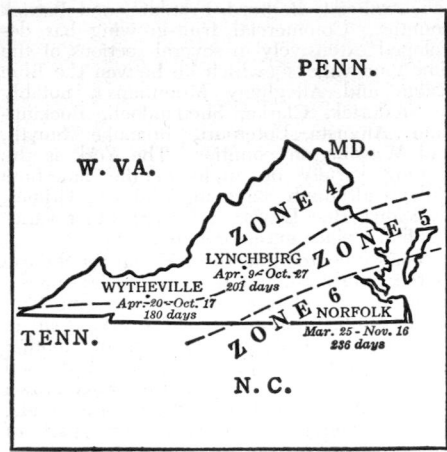

VIRGINIA

The zones of hardiness crossing Virginia are those shown on the map located at ZONE, which should be consulted for details. The dates are the average latest killing frost in spring and the first one in the fall. The figures below the dates show the average length of the growing season.

The principal types of soil in the limestone valleys are Frederick silt loam and Hagerstown loam, and both types are suitable for the growing of fruits, vegetables, and flowers.

GARDENING. The region around Norfolk is one of the most important trucking regions of the United States. Water, railroad, and motor truck transportation place this region in an advantageous position with respect to the great centers of population in our country including the cities of Washington, Baltimore, Philadelphia, New York, and Boston; and truck crops are also shipped to many inland cities. Early potatoes (particularly in Accomac and Northampton counties on the eastern shore), sweet potatoes, cabbage, kale, spinach, and strawberries are grown here on a large scale.

Home gardens are found without exception everywhere in the rural parts of the state, and many of the householders in towns and cities have vegetable gardens. Some of these home gardens have a large assortment of vegetables, in some cases thirty to forty kinds.

FRUIT-GROWING. The growing of apples and peaches on a commercial scale is an important industry in the piedmont plateau region along the foothills of the Blue Ridge Mountains and even in the coves of the mountains. The Albemarle Pippin and Winesap apples made this region famous for fruit-growing in the early history of commercial fruit-growing in the United States. Among the centers of fruit-growing here should be mentioned Rappahannock, Albemarle, Nelson, Amherst, Bedford, Franklin, and Patrick counties. Commercial fruit-growing has developed extensively in several sections of the limestone valleys (which lie betwen the Blue Ridge and Allegheny Mountains), notably in Frederick, Clarke, Shenandoah, Rockingham, Augusta, Botetourt, Roanoke, Smyth, and Washington counties. The York is the leading variety of apple in the limestone valleys, although Stayman, Winesap, Grimes, Delicious, Ben Davis, and many other varieties find a place in the orchards.

Small orchards that furnish fruit for the use of the family are found on about 90% of the farms in the state, and fruit of some kind could readily be grown on every farm in Virginia, for fruit of one sort or another may be grown on practically all of the soil types of the state. Among the fruits grown successfully in home orchards are apple, apricot, cherry, fig (southeastern part of state), peach, pear, plum, quince, grape, persimmon, chestnut (now disappearing), hazelnut, pecan, walnut, blackberry, dewberry, blueberry, cranberry, currant, gooseberry, raspberry, strawberry, and a few others. There is a considerable range of varieties in most of these species from which the farmer may choose the kinds that will serve his needs. The health-giving qualities of fruits make the home orchard a necessary adjunct to the homestead.

ORNAMENTALS. Growing conditions in the state change appreciably with changes in altitude. The coastal plain region has a sufficiently mild and equable climate for the cultivation of live oak, cedar-of-Lebanon, sweet bay magnolia; for shrubs or small trees like Portuguese laurel, yaupon, *Eurya, Osmanthus, Viburnum Tinus, Gardenia,* and the tender azaleas; for vines like *Wistaria,* and Carolina jasmine; for flowers like *Iris,* sea lavender, thrift, rosemary, *Hibiscus,* and Cape fuchsia, also the tea roses.

Most of these plants, were they moved into the less mild climate of the piedmont plateau, would not tolerate the change in exposure without a good deal of protection in winter. Whereas shingle oak, *Cryptomeria* and mimosa, boxwoods, evergreen barberries, evergreen loniceras, American hollies (except yaupon), cherry laurel, and crape myrtle, lavenders, lupines, *Salvia patens,* and pentstemons would probably prove adaptable. The piedmont plateau is well adapted to the growing of willow oaks, swamp maple, *Nyssa,* elm, and hackberries; hollies, bayberries, blueberries, groundsel-bush and gorse; Cherokee, McCartney and Lady Banks' roses; magnolias, azaleas, laurels, jasmines, and gardenias; heathers, lilies, and bulbs in general.

In the limestone valleys, which are bounded on the southeast by the Blue Ridge Mountains and on the northwest by the Allegheny Mountains, the natural growth includes such ornamental species as balsams, white pine, hemlocks, arborvitae, sugar maple, mountain maple, mountain-ash, mountain laurels, rhododendrons, andromedas, hardy azaleas, *Calycanthus,* viburnums, hawthorns, crabapple, hypericums, and hardy roses; bleeding-heart, turk's-cap lily, marsh marigold, celandine, *Mertensia, Gillenia, Tradescantia, Trillium,* and mountain phlox. Most of these are plants so attached to their native region that it is difficult to transplant them to a new environment, but *see,* in this connection, WILD GARDEN. Hardy garden shrubs and perennials are adapted here and many half-hardy sorts will thrive in sheltered spots in soil properly prepared, especially if slight protection is given in winter and early spring.

GARDEN RESTORATIONS. At present, restoration work is being carried on at Woodlawn Plantation near Mount Vernon and Alexandria. Previous restorations have included the grounds and gardens at Kenmore, Fredericksburg; the garden at Stratford Hall in Westmoreland County; the memorial garden at the Lee Chapel, Lexington; the garden at Woodrow Wilson's Birthplace, Staunton; the grounds at Wilton, Richmond; the Rolfe Property in Surry County; Bruton Parish Churchyard, Williamsburg; Mary Washington Monument, Fredericksburg; Thomas Jefferson's garden and walls at Monticello, Charlottesville; completion of Betty Washington Lewis's flower garden at Kenmore; Christ Churchyard, Middlesex County, and the Churchyard at Fincastle; gardens at Gunston Hall, Lorton; grounds of the Barter Theatre Players Home at Abingdon; and the gardens lying between the West Lawn and the West Range at the University of Virginia.

One of the outstanding garden areas in Virginia is Colonial Williamsburg where many of the original buildings and gardens have been restored. Each winter Colonial Williamsburg holds the annual Williamsburg Garden Symposium. At this symposium well-known garden lecturers from all parts of the United States are invited to attend to take part in the various programs and garden tours that are arranged.

Near Williamsburg is Jamestown where recently the Jamestown festival was held. The present plan is to keep the Jamestown Restoration Area open as a public park. Full information about Williamsburg or Jamestown can be obtained by writing to Colonial Williamsburg, Williamsburg, Virginia.

CLIMATE. The state has a long growing season with adequate rainfall well distributed through the year. The following weather records cover 50 years at Norfolk and Lynchburg and 27 years at Wytheville.

SIGNIFICANT FROST DATES

Name of city	Average date of last killing frost in spring	Latest-known killing frost
Norfolk	Mar. 25	Apr. 26
Lynchburg	Apr. 9	May 7
Wytheville	Apr. 20	May 27

* Special articles on the subjects indicated by an asterisk (*) will be found at the words so marked.

SIGNIFICANT FROST DATES

Name of city	Average date of earliest killing frost in fall	Earliest-known killing frost
Norfolk	Nov. 16	Oct. 11
Lynchburg	Oct. 27	Oct. 2
Wytheville	Oct. 17	Sept. 19

RAINFALL IN THREE REGIONS OF THE STATE

Name of city	Average annual rainfall (inches)	Rainfall during growing season (inches)		
		Apr.	May	June
Norfolk	46.43	3.43	3.89	4.24
Lynchburg	41.75	3.11	3.71	3.97
Wytheville	46.71	3.66	3.91	4.11

Name of city	Average annual rainfall (inches)	Rainfall during growing season (inches)		
		July	Aug.	Sept.
Norfolk	46.43	5.83	5.46	3.66
Lynchburg	41.75	4.14	4.07	3.54
Wytheville	46.71	4.44	4.54	3.29

Since the topography of the state ranges in elevation from sea level to about 4000 feet above sea level, there is a corresponding variation in climate which in turn makes possible the growing of many sorts of vegetables, fruits, and ornamental plants.

The address of the Agricultural Experiment Station, which has kindly supplied this information about the state, is Blacksburg, Virginia. The station is always ready to answer gardening questions.

As one of the oldest settled parts of the country, Virginia has long been famous for magnificent estates landscaped upon the English plan, many of which are still among the finest gardens in America. The interest in gardening is so great that garden club activities are very extensive. There are several clubs affiliated with the Garden Club of America, the home office of which is 598 Madison Avenue, New York 22, N.Y. There are also over 500 clubs affiliated with the Virginia Federation of Garden Clubs, and the Garden Club of Virginia.

VIRGINIA COWSLIP = *Mertensia virginica.*

VIRGINIA CREEPER = *Parthenocissus quinquefolia.* See also POISON IVY, for which it is often mistaken.

virginiana, -us, -um (vir-gin-i-ā′na). From Virginia.

VIRGINIA SNAKEROOT = *Aristolochia Serpentaria.*

VIRGINIA STOCK = *Malcomia maritima.*

VIRGINIA WILLOW = *Itea virginica.*

virginica, -us, -um (vir-gin′i-ka). From Virginia.

VIRGIN'S-BOWER. See CLEMATIS.

viridiflora, -us, -um (vi-ri-di-flow′ra). Green-flowered.

viridifolia, -us, -um (vi-ri-di-fō′li-a). Green-leaved.

viridis, -e (vi′ri-dis). Green.

viridissima, -us, -um (vi-ri-diss′i-ma). Very or most green.

Viscaria. An obsolete generic name for plants now included in *Lychnis.*

VISCAYA ART MUSEUM. See No. 6 at GARDEN TOURS.

viscosa, -us, -um (vis-kō′sa). Sticky.

VISITING OTHER GARDENS. See GARDEN TOURS.

VISTA. A vista is a focalized view. This term is used to discriminate between a broad panoramic view and one which is limited in its scope by a frame. A view between hills which fold together, framing a view toward a distant horizon, or an opening through the forest giving glimpses of the landscape beyond are typical natural vistas.

No other element of landscape composition commands as much attention as the vista. Wherever there is a restrained glimpse of something beyond the immediate range of vision the eye quickly focuses on

An open vista

the distant point of interest. The same point of interest might go unnoticed in a panoramic view where there is no vista to pick it out.

Not all vistas terminate with distant views, although this is the origin of the idea. Where property is limited and there is no control over surroundings, similar effects may be created by shortening the vista with an artificial terminus. A fountain playing in the sunlight beyond a shaded avenue of trees, a sculptural figure silhouetted against the sky at the end of an allée, a small garden pavilion or any other feature of architectural interest seen between borders of tall planting, or the view of a specimen tree framed by surrounding trees in the foreground, are all variations of the vista idea.

Aside from its own beauty the vista is a valuable means of arranging other elements in the landscape scheme; it is the backbone or axis on which the skeleton of design is formed. Since it is the most potent means of centering interest the vista is often used as the approach to a garden, as a connecting link between buildings, or as an entrance drive. Wherever a vista appears there is an irresistible impulse to go in that direction. By this means interest may unconsciously lead from one point to another, creating a logical circulation through a city, an estate, a monumental garden, or a modest home grounds.

In cases where it is not possible, because of interfering obstructions, to plan open vistas it may be possible to create an aerial vista. By topping out certain trees in a woodland the vision may be directed over some intervening object to a distant view. The use of aerial vistas often extends the apparent size of a property far beyond its own limits. This scheme also eliminates the "middle ground" which is always the least interesting element of any view. The foreground is usually interesting because of its detail, and the distance because of its simple mass effect. When the foreground is seen silhouetted directly against distance, without the interference of middle ground, a view is always more interesting.

In planning a vista the effect must be visualized in perspective since the picture is always to be viewed that way. The level of the horizon in relation to the observer, the

A closed vista

height of the framework in relation to the height of the terminal feature, as well as the length and breadth of the plan, all must be considered in the design. Beautiful vistas often occur accidentally in nature, but when they are deliberately planned, results are sometimes just as satisfactory as natural vistas. — R. E. G.

vitacea, -us, -um (vy-tay′see-a). Resembling the grape (*Vitis*).

VITACEAE (vy-tay′see-ee). The grape family, nearly always vines in the garden plants, contains about 10 genera and over 600 species, many of which are shrubs or trees in the tropics, but prevailingly woody vines in those from the temperate zone.

From the garden standpoint the grape (*Vitis*) is by far the most important. But *Cissus, Parthenocissus,* and *Ampelopsis* yield many widely cult. vines grown for ornament, especially the Virginia creeper and Boston ivy. *See* VINES. *Leea* is a greenhouse shrub grown for its ornamental foliage.

In all but *Leea,* they are tendril*-bearing vines. Leaves usually alternate,* sometimes a tendril* opposite the leaf, simple or compound. Flowers small, numerous, mostly inconspicuous, sometimes unisexual,* nearly always clustered. Fruit a berry.

Technical flower characters: Calyx* entire or with very small teeth. Petals separate, or united and withering as an apparently tubular flower. Stamens* 4 or 5, opposite the petals. Ovary superior,* mostly 2-celled.

vitalba, -us, -um (vy-tal′ba). A white or white-flowered vine.

VITAMINS. Many of the most important of these essentials of our diet are found in fruits and vegetables. Vitamins A, B, B₁, C, and D are common in nearly all fresh fruits and vegetables. Vitamins are as necessary for plant as for animal growth. All evidence points to the fact that plants generate or produce the vitamins necessary for their own growth, and it is still undemonstrated that the addition of various chemical fertilizers or manure will induce the plant to produce greater or different vitamins necessary for human food.

These two facts should put amateur gardeners in a mood of extreme skepticism as to various nostrums advertised as "vitamin vegetable seeds" and mixtures to add to soil to increase the vitamin content of the crop. Genuine vitamin-deficiencies, from the medical standpoint, have created a wave of so-called vitamin techniques that are still highly controversial as far as their translation into hort. practice is concerned. It is not even certain that commercial fertilizers are any more or less likely to produce vitamins in the crop than stable manure, although much has been written in favor of the latter. This has nothing to do with the merits of stable manure on the soil, which is far better for it than chemical fertilizers. *See* MANURE.

vitellina, -us, -um (vy-tell-eye′na). Dull yellowish-red.

VITEX (vy′tex). Ornamental trees or shrubs comprising about 100 species of the family Verbenaceae, found distributed chiefly in the tropical and warmer regions of the world. Leaves opposite,* compound,* long-stalked, the leaflets 3–7, arranged finger-fashion, sometimes stalked, often grayish-green, and slightly hairy. Flowers small,

* Special articles on the subjects indicated by an asterisk (*) will be found at the words so marked.

white, blue, yellowish, or red in dense, showy, terminal clusters (spikes*). Calyx of 5 sepals. Corolla tubular, 4 of its lobes equal, 1 larger, forming a lip.* Stamens* 4, 2 long, 2 short. Fruit plum-like, 4-seeded. (*Vitex* is an ancient Latin name.)

The shrubby species make good plants for the shrubbery or back of the herbaceous border, and *V. Negundo* is especially grown for bees. In the North the stems are often winter-killed, but the roots send up new shoots which flower the same year. Both species are hardy and do not winter-kill from zone* 5 southward. Propagated by seeds but chiefly by cuttings. Cuttings of young shoots should be inserted in ½ sand and ½ soil, shaded from sun and kept in a humid atmosphere until rooted. They should be kept in a cool greenhouse or cold frame during winter months, before planting out.

Agnus-castus. Chaste tree. Hemp tree. Monk's pepper-tree. Deciduous shrub or small tree, 8–20 ft. high. Leaves long-stalked, the leaflets 5–7, lance-shaped, the middle leaflets to 4 in. long, covered with short gray hairs on the under side, pleasantly scented when bruised. Flowers pale lilac-blue, in dense, showy, terminal spikes, fragrant. Southern Eu. July–Aug. The *var.* **alba** is a white form, while the *var.* **macrophylla** has larger leaves and deep-colored flowers and is the best of the cult. *Vitex.*

latifolia = *Vitex Agnus-castus macrophylla.*

macrophylla = *Vitex Agnus-castus macrophylla.*

Negundo. Deciduous shrub, growing to 15 ft. high, the branches 4-sided. Leaves long-stalked. Leaflets 3–5, broadly lance-shaped, covered with small gray hairs on the under side, the margins sometimes toothed. Flowers deep lavender-blue, ¼ in. long, stalked, in dense, showy, terminal spikes.* China and India. Aug.–Sept. In the *var.* **incisa** (also known as *laciniata*) the leaflets are much cut, and the flowers less showy. It is hardier than the species, being reasonably safe up to zone* 4.

Viticella (vy-ti-sell'a). A diminutive of *Vitis*, the grape; hence a slender vine.

VITICETUM. A plantation of vines.

VITICULTURE. The growing of the grape (which see).

vitifolia, -us, -um (vy-ti-fō′li-a). Having leaves like the grape (*Vitis*).

VITIS (vy′tis). Grape. Woody vines, climbing by tendrils,* belonging to the family Vitaceae, and comprising about 60 species from the north temperate zone. While a few of them are somewhat decorative, the species are of outstanding importance as the source of all the grapes used as fruit or for wine making. They have usually shreddy bark, a brown pith separated by cross partitions, except in *V. rotundifolia.* Tendrils* forked except in *V. rotundifolia.* Leaves alternate,* often lobed finger-fashion, always toothed. Flowers small, greenish, unisexual* or polygamous,* the male and female sometimes on different plants, in small clusters mostly opposite the leaves. For details of flower structure *see* VITACEAE. Fruit the familiar grape (a true berry), 2–4-seeded, the seeds pear-shaped and grooved. (*Vitis* is the Latin name of the grape.)

For the culture and best hort. varieties *see* GRAPE. The vine dimensions given below are for the wild plants, which as ordinarily grown under cult. conditions are very much shorter, due to the different systems described at GRAPE. Many of the cult. varieties are hardier than the wild species from which they have been derived.

aestivalis. Summer grape. Pigeon grape. A high-climbing vine, the leaves broadly oval, deeply 3–5-lobed, 4½–8 in. wide, dull above, rusty beneath. Flower cluster (panicle*) 4½–6 in. long. Fruit black with somewhat of a bloom, usually juicy and sweet, sometimes dryish and sourish. Eastern U.S. June. Hardy from zone* 3 southward.

coignetiae. A strong-growing vine grown for ornament, as its purplish-black, bloomy fruit is inedible. Leaves roundish or ovalish, 4½–9 in. wide, deeply heart-shaped at the base, unequally and shallowly toothed, generally grayish or rusty beneath. Flower cluster (panicle*) short. Jap. June–July. Hardy from zone* 3 southward, and a handsome vine grown mostly for its foliage which turns a bright crimson in the fall. The *var.* **glabrescens,** crimson glory vine, is an especially fine form.

kaempferi = *V. coignetiae.*

Labrusca. Fox grape. A strong-growing vine with a leaf, tendril,* or flower cluster at nearly every joint. Leaves nearly round or broadly ovalish, 3–6½ in. wide, sometimes slightly 3-lobed, green above but whitish or pale-rusty beneath. Flower cluster 2–4½ in. long. Fruit purplish-black (rarely amber), thick-skinned, the pulp sweet but musky. Eastern U.S. June. Hardy from zone* 3 southward. Little grown as a wild plant, but the origin of many fine varieties of American grapes.

rotundifolia. Muscadine or bullace grape; also called scuppernong, and the origin of many grape varieties generally called *rotundifolia* grapes. A strong-growing vine, the stems sometimes 90 ft. long, the tendrils* not forked. Leaves nearly round or broadly oval, 2½–5 in. wide, coarsely and triangularly toothed, green above, yellowish-green beneath. Flower cluster (panicle*) short and dense. Fruit dull purple, thick-skinned, the pulp decidedly musky, Del. to Fla. and westward to Tex., Kan., and Mo. July. Hardy from zones* 4 or 5 southward. Has fine autumnal yellow foliage.

vinifera. The source of all the finer wine grapes, commonly called *vinifera* grapes. A strong-growing vine, the stems 45–60 ft. long. Leaves nearly round, 3½–6 in. wide, heart-shaped at the base, 3–5-lobed, the lobes toothed and often overlapping. Flower cluster (panicle*) long and much-branched. Fruit slightly football-shaped, black and with a bloom, or red or green in many varieties. Originally wild in the Caucasus (?), but cult. for centuries throughout much of Eu. and As., and the leading grape in Calif. While cult. sporadically elsewhere in the U.S., the wine grape is practically confined to Calif. so far as commercial wine production is concerned. *See* GRAPE for varieties and hardiness.

vulpina. Riverbank grape; also called frost grape, chicken, white and raccoon grape. A high-climbing vine. Leaves broadly ovalish, or narrower, 3½–8 in. long, mostly 3-lobed and with a cleft at the base, coarsely toothed. Flower cluster 3½–7 in. long, fragrant. Fruit

---

* Special articles on the subjects indicated by an asterisk (*) will be found at the words so marked.

nearly black, densely covered with a bloom. Eastern N.A., west to Tex. and Mo. June. Hardy from zone* 1 southward.

Vitis-Idaea (vy-tis-eye-dee′a). A specific name meaning, literally, the grape of Mt. Ida (Greece), and applied to the mountain cranberry (*Vaccinium Vitis-Idaea*).

VITTADINIA (vit-a-din′i-a). Perennial herbs or under-shrubs, comprising about 14 species of the family Compositae, and natives of Aust., N.Z., S.A., and the Hawaiian Islands. They are low-growing plants with thick rootstocks. Leaves alternate,* lance-shaped or spoon-shaped, sometimes deeply cut or toothed. Flowers in small heads, solitary, or in loose-branching clusters. Heads surrounded by several rows of overlapping bracts.* Ray florets* white or blue. Disk florets yellow. (Named for Dr. C. Vittadini, Austrian botanist.)

The plant below is grown for ornament, is closely related to *Erigeron,* and often sold under the name of *Erigeron karvinskianus.* Propagated by seeds or division of the rootstocks.

australis. Slightly hairy plant, growing to 1 ft. high, woody at the base. Leaves lance-shaped or spoon-shaped, sometimes cut into 3 lobes. Flowers in solitary heads, the rays white, the disk florets yellow. Aust. and N.Z.

triloba = *Vittadinia australis* or *Erigeron karvinskianus.*

vittata, -us, -um (vit-tay′ta). Striped.

vivipara, -us, -um (vy-vip′a-ra). Viviparous; i.e., freely producing organs of reproduction while still growing on the parent plant. Notable examples are the bulbils* of some onions and lilies, and the sprouting leaf margins of *Bryophyllum* (which see). It also occurs in some water lilies.

volubilis, -e (vol-loo′bill-is). Twining.

vomitoria, -us, -um (vom-i-tor′i-a). Emetic.

VRIESIA (vreez′zi-a). Tropical American tree-perching foliage plants, comprising about 100 species of the pineapple family, with stiff, erect, fleshy, green, often marbled leaves growing in a rosette, which sometimes holds water. Flowers yellow, green, pink, or white in terminal, flattish spikes,* each flower growing in the axil* of a showy, colored bract.* Calyx of 3 colored sepals. Corolla of 3 petals, alternating with the sepals. Stamens* 6. Fruit a 3-celled capsule.* (Named for Dr. W. de Vriese, Dutch botanist.)

Vriesia and the genus *Aechmea* are grown in the greenhouse in a warm, moist atmosphere, in pots or in wire or wooden baskets. Propagated by offshoots. They can be grown in potting mixture* 4, in a winter temperature of 50°–70°. They require plenty of water during summer months while making their growth, and should be shaded from Mar.–Oct.

carinata. Not over 10 in. high, the pale green leaves in a basal rosette, the blades sword-shaped, 7–8 in. long and about ⅔ in. wide. Flower spike flattened, the bracts* keeled, red at the base, yellow above. Flowers yellow, about 2 in. long. Brazil.

saundersi. Leaves many, in a rosette, stiff, fleshy, narrow, recurving, grayish, marked white on the upper side and reddish-brown on the under side. Flowering stalk to 1½ ft. high. Flowers yellow, cylindrical. Brazil.

splendens. Strong-growing, to 3 ft. high. Leaves to 1 ft. long, and 3 in. wide, stiff, fleshy, growing in a rosette, banded brown. Bracts* enclosing the flowers bright red. Flowers yellowish-white. Guiana. Often offered as *V. speciosa.*

vulcanica, -us, -um (vul-kay′ni-ka). Pertaining to a volcano.

vulgaris, -e (vul-gar′is). Common.

vulgata, -us, -um (vul-gay′ta). Common.

vulneraria, -us, -um (vul-ner-rair′i-a). Pertaining to wounds; often an assumed cure for them.

vulpina, -us, -um (vul-py′na). Relating to a fox.

W

WACHENDORFIA (wack-en-dor′fi-a). A genus of 7 species of S. Af. herbs of the family Haemodoraceae, the only commonly cult. one being **W. thyrsiflora.** It is a tuberous-rooted perennial, 18–20 in. high, with sword-shaped, 5-ribbed leaves that are smooth and long-tapering at the tip, nearly 3 ft. long. Flowers yellow, in a loose terminal cluster (panicle*). Cult. outdoors in Calif. and similar climates, but in the East it must be grown in the cool greenhouse, or if planted outdoors, the tuberous roots must be dug and dried off during the winter and replanted about 4 in. deep in the spring. (*Wachendorfia* was named for E. J. Wachendorf, Dutch botanist.)

WAFER ASH = *Ptelea trifoliata.*

WAHLENBERGIA (wall-en-ber′ji-a). Annual or perennial herbs, comprising about 150 species of the family Campanulaceae, widely distributed throughout the world, mostly in the warmer regions. Leaves alternate,* or sometimes opposite,* lance-shaped or ovalish, sometimes heart-shaped at the base. Flowers bell-shaped or tubular, blue, nodding, usually solitary, stalked, terminal or growing in the axils* of the leaves. Corolla funnel-shaped. Stamens* 5. Fruit a capsule.* (Named for George Wahlenberg, Swedish botanist.)

The species generally cult. is used in the

---

* Special articles on the subjects indicated by an asterisk (*) will be found at the words so marked.

rock garden, but may also be grown in the border. Propagated by seeds or division of the roots. Seeds should be sown in a cold frame, ⅛ in. deep, in sandy soil, in early spring. They may be transplanted to permanent positions as soon as large enough to handle.

gracilis. Annual, growing to 1 ft. high. Leaves alternate,* narrowly lance-shaped, to ½ in. long, the margins toothed. Flowers solitary, blue, long-stalked. N.Z., Aust., and S. Af.

WAHOO = *Euonymus atropurpureus.*

WAKEROBIN. See TRILLIUM. *See also* ARUM MACULATUM.

WALDSTEINIA (wald-sty'ni-a). A small genus of strawberry-like herbs of the rose family, and closely related to the strawberry, but with dry, hairy fruits. The only cult. species, **W. fragarioides,** the barren or dry strawberry, is sometimes grown in the wild garden. It looks very like a small strawberry plant, has 3 leaflets and a small cluster (corymb*) of yellow flowers that are about ⅓ in. wide. It is of easy culture in partially shaded places. Eastern N.A. May–June. (Named for Francis Adam, Count of Waldstein-Wartenburg, an Austrian botanist.)

WALKING FERN; WALKING LEAF. *See* CAMPTOSORUS.

WALKING IRIS. See NEOMARICA.

WALL CRESS = *Arabis albida.*

WALL FERN = *Polypodium vulgare.*

WALLFLOWER = *Cheiranthus Cheiri. See also* ERYSIMUM.

WALL GERMANDER = *Teucrium Chamaedrys.*

WALL PEPPER = *Sedum acre.*

WALL-RUE SPLEENWORT = *Asplenium Ruta-muraria.*

WALLS AND WALL GARDENING. As a distinctive structural element in landscape design, a wall may separate or unify space relationships. When its primary purpose is to set up a protective barrier, a wall should induce a sense of security against intrusion; and when it is desirable to segregate an area by an enclosure, a wall materially contributes toward visual unity. The type and style of a wall as well as its height and extent are influenced somewhat by local traditions and environment but more specifically by the requirements of a given problem.

The architectural snap and definition that a wall contributes to a landscape effect should be softened by judicious planting so that the wall will harmonize with the general atmosphere and adjacent surroundings. Plant material for walls might be divided into two general groups: plants to grow within the wall structure, such as rock plants, and secondly, plants to be trained over the surface of the wall, such as espalier trees or climbing or trailing vines.

EARTH WALL. A simple wall of earth suitably planted might be appropriate within the confines of a property when used to define the

A double wall with a topsoil core upon which a hedge or other plants may be grown

limits of an area such as a rock garden or a children's outdoor playroom. This type of wall requires the use of a rich, loamy soil thoroughly tamped and compacted. Turf sods or moss or thick, matted roots of suitable perennials can readily be wired to the slopes of either or both sides. To insure an adequate water supply, a one-inch galvanized iron pipe perforated every few inches might be run along the crest of the wall, and connected to the nearest supply with a control valve. Where a hedge surmounts the earth wall, such irrigation may prove to be a necessity, especially where the side walls as well as the crest are thickly planted.

RIP-RAP WALL. Where large rocks and boulders are available for rip-rap, this type of wall affords an economical way of retaining a steep slope. A liberal batter should be provided and all stones tilted back against the bank to allow rain water to seep into the soil. Rocks should be so placed that they bind on one another, and all voids filled with good topsoil and thoroughly tamped. Native bayberry or dwarf huckleberry or roses, for instance, might be suitable to plant between the rocks along a driveway embankment. Dwarf evergreen creepers such as periwinkle or euonymus would be more suitable where a rich, compact effect is desired.

HA-HA WALL. Suitable for use against pasture land where a definite barrier is required, yet where an uninterrupted view is desired, is a ha-ha wall. It usually takes the form of a dry retaining wall constructed on the near side of a ditch or dry moat so that it is only visible from the outside area. Where one wishes to see only a quiet stretch of lawn from the inside looking out, but would like to see a pleasing bit of color from the outside looking in, this sunken wall would be the suitable type to use.

DRY STONE WALL. A free-standing stone wall laid up dry, with no cement in the joints,

---

* Special articles on the subjects indicated by an asterisk (*) will be found at the words so marked.

requires a more highly skilled mason than a wall whose joints are filled with cement. Where long, flat stones are available, a dry wall may be laid up very effectively. If an old dry stone wall is to be converted into a wall garden, it would be necessary to remove sufficient stone to fill interior voids with topsoil. Plants are liable to dry out from lack of moisture where capillary action cannot take place due to the soil pockets having no direct soil contact with the ground.

DRY DOUBLE WALL. This type is admirably suited to wall gardening, as it provides two stone faces laid up dry with exposed earth pockets as required and with a central core of topsoil to act as a reservoir of cool, moist earth where deep, penetrating roots may feed. A hedge might readily be planted along the top of this type of wall, affording added height and protection. For a low

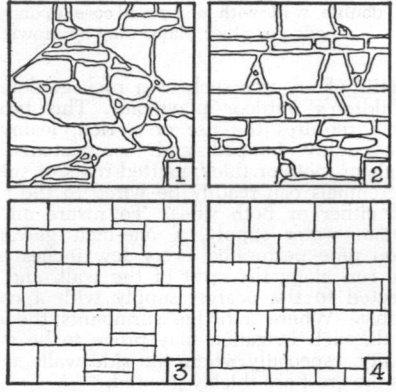

Types of stone garden walls: (1) Random rubble. (2) Random coursed rubble. (3) Broken coursed ashlar. (4) Irregular coursed ashlar. Stone, concrete blocks and brick, if laid with trellis-like air spaces, are very effective and practical in hot climates.

thick tangle, a hedge of *Rosa setigera* would be effective. For a restrained formal hedge, Mugho pines, dwarf evergreen azaleas, or barberry would be suitable. A thorn, beech, or hornbeam hedge would be very formidable on a long run of wall where the element of protection is a factor. Various types of junipers should thrive in such a location, and if provided sufficient moisture, pines and hemlocks should prove very effective. Where both faces of the double dry wall are to be planted, the central core of soil should be adequate to sustain vigorous growth on both sides as well as top. Suitable types for planting in large drifts on both faces might be *Dianthus plumarius, Nepeta mussini, Iberis sempervirens,* or *Euonymus fortunei.*

MASONRY WALL. A masonry wall makes a most suitable background for espalier fruits or flowering trees and shrubs. An easterly exposure is generally considered ideal. Even

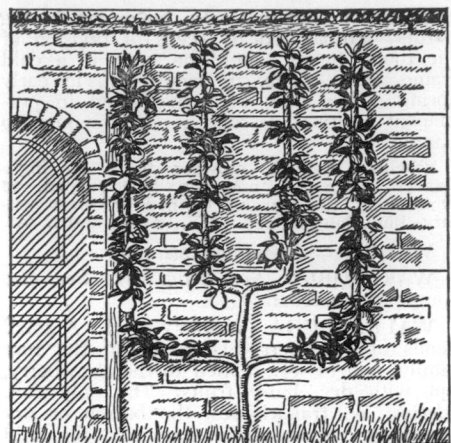

Espaliered fruits on a brick wall

a southern exposure, however, is feasible for this purpose if the lines of supporting wires are run sufficiently far out from the wall surface to prevent the plant from being burned by the reflected heat from the sun. Regular, trained trees and shrubs espaliered against a wall are most suitable for formal effects such as might be required for an entrance court treatment or a garden wall or the plain exposed wall surfaces of a house. Shrubs such as forsythia, cotoneaster, buddleia, and *Euonymus alatus* lend themselves admirably to espalier treatment. Vines, of course, are ideal for softening hard construction lines of masonry wall. Hybrids of the *wichuraiana* rose have good foliage and make excellent cover and can be trained on diagonal wires to give an architectural effect.

STONE VENEER ON CONCRETE WALL. Where laminated stone is laid up in layers facing down a concrete retaining wall, soil pockets may be provided in any location or

Informal wall garden

series of locations desired. A most effective planting display may be created by organizing the material in subtly related rhythmical patterns in form and texture and color.

BRICK WALL. The wall texture of a definitely repeated small unit, such as a brick, creates a background scale of uniform pattern which forms an interesting contrast with the lively lines of branches and more dynamic patterns of living foliage masses. An effective treatment for a brick wall is to divide the wall into a series of panels, possibly varying in width. Alternate panels might be planted with an evergreen vine like English ivy and the wall space or panel between might be embellished with such espaliered material as *Viburnum sieboldi,* or perhaps *Cornus florida* or *Pyracantha coccinea lalandi.* Where protected, buddleia and jasmine are ideal shrubs for training against a wall. See VINES.

CONCRETE WALL. By itself, a concrete wall may be said to lack distinction. It needs planting to give it character. Co-ordinating patterns of evergreens when established on a concrete wall tend to enliven an otherwise dull surface and also tend to integrate the whole lifeless expanse. A flat colortone of soft lavender-pink or a warm beige applied to the concrete enriches the effect. Shrubs such as weigelas, Regel's privet, and forsythias may readily be trained against a concrete wall, and alternate with such vines as wisteria or *Celastrus orbiculatus* to bring new life and light to play on such a static background.

TERRACED WALLS OF TILE OR BLOCK. A wall garden may be constructed of a series of terraced groups of terra-cotta tiles or concrete blocks. They may be laid up in varying patterns, such as pyramidal or winged formations, and filled with topsoil and planted with rock plants, ferns, or dwarf evergreens.

CITY WALLS: The following plants have been successfully grown in backyard gardens trained on walls or fences: *Cotoneaster simondsi, Ilex crenata, Forsythia suspensa, Forsythia intermedia, Ligustrum obtusifolium regelianum.* The following vines also do well on city walls: *Polygonum auberti, Campsis radicans, Wistaria sinensis,* and in shady, protected places, the English ivy will often thrive.

HERBS FOR SUNNY WALL GARDENS: *Ajuga, Alyssum, Aster,* Mauve Cushion, *Campanula, Cerastium, Dianthus, Gypsophila, Helianthemum, Iberis, Phlox subulata, Ceratostigma plumbaginoides, Sedum, Silene, Thymus, Tunica Saxifraga, Veronica.*

PLANTS FOR SHADY WALL GARDENS: *Ajuga, Campanula carpatica, Hypericum, Euonymus fortunei minimus, Potentilla tridentata, Saxifraga, Sedum, Veronica repens, Viola.* — A. F. and G. E.

WALNUT. Valuable nut trees constituting the genus **Juglans** (jug'lanz) of the family Juglandaceae, and comprising only about 15 species found mostly in N.A. and Eurasia,

and including, besides the walnuts, the butternut. They are usually tall trees closely related to the hickory, but not having the shaggy bark of some hickories. Leaves alternate,* compound,* the leaflets arranged feather-fashion, with an odd one at the end. Male and female flowers separate, on the same tree, the male flowers in hanging catkins, the female in few-flowered, erect clusters (racemes*). Petals none. Fruit a large, fleshy, non-splitting drupe,* within which is the seed (the walnut or butternut), commonly but incorrectly called a nut. In some species, especially the butternut, the outer husk of the fruit is aromatic, and the bruised foliage of all species is also aromatic. (*Juglans* is the old Latin name of the English walnut, and means, literally, the acorn of Jupiter.)

For culture *see* below. Nut as used below means nut in the ordinary sense, although it is actually the seed. All species flower with or before the expansion of the leaves.

J. californica. A shrub or small tree, the leaflets 11–15, oblongish, pointed, 1½–3 in. long, smooth. Fruit round, about ¾ in. in diameter, the nut deeply grooved. Southern Calif. Hardy from zone* 6 southward, and of little interest except as breeding stock for English walnut varieties. This and a related Californian tree, *J. hindsi* (which is a street tree in Calif.), have been much used by walnut breeders. *J. hindsi* has 15–19 leaflets, and a faintly grooved nut.

J. cinerea. Butternut; sometimes called white walnut. A round-headed tree, sometimes 90 ft. high, usually less, the bark deeply fissured. Leaflets 11–19, oblongish, 2½–5 in. long, the blade and stalk sticky-hairy. Fruit egg-shaped or football-shaped, about 3½ in. long, the nut ridged and with smaller ridges or furrows between the main ridges, the meat oily, rich, and spicy. Eastern N.A. Hardy from zone* 2 southward.

J. hindsi. *See* JUGLANS CALIFORNICA.

J. nigra. Black walnut. A tall tree, sometimes 150 ft. high, its brown bark deeply fissured, and its timber highly prized. Leaflets 15–23, ovalish or narrower, rounded at the base, 2½–5 in. long, irregularly toothed, minutely hairy but not sticky. Fruit nearly round or slightly pear-shaped, about 2 in. thick, hairy, the nut strongly and irregularly sculptured. Mass. to Fla. west to Tex. and Minn. Hardy from zone* 3 southward. An ornamental tree, but valued chiefly for its fine, rich, oily nuts.

J. regia. English walnut; also, and more correctly, called Persian walnut, as it is native there and not in England. A tree up to 100 ft. high, the bark silvery-gray. Leaflets 5–9, rarely 11, elliptic or oblongish, without marginal teeth except on young leaves. Fruit nearly round, green, smooth, about 2 in. in diameter, the nut much sculptured. Southeastern Eu. and Asia Minor to the Himalayas and China. Hardy, in some of its forms, from zone* 4 southward. Long cult. and the origin, after centuries of breeding, of the modern varieties of the English walnut. *See* below. Its wood is usually called Circassian walnut.

J. sieboldiana. A Japanese walnut of chief interest for breeding with the English walnut, as it is hardier than that species. Leaflets 9–17, ovalish or oblong, minutely toothed. Fruit nearly round, or egg-shaped, but pointed, about

* Special articles on the subjects indicated by an asterisk (*) will be found at the words so marked.

2½ in. long, the nut 8-ridged, and sculptured between the ridges. Hardy from zone° 3 southward. The *var.* cordiformis, the heartnut, has a thin shell and the nut easily slips out of it.

WALNUT CULTURE

Of the important genus *Juglans,* to which the walnuts belong, two representatives are of principal importance in the United States; the English or Persian walnut (*Juglans regia*), which is grown in California and Oregon, and the native black walnut (*Juglans nigra*), grown in the central and eastern U.S. Although, because of the blight disease, commercial culture of the former is restricted to the Pacific Coast, there are hardy and late-blooming varieties which succeed reasonably well in the Middle Atlantic states and Great Lakes region.

ENGLISH WALNUT. On the basis of climatic requirements and tolerances the English walnuts grown in this country are of three kinds: the so-called Santa Barbara group, a hardy sub-tropical type of Chilean origin; the French group, a warm-temperate type; and the Circassin group, a hardy temperate type. The first requires a longer growing season and is less resistant to both heat and cold. Its commercial culture is restricted, therefore, to those parts of the coastal plain area of southern California and adjoining valleys where the equable summer climate favors high quality and the winters are cool enough to break the rest period. The second has a much higher requirement for winter cold and hence its commercial culture is restricted to central and northern California and parts of Oregon. This type is sufficiently hardy to withstand the winters of all save the coldest parts of eastern United States, but bears poorly because of killing of the small fruit-wood. The third is intensely hardy to cold and is late-blooming. All kinds require more winter cold than most pecans, for which reason they do not succeed in the Gulf Coast states.

The English walnut is one of the most exacting of all orchard trees with reference to soil requirements. While the tree itself succeeds reasonably well on a wide variety of soils, and notably so on relatively light soils, good crops of well-filled, high-quality nuts are produced only on deep, fertile soils of medium-heavy texture. It is also intolerant of wet soils, for which reason excellent under-drainage must exist and heavy soils should be avoided. The English walnut is markedly sensitive to alkali, even in low concentration, which requires the avoidance of such soils and the use of irrigation water of the best possible quality. Because of its exacting soil requirement no greater mistake can be made than to plant the walnut on any soil but the best.

All varieties appear to be both self-fertile and cross-fertile, and provision for cross-pollination is ordinarily not made, though there is, in some years, evidence of benefits therefrom. Satisfactory overlapping of the bloom periods of the male and female flowers usually occurs, but not always. The benefits of pollinators are most evident in the central and northern California sections.

Nursery trees are propagated either by whip-grafting year-old seedlings, or patch-budding in summer or fall. The rootstock most employed in the past is the northern California black walnut (*Juglans hindsi*), but the trend is now toward the use of the English walnut seedlings which appear to be immune to the crown-rot disease. Top-grafting orchard trees is of considerable importance for converting seedling trees to standard sorts. The English walnut top-grafts with greater difficulty than the black walnuts. For the former, modified cleft-grafting is the most successful method; for the latter, cutting back and patch-budding the new shoots is equally satisfactory. Successful conversion depends largely on the care with which the follow-up work is done.

The walnut requires wide spacing for satisfactory yield and quality. On good soils the permanent trees should not be closer than 60 to 70 feet apart.

Of soil-management practices irrigation is undoubtedly the most important. An adequate soil moisture supply must be maintained at all times. Failure to wet the soil deeply in winter causes dieback, a form of drought injury. On good soils the response to nitrogen fertilizers is rarely sufficient to pay for the costs. Cultivation is necessary only to turn under weeds and to facilitate irrigation and harvesting. Pruning is of minor importance and is confined to the removal of suckers° and declined lower limbs, and to light thinning of the tops.

Early harvesting and rapid drying enhance the quality of the nuts and are recommended. The nuts are shaken from the trees and are hand-pulled as gathered.

The principal varieties in southern California are Placentia, Eureka, and Ehrhardt. In northern California the major varieties are Concord, Payne, Franquette, and Blackmer. Mayette and Franquette are the hardiest to winter cold and hence best adapted to Oregon. For the eastern United States the Circassin type is safer.

AMERICAN BLACK WALNUT. This nut is a hardy temperate-zone forest tree grown mainly for lumber, though the harvesting of the nuts is an industry of some importance. In recent years small plantings have been made primarily for the nuts, which are of distinctive flavor and are sold mainly in shelled form. Several comparatively thin-shelled varieties have been selected and propagated, of which the most important are Thomas, Ohio, Stabler, and Ten Eyck; the two latter have the thinnest shells and are the most promising. — R. W. H.

INSECT PESTS. Gregarious caterpillars may be controlled by arsenicals. These ugly creatures also attack pecan, hickory, and other trees. English walnuts are attacked by codling moth and should be controlled by arsenicals,

---

° Special articles on the subjects indicated by an asterisk (°) will be found at the words so marked.

pesticide #1 or #17 (*see* SPRAYS AND DUSTS) as at APPLE. Plant lice may be killed by pesticide #1 or #21. A maggot working in the husk of English walnut can be controlled by arsenicals.

DISEASES. Bacterial blight causes black spots on leaves, young shoots, and husks of fruit. Apply pesticide #3 (*see* SPRAYS AND DUSTS) just as blooming starts, again when trees are in full bloom, and again immediately after bloom. In commercial walnut areas several later applications may also be necessary during rainy periods. Recent work in some states indicates that the antibiotic* materials such as streptomycin may prove of value. Contact your state agricultural experiment station for particulars.

A number of wood rots* and cankers* may develop if wounds are not protected with tree-wound dressings.

WALPOLE TEA = *Ceanothus americanus.*

WANDERING JEW = *Tradescantia fluminensis.* See SPIDERWORT. See also ZEBRINA.

WAND-FLOWER. See SPARAXIS.

WAPATOO = *Sagittaria latifolia.*

WARDIAN CASE. See TERRARIUM.

WARMINSTER BROOM = *Cytisus praecox.* See BROOM

WASHINGTON. The state flower is *Rhododendron macrophyllum.* The state lies wholly in zones* 3, 4, 5, and 6, which, instead of running east and west as in most parts of America, run approximately north and south, due to the proximity of high mountains and the warm sea water.

SOILS. In western Washington the most productive soils are the dark silt or sandy loam soils, high in organic matter, found in the alluvial river valleys and the reclaimed tidal flats. In the upland areas the soils, sandy and light yellowish in color, are not quite so productive as the first soil type. East of the Cascade Mountains the soils are predominantly of volcanic origin, modified by ice, water, and wind. In the larger and lower valleys of central Washington the soil is a productive sandy loam. In the southeast section the soil is a deep, fertile, brown silt loam, in many respects resembling a loess* soil. Certain northern areas of the state have been glaciated and such soils vary from a stony, gravelly type to a sandy loam structure.

FRUIT AREAS. The Spokane Valley is the principal fruit district of zone* 3 in the state of Washington. Apples are the leading tree fruit crop with cherries closely following. Midseason and early varieties of apples are primarily grown. Of the small fruits, raspberries and strawberries are grown both commercially and for home use. The Kettle Falls district in the upper Columbia River and the central part of Stevens County around Colville produce some small fruits.

Zone* 4 includes the principal fruit-growing areas with Okanogan on the north and White Salmon on the south. The principal fruits of the Okanogan Valley are apples and pears grown under irrigation near Okanogan,

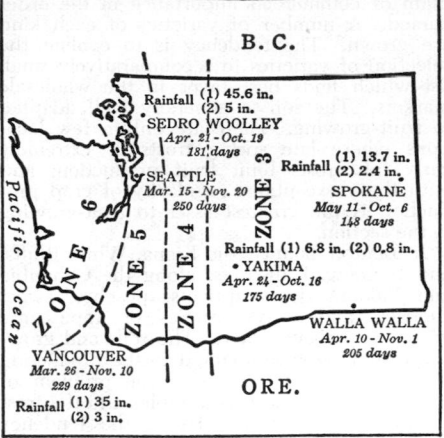

WASHINGTON

The zones of hardiness crossing Washington are those shown on the map located at ZONE, which should be consulted for details. The dates are the average latest killing frost in spring and the first one in the fall. The figures below the dates show the average length of the growing season. Rainfall figures (in inches) show (1) the total annual rainfall and (2) the amount falling in the growing season at the places indicated.

Omak, and Oroville, and in other smaller districts.

The Methow Valley is a small, irrigated apple-growing district in the valley of the Methow River, extending from Pateros to Methow.

The Wenatchee section, extending from Wenatchee to Leavenworth up the Wenatchee River, to Orondo on the east side of the Columbia River and to Rock Island in the southeastern direction from Wenatchee, is a large district confined to the narrow irrigated lands near the rivers. Apples are the leading crop with pears, cherries, apricots, and peaches following in approximately the order named. There are relatively few fruits, chiefly apricots, grown on the non-irrigated lands. Regularity of crop production is one of the principal features of this district.

The Ellensburg and Kittitas community has a commercial orchard area in which fruit of good quality is grown. On the irrigated farms fruit is grown for home use and there is considerable irrigated land devoted to general farming. The apples grown are nearly all of the midseason and early-ripening varieties.

The Yakima fruit district extends from Tieton and Naches, at the upper limits, to Grandview, the lower limit of the section. Fruit-growing is confined almost entirely to the irrigated land and is nearly all on a commercial scale. The apple is the leading crop, with the pear, peach, cherry, apricot, and the

---

* Special articles on the subjects indicated by an asterisk (*) will be found at the words so marked.

plum of commercial importance in the order named. A number of varieties of each kind are grown. The tendency is to confine the selection of varieties to a comparatively small list which finds best favor in the wholesale markets. The soil is generally well adapted to fruit-growing. There are only a few locations where late spring frosts or extremely early fall frosts limit fruit production, and with these exceptions regularity of crop production is the greatest asset to fruit-growing in the section.

In Benton County, the Kiona, White Bluffs, and Kennewick districts, along the Columbia and Yakima rivers apricots, peaches, sweet cherries, and early varieties of apples are grown on irrigated land. The soils and growing season are well adapted to the production of early crops. Because of the problem of codling moth control with apples and the frost hazard with the stone fruits, the tendency has been toward increased production of small fruits and vegetable crops and decreased production of orchard crops.

The Walla Walla and Asotin County districts include the sections near Walla Walla and the areas along the Snake River in which stone fruits, such as peaches, plums, and cherries are the most important. There are relatively small quantities being grown for home use, most of the material being for commercial purposes.

The White Salmon section is a small area in which a large list of fruits are grown for home use, and the commercial production of fruits is confined almost entirely to apples. Only a part of the commercial orchards are irrigated and usually none of the home orchards.

In zone* 6 are found three districts. In Clark County prunes and small fruits, such as raspberries and strawberries, filberts and walnuts are grown. Rainfall is depended upon for the water supply, but the semi-coastal climate has given protection against injury from late spring frosts and early autumn frosts. Rains at blossom time have been the most destructive element of climate.

In the Puyallup district, which extends from Tacoma to near Seattle, raspberries and black-berries form the principal fruit crops. Some pears and sour cherries are also grown. Commercial plantings are successful and also nearly every farm home has a goodly supply of tree and bush fruits for family use.

VEGETABLE AREAS. In zone* 3 the principal vegetable-gardening center is in the Spokane Valley, near the city of Spokane. The vegetables best suited are tomatoes, cabbage, muskmelons, squash, sweet corn, late potatoes, carrots, cucumbers, string beans, and celery. The soils of the Spokane Valley are generally somewhat shallow, with the surface soil tending to be a gravelly loam in character, while the subsoil is somewhat gravelly to very gravelly.

In zone* 4 the principal vegetable-gardening centers are the Yakima Valley, especially around Wapato, Toppenish, Sunnyside, and Kennewick. About Wapato, spinach, carrots, potatoes, string beans, tomatoes, eggplants, peppers, watermelons, muskmelons, cucumbers, and sweet corn are grown. In the Toppenish region, spinach, onions, potatoes, tomatoes, cucumbers, muskmelons, watermelons, and sweet corn are produced. Around Sunnyside, the principal vegetables are asparagus, spinach, onions, potatoes, tomatoes, pumpkins, squash, and sweet corn, while at Kennewick asparagus, head lettuce, potatoes, and muskmelons are important vegetables. The soils of Wapato, Toppenish, and Sunnyside are deep to very deep, with the surface soil tending to be a fine, silty loam and the subsoil a silt. In the Kennewick area the soils are medium in depth with the subsoil tending to be a sandy gravel. Occasionally a hardpan is found near the surface in some of the areas.

Vegetables are also grown in the Walla Walla Valley, around the city of Walla Walla, the principal crops being asparagus, rhubarb, spinach, head lettuce, onions, potatoes, beans, peas, tomatoes, eggplants, peppers, cucumbers, and sweet corn. The soils of the vegetable-producing areas of the Walla Walla Valley are generally deep to very deep and of a silty loam to a silt nature.

Other principal vegetable-growing areas are in the White River Valley, from Puyallup to Seattle, and about the cities of Monroe and Bellingham. In the White River Valley, rhubarb, spinach, celery, head lettuce, cabbage, cauliflower, root crops, green beans, peas, eggplants, peppers, and cucumbers are grown. In the Monroe section any of the market garden crops can be grown except those requiring a high degree of heat, such as tomatoes, melons, and sweet corn, but the principal crops are head lettuce, cabbage, and potatoes. In the vicinity of Bellingham, the vegetables grown are rhubarb, head lettuce, celery, cabbage, cauliflower, carrots, beets, parsnips, beans, peas, eggplants, peppers, and cucumbers.

ORNAMENTAL PLANTS. No extensive study has been made in the state of Washington concerning the preference of ornamental plants for certain soil types. One reason for this is that the soil in most sections where ornamentals are grown is relatively good, reasonably fertile, and sufficiently deep to maintain the plant materials grown. Water and climate, rather than soil, are the two limiting factors in the selection and choice of ornamental plant materials, especially for the eastern section of the state. Thus, the state may be divided into two rather distinct areas from the standpoint of growing ornamental plants. West of the Cascades the winters are relatively mild, with an abundant rainfall. The soils in most of this area give a distinct acid reaction. East of the Cascades the winters are comparatively cold, the summers warm and dry. The soil gives a neutral or in some cases a distinctly alkaline reaction.

Some of the trees which do particularly

well on the coast are: Alaska cedar, arborvitae, Douglas fir, hemlock, incense cedar, juniper, Oregon maple, pine, spruce, vine maple, and white fir.

The shrubs are: azaleas, boxwood, barberry, dogwood, English holly, hydrangea, laurel, madroña, Oregon grape, rose, and rhododendron.

The trees commonly grown east of the Cascades are: ash, birch, black locust, linden, maple, mountain-ash, pine, poplar, Siberian or Chinese elm, spruce, and sycamore.

The shrubs are: barberry, bush honeysuckle, hawthorn, lilac, mock-orange, cream bush, Russian olive, serviceberry, pea tree, snowberry, spirea, and sumac.

CLIMATE. The climate varies widely with the proximity to the Pacific Ocean, the topography, the altitude, and latitude. West of the Cascades, because of the proximity to large bodies of water, the climate is mild and humid, and the rainfall varies from 35 to over 100 inches annually. East of the Cascades the winters are more severe and the day summer temperatures hotter and relative humidity lower than in western Washington. At the extreme lower end of the Yakima Valley the rainfall may average only about 6.5 inches, but in the higher elevations elsewhere east of the Cascades the rainfall may exceed 25 inches per annum.

KILLING FROSTS

Towns	Average date of last killing frost in spring	Latest-known spring killing frost
Spokane	May 11	May 25
Yakima	Apr. 24	May 10
Walla Walla	Apr. 10	May 10
Seattle	Mar. 15	Apr. 20
Sedro Woolley	Apr. 21	May 15
Vancouver	Mar. 26	Apr. 25

Towns	Average date of the earliest killing frost in fall	Earliest-known fall killing frost
Spokane	Oct. 6	Sept. 5
Yakima	Oct. 16	Sept. 5
Walla Walla	Nov. 1	Sept. 20
Seattle	Nov. 20	Nov. 1
Sedro Woolley	Oct. 19	Sept. 15
Vancouver	Nov. 10	Oct. 10

RAINFALL

Places	Total yearly rainfall	Approximate amount falling in June, July, August
Spokane	13.7 in.	2.4 in.
Yakima	6.8 in.	0.8 in.
Walla Walla	15.6 in.	2.2 in.
Seattle	29.6 in.	3.5 in.
Sedro Woolley	45.6 in.	5.0 in.
Vancouver	35.0 in.	3.0 in.

FOG. During the growing season fog occurs quite generally in zones* 5 and 6 throughout the spring and early summer months. By 9:00 to 10:00 o'clock in the morning, however, the fog generally rises. The humidity is unusually high during the summer months.

SNOW COVER. In zone* 4, snow covers the ground during parts of December and January, affording considerable protection to the perennial crops. If it were not for the snowfall, the area would have a deficient water supply.

Zone* 3 depends on irrigation as a source of water supply. The streams from which much of the irrigation water is taken have their origin in the Cascade Mountains. Whether or not there is a water shortage depends on the annual snowfall. Some water for irrigation comes from reservoirs in the mountains which are filled by the melting snows. Little if any snow falls in the area to the west of the Cascades.

CASCADE MOUNTAINS. The chief climatic control is the Cascade range of mountains. The rains from the Pacific fall mostly on the western slopes of the mountains, and that carried over is diverted high into the air and does not begin to fall until it reaches the extreme eastern section of Washington, known as the Palouse region. As a consequence, a great part of eastern Washington is arid.

The address of the Agricultural Experiment Station, which has kindly supplied this information about the state, is the State College of Washington, Pullman, Washington. The station is always ready to answer gardening questions.

Garden club activities include clubs of the Garden Club of America at Tacoma and Seattle. The home office is at 598 Madison Avenue, New York 22, N.Y. There are also many clubs affiliated with the Washington State Federation of Garden Clubs.

WASHINGTON ASPARAGUS. See ASPARAGUS.

WASHINGTON CREEPING BENT. A good variety of creeping bent grass suitable for golf greens and bowling greens. See LAWN.

WASHINGTONIA (wash-ing-tō'ni-a). Fan palms with massive trunks, comprising only 2 (or perhaps 3) species native in Calif., northern Mex., and in southwestern Ariz. and widely planted there; also planted less commonly along the Gulf Coast and in Fla. Trunks unarmed, shaggy in the second species, but densely clothed with a "petticoat" of hanging withered leaves in the first. Leaves fan-like, but cut into numerous narrow segments. Flowers perfect,* nearly stalkless on the flowering branches, which are long, slender, and usually longer than the foliage. Stamens* 6. Fruit 1-seeded, thinfleshed, scarcely ⅛ in. long (a drupe*). The individual flower clusters suggest a corntassel. (Named for General George Wash-

---

* Special articles on the subjects indicated by an asterisk (*) will be found at the words so marked.

ington.) Long known as *Neowashingtonia* and closely related to *Brahea* (which see).

The California fan palms are widely planted and make extremely handsome avenue trees throughout central and southern Calif. While, for palms, they are relatively hardy, they are not safe above zone* 7. *See* PALM.

filifera. A stout palm, 60–80 ft. high, the upper part of the trunk clothed with the long-persistent, withered or dead, hanging leaves. Living leaves long-stalked, erect, the stalks prickly, the blade 3–5 ft. wide, grayish-green, cut to nearly the middle into many, narrow, drooping, thready segments. Moist places near the Colorado Desert, Calif. Less planted than the next species, and less satisfactory near the Calif. coast, but superior in dry soils in Fla.

robusta. California fan palm. Taller than the last, the trunk more slender, usually clothed above with a dense, shaggy, fibrous network, through which protrude the old, spiny leafstalks, but the trunk naked toward the base. Leaf blades cut only about ⅓ of the way to the middle, the stiffish or drooping segments not thready as in *W. filifera.*

washingtoniana, -us, -um (wash-ing-tō-ni-a'na). From the state of Washington.

WASHINGTON LILY = *Lilium washingtonianum.*

WASHINGTON PLANT = *Cabomba caroliniana.*

WASHINGTON'S BOWER = *Lycium halimifolium.*

WASHINGTON THORN = *Crataegus Phaenopyrum.*

WATER. Without water no plant can live and grow, and without water as a landscape feature few gardens are as attractive as they might be. For this purely aesthetic feature of water see the next entry which includes notes on the landscape value of pools, streams, fountains, etc. For the cultivation of aquatic or water plants *see* WATER GARDEN. For supplying water to gardens deficient in it *see* IRRIGATION. For the purely physical water-needs of plants all gardeners should consult the articles on WATERING, SOIL MOISTURE, CULTIVATION, and PLANT FOODS. For the amount of water in some common fruits and vegetables *see* WATER CONTENT.

WATER. Although water has no tangible form of its own, it will assume the shape of any form into which it flows, and may be made to take on a great variety of predictable shapes and characters by the direction of forces upon it. Responsive to such outside influences, water may vary endlessly in type and character as well as in emotional appeal. Whatever form it may take, however, water retains certain constant attributes such as moisture and the ability to reflect light. Throughout all its various manifestations, water retains its identity and unity of spirit, making it an ideal element in landscape design.

Electrical illumination for night lighting effects is an intriguing problem. Blue light seems to have the greatest appeal and yellow follows for colored lighting effects. A crystal white light is most satisfactory for general use, however, and is more symbolic of the attributes of water — refreshing purity and cleanliness. *See* LIGHTING.

LAKE OR POND. With its extended surface area, a lake or pond can reflect greater play of light and shade and color tone and provide wider scope for dramatic mood, than smaller water features.

Introducing aquatic plants in organized groups along the shoreline and backing these up with naturalized masses of shrubby growth whose flowering season synchronizes with the water plants, creates a lovely splash of color in the water, and this effect is greatly strengthened if the shrub growth is supplemented with flowering trees. One should bear in mind an essential principle of landscape design, that a very simple and restrained initial grouping that is rich in color will make the most beautiful reflections in the water. *See* WATER GARDEN.

POOLS AND BASINS. Where the purpose of a pool is to reflect, one should use great restraint in adding supplementary details such as balustrades, hedge-like edgings, or water lilies and other aquatic plants. Should a pool be built under a canopy of trees,

An artificial but skillfully contrived cascade, making a fine site for water plants in a naturalistic setting.

care should be taken to let the light play through onto the water so that there will be reflected light coming up out of darkness. Adjacent planting material might well be evergreen so as to avoid staining and littering the pool by deciduous tree leaves. However, a spreading dogwood tree arching over a pool or basin is most effective.

STREAM AND BROOK. The essential quality of a stream is continuity of flow, and it is very helpful to keep this constantly in mind when constructing an artificial brook or stream. An exaggerated expression of water action should be suggested in the bed and banks of the stream to imply a greater flow in times of freshet. The careful placement of a selected group of waterside plants should produce interesting reflections.

CASCADE. There is a sweetly melancholy aspect about a cascade which is soothing and relaxing. In constructing such a watercourse the source of the water must either be very frankly displayed or very cleverly concealed. Falling in thinly veiled sheets from basin to basin, the water playfully may create a dramatic effect with a small supply. To avoid any tendency toward mechanical setness, one should endeavor to have a slightly different light aspect for each individual waterfall by subtle variations in orientation and height. All lip stones should be undercut to insure a direct fall and prevent the water from dribbling down the underside of the rock.

WATER RAMP. There are interesting possibilities in the treatment of a runnel which follows the course of a ramp. A series of small pools, overflowing to join the runnel again, together with specially constructed sides to create a gurgling sound along the runnel's course, suggest a refreshing tonal symphony.

WATERFALL. Where a fairly large stream is provided, a very satisfying effect is produced by letting it fall directly into the pool below. Where the stream has only a small flow, it is well to make the most of what is given and so distribute the rocks that they catch the falling water and dash and splash it from one face to another, thereby employing the element of light to amplify the interest and playfulness of the waterfall.

WALL FOUNTAIN. A wall fountain usually takes the form of a basin architecturally related to a building or wall and the basin is fed by a spouting sculptural feature of various types and descriptions. Such a fountain would be appropriate on a terrace or in an intimate garden. One of the most attractive uses of fountains is indoors. The water provides a good atmosphere in which to grow plants and the pool into which the water tumbles may be used for aquatics (*see* WATER GARDEN).

FREESTANDING FOUNTAIN. Where a freestanding fountain jet is concerned, it is the architectural effect of the water mass itself that is to be considered primarily. The pool or basin which holds the jet may express to a minor degree the mood the designer wishes to create. The character the fountain is to assume may vary endlessly. Upspringing into the light, and joyously welling up from within, a fountain is usually inspiring and emotionally stimulating. Through sight and sound simultaneously playing together, a reaction of emotional tenseness is stirred within the beholder — if he is sensitive. There seems to be a universal quality about a fountain that recalls all fountains everywhere, and serves to give its eternal message as a symbol of the water of life. — A. F.

WATER-ALOE = *Stratiotes.*

WATER ARUM = *Calla palustris.*

WATER BEECH = *Carpinus caroliniana.* See HORNBEAM.

WATER BLISTER. A usually discolored spot on the leaves of greenhouse plants caused by the concentration of sunlight through a drop of water, or by imperfections in the glass, often called a burn.

WATER CALTROP, WATER CHESTNUT = *Trapa natans.*

WATER CANNA. See THALIA.

WATER CHESTNUT = *Trapa.*

WATER CHINQUAPIN = *Nelumbo lutea.*

WATER CONTENT. The water content of fresh fruits and vegetables is a fair index of the water needs of the plants that produce them. While grains like rice or wheat may be only 12–14% water, fruits and vegetables contain far more than this.

Percentage of water in some common vegetables:

Artichoke	81	Onion	86
Asparagus	93	Parsnip	79
Bean	15	Pea	14
Beet	85	Potato	75
Cabbage	90	Pumpkin	90
Carrot	85	Rutabaga	87
Cauliflower	90	Rhubarb	91
Celery	84	Spinach	92
Cucumber	95	Turnip	92
Lettuce	94		

Percentage of water in some common fruits:

Apple	83	Pear	83
Cherry	82	Plum	83
Gooseberry	90	Strawberry	90
Grape	83		

WATERCRESS (*Nasturtium officinale*). This extremely hardy European perennial can be grown wherever there is standing or quietly flowing water, but it prefers cool to warm water and so does better in the northern part of the country, where it is widely naturalized. It may be gathered from the wild and will easily root from broken-off stems inserted in wet sand, or it often, in quiet pools, begins to grow without attachment to the soil. Often it will completely choke such pools, and this should be kept in mind when introducing it.

If pools are not available, watercress may be planted in wet sand or sandy soil, and the flats put in the cold frame and kept constantly wet.

WATER CULTURE. See SOILLESS GARDENING.

WATER DAFFODIL. See STERNBERGIA.

WATER DOCK = *Orontium aquaticum.*

WATER ELM = *Ulmus americana.* See ELM.

WATER FEATHER = *Myriophyllum proserpinacoides.*

WATER FERN. See CERATOPTERIS.

WATER FLAG = *Iris Pseudacorus.*

---

* Special articles on the subjects indicated by an asterisk (*) will be found at the words so marked.

WATER GARDEN. Under the term water gardening is included the cultivation and grouping of aquatic or waterside plants for the best effect. The value of water gardening lies in its extreme ease of care and culture, and its wide adaptability to all kinds of gardens. Aquatic gardens vary from small tub gardens and artificial or natural brooks to the large formal or informal pools, but in each and every case, they all share the same joyful lack of weeding, cultivation, and spraying. Their only demands are for as much sun as possible, and for proper construction in the first place. With these two factors taken care of, by selecting the plants which are suitable to your own climate and garden, your water garden will be a constant delight all summer long, being of especial value in those localities where the summers are hot and dry, and any water feature of maximum importance.

CONSTRUCTION

The best mixture for concrete brooks or pools is one part Portland cement, two parts sharp sand, and three parts ½-inch gravel. The sand should be well graded, the particles varying in size from the finest up to that which screens through a ½-inch mesh. For every cubic yard needed, this 1–2–3 mixture will require 7 sacks of cement, 14 cubic feet of sand, and 21 cubic feet of gravel. If the sand and gravel are absolutely dry, it will require about 5½ gallons of water to each sack of cement; if moist, 4½ gallons; if wet, 3¾ gallons. Use only pure water.

In order to form a winterproof pool, it should be built on compact ground, with a six-inch layer of cinders or gravel beneath the concrete. The floor and walls must be poured at the same time to avoid any construction joints, and the concrete should be about six inches thick, with a layer of reinforcement in the middle. The reinforcement should be bent to the shape of the pool and raised as the concrete is poured until it is approximately in the center of the six-inch layer.

Allow for ledges or pockets to hold the shallow-growing plants, and be sure that there is plenty of area where the required two feet of depth needed for the growing of water lilies will be available. If you use forms to hold your mixture, oil the sides which come in contact with the concrete. Used motor oil will do for this, and will insure an easy removal of the forms after they have remained in contact with the cement for the required forty-eight hours or more. Smooth down the surface with a brick when the forms are removed, or finish off with a thin coat of cement applied with a trowel or paint brush.

Protect the new concrete from wind and sun, which would otherwise evaporate the water still contained in it and prevent its hardening properly. Moist earth or straw will accomplish this, if it is kept wet for a week or ten days. Walls may have wet canvas or burlap hung over them. If the weather is cold, it is not necessary to maintain the moisture in the protecting layer; merely keep the work covered for a week or ten days. It takes about four weeks for a pool to cure completely — with a minimum of two weeks at least. If possible, wait a month before filling the pool for the first time. *It is very important* to remember that the first water put into a pool will absorb the alkali from the new concrete, and it is absolutely essential to fill the pool at least two weeks to permit the complete absorption of this free alkali into the water. Then drain and refill with fresh water before planting or stocking with fish.

BROOKS

For the small home owner who does not care for the little tub-garden, or wishes something more striking for his small available space, the answer is found in an artificial brook. For satisfactory aquatic culture, a brook, like a pool, should be about two feet deep at least in spots. Both width and depth may vary along its course, simulating nature wherever possible. An inlet and outlet drain are advisable, and in all construction details the artificial brook follows the same rules as the conventional pool.

It is in planting that the most noticeable difference arises. There is no such thing as a formal brook; it must be as natural as space and material permit. For this reason, your choice of material will be decided by your particular geographical location. Water lilies will need a two-foot depth to accommodate the boxes in which they grow and still maintain the required 8 to 12 inches above their bulb crown. The aquatics which do not call for so much water covering may be grown in the shallower portions of the brook, while the submerged oxygenating plants (*see* AQUARIUM) will assist your snails and other scavengers in keeping the water clean and pure for the plants and fish.

The surface of the brook may be still further enhanced by the floating plants like *Salvinia* and *Azolla*, and along the edges and in the bends of the brook the marsh-loving cat-tails, lotus (*Nelumbo*), *Acorus*, *Thalia* (water canna), etc., may be used to bring accent and height. Be sure to confine the roots of these, however, to limited areas, or they will take over your whole brook in a season or two.

WINTER CARE

A well-reinforced pool will not crack over the winter even if left uncovered, but it is safer either to drain the pool or to cover it with boards, topped by leaves, straw, or other mulching material. This is also adequate protection for pools in which hardy lilies, water plants, and fish are left, provided the water level is kept up. If the pool is to be drained, and the plants left in, place a covering of manure, straw, or

---

* Special articles on the subjects indicated by an asterisk (*) will be found at the words so marked.

leaves directly on the soil bottom. The most satisfactory method is to have the lilies in tubs, which can be taken out and covered in a trench or brought into the cool basement and kept covered with moist wrappings of burlap to prevent the destructive dry rot attacking the dormant roots. Tropical lilies can be carried over in heated aquaria, or in greenhouse pools, according to instructions given later under *propagation,* though it is easier to treat them as annuals, replacing them each year. Tub gardens should be drained and covered with leaves and boards, holding the leaves in place. Leave them in the ground if possible, if not, heap up leaves around them.

PLANTING DESIGN

Your arrangement of plants will depend on whether you have decided upon a formal or informal pool. A formal pool is regular in outline, and requires great care in planting to retain the proportion of the pool itself in relation to the rest of the garden. If it is squared or oblong, the corners will be available for tall plantings of water canna, lotus, cat-tails or any of the water plants which grow several feet above the surface of the water. If it is round or oval, any height must be gained from the center. The outline of a formal pool should be a thing of beauty in itself, and never obscured by poor planting. If a fountain is built either at one end or in the center, a very valuable plant will be found in the parrot's-feather (*Myriophyllum proserpinacoides*).

An informal pool must be just as carefully planted as the formal, but with a different end in view. Proportion must be observed, of course, but with the idea of attaining as naturalistic an effect as possible, drawing the pool into its surroundings rather than bringing it into prominence. Conspicuous edgings of upended rock should be avoided. Either lay the rock flat, covering it with rock plants, moss, fern or any other suitable planting; or avoid its use altogether, and bring the turf right down to the brink of the pool. It is usually found advisable to locate a naturalistic pool against a background of shrubbery, rock garden, or some other terminating feature of the garden, unless the garden is of estate proportions, and the pool then becomes a pond. A formal pool may be isolated as a central feature, but a naturalistic pool is seldom successfully handled unless it is closely tied in with the general plan of the marginal planting. Its outline is frequently irregular, and gives plenty of opportunity for the use of the tall water plants in the nooks and pockets of the "shore line" as well as in the background. However, in a small pool, it is necessary to use extreme care with the larger, coarser plant material, to keep the planting in scale. The desired effect is one of harmony with the surroundings, and any too-obvious rock work, or misplaced cat-tail clump will appear definitely grotesque.

PLANT MATERIALS

A. Aquatics, other than lilies.
    I. Hardy aquatics: — 2–4 ft. tall.
        Nelumbo (lotus)
        Thalia dealbata (water canna)
        Pontederia cordata (pickerelweed)
        Typha latifolia (cat-tail)
        Typha angustifolia (cat-tail)
        Sagittaria sagittifolia *fl. pl.*
        Acorus Calamus variegata (sweet flag)
    II. Tender aquatics
        a. *Free-floating*
          Salvinia auriculata
          Azolla caroliniana (azolla)
        b. *Plants that float, but do best if planted in shallow water where they may take root.*
          Eichhornia (water hyacinth)
          Pistia Stratiotes (water lettuce)
          Ceratopteris pteridoides (water fern)
        c. *Plants that must take root in shallow water.*
          Hydrocleis nymphoides (water poppy)
          Myriophyllum proserpinacoides (parrot's-feather)
          Colocasia esculenta (taro)
          Cyperus Papyrus (papyrus)
          Cyperus alternifolius (umbrella plant)
B. Water Lilies (*Nymphaea*); for the species *see* NYMPHAEA; those below are all hort. hybrids. Viviparous* varieties are marked with a dagger (†).
    I. Hardy water lilies
      Red
        Attraction
        Conqueror
        Escarboucle
        Gloriosa
        James Brydon
        James Hudson
      Pink Shades
        Lustrous
        Mme. Chiflot
        Pink Opal
        Rose Arey
        Somptuosa
        Wilfon Gonnere
      Sunset Shades
        Comanche
        Paul Hariot
        Robinsoni
      Yellow
        Chromatella
        Sunrise
      White
        Gladstone
        Gonnere
        Hermine
    II. Tropical water lilies
      a. Day-bloomers
      Blue
        Bagdad†
        Blue Bird
        Bob Trickett
        Henry Shaw

---

* Special articles on the subjects indicated by an asterisk (*) will be found at the words so marked.

Mrs. Edwards Whitaker
Mrs. Wilson gigantea†
Pennsylvania (Blue Beauty)
Purple
   August Koch†
   Dr. George T. Moore
   Judge Hitchcock
   Midnight
Pink Shades
   American Beauty
   Castaliiflora
   Independence
   General Pershing
   Golden West
   Peach Blow†
   Persian Lilac
   Pink Platter†
   Rio Rita†
   Shell Pink
   Talisman†
   Wild Rose†
Yellow
   African Gold
   Aviator Pring†
   St. Louis Gold
   St. Louis
   Sunbeam†
   Yellow Star
White
   Daisy†
   Isabelle Pring†
   Mrs. George H. Pring
  b. Night-bloomers
White
   Juno
   Missouri
Pink
   Emily Grant Hutchings
   James Gurney
   Mrs. George C. Hitchcock
Red
   B. C. Berry
   Frank Trelease
   H. C. Haarstick
III. Pygmies (for tub and small pools)
A wide range of colors is available
in the following types
  N. tetragona — white
  N. tetragona helvola — yellow
  N. tetragona Jo Ann Pring

WATER LILIES

Water lilies will make up the main feature in a water garden, since they bloom all summer long, and are quite capable of providing a lovely spectacle with no help from any other plants. There are the hardy types of lilies, which may be left in the ground all winter long; and there are the tropical lilies, which provide the large, fragrant blooms so much admired in any pool large enough to accommodate their size. A pool 6 to 8 feet will hold three comfortably. The tropical lilies are divided into day- and night-bloomers. When the temperature is above 70° the night-bloomers will be open from 7 P.M. to about 9 A.M., the day-bloomers opening at 8 A.M. and closing at 6 P.M. A cooler temperature and cloudy weather will often keep the day-bloomers asleep, and waken the night-bloomers to full activity all day long . . . so there is no possibility of missing a glorious all-summer display if both types of the tropical lilies are planted.

VIVIPAROUS LILIES. Another division of the tropical lilies is found in the day-blooming class, which is now divided into viviparous and non-viviparous type. Due to the extreme ease of propagation of the viviparous types, they are becoming increasingly popular, particularly since they are now available in a full range of colors. These viviparous day-blooming tropical lilies produce in the center of each mature leaf a tiny new plant, complete from roots to leaves. Details are given in the section on propagation on the treatment of this new plant. Non-viviparous tropical lilies are best treated as annuals, being replaced every spring.

PLANTING. The time for planting will be governed by your geographical location. The water must be at least 70°, as a minimum, since the tropical lilies especially are susceptible to chilling in cooler water, and will become dormant Frequently dealers are blamed for sending poor plants, when in reality the lilies have merely gone back to sleep in water which was too cold.

In planting, the tuber* should be set with the crown just below the surface of the soil. As the lily grows, the water level should be raised until it is a foot above the roots. The plants will bloom about July 1, and continue until killed back by frost. The hardy lilies grow from continuously dividing rhizomes, like iris, and require transplanting every four years. When grown in boxes, fresh soil should be added at the time of removal. Plant the rhizomes* in early spring about 2–3 inches deep.

SOIL. Where the pool is given a natural bottom, the soil should be very well fertilized before the lilies are planted. Both tropical and hardy water lilies are rank feeders, and require plenty of rich food. When a concrete pool has been built, spread about two inches of manure over the bottom, followed by eight inches of sod-soil. The lilies will do well in this, but if the pool is small the gardener is not so likely to be satisfied. It is absolutely essential in a small pool to keep it well stocked with fish to prevent the mosquito menace, and fish will so stir up a pond whose bottom is covered with soil that the water will be constantly muddy. To avoid this, plant your lilies in boxes two to three feet square and a foot deep, or in half-barrels, placing manure in the bottom and filling up with sod soil. The concrete bottom can then be left clear, and the surface of the water covered with floating plants. In the corners and along the edges of the pool it is possible to construct ledges or pockets for the larger plants like lotus and cat-tails, whose root-space must be restricted to keep them from usurping the entire area. By carrying up the wall of the pocket almost to the surface,

---

* Special articles on the subjects indicated by an asterisk (*) will be found at the words so marked.

the roots of the plants may be protected from the nibbling fish.

PROPAGATION. The hardy lilies which grow from a creeping rhizome or underground stem may be propagated merely by dividing the clump in early spring and planting the growing tips, exactly as the familiar garden iris is handled. The tricks of propagation are called into play only with the tropical lilies. Here the old tubers are of little use, and it is actually a waste of time to dig them up. For new lilies, then, it is necessary either to buy new plants or to make use of one of the three available methods for propagating the tropical lilies. These are (1) seeds, (2) leaf propagation, (3) tubers, the second being confined to the viviparous hybrids from *N. micrantha* parentage.

(1) *Seeds.* In view of the mongrel ancestry of our cultivated lilies their seeds will be valueless if you expect them to produce plants like their father or mother. You may obtain a lily worth growing, but you will almost never get one which really resembles one of its immediate parents, even in controlled pollination. However, if you have the space for experimenting and are interested in producing new varieties, you may check up on the vagaries of ancestors by keeping a record of crosses you make and seeing what comes out in the children. Pick out two lilies which you wish to cross, and remove the stamens from the one you decide to use as a seed-bearer. This will prevent self-pollination. The time to place the pollen from the stamens of the one flower on the pistil of the seed-bearing lily from which the stamens have been removed can be judged by the condition of the pistil, and will be somewhere between 10 A.M. and 12 noon on the first day.

After dusting the pollen from the one flower onto the pistil of the other, cover the pollinated flower with thin muslin and attach it to a stake, with enough string to permit the flower lowering itself under the water. This is the natural position for it to assume while the seed is developing. After about three weeks the seed pod will again rise to the surface, and unless the pod has been wrapped with muslin as indicated above, the seeds will have been broadcast over the surface of the water by the natural opening of the seed pod.

In order to disintegrate the fleshy covering of the seeds, place them in a battery jar of water for three or four days to ripen them. When they are fully ripened, the virile seeds will sink to the bottom, and should be removed from the water at once to prevent premature germination. Dry them for two or three days, and when they separate readily, sow them in sandy soil in shallow pans or in glass battery jars half filled with water. Barely cover the seeds with fine sand, and gently firm the soil to prevent the seeds rising when water is placed in the pan or jar. Place the container in tanks heated to about 75° to 80° F., and as soon as the seedlings develop their floating leaves, transplant them to small pots for development, maintaining the same temperature all winter.

(2) *Leaf propagation.* As has been stated, this is limited to the viviparous varieties, but in view of the extreme ease of multiplying lilies in this fashion, it is suggested that the amateur confine his list to these forms for restocking his pool with tropical lilies, until he becomes sufficiently familiar with his plants to use their tubers. The tiny plants formed in the center of each mature leaf may be cut out when the old leaf begins to turn yellow. Remove a small portion of the stem with the little plant, to act as a brace in the pot. The pots may be left in the pool all summer and brought inside into heated tanks at about the end of September.

(3) *Tuber propagation.* This is the only method of producing true type lilies from the non-viviparous tropical forms. The original tubers which are planted out of doors are of no use in carrying the lilies over the winter; but at their base during the summer are formed small nut-like tubers which will bring forth new plants in great numbers if properly handled. At the end of August or early September, remove these tubers from the base of the old one, and place each one of them in sand for two or three weeks to rest. Be sure to keep them in a tin container with a firmly attached top during this resting period, since both rats and mice relish them.

After the resting period, place each tuber in the bottom of a pot filled with sandy soil. The depth of planting will induce the tuber to grow a long radicle* when placed in a tank of water heated to a temperature of about 80°. The young leaves will appear in about two weeks, and when the plants have formed two floating leaves the time is ripe for removing them from their tubers. Dig into the soil with thumb and finger; locate the radicle or stem by feeling the top of the tuber; and pinch off the stem just above the tuber, removing the young plant with roots and all, and potting it up immediately to prevent drying out. Leave the tuber in its pot, and it will continue to send off these young plants.

VICTORIA CRUZIANA (The water platter)

This lily, while belonging to the night-blooming tropical group is so distinctive in habit as to require a separate treatment. It has enormous circular leaves with upturned edges, strengthened underneath by a network of veins which makes it capable of supporting a great weight. The writer, who weighs 160 pounds, has stood upon a leaf on which a cotton pad and wooden frame or composition board was placed to equalize his weight and prevent the leaf from being torn. The exterior of the flowers, stems, leaves and seed pods are covered

---

* Special articles on the subjects indicated by an asterisk (*) will be found at the words so marked.

with dagger-like prickles, which necessitates the use of great care in handling; but as a curiosity it is unequaled in water-gardening, and is worth the trouble it causes.

The flowers bloom at night, being white when opening, and turning gradually to a dark pink. The older blooms have a fragrance similar to the pineapple, and are very large, often measuring a foot or more in diameter. The plant attains a great size when grown in rich soil and given plenty of room, but it will remain small if limited in space and food; so it is possible to grow it even in a small pool. However, to accommodate its full beauty, the pool should be at least 20 feet in diameter, and the soil thoroughly enriched with fertilizer. These plants will frequently produce from eight to ten of their enormous leaves at one time, all growing from the center, and as the stems develop it is necessary to peg them down to prevent the giant leaves from tearing and turning over during wind storms. The flowers are proportionally large and handsome, and it is well worth while to turn over a large pool to one of these tropical beauties.

Since they are a pure species, they will come true from seed, but the growing season is only about four months, except in the southern states, which is not sufficient time to ripen the pods in the pool. When the first light freeze comes, cut off the seed pods and bring them into a tub of water in the greenhouse. In about six weeks the seeds will free themselves from the pod and show a light yellow color, and may then be separated from the pulp and prickles by screening . . . but be even more careful of the prickles than usual, since they are most dangerous in this free state.

Pack the seeds in a covered tin box between layers of moist sand, keeping them at a temperature of about 60°. When the seeds are fully ripened, they will be about the size of an ordinary garden pea, and dark brown or black in color. This process may take as long as two years, but it is essential for them to be fully ripe to germinate. Seeds have germinated in the pool at the Missouri Botanical Garden in St. Louis three years after the plant had been grown in the pond, even though it was drained each winter.

When the seeds are ripe, plant them about March 1 at twice their depth in a medium of half sand and half soil, screened through a ½-inch mesh. Use a shallow pan as a container, submerging it in a tank of water about three inches above the top of the pan, and keeping at a temperature of 80°. In three or four weeks, a needle-like shoot will appear, followed by a submerged, lance-shaped leaf and an ovate floating leaf. When two floating leaves appear, separate the seedlings and plant in 3-inch pots in a mixture of ¾ sod-soil and ¼ sand. When the roots have filled the pot, transplant to a shallow, 8-inch pot, which should be large enough to contain the plant until it may be placed outside.

The period of outdoor planting depends upon your geographical location. The water must be about 75°–80°, which in St. Louis is usually between June 1 and June 15. When a natural pond is available, an area of 100 square feet should be covered with 2 inches of cow manure or one ounce per cubic foot of an inorganic fertilizer consisting of 15 parts of nitrogen, 30 of phosphoric acid, and 15 of potash. Spade in to a depth of one foot, and mound it up slightly at the center of the area to indicate the place of planting. Fertilizing may be done also while the plant is still potted up indoors, and the leaves when brought outside should be about one foot in diameter if the plant is to be forced to a maximum size. With plenty of room for the roots, and the free use of manure, the plant may be brought to giant proportions in eight weeks. — G. H. P.

WATER HAWTHORN = *Aponogeton distachyus.*

WATER HEMLOCK. See Cicuta.

WATER HOLLY = *Mahonia nervosa.*

WATER HYACINTH. Very showy, chiefly South American, floating aquatic plants constituting the genus **Eichhornia** (ike-hor′ni-a) of the family Pontederiaceae, often grown for ornament in warm pools, or outdoors in the Far South, but unable to stand frost. In Fla. and in several tropical countries the water hyacinth has become a major pest, completely choking otherwise navigable streams. This should be kept in mind in planting it.

They have floating leaves, the stalk of *E. crassipes* much inflated and spongy with air chambers, the blade more or less erect. Flowers in a terminal cluster on a fleshy stalk, rising well above the water. Corolla irregular,* of 6 segments, more or less funnel-shaped. Stamens* 6, some of them protruding. Fruit a 3-celled capsule.* (Named for J. A. F. Eichhorn, Prussian minister.) The plants are often known as *Piaropus.*

These extremely attractive aquatics are easily grown in shallow pools or even in tubs of water. They may be propagated by division, but in all warm regions the difficulty is to prevent them from propagating too fast.

E. azurea. Leaves variable, generally broadly oval or roundish, the stalk not inflated. Flower stalk gradually inflated into a hood-like organ, the lavender-blue, purple-centered flowers scattered or in pairs along the hairy stalk. Brazil.

E. crassipes. The common water hyacinth, upon which Fla. has spent thousands of dollars for eradication. Leafstalk much inflated and spongy, the blade ovalish or roundish, 2–5 in. wide. Flower spikes profuse, the flowers violet, the upper lobes blue-patched and yellow-spotted. Throughout tropical America, and naturalized in Fla. An extremely handsome aquatic with fine feathery roots which show attractively in an aquarium. Some prefer to call this *E. speciosa.*

---

* Special articles on the subjects indicated by an asterisk (*) will be found at the words so marked.

WATERING. Water is not only a plant nutrient in itself, but also the conveyor of other food constituents taken up in solution through the medium of the root hairs. Its proper application calls for good judgment on the part of the grower, especially in the cultivation of plants under glass, where it becomes a matter of daily importance. Skill in watering comes from practice and close observation of the conditions which govern the amount of water each plant requires. Neither the amount nor the frequency of its application can be definitely stated, weather conditions alone being too variable.

Large-leaved and actively growing soft-wooded plants require more than those of slower and harder growth, while any plant should be watered less frequently when in a state of rest. Plants get dry much faster under the influence of strong light and dry air, due to the more rapid loss of water by transpiration through the leaves. Subdued light and a moisture-laden atmosphere tend to reduce the amount of water needed at the roots, and are important factors in the growth of many plants. Leaf wilting follows when the soil becomes so dry that the roots are unable to supply enough water to keep the cells distended.

Some plants will recover from an occasional flagging with no apparent injury, but hard-wooded plants in pots may not readily recover if allowed to get so dry. Complete immersion of the pot for a few minutes is the best way to assist recovery, but it is well to avoid the need for such treatment. Strong sunlight following a cloudy period sometimes causes the leaves of fast-growing plants to wilt when there is no lack of water at the roots. In such a case the proper balance is restored by spraying the leaves or otherwise creating atmospheric moisture to check the rate of transpiration, and so avoid overwatering.

Plants set out in beds or benches will not require such frequent watering as those in pots, but in any case it should be well done when needed. Mere surface waterings will not supply the needs. On the other hand, except for aquatics, plants object to soil that is continually saturated. Proper drainage is therefore necessary to allow the free passage of water which the soil does not readily absorb. Benches may be watered by sub-irrigation, in which case the water is distributed through lines of tile laid on watertight bottoms. While effective, it increases construction costs. Plants should be thoroughly soaked before being re-potted. It is generally best to water immediately after, then wait for the soil to get somewhat dry before repeating. Overwatering before the roots get working freely in the new soil is likely to cause trouble.

Excessive moisture about the plants at night during winter is likely to cause trouble, so watering is best done early in the day. In late spring and summer, water may be needed more than once on bright days, but with free ventilation late watering will do no harm. In the watering of seedpans special care is needed. Some prefer to water well before sowing the seeds, and have found boiling water used at this time efficacious in preventing troubles which may bother seedlings, especially those of slow germination. Overhead watering of seed through the fine rose of a carefully handled watering can is generally safe. With very fine seeds it may be safe to water from below by partial immersion of the soil container as required.

A question often asked by those wishing to keep plants in the home is, How often should I water my plants? Conditions are so variable that the only safe reply is, "When needed." One thing is certain, never give water in driblets, but enough to ensure a thorough soaking all the way through. The frequency of watering will depend on the kind of plant, its condition of growth, the temperature of the room, and the moisture content of the air. It is chiefly the hot and dry air of the average room that is so detrimental to the well-being of many plants in the home. Anything that can be done to modify this condition, such as standing the pots on a tray of moist sand or gravel, will be of material help to the plants. On the other hand, except for such moisture-loving plants as the calla lily, it is not good for plants to be kept standing in water in a jardiniere.* Succulent plants are so constructed that they lose moisture very slowly by transpiration, and many of these are excellent plants for the home if placed in good light. While they need to be watered less often than leafy plants, good drainage is essential.

Where pot plants are used to furnish inside window boxes, filling the spaces between the pots with sphagnum moss helps to check dryness. Such boxes may be made with a false bottom, from which surplus water can be drawn off through the stopcock. Window boxes and hanging baskets with devices for watering by sub-irrigation work out very well in places where drip would be a nuisance. Wire hanging baskets lined with moss need to be immersed occasionally to ensure sufficient moisture. Large plants in tubs will need careful attention, especially in exposed positions. A removable outer shell of larger size, to allow of an insulation of damp moss, would be of help in keeping the roots cool and moist.

It has long been known by plantsmen that soft rain-water has a more kindly effect on plants than hard water, and also that they prefer it at about the same temperature in which they are growing. — H. E. D.

WATERING POT. *See* No. 7 at Tools and Implements.

WATERLEAF. *See* Hydrophyllum.

WATER LEMON = *Passiflora laurifolia.*

WATER LETTUCE = *Pistia Stratiotes.*

WATER LILY. *See* Nymphaea. *See also* Water Garden.

WATER LILY TULIP = *Tulipa kaufman-niana.*

WATER LOCUST = *Gleditsia aquatica.* See HONEY LOCUST.

WATERMELON. The common water-melon is the only cult. species of the genus **Citrullus** (sit-trull'us) of the cucumber family. A variety of it is the citron, sometimes called the preserving melon. *Citrullus* contains only 4 or 5 species, all from tropical Africa, but one of them also found in Asia. The watermelon is **C. vulgaris,** a long-running, annual, very tender, prostrate vine with branched tendrils* (the tendrils are unbranched in the closely related muskmelon; *see* CUCUMIS). Leaves alternate,* broad, but divided into segments. Flowers light yellow, about 1½ in. wide, solitary in the leaf axils,* the male and female separate, but on the same plant. Corolla shallowly funnel-shaped, deeply 5-parted. Stamens* 5, but apparently 3 because two pairs are united. Fruit berry-like, but with hard rind (a pepo), green in the familiar watermelon in which the flesh is red or pink and very watery. In the *var.* **citroides,** the citron or preserving melon, the fruit is much smaller and the flesh is hard, white, and useful only when cooked. Tropical and South Africa. (*Citrullus* is a diminutive of *Citrus,* probably in some unknown allusion to the fruit.) For the Chinese watermelon *see* BENINCASA.

WATERMELON CULTURE

The watermelon requires a long, hot growing season; it does not succeed as far north as the cantaloupe, but does well under high humidity and is grown extensively in the southern sections of the U.S. When grown in northern sections, early-maturing varieties must be selected or the plants started under protection and set in the field after frost. A fertile sandy loam is a preferable soil type; it must be well drained and have a pH of 5–6.

The culture of the watermelon is similar to that of the cantaloupe or muskmelon except that it requires more room. *See* MELON.

For highest quality the watermelon should be picked when fully ripe but not overripe. It is difficult to determine the proper stage, as the fruit shows very few external changes in size or color as it ripens. When green, the fruit gives forth a metallic ring when thumped; this sound becomes more muffled or deader with increasing ripeness. It is advisable to test this and other criteria of ripeness by cutting occasional melons in the field to secure the knack of picking at the proper stage.

The most important varieties are:
FOR SHORT-SEASON REGIONS: Golden Honey Cream, New Hampshire Midget,† Early Kansas, Baby Rhode Island Red.†
FOR LONG-SEASON REGIONS: Any of the above and Klondike, Charleston Gray, Icebox.†

Vars. marked with a dagger (†) are the recent so-called midget melons which are seldom over 10 in. in diameter, and roundish.

Pumpkins or squash can have no possible effect on flavor or quality of adjacent melons.

Because of the size and length of the vines watermelons cannot be grown where space is limited. The vines should be at least 6 ft. apart each way.

INSECT PESTS. Control beetles and aphids by pesticide #1 or #20 (*see* SPRAYS AND DUSTS).

DISEASES. The watermelon suffers from the same diseases as cucumber (which see). A fungus wilt* may also be serious on watermelon. Plants wilt and die and brown streaks are present inside the stem. Grow wilt-resistant varieties recommended for your particular area.

WATER-MILFOIL. See MYRIOPHYLLUM.

WATER OAK = *Quercus nigra.* See OAK.

WATER PLANTAIN = *Alisma Plantago-aquatica.*

WATER PLANTS. See WATER GARDEN, BOG GARDEN.

WATER PLATTER. See VICTORIA.

WATER POPPY = *Hydrocleis nymphoides.*

WATER RICE = *Zizania aquatica.*

WATER SHIELD. See CABOMBA and BRASENIA SCHREBERI.

WATER SNOWFLAKE = *Nymphoides indicum.*

WATER-SOLDIER. See STRATIOTES.

WATER SPROUT. See SUCKER.

WATER TABLE. The level at which ground water is found. It varies with topography, being nearest the surface in depressions. Capillarity is responsible for raising the moisture from the water table to the roots of plants.

WATER-WEED = *Anacharis canadensis.*

WATER WILLOW = *Decodon verticillatus.*

WATSONIA (wat-sō'ni-a). Bugle-lily. South African gladiolus-like herbs of the iris family, comprising perhaps 60 species, of which three are cult. for ornament, but better known in Calif. than in the East. They have basal, sword-shaped leaves, sometimes a few on the stem, and rather showy flowers in a terminal cluster (raceme*), the corolla differing from the closely related *Gladiolus* in being nearly regular,* the tube curved. Fruit a 3-celled capsule.* (Named for Sir William Watson, English botanist.)

The culture of watsonias, which are summer-blooming, is the same as for gladiolus (which see).

fulgens. Nearly 4 ft. high. Flowers scarlet, the tube not expanding upward, the segments tapering, about 1 in. long. Often offered as *W. angusta.*

iridifolia. Nearly 4 ft. high. Flowers nearly 3 in. long, pink, the tube longer than the segments. Perhaps only a var. of *W. fulgens.* The *var.* **o'brieni** has white flowers.

rosea. From 3–6 ft. high. Flowers rose-red, the tube flaring toward the top and as

---

* Special articles on the subjects indicated by an asterisk (*) will be found at the words so marked.

long as the segments. Also known as *W. pyramidata.*

WATTLE. *See* ACACIA.

WAUKEGAN JUNIPER = *Juniperus horizontalis douglasi.*

WAX. The chief use of wax is in grafting. For the preparation of the sort so used *see* GRAFTING WAX. The other use of wax is to cover young whips,* buds, cions, etc., with a thin film in packing them for transportation. The wax prevents them from drying out and can easily be removed by melting, without injury to the buds.

WAX BEAN = *Phaseolus vulgaris.* For culture *see* BEAN.

WAXBERRY = *Symphoricarpos albus.*

WAX DOLLS = *Fumaria officinalis.* See FUMITORY.

WAX FLOWER = *Stephanotis floribunda.*

WAX GOURD = *Benincasa hispida.*

WAX MYRTLE = *Myrica cerifera.*

WAX PALM = *Ceroxylon andicola.*

WAX PINK = *Portulaca grandiflora.*

WAX-PLANT = *Hoya carnosa.*

WAX PRIVET = *Ligustrum japonicum.* See PRIVET.

WAXWORK = *Celastrus scandens.*

WAYFARING-TREE = *Viburnum Lantana.*

WAYTHORN = *Rhamnus cathartica.*

WEATHER. *See* CLIMATE.

WEAVER'S BROOM = *Spartium junceum.*

WEEDS AND WEEDING. Weeds are useless plants out of place.

The effects of weeds are many. They flourish more readily than most cultivated plants. They have a direct influence on the devaluation of property — and often the reputation of the owner. The expense of clearing weeds will often adversely impress a prospective buyer. Some weeds are hosts* for fungi, rusts, and insects which may spread to garden plants. Others, like poison ivy and black nightshade, are poisonous either externally or internally.

THE KINDS

Weeds, for the practical gardener, may be put under two main headings, annual* and perennial.* Neither should be tolerated in any garden, and in commercial nurseries or market gardens few are found, for they are a costly extravagance. Because of their different life spans annual and perennial weeds must be treated differently, but for both cultivation* is always right in their early stages, for it leaves the roots exposed. The list of weeds at the end gives special directions for both classes, where cultivation is not sufficient.

ANNUAL WEEDS

Because of their short life span, many gardeners think annual weeds may be neglected because they will soon die out or can be easily exterminated. A dense crop of several generations, however, means a costly clearing not only locally, but whenever the seed has had time to scatter. Annual weeds are the most persistent in cultivated gardens, but are fortunately very easily controlled if cultivation is regular and well done. Even winter annuals,* while more difficult to control, can be destroyed by early spring cultivation.

PERENNIAL WEEDS

These invade and persist in lawns and permanent crops like strawberry, asparagus, and perennial flower borders. When full grown they have to be individually hand-weeded or dug out. In the case of lawn infestation, strong weed killers (*see* below) are necessary.

The most effective means of control in a regularly cropped garden is annual trenching or deep digging of all spare ground. While many weeds have powerful and long-lived rootstocks, the great majority will not survive deep burial. The turned-up soil will reveal any deep-rooted ones which should be picked out whole. Regular cultivation after this will take care of any seed blown from neglected lots, whether annual or perennial, but the cultivation must be prompt to prevent deep-rooted perennials from getting a start.

A continual cutting of the green leaves will effectively remove the most vital source of nourishment to some weed roots and thus starve them out.

Should a plot harbor weeds like thistles and dandelions, the cleanest method to reclaim the soil would be deep plowing or digging.

Weeds in paths, drives, crazy paving, and rock gardens present other problems. In the hands of a careful distributor, the commercial weed killers are easy and effective (*see* Weed Killers below). Weeding annuals from crazy paving and rock gardens may be simple, but perennials follow the half-buried stones so thoroughly that it is often most effective to take up and relay the stones in a crazy path. Around large rocks a constant warfare must be kept up to break the heart of any persistent weed roots, such as sheep's-sorrel, knotweed, or quack grass.

For surface weeds, where weed killers are impossible, a Dutch or "D" hoe is the most effective and quickest tool to use. By working backwards the soil is not trodden down and the weeds in the surface mulch, with their necks broken, do not revive after a shower.

LAWN WEEDS

Weedy lawns present a problem by themselves. Perennials are the main source of trouble, but if annuals like chickweed or crab grass once invade the lawn, they outrun all perennials in exasperating persistency. The latter pest has become most notorious.

---

* Special articles on the subjects indicated by an asterisk (*) will be found at the words so marked.

A condition of high acidity, however, discourages its growth, and this may be secured by the liberal use of peat moss and sheep manure. This not only benefits a poor soil but will also check chickweed, which will often disappear with the use of sheep manure alone. If the lawn is of Kentucky bluegrass, however, the acidity cannot be increased too much. *See* LAWN.

If the lawn grasses are strong, but invaded by deep-rooting dandelions, plantains, or prickly lettuce, the best method would be to apply 2,4-D through a spring gun to the heart of every weed or to dust it on the tender, flat weed leaves. Grass itself is most resistant to this weed killer, owing to the fineness of its blades. Any damaged grass leaves are quickly removed by mowing.

For persistent, shallow-rooted lawn weeds there is a long-handled weeder that grips like long pincers, with two inches of steel thrust on either side of the weed. An asparagus knife is also excellent for such and for dock or dandelion.

One of the main sources of weeds is cheap grass seed and the penalty of one year's bad seeding may be seven years' weeding. Just as clean seed should be used for lawns, equal care should be taken in the use of lawn dressings. (*See* LAWN.) Heat and fermentation are the main destroyers of weed seed, but do not trust too much to farmyard manures. Many new weeds have traveled long distances by way of the manure heap.

WEED KILLERS (HERBICIDES)

Chemical weed killers are most effective in places where cultivation is impossible, as on roadways, tennis courts, and garden paths. They may be used as liquids (plainly labeled "poison") through a rose-spouted watering pot or as a powder dusted on the damp weed foliage. Take care not to pour these poisons within six inches of grass edges or borders with live surface roots. The untreated six inches must be hand-weeded or hoed off. Dwarf shrub borders may be protected from splashes by light boards placed alongside. Apply weed killer after a rain or after wetting the weeds down first. Do not walk from the treated places to borders or the vegetable garden.

Many dangerously poisonous chemicals will kill weeds, but their preparation is troublesome and some are so hazardous to mix (explosive if mixed wrongly) that the average gardener will do well to buy ready-mixed weed killers of which there are many on the market. All the reputable ones have the ingredients on the container and state whether they are selective or not — which means whether they kill everything (useful on a path or drive), or are aimed at a particular type of weed and harmless to other vegetation. It should never be forgotten that all of these prepared weed killers are poisonous to animals, pets, children, birds, etc.

Among the many types of commercially prepared weed killers are the so-called hormone weed killers of which 2,4-D is the best for broad-leaved weeds, but harmless to grass. There are so many others that even listing them is impossible here. The important thing to remember in purchasing any of them is that they are usually aimed at a particular target and it is well to know whether you need a selective one or not.

THE FIFTY WORST GARDEN WEEDS

Of the hundreds of naturalized weeds in America, mostly of European or Asiatic origin, the following appear to be either the most common or most troublesome. It should not be forgotten, however, that they seldom trouble good gardeners who know that constant cultivation will kill all weed seedlings and so prevent permanent infestation.

Those marked with a dagger (†) are annual.* All the rest are perennial,* except a few noted as biennial.*

To aid in identifying them they may be grouped thus:

> Grasses: Numbers 11, 36, 39
> Low or prostrate weeds: Numbers 2, 10, 12, 16, 20, 21, 23, 26, 34, 35, 40, 41, 45, 46, 47
> Obviously creeping or climbing plants: Numbers 3, 15, 16, 17, 32
> Erect weeds prickly on the stems, leaves or flower-cluster: Numbers 6, 7, 18, 33, 38, 44
> Erect weeds of varying heights but never prickly.
> White-flowered: Numbers 4, 24, 43, 50
> Yellow-flowered: Numbers 1, 5, 8, 14, 24, 27, 49
> Blue or purple: Numbers 9, 41
> Red, pink, or orange: Numbers 9, 29, 41, 50
> Greenish, or inconspicuous: Numbers 13, 22, 25, 28, 30, 31, 42, 48

†1. **Beggar-ticks** (*Bidens frondosa*). Called also boot-jack and Spanish needles. Yellow-flowered stout herb with compound* leaves and barbed fruit that sticks to clothing. Tillage is the remedy.

2. **Bird's-foot trefoil** (*Lotus corniculatus*). Low clover-like herb with yellow flower heads. Spray chemical weed killer for lawn infestation; cultivate it out of the garden. *See* LOTUS CORNICULATUS.

†3. **Black bindweed** (*Polygonum Convolvulus*). A rampant twining vine with heart-shaped or halberd-shaped leaves on long stalks. Often called wild buckwheat. Easily killed by cultivation. *See also* 21, 22.

†4. **Black nightshade** (*Solanum nigrum*). Wilted foliage very poisonous. Erect herb with oval leaves, small white flowers in drooping clusters and black fruit. Very common but easily controlled by cultivation. *See also* 18.

5. **Bulbous buttercup** (*Ranunculus bulbosus*). Deep-rooted buttercup with the familiar yellow flowers. Often a serious pest in lawns

---

* Special articles on the subjects indicated by an asterisk (*) will be found at the words so marked.

from which it must be dug. Cultivation will control it in the garden. There are many other species. *See also* 12.

6. **Burdock** (*Arctium Lappa*). A coarse biennial,* resembling a thistle but with only the flower head and fruits prickly. Leaves large, green above and whitish beneath, the stalks deeply furrowed. Flower heads loosely clustered, purplish or whitish. Its bur-like fruit sticks to clothing by minute hooked prickles. Cut it off below ground. Called, also, gobo and great burdock.

7. **Canada thistle** (*Cirsium arvense*). A deep-rooted, smooth-stemmed but prickly-leaved herb with showy purple flowers in a tight head. Perhaps the most pernicious European weed ever introduced into America. Proof against most chemicals, and cultivation does not reach deep enough to kill the root. It must be dug out.

8. **Cat's-ear** (*Hypochaeris radicata*). Called also gosmore and California dandelion. Erect herb with dandelion-like, but smaller, flower heads and leaves like a cat's ear. Cultivate or apply chemical weed killer.

9. **Chicory** (*Cichorium Intybus*). Deep-rooted plant with alternate cut leaves and handsome blue, pink, or purplish flowers in solitary stalkless heads. Must be dug, when old, but cultivation will kill young plants. *See* CICHORIUM INTYBUS.

†10. **Chickweed.** (*Stellaria media*). A general garden pest. Low, with oval leaves on hairy stalks and tiny white flowers with 4 or 5 petals. Cultivation for the garden or spraying with a 2,4-D solution on the lawn. It must sometimes (*i.e.*, in times when the soil is too moist to cult.) be pulled out by hand from seedbeds or borders.

†11. **Crab grass** (*Digitaria*). A bad lawn pest, often called finger-grass. It spreads and roots at the joints, and sends up a long stalk with finger-like, spreading spikes. For control *see* CRAB GRASS in the body of the book.

12. **Creeping buttercup** (*Ranunculus repens*). Low prostrate herb with small yellow flowers. Mostly a lawn weed and there treated with 2,4-D. Called also creeping crowfoot and sitfast. *See also* 5.

13. **Curled dock** (*Rumex crispus*). Deep-rooted, pernicious weed with wavy-margined narrow leaves and a dense terminal cluster of greenish, small flowers. Must be dug out. There are many other species. *See also* 42.

14. **Dandelion** (*Taraxacum officinale*). Golden-headed tramp with a deep root. Apply 2, 4-D in the lawn or dig out. Cultivate it out of the garden.

15. **Field bindweed** (*Convolvulus arvensis*). A creeping vine with arrow-shaped leaves and flowers resembling a small, whitish-pink morning-glory. It has deep white rootstocks which must be dug or killed with 2,4-D. A persistent and pernicious pest. *See also* 17.

16. **Ground ivy** (*Glecoma hederacea*). Creeping plant with roundish, scalloped leaves and small, light blue flowers clustered in the axils.* Easily killed by cultivation. Called

also gill-over-the-ground and field balm. Also known as *Nepeta hederacea.*

17. **Hedge bindweed** (*Convolvulus sepium*). Resembling the field bindweed but with leaves and flowers nearly twice the size and with the leaves roundish. It is sometimes called Rutland beauty. Treatment same as field bindweed (No. 15).

18. **Horse nettle** (*Solanum carolinense*). Deep-rooted, pernicious, prickly pest. Erect or straggling stems, irregularly lobed or cut leaves, potato-like, blue or white flowers followed by yellow berries. Cultivate or kill with chemical weed killer. *See also* 4.

19. **Horsetail** (*Equisetum arvense*). Leafless herb having whorls* of thread-like branches and a terminal yellowish cone. Very persistent and must be frequently cultivated.

†20. **Knawel** (*Scleranthus annuus*). Low, spreading weed with tiny thread-like leaves and very small green flowers. Cultivate or spray with 2,4-D on lawns.

21. **Knotweed** (*Polygonum aviculare*). Prostrate, very wiry herb with bluish-gray, very small leaves and still smaller greenish, pink-margined flowers. Cultivate it out of the garden and pull it out of the lawn, filling the space with white clover. *See also* 3, 22.

†22. **Lady's-thumb** (*Polygonum Persicaria*). Erect herb with a conspicuous dark spot on the leaves and a spike of small, inconspicuous, pinkish-white flowers. Kill it by cultivation. *See also* 3, 21.

23. **Mallow** (*Malva rotundifolia*). Really a biennial.* Low, nearly prostrate herb with alternate, roundish, long-stalked leaves and white solitary flowers in the axils.* Cultivate from garden and spray lawn with 2,4-D. Called also cheeses.

†24. **Mayweed** (*Anthemis Cotula*). Called also dog fennel. A rank-smelling, upright weed with dissected leaves and white-flowered heads with a yellow center. Decorative, but should be exterminated by cultivation.

25. **Mexican tea** (*Chenopodium ambrosioides*). The strongest-smelling of all our weeds. Stout herb (sometimes an annual) with cut or merely toothed, nearly stalkless leaves and a terminal leafy cluster of minute, very numerous, greenish flowers. Cultivation kills it. Common in the garden or dooryards, rare in the lawn. *See also* 30, 48.

26. **Mouse-ear chickweed** (*Cerastium vulgatum*). Low, creeping weed with opposite* leaves and small white flowers on erect stalks. Most common in lawns where it must be dug, or spray with chemical weed killer.

27. **Mouse-ear hawkweed** (*Hieracium Pilosella*). Somewhat resembling the orange hawkweed, but with yellow flowers. Treat as for orange hawkweed, No. 29.

†28. **Orach** (*Atriplex patula*). A dry-soil weed, pale green and often somewhat scurfy or mealy on its slender-stalked, narrowly arrow-shaped leaves. It has inconspicuous flowers in slender, discontinuous spikes. Easily killed by cultivation.

29. **Orange hawkweed** (*Hieracium aurantiacum*). A persistent, very prolific weed in

---

* Special articles on the subjects indicated by an asterisk (*) will be found at the words so marked.

fields and lawns, less common in gardens. It has basal hairy leaves and long-stalked heads of very showy orange flowers. Shallow-rooted and easily controlled by cultivation. Spray lawns with 2,4-D. Called also devil's-paintbrush. *See also* 27.

†30. **Pigweed** (*Chenopodium album*). One of the commonest weeds in America, with mealy, toothed leaves and greenish-white flower spikes in the axils.* Often called lamb's-quarters. Pull up, or, in young state, cultivate. *See also* 25, 48.

31. **Plantain** (*Plantago major* and *P. lanceolata*). One of these has broad leaves; the other, narrow ones, but in both species they are basal and ribbed. Flowers small and inconspicuous, in erect, close clusters. Dig out of the garden and apply chemical weed killer on lawns.

32. **Poison ivy** (*Rhus radicans*). A deep-rooted woody vine, or often shrubby, with glossy, compound* leaves, tiny greenish flowers and white fruit. Poisonous by contact.

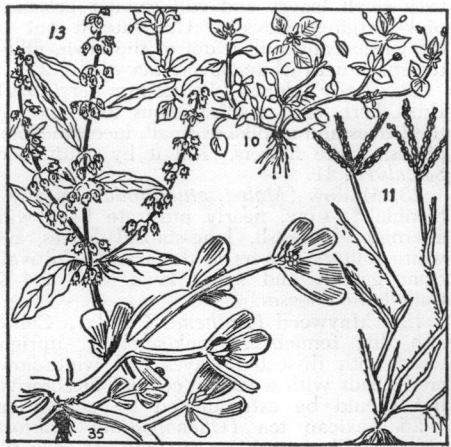

Four common garden weeds, numbered as in the list. No. 10 — Chickweed; No. 11 — Crab grass; No. 13 — Curled dock; No. 35 — Purslane.

Dig out (with gloves on) or burn, in dormant season; 2,4-D, if sprayed on in summer weather, will kill it. Crankcase oil will also kill it. Hogs are said to relish it and to eat it with impunity. For related, and also poisonous, species *see* POISON IVY.

33. **Prickly lettuce** (*Lactuca Scariola*). Nearly five feet high when full grown. Leaves bluish-green, prickly margined and with scattered prickles on the midrib.* Flowers pale yellow in a huge, branched, rather sparse inflorescence.* Dig out, or cut off below ground. It will continue to grow if cut above ground.

†34. **Prostrate pigweed** (*Amaranthus graecizans*). Spreading over the ground, often in dense mats, and very quickly. Nearly stalk-

less green leaves and tiny greenish flowers in the axils.* Cultivation is the only remedy. There are several other species, often erect and coarse.

†35. **Purslane** (*Portulaca oleracea*). Commonly called "pussley." Fleshy-leaved pest, perhaps the most notorious weed in the world. Flowers very small, yellow. Never let it set seed, as they have long-keeping qualities. Cultivation is a sure cure.

36. **Quack grass** (*Agropyron repens*). Also called witch grass. A grass most easily distinguished by its ivory-white, sharp-pointed rootstocks. Perhaps the most troublesome weed known. Only digging out will control it. Broken rootstocks simply make new plants.

†37. **Ragweed** (*Ambrosia artemisiifolia*). A coarse, roughish herb from 3 to 12 ft. high. Leaves large, 3- to 5-lobed. Flowers very numerous in tall, often branching, spike-like clusters, the individual heads turban-shaped and apparently upside down. Its profuse pollen is one of the leading causes of hay fever. Kill by cultivation. There is another species, also annual.

†38. **Russian thistle** (*Salsola pestifer*). A red-stemmed herb that becomes prickly, profusely branched into a dome-shaped plant. Most serious in the Middle and Far West. Cultivate it out of gardens and mow all roadsides and fence-rows to prevent its copious seeding.

†39. **Sandbur** (*Cenchrus pauciflorus*). A spreading grass, easily recognized by its prickly burs. Common in sandy soils, shallow-rooted and easily controlled by cultivation.

†40. **Scarlet pimpernel** (*Anagallis arvensis*). A low, often nearly prostrate herb with tiny bell-shaped, red or white flowers. Called also poor-man's-weatherglass. Cultivate it out.

41. **Self-heal** (*Prunella vulgaris*). Low or sprawling herb with opposite, stalked leaves and head-like, mostly terminal clusters of violet or pinkish flowers. Easily exterminated by cultivation. Called also heal-all.

42. **Sheep's-sorrel** (*Rumex Acetosella*). A bitter-tasting herb with halberd-shaped leaves and slender spikes of small flowers. Cultivating it out of the garden is difficult or almost impossible. Spray 2,4-D on lawn. *See also* 13.

†43. **Shepherd's-purse** (*Capsella Bursa-pastoris*). Erect herb with root leaves clustered, small white flowers in spreading clusters and small, purse-shaped pods that taper toward the base. Easily controlled by cultivation, but a prolific seeder.

†44. **Sow thistle** (*Sonchus oleraceus*). A coarse, leafy herb with smooth stems, yellow, dandelion-like flowers in sparse clusters and cut leaves with a large terminal lobe and finely prickly teeth. Chemical weed killers in fields and cultivation in the garden. There are other, sometimes perennial, species.

45. **Speedwell** (*Veronica officinalis*). Rare in the garden, but common on lawns where spraying with 2,4-D is best. It is a semi-prostrate plant with ascending clusters of small blue flowers.

---

* Special articles on the subjects indicated by an asterisk (*) will be found at the words so marked.

†46. **Spotted spurge** (*Euphorbia maculata*). Hugs the ground in flat mats. Leaves small, with a conspicuous red dot. Cultivation is the remedy. There are many other species, some erect.

†47. **Spurry** (*Spergula arvensis*). A small, nearly prostrate, very common, white-flowered herb with thread-like whorled* leaves. Easily killed by cultivation.

†48. **Strawberry-blite** (*Chenopodium capitatum*). A coarse weed with fleshy red fruit. Cultivation. *See also* 25, 30.

†49. **Wild mustard** (various species of *Brassica*). Serious weed in grain fields and in ill-kept gardens. Various forms are known, all resembling mustard and with yellow flowers. Spray with chemical weed killer, or cultivate.

50. **Yarrow** (*Achillea Millefolium*). Erect herb with finely dissected, strong-smelling leaves and flat-topped clusters of small white flowers. Dig old plants out or cultivate. Spray lawns with chemical weed killer.

Some would add to this list *Galinsoga ciliata*, and *G. parviflora*, tropical American annual weeds that are pests and *Commelina communis*, an annual day-flower, with blue flowers. One of our worst weeds is Bermuda grass. *See* CYNODON. Also, the wild onion (*Allium cernuum*) is often a pest in lawns, but a single spring mowing removes the tops for the season. Its eradication by digging out the bulbs is endless. The Japanese honeysuckle is also an almost ineradicable weed, once it gets started.

WEEPING AMERICAN ELM = *Ulmus americana pendula*. *See* ELM.

WEEPING BEECH = *Fagus sylvatica pendula*. *See* BEECH.

WEEPING BOREE = *Acacia pendula*.

WEEPING GOLDEN BELL = *Forsythia suspensa*.

WEEPING MULBERRY. *See Morus alba* at MULBERRY.

WEEPING MYALL = *Acacia pendula*.

WEEPING TREES. Besides the six just above, and the weeping willow which follows, there are several other shrubs and trees with drooping branches, although they are not all so named. Among the best of them are weeping forms of the white birch, ash, *Sophora japonica pendula*, and *Sorbus Aucuparia pendula* (*see* MOUNTAIN-ASH). Among trees that flower showily the finest weeping tree is probably *Prunus subhirtella pendula* whose weeping branches are loaded with showy bloom in spring. Many of the weeping trees are grafted or budded as standards (*see* STANDARD, 1), which ensures their being kept at the desired height, while the weeping branches often reach the ground. If you need a weeping tree on the lawn, it is well to specify whether you want a natural weeping tree like the weeping beech or weeping willow, or whether one grown as a standard is needed.

WEEPING WILLOW. The common weeping willow is *Salix babylonica*, but *S. blanda*

and *S. elegantissima* both have pendulous branches and are sometimes called weeping willows. *See* WILLOW.

WEIGELA (wy-gee′la). Very handsome, mostly May–June flowering shrubs of the honeysuckle family, comprising about 12 species, closely related to *Diervilla* and by some not considered distinct, but differing in the larger, much more showy flowers. Leaves opposite.* Flowers more or less funnel-shaped, about 1½ in. long, borne very profusely on short shoots of the season, mostly in clusters of 1–3. Corolla slightly irregular.* Stamens* 5. Fruit a rather woody, 2-valved capsule,* splitting from the top downward. All the species are Asiatic and the identity of the cult. sorts is in considerable confusion, as there are many hybrids and named forms. (Named for C. E. Weigel, German physician.)

These very showy bushes are of the easiest cult. in any ordinary garden soil, which fact, with their attractive bloom, accounts for their wide popularity. They root easily from cuttings taken in summer and put in moist sand in the cold frame or in boxes under the trees. Their profuse bloom is borne on shoots of the season which start from last year's twigs. They should only be pruned, therefore, if this is necessary at all, after flowering is over. The Latin names below, while of wide usage, are by no means definitive, and they have no common names. All are hardy from zone* 3 southward.

amabilis. The plants offered as this are usually *Weigela florida*.

floribunda. A shrub 7–10 ft. high. Leaves elliptic or oblongish, 3–4½ in. long, toothed, hairy both sides. Flowers dark crimson, nearly stalkless, the stamens* as long as the corolla, but the style * protruding. Jap.

florida. The most widely planted sort, and a shrub 8–10 ft. high, the branches spreading. Leaves generally elliptic, tapering at the tip, 3–4 in. long, hairy only on the veins beneath. Flowers rose-pink in the typical form, but in the many hort. varieties white, pink, or darker. Northern China and Korea. More than a dozen different names have been applied to this old favorite, among them *amabilis, candida* (white), *rosea, versicolor,* etc.

hortensis. Resembling *W. florida,* but the carmine flowers are distinctly stalked and rather narrowly bell-shaped. Jap.

hybrida. A group name for many named forms of *Weigela,* some of which may belong to *W. florida.* One of the best is Eva Rathke, a fine, red-flowered shrub; others include plants known as Abel Carrière, Dr. Baillon, Madame Lemoine, etc. Some have variegated leaves.

japonica. A shrub 8–10 ft. high, the leaves oblongish, 3–4 in. long, hairy on the under side, especially on the veins. Flowers generally in clusters of 3, narrowly bell-shaped, white at first, ultimately carmine. Jap.

praecox. Plants so named appear to be early-flowering forms of *W. florida.*

rosea = *Weigela florida.*

WEIGHTS AND MEASURES. Here are included the purely arithmetical dimensions of land, or of the contents of containers, useful for ready reference in the garden. Elsewhere are grouped an entirely different set of gar-

---

* Special articles on the subjects indicated by an asterisk (*) will be found at the words so marked.

den statistics having to do with yields, seeds, plants per acre, longevity of seeds, height and age of trees, and many other figures of use in making calculations for planting. *See* GARDEN TABLES.

In the tables below are grouped, according to sections, the following:

1. Acre.
2. Linear, square, and cubic measures.
3. Volume of containers (liquid and dry measures).
4. Standard weights.
5. Contents of cisterns.

1. ACRE

An acre contains 43,560 square ft. or 4840 square yards. It is almost exactly 209 × 209 ft. Hence, some of the ordinary-shaped gardens are:

100 × 200 ft. = ½ acre ⎫
100 × 100 = ¼ acre ⎬ approximately.
50 × 100 = ⅛ acre ⎪
25 × 100 = ⅟₁₆ acre ⎭
33 × 66 = ⅟₂₀ acre exactly

For the number of plants needed for an acre, at intervals of from 1 × 1 in. to 100 × 100 ft., *see* GARDEN TABLES I. There are 640 acres in a square mile.

2. LINEAR, SQUARE, AND CUBIC MEASURES

Linear. 12 in. = 1 ft.   320 rods = 1 mile
        3 ft. = 1 yd.   1760 yds. = 1 mile
        16½ ft. = 1 rod   5280 ft. = 1 mile

Square. 144 square in. = 1 square ft.
         9 " ft. = 1 " yard
         30¼ square yards = 1 " rod
         160½ " rods = 1 acre

Cubic.   1 cubic ft. = 1728 cubic in.
         1 cubic yard = 27 " ft.
         A cubic yard contains 43,656 cubic in.
         A cubic foot of water weighs about 62½ pounds, and is almost 7½ gallons.

3. VOLUMES OF CONTAINERS
(Liquid and Dry Measures)

Liquid Measure:
4 gills = 1 pint, which is just over 1 pound of water
2 pints = 1 quart
4 quarts = 1 gallon, which is 8.34 pounds of water, and contains 231 cubic in.

Dry Measure:
2 pints = 1 quart
8 quarts = 1 peck
4 pecks = 1 bushel, which, in the U.S., should contain 2150 cubic in. For the weight of a bushel see next table.

4. STANDARD WEIGHTS
(avoirdupois)

16 drams = 1 ounce
16 ounces = 1 pound
100 pounds = hundredweight
2000 " = 1 ton
2240 " = 1 long ton

These are some figures of weights that gardeners often find useful.

Bushel of Apples = 48–50 pounds
        Barley = 48 "
        Beets = 56–60 "
        Buckwheat = 42–50 "
        Corn = 56–60 "
        Onions = 52–57 "
        Potatoes = 60 "
        (except in Va., where it is 56)
        Turnips = 55–60 "
        Wheat = 60 "
Gallon of Water = 8.34 pounds
Pint of Water = Just over 1 pound
Cubic foot of water = 62.42 pounds

5. CONTENTS OF CISTERNS
Gallons in Round Tanks

Diameter ft.	3 ft.	4 ft.	5 ft.	6 ft.	7 ft.
4	282	376	470	564	658
5	440	587	734	881	1028
6	634	846	1057	1269	1480
7	863	1151	1439	1727	2015
8	1128	1504	1880	2256	2632
9	1427	1903	2379	2855	3331
10	1762	2350	2937	3525	4112
11	2132	2843	3554	4265	4976
12	2538	3384	4230	5076	5922

Gallons in Round Tanks

Diameter ft.	8 ft.	9 ft.	10 ft.
4	752	846	940
5	1175	1321	1468
6	1692	1903	2115
7	2303	2590	2878
8	3008	3384	3760
9	3807	4282	4758
10	4700	5287	5875
11	5687	6397	7108
12	6768	7614	8460

Gallons in Rectangular Tanks

Size of Tank in Feet	1 Ft. Deep	3 Ft. Deep	4 Ft. Deep	5 Ft. Deep
4 by 4	119	359	478	598
5 by 5	187	561	748	935
6 by 4	179	538	718	897
6 by 6	269	807	1077	1346
7 by 5	261	785	1047	1309
7 by 6	314	942	1256	1570
7 by 7	366	1099	1466	1832
8 by 4	239	718	957	1196
8 by 6	359	1077	1436	1795
8 by 8	478	1436	1915	2393
9 by 6	403	1211	1615	2019
9 by 8	538	1615	2154	2692
9 by 9	605	1817	2423	3029
10 by 5	374	1122	1496	1870
10 by 6	448	1346	1795	2244
10 by 8	598	1795	2393	2992
10 by 10	748	2244	2992	3740
11 by 6	493	1481	1974	2468
11 by 9	740	2221	2962	3702
11 by 11	905	2715	3620	4525
12 by 6	538	1615	2154	2692
12 by 8	718	2154	2872	3590
12 by 10	897	2692	3590	4488
12 by 12	1077	3231	4308	5385

---

* Special articles on the subjects indicated by an asterisk (*) will be found at the words so marked.

WELSH ONION = *Allium fistulosum.*

WELSH POPPY = *Meconopsis cambrica.*

WESTERN HEMLOCK = *Tsuga heterophylla* See HEMLOCK.

WESTERN JUNIPER = *Juniperus occidentalis.*

WESTERN RED CEDAR = *Juniperus scopulorum* and *Thuja plicata.*

WESTERN YELLOW PINE = *Pinus ponderosa.* See PINE.

WEST INDIAN CEDAR = *Cedrela odorata.*

WEST INDIAN GHERKIN = *Cucumis Anguria.*

WEST INDIAN KALE = *Xanthosoma atrovirens.*

WEST INDIAN LIME. See Acid Lime at LIME (the citrus fruit).

WEST INDIAN LOCUST = *Hymenaea Courbaril.*

WEST VIRGINIA. The state lies wholly in zones* 3 and 4, and chose as its state flower the great laurel (*Rhododendron maximum*).

SOILS. The U.S. Bureau of Soils has divided the United States into thirteen soil provinces or regions, three of which are found in West Virginia; viz. Limestone Valleys and Upland Province, Appalachian Mountains and Plateau Province, and the River Flood Plains Province. The Limestone Valleys and Upland Province soils are derived for the most part from limestone, are generally productive and are easily worked. They are found in the eastern panhandle, in the southern part of the state and in restricted areas in the northern panhandle. From the standpoint of a permanent agriculture these soils are the most important in the state. The commercial fruit industry is, for the most part, located on these soils. The Appalachian Mountains and Plateau Province soils are derived from sandstones and shales. They are not very productive, generally heavy in texture, so that they are difficult to cultivate and shallow in depth, particularly where eroded on the hillsides. Soils belonging to this series constitute the hilly, mountainous and high plateau areas of the state and are, therefore, the most important from the standpoint of total area. They are, however, of relatively little importance horticulturally, except in potato production. The soils belonging to the River Flood Plains Province series are alluvial in nature, and generally light in texture. Their productivity varies, depending on the series from which they have been derived. Although limited in area, from the standpoint of vegetable production they are the most important soils of the state.

GARDENING. West Virginia is essentially a rural state with approximately 68 per cent of the population being classified as rural farm or rural non-farm. Hence, vegetable and fruit gardens are grown by about 60 per cent of the families — a total of 300,000 gardens.

Most of the garden soils are somewhat acid and lacking in phosphorus and nitrogen, so liming and fertilization are essential for satisfactory production. The majority of gardens contain one or more kind of beans, tomatoes, sweet corn, potatoes, cabbage, onions, radishes, lettuce, peas, beets, carrots, peppers, and cucumbers. In addition, many gardeners add some of the following: a green such as chard, spinach, or kale, broccoli, sweet potatoes, eggplants, squash, melons, parsnips, cauliflower, rhubarb, and asparagus.

Grapes, strawberries, and black raspberries are often included in the garden, with red raspberries, blackberries, currants, and gooseberries being more rare. Also, a few trees of peaches, cherries, plums, apples, or pears for home use are often found.

Generally speaking, West Virginia is well adapted to growing ornamental plants of this latitude. The altitudes vary from 250 feet at Harpers Ferry to 4860 feet at Spruce Knob. This makes a marked difference in temperature and rainfall which has a profound effect upon the adaptability of the different types of plants. Among the native plants which are used extensively in landscape work are the flowering dogwood (*Cornus florida*), flame azalea (*Azalea calendulacea*), swamp honeysuckle (*Azalea viscosa*), pinxter (*Azalea nudiflora*), great laurel (*Rhododendron maximum*), rose-bay (*Rhododendron catawbiense*), redbud (*Cercis canadensis*), bittersweet (*Celastrus scandens*), and white fringe (*Chionanthus virginicus*).

WEST VIRGINIA

The zones of hardiness crossing West Virginia are those shown on the map located at ZONE, which should be consulted for details. The dates are the latest known killing frost in spring and the average earliest one in the fall. The figures below the dates show the length of the growing season based on this data. Rainfall figures (in inches) are for total annual rainfall in the regions so indicated.

* Special articles on the subjects indicated by an asterisk (*) will be found at the words so marked.

CLIMATE. Due to physical conditions — latitude and particularly altitude — the climate of West Virginia is markedly varied, although genial and healthful. Winters are mild at the low altitudes with occasional periods of prolonged hot weather during the summer. As the altitude increases, the winters increase in severity, approaching those of northern New York at altitudes of 3500 ft. and above. Summers are correspondingly cool and delightful.

The rainfall is ample and well distributed, with periods of severe drought uncommon except at the low altitudes along the Ohio River, and in the eastern panhandle near the foothills of the Alleghenies.

Total annual rainfall corresponds roughly to altitude. Thus, at Martinsburg (435 ft. elavation) the average annual rainfall is 37.59 inches, at Morgantown (1300 ft. elevation) 43.73 inches, while at Davis (3093 ft. elevation) it is 53.62 inches.

FROST DATA

City	Elevation	Latest-known killing frost in spring
Terra Alta	2559	June 8
Elkins	1947	May 26
Martinsburg	435	May 16
Point Pleasant	595	May 23
Charleston	600	May 12

City	Average date of earliest killing frost in fall	Earliest-known killing frost in fall
Terra Alta	Sept. 26	Sept. 7
Elkins	Oct. 12	Sept. 20
Martinsburg	Oct. 16	Sept. 23
Point Pleasant	Oct. 16	Sept. 23
Charleston	Oct. 23	Sept. 26

The address of the Agricultural Experiment Station, which has kindly supplied this information, is Morgantown, W.Va. The station is always ready to answer gardening questions.

Garden club activities include a club of the Garden Club of America, the home office of which is 598 Madison Avenue, New York 22, N.Y. There are also over 300 clubs affiliated with the Federated Garden Club of West Virginia.

WET FEET. That condition in potted plants caused by excessive watering and insufficient drainage. It is most evident in house plants which begin to turn yellow and drop their leaves. *See* POTTING.

WEYMOUTH PINE = *Pinus Strobus.* *See* PINE.

WHEAT. *See* TRITICUM.

WHEELBARROW. *See* No. 5 at TOOLS AND IMPLEMENTS.

WHIN. *See* FURZE.

WHIP. A young, unbranched shoot of a woody plant, especially the first year's growth from a graft or bud. *See also* MAIDEN.

WHISPERING BELLS = *Emmenanthe penduliflora.*

WHITE. As an adjective, *white* is applied to many things in the garden. Those that occur in the ENCYCLOPEDIA OF GARDENING and their proper equivalents are:

White alder (*see* CLETHRA); White alder family (*see* ERICACEAE); White ash = *Fraxinus americana* (*see* ASH); White azalea = *Azalea viscosa;* White baneberry = *Actaea alba;* White bay = *Magnolia virginiana;* Whitebeam = *Sorbus Aria* (*see* MOUNTAIN-ASH); White bedstraw = *Galium Mollugo;* White beech = *Fagus grandifolia* (*see* BEECH); White birch. In America, *Betula papyrifera;* in Europe, *Betula pendula* (*see* BIRCH); White campion = *Lychnis alba;* White cedar = *Thuja occidentalis;* White cedar (*see* TABEBUIA PALLIDA); White cedar = *Libocedrus decurrens* (*see* INCENSE CEDAR); White cedar. In the West, *Chamaecyparis lawsoniana;* in the East, *C. thyoides.* It is also used for *Cupressus macnabiana;* White clover = *Trifolium repens* (*see* CLOVER); White cohosh = *Actaea alba;* White corallita (*see* PORANA PANICULATA); Whitecup = *Nierembergia rivularis;* White daisy = *Layia glandulosa;* White daisy = *Chrysanthemum Leucanthemum;* White Dutch clover = *Trifolium repens* (*see* CLOVER); White Dutch runner = *Phaseolus coccineus albus;* White eardrops = *Dicentra Cucullaria;* White elm = *Ulmus americana* (*see* ELM); White fir = *Abies concolor* (*see* FIR); White-flowered gourd = *Lagenaria siceraria;* White fringed orchis = *Habenaria Blephariglottis;* White garden (*see* first main entry below); White globe lily = *Calochortus albus;* White goldenrod = *Solidago bicolor* (*see* GOLDENROD); White gourd = *Benincasa hispida;* White hellebore = *Veratrum viride;* White holly = *Ilex opaca* (*see* HOLLY); White kerria = *Rhodotypos scandens;* White jasmine = *Jasminum officinale;* White linden = *Tilia tomentosa* (*see* LINDEN); White lotus = *Nymphaea Lotus;* White mariposa lily = *Calochortus venustus;* White melilot = *Melilotus alba;* White mulberry = *Morus alba* (*see* MULBERRY); White mustard = *Brassica hirta;* White oak = *Quercus alba* (*see* OAK); White osier = *Leucothoë racemosa;* White pine. In the East, *Pinus Strobus;* in the West, *P. flexilis* (*see* PINE); White popinac = *Leucaena glauca;* White poplar = *Populus alba;* White rose mallow = *Hibiscus oculiroseus;* White sage = *Audibertia polystachya;* White sapote = *Casimiroa edulis;* White snakeroot = *Eupatorium rugosum;* White Spanish broom (*see* *Cytisus multiflorus* at BROOM); White spruce = *Picea glauca* (*see* SPRUCE); White swamp azalea = *Azalea viscosa;* White tassel-flower = *Petalostemon candidum;* White trumpetlily = *Lilium longiflorum;* White trumpet narcissus = *Narcissus moschatus;* White upland

---

* Special articles on the subjects indicated by an asterisk (*) will be found at the words so marked.

aster = *Aster ptarmicoides;* White walnut = *Juglans cinerea* (*see* WALNUT); White water lily = *Nymphaea odorata;* White willow = *Salix alba* (*see* WILLOW); Whitewood = *Liriodendron Tulipifera* (*see* TULIP-TREE); White wood aster = *Aster divaricatus.*

WHITE GARDEN. A garden, or a section of it, planted wholly with white flowers, has far more distinction and variety than might be supposed. Few flowers are pure white throughout, nearly all being flushed or veined or otherwise marked with green, rose, mauve, or yellow. The effect of a white garden is tranquil and cool and is especially lovely at night. In planting such a garden or border, dark evergreens make the most effective background, and much gray foliage may be used. In the following lists only white-flowered forms of the plants named are intended, so the variety name *alba* has been omitted to save space.

SHRUBS OR SMALL TREES TO BE USED AS ACCENTS OR BACKGROUND

SPRING-FLOWERING: *Amelanchier canadensis,* 10 ft.; *Aronia arbutifolia,* 10 ft.; *Chamaedaphne calyculata,* 3 ft., evergreen; *Cornus florida,* 10–20 ft., *C. Kousa,* 10–15 ft.; *Crataegus Oxyacantha,* hawthorn, 10–20 ft.; *Cytissus albus* (*see* BROOM), 4–8 ft., *C. kewensis,* low-growing; *Deutzia gracilis,* 1½ ft., *D. lemoinei; Exochorda racemosa,* 10 ft.; *Halesia carolina,* 20 ft.; *Leucothoë catesbaei* (evergreen), 4 ft.; *Lonicera bella albida,* 10 ft., *L. fragrantissima,* 8 ft.; *Magnolia soulangeana alba superba,* 20 ft., *M. stellata,* 8–10 ft.; *Philadelphus* (mock-orange) many vars. tall and dwarf, single and double; *Pieris floribunda* and *P. japonica* (evergreen), 3–6 ft.; *Prunus glandulosa* (white flowering almond), 4–5 ft., *P. maritima* (beach plum), 2–5 ft., *P. tomentosa,* 5 ft.; Japanese cherries, 20–30 ft.; *Malus sargenti,* 8 ft., *M. toringoides,* 25 ft.; *Rhododendron carolinianum,* 4–6 ft., many hybrid varieties; *Rhodotypos scandens,* 5–6 ft.; *Rubus deliciosus,* 3–6 ft.; *Spiraea arguta,* 6 ft., *S. prunifolia,* 5 ft., *S. thunbergi,* 3–5 ft., *S. vanhouttei,* 8 ft.; *Viburnum carlesi,* 3–5 ft., *V. Lantana,* 15 ft.

SUMMER- AND AUTUMN-FLOWERING: *Abelia chinensis,* 4 ft.; *Calluna vulgaris,* 15 in.; *Ceanothus americanus,* 2–5 ft.; *Chionanthus virginicus,* 15 ft.; *Clethra alnifolia,* 4–8 ft.; *Cornus nuttalli,* 8–10 ft.; *Deutzia scabra,* 8 ft.; *Hibiscus syriacus* Jeanne d'Arc (double), and Snowstorm (single), 12 ft.; *Hydrangea arborescens grandiflora,* 5 ft., *H. radiata,* 6 ft.; *Itea virginica,* 4 ft.; *Kalmia latifolia* (evergreen), 4–8 ft.; *Lonicera ruprechtiana,* 12 ft.; *L. tatarica,* 10 ft.; *Azalea viscosa,* 4–6 ft.; *Rosa multiflora,* 10 ft., *R. rugosa* and varieties, 5 ft., *R. spinosissima,* 4–5 ft.; *Sambucus canadensis* (elder), 10 ft.; *Syringa* (lilac), many varieties; *Viburnum trilobum,* 12 ft.; *V. cassinoides,* 12 ft., *V. tomentosum,* 8 ft., *V. macrocephalum,* 7–12 ft.; *Weigela florida,* 7 ft.

TALL PLANTS FOR USE AT BACK OF BORDER

SUMMER-FLOWERING: *Althaea rosea* (hollyhock), double and single; *Aruncus sylvester; Macleaya cordata; Campanula lactiflora, C. pyramidalis; C. racemosa; Delphinium; Filipendula camtschatica; Thalictrum aquilegifolium, T. dipterocarpum.*

FALL-FLOWERING: Asters; *Boltonia asteroides; Chrysanthemum uliginosum; Phlox,* several varieties; *Veronicastrum virginicum.*

PLANTS OF MEDIUM HEIGHT

SPRING-FLOWERING: *Aquilegia vulgaris; Astilbe japonica; Dianthus barbatus* (Sweet William); *Hesperis matronalis; Linum perenne; Polemonium caeruleum.*

SUMMER-FLOWERING: *Achillea Ptarmica* Boule de Neige, and Perry's White; *Campanula alliariaefolia, C. latifolia, C. Medium* (Canterbury bells), *C. persicifolia; Centranthus ruber; Centaurea montana; Chrysanthemum maximum* varieties; *Chelone glabra; Clematis recta; Dictamnus albus; Filipendula hexapetala* (dropwort), *F. Ulmaria* (queen-of-the-meadow), *F. purpurea; Galega officinalis; Geranium pratense, G. sanguineum; Gypsophila paniculata,* double and single; *Iris* (bearded), many varieties; *Iris* (Japanese); *Iris sibirica* and varieties; *Lobelia siphilitica; Lupinus polyphyllus; Monarda fistulosa; Papaver orientale* Perry's White; *Paeonia,* double and single, many varieties; *Pentstemon Digitalis; Platycodon grandiflorum; Sidalcea candida; Stenanthium gramineum; Veronica longifolia, V. spicata; Yucca filamentosa.*

FALL-FLOWERING: *Anemone japonica; Aster; Chrysanthemum coreanum; Eupatorium rugosum; Hosta plantaginea.*

LOW-GROWING PLANTS FOR FOREGROUND

SPRING-FLOWERING: *Aquilegia flabellata nana; Arenaria montana; Arabis albida; Asperula odorata; Cerastium tomentosum; Convallaria majalis* (lily-of-the-valley); *Dianthus deltoides; Epimedium grandiflorum; Erinus alpinus; Gypsophila cerastioides; Iberis sempervirens; Iris,* dwarf varieties; *Myosotis; Phlox subulata; Sanguinaria canadensis; Silene alpestris; Armeria maritima* (thrift); *Tiarella cordifolia; Veronica latifolia dubia; Viola cornuta.*

SUMMER-FLOWERING: *Anemone sylvestris; Campanula carpatica; Delphinium grandiflorum; Erigeron coulteri; Galium boreale; Helianthemum; Heuchera* Perry's White; *Lychnis Viscaria; Nierembergia rivularis; Primula japonica; Scabiosa caucasica; Sedum album; Stokesia laevis; Thymus Serpyllum; Tunica Saxifraga.*

AUTUMN-FLOWERING: *Aster ericoides; A. ptarmicoides; Chrysanthemum arcticum; Helleborus niger.*

ANNUALS FOR SUMMER FLOWERING

Ageratum; Lobularia maritima; Antirrhinum, tall and dwarf; *Argemone mexicana;* Asters, tall and dwarf; *Bellis;* Candytuft; Sweet Sultan; Cornflower, double; *Clarkia; Cosmos,* early and late; Chinese Pinks; *Gode-*

tia; *Gypsophila elegans;* Heliotrope; *Lavatera trimestris splendens;* Larkspur; *Lobelia;* Mignonette; *Nicotiana alata grandiflora;* *Omphalodes linifolia;* Pansies; *Petunia,* double and single; *Phlox drummondi;* Poppies; Sweet Peas; Stocks; Verbenas; Zinnias.

SPRING AND SUMMER-FLOWERING BULBS

Allium neapolitanum; Camassia leichtlini; Chionodoxa luciliae; Colchicum autumnale, C. speciosum (autumn); *Crocus biflorus,* and hybrid crocuses (spring-flowering), *C. speciosus* (autumn-flowering); *Eremurus elwesi,* 10–12 ft.; *Erythronium californicum; Fritillaria meleagris; Galanthus* (snowdrop) species; Hyacinths, double and single; *Leucojum aestivum, L. vernum (see* SNOWFLAKE); *Lilium auratum* (summer), *L. browni* (early summer), *L. candidum, L. Martagon, L. speciosum* (late summer); *L. regale* (July); *Narcissus,* many varieties; *Ornithogalum umbellatum;* Tulips, many varieties; *Scilla hispanica, S. nutans, S. sibirica.*

SUMMER-FLOWERING BULBS AND ROOTS TO BE PLANTED IN SPRING

Dahlias, tall and dwarf; Gladioli; *Galtonia candicans;* tuberoses, double and single; *Zephyranthes; Caladium* for foliage effects.

CLIMBERS

Actinidia arguta; Clematis, Duchess of Edinburgh, *C. montana, C. paniculata, C. veitchiana; Calonyction aculeatum* (moonflower); *Lonicera japonica halliana; Lathyrus latifolius; Polygonum auberti;* Roses, many varieties; *Wistaria sinensis.* — L. B. W.

WHITLAVIA = *Phacelia Whitlavia.*

WHITLOW GRASS. *See* DRABA.

WHITSUN GILLYFLOWER. *See* HESPERIS MATRONALIS.

WHORL: WHORLED. Having three or more leaves, flowers, twigs, etc., all inserted at one point and in a circle. This arrangement, known as a whorl, is verticillate. *See* VERTICILLATA.

WHORLED MILKWEED = *Asclepias verticillata. See* MILKWEED.

WHORL-FLOWER = *Morina longifolia.*

WHORTLEBERRY. *See* VACCINIUM.

WICK WATERING. A method of growing potted plants without surface watering. It consists of inserting a fiberglass wick through the hole in the bottom of the flower pot until it is in firm contact with the soil. The other end of the wick is inserted through a hole in a container which holds the water, so as to reach it. Capillarity will bring up water from the container to the soil in the pot according as plant needs and evaporation demand it. By superimposing the hole in the flower pot over the hole in the container, the wick is completely hidden (as the flower pot stands directly on the water container). It saves much effort as the soil always has the correct amount of water in

it, except for succulents for which wick watering is not advised. Plants can be left for considerable periods without attention, so long as the water container is kept supplied. To do this it is best to have another hole in the top of the water container through which water can be poured to the proper level, *i.e.,* to keep the end of the wick submerged. It is a boon to weekenders who can leave house plants with their water needs provided for. To start operations it is best to soak the wick in water before inserting it into the soil.

WICOPY = *Dirca palustris* and *Lyonia mariana.*

WIDOW'S-CROSS = *Sedum pulchellum.*

WIDOW'S-TEAR. *See* SPIDERWORT.

WIEGELA. Incorrect spelling of *Weigela.*

WIER'S CUT-LEAVED MAPLE = *Acer saccharinum wieri. See* MAPLE.

WIGANDIA (wi-gan′di-a). Tropical American foliage plants of the family Hydrophyllaceae, comprising only six species, of which *W. caracasana* is planted for ornament outdoors in southern Calif. and similar climates. It is a bold plant, 7–10 ft. high or more, sometimes nearly tree-like. Leaves (for which it is grown) heart-shaped, nearly 18 in. long, covered with glistening and stinging hairs, coarsely and doubly toothed, long-stalked. Flowers small, tubular, blue or violet, but the tube white, scarcely over ½ in. long, and borne in terminal 1-sided clusters (cymes*). A very handsome foliage plant, especially the *var.* macrophylla, which has still larger leaves, and is fine for the sub-tropical garden. It can be raised from seed sown in winter in the greenhouse, or increased from root cuttings in spring. (Named for Johannes Wigand, a Prussian bishop who wrote on plants.)

WILCOXIA (will-kocks′i-a). Slender-stemmed cacti of Mex. and adjacent Tex., comprising 4 species, of which only *W. poselgeri,* the sacasil, is likely to be in cult. It is a branched cactus from a tuberous, dahlia-like black root, the stems scarcely ½ in. thick and 1–2 ft. long, faintly 8–10-ribbed, the very numerous flattened spines nearly hiding the stems. Each spine cluster consists of a single central, erect spine, and 9–12 widely divaricating lateral spines. Flowers about 2 in. long, purple or pink. For cult. *see* CACTI. (Named for Timothy E. Wilcox, American army officer.)

WILD. As an adjective, *wild* still clings to the name of many garden plants or things to do with the garden. Those occurring here and their proper equivalents are:

Wild balsam apple = *Echinocystis lobata;* **Wild bean** = *Apios americana;* **Wild bergamot** = *Monarda fistulosa;* **Wild black cherry** = *Prunus serotina;* **Wild bleeding-heart** = *Dicentra eximia;* **Wild buckwheat** = Black bindweed (*see* list at WEEDS); **Wild buckwheat** = *Eriogonum fasciculatum;* **Wild calla** = *Calla palustris;* **Wild camomile** (*see* MAT-

---

* Special articles on the subjects indicated by an asterisk (*) will be found at the words so marked.

RICARIA); **Wild carrot** (*see* CARROT); **Wild celery** = *Vallisneria spiralis* (*see* EEL-GRASS); **Wild clove** = *Pimenta acris;* **Wild coffee** (*see* PSYCHOTRIA); **Wild corn** = *Clintonia umbellulata;* **Wild cucumber** = *Echinocystis lobata;* **Wild date** = *Phoenix sylvestris;* **Wild flag** = *Iris versicolor;* **Wild garden** (*see* first main entry below); **Wild geranium** = *Geranium maculatum;* **Wild ginger** = *Asarum;* **Wild ginger family** = Aristolochiaceae; **Wild hoarhound** = *Eupatorium aromaticum;* **Wild hollyhock** = *Sidalcea malvaeflora;* **Wild hyacinth** = *Brodiaea lactea* and *Camassia scilloides;* **Wild hydrangea** = *Hydrangea arborescens;* **Wild indigo** (*see* BAPTISIA); **Wilding** (*see* second main entry below); **Wild ipecac** = *Apocynum androsaemifolium;* also *Triosteum perfoliatum;* **Wild lantana** (*see* ABRONIA); **Wild lilac** (*see* CEANOTHUS); **Wild lily-of-the-valley** = *Maianthemum canadense;* **Wildling** (*see* Wilding, at second main entry below); **Wild lupine** = *Lupinus perennis;* **Wild madder** = *Galium Mollugo;* **Wild marjoram** = *Origanum vulgare;* **Wild monkshood** = *Aconitum uncinatum* (*see* MONKSHOOD); **Wild mulberry** = *Morinda Royoc;* **Wild mustard** (*see* list at WEEDS); **Wild oat** = *Avena fatua;* **Wild oats** = *Uvularia sessilifolia;* **Wild oleander** = *Decodon verticillatus;* **Wild oleaster** = *Shepherdia argentea;* **Wild onion.** *See* the end of the list at WEEDS; **Wild orange** = *Laurocerasus caroliniana;* **Wild passion-flower** = *Passiflora incarnata;* **Wild pennyroyal** = *Mentha arvensis* (*see* MINT); **Wild pink** = *Arethusa bulbosa* and *Silene caroliniana;* **Wild plantain** = *Heliconia Bihai;* **Wild plum** = *Prunus americana;* **Wild pumpkin** = *Cucurbita foetidissima;* **Wild red cherry** = *Prunus pensylvanica;* **Wild rice** (*see* ZIZANIA); **Wild rosemary** = *Ledum palustre;* **Wild rye** (*see* ELYMUS); **Wild sage** = *Artemisia frigida;* **Wild sarsaparilla** = *Aralia nudicaulis;* **Wild senna** = *Cassia marilandica;* **Wild spikenard** = *Smilacina racemosa;* **Wild sunflower** = *Helianthus giganteus* (*see* SUNFLOWER); **Wild sweet pea** = *Tephrosia virginiana;* **Wild sweet potato** = *Ipomoea pandurata;* **Wild Sweet William** = *Phlox divaricata* and *P. maculata;* **Wild wormwood** = *Artemisia canadensis;* **Wild yam** = *Dioscorea villosa.*

WILD GARDEN. Broadly speaking, the term wild gardening signifies the use of native American plants as the dominant note in ornamental planting. In actual practice it is generally construed as applying to the creation of more or less naturalistic effects in which no plant of foreign origin is used, reliance being placed solely on species indigenous to N.A., although not necessarily to that part of the country where the garden in question is located. It is in this second and more specific sense that the term is here used.

Properly conceived and executed plantings of native material, besides being pleasing to the eye, are relatively novel and offer wide scope for the originality of the gardener.

A corner in a real wild garden

They are particularly appropriate to the American scene and American life, especially in country regions, and the less populous suburbs, where it frequently happens that they can be developed with little or no alteration of already existing land characteristics and contours.

Another advantage of this type of planting is its value from the conservation standpoint. Through extension of real estate development and the general opening up of land, the habitats of many species are being altered and the less resistant types of local flora eliminated. Despite efforts to control their depredations, plant vandals continue to destroy stands of the choicer flowers, with the result that over many large areas such formerly abundant species as the trailing arbutus, pink lady's-slipper and the eastern columbine have been completely exterminated. Intelligent wild-flower gardening suggests the possibilities of establishing private sanctuaries where such threatened plants can be perpetuated and may conceivably lead to their large-scale re-establishment in suitable regions.

Native plants of definite merit can be successfully chosen for practically any type of site — wet or dry, sunny or shaded, sloping or level. Among the conifers a wide selection is available, ranging from the low, trailing types of junipers to such forest trees as the Douglas fir, white pine, and the American and Carolina hemlocks. Worth-while deciduous trees are too numerous for even a partial listing in this discussion; a study of any unspoiled natural woodland will disclose many of them. The same can be said of the flowering woody material, although one cannot refrain from specific mention of such outstanding examples as our native rhododendrons, viburnums, flowering dogwood, *Magnolia virginiana,* various hawthorns, redbud, and the incomparable mountain laurel. In vines the choice is more limited,

---

but even so there are many possibilities among the grape, clematis, *Parthenocissus, Passiflora, Gelsemium,* and trumpet-creeper, which are indigenous to various regions.

Wild Flowers

As a rule, the really desirable native plants demand at least approximately the conditions of soil, moisture, and light to which they are accustomed in their natural habitats. It becomes necessary, therefore, to determine definitely what these conditions are in the site of the proposed planting and then either select plants which fit them or change the conditions to conform to the needs of desired plants which are not already met. Failure to provide the right surroundings will lead to disappointment and the loss of plants which would better have been left growing in their wild state.

Soils. Particular attention should be paid to the acidity or alkalinity of the soil, and its physical condition. Many desirable native plants have marked preference for a heavy, a sandy or a leaf-moldy soil and refuse to thrive unless these predilections are satisfied. Similarly, the degree of moisture, especially sub-soil moisture, is a prominent factor in numerous cases. Methods of providing for these various needs are obvious and need not be discussed here. *See* Acid and Alkali Soils.

When it comes to the actual securing of plants for a wild-flower garden, three general courses are open. The first and most obvious plan is to collect them directly from the wild, a perfectly permissible and satisfactory method, with easily transplanted species, of which a plentiful supply exists. Digging may be done in either spring or fall — the former for late summer- and autumn-bloomers, the latter for those which flower in spring and early summer.

Secondly, nursery-grown plants may be secured from reliable concerns which specialize in native material. As a rule these are superior in root development and top growth to those collected from field or woodland. This fact is of special importance in connection with trees and shrubs which, in a natural state, are often poorly rooted and leggy* as a result of the crowded conditions in which they have developed.

The third plan is to propagate the plants yourself from seed, top-growth cuttings, root division or whatever special method may fit the species in question. Comparatively little has been written on the propagation of native plants, so the field is a rich one for original investigation. Certain species are so constituted that they rarely succeed when transplanted from the wild, so that some form of propagation is essential if one is to get them established in the native planting. As a truly constructive conservation move, of course, experimentation along these lines may be invaluable.

In general, a sowing mixture of one-third good garden loam, one-third woods leaf mold and one-third rather coarse, clean sand should be used. Seeds of plants of the heath family may be sown in a mixture of one part sand and two parts Michigan peat. All sowing soils should be finely screened, very thoroughly mixed and firmed down evenly in the flats when somewhat damp. Well-drained wooden flats are the best containers; pots, pans, and other earthenware containers dry out too rapidly and are likely to crack and spill their contents under the influence of the hard winter freezing to which many seeds must be subjected. Some of the tree and shrub seeds, especially, lie dormant for two full years, so substantial containers are obviously necessary.

Use fresh seed — as fresh as possible. Nature has a reason for making seed fall as soon as it is fully ripe. Most seeds should be covered about twice their own depth. In the case of very small ones, broadcast rather than sow in drills, and barely cover them with a dusting of the sowing soil mixture, shaken on through a small-mesh kitchen sifter.

Watering must be carefully done, to avoid washing out some of the seeds and covering others too deeply. It is hard to find a watering can with a rose fine enough to forestall risks like this. A safe job can be done with a compressed-air sprayer of the flit-gun type for one or two flats, or the large plunger pump brand, with rubber hose and trigger nozzle, for more extensive operations. Either of these, used with reasonable care and allowing time for the mist-like spray to sink into the soil, will obviate the need for all the paraphernalia of watering from below. *See* Watering.

When the flats have been sown and watered and installed in the frame, a screen made of laths or laths and cheesecloth is laid over the sash to shade it, the sash itself being left on to protect the seeds from beating rains. The seed of most worth-while native plants takes its time about germinating — two, three, or four weeks, six months, a year or two. During this time the soil in which it lies must not be allowed to become bone-dry; sometimes weekly or semi-weekly watering will be necessary.

There is nothing mysterious or particularly tricky about handling most of the seedlings, once they are up — the procedure is similar to that for regular garden* flowers. In other words, they are pricked* off to other flats or to small individual pots when they have made their second pair of true leaves, kept protected from heavy rains, and in all respects given more than a fair chance to live long and prosper. The soil into which they are shifted must of course match that selected by their parents in the wild — sandy, acid, alkaline, clayey, well furnished with leaf mold, moist or dry, as the case may be. Here again arises the importance of knowing the requirements of the species and following them with reasonable fidelity. The one liberty which can be taken with safety

— with actual benefit — is to give the young plants an occasional dose of weak liquid manure. Most of them like it and will repay the attention with more rapid growth.

In the case of other methods of propagation, such as cuttings, the various forms of division, etc., the accepted nursery procedures should be followed as a basis. *See* PROPAGATION.

As has been intimated, the cultural conditions required by different choice native plants vary widely and are best learned by observation and the study of books. Certain ones may be set down here, however, because of their highly specialized character and the fact that specific data on them are scattered, inadequate, or unrecorded elsewhere.

WILD GARDEN PLANTS

Bearberry (*Arctostaphylos Uva-ursi*). Evergreen trailer, scarlet berries. Sandy, acid or nearly neutral soil, very well drained. Sun or part shade. Very hard to transplant from the wild, unless frozen clumps are used, but not difficult with pot-grown plants. Propagation by late-fall or winter cuttings under glass, or by seeds (very slow) exposed in winter.

Columbine (*Aquilegia canadensis*). Rather poor, dry soil (moisture and feeding promotes too rank growth), strongly acid to neutral. Full sun to ¾ shade. Propagation by seed.

Chimaphila umbellata and *C. maculata*. Very choice, low, half-woody evergreens, fragrant white to pinkish flowers. Shade, good drainage, highly acid, leaf-moldy soil. Practically impossible to transplant; must be pot-grown. Propagation by summer cuttings; difficult.

Bunchberry (*Cornus canadensis*). Dwarf, nearly herbaceous dogwood, only a few inches high. Rich woods soil, highly acid. Shade, good drainage, cool location. May be transplanted in large sods, but pot-grown plants are better.

Pink lady's-slipper (*Cypripedium acaule*). Well-drained woods soil, intensely acid. Full shade. Usually difficult to transplant from the wild, but possible if large amount of soil from the site is taken with it; best seasons after flowering or in early October. In planting, do not cover crown more than ½ in. Satisfactory propagation method unknown. If possible keep well mulched with pine needles. They provide acidity and prevent soil splashing on the leaves, which this plant resents.

Larger yellow lady's-slipper (*see* CYPRIPEDIUM CALCEOLUS). Woods soil, neutral to moderately acid, well drained. Half to full shade. Not difficult to transplant.

Fringed gentian (*Gentiana crinita*). Heavy, somewhat sandy muck soil, preferably neutral. Full sun to half shade, abundant subsoil moisture. Character of root system makes transplanting practically impossible. Propagation by strictly fresh seed broadcast in autumn on prepared soil in suitable location, lightly covered with clean sand and protected for the winter with single thickness of burlap laid on. Remove burlap about mid-April. As species is biennial, sow seed every year. Has been grown successfully in pots. *See G. crinita* at GENTIANA.

Hepatica americana. Acid woods soil, full shade, good drainage. Not difficult to transplant, but takes time to become fully reestablished. Propagation by division or seed.

Trailing arbutus (*Epigaea repens*). Very acid, sandy, leaf-moldy soil, excellent drainage. Full shade (will live in part sun, but foliage is injured and small and plants are stubby). Extremely difficult to transplant. Pot-grown plants move readily and should always be used. Propagation by cuttings or strictly fresh seed.

Mountain laurel (*Kalmia latifolia*). Acid soil containing plenty of humus, good drainage. Shade or sun. Shelter from heavy winds desirable. Nursery-grown plants preferable. Propagation by fall or early spring-sown seed.

Twinflower (*Linnaea borealis*). Very choice evergreen creeper with fragrant blossoms in pairs. Rich, acid, woods soil. Full shade. Propagation by cuttings.

Sand myrtle (*Leiophyllum buxifolium*). Fine evergreen flowering shrublet. Acid, rather sandy soil, half sun. Propagation by cuttings; difficult.

Partridge berry (*Mitchella repens*). Acid woods soil. Can be acclimated to either sun or shade. Transplanted easily.

Phyllodoce glanduliflora. One of the choice northwestern alpine heaths. Withstands eastern conditions if given some winter protection from sun and wind. Acid, gritty soil containing good supply of peat moss.

Gaywings (*Polygala paucifolia*). Very acid leaf-moldy soil, shade, moist or dry. Transplants readily in large sods. Propagation by root division.

Bloodroot (*Sanguinaria canadensis*). Well-drained soil, neutral to acid. Shade to ¾ sun. Transplants readily. Propagation by seed (slow) or root division.

Mountain cranberry (*Vaccinium Vitis-Idaea*). Excellent, low, evergreen ground cover, only a few inches high. Acid, gritty soil, sun to half shade. Propagation by seed or cuttings.

Viola pedata. There is a narrow-leaved and particularly showy form of the always lovely bird's-foot violet. Acid, sandy, well-drained soil, in full sun. Propagation by division.

For the exact definition of the terms acid, very acid, neutral, etc., as applied to soils for the wild garden *see* ACID AND ALKALI SOILS. — R. S. L.

WILDING AND WILDLING. These mean almost exactly the same thing. Both are applied to wild or uncultivated plants of natural origin. But *wildling* is also used for a culti-

---

* Special articles on the subjects indicated by an asterisk (*) will be found at the words so marked.

vated plant that has run wild, otherwise known as an escape (which see).

WILLOW. For the true willows *see* the next entry. Several other plants, however, have *willow* as part of their name. For those in this book *see* CHILOPSIS, DECODON, EPILOBIUM, ITEA, JUSSIAEA, LYTHRUM and the next few entries.

WILLOW. A huge group of quick-growing, often brittle-wooded shrubs and trees, comprising the genus **Salix** (say'licks) of the family Salicaceae. More than 300 species are known, chiefly from the cooler parts of the north temperate zone, but a few in the southern hemisphere, none in Aust. Besides the great number of very similar species there are innumerable natural and induced hybrids, so that exact naming of willows is difficult even for the experts. For this reason only a few of the best-known ones are here included, although others are known to be in cult. in America, where there are over 100 wild species of willow. They are closely related to the poplars, which, however, have mostly drooping catkins, while in willows the catkins are erect. *See* POPULUS.

Leaves alternate,* usually narrow, mostly lance-shaped and tapering both ends. Male and female flowers on separate plants, both in catkins* which bloom before or when the leaves expand. Petals and sepals none, the flowers thus naked, but each flower borne in the axil* of a bract,* the collection of which forms the catkin* (the female is the familiar pussy willow). Fruit a 2-valved capsule.* (*Salix* is the classical Latin name for a willow.)

While most willows grow best in moist places, most of them will do well in any ordinary garden soil and they are probably the easiest of all plants to propagate. Cuttings will root almost anywhere, but best, of course, in moist sand. There are a few dryland species and among the cult. sorts the best of these is *Salix tristis*. While the best-known of the weeping willows is S. *babylonica*, other weeping sorts are S. *blanda* and S. *elegantissima*. Some, like the osier willow, are cult. for basket making, and a few species are useful for the drug salicin, one of the ingredients of aspirin.

S. alba. White willow. A tree 30–60 ft. high. Leaves 3–4 in. long, finely toothed, the under side silky-hairy. Eurasia and northern Af., often an escape * in N.A. Hardy everywhere. There are several varieties, differing mostly in the shape of the leaves and the amount of hairiness of them. Among them is *var.* **vitellina,** which as here treated = S. *vitellina*.

S. amygdaloides. Peach-leaved willow. A tree 30–50 ft. high, the branches upward-pointing, the twigs reddish-orange. Leaves lance-shaped, 4–6 in. long, sharp pointed, finely toothed, pale beneath. Female catkins 2–5 in. long. N.A. Hardy everywhere.

S. babylonica. Weeping willow. A tree up to 40 ft. high, the branches long and pendulous, yellowish-brown when young. Leaves 5–6 in. long, finely toothed, grayish-green beneath. China. Hardy from zone* 3 southward. Often confused with S. *elegantissima*.

S. blanda. Wisconsin weeping willow. A hybrid between the ordinary weeping willow (*S. babylonica*) and a Eurasian species. It is a round-headed tree with long, pendulous branches, the young twigs dull green or brown. Leaves 3½–6 in. long, finely toothed, bluish-green beneath. Hardy from zone* 3 southward.

S. Caprea. Goat willow; also called sallow. Not over 25 ft. high, usually much less and a shrub. Leaves oblongish, or broader, 3–4 in. long, faintly toothed. Catkins bright yellow, conspicuous. Eurasia and northern Persia. Hardy from zone* 3 southward. There is a variegated-leaved form, and another with pendulous branches.

S. discolor. Common pussy willow. A shrub or small tree 10–18 ft. high. Leaves elliptic or oblongish, 3–4 in. long, finely wavy-toothed or without teeth, bluish-green beneath. The female catkins are the familiar pussy willow which can be easily forced by bringing them into a warm room after Jan. 15. Eastern N.A. Hardy everywhere.

S. Elaeagnos. Rosemary willow. A shrub or small tree, not over 30–40 ft., usually less and box-like when trimmed, the twigs gray-hairy when young. Leaves narrowly lance-shaped, pointed, 2–6 in. long, finely toothed, densely white-hairy when young, turning yellow in the autumn. Eurasia. Hardy from zone* 3 southward. Also known as S. *incana* and S. *rosmarinifolia*.

S. elegantissima. Thurlow's weeping willow. A medium-sized tree with long, pendulous branches, the twigs brown. Leaves narrow, 4–6 in. long, sharply toothed, bluish-green beneath. Probably a hybrid. Hardy from zone* 3 southward.

S. gracilistyla. A shrub 4–6 ft. high, the twigs grayish-hairy. Leaves narrow, 2–4 in. long, about one quarter as wide, faintly toothed, bluish-green and softly hairy beneath. Male catkins showy, the anthers* orange. Jap. and Korea. Mar.–Apr. Hardy from zone* 4 southward.

S. Matsudana. A tree not usually over 40 ft. as cult., often less, with olive-green twigs. Leaves narrowly lance-shaped, 2–4 in. long, sharply toothed with glandular* teeth. Most commonly cult. in the *var.* **tortuosa,** the corkscrew willow, with spirally twisted and contorted twigs and leaves. Eastern As. Hardy from zone* 3 southward.

S. nigra. Black willow. A tree up to 35 ft. high, the bark very dark purple, almost black, the branches erect, the twigs yellowish. Leaves narrow, 3–5 in. long, finely toothed, pale beneath. Nearly throughout N.A. Hardy from zone* 2 southward. An extremely effective combination with the nearly black bark of this tree are the white flowers of some of the Japanese flowering cherries or of white crabapples.

S. "niobe." A trade name of a weeping willow, probably a hybrid, and related to S. *blanda*.

S. pentandra. Laurel or bay willow. A tree 40–60 ft. high, the leaves elliptic, shining green, 3–5 in. long and finely toothed. Catkins showy, golden-yellow. Southeastern Eu., sometimes an escape in the eastern U.S. Hardy from zone* 2 southward.

S. purpurea. Purple osier. A shrub 5–8 ft. high, the twigs purplish when young, gray later. Leaves lance-shaped or broader, 2–4 in. long, toothed toward the tip, pale beneath. Mostly cult. in a dwarf form known in the trade (but by no one else) as *var.* **nana.**

---

* Special articles on the subjects indicated by an asterisk (*) will be found at the words so marked.

Eurasia and N. Af. Hardy from zone* 3 southward.

S. rosmarinifolia. A badly mixed-up name for the rosemary willow, properly defined as *S. Elaeagnos.*

S. sepulcralis. A hybrid tree, resembling the weeping willow (*S. babylonica*) in its weeping habit and *S. alba* in its silvery foliage. It is more hardy than the weeping willow. Called by some *S. salamoni.*

S. tristis. A shrub scarcely 2 ft. high, the leaves 1½–2 in. long, without marginal teeth, densely white-felty beneath. In dry, sandy places, eastern U.S. Hardy from zone* 2 southward. *See* SAND GARDEN.

S. Uva-ursi. Bearberry willow. A prostrate shrub, the branches less than 20 in. long. Leaves elliptic, ¼–1 in. long, shining green above, pale beneath and veiny. Arctic and alpine N.A. Can only be grown from zone* 2 or 3 northward.

S. viminalis. Common osier or osier willow. The young twigs densely hairy. Leaves very narrow, 7–10 in. long, practically without teeth. Eurasia, but naturalized in the eastern U.S. Much cult. for basket making, especially the *var. gmelini,* a Siberian form.

S. vitellina. Golden osier. Considered by many to be only a variety of *S. alba,* but its bright yellow twigs make it sufficiently distinct for garden purposes. Its winter and early spring color, due to these showy twigs, is very handsome. Eurasia. Hardy everywhere, and much grown for ornament.

INSECT PESTS. Leaf beetles may cause great damage to foliage. Control with pesticide #1 or #17 (*see* SPRAYS AND DUSTS).

DISEASES. Scab* or blight* cause severe defoliation of willow in some parts of the country. The tree is not usually considered valuable enough to warrant it, but three applications of pesticide #5 (*see* SPRAYS AND DUSTS) will do a good job of control. Apply when new leaves appear and repeat at 10-day intervals.

The bacterial disease crown gall * often causes large swellings on branches or trunk of willow. It may kill small trees, but on large trees it does not appear to cause serious damage. In fact, we feel that it is rather picturesque on large, old willows!

WILLOW CACTUS. *See* RHIPSALIS.

WILLOW-HERB. *See* EPILOBIUM.

WILLOW-LEAVED JASMINE = *Cestrum parqui.*

WILLOW MYRTLE = *Agonis.*

WILLOW OAK = *Quercus Phellos. See* OAK.

WILLOW-WORT = *Lysimachia vulgaris.*

WILT. A plant disease which is caused by various fungi, bacteria, and occasionally a virus. As the name implies, the plants wilt and may die. Most wilt diseases are specific to one group of plants. The fungi and bacteria which cause wilt diseases can live in the soil for several years. For this reason, the gardener should rotate his plantings. For example, if tomato dies from wilt disease, plant some other crop in that area for several years prior to planting tomato again, or use resistant varieties of tomato.

One of the rather common wilt diseases, known as Verticillium wilt, may attack a number of different types of plants, including chrysanthemum, dahlia, eggplant, strawberry, maple, linden, and others. — S. H. D.

WILTING. The flagging of leaves or flowers due to improper moisture conditions, too great heat, or too much wind. Wilting is actually a lack of turgidity in the cells of the plant, which instead of being distended with water become partly dried out, causing leaves or petals to become flaccid.

Reviving wilted plants is often easy if wilting has not gone too far. In the case of potted plants it is usually sufficient to set them in a moist atmosphere for a few hours. If you have no greenhouse, the proper atmosphere can be arranged by standing the pot in a glass-covered carton at the bottom of which is a pail of water. Put a brick in the pan and stand the pot on the brick, as the soil in the pot, while needing moisture, must not get soggy.

Vegetable or flower seedlings set out in the open ground are harder to revive, because one cannot control the atmosphere. See that the flagged plants have plenty of water, and if the plantation is not too extensive cover it for a day or two with lath shades. *See* SHADING. Or they may be covered with cheesecloth or newspaper. The object in all cases is to try to prevent too rapid transpiration* which is the real cause of all wilting. Merely drowning the soil will not answer, because plants, except aquatics, cannot absorb "free water." They can only use the capillary water around each soil particle, and excess water, because it fills up space which should be filled with air, is worse than useless. Instead of reviving wilted plants this excess water is itself the cause of wilting.

Wilted flowers can often be revived by submerging their stems, and making a fresh cut, under water, never allowing the freshly cut stem to come out of the water until the flowers have revived. Some flowers, especially dahlias, poppies, and heliotrope may be revived by making a fresh cut and dipping the end of the flower stalk for a few seconds in hot water (150°–170°). *See also* CUT FLOWERS.

WIND. Even more than too much heat, wind is an unfavorable factor in any garden, and most garden operations should never be attempted in a high wind. Some of the things that should never be done in a high wind are:

Seeding a Lawn	Planting Trees or
Cutting Flowers	Shrubs
Planting Seedlings	Moving Evergreens
Spreading Lime or	or Broad-leaved
Fertilizer	Evergreens

Some of these things can be done in a wind, if you don't mind a thorough dusting from lime or fertilizer, or are resigned to losing much of your grass seed. But planting operations of any sort are far better postponed to a quiet or cloudy day. Wind

---

* Special articles on the subjects indicated by an asterisk (*) will be found at the words so marked.

greatly increases the rate of transpiration, and the shock of transplanting.

Another feature of wind to observe closely, particularly in the prairie states and along the seacoast, is the prevailing direction of the summer and winter winds. If either is violent some protection against them must be provided before a good garden is possible. *See* WINDBREAK. Also, in towns or cities it is equally desirable to watch the prevailing wind direction, in order to avoid if possible the steady fumes of factory smoke. *See* SMOKE.

It is also necessary to exclude as much wind as possible from the wild garden. Plants of the cool, moist forest floor do not tolerate winds, and the wild garden should be screened by planting, even more than most garden sites. *See* WILD GARDEN.

WINDBREAK. In regions of high winds, such as prairies or along the seashore, it is necessary to plant wind-resistant trees to form a screen behind which the better kinds of gardening are possible. Such shelter trees, or in more extensive plantings what are called protection woods, must be spaced so thickly that even in their early years they form some protection against wind. By crowding they also protect each other.

For a small garden one of the best windbreaks is a high, thick hedge, preferably of the California privet. For the details of planting and care *see* HEDGES.

Where higher protection is needed a dense growth of the following trees is by far the best, but they are better adapted to regions from zone* 5 northward than south of this. All are extremely wind-resistant and grow fairly rapidly:

Russian Mulberry	Box-elder (a maple)
Osage Orange	Silver Maple
London Plane	Cottonwood
Pea tree	White Poplar

In regions of more heat, from zones* 6 and 7 southward, very effective shelter belts can be made with *Tamarix aphylla,* or *Cupressus arizonica,* and in Calif. the Monterey cypress is often so used. Also in Calif. various eucalyptus trees will make a good screen against wind. Some fruit crops, especially lemons, demand such protection from wind. In Fla. good wind-resistant trees will be found in the genus *Casuarina,* and a useful shrub for that purpose is *Tephrosia candida.*

Some Californian gardeners, for low (5–6 ft.) windbreaks, use the showy *Lavatera assurgentiflora,* but the plant is not hardy in cold regions.

In regions of very heavy snowfall a windbreak will act as a snow trap, just as the snow guards do along the highway or railroad. If protection from snow is desired the windbreak must be located at right angles to the prevailing direction of the winter winds. Otherwise windbreaks are more often used as a protection for late spring or hot summer winds which, because of normal growth of leaves, are often more destructive than winter winds.

WIND BURN. A withered, apparently blasted condition of foliage, due to violent winds. It is often seen along the seashore or on prairies, and leaves so affected do not usually recover. Wind-burned privet, looking as though fired in Aug., will, however, leaf out the following season with little or no permanent damage to the hedge. The term is also applied, not very accurately, to the bronzed condition of some evergreens in winter, from which they usually recover.

WINDFLOWER = *Anemone.*

WINDMILL PALM = *Trachycarpus fortunei.*

WINDOW BOXES. The common attitude of considering window boxes as merely a poor substitute for a garden is as unfortunate as it is unfair. Actually we are dealing here with a rather distinct type of plant culture because the conditions for the growth of plants in a box are quite different from those in the open ground. In consequence, the treatment of the plants must be different also, and, as soon as this fact is understood, a wide range of new gardening possibilities and pleasures is discovered. The intelligent window-box gardener has no reason to feel apologetic toward a garden owner, because

A simple window box of annuals

he is doing something quite different, and he is able to achieve effects of intimate detail which are not possible in an open garden bed.

For success it is, of course, first of all necessary to understand the principles which are involved. These are the following:

1. *The dimensions of the box.* Confinement and limited space are the main characteristics of a box as far as plants are concerned. This seems to be a disadvantage but becomes an advantage when one takes into account that confinement of the roots

---

* Special articles on the subjects indicated by an asterisk (*) will be found at the words so marked.

causes many annuals to produce a super-abundance of flowers, provided that they receive proper care. The question then arises, To what minimum can this confinement be carried without defeating the purpose by not allowing sufficient room for the development of the plants? Careful tests have established that a box depth of 8 inches is excellent. With a 1-inch drainage layer at the bottom, which is important, it still leaves 7 inches of soil, which is perfectly satisfactory for the growth of one season. More is not necessary and less is insufficient.

A formal window box for a city house or apartment, with evergreens, ivy, etc.

A width of 8 inches is equally good because it allows room for 2 or 3 rows of plants and permits an attractive arrangement without making the box too large. A narrower box is much less satisfactory.

The length of the box is frequently dictated by circumstances, such as the width of the window. However, even if a long space is available, for instance on a balcony or porch railing, it is still not advisable to make the box more than 3 or 4 ft. long. Otherwise it becomes very heavy and awkward to handle, which is necessary whenever the box has to be cleaned and repainted. A row of several 3- or 4-ft.-long boxes has the additional advantage over one very long one that alternating boxes may be planted differently in a rhythmic arrangement or the central 3 or 4 boxes may be treated differently from those on both ends.

The generally most satisfactory dimensions therefore are: 8 in. deep, 8 in. wide, and 3 to 4 ft. long. Smaller boxes are definitely unsatisfactory, not only for the above-mentioned reasons but also because they dry out too fast and are likely to overheat in the sun. Overheating kills or inhibits the soil bacteria, which causes nutritional difficulties for the plants.

2. *Construction of the box.* Metal boxes, because of overheating, never give as good results as wooden ones, especially not in full exposure to the sun. One-inch-thick boards

of pine or cedar wood are most satisfactory, being sufficiently rigid as well as providing much-needed insulation. Thinner boards are likely to warp badly. The boards should be fastened together with brass screws. Iron screws rust, while nails pull out when the boards warp. The bottom board must be provided with 2 rows of drainage holes, about 5 inches apart and each ½ to ¾ inch in diameter.

3. *Painting of the box.* To preserve the wood, the finished box should be painted inside and out with a quick-drying paint. Inside, only one coat of paint is required, and, when this is dry, it should be wiped with a wet cloth to remove any remaining water-soluble and possibly poisonous paint residues. The outside of the box will need 2 or 3 coats of paint for good appearance. The most generally satisfactory color for a window box is cream or yellowish ivory (not white), because it looks pleasing with any combination of flower colors, setting them off to best advantage. Green, which is most frequently chosen, easily clashes with the green tints of the plant leaves.

4. *Soil.* Potting mixture* 3 is suitable for filling the window box, and leaf mold may be replaced by the more readily available peat moss. Dried sheep manure, at the rate of one 5-inch flowerpotful per bushel of soil, replaces cow manure. The soil must be thoroughly mixed as well as moderately moistened before it is put into the box.

5. *Drainage.* Most suitable for the 1-inch drainage layer at the bottom of the box are either leached hard-coal cinders or broken-up brick, because both are porous and will hold some water in reserve. Both should be reduced with a hammer to about bean-size pieces. Ashes and dust must be sifted out. When neither cinders nor brick are available, coarse gravel may be used, but, since this is not porous, it should be covered with a ½-inch layer of sphagnum moss (not peat moss).

6. *Arranging the plants.* The plants may be set out either in alternating rows or in groups of 3 to 5, depending upon the desired effect. Alternating rows should be 3 to 4 inches apart and a distance of 6 to 8 inches between the plants in the row is satisfactory. Eight to 10 inches must be considered as the height limit for a good window-box plant, and in an arrangement the highest plants should be placed either in the back or in the center or on both sides. Hanging plants which more or less cover the box should be planted in front.

7. *Color combinations.* When working out color combinations, one should remember that clear white and clear yellow as well as rose-pink and clear yellow are bad neighbors which must not be put together. Always effective are simple combinations such as white and rose-red, yellow and blue, white and blue, or orange and purple. Very brilliant together are mauve, scarlet, and golden yellow.

---

* Special articles on the subjects indicated by an asterisk (*) will be found at the words so marked.

8. *Choice of plants.* A vast variety of plants, suitable for growing in window boxes, are at our disposal and the ubiquitous petunias are by no means the only ones. A few effective sample combinations may be suggested here, but the imaginative and ambitious window-box gardener will readily be able to work out others:

A. For full sun
    I. Scarlet Sage (a dwarf, early-flowering variety), scarlet
        Dwarf Snapdragon "Baby Orange," orange
        Lobelia "Sapphire," blue
    II. *Phlox drummondi* "Globe mixed"
        Moneywort (*Lysimachia Nummularia*)
    III. Geranium, double white
        Balcony Petunia, dark blue
B. For northern exposure
    I. Coleus, red-leaved
        Potato vine (*Solanum jasminoides*)
    II. Tuberous begonias, salmon and yellow
        Hanging tuberous begonias, scarlet
        Periwinkle (*Vinca minor*), blue
    III. Coleus, yellow-leaved
        Begonia semperflorens, scarlet, red-leaved
        Basket grass (*Oplismenus*)

9. *Care of the window box.* Proper watering when needed — which must be so thorough that the water runs out of the bottom — is particularly important. The best time for watering is in the evening after sundown. Four to 5 weeks after planting, one should start feeding the box once weekly with a complete fertilizer dissolved at the rate of 1 teaspoonful in a gallon of water (not stronger). Without such feeding the plants will quickly decline in health and cease flowering. Young seed pods must be removed together with the faded flowers.

10. *Spring-flowering bulbs.* A 4-ft.-long window box may be equipped with 2 tin inserts of approximately the same depth and width as the window box and each 2 ft. long. The bulbs are planted in these inserts in fall and are buried outside in the ground. In early spring, the inserts are dug out and are placed in the window box where the bulbs flower. When the flowers fade, the inserts are moved back into the garden where the bulbs go to rest. Toward the end of August the inserts are emptied, the bulbs are replanted in fresh soil, and the same routine — which can be continued for many years — commences once more.

11. *Roses and chrysanthemums.* The same type of tin inserts can be used also to grow long-flowering floribunda roses or late summer-flowering cushion chrysanthemums in window boxes. Since this procedure permits one to winter the plants in the garden with proper covering, the same plants will serve for many years.

In the northern parts of the country, neither spring-flowering bulbs nor roses or chrysanthemums will live over winter in the window box itself.

12. *The dripproof window box.* A self-watering window box which can be left alone for 4 or 5 days, and which does not drip, has been designed also and is very satisfactory. This consists of two compartments, the upper one, containing the plants, filled with vermiculite instead of soil. The lower compartment contains a tin tray, holding a fertilizer solution which moves into the upper compartment through capillarity by means of glasswool wicks. The owner of such a box can go away over the weekend without having to worry about his plants, and the controlled nutrition which this procedure provides results in exceptionally healthy growth and abundant flowering. — H. T.

For a much more extensive list of plants suited to window-box culture, too long to include here, the enthusiast should consult *Window Box Gardening,* by Henry Teuscher (N.Y., 1956).

WIND-POLLINATED. Having the pollen carried by wind instead of insects, which is the usual procedure. Plants, such as the pines, grasses, birches, and many others, are wind-pollinated, and are hence often said to be anemophilous.

WIND POPPY = *Meconopsis heterophylla.*

WINEBERRY = *Rubus phoenicolasius.* See also ARISTOTELIA.

WINE PALM. Several palms with a sweet juice are used to make wine, especially in India and the East Indies. Among cult. palms so used and usually called wine palm are *Caryota urens* and *Jubaea spectabilis* (see both genera).

WINE PLANT. The common garden rhubarb (which see).

WING. A membranous or leaf-like appendage found on many fruits as in the stone cress, ash, maple, *Ptela trifoliata,* etc. Wings are often found on leafstalks, as in most citrus fruits. There are also corky-winged twigs, as in the sweet gum and in *Euonymus alatus.*

WINGED ACACIA = *Acacia alata.*

WINGED EVERLASTING = *Ammobium alatum.*

WINGED PEA = *Lotus Tetragonolobus.*

WINGED PETIOLE. A winged leafstalk. See PETIOLE.

WINGED SPINDLE-TREE = *Euonymus alatus.*

WING-NUT = *Pterocarya.*

WINTER. As part of the name of many plants, and not a few garden activities, *winter* is very common. Those that occur here and their proper equivalents are:

Winter aconite = *Eranthis hyemalis;* **Winter annual** (*see* first main entry below); **Winterberry** = *Ilex glabra* and *I. verticillata* (*see* HOLLY); **Winter-bloom** (*see* HAMAMELIS); **Winter bouquet** (*see* DRIED FLOWERS); **Win-**

---

* Special articles on the subjects indicated by an asterisk (*) will be found at the words so marked.

terbud (*see* Buds); Winter cauliflower = *Brassica oleracea botrytis* (for culture *see* Cauliflower); Winter cherry = *Physalis Alkekengi*; Winter cress (*see* Barbarea); Winter crookneck squash = *Cucurbita moschata* (for culture *see* Squash); Winter daffodil = *Sternbergia lutea*; Winter fern (*see* Poison Hemlock); Winter garden (*see* second main entry below); Winter grape = *Vitis cordifolia*; Wintergreen (*see* Wintergreen below); Winter hazel (*see* Corylopsis); Winter heath = *Erica carnea*; Winter heliotrope = *Petasites fragrans*; Wintering (*see* Protecting Plants); Winter jasmine = *Jasminum nudiflorum*; Winter-kill (*see* Winter-kill below); Winter melon (*see* Melon); Winter pink = *Epigaea repens* (*see* Trailing Arbutus); Winter protection (*see* Protecting Plants); Winter purslane = *Montia perfoliata*; Winter radish = *Raphanus sativus longipinnatus* (*see* Radish); Winter rose = *Helleborus niger*; Winter savory = *Satureia montana* (*see* Savory); Winter squash = *Cucurbita maxima* (for cult. *see* Squash); Winter sunscald (*see* Sunscald); Winter-sweet = *Origanum vulgare*; Winter sweet pea (*see* Swainsona galegiflora); Winter vetch = *Vicia villosa*; Winter work (*see* Garden Calendar).

WINTER ANNUAL. An annual plant, sown late in the summer or early fall, which lies dormant over the winter and completes its growth the following season. Such annuals may be protected with a light mulch of straw or leaves, in severe climates, and really approach biennials in their method of handling. Unfortunately many weeds are winter annuals, and in the late fall and early spring are hard to control because the ground is usually too wet for cult.

WINTER GARDEN. It is not usual in northern latitudes to plan for flowers in the open air in winter, yet it is possible to contrive a winter garden even in cold climates that will give shelter from cold winds and refreshment to the eye, and even produce a few flowers during the so-called flowerless months. Evergreens, both broad and narrow-leaved, will play an important part in its furnishing, as will shrubs that have colored bark, and such as carry their berries late.

The choice of a situation must be carefully made. It is imperative that it be open to the south and cut off by some means from the prevailing winter winds. A south-facing wall provides a comfortable back, or the angle of house walls may be utilized for two sides, and if there is a chimney in the wall greater warmth will be furnished. The remaining sides may be made of some close-knit evergreens, such as hemlock or spruce, planted close together and kept clipped so that they will grow the thicker.

If no wall is available an enclosure of evergreens may be made in any part of the grounds and left open to the south so the full force of the sun may enter. It is wise not to make this enclosure too large but to keep it small enough to seem a snug refuge, not only for the plants, but for individuals who enjoy sitting out of doors in the winter sunshine.

If only a very small winter garden is desired one may easily be built into the rock garden, for it is a simple matter to arrange sheltered hollows and heat-retaining surfaces among the rocks.

In connection with the winter garden it must be remembered that while it is warmer in winter than the rest of the garden it is also warmer and probably drier in summer. Plants growing there must be watered during dry periods and the soil kept stirred to form a mulch. Bulbs and herbaceous plants may be scattered about at the base.

Flowering dates given in the following lists are for the neighborhood of New York. Plants marked † are tender in that locality, but may be grown southward.

Flowering Shrubs and Trees

Mahonia japonica, 6 ft., and a broad-leaved evergreen. Yellow flowers. March.

Mahonia bealei, much like the foregoing, but flowers smell of lily-of-the-valley.

†*Chimonanthus praecox*, yellow, blossoms in winter.

Cornus Mas, tree, 15–20 ft., yellow blossoms in February and March.

Corylopsis spicata, yellow cowslip-scented flowers in February–March.

Chaenomeles japonica (flowering quince), scarlet flowers in March–April.

Daphne Mezereum, 3–4 ft., white or pink flowers, fragrant, March–April.

†*Daphne odora*, evergreen, white fragrant flowers in March–April.

Epigaea repens, creeper, pink, March–April.

†*Erica carnea*, 6–8 in., white or rose flowers throughout winter (with protection).

Hamamelis japonica, H. mollis, and *H. vernalis* (witch-hazels), slender shrubs or small trees, with yellow flowers.

Jasminum nudiflorum (winter jasmine), slender and sprawling; yellow flowers in February and March.

Lonicera fragrantissima and *L. standishi*, creamy flowers in March–April.

Magnolia stellata, March.

Pieris floribunda and *P. japonica*, evergreens, creamy flowers in March.

Salix discolor (pussy willow), catkins in February–March.

Herbaceous Plants

Adonis amurensis, 18 in., yellow, March.

Arabis albida (wall cress), trailing, white, March.

Helleborus niger (Christmas rose), white, October onwards.

Petasites fragrans (winter heliotrope), creeper, yellow blossoms, March.

Primula denticulata, purple or white, March; *P. vulgaris* (common primrose).

Pulmonaria angustifolia (lungwort), 10 in., blue, March; *P. saccharata*, pink flowers, spotted leaves.

Anemone vernalis, lavender, March.

Synthyris rotundifolia, 4 in., blue, March.

---

* Special articles on the subjects indicated by an asterisk (*) will be found at the words so marked.

Bergenia lingulata, white or rose-purple, March.

Bulbs

Anemone blanda, blue, pink or white, late March.

Bulbocodium vernum, pinkish, February, March.

Chionodoxa luciliae, C. sardensis, blue, 3 in., March.

Crocus longiflorus; C. pulchellus, flowering in late autumn; *C. biflorus; C. imperati; C. susianus; C. tomassinianus; C. verna,* flowering in February, March, April.

Eranthis hyemalis (winter aconite), yellow, 3 in., February, March.

Galanthus (snowdrop); *G. byzantinus; G. elwesi; G. nivalis,* double and single, Dec., Jan., Feb., Mar.

Hyacinthus ciliatus, pale blue, 3–4 in., March.

Leucojum vernum, white, March, 8 in.

Narcissus cyclamineus, 3 in., March; *N. minor,* 4 in., March.

Scilla sibirica, blue, 3–4 in., March. Shade.

Sisyrinchium douglasi, 10 in., rose, March.

Tulipa kaufmanniana, 8 in., rose and cream, March. — L. B. W.

WINTERGREEN = *Gaultheria procumbens* and *Chimaphila umbellata.* For flowering wintergreen *see* POLYGALA PAUCIFOLIA.

WINTERGREEN BARBERRY = *Berberis julianae.*

WINTER-KILL. The killing of twigs unfit to survive the winter, usually because the wood was not sufficiently ripened to withstand severe weather. Unless very badly winter-killed, most old wood of shrubs and trees will put out new shoots the following year, when the winter-killed twigs should be pruned. The real cause of winter-killing is lack of hardiness (which see). For ways of guarding against winter-killing *see* PROTECTING PLANTS.

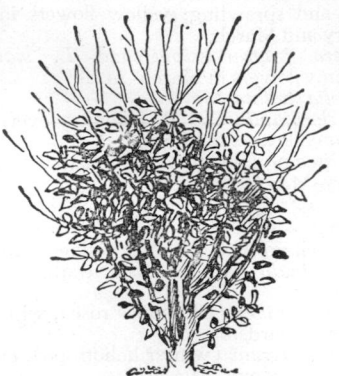

A typically winter-killed shrub as it appears in May before the dead wood has been removed.

WINTER'S-BARK = *Drimys winteri.*

WINTERTHUR. *See* No. 14 at GARDEN TOURS.

WIRE GRASS = *Poa compressa* and *Eleusine indica.* Perhaps the worst wire grass is the pestiferous Bermuda grass. *See* CYNODON.

WIRE-VINE = *Muehlenbeckia complexa.*

WISCONSIN. The state flower is the violet, and the state lies principally in zones* 1 and 2, a small portion in the southeastern corner falling in zone* 3.

CLIMATE. Climatic zone lines in Wisconsin are greatly affected by the water influences of Lakes Michigan and Superior, and the Mississippi and Wisconsin rivers. Plant-hardiness in Wisconsin is not entirely a matter of minimum temperatures, but is influenced by the atmospheric moisture and soil conditions prevailing in a given section, the latter being particularly important in the growing of tree fruits.

Variations in the length of the growing season make a considerable difference in the crops successfully grown in various sections. The average maximum growing season of 170 days is found in the southeastern corner of the state in Kenosha, Racine, and Milwaukee counties; and the shortest, under 100 days, in the extreme north-central part. The shorter season of this section and the lower mean summer temperature make it very difficult and in some cases impossible to grow successfully the long-season crops which require relatively high temperatures.

Dates of killing frosts do not follow latitude lines. Frost lines are irregularly sharply crescent-shaped with the base of the crescent lying in the center of the state east and west. Lines showing the same late frost dates will have the two horns of the crescent 50 to 100 miles north of the base, and the difference in early fall frosts is even greater. For example, Marinette, Portage, and New Richmond have nearly the same date for the last killing frost in spring and first killing frost in fall. The following table gives some significant data as to range of frost occurrence and its variability as to latitude due to water and altitude influence.

Town	Average date of last killing frost in spring	Latest killing frost
Marinette	May 8	May 25
Portage	May 3	June 8
New Richmond	May 10	May 28
Milwaukee	Apr. 26	May 29
Prentice	June 2	June 29
Grantsburg	May 22	June 11

Town	Average date of first killing frost in fall	Earliest killing frost
Marinette	Oct. 7	Sept. 25
Portage	Oct. 5	Sept. 10
New Richmond	Oct. 3	Sept. 10
Milwaukee	Oct. 18	Sept. 25
Prentice	Sept. 9	Aug. 15
Grantsburg	Sept. 19	Aug. 26

* Special articles on the subjects indicated by an asterisk (*) will be found at the words so marked.

RAINFALL. The distribution of rainfall is quite uniform over the entire state. The mean for the state is 31 inches, the average varying for different sections from 28 to 34 inches. The heaviest rainfall is in the elevated sections of the southwestern part of the state, and the smallest in the north-central highlands. Wisconsin is fortunate in the amount of rainfall occurring during the growing season. Nearly 70% of the precipitation is from April to September inclusive, which covers the growing season for most plants. Under ordinary conditions, the summer rainfall is adequate to produce reasonably satisfactory growing conditions for many crops. Irrigation, however, is widely practiced and is becoming increasingly essential for the profitable production of many horticultural crops, especially on lighter soils.

SOILS. A wide variety of soils is found in the state. They range from the very heavy clays to light sands. There are also extensive areas of organic soils, especially in the southeastern, central, and north-central counties. The lighter sandy soils are largely confined to four sections. The largest is the central section, lying mostly in an area bounded by Portage and Wisconsin Dells on the south; Stevens Point and Wisconsin Rapids on the north; Waupaca and Berlin on the east; and Black River Falls and Sparta on the west. A much smaller section is found in the northeastern part of the state, beginning near Shawano and extending northeasterly to the Wisconsin-Michigan state line. The third section is in the northwest corner of the state, beginning in the vicinity of Grantsburg in Burnett County and extending northeasterly into Douglas and Bayfield counties. The fourth area is one in which the sandy lands are interspersed with areas of heavier soil. It lies in parts of Lincoln, Langlade, Oneida, Forest, and Vilas counties.

There is a large area of fine sandy loam soil northwest of Black River Falls extending across Jackson, Eau Claire, Chippewa, and Dunn counties and into southern Barron County. The soils in the remaining portion of the state are largely silt loams, with clay along Lake Superior and Lake Michigan from near Milwaukee north to Algoma, and extending west at Manitowoc to include the area around Lake Winnebago and the Fox River Valley to Green Bay.

GARDENING. Amateur gardening is practiced throughout the state, but it is most highly developed in the southern and eastern counties. Climatic and soil conditions are generally more favorable in these areas and it is here that the principal population centers are located. Earlier and more extensive development of the summer resort possibilities in these areas, accompanied by the establishment of country estates and summer homes with their extensive gardens and landscaped plantings, contribute to the concentration of amateur gardening in these counties.

Amateur flower, vegetable, and fruit growing is practiced throughout the state with

WISCONSIN

The zones of hardiness crossing Wisconsin are those shown on the map located at ZONE, which should be consulted for details. The dates are the average latest killing frost in spring and the first one in the fall. The figures below the dates show the average length of the growing season.

the greatest development found in the urban areas.

COMMERCIAL HORTICULTURE. The production of horticultural crops and the many enterprises closely related to these activities constitute important aspects of Wisconsin's agriculture and related industries. Fruits, flowers, vegetables, and woody ornamentals are grown extensively in the state.

Fruits are grown almost throughout the state. Important commercial production is centered in local areas. Apples are grown largely on the Door Peninsula, along the shore of Lake Michigan, on the Bayfield Peninsula, and in the west-central counties, especially along the Mississippi River. Sour cherries are grown commercially almost exclusively on the Door Peninsula, largely north of Sturgeon Bay. Pears are grown only on a very limited scale in the southeastern and lake-shore counties. Cranberries are grown extensively, especially in the central and north-central counties. Strawberries are grown largely in the southeastern and lake-shore counties, on the Bayfield Peninsula, and in the west-central counties of Jackson, Monroe, Clark, Eau Claire, and Trempealeau. Grapes are not an important commercial crop in Wisconsin. Only varieties which are both winter-hardy and comparatively early may be grown successfully. Varieties ripening with or later than Concord are not recommended. Peaches are not hardy in Wisconsin but trees are occasionally found in home plantings in the southern counties. Plum production is very limited and is confined generally to the southeastern and lake-shore counties. Native blueberries grow extensively in the northern counties; cultivated blueberries are grown only

---

* Special articles on the subjects indicated by an asterisk (*) will be found at the words so marked.

on a very limited scale by amateur gardeners. Raspberries, largely red varieties, are grown on a limited scale near urban centers, especially in the southern and lake-shore counties. Blackberries, gooseberries, and currants are adapted to many areas of Wisconsin but are little grown.

Flowers are grown largely in greenhouses in and near urban centers. Gladiolus and several other flowers are grown out of doors, but not extensively. Perennial flowering plants are an important commercial crop, especially on the Bayfield Peninsula and in nurseries near urban centers throughout the state.

Vegetables are grown throughout the state. Wisconsin is a leading state in the production of vegetables for processing and also produces large quantities for fresh use. Peas, sweet corn, cucumbers for pickles, snap beans, lima beans, beets, carrots, and cabbage for kraut are the leading processing crops. Smaller acreages of tomatoes, asparagus, spinach, squash, and peppers are also grown for processing, and large quantities of potatoes and onions are processed as chips or used in the manufacture of soups and processed mixed vegetables. Only limited quantities of vegetables, largely peas and sweet corn, are frozen in Wisconsin. Principal vegetables grown for fresh market include potatoes, onions, cabbage, snap beans, carrots, cauliflower, celery, cucumbers, head lettuce, muskmelons, peppers, radishes, pumpkin, squash, rutabaga, spinach, sweet corn, tomatoes, and watermelons. Extensive deposits of peat soil are located in Wisconsin and large acreages, especially in the southeastern and south-central counties, are used for the production of onions, carrots, potatoes, mint, beets, cabbage, celery, head lettuce, radish, spinach, and sweet corn.

ORNAMENTAL PLANTS. Both herbaceous and woody ornamentals are grown by florists and nurserymen in and near urban centers throughout the state; principal production is in the southeastern and lake-shore counties. Producers of woody ornamentals ordinarily provide complete or limited landscape service. Many nurserymen are becoming important producers of grass sod for lawns and most of them also produce a limited number of herbaceous perenals.

The address of the Agricultural Experiment Station which has kindly supplied the above information is Madison. The Station is always glad to answer garden questions requiring more detailed information than that given above.

Garden club activities are extensive, especially in the regions of ornamental gardening. They include clubs of the Garden Club of America, the home office of which is 598 Madison Avenue, New York 22, N.Y. There are also many clubs affiliated with the Wisconsin Federation of Garden Clubs and the Wisconsin Garden Club.

WISCONSIN WEEPING WILLOW = *Salix blanda.* See WILLOW.

wisetonensis, -e (wise-to-nen′sis). A name applied by its originator to *Schizanthus wisetonensis* and derived from Wiseton, a village in Nottinghamshire, England.

WISTARIA (wis-tair′i-a). Wisteria (which is the preferred spelling of the common name). Beautiful woody vines of the pea family, two of the species native in the U.S., the other five Asiatic. They are widely planted for their profuse spring bloom and often reach to the housetop when old. Leaves alternate,* compound,* the leaflets arranged feather-fashion, with an odd one at the end, the leaflets also alternate.* Flowers pea-like, in showy, drooping clusters (racemes*). Fruit a stalked, flattened pod (legume*), usually constricted between the seeds. (Named for Casper Wistar, Pennsylvania professor of anatomy.) The plants are sometimes known as *Kraunhia*, and the generic name is occasionally spelled *Wisteria.*

For culture *see* below.

floribunda. Japanese wisteria. A tall-climbing vine, but not usually so high as the Chinese wisteria. Leaflets 13–19, ovalish or oblong, 1¾–3½ in. long. Flowers violet-blue or violet, about ¾ in. long, the cluster nearly 18 in. long. Pod velvety, 4½–7 in. long. Jap. May. Hardy from zone* 3 southward. There are several hort. varieties, one with white or pink flowers, another with variegated leaves, but the most striking is *var.* **macrobotrys,** where the hanging flower cluster may be 3 ft. long. This variety is often offered as *W. multijuga,* and is very popular.

frutescens. A native American wisteria found wild from Va. to Fla. and Ala. It climbs 20–30 ft. high, and has 9–15 elliptic or ovalish leaflets ¾–2 in. long. Flowers about ½ in. long, lilac-purple, the hairy cluster scarcely over 4 in. long. Pod smooth, 2–4 in. long. June–July. Hardy from zone* 4 southward. Not much cult. The plant often listed as the *var.* **magnifica** is W. *macrostachya.*

macrostachya. A native American wisteria found wild from La. and Tex. to Ill. and Mo. Leaflets 9, ovalish, 1–2½ in. long. Flowers lilac-purple, but with a yellow spot, the individual flower stalks sticky-hairy, the clusters nearly 1 ft. long. Pod smooth, 3–6 in. long. June–July. Hardy from zone* 4 southward. Usually offered as *W. frutescens magnifica.*

multijuga = *Wistaria floribunda macrobotrys.*

sinensis. Chinese wisteria, and, with W. *floribunda,* the usual one in cult. It is a high-climbing vine reaching, in old specimens, the tops of trees or houses. Leaflets 7–13 (mostly 11), ovalish or oblong, 2½–4 in. long. Flowers bluish-violet, fragrant, about 1 in. long, the cluster about 12 in. long. Pods 5–7 in. long, densely velvety. China. May. Generally hardy from zone* 3 southward, but not so hardy as W. *floribunda.* The *var.* **alba** has pure white flowers, and there is a double pink form.

WISTERIA CULTURE

These, probably the most desirable of all hardy woody vines, are not difficult to transplant but are quite apt to be without flowers for the first few years unless precautions are taken. In starting, it is always better to buy a small potted and grafted vine from a reliable nurseryman and so avoid the risk of field-dug

---

* Special articles on the subjects indicated by an asterisk (*) will be found at the words so marked.

specimens. While wisteria vines will grow in most ordinary garden soils, it is far better to make a special mixture for such a permanent vine which, if you want it to flower freely, must be richly fed. Dig out enough soil (about a barrelful) and replace with rich garden loam to which about ⅓ its bulk of old, well-rotted manure has been added. Thoroughly mix up the soil, pack it in well and plant the potted wisteria (with of course the pot removed). See that it gets water enough the first season and that you do not injure the roots while planting, nor afterwards by cultivation or otherwise.

The young vine will have to be tied up at first until it begins to twine around its support, for the wisterias have no tendrils.* Later it will look after its own climbing.

Many beautiful old wisteria vines are growing up the trunks of trees. If you pick such a site for your vine, do not start it under a young, vigorous, densely canopied tree, but choose an old, slowly dying one. Wisterias do not like shade, at least the best of the Asiatic species do not. If the vine is to grow against the house see that it is securely fastened for the first few years, or better yet, start it on a trellis.

While many nurserymen offer plants that have already bloomed once or twice, it is not unusual for a wisteria to grow vigorously for a few years and produce no flowers or only a few. While few gardeners take the trouble, more and better bloom will be produced by a careful system of pruning. In the summer prune out the long, straggling growths except those needed for climbing purposes. This is more likely to induce fine bloom than anything else. The straggling shoots should be cut back from ½–⅓ their length, which will induce the production of short spurs upon which next season's flower clusters will be borne. It is also necessary to give the vine an annual mulch of rich manure each fall and to dig it in carefully in the spring.

While normal wisterias are always vines, very beautiful effects can be had by the shrubby, weeping forms. These are the result of long training. The height is held at a definite point by pinching out young shoots, and after a trunk-like stem is produced (it takes years) the leaders are then allowed to droop to the ground.

In choosing wisterias it is well to remember that the finest of them are the two Asiatic species, W. *sinensis* and W. *floribunda*, and that both of them bloom before or with the unfolding of the leaves. The native American W. *frutescens* and W. *macrostachya* bloom later and after the leaves are grown. They are consequently never as showy as the Asiatic kinds, but they do prolong wisteria bloom.

WISTERIA. The preferred spelling of the common name for vines of the genus *Wistaria* (which see).

WITCH-ALDER. See FOTHERGILLA.

WITCHES'-BROOM. An abnormal, bush-like growth caused by a parasitic fungus, found on cedars, blueberries, and several other woody plants. They are not usually serious and the best remedy is to cut them out.

WITCH GRASS = Quack grass. *See* No. 36 in the list at WEEDS AND WEEDING.

WITCH-HAZEL. *See* HAMAMELIS.

WITCH-HOBBLE = *Viburnum alnifolium.*

WITCH'S-TEETH = *Hosackia gracilis.*

WITHE. A slender, whip-like twig, especially a willow twig.

WITHERING. *See* WILTING.

WITHEROD = *Viburnum cassinoides.*

WITHY. Any willow, especially the osier willow.

WITHYWIND = *Clematis Vitalba* and *Solanum Dulcamara.*

WITLOOF. A form of chicory grown as a salad plant. For description *see* CICHORIUM. For culture *see* CELLAR GARDENING. Another name for witloof is French endive.

WOAD. *See* ISATIS.

WOADWAXEN = *Genista tinctoria.*

WOLFBERRY = *Symphoricarpos occidentalis* and *Elaeagnus commutata.*

WOLFSBANE = *Monkshood.*

WOMAN'S-TONGUE TREE = *Albizzia Lebbek.*

WOMEN GARDENERS. The gardening movement in America is very largely in the hands of women. For the chief manifestation of it *see* GARDEN CLUBS. For the training of professional women gardeners and landscape architects *see* GARDEN SCHOOLS.

WONDERBERRY. *See* SOLANUM NIGRUM.

WONGA-WONGA = *Pandorea pandorana.*

WOOD ANEMONE = *Anemone nemorosa* and *A. quinquefolia.*

WOOD ASHES. *See* ASH AND ASHES.

WOOD BETONY. *See* PEDICULARIS; also STACHYS OFFICINALIS.

WOODBINE. A very old name for any number of vines. Those in this book are *Parthenocissus quinquefolia* (the Virginia creeper), and *Lonicera Periclymenum* (an Old World honeysuckle).

WOOD CUDWEED = *Gnaphalium sylvaticum.*

WOOD DAFFODIL = *Uvularia grandiflora.*

WOODEN ROSE. *See* IPOMOEA TUBEROSA.

WOOD HYACINTH = *Scilla nonscripta.*

WOODLAND GARDEN. *See* WILD GARDEN.

WOODLAND STAR = *Lithophragma affinis.*

WOOD LILY = *Lilium philadelphicum.*

WOOD MEADOW GRASS = *Poa nemoralis.*

---

* Special articles on the subjects indicated by an asterisk (*) will be found at the words so marked.

WOOD-OIL TREE. *See* TUNG-OIL TREE.

WOOD ROT. The wood of all trees, living or dead, is subject to decay or disintegration by micro-organisms, among which fungi are the most numerous and of greatest importance. Wood-destroying fungi use the wood as food and the materials which serve to make wood strong and hard are wholly or partly removed in the process, decay being the result. In the case of living trees, decay fungi enter through wounds or other openings in the bark. The reproductive bodies or spores of the wood-rotting fungi are nearly everywhere in the air. The number is naturally greater near heavily forested regions where there is an abundance of decaying wood, but the spores* may be carried for long distances by air currents. The fact that many wood-destroying fungi are the same the world over indicates that the spores* travel widely.

Some time before the final stage in the disintegration of the wood is reached, most decay-producing fungi form fruiting bodies on the outside of the tree or piece of rotting wood. The spores* which serve to perpetuate the fungus are borne on these mature fungi and liberated into the air in enormous numbers in such a way that they are easily carried away by wind and air currents. In this manner, some spores find places favorable for initiating decay anew.

As most of the decay of wood starts at some injured part of the tree, the remedy and prevention is always to see that such injuries are repaired. The details of this will be found at TREE SURGERY.

WOODRUFF = *Asperula*.

WOODSIA (wood'zi-a). Tufted,* mostly rock-inhabiting ferns of the family Polypodiaceae, comprising about 12 species, and natives of the cooler and cold regions, mostly from the northern hemisphere. They have stout rootstocks and numerous fronds which (in ours) are once- or twice-compound and often with a shaggy stalk. Spore cases scattered on the under side of the leaf segments, usually at the forking of the veins. (Named for Joseph Woods, English botanist and architect.)

The cult. woodsias are plants for the hardy fern garden, and prefer rocky, shady places. For culture *see* FERNS AND FERN GARDENING

ilvensis. Rootstocks growing in masses, the plant densely tufted.* Stalk of the frond rusty and chaffy.* Leaves compound,* generally lance-shaped, 5–10 in. long, the stalkless segments coarsely toothed, the teeth themselves toothed, rusty on the under side. Northern N.A. and westward. Also in Greenland and Eurasia, chiefly on exposed rocks.

obtusa. Rootstock slender and creeping, the stalk of the frond smooth. Fronds twice-compound,* 1–3 ft. long, more or less triangular-lance-shaped, pointed at the tip, its main segments cut into sharply toothed ultimate segments which are themselves toothed, the foliage hence fine and feathery. Eastern N.A., mostly in rocky woods.

WOOD SORREL. *See* OXALIS.

WOODWARDIA (wood-war'di-a). Chain fern. Rather coarse marsh ferns of the family Polypodiaceae, comprising perhaps 10 species, with creeping rootstocks,* and often bearing both infertile foliage fronds and other spore*-bearing fertile fronds. The fronds are once- or twice-compound* or divided, the spore cases borne in chain-like lines along the midrib of the fertile fronds. (Named for Thomas J. Woodward, English botanist.)

The cult. chain ferns are not of much hort. importance and present no difficulties in growing. *Woodwardia areolata* grows best in rather acid wet places, but the others are not particular so long as the place is moist. They require less shade than most ferns and in the wild often grow in full sun.

areolata. Rootstock creeping and chaffy. Foliage fronds triangular-ovalish, the segments narrow, minutely toothed on the margins. Fertile or spore-bearing fronds similar but larger than the foliage fronds, the segments narrower, the under side with a double row of chain-like spore cases. Eastern N.A.

virginica. Rootstock creeping, chaffy only at the end. Fronds of one sort, 2–3 ft. high, the stalks polished. Fronds twice-compound,* the main segments narrow, deeply toothed, but the teeth not again toothed. Spore cases in chain-like lines on the lower side of the ultimate segments, mostly along the midrib. Eastern N.A. Sometimes known as *Anchistea virginica*.

WOODY PLANTS. Shrubs, trees, and woody vines are distinguished from all herbaceous plants by the fact that they produce wood, and have buds which survive above ground during the winter. Fleshy-stemmed herbs do neither (except in rare cases), and their buds are underground during the winter. For Woody Vines *see* VINES.

WOOLLY. Covered with soft, loose, somewhat matted hairs, hence resembling wool. The technical term is lanate. *See also* TOMENTOSA.

WOOLLY MANZANITA = *Arctostaphylos tomentosa*.

WOOLLY SUNFLOWER. *See* ERIOPHYLLUM.

WOOLLY THYME = *Thymus Serpyllum lanuginosus*. *See* THYME.

WORM. For true worms *see* EARTHWORMS. For the caterpillars often incorrectly called worms *see* INSECT PESTS.

WORM-GRASS = *Spigelia marilandica* and *Sedum album*.

WORMWOOD. Any species of *Artemisia*, especially *A. Absinthium*.

WORMWOOD SAGE = *Artemisia frigida*.

WOUNDS. *See* TREE SURGERY.

WOUNDWORT = *Anthyllis Vulneraria*. *See also* STACHYS.

WREATH GOLDENROD = *Solidago caesia*. *See* GOLDENROD.

WULFENIA (wool-fen'ia). Eurasian per-

---

* Special articles on the subjects indicated by an asterisk (*) will be found at the words so marked.

ennial herbs of the family Scrophulariaceae, comprising about 8 species, of which only **W. carinthiaca** from the Carinthian Mountains is cult. in the rock garden. It needs a gritty soil, moist in the growing season but not too wet in the winter as the plant rots easily. It is about 9 in. high with basal, oblongish, toothed leaves, 6–8 in. long. Flowers tubular, blue, about ⅓ in. long, in a dense terminal cluster (raceme*-like), the stalk of which may be 2 ft. high. Corolla cylindrical, 4-lobed, the stamens* 2. Fruit a 4-valved capsule. (Named for T. X. von Wulfen, Austrian botanist.)

WYCH ELM = *Ulmus glabra*. See ELM.

WYETHIA (wy-ee'thi-a). Mule-ears. Sunflower-like perennial herbs of the family Compositae, all the 8 known species from western N.A., two of them of some hort. interest, and occasionally planted in the wild garden. They have basal or alternate* stem leaves which are narrow and without marginal teeth. Flower heads yellow, solitary, or a few in a cluster, the ray flowers in a single row. (Named for N. J. Wyeth, American botanical explorer.)

They are plants of similar culture to the sunflower (which see).

amplexicaulis. A smooth herb 1–2 ft. high. Leaves glossy-green, oblongish, 8–12 in. long, the upper nearly stalkless or clasping the stem. Flower heads nearly 3 in. wide, bright yellow. British Columbia to Colo.

angustifolia. Not over 2 ft. high, the stem hairy. Leaves oblongish or narrower, 8–12 in. long, the upper nearly stalkless but not clasping, sometimes stalked. Flower heads about 4 in. wide. Calif.

WYOMING. The state flower is the Indian paintbrush, the state tree the cottonwood, and the state lies wholly in zones* 2 and 3.

SOILS. The Wyoming soils, covering an area of 62.5 million acres, are derived from a great variety of crystalline, shale, sandstone, and limestone rocks which have been weathered by an arid or semi-arid climate and vegetation. Owing to limited rainfall and vegetation, about 44 million acres are best adapted to grazing and livestock production. About 6 million acres, primarily in the eastern portion of the state, could be dry-farmed more or less intensively. Between 1.5 and 2 million acres of land are irrigated. Although several times this area could be irrigated, most of the available water is already pre-empted. Nine million acres are in national forest and 2 million acres in national parks.

The soils of Wyoming have been classified into seven broad groups based on the origin of their parent materials as follows: mountain soils; limy valley alluvial soils; tight gray clays and loams on salty marine shales; friable grayish-brown loam from fresh-water shales; reddish-brown loams on red shale, sandstone, limestone, and scoria; brown sandy loams on loess, limestone, and sandstone; and dune sands. Each of these soil

groups contains from 8 to 30 soil series; hence a considerable variety of texture, color, drainage, reaction, slope, and crop adaptation occurs in each soil group.

Summertime grazing for cattle and sheep is the most general agricultural use made of the mountain soils. Supervised timber cutting is practiced in most of the forest preserves and logging and sawing of timber is let to the highest bidder. Use of timbered mountains for recreation is very popular. Yellowstone Park is one of the most visited tourist areas of the West.

The alluvial, terrace, bench, fan, and bottom soils of the valleys and plains occupy nearly four million acres in the state. Much of the irrigated area is found on this group of soils. This is true in part because stream and reservoir water is adjacent to them, and the level surface encouraged early diversion from nearby streams.

The tight gray soils on salty marine shales are adapted to pasture and the production of native hay. Generally the conversion of these soils into crop production involves slow and expensive processes of both drainage and leaching out of the salts. Irrigated crops are produced on the friable soils from freshwater shales, wherever water is available. However, the larger portion of land in crop production is dry-farmed.

The reddish-colored soils are generally shallow and stony and are in rough areas which make them best adapted to grazing or pasture. In the smoother areas where these soils are deeper they are cropped by either irrigation or dry-farm methods.

The brown sandy loams are found more in the eastern counties of the state where annual rainfall is greater. These soils are dry-farmed quite extensively, and are irrigated where well water is available.

The dune areas occupy small scattered sections of the state and have little agricultural value.

FLOWERS AND SHRUBS. All of the common varieties of flowers, including the columbine, snapdragon, *Phlox, Lychnis, Campanula, Coreopsis,* bleeding-heart, *Delphinium* (both annual and perennial), dahlias, gladioli, peony, *Anchusa, Papaver,* pansy, *Portulaca, Cosmos, Rudbeckia, Alyssum,* and *Centaurea,* as well as iris, chrysanthemums, and asters are adapted in the state. In general they are better adapted at lower elevations, and do more poorly at higher elevations in the mountains.

Ornamental trees for most sections of the state include *Picea pungens, P. glauca, Pinus flexilis, P. ponderosa, Juniperus scopulorum, J. virginiana, Acer Negundo, A. Saccharum, Malus* sp., and *Populus* sp., as well as *Quercus macrocarpa,* Salix sp., *Tilia* sp. and *Ulmus* sp.

Many native shrubs are suitable in all parts of the state. These include *Cercocarpus, Cornus, Ribes, Sambucus, Prunus, Shepherdia, Elaeagnus, Betula, Amelanchier, Potentilla, Symphoricarpos, Acer,* and many of

---

* Special articles on the subjects indicated by an asterisk (*) will be found at the words so marked.

the low-growing species of *Salix*. *Caragana, Syringa, Lonicera, Crataegus, Viburnum* and *Cotoneaster* are dependable introduced shrubs, especially *Caragana,* which is useful on dry sites.

Where there is an ample supply of water available, satisfactory flowers and shrubs may be grown. Cultivation on dry land is the principal precaution against failure in order that every bit of moisture may be conserved and held for the use of the growing plants. There is increasing interest in, and use being made of native trees, shrubs, and flowers.

CLIMATE. The variation in climate of different places in the state is associated for the most part with differences in altitude and terrain.

The length of time between killing frosts is shown for several places in the following table:

Name of Town	Average date of last killing frost in spring	Latest-known killing frost
Casper	May 16	July 3
Cheyenne	May 16	June 13
Douglas	May 17	July 4
Evanston	June 12	July 13
Jackson	June 21	July 13
Laramie	May 29	July 7
Newcastle	May 13	June 5
Powell	May 13	June 13
Riverton	May 16	June 16
Sheridan	May 14	June 2
Torrington	May 12	June 20

Name of Town	Average date of earliest killing frost in fall	Earliest-known killing frost
Casper	Oct. 1	Sept. 7
Cheyenne	Sept. 27	Aug. 25
Douglas	Sept. 23	Aug. 24
Evanston	Sept. 8	Aug. 11
Jackson	Aug. 20	July 17
Laramie	Sept. 19	Aug. 16
Newcastle	Sept. 28	Aug. 25
Powell	Sept. 25	Aug. 25
Riverton	Sept. 21	Aug. 7
Sheridan	Sept. 22	Aug. 25
Torrington	Sept. 27	Sept. 6

RAINFALL

Name of Town	No. years recorded	Yearly total (inches)	Growing-season total (5 mo.) (inches)
Casper	36	15.33	7.33
Cheyenne	85	16.25	9.33
Douglas	10	13.89	7.78
Evanston	55	13.04	5.29
Jackson	31	16.36	6.84
Laramie	74	11.32	6.71
Newcastle	42	15.16	9.86
Powell	46	5.82	3.89
Riverton	36	9.71	5.68
Sheridan	60	16.75	8.89
Torrington	34	14.36	9.03

This information was kindly supplied by the Wyoming Agricultural Experiment Station, Laramie, Wyoming. The station is always ready to answer questions on gardening.

X

xanthina, -us, -um (zan-thy′na). Yellow.

XANTHISMA (zan-this′ma). Texas herbs of the family Compositae, one of the two best known species, **X. texanum**, the Texas star or Star-of-Texas, grown for ornament. It is an annual (or biennial), 2–4 ft. high, with wand-like stems and narrow, alternate* leaves 1½–2½ in. long. Flower heads long-stalked, mostly solitary, about 2½ in. wide, the 18–20 rays yellow. The plant is not much grown, but as it grows naturally on dry, open prairies, it is well suited to open places with poorish soil. Seeds should be sown where wanted as the plant will bloom the first year, although often biennial in habit. (*Xanthisma* is from the Greek for yellow dyed, in allusion to the color of the flowers.)

XANTHOCERAS (zan-tho-seer′ras). A single species of rather handsome Chinese shrubs of the family Sapindaceae, **X. sorbifolium** grown for ornament. It is a shrub 10–15 ft. high with compound* leaves composed of 9–17 narrow, toothed leaflets which are 1–2 in. long and pale beneath. Flowers polygamous,* whitish, about ¾ in. wide, the base of each of the 5 petals with a yellow or reddish blotch. The flower cluster (raceme*) is rather showy, 6–10 in. long, upright, its individual flower stalks slender. Stamens* 8. Fruit a 3-valved capsule. It is an attractive shrub, holding its bright green foliage late in the fall. Not particular as to soils and propagated by root cuttings over bottom-heat,* or by stratified seeds. April–May. Hardy from zone* 3 southward. (*Xanthoceras* is from the Greek for yellow horn, in allusion to the horn-like projections on the receptacle or disk.)

XANTHORHIZA (zan-tho-ry′za). Sometimes spelled *Zanthorhiza*. A single species of low shrubs of the buttercup family, **X. simplicissima**, the yellowroot or shrub yellow-root, a native of the eastern U.S. It is scarcely 2 ft. high and has yellow, bitter roots. Leaves compound,* long-stalked, the usually 5 leaflets ovalish, deeply cut, sometimes 3-lobed, 2–4 in. long. Flowers perfect or unisexual,* brownish-purple, about ⅓ in.

* Special articles on the subjects indicated by an asterisk (*) will be found at the words so marked.

long, in drooping clusters (racemes*). Sepals 5, petal-like. Petals none, but the 5 nectaries 3-lobed and petal-like. Stamens* 5–10. Fruit a collection of 10, 1-seeded, small pods (follicles*). A useful shrub for low, moist, shady banks, but not thriving in open, wind-swept places. N.Y. to Fla. and Ala. April–May. Hardy from zone* 3 southward. Easily propagated by division. (*Xanthorhiza* is from the Greek for yellow root.)

XANTHOSOMA (zan-tho-sō′ma). Tropical American, thick, fleshy-leaved herbs of the arum family, comprising about 40 species, related to the elephant-ear, grown chiefly in the tropics for their starchy, edible rootstocks, but also grown for ornament in warm regions, and in the greenhouse. They have large, arrowhead-shaped leaves, sometimes cut or divided, and thick, channeled leafstalks. Flowers minute, unisexual,* crowded on a spadix* which is usually shorter than the spathe.* (For details see ARACEAE.) A somewhat diversified hort. group of plants as some are only grown for food, and in tropical America replace the taro for that purpose, while *X. lindeni* is an old favorite as a greenhouse foliage plant. (*Xanthosoma* is from the Greek for yellow body, in reference to the yellow stigma.)

Xanthosoma atrovirens and *X. sagittaefolium* are food plants in tropical America and can only be grown outdoors in extreme southern Fla. They need a rich, moist soil and should have frequent top-dressings of well-rotted manure. The two other species are foliage plants for the tropical greenhouse where they need the same conditions as *Caladium* (which see). While not such a showy foliage plant, *Xanthosoma lindeni* is a better house plant than the caladiums.

atrovirens. Malanga; also called West Indian kale. Leaves 2–3 ft. long and nearly 2 ft. wide, green above, bluish-green below, the grooved stalks nearly 2 ft. long. S.A.

lindeni. A handsome foliage plant producing a mass of white-veined leaves which are about 12 in. long, 4–6 in. wide, the stalks nearly 12 in. long. Spathe* nearly 6 in. long, white. Colombia. A good plant for the tropical greenhouse, or it can be used for summer bedding.

sagittaefolium. Tania. Yautia. A tropical American food plant, replacing the taro in the W.I. It has a distinct stem, 2–3 ft. high, but often appears stemless, the leafstalks arising from the ground. Leaves 2–3 ft. wide and long, green both sides, the stalks nearly 3 ft. long. Spathe* 7–9 in. long, greenish-white.

violaceum. A purplish-veined foliage plant, the leaves 18–24 in. long and nearly as wide, the purple stalks even longer. Spathes* about 12 in. long, yellowish-white. Tropical America.

XANTHOXYLUM = *Zanthoxylum*.

XERANTHEMUM (zer-ran′the-mum). Everlasting. A small group of Mediterranean annual herbs of the daisy family, **X. annuum** the common everlasting or immortelle, and perhaps the best-known of all everlastings. It is a white-felty annual, 2–3 ft. high, with oblongish leaves 1–2 in. long, without marginal teeth. Flower heads long-stalked, solitary, about 1½ in. wide, composed wholly of white, purple, or violet disk flowers. Surrounding the head is a collection of small, papery or chaffy bracts,* colored like the heads. There are several varieties, some with double flower heads. Should be grown as a hardy annual, or if wanted especially early, it may be started as a tender annual. See ANNUALS. For the best method of preserving the flowers for winter use see DRIED FLOWERS. (*Xeranthemum* is from the Greek for dry flower.)

XEROPHYLLUM (zer-o-fill′um). Turkey-beard. A group of North American herbs of the lily family, two of the 3 known species grown in the wild garden. They have woody rootstocks and wiry, basal, grass-like leaves. Flowers small, white, in a long-stalked, dense cluster (raceme*) which rises from the leaf rosette. Petals soon withering. Stamens* 6. Fruit a 3-valved capsule.* (*Xerophyllum* is from the Greek for dry leaf, in allusion to the wiry leaves.)

The eastern turkey-beard (*X. asphodeloides*) prefers moist, acid sand such as that found along the edges of pine-barren bogs with a pH of 4–5. The western *X. tenax* is certainly hardy only in its own region.

asphodeloides. Leaves tough, wiry, rough-margined, about 15 in. long and ⅒ in. wide. Flowering stalk 4–5 ft. high, the terminal cluster (raceme*) dense, about 6 in. long. Pine-barrens. N.J. to Ga. June.

tenax. Elk-grass; also known as fire-lily. Leaves nearly 24 in. long, about ⅛ in. wide. Flowering stalk 4–5 ft. high, the terminal cluster (raceme*) nearly 20 in. long, the stamens* violet and longer than the petals. British Columbia to Calif. June–July.

XEROPHYTE. A plant adapted to a deficiency of water or to only periodic occurrence of it. While most xerophytes are desert plants, not all of them store large quantities of water as do the cacti. Many xerophytes have ashy or white foliage, or drop their leaves, or have varnished or tightly rolled leaves — all devices to reduce the plant's water needs. See SUCCULENTS.

Xiphium (zy′fi-um). A group name for a section of *Iris*.

XOLISMA (zo-liz′ma) = *Lyonia*.

XYLOSMA (zy-los′ma). A genus of over 100 species of shrubs and trees of the family Flacourtiaceae, all tropical, with alternate leaves, small unisexual and inconspicuous flowers without petals. Stamens* many, surrounded by a disk. Fruit a 2–8-seeded berry. The only cult. species is **X. senticosa**, from southern China, a low shrub with the twigs brown-hairy. Spines in the leaf axils* slender and sharp. Leaves ovalish, about ½ in. long, bluntly toothed on the margin. Flowers negligible. Grow in the cool greenhouse, in potting mixture* 4, or outdoors from zone* 7 southward.

Xylosteum (zy-los′te-um). Pre-Linnaean* name for some bush honeysuckles. See LONICERA.

xyphioides (zy-fi-oi′deez, but see OïDES). Like the Spanish iris (*Iris Xiphium*).

---

* Special articles on the subjects indicated by an asterisk (*) will be found at the words so marked.

Y

YAM. The true yam is *Dioscorea* (which see). In the southeastern U.S. *yam* is often, but incorrectly, applied to the sweet potato.

YAM BEAN. Tropical herbaceous vines of the pea family, comprising the genus **Pachyrhizus** (pack-i-ry′zus), two of the 3 known species grown for the edible tubers and pods in warm countries but little known in the U.S. They have long, twining stems, often thickened and woody at the base, and compound* leaves with 3, often lobed, leaflets. Flowers pea-like, white or violet, borne in clusters (racemes*) which have swollen joints. Fruit a large, beaked, reddish-hairy pod (legume*), somewhat constricted between the flat seeds. (*Pachyrhizus* is from the Greek for thick root, in allusion to the tubers.)

The vines need support or they will sprawl over the ground. Grown from seeds.

erosus. Common yam bean. Tubers large, the stems 15–20 ft. long. Leaflets 3–6 in. long, the lateral ones somewhat oblique, the central one with angular lobes. Flowers violet or reddish-pink. Pod 4–6 in. long, the seeds 6–8. Tropical regions.

tuberosus. Similar to the above, but the flowers white, the central leaflet scarcely lobed and the pods twice as large. S.A. (?).

YAM FAMILY = Dioscoreaceae.

YAMPEE = *Dioscorea trifida*.

YANGTAO = *Actinidia chinensis*.

YANKEE CORN = *Zea Mays indurata*. See CORN.

YARD-LONG BEAN = *Vigna sesquipedalis*.

YARROW = *Achillea Millefolium*.

YATE-TREE = *Eucalyptus cornuta*.

YAUPON = *Ilex vomitoria;* and sometimes, but less correctly, *I. Cassine*. See HOLLY.

YAUTIA = *Xanthosoma sagittaefolium*.

YAW-WEED = *Morinda Royoc*.

YEDDO HAWTHORN = *Raphiolepis umbellata*.

YEDDO SPRUCE = *Picea jezoensis*. See SPRUCE.

yedoensis, -e (yed-o-en′sis). From Yeddo, the former name of Tokyo, Japan.

YELLOW. As an adjective, *yellow* is part of the name of many plants and things to do with a garden. Those that occur here and their proper equivalents are:

Yellow adder's-tongue = *Erythronium americanum;* **Yellow archangel** = *Lamium Galeobdolon;* **Yellow aster** = Golden aster (*see* CHRYSOPSIS. *See also* note at ASTER); **Yellow bedstraw** = *Galium verum;* **Yellow bell** = *Allamanda neriifolia;* **Yellow bells** = *Emmenanthe penduliflora;* **Yellow birch** = *Betula lutea* (*see* BIRCH); **Yellow buckthorn** = *Rhamnus caro-*

liniana; **Yellow calla lily** = *Zantedeschia elliottiana* (*see* CALLA LILY); **Yellow camomile** = *Anthemis tinctoria;* **Yellow cedar** = *Juniperus occidentalis;* **Yellow cypress** = *Chamaecyparis nootkatensis;* **Yellow daisy** (*see* RUDBECKIA); **Yellow elder** = *Stenolobium Stans;* **Yellow-eyed grass** = *Hypoxis hirsuta;* **Yellow flax** = *Reinwardtia indica;* **Yellow-flowering pea** (*see* CROTALARIA); **Yellow foxglove** = *Digitalis ambigua* (*see* FOXGLOVE); **Yellow fringed orchis** = *Habenaria ciliaris;* **Yellow fritillary** = *Fritillaria pudica;* **Yellow garden** (*see* first main entry below); **Yellow gentian** = *Gentiana lutea;* **Yellow gourds** (*see* CUCURBITA PEPO OVIFERA); **Yellow granadilla** = *Passiflora laurifolia;* **Yellow honeysuckle** = *Lonicera flava;* **Yellow jasmine** = *Gelsemium sempervirens;* **Yellow lady's-slipper** (*see* CYPRIPEDIUM CALCEOLUS); **Yellow locust** = *Robinia Pseudo-acacia* (*see* LOCUST); **Yellow melilot** = *Melilotus officinalis;* **Yellow mombin** = *Spondias Mombin;* **Yellow oak** = *Quercus velutina* (*see* OAK); **Yellow oleander** = *Thevetia nereifolia;* **Yellow perilla** = *Menispermum canadense;* **Yellow pine** = *Pinus ponderosa* (*see* PINE); **Yellow pitcher-plant** = *Sarracenia flava* (*see* PITCHER-PLANT); **Yellow plum** = *Prunus americana;* **Yellow pond lily** = *Nuphar advena;* **Yellow poplar** = *Liriodendron Tulipifera* (*see* TULIP-TREE); **Yellow puccoon** = *Lithospermum incisum;* **Yellow puccoon** = *Hydrastis canadensis* (*see* GOLDENSEAL); **Yellowroot** = *Hydrastis canadensis* (*see* GOLDENSEAL. *See also* XANTHORHIZA SIMPLICISSIMA and COPTIS TRIFOLIA); **Yellow sage** = *Lantana Camara;* **Yellow skunk-cabbage** = *Lysichitum americanum;* **Yellow star** = *Helenium autumnale;* **Yellow stonecrop** = *Sedum reflexum;* **Yellow trillium** = *Trillium viride luteum;* **Yellow trumpet narcissus** (*see* NARCISSUS MINOR); **Yellow tuft** = *Alyssum argenteum;* **Yellow violet** = *Viola pubescens;* **Yellow water flag** = *Iris Pseudacorus;* **Yellow water lily** = *Nymphaea mexicana;* **Yellowweed** = *Solidago canadensis* (*see* GOLDENROD); **Yellow-wood** (*see* CLADRASTIS).

YELLOW GARDEN. Generally speaking, flowers of the yellow scale, ranging from pale yellow to orange, appear best in full sunshine. An evergreen hedge makes a good background for them as does a white stucco wall. Fences, trelliswork, arbors, and furniture may be painted pure white, light or dark green, or gray-blue. Other accessories should be in harmony. Introduced as foils, a few white, sky-blue or deep purple flowers bring about an excellent effect.

SHRUBS OR SMALL TREES TO BE USED AS ACCENTS OR BACKGROUND

SPRING-FLOWERING: *Lindera Benzoin*, 6–10 ft.; *Berberis*, many species, 3–10 ft.; *Cornus*

* Special articles on the subjects indicated by an asterisk (*) will be found at the words so marked.

Mas, 10–15 ft.; *Corylopsis pauciflora,* 4–6 ft., *C. spicata,* 4–6 ft.; *Enkianthus campanulatus,* 6–10 ft.; *Forsythia,* all species, 6–10 ft.; *Hamamelis mollis,* 10–15 ft., *H. vernalis,* 6–10 ft.; *Kerria japonica; Mahonia Aquifolium,* 3–6 ft., *M. repens,* 1–2 ft.; *Azalea calendulacea,* 4–10 ft. and many hybrid azaleas; *Ribes odoratum.*

SUMMER-FLOWERING: *Caragana arborescens,* 10–15 ft.; *Cytisus nigricans,* 3–6 ft., *C. scoparius,* 4–8 ft.; *Genista pilosa,* 2–3 ft., *G. tinctoria,* 2–3 ft.; *Hypericum prolificum,* 4–8 ft.; *Laburnum anagyroides,* 6–10 ft.; *Potentilla fruticosa.* 2–3 ft.; *Rosa hugonis,* 5–6 ft., *R. xanthina* (yellow).

AUTUMN-FLOWERING: *Hamamelis virginiana,* 10–15 ft.

TALL PLANTS FOR USE IN BACKGROUND

SPRING-FLOWERING: *Doronicum plantagineum; Fritillaria imperialis* (bulb).

SUMMER-FLOWERING: *Achillea filipendulina; Althaea ficifolia* (Antwerp hollyhock); *Asphodeline lutea; Baptisia tinctoria; Buphthalmum salicifolium; Dahlia,* many varieties; *Helianthus annuus* (annual sunflower), *H. mollis; Hemerocallis* varieties (*see* DAYLILY); *Inula Helenium; Lilium hansoni, L. henryi, L. superbum; Lysimachia vulgaris; Oenothera biennis; Rudbeckia laciniata; Tagetes erecta* (African marigold); *Thalictrum glaucum; Verbascum chaixi, V. olympicum; Zinnia,* many varieties (annual).

AUTUMN-FLOWERING: *Cosmos* (annual); *Dahlia; Helenium autumnale; Helianthus decapetalus,* single and double, *H. maximiliani, H. scaberrimus; Rudbeckia subtomentosa.*

PLANTS OF MEDIUM HEIGHT, 1½–4 FT.

SPRING-FLOWERING: *Euphorbia epithymoides; Doronicum caucasicum; Trollius asiaticus, T. europaeus.*

SUMMER-FLOWERING: *Aconitum Anthora, A. lycoctonum; Allium Moly* (bulb); *Anthemis tinctoria; Aquilegia chrysantha; Argemone mexicana* (annual); *Asclepias tuberosa; Antirrhinum* (annual), lemon to orange; *Calendula officinalis* (annual), lemon to orange; *Centaurea moschata* (annual); *Chrysanthemum* (annual) varieties; *Coreopsis grandiflora, C. tinctoria* (annual), *C. verticillata; Digitalis ambigua; Dimorphotheca aurantiaca* (annual); *Erysimum perofskianum* (annual); *Gaillardia* varieties; *Gladiolus* varieties; *Glaucium flavum* (biennial); *Helenium autumnale pumilum; Heliopsis helianthoides; Hemerocallis,* species and varieties; *Lilium canadense, L. croceum, L. elegans; Linaria dalmatica; Lysimachia punctata; Oenothera fruticosa; Rudbeckia hirta, R. speciosa.*

AUTUMN-FLOWERING: *Chrysanthemum* (hardy) yellow to orange; *Helenium hoopesi.*

LOW-GROWING PLANTS, 6 IN. TO 1½ FT.

SPRING-FLOWERING: *Adonis amurensis, A. vernalis; Alyssum saxatile; Brodiaea ixioides* (bulb); *Crocus aureus, C. susianus* (Cloth-of-Gold); *Doronicum clusi; Epimedium pin-*

natum colchicum; Eranthis hyemalis (tuber); *Erythronium grandiflorum* (bulb); *Euphorbia Myrsinites; Geum montanum; Helianthemum Nummularium; Hyacinthus orientalis* varieties (bulb); *Lysimachia Nummularia; Lotus corniculatus; Narcissus* (daffodils), many varieties; *Primula Auricula, P. elatior, P. vulgaris;* and garden tulips.

SUMMER-FLOWERING: *Achillea tomentosa; Alyssum argenteum; Arnica montana; Antirrhinum,* low varieties (annual); *Belamcanda chinensis; Coreopsis drummondi* (golden wave, annual); *Corydalis cheilanthifolia, C. lutea; Dianthus knappi; Erigeron aurantiacus; Erysimum pulchellum; Eschscholtzia californica* (annual); *Hemerocallis middendorfi, H. minor; Inula ensifolia; Linum flavum;* nasturtiums (annual); *Nemesia* varieties; *Papaver nudicaule; Phlox drummondi* (annual); *Potentilla pyrenaica; Sanvitalia procumbens; Tagetes.*

AUTUMN-FLOWERING: *Crocus,* several species (bulb); *Sternbergia lutea* (bulb).

CLIMBERS

Clematis orientalis (autumn), *C. tangutica* (summer); *Jasminum nudiflorum* (spring); *Lonicera flava* (summer), *L. japonica halliana* (summer); nasturtiums (climbing annual, summer and autumn); rose, climbing, numerous varieties (summer); sweet pea (summer). — L. B. W.

YELLOWS. A plant disease caused primarily by a virus which is capable of attacking a wide range of plants such as aster, calendula, lettuce, etc. Plants turn yellow and appear "bunchy" and stunted and soon die. The virus yellows is spread by leafhoppers.

Another group of diseases, also known as yellows, is caused by fungi. Cabbage and gladiolus suffer from Fusarium yellows and require rotating crops or using resistant varieties. — S. H. D.

YERBA BUENA = *Micromeria chamissonis.*

YEW. See TAXUS. For the plum-yew *see* CEPHALOTAXUS.

YEW FAMILY = Taxaceae.

yezoensis, -e (yez-o-en'sis). From Yezo, an old name for Hokkaido, Japan.

YIELDS. See GARDEN TABLES I.

YLANG-YLANG = *Cananga odorata.* See *also* ARTABOTRYS.

yodogava, -us, -um (yo-do-ga'va). From Yodogawa, Japan.

YOKOHAMA BEAN = *Stizolobium Hasjoo.*

YORK AND LANCASTER ROSE = *Rosa damascena versicolor.*

yosemitensis, -e (yo-sem-i-ten'sis). From Yosemite National Park, California.

YOUTH-AND-OLD-AGE = *Zinnia elegans.*

YUCCA (yuck'a). Semi-desert plants of the lily family, chiefly Mexican, but a few in the southern states and in the W.I. cult. for their striking flower clusters, and comprising about 40 species. Most of them are stemless

---

* Special articles on the subjects indicated by an asterisk (*) will be found at the words so marked.

with a basal rosette of sword-shaped, tough, leathery leaves, but Y. *brevifolia*, Y. *aloifolia*, and Y. *glauca* have distinct trunks. Flowers white (rarely purple-tinged), waxy, cup-shaped, nodding, usually fragrant at night, some blooming only at night, and borne in showy, erect, terminal clusters (panicles*). Petals (or sepals) 6. Stamens* 6. Fruit usually a capsule.* (*Yucca* is the Latinized version of a Spanish vernacular for some other desert plant.)

The yuccas are bold striking plants which are very common in the southwestern U.S., culminating in the extraordinary Joshua-tree (Y. *brevifolia*) which ranges from Calif. to Utah. It has a grotesquely branching trunk and often is 30–40 ft. high. The other cult. species with an obvious trunk are Y. *glauca* and Y. *aloifolia*. Y. *aloifolia* and Y. *brevifolia* are not hardy in regions of wet slushy winters. They need the same culture as desert cacti.

The other species have no evident trunk and are hardy over much of the U.S. south of zone* 3, and sometimes in zone* 3 if they are protected from too much winter moisture. All of them do best in light, sandy or gritty soils, and may be propagated by seeds or offsets* which are frequently produced. Several Mexican (non-hort.) species yield fibers.

aloifolia. Spanish bayonet. Spanish dagger. Producing a simple or branched trunk, 10–25 ft. high. Leaves stiff, about 2½ ft. long, 2 in. wide, and prolonged into a very sharp point. Flowers nearly 4 in. wide, white, or purple-tinged, the cluster often 2 ft. long and very showy; it is particularly good for its late flowering. Southern U.S. to Mex. and the W.I.

brevifolia. Joshua-tree; also called tree yucca. An extraordinary, grotesquely branching desert plant, often 30–40 ft. high, the leaves in dense terminal rosettes. Leaves 6–9 in. long, toothed. Flowers greenish-white, about 2 in. long, the cluster not over 18 in. long. Calif. to Utah.

filamentosa. Adam's-needle. Bear grass. Spanish bayonet. The commonest yucca in cult. in the East, and native from Del. to Fla. and Miss. It is practically stemless, but the stalk of the flower cluster may be 8–12 ft. high. Leaves 2–2½ ft. long, about 1 in. wide, thready on the margin. Flowers white or cream-white, about 2 in. long. There is also a form with variegated leaves. For hardiness *see* above.

glauca. Bear grass. Trunk short and usually prostrate. Leaves nearly 3 ft. long, scarcely ½ in. wide, white-margined and also finely thready on the margin. Flowers greenish-white, about 2 in. long. New Mex., northward to Iowa and S. D., and one of the hardiest of the yuccas.

gloriosa. Spanish dagger. Stemless, or with a very short trunk in the South. Leaves nearly 2½ ft. long, about 2 in. wide, prolonged into a stiff, sharp point, but not thready on the margin. Flowers nearly 4 in. wide, greenish-white or reddish. N. Car. to Fla.

whipplei = *Hesperoyucca whipplei*.

YULAN = *Magnolia denudata*.

yunnanensis, -e (you-nan-en′sis). From Yunnan, China.

YUQUILLA = *Manihot carthaginensis*.

Z

ZABEL HONEYSUCKLE = *Lonicera korolkowi zabeli*.

ZALUZIANSKYA (zal-oo-zi-an′ski-a). Night phlox. Beautifully fragrant, chiefly night-blooming, South African plants of the family Scrophulariaceae, two of the 40 known species grown in the flower garden as tender annuals. They have opposite* leaves, or the upper ones alternate,* and reduced upward to mere bracts.* Flowers in terminal spikes, the calyx 2-lipped.* Corolla tubular, the tube much longer than the regular, 5-lobed limb.* Fruit an oblong capsule.* (Named for Adam Zaluziansky von Zaluzian, Polish physician.)

Both the cult. species should be grown as tender annuals. *See* ANNUALS.

capensis. Not over 18 in. high, the leaves narrow, about 1½ in. long. Flowers about 1½ in. long, the corolla white inside, but purplish-black and hairy outside. Summer.

villosa. Not over 12 in. high, the stems hairy. Leaves ovalish or broader toward the tip, about 1 in. long. Flowers night-fragrant, white or pale lilac inside, but purple outside and the corolla only slightly hairy, if at all. Summer.

ZAMAN. *See* SAMANEA SAMAN.

ZAMBAC = *Jasminum Sambac*.

ZAMIA (zay′mi-a). Stiff-leaved, fern-like or palm-like plants comprising over 40 species of the family Cycadaceae, all from tropical or sub-tropical America. They have generally underground, woody trunks (obviously above ground in some old specimens), and a terminal crown of evergreen compound* leaves. Flowers none in the usual garden sense, the male and female organs borne in dense, woody cones or close clusters (for details *see* CYCADACEAE). (*Zamia* is a Latin word for a barren pine cone and was adopted by Linnaeus for these plants because of the cone-like inflorescence.)

The zamias are of secondary hort. importance and the two below can only be grown outdoors in zone* 9. Some of the Florida species were used by the Indians to make soap, and the plants are sometimes now grown for ornament or interest. One of them is the source of Florida arrowroot. They do well in the light, sandy soils of southern Fla. If grown in the greenhouse, they re-

---

* Special articles on the subjects indicated by an asterisk (*) will be found at the words so marked.

quire the same conditions as *Cycas* (which see).

floridana. Coontie. Trunk mostly underground. Leaves with 14–20 mostly opposite leaflets, which are slightly arched, rolled on the margin and blunt at the tip. Female cones 5–6 in. long. Southern Fla.

integrifolia. Trunk more obvious, generally above ground and sometimes 12 in. high. Leaflets 14–32, oblongish or narrower, blunt at the tip, mostly without teeth, but sometimes toothed toward the tip. Fla. and the W.I. It is the source of Florida arrowroot, an important food of the Seminole Indians. Also called *Z. media commeliniana.*

ZANTEDESCHIA. See Calla Lily.

ZANTHORHIZA = *Xanthorhiza.*

ZANTHOXYLUM (zan-thocks′i-lum), also spelled *Zanthoxylon* and *Xanthoxylum*. Aromatic, prickly shrubs or trees of the family Rutaceae, comprising about 200 species from both hemispheres, but chiefly tropical, although the cult. species are natives of the U.S. They have alternate,* compound* leaves, the leaflets arranged feather-fashion and opposite each other, with an odd one at the end. Flowers small, greenish, the male and female on different plants, or polygamous* (for details *see* Rutaceae). Fruit a collection of 2-valved, ripened carpels (*see* Pistil), each with 1 shining, black seed. (*Zanthoxylum* is from the Greek for yellow and wood, in allusion to the yellow wood of some species.)

These shrubs present no difficulties and thrive in any ordinary garden soil, although they are hardy only as indicated below. Propagated by seeds, or by root cuttings.

americanum. Prickly ash; also called angelica tree and toothache tree. A shrub or small tree, 10–20 ft. high, the prickles about ½ in. long. Leaflets 5–11, ovalish, about 2 in. long, hairy beneath. Flowers small, blooming before the leaves unfold, in small clusters in the leaf axils.* Eastern N.A. April–May. Hardy from zone* 3 southward.

Clava-Herculis. Hercules′-club; also called prickly ash and toothache tree. A tree 30–50 ft. high, the trunk and branches prickly. Leaflets 7–19, toothed, the stalk and main axis usually prickly. Flowers in rather large, terminal clusters (panicles*). Southern Va. to Fla. and Tex. April. Hardy from zone* 5 southward, sometimes north of this. It is often shrubby in the young state.

zanzibariensis, -e (zan-zi-bar-i-en′sis). From Zanzibar, Africa.

Zapota (za-po′ta). The common name in Latin America for the marmalade plum (*Achras Zapota*).

ZAUSCHNERIA (zaush-near′i-a). A small genus of Californian perennial herbs of the family Onagraceae, **Z. californica**, the California fuchsia or hummingbird′s-trumpet, cult. for its late-blooming, brilliant scarlet flowers. It is a decumbent or partly erect branched herb, 8–15 in. high, the foliage densely hairy. Leaves generally alternate,* oblongish or narrower, ½–1½ in. long. Calyx tubular, scarlet, flaring above. Petals scarlet, not much exceeding the calyx* lobes. Stamens* 8, protruding. Fruit a 4-valved, many-seeded capsule.* A showy garden plant with fuchsia-like flowers, but not certainly hardy in the eastern states. It may be propagated by division or by seeds. In Calif. it is remarkably drought-resistant. (Named for H. Zauschner, once a botanist at Prague.)

ZEA. See Corn.

ZEBRA-GRASS = *Miscanthus sinensis zebrinus.*

ZEBRA-PLANT = *Calathea zebrina.*

ZEBRINA (zee-bry′na). A genus of only 2 species of the family Commelinaceae, one of them, *Z. pendula,* the wandering Jew, a Mexican, watery-juiced herb, widely cult. in greenhouses and often spreading under the benches. It is closely related to *Tradescantia fluminensis* (also called wandering Jew), a Brazilian plant, from which it differs chiefly in having the petals united into a tube (*see* Spiderwort). *Zebrina pendula* is a decumbent or prostrate plant, rooting very easily at the joints and grown mostly for its foliage and handsome reddish-purple flowers from between 2 boat-shaped, unequal bracts.* The *var.* quadricolor, with its leaves striped green, white, and red, is a particularly showy form. The plant will stand no frost, but is a handsome subject for hanging baskets or window boxes. (*Zebrina* is from the Latin for zebra, in allusion to the striped foliage.)

ZELKOVA (zel-ko′va). Elm-like Asiatic shrubs and trees of the family Ulmaceae, comprising about 5 species, the two below of secondary garden interest but cult. for ornament. They have alternate,* toothed leaves which are slightly unequal at the base. Flowers small, polygamous, without petals, not showy, solitary, or the male flowers in small clusters in the leaf axils,* all blooming early in the spring with the opening of the leaves. Fruit a 2-edged, oblique drupe,* winged on the upper half. (*Zelkova* is a Latinized version of a common name in the Caucasus for the first species.)

carpinifolia. A tree up to 80 ft. high in the wild, as cult. usually with a short trunk which splits into several main branches, making a round-headed tree. Leaves elliptic or oblongish, pointed, 1–2 in. long, toothed and hairy on the veins beneath. Fruit about ⅛ in. wide. Caucasus. Hardy from zone* 4 southward. Sometimes offered as *Z. ulmoides.*

serrata. A similar tree, but the leaves more sharply toothed, tapering at the tip, broader and about twice as long, and without hairs on the veins beneath. Jap. Hardy from zone* 3 southward. A good substitute for the American elm, and often offered under the incorrect name of *Planera japonica.*

ZENOBIA (zen-ō′bi-a). A single species of little-known shrubs of the heath family, **Z. pulverulenta** of the southeastern U.S. grown for ornament, and sometimes forced in the greenhouse for its white, bell-shaped flowers. See Forcing. It is a partly evergreen shrub, 4–6 ft. high, the alternate*

---

* Special articles on the subjects indicated by an asterisk (*) will be found at the words so marked.

ovalish leaves very bluish-green, 2–3 in. long. Flowers about ½ in. wide, in a terminal cluster made up of racemes.* Fruit a small capsule.* N. Car. to Fla. May–June. Hardy from zone* 4 southward. It is closely related to *Pieris* and needs the same conditions for growth. *See* PIERIS. (Named for Queen Zenobia of Palmyra.)

ZEPHYRANTHES (zeff-i-ran'theez). Zephyr-flower. Zephyr lily. A genus of 55 species of New World bulbous herbs of the family Amaryllidaceae, a few grown for ornament and of uncertain hardiness over most of the country north of zone* 5. They have narrow, basal leaves, more or less grass-like, usually appearing with the flowers and persistent in some species over the winter, or in others appearing after the flowers. Flower solitary, its stalk hollow, and appearing from a tubular spathe* which is notched at the tip. Corolla erect, more or less funnel-shaped, the segments nearly of equal length, the flower thus faintly irregular. Stamens* 6. Fruit a nearly round, 3-celled capsule.* (*Zephyranthes* is from the Greek for the west-wind flower, in allusion to the plants being wholly American.) They are sometimes known under the genus name *Atamosco*.

The second species is the hardiest and will ordinarily survive the winters up to zone* 4 if given a site not too wet and slushy in the winter months. The others are best planted in the spring, allowed to flower, and dug up and stored over the winter. Storage should not allow the bulbs to dry out, and they should be kept in dry or moistish sand. South of zone* 5 they can stay in the ground all year; they will sometimes survive this treatment northward, but not usually. All the half-hardy species can be grown in the cool greenhouse.

Ajax. A hybrid between Z. *candida* and the non-hort. Z. *citrina*. Leaves evergreen, erect, very narrow, present at flowering time, 8–14 in. long. Flowers about 2½ in. long, yellow, but green-based. June.

Atamasco. Atamasco lily. Fairy lily. Leaves about 12 in. long, very narrow. Flowering stalk nearly 1 ft. long, the flowers white or tinged with purple, nearly 3 in. long. Va. to Fla. and Ala. April–May.

candida. Leaves thick, stiffish, about 1 ft. long. Flowers summer-blooming, about 2 in. long, white or rarely rose-tinged. Argentine.

carinata = Z. *grandiflora*.

citrina. Leaves 8–12 in. long, about ⅛ in. wide, grooved. Flowers yellow, the tube green, about 1½ in. long. British Guiana. June–Sept. Sometimes called Z. *sulphurea*.

grandiflora. Common zephyr lily. Leaves flat, narrow, about 12 in. long. Flowers blooming in late spring and summer, about 3 in. long, red or pink. Tropical America.

rosea. Resembling Z. *grandiflora* and sometimes mistaken for it, but with broader, blunter leaves, and smaller flowers which do not bloom until autumn. Cuba, and the least hardy of the zephyr lilies.

robusta = *Habranthus robustus*.

ZEPHYR-FLOWER; ZEPHYR LILY. *See* ZEPHYRANTHES.

zeylanica, -us, -um (zee-lan'i-ka). From Ceylon.

ZIGADENUS = *Zygadenus*.

ZIGZAG CLOVER = *Trifolium medium*. *See* CLOVER.

ZINEB. *See* FUNGICIDES.

ZINGIBER. *See* GINGER.

ZINGIBERACEAE (zin-ji-ber-ray'see-ee). The ginger family comprises aromatic tropical herbs grown for their flavoring products and for ornament. All require greenhouse culture, or some can be grown outdoors in completely frost-free parts of the country (zone* 9). There are over 40 genera and 800 species, mostly from the Old World tropics. The family was once included in the Scitamineae.

Of the six cult. genera two are the most important, *Zingiber* (*see* GINGER) and *Elettaria* (*see* CARDAMON). The others, grown mostly for ornament, are *Alpinia, Amomum, Curcuma,* and *Hedychium,* the latter including the popular ginger-lily, also called butterfly-lily.

Nearly all are stout herbs with large aromatic rootstocks (ginger). Leaves mostly with sheathing bases or leafstalks, always without marginal teeth, often very large. Flowers irregular, usually in bracted* clusters, often from between sheath-like bracts (a spathe*). Fruit a dry pod (capsule*).

Technical flower characters: Flowers hermaphrodite,* irregular.* Calyx tubular or spathe*-like of 3 segments. Corolla tubular, but unequal, 3-lobed. Stamens 1, but there are often sterile ones and sometimes these are petal-like or form a lip.* Ovary inferior,* mostly 1-celled.

ZINNIA (zin'i-a). Annual or perennial herbs or under-shrubs comprising about 15 species of the family Compositae, chiefly found in Mex., but also from Tex. and Colo. and Chile. They have rather stiff, erect stems covered with short bristly hairs and somewhat woody at the base. Leaves opposite,* ovalish or lance-shaped, usually stemclasping. Flowers in solitary, flattish or cone-shaped, showy heads, each flower growing in the axil of a scale-like bract,* the tip of which is often colored. Ray florets of every shade except blue, the under side often greenish, arranged in 1 to many rows. Disk florets* yellow or purplish-brown. (Named for Johann Gottfried Zinn, Professor of Medicine at Göttingen.) Garden zinnias are of comparatively recent introduction. The tall forms of *Zinnia elegans* were introduced about 1886, while the lower forms, mostly derivatives of *Zinnia angustifolia,* appeared about 1861 in the single form and 1871 for the double-flowered varieties. For cult. and varieties, *see* below.

angustifolia. Stiff-growing, erect annual, up to 18 in. high, covered with short stiff hairs. Leaves broadly lance-shaped, not stalked. Flowers in terminal heads to 1½ in. across. Ray florets orange. Disk florets yellow, red or orange. Mex.

elegans. Youth-and-old-age. Stiff-growing,

---

* Special articles on the subjects indicated by an asterisk (*) will be found at the words so marked.

erect annual to 3 ft. high, covered with short stiff hairs. Leaves ovalish, clasping the stem, prominently veined. Flowers in solitary heads to 4½ in. across. Ray florets purple or reddish-lilac. Disk florets yellow or orange. There are hort. varieties of every shade except blue. Disk florets often absent in hort. forms. Mex.

haageana = *Zinnia angustifolia*.
mexicana = *Zinnia angustifolia*.

ZINNIA CULTURE

Zinnias are among the most popular summer- and autumn-flowering plants. The various shades and heights now obtainable make effective showy plantings for the sunny or semi-shady borders. As they last well in the hot weather they are much grown for cutting. The giant forms of *Zinnia elegans*, growing to 3 ft. high, are especially adapted for the back of the border, while the free-flowering, smaller-flowered Lilliputian varieties, with their cone-shaped heads, growing to 18 in. high, are useful for the front of the border and for table decoration when cut. Zinnias are easily cult. and will grow in almost any soil. Best results are obtained when grown in deep, rich soil which has been well dug and manured. They should be given water freely in hot, dry weather; a mulch of strawy manure or hay placed round the plants will help retain the moisture and keep soil from packing during heavy rains.

Seeds should be sown in cool greenhouse or cold frame in boxes of light, sandy soil, ⅛ in. deep, in early April. When plants are large enough to handle they should be transplanted in the same kind of soil to 3 in. apart in boxes and placed near the glass if grown in greenhouse to keep them from becoming leggy,* but if started in the cold frame they may be transplanted into the frame, keeping the sash closed at night until danger of frost is over when they may be transplanted.

Those started in the greenhouse must be hardened off by admitting air whenever possible and placing boxes outside for a few days before planting. The giant forms should be planted 1½–2 ft. apart; the Lilliputian varieties may be planted 1 ft. apart. Seeds may also be sown outdoors from the end of April to the middle of May, or earlier in the southern states. They may be sown where required to bloom; 3–4 seeds should be planted about 1 ft. apart. When 3 in. high they should be thinned out, leaving the plants about a foot apart each way.

INSECT PESTS. For stalk borers, *see* CALLISTEPHUS. For tarnished plant bug, *see* DAHLIA. Use pesticide #1 (*see* SPRAYS AND DUSTS) on general leaf-feeders.

DISEASES. A leafspot* disease may gradually defoliate plants, starting at the bottom and working up through the plant. When plants are 6 inches tall, apply pesticide #1 or #5 (*see* SPRAYS AND DUSTS) and repeat at 10-day intervals.

If powdery mildew* develops, use pesticide #9 at 10-day intervals.

zinniaeflora, -us, -um (zin-i-ee-flow′ra). With zinnia-like flowers.

ZIRAM. *See* FUNGICIDES.

ZIT-KWA = *Benincasa hispida*.

ZIZANIA (zy-zay′ni-a). Tall, and in ours, annual marsh grasses comprising two American and one Asiatic species, of which Z. aquatica, the wild rice of eastern N.A., is much cult. for its nutritious grain, and for ornament, as it is a handsome grass 7–10 ft. high. It is often called water, Indian, or Canada rice, and besides its use for food is widely grown by sportsmen for wild-fowl food. Leaves grass-like, 12–18 in. long and about 2 in. wide. Flower cluster terminal (a panicle*), nearly 2 ft. long, the upper spikelets furnished with awns* nearly 3 in. long. Grain rice-like, but narrower. The plant grows best in water from 5 in. to 3 ft. deep, but can be made to grow also along the edges of pools, marshes, or bogs. The seed should be soaked in coarse cotton bags, submerged in the water it is to be planted in. Sow the seeds in May on the muddy bottom (not on sandy bottoms), or plant them in mud which can later be flooded, as the plant does better in standing (not running) water than anywhere else. There is a *var.* angustifolia with narrower leaves, which is sometimes offered as Z. palustris. (*Zizania* is a Greek name for some wild grain, but not certainly for this one.)

zizanioides (zy-zay-ni-oy′deez, but *see* OÏDES). Like the wild rice (*Zizania*).

ZIZYPHUS (ziz′i-fuss). A genus of over 40 species of somewhat spiny shrubs and trees of the family Rhamnaceae, one of the three below a little-known fruit in the U.S. — the jujube. The species are natives of the warmer regions of both the Old and New Worlds and are not generally satisfactory in the cooler parts of the country. Leaves alternate,* short-stalked, 3–5-veined from the base. Flowers small, yellowish or greenish-yellow, perfect,* in small clusters (cymes*) in the leaf axils.* For details *see* RHAMNACEAE. Fruit oblong, or nearly round, fleshy (a drupe*). (*Zizyphus* is the old Greek name for the first species.) *See* LOTUS.

The common or Chinese jujube (Z. Jujuba) is the only one of commercial importance, and this is slight as the fruits of the jujube are little known in the U.S. Another species, Z. *mauritiana*, is suited to the warmer parts of Fla. The common jujube is most satisfactory in regions of great summer heat, notably southern Tex., N. Mex., Ariz., and especially Calif. Trees should be planted 20 × 20 ft. apart, and they have a wide soil tolerance, if there is sufficient summer heat, being more alkali-tolerant than most fruit trees. The jujube has not been much troubled with pests. While isolated trees have been grown here for many years, the introduction of the improved Chinese varieties noted below has greatly increased the demand for jujubes. Its use here has been

---

* Special articles on the subjects indicated by an asterisk (*) will be found at the words so marked.

held back by lack of knowledge as to its qualities. It is not the best of all fruits to be eaten fresh, but a very fine confection is made by scoring the skin of the fruit with a sharp knife (or razor blade) just before it is dropped into boiling syrup, where it should stay 20–30 minutes. Cool the fruit and syrup and then repeat the boiling. The fruit is then removed from the syrup and dried about to the consistency of a prune. Sometimes, but not very appropriately, called Chinese date.

Jujuba. Common or Chinese jujube. A shrub or small tree, not over 30 ft. high, one spine of each group of 2, curved. Leaves oblongish, 1–2 in. long, bluntly toothed. Fruits oblong or nearly round or sometimes egg-shaped, about 1 in. long, acid, when ripe brownish. Eurasia. Among the best varieties for Calif. and similar climates, all originating in China where the fruit is highly prized, are: Mu Shing Hong, Lang, Sui Meu, and Li, all of them imported by the U.S. Department of Agriculture.

mauritiana. Indian or cottony jujube. Usually an evergreen shrub or small tree with broadly oval leaves, 1¾–2½ in. long, the under side rusty-hairy. Fruit nearly round, red when ripe, acid, about 1 in. in diameter. India. Suited only to zone* 9, and does well on a variety of soils in southern Fla., but not much known, and with no outstanding hort. forms.

obtusifolia. Texas jujube or buckthorn; also called lote bush. A stiff, spiny, much-branched shrub. Leaves generally ovalish, ¾–1¼ in. long, smooth, a little toothed or without teeth. Fruit about ⅛ in. long, black, edible, but of inferior quality. Tex. and Ariz. to northern Mex.

ZONAL GERANIUM. The common garden geranium. See PELARGONIUM.

zonata, -us, -um (zo-nay′ta). Banded or zoned.

ZONE. As outlined in the article on HARDINESS, the ability of woody plants to grow in any particular place is a combination of many factors. But of these the average minimum temperature of the coldest month is probably the most critical. As a criterion for the hardiness of woody plants in this country it was adopted by the late Alfred Rehder of the Arnold Arboretum, and, with modifications to be explained presently, has been used throughout this book.

The advantage of such a method is that it creates, upon the reasonably accurate basis of the Weather Bureau figures, rather fixed zones of hardiness, within which certain plants will grow and north of which they usually perish. Rehder divided the regions north of a line from northern S. Car. to northern Tex. into 8 zones.

Because the ENCYCLOPEDIA includes all of the U.S. it was necessary to re-zone the country in accordance with the accompanying map — there being 9 zones in all. These zones are all based upon Weather Bureau figures kept for a period of many years, and show the average minimum temperatures of the coldest month.

This enlarged zoning system was devised for the first edition of this book in 1936, and it had never before been done for the whole country. Since that time modifications of it have been suggested, one by the Arnold Arboretum in 1948 and another by the United States Department of Agriculture in 1959. Both these suggest minor, and more detailed changes in the map. But the changes (affecting thousands of entries having to do with hardiness of species and many garden operations) do not seem to be sufficiently significant to warrant the abandonment of the map here used. (Unfortunately the "Plant Hardiness Zone Map" issued by the Department in June 1960 was not available while the Fourth Edition of the ENCYCLOPEDIA was in preparation).

The nine zones and their average minimum temperatures are:

Zone 1.	zero or below	This includes the region of the northern spruce and fir forests in the East, some prairie in the north-central area, and in addition to intense cold has a short growing season.
Zone 2.	zero to 10° above.	In the East this includes the southern edge of the spruce and fir forests as well as much of the red and white pine country. In the central section it cuts across large sections of prairie.
Zone 3.	10°–20°	In the East the heart of the beech-birch-maple forests of the North are found in this zone, which, in the central section, covers a large area of prairie.
Zone 4.	20°–25°	While the natural vegetation is not greatly different from zone 3, the line between zones 3 and 4 seems to be a critical one for many cult. woody plants, especially plants like box and English holly.
Zone 5.	25°–30°	It is in this zone that many southern plants reach about the northern limits of their hardiness.
Zone 6.	30°–40°	This is the upper limit for the commercial culture of cotton and for many garden plants.
Zone 7.	40°–50°	The great cotton belt, and the largest area in the country with such a warm winter temperature. Many plants from zone 8 are safe in zone 7 if local conditions are favorable.
Zone 8.	50°–60°	A limited region, where citrus fruits are relatively safe, confined to central Fla. and extreme southern Calif. and adjacent Ariz. Horticulturally an extremely important

---

* Special articles on the subjects indicated by an asterisk (*) will be found at the words so marked.

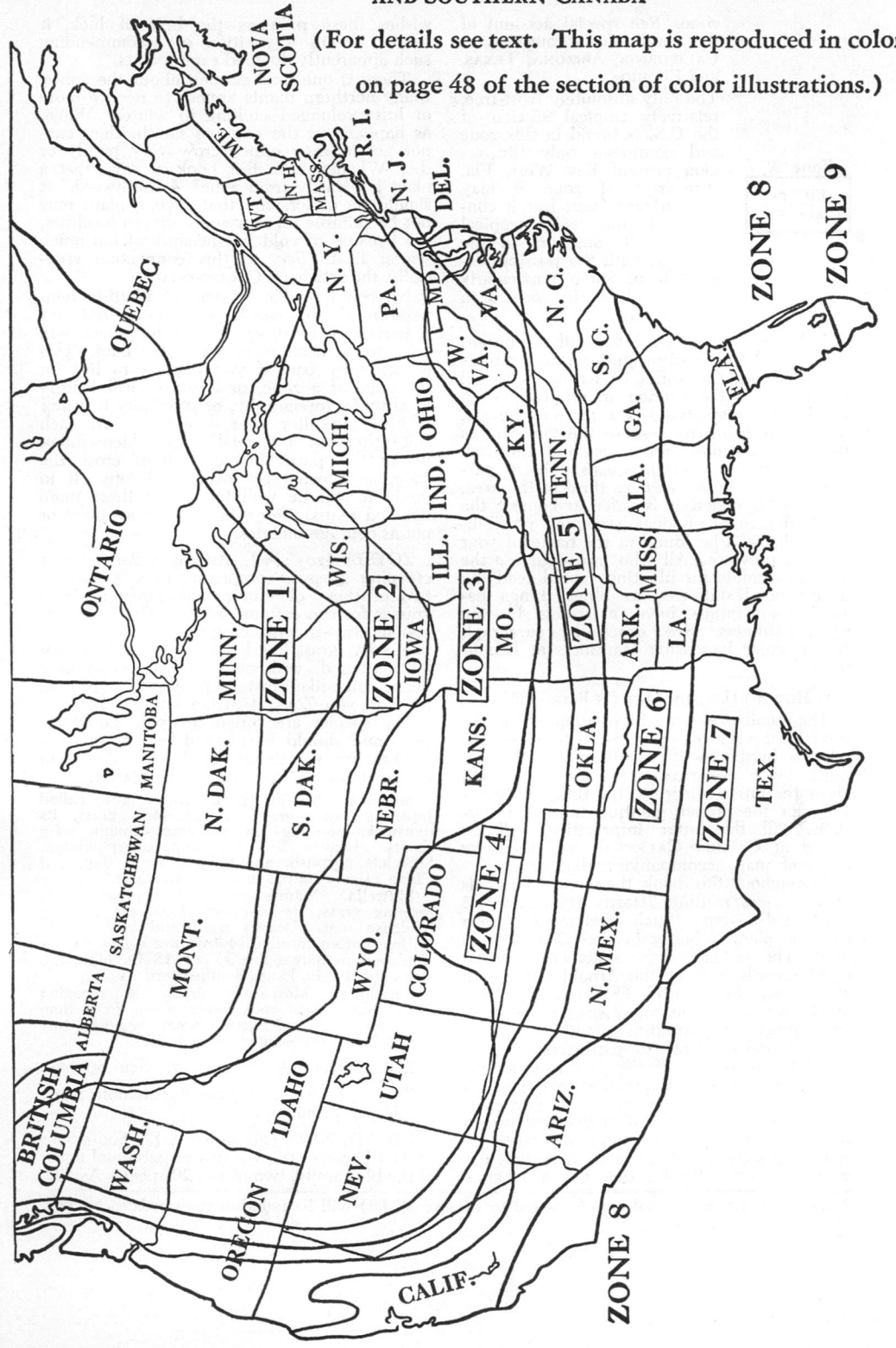

ZONES OF HARDINESS FOR WOODY PLANTS IN THE UNITED STATES AND SOUTHERN CANADA

(For details see text. This map is reproduced in color on page 48 of the section of color illustrations.)

zone. *See* special account of the conditions as outlined at CALIFORNIA, ARIZONA, TEXAS, and FLORIDA.

The only absolutely frost-free, relatively tropical section of the U.S. is found in this zone and comprises only the region around Key West, Fla. The rest of zone 9 may have a rare frost, but it contains all the really tropical plants cult. outdoors in the country, with the possible exception of some particularly favored places in zone 8 in Calif. (which see).

Zone 9.

60° or above.

If North America were flat and the oceans that bathe the eastern and western coasts did not exist, the zones of hardiness would extend across the country in relatively even bands. The map shows how far they deviate from such regularity, where the zones cross the two main mountain ranges and approach the eastern and western oceans. This is particularly true in the western third of the area, and in this region it is safer to consult the detailed account of local gardening possibilities which will be found at the name of your state or province. All who intend to use the map as a guide for planting should read the article on HARDINESS, as other things besides temperature have a strong bearing upon hardiness. *See*, especially, paragraph No. 4 under Increasing Hardiness at HARDINESS.

HOW TO USE THE MAP ON PAGE 1327

The zoning system here adopted is designed for only one purpose — to show the relative hardiness of woody plants as cult. outdoors in America. The map does not show the onset of spring, the time of flowering, nor the proper planting times for gardens. All the latter information will be found at GARDEN CALENDAR and the very different map accompanying that article.

Throughout this book there are thousands of references reading "Hardy from zone* 3 southward" — etc. Such statements mean that the plant is hardy in zone 3 and south of it. The validity of the statement is based upon records kept at the Arnold Arboretum at Boston, the Central Experimental Farm at Ottawa, as well as many scattered records from agricultural experiment stations, botanic gardens, and some private gardeners.

While no scheme of this sort is infallible, wherever there was a doubt as to the hardiness of a particular plant for a particular zone, it has been assigned to the next warmest zone for safety. Venturesome gardeners will always try growing plants in regions unfit for them. While the ENCYCLOPEDIA wishes these pioneers the best of luck, it cannot be in a position of recommending such apparently doomed experiments.

There is one final caution about the zones. Many northern plants appear to need a more or less prolonged chilling in winter. When, as happens in the extreme South, they cannot get it, they either grow very poorly or die. Whenever, in this book, it says that a plant is "Hardy from zone* 4 southward," it should be understood that such a plant may not be suitable for extreme southern localities, not because of cold but because of too much winter heat. *See*, in this connection especially, the article on CALIFORNIA.

No country-wide scheme of plotting temperature records can hope to be accurate for a particular locality, so that judgment will have to be used in applying the map. This is especially true if you happen to live on the edge of a zone, or if some local feature of altitude, topography, or proximity to water is likely to alter your conditions. At each state there is a special map which shows where the particular zone lines cross the state, as affected by local conditions. If in doubt it will be well to consult these more detailed maps, after which you may plant or not as courage dictates.

ZOYSIA (zoy'si-a). Asiatic or Australasian creeping grasses, comprising only 4 species, two of them of minor importance as lawn grasses for the extreme South. They are perennial grasses with creeping rootstocks and fine, wiry, grass-like leaves. Flowering spikelets flattened, without awns,* crowded in a dense spike-like cluster (panicle*). (Named for Karl von Zoys, Austrian botanist.)

The species are suited to open, sandy regions and should be planted by bits of rootstocks. For the details of this *see* Zoysia in the section on southern lawns at LAWN.

japonica. Korean lawn grass; also called Japanese lawn grass. A creeping grass, its rootstocks sending up numerous tough, wiry shoots. Leaves 1–3 in. long, sharp-pointed. Spikelets purplish, about 1 in. long. Jap. and China. Useful in the southeastern states.

Matrella. Manila grass. A compact, turf-forming grass, its creeping rhizomes* forming a dense mat. Leaves rigid and stiff, ½–1½ in. long, often inrolled. Flowering spikes (never produced in mown lawns) 12–18 in. high, the spike about 2 in. long. Southeastern As.

tenuifolia. Mascarene grass. A creeping grass, the shoots and leaves much finer than in *Z. japonica*, and making a flat, beautiful turf in Calif., but little known elsewhere.

ZUCCHINI. A squash var. *See* SQUASH.

Zumi (zoo'mi). Japanese common name for *Malus Zumi*.

ZYGADENUS (zig-a-den'us). Sometimes spelled *Zigadenus*. A genus of perennial herbs of the lily family, two of the 20 species Asiatic,

* Special articles on the subjects indicated by an asterisk (*) will be found at the words so marked.

all the rest from the New World. They are of secondary garden interest, although the three below are planted in the wild garden. They have a collection of basal, long, narrow, grass-like leaves and a tall flowering stalk crowned with a simple or branched cluster (raceme* or panicle*) of white or yellowish-green flowers which soon wither but persist. Corolla of petal-like sepals. Stamens* 6. Fruit a 3-celled capsule.* (*Zygadenus* is from the Greek for yoke and gland, in allusion to the pair of glands found at the base of the sepals.) Sometimes known as *Amianthium.* The foliage and rootstock of most species contain a poisonous juice, and some non-hort. species are deadly. The second species is from Calif. and not certainly hardy in the eastern states. The other two are suited to moist, somewhat acid sites in the wild garden or in the bog.

elegans. Alkali-grass. Leaves tough and wiry, nearly 12 in. long, very bluish-green. Flower stalk 2–3 ft. high, the cluster about 12 in. long and branched. Flowers greenish, about ½ in. wide. Central and western N.A.

fremonti. Leaves about 12 in. long, nearly ½ in. wide, only slightly bluish-green. Flowers similar to those of *Z. elegans,* but the cluster often not branched. Calif.

leimanthoides. With a slender, leafy stem about 4 ft. high, the leaves mostly basal, about 12 in. long and ⅓ in. wide. Flowers greenish-white, about ⅓ in. wide, the cluster branched, nearly 12 in. long. N.Y. to Ala. Summer.

ZYGOCACTUS (zy-go-kak'tus). A single Brazilian species of tree-perching, spineless cacti, **Z. truncatus,** widely grown and popular under the name of crab cactus or Christmas cactus. It is a much-branched, hanging plant, the broad, leaf-like stems or joints sharply cut off at the tip, 1½–2 in. long, about ¾ in. wide, the margins with 1–3 coarse, blunt teeth, the two upper ones a little incurved. Flowers very showy, 2½–3½ in. wide, red and very irregular.* Fruit about ¾ in. in diameter, red and pear-shaped. Often sold as *Epiphyllum truncatum,* and the genus *Zygocactus* is often confused with *Epiphyllum,* but the latter has regular flowers. Unlike most cacti the crab cactus can be easily grown in potting mixture* 3, and is a favorite house plant. It needs more water than other cacti and is a fine plant for the window sill or for hanging baskets. (*Zygocactus* is from the Greek for yoke and *Cactus,* in allusion to the irregular* flowers.) Sometimes offered as *Phyllocactus,* and blooming about Christmastime. Some prefer to call this *Schlumbergera truncata,* a suggestion not adopted here.

There is another plant also known as Christmas cactus, *Schlumbergera bridgesi,* which differs from the above in not having teeth on the margin of the joints. Some consider this the "true" Christmas cactus.

ZYGOMORPHIC. Said of an irregular* flower which can be divided into two similar halves in one plane only. Common examples are the snapdragon, all orchids, the foxglove, and many others. *See* IRREGULAR FLOWER.

ZYGOPETALUM (zy-go-pet'a-lum). Tropical American tree-perching (epiphytic*) orchids, comprising about 20 species, of which **Z. mackayi** of Brazil is often cult. in greenhouses for its showy bloom. It has egg-shaped pseudobulbs,* 2–3 in. long, from which arise 2–3 narrow, sheathing leaves about 12 in. long. Flower stalk about 18 in. long, the 5–8 flowers separate, each about 3 in. wide. Sepals and petals somewhat similar, yellowish-green and white, spotted with purple-brown. Lip* notched, more or less fan-shaped, white, but streaked and spotted with bluish-purple. An extremely handsome orchid of comparatively easy culture. *See* Tropical Orchid Cultivation at ORCHID. The *var.* crinitum has greenish flowers spotted with brown and a hairy, wavy lip.* (*Zygopetalum* is from the Greek for yoke and petal, in allusion to the irregular* flower.)

ZYGOPHYLLACEAE (zy-go-fill-lay'see-ee). A chiefly tropical family of herbs, shrubs, and trees, all of little or no hort. interest except *Larrea,* which see for the only commonly cult. plants in the family Zygophyllaceae.

SOME STATISTICS

Total number of **boldface** entry words 15,753
Plant Families 191
Genera 1,798
Species, varieties and named horticultural forms 9,191
Common or vernacular plant names 4,732
Species names defined and pronounced 2,287
Cross-references and miscellaneous short definitions 7,314
Cultural and special articles 495

* Special articles on the subjects indicated by an asterisk (*) will be found at the words so marked.

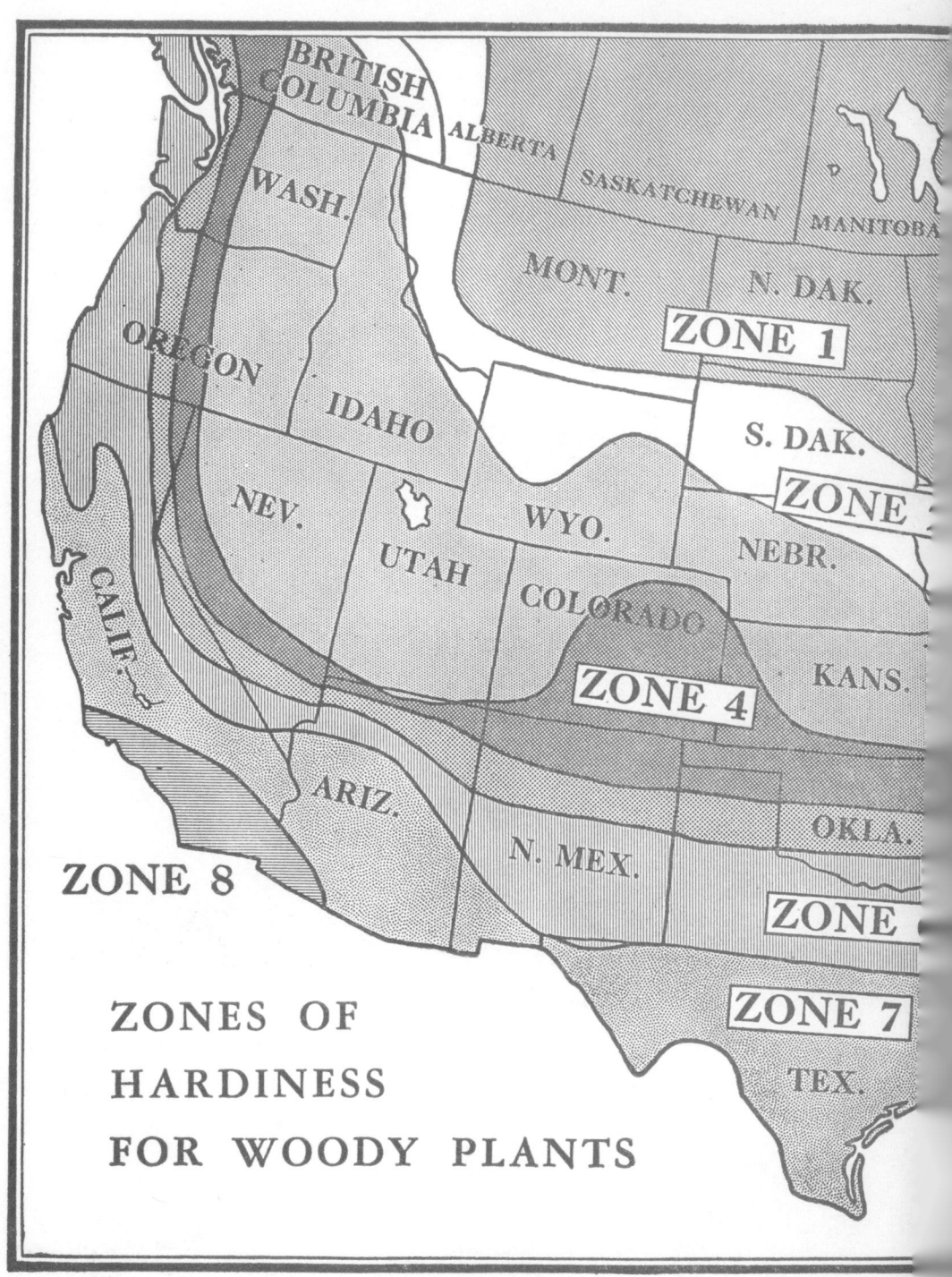

ZONE 8

ZONES OF
HARDINESS
FOR WOODY PLANTS